2002 County and City Extra

11th Edition

2002 County and City Extra

Annual Metro, City, and County Data Book

11th Edition

Editors
Deirdre A. Gaquin
Katherine A. DeBrandt

BERNAN PRESS
Lanham, MD

First edition 1992. 11th edition 2002.

ISBN: 0-89059-597-6

ISSN: 1059-9096

Composed and printed by Automated Graphic Systems, Inc., White Plains, MD, on acid-free paper that meets the American National Standards Institute Z39-48 standard.

2003   2002   4 3 2 1

BERNAN
4611-F Assembly Drive
Lanham, MD 20706
800-274-4447
email: info@bernan.com
www.bernan.com

Contents

ABOUT THE EDITORS

Deirdre Gaquin has been a data use consultant to private organizations, government agencies, and universities for 20 years. Prior to that, she was Director of Data Access Services at Data Use & Access Laboratories, a pioneer in private sector distribution of federal statistical data. A former President of the Association of Public Data Users, Ms. Gaquin has served on numerous boards, panels, and task forces concerned with federal statistical data and has worked on four decennial censuses. She holds a Master of Urban Planning (MUP) degree from Hunter College. Mrs. Gaquin is also an editor of Bernan's *Education Statistics of the United States* and *Places, Towns and Townships*.

Katherine A. DeBrandt is a senior data analyst with Bernan Associates. She received her B.A. in political science from Colgate University. She is also an editor of *State Profiles, The Population and Economy of Each U.S. State* and *Education Statistics of the United States*, also published by Bernan.

ACKNOWLEDGEMENTS

The editors of *2002 County and City Extra* extend their appreciation to George Hall and Courtenay Slater, the originators of this publication, whose contributions continue to enrich this book.

We are extremely grateful to Kara Gottschlich, Bernan's production team leader, and Christopher Jorgenson, her production assistant, for coordinating all production aspects of this project. We also appreciate the assistance of Jacalyn Houston, Bernan's staff editor, for proofreading this volume. Under the direction of managing editor Tamera Wells-Lee and with support from Automated Graphic Systems, Inc. and Bowring Cartographics, Inc., Kara, Chris, and Jacalyn assisted the editors tremendously with finalizing this edition of *County and City Extra*.

As always, we are especially grateful to the many federal agency personnel who assisted us in obtaining the data, provided excellent resources on their Web sites, and patiently answered our questions.

INTRODUCTION

County and City Extra is an annual publication providing the most up-to-date statistical information available for every state, county, metropolitan area, congressional district, and for all cities in the United States with a 2000 population of 25,000 or more. Data for places including towns and cities under 25,000 population are published in a separate companion Bernan Press volume, *Places, Towns, and Townships*. These two volumes are designed to meet the needs of libraries, businesses, and other organizations or individuals who desire convenient and timely sources of the most frequently sought information about geographic entities within the United States. Annual updating of *County and City Extra* ensures its stature as a reliable and authoritative source for statistical information.

County and City Extra and *Places, Towns, and Townships* are large volumes, but not big enough to accommodate the wealth of information from the 2000 Census. The recently published *County and City Extra— Special Decennial Census Edition*, includes additional details from the complete count data. Another forthcoming volume will include social and economic details from the 2000 Census long form.

Changing Data Sources

This edition of *County and City Extra* marks a transition, as 2000 census data begin to replace 1990. This volume includes population and housing characteristics from the complete count of the 2000 Census (the short form), released by the Census Bureau as Summary File 1. Summary File 3, which includes the socio-economic details from the sample survey portion of the 2000 Census (the long form), was being released as this volume was prepared, and will be included in next year's edition. The Census Bureau is phasing in a new survey, the American Community Survey (ACS), which is scheduled to replace the long form in future censuses. Part of the development of the ACS resulted in a new data source that is included in this volume for some housing characteristics at the state level. That new data source, the Census 2000 Supplementary Survey (C2SS), used the ACS questionnaire during the 2000 census year to demonstrate the operational feasibility of collecting long form information at the same time as, but in a separate process, from the decennial census. Estimates from the C2SS were released earlier than the comparable long form data from the census. As we proceed through this decade, the ACS data will become a more important source for *County and City Extra* because the ongoing survey will enable us to provide intercensal estimates

with greater geographic and subject matter detail than has been available in the past.

Updated Information for the 2002 Edition

In addition to the 2000 Census and the C2SS, updated data in this edition include 2001 population estimates for states, counties, and metropolitan areas. Civilian labor force, crimes known to police, residential construction, and federal funds data have all been updated for cities, counties, metropolitan areas, and states. Vital statistics (births and deaths), income and poverty, personal income, educational expenditures, and employment and payroll have been updated for states, counties, and metropolitan areas.

Although some of the state data are also included in Table B (States and Counties), the separate state data table offers several important features:

- Additional data not available at the county level can be found. Examples include population projections, health insurance coverage, number of immigrants, personal tax payments, information on health service firms not subject to federal tax, and exports by state of origin.

- Additional detail that exceeds the space limitations for counties can be found for states. Examples are age of householder, the more detailed information on employment in retail trade and services, and the expanded presentation of federal grants and payments to individuals by type.

- State totals can be found more quickly and compared more readily.

In addition to the new data and special features, users will find in this volume not only a careful selection of the most frequently used data from the 1990 and 2000 Census, but also the latest available data for population estimates, education, vital statistics, employment and unemployment, production by industry, health resources, crime, the distribution of federal funds, city government finances, weather statistics, and many other topics.

Subjects Covered and Volume Organization

Immediately following this introduction (pages **xiii–xv**) is a chart summarizing the **subjects covered** in each of the five tables in this volume. Pages **xvii–xxxiv** show the complete column headings for each table.

The **colored map portfolio** begins on page **7**. **Rankings** of counties, cities, metropolitan areas, and congressional districts on a number of key demographic and economic characteristics begin on page **23**.

The main body of this volume contains five basic tables. **Table A**, which begins on page **79**, contains data for states. **Table B**, beginning on page **107**, contains information for states and counties, while **Table C**, beginning on page **809**, contains similar information for metropolitan areas. The county geography codes include *county typology* or *Beale* codes from the Economic Research Service of the Department of Agriculture. These codes characterize counties by size of the largest place as well as other criteria for nonmetropolitan counties (see Appendix A for the definition of each code). Statistics for cities with a 2000 population of 25,000 or more can be found in **Table D**, which begins on page **895**. **Table E**, beginning on page **1117**, contains data for congressional districts of the 107th Congress. A contents page preceding each of tables B through E lists the page number where the data for a given geographic area begin. Counties and cities are listed alphabetically by state. Metropolitan areas are listed alphabetically, except that Primary Metropolitan Statistical Areas (PMSAs) are listed alphabetically within the Consolidated Metropolitan Statistical Area (CMSA) of which they are components. Congressional districts are listed in numeric order within state.

The Appendices include definitions of geographic concepts (**Appendix A**), sources and definitions of each data item included in this volume (**Appendix F**), a listing of metropolitan areas with their component counties delineated as of June 1999 listed alphabetically (**Appendix B**) and within state (**Appendix C**), a list of cities by county (**Appendix E**), and maps showing counties, metropolitan areas and selected places within each state (**Appendix D**).

Symbols and Terms

The following symbols are used in this volume:

D   Indicates that a figure has been withheld to avoid disclosure of information pertaining to a specific organization or individual, or because it does not meet statistical standards for publication.

NA   Indicates that data are not available.

X   Indicates that data are not applicable or meaningful for this geographic unit.

Figures that are less than half of the unit of measure shown appear in this volume as zero.

Sources

The great majority of the data in this volume have been obtained from federal government sources. A few items are obtained from private sources that are widely recognized as reliable basic sources of those particular data items. Complete source notes for each item are included in **Appendix F**, beginning on page F-1. Data included in this volume meet the publication standards established by the Census Bureau and the other federal statistical agencies from which they were obtained. Every effort has been made to select data that are accurate, meaningful and useful. All data from censuses, surveys, and administrative records are subject to error arising from factors such as sampling variability, reporting errors, incomplete coverage, nonresponse, imputations, and processing error. Responsibility of the editors and publisher of this volume is limited to reasonable care in the reproduction and presentation of data obtained from sources believed to be reliable.

SUBJECTS COVERED, BY TYPE OF AREA

State data begin on page 79
County data begin on page 107
Metropolitan area data begin on page 809
City data begin on page 895
Congressional District data begin on page 1117

Subject	Column Number				
	Table A: States	Table B: States and Counties	Table C: Metropolitan Areas	Table D: Cities	Table E: Congressional Districts
Land area in 2000	1	1	1	1	
Land area in 1990					1
Population:					
Total in 1980	29			7	
Total in 1990	30	21	21	5	
Total in 2001	2	20	20		
Total in 2000	3	2	2	2	2
Rank in 2000	4	3	3	3	
Per Square Kilometer	5	4	4	4	3
Race and Hispanic Origin in 2000	6-10	5-9	5-9	9-15	4-10
Race and Hispanic Origin in 1990	38-43				
Immigrants in 2000	28				
Foreign born population in 1990	44				
Percent U.S. citizen					11
Age Distribution 2000	11-19	10-18	10-18	16-24	12-20
Age Distribution 1990	45-53				
Percent Female	20,54	19	19	25	21
Population Change 1990-2000	33	22	22	6	
Population Change 2000-2001	34	23	23		
Components of Population Change	35-37	24-26	24-26		
Projections to 2025	32				
Households:					
Number in 2000	21	27	27	26	22
Number in 1990	55				
Change	22,56	28	28	27	
Persons per Household	23,57	29	29	28	23
Age of Householder	24-27				
Female-family Householder	58	30	30	29	24
One-person	59	31	31	30	25
Vital Statistics:					
Births, birth rate	60-61	32-33	32-33		
Deaths, death rate	62,64	34,36	34,36		
Age adjusted death rate	65				
Infant deaths, infant death rate	63,66	35,37	35,37		
Health:					
Physicians	67-68	38-39	38-39		
Hospitals	69-71	40-42	40-42		
Persons in group quarters				31-34	26-28
Persons in nursing homes				33	27
Medicare enrollees	72	43	43		
Percent lacking health insurance	96				
Percent of children lacking health insurance	97				
Crime:					
Serious	73-74	44-45	44-45	35-36	
Violent	75	46	46	37	
Property	76	47	47	38	

SUBJECTS COVERED, BY TYPE OF AREA - Continued

State data begin on page 79
County data begin on page 107
Metropolitan area data begin on page 809
City data begin on page 895
Congressional District data begin on page 1117

Subject	Column Number				
	Table A: States	Table B: States and Counties	Table C: Metropolitan Areas	Table D: Cities	Table E: Congressional Districts
Education:					
Enrollment	77-78	48-49	48-49	39-40	29-30
Years of School/Degrees completed	79-82	50-51	50-51	41-42	31-32
Local Government Expenditures	83-84	52-53	52-53		
Income and Personal Taxes					
Money Income, Per capita and Household	85-90,98-101	54-58,62-65	54-57,62-65	43-46	33-35
Poverty	91-94	59	59	47-49	36-37
Children in poverty	95	60-61	60-61		
Personal Income by type	102-110	66-74	66-74		
Personal tax payments	111				
Disposable personal income	112-113				
Earnings by Industry	114-122	75-83	75-83		
Gross state product	123				
Transfer Payments by type	105-110	69-74	69-74		
Social Security recipients	138-139	84-85	84-85		
Supplemental Security Income recipients	140	86	86		
Construction and Housing:					
Housing units in 2000	128,130			50,52-60	
Housing units in 1990	124,126	87,89	87,89		38-43
Percent change in housing units	125,129	88	88	51	
Percent owner-occupied	127,131	90	90	57	40
Median Value, Owner costs	132-134	91-93	91-93		41-43
Median Gross Rent, rent/income ratio	135-136	94-95	94-95		44-45
Substandard units	137	96	96		46
Value of New Residential Construction	279-282	133-134	133-134	69-71	
Labor Force and Employment:					
Civilian labor force, change in labor force	144-146	97-98	97-98	61-62	47
Unemployment, unemployment rate	147-148	99-100	99-100	63-64	48-49
Employment in selected occupations	141-143	101-103	101-103	65-67	50-52
Work disabled persons				68	53
Nonfarm establishments		104	104		
Earnings and employment in manufacturing	151-153				
Employment by Industry	149-150,154-159	105-110	105-110		
Payroll		111-112	111-112		
Agriculture:					
Farms	160-162	113-115	113-115		
Farm Operators	163	116	116		
Acreage	164-168	117-121	117-121		
Value of land and buildings	169-170	122-123	122-123		
Value of machinery and equipment	171	124	124		
Value of agricultural sales	172-177	125-130	125-130		
Land and Water:					
Land owned by the Federal Government	178	131	131		
Developed land	179				
Water use	180	132	132		

SUBJECTS COVERED, BY TYPE OF AREA - Continued

State data begin on page 79
County data begin on page 107
Metropolitan area data begin on page 809
City data begin on page 895
Congressional District data begin on page 1117

Subject	Column Number				
	Table A: States	Table B: States and Counties	Table C: Metropolitan Areas	Table D: Cities	Table E: Congressional Districts
Manufacturing:	181-190 269-270	151-154	151-154	88-91	
Construction:	191-194 267-268				
Wholesale Trade:	195-198 271-272	135-138	135-138	72-75	
Retail Trade:	199-206 273-274	139-142	139-142	76-79	
Transportation and Warehousing:	207-210				
Finance and Insurance:	211-214 275-276				
Real Estate and Rental and Leasing:	215-218 275-276	143-146	143-146	80-83	
Information:	219-226				
Utilities:	227-230				
Professional, Scientific, and Technical Services:	231-238 277-278	147-150	147-150	84-87	
Arts, Entertainment, and Recreation:	239-242			96-99	
Health Care and Social Assistance:	243-254 277-278	159-162	159-162	100-103	
Accommodation and Food Services:	255-259	155-158	155-158	92-95	
Other Services:	260-266 277-278	163-166	163-166	104-107	
Export of goods produced	283-285				
Federal Funds and Grants:					
Payments to Individuals	290-296	168-170	168-170	115-116	
Total, salaries and wages	286-287	167,171	167,171		
Procurement contract awards	288-289	172-173	172-173	108-109	
Grants by purpose	297-302	174-177	174-177	110-114	
Government Finances:					
Revenue	303-310	178-179	178-179	117-119	
Taxes	307-310	180-182	180-182	120-123	
Expenditures	311-319	183-189	183-189	124-136	
Debt outstanding	320-321	190-191	190-191	137-139	
Government Employment:					
Federal civilian and military	322-323	192-193	192-193		
State and/or local	324	194	194	140	
Election results	325-327	195-197	195-197		
Climate				141-147	

COLUMN HEADINGS FOR STATES

Table A. States — **Land Area and Population**

STATE code	STATE	Land area, 2000[1] (sq km)	Population 2001	Population and population characteristics, 2000											
				Population			Race (percent) (one race only)					Age (percent)			
				Total persons	Rank	Per square kilometer	White	Black	American Indian, Alaska Native	Asian and Pacific Islander	Hispanic[2] (percent)	Under 5 years	5 to 17 years	18 to 24 years	25 to 34 years
		1	2	3	4	5	6	7	8	9	10	11	12	13	14

1. Dry land or land partially or temporarily covered by water.   2. Hispanic persons may be of any race.

Table A. States — **Population and Households**

STATE	Population and population characteristics, 2000 (cont'd)						Households, 2000						
	Age (percent) (cont'd)									Age of householder (percent)			
	35 to 44 years	45 to 54 years	55 to 64 years	65 to 74 years	75 years and over	Percent female	Number	Percent change, 1990 to 2000	Persons per household	Under 25 years	25 to 44 years	45 to 64 years	65 years and over
	15	16	17	18	19	20	21	22	23	24	25	26	27

Table A. States — **Immigration and Population Change**

STATE	Immigrants admitted to legal status, 2000	Population, 1980–2025				Population change, 1990–2001				
		Census counts			Projection	Percent change		Components of change, 2000–2001		
		1980	1990	2000	2025	1990–2000	2000–2001	Births	Deaths	Net migration
	28	29	30	31	32	33	34	35	36	37

Table A. States — **Population Characteristics, 1990**

STATE	Population characteristics, 1990 (percent)																
	Race							Age									
	White	Black	American Indian, Eskimo, Aleut	Asian and Pacific Islander	Other race	His- panic[1]	Foreign born	Under 5 years	5 to 17 years	18 to 24 years	25 to 34 years	35 to 44 years	45 to 54 years	55 to 64 years	65 to 74 years	75 years and over	Female
	38	39	40	41	42	43	44	45	46	47	48	49	50	51	52	53	54

1. Hispanic persons may be of any race.

COLUMN HEADINGS FOR STATES

Table A. States — Households 1990, Vital Statistics, and Health Resources

STATE	Households, 1990					Births, 2000		Deaths, 1999					Physicians 2000	
				Percent				Number		Rate				
										Total				
	Number	Percent change, 1980–1990	Persons per house-hold	Female family house-holder[1]	One person	Total	Rate[2]	Total	Infant[3]	Crude[2]	Age-adjusted	Infant[4]	Number	Rate[5]
	55	56	57	58	59	60	61	62	63	64	65	66	67	68

1. No spouse present.   2. Per 1,000 resident population.   3. Deaths of infants under 1 year old.   4. Deaths of infants under 1 year old per 1,000 live births.
5. Per 100,000 resident population as of April 1 of the year shown.

Table A. States — Health Resources, Crime, and Education

STATE	Hospitals, 1998				Serious crimes known to police, 2000[2]				Elementary and secondary school enrollment, 1999–2000		Educational attainment[4] (percent)			
	---	---	---	---	---	---	---	---	---	---	---	---	---	---
		Beds			Total		Rate[3]				1990		2000	
	Total	Number	Rate[1]	Medicare enrollees 2000	Number	Rate[3]	Violent	Property	Total (1,000)	Percent private	High school graduate or more	Bach-elor's degree or more	High school graduate or more	Bach-elor's degree or more
	69	70	71	72	73	74	75	76	77	78	79	80	81	82

1. Per 100,000 resident population as of July 1 of the year shown.   2. Data for serious crimes have not been adjusted for underreporting; this may affect comparability between geographic areas
and over time.   3. Per 100,000 population estimated by the FBI.   4. Persons 25 years old and older.

Table A. States — Education Expenditures, Income, Poverty, and Health Insurance

STATE	Local government ex-penditures for education, 1999–2000		Money income							Percent below poverty level					Average percent lack-ing health insurance, 2000
	---	---	---	---	---	---	---	---	---	---	---	---	---	---
			1999							1999		2000			
				Households						Persons					
				Median											
	Total current expend-itures (mil dol)	Current expend-itures per student (dollars)	Per capita[1] (dollars)	Dollars	Percent change, 1989–1999 (constant 1999 dollars)	Percent with $100,000 or more	Median household income, 1998–2000 average (dollars)	Median income of family of four 2000	Total	Percent change in rate, 1989–1999	Families	Persons	Children under 18 years	Persons	Children under 18 years
	83	84	85	86	87	88	89	90	91	92	93	94	95	96	97

1. Based on population enumerated as of April 1, 2000.

Table A. States — Personal Income

STATE	Personal income, 2001												
	---	---	---	---	---	---	---	---	---	---	---	---	---
					Sources of personal income (mil dol)								
									Transfer payments				
										Government payments to individuals			
		Per capita[1]											
	Total (mil dol)	Percent change, 2000–2001	Dollars	Rank	Wages and salaries[2]	Propri-etors' income	Divi-dends, interest, and rent	Total	Total	Social Security	Medical payments	Income mainte-nance	Unemploy-ment insurance
	98	99	100	101	102	103	104	105	106	107	108	109	110

1. Based on the resident population estimated as of July 1 of the year shown.   2. Includes other labor income.

COLUMN HEADINGS FOR STATES

Table A. States — **Personal Income and Earnings**

STATE	Personal tax payments 2001 (mil dol)	Disposable personal income, 2001		Earnings, 2001									Gross state product (mil dol) 2000
				Total (mil dol)		Percent by selected industries							
							Goods-related[2]		Service-related and other[3]					
		Total (mil dol)	Per capita[1] (dollars)		Farm	Total	Manu-facturing	Total	Retail trade	Finance, insurance, and real estate	Services	Government	
	111	112	113	114	115	116	117	118	119	120	121	122	123

1. Based on the resident population estimated as of July 1 of the year shown. 2. Includes mining, construction, and manufacturing. 3. Includes private sector earnings in agricultural services, forestry, and fisheries; transportation and public utilities; wholesale and retail trade; finance, insurance, and real estate; and services.

Table A. States — **Housing**

STATE	Housing units, 1990				Housing units, 2000									
			Occupied units				Occupied units							
									Owner-occupied				Renter-occupied		
											Owner cost as a percent of income				
	Total	Percent change 1980–1990	Total	Percent owner-occupied	Total	Percent change 1990–2000	Total	Percent	Median value[1] (dollars)	With a mort-gage	Without a mort-gage	Median rent[2] (dollars)	Rent as a per-cent of income	Sub-standard units[3] (percent)
	124	125	126	127	128	129	130	131	132	133	134	135	136	137

1. Specified owner-occupied units. 2. Specified renter-occupied units. 3. Overcrowded or lacking complete plumbing facilities.

Table A. States — **Social Security, Employment, Unemployment, and Labor Force**

STATE	Social Security beneficiaries, December 2000		Supple-mental Security Income recipients, December 2000	Civilian employment and selected occupations, March 2000[2]			Civilian labor force annual average, 2001				
					Percent					Unemployed	
					Profes-sional, managerial, and technical	Precision production, craft, and repair		Percent change, 2000–2001	Employed		
	Number	Rate[1]		Total			Total			Total	Rate[3]
	138	139	140	141	142	143	144	145	146	147	148

1. Per 1,000 resident population estimated as of April 1 of the year shown. 2. Persons 16 years and older. 3. Percent of civilian labor force.

Table A. States — **Nonfarm Employment and Earnings**

STATE	Private nonfarm employment and earnings, 2001										
	Employment		Manufacturing			Employment (1,000)					
				Average earnings of production workers							
	Total (1,000)	Percent change, 2000–2001	Employ-ment (1,000)	Hourly	Weekly	Con-struction	Trans-portation and public utilities	Whole-sale trade	Retail trade	Finance, insurance, and real estate	Services
	149	150	151	152	153	154	155	156	157	158	159

COLUMN HEADINGS FOR STATES

Table A. States — **Agriculture**

STATE	Agriculture, 1997										
	Farms				Land in farms					Value of land and buildings	
		Percent with —		Farm operators whose principal occupation is farming (percent)	Acreage (1,000)	Percent change, 1992–1997	Acres			Average per farm ($1,000)	Average per acre (dollars)
	Number	Less than 50 acres	500 acres and over				Average size of farm	Total irrigated (1,000)	Total cropland (1,000)		
	160	161	162	163	164	165	166	167	168	169	170

Table A. States — **Agriculture, Land, and Water**

STATE	Agriculture, 1997 (cont'd)							Land, 1997		
	Value of machinery and equipment Average per farm ($1,000)	Value of products sold				Percent of farms with sales of —				Water consumption (mil gal per day) 1995
		Total (mil dol)	Average per farm (dollars)	Percent from —		$10,000 or more	$100,000 or more	Owned by Federal Government (percent)	Developed (percent)	
				Crops	Livestock and poultry products					
	171	172	173	174	175	176	177	178	179	180

Table A. States — **Manufactures and Construction**

STATE	Manufactures, 2000										Construction, 1997			
	All employees			Production workers				Value added by manu- facture (mil dol)	Value of ship- ments (mil dol)	Total capital expenditures (mil dol)	Estab- lishments	Value (mil dol)	Paid employees	Annual Payroll (mil dol)
	Number (1,000)	Percent change, 1999–2000	Annual Payroll (mil dol)	Number (1,000)	Work hours (millions)	Wages								
						Total (mil dol)	Average per worker (dollars)							
	181	182	183	184	185	186	187	188	189	190	191	192	193	194

Table A. States — **Wholesale and Retail Trade**

| STATE | Wholesale Trade, 1997 | | | | Retail Trade[1], 1997 | | | | | | | |
| | Number of Establish- ments | Number of Employees | Sales (mil dol) | Annual Payroll (mil dol) | Number of Establish- ments | Number of Employees | | | | | Sales (mil dol) | Annual Payroll (mil dol) |
						Total	Motor Vehicle and Parts Dealers	Food and Beverage Stores	Clothing and Clothing Accessory Stores	General Merchandise Stores		
	195	196	197	198	199	200	201	202	203	204	205	206

1. Establishments with payroll.

COLUMN HEADINGS FOR STATES

Table A. States — **Transportation and Warehousing, Finance and Insurance, and Real Estate**

STATE	Transportation and Warehousing, 1997				Finance and Insurance, 1997				Real Estate and Rental and Leasing, 1997			
	Number of Establishments	Number of Employees	Receipts (mil dol)	Annual Payroll (mil dol)	Number of Establishments	Number of Employees	Receipts (mil dol)	Annual Payroll (mil dol)	Number of Establishments	Number of Employees	Receipts (mil dol)	Annual Payroll (mil dol)
	207	208	209	210	211	212	213	214	215	216	217	218

Table A. States — **Information and Utilities**

STATE	Information, 1997								Utilities, 1997			
	Number of Establishments	Number of Employees					Receipts (mil dol)	Annual Payroll (mil dol)	Number of Establishments	Number of Employees	Receipts (mil dol)	Annual Payroll (mil dol)
		Total	Publishing	Motion Picture and Sound Recording	Broadcast and telecommunications	Information and Data Processing Services						
	219	220	221	222	223	224	225	226	227	228	229	230

Table A. States — **Professional, Scientific, and Technical Services, and Arts, Entertainment, and Recreation**

STATE	Professional, Scientific, and Technical Services,[1] 1997								Arts, Entertainment, and Recreation,[1] 1997			
	Number of Establishments	Number of Employees					Receipts (mil dol)	Annual Payroll (mil dol)	Number of Establishments	Number of Employees	Receipts (mil dol)	Annual Payroll (mil dol)
		Total	Legal Services	Accounting and Related Services	Architectural, Engineering, and Related Services	Computer Systems Design and Related Services						
	231	232	233	234	235	236	237	238	239	240	241	242

1. Firms subject to federal tax.

Table A. States — **Health Care and Social Assistance**

STATE	Health Care and Social Assistance, 1997											
	Subject to Federal Tax						Tax Exempt					
	Number of Establishments	Number of Employees			Receipts (mil dol)	Annual Payroll (mil dol)	Number of Establishments	Number of Employees			Receipts (mil dol)	Annual Payroll (mil dol)
		Total	Ambulatory Health Care Services	Hospitals				Total	Ambulatory Health Care Services	Hospitals		
	243	244	245	246	247	248	249	250	251	252	253	254

COLUMN HEADINGS FOR STATES

Table A. States — **Accommodation and Food Services and Other Services**

STATE	Accommodation and Food Services, 1997					Other Services, 1997						
		Number of Employees						Number of Employees				
	Number of Establishments	Total	Food Services and Drinking Places	Receipts (mil dol)	Annual Payroll (mil dol)	Number of Establishments[1]	Total[1]	Repair and Maintenance[1]	Personal and Laundry Services[1]	Religious, Civic, and Similar Services[2]	Receipts (mil dol)[1]	Annual Payroll (mil dol)[1]
	255	256	257	258	259	260	261	262	263	264	265	266

1. Firms subject to federal tax.

Table A. States — **Economic Census by SIC Code**

STATE	Construction		Manufacturing		Wholesale Trade		Retail Trade		Finance, Insurance, and Real Estate		Service industries, subject to federal tax	
	Paid Employees 1997	Percent change, 1992–1997	Paid Employees 1997	Percent change, 1992–1997	Paid Employees 1997	Percent change, 1992–1997	Paid Employees 1997	Percent change, 1992–1997	Paid Employees 1997	Percent change, 1992–1997	Paid Employees 1997	Percent change, 1992–1997
	267	268	269	270	271	272	273	274	275	276	277	278

Table A. States — **Residential Construction, Exports, and Federal Funds**

STATE	Value of residential construction authorized by building permits, 2001				Exports of goods by state of origin, 2000 (mil dol)			Federal funds and grants, fiscal 2001[1] (mil dol)			
										Procurement contract awards	
	New Construction ($1,000)	Number of housing units	Percent single family	Manufactured housing units put in place 2001 (1,000)	Total	Manufactured	Non-manufactured	Total	Salaries and wages	Defense	Other
	279	280	281	282	283	284	285	286	287	288	289

1. October 1, 2000–September 30, 2001.

Table A. States — **Federal Funds**

STATE	Federal funds and grants, fiscal 2001[1] (mil dol) (cont'd)												
	Direct payments for individuals							Grants					
	Total	Social Security and government retirement	Medicare	Food stamps	Supplemental Security Income	Educational assistance	Housing assistance	Total[2]	Medicaid and other health-related	Nutrition and family welfare	Education	Housing and community development	Energy and environment
	290	291	292	293	294	295	296	297	298	299	300	301	302

1. October 1, 1998 to September 30, 1999.   2. Includes program categories not shown separately.

COLUMN HEADINGS FOR STATES

Table A. States — **State Government Finances**

STATE	State government finances, fiscal 2000											
	General revenue (mil dol)								General expenditures (mil dol)			
	From federal government			From own sources							Direct general expenditures	
					Taxes		Taxes per capita[1] (dollars)					
	Total	Total	Per capita[1] (dollars)	Total	Total	Sales and gross receipts	Total	Sales and gross receipts	Total	To local govern- ments	Total	Per capita[1] (dollars)
	303	304	305	306	307	308	309	310	311	312	313	314

1. Based on the resident population as of April 1 of the year shown.

Table A. States — **State Government Finances, Government Employment, and Elections**

STATE	State government finances, fiscal 2000 (cont'd)							Government employment, 2000			Presidential election, 2000[2] (percent of vote cast)		
	General expenditures (mil dol) (cont'd)					Debt outstanding							
	By selected function (mil dol)												
	Education	Health and hospitals	Highways	Public safety	Public welfare	Total (mil dol)	Per capita[1]	Federal civilian	Federal military	State and local	Demo- cratic	Repub- lican	All other
	315	316	317	318	319	320	321	322	323	324	325	326	327

1. Based on the resident population as of April 1 of the year shown.   2. Data subject to copyright.

COLUMN HEADINGS FOR STATES AND COUNTIES

Table B. States and Counties — **Land Area and Population**

STATE/ County code	MSA/ PMSA/ NECMA code[1]	County Type[2]	STATE County	Land area,[3] (sq km) 2000	Population and population characteristics, 2000													
								Race alone or in combination (percent)					Age (percent)					
					Total persons	Rank	Per square kilometer	White	Black	Am. Indian, Alaska Native	Asian and Pacific Islander	Percent Hispanic[4]	Under 5 years	5 to 17 years	18 to 24 years	25 to 34 years	35 to 44 years	45 to 54 years
				1	2	3	4	5	6	7	8	9	10	11	12	13	14	15

1. MSA = Metropolitan Statistical Area. PMSA = Primary MSA. NECMA = New England County Metropolitan Area. See Appendix A for explanation of these concepts. See Appendix B for list of metropolitan areas identified by type, with component counties.   2. County typology code from the Economic Research Service of USDA. See Appendix A for definition.   3. Dry land or land partially or temporarily covered by water.   4. Hispanic persons may be of any race.

Table B. States and Counties — **Population and Households**

STATE County	Population, 2000 (cont'd)				Population — change and components of change, 1990–2001							Households, 2000				
	Age (percent) (cont'd)				Total persons		Percent change		Components of change, 2000–2001						Percent		
	55 to 64 years	65 to 74 years	75 years and over	Percent female	2001	1990	1990– 2000	2000– 2001	Births	Deaths	Net migration	Number	Percent change, 1990– 2000	Persons per house- hold	Female family house- holder[1]	One person
	16	17	18	19	20	21	22	23	24	25	26	27	28	29	30	31

1. No spouse present.

COLUMN HEADINGS FOR STATES AND COUNTIES

Table B. States and Counties — Vital Statistics, Health Resources, and Crime

STATE County	Births, average 1997–1999		Deaths, average 1997–1999				Physicians,[4] 2000		Hospitals,[4] 1998			Medicare enrollees 2000	Serious crimes known to police, 2000[6]	
			Number		Rate					Beds			Total	
	Total	Rate[1]	Total	Infant[2]	Total[1]	Infant[3]	Number	Rate[5]	Number	Number	Rate[5]		Number	Rate[7]
	32	33	34	35	36	37	38	39	40	41	42	43	44	45

1. Per 1,000 estimated resident population, average 1997–1999.   2. Deaths of infants under 1 year old.   3. Deaths of infants under 1 year old per 1,000 live births.   4. Data subject to copyright.   5. Per 100,000 resident population as of July 1 of the year shown.   6. Data for serious crimes have not been adjusted for underreporting; this may affect comparability between geographic areas and over time.   7. Per 100,000 population estimated by the FBI.

Table B. States and Counties — Crime, Education, Money Income, and Poverty

STATE County	Serious crimes known to police, 2000[1] (cont'd)		Education						Money income				Income and poverty, 1998		
	Rate[2]		School enrollment and attainment, 1990				Local government expenditures, fiscal 1999[5]		1989				Percent below poverty level		
			Enrollment[3]		Attainment[4] (percent)					Households					
										Median					
	Violent	Property	Total	Percent private	High school graduate or more	Bachelor's degree or more	Total current expenditures (mil dol)	Current expenditures per student (dollars)	Per capita[6] (dollars)	Dollars	Percent change, 1979–1989 (constant 1989 dollars)	Percent with $100,000 or more	Median household income	All persons	Persons under 18	Persons 5–17 in families
	46	47	48	49	50	51	52	53	54	55	56	57	58	59	60	61

1. Data for serious crimes have not been adjusted for underreporting; this may affect comparability between geographic areas and over time.   2. Per 100,000 population estimated by the FBI.   3. All persons 3 years old and over enrolled in nursery school through college.   4. Persons 25 years old and over.   5. Elementary and secondary education expenditures, local government fiscal years ending between July 1, 1998 and June 30, 1999.   6. Based on population enumerated as of April 1, 1990.

Table B. States and Counties — Personal Income

STATE County	Personal income, 1999													
			Per capita[1]							Transfer payments				
											Government payments to individuals			
	Total (mil dol)	Percent change, 1998–1999	Dollars	Rank	Wages and salaries[2] (mil dol)	Proprietor's income (mil dol)	Dividends, interest, and rent (mil dol)	Total (mil dol)	Total (mil dol)	Social Security (mil dol)	Medical payments (mil dol)	Income maintenance (mil dol)	Unemployment insurance (mil dol)
	62	63	64	65	66	67	68	69	70	71	72	73	74

1. Based on the resident population estimated as of July 1 of the year shown.   2. Includes other labor income.

Table B. States and Counties — Earnings, Social Security, and Housing

STATE County	Earnings, 1999									Social Security beneficiaries, December 2000		Supplemental Security Income recipients, December 2000	Housing units, 1990	
			Percent by selected industries											
			Goods-related[1]		Service-related and other[2]									
	Total (mil dol)	Farm	Total	Manufacturing	Total	Retail trade	Finance, insurance, and real estate	Services	Government	Number	Rate[3]		Total	Percent change, 1980–1990
	75	76	77	78	79	80	81	82	83	84	85	86	87	88

1. Covers mining, construction, and manufacturing.   2. Covers private sector earnings in agricultural services, forestry, and fisheries; transportation and public utilities; wholesale trade; retail trade; finance, insurance, and real estate; and services.   3. Per 1,000 resident population estimated as of July 1 of the year shown.

COLUMN HEADINGS FOR STATES AND COUNTIES

Table B. States and Counties — Housing, Labor Force, and Employment

STATE County	Housing units, 1990 (cont'd)								Civilian labor force, 2001				Civilian employment, 1990[5]		
	Occupied units										Unemployment			Percent	
	Owner-occupied					Renter-occupied									
				Owner cost as a percent of income											
	Total	Percent	Median value[1]	With a mortgage	Without a mortgage	Median rent[2]	Rent as percent of income	Substandard units[3] (percent)	Total	Percent change, 2000–2001	Total	Rate[4]	Total	Professional, managerial, and technical	Precision production, craft, and repair
	89	90	91	92	93	94	95	96	97	98	99	100	101	102	103

1. Specified owner-occupied units. 2. Specified renter-occupied units. 3. Overcrowded or lacking complete plumbing facilities. 4. Percent of civilian labor force. 5. Persons 16 years and older.

Table B. States and Counties — Nonfarm Employment and Agriculture

STATE County	Private nonfarm establishments, employment and payroll, 1999										Agriculture, 1997			Farm operators
		Employment						Annual payroll		Farms			
											Percent with—		
	Number of establishments	Total	Health Care and Social Assistance	Manufacturing	Retail trade	Finance and Insurance	Professional Scientific and Technical Services	Total (mil dol)	Average per employee (dollars)	Number	Less than 50 acres	500 acres and over	Whose principal occupation is farming (percent)
	104	105	106	107	108	109	110	111	112	113	114	115	116

Table B. States and Counties — Agriculture, Land, and Water

STATE County	Agriculture, 1997 (cont'd)														
	Land in farms					Value of land and buildings			Value of products sold				Percent of farms with sales of —		
			Acres								Percent from —				
	Acreage (1,000)	Percent change, 1992–1997	Average size of farm	Total irrigated (1,000)	Total cropland (1,000)	Average per farm ($1,000)	Average per acre (dollars)	Value of machinery and equipment average per farm ($1,000)	Total (mil dol)	Average per farm (dollars)	Crops	Livestock and poultry products	$10,000 or more	$100,000 or more	Percent of land owned by fed. gov. 1997	Water consumption 1995 (mil gal/ day)
	117	118	119	120	121	122	123	124	125	126	127	128	129	130	131	132

Table B. States and Counties — Residential Construction, Wholesale and Retail Trade, and Real Estate

STATE County	Value of Residential Construction Authorized by Building Permits, 2000		Wholesale Trade, 1997				Retail Trade[1], 1997				Real Estate and Rental and Leasing, 1997			
	New Construction ($1,000)	Number of Housing Units	Number of Establishments	Number of Employees	Sales (mil dol)	Annual Payroll (mil dol)	Number of Establishments	Number of Employees	Sales (mil dol)	Annual Payroll (mil dol)	Number of Establishments	Number of Employees	Receipts (mil dol)	Annual Payroll (mil dol)
	133	134	135	136	137	138	139	140	141	142	143	144	145	146

1. Establishments with payroll.

COLUMN HEADINGS FOR STATES AND COUNTIES

Table B. States and Counties — **Professional, Manufacturing, and Accommodation and Foodservices**

STATE County	Professional, Scientific, and Technical Services[1], 1997				Manufacturing, 1997				Accommodation and Foodservices, 1997			
	Number of Establish-ments	Number of Employees	Receipts (mil dol)	Annual Payroll (mil dol)	Number of Establish-ments	Number of Employees	Receipts (mil dol)	Annual Payroll (mil dol)	Number of Establish-ments	Number of Employees	Sales (mil dol)	Annual Payroll (mil dol)
	147	148	149	150	151	152	153	154	155	156	157	158

1. Firms subject to federal tax.

Table B. States and Counties — **Health and Other Services and Federal Funds**

STATE County	Health Care and Social Assistance[1], 1997				Other Services[1], 1997				Federal funds and grants, fiscal 2001[2]			
										Expenditures (mil dol)		
											Direct payments for individuals[3]	
	Number of Establish-ments	Number of Employees	Receipts (mil dol)	Annual Payroll (mil dol)	Number of Establish-ments	Number of Employees	Receipts (mil dol)	Annual Payroll (mil dol)	Total	Social Security and government retirement	Medicare	Food stamps and Supplemental Security Income
	159	160	161	162	163	164	165	166	167	168	169	170

1. Firms subject to federal tax. 2. October 1, 2000 to September 30, 2001. 3. State totals may include programs not allocated by county.

Table B. States and Counties — **Federal Funds and Local Government Finances**

STATE County	Federal funds and grants, fiscal 2001[1] (cont'd)							Local government finances, 1997				
	Expenditures (mil dol) (cont'd)							General revenue				
	Procurement contract awards			Grants[2]							Taxes	
											Per capita[3] (dollars)	
	Salaries and wages	Defense	Other	Medicaid and other health-related	Nutrition and family welfare	Education	Other	Total (mil dol)	Intergovern-mental (mil dol)	Total (mil dol)	Total	Property
	171	172	173	174	175	176	177	178	179	180	181	182

1. October 1, 2000 to September 30, 2001. 2. State totals may include programs not allocated by county. 3. Based on the resident population estimated as of July 1 of the year shown.

Table B. States and Counties — **Local Government Finances, Government Employment, and Elections**

STATE County	Local government finances, 1997 (cont'd)								Debt outstanding		Government employment, 1999			Presidential election, 2000[2]		
	Direct general expenditure													Percent of vote cast —		
			Percent of total for —													
	Total (mil dol)	Per capita[1] (dollars)	Educa-tion	Health and hospitals	Police protec-tion	Public welfare	High-ways		Total (mil dol)	Per capita[1] (dollars)	Federal civilian	Federal military	State and local	Demo-cratic	Republi-can	All other
	183	184	185	186	187	188	189		190	191	192	193	194	195	196	197

1. Based on the resident population estimated as of July 1 of the year shown. 2. Data subject to copyright.

COLUMN HEADINGS FOR METROPOLITAN AREAS

Table C. Metropolitan Areas — **Land Area and Population**

CMSA/ MSA/ PMSA/ NECMA code[1]	Area Name	Land area,[2] (sq km) 2000	Population and population characteristics, 2000												
						Race alone or in combination (percent)					Age (percent)					
			Total persons	Rank	Per square kilometer	White	Black	Am. Indian, Alaska Native	Asian and Pacific Islander	Percent Hispanic[3]	Under 5 years	5 to 17 years	18 to 24 years	25 to 34 years	35 to 44 years	45 to 54 years
		1	2	3	4	5	6	7	8	9	10	11	12	13	14	15

1. MSA = Metropolitan Statistical Area. CMSA = Consolidated MSA. PMSA = Primary MSA. NECMA = New England County Metropolitan Area. See Appendix A for explanation of these concepts. See Appendix B for list of metropolitan areas identified by type, with component counties. 2. Dry land or land partially or temporarily covered by water. 3. Hispanic persons may be of any race.

Table C. Metropolitan Areas — **Population and Households**

Area Name	Population, 2000 (cont'd)				Population — change and components of change, 1990–2001								Households, 2000				
	Age (percent) (cont'd)				Total persons		Percent change		Components of change, 2000–2001							Percent	
	55 to 64 years	65 to 74 years	75 years and over	Percent female	2001	1990	1990–2000	2000–2001	Births	Deaths	Net migration	Number	Percent change, 1990–2000	Persons per house-hold	Female family house-holder[1]	One person
	16	17	18	19	20	21	22	23	24	25	26	27	28	29	30	31

1. No spouse present.

Table C. Metropolitan Areas — **Vital Statistics, Health Resources, and Crime**

Area Name	Births, average 1997–1999		Deaths, average 1997–1999				Physicians,[4] 1998		Hospitals,[4] 1998			Medicare enrollees 1999	Serious crimes known to police, 2000[6]	
			Number		Rate					Beds			Total	
	Total	Rate[1]	Total	Infant[2]	Total[1]	Infant[3]	Number	Rate[5]	Number	Number	Rate[5]		Number	Rate[7]
	32	33	34	35	36	37	38	39	40	41	42	43	44	45

1. Per 1,000 estimated resident population, average 1997–1999. 2. Deaths of infants under 1 year old. 3. Deaths of infants under 1 year old per 1,000 live births. 4. Data subject to copyright. 5. Per 100,000 resident population as of July 1 of the year shown. 6. Data for serious crimes have not been adjusted for underreporting; this may affect comparability between geographic areas and over time. 7. Per 100,000 population estimated by the FBI.

Table C. Metropolitan Areas — **Crime, Education, Money Income, and Poverty**

Area Name	Serious crimes known to police, 2000[1] (cont'd)		Education							Money income				Income and poverty, 1998		
	Rate[2]		School enrollment and attainment, 1990				Local government expenditures, fiscal 1999[5]			1989				Percent below poverty level		
			Enrollment[3]		Attainment[4] (percent)						Households					
												Median				
	Violent	Property	Total	Percent private	High school grad-uate or more	Bach-elor's degree or more	Total current expendi-tures (mil dol)	Current expendi-tures per student (dollars)	Per capita[6] (dollars)	Dollars	Percent change, 1979–1989 (constant 1989 dollars)	Percent with $100,000 or more	Median house-hold income	All persons	Persons under 18	Persons 5–17 in families
	46	47	48	49	50	51	52	53	54	55	56	57	58	59	60	61

1. Data for serious crimes have not been adjusted for underreporting; this may affect comparability between geographic areas and over time. 2. Per 100,000 population estimated by the FBI. 3. All persons 3 years old and over enrolled in nursery school through college. 4. Persons 25 years old and over. 5. Elementary and secondary education expenditures, local government fiscal years ending between July 1, 1998 and June 30, 1999. 6. Based on population enumerated as of April 1, 1990.

COLUMN HEADINGS FOR METROPOLITAN AREAS

Table C. Metropolitan Areas — **Personal Income**

Area Name	Personal income, 1999												
			Per capita[1]						Transfer payments				
										Government payments to individuals			
	Total (mil dol)	Percent change, 1998–1999	Dollars	Rank	Wages and salaries[2] (mil dol)	Proprietor's income (mil dol)	Dividends, interest, and rent (mil dol)	Total (mil dol)	Total (mil dol)	Social Security (mil dol)	Medical payments (mil dol)	Income mainte-nance (mil dol)	Unemploy-ment insurance (mil dol)
	62	63	64	65	66	67	68	69	70	71	72	73	74

1. Based on the resident population estimated as of July 1 of the year shown.　2. Includes other labor income.

Table C. Metropolitan Areas — **Earnings, Social Security, and Housing**

Area Name	Earnings, 1999									Social Security bene-ficiaries, December 2000			Housing units, 1990	
			Percent by selected industries											
			Goods-related[1]		Service-related and other[2]									
	Total (mil dol)	Farm	Total	Manu-facturing	Total	Retail trade	Finance, insur-ance, and real estate	Services	Govern-ment	Number	Rate[3]	Supple-mental Security Income recipients, December 2000	Total	Percent change, 1980–1990
	75	76	77	78	79	80	81	82	83	84	85	86	87	88

1. Covers mining, construction, and manufacturing.　2. Covers private sector earnings in agricultural services, forestry, and fisheries; transportation and public utilities; wholesale trade; retail trade; finance, insurance, and real estate; and services.　3. Per 1,000 resident population estimated as of July 1 of the year shown.

Table C. Metropolitan Areas — **Housing, Labor Force, and Employment**

Area Name	Housing units, 1990 (cont'd)								Civilian labor force, 2001				Civilian employment, 1990[5]		
			Occupied units								Unemployment			Percent	
			Owner-occupied			Renter-occupied									
				Owner cost as a percent of income											
	Total	Percent	Median value[1]	With a mort-gage	Without a mort-gage	Median rent[2]	Rent as per-cent of income	Sub-stand-ard units[3] (percent)	Total	Percent change, 2000–2001	Total	Rate[4]	Total	Professional, managerial, and technical	Precision production, craft, and repair
	89	90	91	92	93	94	95	96	97	98	99	100	101	102	103

1. Specified owner-occupied units.　2. Specified renter-occupied units.　3. Overcrowded or lacking complete plumbing facilities.　4. Percent of civilian labor force.　5. Persons 16 years and older.

Table C. Metropolitan Areas — **Nonfarm Employment and Agriculture**

Area Name	Private nonfarm establishments, employment and payroll, 1999									Agriculture, 1997			
		Employment						Annual payroll		Farms			Farm operators
											Percent with—		
	Number of establish-ments	Total	Health Care and Social Assistance	Manufac-turing	Retail trade	Finance and Insurance	Professional Scientific and Technical Services	Total (mil dol)	Average per employee (dollars)	Number	Less than 50 acres	500 acres and over	Whose principal occu-pation is farming (percent)
	104	105	106	107	108	109	110	111	112	113	114	115	116

COLUMN HEADINGS FOR METROPOLITAN AREAS

Table C. Metropolitan Areas — Agriculture, Land, and Water

Area Name	Agriculture, 1997 (cont'd)															
	Land in farms					Value of land and buildings		Value of machinery and equipment Average per farm ($1,000)	Value of products sold				Percent of farms with sales of —		Percent of land owned by Fed. Gov. 1997	Water consumption 1995 (mil gal/day)
			Acres								Percent from —					
	Acreage (1,000)	Percent change, 1992–1997	Average size of farm	Total irrigated (1,000)	Total cropland (1,000)	Average per farm ($1,000)	Average per acre (dollars)		Total (mil dol)	Average per farm (dollars)	Crops	Live-stock and poultry products	$10,000 or more	$100,000 or more		
	117	118	119	120	121	122	123	124	125	126	127	128	129	130	131	132

Table C. Metropolitan Areas — Residential Construction, Wholesale and Retail Trade, and Real Estate

Area Name	Value of Residential Construction Authorized by Building Permits, 2000		Wholesale Trade, 1997				Retail Trade[1], 1997				Real Estate and Rental and Leasing, 1997			
	New Construction ($1,000)	Number of Housing Units	Number of Establishments	Number of Employees	Sales (mil dol)	Annual Payroll (mil dol)	Number of Establishments	Number of Employees	Sales (mil dol)	Annual Payroll (mil dol)	Number of Establishments	Number of Employees	Receipts (mil dol)	Annual Payroll (mil dol)
	133	134	135	136	137	138	139	140	141	142	143	144	145	146

1. Establishments with payroll.

Table C. Metropolitan Areas — Professional, Manufacturing, Accommodation and Foodservices, Finance and Insurance

Area Name	Professional, Scientific, and Technical Services[1], 1997				Manufacturing, 1997				Accommodation and Foodservices, 1997			
	Number of Establishments	Number of Employees	Sales (mil dol)	Annual Payroll (mil dol)	Number of Establishments	Number of Employees	Sales (mil dol)	Annual Payroll (mil dol)	Number of Establishments	Number of Employees	Sales (mil dol)	Annual Payroll (mil dol)
	147	148	149	150	151	152	153	154	155	156	157	158

1. Firms subject to federal tax.

Table C. Metropolitan Areas — Health and Other Services and Federal Funds

Area Name	Health Care and Social Assistance[1], 1997				Other Services[1], 1997				Federal funds and grants, fiscal 2001[2]			
									Expenditures (mil dol)			
										Direct payments for individuals		
	Number of Establishments	Number of Employees	Receipts (mil dol)	Annual Payroll (mil dol)	Number of Establishments	Number of Employees	Receipts (mil dol)	Annual Payroll (mil dol)	Total	Social Security and government retirement	Medicare	Food stamps and Supplemental Security Income
	159	160	161	162	163	164	165	166	167	168	169	170

1. Firms subject to federal tax.   2. October 1, 1998 to September 30, 1999.

COLUMN HEADINGS FOR METROPOLITAN AREAS

Table C. Metropolitan Areas — Federal Funds and Local Government Finances

Area Name	Federal funds and grants, fiscal 2001[1] (cont'd)							Local government finances, 1997				
	Expenditures (mil dol) (cont'd)							General revenue				
	Procurement contract awards		Grants[2]							Taxes		
											Per capita[3] (dollars)	
	Salaries and wages	Defense	Other	Medicaid and other health-related	Nutrition and family welfare	Education	Other	Total (mil dol)	Intergovern-mental (mil dol)	Total (mil dol)	Total	Property
	171	172	173	174	175	176	177	178	179	180	181	182

1. October 1, 1998 to September 30, 1999. 2. State totals may include programs not allocated by county. 3. Based on the resident population estimated as of July 1 of the year shown.

Table C. Metropolitan Areas — Local Government Finances, Government Employment, and Elections

Area Name	Local government finances, 1997 (cont'd)									Government employment, 1999			Presidential election, 2000[2]		
	Direct general expenditure							Debt outstanding					Percent of vote cast —		
			Percent of total for —												
	Total (mil dol)	Per capita[1] (dollars)	Educa-tion	Health and hospitals	Police protec-tion	Public welfare	High-ways	Total (mil dol)	Per capita[1] (dollars)	Federal civilian	Federal military	State and local	Demo-cratic	Republi-can	All other
	183	184	185	186	187	188	189	190	191	192	193	194	195	196	197

1. Based on the resident population estimated as of July 1 of the year shown. 2. Data subject to copyright.

COLUMN HEADINGS FOR CITIES

Table D. Cities — Land Area and Population

STATE Place code	City	Land area, 2000[1] (sq km)	Population, 2000			Population				Population characteristics, 2000							
										Percent							
													Race (alone or in combination)				
			Total persons	Rank	Per square kilo-meter	Total persons 1990	Percent change 1990–2000	Total persons 1980	Percent change 1980–1990	White	Black	Am. Indian, Alaska Native	Asian and Pacific Islander	Other race	His-panic[2]	Non-His-panic White
		1	2	3	4	5	6	7	8	9	10	11	12	13	14	15

1. Dry land or land partially or temporarily covered by water. 2. Hispanic persons may be of any race.

Table D. Cities — Population and Households

City	Population characteristics, 2000 (cont'd)										Households, 2000			
	Age of population (percent)												Percent	
	Under 5 years	5 to 17 years	18 to 24 years	25 to 34 years	35 to 44 years	45 to 54 years	55 to 64 years	65 to 74 years	75 years and over	Percent female	Number	Percent change, 1990–2000	Persons per house-hold	Female family house-holder[1]	One-person
	16	17	18	19	20	21	22	23	24	25	26	27	28	29	30

1. No spouse present.

COLUMN HEADINGS FOR CITIES

Table D. Cities — Group Quarters, Crime, Education, and Income

City	Persons in group quarters, 2000				Serious crimes known to police, 2000[2]				Education, 1990				Money income, 1989		
		Institutional			Total		Rate[3]		School enrollment		Attainment[4] (percent)			Households	
															Median
	Total	Total	Persons in nursing homes	Non-Institu- tional[1]	Number	Rate[3]	Violent	Property	Public	Private	High school grad- uate or more	Bach- elor's degree or more	Per capita (dollars)[5]	Dollars	Percent change, 1979– 1989 (constant 1989 dollars)
	31	32	33	34	35	36	37	38	39	40	41	42	43	44	45

1. Persons in emergency shelters and persons visible in street locations. areas and over time. 3. Per 100,000 population estimated by the FBI. 2. Data for serious crimes have not been adjusted for underreporting. This may affect comparability between geographic 4. Persons 25 years old and older. 5. Based on population enumerated as of April 1, 1990.

Table D. Cities — Income, Poverty, and Housing

City	Money income, 1989 (cont'd)					Housing units, 2000									
	House- holds (cont'd)	Percent below poverty, 1989					Vacant units					Occupied units			
		Persons		Fam- ilies											
	Percent with $100,000 or more	Total	Percent change in rate, 1979– 1989	Total	Total	Percent change, 1990– 2000	Vacant units for sale or rent[1]	For seasonal use (percent)	Home owner vacancy rate	Renter vacancy rate	Total	Percent owner occu- pied	Percent renter occu- pied	Average size owner occu- pied	Average size renter occu- pied
	46	47	48	49	50	51	52	53	54	55	56	57	58	59	60

1. Includes units rented or sold but not occupied. 2. Specified owner-occupied units. 3. Specified renter-occupied units. 4. Overcrowded or lacking complete plumbing facilities.

Table D. Cities — Labor Force, Employment, Disability, and Construction

City	Civilian labor force, 2001				Civilian employment, 1990[2]			Disability 1990	Value of residential construction authorized by building permits, 2000		
		Unemployment				Percent					
	Total	Percent change, 2000– 2001	Total	Rate[1]	Total	Professional, managerial, and technical	Precision production, craft, and repair	Work disabled persons[3] (percent)	New construction ($1,000)	Number of housing units	Percent single family
	61	62	63	64	65	66	67	68	69	70	71

1. Percent of civilian labor force. 2. Persons 16 years and older. 3. Persons 16 to 64 years old.

Table D. Cities — Wholesale Trade, Retail Trade, and Real Estate

City	Wholesale Trade, 1997				Retail Trade[1], 1997				Real Estate and Rental and Leasing, 1997			
	Number of Establish- ments	Number of Employees	Sales (mil dol)	Annual Payroll (mil dol)	Number of Establish- ments	Number of Employees	Sales (mil dol)	Annual Payroll (mil dol)	Number of Establish- ments	Number of Employees	Receipts (mil dol)	Annual Payroll (mil dol)
	72	73	74	75	76	77	78	79	80	81	82	83

1. Establishments with payroll.

COLUMN HEADINGS FOR CITIES

Table D. Cities — **Professional Services, Manufacturing, Accommodation and Foodservices**

City	Professional, Scientific, and Technical Services, 1997[1]				Manufacturing, 1997				Accommodation and Foodservices, 1997			
	Number of Establishments	Number of Employees	Receipts (mil dol)	Annual Payroll (mil dol)	Number of Establishments	Number of Employees	Receipts (mil dol)	Annual Payroll (mil dol)	Number of Establishments	Number of Employees	Sales (mil dol)	Annual Payroll (mil dol)
	84	85	86	87	88	89	90	91	92	93	94	95

1. Firms subject to federal tax.

Table D. Cities — **Entertainment, Health Care, and Other Services**

City	Arts, Entertainment, and Recreation[1], 1997				Health Care and Social Assistance[1], 1997				Other Services[1], 1997			
	Number of Establishments	Number of Employees	Receipts (mil dol)	Annual Payroll (mil dol)	Number of Establishments	Number of Employees	Receipts (mil dol)	Annual Payroll (mil dol)	Number of Establishments	Number of Employees	Receipts (mil dol)	Annual Payroll (mil dol)
	96	97	98	99	100	101	102	103	104	105	106	107

1. Firms subject to federal tax.

Table D. Cities — **Federal Funds and City Government Finances**

City	Selected federal funds, fiscal 2001[1] (mil dol)										City government finances, 1999						
	Procurement contracts		Grants					Direct payments for individuals			General revenue						
												Intergovernmental		Taxes			
															Per capita[3] (dollars)		
	Defense	Other	Total[2]	Health and family welfare	Energy and environment	Education	Housing and community development	Educational assistance	Housing assistance	Total (mil dol)	Total (mil dol)	Percent from state government	Total (mil dol)	Total	Property	Sales and gross receipts
	108	109	110	111	112	113	114	115	116	117	118	119	120	121	122	123

1. October 1, 2000 to September 30, 2001.   2. Includes program categories not shown separately. State totals include additional categories not allocated by city.   3. Based on population estimated as of July 1 of the year shown.

Table D. Cities — **City Government Finances**

City	City government finances, 1999 (cont'd)												
	General expenditure												
		Per capita[1] (dollars)		Percent of total for —									
	Total (mil dol)	Total	Capital outlays	Public welfare	Highways	Parking facilities	Education	Health and hospitals	Police protection	Sewerage and sanitation	Parks and recreation	Housing and community development	Interest on debt
	124	125	126	127	128	129	130	131	132	133	134	135	136

1. Based on population estimated as of July 1 of the year shown.

COLUMN HEADINGS FOR CITIES

Table D. Cities — **City Government Finances, City Government Employment, and Climate**

City	City government finances, 1999 (cont'd)			City government employment, 2001	Climate[2]							
	Debt outstanding				Average daily temperature (degrees Fahrenheit)							
					Mean		Limits					
	Total (mil dol)	Per capita[1] (dollars)	Percent utility		January	July	January[3]	July[4]	Annual precipitation (inches)	Heating degree days	Cooling degree days
	137	138	139	140	141	142	143	144	145	146	147

1. Based on the population estimated as of July 1 of the year shown.   2. Represents normal values based on the 30-year period, 1961–1990.   3. Average daily minimum.   4. Average daily maximum.

COLUMN HEADINGS FOR CONGRESSIONAL DISTRICTS

Table E. Congressional Districts 107th Congress — **Land Area and Population**

STATE District	Land area, 2000[1] (sq km)	Population and population characteristics, 2000																
									Percent								
				Race alone or in combination								Age					
		Total persons	Per square kilometer	White	Black	Am. Indian, Alaska Native	Asian and Pacific Islander	Other race	Hispanic[2]	Non-Hispanic White	2 or more races	Under 5 years	5 to 17 years	18 to 24 years	25 to 34 years	35 to 44 years	45 to 54 years	55 to 64 years
	1	2	3	4	5	6	7	8	9	10	11	12	13	14	15	16	17	18

1. Dry land or land partially or temporarily covered by water.   2. Hispanic persons may be of any race.

Table E. Congressional Districts 107th Congress — **Population, Households, Group Quarters, and Education**

STATE District	Population and population characteristics, 2000 (cont'd)			Households, 2000				Persons in correctional institutions 2000	Persons in nursing homes, 2000	Persons in military quarters 2000	Education, 1990	
	Percent (cont'd)				Percent						School enrollment	
	Age (cont'd)											
	65 to 74 years	75 years and over	Percent female	Number	Persons per house-hold	Female family house-holder[1]	One person				Public	Private
	19	20	21	22	23	24	25	26	27	28	29	30

1. No spouse present.

COLUMN HEADINGS FOR CONGRESSIONAL DISTRICTS

Table E. Congressional Districts 107th Congress — **Education, Money Income, Poverty, and Housing**

STATE District	Education, 1990 (cont'd) Attainment[1] (percent)		Money income, 1989	Households		Percent below poverty level, 1989			Housing units, 1990					
						Persons	Families			Occupied units			Owner-occupied	
														Owner cost as a percent of income
	High school graduate or more	Bach-elor's degree or more	Per capita[2]	Median	Percent with $100,000 or more	Total	Total	Total	Total	Percent	Median value[3] (dollars)	With a mortgage	Without a mortgage
	31	32	33	34	35	36	37	38	39	40	41	42	43

1. Persons 25 years old and older.   2. Based on the population enumerated as of April 1, 1990.   3. Specified owner-occupied units.

Table E. Congressional Districts 107th Congress — **Housing, Labor Force, and Employment**

STATE District	Housing units, 1990 (cont'd) Occupied units (cont'd) Renter-occupied			Civilian labor force, 1990	Unemployment		Civilian employment, 1990[4]	Percent		Disability, 1990
	Median rent[1] (dollars)	Rent as a percent of income	Substandard units[2] (percent)	Total	Total	Rate[3]	Total	Professional, managerial, and technical	Precision production, craft, and repair	Work disabled persons[5] (percent)
	44	45	46	47	48	49	50	51	52	53

1. Specified renter-occupied units.   2. Overcrowded or lacking complete plumbing facilities.   3. Percent of total civilian labor force.   4. Persons 16 years old and older.   5. Persons 16 to 64 years of age.

2002 Highlights

Highlights for States, Counties, Cities, and Metropolitan Areas in a New Century

This book contains data for a variety of geographic entities—cities of 25,000 or more population, counties (or their equivalents in states without counties), metropolitan areas (regardless of size), Congressional Districts, states, and the United States as a whole. Such geographic constructs are often the basic building blocks for several forms of government organization and community services. Often they also serve as the root of many social ties within the United States such as which schools our children attend or the boundaries of what we consider our neighborhood. The discussion that follows has been gleaned from data presented in *2002 County and City Extra.*

The 2000 Census

The population of the United States as a whole increased by 13.1 percent between 1990 and 2000, with 19 **states** exceeding this rate and the remainder growing more slowly. States with the fastest population growth in the 1990s were concentrated in the West, with seven out of the 10 fastest growing states located in that region. Heading the list was Nevada, whose population increased by two-thirds during the decade. Every state gained population during the decade, with gains of less than 1 percent in West Virginia and North Dakota, but a population loss only in the District of Columbia—a loss of 5.7 percent.

There is no simple relationship between population size and land area for most of the geographic entities for which data are presented here. At the **state** level, for example, population in 2000 ranged from a high of 33.9 million for California that was almost 69 times the low of 494,000 for Wyoming. (The median population for states—with half having a larger and half a smaller populace—was about 4 million people). While California is also one of our largest states in land area (ranking third), Alaska is by far the largest state in area, more than twice the size of Texas, even though its population rank is close to the bottom (48th). Texas is the second largest state in both land area and total population. At the other end of the geographic size spectrum are many of the New England states (with Rhode Island the smallest), as well as Delaware and Hawaii. As a consequence of the differing area size and population rank, New Jersey is the most densely settled state, with about 438 persons per square kilometer of land,

while Alaska is the least densely settled, with less than one person (.4) per square kilometer. California, which is the state with the largest population and third largest land area, ranks 13th in terms of population density (with about 84 persons per square kilometer).

Within states, the number and physical size of **counties** varies considerably; Delaware has three counties while Texas has over 250 counties. For the approximately 3,140 counties (and county equivalents—see Appendix A) in the United States, population in 2000 ranged from over 9 million in Los Angeles, CA, to 67 in Loving County, TX. Other particularly large counties in terms of population include Cook County, IL (over 5 million population), and Harris County, TX (over 3 million); the former encompassing Chicago and its suburbs, the latter containing Houston. These three counties maintained their top-three rankings from 1990, but the fourth largest county—Maricopa County, AZ (which includes Phoenix)—rose from seventh in population in 1990, while San Diego, CA dropped from fourth to sixth place between 1990 and 2000. There were 34 counties with a population of 1,000,000 or more, which combined contain about one-fourth of the U.S. population. About half of the U.S. population lived in the 150 largest counties, those with a population of about 400,000 or more. At the other extreme, there were 31 counties with fewer than 1,000 people in 2000. The median county population size was just under 25,000.

The nation's fastest growing counties in the 1990s tended to be in or near metropolitan areas in the West or South regions. Douglas County, CO (near Denver), grew by 191 percent, while Forsyth County, GA (near Atlanta), grew by 123 percent. Five counties more than doubled their populations during the decade, all of them near either Denver or Atlanta. The five biggest *numeric* gainers of the decade were Maricopa (AZ), Los Angeles (CA), Clark (NV), Harris (TX), and Orange (CA). Two more California counties (Riverside and San Diego), two Florida counties (Broward and Miami-Dade) and Dallas (TX) complete the top-10 numeric gainers from 1990 to 2000. The largest numeric population loss occurred in Baltimore City (MD), followed closely by two Pennsylvania counties, Philadelphia and Allegheny, which includes Pittsburgh.

In terms of land area, counties range from the nearly 378,000 square kilometers of Yukon-Koyukuk (AK) to New York (NY) with 59 square kilometers, Arlington (VA) with 67 square kilometers and Bristol (RI) with 64 square kilometers.[1] Counties tend to be larger in the western United States (most of the largest 50 are in that region). The median land area for all U.S. counties was about 1,600 square kilometers in 2000.

While New York County (Manhattan) may have one of the smallest land areas, it had by far the highest population density among U.S. counties in 2000, with over 26,000 persons per square kilometer. No other county approached that density (although three other New York City boroughs were among the top-five counties in population density). San Francisco had the highest density outside of New York City, with Boston (Suffolk, MA), Philadelphia, and Washington, DC among the top 10. The median county only had about 16 persons per square kilometer, with only 105 counties having more than 500 persons per square kilometer. The Nation's largest county in terms of population (Los Angeles) had a population density of 905 persons per square kilometer, ranking only 47th among all U.S. counties.

In 2000, nine **cities** had populations over 1 million people, topped by New York City with 8 million, Los Angeles with 3.7 million, and Chicago with 2.9 million. California and Texas each have four cities among the nation's 20 largest: Houston, Dallas, San Antonio, and Austin in Texas; and Los Angeles, San Diego, San Jose, and San Francisco in California. No other state has more than one city among the 20 most populous in the country.

While the majority of these large cities grew in the 1990s, St. Louis lost 12.2 percent of its population, and Baltimore lost 11.5 percent. Also losing more than 10 percent of their populations were Buffalo, NY and Norfolk, VA. Thirteen other large cities lost population in the 1990–2000 period. Large cities are not alone in losing population: about one out of five of the 1,238 U.S. cities with a population of 25,000 or more lost population between 1990 and 2000.

The largest proportionate increase among large cities was in Las Vegas, which grew by more than 85 percent during the decade. This 1990s growth is dwarfed by the percentage increase in many smaller cities, with such places as Gilbert, AZ (near Phoenix, with a 2000 population of

109,697), more than tripling during the 1990–2000 period. Similarly, Henderson, NV, near Las Vegas, nearly doubled in population. Some smaller cities tripled or quadrupled in population. Frisco and Cedar Park, TX, Fishers, IN, and Surprise, AZ had fewer than 10,000 people in 1990, but 10 years later had grown to about 30,000.

Juneau, AK is the nation's largest city in terms of land area, with over 7,000 square kilometers, an area 5.8 times the size of Los Angeles. Twenty cities in the United States have land area larger than New York City (which has a land area of about 785 square kilometers). Cities with very large land area tend to be in the West, but some cities with boundaries coextensive with their respective counties (such as the Nashville-Davidson consolidated city in Tennessee or Indianapolis, IN) also have particularly large land areas. The median land area for all places of 25,000 or more was about 64 square kilometers.

The growth (or declining population) of the largest city in a **metropolitan area** may not correspond to the growth of the metropolitan statistical area (MSA) as a whole. While, for example, Detroit city lost 7.5 percent of its population during the decade, the metropolitan area grew by 4.1 percent between 1990 and 2000. The population of the city of Washington, DC decreased by more than 5 percent while the metropolitan area as a whole grew by over 16 percent during this same period. It was, however, far from the fastest growing metropolitan area during the 1990s. That distinction went to Las Vegas, Nevada-Arizona MSA, whose population increased by 83 percent between 1990 and 2000. The Atlanta metropolitan area was the fastest growing among the largest 10 metropolitan areas; after dropping 7 percent in the 1980s, the city's population grew by nearly 6 percent in the 1990s, but the MSA as a whole had a population increase of 38.9 percent between 1990 and 2000.

However, 24 MSAs did lose population during the decade, representing about one of every 13 metropolitan areas in the United States. As a group those experiencing population loss are geographically dispersed, and tend to be relatively small metropolitan areas, although they may have been metropolitan for decades. They include Pine Bluff, AR; Alexandria, LA; Binghamton, NY; and Muncie, IN, as well as larger metropolitan areas such as Pittsburgh, PA, and Buffalo-Niagara Falls, NY. None of the MSAs that lost population between 1990 and 2000 were in the West region, and about two-thirds of them were in New York, Pennsylvania, and Ohio.

[1]Several independent cities in Virginia, which are treated as counties for tabulation purposes, were excluded here.

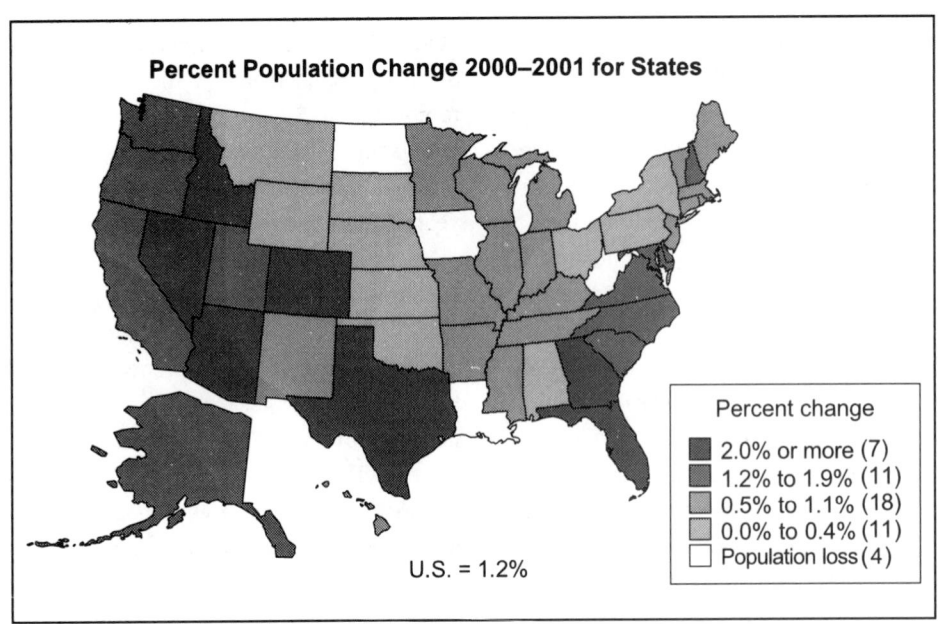

Percent Population Change 2000–2001 for States

Percent change
- 2.0% or more (7)
- 1.2% to 1.9% (11)
- 0.5% to 1.1% (18)
- 0.0% to 0.4% (11)
- Population loss (4)

U.S. = 1.2%

Changes in the New Century

Estimates of the population in 2001 show a national growth rate of 1.2 percent, with Nevada continuing to lead the growth at 5.4 percent, followed closely by its Southwestern neighbors, Arizona (3.4 percent) and Colorado (2.7 percent). Four other states grew more than 2 percent in the first year of the century (Florida, Georgia, Texas, and Idaho), with another 11 states growing at rates higher than the national average. These 11 states were on the East Coast (New Hampshire, North Carolina, Delaware, Virginia, Maryland, and South Carolina), the West Coast (California, Washington, Oregon, and Alaska), and one additional Southwestern state (Utah). A dozen states experienced losses or very little growth, with North Dakota showing the largest decrease at 1.2 percent.

Douglas County, CO (near Denver) was the fastest growing county in the last decade and held its first place in the new century with 13.6 percent growth in just one year. The second highest growth was in Loudoun County, VA (near Washington, DC) which grew 12.6 percent between 2000 and 2001, surpassing Forsyth County, GA (near Atlanta) where the growth rate was still a very high 12.1 percent.

Among the 75 largest counties, Clark County, NV (Las Vegas) continued to lead with 6.5 percent growth between 2000 and 2001. Maricopa County, AZ (Phoenix) dropped from second place in the last decade to third place with a growth rate of 4.0 percent. Riverside County, CA jumped to second place with 5.9 percent growth, while two other California counties rounded out the top five: Sacramento (3.7 percent) and San Bernardino (3.3 percent).

Not surprisingly, Las Vegas, NV-AZ had the highest growth rate (6.5 percent) among the 75 largest metropolitan areas, followed by Austin-San Marcos, TX with 5.1 percent. These two MSA's also topped the list of fast-growing large metropolitan areas in the 1990s. New at the top of this list are Riverside-San Bernardino, CA (4.5 percent) and Sacramento, CA (4.4 percent), both of which experienced slower growth in the 1990s, ranked 15 and 23 respectively. When all metropolitan areas, regardless of size, are included, Greeley, CO jumps to the top with 7.7 percent growth, while Naples, FL and Stockton-Lodi, CA join Las Vegas and Austin-San Marcos to make up the top five.

A Slower Growth in the Labor Force

The U. S. labor force grew by only .7 percent between 2000 and 2001, after exceeding 1 percent growth per year for much of the 1990s. Nevada had the highest labor force growth (3.8 percent) as well as the highest population growth. Other states that experienced growth of more than 2 percent were scattered around the country: Idaho, Arizona, Minnesota, Delaware, and Florida. While no states had experienced declining labor forces in the late 1990s, 19 states and the District of Columbia had no growth or losses between 2000 and 2001. Montana's labor force shrunk the most—2.9 percent, followed by Mississippi with a 2.3 percent loss.

Proportionally large year-to-year labor force changes are not unusual for counties with small populations, but no county's labor force grew more than 20 percent between 2000 and 2001. Among metropolitan counties with over 100,000 population, only Collier County, FL (Naples) and Mojave County, AZ (in the Las Vegas metropolitan area)

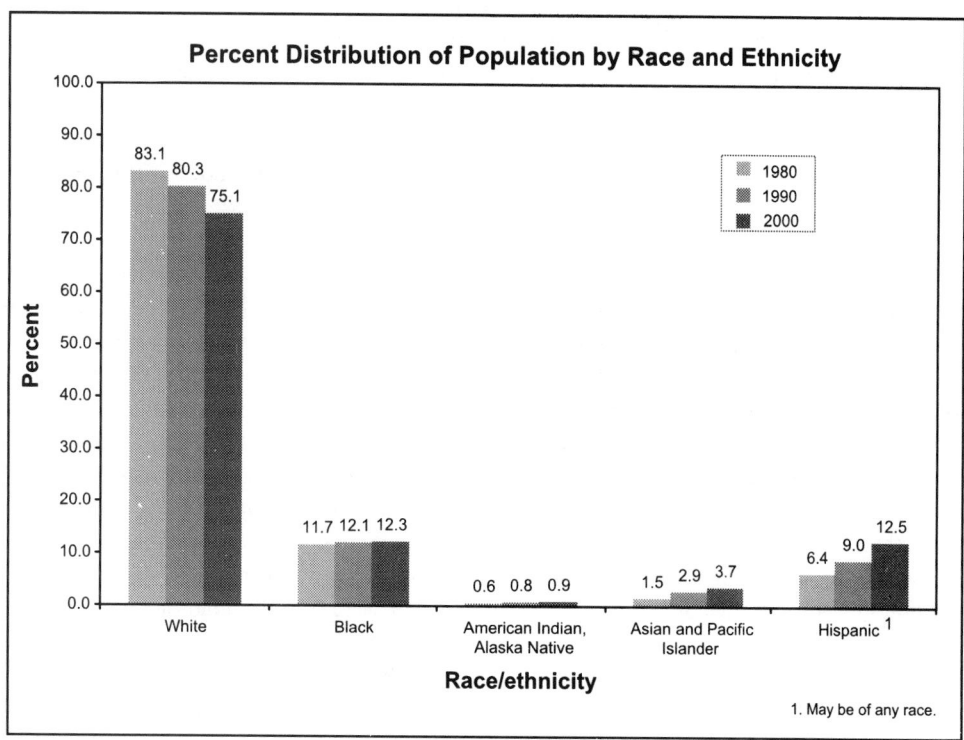

Percent Distribution of Population by Race and Ethnicity

1980
1990
2000

White: 83.1, 80.3, 75.1
Black: 11.7, 12.1, 12.3
American Indian, Alaska Native: 0.6, 0.8, 0.9
Asian and Pacific Islander: 1.5, 2.9, 3.7
Hispanic [1]: 6.4, 9.0, 12.5

1. May be of any race.

experienced labor force increases of more than 5 percent. The labor force decreased in about half of all counties, with Greene County, MS losing 26.2 percent in a single year.

In the Naples, FL metropolitan area, the labor force grew by 7.6 percent, the largest growth of any MSA. In three other Florida MSA's, the labor force grew by 4.0 percent or more (Punta Gorda, Fort Myers-Cape Coral, and West Palm Beach-Boca Raton), a level matched by Las Vegas, NV-AZ, Boise City, ID, Rochester, MN, and St. Joseph, MO. Five MSAs lost 3 percent or more of their labor force, with Decatur, IL and Albany, GA experiencing the largest proportional losses (4.5 percent and 4.4 percent, respectively).

The unemployment rate for the United States in 2001 was 4.8 percent. Eighteen states and the District of Columbia had higher unemployment rates, while lower rates occurred in 32 states. North Dakota, Nebraska, South Dakota, Iowa, and Connecticut were the states with the lowest unemployment rates (3.3 percent or lower). The District of Columbia had the highest unemployment rate at 6.5 percent. Washington, Alaska, Oregon, and Louisiana all had unemployment rates of 6.0 percent or higher. More than 1,500 counties had unemployment rates above the national average of 4.8 percent. Six counties had more than 20 percent unemployment, including three counties in Texas. Of the six counties with the highest unemployment rates, only Yuma (AZ) and Imperial (CA) had populations over 100,000. Only one metropolitan area (Yuma, AZ) had an unemployment rate of more than 20 percent. Eight metropolitan areas, six of them in California, had

unemployment rates over 10 percent. Five metropolitan areas, relatively small MSA's in different parts of the country, had unemployment rates of 2 percent or less.

Increasing Diversity

The census measures ethnicity through two separate questions. The first is "Is this person Spanish/Hispanic/Latino?" and the second "What is this person's race?" These are separate questions, and Hispanic persons can be of any race. Other questions concerning ancestry, primary language, and citizenship were asked only on the long form questionnaire, results from which are not included in this volume.

Individuals can identify with more than one race. In the United States as a whole, 77.1 percent of the people were **white**, alone or in combination with other races; 12.9 percent were **black** alone or in combination; 4.2 percent were **Asian**; 1.5 percent **American Indian or Alaska Native**; .3 percent **Native Hawaiian or other Pacific Islander**; and 6.6 percent checked that they were "**some other race**". This adds to more than 100 percent because of the 2.4 percent of the population who identified with more than one race. The **Hispanic** population is 12.5 percent of the total.

In the 1990 census, each person was asked to select a single racial category. At that time, 80.3 percent considered themselves white, 12.1 percent black, less than 1 percent American Indian or Alaska Native, and 2.9 percent Asian or Pacific Islander. Nine percent were Hispanic. Though all groups increased in population during the 1990s, the white population increased less than the others, resulting in a smaller share of the total.

In 14 **states**, more than 90 percent of the people were **white**. The highest proportions were the New England states of Vermont, Maine, and New Hampshire. In Hawaii and the District of Columbia, fewer than 40 percent of the people were white. About 300 **counties** are 99 percent white. Located in all regions, these counties tend to have small populations—many with fewer than 1000 people— with only two exceeding 50,000. In about 150 counties, fewer than half the people are white. Many of these are small counties in Alaska, Hawaii, and several states in the South and the Southwest, but they also include many large cities such as Philadelphia, St Louis, and the New York Boroughs of Brooklyn, Queens, and the Bronx.

More than half of the **black** population lived in the southern **states**. In nine states and the District of Columbia, 20 percent or more of the people were black alone or in combination, led by the District of Columbia with over 60 percent. In Jefferson and Claiborne **counties** in Mississippi, and Macon and Greene counties in Alabama, more than 80 percent of the people were black. In about a hundred counties, more than half of the people were black. These were mostly in the South and include large urban counties like the District of Columbia and its suburb Prince George's, MD; Baltimore City, MD; Orleans Parish, LA; (New Orleans); DeKalb, GA (Atlanta); and Shelby, TN (Memphis). More than 2000 counties had black populations of less than 5 percent, including such large counties as Maricopa, AZ (Phoenix); Middlesex, MA (near Boston); Bucks, PA (near Philadelphia); and Santa Clara, CA (San Jose). Among large **cities**, Gary, IN and Detroit, MI were more than 80 percent black, with 10 of the 75 largest cities more than half black.

About 42 percent of New Mexico's residents were **Hispanic**, making it the **state** with the highest proportion of persons of Hispanic origin, followed by California and Texas, both about 32 percent, and together accounting for fully half of the nation's Hispanic population. Other states with Hispanic populations larger than the national average included the Southwestern states of Arizona, Nevada, and Colorado, as well as Florida, New York, and New Jersey. In about 20 counties, more than 80 percent of the people were Hispanic. Most of these counties were in Texas, and most were near the Mexican border. Starr County tops the list with a 97.5 percent Hispanic population. Several are populous metropolitan counties such as Webb (Laredo), Hidalgo (McAllen), Cameron (Brownsville), and El Paso. Other big cities with large Hispanic populations include Hialeah and Miami in Florida, and several California cities,

such as Santa Ana, Anaheim, and Los Angeles. Nearly half (46.5 percent) of the population of Los Angeles is Hispanic. In more than 800 counties, fewer than 1 percent of the people are Hispanic. These counties are in all regions, but most are in the Midwest, the Northeast and the South.

In the United States, 2.4 percent of the population identified with two or more races. However, in Hawaii, 21.4 percent were multiracial, with Alaska a distant second at 5.4 percent. Hawaii is the only state with more than 1 percent in the category "Native Hawaiian and Other Pacific Islander" (alone or in combination), 23.3 percent of Hawaii's population. In this volume, the "Native Hawaiian and Other Pacific Islander" category is combined with "Asian", making it comparable with the "Asian/Pacific Islander" group of the 1990 census. Another 58 percent in Hawaii were **Asian**, alone or in combination, making Hawaii by far the state with the highest proportion of Asian/Pacific Islanders (81.3 percent). Nationally, 4.5 percent were in this combined category, while California's population was 13 percent Asian or Pacific Islander, and seven more states were above the national average (Washington, New York, New Jersey, Nevada, Alaska, Maryland, and Virginia.) Hawaii's four major counties top the list of counties, with about three-quarters or more of their populations in the combined Asian/Pacific Islander category. In four large counties in central California—San Francisco, Santa Clara (San Jose), Alameda, and San Mateo—more than one-fifth of the people are Asian/Pacific Islander, alone or in combination with another race. About 30 counties had populations comprising 10 percent or more Asian people, most of them large urban counties in California, Virginia, and New Jersey.

Nationally, fewer than 1 percent of the population indicated that they were American Indian or Alaska Native. Of the states, Alaska has the largest proportion of native peoples at 15.6 percent. New Mexico, South Dakota, Oklahoma, Montana, Arizona, and North Dakota have between 5 percent and 10 percent in this group. In 25 counties, at least half of the people are American Indian or Alaska Native, led by Shannon County, SD and Wade Hampton census area in Alaska, both with 95 percent. The group included 10 additional counties in the Dakotas and eight in Alaska. Most of these counties had fewer than 10,000 people, but Apache, AZ and McKinley, NM had more than 50,000 people each, with more than three-quarters of their populations American Indian. Among the 75 largest cities, 7.3 percent of the people in Anchorage, AK and 4.8 percent of the people in Tulsa, OK were American Indian or Alaska Native. Flagstaff, AZ-UT is the metropolitan area with the largest American Indian or Alaska Native population, at 27 percent.

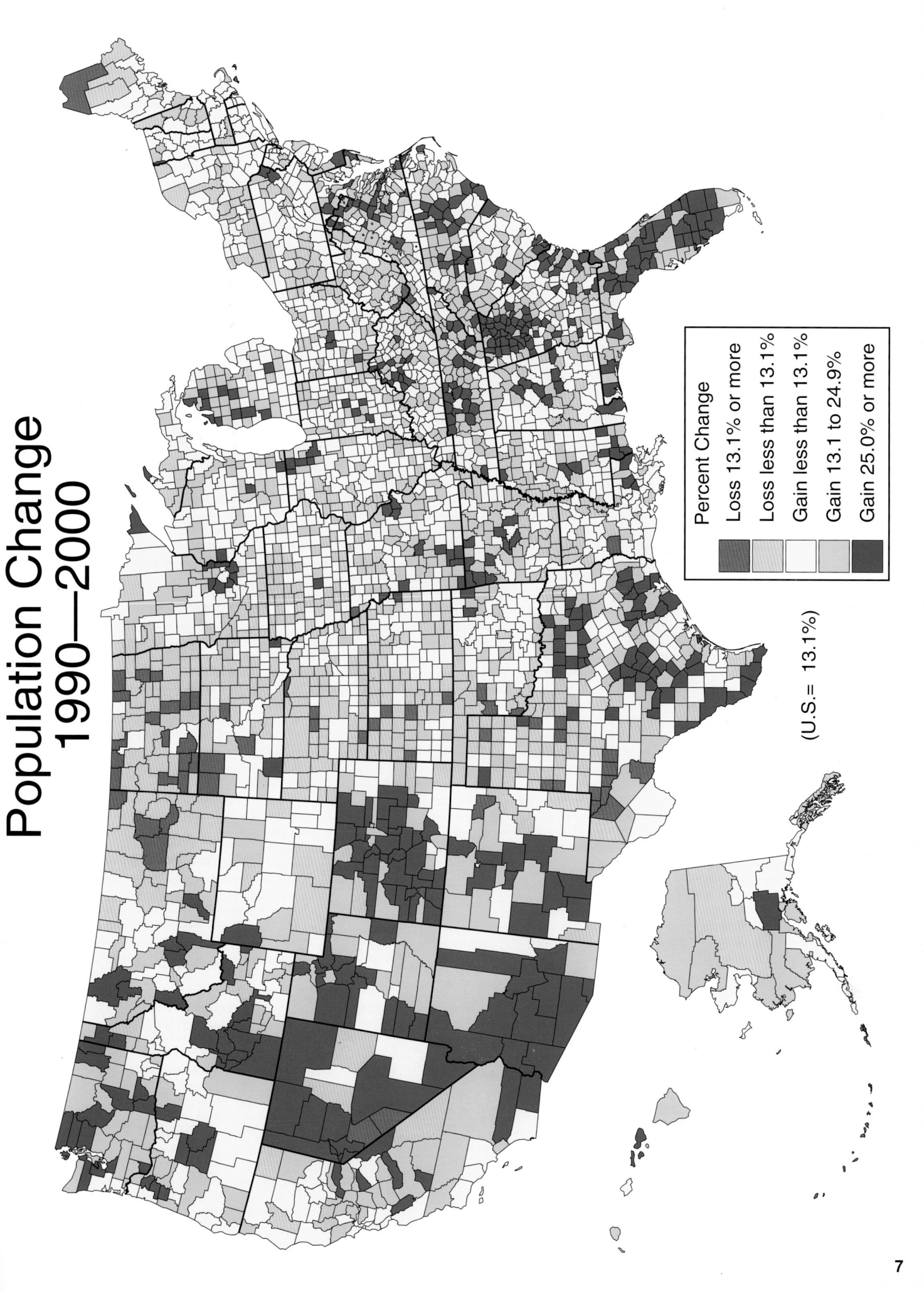

Population Change
1990—2000

Percent Change

Loss 13.1% or more
Loss less than 13.1%
Gain less than 13.1%
Gain 13.1 to 24.9%
Gain 25.0% or more

(U.S. = 13.1%)

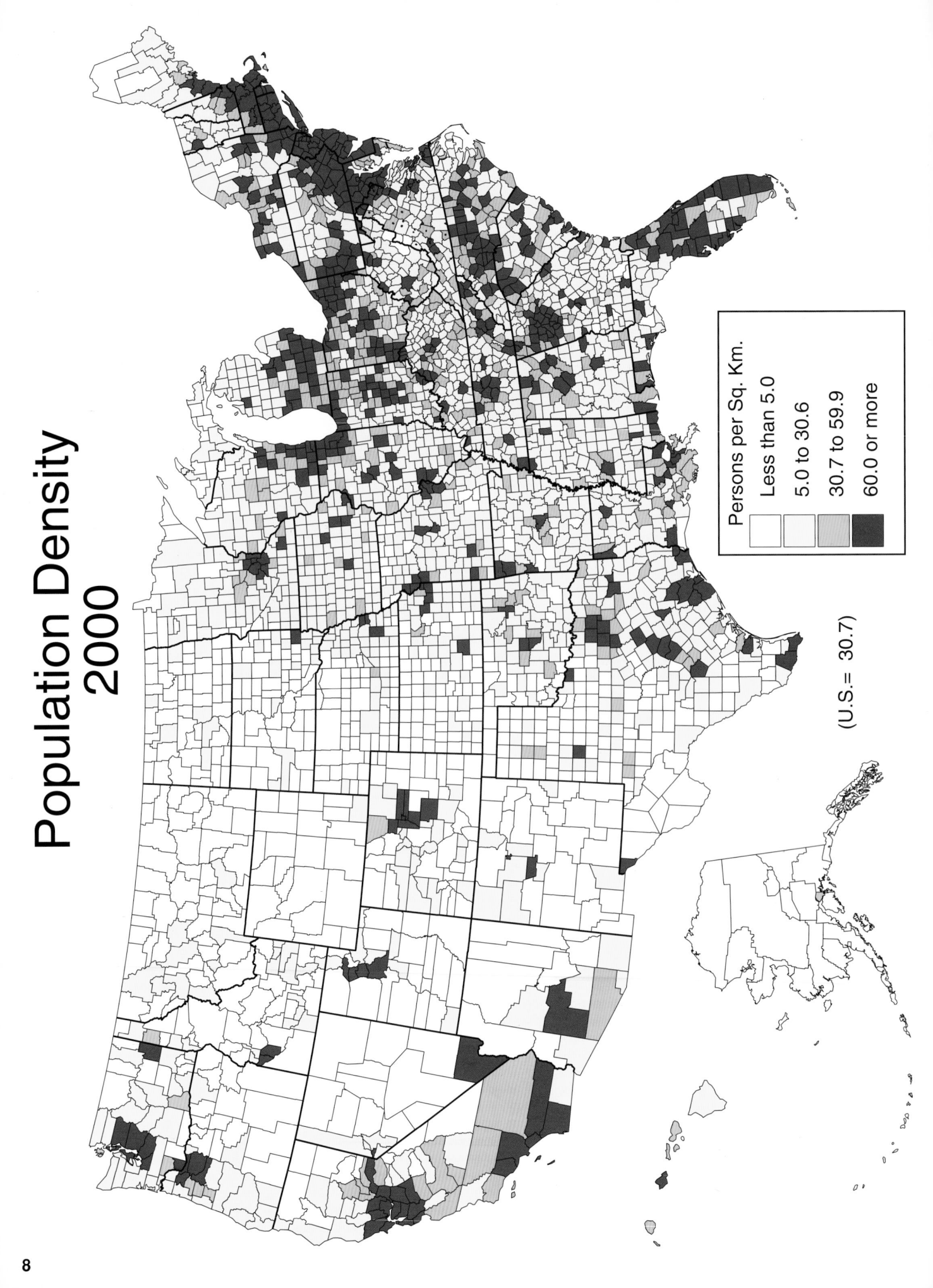

Population Density
2000

Persons per Sq. Km.

| Less than 5.0 | 5.0 to 30.6 | 30.7 to 59.9 | 60.0 or more |

(U.S. = 30.7)

8

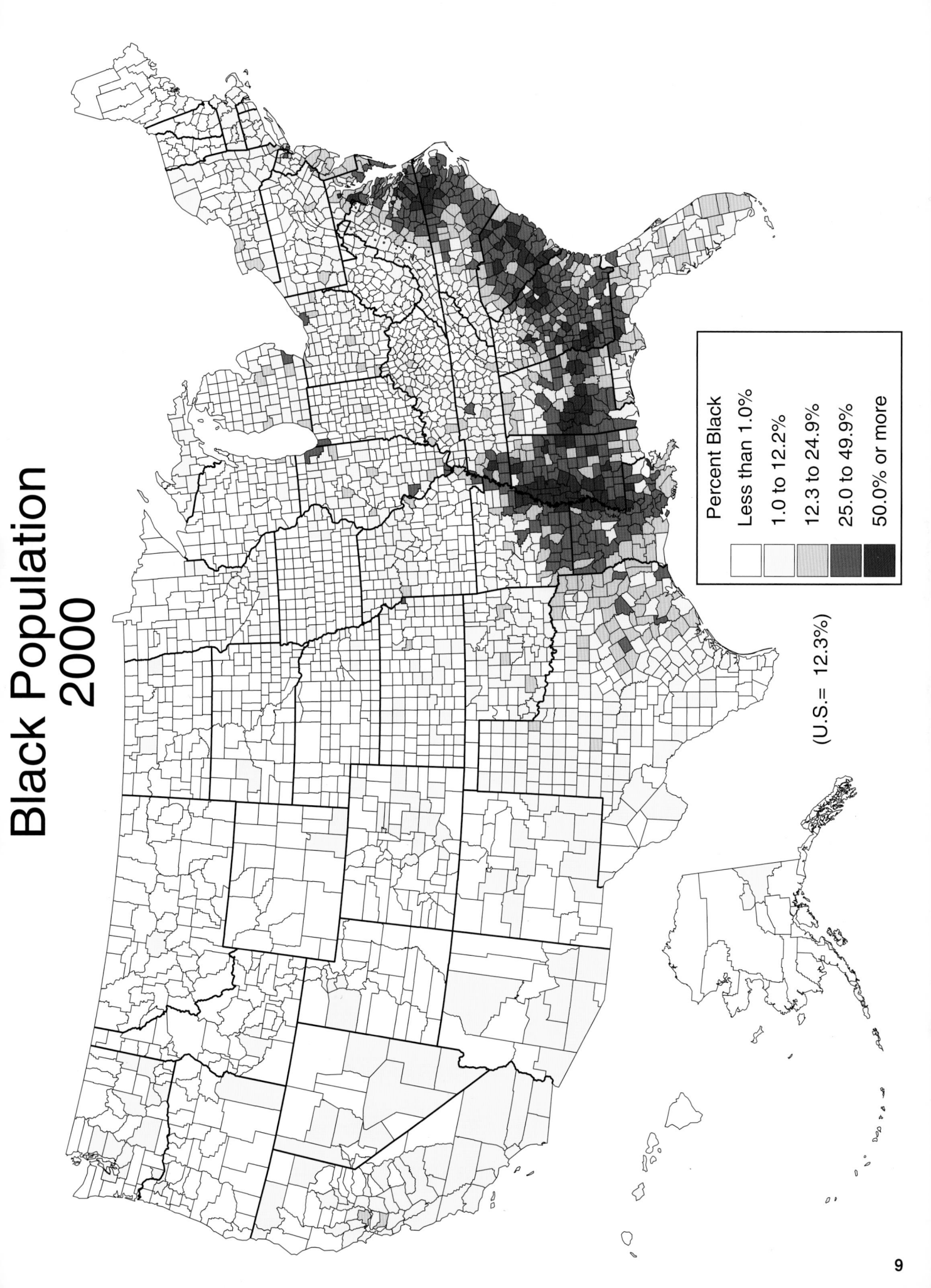

Black Population
2000

Percent Black

Less than 1.0%
1.0 to 12.2%
12.3 to 24.9%
25.0 to 49.9%
50.0% or more

(U.S. = 12.3%)

Hispanic Population 2000

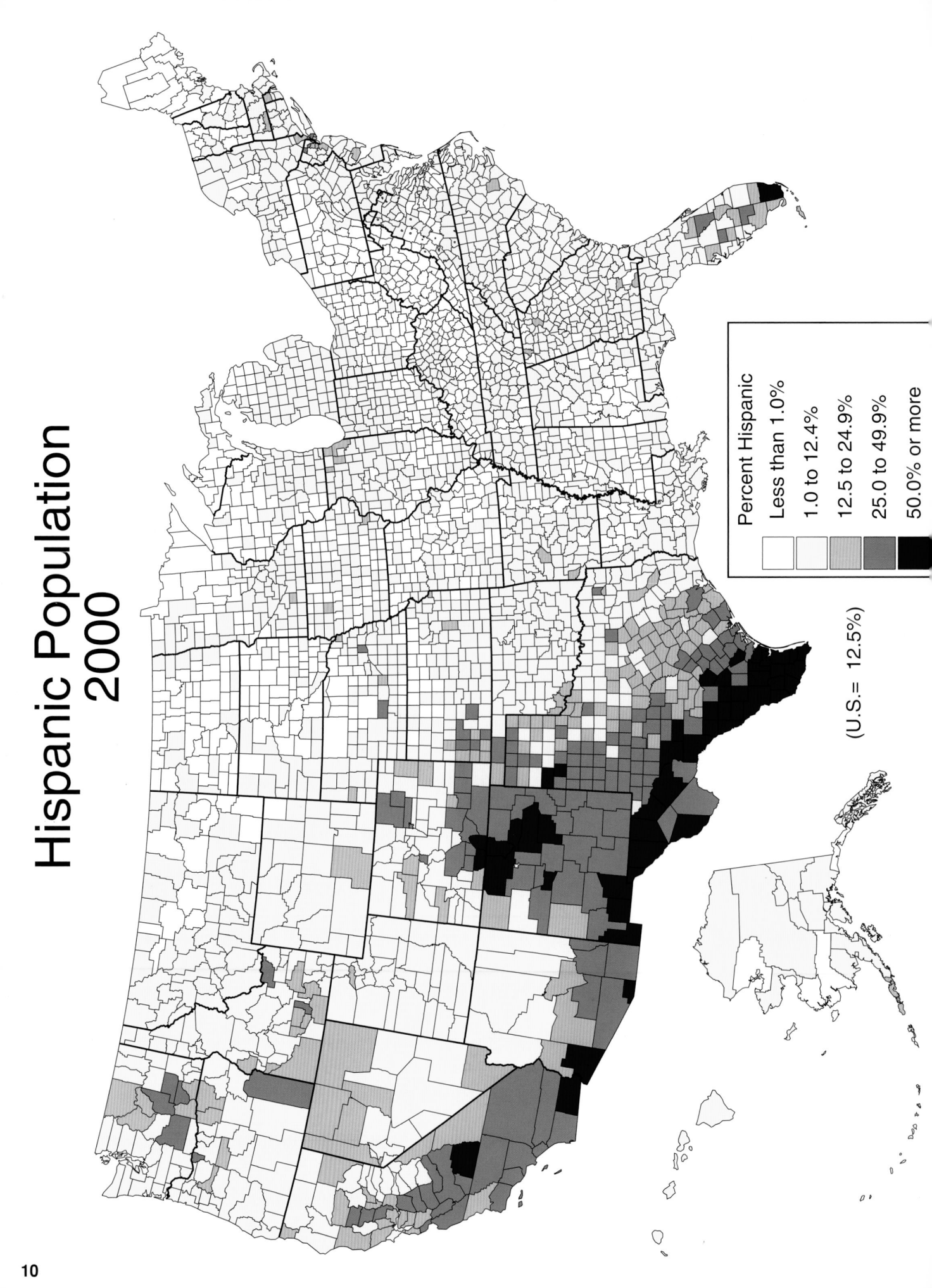

Percent Hispanic

Less than 1.0%

1.0 to 12.4%

12.5 to 24.9%

25.0 to 49.9%

50.0% or more

(U.S. = 12.5%)

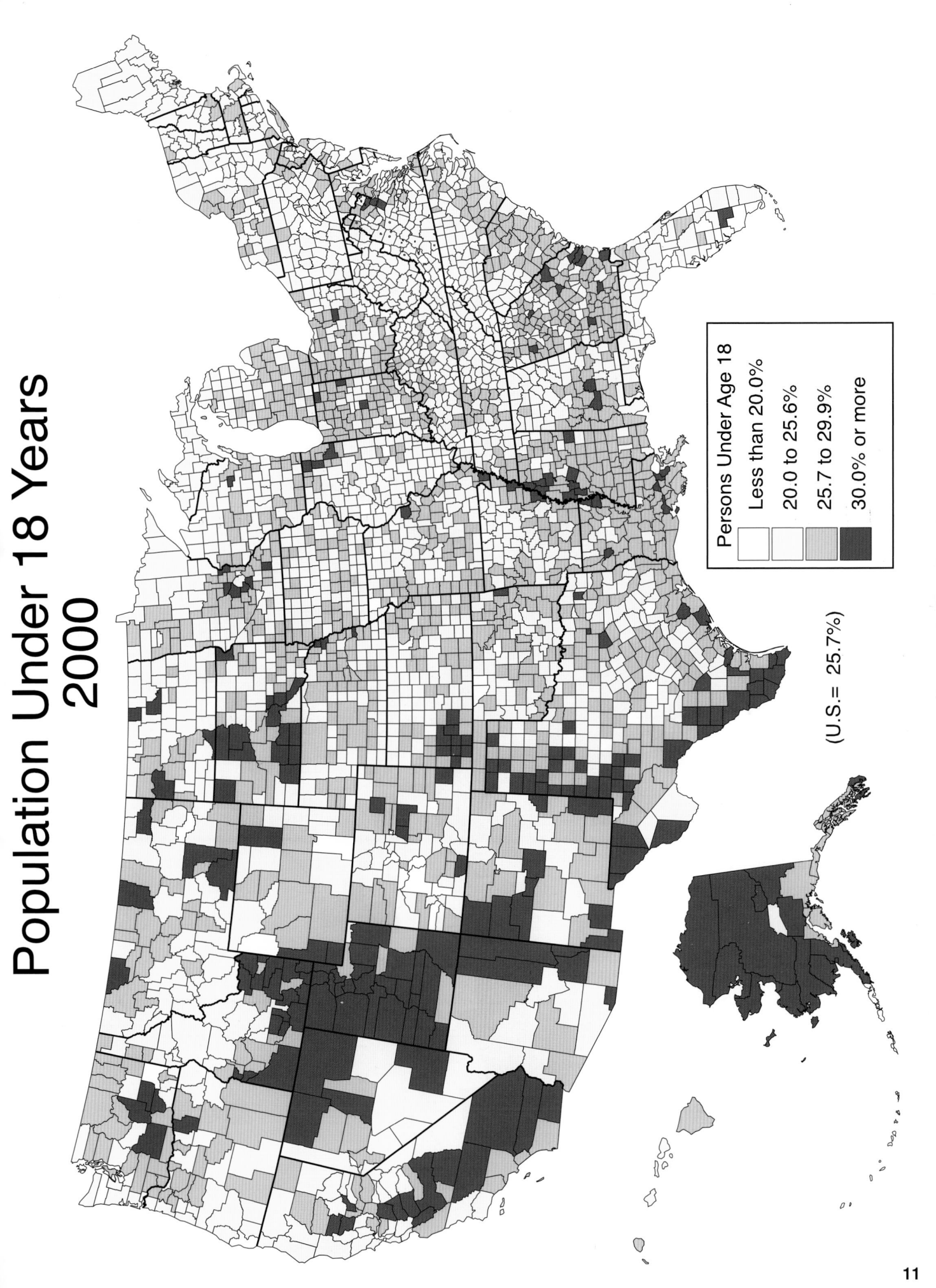

Population Under 18 Years
2000

Persons Under Age 18

Less than 20.0%

20.0 to 25.6%

25.7 to 29.9%

30.0% or more

(U.S. = 25.7%)

11

Population 65 Years and Older
2000

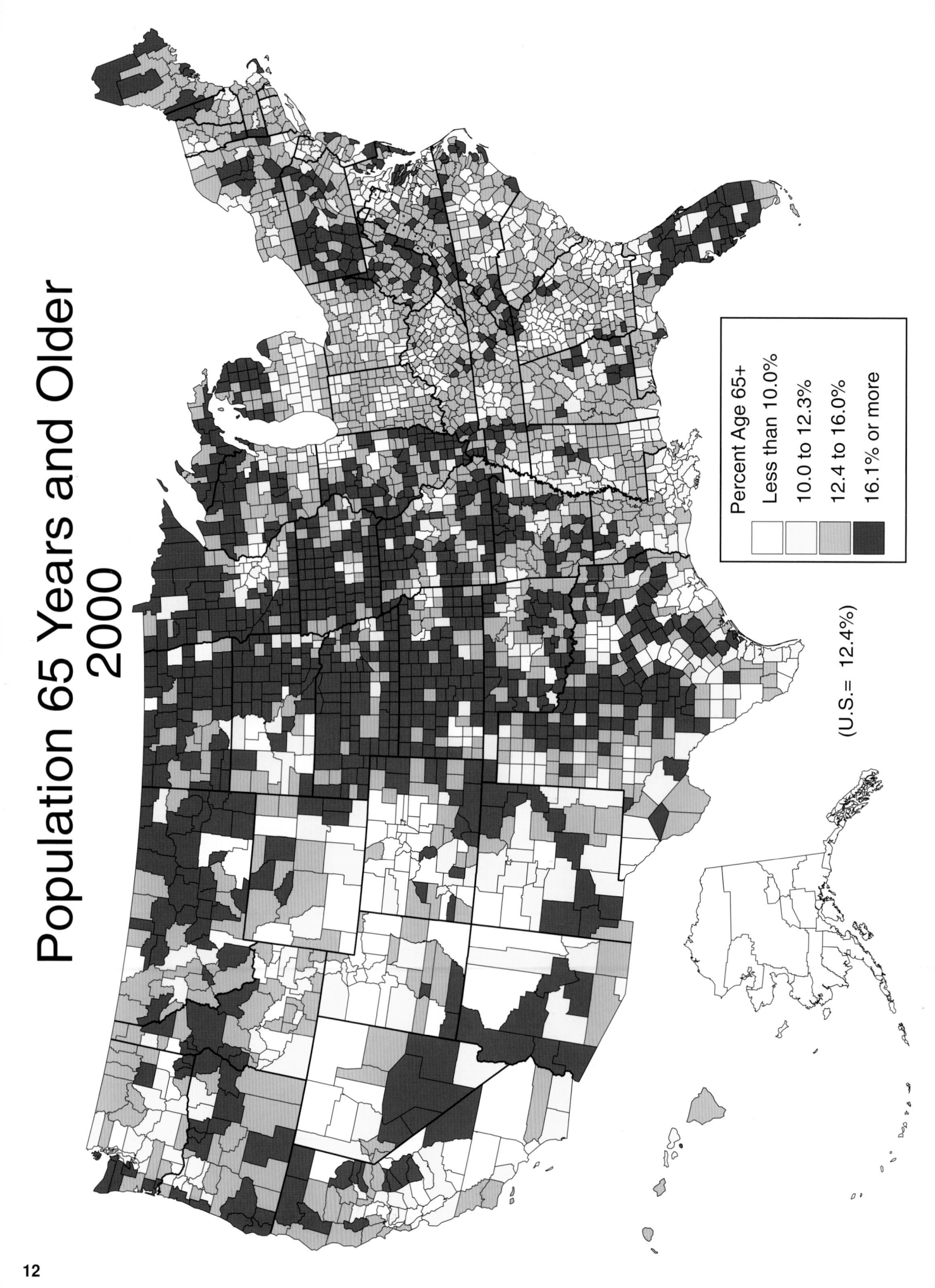

Percent Age 65+

Less than 10.0%
10.0 to 12.3%
12.4 to 16.0%
16.1% or more

(U.S. = 12.4%)

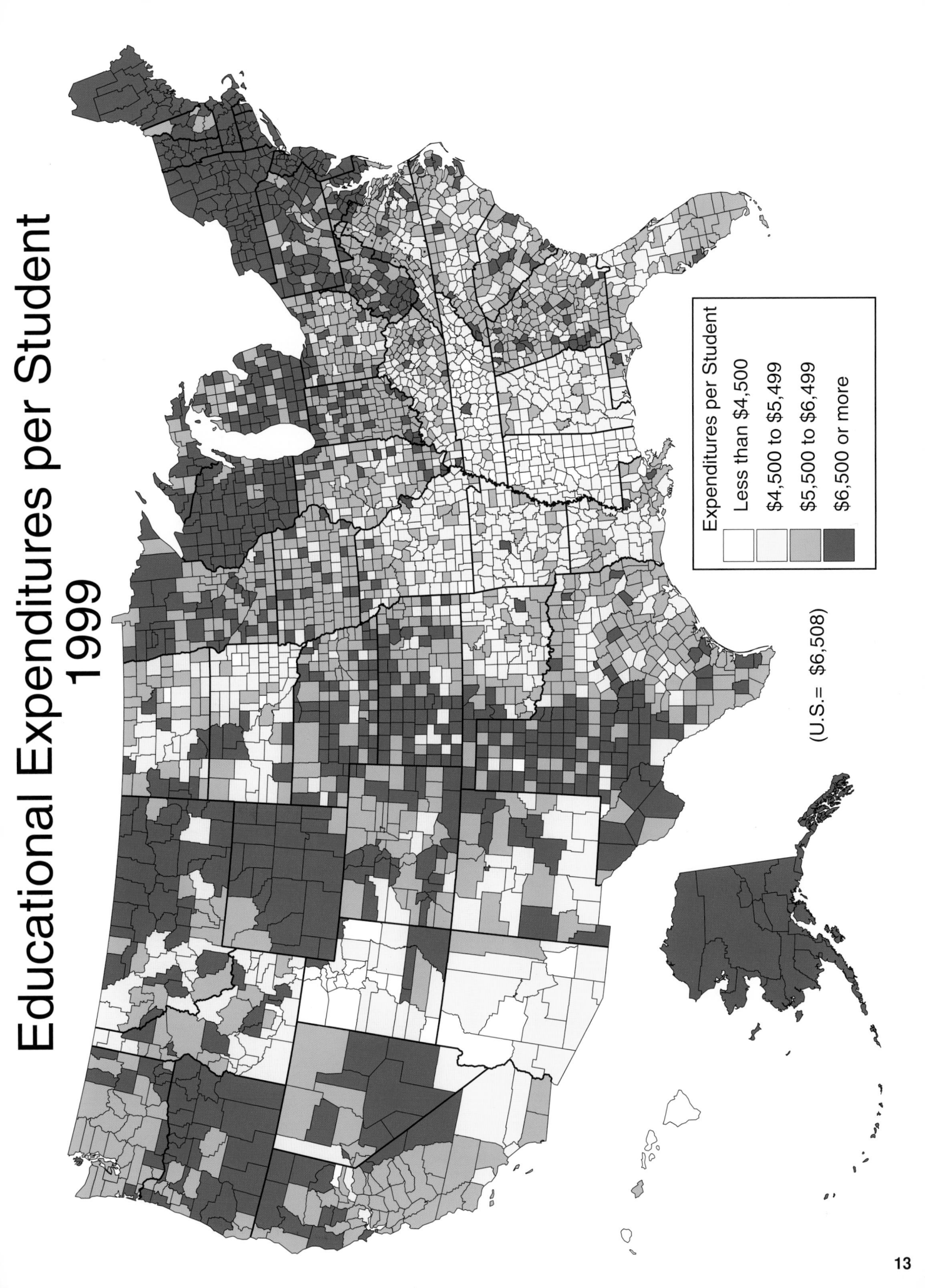

Educational Expenditures per Student
1999

Expenditures per Student

Less than $4,500
$4,500 to $5,499
$5,500 to $6,499
$6,500 or more

(U.S.= $6,508)

13

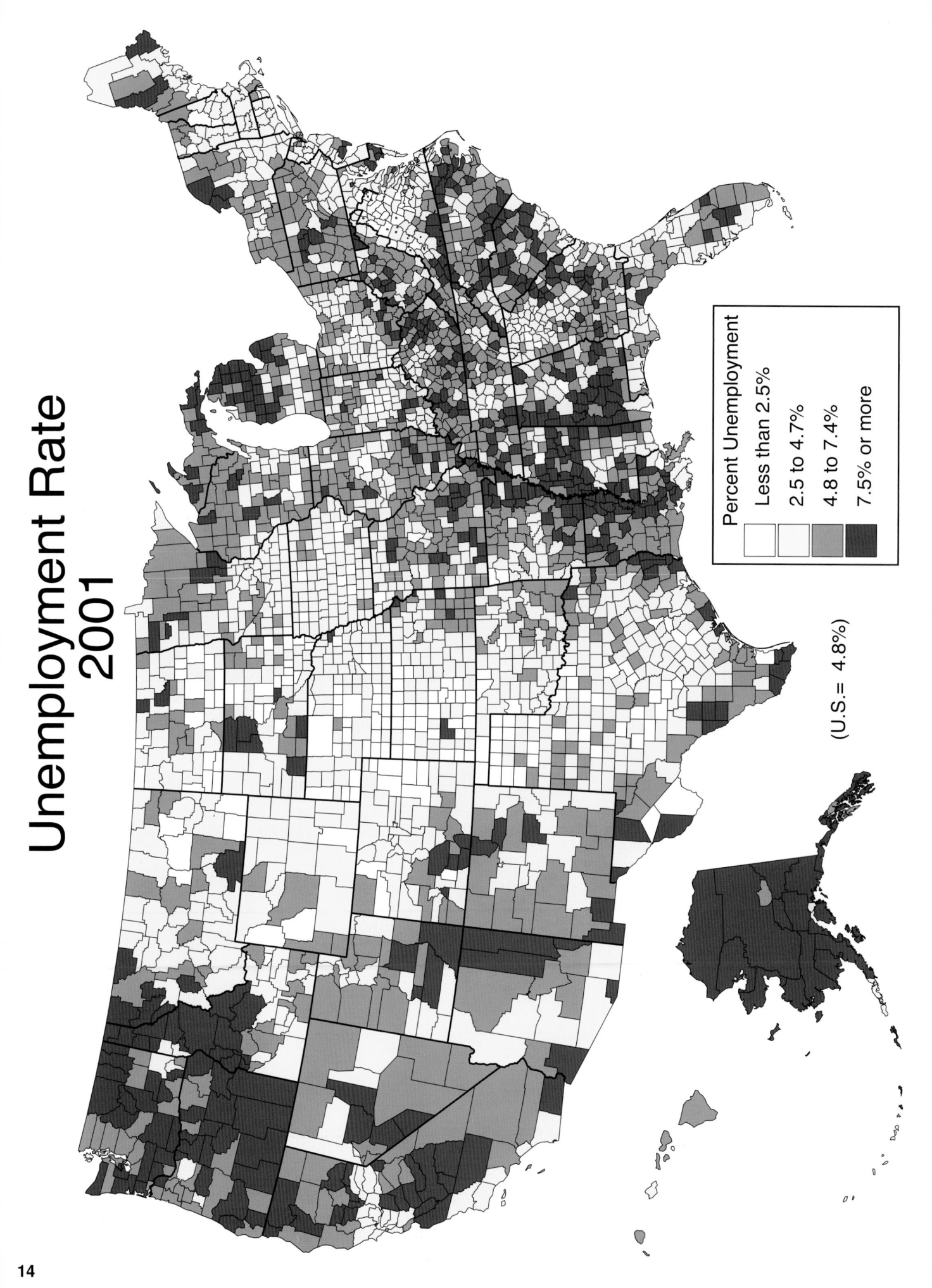

Unemployment Rate
2001

Percent Unemployment

Less than 2.5%

2.5 to 4.7%

4.8 to 7.4%

7.5% or more

(U.S.= 4.8%)

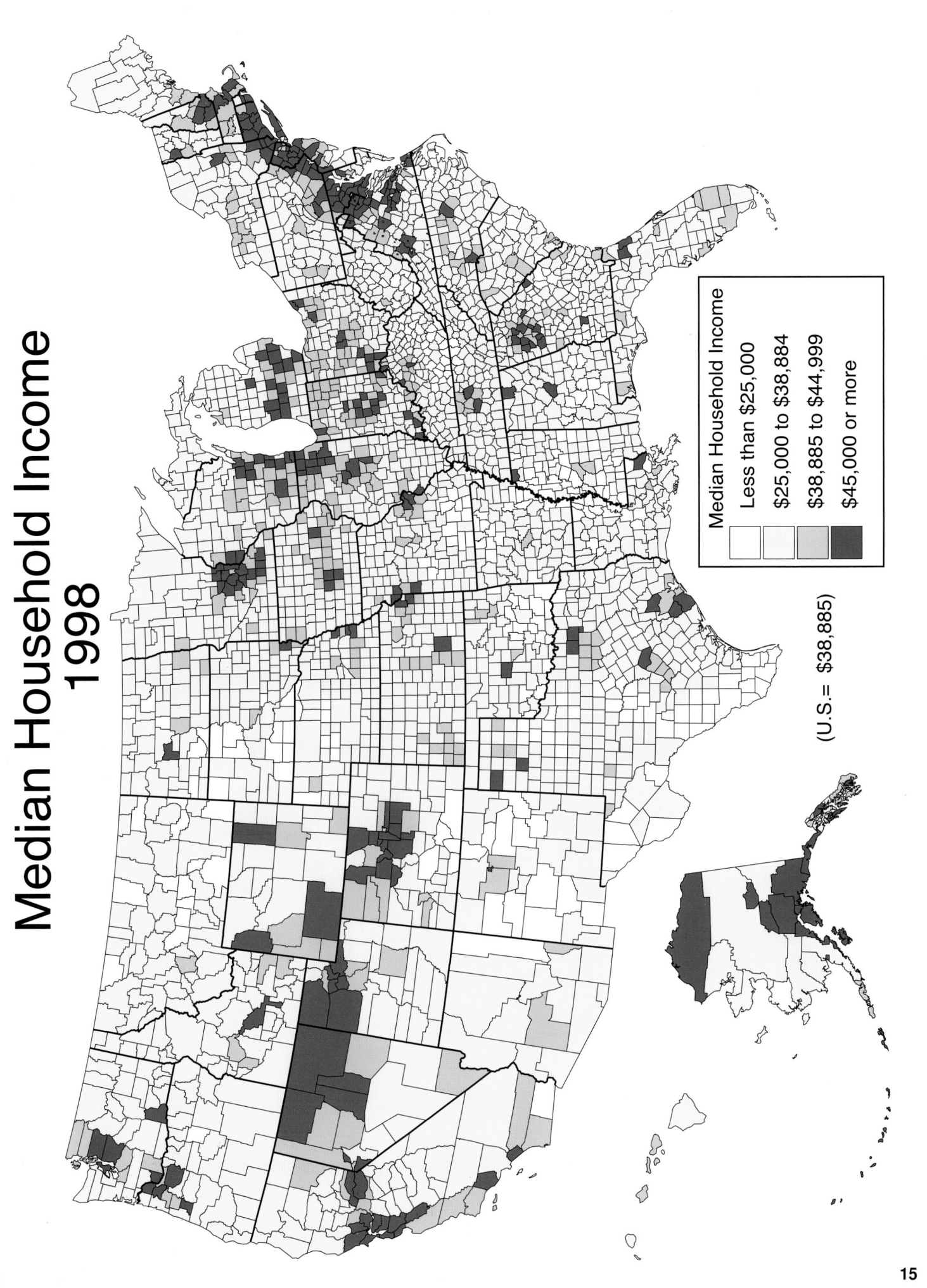

Median Household Income 1998

Median Household Income

Less than $25,000

$25,000 to $38,884

$38,885 to $44,999

$45,000 or more

(U.S.= $38,885)

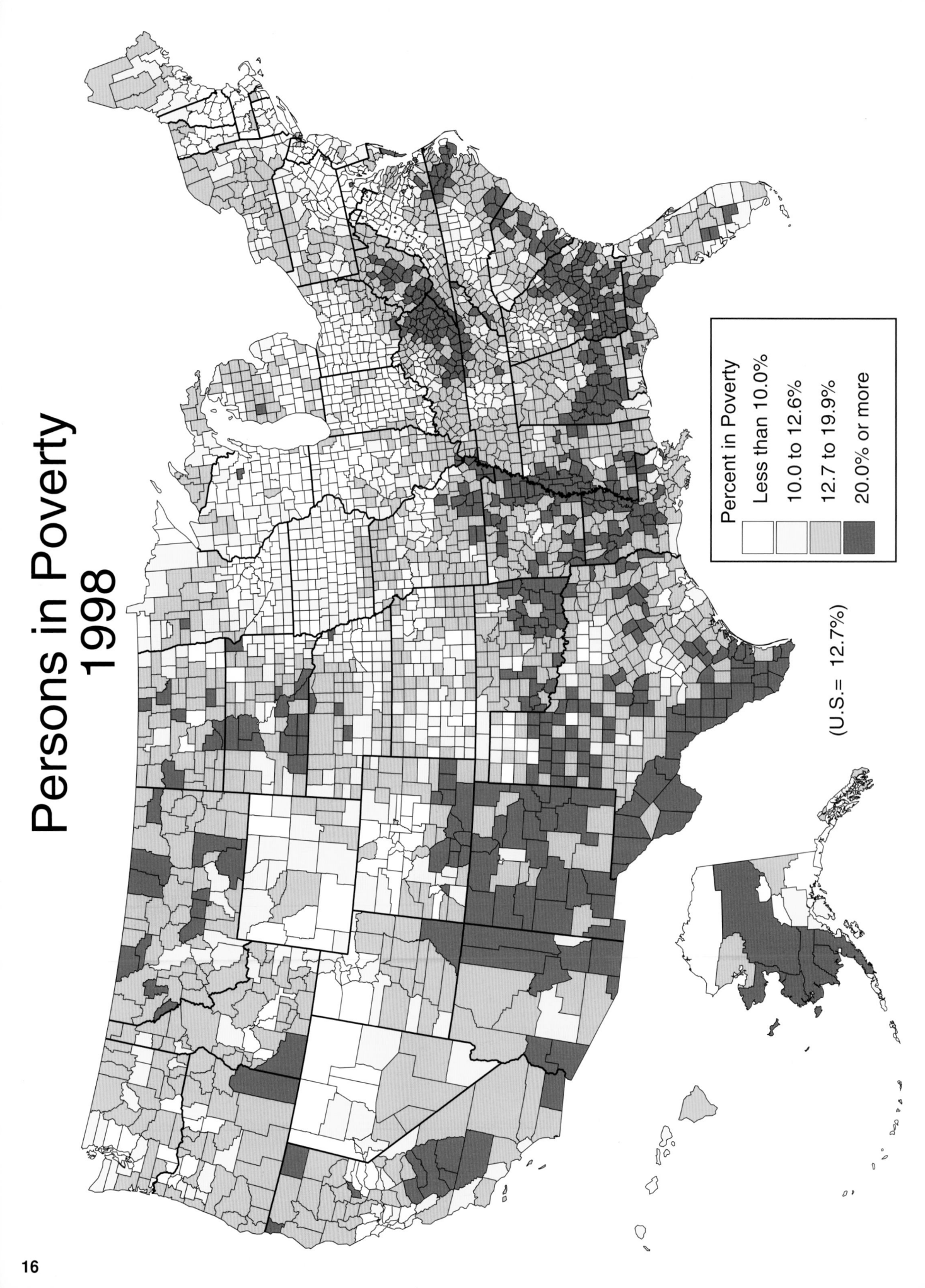

Persons in Poverty
1998

Percent in Poverty

- Less than 10.0%
- 10.0 to 12.6%
- 12.7 to 19.9%
- 20.0% or more

(U.S.= 12.7%)

Land Owned by the Federal Government 1997

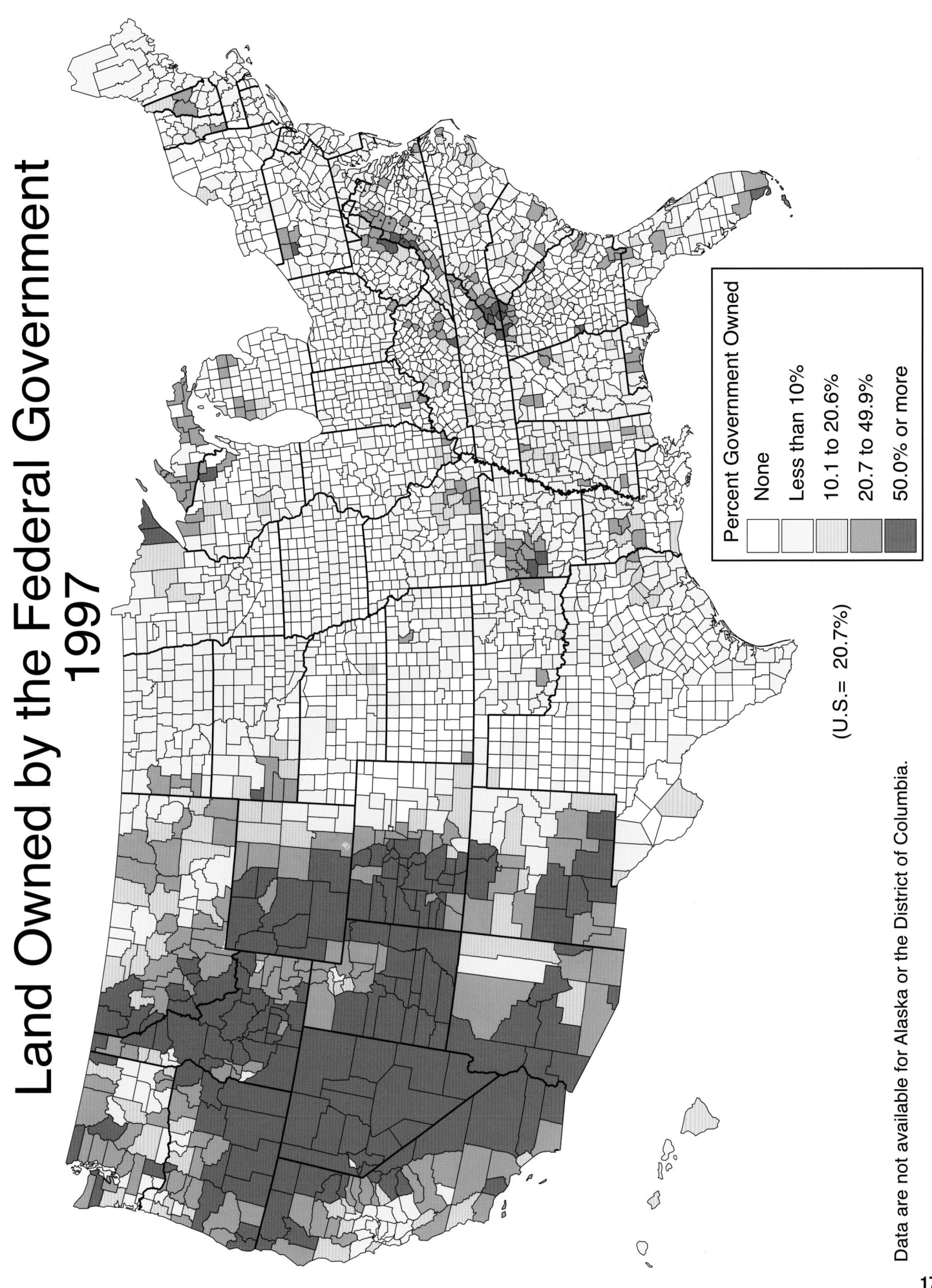

Percent Government Owned

None

Less than 10%

10.1 to 20.6%

20.7 to 49.9%

50.0% or more

(U.S.= 20.7%)

Data are not available for Alaska or the District of Columbia.

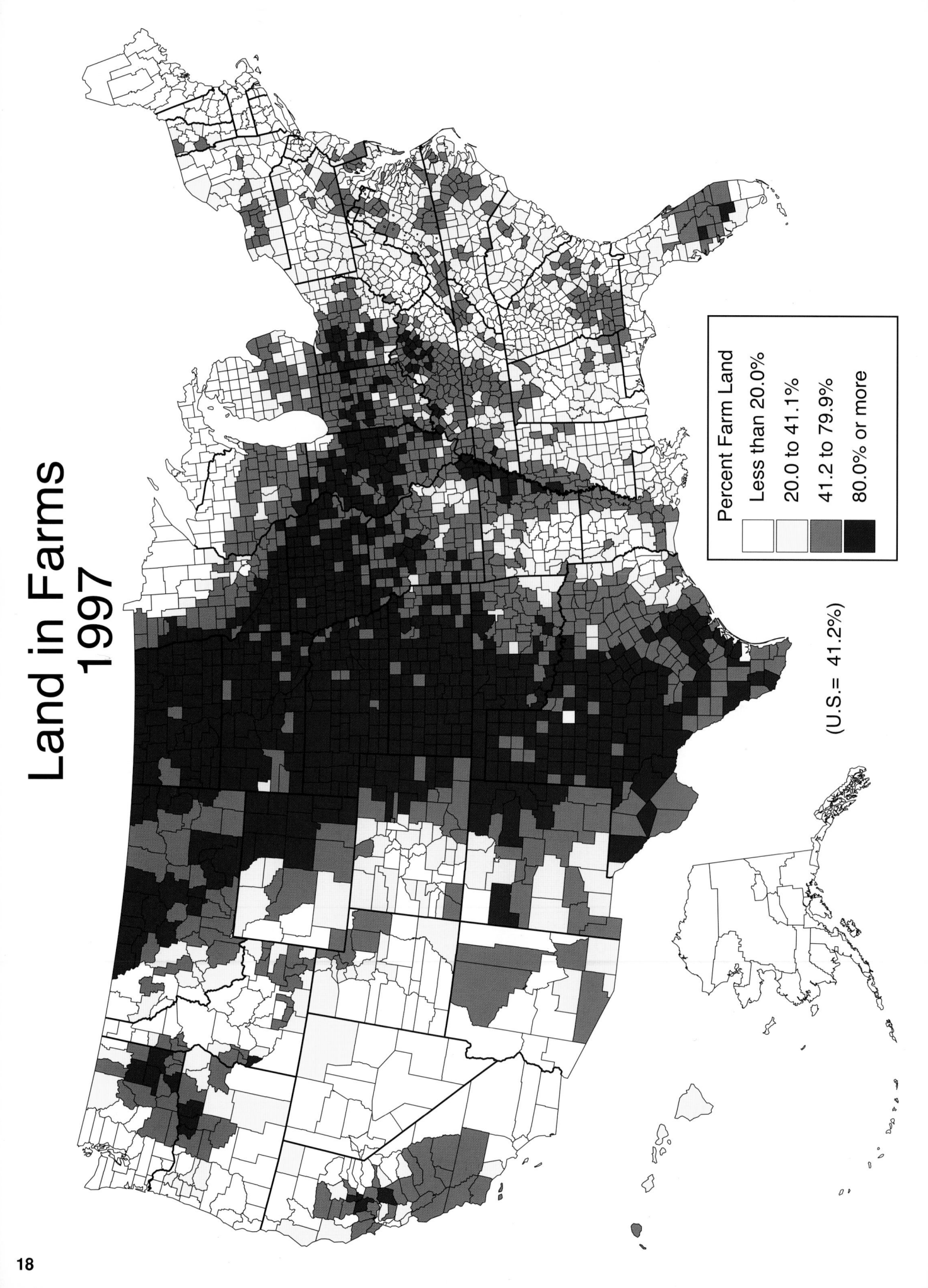

Land in Farms
1997

Percent Farm Land

Less than 20.0%

20.0 to 41.1%

41.2 to 79.9%

80.0% or more

(U.S. = 41.2%)

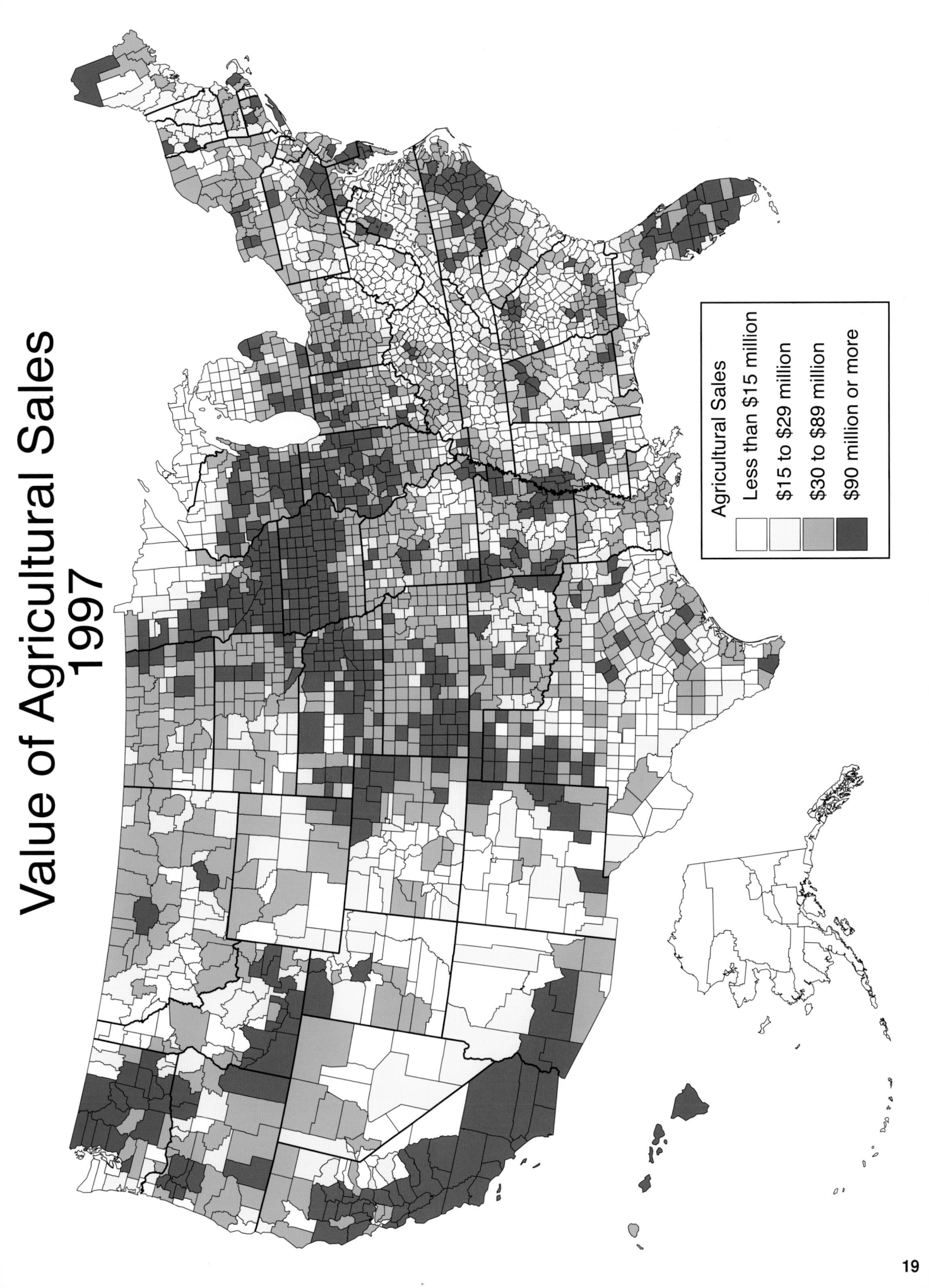

Value of Agricultural Sales
1997

Agricultural Sales

Less than $15 million
$15 to $29 million
$30 to $89 million
$90 million or more

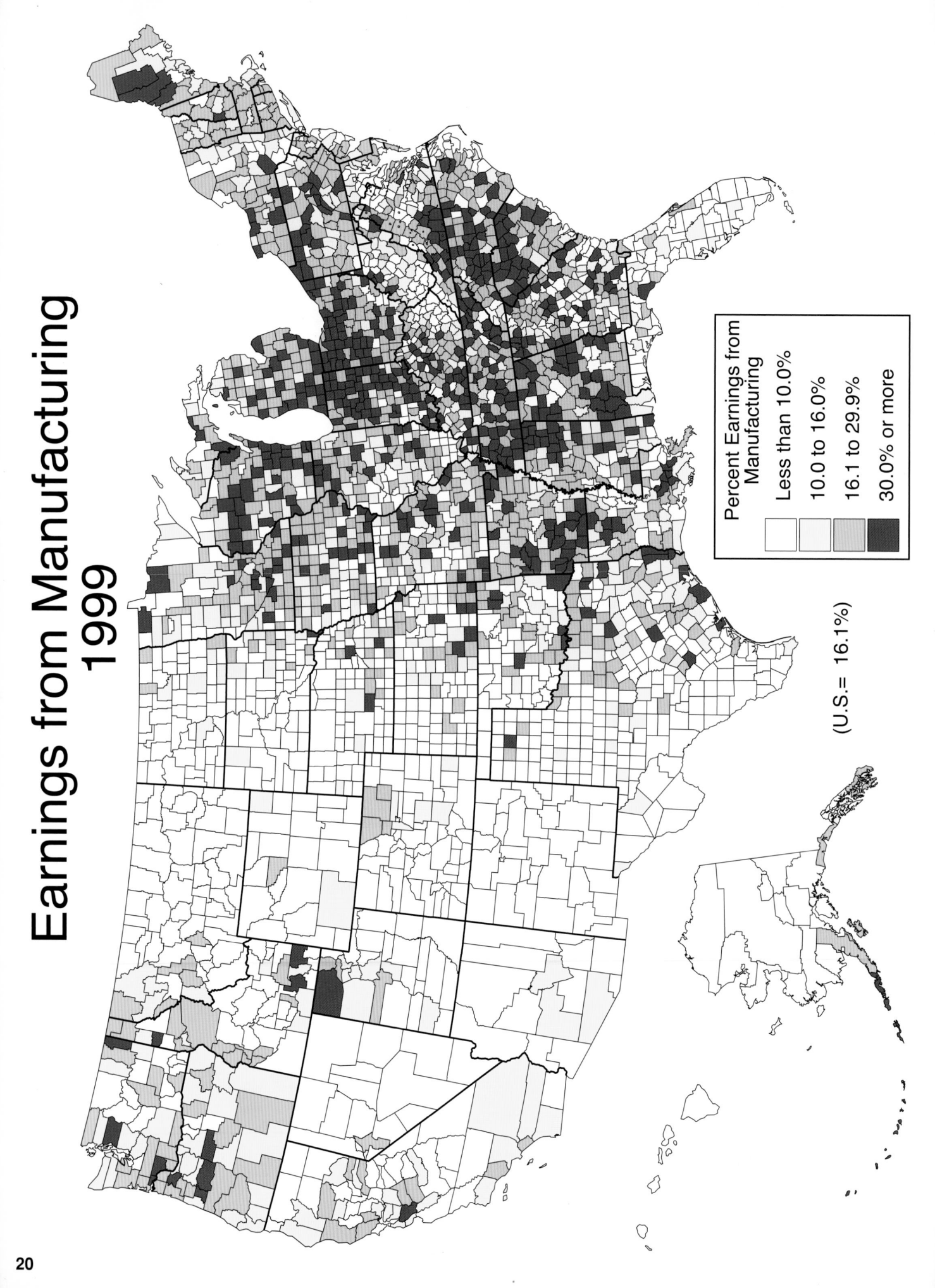

Earnings from Manufacturing 1999

Percent Earnings from Manufacturing

Less than 10.0%

10.0 to 16.0%

16.1 to 29.9%

30.0% or more

(U.S. = 16.1%)

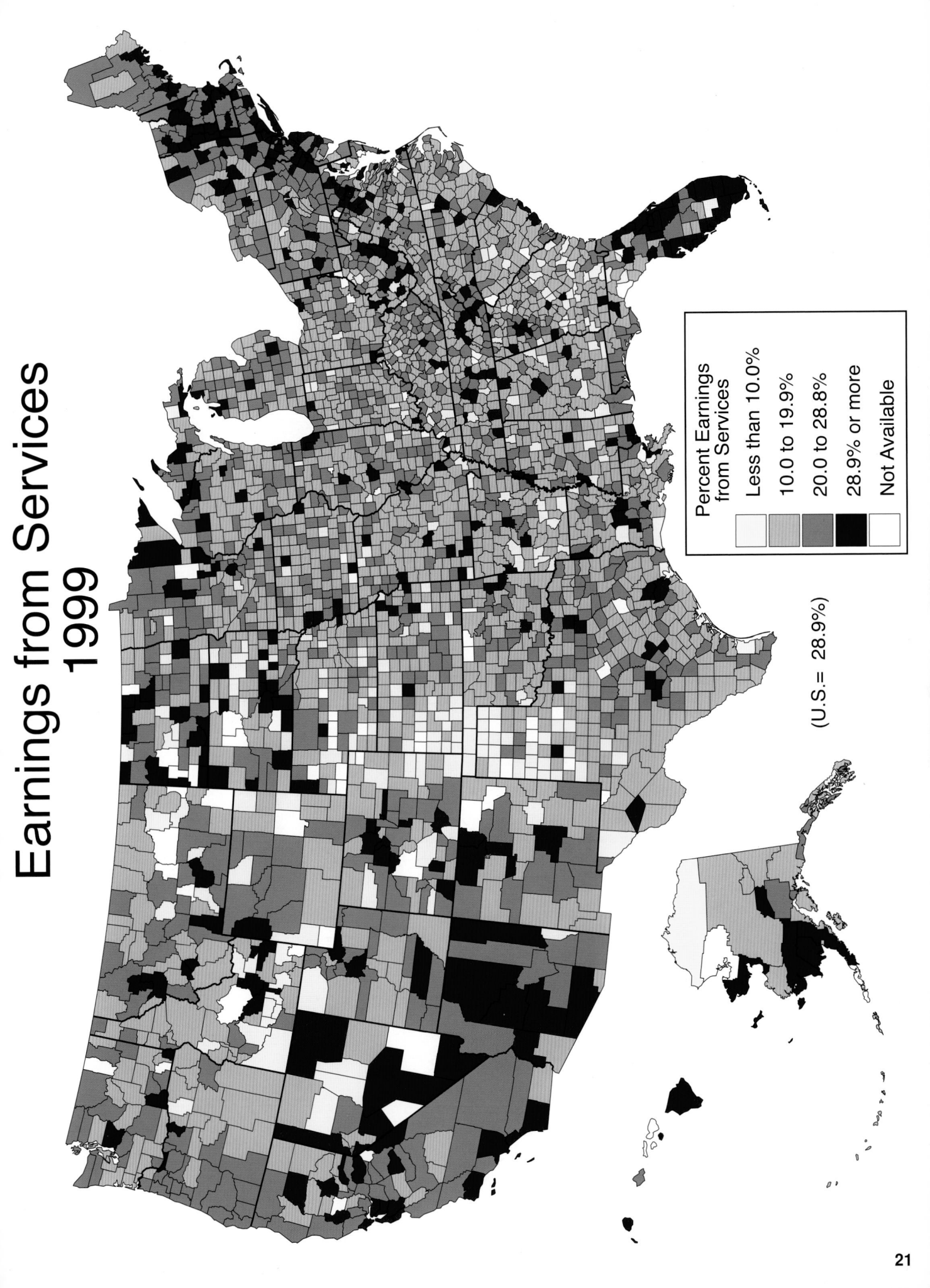

Earnings from Services
1999

Percent Earnings from Services

- Less than 10.0%
- 10.0 to 19.9%
- 20.0 to 28.8%
- 28.9% or more
- Not Available

(U.S. = 28.9%)

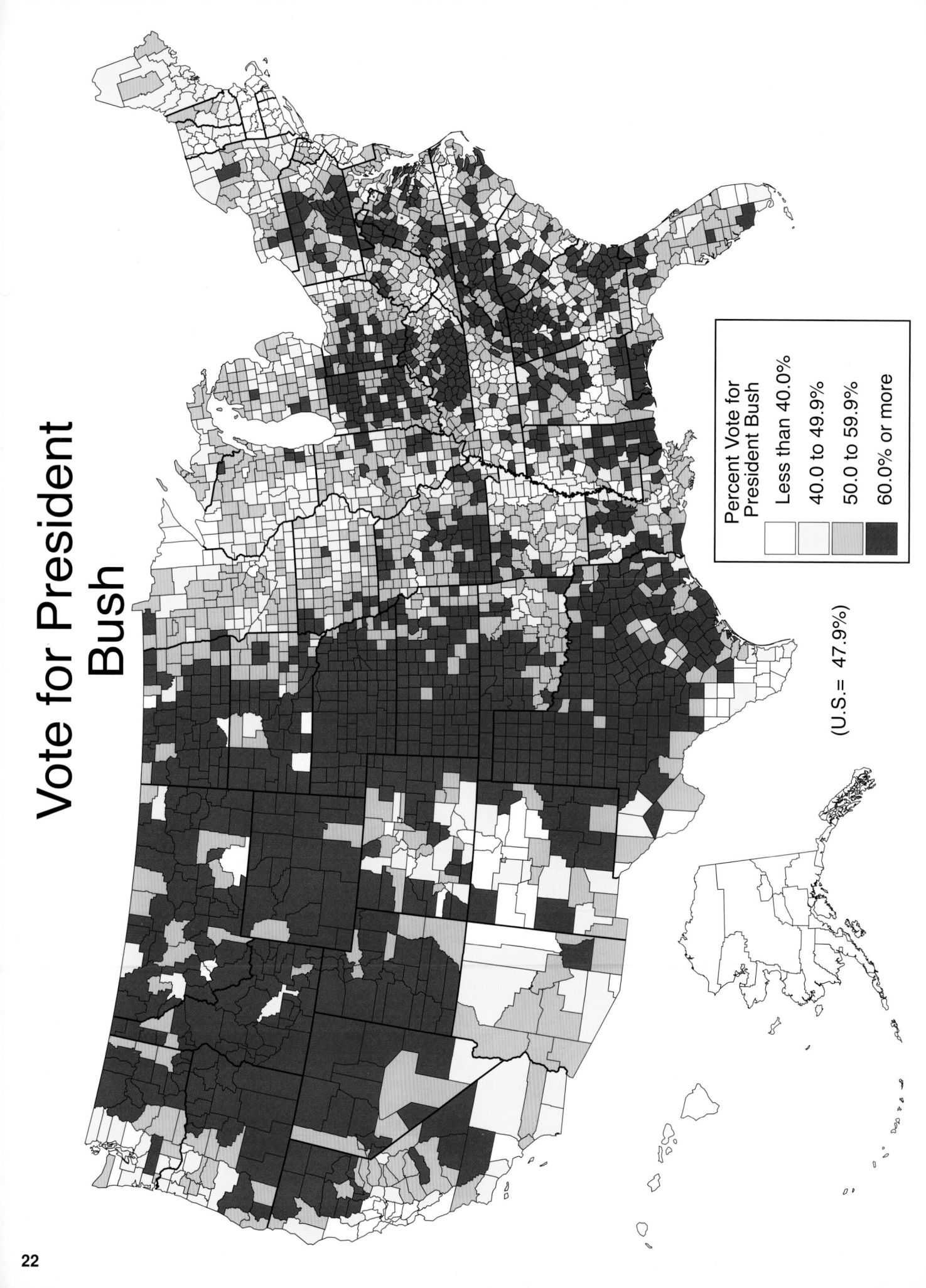

Vote for President Bush

Percent Vote for
President Bush

Less than 40.0%

40.0 to 49.9%

50.0 to 59.9%

60.0% or more

(U.S. = 47.9%)

Area Rankings

Area Rankings

Area Rankings

Area Rankings

TABLE 1—States and the District of Columbia
Selected Rankings

Total Persons, 2000

Population Rank	State	[col 3] Population
X	United States	281 421 906
1	California	33 871 648
2	Texas	20 851 820
3	New York	18 976 457
4	Florida	15 982 378
5	Illinois	12 419 293
6	Pennsylvania	12 281 054
7	Ohio	11 353 140
8	Michigan	9 938 444
9	New Jersey	8 414 350
10	Georgia	8 186 453
11	North Carolina	8 049 313
12	Virginia	7 078 515
13	Massachusetts	6 349 097
14	Indiana	6 080 485
15	Washington	5 894 121
16	Tennessee	5 689 283
17	Missouri	5 595 211
18	Wisconsin	5 363 675
19	Maryland	5 296 486
20	Arizona	5 130 632
21	Minnesota	4 919 479
22	Louisiana	4 468 976
23	Alabama	4 447 100
24	Colorado	4 301 261
25	Kentucky	4 041 769
26	South Carolina	4 012 012
27	Oklahoma	3 450 654
28	Oregon	3 421 399
29	Connecticut	3 405 565
30	Iowa	2 926 324
31	Mississippi	2 844 658
32	Kansas	2 688 418
33	Arkansas	2 673 400
34	Utah	2 233 169
35	Nevada	1 998 257
36	New Mexico	1 819 046
37	West Virginia	1 808 344
38	Nebraska	1 711 263
39	Idaho	1 293 953
40	Maine	1 274 923
41	New Hampshire	1 235 786
42	Hawaii	1 211 537
43	Rhode Island	1 048 319
44	Montana	902 195
45	Delaware	783 600
46	South Dakota	754 844
47	North Dakota	642 200
48	Alaska	626 932
49	Vermont	608 827
50	District of Columbia	572 059
51	Wyoming	493 782

Total Land Area, (square kilometers), 2000

Population Rank	Land Area Rank	State	[col 1] Land Area
X	X	United States	9 161 924
48	1	Alaska	1 481 347
2	2	Texas	678 051
1	3	California	403 933
44	4	Montana	376 979
36	5	New Mexico	314 309
20	6	Arizona	294 312
35	7	Nevada	284 448
24	8	Colorado	268 627
51	9	Wyoming	251 489
28	10	Oregon	248 631
39	11	Idaho	214 314
34	12	Utah	212 751
32	13	Kansas	211 900
21	14	Minnesota	206 189
38	15	Nebraska	199 099
46	16	South Dakota	196 540
47	17	North Dakota	178 647
17	18	Missouri	178 414
27	19	Oklahoma	177 847
15	20	Washington	172 348
10	21	Georgia	149 976
8	22	Michigan	147 121
30	23	Iowa	144 701
5	24	Illinois	143 961
18	25	Wisconsin	140 663
4	26	Florida	139 670
33	27	Arkansas	134 856
23	28	Alabama	131 426
11	29	North Carolina	126 161
3	30	New York	122 283
31	31	Mississippi	121 488
6	32	Pennsylvania	116 074
22	33	Louisiana	112 825
16	34	Tennessee	106 752
7	35	Ohio	106 056
25	36	Kentucky	102 896
12	37	Virginia	102 548
14	38	Indiana	92 895
40	39	Maine	79 931
26	40	South Carolina	77 983
37	41	West Virginia	62 361
19	42	Maryland	25 314
49	43	Vermont	23 956
41	44	New Hampshire	23 227
13	45	Massachusetts	20 306
9	46	New Jersey	19 211
42	47	Hawaii	16 635
29	48	Connecticut	12 548
45	49	Delaware	5 060
43	50	Rhode Island	2 706
50	51	District of Columbia	159

Population Density (per square kilometer), 2000

Population Rank	Density Rank	State	[col 5] Density
X	X	United States	31.1
50	1	District of Columbia	3 596.4
9	2	New Jersey	441.6
43	3	Rhode Island	391.3
13	4	Massachusetts	314.2
29	5	Connecticut	273.0
19	6	Maryland	212.3
45	7	Delaware	157.3
3	8	New York	155.5
4	9	Florida	117.4
7	10	Ohio	107.2
6	11	Pennsylvania	105.9
5	12	Illinois	86.7
1	13	California	85.4
42	14	Hawaii	73.6
12	15	Virginia	70.1
8	16	Michigan	67.9
14	17	Indiana	65.8
11	18	North Carolina	64.9
10	19	Georgia	55.9
41	20	New Hampshire	54.2
16	21	Tennessee	53.8
26	22	South Carolina	52.1
23	23	Louisiana	39.6
25	24	Kentucky	39.5
18	25	Wisconsin	38.4
15	26	Washington	34.7
23	27	Alabama	34.0
17	28	Missouri	31.6
2	29	Texas	31.5
37	30	West Virginia	28.9
49	31	Vermont	25.6
21	32	Minnesota	24.1
31	33	Mississippi	23.5
30	34	Iowa	20.2
33	35	Arkansas	20.0
27	36	Oklahoma	19.5
20	37	Arizona	18.0
24	38	Colorado	16.4
40	39	Maine	16.1
28	40	Oregon	14.0
32	41	Kansas	12.7
34	42	Utah	10.7
38	43	Nebraska	8.6
35	44	Nevada	7.4
39	45	Idaho	6.2
36	46	New Mexico	5.8
46	47	South Dakota	3.8
47	48	North Dakota	3.6
44	49	Montana	2.4
51	50	Wyoming	2.0
48	51	Alaska	0.4

Note: Column numbers refer to Table A. States.

TABLE 1—States and the District of Columbia

Selected Rankings

Percent Population Change, 2000-2001				Projected State Population, 2025				Percent White (one race), 2000			
Popu-lation Rank	Percent Change Rank	State	[col 34] Percent Change	2000 Popu-lation Rank	2025 Popu-lation Rank	State	[col 32] Projected Population 2025	Popu-lation Rank	White Rank	State	[col 6] Percent White
X	X	United States	1.2	X	X	United States	335 048 000	X	X	United States	75.1
35	1	Nevada	5.4	1	1	California	49 285 000	40	1	Maine	96.9
20	2	Arizona	3.4	2	2	Texas	27 183 000	49	2	Vermont	96.8
24	3	Colorado	2.7	4	3	Florida	20 710 000	41	3	New Hampshire	96.0
4	4	Florida	2.6	3	4	New York	19 830 000	37	4	West Virginia	95.0
10	5	Georgia	2.4	5	5	Illinois	13 440 000	30	5	Iowa	93.9
2	6	Texas	2.3	6	6	Pennsylvania	12 683 000	47	6	North Dakota	92.4
39	7	Idaho	2.1	7	7	Ohio	11 744 000	51	7	Wyoming	92.1
1	8	California	1.9	8	8	Michigan	10 078 000	39	8	Idaho	91.0
41	8	New Hampshire	1.9	10	9	Georgia	9 869 000	44	9	Montana	90.6
11	10	North Carolina	1.7	9	10	New Jersey	9 558 000	25	10	Kentucky	90.1
45	11	Delaware	1.6	11	11	North Carolina	9 349 000	38	11	Nebraska	89.6
34	11	Utah	1.6	12	12	Virginia	8 466 000	21	12	Minnesota	89.4
15	11	Washington	1.6	15	13	Washington	7 808 000	34	13	Utah	89.2
19	14	Maryland	1.5	13	14	Massachusetts	6 902 000	18	14	Wisconsin	88.9
28	14	Oregon	1.5	16	15	Tennessee	6 665 000	46	15	South Dakota	88.7
12	14	Virginia	1.5	14	16	Indiana	6 546 000	14	16	Indiana	87.5
48	17	Alaska	1.3	20	17	Arizona	6 412 000	28	17	Oregon	86.6
26	17	South Carolina	1.3	19	18	Maryland	6 274 000	32	18	Kansas	86.1
42	19	Hawaii	1.1	17	19	Missouri	6 250 000	6	19	Pennsylvania	85.4
21	19	Minnesota	1.1	18	20	Wisconsin	5 867 000	7	20	Ohio	85.0
43	21	Rhode Island	1.0	21	21	Minnesota	5 510 000	43	20	Rhode Island	85.0
40	22	Maine	0.9	23	22	Alabama	5 224 000	17	22	Missouri	84.9
16	22	Tennessee	0.9	24	23	Colorado	5 188 000	13	23	Massachusetts	84.5
9	24	New Jersey	0.8	22	24	Louisiana	5 133 000	24	24	Colorado	82.8
33	25	Arkansas	0.7	26	25	South Carolina	4 645 000	15	25	Washington	81.8
49	25	Vermont	0.7	28	26	Oregon	4 349 000	29	26	Connecticut	81.6
18	25	Wisconsin	0.7	25	27	Kentucky	4 314 000	8	27	Michigan	80.2
29	28	Connecticut	0.6	27	28	Oklahoma	4 057 000	16	27	Tennessee	80.2
14	28	Indiana	0.6	29	29	Connecticut	3 739 000	33	29	Arkansas	80.0
25	28	Kentucky	0.6	31	30	Mississippi	3 142 000	4	30	Florida	78.0
17	28	Missouri	0.6	32	31	Kansas	3 108 000	27	31	Oklahoma	76.2
36	28	New Mexico	0.6	33	32	Arkansas	3 055 000	20	32	Arizona	75.5
5	33	Illinois	0.5	30	33	Iowa	3 040 000	35	33	Nevada	75.2
13	33	Massachusetts	0.5	34	34	Utah	2 883 000	45	34	Delaware	74.6
8	33	Michigan	0.5	36	35	New Mexico	2 612 000	5	35	Illinois	73.5
31	33	Mississippi	0.5	35	36	Nevada	2 312 000	9	36	New Jersey	72.6
23	37	Alabama	0.4	38	37	Nebraska	1 930 000	12	37	Virginia	72.3
27	38	Oklahoma	0.3	37	38	West Virginia	1 845 000	11	38	North Carolina	72.1
32	39	Kansas	0.2	42	39	Hawaii	1 812 000	23	39	Alabama	71.1
44	39	Montana	0.2	39	40	Idaho	1 739 000	2	40	Texas	71.0
3	39	New York	0.2	41	41	New Hampshire	1 439 000	48	41	Alaska	69.3
7	39	Ohio	0.2	40	42	Maine	1 423 000	3	42	New York	67.9
46	39	South Dakota	0.2	43	43	Rhode Island	1 141 000	26	43	South Carolina	67.2
38	45	Nebraska	0.1	44	44	Montana	1 121 000	36	44	New Mexico	66.8
51	44	Wyoming	0.1	48	45	Alaska	885 000	10	45	Georgia	65.1
50	47	District of Columbia	0.0	46	46	South Dakota	866 000	19	46	Maryland	64.0
6	46	Pennsylvania	0.0	45	47	Delaware	861 000	22	47	Louisiana	63.9
30	49	Iowa	-0.1	47	48	North Dakota	729 000	31	48	Mississippi	61.4
22	48	Louisiana	-0.1	51	49	Wyoming	694 000	1	49	California	59.5
37	50	West Virginia	-0.4	49	50	Vermont	678 000	50	50	District of Columbia	30.8
47	51	North Dakota	-1.2	50	51	District of Columbia	655 000	42	51	Hawaii	24.3

Note: Column numbers refer to Table A. States.

TABLE 1—States and the District of Columbia
Selected Rankings

Percent Black (one race), 2000				Percent Hispanic, 2000				Net Migration, 2000-2001			
Population Rank	Black Rank	State	[col 7] Percent Black	Population Rank	Hispanic Rank	State	[col 10] Percent Hispanic	Population Rank	Migration Rank	State	[col 37] Net Migration
X	X	United States	12.3	X	X	United States	12.5	X	X	United States	1 339 827
50	1	District of Columbia	60.0	36	1	New Mexico	42.1	4	1	Florida	359 194
31	2	Mississippi	36.3	1	2	California	32.4	1	2	California	255 179
22	3	Louisiana	32.5	2	3	Texas	32.0	2	3	Texas	209 561
26	4	South Carolina	29.5	20	4	Arizona	25.3	20	4	Arizona	121 810
10	5	Georgia	28.7	35	5	Nevada	19.7	10	5	Georgia	106 412
19	6	Maryland	27.9	24	6	Colorado	17.1	35	6	Nevada	87 422
23	7	Alabama	26.0	4	7	Florida	16.8	11	7	North Carolina	76 874
11	8	North Carolina	21.6	3	8	New York	15.1	24	8	Colorado	69 799
12	9	Virginia	19.6	9	9	New Jersey	13.3	12	9	Virginia	54 758
45	10	Delaware	19.2	5	10	Illinois	12.3	15	10	Washington	49 721
16	11	Tennessee	16.4	29	11	Connecticut	9.4	19	11	Maryland	39 542
3	12	New York	15.9	34	12	Utah	9.0	28	12	Oregon	32 923
33	13	Arkansas	15.7	43	13	Rhode Island	8.7	26	13	South Carolina	26 787
5	14	Illinois	15.1	28	14	Oregon	8.0	9	14	New Jersey	21 146
4	15	Florida	14.6	50	15	District of Columbia	7.9	16	15	Tennessee	20 833
8	16	Michigan	14.2	39	15	Idaho	7.9	41	16	New Hampshire	17 926
9	17	New Jersey	13.6	15	17	Washington	7.5	21	17	Minnesota	17 529
7	18	Ohio	11.5	42	18	Hawaii	7.2	39	18	Idaho	14 131
2	18	Texas	11.5	32	19	Kansas	7.0	18	19	Wisconsin	12 137
17	20	Missouri	11.2	13	20	Massachusetts	6.8	40	20	Maine	11 021
6	21	Pennsylvania	10.0	51	21	Wyoming	6.4	17	21	Missouri	9 038
29	22	Connecticut	9.1	38	22	Nebraska	5.5	43	22	Rhode Island	8 167
14	23	Indiana	8.4	10	23	Georgia	5.3	45	23	Delaware	7 540
27	24	Oklahoma	7.6	27	24	Oklahoma	5.2	33	24	Arkansas	5 683
25	25	Kentucky	7.3	45	25	Delaware	4.8	29	25	Connecticut	5 196
35	26	Nevada	6.8	11	26	North Carolina	4.7	25	26	Kentucky	5 181
1	27	California	6.7	12	26	Virginia	4.7	49	27	Vermont	2 981
32	28	Kansas	5.7	19	28	Maryland	4.3	13	28	Massachusetts	1 279
18	28	Wisconsin	5.7	48	29	Alaska	4.1	42	29	Hawaii	269
13	30	Massachusetts	5.4	18	30	Wisconsin	3.6	44	30	Montana	-907
43	31	Rhode Island	4.5	14	31	Indiana	3.5	48	31	Alaska	-993
38	32	Nebraska	4.0	8	32	Michigan	3.3	51	32	Wyoming	-1 950
24	33	Colorado	3.8	33	33	Arkansas	3.2	46	33	South Dakota	-2 240
48	34	Alaska	3.5	6	33	Pennsylvania	3.2	50	34	District of Columbia	-2 757
21	34	Minnesota	3.5	21	35	Minnesota	2.9	14	35	Indiana	-3 178
15	36	Washington	3.2	30	36	Iowa	2.8	37	36	West Virginia	-5 233
37	36	West Virginia	3.2	22	37	Louisiana	2.4	34	37	Utah	-5 549
20	38	Arizona	3.1	26	37	South Carolina	2.4	23	38	Alabama	-5 607
30	39	Iowa	2.1	16	39	Tennessee	2.2	8	39	Michigan	-6 207
36	40	New Mexico	1.9	17	40	Missouri	2.1	36	40	New Mexico	-6 546
42	41	Hawaii	1.8	44	41	Montana	2.0	27	41	Oklahoma	-7 177
28	42	Oregon	1.6	7	42	Ohio	1.9	31	42	Mississippi	-7 558
34	43	Utah	0.8	23	43	Alabama	1.7	6	43	Pennsylvania	-8 095
51	43	Wyoming	0.8	41	43	New Hampshire	1.7	38	44	Nebraska	-9 047
41	45	New Hampshire	0.7	25	45	Kentucky	1.5	47	45	North Dakota	-9 822
47	46	North Dakota	0.6	31	46	Mississippi	1.4	32	46	Kansas	-11 379
46	46	South Dakota	0.6	46	46	South Dakota	1.4	30	47	Iowa	-14 184
40	48	Maine	0.5	47	48	North Dakota	1.2	5	48	Illinois	-35 126
49	48	Vermont	0.5	49	49	Vermont	0.9	7	49	Ohio	-37 015
39	50	Idaho	0.4	40	50	Maine	0.7	22	50	Louisiana	-39 132
44	51	Montana	0.3	37	50	West Virginia	0.7	3	51	New York	-90 510

Note: Column numbers refer to Table A. States.

TABLE 1—States and the District of Columbia
Selected Rankings

Popu-lation Rank	Under 18 Years Rank	State	[cols 11 & 12] Percent Under 18 Years	Popu-lation Rank	65 Years and Over Rank	State	[cols 18 & 19] Percent 65 Years and Over	Popu-lation Rank	Birth Rate Rank	State	[col 61] Birth Rate
X	X	United States	25.7	X	X	United States	12.4	X	X	United States	14.7
34	1	Utah	32.2	4	1	Florida	17.6	34	1	Utah	21.9
48	2	Alaska	30.4	6	2	Pennsylvania	15.6	2	2	Texas	17.8
39	3	Idaho	28.5	37	3	West Virginia	15.3	20	3	Arizona	17.5
2	4	Texas	28.2	30	4	Iowa	14.9	10	4	Georgia	16.7
36	5	New Mexico	28.0	47	5	North Dakota	14.7	35	5	Nevada	16.4
1	6	California	27.3	43	6	Rhode Island	14.5	48	6	Alaska	16.0
22	6	Louisiana	27.3	40	7	Maine	14.3	39	6	Idaho	16.0
31	6	Mississippi	27.3	46	7	South Dakota	14.3	1	8	California	15.8
46	9	South Dakota	26.9	33	9	Arkansas	14.0	24	8	Colorado	15.8
20	10	Arizona	26.7	29	10	Connecticut	13.8	31	8	Mississippi	15.8
10	11	Georgia	26.5	38	11	Nebraska	13.6	36	11	New Mexico	15.6
32	11	Kansas	26.5	13	12	Massachusetts	13.5	22	12	Louisiana	15.5
38	13	Nebraska	26.3	17	12	Missouri	13.5	11	12	North Carolina	15.5
5	14	Illinois	26.2	44	14	Montana	13.4	5	14	Illinois	15.2
8	14	Michigan	26.2	7	15	Ohio	13.3	42	15	Hawaii	14.9
21	14	Minnesota	26.2	42	16	Hawaii	13.2	32	15	Kansas	14.9
51	17	Wyoming	26.1	32	16	Kansas	13.2	50	17	District of Columbia	14.8
14	18	Indiana	25.9	9	16	New Jersey	13.2	38	17	Nebraska	14.8
27	19	Oklahoma	25.8	27	16	Oklahoma	13.2	33	19	Arkansas	14.7
15	20	Washington	25.7	18	20	Wisconsin	13.1	14	19	Indiana	14.7
24	21	Colorado	25.6	23	21	Alabama	13.0	27	19	Oklahoma	14.7
19	21	Maryland	25.6	20	21	Arizona	13.0	45	22	Delaware	14.5
35	21	Nevada	25.6	45	21	Delaware	13.0	23	23	Alabama	14.4
33	24	Arkansas	25.5	3	24	New York	12.9	16	23	Tennessee	14.4
17	24	Missouri	25.5	28	25	Oregon	12.8	26	25	South Carolina	14.3
44	24	Montana	25.5	49	26	Vermont	12.7	19	26	Maryland	14.2
18	24	Wisconsin	25.5	25	27	Kentucky	12.5	3	26	New York	14.2
7	28	Ohio	25.4	14	28	Indiana	12.4	12	26	Virginia	14.2
23	29	Alabama	25.3	8	29	Michigan	12.3	25	29	Kentucky	14.1
26	30	South Carolina	25.2	16	29	Tennessee	12.3	9	29	New Jersey	14.1
30	31	Iowa	25.0	50	31	District of Columbia	12.2	21	31	Minnesota	14.0
41	31	New Hampshire	25.0	5	32	Illinois	12.1	46	31	South Dakota	14.0
47	31	North Dakota	25.0	21	32	Minnesota	12.1	17	33	Missouri	13.9
45	34	Delaware	24.9	26	32	South Carolina	12.1	15	33	Washington	13.9
29	35	Connecticut	24.8	31	35	Mississippi	12.0	7	35	Ohio	13.8
9	35	New Jersey	24.8	11	35	North Carolina	12.0	8	36	Michigan	13.7
3	37	New York	24.7	41	37	New Hampshire	11.9	28	36	Oregon	13.7
28	37	Oregon	24.7	36	38	New Mexico	11.7	4	38	Florida	13.3
25	39	Kentucky	24.6	51	39	Wyoming	11.6	30	38	Iowa	13.3
16	39	Tennessee	24.6	22	40	Louisiana	11.5	13	40	Massachusetts	13.2
42	41	Hawaii	24.5	39	41	Idaho	11.3	18	41	Wisconsin	13.1
12	41	Virginia	24.5	19	41	Maryland	11.3	29	42	Connecticut	13.0
11	43	North Carolina	24.4	12	43	Virginia	11.2	51	42	Wyoming	13.0
49	44	Vermont	24.2	15	43	Washington	11.2	43	44	Rhode Island	12.6
6	45	Pennsylvania	23.8	35	45	Nevada	11.0	44	45	Montana	12.3
13	46	Massachusetts	23.7	1	46	California	10.6	47	46	North Dakota	12.2
40	47	Maine	23.6	2	47	Texas	10.0	6	46	Pennsylvania	12.2
43	47	Rhode Island	23.6	24	48	Colorado	9.7	41	48	New Hampshire	12.0
4	49	Florida	22.8	10	49	Georgia	9.6	37	49	West Virginia	11.6
37	50	West Virginia	22.2	34	50	Utah	8.5	49	50	Vermont	10.9
50	51	District of Columbia	20.1	48	51	Alaska	5.7	40	51	Maine	10.8

Note: Column numbers refer to Table A. States.

TABLE 1—States and the District of Columbia
Selected Rankings

Infant Deaths Per 1,000 Live Births, 1999				Percent College Graduates (Bachelor's or Higher Degree), 2000				Median Household Income, 1998-2000 Average			
Popu-lation Rank	Infant Mortality Rate	State	[col 66] Infant Mortality Rank	Popu-lation Rank	Percent College Graduate Rank	State	[col 82] Percent College Grads	Popu-lation Rank	Median Income Rank	State	[col 89] Median Income (dollars)
X	X	United States	7.1	X	X	United States	25.6	X	X	United States	41 789
50	1	District of Columbia	15.0	50	1	District of Columbia	38.3	19	1	Maryland	52 846
26	2	South Carolina	10.2	24	2	Colorado	34.6	48	2	Alaska	52 492
31	3	Mississippi	10.1	13	3	Massachusetts	32.7	9	3	New Jersey	51 739
23	4	Alabama	9.8	19	4	Maryland	32.3	29	4	Connecticut	50 647
22	5	Louisiana	9.2	12	5	Virginia	31.9	21	5	Minnesota	50 088
11	6	North Carolina	9.1	29	6	Connecticut	31.6	24	6	Colorado	49 216
46	7	South Dakota	8.9	21	7	Minnesota	31.2	41	7	New Hampshire	48 029
5	8	Illinois	8.5	41	8	New Hampshire	30.1	12	8	Virginia	47 701
27	8	Oklahoma	8.5	9	8	New Jersey	30.1	45	9	Delaware	47 438
19	10	Maryland	8.4	49	10	Vermont	28.8	5	10	Illinois	46 649
10	11	Georgia	8.2	3	11	New York	28.7	34	11	Utah	46 539
7	11	Ohio	8.2	15	12	Washington	28.6	15	12	Washington	46 412
8	13	Michigan	8.1	48	13	Alaska	28.1	8	13	Michigan	46 034
33	14	Arkansas	8.0	1	14	California	27.5	13	14	Massachusetts	45 769
14	14	Indiana	8.0	32	15	Kansas	27.3	42	15	Hawaii	45 657
17	16	Missouri	7.8	28	16	Oregon	27.2	18	16	Wisconsin	45 441
16	17	Tennessee	7.7	5	17	Illinois	27.1	1	17	California	45 070
25	18	Kentucky	7.6	43	18	Rhode Island	26.4	17	18	Missouri	44 247
45	19	Delaware	7.4	34	18	Utah	26.4	43	19	Rhode Island	43 428
4	19	Florida	7.4	42	20	Hawaii	26.3	35	20	Nevada	43 262
37	19	West Virginia	7.4	17	21	Missouri	26.2	7	21	Ohio	41 972
32	22	Kansas	7.3	46	22	South Dakota	25.7	28	22	Oregon	41 915
6	22	Pennsylvania	7.3	30	23	Iowa	25.5	30	23	Iowa	41 560
12	22	Virginia	7.3	20	24	Arizona	24.6	10	24	Georgia	41 481
42	25	Hawaii	7.0	38	24	Nebraska	24.6	6	25	Pennsylvania	41 394
36	26	New Mexico	6.9	7	24	Ohio	24.6	14	26	Indiana	41 315
51	26	Wyoming	6.9	6	27	Pennsylvania	24.3	49	27	Vermont	40 908
20	28	Arizona	6.8	40	28	Maine	24.1	3	28	New York	40 822
38	28	Nebraska	6.8	45	29	Delaware	24.0	40	29	Maine	39 815
47	28	North Dakota	6.8	2	30	Texas	23.9	20	30	Arizona	39 653
24	31	Colorado	6.7	44	31	Montana	23.8	2	31	Texas	39 296
39	31	Idaho	6.7	18	31	Wisconsin	23.8	38	32	Nebraska	39 029
44	31	Montana	6.7	36	33	New Mexico	23.6	11	33	North Carolina	38 413
9	31	New Jersey	6.7	11	34	North Carolina	23.2	32	34	Kansas	38 393
18	31	Wisconsin	6.7	10	35	Georgia	23.1	51	35	Wyoming	38 291
35	36	Nevada	6.6	8	36	Michigan	23.0	50	36	District of Columbia	38 005
3	37	New York	6.4	4	37	Florida	22.8	39	37	Idaho	37 760
21	38	Minnesota	6.2	47	38	North Dakota	22.6	4	38	Florida	37 305
2	38	Texas	6.2	22	39	Louisiana	22.5	25	39	Kentucky	36 826
29	40	Connecticut	6.1	27	39	Oklahoma	22.5	26	40	South Carolina	36 671
41	41	New Hampshire	5.8	16	41	Tennessee	22.0	23	41	Alabama	36 268
28	41	Oregon	5.8	51	42	Wyoming	20.6	46	42	South Dakota	35 986
49	41	Vermont	5.8	25	43	Kentucky	20.5	16	43	Tennessee	35 874
48	44	Alaska	5.7	23	44	Alabama	20.4	36	44	New Mexico	34 035
30	44	Iowa	5.7	39	45	Idaho	20.0	27	45	Oklahoma	34 020
43	44	Rhode Island	5.7	35	46	Nevada	19.3	47	46	North Dakota	33 769
1	47	California	5.4	26	47	South Carolina	19.0	44	47	Montana	32 553
13	48	Massachusetts	5.2	31	48	Mississippi	18.7	22	48	Louisiana	32 500
15	49	Washington	5.0	33	49	Arkansas	18.4	31	49	Mississippi	31 963
40	50	Maine	4.8	14	50	Indiana	17.1	33	50	Arkansas	30 082
34	50	Utah	4.8	37	51	West Virginia	15.3	37	51	West Virginia	29 217

Note: Column numbers refer to Table A. States.

TABLE 1—States and the District of Columbia
Selected Rankings

Percent of Persons Below the Poverty Level, 2000				Percent of Children Under 18 Years Below the Poverty Level, 2000				Percent of Persons Lacking Health Insurance, 2000			
Popu-lation Rank	Poverty Rate Rank	State	[col 94] Poverty Rate	Popu-lation Rank	Poverty Rate of Children Under 18 Years Rank	State	[col 95] Poverty Rate of Children Under 18 Years	Popu-lation Rank	Percent Lacking Health Insurance Rank	State	[col 96] Percent Lacking Health Insurance
X	X	United States	11.3	X	X	United States	18.9	X	X	United States	14.0
33	1	Arkansas	17.8	50	1	District of Columbia	45.3	36	1	New Mexico	23.8
22	2	Louisiana	17.3	22	2	Louisiana	29.2	2	2	Texas	21.5
36	3	New Mexico	16.8	36	3	West Virginia	27.5	48	3	Alaska	19.3
44	4	Montana	15.7	20	4	Arizona	26.4	27	3	Oklahoma	19.3
27	5	Oklahoma	15.4	37	5	New Mexico	26.3	22	5	Louisiana	19.1
50	6	District of Columbia	14.9	3	6	New York	24.6	44	6	Montana	18.5
16	7	Tennessee	14.7	23	7	Alabama	24.1	1	7	California	18.1
2	7	Texas	14.7	1	8	California	23.6	4	8	Florida	17.3
23	9	Alabama	14.4	10	9	Georgia	23.4	20	9	Arizona	16.1
37	10	West Virginia	14.0	44	10	Montana	22.6	39	10	Idaho	15.6
3	11	New York	13.4	4	11	Florida	22.3	35	10	Nevada	15.6
39	12	Idaho	12.9	2	12	Texas	22.0	3	12	New York	15.2
31	12	Mississippi	12.9	31	13	Mississippi	21.8	10	13	Georgia	14.6
1	14	California	12.8	28	14	Oregon	21.6	50	14	District of Columbia	14.4
11	15	North Carolina	12.1	11	15	North Carolina	21.5	37	15	West Virginia	14.3
20	16	Arizona	12.0	47	16	North Dakota	20.6	51	15	Wyoming	14.3
25	17	Kentucky	11.9	40	17	Idaho	20.1	33	17	Arkansas	13.9
5	18	Illinois	11.5	27	18	Oklahoma	19.5	28	18	Oregon	13.7
49	19	Vermont	11.3	43	19	Rhode Island	19.4	23	19	Alabama	13.5
10	20	Georgia	11.2	25	20	Kentucky	18.6	5	19	Illinois	13.5
28	20	Oregon	11.2	6	21	Pennsylvania	18.2	34	21	Utah	13.4
51	22	Wyoming	11.0	26	22	South Carolina	18.1	24	22	Colorado	13.3
4	23	Florida	10.6	16	22	Tennessee	18.1	15	22	Washington	13.3
26	23	South Carolina	10.6	7	24	Ohio	18.0	31	24	Mississippi	13.1
13	25	Massachusetts	10.1	33	25	Arkansas	16.7	11	25	North Carolina	13.0
47	25	North Dakota	10.1	38	26	Nebraska	16.2	25	26	Kentucky	12.9
15	25	Washington	10.1	45	27	Delaware	16.1	12	27	Virginia	12.7
8	28	Michigan	10.0	8	28	Michigan	15.6	9	28	New Jersey	12.6
7	28	Ohio	10.0	17	28	Missouri	15.6	14	29	Indiana	12.0
42	30	Hawaii	9.9	30	30	Iowa	15.5	26	30	South Carolina	11.9
32	31	Kansas	9.6	21	31	Minnesota	15.4	46	31	South Dakota	11.8
46	31	South Dakota	9.6	42	32	Hawaii	15.1	32	32	Kansas	11.5
34	31	Utah	9.6	51	33	Wyoming	14.9	40	32	Maine	11.5
18	31	Wisconsin	9.6	41	34	New Hampshire	14.7	47	34	North Dakota	11.4
45	35	Delaware	9.1	39	35	Maine	14.3	7	35	Ohio	10.9
43	35	Rhode Island	9.1	49	35	Vermont	14.3	17	36	Missouri	10.6
38	37	Nebraska	9.0	34	37	Utah	14.0	49	36	Vermont	10.6
6	38	Pennsylvania	8.9	5	38	Illinois	13.8	45	38	Delaware	10.4
14	39	Indiana	8.7	13	38	Massachusetts	13.8	16	39	Tennessee	10.3
35	40	Nevada	8.5	24	40	Colorado	13.7	42	40	Hawaii	10.1
40	41	Maine	8.4	35	40	Nevada	13.7	8	41	Michigan	9.9
48	42	Alaska	8.2	18	42	Wisconsin	13.5	38	41	Nebraska	9.9
24	43	Colorado	8.1	32	43	Kansas	12.9	19	43	Maryland	9.8
17	44	Missouri	8.0	9	44	New Jersey	12.2	13	44	Massachusetts	9.5
9	44	New Jersey	8.0	29	45	Connecticut	12.1	21	45	Minnesota	9.0
12	46	Virginia	7.7	14	46	Indiana	12.0	30	46	Iowa	8.7
19	47	Maryland	7.6	46	47	South Dakota	11.7	29	47	Connecticut	7.9
30	48	Iowa	7.2	15	48	Washington	11.2	6	48	Pennsylvania	7.6
29	49	Connecticut	6.6	48	49	Alaska	10.7	18	49	Wisconsin	7.1
21	50	Minnesota	6.0	12	50	Virginia	9.0	41	50	New Hampshire	6.9
41	51	New Hampshire	5.2	19	51	Maryland	7.5	43	51	Rhode Island	5.9

Note: Column numbers refer to Table A. States.

TABLE 1—States and the District of Columbia
Selected Rankings

Percent of Occupied Units that were Owner-Occupied, 2000				Median Value of Owner-Occupied Housing Units, 2000				Medium Gross Rent of Renter-Occupied Housing Units, 2000			
Population Rank	Rank of Percent Owner-Occupied	State	[col 131] Percent Owner-Occupied	Population Rank	Median Value Rank	State	[col 132] Median Value (dollars)	Population Rank	Median Rent Rank	State	[col 135] Median Rent (dollars)
X	X	United States	66.2	X	X	United States	120 496	X	X	United States	527
37	1	West Virginia	75.2	42	1	Hawaii	288 332	42	1	Hawaii	766
21	2	Minnesota	74.6	1	2	California	216 164	1	2	California	692
8	3	Michigan	73.8	13	3	Massachusetts	192 483	9	3	New Jersey	690
23	4	Alabama	72.5	9	4	New Jersey	173 045	48	4	Alaska	649
39	5	Idaho	72.4	15	5	Washington	169 406	13	5	Massachusetts	645
45	6	Delaware	72.3	24	6	Colorado	168 896	35	6	Nevada	628
30	6	Iowa	72.3	29	7	Connecticut	166 941	24	7	Colorado	625
31	6	Mississippi	72.3	50	8	District of Columbia	164 787	19	8	Maryland	615
26	9	South Carolina	72.2	3	9	New York	150 673	3	8	New York	615
40	10	Maine	71.6	28	10	Oregon	149 729	29	10	Connecticut	600
34	11	Utah	71.5	19	11	Maryland	146 866	15	11	Washington	598
14	12	Indiana	71.4	48	12	Alaska	144 271	41	12	New Hampshire	594
6	13	Pennsylvania	71.3	34	13	Utah	144 036	50	13	District of Columbia	592
25	14	Kentucky	70.8	35	14	Nevada	140 844	45	14	Delaware	565
49	15	Vermont	70.6	41	15	New Hampshire	138 031	4	15	Florida	562
17	16	Missouri	70.3	43	16	Rhode Island	137 907	12	16	Virginia	555
4	17	Florida	70.1	45	17	Delaware	132 942	28	17	Oregon	547
36	18	New Mexico	70.0	5	18	Illinois	130 396	34	18	Utah	543
51	18	Wyoming	70.0	12	19	Virginia	126 526	5	19	Illinois	541
16	20	Tennessee	69.9	21	20	Minnesota	123 960	20	20	Arizona	540
41	21	New Hampshire	69.7	20	21	Arizona	121 688	21	21	Minnesota	535
33	22	Arkansas	69.4	8	22	Michigan	117 360	10	22	Georgia	519
11	22	North Carolina	69.4	49	23	Vermont	115 288	2	23	Texas	489
32	24	Kansas	69.2	10	24	Georgia	113 807	43	24	Rhode Island	484
44	25	Montana	69.1	18	25	Wisconsin	109 688	8	25	Michigan	476
7	25	Ohio	69.1	11	26	North Carolina	108 215	49	26	Vermont	472
27	27	Oklahoma	68.4	4	27	Florida	107 443	18	27	Wisconsin	469
18	27	Wisconsin	68.4	36	28	New Mexico	105 771	11	28	North Carolina	440
46	29	South Dakota	68.2	39	29	Idaho	105 403	14	29	Indiana	436
12	30	Virginia	68.1	26	30	South Carolina	103 882	40	30	Maine	435
20	31	Arizona	68.0	7	31	Ohio	102 822	6	31	Pennsylvania	433
22	32	Louisiana	67.9	40	32	Maine	102 656	26	31	South Carolina	433
19	33	Maryland	67.7	44	33	Montana	98 849	39	33	Idaho	427
10	34	Georgia	67.5	51	34	Wyoming	98 456	7	34	Ohio	424
38	35	Nebraska	67.4	16	35	Tennessee	96 109	16	35	Tennessee	423
24	36	Colorado	67.3	14	36	Indiana	94 767	36	36	New Mexico	419
5	36	Illinois	67.3	6	37	Pennsylvania	94 479	38	37	Nebraska	415
29	38	Connecticut	66.8	17	38	Missouri	91 090	32	38	Kansas	396
47	39	North Dakota	66.6	25	39	Kentucky	89 078	30	39	Iowa	391
9	40	New Jersey	65.6	38	40	Nebraska	85 959	17	40	Missouri	390
15	41	Washington	64.6	23	41	Alabama	85 833	44	41	Montana	389
28	42	Oregon	64.3	22	42	Louisiana	84 460	51	42	Wyoming	385
2	43	Texas	63.8	32	43	Kansas	84 375	47	43	North Dakota	382
48	44	Alaska	62.5	2	44	Texas	83 623	46	44	South Dakota	378
13	45	Massachusetts	61.7	46	45	South Dakota	82 142	25	45	Kentucky	371
35	46	Nevada	60.9	30	46	Iowa	80 366	22	46	Louisiana	369
43	47	Rhode Island	60.0	47	47	North Dakota	75 152	27	47	Oklahoma	360
1	48	California	56.9	31	48	Mississippi	75 053	33	48	Arkansas	358
42	49	Hawaii	56.5	27	49	Oklahoma	73 750	31	49	Mississippi	348
3	50	New York	53.0	33	50	Arkansas	73 480	23	50	Alabama	328
50	51	District of Columbia	40.8	37	51	West Virginia	72 215	37	51	West Virginia	316

Note: Column numbers refer to Table A. States.

TABLE 1—States and the District of Columbia
Selected Rankings

	Unemployment Rate, 2001				Exports of Goods by State of Origin (mil dol), 2000				Value of Residential Construction Authorized by Building Permits, 2001		
Population Rank	Unemployment Rate Rank	State	[col 148] Unemployment Rate	Population Rank	Export Rank	State	[col 283] Exports by State (mil dol)	Population Rank	Value Rank	State	[col 279] Value of Residential Construction (mil dol)
X	X	United States	4.8	X	X	United States	653 632	X	X	United States	196 242 858
50	1	District of Columbia	6.5	1	1	California	111 476	1	1	California	23 649 970
15	2	Washington	6.4	2	2	Texas	60 909	4	2	Florida	19 465 400
48	3	Alaska	6.3	8	3	Michigan	47 971	2	3	Texas	15 761 345
28	3	Oregon	6.3	3	4	New York	45 440	10	4	Georgia	9 461 766
22	5	Louisiana	6.0	15	5	Washington	32 385	11	5	North Carolina	9 226 070
25	6	Kentucky	5.5	5	6	Illinois	30 360	20	6	Arizona	7 782 865
31	6	Mississippi	5.5	7	7	Ohio	27 811	5	7	Illinois	7 141 367
11	6	North Carolina	5.5	9	8	New Jersey	25 540	24	8	Colorado	6 593 250
5	9	Illinois	5.4	6	9	Pennsylvania	22 530	7	9	Ohio	6 452 250
26	9	South Carolina	5.4	4	10	Florida	22 244	8	10	Michigan	6 085 397
23	11	Alabama	5.3	13	11	Massachusetts	18 155	12	11	Virginia	5 715 146
1	11	California	5.3	21	12	Minnesota	16 573	3	12	New York	5 257 031
8	11	Michigan	5.3	11	13	North Carolina	14 009	14	13	Indiana	4 876 861
35	11	Nevada	5.3	14	14	Indiana	13 419	6	14	Pennsylvania	4 804 172
33	15	Arkansas	5.1	29	15	Connecticut	12 659	15	15	Washington	4 689 002
39	16	Idaho	5.0	10	16	Georgia	10 628	21	16	Minnesota	4 576 087
3	17	New York	4.9	18	17	Wisconsin	10 453	18	17	Wisconsin	4 495 419
2	17	Texas	4.9	16	18	Tennessee	10 331	35	18	Nevada	3 742 085
37	17	West Virginia	4.9	12	19	Virginia	10 153	16	19	Tennessee	3 540 178
4	20	Florida	4.8	24	20	Colorado	9 869	26	20	South Carolina	3 469 848
36	20	New Mexico	4.8	20	21	Arizona	9 129	19	21	Maryland	3 228 064
20	22	Arizona	4.7	28	22	Oregon	8 492	9	22	New Jersey	3 016 685
17	22	Missouri	4.7	25	23	Kentucky	7 854	28	23	Oregon	2 997 980
6	22	Pennsylvania	4.7	17	24	Missouri	7 679	17	24	Missouri	2 750 047
43	22	Rhode Island	4.7	26	25	South Carolina	7 450	13	25	Massachusetts	2 688 748
42	26	Hawaii	4.6	45	26	Delaware	5 692	34	26	Utah	2 312 017
44	26	Montana	4.6	23	27	Alabama	5 516	23	27	Alabama	1 822 964
18	26	Wisconsin	4.6	32	28	Kansas	4 803	25	28	Kentucky	1 817 684
16	29	Tennessee	4.5	19	29	Maryland	4 635	32	29	Kansas	1 612 466
14	30	Indiana	4.4	50	30	District of Columbia	4 454	22	30	Louisiana	1 597 626
34	30	Utah	4.4	22	31	Louisiana	3 786	30	31	Iowa	1 480 259
32	32	Kansas	4.3	30	32	Iowa	3 160	27	32	Oklahoma	1 477 528
7	32	Ohio	4.3	27	33	Oklahoma	3 139	39	33	Idaho	1 448 402
9	34	New Jersey	4.2	38	34	Nebraska	3 097	29	34	Connecticut	1 440 308
19	35	Maryland	4.1	34	35	Utah	2 603	36	35	New Mexico	1 186 378
10	36	Georgia	4.0	39	36	Idaho	2 464	33	36	Arkansas	1 019 170
40	36	Maine	4.0	41	37	New Hampshire	2 282	41	37	New Hampshire	950 396
51	38	Wyoming	3.9	33	38	Arkansas	2 012	31	38	Mississippi	894 241
27	39	Oklahoma	3.8	49	39	Vermont	1 782	38	39	Nebraska	834 966
24	40	Colorado	3.7	31	40	Mississippi	1 696	42	40	Hawaii	812 192
13	40	Massachusetts	3.7	40	41	Maine	1 587	40	41	Maine	776 360
21	40	Minnesota	3.7	37	42	West Virginia	1 421	45	42	Delaware	504 014
49	43	Vermont	3.6	35	43	Nevada	1 316	48	43	Alaska	450 421
45	44	Delaware	3.5	43	44	Rhode Island	1 062	46	44	South Dakota	405 260
41	44	New Hampshire	3.5	48	45	Alaska	948	49	45	Vermont	397 422
12	44	Virginia	3.5	47	46	North Dakota	693	37	46	West Virginia	384 877
29	47	Connecticut	3.3	36	47	New Mexico	581	43	47	Rhode Island	306 040
30	47	Iowa	3.3	44	48	Montana	531	51	48	Wyoming	277 173
46	47	South Dakota	3.3	46	49	South Dakota	455	44	49	Montana	266 479
38	50	Nebraska	3.1	42	50	Hawaii	268	47	50	North Dakota	240 815
47	51	North Dakota	2.8	51	51	Wyoming	133	50	51	District of Columbia	60 367

Note: Column numbers refer to Table A. States.

TABLE 1—States and the District of Columbia
Selected Rankings

Value of Agricultural Products Sold (mil dol), 1997				Per Capita State Taxes, 2000				Violent Crime Rate, 2000 (violent crimes known to police per 100,000 population)			
Population Rank	Agricultural Production Rank	State	[col 172] Value of Agricultural Products Sold	Population Rank	Taxes Rank	State	[col 309] State Taxes Per Capita (dollars)	Population Rank	Crime Rate Rank	State	[col 75] Crime Rate
X	X	United States	196 865	X	X	United States	X	X	X	United States	506
1	1	California	23 032	29	1	Connecticut	2 986	50	1	District of Columbia	1 508
2	2	Texas	13 767	42	2	Hawaii	2 751	4	2	Florida	812
30	3	Iowa	11 948	45	3	Delaware	2 720	26	3	South Carolina	805
38	4	Nebraska	9 832	21	4	Minnesota	2 712	19	4	Maryland	787
32	5	Kansas	9 207	13	5	Massachusetts	2 544	36	5	New Mexico	758
5	6	Illinois	8 556	1	6	California	2 474	16	6	Tennessee	707
21	7	Minnesota	8 290	49	7	Vermont	2 435	45	7	Delaware	684
11	8	North Carolina	7 677	18	8	Wisconsin	2 344	22	8	Louisiana	681
4	9	Florida	6 005	8	9	Michigan	2 290	5	9	Illinois	657
18	10	Wisconsin	5 580	48	10	Alaska	2 270	1	10	California	622
33	11	Arkansas	5 480	3	11	New York	2 199	48	11	Alaska	567
17	12	Missouri	5 368	9	12	New Jersey	2 157	8	12	Michigan	555
14	13	Indiana	5 230	15	13	Washington	2 132	3	13	New York	554
10	14	Georgia	4 993	40	14	Maine	2 087	2	14	Texas	545
15	15	Washington	4 768	36	15	New Mexico	2 058	20	15	Arizona	532
7	16	Ohio	4 684	19	16	Maryland	1 955	35	16	Nevada	524
24	17	Colorado	4 534	51	17	Wyoming	1 951	10	17	Georgia	505
27	18	Oklahoma	4 146	43	18	Rhode Island	1 942	11	18	North Carolina	498
6	19	Pennsylvania	3 998	25	19	Kentucky	1 904	27	18	Oklahoma	498
46	20	South Dakota	3 570	11	20	North Carolina	1 903	17	20	Missouri	490
8	21	Michigan	3 568	35	21	Nevada	1 860	23	21	Alabama	486
39	22	Idaho	3 346	37	22	West Virginia	1 849	13	22	Massachusetts	476
31	23	Mississippi	3 127	39	23	Idaho	1 837	33	23	Arkansas	445
23	24	Alabama	3 099	5	24	Illinois	1 835	6	24	Pennsylvania	420
25	25	Kentucky	3 064	6	25	Pennsylvania	1 829	32	25	Kansas	389
28	26	Oregon	2 969	47	26	North Dakota	1 826	9	26	New Jersey	384
47	27	North Dakota	2 869	33	27	Arkansas	1 822	15	27	Washington	370
3	28	New York	2 835	32	28	Kansas	1 804	31	28	Mississippi	361
12	29	Virginia	2 344	12	29	Virginia	1 787	28	29	Oregon	351
16	30	Tennessee	2 178	34	30	Utah	1 782	14	30	Indiana	349
22	31	Louisiana	2 031	30	31	Iowa	1 772	24	31	Colorado	334
20	32	Arizona	1 903	38	32	Nebraska	1 742	7	31	Ohio	334
44	33	Montana	1 871	28	33	Oregon	1 738	38	33	Nebraska	328
36	34	New Mexico	1 618	7	34	Ohio	1 733	29	34	Connecticut	325
26	35	South Carolina	1 588	27	35	Oklahoma	1 692	37	35	West Virginia	317
19	36	Maryland	1 312	14	36	Indiana	1 662	43	36	Rhode Island	298
51	37	Wyoming	899	31	37	Mississippi	1 656	25	37	Kentucky	295
34	38	Utah	877	10	38	Georgia	1 651	12	38	Virginia	282
9	39	New Jersey	697	24	39	Colorado	1 645	21	39	Minnesota	281
45	40	Delaware	691	26	40	South Carolina	1 591	51	40	Wyoming	267
42	41	Hawaii	497	20	41	Arizona	1 579	30	41	Iowa	266
49	42	Vermont	476	44	42	Montana	1 564	34	42	Utah	256
13	43	Massachusetts	454	4	43	Florida	1 553	39	43	Idaho	253
37	44	West Virginia	447	17	44	Missouri	1 532	42	44	Hawaii	244
40	45	Maine	439	22	45	Louisiana	1 457	44	45	Montana	241
29	46	Connecticut	422	23	46	Alabama	1 448	18	46	Wisconsin	237
35	47	Nevada	357	41	47	New Hampshire	1 372	41	47	New Hampshire	175
41	48	New Hampshire	149	16	48	Tennessee	1 360	46	48	South Dakota	167
43	49	Rhode Island	48	2	49	Texas	1 315	49	49	Vermont	114
48	50	Alaska	25	46	50	South Dakota	1 228	40	50	Maine	110
50	51	District of Columbia	0	50	51	District of Columbia	X	47	51	North Dakota	81

Note: Column numbers refer to Table A. States.

TABLE 2—75 Largest Counties by 2000 Population
Selected Rankings

	Total Persons, 2000			Total Land Area (square kilometers), 2000				Population Density (per square kilometer), 2000		
Population Rank	County	[col 2] Population	Population Rank	Land Area Rank	County	[col 1] Land Area	Population Rank	Density Rank	County	[col 4] Density
1	Los Angeles, CA	9 519 338	13	1	San Bernardino, CA	51 936	17	1	New York, NY	26 054.2
2	Cook, IL	5 376 741	4	2	Maricopa, AZ	23 836	7	2	Kings, NY	13 471.7
3	Harris, TX	3 400 578	53	3	Pima, AZ	23 792	27	3	Bronx, NY	12 226.1
4	Maricopa, AZ	3 072 149	25	4	Clark, NV	20 488	9	4	Queens, NY	7 877.7
5	Orange, CA	2 846 289	16	5	Riverside, CA	18 667	62	5	San Francisco, CA	6 419.3
6	San Diego, CA	2 813 833	58	6	Fresno, CA	15 443	74	6	Suffolk, MA	4 538.2
7	Kings, NY	2 465 326	6	7	San Diego, CA	10 878	18	7	Philadelphia, PA	4 335.9
8	Miami-Dade, FL	2 253 362	1	8	Los Angeles, CA	10 518	59	8	Essex, NJ	2 427.0
9	Queens, NY	2 229 379	12	9	King, WA	5 506	2	9	Cook, IL	2 195.5
10	Dallas, TX	2 218 899	31	10	Palm Beach, FL	5 113	26	10	Nassau, NY	1 796.2
11	Wayne, MI	2 061 162	8	11	Miami-Dade, FL	5 040	39	11	Milwaukee, WI	1 501.9
12	King, WA	1 737 034	64	12	Ventura, CA	4 779	46	12	Bergen, NJ	1 456.5
13	San Bernardino, CA	1 709 434	3	13	Harris, TX	4 478	5	13	Orange, CA	1 391.8
14	Santa Clara, CA	1 682 585	71	14	Pierce, WA	4 348	11	14	Wayne, MI	1 295.5
15	Broward, FL	1 623 018	65	15	Worcester, MA	3 919	41	15	Pinellas, FL	1 271.0
16	Riverside, CA	1 545 387	14	16	Santa Clara, CA	3 343	23	16	Cuyahoga, OH	1 174.4
17	New York, NY	1 537 195	24	17	Bexar, TX	3 229	42	17	Du Page, IL	1 046.5
18	Philadelphia, PA	1 517 550	15	18	Broward, FL	3 122	10	18	Dallas, TX	974.1
19	Middlesex, MA	1 465 396	35	19	Hillsborough, FL	2 722	36	19	Fairfax, VA	947.9
20	Tarrant, TX	1 446 219	37	20	Erie, NY	2 704	66	20	Middlesex, NJ	935.4
21	Alameda, CA	1 443 741	75	21	El Paso, TX	2 624	1	21	Los Angeles, CA	905.1
22	Suffolk, NY	1 419 369	56	22	Travis, TX	2 562	50	22	Marion, IN	838.6
23	Cuyahoga, OH	1 393 978	29	23	Sacramento, CA	2 501	40	23	Westchester, NY	823.8
24	Bexar, TX	1 392 931	2	24	Cook, IL	2 449	52	24	Hamilton, OH	801.2
25	Clark, NV	1 375 765	22	25	Suffolk, NY	2 363	32	25	Hennepin, MN	774.1
26	Nassau, NY	1 334 544	45	26	Orange, FL	2 350	34	26	St. Louis, MO	772.9
27	Bronx, NY	1 332 650	10	27	Dallas, TX	2 278	33	27	Franklin, OH	764.6
28	Allegheny, PA	1 281 666	30	28	Oakland, MI	2 260	3	28	Harris, TX	759.4
29	Sacramento, CA	1 223 499	20	29	Tarrant, TX	2 236	21	29	Alameda, CA	755.9
30	Oakland, MI	1 194 156	19	30	Middlesex, MA	2 133	73	30	Jefferson, KY	695.7
31	Palm Beach, FL	1 131 184	5	31	Orange, CA	2 045	19	31	Middlesex, MA	687.0
32	Hennepin, MN	1 116 200	61	32	Duval, FL	2 004	49	32	Montgomery, MD	680.7
33	Franklin, OH	1 068 978	44	33	Shelby, TN	1 954	28	33	Allegheny, PA	677.8
34	St. Louis, MO	1 016 315	21	34	Alameda, CA	1 910	20	34	Tarrant, TX	646.8
35	Hillsborough, FL	998 948	43	35	Salt Lake, UT	1 910	57	35	Prince George's, MD	637.6
36	Fairfax, VA	969 749	51	36	Hartford, CT	1 905	60	36	Macomb, MI	633.6
37	Erie, NY	950 265	28	37	Allegheny, PA	1 891	70	37	San Mateo, CA	608.0
38	Contra Costa, CA	948 816	38	38	Contra Costa, CA	1 865	22	38	Suffolk, NY	600.7
39	Milwaukee, WI	940 164	68	39	Monroe, NY	1 708	67	39	Montgomery, PA	599.6
40	Westchester, NY	923 459	47	40	Fairfield, CT	1 621	55	40	Fulton, GA	596.1
41	Pinellas, FL	921 482	11	41	Wayne, MI	1 591	48	41	Honolulu, HI	564.2
42	Du Page, IL	904 161	54	42	New Haven, CT	1 569	69	42	Essex, MA	557.8
43	Salt Lake, UT	898 387	48	43	Honolulu, HI	1 553	47	43	Fairfield, CT	544.5
44	Shelby, TN	897 472	63	44	Baltimore, MD	1 550	30	44	Oakland, MI	528.4
45	Orange, FL	896 344	32	45	Hennepin, MN	1 442	54	45	New Haven, CT	525.2
46	Bergen, NJ	884 118	33	46	Franklin, OH	1 398	15	46	Broward, FL	519.9
47	Fairfield, CT	882 567	55	47	Fulton, GA	1 369	72	47	Mecklenburg, NC	510.2
48	Honolulu, HI	876 156	72	48	Mecklenburg, NC	1 363	38	48	Contra Costa, CA	508.7
49	Montgomery, MD	873 341	34	49	St. Louis, MO	1 315	14	49	Santa Clara, CA	503.3
50	Marion, IN	860 454	69	50	Essex, MA	1 297	29	50	Sacramento, CA	489.2
51	Hartford, CT	857 183	49	51	Montgomery, MD	1 283	63	51	Baltimore, MD	486.6
52	Hamilton, OH	845 303	57	52	Prince George's, MD	1 257	43	52	Salt Lake, UT	470.4
53	Pima, AZ	843 746	67	53	Montgomery, PA	1 251	44	53	Shelby, TN	459.3
54	New Haven, CT	824 008	60	54	Macomb, MI	1 244	51	54	Hartford, CT	450.0
55	Fulton, GA	816 006	23	55	Cuyahoga, OH	1 187	8	55	Miami-Dade, FL	447.1
56	Travis, TX	812 280	70	56	San Mateo, CA	1 163	24	56	Bexar, TX	431.4
57	Prince George's, MD	801 515	40	57	Westchester, NY	1 121	68	57	Monroe, NY	430.5
58	Fresno, CA	799 407	52	58	Hamilton, OH	1 055	61	58	Duval, FL	388.7
59	Essex, NJ	793 633	50	59	Marion, IN	1 026	45	59	Orange, FL	381.4
60	Macomb, MI	788 149	36	60	Fairfax, VA	1 023	35	60	Hillsborough, FL	367.0
61	Duval, FL	778 879	73	61	Jefferson, KY	997	37	61	Erie, NY	351.4
62	San Francisco, CA	776 733	42	62	Du Page, IL	864	56	62	Travis, TX	317.0
63	Baltimore, MD	754 292	66	63	Middlesex, NJ	802	12	63	King, WA	315.5
64	Ventura, CA	753 197	26	64	Nassau, NY	743	75	64	El Paso, TX	259.0
65	Worcester, MA	750 963	41	65	Pinellas, FL	725	6	65	San Diego, CA	258.7
66	Middlesex, NJ	750 162	39	66	Milwaukee, WI	626	31	66	Palm Beach, FL	221.2
67	Montgomery, PA	750 097	46	67	Bergen, NJ	607	65	67	Worcester, MA	191.6
68	Monroe, NY	735 343	18	68	Philadelphia, PA	350	71	68	Pierce, WA	161.2
69	Essex, MA	723 419	59	69	Essex, NJ	327	64	69	Ventura, CA	157.6
70	San Mateo, CA	707 161	9	70	Queens, NY	283	4	70	Maricopa, AZ	128.9
71	Pierce, WA	700 820	7	71	Kings, NY	183	16	71	Riverside, CA	82.8
72	Mecklenburg, NC	695 454	74	72	Suffolk, MA	152	25	72	Clark, NV	67.1
73	Jefferson, KY	693 604	62	73	San Francisco, CA	121	58	73	Fresno, CA	51.8
74	Suffolk, MA	689 807	27	74	Bronx, NY	109	53	74	Pima, AZ	35.5
75	El Paso, TX	679 622	17	75	New York, NY	59	13	75	San Bernardino, CA	32.9

Note: Column numbers refer to Table B. States and Counties.

TABLE 2—75 Largest Counties by 2000 Population
Selected Rankings

\	Percent Population Change, 2000-2001			\	Percent White (alone or in combination), 2000			\	Percent Black (alone or in combination), 2000		
Popu- lation Rank	Percent Change Rank	County	[col 23] Percent Change	Popu- lation Rank	White Rank	County	[col 5] Percent White	Popu- lation Rank	Black Rank	County	[col 6] Percent Black
25	1	Clark, NV	6.5	60	1	Macomb, MI	94.3	57	1	Prince George's, MD	64.3
16	2	Riverside, CA	5.9	65	2	Worcester, MA	91.1	44	2	Shelby, TN	49.0
4	3	Maricopa, AZ	4.0	43	3	Salt Lake, UT	88.6	55	3	Fulton, GA	45.2
29	4	Sacramento, CA	3.7	69	4	Essex, MA	88.1	18	4	Philadelphia, PA	44.3
13	5	San Bernardino, CA	3.3	19	5	Middlesex, MA	87.6	11	5	Wayne, MI	43.0
72	6	Mecklenburg, NC	3.0	67	6	Montgomery, PA	87.4	59	6	Essex, NJ	42.9
45	6	Orange, FL	3.0	41	7	Pinellas, FL	87.2	27	7	Bronx, NY	38.3
31	6	Palm Beach, FL	3.0	22	8	Suffolk, NY	86.1	7	8	Kings, NY	38.1
15	9	Broward, FL	2.8	42	9	Du Page, IL	85.5	61	9	Duval, FL	28.5
38	9	Contra Costa, CA	2.8	28	10	Allegheny, PA	85.2	72	10	Mecklenburg, NC	28.4
35	9	Hillsborough, FL	2.8	30	11	Oakland, MI	84.4	23	11	Cuyahoga, OH	28.2
20	9	Tarrant, TX	2.8	37	12	Erie, NY	83.2	2	12	Cook, IL	26.7
71	13	Pierce, WA	2.7	71	13	Pierce, WA	82.7	39	13	Milwaukee, WI	25.5
56	14	Travis, TX	2.6	32	14	Hennepin, MN	82.4	50	14	Marion, IN	25.0
53	16	Pima, AZ	2.3	47	15	Fairfield, CT	81.1	74	15	Suffolk, MA	24.4
64	15	Ventura, CA	2.3	54	16	New Haven, CT	81.0	52	16	Hamilton, OH	24.1
49	17	Montgomery, MD	2.1	26	17	Nassau, NY	80.8	15	17	Broward, FL	22.2
58	18	Fresno, CA	2.0	68	18	Monroe, NY	80.6	9	18	Queens, NY	21.8
57	19	Prince George's, MD	1.9	31	19	Palm Beach, FL	80.4	8	19	Miami-Dade, FL	21.6
24	20	Bexar, TX	1.8	46	20	Bergen, NJ	80.2	63	20	Baltimore, MD	20.8
3	20	Harris, TX	1.8	4	21	Maricopa, AZ	79.8	10	20	Dallas, TX	20.8
61	22	Duval, FL	1.7	12	22	King, WA	78.9	34	22	St. Louis, MO	19.6
6	22	San Diego, CA	1.7	73	23	Jefferson, KY	78.6	73	23	Jefferson, KY	19.5
36	24	Fairfax, VA	1.6	51	24	Hartford, CT	78.5	45	23	Orange, FL	19.5
8	24	Miami-Dade, FL	1.6	53	25	Pima, AZ	77.8	33	25	Franklin, OH	19.1
5	24	Orange, CA	1.6	34	25	St. Louis, MO	77.8	3	26	Harris, TX	19.0
60	27	Macomb, MI	1.5	33	27	Franklin, OH	77.1	17	26	New York, NY	19.0
65	27	Worcester, MA	1.5	35	27	Hillsborough, FL	77.1	49	28	Montgomery, MD	16.3
22	29	Suffolk, NY	1.4	75	29	El Paso, TX	76.8	21	29	Alameda, CA	16.2
67	30	Montgomery, PA	1.3	63	30	Baltimore, MD	75.4	35	30	Hillsborough, FL	15.8
10	31	Dallas, TX	1.2	25	31	Clark, NV	75.0	40	31	Westchester, NY	15.2
75	31	El Paso, TX	1.2	52	32	Hamilton, OH	74.0	31	32	Palm Beach, FL	14.9
1	31	Los Angeles, CA	1.2	40	33	Westchester, NY	73.6	68	33	Monroe, NY	14.7
63	34	Baltimore, MD	1.1	20	34	Tarrant, TX	73.4	37	34	Erie, NY	13.6
21	35	Alameda, CA	1.0	64	35	Ventura, CA	73.3	20	35	Tarrant, TX	13.3
69	35	Essex, MA	1.0	36	36	Fairfax, VA	72.9	28	36	Allegheny, PA	13.0
42	37	Du Page, IL	0.9	15	37	Broward, FL	72.4	51	37	Hartford, CT	12.6
66	37	Middlesex, NJ	0.9	8	38	Miami-Dade, FL	72.3	54	38	New Haven, CT	12.2
43	39	Salt Lake, UT	0.7	24	39	Bexar, TX	72.0	29	39	Sacramento, CA	11.4
48	40	Honolulu, HI	0.6	50	40	Marion, IN	71.8	47	40	Fairfield, CT	10.9
40	40	Westchester, NY	0.6	45	41	Orange, FL	70.9	26	41	Nassau, NY	10.8
51	42	Hartford, CT	0.5	56	42	Travis, TX	70.6	30	42	Oakland, MI	10.6
54	42	New Haven, CT	0.5	66	43	Middlesex, NJ	70.3	1	43	Los Angeles, CA	10.5
27	44	Bronx, NY	0.4	6	43	San Diego, CA	70.3	38	44	Contra Costa, CA	10.3
30	44	Oakland, MI	0.4	38	45	Contra Costa, CA	69.7	32	44	Hennepin, MN	10.3
46	46	Bergen, NJ	0.3	16	46	Riverside, CA	69.3	25	46	Clark, NV	10.0
47	46	Fairfield, CT	0.3	23	47	Cuyahoga, OH	68.7	13	46	San Bernardino, CA	10.0
12	46	King, WA	0.3	29	48	Sacramento, CA	68.5	66	48	Middlesex, NJ	9.8
17	46	New York, NY	0.3	5	49	Orange, CA	68.3	56	48	Travis, TX	9.8
41	46	Pinellas, FL	0.3	39	50	Milwaukee, WI	67.4	41	50	Pinellas, FL	9.4
33	51	Franklin, OH	0.2	61	51	Duval, FL	67.3	36	51	Fairfax, VA	9.3
55	52	Fulton, GA	0.1	49	51	Montgomery, MD	67.3	71	52	Pierce, WA	8.6
7	53	Kings, NY	0.0	72	53	Mecklenburg, NC	65.2	62	52	San Francisco, CA	8.6
26	53	Nassau, NY	0.0	70	54	San Mateo, CA	63.5	67	54	Montgomery, PA	8.0
59	55	Essex, NJ	-0.1	13	55	San Bernardino, CA	63.1	24	55	Bexar, TX	7.7
32	55	Hennepin, MN	-0.1	3	56	Harris, TX	61.2	22	55	Suffolk, NY	7.7
73	55	Jefferson, KY	-0.1	10	57	Dallas, TX	60.6	16	57	Riverside, CA	7.0
19	55	Middlesex, MA	-0.1	74	58	Suffolk, MA	60.2	6	58	San Diego, CA	6.6
34	55	St. Louis, MO	-0.1	2	59	Cook, IL	58.3	12	59	King, WA	6.5
68	60	Monroe, NY	-0.2	58	60	Fresno, CA	58.0	58	60	Fresno, CA	5.9
9	60	Queens, NY	-0.2	14	61	Santa Clara, CA	57.6	46	61	Bergen, NJ	5.8
44	60	Shelby, TN	-0.2	17	62	New York, NY	57.1	4	62	Maricopa, AZ	4.3
50	63	Marion, IN	-0.4	11	63	Wayne, MI	53.7	70	63	San Mateo, CA	4.1
2	64	Cook, IL	-0.5	21	64	Alameda, CA	53.1	19	64	Middlesex, MA	4.0
37	65	Erie, NY	-0.6	62	65	San Francisco, CA	53.0	53	65	Pima, AZ	3.7
70	66	San Mateo, CA	-0.7	1	66	Los Angeles, CA	52.8	75	66	El Paso, TX	3.5
62	67	San Francisco, CA	-0.8	55	67	Fulton, GA	49.1	42	67	Du Page, IL	3.4
14	67	Santa Clara, CA	-0.8	44	68	Shelby, TN	48.1	69	67	Essex, MA	3.4
11	67	Wayne, MI	-0.8	9	69	Queens, NY	47.4	48	67	Honolulu, HI	3.4
28	70	Allegheny, PA	-0.9	59	70	Essex, NJ	46.4	14	67	Santa Clara, CA	3.4
39	70	Milwaukee, WI	-0.9	18	70	Philadelphia, PA	46.4	65	71	Worcester, MA	3.2
23	72	Cuyahoga, OH	-1.0	7	72	Kings, NY	43.7	60	72	Macomb, MI	3.1
74	73	Suffolk, MA	-1.1	48	73	Honolulu, HI	35.2	64	73	Ventura, CA	2.4
52	74	Hamilton, OH	-1.2	27	74	Bronx, NY	33.1	5	74	Orange, CA	2.1
18	75	Philadelphia, PA	-1.7	57	75	Prince George's, MD	28.5	43	75	Salt Lake, UT	1.4

Note: Column numbers refer to Table B. States and Counties.

TABLE 2—75 Largest Counties by 2000 Population
Selected Rankings

Percent American Indian, Alaska Native (alone or in combination), 2000				Percent Asian and Pacific Islander, 2000				Percent Hispanic, 2000			
Population Rank	American Indian, Alaska Native Rank	County	[col 7] Percent American Indian, Alaska Native	Population Rank	Asian & Pac. Is. Rank	County	[col 8] Percent Asian & Pac. Is.	Population Rank	Hispanic Rank	County	[col 9] Percent Hispanic
53	1	Pima, AZ	4.0	48	1	Honolulu, HI	83.2	75	1	El Paso, TX	78.2
71	2	Pierce, WA	2.8	62	2	San Francisco, CA	33.4	8	2	Miami-Dade, FL	57.3
58	3	Fresno, CA	2.6	14	3	Santa Clara, CA	28.2	24	3	Bexar, TX	54.3
4	4	Maricopa, AZ	2.5	70	4	San Mateo, CA	24.1	27	4	Bronx, NY	48.4
29	4	Sacramento, CA	2.5	21	5	Alameda, CA	23.8	1	5	Los Angeles, CA	44.6
13	6	San Bernardino, CA	2.2	9	6	Queens, NY	19.6	58	6	Fresno, CA	44.0
16	7	Riverside, CA	2.1	5	7	Orange, CA	15.5	13	7	San Bernardino, CA	39.2
12	8	King, WA	1.9	36	8	Fairfax, VA	14.7	16	8	Riverside, CA	36.2
48	9	Honolulu, HI	1.8	66	8	Middlesex, NJ	14.7	64	9	Ventura, CA	33.4
64	9	Ventura, CA	1.8	29	10	Sacramento, CA	14.1	3	10	Harris, TX	32.9
21	11	Alameda, CA	1.6	38	11	Contra Costa, CA	13.7	5	11	Orange, CA	30.8
38	11	Contra Costa, CA	1.6	1	12	Los Angeles, CA	13.6	10	12	Dallas, TX	29.9
32	11	Hennepin, MN	1.6	12	13	King, WA	13.4	53	13	Pima, AZ	29.3
6	11	San Diego, CA	1.6	49	14	Montgomery, MD	12.5	56	14	Travis, TX	28.2
27	15	Bronx, NY	1.5	46	15	Bergen, NJ	11.4	17	15	New York, NY	27.2
25	15	Clark, NV	1.5	6	15	San Diego, CA	11.4	6	16	San Diego, CA	26.7
1	15	Los Angeles, CA	1.5	17	17	New York, NY	10.4	9	17	Queens, NY	25.0
24	18	Bexar, TX	1.3	58	18	Fresno, CA	9.5	4	18	Maricopa, AZ	24.8
39	18	Milwaukee, WI	1.3	42	19	Du Page, IL	8.6	14	19	Santa Clara, CA	24.0
5	18	Orange, CA	1.3	7	19	Kings, NY	8.6	25	20	Clark, NV	22.0
43	18	Salt Lake, UT	1.3	71	21	Pierce, WA	8.4	70	21	San Mateo, CA	21.9
14	18	Santa Clara, CA	1.3	74	22	Suffolk, MA	7.9	2	22	Cook, IL	19.9
9	23	Queens, NY	1.2	25	23	Clark, NV	7.5	7	23	Kings, NY	19.8
62	23	San Francisco, CA	1.2	19	24	Middlesex, MA	7.0	20	24	Tarrant, TX	19.7
75	25	El Paso, TX	1.1	64	24	Ventura, CA	7.0	21	25	Alameda, CA	19.0
70	25	San Mateo, CA	1.1	13	26	San Bernardino, CA	6.2	45	26	Orange, FL	18.8
20	25	Tarrant, TX	1.1	3	27	Harris, TX	5.8	35	27	Hillsborough, FL	18.0
56	25	Travis, TX	1.1	32	28	Hennepin, MN	5.6	38	28	Contra Costa, CA	17.7
10	29	Dallas, TX	1.0	2	29	Cook, IL	5.4	15	29	Broward, FL	16.7
17	29	New York, NY	1.0	26	29	Nassau, NY	5.4	29	30	Sacramento, CA	16.0
57	29	Prince George's, MD	1.0	56	31	Travis, TX	5.3	40	31	Westchester, NY	15.6
11	29	Wayne, MI	1.0	40	32	Westchester, NY	5.2	74	32	Suffolk, MA	15.5
37	33	Erie, NY	0.9	18	33	Philadelphia, PA	5.1	59	33	Essex, NJ	15.4
33	33	Franklin, OH	0.9	16	33	Riverside, CA	5.1	62	34	San Francisco, CA	14.1
35	33	Hillsborough, FL	0.9	43	35	Salt Lake, UT	4.8	66	35	Middlesex, NJ	13.6
60	33	Macomb, MI	0.9	30	36	Oakland, MI	4.7	31	36	Palm Beach, FL	12.4
74	33	Suffolk, MA	0.9	10	37	Dallas, TX	4.5	47	37	Fairfield, CT	11.9
61	38	Duval, FL	0.8	67	37	Montgomery, PA	4.5	43	38	Salt Lake, UT	11.9
3	38	Harris, TX	0.8	57	37	Prince George's, MD	4.5	51	39	Hartford, CT	11.5
7	38	Kings, NY	0.8	59	40	Essex, NJ	4.4	49	39	Montgomery, MD	11.5
49	38	Montgomery, MD	0.8	45	41	Orange, FL	4.3	69	41	Essex, MA	11.0
30	38	Oakland, MI	0.8	20	41	Tarrant, TX	4.3	36	41	Fairfax, VA	11.0
45	38	Orange, FL	0.8	27	43	Bronx, NY	3.9	22	43	Suffolk, NY	10.5
36	44	Fairfax, VA	0.7	47	44	Fairfield, CT	3.8	46	43	Bergen, NJ	10.3
50	44	Marion, IN	0.7	63	45	Baltimore, MD	3.7	54	45	New Haven, CT	10.1
72	44	Mecklenburg, NC	0.7	33	46	Franklin, OH	3.6	26	46	Nassau, NY	10.0
68	44	Monroe, NY	0.7	72	46	Mecklenburg, NC	3.6	42	47	Du Page, IL	9.0
54	44	New Haven, CT	0.7	61	48	Duval, FL	3.5	39	48	Milwaukee, WI	8.8
18	44	Philadelphia, PA	0.7	55	48	Fulton, GA	3.5	18	49	Philadelphia, PA	8.5
41	44	Pinellas, FL	0.7	39	50	Milwaukee, WI	3.1	57	50	Prince George's, MD	7.1
63	51	Baltimore, MD	0.6	65	50	Worcester, MA	3.1	65	51	Worcester, MA	6.8
2	51	Cook, IL	0.6	15	52	Broward, FL	3.0	48	52	Honolulu, HI	6.7
23	51	Cuyahoga, OH	0.6	4	52	Maricopa, AZ	3.0	72	53	Mecklenburg, NC	6.5
59	51	Essex, NY	0.6	22	52	Suffolk, NY	3.0	55	54	Fulton, GA	5.9
52	51	Hamilton, OH	0.6	51	55	Hartford, CT	2.9	12	55	King, WA	5.5
51	51	Hartford, CT	0.6	35	55	Hillsborough, FL	2.9	71	55	Pierce, WA	5.5
73	51	Jefferson, KY	0.6	68	55	Monroe, NY	2.9	68	57	Monroe, NY	5.3
66	51	Middlesex, NJ	0.6	53	55	Pima, AZ	2.9	19	58	Middlesex, MA	4.6
22	51	Suffolk, NY	0.6	69	59	Essex, MA	2.8	41	58	Pinellas, FL	4.6
40	51	Westchester, NY	0.6	54	59	New Haven, CT	2.8	61	60	Duval, FL	4.1
65	51	Worcester, MA	0.6	34	61	St. Louis, MO	2.7	32	60	Hennepin, MN	4.1
15	62	Broward, FL	0.5	60	62	Macomb, MI	2.6	50	62	Marion, IN	3.9
69	62	Essex, MA	0.5	41	63	Pinellas, FL	2.5	11	63	Wayne, MI	3.7
47	62	Fairfield, CT	0.5	24	64	Bexar, TX	2.4	23	64	Cuyahoga, OH	3.4
55	62	Fulton, GA	0.5	23	65	Cuyahoga, OH	2.2	37	65	Erie, NY	3.3
31	62	Palm Beach, FL	0.5	11	65	Wayne, MI	2.2	44	66	Shelby, TN	2.6
44	62	Shelby, TN	0.5	31	67	Palm Beach, FL	2.1	30	67	Oakland, MI	2.4
34	62	St. Louis, MO	0.5	28	68	Allegheny, PA	2.0	33	68	Franklin, OH	2.3
28	69	Allegheny, PA	0.4	52	68	Hamilton, OH	2.0	67	69	Montgomery, PA	2.0
46	69	Bergen, NJ	0.4	8	68	Miami-Dade, FL	2.0	63	70	Baltimore, MD	1.8
42	69	Du Page, IL	0.4	44	68	Shelby, TN	2.0	73	70	Jefferson, KY	1.8
8	69	Miami-Dade, FL	0.4	50	72	Marion, IN	1.9	60	72	Macomb, MI	1.6
19	69	Middlesex, MA	0.4	37	73	Erie, NY	1.8	34	73	St. Louis, MO	1.4
67	69	Montgomery, PA	0.4	73	73	Jefferson, KY	1.8	52	74	Hamilton, OH	1.1
26	69	Nassau, NY	0.4	75	75	El Paso, TX	1.5	28	75	Allegheny, PA	0.9

Note: Column numbers refer to Table B. States and Counties.

38

TABLE 2—75 Largest Counties by 2000 Population
Selected Rankings

Percent Under 18 Years, 2000				Percent Age 65 and Over, 2000				Percent Female-Headed Family Household, 2000			
Population Rank	Under 18 Years Rank	County	[cols 10 & 11] Percent Under 18 Years	Population Rank	65 Years and Over Rank	County	[cols 17 & 18] Percent Age 65 and Over	Population Rank	Female Householder Rank	County	[col 30] Percent Female Householder
13	1	San Bernardino, CA	32.3	31	1	Palm Beach, FL	23.1	27	1	Bronx, NY	30.4
58	2	Fresno, CA	32.1	41	2	Pinellas, FL	22.5	7	2	Kings, NY	22.3
75	3	El Paso, TX	32.0	28	3	Allegheny, PA	17.8	18	2	Philadelphia, PA	22.3
43	4	Salt Lake, UT	30.5	15	4	Broward, FL	16.1	11	4	Wayne, MI	20.6
16	5	Riverside, CA	30.4	37	5	Erie, NY	15.9	59	5	Essex, NJ	20.4
27	6	Bronx, NY	29.8	23	6	Cuyahoga, OH	15.6	44	6	Shelby, TN	20.1
3	7	Harris, TX	29.0	46	7	Bergen, NJ	15.3	57	7	Prince George's, MD	19.6
24	8	Bexar, TX	28.5	26	8	Nassau, NY	15.0	75	8	El Paso, TX	18.0
64	8	Ventura, CA	28.5	67	9	Montgomery, PA	14.9	8	9	Miami-Dade, FL	17.2
44	10	Shelby, TN	28.2	63	10	Baltimore, MD	14.7	55	10	Fulton, GA	16.5
20	11	Tarrant, TX	28.1	51	11	Hartford, CT	14.6	39	11	Milwaukee, WI	16.3
1	12	Los Angeles, CA	28.0	54	12	New Haven, CT	14.4	74	11	Suffolk, MA	16.3
11	12	Wayne, MI	28.0	53	13	Pima, AZ	14.2	9	13	Queens, NY	16.0
10	14	Dallas, TX	27.9	18	14	Philadelphia, PA	14.1	23	14	Cuyahoga, OH	15.7
29	15	Sacramento, CA	27.6	34	15	St. Louis, MO	14.0	2	15	Cook, IL	15.6
71	16	Pierce, WA	27.2	40	16	Westchester, NY	13.9	61	15	Duval, FL	15.6
4	17	Maricopa, AZ	27.0	69	17	Essex, MA	13.8	24	17	Bexar, TX	15.5
5	17	Orange, CA	27.0	60	18	Macomb, MI	13.7	58	18	Fresno, CA	15.2
7	19	Kings, NY	26.9	62	19	San Francisco, CA	13.6	50	19	Marion, IN	14.9
42	20	Du Page, IL	26.8	52	20	Hamilton, OH	13.5	13	20	San Bernardino, CA	14.8
57	21	Prince George's, MD	26.7	73	20	Jefferson, KY	13.5	73	21	Jefferson, KY	14.7
38	22	Contra Costa, CA	26.6	48	22	Honolulu, HI	13.4	1	21	Los Angeles, CA	14.7
61	23	Duval, FL	26.3	47	23	Fairfield, CT	13.3	52	23	Hamilton, OH	14.3
39	23	Milwaukee, WI	26.3	8	23	Miami-Dade, FL	13.3	10	24	Dallas, TX	14.1
59	25	Essex, NJ	26.1	65	25	Worcester, MA	13.1	29	24	Sacramento, CA	14.1
22	25	Suffolk, NY	26.1	39	26	Milwaukee, WI	13.0	37	26	Erie, NY	13.7
2	27	Cook, IL	26.0	68	26	Monroe, NY	13.0	3	26	Harris, TX	13.7
52	28	Hamilton, OH	25.8	19	28	Middlesex, MA	12.7	45	26	Orange, FL	13.7
50	28	Marion, IN	25.8	9	28	Queens, NY	12.7	54	29	New Haven, CT	13.6
6	28	San Diego, CA	25.8	16	28	Riverside, CA	12.7	51	30	Hartford, CT	13.5
47	31	Fairfield, CT	25.7	70	31	San Mateo, CA	12.4	68	31	Monroe, NY	13.4
65	31	Worcester, MA	25.7	66	32	Middlesex, NJ	12.3	35	32	Hillsborough, FL	13.2
25	33	Clark, NV	25.6	17	33	New York, NY	12.1	21	33	Alameda, CA	13.0
68	33	Monroe, NY	25.6	11	33	Wayne, MI	12.1	33	33	Franklin, OH	13.0
36	35	Fairfax, VA	25.4	35	35	Hillsborough, FL	12.0	63	35	Baltimore, MD	12.8
35	35	Hillsborough, FL	25.4	59	36	Essex, NJ	11.9	34	36	St. Louis, MO	12.7
49	35	Montgomery, MD	25.4	22	37	Suffolk, NY	11.8	17	37	New York, NY	12.6
18	38	Philadelphia, PA	25.3	2	38	Cook, IL	11.7	15	38	Broward, FL	12.5
69	39	Essex, MA	25.2	4	39	Maricopa, AZ	11.6	28	39	Allegheny, PA	12.4
30	39	Oakland, MI	25.2	7	40	Kings, NY	11.5	69	39	Essex, MA	12.4
45	39	Orange, FL	25.2	38	41	Contra Costa, CA	11.3	72	39	Mecklenburg, NC	12.4
34	39	St. Louis, MO	25.2	30	41	Oakland, MI	11.3	48	42	Honolulu, HI	12.3
33	42	Franklin, OH	25.1	49	43	Montgomery, MD	11.2	20	43	Tarrant, TX	12.2
72	42	Mecklenburg, NC	25.1	6	43	San Diego, CA	11.2	40	43	Westchester, NY	12.2
40	45	Westchester, NY	25.0	50	45	Marion, IN	11.1	16	45	Riverside, CA	12.0
23	46	Cuyahoga, OH	24.9	29	45	Sacramento, CA	11.1	25	46	Clark, NV	11.8
8	47	Miami-Dade, FL	24.8	74	45	Suffolk, MA	11.1	71	46	Pierce, WA	11.8
14	47	Santa Clara, CA	24.8	32	48	Hennepin, MN	11.0	53	46	Pima, AZ	11.8
26	49	Nassau, NY	24.7	25	49	Clark, NV	10.7	6	49	San Diego, CA	11.6
51	50	Hartford, CT	24.6	61	50	Duval, FL	10.5	38	50	Contra Costa, CA	11.5
53	50	Pima, AZ	24.6	24	51	Bexar, TX	10.4	47	50	Fairfield, CT	11.5
21	52	Alameda, CA	24.5	12	51	King, WA	10.4	65	52	Worcester, MA	11.4
55	52	Fulton, GA	24.5	21	53	Alameda, CA	10.2	26	53	Nassau, NY	10.9
54	54	New Haven, CT	24.4	71	53	Pierce, WA	10.2	64	53	Ventura, CA	10.9
37	55	Erie, NY	24.3	64	53	Ventura, CA	10.2	66	55	Middlesex, NJ	10.8
73	56	Jefferson, KY	24.2	27	56	Bronx, NY	10.0	22	55	Suffolk, NY	10.8
60	57	Macomb, MI	24.1	58	56	Fresno, CA	10.0	4	57	Maricopa, AZ	10.7
67	57	Montgomery, PA	24.1	45	56	Orange, FL	10.0	5	57	Orange, CA	10.7
32	59	Hennepin, MN	24.0	44	59	Shelby, TN	9.9	49	59	Montgomery, MD	10.5
48	60	Honolulu, HI	23.8	42	60	Du Page, IL	9.8	41	59	Pinellas, FL	10.5
66	61	Middlesex, NJ	23.7	33	60	Franklin, OH	9.8	43	61	Salt Lake, UT	10.4
56	61	Travis, TX	23.7	1	60	Los Angeles, CA	9.8	56	61	Travis, TX	10.4
63	63	Baltimore, MD	23.6	5	60	Orange, CA	9.8	60	63	Macomb, MI	10.1
15	64	Broward, FL	23.5	75	64	El Paso, TX	9.7	70	63	San Mateo, CA	10.1
46	65	Bergen, NJ	23.0	14	65	Santa Clara, CA	9.6	14	65	Santa Clara, CA	10.0
70	66	San Mateo, CA	22.9	72	66	Mecklenburg, NC	8.6	32	66	Hennepin, MN	9.9
9	67	Queens, NY	22.8	13	66	San Bernardino, CA	8.6	19	66	Middlesex, MA	9.9
12	68	King, WA	22.5	55	68	Fulton, GA	8.5	46	68	Bergen, NJ	9.7
19	68	Middlesex, MA	22.5	20	69	Tarrant, TX	8.3	31	68	Palm Beach, FL	9.7
28	70	Allegheny, PA	21.9	43	70	Salt Lake, UT	8.1	30	70	Oakland, MI	9.5
31	71	Palm Beach, FL	21.3	10	71	Dallas, TX	8.0	12	71	King, WA	9.0
74	72	Suffolk, MA	20.2	36	72	Fairfax, VA	7.9	62	72	San Francisco, CA	8.9
41	73	Pinellas, FL	19.2	57	73	Prince George's, MD	7.7	67	73	Montgomery, PA	8.8
17	74	New York, NY	16.7	3	74	Harris, TX	7.4	36	74	Fairfax, VA	8.6
62	75	San Francisco, CA	14.6	56	75	Travis, TX	6.8	42	75	Du Page, IL	7.9

Note: Column numbers refer to Table B. States and Counties.

TABLE 2—75 Largest Counties by 2000 Population
Selected Rankings

Live Birth Rate Per 1,000 Population, 1997-1999 Average				Infant Deaths Per 1,000 Live Births, 1997-1999 Average				Percent College Graduates (Bachelor's or higher degree), 1990			
Population Rank	Birth Rate Rank	County	[col 33] Birth Rate	Population Rank	Infant Mortality Rate	County	[col 37] Infant Mortality Rate	Population Rank	Percent College Graduate Rank	County	[col 51] Percent College Grads
75	1	El Paso, TX	20.6	44	1	Shelby, TN	12.9	49	1	Montgomery, MD	49.9
43	2	Salt Lake, UT	20.2	18	2	Philadelphia, PA	12.8	36	2	Fairfax, VA	49.0
27	3	Bronx, NY	18.8	57	3	Prince George's, MD	12.0	17	3	New York, NY	42.2
10	4	Dallas, TX	18.5	11	4	Wayne, MI	11.0	42	4	Du Page, IL	36.0
58	4	Fresno, CA	18.5	59	5	Essex, NJ	10.4	19	5	Middlesex, MA	35.4
3	6	Harris, TX	18.4	50	5	Marion, IN	10.4	40	6	Westchester, NY	35.3
13	7	San Bernardino, CA	17.7	2	7	Cook, IL	10.3	62	7	San Francisco, CA	35.0
24	8	Bexar, TX	17.3	61	8	Duval, FL	10.1	56	8	Travis, TX	34.7
4	9	Maricopa, AZ	17.2	52	8	Hamilton, OH	10.1	47	9	Fairfield, CT	34.2
20	9	Tarrant, TX	17.2	39	10	Milwaukee, WI	10.0	12	10	King, WA	32.8
56	9	Travis, TX	17.2	23	11	Cuyahoga, OH	9.8	14	11	Santa Clara, CA	32.6
1	12	Los Angeles, CA	17.1	55	11	Fulton, GA	9.8	67	12	Montgomery, PA	32.1
7	13	Kings, NY	16.9	33	13	Franklin, OH	9.2	46	13	Bergen, NJ	31.7
5	14	Orange, CA	16.7	51	14	Hartford, CT	8.3	38	14	Contra Costa, CA	31.6
44	14	Shelby, TN	16.7	34	14	St. Louis, MO	8.3	55	14	Fulton, GA	31.6
50	16	Marion, IN	16.6	35	16	Hillsborough, FL	8.2	32	14	Hennepin, MN	31.6
25	17	Clark, NV	16.5	63	17	Baltimore, MD	8.1	70	17	San Mateo, CA	31.3
55	18	Fulton, GA	16.4	37	17	Erie, NY	8.1	30	18	Oakland, MI	30.2
16	19	Riverside, CA	16.3	7	17	Kings, NY	8.1	26	19	Nassau, NY	30.0
2	20	Cook, IL	16.2	41	20	Pinellas, FL	8.0	34	20	St. Louis, MO	29.2
61	21	Duval, FL	16.0	73	21	Jefferson, KY	7.7	21	21	Alameda, CA	28.8
72	22	Mecklenburg, NC	15.9	13	21	San Bernardino, CA	7.7	72	22	Mecklenburg, NC	28.3
33	23	Franklin, OH	15.6	28	23	Allegheny, PA	7.6	5	23	Orange, CA	27.8
59	24	Essex, NJ	15.5	4	24	Maricopa, AZ	7.4	74	24	Suffolk, MA	27.7
45	24	Orange, FL	15.5	20	24	Tarrant, TX	7.4	33	25	Franklin, OH	26.6
6	24	San Diego, CA	15.5	45	26	Orange, FL	7.3	66	26	Middlesex, NJ	26.5
14	24	Santa Clara, CA	15.5	72	27	Mecklenburg, NC	7.1	10	27	Dallas, TX	26.3
64	24	Ventura, CA	15.5	24	28	Bexar, TX	7.0	68	27	Monroe, NY	26.3
42	29	Du Page, IL	15.4	27	28	Bronx, NY	7.0	69	29	Essex, MA	25.9
39	30	Milwaukee, WI	15.3	15	28	Broward, FL	7.0	51	30	Hartford, CT	25.8
57	31	Prince George's, MD	15.2	58	28	Fresno, CA	7.0	57	31	Prince George's, MD	25.5
9	31	Queens, NY	15.2	48	28	Honolulu, HI	7.0	3	32	Harris, TX	25.4
74	33	Suffolk, MA	15.1	68	28	Monroe, NY	7.0	6	33	San Diego, CA	25.3
35	34	Hillsborough, FL	15.0	32	34	Hennepin, MN	6.8	63	34	Baltimore, MD	25.0
29	35	Sacramento, CA	14.9	25	35	Clark, NV	6.7	48	35	Honolulu, HI	24.6
18	36	Philadelphia, PA	14.8	10	35	Dallas, TX	6.7	54	36	New Haven, CT	24.2
53	36	Pima, AZ	14.8	60	35	Macomb, MI	6.7	59	37	Essex, NJ	24.0
71	38	Pierce, WA	14.7	49	38	Montgomery, MD	6.6	20	37	Tarrant, TX	24.0
11	38	Wayne, MI	14.7	16	38	Riverside, CA	6.6	43	39	Salt Lake, UT	23.8
21	40	Alameda, CA	14.5	29	38	Sacramento, CA	6.6	52	40	Hamilton, OH	23.7
32	41	Hennepin, MN	14.4	54	41	New Haven, CT	6.5	53	41	Pima, AZ	23.3
8	41	Miami-Dade, FL	14.4	9	41	Queens, NY	6.5	29	42	Sacramento, CA	23.0
47	43	Fairfield, CT	14.3	31	43	Palm Beach, FL	6.4	22	42	Suffolk, NY	23.0
48	43	Honolulu, HI	14.3	74	43	Suffolk, MA	6.4	64	42	Ventura, CA	23.0
49	43	Montgomery, MD	14.3	3	45	Harris, TX	6.3	2	45	Cook, IL	22.8
52	46	Hamilton, OH	14.2	30	46	Oakland, MI	6.2	28	46	Allegheny, PA	22.6
36	47	Fairfax, VA	14.1	42	47	Du Page, IL	6.1	1	47	Los Angeles, CA	22.3
22	47	Suffolk, NY	14.1	47	47	Fairfield, CT	6.1	65	48	Worcester, MA	22.2
73	49	Jefferson, KY	14.0	64	47	Ventura, CA	6.1	4	49	Maricopa, AZ	22.1
70	49	San Mateo, CA	14.0	71	50	Pierce, WA	6.0	31	49	Palm Beach, FL	22.1
66	51	Middlesex, NJ	13.9	53	50	Pima, AZ	6.0	50	51	Marion, IN	21.4
69	52	Essex, MA	13.8	17	52	New York, NY	5.9	45	52	Orange, FL	21.2
23	53	Cuyahoga, OH	13.7	43	52	Salt Lake, UT	5.9	44	53	Shelby, TN	20.8
68	53	Monroe, NY	13.7	1	54	Los Angeles, CA	5.8	9	54	Queens, NY	20.6
40	53	Westchester, NY	13.7	67	54	Montgomery, PA	5.8	35	55	Hillsborough, FL	20.2
65	56	Worcester, MA	13.6	22	56	Suffolk, NY	5.7	23	56	Cuyahoga, OH	20.1
15	57	Broward, FL	13.5	65	56	Worcester, MA	5.7	37	57	Erie, NY	20.0
51	57	Hartford, CT	13.5	21	58	Alameda, CA	5.6	24	58	Bexar, TX	19.7
38	59	Contra Costa, CA	13.4	8	58	Miami-Dade, FL	5.6	73	59	Jefferson, KY	19.3
30	60	Oakland, MI	13.3	56	58	Travis, TX	5.6	39	59	Milwaukee, WI	19.3
12	61	King, WA	13.2	38	61	Contra Costa, CA	5.5	15	61	Broward, FL	18.8
54	61	New Haven, CT	13.2	69	61	Essex, MA	5.5	8	61	Miami-Dade, FL	18.8
19	63	Middlesex, MA	13.0	26	63	Nassau, NY	5.4	41	63	Pinellas, FL	18.5
34	64	St. Louis, MO	12.8	6	64	San Diego, CA	5.3	61	64	Duval, FL	18.4
67	65	Montgomery, PA	12.5	75	65	El Paso, TX	5.2	71	65	Pierce, WA	17.5
26	65	Nassau, NY	12.5	12	65	King, WA	5.2	58	66	Fresno, CA	16.9
31	65	Palm Beach, FL	12.5	66	67	Middlesex, NJ	5.1	7	67	Kings, NY	16.6
37	68	Erie, NY	12.4	14	68	Santa Clara, CA	5.0	75	68	El Paso, TX	15.2
60	69	Macomb, MI	12.3	40	68	Westchester, NY	5.0	18	68	Philadelphia, PA	15.2
17	69	New York, NY	12.3	46	70	Bergen, NJ	4.8	13	70	San Bernardino, CA	14.9
63	71	Baltimore, MD	12.2	62	70	San Francisco, CA	4.8	16	71	Riverside, CA	14.6
46	71	Bergen, NJ	12.2	36	72	Fairfax, VA	4.7	25	72	Clark, NV	13.8
28	73	Allegheny, PA	11.3	5	73	Orange, CA	4.6	11	73	Wayne, MI	13.7
41	74	Pinellas, FL	10.6	70	74	San Mateo, CA	4.5	60	74	Macomb, MI	13.5
62	75	San Francisco, CA	10.5	19	75	Middlesex, MA	4.2	27	75	Bronx, NY	12.2

Note: Column numbers refer to Table B. States and Counties.

TABLE 2—75 Largest Counties by 2000 Population
Selected Rankings

Population Rank	Expenditures Rank	County	[col 53] Expenditures Per Student (dollars)	Population Rank	Per Capita Income Rank	County	[col 64] Per Capita Income (dollars)	Population Rank	Median Income Rank	County	[col 58] Median Income (dollars)
40	1	Westchester, NY	12 202	17	1	New York, NY	81 665	36	1	Fairfax, VA	73 337
26	2	Nassau, NY	12 042	47	2	Fairfield, CT	56 643	49	2	Montgomery, MD	65 691
59	3	Essex, NJ	11 608	40	3	Westchester, NY	51 033	42	3	Du Page, IL	64 365
22	4	Suffolk, NY	11 532	62	4	San Francisco, CA	49 464	14	4	Santa Clara, CA	63 298
46	5	Bergen, NJ	11 203	46	5	Bergen, NJ	48 017	30	5	Oakland, MI	62 538
74	6	Suffolk, MA	10 452	36	6	Fairfax, VA	47 241	26	6	Nassau, NY	61 096
66	7	Middlesex, NJ	10 019	70	7	San Mateo, CA	47 146	46	7	Bergen, NJ	60 760
47	8	Fairfield, CT	9 515	14	8	Santa Clara, CA	46 649	70	8	San Mateo, CA	59 771
67	9	Montgomery, PA	9 434	49	9	Montgomery, MD	45 595	67	9	Montgomery, PA	57 837
37	10	Erie, NY	9 015	55	10	Fulton, GA	45 473	38	10	Contra Costa, CA	57 611
68	11	Monroe, NY	8 985	42	11	Du Page, IL	44 793	47	11	Fairfield, CT	57 389
51	12	Hartford, CT	8 965	12	12	King, WA	44 719	40	12	Westchester, NY	56 865
28	13	Allegheny, PA	8 907	67	13	Montgomery, PA	44 446	19	13	Middlesex, MA	54 819
27	14	Bronx, NY	8 818	30	14	Oakland, MI	44 146	66	14	Middlesex, NJ	54 070
7	14	Kings, NY	8 818	26	15	Nassau, NY	43 997	22	15	Suffolk, NY	54 008
17	14	New York, NY	8 818	19	16	Middlesex, MA	42 801	12	16	King, WA	52 435
9	14	Queens, NY	8 818	32	17	Hennepin, MN	42 313	64	17	Ventura, CA	51 710
54	18	New Haven, CT	8 809	31	18	Palm Beach, FL	41 907	60	18	Macomb, MI	51 187
19	19	Middlesex, MA	8 680	74	19	Suffolk, MA	40 748	5	19	Orange, CA	50 986
49	20	Montgomery, MD	8 604	34	20	St. Louis, MO	38 886	57	20	Prince George's, MD	50 050
39	21	Milwaukee, WI	8 323	38	21	Contra Costa, CA	37 994	32	21	Hennepin, MN	49 449
30	22	Oakland, MI	8 267	72	22	Mecklenburg, NC	37 321	34	22	St. Louis, MO	49 412
23	23	Cuyahoga, OH	8 023	10	23	Dallas, TX	36 425	21	23	Alameda, CA	48 445
32	24	Hennepin, MN	7 854	51	24	Hartford, CT	36 016	51	24	Hartford, CT	47 545
69	25	Essex, MA	7 772	56	25	Travis, TX	35 632	62	25	San Francisco, CA	47 239
36	26	Fairfax, VA	7 737	59	26	Essex, NJ	34 824	63	26	Baltimore, MD	46 577
11	27	Wayne, MI	7 714	69	27	Essex, MA	34 405	72	27	Mecklenburg, NC	46 033
2	28	Cook, IL	7 685	66	28	Middlesex, NJ	34 267	54	28	New Haven, CT	46 030
50	29	Marion, IN	7 511	63	29	Baltimore, MD	34 236	43	29	Salt Lake, UT	45 484
65	30	Worcester, MA	7 495	21	30	Alameda, CA	34 131	69	30	Essex, MA	44 969
60	31	Macomb, MI	7 411	52	31	Hamilton, OH	33 953	48	31	Honolulu, HI	44 934
18	32	Philadelphia, PA	7 362	3	32	Harris, TX	33 864	20	32	Tarrant, TX	44 669
55	33	Fulton, GA	7 358	5	33	Orange, CA	33 805	71	33	Pierce, WA	44 389
63	34	Baltimore, MD	7 172	22	34	Suffolk, NY	33 803	56	34	Travis, TX	43 489
34	35	St. Louis, MO	7 165	28	35	Allegheny, PA	33 474	10	35	Dallas, TX	42 736
52	36	Hamilton, OH	7 156	2	36	Cook, IL	33 398	4	36	Maricopa, AZ	42 192
42	37	Du Page, IL	7 141	54	37	New Haven, CT	33 201	68	37	Monroe, NY	41 945
57	38	Prince George's, MD	6 979	23	38	Cuyahoga, OH	32 241	6	38	San Diego, CA	41 909
33	39	Franklin, OH	6 907	41	39	Pinellas, FL	31 658	2	39	Cook, IL	41 815
62	40	San Francisco, CA	6 851	73	40	Jefferson, KY	31 474	29	40	Sacramento, CA	41 657
12	41	King, WA	6 259	33	41	Franklin, OH	30 820	17	41	New York, NY	41 590
72	42	Mecklenburg, NC	6 193	50	42	Marion, IN	30 685	33	42	Franklin, OH	41 267
73	43	Jefferson, KY	6 175	25	43	Clark, NV	30 628	65	43	Worcester, MA	41 142
8	44	Miami-Dade, FL	6 141	68	44	Monroe, NY	30 599	55	44	Fulton, GA	40 878
70	45	San Mateo, CA	6 124	44	45	Shelby, TN	30 524	25	45	Clark, NV	40 720
14	46	Santa Clara, CA	6 111	65	46	Worcester, MA	30 133	3	46	Harris, TX	40 690
48	47	Honolulu, HI	6 082	64	47	Ventura, CA	29 639	59	47	Essex, NJ	40 595
24	48	Bexar, TX	5 986	57	48	Prince George's, MD	29 547	15	48	Broward, FL	40 589
1	49	Los Angeles, CA	5 968	6	49	San Diego, CA	29 489	52	49	Hamilton, OH	40 141
71	50	Pierce, WA	5 924	48	50	Honolulu, HI	29 465	50	50	Marion, IN	40 114
31	51	Palm Beach, FL	5 871	15	51	Broward, FL	29 442	28	51	Allegheny, PA	39 887
21	52	Alameda, CA	5 851	60	52	Macomb, MI	29 192	73	52	Jefferson, KY	39 756
35	52	Hillsborough, FL	5 851	9	53	Queens, NY	29 095	16	53	Riverside, CA	39 428
29	54	Sacramento, CA	5 794	20	54	Tarrant, TX	28 835	31	54	Palm Beach, FL	39 199
6	55	San Diego, CA	5 774	39	55	Milwaukee, WI	28 681	23	55	Cuyahoga, OH	38 522
58	56	Fresno, CA	5 765	1	56	Los Angeles, CA	28 276	45	56	Orange, FL	38 327
15	57	Broward, FL	5 650	4	57	Maricopa, AZ	28 205	13	57	San Bernardino, CA	38 225
75	58	El Paso, TX	5 626	29	58	Sacramento, CA	27 485	39	58	Milwaukee, WI	37 952
56	59	Travis, TX	5 612	43	59	Salt Lake, UT	27 350	74	59	Suffolk, MA	37 931
41	60	Pinellas, FL	5 611	35	60	Hillsborough, FL	27 304	61	60	Duval, FL	37 739
3	61	Harris, TX	5 590	45	61	Orange, FL	27 278	1	61	Los Angeles, CA	37 655
38	62	Contra Costa, CA	5 546	37	62	Erie, NY	27 263	37	62	Erie, NY	37 641
45	63	Orange, FL	5 518	61	63	Duval, FL	26 868	11	63	Wayne, MI	37 525
13	64	San Bernardino, CA	5 460	11	64	Wayne, MI	26 329	35	64	Hillsborough, FL	37 362
64	65	Ventura, CA	5 435	18	65	Philadelphia, PA	25 436	44	65	Shelby, TN	36 610
10	66	Dallas, TX	5 426	71	66	Pierce, WA	25 289	9	66	Queens, NY	36 480
16	67	Riverside, CA	5 420	24	67	Bexar, TX	24 785	41	67	Pinellas, FL	34 741
25	68	Clark, NV	5 402	8	68	Miami-Dade, FL	24 733	24	68	Bexar, TX	34 210
5	69	Orange, CA	5 399	7	69	Kings, NY	24 596	53	69	Pima, AZ	34 049
44	70	Shelby, TN	5 375	53	70	Pima, AZ	23 911	58	70	Fresno, CA	32 023
20	71	Tarrant, TX	5 299	16	71	Riverside, CA	23 271	8	71	Miami-Dade, FL	30 669
61	72	Duval, FL	5 241	58	72	Fresno, CA	21 146	18	72	Philadelphia, PA	29 560
53	73	Pima, AZ	4 962	13	73	San Bernardino, CA	20 949	7	73	Kings, NY	27 556
4	74	Maricopa, AZ	4 768	27	74	Bronx, NY	20 319	75	74	El Paso, TX	26 318
43	75	Salt Lake, UT	4 113	75	75	El Paso, TX	17 216	27	75	Bronx, NY	25 750

Note: Column numbers refer to Table B. States and Counties.

TABLE 2—75 Largest Counties by 2000 Population
Selected Rankings

Percent of Persons Below the Poverty Level, 1998				Percent of Persons Under 18 Years Below the Poverty Level, 1998				Median Value of Owner-Occupied Housing Units, 1990			
Population Rank	Poverty Rate Rank	County	[col 59] Poverty Rate	Population Rank	Poverty Rate Rank for Persons Under 18 yrs.	County	[col 60] Poverty Rate for Persons Under 18 yrs.	Population Rank	Median Value Rank	County	[col 91] Median Value 1990 (dollars)
27	1	Bronx, NY	29.2	27	1	Bronx, NY	38.2	17	1	New York, NY	487 300
75	2	El Paso, TX	26.8	7	2	Kings, NY	35.8	70	2	San Mateo, CA	343 900
7	3	Kings, NY	25.7	75	3	El Paso, TX	35.6	62	3	San Francisco, CA	298 900
58	4	Fresno, CA	24.3	58	4	Fresno, CA	34.1	14	4	Santa Clara, CA	289 400
18	5	Philadelphia, PA	21.1	17	5	New York, NY	33.6	48	5	Honolulu, HI	283 600
17	6	New York, NY	20.0	18	6	Philadelphia, PA	31.0	40	6	Westchester, NY	283 500
8	7	Miami-Dade, FL	19.8	8	7	Miami-Dade, FL	29.6	5	7	Orange, CA	252 700
1	8	Los Angeles, CA	18.9	55	8	Fulton, GA	28.8	47	8	Fairfield, CT	249 800
24	9	Bexar, TX	17.8	1	9	Los Angeles, CA	28.1	64	9	Ventura, CA	245 300
55	10	Fulton, GA	17.4	9	10	Queens, NY	27.2	46	10	Bergen, NJ	227 700
11	11	Wayne, MI	17.3	74	11	Suffolk, MA	26.2	21	11	Alameda, CA	227 200
9	12	Queens, NY	17.2	39	12	Milwaukee, WI	26.0	1	12	Los Angeles, CA	226 400
74	13	Suffolk, MA	17.1	24	13	Bexar, TX	25.6	38	13	Contra Costa, CA	219 400
13	14	San Bernardino, CA	17.0	11	13	Wayne, MI	25.6	36	14	Fairfax, VA	213 800
59	15	Essex, NJ	16.0	29	15	Sacramento, CA	24.6	26	15	Nassau, NY	209 500
39	16	Milwaukee, WI	15.9	53	16	Pima, AZ	24.4	49	16	Montgomery, MD	200 800
53	16	Pima, AZ	15.9	13	17	San Bernardino, CA	23.4	59	17	Essex, NJ	196 100
29	16	Sacramento, CA	15.9	59	18	Essex, NJ	23.3	7	17	Kings, NY	196 100
44	19	Shelby, TN	15.6	35	19	Hillsborough, FL	22.7	19	19	Middlesex, MA	192 800
35	20	Hillsborough, FL	14.3	44	20	Shelby, TN	22.4	9	20	Queens, NY	191 000
37	21	Erie, NY	14.0	37	21	Erie, NY	22.3	6	21	San Diego, CA	186 700
16	21	Riverside, CA	14.0	23	22	Cuyahoga, OH	22.2	69	22	Essex, MA	176 200
3	23	Harris, TX	13.9	68	23	Monroe, NY	20.7	27	23	Bronx, NY	173 900
23	24	Cuyahoga, OH	13.5	45	23	Orange, FL	20.7	51	24	Hartford, CT	168 900
2	25	Cook, IL	13.1	62	25	San Francisco, CA	20.6	22	25	Suffolk, NY	165 900
6	25	San Diego, CA	13.1	16	26	Riverside, CA	20.4	54	26	New Haven, CT	165 200
45	27	Orange, FL	12.9	3	27	Harris, TX	20.2	66	27	Middlesex, NJ	164 700
61	28	Duval, FL	12.8	6	27	San Diego, CA	20.2	74	28	Suffolk, MA	162 100
68	28	Monroe, NY	12.8	2	29	Cook, IL	20.0	67	29	Montgomery, PA	143 400
10	30	Dallas, TX	12.6	41	29	Pinellas, FL	20.0	12	30	King, WA	140 100
73	31	Jefferson, KY	12.0	10	31	Dallas, TX	19.9	65	31	Worcester, MA	140 000
4	31	Maricopa, AZ	12.0	61	32	Duval, FL	19.7	16	32	Riverside, CA	139 100
50	33	Marion, IN	11.9	73	33	Jefferson, KY	19.6	42	33	Du Page, IL	137 100
62	34	San Francisco, CA	11.7	31	34	Palm Beach, FL	19.2	29	34	Sacramento, CA	129 800
41	35	Pinellas, FL	11.6	4	35	Maricopa, AZ	18.6	13	35	San Bernardino, CA	129 200
52	36	Hamilton, OH	11.3	28	36	Allegheny, PA	18.3	57	36	Prince George's, MD	122 600
15	37	Broward, FL	11.0	50	37	Marion, IN	18.2	2	37	Cook, IL	102 100
33	37	Franklin, OH	11.0	15	38	Broward, FL	17.9	63	38	Baltimore, MD	99 900
31	37	Palm Beach, FL	11.0	52	39	Hamilton, OH	17.4	31	39	Palm Beach, FL	98 400
56	40	Travis, TX	10.9	21	40	Alameda, CA	17.3	55	40	Fulton, GA	97 700
21	41	Alameda, CA	10.8	33	41	Franklin, OH	17.1	30	41	Oakland, MI	95 400
28	41	Allegheny, PA	10.8	56	42	Travis, TX	16.7	25	42	Clark, NV	93 300
25	41	Clark, NV	10.8	5	43	Orange, CA	16.4	15	43	Broward, FL	91 800
20	44	Tarrant, TX	10.6	20	44	Tarrant, TX	16.3	32	44	Hennepin, MN	91 000
54	45	New Haven, CT	10.4	64	44	Ventura, CA	16.3	68	45	Monroe, NY	90 700
71	46	Pierce, WA	10.3	54	46	New Haven, CT	16.1	72	46	Mecklenburg, NC	86 900
51	47	Hartford, CT	10.1	51	47	Hartford, CT	16.0	8	47	Miami-Dade, FL	86 500
5	47	Orange, CA	10.1	72	48	Mecklenburg, NC	15.7	4	48	Maricopa, AZ	85 300
64	49	Ventura, CA	10.0	25	49	Clark, NV	15.6	58	49	Fresno, CA	83 600
72	50	Mecklenburg, NC	9.9	69	50	Essex, MA	15.2	34	50	St. Louis, MO	83 500
48	51	Honolulu, HI	9.7	40	50	Westchester, NY	15.2	71	51	Pierce, WA	82 500
69	52	Essex, MA	9.3	32	52	Hennepin, MN	14.7	45	52	Orange, FL	81 400
32	52	Hennepin, MN	9.3	48	53	Honolulu, HI	14.3	10	53	Dallas, TX	79 200
65	52	Worcester, MA	9.3	71	54	Pierce, WA	14.0	56	54	Travis, TX	78 300
43	55	Salt Lake, UT	9.1	65	54	Worcester, MA	14.0	60	55	Macomb, MI	76 800
40	55	Westchester, NY	9.1	38	56	Contra Costa, CA	13.8	53	56	Pima, AZ	76 500
57	57	Prince George's, MD	8.7	14	57	Santa Clara, CA	13.5	37	57	Erie, NY	74 000
14	58	Santa Clara, CA	8.2	57	58	Prince George's, MD	12.7	33	58	Franklin, OH	73 800
38	59	Contra Costa, CA	8.1	43	59	Salt Lake, UT	12.2	41	58	Pinellas, FL	73 800
47	60	Fairfield, CT	7.7	34	59	St. Louis, MO	12.2	35	60	Hillsborough, FL	73 100
12	61	King, WA	7.6	47	61	Fairfield, CT	12.0	20	61	Tarrant, TX	72 900
22	61	Suffolk, NY	7.6	22	62	Suffolk, NY	11.9	52	62	Hamilton, OH	72 200
63	63	Baltimore, MD	7.3	63	63	Baltimore, MD	11.5	23	63	Cuyahoga, OH	72 100
34	63	St. Louis, MO	7.3	12	64	King, WA	11.1	43	64	Salt Lake, UT	71 000
66	65	Middlesex, NJ	6.5	26	65	Nassau, NY	10.6	44	65	Shelby, TN	66 500
19	66	Middlesex, MA	6.2	19	66	Middlesex, MA	9.9	39	66	Milwaukee, WI	65 300
26	66	Nassau, NY	6.2	30	66	Oakland, MI	9.9	61	67	Duval, FL	64 000
30	66	Oakland, MI	6.2	66	68	Middlesex, NJ	9.8	3	68	Harris, TX	63 500
60	69	Macomb, MI	6.0	60	69	Macomb, MI	9.5	50	69	Marion, IN	61 400
70	70	San Mateo, CA	5.9	70	70	San Mateo, CA	9.4	75	70	El Paso, TX	57 300
46	71	Bergen, NJ	5.3	46	71	Bergen, NJ	7.9	28	71	Allegheny, PA	57 100
49	71	Montgomery, MD	5.3	49	71	Montgomery, MD	7.9	73	72	Jefferson, KY	57 000
36	73	Fairfax, VA	4.7	67	73	Montgomery, PA	7.3	24	73	Bexar, TX	56 300
67	73	Montgomery, PA	4.7	36	74	Fairfax, VA	7.0	18	74	Philadelphia, PA	49 400
42	75	Du Page, IL	3.7	42	75	Du Page, IL	5.7	11	75	Wayne, MI	48 500

Note: Column numbers refer to Table B. States and Counties.

TABLE 2—75 Largest Counties by 2000 Population
Selected Rankings

Median Gross Rent of Renter-Occupied Housing Units, 1990				Unemployment Rate, 2001				Manufacturing Employment as a Percent of Total Nonfarm Employment, 1999			
Popu-lation Rank	Median Rate Rank	County	[col 94] Median Rent (dollars)	Popu-lation Rank	Unem-ployment Rate Rank	County	[col 100] Unem-ployment Rate 1999	Popu-lation Rank	Manufac-turing Rank	County	[col 107/col 105] Percent employed in Manufac-turing
36	1	Fairfax, VA	834	58	1	Fresno, CA	13.7	60	1	Macomb, MI	28.2
22	2	Suffolk, NY	802	75	2	El Paso, TX	8.2	14	2	Santa Clara, CA	24.6
5	3	Orange, CA	790	27	3	Bronx, NY	7.4	65	3	Worcester, MA	20.4
14	4	Santa Clara, CA	773	8	4	Miami-Dade, FL	6.9	68	4	Monroe, NY	19.9
70	5	San Mateo, CA	769	7	5	Kings, NY	6.7	69	5	Essex, MA	19.6
64	6	Ventura, CA	754	18	6	Philadelphia, PA	6.4	39	6	Milwaukee, WI	18.0
26	7	Nassau, NY	749	71	6	Pierce, WA	6.4	75	7	El Paso, TX	17.5
49	8	Montgomery, MD	740	17	8	New York, NY	6.0	5	8	Orange, CA	16.9
47	9	Fairfield, CT	709	2	9	Cook, IL	5.9	11	9	Wayne, MI	16.7
46	10	Bergen, NJ	689	11	10	Wayne, MI	5.8	1	10	Los Angeles, CA	16.6
38	11	Contra Costa, CA	675	1	11	Los Angeles, CA	5.7	54	10	New Haven, CT	16.6
19	12	Middlesex, MA	671	39	12	Milwaukee, WI	5.6	37	12	Erie, NY	15.8
66	13	Middlesex, NJ	667	25	13	Clark, NV	5.5	13	13	San Bernardino, CA	15.6
48	14	Honolulu, HI	663	31	13	Palm Beach, FL	5.5	23	14	Cuyahoga, OH	15.2
62	15	San Francisco, CA	653	59	15	Essex, NJ	5.4	20	15	Tarrant, TX	15.1
57	16	Prince George's, MD	642	10	16	Dallas, TX	5.3	19	16	Middlesex, MA	15.0
21	17	Alameda, CA	626	16	17	Riverside, CA	5.2	51	17	Hartford, CT	14.9
1	17	Los Angeles, CA	626	62	17	San Francisco, CA	5.2	21	18	Alameda, CA	14.6
42	19	Du Page, IL	625	37	19	Erie, NY	5.1	73	19	Jefferson, KY	13.9
74	19	Suffolk, MA	625	12	19	King, WA	5.1	12	19	King, WA	13.9
6	21	San Diego, CA	611	9	19	Queens, NY	5.1	34	19	St. Louis, MO	13.9
40	22	Westchester, NY	600	60	22	Macomb, MI	5.0	2	22	Cook, IL	13.8
69	23	Essex, MA	597	15	23	Broward, FL	4.9	64	23	Ventura, CA	13.7
67	24	Montgomery, PA	593	73	24	Jefferson, KY	4.8	16	24	Riverside, CA	13.5
31	25	Palm Beach, FL	587	13	24	San Bernardino, CA	4.8	22	24	Suffolk, NY	13.5
54	26	New Haven, CT	585	23	26	Cuyahoga, OH	4.6	52	26	Hamilton, OH	13.3
15	27	Broward, FL	575	21	27	Alameda, CA	4.5	66	27	Middlesex, NJ	13.2
16	28	Riverside, CA	572	61	27	Duval, FL	4.5	56	28	Travis, TX	13.1
51	29	Hartford, CT	568	3	27	Harris, TX	4.5	58	29	Fresno, CA	12.7
9	30	Queens, NY	560	14	27	Santa Clara, CA	4.5	67	30	Montgomery, PA	12.5
30	31	Oakland, MI	557	64	27	Ventura, CA	4.5	32	31	Hennepin, MN	12.3
13	32	San Bernardino, CA	556	63	32	Baltimore, MD	4.4	50	31	Marion, IN	12.3
63	33	Baltimore, MD	529	68	32	Monroe, NY	4.4	46	33	Bergen, NJ	12.1
59	34	Essex, NJ	528	55	34	Fulton, GA	4.3	47	34	Fairfield, CT	11.9
29	35	Sacramento, CA	527	43	34	Salt Lake, UT	4.3	30	35	Oakland, MI	11.7
65	36	Worcester, MA	522	29	36	Sacramento, CA	4.2	42	36	Du Page, IL	11.6
45	37	Orange, FL	517	44	36	Shelby, TN	4.2	6	37	San Diego, CA	11.5
25	38	Clark, NV	516	20	36	Tarrant, TX	4.2	43	38	Salt Lake, UT	11.3
17	39	New York, NY	513	24	39	Bexar, TX	4.1	4	39	Maricopa, AZ	10.8
12	40	King, WA	510	69	39	Essex, MA	4.1	71	39	Pierce, WA	10.8
60	41	Macomb, MI	493	48	39	Honolulu, HI	4.1	10	41	Dallas, TX	10.6
8	41	Miami-Dade, FL	493	72	39	Mecklenburg, NC	4.1	7	41	Kings, NY	10.6
32	43	Hennepin, MN	487	45	39	Orange, FL	4.1	53	43	Pima, AZ	10.5
34	44	St. Louis, MO	482	57	39	Prince George's, MD	4.1	9	43	Queens, NY	10.5
55	45	Fulton, GA	479	74	39	Suffolk, MA	4.1	59	45	Essex, NJ	10.2
2	46	Cook, IL	478	56	39	Travis, TX	4.1	41	46	Pinellas, FL	10.0
68	46	Monroe, NY	478	65	39	Worcester, MA	4.1	3	47	Harris, TX	9.5
7	48	Kings, NY	477	4	48	Maricopa, AZ	3.9	63	47	Baltimore, MD	9.5
72	49	Mecklenburg, NC	467	30	48	Oakland, MI	3.9	70	49	San Mateo, CA	9.2
4	50	Maricopa, AZ	466	34	48	St. Louis, MO	3.9	44	50	Shelby, TN	8.7
41	51	Pinellas, FL	463	28	51	Allegheny, PA	3.8	33	51	Franklin, OH	8.3
18	52	Philadelphia, PA	452	42	51	Du Page, IL	3.8	28	52	Allegheny, PA	8.1
10	53	Dallas, TX	448	50	51	Marion, IN	3.8	72	53	Mecklenburg, NC	7.8
35	54	Hillsborough, FL	446	66	54	Middlesex, NJ	3.7	29	53	Sacramento, CA	7.8
27	55	Bronx, NY	443	54	54	New Haven, CT	3.7	18	55	Philadelphia, PA	7.3
71	56	Pierce, WA	436	41	54	Pinellas, FL	3.7	24	55	Bexar, TX	7.3
58	57	Fresno, CA	434	46	57	Bergen, NJ	3.6	61	57	Duval, FL	7.1
39	57	Milwaukee, WI	434	52	57	Hamilton, OH	3.6	8	58	Miami-Dade, FL	6.8
61	59	Duval, FL	431	35	57	Hillsborough, FL	3.6	26	58	Nassau, NY	6.8
33	60	Franklin, OH	430	51	60	Hartford, CT	3.5	38	60	Contra Costa, CA	6.3
20	60	Tarrant, TX	430	67	60	Montgomery, PA	3.5	35	60	Hillsborough, FL	6.3
56	62	Travis, TX	416	53	60	Pima, AZ	3.5	15	62	Broward, FL	6.1
50	63	Marion, IN	412	22	60	Suffolk, NY	3.5	45	63	Orange, FL	6.0
11	64	Wayne, MI	406	40	60	Westchester, NY	3.5	27	64	Bronx, NY	5.9
3	65	Harris, TX	405	38	65	Contra Costa, CA	3.3	31	64	Palm Beach, FL	5.9
23	66	Cuyahoga, OH	397	32	66	Hennepin, MN	3.2	55	66	Fulton, GA	5.1
44	67	Shelby, TN	394	6	66	San Diego, CA	3.2	40	67	Westchester, NY	4.9
53	68	Pima, AZ	390	47	68	Fairfield, CT	3.1	57	68	Prince George's, MD	4.7
28	69	Allegheny, PA	389	19	68	Middlesex, MA	3.1	62	69	San Francisco, CA	4.1
37	70	Erie, NY	384	26	68	Nassau, NY	3.1	49	70	Montgomery, MD	3.9
24	71	Bexar, TX	379	5	71	Orange, CA	3.0	17	71	New York, NY	3.5
43	71	Salt Lake, UT	379	33	72	Franklin, OH	2.8	48	71	Honolulu, HI	3.5
52	73	Hamilton, OH	355	70	72	San Mateo, CA	2.8	74	71	Suffolk, MA	3.5
75	74	El Paso, TX	347	36	74	Fairfax, VA	2.3	25	74	Clark, NV	3.1
73	75	Jefferson, KY	346	49	74	Montgomery, MD	2.3	36	75	Fairfax, VA	2.8

Note: Column numbers refer to Table B. States and Counties.

TABLE 2—75 Largest Counties by 2000 Population
Selected Rankings

Employment in Services as a Percent of Total Nonfarm Employment, 1999				Finance, Insurance, and Real Estate Employment as a Percent of Total Nonfarm Employment, 1999				Per Capita Local Government Taxes, 1997			
Population Rank	Services Rank	County	[col 110/ col 105] Percent employed in Services	Population Rank	FIRE Rank	County	[col 109/ col 105] Percent FIRE Employment	Population Rank	Local Taxes Rank	County	[col 181] Local Per Capita Taxes (dollars)
36	1	Fairfax, VA	24.0	17	1	New York, NY	17.1	26	1	Nassau, NY	3 089
49	2	Montgomery, MD	14.7	74	2	Suffolk, MA	15.4	40	2	Westchester, NY	2 843
17	3	New York, NY	13.6	51	3	Hartford, CT	14.0	27	3	Bronx, NY	2 638
62	3	San Francisco, CA	13.6	61	4	Duval, FL	11.9	7	3	Kings, NY	2 638
19	5	Middlesex, MA	11.0	62	5	San Francisco, CA	11.6	17	3	New York, NY	2 638
66	6	Middlesex, NJ	10.8	33	6	Franklin, OH	10.6	9	3	Queens, NY	2 638
55	7	Fulton, GA	10.5	59	7	Essex, NJ	10.3	22	7	Suffolk, NY	2 479
1	7	Los Angeles, CA	10.5	67	8	Montgomery, PA	9.7	55	8	Fulton, GA	2 127
74	7	Suffolk, MA	10.5	32	9	Hennepin, MN	9.1	46	9	Bergen, NJ	1 987
57	10	Prince George's, MD	10.3	72	10	Mecklenburg, NC	8.6	47	10	Fairfield, CT	1 878
30	11	Oakland, MI	10.2	26	11	Nassau, NY	8.5	49	11	Montgomery, MD	1 817
18	12	Philadelphia, PA	9.8	38	12	Contra Costa, CA	8.4	62	12	San Francisco, CA	1 773
14	13	Santa Clara, CA	9.7	47	13	Fairfield, CT	8.1	2	13	Cook, IL	1 742
56	14	Travis, TX	9.1	18	14	Philadelphia, PA	8.0	36	14	Fairfax, VA	1 682
42	15	Du Page, IL	8.4	29	14	Sacramento, CA	8.0	68	15	Monroe, NY	1 681
47	16	Fairfield, CT	8.3	55	16	Fulton, GA	7.9	59	16	Essex, NJ	1 656
6	17	San Diego, CA	8.2	39	16	Milwaukee, WI	7.9	23	17	Cuyahoga, OH	1 632
70	17	San Mateo, CA	8.2	2	18	Cook, IL	7.5	66	18	Middlesex, NJ	1 605
2	17	Cook, IL	8.2	35	19	Hillsborough, FL	7.4	18	19	Philadelphia, PA	1 591
38	20	Contra Costa, CA	8.0	63	20	Baltimore, MD	7.2	42	20	Du Page, IL	1 563
10	21	Dallas, TX	7.9	23	20	Cuyahoga, OH	7.2	33	21	Franklin, OH	1 531
28	21	Allegheny, PA	7.9	10	22	Dallas, TX	7.1	51	22	Hartford, CT	1 526
32	23	Hennepin, MN	7.7	28	23	Allegheny, PA	7.0	10	23	Dallas, TX	1 521
12	23	King, WA	7.7	50	24	Marion, IN	6.9	52	24	Hamilton, OH	1 506
35	23	Hillsborough, FL	7.7	5	26	Orange, CA	6.8	37	25	Erie, NY	1 496
67	26	Montgomery, PA	7.6	4	26	Maricopa, AZ	6.8	31	26	Palm Beach, FL	1 495
3	27	Harris, TX	7.4	43	26	Salt Lake, UT	6.8	56	27	Travis, TX	1 422
59	28	Essex, NJ	7.2	24	28	Bexar, TX	6.7	12	28	King, WA	1 399
26	28	Nassau, NY	7.2	73	28	Jefferson, KY	6.7	54	29	New Haven, CT	1 395
72	30	Mecklenburg, NC	7.1	30	30	Oakland, MI	6.3	67	30	Montgomery, PA	1 375
5	31	Orange, CA	6.9	41	30	Pinellas, FL	6.3	32	31	Hennepin, MN	1 363
22	32	Suffolk, NY	6.8	65	30	Worcester, MA	6.3	74	32	Suffolk, MA	1 356
63	33	Baltimore, MD	6.7	64	33	Ventura, CA	6.2	39	33	Milwaukee, WI	1 328
34	34	St. Louis, MO	6.6	34	34	St. Louis, MO	6.1	3	34	Harris, TX	1 317
52	34	Hamilton, OH	6.6	42	35	Du Page, IL	6.0	28	35	Allegheny, PA	1 311
41	36	Pinellas, FL	6.5	37	35	Erie, NY	6.0	19	36	Middlesex, MA	1 301
21	36	Alameda, CA	6.5	15	37	Broward, FL	5.8	14	37	Santa Clara, CA	1 281
31	36	Palm Beach, FL	6.5	52	37	Hamilton, OH	5.8	21	38	Alameda, CA	1 271
29	39	Sacramento, CA	6.4	66	37	Middlesex, NJ	5.8	50	39	Marion, IN	1 268
4	39	Maricopa, AZ	6.4	48	40	Honolulu, HI	5.6	70	40	San Mateo, CA	1 255
23	41	Cuyahoga, OH	6.3	49	40	Montgomery, MD	5.6	63	41	Baltimore, MD	1 207
46	41	Bergen, NJ	6.3	70	40	San Mateo, CA	5.6	45	42	Orange, FL	1 190
40	43	Westchester, NY	6.2	31	43	Palm Beach, FL	5.3	34	43	St. Louis, MO	1 185
24	44	Bexar, TX	6.1	40	43	Westchester, NY	5.3	20	44	Tarrant, TX	1 182
15	45	Broward, FL	6.0	8	45	Miami-Dade, FL	5.1	15	45	Broward, FL	1 166
33	46	Franklin, OH	5.9	36	46	Fairfax, VA	5.0	8	46	Miami-Dade, FL	1 151
64	47	Ventura, CA	5.8	12	46	King, WA	5.0	57	47	Prince George's, MD	1 093
45	48	Orange, FL	5.7	46	48	Bergen, NJ	4.9	72	48	Mecklenburg, NC	1 090
51	49	Hartford, CT	5.6	56	48	Travis, TX	4.9	30	49	Oakland, MI	1 044
8	49	Miami-Dade, FL	5.6	11	48	Wayne, MI	4.9	69	50	Essex, MA	1 041
43	49	Salt Lake, UT	5.6	1	51	Los Angeles, CA	4.8	41	51	Pinellas, FL	1 016
61	49	Duval, FL	5.6	58	52	Fresno, CA	4.7	38	52	Contra Costa, CA	954
37	53	Erie, NY	5.5	6	52	San Diego, CA	4.7	35	53	Hillsborough, FL	936
50	54	Marion, IN	5.2	44	52	Shelby, TN	4.7	25	54	Clark, NV	931
53	55	Pima, AZ	5.1	3	55	Harris, TX	4.6	44	55	Shelby, TN	929
39	55	Milwaukee, WI	5.1	54	56	New Haven, CT	4.5	73	56	Jefferson, KY	908
48	55	Honolulu, HI	5.1	22	57	Suffolk, NY	4.4	5	57	Orange, CA	895
68	58	Monroe, NY	4.9	69	58	Essex, MA	4.2	1	58	Los Angeles, CA	890
60	59	Macomb, MI	4.8	20	59	Tarrant, TX	4.1	11	59	Wayne, MI	868
44	60	Shelby, TN	4.6	45	60	Orange, FL	4.0	64	60	Ventura, CA	865
69	60	Essex, MA	4.6	71	60	Pierce, WA	4.0	24	61	Bexar, TX	864
73	62	Jefferson, KY	4.5	21	62	Alameda, CA	3.9	4	61	Maricopa, AZ	864
20	62	Tarrant, TX	4.5	68	63	Monroe, NY	3.8	53	63	Pima, AZ	860
11	64	Wayne, MI	4.4	57	63	Prince George's, MD	3.8	43	64	Salt Lake, UT	857
25	65	Clark, NV	4.3	25	65	Clark, NV	3.6	61	65	Duval, FL	834
58	65	Fresno, CA	4.3	7	66	Kings, NY	3.3	65	66	Worcester, MA	830
54	67	New Haven, CT	4.2	19	66	Middlesex, MA	3.3	29	67	Sacramento, CA	784
75	68	El Paso, TX	3.5	13	68	San Bernardino, CA	3.1	71	68	Pierce, WA	776
71	69	Pierce, WA	3.4	75	69	El Paso, TX	3.0	6	69	San Diego, CA	766
65	70	Worcester, MA	3.3	53	69	Pima, AZ	3.0	16	70	Riverside, CA	741
16	71	Riverside, CA	2.8	16	71	Riverside, CA	2.7	75	71	El Paso, TX	724
7	71	Kings, NY	2.8	9	72	Queens, NY	2.6	60	72	Macomb, MI	706
13	73	San Bernardino, CA	2.5	60	73	Macomb, MI	2.2	13	73	San Bernardino, CA	673
9	73	Queens, NY	2.5	14	73	Santa Clara, CA	2.2	58	74	Fresno, CA	640
27	75	Bronx, NY	2.0	27	75	Bronx, NY	1.5	48	75	Honolulu, HI	606

Note: Column numbers refer to Table B. States and Counties.

TABLE 2—75 Largest Counties by 2000 Population
Selected Rankings

Violent Crime Rate (violent crime known to police per 100,000 population), 2000				Percent of County's Land Owned by Federal Government, 1997				Military as a Percent of All Federal Employment, 1999			
Popu-lation Rank	Crime Rate Rank	County	[col 46] Violent Crime Rate	Popu-lation Rank	Fed. Land Rank	County	[col 131] Percent Fed. Land	Popu-lation Rank	Military Rank	County	[col 193/col 192+193] Percent Fed. Employment Military
55	1	Fulton, GA	1 563	25	1	Clark, NV	88.3	6	1	San Diego, CA	71.7
18	2	Philadelphia, PA	1 503	13	2	San Bernardino, CA	74.5	71	2	Pierce, WA	71.0
11	3	Wayne, MI	1 293	16	3	Riverside, CA	55.7	48	3	Honolulu, HI	64.3
8	4	Miami-Dade, FL	1 233	4	4	Maricopa, AZ	53.2	13	4	San Bernardino, CA	62.7
74	5	Suffolk, MA	1 211	64	5	Ventura, CA	50.0	61	5	Duval, FL	59.9
44	6	Shelby, TN	1 145	58	6	Fresno, CA	38.4	75	6	El Paso, TX	57.7
35	7	Hillsborough, FL	1 127	8	7	Miami-Dade, FL	33.4	24	7	Bexar, TX	51.9
72	8	Mecklenburg, NC	1 104	1	8	Los Angeles, CA	29.6	25	8	Clark, NV	51.3
61	9	Duval, FL	1 095	53	9	Pima, AZ	29.0	53	9	Pima, AZ	46.0
45	10	Orange, FL	1 071	71	10	Pierce, WA	28.8	64	10	Ventura, CA	45.7
59	11	Essex, NJ	1 049	12	11	King, WA	23.1	34	11	St. Louis, MO	45.6
1	12	Los Angeles, CA	945	6	12	San Diego, CA	22.9	67	12	Montgomery, PA	44.7
17	12	New York, NY	945	43	13	Salt Lake, UT	20.4	65	12	Worcester, MA	44.7
57	14	Prince George's, MD	924	75	14	El Paso, TX	13.7	4	14	Maricopa, AZ	40.3
62	15	San Francisco, CA	845	5	15	Orange, CA	13.1	35	14	Hillsborough, FL	40.3
10	16	Dallas, TX	843	48	16	Honolulu, HI	12.5	46	16	Bergen, NJ	38.8
63	17	Baltimore, MD	822	31	17	Palm Beach, FL	10.1	43	17	Salt Lake, UT	36.8
50	17	Marion, IN	822	62	18	San Francisco, CA	7.3	7	18	Kings, NY	35.9
41	19	Pinellas, FL	809	57	19	Prince George's, MD	7.1	5	18	Orange, CA	35.9
3	20	Harris, TX	798	36	20	Fairfax, VA	6.3	69	20	Essex, MA	34.5
58	21	Fresno, CA	756	24	21	Bexar, TX	6.1	15	21	Broward, FL	34.2
31	22	Palm Beach, FL	742	7	22	Kings, NY	5.4	66	22	Middlesex, NJ	33.0
75	23	El Paso, TX	705	61	23	Duval, FL	4.6	41	23	Pinellas, FL	32.9
39	24	Milwaukee, WI	671	42	24	Du Page, IL	4.3	68	24	Monroe, NY	32.8
23	25	Cuyahoga, OH	666	9	25	Queens, NY	4.0	16	24	Riverside, CA	32.8
21	26	Alameda, CA	658	21	26	Alameda, CA	3.3	19	26	Middlesex, MA	32.1
53	26	Pima, AZ	658	49	26	Montgomery, MD	3.3	47	27	Fairfield, CT	31.8
71	28	Pierce, WA	654	3	28	Harris, TX	2.6	30	28	Oakland, MI	30.2
33	29	Franklin, OH	636	10	29	Dallas, TX	2.3	31	29	Palm Beach, FL	30.1
24	30	Bexar, TX	631	38	30	Contra Costa, CA	2.0	26	30	Nassau, NY	29.9
16	31	Riverside, CA	621	19	30	Middlesex, MA	2.0	72	31	Mecklenburg, NC	29.0
15	32	Broward, FL	603	65	32	Worcester, MA	1.7	70	32	San Mateo, CA	28.9
25	33	Clark, NV	591	29	33	Sacramento, CA	1.6	3	33	Harris, TX	28.3
29	34	Sacramento, CA	589	18	34	Philadelphia, PA	1.5	8	34	Miami-Dade, FL	28.2
65	35	Worcester, MA	577	69	35	Essex, MA	1.4	39	35	Milwaukee, WI	28.1
4	36	Maricopa, AZ	553	14	35	Santa Clara, CA	1.4	1	36	Los Angeles, CA	27.4
73	37	Jefferson, KY	539	20	37	Tarrant, TX	1.3	42	37	Du Page, IL	27.2
37	38	Erie, NY	537	33	38	Franklin, OH	1.2	32	38	Hennepin, MN	27.0
13	39	San Bernardino, CA	536	67	39	Montgomery, PA	1.1	12	39	King, WA	26.6
32	40	Hennepin, MN	533	23	40	Cuyahoga, OH	1.0	57	40	Prince George's, MD	26.5
20	41	Tarrant, TX	519	50	40	Marion, IN	1.0	20	41	Tarrant, TX	26.1
6	42	San Diego, CA	489	17	40	New York, NY	1.0	21	42	Alameda, CA	26.0
38	43	Contra Costa, CA	478	22	40	Suffolk, NY	1.0	73	42	Jefferson, KY	26.0
52	44	Hamilton, OH	459	60	44	Macomb, MI	0.9	45	44	Orange, FL	25.9
28	45	Allegheny, PA	456	70	45	San Mateo, CA	0.8	29	45	Sacramento, CA	25.8
69	46	Essex, MA	452	74	45	Suffolk, MA	0.8	44	46	Shelby, TN	24.7
56	47	Travis, TX	430	55	47	Fulton, GA	0.7	28	47	Allegheny, PA	24.6
14	48	Santa Clara, CA	429	35	47	Hillsborough, FL	0.7	54	48	New Haven, CT	24.2
12	49	King, WA	428	44	47	Shelby, TN	0.7	9	49	Queens, NY	24.0
54	50	New Haven, CT	382	32	50	Hennepin, MN	0.5	38	50	Contra Costa, CA	23.9
51	51	Hartford, CT	364	56	50	Travis, TX	0.5	14	51	Santa Clara, CA	23.6
47	52	Fairfield, CT	359	63	52	Baltimore, MD	0.4	40	52	Westchester, NY	23.4
43	52	Salt Lake, UT	359	47	53	Fairfield, CT	0.3	51	53	Hartford, CT	23.0
60	54	Macomb, MI	332	52	53	Hamilton, OH	0.3	27	54	Bronx, NY	22.8
30	55	Oakland, MI	312	26	53	Nassau, NY	0.3	50	55	Marion, IN	22.3
5	56	Orange, CA	302	15	56	Broward, FL	0.2	60	56	Macomb, MI	22.2
40	57	Westchester, NY	297	54	56	New Haven, CT	0.2	11	57	Wayne, MI	21.8
68	58	Monroe, NY	284	28	58	Allegheny, PA	0.1	33	58	Franklin, OH	20.3
70	59	San Mateo, CA	282	59	58	Essex, NJ	0.1	10	59	Dallas, TX	20.2
64	60	Ventura, CA	280	45	58	Orange, FL	0.1	37	60	Erie, NY	20.1
48	61	Honolulu, HI	263	46	61	Bergen, NJ	0.0	2	61	Cook, IL	19.5
34	62	St. Louis, MO	256	27	61	Bronx, NY	0.0	56	62	Travis, TX	19.0
66	63	Middlesex, NJ	244	2	61	Cook, IL	0.0	23	63	Cuyahoga, OH	18.8
19	64	Middlesex, MA	242	37	61	Erie, NY	0.0	22	63	Suffolk, NY	18.8
49	65	Montgomery, MD	214	51	61	Hartford, CT	0.0	52	65	Hamilton, OH	18.1
67	66	Montgomery, PA	196	73	61	Jefferson, KY	0.0	36	66	Fairfax, VA	16.6
46	67	Bergen, NJ	127	72	61	Mecklenburg, NC	0.0	59	67	Essex, NJ	16.5
36	68	Fairfax, VA	26	66	61	Middlesex, NJ	0.0	55	68	Fulton, GA	16.4
27		Bronx, NY	NA	39	61	Milwaukee, WI	0.0	49	69	Montgomery, MD	14.9
2		Cook, IL	NA	68	61	Monroe, NY	0.0	63	70	Baltimore, MD	14.8
42		Du Page, IL	NA	30	61	Oakland, MI	0.0	74	70	Suffolk, MA	14.8
7		Kings, NY	NA	41	61	Pinellas, FL	0.0	58	72	Fresno, CA	13.8
26		Nassau, NY	NA	34	61	St. Louis, MO	0.0	18	73	Philadelphia, PA	13.5
9		Queens, NY	NA	11	61	Wayne, MI	0.0	17	74	New York, NY	9.2
22		Suffolk, NY	NA	40	61	Westchester, NY	0.0	62	75	San Francisco, CA	8.0

Note: Column numbers refer to Table B. States and Counties.

TABLE 3—75 Counties with Highest Agricultural Sales, 1997
Selected Rankings

Value of Sales Rank	County	[col 125] Value of Sales (Mil Dol)	Value of Sales Rank	Average Sales Rank	County	[col 126] Average Sales per Farm ($)	Value of Sales Rank	Number of Farms Rank	County	[col 113] Number of Farms
1	Fresno, CA	2 773	38	1	Haskell, KS	1 794 382	1	1	Fresno, CA	6 592
2	Kern, CA	1 969	12	2	Imperial, CA	1 526 662	24	2	San Diego, CA	5 925
3	Tulare, CA	1 921	4	3	Monterey, CA	1 447 268	3	3	Tulare, CA	5 446
4	Monterey, CA	1 750	47	4	Hartley, TX	1 428 449	15	4	Lancaster, PA	4 556
5	Weld, CO	1 287	20	5	Castro, TX	1 366 952	7	5	Stanislaus, CA	4 009
6	Merced, CA	1 273	35	6	Scott, KS	1 347 057	8	6	San Joaquin, CA	3 862
7	Stanislaus, CA	1 209	48	7	Hansford, TX	1 241 020	11	7	Yakima, WA	3 365
8	San Joaquin, CA	1 180	70	8	Grant, KS	1 133 381	9	8	Riverside, CA	3 048
9	Riverside, CA	1 048	28	9	Yuma, AZ	1 122 717	62	9	Stearns, MN	2 982
10	Palm Beach, FL	* 873	67	10	Moore, TX	1 118 443	5	10	Weld, CO	2 959
11	Yakima, WA	873	10	11	Palm Beach, FL	1 020 908	6	11	Merced, CA	2 831
12	Imperial, CA	850	23	12	Deaf Smith, TX	1 014 894	34	12	Sonoma, CA	2 745
13	Ventura, CA	846	66	13	Sherman, TX	1 006 870	55	13	Hillsborough, FL	2 639
14	Grant, WA	804	2	14	Kern, CA	985 735	74	14	Dane, WI	2 595
15	Lancaster, PA	767	33	15	Finney, KS	922 739	36	15	Marion, OR	2 546
16	Duplin, NC	746	27	16	Parmer, TX	919 706	45	16	Washington, AR	2 476
17	Sampson, NC	733	46	17	Dallam, TX	862 291	51	17	Benton, AR	2 323
18	Kings, CA	694	19	18	Texas, OK	850 985	13	18	Ventura, CA	2 214
19	Texas, OK	668	42	19	Gray, KS	810 604	54	19	Cullman, AL	2 151
20	Castro, TX	668	58	20	Hendry, FL	802 575	2	20	Kern, CA	1 997
21	Maricopa, AZ	664	43	21	Swisher, TX	688 268	73	21	Butte, CA	1 942
22	Santa Barbara, CA	660	44	22	Pinal, AZ	671 865	59	22	San Luis Obispo, CA	1 916
23	Deaf Smith, TX	657	18	23	Kings, CA	642 889	60	23	Canyon, ID	1 898
24	San Diego, CA	633	17	24	Sampson, NC	617 925	37	24	Rockingham, VA	1 834
25	Madera, CA	627	16	25	Duplin, NC	609 844	29	25	Sioux, IA	1 752
26	San Bernardino, CA	618	53	26	Phelps, NE	609 402	14	26	Grant, WA	1 699
27	Parmer, TX	551	32	27	Yuma, CO	537 247	25	27	Madera, CA	1 673
28	Yuma, AZ	522	40	28	Morgan, CO	534 842	21	28	Maricopa, AZ	1 643
29	Sioux, IA	508	30	29	Cuming, NE	509 501	68	29	Gonzales, TX	1 629
30	Cuming, NE	507	14	30	Grant, WA	473 368	39	30	Dade, FL	1 576
31	Sussex, DE	500	41	31	Dawson, NE	465 589	26	31	San Bernardino, CA	1 455
32	Yuma, CO	481	57	32	Cassia, ID	456 541	22	32	Santa Barbara, CA	1 451
33	Finney, KS	480	22	33	Santa Barbara, CA	454 680	50	33	Chester, PA	1 424
34	Sonoma, CA	464	6	34	Merced, CA	449 832	31	34	Sussex, DE	1 366
35	Scott, KS	451	61	35	Ford, KS	445 514	71	35	Custer, NE	1 307
36	Marion, OR	438	5	36	Weld, CO	434 821	65	36	Ottawa, MI	1 292
37	Rockingham, VA	438	26	37	San Bernardino, CA	424 628	72	37	Mercer, OH	1 255
38	Haskell, KS	432	1	38	Fresno, CA	420 629	16	38	Duplin, NC	1 224
39	Dade, FL	417	52	39	Wayne, NC	407 604	4	39	Monterey, CA	1 209
40	Morgan, CO	406	21	40	Maricopa, AZ	404 174	17	40	Sampson, NC	1 186
41	Dawson, NE	399	56	41	Franklin, WA	392 612	52	41	Union, NC	1 142
42	Gray, KS	374	13	42	Ventura, CA	381 939	64	42	Renville, MN	1 114
43	Swisher, TX	364	25	43	Madera, CA	374 901	18	43	Kings, CA	1 079
44	Pinal, AZ	363	49	44	Yolo, CA	373 666	63	44	Benton, WA	1 078
45	Washington, AR	359	31	45	Sussex, DE	366 149	30	45	Cuming, NE	995
46	Dallam, TX	357	3	46	Tulare, CA	352 806	49	46	Yolo, CA	923
47	Hartley, TX	350	9	47	Riverside, CA	343 676	28	47	Yuma, AZ	896
48	Hansford, TX	346	69	48	Logan, CO	333 038	69	48	Logan, CO	879
49	Yolo, CA	345	8	49	San Joaquin, CA	305 465	41	49	Dawson, NE	858
50	Chester, PA	343	7	50	Stanislaus, CA	301 453	10	50	Palm Beach, FL	855
51	Benton, AR	338	29	51	Sioux, IA	289 932	56	51	Franklin, WA	848
52	Wayne, NC	337	63	52	Benton, WA	278 785	52	52	Wayne, NC	827
53	Phelps, NE	336	64	53	Renville, MN	269 849	19	53	Texas, OK	785
54	Cullman, AL	334	39	54	Dade, FL	264 278	40	54	Morgan, CO	759
55	Hillsborough, FL	333	11	55	Yakima, WA	259 582	57	55	Cassia, ID	729
56	Franklin, WA	333	75	56	Union, NC	248 304	61	56	Ford, KS	692
57	Cassia, ID	333	50	57	Chester, PA	240 778	23	57	Deaf Smith, TX	647
58	Hendry, FL	323	37	58	Rockingham, VA	238 879	27	58	Parmer, TX	599
59	San Luis Obispo, CA	313	65	59	Ottawa, MI	232 187	12	59	Imperial, CA	557
60	Canyon, ID	311	72	60	Mercer, OH	229 213	53	60	Phelps, NE	552
61	Ford, KS	308	71	61	Custer, NE	220 766	44	61	Pinal, AZ	541
62	Stearns, MN	302	68	62	Gonzales, TX	180 725	43	62	Swisher, TX	529
63	Benton, WA	301	36	63	Marion, OR	172 179	33	63	Finney, KS	520
64	Renville, MN	301	34	64	Sonoma, CA	168 895	20	64	Castro, TX	489
65	Ottawa, MI	300	15	65	Lancaster, PA	168 293	28	65	Yuma, AZ	465
66	Sherman, TX	295	60	66	Canyon, ID	164 066	42	66	Gray, KS	461
67	Moore, TX	294	59	67	San Luis Obispo, CA	163 335	46	67	Dallam, TX	414
68	Gonzales, TX	294	54	68	Cullman, AL	155 345	58	68	Hendry, FL	403
69	Logan, CO	293	73	69	Butte, CA	147 388	35	69	Scott, KS	335
70	Grant, KS	291	51	70	Benton, AR	145 296	66	70	Sherman, TX	293
71	Custer, NE	289	45	71	Washington, AR	145 163	48	71	Hansford, TX	279
72	Mercer, OH	288	55	72	Hillsborough, FL	126 084	67	72	Moore, TX	263
73	Butte, CA	286	74	73	Dane, WI	109 687	70	73	Grant, KS	257
74	Dane, WI	285	24	74	San Diego, CA	106 790	47	74	Hartley, TX	245
75	Union, NC	284	62	75	Stearns, MN	101 356	38	75	Haskell, KS	241

Note: Column numbers refer to Table B. States and Counties.

TABLE 3—75 Counties with Highest Agricultural Sales, 1997
Selected Rankings

Average Size of Farm, 1997				Average Value of Lands and Buildings Per Farm, 1997				Average Value of Land and Buildings Per Acre, 1997			
Value of Sales Rank	Size of Farm Rank	County	[col 119] Average Size of Farm (acres)	Value of Sales Rank	Value of Land and Bldgs per Farm Rank	County	[col 122] Average Value per Farm (thousands of dollars)	Value of Sales Rank	Value of Land and Bldgs per Acre Rank	County	[col 123] Average Value per Acre (Dollars)
47	1	Hartley, TX	3 359	58	1	Hendry, FL	4 289	39	1	Dade, FL	8 047
44	2	Pinal, AZ	2 409	4	2	Monterey, CA	2 685	13	2	Ventura, CA	6 860
46	3	Dallam, TX	2 250	12	3	Imperial, CA	2 614	50	3	Chester, PA	5 658
67	4	Moore, TX	2 112	10	4	Palm Beach, FL	2 398	15	4	Lancaster, PA	5 578
48	5	Hansford, TX	2 086	28	5	Yuma, AZ	2 266	24	5	San Diego, CA	5 504
66	6	Sherman, TX	2 072	2	6	Kern, CA	2 162	34	6	Sonoma, CA	5 211
38	7	Haskell, KS	1 530	44	7	Pinal, AZ	1 891	8	7	San Joaquin, CA	4 667
32	8	Yuma, CO	1 524	18	8	Kings, CA	1 602	9	8	Riverside, CA	4 618
58	9	Hendry, FL	1 500	49	9	Yolo, CA	1 420	7	9	Stanislaus, CA	4 508
33	10	Finney, KS	1 464	21	10	Maricopa, AZ	1 384	28	10	Yuma, AZ	4 496
2	11	Kern, CA	1 428	22	11	Santa Barbara, CA	1 378	36	11	Marion, OR	4 248
35	12	Scott, KS	1 422	38	12	Haskell, KS	1 321	55	12	Hillsborough, FL	4 234
19	13	Texas, OK	1 384	47	13	Hartley, TX	1 240	73	13	Butte, CA	3 589
23	14	Deaf Smith, TX	1 360	46	14	Dallam, TX	1 181	25	14	Madera, CA	3 537
70	15	Grant, KS	1 294	66	15	Sherman, TX	1 166	3	15	Tulare, CA	3 444
69	16	Logan, CO	1 284	25	16	Madera, CA	1 157	10	16	Palm Beach, FL	3 404
4	17	Monterey, CA	1 277	63	17	Benton, WA	1 122	1	17	Fresno, CA	3 334
42	18	Gray, KS	1 206	59	18	San Luis Obispo, CA	1 046	6	18	Merced, CA	3 149
71	19	Custer, NE	1 188	34	19	Sonoma, CA	1 025	37	19	Rockingham, VA	3 069
20	20	Castro, TX	1 142	8	20	San Joaquin, CA	1 017	12	20	Imperial, CA	3 068
40	21	Morgan, CO	976	14	21	Grant, WA	1 001	65	21	Ottawa, MI	3 066
43	22	Swisher, TX	975	1	22	Fresno, CA	971	21	22	Maricopa, AZ	2 944
61	23	Ford, KS	967	56	23	Franklin, WA	969	58	23	Hendry, FL	2 868
27	24	Parmer, TX	913	33	24	Finney, KS	951	72	24	Mercer, OH	2 812
57	25	Cassia, ID	901	6	25	Merced, CA	951	75	25	Union, NC	2 790
12	26	Imperial, CA	879	57	26	Cassia, ID	918	18	26	Kings, CA	2 732
41	27	Dawson, NE	757	64	27	Renville, MN	913	49	27	Yolo, CA	2 732
10	28	Palm Beach, FL	707	32	28	Yuma, CO	891	22	28	Santa Barbara, CA	2 716
53	29	Phelps, NE	686	70	29	Grant, KS	888	54	29	Cullman, AL	2 647
59	30	San Luis Obispo, CA	679	13	30	Ventura, CA	883	51	30	Benton, AR	2 549
56	31	Franklin, WA	665	53	31	Phelps, NE	876	29	31	Sioux, IA	2 445
5	32	Weld, CO	647	48	32	Hansford, TX	856	31	32	Sussex, DE	2 441
14	33	Grant, WA	645	3	33	Tulare, CA	835	4	33	Monterey, CA	2 358
26	34	San Bernardino, CA	635	67	34	Moore, TX	804	16	34	Duplin, NC	2 321
18	35	Kings, CA	609	42	35	Gray, KS	786	45	35	Washington, AR	2 230
49	36	Yolo, CA	581	7	36	Stanislaus, CA	779	60	36	Canyon, ID	2 225
63	37	Benton, WA	568	73	37	Butte, CA	754	63	37	Benton, WA	2 169
22	38	Santa Barbara, CA	563	9	38	Riverside, CA	749	52	38	Wayne, NC	2 025
64	39	Renville, MN	540	19	39	Texas, OK	718	17	39	Sampson, NC	1 971
28	40	Yuma, AZ	511	35	40	Scott, KS	694	74	40	Dane, WI	1 853
11	41	Yakima, WA	500	20	41	Castro, TX	676	64	41	Renville, MN	1 703
68	42	Gonzales, TX	436	50	42	Chester, PA	670	2	42	Kern, CA	1 605
21	43	Maricopa, AZ	431	29	43	Sioux, IA	662	14	43	Grant, WA	1 596
25	44	Madera, CA	383	41	44	Dawson, NE	625	59	44	San Luis Obispo, CA	1 591
30	45	Cuming, NE	361	23	45	Deaf Smith, TX	611	30	45	Cuming, NE	1 571
6	46	Merced, CA	311	11	46	Yakima, WA	605	56	46	Franklin, WA	1 469
1	47	Fresno, CA	285	40	47	Morgan, CO	604	53	47	Phelps, NE	1 376
29	48	Sioux, IA	282	72	48	Mercer, OH	582	11	48	Yakima, WA	1 220
52	49	Wayne, NC	277	5	49	Weld, CO	567	62	49	Stearns, MN	1 099
3	50	Tulare, CA	240	27	50	Parmer, TX	564	57	50	Cassia, ID	932
17	51	Sampson, NC	228	30	51	Cuming, NE	549	41	51	Dawson, NE	859
31	52	Sussex, DE	225	71	52	Custer, NE	547	38	52	Haskell, KS	828
62	53	Stearns, MN	217	52	53	Wayne, NC	542	5	53	Weld, CO	807
8	54	San Joaquin, CA	209	31	54	Sussex, DE	518	68	54	Gonzales, TX	797
34	55	Sonoma, CA	208	69	55	Logan, CO	511	44	55	Pinal, AZ	760
73	56	Butte, CA	208	36	56	Marion, OR	500	26	56	San Bernardino, CA	693
72	57	Mercer, OH	208	61	57	Ford, KS	483	42	57	Gray, KS	663
74	58	Dane, WI	198	15	58	Lancaster, PA	472	70	58	Grant, KS	660
16	59	Duplin, NC	195	26	59	San Bernardino, CA	470	40	59	Morgan, CO	649
60	60	Canyon, ID	187	17	60	Sampson, NC	464	27	60	Parmer, TX	621
7	61	Stanislaus, CA	183	16	61	Duplin, NC	457	33	61	Finney, KS	588
9	62	Riverside, CA	167	43	62	Swisher, TX	445	66	62	Sherman, TX	584
13	63	Ventura, CA	156	75	63	Union, NC	428	20	63	Castro, TX	578
75	64	Union, NC	156	39	64	Dade, FL	408	32	64	Yuma, CO	565
45	65	Washington, AR	135	24	65	San Diego, CA	407	46	65	Dallam, TX	516
65	66	Ottawa, MI	132	60	66	Canyon, ID	399	19	66	Texas, OK	511
51	67	Benton, AR	128	65	67	Ottawa, MI	396	35	67	Scott, KS	510
37	68	Rockingham, VA	126	55	68	Hillsborough, FL	391	61	68	Ford, KS	508
50	69	Chester, PA	123	37	69	Rockingham, VA	383	71	69	Custer, NE	444
36	70	Marion, OR	120	68	70	Gonzales, TX	381	43	70	Swisher, TX	437
55	71	Hillsborough, FL	94	74	71	Dane, WI	367	23	71	Deaf Smith, TX	430
54	72	Cullman, AL	94	45	72	Washington, AR	303	69	72	Logan, CO	427
15	73	Lancaster, PA	86	51	73	Benton, AR	300	48	73	Hansford, TX	424
24	74	San Diego, CA	80	54	74	Cullman, AL	253	67	74	Moore, TX	385
39	75	Dade, FL	54	62	75	Stearns, MN	227	47	75	Hartley, TX	367

Note: Column numbers refer to Table B. States and Counties.

TABLE 4—75 Largest Metropolitan Areas by 2000 Population
Selected Rankings

Total Persons, 2000			Total Land Area (square kilometers), 2000			
Population Rank	Metropolitan Area	[col 2] Population	Population Rank	Land Area Rank	Metropolitan Area	[col 1] Land Area
1	Los Angeles-Long Beach, CA	9 519 338	40	1	Las Vegas, NV-AZ	101 964
2	New York, NY	9 314 235	11	2	Riverside-San Bernardino, CA	70 603
3	Chicago, IL	8 272 768	12	3	Phoenix-Mesa, AZ	37 743
4	Boston-Worcester-Lawrence-Lowell-Brockton, MA-NH	6 057 826	70	4	Tucson, AZ	23 792
5	Philadelphia, PA-NJ	5 100 931	66	5	Fresno, CA	20 975
6	Washington, DC-MD-VA-WV	4 923 153	6	6	Washington, DC-MD-VA-WV	16 859
7	Detroit, MI	4 441 551	4	7	Boston-Worcester-Lawrence-Lowell-Brockton, MA-NH	16 711
8	Houston, TX	4 177 646	17	8	St. Louis, MO-IL	16 555
9	Atlanta, GA	4 112 198	10	9	Dallas, TX	16 021
10	Dallas, TX	3 519 176	9	10	Atlanta, GA	15 861
11	Riverside-San Bernardino, CA	3 254 821	13	11	Minneapolis-St. Paul, MN-WI	15 703
12	Phoenix-Mesa, AZ	3 251 876	75	12	Albuquerque, NM	15 392
13	Minneapolis-St. Paul, MN-WI	2 968 806	8	13	Houston, TX	15 333
14	Orange County, CA	2 846 289	28	14	Kansas City, MO-KS	14 002
15	San Diego, CA	2 813 833	3	15	Chicago, IL	13 111
16	Nassau-Suffolk, NY	2 753 913	27	16	Portland-Vancouver, OR-WA	13 022
17	St. Louis, MO-IL	2 603 607	71	17	Tulsa, OK	12 987
18	Baltimore, MD	2 552 994	22	18	Pittsburgh, PA	11 980
19	Seattle-Bellevue-Everett, WA	2 414 616	19	19	Seattle-Bellevue-Everett, WA	11 457
20	Tampa-St. Petersburg-Clearwater, FL	2 395 997	60	20	Oklahoma City, OK	10 999
21	Oakland, CA	2 392 557	48	21	Austin-San Marcos, TX	10 940
22	Pittsburgh, PA	2 358 695	15	22	San Diego, CA	10 878
23	Miami, FL	2 253 362	35	23	Sacramento, CA	10 569
24	Cleveland-Lorain-Elyria, OH	2 250 871	49	24	Nashville, TN	10 548
25	Denver, CO	2 109 282	1	25	Los Angeles-Long Beach, CA	10 518
26	Newark, NJ	2 032 989	7	26	Detroit, MI	10 093
27	Portland-Vancouver, OR-WA	1 918 009	47	27	Greensboro—Winston-Salem—High Point, NC	10 052
28	Kansas City, MO-KS	1 776 062	5	28	Philadelphia, PA-NJ	9 985
29	San Francisco, CA	1 731 183	25	29	Denver, CO	9 740
30	New Haven-Bridgeport-Stamford-Danbury-Waterbury, CT	1 706 575	37	30	Indianapolis, IN	9 125
31	Fort Worth-Arlington, TX	1 702 625	34	31	Orlando, FL	9 041
32	San Jose, CA	1 682 585	50	32	Raleigh-Durham-Chapel Hill, NC	9 036
33	Cincinnati, OH-KY-IN	1 646 395	58	33	Rochester, NY	8 872
34	Orlando, FL	1 644 561	45	34	New Orleans, LA	8 805
35	Sacramento, CA	1 628 197	43	35	Charlotte-Gastonia-Rock Hill, NC-SC	8 746
36	Fort Lauderdale, FL	1 623 018	33	36	Cincinnati, OH-KY-IN	8 655
37	Indianapolis, IN	1 607 486	38	37	San Antonio, TX	8 615
38	San Antonio, TX	1 592 383	69	38	Albany-Schenectady-Troy, NY	8 345
39	Norfolk-Virginia Beach-Newport News, VA-NC	1 569 541	64	39	Greenville-Spartanburg-Anderson, SC	8 310
40	Las Vegas, NV-AZ	1 563 282	67	40	Birmingham, AL	8 253
41	Columbus, OH	1 540 157	41	41	Columbus, OH	8 136
42	Milwaukee-Waukesha, WI	1 500 741	73	42	Syracuse, NY	7 984
43	Charlotte-Gastonia-Rock Hill, NC-SC	1 499 293	54	43	Memphis, TN-AR-MS	7 787
44	Bergen-Passaic, NJ	1 373 167	62	44	Richmond-Petersburg, VA	7 626
45	New Orleans, LA	1 337 726	31	45	Fort Worth-Arlington, TX	7 557
46	Salt Lake City-Ogden, UT	1 333 914	59	46	Grand Rapids-Muskegon-Holland, MI	7 144
47	Greensboro—Winston-Salem—High Point, NC	1 251 509	24	47	Cleveland-Lorain-Elyria, OH	7 011
48	Austin-San Marcos, TX	1 249 763	57	48	Jacksonville, FL	6 825
49	Nashville, TN	1 231 311	18	49	Baltimore, MD	6 757
50	Raleigh-Durham-Chapel Hill, NC	1 187 941	20	50	Tampa-St. Petersburg-Clearwater, FL	6 615
51	Buffalo-Niagara Falls, NY	1 170 111	74	51	Omaha, NE-IA	6 411
52	Middlesex-Somerset-Hunterdon, NJ	1 169 641	39	52	Norfolk-Virginia Beach-Newport News, VA-NC	6 083
53	Hartford, CT	1 148 618	61	53	Louisville, KY-IN	5 366
54	Memphis, TN-AR-MS	1 135 614	55	54	West Palm Beach-Boca Raton, FL	5 113
55	West Palm Beach-Boca Raton, FL	1 131 184	23	55	Miami, FL	5 040
56	Monmouth-Ocean, NJ	1 126 217	72	56	Ventura, CA	4 779
57	Jacksonville, FL	1 100 491	65	57	Dayton-Springfield, OH	4 360
58	Rochester, NY	1 098 201	46	58	Salt Lake City-Ogden, UT	4 189
59	Grand Rapids-Muskegon-Holland, MI	1 088 514	26	59	Newark, NJ	4 086
60	Oklahoma City, OK	1 083 346	51	60	Buffalo-Niagara Falls, NY	4 059
61	Louisville, KY-IN	1 025 598	53	61	Hartford, CT	3 923
62	Richmond-Petersburg, VA	996 512	42	62	Milwaukee-Waukesha, WI	3 781
63	Providence-Warwick-Pawtucket, RI	962 886	21	63	Oakland, CA	3 775
64	Greenville-Spartanburg-Anderson, SC	962 441	32	64	San Jose, CA	3 343
65	Dayton-Springfield, OH	950 558	30	65	New Haven-Bridgeport-Stamford-Danbury-Waterbury, CT	3 189
66	Fresno, CA	922 516	36	66	Fort Lauderdale, FL	3 122
67	Birmingham, AL	921 106	16	67	Nassau-Suffolk, NY	3 105
68	Honolulu, HI	876 156	2	68	New York, NY	2 957
69	Albany-Schenectady-Troy, NY	875 583	56	69	Monmouth-Ocean, NJ	2 870
70	Tucson, AZ	843 746	52	70	Middlesex-Somerset-Hunterdon, NJ	2 705
71	Tulsa, OK	803 235	29	71	San Francisco, CA	2 630
72	Ventura, CA	753 197	63	72	Providence-Warwick-Pawtucket, RI	2 437
73	Syracuse, NY	732 117	14	73	Orange County, CA	2 045
74	Omaha, NE-IA	716 998	68	74	Honolulu, HI	1 553
75	Albuquerque, NM	712 738	44	75	Bergen-Passaic, NJ	1 086

Note: Column numbers refer to Table C. Metropolitan Areas.

TABLE 4—75 Largest Metropolitan Areas by 2000 Population
Selected Rankings

Population Density (per square kilometer), 2000				Percent Population Change, 2000-2001			
Population Rank	Density Rank	Metropolitan Area	[col 4] Density	Population Rank	Percent Change Rank	Metropolitan Area	[col 23] Percent Change
2	1	New York, NY	3 150.1	40	1	Las Vegas, NV-AZ	6.2
14	2	Orange County, CA	1 392.1	48	2	Austin-San Marcos, TX	5.1
44	3	Bergen-Passaic, NJ	1 264.0	11	3	Riverside-San Bernardino, CA	4.5
1	4	Los Angeles-Long Beach, CA	905.1	35	4	Sacramento, CA	4.4
16	5	Nassau-Suffolk, NY	886.9	12	5	Phoenix-Mesa, AZ	4.1
29	6	San Francisco, CA	658.2	34	6	Orlando, FL	3.8
21	7	Oakland, CA	633.8	9	7	Atlanta, GA	3.7
3	8	Chicago, IL	631.0	50	7	Raleigh-Durham-Chapel Hill, NC	3.7
68	9	Honolulu, HI	564.0	10	9	Dallas, TX	3.6
30	10	New Haven-Bridgeport-Stamford-Danbury-Waterbury, CT	535.1	43	10	Charlotte-Gastonia-Rock Hill, NC-SC	3.0
36	11	Fort Lauderdale, FL	519.9	31	10	Fort Worth-Arlington, TX	3.0
5	12	Philadelphia, PA-NJ	510.9	55	10	West Palm Beach-Boca Raton, FL	3.0
32	13	San Jose, CA	503.3	36	13	Fort Lauderdale, FL	2.8
26	14	Newark, NJ	497.5	57	13	Jacksonville, FL	2.8
23	15	Miami, FL	447.1	8	15	Houston, TX	2.7
7	16	Detroit, MI	440.1	6	16	Washington, DC-MD-VA-WV	2.6
52	17	Middlesex-Somerset-Hunterdon, NJ	432.4	27	17	Portland-Vancouver, OR-WA	2.5
42	18	Milwaukee-Waukesha, WI	396.9	25	18	Denver, CO	2.4
63	19	Providence-Warwick-Pawtucket, RI	395.1	20	19	Tampa-St. Petersburg-Clearwater, FL	2.3
56	20	Monmouth-Ocean, NJ	392.4	70	19	Tucson, AZ	2.3
18	21	Baltimore, MD	377.8	72	19	Ventura, CA	2.3
4	22	Boston-Worcester-Lawrence-Lowell-Brockton, MA-NH	362.5	66	22	Fresno, CA	2.1
20	23	Tampa-St. Petersburg-Clearwater, FL	362.2	56	22	Monmouth-Ocean, NJ	2.1
24	24	Cleveland-Lorain-Elyria, OH	321.1	38	22	San Antonio, TX	2.1
46	25	Salt Lake City-Ogden, UT	318.4	49	25	Nashville, TN	1.7
53	26	Hartford, CT	292.8	21	25	Oakland, CA	1.7
6	27	Washington, DC-MD-VA-WV	292.0	15	25	San Diego, CA	1.7
51	28	Buffalo-Niagara Falls, NY	288.3	64	28	Greenville-Spartanburg-Anderson, SC	1.6
8	29	Houston, TX	272.5	37	28	Indianapolis, IN	1.6
9	30	Atlanta, GA	259.3	23	28	Miami, FL	1.6
15	31	San Diego, CA	258.7	13	28	Minneapolis-St. Paul, MN-WI	1.6
39	32	Norfolk-Virginia Beach-Newport News, VA-NC	258.0	14	28	Orange County, CA	1.6
31	33	Fort Worth-Arlington, TX	225.3	75	33	Albuquerque, NM	1.5
55	34	West Palm Beach-Boca Raton, FL	221.2	28	33	Kansas City, MO-KS	1.5
10	35	Dallas, TX	219.7	59	35	Grand Rapids-Muskegon-Holland, MI	1.4
65	36	Dayton-Springfield, OH	218.0	47	35	Greensboro—Winston-Salem—High Point, NC	1.4
25	37	Denver, CO	216.6	41	37	Columbus, OH	1.3
19	38	Seattle-Bellevue-Everett, WA	210.8	52	37	Middlesex-Somerset-Hunterdon, NJ	1.3
22	39	Pittsburgh, PA	196.9	62	37	Richmond-Petersburg, VA	1.3
61	40	Louisville, KY-IN	191.1	1	40	Los Angeles-Long Beach, CA	1.2
33	41	Cincinnati, OH-KY-IN	190.2	63	41	Providence-Warwick-Pawtucket, RI	1.1
41	42	Columbus, OH	189.3	46	41	Salt Lake City-Ogden, UT	1.1
13	43	Minneapolis-St. Paul, MN-WI	189.1	19	43	Seattle-Bellevue-Everett, WA	1.0
38	44	San Antonio, TX	184.8	39	44	Norfolk-Virginia Beach-Newport News, VA-NC	0.9
34	45	Orlando, FL	181.9	74	44	Omaha, NE-IA	0.9
37	46	Indianapolis, IN	176.2	71	44	Tulsa, OK	0.9
43	47	Charlotte-Gastonia-Rock Hill, NC-SC	171.4	18	47	Baltimore, MD	0.8
57	48	Jacksonville, FL	161.2	67	47	Birmingham, AL	0.8
72	49	Ventura, CA	157.6	3	47	Chicago, IL	0.8
17	50	St. Louis, MO-IL	157.3	53	47	Hartford, CT	0.8
35	51	Sacramento, CA	154.0	54	47	Memphis, TN-AR-MS	0.8
59	52	Grand Rapids-Muskegon-Holland, MI	152.4	60	47	Oklahoma City, OK	0.8
45	53	New Orleans, LA	151.9	4	53	Boston-Worcester-Lawrence-Lowell-Brockton, MA-NH	0.7
27	54	Portland-Vancouver, OR-WA	147.3	33	53	Cincinnati, OH-KY-IN	0.7
54	55	Memphis, TN-AR-MS	145.8	16	53	Nassau-Suffolk, NY	0.7
50	56	Raleigh-Durham-Chapel Hill, NC	131.5	68	56	Honolulu, HI	0.6
62	57	Richmond-Petersburg, VA	130.7	61	57	Louisville, KY-IN	0.5
28	58	Kansas City, MO-KS	126.8	17	57	St. Louis, MO-IL	0.5
47	59	Greensboro—Winston-Salem—High Point, NC	124.5	30	59	New Haven-Bridgeport-Stamford-Danbury-Waterbury, CT	0.4
58	60	Rochester, NY	123.8	26	59	Newark, NJ	0.4
49	61	Nashville, TN	116.7	69	61	Albany-Schenectady-Troy, NY	0.3
64	62	Greenville-Spartanburg-Anderson, SC	115.8	44	61	Bergen-Passaic, NJ	0.3
48	63	Austin-San Marcos, TX	114.2	5	61	Philadelphia, PA-NJ	0.3
74	64	Omaha, NE-IA	111.8	7	64	Detroit, MI	0.2
67	65	Birmingham, AL	111.6	2	64	New York, NY	0.2
69	66	Albany-Schenectady-Troy, NY	104.9	42	66	Milwaukee-Waukesha, WI	0.1
60	67	Oklahoma City, OK	98.5	58	66	Rochester, NY	0.1
73	68	Syracuse, NY	91.7	73	66	Syracuse, NY	0.1
12	69	Phoenix-Mesa, AZ	86.2	24	69	Cleveland-Lorain-Elyria, OH	-0.2
71	70	Tulsa, OK	61.8	45	70	New Orleans, LA	-0.4
75	71	Albuquerque, NM	46.3	65	71	Dayton-Springfield, OH	-0.5
11	72	Riverside-San Bernardino, CA	46.1	22	71	Pittsburgh, PA	-0.5
66	73	Fresno, CA	44.0	51	73	Buffalo-Niagara Falls, NY	-0.6
70	74	Tucson, AZ	35.5	29	73	San Francisco, CA	-0.6
40	75	Las Vegas, NV-AZ	15.3	32	75	San Jose, CA	-0.8

Note: Column numbers refer to Table C. Metropolitan Areas.

TABLE 4—75 Largest Metropolitan Areas by 2000 Population
Selected Rankings

Percent White (alone or in combination), 2000				Percent Black (alone or in combination), 2000			
Population Rank	White Rank	Metropolitan Area	[col 5] Percent White	Population Rank	Black Rank	Metropolitan Area	[col 6] Percent Black
69	1	Albany-Schenectady-Troy, NY	90.6	54	1	Memphis, TN-AR-MS	43.8
22	2	Pittsburgh, PA	90.3	45	2	New Orleans, LA	38.0
73	2	Syracuse, NY	90.3	39	3	Norfolk-Virginia Beach-Newport News, VA-NC	31.9
46	4	Salt Lake City-Ogden, UT	89.7	62	4	Richmond-Petersburg, VA	30.8
56	5	Monmouth-Ocean, NJ	89.5	67	5	Birmingham, AL	30.3
13	6	Minneapolis-St. Paul, MN-WI	87.7	9	6	Atlanta, GA	29.6
27	7	Portland-Vancouver, OR-WA	87.4	18	7	Baltimore, MD	28.1
59	8	Grand Rapids-Muskegon-Holland, MI	87.3	6	8	Washington, DC-MD-VA-WV	27.1
4	9	Boston-Worcester-Lawrence-Lowell-Brockton, MA-NH	87.0	2	9	New York, NY	26.3
74	10	Omaha, NE-IA	86.7	7	10	Detroit, MI	23.5
63	11	Providence-Warwick-Pawtucket, RI	86.3	26	11	Newark, NJ	23.3
58	12	Rochester, NY	85.3	50	11	Raleigh-Durham-Chapel Hill, NC	23.3
33	13	Cincinnati, OH-KY-IN	85.0	36	13	Fort Lauderdale, FL	22.2
51	14	Buffalo-Niagara Falls, NY	84.8	57	13	Jacksonville, FL	22.2
20	15	Tampa-St. Petersburg-Clearwater, FL	84.5	23	15	Miami, FL	21.6
61	16	Louisville, KY-IN	83.9	43	16	Charlotte-Gastonia-Rock Hill, NC-SC	21.0
65	17	Dayton-Springfield, OH	83.6	5	17	Philadelphia, PA-NJ	20.9
16	18	Nassau-Suffolk, NY	83.5	47	18	Greensboro—Winston-Salem—High Point, NC	20.7
37	19	Indianapolis, IN	83.1	3	19	Chicago, IL	19.4
41	20	Columbus, OH	82.7	24	20	Cleveland-Lorain-Elyria, OH	19.2
28	21	Kansas City, MO-KS	82.5	17	21	St. Louis, MO-IL	18.8
53	22	Hartford, CT	82.2	8	22	Houston, TX	17.9
25	23	Denver, CO	81.9	64	23	Greenville-Spartanburg-Anderson, SC	17.8
19	24	Seattle-Bellevue-Everett, WA	81.7	42	24	Milwaukee-Waukesha, WI	16.3
30	25	New Haven-Bridgeport-Stamford-Danbury-Waterbury, CT	81.1	49	25	Nashville, TN	16.0
49	26	Nashville, TN	80.6	10	26	Dallas, TX	15.5
71	27	Tulsa, OK	80.4	65	27	Dayton-Springfield, OH	15.0
55	27	West Palm Beach-Boca Raton, FL	80.4	34	28	Orlando, FL	14.9
64	29	Greenville-Spartanburg-Anderson, SC	79.9	55	28	West Palm Beach-Boca Raton, FL	14.9
12	30	Phoenix-Mesa, AZ	79.4	37	30	Indianapolis, IN	14.5
17	31	St. Louis, MO-IL	79.3	61	30	Louisville, KY-IN	14.5
60	32	Oklahoma City, OK	79.0	41	32	Columbus, OH	14.4
42	33	Milwaukee-Waukesha, WI	78.5	21	33	Oakland, CA	13.8
24	34	Cleveland-Lorain-Elyria, OH	78.2	33	34	Cincinnati, OH-KY-IN	13.5
70	35	Tucson, AZ	77.8	28	35	Kansas City, MO-KS	13.4
40	36	Las Vegas, NV-AZ	77.1	51	36	Buffalo-Niagara Falls, NY	12.3
34	37	Orlando, FL	77.0	31	37	Fort Worth-Arlington, TX	11.6
31	38	Fort Worth-Arlington, TX	76.3	30	38	New Haven-Bridgeport-Stamford-Danbury-Waterbury, CT	11.5
52	39	Middlesex-Somerset-Hunterdon, NJ	75.5	60	39	Oklahoma City, OK	11.4
47	40	Greensboro—Winston-Salem—High Point, NC	75.4	58	40	Rochester, NY	11.0
44	41	Bergen-Passaic, NJ	74.9	20	41	Tampa-St. Petersburg-Clearwater, FL	10.8
48	42	Austin-San Marcos, TX	74.7	53	42	Hartford, CT	10.5
43	43	Charlotte-Gastonia-Rock Hill, NC-SC	74.6	1	42	Los Angeles-Long Beach, CA	10.5
35	44	Sacramento, CA	74.3	71	44	Tulsa, OK	9.5
57	45	Jacksonville, FL	74.1	16	45	Nassau-Suffolk, NY	9.2
38	46	San Antonio, TX	73.6	40	46	Las Vegas, NV-AZ	8.9
5	47	Philadelphia, PA-NJ	73.3	74	46	Omaha, NE-IA	8.9
72	47	Ventura, CA	73.3	44	48	Bergen-Passaic, NJ	8.8
75	49	Albuquerque, NM	73.2	35	48	Sacramento, CA	8.8
7	50	Detroit, MI	73.0	52	50	Middlesex-Somerset-Hunterdon, NJ	8.6
36	51	Fort Lauderdale, FL	72.4	22	50	Pittsburgh, PA	8.6
23	52	Miami, FL	72.3	11	50	Riverside-San Bernardino, CA	8.6
50	53	Raleigh-Durham-Chapel Hill, NC	70.6	48	53	Austin-San Marcos, TX	8.5
15	54	San Diego, CA	70.3	59	54	Grand Rapids-Muskegon-Holland, MI	8.0
10	55	Dallas, TX	69.2	38	55	San Antonio, TX	7.2
18	56	Baltimore, MD	68.5	73	55	Syracuse, NY	7.2
14	57	Orange County, CA	68.3	69	57	Albany-Schenectady-Troy, NY	6.8
67	58	Birmingham, AL	68.0	15	58	San Diego, CA	6.6
3	59	Chicago, IL	67.7	56	59	Monmouth-Ocean, NJ	6.3
26	59	Newark, NJ	67.7	25	60	Denver, CO	6.2
11	61	Riverside-San Bernardino, CA	66.0	13	60	Minneapolis-St. Paul, MN-WI	6.2
62	62	Richmond-Petersburg, VA	65.9	29	62	San Francisco, CA	6.0
9	63	Atlanta, GA	64.2	4	63	Boston-Worcester-Lawrence-Lowell-Brockton, MA-NH	5.8
39	64	Norfolk-Virginia Beach-Newport News, VA-NC	64.1	66	64	Fresno, CA	5.7
8	65	Houston, TX	63.4	63	65	Providence-Warwick-Pawtucket, RI	5.6
6	66	Washington, DC-MD-VA-WV	62.2	19	66	Seattle-Bellevue-Everett, WA	5.3
29	67	San Francisco, CA	62.1	12	67	Phoenix-Mesa, AZ	4.2
21	68	Oakland, CA	59.7	70	68	Tucson, AZ	3.7
66	69	Fresno, CA	59.2	68	69	Honolulu, HI	3.4
45	70	New Orleans, LA	58.4	27	69	Portland-Vancouver, OR-WA	3.4
32	71	San Jose, CA	57.6	32	69	San Jose, CA	3.4
54	72	Memphis, TN-AR-MS	53.6	75	72	Albuquerque, NM	3.1
1	73	Los Angeles-Long Beach, CA	52.8	72	73	Ventura, CA	2.4
2	74	New York, NY	51.6	14	74	Orange County, CA	2.1
68	75	Honolulu, HI	35.2	46	75	Salt Lake City-Ogden, UT	1.5

Note: Column numbers refer to Table C. Metropolitan Areas.

TABLE 4—75 Largest Metropolitan Areas by 2000 Population
Selected Rankings

Percent American Indian, Alaska Native (alone or in combination), 2000				Percent Asian and Pacific Islander, 2000			
Population Rank	American Indian, Alaska Native Rank	Metropolitan Area	[col 7] Percent American Indian, Alaska Native	Population Rank	Asian & Pac. Is. Rank	Metropolitan Area	[col 8] Percent Asian & Pac. Is.
71	1	Tulsa, OK	10.7	68	1	Honolulu, HI	83.2
75	2	Albuquerque, NM	6.6	32	2	San Jose, CA	28.2
60	2	Oklahoma City, OK	6.6	29	3	San Francisco, CA	25.7
70	4	Tucson, AZ	4.0	21	4	Oakland, CA	19.8
66	5	Fresno, CA	2.8	14	5	Orange County, CA	15.5
12	5	Phoenix-Mesa, AZ	2.8	1	6	Los Angeles-Long Beach, CA	13.6
35	7	Sacramento, CA	2.4	52	7	Middlesex-Somerset-Hunterdon, NJ	12.0
11	8	Riverside-San Bernardino, CA	2.1	19	8	Seattle-Bellevue-Everett, WA	11.7
19	9	Seattle-Bellevue-Everett, WA	2.0	35	9	Sacramento, CA	11.6
27	10	Portland-Vancouver, OR-WA	1.9	15	10	San Diego, CA	11.4
68	11	Honolulu, HI	1.8	2	11	New York, NY	10.3
72	11	Ventura, CA	1.8	44	12	Bergen-Passaic, NJ	8.9
25	13	Denver, CO	1.7	66	13	Fresno, CA	8.5
40	13	Las Vegas, NV-AZ	1.7	6	14	Washington, DC-MD-VA-WV	7.8
21	15	Oakland, CA	1.6	72	15	Ventura, CA	7.0
15	15	San Diego, CA	1.6	40	16	Las Vegas, NV-AZ	6.8
1	17	Los Angeles-Long Beach, CA	1.5	27	17	Portland-Vancouver, OR-WA	6.2
13	18	Minneapolis-St. Paul, MN-WI	1.3	8	18	Houston, TX	5.9
14	18	Orange County, CA	1.3	11	19	Riverside-San Bernardino, CA	5.7
46	18	Salt Lake City-Ogden, UT	1.3	3	20	Chicago, IL	5.2
38	18	San Antonio, TX	1.3	13	21	Minneapolis-St. Paul, MN-WI	4.8
32	18	San Jose, CA	1.3	10	22	Dallas, TX	4.6
31	23	Fort Worth-Arlington, TX	1.2	26	22	Newark, NJ	4.6
28	23	Kansas City, MO-KS	1.2	4	24	Boston-Worcester-Lawrence-Lowell-Brockton, MA-NH	4.4
73	23	Syracuse, NY	1.2	48	25	Austin-San Marcos, TX	4.3
48	26	Austin-San Marcos, TX	1.1	16	26	Nassau-Suffolk, NY	4.1
10	26	Dallas, TX	1.1	46	27	Salt Lake City-Ogden, UT	4.0
59	26	Grand Rapids-Muskegon-Holland, MI	1.1	5	28	Philadelphia, PA-NJ	3.9
29	26	San Francisco, CA	1.1	9	29	Atlanta, GA	3.8
51	30	Buffalo-Niagara Falls, NY	1.0	25	29	Denver, CO	3.8
42	30	Milwaukee-Waukesha, WI	1.0	31	29	Fort Worth-Arlington, TX	3.8
2	30	New York, NY	1.0	39	32	Norfolk-Virginia Beach-Newport News, VA-NC	3.7
39	30	Norfolk-Virginia Beach-Newport News, VA-NC	1.0	34	33	Orlando, FL	3.5
74	30	Omaha, NE-IA	1.0	50	34	Raleigh-Durham-Chapel Hill, NC	3.4
63	30	Providence-Warwick-Pawtucket, RI	1.0	30	35	New Haven-Bridgeport-Stamford-Danbury-Waterbury, CT	3.3
7	36	Detroit, MI	0.9	18	36	Baltimore, MD	3.2
41	37	Columbus, OH	0.8	56	36	Monmouth-Ocean, NJ	3.2
8	37	Houston, TX	0.8	60	36	Oklahoma City, OK	3.2
57	37	Jacksonville, FL	0.8	57	39	Jacksonville, FL	3.1
45	37	New Orleans, LA	0.8	36	40	Fort Lauderdale, FL	3.0
34	37	Orlando, FL	0.8	63	40	Providence-Warwick-Pawtucket, RI	3.0
50	37	Raleigh-Durham-Chapel Hill, NC	0.8	12	42	Phoenix-Mesa, AZ	2.9
62	37	Richmond-Petersburg, VA	0.8	70	42	Tucson, AZ	2.9
20	37	Tampa-St. Petersburg-Clearwater, FL	0.8	41	44	Columbus, OH	2.8
6	37	Washington, DC-MD-VA-WV	0.8	7	44	Detroit, MI	2.8
9	46	Atlanta, GA	0.7	53	44	Hartford, CT	2.8
18	46	Baltimore, MD	0.7	42	47	Milwaukee-Waukesha, WI	2.5
43	46	Charlotte-Gastonia-Rock Hill, NC-SC	0.7	45	47	New Orleans, LA	2.5
65	46	Dayton-Springfield, OH	0.7	62	47	Richmond-Petersburg, VA	2.5
47	46	Greensboro—Winston-Salem—High Point, NC	0.7	75	50	Albuquerque, NM	2.4
49	46	Nashville, TN	0.7	20	50	Tampa-St. Petersburg-Clearwater, FL	2.4
58	46	Rochester, NY	0.7	43	52	Charlotte-Gastonia-Rock Hill, NC-SC	2.3
69	53	Albany-Schenectady-Troy, NY	0.6	69	53	Albany-Schenectady-Troy, NY	2.2
67	53	Birmingham, AL	0.6	28	53	Kansas City, MO-KS	2.2
4	53	Boston-Worcester-Lawrence-Lowell-Brockton, MA-NH	0.6	58	53	Rochester, NY	2.2
3	53	Chicago, IL	0.6	38	53	San Antonio, TX	2.2
33	53	Cincinnati, OH-KY-IN	0.6	49	57	Nashville, TN	2.1
24	53	Cleveland-Lorain-Elyria, OH	0.6	55	57	West Palm Beach-Boca Raton, FL	2.1
53	53	Hartford, CT	0.6	23	59	Miami, FL	2.0
37	53	Indianapolis, IN	0.6	74	59	Omaha, NE-IA	2.0
61	53	Louisville, KY-IN	0.6	59	61	Grand Rapids-Muskegon-Holland, MI	1.9
30	53	New Haven-Bridgeport-Stamford-Danbury-Waterbury, CT	0.6	17	62	St. Louis, MO-IL	1.8
17	53	St. Louis, MO-IL	0.6	73	62	Syracuse, NY	1.8
44	64	Bergen-Passaic, NJ	0.5	24	64	Cleveland-Lorain-Elyria, OH	1.7
36	64	Fort Lauderdale, FL	0.5	65	64	Dayton-Springfield, OH	1.7
64	64	Greenville-Spartanburg-Anderson, SC	0.5	47	64	Greensboro—Winston-Salem—High Point, NC	1.7
54	64	Memphis, TN-AR-MS	0.5	54	64	Memphis, TN-AR-MS	1.7
52	64	Middlesex-Somerset-Hunterdon, NJ	0.5	71	64	Tulsa, OK	1.7
16	64	Nassau-Suffolk, NY	0.5	51	69	Buffalo-Niagara Falls, NY	1.6
26	64	Newark, NJ	0.5	37	69	Indianapolis, IN	1.6
5	64	Philadelphia, PA-NJ	0.5	33	71	Cincinnati, OH-KY-IN	1.5
55	64	West Palm Beach-Boca Raton, FL	0.5	64	71	Greenville-Spartanburg-Anderson, SC	1.5
23	73	Miami, FL	0.4	61	73	Louisville, KY-IN	1.4
56	73	Monmouth-Ocean, NJ	0.4	22	73	Pittsburgh, PA	1.4
22	73	Pittsburgh, PA	0.4	67	75	Birmingham, AL	1.1

Note: Column numbers refer to Table C. Metropolitan Areas.

TABLE 4—75 Largest Metropolitan Areas by 2000 Population
Selected Rankings

Percent Hispanic, 2000

Population Rank	Hispanic Rank	Metropolitan Area	[col 9] Percent Hispanic
23	1	Miami, FL	57.3
38	2	San Antonio, TX	51.2
1	3	Los Angeles-Long Beach, CA	44.6
66	4	Fresno, CA	44.0
75	5	Albuquerque, NM	41.6
11	6	Riverside-San Bernardino, CA	37.8
72	7	Ventura, CA	33.4
14	8	Orange County, CA	30.8
8	9	Houston, TX	29.9
70	10	Tucson, AZ	29.3
15	11	San Diego, CA	26.7
48	12	Austin-San Marcos, TX	26.2
2	13	New York, NY	25.1
12	13	Phoenix-Mesa, AZ	25.1
32	15	San Jose, CA	24.0
10	16	Dallas, TX	23.0
40	17	Las Vegas, NV-AZ	20.6
25	18	Denver, CO	18.8
21	19	Oakland, CA	18.5
31	20	Fort Worth-Arlington, TX	18.2
44	21	Bergen-Passaic, NJ	17.3
3	22	Chicago, IL	17.1
29	23	San Francisco, CA	16.8
36	24	Fort Lauderdale, FL	16.7
34	25	Orlando, FL	16.5
35	26	Sacramento, CA	14.4
26	27	Newark, NJ	13.3
55	28	West Palm Beach-Boca Raton, FL	12.4
52	29	Middlesex-Somerset-Hunterdon, NJ	11.2
30	30	New Haven-Bridgeport-Stamford-Danbury-Waterbury, CT	11.0
46	31	Salt Lake City-Ogden, UT	10.8
20	32	Tampa-St. Petersburg-Clearwater, FL	10.4
16	33	Nassau-Suffolk, NY	10.3
53	34	Hartford, CT	9.4
63	35	Providence-Warwick-Pawtucket, RI	9.2
6	36	Washington, DC-MD-VA-WV	8.8
27	37	Portland-Vancouver, OR-WA	7.4
68	38	Honolulu, HI	6.7
60	38	Oklahoma City, OK	6.7
9	40	Atlanta, GA	6.5
59	41	Grand Rapids-Muskegon-Holland, MI	6.3
42	41	Milwaukee-Waukesha, WI	6.3
50	43	Raleigh-Durham-Chapel Hill, NC	6.1
4	44	Boston-Worcester-Lawrence-Lowell-Brockton, MA-NH	6.0
56	45	Monmouth-Ocean, NJ	5.7
74	46	Omaha, NE-IA	5.5
28	47	Kansas City, MO-KS	5.2
19	47	Seattle-Bellevue-Everett, WA	5.2
43	49	Charlotte-Gastonia-Rock Hill, NC-SC	5.1
5	49	Philadelphia, PA-NJ	5.1
47	51	Greensboro—Winston-Salem—High Point, NC	5.0
71	52	Tulsa, OK	4.8
45	53	New Orleans, LA	4.4
58	54	Rochester, NY	4.3
57	55	Jacksonville, FL	3.8
24	56	Cleveland-Lorain-Elyria, OH	3.3
13	56	Minneapolis-St. Paul, MN-WI	3.3
49	56	Nashville, TN	3.3
39	59	Norfolk-Virginia Beach-Newport News, VA-NC	3.1
51	60	Buffalo-Niagara Falls, NY	2.9
7	60	Detroit, MI	2.9
69	62	Albany-Schenectady-Troy, NY	2.7
64	62	Greenville-Spartanburg-Anderson, SC	2.7
37	62	Indianapolis, IN	2.7
54	65	Memphis, TN-AR-MS	2.4
62	66	Richmond-Petersburg, VA	2.3
73	67	Syracuse, NY	2.1
18	68	Baltimore, MD	2.0
67	69	Birmingham, AL	1.8
41	69	Columbus, OH	1.8
61	71	Louisville, KY-IN	1.6
17	72	St. Louis, MO-IL	1.5
65	73	Dayton-Springfield, OH	1.2
33	74	Cincinnati, OH-KY-IN	1.1
22	75	Pittsburgh, PA	0.7

Percent Under 18 Years, 2000

Population Rank	Under 18 Years Rank	Metropolitan Area	[cols 10 & 11] Percent Under 18 Years
66	1	Fresno, CA	31.8
46	2	Salt Lake City-Ogden, UT	31.4
11	3	Riverside-San Bernardino, CA	31.3
8	4	Houston, TX	29.2
72	5	Ventura, CA	28.5
38	6	San Antonio, TX	28.4
59	7	Grand Rapids-Muskegon-Holland, MI	28.3
54	7	Memphis, TN-AR-MS	28.3
10	9	Dallas, TX	28.0
31	9	Fort Worth-Arlington, TX	28.0
1	9	Los Angeles-Long Beach, CA	28.0
35	12	Sacramento, CA	27.3
74	13	Omaha, NE-IA	27.2
3	14	Chicago, IL	27.0
14	14	Orange County, CA	27.0
13	16	Minneapolis-St. Paul, MN-WI	26.8
45	16	New Orleans, LA	26.8
12	16	Phoenix-Mesa, AZ	26.8
71	19	Tulsa, OK	26.7
9	20	Atlanta, GA	26.6
33	20	Cincinnati, OH-KY-IN	26.6
37	20	Indianapolis, IN	26.6
28	20	Kansas City, MO-KS	26.6
7	24	Detroit, MI	26.5
42	25	Milwaukee-Waukesha, WI	26.4
39	25	Norfolk-Virginia Beach-Newport News, VA-NC	26.4
75	27	Albuquerque, NM	26.3
17	27	St. Louis, MO-IL	26.3
57	29	Jacksonville, FL	26.1
25	30	Denver, CO	25.8
15	30	San Diego, CA	25.8
58	32	Rochester, NY	25.7
73	32	Syracuse, NY	25.7
26	34	Newark, NJ	25.6
60	34	Oklahoma City, OK	25.6
41	36	Columbus, OH	25.5
27	36	Portland-Vancouver, OR-WA	25.5
43	38	Charlotte-Gastonia-Rock Hill, NC-SC	25.4
24	38	Cleveland-Lorain-Elyria, OH	25.4
16	38	Nassau-Suffolk, NY	25.4
21	38	Oakland, CA	25.4
5	38	Philadelphia, PA-NJ	25.4
48	43	Austin-San Marcos, TX	25.3
18	43	Baltimore, MD	25.3
40	43	Las Vegas, NV-AZ	25.3
6	43	Washington, DC-MD-VA-WV	25.3
62	47	Richmond-Petersburg, VA	25.2
67	48	Birmingham, AL	25.1
30	48	New Haven-Bridgeport-Stamford-Danbury-Waterbury, CT	25.1
65	50	Dayton-Springfield, OH	24.8
23	50	Miami, FL	24.8
56	50	Monmouth-Ocean, NJ	24.8
49	50	Nashville, TN	24.8
34	50	Orlando, FL	24.8
32	50	San Jose, CA	24.8
61	56	Louisville, KY-IN	24.7
70	57	Tucson, AZ	24.6
51	58	Buffalo-Niagara Falls, NY	24.4
64	58	Greenville-Spartanburg-Anderson, SC	24.4
52	58	Middlesex-Somerset-Hunterdon, NJ	24.4
2	58	New York, NY	24.4
53	62	Hartford, CT	24.2
50	62	Raleigh-Durham-Chapel Hill, NC	24.2
44	64	Bergen-Passaic, NJ	24.1
4	65	Boston-Worcester-Lawrence-Lowell-Brockton, MA-NH	24.0
47	65	Greensboro—Winston-Salem—High Point, NC	24.0
69	67	Albany-Schenectady-Troy, NY	23.9
19	67	Seattle-Bellevue-Everett, WA	23.9
68	69	Honolulu, HI	23.8
63	70	Providence-Warwick-Pawtucket, RI	23.7
36	71	Fort Lauderdale, FL	23.5
22	72	Pittsburgh, PA	22.3
20	73	Tampa-St. Petersburg-Clearwater, FL	22.0
55	74	West Palm Beach-Boca Raton, FL	21.3
29	75	San Francisco, CA	18.8

Note: Column numbers refer to Table C. Metropolitan Areas.

TABLE 4—75 Largest Metropolitan Areas by 2000 Population
Selected Rankings

Percent 65 Years and Over, 2000				Percent Female-Headed Family Households, 2000			
Population Rank	65 Years and Over Rank	Metropolitan Area	[cols 17 & 18] Percent 65 Years and Over	Population Rank	Female Householder Rank	Metropolitan Area	[col 30] Percent Female Householder
55	1	West Palm Beach-Boca Raton, FL	23.1	54	1	Memphis, TN-AR-MS	18.9
20	2	Tampa-St. Petersburg-Clearwater, FL	19.2	45	2	New Orleans, LA	18.2
22	3	Pittsburgh, PA	17.7	2	3	New York, NY	18.1
56	4	Monmouth-Ocean, NJ	16.9	23	4	Miami, FL	17.2
36	5	Fort Lauderdale, FL	16.1	18	5	Baltimore, MD	14.9
51	6	Buffalo-Niagara Falls, NY	15.8	66	5	Fresno, CA	14.9
24	7	Cleveland-Lorain-Elyria, OH	14.6	39	5	Norfolk-Virginia Beach-Newport News, VA-NC	14.9
63	8	Providence-Warwick-Pawtucket, RI	14.5	67	8	Birmingham, AL	14.8
69	9	Albany-Schenectady-Troy, NY	14.3	38	8	San Antonio, TX	14.8
70	10	Tucson, AZ	14.2	1	10	Los Angeles-Long Beach, CA	14.7
44	11	Bergen-Passaic, NJ	14.1	7	11	Detroit, MI	14.6
53	12	Hartford, CT	14.0	26	12	Newark, NJ	14.4
30	13	New Haven-Bridgeport-Stamford-Danbury-Waterbury, CT	13.9	62	12	Richmond-Petersburg, VA	14.4
65	14	Dayton-Springfield, OH	13.5	5	14	Philadelphia, PA-NJ	14.3
5	14	Philadelphia, PA-NJ	13.5	57	15	Jacksonville, FL	14.0
68	16	Honolulu, HI	13.4	24	16	Cleveland-Lorain-Elyria, OH	13.8
16	16	Nassau-Suffolk, NY	13.4	9	17	Atlanta, GA	13.6
23	18	Miami, FL	13.3	61	17	Louisville, KY-IN	13.6
73	18	Syracuse, NY	13.3	51	19	Buffalo-Niagara Falls, NY	13.5
29	20	San Francisco, CA	13.2	17	19	St. Louis, MO-IL	13.5
58	21	Rochester, NY	12.9	11	21	Riverside-San Bernardino, CA	13.4
17	22	St. Louis, MO-IL	12.8	3	22	Chicago, IL	13.3
67	23	Birmingham, AL	12.7	8	23	Houston, TX	13.2
4	23	Boston-Worcester-Lawrence-Lowell-Brockton, MA-NH	12.7	30	24	New Haven-Bridgeport-Stamford-Danbury-Waterbury, CT	13.0
61	25	Louisville, KY-IN	12.6	63	24	Providence-Warwick-Pawtucket, RI	13.0
42	25	Milwaukee-Waukesha, WI	12.6	42	26	Milwaukee-Waukesha, WI	12.9
47	27	Greensboro—Winston-Salem—High Point, NC	12.5	75	27	Albuquerque, NM	12.8
34	28	Orlando, FL	12.4	35	27	Sacramento, CA	12.8
64	29	Greenville-Spartanburg-Anderson, SC	12.3	65	29	Dayton-Springfield, OH	12.7
26	30	Newark, NJ	12.2	64	30	Greenville-Spartanburg-Anderson, SC	12.6
18	31	Baltimore, MD	12.1	36	31	Fort Lauderdale, FL	12.5
7	31	Detroit, MI	12.1	33	32	Cincinnati, OH-KY-IN	12.4
12	33	Phoenix-Mesa, AZ	12.0	21	32	Oakland, CA	12.4
33	34	Cincinnati, OH-KY-IN	11.9	34	32	Orlando, FL	12.4
2	34	New York, NY	11.9	58	32	Rochester, NY	12.4
40	36	Las Vegas, NV-AZ	11.8	6	32	Washington, DC-MD-VA-WV	12.4
52	36	Middlesex-Somerset-Hunterdon, NJ	11.8	47	37	Greensboro—Winston-Salem—High Point, NC	12.3
71	36	Tulsa, OK	11.8	68	37	Honolulu, HI	12.3
35	39	Sacramento, CA	11.5	49	37	Nashville, TN	12.3
28	40	Kansas City, MO-KS	11.4	60	37	Oklahoma City, OK	12.3
45	40	New Orleans, LA	11.4	43	41	Charlotte-Gastonia-Rock Hill, NC-SC	12.1
60	40	Oklahoma City, OK	11.4	10	41	Dallas, TX	12.1
75	43	Albuquerque, NM	11.3	37	41	Indianapolis, IN	12.1
62	44	Richmond-Petersburg, VA	11.2	73	41	Syracuse, NY	12.1
15	44	San Diego, CA	11.2	53	45	Hartford, CT	12.0
57	46	Jacksonville, FL	11.1	41	46	Columbus, OH	11.9
37	47	Indianapolis, IN	10.9	44	47	Bergen-Passaic, NJ	11.8
59	48	Grand Rapids-Muskegon-Holland, MI	10.8	28	47	Kansas City, MO-KS	11.8
3	49	Chicago, IL	10.7	70	47	Tucson, AZ	11.8
21	49	Oakland, CA	10.7	31	50	Fort Worth-Arlington, TX	11.7
38	49	San Antonio, TX	10.7	15	51	San Diego, CA	11.6
74	52	Omaha, NE-IA	10.6	71	52	Tulsa, OK	11.5
11	52	Riverside-San Bernardino, CA	10.6	40	53	Las Vegas, NV-AZ	11.4
27	54	Portland-Vancouver, OR-WA	10.4	74	53	Omaha, NE-IA	11.4
39	55	Norfolk-Virginia Beach-Newport News, VA-NC	10.3	22	53	Pittsburgh, PA	11.4
43	56	Charlotte-Gastonia-Rock Hill, NC-SC	10.2	69	56	Albany-Schenectady-Troy, NY	11.3
19	56	Seattle-Bellevue-Everett, WA	10.2	20	57	Tampa-St. Petersburg-Clearwater, FL	11.2
72	56	Ventura, CA	10.2	4	58	Boston-Worcester-Lawrence-Lowell-Brockton, MA-NH	11.0
66	59	Fresno, CA	10.1	50	58	Raleigh-Durham-Chapel Hill, NC	11.0
41	60	Columbus, OH	10.0	59	60	Grand Rapids-Muskegon-Holland, MI	10.9
49	60	Nashville, TN	10.0	16	60	Nassau-Suffolk, NY	10.9
54	62	Memphis, TN-AR-MS	9.9	72	60	Ventura, CA	10.9
1	63	Los Angeles-Long Beach, CA	9.8	12	63	Phoenix-Mesa, AZ	10.8
14	63	Orange County, CA	9.8	14	64	Orange County, CA	10.7
13	65	Minneapolis-St. Paul, MN-WI	9.6	48	65	Austin-San Marcos, TX	10.2
32	65	San Jose, CA	9.6	25	65	Denver, CO	10.2
6	67	Washington, DC-MD-VA-WV	9.1	46	65	Salt Lake City-Ogden, UT	10.2
25	68	Denver, CO	9.0	32	68	San Jose, CA	10.0
31	69	Fort Worth-Arlington, TX	8.8	27	69	Portland-Vancouver, OR-WA	9.9
50	70	Raleigh-Durham-Chapel Hill, NC	8.6	52	70	Middlesex-Somerset-Hunterdon, NJ	9.7
46	71	Salt Lake City-Ogden, UT	8.3	13	70	Minneapolis-St. Paul, MN-WI	9.7
10	72	Dallas, TX	7.7	55	70	West Palm Beach-Boca Raton, FL	9.7
9	73	Atlanta, GA	7.5	56	73	Monmouth-Ocean, NJ	9.6
8	74	Houston, TX	7.4	29	74	San Francisco, CA	9.3
48	75	Austin-San Marcos, TX	7.3	19	75	Seattle-Bellevue-Everett, WA	9.2

Note: Column numbers refer to Table C. Metropolitan Areas.

TABLE 4—75 Largest Metropolitan Areas by 2000 Population
Selected Rankings

Live Birth Rate Per 1,000 Population, 1997-1999 Average				Infant Deaths Per 1,000 Live Births, 1997-1999 Average			
Population Rank	Birth Rate Rank	Metropolitan Area	[col 33] Birth Rate	Population Rank	Infant Mortality Rate	Metropolitan Area	[col 37] Infant Mortality Rate
46	1	Salt Lake City-Ogden, UT	20.1	54	1	Memphis, TN-AR-MS	12.2
66	2	Fresno, CA	18.3	47	2	Greensboro—Winston-Salem—High Point, NC	9.2
8	3	Houston, TX	17.7	57	2	Jacksonville, FL	9.2
10	4	Dallas, TX	17.6	18	4	Baltimore, MD	8.9
1	5	Los Angeles-Long Beach, CA	17.1	3	4	Chicago, IL	8.9
12	5	Phoenix-Mesa, AZ	17.1	7	6	Detroit, MI	8.7
11	7	Riverside-San Bernardino, CA	17.0	64	7	Greenville-Spartanburg-Anderson, SC	8.6
38	8	San Antonio, TX	16.9	24	8	Cleveland-Lorain-Elyria, OH	8.4
48	9	Austin-San Marcos, TX	16.7	41	9	Columbus, OH	8.2
14	9	Orange County, CA	16.7	5	9	Philadelphia, PA-NJ	8.2
31	11	Fort Worth-Arlington, TX	16.6	50	9	Raleigh-Durham-Chapel Hill, NC	8.2
54	12	Memphis, TN-AR-MS	16.5	17	12	St. Louis, MO-IL	8.1
9	13	Atlanta, GA	16.3	53	13	Hartford, CT	8.0
3	14	Chicago, IL	16.1	20	14	Tampa-St. Petersburg-Clearwater, FL	7.9
40	14	Las Vegas, NV-AZ	16.1	51	15	Buffalo-Niagara Falls, NY	7.8
59	16	Grand Rapids-Muskegon-Holland, MI	15.6	43	16	Charlotte-Gastonia-Rock Hill, NC-SC	7.5
15	17	San Diego, CA	15.5	59	16	Grand Rapids-Muskegon-Holland, MI	7.5
32	17	San Jose, CA	15.5	12	16	Phoenix-Mesa, AZ	7.5
72	17	Ventura, CA	15.5	74	19	Omaha, NE-IA	7.3
25	20	Denver, CO	15.4	26	20	Newark, NJ	7.2
37	20	Indianapolis, IN	15.4	11	20	Riverside-San Bernardino, CA	7.2
2	20	New York, NY	15.4	36	22	Fort Lauderdale, FL	7.0
75	23	Albuquerque, NM	15.3	31	22	Fort Worth-Arlington, TX	7.0
74	23	Omaha, NE-IA	15.3	68	22	Honolulu, HI	7.0
43	25	Charlotte-Gastonia-Rock Hill, NC-SC	15.1	22	25	Pittsburgh, PA	6.9
60	25	Oklahoma City, OK	15.1	25	26	Denver, CO	6.8
50	25	Raleigh-Durham-Chapel Hill, NC	15.1	66	26	Fresno, CA	6.8
71	25	Tulsa, OK	15.1	40	26	Las Vegas, NV-AZ	6.8
39	29	Norfolk-Virginia Beach-Newport News, VA-NC	15.0	2	29	New York, NY	6.7
57	30	Jacksonville, FL	14.9	34	29	Orlando, FL	6.7
49	30	Nashville, TN	14.9	75	31	Albuquerque, NM	6.6
41	32	Columbus, OH	14.8	63	31	Providence-Warwick-Pawtucket, RI	6.6
13	32	Minneapolis-St. Paul, MN-WI	14.8	55	33	West Palm Beach-Boca Raton, FL	6.4
45	32	New Orleans, LA	14.8	30	34	New Haven-Bridgeport-Stamford-Danbury-Waterbury, CT	6.3
70	32	Tucson, AZ	14.8	8	35	Houston, TX	6.2
28	36	Kansas City, MO-KS	14.7	35	36	Sacramento, CA	6.1
6	36	Washington, DC-MD-VA-WV	14.7	72	36	Ventura, CA	6.1
33	38	Cincinnati, OH-KY-IN	14.6	70	38	Tucson, AZ	6.0
27	39	Portland-Vancouver, OR-WA	14.5	10	39	Dallas, TX	5.8
23	40	Miami, FL	14.4	1	39	Los Angeles-Long Beach, CA	5.8
68	41	Honolulu, HI	14.3	46	39	Salt Lake City-Ogden, UT	5.8
26	41	Newark, NJ	14.3	23	42	Miami, FL	5.6
67	43	Birmingham, AL	14.1	56	42	Monmouth-Ocean, NJ	5.6
21	43	Oakland, CA	14.1	16	42	Nassau-Suffolk, NY	5.6
34	43	Orlando, FL	14.1	21	42	Oakland, CA	5.6
35	43	Sacramento, CA	14.1	44	46	Bergen-Passaic, NJ	5.3
42	47	Milwaukee-Waukesha, WI	14.0	15	46	San Diego, CA	5.3
52	48	Middlesex-Somerset-Hunterdon, NJ	13.9	4	48	Boston-Worcester-Lawrence-Lowell-Brockton, MA-NH	5.1
47	49	Greensboro—Winston-Salem—High Point, NC	13.8	27	48	Portland-Vancouver, OR-WA	5.1
30	49	New Haven-Bridgeport-Stamford-Danbury-Waterbury, CT	13.8	19	48	Seattle-Bellevue-Everett, WA	5.1
17	49	St. Louis, MO-IL	13.8	52	51	Middlesex-Somerset-Hunterdon, NJ	5.0
7	52	Detroit, MI	13.7	32	51	San Jose, CA	5.0
61	53	Louisville, KY-IN	13.6	14	53	Orange County, CA	4.6
18	54	Baltimore, MD	13.5	29	54	San Francisco, CA	4.4
44	54	Bergen-Passaic, NJ	13.5	69		Albany-Schenectady-Troy, NY	NA
36	54	Fort Lauderdale, FL	13.5	9		Atlanta, GA	NA
19	54	Seattle-Bellevue-Everett, WA	13.5	48		Austin-San Marcos, TX	NA
24	58	Cleveland-Lorain-Elyria, OH	13.4	67		Birmingham, AL	NA
5	58	Philadelphia, PA-NJ	13.4	33		Cincinnati, OH-KY-IN	NA
4	60	Boston-Worcester-Lawrence-Lowell-Brockton, MA-NH	13.3	65		Dayton-Springfield, OH	NA
64	60	Greenville-Spartanburg-Anderson, SC	13.3	37		Indianapolis, IN	NA
16	60	Nassau-Suffolk, NY	13.3	28		Kansas City, MO-KS	NA
62	60	Richmond-Petersburg, VA	13.3	61		Louisville, KY-IN	NA
58	64	Rochester, NY	13.2	42		Milwaukee-Waukesha, WI	NA
65	65	Dayton-Springfield, OH	13.1	13		Minneapolis-St. Paul, MN-WI	NA
53	65	Hartford, CT	13.1	49		Nashville, TN	NA
56	65	Monmouth-Ocean, NJ	13.1	45		New Orleans, LA	NA
73	68	Syracuse, NY	12.8	39		Norfolk-Virginia Beach-Newport News, VA-NC	NA
63	69	Providence-Warwick-Pawtucket, RI	12.7	60		Oklahoma City, OK	NA
55	70	West Palm Beach-Boca Raton, FL	12.5	62		Richmond-Petersburg, VA	NA
51	71	Buffalo-Niagara Falls, NY	12.3	58		Rochester, NY	NA
20	71	Tampa-St. Petersburg-Clearwater, FL	12.3	38		San Antonio, TX	NA
69	73	Albany-Schenectady-Troy, NY	12.0	73		Syracuse, NY	NA
29	73	San Francisco, CA	12.0	71		Tulsa, OK	NA
22	75	Pittsburgh, PA	11.0	6		Washington, DC-MD-VA-WV	NA

Note: Column numbers refer to Table C. Metropolitan Areas.

TABLE 4—75 Largest Metropolitan Areas by 2000 Population
Selected Rankings

Percent College Graduates (Bachelor's or higher degree), 1990				Median Household Income, 1989			
Population Rank	Percent College Graduate Rank	Metropolitan Area	[col 51] Percent College Grad	Population Rank	Median Income Rank	Metropolitan Area	[col 58] Median Income 1989 (dollars)
6	1	Washington, DC-MD-VA-WV	37.0	16	1	Nassau-Suffolk, NY	51 670
29	2	San Francisco, CA	34.9	52	2	Middlesex-Somerset-Hunterdon, NJ	48 701
32	3	San Jose, CA	32.6	32	3	San Jose, CA	48 115
50	4	Raleigh-Durham-Chapel Hill, NC	31.7	14	4	Orange County, CA	45 921
48	5	Austin-San Marcos, TX	30.7	6	5	Washington, DC-MD-VA-WV	45 900
52	6	Middlesex-Somerset-Hunterdon, NJ	30.2	72	6	Ventura, CA	45 612
21	7	Oakland, CA	29.9	44	7	Bergen-Passaic, NJ	45 039
19	8	Seattle-Bellevue-Everett, WA	29.5	30	8	New Haven-Bridgeport-Stamford-Danbury-Waterbury, CT	43 268
30	9	New Haven-Bridgeport-Stamford-Danbury-Waterbury, CT	29.3	26	9	Newark, NJ	42 174
25	10	Denver, CO	28.9	53	10	Hartford, CT	41 428
4	11	Boston-Worcester-Lawrence-Lowell-Brockton, MA-NH	27.8	21	11	Oakland, CA	40 620
14	11	Orange County, CA	27.8	68	12	Honolulu, HI	40 580
44	13	Bergen-Passaic, NJ	27.3	29	13	San Francisco, CA	40 493
10	14	Dallas, TX	26.9	56	14	Monmouth-Ocean, NJ	39 830
13	14	Minneapolis-St. Paul, MN-WI	26.9	4	15	Boston-Worcester-Lawrence-Lowell-Brockton, MA-NH	38 529
26	14	Newark, NJ	26.9	18	16	Baltimore, MD	36 549
53	17	Hartford, CT	26.5	13	17	Minneapolis-St. Paul, MN-WI	36 467
16	17	Nassau-Suffolk, NY	26.5	3	18	Chicago, IL	36 301
9	19	Atlanta, GA	26.1	19	19	Seattle-Bellevue-Everett, WA	36 126
15	20	San Diego, CA	25.3	9	20	Atlanta, GA	35 606
8	21	Houston, TX	25.0	5	21	Philadelphia, PA-NJ	35 406
75	22	Albuquerque, NM	24.8	15	22	San Diego, CA	35 021
68	23	Honolulu, HI	24.6	1	23	Los Angeles-Long Beach, CA	34 964
2	23	New York, NY	24.6	7	24	Detroit, MI	34 300
3	25	Chicago, IL	24.5	58	25	Rochester, NY	34 001
62	26	Richmond-Petersburg, VA	23.8	62	26	Richmond-Petersburg, VA	33 488
69	27	Albany-Schenectady-Troy, NY	23.6	11	27	Riverside-San Bernardino, CA	33 278
41	28	Columbus, OH	23.3	35	28	Sacramento, CA	33 195
27	28	Portland-Vancouver, OR-WA	23.3	25	29	Denver, CO	32 851
70	28	Tucson, AZ	23.3	10	30	Dallas, TX	32 667
28	31	Kansas City, MO-KS	23.2	55	31	West Palm Beach-Boca Raton, FL	32 523
18	32	Baltimore, MD	23.1	69	32	Albany-Schenectady-Troy, NY	32 427
72	33	Ventura, CA	23.0	42	33	Milwaukee-Waukesha, WI	32 315
58	34	Rochester, NY	22.9	31	34	Fort Worth-Arlington, TX	32 112
46	34	Salt Lake City-Ogden, UT	22.9	50	35	Raleigh-Durham-Chapel Hill, NC	32 046
35	36	Sacramento, CA	22.7	63	36	Providence-Warwick-Pawtucket, RI	31 908
5	37	Philadelphia, PA-NJ	22.6	59	37	Grand Rapids-Muskegon-Holland, MI	31 796
56	38	Monmouth-Ocean, NJ	22.5	17	38	St. Louis, MO-IL	31 718
74	38	Omaha, NE-IA	22.5	2	39	New York, NY	31 658
31	40	Fort Worth-Arlington, TX	22.4	28	40	Kansas City, MO-KS	31 559
1	41	Los Angeles-Long Beach, CA	22.3	8	41	Houston, TX	31 473
55	42	West Palm Beach-Boca Raton, FL	22.1	37	42	Indianapolis, IN	31 314
60	43	Oklahoma City, OK	21.6	43	43	Charlotte-Gastonia-Rock Hill, NC-SC	31 124
49	44	Nashville, TN	21.4	27	44	Portland-Vancouver, OR-WA	31 037
12	44	Phoenix-Mesa, AZ	21.4	46	45	Salt Lake City-Ogden, UT	30 881
42	46	Milwaukee-Waukesha, WI	21.3	39	46	Norfolk-Virginia Beach-Newport News, VA-NC	30 766
73	47	Syracuse, NY	20.8	73	47	Syracuse, NY	30 705
17	48	St. Louis, MO-IL	20.5	41	48	Columbus, OH	30 609
34	49	Orlando, FL	20.4	36	49	Fort Lauderdale, FL	30 570
63	49	Providence-Warwick-Pawtucket, RI	20.4	65	50	Dayton-Springfield, OH	30 471
71	51	Tulsa, OK	20.3	33	51	Cincinnati, OH-KY-IN	30 370
37	52	Indianapolis, IN	20.2	24	52	Cleveland-Lorain-Elyria, OH	30 350
33	53	Cincinnati, OH-KY-IN	19.9	12	52	Phoenix-Mesa, AZ	30 350
39	54	Norfolk-Virginia Beach-Newport News, VA-NC	19.8	74	54	Omaha, NE-IA	30 258
67	55	Birmingham, AL	19.7	49	55	Nashville, TN	30 222
43	56	Charlotte-Gastonia-Rock Hill, NC-SC	19.6	34	56	Orlando, FL	30 211
45	57	New Orleans, LA	19.3	40	57	Las Vegas, NV-AZ	30 022
38	57	San Antonio, TX	19.3	57	58	Jacksonville, FL	29 513
65	59	Dayton-Springfield, OH	19.1	47	59	Greensboro—Winston-Salem—High Point, NC	29 043
51	60	Buffalo-Niagara Falls, NY	18.8	51	60	Buffalo-Niagara Falls, NY	28 083
36	60	Fort Lauderdale, FL	18.8	48	61	Austin-San Marcos, TX	27 956
23	60	Miami, FL	18.8	61	62	Louisville, KY-IN	27 435
47	63	Greensboro—Winston-Salem—High Point, NC	18.7	75	63	Albuquerque, NM	27 317
54	63	Memphis, TN-AR-MS	18.7	64	64	Greenville-Spartanburg-Anderson, SC	27 236
22	63	Pittsburgh, PA	18.7	71	65	Tulsa, OK	26 990
57	66	Jacksonville, FL	18.6	23	66	Miami, FL	26 908
24	67	Cleveland-Lorain-Elyria, OH	18.5	54	67	Memphis, TN-AR-MS	26 899
59	68	Grand Rapids-Muskegon-Holland, MI	17.8	60	68	Oklahoma City, OK	26 882
7	69	Detroit, MI	17.7	22	69	Pittsburgh, PA	26 656
20	70	Tampa-St. Petersburg-Clearwater, FL	17.3	67	70	Birmingham, AL	26 613
61	71	Louisville, KY-IN	17.2	66	71	Fresno, CA	26 481
64	72	Greenville-Spartanburg-Anderson, SC	16.7	38	72	San Antonio, TX	26 048
66	73	Fresno, CA	16.3	20	73	Tampa-St. Petersburg-Clearwater, FL	26 035
11	74	Riverside-San Bernardino, CA	14.8	70	74	Tucson, AZ	25 400
40	75	Las Vegas, NV-AZ	13.3	45	75	New Orleans, LA	24 415

Note: Column numbers refer to Table C. Metropolitan Areas.

TABLE 4—75 Largest Metropolitan Areas by 2000 Population
Selected Rankings

Percent of Persons Below the Poverty Level, 1998				Percent of Persons Under 18 Years Below the Poverty Level, 1998			
Population Rank	Poverty Rate Rank	Metropolitan Area	[col 59] Poverty Rate	Population Rank	Poverty Rate Rank for Persons Under 18 yrs.	Metropolitan Area	[col 60] Poverty Rate for Persons Under 18 yrs.
66	1	Fresno, CA	24.1	66	1	Fresno, CA	34.0
2	2	New York, NY	20.0	2	2	New York, NY	30.1
23	3	Miami, FL	19.8	23	3	Miami, FL	29.6
1	4	Los Angeles-Long Beach, CA	18.9	1	4	Los Angeles-Long Beach, CA	28.1
45	5	New Orleans, LA	17.8	45	5	New Orleans, LA	26.2
38	6	San Antonio, TX	17.1	38	6	San Antonio, TX	24.7
70	7	Tucson, AZ	15.9	70	7	Tucson, AZ	24.4
11	8	Riverside-San Bernardino, CA	15.6	11	8	Riverside-San Bernardino, CA	22.0
54	9	Memphis, TN-AR-MS	15.0	51	9	Buffalo-Niagara Falls, NY	21.9
75	10	Albuquerque, NM	14.3	20	10	Tampa-St. Petersburg-Clearwater, FL	21.6
60	11	Oklahoma City, OK	14.1	75	11	Albuquerque, NM	21.5
35	12	Sacramento, CA	13.8	54	11	Memphis, TN-AR-MS	21.5
51	13	Buffalo-Niagara Falls, NY	13.7	35	13	Sacramento, CA	21.4
15	14	San Diego, CA	13.1	60	14	Oklahoma City, OK	20.8
8	15	Houston, TX	13.0	15	15	San Diego, CA	20.2
20	16	Tampa-St. Petersburg-Clearwater, FL	12.9	67	16	Birmingham, AL	19.8
67	17	Birmingham, AL	12.8	71	17	Tulsa, OK	19.5
73	17	Syracuse, NY	12.8	55	18	West Palm Beach-Boca Raton, FL	19.2
71	19	Tulsa, OK	12.7	73	19	Syracuse, NY	19.1
12	20	Phoenix-Mesa, AZ	12.3	34	20	Orlando, FL	19.0
39	21	Norfolk-Virginia Beach-Newport News, VA-NC	12.1	12	20	Phoenix-Mesa, AZ	19.0
58	22	Rochester, NY	12.0	58	22	Rochester, NY	18.9
34	23	Orlando, FL	11.8	8	23	Houston, TX	18.7
7	24	Detroit, MI	11.5	24	24	Cleveland-Lorain-Elyria, OH	18.3
57	24	Jacksonville, FL	11.5	36	25	Fort Lauderdale, FL	17.9
40	24	Las Vegas, NV-AZ	11.5	42	25	Milwaukee-Waukesha, WI	17.9
24	27	Cleveland-Lorain-Elyria, OH	11.4	7	27	Detroit, MI	17.7
61	28	Louisville, KY-IN	11.1	57	27	Jacksonville, FL	17.7
36	29	Fort Lauderdale, FL	11.0	22	27	Pittsburgh, PA	17.7
64	29	Greenville-Spartanburg-Anderson, SC	11.0	47	30	Greensboro—Winston-Salem—High Point, NC	17.3
42	29	Milwaukee-Waukesha, WI	11.0	64	31	Greenville-Spartanburg-Anderson, SC	17.2
22	29	Pittsburgh, PA	11.0	61	31	Louisville, KY-IN	17.2
55	29	West Palm Beach-Boca Raton, FL	11.0	40	33	Las Vegas, NV-AZ	17.0
5	34	Philadelphia, PA-NJ	10.9	9	34	Atlanta, GA	16.9
63	34	Providence-Warwick-Pawtucket, RI	10.9	69	35	Albany-Schenectady-Troy, NY	16.8
47	36	Greensboro—Winston-Salem—High Point, NC	10.8	63	35	Providence-Warwick-Pawtucket, RI	16.8
69	37	Albany-Schenectady-Troy, NY	10.6	39	37	Norfolk-Virginia Beach-Newport News, VA-NC	16.7
9	38	Atlanta, GA	10.5	14	38	Orange County, CA	16.4
10	38	Dallas, TX	10.5	5	38	Philadelphia, PA-NJ	16.4
31	38	Fort Worth-Arlington, TX	10.5	72	40	Ventura, CA	16.3
43	41	Charlotte-Gastonia-Rock Hill, NC-SC	10.3	10	41	Dallas, TX	16.1
17	41	St. Louis, MO-IL	10.3	65	41	Dayton-Springfield, OH	16.1
3	43	Chicago, IL	10.2	31	41	Fort Worth-Arlington, TX	16.1
62	43	Richmond-Petersburg, VA	10.2	43	44	Charlotte-Gastonia-Rock Hill, NC-SC	15.9
48	45	Austin-San Marcos, TX	10.1	21	44	Oakland, CA	15.9
65	45	Dayton-Springfield, OH	10.1	17	46	St. Louis, MO-IL	15.5
14	45	Orange County, CA	10.1	41	47	Columbus, OH	15.3
18	48	Baltimore, MD	10.0	3	48	Chicago, IL	15.1
72	48	Ventura, CA	10.0	48	49	Austin-San Marcos, TX	14.8
41	50	Columbus, OH	9.9	33	50	Cincinnati, OH-KY-IN	14.6
26	51	Newark, NJ	9.8	26	50	Newark, NJ	14.6
68	52	Honolulu, HI	9.7	50	50	Raleigh-Durham-Chapel Hill, NC	14.6
21	52	Oakland, CA	9.7	62	53	Richmond-Petersburg, VA	14.5
33	54	Cincinnati, OH-KY-IN	9.6	68	54	Honolulu, HI	14.3
49	55	Nashville, TN	9.5	18	55	Baltimore, MD	14.1
50	55	Raleigh-Durham-Chapel Hill, NC	9.5	30	56	New Haven-Bridgeport-Stamford-Danbury-Waterbury, CT	14.0
27	57	Portland-Vancouver, OR-WA	9.4	53	57	Hartford, CT	13.8
37	58	Indianapolis, IN	9.2	29	58	San Francisco, CA	13.7
30	59	New Haven-Bridgeport-Stamford-Danbury-Waterbury, CT	9.0	37	59	Indianapolis, IN	13.6
74	59	Omaha, NE-IA	9.0	49	59	Nashville, TN	13.6
46	61	Salt Lake City-Ogden, UT	8.9	32	61	San Jose, CA	13.5
59	62	Grand Rapids-Muskegon-Holland, MI	8.8	27	62	Portland-Vancouver, OR-WA	13.3
53	62	Hartford, CT	8.8	4	63	Boston-Worcester-Lawrence-Lowell-Brockton, MA-NH	13.1
25	64	Denver, CO	8.6	74	64	Omaha, NE-IA	12.9
28	64	Kansas City, MO-KS	8.6	25	65	Denver, CO	12.8
29	64	San Francisco, CA	8.6	59	65	Grand Rapids-Muskegon-Holland, MI	12.8
4	67	Boston-Worcester-Lawrence-Lowell-Brockton, MA-NH	8.4	28	65	Kansas City, MO-KS	12.8
32	68	San Jose, CA	8.2	44	68	Bergen-Passaic, NJ	11.9
44	69	Bergen-Passaic, NJ	7.8	46	68	Salt Lake City-Ogden, UT	11.9
13	70	Minneapolis-St. Paul, MN-WI	7.6	16	70	Nassau-Suffolk, NY	11.3
6	71	Washington, DC-MD-VA-WV	7.5	13	71	Minneapolis-St. Paul, MN-WI	11.2
19	72	Seattle-Bellevue-Everett, WA	7.3	6	72	Washington, DC-MD-VA-WV	11.0
16	73	Nassau-Suffolk, NY	6.9	19	73	Seattle-Bellevue-Everett, WA	10.5
56	74	Monmouth-Ocean, NJ	6.7	56	74	Monmouth-Ocean, NJ	9.9
52	75	Middlesex-Somerset-Hunterdon, NJ	5.4	52	75	Middlesex-Somerset-Hunterdon, NJ	8.1

Note: Column numbers refer to Table C. Metropolitan Areas.

	Median Value of Owner-Occupied Housing Units, 1990				Median Gross Rent of Renter-Occupied Housing Units, 1990		
Popu-lation Rank	Median Value Rank	Metropolitan Area	[col 91] Median Value in 1990 (dollars)	Popu-lation Rank	Median Rent Rank	Metropolitan Area	[col 94] Median Rent (dollars)
29	1	San Francisco, CA	332 400	14	1	Orange County, CA	789
32	2	San Jose, CA	289 400	16	2	Nassau-Suffolk, NY	777
68	3	Honolulu, HI	283 600	32	3	San Jose, CA	772
14	4	Orange County, CA	252 700	72	4	Ventura, CA	753
72	5	Ventura, CA	245 300	29	5	San Francisco, CA	708
1	6	Los Angeles-Long Beach, CA	226 400	52	6	Middlesex-Somerset-Hunterdon, NJ	679
21	7	Oakland, CA	224 400	68	7	Honolulu, HI	662
44	8	Bergen-Passaic, NJ	214 400	6	8	Washington, DC-MD-VA-WV	658
2	9	New York, NY	209 000	56	9	Monmouth-Ocean, NJ	647
30	10	New Haven-Bridgeport-Stamford-Danbury-Waterbury, CT	198 400	44	10	Bergen-Passaic, NJ	645
26	11	Newark, NJ	188 400	21	11	Oakland, CA	641
16	12	Nassau-Suffolk, NY	187 000	30	12	New Haven-Bridgeport-Stamford-Danbury-Waterbury, CT	630
15	13	San Diego, CA	186 700	1	13	Los Angeles-Long Beach, CA	625
52	14	Middlesex-Somerset-Hunterdon, NJ	173 500	15	14	San Diego, CA	610
53	15	Hartford, CT	169 300	4	15	Boston-Worcester-Lawrence-Lowell-Brockton, MA-NH	595
4	16	Boston-Worcester-Lawrence-Lowell-Brockton, MA-NH	165 200	55	16	West Palm Beach-Boca Raton, FL	586
6	17	Washington, DC-MD-VA-WV	160 939	26	17	Newark, NJ	581
56	18	Monmouth-Ocean, NJ	150 600	53	18	Hartford, CT	576
35	19	Sacramento, CA	136 700	36	19	Fort Lauderdale, FL	574
19	20	Seattle-Bellevue-Everett, WA	135 900	11	20	Riverside-San Bernardino, CA	561
11	21	Riverside-San Bernardino, CA	133 900	35	21	Sacramento, CA	532
63	22	Providence-Warwick-Pawtucket, RI	131 300	9	22	Atlanta, GA	524
3	23	Chicago, IL	109 900	34	23	Orlando, FL	515
18	24	Baltimore, MD	101 200	5	24	Philadelphia, PA-NJ	514
5	25	Philadelphia, PA-NJ	100 400	19	24	Seattle-Bellevue-Everett, WA	514
69	26	Albany-Schenectady-Troy, NY	99 000	40	26	Las Vegas, NV-AZ	511
55	27	West Palm Beach-Boca Raton, FL	98 400	2	27	New York, NY	502
36	28	Fort Lauderdale, FL	91 800	23	28	Miami, FL	492
40	29	Las Vegas, NV-AZ	91 500	3	29	Chicago, IL	491
50	30	Raleigh-Durham-Chapel Hill, NC	89 100	18	30	Baltimore, MD	489
9	31	Atlanta, GA	88 800	63	31	Providence-Warwick-Pawtucket, RI	480
13	32	Minneapolis-St. Paul, MN-WI	88 300	39	32	Norfolk-Virginia Beach-Newport News, VA-NC	479
25	33	Denver, CO	87 800	13	33	Minneapolis-St. Paul, MN-WI	477
39	34	Norfolk-Virginia Beach-Newport News, VA-NC	86 800	58	34	Rochester, NY	462
23	35	Miami, FL	86 500	12	35	Phoenix-Mesa, AZ	461
58	36	Rochester, NY	85 500	62	36	Richmond-Petersburg, VA	458
12	37	Phoenix-Mesa, AZ	84 200	69	37	Albany-Schenectady-Troy, NY	456
66	38	Fresno, CA	83 900	50	37	Raleigh-Durham-Chapel Hill, NC	456
34	39	Orlando, FL	82 500	10	39	Dallas, TX	453
75	40	Albuquerque, NM	82 400	7	39	Detroit, MI	453
10	41	Dallas, TX	81 500	20	41	Tampa-St. Petersburg-Clearwater, FL	447
62	42	Richmond-Petersburg, VA	79 300	42	42	Milwaukee-Waukesha, WI	446
42	43	Milwaukee-Waukesha, WI	76 900	57	43	Jacksonville, FL	438
70	44	Tucson, AZ	76 500	27	44	Portland-Vancouver, OR-WA	436
49	45	Nashville, TN	76 000	66	45	Fresno, CA	432
73	46	Syracuse, NY	75 300	25	46	Denver, CO	431
48	47	Austin-San Marcos, TX	74 800	31	47	Fort Worth-Arlington, TX	428
27	48	Portland-Vancouver, OR-WA	72 400	73	48	Syracuse, NY	426
43	49	Charlotte-Gastonia-Rock Hill, NC-SC	72 300	49	49	Nashville, TN	425
41	49	Columbus, OH	72 300	43	50	Charlotte-Gastonia-Rock Hill, NC-SC	424
24	51	Cleveland-Lorain-Elyria, OH	72 100	28	50	Kansas City, MO-KS	424
31	52	Fort Worth-Arlington, TX	72 000	41	52	Columbus, OH	420
51	53	Buffalo-Niagara Falls, NY	71 900	59	52	Grand Rapids-Muskegon-Holland, MI	420
20	54	Tampa-St. Petersburg-Clearwater, FL	71 300	48	54	Austin-San Marcos, TX	414
46	55	Salt Lake City-Ogden, UT	71 000	17	55	St. Louis, MO-IL	413
47	56	Greensboro—Winston-Salem—High Point, NC	70 700	37	56	Indianapolis, IN	407
33	57	Cincinnati, OH-KY-IN	70 400	8	57	Houston, TX	406
45	58	New Orleans, LA	69 800	75	58	Albuquerque, NM	401
17	58	St. Louis, MO-IL	69 800	24	59	Cleveland-Lorain-Elyria, OH	399
57	60	Jacksonville, FL	67 800	74	59	Omaha, NE-IA	399
7	61	Detroit, MI	67 600	65	61	Dayton-Springfield, OH	398
28	62	Kansas City, MO-KS	66 300	45	62	New Orleans, LA	396
59	63	Grand Rapids-Muskegon-Holland, MI	65 700	47	63	Greensboro—Winston-Salem—High Point, NC	390
65	64	Dayton-Springfield, OH	65 000	70	64	Tucson, AZ	389
54	65	Memphis, TN-AR-MS	64 600	54	65	Memphis, TN-AR-MS	388
8	66	Houston, TX	64 200	51	66	Buffalo-Niagara Falls, NY	380
37	67	Indianapolis, IN	64 100	38	67	San Antonio, TX	379
67	68	Birmingham, AL	60 600	46	68	Salt Lake City-Ogden, UT	377
74	69	Omaha, NE-IA	59 000	60	69	Oklahoma City, OK	368
71	70	Tulsa, OK	58 900	33	70	Cincinnati, OH-KY-IN	364
64	71	Greenville-Spartanburg-Anderson, SC	58 700	22	71	Pittsburgh, PA	362
38	72	San Antonio, TX	57 200	67	72	Birmingham, AL	361
61	73	Louisville, KY-IN	56 100	71	73	Tulsa, OK	360
22	74	Pittsburgh, PA	55 600	64	74	Greenville-Spartanburg-Anderson, SC	358
60	75	Oklahoma City, OK	54 500	61	75	Louisville, KY-IN	345

Note: Column numbers refer to Table C. Metropolitan Areas.

TABLE 4—75 Largest Metropolitan Areas by 2000 Population
Selected Rankings

	Unemployment Rate, 2001				Manufacturing Employment as a Percent of Total Nonfarm Employment, 1999		
Population Rank	Unemployment Rate Rank	Metropolitan Area	[col 100] Unemployment Rate	Population Rank	Manufacturing Rank	Metropolitan Area	[col 107/col 105] Percent employed in Manufacturing
66	1	Fresno, CA	13.5	59	1	Grand Rapids-Muskegon-Holland, MI	29.5
23	2	Miami, FL	6.9	32	2	San Jose, CA	24.6
27	3	Portland-Vancouver, OR-WA	5.9	47	3	Greensboro—Winston-Salem—High Point, NC	24.4
1	4	Los Angeles-Long Beach, CA	5.7	64	4	Greenville-Spartanburg-Anderson, SC	24.2
2	5	New York, NY	5.6	42	5	Milwaukee-Waukesha, WI	21.1
40	6	Las Vegas, NV-AZ	5.5	65	6	Dayton-Springfield, OH	20.7
55	6	West Palm Beach-Boca Raton, FL	5.5	58	7	Rochester, NY	20.6
51	8	Buffalo-Niagara Falls, NY	5.4	24	8	Cleveland-Lorain-Elyria, OH	19.0
3	8	Chicago, IL	5.4	63	9	Providence-Warwick-Pawtucket, RI	18.3
45	10	New Orleans, LA	5.2	51	10	Buffalo-Niagara Falls, NY	17.3
19	10	Seattle-Bellevue-Everett, WA	5.2	7	11	Detroit, MI	17.2
43	12	Charlotte-Gastonia-Rock Hill, NC-SC	5.1	14	12	Orange County, CA	16.9
7	12	Detroit, MI	5.1	43	13	Charlotte-Gastonia-Rock Hill, NC-SC	16.8
59	12	Grand Rapids-Muskegon-Holland, MI	5.1	1	14	Los Angeles-Long Beach, CA	16.6
47	15	Greensboro—Winston-Salem—High Point, NC	5.0	19	15	Seattle-Bellevue-Everett, WA	16.5
11	15	Riverside-San Bernardino, CA	5.0	61	16	Louisville, KY-IN	15.8
36	17	Fort Lauderdale, FL	4.9	73	17	Syracuse, NY	15.6
17	17	St. Louis, MO-IL	4.9	53	18	Hartford, CT	15.5
10	19	Dallas, TX	4.8	31	19	Fort Worth-Arlington, TX	15.4
63	19	Providence-Warwick-Pawtucket, RI	4.8	27	20	Portland-Vancouver, OR-WA	15.3
42	21	Milwaukee-Waukesha, WI	4.7	3	21	Chicago, IL	14.9
73	21	Syracuse, NY	4.7	11	22	Riverside-San Bernardino, CA	14.7
18	23	Baltimore, MD	4.6	71	22	Tulsa, OK	14.7
24	23	Cleveland-Lorain-Elyria, OH	4.6	33	24	Cincinnati, OH-KY-IN	14.5
64	23	Greenville-Spartanburg-Anderson, SC	4.6	13	25	Minneapolis-St. Paul, MN-WI	14.3
58	26	Rochester, NY	4.5	17	25	St. Louis, MO-IL	14.3
32	26	San Jose, CA	4.5	4	27	Boston-Worcester-Lawrence-Lowell-Brockton, MA-NH	14.1
72	26	Ventura, CA	4.5	44	28	Bergen-Passaic, NJ	14.0
28	29	Kansas City, MO-KS	4.4	30	28	New Haven-Bridgeport-Stamford-Danbury-Waterbury, CT	14.0
61	29	Louisville, KY-IN	4.4	37	30	Indianapolis, IN	13.8
44	31	Bergen-Passaic, NJ	4.3	72	31	Ventura, CA	13.7
65	31	Dayton-Springfield, OH	4.3	48	32	Austin-San Marcos, TX	13.5
8	31	Houston, TX	4.3	49	33	Nashville, TN	13.3
26	31	Newark, NJ	4.3	66	34	Fresno, CA	13.2
5	31	Philadelphia, PA-NJ	4.3	46	35	Salt Lake City-Ogden, UT	13.0
22	31	Pittsburgh, PA	4.3	50	36	Raleigh-Durham-Chapel Hill, NC	12.8
46	31	Salt Lake City-Ogden, UT	4.3	26	37	Newark, NJ	12.2
57	38	Jacksonville, FL	4.2	52	38	Middlesex-Somerset-Hunterdon, NJ	12.0
54	38	Memphis, TN-AR-MS	4.2	10	39	Dallas, TX	11.9
31	40	Fort Worth-Arlington, TX	4.1	60	39	Oklahoma City, OK	11.9
68	40	Honolulu, HI	4.1	22	39	Pittsburgh, PA	11.9
21	42	Oakland, CA	4.0	21	42	Oakland, CA	11.8
34	42	Orlando, FL	4.0	62	43	Richmond-Petersburg, VA	11.5
35	42	Sacramento, CA	4.0	15	43	San Diego, CA	11.5
38	42	San Antonio, TX	4.0	67	45	Birmingham, AL	11.1
33	46	Cincinnati, OH-KY-IN	3.9	5	45	Philadelphia, PA-NJ	11.1
60	46	Oklahoma City, OK	3.9	39	47	Norfolk-Virginia Beach-Newport News, VA-NC	11.0
12	46	Phoenix-Mesa, AZ	3.9	12	48	Phoenix-Mesa, AZ	10.9
48	49	Austin-San Marcos, TX	3.8	41	49	Columbus, OH	10.7
56	49	Monmouth-Ocean, NJ	3.8	28	49	Kansas City, MO-KS	10.7
29	49	San Francisco, CA	3.8	70	51	Tucson, AZ	10.5
4	52	Boston-Worcester-Lawrence-Lowell-Brockton, MA-NH	3.7	54	52	Memphis, TN-AR-MS	10.2
20	52	Tampa-St. Petersburg-Clearwater, FL	3.7	16	53	Nassau-Suffolk, NY	10.0
75	54	Albuquerque, NM	3.6	8	54	Houston, TX	9.9
39	54	Norfolk-Virginia Beach-Newport News, VA-NC	3.6	74	54	Omaha, NE-IA	9.9
9	56	Atlanta, GA	3.5	69	56	Albany-Schenectady-Troy, NY	9.7
25	56	Denver, CO	3.5	9	57	Atlanta, GA	9.3
70	56	Tucson, AZ	3.5	75	58	Albuquerque, NM	8.9
67	59	Birmingham, AL	3.4	18	59	Baltimore, MD	8.6
37	59	Indianapolis, IN	3.4	38	60	San Antonio, TX	8.5
30	59	New Haven-Bridgeport-Stamford-Danbury-Waterbury, CT	3.4	45	61	New Orleans, LA	8.0
62	59	Richmond-Petersburg, VA	3.4	35	62	Sacramento, CA	7.9
71	59	Tulsa, OK	3.4	20	63	Tampa-St. Petersburg-Clearwater, FL	7.8
53	64	Hartford, CT	3.3	25	64	Denver, CO	7.3
13	64	Minneapolis-St. Paul, MN-WI	3.3	57	65	Jacksonville, FL	7.2
49	64	Nashville, TN	3.3	23	66	Miami, FL	6.8
16	64	Nassau-Suffolk, NY	3.3	36	67	Fort Lauderdale, FL	6.1
50	64	Raleigh-Durham-Chapel Hill, NC	3.3	34	68	Orlando, FL	6.0
69	69	Albany-Schenectady-Troy, NY	3.2	29	69	San Francisco, CA	5.9
52	69	Middlesex-Somerset-Hunterdon, NJ	3.2	55	69	West Palm Beach-Boca Raton, FL	5.9
74	69	Omaha, NE-IA	3.2	56	71	Monmouth-Ocean, NJ	5.8
15	69	San Diego, CA	3.2	2	72	New York, NY	5.6
6	73	Washington, DC-MD-VA-WV	3.1	6	73	Washington, DC-MD-VA-WV	3.7
14	74	Orange County, CA	3.0	40	74	Las Vegas, NV-AZ	3.6
41	75	Columbus, OH	2.8	68	75	Honolulu, HI	3.5
				68	75	Honolulu, HI	3.5

Note: Column numbers refer to Table C. Metropolitan Areas.

TABLE 4—75 Largest Metropolitan Areas by 2000 Population
Selected Rankings

Population Rank	Services Rank	Professional, Scientific, and Technical Services as a Percent of Total Nonfarm Employment, 1999 — Metropolitan Area	[col 110/col 105] Percent employed in Services	Population Rank	FIRE Rank	Finance, Insurance and Real Estate Employment as a Percent of Total Nonfarm Employment, 1999 — Metropolitan Area	[col 109/col 105] Percent FIRE Employment
6	1	Washington, DC-MD-VA-WV	16.4	53	1	Hartford, CT	13.1
29	2	San Francisco, CA	11.2	2	2	New York, NY	10.9
1	3	Los Angeles-Long Beach, CA	10.5	57	3	Jacksonville, FL	10.4
52	4	Middlesex-Somerset-Hunterdon, NJ	10.4	41	4	Columbus, OH	10.2
32	5	San Jose, CA	9.7	29	5	San Francisco, CA	9.0
75	6	Albuquerque, NM	9.1	62	6	Richmond-Petersburg, VA	8.7
2	6	New York, NY	9.1	74	7	Omaha, NE-IA	8.5
15	8	San Diego, CA	8.2	69	8	Albany-Schenectady-Troy, NY	7.7
5	9	Philadelphia, PA-NJ	8.1	67	9	Birmingham, AL	7.6
48	10	Austin-San Marcos, TX	8.0	13	10	Minneapolis-St. Paul, MN-WI	7.2
18	10	Baltimore, MD	8.0	35	11	Sacramento, CA	7.1
25	12	Denver, CO	7.8	4	12	Boston-Worcester-Lawrence-Lowell-Brockton, MA-NH	7.0
26	12	Newark, NJ	7.8	25	12	Denver, CO	7.0
50	14	Raleigh-Durham-Chapel Hill, NC	7.7	3	14	Chicago, IL	6.9
3	15	Chicago, IL	7.6	26	14	Newark, NJ	6.9
9	16	Atlanta, GA	7.5	37	16	Indianapolis, IN	6.8
4	17	Boston-Worcester-Lawrence-Lowell-Brockton, MA-NH	7.4	28	16	Kansas City, MO-KS	6.8
8	17	Houston, TX	7.4	14	16	Orange County, CA	6.8
10	19	Dallas, TX	7.2	5	16	Philadelphia, PA-NJ	6.8
56	19	Monmouth-Ocean, NJ	7.2	42	20	Milwaukee-Waukesha, WI	6.7
16	21	Nassau-Suffolk, NY	7.0	12	20	Phoenix-Mesa, AZ	6.7
21	21	Oakland, CA	7.0	20	20	Tampa-St. Petersburg-Clearwater, FL	6.7
14	23	Orange County, CA	6.9	10	23	Dallas, TX	6.6
19	23	Seattle-Bellevue-Everett, WA	6.9	52	23	Middlesex-Somerset-Hunterdon, NJ	6.6
20	25	Tampa-St. Petersburg-Clearwater, FL	6.8	16	25	Nassau-Suffolk, NY	6.5
39	26	Norfolk-Virginia Beach-Newport News, VA-NC	6.7	30	25	New Haven-Bridgeport-Stamford-Danbury-Waterbury, CT	6.5
7	27	Detroit, MI	6.6	46	27	Salt Lake City-Ogden, UT	6.4
28	28	Kansas City, MO-KS	6.5	38	27	San Antonio, TX	6.4
30	28	New Haven-Bridgeport-Stamford-Danbury-Waterbury, CT	6.5	43	29	Charlotte-Gastonia-Rock Hill, NC-SC	6.2
55	28	West Palm Beach-Boca Raton, FL	6.5	49	29	Nashville, TN	6.2
69	31	Albany-Schenectady-Troy, NY	6.4	72	29	Ventura, CA	6.2
22	31	Pittsburgh, PA	6.4	24	32	Cleveland-Lorain-Elyria, OH	6.0
12	33	Phoenix-Mesa, AZ	6.3	63	32	Providence-Warwick-Pawtucket, RI	6.0
13	34	Minneapolis-St. Paul, MN-WI	6.1	36	34	Fort Lauderdale, FL	5.8
36	35	Fort Lauderdale, FL	6.0	61	34	Louisville, KY-IN	5.8
35	35	Sacramento, CA	6.0	18	36	Baltimore, MD	5.7
44	37	Bergen-Passaic, NJ	5.9	27	36	Portland-Vancouver, OR-WA	5.7
38	38	San Antonio, TX	5.8	9	38	Atlanta, GA	5.6
72	38	Ventura, CA	5.8	68	38	Honolulu, HI	5.6
33	40	Cincinnati, OH-KY-IN	5.7	17	38	St. Louis, MO-IL	5.6
17	40	St. Louis, MO-IL	5.7	47	41	Greensboro—Winston-Salem—High Point, NC	5.5
23	42	Miami, FL	5.6	22	41	Pittsburgh, PA	5.5
34	42	Orlando, FL	5.6	51	43	Buffalo-Niagara Falls, NY	5.4
27	42	Portland-Vancouver, OR-WA	5.6	21	43	Oakland, CA	5.4
41	45	Columbus, OH	5.4	71	45	Tulsa, OK	5.3
53	45	Hartford, CT	5.4	55	45	West Palm Beach-Boca Raton, FL	5.3
46	45	Salt Lake City-Ogden, UT	5.4	48	47	Austin-San Marcos, TX	5.2
43	48	Charlotte-Gastonia-Rock Hill, NC-SC	5.3	44	48	Bergen-Passaic, NJ	5.1
24	48	Cleveland-Lorain-Elyria, OH	5.3	33	48	Cincinnati, OH-KY-IN	5.1
57	48	Jacksonville, FL	5.3	23	48	Miami, FL	5.1
45	48	New Orleans, LA	5.3	60	48	Oklahoma City, OK	5.1
51	52	Buffalo-Niagara Falls, NY	5.2	73	48	Syracuse, NY	5.1
62	52	Richmond-Petersburg, VA	5.2	75	53	Albuquerque, NM	5.0
67	54	Birmingham, AL	5.1	7	54	Detroit, MI	4.9
65	54	Dayton-Springfield, OH	5.1	19	54	Seattle-Bellevue-Everett, WA	4.9
68	54	Honolulu, HI	5.1	1	56	Los Angeles-Long Beach, CA	4.8
70	54	Tucson, AZ	5.1	15	57	San Diego, CA	4.7
74	58	Omaha, NE-IA	5.0	6	57	Washington, DC-MD-VA-WV	4.7
42	59	Milwaukee-Waukesha, WI	4.9	45	59	New Orleans, LA	4.6
60	59	Oklahoma City, OK	4.9	8	60	Houston, TX	4.5
73	61	Syracuse, NY	4.8	66	61	Fresno, CA	4.4
71	61	Tulsa, OK	4.8	54	61	Memphis, TN-AR-MS	4.4
37	63	Indianapolis, IN	4.7	39	63	Norfolk-Virginia Beach-Newport News, VA-NC	4.2
49	64	Nashville, TN	4.5	50	63	Raleigh-Durham-Chapel Hill, NC	4.2
31	65	Fort Worth-Arlington, TX	4.4	31	65	Fort Worth-Arlington, TX	4.1
58	65	Rochester, NY	4.4	34	65	Orlando, FL	4.1
54	67	Memphis, TN-AR-MS	4.3	56	67	Monmouth-Ocean, NJ	4.0
40	68	Las Vegas, NV-AZ	4.2	40	68	Las Vegas, NV-AZ	3.6
61	68	Louisville, KY-IN	4.2	58	69	Rochester, NY	3.5
66	70	Fresno, CA	4.0	65	70	Dayton-Springfield, OH	3.4
63	71	Providence-Warwick-Pawtucket, RI	3.9	59	70	Grand Rapids-Muskegon-Holland, MI	3.4
64	72	Greenville-Spartanburg-Anderson, SC	3.7	70	72	Tucson, AZ	3.0
59	73	Grand Rapids-Muskegon-Holland, MI	3.6	11	73	Riverside-San Bernardino, CA	2.9
47	74	Greensboro—Winston-Salem—High Point, NC	3.5	64	74	Greenville-Spartanburg-Anderson, SC	2.8
11	75	Riverside-San Bernardino, CA	2.6	32	75	San Jose, CA	2.2

Note: Column numbers refer to Table C. Metropolitan Areas.

TABLE 4—75 Largest Metropolitan Areas by 2000 Population
Selected Rankings

	Per Capita Local Government Taxes, 1997				Violent Crime Rate (violent crimes known to police per 100,000 population), 2000		
Population Rank	Local Taxes Rank	Metropolitan Area	[col 181] Local Per Capita Taxes (dollars)	Population Rank	Crime Rate Rank	Metropolitan Area	[col 46] Violent Crime Rate
16	1	Nassau-Suffolk, NY	2 777	23	1	Miami, FL	1 233
2	2	New York, NY	2 657	18	2	Baltimore, MD	1 072
6	3	Washington, DC-MD-VA-WV	1 840	54	3	Memphis, TN-AR-MS	1 015
26	4	Newark, NJ	1 744	49	4	Nashville, TN	969
44	5	Bergen-Passaic, NJ	1 735	57	5	Jacksonville, FL	954
52	6	Middlesex-Somerset-Hunterdon, NJ	1 713	1	6	Los Angeles-Long Beach, CA	945
30	7	New Haven-Bridgeport-Stamford-Danbury-Waterbury, CT	1 643	75	7	Albuquerque, NM	924
3	8	Chicago, IL	1 632	20	8	Tampa-St. Petersburg-Clearwater, FL	892
56	9	Monmouth-Ocean, NJ	1 628	34	9	Orlando, FL	882
69	10	Albany-Schenectady-Troy, NY	1 562	2	10	New York, NY	854
58	11	Rochester, NY	1 561	43	11	Charlotte-Gastonia-Rock Hill, NC-SC	798
55	12	West Palm Beach-Boca Raton, FL	1 495	45	12	New Orleans, LA	773
51	13	Buffalo-Niagara Falls, NY	1 491	7	13	Detroit, MI	761
73	14	Syracuse, NY	1 483	66	14	Fresno, CA	742
29	15	San Francisco, CA	1 478	55	14	West Palm Beach-Boca Raton, FL	742
53	16	Hartford, CT	1 463	64	16	Greenville-Spartanburg-Anderson, SC	737
24	17	Cleveland-Lorain-Elyria, OH	1 437	8	17	Houston, TX	716
5	18	Philadelphia, PA-NJ	1 354	71	18	Tulsa, OK	666
10	19	Dallas, TX	1 339	70	19	Tucson, AZ	658
25	20	Denver, CO	1 337	5	20	Philadelphia, PA-NJ	654
41	21	Columbus, OH	1 324	10	21	Dallas, TX	652
42	22	Milwaukee-Waukesha, WI	1 321	28	22	Kansas City, MO-KS	627
32	23	San Jose, CA	1 281	36	23	Fort Lauderdale, FL	603
8	24	Houston, TX	1 262	21	24	Oakland, CA	587
48	25	Austin-San Marcos, TX	1 237	38	24	San Antonio, TX	587
63	26	Providence-Warwick-Pawtucket, RI	1 235	67	26	Birmingham, AL	585
19	27	Seattle-Bellevue-Everett, WA	1 224	11	27	Riverside-San Bernardino, CA	576
9	28	Atlanta, GA	1 167	9	28	Atlanta, GA	569
36	29	Fort Lauderdale, FL	1 166	26	29	Newark, NJ	560
33	30	Cincinnati, OH-KY-IN	1 162	40	30	Las Vegas, NV-AZ	559
18	31	Baltimore, MD	1 161	12	31	Phoenix-Mesa, AZ	556
4	32	Boston-Worcester-Lawrence-Lowell-Brockton, MA-NH	1 158	47	32	Greensboro—Winston-Salem—High Point, NC	551
23	33	Miami, FL	1 151	74	33	Omaha, NE-IA	547
28	34	Kansas City, MO-KS	1 147	29	34	San Francisco, CA	531
65	35	Dayton-Springfield, OH	1 146	41	35	Columbus, OH	530
21	36	Oakland, CA	1 145	60	36	Oklahoma City, OK	518
74	37	Omaha, NE-IA	1 134	35	36	Sacramento, CA	518
13	38	Minneapolis-St. Paul, MN-WI	1 113	51	38	Buffalo-Niagara Falls, NY	497
27	39	Portland-Vancouver, OR-WA	1 107	15	39	San Diego, CA	489
31	40	Fort Worth-Arlington, TX	1 101	61	40	Louisville, KY-IN	486
62	41	Richmond-Petersburg, VA	1 092	50	41	Raleigh-Durham-Chapel Hill, NC	474
45	42	New Orleans, LA	1 091	65	42	Dayton-Springfield, OH	470
37	43	Indianapolis, IN	1 086	31	43	Fort Worth-Arlington, TX	469
22	44	Pittsburgh, PA	1 050	39	44	Norfolk-Virginia Beach-Newport News, VA-NC	464
34	45	Orlando, FL	1 024	6	44	Washington, DC-MD-VA-WV	464
39	46	Norfolk-Virginia Beach-Newport News, VA-NC	1 003	4	46	Boston-Worcester-Lawrence-Lowell-Brockton, MA-NH	462
17	46	St. Louis, MO-IL	1 003	62	47	Richmond-Petersburg, VA	458
49	48	Nashville, TN	991	42	48	Milwaukee-Waukesha, WI	449
67	49	Birmingham, AL	934	27	49	Portland-Vancouver, OR-WA	448
40	50	Las Vegas, NV-AZ	929	32	50	San Jose, CA	429
20	51	Tampa-St. Petersburg-Clearwater, FL	919	59	51	Grand Rapids-Muskegon-Holland, MI	402
14	52	Orange County, CA	895	19	52	Seattle-Bellevue-Everett, WA	371
1	53	Los Angeles-Long Beach, CA	890	30	53	New Haven-Bridgeport-Stamford-Danbury-Waterbury, CT	370
7	54	Detroit, MI	871	48	54	Austin-San Marcos, TX	369
72	55	Ventura, CA	865	13	55	Minneapolis-St. Paul, MN-WI	354
12	56	Phoenix-Mesa, AZ	864	25	56	Denver, CO	340
70	57	Tucson, AZ	860	33	57	Cincinnati, OH-KY-IN	336
38	58	San Antonio, TX	850	22	58	Pittsburgh, PA	329
47	59	Greensboro—Winston-Salem—High Point, NC	840	53	59	Hartford, CT	327
50	60	Raleigh-Durham-Chapel Hill, NC	838	73	60	Syracuse, NY	326
43	61	Charlotte-Gastonia-Rock Hill, NC-SC	836	69	61	Albany-Schenectady-Troy, NY	317
54	62	Memphis, TN-AR-MS	834	46	62	Salt Lake City-Ogden, UT	316
35	63	Sacramento, CA	831	14	63	Orange County, CA	302
61	64	Louisville, KY-IN	808	63	64	Providence-Warwick-Pawtucket, RI	298
57	65	Jacksonville, FL	796	72	65	Ventura, CA	280
46	66	Salt Lake City-Ogden, UT	771	68	66	Honolulu, HI	263
15	67	San Diego, CA	766	44	67	Bergen-Passaic, NJ	261
71	68	Tulsa, OK	746	58	68	Rochester, NY	231
60	69	Oklahoma City, OK	735	56	69	Monmouth-Ocean, NJ	189
11	70	Riverside-San Bernardino, CA	705	52	70	Middlesex-Somerset-Hunterdon, NJ	188
59	71	Grand Rapids-Muskegon-Holland, MI	683	3		Chicago, IL	NA
64	72	Greenville-Spartanburg-Anderson, SC	631	24		Cleveland-Lorain-Elyria, OH	NA
66	73	Fresno, CA	630	37		Indianapolis, IN	NA
68	74	Honolulu, HI	606	16		Nassau-Suffolk, NY	NA
75	75	Albuquerque, NM	578	17		St. Louis, MO-IL	NA

Note: Column numbers refer to Table C. Metropolitan Areas.

TABLE 5—75 Metropolitan Areas with Highest Agricultural Sales, 1997
Selected Rankings

Value of Agricultural Sales, 1997			Land in Farms, 1997				
Value of Sales Rank	Metropolitan Area	[col 125] Sales (Mil Dollars)	Value of Sales Rank	Land in Farms Rank	Metropolitan Area	[col 117] Land in Farms (1000 acres)	[col 117] & col 1] Farm Land as % of Total Land Area
1	Fresno, CA	3 400	2	1	Bakersfield, CA	2 851	54.7
2	Bakersfield, CA	1 969	1	2	Fresno, CA	2 523	48.6
3	Visalia-Tulare-Porterville, CA	1 921	35	3	Kansas City, MO-KS	2 256	65.2
4	Salinas, CA	1 750	25	4	St. Louis, MO-IL	2 159	52.7
5	Riverside-San Bernardino, CA	1 665	10	5	Phoenix-Mesa, AZ	2 012	21.6
6	Greeley, CO	1 287	6	6	Greeley, CO	1 914	74.9
7	Merced, CA	1 273	17	7	Minneapolis-St. Paul, MN-WI	1 906	49.1
8	Modesto, CA	1 209	52	8	Grand Forks, ND-MN	1 827	83.7
9	Stockton-Lodi, CA	1 180	12	9	Yakima, WA	1 683	61.2
10	Phoenix-Mesa, AZ	1 028	57	10	Fargo-Moorhead, ND-MN	1 649	91.6
11	West Palm Beach-Boca Raton, FL	873	59	11	Wichita, KS	1 620	85.2
12	Yakima, WA	873	16	12	Chicago, IL	1 590	49.0
13	Ventura, CA	846	4	13	Salinas, CA	1 544	72.6
14	Lancaster, PA	767	5	14	Riverside-San Bernardino, CA	1 433	8.2
15	Portland-Vancouver, OR-WA	734	29	15	Indianapolis, IN	1 423	63.1
16	Chicago, IL	712	48	16	Washington, DC-MD-VA-WV	1 381	33.1
17	Minneapolis-St. Paul, MN-WI	701	3	17	Visalia-Tulare-Porterville, CA	1 310	42.4
18	Fayetteville-Springdale-Rogers, AR	697	55	18	San Luis Obispo-Atascadero-Paso Robles, CA	1 302	61.5
19	Philadelphia, PA-NJ	690	36	19	Omaha, NE-IA	1 271	80.2
20	Santa Barbara-Santa Maria-Lompoc, CA	660	38	20	Columbus, OH	1 204	59.8
21	Grand Rapids-Muskegon-Holland, MI	652	39	21	Fort Wayne, IN	1 193	76.1
22	San Diego, CA	633	23	22	Richland-Kennewick-Pasco, WA	1 176	62.4
23	Richland-Kennewick-Pasco, WA	633	24	23	Lexington, KY	1 058	86.1
24	Lexington, KY	556	27	24	Orlando, FL	1 008	45.1
25	St. Louis, MO-IL	555	30	25	Rochester, NY	968	44.1
26	Salem, OR	529	56	26	Peoria-Pekin, IL	895	77.8
27	Orlando, FL	525	7	27	Merced, CA	882	71.4
28	Yuma, AZ	522	51	28	Davenport-Moline-Rock Island, IA-IL	852	77.9
29	Indianapolis, IN	504	72	29	Des Moines, IA	849	76.7
30	Rochester, NY	478	43	30	St. Cloud, MN	822	73.3
31	Raleigh-Durham-Chapel Hill, NC	465	20	31	Santa Barbara-Santa Maria-Lompoc, CA	817	46.6
32	Santa Rosa, CA	464	9	32	Stockton-Lodi, CA	809	90.3
33	Atlanta, GA	455	45	33	Greensboro—Winston-Salem—High Point, NC	800	32.2
34	Tampa-St. Petersburg-Clearwater, FL	452	8	34	Modesto, CA	733	76.6
35	Kansas City, MO-KS	451	65	35	Rockford, IL	716	71.9
36	Omaha, NE-IA	451	58	36	Detroit, MI	704	28.2
37	Charlotte-Gastonia-Rock Hill, NC-SC	450	62	37	Syracuse, NY	687	34.8
38	Columbus, OH	435	15	38	Portland-Vancouver, OR-WA	670	20.8
39	Fort Wayne, IN	420	31	39	Raleigh-Durham-Chapel Hill, NC	669	29.9
40	Miami, FL	417	21	40	Grand Rapids-Muskegon-Holland, MI	667	37.8
41	Boise City, ID	405	33	41	Atlanta, GA	640	16.3
42	Vallejo-Fairfield-Napa, CA	400	18	42	Fayetteville-Springdale-Rogers, AR	631	54.9
43	St. Cloud, MN	392	71	43	Lakeland-Winter Haven, FL	621	51.7
44	Yuba City, CA	386	11	44	West Palm Beach-Boca Raton, FL	605	46.4
45	Greensboro—Winston-Salem—High Point, NC	370	37	45	Charlotte-Gastonia-Rock Hill, NC-SC	591	27.3
46	Harrisburg-Lebanon-Carlisle, PA	368	41	46	Boise City, ID	586	55.6
47	Boston-Worcester-Lawrence-Lowell-Brockton, MA-NH	348	75	47	Toledo, OH	581	66.5
48	Washington, DC-MD-VA-WV	346	42	48	Vallejo-Fairfield-Napa, CA	575	56.8
49	Yolo, CA	345	69	49	Baltimore, MD	573	34.3
50	Goldsboro, NC	337	32	50	Santa Rosa, CA	571	56.6
51	Davenport-Moline-Rock Island, IA-IL	324	19	51	Philadelphia, PA-NJ	569	23.0
52	Grand Forks, ND-MN	323	67	52	Kalamazoo-Battle Creek, MI	567	47.1
53	Fort Pierce-Port St. Lucie, FL	318	63	53	Appleton-Oshkosh-Neenah, WI	564	63.0
54	Rocky Mount, NC	317	44	54	Yuba City, CA	557	70.5
55	San Luis Obispo-Atascadero-Paso Robles, CA	313	66	55	Sacramento, CA	550	21.0
56	Peoria-Pekin, IL	308	49	56	Yolo, CA	537	82.8
57	Fargo-Moorhead, ND-MN	307	61	57	Madison, WI	513	66.6
58	Detroit, MI	289	26	58	Salem, OR	478	38.8
59	Wichita, KS	287	22	59	San Diego, CA	475	17.6
60	Chico-Paradise, CA	286	70	60	Cleveland-Lorain-Elyria, OH	467	26.9
61	Madison, WI	285	34	61	Tampa-St. Petersburg-Clearwater, FL	464	28.4
62	Syracuse, NY	284	46	62	Harrisburg-Lebanon-Carlisle, PA	455	35.7
63	Appleton-Oshkosh-Neenah, WI	280	53	63	Fort Pierce-Port St. Lucie, FL	411	56.9
64	Naples, FL	277	60	64	Chico-Paradise, CA	404	38.5
65	Rockford, IL	272	68	65	Sarasota-Bradenton, FL	397	47.2
66	Sacramento, CA	268	14	66	Lancaster, PA	392	64.5
67	Kalamazoo-Battle Creek, MI	267	47	67	Boston-Worcester-Lawrence-Lowell-Brockton, MA-NH	379	9.2
68	Sarasota-Bradenton, FL	264	54	68	Rocky Mount, NC	347	51.9
69	Baltimore, MD	262	13	69	Ventura, CA	346	29.3
70	Cleveland-Lorain-Elyria, OH	261	64	70	Naples, FL	277	21.4
71	Lakeland-Winter Haven, FL	253	28	71	Yuma, AZ	238	6.7
72	Des Moines, IA	248	50	72	Goldsboro, NC	229	64.7
73	Reading, PA	248	73	73	Reading, PA	222	40.4
74	Santa Cruz-Watsonville, CA	248	40	74	Miami, FL	85	6.8
75	Toledo, OH	245	74	75	Santa Cruz-Watsonville, CA	71	24.9

Note: Column numbers refer to Table C. Metropolitan Areas.

Value of Average Land and Buildings Per Acre, 1997				Number of Farms, 1997			
Value of Sales Rank	Value per Acre Rank	Metropolitan Area	[col 123] Value per acre (1,000 acres)	Value of Sales Rank	Number of Farms Rank	Metropolitan Area	[col 113] Number of Farms
40	1	Miami, FL	8 047	17	1	Minneapolis-St. Paul, MN-WI	10 460
13	2	Ventura, CA	6 860	35	2	Kansas City, MO-KS	9 774
74	3	Santa Cruz-Watsonville, CA	6 234	15	3	Portland-Vancouver, OR-WA	9 677
42	4	Vallejo-Fairfield-Napa, CA	5 909	25	4	St. Louis, MO-IL	8 702
15	5	Portland-Vancouver, OR-WA	5 804	1	5	Fresno, CA	8 265
47	6	Boston-Worcester-Lawrence-Lowell-Brockton, MA-NH	5 771	48	6	Washington, DC-MD-VA-WV	7 955
14	7	Lancaster, PA	5 578	45	7	Greensboro—Winston-Salem—High Point, NC	6 934
22	8	San Diego, CA	5 504	24	8	Lexington, KY	6 229
19	9	Philadelphia, PA-NJ	5 254	22	9	San Diego, CA	5 925
32	10	Santa Rosa, CA	5 211	33	10	Atlanta, GA	5 572
9	11	Stockton-Lodi, CA	4 667	3	11	Visalia-Tulare-Porterville, CA	5 446
8	12	Modesto, CA	4 508	39	12	Fort Wayne, IN	5 416
28	13	Yuma, AZ	4 496	29	13	Indianapolis, IN	5 113
69	14	Baltimore, MD	3 900	19	14	Philadelphia, PA-NJ	5 077
44	15	Yuba City, CA	3 882	16	15	Chicago, IL	4 878
26	16	Salem, OR	3 877	18	16	Fayetteville-Springdale-Rogers, AR	4 799
34	17	Tampa-St. Petersburg-Clearwater, FL	3 788	38	17	Columbus, OH	4 646
48	18	Washington, DC-MD-VA-WV	3 718	14	18	Lancaster, PA	4 556
16	19	Chicago, IL	3 681	5	19	Riverside-San Bernardino, CA	4 503
73	20	Reading, PA	3 673	47	20	Boston-Worcester-Lawrence-Lowell-Brockton, MA-NH	4 421
60	21	Chico-Paradise, CA	3 589	58	21	Detroit, MI	4 388
33	22	Atlanta, GA	3 514	37	22	Charlotte-Gastonia-Rock Hill, NC-SC	4 253
3	23	Visalia-Tulare-Porterville, CA	3 444	21	23	Grand Rapids-Muskegon-Holland, MI	4 175
11	24	West Palm Beach-Boca Raton, FL	3 404	34	24	Tampa-St. Petersburg-Clearwater, FL	4 151
1	25	Fresno, CA	3 386	31	25	Raleigh-Durham-Chapel Hill, NC	4 112
66	26	Sacramento, CA	3 336	8	26	Modesto, CA	4 009
7	27	Merced, CA	3 149	9	27	Stockton-Lodi, CA	3 862
70	28	Cleveland-Lorain-Elyria, OH	3 103	43	28	St. Cloud, MN	3 816
46	29	Harrisburg-Lebanon-Carlisle, PA	3 070	26	29	Salem, OR	3 693
37	30	Charlotte-Gastonia-Rock Hill, NC-SC	2 803	70	30	Cleveland-Lorain-Elyria, OH	3 675
58	31	Detroit, MI	2 790	69	31	Baltimore, MD	3 622
53	32	Fort Pierce-Port St. Lucie, FL	2 748	30	32	Rochester, NY	3 609
49	33	Yolo, CA	2 732	36	33	Omaha, NE-IA	3 446
45	34	Greensboro—Winston-Salem—High Point, NC	2 731	59	34	Wichita, KS	3 430
20	35	Santa Barbara-Santa Maria-Lompoc, CA	2 716	12	35	Yakima, WA	3 365
29	36	Indianapolis, IN	2 714	41	36	Boise City, ID	3 119
31	37	Raleigh-Durham-Chapel Hill, NC	2 712	46	37	Harrisburg-Lebanon-Carlisle, PA	3 098
56	38	Peoria-Pekin, IL	2 621	27	38	Orlando, FL	3 080
65	39	Rockford, IL	2 524	66	39	Sacramento, CA	3 048
24	40	Lexington, KY	2 469	6	40	Greeley, CO	2 959
68	41	Sarasota-Bradenton, FL	2 465	72	41	Des Moines, IA	2 932
21	42	Grand Rapids-Muskegon-Holland, MI	2 416	63	42	Appleton-Oshkosh-Neenah, WI	2 849
38	43	Columbus, OH	2 392	67	43	Kalamazoo-Battle Creek, MI	2 840
18	44	Fayetteville-Springdale-Rogers, AR	2 380	7	44	Merced, CA	2 831
4	45	Salinas, CA	2 358	51	45	Davenport-Moline-Rock Island, IA-IL	2 761
51	46	Davenport-Moline-Rock Island, IA-IL	2 324	56	46	Peoria-Pekin, IL	2 756
75	47	Toledo, OH	2 275	32	47	Santa Rosa, CA	2 745
39	48	Fort Wayne, IN	2 188	62	48	Syracuse, NY	2 745
71	49	Lakeland-Winter Haven, FL	2 110	61	49	Madison, WI	2 595
41	50	Boise City, ID	2 093	71	50	Lakeland-Winter Haven, FL	2 464
5	51	Riverside-San Bernardino, CA	2 087	65	51	Rockford, IL	2 276
27	52	Orlando, FL	2 037	13	52	Ventura, CA	2 214
50	53	Goldsboro, NC	2 025	75	53	Toledo, OH	2 194
72	54	Des Moines, IA	2 005	10	54	Phoenix-Mesa, AZ	2 184
17	55	Minneapolis-St. Paul, MN-WI	1 977	52	55	Grand Forks, ND-MN	2 134
25	56	St. Louis, MO-IL	1 951	42	56	Vallejo-Fairfield-Napa, CA	2 113
36	57	Omaha, NE-IA	1 943	44	57	Yuba City, CA	2 020
61	58	Madison, WI	1 853	2	58	Bakersfield, CA	1 997
23	59	Richland-Kennewick-Pasco, WA	1 833	60	59	Chico-Paradise, CA	1 942
64	60	Naples, FL	1 796	23	60	Richland-Kennewick-Pasco, WA	1 926
54	61	Rocky Mount, NC	1 746	55	61	San Luis Obispo-Atascadero-Paso Robles, CA	1 916
67	62	Kalamazoo-Battle Creek, MI	1 658	57	62	Fargo-Moorhead, ND-MN	1 806
2	63	Bakersfield, CA	1 605	73	63	Reading, PA	1 586
35	64	Kansas City, MO-KS	1 601	40	64	Miami, FL	1 576
55	65	San Luis Obispo-Atascadero-Paso Robles, CA	1 591	20	65	Santa Barbara-Santa Maria-Lompoc, CA	1 451
63	66	Appleton-Oshkosh-Neenah, WI	1 556	4	66	Salinas, CA	1 209
10	67	Phoenix-Mesa, AZ	1 529	68	67	Sarasota-Bradenton, FL	1 012
30	68	Rochester, NY	1 339	49	68	Yolo, CA	923
12	69	Yakima, WA	1 220	11	69	West Palm Beach-Boca Raton, FL	855
62	70	Syracuse, NY	1 099	50	70	Goldsboro, NC	827
43	71	St. Cloud, MN	1 075	53	71	Fort Pierce-Port St. Lucie, FL	805
59	72	Wichita, KS	976	54	72	Rocky Mount, NC	787
57	73	Fargo-Moorhead, ND-MN	900	74	73	Santa Cruz-Watsonville, CA	722
6	74	Greeley, CO	807	28	74	Yuma, AZ	465
52	75	Grand Forks, ND-MN	780	64	75	Naples, FL	235

Note: Column numbers refer to Table C. Metropolitan Areas.

TABLE 6—75 Largest Cities by 2000 Population
Selected Rankings

Total Persons, 2000			Total Land Area (square kilometers), 2000				Population Density (per square kilometer), 2000			
Popu-lation Rank	City	[col 2] Population	Popu-lation Rank	Land Area Rank	City	[col 1] Land Area	Popu-lation Rank	Density Rank	City	[col 4] Density
1	New York City, NY	8 008 278	65	1	Anchorage city, AK	4 395.8	1	1	New York City, NY	10 194
2	Los Angeles city, CA	3 694 820	14	2	Jacksonville city, FL	1 962.4	13	2	San Francisco city, CA	6 425
3	Chicago city, IL	2 896 016	29	3	Oklahoma City, OK	1 572.1	72	3	Jersey City, NJ	6 219
4	Houston city, TX	1 953 631	4	4	Houston city, TX	1 500.7	3	4	Chicago city, IL	4 923
5	Philadelphia city, PA	1 517 550	22	5	Nashville-Davidson consolidated city, TN	1 300.9	51	5	Santa Ana city, CA	4 808
6	Phoenix city, AZ	1 321 045	6	6	Phoenix city, AZ	1 229.9	20	6	Boston city, MA	4 698
7	San Diego city, CA	1 223 400	2	7	Los Angeles city, CA	1 214.9	75	7	Hialeah, FL	4 547
8	Dallas city, TX	1 188 580	9	8	San Antonio city, TX	1 055.6	63	8	Newark city, NJ	4 441
9	San Antonio city, TX	1 144 646	12	9	Indianapolis consolidated city, IN	949.2	5	9	Philadelphia city, PA	4 337
10	Detroit city, MI	951 270	8	10	Dallas city, TX	887.2	47	10	Miami city, FL	3 923
11	San Jose city, CA	894 943	7	11	San Diego city, CA	840.0	21	11	Washington city, DC	3 598
12	Indianapolis consolidated city, IN	791 926	36	12	Kansas City, MO	812.1	34	12	Long Beach city, CA	3 534
13	San Francisco city, CA	776 733	1	13	New York city, NY	785.6	17	13	Baltimore city, MD	3 111
14	Jacksonville city, FL	735 617	27	14	Fort Worth city, TX	757.7	2	14	Los Angeles city, CA	3 041
15	Columbus city, OH	711 470	64	15	Lexington-Fayette, KY	736.9	58	15	Buffalo city, NY	2 782
16	Austin city, TX	656 562	18	16	Memphis city, TN	723.4	41	16	Oakland city, CA	2 751
17	Baltimore city, MD	651 154	16	17	Austin city, TX	651.4	45	17	Minneapolis city, MN	2 691
18	Memphis city, TN	650 100	23	18	El Paso city, TX	645.1	10	18	Detroit city, MI	2 647
19	Milwaukee city, WI	596 974	38	19	Virginia Beach city, VA	643.1	24	19	Seattle city, WA	2 594
20	Boston city, MA	589 141	26	20	Charlotte city, NC	627.5	55	20	Anaheim city, CA	2 587
21	Washington city, DC	572 059	3	21	Chicago city, IL	588.3	19	21	Milwaukee city, WI	2 399
22	Nashville-Davidson consolidated city, TN	569 891	15	22	Columbus city, OH	544.6	33	22	Cleveland city, OH	2 381
23	El Paso city, TX	563 662	30	23	Tucson city, AZ	504.2	52	23	Pittsburgh city, PA	2 323
24	Seattle city, WA	563 374	48	24	Colorado Springs city, CO	481.1	49	24	St. Louis city, MO	2 171
25	Denver city, CO	554 636	43	25	Tulsa city, OK	473.1	59	25	St. Paul city, MN	2 101
26	Charlotte city, NC	540 828	35	26	Albuquerque city, NM	467.9	11	26	San Jose city, CA	1 976
27	Fort Worth city, TX	534 694	31	27	New Orleans city, LA	467.6	70	27	Stockton city, CA	1 720
28	Portland city, OR	529 121	11	28	San Jose city, CA	452.9	73	28	Norfolk city, VA	1 684
29	Oklahoma City, OK	506 132	60	29	Corpus Christi city, TX	400.5	46	29	Honolulu CDP, HI	1 674
30	Tucson city, AZ	486 699	25	30	Denver city, CO	397.2	54	30	Cincinnati city, OH	1 641
31	New Orleans city, LA	484 674	71	31	Birmingham city, AL	388.3	32	31	Las Vegas city, NV	1 630
32	Las Vegas city, NV	478 434	61	32	Aurora city, CO	369.1	40	32	Sacramento city, CA	1 618
33	Cleveland city, OH	478 403	10	33	Detroit city, MI	359.4	68	33	St. Petersburg city, FL	1 608
34	Long Beach city, CA	461 522	50	34	Wichita city, KS	351.6	66	34	Louisville city, KY	1 593
35	Albuquerque city, NM	448 607	5	35	Philadelphia city, PA	349.9	37	35	Fresno city, CA	1 582
36	Kansas City, MO	441 545	28	36	Portland city, OR	347.9	28	36	Portland city, OR	1 521
37	Fresno city, CA	427 652	39	37	Atlanta city, GA	341.2	56	37	Toledo city, OH	1 502
38	Virginia Beach city, VA	425 257	42	38	Mesa city, AZ	323.7	7	38	San Diego city, CA	1 456
39	Atlanta city, GA	416 474	44	39	Omaha city, NE	299.7	25	39	Denver city, CO	1 396
40	Sacramento city, CA	407 018	62	40	Raleigh city, NC	296.8	53	40	Arlington city, TX	1 342
41	Oakland city, CA	399 484	32	41	Las Vegas city, NV	293.5	8	41	Dallas city, TX	1 340
42	Mesa city, AZ	396 375	69	42	Bakersfield, CA	292.9	15	42	Columbus city, OH	1 306
43	Tulsa city, OK	393 049	57	43	Tampa city, FL	290.2	4	43	Houston city, TX	1 302
44	Omaha city, NE	390 007	37	44	Fresno city, CA	270.3	44	44	Omaha city, NE	1 301
45	Minneapolis city, MN	382 618	40	45	Sacramento city, CA	251.6	67	45	Riverside city, CA	1 261
46	Honolulu CDP, HI	371 657	19	46	Milwaukee city, WI	248.8	42	46	Mesa city, AZ	1 225
47	Miami city, FL	362 470	53	47	Arlington city, TX	248.2	39	47	Atlanta city, GA	1 221
48	Colorado Springs city, CO	360 890	46	48	Honolulu CDP, HI	222.0	74	48	Baton Rouge, LA	1 145
49	St. Louis city, MO	348 189	24	49	Seattle city, WA	217.2	9	49	San Antonio city, TX	1 084
50	Wichita city, KS	344 284	17	50	Baltimore city, MD	209.3	6	50	Phoenix city, AZ	1 074
51	Santa Ana city, CA	337 977	56	51	Toledo city, OH	208.8	57	51	Tampa city, FL	1 046
52	Pittsburgh city, PA	334 563	67	52	Riverside city, CA	202.3	31	52	New Orleans city, LA	1 037
53	Arlington city, TX	332 969	54	53	Cincinnati city, OH	201.9	16	53	Austin city, TX	1 008
54	Cincinnati city, OH	331 285	33	54	Cleveland city, OH	200.9	50	54	Wichita city, KS	979
55	Anaheim city, CA	328 014	74	55	Baton Rouge, LA	199.0	30	55	Tucson city, AZ	965
56	Toledo city, OH	313 619	66	56	Louisville city, KY	160.9	35	56	Albuquerque city, NM	959
57	Tampa city, FL	303 447	49	57	St. Louis city, MO	160.4	62	57	Raleigh city, NC	930
58	Buffalo city, NY	292 648	21	58	Washington city, DC	159.0	18	58	Memphis city, TN	899
59	St. Paul city, MN	287 151	68	59	St. Petersburg city, FL	154.4	23	59	El Paso city, TX	874
60	Corpus Christi city, TX	277 454	41	60	Oakland city, CA	145.2	26	60	Charlotte city, NC	862
61	Aurora city, CO	276 393	52	61	Pittsburgh city, PA	144.0	69	61	Bakersfield, CA	844
62	Raleigh city, NC	276 093	45	62	Minneapolis city, MN	142.2	12	62	Indianapolis consolidated city, IN	834
63	Newark city, NJ	273 546	70	63	Stockton city, CA	141.7	43	63	Tulsa city, OK	831
64	Lexington-Fayette, KY	260 512	73	64	Norfolk city, VA	139.2	48	64	Colorado Springs city, CO	750
65	Anchorage city, AK	260 283	59	65	St. Paul city, MN	136.7	61	65	Aurora city, CO	749
66	Louisville city, KY	256 231	34	66	Long Beach city, CA	130.6	27	66	Fort Worth city, TX	706
67	Riverside city, CA	255 166	55	67	Anaheim city, CA	126.8	60	67	Corpus Christi city, TX	693
68	St. Petersburg city, FL	248 232	20	68	Boston city, MA	125.4	38	68	Virginia Beach city, VA	661
69	Bakersfield, CA	247 057	13	69	San Francisco city, CA	120.9	71	69	Birmingham city, AL	625
70	Stockton city, CA	243 771	58	70	Buffalo city, NY	105.2	36	70	Kansas City, MO	544
71	Birmingham city, AL	242 820	47	71	Miami city, FL	92.4	22	71	Nashville-Davidson consolidated city, TN	438
72	Jersey City, NJ	240 055	51	72	Santa Ana city, CA	70.3	14	72	Jacksonville city, FL	375
73	Norfolk city, VA	234 403	63	73	Newark city, NJ	61.6	64	73	Lexington-Fayette, KY	354
74	Baton Rouge, LA	227 818	75	74	Hialeah, FL	49.8	29	74	Oklahoma City, OK	322
75	Hialeah, FL	226 419	72	75	Jersey City, NJ	38.6	65	75	Anchorage city, AK	59

Note: Column numbers refer to Table D. Cities.

TABLE 6—75 Largest Cities by 2000 Population
Selected Rankings

Percent Population Change, 1990-2000				Percent Non-Hispanic White, 2000				Percent Black, 2000			
Population Rank	Percent Change Rank	City	[col 6] Percent Change	Population Rank	White Rank	City	[col 9] Percent Non-Hispanic White	Population Rank	Black Rank	City	[col 10] Percent Black
32	1	Las Vegas city, NV	85.3	32	1	Lexington-Fayette, KY	79.1	10	1	Detroit city, MI	82.8
69	2	Bakersfield, CA	40.2	26	2	Portland city, OR	75.5	71	2	Birmingham city, AL	74.0
16	3	Austin city, TX	39.1	69	3	Omaha city, NE	75.4	31	3	New Orleans city, LA	67.9
42	4	Mesa city, AZ	37.1	62	4	Colorado Springs city, CO	75.3	17	4	Baltimore city, MD	65.2
6	5	Phoenix city, AZ	34.2	16	5	Mesa city, AZ	73.2	39	5	Atlanta city, GA	62.1
62	6	Raleigh city, NC	30.2	42	6	Wichita city, KS	71.7	18	6	Memphis city, TN	61.9
26	7	Charlotte city, NC	28.9	28	7	Anchorage city, AK	69.9	21	7	Washington city, DC	61.3
48	8	Colorado Springs city, CO	28.7	48	8	Virginia Beach city, VA	69.5	63	8	Newark city, NJ	55.0
53	9	Arlington city, TX	27.2	35	9	St. Petersburg city, FL	68.6	33	9	Cleveland city, OH	52.1
61	10	Aurora city, CO	24.4	64	10	Seattle city, WA	67.9	49	9	St. Louis city, MO	52.1
55	11	Anaheim city, CA	23.1	9	11	Toledo city, OH	67.8	74	11	Baton Rouge, LA	50.4
37	12	Fresno city, CA	20.8	15	12	Indianapolis consolidated city, IN	67.7	73	12	Norfolk city, VA	45.3
75	13	Hialeah, FL	20.4	6	13	Tulsa city, OK	67.1	5	13	Philadelphia city, PA	44.3
27	14	Fort Worth city, TX	19.5	75	14	Columbus city, OH	66.9	54	14	Cincinnati city, OH	44.0
4	15	Houston city, TX	19.3	53	14	Pittsburgh city, PA	66.9	58	15	Buffalo city, NY	38.6
9	16	San Antonio city, TX	19.3	44	16	Nashville-Davidson consolidated city, TN	65.1	19	15	Milwaukee city, WI	38.6
25	17	Denver city, CO	18.6	37	17	Oklahoma City, OK	64.7	41	17	Oakland city, CA	37.6
30	18	Tucson city, AZ	18.3	23	18	St. Paul city, MN	64.0	3	18	Chicago city, IL	37.4
8	19	Dallas city, TX	18.0	30	19	Minneapolis city, MN	62.5	66	19	Louisville city, KY	33.9
35	20	Albuquerque city, NM	16.5	70	20	Jacksonville city, FL	62.2	26	20	Charlotte city, NC	33.4
64	21	Lexington-Fayette, KY	15.6	50	21	Louisville city, KY	61.9	36	21	Kansas City, MO	32.3
70	21	Stockton city, CA	15.6	22	22	Raleigh city, NC	60.3	72	22	Jersey City, NJ	30.0
65	23	Anchorage city, AK	15.0	38	23	Arlington city, TX	59.6	14	23	Jacksonville city, FL	29.7
51	23	Santa Ana city, CA	15.0	12	24	Aurora city, CO	59.2	62	24	Raleigh city, NC	28.6
11	25	San Jose city, CA	14.4	61	25	Las Vegas city, NV	58.0	1	25	New York City, NY	28.4
28	26	Portland city, OR	14.1	18	26	Kansas City, MO	57.6	52	26	Pittsburgh city, PA	28.1
29	27	Oklahoma City, OK	13.8	46	27	Phoenix city, AZ	55.8	20	27	Boston city, MA	27.7
44	27	Omaha city, NE	13.8	7	28	Charlotte city, NC	55.1	57	28	Tampa city, FL	27.2
50	29	Wichita city, KS	13.2	11	29	Tucson city, AZ	54.2	22	29	Nashville-Davidson consolidated city, TN	26.6
67	30	Riverside city, CA	12.6	24	30	Austin city, TX	52.9	8	30	Dallas city, TX	26.5
15	31	Columbus city, OH	12.4	27	31	Cincinnati city, OH	52.5	12	31	Indianapolis consolidated city, IN	26.1
22	32	Nashville-Davidson consolidated city, TN	11.6	14	32	Denver city, CO	51.9	15	32	Columbus city, OH	26.0
40	33	Sacramento city, CA	10.2	4	33	Buffalo city, NY	51.8	4	33	Houston city, TX	25.9
7	33	San Diego city, CA	10.2	60	34	Bakersfield, CA	51.1	56	34	Toledo city, OH	24.8
23	35	El Paso city, TX	9.4	29	35	Tampa city, FL	51.0	47	35	Miami city, FL	24.2
1	35	New York City, NY	9.4	67	36	Albuquerque city, NM	49.9	68	36	St. Petersburg city, FL	23.2
14	37	Jacksonville city, FL	9.3	55	37	Boston city, MA	49.5	27	37	Fort Worth city, TX	20.8
24	38	Seattle city, WA	9.1	1	38	San Diego city, CA	49.4	45	38	Minneapolis city, MN	20.5
57	39	Tampa city, FL	8.4	40	39	Norfolk city, VA	47.0	38	39	Virginia Beach city, VA	20.0
38	40	Virginia Beach city, VA	8.2	65	40	Fort Worth city, TX	45.8	40	40	Sacramento city, CA	17.3
60	41	Corpus Christi city, TX	7.8	13	41	Riverside city, CA	45.6	43	41	Tulsa city, OK	16.5
34	42	Long Beach city, CA	7.5	25	42	Milwaukee city, WI	45.4	29	42	Oklahoma City, OK	16.4
41	43	Oakland city, CA	7.3	57	43	Baton Rouge, LA	44.7	34	43	Long Beach city, CA	16.0
13	43	San Francisco city, CA	7.3	8	44	San Francisco city, CA	43.6	61	44	Aurora city, CO	15.0
43	45	Tulsa city, OK	7.0	72	45	St. Louis city, MO	42.9	53	45	Arlington city, TX	14.5
12	46	Indianapolis consolidated city, IN	6.7	2	46	Philadelphia city, PA	42.5	44	46	Omaha city, NE	14.2
2	47	Los Angeles city, CA	6.0	47	47	Sacramento city, CA	40.5	64	47	Lexington-Fayette, KY	14.1
39	48	Atlanta city, GA	5.7	39	48	Cleveland city, OH	38.8	59	48	St. Paul city, MN	13.4
59	49	St. Paul city, MN	5.5	3	49	Corpus Christi city, TX	38.5	70	49	Stockton city, CA	12.5
18	50	Memphis city, TN	5.1	41	50	Fresno city, CA	37.3	50	50	Wichita city, KS	12.4
72	51	Jersey City, NJ	5.0	43	51	San Jose city, CA	36.0	25	51	Denver city, CO	12.1
3	52	Chicago city, IL	4.0	34	52	Anaheim city, CA	35.9	2	52	Los Angeles city, CA	12.0
45	53	Minneapolis city, MN	3.9	20	53	New York City, NY	35.0	32	53	Las Vegas city, NV	11.3
74	54	Baton Rouge, LA	3.8	74	54	Dallas city, TX	34.6	16	54	Austin city, TX	10.7
68	55	St. Petersburg city, FL	3.3	36	55	Memphis city, TN	33.3	69	55	Bakersfield, CA	10.0
20	56	Boston city, MA	2.6	51	56	Long Beach city, CA	33.1	24	56	Seattle city, WA	9.9
36	57	Kansas City, MO	1.5	68	57	Stockton city, CA	32.2	37	57	Fresno city, CA	9.2
47	58	Miami city, FL	1.1	17	58	San Antonio city, TX	31.8	7	58	San Diego city, CA	8.9
63	59	Newark city, NJ	-0.6	21	59	Atlanta city, GA	31.3	13	59	San Francisco city, CA	8.6
46	60	Honolulu CDP, HI	-1.4	59	59	Chicago city, IL	31.3	67	60	Riverside city, CA	8.4
31	61	New Orleans city, LA	-2.5	56	61	Baltimore city, MD	31.0	28	61	Portland city, OR	7.9
5	62	Philadelphia city, PA	-4.3	54	62	Houston city, TX	30.8	48	62	Colorado Springs city, CO	7.8
66	63	Louisville city, KY	-4.9	5	63	Los Angeles city, CA	29.7	9	63	San Antonio city, TX	7.4
19	64	Milwaukee city, WI	-5.0	19	64	Washington city, DC	27.8	65	64	Anchorage city, AK	7.2
33	65	Cleveland city, OH	-5.4	66	65	New Orleans city, LA	26.6	6	65	Phoenix city, AZ	5.8
21	66	Washington city, DC	-5.7	63	66	Jersey City, NJ	23.6	60	66	Corpus Christi city, TX	5.1
56	67	Toledo city, OH	-5.8	45	67	Birmingham city, AL	23.5	30	66	Tucson city, AZ	5.1
10	68	Detroit city, MI	-7.5	33	67	Oakland city, CA	23.5	11	68	San Jose city, CA	4.1
71	69	Birmingham city, AL	-8.5	52	69	Honolulu CDP, HI	18.7	35	69	Albuquerque city, NM	3.8
54	70	Cincinnati city, OH	-9.0	58	70	El Paso city, TX	18.3	23	70	El Paso city, TX	3.5
52	71	Pittsburgh city, PA	-9.5	73	71	Newark city, NJ	14.2	55	71	Anaheim city, CA	3.2
73	72	Norfolk city, VA	-10.3	31	72	Santa Ana city, CA	12.4	42	72	Mesa city, AZ	3.1
58	73	Buffalo city, NY	-10.8	71	73	Miami city, FL	11.8	75	73	Hialeah, FL	2.9
17	74	Baltimore city, MD	-11.5	10	74	Detroit city, MI	10.5	46	74	Honolulu CDP, HI	2.4
49	75	St. Louis city, MO	-12.2	49	75	Hialeah, FL	8.1	51	75	Santa Ana city, CA	2.1

Note: Column numbers refer to Table D. Cities.

TABLE 6—75 Largest Cities by 2000 Population
Selected Rankings

Population Rank	American Indian, Alaska Native Rank	City	[col 11] Percent American Indian, Alaska Native	Population Rank	Asian and Pac. Is. Rank	City	[col 12] Percent Asian and Pac. Is.	Population Rank	Hispanic Rank	City	[col 14] Percent Hispanic
65	1	Anchorage city, AK	10.4	46	1	Honolulu CDP, HI	83.3	75	1	Hialeah, FL	90.3
43	2	Tulsa city, OK	7.7	13	2	San Francisco city, CA	33.4	23	2	El Paso city, TX	76.6
29	3	Oklahoma City, OK	5.7	11	3	San Jose city, CA	29.6	51	3	Santa Ana city, CA	76.1
35	4	Albuquerque city, NM	4.9	70	4	Stockton city, CA	23.9	47	4	Miami city, FL	65.8
45	5	Minneapolis city, MN	3.3	40	5	Sacramento city, CA	20.6	9	5	San Antonio city, TX	58.7
30	6	Tucson city, AZ	3.2	72	6	Jersey City, NJ	17.9	60	6	Corpus Christi city, TX	54.3
40	7	Sacramento city, CA	2.8	41	7	Oakland city, CA	17.4	55	7	Anaheim city, CA	46.8
6	8	Phoenix city, AZ	2.7	7	8	San Diego city, CA	16.4	2	8	Los Angeles city, CA	46.5
37	9	Fresno city, CA	2.6	24	9	Seattle city, WA	15.9	35	9	Albuquerque city, NM	39.9
69	10	Bakersfield, CA	2.5	34	10	Long Beach city, CA	15.4	37	9	Fresno city, CA	39.9
42	11	Mesa city, AZ	2.3	55	11	Anaheim city, CA	13.9	67	11	Riverside city, CA	38.1
28	11	Portland city, OR	2.3	59	11	St. Paul city, MN	13.9	4	12	Houston city, TX	37.4
70	11	Stockton city, CA	2.3	37	13	Fresno city, CA	13.0	34	13	Long Beach city, CA	35.8
50	11	Wichita city, KS	2.3	2	14	Los Angeles city, CA	11.4	30	14	Tucson city, AZ	35.7
25	15	Denver city, CO	2.2	1	15	New York City, NY	11.1	8	15	Dallas city, TX	35.6
67	16	Riverside city, CA	2.1	51	16	Santa Ana city, CA	9.9	6	16	Phoenix city, AZ	34.1
24	16	Seattle city, WA	2.1	65	17	Anchorage city, AK	8.5	69	17	Bakersfield, CA	32.5
59	16	St. Paul city, MN	2.1	20	18	Boston city, MA	8.4	70	17	Stockton city, CA	32.5
48	19	Colorado Springs city, CO	1.9	28	19	Portland city, OR	8.2	25	19	Denver city, CO	31.7
61	20	Aurora city, CO	1.8	67	20	Riverside city, CA	7.4	16	20	Austin city, TX	30.5
34	21	Long Beach city, CA	1.7	45	21	Minneapolis city, MN	7.2	11	21	San Jose city, CA	30.2
41	21	Oakland city, CA	1.7	32	22	Las Vegas city, NV	6.9	27	22	Fort Worth city, TX	29.8
51	21	Santa Ana city, CA	1.7	53	23	Arlington city, TX	6.8	63	23	Newark city, NJ	29.5
55	24	Anaheim city, CA	1.5	38	24	Virginia Beach city, VA	6.3	72	24	Jersey City, NJ	28.3
32	24	Las Vegas city, NV	1.5	4	25	Houston city, TX	5.9	1	25	New York City, NY	27.0
19	24	Milwaukee city, WI	1.5	61	26	Aurora city, CO	5.7	3	26	Chicago city, IL	26.0
11	24	San Jose city, CA	1.5	16	27	Austin city, TX	5.6	7	27	San Diego city, CA	25.4
58	28	Buffalo city, NY	1.4	69	27	Bakersfield, CA	5.6	32	28	Las Vegas city, NV	23.6
46	28	Honolulu CDP, HI	1.4	3	29	Chicago city, IL	5.1	41	29	Oakland city, CA	21.9
2	28	Los Angeles city, CA	1.4	5	29	Philadelphia city, PA	5.1	40	30	Sacramento city, CA	21.6
9	31	San Antonio city, TX	1.3	50	31	Wichita city, KS	4.7	61	31	Aurora city, CO	19.8
7	31	San Diego city, CA	1.3	48	32	Colorado Springs city, CO	4.3	42	32	Mesa city, AZ	19.7
53	33	Arlington city, TX	1.2	29	33	Oklahoma City, OK	4.2	57	33	Tampa city, FL	19.3
23	33	El Paso city, TX	1.2	15	34	Columbus city, OH	4.0	53	34	Arlington city, TX	18.3
36	33	Kansas City, MO	1.2	26	35	Charlotte city, NC	3.9	20	35	Boston city, MA	14.4
44	33	Omaha city, NE	1.2	73	35	Norfolk city, VA	3.9	13	36	San Francisco city, CA	14.1
13	33	San Francisco city, CA	1.2	62	35	Raleigh city, NC	3.9	48	37	Colorado Springs city, CO	12.0
16	38	Austin city, TX	1.1	25	38	Denver city, CO	3.6	19	37	Milwaukee city, WI	12.0
60	38	Corpus Christi city, TX	1.1	14	38	Jacksonville city, FL	3.6	29	39	Oklahoma City, OK	10.1
27	38	Fort Worth city, TX	1.1	19	40	Milwaukee city, WI	3.5	50	40	Wichita city, KS	9.6
1	38	New York City, NY	1.1	30	40	Tucson city, AZ	3.5	5	41	Philadelphia city, PA	8.5
73	38	Norfolk city, VA	1.1	68	42	St. Petersburg city, FL	3.3	59	42	St. Paul city, MN	7.9
15	43	Columbus city, OH	1.0	8	43	Dallas city, TX	3.2	21	42	Washington city, DC	7.9
8	43	Dallas city, TX	1.0	27	43	Fort Worth city, TX	3.2	45	44	Minneapolis city, MN	7.6
72	43	Jersey City, NJ	1.0	52	43	Pittsburgh city, PA	3.2	58	45	Buffalo city, NY	7.5
38	43	Virginia Beach city, VA	1.0	21	43	Washington city, DC	3.2	44	45	Omaha city, NE	7.5
20	47	Boston city, MA	0.9	35	47	Albuquerque city, NM	3.1	26	47	Charlotte city, NC	7.4
33	47	Cleveland city, OH	0.9	74	48	Baton Rouge, LA	3.0	33	48	Cleveland city, OH	7.3
10	47	Detroit city, MI	0.9	64	49	Lexington-Fayette, KY	2.9	43	49	Tulsa city, OK	7.2
68	47	St. Petersburg city, FL	0.9	22	49	Nashville-Davidson consolidated city, TN	2.9	62	50	Raleigh city, NC	7.0
57	47	Tampa city, FL	0.9	57	49	Tampa city, FL	2.9	36	51	Kansas City, MO	6.9
56	47	Toledo city, OH	0.9	6	52	Phoenix city, AZ	2.8	28	52	Portland city, OR	6.8
17	53	Baltimore city, MD	0.8	31	53	New Orleans city, LA	2.6	65	53	Anchorage city, AK	5.7
54	53	Cincinnati city, OH	0.8	36	54	Kansas City, MO	2.5	56	54	Toledo city, OH	5.5
4	53	Houston city, TX	0.8	42	55	Mesa city, AZ	2.4	24	55	Seattle city, WA	5.3
14	53	Jacksonville city, FL	0.8	49	55	St. Louis city, MO	2.4	10	56	Detroit city, MI	5.0
63	53	Newark city, NJ	0.8	39	57	Atlanta city, GA	2.3	22	57	Nashville-Davidson consolidated city, TN	4.6
62	53	Raleigh city, NC	0.8	9	57	San Antonio city, TX	2.3	39	58	Atlanta city, GA	4.5
49	53	St. Louis city, MO	0.8	43	57	Tulsa city, OK	2.3	46	59	Honolulu CDP, HI	4.4
21	53	Washington city, DC	0.8	44	60	Omaha city, NE	2.2	14	60	Jacksonville city, FL	4.2
26	61	Charlotte city, NC	0.7	17	61	Baltimore city, MD	1.9	68	60	St. Petersburg city, FL	4.2
3	61	Chicago city, IL	0.7	54	61	Cincinnati city, OH	1.9	38	60	Virginia Beach city, VA	4.2
12	61	Indianapolis consolidated city, IN	0.7	60	61	Corpus Christi city, TX	1.9	12	63	Indianapolis consolidated city, IN	3.9
66	61	Louisville city, KY	0.7	58	64	Buffalo city, NY	1.8	73	64	Norfolk city, VA	3.8
22	61	Nashville-Davidson consolidated city, TN	0.7	12	64	Indianapolis consolidated city, IN	1.8	64	65	Lexington-Fayette, KY	3.3
5	61	Philadelphia city, PA	0.7	66	64	Louisville city, KY	1.8	31	66	New Orleans city, LA	3.1
52	61	Pittsburgh city, PA	0.7	18	64	Memphis city, TN	1.8	18	67	Memphis city, TN	3.0
64	68	Lexington-Fayette, KY	0.6	63	64	Newark city, NJ	1.8	15	68	Columbus city, OH	2.5
39	69	Atlanta city, GA	0.5	33	69	Cleveland city, OH	1.7	49	69	St. Louis city, MO	2.0
74	69	Baton Rouge, LA	0.5	23	69	El Paso city, TX	1.7	66	70	Louisville city, KY	1.9
71	69	Birmingham city, AL	0.5	10	71	Detroit city, MI	1.4	17	71	Baltimore city, MD	1.7
18	69	Memphis city, TN	0.5	56	71	Toledo city, OH	1.4	74	71	Baton Rouge, LA	1.7
47	69	Miami city, FL	0.5	71	73	Birmingham city, AL	1.1	71	73	Birmingham city, AL	1.6
31	69	New Orleans city, LA	0.5	47	73	Miami city, FL	1.1	54	74	Cincinnati city, OH	1.3
75	75	Hialeah, FL	0.3	75	75	Hialeah, FL	0.7	52	74	Pittsburgh city, PA	1.3

Note: Column numbers refer to Table D. Cities.

TABLE 6—75 Largest Cities by 2000 Population
Selected Rankings

	Percent Under 18 Years, 2000				Percent 65 Years and Over, 2000				Percent Female-Headed Family Household, 2000		
Popu-lation Rank	Under 18 Years Rank	City	[cols 16 & 17] Percent Under 18 Years	Popu-lation Rank	65 Years And Over Rank	City	[cols 23 & 24] Percent 65 Years and over	Popu-lation Rank	Female House-holder Rank	City	[col 29] Percent Female House-holder
51	1	Santa Ana city, CA	34.2	46	1	Honolulu CDP, HI	17.8	10	1	Detroit city, MI	31.6
37	2	Fresno city, CA	32.9	68	2	St. Petersburg city, FL	17.4	63	2	Newark city, NJ	29.3
69	3	Bakersfield, CA	32.7	47	3	Miami city, FL	17.0	17	3	Baltimore city, MD	25.0
70	4	Stockton city, CA	32.4	75	4	Hialeah, FL	16.6	33	4	Cleveland city, OH	24.8
10	5	Detroit city, MI	31.1	52	5	Pittsburgh city, PA	16.4	71	5	Birmingham city, AL	24.6
23	5	El Paso city, TX	31.1	66	6	Louisville city, KY	14.7	31	6	New Orleans city, LA	24.5
55	7	Anaheim city, CA	30.2	5	7	Philadelphia city, PA	14.1	18	7	Memphis city, TN	23.8
67	8	Riverside city, CA	30.1	49	8	St. Louis city, MO	13.7	58	8	Buffalo city, NY	22.3
65	9	Anchorage city, AK	29.2	13	9	San Francisco city, CA	13.6	5	8	Philadelphia city, PA	22.3
34	9	Long Beach city, CA	29.2	58	10	Buffalo city, NY	13.5	49	10	St. Louis city, MO	21.3
6	11	Phoenix city, AZ	29.0	71	11	Birmingham city, AL	13.4	19	11	Milwaukee city, WI	21.1
19	12	Milwaukee city, WI	28.7	42	12	Mesa city, AZ	13.3	39	12	Atlanta city, GA	20.7
9	13	San Antonio city, TX	28.6	17	13	Baltimore city, MD	13.2	72	13	Jersey City, NJ	20.2
33	14	Cleveland city, OH	28.5	56	14	Toledo city, OH	13.1	66	14	Louisville city, KY	19.2
53	15	Arlington city, TX	28.3	43	15	Tulsa city, OK	12.8	1	15	New York City, NY	19.1
27	15	Fort Worth city, TX	28.3	33	16	Cleveland city, OH	12.5	74	16	Baton Rouge, LA	19.0
60	17	Corpus Christi city, TX	28.2	57	16	Tampa city, FL	12.5	3	17	Chicago city, IL	18.9
63	18	Newark city, NJ	28.0	54	18	Cincinnati city, OH	12.3	21	17	Washington city, DC	18.9
18	19	Memphis city, TN	27.9	21	19	Washington city, DC	12.2	73	19	Norfolk city, VA	18.8
61	20	Aurora city, CO	27.6	24	20	Seattle city, WA	12.0	47	20	Miami city, FL	18.7
38	21	Virginia Beach city, VA	27.5	35	21	Albuquerque city, NM	11.9	54	21	Cincinnati city, OH	18.6
4	22	Houston city, TX	27.4	30	21	Tucson city, AZ	11.9	23	22	El Paso city, TX	18.5
42	23	Mesa city, AZ	27.3	50	21	Wichita city, KS	11.9	41	23	Oakland city, CA	17.7
40	23	Sacramento city, CA	27.3	36	24	Kansas City, MO	11.8	37	24	Fresno city, CA	17.6
59	25	St. Paul city, MN	27.1	44	24	Omaha city, NE	11.8	75	25	Hialeah, FL	17.4
50	25	Wichita city, KS	27.1	31	26	New Orleans city, LA	11.7	70	26	Stockton city, CA	17.3
14	27	Jacksonville city, FL	26.7	1	26	New York City, NY	11.7	56	27	Toledo city, OH	17.2
31	27	New Orleans city, LA	26.7	32	28	Las Vegas city, NV	11.6	52	28	Pittsburgh city, PA	16.5
48	29	Colorado Springs city, CO	26.5	29	29	Oklahoma City, OK	11.5	20	29	Boston city, MA	16.4
8	29	Dallas city, TX	26.5	28	29	Portland city, OR	11.5	9	29	San Antonio city, TX	16.4
2	29	Los Angeles city, CA	26.5	74	31	Baton Rouge, LA	11.4	34	31	Long Beach city, CA	16.1
11	32	San Jose city, CA	26.4	40	31	Sacramento city, CA	11.4	57	31	Tampa city, FL	16.1
58	33	Buffalo city, NY	26.3	25	33	Denver city, CO	11.2	14	33	Jacksonville city, FL	16.0
3	34	Chicago city, IL	26.2	22	33	Nashville-Davidson consolidated city, TN	11.2	36	33	Kansas City, MO	16.0
56	34	Toledo city, OH	26.2	60	35	Corpus Christi city, TX	11.1	69	35	Bakersfield, CA	15.5
32	36	Las Vegas city, NV	25.9	12	36	Indianapolis consolidated city, IN	11.0	60	36	Corpus Christi city, TX	15.4
49	37	St. Louis city, MO	25.7	18	37	Memphis city, TN	10.9	40	36	Sacramento city, CA	15.4
12	38	Indianapolis consolidated city, IN	25.6	19	37	Milwaukee city, WI	10.9	4	38	Houston city, TX	15.3
44	38	Omaha city, NE	25.6	73	37	Norfolk city, VA	10.9	12	39	Indianapolis consolidated city, IN	15.0
29	40	Oklahoma City, OK	25.5	23	40	El Paso city, TX	10.6	8	40	Dallas city, TX	14.9
36	41	Kansas City, MO	25.4	10	41	Detroit city, MI	10.5	67	41	Riverside city, CA	14.8
5	42	Philadelphia city, PA	25.3	41	41	Oakland city, CA	10.5	27	42	Fort Worth city, TX	14.7
71	43	Birmingham city, AL	25.0	7	41	San Diego city, CA	10.5	15	43	Columbus city, OH	14.5
41	43	Oakland city, CA	25.0	20	44	Boston city, MA	10.4	2	43	Los Angeles city, CA	14.5
17	45	Baltimore city, MD	24.8	9	44	San Antonio city, TX	10.4	22	45	Nashville-Davidson consolidated city, TN	14.3
43	45	Tulsa city, OK	24.8	3	46	Chicago city, IL	10.3	59	46	St. Paul city, MN	13.9
26	47	Charlotte city, NC	24.7	14	46	Jacksonville city, FL	10.3	68	47	St. Petersburg city, FL	13.8
72	47	Jersey City, NJ	24.7	59	46	St. Paul city, MN	10.3	30	47	Tucson city, AZ	13.8
57	47	Tampa city, FL	24.7	70	49	Stockton city, CA	10.2	26	49	Charlotte city, NC	13.7
35	50	Albuquerque city, NM	24.6	64	50	Lexington-Fayette, KY	10.0	51	50	Santa Ana city, CA	13.5
54	51	Cincinnati city, OH	24.5	39	51	Atlanta city, GA	9.7	29	51	Oklahoma City, OK	13.2
30	51	Tucson city, AZ	24.5	72	51	Jersey City, NJ	9.7	55	52	Anaheim city, CA	13.1
74	53	Baton Rouge, LA	24.4	2	51	Los Angeles city, CA	9.7	61	52	Aurora city, CO	13.1
1	54	New York City, NY	24.3	48	54	Colorado Springs city, CO	9.6	44	54	Omaha city, NE	13.0
15	55	Columbus city, OH	24.2	27	54	Fort Worth city, TX	9.6	35	55	Albuquerque city, NM	12.9
73	56	Norfolk city, VA	24.1	37	56	Fresno city, CA	9.3	6	55	Phoenix city, AZ	12.9
7	57	San Diego city, CA	24.0	63	56	Newark city, NJ	9.3	43	55	Tulsa city, OK	12.9
66	58	Louisville city, KY	23.6	34	58	Long Beach city, CA	9.1	38	58	Virginia Beach city, VA	12.4
75	59	Hialeah, FL	23.0	45	58	Minneapolis city, MN	9.1	45	59	Minneapolis city, MN	12.3
16	60	Austin city, TX	22.5	67	60	Riverside city, CA	9.0	32	60	Las Vegas city, NV	12.2
39	61	Atlanta city, GA	22.3	26	61	Charlotte city, NC	8.8	46	61	Honolulu CDP, HI	12.1
22	62	Nashville-Davidson consolidated city, TN	22.2	15	61	Columbus city, OH	8.8	53	62	Arlington city, TX	11.8
45	63	Minneapolis city, MN	22.0	69	63	Bakersfield, CA	8.7	11	63	San Jose city, CA	11.7
25	64	Denver city, CO	21.9	8	64	Dallas city, TX	8.6	50	64	Wichita city, KS	11.6
47	65	Miami city, FL	21.8	38	65	Virginia Beach city, VA	8.5	65	65	Anchorage city, AK	11.5
68	66	St. Petersburg city, FL	21.5	4	66	Houston city, TX	8.4	64	65	Lexington-Fayette, KY	11.5
64	67	Lexington-Fayette, KY	21.3	62	66	Raleigh city, NC	8.4	62	67	Raleigh city, NC	11.4
28	68	Portland city, OR	21.1	11	68	San Jose city, CA	8.3	7	67	San Diego city, CA	11.4
62	69	Raleigh city, NC	20.8	55	69	Anaheim city, CA	8.2	16	69	Austin city, TX	10.8
21	70	Washington city, DC	20.1	6	70	Phoenix city, AZ	8.1	25	69	Denver city, CO	10.8
52	71	Pittsburgh city, PA	19.9	61	71	Aurora city, CO	7.4	28	69	Portland city, OR	10.8
20	72	Boston city, MA	19.7	16	72	Austin city, TX	6.7	48	72	Colorado Springs city, CO	10.6
46	73	Honolulu CDP, HI	19.2	53	73	Arlington city, TX	6.1	42	72	Mesa city, AZ	10.6
24	74	Seattle city, WA	15.6	65	74	Anchorage city, AK	5.5	13	74	San Francisco city, CA	8.9
13	75	San Francisco city, CA	14.6	51	74	Santa Ana city, CA	5.5	24	75	Seattle city, WA	8.1

Note: Column numbers refer to Table D. Cities.

TABLE 6—75 Largest Cities by 2000 Population
Selected Rankings

Percent of Households Composed of One Person, 2000				Percent College Graduates (Bachelor's or higher degree), 1990				Median Household Income, 1989			
Population Rank	One person Household Rank	City	[col 30] Percent of All Households	Population Rank	Percent College Graduate Rank	City	[col 42] Percent College Grads	Population Rank	Median Income Rank	City	[col 44] Median Income 1989 (dollars)
21	1	Washington city, DC	43.8	62	1	Raleigh city, NC	40.6	11	1	San Jose city, CA	46 206
54	2	Cincinnati city, OH	42.8	24	2	Seattle city, WA	37.9	65	2	Anchorage city, AK	43 946
24	3	Seattle city, WA	40.8	13	3	San Francisco city, CA	35.0	55	3	Anaheim city, CA	39 620
45	4	Minneapolis city, MN	40.3	16	4	Austin city, TX	34.4	46	4	Honolulu CDP, HI	37 190
49	4	St. Louis city, MO	40.3	21	5	Washington city, DC	33.3	38	5	Virginia Beach city, VA	36 271
52	6	Pittsburgh city, PA	39.4	64	6	Lexington-Fayette, KY	30.6	51	6	Santa Ana city, CA	35 162
25	7	Denver city, CO	39.3	45	7	Minneapolis city, MN	30.3	53	7	Arlington city, TX	35 048
13	8	San Francisco city, CA	38.6	53	8	Arlington city, TX	30.0	67	8	Riverside city, CA	34 801
39	9	Atlanta city, GA	38.5	20	8	Boston city, MA	30.0	7	9	San Diego city, CA	33 686
66	10	Louisville city, KY	37.9	7	10	San Diego city, CA	29.8	13	10	San Francisco city, CA	33 414
58	11	Buffalo city, NY	37.7	25	11	Denver city, CO	29.0	61	11	Aurora city, CO	33 214
20	12	Boston city, MA	37.1	35	12	Albuquerque city, NM	28.4	62	12	Raleigh city, NC	32 451
59	13	St. Paul city, MN	35.9	26	12	Charlotte city, NC	28.4	69	13	Bakersfield, CA	32 154
68	14	St. Petersburg city, FL	35.6	74	14	Baton Rouge, LA	28.3	34	14	Long Beach city, CA	31 938
33	15	Cleveland city, OH	35.2	46	15	Honolulu CDP, HI	27.7	26	15	Charlotte city, NC	31 873
17	16	Baltimore city, MD	34.9	48	16	Colorado Springs city, CO	27.5	2	16	Los Angeles city, CA	30 925
28	17	Portland city, OR	34.6	41	17	Oakland city, CA	27.2	21	17	Washington city, DC	30 727
71	18	Birmingham city, AL	34.4	8	18	Dallas city, TX	27.1	32	18	Las Vegas city, NV	30 590
15	19	Columbus city, OH	34.1	65	19	Anchorage city, AK	26.9	42	19	Mesa city, AZ	30 273
36	19	Kansas City, MO	34.1	39	20	Atlanta city, GA	26.6	1	20	New York City, NY	29 823
43	21	Tulsa city, OK	33.9	59	21	St. Paul city, MN	26.5	24	21	Seattle city, WA	29 353
5	22	Philadelphia city, PA	33.8	61	22	Aurora city, CO	26.3	6	22	Phoenix city, AZ	29 291
57	23	Tampa city, FL	33.7	28	23	Portland city, OR	25.9	20	23	Boston city, MA	29 180
19	24	Milwaukee city, WI	33.5	43	24	Tulsa city, OK	25.8	12	24	Indianapolis consolidated city, IN	29 083
22	25	Nashville-Davidson consolidated city, TN	33.4	38	25	Virginia Beach city, VA	25.5	72	25	Jersey City, NJ	29 054
31	26	New Orleans city, LA	33.2	11	26	San Jose city, CA	25.3	48	26	Colorado Springs city, CO	28 928
62	27	Raleigh city, NC	33.1	4	27	Houston city, TX	25.1	14	27	Jacksonville city, FL	28 513
8	28	Dallas city, TX	32.9	15	28	Columbus city, OH	24.6	22	28	Nashville-Davidson consolidated city, TN	28 377
16	29	Austin city, TX	32.8	22	29	Nashville-Davidson consolidated city, TN	24.4	40	29	Sacramento city, CA	28 183
56	29	Toledo city, OH	32.8	40	30	Sacramento city, CA	23.5	64	30	Lexington-Fayette, KY	28 056
3	31	Chicago city, IL	32.6	34	31	Long Beach city, CA	23.2	50	31	Wichita city, KS	28 024
41	32	Oakland city, CA	32.5	44	32	Omaha city, NE	23.1	35	32	Albuquerque city, NM	27 555
30	33	Tucson city, AZ	32.3	2	33	Los Angeles city, CA	23.0	8	33	Dallas city, TX	27 489
12	34	Indianapolis consolidated city, IN	32.0	1	33	New York City, NY	23.0	41	34	Oakland city, CA	27 095
40	34	Sacramento city, CA	32.0	50	35	Wichita city, KS	22.7	44	35	Omaha city, NE	26 927
1	36	New York City, NY	31.9	31	36	New Orleans city, LA	22.4	70	36	Stockton city, CA	26 876
44	36	Omaha city, NE	31.9	54	37	Cincinnati city, OH	22.2	36	37	Kansas City, MO	26 713
74	38	Baton Rouge, LA	31.7	36	38	Kansas City, MO	22.0	15	38	Columbus city, OH	26 651
64	38	Lexington-Fayette, KY	31.7	12	39	Indianapolis consolidated city, IN	21.9	27	39	Fort Worth city, TX	26 547
50	40	Wichita city, KS	31.2	29	40	Oklahoma City, OK	21.6	59	40	St. Paul city, MN	26 498
29	41	Oklahoma City, OK	30.7	27	41	Fort Worth city, TX	21.5	3	41	Chicago city, IL	26 301
35	42	Albuquerque city, NM	30.5	72	42	Jersey City, NJ	21.4	4	42	Houston city, TX	26 261
18	42	Memphis city, TN	30.5	42	43	Mesa city, AZ	21.0	60	43	Corpus Christi city, TX	25 773
47	44	Miami city, FL	30.4	30	44	Tucson city, AZ	20.7	29	44	Oklahoma City, OK	25 741
73	45	Norfolk city, VA	30.2	52	45	Pittsburgh city, PA	20.1	43	45	Tulsa city, OK	25 708
10	46	Detroit city, MI	29.7	6	46	Phoenix city, AZ	19.9	28	46	Portland city, OR	25 592
46	46	Honolulu CDP, HI	29.7	69	47	Bakersfield, CA	19.6	16	47	Austin city, TX	25 414
4	48	Houston city, TX	29.6	3	48	Chicago city, IL	19.5	45	48	Minneapolis city, MN	25 324
34	48	Long Beach city, CA	29.6	67	49	Riverside city, CA	19.3	25	49	Denver city, CO	25 106
26	50	Charlotte city, NC	29.5	37	50	Fresno city, CA	19.1	37	50	Fresno city, CA	24 923
72	51	Jersey City, NJ	29.2	55	51	Anaheim city, CA	18.8	56	51	Toledo city, OH	24 819
27	52	Fort Worth city, TX	28.6	57	52	Tampa city, FL	18.7	5	52	Philadelphia city, PA	24 603
2	53	Los Angeles city, CA	28.5	68	53	St. Petersburg city, FL	18.6	17	53	Baltimore city, MD	24 045
7	54	San Diego city, CA	28.0	14	54	Jacksonville city, FL	18.4	19	54	Milwaukee city, WI	23 627
61	55	Aurora city, CO	27.4	60	55	Corpus Christi city, TX	17.8	9	55	San Antonio city, TX	23 584
48	56	Colorado Springs city, CO	27.0	9	56	San Antonio city, TX	17.8	68	56	St. Petersburg city, FL	23 577
63	57	Newark city, NJ	26.6	18	57	Memphis city, TN	17.5	73	57	Norfolk city, VA	23 563
14	58	Jacksonville city, FL	26.2	66	58	Louisville city, KY	17.2	23	58	El Paso city, TX	23 460
6	59	Phoenix city, AZ	25.4	73	59	Norfolk city, VA	16.8	75	59	Hialeah, FL	23 443
9	60	San Antonio city, TX	25.1	71	60	Birmingham city, AL	16.2	57	60	Tampa city, FL	22 772
32	61	Las Vegas city, NV	25.0	23	60	El Paso city, TX	16.2	18	61	Memphis city, TN	22 674
53	62	Arlington city, TX	24.7	58	62	Buffalo city, NY	16.0	39	62	Atlanta city, GA	22 275
42	63	Mesa city, AZ	24.2	17	63	Baltimore city, MD	15.5	74	63	Baton Rouge, LA	21 898
65	64	Anchorage city, AK	23.4	49	64	St. Louis city, MO	15.3	30	64	Tucson city, AZ	21 748
37	65	Fresno city, CA	23.3	5	65	Philadelphia city, PA	15.2	63	65	Newark city, NJ	21 650
60	66	Corpus Christi city, TX	23.2	70	66	Stockton city, CA	15.0	54	66	Cincinnati city, OH	21 006
70	67	Stockton city, CA	22.9	19	67	Milwaukee city, WI	14.8	52	67	Pittsburgh city, PA	20 747
69	68	Bakersfield, CA	21.5	56	68	Toledo city, OH	14.1	66	68	Louisville city, KY	20 141
67	68	Riverside city, CA	21.5	32	69	Las Vegas city, NV	13.4	49	69	St. Louis city, MO	19 458
38	70	Virginia Beach city, VA	20.4	47	70	Miami city, FL	12.8	71	70	Birmingham city, AL	19 193
23	71	El Paso city, TX	19.2	51	71	Santa Ana city, CA	10.6	10	71	Detroit city, MI	18 742
11	72	San Jose city, CA	18.4	10	72	Detroit city, MI	9.6	58	72	Buffalo city, NY	18 482
55	73	Anaheim city, CA	18.1	63	73	Newark city, NJ	8.5	31	73	New Orleans city, LA	18 477
75	74	Hialeah, FL	14.7	33	74	Cleveland city, OH	8.1	33	74	Cleveland city, OH	17 822
51	75	Santa Ana city, CA	12.7	75	75	Hialeah, FL	7.3	47	75	Miami city, FL	16 925

Note: Column numbers refer to Table D. Cities.

TABLE 6—75 Largest Cities by 2000 Population
Selected Rankings

Percent of Persons Below the Poverty Level, 1989

Population Rank	Poverty Rate Rank	City	[col 47] Poverty Rate for Persons 1989
10	1	Detroit city, MI	32.4
31	2	New Orleans city, LA	31.6
47	3	Miami city, FL	31.2
33	4	Cleveland city, OH	28.7
39	5	Atlanta city, GA	27.3
63	6	Newark city, NJ	26.3
74	7	Baton Rouge, LA	26.2
58	8	Buffalo city, NY	25.6
23	9	El Paso city, TX	25.3
71	10	Birmingham city, AL	24.8
49	11	St. Louis city, MO	24.6
54	12	Cincinnati city, OH	24.3
37	13	Fresno city, CA	24.0
18	14	Memphis city, TN	23.0
66	15	Louisville city, KY	22.6
9	15	San Antonio city, TX	22.6
19	17	Milwaukee city, WI	22.2
17	18	Baltimore city, MD	21.9
3	19	Chicago city, IL	21.6
52	20	Pittsburgh city, PA	21.4
70	20	Stockton city, CA	21.4
4	22	Houston city, TX	20.7
5	23	Philadelphia city, PA	20.3
30	24	Tucson city, AZ	20.2
60	25	Corpus Christi city, TX	20.0
57	26	Tampa city, FL	19.4
1	27	New York City, NY	19.3
73	27	Norfolk city, VA	19.3
56	29	Toledo city, OH	19.1
72	30	Jersey City, NJ	18.9
2	30	Los Angeles city, CA	18.9
41	32	Oakland city, CA	18.8
20	33	Boston city, MA	18.7
45	34	Minneapolis city, MN	18.5
75	35	Hialeah, FL	18.2
51	36	Santa Ana city, CA	18.1
8	37	Dallas city, TX	18.0
16	38	Austin city, TX	17.9
27	39	Fort Worth city, TX	17.4
15	40	Columbus city, OH	17.2
40	40	Sacramento city, CA	17.2
25	42	Denver city, CO	17.1
21	43	Washington city, DC	16.9
34	44	Long Beach city, CA	16.8
59	45	St. Paul city, MN	16.7
29	46	Oklahoma City, OK	15.9
36	47	Kansas City, MO	15.3
69	48	Bakersfield, CA	15.0
43	48	Tulsa city, OK	15.0
28	50	Portland city, OR	14.5
6	51	Phoenix city, AZ	14.2
64	52	Lexington-Fayette, KY	14.1
35	53	Albuquerque city, NM	14.0
68	54	St. Petersburg city, FL	13.6
7	55	San Diego city, CA	13.4
22	56	Nashville-Davidson consolidated city, TN	13.0
14	57	Jacksonville city, FL	12.8
13	58	San Francisco city, CA	12.7
44	59	Omaha city, NE	12.6
12	60	Indianapolis consolidated city, IN	12.5
50	60	Wichita city, KS	12.5
24	62	Seattle city, WA	12.4
67	63	Riverside city, CA	11.9
62	64	Raleigh city, NC	11.8
32	65	Las Vegas city, NV	11.5
48	66	Colorado Springs city, CO	10.9
26	67	Charlotte city, NC	10.8
55	68	Anaheim city, CA	10.6
42	69	Mesa city, AZ	9.5
11	70	San Jose city, CA	9.3
46	71	Honolulu CDP, HI	8.4
53	72	Arlington city, TX	8.2
61	73	Aurora city, CO	7.4
65	74	Anchorage city, AK	7.1
38	75	Virginia Beach city, VA	5.9

Percent Change in Housing Units, 1990-2000

Population Rank	Percent Change Rank	City	[col 47] Percent Change
32	1	Las Vegas city, NV	73.9
26	2	Charlotte city, NC	35.2
69	3	Bakersfield, CA	33.4
62	4	Raleigh city, NC	30.3
16	5	Austin city, TX	27.5
42	6	Mesa city, AZ	25.1
28	7	Portland city, OR	19.6
48	8	Colorado Springs city, CO	19.5
35	9	Albuquerque city, NM	18.9
64	9	Lexington-Fayette, KY	18.9
9	11	San Antonio city, TX	18.5
15	12	Columbus city, OH	17.7
6	13	Phoenix city, AZ	17.5
75	14	Hialeah, FL	16.0
53	15	Arlington city, TX	15.8
44	16	Omaha city, NE	15.4
37	17	Fresno city, CA	15.2
23	18	El Paso city, TX	14.8
30	19	Tucson city, AZ	14.3
70	20	Stockton city, CA	13.1
50	21	Wichita city, KS	12.6
22	22	Nashville-Davidson consolidated city, TN	10.4
38	22	Virginia Beach city, VA	10.4
12	24	Indianapolis consolidated city, IN	10.0
61	25	Aurora city, CO	9.4
18	26	Memphis city, TN	9.2
46	27	Honolulu CDP, HI	8.8
7	27	San Diego city, CA	8.8
11	29	San Jose city, CA	8.7
24	30	Seattle city, WA	8.6
27	31	Fort Worth city, TX	8.5
14	31	Jacksonville city, FL	8.5
4	33	Houston city, TX	7.7
60	34	Corpus Christi city, TX	7.6
29	35	Oklahoma City, OK	7.4
67	36	Riverside city, CA	7.1
55	37	Anaheim city, CA	7.0
1	37	New York City, NY	7.0
40	39	Sacramento city, CA	6.9
65	40	Anchorage city, AK	6.6
13	41	San Francisco city, CA	5.5
25	42	Denver city, CO	4.9
57	43	Tampa city, FL	4.7
8	44	Dallas city, TX	4.0
72	45	Jersey City, NJ	3.2
2	46	Los Angeles city, CA	2.9
47	47	Miami city, FL	2.7
39	48	Atlanta city, GA	2.3
3	49	Chicago city, IL	1.8
41	49	Oakland city, CA	1.8
43	49	Tulsa city, OK	1.8
34	52	Long Beach city, CA	0.7
20	53	Boston city, MA	0.4
74	54	Baton Rouge, LA	0.3
36	54	Kansas City, MO	0.3
51	56	Santa Ana city, CA	-0.5
68	57	St. Petersburg city, FL	-0.7
17	58	Baltimore city, MD	-1.1
21	59	Washington city, DC	-1.3
59	60	St. Paul city, MN	-1.6
56	60	Toledo city, OH	-1.6
54	62	Cincinnati city, OH	-1.8
5	63	Philadelphia city, PA	-1.9
19	64	Milwaukee city, WI	-2.0
66	65	Louisville city, KY	-2.2
63	66	Newark city, NJ	-2.3
45	67	Minneapolis city, MN	-2.4
33	68	Cleveland city, OH	-3.8
52	69	Pittsburgh city, PA	-4.0
58	70	Buffalo city, NY	-4.2
73	71	Norfolk city, VA	-4.4
31	72	New Orleans city, LA	-4.6
71	73	Birmingham city, AL	-4.9
10	74	Detroit city, MI	-8.5
49	75	St. Louis city, MO	-9.5

Percent Change in Civilian Labor Force, 2000-2001

Population Rank	Percent Change Rank	City	[col 62] Percent Change 2000-2001
32	1	Las Vegas city, NV	4.6
47	2	Miami, FL	3.8
6	2	Phoenix city, AZ	3.8
42	4	Mesa city, AZ	3.5
75	5	Hialeah, FL	3.1
41	5	Oakland city, CA	3.1
45	7	Minneapolis city, MN	3.0
67	8	Riverside city, CA	2.8
59	8	St. Paul city, MN	2.8
8	10	Dallas city, TX	2.7
68	10	St. Petersburg city, FL	2.7
57	12	Tampa city, FL	2.6
15	13	Columbus city, OH	2.5
34	14	Long Beach city, CA	2.4
2	14	Los Angeles city, CA	2.4
16	16	Austin city, TX	2.3
40	16	Sacramento city, CA	2.3
62	18	Raleigh city, NC	2.2
14	19	Jacksonville city, FL	2.1
51	19	Santa Ana city, CA	2.1
30	19	Tucson city, AZ	2.1
27	22	Fort Worth city, TX	2.0
36	22	Kansas City, MO	2.0
70	24	Stockton city, CA	1.9
55	25	Anaheim city, CA	1.8
4	25	Houston city, TX	1.8
73	25	Norfolk city, VA	1.8
48	28	Colorado Springs city, CO	1.7
12	28	Indianapolis consolidated city, IN	1.7
9	28	San Antonio city, TX	1.7
54	31	Cincinnati city, OH	1.6
5	31	Philadelphia city, PA	1.6
7	31	San Diego city, CA	1.6
53	34	Arlington city, TX	1.5
74	34	Baton Rouge, LA	1.5
20	34	Boston city, MA	1.5
19	34	Milwaukee city, WI	1.5
52	34	Pittsburgh city, PA	1.5
46	39	Honolulu CDP, HI	1.3
22	40	Nashville-Davidson consolidated city, TN	1.1
38	40	Virginia Beach city, VA	1.1
29	42	Oklahoma City, OK	1.0
35	43	Albuquerque city, NM	0.9
17	43	Baltimore city, MD	0.9
31	43	New Orleans city, LA	0.9
11	43	San Jose city, CA	0.9
44	47	Omaha city, NE	0.8
49	47	St. Louis city, MO	0.8
26	49	Charlotte city, NC	0.7
18	49	Memphis city, TN	0.7
56	49	Toledo city, OH	0.7
39	52	Atlanta city, GA	0.6
13	52	San Francisco city, CA	0.6
71	54	Birmingham city, AL	0.5
25	54	Denver city, CO	0.5
28	54	Portland city, OR	0.5
65	57	Anchorage city, AK	0.4
43	57	Tulsa city, OK	0.4
61	59	Aurora city, CO	0.3
69	59	Bakersfield, CA	0.3
33	59	Cleveland city, OH	0.3
10	62	Detroit city, MI	0.2
63	63	Newark city, NJ	-0.1
60	64	Corpus Christi city, TX	-0.2
72	65	Jersey City, NJ	-0.3
23	66	El Paso city, TX	-0.4
21	66	Washington city, DC	-0.4
3	68	Chicago city, IL	-0.7
1	69	New York City, NY	-1.5
64	70	Lexington-Fayette, KY	-1.6
24	71	Seattle city, WA	-1.7
58	72	Buffalo city, NY	-1.8
37	73	Fresno city, CA	-1.9
50	74	Wichita city, KS	-2.1
66	75	Louisville city, KY	-2.3

Note: Column numbers refer to Table D. Cities.

TABLE 6—75 Largest Cities by 2000 Population
Selected Rankings

Population Rank	Unemployment Rate Rank	City	[col 64] Unemployment Rate	Population Rank	Local Taxes Rank	City	[col 121] Local Per Capita Taxes (dollars)	Population Rank	Police Exp. Rank	City	[col 132] Percent of City Expenditures
		Unemployment Rate, 2001				**Per Capita Local Government Taxes, 1999**				**Percent of City Expenditures for Police Protection, 1999**	
37	1	Fresno city, CA	12.3	21	1	Washington city, DC	5 684	51	1	Santa Ana city, CA	25.5
70	2	Stockton city, CA	10.3	1	2	New York City, NY	2 902	61	2	Aurora city, CO	23.9
47	3	Miami city, FL	10.0	13	3	San Francisco city, CA	1 844	42	2	Mesa city, AZ	23.9
10	4	Detroit city, MI	9.7	20	4	Boston city, MA	1 590	47	4	Miami city, FL	23.5
63	5	Newark city, NJ	9.2	22	5	Nashville-Davidson consolidated city, TN	1 535	67	5	Riverside city, CA	22.9
33	6	Cleveland city, OH	8.8	74	6	Baton Rouge, LA	1 317	57	6	Tampa city, FL	22.4
58	7	Buffalo city, NY	8.6	46	7	Honolulu CDP, HI	1 295	3	7	Chicago city, IL	22.3
49	8	St. Louis city, MO	8.2	5	8	Philadelphia city, PA	1 268	27	8	Fort Worth city, TX	21.6
17	9	Baltimore city, MD	7.9	73	9	Norfolk city, VA	1 211	19	9	Milwaukee city, WI	21.4
19	9	Milwaukee city, WI	7.9	25	10	Denver city, CO	1 189	70	10	Stockton city, CA	21.0
23	11	El Paso city, TX	7.8	17	11	Baltimore city, MD	1 139	72	11	Jersey City, NJ	20.8
69	12	Bakersfield, CA	7.7	38	12	Virginia Beach city, VA	1 115	33	12	Cleveland city, OH	20.4
72	12	Jersey City, NJ	7.7	65	13	Anchorage city, AK	1 064	23	13	El Paso city, TX	20.2
75	14	Hialeah, FL	7.2	36	14	Kansas City, MO	1 006	60	14	Corpus Christi city, TX	20.1
41	15	Oakland city, CA	7.1	24	15	Seattle city, WA	985	56	14	Toledo city, OH	20.1
3	16	Chicago city, IL	6.9	54	16	Cincinnati city, OH	979	68	16	St. Petersburg city, FL	19.9
28	17	Portland city, OR	6.7	49	17	St. Louis city, MO	957	49	17	St. Louis city, MO	19.7
2	18	Los Angeles city, CA	6.5	71	18	Birmingham city, AL	939	71	18	Birmingham city, AL	19.2
21	18	Washington city, DC	6.5	10	19	Detroit city, MI	842	15	19	Columbus city, OH	19.0
5	20	Philadelphia city, PA	6.4	12	20	Indianapolis consolidated city, IN	828	69	20	Bakersfield, CA	18.9
8	21	Dallas city, TX	6.2	66	21	Louisville city, KY	809	2	20	Los Angeles city, CA	18.9
1	22	New York City, NY	6.1	31	22	New Orleans city, LA	775	37	22	Fresno city, CA	18.8
24	23	Seattle city, WA	6.0	52	23	Pittsburgh city, PA	741	75	23	Hialeah, FL	18.7
74	24	Baton Rouge, LA	5.9	33	24	Cleveland city, OH	733	4	24	Houston city, TX	18.6
31	24	New Orleans city, LA	5.9	64	25	Lexington-Fayette, KY	710	40	24	Sacramento city, CA	18.6
39	26	Atlanta city, GA	5.8	41	26	Oakland city, CA	697	29	26	Oklahoma City, OK	18.1
56	26	Toledo city, OH	5.8	28	27	Portland city, OR	690	26	27	Charlotte city, NC	17.5
60	28	Corpus Christi city, TX	5.7	3	28	Chicago city, IL	678	44	27	Omaha city, NE	17.5
73	28	Norfolk city, VA	5.7	14	29	Jacksonville city, FL	677	46	29	Honolulu CDP, HI	16.9
71	30	Birmingham city, AL	5.5	15	30	Columbus city, OH	674	9	29	San Antonio city, TX	16.9
27	30	Fort Worth city, TX	5.5	63	31	Newark city, NJ	671	30	31	Tucson city, AZ	16.8
32	30	Las Vegas city, NV	5.5	45	32	Minneapolis city, MN	668	35	32	Albuquerque city, NM	16.6
36	33	Kansas City, MO	5.4	29	32	Oklahoma City, OK	668	66	32	Louisville city, KY	16.6
51	33	Santa Ana city, CA	5.4	8	34	Dallas city, TX	627	34	34	Long Beach city, CA	16.5
4	35	Houston city, TX	5.3	43	35	Tulsa city, OK	622	53	35	Arlington city, TX	16.4
34	35	Long Beach city, CA	5.3	11	36	San Jose city, CA	606	32	35	Las Vegas city, NV	16.4
54	37	Cincinnati city, OH	5.2	2	37	Los Angeles city, CA	592	7	37	San Diego city, CA	16.3
67	37	Riverside city, CA	5.2	47	38	Miami city, FL	589	36	38	Kansas City, MO	16.2
13	37	San Francisco city, CA	5.2	39	39	Atlanta city, GA	576	63	39	Newark city, NJ	15.5
11	37	San Jose city, CA	5.2	61	40	Aurora city, CO	573	52	40	Pittsburgh city, PA	14.8
18	41	Memphis city, TN	5.1	4	41	Houston city, TX	569	8	41	Dallas city, TX	14.3
40	41	Sacramento city, CA	5.1	56	42	Toledo city, OH	558	6	41	Phoenix city, AZ	14.3
50	43	Wichita city, KS	4.6	26	43	Charlotte city, NC	551	11	41	San Jose city, CA	14.3
26	44	Charlotte city, NC	4.5	16	44	Austin city, TX	539	43	41	Tulsa city, OK	14.3
48	44	Colorado Springs city, CO	4.5	44	45	Omaha city, NE	524	45	45	Minneapolis city, MN	14.0
25	44	Denver city, CO	4.5	27	46	Fort Worth city, TX	519	31	46	New Orleans city, LA	13.9
14	44	Jacksonville city, FL	4.5	57	47	Tampa city, FL	515	62	47	Raleigh city, NC	13.5
57	44	Tampa city, FL	4.5	55	48	Anaheim city, CA	499	28	48	Portland city, OR	13.1
66	49	Louisville city, KY	4.4	72	48	Jersey City, NJ	499	41	49	Oakland city, CA	12.7
9	49	San Antonio city, TX	4.4	40	50	Sacramento city, CA	491	50	50	Wichita city, KS	12.4
65	51	Anchorage city, AK	4.3	35	51	Albuquerque city, NM	489	54	51	Cincinnati city, OH	12.1
16	51	Austin city, TX	4.3	6	52	Phoenix city, AZ	462	14	51	Jacksonville city, FL	12.1
6	51	Phoenix city, AZ	4.3	30	53	Tucson city, AZ	441	24	53	Seattle city, WA	12.0
68	51	St. Petersburg city, FL	4.3	59	54	St. Paul city, MN	437	55	54	Anaheim city, CA	11.7
29	55	Oklahoma City, OK	4.2	34	55	Long Beach city, CA	433	74	55	Baton Rouge, LA	11.3
20	56	Boston city, MA	4.1	18	56	Memphis city, TN	424	64	56	Lexington-Fayette, KY	11.2
46	56	Honolulu CDP, HI	4.1	7	57	San Diego city, CA	417	59	57	St. Paul city, MN	11.1
59	56	St. Paul city, MN	4.1	68	58	St. Petersburg city, FL	412	17	58	Baltimore city, MD	10.9
52	59	Pittsburgh city, PA	4.0	48	59	Colorado Springs city, CO	403	20	58	Boston city, MA	10.9
12	60	Indianapolis consolidated city, IN	3.9	58	60	Buffalo city, NY	393	5	60	Philadelphia city, PA	10.7
45	60	Minneapolis city, MN	3.9	62	60	Raleigh city, NC	393	39	61	Atlanta city, GA	10.6
62	60	Raleigh city, NC	3.9	75	62	Hialeah, FL	384	18	62	Memphis city, TN	10.5
44	63	Omaha city, NE	3.8	53	63	Arlington city, TX	381	16	63	Austin city, TX	10.1
30	63	Tucson city, AZ	3.8	60	64	Corpus Christi city, TX	356	48	64	Colorado Springs city, CO	9.7
43	65	Tulsa city, OK	3.7	51	65	Santa Ana city, CA	355	25	65	Denver city, CO	9.4
53	66	Arlington city, TX	3.6	42	66	Mesa city, AZ	353	10	66	Detroit city, MI	8.5
55	67	Anaheim city, CA	3.5	70	67	Stockton city, CA	332	12	67	Indianapolis consolidated city, IN	8.1
61	67	Aurora city, CO	3.5	9	68	San Antonio city, TX	324	22	68	Nashville-Davidson consolidated city, TN	7.6
35	69	Albuquerque city, NM	3.4	67	69	Riverside city, CA	323	1	69	New York City, NY	6.8
42	70	Mesa city, AZ	3.3	69	70	Bakersfield, CA	321	13	70	San Francisco city, CA	6.7
7	70	San Diego city, CA	3.3	32	71	Las Vegas city, NV	300	65	71	Anchorage city, AK	6.5
15	72	Columbus city, OH	3.2	37	72	Fresno city, CA	294	21	71	Washington city, DC	6.5
22	73	Nashville-Davidson consolidated city, TN	3.1	23	73	El Paso city, TX	288	58	73	Buffalo city, NY	6.4
64	74	Lexington-Fayette, KY	3.0	50	74	Wichita city, KS	287	38	74	Virginia Beach city, VA	6.2
38	74	Virginia Beach city, VA	3.0	19	75	Milwaukee city, WI	284	73	75	Norfolk city, VA	5.6

Note: Column numbers refer to Table D. Cities.

TABLE 6—75 Largest Cities by 2000 Population
Selected Rankings

Popu-lation Rank	Violent Crime Rate Rank	City	[col 37] Violent Crime Rate	Popu-lation Rank	Precip-itation Rank	City	[col 144] Annual Precip-itation	Popu-lation Rank	Income of $100K or more Rank	City	[col 46] % with Income of $100,000 or more
39	1	Atlanta city, GA	2 781	75	1	Hialeah, FL	63.0	65	1	Anchorage city, AK	9.3
17	2	Baltimore city, MD	2 458	31	2	New Orleans city, LA	61.9	46	2	Honolulu CDP, HI	9.0
10	3	Detroit city, MI	2 324	74	3	Baton Rouge, LA	60.9	11	3	San Jose city, CA	8.0
49	4	St. Louis city, MO	2 279	47	4	Miami city, FL	55.9	2	4	Los Angeles city, CA	7.9
47	5	Miami city, FL	2 173	71	5	Birmingham city, AL	54.6	21	5	Washington city, DC	7.8
57	6	Tampa city, FL	2 103	18	6	Memphis city, TN	52.1	13	6	San Francisco city, CA	7.4
36	7	Kansas City, MO	1 626	4	7	Houston city, TX	50.8	1	7	New York City, NY	6.4
22	8	Nashville-Davidson consolidated city, TN	1 623	39	8	Atlanta city, GA	50.8	39	8	Atlanta city, GA	6.3
68	8	St. Petersburg city, FL	1 623	68	9	St. Petersburg city, FL	48.6	55	9	Anaheim city, CA	6.2
3	10	Chicago city, IL	1 606	1	10	New York City, NY	47.3	8	9	Dallas city, TX	6.2
21	11	Washington city, DC	1 507	62	11	Raleigh city, NC	45.0	7	11	San Diego city, CA	5.9
5	12	Philadelphia city, PA	1 503	73	12	Norfolk city, VA	44.6	34	12	Long Beach city, CA	5.5
63	13	Newark city, NJ	1 496	38	12	Virginia Beach city, VA	44.6	26	13	Charlotte city, NC	5.1
18	14	Memphis city, TN	1 479	64	14	Lexington-Fayette, KY	44.6	41	14	Oakland city, CA	4.9
2	15	Los Angeles city, CA	1 360	66	15	Louisville city, KY	44.4	20	15	Boston city, MA	4.8
8	16	Dallas city, TX	1 350	63	16	Newark city, NJ	44.0	4	15	Houston city, TX	4.8
33	17	Cleveland city, OH	1 263	57	17	Tampa city, FL	43.9	24	15	Seattle city, WA	4.8
41	18	Oakland city, CA	1 261	72	18	Jersey City, NJ	43.5	62	18	Raleigh city, NC	4.7
58	19	Buffalo city, NY	1 250	26	19	Charlotte city, NC	43.1	67	18	Riverside city, CA	4.7
20	20	Boston city, MA	1 243	20	20	Boston city, MA	41.5	43	20	Tulsa city, OK	4.6
70	21	Stockton city, CA	1 219	5	21	Philadelphia city, PA	41.4	69	21	Bakersfield, CA	4.5
71	22	Birmingham city, AL	1 214	17	22	Baltimore city, MD	40.8	53	22	Arlington city, TX	4.4
26	23	Charlotte city, NC	1 201	54	23	Cincinnati city, OH	40.7	64	23	Lexington-Fayette, KY	4.2
72	24	Jersey City, NJ	1 162	43	24	Tulsa city, OK	40.6	38	23	Virginia Beach city, VA	4.2
45	25	Minneapolis city, MN	1 151	21	25	Washington city, DC	38.6	74	25	Baton Rouge, LA	4.0
35	26	Albuquerque city, NM	1 145	58	26	Buffalo city, NY	38.6	25	26	Denver city, CO	3.9
74	27	Baton Rouge, LA	1 129	15	27	Columbus city, OH	38.1	6	26	Phoenix city, AZ	3.9
43	28	Tulsa city, OK	1 122	49	28	St. Louis city, MO	37.9	22	28	Nashville-Davidson consolidated city, TN	3.8
14	29	Jacksonville city, FL	1 116	36	29	Kansas City, MO	37.6	31	29	New Orleans city, LA	3.6
4	30	Houston city, TX	1 100	3	30	Chicago city, IL	37.4	16	30	Austin city, TX	3.5
28	31	Portland city, OR	1 077	24	31	Seattle city, WA	37.2	3	30	Chicago city, IL	3.5
31	32	New Orleans city, LA	1 064	52	32	Pittsburgh city, PA	36.9	72	30	Jersey City, NJ	3.5
19	33	Milwaukee city, WI	957	33	33	Cleveland city, OH	36.6	32	30	Las Vegas city, NV	3.5
52	33	Pittsburgh city, PA	957	28	34	Portland city, OR	36.3	57	34	Tampa city, FL	3.4
1	35	New York City, NY	945	8	35	Dallas city, TX	36.1	35	35	Albuquerque city, NM	3.3
30	36	Tucson city, AZ	933	53	36	Arlington city, TX	33.7	12	35	Indianapolis consolidated city, IN	3.3
37	37	Fresno city, CA	899	27	36	Fort Worth city, TX	33.7	44	35	Omaha city, NE	3.3
12	38	Indianapolis consolidated city, IN	862	29	38	Oklahoma City, OK	33.4	27	38	Fort Worth city, TX	3.2
15	39	Columbus city, OH	843	56	39	Toledo city, OH	33.0	45	38	Minneapolis city, MN	3.2
54	40	Cincinnati city, OH	840	10	40	Detroit city, MI	32.1	70	40	Stockton city, CA	3.1
13	41	San Francisco city, CA	837	16	41	Austin city, TX	31.9	48	41	Colorado Springs city, CO	3.0
59	42	St. Paul city, MN	833	19	42	Milwaukee city, WI	31.1	37	41	Fresno city, CA	3.0
44	43	Omaha city, NE	811	9	43	San Antonio city, TX	31.0	28	41	Portland city, OR	3.0
66	44	Louisville city, KY	796	60	44	Corpus Christi city, TX	30.1	40	41	Sacramento city, CA	3.0
67	45	Riverside city, CA	786	44	45	Omaha city, NE	29.9	51	41	Santa Ana city, CA	3.0
29	46	Oklahoma City, OK	781	50	46	Wichita city, KS	29.3	14	46	Jacksonville city, FL	2.9
23	47	El Paso city, TX	780	45	47	Minneapolis city, MN	28.3	36	46	Kansas City, MO	2.9
24	48	Seattle city, WA	769	59	47	St. Paul city, MN	28.3	18	46	Memphis city, TN	2.9
40	49	Sacramento city, CA	766	41	49	Oakland city, CA	24.3	52	46	Pittsburgh city, PA	2.9
56	50	Toledo city, OH	759	46	50	Honolulu CDP, HI	21.5	29	50	Oklahoma City, OK	2.8
60	51	Corpus Christi city, TX	758	13	51	San Francisco city, CA	19.7	68	50	St. Petersburg city, FL	2.8
62	52	Raleigh city, NC	742	40	52	Sacramento city, CA	17.5	50	50	Wichita city, KS	2.8
6	53	Phoenix city, AZ	738	48	53	Colorado Springs city, CO	16.2	60	53	Corpus Christi city, TX	2.7
75	54	Hialeah, FL	737	65	55	Anchorage city, AK	15.9	54	54	Cincinnati city, OH	2.6
64	55	Lexington-Fayette, KY	725	61	55	Aurora city, CO	15.4	47	54	Miami city, FL	2.6
27	56	Fort Worth city, TX	714	25	55	Denver city, CO	15.4	42	56	Mesa city, AZ	2.5
73	57	Norfolk city, VA	712	2	57	Los Angeles city, CA	14.8	59	56	St. Paul city, MN	2.5
34	58	Long Beach city, CA	697	11	58	San Jose city, CA	14.4	17	58	Baltimore city, MD	2.4
9	59	San Antonio city, TX	691	70	59	Stockton city, CA	14.0	23	58	El Paso city, TX	2.4
53	60	Arlington city, TX	648	55	60	Anaheim city, CA	12.3	9	58	San Antonio city, TX	2.4
42	61	Mesa city, AZ	604	51	60	Santa Ana city, CA	12.3	61	61	Aurora city, CO	2.3
50	61	Wichita city, KS	604	30	62	Tucson city, AZ	12.0	73	62	Norfolk city, VA	2.2
32	63	Las Vegas city, NV	599	34	63	Long Beach city, CA	11.8	5	62	Philadelphia city, PA	2.2
65	64	Anchorage city, AK	586	37	64	Fresno city, CA	10.6	15	64	Columbus city, OH	1.9
7	65	San Diego city, CA	585	7	65	San Diego city, CA	9.9	66	64	Louisville city, KY	1.9
11	66	San Jose city, CA	551	67	66	Riverside city, CA	9.6	56	66	Toledo city, OH	1.6
61	67	Aurora city, CO	547	35	67	Albuquerque city, NM	8.9	63	67	Newark city, NJ	1.5
51	68	Santa Ana city, CA	541	23	68	El Paso city, TX	8.8	30	67	Tucson city, AZ	1.5
25	69	Denver city, CO	520	42	69	Mesa city, AZ	8.5	71	69	Birmingham city, AL	1.4
16	70	Austin city, TX	472	6	70	Phoenix city, AZ	7.7	58	69	Buffalo city, NY	1.4
48	71	Colorado Springs city, CO	455	69	71	Bakersfield, CA	5.7	49	71	St. Louis city, MO	1.3
55	72	Anaheim city, CA	431	32	72	Las Vegas city, NV	4.1	10	72	Detroit city, MI	1.2
69	73	Bakersfield, CA	290	12	73	Indianapolis consolidated city, IN	NA	75	73	Hialeah, FL	1.0
46	74	Honolulu CDP, HI	263	14	74	Jacksonville city, FL	NA	19	73	Milwaukee city, WI	1.0
38	75	Virginia Beach city, VA	222	22	75	Nashville-Davidson consolidated city, TN	NA	33	75	Cleveland city, OH	0.7

Note: Column numbers refer to Table D. Cities.

TABLE 7—Congressional Districts of the 107th Congress
Selected Rankings

Total Persons, 2000			Largest Total Land Area (square kilometers), 2000			Population Density (per square kilometer), 2000		
Popu-lation Rank	State/Congressional District	[col 2] Population	Land Area Rank	State/Congressional District	[col 1] Land Area	Density Rank	State/Congressional District	[col 3] Population Density
1	NV District 2	1 062 153	1	AK At Large	1 481 347	1	NY District 15	24 390.5
2	AZ District 6	1 001 151	2	MT At Large	376 979	2	NY District 11	21 108.6
3	AZ District 3	997 565	3	NV District 2	283 851	3	NY District 14	18 941.3
4	GA District 6	943 373	4	WY At Large	251 489	4	NY District 8	16 774.7
5	NV District 1	936 104	5	SD At Large	196 540	5	NY District 16	16 185.9
6	MT At Large	902 195	6	OR District 2	182 831	6	NY District 12	14 992.2
7	TX District 26	845 541	7	ND At Large	178 647	7	NY District 10	14 449.0
8	GA District 11	836 416	8	NM District 2	174 409	8	NY District 7	11 864.4
9	TX District 3	835 040	9	NE District 3	162 847	9	NY District 17	11 266.9
10	AZ District 1	829 492	10	TX District 23	151 275	10	CA District 8	6 925.9
11	GA District 9	814 305	11	CO District 3	147 722	11	NY District 9	6 881.5
12	CO District 5	810 423	12	KS District 1	145 669	12	NY District 6	6 855.1
13	TX District 21	801 078	13	NM District 3	127 699	13	IL District 4	6 118.7
14	FL District 19	800 902	14	UT District 3	123 331	14	CA District 30	6 038.8
15	AZ District 5	793 256	15	ID District 2	111 878	15	MA District 8	5 389.9
16	VA District 10	792 534	16	AZ District 3	107 779	16	CA District 35	5 389.6
17	TX District 10	791 117	17	AZ District 6	106 755	17	CA District 33	4 852.1
18	FL District 14	790 852	18	CO District 4	104 330	18	CA District 32	4 807.5
19	FL District 21	789 742	19	ID District 1	102 436	19	IL District 5	4 654.6
20	TX District 22	784 759	20	UT District 1	88 233	20	PA District 2	4 527.7
21	DE At Large	783 600	21	TX District 13	82 231	21	NJ District 13	4 435.5
22	FL District 20	783 412	22	CA District 40	77 476	22	IL District 7	4 330.6
23	FL District 8	782 397	23	CA District 2	73 589	23	IL District 9	4 264.6
24	GA District 3	781 694	24	TX District 17	72 843	24	NJ District 10	4 201.0
25	TX District 15	780 310	25	ME District 2	70 563	25	CA District 46	4 078.4
26	TX District 8	776 623	26	MN District 7	68 163	26	NY District 13	3 973.9
27	AZ District 2	773 824	27	MN District 8	66 868	27	IL District 1	3 898.7
28	CA District 48	773 292	28	OK District 6	66 285	28	PA District 3	3 897.1
29	TX District 7	772 147	29	WA District 4	61 408	29	PA District 1	3 799.3
30	UT District 3	765 911	30	MI District 1	58 958	30	CA District 26	3 647.6
31	NC District 4	765 876	31	TX District 19	52 282	31	DC Delegate	3 597.9
32	UT District 1	765 156	32	AR District 4	46 727	32	CA District 37	3 294.7
33	AR District 3	764 853	33	OK District 3	46 520	33	CA District 38	3 231.7
34	TX District 23	762 627	34	IA District 5	46 102	34	CA District 9	3 163.6
35	TX District 6	759 418	35	AZ District 2	45 866	35	CA District 31	3 069.4
36	IL District 13	759 124	36	WA District 5	45 778	36	NY District 4	2 811.0
37	FL District 16	758 365	37	MO District 8	45 243	37	NJ District 9	2 701.3
38	FL District 6	755 939	38	TX District 21	44 845	38	MI District 14	2 662.5
39	SD At Large	754 844	39	WI District 7	43 310	39	CA District 34	2 637.1
40	GA District 7	752 161	40	AR District 1	42 986	40	CA District 45	2 625.5
41	CO District 4	748 228	41	MN District 2	42 183	41	NY District 18	2 549.2
42	GA District 4	744 717	42	OR District 4	41 649	42	MI District 15	2 429.8
43	OR District 1	743 195	43	TX District 14	39 824	43	NJ District 8	2 365.2
44	CA District 44	742 718	44	TX District 2	36 763	44	CA District 39	2 297.8
45	TN District 6	738 663	45	MO District 4	36 519	45	CA District 12	2 219.1
46	CA District 43	736 634	46	KS District 2	36 185	46	FL District 17	2 123.5
47	AZ District 4	735 344	47	IA District 3	35 822	47	MN District 5	2 013.1
48	FL District 4	734 246	48	MO District 6	35 146	48	FL District 18	2 007.2
49	KS District 3	733 606	49	NE District 1	34 701	49	OH District 11	1 970.2
50	SC District 2	731 022	50	LA District 5	33 943	50	WI District 5	1 943.5
51	NC District 2	730 266	51	AZ District 5	32 866	51	IL District 3	1 922.4
52	TN District 7	728 956	52	NY District 24	32 093	52	CA District 29	1 915.6
53	CA District 4	725 180	53	IA District 2	31 754	53	CA District 49	1 913.5
54	IN District 6	724 143	54	MS District 2	31 723	54	MD District 7	1 912.9
55	CO District 3	723 533	55	TX District 28	31 537	55	FL District 22	1 906.8
56	MD District 6	723 196	56	MO District 9	31 455	56	CA District 50	1 844.8
57	FL District 7	722 139	57	FL District 2	30 607	57	WA District 7	1 803.9
58	FL District 9	722 068	58	OK District 2	30 291	58	IL District 2	1 726.6
59	MN District 6	720 995	59	TX District 1	29 949	59	CA District 5	1 710.3
60	IL District 14	720 663	60	AR District 3	29 804	60	NV District 1	1 567.5
61	WA District 2	719 487	61	GA District 8	29 785	61	NY District 5	1 565.6
62	FL District 15	718 294	62	GA District 3	29 679	62	AZ District 1	1 520.3
63	CA District 47	715 625	63	TX District 11	29 262	63	VA District 8	1 497.7
64	KY District 6	715 306	64	KY District 1	29 087	64	FL District 10	1 495.0
65	MD District 5	714 886	65	CA District 4	27 988	65	TX District 18	1 492.2
66	CA District 51	713 746	66	CA District 1	27 978	66	MI District 12	1 489.9
67	CA District 10	713 341	67	IL District 19	27 791	67	AZ District 4	1 468.9
68	CA District 20	711 574	68	WI District 3	27 552	68	NY District 3	1 468.2
69	NJ District 12	709 867	69	PA District 5	27 140	69	OH District 10	1 423.3
70	CA District 19	709 622	70	MS District 1	26 931	70	MA District 7	1 378.4
71	VA District 1	709 060	71	KY District 5	26 744	71	MO District 1	1 363.0
72	TX District 4	707 329	72	LA District 4	26 405	72	MD District 4	1 298.3
73	KY District 2	706 978	73	AL District 2	26 235	73	IL District 6	1 291.5
74	ID District 1	702 521	74	KS District 4	26 029	74	CA District 42	1 288.9
75	CO District 2	702 336	75	MS District 3	25 893	75	FL District 21	1 283.9

Note: Column numbers refer to Table E. Congressional Districts.

TABLE 7—Congressional Districts of the 107th Congress
Selected Rankings

	Percent White, 2000			Percent Black, 2000			Percent American Indian, Alaska Native, 2000	
White Rank	State/Congressional District	[col 4] Percent White	Black Rank	State/Congressional District	[col 5] Percent Black	American Indian, Alaska Native Rank	State/Congressional District	[col 6] Percent American Indian, Alaska Native
1	KY District 5	98.3	1	MI District 14	80.2	1	OK District 2	23.2
2	ME District 2	98.0	2	IL District 2	76.6	2	NM District 3	21.4
3	VT At Large	97.9	3	MD District 7	75.5	3	AK At Large	19.0
4	ME District 1	97.7	4	IL District 1	71.1	4	AZ District 6	16.4
4	PA District 12	97.7	4	NY District 11	71.1	5	OK District 3	15.3
6	PA District 9	97.6	6	MI District 15	71.0	6	SD At Large	9.0
7	WI District 3	97.2	7	AL District 7	70.3	7	OK District 1	8.5
8	NH District 1	97.1	8	LA District 2	67.5	8	MT At Large	7.4
8	WV District 1	97.1	9	TN District 9	66.6	8	NC District 7	7.4
10	TN District 1	97.0	10	MD District 4	66.5	10	OK District 4	7.1
11	NH District 2	96.9	11	NY District 10	66.2	11	OK District 6	6.9
11	WI District 6	96.9	12	OH District 11	65.7	12	OK District 5	6.6
13	IN District 9	96.8	12	PA District 2	65.7	13	ND At Large	5.5
13	PA District 11	96.8	14	MS District 2	65.5	14	AZ District 2	5.2
15	WI District 9	96.7	15	IL District 7	64.0	15	NM District 2	5.0
16	OH District 18	96.6	16	GA District 5	63.7	16	CA District 1	4.5
16	OH District 6	96.6	17	FL District 17	63.4	16	NM District 1	4.5
16	PA District 5	96.6	18	NJ District 10	63.2	18	CA District 2	4.2
19	MN District 8	96.4	19	DC Delegate	61.3	19	WA District 6	3.9
20	IA District 2	96.3	19	SC District 6	61.3	20	MI District 1	3.8
20	IA District 3	96.3	21	MO District 1	60.8	20	WA District 4	3.8
20	MN District 2	96.3	22	FL District 23	58.7	22	WI District 8	3.5
23	KY District 4	96.1	23	VA District 3	57.7	23	MN District 7	3.4
23	MI District 4	96.1	24	PA District 1	56.6	24	AZ District 3	3.3
23	MO District 7	96.1	25	NY District 6	56.5	24	OR District 2	3.3
26	WI District 7	96.0	26	NC District 1	50.9	26	NC District 8	3.2
27	IA District 5	95.9	27	FL District 3	50.8	27	MN District 8	3.0
28	VA District 9	95.8	28	GA District 4	50.6	27	OR District 4	3.0
29	NY District 22	95.7	29	MS District 4	47.2	27	WA District 2	3.0
29	PA District 10	95.7	30	NY District 17	46.2	27	WY At Large	3.0
29	PA District 4	95.7	31	NC District 12	45.3	31	CA District 19	2.9
32	PA District 20	95.6	32	WI District 5	44.6	32	CA District 21	2.8
33	MN District 1	95.5	33	TX District 18	40.9	32	CA District 40	2.8
33	WV District 2	95.5	34	GA District 2	40.8	32	UT District 3	2.8
35	IN District 5	95.4	35	TX District 30	39.8	32	WA District 5	2.8
35	MI District 1	95.4	36	VA District 4	39.7	32	WA District 9	2.8
37	OH District 2	95.3	37	NY District 15	39.4	37	AZ District 1	2.7
37	OH District 5	95.3	38	NY District 16	39.1	37	CA District 3	2.7
39	MI District 10	95.2	39	GA District 10	39.0	39	CA District 5	2.6
39	MN District 7	95.2	40	CA District 35	35.7	39	CO District 3	2.6
39	NE District 3	95.2	41	IN District 10	35.3	39	MN District 5	2.6
42	IN District 6	95.1	42	OH District 1	34.9	39	NV District 2	2.6
42	IN District 7	95.1	43	CA District 32	34.6	43	HI District 2	2.5
42	MO District 6	95.1	44	LA District 4	34.4	44	AR District 3	2.4
42	NY District 23	95.1	45	LA District 6	33.8	44	AZ District 4	2.4
42	NY District 31	95.1	46	LA District 5	32.9	44	CA District 18	2.4
47	TN District 4	95.0	47	GA District 8	32.7	44	CA District 20	2.4
48	MI District 16	94.9	48	MS District 3	32.3	44	KS District 4	2.4
48	OH District 8	94.9	49	GA District 1	31.7	44	OR District 5	2.4
48	WV District 3	94.9	50	GA District 3	31.3	44	WA District 3	2.4
51	MO District 4	94.8	51	SC District 5	31.0	51	CA District 11	2.3
51	OR District 4	94.8	52	MD District 5	30.2	51	CA District 4	2.3
53	OH District 19	94.7	53	AL District 1	28.9	53	OR District 3	2.3
54	IN District 8	94.6	54	AL District 2	28.3	54	CA District 22	2.2
54	MN District 6	94.6	55	SC District 2	28.2	54	CO District 1	2.2
56	IL District 19	94.4	56	CA District 9	27.9	54	ID District 1	2.2
56	NY District 27	94.4	57	MD District 3	27.8	54	KS District 2	2.2
56	PA District 19	94.4	58	NC District 2	27.5	58	CA District 42	2.1
59	PA District 21	94.3	59	MO District 5	27.1	58	CA District 44	2.1
60	IN District 2	94.2	59	NC District 8	27.1	58	CA District 52	2.1
60	MO District 8	94.2	61	AR District 4	27.0	58	LA District 3	2.1
60	MO District 9	94.2	62	CA District 37	26.8	58	NY District 6	2.1
60	NY District 24	94.2	63	FL District 2	25.7	58	WA District 7	2.1
64	OH District 16	94.0	64	AL District 3	25.6	58	WI District 7	2.1
65	WI District 8	93.8	64	LA District 3	25.6	65	AZ District 5	2.0
66	WY At Large	93.7	64	TN District 5	25.6	65	CA District 17	2.0
67	ID District 1	93.5	67	LA District 7	25.4	65	CA District 43	2.0
68	IL District 17	93.4	68	VA District 5	24.5	65	ID District 2	2.0
68	ND At Large	93.4	69	TX District 25	24.4	65	MO District 7	2.0
68	OH District 4	93.4	70	OH District 12	24.2	65	NC District 11	2.0
71	IA District 1	93.3	70	VA District 2	24.2	71	CA District 23	1.9
71	NE District 1	93.3	72	TN District 8	23.8	71	CA District 34	1.9
73	IL District 20	93.2	73	NC District 7	23.5	71	CA District 6	1.9
73	OH District 7	93.2	74	MA District 8	22.6	71	CA District 7	1.9
73	PA District 8	93.2	75	MS District 1	22.6	71	NY District 16	1.9

Note: Column numbers refer to Table E. Congressional Districts.

TABLE 7—Congressional Districts of the 107th Congress
Selected Rankings

Asian Rank	State/Congressional District	[col 7] Percent Asian	Hispanic Rank	State/Congressional District	[col 9] Percent Hispanic	Under 18 Years Rank	State/Congressional District	[cols 12 & 13] Percent Under 18 Years
1	HI District 1	83.9	1	CA District 33	86.0	1	CA District 37	36.2
2	HI District 2	79.1	2	TX District 15	78.9	2	CA District 42	35.3
3	CA District 12	35.0	3	TX District 16	78.0	3	CA District 35	34.6
4	CA District 13	34.5	4	FL District 21	77.5	4	CA District 20	34.3
5	CA District 8	31.0	5	CA District 34	72.4	4	NY District 16	34.3
6	CA District 31	29.6	6	FL District 18	70.5	6	UT District 3	33.7
7	CA District 16	29.5	6	TX District 27	70.5	7	TX District 15	33.2
8	CA District 14	21.7	8	IL District 4	70.1	8	TX District 29	33.1
9	CA District 28	21.2	9	TX District 20	67.0	8	UT District 1	33.1
10	CA District 30	21.0	10	TX District 23	66.3	10	CA District 33	33.0
11	CA District 39	20.5	11	CA District 26	65.4	11	CA District 46	32.5
12	CA District 15	20.1	12	TX District 28	65.0	11	TX District 23	32.5
13	CA District 9	20.0	13	CA District 30	64.3	13	AZ District 2	32.2
14	NY District 5	19.8	14	CA District 20	63.7	14	CA District 18	32.1
15	CA District 5	19.3	15	NY District 16	62.9	15	CA District 43	31.7
16	CA District 7	18.5	16	AZ District 2	62.5	16	CA District 26	31.5
17	NY District 7	18.4	17	CA District 46	62.3	17	CA District 50	31.4
18	CA District 36	17.9	18	TX District 29	60.9	17	MI District 14	31.4
19	NY District 12	17.7	19	CA District 31	59.4	17	TX District 16	31.4
20	CA District 45	17.6	20	CA District 37	57.2	20	TX District 28	31.3
21	CA District 50	17.3	21	CA District 35	54.2	21	IL District 4	31.2
22	CA District 46	16.7	22	CA District 42	50.8	22	CA District 21	31.1
23	CA District 41	16.4	22	CA District 50	50.8	22	IL District 2	31.1
24	WA District 7	16.0	24	NY District 15	50.5	22	TX District 27	31.1
25	CA District 47	15.7	25	NY District 12	48.6	25	CA District 34	30.9
26	CA District 27	14.9	26	NM District 2	48.0	25	CA District 41	30.9
27	NY District 9	14.7	27	NJ District 13	47.2	25	TX District 24	30.9
28	CA District 11	13.9	28	NM District 1	42.8	28	FL District 17	30.8
28	VA District 11	13.9	29	CA District 17	42.6	29	CA District 11	30.6
30	CA District 51	13.4	30	CA District 41	40.9	30	AK At Large	30.4
30	IL District 9	13.4	31	CA District 38	40.1	31	WA District 4	30.2
32	NY District 6	13.2	32	CA District 16	39.8	32	CA District 19	30.1
33	MD District 8	12.6	33	NY District 7	39.1	33	CA District 25	30.0
34	NY District 18	12.2	34	CA District 44	38.5	34	MS District 2	29.9
35	NJ District 9	12.1	35	CA District 23	37.7	35	MN District 6	29.8
36	CA District 10	11.7	36	CA District 32	37.1	36	MI District 15	29.7
37	WA District 9	11.6	37	CA District 18	36.4	37	CA District 40	29.6
38	CA District 29	11.5	38	NY District 17	35.9	37	UT District 2	29.6
39	CA District 38	11.4	39	NM District 3	35.7	39	NY District 10	29.5
39	NY District 8	11.4	40	CA District 43	35.5	40	CA District 31	29.4
41	CA District 37	10.9	41	TX District 30	34.7	40	ID District 2	29.4
41	TX District 22	10.9	42	TX District 24	34.5	40	TX District 25	29.4
43	CA District 49	10.5	43	CO District 1	33.4	43	TX District 22	29.3
43	NY District 13	10.5	43	TX District 18	33.4	43	TX District 30	29.3
43	NY District 14	10.5	45	CA District 19	32.9	45	IL District 14	29.2
43	WA District 1	10.5	46	CA District 28	31.6	45	NM District 3	29.2
47	VA District 8	10.2	47	CA District 21	31.4	47	FL District 23	29.1
48	CA District 34	10.1	48	TX District 25	31.1	48	LA District 3	28.9
48	NJ District 6	10.1	49	CA District 39	30.4	49	CA District 23	28.8
50	WA District 8	9.8	50	CA District 52	29.7	49	NM District 2	28.8
51	CA District 24	9.4	51	TX District 10	28.8	51	CA District 44	28.7
51	NJ District 7	9.4	52	TX District 14	27.9	52	TX District 20	28.6
53	CA District 25	9.3	53	CA District 11	27.8	53	IL District 1	28.5
54	CA District 32	9.2	54	FL District 17	27.4	53	TX District 3	28.5
55	MN District 4	9.1	55	CA District 22	27.0	53	WI District 5	28.5
56	TX District 3	8.8	56	NV District 1	26.6	56	CA District 38	28.4
57	CA District 19	8.7	57	TX District 19	26.1	56	GA District 3	28.4
57	CA District 3	8.7	58	NJ District 8	25.8	58	LA District 2	28.3
59	IL District 6	8.5	59	WA District 4	25.4	58	NY District 11	28.3
59	MA District 8	8.5	60	CA District 25	25.0	60	AZ District 6	28.2
61	NJ District 12	8.4	60	IL District 5	25.0	60	CA District 30	28.2
62	TX District 7	8.2	60	TX District 12	25.0	60	FL District 3	28.2
63	IL District 8	8.1	63	TX District 13	24.6	63	CO District 5	28.1
64	CA District 26	7.6	64	IL District 3	24.3	63	IL District 13	28.1
65	NV District 1	7.5	65	CA District 40	23.8	63	IN District 4	28.1
66	OR District 3	7.3	66	TX District 5	23.6	63	LA District 7	28.1
67	CA District 17	7.2	67	CA District 27	23.1	63	MI District 3	28.1
68	CA District 48	7.0	67	FL District 20	23.1	68	CA District 5	28.0
68	IL District 5	7.0	69	FL District 8	23.0	68	IL District 16	28.0
68	NJ District 11	7.0	69	TX District 5	23.0	68	NY District 17	28.0
71	CA District 23	6.9	71	AZ District 1	22.7	68	WA District 8	28.0
71	NJ District 13	6.9	72	CA District 48	22.5	72	CA District 3	27.9
73	CA District 18	6.8	73	TX District 22	22.3	72	CA District 48	27.9
73	IL District 13	6.8	74	CA District 13	22.1	72	TN District 9	27.9
73	WA District 6	6.8	75	CA District 7	21.6	72	VA District 10	27.9

Note: Column numbers refer to Table E. Congressional Districts.

73

TABLE 7—Congressional Districts of the 107th Congress
Selected Rankings

65 Years and Over Rank	Percent 65 Years and Over, 2000 — State/Congressional District	[cols 19 & 20] Percent 65 Years and Over	Female House-holder Rank	Percent Female-Headed Family Household, 2000 — State/Congressional District	[col 24] Percent Female Householder	One Person House-hold Rank	Percent of Households Composed of One Person, 2000 — State/Congressional District	[col 25] Percent of All House-holds
1	FL District 13	29.4	1	NY District 16	37.5	1	NY District 14	51.3
2	FL District 14	26.6	2	MI District 8	30.5	2	NY District 8	47.1
3	FL District 19	25.3	3	NY District 10	29.2	3	CA District 29	45.8
4	FL District 22	23.5	4	NY District 11	29.1	4	DC Delegate	43.8
5	FL District 16	23.2	5	IL District 2	29.0	5	CA District 8	41.3
6	FL District 5	22.9	6	MI District 15	28.7	6	FL District 22	40.5
7	FL District 10	22.3	7	NY District 15	27.8	7	WA District 7	39.8
8	FL District 15	20.5	7	PA District 1	27.8	8	IL District 9	39.6
9	FL District 6	20.2	9	FL District 17	27.0	9	PA District 2	38.4
10	PA District 18	19.7	9	IL District 1	27.0	10	MN District 5	38.1
11	FL District 9	19.4	9	NY District 17	27.0	11	CO District 1	37.5
12	PA District 11	18.4	12	MD District 7	26.6	12	CA District 49	36.5
13	AZ District 3	18.2	13	AL District 7	26.1	13	MA District 8	36.4
14	PA District 12	17.9	14	NJ District 10	25.8	14	PA District 14	36.2
15	IA District 5	17.8	15	LA District 2	25.7	15	GA District 5	35.2
16	NC District 11	17.6	16	MS District 2	25.6	16	FL District 10	35.1
16	PA District 20	17.6	17	TN District 9	25.3	17	IL District 7	34.9
18	CA District 44	17.3	18	CA District 35	24.7	18	NY District 15	34.7
18	PA District 4	17.3	19	NY District 6	24.3	18	OH District 1	34.7
20	NE District 3	17.2	20	OH District 11	24.0	18	OH District 11	34.7
21	FL District 18	17.1	21	IL District 7	23.9	21	IL District 5	34.4
22	FL District 12	17.0	22	CA District 37	23.6	22	MO District 1	34.3
23	IL District 19	16.9	23	MO District 1	23.1	23	VA District 8	33.8
24	MA District 10	16.8	24	PA District 2	23.0	24	CA District 9	33.7
24	PA District 14	16.8	25	SC District 6	22.5	24	WI District 5	33.7
26	NJ District 3	16.7	26	NY District 12	22.3	26	IN District 10	33.4
26	OH District 17	16.7	27	FL District 3	22.1	27	MI District 15	33.1
26	OH District 19	16.7	28	FL District 23	22.0	28	MD District 7	32.9
26	PA District 10	16.7	29	VA District 3	21.7	28	OH District 10	32.9
30	IL District 17	16.6	30	MD District 4	21.1	30	MO District 5	32.8
31	PA District 6	16.5	31	GA District 5	20.9	31	TN District 5	32.5
32	KS District 1	16.4	32	TX District 30	20.6	32	PA District 1	32.2
33	IA District 2	16.3	32	WI District 5	20.6	33	NY District 21	32.1
34	MI District 1	16.2	34	NC District 1	19.3	34	PA District 18	32.0
34	NJ District 4	16.2	35	MS District 4	19.1	35	IL District 1	31.8
34	PA District 9	16.2	36	TX District 18	19.0	35	MN District 4	31.8
37	IA District 3	16.0	37	DC Delegate	18.9	37	KY District 3	31.7
37	NY District 5	16.0	38	GA District 2	18.8	38	CA District 32	31.3
39	AZ District 5	15.9	38	NC District 12	18.8	39	TN District 9	30.9
39	NY District 18	15.9	40	CA District 32	18.7	40	FL District 11	30.5
39	NY District 9	15.9	41	CA District 50	18.5	41	OH District 15	30.4
42	NY District 23	15.8	42	TX District 16	18.3	41	OH District 3	30.4
42	WV District 1	15.8	43	IN District 10	18.1	41	TX District 10	30.4
44	WV District 3	15.7	44	CA District 33	17.7	41	TX District 18	30.4
45	AR District 4	15.6	44	GA District 10	17.7	45	CA District 36	30.3
45	MO District 8	15.6	46	NJ District 13	17.6	45	RI District 1	30.3
45	NY District 30	15.6	46	TX District 20	17.6	47	NY District 28	30.2
45	PA District 15	15.6	46	TX District 28	17.6	47	NY District 29	30.2
45	PA District 3	15.6	49	CA District 31	17.4	47	VA District 3	30.2
45	PA District 7	15.6	50	OH District 1	17.3	50	NY District 9	30.1
51	PA District 21	15.5	51	CA District 42	17.2	50	PA District 3	30.1
52	FL District 7	15.4	52	CA District 34	16.9	52	MI District 12	29.8
52	MA District 7	15.4	53	GA District 4	16.8	52	NY District 30	29.8
52	RI District 1	15.4	53	PA District 3	16.8	54	WI District 4	29.7
55	CA District 2	15.3	55	LA District 4	16.7	55	MA District 7	29.6
55	NY District 21	15.3	55	LA District 5	16.7	56	CA District 5	29.5
55	NY District 3	15.3	57	AZ District 2	16.6	56	NY District 17	29.5
58	HI District 1	15.2	57	IL District 4	16.6	58	FL District 13	29.4
58	OR District 4	15.2	59	CA District 20	16.5	58	LA District 2	29.4
58	PA District 13	15.2	59	CA District 30	16.5	58	MA District 9	29.4
58	TX District 1	15.2	59	TX District 29	16.5	58	NY District 26	29.4
62	IL District 20	15.1	62	GA District 8	16.4	62	MO District 3	29.3
62	OH District 18	15.1	62	VA District 4	16.4	62	ND At Large	29.3
62	OR District 2	15.1	64	TX District 27	16.2	64	MD District 3	29.2
62	TX District 17	15.1	65	FL District 21	16.1	65	OK District 1	29.1
62	VA District 5	15.1	65	TX District 24	16.1	66	MI District 13	29.0
67	MN District 7	15.0	67	SC District 5	16.0	66	PA District 11	29.0
67	NY District 31	15.0	68	NY District 7	15.9	68	IL District 15	28.9
67	OK District 3	15.0	68	TX District 25	15.9	68	OH District 9	28.9
67	VA District 6	15.0	70	LA District 6	15.7	70	TX District 5	28.8
67	WI District 7	15.0	70	MS District 3	15.7	71	CA District 27	28.6
72	MN District 8	14.9	72	AL District 1	15.6	71	NJ District 9	28.6
72	NJ District 9	14.9	72	IN District 1	15.6	71	NY District 25	28.6
72	PA District 19	14.9	74	CA District 26	15.5	71	OR District 3	28.6
75	ME District 2	14.8	74	CA District 38	15.5	75	FL District 19	28.5
75	NY District 29	14.8	74	GA District 3	15.5	75	IL District 19	28.5
75	OH District 10	14.8	74	NY District 30	15.5	75	NY District 10	28.5

Note: Column numbers refer to Table E. Congressional Districts.

TABLE 7—Congressional Districts of the 107th Congress
Selected Rankings

Percent College Graduates (Bachelor's or higher degree), 1990

Percent College Graduate Rank	State/Congressional District	[col 32] Percent of All Persons 25 Yrs. and Over
1	NY District 14	51.4
2	MD District 8	51.1
3	VA District 8	48.0
4	VA District 11	44.3
5	CA District 14	44.2
6	CA District 29	43.5
7	NY District 8	42.1
8	TX District 26	40.8
9	TX District 7	40.6
10	IL District 10	40.4
11	NJ District 12	39.7
12	GA District 6	39.5
13	NJ District 11	37.4
14	CA District 47	37.1
15	WA District 7	37.0
16	CA District 36	36.8
17	IL District 9	36.6
18	MA District 8	36.0
19	NC District 4	35.9
19	TX District 3	35.9
21	CA District 10	35.8
22	CA District 9	35.4
23	IL District 13	35.0
24	CA District 15	34.8
24	NY District 5	34.8
26	CA District 51	34.5
26	TX District 10	34.5
28	MI District 11	34.4
29	CT District 4	34.0
30	CA District 49	33.9
31	CA District 8	33.8
32	MO District 2	33.6
33	PA District 13	33.5
34	CA District 24	33.4
34	CO District 6	33.4
34	NY District 18	33.4
37	DC Delegate	33.3
38	GA District 4	33.1
39	CA District 6	33.0
40	MN District 3	32.9
41	NJ District 5	32.6
41	TX District 6	32.6
43	NJ District 7	32.4
43	NY District 19	32.4
45	CA District 12	31.6
46	KS District 3	31.5
47	CA District 27	31.4
48	WA District 1	31.2
49	PA District 7	31.0
50	MA District 4	30.9
51	OR District 1	30.8
52	MA District 7	30.6
53	VA District 7	30.5
54	MN District 5	30.3
54	VA District 10	30.3
56	IL District 8	30.2
57	CO District 5	30.1
58	NY District 3	29.9
58	TX District 22	29.9
60	NY District 20	29.6
61	CO District 2	29.5
62	TX District 8	29.2
63	WA District 8	29.0
64	MA District 5	28.8
65	IL District 6	28.6
66	MN District 4	28.1
67	TX District 21	28.0
68	MA District 9	27.8
69	CA District 45	27.7
69	CA District 48	27.7
69	MD District 4	27.7
72	AZ District 1	27.6
73	MA District 6	27.4
73	NY District 28	27.4
75	MI District 13	27.3

Median Household Income, 1989

Household Income Rank	State/Congressional District	[col 34] Median Income (dollars)
1	NJ District 11	57 219
2	MD District 8	56 789
3	NY District 3	56 060
4	NY District 12	54 630
5	VA District 11	54 369
6	NJ District 5	53 433
7	CA District 10	52 378
8	CA District 47	51 554
9	NJ District 7	50 996
10	NY District 4	50 887
11	CA District 15	50 823
12	IL District 10	50 355
13	NY District 19	50 239
14	NY District 5	50 103
15	IL District 13	50 087
16	CA District 14	50 078
17	NY District 2	50 076
18	MI District 11	49 021
19	VA District 8	48 839
20	CA District 36	48 522
21	CA District 24	48 433
22	CT District 4	47 636
23	IL District 8	47 374
24	NY District 20	47 107
25	MD District 5	46 936
26	CA District 25	46 480
27	VA District 10	46 205
28	CA District 39	46 196
29	GA District 6	46 148
30	NY District 1	45 464
31	CA District 51	45 186
32	CA District 45	45 074
33	PA District 13	44 764
34	CA District 12	44 720
35	CA District 41	44 607
36	MN District 3	44 329
37	IL District 6	44 216
38	CT District 5	44 056
39	MO District 2	43 957
40	CA District 13	43 877
41	NY District 18	43 754
42	CA District 28	43 508
43	PA District 8	43 483
44	CA District 23	42 989
45	CT District 6	42 817
46	MA District 5	42 701
47	CA District 48	42 389
48	WA District 8	42 379
49	NJ District 6	42 309
50	CA District 16	42 223
51	NY District 14	42 184
52	MN District 6	42 161
53	PA District 7	41 710
54	TX District 3	41 683
55	AK At Large	41 408
56	MA District 7	41 318
57	NJ District 3	41 257
58	MD District 4	41 081
59	TX District 6	40 930
60	MA District 6	40 836
61	NJ District 9	40 816
62	CA District 6	40 564
63	WA District 1	40 390
64	TX District 7	40 331
65	TX District 26	40 269
66	HI District 1	40 257
67	TX District 22	40 160
68	MD District 2	40 120
69	CT District 1	39 961
70	NJ District 8	39 944
71	CT District 3	39 815
71	IL District 14	39 815
73	MA District 4	39 005
74	VA District 7	38 865
75	MI District 12	38 760

Percentage of Households with Income of $100,000 or more, 1989

Income Rank	State/Congressional District	[col 35] Percent with $100,000 or More Income
1	IL District 10	18.5
2	NY District 14	18.3
3	MD District 8	18.2
4	NJ District 11	18.0
5	CT District 4	17.7
6	NY District 3	17.3
7	NJ District 12	16.9
8	CA District 29	16.8
9	NJ District 5	16.3
10	CA District 24	16.2
10	NY District 5	16.2
12	CA District 47	16.1
13	CA District 14	15.8
14	CA District 36	14.8
15	CA District 10	14.5
16	NY District 19	14.4
17	NY District 18	14.3
18	NJ District 7	13.9
19	MI District 11	13.7
20	NY District 4	13.3
21	VA District 11	12.8
22	NY District 20	12.7
23	CA District 15	12.4
24	PA District 13	12.0
25	NY District 8	11.8
25	VA District 8	11.8
27	TX District 7	11.1
28	TX District 26	11.0
29	GA District 6	10.9
30	CT District 5	10.6
31	CA District 48	10.5
31	IL District 13	10.5
33	CA District 27	10.4
34	VA District 10	10.3
35	CA District 45	10.2
35	CA District 51	10.2
37	NY District 2	10.1
38	CA District 25	10.0
38	CA District 6	10.0
38	MA District 4	10.0
41	CA District 12	9.8
42	CA District 39	9.5
42	IL District 8	9.5
42	NJ District 8	9.5
45	MA District 5	9.3
45	MO District 2	9.3
45	PA District 7	9.3
48	MN District 3	9.1
49	CA District 28	9.0
50	FL District 22	8.8
51	NY District 1	8.7
52	MA District 7	8.6
53	CA District 41	8.5
54	HI District 1	8.3
55	NJ District 9	8.1
56	MA District 6	8.0
57	CT District 6	7.8
57	DC Delegate	7.8
59	AK At Large	7.7
59	PA District 8	7.7
61	IL District 6	7.6
61	MA District 9	7.6
61	TX District 3	7.6
64	CA District 23	7.5
64	NJ District 3	7.5
66	NJ District 6	7.4
67	CT District 1	7.3
68	NY District 13	7.0
68	WA District 8	7.0
70	AZ District 4	6.9
70	CA District 49	6.9
70	CA District 8	6.9
70	CT District 3	6.9
70	MD District 5	6.9
70	TX District 8	6.9

Note: Column numbers refer to Table E. Congressional Districts.

TABLE 7—Congressional Districts of the 107th Congress
Selected Rankings

Percent of Persons Below the Poverty Level, 1989			Median Value of Owner-Occupied Housing Units, 1990			Median Gross Rent of Renter-Occupied Housing Units, 1990		
Poverty Rate Rank	State/Congressional District	[col 36] Poverty Rate for Persons 1989	Median Value Rank	State/Congressional District	[col 41] Median Value in 1990 (dollars)	Median Rent Rank	State/Congressional District	[col 44] Median Rent in 1990 (dollars)
1	NY District 16	41.8	1	CA District 29	500 001	1	CA District 47	845
2	MS District 2	37.7	2	CA District 14	404 400	2	NY District 2	817
3	TX District 15	37.5	3	CA District 36	371 100	3	CA District 45	815
4	MI District 15	36.6	4	CA District 12	324 100	4	CA District 36	812
5	NY District 15	33.0	5	HI District 1	311 200	5	NY District 3	811
6	KY District 5	32.7	6	CA District 24	305 700	6	VA District 11	797
7	AL District 7	31.2	7	CA District 27	296 000	7	CA District 15	794
8	LA District 2	31.0	8	CA District 15	291 500	8	NY District 1	782
9	NY District 12	30.4	9	NY District 18	288 500	9	CA District 12	780
10	TX District 27	29.7	10	CA District 47	280 800	10	CA District 24	779
11	IL District 7	29.5	11	CT District 4	277 400	11	CA District 14	777
11	TX District 23	29.5	12	CA District 10	275 100	11	MD District 8	777
13	NY District 10	28.3	13	CA District 8	274 700	13	CA District 10	746
14	TX District 28	28.2	14	CA District 45	266 300	14	CA District 39	736
15	CA District 33	28.0	15	CA District 6	257 400	15	CA District 23	733
15	PA District 1	28.0	16	NY District 5	256 900	16	CA District 51	730
17	AZ District 2	27.9	17	CA District 39	239 000	16	NJ District 11	730
17	CA District 20	27.9	18	CA District 48	237 300	18	VA District 8	729
17	LA District 5	27.9	19	NY District 14	235 700	19	CA District 13	726
20	SC District 6	27.0	20	CA District 23	235 600	20	CA District 46	719
20	TX District 16	27.0	21	CA District 32	234 800	21	CA District 16	718
22	TX District 18	26.7	22	CA District 16	234 500	22	NJ District 5	717
23	FL District 17	26.6	23	CA District 28	233 700	23	CA District 6	709
24	NC District 1	26.1	24	CA District 51	231 000	24	CT District 4	706
25	MS District 4	25.3	25	CA District 22	230 100	25	CA District 28	705
26	LA District 7	24.7	26	CA District 49	226 000	25	NY District 4	705
27	AR District 1	24.6	27	CA District 38	224 700	27	NJ District 7	699
27	CA District 35	24.6	28	CA District 9	223 900	28	CA District 48	696
27	MI District 14	24.6	29	CA District 13	223 700	28	NJ District 12	696
30	TX District 20	24.4	30	NY District 8	223 000	30	CA District 25	690
31	GA District 2	24.2	31	CA District 17	220 800	31	MA District 7	685
31	TN District 9	24.2	32	NJ District 11	215 600	32	CA District 29	678
33	CA District 30	24.1	33	NJ District 5	214 400	32	NY District 14	678
33	WV District 3	24.1	34	CA District 25	214 100	34	MD District 5	674
35	IL District 1	23.8	35	NY District 9	212 300	35	FL District 19	672
35	IL District 4	23.8	36	VA District 8	209 900	36	CA District 27	671
37	LA District 4	23.7	37	MD District 8	207 200	37	IL District 8	667
38	NM District 3	23.6	38	NY District 7	206 100	38	NY District 5	660
39	NM District 2	23.5	39	NJ District 12	205 700	39	HI District 1	659
40	CA District 37	23.3	40	NY District 3	205 300	39	NY District 20	659
41	LA District 3	22.6	41	CA District 41	204 600	41	VA District 10	657
42	AR District 4	22.4	42	NY District 19	199 200	42	CA District 41	656
42	MO District 8	22.4	43	NY District 4	197 800	43	NY District 19	653
42	OK District 3	22.4	44	NJ District 9	195 700	44	MA District 10	651
45	OH District 11	22.1	45	MA District 7	193 600	44	NJ District 3	651
46	FL District 3	22.0	45	NJ District 8	193 600	46	NJ District 6	645
46	GA District 5	22.0	45	NY District 20	193 600	47	CA District 17	643
46	MS District 3	22.0	48	VA District 11	191 000	47	MD District 4	643
49	TX District 29	21.8	49	HI District 2	190 900	49	NJ District 9	640
49	TX District 30	21.8	50	NY District 13	190 700	50	MI District 11	638
49	VA District 3	21.8	51	MA District 8	189 700	51	CA District 34	637
52	NY District 11	21.7	52	CA District 30	189 000	52	CA District 38	636
53	FL District 23	21.5	53	CA District 46	188 500	52	MA District 8	636
54	MD District 7	21.4	54	NJ District 7	186 900	54	HI District 2	633
55	AZ District 6	21.3	55	CA District 26	186 600	55	CA District 8	631
55	TX District 13	21.3	55	NY District 15	186 600	56	CA District 7	625
57	WI District 5	21.0	57	CT District 5	183 900	57	CA District 26	624
58	AL District 1	20.9	57	NY District 11	183 900	57	FL District 20	624
58	PA District 2	20.9	59	IL District 10	181 400	59	CT District 3	623
60	MS District 5	20.8	60	MA District 6	181 100	60	CA District 31	622
61	TX District 2	20.5	61	CA District 31	180 100	61	CA District 22	621
62	MS District 1	20.1	62	NY District 17	176 400	62	IL District 13	619
62	OH District 6	20.1	63	NY District 12	176 300	63	MA District 6	617
62	TX District 1	20.1	64	CA District 34	174 400	64	MA District 9	616
65	LA District 6	20.0	65	MA District 5	174 200	65	PA District 8	608
65	TX District 14	20.0	66	CT District 3	173 800	66	CA District 49	607
67	OK District 2	19.7	67	MA District 9	172 800	67	IL District 10	605
68	FL District 2	19.5	68	CT District 1	172 000	67	IL District 6	605
69	AL District 3	19.3	69	MA District 4	170 600	69	MA District 5	603
69	GA District 8	19.3	70	CA District 7	168 100	70	PA District 13	600
71	CA District 32	19.2	71	NY District 10	167 900	71	GA District 6	598
72	MO District 1	19.1	72	CT District 6	166 400	72	CA District 43	595
72	TX District 17	19.1	73	MA District 10	163 700	72	NJ District 8	595
72	VA District 9	19.1	74	NJ District 6	160 600	74	NY District 18	594
75	KY District 1	19.0	75	NY District 2	159 600	75	CA District 32	592
			75	NY District 6	159 600	75	FL District 21	592

Note: Column numbers refer to Table E. Congressional Districts.

TABLE 8—Defense Procurement Contracts by Geographic Areas, 2001—75 States, Counties, Metropolitan Areas and Cities with the Largest Contract Amounts

	Defense Contracts in States, 2001				Defense Contracts in Counties, 2001	
Defense Contract Rank	State	[col 288] Defense Contract (Mil Dol)		Defense Contract Rank	County	[col 172] Defense Contract (Mil Dol)
1	California	19 864		1	Los Angeles, CA	7 583.4
2	Virginia	18 597		2	Newport News City, VA	5 919.4
3	Texas	9 460		3	Cobb, GA	4 668.8
4	Florida	6 615		4	Fairfax, VA	4 659.1
5	Georgia	5 990		5	St. Louis city, MO	4 511.6
6	Massachusetts	5 281		6	San Diego, CA	2 863.2
7	Missouri	5 021		7	Santa Clara, CA	2 741.0
8	Maryland	4 909		8	Maricopa, AZ	2 559.0
9	Arizona	4 584		9	Middlesex, MA	2 340.8
10	Pennsylvania	4 214		10	Madison, AL	2 285.8
11	Connecticut	4 206		11	Tarrant, TX	1 768.6
12	Alabama	3 427		12	Pima, AZ	1 765.9
13	Ohio	3 312		13	Orange, CA	1 758.7
14	New York	3 246		14	New London, CT	1 718.0
15	New Jersey	2 800		15	Macomb, MI	1 679.6
16	Washington	2 404		16	Orange, FL	1 641.9
17	Colorado	2 277		17	District of Columbia, DC	1 633.8
18	Michigan	2 263		18	Bexar, TX	1 507.6
19	Indiana	1 750		19	Arlington, VA	1 419.0
20	Illinois	1 716		20	Dallas, TX	1 405.7
21	District of Columbia	1 634		21	Fairfield, CT	1 405.5
22	Oklahoma	1 568		22	King, WA	1 378.9
23	North Carolina	1 556		23	Philadelphia, PA	1 366.1
24	Louisiana	1 474		24	Norfolk City, VA	1 285.7
25	Minnesota	1 379		25	Honolulu, HI	1 182.8
26	Mississippi	1 355		26	Palm Beach, FL	1 146.4
27	Hawaii	1 294		27	Sacramento, CA	1 139.2
28	Utah	1 275		28	Montgomery, MD	1 134.4
29	Kentucky	1 134		29	Essex, MA	1 133.7
30	South Carolina	1 064		30	Hamilton, OH	1 041.8
31	Tennessee	1 028		31	El Paso, CO	1 029.2
32	Kansas	960		32	Brevard, FL	1 005.5
33	Wisconsin	906		33	Fairfax City, VA	973.2
34	Alaska	834		34	Hennepin, MN	972.1
35	New Mexico	761		35	Hartford, CT	951.9
36	Iowa	503		36	Marion, IN	887.8
36	Maine	503		37	Harris, TX	869.9
38	New Hampshire	479		38	Burlington, NJ	849.5
39	Oregon	389		39	St. Mary's, MD	841.9
40	Arkansas	385		40	Oklahoma, OK	838.1
41	Nevada	323		41	Alexandria City, VA	835.4
42	Vermont	307		42	Davis, UT	821.8
43	Rhode Island	283		43	Bristol, MA	763.7
44	Nebraska	190		44	Greene, OH	761.1
45	North Dakota	159		45	Allegheny, PA	738.5
46	Idaho	146		46	Monmouth, NJ	726.6
47	Montana	127		47	Cook, IL	714.5
48	South Dakota	117		48	Orleans, LA	675.8
49	West Virginia	105		49	Jackson, MS	634.4
50	Wyoming	96		50	Denver, CO	629.2
51	Delaware	84		51	Anne Arundel, MD	625.2
				52	Pinellas, FL	609.1
				53	Sedgwick, KS	604.6
				54	Prince George's, MD	585.5
				55	Nassau, NY	573.2
				56	Jefferson, KY	572.4
				57	Charleston, SC	559.6
				58	Norfolk, MA	556.0
				59	Baltimore city, MD	552.3
				60	Winnebago, WI	548.9
				61	York, PA	545.6
				62	Ventura, CA	541.4
				63	Santa Barbara, CA	507.6
				64	Okaloosa, FL	471.5
				65	Austin, TX	461.6
				66	Hunt, TX	461.1
				67	San Bernardino, CA	454.9
				68	Loudoun, VA	433.2
				69	Duval, FL	406.9
				70	Anchorage, AK	399.5
				71	Cumberland, NC	398.4
				72	Suffolk, NY	391.6
				73	Hillsborough, FL	389.0
				74	Manassas City, VA	379.1
				75	Bernalillo, NM	377.3

TABLE 8—Defense Procurement Contracts by Geographic Areas, 2001—75 States, Counties, Metropolitan Areas and Cities with the Largest Contract Amounts

Defense Contracts in Metropolitan Areas, 2001			Defense Contracts in Cities, 2001		
Defense Contract Rank	Metropolitan Area	[col 172] Defense Contract (Mil Dol)	Defense Contract Rank	City	[col 107] Defense Contract (Mil Dol)
1	Washington, DC-MD-VA-WV	13 129.2	1	Newport News, VA	5 842.9
2	Norfolk-Virginia Beach-Newport News, VA	8 226.1	2	Marietta, GA	4 640.0
3	Los Angeles-Long Beach, CA	7 583.4	3	St. Louis, MO	4 511.2
4	Boston-Worcester-Lawrence-Lowell-Brockton, MA-NH	5 461.7	4	Long Beach, CA	3 030.1
5	Atlanta, GA	5 056.3	5	San Diego, CA	2 332.3
6	St. Louis, MO-IL	4 769.5	6	Sunnyvale, CA	2 291.6
7	Philadelphia, PA-NJ	3 024.5	7	Huntsville, AL	2 198.1
8	San Diego, CA	2 863.2	8	Tucson, AZ	1 733.4
9	San Jose, CA	2 741.0	9	Washington, DC	1 633.8
10	Phoenix-Mesa, AZ	2 562.9	10	Fort Worth, TX	1 601.2
11	Huntsville, AL	2 286.0	11	Orlando, FL	1 573.2
12	Dallas, TX	2 206.6	12	Philadelphia, PA	1 362.2
13	Baltimore, MD	1 963.6	13	Sterling Heights, MI	1 344.6
14	Detroit, MI	1 795.6	14	Norfolk, VA	1 281.6
15	Fort Worth-Arlington, TX	1 772.2	15	Seattle, WA	1 168.1
16	Tucson, AZ	1 765.9	16	San Antonio, TX	1 137.1
17	Orange County, CA	1 758.7	17	West Palm Beach, FL	1 122.3
18	New London-Norwich, CT	1 718.0	18	Cincinnati, OH	1 040.5
19	Orlando, FL	1 662.2	19	Lynn, MA	880.9
20	San Antonio, TX	1 510.1	20	Sacramento, CA	873.1
21	Seattle-Bellevue-Everett, WA	1 483.3	21	Indianapolis, IN	854.6
22	New Haven-Bridgeport-Stamford-Danbury-Waterbury, CT	1 471.1	22	Phoenix, AZ	836.4
23	Minneapolis-St. Paul, MN-WI	1 322.7	23	Alexandria, VA	832.5
24	Dayton-Springfield, OH	1 263.5	24	Grand Prairie, TX	798.5
25	Honolulu, HI	1 182.8	25	Mesa, AZ	772.2
26	Sacramento, CA	1 151.1	26	Taunton, MA	734.8
27	West Palm Beach-Boca Raton, FL	1 146.4	27	Palmdale, CA	681.4
28	Chicago, IL	1 115.4	28	New Orleans, LA	650.3
29	Salt Lake City-Ogden, UT	1 100.7	29	Melbourne, FL	640.8
30	Cincinnati, OH-KY-IN	1 084.0	30	Pascagoula, MS	632.7
31	Denver, CO	1 068.9	31	Denver, CO	620.7
32	Colorado Springs, CO	1 029.2	32	Anaheim, CA	616.9
33	Melbourne-Titusville-Palm Bay, FL	1 005.5	33	Clearfield, UT	576.5
34	Tampa-St. Petersburg-Clearwater, FL	1 003.2	34	Louisville, KY	571.8
35	Hartford, CT	979.1	35	Wichita, KS	568.0
36	Nassau-Suffolk, NY	964.8	36	Oshkosh, WI	546.2
37	Oklahoma City, OK	931.1	37	Baltimore, MD	545.8
38	Indianapolis, IN	897.5	38	Colorado Springs, CO	528.7
39	Houston, TX	883.5	39	St. Petersburg, FL	482.3
40	New Orleans, LA	858.2	40	Minneapolis, MN	471.6
41	Biloxi-Gulfport-Pascagoula, MS	829.4	41	Huntington Beach, CA	454.9
42	Pittsburgh, PA	770.3	42	York, PA	453.0
43	Monmouth-Ocean, NJ	766.2	43	Tempe, AZ	427.2
44	Louisville, KY-IN	685.4	44	Los Angeles, CA	420.6
45	Wichita, KS	606.3	45	Oklahoma City, OK	413.0
46	New York, NY	593.7	46	Deer Park, TX	383.4
47	Charleston-North Charleston, SC	582.5	47	Manassas, VA	379.1
48	San Francisco, CA	578.5	48	Dallas, TX	357.9
49	Riverside-San Bernardino, CA	557.8	49	Cedar Rapids, IA	354.7
50	Appleton-Oshkosh-Neenah, WI	555.5	50	Rockville, MD	345.1
51	York, PA	545.6	51	Virginia Beach, VA	322.4
52	Ventura, CA	541.4	52	San Francisco, CA	321.6
53	Austin-San Marcos, TX	520.5	53	Austin, TX	320.1
54	Santa Barbara-Santa Maria-Lompoc, CA	507.6	54	Fort Wayne, IN	317.4
55	Fort Walton Beach, FL	471.5	55	Carson, CA	314.5
56	Jacksonville, FL	441.3	56	Dayton, OH	312.8
57	Richmond-Petersburg, VA	434.0	57	Houston, TX	312.2
58	Binghamton, NY	412.6	58	Chicago, IL	308.9
59	Anchorage, AK	399.5	59	New York, NY	285.9
60	Fayetteville, NC	398.4	60	Jacksonville, FL	283.0
61	Memphis, TN-AR-MS	382.5	61	Scottsdale, AZ	280.2
62	Albuquerque, NM	379.8	62	Warren, MI	277.2
63	Columbus, OH	379.5	63	Beavercreek, OH	276.9
64	El Paso, TX	369.9	64	Cambridge, MA	275.2
65	Bergen-Passaic, NJ	357.8	65	El Paso, TX	267.3
66	Cedar Rapids, IA	355.6	66	Burlington, VT	266.8
67	Fort Wayne, IN	351.5	67	Nashua, NH	266.1
68	Oakland, CA	345.4	68	Albuquerque, NM	261.4
69	Bremerton, WA	306.1	69	Annapolis, MD	259.7
70	Kansas City, MO-KS	300.2	70	Redondo Beach, CA	254.5
71	Vallejo-Fairfield-Napa, CA	298.9	71	Anchorage, AK	251.3
72	Greensboro—Winston-Salem—High Point, NC	297.3	72	Columbus, OH	245.3
73	Montgomery, AL	290.4	73	Charleston, SC	244.5
74	Syracuse, NY	287.1	74	Pittsburgh, PA	242.9
75	Bakersfield, CA	278.9	75	Beaumont, TX	241.3

States

(For explanation of symbols, see page xii)

Table A. States — Land Area and Population

STATE code	STATE	Land area, 2000[1] (sq km)	Population 2001	Population and population characteristics, 2000			Race (percent) (one race only)				Hispanic[2] (percent)	Age (percent)			
				Total persons	Rank	Per square kilometer	White	Black	American Indian, Alaska Native	Asian and Pacific Islander		Under 5 years	5 to 17 years	18 to 24 years	25 to 34 years
		1	2	3	4	5	6	7	8	9	10	11	12	13	14
00	UNITED STATES	9 161 924	284 796 887	281 421 906	X	30.7	75.1	12.3	0.9	3.7	12.5	6.8	18.9	9.7	14.2
01	ALABAMA	131 426	4 464 356	4 447 100	23	33.8	71.1	26.0	0.5	0.7	1.7	6.7	18.6	9.9	13.6
02	ALASKA	1 481 347	634 892	626 932	48	0.4	69.3	3.5	15.6	4.5	4.1	7.6	22.8	9.1	14.3
04	ARIZONA	294 312	5 307 331	5 130 632	20	17.4	75.5	3.1	5.0	1.9	25.3	7.5	19.2	10.0	14.5
05	ARKANSAS	134 856	2 692 090	2 673 400	33	19.8	80.0	15.7	0.7	0.9	3.2	6.8	18.7	9.8	13.2
06	CALIFORNIA	403 933	34 501 130	33 871 648	1	83.9	59.5	6.7	1.0	11.2	32.4	7.3	20.0	9.9	15.4
08	COLORADO	268 627	4 417 714	4 301 261	24	16.0	82.8	3.8	1.0	2.3	17.1	6.9	18.7	10.0	15.4
09	CONNECTICUT	12 548	3 425 074	3 405 565	29	271.4	81.6	9.1	0.3	2.4	9.4	6.6	18.2	8.0	13.3
10	DELAWARE	5 060	796 165	783 600	45	154.9	74.6	19.2	0.3	2.1	4.8	6.6	18.3	9.6	13.9
11	DISTRICT OF COLUMBIA	159	571 822	572 059	50	3 597.9	30.8	60.0	0.3	2.8	7.9	5.7	14.4	12.7	17.8
12	FLORIDA	139 670	16 396 515	15 982 378	4	114.4	78.0	14.6	0.3	1.8	16.8	5.9	16.9	8.3	13.0
13	GEORGIA	149 976	8 383 915	8 186 453	10	54.6	65.1	28.7	0.3	2.2	5.3	7.3	19.2	10.2	15.9
15	HAWAII	16 635	1 224 398	1 211 537	42	72.8	24.3	1.8	0.3	51.0	7.2	6.5	18.0	9.5	14.1
16	IDAHO	214 314	1 321 006	1 293 953	39	6.0	91.0	0.4	1.4	1.0	7.9	7.5	21.0	10.7	13.1
17	ILLINOIS	143 961	12 482 301	12 419 293	5	86.3	73.5	15.1	0.2	3.4	12.3	7.1	19.1	9.8	14.6
18	INDIANA	92 895	6 114 745	6 080 485	14	65.5	87.5	8.4	0.3	1.0	3.5	7.0	18.9	10.1	13.7
19	IOWA	144 701	2 923 179	2 926 324	30	20.2	93.9	2.1	0.3	1.3	2.8	6.4	18.6	10.2	12.4
20	KANSAS	211 900	2 694 641	2 688 418	32	12.7	86.1	5.7	0.9	1.7	7.0	7.0	19.5	10.3	13.0
21	KENTUCKY	102 896	4 065 556	4 041 769	25	39.3	90.1	7.3	0.2	0.7	1.5	6.6	18.0	9.9	14.1
22	LOUISIANA	112 825	4 465 430	4 468 976	22	39.6	63.9	32.5	0.6	1.2	2.4	7.1	20.2	10.6	13.5
23	MAINE	79 931	1 286 670	1 274 923	40	16.0	96.9	0.5	0.6	0.7	0.7	5.5	18.1	8.1	12.4
24	MARYLAND	25 314	5 375 156	5 296 486	19	209.2	64.0	27.9	0.3	4.0	4.3	6.7	18.9	8.5	14.1
25	MASSACHUSETTS	20 306	6 379 304	6 349 097	13	312.7	84.5	5.4	0.2	3.8	6.8	6.3	17.4	9.1	14.6
26	MICHIGAN	147 121	9 990 817	9 938 444	8	67.6	80.2	14.2	0.6	1.8	3.3	6.8	19.4	9.4	13.7
27	MINNESOTA	206 189	4 972 294	4 919 479	21	23.9	89.4	3.5	1.1	2.9	2.9	6.7	19.5	9.6	13.7
28	MISSISSIPPI	121 488	2 858 029	2 844 658	31	23.4	61.4	36.3	0.4	0.7	1.4	7.2	20.1	10.9	13.4
29	MISSOURI	178 414	5 629 707	5 595 211	17	31.4	84.9	11.2	0.4	1.2	2.1	6.6	18.9	9.6	13.2
30	MONTANA	376 979	904 433	902 195	44	2.4	90.6	0.3	6.2	0.6	2.0	6.1	19.4	9.5	11.4
31	NEBRASKA	199 099	1 713 235	1 711 263	38	8.6	89.6	4.0	0.9	1.3	5.5	6.8	19.5	10.2	13.0
32	NEVADA	284 448	2 106 074	1 998 257	35	7.0	75.2	6.8	1.3	4.9	19.7	7.3	18.3	9.0	15.3
33	NEW HAMPSHIRE	23 227	1 259 181	1 235 786	41	53.2	96.0	0.7	0.2	1.3	1.7	6.1	18.9	8.4	13.0
34	NEW JERSEY	19 211	8 484 431	8 414 350	9	438.0	72.6	13.6	0.2	5.7	13.3	6.7	18.1	8.0	14.1
35	NEW MEXICO	314 309	1 829 146	1 819 046	36	5.8	66.8	1.9	9.5	1.2	42.1	7.2	20.8	9.8	12.9
36	NEW YORK	122 283	19 011 378	18 976 457	3	155.2	67.9	15.9	0.4	5.5	15.1	6.5	18.2	9.3	14.5
37	NORTH CAROLINA	126 161	8 186 268	8 049 313	11	63.8	72.1	21.6	1.2	1.4	4.7	6.7	17.7	10.0	15.1
38	NORTH DAKOTA	178 647	634 448	642 200	47	3.6	92.4	0.6	4.9	0.6	1.2	6.1	18.9	11.4	12.0
39	OHIO	106 056	11 373 541	11 353 140	7	107.0	85.0	11.5	0.2	1.2	1.9	6.6	18.8	9.3	13.4
40	OKLAHOMA	177 847	3 460 097	3 450 654	27	19.4	76.2	7.6	7.9	1.5	5.2	6.8	19.0	10.3	13.1
41	OREGON	248 631	3 472 867	3 421 399	28	13.8	86.6	1.6	1.3	3.2	8.0	6.5	18.2	9.6	13.8
42	PENNSYLVANIA	116 074	12 287 150	12 281 054	6	105.8	85.4	10.0	0.1	1.8	3.2	5.9	17.9	8.9	12.7
44	RHODE ISLAND	2 706	1 058 920	1 048 319	43	387.4	85.0	4.5	0.5	2.4	8.7	6.1	17.5	10.2	13.4
45	SOUTH CAROLINA	77 983	4 063 011	4 012 012	26	51.4	67.2	29.5	0.3	0.9	2.4	6.6	18.6	10.2	14.0
46	SOUTH DAKOTA	196 540	756 600	754 844	46	3.8	88.7	0.6	8.3	0.6	1.4	6.8	20.1	10.3	12.1
47	TENNESSEE	106 752	5 740 021	5 689 283	16	53.3	80.2	16.4	0.3	1.0	2.2	6.6	18.0	9.6	14.3
48	TEXAS	678 051	21 325 018	20 851 820	2	30.8	71.0	11.5	0.6	2.8	32.0	7.8	20.4	10.5	15.2
49	UTAH	212 751	2 269 789	2 233 169	34	10.5	89.2	0.8	1.3	2.4	9.0	9.4	22.8	14.2	14.6
50	VERMONT	23 956	613 090	608 827	49	25.4	96.8	0.5	0.4	0.9	0.9	5.6	18.6	9.3	12.2
51	VIRGINIA	102 548	7 187 734	7 078 515	12	69.0	72.3	19.6	0.3	3.8	4.7	6.5	18.0	9.6	14.6
53	WASHINGTON	172 348	5 987 973	5 894 121	15	34.2	81.8	3.2	1.6	5.9	7.5	6.7	19.0	9.5	14.3
54	WEST VIRGINIA	62 361	1 801 916	1 808 344	37	29.0	95.0	3.2	0.2	0.5	0.7	5.6	16.6	9.5	12.7
55	WISCONSIN	140 663	5 401 906	5 363 675	18	38.1	88.9	5.7	0.9	1.7	3.6	6.4	19.1	9.7	13.2
56	WYOMING	251 489	494 423	493 782	51	2.0	92.1	0.8	2.3	0.7	6.4	6.3	19.8	10.1	12.1

1. Dry land or land partially or temporarily covered by water.   2. Hispanic persons may be of any race.

Table A. States — **Population and Households**

STATE	Population and population characteristics, 2000 (cont'd) — Age (percent) (cont'd)						Households, 2000			Age of householder (percent)			
	35 to 44 years	45 to 54 years	55 to 64 years	65 to 74 years	75 years and over	Percent female	Number	Percent change, 1990 to 2000	Persons per house-hold	Under 25 years	25 to 44 years	45 to 64 years	65 years and over
	15	16	17	18	19	20	21	22	23	24	25	26	27
UNITED STATES	16.0	13.4	8.6	6.5	5.9	50.9	105 480 101	14.7	2.59	5.2	40.1	33.7	21.0
ALABAMA	15.4	13.5	9.3	7.1	5.9	51.7	1 737 080	15.3	2.49	6.0	38.0	34.0	22.1
ALASKA	18.2	15.1	7.1	3.6	2.1	48.3	221 600	17.3	2.74	6.0	46.6	37.3	10.2
ARIZONA	15.0	12.2	8.6	7.1	5.9	50.1	1 901 327	38.9	2.64	6.4	39.5	32.1	22.0
ARKANSAS	14.9	13.1	9.6	7.4	6.6	51.2	1 042 696	17.0	2.49	6.3	36.9	33.4	23.5
CALIFORNIA	16.2	12.8	7.7	5.6	5.0	50.2	11 502 870	10.8	2.87	4.7	42.9	33.7	18.8
COLORADO	17.1	14.3	7.9	5.3	4.4	49.6	1 658 238	29.3	2.53	6.4	43.8	33.8	16.0
CONNECTICUT	17.1	14.1	9.1	6.8	7.0	51.6	1 301 670	5.8	2.53	3.4	39.4	34.8	22.4
DELAWARE	16.3	13.3	9.1	7.2	5.8	51.4	298 736	20.7	2.54	4.8	39.9	33.7	21.6
DISTRICT OF COLUMBIA	15.3	13.2	8.7	6.3	5.9	52.9	248 338	-0.5	2.16	6.8	42.0	31.7	19.5
FLORIDA	15.5	12.9	9.8	9.1	8.5	51.2	6 337 929	23.4	2.46	4.5	35.6	32.3	27.5
GEORGIA	16.5	13.2	8.1	5.3	4.3	50.8	3 006 369	27.0	2.65	5.9	44.2	33.4	16.5
HAWAII	15.8	14.1	8.8	7.0	6.2	49.8	403 240	13.2	2.92	4.0	37.0	36.6	22.3
IDAHO	14.9	13.2	8.3	5.9	5.4	49.9	469 645	30.2	2.69	7.2	39.2	33.8	19.8
ILLINOIS	16.0	13.1	8.4	6.2	5.9	51.0	4 591 779	9.3	2.63	4.9	40.9	33.3	20.9
INDIANA	15.8	13.4	8.7	6.5	5.9	51.0	2 336 306	13.1	2.53	6.1	39.7	33.4	20.8
IOWA	15.2	13.4	8.8	7.2	7.7	50.9	1 149 276	8.0	2.46	6.5	36.9	32.4	24.2
KANSAS	15.6	13.2	8.2	6.5	6.7	50.6	1 037 891	9.9	2.51	7.0	38.9	32.2	21.9
KENTUCKY	15.9	13.8	9.2	6.8	5.7	51.1	1 590 647	15.3	2.47	5.9	39.0	34.0	21.1
LOUISIANA	15.5	13.1	8.5	6.3	5.2	51.6	1 656 053	10.5	2.62	6.2	39.2	34.1	20.5
MAINE	16.7	15.1	9.7	7.5	6.8	51.3	518 200	11.4	2.39	4.4	37.5	35.3	22.7
MARYLAND	17.3	14.3	8.9	6.1	5.2	51.7	1 980 859	13.3	2.61	4.1	41.5	35.6	18.8
MASSACHUSETTS	16.7	13.8	8.6	6.7	6.8	51.8	2 443 580	8.7	2.51	3.9	40.3	33.6	22.2
MICHIGAN	16.1	13.8	8.7	6.5	5.8	51.0	3 785 661	10.7	2.56	5.0	39.8	34.2	21.0
MINNESOTA	16.8	13.5	8.2	6.0	6.1	50.5	1 895 127	15.0	2.52	5.7	41.5	32.8	20.0
MISSISSIPPI	15.0	12.7	8.6	6.5	5.5	51.7	1 046 434	14.8	2.63	5.7	38.8	33.8	21.6
MISSOURI	15.9	13.3	9.1	7.0	6.5	51.4	2 194 594	11.9	2.48	5.8	38.8	33.1	22.3
MONTANA	15.7	15.0	9.4	6.9	6.5	50.2	358 667	17.1	2.45	6.3	35.8	35.9	22.0
NEBRASKA	15.4	13.2	8.3	6.8	6.8	50.7	666 184	10.6	2.49	6.9	38.8	31.8	22.5
NEVADA	16.1	13.5	9.5	6.6	4.4	49.1	751 165	61.1	2.62	5.6	41.4	34.9	18.1
NEW HAMPSHIRE	17.9	14.9	8.9	6.3	5.6	50.8	474 606	15.4	2.53	3.9	41.2	35.6	19.3
NEW JERSEY	17.1	13.8	9.0	6.8	6.4	51.5	3 064 645	9.7	2.68	2.7	39.8	35.0	22.4
NEW MEXICO	15.5	13.5	8.7	6.5	5.2	50.8	677 971	24.9	2.63	6.2	38.5	35.0	20.2
NEW YORK	16.2	13.5	8.9	6.7	6.2	51.8	7 056 860	6.3	2.61	3.8	39.8	34.6	21.8
NORTH CAROLINA	16.0	13.5	9.0	6.6	5.4	51.0	3 132 013	24.4	2.49	5.9	40.9	33.4	19.8
NORTH DAKOTA	15.3	13.3	8.3	7.1	7.6	50.1	257 152	6.8	2.41	8.1	36.7	31.4	23.8
OHIO	15.9	13.8	8.9	7.0	6.3	51.4	4 445 773	8.8	2.49	5.4	38.9	33.8	21.9
OKLAHOMA	15.2	13.1	9.2	7.0	6.2	50.9	1 342 293	11.3	2.49	7.0	37.6	33.2	22.2
OREGON	15.4	14.8	8.9	6.4	6.4	50.4	1 333 723	20.9	2.51	6.2	37.9	35.0	20.9
PENNSYLVANIA	15.9	13.9	9.2	7.9	7.7	51.7	4 777 003	6.3	2.48	4.1	36.5	34.0	25.4
RHODE ISLAND	16.2	13.5	8.5	7.0	7.5	52.0	408 424	8.1	2.47	4.8	38.7	32.9	23.6
SOUTH CAROLINA	15.6	13.7	9.3	6.7	5.4	51.4	1 533 854	21.9	2.53	5.6	39.1	34.9	20.4
SOUTH DAKOTA	15.3	12.9	8.3	7.0	7.3	50.4	290 245	12.0	2.50	7.0	37.4	31.7	23.8
TENNESSEE	15.9	13.8	9.4	6.7	5.6	51.3	2 232 905	20.5	2.48	5.8	39.5	34.3	20.5
TEXAS	15.9	12.5	7.7	5.5	4.5	50.4	7 393 354	21.8	2.74	6.6	43.3	32.4	17.6
UTAH	13.4	10.6	6.4	4.5	4.0	49.9	701 281	30.5	3.13	9.0	43.5	30.6	17.0
VERMONT	16.7	15.4	9.3	6.7	6.0	51.0	240 634	14.2	2.44	4.7	38.2	36.5	20.6
VIRGINIA	17.0	14.1	8.9	6.1	5.1	51.0	2 699 173	17.8	2.54	5.1	41.5	34.8	18.6
WASHINGTON	16.5	14.4	8.4	5.7	5.5	50.2	2 271 398	21.3	2.53	5.8	41.3	34.4	18.5
WEST VIRGINIA	15.1	15.0	10.2	8.2	7.1	51.4	736 481	7.0	2.40	5.2	33.8	35.6	25.5
WISCONSIN	16.3	13.7	8.5	6.6	6.5	50.6	2 084 544	14.4	2.50	5.8	39.7	33.0	21.5
WYOMING	16.0	15.0	9.0	6.3	5.3	49.7	193 608	14.7	2.48	7.1	37.4	36.0	19.5

Table A. States — **Immigration and Population Change**

		Population, 1980–2025				Population change, 1990–2001				
		Census counts			Projection	Percent change		Components of change, 2000–2001		
STATE	Immigrants admitted to legal status, 2000	1980	1990	2000	2025	1990–2000	2000–2001	Births	Deaths	Net migration
	28	29	30	31	32	33	34	35	36	37
UNITED STATES	844 036	226 542 204	248 790 925	281 421 906	335 048 000	13.1	1.2	5 042 426	2 999 064	1 339 827
ALABAMA	1 904	3 894 025	4 040 389	4 447 100	5 224 000	10.1	0.4	80 131	56 534	-5 607
ALASKA	1 374	401 851	550 043	626 932	885 000	14.0	1.3	12 624	3 628	-993
ARIZONA	11 980	2 716 546	3 665 339	5 130 632	6 412 000	40.0	3.4	104 781	50 703	121 810
ARKANSAS	1 596	2 286 357	2 350 624	2 673 400	3 055 000	13.7	0.7	47 970	34 843	5 683
CALIFORNIA	217 753	23 667 765	29 811 427	33 871 648	49 285 000	13.6	1.9	660 126	285 733	255 179
COLORADO	8 216	2 889 735	3 294 473	4 301 261	5 188 000	30.6	2.7	79 847	34 144	69 799
CONNECTICUT	11 346	3 107 564	3 287 116	3 405 565	3 739 000	3.6	0.6	53 343	37 832	5 196
DELAWARE	1 570	594 338	666 168	783 600	861 000	17.6	1.6	13 862	8 592	7 540
DISTRICT OF COLUMBIA	2 542	638 432	606 900	572 059	655 000	-5.7	0.0	10 181	7 589	-2 757
FLORIDA	98 391	9 746 961	12 938 071	15 982 378	20 710 000	23.5	2.6	256 107	204 172	359 194
GEORGIA	14 778	5 462 982	6 478 149	8 186 453	9 869 000	26.4	2.4	168 353	79 804	106 412
HAWAII	6 056	964 691	1 108 229	1 211 537	1 812 000	9.3	1.1	23 452	10 357	269
IDAHO	1 922	944 127	1 006 734	1 293 953	1 739 000	28.5	2.1	24 583	11 976	14 131
ILLINOIS	36 180	11 427 409	11 430 602	12 419 293	13 440 000	8.6	0.5	231 194	134 303	-35 126
INDIANA	4 128	5 490 214	5 544 156	6 080 485	6 546 000	9.7	0.6	107 126	69 179	-3 178
IOWA	3 052	2 913 808	2 776 831	2 926 324	3 040 000	5.4	-0.1	46 648	35 033	-14 184
KANSAS	4 582	2 364 236	2 477 588	2 688 418	3 108 000	8.5	0.2	48 712	31 045	-11 379
KENTUCKY	2 989	3 660 324	3 686 892	4 041 769	4 314 000	9.6	0.6	68 762	49 431	5 181
LOUISIANA	3 016	4 206 116	4 221 826	4 468 976	5 133 000	5.9	-0.1	87 433	51 633	-39 132
MAINE	1 133	1 125 043	1 227 928	1 274 923	1 423 000	3.8	0.9	16 505	15 512	11 021
MARYLAND	17 705	4 216 933	4 780 753	5 296 486	6 274 000	10.8	1.5	94 603	54 845	39 542
MASSACHUSETTS	23 483	5 737 093	6 016 425	6 349 097	6 902 000	5.5	0.5	101 062	70 785	1 279
MICHIGAN	16 773	9 262 044	9 295 287	9 938 444	10 078 000	6.9	0.5	169 278	109 292	-6 207
MINNESOTA	8 671	4 075 970	4 375 665	4 919 479	5 510 000	12.4	1.1	82 541	47 363	17 529
MISSISSIPPI	1 083	2 520 770	2 575 475	2 844 658	3 142 000	10.5	0.5	56 970	35 931	-7 558
MISSOURI	6 053	4 916 766	5 116 901	5 595 211	6 250 000	9.3	0.6	94 677	68 762	9 038
MONTANA	493	786 690	799 065	902 195	1 121 000	12.9	0.2	13 320	10 165	-907
NEBRASKA	2 230	1 569 825	1 578 417	1 711 263	1 930 000	8.4	0.1	30 192	18 878	-9 047
NEVADA	7 827	800 508	1 201 675	1 998 257	2 312 000	66.3	5.4	37 234	18 588	87 422
NEW HAMPSHIRE	2 001	920 610	1 109 252	1 235 786	1 439 000	11.4	1.9	17 683	12 137	17 926
NEW JERSEY	40 013	7 365 011	7 747 750	8 414 350	9 558 000	8.6	0.8	138 856	89 267	21 146
NEW MEXICO	3 973	1 303 302	1 515 069	1 819 046	2 612 000	20.1	0.6	33 732	16 862	-6 546
NEW YORK	106 061	17 558 165	17 990 778	18 976 457	19 830 000	5.5	0.2	323 772	197 846	-90 510
NORTH CAROLINA	9 251	5 880 095	6 632 448	8 049 313	9 349 000	21.4	1.7	150 843	89 957	76 874
NORTH DAKOTA	420	652 717	638 800	642 200	729 000	0.5	-1.2	9 452	7 379	-9 822
OHIO	9 263	10 797 603	10 847 115	11 353 140	11 744 000	4.7	0.2	195 720	136 432	-37 015
OKLAHOMA	4 586	3 025 487	3 145 576	3 450 654	4 057 000	9.7	0.3	60 327	43 267	-7 177
OREGON	8 543	2 633 156	2 842 337	3 421 399	4 349 000	20.4	1.5	55 999	36 994	32 923
PENNSYLVANIA	18 148	11 864 720	11 882 842	12 281 054	12 683 000	3.4	0.0	180 121	163 050	-8 095
RHODE ISLAND	2 526	947 154	1 003 464	1 048 319	1 141 000	4.5	1.0	15 375	12 571	8 167
SOUTH CAROLINA	2 267	3 120 729	3 486 310	4 012 012	4 645 000	15.1	1.3	71 330	46 194	26 787
SOUTH DAKOTA	465	690 768	696 004	754 844	866 000	8.5	0.2	12 866	8 822	-2 240
TENNESSEE	4 882	4 591 023	4 877 203	5 689 283	6 665 000	16.7	0.9	99 246	68 953	20 833
TEXAS	63 840	14 225 513	16 986 335	20 851 820	27 183 000	22.8	2.3	447 418	185 621	209 561
UTAH	3 710	1 461 037	1 722 850	2 233 169	2 883 000	29.6	1.6	57 516	15 429	-5 549
VERMONT	810	511 456	562 758	608 827	678 000	8.2	0.7	7 872	6 428	2 981
VIRGINIA	20 087	5 346 797	6 189 197	7 078 515	8 466 000	14.4	1.5	124 540	70 495	54 758
WASHINGTON	18 486	4 132 353	4 866 669	5 894 121	7 808 000	21.1	1.6	99 727	55 046	49 721
WEST VIRGINIA	573	1 950 186	1 793 477	1 808 344	1 845 000	0.8	-0.4	25 477	26 372	-5 233
WISCONSIN	5 057	4 705 642	4 891 954	5 363 675	5 867 000	9.6	0.7	85 327	58 334	12 137
WYOMING	248	469 557	453 589	493 782	694 000	8.9	0.1	7 610	4 956	-1 950

STATE	White	Black	American Indian, Eskimo, Aleut	Asian and Pacific Islander	Other race	His-panic[1]	Foreign born	Under 5 years	5 to 17 years	18 to 24 years	25 to 34 years	35 to 44 years	45 to 54 years	55 to 64 years	65 to 74 years	75 years and over	Female
	38	39	40	41	42	43	44	45	46	47	48	49	50	51	52	53	54
UNITED STATES	80.3	12.1	0.8	2.9	3.9	9.0	7.9	7.4	18.2	10.8	17.4	15.1	10.1	8.5	7.3	5.3	51.3
ALABAMA	73.6	25.3	0.4	0.5	0.1	0.6	1.1	7.0	19.2	11.0	16.0	14.4	10.4	9.0	7.5	5.5	52.1
ALASKA	75.5	4.1	15.6	3.6	1.2	3.2	4.5	10.0	21.4	10.2	20.5	18.7	9.8	5.4	2.8	1.2	47.3
ARIZONA	80.8	3.0	5.6	1.5	9.1	18.8	7.6	8.0	18.8	10.7	17.3	14.4	9.5	8.2	7.9	5.1	50.6
ARKANSAS	82.7	15.9	0.5	0.5	0.3	0.8	1.1	7.0	19.4	10.1	15.3	13.9	10.4	9.1	8.3	6.6	51.8
CALIFORNIA	69.0	7.4	0.8	9.6	13.2	25.8	21.7	8.1	18.0	11.5	19.1	15.6	9.8	7.5	6.2	4.3	49.9
COLORADO	88.2	4.0	0.8	1.8	5.1	12.9	4.3	7.7	18.5	10.2	18.6	17.2	10.2	7.6	5.9	4.1	50.5
CONNECTICUT	87.0	8.3	0.2	1.5	2.9	6.5	8.5	6.9	15.9	10.5	17.8	15.5	10.8	9.0	7.8	5.8	51.5
DELAWARE	80.3	16.9	0.3	1.4	1.1	2.4	3.3	7.3	17.2	11.4	17.9	14.8	10.2	9.0	7.4	4.7	51.5
DISTRICT OF COLUMBIA	29.6	65.8	0.2	1.8	2.5	5.4	9.7	6.2	13.1	13.6	20.0	15.7	10.2	8.4	7.3	5.5	53.4
FLORIDA	83.1	13.6	0.3	1.2	1.8	12.2	12.9	6.6	15.6	9.4	16.4	14.0	10.0	9.8	10.6	7.7	51.6
GEORGIA	71.0	27.0	0.2	1.2	0.7	1.7	2.7	7.6	19.0	11.4	18.1	15.7	10.3	7.7	6.0	4.1	51.5
HAWAII	33.4	2.5	0.5	61.8	1.9	7.3	14.7	7.5	17.8	10.9	18.1	16.1	9.8	8.5	7.1	4.2	49.1
IDAHO	94.4	0.3	1.4	0.9	3.0	5.3	2.9	8.0	22.7	9.8	15.2	14.8	9.8	7.7	6.9	5.1	50.2
ILLINOIS	78.3	14.8	0.2	2.5	4.2	7.9	8.3	7.4	18.4	10.6	17.4	14.9	10.2	8.5	7.2	5.4	51.4
INDIANA	90.6	7.8	0.2	0.7	0.7	1.8	1.7	7.2	19.1	10.9	16.5	14.8	10.3	8.7	7.3	5.3	51.5
IOWA	96.6	1.7	0.3	0.9	0.5	1.2	1.6	7.0	18.9	10.2	15.4	14.2	9.9	9.0	8.2	7.2	51.6
KANSAS	90.1	5.8	0.9	1.3	2.0	3.8	2.5	7.6	19.1	10.3	16.7	14.6	9.5	8.4	7.5	6.4	51.0
KENTUCKY	92.0	7.1	0.2	0.5	0.2	0.6	0.9	6.8	19.1	10.9	16.6	14.9	10.4	8.8	7.3	5.4	51.6
LOUISIANA	67.3	30.8	0.4	1.0	0.5	2.2	2.1	7.9	21.2	11.0	16.7	14.4	9.6	8.1	6.5	4.6	51.9
MAINE	98.4	0.4	0.5	0.5	0.1	0.6	3.0	7.0	18.2	10.1	16.7	15.7	10.2	8.8	7.5	5.8	51.3
MARYLAND	71.0	24.9	0.3	2.9	0.9	2.6	6.6	7.5	16.8	10.6	18.8	16.3	10.9	8.3	6.6	4.2	51.5
MASSACHUSETTS	89.8	5.0	0.2	2.4	2.6	4.8	9.5	6.9	15.6	11.8	18.3	15.3	10.0	8.6	7.6	6.0	52.0
MICHIGAN	83.4	13.9	0.6	1.1	0.9	2.2	3.8	7.6	18.9	10.8	16.9	15.1	10.2	8.5	7.1	4.9	51.5
MINNESOTA	94.4	2.2	1.1	1.8	0.5	1.2	2.6	7.7	19.0	10.1	17.8	15.2	9.8	7.9	6.7	5.8	51.0
MISSISSIPPI	63.5	35.6	0.3	0.5	0.1	0.6	0.8	7.6	21.4	11.4	15.5	13.6	9.6	8.3	7.0	5.5	52.2
MISSOURI	87.7	10.7	0.4	0.8	0.4	1.2	1.6	7.2	18.5	10.1	16.7	14.4	10.2	8.9	7.7	6.3	51.8
MONTANA	92.7	0.3	6.0	0.5	0.5	1.5	1.7	7.4	20.4	8.8	15.4	15.9	10.3	8.6	7.6	5.7	50.5
NEBRASKA	93.8	3.6	0.8	0.8	1.0	2.3	1.8	7.6	19.6	9.9	16.3	14.5	9.5	8.6	7.5	6.7	51.3
NEVADA	84.3	6.6	1.6	3.2	4.4	10.4	8.7	7.7	17.0	9.9	18.5	16.0	11.3	9.0	7.1	3.5	49.1
NEW HAMPSHIRE	98.0	0.6	0.2	0.8	0.3	1.0	3.7	7.6	17.5	10.6	18.5	16.5	10.1	8.0	6.4	4.8	51.0
NEW JERSEY	79.3	13.4	0.2	3.5	3.6	9.6	12.5	6.9	16.4	10.1	17.6	15.5	10.9	9.3	7.9	5.5	51.7
NEW MEXICO	75.6	2.0	8.9	0.9	12.6	38.2	5.3	8.3	21.2	10.0	16.9	15.0	9.7	8.0	6.4	4.3	50.8
NEW YORK	74.4	15.9	0.3	3.9	5.5	12.3	15.9	7.0	16.7	10.9	17.4	15.1	10.6	9.1	7.5	5.6	52.1
NORTH CAROLINA	75.6	22.0	1.2	0.8	0.5	1.2	1.7	6.9	17.3	11.8	17.3	15.2	10.5	8.9	7.3	4.8	51.5
NORTH DAKOTA	94.6	0.6	4.1	0.5	0.3	0.7	1.5	7.5	20.0	10.6	16.3	14.1	8.9	8.4	7.4	6.8	50.2
OHIO	87.8	10.6	0.2	0.8	0.5	1.3	2.4	7.2	18.6	10.5	16.5	14.9	10.3	9.0	7.6	5.3	51.8
OKLAHOMA	82.1	7.4	8.0	1.1	1.3	2.7	2.1	7.2	19.4	10.2	16.2	14.4	10.3	8.9	7.5	6.0	51.3
OREGON	92.8	1.6	1.4	2.4	1.8	4.0	4.9	7.1	18.4	9.4	15.9	16.7	10.4	8.3	7.9	5.9	50.8
PENNSYLVANIA	88.5	9.2	0.1	1.2	1.0	2.0	3.1	6.7	16.8	10.3	16.1	14.7	10.2	9.8	9.0	6.4	52.1
RHODE ISLAND	91.4	3.9	0.4	1.8	2.5	4.6	9.5	6.7	15.8	12.0	17.3	14.7	9.6	8.9	8.5	6.5	52.0
SOUTH CAROLINA	69.0	29.8	0.2	0.6	0.3	0.9	1.4	7.4	19.0	11.7	17.0	15.0	10.2	8.4	7.1	4.3	51.6
SOUTH DAKOTA	91.6	0.5	7.3	0.4	0.2	0.8	1.1	7.8	20.7	9.8	15.7	13.7	9.0	8.6	7.8	6.9	50.8
TENNESSEE	83.0	16.0	0.2	0.7	0.2	0.7	1.2	6.8	18.1	10.8	16.7	15.2	10.8	8.9	7.3	5.4	51.8
TEXAS	75.2	11.9	0.4	1.9	10.6	25.5	9.0	8.2	20.3	11.1	18.2	14.9	9.6	7.6	5.9	4.2	50.7
UTAH	93.8	0.7	1.4	1.9	2.2	4.9	3.4	9.8	26.6	11.6	16.0	13.0	8.0	6.2	5.1	3.6	50.3
VERMONT	98.6	0.3	0.3	0.6	0.1	0.7	3.1	7.3	18.1	11.2	16.9	16.4	10.2	8.0	6.6	5.2	51.0
VIRGINIA	77.4	18.8	0.2	2.6	0.9	2.6	5.0	7.2	17.2	11.6	18.4	16.0	10.7	8.1	6.5	4.3	51.0
WASHINGTON	88.5	3.1	1.7	4.3	2.4	4.4	6.6	7.5	18.4	10.0	17.6	16.5	10.3	7.8	6.9	4.9	50.4
WEST VIRGINIA	96.2	3.1	0.1	0.4	0.1	0.5	0.9	5.9	18.8	10.0	14.6	15.1	10.7	9.9	8.7	6.3	52.0
WISCONSIN	92.2	5.0	0.8	1.1	0.9	1.9	2.5	7.4	19.0	10.5	16.8	14.8	9.8	8.5	7.3	6.0	51.1
WYOMING	94.2	0.8	2.1	0.6	2.3	5.7	1.7	7.7	22.2	9.1	16.4	16.4	10.0	7.8	6.1	4.3	50.0

1. Hispanic persons may be of any race.

Table A. States — Households 1990, Vital Statistics, and Health Resources

STATE	Households, 1990 Number	Percent change, 1980–1990	Persons per household	Percent Female family householder[1]	Percent One person	Births, 2000 Total	Births, 2000 Rate[2]	Deaths, 1999 Number Total	Deaths, 1999 Number Infant[3]	Deaths, 1999 Rate Crude[2]	Deaths, 1999 Rate Age-adjusted	Deaths, 1999 Rate Infant[4]	Physicians 2000 Number	Physicians 2000 Rate[5]
	55	56	57	58	59	60	61	62	63	64	65	66	67	68
UNITED STATES	91 947 410	14.4	2.63	11.6	24.6	4 058 814	14.7	2 391 399	27 937	8.8	8.8	7.1	587 994	209
ALABAMA	1 506 790	12.3	2.62	13.4	23.8	63 299	14.4	44 806	606	10.3	10.2	9.8	7 605	171
ALASKA	188 915	43.7	2.80	9.6	22.1	9 974	16.0	2 708	57	4.4	8.3	5.7	1 087	173
ARIZONA	1 368 843	43.0	2.62	10.4	24.7	85 273	17.5	40 050	548	8.4	8.5	6.8	9 612	187
ARKANSAS	891 179	9.2	2.57	11.1	24.0	37 783	14.7	27 925	292	10.9	10.1	8.0	4 267	160
CALIFORNIA	10 381 206	20.3	2.79	11.5	23.4	531 959	15.8	229 380	2 800	6.9	7.9	5.4	75 739	224
COLORADO	1 282 489	20.8	2.51	9.7	26.6	65 438	15.8	27 114	416	6.7	8.0	6.7	9 342	217
CONNECTICUT	1 230 479	12.5	2.59	11.4	24.2	43 026	13.0	29 446	265	9.0	7.9	6.1	10 162	298
DELAWARE	247 497	19.5	2.61	11.8	23.2	11 051	14.5	6 666	79	8.8	9.0	7.4	1 677	214
DISTRICT OF COLUMBIA	249 634	-1.4	2.26	19.5	41.5	7 666	14.8	6 076	113	11.7	10.8	15.0	4 093	715
FLORIDA	5 134 869	37.1	2.46	10.7	25.5	204 125	13.3	163 224	1 452	10.8	8.3	7.4	33 929	212
GEORGIA	2 366 615	26.4	2.66	13.9	22.7	132 644	16.7	62 028	1 040	8.0	9.8	8.2	17 317	212
HAWAII	356 267	21.2	3.01	10.5	19.4	17 551	14.9	8 270	120	7.0	6.8	7.0	3 138	259
IDAHO	360 723	11.3	2.73	8.0	22.4	20 366	16.0	9 579	134	7.7	8.3	6.7	1 831	142
ILLINOIS	4 202 240	3.9	2.65	12.0	25.7	185 036	15.2	108 436	1 550	8.9	9.0	8.5	25 778	208
INDIANA	2 065 355	7.2	2.61	10.5	24.1	87 699	14.7	55 303	686	9.3	9.4	8.0	10 572	174
IOWA	1 064 325	1.1	2.52	8.0	25.9	38 266	13.3	28 411	215	9.9	8.2	5.7	5 236	179
KANSAS	944 726	8.3	2.53	8.6	25.9	39 666	14.9	24 472	283	9.2	8.5	7.3	4 801	179
KENTUCKY	1 379 782	9.2	2.60	11.6	23.3	56 029	14.1	39 321	411	9.9	10.1	7.6	7 010	173
LOUISIANA	1 499 269	6.2	2.74	15.6	23.7	67 898	15.5	41 238	621	9.4	10.4	9.2	9 061	203
MAINE	465 312	17.7	2.56	9.5	23.3	13 603	10.8	12 261	66	9.8	9.0	4.8	2 816	221
MARYLAND	1 748 991	19.7	2.67	13.3	22.6	74 316	14.2	43 089	601	8.3	9.1	8.4	16 561	313
MASSACHUSETTS	2 247 110	10.5	2.58	12.1	25.8	81 614	13.2	55 840	417	9.0	8.2	5.2	20 757	327
MICHIGAN	3 419 331	7.0	2.66	12.9	23.7	136 171	13.7	87 232	1 077	8.8	9.1	8.1	21 114	212
MINNESOTA	1 647 853	14.0	2.58	8.6	25.1	67 604	14.0	38 537	408	8.1	7.9	6.2	10 124	206
MISSISSIPPI	911 374	10.2	2.75	15.9	23.4	44 075	15.8	28 185	433	10.2	10.6	10.1	4 116	145
MISSOURI	1 961 206	9.4	2.54	10.6	26.0	76 463	13.9	55 931	585	10.2	9.5	7.8	11 883	212
MONTANA	306 163	7.9	2.53	8.6	26.3	10 957	12.3	8 128	72	9.2	8.6	6.7	1 646	182
NEBRASKA	602 363	5.4	2.54	8.3	26.5	24 646	14.8	15 579	163	9.4	8.4	6.8	3 091	181
NEVADA	466 297	53.2	2.53	10.2	25.7	30 829	16.4	15 082	193	8.3	9.7	6.6	2 983	149
NEW HAMPSHIRE	411 186	27.1	2.62	8.5	22.0	14 609	12.0	9 537	82	7.9	8.4	5.8	2 603	211
NEW JERSEY	2 794 711	9.7	2.70	12.1	23.1	115 632	14.1	73 981	766	9.1	8.6	6.7	20 834	248
NEW MEXICO	542 709	22.9	2.74	11.9	23.0	27 223	15.6	13 676	188	7.9	8.8	6.9	3 602	198
NEW YORK	6 639 322	4.7	2.63	13.8	27.2	258 737	14.2	159 927	1 627	8.8	8.4	6.4	58 453	308
NORTH CAROLINA	2 517 026	23.2	2.54	12.3	23.7	120 311	15.5	69 600	1 038	9.1	9.4	9.1	16 441	204
NORTH DAKOTA	240 878	5.8	2.55	7.3	26.5	7 676	12.2	6 103	52	9.6	8.0	6.8	1 355	211
OHIO	4 087 546	6.6	2.59	11.7	25.0	155 472	13.8	108 517	1 244	9.6	9.3	8.2	23 939	211
OKLAHOMA	1 206 135	7.8	2.53	10.4	25.6	49 782	14.7	34 700	417	10.3	9.9	8.5	5 448	158
OREGON	1 103 313	11.3	2.52	9.2	25.3	45 804	13.7	29 422	261	8.9	8.4	5.8	7 338	214
PENNSYLVANIA	4 495 966	6.5	2.57	11.3	25.6	146 281	12.2	130 283	1 058	10.9	9.1	7.3	31 671	258
RHODE ISLAND	377 977	11.6	2.55	11.7	26.2	12 505	12.6	9 708	71	9.8	8.1	5.7	2 859	273
SOUTH CAROLINA	1 258 044	22.1	2.68	14.0	22.4	56 114	14.3	36 053	563	9.3	10.0	10.2	6 704	167
SOUTH DAKOTA	259 034	6.8	2.59	8.0	26.4	10 345	14.0	6 953	94	9.5	8.2	8.9	1 307	173
TENNESSEE	1 853 725	14.5	2.56	12.6	23.9	79 611	14.4	53 765	599	9.8	10.0	7.7	11 281	198
TEXAS	6 070 937	23.2	2.73	11.6	23.9	363 414	17.8	146 858	2 164	7.3	8.9	6.2	35 952	172
UTAH	537 273	19.8	3.15	9.1	18.9	47 353	21.9	12 058	224	5.7	7.9	4.8	3 665	164
VERMONT	210 650	18.1	2.57	9.2	23.4	6 500	10.9	4 993	38	8.4	8.4	5.8	1 535	252
VIRGINIA	2 291 830	23.0	2.61	11.1	22.9	98 938	14.2	55 320	693	8.0	9.1	7.3	14 280	202
WASHINGTON	1 872 431	21.5	2.53	9.4	25.4	81 036	13.9	43 865	400	7.6	8.2	5.0	16 660	283
WEST VIRGINIA	688 557	0.3	2.55	10.7	24.5	20 865	11.6	21 049	154	11.6	10.1	7.4	3 593	199
WISCONSIN	1 822 118	10.3	2.61	9.6	24.3	69 326	13.1	46 672	459	8.9	8.4	6.7	10 763	201
WYOMING	168 839	1.9	2.63	8.3	24.5	6 253	13.0	4 042	42	8.4	9.1	6.9	762	154

1. No spouse present.   2. Per 1,000 resident population.   3. Deaths of infants under 1 year old.   4. Deaths of infants under 1 year old per 1,000 live births.
5. Per 100,000 resident population as of April 1 of the year shown.

Table A. States — Health Resources, Crime, and Education

STATE	Hospitals, 1998 Total	Beds Number	Beds Rate[1]	Medicare enrollees 2000	Serious crimes known to police, 2000[2] Total Number	Total Rate[3]	Rate[3] Violent	Property	Elementary and secondary school enrollment, 1999–2000 Total (1,000)	Percent private	Educational attainment[4] (percent) 1990 High school graduate or more	Bachelor's degree or more	2000 High school graduate or more	Bachelor's degree or more
	69	70	71	72	73	74	75	76	77	78	79	80	81	82
UNITED STATES................	5 214	895 681	331	38 748 879	11 605 751	4 124	506	3 618	52 020	9.9	75.2	20.3	84.1	25.6
ALABAMA	110	17 785	409	685 443	202 159	4 546	486	4 060	814	9.0	66.9	15.7	77.5	20.4
ALASKA	16	1 324	216	42 015	26 641	4 249	567	3 683	141	4.4	86.6	23.0	90.4	28.1
ARIZONA........................	61	10 161	218	675 430	299 092	5 830	532	5 298	897	4.9	78.7	20.3	85.1	24.6
ARKANSAS......................	80	10 107	398	439 371	110 019	4 115	445	3 670	477	5.5	66.3	13.3	81.7	18.4
CALIFORNIA....................	444	90 767	278	3 901 323	1 266 714	3 740	622	3 118	6 658	9.3	76.2	23.4	81.2	27.5
COLORADO....................	68	9 438	238	467 455	171 304	3 983	334	3 649	760	6.9	84.4	27.0	89.7	34.6
CONNECTICUT	35	7 782	238	515 288	110 091	3 233	325	2 908	624	11.2	79.2	27.2	88.2	31.6
DELAWARE	9	1 990	268	112 090	35 090	4 478	684	3 794	136	16.8	77.5	21.4	86.1	24.0
DISTRICT OF COLUMBIA ...	10	4 322	826	75 325	41 626	7 277	1 508	5 769	94	17.8	73.1	33.3	83.2	38.3
FLORIDA........................	214	51 241	344	2 803 961	910 154	5 695	812	4 883	2 672	10.9	74.4	18.3	84.0	22.8
GEORGIA	157	24 637	322	916 067	388 949	4 751	505	4 246	1 539	7.6	70.9	19.3	82.6	23.1
HAWAII	19	3 166	265	165 265	62 987	5 199	244	4 955	218	14.8	80.1	22.9	87.4	26.3
IDAHO..........................	43	3 271	266	165 021	41 228	3 186	253	2 934	256	4.0	79.7	17.7	86.2	20.0
ILLINOIS........................	206	40 475	336	1 635 047	532 315	4 286	657	3 629	2 327	12.9	76.2	21.0	85.5	27.1
INDIANA........................	117	19 596	332	852 228	228 135	3 752	349	3 403	1 094	9.6	75.6	15.6	84.6	17.1
IOWA............................	120	13 473	471	476 719	94 630	3 234	266	2 967	547	9.1	80.1	16.9	89.7	25.5
KANSAS........................	132	11 383	433	390 423	118 527	4 409	389	4 019	515	8.4	81.3	21.1	88.1	27.3
KENTUCKY......................	105	16 966	431	622 908	119 626	2 960	295	2 665	723	10.4	64.6	13.6	78.7	20.5
LOUISIANA......................	133	18 314	419	601 516	242 344	5 423	681	4 742	895	15.4	68.3	16.1	80.8	22.5
MAINE..........................	40	4 371	351	216 459	33 400	2 620	110	2 510	228	8.0	78.8	18.8	89.3	24.1
MARYLAND......................	48	13 611	265	645 450	255 085	4 816	787	4 030	991	14.5	78.4	26.5	85.7	32.3
MASSACHUSETTS	90	20 369	331	960 722	192 131	3 026	476	2 550	1 104	12.0	80.0	27.2	85.1	32.7
MICHIGAN	167	31 719	323	1 403 325	408 456	4 110	555	3 555	1 905	9.4	76.8	17.4	86.2	23.0
MINNESOTA....................	142	17 140	363	654 405	171 611	3 488	281	3 208	947	9.8	82.4	21.8	90.8	31.2
MISSISSIPPI....................	104	12 563	456	418 527	113 910	4 004	361	3 644	552	9.3	64.3	14.7	80.3	18.7
MISSOURI......................	134	21 768	400	860 558	253 338	4 528	490	4 038	1 036	11.8	73.9	17.8	86.6	26.2
MONTANA......................	54	4 084	464	136 726	31 878	3 533	241	3 293	166	5.2	81.0	19.8	89.6	23.8
NEBRASKA......................	89	7 870	473	253 639	70 085	4 096	328	3 768	330	12.8	81.8	18.9	90.4	24.6
NEVADA........................	23	3 716	213	239 746	85 297	4 269	524	3 744	340	4.1	78.8	15.3	82.8	19.3
NEW HAMPSHIRE	26	3 179	268	170 070	30 068	2 433	175	2 258	230	10.2	82.2	24.4	88.1	30.1
NEW JERSEY..................	94	30 258	373	1 203 231	265 935	3 161	384	2 777	1 488	13.3	76.7	24.9	87.3	30.1
NEW MEXICO	36	4 015	231	234 319	100 391	5 519	758	4 761	348	6.6	75.1	20.4	82.2	23.6
NEW YORK......................	235	73 682	405	2 714 837	588 189	3 100	554	2 546	3 364	14.1	74.8	23.1	82.5	28.7
NORTH CAROLINA	121	21 735	288	1 133 419	395 972	4 919	498	4 422	1 372	7.0	70.0	17.4	79.2	23.2
NORTH DAKOTA	46	4 304	674	103 196	14 694	2 288	81	2 207	120	6.0	76.7	18.1	85.5	22.6
OHIO............................	188	39 924	356	1 701 227	458 874	4 042	334	3 708	2 091	12.2	75.7	17.0	87.0	24.6
OKLAHOMA....................	110	11 495	343	507 849	157 302	4 559	498	4 061	658	4.8	74.6	17.8	86.1	22.5
OREGON........................	62	7 352	224	489 312	165 780	4 845	351	4 495	590	7.7	81.5	20.6	88.1	27.2
PENNSYLVANIA................	214	46 466	387	2 095 479	367 858	2 995	420	2 575	2 156	15.7	74.7	17.9	85.7	24.3
RHODE ISLAND	10	2 814	285	171 595	36 444	3 476	298	3 179	181	13.7	72.0	21.3	81.3	26.4
SOUTH CAROLINA	64	11 249	293	567 854	209 482	5 221	805	4 417	722	7.7	68.3	16.6	83.0	19.0
SOUTH DAKOTA	51	4 195	568	119 437	17 511	2 320	167	2 153	140	6.7	77.1	17.2	91.8	25.7
TENNESSEE	135	21 953	404	829 246	278 218	4 890	707	4 183	1 010	9.3	67.1	16.0	79.9	22.0
TEXAS..........................	406	55 695	282	2 265 325	1 033 311	4 956	545	4 410	4 219	5.4	72.1	20.3	79.2	23.9
UTAH............................	39	4 269	203	206 056	99 958	4 476	256	4 220	493	2.6	85.1	22.3	90.7	26.4
VERMONT	15	1 566	265	89 028	18 185	2 987	114	2 873	117	10.4	80.8	24.3	90.0	28.8
VIRGINIA........................	92	18 211	268	893 048	214 348	3 028	282	2 746	1 234	8.1	75.2	24.5	86.6	31.9
WASHINGTON	92	12 093	213	735 648	300 932	5 106	370	4 736	1 081	7.1	83.8	22.9	91.8	28.6
WEST VIRGINIA................	56	8 397	464	337 811	47 067	2 603	317	2 286	308	5.2	66.0	12.3	77.1	15.3
WISCONSIN	126	17 111	328	783 003	172 124	3 209	237	2 972	1 017	13.7	78.6	17.7	86.7	23.8
WYOMING	26	2 309	480	65 437	16 285	3 298	267	3 032	94	2.4	83.0	18.8	90.0	20.6

1. Per 100,000 resident population as of July 1 of the year shown. and over time.   3. Per 100,000 population estimated by the FBI.   2. Data for serious crimes have not been adjusted for underreporting; this may affect comparability between geographic areas.   4. Persons 25 years old and older.

Table A. States — Education Expenditures, Income, Poverty, and Health Insurance

STATE	Local government expenditures for education, 1999–2000		Money income						Percent below poverty level					Average percent lacking health insurance, 2000	
			1999						1999			2000			
			Households						Persons						
			Median												
	Total current expenditures (mil dol)	Current expenditures per student (dollars)	Per capita[1] (dollars)	Dollars	Percent change, 1989–1999 (constant 1999 dollars)	Percent with $100,000 or more	Median household income 1998–2000 average (dollars)	Median income of family of four 2000	Total	Percent change in rate, 1989–1999	Families	Persons	Children under 18 years	Persons	Children under 18 years
	83	84	85	86	87	88	89	90	91	92	93	94	95	96	97
UNITED STATES	323 809	6 911	21 587	41 994	4.0	12.3	41 789	62 228	12.4	-5.3	9.2	11.3	16.1	14.0	11.6
ALABAMA	4 176	5 638	18 189	34 135	7.7	7.6	36 268	51 451	16.1	-12.0	12.5	14.4	20.6	13.5	8.5
ALASKA	1 183	8 806	22 660	51 571	-7.3	16.1	52 492	66 874	6.4	-28.9	6.7	8.2	10.6	19.3	17.7
ARIZONA	4 262	4 999	20 275	40 558	9.6	10.8	39 653	55 663	13.9	-11.5	9.9	12.0	19.6	16.1	12.8
ARKANSAS	2 380	5 277	16 904	32 182	13.3	6.0	30 082	44 537	15.8	-17.3	12.0	17.8	27.3	13.9	11.6
CALIFORNIA	38 129	6 314	22 711	47 493	-1.3	17.3	45 070	63 206	14.2	13.6	10.6	12.8	19.2	18.1	15.4
COLORADO	4 401	6 215	24 049	47 203	16.6	14.2	49 216	66 624	9.3	-20.5	6.2	8.1	10.9	13.3	13.7
CONNECTICUT	5 403	9 753	28 766	53 935	-3.8	20.2	50 647	82 702	7.9	16.2	5.6	6.6	9.2	7.9	2.6
DELAWARE	938	8 310	23 305	47 381	1.1	14.0	47 438	69 360	9.2	5.7	6.5	9.1	16.9	10.4	7.2
DISTRICT OF COLUMBIA	780	10 107	28 659	40 127	-2.8	16.4	38 005	63 406	20.2	19.5	16.7	14.9	23.4	14.4	9.9
FLORIDA	13 886	5 831	21 557	38 819	5.1	10.4	37 305	55 351	12.5	-1.6	9.0	10.6	16.1	17.3	16.5
GEORGIA	9 159	6 437	21 154	42 433	8.8	12.3	41 481	59 489	13.0	-11.6	9.9	11.2	16.4	14.6	8.1
HAWAII	1 214	6 530	21 525	49 820	-4.5	16.6	45 657	65 872	10.7	28.9	7.6	9.9	13.9	10.1	8.3
IDAHO	1 303	5 315	17 841	37 572	10.7	7.3	37 760	53 722	11.8	-11.3	8.3	12.9	18.8	15.6	14.7
ILLINOIS	14 463	7 133	23 104	46 590	7.5	14.4	46 649	68 117	10.7	-10.1	7.8	11.5	17.6	13.5	10.8
INDIANA	7 111	7 192	20 397	41 567	7.4	9.2	41 315	62 079	9.5	-11.2	6.7	8.7	10.5	12.0	13.9
IOWA	3 264	6 564	19 674	39 469	12.0	7.3	41 560	57 921	9.1	-20.9	6.0	7.2	8.7	8.7	6.2
KANSAS	2 972	6 294	20 506	40 624	10.8	9.3	38 393	56 784	9.9	-13.9	6.7	9.6	13.0	11.5	11.3
KENTUCKY	3 838	5 921	18 093	33 672	11.2	7.2	36 826	51 249	15.8	-16.8	12.7	11.9	15.2	12.9	7.7
LOUISIANA	4 391	5 804	16 912	32 566	10.4	7.4	32 500	47 363	19.6	-16.9	15.8	17.3	23.4	19.1	15.7
MAINE	1 604	7 667	19 533	37 240	-0.5	7.1	39 815	56 186	10.9	0.9	7.8	8.4	8.9	11.5	7.8
MARYLAND	6 545	7 731	25 614	52 868	-0.1	18.1	52 846	77 562	8.5	2.4	6.1	7.6	6.9	9.8	7.4
MASSACHUSETTS	8 511	8 761	25 952	50 502	1.7	17.7	45 769	78 025	9.3	4.5	6.7	10.1	13.9	9.5	7.8
MICHIGAN	13 994	8 110	22 168	44 667	7.2	12.7	46 034	68 740	10.5	-19.8	7.4	10.0	13.8	9.9	6.7
MINNESOTA	6 140	7 190	23 198	47 111	13.4	12.6	50 088	70 553	7.9	-22.5	5.1	6.0	8.5	9.0	9.3
MISSISSIPPI	2 510	5 014	15 853	31 330	15.8	6.0	31 963	46 331	19.9	-21.0	16.0	12.9	16.4	13.1	9.2
MISSOURI	5 656	6 187	19 936	37 934	7.1	8.8	44 247	61 173	11.7	-12.0	8.6	8.0	10.6	10.6	8.5
MONTANA	995	6 314	17 151	33 024	6.9	5.6	32 553	46 142	14.6	-9.3	10.5	15.7	24.7	18.5	18.7
NEBRASKA	1 927	6 683	19 613	39 250	12.3	8.1	39 029	57 040	9.7	-12.6	6.7	9.0	12.2	9.9	8.8
NEVADA	1 875	5 760	21 989	44 581	7.0	11.3	43 262	59 614	10.5	2.9	7.5	8.5	11.9	15.6	14.9
NEW HAMPSHIRE	1 419	6 860	23 844	49 467	1.3	13.8	48 029	71 661	6.5	1.6	4.3	5.2	7.7	6.9	7.0
NEW JERSEY	13 328	10 337	27 006	55 146	0.3	21.3	51 739	78 560	8.5	11.8	6.3	8.0	11.1	12.6	9.3
NEW MEXICO	1 890	5 825	17 261	34 133	5.5	7.6	34 035	47 314	18.4	-10.7	14.5	16.8	23.5	23.8	20.2
NEW YORK	28 433	9 846	23 389	43 393	-2.0	15.3	38 413	64 520	14.6	12.3	11.5	13.4	19.0	15.2	10.5
NORTH CAROLINA	7 713	6 045	20 307	39 184	9.4	9.4	38 413	57 203	12.3	-5.4	9.0	12.1	18.5	13.0	10.1
NORTH DAKOTA	639	5 667	17 769	34 604	11.0	5.7	33 769	53 140	11.9	-17.4	8.3	10.1	14.1	11.4	11.9
OHIO	12 975	7 065	21 003	40 956	6.2	9.8	41 972	62 251	10.6	-15.2	7.8	10.0	15.3	10.9	9.5
OKLAHOMA	3 383	5 395	17 646	33 400	5.4	6.6	34 020	48 459	14.7	-12.0	11.2	15.4	23.7	19.3	16.8
OREGON	3 896	7 149	20 940	40 916	11.8	10.0	41 915	58 315	11.6	-6.5	7.9	11.2	18.7	13.7	12.9
PENNSYLVANIA	14 120	7 772	20 880	40 106	2.7	10.3	41 394	65 411	11.0	-0.9	7.8	8.9	11.0	7.6	4.9
RHODE ISLAND	1 393	8 904	21 688	42 090	-2.7	11.5	43 428	68 418	11.9	24.0	8.9	9.1	13.8	5.9	2.5
SOUTH CAROLINA	4 087	6 130	18 795	37 082	5.1	8.1	36 671	56 294	14.1	-8.4	10.7	10.6	16.3	11.9	8.6
SOUTH DAKOTA	738	5 632	17 562	35 282	16.7	5.9	35 986	55 150	13.2	-17.0	9.3	9.6	12.7	11.8	11.6
TENNESSEE	4 932	5 383	19 393	36 360	9.1	8.3	35 874	54 899	13.5	-14.0	10.3	14.7	20.2	10.3	4.7
TEXAS	25 099	6 288	19 617	39 927	10.0	11.5	39 296	53 513	15.4	-14.9	12.0	14.7	20.9	21.5	21.5
UTAH	2 103	4 378	18 185	45 726	15.5	11.2	46 539	57 043	9.4	-17.5	6.5	9.6	11.6	13.4	10.1
VERMONT	870	8 323	20 625	40 856	2.1	8.7	40 908	59 125	9.4	-5.1	6.3	11.3	16.1	10.6	8.5
VIRGINIA	7 758	6 841	23 975	46 677	4.2	15.1	47 701	68 054	9.6	-5.9	7.0	7.7	8.3	12.7	11.7
WASHINGTON	6 400	6 376	22 973	45 776	9.3	12.6	46 412	63 568	10.6	-2.8	7.3	10.1	13.8	13.3	8.1
WEST VIRGINIA	2 087	7 152	16 477	29 696	6.3	5.0	29 217	46 270	17.9	-9.1	13.9	14.0	18.3	14.3	9.8
WISCONSIN	6 852	7 806	21 271	43 791	10.7	9.4	45 441	66 725	8.7	-18.7	5.6	9.6	13.8	7.1	3.7
WYOMING	684	7 425	19 134	37 892	4.1	6.7	38 291	55 859	11.4	-4.2	8.0	11.0	14.6	14.3	12.5

1. Based on population enumerated as of April 1, 2000.

Items 83—97

STATE	Personal income, 2001												
			Per capita[1]		Sources of personal income (mil dol)								
									Transfer payments				
										Government payments to individuals			
	Total (mil dol)	Percent change, 2000–2001	Dollars	Rank	Wages and salaries[2]	Propri-etors' income	Divi-dends, interest, and rent	Total	Total	Social Security	Medical payments	Income mainte-nance	Unemploy-ment insurance
	98	99	100	101	102	103	104	105	106	107	108	109	110
UNITED STATES.............	8 678 255	3.2	30 472	X	4 948 115	729 092	1 637 213	1 171 083	1 111 824	425 167	475 838	110 901	32 408
ALABAMA	109 773	3.6	24 589	43	59 028	8 124	20 098	18 964	18 060	7 433	7 207	1 942	332
ALASKA	19 641	4.4	30 936	14	11 325	1 825	3 231	3 152	3 043	506	853	310	111
ARIZONA	137 314	4.6	25 872	38	78 736	9 975	26 771	18 991	17 971	7 718	6 999	1 519	300
ARKANSAS.....................	61 613	3.9	22 887	48	32 524	5 197	11 437	11 473	10 890	4 499	4 208	1 083	314
CALIFORNIA	1 128 256	2.6	32 702	10	647 222	114 430	211 291	134 103	127 064	40 384	54 521	19 941	3 491
COLORADO.....................	147 860	3.5	33 470	7	88 434	15 745	26 350	12 954	12 117	5 007	4 919	1 020	313
CONNECTICUT	145 341	2.9	42 435	1	81 164	11 893	26 920	15 847	15 161	6 019	6 848	1 272	497
DELAWARE	25 853	4.2	32 472	11	16 466	1 593	5 097	3 152	2 968	1 358	1 151	224	91
DISTRICT OF COLUMBIA ...	22 959	3.5	40 150	X	39 103	2 874	4 685	2 860	2 772	603	1 532	411	76
FLORIDA	474 626	4.3	28 947	22	239 379	29 274	122 125	73 404	70 126	30 475	29 731	5 181	1 042
GEORGIA	240 896	3.6	28 733	25	144 367	21 463	40 708	27 924	25 952	10 179	10 651	2 916	636
HAWAII	35 510	3.4	29 002	21	19 885	2 788	6 895	4 372	4 171	1 752	1 440	615	149
IDAHO............................	32 525	3.7	24 621	42	16 861	3 922	6 197	4 383	4 137	1 829	1 461	299	166
ILLINOIS	412 200	2.7	33 023	9	240 650	32 548	83 170	47 384	44 571	18 410	17 926	4 410	1 927
INDIANA.........................	169 885	2.4	27 783	31	95 207	10 703	32 544	23 612	22 300	9 907	8 976	1 782	600
IOWA.............................	79 893	2.6	27 331	33	43 267	6 723	16 615	11 230	10 555	5 153	3 803	725	316
KANSAS.........................	76 973	3.7	28 565	28	42 667	5 992	15 413	10 082	9 559	4 277	3 718	674	249
KENTUCKY......................	101 326	3.2	24 923	40	55 860	7 131	18 306	17 883	17 014	6 583	6 913	1 879	456
LOUISIANA	109 560	5.2	24 535	44	58 069	8 804	18 772	20 455	19 466	6 252	9 727	2 316	237
MAINE	34 384	4.6	26 723	35	17 975	2 599	6 620	5 875	5 621	2 200	2 367	575	113
MARYLAND	189 142	4.6	35 188	5	98 791	10 611	34 931	19 257	18 105	7 063	7 833	1 619	445
MASSACHUSETTS	248 202	2.8	38 907	2	153 635	18 022	45 038	30 778	29 475	10 168	14 510	2 351	1 364
MICHIGAN	297 609	1.3	29 788	18	173 309	17 796	55 193	42 481	40 430	16 839	16 678	3 912	1 623
MINNESOTA.....................	164 589	3.5	33 101	8	99 764	10 782	33 763	18 749	17 623	7 053	7 484	1 400	666
MISSISSIPPI	62 163	3.7	21 750	50	31 005	4 882	10 375	12 647	12 015	4 377	5 219	1 512	194
MISSOURI	158 906	3.2	28 226	29	90 852	11 901	31 460	24 396	23 268	9 420	10 289	1 898	479
MONTANA	21 673	4.6	23 963	46	10 465	2 170	5 004	3 526	3 335	1 452	1 160	269	83
NEBRASKA.....................	49 489	4.0	28 886	23	27 328	4 689	10 692	6 423	6 086	2 666	2 465	401	88
NEVADA	62 966	4.8	29 897	17	37 022	5 170	13 235	6 577	6 218	2 870	2 247	429	298
NEW HAMPSHIRE..............	42 986	3.2	34 138	6	22 533	3 435	8 099	4 513	4 254	1 971	1 738	258	65
NEW JERSEY...................	326 723	2.9	38 509	3	178 439	26 387	59 951	37 133	35 350	14 230	15 499	2 337	1 589
NEW MEXICO	42 354	6.1	23 155	47	23 044	3 182	7 596	6 966	6 585	2 453	2 611	808	107
NEW YORK	684 774	2.9	36 019	4	411 556	63 650	123 279	106 635	102 526	30 161	52 432	12 548	2 676
NORTH CAROLINA	225 234	3.0	27 514	32	129 670	16 245	42 623	32 185	30 598	12 466	12 821	2 752	982
NORTH DAKOTA...............	16 434	2.5	25 902	37	8 856	1 434	3 489	2 654	2 531	1 022	960	168	37
OHIO.............................	327 745	2.2	28 816	24	188 245	20 830	62 286	49 147	46 365	18 611	18 811	4 013	1 232
OKLAHOMA.....................	86 750	4.3	25 071	39	43 749	10 002	15 586	13 869	13 182	5 433	5 198	1 191	201
OREGON.........................	97 814	2.5	28 165	30	55 157	7 591	21 088	14 238	13 573	5 541	4 870	1 106	673
PENNSYLVANIA.................	377 461	3.3	30 720	15	203 375	33 332	70 671	62 137	59 432	23 285	26 316	4 747	2 254
RHODE ISLAND	31 995	4.0	30 215	16	16 595	1 976	6 021	5 567	5 356	1 822	2 507	493	189
SOUTH CAROLINA	101 110	3.4	24 886	41	55 779	6 496	18 604	16 204	15 361	6 359	6 107	1 524	400
SOUTH DAKOTA................	20 174	3.3	26 664	36	10 049	2 396	4 698	2 820	2 685	1 187	1 039	205	23
TENNESSEE.....................	154 911	2.9	26 988	34	86 643	16 198	24 735	25 349	24 293	9 116	11 172	2 187	612
TEXAS	609 489	3.7	28 581	27	355 124	80 265	91 553	70 763	66 744	24 385	29 636	6 987	1 667
UTAH.............................	54 884	4.1	24 180	45	33 792	4 236	9 189	5 845	5 416	2 300	1 973	412	183
VERMONT........................	17 531	4.8	28 594	26	9 407	1 516	3 610	2 544	2 385	974	989	243	65
VIRGINIA	233 107	4.6	32 431	12	137 840	12 692	41 810	23 144	21 681	9 714	8 194	1 770	381
WASHINGTON	191 763	2.6	32 025	13	110 856	14 273	36 279	24 240	22 862	8 432	8 612	1 814	1 417
WEST VIRGINIA.................	41 230	4.2	22 881	49	20 132	2 720	7 274	9 612	9 255	3 693	3 285	867	147
WISCONSIN	158 116	3.3	29 270	20	89 663	9 106	32 049	20 855	19 698	8 824	7 711	1 473	821
WYOMING	14 544	5.7	29 416	19	7 251	1 502	3 788	1 729	1 620	737	521	112	29

1. Based on the resident population estimated as of July 1 of the year shown.　　2. Includes other labor income.

STATE	Personal tax payments 2001 (mil dol)	Disposable personal income, 2001 Total (mil dol)	Per capita[1] (dollars)	Earnings, 2001 Total (mil dol)	Farm	Goods-related[2] Total	Manu-facturing	Service-related and other[3] Total	Retail trade	Finance, insurance, and real estate	Services	Government	Gross state product (mil dol) 2000
	111	112	113	114	115	116	117	118	119	120	121	122	123
UNITED STATES	1 290 892	7 387 363	25 939	6 242 742	0.6	21.8	14.8	61.7	8.8	9.7	29.7	15.9	9 941 552
ALABAMA	13 096	96 677	21 655	74 541	1.7	25.4	18.0	53.0	9.2	6.0	24.8	19.9	119 921
ALASKA	2 470	17 171	27 045	14 952	0.1	19.0	3.7	49.3	8.6	4.1	22.2	31.7	27 747
ARIZONA	18 307	119 007	22 423	97 060	0.7	20.3	11.8	62.5	10.4	10.0	29.3	16.5	156 303
ARKANSAS	7 421	54 192	20 130	41 724	2.6	26.4	19.8	53.8	11.4	4.8	22.7	17.2	67 724
CALIFORNIA	195 421	932 835	27 038	831 027	0.8	20.1	13.7	63.8	8.8	9.2	33.0	15.4	1 344 623
COLORADO	22 913	124 947	28 283	114 682	0.6	19.7	9.5	64.9	8.9	9.4	30.3	14.8	167 918
CONNECTICUT	28 103	117 239	34 230	101 703	0.2	22.8	17.3	64.5	7.8	16.3	29.1	12.4	159 288
DELAWARE	3 886	21 967	27 591	19 949	0.8	25.0	18.8	60.2	8.4	17.0	26.2	13.4	36 336
DISTRICT OF COLUMBIA	4 177	18 782	32 845	49 171	0.0	3.0	1.9	54.7	2.1	6.0	42.6	40.1	59 397
FLORIDA	64 490	410 136	25 014	296 595	0.6	13.7	7.2	69.7	10.9	9.9	35.0	16.0	472 105
GEORGIA	34 124	206 772	24 663	183 261	1.0	19.6	13.3	63.6	8.9	7.5	27.9	15.8	296 142
HAWAII	4 579	30 930	25 262	25 682	0.7	9.0	3.0	60.7	11.3	7.7	29.9	29.6	42 364
IDAHO	4 285	28 240	21 378	22 779	4.2	25.0	16.1	52.7	10.1	5.2	24.2	18.1	37 031
ILLINOIS	62 710	349 489	27 999	300 076	0.4	22.6	16.4	63.5	7.8	10.8	30.2	13.5	467 284
INDIANA	22 569	147 316	24 092	117 624	0.6	33.7	26.6	51.9	9.1	6.7	23.7	13.9	192 195
IOWA	10 133	69 760	23 864	54 999	2.6	25.8	19.3	55.1	9.3	8.2	24.1	16.5	89 600
KANSAS	10 666	66 307	24 607	53 879	1.2	24.0	17.0	56.9	9.2	6.7	24.0	17.8	85 063
KENTUCKY	13 640	87 686	21 568	70 499	1.4	27.4	19.3	52.5	9.7	5.4	23.4	18.8	118 508
LOUISIANA	12 566	96 994	21 721	74 520	0.4	24.6	12.3	55.5	9.1	5.3	27.2	19.4	137 700
MAINE	4 791	29 593	23 000	22 967	0.5	21.8	14.6	59.4	11.8	7.0	29.1	18.3	35 981
MARYLAND	30 850	158 291	29 449	122 231	0.3	15.2	7.8	61.6	8.5	8.0	33.4	22.9	186 108
MASSACHUSETTS	45 800	202 402	31 728	187 753	0.1	20.0	14.3	68.2	8.0	12.4	36.4	11.7	284 934
MICHIGAN	42 861	254 749	25 498	211 961	0.2	34.2	28.1	51.9	8.4	5.9	26.0	13.7	325 384
MINNESOTA	25 373	139 216	27 998	120 924	0.6	25.0	18.2	61.0	9.1	9.8	27.6	13.4	184 766
MISSISSIPPI	6 384	55 779	19 517	40 192	2.1	24.7	17.8	50.5	9.9	4.7	24.0	22.6	67 315
MISSOURI	21 273	137 633	24 448	113 629	0.5	23.0	15.6	61.0	9.2	8.6	28.0	15.5	178 845
MONTANA	2 673	19 000	21 008	14 068	1.7	17.1	6.8	58.7	11.3	6.1	27.7	22.5	21 777
NEBRASKA	6 621	42 868	25 022	35 236	3.3	19.2	12.7	60.4	8.5	8.0	27.1	17.1	56 072
NEVADA	8 897	54 069	25 673	46 551	0.2	16.3	4.7	68.9	10.1	8.6	39.2	14.7	74 745
NEW HAMPSHIRE	5 982	37 003	29 387	28 318	0.1	26.5	18.9	62.1	11.8	7.7	30.1	11.3	47 708
NEW JERSEY	54 367	272 356	32 101	222 348	0.1	19.1	13.9	67.2	8.0	10.5	31.0	13.6	363 089
NEW MEXICO	5 181	37 173	20 322	29 411	2.3	16.5	6.6	52.9	10.1	5.0	27.5	28.2	54 354
NEW YORK	119 536	565 238	29 732	514 437	0.2	14.2	10.1	72.0	6.4	23.2	31.1	13.6	799 202
NORTH CAROLINA	31 000	194 234	23 727	161 385	1.6	26.5	19.4	53.8	9.4	7.5	24.6	18.1	281 741
NORTH DAKOTA	1 799	14 635	23 068	11 432	2.5	16.4	8.0	58.7	9.5	6.3	26.2	22.4	18 283
OHIO	47 122	280 623	24 673	230 611	0.3	28.7	22.5	55.9	9.5	7.3	26.6	15.1	372 640
OKLAHOMA	10 904	75 846	21 920	59 918	1.2	25.3	14.5	52.3	9.4	5.4	24.3	21.2	91 773
OREGON	14 896	82 917	23 876	69 051	0.9	24.4	17.5	57.9	10.3	6.9	26.6	16.7	118 637
PENNSYLVANIA	53 915	323 546	26 332	258 945	0.3	25.2	18.6	61.6	8.7	8.3	31.4	12.9	403 985
RHODE ISLAND	4 492	27 503	25 973	20 570	0.1	20.4	14.7	61.4	9.7	8.7	32.2	18.2	36 453
SOUTH CAROLINA	12 654	88 456	21 771	69 265	0.8	26.8	19.6	52.1	10.4	6.3	23.2	20.3	113 377
SOUTH DAKOTA	2 125	18 049	23 856	13 752	6.1	18.7	12.2	56.2	10.1	8.0	24.9	19.0	23 192
TENNESSEE	16 669	138 241	24 084	112 761	0.3	24.7	18.0	61.1	10.4	7.3	29.2	13.9	178 362
TEXAS	74 467	535 022	25 089	474 963	0.6	23.8	12.6	61.2	9.0	8.1	27.3	14.4	742 274
UTAH	7 582	47 302	20 840	42 229	0.7	21.2	12.5	59.3	9.7	7.9	28.4	18.8	68 549
VERMONT	2 392	15 139	24 693	12 017	1.1	26.4	19.0	56.3	10.2	5.7	29.7	16.2	18 411
VIRGINIA	37 009	196 098	27 282	169 249	0.3	16.8	10.0	59.7	8.0	7.5	32.2	23.2	261 355
WASHINGTON	28 296	163 467	27 299	137 296	0.8	20.5	13.7	60.5	9.3	6.9	30.8	18.2	219 937
WEST VIRGINIA	4 758	36 472	20 241	25 621	0.0	25.6	13.5	52.4	9.3	4.3	26.6	21.9	42 271
WISCONSIN	22 540	135 576	25 098	109 285	0.5	31.0	24.2	53.7	9.0	7.2	24.9	14.8	173 478
WYOMING	2 125	12 419	25 118	9 645	1.4	28.5	5.0	46.6	9.1	5.0	20.2	23.5	19 294

1. Based on the resident population estimated as of July 1 of the year shown. 2. Includes mining, construction, and manufacturing. 3. Includes private sector earnings in agricultural services, forestry, and fisheries; transportation and public utilities; wholesale and retail trade; finance, insurance, and real estate; and services.

Table A. States — Housing

STATE	Housing units, 1990 Total	Percent change 1980–1990	Occupied units Total	Percent owner-occupied	Housing units, 2000 Total	Percent change, 1990–2000	Occupied units Total	Owner-occupied Percent	Median value[1] (dollars)	Owner cost as a percent of income With a mortgage	Without a mortgage	Renter-occupied Median rent[2] (dollars)	Rent as a percent of income	Sub-standard units[3] (percent)
	124	125	126	127	128	129	130	131	132	133	134	135	136	137
UNITED STATES	102 263 678	15.7	91 947 410	64.2	115 904 641	13.3	105 480 101	66.2	120 496	21.8	9.3	527	26.4	4.7
ALABAMA	1 670 379	13.8	1 506 790	70.5	1 963 711	17.6	1 737 080	72.5	85 833	20.4	8.9	328	26.1	3.3
ALASKA	232 608	42.9	188 915	56.1	260 978	12.2	221 600	62.5	144 271	21.8	7.3	649	23.9	10.0
ARIZONA	1 659 430	49.4	1 368 843	64.2	2 189 189	31.9	1 901 327	68.0	121 688	22.3	8.6	540	28.4	8.0
ARKANSAS	1 000 667	11.4	891 179	69.6	1 173 043	17.2	1 042 696	69.4	73 480	19.6	9.2	358	24.6	3.3
CALIFORNIA	11 182 882	20.5	10 381 206	55.6	12 214 549	9.2	11 502 870	56.9	216 164	25.6	8.2	692	28.7	11.5
COLORADO	1 477 349	23.7	1 282 489	62.2	1 808 037	22.4	1 658 238	67.3	168 896	22.5	7.9	625	27.2	3.6
CONNECTICUT	1 320 850	14.0	1 230 479	65.6	1 385 975	4.9	1 301 670	66.8	166 941	22.3	12.6	600	26.2	2.6
DELAWARE	289 919	21.5	247 497	70.2	343 072	18.3	298 736	72.3	132 942	20.2	7.5	565	23.8	2.3
DISTRICT OF COLUMBIA	278 489	0.5	249 634	38.9	274 845	-1.3	248 338	40.8	164 787	22.9	8.0	592	24.9	5.9
FLORIDA	6 100 262	39.3	5 134 869	67.2	7 302 947	19.7	6 337 929	70.1	107 443	23.6	9.4	562	28.4	4.3
GEORGIA	2 638 418	30.1	2 366 615	64.9	3 281 737	24.4	3 006 369	67.5	113 807	21.3	8.9	519	26.4	4.2
HAWAII	389 810	16.6	356 267	53.9	460 542	18.1	403 240	56.5	288 332	26.9	7.0	766	27.8	12.2
IDAHO	413 327	10.2	360 723	70.1	527 824	27.7	469 645	72.4	105 403	20.7	7.5	427	26.6	4.7
ILLINOIS	4 506 275	4.3	4 202 240	64.2	4 885 615	8.4	4 591 779	67.3	130 396	21.8	9.7	541	25.9	4.1
INDIANA	2 246 046	7.4	2 065 355	70.2	2 532 319	12.7	2 336 306	71.4	94 767	19.6	8.4	436	24.6	2.6
IOWA	1 143 669	1.1	1 064 325	70.0	1 232 511	7.8	1 149 276	72.3	80 366	19.0	9.3	391	24.4	2.2
KANSAS	1 044 112	9.3	944 726	67.9	1 131 200	8.3	1 037 891	69.2	84 375	20.4	8.9	396	23.5	2.1
KENTUCKY	1 506 845	10.1	1 379 782	69.6	1 750 927	16.2	1 590 647	70.8	89 078	19.6	7.9	371	24.6	2.5
LOUISIANA	1 716 241	10.8	1 499 269	65.9	1 847 181	7.6	1 656 053	67.9	84 460	19.8	8.6	369	28.6	3.9
MAINE	587 045	17.2	465 312	70.5	651 901	11.0	518 200	71.6	102 656	21.7	11.7	435	26.7	2.0
MARYLAND	1 891 917	20.4	1 748 991	65.0	2 145 283	13.4	1 980 859	67.7	146 866	21.9	9.0	615	25.2	3.0
MASSACHUSETTS	2 472 711	12.0	2 247 110	59.3	2 621 989	6.0	2 443 580	61.7	192 483	22.0	11.8	645	26.9	2.5
MICHIGAN	3 847 926	7.2	3 419 331	71.0	4 234 279	10.0	3 785 661	73.8	117 360	19.7	9.0	476	25.7	2.6
MINNESOTA	1 848 445	14.6	1 647 853	71.8	2 065 946	11.8	1 895 127	74.6	123 960	19.8	8.8	535	23.9	2.8
MISSISSIPPI	1 010 423	10.8	911 374	71.5	1 161 953	15.0	1 046 434	72.3	75 053	20.1	8.8	348	25.1	3.7
MISSOURI	2 199 129	10.6	1 961 206	68.8	2 442 017	11.0	2 194 594	70.3	91 090	19.7	8.4	390	24.3	2.6
MONTANA	361 155	10.0	306 163	67.3	412 633	14.3	358 667	69.1	98 849	21.9	9.7	389	25.0	2.8
NEBRASKA	660 621	5.7	602 363	66.5	722 668	9.4	666 184	67.4	85 959	19.7	9.8	415	23.7	2.0
NEVADA	518 858	52.6	466 297	54.8	827 457	59.5	751 165	60.9	140 844	24.0	8.6	628	28.3	5.8
NEW HAMPSHIRE	503 904	30.4	411 186	68.2	547 024	8.6	474 606	69.7	138 031	21.8	12.7	594	24.2	1.6
NEW JERSEY	3 075 310	10.9	2 794 711	64.9	3 310 275	7.6	3 064 645	65.6	173 045	23.4	15.5	690	25.6	4.2
NEW MEXICO	632 058	24.5	542 709	67.4	780 579	23.5	677 971	70.0	105 771	21.4	7.9	419	28.0	7.8
NEW YORK	7 226 891	5.2	6 639 322	52.2	7 679 307	6.3	7 056 860	53.0	150 673	23.2	12.6	615	27.0	6.1
NORTH CAROLINA	2 818 193	23.9	2 517 026	68.0	3 523 944	25.0	3 132 013	69.4	108 215	21.4	9.5	440	25.8	3.0
NORTH DAKOTA	276 340	6.8	240 878	65.6	289 677	4.8	257 152	66.6	75 152	19.4	9.7	382	22.6	1.5
OHIO	4 371 945	6.4	4 087 546	67.5	4 783 051	9.4	4 445 773	69.1	102 822	20.7	9.5	424	24.6	1.9
OKLAHOMA	1 406 499	13.7	1 206 135	68.1	1 514 400	7.7	1 342 293	68.4	73 750	19.7	8.9	360	25.3	3.4
OREGON	1 193 567	10.2	1 103 313	63.1	1 452 709	21.7	1 333 723	64.3	149 729	23.7	9.5	547	28.2	4.4
PENNSYLVANIA	4 938 140	7.4	4 495 966	70.6	5 249 750	6.3	4 777 003	71.3	94 479	21.2	11.0	433	25.3	1.9
RHODE ISLAND	414 572	11.2	377 977	59.5	439 837	6.1	408 424	60.0	137 907	21.7	13.3	484	25.6	2.4
SOUTH CAROLINA	1 424 155	23.4	1 258 044	69.8	1 753 670	23.1	1 533 854	72.2	103 882	21.1	8.8	433	26.5	2.4
SOUTH DAKOTA	292 436	5.6	259 034	66.1	323 208	10.5	290 245	68.2	82 142	19.9	9.5	378	24.1	2.2
TENNESSEE	2 026 067	15.9	1 853 725	68.0	2 439 443	20.4	2 232 905	69.9	96 109	21.2	8.6	423	24.9	2.8
TEXAS	7 008 999	26.3	6 070 937	60.9	8 157 575	16.4	7 393 354	63.8	83 623	20.0	9.6	489	25.0	7.3
UTAH	598 388	22.1	537 273	68.1	768 594	28.4	701 281	71.5	144 036	23.1	7.5	543	25.3	4.8
VERMONT	271 214	21.5	210 650	69.0	294 382	8.5	240 634	70.6	115 288	22.2	13.5	472	27.5	2.0
VIRGINIA	2 496 334	23.5	2 291 830	66.3	2 904 192	16.3	2 699 173	68.1	126 526	21.2	8.2	555	25.1	2.9
WASHINGTON	2 032 378	20.3	1 872 431	62.6	2 451 075	20.6	2 271 398	64.6	169 406	24.0	9.0	598	27.1	4.2
WEST VIRGINIA	781 295	4.5	688 557	74.1	844 623	8.1	736 481	75.2	72 215	19.5	7.9	316	26.2	2.3
WISCONSIN	2 055 774	10.3	1 822 118	66.7	2 321 144	12.9	2 084 544	68.4	109 688	21.2	10.4	469	23.7	2.4
WYOMING	203 411	8.1	168 839	67.8	223 854	10.1	193 608	70.0	98 456	19.6	7.7	385	24.7	2.9

1. Specified owner-occupied units.   2. Specified renter-occupied units.   3. Overcrowded or lacking complete plumbing facilities.

Items 124—137

Table A. States — Social Security, Employment, Unemployment, and Labor Force

STATE	Social Security beneficiaries, December 2000 — Number	Rate[1]	Supplemental Security Income recipients, December 2000	Civilian employment and selected occupations, March 2000[2] — Total	Percent — Professional, managerial, and technical	Percent — Precision production, craft, and repair	Civilian labor force annual average, 2001 — Total	Percent change, 2000–2001	Employed	Unemployed — Total	Rate[3]
	138	139	140	141	142	143	144	145	146	147	148
UNITED STATES	45 414 762	161	6 601 686	135 073 000	33.4	11.0	141 815 000	0.7	135 073 000	6 742 000	4.8
ALABAMA	825 773	186	159 486	2 033 192	30.9	12.1	2 147 552	-0.3	2 033 192	114 360	5.0
ALASKA	54 331	87	8 672	301 792	35.8	12.0	321 983	0.0	301 792	20 191	6.0
ARIZONA	795 936	155	81 493	2 306 594	32.6	11.4	2 419 619	3.1	2 306 594	113 025	5.0
ARKANSAS	523 588	196	85 410	1 163 865	28.1	11.5	1 226 661	-0.9	1 163 865	62 796	5.0
CALIFORNIA	4 208 926	124	1 086 333	16 435 173	35.4	10.2	17 362 231	1.6	16 435 173	927 058	5.0
COLORADO	534 196	124	53 776	2 209 598	38.8	11.1	2 294 893	0.9	2 209 598	85 295	4.0
CONNECTICUT	577 972	170	48 767	1 661 290	39.3	9.9	1 717 642	-1.7	1 661 290	56 352	3.0
DELAWARE	132 368	169	11 984	404 114	35.6	10.2	418 819	2.4	404 114	14 705	4.0
DISTRICT OF COLUMBIA	73 703	129	20 073	259 744	51.0	4.9	277 879	-0.4	259 744	18 135	7.0
FLORIDA	3 195 615	200	377 218	7 308 900	31.5	11.3	7 673 565	2.4	7 308 900	364 665	5.0
GEORGIA	1 101 028	134	196 907	3 966 348	31.2	12.5	4 131 569	-1.0	3 966 348	165 221	4.0
HAWAII	183 802	152	21 019	577 443	29.3	8.1	605 524	1.7	577 443	28 081	5.0
IDAHO	195 695	151	18 381	648 392	28.3	12.0	682 228	3.7	648 392	33 836	5.0
ILLINOIS	1 840 206	148	248 777	6 005 978	32.4	10.6	6 348 558	-1.1	6 005 978	342 580	5.0
INDIANA	999 089	164	88 041	2 970 497	29.0	13.0	3 106 388	0.7	2 970 497	135 891	4.0
IOWA	541 304	185	40 282	1 534 836	30.9	11.6	1 587 790	1.6	1 534 836	52 954	3.0
KANSAS	440 531	164	36 282	1 322 160	32.1	11.0	1 381 325	-2.1	1 322 160	59 165	4.0
KENTUCKY	739 585	183	174 349	1 859 668	30.2	10.5	1 967 572	-0.7	1 859 668	107 904	6.0
LOUISIANA	711 631	159	165 577	1 927 933	32.3	12.1	2 050 323	1.0	1 927 933	122 390	6.0
MAINE	250 724	197	29 727	656 764	29.7	12.9	683 907	-0.7	656 764	27 143	4.0
MARYLAND	724 544	137	88 138	2 721 724	40.3	9.0	2 837 433	1.2	2 721 724	115 709	4.0
MASSACHUSETTS	1 060 613	167	167 559	3 163 104	40.5	10.0	3 283 709	1.5	3 163 104	120 605	4.0
MICHIGAN	1 646 864	166	209 539	4 900 723	32.5	11.4	5 175 083	-0.5	4 900 723	274 360	5.0
MINNESOTA	739 824	150	64 059	2 710 298	35.4	11.2	2 814 357	2.8	2 710 298	104 059	4.0
MISSISSIPPI	514 300	181	128 910	1 224 651	27.3	13.1	1 296 193	-2.3	1 224 651	71 542	6.0
MISSOURI	1 008 424	180	112 213	2 830 403	34.3	10.9	2 970 118	1.4	2 830 403	139 715	5.0
MONTANA	157 443	175	13 877	443 904	28.0	11.0	465 223	-2.9	443 904	21 319	5.0
NEBRASKA	285 555	167	21 249	899 429	29.6	10.1	928 297	0.4	899 429	28 868	3.0
NEVADA	286 981	144	25 540	968 759	27.6	11.5	1 023 488	3.8	968 759	54 729	5.0
NEW HAMPSHIRE	199 781	162	11 592	664 293	36.8	12.2	688 657	0.5	664 293	24 364	4.0
NEW JERSEY	1 348 996	160	146 112	4 003 801	36.3	9.5	4 179 451	-0.2	4 003 801	175 650	4.0
NEW MEXICO	277 262	152	46 660	797 978	33.5	11.7	837 780	0.6	797 978	39 802	5.0
NEW YORK	3 007 120	158	616 502	8 402 431	34.4	9.1	8 831 770	-1.2	8 402 431	429 339	5.0
NORTH CAROLINA	1 351 121	168	191 137	3 773 489	30.3	13.1	3 994 789	0.9	3 773 489	221 300	6.0
NORTH DAKOTA	114 627	178	8 166	329 218	28.9	10.3	338 768	0.0	329 218	9 550	3.0
OHIO	1 912 006	168	240 002	5 605 933	33.4	11.4	5 857 254	1.3	5 605 933	251 321	4.0
OKLAHOMA	594 155	172	72 204	1 601 921	29.9	12.1	1 665 427	1.1	1 601 921	63 506	4.0
OREGON	562 381	164	52 046	1 679 869	34.3	10.5	1 793 724	-0.5	1 679 869	113 855	6.0
PENNSYLVANIA	2 356 051	192	283 785	5 785 679	33.9	10.5	6 072 613	1.7	5 785 679	286 934	5.0
RHODE ISLAND	192 680	184	27 729	479 830	36.8	9.9	503 566	-0.2	479 830	23 736	5.0
SOUTH CAROLINA	688 569	172	107 558	1 843 393	31.5	13.1	1 949 210	-1.8	1 843 393	105 817	5.0
SOUTH DAKOTA	136 227	180	12 648	391 625	29.9	9.7	405 088	1.0	391 625	13 463	3.0
TENNESSEE	991 029	174	164 288	2 691 676	32.6	11.4	2 817 654	0.7	2 691 676	125 978	5.0
TEXAS	2 634 620	126	409 502	9 955 270	32.3	11.7	10 462 712	1.3	9 955 270	507 442	5.0
UTAH	241 086	108	20 174	1 066 661	35.4	11.7	1 115 380	1.0	1 066 661	48 719	4.0
VERMONT	104 476	172	12 492	322 674	34.2	11.5	334 695	0.9	322 674	12 021	4.0
VIRGINIA	1 036 281	146	132 064	3 548 047	39.0	10.6	3 675 345	1.8	3 548 047	127 298	4.0
WASHINGTON	844 367	143	100 572	2 804 086	35.1	10.6	2 995 696	-1.6	2 804 086	191 610	6.0
WEST VIRGINIA	393 593	218	71 414	792 367	29.4	12.1	833 315	1.1	792 367	40 948	5.0
WISCONSIN	901 712	168	84 892	2 854 473	28.8	12.3	2 990 578	1.9	2 854 473	136 105	5.0
WYOMING	76 116	154	5 827	260 596	29.1	14.0	271 262	1.6	260 596	10 666	4.0

1. Per 1,000 resident population estimated as of April 1 of the year shown.   2. Persons 16 years and older.   3. Percent of civilian labor force.

	Private nonfarm employment and earnings, 2001										
	Employment		Manufacturing			Employment (1,000)					
				Average earnings of production workers							
STATE	Total (1,000)	Percent change, 2000–2001	Employment (1,000)	Hourly	Weekly	Construction	Transportation and public utilities	Wholesale trade	Retail trade	Finance, insurance, and real estate	Services
	149	150	151	152	153	154	155	156	157	158	159
UNITED STATES	110 990.0	0.0	17 695.0	14.83	603.58	6 685.0	7 065.0	6 776.0	23 522.0	7 712.0	40 970.0
ALABAMA	1 561.3	-1.2	339.8	13.30	543.97	104.6	95.9	94.8	345.0	92.2	480.7
ALASKA	211.6	1.0	13.7	13.27	558.67	14.8	28.0	8.3	49.9	12.7	73.0
ARIZONA	1 889.3	0.7	209.6	13.18	527.20	164.6	111.3	111.0	422.3	150.4	710.6
ARKANSAS	962.7	-0.5	240.5	12.39	491.88	53.2	72.4	50.2	216.5	46.1	279.9
CALIFORNIA	12 313.8	1.2	1 904.4	14.72	603.52	767.4	750.4	811.4	2 524.2	843.5	4 688.4
COLORADO	1 887.0	0.6	199.2	15.37	594.82	167.0	143.9	107.0	422.4	144.1	689.4
CONNECTICUT	1 438.3	-0.9	253.8	16.07	682.98	64.9	78.3	78.8	279.5	142.5	539.6
DELAWARE	338.4	-0.2	55.8	16.63	700.12	D	17.2	15.1	76.0	51.9	122.4
DISTRICT OF COLUMBIA	428.5	0.5	11.3	NA	NA	10.9	17.8	5.5	45.8	32.6	304.5
FLORIDA	6 169.3	1.5	468.9	12.78	534.00	403.0	365.9	370.6	1 411.3	457.8	2 685.5
GEORGIA	3 349.0	-0.1	549.8	13.05	528.53	202.8	265.9	249.7	716.1	207.4	1 149.6
HAWAII	415.0	0.5	17.9	14.19	527.87	D	42.1	20.7	115.5	32.7	186.1
IDAHO	459.0	1.8	75.5	15.28	580.64	37.6	28.0	31.7	109.3	24.2	150.7
ILLINOIS	5 160.8	-0.9	907.8	14.55	587.82	269.3	355.2	348.2	1 007.0	403.8	1 859.5
INDIANA	2 529.3	-2.3	642.4	16.20	660.96	146.6	148.0	140.6	555.5	140.2	749.5
IOWA	1 223.0	-1.0	251.6	14.92	619.18	63.3	71.6	81.9	269.3	88.3	394.9
KANSAS	1 108.0	0.7	205.6	15.30	608.94	64.4	89.4	74.4	242.9	65.9	358.1
KENTUCKY	1 506.4	-0.9	307.2	15.34	633.54	88.0	108.0	85.5	338.5	75.5	483.6
LOUISIANA	1 553.8	0.5	181.8	15.90	670.98	121.8	117.5	94.7	355.7	86.7	542.2
MAINE	507.6	0.7	81.2	15.17	617.42	29.7	24.7	26.9	124.4	33.6	187.0
MARYLAND	2 017.4	0.6	178.2	15.35	620.14	162.1	117.8	111.8	442.2	142.6	861.1
MASSACHUSETTS	2 906.3	0.3	423.5	15.31	626.18	136.7	144.7	167.6	572.2	232.6	1 227.5
MICHIGAN	3 899.9	-2.3	926.4	19.71	817.97	201.8	181.1	220.7	852.5	209.5	1 300.3
MINNESOTA	2 273.6	-0.2	423.4	15.36	611.33	121.9	133.9	153.7	479.7	166.2	788.8
MISSISSIPPI	895.0	-2.7	213.8	12.14	480.74	51.8	56.9	44.6	208.1	43.2	270.9
MISSOURI	2 304.0	-0.8	379.1	14.81	601.29	143.8	175.1	148.7	494.5	170.8	787.0
MONTANA	307.8	0.2	23.9	14.68	571.05	20.6	21.8	18.1	84.2	17.9	115.8
NEBRASKA	753.4	-0.1	117.3	13.39	539.62	42.8	57.8	52.5	160.4	62.2	259.2
NEVADA	927.1	2.4	46.3	14.11	599.68	89.6	57.8	39.1	181.9	49.5	452.9
NEW HAMPSHIRE	542.8	0.8	103.9	13.77	565.95	26.7	21.5	32.6	132.6	33.7	191.3
NEW JERSEY	3 423.7	0.5	450.1	15.88	655.84	161.0	269.8	279.1	648.9	271.5	1 341.7
NEW MEXICO	571.0	1.6	43.1	14.09	545.28	45.9	37.3	26.6	147.1	32.6	222.2
NEW YORK	7 160.1	-0.1	842.8	14.76	593.35	334.2	436.2	431.5	1 303.0	741.2	3 066.5
NORTH CAROLINA	3 277.1	-1.0	733.6	13.29	526.28	228.5	183.2	192.3	697.9	189.5	1 048.1
NORTH DAKOTA	256.1	0.6	25.4	12.69	499.99	15.2	19.1	20.9	60.6	17.1	94.1
OHIO	4 772.2	-1.4	1 027.1	17.13	714.32	237.1	250.2	287.0	1 043.9	312.5	1 601.7
OKLAHOMA	1 213.6	1.0	178.5	12.95	495.99	63.8	85.3	66.7	276.4	74.5	437.0
OREGON	1 327.0	-0.9	236.2	15.72	625.66	78.9	79.3	88.0	302.5	95.0	445.3
PENNSYLVANIA	4 971.4	0.1	892.5	14.85	613.31	248.4	303.3	269.0	1 003.0	328.6	1 907.6
RHODE ISLAND	414.4	0.5	70.0	12.20	490.44	18.3	17.1	18.7	88.9	32.5	168.6
SOUTH CAROLINA	1 515.1	-1.4	332.1	11.19	467.74	110.9	95.7	76.8	355.4	83.8	458.8
SOUTH DAKOTA	306.2	-0.4	46.2	11.45	476.32	18.4	17.2	21.1	72.5	27.8	101.9
TENNESSEE	2 309.3	-0.9	478.5	13.37	524.10	121.2	179.8	144.4	494.2	132.3	754.9
TEXAS	7 929.0	0.7	1 057.6	12.57	536.74	564.9	594.8	533.1	1 733.2	533.1	2 750.8
UTAH	892.0	0.2	127.0	13.88	544.10	70.8	60.5	50.9	199.9	59.9	315.2
VERMONT	248.7	-0.2	47.7	14.32	567.07	14.8	12.2	12.5	55.3	12.7	92.9
VIRGINIA	2 898.0	0.2	371.7	14.28	594.05	214.1	188.0	143.8	622.2	193.3	1 154.8
WASHINGTON	2 192.1	-1.6	338.4	17.59	705.36	154.5	146.3	144.4	490.4	141.0	773.7
WEST VIRGINIA	594.4	0.3	77.4	14.95	608.47	33.8	37.0	29.9	131.7	29.5	232.7
WISCONSIN	2 411.9	-0.6	587.7	15.25	620.68	122.6	133.6	137.5	502.9	150.1	774.7
WYOMING	183.9	3.0	11.2	16.70	641.28	17.8	14.1	8.0	47.2	8.3	57.8

STATE	Farms			Farm operators whose principal occupation is farming (percent)	Land in farms						Value of land and buildings	
		Percent with —					Acres					
	Number	Less than 50 acres	500 acres and over		Acreage (1,000)	Percent change, 1992–1997	Average size of farm	Total irrigated (1,000)	Total cropland (1,000)		Average per farm ($1,000)	Average per acre (dollars)
	160	161	162	163	164	165	166	167	168		169	170
UNITED STATES..............	1 911 859	29.5	18.4	50.3	931 795	-1.5	487	55 058	431 144		450	933
ALABAMA	41 384	33.8	9.2	37.6	8 704	3.0	210	77	4 198		298	1 442
ALASKA	548	35.4	16.4	55.8	881	-4.5	1 608	3	95		487	303
ARIZONA.......................	6 135	44.8	27.1	53.0	26 867	-23.3	4 379	1 014	1 277		1 689	388
ARKANSAS....................	45 142	24.1	16.4	49.4	14 365	1.7	318	3 717	10 062		360	1 151
CALIFORNIA...................	74 126	60.6	11.7	53.0	27 699	-4.4	374	8 713	10 804		941	2 605
COLORADO....................	28 268	28.4	34.2	54.5	32 634	-4.0	1 154	3 430	10 509		707	618
CONNECTICUT	3 687	54.7	2.8	49.5	359	0.0	97	7	181		571	5 949
DELAWARE	2 460	47.6	11.9	60.9	580	-1.6	236	73	487		610	2 660
DISTRICT OF COLUMBIA ...	X	X	X	X	X	X	X	X	X		X	X
FLORIDA........................	34 799	57.9	8.7	45.4	10 454	-2.9	300	1 862	3 640		663	2 241
GEORGIA.......................	40 334	31.4	12.6	43.4	10 671	6.4	265	749	5 371		393	1 505
HAWAII	5 473	89.0	2.6	55.8	1 439	-9.4	263	77	292		632	2 405
IDAHO...........................	22 314	39.0	22.6	54.0	11 830	-12.2	530	3 494	6 309		537	1 017
ILLINOIS........................	73 051	23.1	25.1	57.0	27 205	-0.2	372	350	23 921		773	2 126
INDIANA........................	57 916	31.4	15.1	46.6	15 111	-3.3	261	250	12 849		533	2 064
IOWA............................	90 792	18.3	22.8	62.0	31 167	-0.6	343	125	26 822		567	1 697
KANSAS........................	61 593	14.9	37.9	56.8	46 089	-1.2	748	2 707	30 021		431	577
KENTUCKY.....................	82 273	33.9	5.9	41.1	13 334	-2.4	162	58	8 549		230	1 450
LOUISIANA.....................	23 823	34.1	17.3	47.4	7 877	0.5	331	943	5 331		381	1 206
MAINE..........................	5 810	29.6	9.3	49.4	1 212	-3.7	209	22	540		251	1 190
MARYLAND	12 084	43.3	8.2	51.6	2 155	-3.1	178	69	1 613		564	3 176
MASSACHUSETTS	5 574	56.0	2.7	52.5	518	-1.5	93	25	224		455	5 207
MICHIGAN	46 027	31.9	10.7	47.9	9 873	-2.1	215	393	7 892		358	1 671
MINNESOTA	73 367	18.0	20.8	60.0	25 995	1.3	354	380	21 492		408	1 164
MISSISSIPPI...................	31 318	22.3	14.5	40.7	10 125	-0.6	323	1 076	5 947		337	1 052
MISSOURI......................	98 860	20.1	15.5	45.3	28 826	1.0	292	882	19 229		309	1 069
MONTANA......................	24 279	18.4	53.0	64.7	58 608	-1.7	2 414	1 994	17 629		699	294
NEBRASKA.....................	51 454	14.2	42.2	69.5	45 525	2.6	885	6 939	22 093		567	645
NEVADA	2 829	39.6	26.1	55.1	6 409	-30.8	2 266	765	847		876	388
NEW HAMPSHIRE	2 937	41.2	5.2	42.9	415	7.5	141	3	133		324	2 250
NEW JERSEY...................	9 101	66.5	3.8	43.1	833	-1.8	91	93	595		594	6 642
NEW MEXICO	14 094	37.0	35.5	51.1	45 787	-2.3	3 249	805	2 179		625	195
NEW YORK	31 757	24.3	10.7	58.0	7 254	-2.7	228	69	4 722		287	1 284
NORTH CAROLINA	49 406	39.6	8.2	49.3	9 122	2.1	185	156	5 608		376	2 081
NORTH DAKOTA	30 504	6.4	63.9	74.3	39 359	-0.2	1 290	180	27 025		513	401
OHIO............................	68 591	30.7	10.0	45.2	14 103	-1.0	206	34	11 341		415	2 039
OKLAHOMA....................	74 214	20.5	21.6	44.5	33 219	3.3	448	506	14 844		272	610
OREGON	34 030	56.3	12.9	46.0	17 449	-0.9	513	1 949	5 286		479	960
PENNSYLVANIA................	45 457	29.2	5.4	56.4	7 168	-0.3	158	36	5 032		372	2 390
RHODE ISLAND	735	59.6	2.0	50.3	55	10.5	75	3	26		442	5 885
SOUTH CAROLINA	20 189	34.4	10.6	39.4	4 593	2.7	228	86	2 463		325	1 482
SOUTH DAKOTA	31 284	11.5	52.2	72.6	44 355	-1.1	1 418	344	19 355		487	348
TENNESSEE	76 818	39.5	5.0	36.0	11 122	-0.4	145	46	7 069		261	1 808
TEXAS	194 301	27.6	21.4	42.9	131 308	0.3	676	5 485	37 662		398	593
UTAH	14 181	46.3	16.4	42.2	12 025	24.9	848	1 212	2 070		486	575
VERMONT	5 828	25.0	10.0	56.6	1 262	-1.3	217	3	617		323	1 520
VIRGINIA	41 095	32.0	9.0	44.8	8 228	-0.8	200	85	4 322		385	1 920
WASHINGTON	29 011	51.4	16.2	53.3	15 180	-3.5	523	1 705	7 914		635	1 192
WEST VIRGINIA................	17 772	21.1	7.5	40.2	3 456	5.8	194	3	1 337		213	1 090
WISCONSIN	65 602	19.5	9.2	59.5	14 900	-3.6	227	342	10 353		282	1 244
WYOMING......................	9 232	16.9	50.5	60.5	34 089	3.7	3 692	1 719	2 968		808	222

Table A. States — Agriculture, Land, and Water

STATE	Value of machinery and equipment Average per farm ($1,000)	Value of products sold Total (mil dol)	Value of products sold Average per farm (dollars)	Percent from — Crops	Percent from — Livestock and poultry products	Percent of farms with sales of — $10,000 or more	Percent of farms with sales of — $100,000 or more	Land, 1997 Owned by Federal Government (percent)	Land, 1997 Developed (percent)	Water consumption (mil gal per day) 1995
	171	172	173	174	175	176	177	178	179	180
UNITED STATES..................	58	196 865	102 970	49.8	50.2	49.6	18.1	20.7	5.1	340 751.3
ALABAMA	36	3 099	74 884	20.4	79.6	31.1	11.3	3.0	6.7	7 088.0
ALASKA	53	25	44 982	64.8	35.2	40.1	8.6	NA	NA	211.1
ARIZONA	71	1 903	310 254	64.2	35.8	48.0	22.0	41.7	2	6 815.9
ARKANSAS........................	56	5 480	121 388	39.9	60.1	45.4	22.2	9.1	4.1	8 767.3
CALIFORNIA......................	70	23 032	310 718	74.0	26.0	56.2	26.6	45.9	5.4	36 297.8
COLORADO........................	71	4 534	160 401	29.3	70.7	52.6	16.9	35.7	2.5	13 823.9
CONNECTICUT	41	422	114 361	62.6	37.4	39.8	12.6	0.5	27.4	1 275.1
DELAWARE	76	691	280 811	25.3	74.7	69.8	43.8	2.0	14.7	752.1
DISTRICT OF COLUMBIA ...	X	X	X	X	X	X	X	NA		10.2
FLORIDA...........................	41	6 005	172 550	80.2	19.8	42.4	14.9	10.1	13.8	7 215.0
GEORGIA...........................	44	4 993	123 789	38.5	61.5	39.5	17.8	5.6	10.5	5 754.0
HAWAII	39	497	90 798	80.8	19.2	41.9	8.2	9.3	4.3	1 012.4
IDAHO...............................	78	3 346	149 945	53.0	47.0	53.5	21.5	62.7	1.4	15 141.5
ILLINOIS	90	8 556	117 130	76.8	23.2	68.2	31.7	1.4	8.8	19 896.9
INDIANA............................	64	5 230	90 303	62.1	37.9	56.3	20.8	2.0	9.8	9 139.3
IOWA................................	81	11 948	131 596	51.8	48.2	74.0	34.6	0.5	4.7	3 034.6
KANSAS............................	74	9 207	149 483	35.0	65.0	63.0	21.8	1.0	3.7	5 235.4
KENTUCKY........................	33	3 064	37 247	51.5	48.5	44.0	6.8	4.6	6.7	4 420.2
LOUISIANA........................	59	2 031	85 265	69.5	30.5	40.2	17.6	4.2	5.2	9 847.8
MAINE	49	439	75 503	48.4	51.6	41.2	13.2	1.0	3.4	221.0
MARYLAND........................	60	1 312	108 580	35.0	65.0	50.2	21.5	2.1	15.7	1 452.2
MASSACHUSETTS	40	454	81 522	78.6	21.4	46.4	15.4	1.8	27.7	1 145.7
MICHIGAN	66	3 568	77 516	61.7	38.3	49.1	15.8	8.8	9.5	12 059.3
MINNESOTA.......................	85	8 290	112 997	50.7	49.3	64.4	28.1	6.2	4	3 391.5
MISSISSIPPI	52	3 127	99 859	41.3	58.7	33.4	14.4	5.8	4.8	3 088.0
MISSOURI	41	5 368	54 297	43.0	57.0	44.4	10.8	4.3	5.6	7 029.0
MONTANA	78	1 871	77 051	48.3	51.7	61.6	22.1	28.8	1.1	8 847.2
NEBRASKA........................	85	9 832	191 074	38.6	61.4	77.6	35.4	1.3	2.4	10 543.2
NEVADA............................	70	357	126 039	42.5	57.5	51.8	18.0	84.6	0.5	2 259.3
NEW HAMPSHIRE	38	149	50 891	49.3	50.7	33.0	9.4	12.8	9.9	445.5
NEW JERSEY.....................	48	697	76 627	85.0	15.0	39.0	12.8	2.8	34.1	2 137.5
NEW MEXICO	44	1 618	114 780	28.6	71.4	38.9	12.2	34.0	1.5	3 505.3
NEW YORK........................	60	2 835	89 256	35.3	64.7	54.0	21.6	0.7	10.2	10 277.6
NORTH CAROLINA..............	49	7 677	155 376	33.8	66.2	46.2	20.5	7.4	11.4	7 730.2
NORTH DAKOTA.................	112	2 869	94 064	76.5	23.5	75.1	28.4	3.9	2.2	1 122.4
OHIO.................................	58	4 684	68 293	60.4	39.6	52.3	15.7	1.4	13.7	10 523.3
OKLAHOMA.......................	37	4 146	55 870	21.9	78.1	40.0	8.5	2.6	4.3	1 781.3
OREGON............................	55	2 969	87 252	71.2	28.8	38.2	13.4	50.3	2	7 906.0
PENNSYLVANIA..................	53	3 998	87 942	32.1	67.9	54.1	21.1	2.5	13.7	9 684.9
RHODE ISLAND..................	39	48	65 578	81.8	18.2	46.7	13.2	0.4	24.7	136.2
SOUTH CAROLINA..............	45	1 588	78 665	49.8	50.2	31.0	11.3	5.2	10.5	6 202.9
SOUTH DAKOTA.................	91	3 570	114 114	46.3	53.7	76.9	30.2	6.3	1.9	460.0
TENNESSEE	33	2 178	28 358	52.5	47.5	27.7	5.1	4.6	8.8	10 076.2
TEXAS	40	13 767	70 852	31.2	68.8	33.4	8.7	1.7	5	24 332.9
UTAH	51	877	61 864	28.2	71.8	43.6	11.5	63.1	1.2	4 301.4
VERMONT..........................	49	476	81 734	12.5	87.5	50.9	22.9	6.4	5.2	565.3
VIRGINIA...........................	42	2 344	57 027	33.3	66.7	39.3	10.0	9.8	9.7	5 466.9
WASHINGTON	70	4 768	164 342	68.2	31.8	48.5	23.3	27.1	4.7	8 822.5
WEST VIRGINIA..................	24	447	25 176	14.5	85.5	20.7	3.6	7.8	5.6	4 618.3
WISCONSIN	67	5 580	85 056	29.4	70.6	61.4	24.0	5.1	6.7	7 251.7
WYOMING..........................	61	899	97 327	19.3	80.7	62.6	20.6	45.9	1	7 040.2

STATE	Manufactures, 2000										Construction, 1997			
	All employees			Production workers										
						Wages								
	Number (1,000)	Percent change, 1999–2000	Annual Payroll (mil dol)	Number (1,000)	Work hours (millions)	Total (mil dol)	Average per worker (dollars)	Value added by manufacture (mil dol)	Value of shipments (mil dol)	Total capital expenditures (mil dol)	Establishments	Value (mil dol)	Paid employees	Annual Payroll (mil dol)
	181	182	183	184	185	186	187	188	189	190	191	192	193	194
UNITED STATES	16 681.4	0.0	618 217	11 959	24 006	363 272	30 376	2 002 649	4 217 852	154 917	656 448	845 544	5 664 853	174 185
ALABAMA	336.6	-0.6	10 479	266	523	7 119	26 810	29 998	70 290	3 398	9 586	12 567	95 218	2 476
ALASKA	12.6	0.6	391	11	22	291	27 369	1 169	4 034	113	2 034	2 406	14 114	565
ARIZONA	200.8	3.4	7 730	124	241	3 384	27 329	29 259	47 244	2 466	11 058	18 866	131 871	3 621
ARKANSAS	235.3	2.5	6 531	191	380	4 666	24 372	21 329	47 747	1 681	5 457	5 143	42 033	983
CALIFORNIA	1 846.3	1.5	72 310	1 212	2 387	34 334	28 335	242 667	446 873	16 898	60 162	93 145	561 338	19 148
COLORADO	170.8	1.9	6 816	112	224	3 362	30 049	20 206	39 372	1 944	14 681	19 442	125 228	3 808
CONNECTICUT	238.0	0.0	10 675	145	295	5 012	34 539	27 536	46 604	1 862	9 057	9 729	63 935	2 247
DELAWARE	40.7	-3.9	1 612	31	60	1 051	34 175	6 021	17 115	486	2 294	3 052	20 421	633
DISTRICT OF COLUMBIA	2.9	-7.7	118	2	4	70	33 434	98	210	18	310	1 437	6 356	240
FLORIDA	426.1	0.5	14 145	286	568	7 244	25 335	41 919	80 966	2 917	36 608	50 174	324 844	8 803
GEORGIA	514.4	-1.7	16 480	402	825	11 044	27 451	61 169	134 697	4 257	17 896	28 171	163 981	4 688
HAWAII	14.6	-4.2	420	10	18	234	24 401	1 353	3 732	105	2 335	3 902	21 791	845
IDAHO	65.0	-1.3	2 806	48	94	1 556	32 503	14 229	22 329	1 488	5 360	5 365	40 535	1 131
ILLINOIS	867.6	-0.7	33 650	605	1 230	19 015	31 408	102 040	214 315	7 085	27 953	39 447	240 092	8 885
INDIANA	638.3	0.7	24 608	486	987	16 406	33 731	78 202	162 577	6 101	16 000	19 228	140 520	4 345
IOWA	248.3	2.5	8 518	188	380	5 511	29 383	31 002	66 302	1 832	7 941	7 941	62 146	1 734
KANSAS	196.3	-1.2	6 990	144	299	4 400	30 565	20 869	54 549	1 242	7 115	8 762	61 915	1 756
KENTUCKY	293.1	1.8	10 500	226	459	7 045	31 156	32 795	90 148	2 964	8 878	9 754	76 876	2 001
LOUISIANA	162.9	-0.5	6 299	121	252	4 204	34 838	28 258	95 345	3 482	7 812	11 331	107 773	3 033
MAINE	79.8	-3.1	2 926	60	118	1 847	30 554	8 680	16 805	1 003	4 249	2 812	25 157	662
MARYLAND	167.3	2.3	7 049	107	215	3 578	33 390	18 455	36 490	1 407	14 525	20 881	141 469	4 368
MASSACHUSETTS	389.2	-1.0	16 845	239	486	7 868	32 893	48 638	85 688	3 422	14 959	20 413	107 813	3 869
MICHIGAN	809.9	-0.6	36 758	616	1 268	25 361	41 201	96 411	228 923	8 147	25 399	30 400	187 135	6 281
MINNESOTA	390.2	1.1	14 927	262	515	8 091	30 830	43 007	86 803	2 976	12 993	18 125	103 200	3 604
MISSISSIPPI	214.8	-4.7	5 863	171	338	4 054	23 684	17 893	40 994	1 302	4 824	5 978	47 695	1 155
MISSOURI	362.5	-1.0	12 575	266	527	7 743	29 076	41 083	90 261	2 947	15 020	18 772	130 555	3 978
MONTANA	21.4	2.3	644	16	29	448	28 067	1 687	5 628	180	3 452	2 209	18 096	446
NEBRASKA	110.3	-0.1	3 448	87	182	2 393	27 505	12 377	30 969	774	5 198	5 389	40 363	1 148
NEVADA	39.9	2.5	1 370	28	56	785	28 241	4 529	7 953	280	4 436	11 697	70 168	2 313
NEW HAMPSHIRE	101.3	5.5	3 902	71	146	2 230	31 244	10 350	19 641	857	3 684	3 279	22 690	678
NEW JERSEY	390.6	-0.7	16 009	264	527	8 384	31 777	52 185	101 632	3 691	22 102	24 513	143 627	5 190
NEW MEXICO	36.6	1.3	1 169	27	57	761	28 266	10 176	15 185	1 242	4 673	4 746	39 671	1 027
NEW YORK	738.2	-2.0	27 157	511	1 014	14 960	29 281	85 467	155 355	5 355	36 806	43 891	275 501	9 670
NORTH CAROLINA	744.0	-1.8	22 955	578	1 154	14 790	25 596	92 463	178 017	5 298	23 990	26 506	198 367	5 178
NORTH DAKOTA	23.9	5.6	721	17	34	429	24 580	2 419	5 975	202	2 034	1 802	15 782	408
OHIO	985.8	0.6	38 663	734	1 493	25 435	34 656	117 972	258 645	8 751	26 047	33 175	224 302	7 068
OKLAHOMA	172.4	1.6	5 590	128	254	3 595	27 997	18 198	44 480	1 169	6 751	6 502	50 556	1 256
OREGON	205.5	-2.0	7 330	152	293	4 573	30 171	26 838	49 712	2 675	11 740	12 948	80 041	2 649
PENNSYLVANIA	794.8	-0.5	29 154	572	1 157	17 760	31 045	92 512	187 906	7 043	27 563	33 423	230 026	7 276
RHODE ISLAND	74.1	5.0	2 469	50	101	1 326	26 384	6 223	11 681	378	3 060	3 690	17 070	552
SOUTH CAROLINA	330.7	-1.4	11 071	256	520	7 233	28 209	35 324	78 033	3 387	10 430	10 800	86 200	2 114
SOUTH DAKOTA	41.9	-13.3	1 179	33	66	723	21 993	5 308	12 144	263	2 418	1 721	14 488	355
TENNESSEE	468.2	-1.9	15 324	360	706	9 976	27 732	47 651	104 201	3 647	11 417	17 064	119 458	3 360
TEXAS	979.0	2.2	36 991	673	1 368	19 897	29 556	134 088	344 998	15 270	35 315	59 457	426 765	12 398
UTAH	125.9	2.4	4 203	86	169	2 390	27 943	13 174	27 598	1 373	7 288	8 418	55 801	1 578
VERMONT	43.7	1.7	1 646	30	60	828	27 356	5 140	9 394	908	2 474	1 667	13 101	331
VIRGINIA	351.8	-2.5	12 014	263	529	7 370	28 023	53 191	96 067	2 733	19 537	22 797	179 909	4 837
WASHINGTON	322.2	-1.2	13 316	206	418	7 320	35 540	37 443	89 336	2 581	19 867	21 433	138 194	4 529
WEST VIRGINIA	69.5	-1.1	2 530	52	106	1 687	32 207	8 503	17 316	777	4 506	3 022	31 312	757
WISCONSIN	574.9	0.7	21 013	426	839	13 256	31 149	63 684	131 755	4 363	14 976	16 628	115 488	3 864
WYOMING	10.2	7.6	332	8	16	232	29 430	1 462	3 818	178	2 177	1 522	13 867	345

STATE	Wholesale Trade, 1997				Retail Trade[1], 1997							
						Number of Employees						
	Number of Establishments	Number of Employees	Sales (mil dol)	Annual Payroll (mil dol)	Number of Establishments	Total	Motor Vehicle and Parts Dealers	Food and Beverage Stores	Clothing and Clothing Accessory Stores	General Merchandise Stores	Sales (mil dol)	Annual Payroll (mil dol)
	195	196	197	198	199	200	201	202	203	204	205	206
UNITED STATES..................	453 470	5 796 557	4 059 657.8	214 915.4	1 118 446	13 991 004	1 718 963	2 893 074	1 280 153	2 507 540	2 460 963.0	237 201.0
ALABAMA	6 315	79 229	40 986.3	2 394.7	20 163	231 665	28 935	47 883	20 397	47 697	36 623.3	3 381.7
ALASKA	784	6 860	2 989.8	256.8	2 866	32 502	3 965	7 622	2 463	6 912	6 251.4	670.5
ARIZONA	6 689	80 155	45 899.1	2 748.9	16 283	232 050	34 688	43 818	17 411	38 525	43 960.9	4 223.9
ARKANSAS	3 619	41 385	27 515.4	1 136.6	12 600	132 335	16 255	25 232	9 307	31 801	21 643.7	1 904.4
CALIFORNIA....................	57 841	757 294	548 864.5	29 875.0	106 357	1 354 797	174 669	268 874	144 936	215 325	263 118.3	26 362.7
COLORADO.....................	7 383	88 364	60 310.4	3 282.0	18 299	225 647	28 164	41 242	19 259	37 873	40 536.0	4 163.3
CONNECTICUT	5 283	77 716	76 167.9	3 595.3	14 574	186 935	20 876	43 270	19 413	24 650	34 938.9	3 634.3
DELAWARE	906	13 509	12 585.5	619.5	3 736	47 116	6 082	9 605	4 082	8 412	8 237.0	798.7
DISTRICT OF COLUMBIA ...	348	5 008	3 918.6	223.0	2 075	19 608	482	5 572	3 469	1 452	2 788.8	351.5
FLORIDA.......................	31 214	296 139	187 079.9	9 678.2	66 643	841 814	107 767	196 921	80 667	143 248	151 191.2	14 169.5
GEORGIA	13 978	191 087	163 782.6	7 519.7	33 073	420 676	52 692	92 982	38 596	74 468	72 212.5	6 943.6
HAWAII	1 872	18 532	7 147.5	576.0	5 088	64 218	5 739	12 269	11 409	12 586	11 317.8	1 161.8
IDAHO..........................	1 980	22 828	10 127.8	628.0	5 848	63 732	9 894	10 998	3 936	11 112	11 649.6	1 079.7
ILLINOIS.......................	21 951	325 752	275 968.4	13 324.5	44 568	610 790	69 604	109 745	60 545	113 502	108 002.3	10 596.0
INDIANA.......................	8 896	112 705	66 350.1	3 737.8	24 954	337 867	40 300	59 909	23 949	73 621	57 241.7	5 273.8
IOWA...........................	5 399	63 596	35 453.7	1 820.1	14 695	175 694	22 099	37 582	12 451	30 028	26 723.8	2 633.4
KANSAS	5 085	59 954	42 209.9	1 946.8	12 271	140 412	17 846	28 684	10 423	27 776	22 571.9	2 191.1
KENTUCKY	5 051	69 309	37 242.9	2 071.2	17 369	212 189	26 010	43 623	14 324	44 452	33 332.7	3 128.1
LOUISIANA	6 390	76 350	46 972.3	2 375.2	17 863	224 412	28 561	47 341	18 327	46 951	35 807.9	3 307.9
MAINE..........................	1 726	19 932	7 305.6	616.2	7 074	72 897	8 930	16 636	5 547	11 281	12 737.1	1 164.2
MARYLAND	6 283	92 458	54 906.7	3 656.3	19 798	274 260	33 636	61 969	27 846	45 060	46 428.2	4 914.0
MASSACHUSETTS	9 993	146 827	112 792.4	6 484.8	26 209	335 736	34 301	86 377	36 560	45 293	58 578.0	5 894.8
MICHIGAN	13 936	189 057	158 757.3	7 629.6	39 564	529 441	64 429	96 770	44 447	116 058	93 706.1	8 922.3
MINNESOTA	9 348	131 787	99 444.5	5 024.0	20 883	282 282	31 889	54 634	20 926	50 297	48 077.7	4 525.7
MISSISSIPPI...................	3 173	36 520	18 445.2	1 012.1	12 791	138 372	16 921	30 128	10 476	32 314	20 774.5	1 935.3
MISSOURI......................	9 522	125 929	91 411.9	4 639.8	24 181	297 556	39 365	51 029	22 005	62 480	51 269.9	4 945.0
MONTANA	1 574	14 356	7 596.8	371.6	5 042	48 337	7 261	8 733	2 780	8 231	7 779.1	746.5
NEBRASKA	3 157	41 002	38 015.4	1 170.2	8 295	102 684	11 353	20 126	7 016	18 531	16 529.3	1 554.6
NEVADA	2 253	27 251	12 806.9	918.5	6 222	89 452	11 430	16 587	8 165	15 910	18 220.8	1 798.2
NEW HAMPSHIRE	2 033	22 631	11 371.1	875.0	6 645	84 170	10 384	18 316	7 444	14 470	15 890.1	1 428.2
NEW JERSEY....................	17 812	266 944	227 309.0	11 886.1	34 837	420 724	44 951	109 004	50 706	56 016	79 914.9	7 926.0
NEW MEXICO	2 182	21 344	7 397.6	601.1	7 421	86 300	11 470	14 352	6 777	15 779	14 984.5	1 455.5
NEW YORK......................	37 499	414 249	319 697.6	17 185.8	75 241	805 208	72 275	190 395	102 985	118 379	139 303.9	14 329.8
NORTH CAROLINA.............	12 284	157 774	98 080.1	5 574.1	35 563	416 287	54 750	83 706	38 088	74 486	72 356.8	6 697.4
NORTH DAKOTA	1 604	16 992	8 618.4	454.4	3 569	40 685	6 193	7 505	2 345	7 559	6 702.1	616.1
OHIO...........................	17 322	254 226	160 415.6	9 192.2	44 521	630 098	75 633	125 217	46 151	129 491	102 938.8	9 924.5
OKLAHOMA....................	5 191	59 641	32 132.3	1 756.1	14 352	161 613	23 418	28 420	11 438	35 788	27 065.6	2 406.9
OREGON	5 943	74 790	53 679.1	2 578.7	14 467	178 349	25 422	33 345	14 650	33 171	33 396.8	3 308.8
PENNSYLVANIA................	17 138	237 567	159 354.2	8 588.2	50 208	650 144	79 521	152 042	56 354	105 437	109 948.5	10 561.9
RHODE ISLAND	1 590	18 762	7 602.7	635.2	4 169	45 747	4 725	11 885	4 011	6 974	7 505.8	752.2
SOUTH CAROLINA	5 035	58 910	34 179.8	1 866.8	18 481	209 256	24 983	46 596	21 374	37 949	33 634.3	3 107.2
SOUTH DAKOTA	1 402	15 509	7 874.2	389.8	4 311	45 867	5 866	9 253	2 861	7 759	11 707.1	689.6
TENNESSEE	8 234	120 228	82 626.4	3 975.4	24 808	304 452	38 615	58 824	27 531	64 223	50 813.2	4 810.3
TEXAS	33 346	425 750	323 111.7	15 504.9	74 105	950 848	129 773	183 970	86 657	190 380	182 516.1	16 197.1
UTAH	3 277	44 312	21 271.9	1 420.4	7 656	114 474	14 590	20 592	9 189	21 022	19 964.6	1 856.9
VERMONT	941	10 987	4 731.4	330.6	4 093	36 306	4 453	9 342	2 727	3 420	5 898.6	603.3
VIRGINIA	7 868	106 365	61 046.7	3 784.4	29 032	379 039	47 195	73 141	36 212	65 241	62 569.9	6 202.6
WASHINGTON	10 039	118 810	75 397.8	4 376.0	22 841	283 653	37 408	55 974	24 915	46 693	52 472.9	5 385.9
WEST VIRGINIA	1 956	23 805	10 290.4	681.1	8 082	90 087	11 622	18 509	5 572	18 530	14 057.9	1 309.3
WISCONSIN	8 025	110 309	57 192.9	3 764.9	21 717	305 255	37 641	61 524	19 470	54 081	50 520.5	4 826.2
WYOMING	800	5 761	2 547.1	161.9	2 939	26 934	3 928	5 001	1 564	4 846	4 530.5	426.7

1. Establishments with payroll.

Transportation and Warehousing, Finance and Insurance, and Real Estate

STATE	Transportation and Warehousing, 1997				Finance and Insurance, 1997				Real Estate and Rental and Leasing, 1997			
	Number of Establishments	Number of Employees	Receipts (mil dol)	Annual Payroll (mil dol)	Number of Establishments	Number of Employees	Receipts (mil dol)	Annual Payroll (mil dol)	Number of Establishments	Number of Employees	Receipts (mil dol)	Annual Payroll (mil dol)
	207	208	209	210	211	212	213	214	215	216	217	218
UNITED STATES	178 025	2 920 777	318 245.0	82 346.2	395 203	5 835 214	2 197 808	264 551.4	288 273	1 702 420	240 917.6	41 590.7
ALABAMA	3 024	44 692	4 285.3	1 151.6	5 640	70 679	NA	2 323.1	3 664	20 629	2 130.3	396.7
ALASKA	940	13 562	3 346.9	576.6	666	6 728	NA	253.7	716	4 014	543.2	98.3
ARIZONA	2 257	45 233	4 086.2	1 107.2	6 568	84 970	NA	3 007.9	5 450	32 529	4 110.1	747.4
ARKANSAS	2 330	39 917	3 804.4	1 093.4	3 478	32 597	NA	1 000.8	2 269	9 761	1 001.6	163.2
CALIFORNIA	16 056	317 832	36 610.2	9 344.2	40 503	618 971	NA	29 660.2	37 243	243 168	37 937.4	6 563.7
COLORADO	2 411	38 399	3 626.9	1 017.5	7 400	86 239	NA	3 473.2	6 663	38 224	4 853.5	883.8
CONNECTICUT	1 568	28 540	3 266.1	859.0	5 550	117 684	NA	6 533.0	3 372	20 635	3 522.8	609.3
DELAWARE	585	7 258	594.1	179.6	1 619	44 780	NA	1 942.1	1 101	5 243	5 006.5	118.3
DISTRICT OF COLUMBIA	215	3 356	567.1	91.3	908	16 481	NA	1 318.7	934	7 725	1 354.2	275.4
FLORIDA	9 768	157 343	19 852.1	4 429.8	24 785	317 250	NA	11 928.3	20 388	118 086	15 360.4	2 652.2
GEORGIA	4 733	85 109	8 306.3	2 359.4	11 668	153 755	NA	6 005.3	7 794	47 669	6 912.9	1 308.8
HAWAII	686	16 684	1 249.3	427.7	1 573	21 757	NA	775.1	1 753	12 446	1 824.1	311.9
IDAHO	1 233	10 633	948.0	237.8	1 919	14 583	NA	454.9	1 236	4 870	450.3	73.9
ILLINOIS	8 559	153 788	16 521.6	4 377.2	20 195	334 241	NA	16 014.5	11 411	73 819	12 830.0	2 101.4
INDIANA	4 389	77 568	8 991.9	2 177.4	8 946	108 304	NA	3 727.5	5 427	28 948	3 269.1	572.6
IOWA	3 100	36 220	3 914.1	948.5	5 238	72 895	NA	2 509.3	2 518	12 619	1 457.5	249.0
KANSAS	2 332	32 051	3 220.1	870.2	4 973	53 304	NA	1 827.0	2 602	13 005	1 525.8	259.6
KENTUCKY	2 919	49 545	6 288.7	1 447.9	5 373	60 241	NA	1 860.0	3 227	16 284	1 961.6	314.3
LOUISIANA	3 715	64 767	7 889.9	1 875.5	6 968	66 707	NA	2 143.8	4 151	28 571	3 342.1	642.2
MAINE	1 232	9 199	934.6	223.5	1 657	22 213	NA	805.5	1 343	5 929	601.7	114.2
MARYLAND	3 136	46 415	4 023.3	1 259.6	7 064	103 894	NA	4 436.6	5 065	39 502	4 764.7	971.3
MASSACHUSETTS	3 283	53 297	4 704.3	1 391.8	8 875	212 188	NA	11 427.7	5 834	41 233	5 925.4	1 214.1
MICHIGAN	4 733	77 977	9 249.2	2 493.8	12 249	181 898	NA	6 598.9	8 302	50 941	6 492.7	1 126.2
MINNESOTA	3 810	53 811	5 662.8	1 375.1	7 969	124 827	NA	5 390.5	5 051	30 172	3 886.4	687.2
MISSISSIPPI	2 201	24 411	2 475.5	657.3	4 059	33 400	NA	979.8	2 125	8 354	794.2	132.1
MISSOURI	4 874	69 082	7 681.6	1 725.1	8 738	122 082	NA	4 474.4	5 500	31 301	3 991.1	698.1
MONTANA	967	8 758	948.9	196.2	1 553	12 581	NA	366.8	1 186	4 265	353.4	58.1
NEBRASKA	1 874	24 848	3 475.1	700.7	3 369	50 003	NA	1 576.2	1 587	8 240	891.1	160.8
NEVADA	830	18 368	1 410.5	419.0	2 799	27 162	NA	916.4	2 460	16 890	2 276.5	381.5
NEW HAMPSHIRE	733	13 714	933.3	332.7	1 646	23 143	NA	871.2	1 399	6 639	719.4	151.1
NEW JERSEY	6 632	131 171	14 404.7	4 053.0	10 567	208 318	NA	10 519.9	8 292	47 558	8 881.9	1 376.5
NEW MEXICO	1 009	11 841	1 392.3	293.6	2 453	22 936	NA	662.3	1 887	8 844	893.9	165.2
NEW YORK	10 485	178 698	17 635.2	4 848.9	24 691	611 857	NA	52 522.2	27 214	145 326	27 770.1	4 447.8
NORTH CAROLINA	5 077	77 841	6 625.9	2 123.9	10 831	142 234	NA	5 276.5	7 346	39 349	5 026.0	900.6
NORTH DAKOTA	913	8 297	862.5	191.5	1 364	11 790	NA	336.0	657	3 325	287.0	46.3
OHIO	6 709	117 984	11 722.3	3 531.0	16 208	251 657	NA	9 008.4	9 692	62 628	7 243.7	1 334.6
OKLAHOMA	2 112	30 145	4 590.4	868.8	5 587	54 064	NA	1 697.8	3 344	15 354	1 576.0	284.5
OREGON	2 610	38 544	3 771.3	1 163.5	5 172	63 386	NA	2 317.2	4 556	23 058	2 704.0	470.9
PENNSYLVANIA	6 379	126 839	11 540.6	3 400.0	16 601	287 143	NA	11 173.6	8 684	57 519	7 668.6	1 360.5
RHODE ISLAND	546	5 947	587.2	145.0	1 250	22 920	NA	812.9	922	4 649	573.4	105.4
SOUTH CAROLINA	2 126	35 301	3 303.1	913.0	5 596	57 283	NA	1 801.0	3 541	18 760	2 012.6	377.1
SOUTH DAKOTA	957	7 361	887.1	162.0	1 612	18 869	NA	508.3	719	2 951	245.7	45.1
TENNESSEE	3 945	73 973	7 083.4	2 244.3	8 345	102 124	NA	3 650.4	4 999	29 626	3 732.0	667.3
TEXAS	12 800	209 782	28 532.9	6 137.1	28 074	352 019	NA	13 833.6	20 753	128 915	15 957.4	3 119.2
UTAH	1 167	29 028	2 854.2	799.9	3 167	39 603	NA	1 228.8	2 169	12 318	1 342.6	236.0
VERMONT	512	4 856	390.5	111.8	897	9 228	NA	328.3	701	2 362	240.6	42.2
VIRGINIA	4 482	60 884	6 338.2	1 666.9	9 549	135 689	NA	5 064.4	6 717	43 976	5 749.2	1 028.4
WASHINGTON	3 984	61 576	7 289.5	1 933.2	8 332	91 844	NA	3 697.3	7 544	41 899	5 352.8	935.3
WEST VIRGINIA	1 439	14 526	1 979.3	419.9	2 115	21 144	NA	555.3	1 449	5 812	665.0	100.8
WISCONSIN	5 068	69 166	7 028.7	1 868.2	8 062	129 664	NA	4 785.4	4 598	23 924	2 637.5	464.1
WYOMING	580	4 640	557.5	123.9	782	5 885	NA	169.7	717	2 463	220.8	39.5

STATE	Number of Establishments	Information, 1997 — Number of Employees — Total	Publishing	Motion Picture and Sound Recording	Broadcast and telecommunications	Information and Data Processing Services	Receipts (mil dol)	Annual Payroll (mil dol)	Utilities, 1997 — Number of Establishments	Number of Employees	Receipts (mil dol)	Annual Payroll (mil dol)
	219	220	221	222	223	224	225	226	227	228	229	230
UNITED STATES	114 475	3 066 167	1 006 214	275 981	1 434 455	349 517	623 213.9	129 481.6	15 513	702 703	411 713.3	36 594.7
ALABAMA	1 430	35 476	8 863	1 302	22 528	2 783	6 477.5	1 320.1	455	14 286	6 607.8	798.7
ALASKA	353	5 209	1 247	352	3 439	171	1 038.6	203.1	85	1 670	598.4	102.6
ARIZONA	1 731	42 238	12 643	3 370	22 499	3 726	7 209.4	1 487.1	235	10 546	5 840.3	595.4
ARKANSAS	904	20 101	7 233	1 225	9 405	2 238	3 326.6	583.9	359	7 711	3 423.2	352.7
CALIFORNIA	16 302	450 511	154 837	98 151	163 482	34 041	108 719.1	22 868.5	894	52 662	27 017.6	3 090.5
COLORADO	2 653	76 024	21 109	3 881	43 139	7 895	12 743.0	3 306.3	317	9 771	5 205.7	467.7
CONNECTICUT	1 561	48 173	16 027	1 989	20 893	9 264	9 054.2	2 136.8	145	11 161	5 253.3	666.4
DELAWARE	275	8 701	1 571	316	5 093	1 721	1 652.6	310.0	27	D	D	D
DISTRICT OF COLUMBIA	632	23 787	9 456	1 396	9 880	3 055	6 351.0	1 363.0	33	D	D	D
FLORIDA	5 883	145 025	40 014	10 952	78 187	15 872	27 830.2	5 522.4	524	27 652	12 879.4	1 385.8
GEORGIA	3 163	100 656	24 347	4 781	61 056	10 472	18 939.2	4 176.5	498	21 420	10 729.9	1 053.0
HAWAII	458	8 996	2 066	1 496	5 100	334	1 464.2	318.7	43	D	D	D
IDAHO	526	9 017	3 229	697	4 540	551	1 313.6	257.5	169	3 216	1 261.2	153.9
ILLINOIS	4 994	129 204	50 296	10 037	58 436	10 435	26 496.6	5 488.0	390	33 717	15 364.5	1 989.6
INDIANA	2 032	43 961	16 597	3 273	19 353	4 738	8 130.9	1 406.6	418	18 511	9 070.3	867.6
IOWA	1 502	34 363	13 479	1 732	12 653	6 499	5 433.0	1 016.2	280	8 353	3 422.2	363.0
KANSAS	1 357	32 258	11 785	1 934	16 778	1 761	7 324.2	1 161.9	248	7 811	3 697.9	378.3
KENTUCKY	1 261	29 098	9 516	1 820	12 739	5 023	5 056.1	814.7	328	11 367	8 236.0	505.2
LOUISIANA	1 285	27 271	5 876	2 013	18 008	1 374	4 621.7	907.8	516	12 641	6 797.8	609.4
MAINE	647	9 693	3 503	438	4 753	999	1 303.0	297.4	105	3 766	1 687.8	170.7
MARYLAND	2 026	56 781	16 507	3 213	28 435	8 626	10 618.5	2 302.1	106	11 295	5 065.0	645.7
MASSACHUSETTS	3 282	113 698	57 901	4 921	36 815	14 061	20 548.9	5 395.7	222	15 931	12 081.6	942.2
MICHIGAN	3 273	90 178	26 353	6 184	34 788	22 853	18 878.4	3 362.4	385	25 464	15 044.2	1 486.1
MINNESOTA	2 430	58 855	23 652	4 308	24 185	6 710	9 660.3	2 111.5	240	13 205	4 441.1	675.6
MISSISSIPPI	880	14 259	3 257	683	9 693	626	2 480.8	466.6	617	8 307	3 085.6	340.4
MISSOURI	2 254	75 706	25 662	4 143	38 152	7 749	12 112.4	2 743.6	342	16 685	6 172.1	838.1
MONTANA	568	7 077	2 036	693	3 610	738	1 061.7	177.5	215	3 296	949.3	160.1
NEBRASKA	841	28 950	8 099	1 120	9 413	10 318	4 242.2	984.4	141	D	D	D
NEVADA	660	10 750	2 978	1 203	6 201	368	2 110.9	376.3	86	D	D	D
NEW HAMPSHIRE	669	11 602	6 004	644	4 217	737	1 839.2	483.7	104	3 222	1 484.7	179.5
NEW JERSEY	3 384	131 970	38 059	6 283	78 402	9 226	21 004.9	6 833.3	294	21 147	11 626.2	1 254.4
NEW MEXICO	767	11 265	3 772	1 341	5 696	456	1 905.1	320.2	206	5 868	2 168.7	251.1
NEW YORK	9 454	287 054	99 892	27 891	119 678	39 593	83 185.9	14 837.6	371	59 255	23 107.7	3 019.2
NORTH CAROLINA	2 584	60 047	17 572	4 116	34 127	4 232	11 337.2	2 126.3	390	23 765	9 018.2	1 218.8
NORTH DAKOTA	382	7 710	2 627	332	3 357	1 394	921.6	206.8	129	3 303	1 158.0	154.9
OHIO	3 518	102 414	36 336	8 488	45 595	11 995	18 139.8	3 746.8	533	31 560	16 893.4	1 533.3
OKLAHOMA	1 338	28 871	6 708	1 730	17 353	3 080	5 281.8	926.9	362	9 128	5 170.3	401.9
OREGON	1 631	31 382	13 357	2 618	13 793	1 614	5 839.9	1 181.0	226	7 402	4 568.6	424.6
PENNSYLVANIA	4 168	118 315	44 615	6 468	53 020	14 212	21 854.5	4 272.8	606	38 952	39 604.0	2 080.8
RHODE ISLAND	359	10 611	3 773	444	4 014	2 380	1 441.0	363.7	27	1 963	1 038.7	99.6
SOUTH CAROLINA	1 099	25 054	7 287	1 485	13 414	2 868	4 714.5	845.3	267	12 209	4 353.9	600.1
SOUTH DAKOTA	466	6 243	2 058	421	3 673	91	916.1	155.5	137	2 153	619.7	84.0
TENNESSEE	2 101	45 015	14 213	4 366	23 518	2 918	7 949.7	1 511.9	162	3 771	1 815.0	155.0
TEXAS	7 520	210 654	49 949	15 791	114 361	30 553	40 363.2	8 605.6	1 816	57 717	74 102.3	2 817.5
UTAH	971	24 253	8 758	2 204	10 024	3 267	3 567.7	807.9	152	5 580	3 882.5	293.8
VERMONT	483	6 667	2 829	362	2 751	725	1 724.1	188.7	53	1 838	831.7	93.7
VIRGINIA	2 945	90 346	23 602	4 740	47 411	14 593	20 400.4	4 347.3	291	17 251	10 386.6	916.7
WASHINGTON	2 546	61 830	23 439	4 563	29 996	3 832	14 571.3	3 102.5	339	6 245	3 217.9	291.2
WEST VIRGINIA	605	11 862	3 135	490	7 649	588	1 773.5	305.8	240	7 767	3 263.4	353.8
WISCONSIN	2 009	43 546	16 920	3 227	17 343	6 056	7 733.9	1 362.9	253	13 762	5 486.6	716.3
WYOMING	313	3 440	1 170	354	1 810	106	549.9	82.6	132	2 767	1 012.4	137.9

Table A. States — Professional, Scientific, and Technical Services, and Arts, Entertainment, and Recreation

STATE	Professional, Scientific, and Technical Services,[1] 1997								Arts, Entertainment, and Recreation,[1] 1997			
	Number of Establish-ments	Number of Employees					Receipts (mil dol)	Annual Payroll (mil dol)	Number of Establish-ments	Number of Employees	Receipts (mil dol)	Annual Payroll (mil dol)
		Total	Legal Services	Accounting and Related Services	Architectural, Engineering, and Related Services	Computer Systems Design and Related Services						
	231	232	233	234	235	236	237	238	239	240	241	242
UNITED STATES	615 305	5 212 745	1 012 092	966 533	1 038 317	764 659	579 542.1	225 376.1	79 637	1 207 943	85 129.4	26 115.0
ALABAMA	7 076	54 413	12 773	8 097	14 353	7 904	5 295.6	2 051.4	791	9 381	435.7	105.0
ALASKA	1 437	7 892	2 030	1 146	3 027	418	945.9	370.8	320	3 055	168.3	34.9
ARIZONA	10 163	75 789	14 064	15 992	17 543	9 195	6 669.4	2 724.7	1 071	24 416	2 033.3	475.1
ARKANSAS	4 125	23 094	5 608	5 165	4 303	3 010	1 825.8	719.6	594	5 343	228.7	56.8
CALIFORNIA	78 635	805 856	124 890	242 857	129 826	101 494	89 555.7	35 258.6	12 015	182 004	15 913.8	6 296.6
COLORADO	14 315	103 008	15 384	12 498	23 939	27 261	12 887.7	4 625.1	1 494	30 541	1 909.6	625.0
CONNECTICUT	9 393	71 058	14 748	10 537	10 930	9 377	9 115.8	3 700.1	1 046	27 236	2 526.8	589.2
DELAWARE	1 717	12 382	3 859	1 753	2 548	1 609	1 430.4	553.4	216	4 074	240.1	62.0
DISTRICT OF COLUMBIA	3 760	61 123	28 841	5 430	3 785	4 188	10 365.2	3 935.5	171	1 564	161.9	56.1
FLORIDA	42 403	276 263	67 822	54 881	52 415	31 272	27 231.1	10 803.5	4 763	103 980	7 871.5	1 972.9
GEORGIA	17 810	138 198	23 148	26 704	24 718	27 116	15 266.4	5 908.8	1 653	23 437	1 533.7	408.9
HAWAII	2 480	15 743	4 325	3 155	3 735	906	1 574.0	606.5	386	6 925	409.6	116.6
IDAHO	2 364	19 669	3 386	2 308	10 225	1 009	2 046.1	756.2	457	4 425	174.1	45.2
ILLINOIS	30 378	274 714	51 486	44 700	40 670	41 999	33 855.1	13 105.4	3 097	46 972	3 640.3	1 040.6
INDIANA	9 795	69 393	14 161	15 664	14 409	8 216	5 974.2	2 207.5	1 500	24 903	1 918.3	516.1
IOWA	4 670	31 115	7 332	6 347	4 220	2 876	2 435.6	887.9	875	14 169	919.8	220.3
KANSAS	5 345	39 534	6 737	8 086	10 169	4 736	3 559.3	1 396.0	652	7 618	374.5	91.0
KENTUCKY	6 189	41 991	10 036	8 445	8 708	4 604	3 820.3	1 260.1	906	10 580	550.2	126.3
LOUISIANA	9 077	63 642	18 467	13 162	18 537	3 040	5 754.6	2 159.0	1 016	22 828	1 958.1	412.9
MAINE	2 552	13 747	3 918	2 633	3 654	742	1 215.6	474.8	524	5 456	254.4	64.0
MARYLAND	14 115	146 814	17 537	17 492	36 646	36 640	15 940.2	6 483.8	1 460	19 398	1 412.4	494.8
MASSACHUSETTS	18 086	177 345	28 887	21 727	38 025	32 595	22 744.1	9 261.4	1 781	22 598	1 578.5	518.6
MICHIGAN	18 614	162 971	27 677	28 444	42 085	19 296	16 231.7	6 882.9	2 693	34 161	2 202.8	664.6
MINNESOTA	12 391	96 677	18 445	13 690	15 041	19 384	10 447.9	4 091.3	1 593	27 958	1 469.7	477.9
MISSISSIPPI	3 627	21 671	6 814	4 702	5 444	1 046	1 761.6	662.1	483	21 239	1 394.0	371.7
MISSOURI	10 601	93 792	18 383	16 493	18 076	15 307	9 953.3	3 643.6	1 493	29 484	1 803.9	684.2
MONTANA	2 082	10 735	2 700	2 075	2 710	763	769.4	297.7	639	5 638	306.5	62.2
NEBRASKA	3 076	25 720	4 336	4 767	4 318	3 546	2 273.4	838.0	517	5 957	258.6	58.1
NEVADA	4 171	28 963	6 396	4 064	8 395	1 590	2 974.4	1 171.1	811	23 960	1 667.5	465.8
NEW HAMPSHIRE	3 341	18 268	4 469	4 008	3 214	2 685	1 626.6	713.1	460	6 545	365.0	99.6
NEW JERSEY	25 849	220 238	39 180	36 932	31 200	50 602	25 943.8	10 441.0	2 393	27 187	1 981.2	602.2
NEW MEXICO	3 702	31 535	5 450	3 477	7 147	2 078	3 243.4	1 307.3	440	8 679	520.4	115.4
NEW YORK	45 619	416 892	109 483	78 021	47 439	41 878	57 475.0	21 773.1	7 311	77 057	7 029.0	2 284.6
NORTH CAROLINA	14 351	101 610	17 536	18 315	21 380	14 218	9 760.9	3 693.5	2 090	23 481	1 632.6	470.5
NORTH DAKOTA	1 077	7 076	1 609	1 349	1 340	1 322	418.0	175.7	248	3 154	164.3	32.6
OHIO	21 182	182 805	33 925	29 820	37 298	26 134	18 294.7	6 948.0	2 902	37 210	2 308.6	706.6
OKLAHOMA	7 009	40 633	10 986	7 642	8 958	4 167	3 543.0	1 323.7	746	8 904	531.4	110.3
OREGON	8 117	52 514	10 464	10 662	10 806	6 861	4 734.6	1 925.0	968	16 098	875.8	260.6
PENNSYLVANIA	23 184	235 025	46 483	33 381	58 166	35 029	26 240.3	10 448.3	2 883	40 892	2 439.3	810.6
RHODE ISLAND	2 349	14 866	3 522	3 414	3 149	1 633	1 418.1	541.5	307	3 877	234.8	58.1
SOUTH CAROLINA	6 576	47 679	11 256	8 301	16 571	3 517	6 820.9	1 850.5	1 325	18 499	1 107.1	251.9
SOUTH DAKOTA	1 282	6 228	1 673	1 419	1 050	878	450.4	161.7	432	4 647	299.2	60.2
TENNESSEE	8 812	72 225	12 572	11 830	17 174	6 827	6 911.8	2 686.6	1 755	18 263	1 228.7	394.3
TEXAS	42 492	351 422	70 228	53 143	92 449	50 071	42 044.1	15 906.7	3 894	65 218	3 743.8	1 143.4
UTAH	4 282	36 468	5 861	6 511	8 211	6 730	3 306.1	1 303.1	480	9 444	412.4	137.7
VERMONT	1 622	7 792	1 988	1 051	1 596	1 302	719.1	279.0	293	5 450	226.9	61.4
VIRGINIA	17 539	212 632	21 082	19 896	52 792	66 065	24 151.7	9 729.8	1 613	26 624	1 397.9	392.9
WASHINGTON	13 411	101 848	19 122	14 797	26 137	13 232	10 564.8	4 247.3	1 680	27 971	1 620.1	544.6
WEST VIRGINIA	2 517	15 714	4 814	3 353	3 532	799	1 166.9	395.2	408	4 996	273.3	56.6
WISCONSIN	9 281	70 689	14 887	14 876	14 616	7 321	6 398.9	2 542.3	1 730	22 339	1 327.5	384.3
WYOMING	1 264	5 274	1 312	1 321	1 638	171	388.8	146.9	262	2 108	93.3	23.3

1. Firms subject to federal tax.

STATE	Subject to Federal Tax						Tax Exempt					
	Number of Employees						Number of Employees					
	Number of Establishments	Total	Ambulatory Health Care Services	Hospitals	Receipts (mil dol)	Annual Payroll (mil dol)	Number of Establishments	Total	Ambulatory Health Care Services	Hospitals	Receipts (mil dol)	Annual Payroll (mil dol)
	243	244	245	246	247	248	249	250	251	252	253	254
UNITED STATES	531 069	6 231 768	3 744 279	511 584	418 602.2	182 256.3	114 784	7 329 811	669 335	4 421 454	466 451.8	195 949.4
ALABAMA	7 121	104 492	55 516	16 915	7 116.7	3 104.8	1 375	93 858	8 567	68 868	6 075.5	2 463.9
ALASKA	1 143	8 156	6 222	790	758.1	309.4	427	18 858	1 444	10 400	1 283.2	583.6
ARIZONA	9 155	97 091	58 340	7 344	6 687.9	2 893.3	1 366	89 141	9 554	52 682	6 153.3	2 370.6
ARKANSAS	4 571	59 960	28 478	8 079	3 655.1	1 609.7	1 205	67 065	5 348	41 630	3 642.0	1 429.1
CALIFORNIA	69 857	664 539	422 929	59 673	51 968.0	20 619.3	10 715	586 414	49 193	357 559	48 778.8	17 749.8
COLORADO	8 611	85 370	54 140	3 412	5 790.8	2 538.1	1 709	91 319	9 636	54 858	5 866.8	2 392.0
CONNECTICUT	7 515	100 363	60 395	D	6 849.7	3 199.3	1 828	113 366	12 823	60 723	7 058.3	3 296.7
DELAWARE	1 465	15 980	10 043	D	1 131.6	526.4	365	23 991	2 276	14 149	1 500.3	662.3
DISTRICT OF COLUMBIA	1 464	13 692	8 294	904	1 054.8	476.7	655	45 837	1 645	30 712	3 826.3	1 651.4
FLORIDA	35 568	447 117	254 419	81 958	32 559.1	13 610.7	4 170	294 240	28 422	178 820	19 415.1	7 800.2
GEORGIA	13 960	173 768	96 547	18 587	12 065.1	5 158.0	2 028	161 127	14 284	116 039	11 646.5	4 477.7
HAWAII	2 360	18 221	13 828	D	1 646.3	730.8	581	29 344	3 172	17 876	2 329.1	886.9
IDAHO	2 551	26 365	15 393	2 197	1 548.3	680.1	519	22 760	797	15 906	1 287.2	547.3
ILLINOIS	21 122	248 667	150 878	12 907	16 870.2	7 441.8	4 920	355 013	20 457	221 511	22 905.3	9 350.5
INDIANA	10 236	132 416	77 163	5 945	8 132.3	3 675.3	2 565	167 894	11 713	106 580	9 910.6	4 061.4
IOWA	4 876	56 374	32 156	D	3 183.2	1 540.6	2 319	117 658	6 652	64 543	5 582.4	2 425.5
KANSAS	4 793	66 613	38 032	D	4 116.1	1 771.8	1 621	81 767	3 963	46 923	4 082.2	1 817.1
KENTUCKY	6 805	94 720	48 595	11 593	5 936.2	2 620.3	1 579	100 156	8 609	64 953	6 026.7	2 386.4
LOUISIANA	8 580	129 773	69 375	24 000	7 967.6	3 341.5	1 506	110 849	2 121	80 152	6 477.3	2 625.8
MAINE	2 727	28 944	14 464	D	1 608.4	766.3	1 074	47 404	6 469	23 258	2 641.0	1 119.8
MARYLAND	10 841	116 241	76 315	2 859	8 060.7	3 538.0	2 181	144 008	8 363	87 288	9 405.0	3 816.7
MASSACHUSETTS	11 887	182 902	102 893	8 984	11 361.4	5 310.5	4 537	266 968	37 592	139 988	16 091.6	7 410.6
MICHIGAN	18 943	186 954	128 354	1 638	11 811.5	5 696.8	4 684	301 078	27 857	189 916	19 458.5	8 309.7
MINNESOTA	8 033	106 839	66 962	D	5 864.5	2 946.0	2 929	191 473	32 851	83 648	10 965.4	4 893.3
MISSISSIPPI	4 139	55 529	29 916	7 299	3 632.3	1 547.0	847	68 886	3 245	54 786	4 249.0	1 660.9
MISSOURI	10 213	131 485	69 052	10 901	7 885.5	3 596.7	2 580	184 143	11 577	119 145	10 535.6	4 410.5
MONTANA	2 034	15 673	9 118	D	928.6	412.6	691	29 526	3 450	16 885	1 440.4	619.1
NEBRASKA	3 057	34 763	19 225	D	2 027.7	970.3	914	55 235	1 641	35 363	3 074.8	1 263.6
NEVADA	3 226	39 476	23 312	8 604	3 406.5	1 358.9	361	17 185	931	11 538	1 261.6	506.9
NEW HAMPSHIRE	2 373	28 889	15 341	2 228	1 734.1	836.3	834	37 674	8 075	18 197	2 246.2	878.2
NEW JERSEY	18 905	172 723	120 922	1 122	13 702.4	5 900.2	2 742	227 434	21 103	148 173	14 828.8	6 842.7
NEW MEXICO	2 923	32 824	21 144	3 138	2 057.3	864.3	778	43 501	4 479	25 609	2 412.3	1 089.3
NEW YORK	36 054	358 075	259 094	10 262	26 008.3	10 970.9	9 880	768 835	105 062	407 706	48 759.5	23 372.8
NORTH CAROLINA	12 582	173 770	94 102	8 741	10 708.8	4 859.6	2 794	187 651	13 552	129 016	12 400.3	5 006.8
NORTH DAKOTA	1 013	13 181	8 237	D	904.1	386.4	539	33 578	909	16 585	1 463.7	668.9
OHIO	20 399	261 520	156 386	2 579	15 440.1	7 477.0	4 779	352 454	26 617	214 539	21 423.5	9 093.7
OKLAHOMA	6 991	91 803	47 776	8 847	5 061.4	2 244.0	1 463	76 949	4 052	51 711	4 283.6	1 758.5
OREGON	7 328	68 285	42 060	1 410	4 431.4	1 899.6	1 788	82 517	7 491	45 158	4 869.2	2 097.6
PENNSYLVANIA	24 888	262 603	174 984	6 961	17 633.5	7 994.9	6 624	453 579	37 043	260 036	27 620.1	11 860.5
RHODE ISLAND	2 074	25 368	13 270	D	1 459.3	647.4	606	38 409	4 861	20 710	2 443.0	1 132.3
SOUTH CAROLINA	6 261	78 888	40 632	13 530	5 318.5	2 361.3	1 271	75 881	3 537	53 077	4 729.9	1 922.6
SOUTH DAKOTA	1 314	14 080	8 732	167	881.6	414.3	623	33 920	1 156	19 717	1 646.8	753.3
TENNESSEE	10 113	155 667	84 719	22 103	10 753.0	4 509.3	2 180	129 028	11 485	86 739	8 459.9	3 429.5
TEXAS	37 974	557 007	324 347	89 469	35 620.9	14 725.4	5 546	334 563	24 434	223 849	21 137.9	8 357.4
UTAH	3 851	46 989	27 659	5 700	2 988.8	1 226.7	521	33 973	1 583	23 515	2 070.3	859.6
VERMONT	1 262	11 481	6 146	D	631.6	273.9	592	20 697	4 672	9 772	1 129.0	496.6
VIRGINIA	12 014	150 797	89 453	17 193	9 859.6	4 417.9	2 143	135 917	7 245	87 411	8 975.6	3 539.8
WASHINGTON	12 310	122 813	73 402	2 089	7 797.7	3 390.2	2 575	140 792	21 340	78 274	8 982.2	4 039.8
WEST VIRGINIA	3 266	40 085	21 188	5 172	2 575.0	1 056.9	973	55 653	6 667	33 425	3 250.1	1 350.2
WISCONSIN	9 315	114 562	69 466	587	6 917.4	3 447.3	2 932	175 152	18 639	93 326	9 654.7	4 089.4
WYOMING	1 006	7 875	4 865	555	493.6	210.3	350	15 091	681	8 210	695.9	320.6

STATE	Accommodation and Food Services, 1997					Other Services, 1997						
	Number of Establishments	Number of Employees Total	Number of Employees Food Services and Drinking Places	Receipts (mil dol)	Annual Payroll (mil dol)	Number of Establishments[1]	Total[1]	Number of Employees Repair and Maintenance[1]	Number of Employees Personal and Laundry Services[1]	Religious, Civic, and Similar Services[2]	Receipts (mil dol)[1]	Annual Payroll (mil dol)[1]
	255	256	257	258	259	260	261	262	263	264	265	266
UNITED STATES	545 060	9 451 056	7 754 462	350 389.1	97 003.9	420 950	2 493 574	1 276 389	1 217 185	762 604	163 033.3	48 452.6
ALABAMA	6 955	134 719	120 455	3 881.8	1 059.6	6 329	37 061	19 092	17 969	5 480	2 241.7	659.3
ALASKA	1 763	20 587	15 108	1 065.5	301.5	852	4 364	2 489	1 875	2 127	331.0	93.4
ARIZONA	9 089	184 323	143 326	6 633.0	1 823.2	6 494	43 669	24 677	18 992	9 381	2 794.0	829.6
ARKANSAS	4 663	73 397	63 326	2 179.7	589.9	3 553	18 809	9 759	9 050	3 308	1 113.9	310.5
CALIFORNIA	62 532	1 052 715	866 573	42 261.1	11 437.2	44 642	282 762	158 338	124 424	71 943	20 521.5	5 852.2
COLORADO	10 064	195 126	152 323	6 705.5	1 937.4	6 793	39 363	21 585	17 778	13 958	2 571.1	770.0
CONNECTICUT	6 903	96 556	85 802	3 746.6	1 062.8	6 121	34 089	15 534	18 555	11 215	2 370.2	727.8
DELAWARE	1 605	26 969	24 532	1 009.0	280.8	1 198	7 006	3 349	3 657	3 096	420.5	140.7
DISTRICT OF COLUMBIA	1 700	42 650	27 281	2 263.5	701.4	978	6 218	951	5 267	36 416	404.8	111.1
FLORIDA	28 999	608 834	462 266	24 165.3	6 239.5	26 121	146 360	72 673	73 687	47 246	9 123.6	2 665.7
GEORGIA	13 829	274 322	229 132	9 689.9	2 695.1	11 482	69 422	35 701	33 721	13 418	4 580.7	1 407.5
HAWAII	3 081	88 083	47 978	5 007.9	1 507.5	1 476	10 375	3 941	6 434	7 096	683.2	206.4
IDAHO	2 978	42 067	33 222	1 232.5	345.7	1 858	9 461	5 979	3 482	2 562	550.6	151.7
ILLINOIS	23 984	397 300	345 271	14 826.8	4 018.7	18 806	118 317	61 653	56 664	47 363	8 296.8	2 503.0
INDIANA	11 705	215 710	192 910	6 646.3	1 865.3	9 243	60 711	32 426	28 285	15 556	3 701.4	1 127.8
IOWA	6 830	99 148	85 641	2 762.8	769.5	5 234	24 383	12 589	11 794	8 008	1 486.5	411.3
KANSAS	5 677	91 173	81 206	2 685.7	757.1	4 604	24 081	12 846	11 235	7 737	1 548.4	452.9
KENTUCKY	6 546	129 442	113 557	4 056.1	1 140.6	5 383	31 164	15 971	15 193	5 534	1 870.3	551.4
LOUISIANA	7 151	147 016	118 902	5 259.9	1 408.9	5 998	39 764	23 348	16 416	6 418	2 595.2	767.2
MAINE	3 714	39 624	32 211	1 509.3	428.8	1 923	8 820	4 687	4 133	3 201	612.3	169.6
MARYLAND	9 049	161 273	142 027	5 972.5	1 644.7	7 871	55 241	26 167	29 074	18 724	3 561.3	1 129.2
MASSACHUSETTS	14 800	227 476	198 069	9 269.9	2 575.6	10 806	61 557	28 744	32 813	18 807	4 359.8	1 338.6
MICHIGAN	18 958	320 014	287 623	10 158.7	2 835.8	14 705	93 792	50 987	42 805	22 180	6 159.1	1 893.8
MINNESOTA	9 982	179 487	149 584	5 934.2	1 688.8	7 614	55 723	27 703	28 020	21 512	3 394.6	1 103.6
MISSISSIPPI	4 050	84 834	61 742	3 064.8	814.5	3 491	17 449	9 171	8 278	3 701	1 057.1	299.6
MISSOURI	11 150	203 849	169 646	6 780.8	1 933.3	9 427	52 060	26 216	25 844	14 434	3 203.3	963.1
MONTANA	3 278	38 533	30 120	1 198.9	325.4	1 612	6 986	4 518	2 468	2 278	449.1	117.0
NEBRASKA	4 070	61 048	53 127	1 726.6	488.2	3 288	16 940	9 770	7 170	6 500	1 039.2	297.1
NEVADA	3 632	241 672	51 613	15 322.7	4 665.3	2 175	16 185	8 124	8 061	3 033	1 061.7	328.0
NEW HAMPSHIRE	3 029	43 942	36 251	1 543.5	449.8	2 159	11 379	5 720	5 659	3 271	794.5	236.6
NEW JERSEY	16 974	251 872	180 343	13 407.4	3 608.2	15 077	78 644	35 774	42 870	18 414	5 434.8	1 665.1
NEW MEXICO	3 825	67 134	52 969	2 144.9	599.1	2 318	13 448	7 651	5 797	3 814	759.1	227.2
NEW YORK	38 045	473 327	399 485	21 671.1	6 101.1	30 104	146 365	59 977	86 388	76 173	10 014.6	2 858.7
NORTH CAROLINA	14 579	262 848	229 210	8 625.0	2 393.2	11 483	64 802	33 418	31 384	14 644	4 060.6	1 204.0
NORTH DAKOTA	1 827	26 330	21 495	684.9	189.0	1 281	6 294	3 074	3 220	3 410	364.3	101.3
OHIO	22 631	401 206	365 806	12 411.0	3 444.2	17 314	116 165	58 331	57 834	29 986	7 087.5	2 165.7
OKLAHOMA	6 534	105 934	95 639	3 151.3	856.8	4 572	26 308	13 465	12 843	5 709	1 599.4	458.5
OREGON	8 363	124 425	105 930	4 385.7	1 236.6	4 794	28 185	16 554	11 631	7 463	1 897.5	561.9
PENNSYLVANIA	24 465	365 158	317 321	12 227.2	3 364.1	19 754	107 502	51 109	56 393	36 273	7 085.7	2 049.0
RHODE ISLAND	2 617	34 162	31 264	1 220.9	340.6	1 949	8 602	4 142	4 460	3 325	546.2	167.8
SOUTH CAROLINA	7 775	150 621	126 533	4 835.8	1 313.8	5 672	32 166	17 395	14 771	7 364	1 901.0	563.8
SOUTH DAKOTA	2 258	30 131	23 609	888.0	234.4	1 356	5 828	3 296	2 532	2 670	344.7	90.7
TENNESSEE	9 604	197 881	166 252	6 790.2	1 880.3	7 767	49 204	22 362	26 842	11 871	2 996.7	918.7
TEXAS	34 160	638 333	552 066	22 698.8	6 175.4	29 162	197 113	107 946	89 167	38 747	12 477.7	3 785.0
UTAH	3 780	74 390	58 884	2 309.0	648.8	2 728	17 612	10 403	7 209	3 284	1 090.5	312.6
VERMONT	1 932	27 088	18 000	910.2	277.2	1 171	4 490	2 263	2 227	2 859	304.7	76.4
VIRGINIA	12 343	233 639	192 645	8 281.2	2 320.7	11 301	68 807	33 111	35 696	27 818	4 397.2	1 360.3
WASHINGTON	13 105	194 955	169 685	6 995.1	1 962.9	8 771	49 756	27 517	22 239	14 138	3 492.0	1 033.0
WEST VIRGINIA	3 290	51 529	43 149	1 633.2	462.3	2 512	14 805	7 551	7 254	3 308	867.4	255.9
WISCONSIN	13 252	190 411	163 318	5 641.0	1 548.5	8 648	49 101	23 608	25 493	14 402	2 991.3	886.4
WYOMING	1 751	24 950	17 192	808.9	219.0	980	4 866	2 734	2 132	1 429	422.8	94.8

1. Firms subject to federal tax.

Table A. States — Economic Census by SIC Code

STATE	Construction		Manufacturing		Wholesale Trade		Retail Trade		Finance, Insurance, and Real Estate		Service industries, subject to federal tax	
	Paid Employees 1997	Percent change, 1992–1997	Paid Employees 1997	Percent change, 1992–1997	Paid Employees 1997	Percent change, 1992–1997	Paid Employees 1997	Percent change, 1992–1997	Paid Employees 1997	Percent change, 1992–1997	Paid Employees 1997	Percent change, 1992–1997
	267	268	269	270	271	272	273	274	275	276	277	278
UNITED STATES	5 567 052	19.3	17 557 008	3.6	6 509 333	12.4	21 165 862	15.0	7 314 321	12.4	25 278 399	31.0
ALABAMA	94 525	20.8	364 887	0.0	90 151	12.6	342 835	27.1	86 105	18.7	319 408	28.6
ALASKA	13 911	7.3	13 402	-13.4	D	D	46 235	17.1	9 842	8.0	38 822	21.7
ARIZONA	129 315	49.1	199 959	18.9	93 586	36.0	363 999	26.3	110 539	25.7	488 055	63.1
ARKANSAS	D	D	239 244	7.5	48 274	10.0	189 643	24.7	D	D	174 209	30.5
CALIFORNIA	548 028	7.2	1 867 099	1.1	D	D	D	D	820 011	6.7	3 285 881	24.2
COLORADO	122 733	46.5	186 156	7.0	101 918	21.3	366 950	29.5	119 331	20.6	457 757	43.5
CONNECTICUT	D	D	262 959	-9.3	D	D	264 497	9.8	137 061	-8.9	348 287	27.8
DELAWARE	20 070	13.5	41 969	-3.7	15 805	-1.7	69 887	16.1	52 071	35.5	70 912	30.9
DISTRICT OF COLUMBIA	D	D	11 906	0.4	D	D	D	D	26 621	-6.5	130 661	8.3
FLORIDA	D	D	463 791	2.3	333 153	18.6	1 274 403	15.6	D	D	1 745 657	37.0
GEORGIA	160 111	29.2	552 706	6.1	214 242	19.4	630 376	23.8	190 856	15.4	755 082	50.5
HAWAII	20 985	-35.2	16 412	-17.8	20 809	-10.7	110 892	0.4	35 201	-5.4	120 784	2.4
IDAHO	40 060	80.3	71 274	14.9	27 231	9.4	93 090	25.9	18 741	6.3	88 434	39.2
ILLINOIS	D	D	915 860	4.6	357 606	7.7	931 248	10.1	401 132	6.5	1 150 231	27.5
INDIANA	D	D	637 736	7.6	129 290	11.7	516 853	16.9	D	D	455 626	28.5
IOWA	D	D	244 994	10.4	75 462	8.8	250 724	10.9	82 571	16.9	210 117	29.3
KANSAS	61 345	28.0	203 303	11.9	68 008	10.1	214 819	15.6	64 496	8.7	220 599	36.2
KENTUCKY	76 131	19.4	296 956	11.7	80 672	14.8	315 734	20.9	71 664	14.7	279 646	32.7
LOUISIANA	106 314	15.7	173 489	0.5	87 291	7.4	333 931	15.6	81 495	8.3	391 385	32.0
MAINE	24 902	16.1	88 327	-2.1	23 360	6.8	102 614	14.0	26 289	9.9	87 636	28.8
MARYLAND	139 269	3.8	174 740	-3.4	105 973	5.4	404 802	10.4	140 830	6.7	557 370	33.2
MASSACHUSETTS	D	D	441 770	-0.7	161 894	14.4	522 783	11.3	247 872	14.4	703 699	29.0
MICHIGAN	D	D	850 368	8.6	213 537	15.3	796 730	12.7	226 680	18.8	819 080	33.4
MINNESOTA	D	D	399 756	15.3	147 569	19.8	419 310	12.7	152 750	22.4	468 166	34.1
MISSISSIPPI	47 242	36.7	234 764	-0.1	43 026	7.7	194 483	28.8	39 365	6.6	179 905	66.2
MISSOURI	129 183	33.1	391 945	4.6	144 328	11.3	451 894	15.4	149 584	14.3	478 052	28.0
MONTANA	17 987	34.5	22 526	5.1	17 417	6.2	75 840	17.8	D	D	33 381	13.8
NEBRASKA	40 127	33.3	111 098	16.4	48 010	2.0	149 478	13.1	57 400	18.3	64 191	9.6
NEVADA	68 283	66.4	39 954	48.8	32 203	47.5	137 171	38.2	40 038	41.1	20 265	23.0
NEW HAMPSHIRE	22 371	30.4	102 193	14.4	26 379	28.9	117 518	21.0	28 719	-0.5	42 407	16.7
NEW JERSEY	140 900	7.2	432 049	-9.7	287 964	9.6	585 436	12.1	251 453	10.3	257 500	5.1
NEW MEXICO	38 990	26.2	42 254	9.4	26 259	16.2	135 164	20.3	30 150	16.8	49 430	15.1
NEW YORK	271 483	5.5	860 233	-10.0	450 559	3.9	1 181 372	8.5	771 470	4.8	900 533	3.4
NORTH CAROLINA	195 189	34.1	789 476	1.0	178 604	18.2	628 124	23.7	170 949	30.1	607 654	43.0
NORTH DAKOTA	15 693	33.0	23 218	26.8	20 321	10.1	59 130	14.3	14 314	16.6	46 358	42.3
OHIO	221 240	16.2	1 009 620	5.5	D	D	971 264	15.9	303 312	22.0	950 157	25.3
OKLAHOMA	49 861	14.1	168 926	10.2	D	D	251 502	19.0	67 101	13.2	259 359	32.1
OREGON	78 985	48.4	226 715	12.6	D	D	274 347	21.0	83 852	29.1	275 689	41.1
PENNSYLVANIA	226 488	6.1	857 041	-0.8	269 103	5.8	940 957	9.2	342 807	13.8	978 912	22.8
RHODE ISLAND	16 820	20.3	78 452	-7.2	20 487	4.9	75 777	12.6	26 944	-2.1	84 785	31.6
SOUTH CAROLINA	83 661	20.1	353 858	-0.3	67 606	19.3	328 850	24.6	73 899	18.6	325 235	39.6
SOUTH DAKOTA	14 229	10.9	48 306	38.2	19 329	18.1	66 008	14.8	D	D	48 237	40.0
TENNESSEE	118 094	31.6	495 760	2.2	135 432	17.3	457 976	24.4	123 091	21.6	487 855	34.6
TEXAS	420 823	25.4	985 731	11.0	D	D	1 464 183	19.0	452 103	13.6	1 968 608	37.6
UTAH	54 881	57.0	122 200	20.2	50 823	28.3	167 441	32.6	48 569	34.2	207 939	50.1
VERMONT	12 967	9.2	44 648	0.8	D	D	52 529	14.5	D	D	46 922	26.4
VIRGINIA	176 432	22.8	387 576	0.4	125 191	8.1	555 088	17.0	173 123	13.0	716 667	36.3
WASHINGTON	D	D	347 549	5.4	134 842	10.1	D	D	127 681	10.9	461 505	30.0
WEST VIRGINIA	30 892	23.7	76 772	1.5	27 352	11.8	129 956	16.0	D	D	106 642	27.1
WISCONSIN	114 490	18.3	575 318	12.2	128 690	9.4	453 927	12.1	152 563	14.9	416 814	31.6
WYOMING	13 703	25.2	9 763	8.8	D	D	D	D	D	D	33 771	27.6

STATE	Value of residential construction authorized by building permits, 2001				Exports of goods by state of origin, 2000 (mil dol)			Federal funds and grants, fiscal 2001[1] (mil dol)		Procurement contract awards	
	New Construction ($1,000)	Number of housing units	Percent single family	Manufactured housing units put in place 2001 (1,000)	Total	Manufactured	Non-manufactured	Total	Salaries and wages	Defense	Other
	279	280	281	282	283	284	285	286	287	288	289
UNITED STATES................	196 242 858	1 636 676	75.5	192.0	653 632	602 990	50 642	1 763 896	186 909	148 691	96 693
ALABAMA...........................	1 822 964	17 706	79.3	6.5	5 516	5 111	405	31 700	2 895	3 427	1 777
ALASKA..............................	450 421	2 939	60.8	D	948	294	655	6 403	1 414	834	296
ARIZONA............................	7 782 865	62 496	82.9	5.9	9 129	8 543	586	30 376	2 917	4 584	676
ARKANSAS.........................	1 019 170	10 407	71.7	4.3	2 012	1 937	76	16 632	1 178	385	307
CALIFORNIA........................	23 649 970	146 739	73.2	7.2	111 476	103 617	7 858	188 517	17 858	19 864	9 084
COLORADO.........................	6 593 250	55 007	66.2	3.9	9 869	9 648	221	24 345	3 868	2 277	2 191
CONNECTICUT	1 440 308	9 290	84.3	0.2	12 659	10 565	2 094	22 742	1 375	4 206	528
DELAWARE.........................	504 014	4 814	91.9	0.7	5 692	5 608	84	4 246	428	84	64
DISTRICT OF COLUMBIA ...	60 367	896	14.6	D	4 454	3 841	613	30 941	12 646	1 634	8 629
FLORIDA.............................	19 465 400	231 799	76.1	11.7	22 244	20 871	1 373	99 998	8 415	6 615	2 244
GEORGIA	9 461 766	167 035	71.1	9.7	10 628	10 01.1	617	47 320	6 931	5 990	1 392
HAWAII...............................	812 192	93 059	76.9	D	268	210	58	9 722	2 525	1 294	172
IDAHO................................	1 448 402	4 790	84.0	1.1	2 464	2 313	151	7 529	753	146	1 051
ILLINOIS.............................	7 141 367	11 820	82.4	3.6	30 360	27 698	2 662	65 036	6 252	1 716	2 419
INDIANA.............................	4 876 861	54 839	71.8	4.5	13 419	13 143	276	32 166	2 121	1 750	985
IOWA..................................	1 480 259	39 117	82.8	1.3	3 160	2 968	192	17 401	1 029	503	394
KANSAS.............................	1 612 466	13 085	67.3	1.6	4 803	3 866	937	16 699	1 866	960	423
KENTUCKY.........................	1 817 684	14 530	69.7	6.2	7 854	7 543	311	25 835	2 805	1 134	1 625
LOUISIANA.........................	1 597 626	17 685	84.7	5.9	3 786	2 594	1 192	27 816	2 310	1 474	1 152
MAINE................................	776 360	15 653	84.8	1.0	1 587	1 233	354	8 180	808	503	171
MARYLAND	3 228 064	6 492	91.4	0.8	4 635	4 300	335	48 164	8 921	4 909	5 827
MASSACHUSETTS	2 688 748	29 059	81.6	0.4	18 155	17 395	761	44 179	3 214	5 281	1 570
MICHIGAN..........................	6 085 397	17 034	76.5	8.8	47 971	47 297	674	51 632	3 150	2 263	1 116
MINNESOTA.......................	4 576 087	50 139	80.8	2.5	16 573	11 746	4 827	24 935	1 904	1 379	670
MISSISSIPPI.......................	894 241	34 151	78.8	4.7	1 696	1 565	131	20 212	1 725	1 355	508
MISSOURI	2 750 047	9 908	81.4	4.6	7 679	6 532	1 147	39 191	3 463	5 021	1 720
MONTANA	266 479	24 739	76.0	0.9	531	387	144	6 618	711	127	243
NEBRASKA.........................	834 966	2 604	68.7	0.7	3 097	2 545	552	10 771	1 053	190	257
NEVADA.............................	3 742 085	198 835	76.6	0.7	1 316	1 262	54	9 624	1 019	323	718
NEW HAMPSHIRE	950 396	8 198	79.9	0.7	2 282	2 131	150	6 314	516	479	176
NEW JERSEY......................	3 016 685	36 125	74.8	0.9	25 540	23 544	1 996	46 240	3 782	2 800	1 358
NEW MEXICO	1 186 378	6 624	89.2	3.2	581	530	51	16 587	1 747	761	4 361
NEW YORK	5 257 031	28 267	76.1	4.1	45 440	40 539	4 901	116 366	8 122	3 246	2 922
NORTH CAROLINA	9 226 070	9 989	89.6	15.2	14 009	13 483	526	44 557	5 502	1 556	1 598
NORTH DAKOTA	240 815	45 542	53.0	0.3	693	590	103	5 948	634	159	121
OHIO..................................	6 452 250	82 030	76.4	6.0	27 811	26 883	928	61 705	4 851	3 312	1 812
OKLAHOMA........................	1 477 528	2 687	55.2	4.0	3 139	2 982	156	22 672	3 050	1 568	645
OREGON	2 997 980	49 931	77.6	2.5	8 492	6 982	1 510	18 401	1 592	389	571
PENNSYLVANIA...................	4 804 172	12 352	79.2	4.5	22 530	21 616	914	79 310	5 763	4 214	2 574
RHODE ISLAND..................	306 040	21 322	76.6	D	1 062	936	126	6 989	747	283	109
SOUTH CAROLINA.............	3 469 848	41 403	84.1	7.3	7 450	7 328	122	24 675	2 526	1 064	2 091
SOUTH DAKOTA.................	405 260	2 407	90.8	0.7	455	436	19	5 807	600	117	184
TENNESSEE	3 540 178	30 133	82.2	7.7	10 331	9 157	1 174	36 758	2 935	1 028	4 783
TEXAS	15 761 345	4 455	76.9	20.5	60 909	57 722	3 187	112 530	12 104	9 460	6 188
UTAH.................................	2 312 017	32 370	81.0	0.6	2 603	2 414	189	11 377	1 765	1 275	809
VERMONT	397 422	150 342	74.4	0.3	1 782	1 737	45	3 734	319	307	84
VIRGINIA	5 715 146	18 887	79.4	3.9	10 153	8 836	1 317	71 257	12 345	18 597	8 338
WASHINGTON	4 689 002	2 747	85.5	2.5	32 385	28 949	3 436	36 903	4 945	2 404	3 077
WEST VIRGINIA..................	384 877	52 860	78.9	3.5	1 421	1 263	158	12 541	1 005	105	423
WISCONSIN	4 495 419	38 345	69.7	3.0	10 453	10 171	282	26 645	1 626	906	911
WYOMING	277 173	3 947	88.2	0.9	133	118	15	3 584	435	96	246

1. October 1, 2000–September 30, 2001.

STATE	Federal funds and grants, fiscal 2001[1] (mil dol) (cont'd)												
	Direct payments for individuals							Grants					
	Total	Social Security and government retirement	Medicare	Food stamps	Supplemental Security Income	Educational assistance	Housing assistance	Total[2]	Medicaid and other health-related	Nutrition and family welfare	Education	Housing and community development	Energy and environment
	290	291	292	293	294	295	296	297	298	299	300	301	302
UNITED STATES	997 104	560 020	235 930	15 501	34 367	12 389	31 740	334 496	167 778	51 864	30 676	5 768	5 670
ALABAMA	18 303	10 711	4 204	365	792	212	384	5 298	2 639	628	500	73	86
ALASKA	1 546	839	185	47	40	9	69	2 314	776	212	265	12	96
ARIZONA	17 009	10 355	3 602	280	460	220	240	5 190	2 366	836	653	79	75
ARKANSAS	11 314	6 106	2 289	223	395	119	225	3 448	1 676	424	311	33	39
CALIFORNIA	101 914	55 566	27 327	1 574	5 106	1 410	4 446	39 797	18 760	8 669	3 493	761	503
COLORADO	12 094	7 295	2 394	131	281	161	336	3 916	1 652	560	370	64	103
CONNECTICUT	12 269	6 985	3 418	136	279	79	656	4 364	2 299	690	317	67	101
DELAWARE	2 779	1 700	604	32	64	17	98	892	399	125	94	13	34
DISTRICT OF COLUMBIA	4 012	1 753	667	70	113	45	356	4 020	1 276	259	324	51	157
FLORIDA	69 058	40 261	19 581	771	2 074	779	1 209	13 666	6 421	2 191	1 442	232	156
GEORGIA	25 078	14 490	5 392	515	976	247	710	7 929	3 858	1 364	819	124	104
HAWAII	4 217	2 663	753	150	116	29	156	1 514	508	252	209	26	31
IDAHO	4 074	2 408	683	47	99	57	72	1 505	619	178	141	15	40
ILLINOIS	42 765	22 532	10 413	811	1 512	406	1 587	11 883	5 649	2 085	1 222	264	236
INDIANA	21 462	11 933	4 667	317	498	326	637	5 850	3 093	835	525	103	111
IOWA	12 396	6 090	2 206	107	205	135	222	3 079	1 536	476	264	53	71
KANSAS	10 728	5 428	2 139	92	193	101	153	2 721	1 203	408	318	42	50
KENTUCKY	15 172	9 025	3 291	350	934	185	358	5 100	2 737	722	475	91	52
LOUISIANA	16 708	8 514	4 585	483	862	205	420	6 173	3 405	847	582	140	75
MAINE	4 793	2 919	967	86	144	59	182	1 905	1 074	262	150	23	37
MARYLAND	20 920	11 729	4 371	191	497	140	773	7 586	3 975	827	493	95	120
MASSACHUSETTS	24 395	12 676	7 098	173	812	357	1 613	9 718	5 831	1 177	667	186	262
MICHIGAN	34 217	20 043	8 799	504	1 223	302	811	10 887	5 182	2 043	1 094	222	200
MINNESOTA	15 721	8 355	3 066	173	355	216	459	5 260	2 704	828	454	83	87
MISSISSIPPI	12 377	6 189	2 441	255	624	189	292	4 246	2 189	595	387	52	51
MISSOURI	22 122	12 014	5 076	395	584	279	498	6 865	3 804	882	535	123	116
MONTANA	3 871	1 920	604	54	71	48	99	1 665	529	181	191	17	51
NEBRASKA	7 216	3 343	1 120	63	109	70	129	2 054	953	287	193	29	42
NEVADA	6 121	3 939	1 167	65	137	29	129	1 442	512	222	167	25	60
NEW HAMPSHIRE	3 855	2 498	780	28	62	46	150	1 288	610	139	103	18	48
NEW JERSEY	29 822	16 911	8 070	292	756	210	1 363	8 478	4 390	1 238	727	184	144
NEW MEXICO	6 131	3 698	1 027	137	240	91	154	3 586	1 502	421	460	32	111
NEW YORK	69 180	37 260	19 012	1 365	3 286	1 177	3 795	32 897	19 939	5 446	2 259	647	368
NORTH CAROLINA	26 779	16 470	5 409	425	920	277	583	9 122	5 145	1 271	735	117	117
NORTH DAKOTA	3 750	1 245	483	27	37	46	66	1 284	371	133	133	11	34
OHIO	39 968	22 887	9 861	572	1 422	512	1 520	11 762	6 247	2 176	1 067	236	113
OKLAHOMA	13 290	7 498	2 934	236	369	158	292	4 119	1 897	651	478	62	75
OREGON	11 541	6 932	2 248	238	292	119	280	4 308	2 175	592	360	52	67
PENNSYLVANIA	51 912	28 577	14 572	639	1 592	535	1 515	14 847	8 101	2 171	1 136	347	292
RHODE ISLAND	4 241	2 338	1 028	59	136	64	324	1 607	845	221	121	26	32
SOUTH CAROLINA	14 265	8 906	2 707	269	531	175	352	4 730	2 645	577	433	64	89
SOUTH DAKOTA	3 652	1 546	523	39	62	151	81	1 254	425	150	163	13	35
TENNESSEE	20 985	12 135	4 943	454	823	222	598	7 027	4 179	854	548	79	50
TEXAS	63 102	33 618	14 160	1 270	1 992	862	1 448	21 675	9 950	3 102	2 848	419	401
UTAH	5 284	3 376	903	67	114	130	96	2 244	915	344	226	32	41
VERMONT	1 954	1 202	400	31	53	44	69	1 069	518	144	99	13	28
VIRGINIA	26 069	16 939	4 385	263	672	657	624	5 908	2 343	815	666	79	125
WASHINGTON	19 684	11 768	3 603	261	580	179	442	6 794	3 407	1 024	581	87	114
WEST VIRGINIA	8 038	4 856	1 802	178	394	80	179	2 971	1 404	354	243	40	80
WISCONSIN	17 359	10 317	3 668	153	452	204	454	5 843	2 933	893	533	105	123
WYOMING	1 594	966	299	19	29	21	38	1 213	218	82	103	5	35

1. October 1, 1998 to September 30, 1999.   2. Includes program categories not shown separately.

Table A. States — State Government Finances

	State government finances, fiscal 2000											
	General revenue (mil dol)								General expenditures (mil dol)			
		From federal government		From own sources							Direct general expenditures	
					Taxes		Taxes per capita[1] (dollars)					
STATE	Total	Total	Per capita[1] (dollars)	Total	Total	Sales and gross receipts	Total	Sales and gross receipts	Total	To local govern-ments	Total	Per capita[1] (dollars)
	303	304	305	306	307	308	309	310	311	312	313	314
UNITED STATES	X	X	X	X	X	X	X	X	X	X	X	X
ALABAMA	14 117	4 781	1 075	9 336	6 438	3 770	1 448	848	15 873	3 908	11 964	2 690
ALASKA	7 330	1 202	1 916	6 128	1 423	229	2 270	366	6 611	1 027	5 584	8 906
ARIZONA	14 724	4 441	865	10 283	8 101	4 904	1 579	956	16 574	6 391	10 183	1 985
ARKANSAS	9 118	2 735	1 023	6 383	4 871	2 622	1 822	981	9 589	2 725	6 864	2 568
CALIFORNIA	135 782	36 125	1 067	99 657	83 808	33 311	2 474	983	149 772	65 389	84 383	2 491
COLORADO	12 925	3 301	767	9 624	7 075	3 009	1 645	700	13 930	3 703	10 227	2 378
CONNECTICUT	16 232	3 395	997	12 837	10 171	5 419	2 986	1 591	16 723	3 363	13 361	3 923
DELAWARE	4 333	827	1 055	3 506	2 132	1 066	2 720	1 360	4 211	856	3 355	4 279
DISTRICT OF COLUMBIA	X	X	X	X	X	X	X	X	X	X	X	X
FLORIDA	41 665	10 271	643	31 394	24 817	20 636	1 553	1 291	45 208	7 180	31 134	1 948
GEORGIA	23 395	6 459	789	16 936	13 511	6 213	1 651	759	24 813	158	17 633	2 154
HAWAII	5 729	1 128	931	4 601	3 335	2 163	2 751	1 785	6 605	1 278	6 447	5 319
IDAHO	4 202	1 074	830	3 128	2 377	1 272	1 837	983	4 493	12 050	3 215	2 484
ILLINOIS	38 759	10 214	822	28 545	22 789	12 430	1 835	1 001	41 183	6 736	29 133	2 346
INDIANA	18 857	4 952	814	13 905	10 104	5 282	1 662	869	20 289	3 212	13 554	2 229
IOWA	9 892	2 731	933	7 161	5 185	2 971	1 772	1 015	11 453	2 853	8 241	2 817
KANSAS	8 561	2 401	893	6 160	4 848	2 541	1 804	945	9 124	3 280	6 271	2 333
KENTUCKY	14 648	4 341	1 074	10 307	7 695	4 050	1 904	1 002	15 682	3 722	12 402	3 068
LOUISIANA	14 872	4 785	1 071	10 087	6 512	4 209	1 457	942	16 554	912	12 832	2 871
MAINE	5 274	1 555	1 220	3 719	2 661	1 325	2 087	1 040	5 448	4 356	4 536	3 557
MARYLAND	17 956	4 164	786	13 792	10 354	4 741	1 955	895	19 370	6 241	15 014	2 835
MASSACHUSETTS	27 418	5 787	911	21 631	16 153	5 511	2 544	868	29 478	17 201	23 237	3 660
MICHIGAN	39 491	9 370	943	30 121	22 756	10 993	2 290	1 106	42 749	7 610	25 548	2 571
MINNESOTA	20 971	4 451	905	16 520	13 339	6 752	2 712	1 373	23 326	3 248	15 716	3 195
MISSISSIPPI	9 636	3 470	1 220	6 166	4 712	3 426	1 656	1 204	10 972	4 529	7 724	2 715
MISSOURI	16 486	5 256	939	11 230	8 572	4 607	1 532	823	17 293	761	12 764	2 281
MONTANA	3 496	1 206	1 337	2 290	1 411	467	1 564	518	3 718	1 586	2 958	3 279
NEBRASKA	5 706	1 568	917	4 138	2 981	1 635	1 742	956	5 772	2 250	4 187	2 447
NEVADA	5 473	1 057	529	4 416	3 717	3 516	1 860	1 760	6 047	1 053	3 797	1 900
NEW HAMPSHIRE	3 876	1 157	936	2 719	1 696	698	1 372	565	4 366	8 639	3 313	2 680
NEW JERSEY	32 237	7 743	920	24 494	18 148	8 990	2 157	1 068	34 783	2 447	26 144	3 107
NEW MEXICO	7 888	2 187	1 203	5 701	3 743	2 213	2 058	1 216	8 701	31 273	6 253	3 438
NEW YORK	84 765	32 521	1 714	52 244	41 736	14 277	2 199	752	96 925	9 301	65 652	3 460
NORTH CAROLINA	27 762	8 591	1 067	19 171	15 315	6 684	1 903	830	29 615	590	20 314	2 524
NORTH DAKOTA	2 798	1 002	1 561	1 796	1 172	742	1 826	1 156	2 856	12 932	2 266	3 529
OHIO	36 166	10 074	887	26 092	19 676	10 618	1 733	935	44 631	3 089	31 698	2 792
OKLAHOMA	10 783	3 047	883	7 736	5 840	3 010	1 692	872	10 630	3 920	7 540	2 185
OREGON	14 406	4 685	1 369	9 721	5 946	1 333	1 738	390	15 776	11 370	11 856	3 466
PENNSYLVANIA	41 700	10 584	862	31 116	22 467	12 734	1 829	1 037	47 682	678	36 312	2 957
RHODE ISLAND	4 106	1 163	1 110	2 943	2 035	1 094	1 942	1 044	4 648	3 806	3 970	3 789
SOUTH CAROLINA	13 317	4 379	1 091	8 938	6 381	3 616	1 591	901	16 237	448	12 431	3 098
SOUTH DAKOTA	2 282	793	1 050	1 489	927	851	1 228	1 127	2 403	4 364	1 955	2 589
TENNESSEE	15 928	6 121	1 076	9 807	7 740	6 704	1 360	1 178	16 853	16 231	12 489	2 195
TEXAS	55 312	17 151	823	38 161	27 424	26 026	1 315	1 248	60 425	1 978	44 194	2 119
UTAH	7 697	1 889	846	5 808	3 979	2 062	1 782	924	8 592	932	6 614	2 962
VERMONT	2 943	918	1 508	2 025	1 483	552	2 435	906	3 219	7 132	2 288	3 757
VIRGINIA	22 715	4 466	631	18 249	12 648	4 866	1 787	687	24 314	6 371	17 182	2 427
WASHINGTON	21 254	5 190	881	16 064	12 567	10 292	2 132	1 746	25 902	1 360	19 531	3 314
WEST VIRGINIA	7 032	2 406	1 331	4 626	3 343	1 974	1 849	1 092	7 552	8 171	6 192	3 425
WISCONSIN	21 183	4 734	883	16 449	12 575	5 774	2 344	1 076	23 027	838	14 856	2 770
WYOMING	2 357	855	1 731	1 502	964	566	1 951	1 145	2 553	1 461	1 714	3 470

1. Based on the resident population as of April 1 of the year shown.   2. Data subject to copyright.

STATE	General expenditures (mil dol) (cont'd) — By selected function (mil dol)					Debt outstanding		Government employment, 2000			Presidential election, 2000[2] (percent of vote cast)		
	Education	Health and hospitals	Highways	Public safety	Public welfare	Total (mil dol)	Per capita[1]	Federal civilian	Federal military	State and local	Demo-cratic	Repub-lican	All other
	315	316	317	318	319	320	321	322	323	324	325	326	327
UNITED STATES	X	X	X	X	X	X	X	2 891 000	2 075 000	17 775 000	48.4	47.9	3.7
ALABAMA	6 225	2 042	1 076	397	3 485	5 292	1 190	52 779	38 206	296 848	41.6	56.5	1.9
ALASKA	1 319	35	640	237	915	4 150	6 620	16 971	22 386	53 881	27.7	58.6	13.7
ARIZONA	5 552	160	1 584	921	3 169	3 101	604	48 007	33 326	281 984	44.7	51.0	4.3
ARKANSAS	3 976	768	746	348	1 987	2 746	1 027	22 194	18 692	166 535	45.9	51.3	2.9
CALIFORNIA	49 909	6 670	5 848	5 513	36 468	57 170	1 688	267 834	224 666	2 044 447	53.4	41.7	4.9
COLORADO	4 959	298	1 243	768	2 925	4 431	1 030	54 116	42 559	285 671	42.4	50.8	6.9
CONNECTICUT	3 862	2 252	786	696	3 235	18 456	5 419	23 251	16 617	199 571	55.9	38.4	5.6
DELAWARE	1 409	126	332	294	548	3 261	4 159	5 759	8 744	51 418	55.0	41.9	3.1
DISTRICT OF COLUMBIA	X	X	X	X	X	X	X	185 505	23 908	41 742	85.2	9.0	5.9
FLORIDA	14 361	1 221	3 811	2 589	9 162	18 181	1 138	123 705	103 646	861 093	48.8	48.8	2.3
GEORGIA	10 459	1 336	1 587	1 202	5 469	7 086	866	96 598	94 355	502 646	43.2	54.9	1.8
HAWAII	1 854	384	226	160	1 033	5 592	4 614	30 083	52 776	82 827	55.8	37.5	6.8
IDAHO	1 664	85	470	189	762	2 279	1 761	13 303	9 536	91 646	27.6	67.2	5.2
ILLINOIS	12 061	1 694	2 467	1 716	9 775	28 828	2 321	99 653	57 621	740 432	54.6	42.6	2.8
INDIANA	7 733	478	2 007	757	4 046	7 894	1 298	42 829	22 564	366 439	41.0	56.6	2.3
IOWA	4 181	1 310	1 424	360	2 196	2 362	807	20 670	14 248	218 507	48.5	48.2	3.2
KANSAS	3 713	203	1 355	371	1 316	1 912	711	27 118	29 043	221 599	37.2	58.0	4.7
KENTUCKY	5 180	902	1 526	597	4 081	7 753	1 918	38 676	49 068	256 208	41.4	56.5	2.1
LOUISIANA	5 400	2 752	1 101	775	3 097	7 770	1 739	37 096	40 885	330 353	44.9	52.6	2.6
MAINE	1 285	85	415	138	1 566	4 060	3 185	14 149	10 393	82 922	49.1	44.0	6.9
MARYLAND	5 587	721	1 297	1 222	3 922	11 365	2 146	155 406	50 090	312 726	56.5	40.3	3.3
MASSACHUSETTS	5 650	932	2 788	1 210	6 541	38 961	6 137	57 227	23 431	374 459	59.8	32.5	7.7
MICHIGAN	17 461	2 226	2 625	1 847	8 024	19 445	1 957	59 497	21 732	600 362	51.3	46.1	2.6
MINNESOTA	7 765	445	1 478	507	5 361	5 602	1 139	35 198	19 540	336 203	47.9	45.5	6.6
MISSISSIPPI	3 476	1 198	965	326	2 533	3 222	1 133	27 385	35 453	205 339	40.7	57.6	1.7
MISSOURI	5 950	1 185	1 491	688	4 006	9 820	1 755	62 023	38 782	366 017	47.1	50.4	2.5
MONTANA	1 148	88	434	142	548	2 557	2 835	13 347	8 263	64 201	33.4	58.4	8.1
NEBRASKA	1 999	317	554	234	1 393	1 680	982	16 230	14 864	131 109	33.3	62.2	4.5
NEVADA	2 138	181	583	279	822	2 990	1 497	15 360	11 616	102 035	46.0	49.5	4.5
NEW HAMPSHIRE	1 337	87	352	125	1 073	5 499	4 449	8 162	4 428	72 384	46.8	48.1	5.1
NEW JERSEY	9 609	2 321	1 541	1 567	5 730	28 938	3 439	67 506	28 856	507 816	56.1	40.3	3.6
NEW MEXICO	3 166	714	870	294	1 463	3 625	1 993	30 125	17 168	143 373	47.9	47.8	4.3
NEW YORK	20 705	6 396	3 266	2 915	30 718	78 616	4 143	145 414	57 260	1 280 089	60.2	35.2	4.6
NORTH CAROLINA	11 274	2 495	2 314	1 271	5 827	9 336	1 160	66 321	116 597	559 290	43.1	56.0	0.9
NORTH DAKOTA	879	85	357	43	547	1 520	2 367	9 551	12 395	49 847	33.1	60.7	6.3
OHIO	13 248	2 463	3 013	1 875	9 060	18 087	1 593	86 014	36 789	700 317	46.4	50.0	3.6
OKLAHOMA	4 535	298	1 225	543	912	5 663	1 641	47 351	41 247	233 069	38.4	60.3	1.3
OREGON	4 538	1 848	951	720	3 040	6 235	1 823	31 075	12 914	225 223	47.0	46.5	6.5
PENNSYLVANIA	12 734	3 364	3 514	2 256	13 226	18 595	1 514	112 535	43 074	625 879	50.6	46.4	3.0
RHODE ISLAND	1 175	243	220	176	1 163	5 681	5 421	10 749	9 201	56 619	61.0	31.9	7.1
SOUTH CAROLINA	5 011	1 546	1 178	654	3 458	7 057	1 759	30 997	58 594	293 797	40.9	56.8	2.3
SOUTH DAKOTA	690	88	370	81	477	2 305	3 053	11 237	8 384	51 293	37.6	60.3	2.1
TENNESSEE	5 513	733	1 501	567	5 211	3 292	579	53 094	25 447	340 957	47.3	51.1	1.6
TEXAS	22 914	5 895	4 861	3 111	11 866	19 228	922	184 179	167 855	1 368 080	38.0	59.3	2.8
UTAH	3 591	828	902	320	1 464	3 885	1 740	32 367	16 257	154 217	26.3	66.8	6.9
VERMONT	1 334	6	236	104	710	2 165	3 555	6 019	4 577	41 962	50.6	40.7	8.6
VIRGINIA	8 719	2 867	2 354	1 635	4 022	12 011	1 697	165 251	169 075	473 302	44.5	52.5	3.0
WASHINGTON	8 992	1 363	1 560	977	5 070	11 734	1 991	69 151	72 831	404 587	50.2	44.6	5.2
WEST VIRGINIA	2 296	177	838	209	1 762	3 730	2 063	22 297	10 156	120 524	45.6	51.9	2.4
WISCONSIN	7 469	1 188	1 523	943	3 551	11 454	2 135	32 235	18 821	353 081	47.8	47.6	4.5
WYOMING	789	52	365	93	287	1 250	2 529	7 401	6 064	50 074	28.3	69.2	2.5

1. Based on the resident population as of April 1 of the year shown.   2. Data subject to copyright.

TABLE B:

States and Counties

(For explanation of symbols, see page xii)

Page

Table B. States and Counties — Land Area and Population

STATE/ County code	MSA/ PMSA/ NECMA code[1]	County Type[2]	STATE County	Land area,[3] (sq km) 2000	Population and population characteristics, 2000			Race alone or in combination (percent)					Age (percent)					
					Total persons	Rank	Per square kilometer	White	Black	Am. Indian, Alaska Native	Asian and Pacific Islander	Percent Hispanic[4]	Under 5 years	5 to 17 years	18 to 24 years	25 to 34 years	35 to 44 years	45 to 54 years
				1	2	3	4	5	6	7	8	9	10	11	12	13	14	15
00 000	...	X	UNITED STATES.........	9 161 924	281 421 906	X	30.7	77.1	12.9	1.5	4.5	12.5	6.8	18.9	9.7	14.2	16.0	13.4
01 000	...	X	ALABAMA	131 426	4 447 100	X	33.8	72.0	26.3	1.0	1.0	1.7	6.7	18.6	9.9	13.6	15.4	13.5
01 001	5240	2	Autauga	1 544	43 671	1 022	28.3	81.5	17.3	0.9	0.8	1.4	6.9	21.7	8.0	13.1	17.6	12.9
01 003	5160	2	Baldwin	4 135	140 415	390	34.0	88.1	10.5	1.1	0.5	1.8	6.1	18.3	7.5	12.1	15.6	14.0
01 005	...	6	Barbour	2 292	29 038	1 424	12.7	51.7	46.7	0.8	0.6	1.6	6.2	19.3	9.3	14.0	15.6	13.5
01 007	...	6	Bibb	1 614	20 826	1 743	12.9	77.1	22.3	0.6	0.1	1.0	7.0	18.4	9.5	15.6	15.3	13.1
01 009	1000	2	Blount	1 672	51 024	909	30.5	96.0	1.3	1.1	0.3	5.3	6.9	18.5	8.4	14.0	15.2	13.5
01 011	...	6	Bullock	1 619	11 714	2 318	7.2	25.7	73.5	0.7	0.3	2.7	6.3	19.8	10.3	13.7	15.6	12.8
01 013	...	7	Butler	2 012	21 399	1 718	10.6	58.7	41.0	0.4	0.2	0.7	6.3	20.5	8.6	10.9	14.2	13.5
01 015	0450	3	Calhoun	1 576	112 249	478	71.2	79.7	18.8	0.8	0.9	1.6	6.2	17.4	10.4	12.9	15.0	14.2
01 017	...	5	Chambers	1 547	36 583	1 200	23.6	61.3	38.4	0.4	0.3	0.8	6.6	18.0	8.6	13.0	14.0	13.6
01 019	...	6	Cherokee	1 433	23 988	1 593	16.7	93.6	5.8	0.7	0.4	0.9	6.0	16.2	7.6	13.1	14.5	14.3
01 021	...	6	Chilton	1 797	39 593	1 124	22.0	87.3	10.8	0.7	0.3	2.9	6.9	18.8	9.1	13.8	15.2	13.3
01 023	...	9	Choctaw	2 366	15 922	2 025	6.7	55.5	44.4	0.3	0.1	0.7	6.9	19.1	7.9	12.0	14.2	13.9
01 025	...	7	Clarke	3 207	27 867	1 454	8.7	56.3	43.3	0.5	0.2	0.6	7.5	20.6	8.5	12.7	14.9	12.5
01 027	...	9	Clay	1 567	14 254	2 145	9.1	83.4	15.8	0.9	0.2	1.8	6.2	17.7	8.0	12.7	14.7	13.2
01 029	...	6	Cleburne	1 451	14 123	2 151	9.7	95.5	3.8	0.8	0.2	1.4	6.1	18.2	8.2	13.6	14.9	14.2
01 031	...	4	Coffee	1 759	43 615	1 026	24.8	78.5	18.9	1.7	1.5	2.7	6.2	18.5	8.9	13.0	15.1	14.0
01 033	2650	3	Colbert	1 540	54 984	859	35.7	82.3	16.9	0.9	0.4	1.1	6.1	17.7	8.1	12.7	15.1	13.9
01 035	...	7	Conecuh	2 204	14 089	2 155	6.4	56.0	43.7	0.6	0.3	0.7	6.2	19.7	8.3	11.7	14.1	14.0
01 037	...	8	Coosa	1 690	12 202	2 282	7.2	64.7	34.4	0.8	0.1	1.3	6.2	17.5	8.6	13.5	15.5	13.8
01 039	...	7	Covington	2 678	37 631	1 171	14.1	86.8	12.5	0.9	0.3	0.8	5.9	17.6	8.1	11.6	14.5	13.4
01 041	...	6	Crenshaw	1 579	13 665	2 187	8.7	74.4	25.1	0.8	0.2	0.6	5.9	18.8	7.9	11.9	14.5	13.8
01 043	...	6	Cullman	1 913	77 483	654	40.5	97.8	1.1	1.0	0.4	2.2	6.4	17.9	8.8	13.3	15.1	13.5
01 045	2180	3	Dale	1 453	49 129	928	33.8	76.1	21.0	1.5	1.9	3.3	7.5	19.1	9.6	15.0	15.3	12.6
01 047	...	4	Dallas	2 540	46 365	975	18.3	35.9	63.6	0.3	0.5	0.6	7.4	21.2	9.4	11.6	14.6	12.8
01 049	...	6	De Kalb	2 015	64 452	754	32.0	94.1	1.8	1.9	0.4	5.6	6.8	17.9	9.2	14.1	15.0	13.4
01 051	5240	2	Elmore	1 609	65 874	741	40.9	77.9	21.0	1.0	0.6	1.2	6.6	19.1	8.8	15.1	17.0	13.9
01 053	...	6	Escambia	2 454	38 440	1 151	15.7	65.4	31.0	3.7	0.4	1.0	6.2	17.9	9.7	13.5	15.4	13.5
01 055	2880	3	Etowah	1 385	103 459	514	74.7	83.7	14.9	0.8	0.6	1.7	6.4	17.4	8.7	13.0	14.3	14.1
01 057	...	6	Fayette	1 626	18 495	1 869	11.4	87.4	12.1	0.4	0.2	0.8	6.0	17.9	8.2	12.3	14.2	14.0
01 059	...	6	Franklin	1 646	31 223	1 370	19.0	90.5	4.4	0.7	0.3	7.4	6.4	18.1	9.2	13.7	14.3	13.0
01 061	...	6	Geneva	1 493	25 764	1 525	17.3	87.8	10.8	1.2	0.3	1.8	5.6	18.4	7.5	12.3	14.5	13.8
01 063	...	8	Greene	1 673	9 974	2 449	6.0	19.2	80.5	0.2	0.2	0.6	7.7	21.5	8.9	10.7	14.3	13.3
01 065	...	6	Hale	1 667	17 185	1 941	10.3	40.2	59.3	0.4	0.4	0.9	8.2	21.4	9.1	12.0	14.7	12.6
01 067	...	6	Henry	1 455	16 310	2 003	11.2	66.3	32.5	0.6	0.2	1.5	6.2	17.8	8.4	12.2	13.5	14.8
01 069	2180	3	Houston	1 503	88 787	587	59.1	73.8	24.9	0.8	0.9	1.3	6.8	19.1	8.2	13.2	15.6	13.8
01 071	...	6	Jackson	2 794	53 926	869	19.3	93.8	3.9	3.4	0.4	1.1	6.3	17.9	8.3	13.7	15.0	14.2
01 073	1000	2	Jefferson	2 882	662 047	77	229.7	58.7	39.7	0.5	1.2	1.6	6.5	18.3	9.6	14.0	15.7	13.8
01 075	...	9	Lamar	1 567	15 904	2 027	10.1	87.3	12.2	0.4	0.1	1.3	5.8	17.8	8.7	12.9	14.8	13.3
01 077	2650	3	Lauderdale	1 734	87 966	593	50.7	89.1	10.1	0.7	0.4	1.0	5.9	17.1	10.1	13.0	14.9	13.7
01 079	2030	3	Lawrence	1 796	34 803	1 258	19.4	80.7	13.6	8.2	0.2	1.1	6.3	19.4	8.4	14.3	15.9	13.5
01 081	0580	4	Lee	1 577	115 092	469	73.0	74.9	22.9	0.6	2.0	1.4	6.3	17.0	22.7	14.5	13.6	11.0
01 083	3440	2	Limestone	1 471	65 676	742	44.6	84.6	13.6	0.9	0.6	2.6	6.6	18.3	8.8	14.9	17.2	13.8
01 085	...	8	Lowndes	1 859	13 473	2 195	7.2	26.1	73.7	0.3	0.2	0.6	7.5	22.7	9.1	12.0	15.1	12.3
01 087	...	6	Macon	1 581	24 105	1 590	15.2	14.3	85.3	0.5	0.5	0.7	6.5	18.7	16.9	11.0	12.0	12.4
01 089	3440	2	Madison	2 085	276 700	205	132.7	73.6	23.4	1.7	2.4	1.9	6.8	18.8	9.4	13.8	17.7	13.4
01 091	...	7	Marengo	2 531	22 539	1 668	8.9	47.6	52.0	0.4	0.2	1.0	6.8	21.7	8.0	11.6	14.4	13.1
01 093	...	7	Marion	1 920	31 214	1 371	16.3	95.4	3.8	0.7	0.4	1.2	6.0	16.5	8.2	13.3	14.9	13.6
01 095	...	4	Marshall	1 469	82 231	630	56.0	94.4	1.7	1.1	0.5	5.7	6.7	18.2	8.5	13.7	15.3	13.0
01 097	5160	2	Mobile	3 194	399 843	148	125.2	63.9	33.7	1.1	1.7	1.2	7.3	20.1	10.0	13.3	15.3	13.1
01 099	...	7	Monroe	2 657	24 324	1 582	9.2	58.4	40.4	1.4	0.3	0.8	7.5	20.8	8.6	12.5	14.3	13.1
01 101	5240	2	Montgomery	2 045	223 510	253	109.3	49.5	49.0	0.5	1.4	1.2	6.9	18.9	11.7	14.5	15.3	12.9
01 103	2030	3	Morgan	1 508	111 064	487	73.6	86.2	11.5	1.4	0.7	3.3	6.6	18.8	8.4	13.6	16.4	14.1
01 105	...	7	Perry	1 863	11 861	2 301	6.4	31.1	68.8	0.2	0.4	0.9	7.6	22.2	11.1	10.8	12.7	11.1
01 107	...	6	Pickens	2 283	20 949	1 739	9.2	56.4	43.3	0.4	0.4	0.7	6.8	20.5	8.5	11.6	14.1	12.8
01 109	...	6	Pike	1 738	29 605	1 412	17.0	61.8	37.1	1.5	0.6	1.2	6.5	17.9	15.8	12.7	13.3	12.0
01 111	...	7	Randolph	1 505	22 380	1 674	14.9	77.0	22.4	0.5	0.3	1.2	6.6	18.5	8.7	12.4	14.3	13.2
01 113	1800	2	Russell	1 661	49 756	919	30.0	57.5	41.3	0.8	0.8	1.5	7.1	19.5	9.1	13.7	15.1	12.9
01 115	1000	2	St. Clair	1 641	64 742	751	39.5	90.8	8.3	0.9	0.3	1.1	6.6	18.8	7.9	14.3	16.4	14.1
01 117	1000	2	Shelby	2 058	143 293	380	69.6	90.5	7.5	0.6	1.2	2.0	7.5	18.8	8.2	15.8	17.9	15.0
01 119	...	7	Sumter	2 344	14 798	2 103	6.3	26.2	73.6	0.3	0.2	1.1	7.2	21.9	12.2	11.9	13.5	11.6
01 121	...	4	Talladega	1 915	80 321	639	41.9	67.6	31.8	0.5	0.4	1.0	6.3	18.6	9.0	13.6	15.3	14.0
01 123	...	6	Tallapoosa	1 859	41 475	1 068	22.3	73.9	25.6	0.5	0.3	0.6	6.2	18.0	7.6	12.3	14.5	14.1
01 125	8600	3	Tuscaloosa	3 430	164 875	326	48.1	68.8	29.6	0.6	1.2	1.3	6.4	17.0	16.5	13.9	14.1	13.0
01 127	...	6	Walker	2 057	70 713	702	34.4	93.0	6.3	0.7	0.3	0.9	6.4	17.1	8.6	13.1	14.9	14.2

1. MSA = Metropolitan Statistical Area. PMSA = Primary MSA. NECMA = New England County Metropolitan Area. See Appendix A for explanation of these concepts. See Appendix B for list of metropolitan areas identified by type, with component counties. 2. County typology code from the Economic Research Service of USDA. See Appendix A for definition. 3. Dry land or land partially or temporarily covered by water. 4. Hispanic persons may be of any race.

STATE County	Population, 2000 (cont'd) Age (percent) (cont'd)				Population — change and components of change, 1990–2001 Total persons		Percent change		Components of change, 2000–2001			Households, 2000			Percent	
	55 to 64 years	65 to 74 years	75 years and over	Percent female	2001	1990	1990–2000	2000–2001	Births	Deaths	Net migration	Number	Percent change, 1990–2000	Persons per house-hold	Female family house-holder[1]	One person
	16	17	18	19	20	21	22	23	24	25	26	27	28	29	30	31
UNITED STATES............	8.6	6.5	5.9	50.9	284 796 887	248 790 925	13.1	1.2	5 042 426	2 999 064	1 339 827	105 480 101	14.7	2.59	12.2	25.8
ALABAMA	9.3	7.1	5.9	51.7	4 464 356	4 040 389	10.1	0.4	80 131	56 534	-5 607	1 737 080	15.3	2.49	14.2	26.1
Autauga............................	9.6	6.1	4.1	51.4	44 876	34 222	27.6	2.8	747	482	926	16 003	35.3	2.71	13.1	19.9
Baldwin............................	10.9	8.8	6.7	51.0	145 799	98 280	42.9	3.8	2 167	1 612	4 737	55 336	49.4	2.50	10.2	23.3
Barbour............................	8.8	7.0	6.3	48.4	28 947	25 417	14.2	-0.3	491	366	-209	10 409	12.9	2.53	19.1	26.5
Bibb..................................	9.6	6.4	5.2	48.4	21 108	16 598	25.5	1.4	382	284	187	7 421	29.2	2.64	12.7	22.1
Blount..............................	10.6	7.4	5.5	50.1	52 239	39 248	30.0	2.4	805	591	999	19 265	31.6	2.62	7.9	20.8
Bullock............................	8.3	5.9	7.3	47.6	11 502	11 042	6.1	-1.8	214	173	-256	3 986	5.3	2.56	28.2	28.9
Butler..............................	9.6	8.2	8.2	53.2	21 147	21 892	-2.3	-1.2	414	357	-308	8 398	5.8	2.52	18.2	27.5
Calhoun............................	9.8	8.0	6.2	52.2	111 338	116 032	-3.3	-0.8	2 091	1 550	-1 433	45 307	5.4	2.42	13.4	26.9
Chambers..........................	9.9	8.2	8.0	52.8	36 457	36 876	-0.8	-0.3	617	595	-131	14 522	5.3	2.48	17.4	27.0
Cherokee..........................	12.4	9.4	6.5	50.8	24 147	19 543	22.7	0.7	340	336	161	9 719	30.2	2.43	9.2	23.9
Chilton............................	10.1	7.2	5.6	50.5	39 995	32 458	22.0	1.0	620	535	321	15 287	26.2	2.57	10.5	22.9
Choctaw............................	11.3	7.9	6.7	53.0	15 720	16 018	-0.6	-1.3	273	185	-292	6 363	10.7	2.48	16.0	26.5
Clarke..............................	10.0	7.3	6.2	52.7	27 776	27 240	2.3	-0.3	636	355	-369	10 578	11.3	2.60	15.7	25.5
Clay................................	11.0	8.6	8.0	51.2	14 286	13 252	7.6	0.2	237	215	18	5 765	15.2	2.43	10.5	26.7
Cleburne..........................	11.1	7.8	5.9	50.2	14 298	12 730	10.9	1.2	218	191	152	5 590	17.0	2.51	8.7	23.0
Coffee..............................	10.2	7.7	6.4	51.2	43 349	40 240	8.4	-0.6	716	532	-439	17 421	14.2	2.46	12.1	24.9
Colbert............................	11.0	8.3	7.1	52.1	55 106	51 666	6.4	0.2	889	774	38	22 461	11.8	2.42	12.1	26.1
Conecuh............................	10.3	8.5	7.2	52.7	13 839	14 054	0.2	-1.8	266	254	-265	5 792	10.1	2.42	16.2	30.1
Coosa..............................	10.4	8.3	6.2	48.9	12 143	11 063	10.3	-0.5	183	169	-70	4 682	16.6	2.52	13.5	24.3
Covington..........................	10.9	9.2	8.7	52.2	37 107	36 478	3.2	-1.4	576	643	-451	15 640	8.3	2.37	11.3	28.6
Crenshaw..........................	10.1	8.5	8.6	52.7	13 725	13 635	0.2	0.4	227	235	72	5 577	6.0	2.42	15.4	28.2
Cullman............................	10.4	8.0	6.6	50.7	77 900	67 613	14.6	0.5	1 192	1 022	280	30 706	19.9	2.49	8.7	24.0
Dale................................	9.2	6.8	5.1	50.4	48 985	49 633	-1.0	-0.3	963	529	-554	18 878	7.4	2.51	13.6	24.3
Dallas..............................	9.1	7.4	6.5	54.5	46 029	48 130	-3.7	-0.7	1 146	728	-757	17 841	4.7	2.57	25.4	27.8
De Kalb............................	9.9	7.5	6.3	51.1	65 506	54 651	17.9	1.6	1 092	859	835	25 113	19.8	2.53	9.9	23.8
Elmore..............................	8.8	5.9	4.8	49.4	67 461	49 210	33.9	2.4	1 160	750	1 172	22 737	37.5	2.66	12.0	20.0
Escambia	10.2	7.3	6.4	49.3	38 181	35 518	8.2	-0.7	624	560	-317	14 297	10.8	2.48	15.1	26.4
Etowah............................	10.0	8.5	7.5	52.1	103 014	99 840	3.6	-0.4	1 670	1 642	-432	41 615	7.6	2.44	13.1	26.3
Fayette............................	11.2	8.3	7.8	51.7	18 320	17 962	3.0	-0.9	263	315	-120	7 493	9.2	2.42	10.6	26.6
Franklin............................	10.4	8.2	6.6	50.9	30 914	27 814	12.3	-1.0	527	484	-349	12 259	13.0	2.51	10.4	24.5
Geneva............................	11.5	8.7	7.6	51.4	25 438	23 647	9.0	-1.3	417	378	-365	10 477	13.5	2.43	11.0	26.3
Greene............................	8.9	7.8	6.9	53.1	9 923	10 153	-1.8	-0.5	229	171	-106	3 931	11.9	2.52	27.1	30.8
Hale................................	8.5	6.9	6.6	52.8	17 262	15 498	10.9	0.4	353	276	6	6 415	18.9	2.63	22.0	26.4
Henry..............................	10.6	8.5	7.8	52.5	16 292	15 374	6.1	-0.1	266	238	-43	6 525	13.1	2.47	14.7	25.3
Houston............................	9.6	7.4	6.3	52.5	89 232	81 331	9.2	0.5	1 600	1 061	-50	35 834	16.2	2.45	14.1	26.4
Jackson............................	11.2	7.8	5.6	51.3	54 147	47 796	12.8	0.4	814	677	108	21 615	20.0	2.47	10.5	24.3
Jefferson..........................	8.5	7.1	6.6	52.9	659 743	651 520	1.6	-0.3	12 518	9 390	-5 258	263 265	4.7	2.45	17.2	28.7
Lamar..............................	10.8	8.6	7.3	51.7	15 579	15 715	1.2	-2.0	235	219	-346	6 468	7.7	2.43	10.9	25.4
Lauderdale........................	10.2	8.1	6.9	52.2	87 422	79 661	10.4	-0.6	1 346	1 101	-767	36 088	16.8	2.39	10.8	26.4
Lawrence..........................	10.2	6.9	5.2	51.0	34 928	31 513	10.4	0.4	538	441	44	13 538	18.7	2.55	11.2	22.6
Lee................................	6.8	4.6	3.5	50.8	116 572	87 146	32.1	1.3	1 800	910	629	45 702	38.1	2.42	11.8	27.8
Limestone........................	9.4	6.4	4.7	49.2	66 980	54 135	21.3	2.0	1 081	700	926	24 688	25.4	2.55	10.4	23.4
Lowndes..........................	9.1	6.8	5.4	53.2	13 418	12 658	6.4	-0.4	288	162	-178	4 909	21.0	2.73	25.7	24.6
Macon..............................	8.6	6.8	7.2	54.1	24 006	24 928	-3.3	-0.4	450	345	-199	8 950	5.5	2.44	25.8	33.0
Madison............................	9.2	6.4	4.4	51.2	281 931	238 912	15.8	1.9	4 857	2 663	3 091	109 955	20.6	2.45	11.8	27.2
Marengo............................	9.8	7.8	6.7	53.1	22 367	23 084	-2.4	-0.8	438	323	-284	8 767	7.5	2.55	19.4	26.5
Marion..............................	11.6	8.4	7.4	50.5	30 621	29 830	4.6	-1.9	462	489	-570	12 697	10.2	2.39	9.5	26.5
Marshall............................	10.4	8.0	6.2	51.3	82 329	70 832	16.1	0.1	1 529	1 143	-258	32 547	17.2	2.50	10.7	24.6
Mobile..............................	8.7	6.5	5.5	52.2	399 773	378 643	5.6	0.0	8 257	4 899	-3 331	150 199	9.7	2.61	17.7	24.8
Monroe............................	9.4	7.2	6.6	52.4	24 177	23 968	1.5	-0.6	506	339	-311	9 383	11.5	2.57	16.1	25.7
Montgomery	8.0	6.2	5.6	52.4	221 973	209 085	6.9	-0.7	4 727	2 590	-3 666	86 068	11.5	2.46	18.6	29.5
Morgan............................	9.7	7.0	5.4	51.0	111 429	100 043	11.0	0.3	1 868	1 273	-184	43 602	15.4	2.51	11.2	24.8
Perry................................	9.5	7.8	7.1	54.4	11 676	12 759	-7.0	-1.6	269	200	-256	4 333	3.1	2.63	25.1	27.9
Pickens............................	9.9	8.6	7.1	53.2	20 901	20 699	1.2	-0.2	389	321	-108	8 086	6.8	2.56	18.2	26.4
Pike................................	9.2	6.4	6.2	52.8	29 273	27 595	7.3	-1.1	542	398	-479	11 933	15.7	2.38	16.8	29.8
Randolph..........................	10.3	8.5	7.4	51.7	22 529	19 881	12.6	0.7	370	341	128	8 642	14.4	2.52	12.2	25.6
Russell............................	9.5	7.5	5.6	52.4	49 665	46 860	6.2	-0.2	961	687	-349	19 741	12.8	2.49	18.9	28.0
St. Clair............................	10.2	7.0	4.7	49.6	66 402	49 811	30.0	2.6	1 033	741	1 353	24 143	36.7	2.60	10.0	20.8
Shelby..............................	8.4	5.1	3.4	51.0	149 724	99 363	44.2	4.5	2 686	1 095	4 743	54 631	51.8	2.59	8.1	21.7
Sumter............................	7.9	6.7	7.2	54.1	14 492	16 174	-8.5	-2.1	296	227	-380	5 708	2.9	2.55	23.5	31.2
Talladega..........................	9.8	7.4	5.9	51.1	80 436	74 109	8.4	0.1	1 494	1 051	-296	30 674	16.0	2.50	15.2	25.9
Tallapoosa........................	10.9	8.7	7.9	52.5	41 090	38 826	6.8	-0.9	734	644	-471	16 656	13.3	2.44	14.3	26.5
Tuscaloosa........................	7.8	6.3	5.0	51.9	165 062	150 500	9.6	0.1	2 904	1 791	-877	64 517	16.6	2.42	14.0	28.4
Walker..............................	10.9	8.2	6.6	51.8	70 698	67 670	4.5	0.0	1 124	1 174	70	28 364	11.0	2.46	11.9	25.3

1. No spouse present.

STATE County	Births, average 1997–1999		Deaths, average 1997–1999				Physicians,[4] 2000		Hospitals,[4] 1998			Medicare enrollees 2000	Serious crimes known to police, 2000[6]	
			Number		Rate					Beds			Total	
	Total	Rate[1]	Total	Infant[2]	Total[1]	Infant[3]	Number	Rate[5]	Number	Number	Rate[5]		Number	Rate[7]
	32	33	34	35	36	37	38	39	40	41	42	43	44	45
UNITED STATES..........	3 880 783	14.4	2 347 633	28 118	8.7	7.2	587 994	209	5 214	895 681	331	38 748 879	11 605 751	4 124
ALABAMA	60 927	14.0	44 005	607	10.1	10.0	7 605	171	110	17 785	409	685 443	202 159	4 546
Autauga............................	615	14.6	354	NA	8.4	NA	47	108	0	0	0	5 394	1 731	3 964
Baldwin............................	1 727	13.0	1 272	21	9.6	12.0	186	132	3	235	177	23 329	NA	NA
Barbour............................	357	13.3	285	NA	10.6	NA	20	69	1	52	193	4 347	NA	NA
Bibb..................................	284	14.9	199	NA	10.5	NA	15	72	1	138	729	3 129	NA	NA
Blount..............................	647	14.0	454	NA	9.8	NA	18	35	1	56	121	5 730	1 189	2 384
Bullock............................	176	15.6	137	NA	12.2	NA	7	60	1	62	548	1 973	NA	NA
Butler..............................	294	13.6	272	NA	12.6	NA	12	56	2	91	419	4 036	NA	NA
Calhoun............................	1 556	13.3	1 248	18	10.7	11.4	175	156	3	366	313	20 699	5 420	5 982
Chambers..........................	486	13.3	468	NA	12.8	NA	37	101	1	168	458	6 913	NA	NA
Cherokee..........................	265	12.2	262	NA	12.0	NA	16	67	1	45	206	3 720	NA	NA
Chilton............................	508	13.7	394	NA	10.7	NA	22	56	1	25	68	5 535	NA	NA
Choctaw............................	216	13.7	168	NA	10.7	NA	5	31	0	0	0	2 764	29	222
Clarke..............................	460	16.0	288	NA	10.0	NA	27	97	3	107	375	4 798	NA	NA
Clay..................................	188	13.4	168	NA	12.0	NA	5	35	1	116	830	2 687	70	591
Cleburne..........................	188	13.2	155	NA	10.9	NA	4	28	0	0	0	2 380	216	1 581
Coffee..............................	555	13.2	432	NA	10.2	NA	51	117	2	229	540	6 958	831	2 177
Colbert............................	690	13.0	577	NA	10.9	NA	88	160	2	280	529	10 117	1 633	3 087
Conecuh............................	176	12.6	192	NA	13.8	NA	10	71	1	44	315	2 662	169	1 200
Coosa..............................	146	12.6	124	NA	10.7	NA	1	8	0	0	0	2 055	220	1 803
Covington..........................	490	13.1	487	NA	13.0	NA	36	96	3	177	473	7 831	NA	NA
Crenshaw..........................	168	12.3	188	NA	13.8	NA	8	59	1	55	403	2 787	367	2 686
Cullman............................	947	12.6	781	NA	10.4	NA	81	105	2	215	287	12 974	1 919	2 576
Dale..................................	791	16.1	418	9	8.5	11.8	52	106	2	79	162	9 261	1 266	2 784
Dallas..............................	803	17.1	572	9	12.2	11.6	94	203	2	259	554	8 595	NA	NA
De Kalb............................	797	13.6	662	NA	11.3	NA	29	45	1	103	176	10 153	NA	NA
Elmore..............................	892	14.4	560	NA	9.0	NA	29	44	2	138	223	8 913	1 333	2 216
Escambia..........................	480	13.1	430	7	11.7	15.3	30	78	2	142	386	6 167	NA	NA
Etowah............................	1 312	12.6	1 297	12	12.5	8.9	185	179	2	538	517	19 311	NA	NA
Fayette............................	210	11.6	234	NA	12.9	NA	15	81	1	153	844	3 130	372	2 011
Franklin............................	404	13.6	374	NA	12.6	NA	29	93	2	133	448	5 975	NA	NA
Geneva............................	299	12.0	308	NA	12.3	NA	10	39	1	169	678	5 007	357	1 506
Greene............................	157	16.0	123	NA	12.5	NA	6	60	1	72	729	1 750	NA	NA
Hale..................................	262	15.7	198	NA	11.9	NA	9	52	1	30	179	3 028	NA	NA
Henry..............................	189	12.0	182	NA	11.5	NA	7	43	0	0	0	3 007	399	2 532
Houston............................	1 183	13.8	822	12	9.6	10.4	267	301	2	639	744	11 521	3 508	4 037
Jackson............................	649	12.7	536	NA	10.5	NA	48	89	2	191	372	9 138	1 239	2 584
Jefferson..........................	9 120	13.8	7 352	110	11.1	12.1	2 568	388	13	4 650	705	110 359	36 982	6 181
Lamar..............................	199	12.6	187	NA	11.8	NA	3	19	0	0	0	3 276	NA	NA
Lauderdale........................	1 046	12.4	854	NA	10.1	NA	139	158	2	627	744	15 419	2 124	2 447
Lawrence..........................	454	13.6	321	NA	9.6	NA	12	34	1	51	152	4 354	216	655
Lee..................................	1 372	13.7	699	13	7.0	9.7	138	120	1	289	288	10 539	6 506	5 653
Limestone........................	840	13.5	544	NA	8.8	NA	51	78	1	101	162	8 069	1 200	1 829
Lowndes..........................	229	17.7	131	NA	10.1	NA	2	15	0	0	0	1 743	280	2 277
Macon..............................	334	14.5	268	NA	11.6	NA	39	162	0	0	0	3 583	1 092	4 530
Madison............................	3 979	14.4	2 020	23	7.3	5.7	494	179	3	859	309	34 110	14 892	5 413
Marengo..........................	325	13.9	256	NA	10.9	NA	13	58	1	99	423	3 579	NA	NA
Marion............................	359	11.7	378	NA	12.3	NA	28	90	2	189	610	5 610	482	1 837
Marshall..........................	1 132	14.1	887	11	11.0	9.4	75	91	2	192	239	15 422	NA	NA
Mobile............................	6 224	15.6	3 887	75	9.7	12.1	925	231	6	1 762	441	57 159	25 595	6 554
Monroe............................	366	15.2	247	NA	10.3	NA	14	58	1	65	271	3 832	776	3 190
Montgomery......................	3 407	15.7	2 039	43	9.4	12.6	501	224	5	1 208	555	31 053	17 606	7 877
Morgan............................	1 501	13.8	1 002	16	9.2	10.4	146	131	3	446	408	16 945	NA	NA
Perry..............................	189	14.9	149	NA	11.8	NA	8	67	1	76	600	2 022	NA	NA
Pickens............................	274	13.0	243	NA	11.6	NA	14	67	1	56	266	3 927	164	864
Pike..................................	406	14.2	315	NA	11.0	NA	23	78	1	65	227	4 902	1 247	4 574
Randolph..........................	265	13.2	247	NA	12.3	NA	20	89	2	90	452	4 050	604	2 778
Russell............................	726	14.4	546	7	10.8	10.1	38	76	1	120	238	8 325	1 571	3 157
St. Clair............................	831	13.4	554	NA	8.9	NA	24	37	1	72	116	7 699	NA	NA
Shelby..............................	2 170	15.4	830	17	5.9	8.0	136	95	1	164	117	11 613	NA	NA
Sumter............................	226	14.3	186	NA	11.8	NA	7	47	1	33	209	2 450	NA	NA
Talladega........................	1 059	13.7	858	12	11.1	11.0	71	88	2	237	309	13 777	NA	NA
Tallapoosa........................	548	13.5	510	NA	12.6	NA	46	111	2	103	254	7 284	1 317	3 242
Tuscaloosa........................	2 125	13.2	1 371	22	8.5	10.5	316	192	2	680	423	22 426	14 649	8 912
Walker..............................	904	12.7	888	9	12.5	9.6	52	74	1	267	376	14 274	630	1 169

1. Per 1,000 estimated resident population, average 1997–1999. 2. Deaths of infants under 1 year old. 3. Deaths of infants under 1 year old per 1,000 live births. 4. Data subject to copyright. 5. Per 100,000 resident population as of July 1 of the year shown. 6. Data for serious crimes have not been adjusted for underreporting; this may affect comparability between geographic areas and over time. 7. Per 100,000 population estimated by the FBI.

Table B. States and Counties — Crime, Education, Money Income, and Poverty

STATE County	Serious crimes known to police, 2000[1] (cont'd) Rate[2] Violent	Property	School enrollment and attainment, 1990 Enrollment[3] Total	Percent private	Attainment[4] (percent) High school graduate or more	Bachelor's degree or more	Local government expenditures, fiscal 1999[5] Total current expenditures (mil dol)	Current expenditures per student (dollars)	Money income 1989 Per capita[6] (dollars)	Households Median Dollars	Percent change, 1979–1989 (constant 1989 dollars)	Percent with $100,000 or more	Income and poverty, 1998 Median household income	Percent below poverty level All persons	Persons under 18	Persons 5–17 in families
	46	47	48	49	50	51	52	53	54	55	56	57	58	59	60	61
UNITED STATES..........	506	3 618	64 987 101	15.6	75.2	20.3	302 874.0	6 508	14 420	30 056	6.5	4.4	38 885	12.7	18.9	17.5
ALABAMA	486	4 060	1 056 402	11.0	66.9	15.7	3 880.2	5 188	11 486	23 597	3.0	2.3	33 204	15.7	23.4	21.0
Autauga......................	437	3 526	9 459	12.2	70.0	14.5	38.5	4 540	11 182	28 337	2.3	1.3	38 260	11.3	17.7	15.8
Baldwin......................	NA	NA	23 945	13.3	73.2	16.8	117.9	5 316	12 275	25 712	5.0	2.6	37 162	11.0	16.8	15.1
Barbour......................	NA	NA	6 710	10.2	55.6	11.8	26.2	5 334	9 515	19 389	15.0	2.1	27 603	22.7	31.3	30.3
Bibb...........................	NA	NA	4 201	4.8	51.8	4.7	17.7	4 790	8 973	19 775	-4.1	0.8	29 692	16.9	23.7	23.3
Blount........................	174	2 210	8 631	4.4	60.5	7.0	37.9	4 654	10 168	22 382	5.5	1.1	35 623	12.9	19.8	17.7
Bullock.......................	NA	NA	2 890	14.6	49.0	10.0	10.1	5 187	6 922	14 745	7.2	0.3	22 231	28.0	34.5	35.2
Butler.........................	NA	NA	5 712	11.7	52.8	8.0	19.8	5 144	7 903	16 054	-6.1	1.0	23 988	23.4	31.4	29.9
Calhoun......................	753	5 230	30 580	7.5	67.4	14.2	97.4	5 057	10 704	23 802	3.9	1.2	31 866	16.1	24.6	20.6
Chambers...................	NA	NA	8 735	8.1	54.3	8.9	29.5	5 180	10 000	21 256	3.1	1.2	29 260	16.8	26.0	23.0
Cherokee....................	NA	NA	3 919	2.3	53.5	6.7	19.8	5 038	9 915	21 368	6.2	1.1	29 839	16.1	24.4	22.6
Chilton.......................	NA	NA	7 600	4.5	56.6	7.5	32.6	4 964	9 826	21 627	8.6	1.0	31 970	16.0	22.4	21.7
Choctaw.....................	23	199	4 178	13.5	54.3	8.5	13.1	5 397	9 622	17 115	0.8	1.1	26 723	21.1	28.7	28.1
Clarke........................	NA	NA	7 475	10.1	60.3	10.8	27.7	5 137	9 031	19 067	-5.9	1.7	28 044	20.9	28.6	26.8
Clay...........................	34	557	2 835	2.5	53.8	7.3	12.7	4 979	9 533	19 252	4.6	1.1	28 323	14.5	21.7	19.8
Cleburne....................	51	1 530	2 845	2.4	49.8	6.5	12.5	4 887	9 876	21 158	-1.2	0.8	31 153	14.4	19.9	20.9
Coffee........................	275	1 902	10 543	4.9	67.2	16.5	43.4	5 188	11 286	23 905	0.8	1.6	32 925	14.5	22.4	20.4
Colbert.......................	146	2 942	12 011	6.4	65.2	11.5	50.5	5 894	11 425	22 378	-13.6	2.0	32 190	14.0	22.6	20.4
Conecuh.....................	156	1 043	3 345	7.6	52.7	6.4	11.7	5 422	7 953	15 992	3.6	0.7	24 100	25.7	34.9	34.3
Coosa........................	205	1 598	2 422	6.2	53.9	6.3	9.2	5 075	9 234	20 279	10.3	0.9	27 289	15.8	24.2	22.3
Covington...................	NA	NA	8 551	3.5	57.3	9.1	33.0	4 906	9 315	18 394	-2.1	1.0	26 598	19.7	28.4	27.0
Crenshaw...................	710	1 976	3 087	5.9	51.3	8.4	12.3	5 351	8 848	16 460	10.3	1.6	25 353	20.4	28.7	28.0
Cullman.....................	122	2 454	15 330	4.7	58.8	7.8	61.0	4 979	10 447	21 672	6.7	1.6	32 609	13.2	18.8	17.4
Dale...........................	420	2 364	13 525	6.1	74.2	13.5	38.8	5 100	10 580	24 091	13.8	1.1	31 303	16.9	24.6	24.7
Dallas........................	NA	NA	14 011	10.5	59.6	12.2	49.4	5 235	8 344	16 493	-6.9	1.7	24 005	28.0	37.3	35.5
De Kalb......................	NA	NA	11 794	2.3	53.0	7.1	49.9	4 871	9 604	20 135	4.7	1.2	29 364	16.2	24.2	20.1
Elmore........................	158	2 058	12 590	10.8	66.5	12.8	53.7	4 558	10 677	26 341	4.9	1.2	36 723	12.6	19.2	16.9
Escambia	NA	NA	8 834	6.0	59.9	7.6	34.3	5 314	8 858	18 472	-4.8	1.3	27 350	20.2	28.5	26.1
Etowah.......................	NA	NA	23 854	8.5	64.1	10.2	84.4	5 148	10 997	22 314	0.0	1.5	29 619	16.2	24.1	21.4
Fayette.......................	168	1 844	4 330	3.8	56.6	8.5	14.0	4 930	9 864	19 844	-0.3	1.2	29 473	16.7	25.0	22.0
Franklin......................	NA	NA	5 990	1.6	55.1	6.9	30.1	5 322	9 049	17 907	-11.8	1.1	27 971	17.0	25.6	23.2
Geneva.......................	245	1 261	5 326	3.0	55.4	6.8	20.8	4 837	9 768	20 027	10.0	1.0	27 049	18.6	27.2	25.5
Greene.......................	NA	NA	3 184	8.4	53.8	10.4	11.8	5 960	6 306	11 990	-3.4	0.6	19 050	32.7	41.2	40.5
Hale..........................	NA	NA	4 166	6.0	54.4	8.9	17.3	5 075	8 164	14 508	5.1	1.1	21 976	25.4	33.0	32.1
Henry.........................	343	2 190	3 713	7.7	58.5	8.2	14.8	5 259	9 909	22 130	13.6	1.1	29 084	17.3	26.0	25.1
Houston......................	406	3 631	21 193	10.3	68.3	15.0	82.6	5 375	12 118	24 813	5.2	2.3	33 234	16.2	23.7	21.8
Jackson......................	194	2 390	11 493	2.8	58.1	8.0	50.1	5 449	10 144	21 910	-5.1	1.2	32 272	14.4	21.1	19.3
Jefferson....................	735	5 446	164 480	14.5	73.8	19.9	612.6	5 474	13 277	25 858	-1.5	3.5	36 431	14.1	22.6	17.9
Lamar.........................	NA	NA	3 432	1.5	52.9	6.2	13.5	4 742	9 945	20 618	-3.1	0.8	28 262	17.3	24.9	24.0
Lauderdale..................	194	2 254	19 867	9.7	67.9	16.4	75.6	5 663	11 685	23 690	-6.3	1.8	33 447	13.5	20.6	18.6
Lawrence....................	21	634	7 201	3.7	55.6	6.2	32.4	5 180	9 800	21 519	6.1	0.7	34 180	15.2	22.5	21.5
Lee............................	791	4 862	35 831	5.3	73.2	25.3	92.6	5 408	11 409	21 227	8.7	2.7	33 449	14.6	20.9	18.1
Limestone..................	163	1 666	12 671	7.4	63.1	13.8	60.0	5 496	11 696	26 875	12.7	1.7	38 262	13.0	19.5	17.2
Lowndes.....................	423	1 854	3 682	10.2	56.7	8.2	17.1	6 090	6 848	15 584	10.9	0.8	21 095	28.9	35.4	37.6
Macon........................	344	4 186	8 607	30.8	61.9	18.0	20.2	4 982	7 534	15 642	5.5	0.9	22 410	29.6	39.2	39.8
Madison.....................	551	4 862	65 156	13.1	80.2	30.1	245.5	5 553	15 443	33 048	16.3	4.0	45 339	10.7	17.6	15.0
Marengo.....................	NA	NA	5 863	12.6	61.4	11.5	25.5	5 232	9 242	18 663	6.1	1.0	26 846	22.5	30.7	30.3
Marion........................	130	1 707	6 617	2.6	50.0	6.7	26.1	4 929	9 645	18 455	-8.0	1.2	28 627	16.0	21.1	21.5
Marshall.....................	NA	NA	15 312	4.6	61.5	11.5	76.0	5 169	10 793	21 458	3.0	1.4	31 153	15.6	23.4	21.0
Mobile........................	622	5 932	104 729	18.3	70.1	15.5	326.7	5 001	11 158	22 082	-6.7	2.3	31 430	19.0	27.3	24.2
Monroe.......................	867	2 323	6 774	9.7	59.2	10.8	24.4	5 163	9 299	21 140	8.8	1.0	28 942	20.5	28.2	27.4
Montgomery	753	7 124	60 057	17.0	75.3	24.2	169.1	4 976	12 806	26 551	6.5	3.1	36 008	17.0	26.5	23.1
Morgan.......................	NA	NA	24 459	8.2	69.4	15.5	112.7	5 833	12 830	28 364	7.2	2.2	38 381	11.3	17.2	14.7
Perry..........................	NA	NA	3 924	23.4	51.0	11.5	12.2	5 317	6 879	13 769	4.6	1.0	18 880	33.3	40.0	42.4
Pickens......................	153	712	5 247	10.5	56.2	6.6	20.3	5 289	8 564	17 879	2.2	0.6	25 573	22.1	31.5	30.0
Pike...........................	561	4 013	8 613	6.9	59.0	14.3	25.1	5 511	9 423	17 312	6.0	2.1	25 178	23.1	30.4	31.4
Randolph....................	290	2 489	4 541	2.8	50.3	7.7	18.3	4 848	9 092	19 440	11.6	0.8	27 649	17.5	25.7	23.7
Russell.......................	366	2 792	10 951	9.8	57.0	8.2	47.9	5 358	9 675	20 995	10.4	1.1	29 430	18.0	27.5	26.1
St. Clair.....................	NA	NA	11 798	8.4	61.0	8.5	50.3	4 713	10 596	24 106	-0.7	1.7	35 828	13.2	18.2	18.2
Shelby........................	NA	NA	26 069	18.2	78.2	29.0	104.7	5 450	16 237	36 852	20.3	5.8	55 470	6.5	9.3	8.8
Sumter.......................	NA	NA	5 119	9.7	52.4	11.1	15.6	5 460	8 031	12 811	-16.8	0.8	20 605	29.6	36.3	37.1
Talladega	NA	NA	18 839	7.5	60.7	10.2	69.1	5 036	9 700	21 378	1.0	1.1	27 765	18.6	26.2	24.5
Tallapoosa..................	342	2 900	9 364	3.7	57.8	11.5	36.1	5 140	10 878	22 020	5.3	1.8	28 711	16.1	24.0	22.4
Tuscaloosa.................	802	8 110	49 658	7.9	69.6	20.0	139.5	5 412	11 406	23 056	4.9	2.5	33 374	16.2	24.0	20.8
Walker........................	96	1 072	15 510	7.7	56.0	7.2	65.4	5 873	10 105	20 464	-7.4	1.2	29 017	14.5	21.0	19.5

1. Data for serious crimes have not been adjusted for underreporting; this may affect comparability between geographic areas and over time.   2. Per 100,000 population estimated by the FBI.   3. All persons 3 years old and over enrolled in nursery school through college.   4. Persons 25 years old and over.   5. Elementary and secondary education expenditures, local government fiscal years ending between July 1, 1998 and June 30, 1999.   6. Based on population enumerated as of April 1, 1990.

Table B. States and Counties — Personal Income

STATE County	Total (mil dol)	Percent change, 1998-1999	Per capita[1] Dollars	Per capita[1] Rank	Wages and salaries[2] (mil dol)	Proprietor's income (mil dol)	Dividends, interest, and rent (mil dol)	Transfer payments Total (mil dol)	Government payments to individuals Total (mil dol)	Social Security (mil dol)	Medical payments (mil dol)	Income maintenance (mil dol)	Unemployment insurance (mil dol)
	62	63	64	65	66	67	68	69	70	71	72	73	74
UNITED STATES............	7 784 137	5.4	28 546	X	4 965 514	665 067	1 476 316	1 016 203	964 173	379 905	399 060	104 137	20 765
ALABAMA	100 385	4.3	22 972	X	62 531	7 072	17 872	16 519	15 723	6 554	6 116	1 812	215
Autauga...................	951	8.0	22 033	1 353	305	50	135	125	117	52	41	13	2
Baldwin...................	3 354	8.2	24 692	715	1 254	218	737	464	439	234	147	28	5
Barbour...................	581	10.2	21 744	1 434	322	60	95	115	110	38	46	19	1
Bibb.......................	359	6.8	18 298	2 471	103	20	44	75	71	28	30	9	1
Blount....................	999	7.5	21 075	1 645	250	83	130	150	142	68	50	15	1
Bullock...................	191	4.6	16 830	2 770	81	24	33	52	50	16	21	10	1
Butler....................	376	4.1	17 462	2 655	170	35	60	100	96	35	40	14	3
Calhoun...................	2 388	0.9	20 492	1 837	1 559	116	455	462	441	183	163	49	6
Chambers..................	714	3.2	19 631	2 100	371	37	103	148	142	65	53	16	2
Cherokee..................	392	2.7	17 926	2 552	119	38	67	85	81	39	29	8	1
Chilton...................	744	6.6	19 794	2 062	217	49	91	136	129	54	51	15	1
Choctaw...................	294	5.1	18 914	2 310	210	18	52	70	67	26	26	12	1
Clarke....................	546	4.3	18 989	2 282	284	29	94	124	119	45	47	19	2
Clay......................	271	0.5	19 316	2 203	129	23	39	60	57	24	24	6	1
Cleburne..................	263	0.6	18 177	2 505	87	29	32	49	46	21	18	5	1
Coffee....................	976	4.1	23 165	1 054	374	118	183	167	159	64	63	16	2
Colbert...................	1 185	3.4	22 550	1 205	776	77	201	223	214	104	75	19	4
Conecuh...................	257	1.6	18 721	2 362	126	27	36	70	67	24	26	12	1
Coosa.....................	204	1.7	17 384	2 671	62	10	27	45	43	20	14	6	1
Covington.................	718	3.2	19 105	2 256	359	73	126	172	165	69	67	18	3
Crenshaw..................	278	6.8	20 436	1 857	88	60	41	64	62	23	26	9	1
Cullman...................	1 590	4.6	21 011	1 665	751	196	234	284	270	120	107	25	3
Dale......................	987	3.6	20 082	1 970	875	64	149	182	173	61	69	22	3
Dallas....................	885	4.6	18 970	2 286	474	69	157	239	230	71	92	51	4
De Kalb...................	1 240	5.8	21 043	1 656	639	160	174	229	218	100	82	24	3
Elmore....................	1 401	8.2	22 074	1 342	367	82	188	231	220	82	102	19	2
Escambia..................	683	4.4	18 631	2 383	399	61	118	149	142	60	55	17	2
Etowah....................	2 123	2.2	20 518	1 832	1 112	137	338	455	436	194	169	43	7
Fayette...................	337	2.4	18 612	2 390	149	16	65	76	73	33	26	9	1
Franklin..................	622	9.4	20 938	1 686	300	81	94	133	127	52	54	13	3
Geneva....................	493	5.8	19 752	2 068	144	81	75	113	108	44	43	12	2
Greene....................	153	4.1	15 684	2 930	58	13	22	49	47	14	20	11	1
Hale......................	276	4.8	16 380	2 848	92	28	36	74	71	22	32	13	1
Henry.....................	316	6.2	20 017	1 986	125	32	53	67	64	27	25	8	1
Houston...................	2 077	5.1	24 120	835	1 440	129	396	301	285	131	94	36	4
Jackson...................	1 077	5.8	20 891	1 698	550	76	154	190	180	81	67	20	4
Jefferson.................	18 903	3.8	28 753	271	15 203	1 497	3 946	2 680	2 560	1 092	1 012	260	26
Lamar.....................	288	1.1	17 988	2 541	149	19	43	68	65	28	26	7	1
Lauderdale................	1 774	2.7	21 036	1 659	854	117	369	331	316	155	110	27	5
Lawrence..................	699	7.5	20 691	1 779	287	67	72	110	104	46	38	14	2
Lee.......................	2 012	5.5	19 696	2 086	1 202	126	382	266	248	112	81	29	3
Limestone.................	1 342	4.0	21 294	1 573	866	86	208	183	172	79	60	19	2
Lowndes...................	199	4.4	15 252	2 966	89	16	27	55	53	16	21	13	1
Macon.....................	367	3.2	15 945	2 902	188	16	48	107	103	28	40	20	1
Madison...................	7 584	4.0	27 049	413	6 418	391	1 474	716	665	300	228	65	10
Marengo...................	468	4.8	20 209	1 926	240	47	77	103	98	35	41	18	1
Marion....................	586	2.1	19 243	2 222	362	38	89	127	121	51	50	11	2
Marshall..................	1 607	1.9	19 955	2 004	974	159	286	302	287	118	120	30	5
Mobile....................	8 327	1.9	20 835	1 721	5 809	482	1 476	1 522	1 449	570	581	186	22
Monroe....................	453	3.8	18 907	2 313	313	31	71	97	93	36	37	13	2
Montgomery................	5 914	4.1	27 405	382	4 893	395	1 246	809	770	289	286	110	9
Morgan....................	2 696	2.8	24 585	732	1 654	154	447	418	398	163	182	29	5
Perry.....................	187	4.8	14 843	3 002	75	14	26	67	65	18	28	15	1
Pickens...................	385	6.6	18 323	2 464	113	51	52	101	97	34	42	15	2
Pike......................	600	7.6	21 079	1 644	329	89	89	125	120	40	49	18	2
Randolph..................	375	2.7	18 498	2 413	140	37	59	90	86	37	34	10	1
Russell...................	965	4.7	19 270	2 217	415	61	121	190	181	74	62	26	2
St. Clair.................	1 302	7.6	20 396	1 864	377	70	165	192	181	85	65	16	2
Shelby....................	4 323	9.4	29 528	227	1 753	148	616	315	288	152	96	17	3
Sumter....................	248	4.3	15 861	2 913	119	25	34	71	68	20	26	15	1
Talladega.................	1 444	3.7	18 623	2 388	770	69	212	332	318	132	124	42	4
Tallapoosa................	863	2.3	21 395	1 550	446	53	180	179	171	74	70	17	2
Tuscaloosa................	3 746	4.4	23 207	1 043	2 588	183	668	647	617	225	281	61	6
Walker....................	1 447	3.8	20 284	1 899	538	125	216	339	326	133	133	30	4

1. Based on the resident population estimated as of July 1 of the year shown.   2. Includes other labor income.

Table B. States and Counties — Earnings, Social Security, and Housing

STATE County	Earnings, 1999									Social Security beneficiaries, December 2000			Housing units, 1990	
			Percent by selected industries									Supplemental Security Income recipients, December 2000		
			Goods-related[1]		Service-related and other[2]									
	Total (mil dol)	Farm	Total	Manu-facturing	Total	Retail trade	Finance, insurance, and real estate	Services	Government	Number	Rate[3]		Total	Percent change, 1980–1990
	75	76	77	78	79	80	81	82	83	84	85	86	87	88
UNITED STATES............	5 630 581	0.8	22.8	16.1	60.6	8.9	9.1	28.9	15.8	45 414 762	161	6 601 686	102 263 678	15.7
ALABAMA	69 603	1.9	26.8	19.6	51.2	9.4	5.8	23.3	20.1	825 773	186	159 486	1 670 379	13.8
Autauga..........................	355	3.4	D	30.0	D	15.5	3.7	15.5	17.7	6 836	157	1 211	12 732	16.1
Baldwin..........................	1 473	2.0	21.9	12.4	57.9	16.2	7.9	24.1	18.2	28 305	202	2 624	50 933	53.1
Barbour..........................	382	9.0	42.2	39.1	32.5	7.4	2.9	12.6	16.3	5 423	187	1 689	10 705	14.8
Bibb...............................	123	3.5	D	19.5	D	9.8	2.5	16.1	28.8	3 827	184	905	6 404	11.2
Blount............................	333	13.1	29.1	18.4	41.0	9.8	5.4	16.0	16.8	8 741	171	1 156	15 790	14.0
Bullock..........................	106	19.1	D	D	D	6.9	2.7	14.2	22.1	2 349	201	959	4 458	14.5
Butler............................	205	8.3	30.1	23.8	45.5	12.0	2.7	20.9	16.2	4 898	229	1 315	8 745	7.7
Calhoun..........................	1 676	0.4	24.1	19.6	42.3	10.1	2.8	17.8	33.3	24 228	216	4 411	46 753	9.8
Chambers........................	408	1.1	51.0	45.7	35.8	10.0	1.9	14.9	12.0	7 954	217	1 421	14 910	3.3
Cherokee........................	157	10.1	D	20.4	42.6	12.1	3.7	13.4	21.2	5 024	209	702	9 379	14.4
Chilton..........................	267	5.7	D	16.9	D	16.2	3.8	14.7	18.6	7 176	181	1 260	13 883	7.9
Choctaw..........................	228	2.6	D	54.7	D	4.4	D	8.7	8.2	3 527	222	963	6 789	11.6
Clarke............................	312	0.5	40.5	35.7	39.2	11.8	4.2	14.3	19.8	5 996	215	1 676	10 853	8.3
Clay...............................	152	7.1	49.6	46.0	23.7	5.0	1.9	9.5	19.6	3 322	233	500	5 608	5.3
Cleburne........................	116	11.2	D	29.4	D	8.1	1.7	7.5	20.4	2 963	210	499	5 232	9.0
Coffee............................	492	10.9	26.9	23.4	46.7	12.3	3.6	18.7	15.6	8 456	194	1 482	16 951	16.2
Colbert..........................	853	1.6	31.8	22.9	38.5	8.9	2.7	14.9	28.1	12 481	227	1 833	21 812	4.9
Conecuh..........................	153	6.2	D	20.5	D	5.5	D	14.5	18.2	3 358	238	879	6 207	3.5
Coosa.............................	71	4.8	55.0	50.2	20.4	4.1	0.8	11.0	19.8	2 650	217	533	5 113	3.6
Covington........................	432	7.5	D	21.4	D	10.6	3.1	18.5	15.9	9 067	241	1 630	16 178	6.3
Crenshaw........................	148	26.6	14.3	8.7	46.1	5.5	2.5	14.3	13.1	3 188	233	797	5 938	7.9
Cullman..........................	947	10.1	28.3	22.1	D	13.5	D	19.5	12.4	15 695	203	2 448	28 369	14.7
Dale...............................	938	2.4	D	23.2	D	4.4	1.5	9.3	51.8	8 384	171	1 724	19 432	17.4
Dallas............................	543	4.0	31.2	25.6	47.1	10.3	3.4	22.7	17.7	10 015	216	4 720	19 045	-1.6
De Kalb..........................	799	8.8	D	42.7	D	8.3	2.4	13.6	10.7	13 680	212	2 322	22 939	9.8
Elmore............................	449	1.2	31.2	19.7	42.0	11.5	3.4	17.4	25.7	10 571	160	1 871	19 497	13.3
Escambia........................	460	3.5	35.3	26.2	42.3	10.5	4.0	12.5	18.9	7 768	202	1 412	14 356	5.9
Etowah..........................	1 249	1.9	D	25.1	D	11.3	4.0	27.7	14.5	23 675	229	4 254	41 787	4.8
Fayette..........................	165	0.5	44.3	37.5	32.2	9.4	2.6	11.4	23.1	4 322	234	769	7 555	0.5
Franklin..........................	381	13.6	38.3	35.2	30.0	8.8	2.6	12.8	18.0	6 749	216	1 214	11 772	4.7
Geneva..........................	226	23.6	22.2	17.3	36.1	9.4	2.9	9.5	18.2	6 105	237	1 215	10 416	11.5
Greene............................	71	10.8	19.7	14.1	41.7	6.5	2.0	17.2	27.8	2 127	213	968	4 162	8.5
Hale...............................	120	14.3	31.8	28.7	29.7	6.3	2.1	13.8	24.1	3 260	190	1 210	6 370	14.4
Henry.............................	157	9.1	D	34.0	D	7.9	D	11.9	15.6	3 711	228	757	7 056	13.3
Houston..........................	1 569	1.3	D	15.5	D	12.8	3.8	26.9	15.3	17 143	193	3 412	33 196	16.2
Jackson..........................	625	3.4	D	40.4	D	8.7	2.4	10.3	21.7	10 543	196	1 889	19 768	0.8
Jefferson........................	16 700	0.0	17.5	9.6	67.7	8.8	10.3	30.0	14.8	124 738	188	21 741	273 097	5.1
Lamar.............................	168	2.3	D	47.9	D	6.7	2.5	10.3	12.4	3 733	235	631	6 617	3.7
Lauderdale......................	971	0.7	27.4	20.8	49.3	13.2	5.4	22.2	22.6	18 283	208	2 575	33 522	9.7
Lawrence........................	354	11.9	D	D	D	6.0	1.6	9.8	13.7	6 271	180	1 228	12 212	11.4
Lee................................	1 328	0.8	25.5	19.1	39.0	10.8	4.0	16.8	34.6	14 160	123	2 638	36 636	23.5
Limestone......................	952	2.6	42.9	39.1	D	7.3	1.8	14.4	26.0	10 569	161	1 802	21 455	30.1
Lowndes........................	104	7.8	D	40.1	D	6.3	2.2	9.0	19.9	2 557	190	1 036	4 792	13.5
Macon............................	203	3.3	D	1.0	D	5.4	1.5	33.5	49.9	4 099	170	1 284	9 818	6.4
Madison..........................	6 809	0.1	D	20.9	D	7.2	3.1	31.0	27.6	38 629	140	5 443	97 855	37.6
Marengo..........................	288	3.7	37.4	32.8	40.8	9.5	3.2	11.7	18.2	4 675	207	1 505	9 144	2.6
Marion............................	400	3.0	51.2	48.6	33.2	6.6	3.1	13.8	12.6	6 685	214	1 024	12 597	8.6
Marshall........................	1 133	4.2	D	35.0	D	12.6	3.7	12.6	15.1	15 689	191	3 049	30 225	13.3
Mobile............................	6 292	0.6	24.5	15.2	58.1	10.3	5.2	28.0	16.9	69 790	175	13 620	151 220	14.6
Monroe..........................	344	2.6	D	46.2	D	7.0	2.0	10.0	13.7	4 792	197	1 066	9 633	19.2
Montgomery....................	5 288	0.4	14.5	9.2	54.3	8.3	9.2	25.7	30.8	36 391	163	9 166	84 525	14.6
Morgan..........................	1 808	1.3	44.6	35.8	40.7	9.6	4.2	16.9	13.4	19 715	178	2 962	40 419	19.5
Perry.............................	89	10.1	D	31.4	D	6.3	3.2	18.5	21.9	2 783	235	1 199	4 807	-4.3
Pickens..........................	165	19.6	23.9	18.4	37.9	6.7	3.1	19.0	18.5	4 745	227	1 491	8 379	7.5
Pike...............................	418	12.0	22.9	16.6	46.8	10.1	3.4	13.4	18.3	5 612	190	1 767	11 506	12.8
Randolph........................	177	7.3	36.1	32.8	35.0	10.0	3.1	11.5	21.6	4 891	219	862	8 728	11.2
Russell..........................	476	2.8	44.1	35.6	36.5	10.9	3.2	15.9	16.6	9 360	188	2 037	19 633	10.0
St. Clair.........................	448	1.1	30.4	19.2	50.6	12.1	3.8	18.0	17.9	10 905	168	1 495	20 382	30.5
Shelby............................	1 901	0.5	29.8	17.7	60.2	7.8	7.4	22.0	9.5	17 942	125	1 421	39 201	59.1
Sumter............................	144	11.9	22.6	20.0	D	7.9	D	14.6	28.4	2 918	197	1 240	6 545	7.2
Talladega........................	839	1.3	41.5	33.5	36.7	9.7	2.4	18.0	20.6	16 975	211	4 023	29 861	14.6
Tallapoosa......................	499	0.8	44.9	39.6	40.8	8.4	4.1	22.3	13.5	9 340	225	1 698	17 312	12.8
Tuscaloosa......................	2 772	0.3	35.4	22.1	38.5	9.9	3.6	17.4	25.8	27 726	168	5 674	58 740	16.7
Walker............................	663	1.1	25.8	6.7	56.4	15.1	5.3	23.3	16.7	16 304	231	3 290	28 427	5.1

1. Covers mining, construction, and manufacturing. 2. Covers private sector earnings in agricultural services, forestry, and fisheries; transportation and public utilities; wholesale trade; retail trade; finance, insurance, and real estate; and services. 3. Per 1,000 resident population estimated as of July 1 of the year shown.

Table B. States and Counties — **Housing, Labor Force, and Employment**

STATE County	Housing units, 1990 (cont'd)								Civilian labor force, 2001				Civilian employment, 1990[5]		
	Occupied units										Unemployment			Percent	
	Owner-occupied					Renter-occupied									
				Owner cost as a percent of income											
	Total	Percent	Median value[1]	With a mortgage	Without a mortgage	Median rent[2]	Rent as percent of income	Sub-standard units[3] (percent)	Total	Percent change, 2000–2001	Total	Rate[4]	Total	Professional, managerial, and technical	Precision production, craft, and repair
	89	90	91	92	93	94	95	96	97	98	99	100	101	102	103
UNITED STATES............	91 947 410	64.2	79 100	21.0	12.9	447	26.4	5.3	141 815 000	0.7	6 742 000	4.8	115 681 202	30.1	11.3
ALABAMA	1 506 790	70.5	53 700	18.4	12.8	325	24.8	4.5	2 147 552	-0.3	114 360	5.3	1 741 794	26.1	13.0
Autauga.........................	11 826	79.7	59 200	17.7	12.3	372	23.5	5.3	22 499	-0.1	838	3.7	15 432	23.8	13.2
Baldwin.........................	37 044	78.4	64 200	18.8	12.1	357	23.8	4.4	71 740	0.2	2 934	4.1	43 005	25.1	13.5
Barbour.........................	9 218	70.4	41 400	18.2	13.7	227	21.8	9.7	14 259	2.0	1 094	7.7	10 313	20.9	13.3
Bibb..............................	5 745	78.5	39 500	19.7	13.0	261	23.0	9.8	7 077	-2.0	708	10.0	6 725	14.4	15.3
Blount...........................	14 644	81.8	46 500	19.1	12.4	258	23.9	4.2	24 172	0.1	685	2.8	17 568	17.2	20.6
Bullock.........................	3 787	72.1	32 300	19.5	15.7	177	32.2	9.6	4 571	-0.2	531	11.6	3 753	18.8	12.1
Butler...........................	7 935	72.9	34 000	19.4	13.5	225	24.7	9.7	9 200	-1.8	913	9.9	7 537	16.7	11.8
Calhoun........................	42 983	70.3	51 600	19.3	12.7	310	23.8	2.3	52 206	-2.7	2 916	5.6	46 899	23.6	14.0
Chambers......................	13 786	76.0	37 900	16.4	14.0	260	23.4	6.5	16 144	1.3	1 042	6.5	16 376	17.3	14.7
Cherokee.......................	7 466	79.8	44 700	20.3	12.6	253	21.5	4.6	10 296	0.3	448	4.4	8 444	15.6	14.7
Chilton..........................	12 114	81.2	42 800	20.2	13.4	268	24.4	4.7	18 728	-1.8	948	5.1	13 648	18.8	19.2
Choctaw........................	5 747	84.8	37 200	16.5	14.3	182	26.6	13.7	5 088	-5.4	461	9.1	5 659	15.9	14.3
Clarke...........................	9 506	79.6	40 300	17.8	13.2	261	20.9	11.1	13 167	-4.2	1 531	11.6	10 305	21.6	13.7
Clay..............................	5 003	75.6	35 500	20.3	12.5	180	17.8	6.7	6 620	-1.5	391	5.9	5 784	14.4	17.1
Cleburne........................	4 776	81.7	42 600	18.6	12.6	251	23.8	4.8	7 242	-0.1	397	5.5	5 741	15.5	16.7
Coffee...........................	15 260	70.9	53 300	19.0	12.4	325	23.0	2.9	19 876	-7.5	1 328	6.7	16 963	26.2	13.6
Colbert..........................	20 096	75.3	46 300	17.7	12.7	291	25.8	2.8	25 245	-1.1	2 126	8.4	22 098	21.8	16.3
Conecuh........................	5 259	80.1	33 300	22.1	13.8	203	28.2	11.6	5 731	-3.6	455	7.9	5 118	17.2	11.4
Coosa...........................	4 017	82.7	35 600	19.7	12.2	241	21.7	7.0	5 380	2.9	431	8.0	4 590	15.3	15.5
Covington......................	14 444	75.7	34 800	19.3	12.9	233	26.4	4.7	16 452	-2.9	1 224	7.4	15 388	20.4	12.8
Crenshaw.......................	5 262	74.6	31 200	22.8	12.5	193	25.3	8.5	5 260	-1.2	402	7.6	5 479	17.4	11.7
Cullman.........................	25 605	77.8	48 100	19.7	12.6	276	25.6	3.0	40 061	-1.0	1 685	4.2	29 952	19.0	16.7
Dale..............................	17 574	61.0	49 400	18.0	12.7	326	22.8	3.6	21 445	-0.1	1 133	5.3	18 993	24.6	15.7
Dallas............................	17 033	62.2	43 800	17.1	13.8	253	29.9	11.2	19 329	-2.1	2 255	11.7	16 630	23.4	11.0
De Kalb.........................	20 968	78.2	39 700	18.9	13.2	254	23.9	3.1	34 136	2.0	1 556	4.6	24 643	15.4	15.4
Elmore..........................	16 532	80.3	58 100	17.7	12.3	309	21.9	5.7	30 794	0.4	1 186	3.9	20 610	24.2	14.2
Escambia.......................	12 899	76.4	41 100	21.5	12.5	256	26.3	4.7	17 018	-0.7	985	5.8	13 312	18.8	12.1
Etowah..........................	38 675	74.0	42 700	17.8	12.9	281	24.0	2.6	48 309	-3.1	3 560	7.4	40 902	20.8	14.4
Fayette..........................	6 859	76.8	36 800	17.9	12.4	230	23.6	5.8	7 792	0.6	582	7.5	7 405	16.9	15.8
Franklin.........................	10 850	75.1	38 300	21.0	13.6	233	24.7	2.9	16 018	-3.2	1 343	8.4	11 573	16.7	16.7
Geneva..........................	9 231	78.1	35 800	18.0	12.7	214	22.5	3.9	10 093	-3.9	931	9.2	10 262	15.6	15.4
Greene..........................	3 512	71.1	35 800	24.0	15.1	187	27.1	16.7	2 964	-2.4	316	10.7	3 246	21.0	10.4
Hale..............................	5 397	79.1	34 900	21.3	13.8	164	25.7	14.3	7 255	0.1	705	9.7	5 442	15.5	13.2
Henry............................	5 769	78.4	41 300	16.6	12.7	231	21.4	6.4	6 568	-0.4	427	6.5	6 513	18.6	13.1
Houston.........................	30 844	67.6	52 600	17.0	12.8	308	23.1	4.1	45 533	-0.6	1 921	4.2	38 120	24.9	13.2
Jackson.........................	18 020	76.7	43 200	18.2	12.7	277	23.2	4.0	25 728	-2.6	2 150	8.4	21 337	18.0	15.9
Jefferson.......................	251 479	65.2	58 700	18.2	12.9	358	24.8	3.1	336 619	0.3	12 888	3.8	289 888	30.9	10.1
Lamar............................	6 005	75.6	38 900	18.8	12.8	186	22.3	4.7	7 006	-0.6	738	10.5	6 975	13.7	15.8
Lauderdale.....................	30 905	73.4	52 700	18.3	12.2	299	25.1	2.3	41 135	-0.5	3 331	8.1	34 721	23.9	16.1
Lawrence.......................	11 410	80.8	44 300	18.9	13.5	244	23.7	5.0	16 634	-0.4	1 138	6.8	13 646	13.3	19.9
Lee...............................	33 097	58.1	64 900	16.9	12.4	339	35.1	3.7	50 511	0.9	1 918	3.8	40 043	30.8	10.5
Limestone......................	19 685	76.2	56 300	17.1	12.4	305	21.8	4.1	30 194	2.0	1 327	4.4	24 389	24.0	16.8
Lowndes........................	4 056	80.5	34 800	24.7	13.6	195	29.3	16.5	5 136	-12.6	481	9.4	4 200	15.3	12.9
Macon...........................	8 483	66.9	43 400	21.7	13.7	285	33.5	8.7	7 710	-2.1	482	6.3	8 523	27.8	9.6
Madison.........................	91 208	65.1	77 900	17.3	12.0	408	22.7	2.8	147 888	1.4	4 984	3.4	119 797	42.4	9.9
Marengo........................	8 156	77.1	41 800	18.2	13.3	199	27.3	12.5	11 103	-0.3	592	5.3	8 768	20.2	14.0
Marion...........................	11 521	75.3	38 300	19.4	12.5	208	23.5	3.0	13 559	-9.3	1 423	10.5	12 294	15.6	17.1
Marshall........................	27 761	74.2	48 100	19.6	12.6	290	25.3	2.7	38 796	-0.7	2 388	6.2	31 405	21.5	16.5
Mobile...........................	136 899	66.8	53 300	19.1	13.0	325	26.7	4.7	201 475	0.1	11 992	6.0	155 065	27.7	12.8
Monroe..........................	8 412	77.3	43 200	17.5	12.6	274	21.1	9.2	9 326	-3.0	901	9.7	9 428	17.9	15.4
Montgomery...................	77 173	62.3	62 600	19.8	12.7	379	24.9	5.3	110 996	0.3	4 551	4.1	92 614	31.9	8.6
Morgan..........................	37 799	71.8	60 900	17.1	12.0	341	22.3	2.9	56 955	-0.4	3 147	5.5	46 358	27.0	16.1
Perry.............................	4 201	70.1	31 600	21.7	14.6	188	28.8	14.8	4 250	-6.2	580	14.2	4 254	19.3	11.5
Pickens.........................	7 568	76.9	38 000	20.3	13.2	175	26.6	9.9	8 289	-2.0	946	11.4	7 676	17.2	13.4
Pike..............................	10 314	66.4	43 500	17.0	13.3	246	28.6	5.8	13 111	-4.4	746	5.7	11 441	22.2	12.6
Randolph.......................	7 553	79.0	36 500	19.6	12.9	239	23.5	6.4	9 573	1.5	745	7.8	8 546	14.5	14.2
Russell..........................	17 499	65.0	46 200	19.1	12.9	294	25.8	6.9	25 448	-0.4	1 459	5.7	19 698	17.7	16.6
St. Clair........................	17 666	83.1	53 400	19.0	12.6	316	24.3	4.1	31 795	0.6	1 161	3.7	21 593	19.1	19.1
Shelby...........................	35 985	75.6	88 300	18.7	12.1	457	20.8	3.1	83 623	0.4	1 695	2.0	50 246	36.5	10.4
Sumter..........................	5 545	71.0	34 700	23.0	14.3	196	29.4	13.6	5 012	-7.5	530	10.6	5 308	18.6	10.9
Talladega.......................	26 448	75.2	44 800	17.6	13.0	261	26.5	5.4	34 815	3.1	2 782	8.0	30 069	21.3	14.7
Tallapoosa.....................	14 700	75.1	43 200	17.7	13.0	254	21.6	5.5	20 066	2.2	1 340	6.7	17 702	20.4	13.0
Tuscaloosa....................	55 354	61.5	62 100	18.5	12.7	344	29.5	3.8	84 318	-0.1	2 746	3.3	65 917	29.2	12.5
Walker...........................	25 554	79.3	42 100	18.3	12.9	282	25.9	3.6	28 107	-0.1	2 089	7.4	26 620	17.6	19.5

1. Specified owner-occupied units.　2. Specified renter-occupied units.　3. Overcrowded or lacking complete plumbing facilities.　4. Percent of civilian labor force.　5. Persons 16 years and older.

STATE County	Private nonfarm establishments, employment and payroll, 1999									Agriculture, 1997			
		Employment						Annual payroll		Farms			Farm operators
											Percent with—		
	Number of establishments	Total	Health Care and Social Assistance	Manufac-turing	Retail trade	Finance and Insurance	Professional Scientific and Technical Services	Total (mil dol)	Average per employee (dollars)	Number	Less than 50 acres	500 acres and over	Whose principal occupation is farming (percent)
	104	105	106	107	108	109	110	111	112	113	114	115	116
UNITED STATES............	7 008 444	110 705 661	13 865 014	16 659 930	14 476 628	5 965 174	6 432 422	3 554 693	32 109	1 911 859	29.5	18.4	50.3
ALABAMA	100 507	1 633 909	203 808	341 940	224 493	72 609	69 448	42 454	25 983	41 384	33.8	9.2	37.6
Autauga..............................	775	9 143	727	2 048	2 141	260	252	202	22 148	348	26.1	12.4	48.0
Baldwin..............................	3 837	42 848	4 874	5 935	8 314	1 101	1 517	872	20 344	977	45.8	8.4	42.2
Barbour..............................	610	10 169	752	4 278	1 223	304	120	242	23 844	417	14.9	20.1	40.0
Bibb	341	3 383	356	814	548	114	41	71	21 096	177	21.5	15.8	32.8
Blount................................	738	7 817	783	2 645	1 272	319	154	162	20 688	1 191	39.0	2.7	38.2
Bullock..............................	141	2 393	273	D	252	78	D	45	18 719	277	12.6	33.2	44.4
Butler................................	526	5 753	668	1 605	989	179	82	113	19 718	440	22.5	7.5	37.0
Calhoun.............................	2 568	40 241	5 080	11 024	6 392	1 026	889	864	21 459	629	39.1	3.8	35.3
Chambers...........................	657	11 619	1 140	5 596	1 357	190	107	272	23 390	324	22.2	15.7	36.4
Cherokee............................	365	2 985	243	891	638	150	33	60	20 084	494	24.7	10.7	38.9
Chilton...............................	767	6 611	510	1 229	1 549	254	87	132	19 918	663	34.5	5.0	35.1
Choctaw.............................	311	3 548	215	D	388	90	60	139	39 160	225	29.8	14.2	33.3
Clarke................................	739	8 066	783	2 403	1 410	398	106	181	22 390	248	25.4	11.3	25.0
Clay...................................	228	4 390	577	2 517	394	78	D	88	20 095	397	20.9	6.3	42.1
Cleburne............................	188	2 121	65	882	235	D	D	51	24 000	340	27.9	3.8	47.9
Coffee................................	986	13 416	1 465	4 939	2 325	514	362	249	18 556	788	26.5	10.7	47.5
Colbert...............................	1 356	18 614	1 724	4 832	2 701	466	233	452	24 256	557	37.3	8.4	31.6
Conecuh.............................	265	3 325	332	796	281	69	D	76	22 730	366	22.1	8.5	32.0
Coosa................................	128	1 495	94	927	127	D	D	33	22 138	213	16.9	8.0	32.9
Covington...........................	907	11 159	1 370	3 326	2 019	377	276	237	21 263	899	26.1	7.3	38.9
Crenshaw...........................	262	2 615	448	498	360	77	D	50	19 080	488	19.5	12.9	43.2
Cullman.............................	1 720	23 047	2 795	6 753	3 316	601	389	519	22 536	2 151	47.8	1.8	43.3
Dale...................................	874	10 700	1 269	1 263	1 331	364	313	246	22 981	422	22.5	15.4	42.4
Dallas................................	973	15 288	2 373	5 317	2 250	497	207	343	22 430	435	25.5	29.4	43.0
De Kalb..............................	1 241	20 776	1 675	11 863	2 283	454	468	452	21 763	2 080	42.9	2.9	38.7
Elmore...............................	1 058	9 962	1 139	2 185	1 861	291	250	184	18 428	560	28.2	10.4	36.6
Escambia	865	11 130	1 165	2 891	1 815	402	175	242	21 773	380	35.0	11.6	40.3
Etowah...............................	2 198	33 152	5 181	8 066	4 783	955	643	766	23 095	904	47.3	3.1	31.9
Fayette..............................	359	5 447	725	1 794	627	91	27	126	23 154	305	21.6	8.5	32.8
Franklin.............................	616	9 879	864	5 188	941	347	55	201	20 320	833	26.2	5.0	36.9
Geneva..............................	467	4 425	682	1 382	770	181	89	83	18 850	872	26.5	11.2	51.8
Greene...............................	131	1 304	201	314	200	D	32	24	18 715	261	13.8	30.3	38.3
Hale...................................	224	2 996	462	1 439	321	79	32	60	20 030	411	16.3	18.0	39.9
Henry.................................	320	4 133	342	1 498	584	91	59	89	21 444	334	19.8	28.1	49.4
Houston.............................	2 816	46 376	7 444	8 920	7 606	1 108	1 016	1 136	24 487	690	31.9	16.2	47.7
Jackson..............................	886	13 641	1 703	6 810	1 728	335	210	328	24 057	1 296	37.8	7.5	35.0
Jefferson............................	17 613	359 434	51 293	36 341	42 204	27 963	18 021	10 869	30 240	426	52.3	3.1	30.8
Lamar................................	284	5 141	346	2 420	537	136	D	132	25 609	387	31.0	8.5	29.5
Lauderdale.........................	2 048	31 141	5 188	7 037	5 079	986	835	622	19 963	1 355	40.5	6.0	31.0
Lawrence...........................	421	5 517	524	2 206	819	136	40	194	35 165	1 287	40.0	4.7	33.1
Lee....................................	2 021	30 768	4 470	7 081	5 407	827	668	660	21 465	347	32.9	10.7	31.7
Limestone..........................	1 082	16 713	1 634	6 591	2 465	362	880	568	33 989	1 127	39.5	10.3	33.3
Lowndes............................	159	2 119	85	1 174	249	D	26	82	38 542	330	20.3	30.0	40.3
Macon................................	235	6 287	2 009	47	424	86	61	142	22 649	300	16.7	22.7	31.3
Madison.............................	7 124	123 197	12 589	23 655	16 632	3 590	17 905	3 797	30 823	973	40.8	9.5	38.1
Marengo............................	503	6 353	738	1 765	917	280	61	162	25 428	464	19.4	21.1	35.3
Marion...............................	726	10 498	1 412	5 263	1 163	381	99	234	22 303	677	26.7	3.5	29.7
Marshall............................	2 005	32 870	3 170	13 599	5 074	822	480	704	21 431	1 583	51.0	1.8	36.9
Mobile...............................	9 434	161 541	21 458	21 511	22 004	5 906	7 439	4 099	25 376	755	55.2	7.8	39.6
Monroe..............................	449	8 561	522	2 590	1 024	163	61	227	26 562	422	27.3	14.0	39.3
Montgomery	6 100	109 333	15 886	11 201	15 329	7 784	5 598	2 798	25 596	654	25.2	20.9	36.5
Morgan..............................	2 793	45 719	4 400	14 375	6 505	1 526	1 149	1 209	26 450	1 214	41.8	4.1	30.1
Perry.................................	157	2 475	260	1 096	250	70	D	46	18 518	340	19.1	19.4	40.3
Pickens..............................	346	3 288	670	1 050	609	165	50	60	18 296	454	21.6	12.6	37.9
Pike...................................	694	9 991	845	2 749	1 437	364	146	210	21 031	580	19.5	19.1	43.3
Randolph............................	401	5 009	638	2 263	685	145	81	88	17 661	599	22.5	7.2	39.9
Russell..............................	871	12 411	1 136	4 087	1 928	346	173	299	24 130	246	27.2	21.5	38.2
St. Clair.............................	1 118	11 987	1 267	3 062	1 711	338	277	262	21 890	594	37.5	3.2	37.4
Shelby...............................	3 605	53 329	3 164	6 021	6 423	4 286	3 545	1 768	33 148	435	38.2	7.1	35.6
Sumter...............................	249	3 129	274	726	453	74	18	65	20 832	369	19.0	26.6	38.2
Talladega	1 401	20 589	2 360	7 017	3 049	598	285	492	23 885	523	29.3	9.2	37.3
Tallapoosa.........................	833	27 935	2 242	7 198	1 828	384	182	548	19 622	344	23.5	7.8	27.6
Tuscaloosa.........................	3 956	67 473	10 679	12 460	9 763	1 775	2 252	1 782	26 406	510	30.8	10.0	37.3
Walker...............................	1 447	16 220	3 128	1 974	3 600	681	437	361	22 252	470	44.3	4.3	34.7

Table B. States and Counties — Agriculture, Land, and Water

STATE County	Agriculture, 1997 (cont'd)															
	Land in farms					Value of land and buildings		Value of machinery and equipment average per farm ($1,000)	Value of products sold				Percent of farms with sales of —		Percent of land owned by fed. gov. 1997	Water consumption 1995 (mil gal/day)
			Acres								Percent from —					
	Acreage (1,000)	Percent change, 1992–1997	Average size of farm	Total irrigated (1,000)	Total cropland (1,000)	Average per farm ($1,000)	Average per acre (dollars)		Total (mil dol)	Average per farm (dollars)	Crops	Live-stock and poultry products	$10,000 or more	$100,000 or more		
	117	118	119	120	121	122	123	124	125	126	127	128	129	130	131	132
UNITED STATES	931 795	-1.5	487	55 058	431 144	450	933	58	196 865	102 970	49.8	50.2	49.6	18.1	20.7	340 751.3
ALABAMA	8 704	3.0	210	77	4 198	298	1 442	36	3 099	74 884	20.4	79.6	31.1	11.3	3.0	7 088.0
Autauga	105	-2.1	301	0	46	374	1 289	36	11	32 108	62.0	38.0	29.9	7.5	0.3	40.3
Baldwin	166	-1.4	169	8	117	425	2 534	44	62	63 757	76.7	23.3	32.9	9.5	1.4	41.9
Barbour	154	-13.1	369	1	63	308	934	48	24	58 180	51.8	48.2	42.7	12.2	0.7	15.0
Bibb	47	-2.3	265	D	16	313	1 403	31	2	12 149	11.5	88.5	19.8	1.7	15.1	3.3
Blount	139	1.1	116	0	73	244	2 137	29	138	115 854	3.7	96.3	32.2	15.8	0.0	51.3
Bullock	169	16.4	609	D	59	568	938	39	25	89 138	65.4	34.6	38.6	10.5	0.0	4.8
Butler	97	1.4	221	0	36	204	1 016	32	31	69 940	10.7	89.3	28.9	9.5	0.0	3.7
Calhoun	77	4.6	123	1	39	260	1 896	32	54	85 667	12.5	87.5	22.9	7.6	21.3	26.3
Chambers	94	-14.3	291	0	28	275	921	27	4	13 176	27.8	72.2	23.8	2.8	1.3	12.6
Cherokee	123	0.9	249	1	69	302	1 328	44	49	99 847	47.9	52.1	34.8	11.5	2.2	6.4
Chilton	99	-0.3	149	1	44	231	1 596	33	9	14 252	62.2	37.8	24.1	3.0	5.1	5.6
Choctaw	65	-4.4	289	0	16	240	811	32	7	29 641	8.5	91.5	19.6	3.6	0.5	50.8
Clarke	61	0.7	248	0	17	186	910	24	2	8 055	32.4	67.6	17.3	1.2	0.2	25.6
Clay	75	10.7	190	0	32	225	1 245	27	25	62 290	1.7	98.3	31.5	11.1	16.6	2.7
Cleburne	51	8.0	149	D	21	261	1 485	32	46	134 864	3.6	96.4	38.5	19.4	27.0	2.6
Coffee	187	6.8	237	2	95	282	1 319	46	136	172 947	13.2	86.8	47.8	20.8	3.7	16.3
Colbert	116	-16.3	207	2	70	304	1 464	35	33	58 509	36.1	63.9	26.8	9.3	6.5	91.1
Conecuh	88	7.7	241	0	33	257	1 008	21	6	15 599	35.3	64.7	24.0	3.6	0.0	2.2
Coosa	42	1.7	196	0	15	257	1 356	28	1	6 210	19.6	80.4	16.4	0.0	0.0	0.9
Covington	180	8.5	200	D	81	276	1 342	38	66	73 120	29.7	70.3	30.7	12.9	8.1	12.4
Crenshaw	129	16.6	265	2	51	237	1 077	34	54	110 790	9.3	90.7	39.3	17.4	0.0	2.5
Cullman	203	3.0	94	1	115	253	2 647	32	334	155 345	2.6	97.4	39.7	22.6	0.0	20.3
Dale	131	-3.0	310	1	63	365	1 141	57	34	81 371	33.2	66.8	39.8	14.0	12.4	13.8
Dallas	249	6.7	572	1	98	565	969	50	30	68 537	51.8	48.2	36.6	11.5	0.4	57.2
De Kalb	224	6.0	108	1	130	221	1 973	30	234	112 633	4.7	95.3	32.7	16.5	0.0	9.8
Elmore	124	19.5	222	1	62	378	1 649	35	19	34 677	68.9	31.1	24.6	7.3	0.0	6.3
Escambia	87	1.2	229	1	52	256	1 121	53	18	48 285	80.3	19.7	36.3	11.1	4.6	47.0
Etowah	95	10.4	105	0	47	207	2 253	28	55	60 779	6.2	93.8	25.3	9.4	0.0	264.5
Fayette	63	-3.1	206	0	26	219	1 039	38	8	26 719	23.8	76.2	22.0	5.6	0.0	3.1
Franklin	128	-1.2	154	0	61	196	1 167	25	90	108 477	1.2	98.8	30.3	15.0	0.3	5.3
Geneva	207	5.4	237	2	120	288	1 221	45	108	124 033	25.9	74.1	47.5	21.6	0.1	3.9
Greene	123	-3.7	472	D	47	314	795	50	12	44 137	13.1	86.9	32.6	9.6	1.6	320.4
Hale	158	-6.1	384	0	54	369	947	72	32	78 399	6.3	93.7	40.9	16.3	6.7	39.2
Henry	154	-8.1	460	3	90	442	842	69	27	81 435	85.4	14.6	50.0	20.7	0.4	9.5
Houston	198	3.2	287	10	137	340	1 145	62	56	81 579	67.9	32.1	48.7	15.9	0.1	120.0
Jackson	221	8.4	171	1	131	255	1 529	30	64	49 504	20.6	79.4	28.5	9.3	0.1	1 301.6
Jefferson	41	14.8	97	0	19	289	3 009	27	16	37 673	19.4	80.6	17.1	1.6	0.0	90.6
Lamar	71	27.4	184	1	27	244	1 236	27	5	13 926	20.0	80.0	18.6	2.8	0.0	4.2
Lauderdale	212	4.7	156	0	134	227	1 431	27	29	21 461	48.6	51.4	20.5	5.5	0.5	16.1
Lawrence	205	18.5	159	1	139	261	1 578	33	80	62 090	18.6	81.4	26.1	9.1	21.8	62.1
Lee	76	11.5	218	1	22	409	1 847	47	20	57 226	86.4	13.6	30.5	3.5	0.0	18.9
Limestone	254	22.7	225	5	181	480	2 090	47	53	47 051	43.6	56.4	26.4	8.0	3.1	792.3
Lowndes	173	-13.5	524	1	63	515	1 038	40	31	94 012	17.1	82.9	43.9	14.5	2.5	8.5
Macon	127	-7.7	424	2	43	446	1 077	46	10	31 923	70.0	30.0	27.0	5.7	3.1	6.8
Madison	210	-6.0	216	3	158	452	2 114	37	29	29 969	59.6	40.4	29.8	6.1	7.7	54.0
Marengo	198	-0.3	428	0	68	325	877	45	15	32 044	13.5	86.5	34.9	5.8	0.1	31.9
Marion	98	10.2	145	0	44	148	1 144	32	26	38 616	6.8	93.2	21.7	6.5	0.0	6.6
Marshall	146	2.2	92	0	85	205	2 344	29	201	126 742	2.4	97.6	27.9	13.8	0.0	22.4
Mobile	121	16.7	161	2	61	297	2 108	38	63	82 994	84.5	15.5	30.6	9.9	1.2	1 104.5
Monroe	135	22.3	319	2	57	350	1 253	64	23	54 245	77.8	22.2	40.8	12.1	0.2	63.8
Montgomery	241	4.3	368	1	102	582	1 673	44	33	50 633	29.1	70.9	37.2	7.3	0.6	60.0
Morgan	159	1.7	131	0	95	266	2 112	23	78	64 403	7.4	92.6	25.5	9.1	2.7	140.1
Perry	145	0.4	425	D	58	363	795	28	10	30 040	23.8	76.2	29.4	8.2	6.9	8.3
Pickens	123	16.2	271	1	45	309	1 109	39	61	133 424	4.6	95.4	37.4	23.3	0.7	6.2
Pike	174	-3.1	299	3	80	302	1 142	42	61	104 719	21.7	78.3	44.0	17.1	0.0	11.8
Randolph	108	12.6	181	0	43	215	1 092	32	54	90 670	1.2	98.8	30.1	12.9	0.0	2.2
Russell	96	-15.0	391	2	33	448	1 267	40	8	30 799	74.1	25.9	27.6	5.7	2.8	34.1
St. Clair	77	-1.5	129	2	37	281	2 307	31	52	87 084	12.1	87.9	23.9	10.9	0.0	8.7
Shelby	68	-5.0	157	1	39	449	2 594	34	11	25 784	66.6	33.4	23.9	4.6	0.0	719.9
Sumter	175	4.0	474	0	59	389	834	27	11	30 454	7.9	92.1	31.4	6.2	1.0	9.6
Talladega	110	5.3	209	1	60	297	1 555	42	40	77 134	14.9	85.1	31.4	8.4	9.5	77.2
Tallapoosa	78	-1.0	227	0	27	315	1 216	31	7	21 609	17.2	82.7	20.6	3.5	0.4	13.1
Tuscaloosa	100	4.0	196	1	43	294	1 569	29	21	40 254	30.1	69.9	25.1	6.7	1.5	35.3
Walker	55	9.9	117	D	27	262	1 999	26	55	116 522	1.5	98.5	23.6	11.7	0.0	906.7

Table B. States and Counties — Residential Construction, Wholesale and Retail Trade, and Real Estate

STATE County	Value of Residential Construction Authorized by Building Permits, 2000		Wholesale Trade, 1997				Retail Trade[1], 1997				Real Estate and Rental and Leasing, 1997			
	New Construction ($1,000)	Number of Housing Units	Number of Establishments	Number of Employees	Sales (mil dol)	Annual Payroll (mil dol)	Number of Establishments	Number of Employees	Sales (mil dol)	Annual Payroll (mil dol)	Number of Establishments	Number of Employees	Receipts (mil dol)	Annual Payroll (mil dol)
	133	134	135	136	137	138	139	140	141	142	143	144	145	146
UNITED STATES............	185 743 681	1 592 267	453 471	5 794 312	4 058 480.1	214 915.5	1 118 446	13 991 004	2 460 963.0	237 201.0	288 274	1 702 540	241 268.5	41 597.5
ALABAMA	1 718 032	17 406	6 315	79 229	40 986.3	2 394.7	20 163	231 665	36 623.3	3 381.7	3 664	20 629	2 130.3	396.7
Autauga.........................	9 855	181	29	81	39.7	2.1	161	2 200	367.3	32.1	21	D	D	D
Baldwin.........................	310 387	2 472	151	1 248	493.5	42.9	801	7 850	1 215.3	114.8	195	1 139	81.8	19.6
Barbour........................	4 236	67	32	228	79.6	4.2	129	1 076	163.2	15.0	14	29	2.1	0.4
Bibb..............................	310	4	15	82	53.2	1.9	60	527	77.2	6.7	9	31	2.5	0.2
Blount...........................	9 071	71	51	D	D	D	143	1 328	202.0	17.8	14	42	2.4	0.4
Bullock.........................	53	1	10	D	D	D	38	289	40.3	3.8	3	13	0.7	0.3
Butler...........................	4 196	104	23	148	58.1	3.6	122	1 023	144.2	13.9	16	35	2.0	0.4
Calhoun........................	43 645	336	130	1 688	890.9	47.0	578	6 747	982.0	92.5	73	298	24.5	4.4
Chambers......................	2 081	26	23	158	89.3	3.9	131	1 502	216.0	19.7	20	58	4.0	0.7
Cherokee.......................	1 358	14	22	161	65.2	4.0	88	678	123.1	9.0	10	31	2.8	0.3
Chilton..........................	4 480	45	29	193	64.2	3.8	180	1 510	246.6	21.8	21	37	3.1	0.4
Choctaw........................	75	1	19	191	108.0	5.7	76	386	69.1	6.1	9	34	1.0	0.2
Clarke..........................	1 568	11	23	125	34.3	2.4	188	1 669	233.2	21.4	30	83	5.0	1.1
Clay.............................	662	5	4	D	D	D	49	376	45.7	4.6	6	22	1.1	0.1
Cleburne.......................	2 290	27	13	D	D	D	47	262	54.0	3.6	1	D	D	D
Coffee...........................	10 054	108	47	259	141.0	5.8	223	2 405	411.0	34.6	23	111	7.0	1.4
Colbert.........................	9 854	144	109	1 173	404.3	30.4	273	2 915	527.5	45.0	42	140	14.5	1.8
Conecuh........................	387	5	14	102	57.4	2.3	49	275	39.1	3.8	6	10	1.1	0.1
Coosa...........................	0	0	6	D	D	D	28	130	15.3	1.8	5	8	0.7	0.1
Covington......................	2 269	21	49	585	223.1	12.2	239	1 974	287.9	27.8	23	70	4.8	0.7
Crenshaw......................	320	2	15	D	D	D	54	444	56.6	5.3	5	24	1.1	0.2
Cullman........................	5 242	66	95	637	256.1	16.2	360	3 334	650.9	52.1	51	205	20.1	3.6
Dale.............................	4 073	46	37	537	118.6	8.1	182	1 402	201.8	18.1	33	152	9.0	2.4
Dallas...........................	4 237	65	52	517	213.2	12.0	232	2 430	339.0	31.9	41	110	10.0	1.6
De Kalb.........................	7 590	77	62	602	309.6	12.4	269	2 576	343.0	31.3	42	144	10.2	2.1
Elmore..........................	21 527	254	47	309	116.6	7.1	199	1 780	296.8	23.7	35	D	D	D
Escambia.......................	1 583	16	53	532	117.8	11.6	210	2 097	295.1	28.0	15	85	5.2	1.4
Etowah.........................	22 940	263	135	D	D	D	452	4 935	737.8	65.9	68	273	23.9	4.4
Fayette..........................	720	6	11	D	D	D	82	709	111.1	9.4	6	34	0.7	0.2
Franklin........................	1 124	21	27	287	99.8	6.0	144	1 167	184.5	15.5	17	35	1.8	0.4
Geneva..........................	1 300	22	28	D	D	D	124	813	108.5	10.5	15	29	2.5	0.3
Greene..........................	402	7	10	D	D	D	34	232	31.3	2.7	4	6	0.6	0.1
Hale.............................	3 840	32	5	D	D	D	45	322	52.8	4.1	7	23	3.1	0.4
Henry...........................	2 346	17	15	323	68.0	6.4	81	524	84.6	7.9	8	D	D	D
Houston.........................	31 045	660	206	2 149	705.0	54.8	656	7 801	1 288.2	124.6	94	344	34.4	6.2
Jackson.........................	7 562	103	47	630	203.2	12.8	218	1 849	299.8	25.7	31	94	5.6	1.2
Jefferson.......................	381 361	3 057	1 480	23 438	14 471.2	824.1	3 020	44 165	7 636.8	705.6	650	5 558	811.3	132.8
Lamar...........................	160	2	10	D	D	D	69	445	65.0	5.4	8	15	0.7	0.1
Lauderdale.....................	15 880	180	100	1 959	368.9	45.4	462	5 546	780.8	74.9	79	294	27.4	5.7
Lawrence.......................	1 835	32	19	D	D	D	100	721	116.6	9.6	4	11	1.0	0.1
Lee..............................	59 568	574	86	727	308.0	18.6	425	5 437	774.4	73.7	84	464	35.0	6.9
Limestone......................	15 895	109	49	D	D	D	255	2 539	404.6	37.8	34	112	10.5	1.6
Lowndes........................	290	3	8	82	26.6	1.7	29	215	34.7	3.7	5	10	0.6	0.1
Macon...........................	2 930	70	8	D	D	D	66	437	64.1	6.0	9	D	D	D
Madison........................	51 866	1 101	471	D	D	D	1 224	17 275	2 610.7	253.6	332	1 623	167.7	30.1
Marengo........................	923	8	25	229	91.8	5.0	140	1 060	143.5	13.6	15	42	4.9	0.7
Marion..........................	4 789	65	44	387	243.7	10.8	138	1 063	167.6	14.2	15	48	2.5	0.4
Marshall........................	17 174	153	115	1 424	858.8	39.0	560	5 254	1 008.2	73.6	72	390	32.5	6.4
Mobile..........................	164 463	2 158	699	8 647	3 332.9	252.1	1 681	22 860	3 404.5	338.1	380	2 170	228.7	43.3
Monroe.........................	3 770	61	25	267	85.0	7.1	120	1 086	170.4	15.2	13	58	5.1	1.0
Montgomery	89 089	835	392	5 460	2 938.8	157.0	1 144	15 998	2 482.8	237.8	294	2 189	179.1	39.9
Morgan.........................	39 007	367	180	D	D	D	583	6 426	1 136.5	95.5	100	454	40.3	8.2
Perry............................	165	3	4	D	D	D	41	249	31.7	3.7	5	5	0.4	0.0
Pickens.........................	967	14	16	67	33.8	1.5	96	654	130.6	9.0	10	21	1.1	0.2
Pike.............................	3 222	25	44	472	177.5	9.6	145	1 559	223.2	19.9	22	87	8.8	1.0
Randolph.......................	218	2	14	74	30.6	0.9	89	722	89.4	9.3	10	33	2.9	0.4
Russell..........................	21 807	358	23	D	D	D	168	1 797	229.6	23.1	38	120	13.2	1.5
St. Clair........................	19 841	207	68	D	D	D	205	1 724	270.6	21.5	37	125	8.7	1.4
Shelby..........................	201 479	1 798	372	5 413	3 529.0	186.1	476	5 173	891.3	85.2	114	1 194	122.9	34.2
Sumter..........................	255	7	15	162	47.0	2.9	66	511	69.3	6.0	8	16	1.1	0.2
Talladega.......................	8 322	101	57	618	183.0	17.0	348	3 236	474.7	43.5	51	183	10.5	2.1
Tallapoosa.....................	5 820	87	37	D	D	D	196	1 800	239.0	24.1	32	127	9.1	2.4
Tuscaloosa.....................	71 427	709	185	1 981	858.1	61.1	790	10 852	1 543.2	151.0	161	1 079	82.6	13.7
Walker..........................	4 038	32	69	677	210.8	12.4	359	3 923	679.0	54.7	44	150	11.3	2.2

1. Establishments with payroll.

STATE County	Professional, Scientific, and Technical Services[1], 1997				Manufacturing, 1997				Accommodation and Foodservices, 1997			
	Number of Establish-ments	Number of Employees	Receipts (mil dol)	Annual Payroll (mil dol)	Number of Establish-ments	Number of Employees	Receipts (mil dol)	Annual Payroll (mil dol)	Number of Establish-ments	Number of Employees	Sales (mil dol)	Annual Payroll (mil dol)
	147	148	149	150	151	152	153	154	155	156	157	158
UNITED STATES............	615 305	5 212 745	579 542.1	225 376.0	363 753	16 888 016	3 842 061.4	572 101.1	545 060	9 451 056	350 389.1	97 003.9
ALABAMA	7 076	54 413	5 295.6	2 051.4	5 444	352 618	67 970.1	10 187.8	6 955	134 719	3 881.8	1 059.6
Autauga..........................	38	140	13.2	3.2	38	2 130	366.4	69.2	50	1 036	28.0	8.7
Baldwin..........................	225	981	69.6	29.2	138	5 150	809.5	127.1	303	6 337	224.3	61.0
Barbour..........................	40	110	9.8	2.5	41	3 680	689.7	93.0	42	600	17.3	4.3
Bibb...............................	8	32	2.1	0.8	27	1 218	244.3	23.9	12	D	D	D
Blount............................	34	137	8.3	3.6	60	2 742	403.5	49.5	42	461	13.7	3.3
Bullock...........................	3	D	D	D	6	D	D	D	12	D	D	D
Butler.............................	21	53	2.7	0.7	27	2 044	305.5	41.9	31	595	17.2	4.8
Calhoun..........................	149	702	45.2	13.2	149	10 841	1 504.5	257.8	185	4 262	114.4	31.3
Chambers.......................	23	80	6.5	1.6	40	5 612	765.8	147.2	44	671	18.3	4.6
Cherokee........................	15	34	2.3	0.6	21	1 194	121.2	25.4	26	251	6.9	1.8
Chilton...........................	25	58	3.2	0.8	54	1 488	162.1	30.3	50	744	18.4	5.0
Choctaw.........................	21	68	4.6	0.8	12	D	D	D	15	233	5.6	1.5
Clarke............................	29	96	7.4	1.4	32	2 888	540.1	82.7	41	665	17.2	4.2
Clay...............................	9	26	0.8	0.2	15	2 789	212.4	49.6	11	171	3.2	0.8
Cleburne........................	9	41	1.3	0.3	10	1 108	175.1	19.9	11	D	D	D
Coffee............................	49	286	17.4	5.3	39	4 725	679.8	89.8	63	1 092	26.9	7.2
Colbert...........................	77	223	17.4	5.3	118	5 581	1 491.6	205.8	103	1 766	46.3	12.3
Conecuh..........................	7	13	1.6	0.3	21	821	98.8	17.0	17	279	6.1	1.4
Coosa.............................	4	D	D	D	11	978	123.1	22.3	3	D	D	D
Covington........................	56	250	13.9	5.0	30	3 872	388.0	83.5	58	830	20.1	5.0
Crenshaw........................	8	31	1.8	0.9	15	830	26.1	9.6	11	138	3.8	0.6
Cullman..........................	82	286	17.4	5.0	123	5 994	964.1	147.4	94	1 980	52.8	14.4
Dale...............................	55	209	12.7	4.2	26	1 254	70.0	23.0	82	1 204	26.9	7.0
Dallas.............................	50	355	15.9	7.2	53	5 336	1 064.8	137.6	63	887	26.0	6.3
De Kalb..........................	65	338	25.4	11.6	216	11 774	1 286.0	237.3	100	1 419	40.8	10.7
Elmore............................	55	193	14.4	4.8	51	2 340	280.3	57.1	62	1 117	33.1	9.1
Escambia........................	41	122	9.6	2.6	53	3 145	689.5	79.5	56	905	24.0	6.0
Etowah...........................	122	621	36.6	13.7	136	8 775	1 577.0	277.0	169	3 223	85.0	23.6
Fayette...........................	9	20	4.1	0.3	33	2 617	372.0	55.9	18	D	D	D
Franklin..........................	22	66	3.8	0.9	64	5 348	645.8	97.0	44	529	12.7	3.3
Geneva...........................	20	41	3.3	0.9	26	2 123	171.1	34.1	31	343	6.1	1.7
Greene...........................	6	17	0.7	0.2	NA	NA	NA	NA	5	105	1.3	0.5
Hale...............................	10	24	1.1	0.2	16	1 443	210.0	28.4	12	D	D	D
Henry.............................	15	52	3.6	0.9	18	1 410	382.5	33.9	12	D	D	D
Houston..........................	169	1 171	71.3	26.7	125	9 233	1 457.7	231.9	198	3 945	121.6	31.4
Jackson..........................	49	213	17.5	5.8	83	6 557	1 253.5	182.4	70	848	25.9	6.9
Jefferson........................	1 631	14 700	1 504.0	603.6	817	35 972	7 475.6	1 168.7	1 197	25 250	796.1	225.2
Lamar.............................	12	40	1.7	0.6	22	2 589	313.4	61.3	17	106	3.5	0.9
Lauderdale......................	148	740	50.3	17.2	115	7 545	885.1	169.9	146	2 558	67.2	19.5
Lawrence........................	24	35	3.0	0.6	29	D	D	D	33	524	13.5	3.6
Lee................................	129	589	50.6	16.3	88	7 016	1 232.9	194.9	199	4 165	110.3	29.6
Limestone.......................	62	444	38.7	21.5	69	6 780	1 321.0	309.0	71	1 759	45.9	12.8
Lowndes.........................	7	38	3.9	1.2	10	D	D	D	4	D	D	D
Macon............................	19	65	5.8	2.7	NA	NA	NA	NA	21	393	9.9	2.3
Madison..........................	773	13 046	1 591.0	598.1	335	28 280	6 991.7	1 079.1	513	11 052	345.9	94.6
Marengo.........................	21	57	4.1	0.8	18	1 701	404.8	54.1	34	465	12.6	3.2
Marion............................	27	79	7.2	2.2	53	6 423	964.2	154.8	41	D	D	D
Marshall.........................	98	371	25.0	7.7	152	15 773	2 616.7	338.5	157	2 732	70.7	17.9
Mobile............................	769	5 949	518.6	205.9	445	22 130	5 494.8	835.3	649	12 767	370.1	102.2
Monroe...........................	17	42	3.3	0.7	28	4 748	1 094.0	165.0	34	591	15.2	3.5
Montgomery.....................	553	4 447	418.0	193.5	214	11 343	2 024.6	299.4	422	10 064	279.5	77.1
Morgan...........................	169	949	71.4	28.3	214	D	D	D	185	3 752	101.1	29.0
Perry..............................	7	17	1.2	0.2	8	926	96.9	21.7	11	178	3.0	0.8
Pickens..........................	12	44	2.9	0.6	21	1 051	113.7	18.3	14	D	D	D
Pike...............................	27	105	5.8	2.1	32	2 302	356.1	47.1	58	1 135	25.8	7.2
Randolph........................	16	36	2.2	0.9	28	2 322	218.5	39.0	27	335	8.0	2.2
Russell...........................	41	126	10.2	2.7	49	3 295	1 000.4	107.8	71	938	32.2	8.3
St. Clair.........................	68	181	11.5	4.0	85	3 180	480.2	85.1	78	1 170	31.3	8.4
Shelby............................	340	2 445	289.2	105.0	158	6 076	876.6	174.8	188	3 762	120.1	32.5
Sumter...........................	5	15	1.0	0.5	15	832	89.4	17.4	21	327	7.0	2.0
Talladega........................	69	283	20.3	5.5	100	7 160	1 420.6	201.1	94	1 504	37.9	10.0
Tallapoosa......................	35	129	14.8	3.8	53	5 868	1 074.8	112.8	51	788	21.4	5.7
Tuscaloosa......................	257	1 733	134.0	51.6	160	10 738	2 557.9	378.9	317	7 396	202.5	55.6
Walker............................	76	472	26.2	9.1	72	1 709	381.3	32.8	93	1 650	43.5	10.8

1. Firms subject to federal tax.

Table B. States and Counties — Health and Other Services and Federal Funds

STATE County	Health Care and Social Assistance[1], 1997				Other Services[1], 1997				Federal funds and grants, fiscal 2001[2] Expenditures (mil dol)			
										Direct payments for individuals[3]		
	Number of Establishments	Number of Employees	Receipts (mil dol)	Annual Payroll (mil dol)	Number of Establishments	Number of Employees	Receipts (mil dol)	Annual Payroll (mil dol)	Total	Social Security and government retirement	Medicare	Food stamps and Supplemental Security Income
	159	160	161	162	163	164	165	166	167	168	169	170
UNITED STATES...........	531 069	6 231 768	418 602.2	182 256.3	420 950	2 493 574	163 033.3	48 452.6	1 763 896.0	560 020.4	235 930.1	49 851.1
ALABAMA	7 121	104 492	7 116.7	3 104.8	6 329	37 061	2 241.7	659.3	31 700.5	10 668.1	4 203.9	1 156.7
Autauga........................	43	572	32.7	12.7	43	233	12.2	3.7	209.5	106.9	27.1	8.8
Baldwin........................	222	1 901	105.5	51.8	190	809	49.4	14.7	655.3	396.3	117.3	16.3
Barbour........................	42	446	19.7	7.7	26	93	6.1	1.3	156.3	57.1	32.2	11.3
Bibb.............................	16	140	7.0	2.7	20	194	13.5	3.6	95.3	44.1	21.8	5.4
Blount..........................	30	603	23.3	12.5	62	271	18.0	4.6	165.9	82.0	38.6	7.3
Bullock........................	12	280	12.0	5.3	5	12	0.7	0.1	69.5	23.3	12.7	6.5
Butler..........................	37	669	39.9	14.0	30	144	6.9	1.7	126.3	51.3	28.0	7.9
Calhoun........................	212	2 824	185.1	81.1	206	855	45.3	15.1	938.3	392.1	116.3	32.3
Chambers......................	53	511	29.3	12.0	39	208	9.2	2.3	181.4	90.4	41.8	11.0
Cherokee......................	16	110	9.3	4.3	23	61	5.3	1.0	117.4	53.7	21.7	4.4
Chilton.........................	32	524	29.8	9.9	44	130	9.6	2.2	165.2	78.7	40.1	8.8
Choctaw.......................	17	234	9.8	3.6	20	60	2.9	0.8	106.8	36.6	17.8	6.6
Clarke..........................	42	557	31.5	11.2	47	169	13.5	3.1	149.5	64.0	29.0	10.3
Clay.............................	17	204	8.6	3.7	14	49	2.2	0.6	73.9	37.2	15.9	2.3
Cleburne......................	7	45	2.5	1.0	9	49	3.1	1.0	65.1	33.9	11.2	3.0
Coffee..........................	67	415	26.5	10.2	70	324	14.7	3.9	552.7	147.0	41.7	8.9
Colbert.........................	101	1 401	99.5	44.4	103	587	33.5	9.3	417.2	170.3	58.0	9.2
Conecuh.......................	14	320	14.7	6.1	21	65	6.0	1.1	94.1	34.4	19.3	6.5
Coosa..........................	7	96	4.0	1.8	4	8	1.3	0.2	54.3	28.6	9.9	3.5
Covington.....................	57	1 086	64.5	24.8	56	271	12.7	3.4	251.5	102.0	49.0	11.0
Crenshaw.....................	12	191	8.9	3.5	13	34	2.3	0.5	87.3	34.4	16.8	4.7
Cullman........................	120	1 694	110.0	44.5	109	462	27.6	7.0	346.9	176.5	78.9	13.4
Dale.............................	60	649	28.4	12.7	63	226	8.9	2.4	504.6	146.1	46.8	13.6
Dallas..........................	80	1 394	90.6	35.1	62	281	17.2	4.4	366.6	110.8	56.5	37.5
De Kalb........................	72	986	42.2	19.9	62	213	11.8	2.9	265.6	127.2	54.9	11.3
Elmore.........................	74	829	37.2	15.2	70	235	12.7	3.3	282.6	167.3	45.9	10.6
Escambia	41	537	24.0	10.2	50	171	10.5	2.2	203.1	87.6	39.3	10.9
Etowah.........................	199	4 291	312.8	127.9	132	570	34.8	9.5	565.6	277.3	126.9	26.5
Fayette.........................	21	81	6.0	2.8	22	58	3.3	0.9	91.9	40.4	18.1	4.9
Franklin........................	63	929	50.4	20.0	47	152	8.9	2.6	183.3	75.6	37.6	7.2
Geneva.........................	25	194	9.0	3.3	27	59	4.1	0.8	177.3	73.3	30.5	7.7
Greene.........................	4	34	2.3	0.9	9	43	2.7	0.7	70.9	19.8	11.0	7.5
Hale.............................	10	256	8.6	4.0	11	30	2.9	0.5	104.0	39.2	19.6	6.9
Henry...........................	11	101	3.9	1.7	18	56	4.3	1.4	106.9	42.2	17.5	3.4
Houston........................	223	4 564	374.4	171.6	183	1 047	56.9	17.2	464.3	218.7	68.1	23.8
Jackson	75	743	36.1	15.2	49	157	10.8	2.6	486.9	130.2	50.0	11.6
Jefferson......................	1 364	24 333	1 989.4	863.5	1 185	9 418	641.5	191.2	4 314.9	1 628.1	793.7	177.6
Lamar...........................	13	282	11.1	5.4	13	43	3.5	0.6	83.9	39.8	17.5	3.5
Lauderdale....................	194	2 206	156.7	66.0	131	780	38.0	11.8	426.9	228.8	78.5	16.4
Lawrence......................	19	308	13.3	6.4	25	107	5.1	1.1	144.8	57.6	25.3	7.0
Lee..............................	133	1 478	104.9	51.3	125	661	35.6	10.2	399.8	177.5	53.7	18.8
Limestone.....................	76	797	43.0	15.9	84	347	16.2	5.0	269.7	131.3	42.4	11.3
Lowndes.......................	3	D	D	D	6	10	1.1	0.1	77.1	22.3	10.6	8.4
Macon	18	299	12.9	5.1	21	80	4.3	1.3	224.0	58.6	21.2	11.1
Madison........................	582	6 750	496.1	209.8	446	2 526	136.6	45.8	4 787.9	728.9	153.8	45.3
Marengo.......................	31	264	15.0	5.3	33	111	5.6	1.6	130.4	46.0	25.2	9.2
Marion..........................	59	498	27.8	12.7	36	106	7.6	1.7	174.3	70.8	33.9	5.5
Marshall........................	143	1 600	74.9	31.4	107	519	24.9	6.4	432.6	217.1	83.6	20.3
Mobile..........................	561	10 565	742.2	347.1	648	4 775	305.4	91.0	2 566.6	881.2	396.3	127.3
Monroe.........................	26	257	12.0	5.6	24	85	4.6	1.3	130.3	49.7	24.7	6.9
Montgomery...................	537	8 911	638.5	262.8	386	2 760	143.3	44.8	2 779.8	627.5	182.7	74.1
Morgan.........................	243	2 955	184.3	85.7	172	1 310	69.3	22.4	550.0	254.4	91.7	19.2
Perry............................	8	125	4.0	2.0	8	37	2.7	0.4	82.8	24.5	15.3	9.5
Pickens........................	20	219	9.5	4.3	15	44	3.1	0.8	132.7	50.1	27.0	10.1
Pike.............................	38	702	42.2	16.8	43	136	6.9	2.1	186.7	63.1	32.9	11.7
Randolph......................	34	353	14.1	6.4	23	66	3.6	0.8	129.3	52.8	22.7	5.5
Russell.........................	40	740	35.7	11.7	75	357	20.0	5.9	260.9	138.4	43.1	16.6
St. Clair........................	59	722	27.4	13.6	64	409	36.7	9.0	223.3	124.3	49.4	10.6
Shelby..........................	191	1 886	113.7	50.7	177	1 096	71.3	22.2	330.5	185.9	70.5	11.8
Sumter..........................	7	49	2.7	1.2	10	62	2.2	0.6	106.3	29.1	14.4	9.5
Talladega.......................	90	1 150	68.2	29.3	90	454	31.6	9.0	471.3	198.8	87.7	28.2
Tallapoosa.....................	66	869	43.7	22.0	42	170	12.1	2.9	208.0	102.0	43.3	12.4
Tuscaloosa....................	274	3 580	223.9	116.2	248	1 481	79.3	25.1	839.2	328.7	136.2	41.5
Walker..........................	118	1 521	81.2	36.1	84	598	36.9	10.0	444.9	210.6	95.2	19.5

1. Firms subject to federal tax.   2. October 1, 2000 to September 30, 2001.   3. State totals may include programs not allocated by county.

Table B. States and Counties — **Federal Funds and Local Government Finances**

STATE County	Federal funds and grants, fiscal 2001[1] (cont'd)							Local government finances, 1997				
	Expenditures (mil dol) (cont'd)							General revenue				
	Procurement contract awards			Grants[2]						Taxes		
											Per capita[3] (dollars)	
	Salaries and wages	Defense	Other	Medicaid and other health-related	Nutrition and family welfare	Education	Other	Total (mil dol)	Intergovern-mental (mil dol)	Total (mil dol)	Total	Property
	171	172	173	174	175	176	177	178	179	180	181	182
UNITED STATES............	186 908.6	148 691.1	96 693.4	167 777.5	51 863.9	30 675.7	84 179.7	X	X	X	X	X
ALABAMA	2 895.3	3 427.0	1 777.2	2 639.0	627.8	499.9	1 530.8	X	X	X	X	X
Autauga........................	5.6	1.4	1.1	19.0	1.8	2.2	5.3	58.0	33.7	13.8	333	84
Baldwin.........................	16.2	3.0	4.7	28.7	6.2	4.9	46.6	282.3	88.5	71.8	557	210
Barbour.........................	4.9	0.1	0.9	25.3	3.7	2.8	6.1	55.0	35.2	10.1	376	118
Bibb..............................	3.5	0.0	1.1	11.2	1.8	1.6	3.1	39.0	18.7	4.3	232	80
Blount...........................	5.3	0.0	1.4	18.8	2.1	2.1	4.6	67.7	35.3	10.4	231	150
Bullock..........................	2.2	0.0	0.4	18.1	2.6	1.1	0.7	18.0	13.4	3.0	262	117
Butler...........................	2.9	0.0	0.7	20.6	3.3	2.2	6.4	37.8	25.6	7.6	352	124
Calhoun.........................	107.5	156.5	11.6	55.3	9.2	8.7	27.4	301.6	98.5	51.1	436	125
Chambers......................	3.8	0.4	1.5	21.3	3.9	2.1	2.8	46.6	27.9	11.1	301	101
Cherokee.......................	2.8	12.9	0.6	10.3	1.4	1.4	2.8	30.7	18.7	7.3	336	156
Chilton..........................	4.2	0.4	4.9	18.8	2.3	2.2	2.7	45.7	27.5	11.7	321	164
Choctaw........................	2.0	5.2	8.4	17.7	2.8	1.3	7.8	25.4	16.3	4.1	256	158
Clarke..........................	5.2	3.4	0.6	23.9	4.4	2.2	4.6	50.5	27.0	11.9	416	132
Clay.............................	3.4	0.0	0.5	9.7	1.0	0.7	1.2	46.2	16.6	2.3	167	72
Cleburne.......................	3.3	0.0	0.7	8.3	0.8	0.7	1.2	22.7	15.0	2.8	200	129
Coffee..........................	14.0	262.4	2.0	22.4	3.1	3.5	26.0	69.3	40.2	19.5	464	161
Colbert.........................	84.1	1.3	30.8	26.8	3.9	4.8	9.0	146.0	52.8	23.5	443	142
Conecuh........................	2.2	0.1	0.5	17.2	2.0	1.1	5.4	17.2	12.0	3.2	229	159
Coosa..........................	1.8	1.0	0.4	6.3	1.1	0.7	0.3	13.5	9.9	2.3	201	109
Covington......................	7.8	7.5	1.5	27.5	2.6	3.8	27.1	61.5	36.4	13.5	361	116
Crenshaw.......................	3.1	0.0	0.6	17.4	1.5	1.0	3.6	17.9	12.5	2.3	170	92
Cullman........................	12.8	1.4	2.4	38.1	3.7	4.0	6.7	144.3	58.0	24.8	334	102
Dale.............................	214.8	5.2	29.3	21.7	3.5	3.3	4.8	75.6	44.3	18.5	376	134
Dallas...........................	8.8	28.4	16.9	57.6	12.3	8.0	9.2	83.2	49.4	25.8	548	195
De Kalb........................	9.2	2.9	1.8	40.3	6.1	3.2	1.0	84.9	47.6	18.5	321	104
Elmore..........................	8.5	1.1	1.7	22.0	5.2	2.8	11.0	87.0	49.7	13.9	231	85
Escambia	4.6	1.0	1.0	21.3	4.0	4.0	18.1	79.3	32.9	11.8	323	118
Etowah	16.6	0.5	17.3	63.4	7.1	8.4	6.5	184.1	91.8	58.4	560	152
Fayette.........................	3.0	4.0	0.6	12.6	1.2	1.8	2.5	29.0	15.6	3.5	194	75
Franklin........................	4.6	0.1	0.9	25.2	2.2	2.1	23.7	54.7	37.7	7.8	263	136
Geneva..........................	4.9	0.1	0.9	20.1	2.1	1.3	15.3	34.7	21.2	5.8	232	94
Greene..........................	1.9	0.0	0.4	21.3	3.2	1.3	1.4	21.0	13.2	2.5	250	117
Hale.............................	3.4	0.0	0.6	19.3	3.7	1.7	5.2	27.2	19.4	2.6	159	77
Henry...........................	2.9	1.5	1.4	13.6	2.0	1.0	5.1	31.3	17.3	3.9	250	101
Houston........................	17.0	29.2	3.3	45.4	9.0	7.1	11.6	312.7	73.7	54.4	639	210
Jackson.........................	35.4	1.5	211.3	37.0	3.4	2.6	-6.7	126.1	47.7	17.7	348	120
Jefferson.......................	463.9	101.8	168.4	518.8	71.6	45.1	206.4	1 671.5	584.3	730.5	1 109	421
Lamar...........................	3.5	0.1	1.0	13.1	1.0	1.1	1.6	30.3	16.4	5.0	318	116
Lauderdale	17.0	0.2	3.5	38.4	5.8	3.8	11.0	261.0	65.4	59.4	705	436
Lawrence.......................	4.8	0.2	0.8	23.3	2.5	2.3	7.8	55.9	31.8	5.5	164	79
Lee..............................	23.2	3.4	3.4	35.5	8.7	6.6	49.7	272.4	66.3	53.8	546	170
Limestone......................	8.0	0.3	5.2	26.9	2.7	3.3	7.9	106.2	45.1	14.3	236	70
Lowndes........................	2.0	3.1	0.3	15.6	4.5	1.8	4.3	22.1	17.9	2.5	193	87
Macon	46.9	1.0	5.8	36.5	6.8	6.2	18.5	40.5	26.1	10.8	464	161
Madison.........................	737.5	2 285.8	586.3	75.8	13.3	20.7	94.7	501.6	180.1	183.1	672	261
Marengo........................	4.4	0.4	0.7	25.6	4.4	1.9	5.8	61.0	28.2	9.9	421	206
Marion..........................	5.1	0.0	0.9	19.5	1.6	1.5	31.0	45.9	27.8	9.7	314	96
Marshall........................	17.5	2.4	23.5	45.0	4.1	3.6	1.8	132.7	67.7	33.7	427	119
Mobile..........................	154.3	104.8	480.6	184.9	53.0	31.9	56.0	758.5	332.6	278.8	700	208
Monroe.........................	3.3	0.3	0.7	22.4	3.1	3.4	3.9	41.6	29.2	6.9	284	132
Montgomery	503.9	287.9	44.8	206.9	196.3	160.7	379.7	379.7	177.8	151.6	697	169
Morgan.........................	89.8	6.1	5.1	43.7	7.8	5.6	14.2	286.2	87.3	56.4	521	231
Perry	2.7	0.0	0.3	17.1	4.1	1.7	1.8	23.1	16.3	2.7	215	104
Pickens.........................	3.5	0.0	0.7	25.1	4.0	1.7	6.4	41.2	23.1	4.9	235	108
Pike.............................	6.4	5.4	0.9	28.4	5.8	2.6	6.9	43.8	24.6	11.2	393	115
Randolph.......................	2.8	10.6	5.2	16.9	1.8	1.1	4.5	32.5	17.8	6.6	331	208
Russell	5.9	0.1	1.3	32.6	5.8	3.0	2.9	107.8	51.5	24.0	473	160
St. Clair	7.3	0.6	2.6	17.1	4.4	2.9	2.2	78.5	45.4	21.0	346	121
Shelby..........................	18.7	1.4	3.8	17.4	3.9	4.8	7.1	190.1	76.1	79.1	584	238
Sumter..........................	2.9	0.0	1.4	20.2	5.2	2.3	13.1	28.5	18.3	6.7	420	217
Talladega.......................	25.8	11.3	4.8	51.7	13.1	7.1	30.9	116.1	69.1	25.1	326	115
Tallapoosa......................	5.8	0.0	1.2	23.0	3.6	3.3	8.0	74.7	42.5	16.0	399	155
Tuscaloosa.....................	70.1	14.3	53.6	78.8	18.0	15.9	40.6	476.7	141.7	64.7	402	206
Walker..........................	12.7	0.4	2.8	39.4	6.2	5.3	42.0	100.8	59.9	26.4	373	111

1. October 1, 2000 to September 30, 2001.　　2. State totals may include programs not allocated by county.　　3. Based on the resident population estimated as of July 1 of the year shown.

STATE County	Total (mil dol) 183	Per capita[1] (dollars) 184	Education 185	Health and hospitals 186	Police protection 187	Public welfare 188	Highways 189	Total (mil dol) 190	Per capita[1] (dollars) 191	Federal civilian 192	Federal military 193	State and local 194	Democratic 195	Republican 196	All other 197
UNITED STATES	X	X	X	X	X	X	X	X	X	2 785 000	2 074 000	17 397 000	48.4	47.9	3.7
ALABAMA	X	X	X	X	X	X	X	X	X	52 409	39 930	293 485	41.6	56.5	1.9
Autauga	75.3	1 822	73.0	0.2	4.8	0.4	4.7	67.7	1 638	86	260	1 816	28.7	69.7	1.6
Baldwin	310.0	2 406	37.2	23.2	4.1	0.1	8.3	265.3	2 059	287	831	8 025	24.8	72.4	2.9
Barbour	52.7	1 967	49.7	12.9	5.8	0.3	6.8	34.0	1 270	61	170	2 000	53.4	45.2	1.4
Bibb	38.3	2 062	46.2	32.0	3.4	0.3	4.8	14.9	801	79	118	1 087	38.2	60.2	1.7
Blount	67.3	1 494	56.6	17.8	3.3	0.4	7.2	42.9	951	95	286	1 623	27.7	70.5	1.8
Bullock	15.5	1 376	63.8	11.8	1.2	0.8	9.0	12.5	1 112	38	68	720	69.2	29.2	1.5
Butler	38.2	1 762	55.6	12.0	4.6	0.0	8.4	9.8	450	47	130	1 063	46.2	52.9	0.9
Calhoun	295.2	2 521	33.0	36.3	3.6	0.0	3.0	131.3	1 121	4 403	2 374	7 511	40.6	57.3	2.1
Chambers	58.6	1 592	56.4	0.8	6.5	0.2	7.2	34.7	944	61	220	1 517	47.5	51.0	1.5
Cherokee	31.0	1 434	66.3	0.4	3.4	0.1	10.2	3.8	177	50	132	1 068	44.7	53.1	2.2
Chilton	53.2	1 464	60.3	1.5	4.9	0.1	15.4	24.8	682	66	227	1 513	31.8	66.7	1.5
Choctaw	26.1	1 642	53.7	3.7	4.0	0.0	13.7	23.4	1 474	33	94	604	50.3	48.8	0.9
Clarke	48.8	1 711	61.1	8.5	5.9	0.1	5.3	25.0	876	95	174	1 851	43.5	55.7	0.8
Clay	36.6	2 649	38.9	36.0	5.1	0.1	5.9	10.1	727	47	85	1 026	34.8	63.2	2.0
Cleburne	21.7	1 543	53.7	9.5	2.0	0.1	12.2	3.7	264	81	87	717	32.7	65.5	1.9
Coffee	66.4	1 582	63.8	0.6	6.0	0.7	7.3	20.2	481	151	254	2 247	33.8	64.4	1.8
Colbert	152.8	2 881	34.0	39.1	3.5	0.1	4.5	84.6	1 595	1 351	317	4 257	49.0	48.8	2.2
Conecuh	17.1	1 215	67.4	0.2	6.3	0.0	8.9	10.8	766	46	88	827	50.1	48.6	1.2
Coosa	12.9	1 116	71.9	0.0	3.3	0.3	9.4	0.4	37	26	71	423	46.1	52.2	1.8
Covington	64.0	1 712	53.5	0.4	5.9	0.2	11.6	34.5	925	148	228	2 111	32.6	65.8	1.6
Crenshaw	19.7	1 444	60.3	1.0	4.8	0.1	12.4	5.2	380	46	82	586	40.3	58.2	1.4
Cullman	135.2	1 821	47.0	26.8	4.4	0.1	8.0	138.1	1 860	253	457	3 579	33.0	64.9	2.1
Dale	78.7	1 603	53.0	4.1	6.6	0.2	7.5	40.9	832	2 941	4 432	2 803	31.0	67.0	1.9
Dallas	75.5	1 601	64.5	0.4	4.9	0.1	3.6	28.0	595	166	282	2 942	59.4	39.9	0.7
De Kalb	85.1	1 473	61.4	2.7	5.5	0.6	6.7	81.9	1 418	168	356	2 614	34.8	63.2	2.0
Elmore	89.2	1 481	55.3	16.2	4.7	0.7	7.2	21.3	354	135	383	3 360	27.9	70.5	1.6
Escambia	75.4	2 065	47.6	27.3	4.2	0.5	6.1	20.0	547	75	226	2 766	38.8	59.8	1.4
Etowah	177.1	1 698	49.6	1.9	7.7	0.3	6.0	79.1	758	347	627	5 013	44.3	53.6	2.1
Fayette	31.5	1 732	52.8	17.0	3.2	0.4	3.7	18.6	1 022	51	109	1 260	39.2	58.7	2.1
Franklin	45.3	1 531	64.2	0.1	4.3	0.2	11.1	22.2	749	94	179	2 126	43.2	55.1	1.7
Geneva	38.1	1 534	60.1	7.2	4.4	0.2	8.7	11.4	458	73	151	1 402	29.0	68.9	2.1
Greene	19.7	1 987	58.6	18.0	2.4	0.4	4.7	5.7	573	36	59	710	79.7	19.3	1.0
Hale	28.3	1 724	65.0	12.3	3.2	0.1	9.9	1.8	108	61	102	913	60.2	38.6	1.2
Henry	32.8	2 097	50.4	0.1	4.9	13.5	7.6	10.6	677	69	95	733	40.1	58.5	1.4
Houston	316.3	3 715	24.9	45.5	3.1	0.3	3.1	317.2	3 725	341	522	6 747	29.4	69.1	1.5
Jackson	122.7	2 417	40.9	33.3	4.2	0.5	5.0	88.3	1 739	601	311	3 254	50.6	47.3	2.0
Jefferson	1 657.6	2 517	36.9	8.9	6.7	1.2	4.4	2 297.0	3 487	9 107	4 400	49 732	47.4	50.6	2.0
Lamar	29.0	1 842	47.9	14.8	3.8	0.1	9.2	17.2	1 090	43	97	604	36.6	61.7	1.7
Lauderdale	243.7	2 893	36.7	36.1	3.1	0.0	3.8	90.7	1 076	328	516	6 405	43.2	54.4	2.4
Lawrence	56.8	1 702	57.1	0.6	3.6	0.4	5.9	188.8	5 656	92	204	1 396	51.7	46.5	1.8
Lee	269.9	2 741	40.6	31.9	3.5	0.0	3.9	317.7	3 225	345	704	12 885	38.1	58.6	3.3
Limestone	117.9	1 943	48.4	28.7	3.9	0.4	4.5	85.6	1 409	1 230	381	4 281	38.0	60.1	1.9
Lowndes	20.2	1 571	76.9	0.2	5.0	0.1	6.2	4.5	348	25	79	705	73.0	26.2	0.8
Macon	39.8	1 706	55.9	0.8	6.6	0.4	9.6	26.7	1 144	1 181	155	1 193	86.8	12.4	0.8
Madison	575.0	2 112	41.6	1.9	5.3	0.1	5.0	799.8	2 937	14 016	3 088	20 038	42.5	54.8	2.6
Marengo	71.8	3 055	38.0	36.2	2.6	0.3	4.5	27.0	1 147	73	156	1 727	50.4	48.8	0.8
Marion	42.8	1 390	64.1	0.2	4.1	0.2	6.5	26.7	867	90	184	1 503	39.1	58.8	2.1
Marshall	124.8	1 581	56.8	3.8	6.0	0.2	5.8	110.0	1 395	288	486	5 006	37.1	61.0	1.9
Mobile	725.5	1 822	44.1	4.7	6.0	0.3	6.7	958.2	2 406	2 473	3 184	25 080	42.0	55.9	2.1
Monroe	46.1	1 907	52.6	10.4	4.7	0.0	14.3	18.8	778	59	145	1 518	41.8	57.6	0.6
Montgomery	367.4	1 689	48.2	2.1	8.5	0.2	8.5	365.4	1 679	6 825	6 243	24 281	50.3	48.3	1.4
Morgan	297.4	2 746	36.8	34.7	4.1	0.1	2.9	240.5	2 221	301	663	6 665	37.6	60.4	2.0
Perry	22.7	1 794	58.5	19.8	2.8	0.1	7.7	5.8	461	30	87	593	69.5	29.9	0.6
Pickens	41.0	1 955	51.5	2.6	3.1	0.0	9.4	83.1	3 963	53	127	941	48.5	50.4	1.1
Pike	51.9	1 813	52.5	2.0	5.2	0.2	10.0	37.8	1 323	68	177	2 454	41.3	57.5	1.2
Randolph	33.2	1 668	56.4	13.2	4.7	0.1	7.4	13.1	659	52	122	1 210	39.1	58.9	2.0
Russell	97.2	1 917	46.0	15.7	4.8	0.1	4.4	47.5	936	102	302	2 441	56.8	41.9	1.2
St. Clair	76.9	1 264	69.8	0.4	5.0	0.0	5.7	36.2	595	107	385	2 244	26.9	71.1	2.0
Shelby	175.6	1 296	55.9	2.4	7.0	0.3	6.2	147.5	1 089	268	884	5 045	21.2	76.7	2.1
Sumter	28.3	1 768	53.7	0.9	6.4	0.5	10.3	16.3	1 018	40	94	1 437	72.5	26.8	0.7
Talladega	122.2	1 590	59.2	4.0	4.4	0.1	5.7	87.5	1 138	512	468	4 612	44.3	54.2	1.5
Tallapoosa	75.1	1 871	51.3	13.4	5.1	0.2	4.3	83.0	2 068	100	243	1 944	38.0	60.3	1.6
Tuscaloosa	431.2	2 682	35.6	32.7	3.9	0.0	4.1	333.6	2 075	1 454	1 001	18 678	40.9	56.6	2.5
Walker	104.2	1 473	58.7	0.3	4.8	0.0	7.6	62.4	882	203	431	3 235	45.3	52.6	2.1

1. Based on the resident population estimated as of July 1 of the year shown.   2. Data subject to copyright.

Table B. States and Counties — **Land Area and Population**

STATE/ County code	MSA/ PMSA/ NECMA code[1]	County Type[2]	STATE County	Land area,[3] (sq km) 2000	Total persons	Rank	Per square kilometer	White	Black	Am. Indian, Alaska Native	Asian and Pacific Islander	Percent Hispanic[4]	Under 5 years	5 to 17 years	18 to 24 years	25 to 34 years	35 to 44 years	45 to 54 years
				1	2	3	4	5	6	7	8	9	10	11	12	13	14	15
			ALABAMA—Cont'd															
01 129	...	8	Washington	2 799	18 097	1 893	6.5	65.7	27.1	7.7	0.2	0.9	7.2	21.4	8.6	12.8	14.6	13.3
01 131	...	9	Wilcox	2 302	13 183	2 213	5.7	27.6	72.0	0.3	0.2	0.7	8.1	22.6	9.1	11.9	13.6	12.2
01 133	...	6	Winston	1 591	24 843	1 563	15.6	98.1	0.4	1.0	0.3	1.5	6.2	17.5	7.9	13.6	15.1	14.0
02 000	...	X	ALASKA	1 481 347	626 932	X	0.4	74.0	4.3	19.0	6.1	4.1	7.6	22.8	9.1	14.3	18.2	15.1
02 013	...	NA	Aleutians East Borough	18 099	2 697	3 014	0.1	26.4	1.7	38.6	28.2	12.6	4.3	12.5	10.2	17.4	24.8	19.9
02 016	...	NA	Aleutians West Census Area	11 388	5 465	2 819	0.5	42.8	3.3	22.5	27.1	10.5	4.7	12.5	7.8	22.0	25.6	18.7
02 020	0380	3	Anchorage	4 396	260 283	212	59.2	77.2	7.2	10.4	8.5	5.7	7.7	21.5	9.6	15.4	18.5	14.9
02 050	...	7	Bethel	105 240	16 006	2 021	0.2	15.8	0.7	85.5	1.5	0.9	10.0	29.8	9.7	13.5	15.4	10.6
02 060	...	NA	Bristol Bay	1 308	1 258	3 102	1.0	54.3	0.6	45.1	2.0	0.6	7.1	24.2	5.9	11.4	23.4	17.1
02 068	...	NA	Denali Borough	33 021	1 893	3 074	0.1	90.9	1.5	8.6	2.6	2.5	5.2	18.6	6.7	14.3	22.5	20.7
02 070	...	NA	Dillingham	48 367	4 922	2 854	0.1	27.2	0.5	76.2	1.5	2.3	9.7	28.5	7.7	12.1	16.8	12.7
02 090	...	5	Fairbanks North Star	19 078	82 840	627	4.3	82.6	7.0	9.9	3.8	4.2	8.1	22.0	12.2	16.3	17.0	13.8
02 100	...	9	Haines	6 070	2 392	3 031	0.4	86.9	0.3	15.6	1.3	1.4	5.4	20.3	5.3	10.1	18.1	20.5
02 110	...	5	Juneau	7 036	30 711	1 380	4.4	80.5	1.4	16.6	7.4	3.4	6.5	20.9	8.1	14.0	18.8	18.0
02 122	...	5	Kenai Peninsula	41 474	49 691	922	1.2	89.8	0.8	10.2	2.0	2.2	6.6	23.3	6.9	11.4	18.3	17.6
02 130	...	7	Ketchikan Gateway	3 194	14 070	2 158	4.4	79.2	0.8	19.1	5.7	2.6	6.9	21.3	7.5	12.7	18.7	16.3
02 150	...	7	Kodiak Island	16 990	13 913	2 167	0.8	64.0	1.1	17.6	19.0	6.1	8.9	23.5	8.3	14.8	19.1	14.3
02 164	...	NA	Lake and Peninsula Borough	61 595	1 823	3 078	0.0	25.3	0.2	79.7	0.8	1.2	8.0	29.8	8.5	9.6	18.4	12.5
02 170	...	6	Matanuska-Susitna	63 925	59 322	810	0.9	91.9	1.1	8.6	1.8	2.5	7.0	25.2	7.4	11.7	19.4	16.0
02 180	...	7	Nome	59 572	9 196	2 514	0.2	23.2	0.6	79.1	1.1	1.0	8.6	28.6	9.3	13.3	15.7	12.3
02 185	...	NA	North Slope	230 035	7 385	2 649	0.0	22.4	1.2	73.8	8.5	2.4	9.5	28.6	9.5	13.4	16.7	12.1
02 188	...	NA	Northwest Arctic Borough	92 976	7 208	2 666	0.1	15.6	0.5	85.8	1.4	0.8	10.7	30.8	10.0	14.0	14.1	10.5
02 201	...	NA	Prince of Wales-Outer Ketchikan	19 193	6 146	2 768	0.3	59.6	0.4	45.3	1.5	1.7	7.4	23.6	7.5	11.9	18.1	16.6
02 220	...	NA	Sitka	7 444	8 835	2 541	1.2	75.0	0.8	24.7	5.9	3.3	6.4	20.8	9.4	13.1	17.8	15.5
02 232	...	NA	Skagway-Hoonah-Angoon	20 452	3 436	2 960	0.2	62.7	0.4	39.5	1.5	2.8	5.2	21.6	7.1	11.6	17.9	18.9
02 240	...	NA	Southeast Fairbanks	64 270	6 174	2 765	0.1	83.7	2.3	15.9	1.5	2.7	7.1	25.7	7.6	11.1	16.7	16.0
02 261	...	7	Valdez-Cordova	88 886	10 195	2 429	0.1	81.1	0.5	17.3	5.2	2.8	6.7	23.0	7.0	11.5	19.4	18.5
02 270	...	9	Wade Hampton	44 531	7 028	2 681	0.2	7.0	0.2	94.9	0.3	0.3	10.6	36.0	9.7	13.3	12.4	8.2
02 280	...	7	Wrangell-Petersburg	15 112	6 684	2 719	0.4	80.0	0.6	22.6	3.7	2.0	6.7	23.0	5.7	11.5	17.5	17.0
02 282	...	NA	Yakutat Borough	19 815	808	3 124	0.0	56.7	0.2	46.8	5.9	0.7	4.8	23.3	5.3	11.6	20.9	20.2
02 290	...	NA	Yukon-Koyukuk	377 878	6 551	2 734	0.0	27.9	0.3	74.4	0.8	1.2	7.1	27.9	8.7	10.7	16.2	14.5
04 000	...	X	ARIZONA	294 312	5 130 632	X	17.4	77.9	3.6	5.7	2.6	25.3	7.5	19.2	10.0	14.5	15.0	12.2
04 001	...	5	Apache	29 021	69 423	714	2.4	20.6	0.4	77.8	0.3	4.5	9.1	29.4	9.4	11.5	13.6	11.0
04 003	...	4	Cochise	15 979	117 755	459	7.4	79.8	5.3	2.1	3.0	30.7	6.8	19.6	9.3	11.9	14.1	13.1
04 005	2620	5	Coconino	48 219	116 320	463	2.4	65.1	1.4	29.7	1.3	10.9	7.3	21.5	14.4	14.0	15.2	13.4
04 007	...	4	Gila	12 348	51 335	901	4.2	79.4	0.5	15.8	0.7	16.6	6.1	19.0	6.4	9.2	13.1	13.7
04 009	...	7	Graham	11 990	33 489	1 300	2.8	68.9	2.1	15.6	0.9	27.0	7.8	22.3	12.0	13.5	13.8	10.9
04 011	...	7	Greenlee	4 784	8 547	2 564	1.8	77.4	0.6	2.7	0.4	43.1	8.3	23.4	7.5	12.5	15.7	14.1
04 012	...	7	La Paz	11 655	19 715	1 810	1.7	76.2	1.1	14.2	0.7	22.4	4.9	16.2	6.1	8.6	11.8	12.2
04 013	6200	0	Maricopa	23 836	3 072 149	4	128.9	79.8	4.3	2.5	3.0	24.8	7.9	19.1	10.2	15.9	15.5	11.9
04 015	4120	2	Mohave	34 477	155 032	344	4.5	92.0	0.7	3.3	1.3	11.1	6.0	17.1	6.5	10.0	13.3	13.1
04 017	...	5	Navajo	25 779	97 470	532	3.8	47.6	1.1	48.8	0.6	8.2	8.6	26.9	8.8	11.4	13.9	11.7
04 019	8520	2	Pima	23 792	843 746	53	35.5	77.8	3.7	4.0	2.9	29.3	6.6	18.0	10.9	13.5	14.9	13.1
04 021	6200	1	Pinal	13 907	179 727	307	12.9	72.6	3.1	8.7	1.1	29.9	6.7	18.4	8.7	13.1	14.1	11.9
04 023	...	6	Santa Cruz	3 205	38 381	1 154	12.0	78.4	0.5	1.0	0.8	80.8	8.7	25.0	8.2	12.3	14.4	12.3
04 025	...	4	Yavapai	21 039	167 517	322	8.0	93.7	0.6	2.5	1.0	9.8	5.2	16.0	7.1	9.2	13.2	14.5
04 027	9360	3	Yuma	14 281	160 026	333	11.2	71.1	2.6	2.2	1.7	50.5	7.9	21.0	10.0	12.5	13.1	9.9
05 000	...	X	ARKANSAS	134 856	2 673 400	X	19.8	81.2	16.0	1.4	1.1	3.2	6.8	18.7	9.8	13.2	14.9	13.1
05 001	...	7	Arkansas	2 560	20 749	1 755	8.1	75.7	23.6	0.6	0.6	0.8	6.6	18.3	8.3	11.8	14.5	14.3
05 003	...	7	Ashley	2 386	24 209	1 588	10.1	70.6	27.3	0.6	0.4	3.2	6.7	20.1	8.3	13.1	14.1	13.5
05 005	...	7	Baxter	1 436	38 386	1 153	26.7	98.8	0.2	1.2	0.6	1.0	4.5	14.5	5.8	8.8	12.2	13.2
05 007	2580	3	Benton	2 191	153 406	346	70.0	92.6	0.5	2.7	1.4	8.8	7.6	19.0	8.6	14.3	15.1	11.9
05 009	...	7	Boone	1 531	33 948	1 281	22.2	98.5	0.2	1.3	0.5	1.1	6.3	17.7	8.2	12.3	14.2	13.5
05 011	...	7	Bradley	1 685	12 600	2 255	7.5	64.0	28.9	0.5	0.2	8.3	5.9	17.6	9.7	12.4	14.0	12.5
05 013	...	9	Calhoun	1 627	5 744	2 806	3.5	75.2	23.8	0.8	0.3	1.5	5.3	19.3	7.0	11.7	16.5	13.1
05 015	...	7	Carroll	1 632	25 357	1 550	15.5	95.2	0.2	1.9	0.6	9.7	6.4	17.5	8.1	11.5	14.6	14.5
05 017	...	7	Chicot	1 668	14 117	2 153	8.5	43.8	54.3	0.5	0.8	2.9	6.9	20.5	8.6	12.5	13.8	12.4
05 019	...	7	Clark	2 241	23 546	1 614	10.5	75.3	22.6	1.0	0.9	2.4	6.0	15.7	20.0	11.6	12.2	11.3
05 021	...	7	Clay	1 656	17 609	1 922	10.6	98.9	0.2	1.3	0.2	0.8	6.0	17.1	7.7	11.7	13.6	12.8
05 023	...	6	Cleburne	1 432	24 046	1 592	16.8	99.1	0.2	1.1	0.3	1.2	5.1	16.2	6.6	10.1	14.0	13.0
05 025	...	8	Cleveland	1 548	8 571	2 561	5.5	85.6	13.4	0.7	0.5	1.6	6.5	19.6	7.9	12.9	14.8	13.4
05 027	...	7	Columbia	1 984	25 603	1 531	12.9	62.6	36.4	0.7	0.6	1.1	6.1	19.0	12.3	11.7	13.6	11.9

1. MSA = Metropolitan Statistical Area. PMSA = Primary MSA. NECMA = New England County Metropolitan Area. See Appendix A for explanation of these concepts. See Appendix B for list of metropolitan areas identified by type, with component counties.   2. County typology code from the Economic Research Service of USDA. See Appendix A for definition.   3. Dry land or land partially or temporarily covered by water.   4. Hispanic persons may be of any race.

Table B. States and Counties — Population and Households

STATE County	55 to 64 years	65 to 74 years	75 years and over	Percent female	2001	1990	1990–2000	2000–2001	Births	Deaths	Net migration	Number	Percent change, 1990–2000	Persons per household	Female family householder[1]	One person
	16	17	18	19	20	21	22	23	24	25	26	27	28	29	30	31
ALABAMA—Cont'd																
Washington	9.6	7.0	5.4	51.0	17 868	16 694	8.4	-1.3	316	208	-338	6 705	17.4	2.69	12.5	22.8
Wilcox	8.8	7.1	6.6	53.4	13 130	13 568	-2.8	-0.4	332	205	-178	4 776	8.2	2.70	26.5	27.5
Winston	11.5	8.0	6.2	51.0	24 654	22 053	12.7	-0.8	356	340	-203	10 107	18.3	2.43	9.1	25.6
ALASKA	7.1	3.6	2.1	48.3	634 892	550 043	14.0	1.3	12 624	3 628	-993	221 600	17.3	2.74	10.8	23.5
Aleutians East Borough	8.2	1.9	0.7	35.1	2 597	2 464	9.5	-3.7	28	10	-123	526	-1.3	2.69	14.4	27.4
Aleutians West Census Area	6.4	1.7	0.5	35.7	5 392	9 478	-42.3	-1.3	42	16	-85	1 270	-31.2	2.52	7.6	32.0
Anchorage	7.0	3.4	2.1	49.4	264 937	226 338	15.0	1.8	5 283	1 370	852	94 822	14.7	2.67	11.5	23.4
Bethel	5.8	3.2	2.0	46.9	16 280	13 660	17.2	1.7	596	110	-211	4 226	17.2	3.73	15.2	19.9
Bristol Bay	7.1	2.8	1.0	45.5	1 196	1 410	-10.8	-4.9	25	5	-83	490	20.4	2.57	6.1	31.2
Denali Borough	9.0	2.2	0.9	41.8	1 914	1 682	12.5	1.1	21	6	7	785	NA	2.28	4.5	35.0
Dillingham	6.8	3.7	2.0	47.8	4 938	4 010	22.7	0.3	152	38	-101	1 529	25.8	3.20	15.0	23.3
Fairbanks North Star	6.0	2.9	1.7	47.8	83 694	77 720	6.6	1.0	1 854	429	-522	29 777	11.6	2.68	9.3	23.6
Haines	9.9	6.2	4.3	49.4	2 333	2 117	13.0	-2.5	32	16	-78	991	25.3	2.41	7.3	27.1
Juneau	7.7	3.5	2.6	49.6	30 558	26 752	14.8	-0.5	483	145	-498	11 543	16.6	2.60	10.5	24.4
Kenai Peninsula	8.7	4.8	2.6	48.0	50 556	40 802	21.8	1.7	786	331	415	18 438	29.4	2.62	9.0	24.7
Ketchikan Gateway	8.7	4.5	3.3	48.9	13 782	13 828	1.8	-2.0	240	135	-402	5 399	7.3	2.56	11.3	26.1
Kodiak Island	6.2	3.2	1.6	47.1	13 915	13 309	4.5	0.0	342	72	-272	4 424	8.4	3.07	8.8	19.9
Lake and Peninsula Borough	7.7	3.6	1.9	46.8	1 675	1 666	9.4	-8.1	32	12	-175	588	15.5	3.10	9.7	24.7
Matanuska-Susitna	7.4	4.0	1.9	48.0	62 426	39 683	49.5	5.2	796	329	2 577	20 556	53.5	2.84	9.1	20.3
Nome	6.3	3.5	2.4	46.0	9 240	8 288	11.0	0.5	300	79	-177	2 693	13.6	3.33	15.3	23.2
North Slope	5.9	2.7	1.4	47.1	7 264	5 986	23.4	-1.6	183	54	-256	2 109	26.1	3.45	18.3	21.4
Northwest Arctic Borough	5.0	3.4	1.6	46.6	7 344	6 106	18.0	1.9	265	54	-73	1 780	16.6	3.87	19.7	16.6
Prince of Wales-Outer Ketchikan	9.2	4.0	1.7	45.5	5 864	6 278	-2.1	-4.6	101	25	-368	2 262	9.8	2.68	10.0	26.0
Sitka	8.7	5.1	3.3	49.0	8 716	8 588	2.9	-1.3	142	63	-201	3 278	11.5	2.61	10.3	24.5
Skagway-Hoonah-Angoon	10.4	4.5	2.8	46.2	3 449	3 679	-6.6	0.4	43	30	1	1 369	NA	2.50	8.4	30.1
Southeast Fairbanks	9.8	4.3	1.7	48.3	5 702	5 925	4.2	-7.6	134	32	-588	2 098	9.9	2.80	8.6	23.5
Valdez-Cordova	8.0	3.9	2.2	46.8	10 201	9 920	2.8	0.1	160	54	-102	3 884	13.4	2.58	8.5	27.0
Wade Hampton	4.9	3.2	1.8	47.8	7 077	5 789	21.4	0.7	316	73	-198	1 602	17.1	4.38	20.3	16.0
Wrangell-Petersburg	9.1	5.0	4.5	48.0	6 615	7 042	-5.1	-1.0	101	62	-109	2 587	2.9	2.56	9.2	26.3
Yakutat Borough	8.5	4.0	1.4	40.7	791	725	11.4	-2.1	10	5	-22	265	NA	2.59	12.1	32.1
Yukon-Koyukuk	7.6	4.8	2.5	45.7	6 436	6 798	-3.6	-1.8	157	73	-201	2 309	-16.0	2.81	16.9	30.5
ARIZONA	8.6	7.1	5.9	50.1	5 307 331	3 665 339	40.0	3.4	104 781	50 703	121 810	1 901 327	38.9	2.64	11.1	24.8
Apache	7.7	5.0	3.3	50.4	68 610	61 591	12.7	-1.2	1 858	545	-2 168	19 971	25.0	3.41	21.4	21.2
Cochise	10.6	8.7	6.1	49.6	119 281	97 624	20.6	1.3	2 123	1 372	857	43 893	27.1	2.55	11.1	25.3
Coconino	7.3	4.3	2.7	50.1	117 916	96 591	20.4	1.4	2 424	648	-135	40 448	35.2	2.80	12.2	22.1
Gila	12.7	11.2	8.6	50.8	51 419	40 216	27.6	0.2	939	790	-41	20 140	30.5	2.50	10.8	25.8
Graham	7.9	6.5	5.4	47.1	33 390	26 554	26.1	-0.3	645	372	-368	10 116	27.6	2.99	13.4	20.9
Greenlee	8.5	5.9	4.0	47.8	8 301	8 008	6.7	-2.9	192	84	-361	3 117	11.0	2.73	9.0	24.5
La Paz	14.4	16.6	9.2	48.7	19 759	13 844	42.4	0.2	238	247	63	8 362	56.4	2.32	8.2	26.6
Maricopa	7.8	6.1	5.5	50.0	3 194 798	2 122 101	44.8	4.0	66 298	28 515	84 197	1 132 886	40.3	2.67	10.7	24.5
Mohave	13.6	12.3	8.2	50.3	161 788	93 497	65.8	4.4	2 413	2 361	6 572	62 809	70.7	2.45	9.3	24.1
Navajo	8.7	6.2	3.8	50.3	100 135	77 674	25.5	2.7	2 484	841	1 029	30 043	35.4	3.17	16.3	19.9
Pima	8.8	7.5	6.7	51.1	863 049	666 957	26.5	2.3	15 242	9 053	13 238	332 350	27.0	2.47	11.8	28.5
Pinal	10.8	10.0	6.2	46.7	188 846	116 397	54.4	5.1	3 070	1 883	7 774	61 364	56.7	2.68	11.5	21.1
Santa Cruz	8.5	6.3	4.5	52.2	39 590	29 676	29.3	3.1	982	275	513	11 809	34.1	3.23	15.4	16.5
Yavapai	12.9	12.1	9.9	51.0	175 507	107 714	55.5	4.8	2 164	2 500	8 152	70 171	56.7	2.33	8.1	26.7
Yuma	9.0	10.0	6.6	49.5	164 942	106 895	49.7	3.1	3 709	1 217	2 488	53 848	50.5	2.86	11.2	18.5
ARKANSAS	9.6	7.4	6.6	51.2	2 692 090	2 350 624	13.7	0.7	47 970	34 843	5 683	1 042 696	17.0	2.49	12.1	25.6
Arkansas	10.1	8.2	8.0	52.4	20 588	21 653	-4.2	-0.8	374	340	-191	8 457	0.8	2.41	13.9	26.1
Ashley	10.4	7.3	6.5	51.7	23 979	24 319	-0.5	-1.0	438	368	-297	9 384	5.6	2.55	13.0	23.9
Baxter	14.2	14.2	12.6	52.0	38 590	31 186	23.1	0.5	398	782	589	17 052	26.4	2.21	7.7	27.5
Benton	9.2	8.0	6.4	50.7	159 838	97 530	57.3	4.2	2 739	1 487	5 083	58 212	55.0	2.60	8.2	21.1
Boone	11.2	8.8	7.8	51.8	34 569	28 297	20.0	1.8	523	461	561	13 851	24.4	2.41	8.8	25.6
Bradley	10.4	8.8	8.7	50.6	12 564	11 793	6.8	-0.3	205	218	-18	4 834	6.4	2.45	14.5	27.6
Calhoun	11.2	8.1	7.8	51.9	5 672	5 826	-1.4	-1.3	77	93	-54	2 317	6.0	2.43	11.3	27.3
Carroll	11.5	8.8	7.0	50.7	25 761	18 623	36.2	1.6	438	328	302	10 189	35.0	2.47	8.6	25.2
Chicot	9.8	8.4	7.0	51.5	13 943	15 713	-10.2	-1.2	314	242	-245	5 205	-6.3	2.58	22.0	26.9
Clark	8.6	7.4	7.2	51.9	23 517	21 437	9.8	-0.1	370	322	-70	8 912	12.7	2.38	12.2	27.6
Clay	11.8	10.0	9.4	51.7	17 355	18 107	-2.8	-1.4	254	311	-193	7 417	-1.2	2.35	8.6	28.4
Cleburne	13.9	12.1	9.0	51.6	24 233	19 411	23.9	0.8	299	341	224	10 190	28.6	2.33	7.9	24.4
Cleveland	11.3	7.5	6.1	51.2	8 609	7 781	10.2	0.4	135	104	7	3 273	14.1	2.60	9.9	21.4
Columbia	9.5	8.0	7.9	52.4	25 245	25 691	-0.3	-1.4	441	417	-381	9 981	3.6	2.45	15.1	29.2

1. No spouse present.

Table B. States and Counties — Vital Statistics, Health Resources, and Crime

STATE County	Births, average 1997–1999 Total	Rate[1]	Deaths, average 1997–1999 Number Total	Number Infant[2]	Rate Total[1]	Rate Infant[3]	Physicians,[4] 2000 Number	Rate[5]	Hospitals,[4] 1998 Number	Beds Number	Rate[5]	Medicare enrollees 2000	Serious crimes known to police, 2000[6] Total Number	Rate[7]
	32	33	34	35	36	37	38	39	40	41	42	43	44	45
ALABAMA—Cont'd														
Washington	231	13.1	165	NA	9.4	NA	7	39	1	100	566	2 779	NA	NA
Wilcox	216	16.0	172	NA	12.8	NA	5	38	1	32	238	2 448	127	1 162
Winston	304	12.6	277	NA	11.5	NA	9	36	1	45	186	4 524	246	1 020
ALASKA	9 859	16.0	2 618	64	4.3	6.5	1 087	173	16	1 324	216	42 015	26 641	4 249
Aleutians East Borough	NA	NA	NA	NA	NA	NA	0	0	0	0	0	NA	NA	NA
Aleutians West Census Area	NA	NA	NA	NA	NA	NA	0	0	0	0	0	NA	NA	NA
Anchorage	NA	NA	NA	NA	NA	NA	620	238	2	603	236	16 913	NA	NA
Bethel	NA	NA	NA	NA	NA	NA	15	94	0	0	0	714	NA	NA
Bristol Bay	NA	NA	NA	NA	NA	NA	1	79	0	0	0	605	NA	NA
Denali Borough	NA	NA	NA	NA	NA	NA	0	0	0	0	0	NA	NA	NA
Dillingham	NA	NA	NA	NA	NA	NA	7	142	0	0	0	NA	NA	NA
Fairbanks North Star	NA	NA	NA	NA	NA	NA	161	194	1	224	266	4 817	NA	NA
Haines	NA	NA	NA	NA	NA	NA	4	167	0	0	0	295	NA	NA
Juneau	NA	NA	NA	NA	NA	NA	59	192	1	59	195	2 488	NA	NA
Kenai Peninsula	NA	NA	NA	NA	NA	NA	51	103	3	128	267	NA	NA	NA
Ketchikan Gateway	NA	NA	NA	NA	NA	NA	30	213	1	71	528	1 265	NA	NA
Kodiak Island	NA	NA	NA	NA	NA	NA	23	165	1	49	337	439	NA	NA
Lake and Peninsula Borough	NA	NA	NA	NA	NA	NA	0	0	0	0	0	NA	NA	NA
Matanuska-Susitna	NA	NA	NA	NA	NA	NA	54	91	1	36	64	NA	NA	NA
Nome	NA	NA	NA	NA	NA	NA	7	76	1	35	388	537	NA	NA
North Slope	NA	NA	NA	NA	NA	NA	4	54	0	0	0	NA	NA	NA
Northwest Arctic Borough	NA	NA	NA	NA	NA	NA	3	42	0	0	0	NA	NA	NA
Prince of Wales-Outer Ketchikan	NA	NA	NA	NA	NA	NA	4	65	0	0	0	407	NA	NA
Sitka	NA	NA	NA	NA	NA	NA	21	238	1	28	336	754	NA	NA
Skagway-Hoonah-Angoon	NA	NA	NA	NA	NA	NA	0	0	0	0	0	NA	NA	NA
Southeast Fairbanks	NA	NA	NA	NA	NA	NA	4	65	0	0	0	459	NA	NA
Valdez-Cordova	NA	NA	NA	NA	NA	NA	13	128	2	43	418	NA	NA	NA
Wade Hampton	NA	NA	NA	NA	NA	NA	0	0	0	0	0	389	NA	NA
Wrangell-Petersburg	NA	NA	NA	NA	NA	NA	6	90	2	48	704	680	NA	NA
Yakutat Borough	NA	NA	NA	NA	NA	NA	0	0	0	0	0	NA	NA	NA
Yukon-Koyukuk	NA	NA	NA	NA	NA	NA	0	0	0	0	0	364	NA	NA
ARIZONA	76 877	16.5	38 472	558	8.2	7.3	9 612	187	61	10 161	218	675 430	299 092	5 830
Apache	1 362	19.8	424	10	6.1	7.3	64	92	2	50	73	6 456	619	892
Cochise	1 645	14.6	1 011	12	9.0	7.1	124	105	5	250	222	18 078	4 883	4 147
Coconino	1 811	15.9	503	NA	4.4	NA	208	179	2	141	123	12 836	6 640	5 851
Gila	671	13.7	614	NA	12.6	NA	55	107	2	93	190	11 097	1 861	3 625
Graham	503	15.9	266	NA	8.4	NA	23	69	1	42	133	4 188	738	2 204
Greenlee	143	15.5	64	NA	6.9	NA	4	47	0	0	0	1 023	NA	NA
La Paz	NA	NA	NA	NA	NA	NA	20	101	1	39	262	3 554	684	3 469
Maricopa	47 929	17.2	21 390	357	7.7	7.4	6 038	197	27	6 245	224	363 705	192 271	6 259
Mohave	1 777	13.5	1 793	17	13.7	9.6	170	110	4	283	217	33 275	6 849	4 418
Navajo	1 768	18.3	653	16	6.8	9.0	88	90	2	83	86	11 020	2 793	2 865
Pima	11 691	14.8	7 104	70	9.0	6.0	2 266	269	9	2 078	263	126 234	59 039	6 997
Pinal	2 264	15.4	1 413	20	9.6	9.0	106	59	2	316	215	25 169	8 132	4 608
Santa Cruz	776	20.3	211	NA	5.5	NA	43	112	1	80	210	4 733	1 224	3 189
Yavapai	1 602	10.8	1 874	11	12.6	7.1	247	147	2	186	125	35 327	7 172	4 281
Yuma	2 934	20.6	1 089	19	7.4	6.5	156	97	1	275	208	18 570	5 455	3 770
ARKANSAS	36 381	14.3	27 760	312	10.9	8.6	4 267	160	80	10 107	398	439 371	110 019	4 115
Arkansas	277	13.3	281	NA	13.5	NA	16	77	2	187	900	3 915	655	3 157
Ashley	338	13.9	291	NA	12.0	NA	16	66	1	28	115	4 190	653	2 697
Baxter	314	8.6	608	NA	16.7	NA	68	177	1	207	569	11 219	685	1 785
Benton	2 063	15.3	1 212	15	9.0	7.1	163	106	4	316	236	23 850	3 668	2 391
Boone	431	13.5	375	NA	11.8	NA	47	138	1	125	392	7 181	572	1 685
Bradley	145	12.7	175	NA	15.3	NA	9	71	1	60	525	2 464	267	2 257
Calhoun	66	11.5	78	NA	13.6	NA	2	35	0	0	0	904	58	1 010
Carroll	306	13.6	244	NA	10.8	NA	23	91	2	60	266	4 340	616	2 429
Chicot	218	14.6	185	NA	12.4	NA	13	92	1	35	236	2 699	581	4 116
Clark	270	12.4	256	NA	11.7	NA	23	98	1	57	260	4 053	469	1 992
Clay	201	11.7	265	NA	15.4	NA	5	28	1	35	203	3 993	321	1 823
Cleburne	223	9.7	282	NA	12.3	NA	18	75	1	49	214	5 569	801	3 331
Cleveland	102	12.0	95	NA	11.2	NA	1	12	0	0	0	1 343	70	817
Columbia	339	13.6	337	NA	13.5	NA	15	59	1	71	283	4 886	1 055	4 121

1. Per 1,000 estimated resident population, average 1997–1999. 2. Deaths of infants under 1 year old. 3. Deaths of infants under 1 year old per 1,000 live births. 4. Data subject to copyright. 5. Per 100,000 resident population as of July 1 of the year shown. 6. Data for serious crimes have not been adjusted for underreporting; this may affect comparability between geographic areas and over time. 7. Per 100,000 population estimated by the FBI.

Table B. States and Counties — Crime, Education, Money Income, and Poverty

	Serious crimes known to police, 2000[1] (cont'd)		Education						Money income				Income and poverty, 1998			
	Rate[2]		School enrollment and attainment, 1990				Local government expenditures, fiscal 1999[5]		1989				Percent below poverty level			
			Enrollment[3]		Attainment[4] (percent)					Households							
										Median						
STATE County	Violent	Property	Total	Percent private	High school graduate or more	Bachelor's degree or more	Total current expenditures (mil dol)	Current expenditures per student (dollars)	Per capita[6] (dollars)	Dollars	Percent change, 1979–1989 (constant 1989 dollars)	Percent with $100,000 or more	Median household income	All persons	Persons under 18	Persons 5–17 in families
	46	47	48	49	50	51	52	53	54	55	56	57	58	59	60	61
ALABAMA—Cont'd																
Washington	NA	NA	4 370	5.0	58.2	6.7	18.9	5 101	8 340	20 082	-6.0	0.4	30 186	18.9	26.0	24.8
Wilcox	275	888	4 120	16.1	51.1	10.3	14.7	5 625	6 552	12 437	-10.2	1.5	19 035	33.8	39.9	41.0
Winston	145	875	4 534	2.3	48.8	5.4	23.1	5 032	9 349	17 936	-10.8	1.3	26 744	15.7	22.4	21.6
ALASKA	567	3 683	156 357	9.2	86.6	23.0	1 137.6	8 404	17 610	41 408	-2.8	7.7	47 177	10.8	14.6	13.6
Aleutians East Borough	NA	NA	476	1.5	66.4	12.9	5.6	15 287	17 242	42 384	NA	10.9	40 350	12.1	15.1	17.3
Aleutians West Census Area	NA	NA	1 636	3.9	85.8	14.8	8.5	14 038	15 035	35 187	NA	5.1	45 528	6.2	10.6	9.5
Anchorage	NA	NA	63 357	11.5	90.4	26.9	333.0	6 715	19 620	43 946	-4.2	9.3	53 568	8.7	12.9	10.8
Bethel	NA	NA	4 156	1.4	62.3	13.1	68.7	14 985	8 833	25 402	11.0	3.1	27 371	31.0	31.6	33.5
Bristol Bay	NA	NA	395	4.1	89.8	18.9	15.9	14 317	19 123	51 112	-9.0	8.4	56 849	8.0	10.0	9.6
Denali Borough	NA	NA	NA		NA		4.5	12 515					49 788	6.2	10.7	10.2
Dillingham	NA	NA	1 119	1.7	69.8	15.3	7.1	12 446	12 782	28 779	NA	6.2	35 308	27.1	30.5	33.9
Fairbanks North Star	NA	NA	23 206	8.5	89.8	25.2	135.2	7 651	15 914	37 468	-5.5	5.0	47 552	8.9	11.9	10.5
Haines	NA	NA	518	7.1	78.5	17.6	4.3	9 739	16 204	36 048	2.9	5.6	39 656	12.8	17.3	16.5
Juneau	NA	NA	7 638	10.6	89.9	30.7	43.7	7 546	19 920	47 924	-7.3	8.6	58 883	6.5	9.4	8.3
Kenai Peninsula	NA	NA	11 757	9.4	87.2	17.9	85.4	8 292	18 173	42 403	6.9	8.3	47 602	11.3	15.1	13.2
Ketchikan Gateway	NA	NA	3 737	10.0	85.4	20.1	20.1	7 293	18 789	45 172	-0.2	6.9	52 204	8.3	11.2	10.7
Kodiak Island	NA	NA	3 454	10.9	84.7	21.5	26.3	9 382	19 979	44 815	1.2	10.9	47 200	8.7	11.9	10.8
Lake and Peninsula Borough	NA	NA	459	2.8	60.7	14.4	10.1	17 509	11 560	25 231	NA	6.1	27 422	24.8	25.7	30.0
Matanuska-Susitna	NA	NA	12 099	8.4	87.8	18.1	101.5	7 840	15 898	40 745	3.5	5.6	49 498	10.9	13.5	12.7
Nome	NA	NA	2 573	1.2	65.0	13.8	37.2	13 895	10 701	30 144	23.6	4.0	34 254	23.7	25.7	27.6
North Slope	NA	NA	1 843	1.4	68.5	14.1	51.1	24 345	18 231	50 473	NA	13.4	58 705	6.6	6.5	6.4
Northwest Arctic Borough	NA	NA	1 940	1.6	63.8	11.9	29.9	13 375	10 040	33 313	NA	3.8	38 006	19.5	20.3	22.9
Prince of Wales-Outer Ketchikan	NA	NA	1 635	3.4	77.5	11.4	16.4	11 786	15 510	39 495	7.4	3.9	41 555	14.0	15.2	17.7
Sitka	NA	NA	2 538	15.4	87.0	21.4	14.1	8 220	16 962	43 337	-16.9	4.0	49 027	8.6	10.9	10.1
Skagway-Hoonah-Angoon	NA	NA	NA		NA		5.6	14 410	NA	NA	NA	NA	38 514	9.3	11.4	13.8
Southeast Fairbanks	NA	NA	1 949	13.1	85.9	19.0	6.4	12 453	12 505	30 222	13.4	2.7	34 969	19.1	24.5	24.0
Valdez-Cordova	NA	NA	2 516	8.2	83.9	18.5	23.6	10 660	22 772	47 500	3.2	14.2	51 525	9.4	12.8	11.8
Wade Hampton	NA	NA	1 964	1.4	57.8	10.2	29.6	11 389	6 519	20 586	8.0	2.2	19 827	37.5	35.8	41.3
Wrangell-Petersburg	NA	NA	1 776	5.8	81.0	19.8	12.9	8 767	19 012	42 020	2.7	9.2	44 721	10.2	13.5	13.1
Yakutat Borough	NA	NA	NA				2.4	13 754					45 199	7.9	11.4	14.5
Yukon-Koyukuk	NA	NA	2 424	2.5	73.2	13.8	44.4	8 385	11 554	23 945	15.5	2.8	27 623	22.5	23.4	25.2
ARIZONA	532	5 298	991 122	9.6	78.7	20.3	3 963.4	4 672	13 461	27 540	-0.1	3.4	37 281	14.9	22.6	21.5
Apache	130	762	21 515	5.9	54.7	8.5	96.3	6 165	5 399	14 100	-23.9	0.5	21 283	38.9	43.4	45.2
Cochise	391	3 756	26 371	6.3	75.7	16.1	101.7	4 914	10 716	22 425	-2.1	1.4	31 443	23.1	30.7	31.2
Coconino	428	5 423	37 122	5.9	79.0	24.6	101.6	5 226	10 580	26 112	-2.4	2.4	34 939	19.8	25.3	25.5
Gila	471	3 154	9 215	6.6	68.1	9.7	45.2	4 786	10 297	20 964	-9.5	1.9	29 299	20.8	33.1	32.9
Graham	185	2 019	8 843	3.4	67.6	11.3	26.8	4 372	8 955	18 455	-11.8	0.9	29 107	21.7	25.3	28.9
Greenlee	NA	NA	2 519	4.8	74.2	10.4	10.1	4 915	9 794	27 491	-23.3	0.3	44 351	10.7	13.8	14.4
La Paz	178	3 292	3 064	2.6	63.0	8.5	16.1	5 433	9 240	16 555	NA	1.5	25 107	24.1	38.6	41.3
Maricopa	553	5 706	557 988	10.9	81.5	22.1	2 297.2	4 768	14 970	30 797	3.7	4.2	42 192	12.0	18.6	16.6
Mohave	319	4 099	18 422	6.3	72.8	10.3	90.1	4 126	11 933	24 002	1.1	1.8	29 326	18.0	31.8	31.0
Navajo	290	2 575	25 999	5.1	64.6	10.0	117.6	5 225	7 586	19 452	-14.6	1.1	26 304	37.2	32.1	35.0
Pima	658	6 339	188 198	9.8	80.5	23.3	622.1	4 962	13 177	25 401	-4.1	3.1	34 049	15.9	24.4	23.2
Pinal	613	3 996	30 776	4.9	65.5	8.2	129.1	4 881	9 228	21 301	-12.2	1.1	29 726	18.5	25.6	28.1
Santa Cruz	336	2 853	8 566	5.1	57.2	10.8	43.3	4 735	9 007	22 066	-9.7	2.2	27 934	26.6	36.2	36.3
Yavapai	351	3 930	23 789	13.4	78.9	17.7	96.5	4 441	12 657	22 060	0.7	2.0	32 273	13.3	21.6	20.2
Yuma	466	3 304	28 755	5.9	64.9	12.7	132.7	4 587	10 428	23 635	NA	1.8	28 207	27.3	42.4	37.0
ARKANSAS	445	3 670	582 405	9.0	66.3	13.3	2 241.2	4 956	10 520	21 147	3.3	1.8	29 212	16.4	23.5	20.3
Arkansas	496	2 660	5 510	7.0	61.1	10.3	18.5	4 843	11 169	19 516	-4.5	2.3	30 398	17.8	25.4	22.0
Ashley	355	2 342	6 176	4.8	62.8	9.3	23.3	5 040	9 696	20 609	-3.2	1.5	32 357	18.6	26.7	23.2
Baxter	188	1 597	5 352	5.3	67.9	10.4	24.0	4 725	10 648	18 826	-1.7	1.5	27 769	13.9	23.7	19.8
Benton	138	2 253	21 018	11.7	74.8	14.4	111.8	4 754	12 274	26 021	11.5	2.0	38 224	9.6	15.4	11.8
Boone	144	1 541	6 278	7.1	67.6	10.7	32.6	5 607	10 129	20 656	8.7	1.6	29 798	15.9	23.3	19.4
Bradley	135	2 122	2 532	2.8	56.1	9.8	12.3	5 511	8 824	17 259	2.7	0.7	26 629	20.1	28.5	25.1
Calhoun	157	853	1 345	2.5	63.3	7.4	4.4	5 148	9 464	21 198	28.8	1.5	28 912	15.4	21.2	19.8
Carroll	260	2 169	3 778	5.8	68.4	11.6	16.8	4 696	10 176	20 623	12.9	1.5	27 632	15.8	23.2	20.3
Chicot	390	3 726	4 522	8.8	51.2	8.3	16.4	5 651	7 452	12 680	1.5	1.6	21 465	29.7	36.3	34.9
Clark	119	1 873	7 008	19.9	64.9	17.9	20.3	6 416	9 001	18 068	-6.1	1.1	28 141	18.2	26.7	21.2
Clay	131	1 692	3 384	2.5	47.9	5.2	13.1	4 478	9 018	16 219	3.4	1.3	26 518	16.6	24.2	21.3
Cleburne	320	3 011	3 542	3.4	61.0	9.4	16.8	4 775	10 039	19 438	6.5	1.1	28 773	15.5	25.5	19.9
Cleveland	93	723	1 990	2.4	59.9	7.8	7.4	4 788	9 025	19 703	5.8	0.6	32 805	15.5	22.7	20.0
Columbia	609	3 511	6 843	4.0	64.3	13.1	22.3	4 716	9 425	18 470	-2.9	1.5	28 450	20.9	30.1	26.0

1. Data for serious crimes have not been adjusted for underreporting; this may affect comparability between geographic areas and over time. 2. Per 100,000 population estimated by the FBI. 3. All persons 3 years old and over enrolled in nursery school through college. 4. Persons 25 years old and over. 5. Elementary and secondary education expenditures, local government fiscal years ending between July 1, 1998 and June 30, 1999. 6. Based on population enumerated as of April 1, 1990.

Table B. States and Counties — Personal Income

	Personal income, 1999												
			Per capita[1]						Transfer payments				
										Government payments to individuals			
STATE County	Total (mil dol)	Percent change, 1998–1999	Dollars	Rank	Wages and salaries[2] (mil dol)	Proprietor's income (mil dol)	Dividends, interest, and rent (mil dol)	Total (mil dol)	Total (mil dol)	Social Security (mil dol)	Medical payments (mil dol)	Income mainte- nance (mil dol)	Unemploy- ment insurance (mil dol)
	62	63	64	65	66	67	68	69	70	71	72	73	74
ALABAMA—Cont'd													
Washington	310	1.0	17 471	2 652	213	14	44	71	68	27	26	10	1
Wilcox	200	6.6	14 934	2 993	138	20	33	71	68	19	27	19	1
Winston	470	3.7	19 223	2 226	295	53	65	108	103	38	48	10	2
ALASKA	17 736	3.1	28 629	X	11 754	1 610	3 209	2 669	2 573	423	592	249	123
Aleutians East Borough	61	12.4	27 792	347	53	3	6	9	9	1	1	0	0
Aleutians West Census Area	127	11.9	32 478	140	151	9	15	13	12	1	2	1	1
Anchorage	8 717	3.4	33 813	113	5 897	841	1 536	1 082	1 042	168	237	97	39
Bethel	278	-0.9	17 131	2 711	166	9	28	85	83	6	27	16	3
Bristol Bay	47	-1.0	43 996	29	37	8	7	5	5	1	1	0	0
Denali Borough	72	16.3	38 410	55	91	2	13	13	13	1	5	3	1
Dillingham	118	5.2	25 935	524	78	15	13	21	20	3	5	3	1
Fairbanks North Star	2 200	3.0	26 082	503	1 560	138	401	339	327	51	75	29	16
Haines	70	1.8	30 681	188	28	12	16	12	12	3	3	1	1
Juneau	1 026	2.5	33 974	108	665	72	223	119	115	22	22	8	5
Kenai Peninsula	1 248	2.2	25 478	586	597	155	253	227	219	46	47	16	14
Ketchikan Gateway	457	1.2	32 412	141	277	53	90	67	64	14	15	6	3
Kodiak Island	362	4.7	25 204	638	244	45	74	50	48	7	8	4	3
Lake and Peninsula Bor- ough	34	9.6	19 533	2 129	19	4	4	8	8	1	2	1	0
Matanuska-Susitna	1 079	4.0	18 615	2 389	386	98	207	226	216	44	34	13	14
Nome	189	2.3	21 258	1 581	116	8	22	51	49	5	17	9	2
North Slope	206	0.4	29 025	260	520	8	36	28	27	5	6	2	1
Northwest Arctic Borough	142	1.2	21 090	1 642	118	3	14	40	39	4	15	7	2
Prince of Wales-Outer Ket- chikan	131	3.2	19 548	2 121	74	11	23	27	26	4	5	2	3
Sitka	245	4.3	29 895	215	146	29	59	36	34	8	7	2	2
Skagway-Hoonah-Angoon	90	0.8	25 787	543	46	8	20	17	16	3	4	1	1
Southeast Fairbanks	132	2.2	22 629	1 186	72	8	20	30	29	5	7	4	2
Valdez-Cordova	289	0.2	28 211	304	200	28	55	40	39	7	6	3	3
Wade Hampton	91	4.0	13 029	3 081	44	2	8	42	41	3	16	8	2
Wrangell-Petersburg	186	5.5	27 414	381	91	29	39	34	33	8	8	2	2
Yakutat Borough	20	-4.3	26 478	468	13	1	5	3	3	0	1	0	0
Yukon-Koyukuk	118	2.0	19 126	2 253	65	10	18	45	44	4	17	9	2
ARIZONA	120 287	6.8	25 173	X	76 213	9 087	23 816	16 036	15 173	6 710	5 651	1 383	189
Apache	905	10.3	13 193	3 076	555	38	81	331	319	47	159	77	6
Cochise	2 119	3.5	18 797	2 347	1 178	133	436	446	427	163	162	48	5
Coconino	2 438	5.4	21 297	1 572	1 437	235	557	332	311	93	120	46	8
Gila	932	4.6	19 002	2 277	395	84	210	268	259	112	104	26	3
Graham	471	4.9	14 719	3 011	201	47	69	128	122	41	55	16	2
Greenlee	173	-2.2	19 237	2 223	160	12	17	31	29	11	13	3	1
La Paz	329	3.9	22 133	1 317	138	35	48	78	75	34	28	7	1
Maricopa	80 705	7.3	28 205	306	55 182	5 926	15 010	8 600	8 082	3 724	2 980	633	83
Mohave	2 711	7.1	20 199	1 933	1 000	240	558	617	593	339	173	43	3
Navajo	1 322	6.0	13 440	3 071	731	82	182	380	362	97	143	75	9
Pima	19 215	6.5	23 911	875	10 903	1 281	4 661	2 951	2 806	1 219	1 089	250	21
Pinal	2 522	6.6	16 563	2 819	1 283	213	401	678	651	254	285	63	4
Santa Cruz	646	6.2	16 496	2 830	368	65	149	106	99	37	40	14	2
Yavapai	3 296	5.7	21 545	1 506	1 226	329	1 050	641	613	376	154	34	5
Yuma	2 502	1.8	18 452	2 427	1 457	367	387	449	425	163	145	48	36
ARKANSAS	56 724	5.1	22 233	X	33 480	5 421	10 731	9 869	9 391	4 051	3 454	1 008	189
Arkansas	477	4.1	23 032	1 081	285	64	92	85	81	35	31	10	2
Ashley	506	2.1	20 824	1 724	340	47	76	101	96	40	35	13	3
Baxter	829	4.7	22 612	1 193	362	65	281	196	189	110	56	9	2
Benton	3 659	10.2	26 435	474	2 329	297	809	423	397	235	111	21	5
Boone	692	5.8	21 717	1 445	381	84	152	132	126	63	40	11	3
Bradley	242	1.7	21 206	1 594	100	28	41	70	67	23	33	7	1
Calhoun	95	1.9	16 764	2 787	102	7	14	21	20	10	6	3	1
Carroll	449	5.5	19 943	2 008	214	88	98	82	77	41	24	6	2
Chicot	246	2.1	16 571	2 817	107	29	39	69	66	21	26	15	1
Clark	445	6.4	20 777	1 744	253	31	85	102	98	35	47	7	1
Clay	317	2.8	18 602	2 394	138	38	58	79	76	34	27	9	2
Cleburne	480	6.6	20 602	1 809	160	68	125	104	99	51	31	8	1
Cleveland	170	7.0	19 836	2 046	27	25	20	30	29	12	10	3	1
Columbia	532	2.3	21 564	1 499	287	60	121	107	103	46	34	15	2

1. Based on the resident population estimated as of July 1 of the year shown. 2. Includes other labor income.

STATE County	Earnings, 1999 Total (mil dol)	Farm	Goods-related[1] Total	Manufacturing	Service-related and other[2] Total	Retail trade	Finance, insurance, and real estate	Services	Government	Social Security beneficiaries, December 2000 Number	Rate[3]	Supplemental Security Income recipients, December 2000	Housing units, 1990 Total	Percent change, 1980–1990
	75	76	77	78	79	80	81	82	83	84	85	86	87	88
ALABAMA—Cont'd														
Washington	226	0.7	D	53.4	D	3.2	1.7	5.9	12.6	3 640	201	858	6 625	12.0
Wilcox	158	5.2	52.6	49.0	24.2	5.0	1.6	8.7	18.0	3 016	229	1 814	5 119	1.6
Winston	347	7.2	D	49.2	D	6.3	2.3	10.5	10.2	5 318	214	1 122	10 254	17.9
ALASKA	13 364	0.2	18.0	4.2	49.3	9.3	4.2	21.6	32.5	54 331	87	8 672	232 608	42.9
Aleutians East Borough	56	0.0	D	66.1	D	2.9	1.5	D	16.0	100	37	NA	693	NA
Aleutians West Census Area	160	0.2	D	48.4	D	D	2.5	13.7	14.2	152	28	NA	2 051	NA
Anchorage	6 738	0.0	14.9	1.5	55.8	9.7	5.4	24.9	29.2	20 935	80	4 022	94 153	33.8
Bethel	175	0.0	D	0.7	D	6.1	5.0	29.9	44.9	1 241	78	366	4 362	32.3
Bristol Bay	45	0.0	20.7	16.0	45.2	5.3	3.6	11.1	34.0	116	92	NA	596	61.5
Denali Borough	93	0.0	D	0.0	D	D	D	31.5	24.0	110	58	NA		
Dillingham	92	0.0	D	D	D	5.9	4.3	35.7	23.8	467	95	NA	1 691	-13.4
Fairbanks North Star	1 698	0.1	12.6	1.7	39.8	8.6	2.8	17.5	47.5	6 132	74	877	31 823	40.1
Haines	40	0.0	D	D	D	14.9		24.2	18.4	336	140	30	1 112	49.7
Juneau	736	0.2	D	2.2	D	8.7	3.6	16.8	49.2	2 815	92	368	10 638	38.9
Kenai Peninsula	752	0.1	28.9	9.5	45.1	11.5	2.2	17.9	25.8	5 753	116	175	19 364	64.9
Ketchikan Gateway	331	0.0	22.0	13.2	49.1	10.9	4.0	21.6	28.9	1 555	111	111	5 463	23.3
Kodiak Island	289	0.0	25.3	20.6	40.3	7.5	2.4	15.1	34.5	934	67	111	4 885	37.3
Lake and Peninsula Borough	23	0.0	D	29.5	D	4.5	0.5	31.6	18.5	156	86	NA	991	NA
Matanuska-Susitna	484	4.4	13.0	1.1	55.9	15.7	3.3	24.1	26.8	5 768	97	655	20 953	107.5
Nome	124	0.0	4.0	1.1	D	8.5	5.3	32.0	42.2	863	94	177	3 684	41.3
North Slope	527	0.0	59.7	0.1	21.5	3.9	2.0	9.3	18.8	554	75	NA	2 153	85.9
Northwest Arctic Borough	121	0.0	D	0.3	D	4.6	4.0	D	28.3	647	90	NA	1 998	NA
Prince of Wales-Outer Ketchikan	85	0.0	D	22.2	D	9.2	4.2	11.1	34.2	529	86	NA	2 543	83.6
Sitka	175	0.0	D	4.8	D	9.6	2.4	27.0	32.8	908	103	74	3 222	19.6
Skagway-Hoonah-Angoon	55	0.0	D	14.0	D	14.5	1.8	15.3	31.5	337	98	NA	NA	NA
Southeast Fairbanks	81	0.0	D	0.8	D	10.2	0.6	12.7	56.6	663	107	119	3 149	28.5
Valdez-Cordova	228	0.0	13.2	8.0	61.8	5.9	3.3	15.4	25.0	934	92	NA	5 196	25.4
Wade Hampton	46	0.0	D	D	D	7.6	2.4	12.2	61.4	709	101	204	1 882	60.4
Wrangell-Petersburg	120	0.0	25.8	20.0	41.5	8.5	2.4	7.6	32.7	889	133	55	3 005	27.2
Yakutat Borough	14	0.0	D	20.2	D	6.2	D	24.3	30.5	59	73	NA		
Yukon-Koyukuk	74	0.0	D	4.3	D	7.2	1.8	14.7	53.0	664	101	98	4 899	53.5
ARIZONA	85 300	0.9	21.0	12.6	62.3	10.5	9.7	29.4	15.7	795 936	155	81 493	1 659 430	49.4
Apache	593	0.6	D	1.0	D	5.8	D	33.6	43.8	8 163	118	4 440	26 731	41.6
Cochise	1 310	2.2	7.9	2.0	38.6	8.9	2.5	20.1	51.3	21 732	185	2 351	40 238	23.6
Coconino	1 671	0.6	13.5	5.7	53.2	13.9	3.2	28.9	32.8	12 406	107	2 988	42 914	41.8
Gila	479	0.5	D	11.6	51.2	11.6	6.3	26.4	21.5	13 387	261	1 121	22 961	22.4
Graham	248	5.2	D	2.9	D	14.0	2.2	21.8	40.5	5 045	151	848	9 112	23.1
Greenlee	172	3.1	D	0.1	D	2.3	D	2.4	9.8	1 306	153	109	3 582	-17.5
La Paz	173	7.6	D	6.1	D	16.3	3.2	30.1	21.2	4 275	217	352	10 182	NA
Maricopa	61 108	0.5	21.9	13.9	65.8	10.3	11.7	29.7	11.8	427 713	139	38 557	952 041	55.9
Mohave	1 241	0.5	21.3	8.8	61.1	16.7	6.3	27.6	17.0	40 221	259	2 429	50 822	76.4
Navajo	814	0.6	D	5.6	51.0	12.0	2.2	22.2	28.9	13 712	141	4 250	38 967	37.2
Pima	12 184	0.1	21.1	13.0	56.9	10.2	5.6	32.8	21.9	143 679	170	14 396	298 207	36.4
Pinal	1 496	9.5	23.3	7.3	39.1	9.3	2.1	20.4	28.1	32 138	179	3 387	52 732	54.7
Santa Cruz	433	0.2	D	7.3	D	12.0	2.0	14.9	29.4	5 381	140	1 212	9 595	49.9
Yavapai	1 555	0.9	22.7	7.3	58.4	14.1	5.6	30.0	18.1	44 767	267	2 397	54 805	62.3
Yuma	1 824	12.8	D	3.8	D	9.8	D	18.1	28.0	22 008	138	2 603	46 541	24.1
ARKANSAS	38 902	4.4	27.5	21.2	51.5	11.4	4.8	21.3	16.6	523 588	196	85 410	1 000 667	11.4
Arkansas	348	11.0	32.3	28.2	45.1	8.0	2.8	11.8	11.7	4 332	209	730	9 575	-3.0
Ashley	387	4.1	D	48.7	D	6.5	2.3	9.5	9.4	5 026	208	978	9 820	0.5
Baxter	426	1.6	D	24.2	D	12.1	5.0	32.5	11.2	13 068	340	749	15 549	20.3
Benton	2 626	4.1	25.4	20.0	63.2	33.9	4.1	14.8	7.3	28 437	185	1 786	41 444	28.7
Boone	465	5.1	D	20.3	D	10.8	4.0	14.1	17.8	8 378	247	972	12 380	15.8
Bradley	128	7.8	D	32.8	D	7.2	3.7	17.2	16.9	2 913	231	501	5 092	-8.9
Calhoun	109	0.6	D	67.8	D	1.6	2.2	3.6	13.9	1 317	229	177	2 437	2.7
Carroll	302	16.0	D	D	D	11.8	3.4	18.1	10.0	5 449	215	438	8 740	19.0
Chicot	136	16.3	D	15.7	D	7.6	3.9	12.7	25.5	3 015	214	1 114	6 191	-6.0
Clark	284	2.4	33.5	31.1	42.5	11.0	3.5	18.9	21.5	4 471	190	617	8 807	-0.2
Clay	176	13.2	37.6	32.8	D	7.6	D	8.0	14.5	4 577	260	785	8 362	-3.8
Cleburne	228	7.3	D	29.5	D	11.6	3.9	18.5	11.6	6 727	280	591	10 802	25.8
Cleveland	52	33.2	D	11.4	D	4.4	D	9.4	19.5	1 649	192	247	3 322	7.9
Columbia	347	5.7	44.3	35.2	34.2	8.5	3.9	11.5	15.8	5 869	229	1 153	10 690	2.3

1. Covers mining, construction, and manufacturing. 2. Covers private sector earnings in agricultural services, forestry, and fisheries; transportation and public utilities; wholesale trade; retail trade; finance, insurance, and real estate; and services. 3. Per 1,000 resident population estimated as of July 1 of the year shown.

Table B. States and Counties — Housing, Labor Force, and Employment

STATE County	Housing units, 1990 (cont'd)								Civilian labor force, 2001				Civilian employment, 1990[5]		
	Occupied units										Unemployment			Percent	
			Owner-occupied			Renter-occupied									
				Owner cost as a percent of income											
	Total	Percent	Median value[1]	With a mortgage	Without a mortgage	Median rent[2]	Rent as percent of income	Substandard units[3] (percent)	Total	Percent change, 2000–2001	Total	Rate[4]	Total	Professional, managerial, and technical	Precision production, craft, and repair
	89	90	91	92	93	94	95	96	97	98	99	100	101	102	103
ALABAMA—Cont'd															
Washington	5 709	87.2	34 300	19.8	13.3	230	22.0	8.9	5 766	-2.5	909	15.8	5 954	16.3	18.4
Wilcox	4 415	77.1	34 000	23.0	14.4	179	28.9	19.6	3 678	-1.0	485	13.2	3 672	21.4	11.4
Winston	8 544	79.9	37 700	19.4	12.2	212	22.5	3.5	10 665	-8.6	1 330	12.5	9 219	15.3	15.4
ALASKA	188 915	56.1	94 400	21.5	12.2	559	23.8	12.4	321 983	0.0	20 191	6.3	245 379	34.3	11.2
Aleutians East Borough	533	61.4	85 700	13.5	11.6	602	14.5	6.2	1 521	-1.9	66	4.3	1 432	13.5	14.5
Aleutians West Census Area	1 845	17.9	80 100	20.0	13.9	441	16.0	6.8	2 024	-1.0	187	9.2	3 870	18.8	14.0
Anchorage	82 702	52.8	109 700	22.6	11.4	564	24.8	4.3	144 851	0.4	6 165	4.3	111 242	37.5	9.5
Bethel	3 605	58.8	51 900	21.6	15.8	534	20.7	68.2	6 276	-0.8	667	10.6	4 109	37.3	8.0
Bristol Bay	407	48.6	102 000	17.7	11.0	549	14.6	8.9	490	-3.4	49	10.0	510	42.4	15.5
Denali Borough									1 161	-0.3	102	8.8			
Dillingham	1 215	63.2	63 300	16.5	13.8	592	20.5	38.9	1 791	-0.5	165	9.2	1 243	42.6	7.8
Fairbanks North Star	26 693	49.0	87 300	21.4	11.3	534	26.2	10.3	43 816	0.1	2 498	5.7	31 379	35.4	12.0
Haines	791	65.0	81 000	18.1	12.4	470	17.8	23.1	1 223	-0.2	129	10.5	1 031	25.9	13.9
Juneau	9 902	58.2	113 500	20.3	11.6	653	23.9	6.3	16 868	-1.6	817	4.8	14 482	42.0	8.3
Kenai Peninsula	14 250	67.9	85 100	19.2	11.4	479	20.3	11.5	21 515	-1.1	2 073	9.6	17 137	26.5	16.3
Ketchikan Gateway	5 030	56.0	112 600	20.6	11.5	614	21.6	8.9	7 527	-1.4	576	7.7	6 943	30.9	13.0
Kodiak Island	4 083	50.0	111 500	20.5	13.2	676	23.5	11.9	6 918	-1.4	624	9.0	6 178	25.8	12.0
Lake and Peninsula Borough	509	69.5	67 100	16.7	12.9	535	22.0	48.1	613	-1.0	66	10.8	454	35.5	9.9
Matanuska-Susitna	13 394	73.3	71 500	21.8	11.5	508	23.9	12.2	30 945	0.8	2 370	7.7	15 714	29.5	15.6
Nome	2 371	56.8	56 700	23.8	15.3	698	22.4	51.8	3 435	2.9	392	11.4	2 700	38.1	9.2
North Slope	1 673	40.0	80 700	15.4	12.6	724	15.8	66.9	3 418	2.3	283	8.3	2 522	29.8	15.7
Northwest Arctic Borough	1 526	57.9	62 800	17.8	13.9	762	24.8	65.7	2 273	5.5	335	14.7	1 681	35.3	10.1
Prince of Wales-Outer Ketchikan	2 061	60.5	63 300	15.3	12.1	457	15.5	18.7	3 124	-3.4	383	12.3	2 618	20.1	12.5
Sitka	2 939	55.9	120 000	18.7	10.2	610	23.5	8.9	4 238	-1.7	203	4.8	4 307	27.8	12.8
Skagway-Hoonah-Angoon	NA	NA	NA	NA	NA	NA	NA	NA	2 122	0.0	228	10.7			
Southeast Fairbanks	1 909	60.8	54 900	20.1	12.2	489	19.6	28.7	2 612	-0.4	279	10.7	1 943	29.4	12.7
Valdez-Cordova	3 425	64.5	97 100	14.6	13.0	564	19.7	21.4	5 071	0.2	477	9.4	4 730	27.7	13.1
Wade Hampton	1 368	67.9	42 400	18.0	13.2	443	15.9	79.9	2 222	-1.1	403	18.1	1 316	39.0	6.7
Wrangell-Petersburg	2 514	66.7	91 700	14.8	10.9	520	19.5	14.0	3 486	-1.9	306	8.8	3 352	24.9	10.8
Yakutat Borough									312	-0.6	40	12.8			
Yukon-Koyukuk	2 748	71.1	31 800	16.2	14.1	418	17.4	59.6	2 134	-0.3	308	14.4	2 451	35.3	12.4
ARIZONA	1 368 843	64.2	80 100	22.8	12.4	438	27.5	7.8	2 419 619	3.1	113 025	4.7	1 603 896	30.8	11.4
Apache	15 981	73.2	19 400	17.7	12.7	243	15.5	51.8	19 390	-1.5	2 323	12.0	14 039	26.2	14.9
Cochise	34 546	63.6	60 600	21.4	12.7	356	26.1	5.3	41 013	4.4	1 870	4.6	33 766	30.5	10.9
Coconino	29 918	60.5	82 800	20.8	12.2	431	24.9	19.2	61 627	1.9	3 323	5.4	41 990	28.5	11.7
Gila	15 438	77.4	58 300	19.4	12.7	346	24.0	7.8	17 273	0.3	1 024	5.9	13 601	22.7	15.9
Graham	7 930	73.7	51 300	21.4	13.1	303	29.7	13.2	10 013	-2.1	731	7.3	7 701	24.1	11.1
Greenlee	2 809	49.7	40 900	17.5	13.1	295	12.8	5.8	3 918	-8.9	352	9.0	2 829	16.2	24.7
La Paz	5 348	72.5	57 000	21.1	14.4	337	25.3	12.9	6 417	-6.6	402	6.3	5 215	17.8	10.2
Maricopa	807 560	63.3	85 300	23.2	12.3	466	27.5	6.1	1 558 629	3.7	60 460	3.9	1 005 925	32.1	11.0
Mohave	36 801	72.1	75 600	21.9	11.9	468	27.4	5.6	66 777	5.5	3 002	4.5	37 191	20.8	15.8
Navajo	22 189	74.3	51 900	19.9	12.4	292	21.6	30.9	31 973	2.3	3 354	10.5	22 424	25.1	13.5
Pima	261 792	60.9	76 500	22.2	12.0	390	28.7	6.5	392 593	2.1	13 561	3.5	290 058	33.1	10.8
Pinal	39 154	72.0	53 200	21.5	13.4	376	27.0	11.0	61 431	3.4	3 150	5.1	40 326	19.7	16.3
Santa Cruz	8 808	66.0	71 500	23.1	13.9	366	29.1	16.7	13 257	0.6	1 694	12.8	11 286	22.3	9.7
Yavapai	44 778	72.1	84 500	24.4	12.4	416	28.7	4.2	70 821	4.2	2 063	2.9	40 356	27.0	14.5
Yuma	35 791	66.0	64 000	21.3	13.5	436	27.7	14.6	64 487	-2.2	15 716	24.4	37 189	24.2	10.2
ARKANSAS	891 179	69.6	46 300	20.0	13.4	328	26.5	4.9	1 226 661	-0.9	62 796	5.1	994 289	23.3	12.5
Arkansas	8 389	67.0	40 600	20.8	14.1	293	26.5	4.2	10 315	-0.6	505	4.9	9 228	21.7	10.4
Ashley	8 890	77.0	39 200	19.3	13.9	291	25.9	5.9	10 315	-2.3	936	9.1	9 632	19.7	13.4
Baxter	13 486	80.5	51 800	22.1	12.4	344	28.0	3.1	14 273	-1.6	809	5.7	10 621	23.3	13.3
Benton	37 555	73.1	58 700	19.5	11.8	369	23.9	3.7	71 257	2.7	1 596	2.2	44 371	21.6	13.7
Boone	11 131	76.1	45 900	21.4	12.9	327	26.9	4.2	14 509	-2.2	873	6.0	12 534	21.4	11.4
Bradley	4 545	74.9	30 500	19.1	13.4	217	25.2	6.0	4 655	4.3	422	9.1	4 410	20.0	13.2
Calhoun	2 185	81.2	34 400	16.7	14.5	288	20.3	7.8	2 163	-2.8	155	7.2	2 249	16.6	12.4
Carroll	7 550	75.6	47 700	23.3	12.7	301	24.1	4.9	11 415	-1.7	482	4.2	8 312	18.8	14.8
Chicot	5 557	69.2	28 700	24.6	17.7	266	31.9	9.1	6 132	-2.3	631	10.3	5 004	17.7	8.6
Clark	7 907	68.8	40 000	17.4	13.5	274	28.2	4.1	12 001	0.2	443	3.7	8 992	26.5	8.8
Clay	7 504	74.0	28 900	20.1	14.1	235	22.8	3.5	7 428	-4.5	608	8.2	7 198	16.4	14.6
Cleburne	7 926	81.3	50 700	24.7	12.2	319	26.3	3.5	9 533	-1.0	445	4.7	7 510	17.5	16.4
Cleveland	2 868	83.1	33 900	18.8	14.4	238	27.6	5.8	3 585	-1.0	231	6.4	3 104	16.0	15.5
Columbia	9 638	71.9	39 200	21.1	14.4	282	28.3	8.3	10 914	-3.5	582	5.3	10 347	21.0	13.7

1. Specified owner-occupied units. 2. Specified renter-occupied units. 3. Overcrowded or lacking complete plumbing facilities. 4. Percent of civilian labor force. 5. Persons 16 years and older.

Table B. States and Counties — Nonfarm Employment and Agriculture

	Private nonfarm establishments, employment and payroll, 1999									Agriculture, 1997			
STATE County	Number of establishments	Employment						Annual payroll		Farms			Farm operators
		Total	Health Care and Social Assistance	Manufacturing	Retail trade	Finance and Insurance	Professional Scientific and Technical Services	Total (mil dol)	Average per employee (dollars)	Number	Percent with—		Whose principal occupation is farming (percent)
											Less than 50 acres	500 acres and over	
	104	105	106	107	108	109	110	111	112	113	114	115	116
ALABAMA—Cont'd													
Washington	272	3 443	251	1 722	314	89	49	131	38 066	397	27.2	9.3	37.0
Wilcox	230	2 677	228	D	325	93	34	94	35 213	248	19.0	32.7	34.3
Winston	455	10 482	443	6 931	955	254	69	220	20 945	582	38.7	1.7	33.8
ALASKA	18 433	198 459	30 371	11 828	32 280	7 161	9 612	7 108	35 817	548	35.4	16.4	55.8
Aleutians East Borough	51	2 048	D	D	59	D	0	35	17 057	NA	NA	NA	NA
Aleutians West Census Area	111	4 456	76	2 845	244	D	82	82	18 385	NA	NA	NA	NA
Anchorage	7 929	108 021	15 451	1 741	14 965	4 945	6 888	4 317	39 965	NA	NA	NA	NA
Bethel	225	3 102	1 316	D	739	43	D	86	27 772	NA	NA	NA	NA
Bristol Bay	68	466	D	142	36	D	D	22	46 185	NA	NA	NA	NA
Denali Borough	73	347	D	0	43	0	D	22	63 657				
Dillingham	90	1 200	D	D	160	27	D	40	33 077	NA	NA	NA	NA
Fairbanks North Star	2 192	21 694	4 279	444	4 587	664	947	678	31 259	NA	NA	NA	NA
Haines	126	431	20	1	92	D	7	14	31 401	NA	NA	NA	NA
Juneau	1 098	9 712	1 647	155	1 823	347	467	309	31 800	NA	NA	NA	NA
Kenai Peninsula	1 767	10 975	1 757	1 068	2 272	249	315	341	31 050	89	38.2	12.4	51.7
Ketchikan Gateway	578	5 150	701	324	1 131	194	111	175	34 040	NA	NA	NA	NA
Kodiak Island	446	4 308	453	1 531	625	110	67	119	27 696	NA	NA	NA	NA
Lake and Peninsula Borough	54	205	0	D	23	0	0	10	48 863	NA	NA	NA	NA
Matanuska-Susitna	1 364	9 105	1 474	144	2 265	280	311	253	27 803	NA	NA	NA	NA
Nome	187	1 837	518	D	394	42	D	52	28 323	NA	NA	NA	NA
North Slope	136	1 819	D	40	353	D	D	82	45 272	NA	NA	NA	NA
Northwest Arctic Borough	83	1 496	D	0	263	D	D	68	45 560	NA	NA	NA	NA
Prince of Wales-Outer Ketchikan	167	1 203	66	333	161	D	D	39	32 337	NA	NA	NA	NA
Sitka	390	2 760	806	255	474	77	52	82	29 626	NA	NA	NA	NA
Skagway-Hoonah-Angoon	157	497	8	27	134	D	D	21	41 688				
Southeast Fairbanks	140	639	93	D	144	16	8	14	22 072	NA	NA	NA	NA
Valdez-Cordova	470	2 253	253	280	399	D	50	70	31 140	NA	NA	NA	NA
Wade Hampton	63	597	28	D	312	D	0	8	12 930	NA	NA	NA	NA
Wrangell-Petersburg	284	1 756	199	266	416	40	26	51	28 855	NA	NA	NA	NA
Yakutat Borough	32	243	D	D	21	D	0	7	28 909				
Yukon-Koyukuk	132	552	17	D	145	D	D	13	24 214	NA	NA	NA	NA
ARIZONA	112 545	1 838 277	194 047	192 594	248 866	103 628	104 827	52 955	28 807	6 135	44.8	27.1	53.0
Apache	493	6 425	1 710	288	1 122	119	167	123	19 198	288	30.9	34.7	43.8
Cochise	2 190	21 365	3 760	786	4 835	509	1 950	453	21 212	824	23.7	38.3	57.8
Coconino	3 408	37 502	4 234	2 322	7 063	716	1 037	797	21 241	199	37.2	33.2	43.2
Gila	1 138	13 288	1 783	2 321	2 103	239	230	316	23 793	148	45.9	18.2	56.8
Graham	514	4 966	836	D	1 400	182	113	86	17 256	281	41.3	28.1	54.1
Greenlee	102	3 422	99	D	131	D	D	127	37 113	99	37.4	14.1	59.6
La Paz	359	3 794	423	D	897	D	D	70	18 439	97	24.7	44.3	69.1
Maricopa	70 489	1 305 261	120 024	141 095	158 834	88 570	82 922	40 089	30 713	1 643	67.4	12.5	47.2
Mohave	3 295	33 945	4 483	3 989	7 214	1 226	731	710	20 912	212	34.4	41.5	50.5
Navajo	1 697	16 359	2 004	1 022	3 812	431	307	380	23 245	310	37.7	32.3	42.6
Pima	18 507	278 669	40 371	29 214	40 823	8 241	14 351	7 368	26 440	419	60.1	22.0	45.6
Pinal	1 971	27 776	3 022	4 151	4 532	670	659	671	24 156	541	26.1	44.7	68.2
Santa Cruz	1 070	9 881	620	891	2 212	220	159	206	20 855	156	19.2	34.0	57.7
Yavapai	4 801	43 864	6 217	3 660	7 412	1 426	1 365	931	21 218	453	47.5	26.3	57.2
Yuma	2 489	31 256	4 461	2 164	6 476	964	745	610	19 530	465	44.7	25.6	59.4
ARKANSAS	62 737	954 948	129 260	229 628	131 257	33 064	29 663	23 171	24 264	45 142	24.1	16.4	49.4
Arkansas	587	8 491	915	3 130	1 113	271	83	203	23 911	518	7.9	58.5	78.4
Ashley	521	8 679	698	3 700	867	225	77	255	29 429	299	23.7	31.8	53.8
Baxter	1 044	11 346	2 325	3 088	1 845	371	334	252	22 249	492	22.8	9.8	38.8
Benton	3 502	62 484	4 709	13 219	6 033	1 903	1 846	1 893	30 288	2 323	44.2	3.9	45.7
Boone	937	14 032	1 647	2 768	2 314	379	186	313	22 303	1 259	25.3	8.7	40.9
Bradley	304	3 212	663	430	372	137	25	55	17 196	249	29.3	2.8	42.2
Calhoun	98	771	91	113	85	D	D	14	18 477	112	23.2	3.6	29.5
Carroll	769	8 151	721	3 552	1 316	253	110	157	19 295	1 032	20.7	10.7	48.9
Chicot	300	3 102	553	1 036	537	142	80	53	17 020	361	8.3	47.4	76.7
Clark	583	7 819	832	2 957	913	209	142	158	20 232	376	19.1	14.1	41.0
Clay	358	5 216	476	2 785	556	126	35	88	16 885	611	16.9	36.7	61.2
Cleburne	551	5 699	644	1 862	947	178	90	108	19 031	710	24.4	4.9	43.8
Cleveland	112	759	D	119	98	D	6	13	17 005	222	31.5	4.1	45.9
Columbia	647	8 453	1 045	2 872	1 201	282	185	196	23 216	313	24.0	7.0	46.6

Table B. States and Counties — Agriculture, Land, and Water

STATE County	Agriculture, 1997 (cont'd)													Percent of land owned by fed. gov. 1997	Water consumption 1995 (mil gal/day)
	Land in farms					Value of land and buildings		Value of machinery and equipment average per farm ($1,000)	Value of products sold				Percent of farms with sales of —			
			Acres								Percent from —					
	Acreage (1,000)	Percent change, 1992–1997	Average size of farm	Total irrigated (1,000)	Total cropland (1,000)	Average per farm ($1,000)	Average per acre (dollars)		Total (mil dol)	Average per farm (dollars)	Crops	Live-stock and poultry products	$10,000 or more	$100,000 or more		
	117	118	119	120	121	122	123	124	125	126	127	128	129	130	131	132
ALABAMA—Cont'd																
Washington	87	2.5	220	0	26	274	1 329	31	22	55 127	10.1	89.9	32.2	10.8	0.1	86.4
Wilcox	154	9.3	621	0	39	564	914	43	7	29 106	34.5	65.5	30.2	5.2	0.3	43.0
Winston	59	3.7	102	0	29	181	1 731	28	59	101 564	0.5	99.5	32.1	18.4	23.3	2.7
ALASKA	881	-4.5	1 608	3	95	487	303	53	25	44 982	64.8	35.2	40.1	8.6	NA	211.1
Aleutians East Borough	NA	NA	NA	NA	NA	NA	NA	NA	NA	NA	NA	NA	NA	NA	NA	1.7
Aleutians West Census Area	NA	NA	NA	NA	NA	NA	NA	NA	NA	NA	NA	NA	NA	NA	NA	3.3
Anchorage	NA	NA	NA	NA	NA	NA	NA	NA	NA	NA	NA	NA	NA	NA	NA	45.2
Bethel	NA	NA	NA	NA	NA	NA	NA	NA	NA	NA	NA	NA	NA	NA	NA	0.4
Bristol Bay	NA	NA	NA	NA	NA	NA	NA	NA	NA	NA	NA	NA	NA	NA	NA	0.1
Denali Borough															NA	0.0
Dillingham	NA	NA	NA	NA	NA	NA	NA	NA	NA	NA	NA	NA	NA	NA	NA	0.3
Fairbanks North Star	NA	NA	NA	NA	NA	NA	NA	NA	NA	NA	NA	NA	NA	NA	NA	32.0
Haines	NA	NA	NA	NA	NA	NA	NA	NA	NA	NA	NA	NA	NA	NA	NA	0.5
Juneau	NA	NA	NA	NA	NA	NA	NA	NA	NA	NA	NA	NA	NA	NA	NA	4.7
Kenai Peninsula	56	10.7	635	0	8	477	752	37	1	14 151	71.8	28.2	23.6	2.2	NA	8.6
Ketchikan Gateway	NA	NA	NA	NA	NA	NA	NA	NA	NA	NA	NA	NA	NA	NA	NA	54.1
Kodiak Island	NA	NA	NA	NA	NA	NA	NA	NA	NA	NA	NA	NA	NA	NA	NA	5.3
Lake and Peninsula Borough	NA	NA	NA	NA	NA	NA	NA	NA	NA	NA	NA	NA	NA	NA	NA	0.1
Matanuska-Susitna	NA	NA	NA	NA	NA	NA	NA	NA	NA	NA	NA	NA	NA	NA	NA	5.7
Nome	NA	NA	NA	NA	NA	NA	NA	NA	NA	NA	NA	NA	NA	NA	NA	1.3
North Slope	NA	NA	NA	NA	NA	NA	NA	NA	NA	NA	NA	NA	NA	NA	NA	0.9
Northwest Arctic Borough	NA	NA	NA	NA	NA	NA	NA	NA	NA	NA	NA	NA	NA	NA	NA	6.4
Prince of Wales-Outer Ketchikan	NA	NA	NA	NA	NA	NA	NA	NA	NA	NA	NA	NA	NA	NA	NA	1.5
Sitka	NA	NA	NA	NA	NA	NA	NA	NA	NA	NA	NA	NA	NA	NA	NA	5.1
Skagway-Hoonah-Angoon															NA	0.0
Southeast Fairbanks	NA	NA	NA	NA	NA	NA	NA	NA	NA	NA	NA	NA	NA	NA	NA	2.7
Valdez-Cordova	NA	NA	NA	NA	NA	NA	NA	NA	NA	NA	NA	NA	NA	NA	NA	4.5
Wade Hampton	NA	NA	NA	NA	NA	NA	NA	NA	NA	NA	NA	NA	NA	NA	NA	0.2
Wrangell-Petersburg	NA	NA	NA	NA	NA	NA	NA	NA	NA	NA	NA	NA	NA	NA	NA	2.0
Yakutat Borough															NA	0.0
Yukon-Koyukuk	NA	NA	NA	NA	NA	NA	NA	NA	NA	NA	NA	NA	NA	NA	NA	7.7
ARIZONA	26 867	-23.3	4 379	1 014	1 277	1 689	388	71	1 903	310 254	64.2	35.8	48.0	22.0	41.7	6 815.9
Apache	D	D	D	11	17	2 813	D	18	7	23 375	3.9	96.1	30.2	5.2	10.7	39.0
Cochise	1 260	-33.4	1 529	63	116	546	348	41	60	73 003	68.2	31.8	52.2	15.7	25.3	234.0
Coconino	6 209	3.7	31 203	3	D	4 416	142	33	11	53 702	3.8	96.2	32.7	10.6	38.9	47.3
Gila	D	D	D	1	8	2 777	D	27	3	19 775	2.6	97.4	36.5	2.7	57.2	40.6
Graham	1 245	-32.6	4 430	40	D	1 648	377	92	56	199 306	90.0	10.0	58.0	23.1	37.8	176.4
Greenlee	29	-78.7	297	5	8	210	749	41	5	47 921	30.5	69.5	43.4	9.1	77.0	36.8
La Paz	279	13.4	2 875	101	93	4 311	1 512	176	95	975 925	99.2	0.8	77.3	54.6	77.6	628.6
Maricopa	709	-2.9	431	298	341	1 384	2 944	79	664	404 174	57.6	42.4	44.9	25.9	53.2	2 392.0
Mohave	997	-49.7	4 704	13	19	1 237	257	51	15	70 674	54.5	45.5	39.2	11.3	68.4	140.3
Navajo	3 903	-46.0	12 589	10	19	2 703	219	49	26	82 894	4.1	95.9	28.7	6.5	9.5	63.7
Pima	2 914	-16.1	6 954	29	D	2 346	340	38	47	111 841	80.6	19.4	41.1	13.6	29.0	263.8
Pinal	1 303	-31.5	2 409	228	D	1 891	760	145	363	671 865	52.3	47.7	70.6	51.9	20.6	1 257.1
Santa Cruz	265	-20.6	1 701	6	11	1 352	838	20	4	23 758	D	D	42.3	4.5	54.6	15.4
Yavapai	772	-63.4	1 703	9	24	592	359	37	27	58 825	8.5	91.5	39.3	8.2	50.0	82.4
Yuma	238	3.8	511	196	215	2 266	4 496	145	522	1 122 717	D	D	68.4	43.0	81.5	1 398.6
ARKANSAS	14 365	1.7	318	3 717	10 062	360	1 151	56	5 480	121 388	39.9	60.1	45.4	22.2	9.1	8 767.3
Arkansas	426	3.7	823	309	376	896	1 136	176	142	274 913	99.4	0.6	78.4	63.5	8.5	820.6
Ashley	166	9.8	555	91	138	550	1 078	95	59	198 590	86.4	13.6	51.8	33.8	4.2	134.8
Baxter	105	13.3	214	0	40	239	1 081	25	21	42 776	1.2	98.8	31.3	6.5	18.5	5.5
Benton	297	0.9	128	1	168	300	2 549	34	338	145 296	1.4	98.6	41.5	20.5	3.8	336.3
Boone	258	2.7	205	0	116	251	1 397	26	60	47 583	1.2	98.8	36.6	7.7	0.6	4.6
Bradley	29	-3.7	116	1	15	194	1 690	32	14	57 871	23.5	76.5	35.7	14.5	4.1	1.5
Calhoun	18	-7.3	157	0	10	145	1 069	29	2	15 307	11.0	89.1	25.9	4.5	0.0	1.1
Carroll	242	-1.4	235	0	105	283	1 186	33	146	141 837	0.5	99.5	51.0	22.6	0.9	7.3
Chicot	288	7.0	798	116	254	704	912	156	101	280 472	74.8	25.2	80.9	55.7	0.0	233.5
Clark	96	-2.7	256	2	51	252	965	30	19	49 801	15.4	84.6	34.6	9.6	0.8	5.2
Clay	324	3.1	530	176	296	676	1 351	106	88	144 183	98.0	2.0	66.1	37.8	0.7	176.1
Cleburne	117	8.7	165	0	55	169	1 167	31	46	65 474	1.4	98.6	36.1	15.9	1.6	6.7
Cleveland	33	-3.5	148	0	14	224	1 381	36	51	228 476	0.3	99.7	42.8	28.4	0.0	1.3
Columbia	58	1.2	184	0	26	217	1 327	27	41	130 548	8.0	92.0	35.8	18.5	0.0	6.3

STATE County	Value of Residential Construction Authorized by Building Permits, 2000		Wholesale Trade, 1997				Retail Trade[1], 1997				Real Estate and Rental and Leasing, 1997			
	New Construction ($1,000)	Number of Housing Units	Number of Establish-ments	Number of Employees	Sales (mil dol)	Annual Payroll (mil dol)	Number of Establish-ments	Number of Employees	Sales (mil dol)	Annual Payroll (mil dol)	Number of Establish-ments	Number of Employees	Receipts (mil dol)	Annual Payroll (mil dol)
	133	134	135	136	137	138	139	140	141	142	143	144	145	146
ALABAMA—Cont'd														
Washington	485	5	11	D	D	D	53	319	52.1	4.2	2	D	D	D
Wilcox	0	0	8	36	18.3	0.7	62	331	53.0	5.0	7	9	0.4	0.0
Winston	224	3	37	560	127.2	11.6	108	751	103.8	10.8	16	37	2.8	0.4
ALASKA	332 575	2 147	784	6 860	2 989.8	256.8	2 866	32 502	6 251.4	670.5	716	4 014	543.2	98.3
Aleutians East Borough	85	1	2	D	D	D	6	56	7.2	1.0	2	D	D	D
Aleutians West Census Area	7 317	51	14	110	61.4	3.2	20	197	41.2	4.2	4	55	9.5	2.2
Anchorage	202 855	1 190	434	4 748	1 989.1	181.4	1 001	15 115	3 114.9	319.3	356	2 145	322.2	56.8
Bethel	6 321	50	9	3	1.1	0.2	59	829	77.2	8.5	7	33	5.3	0.7
Bristol Bay	0	0	2	D	D	D	13	91	12.8	2.1	3	15	1.4	0.2
Denali Borough	NA	NA	2	D	D	D	7	D	D	D	1	D	D	D
Dillingham	NA	NA	4	10	4.7	0.5	16	220	33.1	3.6	4	15	1.9	0.5
Fairbanks North Star	12 699	124	75	737	266.0	27.7	359	4 431	927.9	99.5	91	687	79.1	17.3
Haines	824	9	3	D	D	D	26	98	13.1	2.0	4	15	1.1	0.2
Juneau	19 313	98	33	196	96.3	8.2	173	1 807	312.7	37.2	49	249	38.3	4.0
Kenai Peninsula	12 488	109	70	337	242.0	12.6	292	2 219	426.5	45.1	49	219	21.9	4.0
Ketchikan Gateway	4 990	39	31	190	78.8	4.7	119	1 164	205.1	28.6	27	110	13.5	2.9
Kodiak Island	7 157	54	35	87	50.8	4.4	67	590	102.9	11.9	16	49	7.6	0.9
Lake and Peninsula Borough	NA	NA	NA	NA	NA	NA	10	D	D	D	3	6	0.3	0.0
Matanuska-Susitna	12 837	120	22	D	D	D	201	2 149	477.3	46.6	35	169	13.7	2.0
Nome	612	3	1	D	D	D	41	442	57.0	5.8	8	D	D	D
North Slope	1 526	11	4	26	42.5	2.0	22	293	45.0	7.4	3	D	D	D
Northwest Arctic Borough	NA	NA	NA	NA	NA	NA	30	286	40.8	5.4	1	D	D	D
Prince of Wales-Outer Ketchikan	129	1	6	32	21.6	1.0	40	158	26.0	2.7	4	D	D	D
Sitka	3 281	38	9	D	D	D	75	534	78.2	10.3	17	44	4.0	0.8
Skagway-Hoonah-Angoon	2 667	32	2	D	D	D	45	208	25.3	3.2	3	2	0.2	0.1
Southeast Fairbanks	NA	NA	3	D	D	D	30	193	28.4	2.9	4	10	0.4	0.1
Valdez-Cordova	4 836	35	20	D	D	D	78	417	81.7	8.2	15	23	3.8	0.7
Wade Hampton	NA	NA	1	D	D	D	29	353	27.3	3.1	NA	NA	NA	NA
Wrangell-Petersburg	715	9	7	D	D	D	61	406	54.1	8.2	5	10	0.6	0.1
Yakutat Borough	615	6	1	D	D	D	6	30	5.3	0.8	1	D	D	D
Yukon-Koyukuk	NA	NA	NA	NA	NA	NA	40	147	22.3	2.1	4	20	1.9	0.3
ARIZONA	7 157 588	61 485	6 689	80 155	45 763.9	2 748.9	16 283	232 050	43 960.9	4 223.9	5 450	32 529	4 110.1	747.4
Apache	11 141	104	9	D	D	D	126	1 242	170.0	17.0	13	56	6.5	0.8
Cochise	53 631	686	68	468	132.3	11.4	421	4 557	712.1	68.1	96	330	27.9	4.7
Coconino	99 011	683	112	D	D	D	653	7 217	1 081.2	112.1	175	662	75.3	13.0
Gila	39 106	339	42	220	60.7	6.4	176	2 040	329.6	32.9	50	111	16.5	2.1
Graham	5 800	70	25	193	59.1	3.9	110	1 377	205.4	19.4	18	47	4.0	0.7
Greenlee	721	5	7	D	D	D	22	146	20.8	1.8	1	D	D	D
La Paz	2 711	32	14	183	56.4	3.9	79	830	177.5	10.8	14	D	D	D
Maricopa	5 056 806	43 056	4 752	61 594	39 518.5	2 265.9	9 214	144 912	29 331.0	2 792.4	3 391	22 214	3 047.6	553.6
Mohave	174 319	1 938	106	D	D	D	578	6 944	1 236.9	111.1	148	486	50.0	7.6
Navajo	72 197	584	50	266	98.7	7.3	296	3 667	602.7	55.2	67	273	21.6	4.6
Pima	995 002	7 779	929	9 257	2 759.8	266.0	2 785	39 285	6 853.8	693.4	978	6 631	676.6	130.5
Pinal	241 010	2 254	88	690	206.4	18.1	404	4 355	680.8	63.9	111	337	32.3	4.6
Santa Cruz	36 609	440	205	1 859	1 124.9	49.9	207	2 169	320.3	30.7	49	113	11.6	1.9
Yavapai	273 227	2 227	150	1 134	480.6	29.1	757	7 325	1 203.1	120.8	226	737	88.2	15.6
Yuma	96 296	1 288	132	2 376	512.9	41.3	455	5 984	1 035.7	94.5	113	485	48.4	7.0
ARKANSAS	858 615	9 203	3 619	41 385	27 515.4	1 136.6	12 600	132 335	21 643.7	1 904.4	2 269	9 761	1 001.6	163.2
Arkansas	1 031	13	39	485	233.0	15.1	143	1 190	201.1	17.7	12	26	1.9	0.4
Ashley	1 865	25	28	D	D	D	117	961	133.8	12.3	12	43	1.8	0.5
Baxter	9 594	131	27	130	22.9	2.8	227	1 713	298.2	27.1	41	116	13.6	2.0
Benton	122 997	1 159	167	1 886	2 480.5	52.6	548	6 217	1 015.6	93.2	138	523	51.1	8.1
Boone	15 107	151	45	D	D	D	194	2 205	368.9	30.4	44	130	9.9	2.0
Bradley	185	3	11	37	25.6	1.0	62	385	65.1	4.9	5	14	0.5	0.1
Calhoun	218	2	2	D	D	D	22	91	13.3	1.1	1	D	D	D
Carroll	2 526	39	26	126	25.6	3.0	202	1 204	174.9	17.3	23	46	3.9	0.6
Chicot	544	12	23	216	87.6	5.7	80	627	87.1	7.1	10	D	D	D
Clark	1 978	29	25	128	39.1	3.4	116	1 100	171.3	14.8	26	70	3.9	0.6
Clay	792	14	23	350	98.8	7.4	86	632	106.2	8.1	10	19	1.6	0.2
Cleburne	3 062	46	33	255	63.9	5.3	111	982	135.7	12.4	20	44	4.1	0.8
Cleveland	0	0	6	D	D	D	19	94	9.2	0.8	2	D	D	D
Columbia	2 115	12	30	177	47.1	3.7	136	1 205	157.8	14.9	25	94	7.9	1.3

1. Establishments with payroll.

STATE County	Professional, Scientific, and Technical Services[1], 1997				Manufacturing, 1997				Accommodation and Foodservices, 1997			
	Number of Establishments	Number of Employees	Receipts (mil dol)	Annual Payroll (mil dol)	Number of Establishments	Number of Employees	Receipts (mil dol)	Annual Payroll (mil dol)	Number of Establishments	Number of Employees	Sales (mil dol)	Annual Payroll (mil dol)
	147	148	149	150	151	152	153	154	155	156	157	158
ALABAMA—Cont'd												
Washington	11	39	3.1	1.8	12	D	D	D	13	D	D	D
Wilcox	8	13	1.0	0.1	12	D	D	D	17	178	4.5	1.1
Winston	25	71	5.0	1.4	87	6 573	838.7	135.8	33	426	11.1	2.7
ALASKA	1 437	7 892	945.9	370.8	488	10 770	3 305.0	331.2	1 763	20 587	1 065.5	301.5
Aleutians East Borough	NA	NA	NA	NA	2	D	D	D	8	D	D	D
Aleutians West Census Area	1	D	D	D	8	D	D	D	11	165	7.6	3.4
Anchorage	907	5 939	767.2	301.3	187	2 022	322.3	62.9	640	11 364	574.0	165.8
Bethel	4	11	1.3	0.6	NA	NA	NA	NA	12	44	3.2	0.6
Bristol Bay	2	D	D	D	NA	NA	NA	NA	12	71	4.5	1.3
Denali Borough	NA	NA	NA	NA	NA	NA	NA	NA	18	80	8.7	2.6
Dillingham	NA	NA	NA	NA	NA	NA	NA	NA	18	73	8.9	2.2
Fairbanks North Star	167	784	70.5	28.1	NA	NA	NA	NA	184	2 488	112.1	29.4
Haines	4	8	0.5	0.3	NA	NA	NA	NA	19	84	5.3	1.4
Juneau	96	415	44.9	18.5	NA	NA	NA	NA	94	1 117	57.7	16.1
Kenai Peninsula	80	211	19.6	6.6	56	1 246	1 027.0	56.7	213	1 251	65.2	16.2
Ketchikan Gateway	25	84	9.8	3.4	18	762	131.3	31.1	57	476	25.2	7.1
Kodiak Island	20	48	3.4	1.5	25	1 576	204.3	35.4	41	378	18.4	5.3
Lake and Peninsula Borough	NA	NA	NA	NA	NA	NA	NA	NA	16	D	D	D
Matanuska-Susitna	78	251	17.2	7.0	NA	NA	NA	NA	126	928	43.9	10.2
Nome	2	D	D	D	NA	NA	NA	NA	20	215	6.6	2.1
North Slope	3	D	D	D	NA	NA	NA	NA	31	313	32.4	12.0
Northwest Arctic Borough	1	D	D	D	NA	NA	NA	NA	13	159	11.1	4.2
Prince of Wales-Outer Ketchikan	3	D	D	D	NA	NA	NA	NA	25	135	8.2	2.4
Sitka	13	34	2.6	0.6	NA	NA	NA	NA	32	331	15.5	4.4
Skagway-Hoonah-Angoon	1	D	D	D	NA	NA	NA	NA	39	120	9.4	2.7
Southeast Fairbanks	4	D	D	D	NA	NA	NA	NA	28	140	6.6	1.8
Valdez-Cordova	15	39	3.2	0.9	NA	NA	NA	NA	58	315	19.8	4.9
Wade Hampton	NA	NA	NA	NA	NA	NA	NA	NA	2	D	D	D
Wrangell-Petersburg	9	19	0.9	0.2	NA	NA	NA	NA	23	120	6.3	1.7
Yakutat Borough	NA	NA	NA	NA	NA	NA	NA	NA	6	75	2.8	0.9
Yukon-Koyukuk	2	D	D	D	NA	NA	NA	NA	17	38	4.4	0.7
ARIZONA	10 163	75 789	6 669.4	2 724.7	4 917	193 616	43 030.3	6 753.6	9 089	184 323	6 633.0	1 823.2
Apache	26	99	5.6	1.5	NA	NA	NA	NA	65	1 310	37.7	10.0
Cochise	127	1 731	148.2	61.9	53	921	153.8	20.9	270	3 310	94.2	23.9
Coconino	181	777	58.8	21.6	95	D	D	D	477	9 409	407.7	105.8
Gila	63	191	12.8	4.4	34	D	D	D	147	1 660	55.9	14.5
Graham	21	71	3.0	1.2	NA	NA	NA	NA	59	734	19.0	4.8
Greenlee	3	13	0.4	0.1	NA	NA	NA	NA	15	180	3.9	1.1
La Paz	12	39	2.3	0.7	NA	NA	NA	NA	76	795	33.2	6.5
Maricopa	7 158	57 583	5 115.0	2 134.1	3 364	143 683	32 782.1	5 045.0	4 901	112 073	4 196.1	1 170.4
Mohave	138	517	33.0	10.0	156	3 807	760.4	85.2	324	4 516	144.6	39.3
Navajo	59	234	16.2	4.4	45	1 346	275.9	44.2	222	2 890	118.5	26.2
Pima	1 811	12 214	1 124.2	430.9	764	26 746	4 455.2	1 064.7	1 524	32 305	1 041.9	292.2
Pinal	70	468	21.8	7.4	74	4 594	2 530.6	154.8	233	3 995	139.6	36.8
Santa Cruz	42	143	8.9	3.8	35	D	D	D	87	1 374	40.3	11.7
Yavapai	304	1 043	71.1	25.4	189	3 511	445.8	91.3	444	5 614	180.4	48.6
Yuma	148	666	48.1	17.3	66	3 041	389.5	54.6	245	4 158	130.0	31.3
ARKANSAS	4 125	23 094	1 825.8	719.6	3 316	230 153	45 186.0	5 778.4	4 663	73 397	2 179.7	589.9
Arkansas	25	63	3.2	0.9	28	2 768	916.2	66.4	43	340	10.5	2.8
Ashley	25	83	4.5	1.3	24	3 792	921.4	141.7	24	280	9.9	2.3
Baxter	65	312	17.1	6.4	56	3 185	350.8	74.1	106	1 060	32.3	9.1
Benton	250	1 239	155.5	46.2	194	14 220	2 491.8	346.5	230	3 585	98.9	26.9
Boone	54	137	6.8	2.2	67	2 808	495.0	70.4	65	1 015	26.7	7.0
Bradley	16	62	2.6	0.9	9	594	90.0	12.5	16	193	5.0	1.3
Calhoun	2	D	D	D	NA	NA	NA	NA	4	13	0.4	0.1
Carroll	27	76	3.4	1.3	41	3 408	426.5	62.8	157	1 117	41.3	10.9
Chicot	15	49	2.5	1.0	11	1 019	67.1	12.8	23	124	4.0	1.0
Clark	28	140	6.9	2.8	31	2 960	401.1	64.2	45	862	23.3	6.6
Clay	17	27	1.1	0.5	23	2 475	188.6	42.0	17	D	D	D
Cleburne	25	64	4.4	1.5	34	1 687	367.0	39.1	49	735	21.0	6.2
Cleveland	4	D	D	D	NA	NA	NA	NA	2	D	D	D
Columbia	40	153	7.5	3.1	39	2 957	602.3	96.6	50	755	19.5	4.8

1. Firms subject to federal tax.

STATE County	Health Care and Social Assistance[1], 1997				Other Services[1], 1997				Federal funds and grants, fiscal 2001[2]			
									Expenditures (mil dol)			
									Direct payments for individuals[3]			
	Number of Establishments	Number of Employees	Receipts (mil dol)	Annual Payroll (mil dol)	Number of Establishments	Number of Employees	Receipts (mil dol)	Annual Payroll (mil dol)	Total	Social Security and government retirement	Medicare	Food stamps and Supplemental Security Income
	159	160	161	162	163	164	165	166	167	168	169	170
ALABAMA—Cont'd												
Washington	7	D	D	D	7	12	0.6	0.1	92.4	39.2	16.5	6.4
Wilcox	8	144	5.3	2.2	9	25	1.6	0.4	107.6	29.1	14.0	11.8
Winston	25	452	20.6	7.7	33	90	4.5	1.3	179.2	60.1	33.3	6.7
ALASKA	1 143	8 156	758.1	309.4	852	4 364	331.0	93.4	6 403.2	895.9	184.8	86.4
Aleutians East Borough	8	D	D	D	NA	NA	NA	NA	25.9	4.3	0.1	0.2
Aleutians West Census Area	5	22	1.6	0.5	5	42	7.8	2.2	65.0	1.6	0.5	0.1
Anchorage	599	5 053	508.6	203.9	393	2 576	185.8	54.8	2 532.2	399.9	72.0	33.1
Bethel	5	47	2.1	0.6	7	23	2.5	0.4	229.4	9.3	3.6	6.3
Bristol Bay	1	D	D	D	NA	NA	NA	NA	30.3	3.9	0.9	0.0
Denali Borough	1	D	D	D	NA	NA	NA	NA	15.0	1.0	1.1	0.0
Dillingham	1	D	D	D	4	8	0.9	0.1	49.9	7.5	0.0	1.3
Fairbanks North Star	146	1 007	96.4	45.9	129	658	52.2	14.6	970.7	113.2	23.8	7.9
Haines	3	D	D	D	4	5	0.7	0.2	17.3	4.5	1.4	0.3
Juneau	81	437	40.1	16.6	56	240	15.8	4.5	573.1	47.6	11.5	3.3
Kenai Peninsula	97	543	37.3	12.8	80	266	20.1	5.3	212.6	79.5	21.6	5.5
Ketchikan Gateway	24	130	9.9	3.6	21	76	6.6	1.7	103.1	19.5	7.3	0.9
Kodiak Island	14	78	6.7	3.1	20	79	6.7	1.8	150.1	8.3	1.9	1.5
Lake and Peninsula Borough	NA	NA	NA	NA	NA	NA	NA	NA	11.2	2.2	1.3	0.5
Matanuska-Susitna	95	484	33.5	13.6	78	270	20.6	5.5	269.4	87.6	16.8	7.6
Nome	5	27	1.3	0.7	5	14	2.1	0.3	118.2	8.2	1.9	3.0
North Slope	3	11	0.4	0.1	1	D	D	D	59.3	6.7	1.2	0.3
Northwest Arctic Borough	NA	NA	NA	NA	NA	NA	NA	NA	74.7	5.4	1.3	2.2
Prince of Wales-Outer Ketchikan	4	18	1.3	0.3	5	16	1.2	0.3	54.1	6.5	0.8	0.8
Sitka	14	76	5.2	2.3	15	41	2.5	0.6	101.1	13.7	4.2	0.8
Skagway-Hoonah-Angoon	NA	NA	NA	NA	4	3	0.2	0.0	29.2	5.8	1.4	0.3
Southeast Fairbanks	8	46	2.9	1.6	3	D	D	D	66.0	10.8	1.8	1.1
Valdez-Cordova	18	85	4.0	1.5	15	35	3.4	0.7	118.2	12.0	2.7	1.1
Wade Hampton	1	D	D	D	NA	NA	NA	NA	58.5	4.5	1.5	4.7
Wrangell-Petersburg	8	19	1.7	0.3	7	9	1.1	0.2	55.0	11.1	3.7	0.6
Yakutat Borough	NA	NA	NA	NA	NA	NA	NA	NA	3.8	0.2	0.0	0.0
Yukon-Koyukuk	2	D	D	D	NA	NA	NA	NA	128.8	9.6	0.6	2.8
ARIZONA	9 155	97 091	6 687.9	2 893.3	6 494	43 669	2 794.0	829.6	30 375.9	10 614.7	3 602.4	740.8
Apache	24	180	8.1	3.7	18	67	3.6	0.9	761.3	95.4	25.9	36.0
Cochise	145	1 432	79.1	30.7	122	514	25.0	6.7	1 162.8	389.9	79.6	21.4
Coconino	240	1 627	107.5	45.8	183	899	54.7	14.2	692.6	204.4	53.9	24.7
Gila	76	666	37.1	14.8	54	184	10.7	2.6	359.6	161.8	58.6	10.2
Graham	53	501	26.7	10.1	32	210	12.2	3.6	170.3	62.1	19.7	7.1
Greenlee	6	20	1.0	0.3	5	8	0.5	0.2	38.4	14.8	5.2	1.1
La Paz	20	100	7.9	3.8	19	80	5.0	0.8	167.4	50.0	0.0	3.5
Maricopa	5 848	63 697	4 532.2	1 979.0	4 060	30 024	2 012.8	597.3	15 155.1	5 623.9	2 093.8	368.0
Mohave	258	1 950	134.6	55.3	194	1 039	67.4	18.7	820.0	496.6	153.0	24.7
Navajo	108	675	43.0	16.3	91	424	24.5	6.3	634.4	176.5	45.1	31.2
Pima	1 614	19 280	1 283.3	563.9	1 171	7 575	437.9	138.1	6 360.2	2 062.9	676.0	128.3
Pinal	132	1 395	86.4	37.1	108	656	27.7	9.0	861.5	367.7	137.2	31.6
Santa Cruz	30	126	19.5	5.7	48	130	6.4	1.6	190.0	57.3	18.6	8.6
Yavapai	377	3 014	167.5	66.8	231	1 004	59.1	16.1	866.7	548.5	126.0	18.5
Yuma	224	2 428	154.1	60.1	158	855	46.5	13.6	815.4	292.9	109.9	26.0
ARKANSAS	4 571	59 960	3 655.1	1 609.7	3 553	18 809	1 113.9	310.5	16 632.1	6 270.6	2 289.3	618.7
Arkansas	31	362	13.8	6.2	38	138	7.5	1.5	183.8	50.2	23.9	5.9
Ashley	23	325	13.8	6.2	25	103	6.5	1.9	150.1	56.0	26.3	7.9
Baxter	99	796	62.0	28.1	83	466	25.3	8.1	239.7	156.8	48.3	5.7
Benton	207	2 285	121.6	60.2	193	1 162	72.4	22.3	524.4	338.9	88.3	12.7
Boone	64	535	32.5	12.8	54	226	12.6	3.5	180.8	97.9	29.0	6.4
Bradley	19	265	11.1	4.4	23	58	5.0	1.1	71.8	32.2	16.2	2.6
Calhoun	3	D	D	D	3	D	D	D	28.8	11.8	4.3	1.6
Carroll	35	256	12.3	4.8	34	88	5.0	1.2	100.1	59.6	19.4	2.7
Chicot	16	167	7.4	3.2	17	61	2.7	0.8	142.4	31.2	17.0	8.3
Clark	40	380	15.3	6.4	29	115	5.6	1.5	106.9	52.8	22.8	4.4
Clay	18	265	10.1	4.5	20	55	3.3	0.8	155.8	46.8	22.5	4.0
Cleburne	28	304	12.1	5.2	28	138	7.0	2.0	132.0	80.9	24.2	2.6
Cleveland	3	D	D	D	5	10	0.9	0.3	38.5	20.3	7.0	1.8
Columbia	45	375	15.7	7.0	40	165	9.1	2.8	159.1	63.0	26.1	8.6

1. Firms subject to federal tax.   2. October 1, 2000 to September 30, 2001.   3. State totals may include programs not allocated by county.

Table B. States and Counties — **Federal Funds and Local Government Finances**

| | Federal funds and grants, fiscal 2001[1] (cont'd) — Expenditures (mil dol) (cont'd) | | | | | | | Local government finances, 1997 — General revenue | | | | |
| | Procurement contract awards | | | Grants[2] | | | | | | Taxes | | |
STATE County	Salaries and wages	Defense	Other	Medicaid and other health-related	Nutrition and family welfare	Education	Other	Total (mil dol)	Intergovern-mental (mil dol)	Total (mil dol)	Per capita[3] (dollars) Total	Property
	171	172	173	174	175	176	177	178	179	180	181	182
ALABAMA—Cont'd												
Washington	2.3	0.0	0.6	15.1	2.3	1.2	7.7	35.3	18.1	7.3	412	314
Wilcox	4.1	2.2	0.7	26.5	4.3	1.7	9.2	31.2	16.1	3.4	250	95
Winston	5.5	50.3	1.6	14.3	1.4	1.3	4.0	43.1	31.1	5.7	239	97
ALASKA	1 413.6	833.9	296.5	776.4	211.5	264.7	1 061.2	X	X	X	X	X
Aleutians East Borough	1.2	5.8	0.5	5.8	0.7	1.9	2.5	16.3	8.3	5.0	2 142	410
Aleutians West Census Area	2.3	48.7	7.6	0.9	0.6	1.4	1.2	34.0	8.4	14.6	3 121	934
Anchorage	785.0	399.5	118.2	246.6	62.1	34.4	328.5	747.0	306.7	234.7	935	835
Bethel	8.5	2.2	4.0	128.2	12.6	23.0	10.2	35.6	26.1	3.4	212	0
Bristol Bay	2.8	2.1	2.5	13.2	0.1	3.2	1.5	10.6	6.1	2.7	2 022	1 081
Denali Borough	11.3	0.0	0.1	0.0	0.1	0.1	1.2	6.0	4.1	1.7	849	100
Dillingham	2.7	0.2	0.9	19.2	2.7	5.5	1.8	13.4	7.2	1.8	406	0
Fairbanks North Star	357.2	199.2	26.7	70.7	22.2	15.8	100.1	261.4	141.8	58.7	697	631
Haines	0.6	2.1	0.4	2.1	0.2	0.3	4.1	10.5	3.3	4.2	1 909	875
Juneau	57.9	0.4	5.6	50.3	63.4	76.2	244.9	160.4	54.3	50.1	1 671	771
Kenai Peninsula	23.4	2.9	5.5	23.9	5.4	4.7	33.7	181.6	89.3	62.9	1 322	800
Ketchikan Gateway	21.5	2.7	7.2	14.9	2.8	1.2	15.6	90.1	37.3	22.2	1 606	765
Kodiak Island	51.6	15.4	46.7	7.1	3.1	2.3	5.6	60.0	31.3	13.1	882	424
Lake and Peninsula Borough	1.8	0.1	0.3	0.0	0.6	0.2	2.9	17.8	11.5	4.3	2 443	809
Matanuska-Susitna	8.7	3.4	16.7	10.6	7.2	5.3	102.1	147.2	90.7	41.0	755	613
Nome	6.0	2.6	3.1	32.7	7.2	13.4	27.5	34.0	21.8	4.1	463	147
North Slope	1.4	18.8	1.7	8.3	1.2	10.9	5.6	335.6	43.5	224.1	31 157	31 139
Northwest Arctic Borough	3.6	0.8	1.4	35.4	2.4	10.7	5.9	47.9	36.3	1.9	288	0
Prince of Wales-Outer Ketchikan	4.2	1.7	12.0	4.9	0.8	8.4	2.2	20.6	13.0	2.1	289	46
Sitka	17.4	0.0	8.0	27.3	1.5	4.3	6.0	45.5	21.3	9.1	1 070	375
Skagway-Hoonah-Angoon	5.3	0.8	7.4	3.6	0.3	1.8	0.3	12.3	7.2	2.8	730	282
Southeast Fairbanks	11.7	12.8	7.8	10.4	1.2	1.6	5.4	0.2	0.2	0.0	1	1
Valdez-Cordova	9.7	43.1	4.7	6.7	1.8	1.2	30.8	112.3	11.6	19.7	1 895	1 677
Wade Hampton	2.0	4.2	1.0	22.4	1.9	12.7	2.1	6.4	2.9	0.6	91	14
Wrangell-Petersburg	8.5	6.0	3.7	3.5	1.2	1.5	2.4	39.0	17.4	6.5	935	337
Yakutat Borough	0.7	0.6	0.2	0.2	0.1	0.2	0.2	5.0	3.6	0.5	572	159
Yukon-Koyukuk	6.4	57.7	2.4	23.6	4.1	9.5	9.7	13.9	9.3	0.8	125	39
ARIZONA	2 917.0	4 583.6	676.3	2 365.5	835.7	653.3	1 335.8	X	X	X	X	X
Apache	81.4	0.7	30.6	163.8	78.1	75.3	91.7	174.4	115.8	33.5	481	430
Cochise	315.9	146.8	69.0	66.7	16.9	17.2	12.2	259.3	137.4	71.2	635	533
Coconino	123.1	4.6	32.3	86.9	21.4	45.1	65.4	277.5	122.9	94.2	828	569
Gila	20.8	0.1	5.1	34.4	10.5	12.8	37.7	116.4	59.1	41.0	847	667
Graham	15.5	7.1	1.4	24.7	6.2	5.8	10.6	76.4	51.6	12.6	404	260
Greenlee	1.7	1.2	0.4	3.9	1.3	0.5	7.6	29.5	12.4	8.2	875	782
La Paz	6.6	56.2	12.3	0.5	3.3	7.4	19.6	47.5	24.1	10.6	710	597
Maricopa	1 277.0	2 559.0	349.3	1 078.1	464.7	288.8	638.0	6 771.3	2 846.3	2 329.4	864	588
Mohave	26.2	4.3	9.4	22.2	9.7	9.1	57.9	283.3	104.9	121.7	944	765
Navajo	63.9	1.3	15.8	114.7	27.4	57.4	45.7	237.3	151.0	54.4	573	430
Pima	635.8	1 765.9	100.5	496.4	94.8	78.7	207.3	1 850.7	837.9	671.3	860	654
Pinal	38.9	3.9	23.9	117.3	33.9	24.1	30.0	371.0	165.3	123.1	859	700
Santa Cruz	48.6	2.0	1.6	35.6	6.1	5.4	4.6	87.4	48.5	24.6	649	543
Yavapai	55.1	3.1	13.6	38.5	9.6	10.4	34.8	322.9	131.7	135.5	939	677
Yuma	206.5	27.3	10.8	54.2	25.3	14.0	18.1	336.4	182.6	93.8	721	481
ARKANSAS	1 178.3	384.8	306.8	1 675.6	423.5	310.8	1 038.6	X	X	X	X	X
Arkansas	9.0	1.5	6.7	18.1	2.7	1.2	2.1	40.3	16.2	11.7	564	293
Ashley	4.5	0.0	0.9	23.7	3.1	1.8	2.0	43.2	19.1	12.3	503	292
Baxter	8.2	0.3	1.9	9.9	1.5	1.4	2.5	40.7	17.0	16.8	460	288
Benton	21.9	3.0	9.8	22.8	6.5	4.0	7.5	204.5	71.8	79.9	614	356
Boone	10.6	0.5	2.5	14.7	3.2	2.6	6.3	82.3	24.7	14.1	442	237
Bradley	2.6	0.0	0.4	10.8	2.7	0.6	1.6	33.8	11.2	7.2	623	466
Calhoun	0.7	1.4	0.2	7.5	0.7	0.2	0.1	9.2	3.8	4.2	723	657
Carroll	6.9	0.1	1.2	7.3	0.9	1.0	0.1	39.4	12.7	12.4	554	315
Chicot	1.8	3.5	0.3	30.8	4.5	2.0	3.1	35.9	15.8	6.0	396	292
Clark	6.2	0.8	2.1	14.9	2.1	3.2	-12.1	32.5	15.9	11.5	519	253
Clay	3.6	2.2	0.8	21.5	1.7	1.0	3.6	23.4	12.5	5.6	323	233
Cleburne	4.9	1.1	1.0	10.8	1.2	1.3	0.3	25.0	12.4	8.1	359	271
Cleveland	1.0	0.0	0.3	5.8	0.9	0.5	0.0	9.9	7.0	1.9	232	187
Columbia	5.6	16.1	1.5	23.7	3.4	2.4	2.1	44.7	21.1	7.3	289	231

1. October 1, 2000 to September 30, 2001.   2. State totals may include programs not allocated by county.   3. Based on the resident population estimated as of July 1 of the year shown.

STATE County	Direct general expenditure — Total (mil dol)	Per capita[1] (dollars)	Education	Health and hospitals	Police protection	Public welfare	High-ways	Debt outstanding — Total (mil dol)	Per capita[1] (dollars)	Federal civilian	Federal military	State and local	Demo-cratic	Republi-can	All other
	183	184	185	186	187	188	189	190	191	192	193	194	195	196	197
ALABAMA—Cont'd															
Washington	35.6	2 019	55.0	15.9	3.3	0.1	6.8	15.6	888	38	107	964	44.6	54.2	1.2
Wilcox	38.3	2 830	54.0	5.1	1.8	0.1	4.0	93.9	6 934	108	81	807	67.2	32.4	0.4
Winston	44.5	1 859	51.7	21.1	4.2	0.1	8.5	15.8	660	90	149	1 047	28.9	68.8	2.3
ALASKA	X	X	X	X	X	X	X	X	X	16 535	22 291	53 739	27.7	58.6	13.7
Aleutians East Borough	15.0	6 467	42.2	3.4	3.3	0.0	3.5	6.6	2 834	22	15	221	NA	NA	NA
Aleutians West Census Area	32.5	6 923	14.8	0.7	8.5	0.2	12.8	16.9	3 601	31	53	419	NA	NA	NA
Anchorage	796.1	3 171	47.4	3.8	5.0	1.1	7.7	1 314.8	5 237	9 696	10 542	17 704	NA	NA	NA
Bethel	33.6	2 122	0.0	1.0	4.7	0.2	5.7	70.2	4 442	115	112	2 251	NA	NA	NA
Bristol Bay	10.9	8 125	38.7	6.5	7.1	0.0	2.9	1.1	806	44	0	312	NA	NA	NA
Denali Borough	5.2	2 620	92.2	0.4	0.0	0.0	1.0	0.0	0	184	135	120	NA	NA	NA
Dillingham	15.3	3 433	47.5	0.6	6.8	0.0	1.8	0.0	0	49	31	535	NA	NA	NA
Fairbanks North Star	268.4	3 184	53.7	0.3	2.2	0.0	3.7	146.4	1 737	3 191	7 639	6 916	NA	NA	NA
Haines	9.6	4 422	44.1	1.8	10.9	0.1	3.5	3.9	1 783	11	16	173	NA	NA	NA
Juneau	148.3	4 944	35.8	21.0	4.7	1.4	4.7	58.6	1 954	851	411	5 945	NA	NA	NA
Kenai Peninsula	177.8	3 738	50.9	4.9	2.9	0.0	3.5	84.6	1 778	385	430	3 813	NA	NA	NA
Ketchikan Gateway	63.0	4 566	32.4	4.9	4.0	0.1	4.6	44.8	3 246	252	340	1 482	NA	NA	NA
Kodiak Island	58.6	3 944	41.1	4.9	4.4	0.6	2.6	50.9	3 421	179	1 019	933	NA	NA	NA
Lake and Peninsula Borough	20.5	11 550	63.1	0.3	0.6	0.0	1.9	8.5	4 798	27	12	112	NA	NA	NA
Matanuska-Susitna	135.8	2 496	71.2	5.0	2.1	0.0	3.7	30.0	551	146	399	2 807	NA	NA	NA
Nome	40.1	4 512	21.2	0.6	3.5	0.0	2.8	1.1	125	74	85	1 284	NA	NA	NA
North Slope	325.0	45 193	14.3	3.5	5.2	1.9	4.7	893.1	124 196	24	49	1 845	NA	NA	NA
Northwest Arctic Borough	45.0	6 788	74.9	0.2	1.8	0.0	0.5	39.1	5 899	57	46	869	NA	NA	NA
Prince of Wales-Outer Ketchikan	20.4	2 852	39.5	0.6	1.3	0.0	1.0	29.6	4 131	108	46	689	NA	NA	NA
Sitka	35.8	4 227	38.6	17.1	6.6	0.7	2.3	73.4	8 661	194	237	887	NA	NA	NA
Skagway-Hoonah-Angoon	13.5	3 561	60.4	1.5	5.0	0.3	2.9	2.6	693	130	24	318	NA	NA	NA
Southeast Fairbanks	0.2	36	0.0	19.4	0.0	0.0	9.5	0.0	0	305	298	351	NA	NA	NA
Valdez-Cordova	114.5	11 009	11.8	6.1	1.9	0.1	1.9	874.1	84 056	123	176	1 018	NA	NA	NA
Wade Hampton	6.8	998	25.4	4.1	11.0	2.1	1.5	0.0	0	29	48	958	NA	NA	NA
Wrangell-Petersburg	41.7	5 995	31.7	21.2	2.6	0.1	3.1	9.9	1 422	191	73	663	NA	NA	NA
Yakutat Borough	5.5	6 358	40.2	0.4	5.3	0.0	3.3	0.0	0	23	0	76	NA	NA	NA
Yukon-Koyukuk	14.3	2 370	54.0	5.5	4.3	0.0	1.6	1.2	205	94	43	1 038	NA	NA	NA
ARIZONA	X	X	X	X	X	X	X	X	X	46 111	32 373	273 535	44.7	51.0	4.3
Apache	164.2	2 362	72.4	1.2	2.4	0.8	4.0	351.4	5 053	2 749	163	3 640	67.0	30.6	2.4
Cochise	241.3	2 150	46.6	1.4	6.6	6.7	5.3	172.7	1 538	3 976	5 718	5 777	40.2	54.8	5.1
Coconino	262.4	2 307	44.3	1.6	6.3	6.2	5.4	373.3	3 283	3 178	290	11 452	49.6	43.0	7.5
Gila	101.1	2 089	51.0	1.8	5.3	2.7	6.9	42.9	887	511	118	2 565	43.4	51.6	4.9
Graham	81.0	2 605	69.3	1.8	3.6	2.1	4.6	5.6	179	317	76	2 741	34.7	62.2	3.1
Greenlee	30.5	3 242	37.8	3.0	6.2	2.7	5.3	81.9	8 719	37	21	534	41.1	54.7	4.2
La Paz	44.9	3 008	40.0	3.5	8.6	0.4	8.9	23.7	1 587	141	35	941	39.5	56.7	3.8
Maricopa	6 755.5	2 506	36.9	3.4	7.2	7.7	4.2	13 875.8	5 146	19 041	12 878	150 372	43.0	53.3	3.7
Mohave	272.6	2 115	38.6	1.4	7.6	1.1	8.0	363.9	2 823	491	319	5 752	39.6	55.2	5.2
Navajo	229.0	2 412	64.2	2.2	3.4	1.1	5.0	205.3	2 163	1 529	234	5 214	46.9	49.3	3.9
Pima	2 026.7	2 598	36.8	5.1	5.5	7.0	3.9	2 077.0	2 662	8 835	7 512	56 154	51.3	43.3	5.3
Pinal	369.7	2 579	49.1	3.5	5.4	5.8	5.7	338.8	2 364	858	362	12 735	47.6	48.7	3.7
Santa Cruz	100.4	2 652	46.7	1.0	5.6	7.2	8.3	84.4	2 229	947	93	1 946	58.8	37.6	3.5
Yavapai	307.7	2 133	42.8	1.1	6.4	2.3	8.5	247.2	1 713	1 159	373	6 969	35.3	59.0	5.7
Yuma	334.0	2 569	46.4	1.4	6.7	2.1	7.3	266.5	2 049	2 342	4 181	6 743	42.1	54.8	3.1
ARKANSAS	X	X	X	X	X	X	X	X	X	20 410	18 961	162 729	45.9	51.3	2.9
Arkansas	39.9	1 921	46.9	9.6	5.8	0.0	7.9	40.0	1 923	189	115	1 216	45.2	52.6	2.2
Ashley	43.6	1 784	53.2	0.2	3.7	0.0	6.6	90.9	3 721	85	135	1 219	51.4	46.9	1.7
Baxter	45.2	1 237	60.5	0.3	4.3	3.7	10.3	31.9	872	159	205	1 370	39.0	57.1	3.9
Benton	195.6	1 505	55.8	5.9	6.1	0.0	5.0	213.8	1 644	398	769	5 548	32.2	64.9	2.8
Boone	74.6	2 332	34.5	42.9	2.5	0.0	5.0	19.5	609	203	177	2 400	33.0	62.8	4.2
Bradley	30.0	2 597	39.2	41.5	2.9	0.0	4.2	6.4	552	39	65	723	53.3	45.1	1.7
Calhoun	8.0	1 391	61.1	0.0	4.6	0.1	9.9	1.2	205	13	31	583	46.5	51.6	1.9
Carroll	42.3	1 893	40.9	17.5	5.5	0.1	7.7	29.4	1 315	115	125	885	37.5	57.9	4.5
Chicot	34.3	2 267	50.7	26.1	3.8	0.0	4.8	16.8	1 110	45	83	1 194	63.3	35.1	1.5
Clark	30.5	1 381	57.2	0.2	5.6	0.1	9.8	18.8	851	101	119	2 089	54.0	43.8	2.2
Clay	20.9	1 200	62.8	0.3	4.6	0.3	11.4	11.0	631	67	95	880	59.8	38.2	2.0
Cleburne	24.3	1 081	69.4	0.1	5.3	0.4	4.7	21.9	975	108	129	778	40.4	56.1	3.5
Cleveland	10.1	1 214	77.2	0.4	3.3	0.0	7.6	2.5	296	17	48	361	44.5	52.8	2.8
Columbia	47.5	1 884	46.2	24.5	3.1	0.0	3.8	18.6	737	55	137	1 832	43.0	53.9	3.1

1. Based on the resident population estimated as of July 1 of the year shown.   2. Data subject to copyright.

Table B. States and Counties — Land Area and Population

STATE/ County code	MSA/ PMSA/ NECMA code[1]	County Type[2]	STATE County	Land area,[3] (sq km) 2000	Population and population characteristics, 2000												
								Race alone or in combination (percent)				Age (percent)					
					Total persons	Rank	Per square kilometer	White	Black	Am. Indian, Alaska Native	Asian and Pacific Islander	Percent Hispanic[4]	Under 5 years	5 to 17 years	18 to 24 years	25 to 34 years	35 to 44 years	45 to 54 years
					1	2	3	4	5	6	7	8	9	10	11	12	13	14	15

STATE/ County code	MSA code	Type	County	Land area	Total persons	Rank	Per sq km	White	Black	Am. Ind.	Asian	% Hisp.	Under 5	5-17	18-24	25-34	35-44	45-54
			ARKANSAS—Cont'd															
05 029	...	6	Conway	1 440	20 336	1 770	14.1	85.4	13.5	1.1	0.5	1.8	6.5	19.0	8.3	11.7	15.0	13.0
05 031	3700	5	Craighead	1 841	82 148	631	44.6	90.2	8.0	0.8	0.9	2.1	6.9	17.2	14.0	14.4	14.3	12.8
05 033	2720	3	Crawford	1 542	53 247	879	34.5	94.3	1.1	3.5	1.6	3.3	7.4	20.8	8.4	13.2	16.1	13.3
05 035	4920	1	Crittenden	1 580	50 866	912	32.2	51.4	47.3	0.5	0.7	1.4	8.4	22.7	9.4	13.8	15.3	12.3
05 037	...	6	Cross	1 595	19 526	1 816	12.2	75.4	23.9	0.6	0.5	0.9	6.7	21.1	8.5	12.3	15.1	13.0
05 039	...	7	Dallas	1 729	9 210	2 511	5.3	57.4	41.3	0.4	0.4	1.9	6.1	20.0	8.3	10.9	13.6	14.4
05 041	...	7	Desha	1 981	15 341	2 068	7.7	51.1	46.6	0.7	0.6	3.2	7.5	21.4	9.0	11.3	13.9	13.1
05 043	...	7	Drew	2 145	18 723	1 860	8.7	71.0	27.5	0.7	0.6	1.8	6.7	19.1	12.6	12.8	14.4	12.4
05 045	4400	2	Faulkner	1 677	86 014	605	51.3	89.5	8.8	1.1	1.0	1.8	6.9	18.7	15.3	14.6	15.5	12.0
05 047	...	6	Franklin	1 579	17 771	1 913	11.3	97.5	0.7	1.7	0.5	1.7	6.5	19.4	8.5	12.2	14.6	12.8
05 049	...	9	Fulton	1 601	11 642	2 323	7.3	98.8	0.3	1.6	0.3	0.5	5.5	17.3	6.4	10.2	13.4	13.8
05 051	...	4	Garland	1 754	88 068	591	50.2	90.2	8.2	1.4	0.8	2.6	5.5	15.8	7.3	11.1	14.1	13.5
05 053	...	6	Grant	1 636	16 464	1 992	10.1	96.2	2.6	0.9	0.3	1.1	6.4	19.5	8.0	13.3	16.3	14.0
05 055	...	7	Greene	1 496	37 331	1 182	25.0	98.7	0.2	1.5	0.4	1.2	6.7	18.5	9.1	13.8	14.9	13.0
05 057	...	6	Hempstead	1 888	23 587	1 608	12.5	64.6	31.0	1.2	0.4	8.3	7.5	19.8	9.6	12.8	14.5	12.4
05 059	...	6	Hot Spring	1 593	30 353	1 389	19.1	88.5	10.6	1.3	0.4	1.3	6.3	18.8	8.2	11.8	14.6	14.0
05 061	...	7	Howard	1 521	14 300	2 140	9.4	74.3	22.1	0.9	0.6	5.1	6.7	20.1	8.6	12.8	15.1	12.2
05 063	...	7	Independence	1 978	34 233	1 274	17.3	96.1	2.3	1.3	0.9	1.5	6.4	18.1	9.2	12.2	15.4	13.8
05 065	...	9	Izard	1 504	13 249	2 208	8.8	97.5	1.5	1.5	0.3	1.0	5.1	15.8	7.1	11.0	14.0	12.7
05 067	...	7	Jackson	1 641	18 418	1 873	11.2	81.5	17.7	0.8	0.3	1.3	5.7	16.4	11.5	11.5	14.6	13.4
05 069	6240	3	Jefferson	2 292	84 278	617	36.8	49.0	49.9	0.5	0.9	1.0	6.9	19.4	10.8	12.8	15.1	13.4
05 071	...	7	Johnson	1 715	22 781	1 655	13.3	95.0	1.5	1.4	0.6	6.7	6.7	18.5	9.7	13.0	14.6	12.6
05 073	...	8	Lafayette	1 364	8 559	2 563	6.3	62.6	36.7	0.6	0.4	1.0	6.0	19.4	8.1	10.6	13.8	13.2
05 075	...	7	Lawrence	1 519	17 774	1 911	11.7	98.8	0.5	1.3	0.3	0.7	6.3	17.6	9.6	12.1	13.8	12.5
05 077	...	6	Lee	1 558	12 580	2 258	8.1	41.7	57.4	0.3	0.5	2.2	6.4	19.6	10.2	14.4	14.3	12.4
05 079	...	8	Lincoln	1 454	14 492	2 122	10.0	65.6	33.2	0.8	0.2	1.8	5.7	16.5	12.4	15.9	17.3	12.5
05 081	...	6	Little River	1 377	13 628	2 188	9.9	76.1	21.6	2.5	0.3	1.7	6.9	18.3	8.4	12.1	13.7	14.2
05 083	...	6	Logan	1 839	22 486	1 672	12.2	97.7	1.2	1.6	0.3	1.2	6.5	19.4	7.5	12.0	14.7	13.2
05 085	4400	2	Lonoke	1 984	52 828	882	26.6	92.0	6.7	1.0	0.8	1.7	7.1	21.6	8.0	13.7	17.2	12.9
05 087	...	8	Madison	2 167	14 243	2 146	6.6	97.0	0.2	2.1	0.2	3.1	6.4	20.4	7.5	11.6	15.4	14.0
05 089	...	9	Marion	1 548	16 140	2 013	10.4	98.7	0.2	1.8	0.4	0.8	5.0	17.1	6.0	9.2	14.2	14.5
05 091	8360	3	Miller	1 616	40 443	1 106	25.0	75.3	23.4	1.3	0.5	1.6	7.4	19.1	9.7	13.9	14.6	12.9
05 093	...	4	Mississippi	2 326	51 979	893	22.3	65.3	33.2	0.7	0.7	2.2	8.1	21.5	9.9	13.0	14.5	12.3
05 095	...	7	Monroe	1 571	10 254	2 421	6.5	60.3	39.4	0.7	0.4	1.3	6.9	21.0	7.6	10.2	13.6	13.0
05 097	...	9	Montgomery	2 023	9 245	2 508	4.6	96.6	0.4	2.2	0.5	2.5	6.1	17.4	6.2	10.8	14.1	13.3
05 099	...	7	Nevada	1 606	9 955	2 451	6.2	67.4	31.5	0.7	0.2	1.5	6.4	18.8	8.7	12.1	14.0	13.7
05 101	...	9	Newton	2 131	8 608	2 557	4.0	98.7	0.2	1.5	0.3	1.1	5.8	17.1	7.6	10.5	14.5	14.9
05 103	...	7	Ouachita	1 897	28 790	1 428	15.2	60.4	39.0	0.7	0.4	0.7	6.1	19.7	8.0	11.0	14.6	13.9
05 105	...	8	Perry	1 427	10 209	2 427	7.2	96.7	1.9	1.7	0.2	1.2	6.3	19.0	7.4	12.8	15.2	13.5
05 107	...	7	Phillips	1 794	26 445	1 505	14.7	39.7	59.4	0.6	0.5	1.4	8.5	23.7	9.4	10.5	12.8	11.8
05 109	...	9	Pike	1 562	11 303	2 349	7.2	93.1	3.7	1.3	0.2	3.6	6.4	18.6	7.3	12.1	14.3	12.8
05 111	...	6	Poinsett	1 963	25 614	1 530	13.0	91.7	7.3	0.6	0.2	1.4	6.8	19.3	8.9	12.7	14.4	13.1
05 113	...	7	Polk	2 226	20 229	1 778	9.1	96.3	0.2	2.9	0.4	3.5	6.7	18.9	7.9	11.7	13.3	13.0
05 115	...	5	Pope	2 103	54 469	865	25.9	95.0	2.8	1.5	0.9	2.1	6.5	19.0	11.6	13.1	15.1	12.9
05 117	...	8	Prairie	1 673	9 539	2 486	5.7	85.4	14.0	0.8	0.2	0.8	6.0	18.0	7.5	11.4	14.7	13.8
05 119	4400	2	Pulaski	1 996	361 474	163	181.1	65.1	32.5	0.9	1.7	2.4	7.2	18.1	9.6	15.2	15.9	14.2
05 121	...	7	Randolph	1 688	18 195	1 887	10.8	98.1	1.1	1.3	0.3	0.8	6.0	18.6	8.3	11.5	14.2	13.4
05 123	...	6	St. Francis	1 642	29 329	1 420	17.9	49.6	49.4	0.5	0.8	4.9	7.7	20.3	9.9	13.7	15.4	12.8
05 125	4400	2	Saline	1 874	83 529	622	44.6	96.2	2.3	1.1	0.9	1.3	6.4	19.0	7.7	13.7	16.4	13.8
05 127	...	6	Scott	2 315	10 996	2 366	4.7	94.8	0.3	2.3	1.1	5.7	7.3	19.2	8.1	12.1	14.4	12.5
05 129	...	9	Searcy	1 728	8 261	2 585	4.8	98.6	0.1	1.8	0.3	1.0	5.5	17.1	6.9	10.4	14.0	14.5
05 131	2720	3	Sebastian	1 389	115 071	470	82.8	84.7	6.7	3.1	4.0	6.7	7.4	18.7	9.2	14.0	15.5	13.2
05 133	...	6	Sevier	1 461	15 757	2 035	10.8	81.1	5.2	2.8	0.3	19.7	7.8	20.4	9.5	14.2	13.5	12.1
05 135	...	7	Sharp	1 565	17 119	1 948	10.9	98.5	0.6	1.8	0.2	1.0	5.5	16.4	6.3	10.1	12.6	12.8
05 137	...	9	Stone	1 571	11 499	2 335	7.3	98.9	0.2	2.1	0.3	1.1	5.5	16.8	7.1	9.4	14.2	14.4
05 139	...	5	Union	2 691	45 629	988	17.0	66.7	32.3	0.6	0.7	1.1	6.4	19.5	8.3	11.8	15.1	13.4
05 141	...	8	Van Buren	1 843	16 192	2 008	8.8	98.2	0.4	1.8	0.5	1.3	5.1	16.4	6.6	9.8	13.2	12.8
05 143	2580	3	Washington	2 460	157 715	338	64.1	89.9	2.6	2.3	2.6	8.2	7.4	17.7	15.3	15.6	14.6	12.0
05 145	...	4	White	2 678	67 165	731	25.1	94.8	3.9	1.2	0.5	1.9	6.3	18.1	12.8	12.7	14.5	12.6
05 147	...	7	Woodruff	1 519	8 741	2 551	5.8	68.5	31.2	0.7	0.2	0.8	7.0	19.0	8.4	10.8	13.7	14.3
05 149	...	7	Yell	2 403	21 139	1 727	8.8	88.1	1.6	1.4	1.0	12.7	6.5	19.3	8.9	13.6	14.7	12.2
06 000	...	X	CALIFORNIA	403 933	33 871 648	X	83.9	63.4	7.4	1.9	13.0	32.4	7.3	20.0	9.9	15.4	16.2	12.8
06 001	5775	0	Alameda	1 910	1 443 741	21	755.9	53.1	16.2	1.6	23.8	19.0	6.8	17.7	9.6	16.7	17.2	13.9
06 003	...	9	Alpine	1 913	1 208	3 103	0.6	77.1	1.2	22.9	2.1	7.8	5.0	17.8	10.4	10.2	17.3	19.0
06 005	...	6	Amador	1 536	35 100	1 247	22.9	88.0	4.1	3.0	1.7	8.9	4.2	16.4	6.9	9.9	16.3	16.2

1. MSA = Metropolitan Statistical Area. PMSA = Primary MSA. NECMA = New England County Metropolitan Area. See Appendix A for explanation of these concepts. See Appendix B for list of metropolitan areas identified by type, with component counties. 2. County typology code from the Economic Research Service of USDA. See Appendix A for definition. 3. Dry land or land partially or temporarily covered by water. 4. Hispanic persons may be of any race.

Table B. States and Counties — **Population and Households**

STATE County	55 to 64 years	65 to 74 years	75 years and over	Percent female	2001	1990	1990–2000	2000–2001	Births	Deaths	Net migration	Number	Percent change, 1990–2000	Persons per household	Female family householder[1]	One person
	16	17	18	19	20	21	22	23	24	25	26	27	28	29	30	31
ARKANSAS—Cont'd																
Conway	10.5	8.5	7.6	51.5	20 404	19 151	6.2	0.3	325	294	42	7 967	11.0	2.51	11.5	25.4
Craighead	8.6	6.2	5.5	51.6	83 008	68 956	19.1	1.0	1 439	882	335	32 301	22.9	2.46	11.4	25.2
Crawford	9.5	6.5	4.8	50.6	54 246	42 493	25.3	1.9	987	605	623	19 702	29.2	2.68	10.9	20.0
Crittenden	8.2	5.3	4.6	52.4	51 114	49 939	1.9	0.5	1 194	623	-312	18 471	7.9	2.72	21.3	23.7
Cross	9.6	7.2	6.5	51.5	19 596	19 225	1.6	0.4	367	266	-25	7 391	9.4	2.60	14.1	23.5
Dallas	9.7	8.4	8.6	51.5	9 061	9 614	-4.2	-1.6	152	161	-142	3 519	-2.3	2.48	13.8	28.3
Desha	9.6	7.2	7.0	53.3	15 052	16 798	-8.7	-1.9	322	238	-376	5 922	-0.6	2.57	19.9	26.9
Drew	9.1	6.9	5.9	51.5	18 870	17 369	7.8	0.8	339	262	74	7 337	15.7	2.46	14.2	26.0
Faulkner	7.5	5.2	4.3	51.2	88 010	60 006	43.3	2.3	1 508	710	1 200	31 882	49.5	2.57	10.2	22.5
Franklin	10.4	8.0	7.8	50.5	17 867	14 897	19.3	0.5	267	276	108	6 882	23.4	2.51	8.8	24.6
Fulton	13.2	11.4	8.8	51.0	11 650	10 037	16.0	0.1	147	179	41	4 810	20.0	2.39	7.8	24.4
Garland	11.6	11.4	9.8	51.4	89 657	73 397	20.0	1.8	1 321	1 550	1 814	37 813	22.6	2.28	10.1	28.8
Grant	10.3	6.7	5.4	50.4	16 714	13 948	18.0	1.5	244	213	221	6 241	21.9	2.61	8.5	20.4
Greene	10.0	7.6	6.3	51.2	37 763	31 804	17.4	1.2	574	541	403	14 750	19.7	2.49	9.7	24.0
Hempstead	9.3	7.3	6.8	51.6	23 440	21 621	9.1	-0.6	470	318	-301	8 959	9.1	2.60	15.3	25.5
Hot Spring	10.6	8.6	7.2	51.2	30 489	26 115	16.2	0.4	476	389	65	12 004	18.7	2.50	10.6	23.5
Howard	9.5	7.3	7.8	51.2	14 244	13 569	5.4	-0.4	274	254	-75	5 471	10.0	2.55	12.7	25.7
Independence	10.3	7.7	6.8	50.9	34 394	31 192	9.7	0.5	545	466	98	13 467	13.7	2.47	9.2	25.5
Izard	13.1	11.0	10.2	49.3	13 211	11 364	16.6	-0.3	164	288	88	5 440	16.1	2.30	7.5	27.8
Jackson	10.4	8.6	7.9	52.3	17 814	18 944	-2.8	-3.3	271	309	-580	6 971	-5.3	2.40	13.1	27.9
Jefferson	8.7	6.6	6.3	51.1	83 565	85 487	-1.4	-0.8	1 794	1 142	-1 368	30 555	1.8	2.59	18.8	26.2
Johnson	10.2	7.8	7.0	50.3	22 793	18 221	25.0	0.1	398	294	-89	8 738	23.8	2.54	9.5	24.6
Lafayette	11.2	8.8	9.0	51.6	8 339	9 643	-11.2	-2.6	145	143	-227	3 434	-4.2	2.46	14.4	28.4
Lawrence	10.7	8.8	8.6	51.6	17 679	17 455	1.8	-0.5	286	340	-40	7 108	3.7	2.42	9.4	26.7
Lee	8.7	7.1	6.9	47.3	12 361	13 053	-3.6	-1.7	219	193	-249	4 182	-8.7	2.59	23.1	27.2
Lincoln	7.9	5.9	5.9	41.3	14 325	13 690	5.9	-1.2	219	159	-229	4 265	12.4	2.63	14.8	23.5
Little River	11.4	7.9	7.1	51.4	13 484	13 966	-2.4	-1.1	219	198	-163	5 465	6.1	2.46	12.3	26.3
Logan	10.7	8.2	7.8	50.4	22 374	20 557	9.4	-0.5	402	342	-170	8 693	14.0	2.53	10.6	24.4
Lonoke	9.0	5.6	4.8	50.8	54 349	39 268	34.5	2.9	906	587	1 187	19 262	38.9	2.71	10.6	19.0
Madison	10.3	7.6	6.8	50.1	14 470	11 618	22.6	1.6	236	172	166	5 463	24.4	2.59	7.9	22.4
Marion	14.1	11.2	8.8	50.5	16 268	12 001	34.5	0.8	189	210	141	6 776	36.3	2.36	7.4	24.9
Miller	9.2	6.9	6.3	51.3	40 718	38 467	5.1	0.7	796	540	38	15 637	9.6	2.52	16.0	25.6
Mississippi	8.5	6.6	5.7	52.1	51 071	57 525	-9.6	-1.7	1 204	742	-1 379	19 349	-9.2	2.64	17.4	24.7
Monroe	10.4	8.7	8.6	53.1	9 966	11 333	-9.5	-2.8	189	196	-285	4 105	-5.9	2.47	16.7	30.1
Montgomery	13.0	10.5	8.4	51.0	9 244	7 841	17.9	0.0	118	124	5	3 785	23.6	2.41	7.0	24.5
Nevada	10.1	7.9	8.2	51.5	9 865	10 101	-1.4	-0.9	176	160	-106	3 893	2.5	2.48	14.0	27.8
Newton	12.8	7.8	7.0	49.4	8 518	7 666	12.3	-1.0	119	110	-101	3 500	24.2	2.44	7.7	26.0
Ouachita	9.7	8.7	8.2	52.7	28 164	30 574	-5.8	-2.2	491	515	-606	11 613	-0.8	2.45	15.6	28.0
Perry	11.0	8.2	6.5	50.4	10 381	7 969	28.1	1.7	174	143	140	3 989	30.6	2.52	8.7	23.2
Phillips	9.4	7.6	6.4	54.1	25 751	28 830	-8.3	-2.6	730	430	-1 016	9 711	-4.6	2.69	25.1	27.6
Pike	11.7	8.1	8.9	50.7	11 222	10 086	12.1	-0.7	190	167	-104	4 504	16.8	2.47	8.3	25.2
Poinsett	10.6	7.7	6.6	51.4	25 580	24 664	3.9	-0.1	445	386	-84	10 026	7.0	2.52	13.2	24.8
Polk	11.5	9.0	8.0	50.8	20 238	17 347	16.6	0.0	352	340	5	8 047	17.9	2.49	8.4	25.0
Pope	9.0	6.8	6.0	50.9	54 746	45 883	18.7	0.5	903	621	15	20 701	23.0	2.55	10.2	23.0
Prairie	11.4	8.7	8.6	50.8	9 529	9 518	0.2	-0.1	138	144	-6	3 894	6.4	2.41	11.1	25.6
Pulaski	8.5	6.0	5.5	52.1	361 967	349 569	3.4	0.1	7 475	4 093	-2 786	147 942	7.8	2.39	15.1	30.0
Randolph	10.9	9.2	7.8	51.0	18 253	16 558	9.9	0.3	255	274	81	7 265	12.7	2.46	9.9	24.7
St. Francis	8.5	6.4	5.5	48.6	28 952	28 497	2.9	-1.3	686	440	-627	10 043	0.9	2.65	20.8	25.1
Saline	10.4	7.3	5.1	50.5	85 698	64 183	30.1	2.6	1 212	905	1 834	31 778	37.9	2.57	9.7	19.6
Scott	11.8	8.1	6.6	49.5	10 977	10 205	7.8	-0.2	192	164	-42	4 323	9.2	2.52	8.5	24.8
Searcy	12.2	10.3	9.0	50.5	8 189	7 841	5.4	-0.9	112	137	-44	3 523	13.0	2.33	7.7	28.0
Sebastian	9.1	6.6	6.4	51.2	115 674	99 590	15.5	0.5	2 183	1 363	-184	45 300	15.3	2.49	11.3	27.5
Sevier	9.3	6.9	6.3	50.2	15 561	13 637	15.5	-1.2	340	213	-330	5 708	11.5	2.73	10.0	22.8
Sharp	12.7	13.1	10.5	52.0	17 299	14 109	21.3	1.1	192	369	345	7 211	23.9	2.34	8.1	25.6
Stone	14.1	10.9	7.7	50.8	11 596	9 775	17.6	0.8	177	194	117	4 768	23.3	2.38	7.1	24.8
Union	9.4	7.8	8.3	52.2	45 177	46 719	-2.3	-1.0	835	697	-586	17 989	1.0	2.48	15.2	26.9
Van Buren	12.7	12.5	10.8	50.8	16 347	14 008	15.6	1.0	198	273	226	6 825	19.8	2.33	7.7	26.4
Washington	7.5	5.2	4.7	49.9	162 023	113 409	39.1	2.7	3 068	1 372	2 618	60 151	38.7	2.52	9.4	25.8
White	9.3	7.2	6.6	51.2	68 542	54 676	22.8	2.1	1 099	843	1 119	25 148	26.9	2.53	9.5	23.4
Woodruff	10.1	8.1	8.6	52.8	8 691	9 520	-8.2	-0.6	142	181	-7	3 531	-2.7	2.44	16.7	28.2
Yell	9.8	7.7	7.4	50.1	21 077	17 759	19.0	-0.3	375	289	-144	7 922	14.7	2.61	10.1	23.2
CALIFORNIA	7.7	5.6	5.0	50.2	34 501 130	29 811 427	13.6	1.9	660 126	285 733	255 179	11 502 870	10.8	2.87	12.6	23.5
Alameda	7.8	5.2	5.0	50.9	1 458 420	1 304 347	10.7	1.0	27 257	12 555	261	523 366	9.1	2.71	13.0	26.0
Alpine	10.3	6.2	3.7	47.4	1 192	1 113	8.5	-1.3	16	9	-24	483	7.3	2.50	11.0	27.7
Amador	12.1	9.8	8.2	44.9	36 269	30 039	16.8	3.3	354	420	1 215	12 759	21.3	2.39	8.7	23.9

1. No spouse present.

Table B. States and Counties — Vital Statistics, Health Resources, and Crime

STATE County	Births, average 1997–1999 Total	Rate[1]	Deaths, average 1997–1999 Number Total	Number Infant[2]	Rate Total[1]	Rate Infant[3]	Physicians,[4] 2000 Number	Rate[5]	Hospitals,[4] 1998 Number	Beds Number	Beds Rate[5]	Medicare enrollees 2000	Serious crimes known to police, 2000[6] Total Number	Rate[7]
	32	33	34	35	36	37	38	39	40	41	42	43	44	45
ARKANSAS—Cont'd														
Conway	257	12.9	247	NA	12.4	NA	9	44	1	60	301	4 636	308	1 515
Craighead	1 143	14.8	725	8	9.4	7.3	217	264	2	425	548	11 379	3 646	4 438
Crawford	770	15.3	471	NA	9.3	NA	34	64	1	66	131	8 034	1 462	2 746
Crittenden	880	17.6	512	10	10.3	11.4	44	87	1	122	244	6 094	2 728	5 363
Cross	285	14.7	227	NA	11.7	NA	9	46	1	59	302	3 089	483	2 474
Dallas	120	13.3	134	NA	14.8	NA	8	87	1	54	596	1 862	364	3 952
Desha	237	15.7	172	NA	11.4	NA	13	85	2	79	523	2 553	784	5 110
Drew	263	15.0	194	NA	11.0	NA	11	59	1	50	284	2 617	308	1 645
Faulkner	1 149	14.7	563	NA	7.2	NA	87	101	1	116	148	9 617	3 175	3 691
Franklin	229	13.7	206	NA	12.3	NA	10	56	1	39	230	3 159	194	1 092
Fulton	120	11.0	147	NA	13.5	NA	7	60	1	39	358	2 736	163	1 400
Garland	994	11.9	1 211	NA	14.4	NA	205	233	2	441	525	22 536	4 331	4 918
Grant	194	12.3	161	NA	10.2	NA	6	36	0	0	0	2 278	143	869
Greene	470	13.0	425	NA	11.8	NA	39	104	1	129	356	6 159	1 018	2 727
Hempstead	333	15.0	258	NA	11.7	NA	22	93	1	75	339	3 566	851	3 608
Hot Spring	363	12.5	310	NA	10.7	NA	13	43	1	77	265	5 301	932	3 071
Howard	188	13.7	189	NA	13.8	NA	11	77	1	50	364	2 654	279	1 951
Independence	433	13.1	365	NA	11.1	NA	46	134	1	146	442	6 168	1 405	4 104
Izard	145	11.2	216	NA	16.6	NA	6	45	1	27	206	3 316	197	1 487
Jackson	219	12.4	258	NA	14.5	NA	26	141	2	174	978	4 991	615	3 339
Jefferson	1 231	15.1	942	16	11.6	12.7	142	168	1	484	593	12 835	6 879	8 162
Johnson	299	14.0	241	NA	11.3	NA	19	83	1	68	318	3 960	499	2 190
Lafayette	119	13.3	111	NA	12.4	NA	5	58	0	0	0	1 629	68	794
Lawrence	220	12.7	258	NA	14.8	NA	7	39	1	202	1 167	4 034	258	1 452
Lee	163	13.0	151	NA	12.1	NA	8	64	0	0	0	1 988	638	5 072
Lincoln	170	11.9	130	NA	9.1	NA	3	21	0	0	0	1 822	145	1 001
Little River	176	13.3	152	NA	11.5	NA	6	44	1	42	318	2 324	284	2 084
Logan	301	14.2	267	NA	12.6	NA	13	58	2	42	198	4 455	257	1 143
Lonoke	676	13.4	440	NA	8.7	NA	14	27	0	0	0	6 486	1 443	2 732
Madison	172	13.0	146	NA	11.0	NA	3	21	0	0	0	2 434	185	1 299
Marion	139	9.4	175	NA	11.8	NA	10	62	0	0	0	3 298	245	1 518
Miller	595	15.0	421	NA	10.6	NA	17	42	0	0	0	5 861	2 358	5 830
Mississippi	915	18.2	601	8	11.9	9.1	41	79	2	270	533	7 701	3 017	5 804
Monroe	151	14.8	147	NA	14.4	NA	10	98	0	0	0	2 000	111	1 083
Montgomery	105	12.1	109	NA	12.6	NA	4	43	0	0	0	1 814	154	1 666
Nevada	127	12.7	136	NA	13.6	NA	2	20	1	49	488	1 868	115	1 155
Newton	98	12.0	85	NA	10.4	NA	2	23	0	0	0	1 585	75	871
Ouachita	355	12.7	402	NA	14.4	NA	20	69	1	118	423	5 939	1 063	3 692
Perry	116	12.1	118	NA	12.3	NA	2	20	0	0	0	1 931	152	1 489
Phillips	502	18.3	361	NA	13.2	NA	25	95	1	125	457	4 679	933	3 528
Pike	142	13.5	129	NA	12.2	NA	7	62	1	41	387	2 032	35	310
Poinsett	356	14.4	321	NA	13.0	NA	11	43	0	0	0	4 617	1 213	4 736
Polk	297	15.1	268	NA	13.7	NA	27	133	1	38	193	3 967	244	1 206
Pope	754	14.5	481	NA	9.3	NA	74	136	1	157	302	8 041	2 030	3 727
Prairie	109	11.7	119	NA	12.7	NA	2	21	0	0	0	1 730	153	1 604
Pulaski	5 488	15.7	3 261	54	9.3	9.8	1 582	438	8	2 569	733	50 629	28 851	7 981
Randolph	230	12.9	212	NA	11.9	NA	11	60	1	50	281	3 510	511	2 808
St. Francis	489	17.4	328	NA	11.7	NA	23	78	1	90	320	4 567	1 900	6 478
Saline	985	12.7	694	NA	9.0	NA	64	77	1	120	155	8 169	2 808	3 362
Scott	134	12.5	135	NA	12.6	NA	3	27	1	24	225	2 161	219	1 992
Searcy	85	10.9	120	NA	15.4	NA	3	36	0	0	0	2 053	50	605
Sebastian	1 731	16.3	1 121	14	10.5	8.1	323	281	2	722	680	17 307	7 673	6 668
Sevier	241	16.5	172	NA	11.7	NA	19	121	1	77	527	2 357	381	2 418
Sharp	165	9.7	256	NA	15.1	NA	13	76	1	34	200	4 786	241	1 408
Stone	121	10.9	138	NA	12.4	NA	11	96	1	48	430	2 503	147	1 278
Union	631	14.0	565	NA	12.5	NA	87	191	2	378	834	8 771	1 960	4 296
Van Buren	147	9.4	215	NA	13.8	NA	9	56	1	144	926	3 925	145	896
Washington	2 313	16.4	1 105	17	7.8	7.5	312	198	2	419	303	19 057	5 419	3 436
White	850	13.2	689	NA	10.7	NA	72	107	2	253	392	11 213	2 214	3 296
Woodruff	123	13.9	131	NA	14.8	NA	6	69	0	0	0	1 790	43	492
Yell	274	14.4	233	NA	12.2	NA	13	61	2	85	445	4 067	335	1 585
CALIFORNIA	516 576	15.8	226 975	2 970	6.9	5.8	75 739	224	444	90 767	278	3 901 323	1 266 714	3 740
Alameda	20 281	14.5	9 789	114	7.0	5.6	3 488	242	17	3 748	268	157 525	67 823	4 698
Alpine	14	12.0	10	NA	8.1	NA	0	0	0	0	0	130	87	7 202
Amador	276	8.2	352	NA	10.5	NA	59	168	1	89	267	6 830	853	2 500

1. Per 1,000 estimated resident population, average 1997–1999. 2. Deaths of infants under 1 year old. 3. Deaths of infants under 1 year old per 1,000 live births. 4. Data subject to copyright. 5. Per 100,000 resident population as of July 1 of the year shown. 6. Data for serious crimes have not been adjusted for underreporting; this may affect comparability between geographic areas and over time. 7. Per 100,000 population estimated by the FBI.

Table B. States and Counties — Crime, Education, Money Income, and Poverty

STATE County	Serious crimes known to police, 2000[1] (cont'd) Rate[2] Violent	Property	Education — School enrollment and attainment, 1990 — Enrollment[3] Total	Percent private	Attainment[4] (percent) High school graduate or more	Bachelor's degree or more	Local government expenditures, fiscal 1999[5] Total current expenditures (mil dol)	Current expenditures per student (dollars)	Money income 1989 Per capita[6] (dollars)	Households Median Dollars	Percent change, 1979–1989 (constant 1989 dollars)	Percent with $100,000 or more	Income and poverty, 1998 Median household income	Percent below poverty level All persons	Persons under 18	Persons 5–17 in families
	46	47	48	49	50	51	52	53	54	55	56	57	58	59	60	61
ARKANSAS—Cont'd																
Conway	103	1 411	4 477	9.4	64.5	9.8	32.5	9 106	9 126	20 538	4.9	0.5	29 430	16.5	24.0	21.0
Craighead	297	4 141	19 048	5.2	67.5	16.4	64.3	5 019	11 301	22 150	1.3	2.2	33 379	15.2	21.2	17.7
Crawford	265	2 481	10 569	6.4	63.8	7.6	50.1	4 844	9 689	21 574	-0.5	1.4	31 403	15.3	21.2	18.1
Crittenden	1 205	4 158	13 573	8.1	57.6	9.8	51.2	4 742	9 334	20 948	6.9	1.3	28 613	23.5	31.9	27.4
Cross	415	2 059	5 029	3.3	55.8	8.0	19.0	4 656	8 897	19 049	-6.6	1.5	27 475	21.0	27.8	25.2
Dallas	847	3 105	2 169	3.0	59.2	8.8	9.0	5 101	9 101	17 651	-8.2	1.0	26 344	19.4	27.3	26.5
Desha	730	4 380	4 633	4.3	56.5	10.4	18.9	5 189	8 428	15 719	-7.8	2.1	24 994	25.2	33.9	29.6
Drew	240	1 405	4 807	2.4	63.1	13.9	19.7	5 972	9 114	18 906	-5.3	1.2	29 476	18.1	25.3	24.0
Faulkner	236	3 455	18 315	11.6	72.4	17.9	65.6	4 678	10 141	23 663	4.6	1.3	37 983	10.8	15.3	11.9
Franklin	163	928	3 319	4.0	60.1	8.8	18.5	5 091	8 877	18 408	-4.2	0.9	28 507	16.6	22.2	19.8
Fulton	112	1 288	1 956	1.0	54.9	5.4	8.2	4 810	8 240	14 950	-5.6	1.7	21 789	22.1	30.9	30.2
Garland	472	4 445	14 792	8.6	70.2	14.2	64.7	5 069	11 873	20 260	-0.4	1.8	29 627	15.7	26.5	21.7
Grant	49	820	3 230	4.3	68.9	9.3	20.8	4 570	10 344	24 278	1.8	0.5	37 396	11.1	16.5	13.5
Greene	142	2 585	7 058	8.0	58.5	9.1	31.1	4 855	9 757	19 940	3.4	1.2	31 641	13.4	20.0	17.4
Hempstead	424	5 090	5 090	8.3	62.0	9.3	23.0	5 586	8 583	16 986	-9.2	1.0	25 800	20.5	28.8	24.6
Hot Spring	297	2 774	5 961	3.5	64.5	9.0	28.9	5 162	9 164	19 355	-7.0	0.7	28 965	15.5	20.5	19.8
Howard	42	1 909	3 132	5.1	61.8	8.3	15.1	4 875	9 563	21 277	9.5	1.3	27 958	17.5	23.8	21.2
Independence	169	3 935	7 325	11.2	63.1	10.3	30.6	5 180	10 493	20 208	2.5	2.2	30 222	15.9	22.5	18.8
Izard	151	1 336	2 026	2.8	61.1	9.4	11.7	5 807	8 852	16 910	4.9	0.8	23 701	20.0	27.5	27.1
Jackson	472	2 867	4 099	3.4	51.6	6.7	14.3	5 132	8 984	16 641	-9.4	1.2	25 495	22.4	32.3	27.7
Jefferson	1 450	6 712	23 015	6.0	65.9	14.6	80.2	5 189	9 852	21 322	-0.3	1.6	28 609	22.5	31.0	26.0
Johnson	40	2 151	4 347	12.9	63.3	12.0	18.5	4 556	8 924	18 225	3.0	1.2	26 672	18.1	27.2	23.0
Lafayette	82	713	2 466	1.1	51.6	6.9	8.9	5 328	7 573	13 849	-10.5	0.7	23 059	24.4	29.8	31.5
Lawrence	231	1 221	3 945	10.6	53.3	6.1	18.5	5 514	8 231	15 337	-5.5	0.8	25 300	20.4	28.6	25.0
Lee	477	4 595	3 903	9.8	44.2	7.4	11.6	5 811	6 582	11 949	-3.3	1.4	20 616	33.3	36.1	37.5
Lincoln	207	794	3 065	7.3	58.5	5.6	10.7	4 852	7 899	18 457	6.1	1.5	27 740	23.4	25.8	26.0
Little River	147	1 937	3 468	3.9	64.6	8.1	12.0	5 551	9 942	21 791	-3.8	0.7	29 185	18.0	24.9	22.0
Logan	49	1 094	4 835	8.1	58.1	6.8	17.4	4 716	8 283	18 992	13.1	0.4	27 170	17.8	24.5	21.3
Lonoke	218	2 514	10 228	6.2	67.1	10.0	48.1	4 569	10 273	23 831	5.4	1.9	37 993	11.6	16.1	13.2
Madison	442	857	2 459	5.7	59.6	8.2	11.9	4 509	8 548	18 392	7.9	0.8	27 903	18.7	24.9	22.8
Marion	297	1 221	2 240	4.5	64.2	8.0	11.2	4 701	9 339	17 220	3.4	1.2	24 528	17.9	27.0	23.9
Miller	799	5 032	9 781	6.0	63.9	9.5	36.1	5 209	9 663	20 232	-3.6	1.5	28 752	20.0	27.3	25.0
Mississippi	739	5 066	15 874	5.1	60.0	10.5	52.4	5 125	8 691	18 522	-1.4	1.3	27 422	22.9	30.4	27.0
Monroe	263	819	2 955	8.9	52.9	8.4	10.4	5 070	7 587	13 633	-4.5	1.1	21 819	27.9	36.4	34.1
Montgomery	498	1 168	1 601	2.7	60.1	7.0	6.8	4 769	8 343	16 503	0.0	0.8	25 245	20.0	28.7	27.4
Nevada	151	1 005	2 384	1.2	60.6	9.8	9.6	4 831	9 666	18 919	8.7	1.3	26 559	18.9	25.0	22.8
Newton	186	685	1 878	2.3	58.1	6.8	7.6	5 386	7 114	15 139	15.1	0.4	23 064	23.3	28.5	28.0
Ouachita	518	3 175	7 568	4.4	64.8	12.2	30.5	5 377	9 974	21 056	11.1	1.0	27 486	20.1	30.1	25.5
Perry	137	1 352	1 683	5.4	61.1	6.2	9.1	4 851	8 848	17 626	-8.4	0.9	28 054	14.3	20.4	18.8
Phillips	427	3 101	8 596	8.5	51.5	9.2	34.1	5 603	6 692	13 071	-9.1	0.7	20 208	32.6	39.3	37.0
Pike	0	310	2 203	5.6	61.1	8.5	11.1	5 025	9 220	19 240	3.8	1.7	28 490	16.2	20.7	20.5
Poinsett	718	4 017	5 483	2.0	48.9	5.6	26.9	5 533	8 792	16 858	-10.2	1.1	26 249	21.5	29.6	26.9
Polk	148	1 058	3 999	4.1	62.4	9.9	17.6	4 770	8 884	17 789	5.5	1.0	24 976	19.9	27.1	24.5
Pope	191	3 536	12 350	4.3	66.5	14.7	49.5	5 130	10 347	22 326	4.1	1.7	32 170	15.1	20.3	17.7
Prairie	294	1 310	2 121	4.0	56.3	7.2	7.5	4 767	8 642	17 044	0.8	0.8	28 238	17.4	24.3	22.8
Pulaski	779	7 202	89 508	18.1	79.0	23.5	338.4	6 368	13 760	26 883	2.5	3.3	36 249	13.7	21.3	16.7
Randolph	451	2 358	3 724	9.4	54.4	7.9	14.8	4 951	8 219	16 719	-7.5	0.9	25 605	19.1	26.7	24.3
St. Francis	1 132	5 346	8 461	3.8	55.1	8.5	31.9	5 301	7 194	15 029	-7.1	0.6	23 776	27.2	32.7	30.7
Saline	244	3 117	15 304	8.2	72.9	11.9	54.4	4 510	11 677	28 262	-3.8	1.7	40 513	8.6	12.1	11.1
Scott	155	1 837	2 101	3.7	53.8	5.9	7.4	4 408	8 360	16 470	7.9	1.0	25 829	20.9	30.0	27.3
Searcy	109	496	1 711	2.3	52.5	7.5	7.5	5 369	7 209	13 221	3.8	1.5	20 250	25.7	33.3	32.9
Sebastian	578	6 090	23 363	10.4	71.7	14.6	95.0	5 136	12 361	24 037	4.2	2.7	33 727	14.2	21.3	17.3
Sevier	292	2 126	3 185	4.8	59.0	7.2	16.2	5 342	9 060	19 208	-4.4	1.2	27 009	18.6	26.9	23.0
Sharp	105	1 303	2 724	4.8	64.5	8.7	15.0	4 903	8 578	17 362	4.2	0.8	23 111	19.2	26.0	26.2
Stone	139	1 139	2 077	5.7	59.6	9.4	8.7	4 872	7 679	15 655	13.6	0.2	23 135	20.4	27.6	26.3
Union	822	3 474	11 170	6.8	65.9	12.7	43.9	4 997	10 617	21 041	4.5	1.9	31 282	17.7	25.8	21.5
Van Buren	191	704	2 765	4.6	62.6	10.5	11.6	4 772	8 706	17 103	-4.3	0.2	24 325	19.4	28.8	26.4
Washington	311	3 125	33 005	5.9	73.2	20.0	130.2	5 187	11 625	23 124	7.8	2.2	33 831	13.0	17.8	14.9
White	293	3 003	14 775	24.3	62.6	10.9	56.4	4 930	9 902	19 722	4.6	1.5	30 533	15.9	21.0	18.3
Woodruff	0	492	2 437	2.8	48.7	7.5	8.4	5 224	7 583	14 024	-8.1	1.0	21 962	26.4	32.6	33.9
Yell	341	1 244	3 762	3.8	57.2	7.4	18.5	4 715	9 400	19 647	11.6	1.3	26 717	16.4	23.9	20.6
CALIFORNIA	622	3 118	8 300 046	13.5	76.2	23.4	34 379.9	5 801	16 409	35 798	17.1	7.1	41 003	14.9	22.8	21.8
Alameda	658	4 040	351 410	14.5	81.4	28.8	1 254.0	5 851	17 547	37 544	19.8	6.7	48 445	10.8	17.3	16.3
Alpine	828	6 374	257	7.8	87.6	24.0	2.2	17 976	13 799	24 929	-6.5	2.4	31 444	17.9	29.8	39.8
Amador	525	1 975	6 355	11.2	82.5	14.0	28.0	5 630	14 282	30 265	17.5	3.2	39 610	11.3	17.7	18.3

1. Data for serious crimes have not been adjusted for underreporting; this may affect comparability between geographic areas and over time.   2. Per 100,000 population estimated by the FBI.   3. All persons 3 years old and over enrolled in nursery school through college.   4. Persons 25 years old and over.   5. Elementary and secondary education expenditures, local government fiscal years ending between July 1, 1998 and June 30, 1999.   6. Based on population enumerated as of April 1, 1990.

Table B. States and Counties — Personal Income

STATE County	Total (mil dol)	Percent change, 1998–1999	Per capita¹ Dollars	Per capita¹ Rank	Wages and salaries² (mil dol)	Proprietor's income (mil dol)	Dividends, interest, and rent (mil dol)	Transfer payments Total (mil dol)	Government payments to individuals Total (mil dol)	Social Security (mil dol)	Medical payments (mil dol)	Income mainte- nance (mil dol)	Unemploy- ment insurance (mil dol)
	62	63	64	65	66	67	68	69	70	71	72	73	74
ARKANSAS—Cont'd													
Conway	410	3.7	20 642	1 795	192	55	61	87	83	36	31	9	2
Craighead	1 697	5.9	21 853	1 398	1 136	137	295	267	253	105	100	25	4
Crawford	929	7.8	18 074	2 527	434	78	126	173	163	74	58	16	4
Crittenden	1 027	5.0	20 490	1 840	466	86	122	170	161	58	60	35	2
Cross	334	0.5	17 314	2 679	153	37	53	73	70	27	27	10	2
Dallas	189	6.6	21 162	1 613	88	28	26	54	53	17	29	5	1
Desha	277	5.1	18 638	2 381	167	33	47	65	62	21	25	11	2
Drew	348	3.5	19 924	2 018	189	35	56	66	63	25	23	8	2
Faulkner	1 962	10.8	24 517	754	995	112	294	309	294	91	158	15	5
Franklin	310	3.5	18 438	2 431	116	47	54	67	64	28	24	6	1
Fulton	158	5.0	14 310	3 030	40	17	28	50	48	24	15	5	0
Garland	2 094	4.2	24 789	706	927	131	682	425	409	202	149	27	6
Grant	329	5.5	20 559	1 823	109	21	46	49	46	23	14	4	1
Greene	684	4.8	18 804	2 346	383	63	120	128	122	56	41	13	3
Hempstead	440	6.3	19 938	2 012	240	70	69	88	83	34	33	11	2
Hot Spring	508	4.4	17 416	2 662	208	41	83	116	111	52	40	10	2
Howard	308	4.5	22 479	1 218	203	72	45	55	53	22	22	5	1
Independence	692	4.8	20 922	1 689	448	68	124	132	126	55	47	12	3
Izard	222	7.0	16 947	2 743	78	26	46	64	61	30	20	5	1
Jackson	354	1.9	20 213	1 924	160	45	56	97	94	32	43	11	3
Jefferson	1 627	2.9	20 141	1 956	1 117	77	291	320	304	109	100	50	7
Johnson	391	3.9	18 303	2 469	189	53	69	81	77	36	24	8	1
Lafayette	161	9.3	18 192	2 501	49	35	24	39	38	14	14	7	1
Lawrence	300	1.4	17 289	2 686	118	43	52	79	76	31	29	9	2
Lee	197	12.4	15 500	2 944	68	37	30	54	52	16	19	14	1
Lincoln	208	4.2	14 479	3 022	91	35	24	44	41	16	15	7	1
Little River	280	5.5	21 403	1 548	182	40	38	52	49	21	17	5	1
Logan	419	7.4	19 824	2 050	151	59	69	115	111	39	55	9	2
Lonoke	1 139	7.4	22 131	1 318	272	83	149	157	148	60	58	12	2
Madison	251	6.6	18 820	2 341	63	65	39	46	43	22	12	5	1
Marion	254	6.3	17 070	2 723	89	25	64	66	63	32	19	6	1
Miller	760	5.1	19 305	2 207	383	97	131	144	136	54	55	20	1
Mississippi	1 000	3.9	20 032	1 982	662	97	143	197	188	68	65	36	9
Monroe	179	2.5	17 959	2 547	72	23	31	49	48	17	19	9	1
Montgomery	155	4.6	17 713	2 599	37	34	31	38	36	16	13	4	1
Nevada	187	6.4	18 700	2 367	65	28	29	46	44	16	20	5	1
Newton	114	4.1	13 850	3 053	23	12	19	34	32	14	10	5	1
Ouachita	533	1.7	19 399	2 181	223	45	100	128	123	54	43	16	3
Perry	152	4.1	15 706	2 928	29	23	23	36	35	15	12	3	1
Phillips	426	3.3	15 766	2 922	206	36	64	136	131	39	52	34	2
Pike	213	5.1	20 351	1 874	73	45	33	42	40	19	15	4	1
Poinsett	447	2.9	18 193	2 500	177	59	68	102	98	40	37	14	2
Polk	362	5.2	18 470	2 421	153	75	62	81	77	35	25	8	1
Pope	1 103	4.6	20 964	1 675	730	108	185	183	173	78	59	17	4
Prairie	167	3.6	17 956	2 548	47	26	29	40	38	16	14	4	1
Pulaski	10 520	3.5	30 124	206	8 937	760	2 140	1 239	1 175	480	431	117	24
Randolph	285	1.8	15 936	2 903	126	27	50	74	71	32	24	8	2
St. Francis	488	3.3	17 580	2 634	260	50	64	122	117	37	43	27	4
Saline	1 793	8.2	22 884	1 114	505	73	217	305	290	120	141	12	4
Scott	208	4.9	19 515	2 135	75	56	31	43	41	19	14	5	1
Searcy	127	3.5	16 272	2 865	32	24	20	39	37	16	13	5	1
Sebastian	2 765	5.5	26 025	510	2 236	300	558	384	364	168	128	33	8
Sevier	299	4.7	20 371	1 868	136	69	37	53	50	21	19	5	1
Sharp	284	3.9	16 623	2 807	88	30	69	89	85	42	29	8	1
Stone	198	6.5	17 616	2 621	63	38	34	52	49	22	17	5	1
Union	1 118	3.4	24 862	693	631	108	282	195	187	87	65	22	5
Van Buren	263	4.4	16 757	2 788	78	25	65	77	74	38	23	6	1
Washington	3 242	5.8	22 115	1 325	2 352	313	634	400	372	177	114	31	8
White	1 185	5.2	18 207	2 496	641	90	203	229	217	97	75	21	5
Woodruff	154	0.2	17 649	2 612	71	12	25	45	44	14	19	7	1
Yell	361	3.7	19 157	2 244	163	56	57	78	74	34	28	7	1
CALIFORNIA	989 590	7.1	29 856	X	627 536	108 128	182 522	114 051	107 700	35 972	42 783	18 996	2 734
Alameda	48 315	9.7	34 131	105	32 418	3 612	8 021	4 948	4 676	1 436	1 941	858	91
Alpine	30	8.4	25 480	584	21	5	4	6	6	1	3	2	0
Amador	714	5.5	20 915	1 692	290	84	186	140	133	69	43	10	2

1. Based on the resident population estimated as of July 1 of the year shown.   2. Includes other labor income.

Table B. States and Counties — Earnings, Social Security, and Housing

STATE County	Earnings, 1999 Total (mil dol)	Farm	Goods-related[1] Total	Manu-facturing	Service-related and other[2] Total	Retail trade	Finance, insurance, and real estate	Services	Government	Social Security beneficiaries, December 2000 Number	Rate[3]	Supplemental Security Income recipients, December 2000	Housing units, 1990 Total	Percent change, 1980-1990
	75	76	77	78	79	80	81	82	83	84	85	86	87	88
ARKANSAS—Cont'd														
Conway	247	12.2	D	21.6	D	9.8	2.3	16.2	13.7	4 830	238	819	8 009	7.4
Craighead	1 272	2.3	D	22.4	D	10.8	4.4	26.7	15.4	13 252	161	2 496	28 434	17.8
Crawford	512	3.9	D	24.1	D	8.9	3.0	15.0	12.2	10 157	191	1 617	16 711	21.4
Crittenden	552	5.9	D	13.4	D	14.6	3.6	20.9	15.3	7 803	153	2 673	18 875	11.2
Cross	190	10.9	25.8	21.0	45.1	10.7	4.7	13.4	18.2	3 639	186	945	7 254	0.9
Dallas	116	2.2	47.8	43.0	38.7	9.2	1.9	16.8	11.3	2 121	230	464	4 049	-4.4
Desha	200	13.5	D	D	D	8.2	3.2	10.4	16.7	2 839	185	811	6 706	-7.7
Drew	224	5.3	31.4	27.8	40.3	11.1	4.2	13.9	22.9	3 322	177	595	7 159	7.7
Faulkner	1 108	0.9	D	22.6	D	9.4	3.4	31.5	16.1	11 828	138	1 510	23 397	39.2
Franklin	163	17.6	25.2	17.2	32.0	7.4	2.3	12.0	25.1	3 857	217	558	6 228	9.5
Fulton	57	7.0	22.4	13.1	D	9.7	4.3	17.4	25.9	3 409	293	481	4 839	11.0
Garland	1 059	1.5	21.8	12.5	63.0	14.6	5.3	32.8	13.7	24 028	273	2 490	37 966	11.3
Grant	130	2.2	D	41.2	D	7.7	2.5	10.2	18.3	2 875	175	281	5 540	13.0
Greene	446	4.5	D	43.6	D	9.9	2.7	17.1	11.4	7 869	211	1 232	13 216	10.6
Hempstead	310	15.9	36.4	33.4	32.5	7.2	2.4	14.8	15.1	4 391	186	777	9 690	-0.1
Hot Spring	249	1.9	41.0	32.2	38.5	9.9	3.4	14.3	18.6	6 467	213	756	11 378	6.3
Howard	275	17.3	48.5	45.8	25.3	5.9	1.7	8.7	9.0	2 939	206	425	5 600	8.9
Independence	515	3.3	39.7	34.4	45.8	8.8	2.5	20.4	11.2	7 458	218	1 177	12 838	10.4
Izard	104	5.2	D	22.7	D	11.9	4.3	14.6	27.0	3 902	295	448	5 535	9.1
Jackson	205	13.1	D	21.0	D	9.2	D	24.3	12.6	4 118	224	870	8 086	-2.6
Jefferson	1 193	1.7	27.3	24.2	46.1	9.1	3.5	20.6	24.9	14 573	173	3 636	33 311	0.8
Johnson	242	11.4	D	33.4	D	16.7	2.9	15.2	12.7	4 882	214	839	7 984	11.2
Lafayette	85	32.0	25.3	18.2	27.3	6.0	2.9	9.3	15.4	1 891	221	549	4 523	0.5
Lawrence	161	10.9	D	19.9	D	10.5	2.7	12.4	20.8	4 456	251	925	7 692	2.8
Lee	105	32.7	D	10.9	D	6.8	2.0	11.8	26.2	2 493	198	1 021	5 085	-3.5
Lincoln	126	25.3	D	13.4	D	4.2	1.8	8.1	33.4	2 341	162	546	4 295	1.6
Little River	222	9.7	D	48.9	D	4.6	1.6	4.6	10.4	2 729	200	451	6 171	7.7
Logan	209	16.5	D	30.7	D	8.9	3.4	11.4	18.2	5 326	237	803	8 539	8.1
Lonoke	355	9.6	27.9	17.7	45.1	12.7	4.5	16.1	17.4	7 949	150	1 039	15 009	20.6
Madison	128	33.4	27.3	20.7	26.0	6.0	2.6	10.8	13.2	3 129	220	383	5 182	9.2
Marion	114	7.0	D	40.8	D	8.4	4.0	13.4	15.3	4 326	268	462	6 139	13.9
Miller	479	4.2	37.2	29.1	45.5	10.5	2.9	16.0	13.0	7 051	174	1 447	16 172	10.1
Mississippi	759	5.1	D	44.1	D	8.1	2.9	13.3	12.0	9 565	184	3 145	22 232	3.1
Monroe	94	15.2	D	12.9	D	12.9	5.5	14.0	17.3	2 335	228	708	5 063	-11.7
Montgomery	71	25.9	D	17.8	D	7.1	3.1	11.3	20.0	2 291	248	258	4 269	18.6
Nevada	93	16.5	D	34.2	D	6.4	1.6	15.9	11.2	2 222	223	473	4 287	-3.4
Newton	35	5.1	21.3	15.1	D	8.5	D	15.0	39.6	2 125	247	489	3 439	11.6
Ouachita	269	1.5	33.3	27.8	47.2	11.6	3.6	18.3	18.1	6 788	236	1 377	13 204	9.0
Perry	51	23.0	D	5.2	D	7.8	3.2	14.1	24.2	2 189	214	371	3 702	16.6
Phillips	242	7.1	D	15.0	D	10.6	3.7	20.6	21.9	5 697	215	2 507	11 094	-10.5
Pike	117	21.4	25.5	18.3	36.9	10.4	4.5	8.7	16.2	2 551	226	292	4 550	7.0
Poinsett	236	15.1	D	26.9	38.0	7.9	4.3	10.7	15.6	5 617	219	1 362	10 271	0.6
Polk	228	19.7	30.5	26.6	35.9	8.7	2.7	15.2	13.9	4 775	236	604	7 732	10.5
Pope	838	4.5	D	19.0	D	9.9	D	17.8	13.4	10 438	192	1 772	18 430	23.7
Prairie	74	27.3	16.1	11.0	39.6	9.4	2.1	11.8	17.0	2 161	227	312	4 340	6.9
Pulaski	9 696	0.1	13.4	8.4	64.0	8.5	8.5	27.7	22.5	58 526	162	9 821	151 538	14.1
Randolph	153	4.5	D	30.5	D	10.3	4.2	17.5	17.3	4 374	240	675	7 343	9.3
St. Francis	310	8.8	D	20.9	D	9.6	3.2	15.0	24.6	5 146	175	2 189	10 958	2.8
Saline	578	0.2	D	16.3	D	17.2	3.7	21.0	21.0	14 583	175	1 028	24 602	30.5
Scott	131	30.4	35.5	33.2	23.2	5.7	1.5	7.9	11.0	2 787	253	368	4 485	16.8
Searcy	56	6.4	D	14.5	D	10.0	4.0	13.6	24.8	2 395	290	513	3 739	1.5
Sebastian	2 536	0.5	36.8	30.7	53.7	9.3	3.5	30.4	9.0	20 868	181	2 932	43 621	11.5
Sevier	205	22.6	D	30.7	D	6.4	2.5	12.6	12.5	2 789	177	332	5 880	6.4
Sharp	118	10.2	D	7.6	D	14.5	5.5	20.7	18.7	5 365	313	677	7 617	5.7
Stone	101	17.3	27.0	22.1	D	12.9	2.7	15.7	17.9	3 213	279	567	4 548	17.9
Union	739	2.2	45.8	32.0	40.8	8.5	3.2	16.6	11.1	10 365	227	1 949	20 276	2.8
Van Buren	103	3.8	25.2	17.1	D	13.5	5.7	20.0	18.7	4 750	293	479	7 580	25.1
Washington	2 665	3.8	D	21.7	D	10.5	4.1	19.9	17.5	22 588	143	2 613	47 349	23.0
White	731	1.5	D	20.2	D	18.5	2.6	24.6	12.3	12 840	191	1 866	21 658	17.2
Woodruff	83	13.9	21.5	17.5	46.2	5.7	2.7	8.7	17.8	1 994	228	542	4 169	-7.0
Yell	219	14.2	D	34.2	D	6.5	3.3	9.5	17.8	4 763	225	775	7 868	14.4
CALIFORNIA	735 664	1.1	21.0	15.1	62.9	8.9	8.8	32.1	15.0	4 208 926	124	1 086 333	11 182 882	20.5
Alameda	36 030	0.0	22.6	15.9	60.0	9.0	4.8	30.3	17.4	163 915	114	47 991	504 109	13.4
Alpine	26	0.0	11.3	0.0	D	4.7	D	D	17.9	141	117	23	1 319	41.4
Amador	375	0.9	15.4	7.4	56.7	14.3	4.0	28.8	27.0	7 945	226	490	12 814	35.7

1. Covers mining, construction, and manufacturing.   2. Covers private sector earnings in agricultural services, forestry, and fisheries; transportation and public utilities; wholesale trade; retail trade; finance, insurance, and real estate; and services.   3. Per 1,000 resident population estimated as of July 1 of the year shown.

Table B. States and Counties — Housing, Labor Force, and Employment

STATE County	Housing units, 1990 (cont'd) — Occupied units — Owner-occupied			Owner cost as a percent of income		Renter-occupied			Civilian labor force, 2001		Unemployment		Civilian employment, 1990[5]	Percent	
	Total	Percent	Median value[1]	With a mortgage	Without a mortgage	Median rent[2]	Rent as percent of income	Substandard units[3] (percent)	Total	Percent change, 2000–2001	Total	Rate[4]	Total	Professional, managerial, and technical	Precision production, craft, and repair
	89	90	91	92	93	94	95	96	97	98	99	100	101	102	103
ARKANSAS—Cont'd															
Conway	7 179	76.4	38 200	19.8	13.6	299	27.5	5.2	9 021	-1.4	479	5.3	7 821	17.3	14.0
Craighead	26 285	65.4	50 200	19.3	13.1	335	26.8	2.2	42 456	-1.5	1 886	4.4	32 772	23.6	11.2
Crawford	15 251	76.4	43 500	21.1	12.8	298	25.3	5.4	24 572	-1.1	1 014	4.1	18 095	17.7	15.0
Crittenden	17 120	61.0	48 900	20.7	14.6	338	28.6	9.9	22 720	0.2	1 338	5.9	20 049	20.9	11.6
Cross	6 754	69.7	39 100	20.9	14.6	297	26.9	6.1	7 697	-3.5	578	7.5	7 393	16.9	12.1
Dallas	3 600	77.9	33 600	20.1	13.3	265	28.8	6.5	3 529	-0.7	324	9.2	3 757	15.2	12.7
Desha	5 957	66.0	36 700	20.2	14.9	249	34.5	8.5	6 622	-4.9	733	11.1	5 758	19.6	10.6
Drew	6 342	72.0	38 700	18.8	13.8	281	28.5	5.3	9 288	-5.2	942	10.1	7 414	20.9	10.9
Faulkner	21 325	70.5	55 400	20.6	13.0	351	27.3	4.3	42 515	-0.3	2 108	5.0	27 806	25.9	13.3
Franklin	5 578	79.0	36 600	22.8	12.6	268	23.5	5.5	7 512	-0.5	255	3.4	6 161	17.9	16.3
Fulton	4 010	81.7	34 000	22.6	13.5	248	29.1	6.3	4 084	-1.8	225	5.5	3 557	16.9	14.0
Garland	30 836	70.8	53 500	21.2	13.3	327	28.4	2.8	35 544	-0.5	1 528	4.3	29 450	25.1	11.4
Grant	5 118	82.9	43 000	17.3	13.9	312	24.2	4.2	6 890	-5.3	422	6.1	6 269	21.0	16.7
Greene	12 325	73.0	39 400	18.0	12.3	274	25.1	3.1	18 173	-3.8	1 414	7.8	13 831	16.9	14.8
Hempstead	8 212	73.6	34 900	20.3	13.9	288	28.4	6.7	10 927	-2.9	530	4.9	8 839	18.1	15.6
Hot Spring	10 115	77.7	39 200	20.9	13.4	297	24.9	4.5	12 228	0.4	729	6.0	10 264	19.9	14.3
Howard	4 975	73.6	36 200	19.2	13.3	270	21.7	6.0	6 648	-2.9	363	5.5	5 873	14.8	15.6
Independence	11 846	75.3	40 600	19.2	13.5	300	23.7	4.4	16 651	-0.3	1 012	6.1	13 650	20.7	15.2
Izard	4 684	79.8	37 300	22.5	12.9	249	25.4	4.8	4 151	-4.2	274	6.6	3 986	18.4	14.8
Jackson	7 361	68.6	34 100	20.6	13.9	271	27.5	4.8	7 579	-1.7	660	8.7	7 153	19.6	11.3
Jefferson	30 001	67.1	43 300	17.0	15.0	337	28.1	5.7	35 674	-1.2	2 926	8.2	33 236	25.2	11.6
Johnson	7 059	75.2	38 200	18.5	12.6	267	24.6	5.6	10 470	-1.1	447	4.3	7 155	20.8	15.1
Lafayette	3 584	76.3	24 300	20.9	14.6	263	29.4	9.6	3 225	-4.2	169	5.2	3 315	18.2	13.4
Lawrence	6 857	75.1	31 000	20.9	14.0	268	28.4	2.7	7 162	-1.0	574	8.0	6 710	16.5	13.1
Lee	4 578	62.8	31 500	22.2	15.8	234	35.1	13.0	4 599	-2.4	431	9.4	3 853	17.8	9.8
Lincoln	3 796	75.5	30 300	18.7	15.3	253	26.5	9.5	5 190	-2.0	315	6.1	4 045	18.2	11.3
Little River	5 150	76.6	40 100	16.7	12.8	288	25.6	6.4	5 371	-2.1	239	4.4	6 046	19.7	14.7
Logan	7 628	78.2	34 200	19.5	13.1	256	26.5	5.0	9 175	-1.7	492	5.4	8 222	17.8	16.6
Lonoke	13 866	74.4	52 700	22.1	13.8	341	25.9	4.8	25 731	-1.0	911	3.5	17 388	19.5	14.4
Madison	4 392	80.0	34 800	21.5	12.9	265	24.4	8.6	7 007	4.2	209	3.0	5 090	16.0	15.1
Marion	4 970	80.4	41 800	23.1	13.1	287	30.1	4.6	6 189	-0.5	347	5.6	4 363	20.6	12.9
Miller	14 273	68.3	43 200	17.5	14.1	328	26.3	5.5	16 925	-1.2	733	4.3	15 440	20.8	14.3
Mississippi	20 420	54.4	41 800	20.6	15.2	315	26.5	7.1	25 231	-2.9	3 508	13.9	20 907	19.8	13.0
Monroe	4 361	63.1	32 300	23.1	15.5	247	29.6	9.2	3 788	-3.5	282	7.4	3 871	19.1	10.4
Montgomery	3 062	82.5	32 600	23.6	13.6	254	29.0	5.9	3 933	-2.2	164	4.2	3 090	14.5	14.4
Nevada	3 798	76.3	30 000	19.9	13.2	245	25.1	7.5	4 720	-2.9	232	4.9	3 929	16.4	12.9
Newton	2 818	83.2	32 200	17.8	13.3	207	23.4	16.2	2 919	-2.1	196	6.7	2 625	16.8	13.3
Ouachita	11 712	73.2	38 900	17.7	13.9	286	26.4	5.8	11 198	-0.6	1 087	9.7	12 234	23.9	13.4
Perry	3 055	83.6	38 600	23.5	13.3	248	23.0	7.1	3 608	-0.8	261	7.2	3 277	11.0	16.1
Phillips	10 183	53.7	36 900	18.6	16.1	253	34.1	9.2	9 057	-3.4	926	10.2	9 188	21.6	11.8
Pike	3 855	79.9	32 800	22.0	13.3	243	25.0	4.5	4 753	-3.5	262	5.5	4 083	16.7	14.0
Poinsett	9 368	65.2	34 500	19.7	13.9	233	27.6	4.9	10 141	-3.6	962	9.5	9 626	14.7	14.2
Polk	6 827	76.2	36 300	23.1	13.1	255	25.7	5.5	9 165	-1.2	406	4.4	6 841	21.0	15.8
Pope	16 828	70.8	48 000	20.9	13.4	328	25.3	3.0	26 831	-1.2	1 112	4.1	20 347	23.4	14.3
Prairie	3 661	73.2	35 200	19.5	15.9	248	23.4	4.8	3 935	-2.8	190	4.8	3 906	14.5	11.9
Pulaski	137 209	60.3	61 300	19.6	13.1	403	26.4	3.5	188 970	-1.2	7 695	4.1	166 541	32.9	8.9
Randolph	6 445	74.9	31 300	18.4	13.2	262	26.1	5.8	7 983	0.0	687	8.6	6 339	17.7	16.2
St. Francis	9 958	61.1	38 600	22.4	17.3	270	32.6	10.0	11 671	-3.4	1 040	8.9	9 665	20.8	12.4
Saline	23 037	80.6	59 000	18.6	12.5	373	24.4	3.7	41 111	-1.2	1 355	3.3	29 887	24.7	15.4
Scott	3 957	78.0	34 100	23.1	13.2	241	23.2	5.9	4 601	-3.6	163	3.5	4 179	14.2	11.6
Searcy	3 117	79.6	29 400	19.4	14.2	234	31.4	11.9	2 833	-3.8	141	5.0	2 803	16.3	14.6
Sebastian	39 298	65.2	48 600	18.2	12.4	316	23.7	3.5	55 278	-1.0	2 208	4.0	46 226	24.6	13.8
Sevier	5 118	76.3	35 000	19.1	13.1	264	23.2	5.8	6 991	1.4	286	4.1	5 926	16.4	15.8
Sharp	5 819	82.5	37 100	22.0	13.7	282	25.8	4.9	6 100	0.0	413	6.8	4 344	20.6	12.9
Stone	3 866	78.5	36 900	23.1	13.2	238	31.9	8.5	4 951	-3.7	242	4.9	3 788	20.9	11.5
Union	17 819	73.8	40 500	19.2	13.8	311	27.5	5.7	20 896	-0.1	1 119	5.4	18 506	24.1	13.5
Van Buren	5 698	82.3	44 300	25.4	13.1	288	26.2	6.9	6 269	2.3	432	6.9	4 735	19.2	12.4
Washington	43 372	61.6	58 500	19.8	12.4	352	25.8	3.5	81 313	2.5	1 888	2.3	55 567	26.9	11.6
White	19 823	73.3	43 200	20.6	14.0	300	27.7	3.7	31 509	-1.6	1 626	5.2	22 651	21.8	14.3
Woodruff	3 630	63.2	29 700	22.5	15.1	236	28.7	6.2	3 739	-2.8	297	7.9	3 364	15.5	10.3
Yell	6 907	73.5	37 000	21.3	13.5	280	24.4	4.2	9 160	-1.9	298	3.3	7 571	15.0	15.8
CALIFORNIA	10 381 206	55.6	195 500	24.9	11.8	620	29.1	12.0	17 362 231	1.6	927 058	5.3	13 996 309	32.3	11.1
Alameda	479 518	53.3	227 200	25.3	11.9	626	28.6	8.2	754 896	2.2	33 913	4.5	635 840	37.2	10.1
Alpine	450	57.3	113 200	29.2	14.0	413	16.7	7.0	543	9.5	49	9.0	514	31.1	16.7
Amador	10 518	74.6	118 500	23.9	12.2	494	26.1	3.2	14 927	4.4	586	3.9	10 623	25.5	13.1

1. Specified owner-occupied units. 2. Specified renter-occupied units. 3. Overcrowded or lacking complete plumbing facilities. 4. Percent of civilian labor force. 5. Persons 16 years and older.

Table B. States and Counties — Nonfarm Employment and Agriculture

| | Private nonfarm establishments, employment and payroll, 1999 | | | | | | | | | Agriculture, 1997 | | | |
| | Employment | | | | | | Annual payroll | | Farms | | | Farm operators |
STATE County	Number of establishments	Total	Health Care and Social Assistance	Manufacturing	Retail trade	Finance and Insurance	Professional Scientific and Technical Services	Total (mil dol)	Average per employee (dollars)	Number	Percent with— Less than 50 acres	Percent with— 500 acres and over	Whose principal occupation is farming (percent)
	104	105	106	107	108	109	110	111	112	113	114	115	116
ARKANSAS—Cont'd													
Conway	406	5 944	1 251	1 595	869	113	173	149	25 120	729	19.6	8.0	49.7
Craighead	2 252	33 463	5 888	7 758	5 480	893	752	789	23 568	754	21.6	33.8	63.8
Crawford	909	14 795	1 309	3 579	1 710	329	2 267	334	22 574	806	35.7	7.6	40.3
Crittenden	942	14 437	2 104	2 132	2 771	177	403	303	20 964	259	11.2	62.5	77.2
Cross	384	4 587	623	1 414	752	196	D	89	19 322	382	15.2	50.3	74.9
Dallas	262	2 847	597	839	443	69	37	59	20 701	121	15.7	9.9	33.9
Desha	392	4 746	878	1 605	854	166	67	108	22 861	302	12.6	55.0	81.1
Drew	448	7 460	738	2 396	1 018	191	85	144	19 295	342	23.1	20.2	51.2
Faulkner	1 687	28 436	3 189	7 339	3 638	739	705	713	25 075	1 111	29.3	8.8	34.1
Franklin	278	3 162	472	941	473	127	48	62	19 488	783	22.1	9.6	45.3
Fulton	171	1 395	299	374	191	62	D	22	15 710	737	12.2	17.0	41.7
Garland	2 573	30 016	5 981	3 830	5 545	807	804	633	21 098	360	36.1	3.1	33.6
Grant	277	3 043	172	1 452	418	68	D	72	23 692	215	38.6	2.8	30.7
Greene	773	12 736	1 238	5 991	1 756	288	318	271	21 251	733	22.6	23.2	52.0
Hempstead	430	7 389	825	3 583	918	172	79	164	22 194	752	24.2	14.6	52.1
Hot Spring	565	5 910	848	1 841	792	230	70	124	21 025	447	25.1	5.4	41.4
Howard	314	7 192	607	4 893	573	124	64	146	20 267	656	30.5	6.7	54.6
Independence	805	14 183	2 563	4 766	1 729	270	165	313	22 066	1 044	21.6	13.8	41.9
Izard	247	2 169	461	548	437	100	D	42	19 509	703	16.6	13.7	41.4
Jackson	440	4 856	1 213	1 136	757	143	125	101	20 798	461	11.3	38.8	64.9
Jefferson	1 616	27 421	4 330	7 832	4 461	843	639	643	23 449	362	25.7	37.0	60.2
Johnson	393	7 253	600	3 273	852	159	71	138	19 028	606	23.8	6.6	46.5
Lafayette	157	1 371	225	407	160	67	23	28	20 616	261	24.1	19.2	64.0
Lawrence	376	4 261	475	1 525	681	118	52	76	17 748	661	12.7	30.4	62.8
Lee	163	1 267	283	225	265	52	47	23	18 039	273	13.2	47.3	74.7
Lincoln	170	1 579	242	596	237	D	12	30	19 095	292	19.2	34.6	64.0
Little River	231	3 378	288	D	362	99	D	124	36 745	381	19.4	16.0	42.8
Logan	370	4 910	616	2 282	679	187	41	99	20 087	953	23.0	8.6	42.0
Lonoke	901	8 370	1 069	1 652	1 826	350	265	163	19 450	869	22.8	28.2	55.2
Madison	190	1 797	146	828	303	81	35	35	19 490	1 203	16.0	11.0	50.5
Marion	236	3 317	308	1 990	368	102	33	56	16 860	495	16.2	14.5	45.5
Miller	736	10 589	1 025	2 174	1 636	293	235	253	23 883	502	25.7	14.1	44.8
Mississippi	1 002	17 749	1 669	7 115	2 169	423	238	443	24 954	462	14.5	57.8	80.1
Monroe	251	2 069	293	260	434	109	47	33	16 007	245	12.7	58.0	78.0
Montgomery	173	1 018	D	255	141	D	29	17	16 606	417	20.1	6.2	59.0
Nevada	154	1 895	368	638	251	D	36	44	23 233	372	23.1	7.8	44.1
Newton	101	663	82	140	146	D	11	8	12 661	521	15.2	7.9	35.7
Ouachita	616	7 825	1 131	2 496	1 307	173	102	189	24 190	177	35.0	8.5	39.0
Perry	119	790	113	D	165	51	D	17	21 896	391	24.0	7.2	45.8
Phillips	610	5 818	1 295	980	1 140	207	103	113	19 479	323	13.6	50.5	74.6
Pike	256	2 413	243	638	452	119	81	43	17 914	406	26.1	7.4	47.5
Poinsett	421	4 732	503	1 942	763	221	57	93	19 604	570	9.6	54.2	80.5
Polk	494	5 364	598	2 158	808	161	95	97	18 080	850	34.2	6.2	50.6
Pope	1 449	21 579	2 305	4 642	3 473	546	404	515	23 883	917	31.0	5.6	44.2
Prairie	192	1 206	198	D	264	D	24	21	17 474	420	11.2	48.1	71.4
Pulaski	11 973	220 467	35 242	20 387	25 878	12 148	12 223	6 090	27 624	421	40.1	12.6	34.7
Randolph	343	4 619	549	1 852	684	152	68	85	18 455	694	13.3	21.9	47.4
St. Francis	586	6 950	1 122	1 879	1 300	236	126	141	20 304	328	12.5	45.7	63.7
Saline	1 358	15 328	2 290	2 033	3 158	426	329	332	21 667	329	38.0	6.3	33.7
Scott	180	2 801	272	1 535	340	D	21	52	18 651	655	24.4	6.3	51.8
Searcy	119	1 043	246	197	218	D	20	13	12 719	614	15.3	16.1	43.8
Sebastian	3 347	69 316	8 847	23 440	7 927	1 820	1 297	1 767	25 499	724	33.8	6.9	39.6
Sevier	297	4 653	559	1 889	628	118	48	83	17 749	588	27.9	8.2	55.1
Sharp	375	3 156	535	319	668	167	81	55	17 490	618	13.4	12.5	40.0
Stone	242	2 343	303	697	491	68	D	33	14 106	601	19.5	12.3	50.4
Union	1 256	18 410	2 097	5 990	2 402	701	331	480	26 086	281	43.4	3.9	41.3
Van Buren	313	2 826	445	649	594	84	38	49	17 198	578	15.2	10.7	45.3
Washington	4 162	67 608	7 977	15 014	10 325	1 986	2 020	1 623	24 013	2 476	38.1	4.8	44.7
White	1 392	21 110	2 780	4 913	3 186	499	326	478	22 660	1 667	26.3	11.0	37.9
Woodruff	156	1 586	182	389	255	50	D	33	20 881	239	12.1	61.9	76.2
Yell	360	5 934	691	3 062	539	164	D	111	18 692	826	22.3	10.0	48.9
CALIFORNIA	784 935	12 356 363	1 288 744	1 792 190	1 421 434	627 195	975 340	446 547	36 139	74 126	60.6	11.7	53.0
Alameda	35 707	613 225	66 885	89 281	61 345	23 755	40 109	24 360	39 724	458	49.6	16.8	41.0
Alpine	55	1 146	D	0	27	0	D	12	10 839	12	58.3	25.0	33.3
Amador	826	7 473	1 160	857	1 599	233	434	166	22 278	360	41.1	14.2	41.9

Table B. States and Counties — Agriculture, Land, and Water

STATE County	Acreage (1,000) [117]	Percent change, 1992–1997 [118]	Average size of farm [119]	Total irrigated (1,000) [120]	Total cropland (1,000) [121]	Average per farm ($1,000) [122]	Average per acre (dollars) [123]	Value of machinery and equipment average per farm ($1,000) [124]	Total (mil dol) [125]	Average per farm (dollars) [126]	Crops [127]	Live-stock and poultry products [128]	$10,000 or more [129]	$100,000 or more [130]	Percent of land owned by fed. gov. 1997 [131]	Water consumption 1995 (mil gal/day) [132]
ARKANSAS—Cont'd																
Conway	163	-3.1	223	7	96	237	1 099	46	83	114 397	6.6	93.4	46.5	25.2	2.0	28.5
Craighead	363	3.8	482	222	335	612	1 365	119	123	162 763	98.3	1.7	68.4	41.4	0.6	349.6
Crawford	139	-4.9	172	4	78	259	1 617	33	60	74 461	17.5	82.5	32.9	14.3	23.1	15.9
Crittenden	320	-2.2	1 235	96	304	1 239	1 059	216	82	318 153	99.7	0.3	82.2	61.4	1.2	112.4
Cross	344	5.7	900	223	317	922	1 082	203	103	269 240	98.5	1.5	75.9	53.4	0.0	299.2
Dallas	23	10.6	192	0	9	187	1 017	27	2	16 119	33.2	66.8	22.3	2.5	0.0	1.2
Desha	276	5.3	914	159	257	798	930	177	101	334 018	92.9	7.1	83.1	60.9	5.3	330.3
Drew	123	11.4	358	49	94	333	1 157	93	36	104 704	78.4	21.6	47.4	23.7	0.0	71.0
Faulkner	211	0.2	190	3	120	291	1 425	29	21	18 955	27.2	72.8	26.7	4.6	1.9	11.9
Franklin	171	1.4	219	0	86	283	1 357	33	100	127 355	1.7	98.3	42.7	16.3	29.6	12.6
Fulton	228	1.7	309	0	92	238	735	19	15	20 605	4.2	95.8	35.0	5.3	0.2	73.8
Garland	43	1.1	121	0	21	222	1 816	25	25	70 772	6.3	93.7	22.8	5.6	26.1	266.3
Grant	33	-14.4	151	0	16	217	1 314	32	5	21 881	3.0	97.0	23.7	4.2	0.0	2.3
Greene	263	4.3	359	116	230	394	1 184	64	64	87 297	93.6	6.4	49.5	23.5	0.0	153.7
Hempstead	189	12.1	252	1	90	270	924	38	142	188 922	1.1	98.9	50.3	25.3	0.0	9.4
Hot Spring	75	-3.5	168	1	37	190	1 083	25	10	22 673	9.8	90.3	25.3	4.5	0.9	8.1
Howard	108	1.9	165	2	54	241	1 277	47	129	195 924	0.4	99.6	62.0	38.3	2.2	5.9
Independence	283	7.7	271	15	154	254	914	37	73	69 454	18.0	82.0	35.2	10.3	0.0	36.6
Izard	188	2.1	267	0	80	197	735	26	28	39 801	1.5	98.5	30.3	5.8	0.0	2.9
Jackson	335	-8.9	727	155	295	629	966	106	80	173 952	97.3	2.7	71.8	42.3	0.7	298.3
Jefferson	289	2.4	797	147	258	761	976	155	95	263 117	85.0	15.0	60.5	40.3	2.5	454.5
Johnson	115	5.1	189	2	66	264	1 370	37	82	135 766	3.7	96.3	35.5	18.5	40.5	4.2
Lafayette	98	-9.5	374	10	67	357	948	56	72	275 575	13.3	86.7	64.0	41.8	0.3	32.7
Lawrence	294	4.1	444	112	238	440	1 000	78	75	113 296	85.3	14.7	60.4	33.3	0.0	281.4
Lee	280	-6.5	1 024	102	263	856	865	175	80	294 530	98.0	2.0	75.1	49.1	2.8	167.1
Lincoln	184	-1.5	631	98	156	589	989	138	110	375 933	47.6	52.4	61.6	45.5	0.3	151.4
Little River	146	2.3	384	1	83	333	859	41	37	97 454	17.5	82.5	45.9	16.8	0.5	5.0
Logan	199	6.6	209	1	107	229	1 135	30	93	97 184	3.3	96.7	37.8	15.8	23.7	4.9
Lonoke	391	2.0	450	210	327	585	1 305	97	126	144 990	78.9	21.1	50.6	31.2	0.0	372.9
Madison	282	5.3	235	0	125	248	1 176	30	105	86 989	0.8	99.2	44.2	17.2	9.0	3.7
Marion	140	-2.4	282	0	53	238	832	26	22	43 743	1.6	98.4	36.6	5.3	9.0	1.7
Miller	154	-11.4	307	8	105	266	932	43	47	92 816	24.3	75.7	43.4	18.1	0.0	100.4
Mississippi	489	0.9	1 059	163	480	1 287	1 233	236	167	361 061	99.4	0.6	86.6	59.7	2.1	152.8
Monroe	236	7.7	962	128	211	879	918	172	63	257 924	96.9	3.1	77.1	57.6	6.2	194.0
Montgomery	74	-7.2	178	0	36	228	1 201	31	43	103 499	1.0	99.0	49.2	24.2	66.2	1.7
Nevada	73	5.5	196	0	37	213	1 066	32	33	89 393	1.3	98.7	39.8	16.9	0.0	1.7
Newton	109	5.5	209	0	37	214	1 157	19	10	19 057	2.2	97.8	26.7	1.9	46.2	1.0
Ouachita	29	-8.0	166	D	13	179	1 158	28	7	37 807	5.8	94.2	28.8	6.8	0.0	36.4
Perry	73	8.5	186	5	45	286	1 500	34	37	94 079	14.0	86.0	42.7	18.9	26.2	4.4
Phillips	361	1.2	1 118	131	346	1 034	933	163	114	352 013	99.4	0.6	77.4	54.5	4.0	313.7
Pike	73	3.1	180	1	33	217	1 126	33	57	140 568	1.0	99.0	50.5	25.6	1.9	1.9
Poinsett	401	-0.9	704	274	375	786	1 217	168	140	245 117	98.6	1.4	84.7	63.9	1.4	500.5
Polk	133	8.3	157	1	61	205	1 343	26	99	116 782	0.3	99.7	46.2	27.2	35.9	4.9
Pope	152	-2.5	166	2	85	229	1 482	33	110	120 358	2.5	97.5	41.3	19.3	35.9	980.3
Prairie	302	-3.6	719	179	257	780	1 117	149	90	214 481	93.2	6.8	71.7	51.0	0.9	297.1
Pulaski	111	-1.0	263	20	77	334	1 187	40	25	58 816	55.1	44.9	30.2	10.5	1.9	86.3
Randolph	266	4.6	383	47	163	320	837	43	44	63 562	64.1	35.9	40.8	12.7	0.0	80.4
St. Francis	290	-5.0	884	103	244	899	1 006	131	69	210 138	96.0	4.0	70.7	45.4	0.0	201.0
Saline	50	9.2	153	0	26	262	1 956	29	4	12 308	40.1	59.9	24.0	1.2	11.5	9.7
Scott	116	0.6	177	D	56	206	1 196	31	89	135 790	0.4	99.6	44.6	22.0	62.7	2.7
Searcy	188	-3.9	307	0	69	215	653	26	10	16 690	3.1	96.9	31.3	4.2	12.9	1.8
Sebastian	115	0.0	159	0	64	253	1 537	23	37	50 903	4.8	95.2	30.9	8.1	23.2	32.4
Sevier	133	1.9	227	1	63	243	1 005	40	129	218 576	0.4	99.6	54.6	35.5	0.4	4.4
Sharp	174	9.2	281	1	69	220	733	22	33	53 544	2.6	97.4	31.2	8.6	0.0	2.0
Stone	142	4.7	237	0	56	211	765	27	37	62 122	2.0	98.0	43.6	17.3	15.7	1.8
Union	34	10.2	122	D	14	206	1 632	30	50	176 908	0.5	99.5	33.8	23.5	3.1	15.9
Van Buren	132	10.3	229	0	62	234	829	34	20	34 366	2.8	97.2	36.2	9.3	7.3	2.5
Washington	335	-4.9	135	1	175	303	2 230	31	359	145 163	1.1	98.9	38.4	18.6	3.8	27.4
White	394	9.8	237	51	268	289	1 207	38	63	37 689	49.8	50.2	30.2	8.6	2.0	114.0
Woodruff	285	3.5	1 191	159	255	1 128	998	221	74	309 958	98.3	1.7	76.6	60.3	2.9	274.7
Yell	188	-0.8	228	5	107	274	1 086	37	113	137 176	3.5	96.5	49.9	24.3	38.0	9.7
CALIFORNIA	27 699	-4.4	374	8 713	10 804	941	2 605	70	23 032	310 718	74.0	26.0	56.2	26.6	45.9	36 297.8
Alameda	258	-9.8	563	10	42	758	1 504	35	42	91 496	70.4	29.6	46.5	12.9	3.3	237.0
Alpine	4	-21.2	329	3	3	802	2 442	16	0	25 588	D	D	41.7	8.3	90.4	23.7
Amador	204	-13.4	568	12	25	756	1 500	21	21	58 713	44.3	55.7	44.7	7.2	22.1	26.8

Table B. States and Counties — Residential Construction, Wholesale and Retail Trade, and Real Estate

STATE County	New Construction ($1,000)	Number of Housing Units	Wholesale Trade, 1997				Retail Trade[1], 1997				Real Estate and Rental and Leasing, 1997			
			Number of Establishments	Number of Employees	Sales (mil dol)	Annual Payroll (mil dol)	Number of Establishments	Number of Employees	Sales (mil dol)	Annual Payroll (mil dol)	Number of Establishments	Number of Employees	Receipts (mil dol)	Annual Payroll (mil dol)
	133	134	135	136	137	138	139	140	141	142	143	144	145	146
ARKANSAS—Cont'd														
Conway	774	9	23	D	D	D	91	948	157.1	12.3	8	28	1.6	0.3
Craighead	30 695	320	140	1 548	509.7	35.6	480	5 589	854.3	80.8	86	349	41.5	5.9
Crawford	13 286	149	58	373	170.1	9.3	171	1 599	268.5	22.8	38	114	9.9	1.6
Crittenden	27 298	405	64	D	D	D	206	2 722	496.9	33.1	38	137	15.1	2.4
Cross	1 655	31	22	344	102.7	7.1	80	720	129.8	10.5	10	27	2.4	0.2
Dallas	488	3	13	D	D	D	63	480	63.3	6.1	5	D	D	D
Desha	1 679	31	23	D	D	D	99	859	159.4	12.2	15	48	2.3	0.6
Drew	4 458	69	21	170	78.4	4.8	102	952	153.7	12.3	17	87	6.6	1.2
Faulkner	59 557	523	76	826	242.0	17.0	309	3 423	571.2	51.5	66	145	18.6	2.3
Franklin	689	15	8	D	D	D	63	461	71.2	5.9	6	21	0.6	0.2
Fulton	981	9	8	D	D	D	40	184	21.8	1.9	6	6	1.5	0.2
Garland	11 500	105	110	898	966.5	25.5	498	5 023	875.8	74.8	106	285	33.9	5.7
Grant	663	8	14	113	28.7	2.2	54	450	58.5	6.0	6	8	0.9	0.2
Greene	13 544	204	55	571	115.5	9.9	183	1 649	263.2	22.0	22	43	7.2	0.8
Hempstead	1 434	16	17	D	D	D	111	925	134.4	12.0	19	69	4.7	1.0
Hot Spring	850	7	28	170	54.0	4.1	99	787	144.6	11.1	10	36	2.0	0.6
Howard	1 141	17	14	44	12.7	0.7	73	634	88.2	8.0	7	26	0.8	0.1
Independence	2 351	34	50	624	172.5	12.6	195	1 741	284.2	23.2	26	66	5.5	0.9
Izard	1 204	16	9	D	D	D	57	374	71.0	4.8	12	49	2.8	0.4
Jackson	1 417	22	29	D	D	D	108	862	152.4	12.0	15	51	4.7	1.0
Jefferson	8 539	139	77	780	309.8	18.9	393	4 785	726.6	71.8	58	368	23.8	5.8
Johnson	2 553	26	9	D	D	D	104	988	155.5	13.4	16	41	4.0	0.9
Lafayette	860	18	2	D	D	D	40	216	22.1	2.1	8	15	1.5	0.2
Lawrence	2 119	20	21	173	85.2	3.7	88	710	122.0	9.5	8	20	0.6	0.1
Lee	1 094	33	10	95	63.7	2.3	39	273	40.8	3.6	5	11	0.4	0.1
Lincoln	865	9	7	D	D	D	28	228	30.6	2.9	4	11	0.7	0.1
Little River	205	2	16	76	22.5	2.2	57	396	77.4	5.2	10	26	1.3	0.2
Logan	625	8	17	D	D	D	94	707	119.5	9.5	10	14	1.4	0.1
Lonoke	32 950	356	37	321	144.4	7.3	178	1 622	269.1	23.3	27	75	3.8	0.8
Madison	318	5	2	D	D	D	41	282	47.7	4.0	3	10	0.2	0.1
Marion	10 318	179	8	D	D	D	39	360	46.2	4.5	10	D	D	D
Miller	10 736	161	49	D	D	D	167	1 512	254.1	21.0	24	75	4.9	0.8
Mississippi	3 052	40	60	457	237.9	13.1	261	2 117	361.8	29.1	33	138	9.7	1.7
Monroe	968	32	13	65	33.6	1.7	72	488	89.8	7.2	3	D	D	D
Montgomery	NA	NA	12	34	16.6	0.6	36	174	20.9	2.4	9	10	0.9	0.2
Nevada	192	4	5	21	18.2	0.9	40	261	37.0	3.1	NA	NA	NA	NA
Newton	327	3	7	D	D	D	16	121	15.1	1.5	3	10	0.5	0.1
Ouachita	952	8	31	264	121.0	6.8	148	1 380	198.2	19.3	22	156	16.0	3.5
Perry	0	0	3	D	D	D	27	154	19.0	1.7	2	D	D	D
Phillips	928	9	30	D	D	D	151	1 310	187.6	16.9	18	127	9.1	2.2
Pike	NA	NA	13	107	45.5	1.6	60	441	72.7	5.2	5	36	1.0	0.4
Poinsett	4 305	57	24	267	179.0	7.7	111	760	118.1	10.0	14	52	4.3	0.8
Polk	1 374	23	18	65	10.1	0.8	99	828	121.3	10.2	19	50	2.5	0.5
Pope	8 147	135	81	543	193.9	16.6	302	3 168	502.4	45.4	52	177	10.9	2.3
Prairie	335	6	8	53	18.5	1.3	54	246	36.6	3.1	4	8	0.4	0.0
Pulaski	187 152	1 415	882	14 654	9 759.8	455.7	1 847	26 898	4 584.4	415.1	472	3 405	394.4	64.1
Randolph	1 221	42	16	95	28.5	2.2	73	705	96.1	9.1	8	16	0.8	0.1
St. Francis	3 607	80	36	392	303.7	9.1	144	1 485	259.3	21.3	14	29	2.3	0.3
Saline	54 222	444	78	514	204.2	14.1	250	2 860	793.4	51.9	53	125	13.7	1.7
Scott	420	23	8	84	39.4	1.2	40	343	42.2	4.1	4	7	0.6	0.1
Searcy	500	3	7	D	D	D	40	253	31.4	2.6	2	D	D	D
Sebastian	39 518	419	245	2 101	708.5	56.8	659	8 721	1 360.6	128.1	135	670	81.6	12.4
Sevier	530	7	12	88	39.7	3.1	70	710	86.4	8.1	8	18	2.4	0.4
Sharp	776	5	11	D	D	D	91	778	112.6	8.6	17	D	D	D
Stone	632	10	11	D	D	D	63	470	66.3	6.4	3	4	0.2	0.0
Union	892	7	78	511	119.7	12.3	263	2 603	408.6	36.5	38	234	20.3	3.8
Van Buren	0	0	9	17	4.2	0.2	78	536	71.7	6.5	5	53	5.0	1.8
Washington	130 021	1 683	278	3 203	6 815.1	101.4	762	9 555	1 444.9	141.6	184	687	90.7	11.5
White	9 046	122	85	624	243.0	14.2	312	2 997	509.0	42.5	53	162	15.1	2.1
Woodruff	341	6	17	163	112.0	5.3	48	268	34.1	3.2	4	9	0.6	0.1
Yell	1 075	40	19	68	17.0	1.3	70	638	93.2	7.3	15	46	3.0	0.5
CALIFORNIA	23 343 965	145 575	57 842	755 513	551 230.6	29 900.2	106 357	1 354 797	263 118.3	26 362.7	37 244	243 288	38 288.4	6 570.5
Alameda	933 253	4 054	3 232	51 312	47 790.8	2 155.3	4 363	59 289	12 404.9	1 227.8	1 665	10 321	1 645.6	266.1
Alpine	13 346	25	NA	NA	NA	NA	7	28	2.3	0.2	5	18	1.6	0.2
Amador	33 165	253	28	D	D	D	158	1 570	475.0	25.7	36	155	16.8	2.2

1. Establishments with payroll.

B. States and Counties — Professional, Manufacturing, and Accommodation and Foodservices

STATE County	Professional, Scientific, and Technical Services[1], 1997				Manufacturing, 1997				Accommodation and Foodservices, 1997			
	Number of Establishments	Number of Employees	Receipts (mil dol)	Annual Payroll (mil dol)	Number of Establishments	Number of Employees	Receipts (mil dol)	Annual Payroll (mil dol)	Number of Establishments	Number of Employees	Sales (mil dol)	Annual Payroll (mil dol)
	147	148	149	150	151	152	153	154	155	156	157	158
ARKANSAS—Cont'd												
Conway	26	60	3.3	1.0	23	2 108	334.8	49.4	29	342	10.4	2.6
Craighead	148	675	53.4	19.3	122	6 886	1 257.6	184.9	133	2 720	80.2	21.6
Crawford	51	827	26.2	17.3	62	D	D	D	65	961	32.5	7.9
Crittenden	50	300	14.1	4.8	45	2 323	620.6	56.2	84	1 561	51.1	13.3
Cross	19	55	2.3	0.6	15	786	131.3	21.9	10	D	D	D
Dallas	9	31	1.3	0.4	16	1 611	319.2	45.1	35	263	8.0	1.7
Desha	24	57	3.2	0.9	33	2 429	222.0	51.2	31	507	15.3	3.7
Drew	21	72	4.3	1.4								
Faulkner	81	520	42.6	12.3	93	7 556	1 230.5	189.0	112	2 389	69.3	19.0
Franklin	11	30	1.7	0.5	16	1 284	216.0	24.2	27	211	5.9	1.5
Fulton	10	23	0.7	0.3	NA	NA	NA	NA	17	106	3.4	1.0
Garland	167	673	46.3	17.4	108	3 827	795.5	100.0	222	4 005	120.2	36.8
Grant	14	49	3.5	1.4	25	1 481	314.6	42.0	11	D	D	D
Greene	45	269	12.1	6.8	47	5 223	961.3	126.6	54	768	20.8	5.9
Hempstead	22	66	2.8	0.8	32	3 565	558.9	75.9	34	519	14.9	3.8
Hot Spring	29	82	3.5	1.0	47	1 764	315.2	45.3	33	454	13.5	3.6
Howard	14	34	1.8	0.6	26	5 067	1 120.2	94.5	18	224	6.7	1.8
Independence	50	157	11.6	3.3	54	5 168	1 013.3	123.3	48	812	22.6	5.8
Izard	7	7	0.4	0.1	NA	NA	NA	NA	20	88	2.1	0.6
Jackson	30	82	5.2	1.6	23	1 129	199.9	31.5	28	284	8.6	2.3
Jefferson	85	619	38.1	14.5	84	7 774	1 741.5	218.8	131	2 049	57.9	15.0
Johnson	22	58	3.2	0.9	39	3 318	409.4	65.1	36	456	13.7	3.4
Lafayette	7	27	0.7	0.2	NA	NA	NA	NA	9	61	1.6	0.4
Lawrence	18	42	1.9	0.5	37	1 615	215.5	31.2	28	284	7.7	2.1
Lee	9	70	2.6	0.7	NA	NA	NA	NA	8	D	D	D
Lincoln	4	6	0.6	0.1	8	D	D	D	7	63	1.9	0.4
Little River	11	41	2.3	0.8	16	D	D	D	23	D	D	D
Logan	19	36	2.2	0.5	36	2 569	393.0	44.8	33	335	8.7	2.2
Lonoke	57	204	10.7	3.7	39	1 739	269.8	45.4	53	728	21.3	5.3
Madison	12	32	1.8	0.5	19	738	170.7	12.8	9	79	2.1	0.6
Marion	10	22	1.4	0.5	23	1 847	133.7	29.5	30	191	6.1	1.6
Miller	38	167	12.7	4.2	25	2 274	495.6	99.7	79	1 363	45.8	11.6
Mississippi	45	125	8.0	2.7	62	7 644	2 801.7	252.7	74	1 254	36.2	8.6
Monroe	13	55	3.1	1.0	NA	NA	NA	NA	24	430	12.0	2.9
Montgomery	9	18	0.9	0.3	NA	NA	NA	NA	14	148	9.4	2.0
Nevada	8	26	1.4	0.4	8	D	D	D	9	113	3.8	1.2
Newton	3	D	D	D	NA	NA	NA	NA	10	69	1.9	0.5
Ouachita	18	99	6.5	2.6	33	2 961	854.3	96.0	40	626	18.0	4.4
Perry	6	11	0.8	0.2	NA	NA	NA	NA	8	31	1.0	0.2
Phillips	33	94	6.6	1.4	19	983	411.8	24.1	39	369	9.4	2.5
Pike	6	16	0.5	0.2	13	596	121.5	12.0	26	205	4.8	1.3
Poinsett	19	40	2.1	0.5	27	1 895	367.1	42.5	34	249	9.5	2.0
Polk	27	131	14.5	6.0	29	1 933	322.2	38.2	34	435	14.5	3.6
Pope	82	355	19.5	7.4	82	4 940	1 222.1	118.4	106	2 025	50.5	13.8
Prairie	8	20	1.1	0.3	NA	NA	NA	NA	17	132	3.5	0.8
Pulaski	1 217	9 974	918.2	406.5	431	20 557	4 342.4	572.8	801	16 728	508.0	144.7
Randolph	18	59	2.9	0.8	32	1 688	190.5	37.6	27	D	D	D
St. Francis	30	119	7.9	2.4	27	1 606	628.2	41.1	54	822	24.2	6.4
Saline	78	224	19.6	6.3	72	1 827	352.7	56.8	83	1 368	46.3	12.2
Scott	8	14	0.6	0.2	19	1 367	220.7	27.1	17	D	D	D
Searcy	4	13	0.5	0.2	NA	NA	NA	NA	10	88	2.1	0.7
Sebastian	227	1 262	101.0	29.4	233	22 891	4 319.3	582.0	257	4 669	138.9	38.1
Sevier	20	35	1.9	0.7	15	1 985	402.0	37.3	22	D	D	D
Sharp	17	35	1.9	0.7	NA	NA	NA	NA	41	379	10.1	2.6
Stone	12	37	1.5	0.5	26	602	39.8	10.4	21	278	7.6	1.9
Union	67	371	22.8	8.1	63	5 443	2 082.2	158.1	68	1 007	28.1	6.6
Van Buren	15	38	2.0	0.7	15	638	111.5	12.5	27	336	8.9	2.4
Washington	336	1 629	121.3	44.1	193	14 795	2 388.9	357.1	372	6 181	183.4	50.9
White	65	263	16.0	5.5	75	4 149	646.5	103.3	95	1 323	48.1	11.0
Woodruff	6	13	0.5	0.2	9	796	78.4	14.0	6	34	0.9	0.2
Yell	15	185	4.1	2.7	22	2 880	337.7	52.4	18	D	D	D
CALIFORNIA	78 635	805 856	89 555.7	35 258.6	49 418	1 809 667	379 612.4	65 762.8	62 532	1 052 715	42 261.1	11 437.2
Alameda	3 667	30 441	3 875.3	1 498.3	2 507	93 809	22 337.8	3 803.0	2 773	38 360	1 573.2	417.8
Alpine	1	D	D	D	NA	NA	NA	NA	16	148	6.0	1.4
Amador	50	119	9.3	2.7	51	732	136.8	19.5	105	910	29.5	8.1

1. Firms subject to federal tax.

STATE County	Health Care and Social Assistance[1], 1997				Other Services[1], 1997				Federal funds and grants, fiscal 2001[2] Expenditures (mil dol)	Direct payments for individuals[3]		
	Number of Establishments	Number of Employees	Receipts (mil dol)	Annual Payroll (mil dol)	Number of Establishments	Number of Employees	Receipts (mil dol)	Annual Payroll (mil dol)	Total	Social Security and government retirement	Medicare	Food stamps and Supplemental Security Income
	159	160	161	162	163	164	165	166	167	168	169	170
ARKANSAS—Cont'd												
Conway	28	745	21.8	9.7	15	75	4.2	1.3	155.4	58.8	20.8	4.8
Craighead	214	3 357	245.4	115.8	118	623	39.5	10.0	407.4	153.9	53.8	17.5
Crawford	51	957	52.0	21.2	64	364	30.8	6.5	234.7	117.2	37.5	10.0
Crittenden	66	768	42.0	16.7	64	439	25.7	7.3	280.0	80.6	41.2	21.8
Cross	26	299	12.3	5.8	21	74	4.3	1.0	155.1	38.1	16.7	7.0
Dallas	14	707	23.6	11.6	13	56	2.9	0.8	53.9	22.8	12.9	3.1
Desha	21	499	22.0	11.1	17	59	2.6	0.7	171.6	31.6	17.9	6.8
Drew	29	281	14.4	5.2	27	114	7.7	1.4	102.3	34.4	15.8	4.8
Faulkner	137	1 330	74.4	34.5	82	520	27.4	8.1	276.3	155.0	44.1	9.4
Franklin	18	243	9.6	4.8	14	100	3.3	1.2	92.8	44.5	15.8	3.8
Fulton	8	153	5.3	1.7	12	26	1.4	0.3	62.1	35.7	11.5	2.7
Garland	202	3 342	226.8	93.7	133	670	31.1	10.0	570.7	323.2	121.3	18.5
Grant	14	154	6.7	2.6	15	35	2.3	0.5	68.0	35.3	10.7	1.6
Greene	65	421	28.4	10.9	46	202	10.7	2.8	197.2	80.3	28.9	8.1
Hempstead	49	848	38.5	16.9	32	178	12.0	3.2	109.6	45.3	25.1	6.4
Hot Spring	32	331	14.0	5.8	26	78	5.1	1.3	138.7	72.1	30.7	5.8
Howard	31	404	11.8	4.8	17	74	3.9	0.9	70.5	32.9	16.8	3.8
Independence	71	792	41.5	19.2	45	182	12.5	3.3	196.3	81.3	31.0	7.5
Izard	9	336	6.8	2.6	15	25	2.5	0.5	82.5	44.4	14.9	2.8
Jackson	45	922	62.3	18.6	29	97	5.8	1.5	183.1	41.8	36.7	5.8
Jefferson	191	1 709	110.3	48.3	110	750	40.7	12.6	648.8	192.6	70.8	33.4
Johnson	24	278	12.2	5.3	28	99	6.5	1.3	84.3	52.1	18.0	5.3
Lafayette	6	109	4.4	1.8	7	32	1.7	0.5	61.0	19.7	11.8	4.0
Lawrence	16	122	6.4	2.5	26	88	5.7	1.1	145.5	47.6	21.3	5.7
Lee	11	135	4.3	1.5	11	18	1.2	0.2	117.1	20.8	11.7	8.2
Lincoln	9	206	5.2	2.4	11	54	6.3	2.0	91.3	22.0	10.0	4.2
Little River	14	155	4.5	2.0	11	34	2.6	0.7	73.1	36.7	12.7	2.6
Logan	22	238	10.5	4.5	24	100	5.8	1.3	115.6	61.3	19.4	5.0
Lonoke	51	800	29.5	13.9	50	152	8.8	2.2	262.0	122.9	35.8	7.0
Madison	10	47	2.4	1.0	8	30	4.1	1.3	56.7	31.1	8.9	2.1
Marion	8	102	4.0	1.2	12	23	2.4	0.4	78.2	48.8	13.1	3.7
Miller	34	573	23.9	8.9	41	298	14.2	4.5	299.9	85.5	45.4	13.2
Mississippi	72	731	31.3	14.0	51	341	28.0	7.8	346.3	102.9	44.0	23.2
Monroe	11	174	5.4	2.1	15	47	3.7	0.7	112.2	22.9	12.5	5.4
Montgomery	7	19	1.0	0.2	6	13	0.6	0.2	46.2	25.6	9.5	1.5
Nevada	7	193	6.6	3.2	9	33	2.2	0.6	54.7	23.0	13.5	2.6
Newton	1	D	D	D	3	3	0.2	0.0	45.2	20.5	5.7	2.6
Ouachita	40	632	28.3	10.6	37	181	10.2	2.9	186.1	77.7	33.1	10.4
Perry	9	102	3.2	1.4	2	D	D	D	53.0	27.5	9.1	2.3
Phillips	45	449	19.0	7.8	24	86	5.7	1.2	237.6	53.2	29.3	18.6
Pike	11	156	4.5	2.0	5	34	1.8	0.5	52.0	26.1	11.2	2.2
Poinsett	20	315	9.1	4.1	25	49	3.7	0.8	213.8	56.6	26.5	8.7
Polk	36	341	14.4	4.9	33	92	5.6	1.1	102.6	55.7	20.9	4.3
Pope	107	1 999	139.8	54.3	93	458	23.2	6.6	238.7	115.1	34.0	12.0
Prairie	12	207	6.6	3.0	15	48	3.6	0.5	114.4	21.6	11.2	1.9
Pulaski	1 002	12 393	955.6	448.5	698	4 422	273.2	78.7	3 204.7	926.7	299.2	76.4
Randolph	21	293	16.0	6.1	20	47	3.3	0.8	102.6	44.5	15.9	4.4
St. Francis	35	412	19.6	7.5	29	148	7.4	2.1	283.9	52.8	25.3	16.9
Saline	87	1 069	55.0	24.5	83	403	24.3	7.2	209.0	129.5	41.1	8.2
Scott	5	24	1.3	0.7	5	17	1.4	0.3	56.5	29.4	9.4	2.4
Searcy	6	145	3.0	1.2	1	D	D	D	54.4	24.4	8.4	2.8
Sebastian	288	4 698	337.1	152.7	192	1 278	74.3	20.6	515.4	256.7	90.7	21.5
Sevier	27	442	24.3	9.0	22	89	5.3	1.3	71.0	32.2	14.2	2.7
Sharp	21	172	6.6	2.8	15	39	1.8	0.4	110.5	63.5	22.2	4.4
Stone	13	286	19.3	4.9	7	19	1.3	0.3	68.5	34.1	12.0	3.2
Union	95	1 607	100.9	37.0	74	391	25.2	6.1	250.6	116.1	49.0	14.3
Van Buren	11	49	2.7	0.9	15	38	2.5	0.4	91.6	54.7	17.8	3.5
Washington	290	2 938	192.9	92.0	232	1 421	71.8	22.1	596.3	277.3	79.0	18.2
White	97	1 798	122.5	47.4	85	549	28.4	7.8	327.8	154.6	53.2	13.4
Woodruff	10	94	4.6	2.3	5	16	0.9	0.2	102.1	20.1	14.2	4.0
Yell	28	406	16.2	7.4	16	62	3.5	0.7	108.8	54.0	18.9	4.9
CALIFORNIA	69 857	664 539	51 968.0	20 619.3	44 642	282 762	20 521.5	5 852.2	188 516.9	53 200.3	27 327.2	6 679.6
Alameda	3 124	32 552	2 698.7	1 066.4	2 164	14 520	1 186.7	346.2	9 123.6	2 154.2	1 180.7	300.4
Alpine	2	D	D	D	1	D	D	D	7.1	4.1	0.8	0.1
Amador	70	631	26.6	8.9	32	98	8.1	1.6	169.7	97.3	40.0	2.6

1. Firms subject to federal tax.   2. October 1, 2000 to September 30, 2001.   3. State totals may include programs not allocated by county.

STATE County	Federal funds and grants, fiscal 2001[1] (cont'd)							Local government finances, 1997				
	Expenditures (mil dol) (cont'd)							General revenue				
	Procurement contract awards			Grants[2]						Taxes		
											Per capita[3] (dollars)	
	Salaries and wages	Defense	Other	Medicaid and other health-related	Nutrition and family welfare	Education	Other	Total (mil dol)	Intergovernmental (mil dol)	Total (mil dol)	Total	Property
	171	172	173	174	175	176	177	178	179	180	181	182
ARKANSAS—Cont'd												
Conway	3.8	0.0	0.9	17.0	2.2	1.1	40.1	52.2	17.3	31.6	1 581	1 424
Craighead	24.1	0.0	5.4	36.0	11.3	8.1	24.1	110.0	53.7	36.3	471	305
Crawford	6.1	6.9	2.9	18.3	4.7	3.3	21.5	70.4	42.1	15.7	317	239
Crittenden	6.4	0.7	2.2	59.7	8.5	4.4	11.7	90.2	47.5	25.3	509	217
Cross	2.9	8.5	0.6	16.5	3.1	1.4	7.5	35.2	17.2	7.1	366	259
Dallas	1.6	0.0	0.4	8.7	1.4	0.7	1.3	13.9	8.4	3.2	350	266
Desha	6.1	21.3	0.5	20.5	3.7	1.6	19.8	40.0	18.9	8.2	538	393
Drew	4.5	2.3	1.5	13.1	2.0	2.4	2.3	43.9	19.1	7.9	443	240
Faulkner	11.5	0.3	2.4	18.8	6.8	2.7	9.8	99.6	51.6	27.8	363	275
Franklin	10.7	4.5	0.8	7.6	1.0	1.3	0.7	24.3	15.7	5.8	351	307
Fulton	1.7	0.0	0.4	7.6	0.8	0.5	0.2	17.2	8.7	3.0	273	183
Garland	29.9	6.9	7.4	34.1	5.9	8.1	2.9	123.7	45.1	48.8	586	322
Grant	4.9	0.0	0.6	5.3	0.8	1.0	7.6	26.3	17.1	5.9	376	358
Greene	5.3	4.5	1.2	22.3	2.5	1.6	5.4	52.3	27.1	13.7	385	162
Hempstead	5.1	0.1	0.8	15.3	2.8	2.6	0.3	31.5	19.7	7.3	332	193
Hot Spring	5.6	2.0	1.1	12.8	2.5	1.5	1.5	59.5	23.3	10.8	377	254
Howard	3.4	0.2	0.5	8.8	1.3	0.8	0.8	23.9	13.5	7.3	527	304
Independence	9.6	0.2	16.5	23.5	3.2	2.4	9.6	65.8	29.5	17.5	532	371
Izard	2.0	2.6	0.5	9.1	0.9	1.3	1.3	16.1	10.3	3.9	301	234
Jackson	3.2	1.4	0.8	24.7	2.5	1.9	12.9	29.6	12.4	8.4	473	277
Jefferson	65.1	96.6	7.6	76.5	14.8	9.5	18.6	148.9	72.7	47.6	579	343
Johnson	5.1	0.1	0.9	12.4	1.5	1.3	-14.5	42.2	24.4	10.2	482	302
Lafayette	1.8	0.0	0.4	12.0	1.6	0.9	0.8	16.0	10.1	3.7	409	296
Lawrence	4.1	0.1	1.0	18.5	1.8	1.2	-0.7	35.3	16.3	5.6	322	173
Lee	3.1	0.6	0.6	27.3	4.5	1.6	2.9	18.7	12.7	4.4	352	225
Lincoln	1.2	0.3	0.2	15.4	1.8	0.6	12.7	15.3	10.1	2.8	194	140
Little River	2.0	0.7	0.9	8.8	1.3	0.7	2.0	25.5	7.4	9.0	678	383
Logan	7.0	0.3	1.2	14.9	1.8	0.9	0.9	26.3	15.6	6.2	290	197
Lonoke	5.8	8.9	2.9	16.9	2.9	4.7	4.3	69.3	42.6	17.7	359	206
Madison	2.5	0.1	0.8	8.0	0.8	0.6	-0.3	19.4	12.4	4.8	366	207
Marion	1.5	1.3	0.2	6.4	1.0	0.7	0.7	17.8	10.8	5.0	349	234
Miller	3.0	0.7	0.9	25.8	6.2	2.8	97.1	68.8	33.7	19.3	487	305
Mississippi	7.8	-0.2	2.0	54.9	13.3	5.0	34.3	100.3	54.5	25.7	509	206
Monroe	2.2	0.0	0.4	20.7	2.6	1.3	11.4	17.8	10.7	4.3	419	271
Montgomery	2.4	0.0	0.7	5.1	0.5	0.3	0.1	12.2	8.4	2.5	291	187
Nevada	2.4	0.0	0.8	8.4	1.3	0.6	1.2	19.7	8.8	4.0	399	267
Newton	2.6	0.0	0.5	9.7	1.3	0.7	0.6	10.7	7.6	1.7	206	121
Ouachita	7.4	16.4	1.5	28.0	3.8	1.6	2.1	64.3	28.2	10.6	376	272
Perry	2.3	0.0	1.4	6.2	0.6	0.4	1.4	25.2	10.0	9.4	991	160
Phillips	4.3	2.4	0.9	57.6	12.4	3.8	6.9	51.8	33.3	11.9	431	261
Pike	3.2	0.1	1.1	5.8	0.8	0.7	0.2	18.2	9.1	4.5	428	304
Poinsett	4.1	0.4	1.3	31.2	3.5	1.6	7.5	39.4	24.0	9.4	381	230
Polk	4.9	0.0	1.1	8.5	1.6	2.4	0.8	26.7	16.7	6.0	306	183
Pope	14.5	0.5	2.7	24.2	8.3	2.7	14.4	85.0	32.2	35.4	691	333
Prairie	2.5	1.8	0.4	7.7	1.0	0.6	31.2	12.6	6.8	3.8	406	279
Pulaski	581.1	129.3	74.8	253.9	158.0	129.6	479.9	775.2	262.0	288.0	822	477
Randolph	1.9	0.0	0.5	13.0	3.1	0.9	0.5	20.7	12.8	5.1	287	163
St. Francis	19.4	0.0	90.0	48.1	7.7	3.2	-18.7	46.8	29.3	11.0	387	199
Saline	5.9	0.5	1.4	12.4	3.9	2.1	1.0	154.3	60.3	26.7	352	250
Scott	3.7	0.1	1.3	6.2	0.8	0.5	1.7	19.4	9.4	2.0	184	123
Searcy	2.3	0.0	0.3	12.4	0.7	0.5	1.5	10.7	7.0	2.8	357	291
Sebastian	60.6	11.1	7.1	31.8	5.2	4.7	9.3	194.1	72.8	82.5	778	405
Sevier	4.6	0.3	0.7	5.5	1.0	1.5	5.3	21.6	13.5	5.0	337	223
Sharp	3.8	0.0	0.9	10.8	1.6	1.0	1.0	23.5	12.4	6.3	377	249
Stone	2.5	0.0	0.4	11.6	1.0	0.6	1.9	15.1	8.3	5.3	481	334
Union	9.5	1.0	1.8	36.9	8.9	3.2	-0.3	72.3	33.8	24.8	545	272
Van Buren	2.7	0.0	0.7	9.9	1.2	0.6	-0.3	16.8	10.4	4.3	280	217
Washington	62.3	15.7	13.6	32.1	7.9	13.3	54.1	243.4	104.0	87.7	640	383
White	10.7	0.0	2.5	33.8	4.1	4.1	26.9	112.4	48.1	23.8	376	227
Woodruff	1.8	0.3	0.4	18.8	1.8	0.9	2.1	15.4	10.8	2.9	319	226
Yell	6.8	1.9	1.4	13.5	1.4	1.1	0.7	36.8	18.6	5.9	309	271
CALIFORNIA	17 857.6	19 864.2	9 084.4	18 760.2	8 668.8	3 492.7	8 875.4	X	X	X	X	X
Alameda	776.5	172.1	2 057.1	1 154.2	256.5	109.1	580.4	5 667.1	2 317.1	1 742.3	1 271	757
Alpine	0.4	0.0	0.2	0.6	0.3	0.4	0.0	12.2	5.2	3.1	2 579	1 881
Amador	4.9	0.1	2.1	7.6	4.7	0.7	7.5	69.6	32.7	25.4	735	619

1. October 1, 2000 to September 30, 2001.   2. State totals may include programs not allocated by county.   3. Based on the resident population estimated as of July 1 of the year shown.

Table B. States and Counties — Local Government Finances, Government Employment, and Elections

STATE County	Local government finances, 1997 (cont'd) Direct general expenditure Total (mil dol)	Per capita[1] (dollars)	Percent of total for — Education	Health and hospitals	Police protection	Public welfare	Highways	Debt outstanding Total (mil dol)	Per capita[1] (dollars)	Government employment, 1999 Federal civilian	Federal military	State and local	Presidential election, 2000[2] Percent of vote cast — Democratic	Republican	All other
	183	184	185	186	187	188	189	190	191	192	193	194	195	196	197
ARKANSAS—Cont'd															
Conway	30.7	1 535	68.3	0.2	4.2	0.0	5.6	24.6	1 230	69	110	1 161	48.3	49.0	2.7
Craighead	111.5	1 449	60.6	0.5	4.6	0.0	6.7	139.4	1 812	427	436	5 726	49.2	48.3	2.5
Crawford	71.2	1 437	74.0	0.0	4.5	0.0	4.2	58.5	1 180	96	286	1 833	35.7	61.3	3.1
Crittenden	84.3	1 697	56.4	2.1	7.0	0.1	3.9	57.4	1 156	114	279	2 625	54.6	44.3	1.1
Cross	32.9	1 688	57.1	19.8	4.7	0.0	4.8	17.1	878	62	107	1 101	49.8	48.8	1.4
Dallas	14.4	1 572	60.6	0.1	5.5	0.0	8.4	7.1	778	27	50	465	51.4	47.2	1.3
Desha	38.3	2 512	51.1	19.9	5.4	0.0	3.9	30.2	1 979	112	83	1 104	61.8	35.7	2.5
Drew	41.7	2 349	55.5	24.2	3.0	0.2	2.2	20.5	1 156	77	97	1 667	51.7	46.5	1.8
Faulkner	107.8	1 407	65.4	0.1	4.5	0.3	3.7	155.2	2 026	186	450	5 122	40.9	55.0	4.2
Franklin	22.3	1 355	77.6	1.6	2.5	0.1	6.6	16.4	995	154	244	837	43.6	53.4	3.0
Fulton	16.3	1 487	51.2	16.2	2.9	0.1	6.6	7.8	713	35	61	513	48.1	49.6	2.3
Garland	117.1	1 407	53.8	0.3	9.4	0.2	4.7	132.0	1 586	583	472	3 532	44.1	53.1	2.8
Grant	25.0	1 592	81.7	0.1	1.9	0.0	4.3	15.9	1 017	34	89	809	42.2	54.6	3.2
Greene	50.4	1 419	58.1	0.3	4.2	0.0	7.5	64.8	1 822	92	202	1 557	50.6	46.7	2.6
Hempstead	30.8	1 405	66.0	0.2	4.9	0.0	9.2	21.6	983	102	123	1 495	54.0	44.7	1.3
Hot Spring	57.2	2 003	51.3	21.9	2.7	0.2	3.4	79.3	2 776	67	162	1 500	50.3	45.9	3.7
Howard	21.2	1 525	67.6	0.1	3.5	0.0	6.3	19.1	1 379	70	76	766	46.3	52.2	1.5
Independence	65.1	1 978	47.5	0.2	3.6	0.7	5.9	144.6	4 393	193	184	1 680	44.4	53.0	2.6
Izard	16.7	1 295	76.1	0.7	4.5	0.2	6.1	8.7	670	36	73	864	51.4	45.7	2.9
Jackson	25.2	1 421	56.2	1.0	5.3	0.1	7.0	18.6	1 048	55	97	968	60.1	37.5	2.4
Jefferson	150.9	1 835	53.0	0.3	7.5	0.0	4.3	109.7	1 334	1 588	504	6 459	65.1	32.2	2.6
Johnson	41.4	1 957	45.2	28.7	2.6	0.0	7.7	16.3	771	109	119	881	45.7	51.1	3.2
Lafayette	14.1	1 548	63.5	0.2	4.5	0.0	9.4	3.4	370	34	49	474	53.4	45.5	1.2
Lawrence	34.0	1 947	53.0	19.6	4.4	4.7	5.2	9.0	513	74	96	1 192	53.9	43.5	2.6
Lee	17.2	1 376	66.3	3.1	5.8	0.2	8.8	4.9	392	56	72	903	66.2	32.8	1.0
Lincoln	15.6	1 089	68.4	1.7	4.2	0.2	7.4	4.8	331	33	80	1 263	55.2	43.0	1.8
Little River	31.4	2 374	36.6	36.9	2.3	0.0	5.9	100.6	7 616	51	73	805	54.8	43.4	1.9
Logan	28.8	1 356	68.2	3.0	4.9	0.0	8.2	12.1	570	137	117	1 181	40.6	55.4	4.0
Lonoke	67.3	1 366	69.8	0.5	4.4	0.0	6.1	35.9	728	104	286	1 987	38.2	59.1	2.7
Madison	25.8	1 965	47.4	1.5	28.2	0.1	12.1	7.7	586	52	74	515	36.5	60.2	3.3
Marion	16.6	1 154	67.8	3.2	5.4	0.2	11.4	10.8	747	37	83	562	37.1	56.6	6.4
Miller	67.1	1 689	54.7	0.9	7.7	0.2	5.7	90.8	2 288	50	220	1 925	45.7	52.9	1.4
Mississippi	90.7	1 795	55.1	0.1	5.8	0.0	4.3	79.9	1 582	141	278	3 162	56.5	41.3	2.3
Monroe	15.6	1 506	63.7	0.3	5.4	0.1	8.8	8.1	780	46	55	554	58.0	40.4	1.7
Montgomery	9.9	1 169	66.9	0.2	3.7	0.1	9.0	4.5	526	72	49	451	38.5	56.9	4.6
Nevada	19.6	1 958	53.9	16.8	2.6	0.1	5.9	16.2	1 618	32	56	526	49.9	48.0	2.0
Newton	9.9	1 217	78.1	1.5	2.0	0.2	4.6	3.7	462	59	46	458	30.7	64.4	5.0
Ouachita	60.3	1 245	52.3	26.4	3.3	0.1	3.5	35.1	1 250	124	153	1 436	52.6	45.6	1.9
Perry	22.4	2 363	42.0	1.7	9.9	0.0	10.1	57.6	6 091	40	54	421	41.1	52.8	6.1
Phillips	48.5	1 756	67.3	3.9	5.1	0.1	4.0	29.3	1 062	79	150	1 870	64.6	33.9	1.5
Pike	20.9	1 993	70.9	8.0	2.0	0.1	3.9	9.2	880	79	58	631	40.4	57.3	2.3
Poinsett	36.3	1 475	69.9	0.5	5.0	0.0	4.9	21.4	869	74	137	1 268	56.7	41.3	2.0
Polk	28.1	1 428	71.8	0.1	3.8	0.0	8.1	9.6	487	103	109	1 011	32.2	64.0	3.9
Pope	72.9	1 422	60.2	1.1	4.1	0.0	5.6	121.0	2 363	320	302	3 041	36.2	61.0	2.8
Prairie	12.3	1 323	63.2	1.4	6.0	0.0	11.1	6.5	695	42	54	408	44.6	53.1	2.3
Pulaski	779.3	2 224	41.2	6.3	7.1	0.0	5.7	844.4	2 410	9 008	6 468	38 416	53.7	43.9	2.4
Randolph	21.6	1 222	67.5	0.1	6.3	0.2	5.0	17.2	974	42	99	928	51.4	45.5	3.1
St. Francis	48.8	1 720	62.8	0.5	4.3	0.0	4.9	11.5	406	403	154	1 852	58.7	40.2	1.1
Saline	121.4	1 599	43.0	25.9	3.5	0.0	3.9	81.2	1 070	89	435	3 772	39.2	57.5	3.3
Scott	17.0	1 564	43.1	30.5	4.8	0.1	7.5	5.5	504	76	59	398	36.3	60.3	3.5
Searcy	9.3	1 199	75.2	0.2	3.1	0.0	7.2	3.0	387	40	43	454	30.3	64.3	5.4
Sebastian	174.2	1 644	54.0	0.3	5.4	0.0	11.4	104.2	984	1 032	593	5 024	38.7	58.5	2.8
Sevier	21.6	1 456	72.7	0.3	4.7	0.1	6.4	5.0	340	75	81	818	48.8	49.2	2.0
Sharp	22.7	1 366	64.7	0.2	3.6	0.1	8.9	6.2	370	54	95	810	45.4	51.9	2.7
Stone	15.8	1 448	53.2	0.1	3.4	0.2	9.3	3.8	351	67	62	618	42.0	54.0	4.0
Union	68.9	1 515	59.9	0.1	5.9	0.0	7.5	47.5	1 044	201	251	2 500	40.1	55.4	4.5
Van Buren	16.4	1 053	69.3	0.5	4.7	0.4	7.6	6.2	399	50	87	658	45.8	49.9	4.3
Washington	254.3	1 857	48.9	0.4	4.9	0.1	5.0	141.5	1 033	1 168	830	12 128	41.6	54.9	3.5
White	107.5	1 699	50.0	22.5	3.4	0.2	4.3	84.4	1 333	174	363	2 889	37.7	59.5	2.9
Woodruff	15.5	1 735	53.4	0.7	4.9	17.3	8.3	7.0	786	46	48	542	64.1	33.9	2.0
Yell	36.1	1 889	49.0	25.8	3.2	0.0	4.0	18.7	980	164	105	1 135	47.3	49.7	3.0
CALIFORNIA	X	X	X	X	X	X	X	X	X	264 580	223 884	1 964 848	53.4	41.7	4.9
Alameda	5 455.9	3 979	25.9	11.8	5.4	8.6	3.4	7 320.1	5 339	12 316	4 322	107 123	69.4	24.1	6.5
Alpine	12.1	10 029	24.3	5.0	7.0	6.8	16.2	1.2	1 030	13	0	150	45.2	48.0	6.9
Amador	66.4	1 924	35.6	3.9	7.0	8.2	6.6	18.4	533	108	66	2 510	38.2	56.7	5.1

1. Based on the resident population estimated as of July 1 of the year shown.   2. Data subject to copyright.

Table B. States and Counties — Land Area and Population

STATE/ County code	MSA/ PMSA/ NECMA code[1]	County Type[2]	STATE County	Land area,[3] (sq km) 2000	Total persons	Rank	Per square kilometer	White	Black	Am. Indian, Alaska Native	Asian and Pacific Islander	Percent Hispanic[4]	Under 5 years	5 to 17 years	18 to 24 years	25 to 34 years	35 to 44 years	45 to 54 years
				1	2	3	4	5	6	7	8	9	10	11	12	13	14	15
			CALIFORNIA—Cont'd															
06 007	1620	3	Butte	4 246	203 171	270	47.8	88.0	1.9	3.6	4.4	10.5	5.7	18.3	13.6	11.4	13.4	13.2
06 009	...	6	Calaveras	2 642	40 554	1 100	15.3	94.3	1.0	3.5	1.7	6.8	4.4	18.4	5.5	7.7	14.7	16.9
06 011	...	6	Colusa	2 980	18 804	1 855	6.3	68.1	0.7	3.3	2.6	46.5	8.1	23.5	10.3	12.6	14.4	12.0
06 013	5775	0	Contra Costa	1 865	948 816	38	508.7	69.7	10.3	1.6	13.7	17.7	7.0	19.6	7.7	13.3	17.3	15.0
06 015	...	7	Del Norte	2 610	27 507	1 466	10.5	82.6	4.6	9.1	3.3	13.9	5.5	19.5	8.0	14.4	17.7	13.7
06 017	6920	1	El Dorado	4 431	156 299	342	35.3	92.4	0.8	2.2	3.2	9.3	5.7	20.4	6.8	10.0	17.8	17.1
06 019	2840	2	Fresno	15 443	799 407	58	51.8	58.0	5.9	2.6	9.5	44.0	8.5	23.6	11.1	14.0	14.5	11.5
06 021	...	6	Glenn	3 405	26 453	1 503	7.8	75.3	0.8	3.3	4.2	29.6	7.5	23.2	8.7	12.1	14.7	12.1
06 023	...	5	Humboldt	9 253	126 518	429	13.7	88.8	1.4	8.3	2.7	6.5	5.6	17.6	12.4	12.7	14.8	15.7
06 025	...	4	Imperial	10 813	142 361	384	13.2	52.4	4.3	2.4	2.8	72.2	7.7	23.8	9.9	14.7	15.7	11.3
06 027	...	7	Inyo	26 426	17 945	1 902	0.7	83.8	0.4	12.0	1.5	12.6	5.4	19.0	5.8	8.3	15.1	16.2
06 029	0680	2	Kern	21 085	661 645	78	31.4	65.1	6.6	2.6	4.5	38.4	8.4	23.5	10.2	14.1	15.7	11.6
06 031	...	4	Kings	3 603	129 461	414	35.9	57.8	8.9	2.5	4.4	43.6	8.1	20.9	11.8	17.9	17.1	10.8
06 033	...	6	Lake	3 258	58 309	820	17.9	89.4	2.6	4.8	1.7	11.4	5.3	18.8	6.0	9.2	14.4	15.3
06 035	...	6	Lassen	11 803	33 828	1 286	2.9	83.3	9.1	4.6	1.7	13.8	5.0	16.9	10.8	18.1	18.8	14.3
06 037	4480	0	Los Angeles	10 518	9 519 338	1	905.1	52.8	10.5	1.5	13.6	44.6	7.7	20.3	10.3	16.6	15.9	12.1
06 039	2840	2	Madera	5 532	123 109	440	22.3	66.7	4.7	4.0	2.3	44.3	7.7	22.0	9.9	13.7	15.4	12.5
06 041	7360	0	Marin	1 346	247 289	235	183.7	87.1	3.5	1.1	6.2	11.1	5.4	14.9	5.5	12.9	18.0	18.4
06 043	...	8	Mariposa	3 758	17 130	1 947	4.6	92.1	0.8	5.6	1.5	7.8	4.4	17.2	6.9	9.4	15.6	16.1
06 045	...	4	Mendocino	9 088	86 265	603	9.5	84.3	1.0	6.6	2.1	16.5	6.0	19.6	8.1	11.2	14.4	16.9
06 047	4940	3	Merced	4 995	210 554	264	42.2	60.9	4.5	2.3	8.5	45.3	8.9	25.6	10.3	13.4	14.4	10.9
06 049	...	7	Modoc	10 215	9 449	2 491	0.9	88.6	1.0	5.8	1.2	11.5	5.6	20.1	5.7	9.3	14.0	16.0
06 051	...	7	Mono	7 885	12 853	2 243	1.6	86.2	0.7	3.2	2.0	17.7	5.7	17.3	10.3	15.0	18.4	16.1
06 053	7120	2	Monterey	8 604	401 762	147	46.7	60.0	4.5	1.9	8.5	46.8	7.8	20.6	10.9	15.9	15.4	12.3
06 055	8720	0	Napa	1 952	124 279	433	63.7	83.3	1.6	1.8	4.4	23.7	6.1	18.1	8.5	12.5	15.2	14.8
06 057	...	4	Nevada	2 480	92 033	555	37.1	95.9	0.5	2.2	1.6	5.7	4.7	18.4	6.1	8.7	15.3	17.9
06 059	5945	0	Orange	2 045	2 846 289	5	1 391.8	68.3	2.1	1.3	15.5	30.8	7.6	19.4	9.4	16.4	16.8	12.7
06 061	6920	1	Placer	3 637	248 399	233	68.3	91.5	1.1	1.9	4.3	9.7	6.4	20.1	6.9	11.8	17.3	15.2
06 063	...	6	Plumas	6 614	20 824	1 745	3.1	94.3	0.8	4.2	1.1	5.7	4.5	18.2	6.0	8.0	14.6	17.3
06 065	6780	0	Riverside	18 667	1 545 387	16	82.8	69.3	7.0	2.1	5.1	36.2	7.9	22.5	9.2	13.2	15.7	11.4
06 067	6920	0	Sacramento	2 501	1 223 499	29	489.2	68.5	11.4	2.5	14.1	16.0	7.3	20.3	9.5	14.7	16.3	13.1
06 069	...	6	San Benito	3 598	53 234	880	14.8	69.6	1.5	2.2	4.2	47.9	8.8	23.4	8.8	14.6	16.9	12.4
06 071	6780	0	San Bernardino	51 936	1 709 434	13	32.9	63.1	10.0	2.2	6.2	39.2	8.4	23.9	10.3	14.2	15.9	11.9
06 073	7320	0	San Diego	10 878	2 813 833	6	258.7	70.3	6.6	1.6	11.4	26.7	7.1	18.7	11.3	15.7	16.3	12.5
06 075	7360	0	San Francisco	121	776 733	62	6 419.3	53.0	8.6	1.2	33.4	14.1	4.1	10.5	9.1	23.2	17.2	13.9
06 077	8120	2	San Joaquin	3 624	563 598	97	155.5	62.7	7.5	2.3	14.4	30.5	8.0	23.0	10.0	13.4	15.4	12.2
06 079	7460	3	San Luis Obispo	8 558	246 681	236	28.8	87.7	2.4	2.1	3.9	16.3	5.0	16.6	13.6	11.4	15.6	14.7
06 081	7360	0	San Mateo	1 163	707 161	70	608.0	63.5	4.1	1.1	24.1	21.9	6.4	16.5	7.9	15.9	17.4	14.5
06 083	7480	2	Santa Barbara	7 089	399 347	149	56.3	76.4	2.8	2.2	5.6	34.2	6.5	18.4	13.3	13.9	15.1	12.3
06 085	7400	0	Santa Clara	3 343	1 682 585	14	503.3	57.6	3.4	1.3	28.2	24.0	7.1	17.7	9.3	17.8	17.6	13.0
06 087	7485	0	Santa Cruz	1 153	255 602	220	221.7	78.9	1.5	2.1	5.1	26.8	6.1	17.7	11.9	14.4	16.5	15.9
06 089	6690	3	Shasta	9 804	163 256	329	16.7	92.5	1.1	4.8	2.7	5.5	5.9	20.2	8.2	10.3	15.0	14.7
06 091	...	8	Sierra	2 469	3 555	2 949	1.4	96.6	0.3	3.1	0.9	6.0	4.1	19.2	4.8	8.8	15.2	17.2
06 093	...	7	Siskiyou	16 283	44 301	1 010	2.7	90.5	1.6	6.2	1.9	7.6	5.1	18.9	6.7	8.3	14.4	16.8
06 095	8720	0	Solano	2 148	394 542	150	183.7	61.3	16.6	2.0	16.9	17.6	7.3	21.1	9.2	14.2	17.1	14.0
06 097	7500	0	Sonoma	4 082	458 614	125	112.4	85.2	2.0	2.4	4.6	17.3	6.0	18.4	8.8	12.7	16.5	16.1
06 099	5170	2	Stanislaus	3 869	446 997	132	115.5	73.9	3.2	2.5	6.3	31.7	8.0	23.2	9.8	13.6	15.4	12.1
06 101	9340	3	Sutter	1 561	78 930	649	50.6	71.0	2.4	3.0	13.4	22.2	7.3	21.7	9.2	13.2	15.0	12.5
06 103	...	6	Tehama	7 643	56 039	842	7.3	88.0	0.9	3.8	1.4	15.8	6.3	21.1	7.8	10.8	14.8	13.0
06 105	...	6	Trinity	8 233	13 022	2 230	1.6	93.1	0.5	8.1	1.3	4.0	4.2	18.6	5.1	7.9	14.9	18.4
06 107	8780	2	Tulare	12 494	368 021	160	29.5	62.0	2.0	2.5	4.3	50.8	8.9	24.8	10.6	13.6	14.0	11.2
06 109	...	6	Tuolumne	5 790	54 501	863	9.4	92.2	2.3	3.4	1.6	8.2	4.5	16.2	7.6	10.4	15.0	16.3
06 111	8735	0	Ventura	4 779	753 197	64	157.6	73.3	2.4	1.8	7.0	33.4	7.5	21.0	9.0	13.8	16.9	13.6
06 113	9270	0	Yolo	2 624	168 660	321	64.3	72.0	2.6	2.2	12.3	25.9	6.5	18.7	18.3	13.4	14.2	12.0
06 115	9340	3	Yuba	1 633	60 219	803	36.9	75.7	4.0	5.2	9.4	17.4	8.2	22.8	10.7	13.1	14.9	11.7
08 000	...	X	COLORADO	268 627	4 301 261	X	16.0	85.2	4.4	1.9	3.0	17.1	6.9	18.7	10.0	15.4	17.1	14.3
08 001	2080	0	Adams	3 087	363 857	162	117.9	80.3	3.5	2.1	4.1	28.2	8.4	20.1	10.3	17.1	16.9	12.3
08 003	...	7	Alamosa	1 872	14 966	2 093	8.0	74.6	1.3	3.8	1.6	41.4	6.9	20.3	15.9	12.2	14.5	13.1
08 005	2080	0	Arapahoe	2 080	487 967	116	234.6	82.6	8.7	1.4	5.1	11.8	6.9	19.8	8.6	15.5	17.6	15.2
08 007	...	9	Archuleta	3 497	9 898	2 456	2.8	90.9	0.6	2.4	0.5	16.8	5.4	20.0	6.3	9.5	16.6	18.2
08 009	...	9	Baca	6 619	4 517	2 878	0.7	95.5	0.1	2.6	0.3	7.0	5.9	18.6	5.9	9.0	13.7	13.6
08 011	...	9	Bent	3 921	5 998	2 781	1.5	83.0	3.5	3.5	0.9	30.2	5.9	17.8	9.3	13.4	15.8	13.3
08 013	1125	0	Boulder	1 923	291 288	194	151.5	90.5	1.2	1.2	3.9	10.5	6.0	16.9	13.4	16.0	17.6	15.0
08 015	...	7	Chaffee	2 625	16 242	2 005	6.2	92.5	1.7	1.9	0.7	8.6	4.4	15.3	7.7	12.1	15.0	16.0
08 017	...	9	Cheyenne	4 614	2 231	3 049	0.5	93.5	0.5	1.1	0.1	8.1	6.4	22.4	7.1	9.2	17.0	13.8

1. MSA = Metropolitan Statistical Area. PMSA = Primary MSA. NECMA = New England County Metropolitan Area. See Appendix A for explanation of these concepts. See Appendix B for list of metropolitan areas identified by type, with component counties.　2. County typology code from the Economic Research Service of USDA. See Appendix A for definition.　3. Dry land or land partially or temporarily covered by water.　4. Hispanic persons may be of any race.

STATE County	Population, 2000 (cont'd) Age (percent) (cont'd)				Population — change and components of change, 1990–2001								Households, 2000				
					Total persons		Percent change		Components of change, 2000–2001							Percent		
	55 to 64 years	65 to 74 years	75 years and over	Percent female	2001	1990	1990–2000	2000–2001	Births	Deaths	Net migration	Number	Percent change, 1990–2000	Persons per house-hold	Female family house-holder[1]	One person
	16	17	18	19	20	21	22	23	24	25	26	27	28	29	30	31
CALIFORNIA—Cont'd																
Butte	8.6	7.5	8.3	51.0	205 973	182 120	11.6	1.4	2 809	2 679	2 710	79 566	11.0	2.48	11.2	27.2
Calaveras	14.2	10.7	7.5	50.4	42 005	31 998	26.7	3.6	391	506	1 511	16 469	30.2	2.44	8.6	23.3
Colusa	7.8	5.9	5.4	49.2	19 277	16 275	15.5	2.5	389	191	277	6 097	8.6	3.01	9.6	21.5
Contra Costa	8.9	5.8	5.5	51.2	975 532	803 731	18.1	2.8	16 269	8 348	18 904	344 129	14.6	2.72	11.5	22.9
Del Norte	8.5	6.7	5.8	44.8	27 554	23 460	17.3	0.2	403	326	-20	9 170	14.8	2.58	13.6	25.3
El Dorado	9.8	7.0	5.4	50.1	162 586	125 995	24.1	4.0	2 086	1 417	5 533	58 939	25.8	2.63	8.9	20.1
Fresno	6.9	5.2	4.8	49.9	815 734	667 479	19.8	2.0	17 656	6 926	5 913	252 940	14.5	3.09	15.2	20.6
Glenn	8.6	6.8	6.2	49.4	26 558	24 798	6.7	0.4	503	284	-115	9 172	4.0	2.84	10.9	22.0
Humboldt	8.8	6.3	6.1	50.6	126 468	119 118	6.2	0.0	1 843	1 461	-387	51 238	10.4	2.39	11.8	28.9
Imperial	6.8	5.9	4.1	47.8	145 744	109 303	30.2	2.4	3 063	1 093	1 415	39 384	19.9	3.33	17.1	17.1
Inyo	11.1	10.0	9.1	51.2	17 944	18 281	-1.8	0.0	234	228	-5	7 703	1.8	2.31	9.9	31.4
Kern	7.1	5.2	4.2	48.7	676 367	544 981	21.4	2.2	14 327	5 938	6 571	208 652	15.0	3.03	14.5	20.3
Kings	6.1	4.1	3.3	42.6	132 119	101 469	27.6	2.1	2 688	901	946	34 418	18.3	3.18	14.3	17.0
Lake	11.5	10.5	9.0	50.6	60 839	50 631	15.2	4.3	715	1 015	2 753	23 974	15.2	2.39	11.3	29.0
Lassen	7.1	5.0	4.0	37.2	33 830	27 598	22.6	0.0	367	260	-95	9 625	12.7	2.59	10.3	24.5
Los Angeles	7.3	5.2	4.6	50.6	9 637 494	8 863 052	7.4	1.2	199 594	74 407	-6 422	3 133 774	4.8	2.98	14.7	24.6
Madera	7.9	6.2	4.8	52.1	126 415	88 090	39.8	2.7	2 446	1 068	1 957	36 155	27.4	3.18	12.2	16.5
Marin	11.3	6.8	6.7	50.4	247 707	230 096	7.6	0.2	3 262	2 272	-505	100 650	5.9	2.34	8.5	29.8
Mariposa	13.1	9.8	7.4	48.8	17 167	14 302	19.8	0.2	156	233	105	6 613	18.0	2.37	8.0	26.5
Mendocino	10.2	6.9	6.6	50.3	86 860	80 345	7.4	0.7	1 346	1 003	282	33 266	9.4	2.53	11.7	27.0
Merced	7.0	5.3	4.2	50.2	219 096	178 403	18.0	4.1	4 517	1 730	5 742	63 815	15.3	3.25	14.1	17.7
Modoc	11.7	9.6	8.0	49.4	9 333	9 678	-2.4	-1.2	102	139	-77	3 784	2.0	2.39	8.8	28.1
Mono	9.6	5.2	2.4	45.1	12 930	9 956	29.1	0.6	160	46	-36	5 137	29.7	2.43	6.5	26.6
Monterey	7.1	5.3	4.7	48.2	407 629	355 660	13.0	1.5	8 435	2 970	507	121 236	7.3	3.14	11.6	21.2
Napa	9.5	7.0	8.4	50.1	128 145	110 765	12.2	3.1	1 840	1 522	3 546	45 402	9.9	2.62	9.9	25.8
Nevada	11.4	9.1	8.4	50.4	94 361	78 510	17.2	2.5	906	1 081	2 470	36 894	19.9	2.47	8.8	22.8
Orange	7.9	5.2	4.6	50.2	2 890 444	2 410 668	18.1	1.6	58 810	20 628	6 311	935 287	13.1	3.00	10.7	21.1
Placer	9.3	7.0	6.1	50.9	268 512	172 796	43.8	8.1	3 568	2 200	18 219	93 382	45.7	2.63	9.2	21.3
Plumas	13.5	10.2	7.6	50.0	20 942	19 739	5.5	0.6	170	282	223	9 000	10.8	2.29	8.0	27.5
Riverside	7.5	6.7	6.0	50.2	1 635 888	1 170 413	32.0	5.9	29 619	14 771	74 227	506 218	25.9	2.98	12.0	20.7
Sacramento	7.7	5.8	5.3	51.1	1 268 770	1 066 789	14.7	3.7	22 669	11 222	33 600	453 602	15.0	2.64	14.1	26.7
San Benito	6.9	4.5	3.6	49.4	55 098	36 697	45.1	3.5	1 147	349	1 065	15 885	39.1	3.32	10.5	14.1
San Bernardino	6.8	4.8	3.8	50.1	1 766 237	1 418 380	20.5	3.3	35 814	13 299	34 429	528 594	13.7	3.15	14.8	18.4
San Diego	7.3	5.7	5.5	49.7	2 862 819	2 498 016	12.6	1.7	54 974	23 530	19 381	994 677	12.1	2.73	11.6	24.2
San Francisco	8.4	6.9	6.7	49.2	770 723	723 959	7.3	-0.8	10 860	8 840	-8 251	329 700	7.9	2.30	8.9	38.6
San Joaquin	7.4	5.4	5.2	50.0	595 324	480 628	17.3	5.6	11 289	5 453	25 469	181 629	14.8	3.00	14.0	20.7
San Luis Obispo	8.6	7.3	7.1	48.6	250 727	217 162	13.6	1.6	2 915	2 528	3 693	92 739	15.5	2.49	9.1	26.0
San Mateo	9.0	6.3	6.1	50.6	702 020	649 623	8.9	-0.7	13 099	6 357	-12 236	254 103	5.0	2.74	10.1	24.6
Santa Barbara	7.8	6.3	6.4	50.0	399 543	369 608	8.0	0.0	6 927	3 697	-3 025	136 622	5.3	2.80	10.0	24.3
Santa Clara	8.0	5.2	4.4	49.3	1 668 309	1 497 577	12.4	-0.8	34 201	11 487	-38 127	565 863	8.8	2.92	10.0	21.4
Santa Cruz	7.6	4.8	5.1	50.1	254 538	229 734	11.3	-0.4	4 217	2 073	-3 278	91 139	9.1	2.71	10.2	25.1
Shasta	10.5	7.9	7.3	51.3	168 478	147 036	11.0	3.2	2 393	2 159	4 911	63 426	13.3	2.52	11.9	24.7
Sierra	13.0	9.5	8.2	49.5	3 485	3 318	7.1	-2.0	16	37	-53	1 520	13.8	2.32	7.9	29.0
Siskiyou	11.6	9.5	8.6	50.9	44 325	43 531	1.8	0.1	570	587	61	18 556	7.2	2.35	10.1	28.6
Solano	7.6	5.1	4.4	49.6	403 946	339 469	16.2	2.4	7 251	2 998	5 277	130 403	15.0	2.90	13.8	19.6
Sonoma	8.8	6.0	6.7	50.8	464 024	388 222	18.1	1.2	6 838	4 592	3 327	172 403	15.7	2.60	10.4	25.7
Stanislaus	7.4	5.5	5.0	50.8	468 566	370 522	20.6	4.8	8 802	4 204	16 758	145 146	15.8	3.03	13.7	19.4
Sutter	8.8	6.8	5.6	50.5	80 530	64 409	22.5	2.0	1 444	801	997	27 033	17.0	2.87	11.7	21.2
Tehama	10.2	8.4	7.5	50.6	57 101	49 625	12.9	1.9	815	764	1 007	21 013	12.3	2.62	11.6	24.0
Trinity	13.7	10.3	6.9	49.0	13 116	13 063	-0.3	0.7	124	189	155	5 587	8.4	2.29	10.1	29.5
Tulare	7.0	5.2	4.6	50.0	374 249	311 932	18.0	1.7	8 528	3 184	980	110 385	12.8	3.28	14.5	17.1
Tuolumne	11.5	10.2	8.3	47.3	55 521	48 456	12.5	1.9	537	717	1 169	21 004	17.0	2.36	9.6	26.0
Ventura	8.1	5.3	4.9	50.1	770 630	669 016	12.6	2.3	14 435	5 725	9 039	243 234	11.9	3.04	10.9	18.9
Yolo	6.9	4.8	4.6	51.1	174 815	141 212	19.4	3.6	2 717	1 328	4 740	59 375	16.5	2.71	11.1	23.3
Yuba	7.9	6.0	4.7	49.6	60 902	58 234	3.4	1.1	1 243	704	179	20 535	3.8	2.87	13.3	21.7
COLORADO	7.9	5.3	4.4	49.6	4 417 714	3 294 473	30.6	2.7	79 847	34 144	69 799	1 658 238	29.3	2.53	9.6	26.3
Adams	7.1	4.7	3.1	49.3	374 891	265 038	37.3	3.0	7 159	2 547	6 390	128 156	33.0	2.81	12.1	21.2
Alamosa	7.5	5.1	4.5	50.2	14 884	13 617	9.9	-0.5	261	143	-202	5 467	15.8	2.56	11.7	27.3
Arapahoe	7.8	4.6	3.9	50.7	500 785	391 572	24.6	2.6	8 889	3 294	7 315	190 909	23.4	2.53	10.6	27.0
Archuleta	12.2	8.1	3.8	49.3	10 659	5 345	85.2	7.7	138	72	677	3 980	98.0	2.47	8.2	22.1
Baca	10.9	10.6	11.8	50.3	4 495	4 556	-0.9	-0.5	56	85	7	1 905	1.8	2.33	7.5	30.4
Bent	8.5	8.2	7.7	43.7	5 883	5 048	18.8	-1.9	103	79	-143	2 003	7.4	2.53	11.4	27.2
Boulder	7.2	4.2	3.6	49.4	297 686	225 339	29.3	2.2	4 658	1 773	3 573	114 680	29.7	2.47	7.7	26.3
Chaffee	11.5	9.9	7.1	46.8	16 520	12 684	28.1	1.7	178	162	254	6 584	35.8	2.26	6.8	28.4
Cheyenne	7.5	7.4	9.2	49.8	2 204	2 397	-6.9	-1.2	41	29	-40	880	-2.7	2.50	5.7	29.0

1. No spouse present.

Table B. States and Counties — Vital Statistics, Health Resources, and Crime

STATE County	Births, average 1997–1999 Total	Rate[1]	Deaths, average 1997–1999 Number Total	Infant[2]	Rate Total[1]	Infant[3]	Physicians,[4] 2000 Number	Rate[5]	Hospitals,[4] 1998 Number	Beds Number	Rate[5]	Medicare enrollees 2000	Serious crimes known to police, 2000[6] Total Number	Rate[7]
	32	33	34	35	36	37	38	39	40	41	42	43	44	45
CALIFORNIA—Cont'd														
Butte	2 265	11.7	2 161	13	11.1	5.9	383	189	5	661	340	36 252	7 213	3 550
Calaveras	339	8.5	396	NA	10.0	NA	39	96	1	49	123	7 914	1 032	2 545
Colusa	294	15.8	143	NA	7.7	NA	11	58	1	56	302	2 496	453	2 409
Contra Costa	12 259	13.4	6 561	68	7.2	5.5	2 248	237	10	2 081	227	116 829	35 627	3 755
Del Norte	324	12.0	258	NA	9.6	NA	39	142	1	47	174	4 230	936	3 403
El Dorado	1 771	11.2	1 104	6	7.0	3.2	190	122	2	188	119	24 866	3 560	2 278
Fresno	14 015	18.5	5 357	99	7.1	7.0	1 341	168	14	2 118	280	90 028	48 251	6 036
Glenn	397	15.1	223	NA	8.5	NA	19	72	1	28	107	4 011	779	2 945
Humboldt	1 453	11.9	1 162	8	9.5	5.7	262	207	5	332	272	19 244	5 511	4 356
Imperial	2 467	17.1	898	12	6.2	5.0	111	78	3	221	153	17 549	6 156	4 324
Inyo	194	10.7	217	NA	12.0	NA	39	217	2	69	381	3 777	461	2 569
Kern	11 312	17.9	4 590	78	7.3	6.9	869	131	11	1 649	261	73 975	25 533	3 859
Kings	2 092	17.6	722	15	6.1	7.2	119	92	3	175	147	10 639	3 176	2 453
Lake	591	10.7	726	NA	13.2	NA	71	122	2	115	209	12 874	1 754	3 008
Lassen	342	10.3	217	NA	6.5	NA	27	80	1	59	177	3 796	496	1 466
Los Angeles	157 474	17.1	59 833	911	6.5	5.8	22 877	240	114	30 364	330	987 309	379 451	3 986
Madera	1 912	16.6	813	10	7.1	5.4	107	87	2	124	108	17 860	4 596	3 733
Marin	2 535	10.7	1 852	8	7.8	3.3	937	379	3	417	176	34 667	5 874	2 375
Mariposa	144	9.2	174	NA	11.1	NA	13	76	1	34	214	3 055	497	2 901
Mendocino	1 042	12.4	797	NA	9.5	NA	191	221	4	209	250	13 848	2 230	2 585
Merced	3 662	18.6	1 366	24	6.9	6.5	215	102	4	402	203	19 910	8 993	4 271
Modoc	96	10.2	118	NA	12.5	NA	8	85	2	113	1 202	1 736	194	2 053
Mono	146	14.0	44	NA	4.2	NA	20	156	1	15	146	854	577	4 489
Monterey	6 530	17.9	2 290	38	6.3	5.8	673	168	4	675	185	43 021	12 960	3 226
Napa	1 458	12.2	1 272	4	10.7	2.7	376	303	3	1 429	1 198	21 881	2 664	2 144
Nevada	806	8.9	858	NA	9.4	NA	187	203	2	193	211	16 405	1 794	1 949
Orange	45 422	16.7	16 404	208	6.0	4.6	6 371	224	37	6 889	253	290 133	74 298	2 610
Placer	2 741	11.9	1 701	12	7.4	4.3	461	186	2	310	135	32 908	7 239	2 914
Plumas	178	8.7	219	NA	10.7	NA	36	173	4	108	530	3 937	611	2 934
Riverside	24 097	16.3	11 762	159	7.9	6.6	1 990	129	16	3 009	203	202 591	60 653	3 925
Sacramento	17 190	14.9	8 845	114	7.7	6.6	2 913	238	11	3 174	277	151 571	60 508	4 945
San Benito	872	17.8	266	NA	5.4	NA	28	53	1	101	207	4 549	1 451	2 807
San Bernardino	28 891	17.7	10 813	222	6.6	7.7	2 793	163	19	3 704	227	168 532	65 175	3 813
San Diego	43 019	15.5	18 984	230	6.8	5.3	7 062	251	25	6 828	246	341 261	94 408	3 355
San Francisco	7 790	10.5	6 725	37	9.0	4.8	4 539	584	11	4 155	557	117 388	43 162	5 557
San Joaquin	8 797	16.0	4 208	52	7.6	5.9	762	135	8	1 140	207	67 898	29 644	5 260
San Luis Obispo	2 522	10.8	1 988	12	8.5	4.8	581	236	6	636	271	39 210	7 156	2 901
San Mateo	9 766	14.0	4 953	44	7.1	4.5	1 853	262	8	2 036	291	91 884	18 600	2 630
Santa Barbara	5 707	14.7	2 878	28	7.4	5.0	998	250	8	1 314	337	55 067	10 195	2 553
Santa Clara	25 410	15.5	8 984	126	5.5	5.0	4 577	272	15	4 488	273	167 217	44 507	2 645
Santa Cruz	3 529	14.6	1 656	18	6.8	5.1	531	208	2	395	163	28 298	8 690	3 400
Shasta	1 993	12.2	1 694	12	10.3	6.2	379	232	5	656	399	31 379	5 341	3 272
Sierra	25	7.5	39	NA	11.5	NA	3	84	1	40	1 183	696	45	1 266
Siskiyou	435	9.9	480	NA	10.9	NA	62	140	2	137	311	9 533	1 111	2 508
Solano	5 583	14.8	2 360	35	6.2	6.2	703	178	4	522	138	39 475	15 947	4 042
Sonoma	5 481	12.7	3 748	28	8.7	5.1	1 066	232	8	889	205	63 384	13 512	2 946
Stanislaus	6 993	16.4	3 342	48	7.8	6.9	648	145	7	1 478	347	54 896	23 840	5 333
Sutter	1 166	15.1	631	NA	8.2	NA	133	169	1	132	171	10 951	2 965	3 756
Tehama	642	11.9	585	NA	10.8	NA	65	116	1	76	141	9 321	1 830	3 266
Trinity	115	8.8	150	NA	11.5	NA	7	54	1	65	496	2 576	293	2 250
Tulare	6 747	19.0	2 587	41	7.3	6.1	431	117	7	854	240	40 959	16 089	4 372
Tuolumne	452	8.5	538	NA	10.1	NA	109	200	3	223	419	10 881	1 368	2 510
Ventura	11 339	15.5	4 576	69	6.2	6.1	1 299	172	8	1 451	198	84 997	17 512	2 325
Yolo	2 137	13.9	1 032	9	6.7	4.4	327	194	2	169	110	17 554	5 981	3 546
Yuba	1 045	17.5	527	9	8.8	8.6	93	154	1	128	213	8 095	2 807	4 661
COLORADO	58 177	14.6	26 460	404	6.7	6.9	9 342	217	68	9 438	238	467 455	171 304	3 983
Adams	5 307	16.4	1 945	43	6.0	8.2	308	85	4	539	166	38 168	16 862	4 915
Alamosa	236	16.3	111	NA	7.7	NA	41	274	1	70	484	1 708	494	3 301
Arapahoe	6 419	13.6	2 526	47	5.3	7.3	1 177	241	3	605	128	43 046	18 481	4 051
Archuleta	110	12.2	50	NA	5.6	NA	5	51	0	0	0	1 320	317	3 203
Baca	40	9.3	70	NA	16.1	NA	4	89	1	65	1 489	1 057	19	421
Bent	63	11.2	68	NA	12.1	NA	8	133	0	0	0	966	136	2 267
Boulder	3 419	12.8	1 363	17	5.1	5.0	625	215	3	360	135	28 025	9 146	3 140
Chaffee	139	9.1	141	NA	9.2	NA	18	111	1	38	252	3 032	455	2 801
Cheyenne	29	12.7	24	NA	10.4	NA	1	45	1	32	1 364	366	30	1 345

1. Per 1,000 estimated resident population, average 1997–1999.   2. Deaths of infants under 1 year old.   3. Deaths of infants under 1 year old per 1,000 live births.   4. Data subject to copyright.   5. Per 100,000 resident population as of July 1 of the year shown.   6. Data for serious crimes have not been adjusted for underreporting; this may affect comparability between geographic areas and over time.   7. Per 100,000 population estimated by the FBI.

Items 32–45

Table B. States and Counties — Crime, Education, Money Income, and Poverty

	Serious crimes known to police, 2000[1] (cont'd)		Education						Money income				Income and poverty, 1998			
	Rate[2]		School enrollment and attainment, 1990				Local government expenditures, fiscal 1999[5]		1989					Percent below poverty level		
			Enrollment[3]		Attainment[4] (percent)						Households					
											Median					
STATE County					High school grad-uate or more	Bach-elor's degree or more	Total current expendi-tures (mil dol)	Current expendi-tures per student (dollars)	Per capita[6] (dollars)	Dollars	Percent change, 1979–1989 (constant 1989 dollars)	Percent with $100,000 or more	Median house-hold income	All persons	Persons under 18	Persons 5–17 in families
	Violent	Property	Total	Percent private												
	46	47	48	49	50	51	52	53	54	55	56	57	58	59	60	61
CALIFORNIA—Cont'd																
Butte	344	3 206	56 394	5.7	77.6	19.5	216.6	6 139	12 083	22 776	4.4	2.4	30 464	19.4	27.2	29.6
Calaveras	291	2 254	7 030	7.6	81.6	14.4	41.7	6 062	13 497	27 645	8.0	2.7	37 366	11.9	17.7	20.1
Colusa	303	2 106	4 654	3.8	62.9	11.1	30.3	7 061	12 402	24 912	-3.3	3.5	31 049	18.5	27.2	28.6
Contra Costa	478	3 277	213 707	15.2	86.5	31.6	854.1	5 546	20 748	45 087	17.6	10.3	57 611	8.1	13.8	12.6
Del Norte	429	2 974	5 940	9.3	70.9	10.0	29.8	5 657	10 625	22 917	-0.8	2.2	30 420	20.7	27.0	32.7
El Dorado	449	1 829	32 520	7.9	85.9	20.8	165.9	5 748	15 703	35 058	19.4	4.7	47 411	8.6	12.6	13.0
Fresno	756	5 280	204 179	6.6	66.2	16.9	1 028.2	5 765	11 824	26 377	0.1	3.6	32 023	24.3	34.1	33.9
Glenn	302	2 642	6 553	6.3	66.9	9.4	41.0	6 602	10 677	22 831	-7.1	1.8	29 055	19.7	27.7	31.0
Humboldt	338	4 018	36 198	6.0	80.5	20.0	136.5	6 179	12 436	23 586	-4.7	2.2	31 630	17.8	24.0	26.5
Imperial	497	3 828	36 361	5.2	53.2	9.7	201.8	6 134	9 208	22 442	-8.7	2.5	24 430	31.9	44.0	36.9
Inyo	306	2 262	4 093	6.3	81.7	13.5	27.5	8 032	13 397	24 386	-0.2	2.2	35 045	14.3	23.1	24.4
Kern	489	3 370	153 512	7.7	67.6	13.3	880.8	6 131	12 154	28 634	4.4	3.2	33 769	20.5	28.5	28.3
Kings	281	2 172	28 156	8.1	65.6	9.0	147.0	5 876	10 035	25 507	4.8	2.3	31 296	22.8	29.1	30.9
Lake	401	2 607	11 069	7.6	70.9	10.7	64.2	6 479	11 705	21 794	16.4	1.4	28 681	18.6	27.4	31.5
Lassen	216	1 250	7 124	5.7	72.8	11.7	36.6	6 636	12 626	26 764	2.4	1.4	39 247	18.1	22.2	23.8
Los Angeles	945	3 041	2 521 219	15.9	70.0	22.3	9 648.6	5 968	16 149	34 965	18.9	7.9	37 655	18.9	28.1	26.0
Madera	653	3 080	24 840	6.1	63.4	11.7	138.3	5 929	10 856	27 370	6.5	2.4	31 499	22.9	32.9	33.2
Marin	260	2 116	51 962	23.9	91.9	44.0	209.0	7 257	28 381	48 544	18.0	17.0	62 126	6.6	9.7	9.9
Mariposa	759	2 142	2 883	5.5	77.8	16.8	17.2	6 203	13 074	25 272	13.2	2.4	32 760	15.4	25.0	28.1
Mendocino	369	2 216	22 123	9.1	78.7	17.8	109.9	6 959	12 776	26 443	5.1	2.7	32 994	17.5	25.8	28.0
Merced	621	3 650	56 282	6.6	63.1	12.0	295.6	5 943	10 606	25 548	3.9	2.7	29 859	24.7	33.2	35.6
Modoc	402	1 651	2 344	6.8	72.2	11.2	18.2	8 676	10 971	22 029	-1.9	1.6	28 910	21.5	30.5	38.2
Mono	233	4 256	2 096	9.2	87.8	21.9	16.0	7 577	16 120	31 924	12.5	5.1	38 600	11.1	16.7	19.8
Monterey	575	2 651	97 096	10.0	72.9	21.5	421.4	6 060	14 578	33 520	13.3	5.3	40 480	15.4	24.2	22.9
Napa	259	1 884	28 565	16.9	80.7	22.3	113.1	5 858	17 640	36 773	16.2	6.2	46 246	8.7	15.3	14.0
Nevada	173	1 777	18 382	9.1	86.3	22.1	77.4	5 829	15 760	32 200	19.1	4.3	42 386	9.4	14.5	14.4
Orange	302	2 308	666 355	13.5	81.2	27.8	2 545.3	5 399	19 890	45 922	21.5	11.2	50 986	10.1	16.4	14.3
Placer	215	2 700	45 465	12.3	85.1	22.7	283.8	5 426	17 311	37 601	20.1	6.2	52 572	7.1	11.0	10.4
Plumas	303	2 632	5 037	5.8	82.7	15.1	25.6	7 245	12 952	24 299	-4.6	1.8	36 070	13.1	20.4	22.6
Riverside	621	3 304	307 709	10.9	74.1	14.6	1 600.0	5 420	15 265	33 081	23.1	4.7	39 428	14.0	20.4	19.9
Sacramento	589	4 357	289 451	11.4	82.2	23.0	1 211.8	5 794	15 265	32 297	10.8	3.9	41 657	15.9	24.6	24.6
San Benito	652	2 155	10 792	10.8	68.4	14.4	62.7	5 745	13 933	36 473	28.0	4.8	45 989	11.1	16.9	17.7
San Bernardino	536	3 276	405 639	11.7	75.4	14.9	1 992.0	5 460	13 358	33 443	14.3	3.9	38 225	17.0	23.4	23.0
San Diego	489	2 867	678 445	12.5	81.9	25.3	2 716.6	5 774	16 220	35 022	22.2	6.0	41 909	13.1	20.2	18.6
San Francisco	845	4 712	179 009	22.3	78.0	35.0	425.5	6 851	19 695	33 414	25.7	7.4	47 239	11.7	20.6	20.8
San Joaquin	815	4 444	137 025	11.3	68.6	13.2	622.5	5 540	12 705	30 635	13.7	3.5	36 940	17.6	24.8	26.1
San Luis Obispo	283	2 618	65 365	9.3	83.3	22.9	211.9	5 789	15 237	31 164	25.6	4.4	40 032	12.2	17.7	17.8
San Mateo	282	2 349	164 491	19.4	84.1	31.3	569.0	6 124	22 430	46 437	19.6	11.9	59 771	5.9	9.4	8.6
Santa Barbara	329	2 224	109 790	11.8	80.0	26.6	386.8	5 997	17 155	35 677	18.5	7.3	42 806	14.1	21.7	21.5
Santa Clara	429	2 216	429 640	17.4	82.0	32.6	1 548.2	6 111	20 423	48 115	22.8	11.4	63 298	8.2	13.5	12.4
Santa Cruz	464	2 936	67 978	10.7	81.9	29.7	237.4	5 870	17 347	37 112	31.2	7.4	45 267	12.0	18.8	18.4
Shasta	505	2 766	39 216	9.9	78.4	13.7	192.5	6 314	12 381	25 581	3.8	2.4	33 045	17.2	24.8	27.0
Sierra	113	1 153	728	4.3	75.5	15.9	7.9	2 637	13 731	23 657	-2.4	1.3	37 685	10.4	12.7	16.2
Siskiyou	316	2 192	11 087	4.2	77.4	14.2	57.3	7 215	11 610	21 921	-9.6	2.3	29 039	18.4	26.8	29.5
Solano	635	3 407	94 781	11.2	82.7	18.7	374.1	5 224	14 833	39 113	21.1	3.8	47 953	10.6	16.0	15.7
Sonoma	296	2 651	101 892	11.3	84.4	24.5	437.3	6 103	17 239	36 299	22.1	5.2	46 149	8.4	12.5	12.9
Stanislaus	691	4 643	102 957	7.8	68.4	13.0	533.1	5 707	12 731	29 793	10.6	3.5	36 207	17.2	24.2	24.7
Sutter	333	3 423	17 917	7.4	72.3	15.4	96.0	6 108	12 763	27 096	3.1	3.4	34 517	16.9	25.1	26.6
Tehama	485	2 780	12 493	6.2	72.2	10.2	70.1	6 444	10 990	22 436	-0.3	1.6	28 488	19.4	27.2	32.2
Trinity	177	2 073	3 276	7.1	74.2	12.9	20.6	8 955	10 781	20 494	-13.7	1.8	27 816	18.9	25.9	32.9
Tulare	646	3 726	92 825	5.7	60.2	11.8	504.8	5 958	10 302	24 450	3.1	2.6	28 449	26.6	35.3	36.2
Tuolumne	371	2 139	11 301	11.2	80.4	14.7	51.1	6 216	13 224	27 030	13.8	3.2	35 463	13.8	21.1	22.5
Ventura	280	2 045	188 292	14.7	79.4	23.0	729.8	5 435	17 861	45 612	28.2	9.3	51 710	10.0	16.3	15.1
Yolo	565	2 981	51 330	7.6	79.1	30.3	151.0	5 605	13 861	28 866	11.9	4.2	41 169	14.4	21.6	22.2
Yuba	568	4 093	16 537	4.8	68.5	9.5	79.9	6 065	9 874	21 523	6.7	1.3	27 631	23.1	30.5	38.8
COLORADO	334	3 649	896 144	11.9	84.4	27.0	4 140.7	5 923	14 821	30 140	-0.4	3.8	43 402	9.9	14.2	12.9
Adams	410	4 504	69 822	10.3	78.8	13.0	315.8	5 534	12 615	30 522	-6.7	1.5	44 327	10.0	15.2	13.0
Alamosa	367	2 933	4 883	4.1	76.9	24.1	18.9	6 699	9 286	20 265	1.2	1.0	29 121	22.8	27.5	30.2
Arapahoe	376	3 675	107 390	14.7	91.5	35.2	557.2	6 002	18 777	37 234	-6.9	6.5	52 576	6.1	9.6	7.8
Archuleta	30	3 172	1 292	5.0	80.9	19.7	8.0	5 180	10 913	22 894	4.4	2.3	32 609	12.7	15.7	18.0
Baca	111	310	1 031	2.1	72.0	13.6	7.0	7 722	9 571	18 602	0.5	0.5	29 021	19.3	27.0	26.0
Bent	400	1 867	1 099	2.6	72.7	14.6	6.1	5 850	9 170	18 977	-12.8	1.0	26 502	23.8	32.3	34.0
Boulder	268	2 872	72 009	9.7	91.3	42.1	251.4	5 552	17 359	35 322	6.6	6.5	54 503	7.7	10.3	8.7
Chaffee	215	2 586	3 630	9.7	81.0	15.2	13.6	6 185	10 788	21 174	-16.9	1.0	32 962	13.0	17.8	17.1
Cheyenne	134	1 210	635	0.0	80.8	11.9	3.7	8 024	11 382	24 341	23.8	2.7	37 101	11.6	14.7	15.5

1. Data for serious crimes have not been adjusted for underreporting; this may affect comparability between geographic areas and over time. 2. Per 100,000 population estimated by the FBI. 3. All persons 3 years old and over enrolled in nursery school through college. 4. Persons 25 years old and over. 5. Elementary and secondary education expenditures, local government fiscal years ending between July 1, 1998 and June 30, 1999. 6. Based on population enumerated as of April 1, 1990.

Table B. States and Counties — Personal Income

STATE County	Personal income, 1999 Total (mil dol)	Percent change, 1998–1999	Per capita[1] Dollars	Per capita[1] Rank	Wages and salaries[2] (mil dol)	Proprietor's income (mil dol)	Dividends, interest, and rent (mil dol)	Transfer payments Total (mil dol)	Government payments to individuals Total (mil dol)	Social Security (mil dol)	Medical payments (mil dol)	Income mainte- nance (mil dol)	Unemploy- ment insurance (mil dol)
	62	63	64	65	66	67	68	69	70	71	72	73	74
CALIFORNIA—Cont'd													
Butte	4 297	5.7	22 012	1 365	2 023	465	945	918	880	344	309	147	17
Calaveras	830	5.2	20 719	1 769	205	108	207	178	170	82	59	16	3
Colusa	435	15.2	23 085	1 074	207	105	77	66	62	24	22	8	5
Contra Costa	35 454	6.8	37 994	58	15 770	3 403	6 985	3 085	2 906	1 165	1 104	376	58
Del Norte	469	4.5	17 722	2 595	220	66	87	126	121	40	47	25	3
El Dorado	4 597	5.4	28 487	285	1 339	530	801	512	481	222	171	43	12
Fresno	16 136	5.6	21 146	1 619	9 371	1 936	2 595	3 024	2 877	793	1 117	622	165
Glenn	474	6.7	18 015	2 538	226	65	96	105	99	37	36	17	4
Humboldt	2 776	2.9	22 871	1 118	1 410	365	587	552	529	187	192	91	14
Imperial	2 550	2.6	17 550	2 642	1 408	442	298	533	505	147	178	117	37
Inyo	435	3.3	24 212	822	217	38	115	83	80	35	29	9	2
Kern	12 777	2.6	19 886	2 023	7 850	1 377	1 989	2 249	2 126	698	755	434	106
Kings	1 939	5.2	15 732	2 926	1 249	165	276	360	337	97	133	66	18
Lake	1 270	6.0	22 925	1 105	371	120	244	330	319	126	120	50	6
Lassen	578	3.7	17 506	2 646	323	53	101	108	102	32	40	19	3
Los Angeles	263 815	4.8	28 276	297	179 143	32 718	48 089	34 251	32 454	8 687	14 344	7 022	688
Madera	2 144	6.6	18 358	2 455	1 057	252	357	428	406	145	144	74	20
Marin	13 728	5.6	57 982	4	5 092	1 627	3 867	755	709	359	223	62	11
Mariposa	350	4.3	22 452	1 228	145	32	85	75	72	33	26	7	2
Mendocino	1 998	4.7	23 758	908	898	283	481	390	374	133	145	61	11
Merced	3 687	4.8	18 367	2 452	1 780	526	535	791	752	199	316	157	37
Modoc	197	6.8	21 427	1 541	76	31	40	48	46	17	17	8	1
Mono	268	4.9	25 477	587	163	47	54	23	21	9	5	3	2
Monterey	10 927	5.5	29 393	239	5 674	1 894	2 423	1 178	1 107	401	395	157	63
Napa	4 226	9.3	34 935	84	2 106	482	958	454	431	179	175	34	9
Nevada	2 424	6.8	26 341	482	819	336	680	353	336	176	107	26	7
Orange	93 333	6.5	33 805	114	59 062	11 280	17 287	7 411	6 880	2 830	2 541	862	129
Placer	8 375	12.4	34 972	83	3 708	956	1 395	770	724	330	233	69	14
Plumas	508	5.3	24 945	681	216	76	125	98	94	39	33	10	3
Riverside	35 620	7.5	23 271	1 023	14 620	3 205	6 278	5 144	4 850	2 007	1 774	645	125
Sacramento	32 558	6.5	27 485	374	23 616	2 809	5 343	4 824	4 597	1 318	1 897	955	96
San Benito	1 149	9.9	22 402	1 241	457	181	197	122	112	44	38	15	7
San Bernardino	34 984	6.1	20 949	1 682	18 120	3 119	4 536	5 352	5 034	1 579	1 975	991	125
San Diego	83 183	8.3	29 489	229	52 156	8 140	16 838	9 026	8 502	3 122	3 305	1 222	139
San Francisco	36 939	10.8	49 464	11	35 645	5 169	7 412	3 207	3 063	919	1 211	678	52
San Joaquin	12 133	6.2	21 544	1 508	6 455	1 229	1 946	2 262	2 153	622	924	419	69
San Luis Obispo	6 134	5.3	25 888	531	2 926	892	1 575	815	769	377	230	84	14
San Mateo	33 102	6.0	47 146	14	21 456	3 297	7 519	1 977	1 841	902	585	181	30
Santa Barbara	11 817	5.0	30 218	203	6 301	1 378	3 458	1 231	1 156	529	366	141	26
Santa Clara	76 850	15.8	46 649	15	68 466	5 850	11 830	4 539	4 221	1 567	1 592	604	99
Santa Cruz	8 224	8.4	33 539	120	3 622	853	1 652	741	694	269	246	88	31
Shasta	3 764	5.1	22 880	1 116	1 826	548	712	814	782	293	295	117	19
Sierra	82	4.1	24 585	732	38	5	19	14	13	6	4	2	1
Siskiyou	919	2.4	21 092	1 640	387	128	209	234	225	86	81	35	6
Solano	9 711	9.8	25 176	645	4 282	577	1 417	1 135	1 062	370	363	172	38
Sonoma	14 296	8.1	32 492	139	7 003	1 600	3 180	1 477	1 392	625	493	140	28
Stanislaus	9 517	4.6	21 790	1 416	4 981	1 060	1 524	1 621	1 537	511	589	276	71
Sutter	1 900	11.2	24 223	821	692	347	313	307	292	100	105	44	15
Tehama	1 020	8.0	18 879	2 327	462	92	191	244	233	97	80	37	6
Trinity	249	4.1	19 264	2 219	83	25	57	69	67	25	26	9	2
Tulare	6 929	5.0	19 329	2 201	3 429	1 130	1 009	1 412	1 343	370	526	284	96
Tuolumne	1 124	4.7	20 910	1 693	436	116	303	240	230	113	75	24	4
Ventura	22 083	7.2	29 639	224	11 311	2 301	4 054	2 092	1 950	818	692	224	71
Yolo	4 206	4.3	27 037	415	3 219	523	811	502	472	160	178	81	13
Yuba	1 042	4.7	17 485	2 651	689	78	144	305	294	72	126	65	8
COLORADO	127 904	7.9	31 533	X	84 860	13 435	23 741	11 224	10 509	4 428	4 226	945	156
Adams	8 167	9.0	24 670	718	5 187	509	982	929	870	335	391	75	13
Alamosa	308	6.2	21 108	1 635	190	39	50	57	55	14	24	9	1
Arapahoe	19 369	8.3	40 177	43	13 603	2 298	3 325	962	877	454	279	59	16
Archuleta	168	8.5	17 458	2 656	70	24	51	24	23	13	6	2	1
Baca	123	9.6	28 550	280	31	53	23	19	18	9	6	2	0
Bent	99	1.6	17 017	2 731	56	6	19	24	23	7	10	3	0
Boulder	10 248	8.1	37 523	63	7 699	752	2 237	542	494	245	166	37	10
Chaffee	319	7.1	20 474	1 843	151	27	92	59	56	28	21	3	1
Cheyenne	67	15.8	30 122	208	23	26	13	9	8	3	4	1	0

1. Based on the resident population estimated as of July 1 of the year shown.   2. Includes other labor income.

Table B. States and Counties — **Earnings, Social Security, and Housing**

STATE County	Earnings, 1999									Social Security beneficiaries, December 2000		Supplemental Security Income recipients, December 2000	Housing units, 1990	
			Goods-related[1]		Service-related and other[2]									
	Total (mil dol)	Farm	Total	Manufacturing	Total	Retail trade	Finance, insurance, and real estate	Services	Government	Number	Rate[3]		Total	Percent change, 1980–1990
	75	76	77	78	79	80	81	82	83	84	85	86	87	88
CALIFORNIA—Cont'd														
Butte	2 488	2.0	D	8.4	D	12.6	6.2	31.8	21.2	41 551	205	9 092	76 115	24.0
Calaveras	313	-2.0	D	5.2	D	12.5	6.8	23.7	24.6	9 540	235	952	19 153	50.3
Colusa	311	37.0	11.4	8.6	D	8.1	1.7	D	15.0	2 843	151	519	6 295	18.0
Contra Costa	19 172	0.3	20.0	10.4	68.8	9.7	11.6	31.9	11.0	128 173	135	21 362	316 170	25.5
Del Norte	286	4.3	11.2	6.5	45.8	9.8	1.9	21.3	38.6	5 035	183	1 597	9 091	19.9
El Dorado	1 869	0.0	20.0	5.9	62.9	12.5	6.3	36.5	17.1	26 109	167	2 469	61 451	36.6
Fresno	11 307	5.7	15.9	9.3	57.3	10.3	6.3	23.5	21.1	100 961	126	36 187	235 563	21.6
Glenn	291	9.0	24.5	15.5	41.4	7.0	2.0	12.5	25.1	4 723	179	897	9 329	10.7
Humboldt	1 775	1.8	D	13.3	D	12.9	5.3	25.9	22.2	22 446	177	5 858	51 134	12.7
Imperial	1 851	18.6	D	3.4	D	9.6	D	12.8	31.4	21 663	152	8 261	36 559	13.9
Inyo	256	-1.3	13.7	2.9	52.1	15.6	2.2	35.5	42.9	4 183	233	455	8 712	2.7
Kern	9 227	4.2	17.8	5.1	50.4	9.2	3.9	20.4	27.6	88 399	134	25 914	198 636	27.6
Kings	1 414	7.0	D	9.0	D	9.4	D	14.6	42.9	13 050	101	3 852	30 843	20.0
Lake	491	2.9	D	3.9	D	13.5	4.3	30.5	24.5	14 945	256	3 385	28 822	25.3
Lassen	376	0.5	D	7.0	D	8.4	D	14.3	53.7	4 222	125	917	10 358	16.4
Los Angeles	211 861	0.1	18.1	14.0	69.0	8.3	9.6	37.2	12.8	999 598	105	359 866	3 163 343	10.8
Madera	1 309	9.0	D	10.8	D	8.9	D	23.6	20.8	18 345	149	4 214	30 831	25.3
Marin	6 719	0.1	11.3	3.7	D	11.0	14.3	45.9	9.3	37 395	151	3 470	99 757	7.7
Mariposa	176	-3.1	D	3.6	D	8.8	2.5	37.9	39.8	3 908	228	311	7 700	33.6
Mendocino	1 181	2.2	D	16.9	D	14.2	3.5	25.5	18.3	16 104	187	3 600	33 649	16.0
Merced	2 306	13.8	22.3	17.2	44.7	10.5	3.6	16.3	19.2	26 857	128	8 987	58 410	16.7
Modoc	107	15.8	D	3.0	38.3	9.0	3.9	12.6	40.0	2 134	226	345	4 672	25.0
Mono	210	-0.8	D	1.1	D	16.9	8.6	34.0	26.5	1 041	81	103	10 664	27.0
Monterey	7 568	15.0	10.3	5.2	54.0	9.1	6.4	22.8	20.7	49 035	122	8 720	121 224	17.1
Napa	2 588	3.4	D	21.4	D	10.1	5.7	27.8	13.6	21 774	175	1 961	44 199	10.4
Nevada	1 155	0.1	24.9	10.5	59.7	14.5	8.3	29.4	15.6	20 343	221	1 618	37 352	50.9
Orange	70 341	0.3	23.1	16.9	67.4	9.5	12.5	31.0	9.2	309 994	109	56 271	875 072	21.3
Placer	4 664	0.1	29.9	17.3	58.4	13.3	8.1	25.7	11.5	40 442	163	4 029	77 879	44.2
Plumas	292	5.2	22.2	13.9	44.3	10.1	4.1	16.0	28.3	4 662	224	674	11 942	26.4
Riverside	17 825	2.2	23.7	11.6	54.5	12.4	5.6	26.1	19.6	235 533	152	40 579	483 847	64.0
Sacramento	26 424	0.3	14.0	7.6	53.3	8.3	9.5	26.0	32.4	164 355	134	50 865	417 574	29.0
San Benito	638	13.6	D	13.9	D	10.3	4.4	13.6	16.8	5 498	103	824	12 230	39.8
San Bernardino	21 239	1.0	20.3	12.6	56.4	11.8	5.0	24.4	22.3	195 799	115	53 760	542 332	46.5
San Diego	60 296	0.6	17.3	11.4	59.3	8.9	7.9	30.2	22.8	370 870	132	76 889	946 240	31.4
San Francisco	40 814	0.0	D	4.2	D	7.4	22.9	37.5	12.9	105 028	135	46 350	328 471	3.7
San Joaquin	7 684	3.9	20.6	13.1	56.6	10.4	6.3	21.6	18.9	77 655	138	24 799	166 274	22.3
San Luis Obispo	3 818	3.0	17.6	8.0	58.7	13.4	6.0	26.3	20.7	44 075	179	5 186	90 200	35.1
San Mateo	24 753	0.3	19.9	14.0	73.6	8.8	9.1	39.6	6.1	93 648	132	12 687	251 782	8.0
Santa Barbara	7 679	4.8	17.7	10.6	58.2	10.6	6.6	30.7	19.3	61 083	153	9 050	138 149	20.2
Santa Clara	74 315	0.2	41.6	37.3	51.7	5.4	3.8	33.4	6.4	169 766	101	40 971	540 240	14.0
Santa Cruz	4 475	4.3	21.4	13.7	58.9	11.6	5.4	31.6	15.5	31 133	122	5 353	91 878	13.6
Shasta	2 374	0.4	D	8.7	D	12.6	4.0	30.1	19.0	36 125	221	8 117	60 552	27.6
Sierra	43	-5.1	35.4	29.1	D	6.2	D	10.4	50.1	757	213	76	2 166	14.4
Siskiyou	515	1.7	D	9.8	D	12.9	3.7	21.6	27.3	10 726	242	2 228	20 141	15.1
Solano	4 859	0.6	20.8	10.6	49.4	12.6	3.9	23.1	29.2	46 406	118	10 074	119 533	41.8
Sonoma	8 603	1.5	28.5	18.2	56.9	10.9	7.9	27.8	13.1	70 643	154	9 208	161 062	29.7
Stanislaus	6 042	3.9	26.0	18.8	53.8	11.4	4.1	23.6	16.4	63 879	143	18 696	132 027	28.8
Sutter	1 039	13.8	16.1	8.3	54.7	12.6	4.3	23.2	15.3	12 715	161	3 016	24 163	18.3
Tehama	554	3.0	22.9	17.8	54.0	21.2	4.0	19.1	20.1	11 759	210	2 418	20 403	23.2
Trinity	107	0.3	D	11.8	D	10.9	2.4	17.1	43.1	3 147	242	555	7 540	18.7
Tulare	4 559	15.3	D	9.8	D	10.8	D	16.3	21.4	48 818	133	15 792	105 013	18.3
Tuolumne	553	-1.0	20.1	8.9	53.2	13.9	3.9	27.8	27.7	12 878	236	1 558	25 175	30.0
Ventura	13 612	4.1	25.5	18.8	53.7	9.8	6.9	26.3	16.8	95 751	127	14 065	228 478	24.6
Yolo	3 741	4.3	15.1	8.6	50.4	10.9	4.4	16.4	30.3	19 948	118	4 713	53 000	21.5
Yuba	767	3.0	13.7	6.6	34.6	6.6	1.7	16.5	48.8	9 435	157	3 511	21 245	10.4
COLORADO	98 295	0.9	19.5	10.4	64.4	9.2	9.4	29.0	15.1	534 196	124	53 776	1 477 349	23.7
Adams	5 696	0.2	29.3	15.6	57.6	11.8	3.2	17.3	12.9	39 887	110	4 895	106 947	19.8
Alamosa	229	8.0	11.1	1.1	53.9	13.6	4.9	24.5	27.0	1 984	133	529	5 254	18.5
Arapahoe	15 901	0.0	13.0	4.4	79.5	7.9	14.7	30.5	7.4	51 505	106	3 362	168 665	49.0
Archuleta	94	-1.4	23.9	2.4	60.6	17.9	13.9	19.2	16.9	1 633	165	111	3 951	93.3
Baca	83	51.6	D	D	D	7.4	1.7	6.8	19.6	1 164	258	109	2 434	-1.9
Bent	62	4.9	D	D	D	5.6	3.7	13.4	62.1	1 021	170	198	2 332	-1.5
Boulder	8 451	0.1	27.9	22.7	59.6	7.9	5.6	36.5	12.4	27 961	96	2 347	94 621	26.8
Chaffee	178	-0.3	D	4.5	D	18.2	6.8	19.7	29.8	3 469	214	197	6 547	13.3
Cheyenne	49	42.6	D	D	D	4.0	3.5	4.9	16.4	415	186	17	1 083	13.0

1. Covers mining, construction, and manufacturing.   2. Covers private sector earnings in agricultural services, forestry, and fisheries; transportation and public utilities; wholesale trade; retail trade; finance, insurance, and real estate; and services.   3. Per 1,000 resident population estimated as of July 1 of the year shown.

Table B. States and Counties — **Housing, Labor Force, and Employment**

STATE County	Housing units, 1990 (cont'd) — Occupied units — Owner-occupied Total	Percent	Median value[1]	Owner cost as a percent of income — With a mortgage	Owner cost as a percent of income — Without a mortgage	Renter-occupied — Median rent[2]	Rent as percent of income	Sub-standard units[3] (percent)	Civilian labor force, 2001 — Total	Percent change, 2000–2001	Unemployment — Total	Rate[4]	Civilian employment, 1990[5] — Total	Percent — Professional, managerial, and technical	Percent — Precision production, craft, and repair
	89	90	91	92	93	94	95	96	97	98	99	100	101	102	103
CALIFORNIA—Cont'd															
Butte	71 665	60.9	94 000	22.4	11.9	439	32.6	5.1	87 996	0.6	6 191	7.0	70 880	29.6	11.0
Calaveras	12 649	76.1	113 700	24.7	12.8	476	29.3	5.6	15 839	4.8	933	5.9	12 114	24.2	17.8
Colusa	5 612	63.5	68 900	21.2	11.5	354	22.6	12.7	8 544	-4.8	1 503	17.6	6 653	17.0	8.1
Contra Costa	300 288	67.6	219 400	25.3	11.7	675	28.5	4.9	509 770	1.1	16 665	3.3	406 507	38.6	10.3
Del Norte	7 987	65.4	84 600	21.1	11.6	422	28.3	6.9	9 843	-0.6	854	8.7	7 858	22.2	11.4
El Dorado	46 845	70.4	155 000	25.7	12.6	569	29.2	5.0	84 073	2.2	3 158	3.8	58 893	30.0	12.4
Fresno	220 933	54.3	83 600	22.3	12.2	434	29.2	13.7	387 366	-1.9	53 052	13.7	269 826	27.3	9.7
Glenn	8 821	61.8	67 400	20.9	12.7	355	26.5	9.6	10 351	-1.5	1 155	11.2	9 896	17.3	11.6
Humboldt	46 420	58.8	88 000	20.8	11.9	409	29.8	6.0	59 112	-1.6	3 587	6.1	50 831	26.6	11.1
Imperial	32 842	57.6	72 500	21.6	12.6	394	28.9	21.1	55 516	-5.0	11 843	21.3	36 412	22.4	10.4
Inyo	7 565	66.3	115 800	21.4	12.6	412	24.4	5.3	7 343	1.3	357	4.9	7 800	25.8	12.7
Kern	181 480	59.3	82 800	22.5	12.4	440	27.4	10.9	291 683	0.1	30 718	10.5	214 668	26.2	13.3
Kings	29 082	52.9	70 700	21.8	12.2	411	25.8	12.9	46 108	-0.5	6 342	13.8	33 037	19.9	10.9
Lake	20 805	71.2	93 300	24.7	13.5	460	30.7	5.2	23 791	1.6	1 726	7.3	17 143	25.5	15.3
Lassen	8 543	69.4	70 400	20.6	12.4	412	25.2	5.9	10 930	0.1	745	6.8	8 843	26.0	8.9
Los Angeles	2 989 552	48.2	226 400	25.2	11.6	626	29.5	18.9	4 875 237	2.4	277 010	5.7	4 203 792	30.9	11.0
Madera	28 370	64.9	86 500	23.5	12.5	423	27.9	12.0	54 378	-0.9	6 594	12.1	33 263	20.8	11.8
Marin	95 006	62.1	354 200	25.5	11.8	824	29.8	3.0	138 104	-1.0	3 473	2.5	125 886	46.0	7.5
Mariposa	5 604	69.3	99 800	25.4	11.3	392	25.0	5.0	7 198	6.5	456	6.3	5 908	28.1	13.5
Mendocino	30 419	62.1	123 900	24.3	12.0	471	28.4	9.4	42 973	1.0	2 842	6.6	34 983	25.9	12.0
Merced	55 331	54.4	90 800	22.7	12.1	430	28.2	15.6	84 218	-1.5	11 791	14.0	66 116	21.7	11.5
Modoc	3 711	69.6	49 600	20.1	12.2	328	23.8	5.3	3 953	0.4	277	7.0	3 535	20.4	11.4
Mono	3 961	51.9	159 900	25.1	13.4	550	23.4	8.0	6 648	1.5	349	5.2	5 642	29.3	12.2
Monterey	112 965	50.6	198 200	24.8	11.4	625	28.5	14.5	195 850	-0.2	18 133	9.3	146 885	26.8	8.7
Napa	41 312	64.5	183 600	24.4	11.5	632	29.2	5.3	66 612	2.3	2 176	3.3	52 533	31.7	11.7
Nevada	30 758	74.4	154 700	26.0	12.4	598	30.0	3.8	46 271	1.7	1 700	3.7	33 210	32.1	14.0
Orange	827 066	60.1	252 700	25.2	11.4	790	29.0	10.7	1 537 105	1.7	46 277	3.0	1 292 472	35.0	10.3
Placer	64 101	70.7	169 000	25.0	11.9	575	28.8	4.1	127 926	2.8	4 634	3.6	82 920	32.5	12.8
Plumas	8 125	67.5	89 900	22.0	13.0	366	28.9	3.5	9 871	1.1	828	8.4	7 783	25.2	12.7
Riverside	402 067	67.4	139 100	26.6	12.3	572	29.9	9.7	750 634	2.8	39 168	5.2	488 257	26.1	14.4
Sacramento	394 530	56.6	129 800	22.9	11.5	527	29.2	6.1	617 834	2.3	25 792	4.2	485 063	33.3	10.1
San Benito	11 422	61.1	206 600	26.7	12.3	547	25.2	13.0	28 020	2.6	2 312	8.3	16 800	23.6	13.6
San Bernardino	464 737	63.3	129 200	25.1	12.1	556	29.5	9.9	814 531	3.1	38 758	4.8	591 371	27.0	14.4
San Diego	887 403	53.8	186 700	25.9	11.5	611	29.8	9.1	1 424 852	1.6	45 698	3.2	1 145 266	34.5	11.1
San Francisco	305 584	34.5	298 900	24.6	11.8	653	28.0	11.4	436 902	0.6	22 508	5.2	386 530	38.5	6.3
San Joaquin	158 156	57.6	121 700	23.3	11.8	489	28.2	12.4	264 782	1.9	23 134	8.7	195 575	24.2	12.5
San Luis Obispo	80 281	59.8	215 300	27.4	11.3	573	31.8	5.7	118 603	2.2	3 306	2.8	97 417	29.3	12.3
San Mateo	241 914	60.2	343 900	26.0	11.6	769	27.6	8.9	407 903	-0.6	11 422	2.8	352 964	35.6	9.8
Santa Barbara	129 802	54.7	250 000	25.0	11.3	654	31.3	9.6	202 668	-0.7	7 003	3.5	180 217	32.7	10.7
Santa Clara	520 180	59.1	289 400	24.9	11.5	773	27.4	10.5	1 012 671	0.4	45 190	4.5	806 917	41.1	10.6
Santa Cruz	83 566	59.9	256 100	27.2	11.7	713	31.4	9.4	143 814	1.2	8 761	6.1	117 904	36.3	10.7
Shasta	55 966	64.5	91 300	21.7	11.9	432	29.2	5.1	76 487	2.3	5 155	6.7	58 578	26.8	12.6
Sierra	1 336	68.1	79 300	23.5	15.0	423	25.2	5.5	1 453	-11.4	141	9.7	1 333	29.4	9.7
Siskiyou	17 306	67.2	68 300	21.9	12.6	366	27.7	4.9	17 194	-3.6	1 624	9.4	16 505	25.0	10.4
Solano	113 429	62.9	147 300	25.4	12.0	590	27.6	6.6	201 379	2.1	8 273	4.1	151 310	28.4	14.0
Sonoma	149 011	62.9	201 400	26.2	11.7	645	29.5	4.6	262 617	1.3	7 678	2.9	193 296	31.7	12.3
Stanislaus	125 375	60.7	124 300	23.3	11.7	482	28.9	10.4	210 264	2.1	21 472	10.2	151 010	23.8	14.0
Sutter	23 111	58.7	91 900	21.5	12.3	387	27.0	8.9	36 975	-0.6	4 566	12.3	26 359	27.1	12.5
Tehama	18 704	68.6	68 700	22.2	12.2	366	27.8	6.9	25 762	1.6	1 655	6.4	17 898	19.8	13.1
Trinity	5 156	69.6	81 800	23.5	13.6	367	29.3	10.5	5 004	1.9	546	10.9	4 547	25.6	11.0
Tulare	97 861	60.1	73 900	22.6	12.1	403	29.2	14.5	170 908	-0.3	26 396	15.4	118 964	21.8	9.6
Tuolumne	17 959	70.6	120 400	24.4	12.8	500	27.5	4.5	21 474	4.2	1 188	5.5	17 601	26.4	13.7
Ventura	217 298	65.5	245 300	26.2	11.4	754	29.3	10.2	419 863	1.6	18 920	4.5	336 772	33.1	11.7
Yolo	50 972	51.9	137 800	22.2	11.6	510	31.2	7.8	93 198	-0.9	3 955	4.2	66 260	37.1	8.8
Yuba	19 776	52.8	67 600	21.6	11.6	383	28.5	9.7	21 471	0.1	2 522	11.7	18 329	20.7	13.9
COLORADO	1 282 489	62.2	82 700	22.5	12.7	418	26.1	3.0	2 294 893	0.9	85 295	3.7	1 633 281	34.3	9.8
Adams	96 353	65.5	71 500	22.9	12.6	434	26.4	3.6	184 364	0.3	7 005	3.8	132 884	23.5	13.4
Alamosa	4 721	62.5	48 100	21.3	12.8	291	31.5	6.4	8 020	1.7	447	5.6	6 068	29.9	8.3
Arapahoe	154 710	63.6	93 000	22.3	11.8	463	24.6	2.1	286 656	0.2	9 111	3.2	210 935	39.4	7.4
Archuleta	2 010	70.7	79 600	30.6	14.0	385	25.9	7.6	4 744	3.0	204	4.3	2 210	25.3	11.4
Baca	1 872	72.9	31 100	22.1	14.7	235	22.7	3.1	2 151	-1.4	62	2.9	1 903	18.6	6.8
Bent	1 865	69.3	24 300	17.9	14.7	296	23.9	2.1	1 937	-6.1	87	4.5	1 729	28.3	7.4
Boulder	88 402	61.1	102 800	22.3	12.3	502	28.7	2.4	189 963	3.3	6 679	3.5	124 542	45.0	8.1
Chaffee	4 848	70.9	62 900	22.8	11.9	336	26.2	2.8	7 528	-1.4	210	2.8	4 950	25.6	11.1
Cheyenne	904	70.0	38 200	19.0	13.1	297	17.6	2.8	1 200	0.7	28	2.3	1 122	16.9	12.1

1. Specified owner-occupied units. 2. Specified renter-occupied units. 3. Overcrowded or lacking complete plumbing facilities. 4. Percent of civilian labor force. 5. Persons 16 years and older.

Table B. States and Counties — Nonfarm Employment and Agriculture

	Private nonfarm establishments, employment and payroll, 1999									Agriculture, 1997			
	Employment						Annual payroll		Farms			Farm operators
STATE County	Number of establishments	Total	Health Care and Social Assistance	Manufacturing	Retail trade	Finance and Insurance	Professional Scientific and Technical Services	Total (mil dol)	Average per employee (dollars)	Number	Less than 50 acres	500 acres and over	Whose principal occupation is farming (percent)
	104	105	106	107	108	109	110	111	112	113	114	115	116
CALIFORNIA—Cont'd													
Butte	4 534	52 142	10 142	4 512	9 352	1 825	2 556	1 143	21 912	1 942	58.7	9.4	54.8
Calaveras	944	5 582	953	468	984	242	252	118	21 203	457	45.1	23.0	45.5
Colusa	366	3 475	268	709	533	102	D	90	25 887	810	25.7	27.5	64.9
Contra Costa	21 785	300 025	34 651	18 890	39 025	25 180	24 023	11 902	39 671	587	64.6	11.6	49.2
Del Norte	504	4 311	1 034	250	920	106	136	83	19 283	66	45.5	7.6	50.0
El Dorado	3 830	36 640	4 344	2 042	4 871	881	2 311	987	26 933	763	74.2	2.8	41.9
Fresno	15 138	207 810	30 147	26 406	31 478	9 798	8 869	5 567	26 787	6 592	58.6	11.2	62.3
Glenn	484	4 325	368	905	692	151	123	118	27 209	1 189	44.6	16.0	63.4
Humboldt	3 582	36 953	7 211	5 262	6 868	1 181	1 450	830	22 462	792	40.9	20.2	52.7
Imperial	2 260	24 275	3 519	1 506	6 585	795	712	510	20 998	557	24.6	37.7	75.4
Inyo	614	6 484	983	252	1 125	90	131	117	18 033	82	37.8	34.1	53.7
Kern	10 756	146 999	19 597	13 140	24 826	6 641	7 517	3 903	26 550	1 997	35.1	30.3	63.8
Kings	1 517	17 768	2 875	2 948	3 583	583	365	422	23 731	1 079	50.6	18.9	62.2
Lake	1 099	9 292	2 019	338	1 940	390	247	195	20 947	776	66.2	5.4	42.4
Lassen	511	4 112	741	325	976	125	80	86	20 949	365	32.1	33.4	51.5
Los Angeles	222 513	3 747 755	359 599	622 885	355 417	179 710	394 384	130 919	34 933	1 226	84.7	4.7	39.9
Madera	1 852	22 819	2 492	3 964	3 200	379	385	459	20 132	1 673	44.6	13.8	58.4
Marin	10 131	101 281	13 414	4 227	14 737	7 479	9 035	3 877	38 278	276	34.1	34.1	62.3
Mariposa	346	3 276	323	113	398	78	D	71	21 683	252	38.9	27.8	49.6
Mendocino	2 749	24 479	3 705	4 231	4 569	596	659	567	23 159	1 092	45.1	19.3	51.6
Merced	2 931	38 209	5 216	8 322	6 609	975	852	871	22 789	2 831	52.5	10.8	61.9
Modoc	199	1 532	454	0	241	D	D	31	20 519	440	16.1	41.8	64.8
Mono	547	5 796	202	D	751	88	155	104	17 901	63	27.0	39.7	61.9
Monterey	8 519	104 520	12 099	6 755	16 970	4 794	3 714	2 993	28 636	1 209	40.7	29.9	66.3
Napa	3 622	49 785	9 437	10 019	5 928	1 446	1 560	1 510	30 339	1 318	68.2	6.6	44.8
Nevada	2 903	25 130	3 577	2 891	4 282	711	974	604	24 040	412	70.1	8.0	45.6
Orange	76 532	1 330 960	104 096	224 520	137 246	90 695	91 517	47 541	35 719	349	74.8	3.2	49.3
Placer	6 886	88 359	8 263	8 131	13 118	3 933	3 761	2 781	31 471	997	71.8	6.9	43.8
Plumas	689	4 463	924	642	758	175	146	108	24 173	117	32.5	29.9	53.8
Riverside	25 705	366 358	42 058	49 509	59 135	9 981	10 392	9 484	25 888	3 048	79.3	4.8	44.0
Sacramento	25 359	408 586	53 014	31 865	55 234	32 859	26 175	12 861	31 476	1 288	63.0	11.3	51.5
San Benito	926	10 147	969	2 197	1 623	311	295	269	26 461	562	48.0	24.9	55.2
San Bernardino	26 735	440 958	56 782	68 909	62 184	13 620	10 824	11 762	26 673	1 455	78.9	3.2	45.6
San Diego	65 905	1 015 773	107 615	116 648	129 028	47 963	83 377	33 860	33 334	5 925	90.2	2.0	37.2
San Francisco	31 202	536 012	51 480	21 725	40 218	61 927	72 718	26 375	49 207	9	100.0	0.0	22.2
San Joaquin	9 980	147 642	20 034	22 673	21 167	6 170	4 302	4 047	27 411	3 862	62.6	8.3	59.3
San Luis Obispo	6 736	72 677	12 426	6 894	12 020	2 385	3 145	1 832	25 204	1 916	49.3	19.7	48.4
San Mateo	20 267	344 926	25 479	31 803	36 377	19 331	28 306	16 557	48 003	240	60.8	8.3	55.0
Santa Barbara	10 675	135 515	16 737	16 464	20 154	6 191	7 929	4 069	30 027	1 451	59.0	16.1	52.0
Santa Clara	44 909	941 476	71 520	231 338	81 280	21 178	91 218	56 160	59 651	985	74.5	7.8	47.6
Santa Cruz	6 813	75 617	9 548	8 685	12 305	2 035	4 468	2 364	31 259	722	75.8	3.5	59.8
Shasta	4 380	43 952	8 858	3 555	8 200	1 343	1 891	1 109	25 238	850	61.3	14.0	41.6
Sierra	98	652	D	D	72	D	D	19	29 201	47	14.9	31.9	57.4
Siskiyou	1 254	9 231	1 568	864	1 713	344	206	192	20 829	733	32.5	27.3	61.0
Solano	6 359	88 920	14 033	9 202	15 654	2 582	2 917	2 511	28 239	795	57.7	15.5	50.7
Sonoma	13 147	159 421	22 328	26 391	24 643	10 612	7 117	4 953	31 067	2 745	66.3	7.3	49.0
Stanislaus	8 176	117 156	16 354	23 307	18 629	3 454	3 550	3 098	26 447	4 009	65.5	6.5	55.8
Sutter	1 619	17 033	3 412	1 660	3 620	688	461	422	24 784	1 314	45.7	12.8	64.6
Tehama	1 011	11 600	1 717	2 186	1 974	548	368	281	24 197	1 362	57.3	13.1	51.0
Trinity	324	1 486	257	197	310	50	53	30	20 132	116	41.4	19.8	43.1
Tulare	5 862	72 991	10 678	12 048	12 674	3 000	2 089	1 753	24 020	5 446	59.7	8.2	55.5
Tuolumne	1 449	12 025	2 204	930	2 370	433	303	268	22 279	264	43.2	23.5	43.2
Ventura	16 790	224 817	22 778	30 860	32 059	13 898	12 973	7 044	31 332	2 214	73.3	5.6	46.5
Yolo	3 421	55 224	4 463	6 034	6 334	2 731	2 511	1 651	29 897	923	45.6	21.1	56.4
Yuba	835	9 021	1 624	1 213	1 504	252	232	206	22 794	706	49.3	11.2	48.2
COLORADO	133 743	1 821 717	187 962	164 792	240 821	100 979	132 906	59 775	32 813	28 268	28.4	34.2	54.5
Adams	7 102	122 961	7 279	12 655	15 380	2 318	3 024	3 804	30 940	696	36.1	29.2	50.0
Alamosa	506	4 927	1 043	119	1 074	223	172	98	19 841	306	14.7	35.3	62.1
Arapahoe	16 164	277 793	20 683	16 321	32 882	30 133	24 017	11 500	41 396	258	34.5	30.2	45.3
Archuleta	442	2 524	111	21	456	61	59	47	18 630	206	26.2	21.4	44.2
Baca	108	626	D	27	130	49	7	10	16 419	608	3.0	67.6	63.5
Bent	79	1 090	D	D	95	50	D	32	29 735	270	13.7	49.3	70.0
Boulder	10 772	145 191	12 798	25 510	18 073	4 111	22 006	5 897	40 614	657	60.4	6.7	42.0
Chaffee	719	4 538	474	206	818	244	172	86	18 893	189	21.7	19.6	46.6
Cheyenne	63	436	D	D	79	D	D	13	30 326	333	3.0	73.0	69.4

STATE County	Agriculture, 1997 (cont'd)														
	Land in farms				Value of land and buildings		Value of machinery and equipment average per farm ($1,000)	Value of products sold				Percent of farms with sales of —		Percent of land owned by fed. gov. 1997	Water consumption 1995 (mil gal/day)
		Acres								Percent from —					
	Acreage (1,000)	Percent change, 1992–1997	Average size of farm	Total irrigated (1,000)	Total cropland (1,000)	Average per farm ($1,000)	Average per acre (dollars)		Total (mil dol)	Average per farm (dollars)	Crops	Livestock and poultry products	$10,000 or more	$100,000 or more		
	117	118	119	120	121	122	123	124	125	126	127	128	129	130	131	132
CALIFORNIA—Cont'd															
Butte	404	-10.6	208	224	247	754	3 589	73	286	147 388	96.9	3.1	57.3	26.7	14.1	957.7
Calaveras	245	-0.4	536	7	21	722	1 320	20	10	21 535	17.9	82.1	34.6	4.4	19.9	14.7
Colusa	431	-4.2	532	277	317	1 305	2 426	125	277	341 405	97.8	2.2	80.5	53.6	15.0	1 049.1
Contra Costa	148	-9.3	252	30	44	1 046	3 339	29	67	114 256	78.1	21.9	40.7	13.1	2.0	521.0
Del Norte	13	2.3	202	6	8	702	3 480	69	21	315 112	51.9	48.1	40.9	18.2	66.8	19.7
El Dorado	103	0.7	135	5	13	363	2 926	19	13	17 666	74.9	25.1	25.4	3.9	45.2	73.8
Fresno	1 881	6.0	285	1 154	1 251	971	3 334	78	2 773	420 629	76.3	23.7	72.4	35.2	38.4	3 547.7
Glenn	483	1.8	406	220	256	799	2 083	85	228	191 944	78.7	21.3	66.5	34.3	25.6	848.4
Humboldt	585	-2.3	738	18	51	705	1 118	33	75	95 297	32.9	67.1	48.9	17.3	20.8	123.5
Imperial	490	-8.1	879	438	459	2 614	3 068	195	850	1 526 662	69.4	30.6	82.9	62.1	56.8	2 607.7
Inyo	199	-19.9	2 423	19	D	1 975	815	38	5	61 444	20.1	79.9	51.2	19.5	92.1	149.4
Kern	2 851	0.4	1 428	913	1 054	2 162	1 605	189	1 969	985 735	90.8	9.2	66.8	45.6	27.9	2 462.7
Kings	657	-15.3	609	421	526	1 602	2 732	148	694	642 889	53.2	46.8	69.3	43.7	3.2	1 413.4
Lake	138	-15.6	178	17	33	450	2 563	31	40	52 018	95.1	4.9	32.1	11.5	45.0	57.1
Lassen	454	-6.8	1 243	68	118	937	686	79	26	72 325	55.8	44.2	50.7	14.8	56.8	300.9
Los Angeles	131	-28.9	107	27	49	507	4 475	39	238	193 854	94.3	5.7	37.1	14.1	29.6	1 683.0
Madera	642	-14.3	383	309	333	1 157	3 537	76	627	374 901	81.0	19.0	71.4	42.5	36.2	981.0
Marin	150	-11.4	542	1	28	1 315	1 900	44	54	195 212	6.6	93.4	62.0	26.1	20.5	41.0
Mariposa	198	-3.8	787	3	9	598	871	30	6	22 284	6.6	93.4	34.1	6.0	51.8	8.3
Mendocino	639	-11.9	585	25	66	930	1 728	46	117	107 014	87.7	12.3	44.2	15.4	13.3	52.6
Merced	882	-9.9	311	493	532	951	3 149	96	1 273	449 832	45.4	54.6	72.3	38.6	1.9	1 688.4
Modoc	663	-3.5	1 507	159	183	1 055	861	110	64	144 993	63.8	36.2	69.3	28.4	61.8	429.0
Mono	69	-33.2	1 092	31	D	1 119	1 024	67	7	103 208	49.8	50.2	58.7	28.6	85.5	221.4
Monterey	1 544	12.5	1 277	260	389	2 685	2 358	226	1 750	1 447 268	98.0	2.0	69.9	44.4	27.5	632.6
Napa	212	-9.6	161	46	75	1 537	11 629	52	239	181 104	98.0	2.0	65.2	28.8	8.8	67.3
Nevada	63	-12.8	152	7	15	297	3 591	23	4	9 647	45.9	54.1	21.1	0.7	30.4	40.8
Orange	58	-4.7	167	13	17	871	6 010	90	229	655 818	98.6	1.4	53.0	29.2	13.1	517.3
Placer	140	1.2	140	35	62	567	4 765	30	37	37 097	68.4	31.6	25.8	6.4	37.7	200.2
Plumas	109	-9.3	931	29	43	994	1 284	40	23	197 650	70.8	29.2	49.6	12.0	70.3	127.1
Riverside	509	20.1	167	220	280	749	4 618	63	1 048	343 676	55.0	45.0	48.0	19.4	55.7	1 432.3
Sacramento	308	-18.7	239	123	159	718	2 825	52	218	169 272	62.3	37.7	44.5	20.4	1.6	876.1
San Benito	512	-14.7	910	36	73	1 124	1 193	55	157	278 838	84.8	15.2	55.7	21.5	14.3	87.5
San Bernardino	924	-28.2	635	41	58	470	693	63	618	424 628	12.0	88.0	44.1	23.4	74.5	578.1
San Diego	475	-8.3	80	70	113	407	5 504	23	633	106 790	86.6	13.4	34.7	10.9	22.9	776.5
San Francisco	0	0.0	2	0	D	110	46 991	25	1	97 753	100.0	0.0	88.9	33.3	7.3	101.9
San Joaquin	809	3.2	209	519	559	1 017	4 667	82	1 180	305 465	73.4	26.6	65.3	33.6	0.3	1 816.8
San Luis Obispo	1 302	-1.7	679	61	281	1 046	1 591	49	313	163 335	89.5	10.5	47.2	17.6	16.7	188.4
San Mateo	45	-21.8	186	4	15	808	5 653	69	139	577 787	99.1	0.9	60.4	25.0	0.8	111.4
Santa Barbara	817	-2.4	563	104	157	1 378	2 716	82	660	454 680	94.3	5.7	52.9	27.0	49.5	322.2
Santa Clara	319	-7.1	324	19	32	606	2 425	50	188	191 355	89.6	10.4	41.5	13.6	1.4	350.3
Santa Cruz	71	34.2	98	21	28	573	6 234	67	248	343 234	94.9	5.1	57.9	29.8	0.1	72.2
Shasta	317	-18.4	373	39	59	420	1 021	22	31	36 881	58.6	41.4	29.1	5.1	38.0	310.8
Sierra	46	-15.7	986	10	15	1 095	1 110	38	1	27 755	23.9	76.1	55.3	4.3	68.8	40.6
Siskiyou	629	-2.8	858	140	182	1 070	1 139	73	74	101 288	70.3	29.7	55.0	18.0	61.9	474.6
Solano	362	6.5	455	162	210	1 224	2 554	83	161	203 042	83.8	16.2	49.3	25.0	2.6	526.5
Sonoma	571	10.4	208	57	145	1 025	5 211	47	464	168 895	69.1	30.9	53.3	23.8	2.5	126.1
Stanislaus	733	-3.6	183	359	382	779	4 508	61	1 209	301 453	45.5	54.5	63.5	29.4	0.3	1 437.9
Sutter	348	9.5	265	242	297	1 203	4 532	115	280	212 826	97.5	2.5	69.6	37.4	0.7	1 053.9
Tehama	885	-12.9	650	86	127	772	1 106	39	107	78 636	62.4	37.6	49.1	14.2	23.6	399.8
Trinity	118	1.9	1 019	2	7	413	460	24	2	15 494	D	D	21.6	2.6	74.4	25.5
Tulare	1 310	-3.3	240	625	703	835	3 444	68	1 921	352 806	58.4	41.6	67.4	35.7	48.5	2 208.7
Tuolumne	152	10.4	577	3	13	736	1 029	23	19	72 640	6.3	93.7	32.2	8.7	74.0	37.9
Ventura	346	7.9	156	111	132	883	6 860	46	846	381 939	98.0	2.0	57.3	27.5	50.0	372.7
Yolo	537	3.4	581	294	381	1 420	2 732	126	345	373 666	96.9	3.1	62.1	30.6	4.1	1 090.1
Yuba	208	-11.3	295	85	97	763	2 797	63	107	150 972	86.8	13.2	48.2	24.1	17.0	354.7
COLORADO	32 634	-4.0	1 154	3 430	10 509	707	618	71	4 534	160 401	29.3	70.7	52.6	16.9	35.7	13 823.9
Adams	674	-1.8	968	27	530	654	784	67	88	126 062	78.1	21.9	51.0	17.2	(1)2.3	132.2
Alamosa	190	-8.2	621	106	103	763	1 164	166	57	186 912	90.4	9.6	66.7	28.4	19.4	413.8
Arapahoe	333	3.1	1 290	4	169	1 181	818	59	24	91 519	61.7	38.3	43.8	9.7	1.5	86.5
Archuleta	113	-27.3	547	17	18	855	1 654	27	6	29 850	6.4	93.6	36.4	7.3	51.3	48.2
Baca	1 142	-9.1	1 879	65	633	748	427	83	77	127 252	36.1	63.9	61.7	21.7	12.5	105.8
Bent	784	-1.6	2 905	63	D	900	283	78	51	188 798	24.6	75.4	69.3	25.6	1.2	426.0
Boulder	128	-18.4	195	39	59	534	2 054	55	44	66 471	63.9	36.1	34.7	7.8	35.0	173.6
Chaffee	86	1.9	453	24	24	850	1 747	39	5	27 308	40.3	59.7	45.0	6.3	76.9	56.7
Cheyenne	796	-12.9	2 390	21	434	586	237	111	34	101 035	57.0	43.0	71.2	26.4	0.0	26.4

1. Denver County included with Adams County.

STATE County	Value of Residential Construction Authorized by Building Permits, 2000		Wholesale Trade, 1997				Retail Trade[1], 1997				Real Estate and Rental and Leasing, 1997			
	New Construction ($1,000)	Number of Housing Units	Number of Establishments	Number of Employees	Sales (mil dol)	Annual Payroll (mil dol)	Number of Establishments	Number of Employees	Sales (mil dol)	Annual Payroll (mil dol)	Number of Establishments	Number of Employees	Receipts (mil dol)	Annual Payroll (mil dol)
	133	134	135	136	137	138	139	140	141	142	143	144	145	146
CALIFORNIA—Cont'd														
Butte	130 380	1 134	179	1 792	637.9	56.9	777	9 004	1 502.6	154.0	212	1 012	80.5	13.4
Calaveras	84 327	425	27	D	D	D	136	862	135.5	14.0	36	100	10.4	1.6
Colusa	6 812	46	25	318	152.3	8.3	67	545	121.7	10.8	19	49	4.8	0.7
Contra Costa	965 154	5 479	1 159	11 092	14 968.0	518.5	2 705	37 550	7 376.8	752.8	1 056	6 172	972.6	172.2
Del Norte	5 392	45	15	D	D	D	88	982	123.1	12.5	20	58	4.9	0.8
El Dorado	341 284	1 476	108	684	249.7	19.3	546	4 894	926.8	91.1	180	781	68.6	9.9
Fresno	426 595	3 156	971	13 004	5 845.2	415.5	2 492	30 231	5 574.6	548.9	593	3 496	376.5	67.3
Glenn	4 596	41	36	298	125.8	8.6	79	720	98.9	10.5	18	149	7.1	1.4
Humboldt	41 739	532	128	1 306	493.6	37.1	668	6 816	1 024.0	108.7	141	494	47.1	7.9
Imperial	77 292	773	189	1 951	673.7	41.0	521	5 991	989.4	98.8	86	408	33.2	6.5
Inyo	3 637	18	24	D	D	D	145	1 092	171.1	17.8	18	59	4.3	1.1
Kern	371 103	3 070	612	7 930	4 313.9	256.4	1 918	22 792	4 224.4	412.1	419	2 479	220.5	43.8
Kings	44 709	445	60	623	411.6	15.8	316	3 690	629.3	60.0	66	235	20.8	3.3
Lake	31 673	132	39	D	D	D	197	1 954	309.3	30.7	41	89	7.0	1.0
Lassen	11 234	106	11	D	D	D	106	1 032	159.2	15.5	16	56	3.9	0.6
Los Angeles	2 364 387	16 968	21 474	259 217	177 244.9	9 450.4	27 577	343 656	69 534.2	6 769.0	10 932	76 904	13 608.6	2 256.3
Madera	64 176	648	87	623	265.8	18.8	313	3 173	527.3	53.0	60	217	22.3	3.8
Marin	165 778	593	570	4 167	2 414.8	170.4	1 291	14 793	2 775.7	322.0	537	2 978	556.7	91.0
Mariposa	12 060	87	7	D	D	D	78	397	57.4	6.3	14	68	4.3	1.0
Mendocino	23 588	284	108	1 095	308.7	27.0	490	4 572	711.4	76.8	109	445	35.7	5.8
Merced	184 032	1 380	117	1 333	699.9	36.4	551	6 122	1 102.1	108.0	121	461	46.0	5.7
Modoc	0	0	11	D	D	D	46	256	34.3	3.5	6	D	D	D
Mono	36 274	237	2	D	D	D	79	683	84.0	10.2	37	269	13.8	3.4
Monterey	375 397	1 714	473	7 530	4 747.4	267.9	1 558	16 413	3 035.9	327.9	386	1 837	236.4	38.9
Napa	170 427	542	153	1 296	533.0	46.4	525	5 292	952.6	102.8	153	1 068	84.2	15.7
Nevada	129 807	831	90	453	118.7	13.1	430	3 914	654.8	73.7	115	449	57.7	8.2
Orange	1 981 282	12 520	7 029	103 113	94 403.4	3 999.6	9 084	126 575	26 172.8	2 572.0	3 537	29 156	4 714.8	939.1
Placer	1 060 857	6 443	283	3 888	1 792.6	147.7	875	11 769	2 666.6	254.7	302	2 158	204.0	40.7
Plumas	21 876	178	12	D	D	D	119	829	127.5	16.1	26	60	4.8	0.9
Riverside	2 583 927	15 025	1 200	12 649	6 715.6	416.6	4 030	54 433	10 609.0	1 028.9	1 190	6 164	698.6	126.9
Sacramento	1 090 941	7 672	1 287	18 090	8 555.8	626.7	3 587	51 962	9 502.3	990.0	1 180	8 334	909.1	185.4
San Benito	79 180	538	43	752	211.1	21.6	117	1 731	276.8	30.9	34	95	14.5	1.4
San Bernardino	1 043 021	6 471	1 747	24 756	14 254.1	805.8	4 372	60 940	11 342.8	1 100.5	1 134	6 103	753.5	126.0
San Diego	2 732 529	15 592	4 159	53 589	26 543.9	2 273.7	9 109	119 022	22 215.3	2 241.1	3 742	23 069	3 250.0	573.9
San Francisco	413 414	2 766	1 900	17 677	12 219.1	779.8	3 841	39 693	6 795.0	830.6	1 627	14 492	2 721.2	472.9
San Joaquin	828 298	5 392	560	9 751	7 651.7	319.3	1 594	19 957	3 679.6	364.7	436	2 602	257.7	52.3
San Luis Obispo	269 987	1 673	244	1 904	561.5	46.8	1 132	10 917	1 780.7	182.4	319	1 243	149.7	20.9
San Mateo	361 875	2 221	1 687	21 640	14 662.6	1 088.3	2 285	33 757	7 335.4	735.4	1 003	8 940	1 496.0	270.8
Santa Barbara	174 684	867	469	4 282	1 636.0	137.5	1 653	19 187	3 183.5	354.0	558	2 733	708.8	71.0
Santa Clara	936 630	6 639	3 468	66 542	68 095.4	3 891.8	5 278	79 921	16 673.6	1 696.7	1 968	12 585	2 456.4	372.8
Santa Cruz	115 222	545	342	4 472	1 541.8	140.3	986	11 794	1 970.2	215.5	314	1 649	166.5	27.1
Shasta	125 542	970	217	1 786	566.6	51.9	713	8 113	1 354.5	140.3	199	878	80.3	14.6
Sierra	1 992	19	NA	NA	NA	NA	13	64	8.8	0.9	1	D	D	D
Siskiyou	23 130	148	35	D	D	D	233	1 770	256.1	25.4	42	89	6.6	1.0
Solano	393 921	2 233	262	3 909	2 170.1	145.7	1 116	15 046	2 789.4	281.0	321	1 344	164.9	24.5
Sonoma	369 134	2 505	619	7 430	3 069.7	259.4	1 808	22 190	4 146.2	443.7	576	2 394	329.3	48.5
Stanislaus	400 922	3 023	417	5 118	2 264.4	159.1	1 368	17 706	3 282.2	319.2	340	2 033	244.5	42.4
Sutter	37 304	240	90	D	D	D	291	3 604	606.7	61.1	85	488	40.7	6.1
Tehama	32 308	217	40	D	D	D	176	1 953	360.6	33.0	42	149	9.6	1.5
Trinity	4 404	34	6	D	D	D	54	334	38.9	4.6	7	18	0.6	0.2
Tulare	162 800	1 627	343	5 120	2 527.7	135.1	1 107	12 742	2 135.7	211.8	206	809	97.7	12.6
Tuolumne	37 254	279	37	280	96.2	8.8	228	2 343	341.4	38.0	64	198	18.0	2.6
Ventura	815 295	3 960	1 088	13 811	10 402.7	522.6	2 348	30 831	6 476.6	608.7	672	3 254	409.0	73.4
Yolo	184 065	1 202	282	7 829	5 000.2	257.8	458	5 776	1 026.7	110.6	189	1 305	177.9	30.0
Yuba	10 556	82	40	D	D	D	155	1 525	244.6	25.6	33	104	11.2	1.3
COLORADO	6 822 089	54 596	7 383	88 364	60 310.4	3 282.0	18 299	225 647	40 536.0	4 163.3	6 663	38 224	4 853.5	883.8
Adams	512 901	5 479	732	12 884	7 044.5	443.5	952	14 489	2 859.1	308.8	323	2 677	289.6	69.1
Alamosa	4 624	54	30	225	68.8	5.3	97	1 090	167.2	17.2	18	48	4.6	0.8
Arapahoe	748 566	8 140	1 156	15 912	22 395.3	813.5	2 003	30 860	6 353.6	603.5	859	5 109	766.1	157.8
Archuleta	71 820	360	9	13	10.2	0.6	67	370	54.6	5.9	25	109	19.0	4.1
Baca	320	7	11	51	24.1	1.0	27	127	18.6	1.7	2	D	D	D
Bent	1 564	17	2	D	D	D	16	94	11.6	1.1	3	6	0.3	0.1
Boulder	372 872	2 780	539	5 558	3 906.0	234.9	1 275	17 269	2 915.0	309.9	486	2 189	287.9	49.2
Chaffee	20 861	230	25	130	37.4	2.1	112	928	124.4	14.0	31	124	10.0	1.7
Cheyenne	215	3	5	43	39.7	1.1	13	68	11.4	0.9	2	D	D	D

1. Establishments with payroll.

STATE County	Professional, Scientific, and Technical Services[1], 1997				Manufacturing, 1997				Accommodation and Foodservices, 1997			
	Number of Establishments	Number of Employees	Receipts (mil dol)	Annual Payroll (mil dol)	Number of Establishments	Number of Employees	Receipts (mil dol)	Annual Payroll (mil dol)	Number of Establishments	Number of Employees	Sales (mil dol)	Annual Payroll (mil dol)
	147	148	149	150	151	152	153	154	155	156	157	158
CALIFORNIA—Cont'd												
Butte	308	1 513	130.7	45.0	232	4 944	771.6	128.4	380	5 920	156.2	43.3
Calaveras	55	177	13.1	4.5	NA	NA	NA	NA	95	753	21.4	5.7
Colusa	19	37	2.6	0.6	20	651	265.8	20.8	43	508	17.1	4.9
Contra Costa	2 678	19 116	2 487.5	1 020.1	723	19 366	11 644.8	889.0	1 515	23 374	902.1	238.4
Del Norte	33	88	6.0	1.8	NA	NA	NA	NA	82	710	24.1	5.8
El Dorado	262	1 478	165.9	74.4	144	1 775	287.9	56.4	410	5 539	209.0	55.3
Fresno	1 184	11 156	584.1	234.3	696	27 552	5 667.6	704.3	1 256	19 886	631.9	169.6
Glenn	32	108	6.2	1.6	29	946	290.6	29.2	50	549	17.8	4.3
Humboldt	205	981	65.9	23.5	178	5 540	1 041.9	161.4	371	4 312	134.2	36.4
Imperial	113	519	46.2	15.8	61	1 481	241.6	40.6	238	2 723	89.3	23.0
Inyo	32	101	5.8	2.0	NA	NA	NA	NA	100	1 248	54.4	13.5
Kern	753	6 296	525.7	224.6	390	14 306	2 824.6	379.2	1 013	14 724	493.2	129.1
Kings	74	358	26.8	8.6	65	2 796	748.7	90.6	156	2 037	65.1	16.2
Lake	58	159	10.6	3.4	NA	NA	NA	NA	132	978	29.1	6.9
Lassen	22	89	4.9	1.5	NA	NA	NA	NA	68	733	25.8	7.0
Los Angeles	22 194	346 290	31 678.8	12 767.4	17 915	622 302	106 706.4	20 311.3	15 718	267 157	11 074.3	2 991.3
Madera	81	364	42.3	10.7	94	3 913	952.3	120.8	162	2 136	73.0	18.7
Marin	1 495	7 487	881.8	344.4	341	4 605	656.2	160.0	680	10 183	414.7	119.8
Mariposa	19	32	2.9	0.9	NA	NA	NA	NA	56	1 112	80.9	14.8
Mendocino	169	477	33.7	11.6	160	4 287	769.3	124.1	321	3 626	124.6	33.4
Merced	138	668	41.0	15.8	123	8 381	2 431.5	198.2	269	3 265	108.4	27.2
Modoc	6	23	0.9	0.3	NA	NA	NA	NA	27	178	4.9	1.1
Mono	26	115	10.0	3.7	NA	NA	NA	NA	133	3 192	113.3	35.1
Monterey	694	2 998	293.1	109.2	302	7 070	1 329.4	223.7	905	16 869	835.3	226.0
Napa	268	1 752	301.7	132.2	277	8 466	2 139.7	320.7	347	6 250	287.1	80.3
Nevada	220	724	60.3	21.4	174	2 311	372.9	74.1	229	3 968	117.5	33.3
Orange	8 838	75 635	9 728.8	3 540.6	5 767	215 936	39 134.1	7 643.6	5 397	105 298	4 241.7	1 133.2
Placer	526	2 488	260.0	95.9	260	9 244	3 808.4	403.4	546	10 083	334.1	94.0
Plumas	44	102	7.3	1.9	23	643	176.7	21.9	116	512	23.5	5.6
Riverside	1 642	8 798	904.9	277.4	1 420	46 134	7 736.0	1 329.1	2 159	41 940	1 619.4	447.9
Sacramento	2 731	21 959	2 343.5	892.2	910	30 493	8 939.6	1 017.0	2 185	36 413	1 195.3	320.1
San Benito	51	151	13.8	5.2	75	2 160	365.3	64.2	80	962	30.0	7.9
San Bernardino	1 482	8 262	743.8	259.7	1 992	63 448	11 618.7	1 830.4	2 323	37 291	1 279.7	335.0
San Diego	7 144	59 761	7 072.3	2 725.7	3 407	118 868	22 233.6	4 223.5	5 426	105 069	4 237.9	1 157.4
San Francisco	4 984	58 942	9 016.6	3 517.4	1 247	25 037	3 978.9	642.4	3 258	60 113	3 281.1	955.7
San Joaquin	575	3 531	277.7	111.2	553	24 646	5 879.1	749.6	826	11 413	376.9	96.5
San Luis Obispo	529	2 292	212.2	76.7	323	6 322	1 156.3	182.3	674	10 534	382.5	101.7
San Mateo	2 370	21 418	3 235.2	1 313.0	1 019	34 438	6 690.1	1 649.6	1 495	27 990	1 379.0	385.8
Santa Barbara	981	6 344	711.2	270.6	502	14 985	2 770.4	584.2	952	17 195	633.1	177.1
Santa Clara	6 338	71 612	10 440.6	4 424.1	3 464	249 947	72 528.3	13 094.0	3 495	60 330	2 590.7	677.7
Santa Cruz	678	3 073	384.1	132.1	387	10 011	2 135.0	315.2	591	8 223	305.5	80.8
Shasta	304	1 636	127.0	51.6	177	3 526	635.0	118.7	402	5 070	161.7	41.7
Sierra	4	D	D	D	NA	NA	NA	NA	22	86	5.4	1.2
Siskiyou	65	168	12.0	3.0	41	1 016	207.3	30.1	160	1 396	46.9	12.4
Solano	391	2 149	179.3	66.2	277	9 175	3 496.4	331.0	568	8 747	291.1	73.8
Sonoma	1 171	5 682	565.8	239.1	793	24 209	5 119.8	968.8	1 005	13 993	490.2	132.2
Stanislaus	478	2 974	232.5	81.3	435	25 056	6 886.6	823.1	676	9 877	312.7	80.4
Sutter	102	436	26.6	10.4	70	1 589	354.0	49.3	102	1 443	44.9	12.8
Tehama	52	194	17.7	3.8	48	2 228	455.2	62.9	102	1 128	36.7	9.2
Trinity	17	38	1.9	0.6	NA	NA	NA	NA	57	296	11.1	2.5
Tulare	335	1 788	265.6	45.0	282	11 439	3 167.3	314.5	510	7 020	232.3	56.8
Tuolumne	78	240	17.3	5.2	65	880	155.2	22.5	168	1 747	58.4	15.2
Ventura	1 597	10 829	1 229.3	464.9	1 008	33 562	6 163.4	1 136.3	1 200	21 879	775.3	209.4
Yolo	231	1 541	204.1	59.4	175	6 178	1 514.9	212.0	302	4 379	140.1	36.2
Yuba	41	136	10.7	3.9	44	1 203	248.2	26.8	85	940	31.0	9.1
COLORADO	14 315	103 008	12 887.7	4 625.1	5 480	173 069	40 012.8	6 176.8	10 064	195 126	6 705.5	1 937.4
Adams	386	2 568	205.6	86.4	436	13 151	3 045.1	428.4	512	8 990	288.8	79.3
Alamosa	43	157	8.5	3.5	NA	NA	NA	NA	49	938	20.7	5.8
Arapahoe	2 105	19 081	2 225.0	905.6	549	18 852	5 017.3	798.0	914	19 366	683.7	188.7
Archuleta	27	57	5.2	1.6	NA	NA	NA	NA	56	530	15.1	4.4
Baca	3	6	0.3	0.1	NA	NA	NA	NA	7	41	1.3	0.3
Bent	2	D	D	D	NA	NA	NA	NA	8	83	2.2	0.6
Boulder	1 612	15 458	3 081.9	760.2	686	26 225	5 196.3	1 052.1	708	13 824	453.1	131.0
Chaffee	42	178	7.7	2.7	NA	NA	NA	NA	100	969	30.9	8.6
Cheyenne	1	D	D	D	NA	NA	NA	NA	4	D	D	D

1. Firms subject to federal tax.

Table B. States and Counties — Health and Other Services and Federal Funds

STATE County	Health Care and Social Assistance[1], 1997				Other Services[1], 1997				Federal funds and grants, fiscal 2001[2] Expenditures (mil dol)			
										Direct payments for individuals[3]		
	Number of Establishments	Number of Employees	Receipts (mil dol)	Annual Payroll (mil dol)	Number of Establishments	Number of Employees	Receipts (mil dol)	Annual Payroll (mil dol)	Total	Social Security and government retirement	Medicare	Food stamps and Supplemental Security Income
	159	160	161	162	163	164	165	166	167	168	169	170
CALIFORNIA—Cont'd												
Butte	553	5 261	299.4	114.3	261	1 454	147.1	25.3	1 094.0	481.4	222.0	54.8
Calaveras	57	435	22.4	9.5	41	112	22.6	3.2	202.3	115.7	45.2	5.8
Colusa	23	132	7.5	2.6	24	109	6.5	1.8	163.1	31.6	18.2	2.4
Contra Costa	2 034	18 842	1 446.1	631.4	1 201	7 107	526.0	157.5	3 916.8	1 642.4	770.4	129.4
Del Norte	43	369	23.3	7.8	20	56	6.0	1.3	132.5	58.1	24.3	9.3
El Dorado	314	1 781	127.5	47.2	174	692	53.4	13.1	615.5	322.9	135.8	13.4
Fresno	1 614	15 504	1 103.7	463.9	947	6 026	458.9	120.0	3 652.1	1 135.3	454.6	231.2
Glenn	28	236	11.4	4.3	22	68	6.1	1.2	176.3	49.8	25.5	4.0
Humboldt	325	3 003	174.8	68.8	187	828	57.9	14.7	714.2	264.4	112.0	34.2
Imperial	172	1 665	103.7	40.8	107	506	34.5	9.4	674.4	197.9	106.0	38.9
Inyo	46	333	18.5	8.1	33	116	9.9	2.3	276.6	50.1	22.0	2.3
Kern	938	9 631	755.0	278.5	694	4 192	348.6	92.2	3 740.9	1 062.7	517.7	157.8
Kings	142	1 544	99.7	40.9	88	331	25.4	5.8	699.6	165.1	65.9	22.2
Lake	98	759	54.0	18.8	52	150	11.0	2.6	387.1	175.2	99.5	17.4
Lassen	43	348	19.3	5.8	28	78	5.7	1.1	164.7	60.6	20.5	5.2
Los Angeles	20 278	196 543	15 709.6	6 162.8	13 134	86 614	6 086.4	1 734.3	48 957.5	11 382.0	8 544.5	2 330.6
Madera	155	1 238	69.8	26.0	95	386	27.8	7.0	469.4	198.3	89.2	21.5
Marin	841	7 043	494.2	219.1	496	2 608	208.2	62.8	1 031.7	508.8	216.3	18.7
Mariposa	17	148	7.2	2.6	7	57	6.0	1.6	105.8	45.8	17.7	2.4
Mendocino	202	1 310	78.1	30.2	113	429	32.6	7.3	488.7	187.0	85.5	20.6
Merced	323	2 668	167.8	64.2	171	813	49.2	14.3	843.7	320.6	127.3	59.9
Modoc	7	59	2.5	1.2	8	D	D	D	72.9	23.8	9.2	1.8
Mono	15	46	5.7	2.4	10	50	3.3	0.8	45.8	12.7	3.8	0.4
Monterey	708	5 613	430.5	177.7	445	2 416	172.1	48.0	1 894.6	706.7	274.8	46.2
Napa	357	3 272	229.2	90.5	165	916	60.2	17.1	602.1	299.9	157.4	11.0
Nevada	252	1 691	100.9	37.5	107	409	33.0	8.8	527.4	238.3	87.0	7.0
Orange	6 986	66 269	5 571.4	2 170.8	4 249	28 174	2 101.9	600.0	10 905.9	3 884.7	2 097.1	342.3
Placer	585	4 845	380.4	142.6	305	3 164	239.5	83.7	995.1	610.6	153.7	20.4
Plumas	44	269	12.6	5.1	26	99	7.9	1.9	136.6	58.2	24.2	3.4
Riverside	2 307	24 783	1 905.2	707.4	1 499	9 119	620.7	173.1	6 009.7	2 860.8	1 374.8	227.8
Sacramento	2 383	24 874	2 014.7	870.2	1 549	10 484	731.1	214.1	13 835.7	2 807.7	905.6	345.1
San Benito	64	389	20.1	7.7	46	189	17.8	3.1	145.0	59.6	25.2	4.2
San Bernardino	2 314	26 710	2 051.5	798.4	1 720	12 182	804.8	232.9	6 958.3	2 435.4	1 170.0	357.0
San Diego	5 508	53 541	4 232.7	1 656.5	3 811	24 273	1 648.1	466.0	19 825.2	5 542.6	2 300.8	448.1
San Francisco	2 260	14 360	1 209.7	478.5	1 477	8 794	634.9	179.0	6 459.5	1 250.6	863.9	265.9
San Joaquin	949	9 252	664.0	273.5	690	3 838	265.3	74.2	2 439.4	933.2	398.7	158.0
San Luis Obispo	599	5 083	375.3	161.3	294	1 446	96.2	25.9	994.3	519.9	206.4	25.4
San Mateo	1 597	14 194	1 166.2	495.9	1 178	7 290	582.9	172.6	3 052.0	1 232.3	544.9	60.1
Santa Barbara	934	6 609	516.9	199.8	536	3 054	192.1	57.4	2 385.3	771.7	305.2	49.2
Santa Clara	3 742	38 283	3 032.2	1 240.9	2 471	16 850	1 352.9	400.5	9 495.7	2 133.0	1 005.2	265.2
Santa Cruz	631	4 739	309.8	121.7	330	1 614	112.1	31.3	928.7	359.9	190.0	29.5
Shasta	487	5 441	387.9	156.8	241	1 289	86.4	22.8	958.8	443.6	174.8	47.8
Sierra	2	D	D	D	NA	NA	NA	NA	22.4	8.8	4.5	0.3
Siskiyou	86	668	32.0	13.0	57	146	11.7	2.7	307.6	130.8	49.2	11.1
Solano	628	6 046	480.3	199.2	446	3 104	210.4	70.1	2 174.7	869.8	197.3	59.0
Sonoma	1 241	11 357	766.6	319.5	676	3 604	252.0	74.0	1 881.0	884.5	398.4	47.1
Stanislaus	805	9 346	656.1	253.2	538	3 154	210.7	58.7	1 775.3	720.4	337.7	111.0
Sutter	199	1 999	209.0	61.5	105	589	36.9	10.3	407.0	168.7	62.6	15.5
Tehama	89	705	37.3	14.5	62	315	21.3	5.5	294.1	125.4	52.5	13.7
Trinity	18	93	4.5	1.7	18	60	4.0	0.8	94.7	40.1	14.9	2.2
Tulare	588	5 102	334.0	127.8	308	1 544	115.2	28.7	1 459.6	488.7	239.5	90.6
Tuolumne	119	648	47.4	19.8	56	257	16.8	4.4	280.0	153.9	56.2	6.6
Ventura	1 591	13 110	1 086.6	413.1	875	5 577	442.5	126.7	3 663.0	1 257.4	546.1	71.0
Yolo	267	2 432	136.7	58.6	209	1 141	92.3	25.4	998.1	240.3	100.5	27.7
Yuba	53	703	39.1	17.5	43	232	17.0	4.0	496.0	129.4	53.7	22.7
COLORADO	8 611	85 370	5 790.8	2 538.1	6 793	39 363	2 571.1	770.0	24 344.7	7 575.3	2 394.2	411.4
Adams	377	4 049	262.0	117.3	505	3 508	240.0	72.5	1 271.4	476.7	206.8	37.4
Alamosa	27	213	15.8	6.3	34	168	7.6	2.2	75.4	21.4	7.6	3.7
Arapahoe	1 244	15 685	1 250.8	511.9	851	5 400	354.3	110.7	1 923.3	893.5	205.5	27.6
Archuleta	13	34	2.3	0.7	8	36	1.4	0.4	38.2	22.0	2.8	0.7
Baca	4	17	0.6	0.1	13	30	2.2	0.5	57.6	11.8	4.9	0.7
Bent	6	22	0.8	0.2	1	D	D	D	51.7	18.5	4.1	1.5
Boulder	715	6 087	405.5	170.7	482	2 945	192.2	60.9	1 569.4	410.7	133.5	17.2
Chaffee	28	290	11.4	5.2	28	90	6.4	1.3	73.3	43.5	10.8	1.4
Cheyenne	1	D	D	D	3	13	0.8	0.2	33.6	4.2	3.3	0.1

1. Firms subject to federal tax.   2. October 1, 2000 to September 30, 2001.   3. State totals may include programs not allocated by county.

STATE County	Salaries and wages	Defense	Other	Medicaid and other health-related	Nutrition and family welfare	Education	Other	Total (mil dol)	Intergovern-mental (mil dol)	Total (mil dol)	Total	Property
	171	172	173	174	175	176	177	178	179	180	181	182

Column group headers: Federal funds and grants, fiscal 2001[1] (cont'd) — Expenditures (mil dol) (cont'd): Procurement contract awards (171 Salaries and wages; 172 Defense; 173 Other); Grants[2] (174–177). Local government finances, 1997 — General revenue (178 Total; 179 Intergovernmental); Taxes (180 Total (mil dol); Per capita[3] (dollars): 181 Total; 182 Property).

CALIFORNIA—Cont'd

County	171	172	173	174	175	176	177	178	179	180	181	182
Butte	27.9	2.4	22.8	120.5	38.8	16.0	11.1	568.4	340.3	112.7	580	416
Calaveras	6.0	1.1	1.8	12.1	7.0	5.2	1.4	102.5	52.1	31.4	788	696
Colusa	2.9	1.3	2.3	8.6	4.6	1.4	2.9	72.1	37.4	16.7	891	727
Contra Costa	319.8	173.3	134.1	350.8	131.2	41.8	61.0	3 041.2	1 150.9	858.2	954	714
Del Norte	6.8	0.0	2.9	13.3	6.7	2.0	3.6	88.1	58.0	13.5	476	347
El Dorado	35.4	5.3	24.4	30.1	16.2	7.1	16.9	454.4	206.7	126.7	814	661
Fresno	445.1	10.0	123.2	459.2	224.7	86.4	77.0	2 675.7	1 509.5	482.9	640	451
Glenn	12.5	0.1	3.0	11.6	5.9	2.4	7.0	99.2	57.8	16.7	632	501
Humboldt	48.3	28.8	17.1	77.8	29.4	14.6	47.9	377.2	231.6	81.9	664	506
Imperial	87.3	12.2	6.7	92.8	36.5	24.9	33.4	519.5	281.7	81.0	564	422
Inyo	14.1	144.5	10.6	9.5	4.6	3.8	12.6	101.1	32.0	34.0	1 857	1 243
Kern	641.9	278.9	112.8	326.0	141.5	55.2	80.9	2 258.4	1 111.7	475.7	757	618
Kings	181.7	85.0	14.4	59.0	28.7	14.2	9.5	325.1	203.7	53.7	465	334
Lake	7.9	0.7	2.9	41.2	13.0	3.8	19.0	170.7	87.5	35.9	649	544
Lassen	27.5	6.3	14.6	14.8	5.7	2.7	1.6	95.0	63.6	17.7	522	427
Los Angeles	3 074.6	7 583.4	2 949.5	6 248.8	2 348.4	694.4	1 695.2	33 598.5	18 386.9	8 143.3	890	573
Madera	13.8	0.9	3.3	66.7	22.5	8.4	11.7	295.4	170.8	64.8	567	457
Marin	59.4	14.0	34.0	73.1	14.7	8.8	34.7	673.8	220.0	287.2	1 218	923
Mariposa	22.6	3.3	3.2	4.9	3.7	1.0	0.2	53.9	25.5	16.4	1 041	624
Mendocino	17.0	10.0	7.9	57.1	27.9	12.3	44.7	313.8	151.2	72.7	863	667
Merced	29.3	2.2	24.1	116.8	60.1	20.8	30.7	764.1	458.6	102.0	520	413
Modoc	12.2	0.0	2.5	5.3	3.6	2.0	7.1	51.5	28.6	7.6	748	648
Mono	12.5	3.2	1.3	1.4	1.4	0.9	7.6	59.3	16.9	26.8	2 547	1 794
Monterey	357.2	115.5	27.8	132.4	64.7	32.0	85.0	1 447.7	558.4	319.6	883	585
Napa	16.8	2.5	3.9	46.8	13.4	6.4	25.2	325.9	138.7	130.8	1 097	821
Nevada	19.3	55.8	9.3	24.8	8.4	3.4	70.3	263.4	93.2	73.1	807	667
Orange	704.5	1 758.7	462.8	734.5	246.6	129.8	167.2	7 098.7	2 844.4	2 392.0	895	637
Placer	40.6	6.6	15.8	63.7	22.6	9.5	20.8	710.8	253.5	240.0	1 084	778
Plumas	14.8	1.2	8.4	9.0	4.7	1.9	6.9	98.0	40.5	20.4	974	834
Riverside	336.0	102.9	86.2	439.1	195.7	95.9	110.6	4 524.7	2 359.5	1 073.4	741	549
Sacramento	535.0	1 139.2	177.1	1 197.6	2 597.9	1 064.7	2 636.0	3 850.7	1 849.5	882.2	784	512
San Benito	7.1	14.9	2.2	12.7	7.0	3.3	3.8	245.9	68.3	42.2	887	627
San Bernardino	902.4	454.9	284.4	572.1	280.2	119.4	216.1	5 012.4	2 909.6	1 086.7	673	492
San Diego	4 715.6	2 863.2	665.8	1 552.4	425.1	198.3	603.9	8 204.5	3 812.5	2 084.2	766	544
San Francisco	1 074.0	330.1	366.0	1 413.7	121.7	55.7	319.1	4 194.8	1 591.1	1 298.5	1 773	927
San Joaquin	163.3	40.2	54.6	342.5	139.3	41.0	70.2	1 709.9	922.8	354.1	653	458
San Luis Obispo	40.6	12.3	10.4	80.3	31.9	11.7	15.5	676.0	233.4	248.9	1 067	849
San Mateo	281.4	234.4	112.4	273.8	45.9	25.8	137.8	2 114.5	623.0	870.7	1 255	872
Santa Barbara	271.0	507.6	57.0	147.3	48.7	27.1	126.1	1 210.2	497.5	347.8	891	672
Santa Clara	680.2	2 741.0	813.8	822.0	190.3	90.9	374.4	5 453.7	2 104.5	2 060.5	1 281	826
Santa Cruz	33.0	13.2	14.4	115.6	30.8	18.2	57.4	804.9	339.1	228.5	950	629
Shasta	64.2	3.0	24.5	91.2	41.4	14.7	27.3	535.3	281.8	115.6	709	548
Sierra	3.0	0.0	0.7	2.6	0.5	0.2	0.6	27.0	13.0	4.7	1 363	1 214
Siskiyou	29.8	0.4	16.7	27.3	10.8	4.2	13.8	155.6	104.0	26.8	604	467
Solano	430.3	296.4	23.1	120.8	47.3	24.4	30.2	1 155.2	600.9	277.3	748	517
Sonoma	132.5	23.1	34.7	166.2	52.4	22.6	58.3	1 276.7	511.5	384.6	897	665
Stanislaus	70.6	6.4	66.9	246.7	94.6	30.8	25.4	1 342.0	740.0	254.6	604	412
Sutter	9.8	3.5	14.2	33.6	14.9	5.8	12.1	212.9	116.9	49.4	635	492
Tehama	12.4	16.3	0.2	28.4	12.8	7.2	14.7	147.6	94.4	30.6	566	438
Trinity	7.8	0.0	4.2	5.6	3.5	1.2	14.8	63.9	36.5	6.5	490	416
Tulare	56.2	4.5	30.4	260.2	107.3	38.6	51.5	1 468.0	786.8	190.2	539	364
Tuolumne	20.1	0.3	6.5	17.0	8.0	1.7	3.5	152.5	63.3	37.7	706	570
Ventura	643.3	541.4	60.7	204.0	81.7	39.2	114.6	2 111.5	858.6	628.3	865	668
Yolo	150.5	34.3	44.4	154.1	26.4	12.6	122.8	445.1	218.9	121.8	797	490
Yuba	146.1	1.6	5.0	58.5	22.5	13.0	4.5	193.2	130.6	38.0	617	524
COLORADO	3 867.6	2 277.1	2 190.5	1 651.7	559.5	370.2	1 334.1	X	X	X	X	X
Adams	172.9	121.3	38.1	95.7	34.5	15.7	25.2	774.2	274.9	329.1	1 041	644
Alamosa	7.5	0.0	1.6	17.4	4.4	3.2	1.5	43.6	22.9	12.7	883	530
Arapahoe	192.9	296.5	150.9	43.3	19.8	22.2	32.7	1 242.0	356.3	615.4	1 329	924
Archuleta	2.2	0.0	0.7	2.4	0.7	0.4	4.5	29.8	7.4	12.8	1 503	967
Baca	1.8	0.1	0.4	3.3	0.7	0.3	1.7	18.8	7.8	4.9	1 122	1 003
Bent	11.2	0.8	3.1	4.9	1.3	0.4	0.3	22.5	13.7	3.9	707	666
Boulder	193.0	119.3	262.3	82.9	12.6	16.2	287.1	657.8	156.2	368.1	1 407	893
Chaffee	5.1	0.0	2.1	6.8	2.1	0.6	0.4	42.8	11.1	14.9	994	658
Cheyenne	0.8	0.0	0.4	1.2	0.3	0.1	2.3	14.0	3.9	4.5	1 974	1 828

1. October 1, 2000 to September 30, 2001. 2. State totals may include programs not allocated by county. 3. Based on the resident population estimated as of July 1 of the year shown.

STATE County	Total (mil dol) [183]	Per capita[1] (dollars) [184]	Education [185]	Health and hospitals [186]	Police protection [187]	Public welfare [188]	Highways [189]	Total (mil dol) [190]	Per capita[1] (dollars) [191]	Federal civilian [192]	Federal military [193]	State and local [194]	Democratic [195]	Republican [196]	All other [197]
CALIFORNIA—Cont'd															
Butte	588.4	3 031	43.5	4.7	3.8	14.3	2.4	196.0	1 010	558	386	13 779	37.4	54.4	8.1
Calaveras	93.3	2 340	52.7	4.7	3.9	10.6	4.8	72.3	1 814	136	77	2 095	37.6	56.2	6.3
Colusa	68.9	3 666	42.1	4.4	5.6	7.1	5.1	22.7	1 208	78	36	1 369	31.2	64.9	3.9
Contra Costa	3 068.2	3 412	31.4	16.1	5.5	7.1	4.6	3 045.8	3 387	6 275	1 969	38 248	58.8	37.1	4.1
Del Norte	79.8	2 822	38.4	6.6	3.6	13.8	3.5	11.2	394	151	62	2 804	37.6	54.6	7.8
El Dorado	456.2	2 931	39.4	3.9	4.6	6.2	5.0	451.9	2 904	766	310	7 541	36.3	58.3	5.4
Fresno	2 616.2	3 468	40.0	10.8	4.7	13.5	2.8	1 746.2	2 315	9 590	1 535	48 283	43.0	53.1	3.9
Glenn	95.5	3 622	43.7	5.5	3.6	10.3	4.9	33.8	1 283	277	51	1 763	28.7	66.5	4.8
Humboldt	386.9	3 136	40.9	6.2	4.2	13.0	4.5	122.2	990	851	386	9 936	44.4	41.5	14.1
Imperial	510.7	3 554	42.5	19.2	3.9	10.2	3.4	368.8	2 566	1 672	538	11 890	53.5	43.3	3.2
Inyo	105.8	5 783	26.1	37.4	4.1	7.1	3.7	2.7	149	342	35	1 863	33.9	60.3	5.8
Kern	2 097.2	3 336	42.5	10.0	3.9	11.5	2.4	1 046.2	1 664	10 663	5 581	40 054	36.2	60.7	3.1
Kings	318.2	2 755	44.7	7.5	4.3	11.9	2.5	124.5	1 078	1 055	4 964	8 411	39.0	57.8	3.2
Lake	174.2	3 149	36.5	14.0	4.1	14.4	2.7	35.9	649	151	112	3 400	51.2	41.6	7.1
Lassen	91.0	2 681	56.8	2.9	3.3	11.5	5.2	29.9	883	910	78	4 189	28.2	66.9	4.9
Los Angeles	31 842.4	3 482	30.2	8.3	8.9	12.9	2.3	36 250.4	3 964	55 832	21 020	506 753	63.5	32.4	4.2
Madera	294.4	2 576	47.0	6.0	3.6	10.9	3.8	85.5	748	343	225	7 049	34.9	60.7	4.3
Marin	738.4	3 133	32.8	6.6	5.7	5.2	4.3	304.1	1 290	1 045	659	12 577	64.3	28.3	7.4
Mariposa	56.1	3 558	35.1	16.7	5.1	10.6	7.0	9.9	626	596	30	1 054	34.9	58.5	6.6
Mendocino	319.7	3 793	42.8	10.5	3.6	10.5	2.6	176.1	2 089	300	185	5 764	48.3	35.7	16.0
Merced	735.8	3 752	44.4	12.9	3.2	14.4	1.7	149.4	762	466	387	12 306	45.1	51.8	3.1
Modoc	51.6	5 095	37.7	23.7	2.7	8.1	10.0	7.2	714	239	18	1 128	23.0	72.3	4.7
Mono	54.9	5 211	27.9	19.1	6.0	3.3	9.3	27.5	2 614	166	256	1 009	40.9	52.5	6.6
Monterey	1 453.5	4 016	30.8	26.3	4.2	6.0	3.2	538.4	1 488	4 897	5 745	23 857	57.5	37.2	5.2
Napa	328.8	2 757	40.8	5.6	5.8	7.6	3.5	94.8	795	451	233	8 529	54.3	39.9	5.8
Nevada	235.6	2 601	31.9	19.0	5.5	6.4	8.0	154.5	1 705	458	177	4 419	37.2	54.8	8.0
Orange	6 992.4	2 615	37.4	3.2	8.2	7.5	4.5	9 731.1	3 639	12 572	7 039	132 267	40.4	55.8	3.9
Placer	669.7	3 024	39.8	3.8	7.7	6.5	4.9	588.0	2 655	647	473	13 212	36.0	59.3	4.7
Plumas	98.0	4 686	31.9	31.1	3.8	5.8	7.8	6.6	318	366	39	1 992	33.2	61.0	5.8
Riverside	4 415.1	3 050	36.9	8.4	6.1	10.6	4.2	5 007.8	3 459	6 316	3 081	76 835	44.9	51.4	3.7
Sacramento	3 829.3	3 401	36.5	3.6	4.2	13.7	4.3	8 229.3	7 309	13 089	4 562	156 489	49.3	45.3	5.4
San Benito	228.0	4 796	26.8	11.3	2.0	5.7	1.6	122.2	2 569	150	99	2 558	54.3	41.7	4.1
San Bernardino	5 308.7	3 285	38.2	9.1	6.0	12.4	3.0	6 150.8	3 807	10 932	18 386	83 415	47.2	48.7	4.1
San Diego	8 408.2	3 088	34.2	7.9	5.3	9.5	3.2	7 951.5	2 920	41 608	105 281	155 228	45.7	49.6	4.7
San Francisco	4 362.5	5 957	14.1	18.5	6.4	8.3	1.7	5 560.1	7 593	19 544	1 695	73 273	75.5	16.1	8.4
San Joaquin	1 703.2	3 139	38.6	10.0	5.4	13.2	3.4	1 050.8	1 937	3 872	1 122	29 952	47.7	48.9	3.4
San Luis Obispo	664.8	2 850	39.4	8.4	4.8	8.4	4.4	258.3	1 107	682	478	18 934	40.9	52.2	6.9
San Mateo	1 918.8	2 765	29.7	10.5	7.0	7.0	4.5	1 345.0	1 938	3 687	1 499	26 524	64.3	31.0	4.7
Santa Barbara	1 179.2	3 022	36.8	8.6	6.4	7.4	3.8	516.1	1 323	3 823	4 096	27 150	47.4	46.1	6.5
Santa Clara	5 376.2	3 341	32.6	8.6	5.5	9.2	3.5	4 548.0	2 827	12 180	3 771	80 289	60.7	34.4	4.9
Santa Cruz	812.3	3 378	33.2	9.6	5.4	6.7	3.1	432.9	1 800	552	473	16 886	61.5	27.3	11.2
Shasta	520.3	3 189	42.7	6.9	4.7	11.6	4.8	456.1	2 795	1 221	318	10 526	30.2	65.0	4.7
Sierra	24.8	7 213	28.5	31.3	4.9	5.6	10.0	3.5	1 014	81	0	520	29.2	63.5	7.4
Siskiyou	152.4	3 443	46.5	4.1	5.6	10.9	8.3	14.2	321	713	84	3 492	31.9	61.5	6.5
Solano	1 133.1	3 054	35.3	4.6	7.2	10.7	4.4	1 217.8	3 282	4 328	7 949	20 321	57.0	39.2	3.8
Sonoma	1 357.0	3 166	40.4	10.0	5.3	5.9	4.8	947.4	2 210	1 885	1 433	25 132	59.5	32.2	8.2
Stanislaus	1 293.6	3 067	42.7	12.1	4.9	11.6	2.2	1 786.6	4 235	1 216	842	22 857	44.0	52.4	3.6
Sutter	219.7	2 826	39.8	7.2	4.3	7.9	4.6	26.4	340	187	152	3 993	31.7	65.3	3.0
Tehama	145.6	2 697	47.3	7.8	4.7	15.7	4.9	17.8	329	261	104	2 994	31.2	63.6	5.1
Trinity	64.9	4 918	37.8	22.3	2.8	8.1	8.8	20.4	1 549	235	25	1 117	33.3	57.6	9.0
Tulare	1 436.4	4 067	38.3	20.1	3.0	12.0	1.5	565.2	1 600	1 244	689	25 325	36.7	60.2	3.0
Tuolumne	147.0	2 755	33.0	27.4	4.2	8.7	3.7	81.0	1 518	337	103	3 897	39.4	55.5	5.0
Ventura	2 081.2	2 867	37.2	8.8	7.1	6.5	3.7	1 336.7	1 841	8 414	7 074	32 722	47.1	48.2	4.7
Yolo	462.2	3 025	31.9	4.5	5.4	11.7	7.6	253.1	1 657	2 458	307	22 650	54.9	37.5	7.6
Yuba	191.1	3 104	53.8	1.1	3.5	17.6	2.9	123.0	1 998	1 275	3 259	4 445	34.4	61.0	4.6
COLORADO	X	X	X	X	X	X	X	X	X	53 124	41 876	278 321	42.4	50.8	6.9
Adams	712.3	2 254	41.7	0.3	5.8	7.9	6.6	1 298.6	4 109	3 124	1 381	15 073	50.2	44.1	5.7
Alamosa	51.3	3 566	55.7	6.5	4.8	10.7	6.4	15.3	1 064	149	40	1 825	43.4	50.5	6.1
Arapahoe	1 426.5	3 080	41.2	1.4	5.6	3.0	14.6	1 899.4	4 101	2 428	2 312	26 108	43.5	51.5	5.1
Archuleta	25.5	2 990	33.6	21.3	3.1	2.3	13.7	22.6	2 650	50	26	474	30.1	62.8	7.1
Baca	22.1	5 026	32.2	31.5	2.4	11.0	10.0	9.0	2 048	43	12	723	23.3	73.0	3.7
Bent	21.6	3 942	28.9	3.0	2.8	17.4	7.0	14.1	2 580	493	16	496	39.9	55.8	4.2
Boulder	681.5	2 605	38.9	1.0	6.3	3.5	7.7	620.6	2 372	2 649	853	23 567	50.1	36.4	13.4
Chaffee	40.3	2 683	36.9	26.6	3.8	3.8	6.1	20.1	1 338	98	43	1 460	36.4	56.5	7.1
Cheyenne	13.2	5 804	29.8	19.4	2.6	17.3	15.8	0.8	348	19	0	296	17.2	79.0	3.8

1. Based on the resident population estimated as of July 1 of the year shown.   2. Data subject to copyright.

Table B. States and Counties — **Land Area and Population**

STATE/ County code	MSA/ PMSA/ NECMA code¹	County Type²	STATE County	Land area,³ (sq km) 2000	Population and population characteristics, 2000													
								Race alone or in combination (percent)					Age (percent)					
					Total persons	Rank	Per square kilometer	White	Black	Am. Indian, Alaska Native	Asian and Pacific Islander⁴	Percent Hispanic⁴	Under 5 years	5 to 17 years	18 to 24 years	25 to 34 years	35 to 44 years	45 to 54 years
				1	2	3	4	5	6	7	8	9	10	11	12	13	14	15
			COLORADO—Cont'd															
08 019	...	8	Clear Creek	1 024	9 322	2 503	9.1	97.5	0.4	1.3	0.7	3.9	5.7	16.8	5.6	12.0	20.6	21.6
08 021	...	9	Conejos	3 334	8 400	2 573	2.5	76.1	0.3	2.6	0.4	58.9	7.9	24.3	8.5	10.3	13.3	12.4
08 023	...	9	Costilla	3 178	3 663	2 942	1.2	65.5	1.2	4.1	1.8	67.6	5.7	19.4	6.6	9.1	14.2	15.4
08 025	...	8	Crowley	2 043	5 518	2 816	2.7	84.7	7.1	3.6	1.0	22.5	4.4	14.4	9.9	17.9	21.7	13.9
08 027	...	8	Custer	1 914	3 503	2 953	1.8	97.4	0.6	2.1	0.6	2.5	5.5	17.0	4.5	7.1	16.2	19.8
08 029	...	7	Delta	2 958	27 834	1 455	9.4	94.0	0.6	1.7	0.5	11.4	5.8	18.3	6.3	9.6	14.0	14.9
08 031	2080	0	Denver	397	554 636	101	1 397.1	68.3	12.1	2.2	3.6	31.7	6.8	15.1	10.7	20.5	15.6	12.8
08 033	...	9	Dolores	2 763	1 844	3 077	0.7	96.8	0.3	2.6	0.7	3.9	5.0	16.9	6.8	10.8	15.5	15.9
08 035	2080	1	Douglas	2 176	175 766	311	80.8	94.5	1.3	0.8	3.4	5.1	9.6	21.9	4.8	16.3	21.7	14.9
08 037	...	7	Eagle	4 372	41 659	1 064	9.5	87.2	0.5	1.0	1.2	23.2	7.1	16.4	11.4	23.1	19.0	14.0
08 039	...	8	Elbert	4 794	19 872	1 798	4.1	96.9	0.9	1.4	0.9	3.9	6.6	23.6	5.5	10.2	22.6	17.6
08 041	1720	0	El Paso	5 507	516 929	107	93.9	84.5	7.7	2.0	4.1	11.3	7.6	20.0	10.5	14.9	17.6	13.4
08 043	...	6	Fremont	3 970	46 145	979	11.6	91.2	5.5	2.6	0.8	10.3	4.8	15.8	7.5	15.1	18.3	14.5
08 045	...	7	Garfield	7 633	43 791	1 021	5.7	91.7	0.7	1.3	0.9	16.7	7.5	19.7	9.0	15.2	17.8	14.8
08 047	...	8	Gilpin	388	4 757	2 862	12.3	96.1	0.7	2.0	1.1	4.2	5.7	15.5	5.8	16.4	21.0	21.1
08 049	...	9	Grand	4 783	12 442	2 269	2.6	96.3	0.6	0.8	1.0	4.4	5.8	16.0	9.0	16.0	18.7	17.8
08 051	...	7	Gunnison	8 388	13 956	2 164	1.7	96.7	0.7	1.4	0.9	5.0	4.6	13.3	21.1	18.3	14.6	14.1
08 053	...	9	Hinsdale	2 895	790	3 125	0.3	97.8	0.1	1.8	0.3	1.5	6.1	13.4	4.7	10.9	18.6	20.1
08 055	...	6	Huerfano	4 120	7 862	2 617	1.9	84.4	3.0	4.6	0.3	35.1	4.4	16.6	7.3	11.3	16.0	15.3
08 057	...	9	Jackson	4 178	1 577	3 090	0.4	97.5	0.3	1.4	0.3	6.5	5.6	19.9	5.4	10.1	16.8	16.4
08 059	2080	0	Jefferson	2 000	527 056	105	263.5	92.6	1.2	1.5	3.0	10.0	6.3	19.0	8.1	13.6	18.5	16.1
08 061	...	9	Kiowa	4 587	1 622	3 088	0.4	96.7	0.5	1.7	0.2	3.1	6.0	19.9	7.3	9.4	15.3	14.2
08 063	...	7	Kit Carson	5 597	8 011	2 605	1.4	88.1	1.8	0.9	0.4	13.7	6.1	20.6	7.5	11.9	17.1	12.3
08 065	...	7	Lake	976	7 812	2 623	8.0	80.0	0.3	2.2	0.7	36.1	7.8	19.0	12.8	17.7	15.5	13.3
08 067	...	7	La Plata	4 383	43 941	1 018	10.0	89.3	0.6	6.9	0.8	10.4	5.1	17.6	13.9	12.7	16.3	16.4
08 069	2670	3	Larimer	6 737	251 494	227	37.3	93.5	1.0	1.4	2.3	8.3	6.1	17.7	14.2	14.4	16.3	14.2
08 071	...	7	Las Animas	12 361	15 207	2 075	1.2	86.2	0.6	3.7	1.0	41.5	5.6	18.7	7.9	10.1	14.0	15.2
08 073	...	8	Lincoln	6 698	6 087	2 772	0.9	87.8	5.2	1.7	0.7	8.5	5.0	18.9	7.1	14.2	18.8	12.5
08 075	...	7	Logan	4 762	20 504	1 761	4.3	93.0	2.3	1.1	0.7	11.9	6.3	18.4	10.8	12.3	16.0	13.0
08 077	2995	5	Mesa	8 619	116 255	464	13.5	94.2	0.7	1.8	1.0	10.0	6.3	18.8	9.4	11.4	15.4	14.4
08 079	...	9	Mineral	2 268	831	3 121	0.4	99.0	0.4	2.4	0.4	2.0	4.5	16.0	4.7	8.1	16.7	17.1
08 081	...	7	Moffat	12 282	13 184	2 211	1.1	95.3	0.4	1.8	0.5	9.5	6.8	21.7	8.6	12.4	17.5	15.2
08 083	...	7	Montezuma	5 275	23 830	1 598	4.5	84.0	0.3	12.6	0.4	9.5	6.9	20.6	7.1	11.2	15.1	15.0
08 085	...	7	Montrose	5 803	33 432	1 301	5.8	92.1	0.5	2.1	0.7	14.9	6.8	20.0	7.2	10.9	14.9	14.3
08 087	...	6	Morgan	3 329	27 171	1 476	8.2	81.8	0.5	1.4	0.7	31.2	8.5	21.9	8.5	13.1	15.1	11.9
08 089	...	6	Otero	3 271	20 311	1 772	6.2	81.7	1.0	2.5	1.2	37.6	6.5	20.4	8.9	10.6	13.8	13.5
08 091	...	9	Ouray	1 400	3 742	2 937	2.7	98.0	0.2	2.1	0.8	4.1	4.8	17.7	4.1	9.9	17.3	19.7
08 093	...	8	Park	5 700	14 523	2 121	2.5	96.8	0.8	1.9	0.8	4.3	5.7	17.8	5.1	11.2	22.2	20.3
08 095	...	9	Phillips	1 781	4 480	2 883	2.5	94.3	0.4	0.9	0.7	11.8	6.9	20.0	6.3	10.3	15.0	12.7
08 097	...	7	Pitkin	2 513	14 872	2 101	5.9	95.6	0.6	0.7	1.6	6.5	4.1	12.5	7.7	19.5	18.9	19.8
08 099	...	7	Prowers	4 249	14 483	2 123	3.4	80.7	0.4	2.0	0.5	32.9	7.9	22.2	10.7	12.5	14.0	12.4
08 101	6560	3	Pueblo	6 187	141 472	388	22.9	82.4	2.3	2.6	1.2	38.0	6.7	19.1	9.4	12.4	14.8	13.5
08 103	...	9	Rio Blanco	8 342	5 986	2 783	0.7	96.7	0.4	1.6	0.5	4.9	5.7	20.8	9.2	11.2	16.3	15.7
08 105	...	7	Rio Grande	2 361	12 413	2 270	5.3	76.5	0.4	2.1	0.5	41.7	7.0	21.2	8.0	10.7	14.6	14.0
08 107	...	7	Routt	6 116	19 690	1 812	3.2	98.1	0.3	1.1	0.9	3.2	5.5	17.1	10.1	17.3	19.2	18.7
08 109	...	9	Saguache	8 206	5 917	2 792	0.7	74.1	0.3	3.3	0.7	45.3	6.8	21.6	7.9	10.5	15.5	16.6
08 111	...	9	San Juan	1 003	558	3 134	0.6	97.7	0.0	1.3	0.6	7.3	4.7	15.4	4.3	11.8	18.4	27.6
08 113	...	9	San Miguel	3 332	6 594	2 728	2.0	94.6	0.4	1.2	1.1	6.7	4.5	13.1	9.9	23.6	19.7	17.9
08 115	...	9	Sedgwick	1 420	2 747	3 011	1.9	94.7	0.7	0.7	1.0	11.4	5.6	17.1	6.6	10.3	13.2	13.7
08 117	...	9	Summit	1 575	23 548	1 613	15.0	93.8	0.8	0.9	1.3	9.8	5.3	12.0	15.7	25.7	18.5	13.3
08 119	...	6	Teller	1 443	20 555	1 757	14.2	96.8	0.8	2.0	1.1	3.5	5.7	20.2	5.6	9.9	21.3	19.6
08 121	...	9	Washington	6 529	4 926	2 853	0.8	97.0	0.1	1.0	0.4	6.3	6.2	20.3	6.3	10.0	14.8	13.6
08 123	3060	3	Weld	10 340	180 936	305	17.5	84.1	0.8	1.6	1.4	27.0	7.8	20.4	13.2	14.3	15.4	12.6
08 125	...	7	Yuma	6 127	9 841	2 462	1.6	95.3	0.2	0.8	0.2	12.9	6.6	21.7	7.1	11.5	14.5	12.9
09 000	...	X	CONNECTICUT	12 548	3 405 565	X	271.4	83.3	10.0	0.7	2.9	9.4	6.6	18.2	8.0	13.3	17.1	14.1
09 001	5483	2	Fairfield	1 621	882 567	47	544.5	81.1	10.9	0.5	3.8	11.9	7.3	18.4	7.0	13.4	17.5	14.0
09 003	3283	0	Hartford	1 905	857 183	51	450.0	78.5	12.6	0.6	2.9	11.5	6.4	18.2	7.8	13.1	16.6	14.1
09 005	...	4	Litchfield	2 383	182 193	301	76.5	96.8	1.4	0.5	1.5	2.1	5.9	18.8	5.7	11.6	18.1	15.8
09 007	3283	1	Middlesex	956	155 071	343	162.2	92.6	5.1	0.6	2.0	3.0	6.2	17.0	7.3	13.2	17.9	15.3
09 009	5483	2	New Haven	1 569	824 008	54	525.2	81.0	12.2	0.7	2.8	10.1	6.4	18.0	8.7	13.6	16.3	13.7
09 011	5523	2	New London	1 725	259 088	215	150.2	89.1	6.5	1.9	2.7	5.1	6.3	18.1	8.6	13.6	17.6	13.9
09 013	3283	1	Tolland	1 062	136 364	395	128.4	93.5	3.2	0.6	2.7	2.8	5.9	17.2	12.9	12.9	17.8	14.5
09 015	...	4	Windham	1 328	109 091	495	82.1	93.0	2.4	1.2	1.2	7.1	6.1	19.0	9.6	13.1	17.2	14.1

1. MSA = Metropolitan Statistical Area. PMSA = Primary MSA. NECMA = New England County Metropolitan Area. See Appendix A for explanation of these concepts. See Appendix B for list of metropolitan areas identified by type, with component counties.   2. County typology code from the Economic Research Service of USDA. See Appendix A for definition.   3. Dry land or land partially or temporarily covered by water.   4. Hispanic persons may be of any race.

Table B. States and Counties — **Population and Households**

STATE County	Population, 2000 (cont'd) Age (percent) (cont'd)				Population — change and components of change, 1990–2001							Households, 2000				
	55 to 64 years	65 to 74 years	75 years and over	Percent female	Total persons 2001	Total persons 1990	Percent change 1990–2000	Percent change 2000–2001	Births	Deaths	Net migration	Number	Percent change, 1990–2000	Persons per house-hold	Female family house-holder[1]	One person
	16	17	18	19	20	21	22	23	24	25	26	27	28	29	30	31
COLORADO—Cont'd																
Clear Creek	10.6	4.4	2.6	47.9	9 440	7 619	22.4	1.3	130	45	30	4 019	27.5	2.31	6.9	27.2
Conejos	8.5	8.3	6.6	50.4	8 355	7 453	12.7	-0.5	161	91	-115	2 980	19.6	2.80	12.7	23.7
Costilla	12.9	9.8	7.0	50.0	3 647	3 190	14.8	-0.4	64	47	-34	1 503	26.1	2.44	11.3	28.1
Crowley	6.9	5.7	5.1	32.7	5 434	3 946	39.8	-1.5	62	50	-99	1 358	16.6	2.59	11.0	25.7
Custer	15.1	10.1	4.7	49.0	3 693	1 926	81.9	5.4	45	27	170	1 480	92.2	2.36	5.4	23.8
Delta	11.6	10.2	9.5	49.8	28 421	20 980	32.7	2.1	400	416	602	11 058	32.1	2.43	7.9	24.8
Denver	7.2	5.5	5.7	49.5	554 446	467 549	18.6	0.0	13 391	6 059	-7 674	239 235	13.4	2.27	10.8	39.3
Dolores	11.9	9.4	7.7	48.3	1 837	1 504	22.6	-0.4	21	26	-2	785	35.1	2.35	8.5	26.2
Douglas	6.6	2.7	1.4	50.1	199 753	60 391	191.0	13.6	3 825	515	20 063	60 924	192.3	2.88	5.7	13.3
Eagle	6.0	2.1	0.9	45.2	43 027	21 928	90.0	3.3	851	66	590	15 148	81.3	2.73	5.6	20.9
Elbert	7.9	3.7	2.2	49.8	21 445	9 646	106.0	7.9	283	82	1 334	6 770	100.5	2.93	5.7	12.2
El Paso	7.3	4.9	3.8	49.8	533 428	397 014	30.2	3.2	10 615	3 602	9 610	192 409	30.9	2.61	10.2	23.9
Fremont	9.5	7.7	6.8	42.8	47 209	32 273	43.0	2.3	584	607	1 076	15 232	30.0	2.43	9.2	26.9
Garfield	7.3	4.9	3.9	48.6	45 521	29 974	46.1	4.0	892	330	1 155	16 229	44.1	2.65	7.8	22.8
Gilpin	9.0	3.9	1.8	47.0	4 823	3 070	55.0	1.4	58	24	29	2 043	56.2	2.32	5.7	26.8
Grand	9.0	5.4	2.3	47.0	12 711	7 966	56.2	2.2	179	67	152	5 075	60.2	2.37	5.2	24.8
Gunnison	7.0	4.2	2.7	45.8	13 947	10 273	35.9	-0.1	163	63	-107	5 649	46.5	2.30	5.4	27.2
Hinsdale	14.6	8.1	3.5	48.6	800	467	69.2	1.3	11	2	0	359	67.8	2.20	4.7	24.8
Huerfano	12.1	8.3	8.7	45.7	7 845	6 009	30.8	-0.2	92	126	16	3 082	26.0	2.25	10.4	32.8
Jackson	12.7	8.1	5.0	49.7	1 589	1 605	-1.7	0.8	23	14	3	661	4.6	2.37	7.9	28.4
Jefferson	8.8	5.4	4.3	50.2	530 966	438 430	20.2	0.7	8 285	3 906	-305	206 067	23.7	2.52	9.1	24.5
Kiowa	10.4	7.5	10.1	50.0	1 537	1 688	-3.9	-5.2	20	16	-88	665	1.2	2.40	6.6	29.8
Kit Carson	9.9	7.1	7.5	47.1	7 813	7 140	12.2	-2.5	129	92	-241	2 990	7.4	2.50	6.3	27.2
Lake	7.4	4.1	2.5	46.3	7 679	6 007	30.0	-1.7	167	60	-247	2 977	25.0	2.59	8.4	26.3
La Plata	8.7	5.3	4.1	49.1	45 157	32 284	36.1	2.8	553	314	967	17 342	44.8	2.43	8.7	24.8
Larimer	7.6	5.1	4.5	50.0	259 472	186 136	35.1	3.2	3 917	1 832	5 831	97 164	37.9	2.52	7.9	23.4
Las Animas	10.7	8.9	9.1	51.1	15 341	13 765	10.5	0.9	215	231	154	6 173	13.9	2.40	11.6	29.7
Lincoln	9.2	6.9	7.3	43.3	5 927	4 529	34.4	-2.6	68	79	-153	2 058	13.3	2.44	8.4	29.0
Logan	8.7	7.3	7.2	47.2	20 921	17 567	16.7	2.0	332	235	323	7 551	8.2	2.45	8.6	28.5
Mesa	9.3	7.9	7.3	51.0	119 281	93 145	24.8	2.6	1 868	1 314	2 449	45 823	26.4	2.47	9.8	25.1
Mineral	15.6	10.5	6.9	49.0	809	558	48.9	-2.6	4	5	-23	377	52.6	2.20	5.8	28.1
Moffat	8.5	5.2	4.1	48.1	13 154	11 357	16.1	-0.2	218	95	-154	4 983	19.3	2.58	4.2	23.6
Montezuma	10.3	7.7	6.2	50.8	24 035	18 672	27.6	0.9	423	293	85	9 201	36.1	2.54	10.6	24.6
Montrose	10.7	7.8	7.4	50.8	34 572	24 423	36.9	3.4	562	381	946	13 043	38.7	2.52	8.7	24.3
Morgan	8.0	6.5	6.6	49.9	27 543	21 939	23.8	1.4	693	291	-30	9 539	17.2	2.80	9.4	23.0
Otero	9.9	8.6	7.8	51.1	19 972	20 185	0.6	-1.7	374	275	-441	7 920	4.3	2.49	12.0	27.8
Ouray	14.4	8.0	4.2	49.5	3 882	2 295	63.1	3.7	46	32	121	1 576	66.4	2.36	6.5	23.5
Park	10.3	5.2	2.1	48.3	15 580	7 174	102.4	7.3	236	58	851	5 894	112.4	2.45	4.4	21.1
Phillips	9.4	9.1	10.3	51.7	4 472	4 189	6.9	-0.2	80	60	-28	1 781	4.0	2.47	5.6	27.5
Pitkin	10.7	4.7	2.1	46.5	14 810	12 661	17.5	-0.4	185	33	-222	6 807	15.8	2.14	5.3	35.8
Prowers	7.8	6.4	6.3	49.7	14 206	13 347	8.5	-1.9	281	164	-405	5 307	6.5	2.67	10.9	25.4
Pueblo	8.9	8.0	7.2	51.1	144 955	123 051	15.0	2.5	2 514	1 767	2 728	54 579	16.0	2.52	13.3	26.6
Rio Blanco	9.9	6.3	4.9	49.5	5 945	6 051	-1.1	-0.7	97	73	-65	2 306	5.7	2.50	7.4	24.8
Rio Grande	9.8	7.6	7.1	50.7	12 304	10 770	15.3	-0.9	219	144	-186	4 701	19.6	2.59	11.2	24.1
Routt	7.1	3.0	2.1	46.2	20 255	14 088	39.8	2.9	265	87	382	7 953	45.0	2.44	5.8	24.4
Saguache	10.3	6.1	4.7	49.6	6 224	4 619	28.1	5.2	116	52	233	2 300	40.0	2.56	11.0	26.9
San Juan	12.9	4.3	2.7	47.5	586	745	-25.1	5.0	9	6	22	269	-6.3	2.06	8.9	36.8
San Miguel	7.9	2.3	1.0	45.3	6 951	3 653	80.5	5.4	73	14	292	3 015	102.5	2.18	5.4	32.7
Sedgwick	11.3	11.0	11.1	50.0	2 668	2 690	2.1	-2.9	44	47	-78	1 165	2.1	2.31	6.6	29.4
Summit	6.1	2.6	0.7	41.8	24 225	12 881	82.8	2.9	361	57	369	9 120	72.2	2.48	4.4	21.6
Teller	10.1	5.3	2.2	49.3	21 425	12 468	64.9	4.2	268	94	681	7 993	69.3	2.56	6.6	19.6
Washington	10.6	9.7	8.5	49.2	4 861	4 812	2.4	-1.3	79	81	-66	1 989	3.9	2.46	6.4	26.2
Weld	7.4	4.8	4.1	49.9	194 949	131 821	37.3	7.7	3 638	1 387	11 494	63 247	33.2	2.78	9.4	21.0
Yuma	9.3	8.2	8.1	50.8	9 859	8 954	9.9	0.2	175	126	-27	3 800	9.4	2.55	6.8	27.4
CONNECTICUT	9.1	6.8	7.0	51.6	3 425 074	3 287 116	3.6	0.6	53 343	37 832	5 196	1 301 670	5.8	2.53	12.1	26.4
Fairfield	9.2	6.8	6.5	51.7	885 368	827 645	6.6	0.3	15 487	8 924	-3 608	324 232	6.3	2.67	11.5	24.0
Hartford	9.1	7.1	7.5	51.9	861 152	851 783	0.6	0.5	13 198	10 179	1 354	335 098	3.2	2.48	13.5	27.9
Litchfield	9.9	7.0	7.3	51.1	184 460	174 092	4.7	1.2	2 392	2 086	2 003	71 551	7.8	2.51	8.6	25.3
Middlesex	9.5	6.7	6.9	51.3	157 579	143 196	8.3	1.6	2 232	1 670	1 963	61 341	12.2	2.43	8.8	27.2
New Haven	8.7	6.8	7.6	52.0	828 374	804 219	2.5	0.5	12 849	9 869	1 799	319 040	4.7	2.50	13.6	28.2
New London	8.9	6.7	6.3	50.5	259 065	254 957	1.6	0.0	3 830	2 673	-1 051	99 835	7.1	2.48	11.0	26.4
Tolland	8.7	5.4	4.7	49.9	138 914	128 699	6.0	1.9	1 781	1 190	1 963	49 431	11.6	2.54	8.0	23.5
Windham	8.6	6.1	6.2	50.7	110 162	102 525	6.4	1.0	1 574	1 241	773	41 142	9.8	2.56	11.9	24.3

1. No spouse present.

Table B. States and Counties — **Vital Statistics, Health Resources, and Crime**

STATE County	Births, average 1997–1999 Total	Rate[1]	Deaths, average 1997–1999 Number Total	Number Infant[2]	Rate Total[1]	Rate Infant[3]	Physicians,[4] 2000 Number	Rate[5]	Hospitals,[4] 1998 Number	Beds Number	Beds Rate[5]	Medicare enrollees 2000	Serious crimes known to police, 2000[6] Total Number	Rate[7]
	32	33	34	35	36	37	38	39	40	41	42	43	44	45
COLORADO—Cont'd														
Clear Creek	100	11.1	36	NA	4.0	NA	3	32	0	0	0	559	270	2 896
Conejos	132	16.6	73	NA	9.2	NA	4	48	1	49	615	1 407	NA	0
Costilla	50	14.0	39	NA	10.7	NA	0	0	0	0	0	817	86	2 348
Crowley	48	11.1	40	NA	9.1	NA	2	36	0	0	0	652	16	290
Custer	37	10.6	18	NA	5.3	NA	2	57	0	0	0	594	55	1 570
Delta	299	11.3	318	NA	12.0	NA	35	126	1	44	165	6 010	428	1 687
Denver	9 026	18.0	4 715	73	9.4	8.1	3 087	557	8	2 845	570	70 811	26 664	4 807
Dolores	17	9.2	17	NA	9.4	NA	0	0	0	0	0	380	34	1 844
Douglas	2 616	18.5	376	9	2.7	3.4	119	68	0	0	0	5 097	2 106	1 198
Eagle	634	19.0	58	NA	1.7	NA	77	185	1	49	146	1 277	1 648	4 060
Elbert	227	12.2	73	NA	3.9	NA	8	40	0	0	0	1 182	218	1 135
El Paso	7 818	15.9	2 785	68	5.7	8.7	963	186	4	1 008	206	51 952	21 439	4 155
Fremont	422	9.6	469	NA	10.7	NA	40	87	1	277	631	7 448	962	2 085
Garfield	602	15.3	249	NA	6.4	NA	67	153	2	140	356	4 313	1 216	3 448
Gilpin	43	10.1	15	NA	3.5	NA	4	84	0	0	0	182	319	6 706
Grand	126	12.5	48	NA	4.7	NA	13	104	1	21	209	1 047	556	5 118
Gunnison	136	11.0	47	NA	3.8	NA	15	107	1	24	193	1 013	535	3 833
Hinsdale	7	10.1	NA	NA	NA	NA	0	0	0	0	0	82	34	4 304
Huerfano	63	9.3	100	NA	14.8	NA	10	127	1	38	558	1 500	167	2 124
Jackson	19	12.4	12	NA	8.1	NA	0	0	0	0	0	236	26	1 649
Jefferson	6 510	13.0	3 073	32	6.1	4.9	809	153	1	322	64	54 135	17 877	3 396
Kiowa	17	10.2	17	NA	10.6	NA	2	123	1	42	2 572	320	6	370
Kit Carson	92	12.6	71	NA	9.8	NA	3	37	1	24	328	1 244	192	2 397
Lake	114	17.9	38	NA	5.9	NA	6	77	1	22	344	576	117	1 498
La Plata	452	11.1	238	NA	5.9	NA	141	321	1	96	238	4 590	1 565	3 562
Larimer	2 945	12.7	1 371	15	5.9	5.2	433	172	3	375	162	26 632	9 020	3 587
Las Animas	176	12.1	167	NA	11.4	NA	18	118	1	32	220	3 122	NA	NA
Lincoln	53	9.4	56	NA	9.8	NA	4	66	1	56	977	848	42	690
Logan	238	13.2	184	NA	10.2	NA	26	127	1	50	279	3 386	708	3 453
Mesa	1 428	12.6	1 064	15	9.4	10.3	286	246	3	422	374	20 042	4 541	3 919
Mineral	6	9.2	NA	NA	NA	NA	0	0	0	0	0	119	4	481
Moffat	175	14.0	78	NA	6.3	NA	13	99	1	27	215	1 537	388	3 016
Montezuma	308	13.7	217	NA	9.6	NA	34	143	1	137	610	3 715	609	2 556
Montrose	404	13.1	308	NA	10.0	NA	54	162	1	75	244	5 609	927	2 773
Morgan	464	18.4	232	NA	9.2	NA	31	114	2	69	275	3 711	765	2 924
Otero	282	13.6	230	NA	11.1	NA	35	172	1	206	997	4 071	NA	NA
Ouray	33	9.8	20	NA	6.1	NA	10	267	0	0	0	440	NA	NA
Park	148	11.0	49	NA	3.7	NA	5	34	0	0	0	1 058	196	1 427
Phillips	60	14.0	57	NA	13.3	NA	5	112	2	66	1 526	949	16	357
Pitkin	140	10.4	29	NA	2.2	NA	72	484	1	49	365	867	1 005	6 758
Prowers	212	15.4	130	NA	9.4	NA	13	90	1	40	291	2 068	483	3 335
Pueblo	1 838	13.6	1 372	15	10.2	8.0	325	230	2	563	417	25 080	6 338	4 480
Rio Blanco	68	10.9	49	NA	7.9	NA	9	150	2	67	1 069	764	143	2 389
Rio Grande	169	14.8	115	NA	10.1	NA	10	81	0	0	0	1 996	415	3 343
Routt	209	11.9	62	NA	3.5	NA	36	183	1	71	405	1 145	512	2 836
Saguache	102	16.9	43	NA	7.2	NA	2	34	0	0	0	752	100	1 690
San Juan	5	9.4	NA	NA	NA	NA	0	0	0	0	0	62	31	5 556
San Miguel	61	11.3	12	NA	2.2	NA	7	106	0	0	0	270	181	2 745
Sedgwick	28	10.7	40	NA	15.3	NA	0	0	1	58	2 277	668	48	1 747
Summit	263	13.9	41	NA	2.2	NA	30	127	0	0	0	882	2 031	8 625
Teller	219	10.7	79	NA	3.9	NA	13	63	0	0	0	894	295	1 467
Washington	51	11.3	61	NA	13.5	NA	1	20	0	0	0	894	21	426
Weld	2 606	16.3	1 055	19	6.6	7.3	260	144	1	326	204	17 961	6 662	3 877
Yuma	121	12.8	104	NA	11.0	NA	13	132	2	39	415	1 652	141	1 433
CONNECTICUT	43 212	13.2	29 524	294	9.0	6.8	10 162	298	35	7 782	238	515 288	110 091	3 233
Fairfield	12 026	14.3	7 024	73	8.4	6.1	2 512	285	8	1 965	234	124 392	24 990	2 918
Hartford	11 228	13.5	8 160	93	9.8	8.3	2 837	331	9	2 395	289	139 323	32 827	3 924
Litchfield	2 031	11.2	1 652	9	9.1	4.6	313	172	3	279	154	28 343	NA	NA
Middlesex	1 877	12.5	1 291	11	8.6	5.7	372	240	1	158	105	22 789	NA	NA
New Haven	10 459	13.2	7 655	68	9.7	6.5	3 280	398	8	2 268	286	131 334	32 275	4 156
New London	2 794	11.3	1 893	17	7.7	6.2	539	208	2	428	174	38 222	NA	NA
Tolland	1 488	11.3	903	13	6.9	8.7	151	111	2	137	104	15 007	NA	NA
Windham	1 308	12.5	944	10	9.0	7.6	158	145	2	152	145	15 812	NA	NA

1. Per 1,000 estimated resident population, average 1997–1999.   2. Deaths of infants under 1 year old.   3. Deaths of infants under 1 year old per 1,000 live births.   4. Data subject to copyright.   5. Per 100,000 resident population as of July 1 of the year shown.   6. Data for serious crimes have not been adjusted for underreporting; this may affect comparability between geographic areas and over time.   7. Per 100,000 population estimated by the FBI.

Table B. States and Counties — Crime, Education, Money Income, and Poverty

STATE County	Serious crimes known to police, 2000¹ (cont'd) Rate² Violent	Property	Education — School enrollment and attainment, 1990 — Enrollment³ Total	Percent private	High school graduate or more	Bachelor's degree or more	Local government expenditures, fiscal 1999⁵ Total current expenditures (mil dol)	Current expenditures per student (dollars)	Money income 1989 Per capita⁶ (dollars)	Households Median Dollars	Percent change, 1979–1989 (constant 1989 dollars)	Percent with $100,000 or more	Income and poverty, 1998 Median household income	Percent below poverty level All persons	Persons under 18	Persons 5–17 in families
	46	47	48	49	50	51	52	53	54	55	56	57	58	59	60	61
COLORADO—Cont'd																
Clear Creek	429	2 467	1 859	13.0	91.8	31.2	8.1	5 634	16 196	33 149	-6.3	2.8	61 703	7.0	14.1	8.6
Conejos	0	0	2 149	1.2	63.7	10.7	11.1	5 505	6 664	14 188	-7.7	0.3	21 752	28.3	32.0	34.3
Costilla	655	1 693	776	2.1	60.5	10.5	5.4	8 054	7 057	13 057	5.9	0.5	19 815	31.8	38.6	46.5
Crowley	163	127	973	8.7	70.3	8.0	3.5	5 693	6 978	16 088	-3.8	0.8	25 455	29.7	32.5	36.8
Custer	86	1 484	441	4.3	83.8	19.2	2.7	6 449	11 309	20 000	-1.4	2.1	31 809	13.9	18.0	20.3
Delta	154	1 533	4 404	6.2	73.0	13.6	27.1	5 802	9 586	18 532	-2.8	0.9	29 161	16.0	22.1	20.9
Denver	521	4 286	108 999	21.1	79.2	29.0	405.6	5 897	15 590	25 106	-3.4	3.9	38 943	15.6	24.3	23.9
Dolores	108	1 735	328	0.9	71.8	9.8	2.2	6 346	9 784	19 952	-9.6	1.0	29 088	14.0	17.3	18.5
Douglas	46	1 153	16 990	11.7	94.8	40.7	180.2	6 038	21 002	51 718	8.7	11.5	84 645	1.8	2.5	2.1
Eagle	165	3 895	5 173	13.0	89.8	33.0	30.7	7 061	18 202	36 931	3.3	6.0	51 578	5.2	7.5	7.4
Elbert	312	823	2 680	6.9	84.2	19.8	21.7	6 050	14 566	36 273	19.3	4.8	57 910	5.6	7.2	6.8
El Paso	386	3 768	109 787	14.5	88.3	25.8	508.2	5 703	13 664	29 604	8.8	2.9	43 755	9.7	14.3	11.9
Fremont	147	1 937	7 678	10.3	75.4	11.8	34.5	5 218	9 971	19 988	-8.2	1.3	32 201	16.2	20.8	19.2
Garfield	218	3 230	7 740	8.9	85.2	21.6	44.7	4 888	13 086	29 176	-6.9	2.6	43 560	8.2	11.3	11.0
Gilpin	757	5 949	732	6.1	93.0	29.5	2.8	7 375	15 267	31 898	-2.1	1.7	53 136	6.4	11.6	8.9
Grand	166	4 952	1 706	4.8	87.4	30.2	12.6	6 999	13 457	29 991	-3.5	2.0	40 670	7.4	9.4	9.3
Gunnison	193	3 640	3 687	6.7	90.6	36.9	9.7	5 797	11 516	23 013	-10.3	2.2	34 097	12.1	12.9	14.5
Hinsdale	127	4 177	75	17.3	93.0	32.0	0.6	8 879	12 978	26 250	1.2	1.4	36 167	11.2	16.2	18.3
Huerfano	267	1 857	1 479	15.8	65.0	12.6	7.2	5 903	8 212	14 730	-14.5	0.6	24 269	22.1	28.6	31.2
Jackson	63	1 585	379	1.1	82.1	15.3	2.3	7 373	10 858	20 938	-25.9	1.4	30 052	14.4	19.3	20.4
Jefferson	171	3 225	117 385	13.3	89.8	30.7	573.5	6 468	17 310	39 084	-3.0	4.9	55 869	5.5	7.6	7.1
Kiowa	247	123	455	1.3	69.8	9.1	3.2	8 043	10 305	21 417	-6.0	1.7	32 921	14.4	18.3	17.8
Kit Carson	225	2 172	1 681	2.9	73.5	15.8	11.1	6 405	11 385	23 125	0.7	2.3	35 344	12.9	17.3	16.4
Lake	166	1 331	1 566	1.5	81.7	16.2	11.3	8 473	11 269	24 708	-33.6	1.3	36 779	9.9	13.2	14.1
La Plata	271	3 291	10 161	6.8	85.7	28.1	44.7	6 400	12 163	25 759	0.8	2.9	38 458	11.6	14.2	14.2
Larimer	233	3 354	62 261	7.4	88.6	32.3	219.5	5 675	13 968	29 686	3.2	3.0	45 863	8.3	10.5	9.4
Las Animas	NA	NA	3 691	8.9	67.6	12.7	15.7	6 695	8 934	16 284	-13.5	0.7	24 375	22.9	29.8	30.7
Lincoln	82	608	956	3.6	74.5	12.9	8.4	7 983	10 052	20 595	-4.1	1.4	30 380	17.4	22.6	22.5
Logan	298	3 155	4 906	5.8	79.1	14.2	20.3	5 968	10 899	22 065	-13.9	1.4	33 845	14.7	21.4	19.1
Mesa	203	3 716	24 299	7.4	79.5	17.4	104.6	5 261	11 850	23 698	-14.8	1.8	35 405	13.0	18.0	16.0
Mineral	241	241	94	2.1	84.8	17.9	1.3	8 506	11 082	19 830	-22.5	2.8	32 453	11.1	19.7	24.0
Moffat	202	2 814	3 118	6.1	79.9	16.4	16.5	6 103	12 354	31 615	-10.9	2.0	43 611	11.5	14.8	14.5
Montezuma	76	2 480	4 827	4.4	74.8	15.9	26.5	5 638	10 176	22 491	-3.9	2.0	32 319	17.6	22.4	23.0
Montrose	159	2 614	5 584	6.1	74.5	15.4	33.7	5 722	11 092	22 610	-11.7	2.1	33 659	13.2	18.7	16.8
Morgan	111	2 813	5 683	3.5	67.6	11.7	31.2	5 652	10 928	22 849	-9.1	2.6	32 971	14.5	19.8	18.3
Otero	NA	NA	5 508	3.4	69.4	13.0	26.5	6 219	9 573	18 178	-6.5	2.3	26 244	21.9	29.1	29.9
Ouray	NA	NA	496	2.8	87.5	27.9	4.0	7 104	13 208	27 500	15.3	2.9	40 866	8.0	11.1	11.2
Park	22	1 405	1 765	8.0	91.1	22.4	12.7	5 763	14 325	32 102	6.1	2.5	49 712	6.7	9.2	9.3
Phillips	89	268	981	6.3	79.0	14.2	7.7	7 960	10 444	21 484	2.3	0.7	33 433	11.7	16.1	15.7
Pitkin	242	6 516	2 430	19.9	94.7	49.8	9.9	7 674	26 755	39 991	13.7	12.6	53 570	4.2	5.2	5.9
Prowers	69	3 266	3 828	3.7	70.2	12.2	18.1	6 109	9 662	20 625	-3.6	1.9	30 336	20.1	25.7	26.1
Pueblo	720	3 760	32 691	6.1	73.9	14.0	127.8	5 271	10 347	21 553	-16.9	1.3	30 781	17.3	24.0	22.3
Rio Blanco	368	2 021	1 935	4.1	81.2	15.4	10.1	6 730	12 357	29 243	-16.3	1.8	41 399	10.6	13.5	12.6
Rio Grande	193	3 150	2 929	3.1	69.7	17.5	14.9	5 752	9 582	19 193	-12.0	2.4	26 428	26.4	37.6	33.4
Routt	194	2 642	3 779	8.8	91.7	34.7	21.1	7 113	15 429	31 409	-12.8	4.4	45 405	6.7	8.0	8.2
Saguache	186	1 504	1 296	3.3	65.9	14.4	8.0	7 160	8 630	15 853	-4.1	2.6	23 069	23.4	29.7	31.9
San Juan	538	5 018	195	6.7	82.7	24.0	1.3	15 128	11 029	26 167	6.3	1.0	26 077	20.9	22.4	27.1
San Miguel	76	2 669	665	11.7	93.5	40.3	6.9	8 399	16 454	30 578	34.1	4.4	43 090	8.8	11.2	13.8
Sedgwick	218	1 529	583	1.5	70.9	8.6	3.7	7 519	9 901	19 335	-10.3	0.0	29 024	14.6	22.8	20.5
Summit	195	8 430	2 648	10.5	95.5	39.7	16.9	6 692	17 400	35 229	-1.8	4.8	47 456	5.4	7.0	7.8
Teller	139	1 328	3 243	12.0	92.1	26.4	19.0	4 881	13 698	32 209	13.8	1.9	48 476	8.0	10.7	10.8
Washington	102	325	1 075	1.8	75.9	11.8	8.4	8 194	10 473	20 637	-9.8	1.2	31 397	13.2	18.0	17.8
Weld	305	3 572	41 250	6.0	74.9	18.4	156.0	5 532	11 350	25 642	-3.2	2.0	37 659	11.4	15.2	13.5
Yuma	41	1 392	2 354	3.5	78.5	13.4	11.6	5 536	10 713	22 249	12.2	2.2	32 285	13.2	17.7	16.2
CONNECTICUT	325	2 908	805 486	22.2	79.2	27.2	5 075.6	9 318	20 189	41 721	24.0	9.2	49 846	8.7	13.3	13.1
Fairfield	359	2 559	197 636	27.1	81.0	34.2	1 262.3	9 515	26 161	49 891	29.6	17.3	57 389	7.7	12.0	11.4
Hartford	364	3 560	207 561	19.0	77.7	25.8	1 223.8	8 965	18 983	40 609	20.3	7.4	47 545	10.1	16.0	15.6
Litchfield	NA	NA	40 320	16.6	80.9	25.0	241.3	8 732	19 971	42 565	28.2	7.5	53 963	5.3	7.3	7.2
Middlesex	NA	NA	34 794	24.9	82.6	28.2	198.4	8 894	19 660	43 212	26.7	6.3	57 351	5.0	7.6	7.6
New Haven	382	3 774	197 532	25.9	77.5	24.2	1 099.7	8 809	17 666	38 471	24.6	6.3	46 030	10.4	16.1	16.0
New London	NA	NA	61 393	19.8	80.9	21.8	349.0	8 938	16 702	37 488	23.4	4.7	46 311	8.0	11.6	12.1
Tolland	NA	NA	39 989	9.6	84.7	29.2	182.3	8 383	17 849	45 019	26.1	6.1	58 540	5.0	6.6	6.7
Windham	NA	NA	26 261	13.2	71.1	16.8	145.2	8 432	14 520	33 851	24.8	3.0	42 248	9.8	14.0	15.2

1. Data for serious crimes have not been adjusted for underreporting; this may affect comparability between geographic areas and over time. 2. Per 100,000 population estimated by the FBI. 3. All persons 3 years old and over enrolled in nursery school through college. 4. Persons 25 years old and over. 5. Elementary and secondary education expenditures, local government fiscal years ending between July 1, 1998 and June 30, 1999. 6. Based on population enumerated as of April 1, 1990.

STATE County	Total (mil dol)	Percent change, 1998–1999	Per capita[1] Dollars	Per capita[1] Rank	Wages and salaries[2] (mil dol)	Proprietor's income (mil dol)	Dividends, interest, and rent (mil dol)	Transfer payments Total (mil dol)	Government payments to individuals Total (mil dol)	Social Security (mil dol)	Medical payments (mil dol)	Income maintenance (mil dol)	Unemployment insurance (mil dol)
	62	63	64	65	66	67	68	69	70	71	72	73	74
COLORADO—Cont'd													
Clear Creek	285	9.7	31 049	177	97	20	37	18	16	8	5	1	0
Conejos	121	5.4	14 943	2 992	40	15	15	39	38	10	17	9	0
Costilla	63	8.1	17 555	2 639	17	7	9	20	19	6	7	5	0
Crowley	93	19.1	20 989	1 672	34	39	12	18	17	5	8	3	0
Custer	68	4.5	18 970	2 286	18	8	19	11	10	6	3	1	0
Delta	506	4.0	18 591	2 399	184	47	138	120	115	53	46	9	1
Denver	20 419	6.9	40 856	40	21 246	3 469	4 120	2 101	2 012	659	987	231	23
Dolores	37	8.7	19 534	2 126	10	9	7	7	7	3	2	1	0
Douglas	5 561	14.5	35 451	77	1 721	225	831	158	131	88	25	4	2
Eagle	1 374	7.6	39 304	47	919	250	294	32	26	14	6	2	2
Elbert	509	15.5	25 759	547	81	30	57	31	28	14	9	2	1
El Paso	13 627	6.7	27 255	399	9 531	829	2 561	1 301	1 217	481	457	116	18
Fremont	786	5.1	17 595	2 627	406	75	158	155	147	65	55	13	2
Garfield	1 026	8.5	25 233	627	593	134	200	88	81	42	26	5	2
Gilpin	129	8.8	28 945	264	158	6	29	7	6	4	1	1	0
Grand	279	8.4	26 610	451	156	45	62	21	19	10	6	1	0
Gunnison	289	5.1	22 958	1 098	190	33	79	23	21	9	5	2	0
Hinsdale	17	4.9	22 342	1 264	5	3	6	2	2	1	0	0	0
Huerfano	132	2.3	19 406	2 177	50	13	29	40	39	12	17	5	0
Jackson	30	8.7	19 503	2 139	13	3	10	5	5	2	1	0	0
Jefferson	17 844	9.4	35 042	81	8 282	1 319	3 046	1 098	1 008	554	316	58	16
Kiowa	57	0.8	34 822	89	17	26	8	6	6	3	2	1	0
Kit Carson	209	4.9	28 261	299	72	70	48	25	24	12	8	3	0
Lake	161	6.1	25 185	641	53	13	23	16	15	6	7	1	0
La Plata	1 106	5.5	26 878	426	585	145	299	102	95	43	35	8	2
Larimer	6 723	6.8	28 386	290	4 021	579	1 327	564	522	253	188	34	9
Las Animas	273	4.8	18 548	2 404	132	21	57	83	81	25	36	10	1
Lincoln	111	10.2	19 537	2 124	58	15	25	17	16	8	6	1	0
Logan	497	10.6	27 711	355	222	120	97	68	65	31	23	7	1
Mesa	2 712	5.9	23 557	952	1 483	260	593	423	402	183	152	29	5
Mineral	17	7.8	23 099	1 069	9	3	5	2	2	1	1	0	0
Moffat	274	4.2	21 515	1 518	160	26	40	35	33	14	13	3	1
Montezuma	482	3.8	21 254	1 584	237	55	102	79	75	34	28	8	1
Montrose	659	4.7	20 960	1 679	342	71	160	107	102	51	35	9	3
Morgan	590	7.7	23 216	1 039	302	125	103	84	79	34	34	7	1
Otero	432	4.4	20 902	1 676	192	49	72	120	117	30	60	14	1
Ouray	83	6.9	23 900	879	28	13	28	9	8	5	2	1	0
Park	338	13.8	23 761	906	55	27	47	24	21	12	4	2	0
Phillips	106	4.1	25 081	655	39	30	22	17	16	7	7	1	0
Pitkin	874	6.5	65 573	2	559	151	334	19	17	11	4	1	1
Prowers	345	6.9	25 046	663	148	99	53	56	53	18	26	6	1
Pueblo	3 003	4.4	21 924	1 379	1 620	176	531	750	725	212	387	73	6
Rio Blanco	151	7.5	24 280	810	75	48	25	18	17	8	6	1	0
Rio Grande	263	10.9	22 861	1 123	111	59	57	49	47	19	18	8	1
Routt	597	8.9	33 258	125	399	80	145	26	23	12	7	1	1
Saguache	98	•14.9	15 885	2 907	38	25	14	18	17	5	7	4	0
San Juan	12	4.4	22 625	1 188	6	3	2	2	2	1	1	0	0
San Miguel	188	7.9	34 427	95	134	34	52	7	6	3	2	1	0
Sedgwick	71	7.6	27 439	379	22	22	14	14	13	6	5	1	0
Summit	737	8.5	37 603	62	522	92	170	20	17	10	4	1	1
Teller	533	5.1	25 122	651	173	56	96	42	38	21	9	4	1
Washington	120	9.9	27 566	366	36	42	24	17	17	8	6	2	0
Weld	3 789	8.2	22 852	1 124	2 162	526	603	451	422	172	182	38	6
Yuma	231	4.8	24 507	756	87	64	56	32	31	16	10	3	0
CONNECTICUT	129 780	4.7	39 543	X	80 653	10 266	23 483	14 451	13 854	5 406	6 353	1 191	361
Fairfield	47 656	5.5	56 643	5	27 744	4 469	9 377	3 611	3 458	1 338	1 604	291	89
Hartford	29 882	5.2	36 016	72	23 830	2 093	5 227	3 974	3 823	1 441	1 798	358	97
Litchfield	6 100	4.3	33 445	123	2 468	591	1 208	641	608	305	230	31	19
Middlesex	5 287	4.0	34 904	85	2 887	370	911	525	497	245	184	30	16
New Haven	26 336	4.2	33 201	128	15 638	1 693	4 390	3 861	3 717	1 354	1 783	342	87
New London	7 817	2.2	31 771	158	5 428	575	1 412	1 005	962	390	422	78	29
Tolland	3 936	3.8	29 668	222	1 403	274	580	387	363	171	138	22	11
Windham	2 767	2.8	26 290	487	1 255	200	377	446	427	162	195	39	14

1. Based on the resident population estimated as of July 1 of the year shown.   2. Includes other labor income.

STATE County	Total (mil dol)	Farm	Goods-related[1] Total	Manu-facturing	Service-related and other[2] Total	Retail trade	Finance, insur-ance, and real estate	Services	Govern-ment	Number	Rate[3]	Supple-mental Security Income recipients, December 2000	Total	Percent change, 1980-1990
	75	76	77	78	79	80	81	82	83	84	85	86	87	88
COLORADO—Cont'd														
Clear Creek	117	0.0	D	2.8	D	11.6	4.9	19.5	18.4	980	105	39	4 811	14.6
Conejos	55	4.0	D	3.8	D	10.7	2.7	21.4	29.5	1 601	191	480	3 574	14.7
Costilla	24	25.5	D	D	D	5.6	D	9.6	36.4	1 017	278	299	1 743	21.3
Crowley	73	50.3	D	D	D	3.6	1.2	14.8	26.1	746	135	147	1 415	4.0
Custer	26	-8.3	41.9	2.5	D	15.1	8.5	21.9	21.9	721	206	29	2 216	100.0
Delta	230	0.4	D	6.0	D	13.7	5.5	21.6	26.0	6 809	245	492	10 082	9.1
Denver	24 715	0.0	13.1	6.0	73.1	6.0	12.3	32.7	13.8	75 583	136	13 167	239 636	5.2
Dolores	19	20.1	D	D	D	7.5	D	9.1	20.1	443	240	25	947	3.8
Douglas	1 946	0.1	22.1	5.5	66.5	16.9	8.9	27.4	11.5	10 748	61	173	22 291	157.0
Eagle	1 168	0.0	21.5	2.4	71.0	14.2	17.5	32.8	7.4	1 704	41	78	15 226	37.7
Elbert	111	-3.4	27.4	2.6	53.2	10.4	4.7	26.6	22.8	1 768	89	5 583	3 997	46.8
El Paso	10 360	0.0	18.4	12.1	54.3	9.0	6.5	28.2	27.3	60 746	118	40	165 056	40.4
Fremont	481	0.3	16.2	6.7	38.8	10.0	3.1	19.0	44.8	8 602	186	871	13 683	19.1
Garfield	727	0.1	25.1	2.7	59.1	16.2	7.5	26.3	15.7	5 011	114	280	12 517	33.9
Gilpin	164	0.0	5.4	0.5	D	1.7	0.3	84.5	7.4	466	98	11	2 438	21.2
Grand	201	-0.2	D	2.2	D	15.4	11.4	32.1	17.2	1 249	100	68	9 985	38.5
Gunnison	223	-0.7	D	1.5	D	15.9	8.7	D	22.2	1 224	88	52	7 294	27.2
Hinsdale	9	-3.4	D	D	D	22.0	10.5	20.8	19.8	106	134	4	1 254	79.9
Huerfano	63	-2.0	D	5.7	D	15.2	5.2	34.2	20.5	1 680	214	299	3 913	12.9
Jackson	16	-0.9	D	7.2	D	13.0	D	10.0	33.9	276	175	12	1 326	25.0
Jefferson	9 601	0.1	25.4	15.4	58.8	11.0	7.7	28.8	15.7	63 056	120	3 279	178 651	28.9
Kiowa	44	66.8	D	D	D	2.8	D	3.6	14.4	348	215	23	878	5.1
Kit Carson	142	41.5	D	3.5	D	8.1	4.0	11.9	13.7	1 467	183	81	3 224	-2.0
Lake	65	0.0	D	2.0	D	12.5	5.0	26.1	31.5	721	92	400	3 527	-6.0
La Plata	730	-0.2	18.1	3.4	64.8	14.3	7.4	32.9	17.3	5 459	124	48	15 412	26.8
Larimer	4 599	0.5	32.3	23.3	48.0	11.8	5.3	24.1	19.3	30 553	121	1 845	77 811	25.1
Las Animas	153	-2.0	13.1	2.0	58.2	13.1	5.1	21.2	30.7	3 312	218	657	6 975	8.5
Lincoln	74	9.5	D	D	D	14.0	4.5	12.7	41.4	989	162	62	2 204	2.8
Logan	343	16.1	14.4	4.5	51.4	9.9	5.8	18.8	18.1	3 759	183	321	7 824	0.1
Mesa	1 742	0.3	19.8	8.1	62.3	14.1	7.0	28.4	17.6	22 690	195	2 103	39 208	20.4
Mineral	11	-0.7	D	D	D	11.6	D	44.0	22.7	156	188	2	1 201	72.3
Moffat	185	0.5	25.0	1.3	52.1	13.1	3.4	15.9	22.5	1 699	129	165	5 235	-0.6
Montezuma	292	0.1	D	4.3	D	14.6	4.3	25.7	20.0	4 474	188	429	8 050	23.9
Montrose	413	0.1	23.8	9.2	53.9	15.1	4.7	19.6	22.1	6 641	199	534	10 353	10.4
Morgan	427	16.2	28.0	20.7	40.9	7.7	3.2	14.3	14.9	4 253	157	348	9 230	2.3
Otero	241	5.9	12.4	8.1	58.9	10.9	4.8	22.3	22.8	4 227	208	904	8 739	-1.2
Ouray	40	-0.3	D	3.2	D	15.8	7.6	21.6	20.3	570	152	17	1 507	26.7
Park	82	-0.2	23.3	2.1	51.4	9.0	10.3	20.7	25.5	1 474	101	45	7 247	48.7
Phillips	69	35.4	7.5	1.2	D	7.2	2.8	D	20.0	852	190	49	1 960	-2.7
Pitkin	710	0.1	D	1.8	D	15.8	19.6	36.3	9.4	1 177	79	22	9 837	15.7
Prowers	247	29.1	17.0	11.9	35.1	10.2	4.2	11.1	18.8	2 331	161	357	5 855	7.4
Pueblo	1 796	-0.2	19.3	10.7	58.1	15.0	6.7	26.1	22.8	27 702	196	4 869	50 872	3.6
Rio Blanco	123	-1.9	54.3	0.7	23.0	5.5	2.6	7.1	24.6	937	157	51	2 803	11.1
Rio Grande	170	21.7	D	5.7	48.2	8.3	4.2	11.4	17.6	2 696	217	363	5 277	18.8
Routt	479	-0.6	31.3	1.2	58.7	13.8	9.1	26.1	10.6	1 427	72	58	9 252	27.1
Saguache	63	32.1	D	D	D	7.4	2.2	7.9	25.1	552	93	165	2 306	22.4
San Juan	9	0.0	D	D	D	28.2	D	10.6	26.1	83	149	3	481	1.3
San Miguel	168	-0.3	D	2.8	D	14.8	18.5	26.7	12.9	369	56	14	2 635	51.5
Sedgwick	44	49.0	D	D	D	7.9	2.4	7.4	18.7	747	272	39	1 414	-2.3
Summit	614	0.1	D	1.2	D	18.5	12.4	37.2	9.9	1 153	49	33	17 091	66.6
Teller	229	-0.2	D	4.9	D	9.8	10.1	38.5	15.4	2 547	124	91	7 565	48.3
Washington	78	40.2	D	2.6	D	7.4	2.0	5.7	16.8	979	199	47	2 307	-4.4
Weld	2 687	9.4	30.9	19.7	46.0	8.5	7.3	17.2	13.7	22 232	123	2 272	51 138	10.0
Yuma	152	37.1	D	1.7	D	7.4	5.4	10.1	16.1	2 024	206	126	4 082	-1.8
CONNECTICUT	90 918	0.3	24.4	19.3	63.7	7.9	14.4	29.8	11.7	577 972	170	48 767	1 320 850	14.0
Fairfield	32 214	0.0	D	19.8	D	7.2	20.4	29.7	6.7	137 643	156	10 409	324 355	9.9
Hartford	25 923	0.2	D	16.9	D	7.5	18.2	27.5	13.2	155 087	181	15 997	341 812	13.7
Litchfield	3 059	0.9	37.4	25.4	50.5	11.2	3.5	28.2	11.2	32 414	178	1 229	74 274	20.2
Middlesex	3 256	0.6	29.1	23.4	56.2	8.2	12.9	26.3	14.1	26 045	168	1 181	61 593	20.3
New Haven	17 331	0.2	D	19.3	D	8.7	5.8	34.1	13.0	146 152	177	14 320	327 079	13.9
New London	6 003	0.8	27.4	21.8	52.8	8.0	2.7	33.3	19.0	43 359	167	3 166	104 461	15.7
Tolland	1 677	1.4	19.4	10.8	44.6	10.2	3.5	24.3	34.6	18 611	136	579	46 677	22.7
Windham	1 455	1.3	33.8	26.4	47.5	11.7	3.1	23.6	17.3	18 652	171	1 860	40 599	17.2

1. Covers mining, construction, and manufacturing.   2. Covers private sector earnings in agricultural services, forestry, and fisheries; transportation and public utilities; wholesale trade; retail trade; finance, insurance, and real estate; and services.   3. Per 1,000 resident population estimated as of July 1 of the year shown.

Table B. States and Counties — Housing, Labor Force, and Employment

	Housing units, 1990 (cont'd)								Civilian labor force, 2001				Civilian employment, 1990[5]		
	Occupied units										Unemployment			Percent	
			Owner-occupied			Renter-occupied										
				Owner cost as a percent of income											
STATE County	Total	Percent	Median value[1]	With a mortgage	Without a mortgage	Median rent[2]	Rent as percent of income	Substandard units[3] (percent)	Total	Percent change, 2000–2001	Total	Rate[4]	Total	Professional, managerial, and technical	Precision production, craft, and repair
	89	90	91	92	93	94	95	96	97	98	99	100	101	102	103

STATE County	89	90	91	92	93	94	95	96	97	98	99	100	101	102	103
COLORADO—Cont'd															
Clear Creek	3 153	71.9	90 800	22.7	13.2	407	25.0	2.8	4 692	-4.2	178	3.8	4 311	36.4	12.9
Conejos	2 492	79.2	35 400	23.7	14.2	224	26.5	9.3	3 648	2.4	289	7.9	2 662	21.0	11.2
Costilla	1 192	77.3	35 400	28.6	18.9	187	25.2	5.4	1 319	-1.6	124	9.4	1 054	16.1	14.0
Crowley	1 165	69.9	26 500	23.9	14.6	272	28.4	3.5	1 229	-4.9	55	4.5	1 067	17.1	7.7
Custer	770	73.9	58 900	27.4	15.8	332	26.1	6.9	1 923	3.7	67	3.5	771	23.0	12.6
Delta	8 372	74.5	51 200	23.2	14.1	305	28.7	2.7	10 713	1.2	440	4.1	7 440	23.8	13.0
Denver	210 952	49.2	79 000	22.4	13.2	386	26.2	4.2	279 233	0.5	12 443	4.5	233 602	35.4	7.2
Dolores	581	80.0	40 400	18.8	12.7	312	30.7	6.9	648	-6.6	46	7.1	610	18.7	18.9
Douglas	20 844	85.2	119 500	24.4	11.6	597	24.4	1.0	94 083	0.5	2 650	2.8	32 943	45.7	7.7
Eagle	8 354	57.5	135 900	24.2	13.2	620	24.3	5.0	20 941	1.2	585	2.8	13 645	29.8	12.8
Elbert	3 377	82.9	92 400	27.4	15.4	434	25.1	2.5	13 344	3.4	380	2.8	4 961	27.3	15.0
El Paso	146 965	57.4	81 700	22.8	12.2	419	26.0	2.8	263 863	1.7	11 727	4.4	172 530	34.8	10.0
Fremont	11 713	72.9	57 900	21.4	12.9	330	29.0	3.2	17 590	2.2	688	3.9	11 173	26.5	11.6
Garfield	11 266	57.9	90 400	21.4	12.8	407	24.5	3.5	23 740	1.4	598	2.5	15 266	27.7	15.9
Gilpin	1 308	75.5	74 600	24.0	12.0	469	31.1	6.5	2 956	-5.2	92	3.1	1 655	36.2	10.9
Grand	3 168	57.7	81 400	21.8	12.7	457	23.7	3.5	6 032	2.6	184	3.1	4 681	29.5	11.7
Gunnison	3 855	51.3	79 000	22.0	12.7	373	29.0	3.9	7 867	0.0	375	4.8	5 497	32.7	8.8
Hinsdale	214	59.3	84 200	24.4	15.9	335	20.4	4.7	698	1.2	19	2.7	274	31.0	12.4
Huerfano	2 446	70.0	36 100	24.2	15.1	240	27.9	4.9	3 325	-4.4	190	5.7	2 071	21.6	9.6
Jackson	632	65.3	49 800	22.9	12.3	292	17.5	4.3	896	3.2	41	4.6	814	20.1	6.5
Jefferson	166 545	70.1	93 600	22.5	12.0	476	24.9	1.5	308 280	0.1	9 284	3.0	240 911	38.8	9.9
Kiowa	657	68.9	31 300	22.4	16.4	271	18.3	1.2	750	-2.0	19	2.5	745	16.4	7.9
Kit Carson	2 785	71.2	46 700	18.8	13.3	290	20.5	3.5	3 409	-0.5	69	2.0	3 330	20.1	8.7
Lake	2 382	64.4	48 700	17.8	12.8	373	22.9	4.1	3 154	0.7	148	4.7	3 022	25.9	18.4
La Plata	11 976	65.3	85 100	22.5	12.5	425	27.6	4.2	24 072	-0.8	898	3.7	15 601	30.4	11.5
Larimer	70 472	62.9	83 900	22.0	12.5	420	28.4	2.4	146 144	2.6	5 154	3.5	94 102	36.6	10.4
Las Animas	5 421	67.0	44 700	23.1	14.2	247	28.5	5.8	6 496	-0.1	286	4.4	5 023	24.9	11.0
Lincoln	1 817	70.2	43 800	23.5	12.6	302	24.1	3.1	2 607	0.6	41	1.6	2 120	17.5	9.9
Logan	6 978	66.7	43 200	21.0	13.7	279	23.3	3.2	9 938	1.3	330	3.3	8 532	21.1	10.1
Mesa	36 250	64.9	62 700	21.3	12.2	333	25.4	2.7	57 814	-0.1	2 285	4.0	41 219	28.1	11.5
Mineral	247	70.4	53 800	24.0	12.7	293	25.4	1.2	413	-5.9	10	2.4	247	27.1	22.7
Moffat	4 178	66.7	52 900	16.1	11.7	299	19.0	3.2	5 925	-0.6	293	4.9	5 349	21.8	19.7
Montezuma	6 762	74.2	58 100	21.9	13.8	331	26.2	7.0	10 687	-6.0	533	5.0	7 687	27.6	11.9
Montrose	9 405	72.0	60 000	21.6	12.7	338	26.7	3.0	15 404	0.1	749	4.9	10 488	26.2	12.9
Morgan	8 139	62.5	52 000	20.0	13.1	321	24.4	4.6	12 212	-0.5	328	2.7	9 808	19.9	16.1
Otero	7 593	66.9	38 200	21.6	13.7	288	26.3	4.4	8 011	-5.3	403	5.0	7 656	26.1	8.6
Ouray	947	74.6	91 800	25.4	14.3	401	23.0	3.7	1 809	0.2	58	3.2	1 065	29.8	14.0
Park	2 775	80.6	80 100	25.4	12.1	513	32.5	6.0	8 250	-0.8	258	3.1	3 587	27.5	14.8
Phillips	1 712	72.3	41 600	20.7	12.7	252	18.8	2.3	1 986	-0.3	46	2.3	1 824	19.4	11.5
Pitkin	5 877	52.4	452 800	26.5	13.1	732	28.8	4.4	9 070	3.5	296	3.3	8 567	36.6	8.8
Prowers	4 984	65.5	39 400	19.9	13.4	269	21.8	4.7	6 116	-6.8	188	3.1	5 868	21.8	11.1
Pueblo	47 057	67.9	51 300	21.1	12.7	308	27.7	3.7	58 198	-0.4	2 997	5.1	47 431	26.7	10.7
Rio Blanco	2 181	66.1	57 400	21.0	12.6	329	23.0	1.8	3 081	0.6	75	2.4	2 827	22.5	17.9
Rio Grande	3 930	68.3	47 400	22.7	13.7	291	24.6	5.9	4 681	-3.3	368	7.9	4 333	23.8	7.4
Routt	5 483	61.2	94 900	22.8	13.4	492	25.9	3.6	11 506	3.6	255	2.2	8 435	27.9	13.0
Saguache	1 643	67.1	39 000	23.3	14.4	261	29.0	9.2	2 568	-3.4	213	8.3	1 891	17.0	8.1
San Juan	287	61.7	51 000	21.1	14.6	370	23.1	4.8	278	1.5	45	16.2	353	24.4	25.8
San Miguel	1 489	55.5	151 800	22.9	12.5	538	26.6	6.1	4 670	4.5	178	3.8	2 269	30.6	12.4
Sedgwick	1 141	71.1	29 200	19.3	12.1	207	17.6	3.2	1 108	-3.1	33	3.0	1 256	14.7	9.3
Summit	5 295	48.2	121 500	23.6	12.5	553	24.1	4.5	12 907	1.2	346	2.7	8 815	31.7	9.8
Teller	4 720	77.1	83 300	27.0	14.6	495	28.4	2.4	13 312	-2.5	389	2.9	6 262	37.6	13.5
Washington	1 915	72.2	37 100	23.2	14.0	240	20.0	3.2	2 208	-1.5	52	2.4	2 168	16.1	8.5
Weld	47 470	61.2	67 500	22.2	13.0	357	26.6	4.2	88 182	2.7	3 577	4.1	63 113	24.3	12.5
Yuma	3 472	70.2	47 000	19.6	14.1	302	22.7	1.6	4 288	0.7	91	2.1	4 007	16.6	9.5
CONNECTICUT	1 230 479	65.6	177 800	22.9	13.7	598	26.6	2.5	1 717 642	-1.7	56 352	3.3	1 692 874	35.5	11.2
Fairfield	305 011	68.2	249 800	23.2	14.4	709	27.3	3.1	443 727	-2.0	13 654	3.1	430 443	39.5	9.5
Hartford	324 691	62.7	168 900	22.4	13.3	568	26.2	2.8	418 968	-1.5	14 810	3.5	441 123	35.0	10.5
Litchfield	66 371	73.2	166 300	23.3	13.6	575	24.8	1.4	98 964	-1.9	2 959	3.0	93 697	33.4	14.0
Middlesex	54 651	70.4	175 100	22.9	13.1	619	25.1	1.3	83 006	-1.7	2 244	2.7	78 790	36.5	12.6
New Haven	304 730	62.8	165 200	23.2	14.2	585	27.3	2.4	412 932	-1.8	15 210	3.7	407 425	33.6	11.8
New London	93 245	64.7	149 200	23.3	13.0	572	25.8	1.9	132 250	-0.8	3 709	2.8	120 161	33.0	13.6
Tolland	44 309	72.0	165 000	22.4	12.6	598	25.4	1.5	70 295	-1.8	1 644	2.3	70 822	36.7	11.7
Windham	37 471	66.6	126 800	22.9	13.2	488	26.0	2.4	57 500	-0.4	2 122	3.7	50 413	27.4	13.9

1. Specified owner-occupied units.   2. Specified renter-occupied units.   3. Overcrowded or lacking complete plumbing facilities.   4. Percent of civilian labor force.   5. Persons 16 years and older.

Table B. States and Counties — Nonfarm Employment and Agriculture

STATE County	Private nonfarm establishments, employment and payroll, 1999									Agriculture, 1997			Farm operators
		Employment						Annual payroll		Farms			
											Percent with—		
	Number of establishments	Total	Health Care and Social Assistance	Manufacturing	Retail trade	Finance and Insurance	Professional Scientific and Technical Services	Total (mil dol)	Average per employee (dollars)	Number	Less than 50 acres	500 acres and over	Whose principal occupation is farming (percent)
	104	105	106	107	108	109	110	111	112	113	114	115	116

COLORADO—Cont'd

Clear Creek	321	2 800	72	D	254	57	55	69	24 714	12	58.3	25.0	33.3
Conejos	117	931	D	76	175	D	4	15	16 574	429	16.3	30.5	63.9
Costilla	50	175	D	0	D	D	D	2	12 480	171	20.5	29.8	50.3
Crowley	48	487	65	0	100	D	D	9	19 105	203	14.8	42.9	63.5
Custer	129	507	D	D	131	26	18	10	19 897	152	15.1	36.8	53.9
Delta	727	5 459	1 005	398	1 105	243	189	108	19 708	1 041	51.7	9.3	53.1
Denver	21 661	392 072	48 595	24 640	31 684	26 399	32 973	14 725	37 557	16	100.0	0.0	37.5
Dolores	44	225	D	2	60	D	D	5	20 044	160	8.8	49.4	68.1
Douglas	3 834	34 029	1 702	1 790	8 674	2 241	1 868	920	27 047	574	42.9	16.4	36.4
Eagle	2 721	28 367	1 004	357	3 861	560	1 277	716	25 242	124	27.4	33.9	51.6
Elbert	411	1 970	133	64	289	106	116	46	23 537	822	23.5	38.4	44.2
El Paso	13 387	202 377	23 093	22 992	28 749	10 148	14 564	6 037	29 831	851	32.2	32.0	42.0
Fremont	863	7 658	1 356	837	1 479	290	205	153	20 041	561	62.9	16.0	38.5
Garfield	1 912	14 441	1 553	293	2 877	631	649	396	27 441	475	36.2	27.6	53.1
Gilpin	89	4 154	D	D	D	0	13	109	26 200	11	27.3	27.3	45.5
Grand	728	6 281	181	45	770	147	135	105	16 651	161	20.5	50.9	57.1
Gunnison	826	7 058	306	85	1 071	166	187	123	17 417	187	19.3	37.4	55.6
Hinsdale	77	181	D	0	34	D	D	3	18 740	14	0.0	57.1	57.1
Huerfano	194	1 534	357	D	231	232	D	25	16 394	273	14.3	52.7	52.7
Jackson	58	215	13	D	46	D	8	5	22 572	126	15.1	70.6	70.6
Jefferson	15 655	175 422	19 036	17 432	30 399	8 830	16 213	5 507	31 393	377	67.1	11.1	39.5
Kiowa	44	253	D	D	51	D	4	4	17 664	339	0.9	72.0	64.3
Kit Carson	289	2 087	249	90	430	110	41	39	18 808	718	7.8	66.6	67.7
Lake	214	1 385	203	D	198	62	44	25	17 994	20	30.0	45.0	20.0
La Plata	1 970	17 205	2 329	1 301	3 048	524	911	393	22 843	781	33.5	16.6	43.4
Larimer	7 842	90 677	9 874	12 718	15 181	2 806	5 199	2 435	26 853	1 298	50.5	13.0	39.3
Las Animas	370	3 270	481	95	778	144	90	54	16 525	485	10.5	60.4	61.6
Lincoln	134	1 259	221	D	289	50	22	26	20 407	467	6.9	75.4	70.4
Logan	651	5 790	1 037	452	1 165	221	343	119	20 626	879	9.0	53.2	67.6
Mesa	3 622	40 427	6 753	3 837	7 088	1 211	1 604	996	24 625	1 489	64.1	8.3	44.3
Mineral	52	128	D	D	D	D	D	3	21 844	10	20.0	30.0	20.0
Moffat	364	3 246	536	57	691	59	91	93	28 715	389	18.0	44.0	47.3
Montezuma	755	6 571	835	368	1 324	239	283	142	21 609	718	34.8	18.1	46.4
Montrose	1 066	9 813	1 373	1 322	1 889	280	392	212	21 585	866	38.8	14.9	52.9
Morgan	671	8 140	1 084	2 898	1 064	236	117	187	22 948	759	12.1	38.3	69.7
Otero	533	4 934	1 224	393	957	226	121	96	19 544	512	33.2	23.2	56.4
Ouray	221	714	13	D	100	50	38	16	22 213	79	19.0	43.0	60.8
Park	377	1 242	63	63	166	32	75	28	22 300	183	16.9	44.3	45.4
Phillips	150	1 010	274	D	164	55	19	20	20 237	344	7.6	61.6	75.3
Pitkin	1 521	16 087	652	247	2 187	268	826	397	24 654	70	20.0	20.0	42.9
Prowers	438	4 268	514	811	981	215	108	83	19 518	522	12.6	53.3	65.3
Pueblo	3 206	46 711	9 569	4 103	7 320	1 454	1 316	1 040	22 275	664	31.3	34.2	48.3
Rio Blanco	217	1 351	217	32	189	59	D	34	24 899	255	22.0	43.1	56.1
Rio Grande	393	2 854	291	204	504	183	71	60	21 147	348	14.9	37.9	67.8
Routt	1 287	16 436	807	171	1 559	230	418	395	24 011	494	25.9	35.8	44.5
Saguache	117	643	D	105	127	D	9	11	17 185	248	9.7	56.9	74.2
San Juan	46	60	0	0	25	0	D	2	30 833	4	50.0	50.0	25.0
San Miguel	508	4 287	86	116	504	117	154	85	19 827	83	24.1	39.8	50.6
Sedgwick	92	520	132	D	105	25	10	9	16 790	215	4.2	58.6	77.2
Summit	1 761	19 923	460	143	3 378	284	650	376	18 882	35	17.1	40.0	54.3
Teller	640	5 249	183	72	676	229	268	115	21 988	84	35.7	34.5	32.1
Washington	113	749	39	D	157	D	15	15	19 738	792	7.7	62.1	65.0
Weld	3 862	54 202	5 884	10 867	6 960	3 973	1 442	1 566	28 883	2 959	28.6	24.6	57.4
Yuma	344	2 187	464	92	496	108	71	40	18 366	896	8.5	60.3	69.3
CONNECTICUT	92 454	1 530 539	213 240	238 085	194 237	128 290	87 130	62 083	40 563	3 687	54.7	2.8	49.5
Fairfield	28 560	436 325	48 892	51 975	54 864	35 381	36 203	23 021	52 761	255	71.8	0.0	49.4
Hartford	23 261	472 171	62 240	70 243	52 924	66 300	26 500	18 552	39 291	627	58.4	1.9	55.5
Litchfield	5 181	57 742	8 504	15 456	8 455	1 616	1 736	1 798	31 130	689	48.5	4.6	45.3
Middlesex	4 206	59 997	10 640	12 240	8 114	5 930	2 224	2 071	34 525	288	64.2	1.4	43.1
New Haven	20 833	343 145	58 618	56 805	45 438	15 469	14 425	11 683	34 048	423	68.8	1.2	53.7
New London	5 705	103 728	14 350	18 805	13 782	2 052	4 347	3 414	32 908	610	45.4	3.1	51.0
Tolland	2 528	27 166	4 653	4 159	5 902	900	1 209	715	26 312	355	51.8	3.7	46.5
Windham	2 180	30 265	5 343	8 402	4 758	642	486	829	27 395	440	44.8	4.5	48.0

STATE County	Acreage (1,000)	Percent change, 1992–1997	Average size of farm	Total irrigated (1,000)	Total cropland (1,000)	Average per farm ($1,000)	Average per acre (dollars)	Value of machinery and equipment average per farm ($1,000)	Total (mil dol)	Average per farm (dollars)	Crops	Livestock and poultry products	$10,000 or more	$100,000 or more	Percent of land owned by fed. gov. 1997	Water consumption 1995 (mil gal/day)
	117	118	119	120	121	122	123	124	125	126	127	128	129	130	131	132
COLORADO—Cont'd																
Clear Creek	5	-26.9	426	D	D	1 442	3 383	17	0	2 490	0.0	100.0	8.3	0.0	69.3	7.4
Conejos	285	-6.7	664	131	135	450	656	72	25	59 411	54.6	45.4	60.8	15.4	58.6	731.6
Costilla	363	9.7	2 124	44	D	733	345	96	16	93 441	83.7	16.3	55.0	15.2	0.1	196.8
Crowley	390	-8.1	1 920	22	54	1 110	575	53	73	362 007	6.4	93.6	62.6	19.2	0.7	64.8
Custer	144	-8.1	949	20	24	613	561	43	5	31 681	40.6	59.4	48.7	8.6	37.2	41.6
Delta	282	8.0	271	71	75	483	1 925	46	39	37 544	38.8	61.2	39.2	7.5	54.0	704.3
Denver	74	D	5	0	D	D	D	74	2	135 888	99.6	0.4	56.2	25.0	[1]NA	122.5
Dolores	156	-6.7	973	8	68	634	567	63	9	53 753	57.1	42.9	51.9	11.2	60.9	28.5
Douglas	204	-11.5	356	4	40	795	2 126	28	17	29 823	56.5	43.5	25.6	4.4	26.1	28.7
Eagle	185	-13.1	1 492	17	19	1 901	1 356	50	7	59 784	9.6	90.4	41.9	12.9	78.3	137.6
Elbert	1 095	-1.0	1 332	6	179	700	539	43	31	38 016	14.1	85.9	41.7	7.8	0.0	33.8
El Paso	867	1.2	1 019	15	78	410	443	27	30	35 641	41.5	58.5	36.1	6.2	14.9	134.7
Fremont	283	-14.6	505	19	19	730	895	26	12	21 615	28.7	71.3	20.5	2.9	44.9	158.9
Garfield	427	-3.1	899	51	63	970	1 137	48	23	48 035	40.1	59.9	46.9	10.1	62.2	562.6
Gilpin	9	-32.5	797	D	D	1 084	1 360	15	D	D	D		45.5	0.0	41.9	0.5
Grand	251	-16.0	1 560	40	38	1 269	995	51	9	54 861	18.5	81.5	53.4	12.4	67.0	204.2
Gunnison	195	10.2	1 043	51	38	1 436	1 154	70	8	45 114	10.9	89.1	56.1	12.3	77.6	286.4
Hinsdale	9	-1.8	631	2	2	872	1 383	32	0	26 955	D	D	64.3	0.0	94.9	13.2
Huerfano	641	-0.1	2 348	16	28	854	346	41	10	35 461	9.0	91.0	48.0	6.6	20.8	91.3
Jackson	477	1.1	3 786	124	86	2 095	613	104	16	123 754	17.4	82.6	73.0	34.1	52.0	400.6
Jefferson	98	-5.2	259	3	15	615	2 266	35	19	51 655	89.3	10.7	29.2	7.2	21.7	96.7
Kiowa	914	4.1	2 696	6	494	657	264	96	62	182 077	27.8	72.2	69.0	19.5	0.2	14.8
Kit Carson	1 346	0.3	1 874	146	839	754	413	111	177	246 588	39.6	60.4	72.3	35.4	0.0	166.4
Lake	17	22.8	859	4	D	839	976	38	1	25 655	4.1	95.9	35.0	5.0	70.7	26.2
La Plata	580	-1.2	743	72	91	685	1 018	42	16	20 227	31.3	68.7	37.6	3.6	38.6	378.2
Larimer	542	0.4	418	78	127	657	1 602	49	100	77 414	38.1	61.9	37.1	10.2	46.9	270.2
Las Animas	2 215	-3.1	4 567	24	77	886	196	58	20	41 930	10.1	89.9	53.0	9.3	10.4	120.9
Lincoln	1 648	-0.7	3 530	5	D	617	173	86	45	95 873	33.4	66.6	68.1	22.5	0.1	17.6
Logan	1 129	5.9	1 284	109	524	511	427	99	293	333 038	16.8	83.2	74.7	28.1	0.0	335.2
Mesa	417	-0.8	280	88	92	487	2 045	30	50	33 882	39.9	60.1	33.2	5.9	72.1	972.9
Mineral	D	D	D	0	0	460	1 139	28	0	14 551	D	D	50.0	0.0	93.4	2.1
Moffat	1 031	-11.1	2 651	30	104	1 790	668	37	19	48 683	15.4	84.6	46.3	10.3	56.9	206.8
Montezuma	935	12.1	1 303	61	103	576	441	40	22	30 465	59.0	41.0	41.2	6.0	37.5	314.0
Montrose	372	-16.8	429	85	89	508	1 382	53	88	101 933	22.3	77.7	51.3	11.0	67.6	644.2
Morgan	741	-1.5	976	142	342	604	649	99	406	534 842	18.9	81.1	75.8	35.6	0.1	335.5
Otero	580	-8.4	1 132	63	65	473	405	66	100	195 731	21.2	78.8	63.5	21.3	20.3	424.6
Ouray	117	-1.8	1 480	18	15	2 180	1 473	55	3	40 980	17.9	82.1	54.4	11.4	43.9	58.0
Park	311	-20.0	1 700	18	25	936	516	30	4	19 795	20.9	79.1	36.1	3.8	50.8	8.7
Phillips	463	0.7	1 347	88	389	841	625	183	117	340 302	45.8	54.2	77.3	45.9	0.0	86.2
Pitkin	25	-21.2	360	10	10	839	2 329	68	2	21 812	39.5	60.5	50.0	2.9	82.5	46.6
Prowers	863	-14.0	1 653	111	445	679	427	102	151	288 652	28.2	71.8	68.8	28.0	0.1	695.3
Pueblo	823	-8.3	1 239	36	90	533	471	38	34	50 666	42.3	57.7	45.6	10.5	7.9	246.1
Rio Blanco	466	-14.8	1 829	36	56	885	531	52	14	55 239	8.7	91.3	62.4	15.7	73.4	122.8
Rio Grande	232	5.3	666	136	134	908	1 266	144	73	209 246	92.7	7.3	69.8	33.6	58.1	405.4
Routt	521	-9.6	1 054	50	102	935	966	60	23	46 271	15.4	84.6	46.0	10.1	44.3	307.0
Saguache	482	4.2	1 942	207	140	1 242	644	146	50	202 844	81.3	18.7	73.8	35.5	66.2	425.7
San Juan	D	D	D	D	D	D	D	13	D	D	D	D	25.0	0.0	88.3	0.3
San Miguel	162	-19.4	1 951	12	28	1 340	687	51	3	34 907	16.4	83.6	48.2	7.2	58.8	63.0
Sedgwick	294	-5.1	1 368	52	197	744	545	162	55	254 654	45.2	54.8	79.5	41.9	0.0	94.6
Summit	35	-9.1	987	11	7	1 164	1 180	69	2	43 166	52.5	47.5	45.7	11.4	0.0	29.2
Teller	83	-19.8	993	2	5	1 006	1 012	29	1	15 207	21.6	78.4	33.3	3.6	43.8	9.2
Washington	1 394	4.5	1 760	56	853	684	399	106	98	123 608	52.2	47.8	70.2	24.9	0.0	46.1
Weld	1 914	-8.3	647	393	882	567	807	95	1 287	434 821	16.3	83.7	59.8	23.7	8.1	1 161.9
Yuma	1 365	-4.7	1 524	274	633	891	565	161	481	537 247	24.8	75.2	75.6	39.6	0.0	272.7
CONNECTICUT	359	0.0	97	7	181	571	5 949	41	422	114 361	62.6	37.4	39.8	12.6	0.5	1 275.1
Fairfield	12	19.4	47	0	6	636	15 558	31	17	66 026	64.7	35.3	39.6	9.8	0.3	128.0
Hartford	53	-7.2	84	4	33	675	7 695	47	112	178 929	91.3	8.7	50.1	17.9	0.0	93.7
Litchfield	91	4.1	131	0	45	700	5 467	39	27	39 856	38.2	61.8	40.1	9.1	1.2	93.0
Middlesex	19	-6.6	65	1	8	366	7 248	35	34	117 861	92.6	7.4	28.5	6.2	0.1	626.2
New Haven	25	-5.5	58	1	13	643	8 904	39	43	102 326	85.1	14.9	43.0	13.0	0.2	261.0
New London	68	2.9	111	0	30	445	4 220	41	126	206 237	43.8	56.2	34.9	12.5	0.3	41.2
Tolland	36	-7.1	102	0	17	471	4 852	44	27	76 811	39.2	60.8	33.5	10.4	0.5	17.0
Windham	57	2.8	128	0	29	504	3 926	46	35	79 230	16.9	83.1	40.9	17.7	0.7	15.0

1. Denver County included with Adams County.

Table B. States and Counties — Residential Construction, Wholesale and Retail Trade, and Real Estate

STATE County	Value of Residential Construction Authorized by Building Permits, 2000		Wholesale Trade, 1997				Retail Trade[1], 1997				Real Estate and Rental and Leasing, 1997			
	New Construction ($1,000)	Number of Housing Units	Number of Establishments	Number of Employees	Sales (mil dol)	Annual Payroll (mil dol)	Number of Establishments	Number of Employees	Sales (mil dol)	Annual Payroll (mil dol)	Number of Establishments	Number of Employees	Receipts (mil dol)	Annual Payroll (mil dol)
	133	134	135	136	137	138	139	140	141	142	143	144	145	146
COLORADO—Cont'd														
Clear Creek	10 171	58	17	97	30.7	2.7	50	299	39.3	3.9	16	107	3.8	0.7
Conejos	4 936	193	6	57	11.4	0.9	22	139	22.5	2.0	3	9	0.3	0.1
Costilla	NA	NA	NA	NA	NA	NA	11	24	3.6	0.3	2	D	D	D
Crowley	1 110	20	NA	NA	NA	NA	10	87	12.6	1.3	3	6	0.2	0.1
Custer	18 345	143	4	8	1.6	0.1	21	100	13.9	1.4	12	29	1.6	0.4
Delta	7 219	94	26	272	40.8	4.9	129	957	156.8	15.0	24	54	5.5	1.0
Denver	314 704	3 649	1 681	26 604	16 177.1	972.8	2 410	30 080	5 600.9	628.0	1 201	11 339	1 771.9	287.0
Dolores	822	7	6	45	23.7	0.9	6	34	4.5	0.4	5	3	0.4	0.0
Douglas	961 042	6 395	198	967	943.9	34.5	500	8 052	1 212.0	123.5	157	397	69.9	9.6
Eagle	308 345	701	62	242	189.0	8.5	367	3 313	497.2	67.3	175	989	84.8	19.3
Elbert	47 492	317	18	60	39.3	2.8	40	188	34.9	2.8	7	8	0.9	0.2
El Paso	710 778	6 264	498	6 513	1 417.9	213.3	1 901	27 806	5 015.1	503.6	735	3 064	362.3	62.8
Fremont	28 553	385	28	120	42.8	3.0	143	1 311	203.8	21.6	30	101	10.7	1.4
Garfield	106 380	674	52	379	112.8	8.7	277	2 635	552.5	55.7	87	387	30.4	5.9
Gilpin	9 300	83	1	D	D	D	7	27	2.8	0.4	4	30	2.0	0.6
Grand	104 131	544	10	52	12.9	1.0	116	706	95.6	10.5	56	607	34.8	7.5
Gunnison	52 255	330	9	40	9.1	0.7	139	969	135.6	13.6	46	359	15.8	4.1
Hinsdale	1 953	15	1	D	D	D	14	15	5.1	0.5	6	11	1.9	0.2
Huerfano	8 820	96	7	26	2.9	0.6	39	211	33.0	3.3	10	14	1.6	0.1
Jackson	6 310	24	3	25	3.6	0.6	6	50	6.2	0.6	NA	NA	NA	NA
Jefferson	313 754	3 016	771	4 994	2 805.6	178.2	1 986	28 098	5 114.8	509.2	726	3 214	359.1	66.4
Kiowa	0	0	6	16	8.0	0.3	8	52	4.4	0.5	NA	NA	NA	NA
Kit Carson	3 770	32	28	241	122.5	4.8	64	462	100.1	7.6	4	11	1.6	0.2
Lake	6 471	61	4	D	D	D	33	202	25.9	2.7	12	56	4.4	0.7
La Plata	54 454	433	71	511	119.4	15.4	317	2 848	440.6	49.5	108	325	33.0	6.4
Larimer	427 366	3 524	311	2 630	805.6	75.9	1 201	13 810	2 440.5	234.2	360	1 497	190.0	27.8
Las Animas	8 023	83	17	117	33.8	3.3	54	576	84.8	8.0	8	28	4.8	0.5
Lincoln	1 376	13	9	61	20.6	0.9	36	320	58.3	5.1	4	D	D	D
Logan	6 556	73	32	338	97.4	6.4	115	1 149	199.5	16.5	22	61	3.2	0.8
Mesa	128 285	1 316	198	1 461	531.1	42.8	600	6 409	1 152.7	115.0	133	658	62.6	11.6
Mineral	152	14	NA	NA	NA	NA	10	34	3.7	0.5	4	D	D	D
Moffat	4 156	41	28	123	35.6	3.3	77	706	117.4	12.1	11	23	1.9	0.3
Montezuma	3 564	41	23	112	18.4	2.0	136	1 302	228.6	22.4	27	94	6.1	1.4
Montrose	28 963	309	44	377	88.7	6.7	171	1 710	304.1	31.3	44	176	11.4	2.5
Morgan	12 145	116	41	403	416.9	9.0	119	996	157.6	15.0	23	78	4.3	0.8
Otero	4 310	42	34	286	118.9	6.1	101	932	141.2	13.6	17	61	4.1	0.8
Ouray	19 020	66	2	D	D	D	41	99	11.9	1.4	12	25	2.7	0.3
Park	45 744	434	15	D	D	D	35	175	28.2	3.1	13	18	1.9	0.6
Phillips	785	9	15	170	142.3	4.7	23	165	28.4	2.4	3	D	D	D
Pitkin	138 516	274	26	204	79.0	9.3	265	2 264	288.9	41.0	144	644	82.0	18.2
Prowers	1 269	18	25	403	82.0	7.4	93	826	112.9	11.4	17	42	2.0	0.3
Pueblo	106 645	1 098	113	1 101	390.3	27.5	600	7 040	1 180.7	121.7	131	486	58.8	8.2
Rio Blanco	1 434	17	6	23	6.6	0.5	36	201	21.5	2.2	7	10	0.8	0.1
Rio Grande	14 418	123	31	564	98.1	9.1	77	476	96.8	8.6	14	29	3.0	0.5
Routt	116 785	527	31	185	51.4	5.3	184	1 484	190.3	22.5	86	633	33.9	9.1
Saguache	6 933	134	8	92	8.7	1.1	24	118	30.1	2.4	4	D	D	D
San Juan	215	5	NA	NA	NA	NA	18	39	5.1	0.8	1	D	D	D
San Miguel	122 972	142	5	28	2.2	0.6	76	524	44.6	6.5	44	159	17.4	3.4
Sedgwick	620	4	10	71	36.9	1.7	24	129	25.6	2.0	2	D	D	D
Summit	180 898	799	41	191	58.5	4.5	339	2 801	387.9	45.8	156	1 295	100.3	26.4
Teller	44 292	368	15	57	19.5	2.3	72	516	77.6	8.6	42	182	18.3	2.5
Washington	1 269	16	10	147	53.1	3.4	21	162	23.0	2.8	1	D	D	D
Weld	579 174	4 369	247	2 829	1 334.6	84.9	505	6 195	1 155.5	109.2	154	576	65.4	9.5
Yuma	1 344	17	30	239	112.4	4.8	68	529	89.4	8.6	1	D	D	D
CONNECTICUT	1 425 046	9 376	5 283	77 716	75 821.6	3 595.3	14 574	186 935	34 938.9	3 634.3	3 372	20 635	3 522.8	609.3
Fairfield	535 924	2 278	1 768	28 573	48 325.4	1 559.1	4 008	54 012	11 563.9	1 218.0	1 098	7 639	1 748.1	288.2
Hartford	215 159	1 705	1 369	25 741	16 831.0	1 108.2	3 683	51 121	8 829.0	943.6	874	6 243	996.4	181.9
Litchfield	118 515	725	240	2 203	779.0	90.7	816	8 193	1 611.0	158.0	141	409	48.2	9.1
Middlesex	100 569	867	218	2 045	823.0	74.2	742	8 050	1 345.0	143.1	142	765	96.3	14.8
New Haven	215 083	1 918	1 316	15 458	8 028.3	633.3	3 335	41 942	7 725.2	775.9	761	4 030	477.5	89.0
New London	108 777	814	201	2 279	801.6	81.9	1 182	13 923	2 405.0	240.3	188	723	82.4	13.8
Tolland	94 072	693	89	602	246.5	23.2	428	5 028	763.9	81.8	86	484	49.8	8.7
Windham	36 947	376	82	815	333.1	24.7	380	4 666	695.8	73.6	82	342	24.1	3.8

1. Establishments with payroll.

STATE County	Professional, Scientific, and Technical Services[1], 1997				Manufacturing, 1997				Accommodation and Foodservices, 1997			
	Number of Establishments	Number of Employees	Receipts (mil dol)	Annual Payroll (mil dol)	Number of Establishments	Number of Employees	Receipts (mil dol)	Annual Payroll (mil dol)	Number of Establishments	Number of Employees	Sales (mil dol)	Annual Payroll (mil dol)
	147	148	149	150	151	152	153	154	155	156	157	158
COLORADO—Cont'd												
Clear Creek	31	47	5.1	1.9	NA	NA	NA	NA	48	539	18.8	5.2
Conejos	3	8	0.2	0.1	NA	NA	NA	NA	14	44	1.9	0.5
Costilla	3	4	0.3	0.1	NA	NA	NA	NA	7	D	D	D
Crowley	NA	NA	NA	NA	NA	NA	NA	NA	5	D	D	D
Custer	9	59	2.8	0.7	NA	NA	NA	NA	14	103	4.2	1.0
Delta	43	126	5.6	2.1	NA	NA	NA	NA	68	559	15.2	4.2
Denver	3 147	29 056	3 640.3	1 455.0	976	26 320	4 867.8	816.2	1 564	33 749	1 335.2	386.0
Dolores	2	D	D	D	NA	NA	NA	NA	7	D	D	D
Douglas	459	1 143	166.7	43.0	119	1 941	289.7	58.8	178	3 593	109.1	32.1
Eagle	191	755	87.3	34.2	43	502	85.3	14.9	223	7 181	288.1	100.3
Elbert	36	46	4.1	1.7	NA	NA	NA	NA	11	73	2.4	0.7
El Paso	1 384	10 515	1 199.2	467.1	499	21 593	5 698.9	700.6	998	21 480	771.9	216.9
Fremont	37	118	6.6	2.3	47	950	146.9	26.8	82	1 008	29.8	7.6
Garfield	144	508	45.5	17.1	NA	NA	NA	NA	155	1 906	72.6	21.3
Gilpin	8	111	2.5	1.0	NA	NA	NA	NA	9	647	61.1	11.4
Grand	42	99	6.9	2.4	NA	NA	NA	NA	127	1 531	51.9	15.5
Gunnison	45	144	10.4	3.6	NA	NA	NA	NA	114	2 765	84.3	22.6
Hinsdale	4	4	0.6	0.1	NA	NA	NA	NA	18	71	3.7	0.8
Huerfano	13	23	1.3	0.4	NA	NA	NA	NA	28	201	5.9	1.7
Jackson	1	D	D	D	NA	NA	NA	NA	7	48	0.9	0.3
Jefferson	1 979	11 633	1 284.3	490.7	559	17 871	3 711.2	803.0	967	18 968	585.7	172.5
Kiowa	3	4	0.3	0.1	NA	NA	NA	NA	5	D	D	D
Kit Carson	15	42	2.3	0.9	NA	NA	NA	NA	20	360	9.8	2.6
Lake	13	22	1.8	0.9	NA	NA	NA	NA	44	342	8.4	2.1
La Plata	171	639	57.9	22.1	66	752	51.8	19.3	169	4 281	143.2	44.1
Larimer	711	3 815	336.3	134.2	384	15 840	3 890.7	645.0	647	10 779	343.6	95.0
Las Animas	19	83	3.4	1.6	NA	NA	NA	NA	42	462	13.6	3.4
Lincoln	5	16	0.5	0.2	NA	NA	NA	NA	25	238	8.0	2.2
Logan	33	376	17.1	6.8	19	736	163.2	15.2	51	769	20.4	5.8
Mesa	275	1 283	91.3	39.2	167	3 605	484.2	99.2	247	4 555	124.7	36.3
Mineral	NA	NA	NA	NA	NA	NA	NA	NA	11	19	2.0	0.6
Moffat	28	55	3.3	0.9	NA	NA	NA	NA	27	372	12.0	3.4
Montezuma	50	158	11.0	3.3	NA	NA	NA	NA	82	987	27.8	7.8
Montrose	80	259	18.8	7.4	64	1 540	156.0	31.5	76	825	29.3	7.3
Morgan	33	90	5.9	1.6	25	D	D	D	63	789	19.6	5.4
Otero	24	73	4.1	1.1	17	534	36.2	10.7	63	618	15.9	3.8
Ouray	12	30	2.0	0.9	NA	NA	NA	NA	45	223	10.9	2.8
Park	21	49	3.6	1.3	NA	NA	NA	NA	38	270	9.9	2.8
Phillips	8	15	1.2	0.2	NA	NA	NA	NA	10	D	D	D
Pitkin	184	661	81.0	27.3	NA	NA	NA	NA	189	5 720	228.3	81.8
Prowers	28	111	6.5	2.5	20	D	D	D	40	470	12.3	3.5
Pueblo	192	981	49.7	19.3	107	4 688	1 021.3	147.0	321	4 969	142.4	38.1
Rio Blanco	14	37	2.4	0.9	NA	NA	NA	NA	25	182	7.5	2.3
Rio Grande	18	62	3.7	1.7	NA	NA	NA	NA	41	353	10.9	3.0
Routt	102	394	30.8	10.5	NA	NA	NA	NA	108	3 225	98.1	28.1
Saguache	6	11	0.7	0.2	NA	NA	NA	NA	10	D	D	D
San Juan	1	D	D	D	NA	NA	NA	NA	15	6	2.0	0.5
San Miguel	44	110	9.8	3.7	NA	NA	NA	NA	59	848	25.1	8.8
Sedgwick	3	D	D	D	NA	NA	NA	NA	11	D	D	D
Summit	129	531	45.2	18.3	NA	NA	NA	NA	204	7 781	226.6	67.6
Teller	50	155	16.4	5.1	NA	NA	NA	NA	68	1 848	94.8	26.0
Washington	5	16	0.8	0.2	NA	NA	NA	NA	11	D	D	D
Weld	221	964	72.2	27.9	208	10 773	4 338.5	345.4	271	4 047	106.8	29.4
Yuma	15	46	3.1	1.0	NA	NA	NA	NA	24	211	4.6	1.3
CONNECTICUT	9 393	71 058	9 115.8	3 700.1	5 844	252 330	46 938.2	10 452.1	6 903	96 556	3 746.6	1 062.8
Fairfield	3 834	31 051	4 658.6	1 932.2	1 316	57 560	12 115.5	2 495.9	1 772	24 643	1 113.3	311.3
Hartford	2 188	20 638	2 471.2	978.9	1 592	71 982	11 319.8	3 113.1	1 778	28 579	995.4	289.1
Litchfield	381	1 150	133.8	42.5	448	17 288	3 246.8	589.8	369	3 709	150.6	43.2
Middlesex	332	1 747	211.6	76.0	309	13 132	2 999.3	513.5	355	4 231	172.0	49.3
New Haven	1 885	11 285	1 191.0	466.6	1 592	59 380	12 073.9	2 285.0	1 644	21 581	804.7	221.4
New London	463	3 944	338.9	162.2	237	19 888	2 962.8	1 035.1	590	8 652	333.0	95.7
Tolland	200	883	78.1	31.5	152	4 487	739.2	145.8	208	3 148	101.4	32.6
Windham	110	360	32.6	10.2	198	8 613	1 480.9	273.8	187	2 013	76.2	20.2

1. Firms subject to federal tax.

Table B. States and Counties — Health and Other Services and Federal Funds

STATE County	Health Care and Social Assistance[1], 1997				Other Services[1], 1997				Federal funds and grants, fiscal 2001[2] Expenditures (mil dol)			
										Direct payments for individuals[3]		
	Number of Establishments	Number of Employees	Receipts (mil dol)	Annual Payroll (mil dol)	Number of Establishments	Number of Employees	Receipts (mil dol)	Annual Payroll (mil dol)	Total	Social Security and government retirement	Medicare	Food stamps and Supplemental Security Income
	159	160	161	162	163	164	165	166	167	168	169	170
COLORADO—Cont'd												
Clear Creek	7	24	1.5	0.6	9	25	1.8	0.5	21.5	12.2	3.4	0.4
Conejos	4	27	0.9	0.4	5	26	1.0	0.4	51.0	15.2	6.0	2.9
Costilla	NA	NA	NA	NA	1	D	D	D	30.3	11.1	3.1	1.8
Crowley	2	D	D	D	4	7	0.2	0.0	23.5	9.0	3.1	1.1
Custer	2	D	D	D	3	10	0.5	0.1	15.7	10.8	1.6	0.3
Delta	50	551	19.0	8.8	28	91	6.2	1.5	146.9	78.0	26.7	3.4
Denver	1 478	15 938	1 197.2	562.3	1 101	8 212	604.5	172.8	5 379.1	1 116.5	521.8	108.2
Dolores	1	D	D	D	NA	NA	NA	NA	11.6	4.9	1.2	0.2
Douglas	168	1 175	75.0	38.1	169	854	56.7	17.3	184.3	133.2	16.2	0.9
Eagle	79	471	41.5	18.8	78	431	25.0	8.6	50.7	21.9	4.5	0.4
Elbert	11	65	2.9	1.1	20	44	3.5	0.9	44.1	25.8	5.5	0.5
El Paso	1 134	10 522	710.1	311.1	754	4 558	264.9	89.7	4 337.1	1 277.0	240.2	48.2
Fremont	71	771	29.7	13.5	39	158	8.3	2.4	235.0	109.4	31.4	6.3
Garfield	83	686	49.7	21.2	84	479	26.8	8.6	129.2	62.7	18.5	2.5
Gilpin	2	D	D	D	5	D	D	D	6.8	4.2	0.8	0.1
Grand	11	54	3.5	1.2	15	46	3.7	1.4	33.0	17.0	5.9	0.3
Gunnison	29	102	7.0	2.4	25	94	6.3	1.7	90.5	14.9	3.5	0.5
Hinsdale	2	D	D	D	1	D	D	D	2.5	1.4	0.3	0.0
Huerfano	13	117	4.3	1.7	9	18	0.9	0.3	53.0	20.9	11.5	2.0
Jackson	1	D	D	D	2	D	D	D	7.5	3.2	0.8	0.1
Jefferson	1 065	10 148	623.1	271.6	876	4 665	284.7	88.1	2 790.0	750.3	247.5	22.6
Kiowa	1	D	D	D	2	D	D	D	39.0	3.8	2.3	0.1
Kit Carson	11	97	4.5	1.5	15	32	2.5	0.5	86.9	15.1	7.1	0.6
Lake	5	34	2.0	0.6	6	21	1.0	0.2	20.0	8.9	3.7	0.3
La Plata	109	604	46.5	19.9	74	324	19.9	5.1	155.1	67.7	23.0	2.8
Larimer	530	4 957	296.2	133.5	384	2 151	127.6	39.0	906.4	387.6	122.4	13.9
Las Animas	25	137	6.7	2.4	27	80	5.2	1.2	103.3	41.6	15.0	4.1
Lincoln	8	112	4.3	1.7	5	19	1.4	0.5	42.1	10.8	5.7	0.5
Logan	40	416	20.5	9.2	47	200	15.9	3.8	108.4	40.6	17.0	2.3
Mesa	264	2 504	150.7	69.9	188	1 018	73.9	19.1	613.3	283.7	83.9	14.1
Mineral	NA	NA	NA	NA	1	D	D	D	5.9	1.8	0.3	0.0
Moffat	23	263	10.9	4.1	26	67	5.5	1.1	52.3	20.7	8.1	1.2
Montezuma	44	373	19.1	7.6	43	196	12.2	2.7	118.9	51.4	15.9	2.3
Montrose	79	517	30.4	11.3	45	141	10.1	2.6	158.6	79.7	24.3	3.7
Morgan	41	728	44.0	16.0	40	120	7.6	1.8	128.2	44.1	20.5	2.0
Otero	45	239	11.8	5.2	31	126	7.2	1.7	138.1	54.4	22.2	6.1
Ouray	4	3	0.4	0.1	2	D	D	D	10.4	6.6	1.6	0.1
Park	6	16	1.0	0.7	15	31	3.2	0.6	32.9	22.3	2.8	0.5
Phillips	7	79	2.2	1.0	9	19	1.5	0.3	50.9	11.3	6.2	0.3
Pitkin	48	235	20.4	8.1	43	116	9.6	2.6	27.5	13.1	3.0	0.1
Prowers	22	198	9.3	3.7	30	75	6.9	1.5	90.7	24.4	10.5	2.6
Pueblo	299	3 459	203.9	98.4	194	912	47.5	13.9	822.5	369.3	128.7	37.9
Rio Blanco	4	12	1.0	0.2	13	34	2.4	0.6	29.1	10.4	4.5	0.3
Rio Grande	19	198	6.8	2.7	20	62	3.3	0.6	63.1	24.9	7.2	2.9
Routt	44	199	15.2	6.9	43	125	9.0	2.6	46.9	18.9	5.6	0.5
Saguache	NA	NA	NA	NA	2	D	D	D	31.3	9.5	3.0	1.6
San Juan	NA	NA	NA	NA	NA	NA	NA	NA	2.5	1.0	0.2	0.0
San Miguel	11	39	2.3	0.6	8	57	1.9	0.7	16.0	4.5	1.0	0.1
Sedgwick	4	22	0.5	0.2	7	14	1.1	0.2	36.1	8.1	4.4	0.1
Summit	36	168	9.9	4.1	49	200	12.8	3.5	30.2	19.4	2.1	0.2
Teller	26	125	5.8	2.2	28	70	5.5	1.1	60.5	43.3	5.4	0.8
Washington	3	13	0.5	0.2	3	9	0.5	0.1	64.9	10.9	4.8	0.4
Weld	209	2 279	138.2	56.5	215	1 130	67.8	17.9	568.7	240.0	90.9	15.2
Yuma	16	220	8.7	3.4	25	66	4.8	1.0	95.2	19.0	7.9	0.8
CONNECTICUT	7 515	100 363	6 849.7	3 199.3	6 121	34 089	2 370.2	727.8	22 741.8	6 949.2	3 418.4	414.6
Fairfield	2 124	25 229	1 915.4	900.3	1 497	8 289	596.6	192.2	5 288.6	1 647.6	857.3	85.2
Hartford	1 970	28 270	1 925.8	936.4	1 656	10 183	698.7	220.5	6 428.1	1 840.2	909.8	138.2
Litchfield	388	4 258	226.1	97.0	319	1 347	97.5	26.1	741.6	380.6	177.0	8.5
Middlesex	332	4 839	298.1	139.8	297	1 339	111.8	30.9	614.1	311.6	125.1	9.1
New Haven	1 855	26 597	1 750.3	800.2	1 634	9 237	633.4	191.6	4 686.3	1 729.8	933.7	130.4
New London	490	7 493	521.3	227.8	391	2 113	137.6	37.8	3 185.5	597.5	228.2	25.1
Tolland	188	1 657	100.0	41.5	183	1 030	61.4	18.4	450.9	214.8	85.0	3.6
Windham	168	2 020	112.6	56.3	144	551	33.3	10.4	483.3	213.4	102.2	14.5

1. Firms subject to federal tax. 2. October 1, 2000 to September 30, 2001. 3. State totals may include programs not allocated by county.

Table B. States and Counties — **Federal Funds and Local Government Finances**

	Federal funds and grants, fiscal 2001[1] (cont'd)							Local government finances, 1997				
	Expenditures (mil dol) (cont'd)							General revenue				
		Procurement contract awards		Grants[2]							Taxes	
STATE County												Per capita[3] (dollars)
	Salaries and wages	Defense	Other	Medicaid and other health-related	Nutrition and family welfare	Education	Other	Total (mil dol)	Intergovern-mental (mil dol)	Total (mil dol)	Total	Property
	171	172	173	174	175	176	177	178	179	180	181	182
COLORADO—Cont'd												
Clear Creek	1.7	0.2	1.1	1.0	0.4	0.4	0.7	23.0	6.0	14.1	1 577	1 315
Conejos	2.0	0.0	0.4	16.6	2.1	0.8	3.6	22.9	16.1	4.1	530	436
Costilla	0.8	0.0	0.4	9.9	1.2	0.3	0.4	14.0	7.6	4.4	1 215	1 132
Crowley	0.9	0.0	0.2	3.3	0.9	0.2	1.3	7.9	4.4	2.5	594	387
Custer	0.8	0.0	0.4	1.2	0.3	0.2	0.1	6.5	2.2	3.0	906	729
Delta	10.0	0.0	1.8	15.2	3.6	2.1	2.6	71.5	26.2	17.9	694	434
Denver	921.0	629.2	334.7	675.2	254.7	154.7	408.9	2 460.9	611.0	947.2	1 898	752
Dolores	0.5	0.0	0.3	1.1	0.3	0.1	0.8	6.0	3.5	1.7	994	955
Douglas	11.1	5.9	4.8	2.5	1.1	1.6	4.2	351.9	71.6	153.4	1 215	870
Eagle	7.7	0.6	1.9	1.7	1.0	0.7	7.9	149.6	17.9	92.1	2 882	1 718
Elbert	1.9	0.1	0.5	1.7	0.4	0.4	3.0	32.5	16.8	12.0	684	628
El Paso	1 331.2	1 029.2	126.6	105.4	43.2	30.7	51.7	1 187.2	404.2	379.5	791	492
Fremont	50.8	0.0	2.3	20.1	5.3	1.9	5.0	68.5	36.8	22.7	528	341
Garfield	14.4	0.0	3.6	5.8	2.0	3.0	11.0	104.7	34.3	50.9	1 354	962
Gilpin	0.3	0.0	0.1	0.9	0.2	0.1	0.0	32.7	11.5	17.7	4 471	2 192
Grand	4.9	0.0	2.4	0.7	0.5	0.5	0.7	45.7	8.2	23.1	2 349	1 552
Gunnison	6.3	0.3	52.5	1.4	0.5	0.4	7.5	42.2	6.9	22.7	1 859	1 119
Hinsdale	0.2	0.0	0.2	0.2	0.0	0.0	0.1	3.4	1.2	1.7	2 479	1 434
Huerfano	1.1	0.0	0.2	10.3	1.7	0.5	4.2	23.1	12.4	8.0	1 185	1 026
Jackson	1.3	0.0	0.3	0.2	0.1	0.1	1.4	5.4	2.6	2.0	1 272	1 034
Jefferson	539.2	16.1	1 019.9	64.1	21.2	18.7	60.6	1 002.1	321.0	496.0	999	746
Kiowa	0.8	0.0	0.3	0.7	0.2	0.1	3.8	12.8	2.9	4.3	2 553	2 418
Kit Carson	2.3	0.0	0.5	3.5	0.8	0.4	6.0	25.4	10.2	7.9	1 101	913
Lake	2.5	0.0	0.5	1.2	1.0	0.5	0.4	55.7	18.9	19.8	3 137	2 882
La Plata	17.9	0.3	7.3	12.0	4.5	3.2	6.9	102.8	26.8	57.5	1 432	943
Larimer	120.2	6.6	50.8	73.3	15.3	12.8	73.7	708.1	144.5	250.2	1 107	741
Las Animas	3.6	0.5	0.8	22.1	4.0	3.2	1.5	38.2	21.6	10.1	700	522
Lincoln	1.6	0.0	0.4	2.3	1.0	0.5	2.9	25.0	12.6	5.9	1 055	757
Logan	4.0	0.0	5.1	8.7	2.4	1.2	0.3	59.7	26.5	19.7	1 087	766
Mesa	57.5	29.6	48.9	44.2	10.5	6.0	11.9	248.0	103.1	97.9	884	501
Mineral	0.3	0.0	0.0	0.0	0.0	0.0	3.3	4.6	1.6	2.3	3 447	1 705
Moffat	6.4	0.0	1.4	2.4	1.3	0.8	3.7	66.7	7.9	25.9	2 106	1 621
Montezuma	13.6	0.1	4.7	11.2	3.8	2.4	6.7	74.2	28.0	20.4	916	662
Montrose	14.7	0.3	4.5	13.1	3.0	1.6	9.1	107.6	34.1	28.8	950	581
Morgan	6.7	0.0	7.7	11.1	3.7	1.6	6.1	71.4	26.2	28.7	1 141	921
Otero	5.9	0.0	1.2	24.1	9.7	2.4	1.1	58.2	35.5	11.7	559	306
Ouray	0.6	0.0	0.8	0.3	0.2	0.1	0.2	11.7	3.0	5.1	1 581	1 104
Park	2.3	0.0	1.9	0.5	0.6	0.7	1.2	29.2	11.2	12.6	991	947
Phillips	1.4	0.0	0.3	2.1	0.5	0.2	2.2	16.8	6.4	4.2	972	850
Pitkin	4.8	0.0	1.0	0.5	0.1	0.1	4.6	113.0	4.4	63.0	4 640	2 325
Prowers	2.2	0.0	0.5	9.5	2.8	1.3	13.5	39.7	22.1	10.3	753	451
Pueblo	38.2	18.8	11.3	115.5	38.6	12.6	17.4	303.9	144.2	112.1	844	517
Rio Blanco	3.2	0.0	0.8	1.2	0.5	0.4	6.0	40.6	11.9	16.0	2 547	2 326
Rio Grande	5.1	0.2	1.5	10.6	2.5	1.0	0.8	35.5	16.7	11.5	1 011	590
Routt	5.6	0.0	7.8	1.9	0.6	0.6	3.8	66.3	9.5	40.4	2 343	1 455
Saguache	2.0	0.0	0.8	5.4	2.2	1.2	0.4	21.0	12.9	4.0	683	622
San Juan	0.2	0.0	0.2	0.0	0.1	0.2	0.6	3.9	1.3	2.0	3 544	1 785
San Miguel	1.8	0.0	0.5	1.0	0.3	0.2	6.2	36.5	7.0	22.2	4 163	2 898
Sedgwick	1.0	0.0	0.2	2.1	0.4	0.2	5.2	11.3	3.7	3.4	1 309	1 139
Summit	2.9	0.2	0.7	0.9	0.3	0.6	2.3	107.0	9.3	73.2	3 966	1 772
Teller	2.6	0.2	1.8	1.0	1.1	0.6	3.4	50.4	19.0	21.9	1 107	650
Washington	2.2	0.0	0.4	2.3	0.9	0.3	9.7	16.0	8.1	6.3	1 358	1 285
Weld	35.6	0.5	11.2	66.9	19.0	12.8	16.8	385.0	149.5	154.2	991	735
Yuma	2.5	0.0	0.4	3.7	1.2	0.5	5.7	29.8	9.1	13.4	1 433	1 313
CONNECTICUT	1 375.3	4 205.8	528.1	2 298.8	690.4	317.4	1 057.2	X	X	X	X	X
Fairfield	242.1	1 405.5	118.2	454.3	101.5	44.2	161.9	2 356.2	502.0	1 564.8	1 878	1 852
Hartford	377.1	951.9	205.6	704.3	354.6	128.9	553.7	2 202.7	715.6	1 259.4	1 526	1 510
Litchfield	28.8	31.6	8.9	55.8	9.5	6.2	17.5	398.3	104.7	255.6	1 411	1 394
Middlesex	24.1	17.4	7.9	69.0	9.6	6.6	13.4	358.1	94.4	216.6	1 454	1 440
New Haven	333.3	65.6	132.1	785.2	119.0	62.3	159.8	2 067.5	761.1	1 105.2	1 395	1 378
New London	333.0	1 718.0	43.2	114.3	24.1	21.2	36.2	663.2	233.3	332.3	1 314	1 285
Tolland	20.4	9.8	8.0	32.0	6.2	10.2	40.0	270.4	106.6	141.3	1 078	1 067
Windham	16.5	6.0	4.1	67.2	14.5	7.3	7.3	241.0	131.5	90.3	859	849

1. October 1, 2000 to September 30, 2001.   2. State totals may include programs not allocated by county.   3. Based on the resident population estimated as of July 1 of the year shown.

STATE County	Direct general expenditure — Total (mil dol)	Per capita[1] (dollars)	Education	Health and hospitals	Police protection	Public welfare	Highways	Debt outstanding — Total (mil dol)	Per capita[1] (dollars)	Federal civilian	Federal military	State and local	Demo-cratic	Republi-can	All other
	183	184	185	186	187	188	189	190	191	192	193	194	195	196	197
COLORADO—Cont'd															
Clear Creek	23.1	2 593	34.5	2.8	6.8	4.1	14.2	12.7	1 428	43	25	606	44.4	45.6	9.9
Conejos	21.8	2 786	52.3	5.1	2.3	10.6	8.3	5.8	744	47	22	585	47.6	48.3	4.1
Costilla	14.9	4 090	45.3	7.0	4.4	13.2	7.6	4.7	1 284	15	10	383	64.0	30.6	5.5
Crowley	8.0	1 886	53.1	0.8	3.2	11.3	12.1	0.9	213	14	12	512	35.4	59.2	5.4
Custer	6.6	2 014	39.1	17.2	1.1	8.2	10.3	1.2	350	13	10	203	24.0	68.7	7.2
Delta	71.1	2 755	44.4	20.2	3.1	5.8	6.1	29.2	1 131	200	75	1 721	25.7	66.0	8.3
Denver	2 235.7	4 481	17.5	10.2	5.1	8.3	2.6	5 696.5	11 416	15 630	2 782	52 926	61.9	30.9	7.3
Dolores	5.8	3 377	39.6	2.4	5.1	5.1	26.9	0.3	147	14	0	174	25.8	65.3	8.8
Douglas	368.8	2 921	45.5	0.2	2.5	0.6	7.2	756.2	5 990	168	433	5 924	31.4	65.0	3.7
Eagle	152.0	4 756	25.0	2.0	4.8	1.1	8.7	261.8	8 195	151	96	2 283	44.6	47.2	8.3
Elbert	31.2	1 778	68.5	0.3	2.3	3.0	10.2	8.4	481	36	54	851	25.9	68.6	5.5
El Paso	1 144.8	2 385	46.6	14.3	5.3	5.0	5.4	1 299.3	2 707	10 130	29 063	27 281	30.8	63.9	5.3
Fremont	66.4	1 545	52.0	2.7	5.9	6.8	6.3	24.0	558	1 163	123	3 778	33.0	61.7	5.3
Garfield	112.3	2 984	50.1	2.7	3.2	4.1	5.5	177.5	4 716	298	112	2 982	35.6	53.2	11.2
Gilpin	26.8	6 764	10.4	0.6	11.5	2.2	14.9	40.7	10 266	0	12	341	44.6	40.8	14.6
Grand	42.7	4 343	28.9	10.7	6.0	1.9	15.2	23.2	2 360	125	29	941	36.3	56.2	7.5
Gunnison	60.6	4 972	47.4	9.7	3.9	1.1	10.8	39.5	3 240	154	35	1 409	42.3	43.2	14.5
Hinsdale	3.0	4 319	21.7	1.7	6.5	0.1	34.9	0.6	881	0	0	63	33.2	55.8	10.9
Huerfano	21.7	3 223	32.5	1.3	6.3	15.0	15.0	7.1	1 051	20	19	433	47.1	46.2	6.7
Jackson	5.5	3 572	42.6	4.8	3.9	3.6	17.5	4.6	2 985	33	0	158	18.7	73.7	7.5
Jefferson	1 026.6	2 067	49.9	1.1	7.3	3.9	6.7	930.6	1 874	8 661	1 414	23 235	42.9	51.0	6.1
Kiowa	12.3	7 399	24.9	23.6	1.8	24.6	12.2	0.8	453	18	0	234	21.8	75.2	3.0
Kit Carson	27.1	3 782	43.1	15.9	3.3	2.8	13.7	1.8	251	45	20	750	23.4	73.5	3.1
Lake	65.8	10 404	84.8	3.7	1.3	1.0	2.5	1.1	174	58	18	647	49.3	40.2	10.5
La Plata	104.2	2 596	49.5	0.3	4.7	4.2	8.8	62.7	1 561	369	113	3 332	38.4	48.8	12.8
Larimer	577.9	2 557	34.1	17.4	4.7	4.2	8.5	1 031.1	4 562	2 092	690	21 556	38.9	52.7	8.5
Las Animas	40.5	2 792	46.8	2.2	4.5	13.2	7.4	8.1	561	74	41	1 627	53.2	42.2	4.7
Lincoln	22.3	3 972	37.3	11.7	4.5	4.3	24.6	6.7	1 191	30	16	883	23.2	74.1	2.7
Logan	64.4	3 556	57.9	0.5	3.0	5.7	10.3	20.0	1 107	73	49	2 115	28.4	68.3	3.3
Mesa	237.6	2 147	45.0	1.3	6.4	8.4	7.7	240.6	2 174	1 161	319	6 689	30.3	63.5	6.3
Mineral	4.4	6 529	36.2	1.6	7.9	0.0	28.7	0.1	133	0	0	93	34.6	60.5	4.9
Moffat	65.0	5 287	23.0	14.4	3.8	2.4	8.4	245.2	19 948	149	35	1 044	22.9	72.0	5.2
Montezuma	70.2	3 151	42.3	20.9	4.8	4.6	4.5	29.5	1 325	336	63	1 484	27.2	65.6	7.1
Montrose	104.3	3 445	31.4	25.3	3.5	5.4	4.7	58.2	1 922	278	87	2 313	28.4	65.2	6.4
Morgan	77.5	3 081	49.4	0.9	4.3	6.3	8.5	60.1	2 391	130	70	2 135	32.1	63.6	4.3
Otero	65.1	3 123	55.2	1.5	2.9	12.5	5.1	17.5	841	125	57	1 856	40.5	55.8	3.7
Ouray	11.7	3 647	51.8	1.5	6.1	3.5	8.7	4.2	1 313	0	10	279	31.6	57.3	11.1
Park	34.0	2 667	45.3	1.8	3.6	2.7	11.1	13.1	1 032	61	39	631	35.9	55.2	9.0
Phillips	16.9	3 910	50.5	19.3	3.9	2.9	9.7	1.4	316	29	12	513	25.4	70.9	3.8
Pitkin	93.8	6 911	11.5	22.5	6.3	5.3	8.2	89.5	6 590	92	37	1 516	53.0	32.9	14.1
Prowers	39.0	2 858	53.6	1.3	3.6	6.3	7.9	9.5	699	51	38	1 513	30.1	66.9	3.0
Pueblo	298.9	2 249	43.8	1.9	4.8	12.0	5.9	413.0	3 107	707	379	10 569	53.5	42.3	4.1
Rio Blanco	40.0	6 368	51.8	19.0	4.0	3.0	7.6	7.5	1 198	79	17	1 016	19.0	76.5	4.5
Rio Grande	34.7	3 041	50.6	1.5	4.3	10.0	8.1	7.2	630	114	32	825	33.6	61.3	5.0
Routt	62.9	3 653	36.5	5.7	6.3	2.1	9.0	39.3	2 283	132	49	1 448	43.7	46.4	9.9
Saguache	18.1	3 062	46.2	4.8	3.1	8.3	13.9	3.8	635	63	17	555	45.3	42.6	12.1
San Juan	4.0	7 111	30.9	2.9	7.4	0.8	11.3	0.6	1 048	0	0	73	34.2	48.2	17.7
San Miguel	38.8	7 287	15.2	3.5	7.1	1.4	12.3	55.7	10 469	33	15	575	49.1	32.0	18.9
Sedgwick	13.1	5 036	30.7	33.9	2.4	3.5	6.6	6.5	2 484	21	0	319	29.5	67.3	3.2
Summit	109.1	5 909	36.3	2.5	4.2	0.9	10.7	124.4	6 734	67	54	1 668	47.9	40.6	11.4
Teller	47.5	2 402	40.9	4.2	8.6	7.4	8.3	34.3	1 736	48	59	1 018	27.9	65.8	6.3
Washington	16.1	3 472	55.0	0.9	3.6	4.0	15.0	0.4	88	57	12	449	19.5	76.8	3.6
Weld	387.6	2 491	51.6	2.0	5.2	5.1	6.7	205.5	1 321	581	461	10 940	36.3	58.0	5.7
Yuma	31.5	3 364	37.8	21.1	4.9	1.4	15.7	13.1	1 393	53	26	845	24.8	72.4	2.8
CONNECTICUT	X	X	X	X	X	X	X	X	X	22 002	16 342	193 784	55.9	38.4	5.6
Fairfield	2 334.9	2 802	48.1	1.5	5.9	2.2	4.0	1 042.3	1 251	4 444	2 074	39 682	52.3	43.1	4.5
Hartford	2 189.0	2 653	51.8	0.9	6.4	1.8	3.9	1 032.5	1 251	7 219	2 152	61 663	60.2	34.7	5.2
Litchfield	417.6	2 306	63.8	0.7	3.6	0.3	6.3	186.6	1 031	401	446	7 661	47.9	44.9	7.3
Middlesex	385.6	2 588	60.8	1.0	3.9	0.6	5.6	297.4	1 996	327	370	9 040	55.9	37.8	6.2
New Haven	2 132.3	2 692	52.4	1.0	5.9	1.9	3.3	1 353.4	1 708	6 554	2 089	41 828	58.0	36.0	6.0
New London	673.9	2 664	55.5	0.8	5.8	1.1	5.7	441.4	1 745	2 615	8 614	14 293	55.4	37.7	6.9
Tolland	277.7	2 120	64.2	0.4	2.5	0.8	4.6	127.8	976	215	340	13 222	53.5	39.4	7.1
Windham	232.0	2 207	64.3	0.5	1.8	1.0	4.9	128.1	1 218	227	257	6 395	54.6	38.0	7.5

1. Based on the resident population estimated as of July 1 of the year shown.   2. Data subject to copyright.

Table B. States and Counties — **Land Area and Population**

STATE/County code	MSA/PMSA/NECMA code[1]	County Type[2]	STATE County	Land area,[3] (sq km) 2000	Total persons	Rank	Per square kilometer	White	Black	Am. Indian, Alaska Native	Asian and Pacific Islander	Percent Hispanic[4]	Under 5 years	5 to 17 years	18 to 24 years	25 to 34 years	35 to 44 years	45 to 54 years
					1	2	3	4	5	6	7	9	10	11	12	13	14	15
10 000	...	X	DELAWARE	5 060	783 600	X	154.9	75.9	20.1	0.8	2.5	4.8	6.6	18.3	9.6	13.9	16.3	13.3
10 001	2190	3	Kent	1 527	126 697	426	83.0	75.1	21.8	1.3	2.3	3.2	7.2	20.0	10.1	13.5	16.2	12.5
10 003	9160	2	New Castle	1 104	500 265	112	453.1	74.3	21.0	0.6	3.0	5.3	6.7	18.3	10.3	14.8	16.7	13.4
10 005	...	6	Sussex	2 428	156 638	341	64.5	81.3	15.6	1.0	1.0	4.4	5.8	16.8	7.0	11.4	15.0	13.6
11 000	...	X	DISTRICT OF COLUMBIA	159	572 059	X	3 597.9	32.2	61.3	0.8	3.2	7.9	5.7	14.4	12.7	17.8	15.3	13.2
11 001	8840	0	District of Columbia	159	572 059	94	3 597.9	32.2	61.3	0.8	3.2	7.9	5.7	14.4	12.7	17.8	15.3	13.2
12 000	...	X	FLORIDA	139 670	15 982 378	X	114.4	79.7	15.5	0.7	2.3	16.8	5.9	16.9	8.3	13.0	15.5	12.9
12 001	2900	3	Alachua	2 264	217 955	259	96.3	75.1	20.0	0.8	4.2	5.7	5.1	15.0	23.2	14.4	13.3	12.2
12 003	...	6	Baker	1 516	22 259	1 682	14.7	84.9	14.2	0.9	0.7	1.9	7.0	20.5	9.9	14.1	16.6	13.8
12 005	6015	2	Bay	1 978	148 217	366	74.9	85.8	11.2	1.5	2.5	2.4	6.1	18.0	8.7	13.3	16.9	13.7
12 007	...	6	Bradford	759	26 088	1 513	34.4	77.3	21.2	0.8	1.0	2.4	5.5	16.4	9.5	14.8	17.3	13.8
12 009	4900	2	Brevard	2 637	476 230	120	180.6	88.3	9.0	0.9	2.2	4.6	5.2	16.8	6.8	10.6	16.5	13.3
12 011	2680	0	Broward	3 122	1 623 018	15	519.9	72.4	22.2	0.5	3.0	16.7	6.3	17.2	7.2	14.2	17.2	13.3
12 013	...	8	Calhoun	1 469	13 017	2 231	8.9	81.2	16.1	2.0	0.9	3.8	5.9	17.3	9.0	16.0	15.4	12.5
12 015	6580	3	Charlotte	1 796	141 627	387	78.9	93.5	4.8	0.5	1.2	3.3	3.7	12.0	4.5	7.6	11.2	11.8
12 017	...	4	Citrus	1 512	118 085	458	78.1	96.0	2.6	0.9	1.0	2.7	3.8	13.4	4.6	7.7	11.4	12.1
12 019	3600	2	Clay	1 557	140 814	389	90.4	89.1	7.3	1.1	2.8	4.3	6.6	21.4	7.9	12.7	17.6	14.7
12 021	5345	3	Collier	5 246	251 377	228	47.9	87.4	5.5	0.5	0.9	19.6	5.3	14.5	6.6	11.2	13.3	11.7
12 023	...	6	Columbia	2 064	56 513	838	27.4	80.9	17.5	1.2	1.0	2.7	6.4	18.9	9.0	12.3	15.4	13.7
12 027	...	6	De Soto	1 651	32 209	1 341	19.5	74.5	13.1	2.0	0.6	24.9	5.8	16.9	11.2	14.1	12.6	10.4
12 029	...	9	Dixie	1 823	13 827	2 171	7.6	89.7	9.2	1.0	0.4	1.8	5.6	16.5	7.9	11.8	14.8	13.5
12 031	3600	2	Duval	2 004	778 879	61	388.7	67.3	28.5	0.8	3.5	4.1	7.2	19.1	9.6	15.5	16.9	13.3
12 033	6080	2	Escambia	1 715	294 410	192	171.7	74.1	22.0	1.8	3.1	2.7	6.1	17.4	12.2	13.7	15.3	12.9
12 035	2020	2	Flagler	1 256	49 832	918	39.7	88.5	9.4	0.7	1.6	5.1	4.1	13.8	4.8	8.1	12.3	13.2
12 037	...	7	Franklin	1 410	11 057	2 362	7.8	82.4	16.6	1.2	0.4	2.4	4.6	13.4	7.6	14.0	16.8	14.5
12 039	8240	3	Gadsden	1 337	45 087	996	33.7	39.3	57.5	0.5	0.5	6.2	6.7	19.7	9.5	13.3	15.6	13.8
12 041	...	8	Gilchrist	904	14 437	2 127	16.0	91.6	7.3	1.1	0.3	2.8	5.7	18.7	14.2	10.8	14.0	12.5
12 043	...	8	Glades	2 004	10 576	2 391	5.3	78.3	10.8	5.6	0.6	15.1	5.8	16.3	7.6	13.3	13.7	11.5
12 045	...	6	Gulf	1 436	13 332	2 201	9.3	81.1	17.4	1.5	0.8	2.0	5.1	16.7	6.8	12.7	16.7	14.2
12 047	...	9	Hamilton	1 333	13 327	2 203	10.0	59.5	38.2	0.9	0.5	6.4	6.3	17.2	10.8	15.6	16.2	13.8
12 049	...	6	Hardee	1 651	26 938	1 486	16.3	72.1	8.9	1.1	0.5	35.7	7.7	19.9	11.0	14.5	13.7	10.4
12 051	...	6	Hendry	2 985	36 210	1 208	12.1	68.8	15.2	1.2	0.7	39.6	7.8	22.2	13.3	14.8	13.5	10.4
12 053	8280	0	Hernando	1 239	130 802	409	105.6	93.8	4.4	0.7	1.0	5.0	4.5	14.4	5.4	8.4	12.0	11.8
12 055	...	6	Highlands	2 663	87 366	600	32.8	84.7	9.8	0.8	1.3	12.1	4.8	14.3	6.3	8.6	10.8	10.2
12 057	8280	0	Hillsborough	2 722	998 948	35	367.0	77.1	15.8	0.9	2.9	18.0	6.9	18.5	9.3	15.1	16.6	13.3
12 059	...	7	Holmes	1 250	18 564	1 867	14.9	91.2	6.7	2.0	0.6	1.9	5.5	17.5	8.8	14.4	14.9	13.1
12 061	...	4	Indian River	1 303	112 947	476	86.7	88.4	8.6	0.5	1.1	6.5	4.7	14.6	6.0	9.2	13.0	12.2
12 063	...	6	Jackson	2 372	46 755	966	19.7	71.3	27.1	1.4	0.6	2.9	5.5	16.9	9.7	13.9	15.7	13.8
12 065	...	6	Jefferson	1 548	12 902	2 241	8.3	60.2	38.6	0.9	0.6	2.2	5.3	17.4	8.2	12.4	16.5	15.6
12 067	...	9	Lafayette	1 406	7 022	2 683	5.0	80.1	14.7	1.3	0.4	9.1	5.5	16.1	10.7	17.9	16.1	11.9
12 069	5960	1	Lake	2 469	210 528	265	85.3	88.4	8.6	0.7	1.1	5.6	5.2	15.1	5.8	10.2	13.5	11.6
12 071	2700	2	Lee	2 081	440 888	136	211.9	88.9	7.1	0.6	1.1	9.5	5.2	14.4	6.2	10.5	13.4	12.4
12 073	8240	3	Leon	1 727	239 452	240	138.7	67.5	29.7	0.7	2.4	3.5	5.7	15.6	21.4	14.7	14.2	13.1
12 075	...	8	Levy	2 897	34 450	1 266	11.9	87.1	11.2	1.2	0.7	3.9	5.7	17.9	6.9	10.9	14.2	13.7
12 077	...	8	Liberty	2 165	7 021	2 684	3.2	78.4	18.7	2.4	0.4	4.5	5.5	16.3	9.4	18.7	18.9	12.1
12 079	...	7	Madison	1 792	18 733	1 859	10.5	58.3	40.7	0.8	0.5	3.2	5.7	19.5	9.2	13.6	14.7	12.9
12 081	7510	2	Manatee	1 919	264 002	209	137.6	87.5	8.6	0.6	1.2	9.3	5.6	15.1	6.5	11.0	13.7	12.3
12 083	5790	3	Marion	4 089	258 916	217	63.3	85.3	12.0	1.0	1.0	6.0	5.2	16.2	6.4	10.2	13.6	12.1
12 085	2710	2	Martin	1 439	126 731	425	88.1	90.7	5.6	0.6	1.0	7.5	4.4	14.2	5.3	8.9	14.0	13.0
12 086	5000	0	Miami-Dade	5 040	2 253 362	8	447.1	72.3	21.6	0.4	2.0	57.3	6.5	18.3	9.1	15.0	16.1	12.5
12 087	...	4	Monroe	2 582	79 589	644	30.8	92.1	5.2	0.9	1.2	15.8	4.3	12.7	6.3	12.9	18.2	18.4
12 089	3600	2	Nassau	1 688	57 663	828	34.2	91.0	7.9	0.9	0.8	1.5	6.2	18.9	7.2	12.3	16.5	15.0
12 091	2750	3	Okaloosa	2 423	170 498	317	70.4	85.9	9.9	1.4	4.0	4.3	6.4	18.4	9.6	13.9	17.2	13.1
12 093	...	6	Okeechobee	2 005	35 910	1 222	17.9	81.0	8.3	1.0	1.0	18.6	6.3	18.9	9.5	12.8	14.2	11.5
12 095	5960	0	Orange	2 350	896 344	45	381.4	70.9	19.5	0.8	4.3	18.8	6.8	18.4	10.9	16.6	17.1	12.6
12 097	5960	2	Osceola	3 424	172 493	315	50.4	80.0	8.4	0.9	3.0	29.4	6.8	20.0	9.3	14.6	16.3	12.9
12 099	8960	2	Palm Beach	5 113	1 131 184	31	221.2	80.4	14.9	0.5	2.1	12.4	5.6	15.7	6.6	11.8	15.2	12.5
12 101	8280	2	Pasco	1 929	344 765	170	178.7	94.9	2.3	0.9	1.3	5.7	5.3	14.9	5.8	10.4	13.7	12.1
12 103	8280	0	Pinellas	725	921 482	41	1 271.0	87.2	9.4	0.7	2.5	4.6	4.9	14.3	6.4	11.8	15.6	14.0
12 105	3980	2	Polk	4 855	483 924	119	99.7	80.9	14.1	0.8	1.3	9.5	6.4	18.0	8.3	12.3	14.2	12.3
12 107	...	6	Putnam	1 870	70 423	705	37.7	78.9	17.3	0.9	0.7	5.9	6.1	18.4	7.7	10.4	13.8	13.4
12 109	3600	2	St. Johns	1 577	123 135	439	78.1	91.8	6.5	0.6	1.3	2.6	5.4	17.7	7.0	10.8	16.8	15.8
12 111	2710	2	St. Lucie	1 483	192 695	285	129.9	80.3	16.2	0.6	1.3	8.2	5.6	17.0	6.6	10.6	14.5	12.3
12 113	6080	2	Santa Rosa	2 634	117 743	460	44.7	92.5	4.6	1.9	2.1	2.5	6.5	20.0	7.2	13.0	18.2	14.1

1. MSA = Metropolitan Statistical Area. PMSA = Primary MSA. NECMA = New England County Metropolitan Area. See Appendix A for explanation of these concepts. See Appendix B for list of metropolitan areas identified by type, with component counties.　2. County typology code from the Economic Research Service of USDA. See Appendix A for definition.　3. Dry land or land partially or temporarily covered by water.　4. Hispanic persons may be of any race.

STATE County	Age (percent) (cont'd)				Population — change and components of change, 1990-2001							Households, 2000				
					Total persons		Percent change		Components of change, 2000-2001						Percent	
	55 to 64 years	65 to 74 years	75 years and over	Percent female	2001	1990	1990-2000	2000-2001	Births	Deaths	Net migration	Number	Percent change, 1990-2000	Persons per household	Female family householder[1]	One person
	16	17	18	19	20	21	22	23	24	25	26	27	28	29	30	31
DELAWARE	9.1	7.2	5.8	51.4	796 165	666 168	17.6	1.6	13 862	8 592	7 540	298 736	20.7	2.54	13.1	25.0
Kent	8.7	6.6	5.0	51.8	129 066	110 993	14.1	1.9	2 445	1 401	1 364	47 224	19.1	2.61	13.8	23.0
New Castle	8.3	6.2	5.4	51.4	505 829	441 946	13.2	1.1	8 969	5 098	1 945	188 935	15.1	2.56	13.4	25.7
Sussex	12.0	10.9	7.6	51.1	161 270	113 229	38.3	3.0	2 448	2 093	4 231	62 577	43.3	2.45	11.3	24.3
DISTRICT OF COLUMBIA	8.7	6.3	5.9	52.9	571 822	606 900	-5.7	0.0	10 181	7 589	-2 757	248 338	-0.5	2.16	18.9	43.8
District of Columbia	8.7	6.3	5.9	52.9	571 822	606 900	-5.7	0.0	10 181	7 589	-2 757	248 338	-0.5	2.16	18.9	43.8
FLORIDA	9.8	9.1	8.5	51.2	16 396 515	12 938 071	23.5	2.6	256 107	204 172	359 194	6 337 929	23.4	2.46	12.0	26.6
Alachua	7.1	5.0	4.6	51.2	218 795	181 596	20.0	0.4	3 184	2 014	-277	87 509	22.8	2.34	12.3	29.1
Baker	8.9	5.8	3.4	47.5	22 707	18 486	20.4	2.0	467	224	208	7 043	26.8	2.86	13.1	17.1
Bay	10.0	7.9	5.4	50.5	150 316	126 994	16.7	1.4	2 536	1 739	1 354	59 597	21.8	2.43	12.0	26.0
Bradford	9.7	7.0	5.9	44.1	26 423	22 515	15.9	1.3	403	327	262	8 497	18.1	2.58	13.3	22.9
Brevard	11.0	10.9	9.0	51.0	489 522	398 978	19.4	2.8	6 126	6 084	13 117	198 195	22.8	2.35	10.2	26.9
Broward	8.4	7.2	8.9	51.7	1 668 560	1 255 531	29.3	2.8	27 574	20 344	38 431	654 445	23.8	2.45	12.5	29.6
Calhoun	9.8	7.3	6.6	46.0	13 020	11 011	18.2	0.0	196	188	-4	4 468	17.8	2.53	13.5	26.5
Charlotte	14.5	18.4	16.3	52.2	147 009	110 975	27.6	3.8	1 248	2 614	6 631	63 864	31.9	2.18	7.2	26.0
Citrus	14.8	17.4	14.8	52.0	122 470	93 513	26.3	3.7	1 012	2 476	5 742	52 634	29.7	2.20	7.6	26.1
Clay	9.3	5.6	4.2	50.8	147 542	105 986	32.9	4.8	2 231	1 264	5 656	50 243	37.0	2.77	10.7	16.9
Collier	12.7	14.0	10.5	49.9	265 769	152 099	65.3	5.7	3 570	2 694	13 275	102 973	66.9	2.39	7.2	24.5
Columbia	10.3	8.0	5.9	49.3	57 841	42 613	32.6	2.3	981	707	1 049	20 925	34.0	2.56	12.9	23.8
De Soto	10.1	10.6	8.4	43.8	32 438	23 865	35.0	0.7	544	324	8	10 746	30.7	2.70	10.3	21.0
Dixie	12.7	10.7	6.5	46.7	13 992	10 585	30.6	1.2	212	176	130	5 205	32.9	2.44	10.6	23.9
Duval	7.9	5.6	4.9	51.5	792 434	672 971	15.7	1.7	16 263	8 423	5 994	303 747	18.1	2.51	15.6	26.5
Escambia	9.2	7.3	6.1	50.3	293 205	262 445	12.2	-0.4	5 191	3 656	-2 648	111 049	12.6	2.45	15.1	26.9
Flagler	15.1	17.1	11.6	52.1	54 964	28 701	73.6	10.3	446	808	5 338	21 294	79.2	2.32	8.1	21.6
Franklin	13.3	8.9	6.8	43.5	11 202	8 967	23.3	1.3	167	139	115	4 096	12.9	2.28	9.8	28.7
Gadsden	9.2	6.8	5.4	52.4	45 321	41 116	9.7	0.5	991	554	-187	15 867	18.4	2.69	22.5	23.9
Gilchrist	10.3	7.9	5.7	47.1	14 829	9 667	49.3	2.7	215	174	347	5 021	52.9	2.61	11.2	21.1
Glades	13.0	11.9	6.9	45.1	10 750	7 591	39.3	1.6	108	120	181	3 852	33.5	2.51	8.6	22.7
Gulf	11.8	9.6	6.6	46.6	13 417	11 504	15.9	0.6	178	197	106	4 931	14.0	2.42	11.9	25.5
Hamilton	8.9	6.4	4.8	42.5	13 504	10 930	21.9	1.3	232	128	77	4 161	19.3	2.60	16.8	24.1
Hardee	8.4	7.9	6.0	45.6	26 759	19 499	38.2	-0.7	527	304	-408	8 166	27.8	3.06	11.1	18.0
Hendry	7.8	5.9	4.2	44.4	36 562	25 773	40.5	1.0	807	316	-145	10 850	29.1	3.09	12.5	18.6
Hernando	12.6	16.3	14.5	52.5	135 751	101 115	29.4	3.8	1 363	2 602	6 083	55 425	31.0	2.32	8.7	23.3
Highlands	12.0	17.1	15.9	51.2	88 972	68 432	27.7	1.8	1 086	1 533	2 063	37 471	26.8	2.30	8.5	26.3
Hillsborough	8.4	6.4	5.6	51.1	1 027 318	834 054	19.8	2.8	18 751	10 727	20 365	391 357	20.5	2.51	13.2	26.9
Holmes	10.9	7.9	6.9	47.0	18 811	15 778	17.7	1.3	246	303	298	6 921	19.3	2.43	10.8	26.1
Indian River	11.2	14.6	14.6	51.6	116 488	90 208	25.2	3.1	1 335	1 908	4 058	49 137	29.1	2.25	8.9	28.2
Jackson	10.0	7.7	6.8	47.5	46 751	41 375	13.0	0.0	718	723	22	16 620	14.9	2.44	14.4	27.0
Jefferson	10.1	7.7	6.7	49.0	12 946	11 296	14.2	0.3	213	177	12	4 695	17.9	2.53	15.1	25.2
Lafayette	9.4	7.1	5.3	40.2	7 245	5 578	25.9	3.2	98	77	201	2 142	24.5	2.66	9.2	22.0
Lake	12.2	14.4	12.0	51.6	227 598	152 104	38.4	8.1	2 844	3 507	17 229	88 413	39.0	2.34	8.5	24.6
Lee	12.4	13.7	11.7	51.1	462 455	335 113	31.6	4.9	6 003	6 024	21 207	188 599	34.6	2.31	8.7	25.8
Leon	7.0	4.4	3.9	52.3	239 376	192 493	24.4	0.0	4 018	1 788	-2 286	96 521	29.0	2.34	13.0	29.7
Levy	12.8	10.3	7.6	51.6	35 520	25 912	32.9	3.1	485	524	1 093	13 867	37.6	2.44	11.8	24.9
Liberty	8.9	6.2	4.0	40.8	7 067	5 569	26.1	0.7	105	67	7	2 222	30.2	2.51	13.2	25.9
Madison	9.8	7.5	7.0	48.2	18 718	16 569	13.1	-0.1	278	301	14	6 629	20.0	2.57	17.5	25.4
Manatee	10.9	12.5	12.4	51.7	274 523	211 707	24.7	4.0	3 892	4 324	10 779	112 460	23.5	2.29	9.4	28.4
Marion	11.8	12.6	10.9	51.7	267 889	194 835	32.9	3.5	3 565	3 941	9 199	106 755	36.6	2.36	10.7	25.0
Martin	11.9	14.2	14.1	50.9	130 313	100 900	25.6	2.8	1 451	1 979	4 065	55 288	28.5	2.23	7.4	29.0
Miami-Dade	9.2	7.2	6.1	51.7	2 289 683	1 937 194	16.3	1.6	41 489	23 895	18 550	776 774	12.2	2.84	17.2	23.3
Monroe	12.5	8.5	6.1	46.8	78 556	78 024	2.0	-1.3	933	913	-1 065	35 086	4.5	2.23	7.3	28.8
Nassau	11.3	7.9	4.7	50.7	59 830	43 941	31.2	3.8	968	539	1 709	21 980	35.7	2.59	9.9	20.1
Okaloosa	9.3	7.4	4.7	49.5	173 065	143 777	18.6	1.5	2 927	1 585	1 336	66 269	24.3	2.49	10.2	23.5
Okeechobee	10.4	9.5	6.8	46.4	36 385	29 627	21.2	1.3	597	516	406	12 593	23.3	2.69	10.7	21.5
Orange	7.5	5.5	4.5	50.5	923 311	677 491	32.3	3.0	17 151	7 315	17 205	336 286	32.0	2.61	13.7	24.2
Osceola	8.7	6.4	5.0	50.7	181 932	107 728	60.1	5.5	2 939	1 639	7 980	60 977	55.8	2.79	12.8	19.1
Palm Beach	9.6	10.8	12.3	51.7	1 165 049	863 503	31.0	3.0	17 057	16 200	32 835	474 175	29.7	2.34	9.7	29.2
Pasco	11.0	12.9	13.9	52.0	362 658	281 131	22.6	5.2	4 390	6 380	19 465	147 566	21.3	2.30	8.9	27.3
Pinellas	10.4	10.5	12.0	52.4	924 610	851 659	8.2	0.3	12 143	16 418	7 592	414 968	9.0	2.17	10.5	34.1
Polk	10.3	9.9	8.4	50.9	492 751	405 382	19.4	1.8	8 446	6 641	7 075	187 233	20.0	2.52	12.0	24.1
Putnam	11.6	10.8	7.6	50.6	70 880	65 070	8.2	0.6	1 207	1 126	377	27 839	11.0	2.48	12.9	25.1
St. Johns	10.7	8.8	7.1	51.4	131 684	83 829	46.9	6.9	1 552	1 419	8 208	49 614	48.4	2.44	8.9	24.3
St. Lucie	10.7	12.3	10.4	51.2	200 018	150 171	28.3	3.8	2 895	2 713	7 053	76 933	32.2	2.47	11.1	23.5
Santa Rosa	9.9	6.9	4.1	49.8	123 101	81 961	43.7	4.6	1 997	1 112	4 390	43 793	46.5	2.63	10.2	19.3

1. No spouse present.

STATE County	Births, average 1997-1999		Deaths, average 1997-1999				Physicians,[4] 2000		Hospitals,[4] 1998			Medicare enrollees 2000	Serious crimes known to police, 2000[6]	
			Number		Rate					Beds			Total	
	Total	Rate[1]	Total	Infant[2]	Total[1]	Infant[3]	Number	Rate[5]	Number	Number	Rate[5]		Number	Rate[7]
	32	33	34	35	36	37	38	39	40	41	42	43	44	45
DELAWARE	10 377	13.9	6 585	87	8.8	8.4	1 677	214	9	1 990	268	112 090	35 090	4 478
Kent	1 827	14.7	1 032	14	8.3	7.7	184	145	1	190	153	16 236	5 223	4 122
New Castle	6 734	13.9	3 966	57	8.2	8.5	1 234	247	5	1 423	295	64 366	23 904	4 778
Sussex	1 816	13.3	1 587	16	11.6	8.8	259	165	3	377	276	31 377	5 390	3 441
DISTRICT OF COLUMBIA	7 182	13.7	6 086	105	11.6	14.6	4 093	715	10	4 322	826	75 325	41 626	7 277
District of Columbia	7 182	13.7	6 086	105	11.6	14.6	0	0	10	4 322	826	75 325	41 621	7 276
FLORIDA	192 919	12.9	158 629	1 412	10.6	7.3	33 929	212	214	51 241	344	2 803 961	910 154	5 695
Alachua	2 485	12.5	1 494	24	7.5	9.8	1 202	551	3	1 057	532	25 596	14 741	6 763
Baker	305	14.5	173	NA	8.2	NA	21	94	1	93	441	2 526	556	2 498
Bay	1 987	13.5	1 331	19	9.0	9.4	239	161	2	478	325	23 078	7 986	5 388
Bradford	305	12.3	260	NA	10.5	NA	12	46	1	23	93	3 332	888	3 552
Brevard	5 050	10.9	4 771	22	10.3	4.4	819	172	5	1 190	255	95 777	17 204	4 249
Broward	20 321	13.5	15 925	143	10.6	7.0	3 487	215	20	5 538	368	250 023	77 241	4 759
Calhoun	153	12.3	132	NA	10.6	NA	8	61	1	36	290	2 030	NA	NA
Charlotte	1 049	7.8	2 060	4	15.3	3.8	292	206	3	652	483	39 041	3 297	2 328
Citrus	879	7.7	1 883	NA	16.6	NA	201	170	2	299	262	35 572	2 695	2 421
Clay	1 813	13.2	998	15	7.3	8.1	211	150	2	284	207	15 317	5 100	3 766
Collier	2 599	13.0	2 158	20	10.8	7.8	557	222	2	500	251	49 246	9 954	3 960
Columbia	725	13.7	569	NA	10.8	NA	99	175	2	145	274	9 075	NA	NA
De Soto	368	14.9	279	NA	11.3	NA	45	140	1	82	330	5 069	1 244	3 862
Dixie	156	12.1	149	NA	11.6	NA	4	29	0	0	0	2 572	445	3 218
Duval	11 796	16.0	6 425	119	8.7	10.1	1 907	245	7	2 615	355	94 339	54 115	6 962
Escambia	3 933	13.9	2 729	36	9.7	9.2	691	235	3	1 555	551	43 668	11 273	4 733
Flagler	377	8.0	584	NA	12.4	NA	45	90	1	81	171	14 253	1 394	2 797
Franklin	120	11.9	132	NA	13.1	NA	8	72	1	29	288	1 880	263	2 696
Gadsden	654	14.8	433	12	9.8	18.9	52	115	0	0	0	6 880	1 981	4 739
Gilchrist	169	12.3	134	NA	9.7	NA	9	62	0	0	0	2 159	419	2 902
Glades	98	11.5	95	NA	11.1	NA	3	28	0	0	0	915	353	3 338
Gulf	142	10.5	157	NA	11.6	NA	12	90	1	45	334	2 549	310	2 325
Hamilton	164	13.0	115	NA	9.1	NA	4	30	1	42	332	1 878	408	3 495
Hardee	397	18.8	208	NA	9.8	NA	15	56	1	50	238	3 377	1 021	4 036
Hendry	602	20.5	240	NA	8.2	NA	23	64	1	66	225	3 682	1 545	4 267
Hernando	1 099	8.7	1 966	9	15.5	8.5	165	126	3	316	248	41 330	5 360	4 098
Highlands	802	10.7	1 252	NA	16.7	NA	137	157	3	327	435	25 496	3 329	3 810
Hillsborough	13 875	15.0	8 166	114	8.8	8.2	2 411	241	10	2 943	318	134 944	71 448	7 152
Holmes	206	11.1	220	NA	11.8	NA	12	65	1	34	183	3 508	235	1 266
Indian River	998	10.1	1 417	NA	14.3	NA	249	220	2	480	484	31 875	5 025	4 449
Jackson	516	11.4	509	NA	11.2	NA	41	88	2	129	283	8 429	1 308	3 082
Jefferson	152	11.8	140	NA	10.8	NA	6	47	0	0	0	2 079	390	3 023
Lafayette	77	12.2	52	NA	8.1	NA	3	43	0	0	0	700	NA	NA
Lake	2 172	10.7	2 644	15	13.1	6.8	281	133	4	706	349	61 231	8 687	4 126
Lee	4 568	11.6	4 810	35	12.2	7.6	846	192	6	1 707	434	100 842	21 332	4 838
Leon	2 822	13.0	1 409	33	6.5	11.6	461	193	2	812	374	21 742	16 684	6 968
Levy	371	11.7	390	NA	12.3	NA	16	46	1	25	79	6 712	1 652	4 795
Liberty	76	11.3	56	NA	8.3	NA	0	0	0	0	0	908	96	1 367
Madison	225	12.7	192	NA	10.9	NA	10	53	1	57	323	3 126	1 243	6 635
Manatee	2 868	12.0	3 249	19	13.6	6.5	459	174	2	903	377	54 054	13 860	5 250
Marion	2 754	11.4	3 096	23	12.8	8.5	368	142	2	534	221	68 107	11 853	4 578
Martin	1 136	9.8	1 526	9	13.2	8.2	298	235	2	307	265	33 988	4 371	3 449
Miami-Dade	31 072	14.4	18 721	174	8.7	5.6	6 355	282	25	8 657	402	308 583	185 540	8 234
Monroe	812	10.1	716	NA	8.9	NA	188	236	4	342	421	10 996	5 565	6 992
Nassau	715	12.9	466	NA	8.4	NA	41	71	1	48	87	8 093	1 867	3 963
Okaloosa	2 361	14.0	1 213	19	7.2	8.0	298	175	3	433	256	24 355	4 774	3 006
Okeechobee	496	15.7	386	NA	12.2	NA	44	123	1	101	324	6 774	1 564	4 355
Orange	12 437	15.5	5 906	91	7.4	7.3	1 759	196	9	2 816	349	105 029	64 027	7 163
Osceola	2 174	12.9	1 257	15	8.6	6.9	207	120	3	365	251	21 784	10 418	6 040
Palm Beach	12 850	12.5	12 805	82	12.4	6.4	2 784	246	14	3 294	319	241 129	71 962	6 554
Pasco	3 426	10.5	5 081	21	15.6	6.2	509	148	5	941	289	85 079	14 090	4 087
Pinellas	9 289	10.6	12 717	75	14.5	8.0	2 342	254	15	3 931	448	203 728	49 359	5 356
Polk	6 363	14.1	5 086	55	11.2	8.6	714	148	5	1 430	316	89 156	28 140	5 850
Putnam	884	12.6	855	NA	12.2	NA	83	118	1	161	229	13 778	4 389	6 366
St. Johns	1 266	10.9	1 069	9	9.2	7.4	215	175	2	230	198	20 940	4 176	3 391
St. Lucie	2 223	12.4	2 136	17	11.9	7.8	282	146	2	485	271	40 672	8 860	4 598
Santa Rosa	1 562	13.3	827	11	7.1	7.0	93	79	3	237	202	15 124	2 544	2 161

1. Per 1,000 estimated resident population, average 1997-1999. 2. Deaths of infants under 1 year old. 3. Deaths of infants under 1 year old per 1,000 live births. 4. Data subject to copyright. 5. Per 100,000 resident population as of July 1 of the year shown. 6. Data for serious crimes have not been adjusted for underreporting; this may affect comparability between geographic areas and over time. 7. Per 100,000 population estimated by the FBI.

Table B. States and Counties — Crime, Education, Money Income, and Poverty

STATE County	Serious crimes known to police, 2000[1] (cont'd) Rate[2]		Education						Money income 1989				Income and poverty, 1998			
			School enrollment and attainment, 1990				Local government expenditures, fiscal 1999[5]			Households				Percent below poverty level		
			Enrollment[3]		Attainment[4] (percent)						Median						
	Violent	Property	Total	Percent private	High school graduate or more	Bachelor's degree or more	Total current expenditures (mil dol)	Current expenditures per student (dollars)	Per capita[6] (dollars)	Dollars	Percent change, 1979–1989 (constant 1989 dollars)	Percent with $100,000 or more	Median household income	All persons	Persons under 18	Persons 5–17 in families
	46	47	48	49	50	51	52	53	54	55	56	57	58	59	60	61
DELAWARE	684	3 794	171 219	20.9	77.5	21.4	872.8	7 706	15 854	34 875	16.6	4.5	42 662	9.7	15.0	13.7
Kent	638	3 485	29 454	13.8	73.1	15.0	147.4	7 076	12 726	29 497	14.7	2.4	37 538	11.9	17.2	16.6
New Castle	653	4 125	117 099	25.3	80.6	25.2	516.5	7 788	17 442	38 617	17.2	5.6	50 090	8.5	13.1	11.7
Sussex	568	2 874	24 666	9.0	69.7	13.0	189.6	7 535	12 723	26 904	10.8	2.4	34 676	12.1	19.7	18.1
DISTRICT OF COLUMBIA	1 508	5 769	151 248	35.8	73.1	33.3	693.7	9 650	18 881	30 727	13.1	7.8	36 442	18.2	30.5	30.2
District of Columbia	1 507	5 768	151 248	35.8	73.1	33.3	693.4	9 645	18 881	30 727	13.1	7.8	36 442	18.2	30.5	30.2
FLORIDA	812	4 883	2 926 662	16.0	74.4	18.3	13 534.4	5 790	14 698	27 483	11.7	3.9	34 757	13.6	21.9	20.0
Alachua	961	5 802	71 842	7.3	82.7	34.6	165.9	5 592	12 252	22 084	6.7	3.0	33 585	17.1	23.3	23.1
Baker	413	2 085	4 783	3.7	64.1	5.7	24.6	5 207	9 417	25 816	7.0	1.4	33 966	15.9	20.2	20.8
Bay	617	4 771	32 011	9.5	74.7	15.7	137.1	5 285	12 225	24 684	11.0	2.0	33 070	14.6	22.5	22.1
Bradford	592	2 960	4 932	4.8	65.0	8.1	22.2	5 328	10 287	24 625	24.3	1.1	31 413	18.7	23.9	26.7
Brevard	696	3 553	90 909	17.5	82.3	20.4	345.0	5 024	15 093	30 534	8.1	2.8	38 249	10.5	17.5	15.8
Broward	603	4 156	263 345	20.1	76.8	18.8	1 306.1	5 650	16 883	30 571	10.0	4.7	40 589	11.0	17.9	15.4
Calhoun	NA	NA	2 864	5.4	55.9	8.2	11.8	5 182	8 867	18 615	4.2	2.3	26 406	21.3	25.3	29.5
Charlotte	220	2 108	16 107	11.9	75.7	13.4	92.5	5 585	14 431	25 746	16.5	2.6	33 253	9.5	18.3	17.7
Citrus	296	2 126	14 735	8.1	68.6	10.4	84.2	5 756	12 151	21 285	12.8	1.4	28 222	13.6	24.3	24.1
Clay	368	3 398	29 105	11.6	81.2	17.9	135.5	4 954	13 945	34 860	13.0	2.8	45 023	7.7	11.7	10.4
Collier	548	3 412	27 492	11.9	79.0	22.3	197.5	6 415	21 386	34 001	22.1	9.1	42 732	10.3	19.2	18.4
Columbia	NA	NA	10 868	8.3	69.0	11.0	51.2	5 435	10 324	21 961	2.4	1.7	29 565	18.5	26.2	27.3
De Soto	832	3 030	4 711	7.5	54.5	7.6	25.7	5 539	10 286	20 962	10.8	1.7	26 960	22.0	35.4	34.1
Dixie	419	2 799	2 000	4.5	57.7	6.2	12.9	5 392	8 527	15 380	-4.7	1.5	23 852	23.0	32.8	37.0
Duval	1 095	5 868	163 788	16.6	76.9	18.4	667.7	5 241	13 857	28 513	13.9	2.9	37 739	12.8	19.7	17.4
Escambia	766	3 967	68 858	13.8	76.2	18.2	249.8	5 471	12 161	25 158	3.9	2.2	31 891	16.9	25.6	23.7
Flagler	301	2 496	5 340	10.3	78.7	17.3	37.0	6 093	15 124	28 628	17.3	3.2	36 072	9.8	18.8	18.3
Franklin	205	2 491	1 895	7.7	59.5	12.4	9.3	6 166	9 954	17 247	9.0	2.1	25 799	18.4	25.1	28.6
Gadsden	794	3 945	11 311	9.7	59.9	11.2	47.3	5 662	8 597	19 985	7.3	1.3	26 355	23.9	32.7	32.3
Gilchrist	526	2 376	2 140	7.9	63.0	7.4	14.6	5 367	9 690	20 632	14.2	0.4	29 197	16.7	22.8	25.6
Glades	303	3 035	1 577	11.7	57.4	7.1	6.8	5 795	10 719	20 687	22.5	1.2	27 747	17.7	29.7	28.8
Gulf	458	1 868	2 611	4.7	66.4	9.2	13.6	5 912	10 028	21 866	7.9	0.4	29 147	18.1	25.3	28.0
Hamilton	865	2 630	2 774	3.1	58.4	7.0	14.0	6 235	8 851	18 709	5.7	1.2	24 610	24.5	29.2	32.4
Hardee	403	3 633	4 510	3.3	54.8	8.6	28.8	5 563	9 411	22 065	9.5	2.3	27 007	26.7	38.9	36.9
Hendry	748	3 518	6 790	7.3	56.6	10.0	41.8	5 596	10 035	24 904	2.0	2.1	29 775	22.1	32.8	31.6
Hernando	647	3 451	16 891	9.5	70.5	9.7	86.0	5 240	11 864	22 741	9.7	1.4	29 118	12.6	22.6	22.2
Highlands	507	3 303	11 006	9.8	68.2	10.9	65.5	5 903	12 112	21 146	11.8	1.9	27 177	16.4	31.8	29.0
Hillsborough	1 127	6 025	203 572	16.9	75.6	20.2	915.5	5 851	14 203	28 477	14.3	3.5	37 362	14.3	22.7	19.8
Holmes	312	953	3 607	3.7	57.1	7.4	20.9	5 598	8 609	17 241	4.1	0.9	24 687	23.9	33.5	33.8
Indian River	386	4 063	16 602	15.1	76.5	19.1	81.1	5 550	17 825	28 961	14.4	5.8	37 398	11.3	21.2	19.7
Jackson	761	2 321	10 802	6.4	61.6	10.9	43.6	5 569	9 654	19 471	9.2	1.3	26 963	18.9	25.7	25.7
Jefferson	698	2 325	3 014	9.0	64.1	14.7	12.2	6 187	9 744	21 782	32.8	2.6	29 604	20.3	28.1	28.9
Lafayette	NA	NA	1 255	0.7	58.2	5.2	5.9	5 547	8 966	20 744	11.6	1.3	29 621	20.3	24.0	29.9
Lake	873	3 253	26 991	12.8	70.6	12.7	144.4	5 189	12 450	23 395	11.8	1.9	32 898	11.8	21.0	20.0
Lee	590	4 249	59 636	13.1	76.9	16.4	329.5	6 015	15 623	28 448	16.2	4.0	35 520	10.9	19.9	18.4
Leon	1 054	5 913	71 666	9.8	84.9	37.1	180.9	5 724	14 088	27 323	13.5	3.5	39 569	12.8	17.7	16.5
Levy	824	3 971	5 434	6.1	62.8	8.3	33.4	5 354	9 386	18 807	5.0	1.1	25 998	19.1	28.7	28.9
Liberty	256	1 111	1 167	2.3	56.7	7.3	6.8	5 530	11 500	22 253	26.0	0.7	29 562	19.4	24.7	27.3
Madison	710	5 925	3 999	7.1	56.5	9.7	19.6	5 651	9 727	18 153	6.5	1.7	25 875	20.5	27.1	29.6
Manatee	901	4 349	37 553	11.6	75.6	15.5	192.4	5 646	14 444	25 951	14.1	2.9	36 958	11.2	19.6	19.9
Marion	781	3 797	37 941	11.7	69.6	11.5	201.2	5 306	11 782	22 452	13.6	2.0	29 498	15.2	25.3	23.9
Martin	380	3 069	17 470	19.1	79.7	20.3	94.1	5 902	20 328	31 760	20.3	7.6	41 990	10.1	19.5	17.8
Miami-Dade	1 233	7 001	515 611	20.8	65.0	18.8	2 165.1	6 141	13 686	26 909	3.1	4.9	30 669	19.8	29.6	26.3
Monroe	725	6 267	13 043	13.9	79.7	20.3	60.7	6 419	18 869	29 351	27.7	6.4	38 546	10.4	18.5	20.4
Nassau	1 569	2 394	10 571	11.0	71.2	12.5	52.3	5 080	13 288	30 233	6.4	2.6	42 519	9.7	15.2	14.4
Okaloosa	360	2 646	37 715	7.7	83.8	21.0	158.8	5 221	13 147	27 941	10.0	2.0	38 117	10.7	16.5	15.4
Okeechobee	593	3 762	6 842	8.1	59.1	9.8	37.4	5 514	9 792	21 427	5.9	1.5	26 549	19.7	28.7	31.8
Orange	1 071	6 092	161 178	15.1	78.8	21.2	766.3	5 518	14 570	30 252	18.0	3.5	38 327	12.9	20.7	17.8
Osceola	692	5 347	24 293	12.1	73.7	11.2	158.0	5 246	12 268	27 260	25.3	1.6	33 519	13.0	21.1	19.0
Palm Beach	742	5 812	171 097	20.2	78.8	22.1	860.5	5 871	19 937	32 524	16.4	7.2	39 199	11.0	19.2	17.3
Pasco	524	3 562	46 760	11.9	66.9	9.1	259.0	5 622	11 732	21 480	10.1	1.2	30 035	12.8	21.6	20.4
Pinellas	809	4 548	157 458	17.2	78.1	18.5	620.5	5 611	15 712	26 296	17.1	3.4	34 741	11.6	20.0	17.8
Polk	606	5 244	89 009	13.4	68.0	12.9	422.2	5 462	12 392	25 216	5.6	2.4	32 654	15.5	24.9	22.6
Putnam	1 053	5 313	14 792	7.0	64.3	8.3	72.5	5 658	10 079	20 155	5.1	1.4	26 121	21.0	30.9	32.1
St. Johns	476	2 915	18 876	19.9	79.9	23.6	97.6	5 320	17 113	29 926	25.6	6.2	45 345	8.5	13.9	14.1
St. Lucie	752	3 846	31 850	14.0	71.7	13.1	162.5	5 629	13 387	27 710	19.1	2.5	31 625	14.7	24.8	24.0
Santa Rosa	331	1 829	21 043	7.4	78.5	18.6	112.2	5 094	12 656	27 584	9.1	2.6	39 110	11.3	16.8	16.7

1. Data for serious crimes have not been adjusted for underreporting; this may affect comparability between geographic areas and over time. 2. Per 100,000 population estimated by the FBI. 3. All persons 3 years old and over enrolled in nursery school through college. 4. Persons 25 years old and over. 5. Elementary and secondary education expenditures, local government fiscal years ending between July 1, 1998 and June 30, 1999. 6. Based on population enumerated as of April 1, 1990.

Table B. States and Counties — **Personal Income**

STATE County	Total (mil dol)	Percent change, 1998–1999	Per capita¹ Dollars	Per capita¹ Rank	Wages and salaries² (mil dol)	Proprietor's income (mil dol)	Dividends, interest, and rent (mil dol)	Transfer payments Total (mil dol)	Government payments to individuals Total (mil dol)	Social Security (mil dol)	Medical payments (mil dol)	Income mainte-nance (mil dol)	Unemploy-ment insurance (mil dol)
	62	63	64	65	66	67	68	69	70	71	72	73	74
DELAWARE	23 135	6.4	30 701	X	16 570	1 316	4 629	2 692	2 532	1 192	944	207	55
Kent	2 876	3.7	22 819	1 137	1 873	166	471	401	375	166	139	28	12
New Castle	16 933	7.1	34 757	90	13 001	863	3 423	1 626	1 522	708	555	148	32
Sussex	3 325	5.1	23 700	917	1 695	287	735	664	634	318	249	31	11
DISTRICT OF COLUMBIA	20 308	4.0	39 130	X	41 334	2 605	4 180	2 607	2 529	556	1 338	420	63
District of Columbia	20 308	4.0	39 130	48	41 334	2 605	4 180	2 607	2 529	556	1 338	420	63
FLORIDA	419 800	4.6	27 781	X	235 176	26 040	110 286	63 740	60 987	27 281	25 017	4 722	704
Alachua	5 091	3.3	25 648	564	3 596	236	1 026	710	674	231	288	77	5
Baker	389	2.0	18 374	2 449	145	29	50	73	69	24	28	7	1
Bay	3 361	2.9	22 719	1 163	2 023	252	686	567	541	214	214	51	9
Bradford	442	2.0	17 757	2 587	199	22	61	89	85	25	40	12	1
Brevard	11 421	3.4	24 282	809	6 537	501	2 778	2 003	1 917	969	695	99	22
Broward	45 208	4.6	29 442	235	23 588	1 844	12 026	5 945	5 664	2 558	2 468	323	96
Calhoun	219	13.1	17 591	2 628	109	23	29	55	53	17	25	7	1
Charlotte	3 337	4.5	24 356	792	1 019	182	1 316	810	785	450	273	20	3
Citrus	2 379	4.0	20 492	1 837	786	125	793	679	657	378	231	27	5
Clay	3 348	3.5	23 688	920	998	152	549	361	336	161	106	21	4
Collier	9 288	5.1	44 862	21	3 249	845	4 317	916	878	530	287	33	7
Columbia	1 042	2.8	19 395	2 183	565	50	183	224	214	82	89	27	2
De Soto	592	9.5	24 017	853	241	126	108	124	119	49	55	11	1
Dixie	198	2.9	15 321	2 956	70	20	37	60	57	24	21	8	0
Duval	19 841	1.0	26 868	427	17 183	1 228	3 487	2 491	2 361	881	965	260	29
Escambia	6 323	1.8	22 389	1 247	4 617	280	1 284	1 082	1 033	396	400	127	8
Flagler	1 087	6.4	22 144	1 312	306	28	368	237	229	152	63	8	1
Franklin	202	4.0	20 203	1 929	68	25	44	52	50	18	23	6	1
Gadsden	834	4.6	18 922	2 307	396	69	112	183	175	58	70	37	2
Gilchrist	231	4.4	16 416	2 841	63	29	32	50	47	20	20	5	0
Glades	164	9.7	18 905	2 315	32	27	41	29	27	15	7	3	1
Gulf	230	0.3	16 931	2 747	98	14	48	67	65	25	28	6	2
Hamilton	185	3.7	14 460	3 023	140	13	27	48	46	16	19	8	0
Hardee	471	9.8	22 404	1 239	192	110	66	89	85	30	36	13	2
Hendry	732	10.7	24 858	695	341	184	95	107	102	39	42	13	4
Hernando	2 879	4.4	22 412	1 236	807	116	845	788	764	419	274	27	4
Highlands	1 775	5.7	23 734	911	596	201	551	487	473	246	174	26	4
Hillsborough	25 679	4.8	27 304	393	21 395	1 556	4 715	3 332	3 161	1 290	1 226	337	41
Holmes	292	2.5	15 578	2 941	83	34	46	89	85	31	36	11	1
Indian River	3 907	4.8	38 974	50	1 308	232	1 914	593	575	313	210	21	7
Jackson	821	4.7	18 438	2 431	374	58	138	223	215	71	105	25	2
Jefferson	274	5.2	20 916	1 691	71	22	48	52	50	19	19	9	0
Lafayette	109	3.9	16 767	2 786	41	24	14	21	20	9	7	3	0
Lake	4 756	5.3	22 667	1 174	1 731	294	1 430	1 062	1 023	544	381	51	5
Lee	11 160	4.9	27 861	344	5 028	704	4 077	1 959	1 886	1 018	697	76	11
Leon	5 991	4.6	27 748	353	4 830	271	1 028	584	544	212	190	65	6
Levy	593	4.9	18 305	2 468	189	66	121	149	144	68	52	14	1
Liberty	105	4.1	15 699	2 929	49	6	13	22	21	8	8	3	0
Madison	300	4.0	16 720	2 791	134	26	47	79	76	26	32	14	1
Manatee	7 691	4.5	31 582	165	3 310	530	2 409	1 119	1 074	600	360	54	7
Marion	5 440	4.5	22 115	1 325	2 384	359	1 387	1 231	1 186	657	407	80	8
Martin	4 856	3.5	41 114	38	1 588	280	2 426	644	622	348	223	22	6
Miami-Dade	53 811	4.4	24 733	712	37 404	4 114	10 328	9 146	8 748	2 425	4 711	1 212	141
Monroe	2 754	2.8	34 456	93	1 163	193	1 120	269	254	114	101	20	2
Nassau	1 485	3.6	26 141	498	533	74	319	178	168	85	57	12	2
Okaloosa	4 204	3.7	24 720	713	2 911	203	1 051	560	532	218	194	36	6
Okeechobee	625	4.9	19 295	2 212	254	85	115	155	149	59	70	11	2
Orange	22 292	5.9	27 278	396	21 306	1 861	3 604	2 587	2 438	976	1 030	234	28
Osceola	2 973	6.9	19 740	2 075	1 375	161	453	489	462	213	200	33	5
Palm Beach	43 978	4.3	41 907	34	18 150	3 207	17 918	5 153	4 961	2 567	1 963	199	72
Pasco	7 750	6.0	23 435	978	2 051	268	1 740	1 809	1 749	892	676	82	10
Pinellas	27 811	5.7	31 658	162	15 051	1 329	7 438	4 353	4 192	1 975	1 746	216	35
Polk	10 653	5.9	23 294	1 015	5 756	782	2 274	1 890	1 806	889	630	162	21
Putnam	1 269	3.9	18 079	2 524	555	48	237	330	317	136	129	39	3
St. Johns	4 507	7.3	37 654	61	1 216	191	1 161	440	418	213	155	23	3
St. Lucie	4 035	4.7	22 189	1 300	1 502	235	1 121	937	904	443	345	59	18
Santa Rosa	2 743	6.3	22 680	1 171	784	157	462	354	332	149	118	29	4

1. Based on the resident population estimated as of July 1 of the year shown.   2. Includes other labor income.

STATE County	Total (mil dol)	Farm	Goods-related[1] Total	Manu-facturing	Service-related and other[2] Total	Retail trade	Finance, insur-ance, and real estate	Services	Govern-ment	Social Security bene-ficiaries, December 2000 Number	Rate[3]	Supple-mental Security Income recipients, December 2000	Housing units, 1990 Total	Percent change, 1980–1990
	75	76	77	78	79	80	81	82	83	84	85	86	87	88
DELAWARE	17 885	0.7	D	21.2	D	8.7	15.2	24.9	13.8	132 368	169	11 984	289 919	21.5
Kent	2 039	1.3	D	12.6	D	10.7	4.1	19.2	38.8	20 124	159	2 487	42 106	19.1
New Castle	13 864	0.1	D	22.9	D	7.4	17.7	26.1	10.4	75 575	151	7 086	173 560	16.8
Sussex	1 982	4.6	28.2	18.5	55.2	15.6	8.5	22.4	12.0	36 667	234	2 390	74 253	35.8
DISTRICT OF COLUMBIA	43 938	0.0	D	2.3	D	2.1	5.7	40.1	42.1	73 703	129	20 073	278 489	0.5
District of Columbia	43 938	0.0	D	2.3	D	2.1	5.7	40.1	42.1	73 703	129	20 073	278 489	0.5
FLORIDA	261 216	1.3	13.9	7.8	68.1	11.1	9.7	33.4	16.7	3 195 615	200	377 218	6 100 262	39.3
Alachua	3 833	0.6	D	5.2	D	9.5	6.7	30.5	37.3	28 357	130	4 855	79 022	34.1
Baker	174	5.8	10.6	5.3	33.3	9.4	3.1	12.1	50.2	3 214	144	487	5 975	31.4
Bay	2 275	0.1	D	6.5	D	13.3	5.6	27.7	27.9	27 694	187	3 557	65 999	53.8
Bradford	221	2.3	D	10.8	D	9.7	1.8	D	41.8	3 306	127	715	8 099	11.7
Brevard	7 038	0.3	D	19.0	D	9.9	4.4	35.6	17.5	112 990	237	7 736	185 150	62.6
Broward	25 432	0.1	12.8	6.6	72.1	12.6	10.8	33.8	15.0	278 996	172	27 597	628 660	29.3
Calhoun	132	5.5	25.1	17.4	45.2	7.0	2.0	28.0	24.2	2 508	193	515	4 468	25.4
Charlotte	1 200	2.0	D	3.1	D	16.3	6.7	37.8	16.1	50 192	354	1 498	64 641	85.8
Citrus	911	0.3	D	4.7	D	13.1	6.4	33.4	14.9	43 754	371	1 705	49 854	70.8
Clay	1 150	0.8	D	6.3	D	18.1	5.4	32.4	17.4	20 762	147	1 254	40 249	65.4
Collier	4 095	4.2	14.5	2.8	71.6	12.7	14.6	35.3	9.7	56 935	226	1 931	94 165	85.6
Columbia	615	0.9	18.9	11.3	47.8	15.0	2.8	20.4	32.3	10 882	193	2 317	17 818	30.7
De Soto	367	31.0	D	2.1	D	7.0	1.9	10.0	25.9	5 833	181	758	10 310	38.2
Dixie	90	3.0	D	21.1	D	8.8	2.0	11.3	36.0	3 335	241	591	6 445	60.7
Duval	18 411	0.1	13.1	7.3	68.0	9.2	14.6	27.9	18.7	108 653	139	18 446	284 673	25.4
Escambia	4 897	0.1	14.3	7.6	52.5	10.0	4.4	27.6	33.1	51 878	176	8 527	112 230	26.6
Flagler	334	3.7	D	13.9	D	13.8	5.8	32.2	18.7	17 535	352	548	15 215	158.3
Franklin	93	0.0	D	6.0	D	14.9	7.3	21.0	24.0	2 307	209	413	5 891	31.0
Gadsden	464	11.6	D	11.3	D	7.1	1.8	12.1	39.1	8 461	188	2 607	14 859	11.2
Gilchrist	92	18.9	9.0	5.0	32.9	5.3	2.1	13.5	39.2	2 616	181	386	4 071	53.8
Glades	59	38.6	D	D	D	5.0	1.2	13.1	19.8	1 827	173	97	4 624	33.1
Gulf	112	0.0	10.7	5.2	52.5	7.3	4.3	21.7	36.8	3 045	228	409	6 339	33.7
Hamilton	153	3.0	D	D	D	3.7	D	7.3	32.2	2 246	169	595	4 119	23.2
Hardee	303	33.0	D	2.9	37.6	6.1	3.0	12.7	19.8	4 014	149	882	7 941	12.5
Hendry	526	36.1	D	10.2	D	6.5	1.4	7.9	15.8	4 957	137	748	9 945	41.4
Hernando	923	1.0	14.1	5.0	64.4	19.1	6.0	28.6	20.6	47 564	364	2 089	50 018	121.9
Highlands	797	18.8	D	5.4	D	11.6	3.5	24.9	16.4	28 879	331	2 039	40 114	54.3
Hillsborough	22 951	1.1	11.5	6.3	73.5	9.4	11.0	37.3	13.9	156 985	157	26 149	367 740	39.5
Holmes	117	13.4	15.2	7.7	37.0	8.7	2.1	19.0	34.3	4 444	239	712	6 785	18.0
Indian River	1 540	3.8	D	7.8	D	13.6	9.7	32.1	13.3	34 449	305	1 317	47 128	60.2
Jackson	432	4.6	9.2	5.5	38.6	11.9	2.8	13.9	47.6	9 798	210	2 085	16 320	11.9
Jefferson	93	10.8	14.1	5.4	40.5	7.1	6.1	16.8	34.7	2 590	201	683	4 395	14.4
Lafayette	65	30.8	D	6.3	D	4.0	1.7	8.5	32.3	1 134	161	137	2 266	28.5
Lake	2 025	4.3	19.0	6.9	60.7	13.0	7.1	29.6	16.1	63 919	304	3 724	75 707	49.9
Lee	5 732	1.0	15.3	4.3	65.3	15.6	9.8	29.0	18.4	115 298	262	6 086	189 051	70.3
Leon	5 101	0.1	D	2.2	D	8.4	5.7	30.0	42.2	25 388	106	4 008	81 325	36.6
Levy	255	14.7	D	4.5	D	12.4	4.1	15.3	24.5	8 734	254	983	12 307	35.7
Liberty	55	0.6	D	13.1	D	4.8	D	10.0	46.3	1 107	158	217	2 157	6.4
Madison	161	7.3	21.0	19.2	41.0	9.4	2.2	19.6	30.7	3 704	198	1 088	6 275	12.9
Manatee	3 840	4.3	D	14.8	D	11.1	4.9	38.6	11.6	67 433	255	3 520	115 245	37.9
Marion	2 743	2.5	22.5	13.5	56.3	13.9	6.5	24.0	18.7	78 163	302	6 074	94 567	70.9
Martin	1 868	4.0	D	6.9	D	13.6	10.2	33.4	11.0	37 498	296	1 322	54 199	59.4
Miami-Dade	41 518	0.6	9.7	6.1	73.4	9.6	11.0	32.7	16.3	319 860	142	116 250	771 288	15.9
Monroe	1 357	0.0	D	1.4	D	17.8	7.3	34.0	23.7	13 071	164	1 196	46 215	21.3
Nassau	607	2.3	23.5	17.1	48.2	10.7	3.8	23.1	26.0	10 168	176	777	18 726	40.8
Okaloosa	3 114	0.1	8.3	3.8	46.2	10.4	5.0	25.2	45.4	27 883	164	2 402	62 569	45.2
Okeechobee	339	21.6	6.3	1.7	52.5	12.5	2.6	26.2	19.6	7 368	205	879	13 266	38.1
Orange	23 167	0.5	13.7	8.2	75.2	10.2	8.7	41.4	10.6	119 785	134	20 264	282 686	53.0
Osceola	1 536	3.4	12.1	4.9	65.8	17.9	7.3	32.4	18.6	27 454	159	2 800	47 959	101.3
Palm Beach	21 357	2.2	15.0	9.1	71.3	10.2	13.6	35.6	11.5	265 788	235	14 066	461 665	56.1
Pasco	2 319	1.5	13.0	4.7	66.7	15.2	5.9	36.2	18.7	103 176	299	6 453	148 965	47.7
Pinellas	16 380	0.0	D	11.7	D	11.3	10.7	37.5	11.4	221 818	241	15 344	458 341	21.6
Polk	6 538	2.7	22.2	13.3	60.9	15.2	6.1	25.8	14.2	105 981	219	12 260	186 225	38.1
Putnam	603	3.7	29.7	22.4	39.4	12.1	2.7	17.9	27.2	17 196	244	2 696	31 840	34.7
St. Johns	1 407	1.5	D	11.1	D	12.8	7.7	35.1	16.1	24 506	199	1 743	40 712	78.1
St. Lucie	1 737	4.5	D	5.2	D	11.6	5.4	27.8	21.6	50 879	264	4 633	73 843	80.5
Santa Rosa	941	1.3	18.1	6.8	50.9	10.0	6.2	26.5	29.7	19 279	164	1 565	32 831	61.3

1. Covers mining, construction, and manufacturing.   2. Covers private sector earnings in agricultural services, forestry, and fisheries; transportation and public utilities; wholesale trade; retail trade; finance, insurance, and real estate; and services.   3. Per 1,000 resident population estimated as of July 1 of the year shown.

STATE County	Total	Percent	Median value[1]	With a mortgage	Without a mortgage	Median rent[2]	Rent as percent of income	Substandard units[3] (percent)	Total	Percent change, 2000–2001	Total	Rate[4]	Total	Professional, managerial, and technical	Precision production, craft, and repair
	89	90	91	92	93	94	95	96	97	98	99	100	101	102	103
DELAWARE	247 497	70.2	100 100	19.5	12.0	495	24.7	2.5	418 819	2.4	14 705	3.5	335 147	31.0	11.9
Kent	39 655	69.2	80 800	18.8	12.1	422	24.6	3.4	72 364	1.9	2 649	3.7	51 615	25.9	14.0
New Castle	164 161	68.3	110 900	19.8	11.9	524	24.8	2.0	270 059	2.3	9 079	3.4	230 822	34.2	10.4
Sussex	43 681	78.6	79 800	18.8	12.3	383	24.5	3.5	76 396	3.1	2 977	3.9	52 710	22.1	15.9
DISTRICT OF COLUMBIA	249 634	38.9	123 900	20.5	12.8	479	25.4	8.3	277 879	-0.4	18 135	6.5	303 994	44.0	4.5
District of Columbia	249 634	38.9	123 900	20.5	12.8	479	25.4	8.3	277 879	-0.4	18 135	6.5	303 994	44.0	4.5
FLORIDA	5 134 869	67.2	77 100	22.3	12.2	481	28.0	5.7	7 673 565	2.4	364 665	4.8	5 810 467	28.8	11.5
Alachua	71 258	54.1	66 000	20.3	12.4	396	32.8	4.7	107 664	1.0	2 810	2.6	85 785	41.8	7.6
Baker	5 554	79.3	53 400	18.5	12.2	342	26.7	6.7	8 634	-2.4	386	4.5	7 130	19.2	15.3
Bay	48 938	65.5	61 600	20.0	12.3	370	25.2	2.9	65 013	0.4	3 873	6.0	53 222	28.3	11.4
Bradford	7 193	77.0	49 300	18.0	12.8	320	26.0	4.2	9 458	1.7	305	3.2	8 251	21.5	14.0
Brevard	161 365	69.2	75 200	21.0	11.5	483	26.2	2.2	211 968	1.8	9 018	4.3	183 692	34.7	12.8
Broward	528 442	68.0	91 800	23.6	13.1	575	29.0	5.2	811 864	3.7	39 814	4.9	599 119	29.9	11.7
Calhoun	3 793	79.4	33 200	21.6	14.1	244	25.1	6.1	4 353	-4.4	222	5.1	3 865	19.2	11.9
Charlotte	48 433	79.6	77 200	23.7	11.9	500	25.8	2.1	52 044	4.9	1 744	3.4	38 468	26.2	13.8
Citrus	40 573	83.2	66 100	22.5	11.4	382	26.6	2.1	38 479	3.3	2 294	6.0	29 904	24.8	14.9
Clay	36 663	73.4	82 100	21.6	11.1	494	25.7	2.9	74 272	1.9	2 701	3.6	48 601	28.9	12.4
Collier	61 703	70.2	121 400	22.7	11.7	572	26.5	5.5	108 014	7.6	4 221	3.9	68 449	25.9	12.9
Columbia	15 611	73.7	47 300	19.7	12.7	312	26.8	6.2	24 892	2.6	1 603	6.4	17 569	23.5	14.3
De Soto	8 222	74.0	49 600	20.0	11.6	353	26.5	7.2	8 572	-0.8	515	6.0	8 770	17.7	12.0
Dixie	3 916	82.6	37 500	21.6	13.2	264	27.3	6.2	3 690	5.7	246	6.7	3 335	18.2	10.8
Duval	257 245	62.0	64 000	20.6	12.4	431	25.6	4.4	398 854	2.1	17 869	4.5	314 432	28.9	11.1
Escambia	98 608	64.7	57 800	19.9	12.5	387	26.3	3.8	118 476	-0.9	5 921	5.0	108 456	28.9	12.9
Flagler	11 880	76.5	97 500	25.3	11.3	551	26.8	2.4	17 962	1.8	834	4.6	10 542	27.3	12.8
Franklin	3 628	80.5	51 700	26.4	13.3	317	26.4	8.1	4 563	1.1	124	2.7	3 324	21.3	8.2
Gadsden	13 405	75.6	39 500	18.0	13.2	261	24.9	11.6	20 096	1.2	927	4.6	16 215	22.8	9.6
Gilchrist	3 284	85.4	45 900	20.0	12.1	293	26.0	6.6	4 750	6.8	237	5.0	3 572	21.4	16.1
Glades	2 885	78.2	57 200	18.7	11.4	361	28.4	7.5	3 554	-1.1	341	9.6	2 823	21.3	11.2
Gulf	4 324	78.5	43 200	16.9	11.3	301	27.5	3.7	4 721	-1.2	271	5.7	4 531	21.3	16.3
Hamilton	3 488	76.2	36 300	16.3	12.9	242	29.9	9.7	3 209	0.2	335	10.4	3 807	16.6	14.1
Hardee	6 391	75.8	40 300	16.5	12.5	358	27.9	9.2	9 418	0.4	907	9.6	7 773	19.3	11.7
Hendry	8 402	70.8	61 200	17.8	13.7	403	27.0	12.2	14 208	-3.1	1 745	12.3	10 971	20.5	12.7
Hernando	42 300	84.5	71 200	24.1	11.4	426	29.3	2.4	50 428	2.2	2 108	4.2	31 552	22.6	15.8
Highlands	29 544	78.0	58 500	21.3	11.4	371	26.9	3.7	26 026	0.4	1 539	5.9	22 212	23.2	11.3
Hillsborough	324 872	63.1	73 100	22.2	12.5	446	26.4	4.7	581 140	2.4	20 968	3.6	412 188	30.0	10.0
Holmes	5 800	80.8	36 200	20.9	13.0	262	29.9	5.1	6 461	0.3	454	7.0	6 113	19.6	14.4
Indian River	38 057	75.0	78 800	22.0	11.8	505	27.3	2.7	46 700	4.1	3 402	7.3	35 215	27.3	11.9
Jackson	14 465	77.0	41 400	18.3	13.2	257	25.6	4.5	17 012	-1.1	726	4.3	16 422	23.5	9.2
Jefferson	3 982	76.7	43 900	16.0	12.1	311	26.0	10.3	4 725	1.4	278	5.9	4 734	27.6	11.0
Lafayette	1 721	80.7	43 700	19.3	14.3	255	18.6	5.0	2 726	-0.7	102	3.7	2 121	16.3	8.2
Lake	63 616	78.3	67 800	21.6	11.5	387	24.9	2.9	94 566	0.9	3 535	3.7	57 965	22.5	13.1
Lee	140 124	72.1	84 300	22.6	11.8	504	26.2	3.0	192 223	4.9	6 163	3.2	144 465	25.7	13.3
Leon	74 828	56.9	75 200	20.0	12.3	445	30.0	3.9	131 311	0.7	3 783	2.9	103 094	41.2	6.8
Levy	10 079	81.8	49 100	22.4	12.7	297	27.4	5.7	13 895	4.8	698	5.0	9 649	21.6	14.6
Liberty	1 706	80.8	39 600	16.7	11.6	240	22.0	6.3	2 234	0.9	77	3.4	2 024	23.5	10.1
Madison	5 522	76.0	38 800	19.5	15.2	249	27.8	8.9	7 247	-3.3	301	4.2	6 124	20.2	12.1
Manatee	91 060	70.9	79 400	23.1	12.0	488	27.8	3.1	128 383	3.8	4 254	3.3	87 581	25.5	13.3
Marion	78 177	75.6	61 800	22.0	11.7	386	25.4	4.2	98 572	0.0	4 786	4.9	74 958	23.8	12.9
Martin	43 022	76.9	112 700	22.1	11.5	525	25.4	2.9	50 584	2.4	2 821	5.6	41 198	28.9	14.2
Miami-Dade	692 355	54.3	86 500	23.3	13.0	493	31.3	17.6	1 080 432	3.0	74 622	6.9	901 828	27.8	10.7
Monroe	33 583	62.1	151 200	26.1	12.5	589	29.5	6.6	46 280	3.8	1 196	2.6	38 900	27.3	12.1
Nassau	16 192	78.5	72 600	19.1	12.5	415	24.4	4.2	29 937	1.7	1 190	4.0	20 137	23.5	15.7
Okaloosa	53 313	62.2	70 600	21.6	11.5	413	25.5	2.8	83 690	1.7	2 796	3.3	58 554	31.7	11.4
Okeechobee	10 214	72.4	55 600	20.6	12.9	393	26.4	8.4	15 841	1.9	1 112	7.0	12 087	18.1	14.9
Orange	254 852	59.3	81 400	22.5	12.0	517	27.4	4.8	502 753	1.3	20 794	4.1	350 953	29.0	10.6
Osceola	39 150	65.7	75 700	22.8	11.8	526	27.8	5.2	87 445	1.5	3 961	4.5	52 455	21.7	12.9
Palm Beach	365 558	71.9	98 400	23.4	12.4	587	28.1	4.3	540 276	4.0	29 779	5.5	387 274	31.4	11.2
Pasco	121 674	80.9	59 000	23.3	11.6	397	28.1	2.2	144 580	2.7	6 091	4.2	97 682	23.7	14.7
Pinellas	380 635	69.2	73 800	22.6	12.3	463	27.7	2.1	493 556	2.5	18 364	3.7	382 230	30.6	10.8
Polk	155 969	70.5	61 000	19.7	11.9	386	25.4	4.4	205 627	0.8	12 787	6.2	171 677	23.2	13.3
Putnam	25 070	79.0	49 900	18.6	12.3	296	25.8	5.6	26 492	-2.8	1 564	5.9	23 383	20.8	15.8
St. Johns	33 426	70.4	85 800	21.7	12.2	487	25.5	3.3	64 101	1.9	2 223	3.5	39 251	32.2	11.5
St. Lucie	58 174	71.9	73 400	21.6	11.9	512	27.0	4.3	80 116	1.9	6 675	8.3	61 238	23.1	14.8
Santa Rosa	29 900	75.3	65 900	20.8	11.7	367	23.6	3.2	52 196	-1.1	2 296	4.4	34 866	29.4	15.5

1. Specified owner-occupied units.   2. Specified renter-occupied units.   3. Overcrowded or lacking complete plumbing facilities.   4. Percent of civilian labor force.   5. Persons 16 years and older.

Table B. States and Counties — Nonfarm Employment and Agriculture

STATE County	Private nonfarm establishments, employment and payroll, 1999								Agriculture, 1997			Farm operators
	Employment						Annual payroll		Farms			
										Percent with—		Whose principal occupation is farming (percent)
	Number of establishments	Total	Health Care and Social Assistance	Manufacturing	Retail trade	Finance and Insurance	Professional Scientific and Technical Services	Total (mil dol)	Average per employee (dollars)	Number	Less than 50 acres	500 acres and over	
	104	105	106	107	108	109	110	111	112	113	114	115	116
DELAWARE	23 381	360 735	41 163	41 407	50 116	38 190	18 862	12 612	34 962	2 460	47.6	11.9	60.9
Kent	2 979	43 783	5 810	7 339	8 333	2 722	1 541	1 064	24 294	767	40.3	12.0	59.8
New Castle	15 886	268 275	28 305	24 058	31 930	33 818	16 292	10 403	38 776	327	46.8	13.1	51.7
Sussex	4 516	48 677	7 048	10 010	9 853	1 650	1 029	1 146	23 537	1 366	51.9	11.5	63.6
DISTRICT OF COLUMBIA	19 469	404 372	58 299	2 899	18 693	16 504	74 430	18 288	45 225	NA	NA	NA	NA
District of Columbia	19 469	404 372	58 299	2 899	18 693	16 504	74 430	18 288	45 225	NA	NA	NA	NA
FLORIDA	424 089	5 954 982	731 229	420 214	888 690	315 278	338 128	160 962	27 030	34 799	57.9	8.7	45.4
Alachua	5 076	78 917	16 699	5 109	13 401	2 544	4 854	1 889	23 940	1 086	57.9	6.2	40.8
Baker	284	3 620	1 607	D	622	81	54	78	21 654	157	66.2	3.8	45.2
Bay	4 195	53 939	7 622	3 363	10 032	2 783	2 731	1 132	20 992	70	60.0	4.3	40.0
Bradford	396	4 137	1 045	510	886	116	114	74	17 825	274	55.8	4.0	40.5
Brevard	11 358	158 062	20 746	20 127	25 659	4 057	13 050	4 400	27 840	470	74.9	8.7	36.2
Broward	49 501	596 218	75 225	36 232	95 113	34 693	35 920	17 250	28 932	347	86.2	2.3	55.6
Calhoun	232	2 043	441	186	457	67	46	35	17 081	130	33.1	16.2	53.1
Charlotte	2 997	32 143	6 513	677	7 283	1 156	1 380	670	20 836	209	47.8	22.0	47.4
Citrus	2 332	26 340	4 828	1 281	5 150	716	561	574	21 809	294	56.8	8.5	39.8
Clay	2 786	31 647	5 121	2 017	7 312	584	1 127	647	20 433	211	64.0	6.6	44.1
Collier	8 198	87 955	10 422	2 762	16 470	3 422	3 884	2 319	26 370	235	53.6	23.0	46.8
Columbia	1 127	15 078	3 236	1 901	3 093	355	410	340	22 554	600	48.3	6.8	40.2
De Soto	425	4 836	1 775	184	895	166	108	105	21 623	715	53.1	11.9	46.2
Dixie	194	1 313	116	243	318	24	19	24	17 928	155	51.0	10.3	34.8
Duval	20 780	396 912	43 252	28 041	46 436	47 428	22 061	11 297	28 462	320	70.3	6.6	45.9
Escambia	6 696	109 590	17 641	6 871	16 544	3 196	4 805	2 591	23 645	466	59.0	4.5	42.1
Flagler	1 003	9 450	1 064	1 436	1 731	272	356	194	20 510	91	39.6	28.6	53.8
Franklin	302	1 928	D	85	424	107	52	32	16 796	19	57.9	10.5	47.4
Gadsden	597	9 157	3 138	1 677	1 155	247	186	216	23 627	290	37.9	10.3	39.7
Gilchrist	173	1 082	299	114	225	41	31	18	16 821	365	40.0	10.1	45.5
Glades	138	1 480	143	D	366	56	32	30	20 497	188	39.4	28.7	62.8
Gulf	255	2 043	435	221	398	119	64	43	21 146	33	54.5	9.1	27.3
Hamilton	179	2 357	303	D	276	D	17	72	30 574	256	26.2	12.1	39.1
Hardee	364	3 213	734	187	781	181	98	72	22 278	1 045	51.8	9.8	46.5
Hendry	478	4 921	786	713	1 224	202	91	107	21 698	403	40.0	24.8	51.9
Hernando	2 327	24 062	4 830	1 128	5 328	883	638	510	21 187	432	62.7	6.5	39.4
Highlands	1 753	35 560	3 420	1 197	3 915	466	673	597	16 775	779	53.8	13.7	44.4
Hillsborough	26 413	501 962	48 059	31 545	60 395	37 265	38 576	14 909	29 702	2 639	75.8	3.3	45.8
Holmes	256	2 299	675	315	326	48	53	35	15 060	578	28.2	4.5	44.8
Indian River	3 450	37 766	6 067	2 282	8 136	1 382	1 641	883	23 390	437	58.6	10.8	58.6
Jackson	797	8 236	1 388	815	2 106	394	183	150	18 218	844	25.5	14.6	52.6
Jefferson	245	1 706	204	56	384	110	70	30	17 293	342	35.7	13.7	36.8
Lafayette	104	934	133	D	D	42	98	20	21 275	221	27.1	14.0	50.7
Lake	4 446	51 676	9 277	3 434	10 154	1 646	1 861	1 185	22 933	1 389	68.5	6.2	39.8
Lee	12 099	140 147	16 624	5 293	26 933	4 938	8 634	3 379	24 111	509	70.9	10.0	40.3
Leon	6 410	87 961	13 108	2 299	15 777	4 254	7 909	2 210	25 122	243	51.9	6.2	28.8
Levy	630	5 696	434	535	1 413	247	144	107	18 702	549	43.4	13.5	42.3
Liberty	90	734	50	D	67	D	5	16	22 172	47	46.8	4.3	36.2
Madison	324	3 498	554	983	574	57	65	56	16 129	486	20.0	11.1	46.7
Manatee	5 455	112 946	10 163	10 995	12 657	2 300	2 488	2 432	21 535	697	54.1	13.5	51.8
Marion	5 408	71 483	10 583	9 420	13 599	2 291	2 439	1 600	22 382	1 669	62.1	5.0	47.0
Martin	4 219	46 551	6 449	2 688	8 868	1 741	2 393	1 154	24 793	305	59.0	19.0	46.9
Miami-Dade	66 547	863 254	101 724	58 699	113 667	44 184	48 312	25 864	29 961	1 576	87.2	2.9	52.7
Monroe	3 756	32 619	2 383	398	6 989	1 057	1 096	670	20 540	13	61.5	0.0	38.5
Nassau	1 212	12 985	1 388	1 648	2 232	254	444	325	25 049	238	55.5	5.0	39.9
Okaloosa	4 813	57 204	7 023	3 442	10 965	2 200	4 263	1 281	22 386	342	37.1	6.4	36.5
Okeechobee	688	6 871	1 262	153	1 959	222	120	129	18 795	459	35.9	23.1	41.4
Orange	25 874	559 081	43 317	33 494	62 936	22 608	32 003	15 795	28 251	862	77.0	7.0	55.3
Osceola	3 258	47 274	5 131	1 543	8 809	902	948	984	20 814	485	55.9	15.3	49.3
Palm Beach	35 926	427 874	57 929	25 084	65 360	22 886	27 707	13 058	30 519	855	76.0	10.4	57.0
Pasco	6 106	64 050	12 109	4 180	15 027	2 525	2 348	1 352	21 105	951	65.0	6.6	43.2
Pinellas	26 087	408 552	54 270	40 761	54 760	25 877	26 732	11 008	26 945	129	91.5	0.0	41.1
Polk	9 619	157 276	17 356	19 464	22 787	10 998	5 479	3 937	25 032	2 464	62.3	8.6	39.3
Putnam	1 226	12 706	2 002	2 534	2 654	478	277	296	23 280	391	57.0	8.7	46.3
St. Johns	3 306	34 562	4 030	2 363	6 255	1 032	1 457	791	22 895	149	55.0	21.5	61.1
St. Lucie	3 754	39 710	7 295	2 567	7 683	1 463	1 932	915	23 049	500	50.8	13.8	49.6
Santa Rosa	1 944	18 246	2 458	1 687	3 654	643	719	361	19 790	438	43.6	11.6	49.5

Table B. States and Counties — **Agriculture, Land, and Water**

STATE County	Agriculture, 1997 (cont'd)															
	Land in farms					Value of land and buildings		Value of machinery and equipment average per farm ($1,000)	Value of products sold				Percent of farms with sales of —		Percent of land owned by fed. gov. 1997	Water consumption 1995 (mil gal/day)
			Acres								Percent from —					
	Acreage (1,000)	Percent change, 1992–1997	Average size of farm	Total irrigated (1,000)	Total cropland (1,000)	Average per farm ($1,000)	Average per acre (dollars)		Total (mil dol)	Average per farm (dollars)	Crops	Live-stock and poultry products	$10,000 or more	$100,000 or more		
	117	118	119	120	121	122	123	124	125	126	127	128	129	130	131	132
DELAWARE	580	-1.6	236	73	487	610	2 660	76	691	280 811	25.3	74.7	69.8	43.8	2.0	752.1
Kent	195	-1.2	254	21	168	647	2 556	74	154	200 379	40.7	59.3	64.4	29.9	3.7	33.9
New Castle	77	-11.1	236	3	67	908	3 708	84	37	112 976	71.3	28.7	52.0	20.8	0.9	624.7
Sussex	308	0.9	225	49	253	518	2 441	75	500	366 149	17.2	82.8	77.1	57.2	1.3	93.4
DISTRICT OF COLUMBIA	NA	NA	NA	NA	NA	NA	NA	NA	NA	NA	NA	NA	NA	NA	NA	10.2
District of Columbia	NA	NA	NA	NA	NA	NA	NA	NA	NA	NA	NA	NA	NA	NA	NA	10.2
FLORIDA	10 454	-2.9	300	1 862	3 640	663	2 241	41	6 005	172 550	80.2	19.8	42.4	14.9	10.1	7 215.0
Alachua	198	3.8	182	8	75	361	2 209	22	50	46 276	61.9	38.1	32.5	7.7	0.0	48.3
Baker	13	-45.7	83	1	5	247	2 689	37	25	160 535	38.6	61.4	29.3	15.3	22.4	5.4
Bay	7	-25.2	96	0	3	179	1 858	23	3	38 176	91.8	8.2	24.3	4.3	5.1	58.9
Bradford	44	21.1	159	0	10	262	1 680	26	17	63 509	6.7	93.3	27.4	8.0	0.0	7.5
Brevard	277	38.3	588	31	27	909	1 474	33	38	80 758	85.6	14.4	36.0	9.8	12.7	135.5
Broward	31	28.7	89	2	7	414	4 791	33	49	141 280	85.8	14.2	57.6	21.3	0.2	287.3
Calhoun	44	1.9	337	1	27	395	1 298	35	16	124 592	89.5	10.5	47.7	17.7	0.0	4.2
Charlotte	290	27.9	1 389	26	45	1 878	1 359	45	50	240 010	89.4	10.6	51.2	22.0	0.0	49.9
Citrus	49	-30.7	167	1	21	340	2 726	21	6	20 992	59.8	40.2	29.9	4.8	2.2	30.0
Clay	71	-17.6	336	1	8	623	1 992	31	30	142 739	10.9	89.1	22.3	9.5	16.5	21.5
Collier	277	-8.2	1 180	53	69	2 152	1 796	166	277	1 178 401	96.7	3.3	66.8	34.0	35.5	208.2
Columbia	97	0.1	162	3	46	349	1 885	28	22	36 767	46.4	53.6	27.2	5.7	15.8	16.7
De Soto	322	-3.8	451	73	127	1 134	2 510	59	181	253 123	87.6	12.4	52.3	18.9	0.0	70.9
Dixie	34	4.7	216	1	6	211	1 121	17	5	29 844	34.2	65.8	27.1	5.8	6.1	3.4
Duval	36	-11.2	111	1	11	390	3 310	27	26	82 697	36.9	63.1	31.2	8.1	4.6	145.1
Escambia	55	-4.2	117	1	35	248	2 044	36	16	34 727	58.3	41.7	27.0	9.2	3.0	269.6
Flagler	88	68.7	964	8	13	1 236	1 282	84	28	305 906	95.6	4.4	49.5	29.7	0.0	14.2
Franklin	5	0.0	270	0	D	358	1 328	26	D	D		D	52.6	0.0	7.1	2.9
Gadsden	58	-0.1	200	5	24	546	2 521	63	93	319 421	92.2	7.8	36.9	12.1	0.0	16.4
Gilchrist	78	10.0	214	6	44	429	1 911	44	52	311 642	15.0	85.0	38.4	10.7	0.0	9.4
Glades	380	2.8	2 023	26	41	1 663	835	38	59	311 642	64.7	35.3	48.9	23.4	0.0	99.6
Gulf	4	-72.7	116	0	1	132	1 136	16	0	10 876	13.1	86.9	27.3	3.0	0.3	31.1
Hamilton	66	-3.8	259	4	25	303	1 129	30	13	51 094	52.6	47.4	36.3	10.5	0.0	46.2
Hardee	346	5.4	331	54	106	860	2 880	32	155	148 170	75.9	24.1	59.2	18.3	0.0	51.0
Hendry	605	14.1	1 500	184	205	4 289	2 868	178	323	802 575	95.4	4.6	62.3	31.5	0.0	557.0
Hernando	53	-13.1	123	1	21	416	2 963	18	23	53 267	27.6	72.4	28.5	4.6	3.6	41.6
Highlands	490	1.2	628	88	122	1 191	1 909	55	203	260 414	82.4	17.6	54.7	22.7	7.7	119.5
Hillsborough	248	-6.6	94	46	103	391	4 234	31	333	126 084	79.3	20.7	41.0	14.6	0.7	246.3
Holmes	88	0.7	152	0	41	218	1 476	20	32	54 557	16.5	83.5	33.4	13.3	0.0	7.2
Indian River	168	-3.8	385	77	86	1 243	3 169	94	95	217 722	94.7	5.3	59.7	23.6	0.1	212.9
Jackson	245	0.2	290	18	136	300	1 104	41	51	60 965	74.6	25.4	46.6	13.4	0.5	81.1
Jefferson	127	7.3	370	1	33	499	1 429	24	18	52 779	77.4	22.6	35.4	7.6	2.1	11.6
Lafayette	93	-2.7	423	4	22	547	1 207	52	54	245 800	10.8	89.2	54.3	34.8	0.0	7.5
Lake	185	-6.9	133	26	80	407	2 990	27	168	121 049	85.7	14.3	42.4	12.2	12.3	83.1
Lee	129	20.6	253	26	34	724	2 664	38	116	228 678	98.0	2.0	39.9	10.6	0.6	134.0
Leon	68	-33.1	278	3	16	456	1 575	26	3	14 252	38.8	61.2	24.3	1.6	23.4	39.3
Levy	157	-17.6	287	13	68	365	1 325	32	52	94 393	32.0	68.0	43.9	10.6	3.1	23.4
Liberty	7	-39.7	154	0	1	227	1 475	22	1	11 733	7.6	92.6	34.0	0.0	53.2	1.6
Madison	132	-0.3	271	4	54	381	1 397	45	32	65 827	36.5	63.5	31.5	11.3	0.0	9.3
Manatee	268	-10.7	384	58	106	922	2 524	71	240	343 793	91.6	8.4	49.1	17.9	0.0	122.7
Marion	266	-10.3	159	6	100	491	3 094	27	102	60 833	22.6	77.4	31.3	9.3	28.3	52.1
Martin	184	-3.8	602	62	75	1 618	2 704	106	145	475 486	80.5	19.5	53.1	26.2	0.2	170.0
Miami-Dade	85	1.3	54	58	68	408	8 047	49	417	264 278	98.2	1.8	51.2	23.2	33.4	569.3
Monroe	1	0.0	95	0	D	296	3 104	11	D	D		D	7.7	7.7	78.0	1.8
Nassau	35	-21.9	148	0	6	276	2 068	22	28	115 849	2.0	98.0	26.1	12.6	0.0	44.7
Okaloosa	51	-10.8	149	0	21	249	1 608	25	9	25 470	60.9	39.1	21.3	3.8	38.8	29.9
Okeechobee	392	11.3	854	35	73	1 227	1 506	55	138	300 666	24.1	75.9	46.6	17.6	0.0	41.2
Orange	175	26.8	203	25	44	604	3 334	62	248	287 423	98.6	1.4	55.5	27.7	0.1	259.6
Osceola	611	-14.8	1 259	58	51	1 647	1 325	45	89	183 061	68.1	31.9	45.8	16.9	0.0	81.5
Palm Beach	605	-5.2	707	417	529	2 398	3 404	84	873	1 020 908	99.5	0.5	64.1	33.9	10.1	959.8
Pasco	162	-26.7	170	13	58	500	3 149	29	84	88 644	35.8	64.2	35.9	9.1	0.0	141.8
Pinellas	2	-52.6	15	0	1	284	23 143	26	12	91 994	98.7	1.3	41.9	9.3	0.0	44.8
Polk	621	1.7	252	118	187	532	2 110	31	253	102 865	80.5	19.5	48.0	12.5	2.5	391.9
Putnam	86	-19.1	219	7	17	467	2 440	28	34	87 017	89.8	10.2	37.1	11.5	5.1	88.4
St. Johns	50	1.3	333	20	25	749	2 256	141	46	309 042	95.6	4.4	55.0	33.6	0.0	46.4
St. Lucie	227	-24.4	455	139	136	1 183	2 783	60	173	346 274	94.2	5.8	62.4	22.0	0.0	309.9
Santa Rosa	88	11.4	201	5	59	297	1 586	50	30	68 426	93.1	6.9	41.1	17.8	9.9	23.3

STATE County	Value of Residential Construction Authorized by Building Permits, 2000		Wholesale Trade, 1997				Retail Trade[1], 1997				Real Estate and Rental and Leasing, 1997			
	New Construction ($1,000)	Number of Housing Units	Number of Establishments	Number of Employees	Sales (mil dol)	Annual Payroll (mil dol)	Number of Establishments	Number of Employees	Sales (mil dol)	Annual Payroll (mil dol)	Number of Establishments	Number of Employees	Receipts (mil dol)	Annual Payroll (mil dol)
	133	134	135	136	137	138	139	140	141	142	143	144	145	146
DELAWARE	414 088	4 611	906	13 509	12 585.5	619.5	3 736	47 116	8 237.0	798.7	1 101	5 243	5 006.5	118.3
Kent	75 131	858	110	D	D	D	594	7 864	1 325.4	128.3	128	506	49.4	8.0
New Castle	164 782	2 331	637	D	D	D	2 079	30 375	5 367.0	523.1	767	3 712	4 824.3	90.1
Sussex	174 176	1 422	159	1 435	481.2	35.9	1 063	8 877	1 544.5	147.4	206	1 025	132.7	20.1
DISTRICT OF COLUMBIA	53 992	806	348	5 008	3 918.6	223.0	2 075	19 608	2 788.8	351.5	934	7 725	1 354.2	275.4
District of Columbia	53 993	806	348	5 008	3 918.6	223.0	2 075	19 608	2 788.8	351.5	934	7 725	1 354.2	275.4
FLORIDA	17 462 412	155 269	31 214	296 139	187 079.9	9 678.2	66 643	841 814	151 191.2	14 169.5	20 388	118 086	15 360.4	2 652.2
Alachua	164 574	1 973	224	1 824	738.0	54.5	923	12 726	1 934.5	186.2	279	1 630	155.2	28.2
Baker	10 284	111	7	D	D	D	61	630	95.7	7.3	6	26	0.7	0.1
Bay	167 156	1 452	173	1 406	422.1	34.2	832	9 558	1 496.8	148.1	229	1 018	76.8	15.6
Bradford	3 971	59	20	78	31.1	1.7	94	930	151.7	12.7	13	38	3.5	0.4
Brevard	509 727	4 284	577	4 389	1 362.4	136.2	1 856	23 867	3 900.5	370.3	525	2 443	220.0	45.3
Broward	1 486 624	11 970	4 359	38 614	26 122.2	1 414.7	6 804	89 290	17 979.8	1 639.9	2 263	14 394	2 196.6	351.6
Calhoun	1 316	23	13	D	D	D	49	478	81.0	6.4	3	13	0.9	0.1
Charlotte	182 298	1 670	103	446	117.2	11.2	515	6 840	1 063.3	100.4	167	601	60.7	10.1
Citrus	78 697	1 190	88	383	90.4	7.1	429	5 049	800.6	71.8	107	343	33.6	5.7
Clay	162 962	1 528	104	503	220.6	12.7	516	6 956	1 100.5	106.0	114	561	62.3	11.5
Collier	1 188 311	7 970	350	2 076	813.8	63.0	1 343	15 366	2 627.1	274.1	509	2 874	305.2	66.0
Columbia	16 744	289	87	859	286.7	21.6	239	3 132	556.0	49.0	38	94	10.1	1.3
De Soto	14 884	121	19	D	D	D	81	937	197.0	14.9	20	61	5.7	0.8
Dixie	5 782	53	4	D	D	D	42	271	39.2	3.6	6	18	0.6	0.2
Duval	552 244	5 801	1 394	21 860	16 590.0	760.3	3 134	44 276	8 034.1	761.4	886	6 374	918.5	158.4
Escambia	136 707	1 455	388	4 769	1 616.0	128.3	1 301	16 602	2 874.7	261.4	292	1 292	131.8	22.7
Flagler	108 656	1 445	39	272	94.6	7.9	119	1 608	244.1	22.2	53	184	28.3	3.6
Franklin	23 184	131	26	309	64.1	4.4	69	389	57.0	5.6	14	85	6.5	1.4
Gadsden	10 197	80	21	D	D	D	157	1 228	179.8	16.2	15	59	4.0	0.8
Gilchrist	5 656	70	11	D	D	D	34	206	29.9	2.8	6	15	1.0	0.4
Glades	2 385	25	4	D	D	D	27	211	35.2	2.7	11	14	2.7	0.2
Gulf	21 898	188	8	24	28.2	0.6	60	404	48.9	4.7	8	18	1.5	0.2
Hamilton	3 649	36	5	D	D	D	55	393	53.6	4.3	3	33	0.5	0.3
Hardee	4 928	56	21	164	92.4	5.1	79	721	116.8	10.6	9	22	2.5	0.3
Hendry	6 500	75	23	D	D	D	104	1 030	202.6	16.8	22	50	6.8	0.7
Hernando	137 924	1 326	98	513	142.3	13.8	371	5 270	821.5	74.3	97	248	24.2	3.4
Highlands	39 579	450	85	618	184.1	13.1	349	4 035	618.2	57.1	75	249	25.0	3.8
Hillsborough	995 236	11 656	2 233	33 851	23 668.5	1 151.4	3 821	57 038	10 931.6	1 001.4	1 164	8 336	1 034.2	190.0
Holmes	3 141	41	11	D	D	D	55	327	46.3	3.9	6	13	0.9	0.2
Indian River	362 733	2 059	147	D	D	D	667	7 793	1 143.9	121.5	170	714	76.5	12.9
Jackson	16 368	269	42	301	86.0	7.1	221	2 289	376.9	31.6	27	48	4.5	0.7
Jefferson	7 653	70	10	D	D	D	55	426	51.5	4.3	5	19	1.1	0.2
Lafayette	2 624	30	9	D	D	D	17	93	10.0	1.2	2	D	D	D
Lake	437 957	5 231	229	2 137	680.2	48.2	760	9 663	1 514.3	148.2	217	930	82.0	17.3
Lee	1 283 813	9 120	586	4 593	1 450.3	135.3	1 924	25 417	4 367.0	430.5	642	3 328	461.1	72.2
Leon	200 212	2 200	260	D	D	D	1 038	15 478	2 244.4	229.7	301	1 835	202.3	33.1
Levy	15 521	156	21	141	37.7	2.2	132	1 455	234.5	19.2	24	61	4.1	0.8
Liberty	648	6	1	D	D	D	17	83	11.9	1.2	1	D	D	D
Madison	3 757	45	15	128	60.9	2.3	72	567	64.1	6.6	8	25	1.7	0.4
Manatee	411 874	3 452	270	2 348	1 087.6	76.5	938	12 165	2 141.0	194.4	265	1 002	158.6	19.4
Marion	363 776	2 354	309	3 219	999.6	80.0	1 014	13 159	2 221.4	202.1	244	786	88.4	13.8
Martin	248 290	1 384	174	695	423.8	23.7	712	8 425	1 454.0	147.5	211	986	118.6	27.7
Miami-Dade	1 221 757	12 475	8 935	70 050	43 604.4	2 235.9	9 814	110 292	20 720.6	1 995.8	3 378	19 793	2 853.9	465.8
Monroe	26 658	203	131	870	217.5	19.5	707	6 246	914.2	99.5	254	952	108.4	16.1
Nassau	147 037	758	40	238	158.4	8.9	215	2 172	332.2	28.6	43	130	28.0	2.7
Okaloosa	177 457	1 489	139	959	248.3	23.9	931	11 322	1 754.9	165.7	280	1 582	140.3	29.0
Okeechobee	10 828	131	31	D	D	D	149	1 657	270.1	23.6	29	70	8.2	1.5
Orange	907 845	10 239	1 931	25 730	24 089.1	868.5	3 911	53 854	10 450.9	913.6	1 309	14 060	1 952.2	345.5
Osceola	487 061	5 035	108	1 499	1 070.1	41.3	612	8 289	1 349.7	124.8	234	2 884	274.7	60.4
Palm Beach	1 331 563	10 504	2 187	17 864	11 544.5	707.0	4 967	61 563	11 731.2	1 126.1	1 716	9 409	1 323.8	248.3
Pasco	337 234	3 486	243	1 378	351.6	34.1	1 055	14 200	2 247.1	212.5	260	979	116.1	16.9
Pinellas	410 941	2 776	1 730	17 616	11 558.7	609.3	3 895	51 843	10 183.9	911.4	1 238	5 676	630.5	112.9
Polk	330 680	4 746	639	8 329	4 176.2	212.7	1 816	22 751	3 844.3	360.9	431	2 001	217.3	39.8
Putnam	14 913	180	56	D	D	D	250	2 395	397.7	36.1	45	151	12.4	1.9
St. Johns	450 118	2 484	179	1 050	428.0	31.1	549	5 640	862.5	81.0	153	505	83.4	9.6
St. Lucie	193 997	2 093	198	2 262	581.5	53.8	610	7 644	1 387.2	125.1	178	652	85.9	12.1
Santa Rosa	114 447	1 056	82	296	103.1	7.1	319	3 615	561.1	44.2	97	333	27.6	5.1

1. Establishments with payroll.

Items 133—146

	Professional, Scientific, and Technical Services[1], 1997				Manufacturing, 1997				Accommodation and Foodservices, 1997			
STATE County	Number of Establishments	Number of Employees	Receipts (mil dol)	Annual Payroll (mil dol)	Number of Establishments	Number of Employees	Receipts (mil dol)	Annual Payroll (mil dol)	Number of Establishments	Number of Employees	Sales (mil dol)	Annual Payroll (mil dol)
	147	148	149	150	151	152	153	154	155	156	157	158
DELAWARE	1 717	12 382	1 430.4	553.4	675	41 084	13 397.3	1 474.3	1 605	26 969	1 009.0	280.8
Kent	155	1 091	69.4	30.3	82	7 985	1 965.5	209.8	234	3 796	118.4	31.9
New Castle	1 368	10 597	1 314.2	503.2	458	22 610	8 735.0	1 000.1	929	17 837	656.1	187.4
Sussex	194	694	46.8	20.0	135	10 489	2 696.8	264.4	442	5 336	234.5	61.5
DISTRICT OF COLUMBIA	3 760	61 123	10 365.2	3 935.5	200	2 858	320.2	101.1	1 700	42 650	2 263.5	701.4
District of Columbia	3 760	61 123	10 365.2	3 935.5	200	2 858	320.2	101.1	1 700	42 650	2 263.5	701.4
FLORIDA	42 403	276 263	27 231.1	10 803.5	15 992	433 149	77 477.5	13 185.1	28 999	608 834	24 165.3	6 239.5
Alachua	570	3 788	292.8	126.4	151	5 251	1 010.3	157.1	431	8 981	263.0	67.8
Baker	8	32	1.0	0.4	NA	NA	NA	NA	18	380	9.8	2.4
Bay	268	1 730	138.9	56.1	136	3 492	719.0	108.7	483	9 268	336.3	84.8
Bradford	22	72	4.8	1.9	15	698	44.1	10.7	28	698	17.3	4.8
Brevard	1 073	11 192	1 195.6	455.0	494	20 832	3 450.7	753.9	860	16 207	495.3	136.3
Broward	5 625	27 496	2 940.7	1 103.7	1 967	37 134	5 788.3	1 115.4	3 206	61 243	2 474.5	615.5
Calhoun	11	34	1.5	0.5	NA	NA	NA	NA	13	120	4.1	1.1
Charlotte	194	1 083	73.3	37.3	74	587	77.7	13.8	218	3 935	123.5	31.9
Citrus	136	602	38.8	16.0	58	1 025	92.4	18.2	166	2 393	66.3	19.0
Clay	188	685	51.8	19.8	74	1 579	247.2	43.7	195	3 990	114.6	32.7
Collier	743	3 074	414.1	196.5	205	2 305	259.0	62.4	518	11 599	536.7	140.9
Columbia	67	287	21.3	7.8	35	1 798	244.5	46.3	99	2 118	54.1	14.8
De Soto	21	83	4.1	2.0	NA	NA	NA	NA	33	412	12.4	3.0
Dixie	8	14	0.9	0.2	NA	NA	NA	NA	22	152	3.5	0.9
Duval	1 959	17 491	1 552.9	690.0	754	28 237	7 231.0	944.1	1 420	28 354	917.2	244.2
Escambia	547	3 956	306.0	132.3	236	7 526	2 214.1	294.6	493	11 101	350.9	92.3
Flagler	70	242	20.1	7.5	42	1 560	260.7	45.9	88	1 465	42.4	12.8
Franklin	14	48	2.4	0.8	NA	NA	NA	NA	43	393	14.9	3.4
Gadsden	39	133	8.1	2.4	32	1 399	187.8	32.3	39	321	10.7	2.6
Gilchrist	10	38	1.8	0.7	NA	NA	NA	NA	16	D	D	D
Glades	9	34	2.2	0.7	NA	NA	NA	NA	20	129	4.7	1.0
Gulf	15	147	7.5	2.8	12	D	D	D	21	155	4.6	1.2
Hamilton	7	D	D	D	4	D	D	D	13	161	3.7	0.9
Hardee	22	69	3.1	1.4	NA	NA	NA	NA	17	225	7.4	1.6
Hendry	23	71	3.9	1.8	22	724	437.7	26.8	48	644	18.4	5.0
Hernando	132	523	33.0	11.4	72	1 192	235.2	29.4	184	2 772	74.0	19.9
Highlands	106	410	23.4	9.8	54	1 199	191.6	27.0	118	1 817	52.3	13.8
Hillsborough	3 050	34 249	3 859.1	1 403.9	960	30 861	6 019.8	859.3	1 552	34 618	1 248.3	330.4
Holmes	14	53	2.6	0.9	NA	NA	NA	NA	13	160	4.5	1.2
Indian River	281	1 296	103.1	43.3	116	1 825	219.8	55.4	204	3 527	112.4	31.6
Jackson	35	177	11.6	4.6	26	1 344	182.1	27.3	58	931	26.0	7.6
Jefferson	16	36	2.7	0.6	NA	NA	NA	NA	13	121	3.4	0.9
Lafayette	6	D	D	D	NA	NA	NA	NA	13	94	3.1	0.7
Lake	313	1 397	87.7	37.2	164	3 730	578.5	90.2	291	5 161	154.6	42.4
Lee	997	6 053	458.2	197.4	357	5 363	741.8	141.1	824	17 424	699.1	175.2
Leon	838	6 865	702.3	292.9	127	2 676	557.6	68.0	456	9 884	296.8	77.1
Levy	30	104	5.9	2.1	NA	NA	NA	NA	57	809	19.5	5.1
Liberty	1	D	D	D	NA	NA	NA	NA	3	D	D	D
Madison	13	64	3.3	1.2	11	1 114	270.3	25.8	29	433	9.9	2.4
Manatee	445	1 884	147.8	56.1	284	11 156	2 115.7	348.4	390	7 480	241.5	64.5
Marion	361	1 882	132.9	52.8	215	9 620	1 287.8	238.0	363	6 558	200.9	54.1
Martin	409	1 598	141.8	55.5	172	3 274	555.2	101.7	258	4 676	167.8	46.4
Miami-Dade	7 821	42 781	4 640.0	1 856.0	3 031	66 391	8 523.9	1 663.8	3 835	75 597	3 199.5	878.5
Monroe	262	835	72.1	26.6	NA	NA	NA	NA	567	10 939	569.1	151.3
Nassau	65	256	25.9	11.7	34	1 790	630.6	77.3	100	3 102	143.3	37.4
Okaloosa	417	3 181	264.0	113.5	133	3 448	296.5	81.5	401	8 450	261.7	73.0
Okeechobee	28	142	5.9	2.2	NA	NA	NA	NA	60	988	34.8	8.9
Orange	2 878	25 810	2 679.2	1 077.7	889	32 437	5 786.6	1 213.4	1 720	73 124	4 058.7	962.7
Osceola	172	758	50.3	18.8	77	1 295	379.9	37.1	423	12 152	763.0	152.2
Palm Beach	4 211	21 787	2 352.0	985.5	1 051	26 262	6 344.5	1 138.1	2 087	41 031	1 659.8	440.9
Pasco	417	1 931	107.1	41.6	213	4 091	713.3	100.7	437	7 654	246.3	62.6
Pinellas	2 799	26 125	2 187.0	861.6	1 335	40 954	5 732.8	1 256.8	1 965	36 685	1 383.4	367.6
Polk	712	4 006	347.6	135.4	480	20 627	5 999.9	633.5	711	13 383	419.3	113.2
Putnam	67	171	10.8	3.5	48	2 556	730.2	88.9	88	1 318	37.5	9.8
St. Johns	294	961	96.9	34.7	88	2 277	299.6	53.8	332	6 999	263.6	71.1
St. Lucie	257	1 442	91.6	38.6	124	2 230	542.7	60.1	245	3 959	147.6	36.6
Santa Rosa	122	490	34.0	11.4	59	1 895	427.7	41.6	119	1 970	53.8	14.6

1. Firms subject to federal tax.

STATE County	Health Care and Social Assistance[1], 1997				Other Services[1], 1997				Federal funds and grants, fiscal 2001[2]			
									Expenditures (mil dol)			
										Direct payments for individuals[3]		
	Number of Establishments	Number of Employees	Receipts (mil dol)	Annual Payroll (mil dol)	Number of Establishments	Number of Employees	Receipts (mil dol)	Annual Payroll (mil dol)	Total	Social Security and government retirement	Medicare	Food stamps and Supplemental Security Income
	159	160	161	162	163	164	165	166	167	168	169	170
DELAWARE	1 465	15 980	1 131.6	526.4	1 198	7 006	420.5	140.7	4 245.6	1 731.0	604.5	96.4
Kent	192	2 157	137.6	59.6	215	1 016	56.0	16.8	935.8	317.9	74.5	18.0
New Castle	1 016	11 380	846.6	398.1	768	5 051	311.5	108.2	2 263.4	944.6	377.1	60.6
Sussex	257	2 443	147.4	68.6	215	939	53.0	15.7	833.6	465.8	152.9	17.9
DISTRICT OF COLUMBIA	1 464	13 692	1 054.8	476.7	978	6 218	404.8	111.1	30 940.7	1 721.7	666.7	183.2
District of Columbia	1 464	13 692	1 054.8	476.7	978	6 218	404.8	111.1	30 940.7	1 721.7	666.7	183.2
FLORIDA	35 568	447 117	32 559.1	13 610.7	26 121	146 360	9 123.6	2 665.7	99 998.4	40 644.2	19 580.8	2 844.6
Alachua	502	6 499	435.3	201.2	318	1 631	94.1	28.0	1 307.6	395.9	151.3	39.8
Baker	21	299	12.4	4.9	19	57	3.9	0.8	83.5	45.4	14.5	4.5
Bay	317	4 398	315.8	131.2	246	1 569	85.5	27.6	1 460.5	484.3	136.3	26.3
Bradford	27	609	22.2	9.6	17	116	7.4	1.8	116.9	53.7	23.6	6.0
Brevard	1 017	10 631	783.2	358.0	728	3 778	206.4	63.8	4 566.9	1 724.7	524.2	62.8
Broward	4 226	51 708	3 879.0	1 603.0	3 246	19 188	1 397.3	373.4	7 322.5	3 284.0	2 369.1	216.9
Calhoun	13	49	3.0	1.0	8	32	1.6	0.4	64.9	27.2	12.6	3.6
Charlotte	305	4 286	306.9	134.7	189	674	37.4	10.2	884.7	569.3	249.5	10.3
Citrus	228	3 228	205.1	85.0	150	525	29.0	7.5	757.2	484.8	195.1	14.8
Clay	250	3 913	260.4	97.6	193	970	47.8	14.3	561.0	410.8	76.8	11.0
Collier	492	5 124	404.9	175.0	431	2 035	109.6	34.8	1 080.5	691.4	234.3	16.1
Columbia	108	1 406	88.1	35.3	59	227	15.9	3.7	320.5	142.4	50.2	16.5
De Soto	37	253	14.8	5.2	26	100	5.1	1.2	236.9	63.4	41.5	8.5
Dixie	6	60	2.2	1.0	7	31	2.0	0.5	68.0	38.7	13.2	3.7
Duval	1 579	23 107	1 729.8	810.5	1 448	9 054	604.7	184.3	5 408.7	1 707.1	651.1	144.9
Escambia	535	9 282	658.6	301.3	437	3 132	176.5	64.3	2 360.8	946.2	253.5	72.0
Flagler	62	305	21.3	9.8	47	167	10.0	2.2	300.5	222.4	49.7	3.9
Franklin	15	279	8.9	4.0	8	15	1.1	0.2	68.7	27.3	15.5	2.4
Gadsden	26	156	11.5	3.8	37	149	7.3	2.3	237.6	87.3	39.5	17.3
Gilchrist	7	21	1.3	0.4	3	D	D	D	57.7	32.7	10.5	4.8
Glades	2	D	D	D	7	24	2.2	0.9	27.9	15.9	6.3	0.5
Gulf	16	370	20.3	8.3	19	46	3.0	0.5	79.1	41.1	20.2	2.9
Hamilton	14	188	9.0	4.3	12	28	1.9	0.3	87.2	26.9	10.5	4.1
Hardee	27	554	21.9	10.7	22	70	4.0	1.0	101.7	41.5	21.7	7.2
Hendry	28	311	12.7	5.5	29	179	7.4	3.0	135.8	50.9	24.2	6.6
Hernando	252	2 630	181.1	84.2	193	756	38.6	10.8	925.1	578.9	258.1	14.6
Highlands	184	1 759	134.0	47.2	110	431	21.1	5.4	571.3	330.0	155.5	13.8
Hillsborough	2 233	29 728	2 295.7	905.7	1 590	10 820	700.2	209.4	5 346.6	2 075.5	866.5	206.8
Holmes	16	367	25.3	7.2	8	38	2.7	0.8	117.6	52.2	22.1	5.4
Indian River	287	3 388	263.7	96.4	206	944	45.4	13.7	730.1	436.7	206.2	9.6
Jackson	62	701	36.8	14.0	51	218	13.1	3.4	307.6	113.6	47.5	11.6
Jefferson	12	77	3.8	1.2	11	30	1.0	0.2	78.2	27.8	10.9	4.4
Lafayette	4	D	D	D	5	31	2.3	0.4	28.6	10.3	4.2	1.0
Lake	376	3 834	244.4	107.5	300	1 353	71.9	21.3	1 388.1	887.0	305.2	26.6
Lee	825	12 968	954.5	408.4	695	3 599	224.9	68.5	2 334.1	1 400.1	579.0	44.4
Leon	441	6 479	459.0	210.2	390	2 563	144.2	46.7	3 588.9	468.4	112.1	32.1
Levy	33	534	23.8	7.8	32	108	5.9	1.5	172.7	96.4	34.2	7.6
Liberty	8	156	4.5	2.2	2	D	D	D	28.5	12.6	5.1	0.9
Madison	16	179	6.9	3.2	22	93	4.8	1.5	117.6	40.4	18.2	7.5
Manatee	472	9 114	634.7	243.7	316	1 565	84.9	25.8	1 322.1	758.0	326.2	28.2
Marion	466	6 512	466.6	185.9	369	1 680	93.9	29.4	1 495.6	919.2	312.6	45.5
Martin	317	3 142	231.3	101.1	244	1 045	64.9	18.9	740.4	468.3	198.6	7.7
Miami-Dade	6 157	60 718	4 782.5	1 877.5	3 901	22 435	1 391.0	385.8	12 518.6	3 139.0	3 135.0	830.5
Monroe	162	1 416	105.1	40.0	183	674	46.5	11.3	460.3	182.8	80.6	8.9
Nassau	56	683	38.0	16.4	79	321	19.9	6.2	287.4	150.6	39.9	3.7
Okaloosa	356	5 134	412.2	142.7	313	1 531	86.3	25.5	2 219.3	717.8	116.5	17.4
Okeechobee	68	1 153	75.0	27.1	46	184	13.2	3.2	192.1	91.5	56.8	7.2
Orange	1 792	22 044	1 627.8	774.0	1 494	11 286	713.7	216.5	5 230.9	1 629.8	692.2	153.9
Osceola	252	4 024	241.3	103.8	207	923	55.6	16.4	555.7	315.7	137.4	25.4
Palm Beach	3 280	39 623	2 981.7	1 257.5	2 113	11 678	726.5	209.6	7 332.5	3 190.7	1 792.9	114.4
Pasco	676	12 112	849.4	342.5	443	2 124	112.6	31.9	1 882.4	1 009.0	628.3	43.9
Pinellas	2 633	36 006	2 496.2	1 052.0	1 746	9 799	614.7	189.1	6 326.8	2 998.2	1 603.3	123.0
Polk	643	9 886	657.7	279.4	611	3 224	199.6	60.6	2 234.6	1 240.9	463.8	95.1
Putnam	93	1 961	120.3	47.7	74	342	21.5	5.8	386.7	193.6	85.5	21.4
St. Johns	249	2 057	152.3	66.9	139	658	42.5	12.3	621.1	343.3	111.6	12.9
St. Lucie	360	7 250	525.1	193.7	273	1 181	74.2	19.9	1 104.7	643.4	268.8	39.1
Santa Rosa	127	1 881	90.2	42.8	120	540	33.9	9.3	638.6	367.8	71.7	11.9

1. Firms subject to federal tax.　　2. October 1, 2000 to September 30, 2001.　　3. State totals may include programs not allocated by county.

Table B. States and Counties — Federal Funds and Local Government Finances

STATE County	Federal funds and grants, fiscal 2001[1] (cont'd) — Expenditures (mil dol) (cont'd)							Local government finances, 1997 — General revenue				
	Procurement contract awards			Grants[2]							Taxes	
											Per capita[3] (dollars)	
	Salaries and wages	Defense	Other	Medicaid and other health-related	Nutrition and family welfare	Education	Other	Total (mil dol)	Intergovernmental (mil dol)	Total (mil dol)	Total	Property
	171	172	173	174	175	176	177	178	179	180	181	182
DELAWARE	427.7	83.8	64.2	398.8	124.5	94.2	274.0	X	X	X	X	X
Kent	199.9	50.7	4.6	71.9	21.2	49.4	86.4	220.2	144.7	37.8	308	280
New Castle	198.4	32.0	53.8	250.0	75.1	24.5	159.6	942.9	402.1	306.6	646	525
Sussex	29.4	1.1	5.8	76.9	11.1	14.0	24.6	271.1	155.1	68.1	508	433
DISTRICT OF COLUMBIA	12 646.5	1 633.8	8 628.9	1 275.5	259.1	324.2	2 161.5	X	X	X	X	X
District of Columbia	12 646.5	1 633.8	8 628.9	1 275.5	259.1	324.2	2 161.5	5 279.0	1 994.5	2 637.4	4 986	1 322
FLORIDA	8 414.7	6 615.4	2 243.9	6 421.2	2 190.7	1 441.9	3 612.0	X	X	X	X	X
Alachua	160.8	5.9	35.2	193.3	29.2	20.6	200.8	469.0	198.4	135.7	684	581
Baker	2.8	0.0	1.1	6.6	2.9	1.8	0.6	52.2	26.0	8.7	420	296
Bay	288.7	146.2	11.3	47.0	19.0	13.6	8.3	460.6	158.6	108.1	739	475
Bradford	9.1	0.1	0.7	14.2	3.6	1.5	2.0	49.8	31.1	9.1	370	247
Brevard	387.0	1 005.5	633.6	67.9	31.9	23.3	66.5	992.6	322.6	330.2	716	569
Broward	428.3	92.4	137.2	270.1	103.1	68.8	166.7	4 746.9	1 168.5	1 714.5	1 166	921
Calhoun	1.2	0.0	0.4	12.4	2.6	1.2	1.1	22.5	16.3	4.3	351	241
Charlotte	15.9	0.1	4.6	7.1	7.7	3.9	8.7	268.9	54.4	131.5	984	744
Citrus	12.3	15.0	3.3	14.9	7.1	5.1	2.1	196.8	55.8	83.4	742	682
Clay	21.1	4.1	3.1	13.9	6.4	6.0	1.8	245.5	112.9	71.6	529	398
Collier	36.4	5.7	14.3	29.1	17.4	7.4	12.2	502.7	92.3	285.7	1 459	1 257
Columbia	46.5	0.9	7.2	32.1	8.8	3.8	6.6	116.0	63.4	26.8	507	320
De Soto	2.9	0.3	90.4	10.7	4.4	2.4	8.1	53.3	26.8	15.3	583	442
Dixie	1.1	0.0	0.2	5.8	2.4	1.1	0.9	25.1	15.5	5.3	421	326
Duval	1 424.5	406.9	196.1	328.7	110.6	56.5	163.3	1 764.1	657.0	611.2	834	628
Escambia	623.0	116.7	33.2	133.4	49.6	23.8	44.7	659.9	309.9	178.9	633	398
Flagler	7.0	0.0	5.4	3.1	2.5	1.5	3.3	90.5	26.0	44.0	955	859
Franklin	1.5	0.1	1.0	8.1	1.8	0.8	9.3	23.5	9.3	11.0	1 085	963
Gadsden	7.0	1.5	1.3	46.3	16.6	6.1	-0.5	78.6	51.5	15.9	349	261
Gilchrist	1.4	0.0	0.4	4.0	1.5	0.8	0.7	28.1	14.9	5.0	376	298
Glades	0.5	0.4	0.1	1.1	0.8	0.5	0.2	16.5	7.1	6.8	697	628
Gulf	0.8	0.4	0.2	8.9	2.9	1.0	0.3	33.3	12.0	11.6	836	761
Hamilton	1.6	0.0	0.4	11.6	3.0	1.7	25.3	56.8	18.9	27.8	2 224	969
Hardee	3.1	0.1	0.6	12.6	4.8	1.9	4.2	54.0	27.3	17.8	806	666
Hendry	4.5	4.2	0.8	9.8	5.7	2.2	11.2	101.2	40.3	29.4	931	771
Hernando	18.2	1.4	5.7	16.0	10.3	5.3	12.9	311.5	97.6	134.6	1 072	1 010
Highlands	15.2	5.1	3.5	21.7	7.9	4.5	6.2	156.3	67.6	55.9	727	565
Hillsborough	760.3	389.0	130.0	401.5	119.4	72.9	163.9	2 752.7	1 022.1	851.5	936	726
Holmes	3.0	4.0	1.0	19.7	5.0	1.5	-0.3	35.3	26.3	5.1	277	188
Indian River	20.8	10.7	5.4	16.5	9.1	4.5	2.6	350.9	51.9	133.0	1 340	1 093
Jackson	25.1	0.9	3.2	55.9	7.6	3.3	13.5	125.3	58.2	18.7	410	228
Jefferson	1.9	0.0	1.7	16.6	3.1	1.3	5.7	24.3	15.0	6.1	464	340
Lafayette	0.8	1.2	0.2	2.4	0.8	0.4	6.0	12.8	8.8	2.3	369	329
Lake	28.4	10.7	42.4	36.5	16.7	11.4	9.9	348.0	127.2	129.1	658	484
Lee	108.7	6.9	24.6	62.6	28.6	19.3	24.6	1 548.2	259.2	458.5	1 184	1 041
Leon	93.8	27.8	18.2	429.6	559.2	480.6	1 208.0	585.2	208.8	191.1	888	598
Levy	4.9	0.0	1.0	13.7	4.4	3.7	2.3	61.0	32.1	18.0	558	431
Liberty	1.7	0.0	0.7	5.3	1.0	0.5	0.1	12.0	8.5	2.3	343	260
Madison	2.5	0.0	0.6	23.9	4.4	2.0	13.5	43.3	26.9	7.6	434	276
Manatee	64.4	8.2	18.5	41.9	20.4	13.0	21.2	586.6	167.7	222.9	940	788
Marion	37.1	2.9	25.6	70.9	27.7	13.5	13.0	411.8	199.1	119.9	505	446
Martin	16.2	1.1	5.9	13.7	7.9	5.0	9.6	296.6	53.6	161.0	1 387	1 231
Miami-Dade	1 110.0	113.4	256.1	2 519.7	334.1	139.6	247.8	7 614.5	2 402.8	2 454.4	1 151	869
Monroe	89.5	33.8	10.2	26.3	5.5	3.4	9.4	297.6	58.9	141.3	1 724	1 327
Nassau	62.5	2.0	1.6	15.0	5.0	2.3	3.2	115.4	43.2	41.7	771	633
Okaloosa	772.8	471.5	21.1	36.8	14.1	13.6	20.7	354.9	167.7	108.4	647	548
Okeechobee	3.6	4.5	1.0	12.8	4.8	2.8	3.0	65.2	34.7	20.6	623	444
Orange	423.4	1 641.9	105.9	203.2	73.9	46.9	147.8	2 574.5	678.8	932.6	1 190	901
Osceola	17.7	1.4	4.8	13.7	9.8	7.4	13.3	372.6	119.5	143.3	1 008	695
Palm Beach	317.8	1 146.4	132.2	182.1	77.7	39.1	244.7	3 140.0	632.2	1 523.2	1 495	1 256
Pasco	44.2	3.7	12.3	49.9	24.9	13.7	30.1	549.0	226.7	174.7	545	488
Pinellas	373.5	609.1	102.2	175.0	68.6	44.9	136.5	2 106.4	566.2	886.1	1 016	764
Polk	81.2	7.4	23.5	134.0	56.6	29.6	55.8	896.4	388.5	274.6	612	505
Putnam	8.0	0.2	2.4	38.3	14.9	6.9	4.8	240.0	95.3	98.9	1 404	1 312
St. Johns	26.3	28.3	14.8	26.8	7.9	4.9	36.9	243.8	69.7	99.4	882	769
St. Lucie	30.8	1.5	7.2	37.3	19.5	13.1	25.6	471.1	163.9	182.2	1 015	911
Santa Rosa	70.4	51.3	4.4	25.7	11.1	6.0	6.9	201.0	101.1	59.2	517	404

1. October 1, 2000 to September 30, 2001. 2. State totals may include programs not allocated by county. 3. Based on the resident population estimated as of July 1 of the year shown.

Table B. States and Counties — Local Government Finances, Government Employment, and Elections

STATE County	Local government finances, 1997 (cont'd) Direct general expenditure Total (mil dol)	Per capita[1] (dollars)	Percent of total for — Education	Health and hospitals	Police protection	Public welfare	Highways	Debt outstanding Total (mil dol)	Per capita[1] (dollars)	Government employment, 1999 Federal civilian	Federal military	State and local	Presidential election, 2000[2] Percent of vote cast — Democratic	Republican	All other
	183	184	185	186	187	188	189	190	191	192	193	194	195	196	197
DELAWARE	X	X	X	X	X	X	X	X	X	5 313	8 966	50 340	55.0	41.9	3.1
Kent	218.1	1 778	71.3	0.0	5.3	0.2	1.7	105.5	860	1 682	4 610	13 646	47.2	49.9	2.8
New Castle	938.9	1 977	56.5	0.6	6.4	0.1	7.0	968.3	2 039	3 166	3 386	30 465	59.9	36.9	3.2
Sussex	269.8	2 013	65.3	1.2	3.7	0.1	1.7	237.3	1 770	465	970	6 229	44.9	52.2	2.9
DISTRICT OF COLUMBIA	X	X	X	X	X	X	X	X	X	183 671	22 448	41 140	85.2	9.0	5.9
District of Columbia	4 335.8	8 197	15.5	10.2	6.5	27.4	2.7	4 274.6	8 081	183 671	22 448	41 140	85.2	9.0	5.9
FLORIDA	X	X	X	X	X	X	X	X	X	118 191	104 019	841 849	48.8	48.8	2.3
Alachua	479.9	2 420	47.0	1.5	8.0	0.1	2.6	1 023.6	5 161	2 855	511	36 967	55.2	39.8	5.0
Baker	50.2	2 420	49.6	23.3	4.3	0.1	4.0	5.2	253	72	46	2 511	29.3	68.8	1.9
Bay	472.5	3 232	38.8	23.9	6.6	0.0	3.4	247.6	1 693	3 011	4 532	6 955	32.1	65.7	2.2
Bradford	43.3	1 756	65.9	2.0	5.3	0.2	4.7	17.5	712	39	143	2 476	35.5	62.4	2.2
Brevard	964.9	2 093	45.0	7.6	6.9	0.5	4.7	1 111.7	2 412	5 415	3 425	19 851	44.6	52.7	2.7
Broward	4 649.6	3 161	31.9	22.2	8.4	0.6	1.9	4 913.8	3 341	7 202	3 735	75 255	67.4	30.9	1.6
Calhoun	23.3	1 890	50.5	0.8	5.0	1.1	9.2	0.7	58	26	27	952	41.7	55.5	2.9
Charlotte	239.6	1 792	40.7	3.4	7.5	1.5	8.7	365.3	2 732	284	301	5 020	44.3	53.0	2.7
Citrus	199.0	1 770	43.6	1.7	6.9	0.3	6.4	407.5	3 624	201	254	3 799	44.6	52.0	3.3
Clay	234.9	1 737	54.9	1.0	6.7	0.5	6.0	164.6	1 217	322	312	4 792	25.5	72.8	1.7
Collier	530.4	2 710	46.9	2.9	7.6	0.6	6.7	559.5	2 859	622	454	8 977	32.5	65.6	1.9
Columbia	113.0	2 139	58.3	3.0	5.0	0.1	5.4	49.3	933	1 030	118	4 006	38.1	59.2	2.7
De Soto	51.6	1 963	51.9	1.8	11.0	0.0	7.4	8.7	333	56	54	2 781	42.5	54.5	3.0
Dixie	24.5	1 953	55.0	3.4	4.5	0.1	4.5	1.1	89	17	28	1 026	39.1	57.8	3.1
Duval	1 821.6	2 486	42.8	2.8	6.0	0.5	2.3	5 216.9	7 121	16 373	24 420	33 866	40.8	57.5	1.7
Escambia	636.3	2 251	49.3	1.5	6.0	0.8	5.4	1 111.8	3 934	6 728	14 009	16 770	35.1	62.6	2.3
Flagler	78.7	1 706	49.1	3.2	6.7	0.3	9.0	71.7	1 555	97	107	1 899	51.3	46.5	2.2
Franklin	22.7	2 236	45.3	1.7	12.2	0.2	6.7	3.9	387	23	22	668	44.1	52.8	3.1
Gadsden	88.0	1 937	56.8	2.7	9.9	0.1	7.0	24.6	541	125	96	5 234	66.1	32.4	1.5
Gilchrist	28.1	2 102	55.7	17.6	3.7	0.5	3.1	3.8	286	31	31	1 079	35.4	61.2	3.4
Glades	16.4	1 686	45.0	7.3	9.3	0.7	7.9	0.4	40	11	19	378	42.9	54.7	2.5
Gulf	32.7	2 348	41.1	1.8	5.9	0.5	11.0	13.1	940	15	30	1 284	39.0	57.8	3.2
Hamilton	63.3	5 059	25.7	8.8	2.9	0.0	3.4	20.5	1 640	35	28	1 462	43.4	54.1	2.4
Hardee	51.6	2 332	58.3	2.8	6.2	0.1	6.6	14.8	668	52	46	1 701	37.5	60.4	2.1
Hendry	105.5	3 336	50.7	13.1	6.6	0.4	4.3	43.2	1 366	109	64	2 327	39.8	58.3	1.9
Hernando	298.2	2 375	28.6	0.9	4.4	0.1	3.5	726.8	5 790	290	282	4 915	50.1	47.0	3.0
Highlands	152.4	1 983	55.7	2.8	6.7	0.6	6.3	80.2	1 043	295	165	3 593	40.3	57.5	2.3
Hillsborough	2 698.4	2 967	38.0	12.8	6.7	2.2	3.4	3 520.6	3 871	11 094	7 474	56 872	47.1	50.2	2.8
Holmes	33.5	1 821	59.5	3.1	2.3	0.1	7.2	2.5	137	56	41	1 291	29.4	67.8	2.8
Indian River	324.1	3 266	26.7	31.6	6.3	0.9	4.6	440.3	4 438	359	219	4 218	39.8	57.7	2.4
Jackson	124.3	2 720	50.8	24.1	3.0	3.9	4.5	21.5	471	502	101	5 660	42.1	56.1	1.8
Jefferson	24.0	1 813	53.9	2.5	8.3	0.0	7.7	1.8	135	30	29	989	53.9	43.9	2.2
Lafayette	13.0	2 071	65.7	2.4	2.9	0.3	6.2	0.4	65	16	14	628	31.5	66.7	1.8
Lake	327.7	1 670	47.4	2.6	7.6	0.5	4.9	264.3	1 347	520	517	8 692	41.3	56.4	2.2
Lee	1 485.2	3 837	25.8	15.4	3.9	0.4	7.9	2 032.5	5 251	1 910	930	24 096	39.9	57.6	2.5
Leon	579.3	2 693	41.7	0.2	7.8	0.3	4.8	1 208.2	5 615	1 675	628	53 054	59.6	37.9	2.6
Levy	57.1	1 769	57.5	3.0	7.4	0.9	5.8	17.1	530	77	96	1 787	42.4	53.9	3.6
Liberty	11.9	1 771	57.6	1.5	3.6	5.4	9.8	0.8	123	49	15	739	42.2	54.6	3.2
Madison	41.6	2 368	62.6	2.3	4.7	0.6	7.1	13.6	772	50	39	1 500	48.9	49.3	1.8
Manatee	589.2	2 485	48.8	2.4	6.6	0.5	3.9	655.1	2 763	1 152	561	10 151	44.6	52.6	2.8
Marion	416.0	1 753	51.9	0.8	8.5	0.4	9.1	334.0	1 408	690	540	13 917	43.4	53.6	3.1
Martin	284.9	2 454	33.5	2.9	9.1	0.8	5.0	424.6	3 657	288	262	4 872	42.9	54.8	2.3
Miami-Dade	7 843.1	3 679	34.1	9.4	7.5	0.8	1.9	9 180.4	4 306	18 173	7 140	119 901	52.6	46.3	1.2
Monroe	270.0	3 296	30.9	4.5	15.3	1.2	2.6	250.8	3 062	1 256	1 553	4 832	48.6	47.4	4.0
Nassau	106.0	1 960	50.7	3.9	5.8	0.1	5.5	52.5	971	592	124	2 622	29.2	69.0	1.8
Okaloosa	346.9	2 070	61.9	2.2	5.0	0.4	4.2	155.5	928	6 427	15 289	7 425	24.0	73.7	2.3
Okeechobee	66.1	1 996	55.4	1.0	7.4	0.4	6.1	25.9	783	76	71	1 781	46.6	51.3	2.1
Orange	2 576.3	3 286	34.0	2.5	6.3	0.9	6.2	7 335.1	9 356	7 264	2 540	50 838	50.1	48.0	1.9
Osceola	404.5	2 846	46.4	0.7	6.4	1.1	8.2	658.4	4 632	270	329	7 347	50.6	47.1	2.3
Palm Beach	3 052.6	2 997	32.4	4.1	8.0	0.7	3.8	3 439.3	3 377	5 519	2 379	52 139	62.3	35.3	2.4
Pasco	525.8	1 642	52.8	1.7	6.1	2.3	4.9	587.9	1 836	682	724	11 851	48.7	48.0	3.2
Pinellas	2 047.5	2 349	37.7	3.2	8.4	1.6	4.7	2 116.7	2 428	6 033	2 957	37 529	50.3	46.4	3.3
Polk	895.2	1 995	48.6	2.8	7.8	1.0	4.2	1 182.9	2 637	1 411	1 011	25 247	44.6	53.6	1.8
Putnam	154.0	2 187	54.1	2.4	5.9	0.1	5.3	294.1	4 176	151	154	4 546	46.2	51.3	2.5
St. Johns	231.9	2 057	42.9	4.1	6.8	0.6	4.5	292.5	2 595	370	271	5 567	32.1	65.1	2.8
St. Lucie	505.8	2 817	48.7	0.6	7.0	0.8	3.1	931.4	5 187	527	458	9 145	53.3	44.5	2.3
Santa Rosa	199.4	1 741	56.2	1.3	9.1	0.1	4.4	134.8	1 178	758	1 440	4 655	25.4	72.1	2.4

1. Based on the resident population estimated as of July 1 of the year shown. 2. Data subject to copyright.

Table B. States and Counties — **Land Area and Population**

STATE/ County code	MSA/ PMSA/ NECMA code[1]	County Type[2]	STATE County	Land area,[3] (sq km) 2000	Population and population characteristics, 2000													
								Race alone or in combination (percent)					Age (percent)					
					Total persons	Rank	Per square kilometer	White	Black	Am. Indian, Alaska Native	Asian and Pacific Islander	Percent Hispanic[4]	Under 5 years	5 to 17 years	18 to 24 years	25 to 34 years	35 to 44 years	45 to 54 years
				1	2	3	4	5	6	7	8	9	10	11	12	13	14	15
			FLORIDA—Cont'd															
12 115	7510	2	Sarasota	1 480	325 957	177	220.2	93.5	4.5	0.5	1.1	4.3	3.9	12.3	5.0	8.9	12.7	12.8
12 117	5960	0	Seminole	798	365 196	161	457.6	84.2	10.2	0.8	3.1	11.2	6.3	19.0	8.4	14.2	17.8	15.0
12 119	...	6	Sumter	1 413	53 345	876	37.8	83.8	14.1	1.1	0.7	6.3	4.0	12.1	5.9	10.7	12.5	11.3
12 121	...	7	Suwannee	1 781	34 844	1 256	19.6	85.7	12.4	1.1	0.8	4.9	6.0	18.0	8.5	11.1	14.0	13.6
12 123	...	7	Taylor	2 699	19 256	1 830	7.1	79.0	19.3	1.8	0.7	1.5	5.9	18.7	8.2	13.0	15.4	14.3
12 125	...	8	Union	622	13 442	2 197	21.6	74.8	23.3	1.4	0.7	3.5	5.5	16.4	8.7	17.8	21.9	14.7
12 127	2020	2	Volusia	2 857	443 343	135	155.2	87.3	9.7	0.8	1.4	6.6	4.9	15.4	8.2	10.9	14.4	13.3
12 129	...	8	Wakulla	1 571	22 863	1 650	14.6	87.2	11.8	1.2	0.5	1.9	5.9	19.7	7.6	13.4	18.3	14.9
12 131	...	6	Walton	2 739	40 601	1 098	14.8	90.3	7.3	2.6	0.8	2.2	5.3	16.3	7.1	12.2	16.2	14.6
12 133	...	6	Washington	1 502	20 973	1 738	14.0	83.5	14.1	2.8	0.8	2.3	6.0	17.3	7.7	13.1	15.4	13.4
13 000	...	X	**GEORGIA**	149 976	8 186 453	X	54.6	66.1	29.2	0.6	2.5	5.3	7.3	19.2	10.2	15.9	16.5	13.2
13 001	...	7	Appling	1 317	17 419	1 928	13.2	77.3	19.8	0.5	0.4	4.5	7.3	19.8	9.0	13.3	15.3	13.7
13 003	...	9	Atkinson	876	7 609	2 635	8.7	67.5	19.8	0.9	0.3	17.0	9.5	20.9	10.9	15.2	14.4	11.2
13 005	...	7	Bacon	738	10 103	2 437	13.7	82.3	16.1	0.5	0.4	3.4	7.5	18.7	9.9	14.2	13.9	13.7
13 007	...	8	Baker	889	4 074	2 913	4.6	47.9	50.6	0.4	0.1	2.7	7.2	20.1	10.0	12.7	14.2	13.0
13 009	...	4	Baldwin	669	44 700	1 005	66.8	54.6	43.8	0.5	1.3	1.4	5.1	16.6	14.5	14.9	16.3	13.2
13 011	...	8	Banks	605	14 422	2 128	23.8	93.8	3.3	0.7	0.8	3.4	7.5	18.6	8.9	14.5	16.1	13.8
13 013	0520	1	Barrow	420	46 144	980	109.9	85.9	10.1	0.8	2.6	3.2	8.3	20.2	8.5	17.7	16.8	11.9
13 015	0520	1	Bartow	1 190	76 019	659	63.9	88.8	9.0	0.7	0.8	3.3	7.8	20.1	8.3	16.2	16.9	13.1
13 017	...	7	Ben Hill	652	17 484	1 924	26.8	63.9	32.9	0.5	0.4	4.6	7.3	20.2	9.7	13.1	13.9	13.2
13 019	...	7	Berrien	1 172	16 235	2 006	13.9	86.3	11.6	0.8	0.5	2.4	7.1	20.2	8.6	13.9	14.8	12.8
13 021	4680	2	Bibb	647	153 887	345	237.8	50.7	47.7	0.4	1.4	1.3	7.4	19.1	10.1	13.8	15.1	13.3
13 023	...	6	Bleckley	563	11 666	2 321	20.7	73.8	24.8	0.4	1.1	0.9	6.4	20.2	11.3	12.0	14.5	12.4
13 025	...	9	Brantley	1 151	14 629	2 111	12.7	95.4	4.2	1.0	0.3	1.0	7.4	21.0	8.5	13.9	16.0	13.7
13 027	...	7	Brooks	1 278	16 450	1 993	12.9	58.1	39.7	0.9	0.7	3.1	6.5	20.4	8.9	12.6	14.3	12.7
13 029	7520	2	Bryan	1 144	23 417	1 621	20.5	83.8	14.7	0.9	1.5	2.0	7.7	23.4	8.0	13.4	18.6	14.2
13 031	...	6	Bulloch	1 767	55 983	843	31.7	69.3	29.1	0.3	1.1	1.9	5.8	16.5	26.2	12.1	12.7	10.5
13 033	...	6	Burke	2 151	22 243	1 684	10.3	47.7	51.3	0.6	0.6	1.4	8.0	23.3	9.1	12.2	15.1	13.1
13 035	...	6	Butts	483	19 522	1 818	40.4	70.0	29.2	0.8	0.5	1.4	6.3	17.8	9.2	15.1	17.9	14.0
13 037	...	8	Calhoun	726	6 320	2 755	8.7	38.6	60.8	0.3	0.2	3.0	6.0	16.0	11.3	15.6	17.7	13.3
13 039	...	6	Camden	1 631	43 664	1 024	26.8	76.6	20.8	1.0	1.8	3.6	8.7	23.0	12.9	17.2	16.7	10.5
13 043	...	7	Candler	639	9 577	2 482	15.0	66.0	27.4	0.4	0.4	9.2	7.2	19.7	9.4	12.8	13.2	13.0
13 045	0520	1	Carroll	1 292	87 268	601	67.5	81.5	16.8	0.6	0.9	2.6	7.1	18.9	12.9	14.8	15.1	12.5
13 047	1560	2	Catoosa	420	53 282	878	126.9	97.3	1.4	0.8	1.0	1.2	6.8	19.0	8.1	14.7	16.1	13.7
13 049	...	8	Charlton	2 022	10 282	2 419	5.1	69.6	29.7	1.0	0.6	0.8	6.5	20.9	10.6	14.3	17.4	11.5
13 051	7520	2	Chatham	1 135	232 048	248	204.4	56.2	41.0	0.6	2.3	2.3	6.7	18.3	11.2	14.6	15.0	12.8
13 053	1800	2	Chattahoochee	644	14 882	2 100	23.1	60.7	31.6	1.5	3.6	10.4	8.4	20.0	27.9	23.7	12.7	3.5
13 055	...	7	Chattooga	812	25 470	1 541	31.4	87.6	11.6	0.5	0.3	2.1	6.5	16.4	10.0	14.8	15.2	13.0
13 057	0520	1	Cherokee	1 097	141 903	385	129.4	93.6	2.7	0.9	1.2	5.4	8.2	20.0	7.7	15.9	19.8	14.2
13 059	0500	3	Clarke	313	101 489	520	324.2	66.1	27.8	0.5	3.7	6.3	5.2	12.6	31.3	16.4	11.0	9.5
13 061	...	9	Clay	506	3 357	2 967	6.6	38.7	60.9	0.7	0.4	1.0	6.6	19.2	8.0	9.1	11.9	14.9
13 063	0520	0	Clayton	369	236 517	245	641.0	39.2	52.7	0.8	5.2	7.5	8.3	21.6	10.4	18.4	16.9	12.0
13 065	...	7	Clinch	2 096	6 878	2 699	3.3	69.7	29.9	1.0	0.1	0.8	7.3	20.5	8.6	13.7	15.3	13.6
13 067	0520	0	Cobb	881	607 751	89	689.8	73.8	19.5	0.7	3.6	7.7	7.2	18.8	9.0	18.1	18.4	14.2
13 069	...	7	Coffee	1 551	37 413	1 179	24.1	69.0	26.2	0.5	0.8	6.8	7.8	20.4	11.0	15.1	15.3	12.3
13 071	...	7	Colquitt	1 430	42 053	1 057	29.4	68.6	23.8	0.6	0.7	10.8	7.6	19.9	10.3	14.2	13.8	12.3
13 073	0600	2	Columbia	751	89 288	579	118.9	84.0	11.6	0.7	4.2	2.6	6.9	22.7	7.3	12.4	18.6	15.8
13 075	...	7	Cook	593	15 771	2 033	26.6	68.5	29.5	0.5	0.7	3.1	7.7	20.5	9.1	13.6	14.3	12.1
13 077	0520	1	Coweta	1 146	89 215	580	77.8	79.8	18.3	0.6	0.9	3.1	8.2	20.6	7.6	16.2	17.2	13.4
13 079	...	8	Crawford	842	12 495	2 265	14.8	73.7	24.2	0.9	0.4	2.4	6.7	20.9	7.9	14.1	17.5	14.0
13 081	...	6	Crisp	709	21 996	1 693	31.0	54.6	43.8	0.3	1.0	1.7	7.8	21.2	9.2	12.7	14.3	13.1
13 083	1560	2	Dade	451	15 154	2 081	33.6	98.3	0.7	1.1	0.5	0.9	5.9	18.0	11.8	12.9	15.0	14.3
13 085	...	8	Dawson	547	15 999	2 023	29.2	98.1	0.5	1.1	0.5	1.6	7.0	18.0	7.6	14.7	17.7	14.6
13 087	...	8	Decatur	1 546	28 240	1 442	18.3	57.7	40.2	0.5	0.5	3.2	7.7	20.9	9.1	13.2	14.8	12.6
13 089	0520	0	De Kalb	695	665 865	76	958.1	37.0	55.3	0.7	4.6	7.9	7.1	17.5	10.9	19.5	17.2	12.8
13 091	...	7	Dodge	1 296	19 171	1 836	14.8	69.3	29.6	0.4	0.3	1.3	6.2	19.7	8.7	14.1	15.4	13.1
13 093	...	6	Dooly	1 018	11 525	2 332	11.3	46.6	49.8	0.5	0.9	4.7	6.8	18.8	10.3	13.9	15.9	13.6
13 095	0120	3	Dougherty	854	96 065	539	112.5	38.3	60.5	0.5	0.8	1.3	7.6	20.0	12.2	13.8	13.8	12.7
13 097	0520	0	Douglas	516	92 174	553	178.6	78.5	19.2	0.8	1.6	2.9	7.3	20.3	8.9	15.6	17.9	14.2
13 099	...	6	Early	1 324	12 354	2 277	9.3	50.7	48.5	0.6	0.6	1.2	7.1	21.6	7.8	11.6	14.3	12.2
13 101	...	9	Echols	1 047	3 754	2 935	3.6	78.1	7.0	1.7	0.1	19.7	8.0	21.3	12.5	16.4	14.3	11.1
13 103	7520	2	Effingham	1 242	37 535	1 176	30.2	85.6	13.3	0.8	0.8	1.4	7.6	22.3	8.2	14.0	18.1	13.5
13 105	...	6	Elbert	955	20 511	1 759	21.5	67.6	31.0	0.4	0.4	2.4	6.4	19.5	8.4	12.8	14.4	13.6
13 107	...	7	Emanuel	1 776	21 837	1 699	12.3	64.1	33.5	0.3	0.4	3.4	6.8	21.1	10.4	11.9	14.1	13.1
13 109	...	8	Evans	479	10 495	2 398	21.9	62.2	33.1	0.4	0.5	6.0	6.9	20.6	10.2	13.8	15.2	12.2

1. MSA = Metropolitan Statistical Area. PMSA = Primary MSA. NECMA = New England County Metropolitan Area. See Appendix A for explanation of these concepts. See Appendix B for list of metropolitan areas identified by type, with component counties.   2. County typology code from the Economic Research Service of USDA. See Appendix A for definition.   3. Dry land or land partially or temporarily covered by water.   4. Hispanic persons may be of any race.

Table B. States and Counties — Population and Households

STATE County	Age (percent) (cont'd)				Population — change and components of change, 1990–2001							Households, 2000				
					Total persons		Percent change		Components of change, 2000–2001						Percent	
	55 to 64 years	65 to 74 years	75 years and over	Percent female	2001	1990	1990–2000	2000–2001	Births	Deaths	Net migration	Number	Percent change, 1990–2000	Persons per house-hold	Female family house-holder[1]	One person
	16	17	18	19	20	21	22	23	24	25	26	27	28	29	30	31

FLORIDA—Cont'd

STATE County	16	17	18	19	20	21	22	23	24	25	26	27	28	29	30	31
Sarasota	12.8	15.2	16.3	52.6	335 323	277 776	17.3	2.9	3 332	6 277	12 162	149 937	19.5	2.13	7.7	30.4
Seminole	8.7	5.9	4.8	51.0	374 334	287 521	27.0	2.5	5 693	3 121	6 562	139 572	29.6	2.59	11.5	22.9
Sumter	16.1	17.8	9.6	46.9	54 504	31 577	68.9	2.2	546	674	1 218	20 779	71.5	2.27	8.4	23.5
Suwannee	11.8	9.4	7.6	51.2	35 668	26 780	30.1	2.4	608	579	791	13 460	34.1	2.54	11.2	23.3
Taylor	10.5	8.3	5.8	48.9	19 231	17 111	12.5	-0.1	289	246	-66	7 176	12.1	2.51	14.4	24.2
Union	7.5	4.7	2.7	35.3	13 672	10 252	31.1	1.7	219	204	212	3 367	26.7	2.76	15.0	19.5
Volusia	10.9	11.3	10.8	51.4	454 581	370 737	19.6	2.5	5 684	7 131	12 554	184 723	20.4	2.32	10.9	27.9
Wakulla	9.8	6.4	3.9	48.2	24 761	14 202	61.0	8.3	357	238	1 731	8 450	62.2	2.57	12.4	22.0
Walton	12.3	9.6	6.3	48.7	42 644	27 759	46.3	5.0	541	510	1 960	16 548	46.5	2.35	10.1	27.1
Washington	11.2	8.4	7.3	48.6	21 192	16 919	24.0	1.0	287	282	193	7 931	23.1	2.46	11.4	25.1
GEORGIA	8.1	5.3	4.3	50.8	8 383 915	6 478 149	26.4	2.4	168 353	79 804	106 412	3 006 369	27.0	2.65	14.5	23.6
Appling	9.8	6.6	5.2	50.7	17 472	15 744	10.6	0.3	344	217	-69	6 606	13.2	2.60	12.5	23.2
Atkinson	8.6	5.1	4.1	50.5	7 571	6 213	22.5	-0.5	225	88	-178	2 717	22.9	2.78	12.8	23.3
Bacon	9.4	7.5	5.3	51.0	9 993	9 566	5.6	-1.1	174	158	-125	3 833	11.4	2.60	14.1	23.6
Baker	9.0	7.6	6.1	53.7	4 102	3 615	12.7	0.7	61	43	9	1 514	16.5	2.68	19.5	25.1
Baldwin	8.7	6.0	4.6	46.0	44 806	39 530	13.1	0.2	712	521	-74	14 758	21.3	2.50	18.2	25.6
Banks	9.9	6.2	4.3	49.5	14 847	10 308	39.9	2.9	211	130	339	5 364	42.1	2.69	7.9	19.2
Barrow	7.5	4.9	4.1	50.3	48 946	29 721	55.3	6.1	1 010	380	2 125	16 354	53.2	2.79	11.6	18.6
Bartow	8.3	5.5	3.9	50.6	80 026	55 915	36.0	5.3	1 708	772	3 005	27 176	35.3	2.76	11.1	18.7
Ben Hill	9.3	6.7	6.6	52.1	17 242	16 245	7.6	-1.4	431	323	-355	6 673	11.7	2.57	17.4	26.7
Berrien	10.1	6.9	5.5	50.9	16 091	14 153	14.7	-0.9	336	225	-259	6 261	21.6	2.57	11.7	23.6
Bibb	8.4	6.6	6.1	54.0	153 549	150 137	2.5	-0.2	3 505	2 332	-1 498	59 667	6.0	2.49	20.6	28.2
Bleckley	9.7	7.4	6.1	51.8	11 735	10 430	11.9	0.6	217	163	21	4 372	14.6	2.52	15.5	25.5
Brantley	9.5	6.4	3.7	49.8	14 877	11 077	32.1	1.7	136	129	238	5 436	42.6	2.68	10.6	20.4
Brooks	9.6	7.4	7.6	52.0	16 397	15 398	6.8	-0.3	260	220	-87	6 155	14.2	2.61	18.1	25.2
Bryan	7.5	4.3	3.0	50.5	24 552	15 438	51.7	4.8	527	166	762	8 089	59.5	2.88	11.9	16.4
Bulloch	7.0	5.0	4.3	51.3	56 918	43 125	29.8	1.7	894	471	523	20 743	38.4	2.53	11.8	24.6
Burke	8.4	5.8	5.1	52.5	22 591	20 579	8.1	1.6	560	284	75	7 934	12.7	2.77	22.8	23.6
Butts	9.5	5.9	4.3	46.7	20 629	15 326	27.4	5.7	387	191	891	6 455	37.5	2.73	13.9	20.9
Calhoun	7.5	6.2	6.3	43.5	6 307	5 013	26.1	-0.2	138	99	-51	1 962	9.4	2.55	23.2	28.7
Camden	5.8	3.2	2.0	48.3	44 061	30 167	44.7	0.9	845	235	-170	14 705	55.5	2.84	11.7	17.7
Candler	9.5	7.2	8.0	49.8	9 508	7 744	23.7	-0.7	207	146	-132	3 375	19.3	2.72	14.3	23.9
Carroll	8.8	5.5	4.5	51.3	91 956	71 422	22.2	5.4	1 632	916	3 885	31 568	24.4	2.66	12.3	21.2
Catoosa	9.7	7.1	4.8	51.6	55 197	42 464	25.5	3.6	789	512	1 610	20 425	29.7	2.59	11.0	21.3
Charlton	9.1	5.6	4.1	47.1	10 393	8 496	21.0	1.1	173	117	55	3 342	14.8	2.74	15.0	21.8
Chatham	8.6	6.8	6.1	51.8	232 064	216 774	7.0	0.0	5 016	2 919	-2 008	89 865	10.8	2.49	17.0	27.1
Chattahoochee	1.9	1.2	0.6	36.8	15 134	16 934	-12.1	1.7	320	40	33	2 932	1.7	3.41	10.1	8.9
Chattooga	9.9	7.8	6.5	48.4	25 901	22 236	14.5	1.7	423	314	327	9 577	13.1	2.49	12.6	25.2
Cherokee	7.5	3.9	2.7	49.8	152 170	90 204	57.3	7.2	2 744	990	8 299	49 495	58.1	2.85	8.3	16.0
Clarke	5.9	4.1	3.9	51.2	101 800	87 594	15.9	0.3	1 709	807	-583	39 706	19.7	2.35	13.3	29.7
Clay	10.8	10.1	9.4	54.5	3 390	3 364	-0.2	1.0	99	68	4	1 347	11.3	2.45	23.4	27.8
Clayton	6.4	3.6	2.3	51.4	246 779	181 436	30.4	4.3	5 590	1 547	6 153	82 243	25.5	2.84	20.3	21.8
Clinch	9.1	6.8	5.0	50.3	6 833	6 160	11.7	-0.7	132	86	-92	2 512	15.6	2.60	16.9	24.6
Cobb	7.3	4.0	3.0	50.4	631 767	447 745	35.7	4.0	12 296	3 952	15 504	227 487	32.8	2.64	10.7	23.2
Coffee	8.2	5.5	4.4	50.4	37 815	29 592	26.4	1.1	880	399	-68	13 354	26.7	2.69	15.2	22.6
Colquitt	9.0	6.7	6.2	50.5	42 201	36 645	14.8	0.4	875	557	-155	15 495	19.4	2.63	15.5	24.9
Columbia	8.3	4.7	3.3	51.1	92 427	66 031	35.2	3.5	1 489	621	2 238	31 120	42.5	2.85	10.6	15.4
Cook	9.7	7.1	5.9	52.0	15 855	13 456	17.2	0.5	322	237	6	5 882	21.9	2.64	15.3	24.0
Coweta	8.4	4.9	3.6	50.5	94 571	53 853	65.7	6.0	1 765	789	4 276	31 442	66.1	2.81	12.2	17.6
Crawford	9.7	5.4	3.8	49.9	12 559	8 991	39.0	0.5	206	110	-36	4 461	45.4	2.78	12.6	18.8
Crisp	8.7	6.9	6.1	53.0	22 133	20 011	9.9	0.6	527	334	-48	8 337	14.4	2.58	21.6	26.1
Dade	10.2	7.2	4.8	51.0	15 508	13 183	15.0	2.3	229	162	285	5 633	20.9	2.55	9.5	21.7
Dawson	11.0	6.3	3.0	49.8	17 176	9 429	69.7	7.4	302	108	956	6 069	80.9	2.62	8.2	18.6
Decatur	8.6	7.2	6.1	52.4	28 175	25 517	10.7	-0.2	603	355	-311	10 380	15.8	2.65	19.5	24.3
De Kalb	6.9	4.3	3.7	51.5	665 133	546 174	21.9	-0.1	15 141	4 935	-11 170	249 339	19.5	2.62	17.6	26.9
Dodge	9.6	7.1	6.2	48.8	19 143	17 607	8.9	-0.1	296	294	-22	7 062	10.6	2.48	15.2	27.8
Dooly	8.9	6.1	5.7	47.7	11 651	9 901	16.4	1.1	282	125	-29	3 909	9.9	2.62	20.5	25.9
Dougherty	8.2	6.4	5.2	53.4	95 723	96 321	-0.3	-0.4	2 386	1 184	-1 545	35 552	4.1	2.58	23.2	26.8
Douglas	8.2	4.5	3.1	50.9	96 006	71 120	29.6	4.2	1 817	722	2 695	32 822	35.2	2.78	12.7	18.4
Early	9.7	7.8	8.0	53.4	12 282	11 854	4.2	-0.6	263	184	-150	4 695	10.1	2.58	20.8	26.9
Echols	7.2	5.7	3.4	46.3	3 726	2 334	60.8	-0.7	15	20	-27	1 264	54.9	2.97	10.8	18.7
Effingham	8.2	4.7	3.3	50.3	39 616	25 687	46.1	5.5	653	265	1 654	13 151	50.1	2.84	11.1	16.9
Elbert	10.0	8.0	6.9	52.0	20 648	18 949	8.2	0.7	335	330	139	8 004	12.5	2.53	15.7	25.0
Emanuel	9.4	6.8	6.5	51.9	21 859	20 546	6.3	0.1	433	302	-103	8 045	8.4	2.61	17.1	25.0
Evans	8.5	6.6	6.0	51.4	10 738	8 724	20.3	2.3	228	150	165	3 778	20.2	2.62	16.4	25.0

1. No spouse present.

Table B. States and Counties — **Vital Statistics, Health Resources, and Crime**

STATE County	Births, average 1997–1999 Total	Rate[1]	Deaths, average 1997–1999 Number Total	Infant[2]	Rate Total[1]	Infant[3]	Physicians,[4] 2000 Number	Rate[5]	Hospitals,[4] 1998 Number	Beds Number	Rate[5]	Medicare enrollees 2000	Serious crimes known to police, 2000[6] Total Number	Rate[7]
	32	33	34	35	36	37	38	39	40	41	42	43	44	45
FLORIDA—Cont'd														
Sarasota	2 605	8.6	4 780	13	15.8	4.9	952	292	4	1 272	419	103 571	13 583	4 167
Seminole	4 418	12.6	2 418	22	6.9	5.1	523	143	3	706	201	38 740	14 415	3 947
Sumter	436	10.7	516	NA	12.6	NA	21	39	0	0	0	8 435	1 314	2 493
Suwannee	412	12.6	421	NA	12.9	NA	16	46	1	16	49	6 956	1 546	4 437
Taylor	238	12.6	205	NA	10.9	NA	18	93	1	48	255	3 198	721	3 744
Union	138	11.0	163	NA	13.1	NA	14	104	0	0	0	1 205	200	1 488
Volusia	4 500	10.7	5 577	27	13.2	6.0	703	159	8	1 493	353	101 296	21 534	4 857
Wakulla	238	12.7	165	NA	8.8	NA	8	35	0	0	0	2 569	709	3 101
Walton	409	10.9	407	NA	10.9	NA	21	52	1	50	134	5 516	1 492	3 675
Washington	231	11.3	210	NA	10.3	NA	10	48	1	45	222	3 771	299	1 426
GEORGIA	119 885	15.7	60 602	1 032	7.9	8.6	17 317	212	157	24 637	322	916 067	388 949	4 751
Appling	255	15.4	164	NA	9.9	NA	11	63	1	43	261	2 395	295	1 694
Atkinson	154	21.3	68	NA	9.4	NA	1	13	0	0	0	1 034	92	1 209
Bacon	149	14.4	114	NA	11.0	NA	13	129	1	38	366	1 475	126	1 247
Baker	42	11.6	30	NA	8.2	NA	0	0	0	0	0	442	15	465
Baldwin	476	11.3	365	8	8.7	17.5	117	262	1	145	346	5 961	1 742	3 897
Banks	170	13.3	105	NA	8.2	NA	4	28	0	0	0	1 460	472	3 273
Barrow	736	18.2	302	NA	7.5	NA	26	56	1	60	149	5 112	1 884	4 083
Bartow	1 247	17.3	591	8	8.2	6.1	58	76	1	81	113	8 782	2 015	2 675
Ben Hill	281	16.1	213	NA	12.2	NA	14	80	1	60	343	2 964	1 245	7 121
Berrien	261	16.0	171	NA	10.5	NA	9	55	1	167	1 021	2 469	287	1 768
Bibb	2 402	15.4	1 670	34	10.7	14.3	499	324	4	964	618	26 118	13 323	8 658
Bleckley	151	13.5	123	NA	11.0	NA	13	111	1	45	402	1 949	NA	NA
Brantley	137	10.1	111	NA	8.2	NA	2	14	0	0	0	1 819	329	2 249
Brooks	213	13.4	190	NA	11.9	NA	7	43	1	25	156	2 343	486	3 073
Bryan	388	16.4	140	NA	5.9	NA	21	90	0	0	0	2 470	402	1 717
Bulloch	645	12.8	384	NA	7.6	NA	64	114	1	130	257	5 461	NA	NA
Burke	393	17.2	227	NA	9.9	NA	10	45	1	40	175	2 936	1 329	6 100
Butts	244	13.7	158	NA	8.9	NA	14	72	1	28	157	2 777	687	3 519
Calhoun	87	17.3	81	NA	16.1	NA	2	32	1	24	475	1 165	138	2 184
Camden	837	18.0	180	NA	3.9	NA	42	96	1	30	63	2 773	1 625	3 722
Candler	144	16.1	113	NA	12.6	NA	7	73	1	49	540	1 508	381	3 978
Carroll	1 265	15.2	692	8	8.3	6.6	94	108	3	260	313	11 588	3 521	4 035
Catoosa	666	13.1	399	NA	7.9	NA	50	94	1	272	538	5 082	1 948	3 656
Charlton	148	15.7	98	NA	10.4	NA	10	97	1	50	530	1 309	174	1 692
Chatham	3 499	15.5	2 157	27	9.6	7.7	613	264	3	1 159	514	33 408	15 889	6 847
Chattahoochee	229	13.8	30	NA	1.8	NA	28	188	0	0	0	332	81	544
Chattooga	319	13.9	270	NA	11.8	NA	10	39	1	166	728	4 389	120	490
Cherokee	2 266	16.9	712	12	5.3	5.3	87	61	1	84	62	9 842	3 004	2 117
Clarke	1 216	13.4	618	12	6.8	9.9	253	249	2	486	536	10 198	7 510	7 400
Clay	66	18.8	54	NA	15.5	NA	4	119	0	0	0	634	21	626
Clayton	3 723	17.8	1 224	33	5.8	8.9	324	137	1	317	152	17 481	15 561	6 579
Clinch	108	16.2	70	NA	10.5	NA	8	116	1	48	721	1 024	320	4 653
Cobb	8 915	15.7	2 970	61	5.2	6.9	885	146	4	1 016	179	49 873	20 536	3 379
Coffee	611	17.8	296	NA	8.6	NA	42	112	1	114	332	4 605	2 566	6 859
Colquitt	620	15.4	440	10	11.0	16.1	44	105	1	155	386	6 126	2 172	5 207
Columbia	1 243	13.7	467	NA	5.1	NA	178	199	0	0	0	8 481	2 197	2 461
Cook	247	16.5	175	NA	11.7	NA	9	57	1	155	1 033	2 386	183	1 160
Coweta	1 416	16.6	577	8	6.8	5.4	87	98	2	253	298	9 000	2 830	3 219
Crawford	139	13.2	76	NA	7.2	NA	3	24	0	0	0	851	279	2 233
Crisp	338	16.3	250	NA	12.1	NA	29	132	1	65	314	3 295	1 717	7 971
Dade	191	12.8	126	NA	8.4	NA	9	59	1	13	86	2 293	261	1 722
Dawson	230	15.4	83	NA	5.5	NA	6	38	0	0	0	1 779	359	2 334
Decatur	422	15.6	280	NA	10.4	NA	30	106	1	187	692	4 199	1 338	4 874
De Kalb	9 645	16.2	3 924	87	6.6	9.0	2 312	347	5	1 398	235	58 836	37 339	5 608
Dodge	239	13.2	225	NA	12.4	NA	22	115	1	95	525	2 832	618	3 296
Dooly	185	17.8	113	NA	10.8	NA	10	87	2	93	895	1 661	320	2 777
Dougherty	1 621	17.0	876	17	9.2	10.7	214	223	2	601	631	13 745	6 146	6 398
Douglas	1 340	15.0	553	8	6.2	6.2	92	100	2	315	351	8 342	4 137	4 488
Early	188	15.4	154	NA	12.6	NA	9	73	1	176	1 443	2 036	178	1 474
Echols	23	9.5	19	NA	7.6	NA	0	0	0	0	0	147	NA	NA
Effingham	530	14.5	219	NA	6.0	NA	13	35	1	97	266	3 271	1 720	4 582
Elbert	255	13.2	237	NA	12.3	NA	11	54	1	52	269	3 841	290	1 414
Emanuel	315	15.0	245	NA	11.7	NA	17	78	1	119	566	3 837	915	4 190
Evans	156	15.8	110	NA	11.1	NA	8	76	1	36	362	1 585	NA	NA

1. Per 1,000 estimated resident population, average 1997–1999.   2. Deaths of infants under 1 year old.   3. Deaths of infants under 1 year old per 1,000 live births.   4. Data subject to copyright.   5. Per 100,000 resident population as of July 1 of the year shown.   6. Data for serious crimes have not been adjusted for underreporting; this may affect comparability between geographic areas and over time.   7. Per 100,000 population estimated by the FBI.

Table B. States and Counties — Crime, Education, Money Income, and Poverty

STATE County	Serious crimes known to police, 2000[1] (cont'd) Rate[2]		Education						Money income 1989				Income and poverty, 1998		
			School enrollment and attainment, 1990				Local government expenditures, fiscal 1999[5]		Per capita[6] (dollars)	Households Median			Percent below poverty level		
			Enrollment[3]		Attainment[4] (percent)										
	Violent	Property	Total	Percent private	High school graduate or more	Bachelor's degree or more	Total current expenditures (mil dol)	Current expenditures per student (dollars)		Dollars	Percent change, 1979–1989 (constant 1989 dollars)	Percent with $100,000 or more	Median household income	All persons	Persons under 18	Persons 5–17 in families
	46	47	48	49	50	51	52	53	54	55	56	57	58	59	60	61
FLORIDA—Cont'd																
Sarasota	455	3 712	44 114	15.2	81.3	21.9	222.5	6 552	18 441	29 919	18.5	5.2	39 676	8.2	15.6	14.2
Seminole	513	3 434	74 824	15.0	84.6	26.3	297.1	5 108	16 644	35 637	16.3	5.2	44 113	8.8	13.6	12.2
Sumter	518	1 975	6 319	4.5	64.3	7.8	32.4	5 492	9 920	19 584	4.0	1.1	27 360	19.2	28.3	31.6
Suwannee	611	3 826	6 695	6.2	63.8	8.2	31.1	5 352	9 768	19 775	7.6	1.6	27 229	17.0	24.4	25.0
Taylor	753	2 991	4 095	7.4	62.1	9.8	21.7	5 593	10 331	21 380	3.8	1.5	28 824	20.4	28.0	30.9
Union	580	908	2 459	4.9	67.7	7.9	13.0	5 559	9 648	22 831	10.6	0.5	31 996	19.7	21.9	24.2
Volusia	755	4 102	78 296	20.9	75.4	14.8	329.2	5 500	13 288	24 818	19.5	2.4	31 269	12.9	20.4	18.7
Wakulla	455	2 646	3 744	4.9	71.6	10.1	24.4	5 266	10 858	25 019	22.8	2.1	35 903	13.5	20.5	19.7
Walton	697	2 978	5 988	4.3	66.5	11.9	33.1	5 687	11 290	21 297	18.9	2.1	27 971	16.9	23.5	27.4
Washington	100	1 326	4 086	3.2	60.9	7.4	23.6	6 976	8 794	18 266	8.7	0.6	26 444	20.4	27.8	30.7
GEORGIA	505	4 246	1 643 859	12.8	70.9	19.3	8 537.2	6 092	13 631	29 021	15.2	3.8	37 826	14.1	21.8	21.0
Appling	390	1 303	4 088	3.6	57.2	8.2	21.9	6 301	9 901	22 271	24.5	1.0	29 152	19.5	27.7	28.4
Atkinson	171	1 038	1 544	1.6	51.5	6.4	8.4	5 323	7 902	17 685	12.3	0.7	25 912	23.3	31.0	33.3
Bacon	49	1 198	2 370	1.6	58.1	6.6	11.3	5 636	9 137	19 118	4.2	1.7	27 279	20.8	27.4	29.8
Baker	124	341	974	12.3	53.6	9.4	3.8	8 689	8 667	18 489	0.9	1.5	26 189	23.4	33.0	35.2
Baldwin	329	3 568	11 002	12.1	64.7	13.3	37.7	5 903	10 358	25 513	2.6	2.5	31 756	17.9	26.5	24.6
Banks	173	3 099	2 452	3.9	56.6	6.4	11.0	4 844	10 741	24 220	9.2	1.4	34 571	14.0	22.2	20.6
Barrow	290	3 792	6 544	8.4	58.8	9.2	45.8	5 844	11 156	27 538	16.9	1.6	39 843	11.6	17.5	18.0
Bartow	169	2 506	12 761	6.0	58.7	9.0	85.2	5 799	11 748	27 554	13.4	2.0	39 587	11.0	17.7	16.2
Ben Hill	1 195	5 925	4 047	2.9	56.8	7.6	20.3	5 646	9 300	19 106	7.7	0.9	27 225	20.6	28.9	29.2
Berrien	277	1 491	3 407	5.3	57.5	7.5	16.4	5 177	9 403	20 979	2.5	1.1	28 423	19.3	28.7	30.9
Bibb	573	8 085	39 211	23.4	68.2	17.0	150.8	6 127	13 017	25 813	7.3	3.4	33 720	20.3	32.7	30.0
Bleckley	NA	NA	2 812	3.9	60.3	10.3	13.1	5 504	10 775	22 690	-0.9	2.2	31 929	18.0	28.6	27.9
Brantley	205	2 044	2 809	2.4	64.1	5.8	16.0	5 094	9 089	22 087	4.6	0.9	30 977	18.6	27.8	27.3
Brooks	689	2 384	3 821	5.7	58.7	9.1	15.5	5 643	8 522	19 474	22.4	0.9	26 503	23.9	36.7	34.5
Bryan	98	1 618	4 330	8.1	68.5	11.8	27.4	5 353	11 083	28 623	25.3	2.5	41 823	11.3	16.5	16.2
Bulloch	NA	NA	16 551	4.2	67.6	19.9	54.0	6 447	9 635	20 640	-1.3	1.9	32 049	19.4	26.0	27.0
Burke	1 395	4 705	5 564	11.1	55.3	9.6	29.1	5 960	8 185	17 667	-0.3	0.8	24 788	24.7	33.8	33.6
Butts	154	3 365	3 340	4.9	58.4	7.2	17.9	5 641	10 321	24 420	4.5	1.9	33 835	15.4	23.6	22.6
Calhoun	316	1 867	1 427	4.8	52.2	10.1	7.8	9 701	8 244	15 640	-7.9	1.3	23 105	28.8	43.3	42.1
Camden	476	3 245	7 445	7.4	79.5	13.5	50.9	5 249	11 710	28 212	24.9	1.1	40 739	10.9	15.0	16.2
Candler	564	3 414	1 748	5.1	53.2	9.9	10.7	5 541	9 293	19 375	16.9	2.0	25 384	24.3	34.6	36.7
Carroll	364	3 670	19 132	3.9	60.5	12.0	93.5	6 145	11 239	25 607	9.3	1.6	36 455	13.9	21.2	20.3
Catoosa	197	3 459	9 674	8.8	63.8	8.1	48.4	5 286	11 059	25 581	-4.7	1.2	37 596	11.3	17.5	16.8
Charlton	185	1 507	2 031	5.9	56.2	6.4	10.9	5 290	8 894	22 328	1.3	0.5	28 096	18.6	24.6	28.2
Chatham	839	6 008	55 327	20.7	73.7	18.6	216.0	5 882	12 983	26 721	11.9	3.1	35 063	18.2	28.6	26.8
Chattahoochee	60	484	4 671	9.7	88.5	20.2	3.4	6 725	8 673	25 305	12.1	0.1	38 845	14.6	16.0	17.0
Chattooga	8	482	4 728	6.0	50.1	5.9	24.5	5 856	9 281	20 335	-6.0	0.7	29 597	14.8	22.6	22.4
Cherokee	123	1 994	20 407	13.8	75.2	18.4	139.0	5 712	14 849	39 052	31.5	2.9	58 052	6.0	9.4	8.9
Clarke	418	6 982	37 672	6.5	77.1	37.5	87.3	7 780	11 604	20 806	0.3	3.4	33 081	18.2	26.3	25.4
Clay	328	298	827	13.8	51.4	11.2	2.7	7 041	7 678	13 709	11.5	1.6	21 200	30.9	42.3	48.1
Clayton	524	6 055	45 352	10.6	77.2	14.7	252.8	5 737	13 577	33 472	0.1	1.9	39 772	13.4	22.2	19.6
Clinch	1 817	2 835	1 622	2.5	46.2	6.7	9.4	6 179	8 354	18 098	-1.8	1.2	27 116	21.1	26.6	32.2
Cobb	252	3 127	112 101	15.8	85.8	33.0	645.8	6 594	19 166	41 297	15.0	7.3	54 340	6.5	10.7	9.1
Coffee	738	6 121	7 665	4.2	58.0	11.1	41.6	5 568	10 170	20 651	13.6	2.9	29 584	20.3	27.7	28.0
Colquitt	841	4 365	8 833	4.3	57.0	10.0	47.7	5 727	9 878	20 331	2.2	1.6	27 323	21.7	30.5	30.8
Columbia	119	2 342	18 757	12.2	81.1	23.9	92.8	4 983	15 372	40 122	30.4	5.5	53 302	7.6	12.1	10.7
Cook	120	1 040	3 277	3.4	55.2	6.5	17.0	5 432	8 870	19 858	0.7	0.9	27 317	20.4	30.2	30.9
Coweta	262	2 958	12 712	9.0	67.4	13.3	87.8	5 558	13 708	31 925	24.3	3.5	48 365	9.5	14.9	14.9
Crawford	104	2 129	2 263	11.2	60.2	5.7	11.4	5 340	10 003	25 799	4.6	0.5	34 992	14.8	21.4	22.4
Crisp	840	7 131	4 770	6.8	56.2	10.0	28.5	6 172	9 248	17 797	-9.0	1.3	24 609	27.5	39.7	39.9
Dade	79	1 643	3 390	21.5	55.3	8.0	14.7	5 688	9 360	20 176	-8.2	1.2	32 459	13.7	19.5	20.1
Dawson	59	2 475	2 053	3.4	60.1	8.6	14.4	5 836	12 198	28 380	38.4	2.6	42 722	10.5	15.5	17.2
Decatur	532	4 342	6 826	2.7	59.8	11.7	31.9	5 456	9 246	20 854	5.0	1.4	26 911	23.8	33.3	33.9
De Kalb	518	5 090	141 313	20.5	83.9	32.7	627.4	6 544	17 115	35 721	7.3	5.6	43 964	12.9	22.6	18.6
Dodge	427	2 869	4 227	6.2	56.8	8.0	23.0	6 525	8 643	18 244	3.8	0.6	26 630	21.8	30.9	33.0
Dooly	269	2 508	2 538	19.2	54.7	9.5	12.2	6 758	8 413	16 326	-5.6	1.4	24 228	27.6	39.5	36.6
Dougherty	593	5 804	28 313	11.3	67.5	17.0	111.9	6 466	10 888	23 587	-7.9	2.5	29 979	23.9	34.9	33.6
Douglas	307	4 181	17 511	11.6	72.3	12.0	102.1	6 087	14 096	37 138	10.5	2.9	47 461	8.6	13.6	13.1
Early	166	1 308	2 877	5.7	54.1	9.4	16.3	5 679	8 280	16 421	-1.5	1.1	23 897	29.4	41.0	43.5
Echols	NA	NA	574	4.5	61.0	4.7	4.2	5 950	8 915	21 574	11.6	0.6	30 260	19.5	25.6	31.6
Effingham	408	4 175	6 663	5.7	66.0	7.6	41.6	5 166	10 865	29 443	12.9	0.6	44 402	10.5	14.8	15.2
Elbert	93	1 321	4 411	5.4	54.3	8.0	23.0	5 929	9 288	20 501	0.9	1.0	28 608	18.5	28.5	27.8
Emanuel	811	3 380	5 319	5.4	52.6	9.1	27.9	5 591	8 535	17 891	0.7	0.9	23 253	26.3	37.7	36.0
Evans	NA	NA	2 105	6.7	58.5	8.6	10.6	5 223	9 792	19 972	9.7	1.0	26 208	23.6	31.6	35.5

1. Data for serious crimes have not been adjusted for underreporting; this may affect comparability between geographic areas and over time.   2. Per 100,000 population estimated by the FBI.   3. All persons 3 years old and over enrolled in nursery school through college.   4. Persons 25 years old and over.   5. Elementary and secondary education expenditures, local government fiscal years ending between July 1, 1998 and June 30, 1999.   6. Based on population enumerated as of April 1, 1990.

Table B. States and Counties — **Personal Income**

STATE County	Total (mil dol)	Percent change, 1998–1999	Per capita[1] Dollars	Per capita[1] Rank	Wages and salaries[2] (mil dol)	Proprietor's income (mil dol)	Dividends, interest, and rent (mil dol)	Transfer payments Total (mil dol)	Govt. payments Total (mil dol)	Social Security (mil dol)	Medical payments (mil dol)	Income maintenance (mil dol)	Unemployment insurance (mil dol)
	62	63	64	65	66	67	68	69	70	71	72	73	74
FLORIDA—Cont'd													
Sarasota	11 935	3.8	38 934	51	4 648	675	5 098	1 792	1 735	957	656	48	8
Seminole	10 762	7.2	30 113	209	4 625	512	1 658	1 000	934	438	317	61	14
Sumter	740	6.1	17 312	2 682	261	51	169	207	199	85	72	17	1
Suwannee	624	2.2	18 921	2 308	223	96	110	161	155	63	65	16	1
Taylor	342	2.5	17 979	2 544	206	20	55	85	82	32	33	12	1
Union	162	3.1	12 751	3 087	120	14	24	30	28	11	11	4	0
Volusia	9 603	4.1	22 564	1 201	4 020	462	2 801	2 030	1 952	989	733	118	15
Wakulla	494	8.7	25 740	550	129	32	62	62	59	24	23	7	0
Walton	654	5.2	17 159	2 708	280	56	138	140	133	56	48	14	1
Washington	349	4.4	16 941	2 745	171	22	56	98	95	33	42	11	1
GEORGIA	212 806	6.6	27 324	X	145 140	18 512	35 590	23 558	21 888	8 894	8 554	2 747	302
Appling	296	3.1	17 737	2 592	213	34	47	66	63	22	27	10	1
Atkinson	145	5.8	19 843	2 039	56	36	16	28	26	8	12	5	0
Bacon	196	2.7	18 891	2 321	94	24	27	45	42	14	19	7	1
Baker	76	8.2	20 940	1 685	17	15	11	14	14	5	5	3	0
Baldwin	897	2.8	21 267	1 577	541	69	177	194	185	55	103	15	2
Banks	256	1.8	19 408	2 175	68	49	37	36	33	17	11	3	1
Barrow	885	6.9	21 127	1 623	338	84	129	122	113	48	48	12	1
Bartow	1 698	8.0	22 755	1 151	934	134	235	203	187	92	67	16	2
Ben Hill	394	8.4	22 537	1 209	259	53	58	77	73	24	32	10	1
Berrien	305	4.5	18 454	2 426	136	31	52	65	61	21	27	9	1
Bibb	4 181	4.5	26 895	424	3 073	309	828	666	633	221	273	95	8
Bleckley	246	4.0	21 771	1 423	116	13	46	45	43	15	19	6	0
Brantley	242	5.6	17 413	2 663	47	22	27	51	48	18	19	5	1
Brooks	291	7.5	18 037	2 535	81	35	57	67	64	24	24	12	1
Bryan	520	9.0	21 314	1 566	103	39	63	62	56	23	22	6	1
Bulloch	994	5.0	19 582	2 114	572	83	188	152	141	53	55	20	1
Burke	380	5.4	16 386	2 846	216	14	56	89	84	27	35	17	2
Butts	367	6.4	19 994	1 992	144	28	52	64	60	24	27	6	1
Calhoun	107	7.3	21 646	1 473	41	23	16	26	25	7	12	5	0
Camden	795	2.4	16 904	2 754	714	38	114	83	74	30	27	8	1
Candler	176	3.5	19 617	2 127	65	21	30	43	41	13	21	6	0
Carroll	1 783	5.6	21 031	1 660	958	151	278	271	252	110	101	26	3
Catoosa	1 035	8.2	19 871	2 030	398	83	121	146	135	72	42	11	2
Charlton	159	6.0	16 817	2 775	57	12	21	36	34	12	15	4	0
Chatham	6 298	3.3	27 910	338	4 428	405	1 447	874	826	332	317	106	9
Chattahoochee	396	7.9	23 792	899	582	2	31	13	11	3	3	3	0
Chattooga	452	5.3	19 770	2 065	224	31	58	94	89	40	35	9	1
Cherokee	3 670	8.9	25 900	530	976	252	505	252	221	116	75	14	2
Clarke	2 265	4.1	24 985	675	2 071	132	527	253	234	95	86	31	2
Clay	60	6.0	17 082	2 721	17	6	12	17	16	6	6	4	0
Clayton	4 761	6.8	22 277	1 279	4 763	181	575	518	471	180	190	58	7
Clinch	123	2.6	18 379	2 448	74	11	16	31	30	9	15	5	0
Cobb	20 993	7.8	35 974	73	13 165	1 701	3 116	1 147	1 021	512	371	62	15
Coffee	758	5.7	21 686	1 459	509	90	95	126	118	40	51	18	2
Colquitt	794	4.8	19 504	2 138	380	112	130	156	147	55	60	22	2
Columbia	2 140	5.9	22 931	1 102	553	109	426	199	179	82	58	14	2
Cook	278	6.5	18 276	2 477	132	35	38	61	57	20	25	8	1
Coweta	2 167	10.3	24 237	819	807	103	309	222	203	94	79	19	2
Crawford	199	6.1	19 097	2 259	34	15	32	30	28	10	11	4	0
Crisp	420	5.4	20 343	1 877	237	39	72	97	92	29	41	18	1
Dade	287	6.9	18 714	2 364	81	26	39	48	45	20	17	5	1
Dawson	378	11.0	23 691	919	100	41	51	41	37	16	16	3	0
Decatur	539	3.5	19 879	2 026	318	60	91	117	111	38	49	19	1
De Kalb	20 050	5.0	33 592	118	13 901	2 158	3 425	1 600	1 471	621	555	162	25
Dodge	337	4.6	18 581	2 403	145	23	60	76	72	24	32	12	1
Dooly	195	2.2	18 690	2 370	104	19	35	48	46	15	20	9	1
Dougherty	2 162	1.6	22 985	1 094	1 808	156	411	392	371	122	143	72	7
Douglas	2 181	6.4	23 917	874	870	111	256	215	196	88	79	15	2
Early	256	6.8	21 115	1 631	152	45	49	54	52	18	20	11	1
Echols	46	12.2	18 290	2 474	10	6	5	7	7	2	2	1	0
Effingham	835	10.4	21 764	1 428	215	42	81	92	83	38	29	9	1
Elbert	412	4.8	21 302	1 570	191	46	87	87	83	35	33	11	1
Emanuel	386	3.6	18 336	2 460	183	30	70	102	97	33	42	17	2
Evans	200	4.5	19 774	2 064	108	18	34	42	40	14	17	6	0

1. Based on the resident population estimated as of July 1 of the year shown. 2. Includes other labor income.

STATE County	Earnings, 1999									Social Security beneficiaries, December 2000			Housing units, 1990	
			Percent by selected industries											
			Goods-related[1]		Service-related and other[2]							Supplemental Security Income recipients, December 2000		Percent change, 1980–1990
	Total (mil dol)	Farm	Total	Manufacturing	Total	Retail trade	Finance, insurance, and real estate	Services	Government	Number	Rate[3]		Total	
	75	76	77	78	79	80	81	82	83	84	85	86	87	88

STATE County	75	76	77	78	79	80	81	82	83	84	85	86	87	88
FLORIDA—Cont'd														
Sarasota	5 322	0.3	D	6.2	D	13.1	11.4	44.4	9.3	103 539	318	3 192	157 055	38.6
Seminole	5 137	0.3	18.7	8.1	69.7	14.4	9.1	30.6	11.3	51 869	142	4 562	117 845	72.9
Sumter	313	4.9	17.8	8.7	38.7	9.1	2.6	13.0	38.6	17 138	321	1 260	15 298	38.0
Suwannee	319	14.9	D	D	D	12.5	3.9	18.2	18.4	8 484	243	1 116	11 699	33.5
Taylor	226	0.8	D	35.8	D	8.2	2.4	D	21.6	3 979	207	723	7 908	13.3
Union	134	2.7	D	6.3	D	3.1	0.6	7.3	64.7	1 532	114	299	2 975	27.7
Volusia	4 482	1.6	D	8.4	D	14.6	6.4	35.4	17.5	115 262	260	8 746	180 972	45.4
Wakulla	161	1.1	36.5	26.4	34.4	7.3	4.1	15.4	28.0	3 180	139	489	6 587	29.9
Walton	336	2.7	D	7.6	D	16.4	6.8	25.9	23.0	8 291	204	920	18 728	71.5
Washington	193	1.8	D	13.3	D	9.4	2.6	12.2	41.2	4 739	226	855	7 703	28.8
GEORGIA	163 652	1.2	21.2	15.0	61.8	9.0	7.5	26.5	15.7	1 101 028	134	196 907	2 638 418	30.1
Appling	246	6.5	22.5	15.4	D	D	2.2	7.7	14.7	3 041	175	765	6 629	14.1
Atkinson	93	34.4	D	36.4	D	4.6	1.8	4.0	12.0	1 192	157	418	2 449	5.7
Bacon	118	9.7	34.8	32.5	40.8	9.2	3.3	13.3	14.6	1 961	194	531	3 859	13.0
Baker	32	49.2	4.8	1.9	D	2.7	D	17.2	17.9	705	173	225	1 499	17.7
Baldwin	609	0.3	D	17.7	D	10.3	3.6	17.1	42.6	6 845	153	1 362	14 200	16.1
Banks	117	30.2	D	24.2	D	9.7	D	8.0	12.9	2 379	165	254	4 193	27.8
Barrow	422	4.6	D	25.6	D	13.0	4.2	15.1	16.0	6 024	131	1 199	11 812	51.9
Bartow	1 067	1.9	43.7	35.1	41.3	9.8	2.9	14.2	13.1	11 245	148	1 379	21 757	46.7
Ben Hill	312	7.1	50.4	46.3	28.3	7.0	2.8	9.1	14.2	3 260	186	798	6 875	10.9
Berrien	167	7.4	D	31.8	D	14.6	4.9	13.0	13.8	2 965	183	698	5 858	14.4
Bibb	3 382	0.1	D	18.4	D	10.0	9.7	31.3	12.3	28 229	183	6 887	61 462	10.6
Bleckley	129	1.7	D	D	D	7.0	2.4	10.9	22.1	2 196	188	442	4 268	8.8
Brantley	68	9.7	23.1	12.5	38.4	7.7	1.5	12.0	28.8	2 499	171	488	4 404	39.7
Brooks	116	25.7	22.2	17.5	34.7	5.8	2.9	12.7	17.4	3 239	197	734	5 972	11.4
Bryan	142	-0.2	23.4	9.8	51.6	14.4	6.3	19.2	25.1	2 881	123	515	5 549	58.0
Bulloch	654	2.4	D	15.2	D	13.6	3.9	19.6	27.9	7 033	126	1 493	16 541	30.4
Burke	230	-0.5	D	17.2	D	6.6	2.0	13.9	18.3	3 652	164	1 105	8 329	22.3
Butts	172	1.8	D	19.3	D	9.2	4.5	14.9	24.4	3 099	159	525	5 536	11.3
Calhoun	64	28.4	D	D	D	5.3	2.3	9.7	32.1	1 119	177	418	2 061	5.0
Camden	753	0.1	16.7	13.2	23.4	6.1	1.4	12.5	59.8	3 949	90	611	10 885	102.3
Candler	86	5.6	18.1	13.4	53.9	13.0	4.1	18.7	22.4	1 862	194	536	3 203	12.7
Carroll	1 109	2.7	D	30.8	D	9.7	4.0	20.0	15.8	13 761	158	2 334	27 736	36.5
Catoosa	481	2.4	D	28.3	D	14.0	4.5	21.3	12.4	8 633	162	673	16 762	25.1
Charlton	69	2.9	28.4	22.6	43.1	12.6	2.0	20.6	25.5	1 647	160	360	3 222	28.6
Chatham	4 833	0.0	D	18.4	D	10.3	5.1	28.0	18.3	38 258	165	6 481	91 178	17.7
Chattahoochee	584	0.0	D	D	D	D	D	1.9	95.1	400	27	123	3 108	-2.9
Chattooga	255	0.9	53.3	50.2	27.3	10.6	2.2	10.2	18.5	4 970	195	797	9 142	10.3
Cherokee	1 228	1.5	D	10.7	D	13.3	8.2	22.4	14.7	13 761	97	891	33 840	89.1
Clarke	2 203	0.3	D	15.8	D	10.2	4.2	24.0	33.5	11 259	111	2 337	35 971	30.3
Clay	24	17.9	D	D	D	8.5	1.5	10.1	41.2	837	249	236	1 586	18.4
Clayton	4 943	0.0	D	6.1	D	9.9	2.4	17.4	10.6	21 879	93	4 017	71 926	35.7
Clinch	85	3.6	37.9	37.0	39.2	16.6	2.0	8.5	19.3	1 329	193	440	2 423	3.0
Cobb	14 866	0.0	18.4	10.0	74.0	12.2	8.3	31.2	7.6	56 193	92	5 486	189 872	67.6
Coffee	599	7.5	35.0	29.6	45.9	18.0	2.2	16.4	11.5	5 636	151	1 507	11 650	19.0
Colquitt	492	12.0	25.6	20.0	42.3	10.2	3.9	16.8	20.2	7 409	176	1 874	14 350	10.8
Columbia	662	0.7	D	16.1	D	12.6	6.3	26.4	15.8	10 351	116	833	23 745	68.4
Cook	166	12.3	36.2	30.7	37.6	9.5	2.8	13.8	13.9	2 976	189	649	5 340	9.9
Coweta	911	0.3	D	25.0	D	15.6	3.9	21.4	14.6	11 327	127	1 459	20 413	44.6
Crawford	49	16.5	D	8.8	D	5.2	2.4	11.8	26.0	1 436	115	272	3 279	27.4
Crisp	276	5.5	23.2	18.5	53.5	14.7	5.7	17.9	17.9	3 875	176	1 205	8 318	12.7
Dade	108	2.8	35.7	28.5	D	14.6	3.3	19.0	16.3	2 579	170	375	4 998	16.4
Dawson	141	7.3	30.2	14.7	48.2	15.9	6.6	19.5	14.4	2 003	125	290	4 321	80.0
Decatur	378	9.2	D	26.1	D	9.6	3.3	11.1	20.5	5 094	180	11 833	10 120	11.6
De Kalb	16 059	0.0	15.1	8.9	72.9	8.1	8.5	33.4	12.0	69 030	104	1 390	231 520	27.3
Dodge	168	3.7	20.0	14.9	43.4	11.4	3.2	16.7	32.9	3 572	186	911	7 094	10.9
Dooly	123	7.8	34.4	32.2	33.9	6.2	3.4	9.1	24.0	2 276	197	586	4 003	6.1
Dougherty	1 964	0.9	24.9	19.2	D	9.5	D	24.7	22.9	15 760	164	4 859	37 373	7.6
Douglas	981	0.0	D	10.6	D	18.3	3.4	26.0	15.3	10 523	114	1 109	26 495	49.2
Early	197	19.1	38.3	35.7	30.0	4.7	3.3	9.6	12.7	2 508	203	756	4 714	0.7
Echols	17	31.4	D	D	D	2.1	D	4.5	25.8	364	97	66	942	13.9
Effingham	257	1.0	46.2	35.7	31.9	11.0	2.6	9.9	20.9	4 682	125	558	9 492	50.1
Elbert	237	2.0	40.5	33.7	37.1	8.6	3.9	13.9	20.4	4 484	219	963	7 891	11.9
Emanuel	212	2.0	27.4	24.6	40.6	9.6	2.9	15.7	30.0	4 838	222	1 468	8 344	6.9
Evans	125	4.8	43.3	35.1	34.9	10.0	2.8	15.5	17.0	1 967	187	528	3 512	10.1

1. Covers mining, construction, and manufacturing. 2. Covers private sector earnings in agricultural services, forestry, and fisheries; transportation and public utilities; wholesale trade; retail trade; finance, insurance, and real estate; and services. 3. Per 1,000 resident population estimated as of July 1 of the year shown.

Table B. States and Counties — Housing, Labor Force, and Employment

STATE County	Housing units, 1990 (cont'd) Occupied units — Owner-occupied Total	Percent	Median value[1]	Owner cost as a percent of income — With a mortgage	Without a mortgage	Renter-occupied Median rent[2]	Rent as percent of income	Substandard units[3] (percent)	Civilian labor force, 2001 Total	Percent change, 2000–2001	Unemployment Total	Rate[4]	Civilian employment, 1990[5] Total	Percent Professional, managerial, and technical	Precision production, craft, and repair
	89	90	91	92	93	94	95	96	97	98	99	100	101	102	103
FLORIDA—Cont'd															
Sarasota	125 493	76.2	87 200	23.2	11.7	543	28.0	1.6	159 716	3.4	4 414	2.8	114 217	29.8	11.8
Seminole	107 657	66.9	91 500	22.0	11.9	548	26.1	2.7	222 523	0.9	8 301	3.7	151 377	35.3	9.8
Sumter	12 119	80.1	49 900	19.6	12.9	315	25.8	5.1	14 396	1.3	613	4.3	11 081	19.1	13.2
Suwannee	10 034	79.2	45 100	19.6	12.8	277	27.3	5.6	13 472	4.2	749	5.6	10 429	18.0	14.6
Taylor	6 401	78.5	43 600	16.5	12.6	281	25.1	7.5	6 946	-1.5	666	9.6	6 850	21.6	16.3
Union	2 658	69.9	43 800	17.5	13.0	219	19.0	10.0	3 555	5.3	141	4.0	3 332	18.5	8.4
Volusia	153 416	71.9	69 400	23.2	12.2	464	29.2	2.4	177 132	1.4	7 591	4.3	155 529	27.4	12.7
Wakulla	5 210	83.4	51 800	19.7	13.0	331	25.7	8.2	12 094	4.7	413	3.4	7 001	25.6	16.6
Walton	11 294	78.4	49 700	22.8	12.4	324	23.1	3.9	18 113	8.2	601	3.3	11 498	22.5	14.1
Washington	6 443	80.5	40 100	22.0	12.0	269	27.3	6.0	9 336	-1.1	469	5.0	6 417	21.5	12.7
GEORGIA	2 366 615	64.9	71 300	20.9	12.8	433	25.8	4.7	4 131 569	-1.0	165 221	4.0	3 090 276	28.2	11.9
Appling	5 834	76.6	39 200	16.2	13.4	264	23.6	7.8	8 120	-0.1	723	8.9	6 553	18.1	17.3
Atkinson	2 210	72.9	30 300	18.6	14.9	218	22.8	10.0	2 789	-16.6	253	9.1	2 523	15.7	14.5
Bacon	3 442	71.8	40 500	19.8	12.3	219	27.2	5.6	4 209	-3.5	272	6.5	4 138	16.3	18.8
Baker	1 300	73.0	36 600	23.1	12.4	213	24.8	11.0	1 592	-1.8	81	5.1	1 498	17.3	13.0
Baldwin	12 165	68.3	54 900	20.1	12.8	334	24.1	4.2	16 399	-4.8	602	3.7	15 901	28.4	12.1
Banks	3 775	81.2	51 100	20.8	13.0	297	23.7	4.7	6 353	-2.8	241	3.8	5 060	14.0	18.4
Barrow	10 676	72.3	64 000	22.5	12.1	392	24.5	3.8	22 077	1.1	986	4.5	13 875	18.4	17.5
Bartow	20 091	71.7	63 100	20.6	12.5	410	24.7	4.7	41 255	0.1	1 859	4.5	27 377	18.2	16.2
Ben Hill	5 972	66.3	42 300	21.4	13.4	265	27.1	5.1	8 740	-5.5	475	5.4	6 678	17.1	12.9
Berrien	5 149	73.9	40 400	19.3	13.2	259	23.2	5.6	6 193	-5.1	324	5.2	6 438	16.6	15.3
Bibb	56 307	57.6	57 900	18.4	12.7	352	26.7	4.3	68 872	-1.7	2 969	4.3	65 754	28.3	11.2
Bleckley	3 816	75.1	41 000	17.7	13.3	225	21.8	4.7	5 670	-4.3	255	4.5	4 644	22.0	15.3
Brantley	3 811	84.6	36 400	19.9	12.1	285	27.5	5.9	6 313	0.4	353	5.6	4 504	16.6	22.9
Brooks	5 392	72.0	42 200	23.4	14.1	255	25.0	8.8	7 612	-3.3	375	4.9	6 185	18.1	10.6
Bryan	5 070	79.8	70 200	22.9	12.5	328	24.0	5.7	11 128	-1.2	278	2.5	6 582	25.2	16.2
Bulloch	14 984	60.1	59 900	18.3	12.7	330	34.8	6.1	26 186	-3.1	957	3.7	18 839	26.3	11.7
Burke	7 037	70.8	43 500	19.5	13.6	197	29.2	10.8	8 894	-1.7	704	7.9	7 905	20.0	13.3
Butts	4 696	71.8	55 500	20.2	12.5	348	24.6	8.5	8 599	-5.2	430	5.0	6 122	15.0	13.9
Calhoun	1 794	69.1	29 400	16.6	14.2	169	22.2	15.2	2 380	-3.5	165	6.9	1 932	17.2	9.0
Camden	9 459	63.0	66 700	22.8	12.8	416	24.5	6.2	16 823	-0.4	583	3.5	10 805	25.0	14.1
Candler	2 828	71.7	44 700	21.1	15.4	253	20.6	7.3	4 062	3.0	179	4.4	3 266	20.6	11.5
Carroll	25 370	69.4	60 300	20.7	12.3	351	26.0	4.5	46 079	0.7	2 318	5.0	34 189	21.0	15.6
Catoosa	15 745	75.9	56 500	18.5	12.3	358	24.8	3.6	27 372	-0.7	699	2.6	20 146	20.4	13.3
Charlton	2 911	78.8	41 200	20.5	13.1	290	29.3	8.2	3 795	-0.6	149	3.9	3 396	13.3	15.0
Chatham	81 111	58.8	63 300	21.2	13.2	406	27.2	4.2	105 594	-1.4	3 541	3.4	93 969	29.0	11.7
Chattahoochee	2 884	20.2	42 600	22.1	11.2	414	20.2	2.8	2 364	-4.3	142	6.0	2 047	28.9	9.4
Chattooga	8 467	74.7	34 700	16.7	12.5	278	24.0	4.9	10 816	-7.6	477	4.4	9 868	14.7	16.3
Cherokee	31 309	82.5	86 600	22.3	12.7	534	26.2	2.8	83 614	0.0	1 900	2.3	48 237	27.9	15.7
Clarke	33 170	44.2	73 200	20.0	13.2	389	31.1	3.6	46 275	-0.8	1 569	3.4	40 991	37.0	7.5
Clay	1 210	66.4	31 300	19.1	13.1	210	23.2	11.6	1 478	-5.3	86	5.8	1 230	20.8	7.2
Clayton	65 523	58.8	70 100	20.8	12.2	532	26.0	3.5	127 844	0.2	5 145	4.0	96 580	23.3	13.8
Clinch	2 173	68.2	33 600	17.5	13.1	190	22.6	7.7	2 892	-13.5	203	7.0	2 404	15.3	11.8
Cobb	171 288	64.6	97 700	21.0	12.0	575	24.5	1.9	366 575	0.2	10 826	3.0	253 096	38.0	9.0
Coffee	10 541	72.6	45 600	18.5	14.9	273	25.8	6.8	19 358	-6.6	1 035	5.3	13 229	16.2	13.9
Colquitt	12 980	68.5	40 700	19.1	13.4	266	27.5	5.5	18 515	-4.7	1 232	6.7	15 776	19.8	12.2
Columbia	21 841	79.3	83 700	21.0	11.9	442	23.6	3.2	44 362	-2.5	1 106	2.5	32 628	36.9	13.2
Cook	4 825	75.0	39 500	16.7	13.4	276	24.6	5.9	7 781	-3.5	385	4.9	5 987	15.7	12.2
Coweta	18 930	72.8	68 700	21.0	12.4	415	26.5	5.3	47 437	-0.4	1 545	3.3	25 632	23.4	16.2
Crawford	3 069	81.3	49 500	20.3	12.5	252	21.1	10.0	5 900	-1.9	222	3.8	4 113	14.8	18.6
Crisp	7 287	61.1	47 100	19.1	13.6	268	29.6	5.1	9 208	-4.3	559	6.1	8 068	21.4	10.8
Dade	4 661	79.1	45 100	19.1	12.7	301	26.4	4.0	7 590	-0.4	221	2.9	5 851	16.2	15.5
Dawson	3 360	85.2	80 900	26.6	12.1	390	23.2	3.9	9 578	-9.8	245	2.6	4 719	18.2	19.1
Decatur	8 962	72.0	42 700	20.1	14.6	259	25.9	7.4	10 958	-6.9	711	6.5	10 438	21.2	12.3
De Kalb	208 690	57.8	91 600	21.3	12.3	552	26.6	4.1	368 972	0.3	15 574	4.2	299 852	36.9	7.5
Dodge	6 387	74.3	33 700	18.5	13.9	224	25.0	6.7	9 626	-3.3	434	4.5	7 070	19.9	12.8
Dooly	3 557	68.7	39 200	18.3	13.5	215	30.6	9.6	4 343	-4.4	275	6.3	3 713	18.1	10.8
Dougherty	34 163	52.3	57 500	18.5	13.1	334	26.5	6.9	42 478	-4.5	2 574	6.1	38 922	27.4	11.4
Douglas	24 277	77.8	73 400	20.5	12.3	549	25.7	2.8	53 248	-0.2	1 495	2.8	37 431	25.7	15.0
Early	4 263	69.2	40 100	18.9	13.5	232	24.3	10.9	4 765	0.2	279	5.9	4 751	16.1	12.3
Echols	816	81.4	40 000	17.0	13.6	244	19.8	6.8	1 255	-2.2	63	5.0	983	12.8	13.5
Effingham	8 759	78.8	61 300	19.3	12.1	365	21.8	8.0	18 410	-1.2	496	2.7	11 495	19.0	19.3
Elbert	7 115	73.2	44 600	20.4	13.8	253	25.9	6.5	8 822	-3.2	635	7.2	8 182	19.3	16.9
Emanuel	7 420	69.9	35 200	18.1	13.2	230	25.6	7.7	8 125	-5.5	675	8.3	8 263	18.9	13.1
Evans	3 144	67.6	44 100	21.4	14.1	268	25.9	6.5	5 033	-4.4	184	3.7	3 663	17.6	14.4

1. Specified owner-occupied units.   2. Specified renter-occupied units.   3. Overcrowded or lacking complete plumbing facilities.   4. Percent of civilian labor force.   5. Persons 16 years and older.

Table B. States and Counties — Nonfarm Employment and Agriculture

STATE County	Private nonfarm establishments, employment and payroll, 1999									Agriculture, 1997			
		Employment						Annual payroll		Farms			Farm operators
											Percent with—		
	Number of establishments	Total	Health Care and Social Assistance	Manufacturing	Retail trade	Finance and Insurance	Professional Scientific and Technical Services	Total (mil dol)	Average per employee (dollars)	Number	Less than 50 acres	500 acres and over	Whose principal occupation is farming (percent)
	104	105	106	107	108	109	110	111	112	113	114	115	116
FLORIDA—Cont'd													
Sarasota	11 058	146 676	20 796	8 359	21 399	5 268	9 621	3 653	24 908	315	70.5	9.2	37.1
Seminole	10 470	128 422	11 010	8 929	23 420	6 794	8 953	3 523	27 434	344	83.1	2.6	44.2
Sumter	528	5 084	474	803	1 247	139	94	93	18 248	718	49.7	7.9	41.5
Suwannee	614	7 240	1 175	1 754	1 525	263	162	134	18 462	840	37.5	8.1	50.0
Taylor	403	4 994	632	1 953	913	124	74	124	24 776	126	38.1	12.7	38.1
Union	122	1 459	505	D	159	D	12	36	24 332	213	45.1	8.5	36.6
Volusia	10 690	128 550	19 985	10 217	24 192	4 144	5 025	2 754	21 426	910	73.0	4.0	49.7
Wakulla	321	2 464	292	431	463	128	102	47	18 878	88	58.0	8.0	38.6
Walton	871	8 533	635	732	1 801	164	174	169	19 763	476	30.7	5.7	39.5
Washington	352	4 155	776	815	866	97	88	81	19 416	322	28.0	6.8	40.4
GEORGIA	197 759	3 363 797	337 591	530 742	440 893	161 789	185 219	103 837	30 869	40 334	31.4	12.6	43.4
Appling	385	5 603	474	1 061	639	124	D	196	34 992	494	32.8	10.5	40.3
Atkinson	85	1 627	13	1 152	153	44	3	35	21 465	196	20.9	20.4	56.6
Bacon	200	2 807	260	1 249	379	126	51	63	22 318	324	29.3	8.3	46.6
Baker	22	229	D	0	38	D	D	5	23 694	131	21.4	40.5	64.9
Baldwin	823	15 108	5 166	3 128	2 321	381	195	336	22 213	137	24.8	14.6	37.2
Banks	207	3 179	D	1 056	614	D	25	55	17 177	446	40.8	2.5	48.4
Barrow	805	9 112	817	2 865	1 781	269	213	230	25 277	361	46.0	3.0	46.5
Bartow	1 550	26 264	1 701	8 790	3 324	409	491	683	26 009	400	35.2	7.8	38.2
Ben Hill	387	6 984	538	3 970	930	201	86	167	23 884	159	28.9	16.4	57.9
Berrien	276	3 929	399	1 720	476	241	33	91	23 276	399	19.3	19.0	56.9
Bibb	4 577	81 588	13 213	11 423	11 792	7 386	2 758	2 247	27 545	149	34.9	4.7	30.2
Bleckley	209	2 917	352	D	372	79	D	62	21 203	221	23.5	18.1	43.0
Brantley	171	1 299	106	168	284	D	D	25	19 579	207	31.4	4.3	37.7
Brooks	217	2 580	533	901	350	109	D	45	17 510	430	20.0	22.6	47.7
Bryan	402	2 978	290	292	638	141	72	57	19 245	61	44.3	16.4	54.1
Bulloch	1 214	16 508	1 858	3 291	3 231	518	863	338	20 465	524	26.1	21.2	51.5
Burke	320	4 987	439	1 427	657	125	D	149	29 967	346	17.9	30.9	41.3
Butts	341	4 041	446	1 097	575	118	48	93	23 097	148	31.1	6.8	37.2
Calhoun	105	753	147	D	150	37	D	12	15 923	122	13.1	50.0	58.2
Camden	675	7 844	821	1 488	1 782	253	202	148	18 894	46	43.5	17.4	37.0
Candler	204	2 265	449	453	352	110	88	42	18 638	264	15.5	16.7	41.7
Carroll	1 770	26 590	2 968	9 113	3 766	814	617	719	27 058	702	34.0	3.1	42.0
Catoosa	757	10 236	1 766	2 113	2 398	324	257	246	24 074	75	36.0	9.3	28.0
Charlton	173	1 456	205	286	209	42	D	30	20 633	42	45.2	11.9	50.0
Chatham	6 579	105 567	14 860	13 754	15 774	3 147	3 610	2 863	27 120				
Chattahoochee	60	1 597	D	D	42	D	318	47	29 254	13	23.1	15.4	23.1
Chattooga	328	6 298	246	4 050	852	143	56	138	21 968	278	24.8	8.3	32.0
Cherokee	3 068	27 039	2 117	4 116	6 078	1 060	1 482	666	24 645	493	64.9	0.6	41.4
Clarke	2 564	40 851	6 663	7 464	7 593	1 232	1 245	980	23 979	80	48.8	7.5	31.2
Clay	48	363	90	0	110	D	0	6	17 774	56	10.7	44.6	64.3
Clayton	4 381	86 162	6 055	6 220	14 002	2 294	1 652	2 317	26 892	54	50.0	0.0	35.2
Clinch	138	2 588	193	824	198	9	149	48	18 644	93	52.7	8.6	34.4
Cobb	17 564	301 538	19 375	24 212	39 715	14 291	23 095	10 676	35 404	128	63.3	3.1	39.8
Coffee	852	16 529	1 191	6 110	2 175	373	248	360	21 750	656	22.1	7.0	52.7
Colquitt	887	12 092	1 548	4 064	2 286	305	181	230	18 994	634	23.2	20.0	51.4
Columbia	1 798	26 104	5 330	4 906	3 487	704	840	634	24 272	169	42.6	7.7	26.0
Cook	331	4 326	414	1 779	793	132	52	82	18 995	226	31.0	16.8	43.8
Coweta	1 575	23 322	2 399	6 074	3 918	664	432	588	25 196	316	40.2	4.1	38.0
Crawford	80	586	137	D	90	34	D	9	16 027	123	28.5	13.0	44.7
Crisp	559	7 593	993	1 842	1 842	276	99	154	20 295	213	20.7	31.9	59.2
Dade	217	2 442	126	893	532	81	21	48	19 733	175	37.1	5.7	29.7
Dawson	446	3 442	121	378	1 230	99	118	76	21 981	160	53.8	7.5	43.8
Decatur	601	9 145	874	3 655	1 552	399	126	197	21 573	335	20.0	22.4	51.6
De Kalb	17 165	324 395	36 854	23 495	35 636	17 224	21 462	11 030	34 001	46	78.3	2.2	34.8
Dodge	374	4 177	852	919	744	136	79	67	16 124	491	17.3	12.2	36.3
Dooly	189	2 904	240	1 786	238	156	D	59	20 452	259	18.9	34.4	62.9
Dougherty	2 605	45 048	7 163	7 865	7 116	1 379	1 458	1 210	26 854	139	43.9	25.9	47.5
Douglas	2 036	26 885	3 125	2 876	5 667	663	605	627	23 320				
Early	250	2 957	337	1 072	418	170	78	91	30 932	279	16.1	31.5	55.9
Echols	12	30	D	0	D	0	D	0	13 667	67	34.3	9.0	43.3
Effingham	483	5 301	399	1 781	1 221	127	93	154	29 056	203	30.0	12.8	36.0
Elbert	534	5 563	337	2 848	753	107	108	118	21 182	320	20.3	6.2	39.7
Emanuel	414	5 392	804	2 199	870	158	109	96	17 845	441	16.3	19.7	37.2
Evans	232	3 614	377	1 843	419	85	51	77	21 233	183	28.4	14.2	38.3

STATE County	Acreage (1,000)	Percent change, 1992–1997	Average size of farm	Total irrigated (1,000)	Total cropland (1,000)	Average per farm ($1,000)	Average per acre (dollars)	Value of machinery and equipment average per farm ($1,000)	Total (mil dol)	Average per farm (dollars)	Crops	Live-stock and poultry products	$10,000 or more	$100,000 or more	Percent of land owned by fed. gov. 1997	Water con-sumption 1995 (mil gal/day)
	117	118	119	120	121	122	123	124	125	126	127	128	129	130	131	132
FLORIDA—Cont'd																
Sarasota	129	-14.8	408	5	19	900	2 342	27	24	76 657	70.6	29.4	37.1	12.1	0.0	47.9
Seminole	37	-38.0	108	4	7	332	2 870	14	20	58 040	91.3	8.7	35.8	9.3	0.7	69.8
Sumter	183	-27.5	255	2	55	468	1 733	22	34	47 970	27.5	72.5	26.6	7.0	0.0	66.1
Suwannee	158	-2.2	189	15	87	290	1 547	37	121	144 230	33.4	66.6	40.6	19.5	0.0	142.5
Taylor	57	0.0	451	0	6	396	950	15	4	34 226	19.6	80.4	25.4	3.2	0.1	53.1
Union	63	30.2	293	2	16	409	1 347	26	11	51 687	34.2	65.8	30.0	6.6	0.0	2.7
Volusia	112	-19.2	123	10	30	447	4 060	30	120	132 261	94.7	5.3	46.7	18.2	3.2	156.6
Wakulla	11	27.0	130	0	4	223	1 720	30	3	34 798	16.3	83.7	36.4	3.4	61.3	72.5
Walton	79	-18.7	166	1	35	203	1 329	24	20	41 529	24.0	76.0	25.4	8.6	21.0	11.8
Washington	55	22.8	172	0	26	229	1 204	28	9	29 042	38.8	61.2	30.4	6.2	0.0	4.6
GEORGIA	10 671	6.4	265	749	5 371	393	1 505	44	4 993	123 789	38.5	61.5	39.5	17.8	5.6	5 754.0
Appling	108	1.5	218	2	52	298	1 244	42	46	93 875	45.4	54.6	39.7	15.6	0.0	62.9
Atkinson	63	-19.5	320	4	31	304	1 054	50	59	298 910	27.1	72.9	62.8	31.1	0.0	3.0
Bacon	70	-10.8	217	1	25	256	1 245	34	35	107 729	31.9	68.1	50.0	17.3	0.0	3.0
Baker	119	9.4	910	25	63	1 139	1 237	151	39	295 922	69.8	30.2	68.7	42.7	0.0	24.1
Baldwin	30	-8.0	221	0	12	244	1 343	27	3	23 741	7.8	92.2	20.4	4.4	0.0	7.2
Banks	47	-3.2	106	0	21	327	2 829	35	103	231 898	2.6	97.4	48.0	33.0	1.1	2.3
Barrow	41	14.5	114	0	20	369	3 092	25	52	145 011	1.1	98.9	38.8	20.8	0.0	5.7
Bartow	84	-0.8	211	1	36	363	1 855	38	44	111 073	11.5	88.5	35.8	17.8	3.7	58.0
Ben Hill	53	13.5	335	10	34	361	1 160	51	16	103 025	76.3	23.7	56.0	22.0	0.0	17.3
Berrien	131	1.5	328	11	66	410	1 296	48	39	98 642	78.2	21.8	55.4	26.6	0.0	12.9
Bibb	22	29.8	148	0	9	241	1 807	25	5	36 637	18.4	81.6	25.5	5.4	0.5	107.0
Bleckley	71	12.5	321	6	45	325	964	48	12	52 390	89.8	10.2	38.9	14.9	0.0	9.1
Brantley	28	-0.8	134	0	10	177	1 234	18	13	64 950	17.8	82.2	31.9	7.2	0.0	2.5
Brooks	189	12.1	440	14	96	582	1 458	64	59	137 345	73.0	27.0	51.2	23.5	0.0	6.3
Bryan	25	59.2	418	D	6	520	1 246	55	2	29 210	92.1	7.9	31.1	6.6	37.5	2.0
Bulloch	200	-6.6	382	9	132	405	1 149	55	73	138 397	84.1	15.9	53.2	25.6	0.0	17.2
Burke	210	25.6	606	12	119	436	702	71	42	121 948	75.6	24.4	43.6	22.5	0.0	75.5
Butts	27	-5.2	186	0	11	323	1 755	24	3	20 754	20.6	79.4	20.3	3.4	0.1	5.6
Calhoun	129	12.8	1 054	21	65	1 074	1 025	226	40	329 422	71.0	29.0	73.8	45.1	0.0	18.8
Camden	19	5.4	412	D	1	557	1 350	18	1	14 197	88.5	11.5	23.9	2.2	8.6	40.9
Candler	78	37.5	297	2	34	267	938	36	19	70 690	68.6	31.4	37.9	16.7	0.0	3.2
Carroll	78	-6.1	111	1	41	307	2 690	30	90	128 592	3.5	96.5	29.8	14.0	0.0	13.7
Catoosa	22	-24.6	102	0	13	311	2 766	25	25	115 203	7.7	92.3	29.8	14.0	5.5	10.7
Charlton	20	-7.4	271	0	4	563	2 072	28	3	39 187	25.3	74.7	24.0	4.0	35.8	1.8
Chatham	9	-3.4	207	0	2	338	1 635	58	3	69 871	94.3	5.7	42.9	9.5	6.9	605.7
Chattahoochee	4	-32.2	313		1	214	682	33	0	6 083	D	D	23.1	0.0	73.8	13.8
Chattooga	55	4.4	199	D	23	273	1 419	24	5	17 561	16.4	83.6	26.6	0.0	9.7	4.9
Cherokee	32	-5.4	65	0	13	369	5 898	21	55	110 819	10.7	89.3	32.0	17.2	4.5	13.9
Clarke	13	5.5	158	0	5	570	3 601	30	11	142 862	27.6	72.4	30.0	11.2	0.0	18.1
Clay	44	3.0	791	4	24	731	924	122	10	179 821	84.2	15.8	73.2	37.5	0.0	5.6
Clayton	5	-1.6	91	D	3	376	4 126	28	1	14 312	44.2	55.8	25.9	3.7	3.0	5.6
Clinch	16	15.5	174	0	4	356	2 045	39	4	47 149	48.8	51.2	41.9	11.8	1.6	25.6
Cobb	10	-0.9	77	0	4	419	4 227	16	5	38 956	64.7	35.3	18.8	3.1	3.3	1.3
Coffee	204	14.1	311	11	104	448	1 499	48	141	215 585	39.5	60.5	55.6	24.5	4.8	440.1
Colquitt	229	15.8	362	35	136	456	1 373	79	122	192 429	76.3	23.7	57.4	29.0	0.0	39.8
Columbia	29	7.9	172	0	9	472	2 643	25	3	19 836	35.4	64.6	21.9	4.7	1.7	11.9
Cook	84	14.8	371	13	53	443	1 373	82	47	209 607	95.4	4.6	54.9	22.1	0.0	11.9
Coweta	43	1.4	135	0	19	328	3 263	27	7	21 318	65.0	35.0	19.0	2.2	0.0	352.5
Crawford	37	-1.6	304	3	18	357	1 118	54	15	121 089	62.7	37.3	33.3	17.1	0.0	5.9
Crisp	115	4.9	542	15	75	546	1 090	120	43	202 592	75.3	24.7	65.3	35.7	0.0	19.0
Dade	26	-1.1	147	D	11	255	1 668	24	9	51 626	0.9	99.1	28.0	7.4	0.7	1.7
Dawson	19	0.7	120	D	9	460	3 479	25	30	185 252	2.2	97.8	51.9	37.5	5.6	1.5
Decatur	164	-2.7	491	41	102	679	1 454	87	76	227 280	86.8	13.2	53.7	25.7	2.0	64.8
De Kalb	6	106.1	134	0	1	229	1 704	35	2	41 422	50.5	49.6	30.4	8.7	0.0	85.8
Dodge	156	60.5	317	10	64	256	867	42	18	37 089	82.8	17.2	33.2	7.5	0.0	7.5
Dooly	165	4.9	636	15	122	608	1 053	105	55	210 696	79.9	20.1	69.5	42.1	0.0	12.8
Dougherty	83	17.3	599	13	44	738	1 307	142	27	191 552	91.8	8.2	41.7	22.3	1.7	134.1
Douglas	10	22.2	91	0	3	399	3 809	23	1	11 860	44.1	55.9	9.3	2.8	0.5	7.6
Early	173	-6.1	619	31	107	777	1 174	95	45	162 830	94.0	6.0	62.7	32.6	0.1	142.0
Echols	18	11.9	267	1	4	330	1 235	48	5	75 507	93.9	6.1	40.3	16.4	0.0	2.9
Effingham	52	19.3	259	0	25	317	1 340	39	8	40 495	70.4	29.6	30.0	9.4	0.1	145.5
Elbert	57	5.6	178	0	28	256	1 574	26	14	44 989	16.7	83.3	22.5	8.1	5.0	2.8
Emanuel	153	23.6	347	4	61	320	887	97	23	51 078	77.5	22.6	31.3	13.2	0.0	5.6
Evans	43	5.7	237	2	22	346	1 212	45	21	116 048	39.6	60.4	41.0	19.1	14.3	3.3

Table B. States and Counties — Residential Construction, Wholesale and Retail Trade, and Real Estate

STATE County	Value of Residential Construction Authorized by Building Permits, 2000		Wholesale Trade, 1997				Retail Trade[1], 1997				Real Estate and Rental and Leasing, 1997			
	New Construction ($1,000)	Number of Housing Units	Number of Establish-ments	Number of Employees	Sales (mil dol)	Annual Payroll (mil dol)	Number of Establish-ments	Number of Employees	Sales (mil dol)	Annual Payroll (mil dol)	Number of Establish-ments	Number of Employees	Receipts (mil dol)	Annual Payroll (mil dol)
	133	134	135	136	137	138	139	140	141	142	143	144	145	146
FLORIDA—Cont'd														
Sarasota	480 274	3 658	527	3 122	1 035.9	86.2	1 669	20 311	3 606.6	343.8	571	2 320	290.4	48.9
Seminole	569 205	4 419	881	7 301	3 669.7	242.9	1 512	21 219	3 550.1	352.1	440	2 090	338.2	50.4
Sumter	121 107	1 909	18	236	84.4	4.5	111	1 192	185.3	14.8	22	51	6.4	0.8
Suwannee	11 459	125	35	D	D	D	137	1 333	205.0	19.2	20	64	5.3	0.7
Taylor	2 700	47	16	D	D	D	97	945	144.2	12.6	12	40	2.4	0.5
Union	1 997	28	3	D	D	D	28	180	27.2	2.8	2	D	D	D
Volusia	413 095	3 587	488	4 314	1 629.7	105.4	1 865	23 251	3 887.6	360.5	546	2 856	277.6	49.8
Wakulla	24 143	394	15	D	D	D	53	418	57.6	5.0	10	14	2.0	0.3
Walton	269 865	1 464	29	283	98.2	6.6	215	1 959	262.6	27.0	55	588	52.2	10.9
Washington	5 438	79	5	D	D	D	70	742	104.4	9.1	8	34	3.3	0.3
GEORGIA	8 722 246	91 820	13 978	191 078	163 647.5	7 519.7	33 073	420 676	72 212.5	6 943.6	7 794	47 669	6 912.9	1 308.8
Appling	305	3	14	92	41.0	2.8	88	616	116.9	9.7	7	11	1.2	0.2
Atkinson	NA	NA	9	67	11.9	0.9	30	154	20.9	1.9	3	D	D	D
Bacon	423	3	10	141	40.4	2.4	37	291	47.1	4.1	4	D	D	D
Baker	NA	NA	1	D	D	D	5	45	4.4	0.4	NA	NA	NA	NA
Baldwin	13 210	151	23	169	57.6	3.8	218	2 407	372.0	34.3	20	65	6.0	1.0
Banks	12 698	128	12	331	44.6	8.5	69	560	75.7	7.1	2	D	D	D
Barrow	59 536	855	30	223	73.8	5.6	145	1 798	344.8	30.8	23	65	7.7	1.0
Bartow	142 656	1 355	92	814	258.2	23.1	246	3 219	580.0	53.3	56	265	22.4	3.5
Ben Hill	2 368	29	20	D	D	D	93	884	144.0	12.3	13	44	2.5	0.6
Berrien	834	16	24	110	40.5	2.4	62	471	79.3	8.1	9	15	1.0	0.2
Bibb	68 195	794	272	3 545	1 511.7	110.7	912	12 885	1 977.3	194.2	185	1 062	148.8	26.2
Bleckley	4 068	46	4	D	D	D	53	392	59.0	4.8	3	6	0.6	0.1
Brantley	295	3	7	44	6.5	1.2	32	180	26.4	2.1	5	16	0.8	0.1
Brooks	3 001	41	9	36	5.8	0.5	57	349	63.5	5.3	2	D	D	D
Bryan	47 511	341	14	D	D	D	61	537	85.3	7.4	11	D	D	D
Bulloch	39 746	526	54	582	333.4	13.9	259	3 386	471.9	44.0	45	208	15.4	2.4
Burke	5 246	42	19	208	128.0	6.1	81	700	118.6	10.6	8	D	D	D
Butts	24 412	305	12	169	143.4	6.7	71	613	111.9	8.3	15	24	2.5	0.2
Calhoun	185	2	6	44	18.8	1.1	25	212	29.0	2.6	2	D	D	D
Camden	36 328	512	9	63	12.5	1.0	143	1 687	275.7	21.7	28	143	14.0	2.7
Candler	322	2	16	146	54.3	3.2	50	388	74.6	5.5	4	8	0.8	0.1
Carroll	140 130	1 856	84	1 232	1 286.3	48.2	348	3 505	574.5	53.2	62	232	24.1	3.7
Catoosa	49 954	500	39	638	747.7	15.7	172	2 524	406.2	35.4	30	91	8.2	1.6
Charlton	1 400	17	8	37	85.0	0.9	49	201	31.8	3.1	4	12	0.6	0.1
Chatham	182 701	1 922	348	4 347	2 445.1	142.9	1 261	15 625	2 466.9	244.0	280	1 470	195.9	36.0
Chattahoochee	500	4	1	D	D	D	6	26	4.2	0.4	1	D	D	D
Chattooga	521	9	12	54	12.4	1.0	82	922	122.5	11.9	9	13	1.0	0.2
Cherokee	372 334	3 776	201	1 103	490.8	34.7	351	5 202	968.9	86.7	93	276	33.6	5.4
Clarke	69 890	963	81	D	D	D	540	7 760	1 118.8	110.3	131	524	55.8	9.5
Clay	0	0	5	16	3.8	0.3	17	123	10.5	1.2	NA	NA	NA	NA
Clayton	294 519	3 347	316	6 142	3 345.2	217.5	832	16 204	2 731.7	285.3	197	1 326	185.6	30.9
Clinch	0	0	8	60	11.7	1.2	32	220	25.1	2.5	3	4	0.3	0.0
Cobb	736 202	6 642	1 632	24 859	23 231.5	1 270.8	2 234	37 323	6 971.6	663.6	785	5 612	989.9	183.8
Coffee	10 649	126	55	469	183.3	11.2	210	2 120	389.9	33.0	23	112	7.3	1.4
Colquitt	926	9	53	436	156.4	9.8	214	2 026	326.0	29.4	29	102	9.0	1.3
Columbia	120 213	943	91	D	D	D	247	3 731	613.0	60.0	68	285	33.0	6.3
Cook	3 062	37	20	231	86.0	3.9	89	824	121.1	10.7	7	12	0.9	0.1
Coweta	159 637	1 279	79	735	513.5	16.8	259	3 728	550.0	52.7	53	155	21.4	3.2
Crawford	8 120	96	2	D	D	D	14	84	11.2	1.2	NA	NA	NA	NA
Crisp	7 688	88	29	483	266.8	12.5	158	1 859	234.5	23.7	22	96	8.3	1.2
Dade	1 080	9	8	D	D	D	54	476	92.3	5.9	7	44	3.1	0.6
Dawson	43 994	282	19	56	71.0	2.1	106	704	119.4	12.2	7	10	1.0	0.2
Decatur	7 731	94	35	452	341.1	11.0	172	1 656	243.6	21.7	22	90	4.9	1.0
De Kalb	696 193	6 145	1 518	23 560	19 215.9	964.4	2 407	34 901	6 229.3	635.7	867	7 216	906.7	188.1
Dodge	2 602	41	20	D	D	D	84	799	102.4	9.0	8	161	9.3	1.6
Dooly	0	0	15	120	56.7	3.2	51	336	65.7	4.8	3	D	D	D
Dougherty	27 320	396	184	D	D	D	574	7 707	1 154.7	113.9	128	629	82.5	12.4
Douglas	57 004	901	105	1 492	1 100.1	43.7	312	4 781	974.7	82.6	61	263	37.5	5.6
Early	339	5	19	277	133.3	5.7	68	519	69.9	6.4	5	27	1.2	0.4
Echols	NA	NA	1	D	D	D	3	D	D	D	1	D	D	D
Effingham	45 613	445	12	D	D	D	91	1 193	165.8	15.7	21	D	D	D
Elbert	501	14	50	294	68.2	6.6	85	726	130.7	10.5	12	28	1.5	0.4
Emanuel	0	0	25	239	126.3	4.0	102	902	139.6	12.0	9	42	1.7	0.5
Evans	1 174	12	10	74	35.0	1.3	60	444	85.8	7.1	5	15	0.9	0.2

1. Establishments with payroll.

STATE County	Professional, Scientific, and Technical Services[1], 1997				Manufacturing, 1997				Accommodation and Foodservices, 1997			
	Number of Establishments	Number of Employees	Receipts (mil dol)	Annual Payroll (mil dol)	Number of Establishments	Number of Employees	Receipts (mil dol)	Annual Payroll (mil dol)	Number of Establishments	Number of Employees	Sales (mil dol)	Annual Payroll (mil dol)
	147	148	149	150	151	152	153	154	155	156	157	158
FLORIDA—Cont'd												
Sarasota	1 070	5 780	515.2	207.0	379	7 809	872.6	222.9	687	13 051	481.8	132.1
Seminole	1 102	6 182	561.6	210.7	434	9 624	1 582.2	287.1	579	12 966	423.1	117.3
Sumter	21	60	3.1	1.1	30	907	200.9	19.6	48	661	23.6	5.7
Suwannee	35	94	5.4	1.7	19	D	D	D	32	512	15.5	3.7
Taylor	18	61	3.2	1.4	20	1 594	496.1	58.0	36	364	11.9	3.0
Union	3	12	0.5	0.2	NA	NA	NA	NA	5	D	D	D
Volusia	844	4 048	346.4	120.7	392	10 216	1 212.6	263.2	1 051	19 758	635.6	167.0
Wakulla	19	72	3.7	1.4	NA	NA	NA	NA	28	293	9.8	2.3
Walton	54	162	16.4	4.6	35	937	108.7	12.5	87	2 446	107.2	29.4
Washington	19	80	3.5	1.2	14	754	85.8	15.7	22	317	8.8	2.6
GEORGIA	17 810	138 198	15 266.4	5 908.8	9 083	533 830	124 526.8	15 534.1	13 829	274 322	9 689.9	2 695.1
Appling	12	44	2.5	0.8	25	1 160	432.9	28.7	29	350	10.5	2.9
Atkinson	3	3	0.3	0.0	13	1 081	123.8	24.1	7	69	1.7	0.5
Bacon	12	39	2.1	0.7	14	1 373	210.9	27.8	17	D	D	D
Baker	1	D	D	D	NA	NA	NA	NA	3	7	0.2	0.0
Baldwin	52	172	8.1	2.4	20	3 454	624.9	91.2	66	1 507	37.8	9.8
Banks	7	15	1.0	0.2	14	D	D	D	22	372	16.7	4.6
Barrow	39	142	9.7	3.7	64	2 217	509.9	64.0	47	642	24.1	5.7
Bartow	81	315	19.5	8.2	126	10 115	2 918.4	303.1	123	1 827	65.3	17.7
Ben Hill	15	70	4.3	1.4	34	3 621	641.5	93.6	26	D	D	D
Berrien	13	30	1.6	0.5	17	1 987	231.6	45.0	15	169	5.5	1.3
Bibb	358	2 139	190.7	63.0	179	D	D	D	340	7 265	229.8	62.1
Bleckley	14	42	2.3	0.9	6	D	D	D	15	176	5.4	1.5
Brantley	2	D	D	D	NA	NA	NA	NA	10	59	2.1	0.5
Brooks	12	28	1.5	0.6	12	1 077	106.3	17.4	13	D	D	D
Bryan	23	52	4.2	1.2	NA	NA	NA	NA	29	D	D	D
Bulloch	76	353	22.7	7.9	41	3 210	493.4	84.3	99	1 894	52.5	13.5
Burke	11	36	1.2	0.5	16	1 035	84.4	21.3	21	283	7.4	1.9
Butts	13	22	1.4	0.5	18	1 127	181.4	22.3	28	272	10.5	2.8
Calhoun	1	D	D	D	3	D	D	D	8	D	D	D
Camden	41	163	10.6	3.7	21	1 364	528.8	52.7	68	1 220	35.3	9.9
Candler	15	73	3.9	1.4	NA	NA	NA	NA	17	262	7.7	2.0
Carroll	88	429	27.6	11.0	121	9 590	2 156.7	229.6	124	2 196	63.1	16.8
Catoosa	36	130	7.4	2.4	64	2 291	458.5	56.2	57	920	34.3	8.3
Charlton	4	7	0.6	0.1	NA	NA	NA	NA	11	104	3.8	1.1
Chatham	479	2 779	216.1	86.0	207	D	D	D	581	12 599	427.6	116.4
Chattahoochee	4	26	3.0	1.4	NA	NA	NA	NA	2	D	D	D
Chattooga	13	40	4.0	0.8	23	3 996	873.6	91.0	31	378	10.1	2.6
Cherokee	257	893	75.7	32.5	152	3 886	656.7	100.5	139	2 314	75.2	21.0
Clarke	156	943	54.9	22.8	90	9 388	1 368.5	234.9	240	4 371	125.5	33.8
Clay	NA	NA	NA	NA	NA	NA	NA	NA	2	D	D	D
Clayton	227	1 521	118.1	45.0	167	5 901	1 641.6	184.1	376	10 412	422.9	123.2
Clinch	8	35	3.1	1.1	11	918	148.9	18.8	8	D	D	D
Cobb	2 217	17 016	1 854.5	739.9	604	24 499	4 134.7	980.2	1 098	23 334	847.3	236.3
Coffee	52	214	12.1	3.9	45	5 377	773.8	116.1	47	810	26.1	6.5
Colquitt	44	128	9.8	3.5	55	3 503	452.2	67.1	52	754	23.3	6.4
Columbia	147	723	52.1	18.6	77	5 323	1 356.1	154.3	100	1 813	63.3	16.2
Cook	12	49	2.1	0.9	35	1 582	227.4	34.1	30	278	9.7	2.7
Coweta	85	286	22.5	8.7	76	5 589	1 093.2	147.8	103	1 880	58.5	15.2
Crawford	1	D	D	D	NA	NA	NA	NA	2	D	D	D
Crisp	25	76	4.9	1.7	27	2 067	340.5	53.1	51	913	26.2	8.0
Dade	8	30	0.7	0.2	22	907	98.5	19.9	22	319	10.5	2.5
Dawson	15	54	4.5	1.8	NA	NA	NA	NA	16	D	D	D
Decatur	21	64	5.2	1.4	35	3 538	632.8	84.2	30	455	14.0	3.2
De Kalb	2 188	19 674	1 972.8	856.4	697	24 358	8 018.5	942.8	1 232	21 365	809.7	215.4
Dodge	21	79	4.5	1.8	16	867	155.0	17.5	22	324	8.4	2.3
Dooly	5	11	1.6	0.2	12	1 521	186.8	30.4	16	89	3.2	0.8
Dougherty	172	1 327	98.1	37.8	90	8 627	4 275.5	312.0	192	3 736	118.1	31.6
Douglas	127	438	37.7	14.7	95	2 211	371.2	54.5	127	3 049	96.8	25.5
Early	11	31	2.9	1.0	12	1 071	475.2	45.0	17	D	D	D
Echols	1	D	D	D	NA	NA	NA	NA	NA	NA	NA	NA
Effingham	26	77	4.3	1.1	11	D	D	D	31	D	D	D
Elbert	29	103	5.7	1.6	112	2 954	441.7	64.6	34	396	11.6	2.7
Emanuel	22	93	5.9	2.2	36	2 191	253.5	38.4	26	310	9.5	2.5
Evans	13	39	2.6	1.0	14	1 677	184.9	34.2	19	174	6.4	1.8

1. Firms subject to federal tax.

Table B. States and Counties — Health and Other Services and Federal Funds

STATE County	Health Care and Social Assistance[1], 1997				Other Services[1], 1997				Federal funds and grants, fiscal 2001[2] Expenditures (mil dol)			
									Total	Direct payments for individuals[3]		
	Number of Establishments	Number of Employees	Receipts (mil dol)	Annual Payroll (mil dol)	Number of Establishments	Number of Employees	Receipts (mil dol)	Annual Payroll (mil dol)	Total	Social Security and government retirement	Medicare	Food stamps and Supplemental Security Income
	159	160	161	162	163	164	165	166	167	168	169	170
FLORIDA—Cont'd												
Sarasota	1 032	12 069	878.3	369.5	623	3 136	174.8	56.1	2 291.1	1 408.7	632.1	23.5
Seminole	716	8 306	632.6	254.9	625	3 331	198.9	60.5	1 235.6	718.3	234.5	35.1
Sumter	23	332	14.4	6.5	32	116	7.7	1.7	274.9	136.4	52.0	9.9
Suwannee	27	382	21.2	7.4	37	142	13.3	2.5	193.6	103.4	39.1	6.1
Taylor	24	325	16.1	7.8	32	222	12.5	3.2	111.2	45.1	21.9	4.7
Union	6	46	2.8	0.9	6	28	1.4	0.3	39.1	18.5	7.2	2.0
Volusia	906	10 079	596.8	253.3	707	3 094	163.6	47.8	2 575.8	1 405.6	585.0	64.7
Wakulla	8	171	5.8	2.9	14	56	4.6	0.9	73.4	38.2	12.7	3.2
Walton	31	505	27.7	11.1	35	177	9.8	3.4	198.2	107.2	28.4	6.5
Washington	27	289	12.1	5.1	18	77	4.5	1.1	133.1	54.7	26.5	5.3
GEORGIA	13 960	173 768	12 065.1	5 158.0	11 482	69 422	4 580.7	1 407.5	47 320.4	14 601.2	5 392.3	1 491.6
Appling	16	75	3.6	1.4	23	97	6.0	1.5	84.5	30.7	17.1	4.6
Atkinson	6	31	1.1	0.4	2	D	D	D	42.5	12.4	8.6	3.4
Bacon	11	71	3.3	1.1	14	53	3.1	0.7	53.1	18.8	11.9	4.1
Baker	NA	NA	NA	NA	NA	NA	NA	NA	26.4	5.5	3.0	1.4
Baldwin	101	1 868	86.1	35.0	51	329	19.6	5.6	178.1	83.7	34.4	8.7
Banks	7	32	1.3	0.6	5	22	1.8	0.4	54.9	20.7	7.5	1.2
Barrow	43	771	39.7	16.7	47	157	10.0	2.8	171.1	71.5	30.7	9.5
Bartow	98	1 471	105.2	36.6	82	514	36.9	10.0	241.8	132.2	40.5	10.2
Ben Hill	27	227	12.5	5.4	30	85	6.0	1.3	95.0	38.3	18.8	5.2
Berrien	23	505	21.0	10.2	13	40	2.3	0.6	85.8	36.2	17.4	3.8
Bibb	471	8 277	650.9	257.8	305	1 738	105.8	33.4	1 012.9	415.4	181.7	52.6
Bleckley	19	193	7.2	2.9	11	45	2.7	0.6	71.0	34.6	13.1	2.6
Brantley	8	108	5.2	1.8	9	20	1.0	0.2	59.1	30.0	11.5	4.5
Brooks	10	102	5.0	1.9	17	77	3.2	1.1	87.7	30.1	15.2	5.4
Bryan	19	238	11.8	4.7	19	54	3.2	0.9	659.7	48.6	13.5	3.6
Bulloch	97	1 668	110.2	40.7	68	289	14.6	3.7	207.4	75.6	29.6	11.0
Burke	25	364	16.4	7.3	18	53	2.6	0.6	118.1	40.7	18.3	8.4
Butts	24	419	18.7	7.9	19	112	4.3	1.3	82.8	41.7	16.1	4.0
Calhoun	5	69	2.9	1.2	5	16	0.5	0.2	46.8	12.6	7.8	3.9
Camden	63	425	25.0	9.7	37	199	9.1	2.5	447.0	71.9	15.2	4.7
Candler	10	223	6.5	2.9	8	35	2.1	0.6	53.0	17.9	10.6	3.4
Carroll	137	1 800	106.7	47.8	121	484	30.1	7.6	332.7	166.1	70.4	16.6
Catoosa	55	709	43.6	21.7	49	228	14.6	4.5	142.4	78.2	27.5	5.6
Charlton	10	39	1.8	0.6	6	10	0.9	0.1	46.3	20.9	9.7	2.6
Chatham	452	6 348	466.1	235.6	395	2 731	168.6	57.6	1 574.6	530.3	223.4	54.2
Chattahoochee	1	D	D	D	6	100	3.7	1.6	151.6	7.9	1.6	0.7
Chattooga	20	226	12.0	5.2	9	39	2.8	0.6	114.9	56.1	24.9	4.7
Cherokee	152	1 980	126.4	48.4	166	631	47.9	12.2	286.5	172.6	49.5	9.3
Clarke	260	2 017	184.6	91.6	140	817	37.2	12.0	536.9	147.5	54.2	16.1
Clay	4	D	D	D	1	D	D	D	32.8	7.6	2.7	1.7
Clayton	369	4 290	294.0	134.7	312	1 842	131.7	39.4	737.0	345.5	112.3	35.4
Clinch	11	128	5.6	1.9	3	11	0.4	0.2	42.1	13.0	9.3	2.3
Cobb	1 082	12 012	893.9	380.1	1 061	6 802	446.1	154.3	6 253.8	835.0	255.7	39.0
Coffee	61	481	29.4	11.7	52	238	12.9	3.2	156.4	61.0	30.3	10.2
Colquitt	73	616	34.5	15.0	54	321	17.3	5.4	217.2	81.4	37.5	13.2
Columbia	129	1 206	66.0	29.5	142	799	47.1	15.6	626.2	148.6	29.7	5.3
Cook	24	545	19.5	8.5	18	61	3.3	1.0	80.4	31.9	14.1	4.6
Coweta	100	1 638	119.6	53.0	72	284	19.4	5.2	292.6	149.1	54.5	10.8
Crawford	6	127	5.7	1.7	6	33	2.5	0.6	33.3	16.9	6.5	1.8
Crisp	34	293	14.1	5.8	35	118	7.3	1.9	126.5	41.4	23.5	9.1
Dade	12	243	12.2	5.0	10	25	3.0	0.5	70.8	30.7	12.5	2.4
Dawson	18	121	4.6	2.1	13	59	6.7	1.4	47.4	25.7	9.0	1.8
Decatur	44	304	17.7	7.0	41	162	7.5	1.9	140.6	53.2	21.0	9.7
De Kalb	1 360	16 256	1 184.2	486.4	1 101	7 551	535.5	175.6	2 374.8	702.9	389.5	81.2
Dodge	44	484	20.6	8.9	23	65	4.5	0.9	106.9	42.0	20.7	5.5
Dooly	13	170	7.1	2.9	8	42	1.8	0.7	87.4	22.5	11.7	4.0
Dougherty	250	3 277	239.3	110.3	169	1 163	71.1	22.5	709.7	222.7	81.2	39.2
Douglas	139	2 277	125.8	52.9	150	965	63.7	20.4	246.4	143.5	51.4	6.7
Early	10	47	1.8	0.8	10	35	1.2	0.4	83.1	24.6	11.3	4.1
Echols	NA	NA	NA	NA	NA	NA	NA	NA	8.5	2.6	1.4	1.4
Effingham	22	147	9.3	2.9	25	136	12.3	2.6	106.1	59.2	16.3	4.8
Elbert	31	375	19.0	7.7	25	64	4.8	1.0	117.7	49.4	22.5	6.3
Emanuel	40	357	16.2	6.1	24	86	4.8	1.1	136.0	47.3	22.7	8.2
Evans	15	343	17.4	6.4	8	82	5.0	1.8	51.9	21.8	9.5	3.1

1. Firms subject to federal tax.   2. October 1, 2000 to September 30, 2001.   3. State totals may include programs not allocated by county.

STATE County	Federal funds and grants, fiscal 2001[1] (cont'd)							Local government finances, 1997				
	Expenditures (mil dol) (cont'd)							General revenue			Taxes	
	Procurement contract awards			Grants[2]								Per capita[3] (dollars)	
	Salaries and wages	Defense	Other	Medicaid and other health-related	Nutrition and family welfare	Education	Other	Total (mil dol)	Intergovern-mental (mil dol)	Total (mil dol)	Total	Property
	171	172	173	174	175	176	177	178	179	180	181	182
FLORIDA—Cont'd												
Sarasota	52.5	48.9	15.0	37.1	14.8	11.6	32.3	970.3	116.4	328.7	1 090	862
Seminole	89.2	8.3	24.5	53.7	18.5	15.9	17.7	709.8	249.9	297.4	863	620
Sumter	42.7	0.8	7.0	15.8	5.4	2.7	-1.1	66.2	32.4	18.6	472	311
Suwannee	7.0	0.3	1.5	19.7	4.6	2.6	5.6	58.1	33.4	14.7	443	311
Taylor	2.1	13.7	0.6	14.4	4.0	2.1	0.1	44.9	20.3	16.3	870	610
Union	1.2	0.1	0.3	6.3	1.7	0.7	0.5	28.3	21.8	2.9	233	161
Volusia	81.3	150.1	22.2	101.0	30.5	25.6	58.3	1 122.4	316.8	362.7	864	693
Wakulla	3.7	0.2	1.2	6.4	2.6	1.3	2.1	40.0	25.7	8.2	426	328
Walton	8.7	0.1	1.2	19.2	4.6	2.3	10.8	82.1	27.8	42.0	1 107	870
Washington	2.9	0.1	0.6	23.3	3.0	4.3	9.4	61.9	35.3	8.1	403	295
GEORGIA	6 931.0	5 990.4	1 391.8	3 857.5	1 364.2	819.2	1 888.3	X	X	X	X	X
Appling	2.6	0.1	0.5	17.3	2.9	2.1	0.7	55.1	12.8	18.1	1 105	773
Atkinson	1.0	0.5	0.5	9.5	1.6	0.6	0.7	11.8	6.7	4.2	598	362
Bacon	1.4	0.0	0.3	8.3	2.5	0.9	1.1	31.5	13.0	6.7	647	395
Baker	0.3	0.0	0.1	4.7	0.7	0.4	2.1	6.5	3.5	2.4	651	535
Baldwin	5.1	0.1	0.9	23.6	6.2	2.8	2.0	144.5	42.0	29.3	698	366
Banks	0.9	0.0	0.2	6.1	0.7	0.6	16.4	17.7	6.9	9.2	739	390
Barrow	14.2	1.2	1.2	16.8	2.6	2.0	20.3	65.9	27.8	28.2	724	474
Bartow	10.0	2.8	10.1	18.8	7.6	3.6	1.6	141.5	56.8	55.7	805	572
Ben Hill	1.9	0.2	0.4	17.3	3.1	1.3	2.3	51.0	16.3	13.5	781	464
Berrien	1.8	0.0	0.5	11.1	2.0	0.9	2.4	28.2	14.9	10.4	652	380
Bibb	100.0	5.2	38.3	116.4	29.2	14.9	15.1	377.6	142.4	168.9	1 083	648
Bleckley	1.2	0.1	0.3	9.0	1.7	0.7	1.3	26.3	11.0	6.4	578	348
Brantley	1.5	0.0	0.4	6.6	1.4	1.3	1.4	19.7	11.8	6.7	497	359
Brooks	1.6	0.3	0.4	15.2	3.7	1.5	2.0	24.1	13.3	7.8	468	329
Bryan	519.8	58.8	2.8	7.7	2.4	1.2	0.5	38.9	19.3	16.0	691	470
Bulloch	8.3	1.0	1.6	25.5	6.5	4.1	12.6	101.1	53.7	30.1	603	361
Burke	3.5	0.1	1.1	25.3	6.2	2.6	1.9	148.0	12.0	35.1	1 544	1 314
Butts	3.1	0.0	0.6	10.4	4.1	1.0	1.2	31.1	13.4	13.8	803	519
Calhoun	1.2	0.3	0.3	9.6	1.1	0.5	1.9	13.1	7.3	3.6	702	463
Camden	240.3	56.8	3.5	7.8	3.9	7.3	33.7	83.1	38.0	31.7	701	423
Candler	1.3	0.0	0.3	9.2	1.6	0.7	2.6	29.5	10.2	5.7	641	369
Carroll	13.0	0.4	3.0	34.8	7.0	5.7	4.2	134.7	67.1	47.6	585	310
Catoosa	3.9	0.0	1.6	11.4	3.6	2.4	5.3	138.6	32.0	22.9	462	300
Charlton	2.2	0.0	0.9	6.0	1.9	1.2	0.5	25.6	8.2	6.9	739	554
Chatham	272.9	159.8	63.9	127.5	45.2	19.4	30.5	663.3	215.9	301.0	1 332	863
Chattahoochee	0.3	135.6	1.6	2.3	0.4	0.4	0.4	5.9	3.4	1.6	101	32
Chattooga	2.3	0.0	1.2	16.2	3.3	1.8	1.6	38.0	19.2	11.9	518	323
Cherokee	15.3	0.3	4.0	16.9	3.7	3.3	8.9	211.7	81.1	78.8	621	463
Clarke	90.8	5.5	17.8	67.9	18.7	10.0	80.1	367.0	75.0	85.3	937	620
Clay	1.7	7.5	0.1	5.5	1.3	0.4	0.8	5.8	2.8	2.5	711	427
Clayton	60.4	33.7	16.6	31.3	13.2	13.9	32.3	419.5	154.8	178.2	872	579
Clinch	1.0	5.6	0.3	6.8	1.7	0.6	0.8	21.8	8.4	6.7	1 007	755
Cobb	192.3	4 668.8	102.4	52.3	17.5	19.3	40.1	1 114.2	322.0	556.0	1 009	730
Coffee	7.5	0.0	1.3	24.8	5.6	3.1	2.1	65.6	32.0	24.8	731	399
Colquitt	5.3	0.0	1.2	33.5	13.7	3.4	7.0	111.9	40.7	22.0	554	355
Columbia	320.6	94.6	2.5	13.0	4.0	2.4	3.7	141.7	57.8	59.6	671	459
Cook	1.6	0.0	0.4	11.5	2.3	1.8	7.2	25.7	12.8	9.3	634	350
Coweta	11.8	0.3	3.6	24.4	6.3	3.6	17.5	143.8	52.0	69.9	866	559
Crawford	0.6	0.0	0.2	4.6	1.1	0.8	0.2	15.4	8.7	5.6	507	392
Crisp	5.1	0.0	0.7	23.4	5.5	2.6	3.3	49.2	22.0	18.7	905	495
Dade	1.3	0.0	0.4	7.7	1.4	0.8	13.1	20.3	10.5	8.6	584	291
Dawson	2.0	0.0	0.6	5.2	0.8	0.4	1.4	27.6	12.2	12.7	912	637
Decatur	3.7	0.1	1.9	23.3	5.8	3.1	3.2	86.9	36.2	22.3	839	415
De Kalb	740.0	22.4	54.2	140.9	46.2	28.9	91.3	1 883.8	540.6	632.1	1 075	823
Dodge	2.2	0.5	0.6	20.7	3.9	1.3	2.2	43.9	18.3	7.5	409	262
Dooly	2.3	0.0	0.4	14.2	3.3	1.0	7.9	23.3	10.5	8.9	856	622
Dougherty	139.5	42.9	29.6	74.7	31.2	12.0	10.0	263.8	112.2	97.5	1 017	584
Douglas	9.9	0.0	2.7	15.1	4.2	3.5	2.8	155.3	62.3	72.7	839	545
Early	2.1	0.0	1.0	16.4	3.6	1.2	5.1	26.1	12.0	9.0	738	430
Echols	0.1	0.0	0.0	1.9	0.4	0.2	0.1	5.0	2.9	1.9	773	668
Effingham	3.8	0.0	0.9	9.2	2.6	1.5	2.0	67.7	29.8	22.1	630	453
Elbert	7.9	2.0	1.3	18.9	3.5	1.4	1.1	46.2	16.4	11.1	582	365
Emanuel	5.8	0.0	1.6	29.6	6.3	1.8	3.4	60.1	38.2	12.6	599	353
Evans	2.6	0.1	0.4	9.2	1.9	0.9	0.2	20.7	8.8	6.5	664	355

1. October 1, 2000 to September 30, 2001. 2. State totals may include programs not allocated by county. 3. Based on the resident population estimated as of July 1 of the year shown.

Table B. States and Counties — Local Government Finances, Government Employment, and Elections

STATE County	Local government finances, 1997 (cont'd) Direct general expenditure Total (mil dol)	Per capita[1] (dollars)	Percent of total for — Education	Health and hospitals	Police protection	Public welfare	Highways	Debt outstanding Total (mil dol)	Per capita[1] (dollars)	Government employment, 1999 Federal civilian	Federal military	State and local	Presidential election, 2000[2] Percent of vote cast — Democratic	Republican	All other
	183	184	185	186	187	188	189	190	191	192	193	194	195	196	197
FLORIDA—Cont'd															
Sarasota	919.7	3 049	26.1	29.4	5.9	0.3	5.5	856.0	2 838	884	681	11 282	45.3	51.6	3.1
Seminole	721.8	2 094	52.5	0.7	6.5	0.1	9.8	595.0	1 726	1 476	784	13 147	43.0	55.0	2.0
Sumter	72.6	1 842	46.9	0.4	5.9	1.4	5.7	81.3	2 063	779	94	2 092	43.3	54.5	2.3
Suwannee	57.2	1 730	55.6	1.9	5.9	1.0	5.7	21.5	649	127	72	1 557	32.7	64.3	3.0
Taylor	46.4	2 477	51.6	1.5	9.0	0.6	4.9	41.9	2 241	37	42	1 555	38.9	59.6	1.5
Union	25.0	2 025	70.9	1.1	2.5	0.2	4.5	3.6	293	19	28	2 427	36.8	61.0	2.3
Volusia	1 078.3	2 569	35.4	22.7	6.4	0.4	4.3	987.1	2 351	1 292	952	19 731	53.0	44.8	2.2
Wakulla	43.1	2 247	63.2	2.2	5.9	0.1	3.4	15.3	800	79	42	1 313	44.7	52.5	2.7
Walton	79.6	2 099	44.0	5.0	5.7	0.4	18.3	24.5	646	136	114	2 131	30.8	66.5	2.7
Washington	57.0	2 817	45.7	16.7	2.9	0.6	5.6	17.1	843	49	45	2 179	34.9	62.2	2.9
GEORGIA	X	X	X	X	X	X	X	X	X	92 464	93 790	496 132	43.2	54.9	1.8
Appling	52.5	3 202	37.7	29.4	2.6	0.1	4.3	90.4	5 513	47	63	1 202	34.3	64.6	1.0
Atkinson	11.2	1 588	66.9	1.1	4.5	0.9	6.4	0.8	110	20	28	397	39.7	59.3	1.0
Bacon	32.6	3 153	32.9	42.5	2.9	0.2	2.8	9.1	884	34	39	567	31.9	67.2	0.9
Baker	6.7	1 783	56.6	2.4	4.3	0.2	4.2	40.7	970	11	14	205	58.8	40.5	0.7
Baldwin	125.3	2 988	27.6	44.8	3.7	0.6	2.5	9.5	767	16	50	8 068	48.7	49.9	1.4
Banks	16.8	1 354	59.7	1.6	5.4	0.4	8.8	58.8	1 508	134	159	520	27.0	70.9	2.1
Barrow	69.9	1 794	61.8	0.6	4.4	0.6	7.8	254.9	3 685	176	283	2 120	30.4	65.8	3.8
Bartow	157.5	2 277	58.3	0.4	6.1	0.4	4.7	254.9	3 685	176	283	3 957	33.0	64.8	2.2
Ben Hill	49.6	2 861	39.7	25.1	3.6	0.4	3.6	22.6	1 302	35	66	1 549	47.9	51.1	1.0
Berrien	27.3	1 709	57.9	0.8	4.3	2.2	15.2	4.2	264	43	63	754	37.2	61.6	1.2
Bibb	369.6	2 369	41.4	8.2	6.5	0.5	5.3	293.9	1 884	1 471	738	9 525	50.5	48.6	0.9
Bleckley	25.1	2 247	55.4	21.0	6.3	0.6	3.6	2.8	253	33	43	937	34.0	65.0	1.0
Brantley	19.4	1 447	71.6	0.7	2.9	0.5	5.0	5.4	400	26	75	690	30.1	68.4	1.6
Brooks	25.0	1 501	58.0	1.2	5.0	7.5	4.4	5.5	328	37	61	704	46.2	53.0	0.8
Bryan	36.9	1 598	64.0	0.7	6.1	1.0	3.8	3.3	144	44	92	1 243	30.8	68.5	0.7
Bulloch	112.1	2 247	49.2	13.7	3.8	0.1	5.9	33.5	671	149	202	5 042	38.0	61.4	0.6
Burke	145.5	6 401	18.3	6.3	1.7	0.3	2.5	1 117.1	49 157	60	88	1 437	52.2	47.4	0.4
Butts	29.9	1 738	52.3	6.8	7.5	0.2	3.6	9.6	560	36	70	1 271	40.5	56.8	2.6
Calhoun	13.6	2 689	59.7	9.3	4.9	1.4	6.1	1.7	336	24	19	748	58.7	40.7	0.6
Camden	82.5	1 826	53.8	4.7	5.3	0.3	4.2	32.8	726	2 467	5 421	2 252	36.0	63.0	1.0
Candler	25.6	2 873	35.7	32.9	3.3	0.1	5.1	7.3	815	24	34	667	38.7	60.4	1.0
Carroll	138.5	1 702	63.2	0.9	5.4	0.2	8.6	47.0	577	216	323	5 209	34.2	63.8	2.0
Catoosa	149.2	3 011	28.0	56.1	2.5	0.3	3.3	53.4	1 077	73	197	1 860	31.0	68.2	0.9
Charlton	22.2	2 392	45.2	31.7	3.9	0.3	4.4	6.3	681	48	36	575	36.1	63.0	0.9
Chatham	642.5	2 844	38.2	5.2	6.8	0.3	7.0	569.2	2 519	2 584	5 174	14 522	49.5	49.9	0.6
Chattahoochee	5.3	327	55.0	1.5	4.4	0.2	5.3	1.3	81	0	13 032	197	49.9	49.0	1.1
Chattooga	45.3	1 975	53.4	0.7	5.4	0.2	6.7	8.3	362	35	87	1 530	42.2	56.2	1.6
Cherokee	217.0	1 710	62.8	10.6	3.9	0.2	3.9	176.4	1 391	241	537	4 713	23.6	73.1	3.3
Clarke	325.7	3 578	23.7	39.8	5.6	0.8	1.9	212.9	2 339	1 531	693	15 925	54.8	42.8	2.3
Clay	5.6	1 629	49.5	2.5	6.3	0.6	8.0	1.6	458	72	13	242	64.3	35.1	0.6
Clayton	424.7	2 080	54.2	4.6	6.1	0.7	3.0	270.2	1 323	2 094	849	11 971	65.4	32.6	2.0
Clinch	20.0	3 008	44.6	25.1	3.1	0.2	5.1	3.8	579	18	25	586	42.3	56.6	1.1
Cobb	1 260.2	2 287	48.6	2.4	5.4	0.8	10.1	1 600.0	2 904	2 555	3 396	25 470	37.2	60.3	2.4
Coffee	66.3	1 955	59.8	1.8	5.3	0.4	10.6	17.1	503	114	132	2 148	38.1	61.1	0.8
Colquitt	113.8	2 872	40.3	34.6	2.4	0.1	2.7	19.6	496	104	154	3 240	33.1	66.1	0.8
Columbia	136.8	1 540	64.2	0.8	6.9	0.3	5.7	124.6	1 403	95	353	2 923	25.0	74.3	0.7
Cook	27.2	1 861	57.7	1.2	5.4	5.3	6.5	14.5	991	34	58	845	41.6	57.8	0.6
Coweta	141.6	1 755	52.6	2.7	4.0	0.1	6.9	91.5	1 135	194	339	3 829	29.1	68.6	2.3
Crawford	14.8	1 342	66.6	1.3	4.4	0.2	8.1	2.1	191	11	39	461	42.5	55.8	1.7
Crisp	45.0	2 179	57.6	1.1	6.9	0.2	5.8	36.7	1 775	59	78	1 580	40.4	58.6	1.0
Dade	19.3	1 317	65.2	1.1	5.3	0.3	6.3	7.6	517	20	58	587	32.3	66.2	1.4
Dawson	26.8	1 928	69.5	0.8	4.2	0.1	4.4	21.2	1 524	30	60	686	24.8	71.7	3.4
Decatur	80.3	3 018	37.7	40.2	4.5	0.2	3.0	19.5	732	64	103	2 608	44.5	54.8	0.7
De Kalb	1 661.5	2 827	34.6	40.1	4.0	0.3	1.2	1 039.2	1 768	11 087	2 939	29 380	70.9	27.0	2.2
Dodge	44.4	2 439	45.2	36.5	2.8	1.0	3.8	4.3	238	47	69	1 823	39.6	59.1	1.3
Dooly	22.8	2 187	48.9	11.2	4.8	0.1	8.7	7.9	762	50	40	960	54.0	45.1	0.9
Dougherty	262.3	2 738	41.2	13.6	5.2	0.2	1.5	83.0	867	2 687	1 067	8 288	57.4	42.2	0.3
Douglas	157.1	1 812	59.6	4.9	5.1	0.3	2.9	129.8	1 498	168	345	3 848	36.2	61.3	2.4
Early	28.2	2 318	58.0	12.0	4.3	0.1	3.9	6.2	514	51	46	764	45.3	54.1	0.6
Echols	4.9	2 014	77.6	1.6	3.3	0.2	3.9	0.0	7	0	10	171	30.3	68.4	1.3
Effingham	72.3	2 063	55.2	13.7	2.8	0.7	8.0	50.1	1 429	61	145	1 915	30.4	68.9	0.7
Elbert	44.2	2 311	45.8	29.9	4.4	0.5	2.8	7.4	384	150	73	1 416	43.3	55.9	0.9
Emanuel	62.5	2 974	54.3	22.8	2.5	0.2	5.5	12.7	605	99	80	1 977	45.3	53.4	1.3
Evans	21.0	2 151	44.8	22.2	4.2	0.1	6.0	2.4	247	63	38	649	39.5	59.8	0.6

1. Based on the resident population estimated as of July 1 of the year shown.   2. Data subject to copyright.

STATE/ County code	MSA/ PMSA/ NECMA code[1]	County Type[2]	STATE County	Land area,[3] (sq km) 2000	Population and population characteristics, 2000													
								Race alone or in combination (percent)					Age (percent)					
					Total persons	Rank	Per square kilometer	White	Black	Am. Indian, Alaska Native	Asian and Pacific Islander	Percent Hispanic[4]	Under 5 years	5 to 17 years	18 to 24 years	25 to 34 years	35 to 44 years	45 to 54 years
				1	2	3	4	5	6	7	8	9	10	11	12	13	14	15
			GEORGIA—Cont'd															
13 111	...	9	Fannin	999	19 798	1 801	19.8	99.0	0.2	1.3	0.3	0.7	5.4	15.6	7.0	11.2	13.7	15.2
13 113	0520	1	Fayette	510	91 263	564	178.9	84.9	11.9	0.6	2.9	2.8	5.8	23.3	6.5	9.3	18.4	18.2
13 115	...	4	Floyd	1 329	90 565	569	68.1	82.3	13.6	0.7	1.2	5.5	6.6	18.0	10.8	13.6	14.9	12.8
13 117	0520	1	Forsyth	585	98 407	529	168.2	95.9	0.8	0.6	1.0	5.6	9.5	18.4	6.1	16.8	20.3	13.5
13 119	...	8	Franklin	682	20 285	1 775	29.7	90.2	9.1	0.6	0.4	0.9	6.3	17.6	9.6	12.7	14.6	13.0
13 121	0520	0	Fulton	1 369	816 006	55	596.1	49.1	45.2	0.5	3.5	5.9	7.0	17.5	11.0	18.6	16.9	13.4
13 123	...	8	Gilmer	1 105	23 456	1 618	21.2	94.7	0.3	1.3	0.6	7.7	7.2	17.2	8.5	13.6	14.9	13.8
13 125	...	9	Glascock	373	2 556	3 022	6.9	90.8	8.5	0.7	0.5	0.5	6.8	17.1	7.7	12.1	14.7	12.9
13 127	...	5	Glynn	1 094	67 568	725	61.8	71.5	26.9	0.6	1.0	3.0	6.5	18.8	8.2	12.3	15.3	14.4
13 129	...	6	Gordon	921	44 104	1 015	47.9	90.6	3.7	0.7	0.8	7.4	7.2	18.9	9.5	15.8	15.6	13.1
13 131	...	6	Grady	1 187	23 659	1 604	19.9	65.3	30.5	1.3	0.4	5.2	7.0	20.2	9.0	13.0	14.9	13.1
13 133	...	6	Greene	1 006	14 406	2 131	14.3	53.4	44.7	0.5	0.4	2.9	6.7	18.4	8.7	11.0	13.2	14.1
13 135	0520	0	Gwinnett	1 121	588 448	92	524.9	74.3	13.9	0.7	7.9	10.9	8.0	20.2	8.7	17.8	19.7	13.8
13 137	...	7	Habersham	720	35 902	1 223	49.9	89.8	4.8	0.9	2.4	7.7	6.3	17.2	11.1	13.3	15.1	13.1
13 139	...	6	Hall	1 020	139 277	392	136.5	82.7	7.5	0.7	1.7	19.6	8.2	18.7	10.8	16.7	15.5	12.4
13 141	...	9	Hancock	1 226	10 076	2 438	8.2	21.7	78.0	0.3	0.1	0.5	5.8	18.3	9.9	14.7	16.3	13.8
13 143	...	6	Haralson	731	25 690	1 528	35.1	93.8	5.6	0.7	0.4	0.6	6.8	19.2	8.1	14.1	15.1	13.3
13 145	1800	6	Harris	1 201	23 695	1 602	19.7	79.2	19.7	0.8	0.8	1.1	5.9	19.7	6.3	12.0	17.3	16.4
13 147	...	6	Hart	601	22 997	1 642	38.3	79.6	19.6	0.4	0.6	0.9	6.3	17.2	7.7	12.5	14.8	13.8
13 149	...	8	Heard	767	11 012	2 364	14.4	88.1	11.1	0.6	0.3	1.1	7.9	20.8	7.6	15.0	15.6	12.8
13 151	0520	1	Henry	836	119 341	455	142.8	82.3	15.1	0.6	2.2	2.3	8.1	21.1	7.4	16.3	18.6	13.2
13 153	4680	2	Houston	976	110 765	489	113.5	71.9	25.3	0.8	2.3	3.0	7.0	21.2	9.5	14.0	17.8	13.1
13 155	...	7	Irwin	924	9 931	2 455	10.7	72.3	26.0	0.3	0.4	2.0	6.8	22.0	9.2	12.5	13.6	12.2
13 157	...	6	Jackson	887	41 589	1 066	46.9	89.9	8.1	0.6	1.2	3.0	7.3	19.4	8.7	15.3	14.6	13.0
13 159	...	8	Jasper	959	11 426	2 339	11.9	71.7	27.5	0.5	0.2	2.1	7.0	20.3	7.9	13.0	15.6	14.6
13 161	...	7	Jeff Davis	863	12 684	2 248	14.7	81.7	15.2	0.5	0.6	5.1	7.7	19.5	9.3	13.5	14.8	13.8
13 163	...	8	Jefferson	1 367	17 266	1 935	12.6	42.4	56.5	0.3	0.2	1.5	7.2	21.2	9.0	12.7	14.4	12.9
13 165	...	7	Jenkins	906	8 575	2 560	9.5	56.9	40.8	0.4	0.4	3.3	7.1	21.4	9.2	11.8	14.7	13.4
13 167	...	6	Johnson	788	8 560	2 561	10.9	62.7	37.0	0.3	0.2	0.9	6.8	23.3	8.9	11.1	13.2	11.5
13 169	4680	2	Jones	1 020	23 639	1 605	23.2	75.6	23.6	0.5	0.8	0.7	6.5	20.6	7.9	13.2	17.4	14.4
13 171	...	6	Lamar	479	15 912	2 026	33.2	68.5	30.8	0.7	0.4	1.1	6.1	18.4	11.4	13.2	14.7	14.0
13 173	...	9	Lanier	484	7 241	2 661	15.0	72.7	25.9	1.1	0.8	1.7	7.2	20.2	11.0	14.2	16.3	11.8
13 175	...	6	Laurens	2 104	44 874	1 001	21.3	63.9	34.8	0.4	1.0	1.2	6.9	19.9	9.1	12.9	15.0	13.5
13 177	0120	3	Lee	921	24 757	1 565	26.9	82.8	15.7	0.5	1.1	1.2	7.3	23.4	8.5	14.7	18.5	14.7
13 179	...	4	Liberty	1 344	61 610	789	45.8	48.9	44.6	1.1	3.3	8.2	10.4	21.6	17.9	19.1	14.8	8.0
13 181	...	8	Lincoln	547	8 348	2 576	15.3	64.7	34.5	0.7	0.3	1.0	5.4	19.0	7.2	11.9	15.6	14.7
13 183	...	9	Long	1 038	10 304	2 415	9.9	69.9	25.0	1.1	1.4	8.4	11.0	22.1	14.2	16.6	14.4	10.1
13 185	...	5	Lowndes	1 306	92 115	554	70.5	63.0	34.5	0.8	1.7	2.7	7.2	19.0	15.1	15.9	15.4	11.4
13 187	...	7	Lumpkin	737	21 016	1 735	28.5	95.5	1.6	2.0	0.6	3.5	6.4	17.9	15.4	13.6	15.4	12.5
13 189	0600	2	McDuffie	673	21 231	1 723	31.5	61.3	37.9	0.5	0.7	1.3	7.1	20.7	8.6	13.2	15.3	13.9
13 191	...	9	McIntosh	1 123	10 847	2 377	9.7	62.0	37.3	0.8	0.3	0.9	6.6	21.5	7.2	12.3	14.6	14.7
13 193	...	6	Macon	1 045	14 074	2 157	13.5	37.9	59.8	0.6	0.8	2.6	7.1	20.5	9.7	12.4	15.2	13.5
13 195	0500	3	Madison	735	25 730	1 526	35.0	89.9	8.6	0.7	0.6	2.0	6.9	19.4	8.2	14.1	16.5	14.0
13 197	...	8	Marion	951	7 144	2 674	7.5	62.0	34.5	1.2	0.7	5.8	6.5	21.9	8.6	12.7	16.0	14.5
13 199	...	6	Meriwether	1 303	22 534	1 669	17.3	56.7	42.4	0.6	0.4	0.8	6.7	19.9	9.0	12.3	14.8	13.5
13 201	...	9	Miller	733	6 383	2 750	8.7	70.6	29.0	0.4	0.2	0.7	6.0	20.3	7.0	12.0	14.2	12.8
13 205	...	6	Mitchell	1 326	23 932	1 595	18.0	50.1	48.2	0.5	0.5	2.1	7.2	20.1	9.9	14.1	15.3	12.7
13 207	...	6	Monroe	1 025	21 757	1 706	21.2	70.9	28.2	0.7	0.6	1.3	6.3	19.9	8.3	13.1	17.2	15.0
13 209	...	9	Montgomery	635	8 270	2 584	13.0	70.3	27.4	0.3	0.5	3.3	6.8	18.2	12.8	14.5	15.7	12.3
13 211	...	6	Morgan	906	15 457	2 053	17.1	70.3	29.0	0.5	0.6	1.6	6.6	19.9	7.8	12.9	15.8	14.2
13 213	...	7	Murray	892	36 506	1 202	40.9	96.1	0.8	0.7	0.4	5.5	8.1	19.9	9.5	16.4	16.7	12.9
13 215	1800	2	Muscogee	560	186 291	295	332.7	51.8	44.6	0.8	2.3	4.5	7.3	19.5	11.9	14.6	15.2	12.2
13 217	0520	1	Newton	716	62 001	784	86.6	76.1	22.6	0.5	1.0	1.9	7.9	19.7	8.9	16.3	15.8	12.7
13 219	0500	3	Oconee	481	26 225	1 508	54.5	90.3	6.6	0.5	1.8	3.2	6.9	23.3	7.0	12.4	17.8	15.7
13 221	...	8	Oglethorpe	1 142	12 635	2 253	11.1	79.0	20.2	0.6	0.5	1.4	6.9	18.9	7.8	13.3	16.7	13.5
13 223	0520	1	Paulding	812	81 678	636	100.6	91.6	7.3	0.8	0.7	1.7	9.4	21.3	7.6	19.8	18.6	11.0
13 225	4680	2	Peach	391	23 668	1 603	60.5	51.9	45.7	0.6	0.6	4.2	6.5	19.6	14.9	13.2	14.3	12.7
13 227	0520	1	Pickens	601	22 983	1 644	38.2	97.0	1.3	0.9	0.3	2.0	6.3	17.2	7.7	14.0	15.8	13.9
13 229	...	7	Pierce	889	15 636	2 047	17.6	87.5	11.2	0.5	0.4	2.3	6.7	20.0	8.5	13.1	15.0	14.2
13 231	...	8	Pike	566	13 688	2 185	24.2	84.1	15.0	0.5	0.5	1.2	7.0	20.6	8.0	13.2	17.0	13.5
13 233	...	6	Polk	806	38 127	1 161	47.3	81.3	13.7	0.5	0.5	7.7	7.2	18.9	9.7	14.1	14.7	12.6
13 235	...	6	Pulaski	641	9 588	2 481	15.0	63.7	34.6	0.7	0.5	2.8	6.4	16.7	9.3	14.9	16.2	13.4
13 237	...	6	Putnam	892	18 812	1 853	21.1	68.0	30.3	0.6	0.9	2.2	6.1	17.1	7.7	12.5	14.5	14.8
13 239	...	9	Quitman	392	2 598	3 020	6.6	52.5	47.2	0.6	0.0	0.5	6.1	17.9	7.2	9.8	13.8	13.9
13 241	...	9	Rabun	961	15 050	2 088	15.7	95.7	1.0	1.0	0.6	4.5	5.7	16.1	7.0	11.7	13.6	14.6
13 243	...	7	Randolph	1 112	7 791	2 626	7.0	39.3	59.7	0.5	0.5	1.2	7.1	20.2	11.0	10.4	13.8	12.8

1. MSA = Metropolitan Statistical Area. PMSA = Primary MSA. NECMA = New England County Metropolitan Area. See Appendix A for explanation of these concepts. See Appendix B for list of metropolitan areas identified by type, with component counties. 2. County typology code from the Economic Research Service of USDA. See Appendix A for definition. 3. Dry land or land partially or temporarily covered by water. 4. Hispanic persons may be of any race.

STATE County	Population, 2000 (cont'd) Age (percent) (cont'd) 55 to 64 years	65 to 74 years	75 years and over	Percent female	Population — change and components of change, 1990–2001 Total persons 2001	1990	Percent change 1990–2000	2000–2001	Components of change, 2000–2001 Births	Deaths	Net migration	Households, 2000 Number	Percent change, 1990–2000	Persons per household	Percent Female family householder[1]	One person
	16	17	18	19	20	21	22	23	24	25	26	27	28	29	30	31
GEORGIA—Cont'd																
Fannin	13.0	11.1	7.9	51.7	20 661	15 992	23.8	4.4	285	296	852	8 369	32.1	2.35	8.9	25.6
Fayette	9.6	4.9	4.0	51.1	95 542	62 415	46.2	4.7	1 164	671	3 702	31 524	49.7	2.88	8.3	15.0
Floyd	9.3	7.4	6.5	51.6	91 183	81 251	11.5	0.7	1 667	1 250	237	34 028	11.5	2.55	13.0	24.5
Forsyth	8.3	4.3	2.8	49.3	110 296	44 083	123.2	12.1	2 124	621	10 087	34 565	116.9	2.83	6.6	14.8
Franklin	10.8	8.4	6.9	51.5	20 783	16 650	21.8	2.5	320	270	442	7 888	23.9	2.50	10.5	24.6
Fulton	7.3	4.4	4.1	50.8	816 638	648 776	25.8	0.1	18 686	7 970	-10 210	321 242	24.9	2.44	16.5	32.2
Gilmer	11.8	8.3	4.9	49.3	24 349	13 368	75.5	3.8	431	246	695	9 071	78.8	2.57	8.4	22.2
Glascock	10.5	8.5	9.7	52.0	2 583	2 357	8.4	1.1	38	43	31	1 004	15.8	2.44	9.6	26.3
Glynn	10.1	7.8	6.7	52.2	68 217	62 496	8.1	1.0	1 207	941	409	27 208	13.6	2.44	14.6	27.2
Gordon	9.3	6.1	4.5	50.2	45 555	35 067	25.8	3.3	847	462	1 060	16 173	26.6	2.70	11.1	20.3
Grady	9.5	7.0	6.2	52.5	23 714	20 279	16.7	0.2	430	357	-9	8 797	19.6	2.66	16.2	22.4
Greene	13.4	8.4	6.0	52.1	14 914	11 793	22.2	3.5	304	180	378	5 477	34.1	2.59	18.3	23.0
Gwinnett	6.5	3.2	2.2	49.6	621 528	352 910	66.7	5.6	11 886	2 759	23 514	202 317	59.3	2.88	10.0	18.4
Habersham	10.0	7.8	6.0	48.7	37 153	27 622	30.0	3.5	635	426	1 030	13 259	33.0	2.57	9.3	22.4
Hall	8.1	5.4	4.0	49.1	145 664	95 434	45.9	4.6	3 033	1 201	4 517	47 381	36.5	2.89	10.8	19.2
Hancock	9.3	7.0	5.0	46.6	10 065	8 908	13.1	-0.1	193	149	-52	3 237	9.0	2.66	28.2	26.1
Haralson	10.3	7.2	5.8	51.2	26 255	21 966	17.0	2.2	437	359	484	9 826	19.1	2.58	11.3	23.0
Harris	10.5	6.9	5.0	50.6	24 548	17 788	33.2	3.6	370	261	733	8 822	36.7	2.66	10.7	17.9
Hart	11.2	9.3	7.2	50.8	23 087	19 712	16.7	0.4	328	338	108	9 106	22.1	2.47	12.0	24.4
Heard	9.1	6.2	4.8	50.9	11 229	8 628	27.6	2.0	197	128	147	4 043	30.7	2.70	12.1	21.3
Henry	7.8	4.5	2.9	50.7	132 581	58 741	103.2	11.1	2 392	857	11 363	41 373	106.7	2.87	10.3	15.4
Houston	8.2	5.7	3.6	50.8	113 391	89 208	24.2	2.4	2 029	911	1 538	40 911	26.1	2.65	14.0	22.1
Irwin	9.7	7.4	6.6	50.9	10 028	8 649	14.8	1.0	157	143	83	3 644	16.0	2.62	14.4	23.1
Jackson	9.5	5.6	4.8	49.9	44 010	30 005	38.6	5.8	796	452	2 031	15 057	40.4	2.71	10.8	19.7
Jasper	9.8	6.8	5.0	51.0	11 904	8 453	35.2	4.2	195	171	444	4 175	37.5	2.72	13.3	21.4
Jeff Davis	9.6	6.9	5.0	50.9	12 762	12 032	5.4	0.6	314	164	-69	4 828	10.8	2.61	13.6	22.3
Jefferson	8.9	6.8	6.9	52.9	17 090	17 408	-0.8	-1.0	394	259	-314	6 339	4.0	2.65	23.1	25.7
Jenkins	8.9	7.3	6.2	52.1	8 637	8 247	4.0	0.7	185	114	-4	3 214	8.9	2.63	19.7	25.6
Johnson	9.5	8.0	7.6	50.7	8 578	8 329	2.8	0.2	177	139	-16	3 130	4.0	2.53	18.2	26.6
Jones	9.6	6.0	4.3	51.2	24 203	20 739	14.0	2.4	374	269	457	8 659	18.6	2.69	13.3	20.2
Lamar	9.6	7.0	5.6	52.1	16 260	13 038	22.0	2.2	248	200	296	5 712	22.3	2.64	16.3	21.6
Lanier	8.7	6.2	4.5	49.3	7 140	5 531	30.9	-1.4	122	77	-148	2 593	32.0	2.69	13.7	21.8
Laurens	9.3	6.9	6.4	51.9	45 378	39 988	12.2	1.1	876	599	243	17 083	17.7	2.55	17.1	25.7
Lee	6.7	3.8	2.5	49.5	25 539	16 250	52.4	3.2	417	130	490	8 229	58.3	2.91	13.0	14.3
Liberty	4.3	2.4	1.5	47.3	60 107	52 745	16.8	-2.4	2 139	299	-3 331	19 383	28.1	2.93	14.8	16.6
Lincoln	11.6	9.1	5.5	51.3	8 424	7 442	12.2	0.9	106	121	92	3 251	20.3	2.55	15.5	23.7
Long	5.8	3.5	2.3	49.5	10 548	6 202	66.1	2.4	227	68	90	3 574	62.8	2.88	14.5	19.6
Lowndes	7.1	5.0	4.0	50.3	92 250	75 981	21.2	0.1	2 072	911	-1 013	32 654	24.1	2.61	15.9	24.2
Lumpkin	9.1	5.6	4.1	50.9	21 855	14 573	44.2	4.0	306	181	704	7 537	51.5	2.61	9.4	22.0
McDuffie	9.3	6.4	5.5	52.8	21 286	20 119	5.5	0.3	461	315	-81	7 970	9.6	2.62	19.2	23.2
McIntosh	11.4	7.1	4.7	50.5	11 085	8 634	25.6	2.2	206	149	179	4 202	31.9	2.54	14.7	24.2
Macon	8.7	6.7	6.0	50.4	14 133	13 114	7.3	0.4	307	218	-25	4 834	10.2	2.71	24.4	25.2
Madison	9.9	6.3	4.7	50.9	26 214	21 050	22.2	1.9	425	291	351	9 800	26.6	2.61	10.6	21.5
Marion	9.2	5.7	4.8	50.8	7 204	5 590	27.8	0.8	160	89	-11	2 668	36.0	2.65	15.1	24.3
Meriwether	10.1	7.0	6.6	52.2	22 625	22 411	0.5	0.4	419	319	-3	8 248	8.0	2.68	18.4	23.8
Miller	10.7	8.2	8.9	52.9	6 381	6 280	1.6	0.0	111	106	-5	2 487	6.5	2.51	15.5	26.7
Mitchell	8.9	6.3	5.5	49.1	24 053	20 275	18.0	0.5	529	273	-129	8 063	18.6	2.72	22.5	23.3
Monroe	9.8	6.0	4.4	50.2	22 153	17 113	27.1	1.8	383	268	282	7 719	32.2	2.74	13.8	18.9
Montgomery	9.1	6.1	4.5	48.8	8 361	7 379	12.1	1.1	160	89	23	2 919	17.1	2.57	13.5	25.6
Morgan	10.2	6.8	5.7	51.6	16 153	12 883	20.0	4.5	273	206	616	5 558	26.3	2.75	14.6	19.4
Murray	8.6	5.1	2.9	50.0	37 747	26 147	39.6	3.4	567	323	983	13 286	41.9	2.73	11.1	18.8
Muscogee	7.5	6.5	5.2	51.4	184 134	179 280	3.9	-1.2	4 315	2 244	-4 194	69 819	6.0	2.54	19.6	26.7
Newton	8.8	5.7	4.2	51.4	68 047	41 808	48.3	9.8	1 333	610	5 177	21 997	52.7	2.77	14.1	18.3
Oconee	8.3	4.6	3.9	50.7	27 059	17 618	48.9	3.2	371	215	669	9 051	47.0	2.87	9.4	15.5
Oglethorpe	10.5	7.0	5.4	51.4	12 969	9 763	29.4	2.6	171	127	282	4 849	35.4	2.58	11.5	23.0
Paulding	6.4	3.6	2.3	50.0	89 734	41 611	96.3	9.9	1 735	478	6 610	28 089	96.1	2.89	9.0	14.6
Peach	9.0	5.8	4.0	51.6	24 196	21 189	11.7	2.2	507	314	339	8 436	18.1	2.68	19.6	22.6
Pickens	11.9	8.2	5.0	51.1	24 776	14 432	59.3	7.8	362	228	1 614	8 960	66.4	2.54	8.8	20.5
Pierce	10.4	6.8	5.3	50.8	15 698	13 328	17.3	0.4	311	220	-27	5 958	23.9	2.61	11.6	23.1
Pike	9.8	6.2	4.7	50.0	14 253	10 224	33.9	4.1	229	141	468	4 755	34.9	2.81	10.5	17.5
Polk	9.6	7.2	6.0	50.2	38 843	33 815	12.8	1.9	783	567	509	14 012	11.9	2.66	13.1	22.7
Pulaski	9.9	7.0	6.2	57.4	9 598	8 108	18.3	0.1	177	158	-5	3 407	10.0	2.49	15.7	27.9
Putnam	13.1	9.0	5.1	50.8	19 094	14 137	33.1	1.5	343	212	149	7 402	41.6	2.50	12.8	22.0
Quitman	11.5	11.7	8.2	52.9	2 610	2 210	17.6	0.5	39	38	12	1 047	22.2	2.48	18.7	24.9
Rabun	13.1	10.7	7.5	50.7	15 318	11 648	29.2	1.8	196	199	268	6 279	35.6	2.35	8.1	26.8
Randolph	9.1	7.5	8.0	53.8	7 644	8 023	-2.9	-1.9	190	164	-173	2 909	3.3	2.57	22.6	30.0

1. No spouse present.

Table B. States and Counties — **Vital Statistics, Health Resources, and Crime**

STATE County	Births, average 1997–1999 Total	Rate[1]	Deaths, average 1997–1999 Number Total	Number Infant[2]	Rate Total[1]	Rate Infant[3]	Physicians,[4] 2000 Number	Rate[5]	Hospitals,[4] 1998 Number	Beds Number	Beds Rate[5]	Medicare enrollees 2000	Serious crimes known to police, 2000[6] Total Number	Rate[7]
	32	33	34	35	36	37	38	39	40	41	42	43	44	45
GEORGIA—Cont'd														
Fannin	215	11.6	216	NA	11.6	NA	15	76	1	51	274	4 246	216	1 091
Fayette	922	10.4	493	NA	5.6	NA	123	135	0	0	0	8 415	1 540	1 687
Floyd	1 193	14.0	959	9	11.3	7.3	239	264	2	505	593	14 719	5 165	5 703
Forsyth	1 503	17.4	451	8	5.2	5.5	50	51	1	28	33	6 286	2 712	2 756
Franklin	238	12.5	219	NA	11.5	NA	16	79	1	333	1 745	4 084	909	4 481
Fulton	12 125	16.4	6 228	119	8.4	9.8	2 808	344	13	4 287	580	80 154	69 841	8 559
Gilmer	297	15.7	183	NA	9.7	NA	14	60	1	50	268	3 819	259	1 139
Glascock	31	12.4	32	NA	12.8	NA	0	0	0	0	0	546	NA	NA
Glynn	914	13.6	679	NA	10.1	NA	159	235	1	337	501	10 997	5 594	8 279
Gordon	629	15.3	367	NA	8.9	NA	44	100	1	50	122	5 877	1 581	3 585
Grady	308	14.3	247	NA	11.5	NA	17	72	1	49	228	3 404	755	3 191
Greene	199	14.5	138	NA	10.1	NA	12	83	1	58	425	2 460	329	2 385
Gwinnett	8 782	16.8	2 116	54	4.1	6.1	552	94	3	428	82	32 376	17 589	3 064
Habersham	426	13.4	326	NA	10.2	NA	29	81	1	137	430	5 672	665	1 852
Hall	2 174	18.2	928	12	7.8	5.4	213	153	2	447	375	15 711	2 747	1 974
Hancock	126	13.9	103	NA	11.3	NA	5	50	1	52	569	1 518	121	1 201
Haralson	338	13.7	278	NA	11.3	NA	14	54	1	59	239	4 015	399	1 553
Harris	273	12.2	193	NA	8.6	NA	13	55	0	0	0	2 802	186	785
Hart	266	12.2	244	NA	11.2	NA	20	87	1	41	188	3 354	464	2 018
Heard	151	14.8	97	NA	9.5	NA	2	18	0	0	0	1 252	152	1 380
Henry	1 775	16.8	638	11	6.1	6.2	70	59	1	119	114	10 438	3 989	3 643
Houston	1 564	14.8	709	14	6.7	8.7	127	115	2	236	223	11 693	4 945	4 464
Irwin	119	13.2	105	NA	11.7	NA	4	40	1	34	379	1 310	298	3 001
Jackson	587	15.5	349	NA	9.2	NA	17	41	1	233	619	5 540	1 490	3 583
Jasper	127	12.4	101	NA	9.9	NA	9	79	1	68	670	1 391	141	1 234
Jeff Davis	200	15.7	127	NA	9.9	NA	9	71	1	50	392	1 999	607	4 786
Jefferson	272	15.3	190	NA	10.7	NA	14	81	1	37	208	3 133	402	2 649
Jenkins	126	15.0	90	NA	10.7	NA	5	58	1	38	450	1 409	282	3 289
Johnson	130	15.6	96	NA	11.5	NA	3	35	0	0	0	1 424	NA	NA
Jones	293	12.8	183	NA	8.0	NA	7	30	0	0	0	1 793	714	3 020
Lamar	209	14.2	148	NA	10.1	NA	6	38	0	0	0	2 352	326	2 118
Lanier	91	13.2	63	NA	9.2	NA	3	41	1	40	573	808	NA	NA
Laurens	633	14.5	447	10	10.2	15.3	90	201	1	190	434	7 070	1 944	4 332
Lee	319	14.1	100	NA	4.4	NA	3	12	0	0	0	1 633	616	2 488
Liberty	1 526	25.6	242	16	4.1	10.5	54	88	1	49	83	3 046	2 883	4 765
Lincoln	90	10.9	92	NA	11.2	NA	1	12	0	0	0	1 391	123	1 473
Long	186	21.8	58	NA	6.8	NA	0	0	0	0	0	581	197	1 912
Lowndes	1 433	16.8	664	20	7.8	14.2	160	174	2	359	421	10 547	NA	NA
Lumpkin	247	13.0	152	NA	8.0	NA	16	76	1	52	274	2 175	462	2 198
McDuffie	322	14.8	229	NA	10.5	NA	16	75	1	47	216	3 049	838	3 947
McIntosh	145	14.4	103	NA	10.2	NA	4	37	0	0	0	1 566	436	4 020
Macon	198	15.0	157	NA	11.8	NA	9	64	0	0	0	1 847	327	2 412
Madison	353	14.4	219	NA	8.9	NA	2	8	0	0	0	3 719	377	1 494
Marion	95	14.3	66	NA	9.8	NA	4	56	0	0	0	733	161	2 254
Meriwether	315	13.7	257	NA	11.2	NA	9	40	1	96	415	3 323	780	3 461
Miller	78	12.3	69	NA	10.8	NA	3	47	1	135	2 106	1 105	144	2 256
Mitchell	349	16.5	236	NA	11.1	NA	14	58	1	26	123	3 252	631	2 637
Monroe	266	13.5	200	NA	10.2	NA	7	32	1	40	204	2 418	580	2 693
Montgomery	108	13.8	70	NA	9.0	NA	1	12	0	0	0	1 207	NA	NA
Morgan	199	13.3	151	NA	10.0	NA	10	65	1	26	172	2 207	250	1 695
Murray	540	16.4	246	NA	7.5	NA	9	25	1	42	129	3 685	894	2 449
Muscogee	2 987	16.4	1 740	48	9.5	16.2	393	211	3	871	477	25 465	11 922	6 417
Newton	971	16.8	457	NA	7.9	NA	40	65	1	90	156	7 728	1 886	3 042
Oconee	304	12.8	159	NA	6.7	NA	21	80	0	0	0	2 490	679	2 589
Oglethorpe	136	12.0	99	NA	8.7	NA	3	24	0	0	0	1 154	251	1 987
Paulding	1 325	18.0	363	NA	4.9	NA	24	29	1	175	238	4 545	1 684	2 062
Peach	367	15.0	208	NA	8.5	NA	13	55	1	36	147	3 546	952	4 022
Pickens	274	13.9	176	NA	8.9	NA	16	70	1	91	462	3 072	282	1 227
Pierce	227	14.4	156	NA	9.9	NA	7	45	0	0	0	2 557	NA	NA
Pike	180	14.2	118	NA	9.4	NA	2	15	0	0	0	1 839	211	1 541
Polk	558	15.4	422	NA	11.6	NA	24	63	1	35	96	6 565	1 318	3 457
Pulaski	118	14.1	106	NA	12.7	NA	14	146	1	55	655	1 539	92	960
Putnam	231	13.1	160	NA	9.1	NA	9	48	1	50	285	2 710	581	3 088
Quitman	31	12.6	29	NA	11.6	NA	0	0	0	0	0	618	103	3 965
Rabun	165	12.3	166	NA	12.4	NA	25	166	2	66	492	2 878	216	1 658
Randolph	126	15.9	108	NA	13.6	NA	7	90	1	120	1 523	1 376	NA	NA

1. Per 1,000 estimated resident population, average 1997–1999.   2. Deaths of infants under 1 year old.   3. Deaths of infants under 1 year old per 1,000 live births.   4. Data subject to copyright.   5. Per 100,000 resident population as of July 1 of the year shown.   6. Data for serious crimes have not been adjusted for underreporting; this may affect comparability between geographic areas and over time.   7. Per 100,000 population estimated by the FBI.

Table B. States and Counties — Crime, Education, Money Income, and Poverty

STATE County	Serious crimes known to police, 2000[1] (cont'd) Rate[2]		Education						Money income 1989				Income and poverty, 1998			
			School enrollment and attainment, 1990				Local government expenditures, fiscal 1999[5]						Percent below poverty level			
			Enrollment[3]		Attainment[4] (percent)					Households						
										Median						
	Violent	Property	Total	Percent private	High school graduate or more	Bachelor's degree or more	Total current expenditures (mil dol)	Current expenditures per student (dollars)	Per capita[6] (dollars)	Dollars	Percent change, 1979–1989 (constant 1989 dollars)	Percent with $100,000 or more	Median household income	All persons	Persons under 18	Persons 5–17 in families
	46	47	48	49	50	51	52	53	54	55	56	57	58	59	60	61
GEORGIA—Cont'd																
Fannin	10	1 081	3 164	5.0	55.8	7.8	18.3	5 943	9 430	19 023	14.4	0.9	27 379	16.5	25.7	26.5
Fayette	58	1 629	17 522	12.0	86.5	25.8	109.1	5 768	19 025	50 167	17.0	8.3	70 352	3.8	5.9	5.0
Floyd	784	4 919	19 579	20.0	63.9	13.7	95.1	6 225	12 121	25 536	3.8	2.3	35 025	15.3	25.3	23.1
Forsyth	291	2 465	9 689	8.0	67.6	15.6	86.1	6 022	15 763	36 642	29.8	5.2	67 385	4.7	8.1	7.2
Franklin	537	3 944	3 421	13.5	54.1	9.5	20.1	5 721	10 390	21 663	10.3	1.3	30 825	16.5	26.4	25.4
Fulton	1 563	6 996	166 389	20.6	77.8	31.6	928.5	7 358	18 452	29 978	27.9	8.7	40 878	17.4	28.8	26.2
Gilmer	13	1 125	2 677	4.3	52.3	8.6	23.0	6 528	9 676	21 410	14.0	0.8	30 268	15.2	25.3	24.0
Glascock	NA	NA	471	2.1	50.3	5.3	3.0	5 714	9 585	21 806	12.5	0.7	29 283	16.2	26.7	25.7
Glynn	961	7 319	14 394	10.8	74.3	19.9	78.6	6 595	14 055	27 887	10.1	3.3	35 982	15.6	25.7	25.2
Gordon	166	3 419	7 907	8.0	58.4	9.2	47.6	5 759	11 587	26 981	14.4	2.0	35 673	13.0	20.4	19.3
Grady	473	2 718	5 070	7.8	54.9	7.7	27.0	5 723	9 200	19 507	9.2	0.8	26 281	22.8	35.1	32.0
Greene	131	2 255	3 118	10.1	51.2	8.8	16.0	6 491	9 390	20 264	11.8	2.0	28 507	19.8	28.5	30.0
Gwinnett	220	2 844	90 473	12.7	86.7	29.6	588.3	5 841	17 881	43 518	15.0	5.5	57 996	5.4	8.5	7.4
Habersham	170	1 682	6 369	9.7	59.0	12.0	33.7	6 083	10 950	24 386	14.6	1.5	35 402	11.7	18.0	17.1
Hall	172	1 802	21 551	9.8	65.1	15.4	129.4	5 785	13 356	29 774	12.2	3.4	40 526	11.9	19.8	18.2
Hancock	357	844	2 381	8.7	49.5	6.8	10.9	6 135	7 345	17 825	8.4	0.6	23 529	26.7	34.6	37.6
Haralson	163	1 390	4 872	4.6	56.0	7.5	29.1	5 671	9 939	22 775	4.9	0.5	32 100	15.9	23.5	24.9
Harris	131	654	4 129	13.9	65.0	13.6	22.4	5 500	13 135	27 616	8.0	4.3	44 176	10.9	18.9	16.1
Hart	191	1 826	4 089	5.6	56.9	9.1	20.8	6 038	11 187	24 333	19.0	2.0	32 403	14.7	22.3	23.9
Heard	200	1 181	1 918	2.6	49.1	5.7	11.0	5 329	9 218	21 513	0.8	1.4	32 530	16.6	23.9	25.4
Henry	266	3 378	14 087	13.0	72.9	10.7	104.2	5 132	14 167	37 550	18.6	2.4	53 406	6.0	9.9	9.1
Houston	352	4 112	23 336	11.8	79.5	16.0	121.7	5 844	12 939	31 229	0.2	1.6	43 188	11.6	19.6	17.8
Irwin	222	2 779	2 272	4.8	53.1	8.3	12.1	6 091	10 057	20 169	12.7	1.6	28 349	21.6	29.3	29.8
Jackson	221	3 361	6 627	5.2	54.5	9.0	42.2	5 654	10 885	25 418	12.5	1.2	35 708	13.8	20.8	21.0
Jasper	114	1 120	1 868	8.2	64.6	10.8	11.3	5 654	10 761	25 736	20.1	1.6	35 915	16.5	26.6	26.2
Jeff Davis	449	4 336	2 853	6.3	55.2	8.3	14.9	5 598	9 632	21 470	-2.5	1.6	28 959	18.8	27.3	27.7
Jefferson	336	2 313	4 470	11.7	49.7	6.2	20.5	5 348	8 317	17 076	5.7	1.1	23 996	25.2	35.8	35.4
Jenkins	1 259	2 029	2 014	2.5	49.9	7.7	9.5	5 226	8 391	16 967	11.1	0.0	23 616	25.0	33.7	38.0
Johnson	NA	NA	1 900	4.3	52.0	4.9	8.9	6 279	8 550	18 064	1.9	1.1	24 954	24.3	33.0	37.6
Jones	436	2 585	5 387	13.6	70.2	12.0	22.1	4 660	13 543	31 934	15.1	3.8	41 614	10.8	15.8	16.8
Lamar	455	1 663	3 206	10.0	58.0	10.0	14.1	5 346	10 198	23 336	2.8	1.1	31 144	16.6	25.4	25.5
Lanier	NA	NA	1 381	2.0	51.2	5.4	8.4	6 130	8 319	17 618	1.9	1.6	25 853	21.2	29.6	33.5
Laurens	426	3 906	9 841	6.0	61.0	12.0	55.0	6 012	10 423	21 788	5.0	2.0	29 634	20.0	29.9	28.9
Lee	182	2 306	5 023	10.7	69.8	13.7	26.8	5 102	11 106	30 974	4.1	1.4	46 335	10.5	14.1	14.2
Liberty	438	4 327	12 587	6.8	82.1	13.4	56.4	4 942	8 986	21 596	10.4	0.8	29 748	21.5	27.5	29.0
Lincoln	120	1 354	1 774	6.8	59.2	8.2	9.0	5 710	9 628	21 472	-3.7	1.4	28 675	17.7	26.2	27.3
Long	136	1 776	1 413	5.2	63.6	5.2	8.7	4 705	8 815	18 802	3.1	0.6	28 303	20.3	27.6	34.7
Lowndes	NA	NA	22 514	8.2	69.8	16.3	94.1	5 843	10 919	23 295	8.9	2.3	31 365	19.6	27.0	27.8
Lumpkin	119	2 079	4 125	4.0	60.2	11.1	17.8	5 549	10 814	26 116	28.4	1.5	37 593	13.6	19.1	21.5
McDuffie	231	3 716	4 949	9.6	56.1	10.4	27.1	6 048	10 274	21 292	3.1	1.3	29 822	19.7	29.0	29.2
McIntosh	258	3 761	2 000	8.1	56.9	8.7	10.8	5 615	8 878	19 182	11.4	1.1	25 704	21.6	31.6	34.2
Macon	347	2 066	3 650	11.0	53.7	10.1	13.8	5 692	8 101	17 526	2.3	1.2	25 597	26.4	32.7	36.8
Madison	143	1 351	4 555	7.8	59.7	9.7	23.7	5 248	10 997	25 092	17.1	1.3	35 579	14.3	21.3	21.7
Marion	490	1 764	1 418	4.2	54.5	4.6	9.5	5 107	9 779	18 343	3.3	2.0	27 445	20.3	28.5	32.4
Meriwether	355	3 106	5 319	8.3	51.6	6.7	26.4	6 347	8 660	20 212	-1.2	1.1	28 898	19.2	27.0	28.7
Miller	172	2 084	1 496	5.7	57.4	8.2	7.9	6 181	11 096	20 488	13.9	2.7	27 020	23.0	31.8	36.5
Mitchell	180	2 457	5 577	10.3	54.9	7.8	26.5	5 705	8 327	18 926	-3.4	1.5	26 363	25.0	33.7	34.6
Monroe	181	2 512	4 123	16.4	66.2	12.9	21.3	5 696	11 348	27 770	17.8	2.4	35 134	14.0	21.2	21.1
Montgomery	NA	NA	1 940	20.2	57.4	10.1	7.0	5 189	9 283	20 054	17.8	1.8	25 690	23.3	33.0	34.0
Morgan	176	1 519	3 154	8.0	59.6	11.0	18.3	6 283	10 713	26 018	19.6	2.4	34 669	14.6	20.7	22.3
Murray	63	2 386	6 044	5.1	52.1	5.5	33.8	5 284	10 575	26 517	7.2	1.2	35 043	11.4	16.5	16.7
Muscogee	578	5 839	44 639	10.8	71.5	16.6	209.1	6 271	11 949	24 056	7.6	2.6	32 769	19.1	30.0	28.5
Newton	277	2 764	9 963	12.1	59.7	9.5	60.2	5 669	11 641	27 992	7.6	2.4	39 645	12.5	19.7	19.9
Oconee	72	2 517	4 936	11.8	77.1	28.4	27.0	5 338	15 164	34 566	19.7	4.5	51 465	7.6	10.9	11.8
Oglethorpe	602	1 385	2 216	8.5	61.8	12.8	12.2	5 951	10 064	24 667	13.8	0.9	35 114	14.9	21.6	22.8
Paulding	222	1 840	9 143	8.9	64.1	7.6	72.0	5 024	12 322	33 085	28.0	1.4	49 915	7.0	10.3	10.9
Peach	1 141	2 882	6 679	7.8	67.5	15.2	26.0	5 841	10 989	25 604	18.8	2.3	31 163	22.5	31.8	33.4
Pickens	57	1 170	2 874	6.5	56.8	9.0	22.3	6 272	11 442	25 248	20.4	3.1	39 755	11.8	18.7	20.3
Pierce	NA	NA	3 259	3.2	60.0	6.3	16.8	5 230	9 858	20 499	4.7	1.3	29 620	18.5	26.1	27.2
Pike	124	1 417	2 264	12.7	64.9	9.3	11.6	4 618	11 593	27 733	8.1	2.8	36 764	12.1	19.7	18.9
Polk	223	3 234	7 728	6.0	51.8	6.8	37.8	5 482	10 184	22 326	2.5	1.6	31 091	15.4	22.8	23.1
Pulaski	156	803	1 996	4.0	60.6	10.7	10.6	6 421	11 265	21 376	5.2	2.1	30 029	20.2	31.2	30.7
Putnam	425	2 663	3 277	11.3	61.8	11.7	14.8	5 855	11 951	24 325	4.6	2.3	34 133	15.4	24.6	25.1
Quitman	423	3 541	498	6.4	49.5	7.3	2.2	7 989	8 820	15 972	14.6	1.6	22 595	26.3	39.1	48.0
Rabun	223	1 435	2 100	8.2	62.7	11.6	12.6	6 141	11 161	21 177	9.5	2.8	31 252	13.5	22.1	22.3
Randolph	NA	NA	2 212	18.3	49.3	6.0	12.0	6 651	6 991	13 972	-7.1	0.9	21 874	30.9	40.2	44.5

1. Data for serious crimes have not been adjusted for underreporting; this may affect comparability between geographic areas and over time.   2. Per 100,000 population estimated by the FBI.   3. All persons 3 years old and over enrolled in nursery school through college.   4. Persons 25 years old and over.   5. Elementary and secondary education expenditures, local government fiscal years ending between July 1, 1998 and June 30, 1999.   6. Based on population enumerated as of April 1, 1990.

STATE County	Personal income, 1999 Total (mil dol)	Percent change, 1998–1999	Per capita[1] Dollars	Rank	Wages and salaries[2] (mil dol)	Proprietor's income (mil dol)	Dividends, interest, and rent (mil dol)	Transfer payments Total (mil dol)	Government payments to individuals Total (mil dol)	Social Security (mil dol)	Medical payments (mil dol)	Income mainte-nance (mil dol)	Unemploy-ment insurance (mil dol)
	62	63	64	65	66	67	68	69	70	71	72	73	74
GEORGIA—Cont'd													
Fannin	350	4.7	18 495	2 415	113	46	68	91	87	40	32	8	1
Fayette	2 949	7.7	31 922	156	1 012	185	498	187	167	96	51	6	1
Floyd	2 096	5.5	24 509	755	1 303	137	380	351	332	153	131	33	4
Forsyth	3 053	14.2	31 576	166	1 159	145	457	160	139	76	49	8	1
Franklin	434	3.0	22 492	1 217	200	90	65	82	77	33	32	8	1
Fulton	33 869	8.5	45 473	19	38 358	4 507	6 630	2 343	2 182	771	857	379	28
Gilmer	388	5.1	19 635	2 098	171	63	68	81	77	33	34	6	.1
Glascock	50	3.1	19 496	2 142	15	2	8	13	13	4	7	1	0
Glynn	1 895	3.6	27 888	340	1 083	134	531	275	260	115	105	25	2
Gordon	915	6.0	21 812	1 410	616	86	132	133	124	57	49	12	2
Grady	406	6.6	18 794	2 349	145	61	71	83	78	31	28	14	2
Greene	286	6.5	20 292	1 894	142	30	58	59	56	24	22	8	1
Gwinnett	17 402	8.8	31 893	157	11 824	1 029	2 059	821	703	369	246	41	12
Habersham	765	4.6	23 525	959	397	107	150	116	109	52	41	9	1
Hall	3 160	8.2	25 631	567	2 020	274	573	352	326	158	125	26	2
Hancock	152	0.9	16 787	2 783	44	8	23	46	44	13	20	9	1
Haralson	499	7.2	19 923	2 019	178	56	81	95	90	39	37	9	1
Harris	598	7.6	26 403	475	114	44	116	64	59	29	17	6	1
Hart	466	5.7	21 069	1 646	225	46	88	85	80	39	30	8	1
Heard	184	6.6	17 583	2 633	86	23	20	34	32	14	14	3	1
Henry	2 567	12.7	22 630	1 185	908	148	346	238	214	109	77	13	2
Houston	2 466	5.2	22 913	1 108	1 898	136	436	275	253	92	104	31	5
Irwin	191	7.6	20 832	1 723	69	21	32	37	35	13	14	5	0
Jackson	902	5.6	23 095	1 070	400	156	114	126	118	51	49	12	1
Jasper	229	7.2	21 590	1 490	74	17	46	35	33	15	12	4	0
Jeff Davis	233	1.6	18 311	2 467	144	19	39	49	46	19	18	6	0
Jefferson	316	4.2	17 673	2 606	157	22	54	85	81	26	34	16	2
Jenkins	153	7.9	18 174	2 506	72	15	23	38	36	12	16	7	0
Johnson	156	5.5	18 845	2 334	55	14	22	40	38	12	17	6	1
Jones	516	5.8	22 118	1 324	88	30	64	62	57	26	19	6	1
Lamar	283	3.9	18 852	2 332	105	24	49	54	51	23	19	5	1
Lanier	123	8.9	17 675	2 605	30	10	19	27	25	8	12	4	0
Laurens	919	3.5	20 920	1 690	573	59	161	172	163	62	67	23	4
Lee	467	7.5	20 013	1 987	99	32	49	45	40	17	14	5	1
Liberty	962	3.1	16 116	2 883	1 056	56	141	114	105	28	40	20	2
Lincoln	158	4.4	18 992	2 281	40	14	24	31	30	13	11	4	1
Long	120	4.9	13 819	3 056	16	7	17	21	19	6	7	3	0
Lowndes	1 944	4.2	22 760	1 149	1 375	138	347	297	279	94	113	41	4
Lumpkin	444	7.9	22 455	1 226	182	52	71	54	50	23	19	5	0
McDuffie	453	3.4	20 764	1 752	227	32	86	82	77	27	32	13	1
McIntosh	166	4.3	16 450	2 833	51	11	30	41	39	15	17	6	0
Macon	262	5.3	19 927	2 016	123	48	38	59	56	15	27	12	1
Madison	536	5.8	21 260	1 579	94	76	70	83	78	33	31	9	1
Marion	112	5.2	16 481	2 831	55	15	17	22	21	7	8	4	0
Meriwether	447	5.7	19 403	2 180	169	64	64	88	83	32	32	12	1
Miller	141	8.6	22 270	1 281	41	24	26	27	26	10	11	5	0
Mitchell	454	6.6	21 392	1 551	195	86	69	89	84	29	35	17	2
Monroe	434	6.0	21 662	1 465	154	32	68	65	61	27	25	6	1
Montgomery	145	7.0	18 478	2 417	50	12	21	32	30	10	11	4	1
Morgan	361	5.2	23 373	994	166	39	76	51	48	22	18	5	1
Murray	614	4.6	18 098	2 521	355	45	68	87	80	36	32	8	1
Muscogee	4 542	3.8	24 947	680	3 369	247	901	693	653	237	222	104	11
Newton	1 256	8.6	20 737	1 765	567	63	175	181	168	76	69	18	1
Oconee	644	7.8	26 261	488	170	69	97	53	48	25	17	4	0
Oglethorpe	234	5.9	20 257	1 903	43	35	29	34	32	15	11	4	0
Paulding	1 314	10.9	16 505	2 826	337	79	124	134	117	60	40	10	1
Peach	526	7.3	21 028	1 661	250	51	83	91	86	28	31	16	1
Pickens	537	10.0	25 541	577	173	48	101	75	71	35	27	5	1
Pierce	309	4.4	19 534	2 126	89	30	44	63	60	21	23	8	1
Pike	265	7.1	20 188	1 936	52	23	39	39	36	17	14	3	0
Polk	732	7.1	19 990	1 994	279	62	103	154	147	61	57	15	2
Pulaski	194	3.8	23 202	1 045	93	18	38	37	36	12	16	6	1
Putnam	402	4.7	22 108	1 328	189	30	87	66	62	29	24	6	1
Quitman	45	6.1	18 223	2 489	7	2	6	13	12	5	4	2	0
Rabun	304	6.5	22 185	1 302	146	27	85	60	57	27	23	5	0
Randolph	147	6.5	18 298	2 471	66	18	26	38	36	11	14	8	0

1. Based on the resident population estimated as of July 1 of the year shown.   2. Includes other labor income.

STATE County	Earnings, 1999									Social Security bene-ficiaries, December 2000			Housing units, 1990	
			Percent by selected industries									Supple-mental Security Income recipients, December 2000		
			Goods-related[1]		Service-related and other[2]									
							Finance, insur-ance, and real estate							Percent change, 1980–1990
	Total (mil dol)	Farm	Total	Manu-facturing	Total	Retail trade		Services	Govern-ment	Number	Rate[3]		Total	
	75	76	77	78	79	80	81	82	83	84	85	86	87	88
GEORGIA—Cont'd														
Fannin	159	2.4	22.2	14.8	D	17.6	5.0	21.6	16.5	5 139	260	728	8 363	24.3
Fayette	1 197	0.3	D	21.0	D	11.1	8.2	22.7	12.7	10 728	118	412	22 428	133.2
Floyd	1 440	0.7	D	26.6	D	9.4	3.8	29.1	15.0	17 780	196	2 677	32 821	8.5
Forsyth	1 304	2.0	D	21.0	D	8.3	3.3	20.1	8.8	8 989	91	539	17 869	62.9
Franklin	289	17.1	D	21.8	D	14.6	2.3	15.8	10.0	4 549	224	733	7 613	23.0
Fulton	42 865	0.0	11.0	7.9	77.4	5.8	12.5	34.7	11.5	89 559	110	21 006	297 503	20.7
Gilmer	234	12.8	D	32.2	D	10.5	3.5	13.5	12.7	4 302	183	606	6 986	57.9
Glascock	17	-1.7	D	D	D	6.9	D	D	24.8	553	216	89	1 036	13.8
Glynn	1 217	0.0	21.5	15.2	53.7	12.0	5.0	28.4	24.8	13 240	196	1 695	27 724	24.0
Gordon	702	4.0	53.7	49.2	32.1	8.2	2.1	12.3	10.2	7 219	164	944	13 777	26.0
Grady	206	14.9	24.8	19.3	42.0	10.2	3.6	15.7	18.4	4 425	187	1 042	8 129	14.1
Greene	172	5.6	D	29.5	D	8.2	14.9	12.0	15.6	3 139	218	574	4 699	13.3
Gwinnett	12 853	0.0	25.5	16.5	67.0	10.7	7.3	24.9	7.5	43 424	74	3 638	137 608	136.7
Habersham	504	8.0	D	29.0	D	10.1	4.9	15.0	17.4	6 571	183	812	11 076	24.0
Hall	2 294	1.7	D	28.3	D	9.6	6.1	22.1	11.8	19 120	137	2 152	38 315	37.1
Hancock	52	5.2	D	D	D	5.7	3.5	21.0	50.3	1 904	189	531	3 396	7.4
Haralson	233	2.2	38.3	27.5	42.7	11.0	2.2	18.5	16.8	5 020	195	797	9 016	29.0
Harris	158	1.5	26.9	19.0	52.9	11.3	5.0	30.9	18.8	3 688	156	442	7 814	29.1
Hart	271	5.4	D	42.0	D	7.6	2.7	15.4	12.4	4 782	208	604	8 942	18.8
Heard	108	8.3	D	38.6	D	2.2	1.0	4.9	14.3	1 753	159	303	3 536	43.8
Henry	1 056	0.2	D	10.5	D	13.3	5.4	22.6	22.2	13 385	112	1 147	21 275	73.3
Houston	2 034	0.5	12.0	7.7	28.6	8.0	2.1	14.8	58.9	13 720	124	2 259	34 785	26.8
Irwin	89	12.1	24.8	19.1	40.4	4.8	2.8	19.8	22.7	1 919	193	392	3 479	4.1
Jackson	556	18.3	D	24.7	D	11.5	5.3	9.2	12.6	6 567	158	1 157	11 775	29.3
Jasper	91	7.2	D	37.9	D	5.4	1.7	11.7	21.0	2 001	175	281	3 637	18.0
Jeff Davis	163	3.7	42.5	40.5	38.7	10.9	1.5	8.8	15.1	2 552	201	499	4 792	18.4
Jefferson	179	4.2	D	34.3	D	7.6	3.3	9.6	17.6	3 617	209	1 197	7 065	8.4
Jenkins	86	7.2	48.4	45.0	26.1	5.5	2.5	9.6	18.3	1 643	192	504	3 365	0.6
Johnson	69	10.3	20.1	14.5	36.9	4.2	1.6	13.2	32.6	1 743	204	492	3 389	1.9
Jones	118	3.2	D	6.8	D	7.6	3.9	19.2	22.1	3 332	141	330	7 722	32.4
Lamar	129	5.9	40.1	35.6	32.3	9.3	3.5	11.6	21.6	2 908	183	404	5 066	16.9
Lanier	40	7.8	21.9	9.6	D	10.8	D	18.8	27.8	1 149	159	277	2 202	8.2
Laurens	632	1.6	D	24.6	D	13.0	3.2	18.7	24.6	8 399	187	1 948	16 504	22.4
Lee	131	15.1	D	2.7	D	6.8	1.7	14.5	27.3	2 346	95	340	5 537	42.8
Liberty	1 112	0.0	D	4.0	D	3.9	1.8	5.7	79.8	4 075	66	1 024	16 776	55.3
Lincoln	54	4.0	35.0	25.9	D	8.3	2.9	13.0	23.0	1 735	208	284	3 870	25.3
Long	22	9.0	D	D	D	5.9	1.9	10.9	48.6	940	91	175	2 638	52.1
Lowndes	1 513	0.8	D	13.6	D	13.1	3.1	18.6	33.4	12 173	132	2 853	28 906	18.8
Lumpkin	234	6.2	D	19.3	D	9.9	4.6	16.5	25.6	2 985	142	434	5 729	49.4
McDuffie	258	2.8	D	26.7	D	15.9	3.2	14.5	18.9	3 738	176	857	8 043	16.6
McIntosh	62	0.0	10.1	4.4	59.8	19.2	5.6	16.3	30.2	2 058	190	413	4 276	17.4
Macon	171	23.5	34.4	31.0	24.3	5.0	1.2	10.7	17.8	1 991	141	774	4 848	3.7
Madison	170	21.6	D	13.0	D	6.0	2.7	15.2	17.0	4 400	171	789	8 428	30.1
Marion	70	10.4	D	D	D	4.6	1.4	9.9	17.5	982	137	289	2 152	16.9
Meriwether	233	2.1	31.1	25.8	44.3	8.4	4.5	21.3	22.5	4 130	183	979	8 409	10.6
Miller	65	30.3	5.7	1.8	41.0	7.9	5.4	11.3	22.9	1 299	204	315	2 602	1.6
Mitchell	281	21.1	D	D	D	5.9	2.7	11.4	19.4	4 058	170	1 207	7 443	5.6
Monroe	186	3.7	D	9.0	D	6.8	1.8	15.6	26.1	3 469	159	452	6 401	28.1
Montgomery	62	6.8	29.3	14.1	42.3	5.1	6.6	18.2	21.7	1 428	173	383	2 885	13.6
Morgan	205	8.2	35.9	30.5	D	12.2	3.8	11.5	13.7	2 790	181	399	4 814	22.9
Murray	400	2.7	D	59.3	D	6.0	1.7	8.6	10.8	4 890	134	839	10 207	47.0
Muscogee	3 615	0.0	D	16.1	D	9.5	12.2	27.3	22.7	29 740	160	5 805	70 902	11.1
Newton	630	0.3	D	31.1	D	8.9	3.4	19.2	14.3	9 299	150	1 583	15 494	28.6
Oconee	239	6.3	30.1	19.5	D	9.4	7.4	23.4	14.7	3 036	116	294	6 561	45.8
Oglethorpe	77	32.2	18.1	5.4	32.4	5.4	2.2	11.2	17.3	2 069	164	326	3 936	25.0
Paulding	416	0.0	D	12.2	D	16.2	4.0	14.1	22.6	7 511	92	635	15 237	66.2
Peach	301	7.7	D	33.9	D	9.5	3.1	10.1	24.6	4 009	169	885	7 537	13.5
Pickens	220	8.0	D	14.1	D	11.2	8.8	14.5	15.2	4 313	188	404	6 403	32.5
Pierce	119	10.9	22.8	12.6	48.2	10.3	5.8	14.2	18.1	2 978	190	712	5 271	22.7
Pike	76	12.3	D	17.8	D	4.6	7.2	15.0	23.0	2 255	165	280	3 797	22.6
Polk	341	2.3	D	25.8	D	10.0	2.8	17.8	18.0	7 613	200	1 359	13 585	12.6
Pulaski	111	7.8	15.3	12.9	53.9	8.5	2.9	31.2	23.0	1 769	185	402	3 470	1.9
Putnam	219	3.0	41.1	33.9	40.4	6.2	4.1	10.4	15.5	3 556	189	385	7 113	35.3
Quitman	9	-2.1	D	22.3	D	12.9	D	10.7	38.2	618	238	176	1 346	38.1
Rabun	174	3.0	D	32.1	D	11.0	5.2	19.9	13.9	3 382	225	442	7 883	27.9
Randolph	84	9.3	30.0	27.6	35.2	7.2	2.0	13.5	25.4	1 632	209	528	3 225	-9.4

1. Covers mining, construction, and manufacturing. 2. Covers private sector earnings in agricultural services, forestry, and fisheries; transportation and public utilities; wholesale trade; retail trade; finance, insurance, and real estate; and services. 3. Per 1,000 resident population estimated as of July 1 of the year shown.

STATE County	Housing units, 1990 (cont'd)								Civilian labor force, 2001				Civilian employment, 1990[5]		
	Occupied units										Unemployment		Percent		
	Owner-occupied				Renter-occupied										
				Owner cost as a percent of income											
	Total	Percent	Median value[1]	With a mortgage	Without a mortgage	Median rent[2]	Rent as percent of income	Substandard units[3] (percent)	Total	Percent change, 2000–2001	Total	Rate[4]	Total	Professional, managerial, and technical	Precision production, craft, and repair
	89	90	91	92	93	94	95	96	97	98	99	100	101	102	103
GEORGIA—Cont'd															
Fannin	6 334	83.8	48 000	25.4	12.6	253	25.0	4.2	9 002	-1.6	330	3.7	6 461	19.3	14.7
Fayette	21 054	86.1	116 700	22.3	11.9	598	24.3	1.7	51 839	-0.2	1 008	1.9	31 844	36.2	11.2
Floyd	30 518	66.1	50 100	17.5	13.3	325	23.6	2.8	44 482	-0.1	1 906	4.3	38 308	25.5	13.0
Forsyth	15 938	81.9	96 200	22.6	13.0	497	25.0	3.1	56 315	0.5	1 280	2.3	23 266	26.2	16.0
Franklin	6 365	78.0	49 500	20.7	12.3	245	27.3	5.0	10 356	-2.1	527	5.1	7 635	16.3	15.9
Fulton	257 140	49.5	97 700	22.6	13.6	479	27.3	5.0	414 022	0.3	17 627	4.3	320 149	35.5	6.6
Gilmer	5 072	80.4	56 800	23.4	13.1	295	25.8	5.7	8 196	-0.9	288	3.5	6 073	16.5	17.2
Glascock	867	77.9	30 700	18.5	12.3	200	21.4	4.9	979	-0.9	46	4.7	1 041	13.4	16.5
Glynn	23 947	65.1	67 200	20.1	12.4	407	26.2	3.5	35 234	-1.9	1 167	3.3	29 437	29.5	11.2
Gordon	12 778	72.1	53 100	16.4	12.0	350	21.9	4.3	21 220	-4.7	1 402	6.6	17 439	18.2	13.3
Grady	7 354	73.0	41 400	20.5	14.1	270	26.8	6.4	9 038	-4.7	464	5.1	8 852	19.0	13.5
Greene	4 083	77.2	38 800	22.1	13.8	258	21.8	11.0	5 812	-2.1	502	8.6	4 863	15.6	12.0
Gwinnett	126 971	68.4	95 900	22.2	12.0	577	23.8	2.2	349 473	0.4	10 335	3.0	203 387	36.2	10.6
Habersham	9 966	76.7	57 800	20.6	13.2	316	22.5	3.5	15 648	-1.3	703	4.5	13 384	20.1	15.5
Hall	34 721	69.4	75 400	21.2	12.3	424	23.8	4.1	75 161	-0.5	2 212	2.9	49 052	23.3	15.2
Hancock	2 969	77.1	29 200	18.9	14.3	195	26.4	16.4	3 565	-7.5	381	10.7	3 426	16.0	10.6
Haralson	8 248	76.2	47 100	20.0	13.5	299	25.4	4.4	9 742	-0.4	547	5.6	9 769	17.0	19.3
Harris	6 454	82.4	64 500	19.6	12.7	311	22.7	5.8	11 967	-2.2	374	3.1	8 253	24.4	14.6
Hart	7 459	79.3	51 700	20.7	12.1	269	25.0	4.5	9 656	-3.2	679	7.0	9 091	15.1	17.4
Heard	3 093	78.9	43 900	19.7	13.0	263	23.1	8.1	5 087	2.4	282	5.5	3 702	12.3	22.5
Henry	20 012	83.4	81 200	22.0	12.1	531	25.1	3.4	64 466	0.2	1 621	2.5	30 173	24.1	16.2
Houston	32 433	65.1	62 100	17.6	11.9	396	22.9	3.5	49 134	-1.4	1 489	3.0	40 787	30.3	15.8
Irwin	3 142	73.3	40 900	19.2	14.5	227	27.2	6.1	4 695	-4.5	280	6.0	3 615	20.4	12.4
Jackson	10 721	75.1	55 300	20.4	12.4	326	24.5	4.8	22 488	-3.0	886	3.9	14 303	19.0	18.3
Jasper	3 036	76.5	51 100	21.8	12.7	284	20.7	7.6	4 902	-2.0	195	4.0	3 669	18.1	14.3
Jeff Davis	4 357	73.1	39 200	18.4	12.6	269	24.1	5.9	5 071	-2.7	512	10.1	5 529	17.5	13.9
Jefferson	6 093	69.1	38 300	18.6	13.9	218	28.6	10.0	7 039	-3.3	687	9.8	6 780	15.3	12.7
Jenkins	2 951	71.1	39 500	19.5	18.4	224	30.8	12.3	4 194	-8.7	253	6.0	3 344	17.7	14.7
Johnson	3 010	78.0	31 600	17.3	14.3	193	22.8	8.4	3 176	-10.3	230	7.2	3 486	13.3	16.2
Jones	7 300	83.7	63 500	17.4	12.9	337	23.5	4.6	11 386	-2.2	356	3.1	10 139	25.0	17.6
Lamar	4 669	70.0	47 600	22.1	13.7	319	25.8	8.0	6 323	-3.1	381	6.0	5 829	18.9	14.3
Lanier	1 965	71.5	37 500	18.5	12.7	294	22.4	5.4	3 499	-4.5	132	3.8	2 395	16.2	13.7
Laurens	14 514	70.9	46 500	19.0	12.6	282	27.4	5.3	22 244	-1.7	980	4.4	17 535	22.0	13.6
Lee	5 199	77.9	65 300	19.7	14.3	389	21.7	4.8	11 514	-4.1	419	3.6	7 359	28.8	14.5
Liberty	15 136	43.5	60 400	24.5	13.5	399	26.0	6.8	18 687	0.9	921	4.9	12 969	24.5	11.3
Lincoln	2 702	80.3	46 000	20.1	13.1	237	22.5	13.2	2 903	-7.3	349	12.0	3 151	16.9	17.2
Long	2 196	67.1	40 500	23.4	14.8	362	29.3	7.1	4 026	1.2	107	2.7	2 306	21.9	15.5
Lowndes	26 311	59.7	60 800	20.2	13.3	356	25.6	5.3	42 280	-4.3	1 580	3.7	32 401	26.0	10.9
Lumpkin	4 976	76.0	66 400	21.8	12.8	371	24.6	5.3	10 748	-3.0	248	2.3	6 838	20.7	16.6
McDuffie	7 270	68.6	48 000	18.3	12.1	275	27.3	6.9	9 687	-1.0	666	6.9	8 869	21.9	15.7
McIntosh	3 186	83.5	37 500	23.6	15.2	280	24.9	7.9	4 492	-1.5	197	4.4	3 541	19.5	15.1
Macon	4 388	68.7	35 900	18.1	14.1	238	30.6	9.0	5 425	-6.1	416	7.7	5 187	20.5	11.8
Madison	7 740	82.1	53 900	18.3	11.4	322	22.8	5.4	13 643	-0.6	492	3.6	10 419	17.4	20.3
Marion	1 962	78.8	38 400	17.5	13.5	205	27.6	12.2	3 271	-5.4	184	5.6	2 075	19.3	15.4
Meriwether	7 637	74.8	39 900	19.0	13.0	290	26.0	10.0	8 835	-2.0	612	6.9	8 800	15.7	14.3
Miller	2 336	75.7	41 200	19.0	12.7	214	24.9	7.3	3 048	-4.4	137	4.5	2 581	20.8	11.9
Mitchell	6 798	70.1	40 800	19.7	13.8	237	25.2	10.8	11 683	-4.4	603	5.2	8 248	17.3	11.2
Monroe	5 838	74.6	62 400	18.8	14.4	324	20.8	7.4	7 776	-6.8	367	4.7	7 792	24.4	16.8
Montgomery	2 493	74.1	40 100	20.5	14.0	215	23.9	6.1	3 631	-4.3	310	8.5	3 113	18.6	13.8
Morgan	4 399	76.4	55 000	20.9	13.8	319	20.1	8.0	7 347	-2.2	237	3.2	5 851	18.2	13.8
Murray	9 363	75.0	52 000	17.0	12.1	332	21.8	4.9	19 613	-3.0	874	4.5	13 247	13.4	16.0
Muscogee	65 858	53.9	58 900	19.8	12.2	358	25.5	4.5	84 676	-2.5	4 045	4.8	71 922	28.4	10.9
Newton	14 401	70.9	65 400	21.9	12.7	423	27.6	6.1	31 050	0.0	1 097	3.5	19 166	20.7	16.6
Oconee	6 156	77.5	77 900	20.7	12.7	436	24.6	2.8	13 458	-1.2	234	1.7	9 012	35.1	12.3
Oglethorpe	3 581	82.3	52 500	22.5	11.7	261	29.0	7.6	6 234	-2.9	232	3.7	4 739	19.8	15.3
Paulding	14 326	81.5	68 600	21.8	11.8	442	27.6	3.7	43 840	0.0	1 074	2.4	20 732	18.9	20.4
Peach	7 142	69.1	56 700	19.2	12.7	303	30.2	6.7	10 597	-1.9	467	4.4	8 870	27.8	11.2
Pickens	5 386	80.2	59 500	23.2	12.2	341	24.8	5.2	11 339	0.0	336	3.0	7 003	18.9	17.0
Pierce	4 807	80.0	41 700	19.4	13.3	254	23.7	4.8	7 650	-1.6	308	4.0	5 863	17.9	16.7
Pike	3 526	80.7	51 600	19.8	12.5	300	24.4	6.1	6 757	4.3	267	4.0	4 578	20.4	16.3
Polk	12 519	72.4	41 600	19.2	12.8	316	26.0	4.7	17 557	6.2	887	5.1	14 385	16.5	15.1
Pulaski	3 098	70.5	44 900	20.7	14.2	235	27.0	8.7	4 529	-2.1	312	6.9	3 340	23.7	14.9
Putnam	5 229	74.9	59 000	19.2	12.0	296	24.2	7.0	9 741	-1.1	319	3.3	6 558	20.0	14.9
Quitman	857	73.5	36 400	20.4	14.4	183	25.7	13.5	1 284	-9.8	85	6.6	813	18.2	10.9
Rabun	4 630	81.5	65 900	23.7	12.8	292	23.6	4.1	7 375	-4.3	206	2.8	5 478	19.1	20.1
Randolph	2 815	66.7	33 000	25.3	13.7	205	25.7	13.0	3 109	-2.9	288	9.3	2 830	16.3	8.0

1. Specified owner-occupied units. 2. Specified renter-occupied units. 3. Overcrowded or lacking complete plumbing facilities. 4. Percent of civilian labor force. 5. Persons 16 years and older.

Table B. States and Counties — Nonfarm Employment and Agriculture

STATE County	Number of establishments	Total	Health Care and Social Assistance	Manufacturing	Retail trade	Finance and Insurance	Professional Scientific and Technical Services	Total (mil dol)	Average per employee (dollars)	Number	Less than 50 acres	500 acres and over	Whose principal occupation is farming (percent)
	104	105	106	107	108	109	110	111	112	113	114	115	116
GEORGIA—Cont'd													
Fannin	443	4 125	629	891	960	160	113	75	18 126	151	37.1	0.7	40.4
Fayette	2 281	27 858	2 113	5 017	5 437	906	1 017	766	27 499	184	44.6	2.7	34.8
Floyd	2 019	38 069	6 039	10 468	4 856	1 184	861	901	23 679	437	29.1	5.7	34.6
Forsyth	2 259	28 477	1 241	4 900	3 861	442	1 004	818	28 721	699	60.1	1.6	43.3
Franklin	457	6 501	675	1 908	1 030	262	67	146	22 459	257	36.3	2.3	48.5
Fulton	30 590	726 101	59 454	36 892	56 824	57 320	76 543	29 929	41 219	267	56.0	3.9	35.8
Gilmer	424	5 847	434	2 776	809	212	131	117	20 015	76	51.3	1.1	58.4
Glascock	27	207	D	D	D	D	D	3	14 275	36	15.8	14.5	42.1
Glynn	2 386	29 937	4 298	3 534	4 851	930	839	699	23 343	36	55.6	16.7	38.9
Gordon	931	21 092	1 005	11 309	2 286	299	344	494	23 432	535	43.7	4.5	41.3
Grady	400	4 051	465	1 063	827	184	70	77	19 044	462	28.6	13.9	54.5
Greene	310	4 122	331	1 593	471	351	69	91	21 980	198	27.8	14.6	53.0
Gwinnett	17 014	273 909	14 207	27 468	37 904	14 103	19 167	9 633	35 169	303	57.4	2.3	35.0
Habersham	808	12 153	837	4 634	1 792	416	194	277	22 777	407	55.5	1.0	51.1
Hall	3 341	54 746	5 848	18 294	6 731	2 026	1 345	1 474	26 929	666	53.5	1.2	45.6
Hancock	85	830	366	D	151	D	D	13	15 512	103	11.7	14.6	31.1
Haralson	434	5 136	367	1 942	948	122	80	116	22 604	260	36.9	3.5	34.2
Harris	404	4 425	170	1 491	250	77	92	83	18 724	207	33.8	10.6	37.7
Hart	372	6 114	554	2 914	829	109	69	145	23 708	460	33.9	4.8	43.7
Heard	108	1 550	114	365	190	D	15	24	15 657	160	21.2	5.6	40.6
Henry	2 163	25 133	2 418	3 221	4 345	743	837	592	23 555	327	45.6	5.5	34.9
Houston	1 983	25 565	3 670	2 414	5 729	929	2 311	558	21 831	249	39.4	16.1	36.5
Irwin	132	1 975	480	690	179	50	42	38	19 257	288	14.9	26.7	63.9
Jackson	931	13 774	865	4 710	2 017	300	221	331	24 002	719	47.8	3.2	45.2
Jasper	161	1 556	145	676	169	54	D	41	26 530	185	15.7	11.9	36.8
Jeff Davis	314	4 723	283	2 087	689	109	53	99	20 930	220	25.0	16.8	45.9
Jefferson	350	4 782	462	1 828	666	161	47	115	23 968	356	14.6	19.1	43.3
Jenkins	149	2 391	246	1 344	233	47	18	45	18 651	248	12.9	21.4	44.0
Johnson	147	1 467	151	518	177	31	D	29	19 999	288	15.6	13.9	37.8
Jones	238	1 836	296	200	236	76	35	41	22 456	157	27.4	8.3	34.4
Lamar	225	3 167	267	1 405	392	88	36	65	20 399	188	30.9	8.0	37.8
Lanier	107	810	294	58	146	84	12	15	18 849	92	25.0	22.8	42.4
Laurens	1 041	16 724	2 764	5 004	2 738	471	239	368	22 005	688	23.0	12.8	34.0
Lee	205	1 891	237	352	383	44	17	35	18 514	157	29.9	38.9	48.4
Liberty	721	8 799	1 424	883	1 917	369	254	171	19 404	43	25.6	25.6	37.2
Lincoln	160	1 495	28	626	135	40	14	23	15 644	163	27.0	9.2	29.4
Long	47	292	85	0	35	D	0	3	10 493	64	26.6	18.8	38.1
Lowndes	2 367	36 762	5 382	6 282	7 135	888	924	757	20 594	373	40.5	10.2	29.7
Lumpkin	386	3 774	541	812	776	133	86	85	22 581	198	35.4	5.1	43.4
McDuffie	452	6 938	698	1 930	1 462	235	128	151	21 764	217	33.2	10.6	34.1
McIntosh	228	1 966	228	80	881	D	10	34	17 228	24	19.3	8.3	25.0
Macon	220	2 566	389	982	356	83	D	70	27 424	282	19.9	23.4	59.2
Madison	518	7 100	294	3 065	554	226	232	161	22 708	622	38.3	2.4	44.5
Marion	82	2 305	167	D	205	D	44	40	17 312	147	12.2	19.0	38.8
Meriwether	334	5 044	882	2 372	572	147	56	119	23 601	257	24.9	13.6	39.7
Miller	146	1 082	221	10	251	37	20	19	17 460	251	16.3	27.9	64.1
Mitchell	408	3 679	453	479	958	184	107	64	17 488	464	22.4	25.4	53.2
Monroe	397	3 521	479	361	512	89	89	82	23 429	179	25.7	19.0	35.2
Montgomery	100	1 161	D	198	95	86	12	25	21 469	252	20.6	19.8	34.1
Morgan	393	5 845	306	1 547	786	110	111	132	22 635	390	27.2	13.1	40.3
Murray	472	8 913	274	5 369	773	158	143	199	22 298	238	42.9	5.0	33.6
Muscogee	4 333	85 484	9 645	16 302	12 298	6 551	2 352	2 214	25 895	39	43.6	10.3	28.2
Newton	1 140	14 692	1 276	4 766	2 211	357	442	355	24 132	260	40.4	7.7	36.9
Oconee	557	4 865	313	832	1 058	222	303	121	24 824	305	35.1	8.5	42.3
Oglethorpe	143	911	99	129	137	36	70	15	16 552	319	27.0	8.8	42.3
Paulding	910	8 697	732	1 149	2 271	233	259	192	22 074	218	50.9	0.5	35.3
Peach	459	5 910	383	2 827	814	179	56	144	24 430	157	35.0	15.9	40.8
Pickens	450	4 719	517	1 394	692	163	73	118	25 105	194	49.5	0.5	37.6
Pierce	304	2 501	114	463	428	134	45	49	19 567	379	27.2	13.2	50.7
Pike	181	1 217	202	163	124	D	34	26	21 398	252	30.2	9.5	35.3
Polk	623	8 177	702	2 717	1 276	234	137	182	22 228	344	38.4	4.4	32.0
Pulaski	205	2 400	566	489	282	118	77	54	22 661	161	23.6	30.4	46.0
Putnam	341	4 617	295	2 004	701	126	78	118	25 555	152	27.0	8.6	54.6
Quitman	40	228	D	43	49	D	D	4	18 092	17	11.8	47.1	64.7
Rabun	488	5 139	443	1 967	599	157	113	106	20 704	122	51.6	2.5	41.8
Randolph	170	1 562	159	440	224	55	35	33	21 074	119	10.9	47.9	67.2

STATE County	Agriculture, 1997 (cont'd)														Percent of land owned by fed. gov. 1995	Water consumption 1995 (mil gal/day)
	Land in farms					Value of land and buildings		Value of machinery and equipment average per farm ($1,000)	Value of products sold		Percent from —		Percent of farms with sales of —			
		Acres									Livestock and poultry products					
	Acreage (1,000)	Percent change, 1992–1997	Average size of farm	Total irrigated (1,000)	Total cropland (1,000)	Average per farm ($1,000)	Average per acre (dollars)		Total (mil dol)	Average per farm (dollars)	Crops		$10,000 or more	$100,000 or more		
	117	118	119	120	121	122	123	124	125	126	127	128	129	130	131	132
GEORGIA—Cont'd																
Fannin	15	-5.9	100	0	6	308	3 284	29	10	66 368	13.9	86.1	26.5	9.9	53.7	1.9
Fayette	18	-16.6	100	0	9	406	4 117	19	4	21 898	62.9	37.1	24.5	4.3	0.0	13.9
Floyd	83	12.7	191	1	36	388	2 092	31	31	70 958	9.6	90.4	23.1	7.6	2.0	452.3
Forsyth	31	-14.1	71	0	13	406	6 966	23	62	143 406	9.0	91.0	37.8	23.0	2.8	13.7
Franklin	77	3.1	111	0	40	280	2 467	28	148	211 306	0.9	99.1	40.9	24.2	1.0	3.8
Fulton	27	23.5	106	0	10	380	3 642	17	4	15 939	71.2	28.8	17.5	3.5	0.7	226.0
Gilmer	23	-7.8	86	0	9	329	3 745	33	77	288 985	1.6	98.4	54.3	40.4	16.8	3.3
Glascock	20	-30.3	266	0	8	258	969	30	1	12 239	48.8	51.2	26.3	3.9	0.0	0.4
Glynn	8	-22.6	215	0	1	311	1 446	24	0	10 404	30.1	69.6	19.4	2.8	0.1	67.1
Gordon	69	-7.0	129	1	41	376	2 602	34	88	165 101	4.9	95.1	41.5	23.2	3.5	18.1
Grady	127	-7.6	276	6	72	401	1 487	61	70	151 887	77.1	22.9	53.5	18.8	0.0	12.1
Greene	52	11.5	265	D	22	335	1 494	49	29	147 763	D	D	37.9	19.2	10.0	5.1
Gwinnett	31	30.7	103	0	9	546	4 796	34	11	35 021	51.6	48.4	18.8	7.3	0.7	71.8
Habersham	31	-13.1	77	0	15	313	4 146	35	114	279 810	0.8	99.2	54.3	36.1	28.2	10.1
Hall	51	-5.4	77	0	25	409	4 487	28	138	207 017	0.9	99.1	39.3	25.8	4.0	19.8
Hancock	34	-3.8	327	D	7	237	769	21	3	31 777	4.6	95.4	20.4	3.9	0.0	1.1
Haralson	31	-4.0	118	0	14	250	1 820	29	17	63 979	2.7	97.3	22.3	6.9	0.0	2.1
Harris	47	51.4	227	0	13	363	1 483	22	3	14 590	50.4	49.6	22.2	4.3	0.0	10.3
Hart	58	-1.9	126	1	36	274	1 931	33	56	121 576	3.8	96.2	30.0	15.7	3.2	4.2
Heard	28	15.2	173	D	12	254	1 612	37	21	131 628	0.6	99.4	28.8	10.6	3.9	1.1
Henry	45	-2.9	137	0	20	401	3 817	23	7	20 337	72.1	27.9	24.8	3.4	0.0	7.1
Houston	87	19.3	350	6	49	498	1 467	88	28	111 785	57.8	42.2	39.4	16.5	2.5	29.1
Irwin	132	-2.4	457	15	82	480	1 096	84	41	142 154	87.6	12.4	72.9	33.3	0.0	9.8
Jackson	77	-6.6	108	1	38	383	3 134	31	191	265 459	1.3	98.7	44.1	25.7	0.0	6.4
Jasper	52	-14.8	281	0	20	365	1 381	29	14	76 168	3.4	96.6	31.9	8.6	16.9	1.7
Jeff Davis	71	-2.5	324	4	36	380	1 159	39	23	106 017	70.7	29.3	46.8	25.0	0.0	5.0
Jefferson	142	4.4	399	14	84	331	787	56	24	68 524	75.9	24.1	43.0	18.3	1.2	15.5
Jenkins	93	19.4	375	3	44	287	768	41	20	81 249	52.4	47.6	37.1	18.1	0.0	5.5
Johnson	96	35.4	334	1	40	334	984	24	6	22 509	72.8	27.2	29.2	4.5	0.0	3.1
Jones	31	-0.3	197	0	11	301	1 453	32	7	47 187	7.6	92.4	26.8	7.6	17.8	2.4
Lamar	38	-5.3	202	D	20	276	1 642	30	15	78 634	13.7	86.3	30.3	9.6	0.0	4.7
Lanier	43	4.6	466	1	15	470	987	39	7	79 245	90.2	9.8	54.3	20.7	3.0	3.3
Laurens	198	18.1	288	7	85	319	1 137	32	24	34 531	79.7	20.3	27.8	7.8	0.0	32.9
Lee	138	31.4	879	16	76	1 399	1 491	97	38	241 076	79.5	20.5	56.7	32.5	0.0	26.2
Liberty	21	31.2	488		2	419	858	32	1	21 222	78.5	21.5	30.2	4.7	33.8	17.5
Lincoln	31	-5.5	191	0	12	283	1 554	31	2	11 155	4.5	95.5	23.3	1.2	6.7	1.2
Long	19	57.3	295	D	4	285	967	28	6	94 750	13.7	86.3	29.7	14.1	11.2	0.8
Lowndes	72	-1.2	193	3	38	304	1 624	37	23	61 445	88.9	11.1	36.7	12.1	1.3	28.1
Lumpkin	25	9.7	127	0	10	308	2 991	39	64	325 481	1.8	98.2	39.4	28.3	31.7	3.1
McDuffie	41	21.0	190	1	18	277	1 362	29	16	75 097	D	D	25.3	6.5	4.8	3.7
McIntosh	4	-47.4	175	0	1	221	1 261	19	0	6 614	46.5	53.5	16.7	0.0	4.3	1.4
Macon	119	-1.8	421	19	69	386	987	78	99	351 448	24.8	75.2	61.0	35.5	0.2	23.6
Madison	70	12.4	112	0	34	245	2 093	27	107	172 699	1.7	98.3	37.5	20.7	0.0	3.1
Marion	52	14.8	351	1	18	369	976	37	34	228 854	10.3	89.7	42.2	17.7	0.0	3.2
Meriwether	69	-0.2	268	1	22	370	1 270	28	6	24 848	32.7	67.3	29.6	4.3	0.0	5.7
Miller	116	-4.9	462	26	79	478	1 076	85	38	152 124	82.1	17.9	70.5	34.7	0.0	28.8
Mitchell	221	7.3	477	41	135	590	1 288	88	141	304 636	49.0	51.0	56.7	33.8	0.0	32.5
Monroe	57	26.2	317	0	15	491	1 570	36	28	158 360	1.7	98.3	35.3	15.6	0.0	34.8
Montgomery	75	15.5	298	2	22	357	1 143	35	9	36 745	64.4	35.6	25.0	6.7	0.0	4.4
Morgan	88	-5.8	225	1	43	471	2 200	36	43	109 218	5.5	94.5	44.6	21.5	0.1	2.9
Murray	35	5.5	146	0	21	300	2 181	30	44	183 629	3.1	96.9	34.9	16.0	24.1	4.1
Muscogee	8	70.0	218	0	2	347	1 592	19	0	4 824	68.6	31.4	7.7	0.0	35.7	39.5
Newton	46	-0.9	175	0	17	486	3 184	25	10	37 424	9.7	90.3	24.6	5.4	0.0	4.1
Oconee	51	-1.4	168	0	21	406	2 434	32	44	144 348	14.5	85.5	38.4	17.4	1.1	3.1
Oglethorpe	63	13.8	196	0	27	337	2 154	28	57	178 063	2.4	97.6	35.1	16.9	1.3	1.7
Paulding	18	-3.3	84	0	8	347	4 609	19	11	51 241	5.9	94.1	18.8	5.0	0.0	3.5
Peach	51	15.8	325	5	35	499	1 584	66	31	194 444	83.1	16.9	43.3	16.6	1.7	6.8
Pickens	16	-11.5	82	0	7	251	3 921	22	54	278 414	0.3	99.7	37.6	25.8	0.0	2.9
Pierce	100	24.0	265	6	41	364	1 362	40	30	78 211	69.2	30.8	44.6	17.4	0.0	5.8
Pike	48	6.6	190	1	24	425	2 952	26	19	76 138	11.5	88.5	29.4	7.5	0.0	3.1
Polk	50	9.6	147	0	23	190	1 685	25	19	54 281	8.8	91.2	24.4	7.6	0.0	10.6
Pulaski	92	15.5	574	14	64	691	1 223	80	28	171 595	83.2	16.8	49.1	29.8	0.0	12.2
Putnam	31	-10.6	206	0	14	347	1 611	45	21	141 178	1.5	98.5	44.1	27.6	20.4	1 010.5
Quitman	11	-5.4	668	D	6	520	779	80	1	85 914	91.2	8.8	70.6	23.5	0.9	1.9
Rabun	11	-16.4	89	0	5	280	4 198	24	13	106 515	18.0	82.0	32.0	14.8	73.0	4.1
Randolph	94	-1.8	792	15	64	703	897	105	20	171 588	86.0	14.0	61.3	37.8	0.0	10.6

Table B. States and Counties — Residential Construction, Wholesale and Retail Trade, and Real Estate

STATE County	Value of Residential Construction Authorized by Building Permits, 2000		Wholesale Trade, 1997				Retail Trade[1], 1997				Real Estate and Rental and Leasing, 1997			
	New Construction ($1,000)	Number of Housing Units	Number of Establishments	Number of Employees	Sales (mil dol)	Annual Payroll (mil dol)	Number of Establishments	Number of Employees	Sales (mil dol)	Annual Payroll (mil dol)	Number of Establishments	Number of Employees	Receipts (mil dol)	Annual Payroll (mil dol)
	133	134	135	136	137	138	139	140	141	142	143	144	145	146
GEORGIA—Cont'd														
Fannin	86 878	797	16	56	21.1	1.4	103	779	126.7	10.7	12	15	2.0	0.2
Fayette	161 267	938	135	1 236	545.5	42.3	298	4 697	677.6	69.9	91	287	42.0	6.2
Floyd	39 215	382	112	1 163	523.3	35.8	442	4 991	808.1	75.0	56	313	26.8	5.2
Forsyth	381 054	3 389	228	3 138	1 140.8	110.0	255	3 503	653.9	63.5	88	208	44.8	6.5
Franklin	2 121	22	32	208	56.5	3.9	92	937	202.3	15.2	16	43	3.6	0.8
Fulton	839 135	9 621	2 462	40 435	55 915.1	1 823.9	3 569	51 556	9 248.2	990.1	1 496	14 372	2 523.5	516.3
Gilmer	41 045	534	17	170	44.4	2.9	89	778	136.1	11.9	18	69	4.4	0.6
Glascock	0	0	NA	NA	NA	NA	7	30	2.9	0.3	NA	NA	NA	NA
Glynn	112 822	613	118	903	461.5	30.7	504	4 847	716.1	69.6	122	622	51.4	9.9
Gordon	38 259	549	57	675	150.6	16.5	241	2 260	360.1	33.9	24	84	8.1	2.0
Grady	7 329	64	24	272	125.3	5.7	111	824	130.1	12.2	16	33	3.2	0.5
Greene	52 552	194	16	90	102.0	2.2	56	465	66.8	6.2	14	37	5.6	0.7
Gwinnett	1 044 856	12 372	1 959	31 305	29 114.6	1 365.0	2 013	33 639	6 829.0	632.5	580	3 193	492.4	89.2
Habersham	35 847	376	34	203	35.1	4.8	153	1 677	256.3	24.1	21	71	9.7	1.6
Hall	204 173	2 121	238	3 407	1 777.8	100.6	548	6 357	1 240.8	114.6	105	398	44.3	9.0
Hancock	3 106	37	3	D	D	D	24	149	17.0	2.0	1	D	D	D
Haralson	11 067	106	16	121	50.8	4.3	98	845	145.7	11.3	5	21	1.1	0.1
Harris	53 619	301	9	D	D	D	59	259	31.3	3.2	8	D	D	D
Hart	1 347	15	25	113	35.6	2.6	78	778	96.9	9.6	7	24	1.1	0.2
Heard	6 041	56	2	D	D	D	21	117	17.2	1.7	2	D	D	D
Henry	348 868	4 130	84	1 136	377.1	29.1	300	3 580	660.7	58.9	77	313	33.3	4.7
Houston	101 021	1 505	54	454	236.5	14.7	403	5 818	941.2	86.6	88	347	43.4	5.1
Irwin	0	0	10	54	13.3	1.1	31	226	28.3	3.1	2	D	D	D
Jackson	109 811	864	48	867	502.2	25.4	218	1 673	288.4	25.5	24	49	5.4	0.9
Jasper	13 674	153	3	D	D	D	21	148	19.9	2.0	3	12	0.3	0.1
Jeff Davis	52	1	23	228	177.9	6.1	79	660	127.9	9.2	4	19	1.7	0.3
Jefferson	2 771	28	19	188	59.8	3.1	83	681	94.3	10.2	6	33	0.9	0.4
Jenkins	0	0	8	44	10.9	0.7	34	235	38.0	3.2	2	D	D	D
Johnson	0	0	13	56	25.4	0.9	29	250	27.3	2.9	1	D	D	D
Jones	26 523	240	15	D	D	D	36	249	37.7	3.6	8	D	D	D
Lamar	5 765	90	6	63	10.0	1.2	51	440	74.1	6.8	5	6	0.3	0.1
Lanier	1 611	39	3	D	D	D	29	167	24.0	2.3	3	10	0.9	0.1
Laurens	3 011	45	64	390	125.3	9.5	265	2 872	417.5	38.4	35	149	14.8	2.3
Lee	32 245	285	7	D	D	D	39	362	54.0	4.4	5	7	0.9	0.1
Liberty	17 667	221	14	D	D	D	165	1 762	255.0	22.2	39	261	24.7	4.4
Lincoln	5 133	43	6	33	4.1	0.6	21	118	15.9	1.4	1	D	D	D
Long	NA	NA	1	D	D	D	9	37	7.1	0.4	1	D	D	D
Lowndes	46 073	886	135	1 155	452.9	31.5	533	6 187	1 008.5	91.3	88	517	52.4	8.2
Lumpkin	46 917	354	10	42	8.1	0.7	64	740	120.1	11.8	14	34	4.3	0.4
McDuffie	5 603	55	12	D	D	D	112	1 382	312.3	25.0	12	42	2.5	0.5
McIntosh	12 401	91	7	D	D	D	106	732	104.9	9.1	5	D	D	D
Macon	777	14	15	129	63.6	2.6	52	409	57.7	5.5	6	39	1.3	0.2
Madison	17 531	154	47	1 146	514.3	39.3	74	453	76.4	5.9	19	51	4.6	0.8
Marion	NA	NA	4	11	1.2	0.1	23	181	30.1	2.7	3	2	0.2	0.1
Meriwether	16 063	158	8	21	3.1	0.3	85	556	99.4	9.4	8	27	1.9	0.2
Miller	100	3	7	D	D	D	43	286	39.2	3.4	1	D	D	D
Mitchell	8 071	99	39	408	148.5	8.2	107	897	122.3	12.1	12	51	2.8	1.0
Monroe	18 649	146	13	59	26.4	1.0	75	503	70.3	6.7	7	13	1.4	0.2
Montgomery	4 485	37	5	106	36.5	2.7	29	138	20.2	1.9	1	D	D	D
Morgan	21 336	189	17	186	66.7	4.2	71	886	166.3	15.6	6	18	3.2	0.7
Murray	21 258	223	33	320	537.2	10.5	108	743	166.9	13.6	15	45	2.7	0.4
Muscogee	72 220	975	208	2 884	1 316.5	91.3	845	11 718	1 950.9	186.6	224	1 197	142.7	27.3
Newton	179 240	1 918	52	D	D	D	173	2 023	319.8	32.4	33	114	16.1	2.8
Oconee	48 588	241	22	D	D	D	55	799	166.6	14.7	18	86	10.8	1.2
Oglethorpe	NA	NA	10	84	6.3	1.2	25	140	27.9	1.9	2	D	D	D
Paulding	180 510	2 845	45	260	98.6	7.4	124	2 137	390.8	31.4	18	48	3.2	0.7
Peach	11 925	131	18	D	D	D	110	862	146.7	11.5	15	45	7.4	0.9
Pickens	55 686	410	23	D	D	D	74	694	238.5	12.9	22	33	4.8	0.7
Pierce	6 268	66	15	D	D	D	69	417	68.6	6.5	7	15	2.1	0.1
Pike	21 237	212	13	44	14.4	1.4	23	109	15.9	1.4	2	D	D	D
Polk	19 519	266	20	318	121.5	9.5	146	1 377	183.9	18.3	26	90	6.8	1.4
Pulaski	4 433	73	16	215	162.7	5.5	53	319	48.8	4.6	3	6	0.3	0.0
Putnam	27 282	186	8	88	63.7	2.6	56	490	83.7	8.3	8	21	0.9	0.3
Quitman	200	1	2	D	D	D	6	30	4.1	0.4	1	D	D	D
Rabun	19 344	299	8	D	D	D	91	561	97.6	8.7	22	63	7.7	1.2
Randolph	0	0	10	54	33.5	1.2	40	261	27.5	3.3	5	4	0.6	0.2

1. Establishments with payroll.

STATE County	Professional, Scientific, and Technical Services[1], 1997				Manufacturing, 1997				Accommodation and Foodservices, 1997			
	Number of Establishments	Number of Employees	Receipts (mil dol)	Annual Payroll (mil dol)	Number of Establishments	Number of Employees	Receipts (mil dol)	Annual Payroll (mil dol)	Number of Establishments	Number of Employees	Sales (mil dol)	Annual Payroll (mil dol)
	147	148	149	150	151	152	153	154	155	156	157	158
GEORGIA—Cont'd												
Fannin	26	76	3.0	1.2	28	922	146.6	15.7	35	431	11.3	3.3
Fayette	212	719	69.7	27.1	85	5 595	1 345.1	170.2	118	2 750	102.3	27.6
Floyd	131	650	61.6	19.7	120	9 583	1 892.4	280.0	151	2 572	87.8	22.9
Forsyth	206	824	83.2	30.1	129	4 337	701.3	127.7	89	1 523	54.5	15.0
Franklin	18	53	3.3	0.9	46	1 852	281.1	43.2	35	621	16.8	4.3
Fulton	4 614	56 202	7 607.2	2 846.1	897	37 948	14 240.9	1 283.6	2 292	57 973	2 364.4	682.1
Gilmer	28	90	4.4	1.7	34	3 404	303.0	52.3	30	428	11.1	2.9
Glascock	1	D	D	D	NA	NA	NA	NA	2	D	D	D
Glynn	179	579	43.4	16.6	71	3 784	993.6	124.9	214	7 051	251.5	84.3
Gordon	34	235	10.8	4.6	102	10 527	2 419.0	255.4	76	1 201	40.8	11.3
Grady	13	45	2.9	0.8	19	1 402	153.7	29.6	26	300	8.2	2.0
Greene	25	51	3.1	1.3	19	1 533	448.4	33.1	19	208	6.3	1.6
Gwinnett	1 939	12 871	1 326.6	534.3	737	29 121	6 241.7	1 071.3	896	19 623	720.4	199.8
Habersham	37	112	9.8	2.5	69	4 354	681.2	111.8	64	879	26.0	7.3
Hall	217	972	91.6	32.0	226	16 519	4 293.7	443.1	202	4 192	148.5	41.6
Hancock	5	13	2.2	0.3	NA	NA	NA	NA	5	46	1.2	0.3
Haralson	19	75	4.7	1.3	35	2 552	340.0	59.4	31	D	D	D
Harris	16	82	3.9	1.7	19	D	D	D	35	D	D	D
Hart	22	55	4.0	1.5	36	2 540	465.6	61.1	22	268	9.0	2.4
Heard	4	22	0.6	0.2	9	550	77.6	12.8	5	D	D	D
Henry	122	499	48.5	15.4	68	3 392	854.8	106.1	139	2 485	74.5	20.0
Houston	135	1 504	111.5	44.5	66	D	D	D	183	3 753	102.5	28.4
Irwin	5	25	2.0	0.9	7	746	38.5	13.7	9	70	2.0	0.5
Jackson	33	95	8.5	2.0	65	5 896	1 204.5	135.8	53	1 318	65.3	16.7
Jasper	6	19	1.4	0.4	19	737	176.7	21.4	7	78	2.2	0.6
Jeff Davis	15	49	2.4	0.8	23	2 493	304.4	49.0	20	D	D	D
Jefferson	11	36	2.0	1.1	28	1 999	294.2	51.9	17	207	6.4	1.5
Jenkins	7	15	0.7	0.1	4	1 294	154.3	25.0	12	D	D	D
Johnson	4	16	0.8	0.3	8	762	34.9	8.8	7	D	D	D
Jones	12	24	1.4	0.5	NA	NA	NA	NA	8	D	D	D
Lamar	16	27	1.7	0.5	13	1 605	190.9	35.1	18	217	6.6	1.6
Lanier	6	13	0.8	0.1	NA	NA	NA	NA	5	D	D	D
Laurens	44	197	12.4	5.1	43	5 703	888.6	134.2	76	1 448	40.9	10.0
Lee	7	7	0.7	0.1	NA	NA	NA	NA	9	94	2.4	0.8
Liberty	30	182	18.3	3.0	14	1 020	319.0	33.9	65	1 209	35.8	9.0
Lincoln	4	10	0.4	0.2	7	688	55.8	10.9	12	D	D	D
Long	2	D	D	D	NA	NA	NA	NA	6	39	1.1	0.3
Lowndes	132	738	46.2	18.5	98	5 492	1 468.9	146.7	194	3 700	109.3	30.8
Lumpkin	16	34	3.4	1.1	17	879	85.9	21.0	34	465	16.5	4.0
McDuffie	24	105	10.4	4.0	26	1 677	297.8	41.7	34	572	17.8	4.8
McIntosh	6	16	0.7	0.1	NA	NA	NA	NA	23	332	9.0	2.7
Macon	5	17	1.8	0.6	14	1 624	369.0	46.7	15	D	D	D
Madison	58	332	45.7	31.2	31	826	69.0	18.9	50	1 032	33.4	9.8
Marion	2	D	D	D	5	D	D	D	5	D	D	D
Meriwether	15	47	3.4	0.8	22	2 105	273.7	46.1	29	269	9.0	2.5
Miller	7	25	1.2	0.4	NA	NA	NA	NA	7	121	2.7	0.7
Mitchell	21	103	5.1	1.9	17	1 016	72.2	15.4	30	292	11.6	4.0
Monroe	23	63	3.8	1.1	21	515	57.1	10.7	33	616	21.6	4.7
Montgomery	5	13	0.4	0.2	NA	NA	NA	NA	7	90	2.0	0.5
Morgan	21	58	6.3	2.3	20	1 512	262.1	39.8	37	574	16.8	4.4
Murray	19	140	3.9	1.8	100	5 321	1 201.9	121.8	39	493	20.0	5.1
Muscogee	264	1 607	146.2	43.6	158	D	D	D	365	D	D	D
Newton	62	169	13.9	4.0	62	3 976	1 348.8	146.4	58	1 074	30.9	8.2
Oconee	44	158	15.7	5.3	30	746	208.8	20.8	13	134	3.5	0.8
Oglethorpe	10	20	1.4	0.8	NA	NA	NA	NA	8	59	1.4	0.4
Paulding	45	176	10.6	3.8	38	1 161	137.3	26.0	51	D	D	D
Peach	21	63	3.6	1.2	32	D	D	D	44	D	D	D
Pickens	30	69	5.2	2.0	35	1 155	135.8	26.7	25	331	11.3	3.0
Pierce	12	32	2.3	0.8	17	521	77.2	9.1	21	229	5.6	1.8
Pike	13	23	3.2	0.6	NA	NA	NA	NA	10	77	2.1	0.7
Polk	25	110	7.6	2.9	35	2 273	423.1	62.1	43	D	D	D
Pulaski	13	31	2.5	1.1	11	D	D	D	16	326	5.6	1.9
Putnam	21	48	3.4	0.7	24	2 030	424.8	56.8	22	191	6.1	1.3
Quitman	1	D	D	D	NA	NA	NA	NA	1	D	D	D
Rabun	25	72	4.2	1.5	27	1 870	316.0	44.1	47	573	19.0	5.3
Randolph	10	35	3.1	0.9	NA	NA	NA	NA	14	88	2.6	0.6

1. Firms subject to federal tax.

Table B. States and Counties — Health and Other Services and Federal Funds

STATE County	Health Care and Social Assistance[1], 1997				Other Services[1], 1997				Federal funds and grants, fiscal 2001[2] Expenditures (mil dol)			
										Direct payments for individuals[3]		
	Number of Establishments	Number of Employees	Receipts (mil dol)	Annual Payroll (mil dol)	Number of Establishments	Number of Employees	Receipts (mil dol)	Annual Payroll (mil dol)	Total	Social Security and government retirement	Medicare	Food stamps and Supplemental Security Income
	159	160	161	162	163	164	165	166	167	168	169	170
GEORGIA—Cont'd												
Fannin	32	418	29.7	9.2	12	39	2.5	0.6	111.1	61.1	24.1	4.0
Fayette	150	1 197	86.9	37.1	129	777	41.6	13.2	250.6	184.9	34.8	2.1
Floyd	165	4 018	345.6	131.4	95	721	41.6	14.1	396.1	197.9	80.3	18.2
Forsyth	90	1 115	50.4	22.3	105	607	34.8	10.9	163.7	101.9	29.2	3.4
Franklin	20	177	10.4	4.5	33	222	18.2	4.6	115.7	50.8	21.9	4.8
Fulton	2 252	26 639	2 258.3	1 009.7	1 543	12 781	928.9	270.3	7 415.5	1 572.1	597.7	224.8
Gilmer	22	437	23.5	8.8	18	87	6.2	1.7	88.2	53.7	20.2	2.8
Glascock	2	D	D	D	1	D	D	D	15.5	6.7	3.5	0.4
Glynn	205	2 257	149.3	60.7	123	557	36.0	10.5	492.4	178.9	74.5	13.0
Gordon	42	373	26.1	9.9	37	174	12.3	3.1	149.4	80.9	30.4	6.4
Grady	24	263	11.0	4.0	17	84	6.2	1.3	107.4	46.0	16.2	7.2
Greene	13	139	7.3	3.2	15	70	4.1	1.0	78.6	36.7	13.3	3.7
Gwinnett	927	9 585	656.4	265.8	1 032	7 165	510.3	173.4	1 120.9	519.1	140.3	26.1
Habersham	60	488	26.5	10.7	42	149	10.8	2.8	140.7	75.9	28.6	3.2
Hall	245	2 626	230.0	95.8	184	860	56.2	15.3	492.6	225.5	81.9	16.4
Hancock	12	267	8.2	3.3	9	11	1.1	0.2	62.7	25.1	12.5	2.9
Haralson	28	319	12.8	5.3	25	100	8.0	1.7	105.0	54.2	23.0	6.2
Harris	9	D	D	D	13	27	1.9	0.4	84.0	52.2	11.0	2.8
Hart	27	509	24.8	9.2	22	110	8.9	1.8	107.0	45.2	18.9	3.6
Heard	8	111	3.1	1.6	6	12	0.8	0.2	45.3	16.3	7.3	2.1
Henry	127	1 299	66.8	31.8	120	586	34.0	10.3	371.6	200.7	50.7	8.7
Houston	181	1 927	125.5	52.7	162	744	38.3	11.3	1 462.7	344.4	59.7	18.1
Irwin	8	146	4.2	2.1	11	29	1.7	0.3	51.1	16.6	8.1	2.4
Jackson	39	317	19.5	11.1	43	185	10.8	2.8	162.2	77.4	29.3	7.9
Jasper	7	37	1.5	0.5	11	21	1.7	0.3	41.1	21.2	7.2	1.5
Jeff Davis	11	61	2.9	0.8	20	67	4.5	0.9	62.7	27.3	11.7	3.3
Jefferson	22	248	9.7	3.5	19	61	2.8	0.8	114.0	39.0	20.4	7.5
Jenkins	8	60	3.4	1.2	8	20	1.0	0.2	53.1	16.6	10.0	2.7
Johnson	5	136	6.9	3.0	9	21	1.4	0.3	55.2	18.2	10.7	4.4
Jones	16	335	14.8	6.7	15	48	2.3	0.5	67.9	33.2	12.4	2.7
Lamar	16	186	6.8	2.4	14	84	8.1	1.9	67.1	33.6	12.6	2.6
Lanier	8	128	2.7	1.3	5	13	1.1	0.2	35.3	12.7	7.4	1.1
Laurens	96	1 855	135.5	48.9	54	212	11.1	2.9	288.4	106.5	38.4	13.2
Lee	7	142	3.9	1.6	16	51	3.5	1.1	62.6	30.7	7.4	2.7
Liberty	45	586	25.5	9.2	60	379	16.7	5.2	256.8	100.1	17.1	9.8
Lincoln	10	44	3.0	1.3	14	31	2.4	0.4	45.9	20.2	9.5	1.6
Long	3	16	0.2	0.1	2	D	D	D	27.7	13.5	3.4	1.0
Lowndes	185	2 740	162.4	76.4	142	695	37.7	10.6	594.8	179.9	62.7	23.8
Lumpkin	28	456	30.7	9.5	15	69	4.0	0.8	70.5	32.6	10.2	2.5
McDuffie	41	873	29.9	17.2	38	110	7.4	1.6	115.1	46.7	20.4	6.4
McIntosh	5	40	2.3	0.9	13	26	1.4	0.4	52.2	25.3	10.9	3.2
Macon	20	417	22.7	9.0	10	53	4.9	1.5	82.7	23.8	15.9	4.5
Madison	33	311	16.5	7.3	31	256	22.7	4.7	99.8	51.2	18.3	5.1
Marion	5	38	1.8	0.6	2	D	D	D	31.1	10.9	4.0	2.4
Meriwether	24	203	7.4	3.7	15	56	3.7	0.8	104.3	45.5	18.6	6.9
Miller	9	46	1.8	0.7	12	24	1.8	0.5	45.7	12.8	6.3	2.3
Mitchell	14	160	8.6	3.0	26	118	6.1	1.7	246.3	40.4	18.8	8.8
Monroe	20	256	9.8	4.0	20	74	6.8	1.4	73.8	35.9	13.2	3.2
Montgomery	4	12	0.5	0.1	2	D	D	D	41.4	15.8	7.5	2.0
Morgan	16	169	7.9	2.5	12	52	2.5	0.7	70.9	30.5	13.0	2.7
Murray	17	248	17.3	5.8	14	59	4.1	1.4	97.1	50.2	18.7	5.3
Muscogee	343	5 225	439.9	171.5	305	2 004	104.6	35.8	1 689.4	521.2	135.8	51.1
Newton	80	747	40.7	17.9	61	248	19.3	5.8	213.2	113.2	43.9	12.7
Oconee	34	202	11.4	4.9	32	260	12.3	4.9	70.1	40.4	11.9	1.5
Oglethorpe	9	97	4.6	1.8	6	9	0.7	0.1	38.7	16.6	7.0	2.0
Paulding	39	339	13.2	5.5	58	226	14.5	4.7	130.5	76.1	23.2	4.4
Peach	22	196	9.9	3.9	27	122	8.3	1.7	151.9	64.1	18.8	7.8
Pickens	22	476	24.6	9.5	12	30	1.9	0.4	82.1	49.5	15.5	2.0
Pierce	13	106	4.3	2.3	20	61	2.8	0.6	79.3	38.6	13.1	4.7
Pike	5	102	3.3	1.6	4	7	0.6	0.1	56.8	26.8	9.1	3.6
Polk	42	505	24.8	8.8	42	312	24.4	5.3	195.8	94.5	39.1	9.0
Pulaski	18	333	12.5	5.4	10	35	1.6	0.4	60.6	24.5	10.2	1.5
Putnam	14	243	10.8	4.2	14	43	2.6	0.7	79.0	44.4	14.8	3.1
Quitman	1	D	D	D	1	D	D	D	18.4	7.8	3.1	1.3
Rabun	27	276	14.7	5.9	18	41	3.5	0.8	76.6	38.5	17.5	2.1
Randolph	3	27	0.7	0.5	13	34	1.9	0.4	57.7	15.9	8.0	3.7

1. Firms subject to federal tax. 2. October 1, 2000 to September 30, 2001. 3. State totals may include programs not allocated by county.

STATE County	Salaries and wages (171)	Defense (172)	Other (173)	Medicaid and other health-related (174)	Nutrition and family welfare (175)	Education (176)	Other (177)	Total (mil dol) (178)	Intergovern-mental (mil dol) (179)	Total (mil dol) (180)	Per capita Total (181)	Per capita Property (182)
GEORGIA—Cont'd												
Fannin	3.0	0.0	1.0	14.4	2.0	1.1	-0.4	28.5	14.0	11.0	605	334
Fayette	15.0	0.9	1.9	4.5	1.8	1.7	0.9	165.5	59.4	86.5	1 017	808
Floyd	13.7	0.5	3.1	42.4	11.8	5.0	9.2	319.2	89.7	79.3	937	553
Forsyth	9.3	0.3	2.7	11.9	2.0	1.9	0.5	134.6	42.9	74.7	986	635
Franklin	2.9	0.0	0.7	15.5	1.6	1.1	13.3	56.4	14.7	13.2	711	384
Fulton	1 330.5	262.4	666.4	782.9	489.8	317.1	791.3	3 275.8	972.5	1 537.1	2 127	1 387
Gilmer	3.5	0.0	0.7	10.0	1.5	1.0	-6.6	32.3	16.2	12.1	675	492
Glascock	0.6	0.0	0.2	3.3	0.2	0.2	0.2	4.0	2.0	1.5	600	484
Glynn	90.9	3.9	63.8	24.7	11.1	4.3	17.2	283.1	67.1	78.6	1 179	745
Gordon	6.1	0.1	1.3	12.1	3.1	2.2	1.4	78.0	38.4	22.5	559	342
Grady	2.0	0.0	0.5	16.2	3.2	2.1	5.1	38.3	21.5	11.7	545	362
Greene	3.1	0.0	0.6	12.5	2.5	1.1	4.6	26.5	11.2	12.2	914	621
Gwinnett	191.4	60.6	86.7	29.9	10.9	13.5	24.3	1 219.1	341.7	493.6	986	833
Habersham	6.2	0.0	6.0	14.8	1.9	0.7	0.7	76.7	20.7	19.6	627	427
Hall	27.9	6.9	10.2	37.0	22.3	5.0	49.8	258.8	98.1	115.0	991	609
Hancock	0.8	0.0	0.2	14.6	3.6	0.9	0.1	32.1	11.6	8.1	905	771
Haralson	3.0	0.0	0.8	12.5	2.6	1.6	0.6	50.5	22.7	13.7	566	354
Harris	2.7	0.0	0.5	11.0	2.0	0.9	0.5	41.5	20.1	16.8	756	536
Hart	4.5	11.4	0.5	16.2	2.1	1.3	0.8	40.1	19.3	12.2	566	389
Heard	0.8	5.4	0.2	5.5	1.4	0.7	5.0	20.6	8.1	7.8	785	570
Henry	81.7	0.8	5.3	14.7	3.9	2.2	0.3	158.7	53.2	84.1	857	640
Houston	771.9	176.2	26.9	27.6	13.7	5.6	7.9	255.6	83.8	54.7	528	423
Irwin	1.8	0.0	1.0	9.5	1.7	0.7	1.1	16.1	8.7	5.9	658	509
Jackson	6.1	0.0	10.6	20.5	2.7	2.1	3.2	83.6	31.7	26.3	722	432
Jasper	1.3	0.0	0.3	6.3	1.7	0.6	0.5	18.5	8.2	7.8	792	588
Jeff Davis	1.6	0.0	0.4	10.0	1.9	0.7	1.2	33.8	15.3	9.1	722	346
Jefferson	2.0	0.0	0.5	28.1	5.1	1.7	1.5	36.7	17.4	10.1	566	411
Jenkins	1.1	0.0	0.3	12.5	2.2	1.2	1.7	18.7	8.4	5.1	602	363
Johnson	4.8	0.0	0.3	11.3	1.7	0.8	0.4	13.3	7.8	4.1	494	324
Jones	1.6	1.3	0.3	7.8	2.0	1.2	2.7	30.8	16.8	10.8	475	313
Lamar	2.4	0.2	0.5	8.2	1.9	0.8	0.5	24.0	10.2	8.7	590	437
Lanier	0.8	0.0	0.3	6.4	1.3	0.6	3.3	10.5	6.3	3.2	467	302
Laurens	44.0	6.0	8.6	38.5	7.6	3.4	9.7	94.1	56.3	24.0	551	333
Lee	1.6	0.0	0.4	5.9	1.7	0.9	2.8	36.4	20.0	12.1	554	412
Liberty	65.5	21.6	1.2	13.2	7.6	9.7	5.7	111.4	47.3	40.1	668	330
Lincoln	1.0	0.0	0.2	6.1	1.2	0.6	4.9	13.3	7.3	4.4	537	362
Long	0.6	0.0	0.2	3.7	0.9	0.7	3.4	11.5	7.0	3.9	464	392
Lowndes	149.4	69.7	3.7	43.6	14.9	8.0	21.3	298.0	91.2	68.8	819	343
Lumpkin	10.9	0.5	0.7	8.9	1.3	0.6	0.7	30.3	11.0	13.5	743	512
McDuffie	4.2	0.0	0.8	17.5	3.6	1.7	12.4	56.8	23.0	14.5	673	363
McIntosh	1.3	0.1	0.3	7.4	1.9	0.8	0.9	16.4	7.6	7.4	747	441
Macon	1.8	0.8	0.4	17.5	4.6	1.7	2.0	29.5	13.7	10.4	781	522
Madison	3.1	0.0	0.9	14.8	2.1	1.3	1.1	30.4	16.7	10.7	438	291
Marion	1.3	0.0	0.1	8.1	1.2	0.6	1.5	13.2	8.0	3.3	498	322
Meriwether	2.8	0.0	0.7	20.8	4.3	1.9	0.8	40.6	20.6	14.6	638	429
Miller	1.1	0.0	0.5	6.3	1.2	0.5	2.8	11.1	5.9	4.2	671	514
Mitchell	3.5	0.0	0.6	25.7	6.1	2.1	5.6	46.9	27.4	11.4	542	395
Monroe	4.7	0.3	0.6	7.9	1.3	1.0	2.4	61.9	11.6	23.0	1 194	834
Montgomery	1.2	0.0	0.3	9.6	1.2	0.6	0.5	9.7	5.6	3.2	414	253
Morgan	2.2	0.0	0.6	9.2	2.0	0.9	8.3	34.3	12.9	13.6	931	620
Murray	4.9	3.0	2.2	8.1	2.1	1.8	0.2	50.7	25.9	16.0	563	339
Muscogee	766.5	2.4	9.0	93.4	34.2	15.4	26.8	420.3	171.7	182.5	999	589
Newton	9.1	0.2	2.1	19.8	6.1	3.2	1.1	133.1	44.7	40.4	732	484
Oconee	5.0	0.0	3.8	4.8	1.0	0.8	0.2	37.2	16.6	16.9	735	541
Oglethorpe	0.9	0.0	0.2	7.7	1.6	0.8	1.1	17.8	10.8	5.7	506	377
Paulding	5.3	0.1	1.4	11.6	2.9	1.9	2.0	123.4	46.4	39.7	576	386
Peach	5.8	0.5	1.1	14.6	5.6	5.1	18.1	49.7	19.1	16.3	678	414
Pickens	3.0	0.1	0.7	7.9	1.8	0.9	0.1	33.6	17.9	12.4	666	486
Pierce	2.2	0.0	1.1	9.7	1.8	1.0	1.4	24.4	13.9	8.4	546	350
Pike	7.7	0.1	0.5	6.3	0.9	0.6	0.3	16.3	8.9	6.1	492	347
Polk	6.8	8.0	2.4	24.5	4.9	2.2	1.7	63.0	28.4	22.9	639	405
Pulaski	1.2	0.1	0.3	10.3	1.9	0.6	1.9	15.9	8.4	5.5	659	475
Putnam	3.2	0.0	0.6	7.7	2.9	0.9	0.4	45.5	13.8	16.7	990	658
Quitman	0.5	0.0	0.1	4.0	0.7	0.3	0.2	4.8	2.9	1.4	578	466
Rabun	3.0	0.0	1.1	11.5	0.9	0.4	0.9	27.6	7.4	12.3	928	735
Randolph	1.1	0.9	0.3	12.5	3.2	2.5	2.9	25.7	12.3	4.3	542	322

1. October 1, 2000 to September 30, 2001. 2. State totals may include programs not allocated by county. 3. Based on the resident population estimated as of July 1 of the year shown.

Table B. States and Counties — Local Government Finances, Government Employment, and Elections

	Local government finances, 1997 (cont'd)									Government employment, 1999			Presidential election, 2000[2]		
	Direct general expenditure							Debt outstanding					Percent of vote cast —		
				Percent of total for —											
STATE County	Total (mil dol)	Per capita[1] (dollars)	Education	Health and hospitals	Police protection	Public welfare	Highways	Total (mil dol)	Per capita[1] (dollars)	Federal civilian	Federal military	State and local	Democratic	Republican	All other
	183	184	185	186	187	188	189	190	191	192	193	194	195	196	197

GEORGIA—Cont'd

Fannin	26.3	1 454	65.2	0.7	4.0	0.1	8.6	6.0	330	67	72	801	32.7	65.4	1.9
Fayette	180.3	2 120	65.0	0.4	5.3	0.1	4.5	161.5	1 899	217	350	3 945	28.2	69.5	2.2
Floyd	303.5	3 586	29.1	41.9	3.5	0.1	3.6	141.5	1 672	239	337	6 112	38.3	60.4	1.3
Forsyth	154.7	2 042	65.5	0.6	3.3	0.4	3.9	158.5	2 092	148	366	3 007	18.8	78.0	3.2
Franklin	55.5	2 999	30.8	42.1	4.1	0.9	4.3	14.3	771	48	73	972	35.4	63.5	1.1
Fulton	2 693.7	3 728	33.2	6.7	5.8	1.6	2.6	7 810.4	10 810	22 867	4 490	78 008	58.0	40.0	1.9
Gilmer	31.0	1 734	62.6	0.7	4.0	0.0	5.0	9.7	544	74	75	911	30.4	67.4	2.2
Glascock	3.9	1 582	61.6	1.8	3.5	1.1	10.4	0.4	151	12	10	169	24.4	74.8	0.8
Glynn	273.2	4 099	30.3	44.0	4.0	0.3	2.1	141.7	2 126	1 227	264	5 923	34.9	64.5	0.6
Gordon	78.4	1 947	53.9	4.1	3.7	0.3	3.4	31.1	772	98	159	2 075	33.1	65.2	1.7
Grady	41.0	1 906	65.7	1.2	3.6	0.1	4.6	7.3	341	44	82	1 236	40.7	58.2	1.0
Greene	25.2	1 878	55.9	4.7	6.7	1.2	5.4	8.2	612	37	53	872	41.2	57.5	1.3
Gwinnett	1 234.1	2 464	50.5	15.2	3.7	0.4	6.5	1 006.1	2 009	3 475	2 070	19 632	32.4	64.2	3.5
Habersham	75.6	2 424	39.4	32.5	3.0	0.1	4.2	32.5	1 042	133	123	2 522	26.2	72.1	1.7
Hall	262.2	2 259	47.4	8.4	4.2	0.9	2.6	234.4	2 019	458	468	7 265	27.0	70.7	2.2
Hancock	26.2	2 917	38.7	30.3	3.1	0.7	4.6	14.3	1 594	15	34	920	78.3	21.5	0.2
Haralson	53.6	2 220	49.1	18.8	4.5	0.2	4.5	12.7	525	52	95	1 307	35.1	63.1	1.8
Harris	38.7	1 742	67.1	0.9	3.6	1.4	3.3	24.2	1 088	57	86	993	34.1	65.0	0.9
Hart	39.2	1 824	46.6	27.3	3.7	0.2	2.2	12.4	576	100	84	975	42.5	56.4	1.1
Heard	20.7	2 080	52.8	0.6	4.1	3.7	7.5	27.5	2 760	15	40	533	36.9	61.1	2.0
Henry	163.7	1 669	59.4	5.0	5.4	0.6	4.5	216.7	2 208	828	430	4 008	30.8	66.5	2.7
Houston	256.3	2 476	41.7	32.6	4.6	0.0	2.2	107.8	1 041	11 730	4 862	6 554	36.1	62.8	1.1
Irwin	16.0	1 781	66.3	1.2	4.9	0.5	5.8	2.9	324	30	35	684	38.8	60.4	0.8
Jackson	89.9	2 464	50.1	17.1	3.4	0.4	8.0	57.7	1 581	110	148	2 105	29.5	68.0	2.5
Jasper	17.7	1 789	57.5	3.1	7.5	0.2	6.5	7.6	766	23	40	693	39.5	58.3	2.2
Jeff Davis	33.6	2 664	46.0	21.7	3.5	0.2	6.5	5.9	470	30	48	780	32.7	66.3	1.0
Jefferson	38.0	2 128	49.9	19.1	4.7	0.7	3.7	14.2	794	47	68	1 073	53.4	46.0	0.6
Jenkins	19.0	2 262	45.3	22.2	3.7	0.5	10.1	2.5	303	27	32	589	48.3	50.9	0.8
Johnson	14.4	1 731	61.5	1.1	3.5	0.6	7.6	1.2	144	17	31	755	37.0	62.4	0.7
Jones	31.1	1 376	69.9	0.8	5.0	0.0	6.1	20.3	899	30	88	865	38.6	60.3	1.1
Lamar	25.3	1 722	55.7	0.8	4.6	0.1	6.8	15.9	1 086	38	57	873	42.1	55.8	2.1
Lanier	10.5	1 545	71.3	0.9	4.4	0.1	5.2	2.2	324	14	26	358	43.8	55.1	1.1
Laurens	118.2	2 718	44.3	14.7	3.5	0.4	5.2	34.7	797	856	166	3 346	40.8	57.9	1.3
Lee	39.4	1 803	65.5	0.6	3.6	0.2	6.7	18.4	840	34	88	1 141	24.6	74.6	0.9
Liberty	92.2	1 536	55.0	13.7	5.5	0.4	2.4	21.6	360	3 024	15 501	2 738	53.8	44.8	1.4
Lincoln	14.3	1 769	58.1	1.1	3.1	0.9	6.6	7.2	886	19	32	450	41.1	58.2	0.7
Long	10.7	1 288	69.8	1.0	5.9	2.1	5.3	2.5	303	13	33	431	42.2	57.1	0.8
Lowndes	290.3	3 456	27.7	48.8	3.5	0.1	6.1	52.7	628	974	4 184	8 287	42.1	57.3	0.6
Lumpkin	33.3	1 837	48.0	0.8	4.4	0.2	4.4	17.2	946	71	291	1 347	31.4	65.6	3.0
McDuffie	50.3	2 330	47.6	19.3	2.8	1.0	3.6	11.4	528	43	143	1 480	39.4	60.0	0.6
McIntosh	17.7	1 785	57.9	3.7	7.0	0.2	10.5	1.8	185	26	38	663	53.4	46.1	0.5
Macon	30.7	2 320	55.7	1.0	4.6	0.2	3.5	34.8	2 625	33	50	1 016	63.4	36.0	0.7
Madison	32.1	1 315	62.5	1.1	2.7	0.4	7.5	7.5	305	47	95	970	28.7	69.6	1.7
Marion	14.4	2 201	73.2	1.1	2.3	0.4	7.9	6.4	983	36	26	424	45.0	54.3	0.7
Meriwether	38.4	1 676	63.3	1.5	4.9	0.5	3.5	29.9	1 304	47	87	1 717	51.4	47.3	1.3
Miller	11.1	1 775	65.3	1.6	5.2	0.3	4.7	2.6	409	28	24	461	36.4	62.7	0.8
Mitchell	52.6	2 494	53.3	6.3	4.8	0.1	4.7	23.1	1 095	79	80	1 814	51.3	48.2	0.6
Monroe	59.8	3 104	32.7	12.3	5.0	0.2	3.0	248.2	12 883	45	76	1 477	37.7	60.6	1.6
Montgomery	9.5	1 232	68.2	1.3	3.0	1.5	6.2	1.9	242	27	30	430	40.5	58.6	0.9
Morgan	34.6	2 378	49.5	12.9	3.3	0.8	12.3	9.7	663	39	58	926	38.1	60.0	1.9
Murray	53.0	1 659	63.4	2.0	3.0	0.3	8.4	42.5	1 331	101	128	1 274	42.2	55.6	2.2
Muscogee	403.1	2 205	45.6	8.8	6.3	0.2	2.8	423.9	2 319	5 606	4 662	12 145	54.3	45.2	0.5
Newton	134.3	2 436	47.3	20.7	4.8	0.3	3.3	83.7	1 518	121	230	2 735	36.5	60.7	2.8
Oconee	43.5	1 886	65.7	1.0	3.2	0.8	6.6	32.8	1 423	95	93	1 121	28.9	69.1	2.0
Oglethorpe	17.6	1 565	72.2	0.9	2.6	0.8	5.9	0.1	12	16	44	457	35.2	62.7	2.1
Paulding	125.9	1 825	56.0	19.3	3.2	0.3	4.1	104.7	1 518	89	301	2 617	27.8	69.7	2.5
Peach	49.6	2 061	54.6	15.0	5.7	0.2	2.6	16.4	682	101	102	1 986	49.6	49.4	1.0
Pickens	37.6	2 026	71.3	1.3	3.5	0.1	3.6	19.6	1 056	50	80	1 039	30.4	67.0	2.6
Pierce	26.2	1 691	66.5	0.8	3.6	0.1	10.4	6.3	407	45	60	759	27.8	71.6	0.7
Pike	15.6	1 258	65.2	4.1	3.9	0.2	6.3	10.6	860	29	50	552	29.0	68.9	2.1
Polk	62.4	1 741	54.1	8.6	5.5	0.2	4.4	22.0	613	74	139	1 737	40.8	57.9	1.4
Pulaski	17.2	2 059	57.9	1.0	6.8	0.2	6.2	5.3	641	18	32	847	41.6	57.5	1.0
Putnam	50.7	3 007	47.1	14.9	5.0	0.4	3.3	109.8	6 515	79	69	1 053	41.6	57.3	1.1
Quitman	4.5	1 824	60.6	2.0	4.6	0.2	6.4	2.0	822	0	0	121	60.0	38.5	1.5
Rabun	29.3	2 213	35.9	17.7	5.5	0.4	11.4	4.5	342	60	52	786	33.4	65.0	1.6
Randolph	26.6	3 362	47.3	27.9	2.3	0.1	6.0	2.0	257	27	30	780	53.8	45.7	0.5

1. Based on the resident population estimated as of July 1 of the year shown.   2. Data subject to copyright.

STATE/ County code	MSA/ PMSA/ NECMA code[1]	County Type[2]	STATE County	Land area[3] (sq km) 2000	Population and population characteristics, 2000			Race alone or in combination (percent)					Age (percent)					
					Total persons	Rank	Per square kilometer	White	Black	Am. Indian, Alaska Native	Asian and Pacific Islander	Percent Hispanic[4]	Under 5 years	5 to 17 years	18 to 24 years	25 to 34 years	35 to 44 years	45 to 54 years
				1	2	3	4	5	6	7	8	9	10	11	12	13	14	15
			GEORGIA—Cont'd															
13 245	0600	2	Richmond	839	199 775	277	238.1	46.8	50.7	0.7	2.2	2.8	7.1	19.7	12.0	14.8	15.0	12.6
13 247	0520	1	Rockdale	338	70 111	709	207.4	76.8	18.7	0.6	2.2	6.0	6.4	21.1	8.8	13.0	17.5	15.2
13 249	...	9	Schley	434	3 766	2 932	8.7	66.6	31.7	0.8	0.6	2.4	8.5	20.8	8.2	13.5	14.0	13.0
13 251	...	6	Screven	1 679	15 374	2 062	9.2	53.9	45.5	0.3	0.5	1.0	6.6	21.3	8.9	11.5	15.0	13.6
13 253	...	6	Seminole	617	9 369	2 501	15.2	62.1	34.8	0.4	0.2	3.7	7.2	18.9	8.6	11.9	14.5	12.2
13 255	0520	1	Spalding	513	58 417	819	113.9	67.2	31.4	0.5	1.0	1.6	7.5	19.8	9.2	14.1	15.3	13.3
13 257	...	7	Stephens	464	25 435	1 545	54.8	86.6	12.4	0.6	0.9	1.0	6.1	17.3	10.5	12.7	13.9	13.6
13 259	...	8	Stewart	1 188	5 252	2 835	4.4	37.7	62.1	0.6	0.5	1.5	6.4	18.5	8.0	11.7	13.5	13.7
13 261	...	6	Sumter	1 257	33 200	1 308	26.4	48.7	49.3	0.5	0.8	2.7	7.9	19.9	11.9	13.9	13.5	12.5
13 263	...	8	Talbot	1 018	6 498	2 739	6.4	37.3	62.1	0.7	0.4	1.3	5.9	18.2	7.7	11.6	15.3	16.0
13 265	...	9	Taliaferro	506	2 077	3 061	4.1	38.7	60.7	0.1	0.3	0.9	6.3	17.8	7.6	10.9	13.7	12.9
13 267	...	7	Tattnall	1 253	22 305	1 679	17.8	61.3	31.8	0.4	0.5	8.4	6.1	16.8	11.2	17.7	16.9	11.8
13 269	...	8	Taylor	978	8 815	2 544	9.0	56.1	42.9	0.3	0.3	1.8	7.1	19.8	9.0	13.1	15.0	12.6
13 271	...	7	Telfair	1 142	11 794	2 306	10.3	60.0	38.7	0.1	0.4	1.8	6.0	16.5	10.3	14.4	15.6	13.8
13 273	...	6	Terrell	869	10 970	2 369	12.6	38.4	61.0	0.5	0.7	1.2	7.7	20.6	9.5	11.5	14.5	13.0
13 275	...	6	Thomas	1 420	42 737	1 043	30.1	59.6	39.2	0.7	0.7	1.7	6.7	20.4	8.1	12.7	15.5	13.5
13 277	...	7	Tift	686	38 407	1 152	56.0	66.0	28.3	0.5	1.1	7.7	7.7	19.5	11.6	13.9	14.4	12.6
13 279	...	7	Toombs	950	26 067	1 514	27.4	69.7	24.4	0.4	0.6	8.9	7.7	20.8	9.2	13.2	14.6	12.7
13 281	...	9	Towns	432	9 319	2 504	21.6	99.2	0.2	0.4	0.4	0.7	4.4	11.9	9.1	9.6	10.9	13.0
13 283	...	7	Treutlen	520	6 854	2 704	13.2	66.2	33.3	0.2	0.4	1.2	7.4	18.6	11.9	13.6	13.6	12.6
13 285	...	4	Troup	1 072	58 779	816	54.8	66.5	32.2	0.5	0.8	1.7	7.2	20.6	9.2	13.6	14.8	13.6
13 287	...	7	Turner	741	9 504	2 489	12.8	56.6	41.1	0.3	0.4	2.6	7.7	21.7	10.2	12.8	13.5	12.6
13 289	4680	2	Twiggs	933	10 590	2 390	11.4	55.6	43.9	0.6	0.3	1.1	6.7	20.3	9.4	13.1	16.0	13.4
13 291	...	9	Union	835	17 289	1 933	20.7	98.6	0.6	0.7	0.4	0.9	4.8	15.2	6.6	10.3	13.3	13.8
13 293	...	7	Upson	843	27 597	1 464	32.7	71.0	28.1	0.5	0.6	1.2	6.5	19.0	8.3	12.6	15.2	13.4
13 295	1560	2	Walker	1 157	61 053	797	52.8	95.2	4.0	0.7	0.5	0.9	6.6	18.2	8.7	13.2	15.6	13.8
13 297	0520	1	Walton	853	60 687	799	71.1	83.9	14.7	0.7	0.9	1.9	8.1	20.3	8.1	15.4	16.8	13.1
13 299	...	7	Ware	2 337	35 483	1 233	15.2	70.2	28.3	0.4	0.7	1.9	6.4	18.4	9.1	13.6	14.4	13.5
13 301	...	8	Warren	739	6 336	2 753	8.6	39.9	59.7	0.3	0.2	0.8	6.8	19.5	8.7	11.1	14.4	13.7
13 303	...	7	Washington	1 762	21 176	1 726	12.0	46.0	53.5	0.3	0.5	0.6	6.3	20.6	8.8	13.2	17.1	12.7
13 305	...	7	Wayne	1 670	26 565	1 496	15.9	77.5	20.6	0.6	0.6	3.8	6.6	19.3	8.6	14.6	16.1	14.2
13 307	...	8	Webster	543	2 390	3 032	4.4	51.3	47.1	0.6	0.0	2.8	7.1	18.2	8.2	13.0	14.7	14.2
13 309	...	9	Wheeler	771	6 179	2 764	8.0	64.9	33.5	0.5	0.3	3.5	5.9	16.4	10.2	15.4	14.2	14.6
13 311	...	9	White	626	19 944	1 795	31.9	96.2	2.3	1.1	0.8	1.6	6.2	16.9	9.2	12.6	15.2	13.8
13 313	...	4	Whitfield	751	83 525	623	111.2	82.7	4.2	0.7	1.2	22.1	8.2	19.2	10.0	15.7	15.1	12.7
13 315	...	9	Wilcox	985	8 577	2 559	8.7	62.9	36.4	0.2	0.2	1.6	6.2	16.5	9.6	14.6	16.6	14.0
13 317	...	6	Wilkes	1 221	10 687	2 386	8.8	55.9	43.4	0.5	0.4	2.0	5.8	18.1	8.0	11.9	14.8	13.1
13 319	...	8	Wilkinson	1 157	10 220	2 425	8.8	58.4	41.1	0.4	0.3	1.0	7.3	20.0	9.0	12.6	15.5	12.8
13 321	...	6	Worth	1 476	21 967	1 695	14.9	69.2	29.7	0.6	0.3	1.1	7.0	21.6	8.1	12.2	15.2	14.0
15 000	...	X	HAWAII	16 635	1 211 537	X	72.8	39.3	2.8	2.1	81.3	7.2	6.5	18.0	9.5	14.1	15.8	14.1
15 001	...	5	Hawaii	10 433	148 677	363	14.3	52.1	1.2	3.3	78.7	9.5	6.1	20.0	8.2	10.8	15.4	16.4
15 003	3320	2	Honolulu	1 553	876 156	48	564.2	35.2	3.4	1.8	83.2	6.7	6.5	17.3	10.1	14.9	15.7	13.4
15 005	...	NA	Kalawao	34	147	3 140	4.3	31.3	0.0	0.0	68.7	4.1	0.0	2.0	1.4	6.1	12.2	21.1
15 007	...	5	Kauai	1 612	58 463	818	36.3	46.4	0.9	2.4	78.5	8.2	6.2	20.2	7.1	11.6	15.7	16.1
15 009	...	5	Maui	3 002	128 094	422	42.7	48.9	1.0	2.1	73.5	7.8	6.7	18.8	7.7	13.8	17.1	15.5
16 000	...	X	IDAHO	214 314	1 293 953	X	6.0	92.8	0.6	2.1	1.5	7.9	7.5	21.0	10.7	13.1	14.9	13.2
16 001	1080	2	Ada	2 732	300 904	188	110.1	94.9	1.0	1.4	2.7	4.5	7.7	19.6	10.3	15.9	16.7	13.6
16 003	...	9	Adams	3 534	3 476	2 955	1.0	97.3	0.1	2.2	0.3	1.6	4.0	19.9	4.6	7.1	15.5	17.5
16 005	6340	5	Bannock	2 883	75 565	663	26.2	93.1	0.9	3.6	1.8	4.7	8.1	20.0	14.6	13.7	13.5	12.7
16 007	...	7	Bear Lake	2 516	6 411	2 749	2.5	98.1	0.2	0.8	0.2	2.4	6.9	26.0	7.4	8.9	13.6	12.5
16 009	...	8	Benewah	2 010	9 171	2 306	4.6	90.4	0.3	10.3	0.4	1.5	6.5	20.4	6.8	10.7	14.8	15.5
16 011	...	7	Bingham	5 425	41 735	1 061	7.7	84.4	0.4	7.3	1.0	13.3	8.8	26.2	9.7	11.4	13.9	11.8
16 013	...	7	Blaine	6 850	18 991	1 846	2.8	92.1	0.3	0.8	1.3	10.7	5.9	18.2	7.7	14.5	18.1	18.1
16 015	...	8	Boise	4 927	6 670	2 720	1.4	97.2	0.2	2.1	0.9	3.4	6.6	20.3	4.7	9.5	17.6	18.5
16 017	...	6	Bonner	4 501	36 835	1 193	8.2	98.2	0.2	2.0	0.7	1.6	5.7	19.8	6.7	9.6	15.8	17.9
16 019	...	5	Bonneville	4 839	82 522	628	17.1	94.2	0.7	1.2	1.2	6.9	8.2	23.9	9.5	12.2	14.9	13.0
16 021	...	9	Boundary	3 286	9 871	2 459	3.0	96.1	0.2	2.8	0.9	3.4	7.0	22.2	6.9	10.1	14.3	16.5
16 023	...	9	Butte	5 783	2 899	2 999	0.5	96.0	0.8	2.0	0.7	4.1	6.6	22.5	6.3	9.8	14.1	14.1
16 025	...	9	Camas	2 784	991	3 111	0.4	97.3	1.5	1.8	0.9	5.5	4.3	20.4	6.6	10.0	18.2	13.7
16 027	1080	2	Canyon	1 527	131 441	406	86.1	85.5	0.5	1.7	1.6	18.6	9.1	21.8	10.7	14.5	13.8	11.5
16 029	...	7	Caribou	4 574	7 304	2 655	1.6	97.2	0.2	0.5	0.8	4.0	7.5	24.2	8.2	10.1	14.4	13.0
16 031	...	7	Cassia	6 647	21 416	1 717	3.2	86.4	0.2	1.4	0.9	18.7	8.7	25.4	9.0	11.1	13.4	11.5
16 033	...	9	Clark	4 570	1 022	3 110	0.2	75.1	0.5	1.1	0.3	34.2	8.9	26.3	8.0	12.4	15.1	10.2
16 035	...	7	Clearwater	6 375	8 930	2 532	1.4	96.7	0.2	3.3	0.8	1.8	4.8	18.2	5.9	10.4	15.9	16.0

1. MSA = Metropolitan Statistical Area. PMSA = Primary MSA. NECMA = New England County Metropolitan Area. See Appendix A for explanation of these concepts. See Appendix B for list of metropolitan areas identified by type, with component counties. 2. County typology code from the Economic Research Service of USDA. See Appendix A for definition. 3. Dry land or land partially or temporarily covered by water. 4. Hispanic persons may be of any race.

Table B. States and Counties — Population and Households

STATE County	55 to 64 years	65 to 74 years	75 years and over	Percent female	Total persons 2001	Total persons 1990	Percent change 1990–2000	Percent change 2000–2001	Births	Deaths	Net migration	Households Number	Percent change, 1990–2000	Persons per household	Female family householder[1]	One person
	16	17	18	19	20	21	22	23	24	25	26	27	28	29	30	31
GEORGIA—Cont'd																
Richmond	7.9	6.0	4.8	51.8	198 366	189 719	5.3	-0.7	4 504	2 511	-3 347	73 920	7.6	2.55	20.8	27.7
Rockdale	8.8	5.3	3.9	50.3	71 798	54 091	29.6	2.4	1 172	620	1 139	24 052	31.2	2.87	12.4	16.9
Schley	11.0	6.3	4.8	52.1	3 921	3 590	4.9	4.1	79	53	128	1 435	9.1	2.62	15.7	24.8
Screven	9.1	7.4	6.6	52.2	15 177	13 842	11.1	-1.3	279	234	-243	5 797	14.8	2.60	18.3	26.5
Seminole	10.8	8.8	6.9	52.4	9 365	9 010	4.0	0.0	227	126	-101	3 573	13.9	2.54	17.9	24.3
Spalding	9.2	6.3	5.4	51.8	59 066	54 457	7.3	1.1	1 241	795	227	21 519	10.8	2.67	18.2	22.3
Stephens	10.2	8.0	7.6	52.0	25 651	23 436	8.5	0.8	444	386	166	9 951	11.2	2.46	11.1	25.5
Stewart	9.6	8.6	9.9	52.2	5 145	5 654	-7.1	-2.0	83	103	-88	2 007	1.3	2.48	23.1	29.5
Sumter	8.1	6.0	6.4	53.1	33 319	30 232	9.8	0.4	791	478	-192	12 025	14.7	2.64	22.0	25.0
Talbot	10.8	8.7	5.7	53.3	6 703	6 524	-0.4	3.2	130	97	170	2 538	8.2	2.55	20.2	25.4
Taliaferro	11.9	9.5	9.4	51.8	2 034	1 915	8.5	-2.1	35	35	-44	870	19.7	2.36	20.0	33.3
Tattnall	8.2	6.0	5.2	42.4	22 385	17 722	25.9	0.4	425	288	-48	7 057	20.7	2.60	13.4	26.7
Taylor	10.2	6.6	6.7	51.2	8 836	7 642	15.3	0.2	172	130	-15	3 281	17.0	2.56	20.1	27.6
Telfair	8.5	7.4	6.4	47.4	11 692	11 000	7.2	-0.9	214	218	-96	4 140	3.1	2.48	16.7	28.4
Terrell	10.2	6.6	6.4	53.1	10 943	10 653	3.0	-0.2	258	180	-102	4 002	7.1	2.69	24.0	24.3
Thomas	9.4	7.1	6.6	52.9	43 012	38 943	9.7	0.6	958	642	-23	16 309	13.9	2.55	18.4	25.8
Tift	8.5	6.3	5.4	51.4	38 634	34 998	9.7	0.6	837	393	-211	13 919	14.2	2.65	16.9	23.3
Toombs	9.5	6.5	5.7	52.3	26 115	24 072	8.3	0.2	540	401	-93	9 877	12.2	2.59	15.6	27.0
Towns	15.3	14.9	10.9	52.7	9 641	6 754	38.0	3.5	105	145	354	3 998	42.2	2.20	6.3	26.0
Treutlen	9.1	6.8	6.4	50.3	6 787	5 994	14.3	-1.0	121	102	-88	2 531	17.3	2.55	17.3	25.3
Troup	8.3	6.5	6.1	52.3	59 478	55 532	5.8	1.2	1 274	842	289	21 920	7.6	2.61	17.9	24.9
Turner	8.5	6.8	6.2	51.9	9 621	8 703	9.2	1.2	211	172	80	3 435	12.9	2.72	18.6	23.2
Twiggs	9.9	6.6	4.7	52.1	10 589	9 806	8.0	0.0	201	136	-63	3 832	16.3	2.73	17.5	22.3
Union	14.4	12.7	8.9	50.9	17 902	11 993	44.2	3.5	198	278	680	7 159	52.0	2.35	7.1	24.2
Upson	10.1	7.7	7.2	52.5	27 711	26 300	4.9	0.4	482	477	119	10 722	8.2	2.53	16.9	25.2
Walker	10.2	7.7	6.2	51.5	61 884	58 310	4.7	1.4	1 008	851	683	23 605	8.8	2.54	12.0	22.9
Walton	8.6	5.4	4.3	51.3	65 224	38 586	57.3	7.5	1 232	537	3 732	21 307	58.6	2.82	12.8	16.6
Ware	9.1	7.9	7.5	50.6	35 540	35 471	0.0	0.2	659	550	-41	13 475	3.3	2.47	14.8	27.9
Warren	9.7	8.1	8.0	53.6	6 274	6 078	4.2	-1.0	117	132	-46	2 435	14.3	2.55	22.1	27.4
Washington	8.6	6.4	6.2	55.1	21 042	19 112	10.8	-0.6	353	294	-189	7 435	10.3	2.65	21.5	24.8
Wayne	9.2	6.8	4.5	48.0	26 945	22 356	18.8	1.4	440	328	274	9 324	17.7	2.62	14.0	22.6
Webster	9.9	7.9	6.9	49.7	2 301	2 263	5.6	-3.7	34	41	-83	911	14.2	2.62	16.8	23.5
Wheeler	8.5	5.9	6.7	43.8	6 183	4 903	26.0	0.1	105	83	-15	2 011	12.6	2.54	13.0	27.8
White	11.5	8.5	6.1	50.5	21 182	13 006	53.3	6.2	315	259	1 153	7 731	57.6	2.51	8.7	21.7
Whitfield	8.9	5.9	4.4	49.7	85 248	72 462	15.3	2.1	2 112	854	486	29 385	9.4	2.82	10.8	20.6
Wilcox	8.8	6.9	6.6	44.7	8 709	7 008	22.4	1.5	176	138	92	2 785	10.9	2.55	15.0	26.7
Wilkes	11.1	8.6	8.5	52.2	10 688	10 597	0.8	0.0	175	189	20	4 314	7.3	2.45	17.3	28.1
Wilkinson	9.8	7.5	5.5	52.5	10 300	10 228	-0.1	0.8	223	133	-5	3 827	5.7	2.65	18.4	24.1
Worth	9.9	6.6	5.3	52.1	21 938	19 744	11.3	-0.1	394	275	-143	8 106	17.6	2.68	15.7	21.5
HAWAII	8.8	7.0	6.2	49.8	1 224 398	1 108 229	9.3	1.1	23 452	10 357	269	403 240	13.2	2.92	12.4	21.9
Hawaii	9.5	7.3	6.2	49.9	152 083	120 317	23.6	2.3	2 620	1 397	2 208	52 985	27.8	2.75	13.2	23.1
Honolulu	8.7	7.1	6.3	49.7	881 295	836 231	4.8	0.6	17 436	7 346	-4 517	286 450	8.0	2.95	12.3	21.6
Kalawao	25.2	23.8	8.2	50.3	135	130	13.1	-8.2	0	4	-9	115	85.5	1.28	2.6	79.1
Kauai	9.4	7.0	6.8	50.0	59 223	51 177	14.2	1.3	1 031	594	350	20 183	23.9	2.87	12.8	21.4
Maui	8.9	6.0	5.4	49.8	131 662	100 374	27.6	2.8	2 365	1 016	2 237	43 507	31.3	2.91	12.0	21.9
IDAHO	8.3	5.9	5.4	49.9	1 321 006	1 006 734	28.5	2.1	24 583	11 976	14 131	469 645	30.2	2.69	8.7	22.4
Ada	7.2	4.6	4.5	49.9	312 337	205 775	46.2	3.8	5 755	2 120	7 700	113 408	46.4	2.59	9.4	23.8
Adams	15.2	9.9	6.2	48.7	3 428	3 254	6.8	-1.4	33	43	-38	1 421	13.6	2.42	5.7	23.2
Bannock	7.4	5.2	4.9	50.6	75 323	66 026	14.4	-0.3	1 713	750	-1 207	27 192	16.1	2.69	10.0	22.8
Bear Lake	9.2	8.1	7.5	50.4	6 345	6 084	5.4	-1.0	110	85	-92	2 259	12.7	2.81	6.4	22.2
Benewah	11.6	8.2	6.0	49.0	8 995	7 937	15.5	-1.9	138	130	-190	3 580	19.7	2.52	7.7	24.0
Bingham	7.8	5.7	4.6	50.0	42 335	37 583	11.0	1.4	890	356	78	13 317	15.7	3.10	9.8	17.1
Blaine	9.8	5.0	2.8	48.1	19 798	13 552	40.1	4.2	258	109	648	7 780	41.3	2.40	7.2	27.3
Boise	11.8	7.0	4.0	48.7	7 011	3 509	90.1	5.1	107	35	259	2 616	92.8	2.52	5.8	21.8
Bonner	11.4	7.6	5.5	49.9	37 479	26 622	38.4	1.7	446	431	628	14 693	43.1	2.49	7.5	24.0
Bonneville	7.9	5.4	4.7	50.1	83 807	72 207	14.3	1.6	1 724	691	282	28 753	18.4	2.83	9.3	21.4
Boundary	9.7	8.0	5.4	49.6	9 926	8 332	18.5	0.6	145	96	8	3 707	29.8	2.61	7.5	23.1
Butte	11.6	9.0	6.0	49.7	2 856	2 918	-0.7	-1.5	50	42	-52	1 089	9.2	2.64	7.4	23.6
Camas	13.8	7.2	5.9	48.8	1 002	727	36.3	1.1	15	4	-2	396	44.0	2.49	4.5	22.2
Canyon	7.5	5.5	5.5	50.3	139 821	90 076	45.9	6.4	2 852	1 317	6 694	45 018	43.9	2.85	10.1	19.8
Caribou	9.0	7.2	6.4	50.2	7 397	6 963	4.9	1.3	134	62	22	2 560	13.2	2.83	5.2	20.4
Cassia	8.1	6.3	6.4	49.7	21 577	19 532	9.6	0.8	464	236	-63	7 060	10.8	2.99	8.8	19.5
Clark	9.9	5.4	3.8	47.5	971	762	34.1	-5.0	24	12	-66	340	22.7	3.01	7.1	20.0
Clearwater	13.1	8.9	6.7	46.9	8 544	8 505	5.0	-4.3	104	103	-395	3 456	7.6	2.41	6.9	24.0

1. No spouse present.

Table B. States and Counties — Vital Statistics, Health Resources, and Crime

STATE County	Births, average 1997–1999 Total	Births Rate[1]	Deaths, average 1997–1999 Number Total	Deaths Number Infant[2]	Deaths Rate Total[1]	Deaths Rate Infant[3]	Physicians,[4] 2000 Number	Physicians Rate[5]	Hospitals,[4] 1998 Number	Beds Number	Beds Rate[5]	Medicare enrollees 2000	Serious crimes known to police, 2000[6] Total Number	Serious crimes Rate[7]
	32	33	34	35	36	37	38	39	40	41	42	43	44	45
GEORGIA—Cont'd														
Richmond	3 077	16.1	1 855	35	9.7	11.3	1 047	524	4	1 571	821	26 062	12 715	6 365
Rockdale	910	13.4	471	NA	6.9	NA	96	137	1	107	157	7 282	2 508	3 577
Schley	68	17.4	38	NA	9.8	NA	1	27	0	0	0	505	47	1 248
Screven	214	14.8	177	NA	12.2	NA	11	72	1	40	277	2 437	268	1 743
Seminole	137	14.0	99	NA	10.2	NA	11	117	1	62	633	1 754	257	2 743
Spalding	895	15.5	574	11	10.0	12.7	79	135	1	160	278	8 577	4 015	6 873
Stephens	356	14.0	283	NA	11.2	NA	44	173	1	96	378	5 373	670	2 634
Stewart	65	12.0	72	NA	13.3	NA	4	76	1	32	585	957	78	1 485
Sumter	518	16.5	346	NA	11.0	NA	44	133	1	152	485	4 585	NA	NA
Talbot	86	12.5	83	NA	12.0	NA	1	15	0	0	0	1 098	83	1 277
Taliaferro	22	11.4	28	NA	14.5	NA	0	0	0	0	0	422	24	1 156
Tattnall	328	17.2	218	NA	11.4	NA	14	63	1	40	211	3 118	407	2 218
Taylor	115	13.9	100	NA	12.1	NA	2	23	0	0	0	1 512	112	1 271
Telfair	143	12.5	157	NA	13.7	NA	6	51	1	52	450	2 249	273	2 315
Terrell	177	15.9	132	NA	11.9	NA	5	46	0	0	0	1 693	326	3 118
Thomas	660	15.4	470	NA	11.0	NA	125	292	1	264	615	7 674	2 231	5 480
Tift	633	17.2	329	NA	9.0	NA	78	203	1	168	458	5 484	2 145	5 585
Toombs	409	15.8	286	NA	11.1	NA	33	127	1	122	472	4 160	947	4 325
Towns	72	8.5	111	NA	13.0	NA	9	97	1	101	1 184	2 545	150	1 721
Treutlen	81	13.5	80	NA	13.4	NA	3	44	0	0	0	997	72	1 050
Troup	910	15.5	663	9	11.3	9.5	87	148	1	364	619	9 357	3 551	6 041
Turner	150	16.4	120	NA	13.1	NA	3	32	0	0	0	1 588	439	4 619
Twiggs	138	13.7	105	NA	10.5	NA	4	38	0	0	0	1 390	91	859
Union	163	9.9	197	NA	12.0	NA	11	64	1	145	878	3 929	209	1 209
Upson	350	12.9	339	NA	12.5	NA	38	138	1	119	440	4 757	864	3 131
Walker	801	12.8	684	NA	10.9	NA	15	25	0	0	0	11 239	1 686	2 762
Walton	919	16.7	415	NA	7.6	NA	35	58	1	135	248	7 399	1 565	2 579
Ware	502	14.2	416	NA	11.7	NA	66	186	1	125	353	7 082	1 849	5 211
Warren	81	13.4	86	NA	14.2	NA	5	79	0	0	0	1 063	135	2 131
Washington	262	13.1	216	NA	10.8	NA	15	71	1	114	569	3 108	697	3 373
Wayne	371	14.6	247	NA	9.8	NA	36	136	1	123	484	3 792	NA	NA
Webster	27	12.1	26	NA	11.8	NA	0	0	0	0	0	318	NA	NA
Wheeler	72	14.7	57	NA	11.6	NA	3	49	1	40	821	919	NA	NA
White	222	12.7	166	NA	9.5	NA	8	40	0	0	0	3 277	508	2 547
Whitfield	1 449	17.6	647	9	7.9	6.4	137	164	1	282	344	10 978	4 022	4 849
Wilcox	116	15.8	92	NA	12.5	NA	4	47	0	0	0	1 379	NA	NA
Wilkes	130	12.3	142	NA	13.4	NA	12	112	1	44	416	2 198	226	2 115
Wilkinson	159	14.6	101	NA	9.3	NA	3	29	0	0	0	1 750	269	2 803
Worth	311	13.9	205	NA	9.2	NA	10	46	1	50	222	2 468	239	1 104
HAWAII	17 239	14.5	8 084	118	6.8	6.9	3 138	259	19	3 166	265	165 265	62 987	5 199
Hawaii	2 217	15.5	1 229	17	8.6	7.8	272	183	5	435	304	21 389	6 425	4 321
Honolulu	12 494	14.3	5 708	88	6.6	7.0	2 518	287	10	2 316	265	120 506	46 659	5 325
Kalawao	NA	NA	NA	NA	NA	NA	0	0	NA	NA	NA	64	NA	NA
Kauai	760	13.4	430	NA	7.6	NA	101	173	2	240	424	8 253	2 578	4 410
Maui	1 768	14.7	715	9	5.9	5.3	247	193	2	175	145	14 967	7 325	5 718
IDAHO	18 945	15.4	9 237	134	7.5	7.1	1 831	142	43	3 271	266	165 021	41 228	3 186
Ada	4 222	15.3	1 667	22	6.0	5.1	606	201	3	596	216	30 746	11 898	3 954
Adams	35	9.3	38	NA	10.0	NA	3	86	1	26	683	727	55	1 582
Bannock	1 252	16.8	567	9	7.6	7.2	132	175	2	248	331	9 047	2 561	3 389
Bear Lake	87	13.4	68	NA	10.5	NA	4	62	1	58	887	1 095	38	593
Benewah	118	13.1	96	NA	10.6	NA	9	98	1	33	362	1 583	155	1 690
Bingham	706	16.9	287	NA	6.9	NA	25	60	1	120	287	5 042	937	2 245
Blaine	234	13.6	77	NA	4.4	NA	61	321	2	88	512	1 497	414	2 180
Boise	66	12.8	31	NA	6.1	NA	0	0	0	0	0	680	94	1 409
Bonner	400	11.3	301	NA	8.5	NA	42	114	1	62	176	5 485	990	2 688
Bonneville	1 373	17.0	546	10	6.8	7.3	150	182	1	270	335	9 794	3 056	3 703
Boundary	127	12.9	81	NA	8.2	NA	5	51	1	62	633	1 607	154	1 560
Butte	42	13.7	32	NA	10.6	NA	1	34	1	43	1 418	512	39	1 345
Camas	12	13.7	NA	NA	NA	NA	0	0	0	0	0	133	3	303
Canyon	2 174	18.0	955	16	7.9	7.2	144	110	2	274	228	16 360	5 324	4 050
Caribou	92	12.5	55	NA	7.5	NA	5	68	1	65	875	1 091	122	1 670
Cassia	394	18.4	171	NA	8.0	NA	32	149	1	70	328	2 922	746	3 483
Clark	18	20.9	NA	NA	NA	NA	0	0	0	0	0	102	19	1 859
Clearwater	93	9.9	87	NA	9.3	NA	13	146	1	22	236	1 610	143	1 601

1. Per 1,000 estimated resident population, average 1997–1999.   2. Deaths of infants under 1 year old.   3. Deaths of infants under 1 year old per 1,000 live births.   4. Data subject to copyright.   5. Per 100,000 resident population as of July 1 of the year shown.   6. Data for serious crimes have not been adjusted for underreporting; this may affect comparability between geographic areas and over time.   7. Per 100,000 population estimated by the FBI.

Table B. States and Counties — Crime, Education, Money Income, and Poverty

STATE County	Serious crimes known to police, 2000[1] (cont'd) Rate[2] Violent	Property	School enrollment and attainment, 1990 — Enrollment[3] Total	Percent private	Attainment[4] (percent) High school graduate or more	Bachelor's degree or more	Local government expenditures, fiscal 1999[5] Total current expenditures (mil dol)	Current expenditures per student (dollars)	Money income — 1989 Per capita[6] (dollars)	Households Median Dollars	Percent change, 1979–1989 (constant 1989 dollars)	Percent with $100,000 or more	Income and poverty, 1998 Median household income	Percent below poverty level All persons	Persons under 18	Persons 5–17 in families
	46	47	48	49	50	51	52	53	54	55	56	57	58	59	60	61
GEORGIA—Cont'd																
Richmond	384	5 980	49 505	12.7	70.9	17.3	204.7	5 635	11 799	25 265	10.6	2.3	31 167	21.7	33.0	30.8
Rockdale	317	3 261	13 798	11.6	77.7	18.1	79.4	5 984	15 710	39 389	12.7	4.4	49 164	8.3	14.0	13.3
Schley	345	903	907	11.9	56.4	8.0	3.4	5 316	9 747	21 417	11.2	1.6	29 119	20.3	27.4	32.6
Screven	403	1 340	3 535	5.3	58.9	8.6	18.6	5 693	9 269	20 531	30.2	1.1	27 397	21.9	31.2	32.2
Seminole	993	1 750	2 021	6.3	52.7	7.8	11.3	5 868	9 270	18 438	-0.6	1.2	25 961	24.1	35.2	37.3
Spalding	716	6 157	13 169	9.3	60.0	11.1	66.1	6 254	11 073	25 634	12.5	1.3	33 487	16.5	24.5	24.9
Stephens	295	2 339	5 414	19.3	60.1	13.1	26.3	6 027	10 531	22 204	5.3	1.4	30 551	16.1	25.7	25.6
Stewart	590	895	1 349	12.5	51.4	8.0	6.0	6 511	7 772	15 606	12.1	1.1	22 518	26.2	36.3	39.7
Sumter	NA	NA	8 591	14.2	62.8	15.9	34.5	5 888	9 600	20 957	4.5	1.3	29 164	24.4	33.5	34.3
Talbot	108	1 170	1 497	7.5	56.2	7.1	6.6	7 228	8 728	20 489	2.2	0.3	26 666	19.1	27.1	32.3
Taliaferro	385	770	467	12.6	48.6	5.6	1.4	8 968	7 624	14 700	-1.2	0.4	21 628	27.0	39.3	46.9
Tattnall	452	1 765	3 926	7.1	57.4	6.5	19.6	5 776	9 286	20 293	27.7	1.1	27 935	23.8	32.9	33.4
Taylor	374	896	1 908	3.9	51.2	7.1	9.9	5 406	9 182	16 210	-15.6	1.9	24 721	24.9	35.7	38.2
Telfair	399	1 916	2 630	7.3	52.1	8.6	12.4	6 302	8 452	16 573	-1.1	1.2	22 351	25.3	33.7	36.2
Terrell	459	2 659	2 779	16.1	52.4	9.2	12.2	6 476	8 524	18 036	1.2	1.1	24 260	27.1	39.0	40.0
Thomas	447	5 033	9 870	8.5	63.3	13.4	53.1	5 979	10 293	20 901	0.8	2.3	29 040	19.0	25.7	28.3
Tift	745	4 840	9 644	5.7	61.3	14.0	42.5	5 670	10 612	22 421	10.9	2.4	30 717	21.0	30.2	30.1
Toombs	489	3 836	6 003	12.3	59.0	11.4	31.4	6 091	9 775	19 473	7.5	1.8	25 487	23.5	31.4	33.8
Towns	69	1 652	1 429	23.7	58.2	11.4	5.9	5 536	10 777	19 356	21.8	1.7	30 572	13.3	23.1	23.3
Treutlen	292	759	1 355	6.9	52.7	6.3	7.1	5 562	7 865	17 391	1.0	0.8	24 309	25.1	35.2	37.3
Troup	339	5 703	13 802	14.7	60.8	13.6	68.9	6 163	11 581	24 788	13.5	2.2	34 306	15.5	23.3	22.5
Turner	1 031	3 588	2 389	4.3	55.3	7.2	12.6	6 284	7 953	17 766	-2.3	0.5	23 915	28.1	37.7	40.0
Twiggs	208	652	2 477	11.3	48.4	4.8	12.3	6 055	8 510	19 213	-10.6	0.8	28 305	19.7	25.5	30.2
Union	75	1 134	2 194	2.8	58.7	10.1	14.6	5 424	10 975	20 275	30.9	2.3	30 117	13.9	21.4	23.0
Upson	576	2 555	5 938	7.9	54.6	9.0	27.6	5 573	10 554	22 747	5.3	1.5	30 110	16.3	24.8	25.1
Walker	121	2 640	12 824	7.8	58.3	8.4	56.7	5 714	10 575	24 068	2.8	1.1	32 148	12.9	20.0	19.0
Walton	194	2 384	8 983	7.8	57.9	9.4	60.8	5 835	11 932	28 198	21.8	2.2	38 990	11.7	16.8	19.4
Ware	448	4 763	8 784	4.1	61.1	10.4	42.8	6 597	9 712	20 426	2.1	1.3	26 647	22.5	30.7	32.7
Warren	347	1 783	1 381	9.2	42.8	4.2	6.5	6 234	7 864	17 284	-2.5	0.5	24 046	26.3	39.2	41.7
Washington	406	2 966	4 901	13.9	58.1	9.8	24.3	6 069	9 917	21 460	13.0	2.0	29 710	21.6	30.9	32.1
Wayne	NA	NA	5 675	6.0	62.9	9.6	28.7	5 456	9 856	23 311	14.8	1.1	31 515	21.0	29.3	31.2
Webster	NA	NA	544	15.6	50.4	5.5	2.7	6 877	9 202	19 028	17.0	1.5	27 836	19.0	28.6	29.4
Wheeler	NA	NA	1 331	8.6	56.7	8.6	6.4	6 007	9 522	16 585	16.3	1.1	23 662	24.3	32.6	36.9
White	241	2 306	2 787	16.5	62.9	13.6	25.1	8 145	11 277	24 234	12.4	1.7	33 843	12.4	19.9	19.0
Whitfield	345	4 504	16 160	8.2	59.8	12.0	104.9	6 594	13 324	27 797	2.7	2.9	37 178	12.0	19.2	17.1
Wilcox	NA	NA	1 678	6.2	52.8	7.6	7.8	5 856	8 733	16 333	-8.8	1.0	24 416	25.6	35.9	38.8
Wilkes	215	1 900	2 460	11.1	56.6	10.4	12.5	6 281	10 752	18 629	-2.2	2.7	27 313	20.0	31.1	30.5
Wilkinson	761	2 042	2 548	8.6	62.0	8.8	12.7	6 795	10 415	25 166	7.6	0.8	32 242	16.1	23.2	26.1
Worth	65	1 039	5 148	5.3	58.1	6.3	25.2	5 388	9 469	21 312	-2.4	1.6	30 316	20.2	26.7	31.1
HAWAII	244	4 955	290 578	19.5	80.1	22.9	1 143.7	6 081	15 770	38 829	13.2	7.1	41 627	10.5	15.0	13.8
Hawaii	159	4 162	31 939	12.3	77.7	18.5	(7)NA	(7)NA	13 169	29 712	4.4	3.9	34 411	15.1	19.4	19.9
Honolulu	263	5 062	221 821	21.6	81.2	24.6	(7)1 143.9	(7)6 082	16 256	40 581	14.9	7.9	44 934	9.7	14.3	12.5
Kalawao	NA	NA	6	0.0	51.5	4.6	(7)NA	(7)NA	11 281	10 000	3.8	0.0	9 859	0.0	0.0	0.0
Kauai	246	4 163	13 229	11.3	73.1	16.3	(7)NA	(7)NA	14 254	37 425	17.1	5.2	38 553	11.3	15.4	15.5
Maui	212	5 507	23 583	13.8	77.0	17.8	(7)NA	(7)NA	15 616	38 771	14.3	6.0	40 635	10.4	14.1	13.8
IDAHO	253	2 934	295 638	9.2	79.7	17.7	1 239.8	5 066	11 457	25 257	-1.4	2.1	35 863	12.6	17.4	15.0
Ada	284	3 670	57 564	9.4	87.2	24.9	264.1	5 133	14 268	30 246	3.1	3.2	44 772	8.7	12.7	10.1
Adams	115	1 467	718	4.7	75.3	10.8	3.9	6 196	13 732	22 455	-9.4	2.3	29 749	15.8	21.3	22.5
Bannock	282	3 107	23 087	4.3	82.9	19.8	71.7	4 940	10 976	26 275	-10.2	1.6	36 063	13.4	17.4	14.7
Bear Lake	109	484	1 879	0.9	79.8	11.4	7.8	4 674	8 989	21 646	-17.2	0.7	32 883	12.5	15.5	13.4
Benewah	131	1 559	1 956	7.7	74.2	8.8	10.4	5 676	9 921	21 508	-24.4	1.2	33 525	15.2	21.4	19.0
Bingham	208	2 037	12 432	3.4	76.8	13.1	52.0	4 847	9 474	25 158	-2.3	1.5	34 639	15.2	19.6	16.0
Blaine	174	2 006	3 007	13.1	91.7	33.0	20.2	7 134	19 979	31 199	27.4	7.0	47 181	7.0	10.5	9.6
Boise	210	1 199	873	12.6	80.0	14.4	6.2	5 475	11 747	26 048	0.1	2.6	40 031	9.5	14.5	12.8
Bonner	168	2 519	6 325	10.3	78.2	15.2	28.3	4 864	10 527	21 465	5.0	1.8	32 148	14.2	19.4	17.7
Bonneville	238	3 466	22 449	7.4	84.0	23.2	86.3	4 631	12 123	30 462	0.0	2.3	41 170	12.1	16.4	13.7
Boundary	132	1 428	2 187	13.4	74.6	13.3	8.8	5 313	9 054	21 662	3.7	0.5	30 427	16.2	21.1	20.4
Butte	414	931	831	3.1	80.4	13.5	3.5	5 700	10 257	26 292	15.4	1.9	30 863	15.1	17.8	17.0
Camas	0	303	183	5.5	81.8	15.0	1.4	6 885	11 373	24 440	10.5	3.3	35 479	6.0	8.9	7.9
Canyon	329	3 721	24 516	12.6	71.0	12.0	108.9	4 652	9 916	22 979	-0.9	1.6	32 486	15.1	20.5	18.0
Caribou	123	1 547	2 324	1.1	84.3	11.8	11.2	5 703	10 808	29 979	1.1	1.7	42 322	10.1	12.7	11.2
Cassia	350	3 133	6 118	4.0	72.7	14.0	24.5	4 667	9 726	23 381	1.5	2.4	33 260	15.5	21.2	17.1
Clark	98	1 761	244	0.0	74.7	14.1	1.5	6 596	10 608	24 583	28.0	0.7	33 080	10.4	14.9	11.8
Clearwater	157	1 445	1 997	5.6	73.4	11.4	9.5	5 997	11 234	23 925	-17.3	1.5	34 245	15.2	22.7	20.4

1. Data for serious crimes have not been adjusted for underreporting; this may affect comparability between geographic areas and over time.   2. Per 100,000 population estimated by the FBI.   3. All persons 3 years old and over enrolled in nursery school through college.   4. Persons 25 years old and over.   5. Elementary and secondary education expenditures, local government fiscal years ending between July 1, 1998 and June 30, 1999.   6. Based on population enumerated as of April 1, 1990.   7. Hawaii, Kalawao, Kaui, and Maui Counties included with Honolulu County.

Table B. States and Counties — **Personal Income**

	Personal income, 1999												
			Per capita[1]					Transfer payments					
									Government payments to individuals				
STATE County	Total (mil dol)	Percent change, 1998-1999	Dollars	Rank	Wages and salaries[2] (mil dol)	Proprietor's income (mil dol)	Dividends, interest, and rent (mil dol)	Total (mil dol)	Total (mil dol)	Social Security (mil dol)	Medical payments (mil dol)	Income mainte-nance (mil dol)	Unemploy-ment insurance (mil dol)
	62	63	64	65	66	67	68	69	70	71	72	73	74
GEORGIA—Cont'd													
Richmond	4 564	2.0	23 980	864	4 033	182	825	802	763	248	304	116	19
Rockdale	1 757	4.6	25 477	587	1 087	109	279	167	152	78	54	11	1
Schley	75	5.4	18 905	2 315	32	9	8	13	12	4	5	2	0
Screven	277	5.0	19 181	2 234	109	23	48	63	60	21	24	12	1
Seminole	189	7.4	19 247	2 220	63	30	31	45	43	16	18	7	0
Spalding	1 293	4.2	22 354	1 256	641	80	216	209	197	84	78	25	2
Stephens	544	2.6	21 461	1 531	296	49	101	111	105	47	40	10	1
Stewart	101	4.8	18 744	2 356	31	7	14	28	27	7	12	6	0
Sumter	698	4.4	22 246	1 288	410	83	136	130	123	41	50	23	2
Talbot	107	4.9	15 385	2 953	22	6	18	25	24	9	8	4	0
Taliaferro	33	5.4	17 383	2 672	5	3	7	10	10	3	4	2	0
Tattnall	382	3.3	19 943	2 008	157	86	56	77	73	24	32	13	1
Taylor	156	4.6	18 774	2 352	60	22	22	37	35	11	14	7	0
Telfair	211	4.0	18 477	2 418	114	21	36	60	58	18	27	9	1
Terrell	181	3.5	16 153	2 880	67	19	37	47	45	14	18	10	1
Thomas	997	6.2	23 237	1 033	614	101	200	185	175	66	73	25	4
Tift	844	4.0	22 837	1 127	594	73	151	134	126	47	51	19	2
Toombs	502	5.2	19 304	2 208	270	46	89	110	105	36	45	18	2
Towns	195	6.0	22 174	1 305	61	21	55	48	46	23	16	3	0
Treutlen	98	2.5	16 499	2 828	27	8	16	26	25	9	10	4	1
Troup	1 429	6.7	24 306	804	1 087	68	251	216	204	87	75	25	2
Turner	165	4.3	17 831	2 572	60	23	27	39	37	12	15	7	1
Twiggs	169	5.0	16 576	2 816	80	13	20	38	36	14	14	5	1
Union	347	8.6	20 152	1 951	118	42	83	79	75	37	28	6	0
Upson	552	4.1	20 366	1 871	281	47	87	109	104	48	39	11	2
Walker	1 230	5.0	19 532	2 131	421	81	182	243	229	101	97	20	3
Walton	1 119	8.8	19 136	2 248	386	69	151	165	153	64	64	17	2
Ware	695	2.5	19 738	2 078	482	48	123	182	174	52	70	23	2
Warren	107	2.1	17 664	2 607	52	7	16	30	29	9	12	5	1
Washington	471	5.5	23 332	1 005	316	26	95	87	82	28	35	14	2
Wayne	499	5.3	19 483	2 146	272	51	72	102	96	37	41	12	1
Webster	46	7.6	20 728	1 766	12	7	9	8	8	3	3	1	0
Wheeler	92	6.7	18 864	2 331	26	12	12	24	23	8	10	4	1
White	411	5.7	22 598	1 195	149	60	91	68	64	31	22	5	1
Whitfield	2 158	4.1	25 926	525	1 909	148	405	245	227	108	90	20	2
Wilcox	147	5.3	19 834	2 048	37	26	23	36	34	10	17	6	0
Wilkes	228	3.7	21 565	1 497	115	19	46	49	46	18	19	7	1
Wilkinson	214	5.2	19 614	2 108	119	14	28	41	38	16	14	6	1
Worth	425	2.9	18 896	2 319	92	44	57	73	68	26	25	13	1
HAWAII	32 641	2.6	27 533	X	21 115	2 549	6 342	3 933	3 753	1 518	1 293	616	135
Hawaii	2 896	3.6	20 340	1 878	1 620	183	619	578	556	212	175	116	27
Honolulu	25 475	2.0	29 465	233	16 821	1 998	4 915	2 733	2 604	1 076	865	428	89
Kalawao	(3)	(3)	(3)	(3)	(3)	(3)	(3)	(3)	(3)	(3)	(3)	(3)	(3)
Kauai	1 304	4.1	23 061	1 076	778	122	250	212	203	80	79	27	10
Maui	(3)2 966	(3)5.6	(3)24 312	(3)801	(3)1 897	(3)245	(3)557	(3)409	(3)390	(5)150	(3)174	(3)45	(3)9
IDAHO	28 627	6.1	22 871	X	16 826	3 429	5 498	3 671	3 459	1 594	1 145	275	113
Ada	8 904	8.4	31 420	173	6 107	1 159	1 685	719	671	304	218	45	20
Adams	69	2.6	18 212	2 495	25	8	23	14	13	7	3	1	1
Bannock	1 516	4.1	20 252	1 905	893	96	238	223	210	80	64	19	6
Bear Lake	103	2.2	15 647	2 936	35	8	19	21	20	10	6	2	0
Benewah	173	3.2	19 064	2 267	100	24	32	32	31	15	9	3	2
Bingham	742	6.3	17 621	2 618	351	80	117	121	114	50	41	11	4
Blaine	715	6.3	41 259	37	356	109	259	33	30	16	8	1	2
Boise	114	6.6	21 492	1 523	31	8	17	15	14	8	3	1	1
Bonner	684	6.3	18 955	2 293	320	77	176	117	111	55	32	9	6
Bonneville	1 827	4.6	22 408	1 238	1 163	164	333	232	218	99	82	16	6
Boundary	174	4.9	17 410	2 665	94	22	32	33	32	15	10	3	2
Butte	58	1.6	19 376	2 189	327	5	11	11	10	5	4	1	0
Camas	19	0.4	21 585	1 495	6	3	4	2	2	1	1	0	0
Canyon	2 274	5.5	18 271	2 481	1 281	218	366	382	361	148	139	34	11
Caribou	146	1.0	20 068	1 974	118	18	28	20	19	11	5	2	1
Cassia	457	7.8	21 170	1 605	217	105	90	63	59	28	20	6	2
Clark	20	18.5	22 022	1 361	13	6	3	2	2	1	1	0	0
Clearwater	172	2.0	18 429	2 435	96	12	37	37	35	17	10	3	3

1. Based on the resident population estimated as of July 1 of the year shown.   2. Includes other labor income.   3. Kalawao County included with Maui County.

Table B. States and Counties — Earnings, Social Security, and Housing

STATE County	Earnings, 1999 Total (mil dol) [75]	Farm [76]	Goods-related[1] Total [77]	Manu-facturing [78]	Service-related and other[2] Total [79]	Retail trade [80]	Finance, insurance, and real estate [81]	Services [82]	Government [83]	Social Security beneficiaries, December 2000 Number [84]	Rate[3] [85]	Supplemental Security Income recipients, December 2000 [86]	Housing units, 1990 Total [87]	Percent change, 1980–1990 [88]
GEORGIA—Cont'd														
Richmond	4 215	0.0	20.0	14.4	43.3	9.2	3.4	23.0	36.7	31 418	157	6 793	77 288	19.2
Rockdale	1 195	0.0	D	23.9	D	11.6	3.0	19.5	8.8	8 920	127	886	19 963	64.1
Schley	41	10.9	50.8	47.7	D	4.3	D	7.2	11.6	618	164	150	1 447	16.2
Screven	132	4.7	37.6	33.5	D	8.9	2.8	10.2	22.4	2 903	189	844	5 861	6.4
Seminole	93	20.1	D	8.1	D	10.6	3.0	19.2	16.6	2 072	221	508	3 962	2.8
Spalding	721	0.0	D	27.5	D	12.6	3.6	21.4	18.5	10 490	180	1 912	20 702	21.5
Stephens	345	3.5	D	35.7	D	11.2	5.2	16.0	15.9	5 840	230	980	10 254	19.6
Stewart	37	6.2	D	27.4	D	12.9	3.2	19.1	22.0	1 081	206	351	2 156	3.2
Sumter	493	9.3	D	24.1	D	8.8	D	19.4	18.7	5 288	159	1 429	11 726	15.3
Talbot	29	5.2	D	D	D	7.6	4.7	11.9	30.1	1 353	208	368	2 645	10.8
Taliaferro	8	16.0	D	D	D	8.4	D	11.5	35.1	456	220	126	886	1.7
Tattnall	243	26.6	11.0	7.2	29.4	6.2	2.3	8.5	33.0	3 484	156	1 034	6 756	6.4
Taylor	82	14.8	D	4.6	54.3	9.5	4.5	11.8	19.8	1 655	188	567	3 162	10.4
Telfair	134	3.6	41.7	40.4	32.2	7.5	2.5	13.7	22.5	2 602	221	669	4 756	8.5
Terrell	86	14.2	D	18.1	D	9.4	3.0	14.5	23.4	2 098	191	671	4 069	-1.9
Thomas	715	2.7	D	20.7	D	11.4	3.3	31.1	16.8	8 513	199	2 172	15 936	15.5
Tift	667	4.9	25.4	19.0	48.9	14.3	2.7	18.5	20.8	6 297	164	1 475	13 359	21.4
Toombs	316	6.4	22.2	13.6	57.3	13.5	3.6	20.7	14.1	4 925	189	1 526	9 952	17.2
Towns	81	0.0	D	D	D	13.1	7.2	34.2	12.8	2 872	308	243	4 577	34.0
Treutlen	34	8.1	23.0	14.3	36.1	10.2	3.9	13.3	32.8	1 293	189	390	2 437	3.9
Troup	1 155	0.1	D	39.0	D	9.2	3.1	14.7	15.2	10 631	181	2 256	22 426	22.2
Turner	84	17.4	19.0	15.2	43.2	10.1	4.6	9.5	20.4	1 723	181	482	3 426	6.8
Twiggs	92	6.6	60.8	3.0	D	3.1	0.8	6.7	14.7	1 984	187	443	3 648	16.0
Union	161	5.1	D	5.8	D	10.9	10.3	15.7	22.3	4 839	280	470	6 624	50.9
Upson	328	0.8	46.3	40.1	36.9	8.3	3.4	21.8	16.0	5 935	215	863	10 667	9.5
Walker	503	1.7	46.0	38.0	34.2	8.8	2.8	15.3	18.1	11 978	196	1 634	23 347	11.6
Walton	455	2.9	35.9	22.9	42.0	11.1	4.7	16.4	19.2	7 877	130	1 334	14 514	39.0
Ware	529	1.5	21.8	13.2	56.0	13.3	2.6	21.8	20.7	7 006	197	1 879	14 628	6.0
Warren	59	6.2	D	45.6	28.8	4.9	1.6	12.4	14.4	1 312	207	335	2 443	5.1
Washington	342	1.9	44.5	9.9	33.5	7.0	1.7	10.7	20.1	3 751	177	1 004	7 416	11.9
Wayne	324	1.6	38.3	31.4	33.4	12.2	1.8	11.3	26.8	4 653	175	921	8 812	15.3
Webster	19	33.3	D	22.8	D	3.8	D	D	20.2	414	173	100	898	8.2
Wheeler	38	18.9	D	D	D	4.8	2.0	16.1	24.0	1 084	175	317	2 148	11.8
White	209	10.7	28.5	16.2	45.6	16.1	6.1	17.9	15.3	3 980	200	396	6 082	48.7
Whitfield	2 058	0.6	D	50.6	D	7.7	2.3	14.5	8.6	12 978	155	1 723	28 832	20.9
Wilcox	62	34.0	D	5.0	D	5.0	2.9	8.7	30.4	1 506	176	457	2 865	2.5
Wilkes	135	6.2	D	35.5	D	7.6	3.0	12.7	18.6	2 446	229	549	4 548	8.4
Wilkinson	133	0.8	60.7	43.7	27.2	3.8	1.5	6.4	11.4	1 999	196	353	4 151	9.2
Worth	136	17.2	15.8	11.4	43.7	10.1	3.2	18.9	23.2	3 672	167	787	7 597	18.7
HAWAII	23 664	0.8	8.5	2.8	60.1	11.1	8.2	29.0	30.6	183 802	152	21 019	389 810	16.6
Hawaii	1 803	2.6	D	D	D	12.3	6.4	33.2	25.3	25 835	174	3 149	48 253	41.0
Honolulu	18 819	0.3	8.3	2.8	58.2	10.3	8.5	27.2	33.2	130 535	149	15 646	281 683	11.8
Kalawao	(4)	(4)	(4)	(4)	(4)	(4)	(4)	(4)	(4)	NA	NA	NA	101	-16.5
Kauai	899	2.6	D	D	D	14.7	6.0	39.1	20.7	9 603	164	855	17 613	18.8
Maui	(4)2 143	(4)2.7	(4)D	(4)3.2	(4)D	(4)15.6	(4)8.0	(4)37.2	(4)16.1	17 829	139	1 357	42 160	27.6
IDAHO	20 255	4.6	26.3	17.4	51.0	10.2	5.1	22.5	18.0	195 695	151	18 381	413 327	10.2
Ada	7 266	0.5	33.3	23.4	52.2	9.6	6.5	22.5	14.0	36 095	120	3 390	80 849	19.2
Adams	32	-0.5	D	21.8	D	10.1	2.9	8.3	38.8	879	253	43	1 778	12.5
Bannock	989	0.5	D	11.4	D	12.3	5.5	19.8	27.2	9 697	128	1 311	25 694	3.5
Bear Lake	44	7.7	6.8	4.6	D	16.5	4.0	D	35.0	1 231	192	82	2 934	5.1
Benewah	124	0.7	D	30.2	D	7.6	1.2	16.6	17.3	1 887	206	182	3 731	6.6
Bingham	431	12.0	D	17.5	D	8.1	D	13.5	24.2	6 282	151	641	12 664	4.8
Blaine	465	1.2	23.7	3.7	65.4	12.3	10.3	33.1	9.8	1 869	98	47	9 500	29.8
Boise	39	0.2	22.2	7.3	D	6.7	D	22.0	38.9	983	147	49	2 894	22.0
Bonner	397	0.6	26.8	17.3	54.9	16.6	7.8	19.3	17.7	6 997	190	532	15 152	16.1
Bonneville	1 327	1.4	D	4.8	D	11.6	4.1	39.3	14.8	11 835	143	1 217	26 049	10.9
Boundary	116	6.8	D	21.2	D	9.0	D	20.4	22.0	1 907	193	183	3 242	17.7
Butte	332	1.0	0.7	0.1	D	0.8	0.2	94.5	2.2	596	206	51	1 265	-1.2
Camas	9	24.6	D	D	D	8.2	D	10.9	32.3	159	160	7	481	-8.7
Canyon	1 499	5.6	35.1	26.0	46.0	9.7	3.7	19.0	13.3	18 735	143	2 513	33 137	8.2
Caribou	136	5.6	60.8	38.2	20.5	4.9	1.4	6.3	13.1	1 278	175	58	2 867	-7.7
Cassia	323	27.2	17.5	11.1	40.6	11.3	3.1	14.1	14.8	3 488	163	338	7 212	2.9
Clark	19	34.5	D	D	D	3.2	2.1	2.5	23.0	123	120	8	502	12.8
Clearwater	107	0.1	32.2	27.2	D	8.0	D	13.1	37.1	2 126	238	171	3 805	-7.5

1. Covers mining, construction, and manufacturing.   2. Covers private sector earnings in agricultural services, forestry, and fisheries; transportation and public utilities; wholesale trade; retail trade; finance, insurance, and real estate; and services.   3. Per 1,000 resident population estimated as of July 1 of the year shown.   4. Kalawao County included with Maui County.

STATE County	Housing units, 1990 (cont'd)								Civilian labor force, 2001				Civilian employment, 1990[5]		
	Occupied units									Unemployment			Percent		
		Owner-occupied				Renter-occupied									
				Owner cost as a percent of income											
	Total	Percent	Median value[1]	With a mortgage	Without a mortgage	Median rent[2]	Rent as per-cent of income	Sub-stand-ard units[3] (percent)	Total	Percent change, 2000–2001	Total	Rate[4]	Total	Professional, managerial, and technical	Precision production, craft, and repair
	89	90	91	92	93	94	95	96	97	98	99	100	101	102	103
GEORGIA—Cont'd															
Richmond	68 675	56.4	58 500	20.1	12.6	390	26.3	5.0	79 030	-2.6	4 326	5.5	79 382	29.1	12.0
Rockdale	18 337	75.2	86 200	21.4	11.5	555	26.2	2.4	40 206	-0.1	1 099	2.7	28 439	28.5	14.3
Schley	1 315	72.2	40 400	18.9	14.4	246	25.5	8.3	1 833	-3.8	89	4.9	1 504	20.7	14.2
Screven	5 048	73.5	41 800	18.9	13.5	257	27.4	9.5	5 617	-3.3	535	9.5	5 626	16.2	15.2
Seminole	3 137	78.6	42 800	18.6	14.3	239	24.7	8.2	4 683	-3.4	207	4.4	3 855	17.3	15.2
Spalding	19 426	61.4	57 700	19.9	12.7	365	26.1	5.0	30 078	-0.5	1 431	4.8	25 015	20.7	14.1
Stephens	8 949	72.9	49 900	18.8	12.8	292	26.0	3.0	11 530	-1.1	694	6.0	11 097	19.8	15.7
Stewart	1 982	70.8	30 400	21.1	12.7	196	22.6	14.9	2 269	-5.7	165	7.3	2 029	18.2	16.3
Sumter	10 484	64.1	45 300	18.1	12.9	273	26.6	8.1	14 541	-2.9	956	6.6	12 375	25.6	12.1
Talbot	2 345	77.8	35 100	23.9	14.7	180	22.9	12.9	2 757	-3.3	185	6.7	2 706	15.1	14.1
Taliaferro	727	79.4	28 600	20.2	13.7	159	23.3	16.6	725	-1.1	86	11.9	726	13.5	11.3
Tattnall	5 845	68.9	43 500	18.4	12.9	244	26.2	4.9	6 841	-7.0	359	5.2	6 620	17.6	12.4
Taylor	2 804	73.2	35 800	16.8	14.5	229	29.6	9.2	3 775	-1.3	201	5.3	2 935	15.9	15.5
Telfair	4 017	76.5	31 100	18.3	13.0	232	25.8	6.2	4 355	-7.5	583	13.4	4 410	18.4	10.4
Terrell	3 738	63.6	41 200	18.8	12.4	241	28.5	12.5	3 934	-5.5	319	8.1	4 143	17.2	9.6
Thomas	14 323	68.5	46 400	20.2	14.0	317	25.8	6.0	21 541	-0.3	886	4.1	17 173	25.0	10.9
Tift	12 184	66.2	51 600	19.8	12.9	300	24.6	5.8	19 951	-5.0	902	4.5	16 075	24.0	12.1
Toombs	8 804	64.6	49 100	16.6	14.1	276	24.4	5.6	11 820	-6.4	910	7.7	10 080	23.2	12.1
Towns	2 812	87.6	69 400	27.4	12.7	276	23.8	2.2	3 987	-2.4	106	2.7	2 666	22.2	15.1
Treutlen	2 158	72.6	33 300	22.8	13.8	203	22.2	9.2	2 631	-6.5	181	6.9	2 469	16.5	17.6
Troup	20 371	64.1	54 600	20.6	13.3	348	22.0	4.5	31 796	1.1	1 496	4.7	25 071	23.0	14.5
Turner	3 043	66.4	37 000	18.8	15.6	238	27.3	7.9	4 534	9.5	407	9.0	3 197	18.8	9.2
Twiggs	3 296	80.0	37 300	20.2	14.0	251	23.5	12.1	4 049	-0.1	256	6.3	3 767	14.1	18.2
Union	4 709	82.6	58 300	21.9	11.9	313	28.6	3.8	8 023	0.2	209	2.6	4 963	21.5	14.7
Upson	9 911	70.5	41 300	17.1	13.0	272	25.3	5.9	12 011	-2.1	1 256	10.5	11 748	18.0	15.6
Walker	21 697	77.3	45 800	18.0	12.8	332	23.6	3.3	32 217	-0.2	1 272	3.9	26 571	18.6	14.9
Walton	13 433	70.6	66 700	20.6	12.8	386	25.9	6.3	30 671	0.2	1 084	3.5	18 096	18.5	19.3
Ware	13 046	69.7	41 200	20.2	13.2	287	28.2	4.5	14 799	-5.5	789	5.3	13 787	23.0	12.7
Warren	2 130	74.3	33 200	20.5	13.1	224	22.0	11.6	2 705	-2.2	276	10.2	2 409	13.8	13.8
Washington	6 739	72.0	39 600	18.1	13.5	237	21.2	10.9	9 174	-5.2	445	4.9	8 053	21.5	13.3
Wayne	7 922	72.3	44 500	16.9	13.5	264	23.1	6.4	11 064	-6.3	573	5.2	9 387	21.7	17.3
Webster	798	79.8	30 900	21.0	12.8	223	23.3	13.8	1 090	-6.5	52	4.8	951	14.4	16.1
Wheeler	1 786	75.9	29 700	20.1	15.1	177	23.5	7.3	1 759	-9.7	183	10.4	1 926	14.8	12.3
White	4 907	82.0	69 700	21.5	13.0	350	26.2	4.3	9 136	-4.5	302	3.3	6 367	23.0	12.8
Whitfield	26 859	66.9	61 200	17.5	12.0	365	21.3	4.6	46 432	-3.6	1 944	4.2	37 932	20.8	12.1
Wilcox	2 511	76.3	32 000	18.7	14.3	220	24.3	5.9	3 179	-3.8	177	5.6	2 728	18.4	12.0
Wilkes	4 022	77.4	42 200	21.4	14.6	221	21.6	8.8	4 907	-8.0	501	10.2	4 509	20.7	10.6
Wilkinson	3 619	81.1	40 000	19.4	12.2	262	23.6	9.4	4 558	-1.8	214	4.7	4 464	20.5	18.0
Worth	6 895	73.9	45 700	19.8	13.3	276	28.6	8.1	9 421	-0.1	565	6.0	8 475	18.9	14.3
HAWAII	356 267	53.9	245 300	21.4	10.8	650	27.4	15.6	605 524	1.7	28 081	4.6	529 059	29.9	10.5
Hawaii	41 461	61.1	113 000	20.5	10.9	490	27.0	13.2	72 254	3.2	4 949	6.8	54 348	26.0	12.0
Honolulu	265 304	52.0	283 600	21.5	10.7	663	27.6	15.9	429 252	1.3	17 517	4.1	395 811	31.5	9.9
Kalawao	62	0.0	0	0.0	0.0	125	10.0	0.0	NA	NA	NA	NA	41	34.1	0.0
Kauai	16 295	58.8	171 500	21.2	10.9	618	24.1	13.7	29 835	1.5	2 091	7.0	25 241	25.1	12.2
Maui	33 145	57.6	202 100	22.3	11.1	722	27.1	16.7	74 184	2.5	3 524	4.8	53 618	23.5	12.4
IDAHO	360 723	70.1	58 200	19.3	11.8	330	23.8	4.5	682 228	3.7	33 836	5.0	443 703	27.1	11.3
Ada	77 471	69.1	70 500	20.2	11.5	401	24.9	2.6	180 161	4.6	6 313	3.5	104 423	34.3	10.0
Adams	1 251	75.3	43 900	18.6	11.4	254	15.0	4.5	1 646	2.4	223	13.5	1 293	21.3	11.1
Bannock	23 412	68.7	53 300	18.5	11.6	294	24.3	3.8	40 750	3.6	1 932	4.7	29 061	30.2	11.0
Bear Lake	2 005	83.2	38 700	17.5	13.1	276	22.0	4.6	2 829	1.1	142	5.0	2 081	21.8	14.4
Benewah	2 991	76.4	44 500	17.1	12.7	246	19.8	8.1	4 409	0.0	448	10.2	3 044	17.9	11.8
Bingham	11 513	76.7	50 700	17.6	11.7	284	23.0	7.8	22 419	2.9	1 031	4.6	15 003	23.0	12.2
Blaine	5 506	64.2	127 400	22.1	13.7	474	23.1	3.8	12 155	7.7	355	2.9	7 800	30.9	17.4
Boise	1 357	79.2	59 700	18.8	11.0	306	18.0	8.3	2 532	9.2	126	5.0	1 438	27.3	15.2
Bonner	10 269	75.8	60 500	22.5	12.7	318	24.6	7.0	17 548	1.7	1 425	8.1	10 445	23.1	12.9
Bonneville	24 289	71.5	63 700	17.4	11.7	366	23.0	4.1	47 562	2.9	1 585	3.3	32 016	36.7	10.4
Boundary	2 857	78.3	49 500	20.0	12.1	296	21.0	10.0	4 570	3.2	416	9.1	3 045	19.0	11.1
Butte	997	74.6	41 400	15.4	12.0	243	17.0	5.4	1 636	3.1	63	3.9	1 198	20.7	11.3
Camas	275	75.6	35 500	15.0	11.8	235	20.0	3.3	399	1.5	20	5.0	326	18.4	14.4
Canyon	31 288	68.7	51 900	20.1	11.5	306	23.5	6.2	69 082	4.9	3 649	5.3	39 181	21.8	12.6
Caribou	2 262	80.2	48 200	17.9	12.0	249	15.6	3.9	3 396	9.7	197	5.8	2 625	22.4	12.8
Cassia	6 373	71.4	46 100	16.3	12.2	274	21.1	7.0	9 667	2.7	536	5.5	7 708	21.2	11.2
Clark	277	62.8	37 300	14.3	12.8	281	14.6	6.0	658	13.6	29	4.4	416	17.8	8.2
Clearwater	3 213	74.3	43 000	14.4	11.2	268	17.2	2.2	3 776	-3.2	563	14.9	3 061	23.1	10.9

1. Specified owner-occupied units. 2. Specified renter-occupied units. 3. Overcrowded or lacking complete plumbing facilities. 4. Percent of civilian labor force. 5. Persons 16 years and older.

Table B. States and Counties — Nonfarm Employment and Agriculture

| | Private nonfarm establishments, employment and payroll, 1999 | | | | | | | | | Agriculture, 1997 | | | |
| | | Employment | | | | | | Annual payroll | | Farms | | | Farm operators |
STATE County	Number of establishments	Total	Health Care and Social Assistance	Manufacturing	Retail trade	Finance and Insurance	Professional Scientific and Technical Services	Total (mil dol)	Average per employee (dollars)	Number	Percent with— Less than 50 acres	500 acres and over	Whose principal occupation is farming (percent)
	104	105	106	107	108	109	110	111	112	113	114	115	116
GEORGIA—Cont'd													
Richmond	4 533	80 286	15 526	12 201	12 955	2 515	2 319	2 088	26 008	106	49.1	3.8	37.7
Rockdale	1 934	31 080	2 652	6 912	4 844	523	1 077	902	29 031	102	64.7	6.9	35.3
Schley	66	924	D	581	75	D	D	22	23 786	91	19.8	22.0	49.5
Screven	236	2 855	308	1 257	492	106	25	61	21 408	325	14.2	27.4	42.5
Seminole	197	1 400	385	85	380	39	22	26	18 715	183	24.6	28.4	54.6
Spalding	1 210	19 315	2 869	6 088	3 230	544	295	435	22 520	193	40.4	5.2	32.6
Stephens	588	9 610	1 033	3 745	1 150	242	156	208	21 619	188	38.8	2.7	43.1
Stewart	90	841	197	D	111	38	D	19	22 262	77	13.0	33.8	46.8
Sumter	700	12 555	2 711	3 124	2 119	305	158	270	21 473	314	16.9	31.5	57.3
Talbot	62	442	D	D	61	D	9	11	24 172	111	16.2	20.7	36.0
Taliaferro	22	106	D	D	D	D	D	2	14 915	55	12.7	18.2	40.0
Tattnall	300	2 968	489	425	586	185	70	51	17 073	589	31.2	10.5	49.4
Taylor	141	1 393	D	151	281	25	17	31	21 968	196	11.2	20.9	37.8
Telfair	234	4 033	476	2 288	413	93	33	67	16 542	271	13.7	16.2	51.3
Terrell	183	1 960	200	834	331	62	37	38	19 460	174	17.2	43.1	51.7
Thomas	1 082	17 634	2 775	4 232	2 445	519	273	394	22 367	421	31.8	20.9	49.6
Tift	1 118	17 666	2 223	4 541	2 659	498	402	406	22 965	359	30.9	16.7	50.4
Toombs	703	10 389	1 428	2 405	1 611	312	344	201	19 328	401	21.4	13.2	39.2
Towns	270	2 032	305	98	437	113	38	44	21 481	121	45.5	0.0	47.1
Treutlen	93	728	138	222	103	D	D	10	13 790	157	17.8	11.5	29.3
Troup	1 378	29 762	2 906	10 017	3 845	793	382	841	28 252	221	24.4	9.0	30.8
Turner	181	1 721	135	445	216	90	24	33	18 947	230	12.2	26.5	66.1
Twiggs	92	1 574	177	31	140	D	15	57	36 005	98	28.6	14.3	43.9
Union	451	3 531	590	410	629	177	115	69	19 568	256	53.5	2.3	35.5
Upson	516	9 083	1 250	4 436	984	220	81	190	20 891	185	22.7	8.6	27.6
Walker	891	16 067	1 483	6 936	1 842	358	1 282	346	21 547	478	34.3	6.3	34.3
Walton	1 156	10 209	986	2 170	1 709	424	284	247	24 162	493	42.6	4.3	33.1
Ware	983	12 785	2 573	2 167	2 775	452	209	274	21 410	274	34.3	11.3	40.9
Warren	81	1 376	204	776	137	30	4	33	24 326	134	17.2	17.9	46.3
Washington	418	7 052	863	697	904	160	143	230	32 629	327	17.1	19.3	38.8
Wayne	516	7 618	1 606	1 882	1 714	160	93	167	21 933	276	30.8	10.9	41.3
Webster	24	232	D	D	34	0	0	7	29 466	76	10.5	34.2	59.2
Wheeler	70	795	200	19	78	D	8	16	20 020	176	9.1	22.2	36.9
White	547	4 557	331	780	1 016	131	77	91	19 874	284	51.8	2.1	45.1
Whitfield	2 561	54 518	2 932	26 570	7 076	910	754	1 493	27 379	325	42.2	4.3	34.5
Wilcox	102	645	131	155	158	52	D	12	17 944	273	16.1	25.3	54.9
Wilkes	287	3 575	420	1 594	396	97	D	80	22 249	298	15.8	14.4	29.2
Wilkinson	162	2 922	124	1 492	149	58	D	98	33 589	88	11.4	18.2	39.8
Worth	286	2 511	424	559	512	90	D	49	19 565	406	24.6	30.0	59.9
HAWAII	29 569	419 047	49 343	14 512	60 266	19 540	18 137	11 662	27 830	5 473	89.0	2.6	55.8
Hawaii	3 548	41 739	5 392	1 621	7 644	941	1 194	1 011	24 215	3 319	89.0	2.6	55.1
Honolulu	20 583	307 514	37 259	10 806	41 145	17 329	15 605	8 924	29 020	880	93.2	1.7	67.6
Kalawao	NA	NA	NA	NA	NA	NA	NA	NA	NA	NA	NA	NA	NA
Kauai	1 648	19 377	2 308	397	3 433	462	502	464	23 921	468	84.8	3.0	54.5
Maui	3 790	50 417	4 384	1 688	8 044	808	836	1 264	25 064	806	87.0	3.5	46.1
IDAHO	36 975	434 461	51 281	65 992	67 227	17 071	22 432	11 027	25 381	22 314	39.0	22.6	54.0
Ada	9 854	145 958	16 321	19 169	18 190	7 972	6 683	4 310	29 531	1 221	70.7	5.7	38.2
Adams	107	692	D	D	92	41	D	15	21 796	279	40.9	27.6	48.4
Bannock	1 882	23 616	3 245	3 695	4 420	1 444	1 055	551	23 322	664	44.0	20.6	40.5
Bear Lake	120	971	211	74	300	49	D	15	15 900	410	20.2	28.5	47.1
Benewah	292	2 336	326	477	292	47	55	59	25 345	226	26.1	31.4	47.8
Bingham	774	9 003	1 143	2 347	1 529	199	182	185	20 587	1 168	44.6	22.9	52.0
Blaine	1 275	9 791	476	286	1 339	238	620	245	25 060	195	31.3	31.3	57.9
Boise	123	462	10	D	62	D	D	8	17 708	78	25.6	24.4	46.2
Bonner	1 248	10 949	1 040	1 836	2 450	228	284	232	21 149	501	43.3	8.8	43.3
Bonneville	2 632	36 647	4 445	3 047	5 899	1 120	8 372	1 142	31 152	787	44.0	23.8	51.1
Boundary	358	2 321	197	349	372	55	48	52	22 434	312	37.2	11.9	45.2
Butte	63	352	105	D	89	30	D	6	18 301	207	21.3	31.9	63.3
Camas	21	150	D	D	19	D	0	1	8 440	98	10.2	55.1	70.4
Canyon	2 870	37 305	4 599	10 790	4 923	818	794	910	24 392	1 898	56.4	7.5	51.1
Caribou	186	1 938	167	D	352	D	D	70	36 014	427	15.2	46.6	57.8
Cassia	611	6 047	865	1 085	1 277	200	181	123	20 287	729	30.6	35.9	66.9
Clark	19	109	D	0	33	11	0	1	12 862	83	8.4	59.0	63.9
Clearwater	264	2 280	369	435	305	D	61	51	22 391	210	24.3	20.5	46.7

Table B. States and Counties — Agriculture, Land, and Water

STATE County	Land in farms Acreage (1,000) [117]	Percent change, 1992–1997 [118]	Acres Average size of farm [119]	Acres Total irrigated (1,000) [120]	Acres Total cropland (1,000) [121]	Value of land and buildings Average per farm ($1,000) [122]	Value of land and buildings Average per acre (dollars) [123]	Value of machinery and equipment average per farm ($1,000) [124]	Value of products sold Total (mil dol) [125]	Value of products sold Average per farm (dollars) [126]	Percent from Crops [127]	Percent from Livestock and poultry products [128]	Percent of farms with sales of $10,000 or more [129]	Percent of farms with sales of $100,000 or more [130]	Percent of land owned by fed. gov. 1997 [131]	Water consumption 1995 (mil gal/day) [132]
GEORGIA—Cont'd																
Richmond	15	-7.7	139	D	10	194	1 388	25	4	38 749	59.6	40.5	30.2	5.7	21.2	127.3
Rockdale	12	-7.7	118	0	4	418	3 226	22	1	11 825	47.4	52.6	19.6	2.0	0.0	2.3
Schley	41	7.6	449	1	16	703	1 565	50	12	132 136	24.8	75.2	41.8	23.1	0.0	1.8
Screven	165	18.5	507	10	90	497	1 016	59	30	91 820	86.9	13.1	46.5	16.3	0.0	8.1
Seminole	107	-1.5	587	29	68	714	1 227	118	40	217 821	92.3	7.7	66.7	30.1	3.7	23.7
Spalding	27	11.2	138	D	13	405	2 688	20	5	26 127	21.9	78.1	19.7	5.2	0.0	10.1
Stephens	20	22.5	104	D	10	258	2 508	25	41	219 608	1.2	98.8	29.8	16.5	20.3	3.1
Stewart	56	14.7	730	3	17	601	823	62	6	81 196	60.0	40.0	45.5	16.9	0.4	3.5
Sumter	186	9.7	594	30	122	576	1 060	88	92	291 658	80.8	19.2	54.5	30.6	0.0	28.4
Talbot	36	-4.0	329	D	11	415	992	20	2	16 468	10.0	90.0	23.4	1.8	0.0	2.9
Taliaferro	16	-13.9	297		5	279	939	31	3	56 425	2.3	97.7	40.0	12.7	0.0	0.2
Tattnall	137	14.1	232	11	66	301	1 540	37	144	244 885	42.5	57.5	47.7	27.5	2.1	18.4
Taylor	70	28.9	355	1	27	345	948	48	29	148 537	24.7	75.3	37.8	13.3	0.0	2.1
Telfair	86	21.4	318	7	32	345	1 147	41	10	38 349	79.5	20.5	39.5	11.4	0.0	10.4
Terrell	139	-3.1	797	15	88	750	969	83	28	159 838	97.1	2.9	62.6	37.9	0.0	20.8
Thomas	180	3.3	427	5	79	662	1 560	59	38	89 419	87.0	13.0	46.6	22.6	0.0	12.7
Tift	106	-6.9	296	17	67	548	1 704	61	54	149 897	93.8	6.2	57.7	20.9	0.0	34.5
Toombs	100	12.3	249	9	42	269	1 108	35	29	73 244	87.5	12.5	31.7	13.5	0.0	7.0
Towns	9	-12.9	72	D	5	224	2 907	26	1	8 329	15.2	84.7	12.4	1.7	60.4	2.0
Treutlen	42	27.4	268	1	12	198	722	23	3	18 474	88.8	11.2	17.2	4.5	0.0	1.7
Troup	43	4.9	195	D	20	283	1 566	18	4	19 573	24.3	75.7	27.6	4.1	8.0	13.3
Turner	98	-0.8	427	9	63	540	1 320	92	35	150 149	80.3	19.7	74.3	33.5	0.0	19.1
Twiggs	26	-15.5	267	1	11	368	1 029	39	4	37 612	76.9	23.1	31.6	7.1	0.1	23.3
Union	22	0.7	87	0	11	384	4 730	46	17	66 255	D	D	26.6	4.7	46.5	1.4
Upson	38	13.7	203	0	15	269	1 491	27	10	53 462	9.4	90.6	20.5	7.0	0.0	11.1
Walker	86	-3.8	179	D	39	304	1 644	21	28	58 935	4.4	95.6	26.2	6.7	7.3	10.9
Walton	60	6.8	121	1	31	449	3 393	25	29	59 281	26.1	73.9	24.5	8.1	0.0	5.8
Ware	64	19.1	235	2	20	289	1 147	30	18	65 522	57.1	42.9	37.2	13.5	31.4	5.9
Warren	44	-5.4	332	D	15	271	821	29	4	32 791	10.3	89.7	30.6	8.2	0.1	5.0
Washington	111	-1.1	339	5	56	318	876	30	12	35 497	72.2	27.8	34.6	9.8	0.0	24.4
Wayne	65	20.8	236	5	33	407	1 730	44	17	61 724	80.9	19.1	37.7	14.5	0.1	66.0
Webster	58	8.6	758	3	29	810	1 070	90	9	118 219	94.1	5.9	56.6	35.5	0.0	5.4
Wheeler	71	45.5	405	3	20	320	720	42	9	50 299	91.5	8.5	34.7	8.5	0.0	3.1
White	26	9.6	93	0	12	367	3 834	25	53	187 285	1.7	98.3	39.1	23.9	27.5	5.9
Whitfield	39	-0.6	119	0	20	361	2 602	36	46	141 679	2.4	97.6	30.5	13.8	6.1	38.9
Wilcox	123	6.2	451	17	73	382	826	70	52	190 286	47.4	52.6	62.6	27.8	0.0	15.3
Wilkes	95	2.1	319	D	32	325	925	27	22	73 937	4.2	95.8	28.9	6.4	2.1	4.1
Wilkinson	28	-14.0	313		8	233	746	29	1	14 454	45.0	55.0	31.8	2.3	0.0	23.4
Worth	191	-4.6	470	21	122	577	1 215	92	65	159 241	87.2	12.8	62.8	35.5	0.0	29.1
HAWAII	1 439	-9.4	263	77	292	632	2 405	39	497	90 798	80.8	19.2	41.9	8.2	8.7	1 012.4
Hawaii	870	-6.1	262	7	103	574	2 192	22	168	50 651	76.7	23.3	40.7	6.4	10.3	115.8
Honolulu	80	-13.1	91	16	29	565	6 225	33	143	162 460	72.4	27.6	57.5	14.5	12.5	278.9
Kalawao	NA	NA	NA	NA	NA	NA	NA	NA	NA	NA	NA	NA	NA	NA	NA	0.0
Kauai	197	-7.9	421	18	D	848	2 013	81	57	122 808	91.9	8.1	30.8	4.9	0.7	243.8
Maui	292	-18.0	362	35	D	818	2 258	89	128	159 287	90.4	9.6	36.4	10.3	5.3	373.9
IDAHO	11 830	-12.2	530	3 494	6 309	537	1 017	78	3 346	149 945	53.0	47.0	53.5	21.5	62.7	15 141.5
Ada	231	-0.8	189	78	90	362	1 891	40	94	76 756	38.8	61.2	33.8	11.2	42.6	1 098.3
Adams	200	-9.3	719	28	48	535	651	33	8	29 890	13.4	86.6	42.7	6.1	63.9	63.7
Bannock	309	-4.8	466	42	167	257	658	43	25	37 699	62.3	37.7	35.7	8.1	27.4	313.5
Bear Lake	222	-17.6	541	50	121	341	634	34	15	36 284	23.1	76.9	54.6	11.7	44.2	117.3
Benewah	126	12.5	557	0	77	507	960	60	11	50 595	91.9	8.1	31.0	14.2	10.1	8.0
Bingham	796	-42.0	682	322	378	651	932	105	225	193 059	75.0	25.0	55.7	26.2	26.8	1 093.7
Blaine	215	-19.2	1 102	57	70	1 446	1 361	70	24	120 943	53.8	46.2	62.6	25.6	77.0	160.2
Boise	45	-43.2	583	3	7	519	891	34	2	28 885	52.6	47.4	41.0	5.1	73.3	15.2
Bonner	99	-34.2	197	2	37	357	1 781	26	7	14 509	55.4	44.6	24.0	2.8	40.2	35.2
Bonneville	449	-1.0	571	154	312	504	800	85	91	115 106	79.7	20.3	51.0	19.8	47.8	644.9
Boundary	73	-0.4	233	3	51	400	1 892	37	14	43 401	86.5	13.5	43.6	11.2	58.9	2.3
Butte	130	-18.5	626	62	70	492	775	85	22	103 932	69.3	30.7	71.0	28.5	86.8	167.6
Camas	128	-1.2	1 301	12	80	832	639	73	9	89 944	77.3	22.7	73.5	25.5	64.0	27.0
Canyon	355	-9.2	187	221	235	399	2 225	65	311	164 066	50.2	49.8	51.6	21.3	3.4	639.0
Caribou	469	-20.2	1 099	81	265	663	578	76	43	100 510	68.6	31.4	59.5	26.0	40.3	225.4
Cassia	657	-1.4	901	266	378	918	932	155	333	456 541	42.8	57.2	70.4	37.2	53.0	585.5
Clark	215	-25.0	2 594	56	D	1 370	528	159	32	385 897	74.9	25.1	74.7	43.4	65.1	105.8
Clearwater	73	-29.0	348	0	42	310	1 198	30	5	23 091	79.8	20.2	34.3	5.2	51.5	36.4

Table B. States and Counties — Residential Construction, Wholesale and Retail Trade, and Real Estate

STATE County	Value of Residential Construction Authorized by Building Permits, 2000		Wholesale Trade, 1997				Retail Trade[1], 1997				Real Estate and Rental and Leasing, 1997			
	New Construction ($1,000)	Number of Housing Units	Number of Establishments	Number of Employees	Sales (mil dol)	Annual Payroll (mil dol)	Number of Establishments	Number of Employees	Sales (mil dol)	Annual Payroll (mil dol)	Number of Establishments	Number of Employees	Receipts (mil dol)	Annual Payroll (mil dol)
	133	134	135	136	137	138	139	140	141	142	143	144	145	146
GEORGIA—Cont'd														
Richmond	56 865	525	245	2 262	756.9	68.8	912	12 332	1 909.9	189.3	223	1 064	114.0	20.4
Rockdale	62 166	766	124	1 267	1 230.4	47.3	281	4 411	766.0	71.4	58	250	36.6	4.9
Schley	350	4	9	57	21.5	1.5	14	96	9.9	1.1	1	D	D	D
Screven	360	6	8	41	9.8	0.7	56	483	82.1	7.0	7	7	0.6	0.1
Seminole	0	0	14	182	83.0	2.0	61	413	71.5	5.4	5	13	1.0	0.1
Spalding	35 300	430	49	611	338.5	18.4	248	3 119	521.5	52.1	47	170	13.9	2.5
Stephens	10 182	91	28	222	50.8	5.1	121	1 247	203.9	17.8	14	31	4.7	0.5
Stewart	0	0	5	39	9.7	1.2	26	133	14.5	1.3	2	D	D	D
Sumter	3 403	72	42	430	168.9	11.0	162	1 984	283.9	28.1	23	62	6.3	1.0
Talbot	3 815	35	2	D	D	D	13	68	7.1	0.7	NA	NA	NA	NA
Taliaferro	NA	NA	2	D	D	D	4	D	D	D	1	D	D	D
Tattnall	343	4	19	389	58.4	7.3	78	581	76.2	6.7	6	10	1.0	0.1
Taylor	781	14	7	D	D	D	36	227	36.5	2.8	4	3	0.4	0.0
Telfair	300	1	14	237	53.6	4.5	60	407	49.5	4.9	3	7	0.8	0.1
Terrell	1 944	48	17	198	125.8	4.3	57	321	55.3	4.2	2	D	D	D
Thomas	17 787	192	64	701	293.0	21.0	256	2 661	395.8	39.0	32	135	15.9	2.6
Tift	9 723	116	88	1 117	459.4	26.6	260	2 500	440.4	36.1	37	127	11.4	1.7
Toombs	1 963	24	39	333	203.6	8.4	152	1 706	253.7	23.1	17	67	5.7	0.9
Towns	19 465	181	7	D	D	D	52	289	42.4	3.9	13	22	2.6	0.3
Treutlen	0	0	2	D	D	D	23	111	14.2	1.3	3	5	0.2	0.0
Troup	43 685	590	69	681	270.8	22.6	293	3 500	526.0	52.7	45	175	18.9	3.4
Turner	130	4	16	230	203.8	5.8	54	316	58.3	4.4	6	40	4.4	0.6
Twiggs	2 234	22	3	D	D	D	14	116	17.2	1.6	2	D	D	D
Union	42 409	401	15	92	37.3	2.1	75	592	101.8	8.2	16	22	3.7	0.3
Upson	12 010	138	17	112	17.0	1.4	121	1 119	174.5	14.5	12	39	3.3	0.5
Walker	27 133	334	58	D	D	D	180	1 515	240.1	22.4	22	67	4.5	0.9
Walton	125 697	1 241	45	322	239.9	10.4	162	1 567	247.6	25.0	35	108	12.7	1.4
Ware	6 557	67	62	493	169.4	10.4	226	2 628	390.1	35.8	26	131	14.9	2.1
Warren	0	0	3	6	0.8	0.1	22	128	12.5	1.9	1	D	D	D
Washington	1 071	13	24	157	37.8	4.0	108	925	139.3	13.2	12	26	3.4	0.4
Wayne	1 246	13	17	159	50.7	3.9	125	1 145	172.5	16.6	9	57	2.6	0.5
Webster	NA	NA	2	D	D	D	8	80	7.6	0.8	NA	NA	NA	NA
Wheeler	0	0	3	D	D	D	13	64	11.1	0.7	1	D	D	D
White	33 296	315	12	110	23.6	1.8	139	1 028	230.4	18.3	20	36	4.4	0.5
Whitfield	41 433	876	340	4 254	3 475.7	122.9	508	5 908	1 068.1	103.7	87	365	61.3	8.2
Wilcox	0	0	5	D	D	D	30	138	20.1	1.8	2	D	D	D
Wilkes	1 123	13	18	138	61.5	3.1	65	414	56.3	5.2	3	6	0.5	0.1
Wilkinson	NA	NA	7	125	24.8	3.3	29	190	29.5	2.3	NA	NA	NA	NA
Worth	4 356	44	32	308	118.7	7.9	62	461	101.5	8.1	10	24	2.2	0.3
HAWAII	823 363	4 905	1 872	18 532	7 147.5	576.0	5 088	64 218	11 317.8	1 161.8	1 753	12 446	1 824.1	311.9
Hawaii	231 366	1 503	179	1 362	457.3	35.9	688	7 587	1 183.1	128.5	211	1 838	196.9	39.0
Honolulu	288 748	1 969	1 463	15 423	6 079.9	487.0	3 269	44 960	8 264.7	823.6	1 221	7 746	1 219.9	208.4
Kalawao	NA	NA	NA	NA	NA	NA	NA	NA	NA	NA	NA	NA	NA	NA
Kauai	94 392	290	64	423	176.7	11.9	326	3 427	510.7	59.0	108	1 166	131.7	24.8
Maui	208 856	1 143	166	1 324	433.6	41.2	805	8 244	1 359.3	150.7	213	1 696	275.6	39.7
IDAHO	1 358 934	10 915	1 980	22 828	10 127.8	628.0	5 848	63 732	11 649.6	1 079.7	1 236	4 870	450.3	73.9
Ada	567 329	3 999	578	7 610	5 362.7	273.5	1 264	16 663	3 163.2	300.9	379	1 860	197.1	33.5
Adams	7 612	43	1	D	D	D	16	81	13.4	0.9	1	D	D	D
Bannock	23 347	235	104	935	282.6	25.2	343	4 177	705.7	65.1	64	255	23.5	3.5
Bear Lake	7 398	71	3	88	20.2	1.5	34	271	40.2	3.3	7	60	1.2	0.4
Benewah	1 969	18	8	52	17.6	1.2	41	313	50.2	4.9	4	17	0.9	0.3
Bingham	11 475	112	54	974	189.4	18.0	125	1 363	243.8	22.0	14	44	1.8	0.4
Blaine	122 551	397	41	301	172.3	12.3	189	1 372	226.9	26.3	73	292	31.0	4.9
Boise	8 894	88	NA	NA	NA	NA	18	65	6.6	0.5	NA	NA	NA	NA
Bonner	2 182	23	37	256	69.8	6.2	200	2 325	573.8	41.5	46	170	14.4	2.9
Bonneville	48 657	563	181	2 484	808.0	63.2	480	5 615	933.4	90.1	69	368	19 2	3.6
Boundary	4 175	31	12	89	16.7	2.9	54	373	61.6	6.1	8	22	1.8	0.3
Butte	0	0	3	D	D	D	15	81	10.6	0.9	NA	NA	NA	NA
Camas	2 744	21	1	D	D	D	4	11	3.0	0.1	NA	NA	NA	NA
Canyon	209 920	2 043	157	1 512	555.2	38.4	429	4 724	1 014.1	88.9	88	268	22.9	3.6
Caribou	2 426	24	15	64	25.3	1.6	42	301	57.8	4.5	3	7	0.3	0.1
Cassia	5 990	43	40	271	218.6	6.3	116	1 144	193.0	19.2	17	39	3.0	0.6
Clark	0	0	1	D	D	D	4	40	4.5	0.3	NA	NA	NA	NA
Clearwater	3 407	52	5	D	D	D	45	331	56.8	5.0	6	D	D	D

1. Establishments with payroll.

STATE County	Professional, Scientific, and Technical Services[1], 1997				Manufacturing, 1997				Accommodation and Foodservices, 1997			
	Number of Establishments	Number of Employees	Receipts (mil dol)	Annual Payroll (mil dol)	Number of Establishments	Number of Employees	Receipts (mil dol)	Annual Payroll (mil dol)	Number of Establishments	Number of Employees	Sales (mil dol)	Annual Payroll (mil dol)
	147	148	149	150	151	152	153	154	155	156	157	158
GEORGIA—Cont'd												
Richmond	324	1 931	147.2	58.3	134	12 084	4 092.6	423.4	400	8 301	255.6	70.4
Rockdale	141	777	55.7	22.2	116	6 730	1 625.1	200.0	122	2 657	86.6	23.5
Schley	2	D	D	D	9	589	115.4	14.6	4	6	0.3	0.1
Screven	12	28	1.2	0.4	13	1 289	127.8	33.9	18	89	4.0	0.9
Seminole	8	30	1.5	0.5	NA	NA	NA	NA	10	82	2.9	0.6
Spalding	65	302	23.2	8.0	70	6 328	1 118.8	150.7	92	1 524	46.7	12.6
Stephens	33	111	7.9	2.4	64	3 970	634.8	88.4	44	844	21.3	5.7
Stewart	1	D	D	D	NA	NA	NA	NA	6	30	1.7	0.4
Sumter	31	136	9.5	3.3	38	3 163	475.4	71.3	51	770	23.5	6.2
Talbot	3	7	0.3	0.1	NA	NA	NA	NA	6	D	D	D
Taliaferro	NA	NA	NA	NA	NA	NA	NA	NA	1	D	D	D
Tattnall	12	51	2.4	0.8	12	762	62.9	8.4	19	241	6.6	1.6
Taylor	8	21	1.0	0.4	NA	NA	NA	NA	6	48	1.3	0.3
Telfair	12	19	1.0	0.3	14	1 946	566.3	37.0	19	175	4.9	1.1
Terrell	5	41	2.1	0.8	13	786	141.6	15.1	9	D	D	D
Thomas	45	221	18.1	6.6	72	4 926	933.7	108.6	64	1 100	36.9	9.6
Tift	55	297	25.1	8.6	51	4 449	613.3	103.7	80	1 434	44.3	12.8
Toombs	39	174	13.5	4.5	38	2 516	169.3	41.6	60	814	22.8	5.7
Towns	9	34	1.5	0.7	NA	NA	NA	NA	24	381	14.8	4.8
Treutlen	4	12	0.5	0.2	NA	NA	NA	NA	8	131	2.3	0.7
Troup	71	301	21.0	8.6	101	9 369	1 807.7	284.2	111	1 757	50.6	12.8
Turner	7	16	0.7	0.2	10	686	66.1	11.8	16	194	6.0	0.9
Twiggs	4	7	0.4	0.2	NA	NA	NA	NA	4	D	D	D
Union	25	69	3.9	1.8	NA	NA	NA	NA	27	272	8.4	2.3
Upson	24	57	4.0	0.9	26	4 241	555.1	82.9	46	502	14.6	3.8
Walker	46	197	12.7	4.6	77	6 555	1 207.7	159.9	51	658	20.0	5.1
Walton	62	160	10.9	3.7	55	2 611	441.5	70.4	45	D	D	D
Ware	55	161	10.2	3.5	42	2 121	287.4	55.8	63	1 180	34.4	9.9
Warren	2	D	D	D	6	798	131.0	20.0	1	D	D	D
Washington	18	132	6.0	2.9	18	917	131.7	22.3	20	D	D	D
Wayne	25	74	4.1	1.4	23	1 816	460.6	56.0	34	555	15.7	4.1
Webster	NA	NA	NA	NA	NA	NA	NA	NA	NA	NA	NA	NA
Wheeler	2	D	D	D	NA	NA	NA	NA	3	8	0.4	0.0
White	20	49	2.7	0.7	28	952	172.8	27.0	73	666	25.3	6.6
Whitfield	144	856	64.4	29.3	379	27 373	6 166.5	687.5	143	2 565	92.0	25.4
Wilcox	NA	NA	NA	NA	NA	NA	NA	NA	1	D	D	D
Wilkes	10	35	1.6	0.3	23	1 584	315.4	36.8	13	D	D	D
Wilkinson	6	15	1.0	0.3	14	1 307	391.2	49.7	8	D	D	D
Worth	10	26	1.4	0.5	NA	NA	NA	NA	18	D	D	D
HAWAII	2 480	15 743	1 574.0	606.5	921	15 109	3 192.5	405.0	3 081	88 083	5 007.9	1 507.5
Hawaii	246	933	73.3	24.9	106	1 588	192.5	37.5	326	10 441	546.6	188.1
Honolulu	1 917	13 729	1 400.6	546.8	685	11 161	2 692.2	300.9	2 125	53 916	3 036.8	852.8
Kalawao	NA	NA	NA	NA	NA	NA	NA	NA	NA	NA	NA	NA
Kauai	90	327	25.0	9.0	NA	NA	NA	NA	210	5 775	293.8	102.3
Maui	227	754	75.2	25.7	100	1 919	259.6	51.3	420	17 951	1 130.7	364.4
IDAHO	2 364	19 669	2 046.1	756.2	1 647	66 184	16 952.9	2 099.8	2 978	42 067	1 232.5	345.7
Ada	805	6 419	903.2	264.2	395	20 850	6 318.4	862.6	648	12 105	370.1	103.9
Adams	2	D	D	D	NA	NA	NA	NA	14	134	3.4	1.7
Bannock	108	934	47.4	22.5	62	3 482	775.1	119.2	188	2 792	75.3	20.5
Bear Lake	2	D	D	D	NA	NA	NA	NA	13	90	2.8	0.7
Benewah	13	44	1.6	0.7	8	586	141.8	20.2	26	181	4.2	1.3
Bingham	26	110	6.4	2.6	44	2 413	366.1	64.2	51	583	12.6	3.7
Blaine	102	524	55.0	19.2	NA	NA	NA	NA	131	3 365	115.3	34.3
Boise	5	13	1.5	0.4	NA	NA	NA	NA	23	110	3.1	0.7
Bonner	86	214	13.6	5.5	86	1 898	382.1	56.8	115	1 385	33.6	11.1
Bonneville	210	7 327	748.5	338.6	115	2 550	267.9	55.8	180	3 381	90.3	25.9
Boundary	11	31	1.3	0.5	NA	NA	NA	NA	24	276	13.3	2.5
Butte	1	D	D	D	NA	NA	NA	NA	9	50	1.5	0.3
Camas	NA	NA	NA	NA	NA	NA	NA	NA	5	D	D	D
Canyon	128	553	35.4	12.7	176	9 817	3 581.7	268.2	188	2 619	71.4	19.1
Caribou	14	26	1.2	0.3	7	D	D	D	16	129	2.7	0.7
Cassia	30	D	D	D	24	D	D	D	48	653	17.9	4.8
Clark	NA	NA	NA	NA	NA	NA	NA	NA	3	D	D	D
Clearwater	9	40	1.7	0.6	NA	NA	NA	NA	31	186	4.7	1.3

1. Firms subject to federal tax.

Table B. States and Counties — Health and Other Services and Federal Funds

STATE County	Health Care and Social Assistance[1], 1997				Other Services[1], 1997				Federal funds and grants, fiscal 2001[2] Expenditures (mil dol)			
										Direct payments for individuals[3]		
	Number of Establishments	Number of Employees	Receipts (mil dol)	Annual Payroll (mil dol)	Number of Establishments	Number of Employees	Receipts (mil dol)	Annual Payroll (mil dol)	Total	Social Security and government retirement	Medicare	Food stamps and Supplemental Security Income
	159	160	161	162	163	164	165	166	167	168	169	170
GEORGIA—Cont'd												
Richmond	500	5 944	498.0	212.2	282	1 997	102.3	33.3	1 309.4	577.7	153.3	60.0
Rockdale	127	1 615	94.8	43.0	109	518	35.0	9.4	181.9	114.6	35.5	7.4
Schley	2	D	D	D	2	D	D	D	23.0	6.6	3.3	1.2
Screven	13	173	6.4	2.9	13	36	2.9	0.7	86.6	30.3	15.6	5.3
Seminole	15	95	5.8	2.8	17	60	3.6	1.0	60.2	23.5	9.6	3.9
Spalding	103	1 979	107.0	45.3	71	438	28.3	8.5	254.6	119.1	50.5	14.3
Stephens	36	531	32.4	10.2	38	116	8.7	1.8	135.3	68.0	28.2	6.9
Stewart	3	140	6.9	2.2	4	9	0.8	0.1	38.3	11.9	7.5	2.2
Sumter	64	787	38.5	17.5	39	195	10.8	3.0	175.4	58.8	26.8	10.8
Talbot	3	19	1.7	0.6	5	12	0.4	0.1	36.6	18.9	5.1	2.2
Taliaferro	2	D	D	D	2	D	D	D	15.5	4.9	3.2	0.7
Tattnall	19	518	17.2	7.5	18	52	3.7	0.8	105.0	45.1	18.7	7.3
Taylor	1	D	D	D	10	22	1.7	0.3	54.3	21.5	8.6	4.5
Telfair	16	464	19.3	8.3	14	62	4.4	1.1	83.5	34.0	17.1	3.7
Terrell	13	127	4.7	1.7	15	52	2.8	0.6	75.0	21.1	11.2	5.0
Thomas	86	960	70.2	33.6	74	282	17.6	4.6	231.0	98.9	40.8	14.1
Tift	83	1 157	69.5	37.1	57	584	43.3	12.3	199.8	71.9	29.8	10.0
Toombs	67	804	35.1	15.7	37	263	10.6	4.1	133.9	53.4	24.1	10.4
Towns	14	284	14.6	6.3	8	18	0.9	0.2	56.5	35.1	10.0	1.2
Treutlen	9	79	2.8	1.2	4	D	D	D	34.1	12.5	5.7	2.4
Troup	91	1 173	73.7	36.9	94	410	26.5	8.1	269.1	122.9	50.4	15.0
Turner	6	104	3.7	1.5	13	34	2.8	0.5	60.7	18.7	10.7	3.2
Twiggs	5	143	5.2	2.1	7	8	0.9	0.1	46.4	20.5	8.0	3.2
Union	30	171	9.4	4.5	19	59	6.3	1.0	94.6	56.4	17.3	2.5
Upson	48	515	26.9	11.9	39	140	9.6	2.5	129.7	63.4	25.5	4.3
Walker	52	507	25.5	11.2	64	377	22.6	6.3	280.2	148.8	67.8	10.8
Walton	59	639	28.4	12.2	49	152	12.0	3.2	207.0	109.2	40.8	8.6
Ware	90	1 100	62.7	29.8	60	292	16.6	4.4	231.7	100.3	43.3	12.9
Warren	7	234	6.0	3.5	6	19	0.9	0.1	42.0	13.3	8.6	2.4
Washington	41	508	20.6	9.3	30	95	5.9	1.4	105.3	39.6	22.7	4.5
Wayne	46	530	30.1	11.9	26	118	8.3	2.4	156.6	55.6	26.8	6.7
Webster	NA	NA	NA	NA	1	D	D	D	15.5	3.7	2.1	0.7
Wheeler	6	164	9.7	3.3	2	D	D	D	32.2	10.5	6.2	1.8
White	24	269	14.5	4.6	20	69	4.8	1.0	78.7	47.2	13.3	2.0
Whitfield	129	1 442	114.0	52.5	123	672	47.2	14.6	301.3	144.8	58.8	11.9
Wilcox	5	208	6.4	3.0	8	18	0.7	0.2	55.7	19.1	9.6	2.6
Wilkes	22	159	8.6	3.4	21	64	5.4	1.6	65.2	26.9	14.7	3.1
Wilkinson	6	108	4.6	1.6	8	30	1.9	0.5	54.9	26.6	10.8	2.7
Worth	21	316	15.4	5.8	16	51	3.1	0.9	105.6	35.7	14.5	6.0
HAWAII	2 360	18 221	1 646.3	730.8	1 476	10 375	683.2	206.4	9 722.2	2 682.0	752.7	265.9
Hawaii	321	2 441	224.8	76.2	157	808	50.3	14.5	730.7	313.6	89.8	52.5
Honolulu	1 730	13 474	1 231.7	563.1	1 097	8 402	560.8	170.7	7 775.6	2 046.2	555.7	183.5
Kalawao	NA	NA	NA	NA	NA	NA	NA	NA	0.7	0.0	0.7	0.0
Kauai	79	745	51.4	27.6	59	281	17.9	5.1	326.8	110.0	39.4	11.7
Maui	230	1 561	138.4	63.9	163	884	54.2	16.2	474.6	206.2	67.1	18.2
IDAHO	2 551	26 365	1 548.3	680.1	1 858	9 461	550.6	151.7	7 528.9	2 509.7	683.2	146.2
Ada	711	6 993	484.7	228.8	462	3 185	171.1	51.3	1 630.4	530.5	125.2	25.7
Adams	2	D	D	D	1	D	D	D	40.7	11.4	2.2	0.4
Bannock	157	1 421	79.8	39.1	108	564	33.5	9.5	327.1	144.7	36.8	12.4
Bear Lake	7	33	1.6	0.6	6	10	1.3	0.2	41.8	15.1	4.1	0.6
Benewah	9	9	1.4	0.4	15	136	7.2	2.0	60.0	24.0	8.0	1.6
Bingham	51	391	17.2	7.9	39	215	15.7	4.2	193.6	68.5	18.2	5.2
Blaine	52	239	21.1	10.0	44	188	11.8	3.3	45.5	23.0	5.9	0.8
Boise	NA	NA	NA	NA	3	D	D	D	37.6	14.4	2.5	0.4
Bonner	70	535	26.3	10.0	54	166	11.4	3.0	162.3	88.6	21.4	4.7
Bonneville	241	3 151	229.1	91.6	140	709	49.5	13.0	1 136.3	147.2	43.6	10.1
Boundary	16	48	2.2	0.6	17	43	4.1	0.9	52.1	23.2	4.7	1.6
Butte	3	27	1.0	0.3	3	17	1.3	0.2	31.6	6.8	2.6	0.1
Camas	1	D	D	D	NA	NA	NA	NA	6.0	2.1	0.3	0.0
Canyon	182	2 692	161.3	74.9	158	697	39.0	10.9	464.9	224.9	67.9	19.1
Caribou	14	76	3.5	1.2	13	37	1.9	0.4	38.8	14.8	3.6	0.4
Cassia	56	421	20.6	6.4	44	176	10.7	2.7	101.2	37.2	13.0	2.8
Clark	2	D	D	D	NA	NA	NA	NA	21.4	1.6	0.5	0.0
Clearwater	9	94	3.9	1.3	13	39	2.6	0.8	62.7	24.8	7.1	1.4

1. Firms subject to federal tax.   2. October 1, 2000 to September 30, 2001.   3. State totals may include programs not allocated by county.

STATE County	Salaries and wages (171)	Defense (172)	Other (173)	Medicaid and other health-related (174)	Nutrition and family welfare (175)	Education (176)	Other (177)	Total (mil dol) (178)	Intergovern-mental (mil dol) (179)	Total (mil dol) (180)	Total (181)	Property (182)
GEORGIA—Cont'd												
Richmond	202.9	14.3	26.9	147.2	43.5	15.7	22.3	431.8	189.9	153.7	796	401
Rockdale	7.6	0.0	1.9	10.8	3.1	2.5	-4.1	137.6	45.8	65.7	980	763
Schley	0.4	0.5	0.1	3.6	0.7	0.4	4.8	6.2	2.5	2.0	530	420
Screven	2.2	0.0	0.5	17.0	3.3	1.2	3.8	32.0	14.8	9.4	652	449
Seminole	1.0	0.0	0.3	9.6	1.9	0.9	2.3	16.3	9.2	5.4	548	321
Spalding	7.7	0.9	1.5	35.2	8.1	4.4	1.4	127.7	58.6	45.9	805	490
Stephens	4.2	0.5	0.8	16.6	2.5	2.0	1.7	45.4	17.2	19.6	776	504
Stewart	0.6	0.0	0.2	10.0	2.0	0.5	1.0	10.3	5.6	3.1	572	459
Sumter	10.0	0.3	1.7	27.6	7.9	3.1	5.4	120.4	49.6	23.0	726	413
Talbot	0.9	0.0	0.2	6.5	1.5	0.5	0.3	10.6	4.9	4.3	622	483
Taliaferro	0.4	0.0	0.1	3.8	0.5	0.2	1.4	2.9	1.1	1.6	844	728
Tattnall	2.1	0.1	0.6	20.1	4.0	1.2	1.2	31.5	15.9	10.7	559	364
Taylor	1.2	0.0	0.3	10.6	2.0	0.8	2.5	15.4	9.3	4.3	529	311
Telfair	1.7	0.4	0.5	15.9	2.9	1.1	3.3	25.8	11.4	7.8	680	399
Terrell	3.7	0.0	0.8	15.5	3.0	1.0	3.1	22.3	12.7	7.1	638	374
Thomas	9.8	0.0	1.6	38.2	7.4	4.1	3.7	90.8	48.5	19.5	457	261
Tift	11.2	0.0	1.4	25.4	5.7	2.9	29.2	144.2	41.1	27.3	741	389
Toombs	3.8	0.1	0.8	23.8	4.9	2.1	2.4	54.5	25.0	14.3	560	212
Towns	1.6	0.0	1.2	5.6	0.6	0.3	0.5	9.7	4.5	3.7	456	280
Treutlen	0.7	0.0	0.2	9.2	1.4	0.5	0.5	10.5	6.3	2.4	402	285
Troup	7.5	6.6	2.4	39.3	10.3	4.0	3.2	196.3	59.3	44.5	761	538
Turner	1.4	0.0	0.3	9.2	2.6	0.9	5.5	19.8	10.3	7.0	762	505
Twiggs	0.7	0.0	0.3	8.2	2.3	0.9	0.6	16.5	8.7	6.9	702	511
Union	3.3	0.0	0.9	10.1	1.1	0.5	0.4	38.2	10.3	9.4	601	355
Upson	4.1	0.2	0.9	18.5	4.6	1.6	0.6	41.5	20.0	15.9	585	415
Walker	6.8	0.0	2.0	25.6	5.9	4.8	0.7	95.5	52.2	29.0	469	286
Walton	7.7	0.2	2.0	19.3	3.9	3.0	8.8	107.5	36.3	34.5	670	521
Ware	8.9	0.1	2.1	35.7	11.5	3.7	6.2	90.9	51.4	28.6	799	417
Warren	1.1	0.0	0.3	10.8	1.7	0.9	2.2	12.0	5.5	4.4	726	502
Washington	2.3	0.0	0.6	22.5	5.0	1.6	0.9	57.0	17.1	18.3	916	594
Wayne	18.5	11.8	4.6	19.6	4.1	1.9	1.2	89.1	20.3	17.7	704	531
Webster	0.6	0.0	0.1	2.4	0.5	0.1	1.3	4.0	2.3	1.3	578	517
Wheeler	0.6	0.0	0.2	7.9	1.5	0.4	1.2	8.5	5.8	2.1	421	259
White	2.6	0.0	0.7	6.9	0.9	2.8	0.8	37.2	16.1	16.5	981	606
Whitfield	10.9	1.3	5.7	28.9	6.7	6.0	7.6	314.5	75.0	85.5	1 051	795
Wilcox	1.3	0.0	0.3	10.2	1.5	0.7	3.5	13.3	8.4	4.0	550	394
Wilkes	2.1	0.0	0.4	11.9	2.3	0.8	0.6	34.3	9.1	8.5	806	542
Wilkinson	1.3	0.2	0.4	7.9	2.1	0.9	0.7	19.4	7.9	9.8	898	580
Worth	2.0	0.0	0.5	14.3	4.4	2.2	4.4	35.4	20.3	11.2	499	336
HAWAII	2 525.0	1 294.4	172.5	508.4	252.4	209.4	543.4	X	X	X	X	X
Hawaii	48.0	6.0	10.6	45.4	25.9	8.5	95.9	178.0	56.7	102.2	723	611
Honolulu	2 424.9	1 182.8	127.3	403.4	173.4	145.5	385.5	996.0	150.0	526.9	606	476
Kalawao	0.0	0.0	0.0	0.0	0.0	0.0	0.0	NA	NA	NA	NA	NA
Kauai	24.6	73.9	5.3	21.8	5.7	0.2	17.9	94.0	42.2	39.8	705	581
Maui	27.6	31.8	29.3	30.7	12.8	0.9	30.3	181.1	48.6	91.9	773	624
IDAHO	753.2	145.9	1 051.2	619.0	177.8	141.1	567.5	X	X	X	X	X
Ada	257.8	38.6	110.5	120.0	61.7	54.1	258.0	529.1	198.1	205.2	768	709
Adams	3.6	0.0	13.8	1.3	1.9	0.1	2.7	10.4	5.1	2.0	524	502
Bannock	24.6	0.0	9.0	43.6	4.3	3.2	16.7	177.4	69.3	39.1	530	505
Bear Lake	2.0	0.0	0.4	3.4	4.7	0.1	7.7	19.5	8.6	4.3	655	631
Benewah	3.4	0.0	0.6	5.7	3.6	1.4	3.7	26.0	9.1	5.6	627	604
Bingham	11.6	0.5	12.0	24.4	4.6	4.8	17.0	90.8	49.1	18.8	451	433
Blaine	4.8	0.0	1.6	1.8	0.8	0.3	3.4	65.8	13.5	27.5	1 595	1 356
Boise	4.1	4.8	2.2	1.3	0.8	0.1	6.0	15.5	6.7	3.9	768	749
Bonner	10.2	2.2	2.0	16.3	1.6	0.9	13.1	62.4	24.6	20.5	589	564
Bonneville	47.2	26.4	790.7	31.2	6.7	1.4	8.5	154.0	83.7	45.4	565	541
Boundary	4.8	0.0	1.2	5.3	0.8	0.3	6.6	24.7	9.2	4.3	436	430
Butte	8.2	0.0	0.2	4.3	6.0	0.1	0.7	12.3	4.1	2.7	851	849
Camas	0.8	0.0	0.2	0.4	1.0	0.0	0.3	2.7	1.8	0.7	808	778
Canyon	20.0	0.7	7.1	85.7	10.8	4.1	9.0	187.4	99.0	53.7	461	431
Caribou	2.1	0.0	0.8	1.3	1.7	0.2	3.7	24.7	11.5	6.9	934	864
Cassia	7.7	0.0	1.7	9.0	2.0	0.6	2.5	46.5	24.1	12.1	563	537
Clark	1.6	0.0	6.1	0.0	8.5	0.0	0.1	3.6	1.9	0.9	1 016	962
Clearwater	10.8	0.3	2.1	9.0	0.8	0.2	4.5	30.2	13.6	5.6	591	570

1. October 1, 2000 to September 30, 2001.   2. State totals may include programs not allocated by county.   3. Based on the resident population estimated as of July 1 of the year shown.

STATE County	Local government finances, 1997 (cont'd)									Government employment, 1999			Presidential election, 2000[2]		
	Direct general expenditure							Debt outstanding					Percent of vote cast —		
			Percent of total for —												
	Total (mil dol)	Per capita[1] (dollars)	Education	Health and hospitals	Police protection	Public welfare	Highways	Total (mil dol)	Per capita[1] (dollars)	Federal civilian	Federal military	State and local	Democratic	Republican	All other
	183	184	185	186	187	188	189	190	191	192	193	194	195	196	197
GEORGIA—Cont'd															
Richmond	445.7	2 308	45.6	8.0	5.4	0.2	3.7	402.2	2 083	5 777	9 787	22 381	54.8	44.4	0.8
Rockdale	176.1	2 627	47.6	0.4	3.1	0.5	9.1	247.8	3 696	133	261	3 070	33.9	63.0	3.1
Schley	6.5	1 705	65.6	1.4	5.0	0.3	4.4	3.6	944	0	15	178	39.1	60.1	0.8
Screven	32.3	2 241	56.9	14.3	3.8	0.5	3.9	9.4	655	44	55	957	47.3	52.2	0.5
Seminole	16.8	1 713	64.6	1.1	3.4	2.2	4.1	0.3	30	21	37	503	45.6	53.4	0.9
Spalding	130.8	2 295	46.6	11.0	9.4	0.3	2.8	107.3	1 883	130	219	3 867	37.9	60.3	1.8
Stephens	48.3	1 916	48.9	10.6	4.0	0.3	4.3	9.8	387	68	96	1 670	34.3	64.2	1.5
Stewart	10.6	1 951	54.7	1.0	5.9	0.2	3.3	1.6	290	15	20	298	64.8	34.5	0.6
Sumter	115.6	3 648	27.8	42.0	3.5	0.2	1.5	29.7	938	130	119	2 929	49.2	50.2	0.6
Talbot	10.4	1 507	54.3	1.0	4.5	1.0	12.3	4.1	587	16	26	320	65.8	33.4	0.8
Taliaferro	2.3	1 251	51.7	5.1	6.4	2.7	6.8	0.1	52	0	0	106	67.0	32.7	0.4
Tattnall	32.0	1 681	50.7	9.0	2.7	1.6	6.2	9.9	521	34	73	2 612	35.0	64.1	0.9
Taylor	15.5	1 889	56.7	1.3	5.4	0.5	5.9	4.1	497	24	31	539	48.2	50.8	0.9
Telfair	22.9	1 995	51.9	16.2	5.5	0.8	4.0	6.6	576	39	43	1 018	50.9	48.5	0.6
Terrell	22.3	2 011	54.4	1.3	5.1	0.3	6.2	3.1	277	77	42	558	50.9	48.3	0.7
Thomas	96.0	2 255	50.0	14.0	4.2	0.1	4.4	7.1	168	194	163	3 598	40.5	59.0	0.5
Tift	164.7	4 464	29.6	46.7	2.3	0.1	2.2	46.3	1 256	197	140	4 136	34.4	64.8	0.8
Toombs	53.8	2 100	58.1	1.9	5.1	0.1	3.5	16.5	643	70	98	1 440	36.7	62.3	0.9
Towns	10.4	1 279	53.7	6.5	4.5	3.3	8.6	4.5	551	24	33	355	33.5	65.0	1.5
Treutlen	10.4	1 746	60.8	1.5	6.6	0.8	7.0	0.2	31	14	22	372	44.8	54.2	1.0
Troup	204.2	3 488	35.6	38.8	3.6	0.1	2.2	73.9	1 263	146	223	5 115	36.0	63.2	0.8
Turner	19.5	2 136	59.4	1.0	5.0	0.3	8.8	11.2	1 225	32	35	482	47.6	51.3	1.1
Twiggs	15.7	1 587	69.6	1.5	4.5	1.0	5.1	1.7	174	11	39	496	54.7	43.5	1.8
Union	38.1	2 428	34.0	43.7	1.9	0.0	5.7	2.1	131	77	65	1 165	32.3	66.2	1.5
Upson	42.4	1 559	57.8	2.4	5.7	0.2	5.8	19.7	724	48	103	1 657	38.2	60.7	1.1
Walker	92.8	1 501	61.5	11.2	5.7	0.2	4.9	38.1	617	141	238	2 782	33.6	65.2	1.2
Walton	105.9	2 056	49.6	19.0	3.7	0.4	4.3	41.5	805	119	222	2 437	28.8	68.1	3.1
Ware	93.6	2 614	42.4	20.8	4.4	0.1	9.6	28.5	797	154	133	3 389	36.1	63.3	0.5
Warren	11.1	1 846	54.0	1.1	3.9	0.9	6.7	9.5	1 566	19	23	302	55.8	43.5	0.7
Washington	64.9	3 244	44.5	31.2	3.3	0.1	6.7	22.3	1 113	49	76	2 229	52.0	47.3	0.7
Wayne	66.6	2 656	38.1	37.5	3.6	0.1	4.8	25.0	997	373	97	2 243	34.2	65.2	0.6
Webster	3.9	1 743	55.5	2.0	4.2	0.4	17.9	0.2	100	14	0	141	59.6	39.5	0.9
Wheeler	9.2	1 866	63.4	1.3	3.9	4.4	4.5	0.6	114	12	18	334	47.8	51.7	0.5
White	46.2	2 743	52.9	0.9	4.0	0.1	22.8	13.6	806	43	69	898	28.8	69.4	1.8
Whitfield	271.3	3 336	35.1	41.0	2.6	0.2	3.8	100.5	1 235	181	315	4 978	30.4	68.4	1.2
Wilcox	14.5	1 982	70.2	0.9	4.5	0.8	5.0	2.7	368	31	28	647	40.7	58.4	0.9
Wilkes	32.9	3 115	34.8	40.2	4.1	0.5	3.1	4.7	448	41	40	845	48.3	50.9	0.8
Wilkinson	18.4	1 697	63.6	2.2	6.3	0.5	7.5	1.5	135	21	41	536	50.4	48.2	1.4
Worth	36.7	1 643	66.9	0.7	4.0	0.2	10.6	7.2	324	43	85	1 154	36.6	62.6	0.8
HAWAII	X	X	X	X	X	X	X	X	X	29 768	53 284	81 933	55.8	37.5	6.8
Hawaii	195.8	1 384	0.1	4.1	14.3	0.0	7.1	168.0	1 187	963	1 304	9 727	56.4	33.5	10.2
Honolulu	972.6	1 118	0.0	1.3	13.4	0.0	2.6	1 698.5	1 953	27 908	50 274	61 100	54.5	39.6	5.9
Kalawao	NA	NA	NA	NA	NA	NA	NA	NA	NA	(3)	(3)	(3)	0.0	0.0	0.0
Kauai	84.6	1 499	0.0	0.0	10.5	0.0	7.9	51.9	920	384	607	3 721	61.9	30.2	7.9
Maui	187.5	1 578	0.0	0.4	12.0	6.7	15.1	208.2	1 753	(3)513	(3)1 099	(3)7 385	59.8	32.8	7.4
IDAHO	X	X	X	X	X	X	X	X	X	12 666	9 718	88 442	27.6	67.2	5.2
Ada	561.7	2 102	48.4	1.7	6.5	0.9	6.2	227.5	852	4 477	1 296	21 317	32.9	60.8	6.3
Adams	9.0	2 344	43.6	22.2	4.9	0.9	9.8	0.8	217	121	16	263	17.6	77.3	5.1
Bannock	171.1	2 317	40.7	26.7	5.0	0.7	4.2	43.1	584	523	329	7 565	35.3	59.1	5.6
Bear Lake	18.4	2 796	40.9	28.1	3.5	0.2	4.3	1.0	149	51	28	522	17.8	79.2	3.0
Benewah	24.5	2 730	43.7	27.8	2.5	0.5	4.6	6.2	693	69	39	654	24.3	70.7	5.0
Bingham	91.4	2 195	58.2	15.0	4.2	0.4	5.4	20.9	501	325	182	2 899	22.9	73.5	3.6
Blaine	66.3	3 854	32.9	25.0	4.1	0.5	6.1	28.4	1 649	94	75	1 226	47.2	44.4	8.3
Boise	15.6	3 101	41.8	28.4	4.5	0.7	9.5	4.9	974	143	23	342	24.4	66.1	9.5
Bonner	63.9	1 837	43.5	0.9	5.8	1.6	12.8	19.6	562	275	156	1 877	29.7	61.5	8.8
Bonneville	156.7	1 952	54.1	3.7	6.4	0.5	3.9	106.6	1 328	729	352	4 487	21.6	74.5	4.0
Boundary	22.0	2 223	39.2	22.3	6.5	4.0	10.1	6.5	659	128	43	703	21.4	72.0	6.6
Butte	11.7	3 722	31.4	36.1	2.7	0.7	7.0	0.6	183	42	18	192	24.2	72.2	3.6
Camas	3.0	3 550	50.1	1.0	4.7	0.7	18.7	0.8	940	21	0	87	22.3	70.8	6.9
Canyon	210.3	1 802	59.5	1.8	4.3	0.9	5.5	103.5	887	355	541	5 889	24.6	71.1	4.3
Caribou	26.3	3 568	47.7	14.4	5.3	0.6	11.5	10.1	1 375	46	31	575	15.0	81.9	3.2
Cassia	51.2	2 387	61.4	0.4	5.2	0.7	7.9	34.3	1 599	164	93	1 389	14.9	82.2	2.9
Clark	3.6	4 266	39.4	1.6	4.3	0.3	17.4	0.8	976	36	0	118	16.5	81.4	2.1
Clearwater	31.4	3 322	31.0	18.9	4.0	0.5	24.0	8.8	935	274	40	925	21.6	74.1	4.4

1. Based on the resident population estimated as of July 1 of the year shown.   2. Data subject to copyright.   3. Kalawao County included with Maui County.

Table B. States and Counties — **Land Area and Population**

STATE/ County code	MSA/ PMSA/ NECMA code[1]	County Type[2]	STATE County	Land area[3] (sq km) 2000	Population and population characteristics, 2000														
								Race alone or in combination (percent)					Age (percent)						
					Total persons	Rank	Per square kilometer	White	Black	Am. Indian, Alaska Native	Asian and Pacific Islander	Percent Hispanic[4]	Under 5 years	5 to 17 years	18 to 24 years	25 to 34 years	35 to 44 years	45 to 54 years
				1	2	3	4	5	6	7	8	9	10	11	12	13	14	15
			IDAHO—Cont'd															
16 037	...	9	Custer	12 757	4 342	2 893	0.3	98.2	0.0	1.4	0.1	4.2	5.4	20.2	4.8	9.7	16.2	16.9
16 039	...	6	Elmore	7 971	29 130	1 423	3.7	88.3	3.8	1.8	3.1	12.0	8.4	19.6	13.9	18.7	17.3	9.1
16 041	...	7	Franklin	1 723	11 329	2 348	6.6	95.9	0.1	0.6	0.3	5.2	10.0	27.4	9.3	11.7	12.5	10.1
16 043	...	7	Fremont	4 835	11 819	2 303	2.4	92.9	0.4	1.1	0.7	10.6	8.5	24.7	9.3	11.0	13.7	11.5
16 045	...	6	Gem	1 457	15 181	2 077	10.4	95.4	0.2	1.6	0.9	6.9	7.0	20.9	7.6	11.0	14.3	13.3
16 047	...	7	Gooding	1 893	14 155	2 149	7.5	90.3	0.5	1.3	0.6	17.1	7.8	21.9	8.7	11.5	13.6	11.8
16 049	...	7	Idaho	21 976	15 511	2 052	0.7	95.7	0.1	4.0	0.6	1.6	5.3	19.7	6.3	8.3	15.0	16.0
16 051	...	7	Jefferson	2 836	19 155	1 839	6.8	92.1	0.3	0.9	0.7	10.0	8.9	27.4	9.6	11.0	14.5	11.8
16 053	...	7	Jerome	1 554	18 342	1 878	11.8	88.8	0.3	1.4	0.5	17.2	8.2	23.3	8.9	12.2	14.8	12.3
16 055	...	4	Kootenai	3 225	108 685	496	33.7	97.4	0.3	2.1	1.0	2.3	6.9	20.3	8.7	12.6	15.5	14.5
16 057	...	7	Latah	2 789	34 935	1 251	12.5	95.6	0.8	1.4	2.8	2.1	5.4	14.9	24.5	14.6	12.4	11.9
16 059	...	7	Lemhi	11 821	7 806	2 625	0.7	98.2	0.2	1.5	0.6	2.2	5.1	20.4	5.5	8.0	14.7	16.7
16 061	...	9	Lewis	1 241	3 747	2 936	3.0	94.2	0.4	5.0	0.6	1.9	4.8	20.6	5.3	8.8	15.0	14.0
16 063	...	9	Lincoln	3 122	4 044	2 917	1.3	88.4	0.7	2.3	0.6	13.4	7.5	22.8	9.0	11.6	13.9	13.3
16 065	...	7	Madison	1 221	27 467	1 469	22.5	96.4	0.3	0.6	1.2	3.9	7.1	19.0	39.9	7.6	8.3	7.1
16 067	...	7	Minidoka	1 967	20 174	1 782	10.3	80.4	0.4	1.6	0.8	25.5	8.0	23.6	9.1	11.0	14.1	12.0
16 069	...	5	Nez Perce	2 199	37 410	1 180	17.0	93.1	0.4	6.3	1.1	1.9	6.0	17.7	10.0	12.0	14.7	13.7
16 071	...	9	Oneida	3 109	4 125	2 906	1.3	98.0	0.1	0.4	0.6	2.3	7.4	24.6	7.7	9.2	13.9	12.6
16 073	...	8	Owyhee	19 886	10 644	2 388	0.5	79.4	0.3	4.5	0.8	23.1	7.8	24.1	8.5	12.1	14.4	12.0
16 075	...	7	Payette	1 055	20 578	1 756	19.5	92.5	0.3	1.8	1.5	11.9	7.6	23.1	7.9	12.3	14.3	12.1
16 077	...	7	Power	3 640	7 538	2 640	2.1	84.9	0.2	3.7	0.6	21.7	8.4	25.4	8.4	11.8	13.6	13.6
16 079	...	7	Shoshone	6 822	13 771	2 175	2.0	97.5	0.2	2.7	0.7	1.9	5.6	17.3	6.7	10.3	15.2	15.4
16 081	...	9	Teton	1 166	5 999	2 780	5.1	92.1	0.2	0.9	0.5	11.8	8.5	23.3	8.1	16.2	17.6	13.3
16 083	...	5	Twin Falls	4 986	64 284	759	12.9	94.4	0.3	1.4	1.2	9.4	7.3	20.6	10.4	11.8	14.2	12.8
16 085	...	9	Valley	9 526	7 651	2 633	0.8	97.8	0.1	1.3	0.7	2.0	4.3	19.3	4.4	8.4	16.5	18.6
16 087	...	7	Washington	3 772	9 977	2 448	2.6	89.8	0.2	1.5	1.6	13.8	6.7	20.7	7.2	9.7	13.6	13.5
17 000		X	ILLINOIS	143 961	12 419 293	X	86.3	75.1	15.6	0.6	3.9	12.3	7.1	19.1	9.8	14.6	16.0	13.1
17 001	...	5	Adams	2 219	68 277	721	30.8	96.0	3.5	0.4	0.5	0.8	6.2	18.7	8.8	11.7	14.1	13.0
17 003	...	7	Alexander	612	9 590	2 480	15.7	63.7	35.4	0.7	0.5	1.4	6.3	19.6	7.7	12.3	14.3	13.1
17 005	...	6	Bond	985	17 633	1 921	17.9	91.4	7.6	0.8	0.5	1.4	5.6	16.3	11.6	13.8	15.6	13.5
17 007	6880	2	Boone	728	41 786	1 059	57.4	91.5	1.2	0.7	0.8	12.5	7.6	22.2	7.7	13.3	16.6	13.0
17 009	...	9	Brown	792	6 950	2 691	8.8	80.8	18.3	0.3	0.4	3.9	4.0	13.7	12.6	19.2	18.3	11.7
17 011	...	7	Bureau	2 250	35 503	1 232	15.8	97.6	0.5	0.5	0.7	4.9	5.9	18.8	7.4	11.3	14.9	13.9
17 013	...	8	Calhoun	657	5 084	2 846	7.7	99.3	0.1	0.8	0.2	0.6	5.3	17.6	7.6	11.0	14.9	12.8
17 015	...	7	Carroll	1 151	16 674	1 976	14.5	97.9	0.7	0.7	0.8	2.0	5.5	18.7	6.6	10.5	14.9	13.7
17 017	...	6	Cass	974	13 695	2 184	14.1	95.7	0.5	0.5	0.4	8.5	6.8	18.5	8.4	12.9	14.9	13.0
17 019	1400	3	Champaign	2 582	179 669	308	69.6	80.4	12.0	0.7	7.2	2.9	5.8	15.3	23.1	14.7	13.5	11.4
17 021	...	6	Christian	1 836	35 372	1 238	19.3	96.8	2.3	0.4	0.5	1.0	6.1	18.0	7.6	12.2	15.9	13.1
17 023	...	6	Clark	1 299	17 008	1 952	13.1	99.4	0.4	0.4	0.3	0.3	6.0	18.9	7.4	11.4	15.2	12.9
17 025	...	7	Clay	1 215	14 560	2 116	12.0	98.9	0.2	0.5	0.5	0.6	5.9	18.0	8.0	11.6	14.3	13.0
17 027	7040	1	Clinton	1 228	35 535	1 230	28.9	94.7	4.0	0.4	0.6	1.6	6.1	18.8	9.3	13.1	17.0	12.6
17 029	...	5	Coles	1 316	53 196	881	40.4	96.2	2.6	0.5	1.1	1.4	5.3	14.4	23.5	11.1	12.7	11.8
17 031	1600	0	Cook	2 449	5 376 741	2	2 195.5	58.3	26.7	0.6	5.4	19.9	7.2	18.8	9.9	16.2	15.5	12.5
17 033	...	7	Crawford	1 149	20 452	1 763	17.8	94.3	4.8	0.5	0.5	1.7	5.5	17.3	8.6	13.0	15.9	13.3
17 035	...	9	Cumberland	896	11 253	2 353	12.6	99.3	0.2	0.5	0.3	0.6	6.3	20.1	8.0	12.5	15.0	12.9
17 037	1600	1	De Kalb	1 642	88 969	585	54.2	89.8	5.0	0.6	2.8	6.6	6.2	16.9	22.0	13.5	14.1	10.8
17 039	...	6	De Witt	1 030	16 798	1 970	16.3	98.5	0.7	0.5	0.4	1.3	6.2	18.4	7.8	12.3	16.0	13.2
17 041	...	6	Douglas	1 080	19 922	1 797	18.4	97.9	0.4	0.4	0.4	3.5	6.9	20.1	8.0	11.4	15.4	12.7
17 043	1600	0	Du Page	864	904 161	42	1 046.5	85.5	3.4	0.4	8.6	9.0	7.3	19.5	8.2	14.6	17.8	14.5
17 045	...	6	Edgar	1 615	19 704	1 811	12.2	97.5	1.9	0.4	0.2	0.8	5.7	18.1	8.3	11.6	15.4	13.9
17 047	...	9	Edwards	576	6 971	2 688	12.1	99.2	0.2	0.3	0.6	0.5	5.7	17.4	8.0	11.5	14.6	13.9
17 049	...	7	Effingham	1 240	34 264	1 272	27.6	99.1	0.2	0.4	0.4	0.7	7.2	21.4	8.2	12.1	16.1	12.6
17 051	...	6	Fayette	1 856	21 802	1 702	11.7	94.6	5.0	0.4	0.3	0.8	6.1	17.7	9.0	13.3	16.1	12.5
17 053	...	6	Ford	1 258	14 241	2 147	11.3	98.9	0.4	0.4	0.4	1.2	6.4	19.4	6.9	10.7	15.6	12.4
17 055	...	7	Franklin	1 067	39 018	1 138	36.6	99.3	0.2	0.6	0.3	0.6	5.6	17.3	7.9	11.8	14.3	13.4
17 057	...	6	Fulton	2 242	38 250	1 159	17.1	95.7	3.7	0.4	0.3	1.2	5.6	16.4	8.7	13.0	15.0	13.3
17 059	...	8	Gallatin	838	6 445	2 743	7.7	98.8	0.4	0.9	0.2	0.9	5.2	17.0	8.2	11.5	13.9	14.3
17 061	...	6	Greene	1 407	14 761	2 105	10.5	98.6	0.9	0.6	0.3	0.5	6.2	19.2	8.8	11.5	14.9	12.2
17 063	1600	1	Grundy	1 088	37 535	1 176	34.5	97.9	0.3	0.5	0.5	4.1	6.6	20.0	8.3	13.1	17.1	13.8
17 065	...	7	Hamilton	1 127	8 621	2 556	7.6	98.8	0.8	0.5	0.4	0.6	5.9	18.0	7.9	10.5	14.2	13.5
17 067	...	7	Hancock	2 058	20 121	1 785	9.8	99.2	0.3	0.5	0.4	0.5	5.6	19.0	7.1	10.8	14.7	14.3
17 069	...	9	Hardin	462	4 800	2 859	10.4	96.0	2.9	0.5	0.7	1.1	5.5	15.0	7.8	11.3	15.0	15.1
17 071	...	9	Henderson	981	8 213	2 590	8.4	99.3	0.4	0.4	0.3	0.9	5.7	17.4	7.5	10.4	15.8	14.1
17 073	1960	2	Henry	2 132	51 020	910	23.9	97.1	1.5	0.4	0.4	2.9	6.0	19.3	7.7	11.0	15.4	14.3
17 075	...	6	Iroquois	2 892	31 334	1 365	10.8	96.7	0.8	0.5	0.5	3.9	6.1	19.3	7.1	10.7	15.0	13.3

1. MSA = Metropolitan Statistical Area. PMSA = Primary MSA. NECMA = New England County Metropolitan Area. See Appendix A for explanation of these concepts. See Appendix B for list of metropolitan areas identified by type, with component counties.   2. County typology code from the Economic Research Service of USDA. See Appendix A for definition.   3. Dry land or land partially or temporarily covered by water.   4. Hispanic persons may be of any race.

Table B. States and Counties — **Population and Households**

STATE County	| Population, 2000 (cont'd) Age (percent) (cont'd) 55 to 64 years	65 to 74 years	75 years and over	Percent female	Population — change and components of change, 1990–2001 Total persons 2001	1990	Percent change 1990–2000	2000–2001	Components of change, 2000–2001 Births	Deaths	Net migration	Households, 2000 Number	Percent change, 1990–2000	Persons per household	Percent Female family house-holder[1]	One person
	16	17	18	19	20	21	22	23	24	25	26	27	28	29	30	31
IDAHO—Cont'd																
Custer	12.4	8.3	6.2	48.9	4 292	4 133	5.1	-1.2	57	50	-57	1 770	13.4	2.41	4.4	27.7
Elmore	5.9	4.1	3.0	44.8	29 157	21 205	37.4	0.1	638	186	-414	9 092	27.4	2.76	7.5	20.7
Franklin	7.4	5.5	6.2	50.2	11 590	9 232	22.7	2.3	270	126	120	3 476	23.1	3.24	5.8	16.0
Fremont	9.0	7.1	5.3	48.6	11 822	10 937	8.1	0.0	259	106	-151	3 885	12.5	2.96	6.9	19.5
Gem	10.2	7.7	7.9	50.3	15 482	11 844	28.2	2.0	247	223	275	5 539	25.2	2.70	8.4	20.8
Gooding	9.4	7.8	7.6	49.0	14 207	11 633	21.7	0.4	293	159	-81	5 046	16.8	2.76	7.6	22.0
Idaho	12.3	9.4	7.6	49.1	15 423	13 768	12.7	-0.6	171	190	-66	6 084	17.3	2.46	6.3	25.3
Jefferson	7.5	5.1	4.2	49.4	19 578	16 543	15.8	2.2	419	142	154	5 901	21.1	3.23	6.8	15.2
Jerome	7.9	6.5	5.8	48.9	18 449	15 138	21.2	0.6	405	175	-125	6 298	18.3	2.89	7.6	19.5
Kootenai	9.4	6.6	5.7	50.5	112 297	69 795	55.7	3.3	1 859	1 015	2 721	41 308	53.3	2.60	9.2	21.9
Latah	7.0	4.5	5.0	48.2	34 476	30 617	14.1	-1.3	559	266	-763	13 059	16.3	2.38	6.1	26.3
Lemhi	12.8	8.7	8.1	50.2	7 606	6 899	13.1	-2.6	87	121	-168	3 275	18.3	2.38	6.9	27.7
Lewis	13.1	9.6	8.9	49.5	3 625	3 516	6.6	-3.3	41	51	-115	1 554	11.6	2.39	6.4	28.1
Lincoln	8.8	7.1	5.9	48.4	4 132	3 308	22.2	2.2	74	37	51	1 447	21.5	2.77	5.5	22.9
Madison	4.8	3.1	3.0	52.4	27 327	23 674	16.0	-0.5	603	118	-635	7 129	22.9	3.66	5.7	12.7
Minidoka	8.9	6.8	6.4	50.0	19 677	19 361	4.2	-2.5	463	230	-749	6 973	7.7	2.87	8.2	20.0
Nez Perce	9.3	8.0	8.5	50.8	37 095	33 754	10.8	-0.8	608	499	-422	15 286	12.2	2.40	9.3	26.7
Oneida	8.7	7.3	8.6	49.2	4 210	3 492	18.1	2.1	83	37	38	1 430	23.4	2.85	4.5	22.5
Owyhee	8.9	6.6	5.5	47.8	11 008	8 392	26.8	3.4	228	100	235	3 710	31.6	2.85	8.7	21.8
Payette	9.5	6.7	6.5	50.4	20 868	16 434	25.2	1.4	353	210	153	7 371	22.0	2.78	9.3	20.6
Power	8.4	5.6	4.7	49.8	7 468	7 086	6.4	-0.9	135	59	-151	2 560	8.0	2.92	8.8	20.3
Shoshone	12.0	9.1	8.3	50.1	13 443	13 931	-1.1	-2.4	207	242	-299	5 906	3.8	2.30	8.1	29.4
Teton	5.6	4.2	3.3	47.0	6 419	3 439	74.4	7.0	137	41	316	2 078	85.0	2.87	5.8	21.3
Twin Falls	8.6	6.9	7.4	50.9	64 731	53 580	20.0	0.7	1 175	744	31	23 853	20.9	2.64	9.2	23.6
Valley	13.6	9.1	5.8	48.6	7 716	6 109	25.2	0.8	75	65	50	3 208	33.4	2.36	5.4	24.8
Washington	10.8	9.0	8.7	51.1	9 956	8 550	16.7	-0.2	175	162	-31	3 762	15.5	2.61	8.2	23.5
ILLINOIS	8.4	6.2	5.9	51.0	12 482 301	11 430 602	8.6	0.5	231 194	134 303	-35 126	4 591 779	9.3	2.63	12.3	26.8
Adams	9.3	8.2	9.4	51.9	67 937	66 090	3.3	-0.5	1 071	1 038	-358	26 860	5.3	2.44	9.8	28.5
Alexander	9.8	8.6	8.3	50.4	9 544	10 626	-9.7	-0.5	173	154	-62	3 808	-10.1	2.36	17.5	32.3
Bond	8.8	7.5	7.3	46.2	17 758	14 991	17.6	0.7	226	204	105	6 155	8.9	2.47	8.1	25.6
Boone	9.0	5.8	4.9	50.0	43 472	30 806	35.6	4.0	699	364	1 334	14 597	33.3	2.84	8.7	19.0
Brown	7.8	6.0	6.7	36.4	6 897	5 836	19.1	-0.8	61	70	-43	2 108	5.9	2.36	6.8	30.8
Bureau	10.0	8.2	9.5	51.4	35 280	35 688	-0.5	-0.6	503	524	-189	14 182	2.8	2.47	8.0	27.0
Calhoun	11.6	10.0	9.2	49.8	5 082	5 322	-4.5	0.0	73	99	26	2 046	-0.1	2.46	5.7	26.5
Carroll	10.7	10.0	9.3	50.6	16 526	16 805	-0.8	-0.9	239	263	-123	6 794	2.4	2.42	7.4	27.3
Cass	9.7	7.7	8.0	50.3	13 508	13 437	1.9	-1.4	227	185	-232	5 347	2.9	2.52	9.2	26.1
Champaign	6.6	5.1	4.7	49.7	179 643	173 025	3.8	0.0	2 781	1 301	-1 473	70 597	10.5	2.33	9.2	31.4
Christian	9.8	8.3	8.9	50.1	35 350	34 418	2.8	-0.1	492	521	25	13 932	2.4	2.41	9.1	28.4
Clark	10.2	8.6	9.4	51.4	16 964	15 921	6.8	-0.3	233	276	8	6 971	9.0	2.40	8.7	28.1
Clay	10.0	8.7	10.4	51.0	14 262	14 460	0.7	-2.0	222	245	-277	5 839	2.3	2.41	8.6	27.5
Clinton	8.7	7.7	6.8	48.4	35 658	33 944	4.7	0.3	485	446	102	12 754	10.1	2.60	8.4	24.2
Coles	7.9	6.6	6.7	52.3	52 629	51 644	3.0	-1.1	755	621	-699	21 043	11.0	2.31	8.3	31.2
Cook	8.2	6.1	5.6	51.6	5 350 269	5 105 044	5.3	-0.5	109 813	59 305	-78 704	1 974 181	5.0	2.68	15.6	29.4
Crawford	9.8	8.5	8.1	48.2	20 251	19 464	5.1	-1.0	266	324	-137	7 842	0.6	2.41	8.6	26.8
Cumberland	9.3	7.7	8.2	51.1	11 173	10 670	5.5	-0.7	163	143	-98	4 368	8.4	2.55	7.6	25.5
De Kalb	6.6	4.8	5.0	50.4	89 743	77 932	14.2	0.9	1 327	727	207	31 674	19.9	2.56	8.5	25.5
De Witt	10.3	7.7	8.2	51.1	16 708	16 516	1.7	-0.5	224	230	-78	6 770	4.3	2.44	8.5	26.8
Douglas	9.4	8.1	7.8	51.4	19 887	19 464	2.4	-0.2	346	250	-126	7 574	5.1	2.59	7.9	24.7
Du Page	8.2	5.0	4.8	50.7	912 044	781 689	15.7	0.9	16 711	6 982	-1 707	325 601	16.6	2.73	7.9	22.9
Edgar	9.8	8.3	9.4	51.3	19 410	19 595	0.6	-1.5	264	310	-247	7 874	0.2	2.40	9.6	28.5
Edwards	10.4	9.0	9.5	51.6	6 848	7 440	-6.3	-1.8	85	115	-93	2 905	-3.7	2.37	8.2	27.5
Effingham	8.5	6.9	7.0	50.5	34 352	31 704	8.1	0.3	588	375	-110	13 001	13.4	2.60	9.1	26.1
Fayette	9.4	8.0	7.9	47.9	21 710	20 893	4.4	-0.4	340	292	-132	8 146	5.5	2.46	8.5	27.2
Ford	9.1	8.9	10.5	52.1	14 159	14 275	-0.2	-0.6	225	269	-31	5 639	0.7	2.45	8.0	29.8
Franklin	10.9	8.9	9.8	52.1	38 796	40 319	-3.2	-0.6	579	699	-88	16 408	-0.9	2.34	10.1	29.8
Fulton	9.8	8.7	9.6	48.7	37 875	38 080	0.4	-1.0	485	616	-227	14 877	-0.1	2.40	8.8	27.5
Gallatin	12.7	8.9	9.3	51.5	6 318	6 909	-6.7	-2.0	68	102	-92	2 726	-2.1	2.34	9.8	29.4
Greene	9.6	8.6	8.9	50.9	14 573	15 317	-3.6	-1.3	227	232	-180	5 757	-2.6	2.51	9.2	25.7
Grundy	8.7	6.1	6.2	50.3	38 331	32 337	16.1	2.1	591	402	608	14 293	19.3	2.60	8.6	23.5
Hamilton	10.8	9.3	9.9	51.7	8 450	8 499	1.4	-2.0	106	133	-145	3 462	-0.4	2.43	7.9	27.3
Hancock	10.2	8.9	9.4	51.5	19 909	21 373	-5.9	-1.1	266	294	-180	8 069	-4.0	2.45	7.6	26.9
Hardin	11.8	9.9	8.7	49.9	4 824	5 189	-7.5	0.5	58	90	54	1 987	-3.0	2.30	8.8	28.6
Henderson	12.4	9.2	7.5	50.6	8 205	8 096	1.4	-0.1	95	88	-13	3 365	4.0	2.42	7.1	25.3
Henry	10.0	8.0	8.3	51.0	50 773	51 159	-0.3	-0.5	734	665	-297	20 056	2.8	2.51	8.0	25.1
Iroquois	10.3	8.7	9.4	51.0	30 874	30 787	1.8	-1.5	451	466	-441	12 220	3.7	2.51	8.5	25.2

1. No spouse present.

Table B. States and Counties — **Vital Statistics, Health Resources, and Crime**

STATE County	Births, average 1997–1999		Deaths, average 1997–1999				Physicians,[4] 2000		Hospitals,[4] 1998			Medicare enrollees 2000	Serious crimes known to police, 2000[6]	
			Number		Rate					Beds			Total	
	Total	Rate[1]	Total	Infant[2]	Total[1]	Infant[3]	Number	Rate[5]	Number	Number	Rate[5]		Number	Rate[7]
	32	33	34	35	36	37	38	39	40	41	42	43	44	45
IDAHO—Cont'd														
Custer	52	12.5	41	NA	9.9	NA	1	23	0	0	0	693	52	1 198
Elmore	524	20.8	148	NA	5.9	NA	26	89	1	78	310	2 270	755	2 592
Franklin	213	19.1	93	NA	8.3	NA	3	26	1	65	585	1 442	86	759
Fremont	198	16.7	82	NA	6.9	NA	5	42	0	0	0	1 714	108	914
Gem	201	13.6	157	NA	10.6	NA	4	26	1	24	162	2 531	191	1 258
Gooding	221	16.2	122	NA	8.9	NA	6	42	1	27	198	2 357	186	1 314
Idaho	152	10.1	153	NA	10.2	NA	12	77	2	41	272	2 735	219	1 503
Jefferson	345	17.8	111	NA	5.8	NA	2	10	0	0	0	2 147	270	1 410
Jerome	286	16.0	137	NA	7.7	NA	13	71	1	73	406	2 458	579	3 157
Kootenai	1 382	13.6	786	11	7.7	8.0	156	144	1	187	184	15 546	4 270	4 111
Latah	421	13.0	215	NA	6.6	NA	30	86	1	40	125	3 703	739	2 115
Lemhi	93	11.6	83	NA	10.4	NA	6	77	1	28	349	1 507	NA	NA
Lewis	43	10.9	41	NA	10.4	NA	1	27	0	0	0	1 184	43	1 148
Lincoln	49	12.8	35	NA	9.1	NA	0	0	0	0	0	543	NA	NA
Madison	425	17.7	109	NA	4.5	NA	30	109	1	52	221	1 806	391	1 424
Minidoka	361	17.7	169	NA	8.3	NA	11	55	1	103	510	3 016	390	1 933
Nez Perce	439	11.9	386	NA	10.5	NA	92	246	1	120	326	6 843	1 375	3 790
Oneida	62	15.4	34	NA	8.5	NA	2	48	1	52	1 284	682	71	1 721
Owyhee	175	17.1	76	NA	7.4	NA	0	0	0	0	0	1 263	278	2 612
Payette	313	15.3	181	NA	8.8	NA	10	49	0	0	0	3 057	589	2 862
Power	131	15.8	53	NA	6.4	NA	7	93	1	41	493	793	200	2 653
Shoshone	165	11.9	177	NA	12.8	NA	20	145	2	69	497	2 930	339	2 462
Teton	102	18.5	22	NA	4.1	NA	6	100	1	13	237	564	228	3 801
Twin Falls	933	15.0	587	9	9.4	10.0	134	208	2	171	275	9 848	2 656	4 132
Valley	82	10.3	57	NA	7.1	NA	17	222	2	23	287	1 383	233	3 045
Washington	132	12.9	115	NA	11.3	NA	5	50	1	27	265	1 925	179	1 794
ILLINOIS	179 990	14.9	105 277	1 537	8.7	8.5	25 778	208	206	40 475	336	1 635 047	532 315	4 286
Adams	824	12.3	783	NA	11.7	NA	126	185	2	500	745	12 662	NA	NA
Alexander	140	14.2	130	NA	13.2	NA	4	42	0	0	0	1 935	NA	NA
Bond	187	11.5	179	NA	11.0	NA	7	40	1	50	315	2 803	NA	NA
Boone	550	14.2	292	NA	7.5	NA	33	79	2	129	333	4 625	NA	NA
Brown	54	8.1	56	NA	8.4	NA	0	0	0	0	0	969	NA	NA
Bureau	398	11.2	401	NA	11.3	NA	41	115	2	214	602	6 702	NA	NA
Calhoun	46	9.3	71	NA	14.3	NA	2	39	0	0	0	1 031	NA	NA
Carroll	173	10.2	201	NA	11.9	NA	9	54	0	0	0	3 538	NA	NA
Cass	178	13.4	161	NA	12.1	NA	5	37	0	0	0	2 456	NA	NA
Champaign	2 219	13.1	1 058	17	6.3	7.5	393	219	2	555	331	18 968	NA	NA
Christian	423	12.1	411	NA	11.8	NA	31	88	2	165	478	6 695	NA	NA
Clark	191	11.6	209	NA	12.7	NA	7	41	0	0	0	3 320	NA	NA
Clay	171	11.9	194	NA	13.5	NA	7	48	1	40	276	2 984	NA	NA
Clinton	409	11.5	330	NA	9.3	NA	22	62	1	54	152	4 895	NA	NA
Coles	562	10.9	498	NA	9.7	NA	86	162	1	176	344	7 834	NA	NA
Cook	84 033	16.2	46 439	865	8.9	10.3	15 095	281	63	19 465	375	671 582	NA	NA
Crawford	226	10.8	251	NA	12.0	NA	21	103	1	102	487	3 878	NA	NA
Cumberland	135	12.1	121	NA	10.9	NA	2	18	0	0	0	1 825	NA	NA
De Kalb	1 064	12.5	576	NA	6.8	NA	102	115	3	221	263	9 957	NA	NA
De Witt	200	11.9	181	NA	10.8	NA	11	65	1	36	214	2 974	NA	NA
Douglas	265	13.3	197	NA	9.9	NA	11	55	0	0	0	2 864	NA	NA
Du Page	13 558	15.4	5 344	83	6.1	6.1	2 064	228	8	1 880	214	94 857	NA	NA
Edgar	218	11.1	253	NA	12.9	NA	10	51	1	49	249	3 704	NA	NA
Edwards	72	10.4	86	NA	12.4	NA	2	29	0	0	0	1 298	NA	NA
Effingham	507	15.1	311	NA	9.3	NA	72	210	1	143	427	5 502	NA	NA
Fayette	255	11.6	234	NA	10.7	NA	10	46	1	170	774	3 720	NA	NA
Ford	167	11.8	194	NA	13.8	NA	12	84	1	56	398	2 726	NA	NA
Franklin	439	10.8	557	NA	13.8	NA	28	72	2	150	371	8 600	NA	NA
Fulton	407	10.5	469	NA	12.1	NA	36	94	1	124	320	7 660	NA	NA
Gallatin	66	10.0	85	NA	12.9	NA	1	16	0	0	0	1 389	NA	NA
Greene	182	11.7	182	NA	11.6	NA	8	54	1	73	469	2 987	NA	NA
Grundy	472	12.9	315	NA	8.6	NA	50	133	1	82	224	5 177	NA	NA
Hamilton	90	10.4	114	NA	13.3	NA	7	81	1	91	1 057	1 802	NA	NA
Hancock	217	10.3	228	NA	10.8	NA	13	65	1	67	318	4 155	NA	NA
Hardin	48	9.8	71	NA	14.3	NA	3	63	1	48	979	944	NA	NA
Henderson	91	10.6	89	NA	10.3	NA	6	73	0	0	0	1 382	NA	NA
Henry	560	10.9	537	NA	10.4	NA	39	76	2	168	326	8 851	NA	NA
Iroquois	358	11.5	376	NA	12.0	NA	23	73	2	99	317	6 202	NA	NA

1. Per 1,000 estimated resident population, average 1997–1999.   2. Deaths of infants under 1 year old.   3. Deaths of infants under 1 year old per 1,000 live births.   4. Data subject to copyright.   5. Per 100,000 resident population as of July 1 of the year shown.   6. Data for serious crimes have not been adjusted for underreporting; this may affect comparability between geographic areas and over time.   7. Per 100,000 population estimated by the FBI.

STATE County	Serious crimes known to police, 2000[1] (cont'd) Rate[2]		Education School enrollment and attainment, 1990				Local government expenditures, fiscal 1999[5]		Money income 1989				Income and poverty, 1998			
			Enrollment[3]		Attainment[4] (percent)					Households Median			Percent below poverty level			
	Violent	Property	Total	Percent private	High school graduate or more	Bachelor's degree or more	Total current expenditures (mil dol)	Current expenditures per student (dollars)	Per capita[6] (dollars)	Dollars	Percent change, 1979–1989 (constant 1989 dollars)	Percent with $100,000 or more	Median household income	All persons	Persons under 18	Persons 5–17 in families
	46	47	48	49	50	51	52	53	54	55	56	57	58	59	60	61
IDAHO—Cont'd																
Custer	184	1 013	1 036	5.3	81.7	15.6	5.6	6 052	11 607	24 393	23.9	1.8	35 038	12.8	16.5	15.8
Elmore	312	2 279	5 856	5.8	83.1	15.8	24.8	4 782	9 981	23 750	6.2	0.6	34 813	12.7	18.2	16.8
Franklin	26	733	3 106	2.4	82.2	14.3	12.2	4 096	8 532	25 446	5.2	1.2	35 125	12.0	15.2	12.9
Fremont	102	812	3 460	7.5	75.6	11.1	13.9	5 480	8 674	23 498	6.2	1.3	30 668	15.9	20.8	17.0
Gem	125	1 133	2 867	6.2	70.1	8.6	13.8	4 630	10 450	21 495	-3.9	1.6	31 633	14.1	20.1	18.1
Gooding	113	1 201	3 143	3.1	72.5	13.3	15.4	5 135	9 625	19 823	-1.9	1.6	31 820	14.4	20.3	17.9
Idaho	144	1 359	3 312	5.7	75.1	12.7	13.6	5 673	10 527	22 093	-9.0	1.4	30 816	17.1	23.5	21.2
Jefferson	167	1 242	5 708	6.3	77.6	11.8	25.5	4 622	9 055	24 421	2.8	1.9	35 190	13.3	16.9	14.5
Jerome	305	2 851	4 158	3.7	72.4	11.0	17.0	4 528	9 727	21 209	-8.2	2.4	32 724	15.3	21.1	18.5
Kootenai	404	3 707	18 166	9.4	81.1	16.0	79.6	4 543	12 330	25 593	0.8	2.2	37 516	11.3	17.1	14.2
Latah	74	2 041	13 452	6.2	86.6	35.8	29.3	6 402	10 892	22 635	-3.7	1.4	36 494	13.0	16.7	14.2
Lemhi	NA	NA	1 590	5.0	73.9	11.8	7.3	4 942	10 624	19 697	-6.1	1.0	29 031	16.0	22.2	20.7
Lewis	80	1 068	786	0.8	78.8	13.2	7.3	6 505	9 780	20 926	-11.7	1.1	29 323	15.8	23.4	22.3
Lincoln	NA	NA	885	2.7	79.8	11.9	5.5	6 232	9 339	21 640	7.5	0.7	30 857	14.1	22.1	16.8
Madison	51	1 373	12 995	51.1	87.6	19.2	25.7	4 653	7 385	23 000	5.2	2.1	36 251	13.8	14.8	12.6
Minidoka	188	1 745	5 728	3.6	68.5	9.0	21.4	4 408	10 110	23 327	-5.0	2.3	30 807	14.9	18.2	17.7
Nez Perce	168	3 622	8 769	6.3	79.9	15.6	36.6	6 181	12 476	25 219	-5.1	1.9	36 643	12.3	19.3	16.7
Oneida	145	1 576	1 031	3.5	78.7	12.9	4.9	4 889	8 824	22 582	17.6	0.4	33 326	13.5	16.7	16.4
Owyhee	301	2 311	2 293	6.7	62.0	8.7	14.0	5 442	9 786	18 595	4.8	1.5	27 934	21.5	28.3	27.8
Payette	199	2 663	4 226	7.1	67.4	9.8	20.0	4 606	9 400	20 367	4.3	1.5	31 843	15.8	22.0	20.7
Power	252	2 401	2 305	5.2	72.1	11.1	12.2	6 555	9 951	24 771	-5.8	1.2	34 013	14.9	19.3	19.4
Shoshone	276	2 186	3 222	4.0	70.1	9.0	16.6	6 674	10 373	20 980	-25.8	0.6	29 272	18.7	27.3	25.0
Teton	167	3 634	907	4.1	80.2	17.4	6.1	4 759	8 983	22 799	17.6	1.1	33 463	10.2	13.3	12.5
Twin Falls	300	3 831	14 332	5.9	75.4	13.3	56.9	4 605	11 096	23 520	-3.4	2.2	33 008	13.5	18.9	15.9
Valley	549	2 496	1 432	5.4	83.8	19.4	9.7	6 555	12 344	24 232	-8.5	3.3	34 636	11.9	15.4	15.5
Washington	180	1 614	2 183	6.1	72.7	10.3	11.0	5 505	9 088	17 917	-1.3	0.8	28 460	17.7	23.0	22.3
ILLINOIS	657	3 629	3 031 673	19.5	76.2	21.0	13 603.0	6 762	15 201	32 252	-0.4	4.9	43 141	10.6	15.4	13.9
Adams	NA	NA	16 253	23.2	75.1	13.7	64.9	6 152	11 601	23 317	-9.8	2.1	36 597	12.1	16.3	15.8
Alexander	NA	NA	2 677	4.6	59.7	7.8	12.6	7 198	8 846	14 786	-7.8	1.4	22 261	27.0	32.2	39.7
Bond	NA	NA	3 862	17.1	69.3	12.7	11.9	4 981	10 407	23 756	-0.2	0.7	35 077	11.7	14.6	14.6
Boone	NA	NA	7 840	15.1	75.5	12.0	35.7	4 912	14 355	35 103	1.0	3.8	51 925	6.2	9.8	8.7
Brown	NA	NA	1 400	16.4	68.9	9.8	4.3	5 403	8 894	20 445	3.2	1.2	33 862	12.9	12.8	14.2
Bureau	NA	NA	8 505	9.0	76.6	12.5	39.0	6 159	11 915	26 248	-9.5	1.1	37 599	8.9	12.3	11.8
Calhoun	NA	NA	1 196	25.4	62.8	7.0	4.6	5 980	9 815	21 163	1.5	0.9	33 794	11.1	13.6	13.6
Carroll	NA	NA	3 865	3.7	76.0	10.6	18.2	5 644	12 358	25 758	-2.4	2.0	37 035	9.7	13.9	13.7
Cass	NA	NA	3 230	8.5	72.3	10.6	13.0	5 570	10 850	23 642	-13.2	1.4	34 365	11.3	15.8	15.2
Champaign	NA	NA	67 446	5.9	82.6	34.1	147.3	6 177	13 130	26 541	-3.7	3.0	40 519	11.3	14.9	14.7
Christian	NA	NA	7 710	9.1	73.1	9.3	42.9	6 477	11 676	24 506	-8.1	1.3	36 105	11.0	15.9	14.9
Clark	NA	NA	3 450	2.7	71.3	9.2	15.1	4 764	11 176	23 281	-1.3	0.9	33 488	11.2	16.1	16.0
Clay	NA	NA	3 279	4.4	65.6	7.6	15.0	5 366	9 590	20 006	-1.8	1.1	30 440	12.7	16.2	16.4
Clinton	NA	NA	8 786	16.7	67.2	9.2	29.2	5 141	11 422	29 890	5.5	1.0	41 346	8.2	10.9	10.1
Coles	NA	NA	18 652	2.9	76.1	18.7	50.4	6 970	11 315	24 153	-4.6	1.9	36 435	12.8	16.9	16.0
Cook	NA	NA	1 324 299	25.6	73.4	22.8	6 089.0	7 685	15 697	32 673	1.6	5.5	41 815	13.1	20.0	17.2
Crawford	NA	NA	4 506	4.1	76.0	9.5	19.7	5 394	11 768	23 912	-8.5	1.8	34 146	11.6	15.8	15.8
Cumberland	NA	NA	2 695	3.9	72.2	8.2	9.8	4 727	10 486	23 623	-3.5	1.2	34 247	11.6	15.7	16.1
De Kalb	NA	NA	31 177	5.7	83.9	26.1	97.9	6 573	12 657	30 864	0.4	2.5	46 964	7.6	9.6	8.6
De Witt	NA	NA	3 822	6.0	74.6	11.8	22.1	6 521	12 833	27 196	-8.0	2.4	39 289	10.5	15.1	15.4
Douglas	NA	NA	4 509	5.9	74.0	11.4	16.4	5 165	11 461	26 758	-11.4	1.1	37 629	9.3	13.6	12.9
Du Page	NA	NA	210 271	23.5	88.6	36.0	1 072.0	7 141	21 155	48 876	6.0	10.2	64 365	3.7	5.7	4.2
Edgar	NA	NA	4 570	5.2	73.5	11.0	22.1	5 853	11 190	21 657	-7.0	1.2	32 234	13.2	18.3	18.5
Edwards	NA	NA	1 782	3.3	69.7	8.4	5.0	4 765	10 713	21 238	-7.9	1.2	30 994	11.2	15.6	15.4
Effingham	NA	NA	7 923	13.1	75.0	13.0	31.7	4 852	11 977	27 245	-4.3	1.7	38 960	9.0	12.0	11.7
Fayette	NA	NA	4 674	6.7	68.8	8.5	19.4	5 763	10 496	22 029	-2.7	1.3	30 942	13.7	17.3	17.9
Ford	NA	NA	3 390	5.2	77.2	12.1	19.8	7 983	11 895	25 801	-9.4	1.2	37 539	8.8	12.8	11.9
Franklin	NA	NA	9 597	4.0	66.7	8.2	43.6	6 632	10 204	18 698	-11.6	0.9	26 633	17.1	23.8	24.0
Fulton	NA	NA	8 982	4.3	73.8	9.5	44.2	5 957	10 720	21 701	-20.7	0.8	32 316	12.8	17.8	17.1
Gallatin	NA	NA	1 507	3.5	58.4	7.4	6.5	6 399	10 367	19 105	-5.3	1.3	27 892	17.7	24.1	27.0
Greene	NA	NA	3 350	8.2	69.0	9.0	13.5	5 282	9 884	20 752	-3.2	0.6	29 530	13.8	18.1	19.1
Grundy	NA	NA	8 101	9.7	79.0	12.5	55.2	6 819	14 474	35 728	-1.7	2.4	52 469	5.4	7.7	6.9
Hamilton	NA	NA	1 888	1.3	60.0	7.6	8.6	6 048	9 984	18 274	-5.9	1.4	28 314	14.9	20.0	21.2
Hancock	NA	NA	5 060	7.6	77.5	14.4	21.4	5 124	11 358	24 036	-5.3	1.7	35 566	10.6	14.3	13.9
Hardin	NA	NA	1 226	0.8	59.7	7.0	5.4	7 136	8 314	15 498	-11.1	0.9	26 552	17.4	21.2	25.1
Henderson	NA	NA	1 828	5.5	73.3	9.5	7.4	5 712	10 638	22 165	-17.2	0.7	35 221	10.8	15.1	15.7
Henry	NA	NA	13 143	8.5	77.2	11.8	52.9	5 436	12 260	26 198	-17.5	1.7	39 730	8.4	11.5	11.4
Iroquois	NA	NA	7 066	8.2	73.4	10.1	29.5	5 135	11 653	25 435	-7.4	1.4	34 827	9.8	14.4	13.4

1. Data for serious crimes have not been adjusted for underreporting; this may affect comparability between geographic areas and over time. 2. Per 100,000 population estimated by the FBI. 3. All persons 3 years old and over enrolled in nursery school through college. 4. Persons 25 years old and over. 5. Elementary and secondary education expenditures, local government fiscal years ending between July 1, 1998 and June 30, 1999. 6. Based on population enumerated as of April 1, 1990.

Table B. States and Counties — **Personal Income**

STATE County	Personal income, 1999 Total (mil dol)	Percent change, 1998–1999	Per capita[1] Dollars	Per capita[1] Rank	Wages and salaries[2] (mil dol)	Proprietor's income (mil dol)	Dividends, interest, and rent (mil dol)	Transfer payments Total (mil dol)	Government payments to individuals Total (mil dol)	Social Security (mil dol)	Medical payments (mil dol)	Income mainte- nance (mil dol)	Unemploy- ment insurance (mil dol)
	62	63	64	65	66	67	68	69	70	71	72	73	74
IDAHO—Cont'd													
Custer	94	3.0	23 087	1 073	40	13	24	12	12	6	3	1	1
Elmore	561	6.9	21 907	1 387	362	53	79	53	49	20	12	5	2
Franklin	175	3.9	15 451	2 947	56	35	28	27	25	14	7	2	0
Fremont	186	3.4	15 670	2 932	74	25	40	32	30	16	8	3	1
Gem	274	5.1	18 078	2 525	87	19	50	52	50	24	16	4	2
Gooding	349	7.1	25 420	597	121	124	52	45	42	21	14	4	1
Idaho	266	2.8	17 690	2 603	120	22	73	59	56	28	18	5	2
Jefferson	338	4.7	16 947	2 743	109	40	50	46	42	21	13	4	2
Jerome	424	6.5	23 434	979	161	141	54	53	50	23	18	4	1
Kootenai	2 361	6.9	22 527	1 211	1 139	205	468	335	317	155	101	20	13
Latah	695	3.3	21 391	1 552	380	44	161	84	79	36	22	5	1
Lemhi	151	0.8	18 886	2 324	66	16	42	32	30	14	10	2	1
Lewis	75	3.1	19 074	2 265	26	9	23	19	18	9	7	2	0
Lincoln	76	6.5	19 877	2 027	31	15	15	13	12	6	3	1	0
Madison	369	8.4	14 861	3 000	233	60	59	46	42	18	18	3	1
Minidoka	344	4.9	16 955	2 742	200	47	50	59	56	25	19	5	3
Nez Perce	905	5.0	24 519	752	658	73	179	152	146	69	51	11	3
Oneida	63	1.2	15 412	2 950	20	7	12	13	13	6	5	1	0
Owyhee	172	2.0	16 504	2 827	55	32	25	28	27	12	9	3	0
Payette	378	7.1	18 128	2 516	148	41	67	63	60	30	19	6	1
Power	152	8.7	18 027	2 537	130	25	24	20	19	9	6	2	1
Shoshone	265	0.5	19 426	2 166	134	20	52	67	65	31	22	6	2
Teton	86	7.1	15 020	2 987	35	7	21	12	11	5	4	1	0
Twin Falls	1 343	3.2	21 322	1 562	747	191	286	202	191	93	65	14	4
Valley	192	4.1	24 390	783	83	25	59	31	29	14	7	1	2
Washington	166	-0.4	16 075	2 892	77	19	37	37	35	18	11	3	1
ILLINOIS	377 650	4.3	31 138	X	246 148	31 286	75 431	42 054	39 567	16 726	15 610	4 286	1 176
Adams	1 642	1.8	24 523	751	943	129	422	255	242	121	80	21	5
Alexander	167	1.8	16 828	2 771	69	13	26	51	49	17	19	10	1
Bond	347	1.8	20 249	1 907	125	32	69	60	57	27	20	5	1
Boone	1 140	6.3	28 829	270	641	65	208	104	96	53	31	5	4
Brown	111	-4.9	16 045	2 894	71	12	22	19	18	8	6	2	0
Bureau	786	2.2	22 242	1 289	349	41	192	129	122	67	41	6	4
Calhoun	106	0.8	21 762	1 429	24	12	22	20	19	9	7	2	1
Carroll	395	0.0	23 692	918	154	55	93	67	63	30	21	4	2
Cass	307	1.0	23 174	1 053	157	36	65	52	50	23	19	3	2
Champaign	4 296	4.6	25 233	627	3 084	197	1 042	416	381	170	126	41	12
Christian	800	1.2	22 335	1 265	306	57	176	157	150	73	55	10	4
Clark	344	3.2	20 772	1 747	136	29	76	65	62	32	21	4	1
Clay	308	2.0	21 542	1 510	163	26	62	68	65	27	27	5	2
Clinton	836	3.4	23 442	976	308	67	168	123	115	52	48	6	3
Coles	1 170	1.1	22 587	1 198	823	74	251	184	173	73	69	13	3
Cook	173 415	3.9	33 398	124	128 404	17 049	35 151	20 189	19 121	6 887	8 360	2 666	525
Crawford	405	1.0	19 407	2 176	218	30	103	77	73	38	23	5	3
Cumberland	234	1.2	21 121	1 625	48	28	42	38	36	17	13	3	1
De Kalb	2 324	9.0	26 717	438	1 079	124	467	221	203	97	70	11	6
De Witt	382	1.9	22 884	1 114	250	24	76	67	64	29	21	5	2
Douglas	449	3.4	22 613	1 191	240	35	95	69	65	35	21	4	2
Du Page	39 980	5.3	44 793	23	27 954	4 200	7 441	2 210	2 027	1 101	697	85	67
Edgar	418	-2.2	21 418	1 545	170	48	89	79	75	36	27	6	2
Edwards	137	1.4	20 002	1 989	86	11	38	26	24	13	7	2	1
Effingham	833	1.8	24 669	719	570	74	197	109	102	51	36	7	4
Fayette	397	2.0	18 044	2 534	160	37	86	84	80	36	30	7	3
Ford	335	1.6	23 820	893	121	23	81	55	52	27	19	3	1
Franklin	708	2.0	17 551	2 641	266	45	151	200	191	83	68	19	5
Fulton	793	2.0	20 503	1 833	226	37	166	170	162	76	64	11	4
Gallatin	128	1.5	19 452	2 158	49	12	31	31	30	13	11	4	1
Greene	255	0.3	16 197	2 876	69	19	57	62	58	27	20	6	1
Grundy	1 081	5.1	29 081	258	592	42	210	113	105	55	36	4	6
Hamilton	153	1.0	17 872	2 563	39	14	34	39	37	16	14	4	1
Hancock	467	1.2	22 285	1 278	158	49	101	77	72	37	22	6	1
Hardin	87	3.8	17 752	2 588	30	9	18	25	24	10	10	2	0
Henderson	169	-0.4	19 631	2 100	28	9	31	28	27	14	8	2	0
Henry	1 224	1.2	23 595	943	397	68	273	178	167	90	53	11	7
Iroquois	665	1.0	21 311	1 567	232	66	163	126	120	62	42	7	3

1. Based on the resident population estimated as of July 1 of the year shown.　2. Includes other labor income.

STATE County	Earnings, 1999									Social Security beneficiaries, December 2000		Housing units, 1990	
					Percent by selected industries								
			Goods-related[1]		Service-related and other[2]							Supplemental Security Income recipients, December 2000		
	Total (mil dol)	Farm	Total	Manufacturing	Total	Retail trade	Finance, insurance, and real estate	Services	Government	Number	Rate[3]		Total	Percent change, 1980–1990
	75	76	77	78	79	80	81	82	83	84	85	86	87	88
IDAHO—Cont'd														
Custer	53	3.1	D	D	D	9.6	2.2	D	27.6	834	192	66	2 437	16.0
Elmore	415	10.0	D	2.1	D	6.0	1.8	6.7	66.3	2 765	95	243	8 430	4.7
Franklin	90	27.0	D	9.2	D	9.0	D	11.5	21.4	1 762	156	111	3 240	6.3
Fremont	99	13.9	D	3.1	D	8.6	D	11.0	32.8	2 041	173	136	5 961	10.9
Gem	106	3.8	D	22.3	D	9.6	D	14.6	22.7	3 058	201	201	4 725	3.2
Gooding	245	53.7	10.7	7.6	24.3	4.2	1.7	5.9	11.4	2 701	191	198	4 800	4.6
Idaho	142	-2.3	26.6	17.7	41.9	10.0	4.1	14.6	33.7	3 616	233	339	6 346	0.0
Jefferson	149	16.6	D	10.9	D	7.8	D	7.9	21.0	2 673	140	188	5 353	7.2
Jerome	301	41.6	12.5	7.9	37.6	6.7	1.5	9.5	8.3	2 960	161	285	5 886	6.4
Kootenai	1 344	0.0	24.3	13.5	57.1	14.3	6.6	25.1	18.6	18 889	174	1 552	31 964	18.6
Latah	424	0.2	D	6.7	D	11.2	2.6	18.4	48.6	4 200	120	248	11 870	7.8
Lemhi	82	0.2	D	6.6	D	12.7	2.6	18.6	35.3	1 826	234	142	3 752	8.7
Lewis	35	-1.5	D	13.4	50.5	12.0	2.7	10.3	31.0	1 132	302	141	1 681	-7.0
Lincoln	46	25.8	D	D	D	3.1	D	8.3	32.5	798	197	52	1 386	3.2
Madison	293	6.4	D	8.6	D	9.6	7.5	36.1	14.9	2 240	82	164	6 133	10.8
Minidoka	247	16.3	D	25.5	D	5.2	D	9.1	16.0	3 264	162	308	7 044	2.4
Nez Perce	731	0.1	30.4	25.5	55.1	11.3	6.9	24.7	14.3	7 967	213	754	14 463	7.1
Oneida	27	10.9	D	3.8	D	8.6	4.2	11.0	36.3	787	191	52	1 496	1.4
Owyhee	87	34.3	D	4.5	D	7.2	D	7.5	19.3	1 649	155	134	3 332	10.5
Payette	188	12.6	D	23.9	D	8.2	D	14.7	15.5	3 843	187	384	6 520	6.6
Power	154	16.5	50.7	47.0	D	2.8	D	4.4	11.8	1 030	137	78	2 701	5.6
Shoshone	154	0.1	37.0	5.8	38.8	15.4	2.7	14.6	24.3	3 471	252	382	6 923	-9.8
Teton	42	10.0	D	3.1	D	13.8	D	16.0	28.1	707	118	30	1 645	32.1
Twin Falls	939	9.1	18.5	11.0	54.9	13.7	4.7	21.3	17.5	11 311	176	1 076	21 158	3.1
Valley	108	1.6	D	6.5	D	13.9	6.9	17.5	33.3	1 713	224	79	6 640	30.0
Washington	96	7.8	25.5	19.0	45.9	8.4	4.6	11.8	20.8	2 291	230	206	3 685	2.2
ILLINOIS	277 433	0.2	23.5	17.7	63.1	7.8	10.4	30.0	13.2	1 840 206	148	248 777	4 506 275	4.3
Adams	1 072	1.0	30.6	23.9	55.0	11.4	4.5	25.1	13.4	14 202	208	1 097	28 021	-2.0
Alexander	82	-0.7	D	16.1	D	6.7	1.4	19.1	26.6	2 243	234	626	4 902	-6.9
Bond	157	8.5	18.8	15.5	46.1	7.2	3.5	19.6	26.5	3 226	183	232	6 136	-3.8
Boone	705	1.4	D	53.2	D	6.5	2.4	9.8	7.2	5 897	141	201	11 477	14.1
Brown	83	7.4	D	0.0	D	4.1	3.2	8.5	23.3	1 076	155	94	2 357	-1.2
Bureau	391	1.0	D	23.0	D	8.7	4.5	20.8	18.5	7 326	206	251	14 762	-2.6
Calhoun	36	15.0	D	D	D	16.1	7.1	14.3	21.8	1 182	232	85	2 951	-2.5
Carroll	209	11.7	26.4	19.6	43.1	7.4	4.1	10.3	18.8	3 741	224	192	7 481	-1.8
Cass	194	7.9	D	D	D	6.3	3.2	12.6	12.5	2 684	196	194	5 698	-6.3
Champaign	3 281	0.1	18.5	12.8	46.1	9.4	4.5	23.7	35.2	21 055	117	2 205	68 416	9.4
Christian	363	3.3	D	13.5	D	11.9	4.1	22.3	15.8	8 183	231	581	14 640	0.3
Clark	165	0.3	45.6	37.5	40.3	9.2	3.9	11.7	13.7	3 747	220	246	7 115	-1.8
Clay	188	1.9	D	43.6	D	6.2	3.5	11.0	15.0	3 385	232	309	6 270	-3.3
Clinton	374	7.2	22.5	10.0	47.5	12.4	3.3	18.0	22.8	6 428	181	298	12 746	7.1
Coles	896	0.4	29.3	23.7	49.0	9.2	2.8	26.6	21.3	8 508	160	981	20 329	1.3
Cook	145 453	0.0	19.8	15.5	68.4	6.6	13.5	33.3	11.8	741 746	138	154 483	2 021 833	1.4
Crawford	248	-2.1	D	39.6	D	8.7	4.2	16.0	16.3	4 423	216	275	8 464	-2.7
Cumberland	77	9.1	14.4	8.2	D	16.6	4.1	16.6	19.1	2 166	192	158	4 448	0.9
De Kalb	1 203	1.9	28.8	21.5	39.0	8.5	4.5	17.6	30.3	10 831	122	452	27 351	8.1
De Witt	274	-0.3	26.2	17.9	59.8	7.6	3.0	10.4	14.3	3 261	194	231	6 942	-5.3
Douglas	275	0.2	D	40.7	D	13.6	3.6	10.0	9.3	4 021	202	155	7 607	-1.7
Du Page	32 154	0.0	20.9	14.6	72.8	8.9	7.9	37.1	6.3	112 643	125	5 441	292 537	24.6
Edgar	219	11.3	27.9	23.2	D	7.5	4.6	16.1	20.4	4 202	213	383	8 733	-4.3
Edwards	97	0.1	D	D	D	5.2	2.3	6.4	9.1	1 616	232	83	3 260	-4.2
Effingham	644	1.0	37.1	30.0	51.2	12.3	3.0	22.3	10.7	6 097	178	387	12 189	4.3
Fayette	196	5.5	27.6	21.6	45.1	11.4	3.7	16.9	21.8	4 478	205	457	8 551	-4.2
Ford	144	1.6	24.8	15.9	D	10.6	D	19.8	17.1	3 121	219	135	6 118	-3.3
Franklin	311	0.1	D	16.9	D	14.7	2.3	22.7	24.1	9 685	248	1 288	18 430	-2.7
Fulton	262	0.3	10.8	4.1	60.4	15.2	4.3	24.9	28.5	8 581	224	571	16 480	-6.0
Gallatin	61	5.5	D	5.8	D	6.4	1.0	D	15.8	1 596	248	253	3 197	0.2
Greene	88	5.1	D	10.3	D	12.7	7.6	17.5	26.1	3 302	224	336	6 575	-3.5
Grundy	634	-1.0	22.6	15.0	67.5	7.6	2.3	19.6	10.9	5 903	157	127	12 652	9.7
Hamilton	54	7.0	D	4.2	D	10.9	D	13.8	34.4	2 069	240	238	4 013	-3.9
Hancock	208	9.5	D	D	D	6.3	3.4	13.9	15.8	4 453	221	243	9 692	-3.1
Hardin	39	3.7	D	D	D	5.2	2.0	18.1	24.8	1 181	246	165	2 403	-2.9
Henderson	37	3.8	D	D	D	9.5	5.8	17.2	35.0	1 623	198	96	4 089	-3.9
Henry	465	0.6	D	15.6	D	14.6	4.9	16.1	20.5	10 165	199	409	20 881	-3.6
Iroquois	298	5.7	D	14.0	D	8.3	5.7	21.5	15.2	7 070	226	357	12 819	-4.9

1. Covers mining, construction, and manufacturing.   2. Covers private sector earnings in agricultural services, forestry, and fisheries; transportation and public utilities; wholesale trade; retail trade; finance, insurance, and real estate; and services.   3. Per 1,000 resident population estimated as of July 1 of the year shown.

STATE County	Housing units, 1990 (cont'd)								Civilian labor force, 2001				Civilian employment, 1990[5]		
	Occupied units										Unemployment			Percent	
		Owner-occupied				Renter-occupied									
				Owner cost as a percent of income											
	Total	Percent	Median value[1]	With a mortgage	Without a mortgage	Median rent[2]	Rent as percent of income	Sub-standard units[3] (percent)	Total	Percent change, 2000–2001	Total	Rate[4]	Total	Professional, managerial, and technical	Precision production, craft, and repair
	89	90	91	92	93	94	95	96	97	98	99	100	101	102	103

IDAHO—Cont'd

STATE County	89	90	91	92	93	94	95	96	97	98	99	100	101	102	103
Custer	1 561	71.0	49 800	14.9	13.3	317	17.7	3.4	2 206	8.9	168	7.6	1 861	25.3	14.5
Elmore	7 136	54.4	57 900	21.9	11.4	295	22.5	3.8	9 610	5.4	580	6.0	7 373	26.2	13.4
Franklin	2 824	80.2	46 800	18.5	12.4	309	15.7	5.4	4 954	5.3	191	3.9	3 375	17.1	14.4
Fremont	3 453	80.2	46 200	20.9	12.6	273	21.7	6.2	4 758	2.2	308	6.5	4 317	20.2	8.1
Gem	4 424	77.7	46 700	20.0	12.3	265	21.8	5.3	6 601	6.2	522	7.9	4 757	17.0	13.9
Gooding	4 320	69.9	40 600	20.0	12.2	257	20.2	4.0	6 964	4.9	244	3.5	5 033	17.7	10.2
Idaho	5 187	75.5	45 700	17.1	11.4	267	19.7	5.8	6 252	2.0	596	9.5	5 272	22.6	12.4
Jefferson	4 871	80.5	54 300	18.8	12.8	314	21.5	10.0	10 497	2.8	391	3.7	6 589	22.6	10.5
Jerome	5 325	70.4	42 100	20.0	12.9	275	21.5	4.8	9 363	4.6	358	3.8	6 660	17.5	10.2
Kootenai	26 942	71.3	64 800	21.4	11.8	368	26.5	3.2	56 817	2.8	4 306	7.6	30 695	26.4	13.1
Latah	11 229	56.4	63 500	16.3	11.1	314	27.7	2.8	14 971	-0.3	498	3.3	14 060	36.7	6.7
Lemhi	2 769	73.6	47 500	20.0	13.0	258	21.2	4.2	3 759	3.1	285	7.6	2 776	20.9	14.0
Lewis	1 393	71.2	38 500	18.1	11.3	232	19.8	2.0	1 568	2.6	118	7.5	1 315	21.7	10.0
Lincoln	1 191	72.0	37 000	17.5	11.3	238	18.4	5.3	1 934	6.4	76	3.9	1 587	17.1	9.8
Madison	5 801	59.9	68 700	20.6	11.7	299	26.1	15.0	11 552	6.1	234	2.0	8 592	24.0	7.1
Minidoka	6 472	74.5	41 400	16.8	11.9	269	20.3	6.6	9 828	2.5	629	6.4	8 186	16.4	12.0
Nez Perce	13 618	66.2	56 700	16.5	11.6	304	22.9	1.4	23 147	1.0	910	3.9	15 295	25.1	13.0
Oneida	1 159	81.8	43 100	18.3	12.7	319	23.0	5.6	1 758	3.4	63	3.6	1 327	20.0	12.4
Owyhee	2 820	68.4	39 900	22.5	12.4	244	19.3	8.2	4 337	3.0	197	4.5	3 602	14.4	10.3
Payette	6 040	70.9	43 800	18.8	12.4	280	24.3	6.3	9 955	0.5	838	8.4	6 802	18.3	12.5
Power	2 370	73.8	50 400	20.8	11.9	267	20.2	6.8	3 446	-1.3	247	7.2	3 029	14.5	9.8
Shoshone	5 691	70.9	32 500	13.5	11.9	240	21.5	3.2	6 736	3.7	807	12.0	5 310	20.6	23.2
Teton	1 123	74.0	59 000	17.7	13.9	333	23.1	8.0	3 681	11.7	93	2.5	1 596	17.9	14.3
Twin Falls	19 737	67.8	50 700	18.0	11.7	307	22.9	3.6	33 744	4.9	1 389	4.1	24 359	21.2	10.6
Valley	2 404	70.6	70 700	20.4	12.2	326	24.1	5.3	4 102	0.9	342	8.3	2 548	28.8	13.8
Washington	3 257	72.5	43 700	20.1	12.2	256	26.7	3.9	4 498	-1.0	396	8.8	3 223	22.8	9.1
ILLINOIS	4 202 240	64.2	80 900	20.2	12.7	445	25.9	4.2	6 348 558	-1.1	342 580	5.4	5 417 967	30.0	10.7
Adams	25 515	71.1	43 400	17.1	12.4	275	24.2	2.2	36 492	-1.5	1 579	4.3	30 089	24.8	11.2
Alexander	4 234	68.4	23 900	21.2	13.8	174	29.1	4.7	4 212	-1.6	373	8.9	3 418	21.1	8.7
Bond	5 652	77.8	40 400	19.3	14.0	271	25.9	2.5	8 398	1.3	423	5.0	6 640	19.5	12.1
Boone	10 950	72.3	67 900	17.6	11.8	378	21.9	3.0	22 025	-1.8	1 620	7.4	15 239	20.9	16.2
Brown	1 991	73.7	30 600	16.8	14.0	251	22.3	1.1	3 012	-2.2	90	3.0	2 152	19.3	9.9
Bureau	13 790	72.7	41 800	16.3	13.1	326	22.2	1.4	19 219	-0.8	1 060	5.5	16 211	20.3	11.9
Calhoun	2 048	80.2	35 000	18.2	14.6	246	24.5	4.7	3 320	0.6	186	5.6	1 954	18.1	14.3
Carroll	6 638	71.8	38 300	16.4	12.4	286	20.7	1.9	8 571	-2.3	716	8.4	7 667	19.2	12.9
Cass	5 195	74.1	32 900	16.3	12.6	294	22.2	2.1	7 276	0.9	330	4.5	6 007	18.8	15.3
Champaign	63 900	54.5	67 700	20.1	12.2	411	29.6	2.6	99 009	-0.2	2 755	2.8	87 114	39.0	7.4
Christian	13 591	73.9	37 400	16.4	12.9	313	24.5	2.5	18 517	-2.7	982	5.3	15 021	20.2	13.8
Clark	6 394	78.2	34 200	16.2	12.1	264	23.4	1.7	10 256	-2.6	580	5.7	7 026	17.5	14.0
Clay	5 708	78.9	31 900	20.8	13.2	246	25.8	2.9	7 292	-0.7	561	7.7	5 903	18.7	15.4
Clinton	11 583	79.5	55 000	20.4	12.3	330	22.5	3.1	17 267	-1.5	870	5.0	15 025	20.0	12.6
Coles	18 957	64.7	44 600	17.6	12.7	332	26.8	2.2	27 416	-1.6	1 451	5.3	24 092	24.9	9.5
Cook	1 879 488	55.5	102 100	20.9	12.8	478	26.6	6.4	2 675 531	-0.8	157 274	5.9	2 414 964	31.0	9.6
Crawford	7 792	78.4	36 700	15.3	11.9	282	23.5	2.4	10 032	0.1	656	6.5	8 092	17.8	15.0
Cumberland	4 029	80.7	37 700	17.0	12.8	268	23.3	4.7	5 620	-0.9	396	7.0	4 674	16.3	12.7
De Kalb	26 413	58.1	81 200	20.2	12.8	424	27.4	2.5	47 995	-1.0	2 079	4.3	40 120	29.4	11.3
De Witt	6 488	70.9	43 700	16.2	12.5	305	22.1	1.0	7 503	-5.1	476	6.3	7 461	20.8	13.0
Douglas	7 206	74.5	44 000	16.0	12.3	309	22.2	3.8	12 656	-2.8	497	3.9	9 069	18.7	13.6
Du Page	279 344	74.4	137 100	22.4	12.6	625	24.6	1.9	526 376	-0.9	19 804	3.8	432 730	39.9	9.2
Edgar	7 859	72.8	33 200	18.4	13.4	282	26.0	2.1	10 599	-1.5	502	4.7	8 307	21.8	12.4
Edwards	3 016	81.2	32 000	20.2	12.6	245	23.9	1.8	3 625	-5.3	178	4.9	3 220	16.1	13.3
Effingham	11 465	76.5	44 400	17.4	12.0	299	20.9	3.0	18 087	-2.1	918	5.1	14 996	20.3	11.6
Fayette	7 719	77.3	34 600	17.6	12.9	279	24.5	3.7	10 525	-2.6	773	7.3	8 285	17.3	11.4
Ford	5 602	73.3	42 500	17.4	11.8	296	22.9	1.7	6 803	1.4	320	4.7	6 560	21.7	11.8
Franklin	16 564	76.4	30 000	19.1	14.0	295	29.0	2.5	17 169	-0.3	1 482	8.6	14 305	21.4	17.7
Fulton	14 893	72.2	31 100	16.3	12.7	296	25.8	1.6	13 769	-1.6	1 126	8.2	14 595	21.1	13.3
Gallatin	2 784	78.8	32 600	19.6	13.7	237	31.9	3.2	2 730	-2.5	164	6.0	2 644	15.8	14.3
Greene	5 910	74.2	29 000	16.9	13.5	248	24.3	3.4	7 337	-2.8	402	5.5	6 314	19.1	13.2
Grundy	11 979	69.8	71 900	16.5	12.1	410	20.9	1.7	19 077	-1.3	1 246	6.5	15 126	24.6	17.1
Hamilton	3 476	79.4	29 400	19.4	13.4	231	29.3	4.8	3 699	-0.2	257	6.9	3 086	22.1	12.8
Hancock	8 409	76.2	34 500	16.5	12.6	276	20.5	1.4	12 416	-0.4	773	6.2	9 868	21.2	12.7
Hardin	2 049	78.4	25 100	21.0	12.5	214	30.1	6.6	1 835	-1.2	138	7.5	1 762	19.8	18.4
Henderson	3 237	76.3	32 900	14.8	12.4	273	25.6	1.9	5 253	3.1	248	4.7	3 740	17.3	13.1
Henry	19 514	75.1	40 500	16.8	12.9	315	23.7	1.5	26 803	-2.4	1 621	6.0	23 243	20.7	13.0
Iroquois	11 788	73.8	40 100	15.6	11.9	306	21.3	1.7	15 855	-0.8	1 011	6.4	14 212	19.0	12.4

1. Specified owner-occupied units.   2. Specified renter-occupied units.   3. Overcrowded or lacking complete plumbing facilities.   4. Percent of civilian labor force.   5. Persons 16 years and older.

Table B. States and Counties — **Nonfarm Employment and Agriculture**

STATE County	Private nonfarm establishments, employment and payroll, 1999									Agriculture, 1997			
		Employment						Annual payroll		Farms			Farm operators
												Percent with—	Whose principal occupation is farming (percent)
	Number of establishments	Total	Health Care and Social Assistance	Manufacturing	Retail trade	Finance and Insurance	Professional Scientific and Technical Services	Total (mil dol)	Average per employee (dollars)	Number	Less than 50 acres	500 acres and over	
	104	105	106	107	108	109	110	111	112	113	114	115	116
IDAHO—Cont'd													
Custer	151	812	81	D	101	25	11	16	19 670	268	26.5	32.8	54.1
Elmore	406	3 741	817	409	927	160	53	71	18 922	301	34.6	32.6	56.8
Franklin	240	1 498	252	191	379	56	17	27	18 001	655	31.1	22.0	49.9
Fremont	263	1 453	162	D	288	D	D	27	18 462	493	32.3	30.6	58.0
Gem	299	2 327	392	463	380	61	34	51	21 765	552	50.5	10.7	48.4
Gooding	327	2 368	321	246	495	75	72	44	18 464	675	44.7	13.0	59.6
Idaho	445	2 629	403	406	544	91	87	57	21 573	661	20.9	42.4	58.9
Jefferson	334	3 277	146	730	397	66	48	59	18 146	773	41.9	19.9	50.6
Jerome	424	3 811	360	728	758	75	76	83	21 719	683	41.7	15.4	62.1
Kootenai	3 591	33 728	4 216	4 340	6 086	1 063	1 366	796	23 609	598	48.0	13.0	46.3
Latah	910	7 735	1 078	425	1 868	243	284	142	18 356	659	26.6	29.1	47.5
Lemhi	293	1 563	227	128	369	D	52	32	20 164	308	33.8	33.4	61.4
Lewis	129	767	17	208	143	24	D	15	20 095	182	12.6	52.7	64.8
Lincoln	68	621	76	D	110	D	D	11	18 229	281	18.5	24.9	69.0
Madison	546	10 575	785	1 530	1 393	191	136	163	15 375	470	40.2	23.4	50.2
Minidoka	376	5 248	453	1 852	873	46	102	114	21 714	674	42.4	18.2	64.7
Nez Perce	1 223	16 253	2 536	3 132	2 833	1 001	418	440	27 059	383	27.2	43.9	59.5
Oneida	73	574	132	D	168	43	D	9	16 439	387	19.4	39.3	54.5
Owyhee	153	1 468	47	545	210	D	16	38	25 796	570	29.5	28.6	68.4
Payette	430	4 050	353	1 369	556	108	109	80	19 821	564	55.0	7.3	52.1
Power	156	2 023	154	783	234	40	27	39	19 235	323	17.3	55.7	65.6
Shoshone	393	3 606	514	169	699	91	220	87	24 173	44	50.0	2.3	50.0
Teton	211	912	143	D	220	D	44	18	20 146	270	22.2	28.9	57.8
Twin Falls	2 113	27 721	3 517	3 313	4 492	779	668	550	19 825	1 439	38.3	15.6	60.9
Valley	480	2 308	257	146	459	62	81	40	17 452	119	36.1	32.8	51.3
Washington	231	2 375	237	530	302	60	70	39	16 346	489	36.8	29.4	59.3
ILLINOIS	306 899	5 342 675	622 309	861 541	635 558	346 596	337 445	188 020	35 192	73 051	23.1	25.1	57.0
Adams	1 905	29 912	4 530	6 224	4 649	1 228	684	767	25 647	1 415	20.8	20.4	54.3
Alexander	169	1 719	322	390	217	58	D	36	21 202	166	16.9	22.9	51.2
Bond	347	3 860	528	764	514	140	68	80	20 628	616	27.8	19.8	49.0
Boone	733	11 872	840	5 630	1 180	317	105	482	40 623	490	35.1	19.6	54.1
Brown	125	1 867	164	D	139	D	18	44	23 789	377	19.1	24.4	47.5
Bureau	857	10 281	2 044	2 723	1 286	488	268	259	25 219	1 155	15.3	31.6	63.1
Calhoun	114	676	86	D	130	74	D	12	17 422	433	22.4	10.6	43.9
Carroll	451	3 754	418	914	495	241	61	84	22 414	625	18.6	24.8	67.0
Cass	305	4 565	417	2 195	545	166	62	97	21 295	417	21.8	32.6	61.6
Champaign	4 101	68 571	9 709	9 745	10 860	2 990	3 041	1 673	24 393	1 371	17.4	31.1	63.8
Christian	808	10 021	1 836	1 846	1 668	455	159	207	20 656	820	23.3	34.9	64.9
Clark	379	4 574	372	2 041	561	163	65	101	22 141	603	25.2	31.3	54.9
Clay	383	5 044	689	2 168	451	151	70	118	23 328	627	21.2	26.6	52.6
Clinton	826	7 856	1 369	1 079	1 342	333	233	162	20 631	860	23.1	14.2	55.5
Coles	1 308	21 197	3 072	5 965	3 135	692	780	539	25 408	681	26.6	28.3	56.5
Cook	127 634	2 501 517	292 152	345 873	250 753	187 897	204 313	97 523	38 986	237	53.6	11.0	43.5
Crawford	466	7 058	715	2 628	845	316	141	206	29 139	473	24.5	30.4	55.0
Cumberland	180	1 447	371	340	256	D	D	26	17 827	547	23.9	21.4	49.9
De Kalb	1 934	24 829	3 361	6 891	3 951	963	551	648	26 097	828	19.4	30.6	68.1
De Witt	397	5 271	510	1 150	755	168	82	197	37 335	463	23.3	33.3	62.9
Douglas	628	7 348	359	2 845	1 533	210	81	177	24 113	630	27.0	29.8	67.6
Du Page	32 187	606 653	41 972	70 166	67 934	36 373	50 708	24 293	40 045	93	59.1	10.8	41.9
Edgar	406	5 018	826	1 747	654	221	151	108	21 459	766	17.2	33.7	64.1
Edwards	168	2 829	105	D	164	72	D	69	24 542	329	24.3	23.1	52.0
Effingham	1 119	18 799	2 368	5 308	2 938	472	366	456	24 254	1 035	25.1	13.9	47.7
Fayette	480	4 962	786	1 365	895	190	113	100	20 180	1 119	26.1	18.4	45.6
Ford	416	4 099	651	885	701	145	72	85	20 654	550	11.1	43.8	67.6
Franklin	890	9 164	1 619	1 946	1 626	263	147	204	22 298	658	33.6	13.8	40.0
Fulton	728	7 699	2 005	382	1 808	383	131	135	17 525	1 101	20.8	26.2	56.0
Gallatin	137	1 177	95	72	148	D	D	28	24 043	238	20.2	39.9	65.1
Greene	307	1 958	327	250	477	149	99	34	17 588	720	20.6	28.6	61.1
Grundy	900	10 704	1 172	1 555	1 995	446	242	359	33 564	463	17.5	30.9	61.3
Hamilton	194	1 132	367	51	204	67	28	19	16 402	563	22.6	20.2	45.6
Hancock	489	4 918	671	1 970	657	230	65	103	20 871	1 137	17.2	28.2	63.1
Hardin	76	841	371	D	67	31	D	17	19 918	172	16.9	7.0	32.6
Henderson	130	640	117	D	143	83	D	11	16 872	414	16.7	36.7	70.8
Henry	1 174	13 725	1 305	4 493	2 452	575	289	297	21 630	1 344	21.6	24.0	63.8
Iroquois	723	7 472	1 461	1 628	1 104	373	99	154	20 600	1 393	14.0	37.6	69.2

	Agriculture, 1997 (cont'd)														
STATE County	Land in farms				Value of land and buildings		Value of machinery and equipment average per farm ($1,000)	Value of products sold				Percent of farms with sales of —		Percent of land owned by fed. gov. 1997	Water consumption 1995 (mil gal/day)
	Acreage (1,000)	Percent change, 1992–1997	Acres							Percent from —					
			Average size of farm	Total irrigated (1,000)	Total cropland (1,000)	Average per farm ($1,000)	Average per acre (dollars)		Total (mil dol)	Average per farm (dollars)	Crops	Livestock and poultry products	$10,000 or more	$100,000 or more		
	117	118	119	120	121	122	123	124	125	126	127	128	129	130	131	132
IDAHO—Cont'd																
Custer	148	4.9	552	62	68	596	1 155	48	18	65 511	20.6	79.4	56.7	19.8	92.3	141.8
Elmore	356	0.4	1 181	91	127	682	626	142	220	731 298	D	D	51.8	28.2	69.7	327.4
Franklin	246	7.0	376	55	148	289	869	64	57	87 346	19.3	80.7	56.0	19.7	32.2	177.7
Fremont	334	-12.3	678	119	193	568	882	112	81	164 308	85.9	14.1	57.8	27.4	57.9	338.4
Gem	183	-7.1	331	37	48	382	910	38	30	53 634	38.2	61.8	44.9	9.4	36.9	135.6
Gooding	220	-2.9	326	113	D	496	1 567	101	249	369 535	20.7	79.3	64.6	30.4	57.0	1 288.6
Idaho	650	-12.7	983	2	226	625	686	55	33	49 248	58.2	41.8	54.3	16.3	83.2	30.3
Jefferson	333	6.9	430	208	234	513	1 186	87	136	176 108	61.8	38.2	59.4	23.4	49.8	1 544.1
Jerome	194	-6.8	284	152	160	566	1 915	124	250	366 580	33.3	66.7	68.5	34.4	37.6	1 108.5
Kootenai	131	-0.1	219	16	77	406	2 203	45	14	22 711	80.9	19.1	25.9	5.2	30.5	47.1
Latah	325	-6.2	494	0	238	512	955	58	38	56 967	91.5	8.5	39.6	17.0	15.8	11.7
Lemhi	197	1.3	638	82	84	512	830	56	19	60 981	8.6	91.4	61.0	19.8	90.3	123.7
Lewis	194	-8.3	1 064	D	140	822	781	100	20	110 753	93.5	6.5	67.6	38.5	2.5	1.1
Lincoln	131	-0.4	468	73	D	430	1 030	88	44	156 215	61.1	38.9	69.0	26.3	75.8	420.6
Madison	223	-0.5	474	129	174	949	1 824	118	80	171 223	90.9	9.1	58.5	28.1	19.4	295.3
Minidoka	207	-0.5	307	181	D	538	1 856	129	152	225 836	75.4	24.6	66.2	37.2	50.2	526.8
Nez Perce	339	-29.0	886	0	208	877	901	114	38	98 580	87.7	12.3	55.9	27.7	3.7	18.6
Oneida	271	0.0	701	33	188	439	638	53	15	39 183	60.1	39.9	56.1	10.1	52.8	103.3
Owyhee	683	-9.2	1 198	132	158	705	623	71	103	180 656	45.6	54.4	65.8	30.7	78.4	474.0
Payette	148	-0.4	263	53	D	315	1 153	54	49	86 526	55.6	44.4	50.4	17.4	25.6	254.1
Power	424	-2.5	1 313	118	354	1 069	916	246	121	374 535	72.0	28.0	67.8	39.9	30.1	305.5
Shoshone	4	2.5	93	D	2	326	3 499	18	0	8 809	D	D	6.8	2.3	74.5	9.9
Teton	133	-1.7	491	57	102	822	1 631	75	23	84 682	74.1	25.9	60.4	19.3	33.2	116.3
Twin Falls	456	-6.9	317	276	308	494	1 548	78	239	166 372	56.3	43.7	66.2	28.2	50.1	1 890.6
Valley	64	-18.6	540	24	23	729	1 513	38	8	63 931	17.1	82.9	44.5	10.1	84.7	28.1
Washington	443	-20.3	906	45	107	504	550	62	39	79 379	60.8	39.2	53.8	18.2	37.4	83.4
ILLINOIS	27 205	-0.2	372	350	23 921	773	2 126	90	8 556	117 130	76.8	23.2	68.2	31.7	1.4	19 896.9
Adams	442	-4.9	312	2	340	440	1 428	62	121	85 362	61.6	38.4	64.5	24.1	1.8	23.5
Alexander	71	3.3	429	3	58	544	1 121	99	13	79 596	95.8	4.2	48.2	19.9	16.4	2.5
Bond	180	-1.6	292	0	156	423	1 729	58	46	74 326	73.5	26.5	56.0	24.7	0.0	2.4
Boone	141	4.8	289	2	130	651	2 825	68	54	109 577	75.2	24.8	64.3	30.4	0.0	6.3
Brown	152	5.7	404	D	101	447	1 189	57	30	80 520	69.6	30.4	53.8	20.2	0.0	0.4
Bureau	484	0.4	419	5	441	924	2 252	111	199	172 197	82.2	17.8	82.9	43.8	0.0	8.1
Calhoun	99	-0.5	230	0	59	236	1 383	31	19	42 765	70.6	29.4	43.2	8.1	5.5	8.3
Carroll	243	1.8	389	9	214	802	2 152	103	123	196 895	49.7	50.3	74.6	44.0	1.1	8.5
Cass	192	-8.1	461	9	160	862	1 857	106	74	177 869	56.1	43.9	67.4	37.9	0.4	9.5
Champaign	568	-0.8	414	6	549	1 201	2 940	117	190	138 614	96.2	3.8	85.7	42.0	0.3	36.1
Christian	390	0.0	476	D	366	1 172	2 530	113	123	150 070	93.7	6.3	75.7	42.6	0.0	775.6
Clark	269	3.4	446	6	225	651	1 499	116	63	104 874	87.2	12.8	62.0	30.8	0.0	4.2
Clay	239	6.6	381	D	207	508	1 407	90	49	78 538	87.2	12.8	60.9	23.9	0.0	1.7
Clinton	234	2.0	272	1	211	476	1 646	87	107	124 038	38.5	61.5	74.9	29.0	1.7	7.5
Coles	257	-2.3	377	D	237	892	2 373	92	73	107 021	93.5	6.5	66.7	33.9	0.0	7.7
Cook	39	-3.9	166	0	30	549	3 791	43	21	90 238	97.2	2.8	41.8	17.3	0.0	1 691.5
Crawford	209	-6.7	442	6	183	623	1 417	97	52	109 948	81.6	18.4	67.9	32.8	0.0	57.6
Cumberland	170	-3.5	310	0	148	597	1 822	73	54	98 472	67.1	32.9	69.3	28.3	0.0	1.9
De Kalb	368	-2.6	445	1	355	1 440	3 369	123	183	221 493	61.7	38.3	84.2	48.2	0.0	12.0
De Witt	205	-0.5	443	1	197	1 082	2 417	69	148	660	93.8	6.2	77.3	44.7	0.0	712.0
Douglas	250	-3.6	396	0	239	1 101	2 831	97	80	127 598	89.2	10.8	76.7	39.2	0.0	5.7
Du Page	17	-5.0	184	0	14	766	4 164	85	18	189 644	96.7	3.3	54.8	25.8	4.3	18.3
Edgar	352	-0.5	460	D	322	1 093	2 390	110	165	215 908	54.5	45.5	74.9	37.6	0.0	2.8
Edwards	113	-2.7	343	0	95	483	1 408	74	28	84 218	67.4	32.6	60.8	26.1	0.0	1.2
Effingham	257	-0.5	248	D	222	497	2 085	62	79	76 363	57.1	42.9	68.4	22.6	0.0	5.9
Fayette	333	-2.3	298	0	276	395	1 412	52	72	64 320	85.1	14.9	52.1	18.8	1.3	5.7
Ford	315	4.9	572	1	300	1 257	2 300	128	100	181 983	89.7	10.3	89.3	50.7	0.0	3.9
Franklin	180	11.5	273	D	152	297	1 112	54	32	48 082	78.4	21.6	38.4	13.1	4.1	15.5
Fulton	425	-1.4	386	0	319	584	1 534	81	99	89 785	80.9	19.1	67.9	25.7	0.0	273.4
Gallatin	191	11.1	803	19	165	1 271	1 441	165	45	189 965	94.1	5.9	69.3	39.1	5.0	10.0
Greene	328	7.8	455	1	261	690	1 575	85	106	146 875	62.3	37.7	68.3	33.2	0.3	3.1
Grundy	201	-10.9	435	0	190	1 317	2 974	117	59	127 933	93.7	6.3	84.0	40.8	0.0	2 560.5
Hamilton	215	6.3	381	D	181	393	1 109	63	39	68 934	93.5	6.5	45.3	17.6	0.0	0.5
Hancock	438	1.2	386	2	354	616	1 644	87	126	110 764	74.3	25.7	71.2	33.2	0.0	3.2
Hardin	39	3.3	228		24	224	961	24	3	18 372	34.4	65.6	23.3	2.3	23.1	2.8
Henderson	202	-0.9	488	10	169	866	1 835	97	60	145 435	81.1	18.9	82.1	44.9	0.5	15.1
Henry	457	0.6	340	5	413	712	2 246	96	179	133 231	57.8	42.2	77.2	37.4	0.0	9.1
Iroquois	667	0.6	479	4	634	1 109	2 309	123	240	172 320	81.1	18.9	87.4	49.6	0.0	4.4

Table B. States and Counties — **Residential Construction, Wholesale and Retail Trade, and Real Estate**

STATE County	New Construction ($1,000)	Number of Housing Units	Number of Establishments	Number of Employees	Sales (mil dol)	Annual Payroll (mil dol)	Number of Establishments	Number of Employees	Sales (mil dol)	Annual Payroll (mil dol)	Number of Establishments	Number of Employees	Receipts (mil dol)	Annual Payroll (mil dol)
	Value of Residential Construction Authorized by Building Permits, 2000		Wholesale Trade, 1997				Retail Trade[1], 1997				Real Estate and Rental and Leasing, 1997			
	133	134	135	136	137	138	139	140	141	142	143	144	145	146
IDAHO—Cont'd														
Custer	133	3	3	D	D	D	25	106	14.7	1.2	4	D	D	D
Elmore	14 411	195	11	64	20.1	1.6	84	894	231.0	17.3	10	43	3.7	0.5
Franklin	8 185	81	19	122	30.1	2.9	45	383	55.1	4.8	5	13	0.6	0.1
Fremont	13 241	85	17	235	83.0	4.2	50	285	53.0	4.2	4	D	D	D
Gem	10 055	113	18	155	35.7	3.0	42	326	49.5	5.4	9	22	1.2	0.2
Gooding	8 166	83	13	197	58.5	3.3	54	480	66.8	6.5	10	31	0.9	0.3
Idaho	1 266	11	15	168	38.6	2.8	81	540	75.2	8.0	7	16	0.6	0.2
Jefferson	10 997	102	30	511	101.2	8.0	48	438	59.9	5.7	7	8	0.7	0.1
Jerome	5 413	53	37	312	251.9	6.1	57	624	107.6	10.3	4	4	0.6	0.1
Kootenai	135 730	1 174	121	1 171	402.9	35.7	545	5 590	1 022.7	100.5	143	379	47.7	6.1
Latah	12 586	127	44	255	111.6	6.0	176	1 982	253.8	26.7	39	185	12.8	2.4
Lemhi	2 497	45	10	28	8.0	0.6	54	384	54.5	5.1	8	12	1.7	0.2
Lewis	384	5	8	87	27.2	1.8	27	137	21.0	2.5	3	16	0.9	0.2
Lincoln	2 184	19	1	D	D	D	12	57	11.2	0.7	1	D	D	D
Madison	9 121	83	40	605	94.3	8.4	93	1 286	211.9	18.9	19	80	5.6	0.6
Minidoka	2 505	21	42	776	158.4	16.8	76	775	130.4	12.1	6	22	1.3	0.3
Nez Perce	10 808	129	66	725	214.1	16.9	231	2 832	464.3	48.7	39	178	11.5	2.5
Oneida	2 791	33	1	D	D	D	11	78	10.3	0.9	3	11	0.4	0.1
Owyhee	4 363	46	13	161	40.6	4.0	33	202	31.6	2.9	4	D	D	D
Payette	8 300	112	25	308	58.0	5.0	66	490	89.5	8.8	10	18	2.0	0.3
Power	1 126	12	11	143	72.9	3.2	23	191	35.9	3.1	1	D	D	D
Shoshone	1 395	13	13	95	33.1	2.6	76	687	243.5	12.8	16	58	3.3	0.5
Teton	17 892	216	4	6	0.5	0.1	37	217	34.7	3.0	8	16	2.1	0.1
Twin Falls	25 159	288	159	1 600	450.7	37.9	378	4 721	837.9	76.8	65	241	25.9	4.0
Valley	23 754	159	9	21	3.8	0.9	65	436	66.2	6.7	25	49	5.5	0.6
Washington	2 781	18	9	322	46.7	4.2	40	341	58.7	5.5	7	22	1.1	0.2
ILLINOIS	6 527 956	51 944	21 956	325 847	275 978.4	13 325.5	44 568	610 790	108 002.0	10 596.0	11 411	73 819	12 830.0	2 101.4
Adams	12 433	100	127	1 650	686.7	45.7	341	4 752	669.5	68.2	60	256	25.3	3.7
Alexander	60	2	10	D	D	D	35	237	29.1	2.9	5	14	1.0	0.3
Bond	8 312	106	19	264	143.4	6.5	60	496	97.7	7.1	12	20	1.8	0.2
Boone	48 782	365	43	D	D	D	91	1 156	198.7	19.4	34	86	10.9	1.5
Brown	1 180	17	11	D	D	D	21	138	16.5	1.5	5	14	0.4	0.2
Bureau	9 279	99	58	D	D	D	145	1 379	229.5	20.7	16	41	3.3	0.5
Calhoun	1 251	13	4	D	D	D	24	134	26.8	2.0	4	D	D	D
Carroll	10 782	70	26	190	111.6	5.0	72	560	81.4	7.1	9	24	1.4	0.2
Cass	767	11	20	193	240.0	5.4	59	520	68.3	6.3	5	18	1.7	0.4
Champaign	105 873	1 049	199	3 737	2 419.0	111.5	675	10 645	1 556.7	151.9	203	1 356	179.7	27.3
Christian	8 485	99	51	482	363.6	15.0	156	1 644	283.1	24.7	20	67	5.9	0.9
Clark	1 158	14	22	199	104.8	4.6	77	627	106.7	8.5	6	14	0.5	0.1
Clay	1 116	11	31	316	84.2	6.1	66	662	92.1	7.4	9	38	1.7	0.5
Clinton	12 771	98	54	D	D	D	136	1 373	243.8	30.9	18	136	9.7	3.2
Coles	5 542	101	67	663	327.2	15.4	233	3 210	526.5	46.2	49	195	14.3	3.2
Cook	1 400 301	11 877	9 574	149 994	120 551.8	6 467.2	17 318	240 539	42 547.2	4 369.9	5 614	42 649	8 711.0	1 393.7
Crawford	545	5	24	151	246.8	3.4	93	907	136.4	12.5	16	30	2.5	0.3
Cumberland	1 109	11	16	87	48.7	1.9	42	253	37.2	3.3	4	9	0.5	0.0
De Kalb	60 237	576	75	835	871.8	32.2	309	4 008	642.3	63.1	63	275	34.4	3.9
De Witt	6 845	53	22	127	138.0	5.5	70	756	142.0	12.4	9	16	1.0	0.1
Douglas	4 110	32	33	370	203.4	8.6	165	1 299	185.8	16.7	10	46	4.1	0.6
Du Page	694 045	3 931	3 351	64 415	74 318.8	2 918.5	3 625	64 962	12 825.3	1 231.1	1 134	9 484	1 480.5	293.4
Edgar	3 939	68	31	260	163.8	5.4	68	721	108.3	9.8	12	33	1.4	0.2
Edwards	NA	NA	15	188	105.7	6.1	34	235	28.4	2.4	2	D	D	D
Effingham	6 851	57	58	879	265.9	29.6	236	3 205	561.3	50.2	27	119	8.6	1.3
Fayette	994	11	27	372	186.3	8.8	103	933	153.3	12.7	12	24	1.7	0.3
Ford	3 431	37	33	335	298.9	11.4	93	716	120.2	9.6	12	13	1.2	0.1
Franklin	2 480	29	47	258	72.6	6.1	192	1 707	276.9	27.1	22	62	9.1	0.8
Fulton	6 684	73	36	235	95.4	5.0	156	1 718	248.4	24.8	21	52	3.3	0.5
Gallatin	0	0	8	D	D	D	29	144	23.4	2.0	NA	NA	NA	NA
Greene	536	6	22	108	70.1	2.4	70	480	71.1	6.6	5	D	D	D
Grundy	30 855	227	40	347	387.3	12.3	137	1 604	288.0	27.2	39	199	16.7	4.2
Hamilton	NA	NA	13	68	54.3	1.4	37	207	37.7	2.7	2	D	D	D
Hancock	1 546	22	32	220	211.9	5.1	101	601	101.5	8.8	7	33	4.0	1.1
Hardin	0	0	NA	NA	NA	NA	15	60	8.6	0.8	1	D	D	D
Henderson	850	18	10	40	21.6	0.7	23	125	21.0	1.7	2	D	D	D
Henry	13 567	107	81	775	521.6	19.9	217	2 583	371.9	37.1	28	83	4.9	1.3
Iroquois	6 364	69	65	524	405.3	12.8	118	1 139	176.1	17.2	11	25	2.5	0.3

1. Establishments with payroll.

STATE County	Professional, Scientific, and Technical Services[1], 1997				Manufacturing, 1997				Accommodation and Foodservices, 1997			
	Number of Establishments	Number of Employees	Receipts (mil dol)	Annual Payroll (mil dol)	Number of Establishments	Number of Employees	Receipts (mil dol)	Annual Payroll (mil dol)	Number of Establishments	Number of Employees	Sales (mil dol)	Annual Payroll (mil dol)
	147	148	149	150	151	152	153	154	155	156	157	158
IDAHO—Cont'd												
Custer	8	18	0.9	0.2	NA	NA	NA	NA	26	131	5.8	1.7
Elmore	11	40	1.8	0.7	NA	NA	NA	NA	53	479	13.5	3.9
Franklin	9	16	0.7	0.1	NA	NA	NA	NA	14	171	3.3	0.9
Fremont	5	10	0.4	0.0	NA	NA	NA	NA	32	172	8.6	2.0
Gem	16	50	1.8	0.5	NA	NA	NA	NA	22	189	5.4	1.2
Gooding	13	45	2.6	1.0	NA	NA	NA	NA	28	254	5.0	1.5
Idaho	21	70	3.1	1.0	NA	NA	NA	NA	56	323	9.7	2.5
Jefferson	16	39	2.0	0.6	17	664	94.4	11.9	18	D	D	D
Jerome	17	54	3.9	1.4	19	803	176.3	15.9	30	210	6.9	1.7
Kootenai	245	1 121	81.8	32.8	195	4 472	592.1	116.9	298	4 086	137.7	37.9
Latah	69	230	13.3	5.2	NA	NA	NA	NA	91	1 348	33.5	8.6
Lemhi	21	45	2.6	0.7	NA	NA	NA	NA	36	209	6.5	2.0
Lewis	5	13	0.6	0.2	NA	NA	NA	NA	18	109	4.2	1.2
Lincoln	1	D	D	D	NA	NA	NA	NA	7	63	1.5	0.4
Madison	23	158	10.7	5.2	21	1 326	141.4	25.5	40	D	D	D
Minidoka	16	69	3.5	1.1	18	1 638	425.7	44.3	25	274	5.7	1.9
Nez Perce	69	349	24.0	9.4	55	3 263	769.1	128.0	103	1 439	43.0	12.5
Oneida	1	D	D	D	NA	NA	NA	NA	7	D	D	D
Owyhee	4	15	0.7	0.2	5	613	225.2	12.2	18	107	2.4	0.7
Payette	27	90	5.8	1.9	24	D	D	D	25	208	4.7	1.1
Power	6	17	0.6	0.2	8	889	155.3	21.3	16	76	2.3	0.6
Shoshone	24	132	9.2	4.2	NA	NA	NA	NA	49	326	8.1	2.3
Teton	11	33	4.1	0.8	NA	NA	NA	NA	19	104	4.1	1.1
Twin Falls	140	574	41.2	16.7	95	3 588	723.3	82.9	148	2 303	62.7	18.1
Valley	22	61	3.7	1.4	NA	NA	NA	NA	65	484	13.9	3.9
Washington	12	39	2.0	0.6	NA	NA	NA	NA	21	D	D	D
ILLINOIS	30 378	274 714	33 855.1	13 105.4	17 953	887 350	200 020.0	31 837.9	23 984	397 300	14 826.8	4 018.7
Adams	112	504	42.2	13.9	85	5 707	1 868.3	190.4	139	2 204	65.9	18.2
Alexander	11	35	1.6	0.7	NA	NA	NA	NA	23	130	4.3	1.0
Bond	14	51	2.3	0.8	16	695	166.0	19.2	36	407	11.0	3.1
Boone	34	D	D	D	63	5 846	2 300.0	283.9	53	556	18.6	4.7
Brown	7	15	0.6	0.1	NA	NA	NA	NA	12	77	1.8	0.5
Bureau	39	198	9.8	3.9	41	2 499	413.7	72.0	86	766	20.7	5.4
Calhoun	6	9	0.4	0.1	NA	NA	NA	NA	18	96	3.6	0.8
Carroll	18	42	2.2	0.6	33	1 015	235.2	27.0	55	317	9.0	2.1
Cass	16	44	2.4	0.5	13	D	D	D	36	237	7.7	1.8
Champaign	336	2 660	263.2	91.6	152	10 857	2 689.5	292.4	449	8 944	248.6	70.6
Christian	35	140	6.9	2.3	30	1 388	479.3	53.2	76	763	21.6	5.4
Clark	20	61	3.6	1.4	24	1 682	435.5	44.6	40	530	12.4	3.2
Clay	18	60	5.2	1.6	23	2 453	480.1	62.8	30	216	5.8	1.6
Clinton	34	197	8.6	3.7	39	963	175.9	22.4	92	D	D	D
Coles	77	387	37.5	12.2	57	5 754	1 455.6	182.9	136	2 058	59.8	15.4
Cook	15 689	178 223	23 915.1	9 267.6	7 966	362 364	74 563.3	13 032.0	9 912	177 351	7 770.0	2 092.4
Crawford	27	108	8.4	2.5	20	2 547	2 175.4	90.4	34	D	D	D
Cumberland	6	11	0.9	0.2	NA	NA	NA	NA	14	D	D	D
De Kalb	106	321	28.2	7.8	137	6 957	1 511.7	207.7	190	2 664	73.2	17.8
De Witt	21	63	4.5	1.5	15	1 300	267.1	39.6	42	384	11.1	2.9
Douglas	23	58	3.3	1.1	65	2 711	481.7	79.2	47	692	17.3	4.8
Du Page	4 099	32 018	4 200.8	1 475.6	2 033	71 351	11 938.5	2 503.0	1 698	37 452	1 495.4	405.7
Edgar	29	127	7.4	2.2	27	1 539	248.7	36.9	31	264	6.1	1.6
Edwards	8	15	0.7	0.1	8	D	D	D	7	D	D	D
Effingham	47	560	72.5	15.4	59	5 660	978.7	148.7	90	2 061	59.2	15.8
Fayette	18	93	4.0	1.8	22	1 529	277.9	37.8	39	477	12.5	3.5
Ford	21	52	3.1	1.0	22	951	322.4	23.7	32	290	7.5	2.0
Franklin	40	133	8.9	2.3	43	1 632	233.7	36.6	82	983	26.7	7.5
Fulton	25	90	5.2	1.8	NA	NA	NA	NA	81	837	20.4	5.8
Gallatin	7	14	0.7	0.3	NA	NA	NA	NA	8	45	1.3	0.3
Greene	14	56	2.0	0.8	NA	NA	NA	NA	31	D	D	D
Grundy	53	194	17.3	6.6	33	2 015	875.4	87.8	72	999	32.8	8.4
Hamilton	10	23	1.3	0.3	NA	NA	NA	NA	7	88	2.1	0.5
Hancock	14	43	2.9	0.7	28	1 862	193.2	42.5	44	321	7.8	2.0
Hardin	5	9	0.3	0.1	NA	NA	NA	NA	6	D	D	D
Henderson	5	15	0.7	0.1	NA	NA	NA	NA	12	83	2.0	0.3
Henry	52	185	11.0	4.0	53	4 019	1 288.0	124.3	113	1 309	32.9	9.1
Iroquois	27	68	5.1	1.4	30	1 723	296.9	43.0	67	435	14.5	3.3

1. Firms subject to federal tax.

STATE County	Health Care and Social Assistance[1], 1997				Other Services[1], 1997				Federal funds and grants, fiscal 2001[2] Expenditures (mil dol)			
									Total	Direct payments for individuals[3]		
	Number of Establishments	Number of Employees	Receipts (mil dol)	Annual Payroll (mil dol)	Number of Establishments	Number of Employees	Receipts (mil dol)	Annual Payroll (mil dol)		Social Security and government retirement	Medicare	Food stamps and Supplemental Security Income
	159	160	161	162	163	164	165	166	167	168	169	170
IDAHO—Cont'd												
Custer	8	62	1.2	0.6	3	5	0.3	0.1	23.6	9.9	3.2	0.4
Elmore	27	195	8.7	3.0	35	152	7.9	1.9	314.4	60.5	9.0	1.7
Franklin	11	86	3.1	1.1	10	33	2.1	0.3	40.2	19.7	5.6	0.9
Fremont	16	78	4.0	1.8	9	20	1.5	0.3	56.3	22.5	6.1	1.2
Gem	19	293	9.0	4.1	22	76	3.6	1.0	66.2	36.6	10.0	0.7
Gooding	19	207	6.9	3.1	17	69	4.0	0.9	63.5	30.1	9.7	2.6
Idaho	26	147	6.7	1.9	21	62	4.4	0.8	115.2	38.5	11.6	2.5
Jefferson	19	127	4.7	1.8	12	26	2.2	0.4	71.8	30.4	8.9	1.4
Jerome	15	102	5.4	2.8	23	83	4.8	1.3	78.6	31.7	10.7	2.0
Kootenai	267	2 561	137.1	55.6	176	836	47.5	12.9	467.6	251.7	61.5	11.2
Latah	57	389	22.8	10.9	38	201	13.6	3.8	179.5	56.2	14.2	2.1
Lemhi	20	162	6.3	2.7	14	39	2.8	0.6	58.6	22.7	8.3	1.0
Lewis	6	8	0.7	0.1	2	D	D	D	48.4	16.6	4.0	0.8
Lincoln	5	63	3.4	1.3	2	D	D	D	18.8	7.0	2.2	0.2
Madison	49	463	21.9	7.3	27	109	5.2	1.2	75.6	24.9	7.2	1.4
Minidoka	26	185	7.8	3.2	23	117	11.5	2.2	88.6	36.5	14.0	2.5
Nez Perce	111	1 454	82.2	34.0	87	534	28.4	8.1	235.0	96.6	33.3	5.9
Oneida	5	35	1.3	0.5	5	7	0.9	0.1	34.7	8.9	2.9	0.4
Owyhee	5	180	4.2	2.4	6	6	0.6	0.1	41.7	16.6	4.3	1.4
Payette	33	466	12.4	4.5	18	67	3.1	0.7	85.9	40.8	12.0	2.6
Power	7	29	1.7	0.7	15	64	3.3	1.0	52.0	10.9	3.1	0.7
Shoshone	25	308	11.1	4.8	26	56	3.7	1.0	91.3	42.6	15.7	3.8
Teton	7	15	1.4	0.4	4	7	0.8	0.1	23.5	7.6	3.1	0.1
Twin Falls	154	2 301	116.0	52.5	114	630	31.9	9.3	287.8	131.2	41.6	8.0
Valley	19	130	6.3	2.5	20	41	2.8	0.7	54.5	28.0	6.1	1.8
Washington	12	178	7.7	3.1	9	32	2.4	0.6	52.9	26.2	7.5	2.6
ILLINOIS	21 122	248 667	16 870.2	7 441.8	18 806	118 317	8 296.8	2 503.0	65 035.6	22 163.3	10 412.9	2 322.5
Adams	122	1 605	96.3	50.9	146	749	43.3	13.2	350.6	155.6	59.9	10.0
Alexander	2	D	D	D	5	16	0.9	0.2	80.4	24.1	12.6	6.2
Bond	20	217	7.2	3.7	32	79	5.9	1.4	96.6	35.2	14.8	1.8
Boone	34	535	21.9	10.1	53	248	17.6	6.1	123.0	65.5	20.4	2.5
Brown	4	109	3.0	1.7	10	23	1.2	0.3	32.0	11.2	4.4	0.7
Bureau	54	629	30.7	15.4	57	197	10.4	2.5	197.4	84.0	35.2	3.0
Calhoun	5	72	3.8	1.1	5	38	1.8	1.0	35.6	12.2	5.9	0.7
Carroll	20	159	5.2	2.6	30	101	6.2	1.4	117.6	47.9	16.8	1.9
Cass	20	283	7.7	4.0	20	87	4.5	1.2	77.0	31.7	13.7	1.7
Champaign	204	4 973	367.9	182.4	244	1 241	65.0	21.0	930.7	262.1	80.4	21.2
Christian	45	798	30.5	11.8	63	195	12.4	2.7	199.2	87.0	41.0	4.6
Clark	17	102	5.3	1.8	27	74	4.2	0.8	94.7	40.9	17.5	2.0
Clay	23	249	12.6	3.9	24	67	5.8	1.3	91.3	35.2	16.9	1.7
Clinton	51	699	27.3	11.1	47	147	10.9	2.6	152.2	75.3	29.6	2.1
Coles	90	1 224	61.2	27.9	85	428	25.7	6.9	226.2	93.9	42.0	7.3
Cook	9 558	108 873	7 974.7	3 416.1	7 707	55 223	4 042.9	1 211.5	27 878.9	8 698.4	5 280.6	1 486.9
Crawford	37	354	14.6	5.5	33	117	6.6	2.0	102.6	50.3	19.1	2.4
Cumberland	5	84	2.5	1.5	13	35	2.4	0.4	55.4	22.1	9.2	1.5
De Kalb	104	1 453	87.5	40.2	131	495	31.6	8.4	296.1	128.8	49.9	4.3
De Witt	23	218	9.9	4.9	22	65	5.8	1.3	93.2	40.6	15.8	2.1
Douglas	30	399	12.7	5.2	26	117	11.4	2.7	92.9	37.4	13.9	1.3
Du Page	2 117	23 540	1 852.3	807.3	1 706	12 714	931.0	310.5	2 645.7	1 359.4	525.6	40.7
Edgar	24	270	11.5	4.6	22	64	4.5	0.9	121.1	47.2	20.0	3.5
Edwards	10	88	2.5	1.2	16	27	1.6	0.3	37.3	16.1	6.6	0.7
Effingham	90	895	63.5	25.7	70	426	26.4	6.1	160.3	69.3	27.0	2.2
Fayette	33	321	11.7	5.1	31	129	17.7	2.6	109.5	45.4	19.6	4.5
Ford	20	271	12.5	5.0	20	64	4.3	1.0	93.3	37.3	13.2	1.2
Franklin	63	474	19.2	7.1	55	168	11.2	2.8	282.3	118.2	47.8	11.0
Fulton	44	1 104	43.1	21.8	38	154	9.7	2.2	218.5	94.0	47.5	5.5
Gallatin	3	148	2.7	1.4	3	D	D	D	64.2	17.9	8.2	2.3
Greene	21	172	5.1	2.3	18	35	2.4	0.4	95.0	37.1	16.7	2.5
Grundy	62	670	34.5	15.0	58	300	21.1	5.2	187.1	72.7	30.4	1.4
Hamilton	8	70	3.2	1.5	11	28	2.5	0.3	59.5	21.3	9.6	1.9
Hancock	30	238	10.8	4.4	25	52	4.0	0.8	138.3	50.8	18.5	2.1
Hardin	8	76	2.2	0.8	2	D	D	D	28.6	12.4	6.7	1.0
Henderson	7	29	1.5	0.8	7	20	0.6	0.3	52.2	18.3	6.3	0.7
Henry	50	399	16.7	6.2	84	273	19.3	4.2	255.5	118.9	43.2	5.2
Iroquois	35	208	13.3	6.2	45	129	10.7	2.4	212.7	78.7	29.9	3.0

1. Firms subject to federal tax.   2. October 1, 2000 to September 30, 2001.   3. State totals may include programs not allocated by county.

Table B. States and Counties — Federal Funds and Local Government Finances

	Federal funds and grants, fiscal 2001[1] (cont'd)							Local government finances, 1997				
	Expenditures (mil dol) (cont'd)							General revenue				
	Procurement contract awards			Grants[2]						Taxes		
STATE County	Salaries and wages	Defense	Other	Medicaid and other health-related	Nutrition and family welfare	Education	Other	Total (mil dol)	Intergovernmental (mil dol)	Total (mil dol)	Per capita[3] (dollars) Total	Property
	171	172	173	174	175	176	177	178	179	180	181	182
IDAHO—Cont'd												
Custer	4.8	0.0	0.9	1.3	0.9	0.1	1.7	9.6	5.3	2.8	667	640
Elmore	167.4	49.7	1.8	5.8	1.6	3.4	8.1	44.0	25.2	9.8	396	378
Franklin	2.6	0.0	0.6	3.0	0.7	0.2	1.9	21.3	12.3	3.8	354	344
Fremont	4.5	0.0	2.0	4.7	0.8	0.3	1.8	26.0	13.7	7.4	624	586
Gem	4.6	0.0	1.9	8.2	1.5	0.4	1.0	23.7	12.4	5.7	391	334
Gooding	3.2	0.0	0.5	9.9	1.0	1.4	1.3	28.0	14.3	7.3	541	529
Idaho	15.6	0.1	14.1	10.7	1.4	1.9	7.2	31.5	19.5	5.8	382	365
Jefferson	2.7	0.0	2.6	5.2	1.7	0.6	5.9	34.4	23.9	7.6	403	379
Jerome	2.8	0.1	0.7	9.9	1.2	0.6	10.7	30.7	17.6	7.8	442	431
Kootenai	33.6	5.5	17.5	43.1	4.8	1.9	24.5	212.8	76.2	73.7	746	685
Latah	11.9	1.0	7.3	12.4	4.6	8.4	33.8	64.2	24.8	20.3	624	606
Lemhi	10.2	0.0	4.2	4.3	0.6	0.3	5.4	18.6	7.8	3.1	388	371
Lewis	1.5	0.0	0.5	8.1	2.6	0.3	1.8	13.6	7.8	3.1	754	746
Lincoln	3.3	0.0	0.7	0.9	0.4	0.1	0.2	9.6	5.9	2.5	647	618
Madison	3.0	8.9	1.2	3.5	1.6	0.5	5.4	52.2	25.6	8.7	372	352
Minidoka	3.9	0.0	7.3	8.2	1.6	0.8	1.5	60.6	22.1	8.8	426	414
Nez Perce	10.3	0.5	5.8	32.0	5.9	3.7	16.4	77.1	27.1	32.8	892	848
Oneida	0.9	0.0	0.2	1.3	1.8	0.1	11.1	11.5	5.5	2.7	672	613
Owyhee	2.5	0.0	1.1	6.0	0.9	0.6	1.8	21.0	13.3	3.9	384	374
Payette	1.8	0.0	1.9	14.4	4.2	0.6	1.0	33.8	18.2	9.7	481	437
Power	1.3	0.0	3.6	2.2	0.5	0.6	7.3	25.3	10.0	8.3	999	990
Shoshone	3.6	6.4	2.5	10.3	0.8	0.5	1.9	34.8	17.4	8.5	610	595
Teton	1.2	0.0	0.3	4.3	0.5	0.1	2.8	12.2	4.4	2.7	515	484
Twin Falls	18.1	0.1	6.9	35.6	7.7	1.9	12.3	186.4	75.2	36.0	588	554
Valley	10.3	0.0	2.1	2.2	0.6	0.2	3.2	37.0	11.7	10.3	1 270	1 218
Washington	2.3	0.0	0.9	7.3	0.9	0.3	1.4	28.0	12.3	6.1	608	591
ILLINOIS	6 251.9	1 716.4	2 418.8	5 648.7	2 084.5	1 221.7	2 928.5	X	X	X	X	X
Adams	18.8	5.8	11.1	34.8	6.0	2.6	11.5	134.8	68.6	39.8	587	507
Alexander	2.0	0.0	0.4	20.5	2.9	0.9	4.7	21.6	12.9	4.6	456	315
Bond	16.6	0.0	0.9	6.4	1.2	0.4	2.2	23.8	12.6	6.9	403	378
Boone	4.6	0.3	1.4	4.2	1.5	0.6	5.0	67.9	21.9	32.7	862	832
Brown	1.8	0.0	0.3	1.5	1.1	0.2	0.0	10.2	4.9	3.1	490	437
Bureau	9.0	1.7	1.7	5.2	1.9	0.8	1.8	92.2	33.8	27.1	760	744
Calhoun	1.5	4.6	0.7	2.9	0.4	0.1	0.5	13.7	10.2	2.1	417	386
Carroll	3.9	13.8	1.6	3.8	1.1	0.7	2.1	30.7	13.4	13.3	784	739
Cass	4.3	0.0	0.7	4.5	1.0	0.4	1.2	26.5	14.1	9.2	698	588
Champaign	76.5	36.7	16.1	90.3	15.3	12.4	223.0	372.4	147.4	150.3	892	780
Christian	5.1	0.0	1.5	11.2	2.4	0.9	0.8	69.8	36.4	22.3	644	635
Clark	3.1	0.0	0.9	5.2	1.0	0.5	3.1	29.2	14.3	9.2	524	459
Clay	3.0	0.0	0.7	9.2	1.2	0.5	4.8	29.8	14.2	6.6	455	429
Clinton	5.0	5.9	1.2	5.3	1.9	0.7	5.2	47.9	23.6	16.4	463	411
Coles	9.9	0.1	2.2	16.4	3.0	2.5	12.6	117.9	54.0	37.7	735	679
Cook	2 725.6	714.5	1 334.1	3 609.5	877.6	281.9	1 370.9	17 600.0	5 704.9	8 846.2	1 742	1 284
Crawford	3.2	0.0	0.8	6.3	1.2	0.6	0.6	48.6	15.3	12.3	582	576
Cumberland	1.7	0.2	0.4	3.2	2.2	0.3	0.1	20.6	10.8	6.5	581	572
De Kalb	12.5	0.0	3.1	13.1	2.9	10.0	5.1	194.4	58.2	98.2	1 175	993
De Witt	3.2	0.0	0.8	3.9	1.0	0.5	3.5	49.7	11.4	25.5	1 522	1 512
Douglas	3.3	0.1	0.9	3.2	1.0	0.6	4.2	32.5	12.6	15.5	783	649
Du Page	327.2	80.3	98.0	71.7	13.1	12.9	22.6	2 338.6	494.5	1 360.3	1 563	1 383
Edgar	4.2	0.3	1.0	6.8	1.6	0.8	1.6	37.3	17.5	12.5	630	597
Edwards	1.4	0.0	0.4	1.7	0.6	0.1	1.0	11.4	5.9	2.8	392	367
Effingham	10.3	0.1	2.4	8.1	4.3	0.9	13.9	59.3	33.9	18.7	561	551
Fayette	3.7	0.1	0.9	8.4	1.7	0.7	0.7	33.2	18.1	9.3	429	423
Ford	2.9	0.0	0.7	2.3	0.9	0.4	3.6	35.9	16.2	13.1	936	830
Franklin	10.5	1.3	46.3	23.8	4.4	3.6	2.7	70.0	42.0	15.1	371	356
Fulton	7.4	0.6	9.9	9.5	3.6	1.8	7.6	85.0	46.8	24.2	631	600
Gallatin	1.4	0.0	7.9	5.9	0.8	0.3	1.9	12.5	7.0	3.4	507	459
Greene	3.1	0.0	0.8	8.8	1.6	0.6	2.2	26.2	14.7	6.8	436	398
Grundy	6.4	0.0	1.4	2.5	1.1	0.5	46.5	92.9	18.9	56.0	1 545	1 481
Hamilton	1.9	0.0	0.7	5.5	0.8	0.3	0.7	23.7	10.3	4.0	462	381
Hancock	4.6	0.0	1.2	5.8	1.4	0.6	18.9	42.0	20.1	15.0	711	685
Hardin	0.9	0.0	0.2	5.0	0.7	0.3	0.4	7.9	6.0	0.9	177	172
Henderson	2.0	0.1	0.5	2.6	0.7	0.2	0.5	15.3	8.4	5.0	575	557
Henry	9.3	1.3	1.9	6.5	3.0	1.2	13.4	114.1	47.7	32.2	626	589
Iroquois	6.5	0.0	3.0	4.2	1.7	0.8	19.2	57.8	25.2	23.5	748	731

1. October 1, 2000 to September 30, 2001. 2. State totals may include programs not allocated by county. 3. Based on the resident population estimated as of July 1 of the year shown.

Table B. States and Counties — Local Government Finances, Government Employment, and Elections

	Local government finances, 1997 (cont'd)										Government employment, 1999			Presidential election, 2000[2]		
	Direct general expenditure							Debt outstanding						Percent of vote cast —		
			Percent of total for —													
STATE County	Total (mil dol)	Per capita[1] (dollars)	Education	Health and hospitals	Police protection	Public welfare	Highways	Total (mil dol)	Per capita[1] (dollars)	Federal civilian	Federal military	State and local	Democratic	Republican	All other
	183	184	185	186	187	188	189	190	191	192	193	194	195	196	197
IDAHO—Cont'd															
Custer	9.0	2 131	62.5	3.2	3.8	2.7	10.0	2.2	519	136	18	319	17.9	77.0	5.2
Elmore	50.2	2 018	58.8	10.9	3.8	1.1	7.2	16.3	656	1 017	4 278	1 272	26.4	70.2	3.4
Franklin	23.8	2 200	63.2	14.2	2.5	1.8	5.4	6.3	584	37	49	724	12.1	84.7	3.2
Fremont	29.8	2 524	59.7	1.7	2.7	4.9	6.9	25.5	2 157	123	51	854	13.7	83.4	2.9
Gem	23.9	1 653	53.1	15.9	6.0	1.1	5.8	4.1	280	87	65	683	22.5	73.1	4.4
Gooding	26.5	1 953	54.0	1.9	2.8	2.8	10.2	20.7	1 524	62	59	997	25.5	69.7	4.8
Idaho	33.1	2 193	42.6	0.2	4.5	3.7	23.0	11.5	764	459	65	930	15.9	77.9	6.2
Jefferson	34.0	1 794	77.8	0.3	2.7	0.6	5.6	9.9	523	48	86	1 117	14.0	82.7	3.3
Jerome	28.9	1 634	57.3	0.4	5.1	2.3	10.3	10.5	594	52	78	831	22.6	73.5	3.8
Kootenai	205.4	2 079	49.7	3.3	5.2	0.6	7.9	84.1	851	654	454	6 808	30.8	64.3	4.9
Latah	65.6	2 016	44.7	6.9	5.6	9.3	12.2	8.2	252	229	194	5 832	37.0	53.3	9.7
Lemhi	17.2	2 127	41.3	18.9	4.2	1.8	7.9	9.8	1 214	260	34	533	18.1	78.5	3.4
Lewis	15.5	3 799	62.3	0.6	4.1	2.3	15.9	3.0	737	36	17	366	19.8	76.7	3.4
Lincoln	9.1	2 385	59.0	0.2	3.4	1.3	13.0	3.5	926	92	17	376	27.8	66.6	5.6
Madison	51.7	2 200	47.6	24.5	3.0	0.3	5.3	16.6	705	53	107	1 500	9.1	88.5	2.4
Minidoka	61.6	2 983	35.5	32.2	4.6	5.9	4.5	10.9	528	72	87	1 340	20.6	75.3	4.1
Nez Perce	81.4	2 212	44.5	0.3	5.5	0.6	9.5	44.6	1 212	201	162	2 871	31.2	66.0	2.8
Oneida	13.4	3 347	54.2	13.4	3.8	0.1	6.7	5.1	1 269	29	18	386	17.1	79.3	3.6
Owyhee	20.4	1 995	63.4	0.3	3.1	0.0	8.0	8.9	871	36	45	598	19.5	76.9	3.6
Payette	31.8	1 573	62.0	0.9	5.1	1.0	5.6	16.2	800	43	90	999	24.0	72.3	3.7
Power	26.0	3 130	41.8	16.7	3.8	0.6	10.1	13.7	1 657	28	39	660	27.9	69.1	3.0
Shoshone	36.2	2 587	46.3	1.9	5.3	1.8	11.4	9.1	653	127	59	1 081	41.3	53.5	5.2
Teton	13.0	2 444	50.5	28.8	1.8	0.1	4.1	10.5	1 986	41	25	362	27.0	65.3	7.7
Twin Falls	194.3	3 170	47.0	27.8	2.9	0.9	6.2	41.3	674	537	273	4 565	25.6	70.1	4.3
Valley	35.7	4 409	27.7	20.4	14.0	1.0	10.2	17.9	2 215	273	34	756	28.4	64.1	7.6
Washington	27.8	2 758	38.4	14.9	5.4	0.9	7.3	6.1	604	61	44	652	24.1	71.2	4.7
ILLINOIS	X	X	X	X	X	X	X	X	X	95 061	58 126	731 615	54.6	42.6	2.8
Adams	130.3	1 921	53.1	1.9	5.1	0.2	9.6	78.8	1 161	314	149	4 228	40.5	57.6	1.9
Alexander	19.1	1 908	58.6	0.7	11.5	3.2	7.3	2.3	228	40	22	587	58.6	39.5	1.9
Bond	24.4	1 428	49.2	7.3	4.7	0.1	12.1	16.7	978	345	38	669	43.5	54.1	2.4
Boone	62.3	1 643	52.5	1.0	4.5	3.9	7.7	35.8	943	83	88	1 418	41.8	55.5	2.7
Brown	9.4	1 482	40.1	3.3	5.3	0.2	22.9	2.3	360	40	15	519	40.5	57.5	2.0
Bureau	92.1	2 587	43.7	24.7	3.0	3.7	7.6	24.5	688	154	78	2 324	46.1	50.7	3.3
Calhoun	13.3	2 672	31.0	0.0	2.1	5.3	21.3	0.2	46	32	11	255	50.3	47.2	2.4
Carroll	28.1	1 659	61.3	1.0	4.1	0.1	12.2	13.4	788	258	38	828	43.4	53.4	3.1
Cass	24.6	1 857	46.4	6.6	3.7	0.2	16.4	8.2	620	78	29	786	47.3	50.3	2.4
Champaign	353.7	2 099	49.8	0.6	5.7	2.7	6.9	124.5	739	1 371	444	31 076	47.8	46.6	5.6
Christian	68.2	1 972	55.2	3.5	3.6	0.3	9.1	12.7	366	100	79	1 811	46.0	51.0	2.9
Clark	28.2	1 608	50.7	2.6	6.5	0.2	16.8	5.4	308	58	37	790	39.0	58.5	2.4
Clay	28.5	1 972	48.6	16.8	3.9	0.2	7.9	6.3	439	57	32	871	36.1	61.8	2.2
Clinton	44.7	1 263	55.9	1.4	5.6	0.4	11.9	31.1	878	118	79	2 479	41.7	55.7	2.6
Coles	110.0	2 144	62.1	1.4	6.1	0.3	4.8	42.2	822	150	121	6 293	44.3	52.2	3.4
Cook	16 158.6	3 183	36.8	5.1	8.1	1.1	4.4	18 276.7	3 600	48 927	11 868	297 146	68.6	28.6	2.8
Crawford	46.2	2 193	39.5	32.4	2.7	0.2	10.7	5.6	265	64	46	1 390	39.2	58.5	2.3
Cumberland	26.2	2 344	32.8	3.2	2.4	0.2	12.4	7.0	623	38	25	480	37.6	59.6	2.8
De Kalb	183.3	2 192	47.9	1.3	5.1	4.4	8.9	100.7	1 204	230	198	11 307	44.5	51.6	3.9
De Witt	44.7	2 664	44.3	13.4	6.2	5.0	9.9	4.8	283	57	37	1 184	40.7	56.3	3.0
Douglas	30.0	1 518	53.7	0.3	5.7	1.9	11.3	15.9	805	66	44	757	39.4	58.1	2.5
Du Page	2 228.8	2 561	50.8	1.2	5.6	1.6	6.9	1 945.5	2 235	5 303	1 980	40 911	41.9	55.2	3.0
Edgar	35.4	1 778	56.0	5.0	4.1	0.2	9.5	11.3	568	73	43	1 179	39.1	58.7	2.3
Edwards	9.8	1 392	44.8	0.0	3.4	0.4	5.1	6.8	969	25	15	270	30.0	67.9	2.2
Effingham	58.5	1 757	55.3	0.3	4.4	1.2	14.9	36.9	1 108	177	76	1 848	29.2	68.0	2.8
Fayette	29.3	1 357	51.3	5.0	4.5	1.9	15.6	9.1	423	74	49	1 275	41.6	55.7	2.7
Ford	34.9	2 484	49.5	1.1	4.0	5.2	10.1	3.5	251	57	31	779	34.0	63.2	2.8
Franklin	67.7	1 665	56.3	5.3	6.1	1.3	6.5	35.6	876	246	89	1 957	53.1	44.2	2.7
Fulton	79.5	2 070	62.3	3.3	3.8	1.8	8.5	17.2	448	121	86	2 423	54.9	42.6	2.5
Gallatin	11.6	1 735	46.8	0.2	4.1	3.0	19.4	7.6	1 143	32	15	297	52.8	44.7	2.5
Greene	24.9	1 593	50.9	8.7	3.0	0.4	12.9	4.8	306	63	35	736	43.2	54.3	2.6
Grundy	93.3	2 574	60.3	0.9	4.5	4.6	8.0	42.9	1 183	118	82	1 883	45.3	52.5	2.1
Hamilton	22.0	2 552	37.3	33.3	1.0	0.5	11.9	6.3	726	41	19	622	42.4	54.9	2.7
Hancock	41.4	1 960	51.2	4.2	3.3	1.1	12.3	14.2	671	92	46	1 212	43.9	53.0	3.1
Hardin	7.4	1 498	67.5	1.5	2.8	1.6	10.5	2.4	478	12	11	297	44.9	51.8	3.3
Henderson	15.2	1 758	42.5	7.2	3.1	0.2	20.8	5.6	647	45	19	445	52.5	44.2	3.3
Henry	107.2	2 084	45.5	14.6	4.0	4.4	8.3	34.7	675	168	115	3 142	50.8	46.4	2.8
Iroquois	57.4	1 827	50.3	4.8	3.6	0.9	13.2	16.5	527	126	69	1 502	32.8	64.7	2.5

1. Based on the resident population estimated as of July 1 of the year shown.   2. Data subject to copyright.

STATE/ County code	MSA/ PMSA/ NECMA code[1]	County Type[2]	STATE County	Land area,[3] (sq km) 2000	Population and population characteristics, 2000			Race alone or in combination (percent)				Percent Hispanic[4]	Age (percent)					
					Total persons	Rank	Per square kilometer	White	Black	Am. Indian, Alaska Native	Asian and Pacific Islander		Under 5 years	5 to 17 years	18 to 24 years	25 to 34 years	35 to 44 years	45 to 54 years
				1	2	3	4	5	6	7	8	9	10	11	12	13	14	15
			ILLINOIS—Cont'd															
17 077	...	5	Jackson	1 523	59 612	806	39.1	82.3	13.7	0.9	3.5	2.4	5.0	14.2	26.0	14.2	11.7	10.9
17 079	...	7	Jasper	1 280	10 117	2 435	7.9	99.4	0.1	0.2	0.3	0.5	5.7	20.2	8.6	10.8	15.7	13.3
17 081	...	7	Jefferson	1 479	40 045	1 113	27.1	90.9	8.2	0.7	0.7	1.3	5.9	18.4	8.8	13.1	15.3	13.8
17 083	7040	1	Jersey	956	21 668	1 709	22.7	98.8	0.7	0.6	0.4	0.7	5.9	19.5	9.9	11.3	16.3	13.1
17 085	...	6	Jo Daviess	1 557	22 289	1 681	14.3	99.2	0.3	0.4	0.3	1.5	5.6	17.6	6.7	10.6	14.7	14.7
17 087	...	9	Johnson	893	12 878	2 242	14.4	84.3	14.3	0.7	0.4	2.9	4.7	13.7	11.4	17.4	16.7	12.4
17 089	1600	0	Kane	1 348	404 119	146	299.8	81.2	6.3	0.6	2.3	23.7	8.7	21.5	9.1	15.0	16.8	13.2
17 091	3740	3	Kankakee	1 753	103 833	511	59.2	81.1	16.0	0.6	1.0	4.8	7.0	20.1	9.7	12.9	15.3	13.2
17 093	1600	1	Kendall	830	54 544	862	65.7	94.1	1.6	0.5	1.2	7.5	8.0	21.5	7.5	14.6	17.8	13.8
17 095	...	4	Knox	1 855	55 836	845	30.1	91.1	7.0	0.6	0.8	3.4	5.8	16.3	9.8	12.0	14.4	14.1
17 097	1600	0	Lake	1 159	644 356	84	556.0	81.8	7.5	0.6	4.5	14.4	8.2	21.2	8.9	13.7	17.9	13.9
17 099	...	4	La Salle	2 939	111 509	484	37.9	96.0	1.8	0.5	0.7	5.2	6.3	18.8	8.1	11.9	16.1	13.1
17 101	...	7	Lawrence	963	15 452	2 054	16.0	98.7	1.0	0.5	0.2	0.9	5.5	17.2	7.6	11.3	14.8	13.4
17 103	...	7	Lee	1 879	36 062	1 214	19.2	93.6	5.2	0.5	0.8	3.2	5.5	18.7	7.8	12.9	17.4	14.0
17 105	...	6	Livingston	2 703	39 678	1 120	14.7	93.1	5.3	0.4	0.5	2.7	6.0	19.0	8.2	13.1	16.4	13.2
17 107	...	6	Logan	1 601	31 183	1 372	19.5	92.2	6.8	0.4	0.8	1.6	5.4	16.5	11.6	13.5	16.1	12.9
17 109	...	5	McDonough	1 526	32 913	1 322	21.6	93.8	3.8	0.5	2.4	1.5	4.4	13.3	27.6	10.3	11.2	11.2
17 111	1600	0	McHenry	1 563	260 077	213	166.4	94.9	0.8	0.4	1.8	7.5	8.1	22.1	7.1	14.1	19.3	13.8
17 113	1040	3	McLean	3 065	150 433	357	49.1	90.4	6.8	0.5	2.4	2.5	6.5	17.0	18.6	14.2	15.0	12.2
17 115	2040	3	Macon	1 504	114 706	472	76.3	84.7	14.9	0.5	0.8	1.0	6.4	18.2	9.8	11.6	14.8	14.4
17 117	...	6	Macoupin	2 237	49 019	931	21.9	98.6	0.9	0.5	0.4	0.6	5.7	18.9	8.3	11.3	15.3	13.5
17 119	7040	0	Madison	1 878	258 941	216	137.9	91.2	7.7	0.7	0.9	1.5	6.3	18.6	9.4	12.9	16.0	13.4
17 121	...	7	Marion	1 482	41 691	1 063	28.1	95.0	4.3	0.7	0.8	0.9	6.4	19.1	8.1	11.5	15.0	13.3
17 123	...	6	Marshall	1 000	13 180	2 214	13.2	98.9	0.5	0.5	0.4	1.0	5.5	18.0	7.2	11.1	14.5	14.4
17 125	...	6	Mason	1 396	16 038	2 019	11.5	99.3	0.2	0.6	0.3	0.5	5.7	18.7	7.7	11.3	15.0	13.7
17 127	...	7	Massac	619	15 161	2 079	24.5	93.6	6.0	0.7	0.4	0.8	6.2	16.8	7.9	12.2	15.3	13.0
17 129	7880	3	Menard	814	12 486	2 266	15.3	99.0	0.5	0.4	0.3	0.8	5.8	20.8	6.8	11.2	17.7	14.6
17 131	...	6	Mercer	1 453	16 957	1 955	11.7	99.0	0.4	0.4	0.3	1.3	5.7	19.1	7.3	11.0	15.6	14.5
17 133	7040	1	Monroe	1 006	27 619	1 461	27.5	99.2	0.1	0.4	0.4	0.7	6.5	19.9	7.4	12.0	18.6	13.5
17 135	...	6	Montgomery	1 823	30 652	1 383	16.8	95.3	3.8	0.4	0.4	1.1	5.8	18.0	8.3	13.4	16.0	12.8
17 137	...	4	Morgan	1 473	36 616	1 198	24.9	93.2	5.8	0.5	0.6	1.4	5.4	17.3	11.1	11.8	15.3	13.6
17 139	...	6	Moultrie	869	14 287	2 141	16.4	99.4	0.3	0.4	0.3	0.5	6.5	19.2	7.9	11.0	14.9	13.3
17 141	6880	2	Ogle	1 965	51 032	908	26.0	96.3	0.7	0.5	0.7	6.0	6.3	21.1	7.2	12.0	16.8	13.6
17 143	6120	2	Peoria	1 605	183 433	298	114.3	80.8	17.1	0.6	2.0	2.1	6.9	18.3	10.4	13.2	14.4	13.8
17 145	...	7	Perry	1 142	23 094	1 639	20.2	90.3	8.3	0.6	0.5	1.8	5.3	16.7	10.3	13.5	15.6	13.2
17 147	...	6	Piatt	1 140	16 365	1 999	14.4	99.4	0.3	0.4	0.2	0.6	6.2	19.0	6.8	10.7	16.9	14.5
17 149	...	7	Pike	2 150	17 384	1 929	8.1	97.9	1.6	0.5	0.4	0.5	5.8	18.3	7.8	11.6	14.1	13.4
17 151	...	9	Pope	961	4 413	2 886	4.6	94.6	4.1	1.8	0.4	0.9	4.8	16.7	10.2	9.7	14.1	14.0
17 153	...	9	Pulaski	520	7 348	2 652	14.1	67.4	31.7	0.6	1.0	1.5	6.1	21.0	8.3	10.6	14.7	12.6
17 155	...	9	Putnam	414	6 086	2 773	14.7	98.1	0.9	0.5	0.4	2.8	5.9	19.2	7.0	10.7	16.0	14.1
17 157	...	6	Randolph	1 498	33 893	1 284	22.6	89.4	9.6	0.5	0.5	1.5	5.4	16.7	9.6	14.2	16.2	13.4
17 159	...	7	Richland	933	16 149	2 012	17.3	98.7	0.4	0.3	0.9	0.8	6.1	18.4	8.3	11.4	15.2	12.5
17 161	1960	2	Rock Island	1 105	149 374	361	135.2	87.2	8.3	0.7	1.4	8.6	6.4	17.4	10.0	12.3	15.0	14.1
17 163	7040	0	St. Clair	1 719	256 082	219	149.0	69.0	29.3	0.6	1.4	2.2	6.9	20.8	8.9	12.9	16.3	13.1
17 165	...	7	Saline	993	26 733	1 493	26.9	95.0	4.5	0.7	0.3	1.0	5.8	18.2	8.2	10.9	14.2	13.1
17 167	7880	3	Sangamon	2 249	188 951	292	84.0	88.5	10.3	0.6	1.4	1.1	6.4	18.5	8.1	13.3	16.5	14.8
17 169	...	7	Schuyler	1 133	7 189	2 667	6.3	99.3	0.2	0.5	0.2	0.5	5.8	17.3	7.1	11.4	14.9	13.9
17 171	...	9	Scott	650	5 537	2 814	8.5	99.7	0.1	0.3	0.1	0.2	6.3	18.8	7.8	11.3	16.0	13.0
17 173	...	6	Shelby	1 965	22 893	1 649	11.7	99.3	0.2	0.4	0.3	0.5	5.8	19.2	7.6	11.0	15.2	13.1
17 175	...	8	Stark	746	6 332	2 754	8.5	99.4	0.1	0.7	0.3	0.9	6.3	18.8	6.8	11.2	14.0	13.6
17 177	...	4	Stephenson	1 461	48 979	934	33.5	90.7	8.5	0.4	1.0	1.5	6.1	19.1	7.6	11.9	15.7	13.4
17 179	6120	2	Tazewell	1 681	128 485	420	76.4	98.1	1.0	0.6	0.6	1.0	6.2	18.2	8.1	12.8	15.8	14.4
17 181	...	7	Union	1 078	18 293	1 881	17.0	97.3	1.0	0.9	0.5	2.6	5.2	17.9	7.5	11.4	15.3	13.8
17 183	...	4	Vermilion	2 329	83 919	620	36.0	87.0	11.2	0.6	0.7	3.0	6.6	18.3	8.4	12.4	14.8	13.5
17 185	...	7	Wabash	579	12 937	2 237	22.3	98.7	0.6	0.5	0.7	0.7	5.7	18.5	9.1	10.8	15.5	14.1
17 187	...	7	Warren	1 405	18 735	1 858	13.3	96.6	2.1	0.4	0.6	2.7	5.6	17.5	12.4	10.7	13.9	13.8
17 189	...	6	Washington	1 457	15 148	2 082	10.4	99.1	0.4	0.5	0.3	0.7	5.7	19.7	7.6	11.2	16.1	13.4
17 191	...	7	Wayne	1 849	17 151	1 946	9.3	99.2	0.3	0.5	0.4	0.6	6.0	17.7	7.9	11.4	14.4	13.0
17 193	...	6	White	1 282	15 371	2 063	12.0	99.1	0.4	0.4	0.3	0.7	5.1	16.4	7.7	10.2	15.0	13.6
17 195	...	4	Whiteside	1 774	60 653	800	34.2	94.1	1.4	0.6	0.6	8.8	6.4	18.6	8.2	11.8	15.2	14.0
17 197	1600	0	Will	2 168	502 266	111	231.7	83.2	11.0	0.6	2.7	8.7	8.4	21.6	8.1	14.8	18.1	13.2
17 199	...	5	Williamson	1 097	61 296	794	55.9	96.3	2.8	0.7	0.8	1.2	6.0	17.0	8.6	12.9	15.0	13.6
17 201	6880	2	Winnebago	1 331	278 418	203	209.2	84.1	11.2	0.7	2.1	6.9	7.1	19.3	8.4	13.8	16.0	13.8
17 203	6120	2	Woodford	1 367	35 469	1 234	25.9	99.1	0.4	0.5	0.5	0.7	6.6	20.1	8.7	10.6	15.6	14.6

1. MSA = Metropolitan Statistical Area. PMSA = Primary MSA. NECMA = New England County Metropolitan Area. See Appendix A for explanation of these concepts. See Appendix B for list of metropolitan areas identified by type, with component counties. 2. County typology code from the Economic Research Service of USDA. See Appendix A for definition. 3. Dry land or land partially or temporarily covered by water. 4. Hispanic persons may be of any race.

Table B. States and Counties — **Population and Households**

STATE County	55 to 64 years (16)	65 to 74 years (17)	75 years and over (18)	Percent female (19)	Total persons 2001 (20)	Total persons 1990 (21)	Percent change 1990–2000 (22)	Percent change 2000–2001 (23)	Births (24)	Deaths (25)	Net migration (26)	Households 2000 Number (27)	Percent change, 1990–2000 (28)	Persons per household (29)	Female family householder[1] (30)	One person (31)
ILLINOIS—Cont'd																
Jackson	6.9	5.5	5.5	49.0	58 838	61 067	-2.4	-1.3	875	628	-1 027	24 215	3.2	2.21	9.7	34.9
Jasper	9.3	7.8	8.6	50.6	10 037	10 609	-4.6	-0.8	141	136	-87	3 930	-0.8	2.55	7.0	24.7
Jefferson	9.5	7.4	7.9	49.0	40 113	37 020	8.2	0.2	580	537	45	15 374	5.3	2.44	9.9	27.6
Jersey	9.7	7.5	6.9	51.1	21 832	20 539	5.5	0.8	327	292	137	8 096	10.2	2.57	9.1	23.9
Jo Daviess	12.1	9.6	8.3	49.9	22 356	21 821	2.1	0.3	293	262	41	9 218	10.1	2.40	6.5	27.5
Johnson	10.3	7.6	6.0	40.2	13 089	11 347	13.5	1.6	144	142	203	4 183	12.3	2.43	7.1	24.2
Kane	7.2	4.4	4.0	49.7	425 545	317 471	27.3	5.3	8 964	2 957	15 198	133 901	24.9	2.97	10.0	19.6
Kankakee	8.8	6.7	6.3	51.1	104 122	96 255	7.9	0.3	1 897	1 333	-238	38 182	10.3	2.61	13.1	24.9
Kendall	8.3	4.5	4.0	50.3	58 227	39 413	38.4	6.8	955	339	2 992	18 798	41.3	2.89	7.5	16.4
Knox	10.0	8.5	9.1	50.2	55 314	56 393	-1.0	-0.9	808	844	-468	22 056	0.7	2.33	10.6	29.6
Lake	7.7	4.8	3.8	49.7	661 111	516 418	24.8	2.6	13 101	4 641	8 546	216 297	24.3	2.88	9.2	19.7
La Salle	9.2	7.9	8.5	50.5	111 580	106 913	4.3	0.1	1 724	1 502	-100	43 417	5.2	2.49	9.2	27.4
Lawrence	10.0	9.3	10.8	52.4	15 287	15 972	-3.3	-1.1	224	316	-65	6 309	-0.2	2.36	9.0	29.2
Lee	9.0	7.5	7.2	48.7	35 971	34 392	4.9	-0.3	462	465	-71	13 253	6.2	2.49	9.3	26.5
Livingston	8.7	7.4	7.9	50.6	39 441	39 301	1.0	-0.6	570	534	-259	14 374	4.6	2.51	8.8	26.8
Logan	8.9	7.1	7.9	50.0	30 805	30 798	1.3	-1.2	411	438	-345	11 113	0.7	2.42	9.3	27.8
McDonough	7.9	6.7	7.5	51.2	32 575	35 244	-6.6	-1.0	380	351	-361	12 360	0.9	2.28	7.5	31.8
McHenry	7.5	4.4	3.7	49.8	270 504	183 241	41.9	4.0	4 892	1 901	7 320	89 403	42.0	2.89	7.6	18.0
McLean	6.9	5.0	4.7	51.7	151 878	129 180	16.5	1.0	2 429	1 252	331	56 746	21.3	2.45	8.8	27.6
Macon	9.6	7.9	7.3	52.3	112 964	117 206	-2.1	-1.5	1 911	1 486	-2 179	46 561	1.2	2.39	12.2	28.8
Macoupin	9.4	8.4	9.1	51.3	48 924	47 679	2.8	-0.2	701	792	22	19 253	5.9	2.48	8.9	25.6
Madison	9.1	7.4	6.8	51.8	260 259	249 238	3.9	0.5	4 101	3 410	752	101 953	7.5	2.48	11.8	26.3
Marion	10.0	7.8	8.8	51.8	41 446	41 561	0.3	-0.6	627	621	-235	16 619	2.1	2.45	11.6	27.2
Marshall	10.5	9.0	9.8	51.0	12 971	12 846	2.6	-1.6	174	185	-197	5 225	6.6	2.47	6.7	25.0
Mason	10.5	8.4	8.9	51.0	15 960	16 269	-1.4	-0.5	216	245	-42	6 389	0.7	2.48	9.0	24.9
Massac	10.8	8.6	9.2	52.2	15 081	14 752	2.8	-0.5	233	314	7	6 261	6.0	2.37	10.0	28.0
Menard	10.0	6.6	6.6	51.0	12 556	11 164	11.8	0.6	152	146	68	4 873	16.1	2.52	9.1	23.8
Mercer	10.9	7.9	8.1	50.8	16 971	17 290	-1.9	0.1	224	230	27	6 624	0.8	2.53	7.2	22.8
Monroe	8.7	7.2	6.2	50.8	28 507	22 422	23.2	3.2	396	267	748	10 275	25.5	2.65	7.3	21.3
Montgomery	8.9	8.0	9.0	48.4	30 462	30 728	-0.2	-0.6	419	508	-88	11 507	0.2	2.44	8.9	27.8
Morgan	9.7	7.6	8.0	50.3	36 221	36 397	0.6	-1.1	514	478	-428	14 039	2.6	2.37	10.0	29.3
Moultrie	9.5	8.2	9.5	51.8	14 307	13 930	2.6	0.1	226	260	54	5 405	5.5	2.56	7.1	23.6
Ogle	9.5	6.9	6.5	50.4	51 729	45 957	11.0	1.4	782	561	493	19 278	12.5	2.62	8.3	22.5
Peoria	8.9	7.0	7.1	51.9	181 676	182 827	0.3	-1.0	3 380	2 316	-2 823	72 733	2.7	2.43	12.9	29.7
Perry	9.3	7.8	8.2	46.9	22 972	21 412	7.9	-0.5	309	308	-114	8 504	2.4	2.43	9.7	27.9
Piatt	10.4	7.9	7.6	51.2	16 315	15 548	5.3	-0.3	219	202	-61	6 475	9.1	2.50	6.8	23.7
Pike	9.8	8.6	10.6	50.5	17 199	17 577	-1.1	-1.1	222	292	-108	6 876	-2.0	2.42	7.8	27.8
Pope	12.7	9.4	8.3	49.4	4 341	4 373	0.9	-1.6	43	63	-53	1 769	9.8	2.33	7.6	27.9
Pulaski	9.1	8.6	8.8	52.2	7 167	7 523	-2.3	-2.5	135	150	-169	2 893	-2.2	2.44	15.8	30.0
Putnam	11.2	8.2	7.6	50.6	6 124	5 730	6.2	0.6	76	71	33	2 415	9.6	2.52	7.0	24.6
Randolph	8.9	7.4	8.2	46.2	33 830	34 583	-2.0	-0.2	489	478	-59	12 084	1.1	2.46	9.2	26.9
Richland	10.4	8.8	8.8	51.7	16 042	16 545	-2.4	-0.7	254	237	-119	6 660	2.4	2.40	8.8	27.7
Rock Island	9.7	7.6	7.5	51.4	148 379	148 723	0.4	-0.7	2 564	1 923	-1 623	60 712	2.4	2.38	11.6	30.2
St. Clair	8.0	7.0	6.2	52.2	256 599	262 852	-2.6	0.2	4 893	3 236	-1 014	96 810	1.5	2.59	17.1	25.9
Saline	10.5	9.1	9.9	51.9	26 325	26 551	0.7	-1.5	398	524	-275	10 992	1.4	2.32	10.2	31.3
Sangamon	8.9	6.8	6.7	52.3	189 379	178 386	5.9	0.2	3 109	2 231	-364	78 722	9.1	2.36	11.7	31.0
Schuyler	10.3	9.5	9.9	50.4	7 059	7 498	-4.1	-1.8	89	117	-103	2 975	-0.9	2.38	7.1	27.3
Scott	10.2	8.2	8.3	51.7	5 500	5 644	-1.9	-0.7	71	71	-35	2 222	1.5	2.47	8.3	26.1
Shelby	10.3	8.9	8.9	50.6	22 681	22 261	2.8	-0.9	311	278	-241	9 056	5.8	2.50	7.1	25.4
Stark	10.2	8.7	10.4	51.8	6 323	6 534	-3.1	-0.1	99	122	14	2 525	0.5	2.46	7.0	27.1
Stephenson	9.9	8.0	8.4	51.8	48 401	48 052	1.9	-1.2	753	680	-654	19 785	4.6	2.43	9.5	27.6
Tazewell	9.6	8.0	6.9	50.8	128 315	123 692	3.9	-0.1	1 965	1 462	-625	50 327	6.7	2.49	8.7	24.8
Union	11.4	8.2	9.3	51.4	18 263	17 619	3.8	-0.2	272	315	23	7 290	6.6	2.38	9.5	28.4
Vermilion	9.9	8.2	7.8	50.8	83 300	88 257	-4.9	-0.7	1 471	1 287	-783	33 406	-2.0	2.42	12.2	28.9
Wabash	9.2	8.4	8.6	51.2	12 784	13 111	-1.3	-1.2	181	198	-134	5 192	3.2	2.46	8.7	27.0
Warren	9.8	8.0	8.3	51.6	18 374	19 181	-2.3	-1.9	255	288	-328	7 166	-3.1	2.44	8.8	26.7
Washington	9.6	7.9	8.9	50.6	15 157	14 965	1.2	0.1	201	228	44	5 848	3.4	2.55	7.1	24.3
Wayne	10.8	9.2	9.6	51.3	17 076	17 241	-0.5	-0.4	251	287	-30	7 143	3.0	2.37	8.3	27.6
White	11.0	9.7	11.2	52.3	15 264	16 522	-7.0	-0.7	204	310	8	6 534	-4.5	2.29	7.6	29.8
Whiteside	9.8	8.1	8.0	51.0	60 495	60 186	0.8	-0.3	948	804	-291	23 684	4.2	2.51	9.5	25.1
Will	7.4	4.5	3.8	50.1	536 416	357 313	40.6	6.8	9 500	3 649	27 604	167 542	43.3	2.94	9.6	17.8
Williamson	10.5	8.1	8.4	51.6	61 794	57 733	6.2	0.8	867	918	562	25 358	9.7	2.35	10.2	28.9
Winnebago	8.9	6.6	6.1	51.1	279 943	252 913	10.1	0.5	5 037	3 036	-367	107 980	11.6	2.53	11.8	26.3
Woodford	9.1	6.8	8.0	51.2	35 833	32 653	8.6	1.0	523	429	278	12 797	12.3	2.69	6.6	20.5

1. No spouse present.

STATE County	Births, average 1997–1999 Total	Rate[1]	Deaths, average 1997–1999 Number Total	Number Infant[2]	Rate Total[1]	Rate Infant[3]	Physicians,[4] 2000 Number	Rate[5]	Hospitals,[4] 1998 Number	Beds Number	Beds Rate[5]	Medicare enrollees 2000	Serious crimes known to police, 2000[6] Total Number	Rate[7]
	32	33	34	35	36	37	38	39	40	41	42	43	44	45
ILLINOIS—Cont'd														
Jackson	651	10.7	470	NA	7.8	NA	121	203	2	192	318	7 612	NA	NA
Jasper	115	10.8	105	NA	9.9	NA	1	10	0	0	0	1 733	NA	NA
Jefferson	467	12.3	420	NA	11.1	NA	54	135	2	207	554	6 608	NA	NA
Jersey	246	11.5	233	NA	10.9	NA	16	74	1	67	313	2 929	NA	NA
Jo Daviess	240	11.1	219	NA	10.2	NA	10	45	1	85	396	4 271	NA	NA
Johnson	111	8.3	125	NA	9.4	NA	2	16	0	0	0	2 238	NA	NA
Kane	7 049	18.0	2 363	50	6.0	7.1	561	139	4	850	217	40 263	NA	NA
Kankakee	1 506	14.7	1 056	11	10.3	7.5	172	166	2	482	472	16 269	NA	NA
Kendall	726	14.0	282	NA	5.4	NA	16	29	0	0	0	4 032	NA	NA
Knox	618	11.1	667	NA	12.0	NA	80	143	2	330	594	10 835	NA	NA
Lake	10 307	17.0	3 557	55	5.9	5.3	1 157	180	7	1 473	243	60 218	NA	NA
La Salle	1 382	12.6	1 194	8	10.8	6.0	117	105	4	466	423	20 116	NA	NA
Lawrence	160	10.4	250	NA	16.3	NA	7	45	1	59	385	3 305	NA	NA
Lee	406	11.3	383	NA	10.7	NA	52	144	1	101	280	6 072	NA	NA
Livingston	459	11.5	418	NA	10.5	NA	28	71	1	84	212	6 167	NA	NA
Logan	332	10.6	340	NA	10.8	NA	20	64	1	66	211	5 289	NA	NA
McDonough	298	8.7	289	NA	8.4	NA	55	167	1	144	425	4 990	NA	NA
McHenry	3 868	16.0	1 494	24	6.2	6.2	238	92	3	378	157	24 483	NA	NA
McLean	1 905	13.3	971	15	6.8	8.1	242	161	2	322	226	16 392	NA	NA
Macon	1 485	13.1	1 212	15	10.7	10.1	198	173	2	581	511	19 999	NA	NA
Macoupin	534	10.9	605	NA	12.4	NA	16	33	2	90	184	9 713	NA	NA
Madison	3 328	12.8	2 675	29	10.3	8.8	325	126	6	961	371	42 313	NA	NA
Marion	539	12.9	513	NA	12.2	NA	56	134	2	324	774	8 809	NA	NA
Marshall	144	11.1	159	NA	12.3	NA	8	61	0	0	0	2 384	NA	NA
Mason	188	11.2	199	NA	11.8	NA	11	69	1	36	214	3 304	NA	NA
Massac	180	11.6	222	NA	14.3	NA	8	53	1	53	340	2 991	NA	NA
Menard	141	11.2	114	NA	9.1	NA	2	16	0	0	0	1 793	NA	NA
Mercer	189	10.7	179	NA	10.2	NA	4	24	1	45	255	2 752	NA	NA
Monroe	321	12.1	228	NA	8.6	NA	14	51	0	0	0	3 909	NA	NA
Montgomery	343	11.0	383	NA	12.3	NA	17	55	2	189	602	5 898	NA	NA
Morgan	407	11.5	396	NA	11.2	NA	57	156	1	159	450	6 452	NA	NA
Moultrie	175	12.1	208	NA	14.4	NA	8	56	0	0	0	3 009	NA	NA
Ogle	638	12.6	454	NA	9.0	NA	25	49	1	42	83	7 181	NA	NA
Peoria	2 565	14.1	1 752	25	9.6	9.7	612	334	3	1 074	591	29 405	NA	NA
Perry	252	11.9	255	NA	12.1	NA	14	61	2	125	594	4 151	NA	NA
Piatt	189	11.4	152	NA	9.2	NA	12	73	1	18	110	2 934	NA	NA
Pike	192	11.1	223	NA	12.9	NA	10	58	1	59	340	3 629	NA	NA
Pope	46	9.5	45	NA	9.5	NA	2	45	0	0	0	745	NA	NA
Pulaski	90	12.4	107	NA	14.7	NA	0	0	0	0	0	1 476	NA	NA
Putnam	64	11.0	61	NA	10.5	NA	0	0	0	0	0	1 076	NA	NA
Randolph	371	11.0	376	NA	11.2	NA	41	121	3	199	594	5 947	NA	NA
Richland	211	12.6	198	NA	11.8	NA	34	211	1	134	799	3 239	NA	NA
Rock Island	1 970	13.3	1 523	18	10.3	9.0	255	171	3	648	439	25 150	NA	NA
St. Clair	3 779	14.4	2 567	34	9.8	8.9	400	156	4	965	368	38 193	NA	NA
Saline	313	12.0	405	NA	15.5	NA	37	138	2	130	497	5 714	NA	NA
Sangamon	2 515	13.1	1 774	22	9.3	8.7	643	340	3	1 336	698	28 956	NA	NA
Schuyler	81	10.6	94	NA	12.4	NA	4	56	1	53	694	1 398	NA	NA
Scott	65	11.6	61	NA	10.8	NA	1	18	0	0	0	926	NA	NA
Shelby	261	11.5	240	NA	10.6	NA	8	35	1	53	233	4 258	NA	NA
Stark	72	11.4	91	NA	14.4	NA	1	16	0	0	0	1 284	NA	NA
Stephenson	606	12.4	511	NA	10.4	NA	66	135	1	166	339	9 124	NA	NA
Tazewell	1 550	12.1	1 175	11	9.1	7.1	94	73	2	154	120	21 336	NA	NA
Union	207	11.5	244	NA	13.5	NA	25	137	1	94	522	3 583	NA	NA
Vermilion	1 118	13.3	980	NA	11.6	NA	141	168	2	233	277	15 638	NA	NA
Wabash	140	11.1	144	NA	11.4	NA	9	70	1	56	443	2 320	NA	NA
Warren	211	11.2	217	NA	11.5	NA	14	75	1	77	409	3 271	NA	NA
Washington	164	10.7	170	NA	11.1	NA	5	33	1	61	397	2 648	NA	NA
Wayne	198	11.7	226	NA	13.3	NA	10	58	1	81	477	3 394	NA	NA
White	158	10.1	249	NA	15.9	NA	11	72	1	126	805	3 704	NA	NA
Whiteside	798	13.4	628	NA	10.5	NA	56	92	2	182	305	11 167	NA	NA
Will	7 197	15.6	2 756	61	6.0	8.5	432	86	2	646	141	44 385	NA	NA
Williamson	700	11.5	730	7	12.0	10.0	104	170	2	181	298	10 909	NA	NA
Winnebago	3 878	14.5	2 410	28	9.0	7.2	619	222	3	897	335	40 078	NA	NA
Woodford	414	11.8	343	NA	9.7	NA	21	59	1	34	97	4 861	NA	NA

1. Per 1,000 estimated resident population, average 1997–1999.   2. Deaths of infants under 1 year old.   3. Deaths of infants under 1 year old per 1,000 live births.   4. Data subject to copyright.   5. Per 100,000 resident population as of July 1 of the year shown.   6. Data for serious crimes have not been adjusted for underreporting; this may affect comparability between geographic areas and over time.   7. Per 100,000 population estimated by the FBI.

STATE County	Serious crimes known to police, 2000[1] (cont'd) Rate[2] Violent	Property	Education School enrollment and attainment, 1990 Enrollment[3] Total	Percent private	Attainment[4] (percent) High school graduate or more	Bachelor's degree or more	Local government expenditures, fiscal 1999[5] Total current expenditures (mil dol)	Current expenditures per student (dollars)	Money income 1989 Per capita[6] (dollars)	Households Median Dollars	Percent change, 1979–1989 (constant 1989 dollars)	Percent with $100,000 or more	Income and poverty, 1998 Median household income	Percent below poverty level All persons	Persons under 18	Persons 5–17 in families
	46	47	48	49	50	51	52	53	54	55	56	57	58	59	60	61
ILLINOIS—Cont'd																
Jackson	NA	NA	27 965	4.2	78.8	29.5	54.3	6 780	10 003	17 567	-10.9	1.6	28 847	19.3	23.5	24.8
Jasper	NA	NA	2 505	7.9	69.7	8.1	14.7	7 728	10 298	22 751	-7.1	1.1	31 965	12.7	16.7	17.6
Jefferson	NA	NA	8 735	4.5	69.9	11.3	39.0	5 697	11 279	22 397	-9.5	1.8	33 065	15.9	20.6	21.2
Jersey	NA	NA	5 603	25.3	71.9	9.3	17.5	5 298	11 132	27 126	-6.7	1.0	38 918	10.3	14.4	13.3
Jo Daviess	NA	NA	5 216	15.6	74.1	12.1	22.3	6 398	12 497	26 882	-4.5	2.0	39 444	8.1	10.8	10.3
Johnson	NA	NA	2 650	4.2	66.2	9.1	9.9	5 472	9 170	21 953	5.3	0.5	32 976	14.4	17.8	18.6
Kane	NA	NA	88 277	18.4	77.7	21.4	567.9	6 036	15 890	40 080	8.2	5.9	57 033	5.8	7.9	8.2
Kankakee	NA	NA	26 064	17.1	73.1	11.9	112.9	6 074	12 142	28 284	-2.9	1.8	38 294	12.3	17.2	16.6
Kendall	NA	NA	11 335	11.9	83.7	17.8	55.4	5 689	16 115	42 834	4.3	4.4	63 020	3.4	4.5	4.2
Knox	NA	NA	13 887	13.8	76.6	12.7	50.2	5 963	11 973	24 523	-14.4	1.7	34 382	12.3	17.3	16.7
Lake	NA	NA	138 258	19.6	84.7	32.0	869.0	7 370	21 765	46 047	9.0	13.7	63 467	5.6	8.3	7.5
La Salle	NA	NA	25 539	13.5	73.1	10.5	113.8	6 472	12 337	27 093	-13.1	1.8	38 933	9.7	13.7	12.4
Lawrence	NA	NA	3 490	3.9	69.2	6.3	14.5	5 710	10 120	19 688	-16.3	0.5	30 187	14.8	20.9	21.6
Lee	NA	NA	8 623	10.4	76.3	11.8	33.0	5 898	12 050	28 284	-9.0	1.8	39 907	8.4	11.3	10.7
Livingston	NA	NA	8 930	8.5	74.1	9.4	48.5	6 172	12 124	29 848	-7.5	1.5	42 255	9.5	12.8	12.6
Logan	NA	NA	7 413	22.3	75.9	12.5	24.9	6 197	11 576	27 528	-4.5	0.8	38 896	10.8	14.0	13.8
McDonough	NA	NA	15 236	3.3	80.3	23.2	26.6	6 261	10 089	21 774	-8.0	1.5	34 546	14.3	17.4	17.3
McHenry	NA	NA	48 681	13.5	84.5	21.0	246.6	5 942	17 271	43 471	10.5	6.4	62 106	3.5	4.7	4.3
McLean	NA	NA	45 875	11.4	84.7	29.0	136.6	5 961	14 138	31 366	0.9	3.2	48 636	8.2	10.9	10.1
Macon	NA	NA	29 951	15.7	76.2	14.8	107.4	5 723	13 762	28 598	-8.7	2.5	40 676	13.5	20.3	19.3
Macoupin	NA	NA	11 697	9.9	72.8	9.2	50.1	5 066	11 365	23 913	-8.4	1.1	35 362	11.4	15.6	15.4
Madison	NA	NA	64 379	14.0	75.8	14.4	257.5	5 902	13 272	29 861	-3.0	2.3	40 871	10.5	15.0	13.9
Marion	NA	NA	9 961	7.2	70.1	9.6	49.8	6 118	11 500	22 813	-6.3	1.7	32 201	14.7	19.6	19.9
Marshall	NA	NA	3 053	5.4	77.8	10.3	9.7	5 712	12 109	26 450	-14.2	1.3	39 901	9.3	14.4	12.4
Mason	NA	NA	3 920	4.1	72.6	8.8	21.0	5 919	11 036	22 434	-19.7	0.8	35 280	12.2	18.1	17.5
Massac	NA	NA	3 279	3.8	65.3	8.0	14.5	5 351	10 136	19 632	-10.9	0.8	30 904	14.6	21.4	22.0
Menard	NA	NA	2 703	3.4	77.3	13.8	13.9	4 906	12 954	29 326	-7.1	1.9	44 158	8.9	12.7	12.9
Mercer	NA	NA	4 198	5.7	77.4	11.3	18.3	4 997	12 058	26 606	-11.6	1.7	40 244	8.9	12.2	11.7
Monroe	NA	NA	5 594	20.5	75.9	13.7	22.5	5 108	13 886	35 086	4.4	1.8	52 581	4.6	6.2	5.9
Montgomery	NA	NA	7 352	8.0	72.2	8.1	29.9	5 391	10 724	23 879	-3.8	1.4	33 950	13.2	17.2	17.2
Morgan	NA	NA	8 978	23.3	75.9	16.0	35.3	6 325	12 372	26 403	-2.8	2.3	36 838	11.8	16.1	15.9
Moultrie	NA	NA	3 174	8.8	70.3	9.5	9.7	5 164	11 840	26 852	-7.6	1.6	39 377	8.0	10.4	11.2
Ogle	NA	NA	11 394	5.9	77.6	12.1	65.8	6 325	12 880	30 958	-3.6	1.3	44 087	7.1	9.6	8.9
Peoria	NA	NA	50 947	23.7	77.9	19.5	176.3	6 340	13 924	28 193	-13.3	3.3	40 569	13.3	19.8	18.3
Perry	NA	NA	5 263	12.2	67.8	7.3	17.9	5 629	10 751	22 979	-15.5	0.8	31 588	13.9	17.7	18.3
Piatt	NA	NA	3 825	5.8	83.0	15.9	18.7	5 403	13 690	31 369	-3.7	2.1	45 299	6.3	8.5	8.5
Pike	NA	NA	3 853	5.8	69.9	8.1	17.9	5 639	10 200	20 527	-1.2	1.1	30 441	14.3	18.5	19.3
Pope	NA	NA	1 161	2.0	65.2	6.3	4.1	6 064	8 977	19 031	-5.3	0.7	29 971	14.7	17.7	23.6
Pulaski	NA	NA	2 178	2.5	59.8	6.1	12.7	8 152	8 479	15 625	-1.1	0.8	23 195	23.6	29.5	33.2
Putnam	NA	NA	1 361	10.8	75.8	9.8	5.6	5 410	13 672	30 136	-11.1	2.1	43 433	6.9	9.6	10.8
Randolph	NA	NA	8 187	14.1	64.2	8.3	28.5	5 863	11 155	25 859	-12.6	1.1	35 199	11.6	14.8	15.2
Richland	NA	NA	4 117	12.5	73.5	11.9	15.3	5 396	11 692	23 013	-4.8	2.0	31 644	13.8	18.8	19.3
Rock Island	NA	NA	38 550	17.5	77.4	15.0	143.1	6 157	13 214	26 803	-19.8	2.2	38 417	11.0	16.7	15.6
St. Clair	NA	NA	73 302	15.6	72.6	14.7	286.1	6 208	11 916	26 813	-0.7	2.2	36 188	15.1	21.3	20.7
Saline	NA	NA	6 041	2.4	63.2	9.4	25.4	5 661	10 066	18 349	-11.7	1.3	26 956	17.9	24.6	25.8
Sangamon	NA	NA	44 847	17.9	81.8	22.4	181.5	6 276	14 947	30 350	0.1	2.8	42 954	9.8	14.7	13.9
Schuyler	NA	NA	1 704	3.9	69.4	10.7	6.7	5 409	10 080	21 080	-11.4	0.7	33 136	10.6	13.6	14.8
Scott	NA	NA	1 205	7.8	73.6	9.2	5.8	5 463	10 505	23 642	-4.0	1.0	34 904	10.4	13.4	15.7
Shelby	NA	NA	5 209	6.1	72.7	9.8	17.5	5 191	11 608	26 040	-2.2	1.5	35 532	9.7	12.5	13.3
Stark	NA	NA	1 592	3.2	77.0	10.8	7.4	5 945	11 241	25 130	-12.7	0.9	36 423	10.0	14.9	14.4
Stephenson	NA	NA	11 418	9.3	76.7	13.6	45.7	5 686	13 156	28 340	-4.0	2.1	41 247	9.4	13.8	13.0
Tazewell	NA	NA	31 276	10.7	78.6	13.6	122.4	6 011	13 681	30 933	-12.7	2.1	44 509	8.0	11.8	10.5
Union	NA	NA	4 006	3.4	64.2	10.9	19.7	5 522	10 180	20 173	-11.0	1.3	30 412	15.8	22.8	23.7
Vermilion	NA	NA	21 697	9.4	72.8	11.1	90.9	6 303	11 771	23 841	-12.2	1.6	33 216	14.0	19.5	19.2
Wabash	NA	NA	3 324	8.8	74.9	12.6	12.3	5 491	12 072	26 021	-4.8	2.4	33 263	12.3	16.6	16.8
Warren	NA	NA	5 154	19.0	76.3	14.5	13.1	5 193	10 591	22 259	-16.8	1.1	32 636	12.3	14.9	16.7
Washington	NA	NA	3 459	14.9	65.7	8.7	13.1	5 595	11 539	25 387	-3.2	1.7	38 372	7.6	9.6	9.5
Wayne	NA	NA	3 946	5.6	63.1	8.7	17.0	5 627	10 139	20 659	-5.2	1.1	30 978	12.6	16.4	17.5
White	NA	NA	3 693	3.1	66.2	9.5	22.0	7 647	11 332	20 662	-10.8	1.5	30 214	15.3	21.9	22.8
Whiteside	NA	NA	15 402	10.9	73.3	9.9	66.0	6 250	12 245	27 085	-19.6	1.4	38 789	9.1	12.8	12.1
Will	NA	NA	101 606	18.6	80.4	18.0	427.4	5 774	15 186	41 195	5.4	4.5	57 156	5.7	7.8	7.3
Williamson	NA	NA	14 003	4.9	71.8	14.2	54.1	5 720	11 254	22 043	-8.1	1.1	32 506	14.4	20.2	20.4
Winnebago	NA	NA	62 777	18.5	76.3	16.7	297.8	6 785	14 516	31 336	-7.5	3.0	42 267	10.0	14.8	13.9
Woodford	NA	NA	9 138	12.8	80.0	15.4	42.1	5 436	13 516	34 375	-3.4	2.5	50 391	5.9	7.6	7.7

1. Data for serious crimes have not been adjusted for underreporting; this may affect comparability between geographic areas and over time.   2. Per 100,000 population estimated by the FBI.   3. All persons 3 years old and over enrolled in nursery school through college.   4. Persons 25 years old and over.   5. Elementary and secondary education expenditures, local government fiscal years ending between July 1, 1998 and June 30, 1999.   6. Based on population enumerated as of April 1, 1990.

STATE County	Total (mil dol)	Percent change, 1998–1999	Per capita[1] Dollars	Per capita[1] Rank	Wages and salaries[2] (mil dol)	Proprietor's income (mil dol)	Dividends, interest, and rent (mil dol)	Transfer payments Total (mil dol)	Government payments to individuals Total (mil dol)	Social Security (mil dol)	Medical payments (mil dol)	Income mainte-nance (mil dol)	Unemploy-ment insurance (mil dol)
	62	63	64	65	66	67	68	69	70	71	72	73	74
ILLINOIS—Cont'd													
Jackson	1 241	3.9	20 465	1 846	845	87	252	202	190	64	64	26	4
Jasper	197	-1.5	18 683	2 372	82	20	52	35	33	17	11	3	1
Jefferson	841	2.4	21 449	1 535	543	71	172	159	151	63	60	15	4
Jersey	469	3.4	21 744	1 434	124	21	96	74	69	37	24	4	2
Jo Daviess	616	2.2	28 591	276	220	82	177	76	72	43	20	4	2
Johnson	200	4.4	14 741	3 010	69	21	43	44	41	19	13	4	1
Kane	11 283	6.4	28 024	332	6 765	437	1 905	901	819	358	325	63	40
Kankakee	2 389	3.6	23 256	1 028	1 364	99	442	416	395	164	160	42	11
Kendall	1 548	8.3	28 848	268	599	52	232	105	94	58	22	5	4
Knox	1 291	1.3	23 316	1 011	770	90	257	254	242	102	96	17	6
Lake	28 019	5.9	45 341	20	15 264	2 132	5 955	1 442	1 320	660	479	81	50
La Salle	2 615	3.7	23 715	915	1 430	188	581	415	392	214	124	21	18
Lawrence	340	-2.8	22 418	1 234	110	35	97	78	75	32	33	6	2
Lee	785	3.4	21 956	1 374	407	45	184	129	121	61	46	7	4
Livingston	951	4.7	23 988	861	515	68	191	135	126	68	44	7	3
Logan	627	0.3	19 745	2 073	295	40	144	115	108	52	41	6	2
McDonough	696	1.6	19 755	2 067	450	47	154	108	101	49	31	9	2
McHenry	7 920	7.5	32 090	152	3 143	357	1 217	527	477	264	149	21	27
McLean	4 211	7.7	28 947	263	3 261	231	749	357	328	168	98	23	9
Macon	3 078	5.2	27 188	403	2 199	163	618	464	440	203	146	48	11
Macoupin	1 146	6.0	23 387	989	322	86	221	200	190	92	71	13	5
Madison	6 563	3.6	25 297	613	3 220	331	1 244	997	944	432	352	83	19
Marion	937	2.7	22 420	1 233	522	73	192	210	202	70	92	17	5
Marshall	302	0.4	23 274	1 020	86	21	77	51	48	26	16	3	1
Mason	364	1.5	21 689	1 458	107	34	79	73	70	34	25	6	2
Massac	306	0.7	19 852	2 035	155	17	61	71	68	30	28	7	1
Menard	333	5.7	26 187	494	58	26	61	40	37	19	13	3	1
Mercer	394	0.0	22 353	1 258	84	24	74	61	58	31	18	4	3
Monroe	751	5.3	27 502	373	196	33	159	82	76	40	26	3	1
Montgomery	639	1.7	20 405	1 861	307	43	154	128	121	57	46	9	4
Morgan	829	3.3	23 570	947	462	59	189	141	134	64	49	11	3
Moultrie	311	4.3	21 371	1 553	108	31	59	55	52	26	20	3	1
Ogle	1 246	6.0	24 461	766	605	83	234	149	139	78	43	8	5
Peoria	5 162	3.8	28 501	282	3 796	240	1 147	687	649	304	224	75	18
Perry	401	2.1	18 805	2 345	167	24	89	92	87	40	30	7	3
Piatt	436	5.1	26 220	492	102	44	79	54	51	27	18	2	1
Pike	324	-1.8	18 796	2 348	110	36	76	73	69	33	26	6	2
Pope	77	6.5	15 904	2 905	29	7	13	18	17	8	6	2	0
Pulaski	123	0.1	16 845	2 767	57	6	20	36	35	13	13	6	1
Putnam	147	4.6	25 138	649	88	7	33	20	19	11	5	1	1
Randolph	659	3.1	19 611	2 109	390	41	155	126	119	58	43	8	3
Richland	372	0.4	22 320	1 270	203	30	86	70	66	31	23	5	2
Rock Island	3 953	0.7	26 798	430	3 088	262	908	538	508	255	163	46	18
St. Clair	6 085	2.3	23 400	986	3 257	261	1 216	1 055	1 002	368	388	151	18
Saline	523	2.2	20 073	1 973	266	47	115	139	133	54	53	14	3
Sangamon	5 380	3.5	28 121	316	3 893	331	1 157	652	612	292	215	60	15
Schuyler	149	2.4	19 845	2 038	52	16	32	27	25	13	8	2	1
Scott	99	-1.6	17 550	2 642	69	4	22	20	19	10	6	2	1
Shelby	465	2.9	20 654	1 791	155	54	92	84	79	37	30	5	3
Stark	140	0.5	22 353	1 258	35	15	36	28	26	14	10	1	1
Stephenson	1 300	0.0	26 648	446	747	106	306	179	169	89	55	12	6
Tazewell	3 414	1.7	26 302	485	2 271	224	716	450	424	223	144	25	14
Union	368	4.0	20 400	1 863	152	31	73	85	81	31	35	8	3
Vermilion	1 775	1.8	21 182	1 601	1 061	92	363	349	332	153	108	38	9
Wabash	248	1.4	19 831	2 049	119	17	68	50	48	23	17	4	1
Warren	346	0.0	18 285	2 476	141	35	73	65	61	29	22	6	1
Washington	365	1.7	24 020	852	187	38	83	58	55	26	22	3	1
Wayne	336	0.0	19 811	2 057	124	40	81	72	68	32	25	5	2
White	344	1.4	22 122	1 321	133	49	87	75	72	35	28	6	2
Whiteside	1 419	-0.2	23 813	895	721	91	316	238	226	114	84	12	7
Will	12 669	7.9	26 483	466	5 201	560	1 846	1 113	1 015	477	363	73	50
Williamson	1 339	4.1	21 755	1 432	651	115	267	250	238	109	79	23	8
Winnebago	7 111	2.7	26 522	462	5 171	367	1 385	911	856	434	290	79	30
Woodford	881	2.0	24 794	703	281	52	177	102	95	53	31	4	3

1. Based on the resident population estimated as of July 1 of the year shown. 2. Includes other labor income.

Table B. States and Counties — Earnings, Social Security, and Housing

STATE County	Earnings, 1999									Social Security beneficiaries, December 2000		Supplemental Security Income recipients, December 2000	Housing units, 1990	
			Goods-related[1]		Service-related and other[2]									
	Total (mil dol)	Farm	Total	Manufacturing	Total	Retail trade	Finance, insurance, and real estate	Services	Government	Number	Rate[3]		Total	Percent change, 1980–1990
	75	76	77	78	79	80	81	82	83	84	85	86	87	88
ILLINOIS—Cont'd														
Jackson	932	0.9	9.9	4.1	42.9	10.1	3.4	22.7	46.4	7 932	133	1 402	25 539	4.3
Jasper	102	8.8	16.5	10.8	52.4	7.3	4.1	9.1	22.2	2 139	211	147	4 297	-3.1
Jefferson	614	0.8	29.0	18.2	57.5	14.8	4.8	25.8	12.7	7 560	189	899	16 075	4.6
Jersey	145	-1.5	D	2.4	D	16.5	4.0	28.8	27.4	4 204	194	244	8 216	3.4
Jo Daviess	301	4.7	D	23.4	D	11.5	3.4	21.9	11.5	5 021	225	133	10 757	11.2
Johnson	90	2.3	D	2.2	D	8.0	2.7	12.8	48.2	2 470	192	286	4 671	11.6
Kane	7 201	0.1	32.5	24.6	52.5	8.3	6.5	25.4	14.9	38 286	95	3 628	111 496	13.1
Kankakee	1 463	0.7	D	21.9	D	11.5	4.5	24.6	16.0	18 608	179	2 571	37 001	-1.6
Kendall	652	0.0	D	43.6	D	9.2	3.6	10.4	11.5	6 323	116	105	13 747	9.8
Knox	860	2.1	28.5	23.9	55.8	9.7	2.8	24.6	13.6	11 426	205	1 118	23 722	-3.7
Lake	17 396	0.0	D	21.6	D	8.4	9.3	24.8	15.7	69 461	108	1 040	183 283	21.8
La Salle	1 618	0.1	27.3	18.7	58.9	12.3	4.0	19.9	13.7	23 073	207	4 445	43 827	0.8
Lawrence	145	2.5	D	4.0	D	8.3	10.5	10.5	17.0	3 838	248	336	6 980	-5.1
Lee	452	0.6	34.7	29.6	44.2	7.7	3.6	22.2	20.4	6 897	191	490	13 314	-0.3
Livingston	583	2.5	42.2	36.8	36.1	7.4	3.1	15.5	19.2	7 423	187	407	14 365	-4.1
Logan	335	1.0	D	10.4	50.9	13.2	4.1	18.3	29.4	5 851	188	370	11 638	-3.4
McDonough	497	1.7	18.5	13.9	42.5	20.0	3.2	12.0	37.3	5 946	181	495	13 257	-4.9
McHenry	3 501	0.2	42.0	28.7	46.9	8.9	4.4	20.7	10.9	28 351	109	949	65 985	24.6
McLean	3 492	0.1	19.3	13.1	67.9	8.0	31.3	19.8	12.9	18 508	123	1 269	49 164	8.3
Macon	2 362	0.1	39.5	31.5	51.1	9.1	3.6	21.2	9.3	22 322	195	2 899	50 049	-3.0
Macoupin	409	1.2	27.6	12.3	53.1	10.0	4.4	18.1	18.1	10 474	214	823	20 068	-0.1
Madison	3 551	0.1	35.7	27.1	47.7	9.8	4.4	22.5	16.5	48 417	187	4 523	101 098	7.9
Marion	594	1.9	37.9	32.2	45.5	6.8	2.4	21.0	14.7	8 571	206	1 061	18 123	1.7
Marshall	107	5.7	D	27.5	D	9.3	4.5	19.8	11.5	2 953	224	99	5 317	-6.5
Mason	140	12.0	D	12.0	47.4	10.7	4.3	11.5	24.6	3 906	244	259	7 684	-9.3
Massac	172	0.6	D	21.8	D	7.7	3.6	25.7	15.8	3 524	232	458	6 446	3.7
Menard	85	9.0	D	D	D	10.6	6.0	16.7	25.3	2 188	175	114	4 650	0.9
Mercer	109	5.6	21.3	12.7	41.2	8.7	3.7	14.0	32.0	3 566	210	150	7 244	-4.7
Monroe	229	1.6	20.5	5.0	60.6	14.9	5.5	22.8	17.3	4 527	164	173	8 774	17.8
Montgomery	349	1.8	23.9	15.6	54.5	10.1	4.3	22.3	19.9	6 594	215	582	12 456	-3.6
Morgan	521	0.2	D	26.5	D	9.8	4.6	24.3	16.5	7 336	200	772	14 724	1.1
Moultrie	139	1.6	37.0	26.4	48.0	10.0	3.3	17.9	13.4	2 924	205	117	5 384	-1.9
Ogle	688	1.1	36.4	30.4	49.4	6.1	3.2	15.1	13.0	8 691	170	283	18 052	4.4
Peoria	4 036	0.2	D	18.8	D	9.3	6.7	36.7	11.5	32 987	180	4 593	75 211	-5.2
Perry	191	0.9	D	26.9	D	10.1	3.7	14.2	22.8	4 520	196	376	9 235	2.5
Piatt	146	0.0	D	11.9	D	9.4	4.6	27.5	19.8	2 962	181	101	6 227	-1.4
Pike	146	10.2	D	5.6	D	13.4	5.0	18.8	19.9	3 980	229	353	8 057	-2.6
Pope	35	1.0	D	7.5	D	4.5	0.7	15.3	40.7	1 001	227	108	2 154	11.5
Pulaski	63	0.4	D	3.9	D	4.8	1.8	17.4	40.6	1 704	232	388	3 410	-6.8
Putnam	95	0.4	67.8	59.0	D	3.6	2.5	D	7.9	1 206	198	49	2 600	5.6
Randolph	431	1.6	33.4	22.1	37.6	8.8	3.0	13.5	27.3	6 604	195	425	13 179	2.0
Richland	232	2.9	25.7	18.9	52.9	16.5	4.7	20.6	18.5	3 805	236	347	7 142	-4.0
Rock Island	3 349	0.1	27.6	21.3	51.0	8.0	5.4	23.0	21.3	28 381	190	2 646	63 327	-0.3
St. Clair	3 518	0.2	15.0	8.8	54.5	10.7	5.1	26.3	30.3	43 120	168	8 383	103 432	6.1
Saline	313	1.6	29.0	3.6	48.2	9.4	3.7	20.4	21.2	6 481	242	1 134	12 350	0.2
Sangamon	4 224	0.2	9.4	3.7	58.2	7.5	9.4	30.6	32.2	33 590	178	4 672	76 873	5.5
Schuyler	68	5.6	D	3.9	D	9.5	2.9	16.4	22.0	1 606	223	97	3 329	-7.7
Scott	73	-0.9	52.9	2.1	D	3.9	2.3	D	13.3	1 139	206	75	2 442	-3.7
Shelby	209	7.4	D	20.3	D	9.2	3.7	18.9	16.5	4 391	192	278	9 329	-5.6
Stark	50	18.0	D	11.0	D	8.7	5.3	13.7	19.1	1 568	248	68	2 716	-5.5
Stephenson	853	4.7	45.9	36.9	39.1	6.3	9.5	16.3	10.3	10 084	206	695	20 378	5.5
Tazewell	2 495	0.8	51.8	45.9	38.4	7.2	3.6	12.5	9.0	23 998	187	1 549	49 315	0.9
Union	184	4.1	D	9.9	D	9.9	3.2	18.3	37.6	4 058	222	721	7 408	4.8
Vermilion	1 153	0.1	D	25.1	D	10.6	5.3	17.8	21.2	17 667	211	2 493	37 061	-3.4
Wabash	136	-2.8	45.3	20.6	39.2	9.4	4.5	13.8	18.3	2 668	206	197	5 572	-2.4
Warren	176	3.3	D	23.4	D	9.8	4.2	23.8	17.0	3 165	169	279	8 229	-4.0
Washington	225	6.4	D	23.9	D	10.1	3.1	12.7	11.7	3 067	202	110	6 261	-0.1
Wayne	164	3.2	35.2	25.1	45.2	9.6	2.8	17.0	16.4	3 941	230	276	7 622	-2.2
White	182	3.9	29.8	5.1	47.0	12.4	4.3	15.1	19.3	4 117	268	405	7 797	-0.6
Whiteside	812	1.4	D	35.7	D	9.5	4.6	16.4	15.8	12 663	209	833	24 000	-0.4
Will	5 761	0.2	30.0	17.0	54.4	9.1	4.4	24.1	15.4	53 659	107	3 452	122 870	12.0
Williamson	767	0.0	D	13.1	D	11.7	5.4	20.8	26.6	13 013	212	1 357	25 183	3.7
Winnebago	5 538	0.2	41.3	35.7	48.6	8.2	5.8	23.7	9.9	46 826	168	5 001	101 666	9.1
Woodford	333	1.3	33.8	25.8	48.3	9.8	3.1	17.8	16.6	5 809	164	151	11 932	1.1

1. Covers mining, construction, and manufacturing. 2. Covers private sector earnings in agricultural services, forestry, and fisheries; transportation and public utilities; wholesale trade; retail trade; finance, insurance, and real estate; and services. 3. Per 1,000 resident population estimated as of July 1 of the year shown.

STATE County	Total (89)	Percent (90)	Median value[1] (91)	With a mortgage (92)	Without a mortgage (93)	Median rent[2] (94)	Rent as percent of income (95)	Substandard units[3] (percent) (96)	Total (97)	Percent change, 2000–2001 (98)	Total (99)	Rate[4] (100)	Total (101)	Professional, managerial, and technical (102)	Precision production, craft, and repair (103)
ILLINOIS—Cont'd															
Jackson	23 466	52.7	47 100	19.7	13.1	314	35.1	3.6	30 298	-1.5	1 082	3.6	26 855	34.0	7.3
Jasper	3 962	82.6	39 400	16.3	12.8	259	25.2	2.9	3 818	0.4	331	8.7	4 600	16.3	13.2
Jefferson	14 606	73.0	41 500	20.3	14.8	300	26.6	3.6	18 870	-0.7	1 294	6.9	15 038	23.9	13.0
Jersey	7 344	76.1	45 400	18.5	12.9	318	24.0	3.1	10 594	-1.7	628	5.9	9 139	21.1	14.0
Jo Daviess	8 371	74.9	48 700	17.3	12.6	306	22.3	2.1	13 117	-1.3	733	5.6	10 768	17.9	13.4
Johnson	3 725	81.7	36 800	20.2	13.6	235	22.0	3.3	5 053	-2.3	276	5.5	3 639	23.9	10.0
Kane	107 176	69.5	102 500	21.5	12.8	508	24.4	5.0	220 696	-0.8	11 431	5.2	160 944	29.0	12.7
Kankakee	34 623	66.8	54 700	16.9	12.8	376	24.2	3.3	51 935	-1.0	3 026	5.8	42 205	25.2	12.1
Kendall	13 301	76.9	99 700	19.8	11.9	495	22.3	2.1	30 163	-0.9	1 198	4.0	20 751	26.1	14.5
Knox	21 909	69.1	37 100	16.5	12.9	298	26.1	1.3	28 946	-1.5	1 639	5.7	25 053	22.7	11.8
Lake	173 966	74.2	136 700	22.3	13.1	558	25.7	2.9	331 799	-1.1	15 264	4.6	258 003	37.3	10.2
La Salle	41 284	73.2	50 500	16.6	12.4	324	23.3	1.6	57 324	-0.2	3 763	6.6	45 938	22.2	13.5
Lawrence	6 320	76.5	32 800	18.5	12.2	275	27.8	2.7	7 434	4.7	502	6.8	6 134	19.0	12.8
Lee	12 475	69.6	46 600	16.3	12.3	331	21.5	1.4	17 798	-1.1	928	5.2	15 232	22.0	12.7
Livingston	13 737	70.9	46 700	16.6	11.8	340	23.6	1.6	20 377	-0.9	872	4.3	16 800	18.5	12.0
Logan	11 033	67.8	48 700	17.7	12.5	327	21.2	1.2	13 689	-2.6	564	4.1	13 884	23.4	9.9
McDonough	12 255	62.2	36 000	16.4	12.6	289	29.5	2.1	18 757	-3.1	575	3.1	15 637	27.0	9.2
McHenry	62 940	79.9	111 000	22.7	12.9	537	24.3	1.8	138 554	-0.7	6 350	4.6	95 736	30.5	14.9
McLean	46 796	63.5	65 900	17.3	11.8	387	24.8	1.5	91 903	-0.6	2 250	2.4	68 058	29.5	8.4
Macon	45 996	70.2	45 400	15.5	12.5	340	25.0	1.6	57 687	-4.5	3 647	6.3	52 639	26.3	11.7
Macoupin	18 176	77.4	39 700	18.1	12.9	322	26.2	2.4	23 839	1.1	1 409	5.9	20 253	19.5	14.9
Madison	94 857	72.0	51 400	17.2	12.8	384	26.4	2.6	129 412	-1.6	7 208	5.6	113 082	27.3	12.4
Marion	16 272	76.2	36 000	18.8	13.5	295	27.1	2.8	20 257	-3.8	2 188	10.8	17 481	21.6	11.2
Marshall	4 900	76.1	44 000	16.1	12.0	297	23.4	1.5	6 697	0.9	327	4.9	5 811	18.8	13.1
Mason	6 342	73.8	35 800	16.8	13.1	298	23.9	2.4	8 609	0.3	581	6.7	6 702	19.1	11.4
Massac	5 908	77.6	35 700	19.5	13.0	271	30.7	2.1	8 080	-1.1	393	4.9	5 757	20.9	13.0
Menard	4 199	76.6	51 500	18.6	12.2	320	23.6	2.2	6 272	-0.8	277	4.4	5 383	25.7	11.3
Mercer	6 572	74.7	34 900	17.5	12.1	304	23.0	1.3	9 175	-2.3	595	6.5	7 721	20.2	12.5
Monroe	8 189	78.6	72 100	18.2	12.5	376	19.4	2.7	14 310	-1.5	579	4.0	10 867	23.0	13.8
Montgomery	11 480	76.6	35 300	17.3	13.3	302	25.3	2.2	15 191	-2.5	1 011	6.7	12 425	18.7	13.0
Morgan	13 678	67.7	47 700	17.7	12.7	321	24.3	2.0	18 461	-2.9	807	4.4	17 096	26.3	10.8
Moultrie	5 122	75.8	41 200	16.1	13.2	315	20.2	2.4	8 259	-1.7	369	4.5	6 157	19.3	13.7
Ogle	17 132	71.2	57 200	17.1	12.0	343	20.1	2.0	27 551	-2.8	1 491	5.4	22 541	21.1	14.2
Peoria	70 797	64.0	49 100	16.0	12.6	359	23.8	2.0	94 206	-1.4	4 767	5.1	81 671	31.3	9.7
Perry	8 306	78.1	40 400	19.4	12.9	272	26.3	3.0	8 832	-2.2	774	8.8	8 414	17.4	16.9
Piatt	5 934	76.5	51 200	19.6	12.0	350	22.7	1.6	8 480	1.0	322	3.8	7 600	25.8	12.7
Pike	7 016	73.7	28 500	17.3	12.8	230	22.2	3.0	9 010	-2.3	513	5.7	7 572	18.4	12.2
Pope	1 611	75.5	29 700	21.4	12.4	194	29.6	4.5	1 764	-1.5	151	8.6	1 440	19.1	16.5
Pulaski	2 957	75.8	24 000	19.2	14.3	212	30.2	7.3	3 139	-1.3	296	9.4	2 434	19.7	11.6
Putnam	2 204	77.5	48 400	15.4	11.7	310	22.1	2.3	3 259	0.1	202	6.2	2 647	17.0	17.9
Randolph	11 949	78.5	45 000	19.6	12.4	306	23.8	2.6	14 080	-1.3	799	5.7	13 735	19.0	15.1
Richland	6 503	76.6	35 800	18.1	12.1	261	26.6	3.7	8 130	-4.6	554	6.8	7 378	24.6	12.0
Rock Island	59 317	66.9	47 800	16.2	12.3	331	24.9	1.8	74 200	-2.6	3 984	5.4	66 235	25.6	11.3
St. Clair	95 333	64.7	55 500	19.3	13.3	399	28.6	4.4	115 603	-2.1	7 196	6.2	105 544	26.6	10.9
Saline	10 839	75.2	33 400	20.0	13.7	269	33.5	2.5	10 238	-3.1	726	7.1	9 523	23.7	16.2
Sangamon	72 146	66.5	60 900	16.6	12.0	382	23.4	1.8	100 299	-1.2	3 936	3.9	91 949	34.9	8.5
Schuyler	3 002	76.0	35 100	17.2	13.7	265	28.7	4.1	4 261	-0.4	186	4.4	3 219	17.5	12.7
Scott	2 190	73.9	32 800	15.8	12.6	249	20.7	3.1	2 849	-3.0	154	5.4	2 534	16.8	14.2
Shelby	8 563	78.9	39 100	15.9	12.6	296	22.9	2.4	11 263	-1.8	687	6.1	9 737	16.8	15.0
Stark	2 512	74.2	31 200	16.2	12.7	299	20.3	2.2	2 921	1.0	233	8.0	2 795	18.2	11.7
Stephenson	18 920	71.2	50 700	18.3	12.1	321	23.5	1.2	24 348	-2.0	1 733	7.1	23 202	21.7	14.4
Tazewell	47 171	71.6	48 700	14.8	12.2	337	22.0	1.7	70 238	-1.3	3 144	4.5	57 839	25.9	12.0
Union	6 838	72.2	36 700	17.5	13.9	251	26.7	2.5	8 381	-2.5	469	5.6	7 061	26.1	10.1
Vermilion	34 072	71.2	38 700	16.6	12.9	324	27.1	2.2	38 236	-1.9	2 846	7.4	37 147	23.1	12.3
Wabash	5 032	75.8	42 200	17.6	12.0	266	25.2	2.9	4 744	-2.9	405	8.5	5 721	25.0	16.0
Warren	7 393	69.4	33 700	19.8	12.5	295	25.0	1.3	9 863	-2.4	436	4.4	8 604	21.8	12.3
Washington	5 658	80.2	46 000	19.1	14.3	329	20.4	3.0	8 952	1.5	378	4.2	6 746	20.6	12.9
Wayne	6 935	79.1	34 500	20.6	12.4	248	27.6	2.3	7 916	-4.1	534	6.7	7 247	18.4	13.7
White	6 845	74.8	34 500	18.0	13.1	265	26.3	2.3	7 287	0.3	384	5.3	6 390	20.7	15.5
Whiteside	22 740	71.7	44 400	15.3	12.1	335	23.6	1.9	31 112	-3.1	2 181	7.0	27 655	20.3	14.1
Will	116 933	77.4	89 900	21.4	12.6	453	24.4	2.8	250 597	-0.9	13 045	5.2	173 060	28.0	13.8
Williamson	23 120	73.7	40 800	19.1	13.2	300	27.2	2.1	28 839	-2.5	1 644	5.7	23 287	26.8	14.1
Winnebago	96 727	68.0	60 600	17.4	12.8	377	23.8	2.4	148 021	-2.1	9 823	6.6	125 014	27.3	13.1
Woodford	11 395	78.3	57 700	15.3	11.7	337	21.2	1.3	18 999	-1.8	576	3.0	15 307	25.6	13.0

1. Specified owner-occupied units.   2. Specified renter-occupied units.   3. Overcrowded or lacking complete plumbing facilities.   4. Percent of civilian labor force.   5. Persons 16 years and older.

Table B. States and Counties — **Nonfarm Employment and Agriculture**

STATE County	Private nonfarm establishments, employment and payroll, 1999									Agriculture, 1997			
		Employment						Annual payroll		Farms			Farm operators
												Percent with—	
	Number of establishments	Total	Health Care and Social Assistance	Manufacturing	Retail trade	Finance and Insurance	Professional Scientific and Technical Services	Total (mil dol)	Average per employee (dollars)	Number	Less than 50 acres	500 acres and over	Whose principal occupation is farming (percent)
	104	105	106	107	108	109	110	111	112	113	114	115	116
ILLINOIS—Cont'd													
Jackson	1 408	18 028	3 574	947	4 089	686	824	364	20 178	680	24.0	14.3	42.6
Jasper	250	3 119	119	964	347	125	106	80	25 747	729	22.2	27.8	57.8
Jefferson	1 088	15 955	2 731	2 686	2 853	447	416	401	25 154	962	28.4	11.5	37.5
Jersey	420	4 511	733	89	957	228	123	80	17 742	481	24.7	22.7	48.9
Jo Daviess	764	7 406	509	1 894	806	224	172	152	20 545	941	18.5	15.0	57.6
Johnson	183	1 060	128	D	263	D	68	18	16 719	515	21.2	8.2	32.8
Kane	10 123	170 591	17 687	40 547	21 689	9 198	9 352	5 326	31 221	650	36.3	21.5	58.3
Kankakee	2 305	55 090	5 642	6 759	5 852	1 483	677	1 491	27 060	831	21.8	31.0	61.1
Kendall	1 135	11 882	667	2 393	2 175	521	256	312	26 294	441	23.4	25.9	62.1
Knox	1 305	21 137	4 199	5 229	3 554	542	344	491	23 227	928	22.2	27.4	62.4
Lake	18 057	305 529	27 142	59 746	43 991	21 493	19 094	12 450	40 750	335	65.4	6.6	39.7
La Salle	2 957	37 805	5 255	6 215	6 947	1 420	993	986	26 076	1 581	17.0	26.2	60.2
Lawrence	370	3 697	1 046	259	482	439	80	76	20 481	376	25.5	31.1	58.5
Lee	783	10 951	2 059	3 881	1 275	281	229	279	25 477	904	16.2	30.3	61.7
Livingston	966	12 605	1 452	4 903	1 864	555	226	360	28 541	1 380	12.3	36.9	66.4
Logan	719	8 780	1 380	1 551	1 222	368	154	194	22 069	739	15.3	40.5	69.1
McDonough	789	10 381	1 664	2 076	1 775	328	209	197	19 005	824	22.5	28.4	58.4
McHenry	6 649	82 855	6 684	21 978	11 800	2 224	3 370	2 514	30 345	921	42.6	14.8	54.0
McLean	3 533	80 254	7 266	8 271	9 700	20 824	2 023	2 566	31 973	1 475	18.0	35.5	66.0
Macon	2 745	54 983	6 836	10 930	6 906	1 606	1 032	1 641	29 850	665	24.7	36.7	62.1
Macoupin	1 046	10 071	1 589	780	1 697	536	374	228	22 647	1 206	24.3	22.3	56.5
Madison	5 890	84 064	12 710	17 379	11 639	2 845	2 478	2 294	27 292	1 195	34.9	14.6	45.0
Marion	1 155	15 433	3 032	5 537	2 019	405	316	381	24 689	882	24.5	17.6	45.0
Marshall	301	2 828	325	889	437	128	D	64	22 693	494	12.3	30.6	64.4
Mason	362	2 890	525	442	576	210	53	57	19 590	486	15.4	45.5	71.0
Massac	284	4 591	782	700	429	148	D	122	26 575	400	27.5	13.0	49.0
Menard	259	1 419	152	D	323	96	52	30	21 385	352	21.3	34.1	60.5
Mercer	344	2 414	379	410	600	145	D	48	19 893	754	21.9	28.5	61.9
Monroe	632	5 793	572	238	1 049	276	432	138	23 827	556	29.0	21.0	53.6
Montgomery	794	8 523	1 456	1 506	1 359	408	221	197	23 130	980	19.6	27.3	58.1
Morgan	944	14 995	2 555	3 740	2 071	631	258	353	23 561	780	21.5	27.7	63.1
Moultrie	295	3 308	751	881	343	145	86	67	20 309	464	29.1	25.6	59.5
Ogle	1 005	15 361	1 177	5 693	1 562	510	231	429	27 943	1 099	24.1	23.1	56.7
Peoria	4 877	108 278	16 951	13 519	11 593	4 488	5 332	3 535	32 648	924	28.8	19.2	49.9
Perry	455	5 294	958	1 526	743	167	91	115	21 649	551	25.2	21.1	49.9
Piatt	374	2 583	279	384	492	189	106	59	22 824	448	14.1	44.9	71.2
Pike	395	3 304	696	256	767	209	75	60	18 049	1 028	16.4	26.4	55.5
Pope	60	382	104	D	43	D	D	10	26 188	282	13.1	12.1	40.8
Pulaski	130	1 373	263	D	123	46	6	36	26 049	239	18.4	19.2	47.3
Putnam	130	1 720	24	960	132	51	19	64	37 258	190	18.9	29.5	60.5
Randolph	767	10 968	2 219	2 759	1 539	359	117	257	23 434	843	23.5	18.4	53.9
Richland	509	6 330	1 017	1 123	1 128	239	81	119	18 827	495	24.8	26.7	53.1
Rock Island	3 688	67 753	8 021	9 676	8 963	3 397	2 392	2 106	31 087	618	32.7	18.3	51.5
St. Clair	5 498	75 199	12 853	6 801	12 862	3 433	3 712	1 863	24 772	844	29.1	18.5	49.6
Saline	684	7 832	2 068	498	1 356	336	147	163	20 864	441	32.9	16.8	44.9
Sangamon	5 350	82 497	17 975	4 042	12 009	7 094	4 153	2 208	26 764	993	31.4	31.1	60.4
Schuyler	160	1 379	296	122	271	57	53	28	20 372	477	13.2	28.9	57.2
Scott	102	890	9	D	109	66	D	48	54 201	327	24.5	30.3	63.9
Shelby	489	4 725	739	1 334	547	209	123	102	21 536	1 250	23.9	21.9	55.3
Stark	136	988	178	262	128	78	44	19	18 772	354	17.8	39.0	77.1
Stephenson	1 126	21 015	2 453	7 404	2 476	2 050	337	592	28 177	1 081	24.4	15.1	66.9
Tazewell	2 844	42 542	4 427	6 944	7 209	1 832	864	1 231	28 928	909	26.2	27.0	57.5
Union	369	4 663	2 090	461	674	143	76	99	21 187	591	23.0	11.7	37.1
Vermilion	1 835	29 700	4 593	6 980	4 187	1 450	542	756	25 457	984	22.1	36.1	63.3
Wabash	331	3 910	754	604	531	152	106	81	20 682	212	28.3	40.6	64.2
Warren	378	4 544	760	1 188	602	D	86	87	19 128	710	16.5	34.2	67.7
Washington	410	6 155	733	2 698	687	191	93	163	26 427	777	16.6	25.6	58.6
Wayne	393	3 739	554	D	686	192	80	80	21 498	972	22.4	20.0	47.7
White	424	3 398	619	387	661	138	105	70	20 727	432	22.5	29.4	55.6
Whiteside	1 469	21 626	3 475	7 043	3 353	731	442	539	24 943	1 039	22.7	24.4	65.4
Will	9 680	132 669	12 466	25 084	18 558	4 636	4 802	4 619	34 815	910	32.7	20.7	55.6
Williamson	1 579	21 631	3 689	2 693	3 406	1 684	460	459	21 238	585	33.3	6.0	32.1
Winnebago	7 060	132 980	17 093	38 409	16 859	5 570	4 916	3 909	29 392	687	35.1	18.0	54.0
Woodford	725	8 526	1 093	2 272	981	248	186	213	25 033	923	22.5	22.2	56.3

Table B. States and Counties — Agriculture, Land, and Water

STATE County	Agriculture, 1997 (cont'd)														Percent of land owned by fed. gov. 1997	Water consumption 1995 (mil gal/day)
	Land in farms					Value of land and buildings		Value of machinery and equipment average per farm ($1,000)	Value of products sold				Percent of farms with sales of —			
			Acres								Percent from —					
	Acreage (1,000)	Percent change, 1992–1997	Average size of farm	Total irrigated (1,000)	Total cropland (1,000)	Average per farm ($1,000)	Average per acre (dollars)		Total (mil dol)	Average per farm (dollars)	Crops	Livestock and poultry products	$10,000 or more	$100,000 or more		
	117	118	119	120	121	122	123	124	125	126	127	128	129	130	131	132
ILLINOIS—Cont'd																
Jackson	203	8.9	298	0	161	393	1 452	61	37	54 434	74.7	25.3	41.2	12.9	12.9	190.9
Jasper	252	-2.2	346	0	225	687	1 881	100	86	117 947	61.3	38.7	73.4	32.9	0.0	531.1
Jefferson	230	5.8	239	0	184	285	1 075	61	35	36 608	80.0	20.0	39.6	9.8	0.8	2.8
Jersey	164	-9.3	341	0	131	579	1 711	69	40	83 817	80.1	19.9	61.1	24.5	1.6	7.3
Jo Daviess	276	-4.9	293	0	189	408	1 399	75	73	77 131	37.9	62.1	64.5	24.9	3.5	8.6
Johnson	104	9.8	203	D	70	196	953	33	11	20 815	56.9	43.1	26.4	4.7	8.7	2.0
Kane	210	2.9	323	2	197	1 259	4 023	117	123	188 822	84.7	15.3	69.8	36.6	0.4	53.4
Kankakee	352	-2.1	423	14	338	1 102	2 759	132	133	159 906	89.0	11.0	82.6	40.2	0.0	29.0
Kendall	167	-5.9	380	0	158	1 561	3 994	120	59	133 238	85.6	14.4	79.4	35.1	0.0	5.5
Knox	390	1.0	420	0	318	737	1 923	91	130	140 413	69.6	30.4	71.7	35.3	0.0	8.7
Lake	51	-30.3	152	0	42	723	3 993	79	32	96 256	87.1	12.9	46.6	19.1	0.5	2 449.3
La Salle	588	-4.0	372	1	552	1 013	2 855	99	183	115 843	90.1	9.9	81.2	36.7	0.0	888.2
Lawrence	183	8.0	485	7	162	621	1 210	94	55	146 824	66.1	33.9	62.5	32.2	0.0	6.7
Lee	393	-5.1	435	13	369	947	2 313	107	136	150 681	81.9	18.1	84.4	43.1	0.0	15.6
Livingston	614	-3.8	445	0	589	1 111	2 554	109	214	154 814	77.5	22.5	88.8	50.3	0.0	7.2
Logan	381	3.0	515	1	361	1 372	2 663	135	133	180 310	84.1	15.9	85.8	51.8	0.0	4.8
McDonough	340	-1.4	413	0	292	759	1 878	91	97	117 497	84.1	15.9	72.0	35.2	0.0	4.6
McHenry	242	-2.6	263	8	220	1 038	4 072	96	109	118 509	71.4	28.6	60.2	28.0	0.0	39.8
McLean	697	-1.8	472	1	666	1 278	2 657	130	238	161 521	89.0	11.0	81.9	46.8	0.0	17.0
Macon	323	3.8	486	D	303	1 354	2 803	125	106	158 998	96.0	4.0	74.3	44.1	0.0	46.6
Macoupin	396	-1.6	328	1	336	645	2 028	79	121	100 092	71.2	28.8	65.7	27.4	0.0	10.5
Madison	284	-5.5	237	2	248	510	2 155	70	86	72 054	79.0	21.0	55.4	18.3	0.7	308.1
Marion	249	-1.8	283	0	203	298	1 193	54	56	63 037	65.3	34.7	50.6	16.3	0.0	5.7
Marshall	228	11.5	461	4	197	1 000	2 193	103	68	136 931	88.7	11.3	82.4	44.3	0.4	4.4
Mason	292	3.4	600	85	264	1 054	1 912	145	84	173 629	90.9	9.1	75.9	47.5	0.3	119.0
Massac	104	4.8	259	4	84	280	1 238	46	20	49 797	69.5	30.5	46.8	13.8	1.6	592.2
Menard	170	3.8	484	1	153	963	2 112	95	52	148 808	81.4	18.6	74.1	42.3	0.0	1.9
Mercer	310	-0.8	411	4	261	661	1 693	89	92	122 212	76.2	23.8	69.0	34.0	0.8	4.6
Monroe	187	-0.1	336	2	154	632	1 943	105	49	88 821	65.3	34.7	61.2	24.5	0.0	2.8
Montgomery	361	-3.0	368	0	324	686	1 985	82	109	111 381	78.2	21.8	71.9	34.4	0.0	333.7
Morgan	306	-1.7	392	2	267	887	2 319	101	96	123 266	78.0	21.9	74.7	33.1	0.3	159.1
Moultrie	173	-6.7	372	0	165	1 149	2 909	111	56	120 583	86.9	13.1	72.0	33.0	6.3	2.6
Ogle	379	-3.5	345	1	343	834	2 458	89	149	135 493	65.9	34.1	72.4	36.8	0.0	30.8
Peoria	267	2.4	289	3	224	609	2 253	64	77	83 538	86.3	13.7	62.8	23.3	0.0	110.4
Perry	172	2.4	312	0	145	310	1 056	69	29	51 756	81.0	19.0	58.1	15.8	0.0	11.3
Piatt	253	0.9	565	0	245	1 579	2 905	163	83	186 248	93.7	6.3	87.7	51.8	0.0	3.3
Pike	461	4.1	449	1	342	645	1 394	82	124	120 469	65.2	34.8	64.3	27.2	1.1	23.4
Pope	72	6.2	256	0	43	202	834	26	5	16 738	60.7	39.3	27.3	3.5	38.9	0.5
Pulaski	83	1.4	348	D	71	400	1 257	56	15	64 134	83.7	16.3	51.0	16.7	4.4	1.3
Putnam	77	-1.3	405	D	65	1 126	2 428	151	42	220 931	89.8	10.2	80.5	40.5	0.0	166.7
Randolph	262	-3.1	311	0	208	450	1 529	69	50	59 596	70.5	29.5	58.5	17.2	0.0	1 179.4
Richland	197	4.4	398	D	175	614	1 566	98	59	120 024	65.5	34.5	66.1	29.5	0.0	2.3
Rock Island	170	-3.4	275	4	135	499	1 907	58	50	80 565	72.9	27.1	59.9	22.7	2.4	924.9
St. Clair	265	0.2	313	1	239	669	2 228	83	78	92 646	81.5	18.5	66.2	23.3	0.6	46.8
Saline	131	-8.0	296	0	115	301	1 084	67	33	75 091	62.8	37.2	45.4	19.3	5.9	0.5
Sangamon	467	4.5	470	0	436	1 165	2 570	118	163	163 710	88.6	11.4	66.2	37.6	0.0	336.9
Schuyler	209	0.9	438	D	144	432	993	66	40	83 327	79.0	21.0	63.9	22.6	0.0	2.2
Scott	146	12.8	445	4	117	694	1 663	69	35	106 817	84.3	15.7	63.9	32.4	0.0	6.3
Shelby	419	4.2	335	0	376	651	2 061	74	112	89 973	78.1	21.9	65.1	27.0	2.3	4.4
Stark	180	5.7	508	D	165	1 113	2 433	95	65	184 888	84.8	15.2	83.1	52.8	0.0	1.4
Stephenson	309	-2.0	285	0	277	547	1 978	86	142	131 374	41.6	58.4	73.2	39.2	0.0	10.9
Tazewell	328	-2.3	361	30	305	1 006	2 824	94	123	135 493	76.0	24.0	73.3	36.7	0.1	798.5
Union	136	14.3	230	1	95	341	1 229	48	21	35 059	77.8	22.2	33.5	6.1	16.0	3.8
Vermilion	485	-0.6	493	0	458	1 183	2 397	146	140	142 438	95.7	4.3	75.2	41.4	0.1	16.3
Wabash	122	4.9	574	D	112	1 200	1 856	162	31	145 209	91.9	8.1	69.3	42.5	0.0	6.6
Warren	315	-0.6	444	D	278	1 041	2 345	97	105	148 004	80.0	20.0	82.3	42.3	0.0	3.6
Washington	309	3.9	397	1	279	629	1 630	99	88	113 197	62.7	37.3	76.3	31.5	0.0	2.8
Wayne	321	-3.7	330	D	274	325	994	58	71	72 963	70.0	30.0	52.6	18.0	0.0	3.7
White	256	9.1	594	6	224	809	1 409	113	61	141 834	86.9	13.1	60.9	28.2	0.0	4.0
Whiteside	385	-3.6	370	34	353	784	2 125	99	157	151 099	64.4	35.6	77.3	41.2	0.2	33.0
Will	294	-9.7	323	4	275	1 091	3 714	80	107	117 724	92.0	8.0	69.9	28.8	4.9	3 907.9
Williamson	92	2.5	158	0	67	214	1 476	40	11	19 524	70.0	30.0	27.9	5.0	12.3	13.7
Winnebago	196	-3.6	285	1	178	585	2 435	70	69	100 297	73.1	26.9	62.7	28.8	0.0	46.6
Woodford	300	1.3	325	0	275	954	2 728	99	107	116 202	78.6	21.4	75.9	33.0	0.0	10.8

Table B. States and Counties — Residential Construction, Wholesale and Retail Trade, and Real Estate

STATE County	Value of Residential Construction Authorized by Building Permits, 2000 — New Construction ($1,000)	Number of Housing Units	Wholesale Trade, 1997 — Number of Establishments	Number of Employees	Sales (mil dol)	Annual Payroll (mil dol)	Retail Trade[1], 1997 — Number of Establishments	Number of Employees	Sales (mil dol)	Annual Payroll (mil dol)	Real Estate and Rental and Leasing, 1997 — Number of Establishments	Number of Employees	Receipts (mil dol)	Annual Payroll (mil dol)
	133	134	135	136	137	138	139	140	141	142	143	144	145	146
ILLINOIS—Cont'd														
Jackson	5 915	112	45	289	78.4	7.6	287	3 992	551.9	60.7	81	414	29.2	5.3
Jasper	140	2	22	206	120.1	5.1	45	366	78.5	5.9	6	D	D	D
Jefferson	6 361	87	64	667	362.9	18.5	216	2 678	385.2	36.8	31	98	6.4	1.1
Jersey	11 965	103	28	D	D	D	82	1 031	171.0	14.2	3	4	0.3	0.0
Jo Daviess	21 412	134	31	176	130.4	5.5	144	897	150.2	12.4	24	64	8.9	1.2
Johnson	NA	NA	12	90	38.5	1.7	34	235	42.8	4.1	2	D	D	D
Kane	847 885	5 784	787	9 948	8 557.1	392.4	1 353	19 688	3 116.6	331.1	318	1 620	212.1	35.8
Kankakee	50 466	389	126	1 628	809.3	47.2	388	5 594	907.0	88.5	85	348	34.9	5.9
Kendall	113 690	863	61	585	348.0	18.6	118	1 755	371.0	36.6	34	127	15.1	2.0
Knox	11 599	110	75	933	381.7	25.2	252	3 785	489.9	52.5	40	164	12.6	2.0
Lake	638 452	4 134	1 411	20 149	19 079.1	932.4	2 391	38 002	8 562.3	785.9	626	3 563	725.4	95.7
La Salle	45 186	494	168	1 729	1 292.6	55.8	502	6 352	1 047.7	96.8	72	296	23.3	4.0
Lawrence	400	3	16	248	64.0	6.7	63	535	71.8	6.9	4	D	D	D
Lee	12 093	118	55	525	248.5	14.7	138	1 379	234.8	23.6	28	133	7.1	1.5
Livingston	9 137	95	48	431	255.6	11.1	186	1 909	336.3	28.7	20	72	3.1	0.6
Logan	2 548	27	45	433	252.3	12.2	140	1 283	238.0	20.3	33	87	8.6	0.9
McDonough	7 958	152	37	233	164.8	5.6	167	1 870	246.6	24.8	29	205	9.5	2.6
McHenry	473 430	3 522	497	5 381	2 874.1	210.7	813	10 457	2 034.6	188.3	184	807	106.8	15.2
McLean	78 742	909	212	2 268	1 348.4	87.1	632	9 242	1 474.6	142.3	134	704	99.8	14.6
Macon	38 745	361	158	1 815	3 249.3	57.4	506	6 967	1 129.6	110.4	98	515	39.9	8.5
Macoupin	5 474	59	76	749	238.9	19.6	188	1 695	309.4	26.0	27	68	5.7	0.9
Madison	136 641	1 165	259	2 860	2 264.4	91.6	969	11 722	2 057.0	181.4	190	885	106.9	14.0
Marion	1 157	17	53	474	166.7	11.8	226	2 119	309.4	30.2	28	153	8.1	1.4
Marshall	1 717	17	16	127	232.5	3.9	49	395	68.7	6.4	10	16	0.9	0.1
Mason	1 369	15	32	225	305.2	5.6	59	601	98.4	9.5	4	D	D	D
Massac	412	5	6	D	D	D	55	414	79.7	6.4	7	19	1.1	0.2
Menard	9 028	79	15	104	74.7	2.7	41	320	58.3	4.6	11	48	2.2	0.4
Mercer	4 212	41	21	103	102.2	3.1	57	586	88.5	8.6	7	12	0.3	0.2
Monroe	38 212	268	29	D	D	D	85	858	175.2	15.4	22	56	5.1	0.8
Montgomery	1 561	17	46	351	215.1	9.0	142	1 344	236.6	19.3	17	37	2.3	0.3
Morgan	2 005	22	45	D	D	D	192	2 207	344.7	31.9	20	65	6.0	1.0
Moultrie	4 739	47	28	211	103.2	5.1	46	303	42.5	3.9	6	16	0.8	0.1
Ogle	24 678	207	54	D	D	D	150	1 491	268.3	24.0	35	80	8.3	0.9
Peoria	88 418	938	299	4 755	5 876.5	171.6	801	11 817	1 847.4	182.6	192	1 163	115.3	20.6
Perry	NA	NA	14	D	D	D	98	789	113.8	14.3	9	22	1.1	0.2
Piatt	9 951	69	29	335	332.4	7.6	55	432	99.4	7.8	8	37	2.0	0.4
Pike	2 955	46	37	319	175.1	8.0	85	725	119.9	10.6	6	17	1.1	0.2
Pope	185	2	2	D	D	D	12	36	7.5	0.5	3	5	0.2	0.0
Pulaski	140	3	9	D	D	D	27	127	15.5	1.4	3	4	0.4	0.0
Putnam	4 002	40	7	D	D	D	22	126	23.4	1.9	2	D	D	D
Randolph	5 686	64	32	641	266.2	14.0	140	1 601	261.7	27.3	17	45	2.4	0.3
Richland	4 519	45	38				94	940	149.0	13.8	10	45	1.1	0.3
Rock Island	32 130	220	239	4 530	2 042.8	148.4	623	8 593	1 427.4	142.2	136	650	81.8	13.6
St. Clair	122 792	1 102	214	2 169	1 615.1	64.2	965	12 887	2 048.5	197.7	207	961	90.5	18.9
Saline	0	0	26	D	D	D	154	1 404	232.5	32.3	14	56	2.7	0.5
Sangamon	86 629	850	259	3 517	1 513.4	119.7	836	12 054	1 991.9	187.0	204	837	85.3	14.3
Schuyler	NA	NA	8	93	62.5	2.3	37	303	45.5	4.3	6	22	0.5	0.1
Scott	0	0	13	123	152.5	3.4	13	113	20.5	1.5	2	D	D	D
Shelby	5 951	60	37	237	153.1	5.6	86	554	123.9	7.7	9	22	0.8	0.2
Stark	1 609	17	12	73	52.0	1.6	23	124	27.4	2.4	1	D	D	D
Stephenson	16 316	141	54	429	129.6	10.0	191	2 522	414.6	40.3	30	111	9.7	1.7
Tazewell	57 556	445	140	D	D	D	473	6 813	1 275.2	112.1	82	419	45.2	9.6
Union	4 444	48	14	93	25.0	2.6	66	641	96.8	9.4	12	30	1.9	0.5
Vermilion	6 587	70	102	2 221	1 257.5	68.5	351	4 505	639.2	64.4	63	265	17.6	4.2
Wabash	1 567	13	21	116	52.3	2.8	49	508	75.6	6.7	6	16	1.0	0.2
Warren	3 872	38	23	274	164.4	7.3	67	632	97.7	9.1	7	31	1.7	0.4
Washington	7 438	71	27	245	128.9	6.9	83	662	157.1	13.0	5	16	1.0	0.1
Wayne	2 544	54	32	176	113.3	4.2	80	703	103.6	9.9	10	17	1.1	0.1
White	216	2	33	152	104.7	3.7	84	644	109.7	9.3	10	22	1.2	0.2
Whiteside	16 523	136	75	522	481.9	15.3	241	3 303	515.4	54.1	55	181	13.3	2.4
Will	838 314	7 159	577	6 563	3 946.2	230.2	1 157	17 267	3 286.2	301.3	287	1 191	129.0	23.0
Williamson	14 227	145	80	629	189.3	15.0	306	3 405	576.2	51.1	39	185	16.3	2.4
Winnebago	92 528	1 263	510	6 308	2 530.0	216.5	1 090	17 044	2 754.5	270.3	217	1 169	160.4	24.2
Woodford	20 456	181	55	D	D	D	101	1 009	229.4	16.8	15	66	3.5	1.1

1. Establishments with payroll.

Items 133—146

Table B. States and Counties — **Professional, Manufacturing, and Accommodation and Foodservices**

STATE County	Professional, Scientific, and Technical Services[1], 1997				Manufacturing, 1997				Accommodation and Foodservices, 1997			
	Number of Establishments	Number of Employees	Receipts (mil dol)	Annual Payroll (mil dol)	Number of Establishments	Number of Employees	Receipts (mil dol)	Annual Payroll (mil dol)	Number of Establishments	Number of Employees	Sales (mil dol)	Annual Payroll (mil dol)
	147	148	149	150	151	152	153	154	155	156	157	158
ILLINOIS—Cont'd												
Jackson	96	664	37.2	14.6	35	1 062	151.8	29.0	156	2 379	65.4	17.8
Jasper	9	72	2.7	1.7	15	874	66.4	15.2	18	87	2.3	0.5
Jefferson	61	386	29.1	12.2	44	2 922	743.1	104.5	72	1 270	41.9	11.3
Jersey	20	85	6.3	3.1	NA	NA	NA	NA	50	612	16.0	4.6
Jo Daviess	46	116	14.0	4.0	33	1 590	312.6	46.2	101	1 755	61.8	16.0
Johnson	12	55	3.1	0.9	NA	NA	NA	NA	15	111	3.6	1.1
Kane	955	6 298	541.4	225.7	877	40 200	8 226.1	1 443.8	633	11 078	367.0	106.3
Kankakee	132	507	32.7	12.7	116	6 937	2 253.2	263.8	229	3 563	100.4	27.4
Kendall	48	135	7.6	2.8	66	2 303	369.6	69.5	76	869	28.2	6.6
Knox	52	263	19.6	7.1	56	5 528	1 058.8	165.0	132	1 863	54.5	14.8
Lake	2 204	14 385	1 676.3	697.1	969	62 535	13 686.2	2 660.2	1 245	20 090	775.8	210.3
La Salle	154	877	56.0	24.0	152	6 752	1 732.6	232.1	332	3 830	109.7	30.8
Lawrence	20	75	4.8	1.9	NA	NA	NA	NA	24	199	5.6	1.5
Lee	35	186	14.5	6.2	35	3 798	739.4	115.3	68	638	20.1	5.0
Livingston	49	154	10.5	4.0	51	4 573	1 055.8	170.5	86	1 001	26.5	7.2
Logan	32	101	7.6	2.0	24	1 401	318.2	44.9	77	864	24.0	6.4
McDonough	39	169	10.1	2.6	30	1 956	255.9	61.2	78	1 303	29.8	8.1
McHenry	594	2 115	176.6	65.5	583	22 949	3 930.4	760.4	409	5 347	175.8	46.4
McLean	234	1 382	111.6	57.9	112	8 388	3 870.3	357.7	336	7 104	200.5	58.3
Macon	156	1 101	90.0	36.1	134	11 616	6 114.2	479.4	233	4 105	123.6	35.7
Macoupin	46	254	23.3	7.0	35	697	156.5	18.9	90	783	24.7	5.7
Madison	392	2 162	167.1	73.2	224	19 074	7 676.5	743.8	537	8 326	253.8	68.1
Marion	56	238	18.4	5.3	65	5 220	768.3	152.6	95	1 056	31.4	8.5
Marshall	16	56	3.9	1.4	18	921	179.6	28.2	31	422	7.7	2.1
Mason	13	33	2.1	0.6	NA	NA	NA	NA	48	294	8.3	2.1
Massac	13	57	2.1	0.9	12	732	191.5	31.2	38	343	10.3	2.6
Menard	18	40	3.2	1.2	NA	NA	NA	NA	24	D	D	D
Mercer	14	29	1.7	0.4	NA	NA	NA	NA	34	215	5.6	1.5
Monroe	42	245	18.1	9.1	NA	NA	NA	NA	51	D	D	D
Montgomery	41	203	12.1	5.1	37	1 752	300.7	48.3	77	924	25.7	6.5
Morgan	42	223	15.4	7.4	36	3 566	1 213.4	110.6	78	1 165	34.0	9.5
Moultrie	20	57	4.1	0.9	20	796	210.8	19.8	27	283	6.2	1.9
Ogle	52	D	D	D	70	5 859	1 020.5	166.2	93	999	27.6	7.2
Peoria	361	4 635	378.4	167.7	177	14 351	4 392.7	610.6	494	8 204	246.3	70.7
Perry	24	77	3.7	1.2	22	1 481	262.3	35.3	34	428	10.4	2.9
Piatt	25	90	4.6	2.2	NA	NA	NA	NA	28	D	D	D
Pike	16	52	2.0	0.8	NA	NA	NA	NA	39	389	9.3	2.4
Pope	3	D	D	D	NA	NA	NA	NA	8	36	1.8	0.4
Pulaski	4	D	D	D	NA	NA	NA	NA	10	64	1.6	0.4
Putnam	5	22	1.0	0.3	9	D	D	D	11	D	D	D
Randolph	33	99	6.0	2.2	32	2 353	398.6	51.8	75	749	20.4	5.3
Richland	24	67	3.9	1.4	34	1 814	218.3	37.0	34	439	12.9	3.4
Rock Island	238	2 124	164.9	72.3	197	10 675	3 508.8	493.8	373	5 780	161.4	43.9
St. Clair	395	3 109	284.7	119.2	198	7 123	1 763.5	249.3	477	8 481	245.0	66.7
Saline	39	134	11.2	2.9	NA	NA	NA	NA	58	709	19.7	5.1
Sangamon	471	3 283	277.1	117.6	134	D	D	D	497	D	D	D
Schuyler	9	56	3.6	1.8	NA	NA	NA	NA	15	D	D	D
Scott	6	15	0.6	0.1	NA	NA	NA	NA	9	90	1.2	0.3
Shelby	24	97	5.7	2.0	14	1 191	205.7	32.4	40	473	15.4	4.2
Stark	7	64	1.8	0.7	NA	NA	NA	NA	6	D	D	D
Stephenson	62	243	17.5	6.8	62	8 386	1 239.2	300.3	103	1 259	37.1	8.7
Tazewell	153	731	53.9	26.7	118	7 015	2 512.9	311.1	265	4 329	115.8	33.7
Union	17	65	3.8	1.5	11	616	132.2	17.0	26	D	D	D
Vermilion	94	331	27.9	8.6	104	7 055	1 696.1	228.9	185	2 570	68.5	20.0
Wabash	22	93	7.3	2.4	15	611	55.8	20.5	24	367	7.9	2.4
Warren	17	42	2.7	0.6	19	D	D	D	37	334	9.8	2.7
Washington	14	63	3.7	1.7	16	1 397	222.4	44.5	43	380	10.9	2.6
Wayne	23	77	4.6	1.4	20	D	D	D	20	D	D	D
White	20	80	3.4	1.1	NA	NA	NA	NA	28	404	10.7	3.3
Whiteside	56	236	19.2	7.6	102	7 374	1 381.8	245.0	112	1 567	42.9	10.9
Will	689	2 966	285.4	113.7	527	24 090	7 594.7	988.2	646	9 054	291.6	75.2
Williamson	89	381	29.5	8.6	51	2 551	425.1	69.2	135	2 155	68.1	18.1
Winnebago	567	5 447	327.5	128.6	779	39 740	6 608.4	1 483.6	556	9 693	306.3	84.1
Woodford	35	144	14.6	6.1	55	2 272	644.9	74.7	63	789	18.8	4.7

1. Firms subject to federal tax.

STATE County	Health Care and Social Assistance[1], 1997				Other Services[1], 1997				Federal funds and grants, fiscal 2001[2] Expenditures (mil dol)		Direct payments for individuals[3]	
	Number of Establishments	Number of Employees	Receipts (mil dol)	Annual Payroll (mil dol)	Number of Establishments	Number of Employees	Receipts (mil dol)	Annual Payroll (mil dol)	Total	Social Security and government retirement	Medicare	Food stamps and Supplemental Security Income
	159	160	161	162	163	164	165	166	167	168	169	170
ILLINOIS—Cont'd												
Jackson	118	1 698	96.9	46.9	85	338	20.3	4.7	263.5	95.5	38.4	12.9
Jasper	8	109	3.6	1.7	21	62	4.7	0.8	56.9	20.0	8.5	1.1
Jefferson	92	1 088	69.7	23.8	64	384	24.9	7.7	206.1	85.6	42.8	8.9
Jersey	28	387	15.4	6.1	28	63	4.4	0.9	89.8	42.0	17.0	2.0
Jo Daviess	26	224	9.6	4.6	41	130	11.6	1.9	106.8	57.1	18.5	1.2
Johnson	12	112	3.7	1.5	8	21	2.2	0.4	59.3	29.6	10.2	2.0
Kane	620	6 731	522.4	241.2	604	3 897	259.3	84.5	1 495.8	566.8	222.7	35.2
Kankakee	168	1 730	107.6	53.0	162	954	59.8	18.3	498.9	213.6	106.4	21.9
Kendall	43	464	20.9	8.9	69	391	26.3	7.1	126.6	63.0	17.9	0.9
Knox	72	1 213	71.7	27.1	86	390	24.4	6.4	308.1	142.3	59.3	9.0
Lake	1 210	12 163	896.3	414.7	975	5 862	468.9	140.9	3 098.9	947.9	324.4	38.8
La Salle	199	1 663	93.8	38.9	208	933	65.7	16.9	510.3	260.0	99.7	10.0
Lawrence	31	533	18.9	7.4	20	58	4.4	1.0	97.8	41.4	19.4	2.4
Lee	47	537	39.8	16.5	56	245	15.0	3.9	180.7	76.0	29.1	3.4
Livingston	41	265	15.3	7.0	59	206	14.1	3.7	204.9	77.9	34.4	3.4
Logan	31	366	17.4	5.8	37	133	7.7	1.9	164.7	66.7	28.1	3.0
McDonough	58	480	25.5	12.4	64	230	12.6	3.2	151.4	56.7	24.3	4.3
McHenry	410	4 539	226.2	108.2	401	2 001	126.7	38.8	594.0	359.3	122.8	7.8
McLean	228	2 901	190.8	91.6	226	1 433	85.6	26.8	551.2	218.2	73.6	11.9
Macon	204	2 546	155.6	70.3	189	1 456	86.0	28.7	600.1	268.0	98.2	25.7
Macoupin	65	943	29.1	12.4	65	208	13.4	3.1	262.5	127.4	55.6	7.3
Madison	501	5 457	307.2	141.5	438	2 526	158.9	45.8	1 329.3	622.0	251.2	44.3
Marion	96	1 070	62.4	23.6	71	242	13.3	3.5	269.7	118.4	60.5	9.0
Marshall	19	255	9.8	4.7	14	33	1.7	0.3	73.9	30.0	11.8	1.1
Mason	20	157	6.7	2.2	21	54	3.9	0.9	100.0	42.1	20.5	2.5
Massac	23	320	11.7	5.6	18	61	3.9	1.0	87.1	38.7	19.1	3.6
Menard	14	146	4.3	2.1	15	67	3.9	1.0	63.3	25.8	9.5	1.1
Mercer	15	132	5.5	2.6	21	66	3.8	0.8	90.6	37.7	13.7	1.3
Monroe	34	366	14.5	6.7	48	297	13.7	4.8	109.5	57.3	17.9	1.0
Montgomery	47	634	27.8	10.9	48	188	14.8	2.9	170.7	73.7	31.3	4.8
Morgan	75	792	33.0	14.7	58	246	15.6	4.5	210.6	80.7	32.9	5.9
Moultrie	16	195	8.2	2.8	15	49	3.5	0.7	79.0	37.9	14.4	0.8
Ogle	58	564	22.9	9.2	75	264	16.6	4.3	193.7	93.0	31.7	3.3
Peoria	365	4 477	369.3	193.7	291	2 391	172.4	56.2	1 062.6	397.8	159.2	44.5
Perry	35	368	13.4	5.1	31	106	7.0	1.7	108.9	55.8	22.3	4.0
Piatt	14	159	6.5	2.8	20	66	4.5	1.3	93.2	39.5	14.0	0.9
Pike	20	348	11.8	5.2	28	67	4.8	1.1	112.5	41.8	18.9	2.9
Pope	2	D	D	D	2	D	D	D	27.5	10.4	4.7	1.2
Pulaski	2	D	D	D	9	19	1.5	0.3	116.2	18.2	9.0	3.2
Putnam	4	13	0.5	0.1	6	8	0.7	0.1	32.4	14.2	5.0	0.4
Randolph	53	608	22.8	9.8	57	170	10.3	2.7	157.9	78.4	33.3	3.3
Richland	24	403	19.8	9.9	37	124	8.3	1.7	97.5	39.7	14.9	2.9
Rock Island	290	3 073	192.2	87.6	255	1 782	114.3	31.9	939.5	368.8	128.7	24.9
St. Clair	469	6 013	346.2	156.5	423	2 147	124.4	40.7	1 977.6	652.5	248.0	83.3
Saline	55	1 048	42.5	19.7	42	100	7.2	1.7	185.0	75.2	29.5	8.6
Sangamon	356	7 594	478.1	204.4	347	2 285	142.3	46.4	2 735.4	534.2	165.1	39.2
Schuyler	9	129	4.2	1.8	9	11	1.6	0.1	44.7	16.5	6.3	0.9
Scott	3	6	0.2	0.1	6	12	2.1	0.1	36.2	12.2	4.9	0.6
Shelby	26	337	14.9	5.8	33	123	9.5	2.1	131.3	53.4	24.0	2.3
Stark	5	25	0.6	0.2	4	14	1.3	0.2	50.9	15.4	8.0	0.6
Stephenson	67	713	37.8	19.4	86	395	21.8	6.4	225.6	115.3	38.7	6.3
Tazewell	152	1 931	88.1	40.6	221	1 122	72.3	22.3	503.8	270.1	104.0	11.2
Union	35	930	22.9	9.6	16	66	4.7	1.0	98.5	42.7	18.0	5.3
Vermilion	103	1 343	83.4	38.6	133	627	33.3	9.9	521.8	224.9	78.6	21.9
Wabash	22	499	9.3	3.9	19	91	6.0	1.5	67.8	30.2	11.7	1.9
Warren	17	331	10.0	3.9	23	83	4.1	0.9	126.5	41.3	17.0	2.7
Washington	17	295	10.9	4.6	29	94	5.4	1.3	92.4	35.1	18.4	0.9
Wayne	20	129	5.5	2.1	22	72	4.9	1.1	113.6	40.6	19.0	2.1
White	24	265	8.2	3.7	19	59	5.2	0.8	122.5	46.2	19.9	3.0
Whiteside	71	1 087	66.0	27.2	135	691	37.5	10.1	303.0	145.1	55.1	6.4
Will	558	5 682	377.4	173.6	617	3 523	251.6	76.8	1 226.5	666.7	233.9	32.3
Williamson	122	2 043	123.4	38.9	59	430	25.3	6.4	415.8	155.4	56.2	12.4
Winnebago	433	5 688	458.3	222.2	479	3 651	225.9	72.3	1 125.8	532.1	180.7	43.7
Woodford	27	265	10.3	4.8	47	159	10.5	2.8	134.8	60.6	23.5	1.7

1. Firms subject to federal tax.　2. October 1, 2000 to September 30, 2001.　3. State totals may include programs not allocated by county.

STATE County	Salaries and wages	Defense	Other	Medicaid and other health-related	Nutrition and family welfare	Education	Other	Total (mil dol)	Intergovern-mental (mil dol)	Total (mil dol)	Total	Property
	171	172	173	174	175	176	177	178	179	180	181	182
ILLINOIS—Cont'd												
Jackson	18.6	3.7	5.7	31.1	6.3	5.7	8.6	114.5	57.6	30.6	504	429
Jasper	2.3	0.0	0.6	3.2	0.7	0.4	0.1	21.3	10.3	8.7	824	739
Jefferson	9.6	0.2	1.6	20.3	4.0	2.5	11.7	92.2	49.7	27.6	708	525
Jersey	2.6	0.0	0.7	6.9	1.1	0.6	1.7	45.8	19.9	7.9	372	335
Jo Daviess	4.3	0.0	1.2	3.6	1.0	0.3	1.8	48.9	14.9	21.4	988	885
Johnson	3.7	0.0	0.7	6.1	0.9	0.4	1.9	14.4	9.6	3.0	231	231
Kane	149.7	19.6	324.6	58.1	24.4	9.7	13.5	1 062.1	293.5	569.6	1 496	1 399
Kankakee	24.8	0.4	4.3	45.2	14.9	5.1	11.0	227.2	107.0	80.9	793	721
Kendall	13.3	0.1	1.4	1.7	0.8	0.7	8.5	89.6	27.2	52.4	1 051	977
Knox	11.5	0.0	2.9	17.3	4.7	3.3	14.8	121.3	57.7	36.1	650	517
Lake	1 145.4	274.7	82.6	83.3	26.0	29.3	22.0	1 662.8	363.7	967.2	1 626	1 500
La Salle	21.0	0.2	9.1	24.6	5.8	3.4	6.8	224.1	88.5	98.0	895	860
Lawrence	3.2	0.0	0.6	7.4	1.3	0.8	4.3	24.1	15.0	5.5	354	328
Lee	5.8	0.0	3.0	7.5	1.7	0.8	8.9	78.0	32.5	29.3	819	783
Livingston	6.4	0.0	1.6	5.6	2.1	1.0	6.2	89.0	37.7	36.4	903	891
Logan	6.6	0.1	1.3	6.9	2.8	2.1	3.1	56.6	20.7	24.3	776	769
McDonough	6.0	1.8	1.3	7.4	2.2	7.1	0.7	95.6	27.9	20.1	589	580
McHenry	32.5	4.0	9.4	16.2	4.3	2.0	4.3	488.0	118.1	268.3	1 132	1 042
McLean	48.0	1.6	12.1	25.5	7.8	6.0	49.2	287.4	91.3	149.2	1 060	903
Macon	23.2	0.0	44.4	51.4	12.3	5.5	18.3	270.8	134.0	79.6	697	658
Macoupin	8.2	0.9	2.3	13.3	4.2	1.6	4.2	81.4	47.0	26.3	535	434
Madison	40.7	45.9	81.3	102.3	32.3	14.8	35.5	536.5	250.4	179.6	695	619
Marion	11.2	0.0	3.1	20.8	6.3	2.1	14.8	120.6	53.0	25.1	596	542
Marshall	2.5	0.0	0.6	1.7	0.6	0.2	3.2	19.8	8.8	8.6	666	646
Mason	3.2	0.1	0.8	5.2	1.7	0.7	0.3	49.0	18.4	16.2	958	886
Massac	2.3	0.0	2.2	10.5	1.6	0.6	0.4	32.6	13.4	7.1	459	434
Menard	1.9	0.0	0.5	4.4	0.7	0.3	0.7	25.3	12.0	8.0	644	639
Mercer	3.2	0.0	0.7	2.7	1.2	0.4	0.9	41.0	17.9	10.6	604	583
Monroe	3.7	4.8	1.0	6.0	0.7	0.3	3.0	47.0	19.8	15.2	585	509
Montgomery	6.9	1.1	1.4	10.2	2.2	1.4	4.0	56.7	27.2	20.2	651	570
Morgan	6.0	0.3	1.6	20.9	2.4	1.1	23.4	58.4	26.5	21.7	601	541
Moultrie	2.5	0.0	0.5	2.7	0.6	0.2	0.0	20.7	9.0	8.9	617	615
Ogle	8.4	0.7	7.0	6.1	2.1	0.8	0.5	122.7	38.8	63.6	1 268	1 217
Peoria	138.2	79.5	27.2	63.5	21.8	7.9	35.3	395.6	173.7	146.4	801	619
Perry	3.0	0.0	0.8	7.5	1.7	0.7	1.5	30.1	19.3	6.6	308	283
Piatt	3.0	0.0	0.8	2.4	0.8	0.3	1.4	36.6	16.2	14.7	893	870
Pike	3.8	0.0	1.0	7.9	1.5	0.7	5.4	32.3	17.2	9.9	573	526
Pope	3.2	0.0	1.4	2.5	0.5	0.2	0.9	5.9	3.6	1.6	346	326
Pulaski	3.1	52.8	0.8	12.6	5.5	1.6	1.8	16.2	12.1	2.1	295	268
Putnam	1.5	0.0	0.4	0.4	0.3	0.1	2.8	10.3	5.0	3.9	662	653
Randolph	6.6	1.0	5.3	9.0	2.8	0.9	2.0	76.1	26.3	15.4	451	372
Richland	3.3	0.0	0.9	7.5	1.3	1.7	4.7	75.3	31.5	8.0	473	463
Rock Island	225.6	43.6	11.3	40.5	16.0	6.0	17.2	338.4	141.7	119.4	805	718
St. Clair	456.2	103.1	68.7	205.2	45.7	20.4	21.5	607.9	328.6	164.8	624	488
Saline	6.2	4.8	17.9	23.2	2.6	1.5	2.0	59.5	33.5	15.1	572	565
Sangamon	131.3	19.6	21.6	264.6	701.8	324.9	439.1	397.2	159.8	166.8	871	763
Schuyler	1.6	0.0	0.4	3.1	0.6	0.2	0.1	20.5	5.8	5.3	691	621
Scott	0.9	0.3	0.2	3.1	0.5	0.2	1.8	11.6	5.8	3.3	588	567
Shelby	5.0	0.4	1.1	7.3	1.3	0.3	0.4	36.8	16.2	15.2	674	600
Stark	1.7	0.0	0.4	1.5	0.5	0.2	0.8	14.7	5.5	7.0	1 108	1 087
Stephenson	8.9	0.5	2.1	14.0	3.8	2.2	3.8	104.9	45.0	37.5	760	737
Tazewell	25.9	2.3	3.6	25.6	8.5	3.7	2.7	289.5	124.2	105.4	820	753
Union	2.9	0.0	0.6	17.3	1.6	0.8	3.1	45.6	23.1	7.2	399	393
Vermilion	59.6	6.9	13.9	36.7	11.6	4.4	2.9	190.2	95.3	51.5	606	572
Wabash	1.7	0.0	0.5	4.2	1.0	0.4	3.6	40.5	11.4	9.5	747	679
Warren	4.3	0.0	1.3	6.9	3.4	0.7	15.1	44.7	16.6	12.9	685	645
Washington	3.1	0.1	0.7	4.0	0.7	0.2	7.5	31.6	12.2	9.3	606	525
Wayne	3.6	0.0	0.9	7.6	1.4	0.5	11.2	28.8	16.5	8.0	471	411
White	3.3	0.0	11.5	10.2	3.4	0.8	1.7	40.4	20.7	8.9	569	453
Whiteside	9.9	0.1	2.4	12.2	6.0	1.5	17.9	194.4	51.4	43.1	633	592
Will	52.5	22.1	17.1	53.5	23.1	10.0	63.1	915.2	273.2	465.8	1 048	892
Williamson	55.7	73.9	6.4	31.5	4.3	2.6	4.6	154.5	67.1	36.2	591	496
Winnebago	64.3	77.1	25.3	83.9	21.1	13.2	22.7	617.9	241.2	271.4	1 018	973
Woodford	4.2	0.0	1.1	3.6	1.5	0.6	3.8	68.3	30.1	30.9	888	850

1. October 1, 2000 to September 30, 2001.   2. State totals may include programs not allocated by county.   3. Based on the resident population estimated as of July 1 of the year shown.

STATE County	Local government finances, 1997 (cont'd) Direct general expenditure Total (mil dol)	Per capita[1] (dollars)	Percent of total for — Education	Health and hospitals	Police protection	Public welfare	Highways	Debt outstanding Total (mil dol)	Per capita[1] (dollars)	Government employment, 1999 Federal civilian	Federal military	State and local	Presidential election, 2000[2] Percent of vote cast — Democratic	Republican	All other
	183	184	185	186	187	188	189	190	191	192	193	194	195	196	197
ILLINOIS—Cont'd															
Jackson	106.6	1 756	45.7	4.3	6.1	6.6	4.7	78.7	1 296	331	152	13 140	51.0	42.5	6.5
Jasper	23.2	2 196	53.8	5.7	4.2	0.9	17.6	3.7	347	47	23	702	36.1	62.1	1.7
Jefferson	79.4	2 036	62.0	0.0	4.7	0.3	11.2	17.4	447	171	88	2 193	43.5	54.4	2.1
Jersey	42.8	2 014	34.3	31.0	4.0	0.1	3.9	3.0	141	51	48	1 124	46.3	49.9	3.9
Jo Daviess	46.5	2 146	49.4	11.7	4.1	0.2	11.9	10.1	465	90	48	1 114	44.4	51.4	4.2
Johnson	13.4	1 022	67.1	0.0	3.7	0.3	10.5	6.5	499	84	30	1 022	36.0	61.3	2.7
Kane	1 114.6	2 927	55.4	0.5	6.5	0.2	6.0	1 084.3	2 847	1 861	892	22 512	42.5	54.5	3.0
Kankakee	215.3	2 111	58.1	1.3	6.2	0.4	8.2	128.2	1 257	343	227	6 181	47.7	49.9	2.4
Kendall	91.0	1 824	63.6	0.0	2.1	2.5	4.9	60.5	1 214	91	119	2 005	37.1	60.1	2.8
Knox	123.9	2 230	49.0	0.0	5.6	6.3	7.1	56.5	1 017	214	122	3 392	54.3	42.8	3.0
Lake	1 651.8	2 777	56.9	1.6	5.5	1.1	5.1	1 373.3	2 309	6 124	26 327	30 208	47.5	50.0	2.5
La Salle	217.5	1 986	58.6	1.4	4.7	2.2	8.6	129.4	1 181	371	244	6 033	50.8	46.2	3.0
Lawrence	22.5	1 442	61.5	0.1	4.3	0.3	13.9	4.4	280	49	34	1 004	42.9	54.6	2.4
Lee	73.7	2 061	59.8	1.6	4.9	3.5	8.5	21.3	595	105	79	2 431	41.8	55.2	3.0
Livingston	90.9	2 255	56.1	4.0	3.5	0.9	8.5	34.7	861	121	88	3 005	37.8	59.6	2.6
Logan	49.4	1 577	46.6	4.2	5.5	0.1	9.4	9.0	288	122	70	2 447	35.2	62.3	2.5
McDonough	88.4	2 593	30.3	36.0	2.8	3.4	6.7	32.9	967	106	83	6 522	46.7	49.7	3.6
McHenry	525.3	2 217	55.4	2.0	5.5	0.9	6.5	417.5	1 762	563	547	10 190	38.3	58.5	3.2
McLean	271.8	1 931	47.3	1.5	6.8	1.7	7.9	221.9	1 576	973	332	12 968	40.9	55.8	3.2
Macon	264.6	2 316	45.5	2.0	5.7	0.6	6.7	167.2	1 463	371	260	6 144	49.0	48.1	2.9
Macoupin	76.9	1 562	61.8	1.4	6.1	0.3	10.2	31.4	637	152	108	2 513	51.5	45.6	2.9
Madison	521.0	2 014	53.5	3.6	5.4	2.6	5.4	255.0	986	771	602	15 776	53.2	43.9	2.9
Marion	114.5	2 724	53.8	12.2	3.1	0.3	4.2	33.7	801	216	92	2 445	48.4	49.5	2.1
Marshall	18.5	1 442	50.8	0.9	5.0	1.0	15.2	11.5	893	47	29	391	43.5	53.2	3.3
Mason	49.1	2 909	42.0	20.2	2.4	0.3	7.9	21.6	1 277	69	37	1 132	47.1	50.4	2.5
Massac	30.9	2 004	42.6	26.6	4.1	1.1	5.1	8.1	523	50	34	868	43.2	54.5	2.3
Menard	24.3	1 966	60.8	2.2	5.9	9.2	4.2	19.2	1 551	41	28	757	34.9	62.3	2.9
Mercer	37.5	2 138	44.5	22.5	3.1	0.1	9.4	7.5	425	72	39	1 198	52.9	44.3	2.8
Monroe	43.6	1 681	46.7	1.6	4.8	8.4	6.0	17.7	684	65	60	1 218	42.0	55.3	2.7
Montgomery	53.5	1 726	57.7	1.9	5.5	0.1	8.3	25.0	805	119	69	1 882	50.0	47.6	2.5
Morgan	56.5	1 566	56.8	1.3	5.7	1.7	7.6	16.7	462	118	78	2 367	41.2	56.2	2.7
Moultrie	20.8	1 444	47.0	1.3	2.2	0.1	16.2	7.3	503	42	32	561	44.2	53.4	2.4
Ogle	121.6	2 422	62.8	1.1	3.7	0.5	7.1	57.7	1 150	161	113	2 526	37.2	59.8	3.0
Peoria	382.4	2 094	41.8	1.9	5.1	2.3	6.9	229.8	1 258	1 805	445	9 375	50.3	47.4	2.3
Perry	28.4	1 329	58.3	4.3	4.3	0.2	6.5	11.3	527	58	47	1 195	48.9	48.3	2.8
Piatt	35.9	2 175	51.4	0.7	3.9	9.9	11.1	16.3	987	57	37	982	41.6	55.1	3.3
Pike	32.9	1 903	57.3	6.4	2.9	1.4	8.7	14.1	817	77	38	919	39.4	58.0	2.5
Pope	5.7	1 221	61.7	1.1	4.0	0.3	4.1	3.7	781	90	12	299	39.8	57.8	2.4
Pulaski	17.2	2 380	69.9	1.8	2.5	0.6	7.6	1.7	237	65	16	854	50.3	47.4	2.2
Putnam	10.0	1 709	56.7	0.7	5.8	0.1	13.3	2.6	437	26	13	278	52.1	45.2	2.6
Randolph	69.4	2 036	38.0	29.1	3.8	4.1	8.3	24.4	715	114	74	2 950	47.6	49.9	2.6
Richland	76.7	4 554	49.8	30.4	1.1	0.0	7.0	4.6	273	69	37	1 463	33.5	63.5	2.9
Rock Island	311.1	2 098	53.0	1.0	6.6	2.6	4.9	180.0	1 214	6 016	484	8 815	58.3	38.7	3.0
St. Clair	575.1	2 179	52.8	1.8	4.9	1.1	4.8	387.0	1 467	4 593	6 126	12 104	55.7	42.1	2.2
Saline	57.7	2 191	59.1	4.0	3.9	1.0	7.3	24.8	941	135	58	1 951	46.6	50.9	2.5
Sangamon	382.5	1 997	50.5	1.3	7.9	0.4	6.5	439.7	2 295	2 164	439	27 786	42.0	55.1	3.0
Schuyler	20.7	2 714	39.3	35.4	1.0	0.1	5.7	5.0	655	34	17	497	42.1	55.1	2.9
Scott	12.0	2 139	48.3	0.0	3.6	12.8	10.0	1.1	201	21	12	353	38.6	59.1	2.4
Shelby	35.1	1 552	44.8	2.1	3.9	0.1	18.0	5.8	255	114	50	1 133	39.5	57.6	2.9
Stark	14.5	2 288	51.0	0.4	2.6	0.2	10.6	1.7	275	34	14	313	40.5	56.7	2.8
Stephenson	114.7	2 324	60.1	0.9	3.6	4.6	5.8	41.0	831	151	109	2 615	41.6	55.3	3.1
Tazewell	272.1	2 117	60.9	0.9	4.5	0.1	5.3	142.8	1 111	530	287	6 431	43.5	54.0	2.5
Union	44.1	2 443	62.2	21.6	2.0	0.8	3.0	14.7	813	69	40	2 079	46.0	50.8	3.3
Vermilion	174.4	2 049	55.7	1.9	5.7	4.4	5.7	72.5	852	1 551	186	4 512	48.0	49.2	2.9
Wabash	37.3	2 926	28.9	40.6	3.2	1.2	3.3	10.1	792	40	28	766	36.1	61.8	2.1
Warren	38.8	2 065	41.3	21.3	3.8	0.1	10.1	18.0	956	82	42	885	46.2	51.1	2.7
Washington	26.6	1 739	41.0	26.0	3.5	0.0	7.9	10.0	655	66	34	916	37.0	61.0	2.0
Wayne	27.0	1 590	58.1	1.2	4.0	1.2	13.8	3.0	179	74	38	868	28.7	69.5	1.8
White	39.6	2 528	51.7	18.8	3.4	0.7	10.7	6.6	423	65	34	1 097	38.7	59.2	2.1
Whiteside	192.3	2 824	32.8	40.0	2.8	1.0	4.8	52.8	776	194	132	3 635	51.9	45.3	2.8
Will	926.1	2 084	50.8	1.8	6.1	1.0	6.2	729.6	1 642	861	1 074	21 918	47.4	50.0	2.6
Williamson	150.3	2 458	50.4	18.7	3.0	0.6	4.8	68.2	1 115	1 215	136	4 055	45.3	52.0	2.8
Winnebago	617.2	2 315	49.7	1.1	7.1	2.7	5.7	433.9	1 627	1 152	596	12 961	47.6	49.2	3.2
Woodford	59.4	1 709	67.7	0.4	4.0	0.8	9.6	13.4	385	75	79	1 663	32.9	64.9	2.2

1. Based on the resident population estimated as of July 1 of the year shown. 2. Data subject to copyright.

Table B. States and Counties — Land Area and Population

STATE/County code	MSA/PMSA/NECMA code[1]	County Type[2]	STATE County	Land area[3] (sq km) 2000	Population and population characteristics, 2000			Race alone or in combination (percent)					Age (percent)					
					Total persons	Rank	Per square kilometer	White	Black	Am. Indian, Alaska Native	Asian and Pacific Islander	Percent Hispanic[4]	Under 5 years	5 to 17 years	18 to 24 years	25 to 34 years	35 to 44 years	45 to 54 years
				1	2	3	4	5	6	7	8	9	10	11	12	13	14	15
18 000	...	X	INDIANA	92 895	6 080 485	X	65.5	88.6	8.8	0.6	1.3	3.5	7.0	18.9	10.1	13.7	15.8	13.4
18 001	2760	2	Adams	879	33 625	1 295	38.3	98.0	0.2	0.4	0.4	3.3	8.0	23.1	9.1	12.3	14.0	12.0
18 003	2760	2	Allen	1 702	331 849	176	195.0	84.7	12.1	0.8	1.8	4.2	7.7	20.0	9.4	14.2	15.8	13.6
18 005	...	4	Bartholomew	1 054	71 435	692	67.8	95.0	2.2	0.4	2.2	2.2	7.4	19.2	7.7	13.9	15.8	14.2
18 007	...	8	Benton	1 052	9 421	2 493	9.0	98.2	0.4	1.0	0.3	2.6	6.6	21.2	7.1	12.5	15.4	12.1
18 009	...	6	Blackford	428	14 048	2 160	32.8	99.2	0.3	0.9	0.2	0.6	6.5	18.2	7.5	12.7	14.8	14.2
18 011	3480	1	Boone	1 095	46 107	982	42.1	98.5	0.5	0.5	0.6	1.2	7.3	21.0	6.3	12.1	18.0	14.5
18 013	...	8	Brown	809	14 957	2 094	18.5	98.9	0.4	0.7	0.4	0.9	5.3	18.0	6.3	11.1	16.8	17.1
18 015	...	6	Carroll	964	20 165	1 783	20.9	98.2	0.3	0.4	0.1	2.9	6.8	19.5	7.4	12.8	15.9	13.8
18 017	...	6	Cass	1 069	40 930	1 082	38.3	94.5	1.5	0.6	0.8	7.1	7.0	18.9	8.7	12.9	15.5	13.2
18 019	4520	2	Clark	971	96 472	536	99.4	91.6	7.3	0.7	0.9	1.9	6.7	17.5	9.0	14.4	16.3	14.5
18 021	8320	3	Clay	926	26 556	1 499	28.7	99.0	0.5	0.6	0.3	0.6	6.6	19.5	8.6	12.3	15.5	13.2
18 023	3920	3	Clinton	1 049	33 866	1 285	32.3	95.1	0.4	0.4	0.4	7.3	7.1	20.2	8.8	13.0	15.4	12.7
18 025	...	8	Crawford	792	10 743	2 380	13.6	98.8	0.2	0.6	0.3	0.9	6.3	19.2	8.4	12.4	16.0	14.6
18 027	...	7	Daviess	1 115	29 820	1 402	26.7	98.0	0.6	0.5	0.4	2.1	7.6	21.3	8.6	11.8	14.4	12.7
18 029	1640	1	Dearborn	790	46 109	981	58.4	98.7	0.8	0.5	0.4	0.6	6.8	20.8	7.7	12.6	17.5	14.3
18 031	...	6	Decatur	965	24 555	1 573	25.4	99.0	0.1	0.4	0.8	0.5	7.5	18.8	8.9	13.7	15.6	13.0
18 033	2760	2	De Kalb	940	40 285	1 108	42.9	98.5	0.4	0.5	0.5	1.7	7.6	20.4	8.6	13.7	16.6	13.3
18 035	5280	3	Delaware	1 019	118 769	456	116.6	91.8	7.2	0.6	1.0	1.1	5.9	16.2	16.9	12.4	13.2	12.5
18 037	...	7	Dubois	1 114	39 674	1 121	35.6	98.0	0.2	0.3	0.3	2.8	7.2	20.2	7.9	12.9	16.9	13.4
18 039	2330	3	Elkhart	1 201	182 791	299	152.2	88.0	5.8	0.7	1.3	8.9	8.1	20.8	9.5	14.5	15.3	12.8
18 041	...	7	Fayette	557	25 588	1 535	45.9	97.8	1.9	0.4	0.4	0.5	6.4	17.9	8.6	12.8	14.3	14.7
18 043	4520	2	Floyd	383	70 823	701	184.9	94.3	5.0	0.6	0.8	1.1	6.5	19.3	8.4	12.8	17.1	14.6
18 045	...	6	Fountain	1 025	17 954	1 901	17.5	99.2	0.2	0.5	0.3	1.1	6.6	19.6	7.2	12.5	15.4	12.6
18 047	...	6	Franklin	1 000	22 151	1 685	22.2	99.5	0.1	0.4	0.3	0.5	7.0	21.2	7.6	12.8	16.4	13.6
18 049	...	7	Fulton	954	20 511	1 759	21.5	97.4	1.0	0.8	0.6	2.3	6.6	19.4	7.7	12.0	15.6	13.1
18 051	...	6	Gibson	1 266	32 500	1 332	25.7	97.1	2.3	0.4	0.6	0.7	6.4	18.4	8.4	12.3	15.9	13.6
18 053	...	4	Grant	1 072	73 403	681	68.5	90.6	7.9	0.9	0.8	2.4	5.9	17.7	11.8	11.5	14.3	13.6
18 055	...	6	Greene	1 403	33 157	1 311	23.6	99.2	0.2	0.5	0.3	0.8	6.2	18.5	7.7	12.6	15.6	13.9
18 057	3480	0	Hamilton	1 031	182 740	300	177.2	95.2	1.8	0.4	2.9	1.6	9.1	21.7	5.6	15.2	19.7	13.9
18 059	3480	1	Hancock	793	55 391	851	69.8	99.0	0.2	0.5	0.5	0.9	6.8	19.8	6.8	12.5	17.5	15.3
18 061	4520	2	Harrison	1 257	34 325	1 270	27.3	98.9	0.5	0.6	0.3	1.0	6.5	19.5	8.7	12.5	17.7	14.5
18 063	3480	1	Hendricks	1 058	104 093	508	98.4	97.5	1.3	0.6	1.0	1.1	7.3	20.7	7.0	13.8	18.5	14.2
18 065	...	6	Henry	1 018	48 508	939	47.7	98.5	1.0	0.4	0.3	0.8	6.2	17.9	7.5	12.6	15.2	14.3
18 067	3850	3	Howard	759	84 964	614	111.9	91.1	7.2	0.8	1.3	2.0	7.0	18.6	8.3	13.1	15.1	14.3
18 069	2760	2	Huntington	991	38 075	1 162	38.4	98.8	0.3	0.7	0.4	1.0	6.7	19.5	9.9	12.3	15.8	13.1
18 071	...	7	Jackson	1 319	41 335	1 070	31.3	96.8	0.7	0.5	1.0	2.7	7.0	18.5	8.8	14.5	15.8	12.9
18 073	...	6	Jasper	1 450	30 043	1 395	20.7	98.6	0.4	0.5	0.3	2.4	6.9	20.5	10.1	12.5	15.3	13.2
18 075	...	6	Jay	994	21 806	1 700	21.9	98.3	0.3	0.5	0.6	1.8	7.3	19.7	7.7	12.9	14.4	13.1
18 077	...	6	Jefferson	936	31 705	1 352	33.9	97.3	1.8	0.7	0.9	1.0	6.2	18.2	10.6	12.5	16.0	13.6
18 079	...	7	Jennings	977	27 554	1 465	28.2	98.5	1.0	0.6	0.4	0.7	7.5	20.2	8.2	14.7	15.7	13.5
18 081	3480	0	Johnson	829	115 209	468	139.0	97.6	1.0	0.4	1.1	1.4	7.5	19.7	8.7	14.2	16.6	13.2
18 083	...	5	Knox	1 336	39 256	1 132	29.4	97.0	2.1	0.5	0.7	0.8	5.9	17.1	13.6	11.0	14.4	13.2
18 085	...	6	Kosciusko	1 392	74 057	673	53.2	95.6	0.8	0.6	0.7	5.0	7.5	20.3	8.7	13.4	15.6	13.4
18 087	...	8	Lagrange	983	34 909	1 252	35.5	97.5	0.3	0.5	0.4	3.1	9.8	24.0	10.3	12.9	13.3	11.5
18 089	2960	0	Lake	1 287	484 564	118	376.5	68.3	25.9	0.7	1.2	12.2	7.1	19.6	9.3	12.7	15.6	13.7
18 091	...	4	La Porte	1 549	110 106	493	71.1	87.6	10.8	0.8	0.7	3.1	6.5	18.1	8.6	13.6	16.1	14.5
18 093	...	6	Lawrence	1 162	45 922	986	39.5	98.7	0.5	0.7	0.4	0.9	6.5	18.1	7.7	12.9	15.2	14.5
18 095	3480	3	Madison	1 171	133 358	402	113.9	90.8	8.3	0.7	0.5	1.5	6.4	17.4	9.1	13.3	15.0	13.9
18 097	3480	0	Marion	1 026	860 454	50	838.6	71.8	25.0	0.7	1.9	3.9	7.4	18.4	10.0	16.5	16.5	12.7
18 099	...	6	Marshall	1 151	45 128	994	39.2	96.5	0.5	0.6	0.5	5.9	7.3	20.8	8.7	12.5	15.5	13.3
18 101	...	7	Martin	871	10 369	2 407	11.9	99.5	0.3	0.4	0.3	0.4	6.3	18.9	7.4	12.3	15.2	15.1
18 103	...	6	Miami	973	36 082	1 211	37.1	95.0	3.4	1.9	0.7	1.3	6.4	19.5	8.1	13.5	16.4	14.1
18 105	1020	3	Monroe	1 021	120 563	450	118.1	92.3	3.5	0.7	4.0	1.9	5.1	12.9	27.7	14.7	12.6	11.1
18 107	...	6	Montgomery	1 307	37 629	1 172	28.8	97.4	0.9	0.5	0.7	1.6	6.7	19.3	9.0	12.5	16.0	12.8
18 109	3480	1	Morgan	1 053	66 689	733	63.3	99.3	0.2	0.7	0.4	0.7	7.2	20.0	7.7	13.5	17.1	14.3
18 111	...	8	Newton	1 041	14 566	2 115	14.0	98.1	0.2	0.7	0.4	2.9	6.2	20.2	7.9	12.2	16.2	14.2
18 113	...	6	Noble	1 065	46 275	977	43.5	94.9	0.5	0.6	0.6	7.1	8.0	21.0	9.2	14.3	15.7	12.9
18 115	1640	1	Ohio	225	5 623	2 812	25.0	99.1	0.6	0.4	0.3	0.4	5.9	19.0	7.8	11.8	16.8	14.2
18 117	...	7	Orange	1 035	19 306	1 828	18.7	98.6	0.8	0.7	0.2	0.6	6.7	19.0	8.0	12.4	15.6	13.4
18 119	...	6	Owen	998	21 786	1 705	21.8	99.0	0.4	0.8	0.3	0.8	6.3	20.3	7.2	11.9	16.9	14.3
18 121	...	6	Parke	1 152	17 241	1 938	15.0	97.1	2.2	0.7	0.3	0.6	5.5	18.4	7.3	12.2	16.5	14.3
18 123	...	7	Perry	988	18 899	1 849	19.1	98.0	1.6	0.4	0.3	0.7	5.4	17.5	9.8	12.5	16.6	14.2
18 125	...	8	Pike	871	12 837	2 244	14.7	99.5	0.2	0.3	0.2	0.6	6.1	17.8	7.7	12.2	16.0	13.8
18 127	2960	1	Porter	1 083	146 798	370	135.5	96.6	1.1	0.7	1.3	4.8	6.5	19.3	9.8	12.5	16.4	15.5
18 129	2440	2	Posey	1 058	27 061	1 480	25.6	98.5	1.1	0.5	0.3	0.4	6.3	21.0	7.4	11.4	17.6	14.5
18 131	...	9	Pulaski	1 123	13 755	2 176	12.2	98.2	1.0	0.6	0.4	1.4	6.1	20.8	7.4	11.6	15.7	13.3

1. MSA = Metropolitan Statistical Area. PMSA = Primary MSA. NECMA = New England County Metropolitan Area. See Appendix A for explanation of these concepts. See Appendix B for list of metropolitan areas identified by type, with component counties. 2. County typology code from the Economic Research Service of USDA. See Appendix A for definition. 3. Dry land or land partially or temporarily covered by water. 4. Hispanic persons may be of any race.

Table B. States and Counties — **Population and Households**

STATE County	Age (percent) (cont'd) 55 to 64 years	65 to 74 years	75 years and over	Percent female	Population — change and components of change, 1990–2001 Total persons 2001	1990	Percent change 1990–2000	2000–2001	Components of change, 2000–2001 Births	Deaths	Net migration	Households, 2000 Number	Percent change, 1990–2000	Persons per household	Female family householder[1]	One person
	16	17	18	19	20	21	22	23	24	25	26	27	28	29	30	31
INDIANA	8.7	6.5	5.9	51.0	6 114 745	5 544 156	9.7	0.6	107 126	69 179	-3 178	2 336 306	13.1	2.53	11.1	25.9
Adams	8.1	6.0	7.4	50.6	33 441	31 095	8.1	-0.5	708	362	-530	11 818	12.9	2.81	8.3	24.0
Allen	7.9	5.9	5.5	51.1	333 628	300 836	10.3	0.5	6 352	3 374	-1 077	128 745	13.6	2.53	11.7	27.4
Bartholomew	9.8	6.6	5.5	50.9	71 573	63 657	12.2	0.2	1 358	790	-418	27 936	15.5	2.52	9.7	24.0
Benton	9.4	7.3	8.3	50.4	9 279	9 441	-0.2	-1.5	144	130	-156	3 558	1.0	2.59	8.5	24.5
Blackford	10.7	8.3	7.1	50.8	13 852	14 067	-0.1	-1.4	222	206	-212	5 690	4.7	2.44	10.0	25.9
Boone	8.9	5.8	6.0	51.2	47 408	38 147	20.9	2.8	740	484	1 035	17 081	22.7	2.65	7.8	21.1
Brown	12.5	7.6	5.2	49.8	15 124	14 080	6.2	1.1	205	151	106	5 897	9.8	2.51	6.5	20.6
Carroll	9.9	7.2	6.7	50.1	20 257	18 809	7.2	0.5	303	243	38	7 718	9.2	2.59	6.5	22.8
Cass	9.4	7.3	7.2	49.7	40 927	38 413	6.6	0.0	723	548	-163	15 715	7.2	2.53	9.4	25.9
Clark	9.4	6.8	5.6	51.4	97 364	87 774	9.9	0.9	1 595	1 179	513	38 751	16.4	2.45	12.5	26.3
Clay	9.3	7.6	7.5	51.5	26 602	24 705	7.5	0.2	436	362	-16	10 216	8.9	2.57	9.4	23.8
Clinton	8.4	6.9	7.5	50.7	33 749	30 974	9.3	-0.3	594	490	-213	12 545	9.6	2.63	9.0	23.6
Crawford	10.4	7.2	5.4	49.7	10 920	9 914	8.4	1.6	151	135	162	4 181	14.2	2.55	9.5	22.5
Daviess	9.0	7.2	7.5	50.7	29 652	27 533	8.3	-0.6	547	406	-307	10 894	8.8	2.69	8.7	25.0
Dearborn	9.0	6.3	4.9	50.5	46 806	38 835	18.7	1.5	650	443	497	16 832	23.4	2.71	9.6	20.1
Decatur	9.3	7.0	6.3	50.6	24 493	23 645	3.8	-0.3	488	307	-239	9 389	11.4	2.58	9.2	22.8
De Kalb	8.3	5.9	5.5	50.2	40 398	35 324	14.0	0.3	722	442	-155	15 134	18.9	2.63	8.8	23.4
Delaware	9.4	7.1	6.4	52.0	118 531	119 659	-0.7	-0.2	1 799	1 491	-503	47 131	4.3	2.37	10.9	28.2
Dubois	8.7	6.7	6.2	50.5	39 805	36 616	8.4	0.3	664	444	-72	14 813	13.7	2.63	7.4	23.5
Elkhart	8.1	5.6	5.2	50.3	184 186	156 198	17.0	0.8	3 801	1 719	-640	66 154	16.6	2.72	10.5	22.6
Fayette	9.9	8.1	7.3	51.5	25 306	26 015	-1.6	-1.1	401	372	-305	10 199	2.6	2.46	10.2	25.8
Floyd	8.9	6.5	5.8	51.8	71 348	64 404	10.0	0.7	1 084	891	352	27 511	14.2	2.54	12.4	23.5
Fountain	10.5	8.2	7.4	50.4	17 815	17 808	0.8	-0.8	284	290	-129	7 041	2.7	2.52	8.0	24.8
Franklin	9.0	6.8	5.7	50.1	22 284	19 580	13.1	0.6	283	209	65	7 868	18.6	2.77	8.0	19.0
Fulton	10.2	8.0	7.3	50.6	20 664	18 840	8.9	0.7	344	255	74	8 082	10.0	2.52	7.5	24.9
Gibson	9.5	8.0	7.5	51.1	32 716	31 913	1.8	0.7	513	442	156	12 847	4.5	2.48	9.2	25.7
Grant	10.3	8.0	6.9	52.0	72 605	74 169	-1.0	-1.1	1 105	1 006	-886	28 319	2.2	2.43	11.5	26.7
Greene	10.1	7.8	7.4	50.8	33 171	30 410	9.0	0.0	447	456	36	13 372	12.3	2.44	8.4	26.5
Hamilton	7.3	4.2	3.2	50.8	197 477	108 936	67.7	8.1	3 551	1 090	11 950	65 933	69.8	2.75	7.0	18.6
Hancock	10.2	6.4	4.9	50.6	57 160	45 527	21.7	3.2	886	531	1 393	20 718	29.8	2.65	7.4	18.8
Harrison	9.2	6.5	5.0	50.2	34 929	29 890	14.8	1.8	549	379	435	12 917	21.7	2.63	8.8	20.7
Hendricks	8.7	5.4	4.4	49.9	110 784	75 717	37.5	6.4	1 514	858	5 875	37 275	42.8	2.71	7.7	18.3
Henry	10.5	8.3	7.4	51.8	48 408	48 139	0.8	-0.2	772	616	-241	19 486	4.5	2.45	9.9	24.8
Howard	10.3	7.3	6.0	51.6	84 944	80 827	5.1	0.0	1 493	1 021	-471	34 800	10.4	2.41	11.5	28.2
Huntington	8.7	6.6	7.5	51.3	38 024	35 427	7.5	-0.1	649	500	-195	14 242	11.0	2.57	9.1	23.6
Jackson	9.2	7.0	6.3	50.7	41 258	37 730	9.6	-0.2	719	496	-291	16 052	14.4	2.54	9.9	23.5
Jasper	9.1	6.8	5.7	50.4	30 551	24 823	21.0	1.7	505	342	349	10 686	25.3	2.72	7.7	19.9
Jay	10.2	7.5	7.2	51.0	21 769	21 512	1.4	-0.2	418	310	-137	8 405	3.0	2.57	9.1	24.8
Jefferson	9.8	7.1	6.0	50.5	32 051	29 797	6.4	1.1	458	387	276	12 148	11.5	2.46	10.6	25.7
Jennings	9.5	6.1	4.6	50.3	28 097	23 661	16.5	2.0	518	296	322	10 134	21.4	2.67	9.5	20.6
Johnson	8.6	5.7	5.3	51.0	119 240	88 109	30.8	3.5	2 026	1 105	3 059	42 434	35.3	2.63	9.0	21.2
Knox	9.5	7.6	7.7	50.4	38 822	39 884	-1.6	-1.1	575	633	-367	15 552	2.7	2.36	10.2	29.7
Kosciusko	9.2	6.2	5.7	50.1	74 605	65 294	13.4	0.7	1 389	742	-73	27 283	16.4	2.66	8.3	21.9
Lagrange	8.3	5.7	4.4	49.4	35 309	29 477	18.4	1.1	899	296	-193	11 225	21.9	3.09	6.9	18.0
Lake	8.9	7.0	6.0	51.8	485 448	475 594	1.9	0.2	9 220	5 822	-2 369	181 633	6.4	2.64	16.6	25.8
La Porte	9.2	7.1	6.4	48.7	110 585	107 066	2.8	0.4	1 826	1 280	-14	41 050	6.7	2.52	11.7	25.2
Lawrence	10.4	8.1	6.7	51.3	46 020	42 836	7.2	0.2	696	623	45	18 535	14.2	2.44	9.0	25.5
Madison	10.0	7.8	7.1	50.7	132 352	130 669	2.1	-0.8	2 215	1 830	-1 360	53 052	6.5	2.41	11.8	27.2
Marion	7.6	5.8	5.3	51.7	856 938	797 159	7.9	-0.4	18 098	9 726	-11 932	352 164	10.2	2.39	14.9	31.8
Marshall	8.7	6.9	6.4	50.3	45 796	42 182	7.0	1.5	846	492	326	16 519	9.1	2.69	8.3	22.3
Martin	10.5	7.8	6.4	49.4	10 383	10 369	0.0	0.1	187	138	-31	4 183	9.0	2.45	8.2	27.6
Miami	9.2	7.0	5.9	49.2	36 269	36 897	-2.2	0.5	556	394	33	13 716	1.7	2.52	9.8	24.6
Monroe	6.7	4.9	4.3	50.9	119 880	108 978	10.6	-0.6	1 611	910	-1 385	46 898	19.2	2.27	8.1	32.4
Montgomery	9.8	7.2	6.7	50.1	37 840	34 436	9.3	0.6	619	483	91	14 595	10.3	2.50	8.6	25.3
Morgan	9.5	6.2	4.5	50.3	67 513	55 920	19.3	1.2	1 186	630	293	24 437	24.7	2.70	8.6	18.4
Newton	10.2	6.8	6.0	50.3	14 436	13 551	7.5	-0.9	236	179	-186	5 340	10.4	2.69	7.8	20.9
Noble	7.9	5.8	5.2	49.6	46 926	37 877	22.2	1.4	942	493	223	16 696	24.4	2.73	9.0	21.9
Ohio	10.8	7.6	6.1	50.8	5 726	5 315	5.8	1.8	68	48	83	2 201	11.2	2.53	8.5	23.2
Orange	10.1	7.9	6.9	50.8	19 442	18 409	4.9	0.7	293	284	134	7 621	9.7	2.49	8.6	26.2
Owen	10.3	7.6	5.3	50.3	22 115	17 281	26.1	1.5	304	234	262	8 282	29.5	2.60	8.5	21.3
Parke	11.2	8.1	6.6	52.3	17 233	15 410	11.9	0.0	215	201	-21	6 415	9.8	2.51	8.3	24.1
Perry	9.1	7.7	7.2	48.3	18 878	19 107	-1.1	-0.1	270	256	-26	7 270	6.2	2.45	9.0	26.7
Pike	11.0	8.1	7.2	50.0	12 928	12 509	2.6	0.7	212	188	69	5 119	3.9	2.47	8.4	24.9
Porter	9.2	5.9	5.0	50.9	148 769	128 932	13.9	1.3	2 170	1 434	1 267	54 649	21.0	2.62	9.2	22.2
Posey	9.4	6.8	5.6	50.2	27 067	25 968	4.2	0.0	346	272	-58	10 205	7.3	2.63	7.8	22.1
Pulaski	9.7	7.8	7.5	49.6	13 988	12 780	7.6	1.7	246	191	179	5 170	9.5	2.59	7.3	23.5

1. No spouse present.

Table B. States and Counties — Vital Statistics, Health Resources, and Crime

STATE County	Births, average 1997–1999		Deaths, average 1997–1999				Physicians,[4] 2000		Hospitals,[4] 1998			Medicare enrollees 2000	Serious crimes known to police, 2000[6]	
			Number		Rate					Beds			Total	
	Total	Rate[1]	Total	Infant[2]	Total[1]	Infant[3]	Number	Rate[5]	Number	Number	Rate[5]		Number	Rate[7]
	32	33	34	35	36	37	38	39	40	41	42	43	44	45
INDIANA	83 838	14.2	53 970	672	9.1	8.0	10 572	174	117	19 596	332	852 228	228 135	3 752
Adams	593	18.0	264	NA	8.0	NA	17	51	1	87	263	4 560	NA	NA
Allen	4 983	15.8	2 577	42	8.2	8.4	681	205	3	1 042	332	42 553	14 726	4 438
Bartholomew	1 006	14.5	609	9	8.8	8.6	157	220	2	237	341	9 819	2 788	3 919
Benton	141	14.5	96	NA	9.9	NA	2	21	0	0	0	1 704	NA	NA
Blackford	182	13.1	157	NA	11.3	NA	7	50	1	28	201	2 413	262	1 865
Boone	597	13.6	398	NA	9.1	NA	78	169	1	49	112	5 510	NA	NA
Brown	149	9.4	121	NA	7.6	NA	7	47	0	0	0	1 308	225	1 504
Carroll	265	13.3	192	NA	9.6	NA	10	50	0	0	0	2 599	NA	NA
Cass	568	14.6	409	NA	10.5	NA	65	159	1	112	290	6 717	NA	NA
Clark	1 220	13.0	938	13	10.0	10.4	147	152	2	376	401	14 339	5 238	5 430
Clay	341	12.8	280	NA	10.5	NA	20	75	1	55	206	4 923	452	1 702
Clinton	484	14.6	375	NA	11.3	NA	20	59	1	53	160	5 206	921	2 720
Crawford	137	13.0	107	NA	10.1	NA	2	19	0	0	0	1 858	NA	NA
Daviess	427	14.7	311	NA	10.8	NA	22	74	1	85	293	4 462	NA	NA
Dearborn	645	13.7	358	NA	7.6	NA	44	95	1	76	161	6 141	595	1 436
Decatur	374	14.6	233	NA	9.1	NA	20	81	1	73	286	3 846	NA	NA
De Kalb	598	15.2	343	NA	8.7	NA	31	77	1	45	114	5 155	NA	NA
Delaware	1 412	12.1	1 134	10	9.7	6.8	267	225	1	428	366	18 270	1 293	1 089
Dubois	569	14.4	354	NA	8.9	NA	52	131	2	191	481	5 579	NA	NA
Elkhart	2 943	17.1	1 369	23	7.9	7.9	228	125	2	476	276	22 082	9 718	5 316
Fayette	342	13.2	291	NA	11.2	NA	19	74	1	140	539	4 664	NA	NA
Floyd	902	12.6	655	NA	9.1	NA	114	161	1	174	242	10 218	3 556	5 021
Fountain	251	13.7	232	NA	12.7	NA	5	28	0	0	0	3 546	NA	NA
Franklin	268	12.3	170	NA	7.8	NA	12	54	0	0	0	2 779	NA	NA
Fulton	272	13.2	200	NA	9.7	NA	21	102	1	49	238	3 483	NA	NA
Gibson	403	12.6	329	NA	10.2	NA	23	71	2	135	420	5 642	332	1 110
Grant	892	12.3	784	9	10.8	9.7	126	172	1	212	292	12 736	1 330	1 812
Greene	396	11.9	353	NA	10.6	NA	18	54	1	76	227	5 665	NA	NA
Hamilton	2 623	16.1	822	16	5.0	6.1	312	171	2	199	122	13 729	NA	NA
Hancock	710	13.0	427	NA	7.8	NA	67	121	1	70	128	6 793	591	1 067
Harrison	428	12.3	271	NA	7.8	NA	29	84	1	45	130	4 868	727	2 118
Hendricks	1 223	12.8	666	NA	7.0	NA	107	103	1	127	133	10 559	NA	NA
Henry	590	12.1	515	NA	10.6	NA	47	97	1	107	219	8 833	2 462	5 075
Howard	1 160	13.9	795	NA	9.5	NA	143	168	2	300	359	13 418	3 310	3 896
Huntington	511	13.7	379	NA	10.2	NA	22	58	1	75	201	6 172	626	1 644
Jackson	586	14.3	405	NA	9.8	NA	37	90	1	107	261	6 593	NA	NA
Jasper	383	13.1	247	NA	8.5	NA	17	57	1	69	236	4 333	NA	NA
Jay	324	14.9	240	NA	11.0	NA	12	55	1	71	327	3 833	NA	NA
Jefferson	395	12.5	316	NA	10.0	NA	43	136	1	119	378	4 957	482	1 520
Jennings	395	14.2	239	NA	8.6	NA	10	36	1	34	122	3 815	NA	NA
Johnson	1 500	13.7	860	NA	7.8	NA	107	93	2	180	165	14 106	NA	NA
Knox	461	11.7	477	NA	12.1	NA	77	196	1	301	764	7 020	NA	NA
Kosciusko	1 112	15.7	606	11	8.5	9.6	56	76	1	113	159	9 753	1 494	2 132
Lagrange	694	20.8	211	NA	6.3	NA	12	34	1	62	185	3 424	NA	NA
Lake	6 941	14.5	4 651	69	9.7	10.0	912	188	8	2 289	479	71 970	18 469	4 739
La Porte	1 440	13.2	1 012	10	9.2	6.9	160	145	3	468	428	16 338	5 239	4 822
Lawrence	589	12.9	474	NA	10.4	NA	45	98	2	245	537	7 573	944	2 283
Madison	1 676	12.7	1 399	21	10.6	12.3	171	128	3	659	502	22 585	NA	NA
Marion	13 535	16.6	7 696	141	9.5	10.4	3 152	366	11	4 037	496	111 961	40 511	4 708
Marshall	693	15.2	392	NA	8.6	NA	44	98	2	63	139	6 562	NA	NA
Martin	144	13.7	109	NA	10.4	NA	3	29	0	0	0	1 853	150	1 447
Miami	477	14.3	322	NA	9.6	NA	28	78	1	135	402	5 270	NA	NA
Monroe	1 277	11.0	703	9	6.1	7.3	235	195	1	265	230	12 644	4 316	3 580
Montgomery	496	13.6	381	NA	10.5	NA	54	144	1	120	330	5 814	904	2 402
Morgan	919	14.0	504	NA	7.7	NA	53	79	2	191	292	8 084	NA	NA
Newton	171	11.6	133	NA	9.0	NA	7	48	0	0	0	1 860	173	1 188
Noble	698	16.4	374	NA	8.8	NA	27	58	1	51	120	5 650	NA	NA
Ohio	63	11.7	53	NA	9.8	NA	1	18	0	0	0	776	NA	NA
Orange	248	12.7	221	NA	11.3	NA	14	73	1	37	189	3 259	170	881
Owen	242	11.9	183	NA	9.0	NA	3	14	0	0	0	2 794	NA	NA
Parke	185	11.1	159	NA	9.5	NA	11	64	0	0	0	2 788	NA	NA
Perry	211	11.0	192	NA	10.0	NA	11	58	1	44	227	3 179	NA	NA
Pike	159	12.3	143	NA	11.1	NA	5	39	0	0	0	2 184	NA	NA
Porter	1 775	12.2	1 106	14	7.6	7.7	176	120	1	367	252	17 188	3 988	2 717
Posey	305	11.6	228	NA	8.7	NA	10	37	0	0	0	3 626	NA	NA
Pulaski	174	13.1	138	NA	10.4	NA	8	58	1	47	355	2 329	89	647

1. Per 1,000 estimated resident population, average 1997–1999. 2. Deaths of infants under 1 year old. 3. Deaths of infants under 1 year old per 1,000 live births. 4. Data subject to copyright. 5. Per 100,000 resident population as of July 1 of the year shown. 6. Data for serious crimes have not been adjusted for underreporting; this may affect comparability between geographic areas and over time. 7. Per 100,000 population estimated by the FBI.

Table B. States and Counties — Crime, Education, Money Income, and Poverty

STATE County	Serious crimes known to police, 2000[1] (cont'd) Rate[2] Violent	Property	Education — Enrollment[3] Total	Percent private	High school graduate or more	Bachelor's degree or more	Local government expenditures, fiscal 1999[5] Total current expenditures (mil dol)	Current expenditures per student (dollars)	Money income 1989 Per capita[6] (dollars)	Households Median Dollars	Percent change, 1979–1989 (constant 1989 dollars)	Percent with $100,000 or more	Income and poverty, 1998 Median household income	Percent below poverty level All persons	Persons under 18	Persons 5–17 in families
	46	47	48	49	50	51	52	53	54	55	56	57	58	59	60	61
INDIANA	349	3 403	1 436 188	14.1	75.6	15.6	6 697.5	6 772	13 149	28 797	-2.3	2.5	39 719	10.0	14.1	12.6
Adams	NA	NA	7 979	17.4	74.4	10.7	31.3	5 992	11 655	28 792	-2.3	2.2	39 849	10.7	15.8	14.0
Allen	288	4 149	80 225	21.1	81.2	19.0	349.4	6 773	14 631	31 835	-0.5	3.1	44 141	9.0	13.3	11.2
Bartholomew	129	3 790	15 078	10.7	76.9	16.9	74.2	6 031	14 216	30 971	-5.3	3.0	45 190	7.9	11.9	10.2
Benton	NA	NA	2 279	8.3	77.1	9.2	14.7	6 869	12 024	26 860	-3.0	2.0	38 126	8.3	11.5	10.5
Blackford	71	1 794	3 103	6.7	73.0	8.9	15.3	6 254	11 151	25 523	-2.9	0.8	35 894	10.9	17.2	14.6
Boone	NA	NA	9 325	9.0	82.5	22.2	47.9	5 790	16 674	34 652	6.4	6.0	53 811	5.6	8.2	6.9
Brown	87	1 417	2 780	9.2	76.4	15.2	16.1	6 357	13 048	29 425	6.5	1.5	44 673	8.1	12.7	10.9
Carroll	NA	NA	4 493	6.4	76.2	10.0	16.5	5 655	12 165	28 506	-1.8	1.2	42 324	7.7	11.6	9.5
Cass	NA	NA	8 934	6.6	75.9	9.0	49.1	7 247	11 860	25 963	-11.8	1.6	36 311	10.0	14.2	12.8
Clark	369	5 061	21 453	9.8	72.8	11.2	94.9	6 639	12 068	27 386	-4.0	1.3	37 991	9.6	14.4	12.8
Clay	147	1 555	5 854	5.6	75.9	9.8	27.8	5 901	10 538	23 470	-5.9	1.1	34 875	11.3	16.5	14.0
Clinton	145	2 575	7 223	7.0	76.2	11.0	37.8	5 835	11 849	26 148	-3.4	1.6	39 345	8.8	12.1	11.2
Crawford	NA	NA	2 224	6.5	59.6	5.7	12.0	6 328	8 837	20 367	3.5	0.4	30 630	15.1	19.6	21.1
Daviess	NA	NA	6 186	16.6	66.2	7.6	28.4	6 291	10 176	22 801	8.2	1.2	32 441	13.9	18.9	17.7
Dearborn	111	1 325	9 677	11.0	73.5	10.7	53.0	6 018	12 542	31 398	5.8	2.1	45 526	7.2	10.0	8.8
Decatur	NA	NA	5 816	8.2	72.3	9.7	26.6	6 119	11 930	27 701	5.2	2.1	40 880	8.9	12.1	10.7
De Kalb	NA	NA	8 630	7.5	77.5	9.0	48.7	6 526	12 665	30 970	1.4	2.2	44 637	5.9	8.1	7.1
Delaware	93	996	37 870	5.0	74.5	16.5	121.7	7 177	12 168	24 436	-11.4	2.0	35 299	13.6	18.5	16.8
Dubois	NA	NA	8 723	10.3	72.2	10.9	48.9	6 552	12 942	31 227	5.5	2.8	46 041	5.1	6.9	6.0
Elkhart	408	4 908	36 915	15.3	72.8	14.2	215.8	6 747	13 825	30 973	5.0	3.2	42 199	8.9	13.4	11.7
Fayette	NA	NA	6 278	7.5	63.9	8.1	35.6	7 821	11 577	25 565	0.9	1.1	36 156	11.2	14.6	14.2
Floyd	364	4 657	16 375	10.0	73.2	15.1	81.4	7 055	13 203	28 460	-1.8	2.2	40 608	9.6	13.6	12.6
Fountain	NA	NA	3 891	4.9	73.0	7.6	20.6	6 057	11 470	24 772	-7.0	1.3	36 311	9.8	14.2	12.7
Franklin	NA	NA	4 932	15.0	65.3	8.2	16.6	5 579	11 295	27 734	5.7	2.0	40 904	8.9	13.4	10.2
Fulton	NA	NA	4 208	6.0	75.3	9.4	15.3	5 380	11 164	26 141	-1.4	0.9	36 706	9.6	13.6	12.4
Gibson	207	903	7 666	13.6	72.8	9.1	36.3	7 123	11 615	25 985	-5.8	1.1	36 764	9.1	12.4	10.8
Grant	148	1 663	18 682	18.8	71.8	11.2	79.0	6 721	12 308	26 248	-8.0	1.7	35 355	13.3	19.7	17.5
Greene	NA	NA	7 097	4.8	71.6	9.9	38.3	6 458	10 798	23 139	4.2	0.5	34 109	10.8	14.6	13.9
Hamilton	NA	NA	29 183	15.8	88.7	36.2	200.8	6 467	20 426	45 748	11.8	10.3	72 530	3.2	4.6	3.7
Hancock	43	1 024	11 722	8.7	80.1	14.9	62.0	6 223	15 059	37 333	2.5	3.6	53 737	5.0	7.2	5.9
Harrison	87	2 031	7 389	8.5	71.1	8.4	36.6	5 936	11 159	27 238	0.3	1.1	40 055	9.3	12.2	11.6
Hendricks	NA	NA	19 683	12.9	84.1	18.2	101.9	5 704	15 526	39 892	5.0	3.8	58 323	4.3	6.3	5.2
Henry	49	5 026	10 733	4.9	71.4	9.2	58.9	6 826	11 914	25 668	-5.3	0.9	36 947	10.5	15.4	13.2
Howard	324	3 572	20 658	9.5	78.5	14.3	101.9	7 283	14 346	31 511	-2.2	2.2	45 037	10.3	15.9	13.7
Huntington	92	1 552	8 791	14.5	78.6	11.8	40.4	6 023	12 509	29 681	3.9	1.3	41 060	7.5	10.2	9.2
Jackson	NA	NA	8 630	9.8	69.3	8.7	37.6	5 724	11 562	25 767	-2.4	1.4	37 236	9.4	12.6	12.2
Jasper	NA	NA	7 012	22.0	75.5	10.8	29.0	5 894	11 256	28 546	-9.5	1.4	42 769	7.8	10.4	9.1
Jay	NA	NA	4 734	4.7	68.9	8.2	26.6	6 687	10 331	23 705	-3.4	0.7	33 325	10.6	15.0	13.6
Jefferson	107	1 413	7 804	20.8	70.3	13.3	37.3	7 562	11 631	24 820	0.6	1.7	34 426	11.8	16.5	15.1
Jennings	NA	NA	5 283	7.4	64.1	6.5	26.7	5 536	10 333	24 617	-7.9	0.9	33 375	10.1	13.5	12.8
Johnson	NA	NA	22 431	14.1	80.4	16.7	116.9	5 857	14 992	35 035	0.5	3.6	51 221	6.0	8.4	7.0
Knox	NA	NA	11 715	6.8	74.5	11.1	39.5	6 408	11 077	21 550	-2.5	2.2	31 672	15.0	19.9	18.9
Kosciusko	117	2 015	16 151	14.0	77.5	14.4	90.0	6 347	13 323	31 666	12.8	2.7	43 973	6.5	9.1	7.9
Lagrange	NA	NA	7 151	23.1	56.7	7.3	37.1	5 788	10 011	27 296	4.3	1.4	40 983	8.7	12.2	11.2
Lake	610	4 129	130 444	15.0	73.5	12.8	606.6	7 209	12 663	30 439	-14.8	2.1	40 030	13.0	19.0	16.4
La Porte	246	4 576	25 986	12.3	73.9	11.7	119.8	6 641	12 973	28 469	-9.2	2.3	40 113	10.4	15.1	13.2
Lawrence	80	2 203	9 248	6.7	69.7	9.4	46.8	6 225	11 492	25 764	4.2	0.6	37 532	9.5	13.3	11.9
Madison	NA	NA	31 071	14.2	73.5	11.7	132.2	6 493	12 811	27 435	-8.5	1.8	37 048	11.4	17.1	15.0
Marion	822	3 886	188 566	18.8	76.8	21.4	940.3	7 511	14 614	29 152	0.0	3.1	40 114	11.9	18.2	15.6
Marshall	NA	NA	10 517	10.1	74.0	12.3	52.8	6 623	12 428	28 311	2.3	1.8	41 629	7.5	10.2	9.3
Martin	164	1 283	2 466	7.0	64.4	8.6	11.2	5 818	10 177	23 344	0.0	0.4	35 337	11.2	16.0	15.7
Miami	NA	NA	9 139	6.6	76.4	9.7	45.8	5 983	10 862	24 441	-6.8	0.8	36 920	10.8	14.8	14.3
Monroe	173	3 407	47 386	4.6	82.1	32.9	86.3	6 486	12 017	24 781	7.8	2.9	37 333	11.7	13.5	13.0
Montgomery	48	2 355	8 081	15.3	80.0	12.8	42.3	6 372	12 419	28 020	-0.2	1.4	39 899	9.1	12.1	11.7
Morgan	NA	NA	13 660	7.8	73.6	10.0	65.7	5 748	13 068	32 762	-1.0	1.7	45 999	7.5	9.8	9.6
Newton	172	1 016	3 399	8.2	72.4	8.1	17.9	6 131	11 925	28 624	-5.3	1.8	38 358	9.6	11.8	13.2
Noble	NA	NA	9 306	6.7	72.1	8.0	45.5	5 765	11 772	29 845	8.2	1.3	42 047	7.0	9.8	8.8
Ohio	NA	NA	1 285	3.3	67.7	6.0	5.5	5 364	10 786	26 237	2.2	0.3	41 513	7.0	9.6	9.0
Orange	104	777	4 123	4.1	64.9	6.0	21.3	6 216	9 222	21 015	2.1	0.5	30 971	13.4	17.3	18.0
Owen	NA	NA	3 883	5.4	66.3	7.1	18.5	5 903	10 572	23 404	-0.3	0.7	34 929	11.1	14.0	15.8
Parke	NA	NA	3 391	7.0	76.7	10.1	15.3	5 545	11 058	24 514	-1.1	1.7	34 149	12.6	16.9	17.2
Perry	NA	NA	4 152	4.6	65.4	6.8	20.4	6 060	10 567	24 158	-4.6	0.8	36 229	9.1	10.9	10.6
Pike	NA	NA	2 784	4.8	65.5	8.5	14.1	6 334	10 934	23 096	-7.2	1.2	34 083	10.4	14.4	14.7
Porter	95	2 621	36 980	19.7	82.4	18.5	169.9	6 580	15 059	37 142	-8.4	3.7	52 869	6.1	8.0	7.1
Posey	NA	NA	6 522	14.6	76.3	11.0	34.1	7 225	12 879	31 530	0.1	1.8	46 605	8.2	11.2	10.2
Pulaski	153	494	3 124	4.2	71.9	8.9	16.0	6 179	11 107	25 418	1.4	1.5	36 861	10.0	13.3	13.1

1. Data for serious crimes have not been adjusted for underreporting; this may affect comparability between geographic areas and over time.   2. Per 100,000 population estimated by the FBI.   3. All persons 3 years old and over enrolled in nursery school through college.   4. Persons 25 years old and over.   5. Elementary and secondary education expenditures, local government fiscal years ending between July 1, 1998 and June 30, 1999.   6. Based on population enumerated as of April 1, 1990.

Table B. States and Counties — **Personal Income**

STATE County	Personal income, 1999		Per capita[1]					Transfer payments		Government payments to individuals				
	Total (mil dol)	Percent change, 1998–1999	Dollars	Rank	Wages and salaries[2] (mil dol)	Proprietor's income (mil dol)	Dividends, interest, and rent (mil dol)	Total (mil dol)	Total (mil dol)	Social Security (mil dol)	Medical payments (mil dol)	Income mainte-nance (mil dol)	Unemploy-ment insurance (mil dol)
	62	63	64	65	66	67	68	69	70	71	72	73	74
INDIANA	155 448	4.7	26 157	X	101 117	9 412	28 862	20 001	18 844	8 926	7 254	1 469	266
Adams	757	5.4	22 812	1 141	451	43	144	94	88	49	31	5	1
Allen	9 173	4.0	28 985	261	6 983	519	1 885	983	921	456	341	71	12
Bartholomew	2 041	3.7	29 271	246	1 697	121	430	217	203	106	76	14	1
Benton	220	2.8	22 518	1 213	74	15	47	32	30	17	10	2	0
Blackford	285	3.4	20 456	1 848	130	14	55	53	50	27	18	4	1
Boone	1 549	6.3	34 544	91	420	90	350	128	120	64	45	5	1
Brown	416	5.3	25 990	517	66	30	91	44	41	25	11	2	1
Carroll	470	2.2	23 483	965	153	34	98	60	56	33	17	3	1
Cass	910	3.5	23 362	998	514	47	160	158	150	66	64	8	1
Clark	2 374	5.9	24 955	679	1 430	137	394	341	322	143	133	24	5
Clay	552	5.5	20 520	1 830	213	41	101	105	99	47	39	7	1
Clinton	743	1.7	22 540	1 207	346	37	140	111	105	51	39	7	1
Crawford	202	9.0	18 841	2 335	52	16	26	42	40	17	16	4	1
Daviess	607	5.6	20 882	1 705	269	54	132	107	101	39	43	8	2
Dearborn	1 173	6.4	24 441	773	441	68	182	140	130	68	48	8	2
Decatur	633	5.7	24 638	726	404	32	123	80	75	38	28	5	1
De Kalb	984	3.9	24 808	700	798	55	161	111	103	53	38	5	1
Delaware	2 813	3.6	24 362	791	1 744	162	522	453	430	196	162	40	6
Dubois	1 180	3.8	29 424	238	895	62	320	122	114	57	48	4	2
Elkhart	4 605	5.9	26 360	480	4 203	245	863	500	466	235	170	34	7
Fayette	577	3.3	22 307	1 272	394	31	112	114	109	49	46	9	2
Floyd	1 951	5.9	27 009	416	844	116	362	245	231	103	91	19	4
Fountain	382	2.3	20 773	1 746	162	32	72	66	63	33	23	4	1
Franklin	476	3.5	21 512	1 519	103	34	114	64	60	33	19	4	1
Fulton	434	1.9	20 776	1 745	214	38	86	70	66	36	22	4	1
Gibson	743	4.5	23 042	1 078	363	39	152	121	115	56	42	6	2
Grant	1 604	4.8	22 247	1 287	1 058	80	279	308	294	134	119	23	3
Greene	637	3.0	19 220	2 228	219	36	125	118	112	51	43	8	3
Hamilton	6 959	9.6	40 435	42	3 097	473	1 354	335	301	165	109	11	3
Hancock	1 628	9.5	29 269	247	578	99	277	151	140	75	51	6	2
Harrison	830	10.8	23 459	969	308	39	125	104	97	47	36	7	1
Hendricks	2 886	7.9	29 200	250	884	141	440	237	218	117	78	8	3
Henry	1 150	3.2	23 773	903	520	53	194	194	185	93	70	13	3
Howard	2 313	5.6	27 623	360	2 246	93	389	313	297	147	115	22	3
Huntington	904	3.4	24 185	824	478	42	166	119	111	59	38	5	1
Jackson	921	6.8	22 301	1 274	638	47	143	137	129	65	49	9	1
Jasper	594	2.5	20 173	1 942	310	51	119	90	84	45	28	5	2
Jay	414	3.1	19 079	2 263	211	36	66	78	74	38	28	5	1
Jefferson	643	4.7	20 207	1 927	377	42	130	122	116	50	51	9	2
Jennings	598	7.7	21 262	1 578	249	38	64	118	112	38	63	6	1
Johnson	3 182	7.0	28 230	303	1 111	162	540	300	278	146	102	13	3
Knox	889	3.0	22 759	1 150	481	71	181	180	173	67	78	15	2
Kosciusko	1 842	3.3	25 826	538	1 193	95	395	207	193	105	68	9	4
Lagrange	653	6.6	19 215	2 229	432	51	111	74	68	37	22	5	2
Lake	12 173	4.2	25 328	608	7 378	520	2 024	1 911	1 818	789	709	218	28
La Porte	2 588	2.6	23 538	956	1 464	168	495	381	360	176	137	25	5
Lawrence	989	2.5	21 620	1 476	502	70	169	171	162	73	68	10	3
Madison	3 112	4.6	23 759	907	1 652	162	526	524	499	246	192	38	7
Marion	24 884	3.5	30 685	187	24 928	1 788	4 722	2 889	2 731	1 150	1 106	267	39
Marshall	1 075	5.6	23 314	1 013	604	71	200	135	126	68	45	7	2
Martin	214	1.1	20 595	1 813	362	15	45	36	34	15	14	3	1
Miami	696	3.3	20 718	1 770	327	27	123	121	115	49	43	9	2
Monroe	2 801	4.6	23 957	868	1 905	200	584	304	281	133	102	21	5
Montgomery	848	1.7	23 184	1 051	576	56	167	129	122	61	48	7	2
Morgan	1 638	6.8	24 442	772	428	74	199	186	173	87	64	12	3
Newton	280	1.8	18 835	2 336	109	26	41	45	42	21	15	3	1
Noble	999	3.9	23 095	1 070	640	45	144	122	114	60	41	6	2
Ohio	121	2.1	22 220	1 295	57	7	18	17	16	8	6	1	0
Orange	377	2.1	18 999	2 279	182	33	65	75	71	30	31	6	2
Owen	370	3.7	17 944	2 550	115	32	51	65	61	30	22	5	1
Parke	338	5.3	19 985	1 996	87	24	58	61	58	28	22	4	1
Perry	397	4.4	20 788	1 740	177	19	84	66	62	32	23	4	2
Pike	278	4.5	21 369	1 555	110	15	47	52	49	22	20	3	1
Porter	4 223	5.8	28 584	277	2 022	221	670	419	390	202	145	17	8
Posey	703	3.3	26 748	435	387	43	145	85	79	39	29	6	1
Pulaski	298	1.9	22 030	1 355	142	33	67	48	45	24	16	3	1

1. Based on the resident population estimated as of July 1 of the year shown.   2. Includes other labor income.

STATE County	Earnings, 1999									Social Security beneficiaries, December 2000			Housing units, 1990	
			Goods-related[1]		Service-related and other[2]							Supplemental Security Income recipients, December 2000		Percent change, 1980–1990
	Total (mil dol)	Farm	Total	Manu-facturing	Total	Retail trade	Finance, insurance, and real estate	Services	Govern-ment	Number	Rate[3]		Total	
	75	76	77	78	79	80	81	82	83	84	85	86	87	88
INDIANA	110 529	0.2	36.5	29.5	50.0	9.3	6.2	22.3	13.3	999 089	164	88 041	2 246 046	7.4
Adams	493	-0.5	D	54.6	D	9.3	2.9	9.6	11.5	5 300	158	219	10 931	7.2
Allen	7 502	0.0	34.3	27.8	56.8	8.3	9.3	24.0	8.9	49 950	151	4 378	122 923	11.0
Bartholomew	1 818	0.0	55.3	50.3	34.6	7.1	6.2	13.8	10.2	11 770	165	983	25 432	6.0
Benton	89	1.4	D	20.2	D	9.1	5.0	16.9	22.6	1 795	191	90	3 833	-3.1
Blackford	143	-1.0	D	46.3	D	8.6	3.2	11.8	17.3	2 960	211	172	5 856	-3.6
Boone	510	2.0	30.9	16.5	52.1	9.6	5.7	21.2	15.0	6 824	148	256	14 516	7.7
Brown	97	0.0	20.8	8.0	D	15.8	5.0	27.5	22.8	2 861	191	76	6 997	16.0
Carroll	187	4.8	D	39.4	D	7.2	4.0	11.6	13.9	3 724	185	94	8 431	0.4
Cass	560	0.7	D	37.7	D	9.0	3.3	12.7	20.4	7 430	182	594	15 633	-0.9
Clark	1 566	0.1	D	18.8	D	13.1	3.3	19.0	18.8	16 733	173	1 660	35 313	6.7
Clay	254	1.7	D	38.6	D	12.6	3.6	12.1	16.4	5 473	206	498	10 606	3.1
Clinton	382	1.1	51.9	45.9	32.7	7.6	3.2	15.2	14.2	5 707	169	362	12 100	-0.5
Crawford	68	0.1	D	21.2	D	11.5	3.6	D	23.7	2 188	204	273	4 374	6.0
Daviess	323	2.9	37.3	18.2	42.9	10.9	3.4	12.7	16.9	5 169	173	436	10 985	4.1
Dearborn	509	0.1	29.8	20.5	54.3	10.8	4.3	27.3	16.0	7 663	166	434	14 532	17.1
Decatur	437	0.3	D	49.0	D	8.1	3.0	16.3	10.3	4 461	182	284	9 098	4.0
De Kalb	853	0.7	66.6	62.0	25.3	5.6	2.0	10.8	7.4	6 024	150	328	13 601	10.7
Delaware	1 906	0.6	D	24.0	D	10.4	4.5	26.8	18.2	21 646	182	2 613	48 793	2.5
Dubois	957	0.7	55.8	50.0	36.3	9.5	2.5	14.0	7.2	6 530	165	266	13 964	18.2
Elkhart	4 448	0.0	D	55.9	D	7.0	2.8	12.9	6.1	25 650	140	1 991	60 182	16.0
Fayette	425	-0.2	D	56.1	D	7.1	2.1	16.0	12.0	5 492	215	519	10 525	-1.0
Floyd	960	0.1	D	26.7	D	8.9	5.1	22.3	18.4	11 889	168	1 253	25 238	10.8
Fountain	194	0.0	D	47.2	D	8.8	3.6	10.6	14.6	3 825	213	256	7 344	-5.0
Franklin	137	-2.2	D	13.6	D	11.9	5.6	25.4	20.9	4 203	190	237	7 176	7.5
Fulton	252	1.0	D	38.8	D	10.7	4.4	12.9	14.1	4 128	201	173	8 656	0.3
Gibson	402	1.1	44.3	37.8	44.2	10.4	2.5	14.3	10.4	6 385	196	377	13 454	3.0
Grant	1 138	0.1	D	40.0	D	9.4	4.1	20.1	15.4	15 187	207	1 526	29 904	-0.9
Greene	255	-1.7	32.5	8.6	44.2	11.2	3.6	17.1	25.0	6 468	195	557	13 337	5.6
Hamilton	3 570	0.1	22.4	13.2	69.1	11.3	21.0	23.6	8.4	17 963	98	606	41 074	41.3
Hancock	677	0.1	43.8	31.8	40.2	8.7	5.1	15.7	16.1	8 394	152	287	16 495	8.8
Harrison	347	-0.9	32.3	24.6	52.0	10.2	3.7	28.5	16.7	5 927	173	446	11 456	14.9
Hendricks	1 025	0.0	D	7.3	D	15.3	3.5	20.2	20.2	13 002	125	353	26 962	14.1
Henry	573	0.2	D	41.2	D	10.7	3.4	14.4	17.7	10 539	217	749	19 835	-0.8
Howard	2 338	0.2	D	63.5	D	6.9	2.4	11.4	8.3	15 810	186	1 502	33 820	2.7
Huntington	519	0.5	48.5	42.3	37.9	10.7	4.0	15.1	13.1	6 715	176	312	13 629	2.6
Jackson	685	0.6	D	40.9	D	16.2	3.2	11.5	11.8	7 588	184	659	14 820	6.7
Jasper	361	1.5	29.4	17.7	54.2	12.0	2.8	14.0	14.9	5 108	170	232	8 984	2.7
Jay	247	2.4	D	43.7	D	9.9	3.7	14.7	15.3	4 358	200	322	8 905	-1.8
Jefferson	418	-0.4	D	30.0	D	11.9	3.0	24.3	16.7	5 985	189	669	11 921	6.8
Jennings	287	-0.3	D	29.5	D	12.2	2.1	15.7	22.8	4 720	171	432	9 129	16.8
Johnson	1 273	0.0	30.8	20.8	54.0	17.6	6.0	21.1	15.2	16 370	142	700	33 289	22.3
Knox	552	2.6	17.3	11.1	50.1	10.2	4.9	19.7	30.0	8 090	206	990	16 730	1.9
Kosciusko	1 288	1.0	D	55.8	D	7.6	3.1	13.5	7.6	11 756	159	486	30 516	4.0
Lagrange	483	2.3	D	58.1	D	8.0	2.2	9.0	9.3	4 293	123	165	12 218	15.5
Lake	7 898	0.1	34.5	26.2	52.2	9.4	3.8	26.7	13.2	84 666	175	10 531	183 014	-1.8
La Porte	1 632	0.5	D	28.1	D	10.6	3.4	22.8	15.7	19 100	173	1 507	42 268	4.2
Lawrence	572	0.0	D	41.4	D	11.3	3.1	16.2	15.0	8 966	195	828	17 587	6.1
Madison	1 815	0.2	D	37.7	D	10.4	4.1	22.9	13.5	26 445	198	2 474	53 353	0.0
Marion	26 716	0.1	26.7	21.1	61.2	8.4	9.2	27.7	12.0	127 169	148	16 426	349 403	12.9
Marshall	675	0.9	D	46.0	D	8.4	4.4	14.9	10.8	7 626	169	302	16 820	9.4
Martin	377	0.2	D	6.3	D	2.0	1.0	4.1	74.2	2 042	197	199	4 116	0.0
Miami	355	-1.3	D	28.8	D	9.6	3.2	11.9	31.7	5 722	159	506	14 639	0.2
Monroe	2 105	0.0	23.9	17.2	46.3	10.1	5.3	23.2	29.9	14 746	122	1 300	41 948	15.8
Montgomery	632	1.4	D	48.3	D	8.4	3.1	15.6	10.0	6 884	183	444	13 957	1.4
Morgan	502	0.0	32.8	19.7	48.3	13.2	4.4	19.5	18.9	9 803	147	643	20 500	12.3
Newton	136	3.4	D	36.7	D	6.3	3.8	8.5	18.0	2 436	167	104	5 276	-4.1
Noble	685	0.1	D	61.4	D	6.2	2.1	9.9	10.2	6 905	149	382	15 516	7.6
Ohio	64	-1.1	D	D	D	4.5	2.1	D	14.7	914	163	36	2 161	-0.4
Orange	215	0.0	47.9	30.8	36.0	9.4	3.1	15.7	16.1	3 996	207	442	7 732	3.8
Owen	147	-1.3	D	37.1	D	8.3	4.4	14.1	17.6	3 651	168	235	8 011	14.8
Parke	111	-0.4	D	20.9	D	10.5	3.8	18.7	29.8	3 299	191	334	7 189	-3.5
Perry	196	-1.0	D	35.9	D	10.0	3.9	13.0	24.4	3 684	195	289	7 404	0.9
Pike	125	1.7	31.5	5.9	51.5	6.1	2.2	9.4	15.3	2 617	204	243	5 487	0.9
Porter	2 243	0.2	D	32.4	D	9.4	3.8	20.3	13.4	21 488	146	1 110	47 240	13.8
Posey	430	0.2	D	48.1	D	4.5	2.0	12.5	10.4	4 494	166	327	10 401	4.7
Pulaski	174	6.3	D	35.4	D	7.0	3.6	11.4	18.4	2 725	198	177	5 541	2.3

1. Covers mining, construction, and manufacturing. 2. Covers private sector earnings in agricultural services, forestry, and fisheries; transportation and public utilities; wholesale trade; retail trade; finance, insurance, and real estate; and services. 3. Per 1,000 resident population estimated as of July 1 of the year shown.

STATE County	Housing units, 1990 (cont'd)								Civilian labor force, 2001		Unemployment		Civilian employment, 1990[5]		
	Occupied units												Percent		
		Owner-occupied				Renter-occupied									
				Owner cost as a percent of income											
	Total	Percent	Median value[1]	With a mortgage	Without a mortgage	Median rent[2]	Rent as percent of income	Sub-standard units[3] (percent)	Total	Percent change, 2000–2001	Total	Rate[4]	Total	Professional, managerial, and technical	Precision production, craft, and repair
	89	90	91	92	93	94	95	96	97	98	99	100	101	102	103
INDIANA	2 065 355	70.2	53 900	16.7	12.3	374	24.3	2.6	3 106 388	0.7	135 891	4.4	2 628 695	25.6	12.9
Adams	10 470	78.4	51 100	15.6	11.2	319	22.3	6.0	16 449	0.5	904	5.5	14 121	18.9	15.4
Allen	113 333	70.2	59 900	16.2	11.7	393	23.7	2.1	173 346	0.0	7 993	4.6	152 304	29.8	11.4
Bartholomew	24 192	73.2	57 200	16.6	11.8	396	24.0	1.9	37 937	-1.5	1 449	3.8	31 464	28.4	13.2
Benton	3 524	72.9	38 100	16.9	13.9	316	18.7	1.3	5 117	-1.4	181	3.5	4 429	18.1	13.0
Blackford	5 436	77.3	32 300	14.2	13.7	283	20.6	2.6	6 278	0.7	432	6.9	6 431	18.2	12.2
Boone	13 922	76.2	71 100	17.6	11.8	388	23.7	1.7	25 443	1.4	589	2.3	19 550	29.4	12.4
Brown	5 370	82.6	64 900	20.3	12.2	378	21.5	5.9	8 439	-1.9	293	3.5	6 773	24.9	17.5
Carroll	7 067	78.0	45 400	15.2	12.2	307	21.1	2.6	12 078	0.1	468	3.9	9 012	19.2	14.7
Cass	14 659	74.4	40 300	15.4	12.0	299	22.2	1.5	19 777	0.4	1 066	5.4	17 360	19.4	16.0
Clark	33 292	68.4	50 000	17.4	12.4	362	25.0	2.4	53 865	0.6	2 051	3.8	42 447	22.3	12.0
Clay	9 382	79.3	35 500	15.7	13.4	295	26.3	3.5	12 569	0.6	762	6.1	10 495	19.3	13.8
Clinton	11 450	72.0	40 900	15.1	12.8	326	23.3	2.4	15 908	1.4	618	3.9	13 916	19.7	15.6
Crawford	3 660	85.2	31 800	22.2	13.3	241	29.5	7.2	5 968	9.8	324	5.4	3 905	14.8	17.4
Daviess	10 012	78.0	40 600	16.7	13.0	277	22.6	4.2	13 580	0.3	538	4.0	11 734	18.7	15.0
Dearborn	13 642	78.3	59 900	17.2	12.2	321	22.9	3.4	24 010	1.4	849	3.5	17 649	23.3	16.2
Decatur	8 427	75.6	44 900	15.8	12.5	357	21.6	3.7	16 448	-1.3	428	2.6	11 214	17.3	14.7
De Kalb	12 725	81.2	49 700	16.0	12.2	345	21.0	1.8	21 806	0.7	1 230	5.6	17 747	17.7	15.2
Delaware	45 177	66.8	42 300	15.5	12.7	334	27.5	2.0	59 735	1.8	2 734	4.6	55 097	25.1	12.0
Dubois	13 023	78.7	58 000	17.1	11.8	316	18.1	2.7	22 843	0.3	629	2.8	19 280	19.0	14.5
Elkhart	56 713	71.8	62 300	17.0	11.6	405	23.3	2.3	94 834	-2.5	5 142	5.4	80 588	22.6	13.8
Fayette	9 945	69.9	41 100	14.3	12.4	304	23.7	3.1	10 569	-0.7	925	8.8	11 315	18.1	14.3
Floyd	24 085	71.8	57 600	17.6	12.5	349	25.1	2.3	39 543	0.3	1 252	3.2	30 306	28.1	12.9
Fountain	6 858	76.7	37 000	16.2	12.4	290	19.9	2.5	8 605	1.9	431	5.0	7 881	18.0	15.4
Franklin	6 636	79.5	53 300	18.0	11.4	284	23.9	4.8	11 625	3.5	512	4.4	8 857	16.4	15.6
Fulton	7 345	77.3	42 200	15.6	12.7	325	23.0	1.9	9 578	-1.7	715	7.5	8 754	16.3	15.6
Gibson	12 299	78.6	44 400	16.6	12.4	294	23.7	2.3	18 100	2.3	687	3.8	14 674	19.6	16.9
Grant	27 701	71.3	40 400	15.6	12.2	318	25.1	2.3	32 314	1.0	2 198	6.8	33 810	21.5	14.1
Greene	11 910	80.4	36 800	15.5	12.4	274	23.2	2.8	13 987	2.3	1 140	8.2	12 920	22.6	16.0
Hamilton	38 834	76.9	106 500	19.2	12.0	505	22.3	1.1	101 059	1.3	1 979	2.0	57 985	38.8	8.9
Hancock	15 959	80.0	72 000	16.1	11.8	386	22.6	2.2	31 372	1.3	833	2.7	23 112	27.7	14.7
Harrison	10 618	85.3	51 800	18.2	12.0	314	20.8	4.4	19 218	0.6	643	3.3	13 934	18.8	15.2
Hendricks	26 109	82.4	75 700	16.9	11.5	428	22.9	1.6	55 967	1.5	1 330	2.4	38 702	30.6	14.8
Henry	18 642	75.2	36 800	15.1	12.8	301	23.8	1.7	23 625	-0.3	1 199	5.1	21 215	21.4	14.2
Howard	31 523	72.1	51 700	14.6	12.2	364	25.0	1.8	41 546	0.1	2 622	6.3	37 041	23.9	16.1
Huntington	12 830	76.7	44 200	16.2	11.6	344	23.6	1.9	20 244	-0.2	1 057	5.2	17 621	20.4	14.7
Jackson	14 032	77.1	43 900	16.0	12.7	333	23.1	3.5	22 576	4.2	953	4.2	17 331	19.2	12.8
Jasper	8 527	75.4	55 100	16.5	12.0	326	21.0	2.2	14 704	2.2	803	5.5	11 217	19.4	15.8
Jay	8 161	77.6	32 400	15.8	12.8	281	20.0	2.6	10 803	3.0	706	6.5	9 999	16.1	15.6
Jefferson	10 897	73.2	44 900	19.3	12.2	295	22.1	3.9	13 570	1.2	636	4.7	13 710	24.1	14.4
Jennings	8 351	80.0	43 700	16.0	12.7	322	27.4	4.2	14 242	-0.9	702	4.9	10 765	17.5	17.1
Johnson	31 354	74.0	72 200	18.6	11.8	414	24.2	1.6	64 629	1.3	1 569	2.4	45 570	27.0	13.9
Knox	15 145	70.6	39 800	17.1	13.4	310	28.4	1.7	18 876	0.3	631	3.3	17 167	22.9	11.0
Kosciusko	23 449	79.0	60 600	16.3	11.8	378	22.2	3.3	38 382	0.1	1 818	4.7	32 769	20.9	14.3
Lagrange	9 209	81.4	55 100	17.2	12.7	338	19.6	6.8	16 766	-0.5	1 004	6.0	13 200	13.8	16.1
Lake	170 748	67.8	54 800	16.7	13.3	393	25.0	4.2	219 323	0.1	12 002	5.5	203 966	24.4	14.0
La Porte	38 488	73.1	52 700	16.6	13.4	368	23.3	2.4	54 228	2.3	2 684	4.9	48 306	22.1	13.7
Lawrence	16 235	79.7	42 000	16.6	12.3	311	23.7	2.9	22 747	2.0	1 851	8.1	19 193	22.5	15.3
Madison	49 804	73.1	43 700	14.9	12.2	339	24.9	1.8	67 093	2.1	3 070	4.6	59 046	21.2	13.4
Marion	319 471	57.0	61 400	17.6	12.3	412	24.2	2.5	458 962	1.7	17 592	3.8	401 124	30.9	9.9
Marshall	15 146	76.7	49 600	17.1	12.3	362	22.0	2.0	23 661	-2.2	1 073	4.5	20 824	21.1	13.3
Martin	3 836	81.7	38 700	16.6	12.3	264	24.6	5.7	5 074	1.1	259	5.1	4 572	19.9	15.8
Miami	13 484	70.6	40 300	16.3	11.9	318	22.2	1.7	16 265	2.2	1 033	6.4	14 893	18.2	15.7
Monroe	39 351	54.8	66 600	18.5	12.0	401	32.2	2.5	61 386	1.1	1 915	3.1	52 564	36.6	9.2
Montgomery	13 235	72.2	48 100	15.2	12.0	323	23.9	1.9	17 522	-0.6	678	3.9	16 682	20.0	13.8
Morgan	19 600	78.9	59 700	16.8	11.9	380	23.0	3.4	36 673	1.5	1 151	3.1	27 409	20.8	18.4
Newton	4 839	76.9	43 300	17.0	13.0	322	18.6	2.8	6 381	0.0	331	5.2	6 073	18.3	15.6
Noble	13 418	78.1	49 100	15.3	11.4	332	21.8	3.2	24 904	-0.3	1 666	6.7	18 504	17.1	16.0
Ohio	1 980	78.6	45 400	17.5	13.3	272	20.9	3.7	2 695	0.9	95	3.5	2 385	17.2	20.9
Orange	6 950	78.1	37 400	20.0	13.2	273	24.2	5.2	8 579	0.9	780	9.1	7 783	17.1	14.4
Owen	6 394	83.0	43 000	16.0	12.9	322	25.7	5.9	11 172	1.9	527	4.7	7 587	17.3	19.4
Parke	5 845	79.0	37 900	16.6	12.8	278	21.2	4.4	7 604	0.9	356	4.7	6 594	19.2	14.3
Perry	6 845	79.8	42 600	16.5	11.9	260	21.8	3.4	8 896	-2.3	531	6.0	7 809	14.3	16.1
Pike	4 925	82.6	35 700	16.1	12.6	277	23.0	2.7	6 254	-0.5	255	4.1	5 477	18.1	16.6
Porter	45 159	75.2	69 600	15.8	12.0	431	23.6	1.6	74 269	0.1	3 006	4.0	61 823	28.6	16.1
Posey	9 508	80.3	58 800	17.1	11.9	309	22.5	2.7	13 914	1.1	437	3.1	12 058	24.7	14.8
Pulaski	4 722	77.5	40 300	16.5	13.3	306	21.3	1.7	5 762	-1.0	353	6.1	5 500	15.7	13.5

1. Specified owner-occupied units.   2. Specified renter-occupied units.   3. Overcrowded or lacking complete plumbing facilities.   4. Percent of civilian labor force.   5. Persons 16 years and older.

| | Private nonfarm establishments, employment and payroll, 1999 | | | | | | | | | Agriculture, 1997 | | | |
| | Employment | | | | | | Annual payroll | | Farms | | | Farm operators |
STATE County	Number of establish-ments	Total	Health Care and Social Assistance	Manufac-turing	Retail trade	Finance and Insurance	Professional Scientific and Technical Services	Total (mil dol)	Average per employee (dollars)	Number	Percent with— Less than 50 acres	500 acres and over	Whose principal occu-pation is farming (percent)
	104	105	106	107	108	109	110	111	112	113	114	115	116
INDIANA	146 528	2 580 408	314 164	637 426	347 998	112 357	85 974	75 592	29 295	57 916	31.4	15.1	46.6
Adams	774	13 592	1 121	6 862	1 823	288	123	349	25 695	1 093	41.6	10.4	45.3
Allen	8 848	179 644	21 736	37 209	22 269	10 896	8 502	5 408	30 105	1 440	36.4	9.5	41.4
Bartholomew	1 974	35 703	3 810	12 615	4 566	1 156	875	1 022	28 639	577	33.6	19.1	48.7
Benton	256	2 020	178	534	491	117	D	41	20 216	433	10.2	42.0	73.7
Blackford	285	3 749	395	1 800	481	137	39	91	24 205	303	36.3	14.5	42.2
Boone	1 219	11 971	1 627	1 928	1 844	188	456	289	24 135	611	33.6	25.4	53.5
Brown	397	2 104	212	186	398	D	103	35	16 664	173	34.7	1.7	31.8
Carroll	413	4 826	263	2 390	614	158	112	101	20 944	563	28.8	24.9	58.4
Cass	872	16 224	2 675	6 978	2 028	355	214	387	23 838	700	34.6	17.7	47.6
Clark	2 440	40 940	4 605	7 212	7 694	661	841	1 012	24 726	647	33.1	7.3	43.0
Clay	543	5 961	580	2 117	1 121	196	134	124	20 734	520	26.9	20.8	51.0
Clinton	684	10 583	1 311	5 043	1 117	281	137	260	24 599	585	25.6	26.8	59.7
Crawford	148	1 299	142	D	331	61	D	22	17 137	410	19.8	3.9	31.7
Daviess	764	8 996	1 405	1 974	1 621	232	122	175	19 404	1 101	41.9	10.9	47.5
Dearborn	983	12 999	1 574	2 103	2 022	403	245	330	25 377	679	24.0	2.2	33.0
Decatur	633	12 247	925	5 893	1 459	224	765	302	24 635	654	24.0	19.9	59.3
De Kalb	985	22 234	1 317	13 706	1 722	308	440	689	30 976	785	27.3	9.8	36.6
Delaware	2 764	47 613	7 194	9 391	7 420	1 696	1 729	1 240	26 041	635	38.0	13.7	47.7
Dubois	1 253	29 770	2 562	14 715	3 190	562	465	810	27 209	812	22.2	11.3	49.5
Elkhart	5 016	114 299	7 625	58 940	11 353	1 749	1 658	3 303	28 895	1 335	45.9	6.2	46.7
Fayette	548	9 702	1 407	4 494	1 148	206	132	322	33 167	420	29.8	15.0	47.4
Floyd	1 730	26 321	3 839	7 172	2 973	651	973	658	24 986	310	47.1	3.2	36.5
Fountain	377	4 985	377	2 553	685	183	77	115	23 058	550	23.8	26.5	53.8
Franklin	376	3 878	447	831	455	181	66	83	21 381	776	23.3	7.2	43.2
Fulton	500	6 598	535	2 835	939	180	92	158	23 875	622	29.4	17.7	48.9
Gibson	741	11 306	1 171	3 354	1 556	234	224	305	26 943	579	27.8	25.4	54.2
Grant	1 555	31 456	5 003	9 322	3 647	774	472	827	26 292	575	28.9	23.5	52.7
Greene	647	6 099	1 025	1 020	1 268	246	257	107	17 544	878	25.1	11.3	37.9
Hamilton	5 190	75 366	6 828	6 604	9 961	10 618	4 309	2 745	36 419	591	47.9	14.6	42.5
Hancock	1 225	13 431	1 849	2 782	1 651	313	313	415	30 880	549	39.5	17.1	49.2
Harrison	653	7 979	949	2 570	1 480	318	141	171	21 420	1 108	32.5	4.9	37.1
Hendricks	2 116	24 440	3 129	2 065	5 100	681	868	596	24 376	631	38.0	13.5	50.4
Henry	964	12 979	2 200	3 859	2 270	439	268	388	29 873	770	39.6	11.8	41.4
Howard	2 014	43 592	4 447	18 968	5 980	1 136	553	1 862	42 704	486	28.4	19.5	55.1
Huntington	888	15 399	1 529	6 239	1 948	297	303	364	23 669	651	29.5	18.7	49.0
Jackson	1 091	18 918	2 025	6 375	2 481	515	300	492	26 004	809	30.7	15.9	49.4
Jasper	771	9 285	850	1 622	1 571	233	155	235	25 269	618	24.4	34.3	65.0
Jay	432	6 998	824	3 475	685	184	158	157	22 497	839	32.9	10.8	40.0
Jefferson	737	11 388	2 012	3 407	1 917	252	154	287	25 217	796	33.3	5.0	36.1
Jennings	432	6 433	606	2 448	780	137	73	155	24 045	605	33.7	10.4	40.3
Johnson	2 646	37 382	4 685	6 551	8 320	1 683	975	888	23 755	526	41.4	17.7	47.1
Knox	1 048	14 117	3 454	2 548	2 548	440	274	313	22 152	584	22.3	27.6	64.0
Kosciusko	1 878	30 955	2 339	14 924	3 585	835	445	936	30 251	1 130	35.8	12.0	40.6
Lagrange	696	10 968	605	5 994	1 305	218	165	308	28 065	1 392	38.2	5.3	48.2
Lake	10 129	175 548	25 807	35 019	26 546	5 873	5 986	5 233	29 812	442	32.6	20.1	49.5
La Porte	2 671	39 448	4 888	9 973	6 684	846	988	1 027	26 039	749	30.4	21.8	53.7
Lawrence	904	13 770	1 962	4 996	2 221	412	218	373	27 056	875	26.1	8.3	33.8
Madison	2 774	42 338	6 024	10 279	6 561	1 541	1 340	1 165	27 512	738	37.1	19.9	48.6
Marion	24 410	543 952	71 478	66 866	60 888	37 268	28 046	19 125	35 159	225	62.2	8.0	40.4
Marshall	1 135	18 864	1 676	8 582	2 099	361	250	472	24 997	865	31.9	11.9	46.8
Martin	247	2 486	155	806	330	104	193	55	22 157	335	28.7	9.6	42.7
Miami	687	7 505	898	2 218	1 136	269	103	171	22 731	678	27.4	18.0	51.3
Monroe	2 929	45 718	6 416	8 143	7 482	1 526	1 747	1 129	24 693	473	33.4	5.5	35.1
Montgomery	912	15 267	1 431	6 651	1 912	393	193	420	27 502	681	28.5	27.5	55.9
Morgan	1 293	13 321	1 852	2 833	2 427	398	230	308	23 093	601	41.9	12.5	41.8
Newton	282	3 064	129	1 416	455	100	D	72	23 524	381	20.5	36.7	63.0
Noble	928	19 209	1 246	11 501	1 817	242	268	506	26 344	942	31.7	10.1	38.7
Ohio	74	1 797	70	D	121	D	D	41	22 761	252	27.0	1.6	31.0
Orange	401	7 067	889	2 745	717	146	67	152	21 478	531	21.3	12.6	42.6
Owen	319	3 342	264	1 415	486	139	62	70	20 920	569	27.8	8.8	38.3
Parke	300	2 498	349	584	398	98	D	46	18 559	471	26.3	23.1	51.6
Perry	408	4 595	645	1 390	890	212	70	103	22 342	484	19.8	5.4	35.1
Pike	202	1 926	259	183	262	D	D	57	29 399	288	26.0	18.1	46.2
Porter	3 300	49 728	5 143	12 210	6 473	1 225	1 383	1 537	30 911	476	31.5	19.7	49.4
Posey	554	7 845	528	2 961	912	207	273	261	33 265	437	25.9	27.5	61.8
Pulaski	333	3 841	554	1 414	532	145	57	93	24 338	531	21.5	29.2	63.1

STATE County	Land in farms Acreage (1,000) [117]	Percent change, 1992–1997 [118]	Average size of farm [119]	Total irrigated (1,000) [120]	Total cropland (1,000) [121]	Value of land and buildings Average per farm ($1,000) [122]	Average per acre (dollars) [123]	Value of machinery and equipment average per farm ($1,000) [124]	Value of products sold Total (mil dol) [125]	Average per farm (dollars) [126]	Percent from — Crops [127]	Live-stock and poultry products [128]	Percent of farms with sales of — $10,000 or more [129]	$100,000 or more [130]	Percent of land owned by fed. gov. 1997 [131]	Water consumption 1995 (mil gal/day) [132]
INDIANA	15 111	-3.3	261	250	12 849	533	2 064	64	5 230	90 303	62.1	37.9	56.3	20.8	2.0	9 139.3
Adams	209	5.4	191	0	191	387	2 290	56	95	87 134	48.0	52.0	66.6	23.6	0.0	7.4
Allen	276	-3.4	192	1	247	487	2 699	50	90	62 414	69.3	30.7	56.0	16.7	0.0	54.8
Bartholomew	167	1.0	289	6	146	674	2 355	79	47	80 939	82.0	18.0	56.3	23.1	10.2	21.8
Benton	257	-5.2	593	D	248	1 378	2 394	151	79	183 310	95.7	4.3	88.5	56.6	0.0	1.9
Blackford	86	-1.2	284		77	475	1 839	60	25	83 481	72.4	27.6	55.1	19.8	0.0	2.2
Boone	228	2.4	374	D	212	912	2 519	83	82	133 419	74.0	26.0	66.0	31.3	0.0	5.4
Brown	22	-5.6	125	0	10	287	2 390	25	2	12 733	52.0	48.0	24.3	1.2	13.0	0.6
Carroll	218	-0.8	388	1	198	892	2 282	94	117	207 704	52.1	47.9	74.2	39.1	0.0	4.7
Cass	205	-9.9	293	2	179	609	2 088	62	78	110 799	69.0	31.0	62.0	25.0	0.1	29.2
Clark	109	2.6	168	0	76	378	2 458	33	22	33 815	71.2	28.8	40.2	9.0	5.1	31.2
Clay	159	-1.6	307	D	135	489	1 625	66	43	81 824	71.6	28.4	61.2	23.5	0.0	2.1
Clinton	236	0.1	404	0	223	878	2 178	113	106	181 203	60.5	39.5	79.1	42.4	0.0	6.5
Crawford	61	2.2	150	0	30	219	1 471	21	4	8 541	31.1	68.9	16.8	1.0	16.7	6.3
Daviess	217	-2.2	197	2	189	362	1 973	59	118	107 075	34.0	66.0	59.9	21.7	0.0	9.0
Dearborn	81	-5.4	120	0	45	315	2 725	25	9	13 203	58.3	41.7	23.3	2.1	0.0	621.8
Decatur	199	-1.7	304	0	171	687	2 343	82	83	126 719	52.8	47.2	70.6	30.1	0.0	4.4
De Kalb	163	6.5	208	1	135	355	1 739	43	39	49 261	65.9	34.1	43.7	11.7	0.0	7.5
Delaware	173	2.6	273	0	160	585	2 219	65	53	82 874	84.3	15.7	57.2	19.8	0.0	18.8
Dubois	191	-1.0	235	0	138	393	1 686	61	144	177 526	15.5	84.5	61.5	28.8	1.7	9.5
Elkhart	183	-4.8	137	24	160	376	2 738	48	124	92 912	28.0	72.0	64.6	24.7	0.0	43.4
Fayette	107	-4.7	254	D	85	455	1 858	53	26	62 903	64.9	35.1	59.0	19.5	0.0	4.5
Floyd	29	-4.3	93	0	18	345	5 019	30	4	11 986	71.7	28.3	20.6	2.3	0.0	271.5
Fountain	205	-10.7	372	0	177	756	1 882	99	49	89 765	85.9	14.1	61.1	27.1	0.0	3.7
Franklin	139	-7.0	179	0	92	351	2 085	47	31	40 253	48.1	51.9	50.6	11.2	2.0	2.7
Fulton	171	-12.0	274	10	151	415	1 532	68	55	89 151	70.8	29.2	68.0	23.6	0.0	8.2
Gibson	233	-3.4	402	2	212	745	1 910	103	69	119 268	81.3	18.7	71.5	31.1	0.0	49.1
Grant	192	-2.4	334	0	178	767	2 224	98	63	108 781	83.2	16.8	62.6	30.6	0.7	13.6
Greene	206	-1.1	234	1	147	327	1 360	47	77	88 249	30.3	69.7	39.7	11.5	0.9	24.2
Hamilton	141	-13.6	238	1	127	788	3 478	62	59	100 662	87.2	12.8	57.2	18.6	0.0	76.1
Hancock	164	0.4	298	1	155	820	2 670	88	56	101 634	79.8	20.2	59.4	25.0	0.0	5.5
Harrison	161	-0.4	146	0	110	247	1 744	37	46	41 561	30.0	70.0	31.7	6.0	0.0	2.8
Hendricks	167	-10.6	265	0	150	757	2 770	67	49	77 899	81.7	18.3	55.2	18.9	0.0	9.9
Henry	178	-7.0	231	1	161	434	1 915	47	52	67 763	81.0	19.0	55.8	19.1	0.0	11.8
Howard	148	-0.8	304	0	138	773	2 657	81	63	128 779	69.2	30.8	71.6	35.0	0.0	22.9
Huntington	184	-2.1	283	0	169	517	1 857	80	70	107 146	63.6	36.4	66.1	25.0	5.3	5.2
Jackson	201	-1.0	248	1	157	442	1 728	65	93	114 599	35.5	64.5	56.7	20.1	8.5	10.0
Jasper	283	-6.3	458	17	258	812	1 872	95	111	179 636	66.9	33.1	76.7	42.7	0.0	31.0
Jay	180	-1.8	214	0	157	388	1 902	46	83	99 215	42.4	57.6	54.7	20.4	0.0	3.8
Jefferson	126	-3.5	159	0	81	233	1 628	35	23	29 453	76.9	23.1	43.7	6.5	7.4	1 317.8
Jennings	130	4.3	215	1	91	323	1 535	64	45	74 734	43.6	56.4	39.5	10.9	4.9	4.0
Johnson	136	-3.2	258	1	121	724	2 896	66	46	88 103	80.7	19.3	55.1	21.5	2.6	13.1
Knox	281	-8.3	481	14	256	945	1 923	112	101	173 280	70.7	29.3	76.4	35.8	0.0	61.0
Kosciusko	247	-2.0	219	12	210	402	1 870	50	146	129 259	33.4	66.6	56.0	20.0	0.0	23.1
Lagrange	190	1.0	136	23	156	332	2 418	36	103	74 194	36.2	63.8	66.9	13.2	0.0	11.7
Lake	149	3.4	337	6	139	937	2 716	65	48	108 206	89.4	10.6	62.4	26.5	0.2	2 173.7
La Porte	248	-7.6	331	27	227	736	2 069	91	96	127 922	71.0	29.0	65.6	29.2	0.3	85.5
Lawrence	171	7.4	195	3	100	258	1 478	40	22	25 506	46.7	53.3	31.8	4.2	4.3	8.8
Madison	224	0.3	303	1	209	744	2 423	82	78	105 030	88.0	12.0	62.2	24.8	0.0	21.6
Marion	29	-25.6	129	0	24	679	4 369	42	33	145 247	59.5	40.5	47.1	17.8	1.0	318.5
Marshall	202	-7.9	233	5	177	439	1 992	51	62	71 892	69.6	30.4	60.8	19.0	0.0	7.5
Martin	70	-2.6	209	0	46	316	1 421	40	24	71 632	26.6	73.4	37.9	14.6	31.9	2.9
Miami	197	4.3	291	2	175	551	1 926	65	75	110 270	58.4	41.6	64.5	27.3	1.3	7.4
Monroe	62	5.3	131	0	36	296	2 344	27	8	17 771	58.5	41.5	25.8	4.4	8.7	14.6
Montgomery	273	-3.4	401	1	244	782	2 005	88	85	124 935	73.1	26.9	67.7	30.8	0.0	6.6
Morgan	134	-4.3	223	0	111	556	2 567	54	34	57 096	82.1	17.9	43.6	14.0	0.0	151.2
Newton	207	0.2	544	7	193	1 056	1 946	126	84	221 262	68.4	31.6	78.5	44.9	0.0	4.4
Noble	182	-1.1	193	4	147	355	1 886	45	59	62 464	51.8	48.2	50.2	15.1	0.0	10.0
Ohio	30	-6.6	119	0	16	236	2 118	21	4	14 935	71.8	28.2	27.8	2.0	0.0	0.7
Orange	123	6.3	232	D	78	262	1 288	43	22	41 700	44.2	55.8	32.2	7.9	14.5	2.8
Owen	107	-5.1	189	0	70	325	1 457	34	16	28 853	62.2	37.8	32.9	6.3	1.2	2.2
Parke	189	3.7	401	1	146	691	1 600	73	43	92 110	79.8	20.2	59.2	24.2	0.2	1.9
Perry	84	5.3	174	0	44	230	1 214	35	13	27 240	28.0	72.0	31.4	5.4	23.5	2.4
Pike	84	-0.9	292	D	70	377	1 455	59	20	69 620	68.8	31.2	52.8	20.5	0.0	472.6
Porter	135	-5.3	283	7	123	651	2 344	71	42	88 712	86.3	13.7	61.1	28.4	4.8	678.9
Posey	195	-11.6	447	3	180	740	1 718	139	60	136 774	84.3	15.7	73.9	35.9	0.7	19.5
Pulaski	236	-2.7	445	11	216	727	1 591	96	98	184 665	62.4	37.6	77.0	37.7	0.0	9.9

STATE County	Value of Residential Construction Authorized by Building Permits, 2000		Wholesale Trade, 1997				Retail Trade[1], 1997				Real Estate and Rental and Leasing, 1997			
	New Construction ($1,000)	Number of Housing Units	Number of Establish-ments	Number of Employees	Sales (mil dol)	Annual Payroll (mil dol)	Number of Establish-ments	Number of Employees	Sales (mil dol)	Annual Payroll (mil dol)	Number of Establish-ments	Number of Employees	Receipts (mil dol)	Annual Payroll (mil dol)
	133	134	135	136	137	138	139	140	141	142	143	144	145	146
INDIANA	4 414 439	37 903	8 896	112 705	66 350.1	3 737.8	24 954	337 867	57 241.6	5 273.8	5 427	28 948	3 269.1	572.6
Adams	11 565	121	43	314	151.3	7.5	172	1 824	344.6	27.9	14	54	5.3	0.9
Allen	272 687	1 791	686	10 861	6 586.2	357.8	1 320	21 917	3 534.6	351.1	336	1 988	254.8	43.2
Bartholomew	29 614	212	114	910	714.3	29.8	397	4 658	680.6	66.1	68	268	37.2	5.8
Benton	1 545	28	27	181	109.0	4.3	59	413	70.0	7.0	6	D	D	D
Blackford	5 661	96	15	110	20.8	2.9	56	515	82.9	6.8	14	29	2.5	0.4
Boone	96 430	678	94	629	500.9	18.8	173	1 632	261.0	25.3	33	135	11.2	2.0
Brown	8 184	140	9	D	D	D	102	432	42.1	5.3	9	34	2.8	0.6
Carroll	6 525	92	33	224	145.8	6.4	61	574	90.9	8.8	17	47	2.7	0.5
Cass	10 225	87	49	453	220.0	13.7	169	2 046	339.1	31.5	22	76	4.4	0.9
Clark	77 342	793	128	1 486	686.5	37.8	471	7 887	1 261.0	114.9	98	477	59.4	8.2
Clay	4 368	62	18	D	D	D	105	1 076	190.1	16.1	16	42	4.5	0.5
Clinton	8 673	77	47	D	D	D	126	1 200	193.5	18.8	23	70	5.8	1.1
Crawford	425	6	4	D	D	D	36	322	36.3	4.0	6	8	1.1	0.3
Daviess	4 137	22	22	233	76.6	6.0	145	1 490	260.5	21.4	15	60	4.3	0.7
Dearborn	44 774	374	37	D	D	D	158	1 896	344.3	29.0	37	D	D	D
Decatur	10 887	100	36	423	231.2	10.4	128	1 414	230.9	20.2	19	46	4.6	0.8
De Kalb	24 664	192	49	413	254.5	15.6	152	1 667	291.8	25.1	27	112	10.4	2.3
Delaware	51 957	402	119	1 501	653.4	45.8	548	7 340	1 118.7	105.4	119	433	46.9	8.4
Dubois	31 302	250	72	1 417	781.8	52.1	231	2 951	551.7	50.7	36	184	9.8	2.2
Elkhart	125 684	1 296	382	5 031	2 246.1	160.0	751	10 866	1 973.6	179.6	171	884	78.1	13.9
Fayette	6 248	88	19	227	69.5	6.2	94	1 202	193.4	16.8	24	83	4.9	1.0
Floyd	55 056	425	97	1 076	298.0	30.1	231	2 366	331.0	36.8	54	233	20.7	3.7
Fountain	1 042	8	22	D	D	D	75	675	120.4	8.9	9	30	1.0	0.2
Franklin	11 601	88	14	81	28.1	2.1	63	443	66.5	6.5	7	23	1.5	0.4
Fulton	3 536	32	35	175	70.0	4.0	91	936	143.8	11.6	15	39	2.5	0.9
Gibson	8 234	179	38	D	D	D	148	1 694	252.0	21.9	12	33	3.3	0.4
Grant	21 549	237	72	770	200.2	20.4	318	3 864	629.5	54.8	56	284	24.9	4.9
Greene	0	0	30	145	89.2	3.1	135	1 252	178.5	16.7	19	66	2.4	0.4
Hamilton	649 859	4 282	508	5 552	5 171.0	223.2	574	9 896	1 786.5	176.8	168	1 267	172.7	29.9
Hancock	89 929	699	62	665	258.7	17.9	149	1 639	341.4	25.4	39	121	12.5	2.1
Harrison	26 271	204	27	264	70.9	6.0	133	1 540	234.9	20.6	24	54	5.8	0.8
Hendricks	225 910	1 901	100	725	263.9	23.2	289	4 363	756.5	65.5	72	348	27.7	4.6
Henry	20 130	209	46	498	197.3	13.8	189	2 107	426.6	33.4	24	63	6.9	0.9
Howard	54 297	408	110	D	D	D	409	6 078	959.6	89.1	84	306	38.5	5.4
Huntington	16 656	153	54	485	265.1	12.9	169	1 943	312.8	28.1	28	86	7.2	1.3
Jackson	19 358	203	46	553	206.0	14.7	242	2 444	389.5	36.6	41	115	9.9	1.8
Jasper	22 353	270	43	299	283.7	8.6	149	1 718	278.5	24.7	20	113	29.2	2.6
Jay	5 349	65	21	231	122.7	5.2	82	707	115.0	17.0	20	99	3.4	0.6
Jefferson	14 185	169	27	226	40.3	4.8	167	1 766	281.2	24.5	24	76	7.8	1.1
Jennings	16 302	208	16	115	39.9	2.7	72	764	136.0	12.1	18	37	3.4	0.4
Johnson	203 450	1 480	113	788	659.9	26.6	490	7 338	1 171.2	109.2	99	362	42.1	6.1
Knox	5 901	64	68	842	373.7	19.3	234	2 668	399.9	36.7	28	120	10.9	1.7
Kosciusko	53 390	433	105	737	372.3	22.4	333	3 460	551.9	55.3	64	169	18.0	2.7
Lagrange	16 818	217	31	479	132.4	9.6	145	1 184	203.9	17.6	16	44	3.0	0.6
Lake	248 414	1 928	547	7 094	3 876.3	249.7	1 736	25 503	4 380.6	398.6	403	2 001	240.6	44.1
La Porte	44 614	440	135	1 525	658.5	44.6	552	6 312	1 041.7	95.7	95	313	31.0	4.9
Lawrence	3 217	41	26	228	54.7	5.3	207	2 108	372.1	31.6	24	179	22.3	4.2
Madison	43 903	356	105	1 157	428.6	31.3	521	6 790	1 123.4	101.3	112	439	35.0	7.0
Marion	614 579	5 216	1 953	32 619	21 284.8	1 245.4	3 654	59 830	10 757.4	1 038.3	1 106	9 086	1 137.7	212.1
Marshall	19 754	286	71	696	265.5	18.4	202	2 103	367.9	31.2	38	149	15.8	3.4
Martin	632	7	6	D	D	D	52	385	58.6	4.7	7	D	D	D
Miami	11 359	115	41	564	270.9	16.4	121	1 068	205.0	17.9	24	52	3.6	0.5
Monroe	73 296	620	102	D	D	D	514	6 846	1 073.7	97.5	162	869	83.1	15.3
Montgomery	11 549	116	56	271	176.4	8.9	167	1 947	293.8	27.2	30	97	8.8	1.2
Morgan	63 742	583	56	303	150.5	8.8	207	2 372	432.9	35.7	52	185	16.9	2.8
Newton	8 028	98	24	131	82.4	4.1	53	418	70.6	5.7	6	12	2.3	0.3
Noble	25 060	244	39	392	208.3	13.0	157	1 642	258.3	23.5	23	73	4.0	0.7
Ohio	2 152	23	NA	NA	NA	NA	12	108	13.7	1.4	2	D	D	D
Orange	327	5	19	109	33.4	2.0	89	574	103.2	9.0	6	47	2.9	0.5
Owen	397	5	15	60	13.0	1.4	59	510	71.3	6.1	8	D	D	D
Parke	3 533	43	12	67	21.0	1.1	50	367	48.8	4.8	8	33	3.2	0.6
Perry	5 961	56	15	178	77.3	5.8	85	974	131.2	11.7	16	35	4.3	0.5
Pike	6 203	73	12	113	37.1	3.2	38	266	41.1	3.1	1	D	D	D
Porter	142 002	1 107	174	1 823	941.7	56.1	436	6 231	1 040.3	98.6	133	593	74.4	10.2
Posey	13 287	97	30	D	D	D	95	906	151.5	13.9	8	27	1.5	0.2
Pulaski	7 235	73	36	356	167.3	9.7	58	419	73.9	6.9	15	36	1.5	0.3

1. Establishments with payroll.

STATE County	Professional, Scientific, and Technical Services[1], 1997				Manufacturing, 1997				Accommodation and Foodservices, 1997			
	Number of Establishments	Number of Employees	Receipts (mil dol)	Annual Payroll (mil dol)	Number of Establishments	Number of Employees	Receipts (mil dol)	Annual Payroll (mil dol)	Number of Establishments	Number of Employees	Sales (mil dol)	Annual Payroll (mil dol)
	147	148	149	150	151	152	153	154	155	156	157	158
INDIANA	9 795	69 393	5 974.2	2 207.5	9 303	625 692	142 270.7	22 121.4	11 705	215 710	6 646.3	1 865.3
Adams	39	115	6.7	2.1	67	6 536	1 428.9	189.6	61	1 103	27.4	7.9
Allen	658	5 508	463.9	162.4	576	36 585	9 182.2	1 362.0	626	13 472	414.0	122.2
Bartholomew	152	777	58.5	24.7	145	13 311	3 096.7	412.1	135	3 114	102.4	28.4
Benton	14	37	1.6	0.6	16	562	58.8	12.6	19	D	D	D
Blackford	14	32	2.0	0.5	28	2 081	299.2	58.6	21	D	D	D
Boone	76	245	26.4	7.7	73	1 769	190.9	48.5	85	1 303	37.5	11.0
Brown	36	107	5.8	2.5	NA	NA	NA	NA	46	623	18.4	6.1
Carroll	21	73	3.9	1.1	33	2 191	500.8	50.3	26	339	9.8	3.0
Cass	35	141	10.8	3.2	60	6 129	994.3	157.9	88	1 125	30.7	9.0
Clark	138	563	43.5	12.8	163	D	D	D	192	3 876	121.7	34.8
Clay	24	105	4.0	1.7	34	D	D	D	50	516	13.7	3.8
Clinton	35	104	6.0	1.6	49	4 959	1 565.1	148.1	63	753	19.4	5.2
Crawford	8	13	0.7	0.2	NA	NA	NA	NA	18	D	D	D
Daviess	30	127	6.1	1.8	51	1 947	350.0	37.4	59	899	20.4	5.6
Dearborn	46	149	8.8	2.9	39	D	D	D	79	1 068	31.7	8.6
Decatur	26	486	11.8	7.9	52	4 926	847.9	155.6	47	765	19.6	5.7
De Kalb	52	255	12.2	4.0	119	11 000	2 040.2	364.3	78	1 008	34.0	8.8
Delaware	153	1 691	87.8	37.3	176	9 972	1 764.5	402.6	228	4 981	126.7	35.6
Dubois	61	236	16.1	6.1	114	12 450	1 637.0	327.9	91	1 480	39.4	11.5
Elkhart	246	1 465	111.6	36.0	894	56 087	8 999.9	1 610.8	354	6 202	189.4	51.7
Fayette	32	132	6.7	2.8	36	4 809	1 254.3	217.0	49	759	22.0	5.9
Floyd	146	975	77.7	28.3	135	7 499	1 243.2	204.0	107	1 830	54.9	15.8
Fountain	12	47	2.6	0.7	22	2 616	282.8	67.8	48	546	16.4	5.1
Franklin	18	45	3.8	0.9	19	812	134.5	23.3	38	554	12.6	3.5
Fulton	23	56	4.6	1.0	52	3 004	424.4	79.1	46	551	14.2	3.9
Gibson	37	193	11.6	5.2	42	2 142	336.1	54.3	62	894	21.0	6.3
Grant	66	360	16.0	5.6	80	9 375	1 784.4	395.2	140	2 579	74.3	20.2
Greene	31	343	21.1	9.0	26	1 136	171.7	18.5	49	D	D	D
Hamilton	515	4 169	435.2	168.7	191	5 687	836.3	185.8	252	5 154	165.6	49.2
Hancock	81	247	21.9	6.9	66	2 564	712.9	88.4	79	1 470	41.5	11.0
Harrison	24	92	4.2	1.7	38	D	D	D	44	690	21.4	5.5
Hendricks	148	507	33.2	12.1	80	1 537	248.4	48.5	127	2 581	72.2	20.9
Henry	46	205	15.1	4.3	57	3 516	688.7	164.8	68	1 082	30.4	8.3
Howard	98	410	30.8	10.3	80	20 018	4 732.2	1 077.9	182	3 913	115.1	31.7
Huntington	33	239	14.3	6.7	78	7 451	1 245.5	207.8	85	1 260	32.3	9.0
Jackson	43	284	15.8	6.1	90	5 848	1 182.7	179.4	72	1 042	35.3	10.1
Jasper	28	107	5.8	1.6	33	1 479	279.4	35.2	57	810	24.1	6.6
Jay	19	99	3.7	1.2	39	3 751	539.1	86.6	41	528	14.4	3.8
Jefferson	29	124	7.9	2.4	51	3 655	548.9	97.3	77	1 068	29.6	8.7
Jennings	12	54	2.2	0.7	42	2 410	263.2	55.7	31	392	10.0	2.7
Johnson	187	890	54.9	22.1	126	6 486	1 305.5	204.6	214	4 190	121.6	34.9
Knox	47	189	12.1	3.6	44	1 715	289.1	46.2	80	1 375	36.1	10.3
Kosciusko	96	395	27.1	8.3	186	14 949	2 969.2	514.1	152	2 116	58.7	16.6
Lagrange	38	97	5.1	1.6	77	4 765	887.4	154.3	60	702	24.0	6.9
Lake	728	5 402	455.5	154.3	423	37 109	14 297.9	1 748.3	931	15 407	463.1	126.0
La Porte	145	707	40.1	13.9	189	10 835	2 007.9	351.2	234	3 394	106.1	29.0
Lawrence	37	175	9.6	3.6	75	5 322	1 063.0	195.0	74	1 321	38.0	10.5
Madison	187	1 152	62.2	31.9	133	12 144	2 256.8	534.3	244	4 794	139.8	38.4
Marion	2 264	23 108	2 423.6	899.9	1 194	66 571	19 561.3	2 898.6	1 893	43 946	1 523.7	432.4
Marshall	51	250	13.2	4.6	143	8 588	1 516.0	230.2	97	1 418	37.1	10.0
Martin	13	87	5.5	2.7	9	575	133.4	17.7	21	D	D	D
Miami	27	94	5.0	1.4	50	2 491	385.9	64.0	58	706	18.2	5.1
Monroe	196	1 360	97.0	34.0	122	8 817	2 444.2	302.6	302	6 312	176.6	48.8
Montgomery	44	137	9.5	3.5	67	7 634	1 878.7	264.1	88	1 054	33.7	8.6
Morgan	61	193	12.5	4.7	65	2 869	472.3	78.7	80	1 411	45.1	13.3
Newton	11	33	1.4	0.4	29	1 474	176.5	34.4	28	D	D	D
Noble	45	243	19.9	4.5	143	10 818	1 821.7	309.2	69	961	29.8	7.7
Ohio	3	8	0.3	0.2	NA	NA	NA	NA	9	D	D	D
Orange	22	39	2.3	0.7	34	2 478	296.4	55.3	35	610	10.0	3.1
Owen	15	55	2.2	0.7	24	1 242	109.2	31.5	20	D	D	D
Parke	16	48	2.5	0.9	17	641	92.1	13.7	34	D	D	D
Perry	19	55	2.8	0.7	27	1 211	141.1	33.6	44	465	14.1	3.6
Pike	9	30	1.2	0.4	NA	NA	NA	NA	12	D	D	D
Porter	237	1 217	109.8	42.1	146	12 353	4 353.6	624.5	259	4 385	126.5	35.9
Posey	35	247	18.0	9.3	31	D	D	D	35	D	D	D
Pulaski	25	82	3.3	0.8	20	1 353	218.1	41.1	22	D	D	D

1. Firms subject to federal tax.

Table B. States and Counties — Health and Other Services and Federal Funds

STATE County	Health Care and Social Assistance[1], 1997				Other Services[1], 1997				Federal funds and grants, fiscal 2001[2] Expenditures (mil dol)			
									Total	Direct payments for individuals[3]		
	Number of Establishments	Number of Employees	Receipts (mil dol)	Annual Payroll (mil dol)	Number of Establishments	Number of Employees	Receipts (mil dol)	Annual Payroll (mil dol)		Social Security and government retirement	Medicare	Food stamps and Supplemental Security Income
	159	160	161	162	163	164	165	166	167	168	169	170
INDIANA	10 236	132 416	8 132.3	3 675.3	9 243	60 711	3 701.4	1 127.8	32 166.1	12 090.8	4 667.0	815.5
Adams	35	238	14.6	6.5	58	223	12.9	3.2	131.1	58.1	23.6	2.4
Allen	580	9 292	618.5	281.0	584	4 490	272.7	86.3	1 625.7	589.9	203.9	42.1
Bartholomew	142	1 633	106.6	57.3	101	703	39.4	13.8	318.8	137.5	50.5	7.4
Benton	11	191	5.5	2.8	10	43	2.4	0.7	61.9	21.4	8.4	0.8
Blackford	18	209	10.7	3.5	18	54	3.0	1.0	64.2	33.0	11.9	1.9
Boone	71	686	40.3	19.1	67	303	26.2	6.2	159.6	78.0	30.6	2.1
Brown	12	177	6.4	3.2	8	18	1.1	0.2	33.9	21.4	5.5	0.9
Carroll	23	194	8.1	3.0	20	50	3.8	1.1	85.1	35.3	12.4	0.8
Cass	56	777	36.0	18.5	58	226	11.3	3.3	198.8	91.6	35.5	5.1
Clark	155	2 188	119.7	52.0	157	1 165	63.3	21.3	535.7	217.8	87.8	14.4
Clay	34	257	10.7	3.8	40	132	6.6	1.9	143.6	68.3	26.8	3.6
Clinton	31	237	12.8	4.7	46	176	11.4	3.0	148.1	69.0	27.4	3.3
Crawford	5	90	3.4	1.4	5	18	1.3	0.4	57.7	25.4	9.9	2.1
Daviess	59	700	31.5	12.9	52	257	42.4	6.9	154.7	68.5	25.9	3.5
Dearborn	66	759	38.1	17.2	62	182	13.5	3.1	153.8	87.0	30.9	3.4
Decatur	29	406	14.3	6.5	39	153	8.7	2.6	111.4	50.9	18.4	2.6
De Kalb	55	695	37.3	15.6	51	208	12.0	3.7	138.7	70.0	23.4	2.5
Delaware	223	3 304	200.9	94.2	186	1 530	98.7	24.4	539.7	249.0	93.4	23.0
Dubois	86	798	49.6	18.1	69	341	27.5	6.4	163.7	73.9	28.3	1.4
Elkhart	233	3 281	187.7	78.0	345	2 427	164.1	47.3	536.7	298.7	94.9	16.5
Fayette	55	667	27.4	12.4	42	214	11.5	3.4	132.6	62.6	25.6	5.5
Floyd	154	1 835	109.0	45.7	108	628	35.9	11.6	300.8	149.8	59.9	10.8
Fountain	19	298	9.5	4.1	24	81	7.4	1.2	104.5	48.1	17.0	2.0
Franklin	22	230	8.7	3.7	16	70	3.1	1.4	75.0	35.7	12.2	1.9
Fulton	22	133	9.7	3.4	34	104	6.5	2.2	93.5	45.3	16.8	1.7
Gibson	54	556	23.7	9.0	40	153	8.2	2.5	184.0	74.6	30.6	3.1
Grant	124	1 834	80.6	37.2	106	573	32.6	9.2	429.3	186.8	65.7	14.0
Greene	52	739	19.0	7.6	41	101	6.9	1.5	178.2	88.6	27.7	4.2
Hamilton	341	3 816	244.6	108.6	245	1 499	100.2	30.5	377.2	229.7	59.1	4.8
Hancock	78	849	43.8	20.0	80	398	21.4	6.2	185.2	110.8	32.2	2.8
Harrison	40	341	16.0	6.7	24	93	5.9	1.6	129.8	71.2	23.2	3.6
Hendricks	149	1 959	101.8	48.7	131	610	36.0	11.3	275.1	167.1	49.4	3.1
Henry	70	986	43.0	23.3	61	264	13.8	3.9	233.2	117.4	45.3	7.0
Howard	162	1 947	115.9	53.3	131	961	44.4	14.1	394.4	194.8	75.4	14.0
Huntington	46	604	25.0	10.8	58	247	12.2	3.5	149.5	82.3	24.7	3.0
Jackson	59	598	34.0	15.7	64	304	19.0	5.0	180.7	86.7	29.3	5.4
Jasper	33	161	10.9	4.2	40	205	10.9	3.1	127.9	60.0	21.9	1.9
Jay	24	397	18.1	7.0	28	79	4.8	1.4	107.7	48.2	20.0	3.3
Jefferson	51	671	38.8	16.7	36	183	8.5	2.5	153.5	70.9	28.3	4.8
Jennings	23	255	10.8	5.1	21	67	6.8	1.1	103.5	52.9	16.6	3.8
Johnson	158	2 065	123.1	53.3	174	1 031	62.3	20.2	385.4	212.3	65.4	6.9
Knox	81	1 315	65.7	31.0	63	404	24.0	7.2	239.9	94.1	44.8	7.2
Kosciusko	79	851	48.9	22.4	138	708	44.6	13.5	230.8	130.8	40.6	4.0
Lagrange	26	468	24.9	9.2	41	151	14.3	2.7	82.8	46.2	15.1	1.6
Lake	1 013	10 528	697.3	317.5	740	6 006	373.9	123.8	2 463.5	1 019.3	503.4	116.1
La Porte	181	1 995	137.2	64.5	189	929	49.9	17.3	463.4	224.6	95.8	17.2
Lawrence	73	627	28.5	12.6	58	252	14.2	4.5	242.3	114.0	40.3	5.8
Madison	206	2 232	119.4	53.5	199	1 133	60.5	19.2	677.1	334.7	133.4	23.6
Marion	1 847	27 477	1 891.6	876.8	1 442	12 491	742.6	236.4	6 624.2	1 732.7	739.8	162.3
Marshall	53	775	37.0	14.3	65	301	19.5	5.7	157.8	84.8	27.2	2.9
Martin	19	145	5.0	2.0	14	29	1.8	0.3	268.6	31.1	9.2	1.7
Miami	39	352	16.1	6.5	40	162	6.8	1.8	199.6	82.9	27.9	5.0
Monroe	243	2 384	162.1	76.2	160	1 124	64.3	20.0	541.5	181.6	57.5	11.3
Montgomery	61	1 161	70.6	26.5	67	540	37.3	10.8	169.3	76.8	30.0	3.5
Morgan	86	877	48.2	23.3	94	472	26.7	7.8	224.8	118.0	42.3	5.7
Newton	6	44	1.7	0.7	11	26	1.9	0.3	65.1	24.4	10.8	1.0
Noble	50	392	21.4	8.9	71	258	16.9	4.8	151.5	75.2	27.7	2.8
Ohio	3	60	3.0	1.0	6	20	0.7	0.2	20.4	10.8	4.1	0.2
Orange	28	431	15.5	6.5	17	54	3.7	0.8	95.0	43.8	16.8	2.4
Owen	14	212	9.1	4.4	24	92	6.0	1.3	72.8	39.4	11.6	2.3
Parke	20	323	12.2	5.7	18	50	8.5	0.9	84.8	37.2	13.0	2.4
Perry	21	216	10.2	4.3	24	72	4.9	1.1	96.1	40.6	16.3	2.3
Pike	14	188	6.7	3.1	14	44	3.6	0.6	67.4	30.6	13.0	1.8
Porter	263	2 434	158.6	74.5	239	1 330	77.3	24.2	499.0	255.7	95.9	9.9
Posey	25	317	13.4	4.6	31	90	4.9	1.2	138.6	48.6	20.6	2.8
Pulaski	18	137	5.3	2.6	24	76	9.1	1.4	72.7	31.3	11.1	1.1

1. Firms subject to federal tax. 2. October 1, 2000 to September 30, 2001. 3. State totals may include programs not allocated by county.

Table B. States and Counties — Federal Funds and Local Government Finances

	Federal funds and grants, fiscal 2001[1] (cont'd)							Local government finances, 1997				
	Expenditures (mil dol) (cont'd)							General revenue				
	Procurement contract awards		Grants[2]							Taxes		
STATE County	Salaries and wages	Defense	Other	Medicaid and other health-related	Nutrition and family welfare	Education	Other	Total (mil dol)	Intergovernmental (mil dol)	Total (mil dol)	Per capita[3] (dollars) Total	Property
	171	172	173	174	175	176	177	178	179	180	181	182
INDIANA	2 120.8	1 749.7	984.6	3 092.5	835.1	525.2	1 396.8	X	X	X	X	X
Adams	3.8	0.0	3.2	17.7	1.5	0.9	2.0	81.1	25.2	23.3	710	663
Allen	137.9	319.0	73.0	121.8	30.7	8.9	38.6	673.0	233.8	326.6	1 046	965
Bartholomew	20.2	7.3	3.0	33.3	8.6	1.0	25.0	252.6	52.2	78.7	1 145	1 010
Benton	1.9	0.0	0.5	3.0	0.3	0.2	0.6	23.6	9.1	11.2	1 172	1 092
Blackford	1.9	0.0	0.5	5.9	1.2	0.3	1.2	43.6	21.1	11.8	840	757
Boone	5.7	0.2	1.4	6.7	1.3	0.4	7.9	117.4	32.3	44.9	1 044	846
Brown	1.1	0.0	0.3	3.0	0.9	0.2	0.1	28.0	11.6	12.7	812	685
Carroll	3.9	0.0	0.7	4.8	1.0	0.3	5.5	41.9	14.4	21.6	1 082	988
Cass	6.7	10.9	2.0	17.0	4.9	0.8	5.2	104.6	33.9	29.4	762	671
Clark	95.8	3.1	6.0	46.6	9.9	2.4	27.1	259.1	78.3	77.2	828	815
Clay	4.9	0.0	1.1	18.5	1.7	0.5	5.3	59.3	22.3	19.3	727	649
Clinton	4.1	0.1	1.0	12.2	2.4	0.6	2.0	83.8	29.0	27.3	821	732
Crawford	2.2	0.0	0.6	11.1	0.9	1.5	1.9	19.8	11.8	5.7	541	533
Daviess	4.8	0.0	1.0	14.4	2.1	1.0	10.9	65.0	22.6	16.5	571	485
Dearborn	5.1	0.1	1.5	16.3	3.5	0.8	1.1	127.3	45.8	37.3	800	731
Decatur	3.1	0.0	0.8	11.5	1.6	0.5	0.3	60.2	19.3	19.3	759	673
De Kalb	4.7	0.1	1.1	8.9	2.1	0.4	13.8	108.4	33.8	36.1	933	825
Delaware	23.4	0.0	8.2	77.5	14.4	4.5	11.5	214.2	97.2	86.0	731	670
Dubois	6.7	7.4	17.7	6.3	1.9	0.3	4.0	78.6	30.7	34.0	868	783
Elkhart	17.4	3.0	6.1	51.0	9.5	4.0	6.3	350.5	135.9	161.4	946	814
Fayette	3.2	0.0	0.8	17.7	3.4	0.6	2.3	59.2	27.5	25.4	971	747
Floyd	10.4	0.2	4.0	44.7	6.8	1.3	3.4	194.3	54.5	45.4	635	617
Fountain	3.4	0.1	0.9	7.4	2.3	0.3	2.6	33.9	15.4	13.6	744	660
Franklin	2.4	0.1	0.6	11.1	0.9	0.3	1.8	31.3	15.6	11.1	515	422
Fulton	2.8	0.0	0.7	4.8	1.1	0.3	4.6	50.2	14.9	15.6	769	694
Gibson	4.8	0.2	1.2	13.2	2.2	1.3	25.0	62.5	25.0	25.5	799	794
Grant	40.8	0.0	26.6	45.5	9.4	2.4	5.3	150.9	66.8	65.1	895	774
Greene	5.2	16.7	1.2	16.6	1.9	0.9	2.6	71.8	29.6	19.9	601	503
Hamilton	21.8	0.8	6.3	20.2	3.0	0.8	12.6	406.0	106.0	189.8	1 226	997
Hancock	6.9	0.0	1.7	8.1	1.8	0.5	5.3	138.9	40.8	40.5	764	647
Harrison	6.2	0.0	1.3	14.1	2.2	0.6	1.4	61.8	27.1	18.0	529	476
Hendricks	10.9	2.9	2.9	11.1	2.2	0.8	7.3	241.4	64.0	82.7	896	757
Henry	6.0	0.2	1.4	29.6	5.4	1.1	1.2	127.6	44.6	34.4	704	599
Howard	18.9	0.1	4.8	40.3	9.6	2.0	8.9	282.0	77.9	104.5	1 250	1 151
Huntington	5.4	0.5	1.4	7.8	2.0	0.5	5.7	66.7	29.3	26.2	704	614
Jackson	6.3	0.1	2.1	20.0	3.2	0.8	6.8	108.9	30.0	32.8	803	709
Jasper	4.8	0.4	1.3	7.0	1.4	0.4	1.3	81.0	19.7	30.0	1 047	964
Jay	2.8	0.0	0.7	11.5	3.5	0.5	1.2	52.9	20.3	14.8	682	595
Jefferson	6.0	2.9	1.1	23.3	4.4	0.8	0.9	62.3	27.3	23.2	742	734
Jennings	3.4	-0.2	0.7	15.5	1.4	0.6	0.4	38.7	22.0	11.3	414	346
Johnson	17.8	0.0	25.0	26.3	3.8	1.2	7.4	213.2	74.2	80.1	750	640
Knox	9.3	1.2	1.6	29.6	6.8	2.8	2.5	159.7	32.9	27.0	681	677
Kosciusko	11.7	0.0	3.6	11.1	4.7	0.9	2.8	190.2	57.4	69.2	984	897
Lagrange	3.5	0.1	0.9	4.8	0.6	1.1	0.2	61.9	25.5	29.1	888	797
Lake	97.6	76.7	23.7	352.7	95.4	19.9	62.4	1 398.6	542.2	639.6	1 334	1 315
La Porte	14.3	2.4	3.9	42.9	10.4	3.2	10.3	268.9	94.5	117.3	1 076	963
Lawrence	8.9	5.9	3.1	26.7	3.9	0.9	21.0	160.2	38.1	33.6	739	633
Madison	19.1	1.4	11.0	79.1	13.1	3.5	20.4	244.0	118.1	93.9	712	629
Marion	776.2	887.8	199.6	636.4	355.2	193.4	558.0	2 332.3	829.0	1 031.6	1 268	1 127
Marshall	5.7	1.6	2.3	9.6	3.3	0.8	3.3	91.4	35.5	40.8	900	814
Martin	169.2	43.8	0.4	8.5	1.1	0.4	0.2	20.7	10.3	8.2	779	687
Miami	32.8	15.4	1.2	12.9	2.8	1.0	0.8	92.6	39.5	28.2	848	779
Monroe	25.2	1.0	13.3	146.1	7.5	8.8	54.8	209.9	67.1	83.6	716	589
Montgomery	6.4	0.1	1.3	13.7	1.7	2.8	3.1	89.3	29.9	47.4	1 307	1 178
Morgan	7.4	3.3	1.8	22.9	3.3	0.9	4.3	119.7	49.8	39.1	604	505
Newton	2.2	0.0	0.6	3.0	0.9	0.3	0.3	32.1	13.6	13.0	883	805
Noble	15.9	0.1	1.3	10.0	1.4	0.6	4.2	107.7	37.7	36.6	872	774
Ohio	0.8	0.0	0.2	3.0	0.3	0.1	0.0	12.2	5.6	3.5	635	390
Orange	2.6	0.2	0.9	15.5	1.7	0.6	3.3	44.0	16.9	10.6	547	476
Owen	2.6	0.2	0.7	8.5	1.1	0.5	1.0	31.2	16.3	11.8	582	508
Parke	3.2	0.1	0.7	8.9	3.5	0.4	0.9	30.1	15.0	12.2	742	664
Perry	4.5	1.3	2.2	11.8	2.0	0.4	11.2	47.2	18.8	13.1	678	533
Pike	1.9	0.0	0.5	8.1	0.9	0.4	2.3	33.4	8.9	10.6	829	822
Porter	23.5	1.2	12.7	27.0	6.8	1.6	40.9	433.4	109.3	146.2	1 015	971
Posey	3.8	3.1	0.9	9.2	1.7	0.4	25.5	62.1	18.3	32.4	1 218	1 215
Pulaski	2.4	0.0	0.6	4.8	0.7	0.2	1.4	39.9	13.7	13.3	1 008	923

1. October 1, 2000 to September 30, 2001. 2. State totals may include programs not allocated by county. 3. Based on the resident population estimated as of July 1 of the year shown.

Table B. States and Counties — Local Government Finances, Government Employment, and Elections

STATE County	Local government finances, 1997 (cont'd) Direct general expenditure Total (mil dol)	Per capita[1] (dollars)	Percent of total for — Educa-tion	Health and hospitals	Police protec-tion	Public welfare	High-ways	Debt outstanding Total (mil dol)	Per capita[1] (dollars)	Government employment, 1999 Federal civilian	Federal military	State and local	Presidential election, 2000[2] Percent of vote cast — Demo-cratic	Republi-can	All other
	183	184	185	186	187	188	189	190	191	192	193	194	195	196	197
INDIANA	X	X	X	X	X	X	X	X	X	38 843	21 906	361 106	41.0	56.6	2.3
Adams	78.0	2 375	39.4	25.1	2.0	2.9	4.2	21.2	646	73	115	1 883	30.0	68.0	2.1
Allen	624.2	2 000	54.5	1.6	5.3	4.2	4.0	251.6	806	2 147	1 117	15 731	36.4	61.6	2.0
Bartholomew	239.0	3 477	35.6	36.9	2.1	1.8	2.8	127.2	1 851	226	243	5 063	35.0	62.9	2.1
Benton	22.9	2 395	61.7	0.3	2.1	4.2	9.1	3.7	386	34	34	630	34.3	63.0	2.7
Blackford	31.9	2 277	44.0	19.7	3.0	3.4	4.4	9.8	701	31	48	756	43.0	55.1	1.9
Boone	104.5	2 432	47.6	17.4	3.1	1.8	4.5	69.0	1 604	110	156	2 038	25.9	71.5	2.6
Brown	25.4	1 626	58.7	1.5	2.0	2.0	7.5	14.6	938	18	56	728	38.3	56.8	5.0
Carroll	46.0	2 301	53.5	1.2	2.0	1.7	6.7	29.0	1 449	69	70	764	35.9	61.7	2.5
Cass	105.3	2 729	45.0	25.9	2.6	2.1	3.4	55.7	1 444	117	136	3 407	35.8	61.6	2.6
Clark	238.3	2 556	39.3	33.3	3.0	1.9	2.4	85.3	915	2 947	333	5 321	46.5	52.0	1.5
Clay	66.9	2 523	56.2	14.3	1.4	1.2	3.6	16.3	615	83	94	1 244	35.5	62.9	1.6
Clinton	84.5	2 543	44.2	17.7	2.8	3.0	5.3	45.4	1 367	80	115	1 473	33.1	65.0	1.9
Crawford	18.2	1 732	64.9	0.6	0.8	1.8	7.8	3.3	312	33	37	494	43.2	55.3	1.5
Daviess	69.4	2 405	44.1	28.5	1.6	2.6	6.6	32.7	1 133	82	101	1 504	27.6	70.4	2.0
Dearborn	119.3	2 562	43.8	26.0	2.1	1.4	3.0	86.4	1 855	81	167	2 105	34.1	64.9	1.0
Decatur	56.0	2 206	45.6	24.9	2.1	2.5	5.4	23.3	918	72	89	1 271	31.5	66.7	1.8
De Kalb	107.1	2 767	46.1	21.0	2.6	2.1	4.2	49.0	1 266	88	138	1 750	34.6	63.1	2.2
Delaware	213.6	1 816	55.4	1.0	4.1	6.3	4.1	77.7	660	426	413	9 695	47.4	50.2	2.5
Dubois	81.5	2 083	58.2	0.7	2.5	1.2	7.3	51.3	1 312	116	139	1 803	32.8	65.4	1.8
Elkhart	364.3	2 134	60.9	1.3	4.8	4.8	3.5	157.6	923	308	609	6 889	30.1	67.5	2.4
Fayette	61.7	2 362	56.9	1.4	2.8	5.8	6.4	4.3	165	57	90	1 356	39.5	58.5	2.0
Floyd	195.5	2 736	43.2	34.8	2.7	1.7	1.8	53.1	743	179	251	5 027	44.0	54.9	1.1
Fountain	32.9	1 802	58.1	0.8	2.3	2.5	9.0	18.7	1 025	60	64	832	37.3	60.5	2.1
Franklin	28.5	1 321	58.4	0.5	1.2	2.8	11.7	30.2	1 398	53	77	831	31.1	67.0	1.9
Fulton	47.1	2 316	36.5	30.5	3.1	2.7	6.2	28.3	1 393	56	73	1 020	35.5	62.7	1.7
Gibson	67.8	2 121	57.9	1.3	2.1	2.5	6.2	140.1	4 385	90	112	1 092	42.1	56.2	1.8
Grant	135.6	1 862	55.3	0.5	5.3	5.1	4.8	38.9	534	1 027	252	3 265	36.8	61.2	2.0
Greene	71.1	2 149	50.6	17.7	1.7	3.5	5.1	33.5	1 013	84	115	1 856	38.8	59.1	2.2
Hamilton	397.1	2 565	50.1	12.6	3.5	0.7	6.9	216.0	1 395	367	599	7 407	23.7	74.3	2.1
Hancock	152.1	2 865	49.4	29.4	1.7	1.0	4.9	37.9	713	115	194	3 018	28.3	69.5	2.1
Harrison	62.8	1 848	58.4	18.7	1.6	2.1	5.5	40.1	1 178	116	123	1 596	39.4	58.5	2.1
Hendricks	225.3	2 441	52.3	21.4	2.6	1.4	2.7	113.7	1 232	174	344	5 666	26.8	71.2	1.9
Henry	125.6	2 570	45.9	23.7	1.7	1.4	4.3	74.9	1 533	108	168	3 006	41.8	56.4	1.7
Howard	241.9	2 895	40.9	22.3	4.3	2.2	3.7	116.8	1 397	332	292	5 388	37.8	59.6	2.5
Huntington	66.9	1 801	58.7	0.3	3.2	3.5	6.6	28.2	760	94	130	1 806	28.2	69.2	2.6
Jackson	105.1	2 571	43.3	30.7	2.3	1.6	3.1	47.5	1 161	110	144	2 203	36.5	62.0	1.5
Jasper	74.5	2 597	39.3	22.2	3.0	1.5	3.8	140.0	4 878	83	103	1 617	33.5	64.6	1.9
Jay	55.3	2 547	42.4	21.7	2.5	3.2	7.3	10.9	504	50	75	1 162	39.4	58.4	2.2
Jefferson	61.2	1 956	59.9	0.9	2.7	2.4	4.9	34.5	1 103	101	111	2 224	42.9	55.2	1.9
Jennings	37.4	1 375	63.9	1.5	2.9	3.9	6.9	11.9	438	63	98	1 982	37.4	60.4	2.2
Johnson	236.1	2 290	56.6	14.9	2.8	0.7	3.4	193.4	1 809	336	392	5 069	28.3	69.5	2.2
Knox	172.9	4 356	22.5	51.4	1.2	1.4	2.0	37.7	951	180	137	5 124	41.8	56.4	1.8
Kosciusko	188.8	2 683	50.4	21.7	2.2	0.8	3.6	119.8	1 702	185	248	2 612	22.9	75.3	1.9
Lagrange	56.6	1 730	68.2	0.5	1.2	2.9	5.4	46.9	1 434	60	118	1 240	32.8	65.2	1.9
Lake	1 347.7	2 812	46.5	0.9	4.4	10.4	2.7	693.3	1 446	2 011	1 680	26 816	62.0	36.0	2.0
La Porte	247.9	2 273	56.6	1.8	3.0	5.1	3.6	119.9	1 099	233	401	7 327	49.7	47.8	2.5
Lawrence	137.1	3 011	36.1	43.3	2.1	0.4	4.0	40.8	896	164	159	2 303	31.4	66.1	2.4
Madison	263.9	2 002	52.5	0.7	4.6	3.8	4.0	78.7	597	320	457	6 273	44.8	53.5	1.6
Marion	2 401.0	2 951	40.3	11.2	4.5	3.8	2.8	3 747.8	4 606	13 151	3 775	60 151	47.9	49.2	2.9
Marshall	92.5	2 039	59.4	1.2	3.5	3.2	4.5	44.3	978	105	160	2 091	34.3	63.6	2.1
Martin	17.3	1 644	61.4	0.7	2.4	3.5	8.7	4.8	461	3 746	92	468	32.9	65.3	1.8
Miami	88.2	2 656	52.7	18.7	1.7	2.6	3.2	21.7	652	760	124	2 000	32.1	65.0	2.8
Monroe	196.8	1 687	48.0	1.2	3.0	4.3	4.4	139.5	1 196	413	425	19 097	43.6	47.6	8.8
Montgomery	74.2	2 044	60.7	0.5	2.6	2.5	6.9	54.1	1 492	103	127	1 837	29.8	67.9	2.4
Morgan	121.6	1 877	53.3	18.0	2.5	1.6	4.0	64.4	994	124	233	2 619	28.3	69.4	2.4
Newton	31.9	2 175	62.3	0.6	1.8	3.6	7.5	9.9	673	42	52	759	38.1	59.0	2.9
Noble	97.6	2 327	48.2	20.9	2.8	1.3	5.2	51.3	1 225	92	150	2 033	33.9	64.0	2.1
Ohio	12.4	2 271	39.7	0.8	3.5	2.0	8.0	0.3	60	15	19	297	38.2	60.8	1.0
Orange	44.5	2 296	45.8	25.5	1.5	1.3	5.7	20.4	1 051	48	69	995	34.9	62.8	2.3
Owen	28.9	1 427	61.4	1.9	1.6	3.2	7.9	5.0	247	43	72	813	34.6	61.8	3.5
Parke	26.6	1 615	59.8	1.6	2.0	1.9	10.1	10.2	621	59	59	1 118	38.5	59.6	1.9
Perry	43.8	2 267	42.7	23.1	1.8	1.3	4.7	31.1	1 609	81	66	1 441	51.8	46.9	1.4
Pike	31.1	2 440	39.2	1.3	1.2	3.4	5.0	135.3	10 603	38	45	611	41.3	56.6	1.9
Porter	418.3	2 903	40.9	29.5	2.1	0.9	3.5	222.0	1 540	438	515	8 158	45.1	52.5	2.4
Posey	64.4	2 417	56.4	1.4	1.8	2.9	6.6	114.4	4 296	86	91	1 176	39.9	58.5	1.7
Pulaski	40.3	3 050	37.1	24.0	1.9	2.6	5.3	11.4	860	45	47	949	34.8	63.4	1.8

1. Based on the resident population estimated as of July 1 of the year shown.   2. Data subject to copyright.

STATE/County code	MSA/PMSA/NECMA code[1]	County Type[2]	STATE County	Land area[3] (sq km) 2000	Population and population characteristics, 2000			Race alone or in combination (percent)				Percent Hispanic[4]	Age (percent)					
					Total persons	Rank	Per square kilometer	White	Black	Am. Indian, Alaska Native	Asian and Pacific Islander		Under 5 years	5 to 17 years	18 to 24 years	25 to 34 years	35 to 44 years	45 to 54 years
				1	2	3	4	5	6	7	8	9	10	11	12	13	14	15
			INDIANA—Cont'd															
18 133	...	6	Putnam	1 244	36 019	1 216	29.0	95.7	3.2	0.7	0.8	1.1	6.1	17.4	13.2	13.0	16.3	12.3
18 135	...	6	Randolph	1 173	27 401	1 470	23.4	98.8	0.4	0.5	0.3	1.2	6.7	18.5	7.9	12.3	15.0	13.6
18 137	...	6	Ripley	1 156	26 523	1 501	22.9	98.7	0.1	0.6	0.5	0.9	7.4	20.7	7.7	13.2	15.7	12.8
18 139	...	6	Rush	1 057	18 261	1 882	17.3	98.5	0.8	0.6	0.6	0.5	6.8	19.9	7.5	12.9	16.0	13.1
18 141	7800	3	St. Joseph	1 185	265 559	208	224.1	84.1	12.3	0.9	1.8	4.7	7.0	18.7	11.8	13.2	14.8	13.1
18 143	4520	2	Scott	493	22 960	1 645	46.6	99.1	0.1	0.4	0.3	1.0	7.4	18.9	9.2	14.5	15.8	13.5
18 145	3480	1	Shelby	1 069	43 445	1 029	40.6	97.9	0.9	0.5	0.8	1.1	6.8	19.9	8.0	13.2	17.4	13.6
18 147	...	8	Spencer	1 033	20 391	1 767	19.7	98.2	0.7	0.5	0.3	1.5	6.3	20.2	7.3	12.4	16.7	14.3
18 149	...	6	Starke	801	23 556	1 611	29.4	98.5	0.3	0.7	0.4	2.2	6.5	20.3	8.0	12.3	15.5	13.2
18 151	...	6	Steuben	800	33 214	1 306	41.5	98.0	0.5	0.7	0.5	2.1	6.6	19.0	10.4	13.1	15.4	13.9
18 153	...	6	Sullivan	1 158	21 751	1 707	18.8	94.9	4.5	0.8	0.3	0.8	5.6	17.0	9.4	14.3	16.2	14.1
18 155	...	8	Switzerland	573	9 065	2 523	15.8	99.2	0.3	0.5	0.1	0.9	6.3	20.0	8.5	12.2	15.8	13.8
18 157	3920	3	Tippecanoe	1 294	148 955	362	115.1	90.1	2.8	0.7	4.9	5.3	5.9	15.1	25.4	14.6	12.5	10.9
18 159	3850	3	Tipton	674	16 577	1 985	24.6	99.0	0.2	0.4	0.5	1.2	6.1	18.9	7.2	12.7	15.4	14.8
18 161	...	8	Union	418	7 349	2 651	17.6	99.1	0.3	0.5	0.4	0.3	7.0	20.3	7.7	12.9	15.6	13.3
18 163	2440	2	Vanderburgh	608	171 922	316	282.8	90.3	8.8	0.5	1.1	1.0	6.2	16.9	11.5	12.7	15.4	13.3
18 165	8320	3	Vermillion	665	16 788	1 971	25.2	99.2	0.4	0.7	0.4	0.6	6.3	17.5	8.1	12.6	14.9	14.7
18 167	8320	3	Vigo	1 045	105 848	501	101.3	91.9	6.7	0.7	1.6	1.2	6.1	16.8	14.3	12.9	14.3	12.9
18 169	...	7	Wabash	1 070	34 960	1 250	32.7	98.1	0.5	1.0	0.6	1.2	5.9	18.6	10.3	11.7	14.5	13.6
18 171	...	8	Warren	945	8 419	2 571	8.9	99.5	0.1	0.4	0.2	0.4	6.0	20.0	6.6	12.4	15.5	14.3
18 173	2440	2	Warrick	995	52 383	892	52.6	98.0	1.2	0.3	0.9	0.6	6.6	20.3	7.2	12.2	17.5	15.7
18 175	...	6	Washington	1 332	27 223	1 474	20.4	99.3	0.2	0.5	0.2	0.7	6.7	19.8	8.7	13.5	16.2	13.7
18 177	...	5	Wayne	1 045	71 097	699	68.0	93.4	5.9	0.6	0.8	1.4	6.2	18.0	9.2	12.7	14.8	13.5
18 179	2760	2	Wells	958	27 600	1 462	28.8	99.0	0.3	0.5	0.3	1.4	6.6	20.7	8.3	11.5	16.6	13.3
18 181	...	6	White	1 309	25 267	1 556	19.3	96.1	0.2	0.6	0.4	5.3	6.4	19.4	7.8	12.4	15.3	13.8
18 183	2760	2	Whitley	869	30 707	1 381	35.3	98.9	0.3	0.7	0.4	0.9	6.8	19.9	8.1	12.4	16.4	14.5
19 000	...	X	**IOWA**	144 701	2 926 324	X	20.2	94.9	2.5	0.6	1.6	2.8	6.4	18.6	10.2	12.4	15.2	13.4
19 001	...	8	Adair	1 474	8 243	2 587	5.6	99.4	0.1	0.3	0.3	0.7	5.4	18.5	6.9	9.3	15.1	12.9
19 003	...	9	Adams	1 097	4 482	2 882	4.1	99.3	0.1	0.5	0.2	0.6	5.5	18.4	6.3	9.5	14.6	13.2
19 005	...	7	Allamakee	1 656	14 675	2 110	8.9	96.5	0.2	0.4	0.6	3.5	5.9	19.6	7.0	10.6	15.0	13.1
19 007	...	7	Appanoose	1 285	13 721	2 181	10.7	98.8	0.5	0.6	0.3	1.0	5.6	18.2	7.8	10.7	14.4	13.0
19 009	...	7	Audubon	1 148	6 830	2 707	5.9	99.5	0.3	0.3	0.2	0.5	5.8	20.1	5.0	9.2	13.5	12.3
19 011	...	6	Benton	1 855	25 308	1 552	13.6	99.3	0.4	0.4	0.2	0.6	6.5	20.9	6.8	12.0	17.3	12.4
19 013	8920	3	Black Hawk	1 469	128 012	423	87.1	89.8	8.6	0.5	1.3	1.8	6.1	17.0	15.7	11.9	13.3	13.6
19 015	...	6	Boone	1 480	26 224	1 509	17.7	98.9	0.5	0.4	0.3	0.8	6.0	18.8	8.4	11.5	15.6	14.2
19 017	...	6	Bremer	1 134	23 325	1 628	20.6	98.8	0.7	0.2	0.7	0.6	5.5	18.6	12.0	9.9	14.0	13.6
19 019	...	6	Buchanan	1 480	21 093	1 732	14.3	98.9	0.4	0.5	0.5	0.6	6.9	21.7	8.1	11.2	15.1	13.4
19 021	...	7	Buena Vista	1 489	20 411	1 765	13.7	89.1	0.6	0.3	4.8	12.5	5.9	19.5	12.2	10.7	14.7	12.7
19 023	...	8	Butler	1 503	15 305	2 071	10.2	99.5	0.2	0.3	0.4	0.6	5.5	18.9	6.4	10.5	14.4	14.4
19 025	...	9	Calhoun	1 477	11 115	2 357	7.5	98.5	0.9	0.4	0.3	0.9	5.1	17.9	6.4	9.9	14.9	13.5
19 027	...	7	Carroll	1 475	21 421	1 716	14.5	99.2	0.3	0.2	0.4	0.5	6.0	20.9	7.4	10.3	15.6	12.4
19 029	...	6	Cass	1 462	14 684	2 108	10.0	99.2	0.4	0.3	0.1	0.7	5.4	18.3	6.8	9.7	15.1	13.4
19 031	...	6	Cedar	1 501	18 187	1 889	12.1	99.0	0.3	0.4	0.5	0.9	6.1	19.3	6.9	11.3	16.4	14.3
19 033	...	5	Cerro Gordo	1 472	46 447	974	31.6	97.4	1.2	0.4	1.0	2.8	5.9	17.8	9.0	11.0	15.4	14.0
19 035	...	7	Cherokee	1 495	13 035	2 229	8.7	98.7	0.4	0.3	0.6	1.0	5.5	19.1	6.8	8.9	15.1	14.3
19 037	...	7	Chickasaw	1 307	13 095	2 221	10.0	99.3	0.1	0.3	0.4	0.6	5.7	20.4	6.9	10.0	15.7	13.0
19 039	...	6	Clarke	1 117	9 133	2 519	8.2	97.2	0.2	0.6	0.5	4.0	6.4	19.9	7.6	11.0	15.5	13.4
19 041	...	7	Clay	1 473	17 372	1 930	11.8	98.6	0.3	0.3	1.1	1.1	6.1	18.6	8.0	11.1	15.8	13.8
19 043	...	9	Clayton	2 017	18 678	1 862	9.3	99.3	0.2	0.4	0.2	0.8	5.8	19.6	6.5	10.6	15.5	13.7
19 045	...	4	Clinton	1 800	50 149	914	27.9	96.9	2.3	0.6	0.7	1.3	6.4	19.2	8.2	11.4	15.7	13.5
19 047	...	7	Crawford	1 850	16 942	1 956	9.2	93.8	0.9	0.6	0.6	8.7	6.4	20.2	8.1	10.9	14.9	12.9
19 049	2120	2	Dallas	1 519	40 750	1 090	26.8	95.5	1.0	0.4	1.0	5.4	8.3	19.9	6.9	14.7	17.5	13.6
19 051	...	7	Davis	1 303	8 541	2 565	6.6	99.1	0.3	0.7	0.4	0.7	7.1	20.1	7.4	10.7	14.5	12.9
19 053	...	9	Decatur	1 377	8 689	2 552	6.3	97.5	1.2	0.7	1.4	1.7	5.5	17.5	16.3	9.2	12.4	12.0
19 055	...	6	Delaware	1 497	18 404	1 874	12.3	99.6	0.1	0.2	0.2	0.7	6.4	22.6	7.0	10.9	16.7	12.3
19 057	...	5	Des Moines	1 078	42 351	1 048	39.3	94.8	4.2	0.6	0.9	1.7	6.3	18.1	8.5	11.6	14.6	14.6
19 059	...	7	Dickinson	987	16 424	1 996	16.6	99.3	0.3	0.4	0.2	0.7	5.3	16.6	6.6	9.9	14.0	15.6
19 061	2200	3	Dubuque	1 575	89 143	583	56.6	97.8	1.1	0.4	0.8	1.2	6.6	18.9	10.2	12.0	15.3	13.4
19 063	...	7	Emmet	1 025	11 027	2 363	10.8	97.9	0.4	0.5	0.4	4.3	5.5	18.8	10.1	9.9	13.9	13.3
19 065	...	6	Fayette	1 893	22 008	1 691	11.6	98.4	0.7	0.4	0.4	1.5	6.0	19.0	8.6	10.3	14.7	12.6
19 067	...	7	Floyd	1 296	16 900	1 959	13.0	98.6	0.4	0.3	0.8	1.3	6.2	18.9	7.0	10.8	13.7	13.7
19 069	...	7	Franklin	1 508	10 704	2 383	7.1	95.4	0.2	0.4	0.2	6.0	5.6	18.6	7.3	10.0	14.1	13.9
19 071	...	9	Fremont	1 324	8 010	2 606	6.0	98.5	0.1	0.5	0.3	2.2	5.6	19.5	6.0	10.0	14.3	14.6
19 073	...	7	Greene	1 472	10 366	2 408	7.0	98.8	0.3	0.4	0.3	1.7	5.8	19.8	6.1	9.5	14.8	13.1
19 075	...	8	Grundy	1 302	12 369	2 275	9.5	99.5	0.1	0.2	0.4	0.6	5.4	19.8	6.3	9.8	15.3	13.7

1. MSA = Metropolitan Statistical Area. PMSA = Primary MSA. NECMA = New England County Metropolitan Area. See Appendix A for explanation of these concepts. See Appendix B for list of metropolitan areas identified by type, with component counties. 2. County typology code from the Economic Research Service of USDA. See Appendix A for definition. 3. Dry land or land partially or temporarily covered by water. 4. Hispanic persons may be of any race.

Table B. States and Counties — Population and Households

STATE County	55 to 64 years (16)	65 to 74 years (17)	75 years and over (18)	Percent female (19)	Total persons 2001 (20)	Total persons 1990 (21)	Percent change 1990–2000 (22)	Percent change 2000–2001 (23)	Births (24)	Deaths (25)	Net migration (26)	Households Number (27)	Percent change, 1990–2000 (28)	Persons per household (29)	Percent Female family householder[1] (30)	Percent One person (31)
INDIANA—Cont'd																
Putnam	9.3	7.0	5.3	48.0	36 331	30 315	18.8	0.9	580	351	94	12 374	23.8	2.56	7.7	22.4
Randolph	10.2	8.3	7.5	51.0	27 364	27 148	0.9	-0.1	453	357	-121	10 937	4.7	2.48	8.7	25.0
Ripley	9.2	6.9	6.5	50.9	26 976	24 616	7.7	1.7	451	319	323	9 842	12.1	2.66	8.7	22.7
Rush	9.1	7.7	7.1	50.9	17 980	18 129	0.7	-1.5	293	263	-311	6 923	6.4	2.60	8.4	23.3
St. Joseph	7.8	6.7	6.9	51.7	264 779	247 052	7.5	-0.3	4 929	3 101	-2 565	100 743	9.1	2.50	12.4	27.9
Scott	9.7	6.3	4.7	50.4	23 247	20 991	9.4	1.3	367	303	225	8 832	16.3	2.58	11.3	22.5
Shelby	9.0	6.5	5.7	50.5	43 580	40 307	7.8	0.3	724	499	-76	16 561	12.2	2.58	9.3	22.7
Spencer	9.9	7.2	5.7	49.9	20 276	19 490	4.6	-0.6	314	206	-218	7 569	8.7	2.65	7.2	20.8
Starke	10.3	7.8	6.1	50.5	21 805	22 747	3.6	-7.4	375	323	-1 852	8 740	7.4	2.66	9.9	22.4
Steuben	9.7	6.6	5.3	49.5	33 404	27 446	21.0	0.6	480	394	119	12 738	25.0	2.53	8.5	24.3
Sullivan	9.4	7.2	6.9	46.5	21 818	18 993	14.5	0.3	282	327	119	7 819	6.2	2.49	9.3	25.3
Switzerland	10.8	7.2	5.4	49.6	9 374	7 738	17.1	3.4	145	86	242	3 435	21.0	2.61	10.2	21.7
Tippecanoe	6.5	4.6	4.5	48.7	149 036	130 598	14.1	0.1	2 323	1 294	-932	55 226	21.1	2.42	8.3	28.0
Tipton	10.4	7.1	7.4	51.1	16 520	16 119	2.8	-0.3	233	210	-75	6 469	7.4	2.53	7.7	23.1
Union	10.3	6.9	6.0	50.4	7 313	6 976	5.3	-0.5	82	76	-40	2 793	8.4	2.60	8.2	22.4
Vanderburgh	8.7	7.6	7.7	52.6	171 268	165 058	4.2	-0.4	2 856	2 509	-938	70 623	5.8	2.33	11.9	31.0
Vermillion	10.2	7.7	8.1	51.3	16 581	16 773	0.1	-1.2	271	239	-239	6 762	1.9	2.44	9.0	26.6
Vigo	8.4	6.9	7.3	50.9	104 778	106 107	-0.2	-1.0	1 700	1 484	-1 276	40 998	3.0	2.38	11.7	30.0
Wabash	9.7	7.6	8.1	51.5	34 704	35 069	-0.3	-0.7	529	512	-276	13 215	4.6	2.50	8.5	24.9
Warren	11.2	7.5	6.4	49.3	8 614	8 176	3.0	2.3	108	99	183	3 219	6.8	2.58	6.8	21.2
Warrick	9.7	5.8	5.0	50.9	53 080	44 920	16.6	1.3	739	561	522	19 438	22.9	2.66	8.2	18.6
Washington	9.3	6.4	5.6	50.0	27 585	23 717	14.8	1.3	431	314	249	10 264	18.5	2.62	9.2	22.2
Wayne	9.9	8.2	7.5	52.0	70 515	71 951	-1.2	-0.8	1 143	1 012	-698	28 469	3.2	2.42	11.4	27.4
Wells	8.9	7.0	7.1	50.7	27 689	25 948	6.4	0.3	419	327	11	10 402	10.2	2.61	8.3	23.3
White	10.0	7.9	6.9	50.8	25 165	23 265	8.6	-0.4	439	326	-211	9 727	9.0	2.57	8.4	22.6
Whitley	8.8	6.7	6.3	50.4	31 099	27 651	11.1	1.3	514	350	236	11 711	17.0	2.58	8.3	22.4
IOWA	8.8	7.2	7.7	50.9	2 923 179	2 776 831	5.4	-0.1	46 648	35 033	-14 184	1 149 276	8.0	2.46	8.6	27.2
Adair	9.8	9.4	12.7	51.0	8 069	8 409	-2.0	-2.1	89	148	-115	3 398	-0.6	2.37	5.7	28.1
Adams	11.0	10.0	11.4	50.8	4 395	4 866	-7.9	-1.9	66	76	-76	1 867	-6.9	2.34	5.5	30.0
Allamakee	10.5	8.9	9.5	49.9	14 426	13 855	5.9	-1.7	232	215	-270	5 722	8.6	2.49	6.6	27.5
Appanoose	10.5	9.3	10.7	52.2	13 594	13 743	-0.2	-0.9	203	202	-125	5 779	3.0	2.34	8.8	29.9
Audubon	10.6	10.6	12.9	52.1	6 715	7 334	-6.9	-1.7	95	105	-106	2 773	-5.6	2.40	5.6	28.2
Benton	8.7	7.5	8.0	50.0	25 931	22 429	12.8	2.5	365	273	526	9 746	14.4	2.56	6.5	23.4
Black Hawk	8.4	6.8	7.2	52.0	126 483	123 798	3.4	-1.2	1 961	1 388	-2 115	49 683	5.9	2.45	10.8	27.1
Boone	9.1	7.8	8.6	51.0	26 281	25 186	4.1	0.2	381	375	61	10 374	5.6	2.44	7.8	26.7
Bremer	10.3	7.3	8.7	51.7	23 368	22 813	2.2	0.2	260	266	54	8 860	5.6	2.47	6.2	24.7
Buchanan	9.1	7.0	7.5	50.3	20 913	20 844	1.2	-0.9	354	258	-273	7 933	5.7	2.61	7.4	24.7
Buena Vista	7.5	7.9	9.0	49.9	20 023	19 965	2.2	-1.9	326	282	-437	7 499	-0.2	2.54	7.2	27.0
Butler	9.8	9.1	11.0	51.0	15 145	15 731	-2.7	-1.0	188	226	-116	6 175	2.3	2.43	6.3	25.0
Calhoun	10.1	9.8	12.3	50.5	10 916	11 508	-3.4	-1.8	131	184	-147	4 513	-3.7	2.31	6.6	30.5
Carroll	8.6	8.7	9.9	51.3	21 128	21 423	0.0	-1.4	314	314	-289	8 486	6.6	2.46	6.8	29.6
Cass	10.5	9.6	11.2	51.5	14 559	15 128	-2.9	-1.4	185	268	-40	6 120	-0.9	2.32	7.2	29.8
Cedar	9.5	7.6	8.7	50.6	18 144	17 444	4.3	-0.2	234	207	-63	7 147	6.9	2.51	6.7	23.7
Cerro Gordo	9.2	8.7	9.0	51.9	45 638	46 733	-0.6	-1.7	669	646	-835	19 374	1.6	2.32	9.1	30.9
Cherokee	10.0	10.0	10.3	50.7	12 885	14 098	-7.5	-1.2	174	209	-111	5 378	-2.5	2.35	6.5	29.5
Chickasaw	10.4	8.6	9.3	50.0	13 050	13 295	-1.5	-0.3	164	163	-41	5 192	3.0	2.48	6.3	26.1
Clarke	9.1	8.2	8.8	50.8	9 143	8 287	10.2	0.1	126	125	8	3 584	7.2	2.50	8.3	25.9
Clay	8.7	8.5	9.5	51.7	17 074	17 585	-1.2	-1.7	212	230	-279	7 259	2.6	2.35	6.8	29.8
Clayton	9.9	9.2	9.4	50.6	18 539	19 054	-2.0	-0.7	246	299	-78	7 375	2.2	2.47	6.1	26.3
Clinton	9.8	7.7	8.1	51.5	49 962	51 040	-1.7	-0.4	848	706	-313	20 105	1.8	2.44	9.8	27.4
Crawford	9.6	8.2	9.0	49.8	16 908	16 775	1.0	-0.2	247	225	-51	6 441	0.7	2.53	7.0	26.2
Dallas	8.0	5.5	5.6	50.6	42 914	29 755	37.0	5.3	618	407	1 905	15 584	39.1	2.59	8.0	23.6
Davis	10.0	8.4	9.0	50.5	8 628	8 312	2.8	1.0	131	125	81	3 207	3.7	2.61	5.2	25.0
Decatur	9.5	8.6	9.6	51.1	8 645	8 338	4.2	-0.5	119	131	-29	3 337	4.1	2.37	7.2	30.3
Delaware	9.2	7.5	7.5	50.4	18 325	18 035	2.0	-0.4	274	197	-151	6 834	7.0	2.66	6.2	23.0
Des Moines	9.7	7.9	8.8	51.7	41 743	42 614	-0.6	-1.4	649	559	-697	17 270	2.3	2.40	10.5	28.6
Dickinson	11.2	10.7	9.9	51.3	16 523	14 909	10.2	0.6	229	231	107	7 103	15.3	2.27	6.7	28.6
Dubuque	8.9	7.3	7.4	51.4	88 856	86 403	3.2	-0.3	1 386	1 114	-533	33 690	9.4	2.51	8.7	26.7
Emmet	9.3	8.6	10.8	51.4	10 813	11 569	-4.7	-1.9	151	162	-204	4 450	-0.2	2.36	7.8	30.3
Fayette	9.8	9.0	10.0	50.6	21 822	21 843	0.8	-0.8	298	323	-157	8 778	3.4	2.41	7.4	28.2
Floyd	10.5	8.6	10.6	51.7	16 601	17 058	-0.9	-1.8	257	262	-296	6 828	1.6	2.40	7.7	28.0
Franklin	10.0	8.8	10.7	50.9	10 599	11 364	-5.8	-1.0	135	176	-60	4 356	-4.9	2.41	6.4	27.6
Fremont	10.2	9.3	10.6	51.2	7 886	8 226	-2.6	-1.5	109	140	-91	3 199	-0.6	2.45	8.2	26.3
Greene	9.3	9.6	12.0	51.2	10 169	10 045	3.2	-1.9	137	182	-149	4 205	0.2	2.41	7.2	29.1
Grundy	10.4	8.8	10.4	51.1	12 305	12 029	2.8	-0.5	142	165	-38	4 984	4.4	2.45	5.5	25.5

1. No spouse present.

STATE County	Births, average 1997–1999 Total	Rate[1]	Deaths, average 1997–1999 Number Total	Infant[2]	Rate Total[1]	Infant[3]	Physicians,[4] 2000 Number	Rate[5]	Hospitals,[4] 1998 Number	Beds Number	Rate[5]	Medicare enrollees 2000	Serious crimes known to police, 2000[6] Total Number	Rate[7]
	32	33	34	35	36	37	38	39	40	41	42	43	44	45
INDIANA—Cont'd														
Putnam	418	12.2	283	NA	8.2	NA	16	44	1	85	247	4 716	NA	NA
Randolph	351	12.8	292	NA	10.6	NA	18	66	1	27	98	4 931	334	1 219
Ripley	415	15.2	263	NA	9.6	NA	27	102	1	73	268	4 494	NA	NA
Rush	250	13.6	208	NA	11.4	NA	14	77	1	44	240	2 875	NA	NA
St. Joseph	3 821	14.8	2 445	36	9.5	9.5	542	204	4	836	324	40 827	15 492	5 834
Scott	337	14.6	233	NA	10.1	NA	12	52	1	46	201	3 647	NA	NA
Shelby	574	13.2	370	NA	8.5	NA	29	67	1	59	136	5 641	NA	NA
Spencer	269	12.8	171	NA	8.2	NA	5	25	0	0	0	3 038	NA	NA
Starke	311	13.1	257	NA	10.8	NA	10	42	1	35	146	3 588	443	2 233
Steuben	444	14.1	291	NA	9.3	NA	18	54	1	57	181	4 776	1 204	3 625
Sullivan	231	11.5	256	NA	12.7	NA	12	55	1	53	275	3 657	NA	NA
Switzerland	108	12.2	82	NA	9.3	NA	2	22	0	0	0	1 231	NA	NA
Tippecanoe	1 828	13.1	975	9	7.0	4.9	288	193	2	477	343	14 991	5 192	3 486
Tipton	197	11.8	163	NA	9.8	NA	19	115	1	116	694	2 475	271	1 635
Union	98	13.4	60	NA	8.2	NA	0	0	0	0	0	1 096	NA	NA
Vanderburgh	2 234	13.3	1 889	17	11.3	7.5	540	314	3	1 127	670	30 223	7 602	4 422
Vermillion	203	12.0	194	NA	11.5	NA	6	36	1	56	331	2 873	NA	NA
Vigo	1 347	12.8	1 169	14	11.1	10.1	220	208	2	550	523	17 294	NA	NA
Wabash	413	11.9	375	NA	10.8	NA	43	123	1	69	200	6 168	NA	NA
Warren	105	12.7	81	NA	9.8	NA	3	36	1	35	424	1 009	NA	NA
Warrick	645	12.5	410	NA	7.9	NA	53	101	1	34	66	6 180	806	1 539
Washington	340	12.2	255	NA	9.2	NA	12	44	1	68	244	3 805	NA	NA
Wayne	883	12.4	791	10	11.1	11.3	138	194	1	250	351	13 164	3 117	4 384
Wells	380	14.2	269	NA	10.0	NA	60	217	2	144	536	3 799	343	1 243
White	335	13.2	234	NA	9.3	NA	17	67	1	59	233	4 692	NA	NA
Whitley	425	14.0	264	NA	8.7	NA	25	81	1	100	328	4 683	NA	NA
IOWA	36 774	12.8	28 156	230	9.8	6.3	5 236	179	120	13 473	471	476 719	94 630	3 234
Adair	82	10.2	115	NA	14.3	NA	5	61	1	34	422	1 578	53	643
Adams	46	10.4	63	NA	14.5	NA	4	89	1	22	506	998	72	1 606
Allamakee	169	12.1	169	NA	12.0	NA	6	41	0	0	0	2 866	NA	NA
Appanoose	149	11.0	176	NA	13.0	NA	11	80	1	60	441	3 075	583	4 249
Audubon	80	11.7	78	NA	11.5	NA	2	29	1	29	427	1 625	31	454
Benton	314	12.4	219	NA	8.6	NA	7	28	1	116	456	4 033	141	557
Black Hawk	1 545	12.8	1 161	11	9.6	7.1	283	221	3	609	503	19 909	5 501	4 297
Boone	297	11.3	312	NA	11.9	NA	27	103	1	65	248	4 406	371	1 415
Bremer	218	9.3	226	NA	9.7	NA	13	56	2	74	316	4 129	235	1 008
Buchanan	298	14.1	219	NA	10.3	NA	19	90	1	109	514	3 452	448	2 124
Buena Vista	244	12.5	222	NA	11.4	NA	17	83	1	41	211	3 777	382	1 872
Butler	162	10.4	188	NA	12.0	NA	1	7	0	0	0	3 363	51	333
Calhoun	110	9.7	165	NA	14.5	NA	7	63	1	49	431	2 602	127	1 143
Carroll	249	11.5	255	NA	11.8	NA	28	131	2	181	834	4 356	366	1 709
Cass	159	10.9	203	NA	13.9	NA	16	109	1	71	487	3 309	337	2 295
Cedar	201	11.2	183	NA	10.2	NA	10	55	0	0	0	2 935	234	1 287
Cerro Gordo	539	11.7	526	NA	11.4	NA	135	291	1	285	617	9 138	2 593	5 583
Cherokee	145	11.0	170	NA	12.9	NA	17	130	1	67	508	2 831	215	1 649
Chickasaw	153	11.4	136	NA	10.1	NA	3	23	1	55	409	2 534	64	489
Clarke	93	11.2	96	NA	11.6	NA	5	55	1	48	574	1 580	362	3 964
Clay	197	11.3	185	NA	10.6	NA	30	173	1	86	491	3 242	415	2 389
Clayton	214	11.4	229	NA	12.3	NA	9	48	2	54	288	3 748	9	48
Clinton	630	12.6	560	NA	11.2	NA	69	138	2	250	501	8 894	NA	NA
Crawford	195	11.9	174	NA	10.6	NA	9	53	1	72	438	3 156	157	927
Dallas	500	13.5	319	NA	8.6	NA	39	96	1	53	144	5 112	661	1 622
Davis	111	13.2	91	NA	10.8	NA	8	94	1	80	952	1 520	7	82
Decatur	91	11.0	112	NA	13.5	NA	8	92	1	50	608	1 723	5	58
Delaware	230	12.4	150	NA	8.1	NA	12	65	1	49	264	2 787	165	897
Des Moines	519	12.3	448	NA	10.7	NA	75	177	1	388	925	7 733	1 927	4 550
Dickinson	168	10.3	178	NA	11.0	NA	17	104	1	49	302	3 675	NA	NA
Dubuque	1 128	12.8	851	NA	9.7	NA	179	201	3	670	763	14 484	2 298	2 578
Emmet	117	10.8	132	NA	12.2	NA	9	82	1	58	533	2 307	209	1 895
Fayette	251	11.5	262	NA	12.1	NA	21	95	3	119	547	4 344	119	541
Floyd	195	11.9	209	NA	12.7	NA	13	77	1	20	122	3 515	221	1 308
Franklin	118	10.9	137	NA	12.6	NA	6	56	1	92	847	2 090	117	1 093
Fremont	89	11.5	114	NA	14.7	NA	5	62	1	36	465	1 634	0	0
Greene	103	10.2	141	NA	14.0	NA	8	77	1	115	1 143	2 344	NA	NA
Grundy	133	10.9	137	NA	11.2	NA	8	65	1	88	722	2 401	96	776

1. Per 1,000 estimated resident population, average 1997–1999.   2. Deaths of infants under 1 year old.   3. Deaths of infants under 1 year old per 1,000 live births.   4. Data subject to copyright.   5. Per 100,000 resident population as of July 1 of the year shown.   6. Data for serious crimes have not been adjusted for underreporting; this may affect comparability between geographic areas and over time.   7. Per 100,000 population estimated by the FBI.

Table B. States and Counties — Crime, Education, Money Income, and Poverty

	Serious crimes known to police, 2000[1] (cont'd)		Education							Money income					Income and poverty, 1998		
	Rate[2]		School enrollment and attainment, 1990				Local government expenditures, fiscal 1999[5]		1989						Percent below poverty level		
			Enrollment[3]		Attainment[4] (percent)						Households						
											Median						
STATE County	Violent	Property	Total	Percent private	High school graduate or more	Bachelor's degree or more	Total current expenditures (mil dol)	Current expenditures per student (dollars)	Per capita[6] (dollars)	Dollars	Percent change, 1979-1989 (constant 1989 dollars)	Percent with $100,000 or more	Median household income	All persons	Persons under 18	Persons 5-17 in families
	46	47	48	49	50	51	52	53	54	55	56	57	58	59	60	61

INDIANA—Cont'd

Putnam	NA	NA	8 429	30.4	76.1	11.3	46.0	6 854	11 154	27 708	-4.5	1.7	40 081	8.8	11.7	10.8
Randolph	91	1 128	6 227	4.9	71.9	8.6	31.7	6 405	11 241	24 773	-5.6	1.0	34 405	11.5	16.3	15.3
Ripley	NA	NA	6 002	11.5	68.8	9.8	34.9	6 420	11 563	26 608	7.6	1.7	38 997	8.4	8.9	11.2
Rush	NA	NA	4 417	9.6	73.6	8.7	16.7	6 074	10 869	25 111	-3.4	1.6	36 506	9.7	12.2	12.4
St. Joseph	442	5 392	67 863	31.6	76.1	19.2	276.6	7 056	13 277	28 235	-4.1	2.6	38 832	11.0	16.2	14.2
Scott	NA	NA	4 895	3.6	60.0	6.6	24.0	5 864	9 766	21 723	-11.0	0.9	32 993	13.9	18.2	18.8
Shelby	NA	NA	9 626	8.6	74.1	9.9	46.1	5 933	12 935	30 366	0.5	1.8	41 844	7.5	10.0	9.8
Spencer	NA	NA	4 562	8.5	71.9	9.2	23.3	5 942	11 462	28 777	4.5	1.4	40 889	8.5	11.4	10.5
Starke	227	2 007	5 310	6.2	59.9	6.0	26.3	5 892	9 980	22 784	-8.7	1.0	30 738	14.1	20.2	18.3
Steuben	181	3 444	6 899	14.5	79.0	12.5	31.0	6 133	12 399	29 203	6.4	1.2	41 382	6.9	9.3	8.8
Sullivan	NA	NA	4 456	5.6	74.1	10.0	23.2	6 376	10 668	22 940	-4.4	0.9	32 470	13.9	17.8	17.3
Switzerland	NA	NA	1 741	6.0	65.8	5.6	9.7	5 884	10 201	23 871	18.1	0.5	32 241	12.3	15.3	17.2
Tippecanoe	172	3 314	53 925	7.1	85.2	30.7	125.1	6 669	12 570	27 630	0.4	3.0	41 749	9.7	11.7	10.7
Tipton	187	1 448	4 027	8.7	77.0	9.8	17.8	6 035	13 669	31 198	-0.9	1.9	44 182	7.0	9.6	9.5
Union	NA	NA	1 810	7.6	71.3	8.4	8.7	5 525	10 700	24 635	-0.2	1.6	37 826	9.5	11.4	14.5
Vanderburgh	447	3 974	39 087	23.2	75.2	16.0	160.2	6 869	13 434	25 798	-4.2	2.8	36 794	12.1	18.5	16.9
Vermillion	NA	NA	3 947	5.4	72.1	7.8	18.4	6 248	11 217	22 339	-5.6	1.1	35 029	10.3	14.5	13.4
Vigo	NA	NA	30 437	10.5	76.0	18.1	102.9	6 103	11 973	23 505	-7.9	2.1	33 154	14.9	20.1	18.5
Wabash	NA	NA	8 643	18.1	74.4	11.7	42.3	6 839	11 511	26 724	-3.2	1.5	38 261	8.4	10.7	9.9
Warren	NA	NA	1 787	3.8	71.6	9.4	8.0	5 918	10 911	25 680	-10.8	1.0	38 668	8.6	11.9	12.2
Warrick	296	1 243	11 956	12.1	80.1	16.2	50.5	5 546	14 037	34 069	-4.9	3.0	50 013	6.4	8.7	7.9
Washington	NA	NA	5 588	3.2	66.2	6.8	30.8	6 422	10 187	22 897	-0.3	1.2	33 458	11.8	15.1	14.9
Wayne	312	4 072	17 529	12.6	71.2	11.3	75.3	6 366	11 535	23 475	-10.5	1.9	35 512	13.1	18.4	16.9
Wells	43	1 199	6 281	6.3	79.0	12.1	34.0	6 442	12 765	31 261	2.1	1.6	43 603	5.9	7.8	7.6
White	NA	NA	5 459	6.2	77.9	10.7	32.7	5 817	12 111	26 610	-3.7	1.3	37 368	8.7	11.3	11.4
Whitley	NA	NA	6 806	8.1	78.9	8.8	31.0	6 171	12 605	31 128	1.5	1.4	44 961	5.6	7.2	6.7
IOWA	266	2 967	737 729	15.0	80.1	16.9	3 110.6	6 243	12 422	26 229	-6.8	2.1	38 159	9.5	13.8	12.1
Adair	36	607	1 858	3.2	77.5	9.8	7.5	6 052	10 565	21 426	2.1	1.2	33 904	10.8	14.6	13.7
Adams	89	1 517	1 068	3.6	77.1	9.4	4.3	5 864	10 110	20 570	-4.4	1.5	28 832	15.5	23.5	20.5
Allamakee	NA	NA	3 255	8.9	75.9	8.9	15.2	5 521	10 232	21 098	-3.9	1.7	31 888	11.2	15.5	13.8
Appanoose	343	3 906	3 307	7.4	72.1	11.5	14.4	6 002	9 748	17 833	-6.3	1.0	28 107	16.8	22.5	21.4
Audubon	15	439	1 612	6.6	71.7	9.8	6.7	5 830	11 210	21 501	-6.5	1.6	31 345	11.7	18.3	15.5
Benton	20	537	5 494	7.5	78.2	9.6	23.6	5 429	11 373	25 959	-7.5	0.9	42 527	7.2	10.6	9.0
Black Hawk	374	3 923	37 637	12.4	80.4	17.3	132.6	7 932	12 321	25 683	-21.4	2.0	36 770	11.8	17.6	15.4
Boone	50	1 365	5 989	9.0	80.8	13.7	24.4	5 852	12 031	26 110	-5.4	1.5	39 383	7.8	12.5	10.1
Bremer	73	935	6 448	24.0	78.5	15.1	26.5	4 985	11 626	27 326	-9.9	1.4	42 889	6.9	9.3	7.9
Buchanan	24	2 100	5 437	12.2	78.4	11.2	18.2	5 515	10 925	23 386	-13.1	1.4	37 652	10.8	16.0	13.8
Buena Vista	122	1 749	5 334	27.1	82.1	15.2	23.0	5 886	11 423	25 311	-6.9	1.8	35 462	10.1	15.0	13.0
Butler	52	281	3 861	4.0	71.8	9.4	12.1	5 645	10 803	23 292	-11.5	1.2	36 466	8.5	12.1	10.6
Calhoun	108	1 035	2 613	6.8	78.9	11.6	15.2	5 986	11 405	22 496	-10.7	1.6	32 242	11.3	15.6	13.8
Carroll	14	1 695	5 492	35.3	74.6	11.3	19.2	5 560	11 301	24 391	-9.7	1.8	37 016	9.1	12.3	10.7
Cass	68	2 227	3 420	5.9	80.7	12.5	17.4	5 682	11 059	21 801	-8.0	1.4	32 638	10.8	14.8	13.8
Cedar	38	1 248	4 343	5.6	79.3	12.8	20.2	5 552	12 113	27 713	-4.4	1.6	42 250	7.6	11.3	9.1
Cerro Gordo	168	5 415	11 418	11.2	81.3	15.5	50.6	6 984	12 304	25 116	-8.9	1.6	36 631	9.3	13.6	11.7
Cherokee	46	1 603	3 260	4.6	81.3	10.8	14.0	5 922	10 909	22 967	-12.2	1.4	35 472	8.9	12.8	10.7
Chickasaw	31	458	3 312	10.6	75.2	9.9	14.1	5 249	10 919	24 656	-5.3	0.9	36 596	8.6	11.7	10.4
Clarke	197	3 767	1 890	4.6	77.6	8.8	10.4	5 546	11 380	21 735	6.7	1.9	32 303	12.5	18.1	16.5
Clay	29	2 360	4 328	10.8	84.8	14.5	16.6	5 613	12 314	25 028	-7.9	2.2	37 353	8.8	12.5	11.1
Clayton	0	48	4 674	10.8	74.5	9.0	35.0	9 707	9 813	21 406	-4.4	1.1	32 660	10.5	14.5	12.2
Clinton	NA	NA	13 116	11.4	77.4	12.9	52.4	5 904	11 795	25 410	-18.1	1.0	37 106	10.8	15.9	13.7
Crawford	24	903	3 998	10.3	72.5	9.8	15.7	5 942	10 056	22 209	-15.2	0.6	33 085	12.6	17.4	15.9
Dallas	56	1 566	7 613	10.4	83.6	16.3	45.8	5 632	13 364	28 874	-7.7	2.2	49 598	5.6	8.2	6.8
Davis	0	82	2 005	9.1	71.9	10.5	7.2	5 776	9 965	20 054	-8.1	0.4	30 487	14.9	22.2	19.6
Decatur	0	58	2 334	32.3	71.8	12.3	9.2	6 283	8 918	18 105	-2.5	0.5	25 959	18.1	23.0	22.3
Delaware	136	761	4 577	11.9	78.3	11.0	19.6	5 308	11 515	25 757	-3.9	2.6	37 078	10.2	13.7	12.0
Des Moines	380	4 170	10 650	8.5	78.9	12.7	48.1	6 745	12 246	26 536	-8.2	1.3	38 617	11.0	17.5	15.4
Dickinson	NA	NA	3 341	6.3	84.1	17.5	16.2	5 614	13 669	25 211	-6.2	3.5	37 716	8.2	12.5	11.1
Dubuque	165	2 413	23 997	41.1	77.7	16.8	76.2	6 167	12 331	28 276	-13.0	2.4	40 042	8.9	12.9	10.4
Emmet	163	1 732	3 096	4.7	78.3	11.0	12.6	6 198	10 402	22 790	-16.8	1.1	33 777	10.7	15.5	13.8
Fayette	9	532	5 282	14.6	76.6	11.8	26.4	6 005	10 226	21 109	-15.0	1.5	32 457	12.0	16.4	15.1
Floyd	83	1 225	4 123	7.4	79.0	12.2	18.6	6 113	11 307	23 344	-13.1	1.7	32 700	12.0	17.1	16.0
Franklin	19	1 074	2 599	3.7	79.4	12.3	11.7	5 888	11 691	23 741	-7.8	1.3	36 010	9.6	14.2	12.2
Fremont	0	0	1 969	4.9	77.7	11.3	9.4	5 690	10 674	22 948	3.7	1.2	33 503	12.3	18.0	15.5
Greene	NA	NA	2 318	6.0	81.2	13.7	12.0	5 684	11 164	22 320	-7.9	1.0	33 346	10.9	16.9	14.7
Grundy	32	744	2 815	5.0	79.5	12.3	14.6	5 734	12 898	26 314	-12.8	1.5	41 051	6.9	10.1	8.6

1. Data for serious crimes have not been adjusted for underreporting; this may affect comparability between geographic areas and over time. 2. Per 100,000 population estimated by the FBI. 3. All persons 3 years old and over enrolled in nursery school through college. 4. Persons 25 years old and over. 5. Elementary and secondary education expenditures, local government fiscal years ending between July 1, 1998 and June 30, 1999. 6. Based on population enumerated as of April 1, 1990.

Table B. States and Counties — **Personal Income**

STATE County	Total (mil dol)	Percent change, 1998–1999	Per capita[1] Dollars	Rank	Wages and salaries[2] (mil dol)	Proprietor's income (mil dol)	Dividends, interest, and rent (mil dol)	Transfer payments Total (mil dol)	Government payments to individuals Total (mil dol)	Social Security (mil dol)	Medical payments (mil dol)	Income maintenance (mil dol)	Unemployment insurance (mil dol)
	62	63	64	65	66	67	68	69	70	71	72	73	74
INDIANA—Cont'd													
Putnam	722	5.7	20 743	1 761	350	42	128	102	95	51	34	5	1
Randolph	591	3.9	21 545	1 506	231	48	100	101	96	50	34	7	1
Ripley	674	9.0	24 372	786	433	38	114	85	80	38	33	5	1
Rush	392	4.7	21 542	1 510	170	24	63	63	60	30	23	4	1
St. Joseph	6 919	3.9	26 761	434	4 402	434	1 422	906	855	419	327	72	10
Scott	468	6.3	19 990	1 994	205	27	60	86	81	35	34	9	1
Shelby	1 067	4.4	24 447	770	578	45	155	137	128	62	53	7	2
Spencer	459	3.9	21 654	1 470	261	20	81	64	59	30	22	4	1
Starke	396	1.8	16 793	2 780	118	30	60	87	82	40	30	7	1
Steuben	790	4.2	24 878	689	530	50	146	95	89	48	32	5	1
Sullivan	418	3.2	19 420	2 169	158	30	73	84	80	36	33	6	2
Switzerland	146	3.4	16 295	2 860	43	6	18	30	28	12	11	2	1
Tippecanoe	3 444	4.0	24 175	825	2 748	163	690	350	322	158	103	22	4
Tipton	421	4.7	25 269	621	132	28	62	55	52	28	18	2	1
Union	137	3.5	18 730	2 360	37	12	20	22	21	10	8	2	0
Vanderburgh	4 743	3.9	28 247	302	3 686	387	1 087	706	673	307	267	55	9
Vermillion	366	3.6	21 599	1 489	212	15	65	65	61	30	22	4	1
Vigo	2 368	3.9	22 689	1 170	1 627	129	518	429	408	172	163	34	6
Wabash	799	2.9	23 144	1 060	431	85	153	130	124	64	48	6	1
Warren	160	1.7	19 157	2 244	44	13	25	26	25	14	8	2	0
Warrick	1 399	6.6	26 616	449	486	79	234	147	137	68	53	8	2
Washington	563	5.7	19 940	2 011	183	40	74	90	85	39	33	8	2
Wayne	1 717	3.8	24 134	833	1 119	141	311	294	280	134	109	23	3
Wells	671	3.3	25 016	668	357	47	118	80	74	42	27	3	1
White	562	3.4	22 027	1 359	291	43	103	89	84	44	32	4	1
Whitley	760	5.9	24 657	722	378	33	121	92	86	47	31	3	1
IOWA	73 453	3.3	25 598	X	44 952	5 774	15 671	9 945	9 345	4 698	3 251	694	191
Adair	182	2.7	22 565	1 200	75	18	49	30	29	15	10	2	1
Adams	89	0.7	20 260	1 902	41	8	22	20	19	9	8	1	0
Allamakee	291	3.1	20 688	1 780	123	49	72	50	47	25	16	3	1
Appanoose	266	3.2	19 750	2 070	122	25	60	62	59	27	19	7	1
Audubon	137	-5.5	20 163	1 948	44	16	43	28	26	15	9	1	0
Benton	592	4.1	22 929	1 104	145	44	127	78	72	41	22	5	2
Black Hawk	2 988	0.6	24 905	686	2 140	170	618	473	448	208	157	44	13
Boone	666	2.3	25 334	606	271	35	153	118	113	46	54	5	1
Bremer	571	0.9	24 345	794	257	55	128	81	76	39	28	4	2
Buchanan	448	-2.0	21 168	1 608	170	49	105	67	63	33	21	5	2
Buena Vista	459	1.4	23 648	926	256	56	109	72	68	36	24	4	1
Butler	313	-2.9	20 195	1 934	83	40	73	59	56	30	19	3	2
Calhoun	239	4.6	21 123	1 624	75	30	66	50	48	25	18	2	1
Carroll	527	-0.5	24 474	761	294	55	138	80	75	40	29	4	1
Cass	325	0.5	22 395	1 245	162	37	84	62	59	31	22	4	1
Cedar	440	1.2	24 396	782	128	35	121	56	52	30	15	3	1
Cerro Gordo	1 189	3.4	26 046	506	743	95	268	185	176	91	60	10	3
Cherokee	302	1.5	23 132	1 065	150	37	80	52	49	28	15	3	1
Chickasaw	316	5.1	23 545	953	153	48	68	47	44	24	14	3	1
Clarke	182	9.0	21 957	1 373	98	20	34	32	30	15	11	3	1
Clay	441	1.3	25 559	575	243	62	104	60	57	32	17	4	1
Clayton	399	0.1	21 477	1 526	183	43	106	70	66	33	24	4	2
Clinton	1 178	2.1	23 742	909	637	94	233	197	187	90	67	15	4
Crawford	337	0.3	20 486	1 841	181	38	78	61	57	29	21	4	1
Dallas	1 075	6.9	28 145	314	395	78	193	101	93	50	30	5	2
Davis	151	-0.5	17 770	2 582	55	18	32	30	29	13	11	3	1
Decatur	137	4.0	16 436	2 837	55	14	29	33	31	15	11	3	1
Delaware	373	-0.5	20 181	1 938	150	52	85	55	51	26	17	4	2
Des Moines	1 059	2.7	25 251	624	763	68	231	168	159	78	53	14	4
Dickinson	461	3.0	28 319	293	220	57	129	63	59	36	17	3	1
Dubuque	2 237	2.2	25 385	600	1 544	175	559	300	282	144	98	19	7
Emmet	252	-1.8	23 666	922	120	31	54	48	46	22	17	2	1
Fayette	436	-0.8	20 239	1 912	193	56	99	84	79	40	26	6	2
Floyd	363	1.0	22 329	1 266	151	28	96	73	70	35	26	4	1
Franklin	237	-5.5	21 995	1 369	102	23	66	42	40	22	13	2	1
Fremont	166	3.1	21 553	1 504	90	11	49	34	32	16	12	3	0
Greene	215	-0.4	21 429	1 540	83	19	63	41	39	23	12	3	1
Grundy	315	0.3	25 655	561	104	41	79	43	41	26	11	2	1

1. Based on the resident population estimated as of July 1 of the year shown.   2. Includes other labor income.

STATE County	Earnings, 1999									Social Security beneficiaries, December 2000			Housing units, 1990	
			Percent by selected industries											
			Goods-related[1]		Service-related and other[2]							Supplemental Security Income recipients, December 2000		
	Total (mil dol)	Farm	Total	Manufacturing	Total	Retail trade	Finance, insurance, and real estate	Services	Government	Number	Rate[3]		Total	Percent change, 1980–1990
	75	76	77	78	79	80	81	82	83	84	85	86	87	88
INDIANA—Cont'd														
Putnam	392	-0.2	31.8	25.9	47.3	15.5	3.1	20.0	21.1	5 803	161	341	10 981	7.1
Randolph	278	0.4	D	38.3	D	7.4	2.9	11.3	17.7	5 747	210	355	11 327	-1.8
Ripley	471	-0.8	D	50.6	D	7.0	5.9	14.7	9.4	4 530	171	332	9 587	4.4
Rush	194	-0.2	D	34.1	D	8.8	D	16.5	19.6	3 422	187	208	7 014	-1.7
St. Joseph	4 837	0.1	D	21.0	D	9.8	6.3	32.3	10.3	44 888	169	3 933	97 956	7.4
Scott	232	0.2	D	41.1	D	11.6	2.7	14.7	17.6	4 364	190	709	8 078	11.0
Shelby	623	0.3	51.0	42.5	35.7	8.2	2.0	13.1	13.0	7 043	162	467	15 654	4.8
Spencer	280	-0.3	32.8	26.9	56.3	5.6	1.4	17.7	11.1	3 610	177	239	7 636	9.5
Starke	148	2.8	D	24.4	D	12.7	2.4	19.5	21.1	4 858	206	430	9 888	7.0
Steuben	580	0.5	D	47.2	D	11.0	2.6	13.5	8.4	5 460	164	283	15 768	5.1
Sullivan	187	2.9	18.0	9.5	45.5	8.6	5.4	13.1	33.6	4 291	197	344	8 487	-3.8
Switzerland	49	-13.2	D	35.1	D	8.7	4.4	17.8	28.1	1 558	172	168	3 732	16.5
Tippecanoe	2 911	0.0	D	30.2	D	8.7	5.1	20.3	24.2	17 351	116	1 219	48 134	11.6
Tipton	160	3.0	37.7	31.8	36.9	10.0	2.5	13.5	22.4	3 021	182	124	6 427	-0.2
Union	49	0.2	D	11.1	D	13.2	8.1	13.6	24.2	1 147	156	102	2 813	7.1
Vanderburgh	4 074	0.0	32.8	19.6	58.2	10.5	6.5	29.0	9.1	34 073	198	3 687	72 637	7.6
Vermillion	226	-2.2	D	D	D	9.4	1.8	14.9	10.7	3 430	204	228	7 288	-2.4
Vigo	1 756	0.1	28.2	20.9	53.4	14.6	4.2	25.2	18.3	19 851	188	2 550	44 203	2.6
Wabash	516	0.6	51.1	44.6	35.4	8.8	3.6	14.9	12.9	7 220	207	448	13 394	-0.5
Warren	57	10.0	D	16.2	D	6.0	3.2	17.3	21.3	1 587	189	81	3 275	-3.7
Warrick	565	-0.3	52.1	39.3	36.7	6.7	5.1	15.4	11.4	7 748	148	449	16 926	14.7
Washington	223	0.2	D	37.4	D	11.4	3.3	13.0	20.0	4 865	179	517	9 520	11.8
Wayne	1 260	-0.4	D	30.9	D	10.4	4.1	12.5	12.5	15 083	212	1 548	29 586	1.0
Wells	404	1.2	D	36.6	D	14.0	2.5	18.0	12.5	4 630	168	138	9 928	4.5
White	334	3.6	D	35.5	D	10.6	D	12.1	14.5	4 925	195	240	11 875	6.4
Whitley	410	-0.3	54.3	48.0	34.0	8.7	2.7	15.6	11.9	5 152	168	163	10 852	6.2
IOWA	50 726	2.1	26.9	20.3	54.9	9.5	7.8	23.0	16.1	541 304	185	40 282	1 143 669	1.1
Adair	92	7.5	D	23.3	D	9.1	3.9	13.8	16.2	1 878	228	80	3 714	-6.3
Adams	49	1.9	D	25.6	D	7.6	3.5	24.9	16.7	1 174	262	99	2 234	-9.8
Allamakee	172	8.9	D	22.9	D	10.9	4.2	14.4	15.6	3 187	217	161	6 603	0.4
Appanoose	147	0.9	D	30.9	D	10.3	3.4	19.3	17.8	3 449	251	418	6 402	-4.5
Audubon	60	2.0	D	8.1	D	10.4	5.0	20.7	21.6	1 866	273	82	3 247	-7.9
Benton	189	2.6	D	14.0	D	10.2	5.9	14.3	23.6	4 744	187	221	9 125	0.4
Black Hawk	2 311	0.6	D	26.9	D	9.8	5.2	25.2	16.7	23 010	180	2 749	49 688	-1.2
Boone	306	1.4	D	11.2	D	15.1	3.1	16.5	23.7	5 261	201	287	10 371	-0.5
Bremer	312	7.5	D	21.2	D	7.8	14.4	19.5	13.3	4 443	190	175	8 847	0.4
Buchanan	220	4.2	D	19.6	D	10.8	4.8	12.5	23.0	3 852	183	281	8 272	0.6
Buena Vista	312	8.2	31.5	25.8	45.9	9.8	5.0	18.8	14.3	4 062	199	247	8 140	-0.7
Butler	124	11.4	D	14.0	D	8.3	4.6	16.4	16.8	2 975	239	146	6 483	-4.4
Calhoun	106	13.3	D	6.4	D	7.5	5.3	24.6	24.0	2 975	268	150	5 362	-7.3
Carroll	349	1.7	D	13.0	D	10.5	8.2	22.5	10.8	4 700	219	255	8 356	-0.3
Cass	199	2.4	D	18.3	D	9.7	4.5	22.0	20.7	3 673	250	280	6 788	-3.4
Cedar	163	6.4	24.8	17.3	49.7	9.9	4.5	19.1	19.1	3 526	194	120	7 146	-2.3
Cerro Gordo	837	2.2	D	19.2	D	11.2	6.3	31.8	12.1	10 296	222	732	20 954	0.1
Cherokee	187	8.4	D	20.1	D	13.3	4.4	16.5	18.4	3 196	245	136	5 973	-7.8
Chickasaw	201	10.9	D	32.3	D	6.7	3.1	14.3	10.3	3 017	230	145	5 486	-3.8
Clarke	117	6.0	D	32.6	D	9.4	3.7	14.0	19.3	1 858	203	132	3 599	-3.1
Clay	304	4.8	D	13.9	D	13.5	4.3	21.4	15.2	3 758	216	209	7 659	-4.8
Clayton	226	6.7	D	17.7	D	8.4	D	19.3	18.1	4 349	233	293	8 344	-2.5
Clinton	731	3.0	D	31.7	D	9.4	3.7	23.9	11.5	10 205	203	887	21 296	-0.3
Crawford	219	2.2	D	28.8	D	9.3	3.7	16.2	16.9	3 580	211	206	6 920	-2.5
Dallas	473	4.1	D	15.2	D	7.0	D	23.6	13.1	5 661	139	280	11 812	2.2
Davis	73	-0.5	D	19.4	D	9.6	3.7	18.7	24.7	1 711	200	152	3 365	-6.0
Decatur	69	5.0	D	9.3	D	7.4	2.0	29.2	26.2	1 908	220	214	3 692	-7.1
Delaware	202	8.0	D	23.7	D	9.7	5.7	13.8	17.3	3 345	182	242	7 408	13.2
Des Moines	831	0.5	D	34.3	D	10.6	3.2	20.8	10.7	8 631	204	813	18 248	-1.7
Dickinson	276	1.8	D	27.8	D	14.2	6.1	21.3	11.5	4 213	257	145	9 723	-4.6
Dubuque	1 719	1.3	34.8	28.5	56.0	9.6	4.7	29.8	7.9	16 579	186	1 310	32 053	1.7
Emmet	151	7.9	D	18.4	D	8.7	3.2	20.2	17.3	2 506	227	125	4 914	-6.7
Fayette	249	11.1	D	16.8	D	9.5	4.2	23.8	15.5	4 959	225	343	9 262	-4.7
Floyd	179	3.4	31.4	21.9	47.0	10.8	4.9	19.5	18.2	4 111	243	296	7 233	-4.7
Franklin	125	4.7	D	24.1	D	8.0	3.8	19.9	17.1	2 581	241	110	5 018	-7.4
Fremont	101	5.4	D	42.4	D	6.8	3.8	13.6	14.0	1 917	239	134	3 607	-10.2
Greene	102	6.3	D	17.5	D	8.6	5.2	15.5	24.8	2 646	255	174	4 707	-6.2
Grundy	144	18.4	24.6	13.5	D	6.8	5.1	16.0	13.8	2 865	232	55	5 158	-5.9

1. Covers mining, construction, and manufacturing.   2. Covers private sector earnings in agricultural services, forestry, and fisheries; transportation and public utilities; wholesale trade; retail trade; finance, insurance, and real estate; and services.   3. Per 1,000 resident population estimated as of July 1 of the year shown.

STATE County	Total	Percent	Median value[1]	With a mortgage	Without a mortgage	Median rent[2]	Rent as percent of income	Substandard units[3] (percent)	Total	Percent change, 2000-2001	Total	Rate[4]	Total	Professional, managerial, and technical	Precision production, craft, and repair
	89	90	91	92	93	94	95	96	97	98	99	100	101	102	103
INDIANA—Cont'd															
Putnam	9 996	75.9	51 600	18.2	11.7	345	23.8	3.0	17 426	0.7	515	3.0	12 988	22.6	13.3
Randolph	10 451	75.6	35 500	15.2	12.0	279	23.5	2.3	11 477	2.4	755	6.6	12 023	18.7	14.4
Ripley	8 778	75.9	49 000	17.1	12.1	299	20.2	3.9	14 280	3.5	503	3.5	11 039	18.4	15.7
Rush	6 504	71.9	41 200	15.2	13.3	297	19.8	2.3	9 649	2.5	357	3.7	8 314	18.3	12.9
St. Joseph	92 365	72.0	50 800	17.1	12.4	402	25.3	2.2	135 359	0.4	6 245	4.6	117 132	28.9	10.8
Scott	7 593	77.2	38 000	18.9	13.2	301	29.9	4.5	11 433	1.9	559	4.9	8 648	15.7	14.7
Shelby	14 761	73.5	51 300	15.2	12.0	369	23.1	2.5	24 107	1.8	896	3.7	19 825	19.9	15.2
Spencer	6 962	81.3	47 000	16.4	11.6	284	21.2	2.8	10 971	-8.3	518	4.7	8 858	17.2	16.2
Starke	8 141	77.9	40 900	18.4	12.8	329	23.2	2.8	10 340	-2.3	724	7.0	9 346	16.6	15.6
Steuben	10 194	79.0	59 800	16.8	11.9	359	21.2	2.6	16 743	-3.6	1 025	6.1	13 642	20.5	12.7
Sullivan	7 364	80.0	32 300	15.9	13.7	261	21.6	2.7	9 295	-0.6	533	5.7	7 810	21.7	16.8
Switzerland	2 839	79.1	37 700	15.8	14.7	260	23.0	7.1	4 170	17.9	198	4.7	3 349	15.9	18.3
Tippecanoe	45 618	57.1	66 000	17.6	11.7	401	27.1	3.4	74 518	1.1	2 342	3.1	64 082	35.2	9.1
Tipton	6 026	76.9	50 900	15.0	11.7	325	21.0	2.0	8 599	-0.3	452	5.3	7 780	22.5	15.4
Union	2 576	72.3	41 800	17.8	11.9	289	21.8	2.0	3 768	-0.5	180	4.8	3 198	19.0	13.5
Vanderburgh	66 780	64.8	52 100	17.6	12.5	343	25.5	1.9	91 453	1.5	3 295	3.6	78 494	27.6	11.1
Vermillion	6 638	80.2	32 300	14.5	13.2	305	27.4	3.1	7 713	-0.7	453	5.9	6 952	20.6	14.5
Vigo	39 804	69.3	40 000	15.8	12.5	308	25.9	2.6	49 617	0.0	2 680	5.4	46 198	28.0	11.1
Wabash	12 630	74.3	43 400	15.3	12.1	303	22.6	1.8	17 403	0.8	1 013	5.8	16 882	18.2	13.9
Warren	3 015	78.6	39 700	16.7	12.6	273	18.8	2.3	3 894	0.6	142	3.6	3 655	16.8	14.7
Warrick	15 817	81.7	64 800	17.5	11.8	362	23.4	2.5	29 340	0.8	926	3.2	21 998	25.5	15.3
Washington	8 664	80.0	40 000	18.3	13.2	302	25.5	3.7	11 970	2.0	824	6.9	10 651	15.1	15.1
Wayne	27 587	67.6	42 400	15.8	12.6	300	24.5	1.8	36 489	-0.8	1 868	5.1	32 650	23.9	12.3
Wells	9 438	78.9	53 000	15.3	11.9	323	20.8	1.9	14 425	0.1	626	4.3	12 941	20.5	13.6
White	8 926	76.0	46 900	17.2	12.8	335	21.7	1.9	13 614	2.5	711	5.2	10 969	20.9	14.0
Whitley	10 010	82.5	57 300	16.1	11.8	321	21.0	1.5	16 650	0.9	886	5.3	13 708	19.0	16.5
IOWA	1 064 325	70.0	45 900	17.3	12.8	336	24.1	1.9	1 587 790	1.6	52 954	3.3	1 340 242	25.3	10.5
Adair	3 419	73.5	29 400	16.1	12.0	240	21.6	1.3	4 448	-0.2	104	2.3	3 847	17.6	8.9
Adams	2 005	72.5	28 700	16.0	12.2	239	21.8	1.5	2 070	-1.3	98	4.7	2 314	17.0	7.4
Allamakee	5 268	75.8	39 700	18.7	14.2	243	18.5	2.1	7 771	6.4	365	4.7	6 500	16.7	12.1
Appanoose	5 609	74.5	25 600	19.9	13.6	254	27.9	3.8	6 582	2.1	330	5.0	5 657	22.1	10.4
Audubon	2 936	76.1	25 300	17.6	13.6	254	22.5	0.8	3 431	4.1	114	3.3	3 391	17.3	7.1
Benton	8 518	74.8	38 600	16.2	13.1	281	22.7	1.8	12 122	4.4	431	3.6	10 265	18.0	13.5
Black Hawk	46 932	67.3	44 100	15.6	12.9	326	26.2	2.2	67 628	0.7	2 548	3.8	56 595	26.2	11.0
Boone	9 827	71.9	40 300	16.4	13.0	301	22.6	1.5	14 242	0.5	414	2.9	11 815	21.7	12.2
Bremer	8 394	75.0	45 900	15.6	13.0	288	21.6	1.3	12 498	0.9	356	2.8	10 809	24.1	12.1
Buchanan	7 506	75.0	36 300	15.8	12.2	271	24.3	3.7	10 865	1.4	476	4.4	8 746	20.5	13.8
Buena Vista	7 515	67.8	41 400	17.3	12.8	298	20.2	1.8	11 050	3.7	272	2.5	9 575	21.3	14.2
Butler	6 036	77.6	31 600	15.2	13.2	279	21.8	2.1	7 497	3.8	395	5.3	6 902	17.4	11.0
Calhoun	4 684	71.7	26 700	17.6	13.5	255	20.5	1.6	4 634	-0.5	155	3.3	4 764	21.6	10.0
Carroll	7 964	73.4	42 000	17.2	13.1	283	21.9	1.2	12 643	3.6	325	2.6	9 818	20.3	10.4
Cass	6 177	71.8	34 700	17.8	12.4	273	22.1	1.4	7 240	0.5	329	4.5	6 845	22.3	10.8
Cedar	6 684	73.1	45 700	17.1	12.7	316	21.4	1.3	9 580	3.1	292	3.0	8 510	19.3	10.7
Cerro Gordo	19 061	68.8	45 400	17.6	13.0	321	24.2	1.1	25 426	-0.1	882	3.5	22 847	25.9	9.3
Cherokee	5 514	70.8	32 500	16.0	12.9	247	18.8	1.0	7 012	4.0	198	2.8	6 374	18.5	11.3
Chickasaw	5 040	78.4	37 200	18.3	13.1	262	18.7	2.6	6 810	-3.5	489	7.2	6 100	17.7	11.8
Clarke	3 343	72.4	36 400	17.0	13.2	286	23.9	2.3	5 084	-0.5	216	4.2	3 839	18.1	12.5
Clay	7 074	65.4	41 000	16.6	12.4	265	21.7	1.4	10 239	0.6	306	3.0	8 506	21.6	11.1
Clayton	7 218	74.9	37 200	17.2	13.0	241	20.9	1.9	10 517	4.8	555	5.3	8 566	15.9	12.2
Clinton	19 757	71.2	39 100	15.3	12.7	306	23.7	1.7	26 565	1.8	1 221	4.6	23 025	20.6	12.5
Crawford	6 397	71.5	33 900	17.3	12.6	272	20.1	1.9	8 926	2.7	252	2.8	7 732	18.1	11.5
Dallas	11 204	74.4	50 100	18.7	13.6	336	22.9	1.5	21 030	1.5	451	2.1	14 965	24.2	10.4
Davis	3 093	77.6	28 900	20.7	13.3	275	22.5	5.8	4 259	3.2	150	3.5	3 591	18.4	10.2
Decatur	3 207	70.8	22 700	18.9	13.9	220	24.2	3.2	3 689	4.9	164	4.4	3 680	21.8	8.9
Delaware	6 389	75.7	44 600	18.2	12.5	283	21.4	1.6	9 843	5.2	450	4.6	8 158	16.2	12.5
Des Moines	16 874	72.8	41 600	15.8	12.4	321	23.6	1.9	22 748	-1.4	1 121	4.9	20 136	24.0	13.9
Dickinson	6 160	75.8	49 400	17.3	12.3	292	22.3	1.2	9 760	0.1	278	2.8	7 049	24.0	11.3
Dubuque	30 799	71.2	53 600	16.2	12.1	315	23.8	1.7	48 237	-0.2	2 061	4.3	42 025	25.3	10.5
Emmet	4 461	72.0	27 800	15.6	12.3	247	23.7	1.6	5 627	3.2	216	3.8	5 084	20.8	10.4
Fayette	8 490	74.4	30 100	15.2	13.2	250	22.7	1.4	11 294	4.3	596	5.3	9 631	19.5	10.7
Floyd	6 721	73.2	36 200	17.7	12.8	265	23.8	1.4	7 916	3.2	384	4.9	7 886	22.7	9.2
Franklin	4 579	72.0	30 500	15.2	14.3	280	22.1	1.3	5 947	5.2	203	3.4	5 204	20.7	8.5
Fremont	3 217	72.3	32 000	15.6	13.5	262	22.6	1.7	4 421	12.4	115	2.6	3 555	19.8	12.3
Greene	4 195	71.7	27 200	16.1	12.7	265	20.9	1.6	4 804	0.3	193	4.0	4 551	22.7	9.9
Grundy	4 776	74.4	38 100	15.0	13.4	271	20.4	0.4	6 386	6.1	147	2.3	5 420	21.4	10.5

1. Specified owner-occupied units. 2. Specified renter-occupied units. 3. Overcrowded or lacking complete plumbing facilities. 4. Percent of civilian labor force. 5. Persons 16 years and older.

Table B. States and Counties — **Nonfarm Employment and Agriculture**

	Private nonfarm establishments, employment and payroll, 1999									Agriculture, 1997			Farm operators
	Employment						Annual payroll		Farms		Percent with—	
STATE County	Number of establishments	Total	Health Care and Social Assistance	Manufacturing	Retail trade	Finance and Insurance	Professional Scientific and Technical Services	Total (mil dol)	Average per employee (dollars)	Number	Less than 50 acres	500 acres and over	Whose principal occupation is farming (percent)
	104	105	106	107	108	109	110	111	112	113	114	115	116
INDIANA—Cont'd													
Putnam	684	10 958	1 533	2 483	1 245	285	137	226	20 589	794	34.0	14.4	42.9
Randolph	549	6 865	521	3 520	871	219	111	160	23 318	851	29.8	16.2	45.8
Ripley	754	11 420	1 268	3 771	1 151	618	153	376	32 951	821	28.7	8.4	43.1
Rush	416	4 552	668	1 312	719	146	101	99	21 791	663	22.5	24.6	64.6
St. Joseph	6 585	123 952	14 574	21 236	18 431	5 382	5 378	3 423	27 616	666	41.3	13.7	45.6
Scott	441	6 437	719	2 538	1 123	148	73	141	21 925	348	40.2	6.9	35.1
Shelby	948	16 396	1 424	7 349	1 817	249	234	442	26 943	641	34.9	20.7	52.4
Spencer	413	6 097	315	1 772	743	132	90	171	28 092	638	27.3	13.0	41.5
Starke	360	3 820	683	1 418	737	84	D	77	20 041	410	30.5	19.5	49.8
Steuben	1 033	21 558	966	7 890	2 459	241	250	511	23 711	581	24.3	9.1	34.6
Sullivan	392	3 976	591	604	677	187	102	99	24 826	473	28.5	21.6	47.6
Switzerland	117	959	133	267	128	D	28	18	19 209	541	34.9	2.6	35.9
Tippecanoe	3 161	63 353	7 365	17 213	9 987	3 335	1 878	1 799	28 391	665	35.8	23.9	46.2
Tipton	335	3 733	576	1 092	471	101	79	97	25 906	415	28.4	25.1	59.3
Union	137	976	D	D	209	90	D	18	18 623	268	17.9	23.1	56.0
Vanderburgh	5 284	108 459	16 526	17 556	14 710	4 640	4 231	2 988	27 549	271	36.5	14.0	48.0
Vermillion	285	4 678	634	1 448	686	107	D	143	30 595	249	18.9	29.3	56.2
Vigo	2 686	46 685	7 177	8 098	10 278	1 440	1 080	1 145	24 523	455	40.2	14.9	46.6
Wabash	843	12 901	1 866	5 322	1 862	314	207	320	24 784	762	27.0	14.3	50.3
Warren	110	997	D	330	93	D	20	22	21 746	378	22.2	31.7	54.5
Warrick	1 040	11 294	1 352	3 363	1 424	347	340	307	27 188	356	28.7	16.0	46.1
Washington	466	5 838	653	2 827	767	153	88	125	21 375	914	25.3	9.4	42.2
Wayne	1 739	32 489	4 743	8 798	4 316	1 020	471	811	24 977	814	29.2	12.2	43.7
Wells	610	11 088	1 745	3 573	1 140	216	140	280	25 222	660	28.9	19.5	48.5
White	696	8 790	677	3 923	1 235	212	141	207	23 563	620	26.5	31.6	57.7
Whitley	717	11 706	1 123	4 849	1 553	271	142	284	24 228	787	32.9	9.5	36.5
IOWA	81 213	1 239 354	175 284	246 016	179 815	80 441	37 151	32 027	25 841	90 792	18.3	22.8	62.0
Adair	216	2 274	423	538	290	80	51	51	22 390	792	13.0	29.0	62.9
Adams	126	934	259	174	D	50	22	17	18 184	573	14.0	27.6	60.6
Allamakee	423	4 563	796	1 516	714	144	97	86	18 854	958	15.0	18.6	63.7
Appanoose	354	4 014	671	1 325	733	126	130	78	19 470	797	17.4	19.4	50.4
Audubon	217	1 444	343	213	233	67	48	25	17 254	649	15.9	28.5	69.0
Benton	624	4 599	638	536	884	263	79	96	20 979	1 210	20.0	24.0	60.8
Black Hawk	3 178	59 199	9 062	13 132	9 238	2 804	1 737	1 514	25 566	1 002	25.1	18.2	52.5
Boone	588	6 917	1 752	867	1 251	197	143	155	22 396	863	22.4	27.0	62.2
Bremer	641	7 819	1 102	1 849	1 021	1 017	144	182	23 321	982	24.5	13.2	54.1
Buchanan	544	5 330	952	1 294	999	246	89	118	22 099	1 136	21.3	19.1	63.6
Buena Vista	616	8 605	1 068	2 859	1 371	306	159	181	21 047	867	15.3	31.3	75.9
Butler	376	2 260	352	525	400	130	68	43	19 079	1 085	21.4	16.8	60.2
Calhoun	310	2 365	932	160	468	147	44	40	16 838	793	16.0	33.5	70.0
Carroll	842	10 101	1 573	1 349	1 707	957	178	202	20 017	1 102	17.1	20.4	69.4
Cass	502	5 775	1 081	1 394	967	266	112	129	22 339	804	16.4	32.7	66.8
Cedar	499	3 887	489	797	604	170	239	77	19 899	965	19.4	24.8	64.6
Cerro Gordo	1 471	22 862	5 592	4 013	3 698	1 258	469	548	23 960	822	22.7	26.5	64.5
Cherokee	390	4 326	954	834	820	165	84	101	23 376	890	14.8	26.5	69.9
Chickasaw	398	4 440	485	1 924	521	153	54	100	22 541	926	19.3	18.6	67.0
Clarke	227	3 343	401	1 351	435	91	32	68	20 326	678	14.6	18.6	52.2
Clay	639	8 049	1 240	1 381	1 640	278	158	173	21 452	668	15.9	32.8	68.6
Clayton	556	5 865	940	1 566	689	267	106	115	19 686	1 638	14.2	14.7	64.5
Clinton	1 303	18 877	2 820	4 915	2 748	716	247	435	23 051	1 268	20.0	19.7	59.2
Crawford	475	5 572	848	1 993	858	186	123	115	20 559	1 107	18.8	26.4	64.0
Dallas	849	9 499	1 510	2 268	1 496	408	205	238	25 070	918	28.0	24.2	53.7
Davis	175	1 578	454	346	282	51	57	31	19 669	884	16.1	17.3	48.4
Decatur	174	2 406	338	264	238	45	37	33	13 709	730	17.1	22.5	49.6
Delaware	466	4 930	580	1 859	770	174	96	108	21 879	1 278	14.7	11.0	72.9
Des Moines	1 229	20 848	2 572	7 078	3 393	526	298	523	25 073	650	22.3	18.8	53.5
Dickinson	703	7 337	753	2 262	1 094	185	145	170	23 176	512	16.8	29.1	67.2
Dubuque	2 627	48 230	6 382	11 562	6 672	2 020	1 056	1 202	24 914	1 579	17.9	7.3	64.1
Emmet	307	3 502	849	811	535	118	73	75	21 349	519	15.2	36.2	72.6
Fayette	671	7 258	1 183	1 533	1 120	242	144	137	18 932	1 295	18.0	18.5	67.5
Floyd	456	4 395	972	993	750	181	78	92	21 035	850	19.5	24.7	63.1
Franklin	339	3 093	529	868	440	105	71	71	22 964	856	16.1	30.8	70.4
Fremont	196	1 524	335	244	310	106	71	31	20 342	568	10.9	38.7	68.8
Greene	311	2 664	709	605	321	139	66	53	20 010	763	14.7	35.1	69.1
Grundy	312	2 766	337	506	407	167	60	67	24 288	754	18.0	27.9	68.3

Table B. States and Counties — Agriculture, Land, and Water

STATE County	Land in farms Acreage (1,000)	Percent change, 1992–1997	Acres Average size of farm	Total irrigated (1,000)	Total cropland (1,000)	Value of land and buildings Average per farm ($1,000)	Average per acre (dollars)	Value of machinery and equipment average per farm ($1,000)	Value of products sold Total (mil dol)	Average per farm (dollars)	Percent from — Crops	Live-stock and poultry products	Percent of farms with sales of — $10,000 or more	$100,000 or more	Percent of land owned by fed. gov. 1997	Water con-sump-tion 1995 (mil gal/day)
	117	118	119	120	121	122	123	124	125	126	127	128	129	130	131	132
INDIANA—Cont'd																
Putnam	195	-4.2	246	0	153	518	2 131	48	49	61 427	70.0	30.0	47.0	16.2	0.9	8.0
Randolph	224	-5.2	263	0	202	486	1 784	67	68	79 631	70.2	29.8	63.9	20.8	0.0	4.2
Ripley	159	-2.8	194	0	124	347	1 802	48	57	69 317	46.9	53.1	50.9	11.0	9.3	4.1
Rush	228	-2.2	344	D	207	836	2 441	85	86	129 605	65.4	34.6	76.3	35.4	0.0	3.3
St. Joseph	154	-10.4	231	13	140	537	2 258	68	55	82 849	72.6	27.4	56.5	18.8	0.0	94.3
Scott	57	-8.9	165	0	41	299	1 624	35	9	26 388	83.8	16.2	35.3	6.0	0.0	4.2
Shelby	201	-7.5	313	2	186	794	2 451	92	67	104 425	78.8	21.2	64.0	27.8	0.0	8.5
Spencer	173	-1.3	271	0	142	411	1 615	69	52	81 341	56.5	43.5	53.8	19.1	0.0	31.6
Starke	136	0.5	331	11	116	522	1 519	78	33	80 825	96.2	3.8	51.2	20.5	0.0	7.3
Steuben	124	1.6	213	1	99	380	1 692	41	26	44 133	65.4	34.6	44.6	12.9	0.0	4.3
Sullivan	177	-2.3	374	6	154	603	1 636	90	44	92 614	87.2	12.8	63.2	25.4	0.0	450.3
Switzerland	68	-14.1	125	0	34	238	1 817	25	13	24 641	70.2	29.8	44.0	3.7	0.0	4.3
Tippecanoe	242	-6.0	363	4	221	955	2 595	74	80	119 552	77.1	22.9	64.5	27.7	0.0	44.8
Tipton	158	-1.6	382	D	148	1 093	2 895	115	66	158 646	79.7	20.3	77.1	36.6	0.0	2.2
Union	82	3.1	308	0	69	563	2 018	80	26	95 929	68.9	31.1	69.8	29.5	5.2	0.9
Vanderburgh	72	-11.0	266	D	67	662	2 533	80	21	77 030	88.9	11.1	58.3	22.5	0.0	29.5
Vermillion	118	-0.8	474	D	101	728	1 524	110	30	122 449	73.6	26.4	64.3	26.1	5.0	469.7
Vigo	115	-20.8	253	0	99	532	2 006	67	26	57 180	87.1	12.9	50.3	14.9	0.4	328.0
Wabash	188	-4.9	247	1	163	546	2 285	89	98	128 276	42.7	57.3	62.2	24.3	4.1	10.4
Warren	185	-8.6	489	D	162	937	1 914	108	58	153 429	70.8	29.2	67.2	32.8	0.0	6.2
Warrick	99	2.7	277	0	81	495	1 616	71	24	66 491	80.9	19.1	50.8	21.1	0.0	709.0
Washington	181	-4.1	198	0	125	270	1 462	41	40	43 894	41.2	58.8	40.8	10.3	0.0	4.3
Wayne	173	-8.5	212	0	142	412	1 939	54	51	62 680	63.7	36.3	54.8	17.8	0.0	16.2
Wells	196	-1.6	297	0	182	651	2 193	88	74	112 567	67.3	32.7	72.7	30.3	0.5	4.1
White	272	-4.5	439	2	253	957	2 227	102	119	191 296	62.0	38.0	75.6	40.6	0.0	6.4
Whitley	165	1.9	210	1	139	394	2 004	49	52	65 985	59.0	41.0	50.2	16.5	0.0	4.0
IOWA	31 167	-0.6	343	125	26 822	567	1 697	81	11 948	131 596	51.8	48.2	74.0	34.6	0.5	3 034.6
Adair	336	2.1	424	D	284	380	1 003	68	83	104 223	51.9	48.1	74.9	29.8	0.0	2.0
Adams	235	-1.9	411	D	185	380	905	68	50	86 635	51.8	48.2	66.3	23.9	0.0	1.7
Allamakee	296	-8.1	309	D	180	296	974	69	81	84 370	26.7	73.3	67.7	27.6	1.4	212.4
Appanoose	241	0.9	303	D	176	193	649	45	29	36 082	53.8	46.2	54.0	8.0	1.4	5.4
Audubon	272	1.2	420		248	651	1 587	88	114	175 824	46.0	54.0	79.2	39.8	0.0	1.8
Benton	418	-2.0	346	0	376	707	1 999	91	158	130 559	65.1	34.9	76.6	38.0	1.4	3.5
Black Hawk	286	-4.7	285	1	263	622	2 321	82	128	127 636	60.4	39.6	76.6	35.9	0.0	57.3
Boone	329	-0.3	381	0	297	771	2 160	97	120	139 045	71.4	28.6	75.0	38.0	2.1	3.4
Bremer	239	0.6	243	0	211	480	2 094	73	102	103 437	55.1	44.9	75.4	30.1	0.0	4.8
Buchanan	337	1.2	297	D	304	513	1 839	77	137	120 747	57.7	42.3	81.2	35.4	0.0	3.8
Buena Vista	357	4.3	411	D	326	846	2 242	99	210	242 317	43.4	56.6	90.4	53.7	0.0	5.4
Butler	324	2.9	299	0	295	519	1 781	68	131	121 174	56.2	43.8	75.8	34.4	0.0	7.8
Calhoun	337	-2.7	424	D	317	1 005	2 426	116	140	176 853	63.7	36.3	87.1	49.6	0.0	2.3
Carroll	353	-2.0	320	1	324	604	1 814	104	221	200 960	35.1	64.9	87.8	44.7	0.0	5.5
Cass	331	-4.5	412	D	288	518	1 318	74	94	117 040	56.4	43.6	75.6	33.7	0.0	3.6
Cedar	326	-3.9	338	D	292	696	2 071	97	129	133 229	61.9	38.1	76.0	39.6	0.0	3.0
Cerro Gordo	301	-2.3	366	0	282	680	1 946	96	121	146 739	67.5	32.5	74.3	42.5	0.6	9.4
Cherokee	330	-1.7	371		287	687	1 922	90	146	163 881	48.9	51.1	87.1	46.2	0.0	4.7
Chickasaw	272	-1.0	294	1	243	446	1 515	82	122	131 891	46.6	53.4	77.9	37.6	0.0	2.7
Clarke	222	-6.0	327	0	151	251	711	43	39	56 835	33.8	66.2	55.9	10.8	0.2	1.6
Clay	286	-9.3	428	1	263	794	1 927	110	121	180 574	56.5	43.5	82.3	45.7	0.2	3.3
Clayton	452	-1.1	276	0	337	386	1 457	69	171	104 665	31.4	68.6	70.8	32.5	1.3	5.1
Clinton	368	0.0	290	0	325	495	1 788	72	148	117 025	57.9	42.1	74.8	34.4	1.3	279.1
Crawford	432	4.0	390	0	375	560	1 500	89	143	129 188	56.4	43.6	77.2	35.0	0.0	3.7
Dallas	324	3.7	353	1	288	841	2 418	85	118	128 128	65.8	34.2	66.1	29.5	0.8	6.1
Davis	267	-3.1	301	D	189	254	838	39	56	63 178	33.1	66.9	57.0	11.8	0.0	1.3
Decatur	262	0.4	359	0	171	208	608	43	54	74 450	26.5	73.5	52.5	11.4	0.0	1.7
Delaware	326	-2.9	255	0	287	451	1 824	91	196	153 300	26.3	73.7	83.7	49.7	0.0	5.7
Des Moines	192	0.0	296	2	156	455	1 584	70	70	107 337	62.2	37.8	66.8	28.8	7.0	115.2
Dickinson	201	-0.4	393	D	181	667	1 744	81	73	142 294	57.1	42.9	74.6	38.3	1.4	3.0
Dubuque	336	-2.2	213	0	258	336	1 623	69	172	108 709	18.0	82.0	76.0	34.6	0.4	81.5
Emmet	220	-2.1	424	D	205	728	1 744	108	91	176 000	59.0	41.0	78.6	48.2	0.5	2.4
Fayette	404	0.6	312	1	344	469	1 536	86	181	139 874	42.4	57.6	78.5	39.8	0.0	4.9
Floyd	300	4.3	353	2	274	629	1 784	91	114	133 569	67.8	32.2	77.3	38.7	0.0	3.7
Franklin	344	0.4	402	D	316	754	2 014	105	180	210 504	48.0	52.0	84.2	46.1	0.0	2.5
Fremont	318	5.4	560	2	268	721	1 293	93	88	155 256	74.3	25.7	78.5	42.3	0.0	6.3
Greene	343	-6.4	450	1	317	852	2 024	94	122	160 203	71.3	28.7	83.4	49.8	0.1	2.1
Grundy	321	1.4	426	D	299	967	2 289	123	149	197 769	61.5	38.5	86.3	51.5	0.0	2.2

STATE County	New Construction ($1,000)	Number of Housing Units	Wholesale Trade, 1997 Number of Establishments	Number of Employees	Sales (mil dol)	Annual Payroll (mil dol)	Retail Trade[1], 1997 Number of Establishments	Number of Employees	Sales (mil dol)	Annual Payroll (mil dol)	Real Estate and Rental and Leasing, 1997 Number of Establishments	Number of Employees	Receipts (mil dol)	Annual Payroll (mil dol)
	133	134	135	136	137	138	139	140	141	142	143	144	145	146
INDIANA—Cont'd														
Putnam	3 731	40	24	110	39.2	2.7	126	1 278	186.0	18.4	30	65	4.6	0.9
Randolph	5 381	60	21	120	76.5	3.1	111	978	152.2	13.7	8	19	1.0	0.1
Ripley	15 473	210	34	532	108.0	25.5	130	1 124	197.4	18.4	23	104	4.3	1.3
Rush	6 737	77	30	189	119.0	3.9	75	678	114.8	10.3	12	30	4.6	0.4
St. Joseph	162 876	1 665	472	7 080	3 389.0	230.7	1 069	16 822	2 782.9	249.0	215	1 274	127.8	25.5
Scott	9 747	205	15	83	13.9	1.8	105	1 134	168.2	15.9	11	52	5.9	1.0
Shelby	20 103	161	49	530	215.6	18.4	146	1 577	310.8	26.3	34	89	11.8	1.2
Spencer	12 914	147	24	308	217.5	8.4	80	661	94.6	9.7	13	49	2.1	0.6
Starke	8 360	111	20	127	75.8	3.2	95	812	110.3	11.2	13	54	3.7	1.0
Steuben	35 051	275	39	252	98.7	5.9	238	2 280	397.5	35.5	31	87	14.7	1.5
Sullivan	1 700	21	23	155	113.6	3.7	68	648	95.3	8.6	10	D	D	D
Switzerland	7 108	122	3	D	D	D	20	125	17.1	1.4	1	D	D	D
Tippecanoe	140 084	1 710	117	D	D	D	564	9 688	1 479.8	137.8	148	748	81.0	12.0
Tipton	8 099	53	20	D	D	D	52	478	118.1	7.3	11	23	1.2	0.2
Union	3 878	39	10	94	44.9	1.7	31	221	28.9	3.5	3	D	D	D
Vanderburgh	66 089	1 040	352	D	D	D	932	14 807	2 282.8	229.6	222	1 495	170.5	27.2
Vermillion	4 494	41	15	D	D	D	61	726	123.8	9.4	3	23	1.0	0.2
Vigo	34 257	312	143	1 646	682.4	43.0	509	9 685	2 321.3	158.4	87	480	39.5	8.6
Wabash	10 157	88	38	233	86.4	6.0	169	1 853	289.8	27.5	43	136	13.0	1.8
Warren	4 470	67	12	129	74.8	3.5	16	101	19.8	1.4	4	6	0.7	0.0
Warrick	58 804	439	48	D	D	D	170	1 438	219.1	20.2	33	139	14.7	2.0
Washington	2 830	35	16	D	D	D	88	731	176.1	11.8	15	47	5.2	0.6
Wayne	15 123	146	96	1 657	1 256.3	53.8	338	4 233	690.6	64.3	61	226	23.1	4.1
Wells	15 854	123	38	1 735	455.3	37.9	116	1 113	164.0	16.1	29	97	15.9	1.5
White	12 490	134	46	358	196.7	8.5	131	1 173	209.7	19.6	16	64	4.0	0.8
Whitley	25 641	212	29	240	168.0	6.1	108	1 657	221.0	22.8	21	66	9.1	1.3
IOWA	1 333 184	12 500	5 399	63 596	35 453.7	1 820.1	14 695	175 694	26 723.8	2 633.4	2 518	12 619	1 457.5	249.0
Adair	4 459	61	16	142	83.1	3.7	49	320	46.2	3.7	1	D	D	D
Adams	275	2	9	52	18.5	0.9	22	131	16.0	1.5	1	D	D	D
Allamakee	4 768	75	34	512	158.2	9.8	95	652	101.2	8.1	9	24	1.5	0.1
Appanoose	938	16	12	65	25.7	1.0	73	702	92.4	9.4	7	57	1.3	0.6
Audubon	210	2	24	169	76.2	3.5	34	254	51.9	4.0	3	11	0.7	0.1
Benton	12 249	95	40	506	186.3	12.5	101	789	144.1	12.2	11	39	1.3	0.4
Black Hawk	39 574	379	169	2 690	952.7	77.0	598	9 386	1 344.8	139.3	126	549	60.9	10.3
Boone	10 707	102	25	216	155.2	5.2	98	1 134	173.2	15.5	11	23	2.6	0.3
Bremer	17 079	138	42	293	151.8	6.0	115	1 037	144.7	13.7	14	26	2.9	0.5
Buchanan	4 250	42	38	311	222.7	8.4	106	911	154.9	13.8	16	32	1.3	0.2
Buena Vista	2 858	22	42	392	287.3	11.3	122	1 450	192.1	20.1	18	45	2.5	0.6
Butler	2 233	21	42	257	158.5	6.1	86	428	67.6	5.5	2	D	D	D
Calhoun	1 365	11	15	222	184.9	6.3	71	484	81.3	6.1	8	32	1.3	0.4
Carroll	6 075	41	53	868	354.5	21.4	176	1 706	226.0	22.9	23	122	10.9	1.9
Cass	2 894	31	41	D	D	D	99	927	122.3	11.9	11	21	2.8	0.4
Cedar	9 232	76	39	370	137.8	8.3	85	689	100.8	8.6	11	24	1.0	0.2
Cerro Gordo	9 994	80	85	875	489.6	24.5	292	3 995	609.9	54.9	52	164	16.2	2.3
Cherokee	1 959	17	22	184	59.1	3.9	83	787	107.7	10.3	5	7	0.9	0.1
Chickasaw	1 303	9	32	362	179.2	9.6	62	480	73.4	6.4	6	D	D	D
Clarke	2 488	20	8	D	D	D	39	402	51.3	5.3	7	9	2.2	0.2
Clay	4 480	45	58	612	246.8	14.8	141	1 529	215.0	25.7	19	69	4.8	0.8
Clayton	6 867	96	52	335	269.9	7.1	120	670	133.4	10.4	11	20	1.1	0.3
Clinton	14 474	136	68	492	217.7	12.1	227	2 523	418.3	43.3	50	177	12.2	1.9
Crawford	3 460	35	27	309	191.4	6.0	97	919	111.7	9.9	9	14	0.9	0.1
Dallas	47 022	283	53	D	D	D	134	1 371	220.7	21.1	10	20	1.8	0.3
Davis	510	8	15	136	62.6	2.4	42	294	43.4	4.2	5	12	0.7	0.1
Decatur	1 158	10	11	129	68.3	2.0	35	205	24.8	2.4	1	D	D	D
Delaware	1 853	17	39	444	250.5	10.0	80	726	110.8	10.7	2	D	D	D
Des Moines	5 897	49	67	618	375.8	14.5	238	3 724	499.9	51.7	43	422	48.5	10.2
Dickinson	18 204	138	26	738	176.1	17.6	143	1 087	172.2	17.0	38	236	21.5	4.7
Dubuque	44 983	341	157	1 845	926.5	50.8	525	6 583	935.5	100.2	89	341	32.8	4.9
Emmet	2 888	33	14	260	56.8	4.5	61	550	79.2	7.7	1	D	D	D
Fayette	3 050	32	41	D	D	D	133	1 089	174.3	16.6	10	39	1.3	0.3
Floyd	1 095	9	31	258	112.2	5.3	95	839	119.3	10.5	12	33	3.9	0.3
Franklin	888	8	24	241	144.8	5.2	65	459	61.1	5.8	15	27	2.1	0.2
Fremont	2 083	23	15	108	97.4	3.6	32	212	26.8	2.5	2	D	D	D
Greene	2 080	15	19	207	116.8	4.7	47	381	53.1	4.8	5	17	2.7	0.3
Grundy	6 456	60	20	231	171.9	8.2	49	377	61.4	5.3	7	37	9.3	2.2

1. Establishments with payroll.

STATE County	Professional, Scientific, and Technical Services[1], 1997				Manufacturing, 1997				Accommodation and Foodservices, 1997			
	Number of Establish-ments	Number of Employees	Receipts (mil dol)	Annual Payroll (mil dol)	Number of Establish-ments	Number of Employees	Receipts (mil dol)	Annual Payroll (mil dol)	Number of Establish-ments	Number of Employees	Sales (mil dol)	Annual Payroll (mil dol)
	147	148	149	150	151	152	153	154	155	156	157	158
INDIANA—Cont'd												
Putnam	34	123	7.3	2.8	25	2 482	421.7	64.8	75	1 022	27.8	7.5
Randolph	25	79	3.6	1.1	54	3 080	361.0	86.5	44	438	11.9	3.1
Ripley	27	117	7.5	2.6	35	3 168	755.2	109.9	58	787	19.8	5.2
Rush	22	81	3.8	1.2	32	1 081	289.1	32.4	30	D	D	D
St. Joseph	520	4 003	369.9	154.8	457	20 435	4 149.7	698.9	537	10 620	305.2	86.9
Scott	20	51	2.7	0.9	34	D	D	D	38	716	19.6	5.9
Shelby	63	228	15.3	5.3	86	6 656	1 188.8	218.5	57	1 059	31.2	9.3
Spencer	15	54	3.0	0.9	19	1 369	134.0	36.3	28	D	D	D
Starke	13	40	1.8	0.5	19	1 357	143.3	29.7	37	D	D	D
Steuben	47	172	10.0	2.8	110	6 774	1 056.5	189.0	88	1 300	41.6	11.8
Sullivan	24	88	4.4	1.4	18	579	73.0	14.3	28	D	D	D
Switzerland	4	11	0.6	0.1	6	619	58.7	10.7	9	D	D	D
Tippecanoe	207	1 232	104.4	36.5	113	16 695	7 519.0	692.2	312	6 722	194.3	56.0
Tipton	24	93	4.6	1.4	22	954	199.3	30.5	25	319	9.2	2.5
Union	4	6	0.3	0.1	NA	NA	NA	NA	10	D	D	D
Vanderburgh	404	3 594	258.6	99.3	271	17 536	3 824.6	607.7	426	8 841	267.3	78.5
Vermillion	9	12	1.0	0.2	10	D	D	D	35	463	13.7	3.4
Vigo	160	955	70.4	21.3	137	7 464	1 891.8	255.2	268	5 027	148.9	42.7
Wabash	39	130	10.0	3.2	77	5 300	812.8	156.3	71	D	D	D
Warren	6	14	0.7	0.2	NA	NA	NA	NA	7	D	D	D
Warrick	67	254	12.3	4.3	53	D	D	D	68	D	D	D
Washington	26	81	4.3	1.4	40	2 824	298.7	66.9	31	D	D	D
Wayne	76	420	26.5	11.8	132	8 940	1 598.7	270.0	145	2 808	83.7	24.2
Wells	24	127	8.8	2.8	49	3 615	490.2	106.2	36	597	15.3	4.4
White	40	126	16.8	4.8	56	3 402	638.0	90.6	66	459	17.2	4.6
Whitley	32	92	6.1	2.1	66	4 327	908.8	117.3	61	871	23.3	6.6
IOWA	4 670	31 115	2 435.6	887.9	3 749	235 880	62 413.7	7 573.3	6 830	99 148	2 762.8	769.5
Adair	13	39	1.9	0.7	8	527	101.9	15.1	19	246	5.4	1.4
Adams	5	19	0.7	0.2	NA	NA	NA	NA	9	55	1.2	0.3
Allamakee	20	62	2.3	0.9	26	1 505	209.7	27.4	42	293	6.1	1.5
Appanoose	16	43	1.9	0.6	15	1 070	156.5	30.1	35	284	7.4	1.8
Audubon	10	23	1.4	0.4	NA	NA	NA	NA	16	D	D	D
Benton	24	64	3.0	1.1	NA	NA	NA	NA	43	249	6.1	1.6
Black Hawk	193	1 530	100.9	44.9	165	13 542	5 133.1	555.7	293	5 544	135.8	39.2
Boone	27	92	8.1	2.4	26	914	131.9	22.5	48	574	15.1	4.4
Bremer	35	82	6.3	1.7	39	1 993	446.3	58.6	47	578	13.6	4.0
Buchanan	22	66	4.1	1.4	35	1 230	277.7	31.7	38	D	D	D
Buena Vista	34	147	9.3	3.7	28	2 546	688.6	55.2	47	604	15.0	4.0
Butler	19	51	2.6	0.6	23	601	70.7	16.3	29	D	D	D
Calhoun	10	20	1.1	0.2	NA	NA	NA	NA	17	D	D	D
Carroll	37	124	7.6	2.3	39	1 588	423.8	41.7	64	785	19.3	4.9
Cass	20	86	5.6	2.3	25	1 112	150.7	29.8	43	443	10.2	2.8
Cedar	21	211	7.2	3.3	25	810	122.3	19.4	37	375	8.1	1.9
Cerro Gordo	78	376	27.5	10.5	61	3 703	719.8	98.9	139	2 286	61.0	16.7
Cherokee	15	58	2.9	1.1	15	904	188.5	24.6	35	350	8.3	2.2
Chickasaw	16	43	3.0	0.7	25	1 674	414.4	42.2	33	D	D	D
Clarke	12	30	1.4	0.4	19	1 152	209.4	21.4	26	399	12.2	2.8
Clay	28	145	11.1	3.1	28	1 180	202.3	34.9	53	682	17.2	4.8
Clayton	22	66	3.9	1.4	31	1 538	184.6	28.6	51	266	7.2	1.5
Clinton	57	183	12.3	3.8	59	5 148	2 106.9	175.6	132	1 516	39.3	10.9
Crawford	19	120	6.7	2.8	22	1 879	908.9	49.5	49	477	11.4	2.9
Dallas	38	135	8.5	2.8	41	2 489	451.2	59.7	55	596	13.1	3.9
Davis	8	62	2.2	1.0	NA	NA	NA	NA	13	126	2.6	0.7
Decatur	8	22	0.7	0.2	NA	NA	NA	NA	16	110	2.2	0.6
Delaware	19	68	3.8	1.7	34	1 144	327.5	33.7	34	269	5.6	1.3
Des Moines	61	240	16.7	5.2	66	6 772	1 320.8	228.8	109	1 841	47.8	13.4
Dickinson	33	145	10.1	3.0	31	2 386	353.4	60.3	98	857	29.1	8.3
Dubuque	117	802	56.4	23.5	133	10 687	3 074.9	386.9	233	3 838	94.7	27.4
Emmet	18	76	4.9	1.7	15	752	115.8	18.2	25	218	5.5	1.4
Fayette	34	120	6.1	2.1	24	1 539	262.4	38.9	50	504	10.8	3.0
Floyd	24	75	3.9	1.1	17	591	94.5	16.6	37	368	8.9	2.0
Franklin	14	63	2.7	1.2	22	790	83.9	21.6	19	164	3.1	0.9
Fremont	9	58	2.0	0.7	NA	NA	NA	NA	18	83	2.6	0.6
Greene	12	67	3.2	1.4	17	525	83.4	14.4	22	D	D	D
Grundy	15	50	3.2	1.2	NA	NA	NA	NA	23	D	D	D

1. Firms subject to federal tax.

STATE County	Health Care and Social Assistance[1], 1997				Other Services[1], 1997				Federal funds and grants, fiscal 2001[2] Expenditures (mil dol)			
										Direct payments for individuals[3]		
	Number of Establishments	Number of Employees	Receipts (mil dol)	Annual Payroll (mil dol)	Number of Establishments	Number of Employees	Receipts (mil dol)	Annual Payroll (mil dol)	Total	Social Security and government retirement	Medicare	Food stamps and Supplemental Security Income
	159	160	161	162	163	164	165	166	167	168	169	170
INDIANA—Cont'd												
Putnam	40	436	17.7	7.6	37	149	10.4	2.4	134.0	65.5	22.6	2.9
Randolph	23	241	9.2	4.1	34	124	8.4	1.8	136.8	65.0	23.8	3.3
Ripley	56	501	21.8	10.7	53	177	11.0	2.8	124.9	59.1	23.0	2.4
Rush	26	442	15.2	6.4	20	75	5.8	1.4	94.0	37.0	16.8	1.7
St. Joseph	496	5 999	458.0	212.7	452	3 851	256.3	81.0	1 723.3	530.0	211.4	38.1
Scott	28	224	11.7	4.6	25	76	5.4	1.3	118.9	51.3	21.7	6.2
Shelby	61	830	39.5	18.4	57	387	18.6	5.5	173.7	80.9	33.1	4.0
Spencer	14	245	9.8	4.2	21	54	3.7	1.0	95.5	40.4	15.0	2.0
Starke	16	176	6.8	2.9	18	41	2.9	0.8	105.2	50.4	15.7	3.7
Steuben	57	454	25.4	9.7	50	381	15.7	5.6	119.9	64.0	23.4	2.5
Sullivan	25	369	15.4	6.3	27	66	4.1	0.9	115.7	50.5	24.1	2.8
Switzerland	6	D	D	D	4	D	D	D	38.5	17.0	7.1	1.3
Tippecanoe	181	2 830	217.1	103.0	227	1 619	102.3	30.6	592.0	215.4	68.5	11.6
Tipton	27	216	11.6	4.2	21	129	6.8	2.3	74.9	34.1	15.0	1.3
Union	8	100	3.0	1.4	9	23	1.4	0.3	35.6	14.5	5.1	1.1
Vanderburgh	396	7 805	496.6	237.0	338	2 995	179.7	56.2	919.6	400.9	166.9	33.2
Vermillion	19	304	10.5	4.7	12	33	1.4	0.4	112.4	40.5	15.1	1.9
Vigo	249	3 340	243.7	76.8	170	1 395	66.2	20.2	627.5	233.1	111.0	19.8
Wabash	44	712	28.5	11.8	53	170	10.6	3.4	148.0	80.4	24.1	2.9
Warren	4	D	D	D	4	D	D	D	47.7	13.9	6.1	0.7
Warrick	73	931	44.7	18.5	57	275	16.6	5.2	161.5	93.0	29.6	3.2
Washington	31	335	12.9	4.8	33	98	4.5	1.1	110.7	52.4	18.6	4.1
Wayne	134	1 754	95.8	47.4	118	564	29.2	9.3	374.1	171.6	63.8	14.1
Wells	28	484	33.4	17.5	53	237	17.2	4.9	101.5	49.5	18.1	1.4
White	35	285	9.4	3.6	35	89	6.6	1.3	134.0	62.8	22.8	1.9
Whitley	30	314	16.1	7.1	46	302	16.4	6.0	143.7	64.0	20.7	3.3
IOWA	4 876	56 374	3 183.2	1 540.6	5 234	24 383	1 486.5	411.3	17 401.3	6 232.2	2 205.8	312.0
Adair	14	208	5.6	2.9	16	31	1.8	0.4	68.9	18.1	7.1	0.6
Adams	7	92	1.9	1.0	8	16	1.3	0.2	35.4	11.3	4.7	0.6
Allamakee	22	159	6.7	2.8	34	82	6.8	1.1	75.9	31.2	9.4	0.9
Appanoose	18	155	8.3	3.0	26	80	4.7	1.0	92.4	37.3	13.4	3.2
Audubon	8	117	3.5	1.7	20	50	2.9	0.6	55.2	17.3	7.3	0.5
Benton	23	150	5.5	2.3	43	99	6.3	1.3	156.6	50.3	17.9	1.7
Black Hawk	228	2 173	167.9	83.0	213	1 513	80.2	25.9	605.4	265.8	102.9	22.2
Boone	32	287	13.9	6.9	38	122	6.8	1.9	137.2	60.1	19.6	1.7
Bremer	41	333	16.1	7.0	59	153	10.1	2.3	114.3	51.6	19.2	1.4
Buchanan	20	235	8.9	3.5	40	115	7.8	1.7	110.1	43.3	16.7	1.6
Buena Vista	28	397	16.5	8.0	45	145	8.3	1.8	123.2	43.7	17.7	1.6
Butler	19	317	9.1	4.5	25	61	4.5	0.9	100.3	38.5	16.1	1.1
Calhoun	16	272	8.6	4.2	19	58	2.5	0.5	89.6	31.1	12.2	0.9
Carroll	44	305	20.6	8.4	47	174	11.1	2.3	134.9	49.8	18.1	1.6
Cass	27	294	13.5	5.5	43	102	7.3	1.4	102.7	38.8	16.5	2.0
Cedar	31	114	5.1	2.0	29	70	6.7	1.5	97.5	35.9	13.0	0.9
Cerro Gordo	80	1 328	81.5	50.1	97	437	20.3	6.6	257.2	114.5	40.3	5.3
Cherokee	25	250	8.8	4.6	28	53	4.4	1.0	96.8	34.7	12.3	0.8
Chickasaw	17	349	11.6	4.5	38	79	6.9	1.2	83.5	29.6	11.1	1.1
Clarke	12	46	3.9	1.5	18	36	2.4	0.5	45.2	17.8	7.2	0.7
Clay	31	315	24.1	11.4	37	224	11.6	3.4	116.7	39.8	13.2	1.5
Clayton	25	195	9.1	4.3	39	78	4.8	1.0	110.7	42.6	16.1	1.6
Clinton	95	922	46.4	18.0	97	374	21.8	6.1	253.9	118.0	46.8	7.6
Crawford	25	362	14.8	6.7	34	79	5.7	1.1	119.5	36.2	15.1	1.6
Dallas	61	693	39.5	21.5	50	130	10.2	1.7	144.4	69.4	23.8	1.9
Davis	18	210	8.4	3.3	7	20	1.2	0.3	47.9	18.0	6.7	1.0
Decatur	10	136	4.9	2.0	5	11	1.5	0.5	56.3	19.0	6.4	1.8
Delaware	20	127	7.0	2.7	39	96	5.4	1.2	92.2	32.1	11.1	1.5
Des Moines	100	910	54.1	24.0	62	345	16.6	4.5	247.7	102.7	37.8	6.7
Dickinson	37	373	17.5	8.6	37	116	6.5	1.6	91.2	45.8	13.7	1.0
Dubuque	124	2 376	185.8	89.3	172	889	51.2	14.9	402.0	186.9	70.5	8.5
Emmet	27	360	13.3	6.4	20	63	3.3	0.9	79.3	28.2	11.2	1.0
Fayette	44	534	17.8	8.2	50	180	12.7	3.4	133.1	50.5	19.4	2.1
Floyd	30	394	16.5	8.1	34	137	9.0	2.0	119.8	44.9	17.1	1.8
Franklin	16	166	6.0	2.9	23	67	7.4	1.7	79.5	24.8	9.0	0.7
Fremont	13	267	9.5	5.2	12	27	2.3	0.4	63.4	21.1	9.4	0.9
Greene	15	137	7.6	3.1	26	68	4.5	0.8	83.8	27.9	9.2	1.1
Grundy	15	181	6.3	2.6	26	55	4.8	0.8	89.9	29.3	10.5	0.4

1. Firms subject to federal tax. 2. October 1, 2000 to September 30, 2001. 3. State totals may include programs not allocated by county.

	Federal funds and grants, fiscal 2001[1] (cont'd)							Local government finances, 1997				
	Expenditures (mil dol) (cont'd)							General revenue				
	Procurement contract awards			Grants[2]						Taxes		
STATE County	Salaries and wages	Defense	Other	Medicaid and other health-related	Nutrition and family welfare	Education	Other	Total (mil dol)	Intergovernmental (mil dol)	Total (mil dol)	Per capita[3] (dollars) Total	Property
	171	172	173	174	175	176	177	178	179	180	181	182
INDIANA—Cont'd												
Putnam	4.5	0.3	1.0	10.7	1.6	0.6	7.4	81.8	31.2	28.5	847	761
Randolph	4.7	0.1	1.1	13.3	2.5	0.8	4.8	62.2	26.3	18.3	664	553
Ripley	4.7	0.9	5.2	14.4	1.8	0.6	1.3	53.5	24.0	22.0	811	689
Rush	2.9	0.0	1.1	8.5	1.1	0.3	2.1	41.4	14.1	14.3	783	698
St. Joseph	68.0	175.6	414.5	129.6	24.2	9.9	40.5	544.7	219.9	204.9	794	776
Scott	3.6	3.0	0.7	20.7	3.2	1.0	2.6	51.1	22.0	14.7	644	491
Shelby	10.4	1.1	1.4	15.9	2.2	0.6	2.1	110.6	37.3	29.5	683	587
Spencer	3.8	1.4	1.0	9.2	0.9	0.3	9.5	44.7	15.6	23.9	1 153	1 135
Starke	3.0	0.0	0.7	11.5	2.4	0.8	5.1	56.5	22.9	14.6	613	579
Steuben	4.7	1.4	1.5	7.4	2.0	0.4	2.9	64.8	21.7	31.4	1 009	908
Sullivan	3.7	1.5	1.2	12.6	1.3	0.6	1.4	56.5	16.7	17.0	840	837
Switzerland	1.4	0.0	0.4	7.8	0.4	0.3	0.7	14.5	8.7	4.6	532	485
Tippecanoe	33.2	7.6	9.8	66.0	8.2	7.1	101.1	242.6	92.4	112.5	813	713
Tipton	2.1	0.1	0.9	5.2	0.7	0.2	0.0	51.0	13.1	14.5	883	770
Union	0.8	0.0	0.2	3.0	1.0	0.2	2.5	16.9	7.4	7.3	1 000	913
Vanderburgh	53.9	53.0	13.7	117.1	20.8	4.9	14.3	367.0	142.9	153.0	917	775
Vermillion	3.9	29.7	1.0	8.5	1.5	0.4	3.4	35.8	13.1	18.4	1 084	1 081
Vigo	76.9	16.0	13.8	80.7	12.9	5.2	28.0	178.1	80.8	74.8	712	703
Wabash	4.7	0.1	1.1	16.6	2.2	0.5	-2.9	87.3	30.5	25.4	735	632
Warren	1.4	0.0	0.3	2.6	0.5	0.1	3.1	16.7	7.2	7.1	868	742
Warrick	6.8	1.3	1.6	14.8	2.7	0.7	-3.0	101.5	34.1	51.1	1 005	924
Washington	3.6	0.1	0.8	17.0	2.3	0.8	0.7	56.8	24.4	13.9	511	417
Wayne	9.3	1.3	2.9	57.7	11.2	2.1	10.7	148.3	67.4	61.3	854	758
Wells	3.8	0.2	1.3	6.3	1.6	0.3	0.9	64.3	23.8	19.8	740	647
White	4.3	0.0	1.2	7.0	2.1	0.5	5.2	72.7	21.6	32.0	1 276	1 160
Whitley	4.3	31.7	1.2	5.5	1.0	0.3	0.3	59.5	23.5	27.2	908	813
IOWA	1 029.3	503.3	393.5	1 536.1	475.5	263.7	803.9	X	X	X	X	X
Adair	1.5	0.0	0.3	7.0	0.8	0.3	10.8	16.5	8.0	6.5	787	762
Adams	1.3	0.0	0.3	2.1	0.5	0.2	0.2	8.7	4.1	3.6	805	801
Allamakee	3.5	0.0	1.6	7.0	1.4	0.4	3.4	34.6	14.4	11.3	805	752
Appanoose	4.2	0.1	0.7	15.7	2.4	0.8	3.9	28.4	16.4	8.9	659	644
Audubon	1.8	0.0	0.4	2.2	0.5	0.2	1.5	15.1	7.1	6.0	880	869
Benton	3.5	0.0	33.7	6.4	1.9	0.5	0.6	44.7	22.8	16.1	642	638
Black Hawk	34.2	1.9	0.9	73.8	19.9	10.4	15.4	351.5	147.2	104.2	857	735
Boone	8.2	0.2	1.0	9.1	2.3	0.5	2.9	59.1	20.3	18.8	720	611
Bremer	3.4	0.0	0.9	6.1	1.7	0.6	3.3	60.2	24.3	18.6	798	755
Buchanan	3.5	0.0	0.9	7.3	2.0	1.5	1.4	42.2	17.3	13.7	647	603
Buena Vista	6.6	0.2	0.9	7.3	1.6	0.7	3.2	57.3	19.8	16.9	861	793
Butler	2.6	0.0	0.6	7.9	1.2	0.5	0.6	25.8	11.6	10.2	647	622
Calhoun	2.4	0.0	0.6	4.9	1.0	0.3	0.4	29.4	14.1	11.3	989	987
Carroll	5.6	0.2	2.6	10.4	2.8	0.4	6.8	43.4	16.4	17.1	789	774
Cass	4.4	0.0	0.8	6.7	1.6	0.5	4.3	50.6	15.9	13.4	912	895
Cedar	4.8	0.0	1.1	4.9	1.2	0.4	0.5	37.9	16.8	15.0	836	807
Cerro Gordo	10.0	0.5	4.9	25.0	6.0	1.5	8.2	119.0	50.1	41.9	903	772
Cherokee	2.6	0.0	0.7	5.8	1.1	0.5	2.2	32.5	16.3	10.8	802	766
Chickasaw	2.8	0.0	0.5	4.9	1.0	0.3	5.3	26.3	12.7	9.3	691	684
Clarke	1.7	0.0	0.4	4.6	1.1	0.3	0.4	24.4	10.3	7.7	929	921
Clay	4.8	0.0	1.0	8.5	1.7	0.3	2.1	64.4	17.9	14.2	804	786
Clayton	5.0	0.0	1.1	11.8	1.7	0.5	1.5	45.4	23.1	15.2	810	722
Clinton	7.6	0.6	1.8	17.7	5.6	2.1	3.9	110.7	49.9	43.4	863	736
Crawford	7.2	0.0	9.7	8.8	1.8	0.6	0.8	40.6	15.4	12.2	747	727
Dallas	5.7	0.0	1.4	7.7	2.5	0.6	2.9	82.9	33.6	31.3	875	856
Davis	1.8	0.0	0.4	5.5	0.8	0.4	0.6	23.8	8.1	5.0	594	586
Decatur	2.3	0.0	0.5	7.3	2.8	1.4	1.3	21.4	9.2	5.7	696	671
Delaware	2.9	0.0	0.7	7.0	1.6	0.4	0.4	48.2	19.1	14.5	788	718
Des Moines	10.1	29.1	2.0	18.9	6.0	2.0	6.6	108.7	49.8	35.6	846	739
Dickinson	2.7	0.0	0.7	5.5	1.1	0.3	0.0	43.2	11.5	16.9	1 057	1 019
Dubuque	18.4	0.6	4.4	40.5	9.2	2.4	22.0	195.7	82.2	72.6	824	688
Emmet	2.6	0.0	2.8	5.2	1.3	1.5	0.6	43.0	21.4	8.1	743	706
Fayette	5.0	0.0	1.1	10.3	2.4	1.0	0.1	44.7	21.9	16.2	738	685
Floyd	3.1	0.0	1.6	13.3	1.7	0.5	6.8	46.2	17.2	13.3	807	781
Franklin	2.3	0.0	0.6	5.2	0.9	0.3	0.7	28.1	10.5	10.2	939	855
Fremont	1.9	0.0	0.5	5.2	0.9	0.2	0.5	18.9	9.3	7.5	952	888
Greene	2.5	0.0	1.5	6.1	0.9	0.3	1.1	32.3	10.8	9.7	966	942
Grundy	2.1	0.0	0.6	2.8	0.6	0.3	10.2	36.9	15.4	12.7	1 036	1 001

1. October 1, 2000 to September 30, 2001.   2. State totals may include programs not allocated by county.   3. Based on the resident population estimated as of July 1 of the year shown.

	Local government finances, 1997 (cont'd)									Government employment, 1999			Presidential election, 2000[2]		
	Direct general expenditure							Debt outstanding					Percent of vote cast —		
			Percent of total for —												
STATE County	Total (mil dol)	Per capita[1] (dollars)	Educa- tion	Health and hospitals	Police protec- tion	Public welfare	High- ways	Total (mil dol)	Per capita[1] (dollars)	Federal civilian	Federal military	State and local	Demo- cratic	Republi- can	All other
	183	184	185	186	187	188	189	190	191	192	193	194	195	196	197
INDIANA—Cont'd															
Putnam	86.8	2 574	49.8	21.2	1.1	1.7	5.5	75.2	2 231	85	121	2 531	34.7	61.9	3.3
Randolph	62.2	2 265	46.8	19.4	2.0	3.7	6.4	22.0	801	84	95	1 478	38.6	59.4	2.0
Ripley	48.3	1 777	68.5	0.4	1.9	1.2	6.8	28.9	1 062	87	96	1 195	32.8	65.5	1.8
Rush	38.0	2 083	43.2	24.8	3.6	2.0	7.2	3.4	189	58	63	1 180	32.5	65.2	2.3
St. Joseph	554.5	2 149	48.9	1.0	4.1	4.8	4.3	394.6	1 529	1 186	952	12 554	48.9	48.8	2.2
Scott	49.9	2 189	46.8	22.1	3.1	1.6	3.6	16.7	730	59	82	1 193	49.9	47.9	2.2
Shelby	107.6	2 494	51.6	19.6	2.9	1.5	3.2	31.3	726	150	152	2 150	35.1	62.6	2.3
Spencer	38.0	1 836	60.9	0.5	2.0	2.5	7.5	28.7	1 387	80	74	900	41.7	56.7	1.6
Starke	52.7	2 219	50.2	24.2	1.7	1.1	5.0	19.8	834	55	82	932	47.5	49.9	2.5
Steuben	60.9	1 957	56.3	1.7	2.9	3.5	5.1	37.8	1 215	76	110	1 497	36.4	61.7	2.0
Sullivan	57.9	2 856	41.8	0.2	0.8	2.0	5.4	249.9	12 323	69	75	2 047	46.4	52.3	1.2
Switzerland	14.9	1 726	71.6	2.4	1.3	1.6	6.4	10.2	1 180	29	31	420	41.2	56.5	2.3
Tippecanoe	238.3	1 723	56.1	0.5	5.0	6.7	4.3	75.1	543	529	535	19 705	39.3	56.3	4.5
Tipton	49.8	3 035	35.9	36.2	1.6	1.2	5.3	9.5	577	37	58	1 145	32.7	65.4	1.9
Union	15.1	2 075	59.6	0.9	2.5	2.2	8.0	12.8	1 765	16	25	410	32.8	65.0	2.2
Vanderburgh	352.1	2 110	45.8	1.7	7.1	3.7	4.1	115.3	691	935	598	8 723	44.1	54.1	1.8
Vermillion	34.3	2 016	61.1	0.3	1.1	1.6	5.6	28.3	1 664	54	66	691	50.8	47.2	2.0
Vigo	206.6	1 969	65.8	0.8	2.9	2.3	3.3	91.4	871	1 223	386	7 904	48.5	49.7	1.7
Wabash	91.8	2 658	46.8	23.2	2.5	2.4	3.6	51.0	1 477	89	120	1 964	33.2	64.6	2.2
Warren	15.5	1 892	57.1	2.4	1.7	2.5	11.0	6.5	796	26	29	348	39.0	58.9	2.1
Warrick	94.8	1 866	57.0	1.4	2.6	2.0	4.2	102.5	2 016	130	183	1 611	39.2	59.2	1.6
Washington	54.7	2 014	50.4	18.0	1.4	1.5	7.3	18.0	665	63	98	1 297	37.5	59.9	2.6
Wayne	142.3	1 982	53.3	1.0	4.4	2.9	4.9	38.6	537	170	248	4 696	40.8	56.7	2.4
Wells	69.2	2 586	46.9	18.3	2.4	2.7	5.1	34.1	1 275	63	93	1 480	29.4	68.7	1.9
White	71.9	2 873	61.6	15.1	1.1	1.1	4.8	27.0	1 077	75	89	1 466	36.9	61.0	2.1
Whitley	51.3	1 711	60.0	2.2	2.8	2.5	5.7	17.9	598	77	107	1 309	33.0	65.0	1.9
IOWA	X	X	X	X	X	X	X	X	X	19 925	13 817	216 032	48.5	48.2	3.2
Adair	17.0	2 065	43.8	7.6	4.2	0.3	25.1	7.5	914	35	37	542	42.5	55.2	2.3
Adams	8.3	1 882	52.4	6.2	4.6	0.8	15.1	1.2	268	30	20	272	41.8	54.5	3.7
Allamakee	32.0	2 287	45.9	20.1	3.5	1.1	11.1	7.9	568	74	65	954	44.6	50.7	4.7
Appanoose	27.8	2 059	55.9	6.8	5.6	0.9	12.9	9.3	688	82	62	731	44.9	52.5	2.6
Audubon	15.6	2 282	48.8	6.4	2.8	0.3	20.4	3.8	564	38	32	439	47.0	50.4	2.5
Benton	42.2	1 688	53.9	4.2	3.9	0.7	15.1	26.4	1 055	76	120	1 421	50.3	46.5	3.3
Black Hawk	380.5	3 131	44.8	7.7	4.1	4.2	7.8	232.1	1 910	563	578	11 065	54.7	42.6	2.8
Boone	57.7	2 206	41.9	27.4	3.3	1.2	9.2	41.2	1 574	118	122	2 066	51.2	45.9	2.9
Bremer	55.9	2 397	51.5	18.1	4.1	0.7	8.7	22.5	964	70	109	1 369	46.3	50.8	2.9
Buchanan	39.0	1 843	45.8	17.4	5.0	0.2	13.7	8.3	394	102	98	1 540	53.6	43.5	2.9
Buena Vista	57.4	2 933	45.5	23.9	5.6	0.2	7.8	22.9	1 173	97	90	1 488	40.7	57.1	2.3
Butler	25.0	1 592	52.2	5.5	4.4	0.1	15.4	9.0	575	57	72	720	42.3	55.1	2.6
Calhoun	28.1	2 462	57.6	8.3	3.9	4.2	12.7	3.9	340	51	53	819	42.3	55.1	2.6
Carroll	44.6	2 053	48.3	4.5	4.9	5.1	13.1	25.3	1 166	105	100	1 178	46.6	51.0	2.3
Cass	53.5	3 631	34.7	39.5	2.8	0.4	11.6	23.8	1 616	87	67	1 260	36.1	61.1	2.8
Cedar	37.3	2 076	53.8	5.8	3.3	1.8	15.3	10.2	569	116	84	933	48.3	48.3	3.3
Cerro Gordo	125.8	2 713	58.1	1.7	4.1	2.4	6.6	67.3	1 452	178	212	2 847	55.0	42.4	2.6
Cherokee	31.1	2 315	44.7	3.4	3.5	1.7	16.7	8.4	623	56	61	1 054	43.2	52.5	4.3
Chickasaw	25.7	1 912	50.8	5.7	3.3	1.3	15.5	4.7	351	62	62	648	52.2	44.6	3.2
Clarke	24.6	2 984	39.1	27.1	3.3	1.1	10.7	9.4	1 145	39	38	698	49.8	47.5	2.7
Clay	60.7	3 451	28.1	37.7	2.6	4.2	8.4	7.2	407	87	80	1 313	43.5	52.7	3.9
Clayton	53.3	2 838	64.1	2.6	2.6	2.2	10.3	17.0	904	109	86	1 164	49.4	47.1	3.5
Clinton	110.1	2 192	50.5	5.4	6.3	0.7	12.7	88.7	1 766	143	230	2 586	55.3	41.6	3.0
Crawford	40.4	2 462	38.0	22.5	3.5	0.8	15.9	8.2	499	103	76	1 079	43.3	53.1	3.6
Dallas	90.6	2 533	57.4	14.0	3.6	0.9	8.4	57.7	1 612	108	177	1 943	44.3	53.3	2.4
Davis	23.9	2 841	30.2	41.1	2.0	0.4	11.0	6.4	757	43	40	582	45.0	52.0	3.0
Decatur	21.3	2 596	42.5	26.5	2.4	1.2	12.6	5.7	702	47	39	614	45.1	51.3	3.5
Delaware	49.4	2 679	39.9	26.1	2.8	0.4	14.8	13.2	717	68	86	1 079	45.6	51.2	3.2
Des Moines	111.8	2 653	61.6	3.2	4.6	1.2	7.7	46.5	1 104	200	199	2 421	58.6	38.1	3.2
Dickinson	42.4	2 650	37.6	26.5	3.3	0.6	14.6	26.0	1 624	55	76	1 008	45.1	52.0	2.9
Dubuque	191.6	2 175	38.1	5.8	4.4	5.3	10.5	52.5	596	297	433	3 564	55.4	40.8	3.7
Emmet	44.2	4 041	72.5	3.5	2.9	0.5	7.6	8.8	804	47	49	825	46.8	50.3	2.9
Fayette	43.6	1 981	57.9	6.5	3.3	1.4	5.2	10.4	472	101	100	1 247	48.2	49.3	2.4
Floyd	41.1	2 498	43.4	24.6	4.1	1.2	8.4	10.0	606	59	75	1 043	52.9	44.1	3.0
Franklin	28.4	2 609	40.3	21.3	3.9	3.0	12.6	5.3	484	49	50	732	43.0	53.8	3.2
Fremont	17.4	2 220	53.9	4.9	1.8	1.0	17.6	6.4	820	43	36	474	40.3	57.2	2.4
Greene	33.0	3 283	37.4	24.9	3.2	6.0	12.3	14.6	1 459	44	47	884	48.8	48.4	2.8
Grundy	35.2	2 870	50.6	12.6	3.1	3.2	12.8	7.6	616	44	57	682	35.0	63.0	1.9

1. Based on the resident population estimated as of July 1 of the year shown.   2. Data subject to copyright.

STATE/ County code	MSA/ PMSA/ NECMA code[1]	County Type[2]	STATE County	Land area[3] (sq km) 2000	Total persons	Rank	Per square kilometer	White	Black	Am. Indian, Alaska Native	Asian and Pacific Islander	Percent Hispanic[4]	Under 5 years	5 to 17 years	18 to 24 years	25 to 34 years	35 to 44 years	45 to 54 years
				1	2	3	4	5	6	7	8	9	10	11	12	13	14	15
			IOWA—Cont'd															
19 077	...	8	Guthrie	1 530	11 353	2 346	7.4	99.2	0.2	0.4	0.4	1.1	5.5	18.0	6.3	9.6	15.2	14.0
19 079	...	7	Hamilton	1 494	16 438	1 994	11.0	97.4	0.4	0.4	1.7	1.4	6.4	19.0	7.1	11.3	15.8	13.1
19 081	...	7	Hancock	1 479	12 100	2 290	8.2	98.1	0.1	0.2	0.5	2.5	6.1	20.4	6.6	9.9	15.6	13.9
19 083	...	7	Hardin	1 474	18 812	1 853	12.8	97.6	0.7	0.3	0.5	2.4	5.7	19.0	8.4	9.4	14.4	12.9
19 085	...	6	Harrison	1 805	15 666	2 042	8.7	99.3	0.3	0.6	0.3	0.7	6.0	20.2	6.8	10.9	16.1	12.8
19 087	...	7	Henry	1 125	20 336	1 770	18.1	95.7	1.8	0.6	2.3	1.3	6.0	18.7	9.0	13.0	16.2	13.7
19 089	...	7	Howard	1 226	9 932	2 453	8.1	99.5	0.2	0.2	0.3	0.6	6.0	20.3	6.8	10.5	14.9	12.0
19 091	...	7	Humboldt	1 125	10 381	2 404	9.2	99.0	0.2	0.2	0.5	1.0	5.4	19.4	7.0	9.0	15.6	12.8
19 093	...	8	Ida	1 118	7 837	2 620	7.0	99.4	0.2	0.2	0.4	0.5	5.5	20.0	6.1	9.4	14.6	13.5
19 095	...	8	Iowa	1 519	15 671	2 041	10.3	99.0	0.2	0.2	0.4	1.0	6.2	20.2	6.3	11.1	16.8	13.1
19 097	...	6	Jackson	1 647	20 296	1 773	12.3	99.4	0.2	0.3	0.3	0.6	5.9	20.1	7.0	10.7	15.9	13.2
19 099	...	6	Jasper	1 891	37 213	1 186	19.7	98.1	1.0	0.5	0.7	1.0	6.2	18.4	7.4	12.5	16.1	13.8
19 101	...	7	Jefferson	1 128	16 181	2 010	14.3	96.8	0.8	0.4	2.0	1.8	5.4	19.0	7.6	10.2	14.2	21.1
19 103	3500	3	Johnson	1 591	111 006	488	69.8	91.5	3.4	0.6	4.7	2.5	5.8	14.3	23.4	16.6	14.1	12.2
19 105	...	6	Jones	1 490	20 221	1 779	13.6	97.4	2.1	0.6	0.3	1.1	5.6	18.5	7.9	12.4	16.5	13.7
19 107	...	9	Keokuk	1 500	11 400	2 341	7.6	99.3	0.1	0.3	0.4	0.5	5.9	19.8	7.0	10.3	15.2	12.4
19 109	...	7	Kossuth	2 520	17 163	1 944	6.8	99.1	0.2	0.3	0.4	0.8	5.4	20.4	6.1	9.0	15.3	13.4
19 111	...	5	Lee	1 340	38 052	1 163	28.4	95.4	3.4	0.7	0.6	2.4	6.0	18.4	7.8	11.0	15.7	14.8
19 113	1360	3	Linn	1 858	191 701	286	103.2	95.2	3.3	0.6	1.8	1.4	7.0	18.3	10.1	14.3	15.9	13.6
19 115	...	8	Louisa	1 041	12 183	2 284	11.7	94.8	0.4	0.4	0.3	12.6	7.2	20.5	7.9	12.9	15.7	12.5
19 117	...	6	Lucas	1 115	9 422	2 492	8.5	99.1	0.1	0.3	0.3	0.9	6.0	19.3	7.3	10.4	14.2	12.6
19 119	...	6	Lyon	1 522	11 763	2 312	7.7	99.5	0.2	0.4	0.3	0.4	6.7	21.3	7.6	10.6	14.1	12.7
19 121	...	6	Madison	1 453	14 019	2 162	9.6	99.2	0.2	0.7	0.4	0.7	7.0	20.1	6.9	11.9	15.5	14.2
19 123	...	7	Mahaska	1 479	22 335	1 677	15.1	97.9	0.8	0.5	1.1	0.9	6.6	19.1	9.4	11.9	14.9	13.1
19 125	...	6	Marion	1 435	32 052	1 344	22.3	98.1	0.6	0.5	1.3	0.8	6.3	19.1	10.2	11.4	15.1	13.0
19 127	...	5	Marshall	1 482	39 311	1 129	26.5	91.7	1.3	0.6	1.1	9.0	6.5	18.8	8.1	11.9	14.4	14.3
19 129	...	6	Mills	1 131	14 547	2 118	12.9	98.8	0.4	0.8	0.4	1.2	6.3	20.4	7.0	11.5	16.7	15.8
19 131	...	7	Mitchell	1 215	10 874	2 375	8.9	99.5	0.2	0.1	0.2	0.6	6.1	20.4	6.1	9.4	14.8	11.9
19 133	...	7	Monona	1 795	10 020	2 443	5.6	98.9	0.2	1.0	0.2	0.7	5.3	17.9	6.2	9.1	14.2	12.7
19 135	...	7	Monroe	1 123	8 016	2 603	7.1	98.9	0.4	0.6	0.5	0.5	6.4	19.0	7.2	11.1	13.9	13.0
19 137	...	6	Montgomery	1 098	11 771	2 310	10.7	98.6	0.1	0.6	0.3	1.3	6.1	18.9	6.5	11.0	14.5	13.0
19 139	...	4	Muscatine	1 136	41 722	1 062	36.7	92.0	0.9	0.7	1.1	11.9	6.9	20.0	8.6	12.9	15.9	13.9
19 141	...	7	O'Brien	1 484	15 102	2 084	10.2	98.4	0.4	0.3	0.7	1.8	5.9	18.9	7.8	9.6	14.5	12.9
19 143	...	7	Osceola	1 033	7 003	2 686	6.8	98.6	0.2	0.4	0.3	1.8	5.9	20.2	7.2	9.8	16.4	12.1
19 145	...	7	Page	1 385	16 976	1 954	12.3	96.8	1.8	0.8	0.7	1.6	5.6	17.7	7.9	11.4	14.9	13.5
19 147	...	7	Palo Alto	1 460	10 147	2 434	7.0	99.2	0.2	0.5	0.4	0.8	5.4	18.6	9.5	9.1	14.1	12.3
19 149	...	6	Plymouth	2 237	24 849	1 562	11.1	98.7	0.5	0.3	0.5	1.3	6.6	21.7	7.2	10.8	15.7	13.6
19 151	...	9	Pocahontas	1 496	8 662	2 554	5.8	99.0	0.4	0.4	0.4	0.9	4.9	20.5	5.3	7.9	15.6	13.6
19 153	2120	2	Polk	1 475	374 601	156	254.0	89.8	5.4	0.6	3.1	4.4	7.5	18.2	9.4	15.8	16.4	13.5
19 155	5920	2	Pottawattamie	2 472	87 704	596	35.5	97.0	1.1	0.8	0.8	3.3	6.6	19.4	9.1	12.7	15.9	13.7
19 157	...	7	Poweshiek	1 515	18 815	1 852	12.4	97.6	0.8	0.5	1.5	1.2	5.5	17.1	12.8	10.0	14.4	13.0
19 159	...	9	Ringgold	1 393	5 469	2 818	3.9	99.5	0.2	0.4	0.2	0.2	5.9	18.2	6.9	8.2	13.2	12.6
19 161	...	9	Sac	1 491	11 529	2 331	7.7	99.1	0.4	0.2	0.4	1.0	5.6	18.5	6.9	9.3	14.3	13.2
19 163	1960	2	Scott	1 186	158 668	334	133.8	90.2	6.9	0.8	2.0	4.1	6.9	19.6	9.3	13.7	15.7	14.3
19 165	...	6	Shelby	1 530	13 173	2 215	8.6	99.1	0.2	0.5	0.4	0.7	5.9	20.5	5.7	9.4	15.8	13.0
19 167	...	7	Sioux	1 989	31 589	1 357	15.9	97.8	0.3	0.3	0.7	2.6	6.6	20.5	15.2	9.9	13.6	11.4
19 169	...	4	Story	1 484	79 981	642	53.9	92.1	2.1	0.4	5.7	1.5	5.2	13.9	28.3	13.4	12.0	10.9
19 171	...	6	Tama	1 868	18 103	1 892	9.7	91.5	0.4	6.8	0.3	3.8	6.9	19.6	7.0	11.0	14.2	12.6
19 173	...	9	Taylor	1 383	6 958	2 690	5.0	98.4	0.0	0.3	0.5	3.8	5.5	18.4	7.5	9.7	13.7	12.7
19 175	...	7	Union	1 099	12 309	2 279	11.2	99.0	0.3	0.4	0.3	1.0	5.9	17.4	8.7	10.6	14.1	14.1
19 177	...	9	Van Buren	1 256	7 809	2 624	6.2	99.2	0.2	0.6	0.4	0.8	5.6	19.2	7.0	10.3	14.1	13.8
19 179	2120	5	Wapello	1 118	36 051	1 215	32.2	97.0	1.1	0.6	0.8	2.2	5.9	17.3	9.7	11.4	14.6	13.7
19 181	2120	2	Warren	1 481	40 671	1 094	27.5	98.8	0.4	0.5	0.6	1.1	6.8	20.2	9.7	11.7	16.5	14.2
19 183	...	6	Washington	1 473	20 670	1 753	14.0	97.7	0.5	0.4	0.4	2.7	6.7	19.4	7.0	11.2	15.6	13.4
19 185	...	9	Wayne	1 361	6 730	2 716	4.9	99.4	0.2	0.4	0.4	0.7	5.0	18.8	5.9	8.9	14.5	12.1
19 187	...	5	Webster	1 852	40 235	1 109	21.7	94.5	3.9	0.7	0.9	2.3	6.3	18.2	11.1	11.0	14.5	13.0
19 189	...	7	Winnebago	1 037	11 723	2 316	11.3	97.8	0.3	0.3	1.0	2.0	5.6	18.5	9.8	9.7	14.5	14.3
19 191	...	7	Winneshiek	1 786	21 310	1 721	11.9	98.3	0.6	0.3	0.9	0.8	5.1	17.9	16.7	9.4	14.8	11.9
19 193	7720	3	Woodbury	2 260	103 877	510	46.0	89.2	2.7	2.4	2.9	9.1	7.6	19.7	10.2	13.6	14.7	13.0
19 195	...	9	Worth	1 036	7 909	2 614	7.6	99.1	0.4	0.5	0.2	1.6	5.7	18.6	6.5	10.5	15.8	13.8
19 197	...	7	Wright	1 504	14 334	2 137	9.5	96.5	0.3	0.4	0.3	4.9	5.7	18.8	6.5	10.0	14.6	13.7
20 000	...	X	**KANSAS**	211 900	2 688 418	X	12.7	87.9	6.3	1.8	2.2	7.0	7.0	19.5	10.3	13.0	15.6	13.2
20 001	...	7	Allen	1 303	14 385	2 134	11.0	96.3	2.1	1.8	0.5	1.9	5.9	19.3	9.8	9.9	14.2	13.3
20 003	...	6	Anderson	1 510	8 110	2 597	5.4	98.3	0.6	1.3	0.4	1.1	6.2	20.0	7.0	10.0	14.6	11.7
20 005	...	6	Atchison	1 120	16 774	1 972	15.0	93.1	6.1	1.3	0.7	1.9	6.4	20.3	11.3	10.6	13.8	12.1

1. MSA = Metropolitan Statistical Area. PMSA = Primary MSA. NECMA = New England County Metropolitan Area. See Appendix A for explanation of these concepts. See Appendix B for list of metropolitan areas identified by type, with component counties. 2. County typology code from the Economic Research Service of USDA. See Appendix A for definition. 3. Dry land or land partially or temporarily covered by water. 4. Hispanic persons may be of any race.

Table B. States and Counties — **Population and Households**

	Population, 2000 (cont'd)				Population — change and components of change, 1990–2001							Households, 2000				
	Age (percent) (cont'd)				Total persons		Percent change		Components of change, 2000–2001							Percent	
STATE County	55 to 64 years	65 to 74 years	75 years and over	Percent female	2001	1990	1990–2000	2000–2001	Births	Deaths	Net migration	Number	Percent change, 1990–2000	Persons per house-hold	Female family house-holder[1]	One person
	16	17	18	19	20	21	22	23	24	25	26	27	28	29	30	31

IOWA—Cont'd

Guthrie	10.9	10.2	10.3	50.6	11 323	10 935	3.8	-0.3	171	183	-14	4 641	5.3	2.39	6.6	26.1
Hamilton	9.3	8.7	9.3	50.5	16 380	16 071	2.3	-0.4	251	215	-87	6 692	5.3	2.43	7.6	27.5
Hancock	9.5	8.1	9.8	50.8	11 858	12 638	-4.3	-2.0	165	161	-247	4 795	-1.5	2.48	6.0	26.5
Hardin	9.5	9.0	11.6	51.1	18 537	19 094	-1.5	-1.5	249	339	-181	7 628	0.2	2.35	6.5	29.4
Harrison	9.6	8.5	9.2	50.9	15 626	14 730	6.4	-0.3	206	267	25	6 115	8.1	2.51	7.6	26.1
Henry	8.8	6.7	8.0	49.4	20 309	19 226	5.8	-0.1	320	257	-83	7 626	7.6	2.46	8.2	26.8
Howard	9.3	9.2	11.0	50.8	9 856	9 809	1.3	-0.8	140	186	-25	3 974	3.1	2.43	6.6	29.5
Humboldt	9.7	9.7	11.3	51.1	10 292	10 756	-3.5	-0.9	138	143	-79	4 295	-1.0	2.38	6.4	29.8
Ida	9.2	10.2	11.6	51.6	7 651	8 365	-6.3	-2.4	93	137	-141	3 213	-0.3	2.39	5.9	29.3
Iowa	9.3	7.9	9.2	51.3	15 901	14 630	7.1	1.5	225	220	228	6 163	7.9	2.50	6.6	25.9
Jackson	10.0	8.7	8.6	50.7	20 207	19 950	1.7	-0.4	286	259	-109	8 078	7.3	2.47	7.7	27.0
Jasper	9.6	8.2	7.8	49.6	37 296	34 795	6.9	0.2	537	429	-15	14 689	7.8	2.42	7.4	26.1
Jefferson	8.7	6.3	7.5	51.1	16 029	16 310	-0.8	-0.9	208	174	-184	6 649	5.4	2.34	8.0	30.4
Johnson	6.1	3.9	3.5	50.2	111 230	96 119	15.5	0.2	1 641	608	-797	44 080	22.2	2.34	6.8	30.2
Jones	9.5	8.0	7.8	47.8	20 065	19 444	4.0	-0.8	229	220	-162	7 560	9.3	2.47	7.9	25.3
Keokuk	9.1	9.1	11.0	51.5	11 403	11 624	-1.9	0.0	165	148	-10	4 586	0.3	2.45	6.5	27.8
Kossuth	10.2	9.6	10.5	51.2	16 788	18 591	-7.7	-2.2	218	242	-351	6 974	-3.1	2.42	5.8	28.7
Lee	9.9	8.0	8.6	50.5	37 313	38 687	-1.6	-1.9	562	522	-786	15 161	1.5	2.41	10.3	28.3
Linn	8.5	6.2	6.1	51.0	193 165	168 767	13.6	0.8	3 373	1 823	5	76 753	17.2	2.43	9.0	27.5
Louisa	9.2	7.2	6.8	50.3	12 245	11 592	5.1	0.5	210	137	-8	4 519	5.2	2.66	8.2	22.5
Lucas	10.8	9.1	10.2	51.4	9 470	9 070	3.9	0.5	136	161	74	3 811	1.2	2.42	7.0	28.7
Lyon	8.2	9.1	9.7	50.4	11 750	11 952	-1.6	-0.1	185	148	-47	4 428	3.2	2.61	4.4	24.3
Madison	9.3	6.7	8.4	50.7	14 190	12 483	12.3	1.2	224	202	148	5 326	13.0	2.58	7.0	22.7
Mahaska	8.6	7.6	8.8	50.2	22 123	21 532	3.7	-0.9	385	267	-330	8 880	6.9	2.45	7.5	26.6
Marion	9.1	7.3	8.6	50.4	32 610	30 001	6.8	1.7	501	405	466	12 017	11.1	2.50	6.9	25.6
Marshall	9.6	8.0	8.4	50.2	39 438	38 276	2.7	0.3	694	642	80	15 338	3.0	2.48	9.3	26.9
Mills	9.7	6.5	6.1	49.8	14 651	13 202	10.2	0.7	216	167	58	5 324	14.1	2.60	8.9	22.3
Mitchell	9.7	9.8	11.8	51.1	10 842	10 928	-0.5	-0.3	162	181	-9	4 294	1.0	2.47	5.7	27.6
Monona	10.6	10.7	13.2	51.5	9 882	10 034	-0.1	-1.4	125	195	-65	4 211	2.8	2.31	7.1	31.0
Monroe	10.0	9.1	10.5	51.3	7 839	8 114	-1.2	-2.2	103	113	-169	3 228	1.0	2.43	8.6	28.0
Montgomery	8.9	9.4	10.9	52.6	11 536	12 076	-2.5	-2.0	215	209	-244	4 886	-1.4	2.36	8.7	29.5
Muscatine	8.9	6.5	6.5	50.5	41 831	39 907	4.5	0.3	781	502	-156	15 847	7.0	2.59	9.3	24.1
O'Brien	9.2	9.7	11.4	51.1	14 954	15 444	-2.2	-1.0	221	232	-135	6 001	0.4	2.42	4.9	28.0
Osceola	9.5	9.0	9.9	51.3	6 935	7 267	-3.6	-1.0	88	107	-46	2 778	-1.4	2.48	5.1	27.6
Page	9.3	9.2	10.6	49.3	16 682	16 870	0.6	-1.7	241	312	-220	6 708	0.3	2.32	8.1	29.9
Palo Alto	9.6	10.3	11.0	51.4	10 015	10 669	-4.9	-1.3	137	179	-88	4 119	-1.5	2.37	5.9	30.4
Plymouth	8.5	7.9	10.3	50.3	24 876	23 388	6.2	0.1	353	308	-6	9 372	11.3	2.61	6.2	24.0
Pocahontas	10.5	9.7	12.0	50.9	8 473	9 525	-9.1	-2.2	88	136	-139	3 617	-5.3	2.35	5.9	30.2
Polk	8.0	5.7	5.4	51.5	379 029	327 140	14.5	1.2	7 470	3 423	560	149 112	15.4	2.45	10.3	28.1
Pottawattamie	9.0	7.4	6.3	51.1	87 854	82 628	6.1	0.2	1 442	985	-278	33 844	8.3	2.54	11.8	24.9
Poweshiek	9.5	8.1	9.6	52.0	18 899	19 033	-1.1	0.4	232	285	145	7 398	3.4	2.35	7.4	29.2
Ringgold	11.1	11.3	12.7	51.5	5 376	5 420	-0.9	-1.7	69	88	-75	2 245	1.2	2.37	5.5	28.6
Sac	9.6	10.2	12.5	51.1	11 331	12 324	-6.5	-1.7	139	227	-108	4 746	-3.4	2.37	6.2	29.4
Scott	8.7	6.1	5.7	51.1	158 489	150 973	5.1	-0.1	2 930	1 710	-1 367	62 334	8.5	2.49	11.4	26.9
Shelby	9.3	9.5	10.9	51.1	13 182	13 230	-0.4	0.1	177	182	20	5 173	3.0	2.49	6.8	25.2
Sioux	7.7	7.1	7.9	51.0	31 596	29 903	5.6	0.0	478	301	-159	10 693	7.7	2.71	4.2	22.2
Story	6.4	4.7	5.1	48.9	79 462	74 252	7.7	-0.6	1 115	583	-1 050	29 383	13.3	2.39	5.9	26.7
Tama	9.9	8.8	9.9	50.9	18 045	17 419	3.9	-0.3	303	242	-116	7 018	3.7	2.51	8.0	25.3
Taylor	10.1	9.7	12.7	51.5	6 880	7 114	-2.2	-1.1	78	119	-36	2 824	-1.2	2.40	5.9	27.8
Union	9.8	8.5	10.1	52.1	12 240	12 750	-3.5	-0.6	179	191	-52	5 242	1.3	2.29	8.0	31.3
Van Buren	11.0	8.8	10.3	50.1	7 768	7 676	1.7	-0.5	106	130	-12	3 181	4.1	2.41	6.0	28.0
Wapello	9.5	8.7	9.0	51.3	35 794	35 696	1.0	-0.7	471	556	-157	14 784	1.6	2.37	9.9	28.2
Warren	9.0	6.0	5.9	51.4	41 149	36 033	12.9	1.2	604	375	264	14 708	16.2	2.65	8.8	19.9
Washington	8.9	7.8	10.1	51.8	21 010	19 612	5.4	1.6	349	269	264	8 056	8.1	2.50	6.7	26.4
Wayne	10.9	10.6	13.2	52.2	6 639	7 067	-4.8	-1.4	84	147	-27	2 821	-4.5	2.34	6.4	29.8
Webster	8.6	8.3	9.1	49.9	39 806	40 342	-0.3	-1.1	633	572	-485	15 878	-0.5	2.38	9.5	30.3
Winnebago	8.8	8.5	10.5	51.1	11 565	12 122	-3.3	-1.3	151	190	-123	4 749	1.0	2.36	7.2	29.4
Winneshiek	8.5	7.4	8.3	50.8	21 423	20 847	2.2	0.5	239	221	103	7 734	6.6	2.46	5.5	27.6
Woodbury	7.8	6.7	6.7	51.0	103 033	98 276	5.7	-0.8	2 137	1 174	-1 830	39 151	6.1	2.58	11.3	26.6
Worth	9.7	8.8	10.6	50.4	7 810	7 991	-1.0	-1.3	107	127	-79	3 278	1.2	2.38	7.3	27.6
Wright	9.6	9.2	12.0	51.0	14 110	14 269	0.5	-1.6	208	236	-194	5 940	0.7	2.36	6.2	30.2
KANSAS	8.2	6.5	6.7	50.6	2 694 641	2 477 588	8.5	0.2	48 712	31 045	-11 379	1 037 891	9.9	2.51	9.3	27.0
Allen	9.6	8.4	9.6	51.1	14 193	14 638	-1.7	-1.3	202	258	-135	5 775	1.2	2.43	8.9	28.5
Anderson	10.4	9.1	11.0	50.8	8 190	7 803	3.9	1.0	131	112	61	3 221	5.0	2.48	6.9	26.8
Atchison	9.3	7.9	8.4	51.7	16 687	16 932	-0.9	-0.5	268	261	-88	6 275	2.4	2.51	10.0	27.6

1. No spouse present.

STATE County	Births, average 1997–1999 Total	Rate[1]	Deaths, average 1997–1999 Number Total	Number Infant[2]	Rate Total[1]	Rate Infant[3]	Physicians,[4] 2000 Number	Rate[5]	Hospitals,[4] 1998 Number	Beds Number	Beds Rate[5]	Medicare enrollees 2000	Serious crimes known to police, 2000[6] Total Number	Rate[7]
	32	33	34	35	36	37	38	39	40	41	42	43	44	45
IOWA—Cont'd														
Guthrie	121	10.5	133	NA	11.5	NA	9	79	1	26	225	2 555	67	590
Hamilton	203	12.7	175	NA	10.9	NA	19	116	1	42	262	3 124	349	2 123
Hancock	139	11.6	127	NA	10.5	NA	5	41	1	26	216	2 242	134	1 107
Hardin	194	10.5	262	NA	14.2	NA	12	64	2	76	412	4 286	374	1 988
Harrison	172	11.2	201	NA	13.1	NA	8	51	1	37	241	2 969	245	1 564
Henry	234	11.7	198	NA	9.9	NA	21	103	1	61	305	3 339	183	900
Howard	125	12.9	142	NA	14.7	NA	6	60	1	32	330	1 995	233	2 346
Humboldt	111	10.7	119	NA	11.5	NA	9	87	1	49	475	2 260	161	1 551
Ida	97	12.2	104	NA	13.0	NA	4	51	1	36	455	1 738	32	408
Iowa	185	11.9	171	NA	11.0	NA	10	64	1	44	283	2 788	87	555
Jackson	239	11.9	224	NA	11.1	NA	14	69	1	67	334	3 749	237	1 168
Jasper	422	11.7	351	NA	9.7	NA	33	89	1	61	170	6 236	733	1 970
Jefferson	172	10.2	150	NA	8.9	NA	23	142	1	83	485	2 344	529	3 269
Johnson	1 295	12.6	496	9	4.8	6.9	1 045	941	2	1 002	975	9 230	3 460	3 117
Jones	206	10.2	176	NA	8.7	NA	14	69	1	38	187	3 359	218	1 078
Keokuk	134	11.7	133	NA	11.6	NA	1	9	1	33	287	2 629	1	9
Kossuth	186	10.5	211	NA	11.9	NA	8	47	1	24	135	3 609	193	1 125
Lee	446	11.6	433	NA	11.3	NA	53	139	2	155	403	6 730	1 201	3 156
Linn	2 556	14.0	1 400	14	7.6	5.6	353	184	2	877	480	26 448	7 240	3 909
Louisa	172	14.4	104	NA	8.7	NA	2	16	0	0	0	1 845	173	1 420
Lucas	102	11.2	124	NA	13.6	NA	6	64	1	83	907	2 028	255	2 706
Lyon	152	12.7	123	NA	10.2	NA	3	26	1	30	250	2 261	122	1 037
Madison	171	12.3	169	NA	12.1	NA	5	36	1	23	166	2 206	NA	NA
Mahaska	274	12.5	211	NA	9.6	NA	18	81	1	53	242	3 866	510	2 283
Marion	368	11.7	327	NA	10.4	NA	48	150	2	215	686	5 468	626	1 953
Marshall	478	12.3	505	NA	13.0	NA	74	188	1	158	408	7 118	1 461	3 717
Mills	172	11.8	136	NA	9.4	NA	10	69	0	0	0	2 343	372	2 557
Mitchell	126	11.4	145	NA	13.1	NA	5	46	1	30	272	2 541	87	800
Monona	103	10.2	157	NA	15.5	NA	10	100	1	48	475	2 405	233	2 325
Monroe	87	10.8	96	NA	12.0	NA	5	62	1	46	572	1 637	104	1 297
Montgomery	131	11.1	170	NA	14.4	NA	10	85	1	40	336	2 589	354	3 007
Muscatine	605	14.7	374	NA	9.1	NA	24	58	1	80	195	6 233	1 401	3 358
O'Brien	171	11.5	182	NA	12.3	NA	7	46	2	121	812	3 441	201	1 331
Osceola	84	12.0	83	NA	11.9	NA	4	57	1	32	458	1 408	82	1 171
Page	175	10.2	246	NA	14.3	NA	17	100	2	137	793	3 714	397	2 339
Palo Alto	114	11.4	144	NA	14.4	NA	6	59	1	54	539	2 349	NA	NA
Plymouth	316	12.7	246	NA	9.9	NA	15	60	1	44	177	4 219	340	1 368
Pocahontas	83	9.5	113	NA	12.9	NA	3	35	1	20	228	2 077	30	346
Polk	5 666	15.7	2 772	41	7.7	7.3	1 049	280	6	1 879	522	46 789	19 882	5 308
Pottawattamie	1 173	13.6	826	9	9.6	8.0	115	131	2	545	632	13 915	5 936	6 768
Poweshiek	195	10.4	225	NA	12.0	NA	31	165	1	46	244	3 463	544	2 891
Ringgold	55	10.2	81	NA	15.2	NA	8	146	1	36	672	1 277	44	805
Sac	128	10.8	173	NA	14.6	NA	6	52	1	54	453	2 731	84	729
Scott	2 269	14.3	1 310	16	8.3	7.2	314	198	3	660	416	21 218	9 316	5 871
Shelby	143	11.0	165	NA	12.8	NA	5	38	1	52	401	2 761	NA	NA
Sioux	408	13.1	249	NA	8.0	NA	28	89	4	295	943	5 082	NA	NA
Story	869	11.6	452	NA	6.0	NA	144	180	2	338	449	8 645	2 339	2 924
Tama	229	12.9	203	NA	11.4	NA	10	55	0	0	0	3 609	280	1 821
Taylor	74	10.4	103	NA	14.5	NA	3	43	0	0	0	1 669	65	934
Union	146	11.6	155	NA	12.4	NA	6	49	1	53	422	2 653	NA	NA
Van Buren	92	11.7	103	NA	13.1	NA	7	90	1	40	507	1 780	90	1 153
Wapello	419	11.8	448	NA	12.6	NA	71	197	1	137	387	7 442	1 792	4 971
Warren	506	12.6	309	NA	7.7	NA	23	57	0	0	0	4 872	919	2 260
Washington	273	13.0	225	NA	10.7	NA	17	82	1	83	396	4 062	0	0
Wayne	60	9.0	116	NA	17.4	NA	3	45	1	28	420	1 712	125	1 857
Webster	509	13.1	478	NA	12.3	NA	73	181	1	182	470	7 792	2 327	5 784
Winnebago	134	11.2	150	NA	12.6	NA	5	43	0	0	0	2 495	76	648
Winneshiek	215	10.3	181	NA	8.7	NA	22	103	1	83	396	3 423	185	868
Woodbury	1 604	15.7	958	15	9.4	9.1	227	219	2	681	670	15 913	6 071	5 844
Worth	86	11.1	106	NA	13.7	NA	2	25	0	0	0	1 529	89	1 125
Wright	158	11.3	197	NA	14.1	NA	7	49	2	54	386	3 256	184	1 284
KANSAS	37 698	14.3	24 093	276	9.2	7.3	0	0	132	11 383	433	390 423	118 527	4 409
Allen	178	12.3	189	NA	13.0	NA	15	104	1	40	275	2 826	498	3 462
Anderson	99	12.3	98	NA	12.2	NA	5	62	1	60	744	1 785	214	2 775
Atchison	220	13.2	192	NA	11.5	NA	17	101	1	160	946	2 916	490	2 921

1. Per 1,000 estimated resident population, average 1997–1999.   2. Deaths of infants under 1 year old.   3. Deaths of infants under 1 year old per 1,000 live births.   4. Data subject to copyright.   5. Per 100,000 resident population as of July 1 of the year shown.   6. Data for serious crimes have not been adjusted for underreporting; this may affect comparability between geographic areas and over time.   7. Per 100,000 population estimated by the FBI.

Table B. States and Counties — Crime, Education, Money Income, and Poverty

STATE County	Serious crimes known to police, 2000¹ Rate² Violent	Property	Education — Enrollment³ 1990 Total	Percent private	Attainment⁴ HS graduate or more	Bachelor's degree or more	Local govt expenditures FY1999⁵ Total current (mil dol)	Current expend. per student (dollars)	Money income 1989 Per capita⁶ (dollars)	Households Median Dollars	Percent change 1979–1989 (constant 1989 dol)	Percent with $100,000 or more	Income and poverty 1998 Median household income	Pct below poverty All persons	Persons under 18	Persons 5–17 in families
	46	47	48	49	50	51	52	53	54	55	56	57	58	59	60	61
IOWA—Cont'd																
Guthrie	0	590	2 355	3.4	78.0	9.9	13.4	5 725	11 201	23 356	4.4	1.2	35 432	9.4	13.3	12.1
Hamilton	79	2 044	3 761	6.0	79.5	12.8	17.6	5 801	11 879	25 847	-5.4	1.2	38 502	7.7	11.3	10.0
Hancock	140	967	3 238	8.6	78.4	10.3	12.8	6 076	11 064	25 445	-4.9	1.4	36 541	7.7	10.6	9.5
Hardin	149	1 839	4 727	6.3	78.5	12.4	21.2	6 060	11 356	23 457	-9.9	1.4	35 895	9.4	13.2	12.2
Harrison	51	1 513	3 461	6.3	76.2	9.1	19.0	5 555	10 411	22 258	-4.4	1.0	35 331	10.7	14.9	13.6
Henry	59	841	4 878	16.1	79.1	14.5	20.8	5 385	11 355	24 952	-4.9	1.6	33 888	9.6	13.0	11.2
Howard	131	2 215	2 177	14.3	72.9	8.2	12.0	5 659	9 960	21 913	-5.2	1.7	33 387	10.9	15.1	12.8
Humboldt	29	1 522	2 445	5.8	80.0	11.6	10.7	5 527	12 167	24 557	-7.5	2.1	37 801	8.3	12.7	11.1
Ida	0	408	1 931	4.5	75.9	11.0	8.7	5 832	10 993	22 859	0.1	1.9	34 639	10.8	14.8	13.9
Iowa	108	447	3 338	7.9	76.4	11.1	16.3	5 605	12 139	26 579	-7.1	1.6	41 348	6.7	9.2	8.3
Jackson	10	1 158	4 859	16.3	72.2	10.0	21.9	6 081	10 467	22 487	-17.7	0.9	33 565	10.9	14.2	13.3
Jasper	43	1 927	7 863	9.7	77.6	12.7	35.9	5 543	12 877	28 702	0.8	1.6	44 848	7.3	11.0	9.2
Jefferson	260	3 010	4 385	33.7	82.3	26.5	12.3	5 582	11 664	22 630	-4.7	2.0	36 028	12.7	15.8	14.9
Johnson	403	2 714	40 420	6.1	90.6	44.0	76.0	5 814	14 113	27 862	2.3	4.6	44 792	8.5	10.2	9.2
Jones	45	1 034	4 755	14.9	78.7	10.6	19.8	5 732	10 403	24 480	-10.4	1.3	36 309	9.6	12.4	11.8
Keokuk	0	9	2 663	4.8	76.8	9.4	14.2	5 804	10 427	22 234	-1.7	0.9	32 508	12.6	18.2	16.8
Kossuth	70	1 055	4 756	21.1	79.1	11.8	17.2	6 543	11 247	23 321	-9.5	1.5	34 371	10.5	14.3	12.7
Lee	342	2 815	8 965	16.8	77.5	10.7	36.5	5 842	11 488	24 671	-11.3	1.4	36 454	11.7	17.0	15.3
Linn	221	3 688	44 286	18.3	84.9	21.5	187.2	5 791	14 902	32 137	-4.5	2.9	47 501	7.3	11.2	9.4
Louisa	8	1 412	2 840	3.3	76.3	9.2	17.5	6 056	11 226	25 590	-8.4	1.3	37 998	10.2	16.4	13.4
Lucas	127	2 579	1 830	3.7	77.1	9.5	8.7	5 523	11 048	21 316	5.3	1.4	32 046	13.1	17.9	17.4
Lyon	230	808	2 951	16.2	70.4	10.2	12.3	5 843	9 871	22 676	-8.4	1.0	34 874	9.6	13.2	11.7
Madison	NA	NA	2 899	7.5	81.6	12.0	16.1	5 312	11 620	26 644	2.0	1.2	41 302	7.4	9.8	8.7
Mahaska	179	2 104	5 385	21.5	74.8	13.1	18.0	5 362	10 819	23 115	-3.2	1.4	37 847	11.1	15.2	13.5
Marion	181	1 772	8 069	30.1	73.7	12.9	32.2	5 427	11 945	27 991	0.9	2.0	44 199	7.7	10.7	9.4
Marshall	621	3 096	9 378	7.8	81.8	15.8	49.0	6 907	13 231	28 333	-5.3	1.7	38 959	9.8	15.5	13.0
Mills	247	2 310	3 421	5.7	76.1	12.6	17.0	6 178	11 140	27 420	-0.3	1.0	38 211	9.0	12.9	11.6
Mitchell	55	745	2 417	11.3	76.0	11.1	10.8	5 787	11 035	24 519	1.2	0.7	36 023	8.4	12.7	11.2
Monona	220	2 106	2 139	5.6	73.0	10.3	10.1	5 918	10 584	20 714	-8.0	2.2	30 627	12.4	18.0	16.7
Monroe	324	973	1 844	3.3	75.6	8.0	7.8	5 689	10 046	20 745	-6.2	1.1	31 777	13.5	18.8	17.6
Montgomery	170	2 837	2 619	4.9	80.0	12.8	12.1	5 766	11 595	23 312	-6.2	1.4	33 025	11.2	16.3	15.0
Muscatine	570	2 787	10 320	7.6	75.0	13.0	43.6	5 776	12 802	29 786	-2.5	1.8	42 636	10.0	14.1	13.2
O'Brien	46	1 285	3 759	21.6	73.5	12.6	16.3	5 671	10 842	23 125	-6.3	1.0	35 805	9.0	12.9	11.1
Osceola	0	1 171	1 647	11.5	72.1	10.0	5.7	5 326	11 508	23 037	-9.7	1.8	35 498	8.1	11.5	11.4
Page	118	2 221	4 041	6.6	78.2	13.5	17.8	5 833	11 122	22 050	-4.7	1.3	35 301	11.8	15.7	15.1
Palo Alto	NA	NA	2 758	13.7	76.9	12.8	17.8	9 107	10 749	21 223	-13.2	1.3	32 600	10.8	15.0	13.4
Plymouth	32	1 336	6 229	25.5	78.0	15.0	24.6	5 382	11 507	26 796	0.6	2.0	41 040	7.4	9.8	8.6
Pocahontas	35	312	2 136	11.5	80.1	12.8	8.3	5 862	11 531	23 517	-4.0	1.2	34 742	9.7	14.2	12.9
Polk	282	5 025	82 174	19.7	85.4	23.9	418.6	6 908	15 365	31 221	-1.2	3.6	45 776	8.2	12.8	10.6
Pottawattamie	572	6 196	20 448	10.3	77.1	11.0	106.9	6 201	11 734	26 639	-6.1	1.5	36 908	10.5	15.8	14.1
Poweshiek	165	2 727	5 224	26.2	81.6	16.2	17.8	5 729	12 066	26 063	-0.1	2.1	39 895	8.8	12.0	11.1
Ringgold	0	805	1 250	1.0	78.0	10.3	6.7	6 979	9 773	20 761	23.7	1.3	28 132	15.9	22.1	21.3
Sac	61	668	2 856	5.7	77.3	12.7	12.8	5 632	10 852	21 818	-11.9	1.4	32 727	10.8	15.2	14.1
Scott	1 080	4 792	41 790	18.7	81.4	21.9	191.7	6 837	13 625	29 979	-13.9	2.5	42 754	10.7	15.8	13.8
Shelby	NA	NA	3 235	14.9	79.0	12.8	16.4	6 425	10 720	22 702	-11.0	2.2	34 668	9.4	13.0	11.4
Sioux	NA	NA	9 408	50.6	71.7	14.4	28.9	6 603	10 411	25 692	-5.2	2.3	40 919	7.1	10.1	8.3
Story	136	2 788	33 981	3.6	91.0	38.4	66.1	5 957	11 958	26 668	-6.4	2.5	43 220	8.3	9.5	8.5
Tama	488	1 334	4 196	4.7	75.8	11.2	23.7	5 412	11 362	24 297	-6.2	1.5	36 063	8.5	11.3	10.7
Taylor	14	920	1 666	2.5	75.0	8.7	8.4	6 284	8 834	18 641	-5.3	0.2	28 500	15.1	19.6	18.7
Union	NA	NA	3 306	7.6	79.0	12.8	18.3	8 140	10 247	21 550	-5.9	0.8	31 648	11.5	15.5	15.2
Van Buren	77	1 076	1 682	7.9	74.7	9.6	8.7	6 101	9 348	19 244	-0.8	0.7	30 388	12.6	16.9	17.5
Wapello	566	4 405	8 262	5.9	74.2	11.0	46.7	7 038	11 055	21 060	-15.8	1.4	31 498	13.4	20.1	19.4
Warren	86	2 174	10 075	15.2	87.0	16.2	43.0	5 593	12 732	32 452	-3.6	2.0	48 238	5.9	7.7	6.9
Washington	0		4 417	11.6	76.9	11.7	20.8	5 871	11 387	25 822	2.4	1.2	37 508	8.9	14.9	13.0
Wayne	89	1 768	1 416	3.3	71.7	8.4	7.1	6 041	9 225	17 599	-3.0	0.3	27 018	15.9	22.6	21.3
Webster	457	5 326	9 603	16.6	78.4	13.7	44.8	7 651	11 358	23 692	-13.6	1.1	35 770	11.4	16.6	14.9
Winnebago	145	503	3 185	18.3	78.6	14.0	16.2	5 548	10 775	23 480	-5.8	1.4	38 372	8.6	12.3	10.8
Winneshiek	38	831	6 499	43.6	76.4	17.1	16.5	5 807	10 503	24 383	6.1	1.6	37 469	8.7	10.2	9.5
Woodbury	593	5 251	26 130	23.1	78.4	16.7	122.9	6 637	12 218	25 186	-6.4	0.9	37 469	10.5	15.6	13.3
Worth	101	1 024	1 901	7.5	77.9	10.9	6.7	5 608	11 443	22 902	-12.5	1.5	35 612	8.1	11.2	10.6
Wright	49	1 235	3 197	4.8	77.6	11.3	18.0	5 935	11 969	24 582	-6.2	1.7	36 757	8.6	13.1	11.9
KANSAS	389	4 019	668 365	11.2	81.3	21.1	2 841.1	6 015	13 300	27 291	-0.5	2.8	38 553	10.5	14.4	13.4
Allen	306	3 156	3 995	4.4	74.2	12.4	14.9	5 493	9 889	20 774	-3.7	1.2	30 854	14.7	19.1	18.9
Anderson	324	2 450	1 725	17.6	70.2	8.1	8.6	5 763	10 190	21 956	6.3	1.2	31 114	13.7	18.1	17.2
Atchison	215	2 707	4 474	25.7	77.5	13.3	16.2	6 414	10 144	22 339	-6.9	1.4	34 406	13.8	19.8	19.1

1. Data for serious crimes have not been adjusted for underreporting; this may affect comparability between geographic areas and over time. 2. Per 100,000 population estimated by the FBI. 3. All persons 3 years old and over enrolled in nursery school through college. 4. Persons 25 years old and over. 5. Elementary and secondary education expenditures, local government fiscal years ending between July 1, 1998 and June 30, 1999. 6. Based on population enumerated as of April 1, 1990.

Table B. States and Counties — **Personal Income**

| | Personal income, 1999 | | | | | | | | | | | | |
STATE County	Total (mil dol)	Percent change, 1998–1999	Per capita[1] Dollars	Per capita[1] Rank	Wages and salaries[2] (mil dol)	Proprietor's income (mil dol)	Dividends, interest, and rent (mil dol)	Transfer payments Total (mil dol)	Government payments to individuals Total (mil dol)	Social Security (mil dol)	Medical payments (mil dol)	Income mainte-nance (mil dol)	Unemploy-ment insurance (mil dol)
	62	63	64	65	66	67	68	69	70	71	72	73	74
IOWA—Cont'd													
Guthrie	258	2.2	22 248	1 286	72	25	60	46	43	24	14	3	1
Hamilton	403	0.1	25 365	603	230	33	98	57	54	31	16	3	1
Hancock	263	1.9	21 851	1 399	216	26	61	42	40	22	13	2	0
Hardin	426	-3.3	23 483	965	213	46	100	78	75	40	25	4	1
Harrison	313	2.4	20 558	1 824	97	24	58	62	59	27	23	4	1
Henry	460	1.4	22 841	1 126	319	29	96	64	59	32	19	4	2
Howard	228	1.0	23 769	904	108	29	62	37	35	19	12	2	1
Humboldt	243	-0.3	23 789	900	108	27	62	42	40	23	13	2	1
Ida	173	0.4	21 807	1 411	101	20	44	30	28	16	9	2	0
Iowa	441	5.7	28 121	316	352	38	94	49	46	28	13	2	1
Jackson	418	3.1	20 721	1 767	143	46	100	77	73	35	28	5	2
Jasper	955	4.4	26 064	505	500	63	198	128	120	67	41	7	2
Jefferson	384	-1.6	22 892	1 112	256	41	102	51	47	23	17	4	2
Johnson	3 055	6.5	29 425	237	2 221	206	606	218	196	99	61	15	4
Jones	394	3.2	19 620	2 105	152	44	88	64	60	34	19	4	1
Keokuk	227	2.5	20 033	1 981	66	25	62	46	44	23	15	3	1
Kossuth	382	-1.9	21 666	1 464	155	58	102	66	62	37	18	4	1
Lee	878	1.9	22 908	1 110	572	74	198	152	144	67	51	12	4
Linn	5 719	6.0	30 932	179	4 428	318	1 101	571	532	280	175	37	12
Louisa	250	2.0	20 901	1 694	92	26	49	38	36	19	12	3	1
Lucas	194	5.1	21 277	1 575	86	17	48	40	38	18	13	3	1
Lyon	235	-0.7	19 533	2 129	79	39	58	39	36	21	12	2	0
Madison	340	5.1	24 107	839	92	22	62	46	43	22	16	2	1
Mahaska	512	2.6	23 324	1 009	224	33	115	78	74	38	24	7	1
Marion	817	7.3	25 923	526	604	43	172	103	97	51	30	6	1
Marshall	965	2.9	24 891	687	590	62	215	157	149	72	52	10	2
Mills	398	5.9	27 041	414	108	22	55	100	97	22	68	3	0
Mitchell	251	-1.4	22 629	1 186	93	34	67	41	39	22	13	2	1
Monona	211	4.1	20 934	1 688	81	26	50	48	46	22	19	3	1
Monroe	182	3.7	22 739	1 154	95	15	39	36	34	15	13	2	1
Montgomery	272	0.1	23 209	1 042	130	26	68	53	51	25	20	3	1
Muscatine	1 079	2.7	26 192	493	781	51	248	129	121	63	40	11	3
O'Brien	341	-1.8	23 292	1 016	145	47	91	62	59	32	21	3	1
Osceola	156	3.0	22 538	1 208	60	34	33	23	22	13	6	1	0
Page	391	4.2	22 816	1 139	199	44	90	73	69	34	26	5	1
Palo Alto	218	-0.5	22 028	1 358	92	32	48	42	39	21	14	2	1
Plymouth	575	3.2	23 165	1 054	261	78	132	76	71	41	21	4	2
Pocahontas	192	-2.5	21 910	1 386	73	38	47	38	36	19	13	2	1
Polk	11 736	6.0	32 182	149	9 814	714	2 217	1 103	1 027	492	367	87	23
Pottawattamie	2 004	4.5	23 187	1 049	1 003	90	329	311	293	128	100	26	3
Poweshiek	473	2.8	25 319	610	289	50	109	66	62	34	20	4	1
Ringgold	105	3.3	19 534	2 126	36	13	26	24	23	11	9	2	0
Sac	243	1.1	20 619	1 802	84	28	68	46	43	25	14	2	1
Scott	4 220	2.1	26 462	470	2 806	232	897	493	460	219	156	52	10
Shelby	282	1.2	22 099	1 334	113	35	77	53	50	26	18	3	1
Sioux	712	1.0	22 721	1 158	383	109	173	91	85	48	27	4	1
Story	2 006	5.0	26 616	449	1 369	138	417	192	176	89	56	10	2
Tama	385	1.5	21 638	1 474	151	46	84	64	61	34	20	4	1
Taylor	129	2.1	18 373	2 450	42	17	31	29	27	14	9	2	0
Union	271	3.9	21 465	1 529	155	30	57	50	47	22	16	4	1
Van Buren	149	-1.7	18 878	2 328	57	9	32	31	29	15	10	3	1
Wapello	760	2.1	21 443	1 536	429	45	149	162	155	70	55	15	4
Warren	989	5.7	24 363	790	223	56	141	108	99	53	33	5	2
Washington	491	1.2	23 205	1 044	172	61	122	75	71	38	25	5	1
Wayne	120	1.9	18 261	2 482	42	16	30	31	29	14	10	3	0
Webster	954	4.4	24 557	743	585	59	213	164	156	78	54	12	3
Winnebago	265	0.3	22 136	1 313	131	28	59	41	38	22	13	2	0
Winneshiek	487	3.7	23 269	1 024	277	57	108	63	58	31	18	3	2
Woodbury	2 623	3.2	25 856	535	1 590	197	513	350	329	154	119	29	6
Worth	159	-4.8	20 818	1 727	45	20	39	27	26	15	8	1	1
Wright	337	-0.2	24 290	807	164	29	97	64	61	31	24	3	1
KANSAS	70 876	4.9	26 705	X	43 701	6 377	14 192	8 701	8 226	3 862	2 965	657	155
Allen	293	2.6	20 302	1 889	158	27	62	58	56	27	21	5	1
Anderson	143	4.2	17 569	2 637	48	14	36	32	30	16	10	2	1
Atchison	333	1.7	19 780	2 063	185	20	69	61	58	27	22	5	1

1. Based on the resident population estimated as of July 1 of the year shown.   2. Includes other labor income.

Table B. States and Counties — Earnings, Social Security, and Housing

STATE County	Earnings, 1999									Social Security beneficiaries, December 2000		Supplemental Security Income recipients, December 2000	Housing units, 1990	
			Percent by selected industries											
			Goods-related[1]		Service-related and other[2]									
	Total (mil dol)	Farm	Total	Manufacturing	Total	Retail trade	Finance, insurance, and real estate	Services	Government	Number	Rate[3]		Total	Percent change, 1980–1990
	75	76	77	78	79	80	81	82	83	84	85	86	87	88

IOWA—Cont'd

Guthrie	96	5.6	D	1.4	D	10.7	8.1	17.1	22.7	2 893	255	132	5 179	-2.0
Hamilton	263	5.3	D	40.1	D	6.2	3.6	11.4	14.1	3 545	216	194	6 879	-3.7
Hancock	243	4.4	D	63.4	D	3.7	2.3	6.8	8.9	2 605	215	123	5 236	-3.2
Hardin	260	7.2	24.2	15.2	48.5	8.6	4.1	14.2	20.1	4 509	240	198	8 419	-4.3
Harrison	121	2.8	D	7.0	D	14.8	3.8	20.3	21.3	3 301	211	253	6 175	-2.9
Henry	348	-0.2	34.4	29.3	48.8	20.9	2.3	17.2	17.0	3 707	182	220	7 507	3.7
Howard	137	8.6	43.1	37.4	32.4	7.6	4.1	10.1	15.8	2 390	241	112	4 155	-2.7
Humboldt	135	5.9	32.3	26.7	D	8.4	D	11.7	15.7	2 598	250	121	4 670	-6.9
Ida	121	6.5	41.7	33.9	40.4	7.2	4.0	13.5	11.5	1 934	247	61	3 473	-4.4
Iowa	390	2.2	47.6	43.1	43.2	8.5	2.3	8.2	7.0	3 235	206	112	6 003	2.2
Jackson	189	3.5	D	19.0	D	11.9	4.9	19.3	19.8	4 342	214	313	8 426	-1.6
Jasper	563	4.5	D	44.5	D	9.5	2.6	11.0	15.1	7 369	198	361	14 338	-0.8
Jefferson	297	0.6	26.2	22.5	61.5	8.3	6.7	23.1	11.8	2 736	169	235	6 739	11.7
Johnson	2 427	0.3	D	8.5	D	8.7	3.9	20.2	45.3	10 887	98	907	37 210	17.8
Jones	197	7.5	D	18.6	D	10.3	4.1	14.9	22.7	4 000	198	172	7 366	0.2
Keokuk	91	4.7	D	13.1	D	8.3	5.2	14.1	18.1	2 737	240	199	5 024	-6.9
Kossuth	213	7.3	D	15.0	D	10.0	8.5	17.3	15.3	4 334	253	190	7 765	-5.8
Lee	646	0.1	D	37.2	D	8.6	2.7	18.5	12.8	7 609	200	710	16 443	-1.4
Linn	4 746	0.2	31.9	25.1	58.7	8.4	7.1	25.7	9.2	30 447	159	2 099	68 357	5.5
Louisa	118	8.1	D	D	D	5.8	3.0	11.4	18.9	2 201	181	128	5 044	4.5
Lucas	103	1.8	14.0	8.1	D	38.0	5.2	D	20.6	2 186	232	220	4 179	-7.2
Lyon	118	18.4	D	15.5	D	6.6	4.1	16.6	14.8	2 509	213	63	4 561	-4.5
Madison	114	-0.7	D	13.6	D	12.5	5.4	18.7	23.7	2 570	183	138	4 995	0.6
Mahaska	256	3.1	D	19.0	D	10.3	4.4	20.1	14.3	4 516	202	367	8 977	-3.7
Marion	647	0.4	D	50.6	D	5.2	2.0	14.9	14.9	6 228	194	330	11 420	3.6
Marshall	651	1.7	D	35.6	D	8.8	3.2	18.4	15.8	7 996	203	523	15 862	-2.9
Mills	130	1.1	D	4.6	D	7.9	5.2	21.1	41.2	2 681	184	290	5 004	3.6
Mitchell	127	14.4	D	21.6	D	7.3	4.6	16.5	15.8	2 570	236	113	4 514	-4.7
Monona	107	9.9	12.8	5.0	60.0	10.9	4.9	30.3	17.3	2 648	264	164	4 555	-6.6
Monroe	111	0.8	53.1	43.4	D	7.1	2.5	13.1	13.7	1 918	239	159	3 740	-2.1
Montgomery	156	4.4	D	21.1	D	8.3	D	16.9	18.5	2 875	244	177	5 363	-7.5
Muscatine	832	0.7	D	49.0	D	6.5	3.2	15.4	11.3	7 048	169	469	16 044	5.2
O'Brien	192	9.0	D	11.7	D	9.1	5.7	22.5	16.2	3 755	249	209	6 476	-2.7
Osceola	94	26.3	D	19.7	D	5.8	D	11.3	11.2	1 579	225	60	2 998	-8.2
Page	244	1.5	D	27.1	D	14.5	2.9	18.7	19.5	4 114	242	344	7 339	-9.1
Palo Alto	124	14.2	18.6	15.0	43.5	8.2	3.9	17.9	23.7	2 506	247	171	4 826	-8.0
Plymouth	339	11.3	D	D	D	8.5	4.8	12.7	11.7	4 845	195	170	8 806	-0.6
Pocahontas	112	20.6	D	21.6	D	5.9	3.6	12.2	16.2	2 199	254	108	4 193	-10.0
Polk	10 528	0.1	14.5	8.9	72.5	8.6	19.5	26.3	13.0	53 925	144	5 277	135 979	11.3
Pottawattamie	1 093	0.1	D	11.9	D	13.8	5.0	33.0	16.2	15 245	174	1 509	32 831	1.3
Poweshiek	339	4.3	D	20.0	D	7.7	9.3	28.8	8.5	3 887	207	167	8 199	1.5
Ringgold	50	9.4	D	7.2	D	10.1	D	D	28.4	1 401	256	124	2 713	-8.8
Sac	112	11.0	D	7.9	D	9.8	4.8	18.9	18.7	2 947	256	116	5 648	-7.0
Scott	3 038	0.3	D	22.3	D	11.4	4.6	28.3	10.5	24 600	155	2 761	61 379	2.7
Shelby	147	7.0	15.8	5.5	58.4	11.6	5.7	20.4	18.8	3 104	236	175	5 430	-3.2
Sioux	492	10.9	D	25.2	D	8.5	4.2	16.8	10.9	5 701	180	222	10 333	-0.8
Story	1 507	1.0	D	13.5	D	8.3	3.3	16.9	44.9	9 557	119	481	26 847	6.7
Tama	196	8.5	20.8	15.2	53.3	7.1	3.9	28.8	17.4	3 964	219	169	7 417	-3.9
Taylor	58	15.0	D	19.2	D	7.5	3.4	12.9	22.3	1 811	260	130	3 307	-10.2
Union	185	2.6	D	22.8	D	10.8	3.4	18.2	21.2	2 828	230	285	5 622	-2.2
Van Buren	66	-1.1	D	32.1	36.3	6.2	4.1	11.1	26.4	1 956	250	171	3 529	1.3
Wapello	474	0.1	30.0	23.0	51.4	11.7	3.0	25.5	18.4	8 250	229	1 086	15 640	-4.3
Warren	279	0.7	D	7.1	D	14.6	4.6	26.9	21.0	5 990	147	190	13 157	8.0
Washington	234	5.5	D	16.7	D	10.7	3.6	18.0	16.1	4 462	216	232	7 866	2.2
Wayne	58	6.8	23.6	19.7	43.1	8.4	4.7	14.9	26.5	1 908	284	162	3 334	-13.4
Webster	644	0.7	D	19.7	D	11.4	4.0	25.5	16.4	8 833	220	761	17 063	-4.1
Winnebago	159	3.5	D	26.1	D	9.1	4.9	20.1	14.4	2 696	230	119	5 030	-4.2
Winneshiek	334	6.1	33.7	22.8	44.2	8.8	3.2	22.4	15.9	3 905	183	188	7 726	4.1
Woodbury	1 787	0.5	D	15.2	D	10.6	5.2	31.6	13.4	17 651	170	1 873	39 071	0.1
Worth	66	17.1	D	22.2	D	6.0	4.9	13.1	17.1	1 733	219	80	3 443	-7.5
Wright	193	7.0	D	25.5	D	7.1	D	17.5	15.6	3 481	243	171	6 636	-4.4
KANSAS	50 078	2.7	24.5	17.6	55.7	9.6	6.1	23.2	17.2	440 531	164	36 282	1 044 112	9.3
Allen	185	-2.7	D	29.0	D	19.0	3.5	14.6	20.5	3 283	228	314	6 454	-5.6
Anderson	62	2.2	20.5	9.4	54.1	11.6	5.4	19.9	23.2	1 982	244	97	3 514	-3.1
Atchison	205	0.9	35.7	29.2	48.1	10.1	2.9	21.7	15.3	3 284	196	296	6 691	-3.2

1. Covers mining, construction, and manufacturing.   2. Covers private sector earnings in agricultural services, forestry, and fisheries; transportation and public utilities; wholesale trade; retail trade; finance, insurance, and real estate; and services.   3. Per 1,000 resident population estimated as of July 1 of the year shown.

Table B. States and Counties — Housing, Labor Force, and Employment

STATE County	Housing units, 1990 (cont'd) Occupied units — Owner-occupied Total	Percent	Median value[1]	Owner cost as a percent of income With a mortgage	Without a mortgage	Renter-occupied Median rent[2]	Rent as percent of income	Sub-standard units[3] (percent)	Civilian labor force, 2001 Total	Percent change, 2000–2001	Unemployment Total	Rate[4]	Civilian employment, 1990[5] Total	Percent Professional, managerial, and technical	Precision production, craft, and repair
	89	90	91	92	93	94	95	96	97	98	99	100	101	102	103
IOWA—Cont'd															
Guthrie	4 407	75.5	29 200	17.0	13.2	289	25.8	2.2	5 876	1.1	177	3.0	4 933	19.2	13.1
Hamilton	6 358	71.0	39 900	17.9	12.8	295	23.9	1.1	8 261	-2.7	249	3.0	7 715	19.4	11.2
Hancock	4 867	73.0	36 800	18.8	14.0	291	18.6	1.8	6 870	-0.3	161	2.3	5 777	19.4	10.7
Hardin	7 611	71.9	33 800	16.1	13.0	287	22.8	0.5	9 189	3.3	317	3.4	8 505	22.5	10.4
Harrison	5 656	74.5	33 600	18.8	13.5	277	24.5	2.3	7 813	1.1	295	3.8	6 680	19.0	11.2
Henry	7 089	73.5	43 800	16.9	12.5	308	22.5	1.7	10 578	-1.6	405	3.8	9 134	20.3	11.7
Howard	3 856	78.0	30 400	17.7	13.3	233	21.5	2.4	5 653	2.8	174	3.1	4 296	17.6	9.5
Humboldt	4 339	72.8	34 600	16.5	12.0	270	22.4	1.0	5 394	1.2	169	3.1	4 616	20.0	11.9
Ida	3 222	71.7	29 900	16.5	12.7	268	21.0	1.1	4 035	3.8	110	2.7	3 682	20.4	10.9
Iowa	5 713	76.1	43 600	16.5	13.6	295	19.2	1.5	9 367	2.4	182	1.9	7 463	19.6	12.2
Jackson	7 527	73.7	41 200	17.1	13.5	272	22.0	2.1	10 357	1.4	593	5.7	9 030	17.4	14.4
Jasper	13 632	74.6	46 000	15.4	12.2	305	20.0	1.6	19 722	3.5	557	2.8	16 785	20.2	13.8
Jefferson	6 309	66.7	47 000	18.8	14.2	339	25.9	2.2	9 356	-0.2	476	5.1	7 949	30.8	11.8
Johnson	36 067	52.7	76 900	19.0	12.2	412	28.3	2.9	70 883	3.7	1 723	2.4	54 591	40.8	6.3
Jones	6 917	73.6	40 800	14.6	13.5	278	18.5	1.9	9 857	4.0	397	4.0	8 678	18.2	12.2
Keokuk	4 573	78.0	23 900	15.4	12.2	250	23.0	2.3	5 239	5.9	265	5.1	4 930	17.3	12.2
Kossuth	7 194	73.1	33 900	16.5	12.3	260	22.7	1.6	8 596	3.7	264	3.1	8 153	19.1	9.3
Lee	14 936	74.1	36 300	16.9	13.3	293	25.9	1.8	18 215	-1.1	1 250	6.9	17 072	19.7	12.3
Linn	65 501	70.4	58 500	16.5	12.1	369	23.2	1.4	114 357	-0.7	3 204	2.8	87 606	30.8	10.8
Louisa	4 296	74.5	39 400	16.5	13.0	304	19.8	2.5	5 640	5.7	217	3.8	5 382	16.8	14.7
Lucas	3 766	74.3	30 200	16.5	12.6	258	22.6	2.0	4 198	5.2	154	3.7	3 941	17.4	8.8
Lyon	4 289	77.1	31 800	16.5	12.6	252	18.1	1.8	5 584	3.9	150	2.7	5 356	18.4	9.6
Madison	4 715	73.5	42 800	17.7	12.4	294	22.2	2.1	7 390	2.4	263	3.6	5 945	21.4	13.4
Mahaska	8 306	70.0	36 400	17.4	12.8	289	24.4	1.0	11 430	3.5	390	3.4	9 896	21.3	10.2
Marion	10 815	73.9	48 200	17.1	12.1	323	23.9	2.0	19 105	2.0	636	3.3	14 449	23.4	9.9
Marshall	14 890	71.2	42 100	16.5	12.6	321	23.0	1.3	20 322	2.0	597	2.9	18 622	25.3	11.8
Mills	4 665	74.8	47 000	16.6	13.0	319	23.9	1.9	6 286	0.1	179	2.8	6 037	23.6	11.4
Mitchell	4 253	78.3	34 700	14.2	12.6	232	20.9	2.3	5 446	2.8	150	2.8	4 877	17.5	10.9
Monona	4 098	74.2	27 400	19.6	13.1	243	23.7	1.2	4 917	2.4	180	3.7	4 193	20.6	10.6
Monroe	3 196	76.9	27 800	18.3	13.0	272	27.5	3.4	4 092	-1.0	172	4.2	3 366	17.0	12.4
Montgomery	4 955	71.7	35 200	18.2	12.7	254	20.6	0.7	5 929	3.4	303	5.1	5 682	21.5	10.6
Muscatine	14 806	72.0	50 600	16.8	12.5	343	22.0	2.4	21 984	1.7	807	3.7	19 093	20.6	12.8
O'Brien	5 980	75.0	32 700	15.3	12.5	249	22.5	1.2	7 856	3.3	185	2.4	6 953	21.7	10.4
Osceola	2 817	74.7	28 000	13.0	12.4	262	18.8	2.4	3 708	2.1	115	3.1	3 327	19.1	9.3
Page	6 687	70.6	33 700	15.8	13.4	253	23.4	1.2	8 052	-9.5	385	4.8	7 658	21.3	10.9
Palo Alto	4 183	70.9	28 000	17.6	12.5	245	23.5	3.0	5 269	3.2	205	3.9	4 609	18.7	10.1
Plymouth	8 417	74.8	48 800	16.6	13.2	298	21.7	1.5	13 581	3.8	413	3.0	10 990	20.5	10.1
Pocahontas	3 820	74.3	27 000	14.5	12.2	246	18.8	0.8	3 934	6.1	149	3.8	4 153	19.5	9.3
Polk	129 237	65.2	59 700	19.8	13.3	437	25.0	2.4	216 417	1.6	5 727	2.6	176 499	31.5	8.2
Pottawattamie	31 262	71.1	46 900	18.9	13.4	371	24.7	2.2	48 845	1.3	1 473	3.0	40 343	21.8	11.7
Poweshiek	7 158	70.5	47 500	18.1	13.1	303	21.7	1.3	10 700	5.0	380	3.6	9 299	23.3	10.8
Ringgold	2 218	75.4	22 000	17.1	13.3	262	24.4	2.6	2 636	3.7	78	3.0	2 374	20.3	10.2
Sac	4 914	72.5	27 100	16.4	12.3	250	22.1	1.2	5 937	4.2	170	2.9	5 452	18.7	10.9
Scott	57 438	66.4	54 400	17.5	12.8	361	25.0	1.6	84 322	-0.1	2 931	3.5	72 497	29.1	10.8
Shelby	5 024	73.8	36 500	17.9	13.0	261	23.0	0.9	7 009	5.0	189	2.7	5 972	19.8	9.5
Sioux	9 925	78.2	44 700	17.1	12.1	268	21.4	1.7	18 247	4.4	500	2.7	14 668	20.9	10.0
Story	25 941	56.0	63 900	18.4	12.2	392	28.2	2.3	45 940	0.1	1 133	2.5	39 384	39.9	6.8
Tama	6 768	75.2	32 100	16.5	13.7	304	22.0	3.0	8 928	3.7	321	3.6	7 694	18.4	12.5
Taylor	2 859	75.8	23 000	15.5	13.4	235	27.2	1.8	3 389	1.1	146	4.3	2 952	15.0	10.8
Union	5 173	68.7	32 900	15.4	13.4	291	25.4	1.5	6 645	5.0	234	3.5	5 655	22.5	11.5
Van Buren	3 056	77.7	21 300	18.3	13.2	240	21.6	4.3	3 979	-1.3	182	4.6	3 406	17.8	14.5
Wapello	14 555	75.6	27 000	15.5	12.0	276	26.6	1.8	17 842	3.7	826	4.6	15 340	21.1	12.3
Warren	12 659	76.8	59 300	17.7	12.4	348	22.2	1.9	23 533	1.4	549	2.3	19 042	24.7	10.9
Washington	7 454	71.8	43 000	16.8	12.1	297	20.5	2.5	11 604	5.8	311	2.7	9 612	18.8	10.8
Wayne	2 953	75.8	19 900	18.0	13.9	233	26.1	1.6	2 963	3.7	100	3.4	3 014	19.1	9.2
Webster	15 963	68.9	37 000	17.4	12.5	296	24.2	1.3	20 296	2.9	694	3.4	18 044	23.9	11.3
Winnebago	4 704	74.6	39 300	16.9	12.8	271	21.2	0.9	6 559	3.0	186	2.8	5 596	23.7	9.8
Winneshiek	7 256	71.0	49 700	18.7	13.2	276	20.4	2.6	12 460	2.7	441	3.5	10 489	21.0	9.7
Woodbury	36 899	68.5	41 000	17.4	13.1	325	25.1	2.6	53 605	1.7	1 755	3.3	46 324	25.6	12.3
Worth	3 239	76.3	33 500	16.6	13.2	254	20.1	1.0	3 960	-0.3	144	3.6	3 622	16.5	10.8
Wright	5 899	72.2	32 700	16.0	12.6	282	24.1	1.1	6 806	-0.3	220	3.2	6 563	19.2	10.0
KANSAS	944 726	67.9	52 200	19.1	12.6	372	24.5	2.7	1 381 325	-2.1	59 165	4.3	1 172 214	28.7	11.5
Allen	5 705	75.1	27 600	15.8	12.8	251	25.8	3.4	7 010	-1.2	522	7.4	6 381	22.8	13.4
Anderson	3 067	77.9	27 200	15.0	12.7	256	24.5	2.7	3 933	-1.9	232	5.9	3 409	15.9	10.7
Atchison	6 129	73.1	32 400	17.3	12.3	285	25.2	2.2	8 575	-1.0	426	5.0	7 295	23.9	11.6

1. Specified owner-occupied units.   2. Specified renter-occupied units.   3. Overcrowded or lacking complete plumbing facilities.   4. Percent of civilian labor force.   5. Persons 16 years and older.

Table B. States and Counties — Nonfarm Employment and Agriculture

	Private nonfarm establishments, employment and payroll, 1999									Agriculture, 1997			
		Employment						Annual payroll		Farms			Farm operators
											Percent with—		
STATE County	Number of establish-ments	Total	Health Care and Social Assistance	Manufac-turing	Retail trade	Finance and Insurance	Professional Scientific and Technical Services	Total (mil dol)	Average per employee (dollars)	Number	Less than 50 acres	500 acres and over	Whose principal occu-pation is farming (percent)
	104	105	106	107	108	109	110	111	112	113	114	115	116

IOWA—Cont'd

Guthrie	296	1 868	352	151	363	134	64	32	16 952	847	17.7	24.0	58.1
Hamilton	447	6 502	570	2 811	784	183	94	163	25 064	790	16.8	32.2	70.3
Hancock	350	3 051	399	1 225	428	122	44	65	21 278	849	14.7	29.6	70.0
Hardin	661	7 208	1 176	1 685	979	264	127	151	20 886	857	20.8	29.6	68.7
Harrison	364	3 182	675	294	672	150	61	57	17 919	876	17.0	30.8	63.4
Henry	556	12 212	1 070	2 822	940	161	109	277	22 642	835	18.4	17.2	53.5
Howard	291	3 434	521	1 523	352	107	61	75	21 796	862	16.1	17.3	67.1
Humboldt	331	3 594	432	1 331	474	106	46	80	22 201	600	12.3	33.3	71.5
Ida	265	3 249	435	1 139	381	115	38	78	24 085	637	17.3	27.5	70.5
Iowa	514	9 450	520	5 183	1 298	109	69	254	26 893	976	17.2	18.8	55.6
Jackson	583	5 417	933	1 446	921	234	100	88	16 308	1 280	17.0	13.4	56.3
Jasper	852	13 765	1 344	4 835	1 728	309	599	378	27 458	1 204	21.3	25.4	60.4
Jefferson	713	7 889	743	1 913	1 305	268	626	196	24 898	765	16.3	17.1	55.0
Johnson	2 677	48 632	12 411	4 961	8 207	1 427	1 487	1 188	24 437	1 261	24.0	13.3	55.7
Jones	514	4 441	622	931	806	173	106	87	19 487	1 029	18.8	20.9	61.6
Keokuk	271	1 790	344	198	418	115	46	34	19 176	968	15.4	22.4	56.3
Kossuth	550	5 601	734	1 415	959	415	145	109	19 527	1 404	11.8	29.6	73.9
Lee	1 051	16 912	2 021	6 243	2 140	432	198	422	24 973	861	19.0	20.6	52.6
Linn	5 317	109 920	11 278	20 752	13 359	6 171	4 447	3 529	32 105	1 480	28.9	11.6	51.8
Louisa	218	2 643	290	1 332	219	90	52	55	20 934	593	16.9	23.3	56.0
Lucas	214	2 627	429	235	384	110	23	63	23 928	706	16.6	18.3	49.7
Lyon	369	2 317	311	407	446	111	90	43	18 427	1 149	20.5	18.9	68.8
Madison	336	2 769	575	497	525	121	129	55	19 950	986	18.6	19.3	46.2
Mahaska	590	6 226	722	997	1 282	239	113	125	20 044	1 022	15.2	21.4	61.9
Marion	816	17 130	2 473	7 796	1 576	255	176	463	27 045	971	20.2	18.3	45.5
Marshall	933	15 482	2 014	5 219	2 352	424	249	397	25 667	912	21.3	24.7	60.3
Mills	231	2 713	1 398	40	341	78	50	63	23 356	496	15.3	34.5	63.9
Mitchell	347	3 069	549	952	474	128	51	63	20 682	824	21.7	22.8	64.9
Monona	290	2 663	779	146	538	116	53	48	18 008	697	11.5	36.3	67.9
Monroe	209	2 669	458	1 063	344	61	19	61	22 897	691	12.4	19.0	50.9
Montgomery	342	4 545	735	1 351	556	183	84	96	21 136	577	12.9	31.2	68.8
Muscatine	996	20 474	1 867	7 697	2 369	414	1 010	633	30 900	783	25.4	17.9	55.6
O'Brien	565	5 211	1 162	764	952	231	111	98	18 818	977	13.8	26.4	73.1
Osceola	216	1 798	300	523	188	82	33	36	20 260	649	14.6	26.7	71.6
Page	502	6 767	1 262	2 311	1 119	140	132	164	24 252	845	16.1	26.7	58.1
Palo Alto	328	2 698	576	475	674	117	41	46	17 193	787	13.6	32.7	70.8
Plymouth	662	8 418	862	1 634	1 095	331	133	215	25 532	1 490	18.5	22.6	67.9
Pocahontas	283	2 498	391	734	458	90	64	46	18 522	778	9.8	37.1	77.1
Polk	11 510	239 931	27 831	19 272	29 254	41 930	10 482	7 498	31 251	800	36.9	18.0	46.4
Pottawattamie	1 883	28 556	3 167	4 235	6 288	617	846	626	21 936	1 325	21.2	30.6	67.4
Poweshiek	573	8 493	999	1 688	1 008	810	202	217	25 572	934	15.8	25.5	54.5
Ringgold	138	1 015	302	144	208	42	19	20	19 523	671	13.3	24.6	60.1
Sac	381	2 671	647	231	523	139	86	47	17 709	813	15.0	28.3	69.9
Scott	4 518	79 704	9 745	13 139	12 148	2 591	2 671	2 183	27 386	799	24.8	18.4	61.1
Shelby	429	4 480	864	298	688	203	113	86	19 211	921	14.0	26.6	75.0
Sioux	1 097	14 595	1 473	4 711	1 653	482	287	300	20 532	1 752	24.2	16.8	67.1
Story	1 893	27 209	4 095	3 884	5 120	860	1 573	620	22 793	946	23.4	25.4	56.7
Tama	408	4 747	492	889	642	139	65	96	20 127	1 152	18.1	22.3	60.5
Taylor	173	1 261	192	373	199	55	36	23	18 417	746	11.1	23.1	55.2
Union	362	4 815	895	953	853	145	82	93	19 407	671	19.8	21.0	50.5
Van Buren	175	1 677	356	730	161	67	33	36	21 655	807	13.8	19.2	48.5
Wapello	887	13 126	2 451	2 858	2 410	322	249	299	22 742	781	20.2	16.4	47.4
Warren	772	7 230	1 048	335	1 444	203	156	131	18 155	1 214	27.5	13.3	44.6
Washington	714	5 965	1 175	1 349	1 077	229	138	117	19 550	1 061	19.4	19.0	65.8
Wayne	181	1 471	316	429	251	63	39	25	17 036	729	12.2	27.2	56.5
Webster	1 207	16 552	2 641	2 251	3 268	516	373	410	24 790	937	15.3	30.5	71.0
Winnebago	359	7 894	688	4 539	557	176	73	202	25 623	607	20.8	28.2	65.1
Winneshiek	604	9 523	1 353	2 056	1 078	221	154	196	20 588	1 450	18.3	12.6	60.5
Woodbury	2 927	47 671	7 697	7 131	7 544	1 491	1 089	1 147	24 056	1 306	20.8	24.2	60.0
Worth	185	1 391	199	516	181	67	28	26	18 751	608	20.1	30.1	65.8
Wright	442	4 983	649	1 270	613	188	207	107	21 491	717	14.6	39.2	71.5
KANSAS	74 486	1 111 884	152 261	196 166	149 998	53 828	52 418	30 600	27 521	61 593	14.9	37.9	56.8
Allen	410	5 182	616	2 056	667	133	109	103	19 842	604	17.1	25.3	52.2
Anderson	235	1 449	306	194	245	104	40	26	17 665	688	15.4	33.3	55.8
Atchison	398	5 918	1 028	1 883	672	148	72	135	22 884	632	16.6	21.8	53.5

Table B. States and Counties — **Agriculture, Land, and Water**

STATE County	Land in farms — Acreage (1,000) [117]	Percent change, 1992–1997 [118]	Acres — Average size of farm [119]	Total irrigated (1,000) [120]	Total cropland (1,000) [121]	Value of land and buildings — Average per farm ($1,000) [122]	Average per acre (dollars) [123]	Value of machinery and equipment average per farm ($1,000) [124]	Value of products sold — Total (mil dol) [125]	Average per farm (dollars) [126]	Percent from — Crops [127]	Livestock and poultry products [128]	Percent of farms with sales of — $10,000 or more [129]	$100,000 or more [130]	Percent of land owned by fed. gov. 1997 [131]	Water consumption 1995 (mil gal/day) [132]
IOWA—Cont'd																
Guthrie	304	-7.5	359	D	242	481	1 281	67	96	113 080	46.3	53.7	66.5	24.9	0.1	2.2
Hamilton	349	5.0	441	D	330	949	2 373	121	227	287 619	42.2	57.8	85.9	49.7	0.0	3.1
Hancock	334	1.5	393	0	315	829	2 121	107	141	165 679	61.2	38.8	84.3	46.4	0.1	3.6
Hardin	340	2.4	397	D	314	777	1 990	95	202	235 563	43.0	57.0	82.5	44.5	0.0	5.0
Harrison	393	-1.6	448	21	342	635	1 508	102	113	128 974	72.3	27.7	76.8	36.5	0.8	11.7
Henry	245	8.3	293	D	201	482	1 570	76	77	92 319	60.1	39.9	63.5	26.2	0.0	2.6
Howard	270	3.4	313	D	241	432	1 414	74	95	110 359	57.8	42.2	75.5	32.0	0.0	2.0
Humboldt	257	-8.4	429	D	245	924	2 284	137	101	167 533	72.2	27.8	89.3	50.8	0.0	3.6
Ida	253	-7.2	398	D	231	658	1 745	89	96	150 212	57.8	42.2	83.5	43.2	0.0	1.8
Iowa	332	3.4	340	0	272	472	1 406	73	105	107 443	51.0	49.0	67.1	28.2	2.8	3.4
Jackson	335	-3.5	262	0	234	297	1 254	57	97	75 515	27.7	72.3	66.2	22.7	1.6	8.5
Jasper	421	-2.4	349	D	366	540	1 605	73	154	127 776	58.0	42.0	73.3	36.2	0.9	7.5
Jefferson	228	0.4	298	D	178	328	1 175	51	58	75 190	60.9	39.1	59.6	20.8	0.0	2.5
Johnson	288	1.1	229	1	249	416	1 816	56	100	79 613	50.6	49.4	64.0	24.0	4.0	62.9
Jones	322	0.0	313	D	267	484	1 607	76	137	133 077	44.3	55.7	76.8	35.8	0.4	4.0
Keokuk	323	0.3	334	0	263	523	1 535	75	97	99 932	52.9	47.1	65.2	28.1	0.0	2.5
Kossuth	581	-5.5	414	1	548	885	2 216	109	243	172 917	62.9	37.1	91.2	51.7	0.2	3.4
Lee	257	-3.5	298	1	190	381	1 332	71	77	89 847	54.1	45.9	60.3	25.0	0.0	18.5
Linn	339	-2.8	229	0	292	526	2 347	60	113	76 662	66.2	33.8	60.6	20.8	0.0	259.9
Louisa	201	5.4	340	5	168	482	1 516	86	81	137 093	52.1	47.9	68.1	31.4	2.2	10.2
Lucas	227	3.7	322	D	157	246	732	43	29	41 602	46.1	53.9	51.3	10.3	1.6	1.4
Lyon	348	0.1	303	1	315	566	1 923	78	199	173 016	35.5	64.5	86.2	45.4	0.0	4.4
Madison	317	3.5	321	0	229	427	1 251	55	74	74 594	48.8	51.2	57.4	15.7	0.0	2.2
Mahaska	329	4.5	322	D	274	466	1 606	74	157	153 348	38.3	61.7	71.8	34.5	0.0	3.7
Marion	286	6.2	294	0	219	408	1 435	55	73	75 298	60.9	39.1	56.1	20.9	2.6	5.7
Marshall	319	2.0	350	0	290	663	2 029	82	118	128 992	67.6	32.4	71.9	34.9	0.0	11.1
Mills	232	-2.5	468	D	205	685	1 588	84	59	119 334	84.5	15.5	75.2	42.3	0.0	2.5
Mitchell	265	0.8	322	0	243	574	1 874	84	161	194 868	38.3	61.7	81.9	45.4	0.0	2.3
Monona	368	-6.5	527	41	317	692	1 317	89	101	144 267	67.1	32.9	80.5	40.7	0.0	12.2
Monroe	217	-3.0	314	D	151	254	827	43	39	56 907	37.0	63.0	60.1	12.4	0.0	1.3
Montgomery	243	1.1	421	D	209	535	1 227	93	83	143 157	56.9	43.1	72.6	34.5	0.0	1.9
Muscatine	219	-0.5	280	6	190	444	1 711	86	74	94 298	63.8	36.2	67.3	26.6	0.3	270.1
O'Brien	358	-1.0	367	D	330	795	2 253	109	180	184 274	49.7	50.3	93.9	51.2	0.0	3.7
Osceola	241	-7.8	371	1	222	729	1 829	102	140	215 627	39.9	60.1	90.4	47.5	0.0	2.8
Page	309	-3.1	366	0	260	402	1 150	69	79	93 986	65.7	34.3	72.2	30.5	0.0	3.1
Palo Alto	328	-3.3	416	4	306	791	1 962	91	156	197 925	52.5	47.5	84.5	48.9	0.1	2.9
Plymouth	512	-1.2	344	2	456	638	1 950	79	238	159 994	41.4	58.6	80.2	41.1	0.0	6.4
Pocahontas	357	-0.6	459	0	339	990	2 288	128	139	178 147	71.9	28.1	92.4	55.9	0.0	1.7
Polk	226	-1.9	282	0	201	603	2 052	74	71	89 026	86.2	13.8	57.9	24.2	3.6	56.5
Pottawattamie	537	-1.2	405	2	483	732	1 946	89	190	143 397	65.1	34.9	76.0	39.2	0.2	468.8
Poweshiek	335	-1.7	359	0	293	498	1 433	73	107	114 963	59.0	41.0	68.3	32.0	0.0	3.0
Ringgold	264	-10.0	393	D	210	274	741	55	49	72 526	38.2	61.8	60.4	14.3	0.0	1.3
Sac	345	-5.2	424	1	312	841	2 125	102	191	234 870	43.1	56.9	88.8	49.3	0.0	3.5
Scott	225	-3.3	282	1	206	852	2 797	102	95	119 029	64.9	35.1	74.8	34.3	0.9	100.8
Shelby	342	-3.3	372	0	315	609	1 627	80	133	144 237	57.5	42.5	87.6	42.9	0.0	2.6
Sioux	494	-0.5	282	8	453	662	2 445	93	508	289 932	21.7	78.3	89.6	53.3	0.0	15.6
Story	341	3.0	360	0	317	801	2 234	98	131	138 300	71.7	28.3	77.4	36.5	0.2	12.8
Tama	396	-1.4	344	0	348	609	1 911	77	128	110 952	67.5	32.5	72.7	32.7	1.1	4.8
Taylor	291	4.5	391	0	229	354	957	40	62	83 378	49.0	51.0	65.7	17.3	0.0	1.4
Union	225	-4.6	336	0	169	311	909	47	39	58 169	51.1	48.9	59.8	15.8	0.0	3.3
Van Buren	257	6.7	319	0	172	240	851	50	43	53 318	57.5	42.5	54.8	14.6	0.0	1.3
Wapello	208	6.8	267	0	160	355	1 392	63	45	57 112	65.0	35.0	46.0	16.1	0.0	20.2
Warren	300	-0.7	247	0	220	352	1 523	49	60	49 106	64.3	35.7	48.6	12.6	1.5	7.5
Washington	318	2.5	299	D	274	546	1 777	83	174	164 171	33.7	66.3	76.0	39.2	0.0	3.9
Wayne	286	1.2	393	D	219	253	630	48	37	50 157	59.3	40.7	62.0	14.4	1.0	0.9
Webster	413	1.1	440	0	386	1 070	2 330	112	166	177 436	68.0	32.0	85.9	45.1	0.0	8.8
Winnebago	242	4.1	398	0	227	718	1 814	109	78	129 088	81.7	18.3	77.1	43.0	0.1	1.9
Winneshiek	361	0.8	249	0	287	321	1 358	61	131	90 559	32.7	67.3	69.3	28.3	0.0	5.4
Woodbury	497	12.5	381	8	428	507	1 332	79	151	115 869	59.3	40.7	68.8	30.9	0.5	672.2
Worth	228	1.3	375	0	209	640	1 645	100	77	126 030	75.0	25.0	77.6	42.9	0.2	5.3
Wright	350	-1.2	488	D	330	1 056	2 226	137	175	244 136	54.7	45.3	85.4	51.6	0.2	3.3
KANSAS	46 089	-1.2	748	2 707	30 021	431	577	74	9 207	149 483	35.0	65.0	63.0	21.8	1.0	5 235.4
Allen	271	-4.2	449	D	182	316	698	51	33	54 688	65.7	34.3	54.8	12.9	0.0	2.9
Anderson	367	-3.2	533	1	242	312	558	59	53	77 407	57.1	42.9	62.1	19.3	0.0	1.7
Atchison	242	-1.2	383	D	178	342	932	54	36	56 420	66.5	33.5	62.3	15.5	0.0	5.9

STATE County	Value of Residential Construction Authorized by Building Permits, 2000		Wholesale Trade, 1997				Retail Trade[1], 1997				Real Estate and Rental and Leasing, 1997			
	New Construction ($1,000)	Number of Housing Units	Number of Establish-ments	Number of Employees	Sales (mil dol)	Annual Payroll (mil dol)	Number of Establish-ments	Number of Employees	Sales (mil dol)	Annual Payroll (mil dol)	Number of Establish-ments	Number of Employees	Receipts (mil dol)	Annual Payroll (mil dol)
	133	134	135	136	137	138	139	140	141	142	143	144	145	146
IOWA—Cont'd														
Guthrie	9 416	59	14	121	70.6	2.1	53	359	57.9	5.0	11	31	2.1	0.4
Hamilton	4 567	35	36	D	D	D	82	747	90.8	9.0	11	28	1.3	0.2
Hancock	4 624	42	30	285	179.8	6.7	55	425	55.4	4.4	9	30	1.5	0.2
Hardin	2 240	23	63	1 095	554.5	31.5	114	1 097	151.0	13.6	14	46	2.3	0.5
Harrison	7 203	73	26	228	106.5	5.1	78	647	166.9	11.5	14	42	2.3	0.3
Henry	6 850	55	34	246	93.6	5.4	88	970	161.8	13.5	18	82	5.8	1.3
Howard	1 365	16	22	159	102.6	3.9	54	361	54.4	4.0	8	D	D	D
Humboldt	5 292	61	37	285	199.0	7.7	56	496	71.3	7.3	8	19	1.7	0.4
Ida	1 198	8	23	166	211.1	5.0	44	389	52.8	4.6	9	20	1.5	0.3
Iowa	3 105	37	28	217	112.4	4.8	164	1 250	153.6	14.7	4	3	0.8	0.1
Jackson	5 387	67	35	197	73.7	4.3	110	889	165.5	12.0	13	32	1.8	0.2
Jasper	9 966	80	47	465	465.2	11.3	175	1 703	232.3	25.2	21	73	4.5	0.6
Jefferson	1 958	18	50	275	78.3	6.6	107	1 165	279.2	38.5	14	29	1.9	0.4
Johnson	122 604	1 151	89	D	D	D	467	6 924	990.9	104.7	120	566	66.7	10.2
Jones	2 945	35	34	236	101.6	5.6	90	771	124.4	11.4	10	12	1.1	0.1
Keokuk	1 038	13	21	178	90.8	3.9	55	449	94.3	6.6	5	D	D	D
Kossuth	1 531	11	32	279	176.3	6.7	118	1 091	152.2	13.6	15	28	2.2	0.3
Lee	3 133	44	50	486	178.8	11.9	194	2 166	344.2	34.0	37	101	5.5	1.1
Linn	131 869	1 679	375	5 653	2 324.1	166.0	874	13 337	2 040.9	213.9	199	1 135	128.8	25.6
Louisa	2 321	17	14	185	70.9	5.1	39	256	45.7	3.6	6	D	D	D
Lucas	120	1	14	134	35.0	2.8	45	399	50.2	4.8	3	4	0.4	0.0
Lyon	2 190	21	24	243	133.7	5.7	62	476	63.8	5.5	3	D	D	D
Madison	10 649	103	15	89	62.8	2.3	61	522	82.8	7.1	11	26	1.7	0.2
Mahaska	4 007	32	43	374	192.8	10.3	114	1 246	190.8	17.1	21	57	3.8	0.5
Marion	24 046	238	42	510	98.6	7.2	156	1 519	243.1	22.4	23	78	5.4	0.9
Marshall	7 702	61	58	488	227.6	16.6	182	2 457	319.9	33.9	32	247	20.6	6.1
Mills	1 345	20	15	110	51.1	2.8	41	322	52.8	4.4	5	19	4.1	0.2
Mitchell	578	6	24	D	D	D	91	541	71.0	6.0	3	7	0.2	0.0
Monona	4 318	41	22	159	88.1	4.3	61	576	95.4	8.4	6	15	0.8	0.1
Monroe	441	5	11	73	20.9	1.4	43	363	51.7	4.7	1	D	D	D
Montgomery	898	9	30	214	151.3	5.1	68	581	82.8	7.4	6	14	0.7	0.2
Muscatine	11 433	111	63	381	264.1	10.1	177	2 390	337.6	34.5	36	140	11.4	2.4
O'Brien	4 235	40	41	367	201.1	8.9	111	976	169.5	14.0	7	28	3.1	0.6
Osceola	518	4	13	128	65.8	4.8	36	211	32.0	2.6	4	7	0.3	0.0
Page	1 949	22	26	223	87.4	5.0	108	1 185	148.5	14.3	11	42	6.8	1.0
Palo Alto	2 090	16	22	172	164.6	4.2	60	479	75.4	6.5	7	8	0.9	0.2
Plymouth	13 771	101	39	938	401.8	27.2	118	1 052	194.9	16.2	17	63	6.3	0.7
Pocahontas	0	0	18	277	197.4	6.8	46	301	43.4	3.4	5	9	0.5	0.1
Polk	310 704	2 370	901	D	D	D	1 680	28 123	4 454.0	461.4	456	3 433	584.7	84.4
Pottawattamie	57 682	663	101	D	D	D	382	5 742	978.5	87.1	63	D	D	D
Poweshiek	8 147	87	36	298	124.9	8.0	103	1 122	190.6	15.4	20	38	2.7	0.4
Ringgold	255	3	8	35	19.6	0.9	28	214	38.2	2.7	2	D	D	D
Sac	1 315	14	37	230	144.5	6.6	76	491	83.7	6.2	6	12	0.8	0.1
Scott	74 420	701	389	4 535	3 366.3	151.6	747	11 397	1 831.5	187.3	165	1 424	144.1	33.3
Shelby	3 645	29	27	D	D	D	80	645	117.4	9.6	5	18	0.9	0.1
Sioux	14 612	133	92	1 144	470.8	27.7	182	1 557	285.2	21.4	19	49	4.2	0.8
Story	45 561	674	95	772	321.2	21.7	359	4 729	631.3	65.8	68	366	24.4	5.6
Tama	5 649	53	31	221	215.9	4.9	90	646	90.8	8.1	8	22	1.3	0.2
Taylor	672	7	15	72	26.2	1.4	34	193	24.8	2.3	2	D	D	D
Union	1 765	17	24	318	108.9	5.6	72	800	114.6	11.5	22	63	5.3	1.1
Van Buren	415	6	8	69	35.2	0.5	34	154	19.8	1.9	3	5	0.4	0.1
Wapello	4 570	53	38	321	140.6	9.1	185	2 538	330.9	32.7	31	79	11.8	0.9
Warren	36 255	364	54	D	D	D	113	1 314	244.8	20.8	22	47	5.0	0.7
Washington	6 695	54	40	298	134.2	6.5	128	1 036	155.6	16.2	16	28	1.3	0.2
Wayne	277	4	17	130	53.5	2.2	38	252	31.6	3.5	1	D	D	D
Webster	9 167	82	71	885	710.2	31.4	252	3 142	438.7	44.9	47	168	13.3	2.4
Winnebago	2 684	32	17	D	D	D	74	573	81.6	6.2	7	15	1.0	0.1
Winneshiek	9 184	80	39	449	131.4	10.5	124	1 113	180.1	15.0	10	16	3.0	0.4
Woodbury	25 092	204	209	2 476	1 222.1	70.5	523	7 771	1 143.5	116.0	111	D	D	D
Worth	795	7	17	97	85.6	2.6	41	213	28.8	2.3	3	9	0.1	0.0
Wright	1 579	12	28	D	D	D	83	639	73.9	7.8	13	49	2.0	0.4
KANSAS	1 397 043	12 542	5 085	59 954	42 209.9	1 946.8	12 271	140 412	22 571.9	2 191.1	2 602	13 005	1 525.8	259.6
Allen	1 215	14	18	186	35.5	3.2	83	590	85.3	8.1	7	20	1.3	0.2
Anderson	687	5	12	77	48.4	1.4	38	207	43.0	2.9	3	9	0.3	0.0
Atchison	1 337	11	17	449	270.8	9.9	68	659	86.1	7.9	14	45	3.5	0.6

1. Establishments with payroll.

STATE County	Professional, Scientific, and Technical Services[1], 1997				Manufacturing, 1997				Accommodation and Foodservices, 1997			
	Number of Establish-ments	Number of Employees	Receipts (mil dol)	Annual Payroll (mil dol)	Number of Establish-ments	Number of Employees	Receipts (mil dol)	Annual Payroll (mil dol)	Number of Establish-ments	Number of Employees	Sales (mil dol)	Annual Payroll (mil dol)
	147	148	149	150	151	152	153	154	155	156	157	158
IOWA—Cont'd												
Guthrie	11	58	1.7	0.5	NA	NA	NA	NA	30	158	5.8	1.4
Hamilton	24	103	4.8	1.7	30	2 861	472.0	75.8	35	311	8.4	2.2
Hancock	12	33	1.5	0.4	27	1 126	221.2	29.7	22	199	3.9	0.9
Hardin	27	111	5.5	2.0	39	1 580	375.8	34.8	43	371	9.4	2.4
Harrison	12	36	1.5	0.6	NA	NA	NA	NA	30	318	8.6	2.5
Henry	24	94	4.5	2.0	34	2 839	717.4	85.2	44	612	16.7	4.5
Howard	15	45	2.5	0.9	20	1 405	177.7	29.2	29	D	D	D
Humboldt	13	40	2.5	0.7	28	1 257	159.7	31.8	21	210	4.5	1.3
Ida	12	28	1.8	0.5	9	1 112	165.0	32.5	22	D	D	D
Iowa	18	40	4.9	0.9	31	4 698	678.8	144.7	54	999	30.4	8.5
Jackson	26	74	3.6	0.9	34	1 208	194.5	25.7	58	515	11.4	2.6
Jasper	41	586	124.4	13.1	46	3 702	740.0	132.4	74	961	25.9	7.3
Jefferson	122	538	51.0	20.9	37	1 751	256.6	56.4	41	365	10.7	2.7
Johnson	164	1 085	81.9	29.3	89	3 639	2 510.4	121.1	271	5 496	144.3	40.8
Jones	21	78	4.5	1.5	23	889	170.1	23.5	37	366	7.7	1.9
Keokuk	7	25	0.8	0.3	NA	NA	NA	NA	20	86	1.7	0.5
Kossuth	23	89	5.6	1.3	30	1 126	207.3	33.7	42	417	9.2	2.2
Lee	50	182	11.7	3.4	70	6 397	1 671.5	209.0	108	1 257	33.0	8.8
Linn	369	2 936	268.6	106.7	239	22 877	6 376.1	935.0	439	7 853	240.1	68.2
Louisa	10	40	1.5	0.5	11	D	D	D	27	191	4.0	1.0
Lucas	9	23	1.0	0.3	NA	NA	NA	NA	18	148	3.5	0.8
Lyon	15	80	5.8	2.6	NA	NA	NA	NA	26	D	D	D
Madison	19	65	3.8	1.5	NA	NA	NA	NA	21	154	4.8	1.3
Mahaska	24	98	6.5	2.9	26	1 020	230.6	26.3	43	656	15.6	4.3
Marion	35	144	7.9	3.1	44	6 687	1 388.5	229.8	59	900	20.5	5.4
Marshall	50	201	13.4	4.9	44	5 363	1 413.2	174.0	86	1 070	29.7	8.4
Mills	9	43	2.1	0.8	NA	NA	NA	NA	23	221	5.7	1.6
Mitchell	7	37	1.7	0.6	16	1 021	186.3	27.4	21	D	D	D
Monona	15	53	3.5	1.1	NA	NA	NA	NA	36	267	6.4	1.6
Monroe	11	26	1.5	0.3	18	863	593.2	32.8	18	D	D	D
Montgomery	19	48	2.7	1.1	11	1 365	185.0	32.4	32	291	7.0	1.8
Muscatine	53	1 020	75.8	22.7	70	6 523	2 631.1	252.7	85	1 057	29.3	8.0
O'Brien	25	76	5.1	1.4	NA	NA	NA	NA	44	392	8.1	1.9
Osceola	7	35	1.7	0.3	NA	NA	NA	NA	14	117	2.3	0.5
Page	19	143	3.7	1.5	27	2 271	477.3	78.0	41	466	10.1	3.1
Palo Alto	12	31	2.1	0.5	NA	NA	NA	NA	30	D	D	D
Plymouth	29	108	5.6	2.0	26	D	D	D	57	D	D	D
Pocahontas	19	46	2.4	0.7	19	821	91.8	20.3	25	179	3.0	0.8
Polk	954	10 594	845.8	346.1	410	19 790	5 054.9	688.6	897	17 068	534.4	156.1
Pottawattamie	99	656	47.0	16.4	59	4 109	888.7	113.2	197	3 782	186.1	48.4
Poweshiek	33	115	7.2	2.0	32	1 533	226.6	42.7	43	677	13.2	4.1
Ringgold	3	10	0.3	0.1	NA	NA	NA	NA	9	64	1.3	0.3
Sac	20	65	3.3	1.0	NA	NA	NA	NA	25	207	3.9	1.1
Scott	315	1 999	177.4	58.0	210	11 845	4 614.8	478.3	378	8 050	234.2	70.0
Shelby	19	80	3.8	1.5	NA	NA	NA	NA	34	343	7.4	2.1
Sioux	43	192	12.7	4.2	67	4 610	822.0	104.6	71	1 098	19.8	5.0
Story	148	970	97.9	34.7	75	3 577	988.6	108.4	202	3 598	89.1	24.5
Tama	15	48	2.4	0.5	14	911	236.1	22.5	33	311	7.8	1.8
Taylor	10	26	1.1	0.4	NA	NA	NA	NA	11	77	1.4	0.3
Union	18	64	3.2	1.6	19	1 031	113.2	24.6	28	379	10.0	2.7
Van Buren	11	31	1.4	0.7	14	653	54.4	14.8	10	83	2.0	0.3
Wapello	45	206	12.9	4.2	22	2 701	741.8	92.5	85	1 076	29.8	7.8
Warren	35	108	6.2	2.0	NA	NA	NA	NA	58	809	18.3	5.1
Washington	33	133	5.8	1.7	32	1 441	196.2	41.2	42	506	10.8	3.1
Wayne	8	28	2.2	0.3	13	D	D	D	17	99	1.7	0.4
Webster	69	319	22.8	8.5	60	2 554	1 110.9	81.7	93	1 322	37.1	10.5
Winnebago	19	83	4.8	1.4	13	4 006	640.5	105.5	28	259	6.2	1.4
Winneshiek	21	90	5.6	2.6	29	1 453	215.0	38.0	51	573	14.5	4.0
Woodbury	178	946	73.6	23.9	113	D	D	D	246	3 812	109.2	29.9
Worth	6	18	0.8	0.1	12	596	49.2	12.5	9	D	D	D
Wright	27	173	8.8	2.5	25	1 318	546.5	39.2	40	292	7.3	1.8
KANSAS	5 345	39 534	3 559.3	1 396.0	3 309	193 742	46 296.4	6 532.5	5 677	91 173	2 685.7	757.1
Allen	25	94	4.5	1.8	28	1 722	277.3	45.7	38	534	13.7	4.1
Anderson	12	28	1.9	0.4	NA	NA	NA	NA	22	206	4.9	1.1
Atchison	16	48	2.7	1.0	24	1 753	360.1	53.7	32	340	8.2	2.2

1. Firms subject to federal tax.

Table B. States and Counties — Health and Other Services and Federal Funds

	Health Care and Social Assistance[1], 1997				Other Services[1], 1997				Federal funds and grants, fiscal 2001[2]			
									Expenditures (mil dol)			
										Direct payments for individuals[3]		
STATE County	Number of Establishments	Number of Employees	Receipts (mil dol)	Annual Payroll (mil dol)	Number of Establishments	Number of Employees	Receipts (mil dol)	Annual Payroll (mil dol)	Total	Social Security and government retirement	Medicare	Food stamps and Supplemental Security Income
	159	160	161	162	163	164	165	166	167	168	169	170
IOWA—Cont'd												
Guthrie	17	36	2.6	0.6	13	36	2.2	0.5	76.3	29.4	10.5	0.9
Hamilton	30	292	14.8	7.3	23	86	5.9	1.2	105.3	37.5	16.4	1.4
Hancock	11	244	7.8	3.7	29	71	4.2	1.1	78.8	27.1	9.8	0.5
Hardin	24	257	8.9	4.0	41	103	7.0	1.5	150.5	51.6	19.0	1.6
Harrison	14	289	10.0	5.4	23	49	4.2	0.8	106.7	38.7	15.3	1.7
Henry	38	487	18.0	8.1	31	93	6.8	1.1	110.9	41.9	13.6	1.9
Howard	13	182	5.0	2.9	16	32	3.6	0.5	64.9	21.4	8.8	0.8
Humboldt	14	199	6.9	2.9	21	52	4.9	1.0	75.7	27.4	10.4	0.9
Ida	15	192	7.0	3.0	18	50	2.4	0.6	66.5	19.4	7.2	0.4
Iowa	22	244	8.4	4.1	22	73	4.2	1.2	83.6	33.9	11.7	0.8
Jackson	34	424	14.4	6.7	43	114	9.4	1.6	118.7	46.2	18.3	2.4
Jasper	42	664	22.5	12.4	58	198	11.9	3.1	174.7	80.2	28.8	2.6
Jefferson	37	466	17.7	8.4	30	78	5.5	1.2	77.6	28.5	11.3	2.0
Johnson	181	1 907	97.5	41.4	152	767	43.3	12.5	595.6	136.8	38.3	6.1
Jones	22	299	12.1	5.0	34	91	5.7	1.2	108.7	39.8	13.6	1.2
Keokuk	12	201	5.5	2.7	15	29	2.4	0.4	88.8	30.1	12.2	1.4
Kossuth	24	321	7.9	2.7	43	106	6.6	1.4	135.4	42.9	14.6	1.3
Lee	87	1 008	40.8	18.4	68	308	18.4	4.6	186.5	88.4	37.1	4.8
Linn	340	3 925	267.5	138.3	350	2 296	143.5	43.3	1 115.3	363.9	108.7	17.1
Louisa	10	193	5.6	2.7	11	31	1.7	0.3	65.1	24.2	7.3	1.2
Lucas	15	78	4.0	1.8	5	15	1.3	0.3	58.3	24.2	8.7	1.6
Lyon	16	113	4.6	1.8	26	59	4.6	1.0	72.2	24.5	8.8	0.6
Madison	17	305	8.4	4.4	24	53	3.0	0.7	67.9	28.9	11.7	1.0
Mahaska	28	249	11.2	5.5	46	143	10.3	2.0	119.4	46.6	16.9	2.8
Marion	41	479	16.6	7.6	56	208	10.5	2.9	179.2	81.7	22.9	2.7
Marshall	60	612	35.9	17.4	57	250	15.0	3.9	217.2	96.2	28.7	4.3
Mills	14	452	8.5	5.6	29	163	9.4	2.8	80.8	32.9	12.2	1.4
Mitchell	15	97	6.0	2.6	26	95	5.1	1.2	74.2	28.6	10.9	0.8
Monona	17	448	13.9	7.4	21	51	3.9	0.8	90.1	28.3	14.0	1.1
Monroe	12	144	4.2	2.0	10	29	1.6	0.4	52.8	21.6	9.7	1.1
Montgomery	18	231	12.9	4.5	31	76	6.0	1.2	80.5	30.9	14.5	1.5
Muscatine	60	606	28.7	14.8	61	296	17.6	5.5	185.3	83.5	25.1	6.0
O'Brien	33	275	11.2	4.8	45	146	8.5	1.9	106.7	39.2	14.5	1.1
Osceola	11	150	4.4	1.9	14	41	2.6	0.5	50.4	15.9	6.2	0.4
Page	33	569	26.0	10.3	41	105	7.7	1.7	105.7	43.7	16.7	2.3
Palo Alto	24	304	10.3	4.7	16	31	1.8	0.5	87.8	27.5	10.5	1.1
Plymouth	35	436	15.6	7.5	48	176	12.5	2.5	138.5	48.7	17.5	1.1
Pocahontas	17	190	6.1	2.9	17	26	1.8	0.4	78.0	24.6	10.3	0.7
Polk	766	9 160	632.7	311.0	674	4 664	294.6	90.9	2 316.5	716.2	237.8	47.9
Pottawattamie	103	1 322	74.8	41.9	142	684	43.8	12.5	430.9	198.8	68.5	12.4
Poweshiek	39	328	18.8	8.1	30	91	6.1	1.6	104.7	43.4	15.9	1.3
Ringgold	7	149	4.4	1.8	9	23	1.9	0.4	43.7	13.5	5.4	0.7
Sac	14	178	6.6	3.0	27	75	4.2	1.1	87.7	30.9	11.6	0.8
Scott	324	3 126	236.5	111.7	296	2 042	115.7	37.8	722.1	348.0	95.0	26.9
Shelby	19	218	6.7	3.1	29	79	5.4	0.9	103.1	31.7	15.6	1.0
Sioux	50	356	16.7	7.4	75	233	18.9	3.9	159.7	57.1	20.2	1.3
Story	91	1 545	88.0	47.2	107	617	33.9	9.3	439.0	120.8	40.6	4.1
Tama	18	247	7.9	3.8	27	93	6.1	0.9	118.6	41.6	15.4	1.2
Taylor	7	107	2.6	1.2	10	26	1.4	0.3	52.1	17.7	7.0	0.9
Union	17	283	11.1	5.7	20	86	8.3	1.8	82.1	32.4	11.6	1.8
Van Buren	5	9	0.5	0.1	10	13	1.8	0.2	49.7	20.4	7.8	1.0
Wapello	66	723	45.9	22.9	62	284	15.7	4.0	215.8	95.3	37.0	8.0
Warren	49	532	22.3	8.9	48	140	9.1	2.0	137.7	69.2	21.3	1.7
Washington	39	486	16.6	7.8	36	120	11.3	2.0	119.6	48.5	17.0	1.8
Wayne	7	82	2.9	1.3	14	38	2.2	0.6	58.5	19.1	8.7	1.0
Webster	85	809	53.3	25.5	80	448	24.0	7.2	256.0	99.3	40.1	5.6
Winnebago	22	236	8.6	3.8	18	37	3.2	0.6	77.0	28.6	10.3	0.7
Winneshiek	28	219	13.0	5.2	40	102	6.5	1.5	107.1	38.1	13.3	1.1
Woodbury	223	2 111	186.1	89.6	181	1 319	66.4	21.2	533.1	207.9	81.0	13.4
Worth	6	31	1.4	0.9	7	17	1.7	0.3	54.6	17.9	7.0	0.5
Wright	20	310	10.2	4.5	22	91	3.5	0.8	107.6	39.5	15.3	1.1
KANSAS	4 793	66 613	4 116.1	1 771.8	4 604	24 081	1 548.4	452.9	16 698.8	5 667.3	2 138.9	284.8
Allen	28	312	9.1	4.4	24	94	6.3	1.6	83.1	35.7	13.9	2.4
Anderson	14	152	4.7	2.2	14	31	2.4	0.4	51.5	21.8	8.8	0.7
Atchison	35	230	12.8	5.9	23	82	4.7	1.5	89.9	38.4	16.4	2.5

1. Firms subject to federal tax.　2. October 1, 2000 to September 30, 2001.　3. State totals may include programs not allocated by county.

	Federal funds and grants, fiscal 2001[1] (cont'd)							Local government finances, 1997				
	Expenditures (mil dol) (cont'd)							General revenue				
	Procurement contract awards		Grants[2]							Taxes		
											Per capita[3] (dollars)	
STATE County	Salaries and wages	Defense	Other	Medicaid and other health-related	Nutrition and family welfare	Education	Other	Total (mil dol)	Intergovern-mental (mil dol)	Total (mil dol)	Total	Property
	171	172	173	174	175	176	177	178	179	180	181	182
IOWA—Cont'd												
Guthrie	3.0	0.0	0.7	5.8	1.1	0.4	0.6	28.5	11.9	10.3	897	881
Hamilton	3.1	0.2	0.8	6.4	1.3	0.3	2.9	50.9	15.6	15.9	988	953
Hancock	2.7	0.0	0.6	2.8	0.8	0.2	0.8	30.7	12.6	11.1	922	853
Hardin	4.5	0.0	17.4	8.2	1.7	0.6	11.6	53.1	18.2	17.5	946	860
Harrison	4.6	0.0	0.8	8.1	1.6	0.5	3.0	47.1	17.9	14.6	949	893
Henry	3.9	0.0	1.8	7.3	1.4	1.1	12.7	54.3	19.3	15.2	760	667
Howard	1.7	0.2	0.4	6.4	1.0	0.6	0.3	27.8	11.5	9.5	975	865
Humboldt	3.0	0.1	0.8	4.3	0.8	0.3	0.0	27.2	9.4	9.4	905	888
Ida	1.8	0.0	0.4	3.1	0.6	0.2	1.8	16.8	7.6	6.5	816	793
Iowa	3.6	0.0	0.8	4.0	0.8	0.3	0.6	35.0	13.8	13.3	860	697
Jackson	4.2	7.9	0.9	11.8	2.3	0.6	1.2	48.1	19.0	13.8	688	598
Jasper	5.9	0.1	1.7	12.8	3.0	0.6	1.3	101.0	37.4	30.0	840	794
Jefferson	4.8	0.2	0.9	7.4	1.1	0.7	1.2	35.6	11.4	10.6	621	589
Johnson	73.4	1.7	73.1	174.4	4.1	5.9	32.4	199.1	69.1	84.8	829	768
Jones	3.2	0.0	0.8	6.8	1.7	0.5	11.3	34.1	16.2	13.0	639	612
Keokuk	3.2	0.0	0.8	6.7	1.0	0.4	2.9	26.7	12.4	9.6	834	808
Kossuth	4.6	0.0	1.0	8.5	1.1	0.4	0.9	43.5	14.6	15.0	837	788
Lee	7.3	0.4	1.3	17.0	4.5	1.4	5.4	83.1	39.5	30.9	798	670
Linn	60.4	355.6	32.5	68.3	20.0	6.4	25.6	464.3	173.9	175.0	963	924
Louisa	2.7	0.0	1.7	5.5	1.3	0.9	0.2	38.9	15.2	11.4	959	945
Lucas	2.3	0.0	0.4	7.9	1.3	0.4	0.7	25.6	8.5	6.6	727	701
Lyon	2.0	0.0	0.5	4.0	0.7	0.4	0.3	24.8	11.8	8.8	739	687
Madison	2.5	0.0	0.6	6.1	1.1	0.3	0.8	34.5	13.7	10.1	733	710
Mahaska	4.2	0.0	0.8	12.5	2.2	0.6	0.7	52.4	18.5	17.2	787	709
Marion	31.3	0.1	2.4	13.1	2.5	1.6	0.5	56.2	26.6	21.2	679	649
Marshall	7.3	0.1	4.4	18.9	4.3	1.0	15.3	104.6	47.9	35.0	903	888
Mills	2.8	0.0	0.6	9.1	1.3	0.3	-0.2	27.8	13.9	10.9	757	744
Mitchell	2.2	0.0	0.6	4.0	0.7	0.3	0.3	31.2	10.1	9.3	838	760
Monona	2.5	0.1	0.6	8.8	1.3	0.5	0.8	22.8	10.9	9.0	901	811
Monroe	1.6	0.0	0.3	7.0	1.1	0.4	0.1	20.7	8.4	5.4	676	669
Montgomery	3.2	0.0	0.7	6.1	1.2	0.3	2.4	38.9	12.0	9.9	829	807
Muscatine	6.9	3.5	3.1	13.4	5.0	1.5	12.6	119.7	37.6	37.2	903	782
O'Brien	3.6	0.0	0.8	9.7	1.0	1.0	2.1	43.0	18.0	13.9	930	865
Osceola	1.5	0.0	0.3	2.5	0.4	0.1	0.3	13.1	5.8	5.3	756	727
Page	3.8	0.0	1.0	11.2	1.8	0.7	0.9	42.1	16.9	13.6	794	713
Palo Alto	2.3	0.0	1.3	8.5	2.5	0.3	2.5	32.0	12.3	9.7	964	936
Plymouth	5.5	0.0	1.1	7.0	2.5	0.5	5.2	55.5	20.8	17.3	702	688
Pocahontas	2.6	0.0	0.5	4.0	0.8	0.2	0.6	21.4	8.1	7.2	817	804
Polk	317.9	34.7	69.3	230.2	178.3	89.4	297.3	1 055.8	352.4	401.6	1 134	1 079
Pottawattamie	12.8	0.1	2.6	52.1	10.5	2.9	9.1	214.5	94.2	76.5	896	754
Poweshiek	3.0	0.0	0.9	5.5	1.3	0.4	2.9	35.1	15.2	12.8	672	661
Ringgold	1.7	0.0	0.4	3.9	0.8	0.2	2.8	19.8	8.5	5.1	960	950
Sac	2.6	0.0	0.6	4.0	1.1	0.4	1.1	24.8	12.1	9.6	811	805
Scott	31.9	50.6	6.0	69.3	23.7	7.0	11.7	405.3	165.7	152.0	966	831
Shelby	2.9	0.0	0.7	7.9	3.1	0.4	3.0	41.0	14.8	12.1	922	903
Sioux	5.2	0.0	3.5	16.8	1.4	0.6	2.6	66.1	21.7	20.4	657	598
Story	48.9	4.5	38.7	24.3	5.9	3.4	96.6	229.1	55.9	62.2	834	724
Tama	4.1	0.1	5.9	7.9	1.6	0.8	0.9	37.9	19.4	13.7	779	754
Taylor	2.0	0.0	0.5	5.2	1.1	0.3	0.8	16.1	8.7	5.0	695	647
Union	4.2	0.0	0.8	10.0	2.5	0.8	0.4	53.8	23.2	10.5	846	838
Van Buren	2.3	0.0	0.5	3.7	0.8	0.4	0.8	22.0	9.4	5.2	659	633
Wapello	7.8	0.1	1.7	33.4	6.9	2.3	3.7	108.1	51.1	30.0	849	831
Warren	5.9	0.0	1.3	10.1	2.6	0.8	3.4	72.8	35.8	25.8	649	631
Washington	3.8	0.0	0.8	7.3	1.3	1.7	5.9	50.8	18.7	15.9	763	737
Wayne	2.1	0.0	0.5	8.2	1.1	0.5	0.6	18.8	7.9	4.4	643	625
Webster	18.6	6.4	2.9	23.1	5.4	1.6	4.5	101.2	45.7	34.9	904	883
Winnebago	2.8	0.0	1.1	6.4	0.8	0.3	0.8	30.4	14.1	11.3	938	877
Winneshiek	4.8	0.1	0.9	6.2	3.0	1.6	4.7	67.1	24.1	17.1	819	720
Woodbury	51.1	3.2	6.8	55.7	14.8	7.6	29.1	261.2	120.8	90.1	882	809
Worth	1.7	0.0	0.5	3.0	0.6	0.2	1.4	14.2	6.3	6.3	809	799
Wright	4.5	0.0	1.0	6.4	1.3	0.3	0.9	42.9	15.6	16.2	1 144	1 123
KANSAS	1 866.3	960.0	422.9	1 203.1	408.4	318.0	791.7	X	X	X	X	X
Allen	3.5	0.0	0.6	13.1	1.5	0.5	1.7	34.1	16.2	11.4	786	637
Anderson	2.1	0.0	0.5	2.5	0.6	0.2	2.6	16.3	7.1	6.5	812	758
Atchison	3.0	1.0	0.8	8.4	2.1	1.0	3.1	32.0	14.6	12.0	734	565

1. October 1, 2000 to September 30, 2001. 2. State totals may include programs not allocated by county. 3. Based on the resident population estimated as of July 1 of the year shown.

STATE County	Total (mil dol)	Per capita[1] (dollars)	Education	Health and hospitals	Police protection	Public welfare	Highways	Total (mil dol)	Per capita[1] (dollars)	Federal civilian	Federal military	State and local	Democratic	Republican	All other
	Local government finances, 1997 (cont'd)									Government employment, 1999			Presidential election, 2000[2]		
	Direct general expenditure							Debt outstanding					Percent of vote cast —		
					Percent of total for —										
	183	184	185	186	187	188	189	190	191	192	193	194	195	196	197
IOWA—Cont'd															
Guthrie	28.3	2 474	48.7	17.0	2.7	1.9	12.2	12.3	1 079	63	54	757	45.6	51.9	2.5
Hamilton	53.6	3 337	43.7	26.5	3.1	0.7	8.3	21.7	1 354	61	74	1 196	45.0	52.4	2.7
Hancock	29.6	2 461	43.7	18.4	4.3	2.5	13.8	7.1	593	56	56	716	41.9	54.9	3.1
Hardin	52.9	2 857	42.4	20.7	2.9	0.3	9.6	18.5	1 000	88	84	1 721	44.3	53.2	2.6
Harrison	46.9	3 056	43.9	24.0	2.9	1.0	9.9	19.9	1 297	89	71	806	39.0	58.1	2.9
Henry	54.3	2 721	40.1	28.7	3.2	0.4	9.1	29.3	1 469	75	94	1 743	45.1	51.6	3.3
Howard	27.3	2 813	45.4	21.6	2.9	0.3	11.6	9.1	934	41	44	810	54.0	42.8	3.2
Humboldt	26.7	2 569	42.2	25.1	3.7	0.5	12.2	3.7	355	63	47	668	39.5	57.6	2.9
Ida	18.9	2 379	52.7	3.0	5.3	3.0	17.0	5.9	747	42	37	461	40.4	56.4	3.2
Iowa	33.9	2 189	47.2	17.3	4.2	1.9	15.3	15.5	999	72	73	905	43.6	52.5	3.9
Jackson	47.0	2 339	45.6	23.9	3.2	1.0	7.9	10.2	505	86	94	1 187	54.7	41.7	3.5
Jasper	99.0	2 772	37.1	30.4	3.5	2.5	7.5	40.3	1 130	120	170	2 555	48.8	48.9	2.3
Jefferson	34.9	2 053	36.7	33.6	4.4	0.4	9.4	9.7	567	86	78	1 020	37.9	43.0	19.0
Johnson	217.3	2 124	38.7	3.8	4.5	3.4	13.1	200.7	1 961	1 572	504	26 180	59.1	33.9	7.0
Jones	35.5	1 751	58.2	7.5	3.2	1.7	11.2	23.3	1 148	61	93	1 324	51.3	45.9	2.7
Keokuk	25.4	2 208	56.5	11.8	2.7	0.2	13.7	10.2	884	70	53	520	44.1	52.0	3.9
Kossuth	42.7	2 386	39.3	24.2	3.1	1.9	15.2	6.3	352	87	82	1 094	44.6	51.9	3.4
Lee	76.9	1 991	48.1	9.2	5.8	1.4	11.0	47.9	1 240	112	217	2 268	58.1	38.3	3.7
Linn	450.7	2 480	51.4	4.5	6.3	1.2	6.9	272.4	1 499	1 148	867	10 503	53.1	43.9	3.0
Louisa	38.2	3 202	45.1	4.9	3.0	0.6	7.7	129.1	10 815	64	55	679	49.5	47.6	2.9
Lucas	24.9	2 750	34.9	36.1	2.9	0.6	10.8	12.5	1 377	43	42	692	44.9	52.6	2.5
Lyon	28.6	2 391	62.3	2.9	1.7	0.2	14.9	7.6	635	47	56	574	24.6	73.3	2.1
Madison	35.7	2 598	49.1	24.6	3.0	0.4	9.4	24.3	1 769	55	66	799	44.4	52.5	3.0
Mahaska	54.6	2 503	34.2	25.1	2.6	1.1	11.3	29.5	1 354	81	102	1 105	35.3	62.6	2.1
Marion	60.8	1 946	62.0	3.5	4.6	0.7	10.4	46.2	1 477	829	146	1 501	39.8	58.0	2.1
Marshall	105.8	2 727	63.1	1.7	3.9	5.5	6.7	46.3	1 194	138	180	3 096	47.2	49.8	2.9
Mills	26.0	1 807	59.5	6.5	4.1	0.9	10.8	4.8	334	58	68	1 589	34.5	62.3	3.2
Mitchell	29.3	2 649	38.6	28.1	3.7	1.2	11.5	6.6	601	51	52	649	51.3	46.3	2.4
Monona	22.6	2 260	46.2	3.7	4.6	0.4	17.9	2.4	235	54	47	611	45.7	50.5	3.7
Monroe	20.3	2 525	36.3	27.8	3.7	0.8	16.1	10.0	1 244	35	37	482	46.6	50.9	2.5
Montgomery	35.1	2 949	33.2	35.3	3.0	0.1	12.1	11.3	950	60	54	902	34.1	63.3	2.6
Muscatine	110.6	2 685	40.5	24.4	4.4	0.9	4.7	177.0	4 296	129	191	2 590	50.1	46.5	3.3
O'Brien	41.1	2 756	58.7	9.0	2.0	0.4	11.8	12.9	865	67	68	1 069	30.8	66.4	2.8
Osceola	12.8	1 823	43.7	4.6	7.9	0.5	17.3	2.3	332	34	32	323	29.8	67.4	2.8
Page	45.6	2 664	43.1	18.0	4.0	0.3	10.8	19.4	1 131	80	80	1 487	32.5	65.0	2.6
Palo Alto	37.4	3 715	47.1	18.3	2.3	0.6	17.4	5.7	569	54	46	1 022	48.2	48.5	3.3
Plymouth	58.3	2 366	43.5	19.1	2.7	3.0	12.4	25.7	1 041	81	115	1 274	34.6	61.2	4.3
Pocahontas	21.7	2 460	41.5	21.5	4.2	1.2	13.4	4.6	522	49	41	597	41.9	54.1	4.0
Polk	1 021.4	2 884	46.5	10.4	4.8	1.3	5.0	904.5	2 553	5 637	2 019	26 167	51.5	45.9	2.6
Pottawattamie	228.0	2 670	61.2	2.5	4.4	0.3	6.8	107.5	1 258	225	402	4 841	42.7	54.5	2.8
Poweshiek	35.8	1 884	55.1	4.0	3.9	0.8	13.6	19.9	1 050	66	87	961	47.0	49.0	4.0
Ringgold	19.4	3 634	36.4	28.8	1.5	0.4	14.7	2.0	370	40	25	457	46.3	50.9	2.8
Sac	23.0	1 933	58.4	7.6	4.2	0.3	14.4	4.5	376	58	55	712	41.7	55.2	3.1
Scott	413.7	2 628	55.2	3.5	2.9	0.8	9.0	317.1	2 014	1 028	742	7 487	50.8	46.5	2.7
Shelby	40.9	3 121	38.8	26.5	2.7	0.2	12.7	22.6	1 726	57	59	928	36.3	60.8	2.9
Sioux	72.0	2 316	44.3	22.3	2.9	0.3	9.6	38.2	1 230	104	146	1 776	14.6	83.3	2.1
Story	220.0	2 950	31.5	38.3	3.4	0.7	7.2	136.1	1 825	987	384	18 583	49.4	45.9	4.7
Tama	37.3	2 116	56.4	5.5	4.5	0.5	17.2	9.8	554	89	83	988	48.6	48.5	2.8
Taylor	15.9	2 229	51.0	3.2	3.5	4.6	18.1	4.7	659	47	33	455	40.3	57.2	2.6
Union	56.8	4 554	46.9	26.1	2.3	0.1	5.5	12.4	992	86	59	1 204	44.3	52.3	3.5
Van Buren	24.6	3 141	33.9	39.8	2.3	0.8	11.7	4.8	611	46	37	631	40.4	56.6	2.9
Wapello	117.1	3 311	64.1	4.7	2.4	0.3	6.3	74.5	2 106	146	165	2 633	55.2	41.7	3.1
Warren	76.7	1 932	61.3	3.8	3.6	0.7	8.7	48.5	1 222	114	189	1 772	48.4	49.0	2.6
Washington	48.0	2 302	43.7	26.1	3.4	0.4	10.7	15.8	758	78	98	1 247	43.2	53.1	3.7
Wayne	19.5	2 855	40.5	28.9	2.5	0.2	12.3	6.1	896	45	31	516	43.0	55.1	1.8
Webster	107.2	2 777	63.7	5.9	3.0	0.9	7.6	31.6	818	295	182	2 748	49.7	47.9	2.4
Winnebago	28.5	2 360	60.5	4.6	5.2	1.7	10.2	15.8	1 312	54	56	745	48.7	48.2	3.2
Winneshiek	68.2	3 266	53.5	20.7	2.2	0.5	10.7	24.5	1 173	91	97	1 733	46.1	49.3	4.5
Woodbury	273.1	2 675	50.4	2.3	4.5	0.9	6.8	169.0	1 656	824	479	5 401	46.7	49.8	3.5
Worth	13.9	1 787	46.6	5.9	3.3	3.4	26.5	6.5	840	40	36	342	55.1	41.4	3.4
Wright	42.0	2 963	45.4	18.4	2.9	0.2	13.2	13.0	916	84	65	946	44.1	53.4	2.5
KANSAS	X	X	X	X	X	X	X	X	X	25 722	29 009	218 454	37.2	58.0	4.7
Allen	32.7	2 263	64.3	1.6	2.3	0.0	5.2	17.9	1 236	58	69	1 489	37.0	58.6	4.4
Anderson	15.3	1 904	55.9	1.9	3.6	0.0	9.8	16.3	2 032	37	39	547	38.2	57.0	4.8
Atchison	31.2	1 909	52.5	5.8	5.2	0.0	7.9	19.8	1 216	49	81	1 159	46.0	49.0	5.1

1. Based on the resident population estimated as of July 1 of the year shown. 2. Data subject to copyright.

Table B. States and Counties — **Land Area and Population**

STATE/ County code	MSA/ PMSA/ NECMA code[1]	County Type[2]	STATE County	Land area[3] (sq km) 2000	Population and population characteristics, 2000												
					Total persons	Rank	Per square kilometer	Race alone or in combination (percent)				Percent Hispanic[4]	Age (percent)					
								White	Black	Am. Indian, Alaska Native	Asian and Pacific Islander		Under 5 years	5 to 17 years	18 to 24 years	25 to 34 years	35 to 44 years	45 to 54 years
				1	2	3	4	5	6	7	8	9	10	11	12	13	14	15
			KANSAS—Cont'd															
20 007	...	9	Barber	2 937	5 307	2 829	1.8	98.1	0.6	1.1	0.2	2.0	5.0	19.9	5.8	8.3	14.9	14.1
20 009	...	7	Barton	2 315	28 205	1 445	12.2	94.5	1.5	1.0	0.3	8.3	6.4	19.6	9.0	9.9	15.3	12.9
20 011	...	7	Bourbon	1 650	15 379	2 061	9.3	95.3	3.4	1.6	0.6	1.3	6.1	19.6	9.5	10.6	13.5	12.9
20 013	...	7	Brown	1 478	10 724	2 381	7.3	88.7	2.0	9.9	0.3	2.3	6.4	20.0	7.4	10.0	14.1	13.3
20 015	9040	2	Butler	3 698	59 482	808	16.1	96.6	1.7	1.9	0.7	2.2	6.9	21.7	8.3	11.6	17.2	13.9
20 017	...	9	Chase	2 010	3 030	2 992	1.5	97.7	1.2	1.1	0.2	1.7	6.0	18.1	6.5	10.7	15.8	13.9
20 019	...	9	Chautauqua	1 662	4 359	2 891	2.6	95.7	0.5	5.0	0.3	1.4	4.5	18.9	6.1	7.9	13.0	12.3
20 021	...	6	Cherokee	1 521	22 605	1 665	14.9	95.1	0.9	6.0	0.4	1.3	6.9	19.6	8.4	12.1	14.8	12.8
20 023	...	9	Cheyenne	2 641	3 165	2 981	1.2	98.3	0.1	0.3	0.8	2.6	4.7	19.1	5.1	9.0	13.8	13.2
20 025	...	9	Clark	2 524	2 390	3 032	0.9	96.7	0.4	1.6	0.1	4.0	6.1	20.5	4.9	9.3	13.8	13.4
20 027	...	7	Clay	1 668	8 822	2 543	5.3	98.6	0.7	0.9	0.4	0.8	5.4	19.6	6.7	10.0	13.9	14.3
20 029	...	7	Cloud	1 853	10 268	2 420	5.5	99.0	0.4	0.7	0.3	0.6	4.9	17.4	10.4	9.1	12.7	12.4
20 031	...	7	Coffey	1 631	8 865	2 537	5.4	98.4	0.4	1.5	0.5	1.5	5.9	20.9	6.5	10.4	16.0	14.4
20 033	...	9	Comanche	2 042	1 967	3 066	1.0	98.6	0.2	0.7	0.6	1.8	5.6	16.5	4.5	8.3	12.8	13.8
20 035	...	4	Cowley	2 917	36 291	1 205	12.4	92.2	3.2	3.3	1.9	3.6	6.4	19.7	9.9	11.3	14.7	12.9
20 037	...	4	Crawford	1 536	38 242	1 160	24.9	94.8	2.2	1.8	1.4	2.4	6.4	16.5	16.4	12.2	12.9	11.9
20 039	...	9	Decatur	2 314	3 472	2 956	1.5	98.7	0.5	0.6	0.4	1.0	4.5	19.1	4.7	8.3	14.6	12.9
20 041	...	7	Dickinson	2 196	19 344	1 826	8.8	97.7	0.8	1.1	0.6	2.3	5.7	20.0	6.3	10.2	16.1	13.2
20 043	...	8	Doniphan	1 016	8 249	2 586	8.1	96.0	2.4	1.9	0.4	1.2	6.4	18.9	10.7		14.0	13.6
20 045	4150	3	Douglas	1 183	99 962	525	84.5	88.5	5.2	3.6	3.9	3.3	5.6	14.8	26.4	15.2	13.1	11.2
20 047	...	9	Edwards	1 611	3 449	2 959	2.1	93.3	0.4	0.7	0.3	9.7	5.9	18.8	6.7	10.4	14.7	12.4
20 049	...	8	Elk	1 676	3 261	2 976	1.9	97.3	0.3	2.9	0.5	2.2	4.2	18.2	5.8	7.9	12.1	13.8
20 051	...	7	Ellis	2 331	27 507	1 466	11.8	96.9	1.0	0.6	0.9	2.4	5.8	16.7	18.4	11.6	13.6	12.3
20 053	...	9	Ellsworth	1 854	6 525	2 737	3.5	94.7	3.9	1.2	0.4	3.6	4.2	17.2	7.3	10.6	16.5	14.0
20 055	...	5	Finney	3 372	40 523	1 103	12.0	71.5	1.6	1.5	3.4	43.3	10.5	23.8	11.0	15.9	15.2	10.7
20 057	...	5	Ford	2 845	32 458	1 334	11.4	77.1	2.0	1.2	2.4	37.7	9.4	21.7	11.2	15.4	14.0	10.7
20 059	...	6	Franklin	1 486	24 784	1 564	16.7	96.7	1.6	2.1	0.4	2.6	6.8	20.7	8.9	12.0	16.2	12.4
20 061	...	9	Geary	996	27 947	1 453	28.1	68.2	24.6	1.8	5.6	8.5	9.4	20.2	13.6	15.2	14.8	10.6
20 063	...	9	Gove	2 775	3 068	2 987	1.1	98.9	0.3	0.7	0.2	1.2	5.9	20.2	5.4	7.7	14.3	13.7
20 065	...	9	Graham	2 327	2 946	2 995	1.3	95.6	3.5	1.0	0.4	0.8	4.5	18.0	5.3	7.3	15.8	12.9
20 067	...	7	Grant	1 489	7 909	2 614	5.3	78.9	0.3	1.5	0.5	34.7	8.7	24.1	8.7	13.2	15.5	13.0
20 069	...	9	Gray	2 250	5 904	2 793	2.6	93.7	0.3	1.0	0.4	9.8	7.8	23.8	8.3	12.7	14.5	12.5
20 071	...	9	Greeley	2 015	1 534	3 093	0.8	94.1	0.4	0.6	0.2	11.5	6.7	21.5	6.8	8.5	18.8	12.1
20 073	...	6	Greenwood	2 952	7 673	2 632	2.6	98.1	0.3	1.9	0.2	1.7	5.5	18.2	6.5	9.1	14.1	13.3
20 075	...	9	Hamilton	2 581	2 670	3 017	1.0	83.2	0.6	0.9	0.8	20.6	6.9	21.5	7.2	11.0	14.3	12.1
20 077	...	7	Harper	2 076	6 536	2 736	3.1	98.3	0.4	1.5	0.3	1.1	5.6	19.0	6.6	8.6	13.4	13.1
20 079	9040	2	Harvey	1 397	32 869	1 323	23.5	93.0	2.2	1.2	0.8	8.0	6.6	19.4	9.1	11.3	15.2	13.1
20 081	...	9	Haskell	1 495	4 307	2 895	2.9	87.2	0.2	1.3	0.9	23.6	9.1	23.8	9.1	12.7	15.2	12.3
20 083	...	9	Hodgeman	2 227	2 085	3 059	0.9	98.4	1.2	0.7	0.0	2.7	4.8	24.1	4.7	8.5	16.7	12.9
20 085	...	6	Jackson	1 698	12 657	2 251	7.5	92.0	0.7	8.3	0.3	1.5	6.9	21.3	6.8	11.3	15.4	13.8
20 087	...	8	Jefferson	1 389	18 426	1 871	13.3	98.1	0.5	1.8	0.4	1.3	6.4	21.0	7.0	10.8	17.1	14.7
20 089	...	9	Jewell	2 355	3 791	2 928	1.6	99.4	0.1	0.9	0.2	0.7	4.6	17.4	4.4	7.5	13.9	15.3
20 091	3760	0	Johnson	1 235	451 086	131	365.3	92.5	3.0	0.8	3.3	4.0	7.5	19.6	7.6	15.0	17.8	14.8
20 093	...	9	Kearny	2 256	4 531	2 876	2.0	82.4	0.9	1.3	0.5	26.6	8.8	25.5	8.3	11.7	15.3	11.9
20 095	...	6	Kingman	2 236	8 673	2 553	3.9	98.5	0.2	1.5	0.4	1.4	6.1	21.3	5.8	9.3	15.5	12.5
20 097	...	9	Kiowa	1 871	3 278	2 975	1.8	97.9	0.4	1.1	0.5	2.0	5.5	18.5	8.2	8.8	13.0	15.1
20 099	...	7	Labette	1 680	22 835	1 651	13.6	91.7	5.4	3.4	0.5	3.1	6.2	19.5	8.7	11.2	14.6	13.1
20 101	...	9	Lane	1 858	2 155	3 055	1.2	99.1	0.2	1.1	0.4	1.4	5.3	20.1	5.4	9.7	14.9	13.7
20 103	3760	1	Leavenworth	1 200	68 691	718	57.2	86.0	11.2	1.6	1.8	3.8	7.0	19.7	8.2	13.8	19.3	14.1
20 105	...	9	Lincoln	1 862	3 578	2 945	1.9	99.0	0.2	1.1	0.3	1.0	5.2	18.3	5.5	8.5	14.4	14.6
20 107	...	8	Linn	1 551	9 570	2 483	6.2	98.5	0.9	1.1	0.3	0.9	6.3	18.7	6.7	9.7	14.5	14.4
20 109	...	9	Logan	2 779	3 046	2 991	1.1	98.3	0.9	0.8	0.5	1.6	6.4	19.0	7.2	9.4	15.0	13.1
20 111	...	5	Lyon	2 204	35 935	1 220	16.3	85.2	2.7	1.1	2.4	16.7	6.9	18.9	16.2	12.8	14.4	11.8
20 113	...	7	McPherson	2 330	29 554	1 413	12.7	97.6	1.1	0.9	0.7	1.9	5.9	19.5	10.3	10.1	15.1	13.2
20 115	...	6	Marion	2 443	13 361	2 200	5.5	98.1	0.7	1.1	0.5	1.9	5.5	19.3	7.9	9.0	14.5	12.5
20 117	...	7	Marshall	2 338	10 965	2 370	4.7	98.9	0.3	0.8	0.5	0.8	5.0	20.0	6.6	8.3	15.3	13.2
20 119	...	9	Meade	2 534	4 631	2 871	1.8	92.6	0.6	1.3	0.2	10.9	7.9	21.6	6.9	12.4	14.2	11.1
20 121	3760	1	Miami	1 494	28 351	1 436	19.0	97.2	1.9	1.3	0.3	1.6	6.9	21.1	7.3	12.0	17.8	13.9
20 123	...	7	Mitchell	1 813	6 932	2 692	3.8	98.4	0.7	1.0	0.4	0.9	5.1	19.4	8.5	8.6	14.0	13.7
20 125	...	5	Montgomery	1 671	36 252	1 207	21.7	88.8	6.8	5.6	0.7	3.1	6.0	19.0	8.6	10.8	13.9	13.3
20 127	...	9	Morris	1 806	6 104	2 770	3.4	98.3	0.4	0.9	0.4	2.2	5.7	19.6	5.6	9.2	14.7	14.2
20 129	...	9	Morton	1 890	3 496	2 954	1.8	90.0	0.4	1.5	1.3	14.1	8.1	21.3	8.0	11.4	15.9	12.0
20 131	...	9	Nemaha	1 860	10 717	2 382	5.8	98.9	0.7	0.5	0.2	0.7	7.1	21.4	6.0	9.5	14.6	11.2
20 133	...	7	Neosho	1 481	16 997	1 953	11.5	96.7	1.2	2.1	0.6	2.9	6.0	19.7	8.9	10.7	14.7	12.9
20 135	...	9	Ness	2 784	3 454	2 958	1.2	99.1	0.1	0.9	0.2	1.5	5.1	17.8	4.6	8.0	16.0	13.7
20 137	...	7	Norton	2 274	5 953	2 788	2.6	94.0	4.1	0.8	0.7	2.4	4.8	17.3	7.7	11.9	16.4	12.9

1. MSA = Metropolitan Statistical Area. PMSA = Primary MSA. NECMA = New England County Metropolitan Area. See Appendix A for explanation of these concepts. See Appendix B for list of metropolitan areas identified by type, with component counties. 2. County typology code from the Economic Research Service of USDA. See Appendix A for definition. 3. Dry land or land partially or temporarily covered by water. 4. Hispanic persons may be of any race.

STATE County	Age (percent) (cont'd)				Total persons		Percent change		Components of change, 2000–2001			Households, 2000			Percent	
	55 to 64 years	65 to 74 years	75 years and over	Percent female	2001	1990	1990–2000	2000–2001	Births	Deaths	Net migration	Number	Percent change, 1990–2000	Persons per household	Female family householder[1]	One person
	16	17	18	19	20	21	22	23	24	25	26	27	28	29	30	31
KANSAS—Cont'd																
Barber	10.5	10.4	11.1	52.0	5 163	5 874	-9.7	-2.7	67	107	-105	2 235	-5.2	2.35	6.5	29.9
Barton	9.1	8.8	9.1	51.6	27 810	29 382	-4.0	-1.4	482	416	-463	11 393	-1.5	2.41	7.8	30.2
Bourbon	9.4	8.5	9.7	51.8	15 371	14 966	2.8	-0.1	226	273	44	6 161	4.5	2.44	9.2	29.0
Brown	9.4	8.4	11.0	51.7	10 630	11 128	-3.6	-0.9	164	184	-71	4 318	-0.7	2.44	9.2	28.8
Butler	7.8	6.3	6.3	49.8	60 194	50 580	17.6	1.2	970	636	399	21 527	16.4	2.67	8.3	21.9
Chase	10.2	8.8	9.9	49.0	3 033	3 021	0.3	0.1	62	70	11	1 246	2.6	2.34	7.6	31.1
Chautauqua	13.0	10.4	13.9	51.7	4 270	4 407	-1.1	-2.0	44	74	-57	1 796	-2.1	2.34	7.9	29.4
Cherokee	10.2	7.3	7.8	51.5	22 333	21 374	5.8	-1.2	350	331	-288	8 875	5.7	2.51	9.7	26.3
Cheyenne	8.6	12.7	13.9	50.7	3 114	3 243	-2.4	-1.6	36	39	-48	1 360	-2.1	2.29	5.1	30.8
Clark	10.2	9.6	12.2	51.1	2 371	2 418	-1.2	-0.8	33	41	-10	979	-2.7	2.39	6.2	29.6
Clay	9.4	9.3	11.5	50.2	8 771	9 158	-3.7	-0.6	129	140	-35	3 617	-0.7	2.39	6.1	27.7
Cloud	9.8	9.3	14.0	52.5	9 985	11 023	-6.8	-2.8	129	208	-204	4 163	-7.1	2.31	6.6	30.8
Coffey	9.6	7.1	9.1	51.0	8 815	8 404	5.5	-0.6	107	126	-28	3 489	5.4	2.49	6.9	26.0
Comanche	12.7	10.9	14.9	51.7	1 961	2 313	-15.0	-0.3	27	42	8	872	-8.2	2.18	6.2	35.9
Cowley	9.3	7.7	8.2	51.1	35 929	36 915	-1.7	-1.0	573	546	-384	14 039	-0.1	2.46	9.6	27.9
Crawford	8.3	6.5	8.9	51.3	37 927	35 582	7.5	-0.8	678	582	-407	15 504	6.1	2.35	9.3	30.6
Decatur	9.6	12.6	13.6	50.6	3 432	4 021	-13.7	-1.2	33	65	-9	1 494	-9.5	2.24	5.6	32.8
Dickinson	9.9	9.1	9.5	51.3	19 155	18 958	2.0	-1.0	280	349	-112	7 903	4.8	2.40	7.7	28.1
Doniphan	8.4	7.7	8.5	50.3	8 303	8 134	1.4	0.7	131	108	33	3 173	3.2	2.48	8.7	27.6
Douglas	5.8	4.1	3.9	50.3	100 005	81 798	22.2	0.0	1 503	661	-796	38 486	27.7	2.37	8.5	28.5
Edwards	10.4	9.8	11.0	50.6	3 325	3 787	-8.9	-3.6	54	74	-106	1 455	-8.2	2.33	6.0	32.0
Elk	12.6	11.7	13.6	52.2	3 189	3 327	-2.0	-2.2	38	84	-27	1 412	-1.7	2.25	6.1	32.9
Ellis	7.3	7.1	7.2	51.1	27 247	26 004	5.8	-0.9	407	296	-368	11 193	10.9	2.35	7.8	30.1
Ellsworth	9.8	8.9	11.5	47.2	6 488	6 586	-0.9	-0.6	77	118	6	2 481	-1.6	2.30	6.2	31.4
Finney	6.0	3.7	3.3	49.0	40 082	33 070	22.5	-1.1	1 139	236	-1 396	12 948	19.5	3.09	10.5	19.6
Ford	6.6	5.2	5.8	48.3	32 314	27 463	18.2	-0.4	845	343	-672	10 852	9.9	2.92	9.2	22.7
Franklin	8.9	6.9	7.1	50.4	24 943	21 994	12.7	0.6	439	315	47	9 452	13.8	2.56	8.9	24.8
Geary	6.8	5.1	4.3	50.7	26 799	30 453	-8.2	-4.1	804	299	-1 672	10 458	-2.0	2.61	12.3	22.5
Gove	10.0	11.1	11.5	51.2	3 008	3 231	-5.0	-2.0	44	62	-42	1 245	-3.0	2.42	3.5	29.7
Graham	12.5	12.2	11.5	51.3	2 845	3 543	-16.9	-3.4	33	50	-87	1 263	-12.0	2.28	5.9	30.1
Grant	7.2	5.5	4.1	49.8	7 790	7 159	10.5	-1.5	194	66	-254	2 742	14.6	2.86	7.1	21.0
Gray	7.7	5.7	7.0	50.0	5 946	5 396	9.4	-0.2	128	57	-29	2 045	6.9	2.82	5.6	21.2
Greeley	7.9	9.3	8.4	50.4	1 503	1 774	-13.5	-2.0	26	22	-36	602	-8.2	2.50	4.5	28.6
Greenwood	10.4	11.0	11.8	51.2	7 771	7 847	-2.2	1.3	95	169	171	3 234	-1.6	2.31	6.6	30.3
Hamilton	8.7	9.0	9.4	50.6	2 671	2 388	11.8	0.0	53	43	-9	1 054	6.9	2.49	7.6	29.4
Harper	10.4	9.9	13.3	51.6	6 335	7 124	-8.3	-3.1	86	113	-175	2 773	-7.8	2.30	6.9	32.1
Harvey	8.5	7.8	9.0	51.4	33 031	31 028	5.9	0.5	546	461	86	12 581	8.6	2.50	7.7	25.8
Haskell	7.3	5.9	4.7	49.2	4 285	3 886	10.8	-0.5	95	35	-85	1 481	7.9	2.88	5.9	20.1
Hodgeman	9.2	9.3	9.7	50.7	2 154	2 177	-4.2	3.3	30	39	77	796	-3.6	2.58	4.4	24.7
Jackson	9.6	7.4	7.5	50.8	12 742	11 525	9.8	0.7	190	162	57	4 727	10.5	2.63	8.2	22.7
Jefferson	10.2	6.6	6.2	49.3	18 610	15 905	15.9	1.0	268	193	112	6 830	18.2	2.66	7.0	20.1
Jewell	10.9	12.9	13.0	50.5	3 591	4 251	-10.8	-5.3	38	72	-170	1 695	-6.1	2.21	4.8	32.4
Johnson	7.7	5.1	4.9	51.2	465 058	355 021	27.1	3.1	8 135	3 313	9 096	174 570	28.0	2.56	7.8	24.5
Kearny	7.3	5.9	5.2	48.9	4 562	4 027	12.5	0.7	96	49	-18	1 542	11.8	2.91	8.3	20.2
Kingman	10.0	8.8	10.8	51.0	8 512	8 292	4.6	-1.9	114	133	-143	3 371	6.2	2.51	7.1	26.0
Kiowa	9.5	10.6	10.7	50.9	3 132	3 660	-10.4	-4.5	48	43	-156	1 365	-6.9	2.32	5.3	30.5
Labette	9.4	7.9	9.5	51.1	22 483	23 693	-3.6	-1.5	370	372	-349	9 194	-2.0	2.39	10.2	29.8
Lane	10.4	9.3	11.2	49.9	2 091	2 375	-9.3	-3.0	28	36	-57	910	-5.8	2.34	5.1	30.3
Leavenworth	8.1	5.3	4.5	46.8	70 261	64 371	6.7	2.3	1 081	666	1 174	23 071	17.0	2.69	9.5	21.7
Lincoln	9.9	10.9	12.6	51.0	3 547	3 653	-2.1	-0.9	34	60	-3	1 529	-0.1	2.29	6.4	29.6
Linn	11.3	9.6	8.7	50.0	9 685	8 254	15.9	1.2	147	171	141	3 807	18.4	2.48	6.2	24.0
Logan	9.2	8.9	10.9	51.6	2 957	3 081	-1.1	-2.9	45	44	-92	1 243	1.8	2.40	6.3	28.6
Lyon	7.3	5.4	6.3	50.7	35 560	34 732	3.5	-1.0	639	362	-662	13 691	4.8	2.51	8.4	28.5
McPherson	8.5	7.6	9.7	51.0	29 618	27 268	8.4	0.2	415	439	93	11 205	9.5	2.49	6.0	25.5
Marion	10.2	9.3	11.8	51.3	13 423	12 888	3.7	0.5	183	248	130	5 114	2.8	2.46	5.5	25.2
Marshall	9.6	10.0	12.0	50.8	10 772	11 705	-6.3	-1.8	157	209	-139	4 458	-4.9	2.40	5.4	29.5
Meade	8.1	8.9	9.0	50.5	4 647	4 247	9.0	0.3	86	74	5	1 728	3.7	2.61	4.9	25.6
Miami	9.2	6.3	5.6	50.5	28 780	23 466	20.8	1.5	474	315	274	10 365	23.4	2.66	8.0	21.0
Mitchell	9.3	9.8	11.6	50.7	6 778	7 203	-3.8	-2.2	73	138	-90	2 850	0.1	2.31	5.3	31.2
Montgomery	10.0	8.4	9.9	51.8	35 520	38 816	-6.6	-2.0	574	633	-673	14 903	-4.9	2.37	10.1	29.7
Morris	10.1	10.1	11.0	50.8	6 112	6 198	-1.5	0.1	83	99	28	2 539	0.4	2.37	6.6	28.0
Morton	9.4	7.5	6.4	51.4	3 385	3 480	0.5	-3.2	64	29	-150	1 306	1.2	2.63	6.8	24.3
Nemaha	8.2	9.2	12.8	50.8	10 516	10 446	2.6	-1.9	206	178	-230	3 959	-0.9	2.58	5.1	28.0
Neosho	9.6	8.5	9.1	51.7	16 759	17 035	-0.2	-1.4	226	252	-212	6 739	-0.1	2.45	8.5	27.1
Ness	10.5	10.8	13.5	50.4	3 340	4 033	-14.4	-3.3	37	53	-99	1 516	-9.2	2.23	4.7	33.5
Norton	9.4	8.6	11.0	45.0	5 841	5 947	0.1	-1.9	56	116	-52	2 266	-2.7	2.28	7.0	32.3

1. No spouse present.

Table B. States and Counties — **Vital Statistics, Health Resources, and Crime**

STATE County	Births, average 1997–1999		Deaths, average 1997–1999				Physicians,[4] 2000		Hospitals,[4] 1998			Medicare enrollees 2000	Serious crimes known to police, 2000[6]	
			Number		Rate					Beds			Total	
	Total	Rate[1]	Total	Infant[2]	Total[1]	Infant[3]	Number	Rate[5]	Number	Number	Rate[5]		Number	Rate[7]
	32	33	34	35	36	37	38	39	40	41	42	43	44	45
KANSAS—Cont'd														
Barber	55	10.4	85	NA	16.0	NA	5	94	2	66	1 235	1 258	52	980
Barton	382	13.6	323	NA	11.5	NA	39	138	3	238	861	5 383	1 092	3 921
Bourbon	199	13.1	209	NA	13.8	NA	23	150	1	114	747	3 099	612	3 979
Brown	134	12.2	148	NA	13.5	NA	11	103	2	70	632	2 235	221	2 061
Butler	784	12.7	490	NA	7.9	NA	38	64	2	234	378	7 773	1 641	2 789
Chase	48	16.6	46	NA	15.8	NA	0	0	0	0	0	566	37	1 221
Chautauqua	41	9.4	72	NA	16.7	NA	4	92	2	73	1 674	1 045	110	2 524
Cherokee	287	12.8	270	NA	12.0	NA	7	31	1	39	173	3 824	801	3 543
Cheyenne	32	10.0	39	NA	12.2	NA	2	63	1	23	725	841	30	948
Clark	23	9.8	41	NA	17.1	NA	3	126	2	63	2 668	548	3	126
Clay	97	10.7	127	NA	13.9	NA	8	91	1	32	350	1 912	194	2 199
Cloud	102	10.1	153	NA	15.2	NA	18	175	1	39	389	2 534	171	1 665
Coffey	98	11.3	97	NA	11.1	NA	3	34	1	26	299	1 555	169	2 200
Comanche	23	11.5	36	NA	17.9	NA	1	51	1	14	696	519	NA	NA
Cowley	447	12.2	431	NA	11.8	NA	38	105	2	178	490	6 480	915	2 561
Crawford	489	13.4	471	NA	12.9	NA	61	160	2	175	481	6 642	859	2 272
Decatur	36	10.6	57	NA	16.7	NA	6	173	1	74	2 141	933	51	1 469
Dickinson	211	10.7	259	NA	13.1	NA	9	47	2	102	517	3 916	590	3 253
Doniphan	95	12.1	85	NA	10.8	NA	4	48	0	0	0	1 407	92	1 115
Douglas	1 143	12.1	483	NA	5.1	NA	135	135	1	167	179	9 069	743	743
Edwards	39	11.7	53	NA	15.8	NA	4	116	1	49	1 479	773	53	1 537
Elk	32	9.5	53	NA	15.9	NA	0	0	0	0	0	834	84	2 576
Ellis	314	11.9	236	NA	9.0	NA	73	265	1	104	395	4 215	895	3 403
Ellsworth	54	8.7	87	NA	13.9	NA	6	92	1	22	350	1 330	137	2 483
Finney	888	24.2	201	NA	5.5	NA	45	111	1	93	255	3 509	2 856	7 048
Ford	625	21.3	260	NA	8.9	NA	40	123	1	105	357	3 736	2 300	7 268
Franklin	359	14.5	267	NA	10.8	NA	16	65	1	45	182	3 954	815	3 288
Geary	609	24.2	216	12	8.6	20.3	43	154	1	49	193	2 911	2 279	8 155
Gove	36	11.7	46	NA	15.2	NA	5	163	1	123	4 028	729	NA	NA
Graham	25	8.0	38	NA	12.1	NA	2	68	1	42	1 311	694	30	1 018
Grant	145	18.3	58	NA	7.3	NA	7	89	1	45	562	833	176	2 225
Gray	92	16.6	45	NA	8.2	NA	2	34	0	0	0	837	22	373
Greeley	21	12.4	21	NA	12.2	NA	1	65	1	50	2 934	299	7	456
Greenwood	83	10.4	137	NA	17.1	NA	6	78	1	46	565	1 947	148	1 929
Hamilton	35	15.2	31	NA	13.3	NA	2	75	1	77	3 286	501	84	3 146
Harper	67	10.4	103	NA	16.0	NA	12	184	2	50	778	1 508	86	1 316
Harvey	414	12.2	346	NA	10.2	NA	91	277	2	221	643	5 995	1 081	3 427
Haskell	76	18.9	29	NA	7.2	NA	3	70	1	42	1 056	467	72	1 672
Hodgeman	20	9.2	25	NA	11.3	NA	1	48	1	54	2 445	391	66	3 165
Jackson	154	12.7	146	NA	12.1	NA	3	24	1	17	140	2 005	265	2 094
Jefferson	205	11.3	153	NA	8.4	NA	10	54	1	118	647	2 690	589	3 197
Jewell	32	8.2	57	NA	14.8	NA	1	0	1	57	1 474	997	7	185
Johnson	6 361	14.8	2 495	32	5.8	5.0	1 116	247	4	849	198	47 778	9 788	2 382
Kearny	68	16.4	41	NA	9.8	NA	2	44	1	20	479	531	151	3 333
Kingman	99	11.6	103	NA	12.0	NA	6	69	1	49	574	1 696	169	1 949
Kiowa	39	11.5	39	NA	11.5	NA	2	61	1	24	692	785	57	1 739
Labette	285	12.4	291	NA	12.6	NA	32	140	2	91	395	4 423	626	2 741
Lane	25	11.2	25	NA	11.5	NA	2	93	1	31	1 369	486	51	2 367
Leavenworth	861	12.1	509	7	7.2	8.5	87	127	2	136	191	6 895	2 159	3 143
Lincoln	30	9.0	51	NA	15.4	NA	2	56	1	34	1 019	856	30	838
Linn	96	10.5	125	NA	13.6	NA	2	21	0	0	0	1 934	238	2 487
Logan	32	10.8	40	NA	13.3	NA	1	33	1	51	1 707	711	85	2 791
Lyon	484	14.3	290	NA	8.6	NA	43	120	1	152	448	4 690	2 140	6 115
McPherson	368	13.0	330	NA	11.6	NA	27	91	3	83	290	5 412	534	1 807
Marion	140	10.3	177	NA	13.1	NA	11	82	2	152	1 118	2 909	151	1 261
Marshall	115	10.5	165	NA	15.0	NA	9	82	1	55	500	2 545	98	894
Meade	62	14.1	58	NA	13.1	NA	2	43	1	26	588	852	3	65
Miami	326	12.2	243	NA	9.1	NA	26	92	1	22	83	3 590	775	2 734
Mitchell	76	10.9	107	NA	15.3	NA	7	101	1	89	1 283	1 584	166	2 589
Montgomery	465	12.6	483	NA	13.0	NA	44	121	2	182	491	7 618	1 027	2 833
Morris	70	11.3	80	NA	12.9	NA	6	98	1	22	357	1 329	130	2 130
Morton	46	13.3	30	NA	8.6	NA	8	229	1	100	2 907	534	55	1 573
Nemaha	149	14.6	146	NA	14.3	NA	8	75	2	51	503	2 282	167	1 558
Neosho	204	12.1	202	NA	12.0	NA	16	94	1	60	358	3 324	671	3 948
Ness	33	9.1	46	NA	12.8	NA	3	87	2	104	2 883	920	NA	NA
Norton	59	10.3	82	NA	14.3	NA	6	101	1	43	748	1 264	76	1 277

1. Per 1,000 estimated resident population, average 1997–1999.   2. Deaths of infants under 1 year old.   3. Deaths of infants under 1 year old per 1,000 live births.   4. Data subject to copyright.   5. Per 100,000 resident population as of July 1 of the year shown.   6. Data for serious crimes have not been adjusted for underreporting; this may affect comparability between geographic areas and over time.   7. Per 100,000 population estimated by the FBI.

Table B. States and Counties — Crime, Education, Money Income, and Poverty

STATE County	Serious crimes known to police, 2000 (cont'd) Rate[2] Violent	Property	Education — School enrollment and attainment, 1990 Enrollment[3] Total	Percent private	Attainment[4] (percent) High school graduate or more	Bachelor's degree or more	Local government expenditures, fiscal 1999[5] Total current expenditures (mil dol)	Current expenditures per student (dollars)	Money income 1989 Per capita[6] (dollars)	Households Median Dollars	Percent change, 1979–1989 (constant 1989 dollars)	Percent with $100,000 or more	Income and poverty, 1998 Median house-hold income	Percent below poverty level All persons	Persons under 18	Persons 5–17 in families
	46	47	48	49	50	51	52	53	54	55	56	57	58	59	60	61
KANSAS—Cont'd																
Barber	75	904	1 446	3.9	79.4	12.9	6.8	6 037	10 664	21 476	-12.1	1.4	30 719	13.0	16.8	16.2
Barton	409	3 512	7 878	7.0	78.0	13.6	29.8	5 932	11 394	23 432	-14.2	1.3	33 973	12.3	16.9	16.1
Bourbon	442	3 537	3 757	7.5	73.9	14.0	13.7	5 016	9 958	20 367	0.2	1.5	29 705	17.9	24.0	23.3
Brown	121	1 940	2 694	2.3	78.4	12.5	10.9	5 754	10 299	20 392	-1.3	1.6	31 429	14.9	20.7	19.3
Butler	185	2 604	13 618	7.6	81.0	17.0	73.9	5 503	13 260	31 012	0.3	2.0	47 894	7.8	10.3	9.4
Chase	165	1 056	677	3.4	77.9	13.6	3.5	6 871	10 258	20 128	-10.8	0.7	31 014	14.8	18.9	19.8
Chautauqua	413	2 111	942	3.5	70.5	10.6	4.7	6 248	9 043	17 067	-10.1	0.6	25 736	19.8	27.8	26.1
Cherokee	234	3 309	5 256	2.4	70.2	10.3	22.6	5 577	9 705	19 001	-6.5	0.7	29 322	17.2	24.1	22.9
Cheyenne	95	853	694	2.7	74.2	13.3	4.4	6 740	11 165	21 750	0.0	0.5	29 760	13.3	18.4	17.9
Clark	42	84	565	9.7	83.5	17.5	4.2	7 657	11 804	24 003	-2.4	0.4	35 623	9.6	12.5	12.5
Clay	181	2 018	2 135	6.5	77.8	13.3	10.3	6 286	11 431	21 896	1.3	2.1	34 837	11.4	16.7	15.3
Cloud	127	1 539	2 678	2.8	76.0	13.8	11.8	7 162	10 853	20 782	2.8	0.6	30 511	13.6	18.7	17.2
Coffey	143	2 056	2 041	6.1	76.9	13.5	13.9	7 193	11 451	24 435	4.8	1.3	34 915	11.2	14.0	13.1
Comanche	NA	NA	497	3.6	78.0	14.9	3.0	8 105	10 587	19 421	-18.8	1.3	27 552	13.2	16.5	17.8
Cowley	274	2 287	9 487	10.8	76.9	14.9	40.8	6 025	11 624	25 047	-0.3	1.4	35 621	12.6	16.8	16.4
Crawford	249	2 023	10 622	6.3	74.7	18.7	40.9	6 787	10 507	19 616	1.9	1.2	29 906	16.3	21.2	20.9
Decatur	202	1 267	913	4.4	78.5	13.6	4.6	6 874	10 609	20 131	-11.2	1.4	30 072	13.5	18.5	18.3
Dickinson	237	3 016	4 503	7.1	79.7	11.9	23.9	5 506	11 407	22 953	0.2	0.7	35 200	10.1	13.9	12.8
Doniphan	73	1 043	2 046	4.2	73.0	9.7	10.8	6 418	9 465	22 102	-0.1	1.2	33 879	14.2	18.3	18.5
Douglas	35	708	36 059	6.7	88.8	38.4	77.6	6 027	12 003	25 244	6.4	2.7	39 017	11.4	13.7	13.1
Edwards	116	1 421	909	5.3	76.3	13.1	4.0	6 978	11 895	21 904	1.1	2.3	33 200	13.5	19.1	18.8
Elk	184	2 392	639	2.3	67.3	10.5	6.6	8 396	10 390	17 730	2.9	1.2	24 335	19.1	24.3	28.4
Ellis	183	3 221	8 919	8.4	80.6	23.4	28.0	6 524	11 459	22 466	-14.2	1.7	34 499	10.5	12.6	11.7
Ellsworth	163	2 320	1 438	3.4	76.6	12.8	8.8	6 505	9 801	20 064	-3.1	0.8	33 903	11.0	13.0	12.1
Finney	600	6 448	10 118	7.3	70.9	14.4	46.7	5 452	11 278	27 645	-5.8	2.7	38 354	10.8	14.4	13.9
Ford	604	6 665	7 587	15.9	76.6	18.1	28.2	4 703	11 114	25 041	-9.5	2.0	36 360	12.3	17.4	16.8
Franklin	291	2 998	5 561	12.4	77.1	12.9	26.6	5 458	11 483	24 981	4.8	1.6	36 761	11.4	14.9	15.2
Geary	902	7 253	7 197	7.7	83.4	14.6	35.3	5 455	9 996	21 905	2.4	1.0	30 562	16.9	28.5	23.7
Gove	NA	NA	709	3.7	79.1	13.6	5.9	7 802	10 859	23 377	13.6	0.5	32 414	11.9	16.3	14.1
Graham	68	950	873	1.1	77.5	14.2	4.1	7 616	11 472	22 047	5.3	1.9	30 824	14.9	19.8	18.6
Grant	367	1 859	2 058	4.4	75.1	13.6	9.9	5 367	10 757	30 173	-0.3	0.9	43 619	10.6	14.2	14.2
Gray	17	356	1 407	10.6	69.4	12.6	8.5	6 515	11 669	25 872	-5.8	3.1	40 987	9.8	13.1	11.7
Greeley	65	391	465	2.8	82.4	16.8	2.3	6 867	11 641	25 709	-4.0	2.5	38 137	8.5	10.0	11.2
Greenwood	117	1 812	1 695	3.9	75.1	10.4	8.5	6 843	10 694	19 481	-3.8	1.0	28 001	16.3	21.0	22.2
Hamilton	187	2 959	525	8.2	73.4	12.9	3.5	6 629	12 366	22 500	-1.0	1.8	36 567	13.0	19.7	19.2
Harper	76	1 239	1 560	2.3	78.2	10.9	7.6	5 851	10 717	21 226	-7.2	1.0	31 550	13.2	18.1	18.4
Harvey	193	3 234	8 200	21.3	81.2	20.3	35.6	5 908	12 725	27 539	-2.3	2.0	41 545	8.8	12.1	11.2
Haskell	163	1 509	1 055	10.0	76.1	13.4	6.6	6 765	10 990	26 761	-2.7	1.7	43 949	10.3	12.9	13.8
Hodgeman	0	3 165	516	3.3	84.9	17.3	3.4	6 940	10 347	23 788	-7.5	0.5	35 517	8.9	11.3	11.5
Jackson	182	1 912	2 859	3.3	80.8	10.4	16.7	6 795	10 891	25 398	-3.6	1.4	37 643	10.9	14.7	13.1
Jefferson	342	2 855	3 857	3.3	81.0	13.5	26.1	5 948	12 267	29 048	0.6	2.0	43 421	8.2	11.4	10.7
Jewell	26	158	843	2.0	80.8	11.7	5.1	7 448	9 698	18 839	-1.6	0.6	29 853	14.2	19.0	18.6
Johnson	171	2 211	94 679	18.5	92.9	40.5	437.9	5 956	20 592	42 741	1.3	8.7	62 821	3.9	5.5	4.5
Kearny	132	3 200	1 100	1.9	73.8	12.5	7.9	6 940	11 412	29 303	2.5	2.0	41 118	11.1	15.5	15.8
Kingman	161	1 787	2 066	10.2	77.5	11.9	8.9	5 453	10 676	22 763	-8.8	0.8	35 759	11.1	14.9	13.8
Kiowa	31	1 708	866	11.4	78.0	14.6	4.5	7 504	10 607	22 628	-5.2	0.8	33 347	12.0	16.2	16.2
Labette	276	2 466	6 316	4.4	74.2	12.1	22.7	5 100	10 815	21 871	-2.1	1.1	30 592	14.8	19.9	19.5
Lane	93	2 274	576	3.5	81.1	17.8	3.4	7 458	12 159	23 532	0.3	2.0	35 422	11.4	14.8	14.9
Leavenworth	330	2 813	17 505	13.8	84.5	23.9	66.2	5 505	12 822	32 500	4.8	1.6	45 823	8.9	11.4	10.4
Lincoln	224	615	798	6.5	77.6	11.6	4.2	6 423	9 668	18 652	-6.0	0.8	30 238	12.1	16.8	15.2
Linn	178	2 309	1 841	1.2	73.9	10.4	13.4	6 668	11 001	21 287	4.5	1.5	31 218	14.2	18.5	18.5
Logan	98	2 692	727	11.1	78.3	15.9	4.9	7 936	10 878	22 126	-6.1	1.6	33 783	10.5	15.2	14.3
Lyon	306	5 809	11 506	5.0	81.9	21.4	39.8	6 384	11 251	24 050	-9.9	1.6	34 570	13.4	17.2	16.8
McPherson	118	1 688	7 272	23.4	78.2	17.4	32.8	6 225	11 970	27 003	-0.3	1.1	41 609	7.6	10.4	9.3
Marion	100	1 161	2 966	20.5	73.8	14.9	15.7	5 895	10 428	21 725	-3.4	1.3	33 821	10.5	13.9	12.6
Marshall	82	812	2 683	10.8	77.5	10.2	16.7	6 537	10 166	20 597	-2.5	1.0	33 411	12.3	16.6	15.6
Meade	0	65	921	3.0	79.5	17.1	4.6	7 207	10 887	23 403	1.1	1.2	38 212	8.4	11.5	10.7
Miami	222	2 511	5 983	11.0	78.5	13.2	30.1	6 262	12 563	29 259	4.8	2.3	42 530	8.0	10.0	9.9
Mitchell	94	2 496	1 689	12.1	82.6	15.8	11.5	8 158	10 465	22 159	0.2	1.6	35 092	10.0	13.0	12.3
Montgomery	226	2 607	9 686	7.8	73.0	13.6	30.4	4 790	10 837	20 864	-9.5	1.2	30 752	15.1	21.2	20.2
Morris	164	1 966	1 349	1.0	80.8	12.5	5.7	5 333	11 451	22 202	8.7	1.6	32 144	11.4	15.4	14.8
Morton	257	1 316	871	2.5	75.8	16.2	6.3	7 784	12 669	25 659	-6.5	2.6	39 353	11.4	16.4	15.8
Nemaha	47	1 512	2 489	9.5	75.7	12.3	12.4	6 416	10 738	22 144	7.4	1.8	34 096	11.0	14.1	13.4
Neosho	318	3 630	4 379	4.0	77.2	11.5	16.3	5 036	10 402	22 299	-4.4	0.7	31 173	14.5	19.1	19.0
Ness	NA	NA	939	15.7	78.0	12.3	5.4	7 878	11 034	23 594	5.1	1.1	33 989	9.8	12.9	12.5
Norton	134	1 142	1 179	6.1	76.9	12.8	7.1	6 549	10 912	21 259	7.9	1.5	33 365	12.4	17.6	15.9

1. Data for serious crimes have not been adjusted for underreporting; this may affect comparability between geographic areas and over time.   2. Per 100,000 population estimated by the FBI.   3. All persons 3 years old and over enrolled in nursery school through college.   4. Persons 25 years old and over.   5. Elementary and secondary education expenditures, local government fiscal years ending between July 1, 1998 and June 30, 1999.   6. Based on population enumerated as of April 1, 1990.

Table B. States and Counties — **Personal Income**

STATE County	Personal income, 1999		Per capita[1]					Transfer payments					
									Government payments to individuals				
	Total (mil dol)	Percent change, 1998–1999	Dollars	Rank	Wages and salaries[2] (mil dol)	Proprietor's income (mil dol)	Dividends, interest, and rent (mil dol)	Total (mil dol)	Total (mil dol)	Social Security (mil dol)	Medical payments (mil dol)	Income mainte-nance (mil dol)	Unemploy-ment insurance (mil dol)
	62	63	64	65	66	67	68	69	70	71	72	73	74
KANSAS—Cont'd													
Barber	107	2.3	20 438	1 856	47	8	31	26	25	12	10	1	0
Barton	642	1.4	22 400	1 242	341	64	160	109	104	54	36	8	2
Bourbon	319	1.0	21 268	1 576	157	32	73	66	63	29	24	5	1
Brown	234	0.7	21 425	1 542	116	25	56	48	46	20	18	4	2
Butler	1 516	4.3	24 157	827	431	125	221	174	163	85	55	10	3
Chase	76	8.3	26 579	454	18	24	16	12	12	5	4	1	0
Chautauqua	79	3.5	18 443	2 429	22	7	24	23	22	10	9	2	0
Cherokee	417	2.7	18 630	2 385	177	26	76	93	89	38	35	11	1
Cheyenne	77	14.3	23 944	870	25	23	19	15	14	8	5	1	0
Clark	59	5.9	25 062	660	23	6	17	10	10	5	3	1	0
Clay	207	3.6	23 059	1 077	71	33	54	35	33	18	11	2	1
Cloud	216	0.9	21 563	1 500	87	26	58	48	46	23	18	3	0
Coffey	187	3.6	21 416	1 546	140	16	47	34	32	16	12	2	1
Comanche	43	6.4	21 872	1 396	14	7	13	10	9	5	4	0	0
Cowley	759	4.1	20 536	1 825	403	63	145	144	138	64	51	11	2
Crawford	803	5.6	22 088	1 340	470	39	175	159	152	61	61	13	2
Decatur	85	4.2	25 349	604	25	16	29	16	16	9	6	1	0
Dickinson	417	2.8	21 216	1 593	174	46	91	74	70	34	22	5	1
Doniphan	176	6.0	22 105	1 330	84	29	27	32	30	14	11	3	1
Douglas	2 130	5.6	21 658	1 469	1 307	112	434	218	201	92	69	17	5
Edwards	92	3.4	28 024	332	28	28	20	16	16	7	7	1	0
Elk	60	3.4	17 587	2 631	14	7	13	18	17	8	7	1	0
Ellis	650	3.7	24 669	719	373	79	127	89	85	40	31	5	1
Ellsworth	138	4.3	22 157	1 307	61	18	35	29	28	13	12	1	0
Finney	816	5.8	21 826	1 408	552	118	121	80	73	33	28	7	2
Ford	687	4.7	23 224	1 037	449	83	127	85	80	38	28	7	1
Franklin	533	6.2	21 193	1 597	235	36	88	84	79	38	28	7	1
Geary	543	3.9	21 795	1 414	782	27	108	76	73	26	23	12	2
Gove	86	16.4	28 310	294	28	30	19	13	12	6	5	1	0
Graham	73	-2.5	23 367	996	25	19	15	15	15	7	6	1	0
Grant	170	0.9	21 557	1 502	106	29	32	20	18	9	7	2	1
Gray	156	4.7	27 873	342	62	54	24	16	15	8	5	1	0
Greeley	50	10.9	30 124	206	16	21	8	6	6	3	2	0	0
Greenwood	154	3.7	19 302	2 210	42	21	39	38	37	18	14	3	1
Hamilton	80	9.5	33 738	116	24	33	14	10	10	5	4	0	0
Harper	145	3.1	23 021	1 084	51	22	35	32	31	15	12	2	0
Harvey	858	3.1	25 041	665	390	99	145	120	114	52	42	6	2
Haskell	151	11.9	37 282	67	40	78	21	10	10	5	3	1	0
Hodgeman	54	10.6	24 313	800	15	18	12	8	8	4	3	0	0
Jackson	279	4.9	22 886	1 113	99	20	46	41	38	20	12	3	1
Jefferson	414	5.3	22 824	1 133	80	27	60	55	52	27	16	3	1
Jewell	86	-1.5	22 754	1 152	21	22	23	17	16	9	4	1	0
Johnson	18 293	8.9	41 557	36	11 335	1 437	3 830	1 021	942	514	309	38	17
Kearny	106	8.4	25 672	560	32	28	21	12	12	6	4	1	0
Kingman	180	3.2	20 862	1 710	65	18	42	35	34	17	13	2	0
Kiowa	79	4.9	23 666	922	29	11	23	16	16	8	6	1	0
Labette	452	3.1	19 701	2 085	269	39	83	98	94	40	36	9	1
Lane	64	2.2	29 233	248	20	19	17	9	9	5	3	0	0
Leavenworth	1 486	4.4	20 712	1 772	888	89	275	177	165	69	60	13	3
Lincoln	69	-0.6	20 629	1 799	21	10	19	15	14	8	5	1	0
Linn	172	5.0	18 462	2 423	64	11	37	39	37	18	13	3	1
Logan	70	3.4	23 709	916	28	12	18	12	12	7	4	1	0
Lyon	757	4.2	22 388	1 248	484	57	150	110	104	42	38	9	2
McPherson	718	4.9	24 914	684	395	96	148	104	99	57	32	4	1
Marion	250	4.1	18 459	2 425	89	31	54	51	49	27	16	3	1
Marshall	280	2.6	25 691	558	128	35	73	55	53	21	24	4	1
Meade	124	8.5	28 107	321	40	40	22	17	16	8	6	1	0
Miami	639	5.4	23 578	944	221	38	96	88	83	36	34	5	1
Mitchell	170	2.0	24 466	764	90	32	37	28	27	15	9	1	0
Montgomery	744	2.0	20 226	1 919	436	49	150	165	158	73	59	15	3
Morris	122	4.6	19 748	2 072	41	13	31	26	25	12	8	2	0
Morton	79	6.0	22 639	1 181	46	7	19	12	12	5	5	1	0
Nemaha	251	1.8	24 612	728	111	30	76	40	38	20	14	2	1
Neosho	360	3.9	21 617	1 479	199	33	69	74	71	30	29	5	1
Ness	86	-0.6	24 114	836	31	14	25	17	16	8	6	1	0
Norton	134	2.1	23 848	888	63	18	36	24	23	12	9	2	0

1. Based on the resident population estimated as of July 1 of the year shown. 2. Includes other labor income.

Table B. States and Counties — Earnings, Social Security, and Housing

STATE County	Earnings, 1999 Total (mil dol)	Farm	Goods-related¹ Total	Manufacturing	Service-related and other² Total	Retail trade	Finance, insurance, and real estate	Services	Government	Social Security beneficiaries, December 2000 Number	Rate³	Supplemental Security Income recipients, December 2000	Housing units, 1990 Total	Percent change, 1980-1990
	75	76	77	78	79	80	81	82	83	84	85	86	87	88
KANSAS—Cont'd														
Barber	56	-1.2	D	D	D	9.2	5.1	13.9	30.3	1 364	257	76	3 120	2.9
Barton	405	3.7	26.0	11.8	54.8	11.5	3.8	25.6	15.4	5 888	209	340	13 144	2.1
Bourbon	188	0.2	26.8	21.4	56.3	16.7	4.8	23.3	16.7	3 572	232	331	6 920	-3.8
Brown	141	7.4	D	14.1	D	8.1	3.3	36.3	17.3	2 487	232	222	4 890	-6.4
Butler	557	1.2	26.2	14.6	49.3	12.4	5.4	20.8	23.2	9 454	159	433	20 072	16.4
Chase	42	39.4	D	1.8	D	D	4.5	9.9	16.2	659	217	36	1 547	-1.3
Chautauqua	29	3.4	D	3.5	D	8.7	3.9	28.3	24.6	1 279	293	106	2 249	-3.1
Cherokee	202	0.3	D	32.2	D	8.1	2.9	13.9	17.5	4 629	205	620	9 428	1.2
Cheyenne	48	37.3	D	1.0	D	6.7	4.1	14.6	14.0	934	295	24	1 687	-5.3
Clark	29	25.2	D	D	D	8.4	6.3	8.0	33.0	564	236	25	1 327	3.8
Clay	104	14.8	19.9	11.8	45.4	11.3	4.8	13.9	19.9	2 110	239	97	4 138	-2.6
Cloud	113	8.5	D	9.4	D	11.6	3.8	23.1	19.7	2 752	268	164	5 198	-5.4
Coffey	156	0.2	D	6.5	D	6.2	2.5	6.3	18.5	1 922	217	139	3 712	-3.9
Comanche	20	11.9	D	6.4	D	9.0	7.2	18.8	27.8	547	278	19	1 256	7.3
Cowley	466	2.9	37.0	30.0	39.7	9.6	4.0	17.6	20.4	7 290	201	724	15 569	2.9
Crawford	510	0.2	D	21.7	D	11.0	3.0	22.0	24.5	7 318	191	876	16 526	-1.8
Decatur	41	28.5	7.1	1.5	46.0	6.7	3.9	21.7	18.4	1 047	302	44	2 063	-4.2
Dickinson	219	8.5	D	14.4	D	16.2	4.1	13.4	18.4	4 187	216	227	8 415	-3.1
Doniphan	113	16.1	D	31.5	D	4.7	3.1	8.7	17.0	1 637	198	153	3 337	-12.3
Douglas	1 418	0.1	21.1	13.6	47.7	12.4	6.2	21.5	31.1	10 307	103	909	31 782	24.7
Edwards	56	43.5	D	9.8	D	4.9	1.8	10.4	12.8	833	242	43	1 867	-6.2
Elk	21	4.6	D	D	D	9.0	3.7	9.6	45.7	948	291	63	1 743	-11.7
Ellis	452	2.5	D	7.3	D	12.7	3.9	32.2	21.3	4 679	170	332	11 115	8.5
Ellsworth	80	11.3	D	12.5	D	6.3	4.2	17.9	26.0	1 487	228	57	3 317	1.4
Finney	670	6.0	33.7	23.8	46.4	9.9	3.8	18.6	13.8	3 723	92	427	11 696	30.0
Ford	532	6.0	D	29.7	D	10.9	3.1	17.6	14.0	4 201	129	354	10 842	10.3
Franklin	270	0.6	D	13.6	D	29.0	2.8	15.2	19.3	4 555	184	416	8 926	1.9
Geary	809	0.1	5.2	2.9	19.0	6.7	1.7	7.8	75.7	3 531	126	456	11 952	7.8
Gove	58	40.9	D	3.4	D	7.9	D	12.9	18.1	756	246	19	1 494	-6.4
Graham	43	29.2	D	0.5	D	7.6	3.8	13.2	23.2	893	303	53	1 753	-3.1
Grant	136	14.2	26.6	5.0	44.0	6.5	3.4	15.6	15.1	987	125	87	2 599	-0.1
Gray	116	43.8	8.3	1.8	31.5	3.8	4.6	7.9	16.4	915	155	27	2 114	5.2
Greeley	37	59.3	D	D	D	4.0	1.4	D	11.7	325	212	7	801	-1.7
Greenwood	63	10.2	19.5	2.9	47.3	10.7	4.0	21.1	23.0	2 098	273	187	4 243	-4.7
Hamilton	57	60.5	D	D	D	3.2	3.5	5.0	15.3	533	200	26	1 214	-4.6
Harper	73	12.1	D	12.0	D	10.3	4.8	11.2	27.2	1 673	256	81	3 481	-2.3
Harvey	489	3.8	34.8	26.3	50.5	9.9	3.4	26.7	10.9	5 813	177	306	12 290	6.3
Haskell	118	63.8	D	1.7	D	2.3	D	4.1	10.5	568	132	28	1 586	6.1
Hodgeman	33	45.8	D	D	D	5.5	3.0	6.2	23.1	462	222	4	1 022	-3.0
Jackson	118	-3.5	D	7.0	D	11.5	4.9	40.7	21.8	2 581	204	97	4 564	1.6
Jefferson	107	3.2	D	3.0	D	8.8	3.9	17.5	29.5	3 204	174	122	6 314	8.5
Jewell	43	36.5	D	D	D	6.4	5.2	8.5	25.9	1 125	297	48	2 409	-13.7
Johnson	12 772	0.1	14.4	8.2	77.5	10.1	10.8	30.4	7.9	53 673	119	2 037	144 155	40.2
Kearny	60	44.4	D	D	26.1	3.2	2.6	5.1	25.7	635	140	40	1 561	10.8
Kingman	82	6.8	27.6	15.3	D	9.1	5.7	20.2	19.0	1 983	229	69	3 645	-1.0
Kiowa	40	17.5	D	D	D	7.6	3.5	16.6	25.5	847	258	44	1 738	1.5
Labette	309	0.5	D	27.4	D	10.3	3.4	17.2	25.4	4 913	215	599	10 641	0.2
Lane	39	43.4	D	D	D	5.0	D	5.7	17.6	539	250	19	1 117	-3.6
Leavenworth	977	0.3	12.5	5.2	30.9	6.2	4.0	17.0	56.2	8 821	128	531	21 264	15.3
Lincoln	31	15.2	D	D	D	9.6	5.0	10.6	34.6	958	268	39	1 864	-11.7
Linn	75	1.0	19.3	5.1	D	7.5	6.1	9.3	23.7	2 149	225	152	4 811	21.0
Logan	40	19.1	D	D	49.7	10.6	5.2	13.5	25.2	720	236	23	1 466	-9.3
Lyon	541	1.5	35.9	31.7	39.4	9.4	2.7	14.8	23.2	4 963	138	494	14 346	2.6
McPherson	491	4.7	D	28.0	D	7.7	5.6	19.0	10.8	6 236	211	220	10 941	4.6
Marion	120	10.1	14.3	7.9	53.9	9.9	5.3	24.2	21.7	3 210	240	137	5 659	-3.5
Marshall	162	10.7	22.1	17.2	54.5	9.2	6.2	15.8	12.7	2 671	244	162	5 269	-5.6
Meade	79	48.9	5.8	0.9	D	D	2.8	8.8	15.3	938	203	28	2 049	0.0
Miami	259	-0.2	24.5	8.5	53.0	10.6	6.4	18.7	22.8	4 319	152	351	8 971	6.1
Mitchell	122	16.7	15.6	11.6	49.3	8.8	2.9	16.7	18.4	1 666	240	63	3 359	-4.3
Montgomery	485	0.4	38.9	34.2	45.8	9.4	3.5	21.2	15.0	8 573	236	928	17 920	-1.3
Morris	54	4.2	D	12.0	D	11.4	D	15.7	24.1	1 521	249	66	3 149	-1.2
Morton	53	10.0	D	D	D	7.0	4.7	7.1	32.2	610	174	38	1 515	4.2
Nemaha	141	12.9	24.3	18.5	48.5	7.8	3.9	17.8	14.4	2 463	230	120	4 319	-2.5
Neosho	232	-0.5	D	26.7	D	10.2	4.1	17.2	20.3	3 699	218	318	7 726	-2.0
Ness	45	4.3	D	1.6	D	7.4	5.4	12.3	27.8	945	274	29	2 048	-2.8
Norton	81	12.3	D	6.7	D	7.6	5.4	14.9	31.0	1 337	225	55	2 798	-6.2

1. Covers mining, construction, and manufacturing. 2. Covers private sector earnings in agricultural services, forestry, and fisheries; transportation and public utilities; wholesale trade; retail trade; finance, insurance, and real estate; and services. 3. Per 1,000 resident population estimated as of July 1 of the year shown.

Table B. States and Counties — **Housing, Labor Force, and Employment**

STATE County	Housing units, 1990 (cont'd) Occupied units Owner-occupied Total	Percent	Median value[1]	Owner cost as a percent of income With a mortgage	Without a mortgage	Renter-occupied Median rent[2]	Rent as percent of income	Sub-standard units[3] (percent)	Civilian labor force, 2001 Total	Percent change, 2000–2001	Unemployment Total	Rate[4]	Civilian employment, 1990[5] Total	Percent Professional, managerial, and technical	Precision production, craft, and repair
	89	90	91	92	93	94	95	96	97	98	99	100	101	102	103
KANSAS—Cont'd															
Barber	2 358	75.1	28 400	20.7	13.1	276	21.2	1.7	2 234	-6.2	73	3.3	2 645	17.4	11.2
Barton	11 561	72.3	37 700	18.2	12.4	299	21.9	2.2	13 682	-3.4	375	2.7	14 001	22.5	14.6
Bourbon	5 897	73.8	29 800	21.0	13.8	264	25.9	3.2	6 952	-1.2	330	4.7	6 172	23.8	9.3
Brown	4 347	70.6	28 000	15.1	12.3	240	22.0	1.7	5 357	-3.7	333	6.2	4 737	23.7	10.0
Butler	18 488	75.4	51 800	18.6	12.7	352	22.5	2.9	30 879	-2.3	1 162	3.8	24 054	27.8	17.1
Chase	1 214	75.6	22 400	19.4	12.1	247	23.3	1.0	1 411	-2.1	60	4.3	1 274	22.2	10.5
Chautauqua	1 835	79.9	18 900	20.6	14.0	263	22.8	4.1	1 594	-4.3	85	5.3	1 606	21.3	11.5
Cherokee	8 396	76.5	27 000	18.0	12.3	260	27.7	3.5	9 483	-4.1	641	6.8	8 740	20.6	14.3
Cheyenne	1 389	75.6	31 900	18.7	12.8	224	19.7	5.3	1 372	-8.8	26	1.9	1 425	16.6	8.6
Clark	1 006	75.3	29 500	14.4	13.2	288	18.7	2.0	1 266	-4.0	21	1.7	1 204	17.0	11.0
Clay	3 641	73.4	33 800	20.7	11.9	231	21.3	2.5	4 569	-1.5	176	3.9	3 984	19.6	13.2
Cloud	4 483	72.4	25 600	14.2	12.3	230	18.9	1.5	4 451	-6.0	151	3.4	5 001	22.7	10.0
Coffey	3 311	77.3	34 800	18.2	12.1	288	20.1	2.6	4 113	0.2	269	6.5	3 867	21.2	13.2
Comanche	950	71.8	24 300	16.1	12.5	227	21.2	2.9	951	-2.5	14	1.5	1 044	16.7	9.5
Cowley	14 047	71.2	37 500	18.2	12.7	321	23.3	2.0	16 851	-7.2	698	4.1	16 476	23.4	15.0
Crawford	14 606	67.5	30 700	18.3	13.0	299	29.6	2.1	18 109	-2.0	904	5.0	14 905	26.8	11.2
Decatur	1 651	75.1	28 800	17.8	14.6	249	21.9	1.6	1 517	-4.0	35	2.3	1 854	18.4	8.4
Dickinson	7 542	73.5	35 600	19.0	12.3	280	22.5	1.4	9 852	-3.5	353	3.6	8 579	21.8	11.3
Doniphan	3 074	75.4	29 200	16.6	13.2	260	21.8	3.8	3 840	-4.6	379	9.9	3 467	18.4	10.9
Douglas	30 138	52.5	68 000	19.7	12.3	413	33.8	3.0	56 150	1.4	2 474	4.4	41 086	35.1	8.1
Edwards	1 585	75.3	24 900	16.4	13.1	242	18.9	1.4	1 485	-4.0	28	1.9	1 714	19.7	11.4
Elk	1 436	80.0	14 999	19.3	13.4	188	25.4	2.3	1 377	1.0	67	4.9	1 354	19.7	12.4
Ellis	10 096	64.4	49 600	19.9	12.9	291	25.3	1.2	16 196	-1.0	422	2.6	13 255	27.1	10.3
Ellsworth	2 522	77.4	28 300	16.4	13.6	258	18.6	1.6	2 555	-8.4	65	2.5	2 688	23.6	11.5
Finney	10 836	61.5	50 800	18.7	12.8	383	22.6	7.9	18 672	-4.8	1 789	9.6	16 424	20.1	20.3
Ford	9 872	64.9	48 900	19.0	12.5	337	23.8	5.1	15 056	-3.2	405	2.7	13 258	23.8	14.4
Franklin	8 308	72.7	37 700	18.1	12.7	311	23.9	2.2	12 072	-5.1	644	5.3	10 075	22.7	13.9
Geary	10 676	45.5	55 400	20.4	12.6	366	26.6	4.4	9 890	-1.8	702	7.1	9 714	26.0	10.2
Gove	1 284	79.7	30 300	18.8	12.4	246	13.9	1.4	1 443	-3.9	23	1.6	1 404	19.2	10.1
Graham	1 435	76.8	24 900	16.2	13.2	245	18.0	2.5	1 365	-7.5	31	2.3	1 631	20.7	11.6
Grant	2 393	69.2	53 200	18.3	11.3	319	22.8	4.4	3 542	-3.7	96	2.7	3 425	16.9	17.8
Gray	1 913	72.4	45 500	18.9	11.6	287	17.0	4.1	3 059	-5.2	71	2.3	2 487	15.4	11.5
Greeley	656	70.1	39 500	23.1	14.5	297	17.2	3.2	856	3.1	31	3.6	868	18.5	9.4
Greenwood	3 285	74.2	21 900	16.8	13.2	265	25.6	1.6	3 152	-4.8	178	5.6	3 250	17.9	12.9
Hamilton	986	70.8	37 800	17.6	13.5	268	21.5	2.0	1 222	-3.9	22	1.8	1 175	17.7	9.8
Harper	3 007	73.3	32 300	17.6	13.0	264	24.4	1.4	2 803	-5.1	98	3.5	3 125	18.7	14.0
Harvey	11 581	68.4	47 100	17.7	12.4	326	22.8	2.3	17 063	-2.3	576	3.4	14 999	27.5	13.3
Haskell	1 372	70.0	45 900	17.6	12.3	330	19.4	5.1	1 941	-6.2	47	2.4	1 887	14.9	10.3
Hodgeman	826	81.0	26 800	14.9	12.3	252	17.5	2.9	954	-9.2	26	2.7	900	22.8	7.2
Jackson	4 277	81.4	34 300	17.1	13.2	249	26.5	4.7	9 249	3.0	340	3.7	5 250	21.5	12.9
Jefferson	5 778	83.9	47 100	16.6	12.8	327	22.5	4.4	8 812	-9.3	390	4.4	7 528	23.0	12.7
Jewell	1 806	78.7	14 999	15.3	12.9	201	18.0	1.3	1 846	-4.2	31	1.7	1 948	18.1	10.3
Johnson	136 433	69.4	91 500	20.2	11.8	515	23.5	1.1	266 953	-1.0	8 969	3.4	196 066	42.2	6.8
Kearny	1 379	69.4	45 900	18.8	12.4	341	20.5	6.3	1 872	-9.8	85	4.5	1 915	18.2	16.1
Kingman	3 175	75.6	34 600	17.9	13.5	287	19.0	1.4	3 875	-6.6	131	3.4	3 651	19.1	13.3
Kiowa	1 466	71.6	33 600	16.5	12.4	256	21.5	1.1	1 594	-4.7	33	2.1	1 650	19.4	10.2
Labette	9 377	73.3	29 000	16.8	13.3	290	23.4	2.4	11 380	-1.8	633	5.6	10 421	24.9	11.1
Lane	966	74.9	32 600	18.0	13.8	249	16.5	0.7	987	-6.4	38	3.9	1 050	19.6	9.5
Leavenworth	19 715	65.2	64 000	20.8	12.8	426	22.2	2.7	29 042	-0.7	1 537	5.3	23 248	28.8	11.7
Lincoln	1 531	78.8	17 200	17.8	12.9	195	20.2	1.8	1 493	-11.1	43	2.9	1 673	20.6	7.2
Linn	3 215	80.2	28 800	16.9	13.5	256	25.9	3.8	3 124	-3.8	299	9.6	3 046	21.2	18.9
Logan	1 221	76.7	30 800	16.9	12.8	238	19.8	2.3	1 433	-11.4	36	2.5	1 472	16.8	8.9
Lyon	13 059	61.3	45 800	18.5	13.1	301	25.8	3.4	19 170	-2.1	914	4.8	16 719	23.1	15.2
McPherson	10 230	73.1	47 900	18.0	12.2	300	21.1	1.7	15 807	-2.8	482	3.0	13 640	23.4	13.2
Marion	4 975	79.1	30 700	17.3	11.9	261	21.9	2.0	6 747	-3.3	175	2.6	5 896	20.2	11.9
Marshall	4 689	78.0	26 300	16.0	12.4	241	22.7	2.7	5 941	-2.0	208	3.5	5 033	19.9	10.5
Meade	1 667	72.5	34 800	15.9	12.4	280	18.0	2.7	1 923	-9.4	40	2.1	2 065	23.2	10.3
Miami	8 402	77.1	47 700	18.9	13.0	328	23.7	2.9	14 188	-1.0	602	4.2	11 093	22.5	15.8
Mitchell	2 846	74.0	28 800	16.5	13.1	257	24.7	1.5	3 676	-0.4	90	2.4	3 251	22.3	9.2
Montgomery	15 670	72.3	29 400	19.0	13.4	290	24.6	1.9	18 381	-3.3	1 186	6.5	16 545	23.4	15.2
Morris	2 528	75.8	33 500	16.7	12.4	259	21.3	2.2	3 048	-4.4	106	3.5	2 725	20.4	10.4
Morton	1 290	72.7	44 700	17.0	12.4	300	21.3	3.7	1 609	-2.9	39	2.4	1 547	20.7	11.4
Nemaha	3 996	80.6	35 400	19.1	13.0	241	21.8	3.4	5 124	-6.0	169	3.3	4 820	21.3	10.5
Neosho	6 748	74.8	28 600	17.9	13.0	273	23.2	1.9	8 223	-3.0	476	5.8	7 553	22.7	13.2
Ness	1 670	80.0	29 900	17.4	13.6	249	17.6	0.7	1 875	0.5	33	1.8	1 882	20.6	9.9
Norton	2 330	74.9	25 700	12.8	12.4	242	19.6	1.3	2 939	-4.0	47	1.6	2 715	23.7	9.9

1. Specified owner-occupied units. 2. Specified renter-occupied units. 3. Overcrowded or lacking complete plumbing facilities. 4. Percent of civilian labor force. 5. Persons 16 years and older.

Table B. States and Counties — Nonfarm Employment and Agriculture

	Private nonfarm establishments, employment and payroll, 1999									Agriculture, 1997			
	Employment						Annual payroll		Farms			Farm operators
										Percent with—		
STATE County	Number of establishments	Total	Health Care and Social Assistance	Manufacturing	Retail trade	Finance and Insurance	Professional Scientific and Technical Services	Total (mil dol)	Average per employee (dollars)	Number	Less than 50 acres	500 acres and over	Whose principal occupation is farming (percent)
	104	105	106	107	108	109	110	111	112	113	114	115	116

KANSAS—Cont'd

Barber	213	1 471	328	D	340	77	29	29	19 650	433	8.5	54.7	64.9
Barton	1 046	10 762	1 793	1 736	1 785	403	392	234	21 700	742	10.9	44.9	64.3
Bourbon	431	6 514	1 067	1 353	614	642	126	135	20 666	805	14.8	24.1	45.7
Brown	278	3 538	658	510	445	138	96	66	18 751	599	15.5	33.6	62.3
Butler	1 265	11 735	1 867	1 875	2 065	496	310	261	22 274	1 256	20.9	26.7	45.0
Chase	72	422	D	D	100	D	D	7	16 408	285	11.6	48.8	58.6
Chautauqua	91	560	221	D	83	34	10	8	14 998	376	12.2	43.1	55.9
Cherokee	404	5 430	615	2 280	620	129	131	128	23 615	725	26.3	19.0	49.5
Cheyenne	113	551	154	D	105	31	19	10	17 550	398	4.8	61.1	70.1
Clark	79	433	149	D	56	49	15	9	20 843	260	7.3	56.5	65.0
Clay	296	2 540	511	369	503	118	51	45	17 657	546	11.5	44.0	67.2
Cloud	361	3 093	705	347	593	153	69	58	18 772	545	14.3	44.0	60.0
Coffey	258	2 892	421	269	406	85	D	97	33 446	555	11.0	32.1	54.2
Comanche	71	439	133	62	64	38	D	7	15 428	256	5.5	65.6	74.2
Cowley	854	12 082	2 428	3 604	1 640	355	150	266	21 979	962	16.5	27.3	50.4
Crawford	1 011	14 506	2 264	3 590	1 940	408	340	305	21 047	787	21.9	21.0	48.2
Decatur	120	751	206	D	89	37	39	11	15 220	396	10.1	60.1	70.2
Dickinson	542	5 683	869	1 214	846	198	127	111	19 502	893	13.0	38.1	60.2
Doniphan	169	2 233	170	1 002	277	77	25	53	23 715	507	17.6	29.4	57.8
Douglas	2 594	36 795	4 629	4 315	6 211	1 325	1 791	780	21 210	839	30.3	13.8	42.9
Edwards	109	760	175	225	56	44	11	14	18 642	302	3.0	59.9	72.2
Elk	66	242	D	D	D	D	D	3	13 715	383	12.0	41.0	53.8
Ellis	1 016	12 037	3 184	1 087	2 070	374	808	241	19 991	674	8.2	42.4	54.5
Ellsworth	194	1 635	376	249	261	70	120	34	21 078	424	6.6	50.9	64.4
Finney	1 003	16 073	1 549	5 795	2 482	441	448	367	22 859	520	9.4	62.3	69.0
Ford	858	13 105	1 267	4 800	2 102	306	501	308	23 486	692	11.1	49.3	58.1
Franklin	600	7 351	982	941	1 123	198	149	170	23 140	956	22.7	16.9	42.9
Geary	574	8 086	1 207	897	1 132	246	202	148	18 303	223	17.5	41.7	60.1
Gove	133	789	238	95	188	25	8	13	16 649	439	5.9	62.0	74.7
Graham	112	706	237	D	142	56	9	11	15 711	382	6.5	56.0	64.1
Grant	258	2 242	153	170	414	115	46	57	25 411	257	6.2	62.6	70.0
Gray	205	1 214	137	39	157	115	36	27	22 360	461	5.4	66.4	74.8
Greeley	60	346	113	0	62	16	D	6	17 850	273	2.9	62.3	66.7
Greenwood	234	1 545	408	93	252	71	40	26	16 997	593	11.1	39.0	56.3
Hamilton	84	599	D	0	112	38	13	10	17 052	267	4.1	70.0	68.2
Harper	221	1 416	259	225	217	96	31	26	18 438	529	9.6	46.3	61.6
Harvey	804	12 173	2 585	3 212	1 710	284	162	273	22 451	779	23.2	27.5	56.5
Haskell	113	718	D	D	72	65	18	17	24 292	241	3.3	70.5	78.8
Hodgeman	45	315	D	D	55	D	9	6	18 670	359	4.5	67.7	67.7
Jackson	283	3 159	383	150	490	95	39	56	17 879	1 050	18.1	17.1	41.3
Jefferson	352	2 161	403	177	407	97	71	43	19 828	1 018	22.1	13.6	41.2
Jewell	109	531	D	D	91	59	12	7	13 953	579	7.4	47.5	73.2
Johnson	15 507	270 599	21 184	21 175	35 906	20 659	23 567	8 948	33 067	604	41.6	11.9	37.7
Kearny	88	530	111	0	63	44	9	13	24 753	271	2.6	66.8	76.0
Kingman	213	2 025	485	470	264	112	40	42	20 955	759	11.7	40.8	58.1
Kiowa	119	954	282	D	145	35	11	17	18 036	318	3.8	58.2	62.3
Labette	529	8 003	2 117	2 444	1 053	312	134	174	21 760	901	17.8	22.3	46.1
Lane	91	386	D	D	56	31	D	8	20 174	287	5.9	65.5	67.6
Leavenworth	1 104	14 314	3 098	723	2 094	770	811	354	24 726	1 046	33.0	8.3	41.1
Lincoln	111	737	176	D	100	37	23	12	15 626	454	8.1	51.8	70.0
Linn	201	1 323	122	148	190	76	48	37	27 683	757	16.0	21.4	45.6
Logan	138	688	145	D	141	49	25	13	19 507	326	5.5	66.6	69.3
Lyon	919	15 177	1 782	5 864	2 237	344	248	332	21 891	855	15.3	29.2	49.1
McPherson	947	12 905	1 808	3 909	1 367	648	198	309	23 943	1 163	16.2	30.8	56.7
Marion	340	3 057	650	306	571	126	97	51	16 726	968	16.2	36.3	60.6
Marshall	400	3 534	632	810	491	273	174	72	20 307	922	13.8	66.4	66.4
Meade	153	860	169	15	181	49	31	17	19 492	416	6.5	62.0	63.9
Miami	619	6 454	1 680	634	1 370	268	164	139	21 603	1 245	33.5	10.5	34.9
Mitchell	278	2 548	469	399	449	116	87	51	19 962	487	11.5	54.2	72.7
Montgomery	1 029	14 178	1 963	5 282	1 955	373	248	311	21 902	964	19.7	16.2	40.9
Morris	161	1 212	218	252	239	59	48	21	17 732	489	13.3	41.3	61.1
Morton	117	931	D	D	100	37	D	21	22 631	233	3.4	59.2	67.0
Nemaha	388	3 825	737	1 031	500	150	109	82	21 545	1 007	12.3	28.6	63.0
Neosho	536	6 443	1 018	2 100	940	217	130	134	20 725	722	18.8	26.0	47.2
Ness	157	956	243	36	106	53	28	18	18 910	516	3.1	62.6	69.0
Norton	218	1 772	398	164	244	97	66	34	19 141	399	10.5	56.6	63.7

			Agriculture, 1997 (cont'd)												
	Land in farms				Value of land and buildings			Value of products sold				Percent of farms with sales of —			
STATE County			Acres				Value of machinery and equipment average per farm ($1,000)			Percent from —				Percent of land owned by fed. gov. 1997	Water consumption 1995 (mil gal/day)
	Acreage (1,000)	Percent change, 1992–1997	Average size of farm	Total irrigated (1,000)	Total cropland (1,000)	Average per farm ($1,000)	Average per acre (dollars)		Total (mil dol)	Average per farm (dollars)	Crops	Livestock and poultry products	$10,000 or more	$100,000 or more		
	117	118	119	120	121	122	123	124	125	126	127	128	129	130	131	132
KANSAS—Cont'd																
Barber	595	-6.9	1 374	5	194	484	353	75	48	111 277	34.9	65.1	73.0	27.3	0.0	4.7
Barton	613	5.6	826	43	488	465	573	84	186	250 210	28.5	71.5	73.2	25.1	0.0	38.2
Bourbon	329	-2.2	409	D	158	212	493	36	30	36 775	42.0	58.0	49.2	8.7	0.0	3.3
Brown	333	-1.8	556	D	267	538	961	104	70	117 284	67.0	33.0	75.0	29.4	0.0	2.1
Butler	759	-0.9	604	1	314	420	715	42	133	106 255	21.7	78.3	49.1	15.4	0.3	12.8
Chase	409	16.3	1 436	D	88	671	490	65	65	227 296	11.7	88.3	72.3	29.1	0.0	0.9
Chautauqua	391	1.1	1 041	D	61	439	414	33	29	77 171	23.5	76.5	54.5	15.4	0.4	1.2
Cherokee	269	-0.6	371	D	208	284	752	66	52	71 982	57.0	43.0	50.6	15.2	0.0	92.3
Cheyenne	562	-5.0	1 413	46	368	675	473	100	54	134 530	54.3	45.7	75.1	28.9	0.0	38.0
Clark	546	-3.4	2 098	17	196	1 059	499	84	105	405 162	12.0	88.0	73.1	28.8	0.0	5.3
Clay	369	-3.3	675	15	258	383	608	85	64	117 455	51.8	48.2	74.7	30.6	2.2	14.5
Cloud	393	-3.4	722	15	280	401	570	82	46	84 095	73.3	26.7	67.7	26.6	0.0	15.2
Coffey	307	-13.1	553	0	201	334	610	70	39	70 825	59.4	40.6	63.6	19.6	3.3	23.5
Comanche	504	3.5	1 969	6	168	805	390	66	29	113 712	40.0	60.0	78.9	32.4	0.0	7.7
Cowley	643	2.3	668	2	276	354	540	45	68	70 197	34.5	65.5	57.5	14.1	0.6	9.6
Crawford	291	-4.1	369	1	189	221	638	47	35	44 735	66.0	34.0	50.1	11.9	0.0	6.8
Decatur	515	-2.1	1 301	12	322	558	434	101	68	170 679	37.8	62.2	81.6	31.3	0.0	13.2
Dickinson	514	0.0	576	3	381	373	638	79	92	102 847	47.3	52.7	68.2	25.3	0.3	5.2
Doniphan	222	9.9	438	1	174	458	1 161	73	47	92 913	84.6	15.4	67.9	27.2	0.0	0.9
Douglas	219	-1.6	260	2	147	297	1 135	53	39	46 347	55.6	44.4	39.8	10.1	3.1	21.6
Edwards	357	-11.5	1 181	77	283	671	495	123	82	271 217	50.2	49.8	77.8	42.4	0.0	95.5
Elk	331	2.1	864	0	78	368	428	31	21	53 571	20.4	79.6	55.1	13.1	0.0	1.4
Ellis	507	-7.3	753	2	313	320	403	63	50	74 479	30.9	69.1	63.1	10.8	0.0	4.9
Ellsworth	376	-15.0	886	1	234	344	432	71	29	68 823	62.4	37.6	74.5	24.3	2.2	2.8
Finney	761	2.2	1 464	230	631	951	588	195	480	922 739	21.7	78.3	77.1	49.8	0.0	295.3
Ford	669	-0.3	967	70	524	483	508	130	308	445 514	15.8	84.2	70.2	29.6	0.0	103.7
Franklin	303	-4.1	317	1	193	317	975	38	47	49 466	51.0	49.0	45.5	11.1	0.0	3.2
Geary	154	-6.1	690	3	74	375	517	51	19	85 257	36.9	63.1	59.6	20.2	8.2	8.5
Gove	649	-3.5	1 478	14	389	682	477	116	122	277 233	24.2	75.8	81.5	34.9	0.0	20.1
Graham	486	-5.3	1 271	9	304	458	333	79	42	109 256	45.2	54.8	72.3	22.0	0.0	10.8
Grant	333	-2.7	1 294	109	277	888	660	175	291	1 133 381	14.8	85.2	76.7	49.4	0.0	173.0
Gray	556	7.3	1 206	165	469	786	663	172	374	810 604	20.8	79.2	84.2	55.5	0.0	225.6
Greeley	442	4.2	1 618	18	399	720	444	119	123	449 010	21.0	79.0	72.2	32.6	0.0	26.4
Greenwood	634	5.0	1 069	0	153	516	475	54	58	97 740	14.8	85.2	58.0	18.5	2.1	2.0
Hamilton	528	-1.0	1 976	22	397	711	353	117	176	658 671	12.5	87.5	68.9	36.3	0.0	47.4
Harper	461	-7.6	871	1	319	459	494	65	55	104 318	56.9	43.1	72.8	29.1	0.0	3.1
Harvey	321	0.3	412	28	282	449	1 001	85	71	91 652	58.4	41.6	63.4	24.6	0.0	41.9
Haskell	369	0.5	1 530	176	327	1 321	828	241	432	1 794 382	17.4	82.6	83.0	66.0	0.0	291.1
Hodgeman	485	1.0	1 351	24	344	536	423	89	96	268 587	20.2	79.8	77.2	30.4	0.0	32.8
Jackson	321	-5.5	306	D	190	206	660	31	29	27 536	47.9	52.1	47.0	7.2	0.0	2.0
Jefferson	269	-1.1	264	2	176	239	844	38	35	34 126	55.4	44.6	39.1	9.2	4.6	3.1
Jewell	459	-5.3	793	8	315	418	541	89	51	88 470	62.6	37.4	76.2	26.8	0.4	78.1
Johnson	136	-3.7	225	1	88	488	2 349	37	37	61 808	39.7	60.3	37.7	9.6	3.2	12.3
Kearny	526	1.7	1 940	80	381	890	468	148	185	681 602	24.5	75.5	75.3	42.4	0.0	192.3
Kingman	521	-4.3	686	12	351	366	532	72	56	73 880	61.4	38.6	68.5	22.5	0.1	16.4
Kiowa	442	10.5	1 390	40	268	640	446	91	47	149 012	57.5	42.5	72.0	28.0	0.0	51.2
Labette	331	-4.5	368	D	212	229	628	48	59	64 989	35.4	64.6	49.1	10.9	3.3	4.6
Lane	435	3.9	1 517	14	321	595	410	97	134	468 159	16.2	83.8	81.9	36.2	0.0	20.5
Leavenworth	202	-2.5	193	0	126	335	1 724	31	42	40 615	66.2	33.8	36.6	5.9	2.2	9.7
Lincoln	428	-11.3	942	1	248	481	514	60	34	75 796	67.8	32.2	74.9	24.2	0.3	1.3
Linn	278	1.5	367	0	157	217	669	31	30	39 646	46.9	53.1	41.9	8.9	1.6	727.2
Logan	628	4.1	1 926	16	362	647	341	86	36	111 259	62.9	37.1	78.8	28.8	0.0	8.0
Lyon	496	2.0	580	D	257	333	573	61	77	90 555	30.8	69.2	59.6	13.5	1.0	8.9
McPherson	523	-2.8	449	29	412	346	847	64	113	97 196	53.4	46.6	73.0	23.5	0.1	29.9
Marion	563	-4.3	582	2	368	394	717	70	81	83 990	45.6	54.4	70.8	22.6	0.8	3.3
Marshall	514	-10.3	558	1	358	401	718	70	70	76 208	63.1	36.9	72.5	24.6	1.0	3.1
Meade	555	-7.0	1 333	115	349	606	470	124	113	270 837	45.9	54.1	77.4	38.5	0.0	157.5
Miami	280	-2.5	225	1	175	321	1 440	41	40	32 050	45.2	54.8	34.4	5.9	1.3	4.0
Mitchell	455	-5.1	933	5	357	533	598	116	87	177 710	49.3	50.7	78.4	36.6	2.7	12.2
Montgomery	328	1.3	341	1	184	217	627	53	46	47 225	37.3	62.7	37.8	7.0	2.8	8.7
Morris	396	-3.4	810	0	186	386	516	71	47	96 583	37.1	62.9	71.4	21.1	0.5	1.8
Morton	422	-1.1	1 813	42	268	653	374	178	58	247 839	35.4	64.6	68.2	29.6	22.0	55.6
Nemaha	418	-5.3	415	0	305	301	738	60	91	89 977	37.0	63.0	73.9	23.7	0.0	3.0
Neosho	345	5.5	478	D	221	272	536	53	38	52 556	52.3	47.7	47.5	13.0	0.0	3.2
Ness	623	-6.7	1 208	3	414	380	334	73	34	66 584	56.2	43.8	78.9	20.0	0.0	5.6
Norton	479	2.7	1 200	8	289	621	432	81	42	104 447	50.0	50.0	73.7	30.3	0.9	12.2

Table B. States and Counties — **Residential Construction, Wholesale and Retail Trade, and Real Estate**

STATE County	Value of Residential Construction Authorized by Building Permits, 2000		Wholesale Trade, 1997				Retail Trade[1], 1997				Real Estate and Rental and Leasing, 1997			
	New Construction ($1,000)	Number of Housing Units	Number of Establish-ments	Number of Employees	Sales (mil dol)	Annual Payroll (mil dol)	Number of Establish-ments	Number of Employees	Sales (mil dol)	Annual Payroll (mil dol)	Number of Establish-ments	Number of Employees	Receipts (mil dol)	Annual Payroll (mil dol)
	133	134	135	136	137	138	139	140	141	142	143	144	145	146
KANSAS—Cont'd														
Barber	92	1	12	97	35.7	2.0	39	271	35.1	3.9	2	D	D	D
Barton	1 396	12	92	737	206.2	18.2	185	1 803	282.8	28.7	17	48	3.4	1.0
Bourbon	820	17	24	475	233.2	9.8	69	606	95.2	8.8	11	38	2.4	0.6
Brown	1 811	32	27	152	73.6	3.7	51	407	67.1	5.4	5	12	1.0	0.2
Butler	57 731	522	67	368	136.2	8.8	194	1 875	350.3	29.3	38	96	7.0	1.4
Chase	0	0	2	D	D	D	14	103	8.3	0.8	NA	NA	NA	NA
Chautauqua	NA	NA	7	39	9.3	0.8	19	98	10.9	0.9	NA	NA	NA	NA
Cherokee	924	18	18	134	210.5	3.4	91	621	93.2	7.8	9	26	0.8	0.2
Cheyenne	240	1	11	118	57.8	2.7	30	125	17.7	1.4	3	4	0.3	0.1
Clark	908	7	5	D	D	D	19	62	7.6	0.8	NA	NA	NA	NA
Clay	1 930	25	18	140	55.4	3.2	61	487	63.4	6.3	5	12	1.1	0.1
Cloud	0	0	22	238	110.5	5.5	71	608	83.2	7.7	8	D	D	D
Coffey	3 088	34	9	76	38.5	2.1	50	418	58.8	5.2	6	11	0.4	0.1
Comanche	0	0	4	D	D	D	14	71	8.4	0.8	NA	NA	NA	NA
Cowley	9 104	108	38	343	118.9	8.9	173	1 682	255.5	24.2	22	67	4.7	1.5
Crawford	10 708	146	53	624	173.3	17.0	180	2 132	296.5	27.7	29	112	9.2	1.5
Decatur	0	0	15	144	74.3	2.9	23	108	10.2	1.1	5	3	1.4	0.2
Dickinson	4 692	48	25	365	220.6	8.8	110	900	125.0	11.4	10	D	D	D
Doniphan	1 337	15	11	D	D	D	27	322	43.2	4.0	4	7	0.6	0.0
Douglas	83 869	803	88	777	248.8	21.0	453	5 664	758.5	80.3	122	434	46.4	6.6
Edwards	0	0	8	87	57.6	2.6	15	64	7.6	0.7	NA	NA	NA	NA
Elk	NA	NA	6	18	10.9	0.4	8	30	3.7	0.2	2	D	D	D
Ellis	3 457	35	46	411	93.1	8.3	216	2 207	326.7	32.3	36	122	10.3	1.8
Ellsworth	746	10	12	D	D	D	41	242	30.3	2.5	3	3	0.1	0.0
Finney	4 355	62	84	791	495.5	26.2	186	2 502	405.0	38.3	45	147	16.2	3.1
Ford	6 722	66	55	607	347.8	17.3	169	2 016	367.4	31.9	37	114	11.0	1.7
Franklin	17 163	149	29	487	298.4	11.4	89	1 114	167.2	15.3	16	47	2.5	0.5
Geary	4 322	43	18	153	60.1	2.7	99	1 174	181.1	17.9	33	121	10.7	1.6
Gove	0	0	11	74	31.8	1.7	22	122	19.3	1.4	1	D	D	D
Graham	0	0	9	39	16.9	1.0	21	133	25.3	2.1	NA	NA	NA	NA
Grant	772	7	20	165	97.8	4.9	39	371	60.1	6.1	5	26	1.8	0.3
Gray	806	10	23	189	126.5	6.0	28	163	33.2	2.7	2	D	D	D
Greeley	70	1	3	D	D	D	11	59	9.2	0.9	2	D	D	D
Greenwood	147	2	14	70	6.2	0.7	41	215	36.6	2.9	5	10	0.3	0.0
Hamilton	376	3	11	136	53.8	3.0	16	81	14.3	1.0	2	D	D	D
Harper	605	6	18	168	76.8	3.8	39	266	38.7	2.9	3	8	0.2	0.1
Harvey	14 776	124	35	280	181.2	7.7	156	1 608	185.8	19.1	27	56	4.7	0.7
Haskell	0	0	13	146	92.3	4.7	15	84	10.6	0.9	NA	NA	NA	NA
Hodgeman	NA	NA	4	D	D	D	9	55	11.3	0.6	NA	NA	NA	NA
Jackson	4 708	58	12	45	25.0	0.8	50	489	73.9	6.4	6	D	D	D
Jefferson	11 411	121	10	30	9.6	0.5	60	353	51.4	4.2	8	D	D	D
Jewell	0	0	8	76	50.2	1.2	27	89	9.3	0.9	1	D	D	D
Johnson	656 481	5 468	1 502	19 597	21 107.6	789.6	1 903	30 545	5 418.8	543.2	646	4 947	681.3	119.5
Kearny	1 165	19	7	35	24.1	1.0	14	69	5.8	0.6	1	D	D	D
Kingman	2 768	25	15	129	51.6	3.7	41	290	36.2	3.6	4	12	0.4	0.1
Kiowa	0	0	7	50	30.2	1.4	21	176	20.2	1.9	NA	NA	NA	NA
Labette	3 831	66	29	214	81.7	4.6	120	1 021	147.5	14.1	10	37	3.4	0.6
Lane	0	0	9	69	36.0	1.6	17	62	8.9	0.8	NA	NA	NA	NA
Leavenworth	44 124	431	24	D	D	D	178	2 081	359.2	31.6	39	152	16.0	2.2
Lincoln	85	2	15	93	37.5	1.4	22	104	14.6	1.2	1	D	D	D
Linn	3 569	26	6	24	8.6	0.4	34	241	30.1	2.7	2	D	D	D
Logan	0	0	8	72	30.6	1.5	28	249	43.9	3.1	NA	NA	NA	NA
Lyon	2 735	34	41	571	197.3	14.0	172	1 982	285.5	29.3	32	118	7.7	1.6
McPherson	13 193	107	52	337	165.6	9.4	155	1 378	213.7	19.4	20	50	3.8	0.7
Marion	4 463	52	17	215	79.0	4.6	80	482	97.3	7.8	5	12	0.8	0.1
Marshall	337	3	24	206	115.2	5.6	74	490	76.5	6.0	5	5	0.2	0.0
Meade	200	2	10	87	66.8	2.4	32	171	21.3	2.0	3	D	D	D
Miami	23 812	156	21	D	D	D	91	1 163	170.6	16.3	17	65	6.2	0.9
Mitchell	258	2	25	247	133.5	6.1	41	448	79.7	6.7	3	11	0.3	0.0
Montgomery	814	14	52	472	124.4	10.9	223	2 013	264.2	25.4	36	130	7.0	1.7
Morris	565	9	6	24	8.0	0.5	39	239	40.1	2.9	3	9	0.5	0.1
Morton	0	0	13	146	78.8	3.7	19	84	10.8	1.2	NA	NA	NA	NA
Nemaha	3 234	28	21	135	58.5	3.0	82	490	88.1	6.5	5	D	D	D
Neosho	1 477	16	37	297	125.2	8.2	107	925	149.1	12.7	8	18	1.2	0.2
Ness	136	3	18	118	39.4	2.9	25	103	13.3	1.2	1	D	D	D
Norton	216	2	15	92	66.1	1.5	37	263	32.7	2.8	2	D	D	D

1. Establishments with payroll.

STATE County	Professional, Scientific, and Technical Services[1], 1997				Manufacturing, 1997				Accommodation and Foodservices, 1997			
	Number of Establish-ments	Number of Employees	Receipts (mil dol)	Annual Payroll (mil dol)	Number of Establish-ments	Number of Employees	Receipts (mil dol)	Annual Payroll (mil dol)	Number of Establish-ments	Number of Employees	Sales (mil dol)	Annual Payroll (mil dol)
	147	148	149	150	151	152	153	154	155	156	157	158
KANSAS—Cont'd												
Barber	7	27	1.7	0.4	NA	NA	NA	NA	16	121	2.4	0.7
Barton	65	699	26.0	13.5	45	1 608	308.1	34.0	71	959	26.8	7.2
Bourbon	23	111	7.0	3.4	29	1 295	149.0	29.4	60	D	D	D
Brown	12	70	4.3	1.8	18	820	75.8	18.0	20	248	5.4	1.4
Butler	63	198	11.2	3.9	52	1 704	1 132.7	58.8	96	1 400	37.6	10.6
Chase	4	9	0.4	0.1	NA	NA	NA	NA	8	D	D	D
Chautauqua	5	6	0.3	0.1	NA	NA	NA	NA	10	58	1.0	0.2
Cherokee	21	86	8.2	1.8	44	2 291	343.5	59.6	29	285	7.3	2.0
Cheyenne	4	11	0.7	0.2	NA	NA	NA	NA	9	51	1.2	0.3
Clark	5	12	0.4	0.2	NA	NA	NA	NA	6	D	D	D
Clay	10	41	1.6	0.7	NA	NA	NA	NA	21	256	4.6	1.3
Cloud	9	55	2.3	1.2	NA	NA	NA	NA	28	314	7.9	2.0
Coffey	11	20	0.8	0.3	NA	NA	NA	NA	21	172	4.6	1.2
Comanche	3	4	0.1	0.0	NA	NA	NA	NA	10	32	1.0	0.2
Cowley	36	148	8.2	3.2	47	3 793	1 176.7	107.3	74	1 002	25.6	6.5
Crawford	53	354	18.1	7.2	74	3 206	519.3	77.2	96	1 623	50.7	14.0
Decatur	7	43	1.9	0.7	NA	NA	NA	NA	7	D	D	D
Dickinson	24	95	7.9	1.7	25	1 161	160.9	24.6	49	494	12.6	3.6
Doniphan	7	24	0.7	0.2	8	D	D	D	10	51	1.3	0.4
Douglas	192	1 280	84.5	33.1	76	4 240	728.8	120.0	240	4 627	120.7	34.2
Edwards	5	14	0.4	0.1	NA	NA	NA	NA	11	D	D	D
Elk	4	4	0.2	0.1	NA	NA	NA	NA	8	D	D	D
Ellis	58	262	17.7	6.3	28	1 061	95.1	20.6	89	1 717	43.6	11.8
Ellsworth	8	77	4.7	2.1	NA	NA	NA	NA	16	122	3.5	0.9
Finney	59	450	22.3	9.2	38	5 416	2 420.2	123.4	68	1 310	40.2	11.1
Ford	49	439	27.6	12.5	29	D	D	D	69	1 102	35.4	9.6
Franklin	31	123	7.1	2.4	25	806	151.0	22.0	43	603	17.1	4.7
Geary	23	136	7.6	2.8	NA	NA	NA	NA	77	1 128	28.7	9.5
Gove	4	4	0.2	0.0	NA	NA	NA	NA	7	D	D	D
Graham	4	13	0.4	0.2	NA	NA	NA	NA	10	108	1.4	0.3
Grant	10	26	1.9	0.4	NA	NA	NA	NA	23	243	7.0	1.6
Gray	12	41	1.7	0.6	NA	NA	NA	NA	9	44	1.0	0.3
Greeley	2	D	D	D	NA	NA	NA	NA	5	30	0.5	0.1
Greenwood	13	29	1.0	0.3	NA	NA	NA	NA	27	D	D	D
Hamilton	7	18	0.9	0.2	NA	NA	NA	NA	7	59	1.2	0.3
Harper	12	33	1.3	0.4	NA	NA	NA	NA	22	172	4.4	1.1
Harvey	40	140	9.4	3.8	55	2 855	446.6	87.9	65	942	25.5	7.5
Haskell	3	11	0.7	0.3	NA	NA	NA	NA	8	51	1.2	0.3
Hodgeman	3	5	0.1	0.0	NA	NA	NA	NA	4	D	D	D
Jackson	11	39	1.4	0.4	NA	NA	NA	NA	20	271	5.8	1.6
Jefferson	16	35	1.5	0.5	NA	NA	NA	NA	33	148	4.2	0.7
Jewell	4	11	0.6	0.2	NA	NA	NA	NA	11	75	1.2	0.4
Johnson	1 780	18 416	2 032.6	810.1	551	20 590	3 659.3	662.8	827	19 029	636.3	188.5
Kearny	2	D	D	D	NA	NA	NA	NA	6	47	1.1	0.2
Kingman	12	44	1.9	0.8	NA	NA	NA	NA	18	197	4.4	1.2
Kiowa	5	9	0.3	0.1	NA	NA	NA	NA	11	89	1.8	0.6
Labette	23	103	5.6	2.6	40	2 298	254.5	64.4	45	548	13.3	3.7
Lane	4	9	0.4	0.1	NA	NA	NA	NA	4	D	D	D
Leavenworth	71	680	75.5	20.2	36	645	62.3	16.2	85	1 409	37.4	10.8
Lincoln	7	18	0.6	0.2	NA	NA	NA	NA	7	62	1.0	0.2
Linn	12	21	1.0	0.4	NA	NA	NA	NA	12	54	1.8	0.4
Logan	5	8	0.3	0.1	NA	NA	NA	NA	11	77	2.1	0.5
Lyon	38	200	9.6	4.3	40	6 478	2 054.1	167.1	104	1 633	37.3	10.0
McPherson	47	154	9.3	2.6	68	3 845	1 633.5	131.2	64	992	22.9	6.3
Marion	17	81	19.7	1.8	NA	NA	NA	NA	34	264	5.4	1.5
Marshall	10	37	1.7	0.6	21	880	106.8	23.0	36	257	6.1	1.5
Meade	6	20	0.8	0.2	NA	NA	NA	NA	8	62	1.4	0.3
Miami	32	95	6.9	2.0	31	682	58.2	19.1	36	456	11.2	3.3
Mitchell	12	35	2.3	0.6	NA	NA	NA	NA	24	274	5.1	1.5
Montgomery	59	209	12.7	4.4	61	4 590	1 482.9	121.6	87	1 164	30.3	8.5
Morris	8	51	2.4	0.6	NA	NA	NA	NA	10	D	D	D
Morton	6	19	1.0	0.3	NA	NA	NA	NA	10	90	2.4	0.6
Nemaha	20	62	3.9	1.7	19	1 047	209.5	30.3	31	256	5.0	1.4
Neosho	30	119	5.8	2.2	40	2 281	289.0	53.7	41	497	11.1	3.0
Ness	7	24	1.1	0.3	NA	NA	NA	NA	14	D	D	D
Norton	11	41	2.3	0.6	NA	NA	NA	NA	14	157	4.0	0.9

1. Firms subject to federal tax.

STATE County	Health Care and Social Assistance[1], 1997				Other Services[1], 1997				Federal funds and grants, fiscal 2001[2] Expenditures (mil dol)			
										Direct payments for individuals[3]		
	Number of Establishments	Number of Employees	Receipts (mil dol)	Annual Payroll (mil dol)	Number of Establishments	Number of Employees	Receipts (mil dol)	Annual Payroll (mil dol)	Total	Social Security and government retirement	Medicare	Food stamps and Supplemental Security Income
	159	160	161	162	163	164	165	166	167	168	169	170
KANSAS—Cont'd												
Barber	8	87	2.5	1.2	13	28	2.3	0.4	39.3	15.8	7.7	0.5
Barton	72	723	38.8	18.6	66	275	19.3	5.2	145.6	67.2	29.2	3.5
Bourbon	32	509	20.9	11.7	19	52	3.8	0.7	93.0	39.0	18.9	2.1
Brown	18	226	9.0	4.4	20	41	3.7	0.7	85.7	27.3	11.6	1.5
Butler	82	966	45.9	19.3	81	263	17.3	3.9	211.7	115.5	36.1	4.3
Chase	2	D	D	D	5	8	0.7	0.1	18.1	7.4	3.5	0.3
Chautauqua	8	165	3.9	2.2	2	D	D	D	29.8	13.2	6.0	0.7
Cherokee	21	290	9.2	4.1	14	37	2.4	0.6	127.7	51.4	23.7	5.1
Cheyenne	7	27	1.2	0.5	3	3	0.4	0.0	41.7	9.4	4.7	0.1
Clark	4	D	D	D	6	18	0.8	0.2	21.0	6.8	3.6	0.2
Clay	14	191	6.4	3.4	22	65	3.9	0.7	63.5	25.7	10.2	0.7
Cloud	23	149	7.5	3.6	19	93	6.6	2.0	83.0	29.7	14.9	1.0
Coffey	13	125	3.6	1.5	15	25	2.3	0.4	51.3	20.0	10.4	0.7
Comanche	5	D	D	D	5	31	1.1	0.3	18.2	6.6	2.8	0.1
Cowley	57	801	34.7	14.6	52	197	11.2	2.5	244.0	87.2	32.0	5.4
Crawford	82	1 022	38.8	17.0	59	519	48.0	12.7	214.3	87.6	39.9	6.3
Decatur	6	37	2.1	1.0	4	5	0.8	0.2	39.6	11.0	4.8	0.3
Dickinson	35	237	8.5	3.8	37	115	10.9	1.5	120.0	58.0	18.3	1.7
Doniphan	8	129	2.6	1.6	10	26	2.3	0.5	53.7	17.2	7.7	1.1
Douglas	175	1 648	88.7	41.8	132	782	42.5	13.5	349.5	136.2	39.4	7.1
Edwards	7	72	3.6	1.3	9	20	1.2	0.3	41.0	8.9	5.6	0.3
Elk	NA	NA	NA	NA	5	13	0.8	0.2	23.7	10.0	4.7	0.5
Ellis	70	623	42.9	19.4	71	302	23.1	5.2	127.3	52.3	24.2	2.2
Ellsworth	10	145	6.7	3.0	11	27	1.9	0.3	42.7	15.8	9.4	0.3
Finney	48	576	40.4	19.0	75	399	23.1	6.8	138.3	46.7	16.9	3.4
Ford	60	774	65.7	24.5	51	227	13.6	3.6	136.8	49.3	19.6	3.0
Franklin	41	417	17.7	8.4	33	126	8.8	2.1	152.2	52.9	23.0	3.2
Geary	39	283	13.0	5.4	54	529	20.8	10.3	542.2	78.4	9.7	4.4
Gove	2	D	D	D	13	30	2.6	0.4	35.3	7.9	4.3	0.1
Graham	7	25	2.1	0.5	6	15	1.2	0.2	33.9	8.8	4.5	0.2
Grant	9	35	3.3	1.1	15	59	5.3	1.1	44.2	10.8	4.3	0.7
Gray	5	D	D	D	11	22	2.9	0.4	53.8	10.3	3.6	0.2
Greeley	2	D	D	D	6	19	1.7	0.3	34.0	4.0	1.2	0.0
Greenwood	8	186	6.7	3.2	16	32	2.4	0.4	50.8	24.0	11.2	1.3
Hamilton	2	D	D	D	9	23	1.4	0.2	32.9	6.0	3.4	0.2
Harper	11	66	2.6	1.0	17	35	2.0	0.5	54.0	18.8	9.3	0.5
Harvey	51	1 052	66.3	33.2	45	205	12.4	3.7	152.4	80.0	30.2	2.6
Haskell	6	9	0.6	0.0	8	26	3.2	0.4	45.7	6.3	2.4	0.3
Hodgeman	1	D	D	D	3	6	0.2	0.1	25.6	5.1	2.8	0.0
Jackson	16	148	4.0	2.0	23	92	6.5	1.2	62.3	28.5	8.5	1.0
Jefferson	18	231	6.8	3.0	22	63	4.6	1.2	73.5	41.8	11.5	1.1
Jewell	2	D	D	D	10	27	1.7	0.3	51.0	11.4	4.3	0.3
Johnson	1 050	14 539	1 046.2	449.9	765	5 116	347.7	107.9	1 550.8	744.5	256.4	14.9
Kearny	5	17	1.2	0.4	8	16	1.2	0.2	37.3	7.3	3.1	0.3
Kingman	10	189	4.6	2.2	11	24	1.5	0.2	56.4	21.5	10.2	0.6
Kiowa	3	60	1.6	0.7	7	17	1.0	0.2	31.7	9.4	5.1	0.2
Labette	37	430	20.8	8.8	31	262	15.9	4.8	135.0	55.9	26.3	4.0
Lane	3	D	D	D	5	7	0.5	0.1	29.5	6.2	3.0	0.1
Leavenworth	87	906	44.8	20.7	82	545	22.7	7.4	604.4	179.3	41.5	5.4
Lincoln	7	71	1.6	0.8	5	12	0.6	0.1	30.6	10.1	4.0	0.2
Linn	14	127	2.8	1.1	9	18	1.9	0.3	59.2	25.3	11.6	1.1
Logan	5	55	2.6	1.1	9	50	2.4	0.6	36.5	8.2	3.8	0.1
Lyon	67	754	33.8	17.2	64	289	14.5	4.2	140.0	62.4	23.0	4.0
McPherson	47	489	19.7	8.2	70	297	21.6	5.7	133.6	66.8	24.5	1.1
Marion	20	193	7.4	3.3	19	47	2.9	0.5	94.2	34.8	14.3	0.7
Marshall	28	190	8.6	4.1	33	74	5.0	0.9	86.9	31.3	12.4	1.0
Meade	3	18	1.1	0.3	9	14	1.2	0.2	42.0	10.5	5.4	0.2
Miami	39	623	22.0	9.7	41	112	7.7	1.8	140.8	50.6	22.5	2.2
Mitchell	12	235	6.6	3.5	19	81	3.6	1.1	62.0	18.5	8.4	0.4
Montgomery	80	1 233	49.5	22.8	58	211	11.6	3.3	220.0	98.3	41.6	6.8
Morris	9	109	4.4	1.5	15	23	1.9	0.3	42.3	19.0	6.6	0.6
Morton	6	17	1.1	0.5	8	13	1.2	0.2	31.8	7.0	3.7	0.2
Nemaha	25	367	8.3	3.2	24	75	5.4	1.1	68.1	25.0	10.7	0.4
Neosho	32	513	21.5	8.7	33	132	9.5	2.3	92.1	42.8	17.5	2.4
Ness	6	18	0.9	0.4	10	28	2.1	0.4	37.3	10.3	6.3	0.1
Norton	14	76	4.1	1.4	14	32	3.5	0.6	49.1	14.9	6.5	0.2

1. Firms subject to federal tax.   2. October 1, 2000 to September 30, 2001.   3. State totals may include programs not allocated by county.

	Federal funds and grants, fiscal 2001[1] (cont'd)							Local government finances, 1997				
	Expenditures (mil dol) (cont'd)							General revenue				
	Procurement contract awards			Grants[2]							Taxes	
STATE County											Per capita[3] (dollars)	
	Salaries and wages	Defense	Other	Medicaid and other health-related	Nutrition and family welfare	Education	Other	Total (mil dol)	Intergovern-mental (mil dol)	Total (mil dol)	Total	Property
	171	172	173	174	175	176	177	178	179	180	181	182
KANSAS—Cont'd												
Barber	1.4	0.0	1.6	1.9	0.3	0.2	0.4	19.7	7.4	7.6	1 411	1 302
Barton	5.6	0.1	1.2	6.9	2.7	2.1	3.2	69.9	27.6	27.0	968	780
Bourbon	5.4	0.0	2.2	10.6	1.7	1.2	3.4	33.4	17.0	10.4	684	579
Brown	4.1	1.1	1.5	5.8	3.8	0.6	3.7	24.1	12.5	8.2	744	631
Butler	7.8	1.4	2.7	13.4	4.5	1.0	5.7	140.2	68.7	43.0	715	643
Chase	1.4	0.0	0.3	1.2	0.2	0.1	0.2	7.3	3.5	3.1	1 064	1 023
Chautauqua	0.9	0.0	0.2	3.4	0.5	0.2	2.7	9.4	4.7	3.5	802	725
Cherokee	3.0	0.7	0.8	22.1	3.3	1.8	3.2	37.9	20.5	10.1	447	364
Cheyenne	0.7	0.0	0.2	1.6	0.2	0.1	2.9	7.5	3.3	3.1	962	870
Clark	0.4	0.0	0.1	0.6	0.1	0.0	1.6	12.8	2.7	4.6	1 898	1 748
Clay	2.1	0.0	0.5	3.1	1.0	0.3	3.1	29.6	11.5	7.0	758	620
Cloud	2.5	0.0	0.6	8.4	0.8	0.5	3.7	31.9	16.0	9.7	955	824
Coffey	2.2	0.5	0.4	2.5	0.5	0.5	2.7	61.1	9.4	39.6	4 536	4 520
Comanche	0.4	0.0	0.1	0.9	0.1	0.1	0.1	7.8	2.3	3.3	1 644	1 598
Cowley	5.7	59.5	4.5	18.3	4.3	3.7	5.3	112.9	36.5	29.1	792	679
Crawford	7.7	0.0	1.6	32.0	7.7	3.1	8.9	76.2	34.0	26.1	724	479
Decatur	1.1	0.0	0.3	1.2	0.2	0.1	2.4	9.4	3.8	3.9	1 116	983
Dickinson	5.4	0.4	1.3	8.7	1.7	0.6	2.7	46.1	21.1	13.9	705	563
Doniphan	2.0	0.1	0.4	6.0	0.9	0.5	1.7	26.1	13.7	6.4	836	734
Douglas	30.9	2.1	7.1	41.5	6.6	23.4	31.1	214.2	55.5	76.4	839	656
Edwards	1.2	0.0	0.0	2.8	0.3	0.1	1.1	9.6	3.6	4.9	1 433	1 372
Elk	1.1	0.0	0.3	2.8	0.4	0.2	1.4	17.6	9.4	3.0	885	825
Ellis	9.1	0.1	1.3	10.0	1.7	2.7	5.0	50.2	19.0	22.6	858	747
Ellsworth	1.3	0.0	1.9	1.6	0.4	0.1	2.1	20.2	10.5	7.7	1 222	1 133
Finney	7.6	0.0	0.9	11.7	3.2	4.6	2.9	99.9	35.5	44.0	1 224	991
Ford	11.6	0.0	1.3	7.8	3.4	2.3	4.9	76.8	30.0	31.3	1 070	821
Franklin	4.7	0.0	0.8	11.5	3.2	0.7	38.0	60.8	22.6	17.2	724	565
Geary	381.3	32.3	1.2	12.7	5.0	9.6	1.6	75.8	31.1	17.7	701	493
Gove	1.0	0.0	0.2	0.6	0.1	0.1	1.0	14.7	7.2	3.7	1 206	1 114
Graham	1.1	0.0	0.2	1.9	0.2	0.1	1.0	13.0	3.6	4.9	1 502	1 490
Grant	1.0	0.0	0.9	0.9	0.7	0.5	2.9	33.3	2.8	24.3	3 078	2 973
Gray	1.1	0.0	0.2	1.9	0.3	0.1	0.3	15.4	6.9	6.8	1 239	1 169
Greeley	0.4	0.0	0.1	1.7	0.1	0.0	1.7	5.4	1.6	3.2	1 870	1 795
Greenwood	2.4	0.0	0.5	5.6	0.8	0.2	0.7	16.9	8.1	6.8	851	769
Hamilton	0.5	0.0	0.1	0.6	0.2	0.1	0.7	8.8	2.3	5.7	2 483	2 359
Harper	1.9	0.0	0.5	2.5	0.5	0.2	0.8	26.0	7.1	7.5	1 147	1 072
Harvey	4.5	0.3	1.2	6.5	2.5	1.0	4.5	69.7	27.8	24.8	784	612
Haskell	0.8	0.0	0.1	0.9	0.3	0.5	0.2	19.8	2.4	10.4	2 593	2 515
Hodgeman	0.7	0.0	0.2	0.6	0.1	0.0	0.7	10.1	3.0	3.5	1 564	1 436
Jackson	3.4	0.4	0.9	4.9	1.3	1.1	3.5	27.7	15.3	7.0	579	518
Jefferson	3.6	0.2	0.7	3.4	1.1	0.4	1.4	39.7	23.9	12.0	668	584
Jewell	1.8	0.0	0.4	3.1	0.3	0.1	5.2	10.2	4.6	4.1	1 022	960
Johnson	228.2	49.1	145.7	46.4	10.6	3.2	18.1	1 046.2	249.2	541.1	1 297	1 029
Kearny	0.5	0.0	0.1	1.6	0.4	0.2	2.1	22.9	2.0	16.4	3 905	3 863
Kingman	2.0	0.0	0.5	2.2	0.6	0.2	1.9	16.4	6.5	8.0	936	919
Kiowa	1.2	0.0	0.3	1.2	0.3	0.1	0.2	9.7	3.2	5.2	1 522	1 456
Labette	4.7	3.2	0.9	20.6	2.8	1.9	3.1	68.3	24.3	12.0	523	455
Lane	0.5	0.0	0.1	2.2	0.1	0.1	0.5	7.5	2.6	3.6	1 634	1 558
Leavenworth	224.5	92.9	9.6	18.4	4.7	9.6	3.2	113.8	61.0	34.7	495	419
Lincoln	1.5	0.1	0.3	1.2	0.2	0.1	0.7	11.7	4.0	4.0	1 194	1 128
Linn	2.3	0.0	0.6	6.5	0.8	0.9	1.9	25.3	7.7	13.9	1 532	1 495
Logan	0.8	0.0	0.2	0.6	0.9	0.1	1.4	11.5	3.8	4.0	1 312	1 242
Lyon	8.2	0.5	1.4	8.8	2.5	3.6	7.5	108.2	32.5	24.5	717	590
McPherson	4.4	1.5	1.1	5.9	1.6	0.4	0.6	63.5	24.4	26.2	950	820
Marion	3.4	0.3	0.8	4.4	0.7	0.3	17.3	26.3	14.0	8.0	619	540
Marshall	3.6	0.1	0.8	6.5	0.8	0.3	4.1	27.0	14.7	9.0	805	780
Meade	0.6	0.0	0.1	1.6	0.2	0.1	0.0	22.2	3.5	7.7	1 746	1 653
Miami	3.7	0.2	1.2	9.4	1.6	0.4	41.4	49.1	20.8	14.8	564	429
Mitchell	1.9	0.0	0.5	3.1	0.5	0.2	4.8	20.0	8.9	6.7	959	813
Montgomery	9.1	0.1	10.5	31.5	4.9	2.1	2.6	99.2	31.5	31.7	854	640
Morris	1.8	0.1	0.5	2.5	0.5	0.5	1.7	11.3	5.3	4.4	705	630
Morton	0.7	0.0	0.1	0.6	0.3	0.1	2.9	25.2	3.0	12.6	3 743	3 590
Nemaha	3.3	0.1	0.7	4.4	0.6	0.3	1.9	21.9	11.1	7.5	736	660
Neosho	3.3	1.1	0.8	9.0	1.7	1.7	1.8	57.6	16.3	12.4	732	613
Ness	1.3	0.1	0.3	0.9	0.2	0.1	0.6	16.0	3.8	6.0	1 645	1 613
Norton	1.7	0.2	0.3	1.9	0.3	0.1	5.4	18.8	6.9	5.4	920	857

1. October 1, 2000 to September 30, 2001.　2. State totals may include programs not allocated by county.　3. Based on the resident population estimated as of July 1 of the year shown.

Table B. States and Counties — Local Government Finances, Government Employment, and Elections

STATE County	Local government finances, 1997 (cont'd) Direct general expenditure — Total (mil dol)	Per capita[1] (dollars)	Percent of total for — Education	Health and hospitals	Police protection	Public welfare	Highways	Debt outstanding Total (mil dol)	Per capita[1] (dollars)	Government employment, 1999 Federal civilian	Federal military	State and local	Presidential election, 2000[2] Percent of vote cast — Democratic	Republican	All other
	183	184	185	186	187	188	189	190	191	192	193	194	195	196	197
KANSAS—Cont'd															
Barber	20.7	3 816	34.6	25.8	3.9	0.0	11.1	1.8	337	30	25	706	25.5	70.3	4.2
Barton	71.0	2 540	63.9	1.9	4.6	0.0	6.1	34.9	1 248	93	137	2 338	29.6	66.7	3.8
Bourbon	33.5	2 197	63.7	0.7	3.5	0.0	7.0	14.1	923	101	72	1 117	35.1	61.1	3.9
Brown	22.1	2 005	51.4	1.9	2.7	0.0	7.4	12.4	1 125	73	54	864	32.2	63.6	4.1
Butler	138.1	2 293	68.5	1.4	2.9	0.0	5.8	138.6	2 300	130	300	4 646	32.2	63.7	4.1
Chase	7.1	2 458	50.6	2.3	3.4	0.0	10.2	4.8	1 653	27	14	264	29.7	64.4	5.9
Chautauqua	9.6	2 173	59.9	4.0	3.4	0.0	11.8	1.9	428	20	20	284	23.6	71.6	4.8
Cherokee	37.2	1 648	63.8	9.3	4.0	0.0	3.2	10.4	461	57	107	1 286	41.4	54.9	3.6
Cheyenne	7.3	2 262	64.4	0.3	3.5	0.0	10.9	0.2	55	19	15	291	20.3	76.0	3.8
Clark	12.1	4 971	34.3	39.4	2.9	0.0	6.8	1.6	667	16	11	406	23.2	73.4	3.4
Clay	29.6	3 212	35.8	22.0	2.5	0.0	8.9	13.5	1 465	39	43	864	23.3	73.3	3.4
Cloud	34.5	3 382	66.4	2.3	3.2	0.0	5.6	7.8	765	46	48	948	29.2	64.8	6.0
Coffey	59.7	6 826	50.8	13.6	1.6	0.0	12.4	17.7	2 029	47	42	1 150	29.6	66.8	3.6
Comanche	8.8	4 350	48.0	18.9	3.4	0.0	9.2	1.5	749	0	0	285	21.0	75.5	3.5
Cowley	111.9	3 048	46.2	26.4	3.1	0.0	4.2	52.2	1 422	103	177	3 373	39.0	56.9	4.2
Crawford	74.7	2 076	53.1	12.5	4.6	0.0	5.5	38.6	1 072	125	178	4 562	47.1	47.6	5.3
Decatur	8.9	2 509	52.5	3.8	2.9	0.6	11.5	2.1	583	25	16	320	24.1	71.3	4.5
Dickinson	45.8	2 324	54.6	13.4	3.6	0.0	8.3	16.1	817	112	94	1 528	29.8	64.8	5.4
Doniphan	25.9	3 374	75.8	1.9	1.4	0.0	5.6	7.1	924	39	38	782	31.1	64.4	4.5
Douglas	204.5	2 245	35.9	26.7	5.0	0.3	4.3	182.6	2 004	561	509	14 751	42.8	42.8	11.4
Edwards	9.9	2 880	43.8	6.6	4.4	0.0	11.8	1.6	454	26	16	274	28.6	67.9	3.5
Elk	17.4	5 176	38.0	5.9	1.4	0.0	5.0	11.8	3 501	23	16	442	25.9	69.7	4.4
Ellis	49.2	1 867	55.8	3.1	4.8	0.0	8.3	23.2	880	158	126	3 329	35.2	58.4	6.4
Ellsworth	19.7	3 140	47.5	2.6	3.0	0.0	4.1	18.6	2 966	24	30	789	29.1	65.0	6.0
Finney	100.2	2 789	58.0	2.0	5.4	0.0	5.3	80.2	2 232	161	179	2 811	26.6	70.4	3.0
Ford	71.0	2 427	59.6	2.1	4.5	0.0	4.5	49.2	1 682	215	141	2 279	28.8	67.8	3.4
Franklin	58.8	2 473	46.6	25.8	2.8	2.5	1.6	37.7	1 586	87	120	1 762	34.4	61.3	4.3
Geary	81.2	3 207	40.1	20.0	5.5	0.0	3.3	66.2	2 615	2 138	10 504	2 247	38.7	57.9	3.3
Gove	13.8	4 457	42.1	17.3	1.3	0.0	6.6	1.7	559	23	14	436	19.8	75.1	5.2
Graham	12.9	3 976	34.5	31.6	2.7	0.0	11.8	3.6	1 098	25	15	422	23.5	71.8	4.7
Grant	30.5	3 860	48.1	8.7	3.2	0.0	14.8	1.6	206	26	38	771	23.9	74.4	1.6
Gray	15.5	2 817	61.2	1.6	3.1	0.0	11.6	6.6	1 207	24	27	843	22.3	75.5	2.2
Greeley	5.4	3 097	44.5	4.2	4.5	0.0	15.0	2.5	1 473	13	0	195	17.8	78.2	4.0
Greenwood	15.7	1 953	56.1	1.6	5.6	0.0	12.8	2.8	343	50	38	522	28.8	67.2	4.0
Hamilton	8.5	3 728	38.8	2.6	10.6	0.0	13.9	1.0	435	10	11	357	22.1	75.6	2.3
Harper	24.2	3 732	30.7	44.3	2.1	0.0	8.4	0.6	94	39	30	883	28.4	68.0	3.6
Harvey	67.6	2 138	52.5	2.3	4.0	0.0	7.8	86.2	2 729	79	164	1 767	33.6	60.4	6.0
Haskell	18.3	4 564	46.1	23.4	0.8	0.0	11.6	1.2	302	18	19	468	16.3	81.9	1.9
Hodgeman	9.9	4 454	35.3	29.8	1.9	3.0	9.1	1.2	532	18	11	333	19.9	76.7	3.3
Jackson	28.4	2 362	58.3	9.9	2.5	0.0	8.5	13.7	1 141	56	58	921	37.9	57.2	4.9
Jefferson	38.3	2 135	67.7	4.1	4.7	0.0	7.9	20.2	1 129	71	87	1 164	38.1	56.2	5.8
Jewell	9.5	2 388	54.8	3.1	2.4	0.0	14.8	2.9	726	37	18	470	20.2	74.6	5.2
Johnson	1 079.0	2 585	44.8	2.8	8.0	1.1	8.9	1 773.0	4 248	3 939	2 108	21 519	36.4	59.7	3.9
Kearny	20.8	4 950	52.0	14.2	4.0	0.0	8.5	5.3	1 268	20	20	649	22.3	75.5	2.2
Kingman	16.3	1 915	57.1	3.4	4.3	0.0	14.0	9.7	1 136	44	41	603	26.0	70.2	3.8
Kiowa	9.5	2 767	53.9	5.1	4.0	0.0	13.2	1.0	289	23	16	447	18.3	78.5	3.2
Labette	62.6	2 738	46.3	22.8	3.4	0.0	5.2	17.3	759	88	110	2 815	43.9	52.4	3.7
Lane	7.4	3 382	52.8	2.5	3.9	0.0	9.0	1.6	740	14	10	335	22.2	74.7	3.1
Leavenworth	115.2	1 642	57.3	2.3	5.0	2.8	8.3	52.6	750	3 334	3 315	3 705	41.8	54.1	4.1
Lincoln	11.6	3 474	42.1	7.4	1.9	13.9	11.9	4.2	1 256	39	16	426	24.8	68.5	6.7
Linn	25.1	2 765	58.2	0.7	3.1	0.0	8.3	38.6	4 256	39	44	683	37.3	59.0	3.7
Logan	12.7	4 163	40.6	21.4	2.2	0.0	12.4	0.7	213	24	14	494	16.5	77.9	5.6
Lyon	103.6	3 039	37.6	29.4	3.7	2.7	5.7	59.2	1 738	144	161	4 327	41.7	53.4	4.9
McPherson	68.8	2 491	47.1	2.2	3.6	0.0	13.1	104.6	3 790	97	138	1 797	26.3	68.2	5.5
Marion	25.2	1 952	63.9	1.4	2.9	0.0	4.3	24.0	1 860	70	65	1 130	25.0	70.4	4.6
Marshall	27.3	2 450	61.3	1.3	2.7	0.0	11.6	11.4	1 025	67	52	855	35.8	59.9	4.3
Meade	16.7	3 808	28.6	32.6	2.8	0.0	11.1	4.1	932	13	21	536	19.5	78.1	2.4
Miami	45.6	1 742	62.5	12.0	4.9	0.0	2.1	40.7	1 555	75	129	1 970	39.2	57.0	3.8
Mitchell	19.9	2 846	56.7	4.6	3.3	0.0	9.1	10.3	1 467	38	33	825	23.0	72.0	5.1
Montgomery	94.9	2 554	49.6	22.7	3.1	0.0	4.6	39.5	1 062	151	176	2 629	34.7	61.8	3.5
Morris	11.2	1 814	53.3	1.5	1.4	0.0	14.6	4.6	743	37	29	494	33.4	60.5	6.1
Morton	22.9	6 782	36.9	26.2	1.9	7.2	9.6	4.1	1 210	23	17	634	20.6	77.3	2.1
Nemaha	21.5	2 099	56.7	1.1	3.3	0.0	13.5	12.0	1 170	64	49	716	28.2	67.6	4.1
Neosho	56.7	3 348	41.6	30.0	2.1	0.0	4.1	47.9	2 824	62	80	1 585	37.6	58.3	4.1
Ness	16.1	4 419	36.6	35.6	1.4	0.0	11.4	4.0	1 107	33	17	525	20.4	75.7	3.9
Norton	17.9	3 084	41.2	27.5	2.3	0.0	6.5	3.1	525	32	27	910	24.4	71.2	4.4

1. Based on the resident population estimated as of July 1 of the year shown.   2. Data subject to copyright.

Table B. States and Counties — **Land Area and Population**

STATE/County code	MSA/PMSA/NECMA code[1]	County Type[2]	STATE County	Land area,[3] (sq km) 2000	Population and population characteristics, 2000			Race alone or in combination (percent)					Age (percent)					
					Total persons	Rank	Per square kilometer	White	Black	Am. Indian, Alaska Native	Asian and Pacific Islander	Percent Hispanic[4]	Under 5 years	5 to 17 years	18 to 24 years	25 to 34 years	35 to 44 years	45 to 54 years
				1	2	3	4	5	6	7	8	9	10	11	12	13	14	15
			KANSAS—Cont'd															
20 139	...	6	Osage	1 822	16 712	1 975	9.2	98.4	0.4	1.4	0.5	1.5	6.5	20.6	6.4	10.3	16.7	13.5
20 141	...	9	Osborne	2 311	4 452	2 885	1.9	99.4	0.2	0.5	0.3	0.4	4.6	19.2	5.5	7.6	14.7	12.7
20 143	...	9	Ottawa	1 868	6 163	2 766	3.3	98.6	0.8	0.8	0.3	1.3	5.7	20.0	5.8	10.2	16.5	13.8
20 145	...	7	Pawnee	1 953	7 233	2 662	3.7	92.2	5.5	1.3	0.7	4.2	5.6	18.5	7.3	10.4	15.0	14.4
20 147	...	7	Phillips	2 295	6 001	2 779	2.6	98.9	0.3	0.8	0.5	0.7	5.5	19.0	5.7	9.5	13.6	14.4
20 149	...	6	Pottawatomie	2 187	18 209	1 886	8.3	97.7	1.0	1.4	0.6	2.3	7.4	22.0	7.7	11.7	16.1	13.3
20 151	...	7	Pratt	1 904	9 647	2 474	5.1	96.3	1.2	0.9	0.7	3.1	5.9	18.6	9.4	9.2	14.8	13.6
20 153	...	9	Rawlins	2 770	2 966	2 994	1.1	99.2	0.5	0.7	0.2	0.8	4.5	19.5	3.8	7.1	14.4	14.1
20 155	...	4	Reno	3 249	64 790	749	19.9	93.2	3.4	1.3	0.7	5.7	6.4	18.1	9.3	11.6	15.3	13.7
20 157	...	7	Republic	1 855	5 835	2 799	3.1	99.0	0.4	0.5	0.2	0.9	4.5	17.8	4.5	7.8	14.3	14.1
20 159	...	7	Rice	1 882	10 761	2 379	5.7	96.0	1.4	1.2	0.4	5.6	5.8	18.8	13.3	9.1	13.7	11.9
20 161	...	5	Riley	1 579	62 843	774	39.8	86.8	7.7	1.3	4.4	4.6	5.7	13.1	34.5	15.1	10.7	8.5
20 163	...	9	Rooks	2 301	5 685	2 809	2.5	97.8	1.3	0.8	0.4	1.1	5.6	19.6	6.4	10.3	15.3	11.9
20 165	...	9	Rush	1 860	3 551	2 950	1.9	99.0	0.4	0.8	0.2	1.0	4.8	17.3	5.5	8.9	14.1	13.9
20 167	...	7	Russell	2 291	7 370	2 650	3.2	98.3	0.7	1.1	0.4	0.9	5.0	17.4	5.8	8.8	14.5	13.4
20 169	...	5	Saline	1 864	53 597	871	28.8	91.1	3.9	1.3	2.1	6.0	6.9	19.3	9.4	12.9	15.6	13.4
20 171	...	7	Scott	1 858	5 120	2 842	2.8	96.4	0.3	0.7	0.2	6.3	6.1	21.1	6.6	10.1	15.2	14.6
20 173	9040	2	Sedgwick	2 588	452 869	130	175.0	81.8	10.0	2.2	4.1	8.0	7.9	20.3	9.5	14.2	16.1	13.1
20 175	...	7	Seward	1 656	22 510	1 670	13.6	68.1	4.3	1.5	3.5	42.1	9.6	22.4	11.7	15.7	14.7	10.6
20 177	8440	3	Shawnee	1 424	169 871	319	119.3	85.2	10.2	2.2	1.4	7.3	6.8	18.5	8.8	12.8	15.6	14.6
20 179	...	9	Sheridan	2 322	2 813	3 005	1.2	99.2	0.2	0.2	0.2	1.5	5.0	21.4	5.8	8.0	15.7	13.8
20 181	...	7	Sherman	2 735	6 760	2 714	2.5	94.8	0.5	0.8	0.6	8.4	6.1	18.5	11.8	10.4	13.5	12.8
20 183	...	9	Smith	2 319	4 536	2 875	2.0	99.2	0.2	0.6	0.1	0.7	4.3	17.4	4.7	7.7	14.4	13.1
20 185	...	9	Stafford	2 051	4 789	2 861	2.3	96.4	0.4	1.0	0.4	5.4	5.7	20.6	5.4	8.9	15.6	12.8
20 187	...	9	Stanton	1 761	2 406	3 029	1.4	85.3	0.6	1.5	0.5	23.7	7.9	23.0	8.4	12.6	15.8	11.3
20 189	...	7	Stevens	1 884	5 463	2 820	2.9	84.5	1.2	1.5	0.3	21.7	8.2	23.0	8.3	12.0	15.8	11.1
20 191	...	6	Sumner	3 061	25 946	1 519	8.5	96.6	0.9	2.3	0.4	3.6	6.6	21.9	7.5	10.3	15.9	13.7
20 193	...	7	Thomas	2 784	8 180	2 595	2.9	98.0	0.6	0.8	0.4	1.8	6.7	19.6	13.5	9.9	14.5	12.9
20 195	...	9	Trego	2 301	3 319	2 971	1.4	98.7	0.2	1.3	0.6	0.8	5.1	18.8	5.5	7.9	15.6	13.2
20 197	...	8	Wabaunsee	2 065	6 885	2 696	3.3	98.2	0.7	1.0	0.3	1.9	6.2	20.5	6.2	10.1	16.6	14.5
20 199	...	9	Wallace	2 367	1 749	3 083	0.7	95.7	1.0	1.4	0.4	4.8	5.6	23.5	6.5	8.3	15.2	13.7
20 201	...	9	Washington	2 327	6 483	2 740	2.8	99.4	0.3	0.5	0.2	0.6	5.7	18.0	5.4	8.9	14.0	12.4
20 203	...	9	Wichita	1 861	2 531	3 024	1.4	88.5	0.2	1.3	0.4	18.4	8.3	20.4	7.3	11.7	13.9	13.0
20 205	...	7	Wilson	1 486	10 332	2 411	7.0	97.9	0.5	1.7	0.5	1.7	5.8	19.6	7.4	9.6	14.2	13.2
20 207	...	9	Woodson	1 297	3 788	2 929	2.9	98.0	1.0	1.6	0.1	1.4	5.0	16.7	7.4	8.5	13.6	13.9
20 209	3760	0	Wyandotte	392	157 882	337	402.8	60.5	29.4	1.7	2.1	16.0	8.1	20.4	10.4	14.5	15.0	12.1
21 000	...	X	KENTUCKY	102 896	4 041 769	X	39.3	91.0	7.7	0.6	1.0	1.5	6.6	18.0	9.9	14.1	15.9	13.8
21 001	...	7	Adair	1 054	17 244	1 936	16.4	96.7	2.8	0.6	0.3	0.8	6.1	17.4	10.7	13.0	14.8	13.1
21 003	...	7	Allen	896	17 800	1 910	19.9	98.2	1.3	0.5	0.2	0.8	6.6	19.3	8.9	13.4	15.0	13.1
21 005	...	6	Anderson	525	19 111	1 842	36.4	97.2	2.6	0.5	0.2	0.8	7.5	19.1	7.4	15.0	17.4	13.8
21 007	...	9	Ballard	651	8 286	2 581	12.7	96.7	3.1	1.1	0.3	0.6	6.0	17.0	7.6	12.6	15.1	14.2
21 009	...	7	Barren	1 272	38 033	1 164	29.9	94.9	4.4	0.4	0.5	0.9	6.4	17.8	8.2	13.1	15.7	13.6
21 011	...	8	Bath	724	11 085	2 359	15.3	97.5	2.1	0.6	0.1	0.8	6.6	17.5	8.6	13.4	15.4	14.0
21 013	...	7	Bell	934	30 060	1 394	32.2	96.8	2.6	0.7	0.6	0.6	6.1	18.3	9.0	13.5	15.2	13.9
21 015	1640	0	Boone	638	85 991	607	134.8	96.1	1.8	0.6	1.6	2.0	8.0	20.7	8.5	15.5	18.0	13.6
21 017	4280	2	Bourbon	755	19 360	1 825	25.6	91.4	7.4	0.5	0.4	2.6	6.5	18.6	8.1	12.7	15.9	14.7
21 019	3400	2	Boyd	415	49 752	920	119.9	96.8	2.9	0.6	0.4	1.1	5.5	16.3	8.3	13.0	15.7	14.8
21 021	...	7	Boyle	471	27 697	1 458	58.8	88.8	10.2	0.6	0.8	1.4	5.6	17.1	11.0	13.3	15.3	14.2
21 023	...	8	Bracken	526	8 279	2 583	15.7	99.8	0.7	0.4	0.1	0.5	6.6	18.4	8.0	13.4	16.1	13.2
21 025	...	9	Breathitt	1 283	16 100	2 016	12.5	99.1	0.4	0.4	0.4	0.7	5.8	19.7	10.0	13.1	15.9	14.3
21 027	...	9	Breckinridge	1 483	18 648	1 863	12.6	96.7	3.2	0.7	0.1	0.7	6.3	18.6	8.2	11.7	15.0	15.0
21 029	4520	2	Bullitt	775	61 236	796	79.0	98.8	0.5	0.8	0.4	0.6	7.2	19.9	8.6	15.1	17.6	14.4
21 031	...	9	Butler	1 109	13 010	2 232	11.7	98.5	0.6	0.6	0.3	1.0	6.3	19.0	9.5	13.3	15.9	13.1
21 033	...	6	Caldwell	899	13 060	2 226	14.5	94.4	5.0	0.4	0.4	0.6	5.5	16.9	7.0	12.1	14.2	14.8
21 035	...	7	Calloway	1 000	34 177	1 276	34.2	94.3	3.8	0.5	1.7	1.4	4.9	13.8	19.8	12.1	12.6	12.0
21 037	1640	0	Campbell	393	88 616	588	225.5	97.3	1.8	0.5	0.8	0.9	6.9	18.7	9.8	14.2	16.4	13.0
21 039	...	9	Carlisle	499	5 351	2 825	10.7	98.3	1.1	0.8	0.1	0.8	5.9	17.4	7.8	12.6	13.8	14.0
21 041	...	6	Carroll	337	10 155	2 431	30.1	96.1	2.3	0.6	0.4	3.2	6.7	18.7	9.1	14.0	15.9	13.8
21 043	3400	2	Carter	1 063	26 889	1 488	25.3	99.4	0.2	0.5	0.2	0.6	6.4	18.1	10.8	13.5	14.9	13.5
21 045	...	9	Casey	1 154	15 447	2 055	13.4	99.0	0.4	0.6	0.3	1.3	6.3	18.2	8.2	13.0	14.5	13.9
21 047	1660	3	Christian	1 868	72 265	688	38.7	71.8	24.8	1.1	1.9	4.8	9.9	18.4	15.8	17.6	12.5	9.3
21 049	4280	2	Clark	659	33 144	1 313	50.3	94.3	5.0	0.5	0.3	1.2	6.5	18.3	8.1	14.1	16.2	14.7
21 051	...	9	Clay	1 220	24 556	1 572	20.1	94.6	5.0	0.6	0.2	1.4	5.7	19.7	9.2	16.0	16.5	13.4
21 053	...	9	Clinton	511	9 634	2 475	18.9	99.4	0.1	0.5	0.2	1.2	6.3	16.4	8.6	12.7	15.0	13.8
21 055	...	7	Crittenden	938	9 384	2 498	10.0	99.0	0.8	0.6	0.2	0.5	5.4	17.8	8.0	11.4	14.7	13.9

1. MSA = Metropolitan Statistical Area. PMSA = Primary MSA. NECMA = New England County Metropolitan Area. See Appendix A for explanation of these concepts. See Appendix B for list of metropolitan areas identified by type, with component counties.   2. County typology code from the Economic Research Service of USDA. See Appendix A for definition.   3. Dry land or land partially or temporarily covered by water.   4. Hispanic persons may be of any race.

Table B. States and Counties — Population and Households

STATE County	55 to 64 years	65 to 74 years	75 years and over	Percent female	2001	1990	1990–2000	2000–2001	Births	Deaths	Net migration	Number	Percent change, 1990–2000	Persons per household	Female family householder[1] Percent	One person
	16	17	18	19	20	21	22	23	24	25	26	27	28	29	30	31
KANSAS—Cont'd																
Osage	10.2	7.8	8.0	51.0	16 903	15 248	9.6	1.1	234	219	179	6 490	11.8	2.54	8.1	23.5
Osborne	10.0	10.6	15.1	50.8	4 345	4 867	-8.5	-2.4	52	97	-59	1 940	-5.7	2.23	5.2	35.2
Ottawa	10.4	8.5	9.1	50.0	6 190	5 634	9.4	0.4	87	94	37	2 430	7.2	2.46	6.3	25.7
Pawnee	10.2	8.4	10.1	47.2	6 979	7 555	-4.3	-3.5	98	111	-246	2 739	-6.3	2.31	7.3	32.2
Phillips	10.4	9.6	12.2	51.3	5 873	6 590	-8.9	-2.1	73	94	-105	2 496	-7.4	2.35	5.5	28.6
Pottawatomie	8.3	6.7	6.8	50.5	18 336	16 128	12.9	0.7	313	215	37	6 771	14.0	2.65	7.2	23.2
Pratt	9.2	8.9	10.3	51.5	9 544	9 702	-0.6	-1.1	136	154	-80	3 963	0.7	2.35	7.5	30.4
Rawlins	11.0	12.1	13.5	50.0	2 918	3 404	-12.9	-1.6	33	55	-26	1 269	-6.8	2.29	4.9	31.4
Reno	9.2	7.9	8.4	49.8	64 237	62 389	3.8	-0.9	1 023	890	-671	25 498	5.2	2.41	8.7	27.9
Republic	10.9	11.4	14.7	51.8	5 646	6 482	-10.0	-3.2	69	145	-113	2 557	-7.7	2.23	4.8	31.8
Rice	9.4	8.8	9.2	52.0	10 588	10 610	1.4	-1.6	154	187	-141	4 050	-2.8	2.44	7.2	27.8
Riley	4.8	3.6	3.9	46.7	60 368	67 139	-6.4	-3.9	1 167	369	-3 307	22 137	4.0	2.42	6.8	27.5
Rooks	9.6	9.9	11.5	50.5	5 614	6 039	-5.9	-1.2	75	100	-46	2 362	-3.4	2.32	7.2	31.8
Rush	10.3	11.9	13.4	51.5	3 488	3 842	-7.6	-1.8	34	80	-17	1 548	-5.7	2.24	5.8	31.7
Russell	10.9	11.1	13.0	51.9	7 166	7 835	-5.9	-2.8	102	136	-171	3 207	-4.9	2.23	7.1	32.8
Saline	8.6	7.1	6.8	50.7	53 646	49 301	8.7	0.1	955	604	-288	21 436	8.1	2.43	9.7	28.3
Scott	9.8	7.6	8.9	50.7	5 002	5 289	-3.2	-2.3	91	76	-136	2 045	1.1	2.46	6.7	27.3
Sedgwick	7.5	5.9	5.4	50.6	455 516	403 662	12.2	0.6	9 539	4 582	-2 193	176 444	12.7	2.53	10.9	28.2
Seward	6.3	4.6	4.3	48.7	22 434	18 743	20.1	-0.3	628	169	-561	7 419	12.2	2.98	12.0	20.6
Shawnee	9.1	7.1	6.6	51.6	170 080	160 976	5.5	0.1	3 027	2 177	-581	68 920	8.1	2.39	11.6	29.8
Sheridan	10.1	10.6	9.6	50.0	2 726	3 043	-7.6	-3.1	34	51	-70	1 124	-4.0	2.46	4.5	27.6
Sherman	10.0	8.7	8.3	48.9	6 528	6 926	-2.4	-3.4	114	95	-258	2 758	0.9	2.40	6.0	29.2
Smith	10.5	12.2	15.7	51.9	4 436	5 078	-10.7	-2.2	41	92	-48	1 953	-9.8	2.27	4.7	30.2
Stafford	9.7	10.0	11.2	51.2	4 755	5 365	-10.7	-0.7	96	104	-23	2 010	-8.8	2.34	5.9	33.0
Stanton	8.1	7.6	5.3	49.0	2 408	2 333	3.1	0.1	47	26	-20	858	3.2	2.74	6.8	22.6
Stevens	8.3	6.4	7.0	51.2	5 379	5 048	8.2	-1.5	105	44	-150	1 988	5.5	2.72	7.1	24.3
Sumner	8.7	7.5	8.0	50.8	25 749	25 841	0.4	-0.8	415	386	-222	9 888	2.1	2.58	8.0	25.6
Thomas	8.2	7.1	7.6	51.4	8 080	8 258	-0.9	-1.2	125	99	-127	3 226	3.3	2.45	6.9	28.4
Trego	10.1	11.0	13.0	52.3	3 195	3 694	-10.2	-3.7	41	74	-93	1 412	-3.6	2.27	6.3	31.4
Wabaunsee	10.3	8.4	7.2	49.4	6 843	6 603	4.3	-0.6	104	93	-51	2 633	6.1	2.57	6.3	23.0
Wallace	9.0	9.0	9.0	50.3	1 706	1 821	-4.0	-2.5	34	21	-58	674	-0.4	2.56	4.0	27.6
Washington	10.6	10.8	14.3	49.8	6 321	7 073	-8.3	-2.5	87	123	-125	2 673	-6.6	2.35	4.2	31.2
Wichita	9.3	8.0	8.0	48.9	2 538	2 758	-8.2	0.3	45	24	-16	967	-2.9	2.59	5.8	23.7
Wilson	10.3	9.4	10.6	51.5	10 235	10 289	0.4	-0.9	173	210	-57	4 203	0.2	2.40	7.8	29.1
Woodson	10.0	11.5	13.3	50.8	3 758	4 116	-8.0	-0.8	47	75	-1	1 642	-3.4	2.24	7.4	33.3
Wyandotte	7.7	6.2	5.6	51.2	157 461	162 026	-2.6	-0.3	3 689	2 004	-2 132	59 700	-2.9	2.62	17.8	28.9
KENTUCKY	9.2	6.8	5.7	51.1	4 065 556	3 686 892	9.6	0.6	68 762	49 431	5 181	1 590 647	15.3	2.47	11.8	26.0
Adair	10.3	7.9	6.7	51.5	17 291	15 360	12.3	0.3	267	207	-9	6 747	16.3	2.44	10.2	26.2
Allen	10.0	7.6	6.1	51.0	18 056	14 628	21.7	1.4	305	227	177	6 910	23.5	2.55	9.8	23.1
Anderson	8.9	5.8	5.0	51.1	19 564	14 571	31.2	2.4	307	196	341	7 320	34.6	2.59	9.2	20.5
Ballard	11.2	8.4	7.8	50.6	8 158	7 902	4.9	-1.5	112	149	-92	3 395	6.4	2.39	8.0	25.8
Barren	10.2	7.9	7.1	51.9	38 592	34 001	11.9	1.5	595	491	461	15 346	16.8	2.44	9.8	25.6
Bath	9.8	7.8	6.9	50.6	11 355	9 692	14.4	2.4	201	146	216	4 445	21.5	2.47	10.3	25.3
Bell	10.3	7.4	6.4	52.2	29 873	31 506	-4.6	-0.6	450	420	-208	12 004	4.3	2.44	15.7	26.8
Boone	7.7	4.9	3.2	50.6	90 489	57 589	49.3	5.2	1 575	641	3 480	31 258	55.3	2.73	9.8	20.2
Bourbon	10.1	7.2	6.4	51.4	19 478	19 236	0.6	0.6	305	252	70	7 681	5.9	2.49	12.3	24.8
Boyd	10.8	8.7	6.9	51.0	49 727	51 096	-2.6	-0.1	697	740	30	20 010	0.7	2.38	11.6	26.5
Boyle	9.5	7.4	6.7	50.4	27 612	25 590	8.2	-0.3	398	403	-72	10 574	11.5	2.38	12.5	27.1
Bracken	9.8	7.5	6.0	50.5	8 441	7 766	6.6	2.0	130	131	162	3 228	12.4	2.55	10.7	23.9
Breathitt	9.7	6.7	4.9	50.7	16 024	15 703	2.5	-0.5	205	226	-49	6 170	11.1	2.54	14.2	23.8
Breckinridge	11.0	8.2	6.0	50.4	18 871	16 312	14.3	1.2	299	238	158	7 324	18.9	2.51	8.9	24.6
Bullitt	9.3	5.1	2.8	50.3	63 043	47 567	28.7	3.0	968	466	1 289	22 171	38.9	2.75	10.4	16.4
Butler	10.2	6.9	6.0	50.3	13 131	11 245	15.7	0.9	212	191	102	5 059	21.0	2.52	9.3	23.7
Caldwell	11.5	9.3	8.7	51.9	12 898	13 232	-1.3	-1.2	183	235	-108	5 431	3.0	2.36	9.8	27.5
Calloway	9.8	7.3	7.7	51.8	34 206	30 735	11.2	0.1	440	413	14	13 862	19.4	2.25	8.1	29.7
Campbell	8.4	6.7	5.9	51.8	88 362	83 866	5.7	-0.3	1 525	1 113	-644	34 742	11.5	2.49	12.3	28.6
Carlisle	10.1	9.6	8.7	51.2	5 345	5 238	2.2	-0.1	83	94	8	2 208	4.8	2.40	9.3	26.3
Carroll	9.4	7.0	5.4	49.7	10 133	9 292	9.3	-0.2	160	123	-57	3 940	12.4	2.51	11.7	25.3
Carter	10.3	7.1	5.4	51.0	27 024	24 340	10.5	0.5	453	384	75	10 342	19.2	2.54	10.7	22.3
Casey	10.8	8.3	6.8	51.1	15 726	14 211	8.7	1.8	266	243	255	6 260	15.2	2.44	10.8	26.8
Christian	6.7	5.2	4.5	48.4	71 649	68 941	4.9	-0.9	1 979	758	-1 778	24 857	14.9	2.66	13.6	22.5
Clark	9.7	6.9	5.6	51.7	33 409	29 496	12.4	0.8	565	377	90	13 015	18.6	2.51	12.1	22.8
Clay	9.1	5.9	4.4	47.2	24 506	21 746	12.9	-0.2	396	275	-164	8 556	16.1	2.62	12.4	22.5
Clinton	12.2	8.2	6.8	51.8	9 616	9 135	5.5	-0.2	182	140	-55	4 086	13.8	2.34	9.7	28.4
Crittenden	12.5	8.3	8.0	51.6	9 281	9 196	2.0	-1.1	128	170	-61	3 829	5.0	2.42	8.9	27.0

1. No spouse present.

STATE County	Births, average 1997–1999 Total	Rate[1]	Deaths, average 1997–1999 Number Total	Number Infant[2]	Rate Total[1]	Rate Infant[3]	Physicians,[4] 2000 Number	Rate[5]	Hospitals,[4] 1998 Number	Beds Number	Beds Rate[5]	Medicare enrollees 2000	Serious crimes known to police, 2000[6] Total Number	Rate[7]
	32	33	34	35	36	37	38	39	40	41	42	43	44	45
KANSAS—Cont'd														
Osage	204	11.9	180	NA	10.5	NA	6	36	0	0	0	2 937	362	2 376
Osborne	46	10.0	75	NA	16.2	NA	3	67	1	29	615	1 190	NA	NA
Ottawa	63	10.7	81	NA	13.8	NA	3	49	1	53	898	1 112	98	1 590
Pawnee	74	10.0	87	NA	11.8	NA	29	401	1	79	1 062	1 406	284	3 926
Phillips	60	9.9	86	NA	14.2	NA	7	117	1	62	1 020	1 416	444	2 498
Pottawatomie	260	14.0	169	NA	9.1	NA	11	60	3	109	583	2 532	NA	NA
Pratt	110	11.4	118	NA	12.3	NA	17	176	1	99	1 021	1 892	358	3 711
Rawlins	31	10.1	41	NA	13.1	NA	3	101	1	28	896	785	NA	NA
Reno	815	12.9	675	NA	10.6	NA	112	173	1	160	253	11 502	3 585	5 652
Republic	57	9.4	103	NA	16.9	NA	5	86	1	86	1 409	1 556	88	1 508
Rice	122	12.0	130	NA	12.8	NA	6	56	1	44	425	2 186	226	2 260
Riley	908	14.3	282	NA	4.4	NA	99	158	2	155	244	5 155	2 306	3 669
Rooks	69	12.1	82	NA	14.5	NA	5	88	1	27	477	1 313	65	1 143
Rush	30	8.9	60	NA	17.6	NA	2	56	1	76	2 227	989	NA	NA
Russell	73	9.6	104	NA	13.7	NA	4	54	1	60	794	1 954	173	2 347
Saline	731	14.2	505	NA	9.8	NA	111	207	1	187	362	8 337	3 334	6 272
Scott	61	12.2	57	NA	11.4	NA	4	78	1	27	538	489	122	2 383
Sedgwick	7 349	16.5	3 531	64	7.9	8.7	1 007	222	5	1 770	395	57 834	23 243	5 812
Seward	426	21.2	133	NA	6.6	NA	28	124	1	77	385	2 097	1 257	5 584
Shawnee	2 338	14.0	1 645	23	9.8	10.0	479	282	2	642	388	27 328	14 477	8 643
Sheridan	27	10.0	35	NA	12.8	NA	0	0	1	69	2 517	540	6	213
Sherman	99	15.1	74	NA	11.4	NA	6	89	1	49	753	1 231	284	4 201
Smith	38	8.2	79	NA	17.2	NA	4	88	1	54	1 177	1 272	NA	NA
Stafford	58	11.6	82	NA	16.2	NA	1	21	1	25	500	1 084	103	2 151
Stanton	46	20.5	20	NA	8.7	NA	1	42	1	46	2 031	341	11	457
Stevens	87	16.2	44	NA	8.2	NA	5	92	1	17	317	790	147	2 691
Sumner	339	12.5	298	NA	11.0	NA	16	62	2	118	436	4 680	692	2 723
Thomas	108	13.3	81	NA	10.0	NA	8	98	1	40	498	1 262	250	3 056
Trego	28	8.6	53	NA	16.2	NA	7	211	1	73	2 224	777	42	1 265
Wabaunsee	71	10.8	74	NA	11.2	NA	3	44	0	0	0	1 130	180	2 614
Wallace	26	14.2	20	NA	11.3	NA	1	57	0	0	0	350	3	172
Washington	70	10.8	98	NA	15.0	NA	2	31	2	75	1 156	1 753	57	879
Wichita	40	15.0	19	NA	7.1	NA	2	79	1	43	1 627	422	39	1 541
Wilson	122	11.9	152	NA	14.8	NA	9	87	2	80	783	2 120	133	1 287
Woodson	35	8.8	59	NA	14.8	NA	4	106	0	0	0	1 030	59	1 558
Wyandotte	2 631	17.3	1 594	24	10.5	9.2	499	316	3	1 102	723	22 401	NA	NA
KENTUCKY	53 384	13.6	38 384	402	9.7	7.5	7 010	173	105	16 966	431	622 908	119 626	2 960
Adair	207	12.6	177	NA	10.7	NA	18	104	1	85	517	2 975	NA	NA
Allen	222	13.4	186	NA	11.2	NA	6	34	1	62	375	2 816	NA	NA
Anderson	253	13.7	156	NA	8.5	NA	11	58	0	0	0	2 342	NA	NA
Ballard	93	11.0	115	NA	13.6	NA	2	24	0	0	0	1 893	NA	NA
Barren	454	12.3	394	NA	10.6	NA	43	113	1	194	525	6 510	NA	NA
Bath	144	13.7	121	NA	11.5	NA	7	63	0	0	0	2 017	NA	NA
Bell	381	13.0	351	NA	12.0	NA	44	146	2	247	848	6 160	NA	NA
Boone	1 279	16.0	487	NA	6.1	NA	85	99	1	155	195	8 530	2 498	2 905
Bourbon	254	13.1	206	NA	10.7	NA	24	124	1	68	351	2 968	NA	NA
Boyd	564	11.4	612	NA	12.4	NA	115	231	2	539	1 088	10 077	NA	NA
Boyle	304	11.2	294	NA	10.8	NA	61	220	1	168	618	4 724	NA	NA
Bracken	105	12.5	92	NA	10.9	NA	2	24	0	0	0	1 385	NA	NA
Breathitt	200	12.8	175	NA	11.1	NA	20	124	1	59	376	2 765	NA	NA
Breckinridge	212	12.1	184	NA	10.5	NA	12	64	1	45	258	3 187	NA	NA
Bullitt	816	13.8	352	NA	5.9	NA	13	21	0	0	0	5 195	NA	NA
Butler	152	12.7	144	NA	12.1	NA	5	38	0	0	0	1 892	NA	NA
Caldwell	162	12.1	187	NA	14.0	NA	12	92	1	50	376	2 730	NA	NA
Calloway	347	10.4	344	NA	10.3	NA	39	114	1	360	1 075	5 692	NA	NA
Campbell	1 330	15.2	849	9	9.7	6.5	107	121	1	267	306	12 631	NA	NA
Carlisle	60	11.3	72	NA	13.4	NA	1	19	0	0	0	1 123	NA	NA
Carroll	131	13.6	102	NA	10.6	NA	10	98	1	53	552	1 632	NA	NA
Carter	358	13.3	268	NA	10.0	NA	9	33	0	0	0	4 467	NA	NA
Casey	190	12.9	174	NA	11.8	NA	8	52	0	0	0	2 554	NA	NA
Christian	1 422	19.6	573	10	7.9	7.0	92	127	1	226	312	8 106	NA	NA
Clark	426	13.3	300	NA	9.4	NA	29	87	1	109	341	4 941	NA	NA
Clay	300	13.2	224	NA	9.9	NA	17	69	1	62	272	3 624	NA	NA
Clinton	115	12.3	104	NA	11.1	NA	4	42	1	36	385	2 054	NA	NA
Crittenden	111	11.7	120	NA	12.7	NA	8	85	1	46	480	1 751	NA	NA

1. Per 1,000 estimated resident population, average 1997–1999. 2. Deaths of infants under 1 year old. 3. Deaths of infants under 1 year old per 1,000 live births. 4. Data subject to copyright. 5. Per 100,000 resident population as of July 1 of the year shown. 6. Data for serious crimes have not been adjusted for underreporting; this may affect comparability between geographic areas and over time. 7. Per 100,000 population estimated by the FBI.

STATE County	Serious crimes known to police, 2000[1] (cont'd) Rate[2] Violent	Property	Education School enrollment and attainment, 1990 Enrollment[3] Total	Percent private	Attainment[4] (percent) High school graduate or more	Bachelor's degree or more	Local government expenditures, fiscal 1999[5] Total current expenditures (mil dol)	Current expenditures per student (dollars)	Money income 1989 Per capita[6] (dollars)	Households Median Dollars	Percent change, 1979–1989 (constant 1989 dollars)	Percent with $100,000 or more	Income and poverty, 1998 Percent below poverty level Median household income	All persons	Persons under 18	Persons 5–17 in families
	46	47	48	49	50	51	52	53	54	55	56	57	58	59	60	61
KANSAS—Cont'd																
Osage	210	2 166	3 705	3.2	76.9	9.3	19.1	5 688	10 823	24 867	-2.4	0.5	37 301	10.3	14.1	13.4
Osborne	NA	NA	971	2.8	76.1	11.0	3.1	5 979	9 913	18 365	-5.1	1.0	28 883	13.0	17.0	18.3
Ottawa	162	1 428	1 343	7.3	81.0	14.0	8.1	5 968	10 358	21 852	3.7	1.2	38 959	8.8	13.7	10.9
Pawnee	664	3 263	1 978	8.5	82.1	16.7	10.8	8 502	12 531	23 898	-1.5	1.7	35 613	11.3	15.2	15.8
Phillips	163	2 335	1 348	3.1	73.9	10.9	11.0	9 619	10 270	20 918	-5.2	0.9	33 730	13.5	18.3	17.0
Pottawatomie	NA	NA	4 455	8.7	81.8	15.6	25.4	6 666	10 984	25 305	1.3	1.5	40 778	8.8	12.5	11.1
Pratt	280	3 431	2 522	8.7	82.4	19.5	9.6	5 443	12 488	23 865	-7.8	1.9	36 143	11.3	15.1	14.8
Rawlins	NA	NA	802	1.9	80.4	14.4	4.0	7 297	10 468	21 332	2.1	1.3	30 606	14.3	19.4	18.5
Reno	386	5 265	15 511	9.1	77.4	14.9	59.3	5 485	12 074	24 665	-7.7	1.7	37 063	12.0	17.0	15.6
Republic	103	1 405	1 286	1.6	78.3	10.3	7.7	7 039	10 890	20 224	10.0	1.2	28 877	13.2	17.9	18.0
Rice	350	1 910	2 718	13.6	81.2	18.7	14.6	7 320	10 139	21 088	-18.7	0.5	33 931	13.3	17.8	17.7
Riley	313	3 356	28 488	3.4	91.7	34.3	42.0	5 984	10 067	21 700	4.8	1.5	36 174	12.3	11.3	13.4
Rooks	123	1 020	1 368	2.8	74.1	11.0	7.5	6 775	10 223	20 113	-13.0	0.9	31 201	13.7	18.0	17.8
Rush	NA	NA	795	1.5	72.6	11.5	4.9	6 874	10 516	19 356	-8.3	1.3	29 447	14.2	20.4	19.6
Russell	204	2 144	1 658	2.8	74.5	14.1	9.0	6 621	11 338	20 843	-8.5	2.3	28 264	13.9	18.6	18.9
Saline	350	5 922	11 801	15.8	82.4	17.7	54.7	6 215	13 153	25 728	-5.2	2.4	39 005	10.7	15.4	14.4
Scott	195	2 188	1 284	6.6	77.2	13.8	6.2	5 332	11 332	25 474	-1.7	1.2	39 899	8.7	10.2	10.4
Sedgwick	545	5 267	106 048	14.7	82.4	22.2	419.5	5 541	14 555	30 216	-1.1	3.1	43 644	10.5	15.2	13.1
Seward	697	4 887	5 073	6.0	72.2	11.6	26.2	5 256	11 341	26 055	-11.8	2.6	37 195	13.2	18.2	17.6
Shawnee	845	7 798	40 682	12.8	84.4	22.3	162.4	6 023	14 091	29 879	0.6	2.5	41 275	10.4	15.8	14.6
Sheridan	0	213	761	4.9	81.5	13.3	3.5	7 670	9 889	21 540	1.2	1.3	35 636	12.1	15.3	14.1
Sherman	547	3 654	1 681	4.1	75.0	12.5	7.2	6 022	10 356	21 138	-11.3	0.6	32 191	14.1	19.0	20.5
Smith	NA	NA	965	3.0	74.0	10.0	5.4	6 674	9 574	18 834	3.3	0.5	28 966	13.4	17.0	17.4
Stafford	167	1 984	1 312	4.6	78.7	16.5	7.5	6 758	10 496	19 778	-10.3	0.5	30 615	15.2	19.4	20.9
Stanton	166	291	622	3.1	76.9	16.9	3.9	6 618	11 025	24 545	3.5	2.6	39 446	10.2	13.8	14.9
Stevens	238	2 453	1 363	4.0	78.4	14.1	8.0	6 625	11 584	27 549	-3.2	2.6	42 839	10.1	13.2	13.9
Sumner	146	2 578	6 636	6.5	77.1	11.3	28.3	5 767	11 944	26 885	-3.7	1.3	41 137	8.7	10.8	11.0
Thomas	147	2 910	2 616	6.1	85.4	15.7	9.6	6 360	10 551	22 247	-12.9	1.9	36 426	11.5	14.4	14.6
Trego	60	1 205	832	3.5	72.9	12.1	4.1	6 853	10 464	19 921	-14.4	1.8	30 103	11.5	13.8	14.5
Wabaunsee	232	2 382	1 588	5.5	83.8	12.6	8.2	6 555	11 280	27 727	13.0	0.7	38 520	7.7	9.3	9.2
Wallace	0	172	464	4.1	77.8	12.5	3.2	7 069	9 366	20 417	-1.3	1.2	32 308	14.3	20.3	19.9
Washington	31	848	1 631	9.9	69.6	11.2	9.8	6 751	9 595	19 424	1.0	0.8	29 074	12.9	15.5	16.0
Wichita	356	1 185	719	2.9	71.7	12.5	3.1	6 213	10 196	23 395	-5.2	1.8	37 355	12.8	16.3	17.5
Wilson	184	1 103	2 338	4.1	74.6	11.4	12.7	6 105	9 734	18 776	-7.8	1.2	28 613	14.8	19.5	19.7
Woodson	79	1 478	964	4.5	70.6	8.4	4.0	6 301	10 424	19 637	4.8	0.8	25 810	15.0	18.4	20.4
Wyandotte	NA	NA	41 959	12.3	69.9	10.3	183.1	6 441	10 656	23 780	-8.2	0.8	31 197	17.3	24.4	22.7
KENTUCKY	295	2 665	918 315	12.0	64.6	13.6	3 645.6	5 560	11 153	22 534	-3.7	2.0	33 955	15.3	21.2	19.2
Adair	NA	NA	3 394	14.7	46.3	7.4	15.8	5 980	8 596	15 809	0.5	1.4	22 088	22.6	30.2	27.3
Allen	NA	NA	2 863	1.4	51.1	4.6	14.5	4 759	8 361	17 915	-1.7	0.8	31 197	14.5	22.1	17.3
Anderson	NA	NA	3 365	6.1	66.7	9.9	16.4	4 690	12 320	27 747	4.0	1.6	43 185	7.7	12.6	9.8
Ballard	NA	NA	1 754	1.7	64.2	8.7	7.9	5 251	10 262	19 371	-7.5	1.1	33 112	13.2	19.4	17.1
Barren	NA	NA	7 273	2.9	54.5	8.3	37.3	5 449	9 876	19 546	-6.5	1.1	31 523	16.0	22.5	19.1
Bath	NA	NA	2 038	1.3	46.3	6.2	10.7	5 555	8 034	15 940	-4.3	0.6	26 121	22.0	30.7	28.0
Bell	NA	NA	7 938	8.3	46.7	9.3	32.0	5 512	7 037	13 078	-20.9	1.0	21 401	27.7	33.5	33.9
Boone	170	2 735	14 796	17.5	76.4	15.3	73.2	5 321	13 576	34 485	0.4	2.7	51 323	6.2	9.7	7.6
Bourbon	NA	NA	4 392	3.8	64.0	11.8	21.3	5 970	10 858	22 445	6.7	2.1	35 195	13.9	21.1	17.8
Boyd	NA	NA	12 129	5.9	68.9	11.9	45.2	5 676	12 012	23 835	-12.7	2.1	33 592	16.3	25.4	20.9
Boyle	NA	NA	6 182	14.1	65.4	14.4	25.7	5 601	11 029	23 125	1.1	1.4	35 720	13.2	19.3	16.7
Bracken	NA	NA	1 723	3.4	56.0	6.5	7.8	5 210	9 297	19 684	-7.4	0.7	31 711	15.1	21.3	18.2
Breathitt	NA	NA	3 843	9.4	47.8	8.6	18.7	6 000	6 905	12 383	-21.1	0.5	19 716	31.4	37.8	37.0
Breckinridge	NA	NA	3 477	15.4	56.7	6.3	17.6	5 582	9 157	17 687	-2.6	1.4	28 847	18.1	26.5	21.3
Bullitt	NA	NA	12 462	8.5	64.7	6.3	57.8	5 372	10 907	29 455	-3.0	0.8	42 421	9.2	12.9	10.7
Butler	NA	NA	2 459	5.8	46.5	5.1	13.4	5 752	8 108	17 514	-2.6	0.6	27 378	19.3	26.3	24.1
Caldwell	NA	NA	2 921	2.5	61.9	8.2	10.9	5 114	9 658	17 997	-14.5	0.9	29 274	17.0	26.1	22.1
Calloway	NA	NA	10 207	2.4	69.1	19.4	30.4	6 485	10 434	19 408	-8.9	1.7	32 419	13.7	18.6	16.7
Campbell	NA	NA	21 324	21.2	71.0	14.9	71.7	5 615	12 603	29 228	3.2	2.1	40 912	9.6	14.7	12.8
Carlisle	NA	NA	1 130	2.8	62.3	6.6	4.6	5 267	9 735	19 404	-8.2	0.1	29 971	14.3	22.7	19.7
Carroll	NA	NA	2 311	8.7	59.6	10.7	12.2	6 817	10 202	20 179	-3.8	1.4	30 955	16.6	25.0	22.1
Carter	NA	NA	6 039	8.1	51.3	7.6	26.7	5 602	7 996	17 083	-5.1	0.6	25 862	22.5	29.5	27.7
Casey	NA	NA	2 906	7.4	43.1	6.5	14.1	5 734	7 719	14 993	7.5	0.5	23 701	22.4	30.5	26.5
Christian	NA	NA	16 280	7.1	72.2	10.4	51.4	5 607	9 708	21 032	4.0	1.0	29 105	17.5	25.0	21.5
Clark	NA	NA	6 882	9.8	65.1	13.0	28.3	5 373	11 655	25 323	-5.1	2.2	37 389	13.5	20.3	17.5
Clay	NA	NA	5 475	7.9	38.9	7.4	26.2	5 982	6 084	12 732	-3.8	0.7	20 579	30.9	33.5	37.5
Clinton	NA	NA	1 886	2.6	44.4	6.6	10.7	6 828	6 838	11 348	-6.5	1.1	19 150	28.5	37.4	35.8
Crittenden	NA	NA	1 923	10.8	59.6	5.1	8.4	5 472	9 807	18 566	-8.8	0.5	28 480	15.9	21.8	22.5

1. Data for serious crimes have not been adjusted for underreporting; this may affect comparability between geographic areas and over time. 2. Per 100,000 population estimated by the FBI. 3. All persons 3 years old and over enrolled in nursery school through college. 4. Persons 25 years old and over. 5. Elementary and secondary education expenditures, local government fiscal years ending between July 1, 1998 and June 30, 1999. 6. Based on population enumerated as of April 1, 1990.

Table B. States and Counties — **Personal Income**

STATE County	Personal income, 1999 Total (mil dol)	Percent change, 1998–1999	Per capita[1] Dollars	Per capita[1] Rank	Wages and salaries[2] (mil dol)	Proprietor's income (mil dol)	Dividends, interest, and rent (mil dol)	Transfer payments Total (mil dol)	Government payments to individuals Total (mil dol)	Social Security (mil dol)	Medical payments (mil dol)	Income mainte-nance (mil dol)	Unemploy-ment insurance (mil dol)
	62	63	64	65	66	67	68	69	70	71	72	73	74
KANSAS—Cont'd													
Osage	341	3.3	19 836	2 046	84	19	66	60	57	27	20	4	1
Osborne	96	0.1	20 849	1 717	32	16	26	22	21	11	8	1	0
Ottawa	128	5.4	21 789	1 417	32	16	35	22	21	11	7	1	0
Pawnee	170	5.0	23 638	931	84	26	35	27	26	15	8	2	0
Phillips	148	0.0	24 811	699	63	24	41	27	26	13	10	1	0
Pottawatomie	397	5.2	20 970	1 674	200	31	88	54	50	24	18	3	1
Pratt	225	1.8	23 637	932	109	31	53	39	38	19	13	2	0
Rawlins	73	8.0	24 294	806	21	19	20	13	13	7	4	1	0
Reno	1 522	3.4	23 888	883	879	104	350	242	230	117	80	18	4
Republic	127	2.2	21 218	1 592	52	17	33	26	25	14	8	2	0
Rice	221	6.5	21 588	1 492	81	42	48	42	40	21	13	3	1
Riley	1 404	5.5	22 045	1 350	688	75	243	126	115	48	32	12	3
Rooks	122	-1.1	21 600	1 487	51	15	31	25	24	13	9	1	0
Rush	72	-2.0	21 326	1 561	31	3	21	18	17	9	6	1	0
Russell	167	0.8	22 363	1 253	61	25	46	40	38	18	17	2	0
Saline	1 471	4.3	28 624	275	892	255	268	174	165	82	56	12	3
Scott	150	12.9	30 387	199	54	47	31	15	15	9	4	1	0
Sedgwick	12 395	2.1	27 442	378	9 394	904	2 482	1 420	1 339	612	498	127	30
Seward	467	2.3	23 229	1 035	350	62	72	53	49	22	18	6	1
Shawnee	4 507	3.9	26 394	476	3 397	245	922	617	587	257	189	50	10
Sheridan	83	1.6	30 930	180	22	32	18	11	10	6	3	1	0
Sherman	179	9.1	27 473	376	80	38	32	31	29	12	13	2	0
Smith	106	5.6	23 195	1 046	32	23	30	22	22	12	8	1	0
Stafford	125	7.3	25 009	670	37	36	28	26	26	11	12	1	0
Stanton	74	11.0	33 228	126	24	30	15	7	6	3	2	1	0
Stevens	152	4.6	28 141	315	57	43	32	17	16	9	5	1	0
Sumner	653	5.0	24 038	850	200	55	93	95	91	43	32	5	2
Thomas	205	7.1	25 709	553	98	57	37	27	25	13	9	1	0
Trego	66	1.4	20 296	1 890	24	8	17	15	15	7	6	1	0
Wabaunsee	149	4.0	22 678	1 173	30	13	26	23	22	11	7	1	0
Wallace	44	8.3	24 436	774	13	14	11	7	7	3	3	1	0
Washington	129	-0.4	19 913	2 020	44	18	32	30	29	15	10	2	0
Wichita	92	12.5	35 786	74	25	46	13	9	9	4	3	1	0
Wilson	200	4.3	19 308	2 205	108	17	39	45	43	21	15	4	1
Woodson	70	5.7	17 985	2 542	17	13	17	18	18	9	6	1	0
Wyandotte	3 072	2.5	20 292	1 894	3 197	112	424	633	606	215	251	80	15
KENTUCKY	92 000	4.6	23 227	X	58 072	6 067	17 111	15 542	14 807	5 893	5 783	1 748	262
Adair	264	1.1	16 064	2 893	104	18	47	80	77	24	36	10	2
Allen	288	2.0	17 074	2 722	147	16	58	63	60	25	25	6	1
Anderson	427	4.4	22 707	1 166	124	15	74	50	46	25	15	3	1
Ballard	207	5.9	24 259	813	136	16	31	37	36	15	16	3	1
Barren	820	2.1	21 948	1 376	545	71	135	143	136	57	54	15	4
Bath	182	2.3	16 973	2 737	52	9	30	45	43	15	16	8	1
Bell	472	4.2	16 260	2 866	260	27	77	176	171	53	71	32	1
Boone	2 247	8.7	26 961	419	2 427	119	304	197	181	89	61	10	4
Bourbon	513	2.1	26 500	463	195	78	97	66	62	28	23	7	1
Boyd	1 210	2.0	24 767	710	992	62	266	242	233	97	88	24	4
Boyle	642	3.1	23 474	967	488	39	147	102	97	44	35	9	1
Bracken	146	1.4	17 272	2 687	39	9	22	29	28	12	11	3	0
Breathitt	237	5.8	15 049	2 984	90	14	35	95	92	25	38	23	1
Breckinridge	299	1.2	16 870	2 761	73	19	68	70	67	27	26	8	2
Bullitt	1 312	7.9	21 516	1 517	315	66	162	153	142	67	47	11	3
Butler	200	5.6	16 600	2 810	100	13	29	50	47	17	21	6	1
Caldwell	265	3.3	19 795	2 061	109	18	58	59	57	25	22	5	1
Calloway	786	5.5	23 622	937	428	104	162	127	120	55	43	9	2
Campbell	2 125	3.8	24 373	785	828	77	383	302	286	129	107	22	6
Carlisle	117	3.2	21 716	1 446	22	12	23	22	22	10	8	2	0
Carroll	202	3.8	20 702	1 775	202	8	34	39	37	16	15	4	1
Carter	449	6.6	16 564	2 818	127	24	52	116	111	38	43	18	3
Casey	228	1.9	15 279	2 961	78	23	35	67	64	21	27	11	2
Christian	1 295	0.0	18 005	2 539	1 912	81	268	198	191	74	77	24	3
Clark	780	3.6	24 040	849	406	49	147	113	107	47	40	11	2
Clay	341	5.3	14 977	2 989	131	23	39	127	123	29	51	34	1
Clinton	155	11.2	16 391	2 845	68	12	19	57	55	15	28	9	1
Crittenden	155	3.1	16 234	2 870	56	13	25	42	40	18	16	4	1

1. Based on the resident population estimated as of July 1 of the year shown.   2. Includes other labor income.

Table B. States and Counties — Earnings, Social Security, and Housing

STATE County	Earnings, 1999									Social Security bene-ficiaries, December 2000		Housing units, 1990	
			Goods-related[1]		Service-related and other[2]								
	Total (mil dol)	Farm	Total	Manu-facturing	Total	Retail trade	Finance, insur-ance, and real estate	Services	Govern-ment	Number	Rate[3]	Supple-mental Security Income recipients, December 2000	Total	Percent change, 1980–1990
	75	76	77	78	79	80	81	82	83	84	85	86	87	88
KANSAS—Cont'd														
Osage	103	-2.4	D	D	D	12.9	4.8	29.0	29.6	3 271	196	215	6 324	2.8
Osborne	48	12.6	D	10.6	D	11.6	6.5	16.7	18.8	1 281	288	42	2 496	-10.0
Ottawa	48	16.7	D	5.9	D	5.7	7.0	22.6	23.4	1 290	209	58	2 591	-2.8
Pawnee	110	14.6	D	1.5	D	5.7	4.4	12.6	45.6	1 584	219	91	3 412	-0.9
Phillips	88	11.9	D	D	D	7.4	6.2	13.8	20.8	1 594	266	77	3 264	-6.8
Pottawatomie	231	2.3	D	18.4	D	11.7	3.5	19.8	15.4	3 058	168	154	6 472	7.3
Pratt	140	6.6	10.5	2.6	61.6	10.5	4.5	24.0	21.3	2 121	220	93	4 620	3.8
Rawlins	41	33.9	D	1.1	D	4.5	4.6	12.2	22.6	854	288	41	1 744	-4.5
Reno	983	2.2	29.1	21.0	53.5	15.2	4.0	24.4	15.2	13 121	203	1 061	26 607	0.1
Republic	68	9.6	D	11.5	D	9.0	6.9	15.5	22.6	1 686	289	67	3 283	-13.6
Rice	122	20.9	15.8	8.4	43.2	6.6	3.4	14.1	20.1	2 435	226	121	4 868	-2.1
Riley	763	0.2	D	2.5	D	11.1	7.9	22.8	42.3	5 536	88	473	22 868	9.6
Rooks	67	5.8	D	4.7	D	8.5	4.1	8.2	24.9	1 465	258	61	2 979	-5.0
Rush	35	0.0	D	26.9	D	5.7	4.2	12.2	28.0	1 075	303	65	1 999	-4.8
Russell	86	6.7	27.9	12.4	46.2	10.7	3.6	20.8	19.2	2 110	286	132	4 079	-1.2
Saline	1 147	0.3	D	20.9	D	10.6	3.8	28.6	10.8	9 430	176	837	21 129	4.0
Scott	102	44.6	4.3	0.4	37.8	5.3	3.8	9.2	13.4	983	192	46	2 305	-1.7
Sedgwick	10 298	0.1	40.3	34.0	48.2	8.4	4.7	23.9	11.4	66 956	148	7 268	170 159	16.9
Seward	412	4.3	D	D	D	9.7	2.5	14.7	15.5	2 472	110	276	7 572	12.9
Shawnee	3 642	0.0	18.2	11.8	59.0	11.2	8.3	26.1	22.8	29 837	176	3 532	68 991	7.1
Sheridan	55	45.5	5.0	0.8	35.4	6.6	4.8	9.1	14.0	653	232	18	1 324	-8.3
Sherman	118	23.6	D	2.9	D	10.5	5.1	20.4	17.7	1 347	199	103	3 177	-3.5
Smith	55	29.1	12.8	8.4	42.4	7.7	4.8	16.1	15.7	1 386	306	59	2 615	-7.1
Stafford	72	36.6	8.4	2.2	35.2	4.8	4.7	11.7	19.9	1 217	254	56	2 666	-1.6
Stanton	54	59.1	D	D	D	2.5	D	4.8	14.9	381	158	9	956	-0.4
Stevens	100	35.8	D	D	D	5.8	D	6.4	19.1	954	175	36	2 116	7.0
Sumner	255	5.5	D	19.7	D	9.4	4.7	19.1	21.4	4 779	184	279	10 769	4.0
Thomas	155	25.7	D	D	D	13.1	3.5	16.8	17.8	1 448	177	81	3 534	1.1
Trego	33	0.4	D	2.5	D	11.1	5.8	21.1	29.2	872	263	42	1 851	-7.0
Wabaunsee	43	1.4	D	6.1	D	9.0	5.1	20.9	27.8	1 410	205	53	2 853	-1.3
Wallace	27	42.8	D	D	D	5.6	2.4	8.8	15.4	360	206	12	840	-5.8
Washington	62	18.8	D	3.7	D	8.3	5.5	12.4	28.8	1 894	292	91	3 355	-6.3
Wichita	72	63.8	D	D	D	3.0	2.0	D	9.5	492	194	12	1 190	-8.0
Wilson	125	-2.4	D	32.8	D	5.5	3.1	15.4	19.5	2 498	242	215	5 091	-5.2
Woodson	29	13.9	D	4.7	D	9.8	4.1	11.3	21.5	1 070	282	76	2 199	-4.1
Wyandotte	3 309	0.0	D	22.3	D	6.0	2.2	15.4	22.1	24 836	157	4 323	69 102	0.9
KENTUCKY	64 139	1.0	28.7	20.6	52.0	10.1	5.0	23.0	18.3	739 585	183	174 349	1 506 845	10.1
Adair	122	2.7	D	10.6	D	9.9	3.4	33.8	22.2	3 751	218	1 185	6 434	4.4
Allen	163	-2.1	D	38.2	D	23.7	3.7	13.8	13.5	3 527	198	827	6 381	6.2
Anderson	139	-2.7	D	43.1	D	9.9	2.9	13.8	17.5	3 006	157	322	5 804	20.8
Ballard	152	4.6	58.2	36.2	D	4.1	1.4	9.7	8.8	1 830	221	248	3 553	0.3
Barren	616	1.4	48.3	42.7	39.9	9.8	2.3	19.6	10.5	8 000	210	1 747	14 202	5.2
Bath	60	-2.8	36.9	22.5	D	11.0	4.2	13.9	27.2	2 349	212	935	4 021	8.8
Bell	287	0.1	25.7	10.2	53.7	14.6	3.5	24.6	20.7	7 367	245	3 456	12 568	4.3
Boone	2 546	0.0	D	23.7	D	10.7	6.0	13.5	6.9	10 532	122	982	21 476	33.6
Bourbon	273	23.5	D	18.8	D	6.5	D	11.2	11.8	3 621	187	657	7 781	7.9
Boyd	1 053	0.0	D	22.5	D	10.1	3.5	31.7	11.7	10 955	220	2 300	21 365	-0.4
Boyle	527	0.0	D	29.2	D	10.0	2.8	27.6	11.8	5 472	198	1 085	10 191	7.1
Bracken	48	-1.0	D	D	D	7.2	4.1	19.6	23.3	1 635	197	314	3 166	6.2
Breathitt	104	-0.6	D	3.2	D	15.4	4.0	26.2	34.8	3 594	223	2 468	6 127	10.5
Breckinridge	92	-1.3	D	7.0	D	15.5	5.3	21.1	28.3	3 670	197	804	8 261	15.6
Bullitt	381	-0.9	D	24.5	D	12.4	4.3	14.2	19.1	8 202	134	865	16 629	21.7
Butler	112	-1.1	D	39.0	D	6.9	2.4	13.0	18.7	2 511	193	586	4 698	9.9
Caldwell	127	0.0	D	24.6	D	15.9	4.7	16.5	21.0	3 146	241	519	5 794	8.2
Calloway	532	5.2	24.5	17.7	44.4	13.8	2.3	14.4	25.9	6 593	193	711	13 242	10.3
Campbell	905	-0.3	28.8	19.7	51.8	12.1	3.9	27.3	19.6	14 557	164	1 891	32 910	8.7
Carlisle	33	13.5	23.6	12.9	D	9.7	5.0	14.3	22.1	1 306	244	171	2 295	3.8
Carroll	210	0.1	61.7	58.3	D	8.2	D	8.0	10.3	1 988	196	465	3 870	1.3
Carter	151	-1.6	D	15.5	D	18.6	4.1	18.7	26.1	5 192	193	1 831	9 290	5.9
Casey	101	2.6	D	26.1	D	11.1	2.4	19.3	19.5	3 322	215	1 345	6 046	4.0
Christian	1 992	0.0	D	11.5	D	4.2	1.3	8.7	68.1	9 712	134	2 120	23 429	10.5
Clark	455	1.3	D	32.3	D	10.9	2.7	18.5	11.3	5 919	179	1 127	11 635	11.7
Clay	153	-0.8	D	11.6	D	13.1	2.3	20.0	42.1	4 492	183	3 752	7 930	7.1
Clinton	80	2.7	D	31.0	D	9.8	2.3	18.7	20.2	2 415	251	1 099	4 189	3.9
Crittenden	69	2.2	32.4	24.2	47.2	9.4	3.6	25.4	18.2	2 189	233	341	4 039	5.5

1. Covers mining, construction, and manufacturing. 2. Covers private sector earnings in agricultural services, forestry, and fisheries; transportation and public utilities; wholesale trade; retail trade; finance, insurance, and real estate; and services. 3. Per 1,000 resident population estimated as of July 1 of the year shown.

Table B. States and Counties — Housing, Labor Force, and Employment

STATE County	Housing units, 1990 (cont'd)								Civilian labor force, 2001				Civilian employment, 1990[5]		
	Occupied units							Sub-standard units[3] (percent)			Unemployment			Percent	
	Owner-occupied					Renter-occupied									
				Owner cost as a percent of income											
	Total	Percent	Median value[1]	With a mort-gage	Without a mort-gage	Median rent[2]	Rent as per-cent of income		Total	Percent change, 2000–2001	Total	Rate[4]	Total	Professional, managerial, and technical	Precision production, craft, and repair
	89	90	91	92	93	94	95	96	97	98	99	100	101	102	103
KANSAS—Cont'd															
Osage	5 806	79.2	38 300	18.6	12.8	280	22.8	2.1	9 295	-4.9	437	4.7	6 730	20.5	15.5
Osborne	2 057	78.6	18 400	17.3	12.8	206	22.5	1.9	2 229	-2.3	69	3.1	2 272	16.3	8.7
Ottawa	2 266	78.7	27 500	15.4	12.3	253	20.0	2.0	3 082	-2.9	107	3.5	2 536	21.6	13.2
Pawnee	2 923	71.3	35 300	17.9	12.1	282	21.5	1.2	3 568	-1.4	59	1.7	3 414	25.7	10.0
Phillips	2 695	76.4	26 800	13.5	13.7	234	22.1	1.8	3 095	-3.2	63	2.0	2 954	18.7	12.3
Pottawatomie	5 938	77.4	46 400	18.8	11.9	298	23.5	2.5	10 856	-2.1	357	3.3	7 730	22.7	14.8
Pratt	3 937	73.9	37 500	16.5	12.0	313	21.1	1.2	4 460	-5.9	91	2.0	4 546	26.6	12.0
Rawlins	1 361	76.3	27 500	19.5	13.0	234	20.6	3.0	1 485	-4.7	37	2.5	1 555	17.3	8.4
Reno	24 239	69.9	40 100	16.3	12.3	306	22.7	2.1	31 203	-3.0	1 337	4.3	28 858	22.8	12.9
Republic	2 769	78.4	18 900	20.2	11.8	212	19.3	1.2	2 811	-5.5	64	2.3	2 991	19.5	10.4
Rice	4 165	75.2	27 200	15.3	12.0	250	20.1	1.4	4 665	-0.4	164	3.5	4 602	20.6	12.7
Riley	21 280	44.1	63 500	20.3	12.2	379	30.0	3.9	30 050	-2.5	1 110	3.7	26 375	36.6	7.5
Rooks	2 444	77.6	25 800	20.1	13.2	233	21.3	1.8	2 774	-8.7	77	2.8	2 568	17.9	16.5
Rush	1 642	81.0	19 200	16.3	12.9	237	20.7	2.2	1 738	-5.3	40	2.3	1 742	18.6	11.0
Russell	3 371	75.8	28 000	20.4	13.3	257	21.9	2.6	3 200	-5.3	145	4.5	3 443	22.9	11.6
Saline	19 826	66.7	45 500	17.1	12.7	327	23.7	1.7	29 821	-2.9	1 051	3.5	24 601	24.9	12.7
Scott	2 022	73.9	44 000	19.8	12.7	317	23.4	1.4	2 584	-4.0	47	1.8	2 505	20.5	10.3
Sedgwick	156 571	63.7	58 500	19.7	12.5	399	25.1	3.6	230 420	-2.1	9 714	4.2	198 134	31.4	13.6
Seward	6 614	64.6	48 800	19.6	13.2	362	22.1	6.3	10 606	-1.8	376	3.5	8 992	19.3	18.4
Shawnee	63 768	66.6	55 700	18.4	12.1	386	24.5	2.2	88 744	-1.9	3 595	4.1	80 143	32.4	8.6
Sheridan	1 171	79.6	27 600	14.4	13.5	212	18.8	3.0	1 382	-3.4	24	1.7	1 415	19.1	10.7
Sherman	2 733	69.7	37 900	19.4	12.2	276	24.0	2.5	4 131	-0.9	101	2.4	3 292	21.4	9.4
Smith	2 165	79.6	20 700	17.2	12.3	195	21.5	1.6	2 194	-4.4	41	1.9	2 345	16.4	8.8
Stafford	2 203	75.7	24 000	18.3	12.7	252	20.6	1.6	2 282	-4.6	53	2.3	2 253	23.2	8.3
Stanton	831	64.6	44 500	18.8	12.8	286	19.1	4.3	1 201	3.4	25	2.1	1 065	20.2	8.7
Stevens	1 885	74.1	48 800	15.7	12.9	305	21.4	3.7	2 502	-6.9	70	2.8	2 326	22.0	12.0
Sumner	9 689	76.6	39 300	17.2	12.8	299	21.4	2.6	13 740	1.0	562	4.1	11 408	21.0	19.1
Thomas	3 124	68.2	45 400	20.1	12.7	279	22.2	1.5	4 504	-4.3	91	2.0	3 992	21.9	9.6
Trego	1 464	78.8	27 900	21.7	14.8	246	18.3	2.0	1 696	-3.3	38	2.2	1 680	15.0	11.4
Wabaunsee	2 482	80.8	34 600	17.1	11.7	247	21.9	3.9	3 720	2.7	135	3.6	3 082	21.4	12.9
Wallace	677	74.0	28 400	19.0	14.1	257	23.8	2.2	834	0.1	25	3.0	845	16.6	8.6
Washington	2 862	78.3	18 500	15.6	12.4	193	20.3	3.2	3 241	-3.3	100	3.1	3 216	20.4	7.8
Wichita	996	70.6	37 900	21.1	12.6	294	22.4	4.2	1 169	-4.8	37	3.2	1 208	13.1	10.2
Wilson	4 194	77.7	23 500	21.3	14.2	268	27.9	2.3	5 311	-4.0	289	5.4	4 255	21.1	14.6
Woodson	1 699	78.0	18 800	16.5	14.2	257	24.6	4.1	1 500	-2.0	115	7.7	1 557	17.1	11.8
Wyandotte	61 514	62.9	42 300	19.8	13.9	375	26.8	4.5	76 074	-0.5	6 331	8.3	70 343	20.3	11.6
KENTUCKY	1 379 782	69.6	50 500	18.0	12.3	319	24.9	4.7	1 967 572	-0.7	107 904	5.5	1 563 960	24.7	12.9
Adair	5 800	79.9	35 100	20.0	12.8	234	25.9	6.9	7 907	2.6	388	4.9	6 611	15.3	11.2
Allen	5 595	76.7	35 600	20.7	13.1	230	24.5	7.2	8 850	3.5	646	7.3	5 984	12.5	15.9
Anderson	5 438	82.1	51 500	16.8	12.2	328	22.2	3.8	10 184	0.5	554	5.4	7 429	21.8	14.3
Ballard	3 191	82.3	33 000	17.5	12.2	216	22.2	2.6	4 247	-1.7	316	7.4	3 222	18.6	17.0
Barren	13 136	70.8	43 300	16.9	12.9	257	23.7	4.0	18 242	-2.2	999	5.5	14 405	19.2	13.6
Bath	3 659	76.5	31 000	18.0	12.8	207	25.2	10.5	6 156	1.0	468	7.6	3 799	15.3	15.7
Bell	11 512	65.8	34 200	19.5	12.6	227	27.0	8.8	10 324	-1.1	909	8.8	9 129	23.9	17.2
Boone	20 127	72.0	74 500	17.9	11.6	421	24.0	2.3	46 487	-1.0	1 925	4.1	28 991	27.9	11.7
Bourbon	7 250	62.6	51 300	18.9	12.8	317	28.2	3.3	10 130	-0.7	428	4.2	8 783	20.9	11.7
Boyd	19 876	72.7	45 400	15.8	12.0	297	24.2	1.7	22 026	-0.9	1 443	6.6	20 071	25.7	14.3
Boyle	9 483	68.5	54 700	18.4	12.2	301	26.1	2.7	15 288	-0.2	785	5.1	11 193	24.5	12.7
Bracken	2 872	75.4	39 400	17.8	13.4	229	21.5	8.8	3 839	-0.6	185	4.8	3 083	16.3	14.2
Breathitt	5 555	71.8	28 700	21.6	12.9	205	26.5	20.0	4 210	-0.8	420	10.0	4 405	22.3	14.1
Breckinridge	6 159	80.5	37 700	19.9	13.6	240	26.1	6.5	7 886	-0.2	661	8.4	6 227	17.2	15.3
Bullitt	15 965	84.3	51 000	18.2	11.6	334	22.3	4.0	34 293	-1.9	1 447	4.2	22 743	16.6	17.5
Butler	4 180	79.3	33 700	20.5	13.6	204	24.7	6.4	6 012	1.2	412	6.9	4 547	12.4	21.0
Caldwell	5 274	75.5	33 800	20.2	13.2	229	24.0	4.8	6 381	-2.3	319	5.0	5 303	19.8	13.2
Calloway	11 607	72.4	51 800	17.5	13.4	272	26.6	2.5	17 736	0.1	928	5.2	13 706	26.6	9.8
Campbell	31 169	68.2	62 300	16.6	11.9	368	25.2	3.3	45 825	-1.2	1 996	4.4	39 693	27.3	12.3
Carlisle	2 106	84.3	30 300	15.9	13.9	235	21.3	2.9	2 740	-1.4	167	6.1	2 211	18.8	14.9
Carroll	3 505	65.6	41 700	15.3	11.9	261	24.1	7.3	5 579	5.1	388	7.0	3 857	21.0	16.0
Carter	8 679	80.0	37 100	18.7	12.4	272	28.4	8.9	12 123	4.2	1 780	14.7	8 648	18.3	15.1
Casey	5 436	80.0	30 900	17.2	13.2	207	23.4	13.4	6 728	1.0	588	8.7	5 552	13.4	15.3
Christian	21 636	53.4	42 400	18.4	12.6	329	23.9	5.0	29 534	1.7	2 128	7.2	21 813	23.1	12.3
Clark	10 973	68.3	56 900	17.8	12.3	325	24.9	4.2	16 898	-0.1	932	5.5	13 222	23.7	14.8
Clay	7 367	71.6	27 800	19.7	12.3	201	28.3	15.7	7 503	1.1	513	6.8	5 796	21.7	16.4
Clinton	3 591	75.9	27 400	20.9	13.6	198	29.0	11.2	6 396	2.7	328	5.1	3 418	15.0	12.8
Crittenden	3 646	79.2	30 900	15.4	11.9	232	26.5	4.8	4 109	-1.2	444	10.8	3 514	17.2	21.3

1. Specified owner-occupied units. 2. Specified renter-occupied units. 3. Overcrowded or lacking complete plumbing facilities. 4. Percent of civilian labor force. 5. Persons 16 years and older.

Table B. States and Counties — Nonfarm Employment and Agriculture

STATE County	Number of establishments	Total	Health Care and Social Assistance	Manufacturing	Retail trade	Finance and Insurance	Professional Scientific and Technical Services	Total (mil dol)	Average per employee (dollars)	Number	Less than 50 acres	500 acres and over	Whose principal occupation is farming (percent)
	104	105	106	107	108	109	110	111	112	113	114	115	116
KANSAS—Cont'd													
Osage	345	3 923	1 898	D	475	242	D	53	13 486	890	18.4	22.2	45.4
Osborne	172	1 224	263	182	212	78	34	20	16 500	465	6.0	55.5	72.3
Ottawa	139	883	278	30	123	110	22	17	18 726	498	12.9	45.0	58.0
Pawnee	193	2 182	949	84	374	114	41	43	19 492	425	6.8	51.3	68.7
Phillips	241	1 585	288	312	249	115	56	33	21 121	501	10.6	54.1	67.1
Pottawatomie	512	5 563	1 301	665	1 048	187	125	122	21 989	787	15.1	32.8	48.4
Pratt	372	3 044	620	104	648	123	110	62	20 346	434	6.5	52.3	62.7
Rawlins	102	577	160	33	115	54	17	10	17 459	431	3.9	70.8	77.5
Reno	1 723	24 952	3 642	5 445	3 735	925	522	623	24 960	1 363	18.6	29.9	53.3
Republic	209	1 875	341	467	282	99	26	32	17 130	684	9.1	42.0	68.3
Rice	302	2 537	330	337	314	147	49	49	19 279	519	12.1	47.8	61.5
Riley	1 404	18 604	2 900	689	3 550	975	1 183	354	19 027	468	20.9	31.2	54.5
Rooks	212	1 344	87	406	228	75	25	27	19 894	435	9.4	53.6	60.2
Rush	109	892	185	189	72	41	34	19	21 374	486	4.7	47.3	66.7
Russell	293	2 131	222	276	393	81	D	40	18 919	494	7.1	45.3	62.8
Saline	1 683	27 500	3 579	6 921	4 312	727	1 023	672	24 442	720	15.3	33.1	51.4
Scott	216	1 412	279	D	275	94	52	30	21 077	335	10.1	63.0	67.8
Sedgwick	11 831	236 761	29 092	60 309	27 285	8 231	9 526	7 340	31 003	1 395	30.9	21.9	47.0
Seward	675	9 182	1 059	D	1 560	243	211	218	23 732	251	10.4	59.4	64.9
Shawnee	4 605	84 717	16 202	7 643	10 908	5 420	4 400	2 263	26 715	823	30.6	14.2	40.8
Sheridan	103	625	135	D	115	49	21	12	18 995	442	5.2	63.1	70.4
Sherman	266	2 075	381	D	579	143	51	38	18 191	478	4.8	63.0	68.0
Smith	166	1 149	257	184	232	68	21	17	15 131	557	11.7	54.9	67.0
Stafford	151	912	243	63	128	76	15	17	18 390	475	7.2	52.4	65.5
Stanton	78	417	D	D	62	D	17	9	22 379	253	4.3	68.0	75.5
Stevens	181	1 121	140	D	177	63	42	25	22 290	304	6.2	62.5	68.1
Sumner	556	5 071	1 115	1 201	790	292	91	111	21 949	1 064	15.1	39.1	55.5
Thomas	350	2 620	363	D	535	149	60	47	17 755	553	6.1	61.5	63.7
Trego	130	761	D	21	164	29	D	12	15 583	399	4.8	63.7	69.2
Wabaunsee	127	704	125	84	145	50	6	12	16 812	597	12.7	36.2	47.7
Wallace	60	329	D	0	61	24	D	5	16 480	277	6.5	57.4	66.8
Washington	243	1 562	444	76	219	63	49	22	13 784	780	14.6	41.0	67.1
Wichita	95	492	D	35	108	38	D	9	18 315	310	7.1	67.4	74.2
Wilson	262	3 071	473	1 419	298	90	36	70	22 768	541	12.6	33.6	51.4
Woodson	114	542	81	D	104	30	13	8	14 860	371	14.6	38.8	59.3
Wyandotte	3 098	62 368	9 209	14 452	5 367	1 553	1 144	2 129	34 141	189	57.7	3.7	27.5
KENTUCKY	89 946	1 469 315	199 385	292 206	216 211	61 430	50 705	39 541	26 911	82 273	33.9	5.9	41.1
Adair	288	3 076	839	334	471	105	49	63	20 547	1 350	34.6	2.4	44.2
Allen	212	4 242	324	2 085	401	132	47	91	21 358	1 097	30.5	4.3	39.9
Anderson	289	3 428	225	1 431	558	78	59	87	25 370	691	32.9	2.0	26.9
Ballard	161	1 871	132	774	263	66	57	62	33.069	482	29.7	12.4	39.0
Barren	870	15 447	1 987	5 754	2 287	360	379	371	24 012	2 000	36.4	4.0	45.0
Bath	177	1 407	184	434	229	86	37	28	20 251	799	30.0	6.4	50.7
Bell	629	7 797	1 369	916	1 854	256	170	165	21 123	54	44.4	0.0	18.5
Boone	2 319	54 618	2 681	9 387	8 688	2 047	1 011	1 489	27 271	691	49.1	3.5	34.7
Bourbon	396	5 258	469	1 539	757	188	109	130	24 654	910	33.8	10.3	52.7
Boyd	1 535	26 062	4 940	4 220	4 683	750	989	818	31 368	207	35.7	2.9	22.7
Boyle	769	15 290	1 845	5 297	2 000	358	300	376	24 584	673	40.1	4.9	40.3
Bracken	115	1 050	D	D	116	40	14	20	18 770	656	26.4	3.0	44.4
Breathitt	236	2 322	736	32	551	128	49	43	18 585	193	33.2	9.3	29.0
Breckinridge	295	2 167	374	264	526	135	48	38	17 437	1 379	28.1	7.0	40.8
Bullitt	919	10 211	507	3 075	1 830	257	170	220	21 550	564	49.8	2.5	38.1
Butler	203	3 189	228	1 645	263	90	35	59	18 495	700	20.0	9.7	34.6
Caldwell	285	3 175	468	751	787	120	48	62	19 430	608	19.2	12.5	35.2
Calloway	801	11 776	1 678	2 899	2 112	295	411	258	21 907	749	39.3	9.9	40.7
Campbell	1 621	21 810	2 535	3 255	4 213	551	736	618	28 352	503	36.4	0.6	30.8
Carlisle	77	648	77	180	150	59	8	11	17 255	323	26.6	9.9	41.8
Carroll	232	5 095	312	2 471	532	54	41	167	32 769	324	25.9	6.5	43.2
Carter	434	4 208	519	422	1 251	194	90	64	15 186	872	31.0	2.5	33.9
Casey	206	2 338	208	734	359	81	D	40	17 312	1 332	32.0	4.5	43.5
Christian	1 352	22 207	4 891	4 826	2 868	641	443	508	22 896	1 158	25.0	12.3	47.9
Clark	743	11 603	1 041	4 235	1 875	210	295	291	25 107	847	41.3	7.9	45.5
Clay	310	2 991	731	441	653	103	72	54	18 161	402	33.3	6.0	40.5
Clinton	194	2 616	274	1 413	347	69	20	45	17 122	639	38.0	2.8	41.9
Crittenden	175	1 858	431	479	264	77	38	37	20 158	599	18.2	9.2	37.2

STATE County	Land in farms — Acreage (1,000)	Land in farms — Percent change, 1992–1997	Acres — Average size of farm	Acres — Total irrigated (1,000)	Acres — Total cropland (1,000)	Value of land and buildings — Average per farm ($1,000)	Value of land and buildings — Average per acre (dollars)	Value of machinery and equipment average per farm ($1,000)	Value of products sold — Total (mil dol)	Value of products sold — Average per farm (dollars)	Percent from — Crops	Percent from — Livestock and poultry products	Percent of farms with sales of — $10,000 or more	Percent of farms with sales of — $100,000 or more	Percent of land owned by fed. gov. 1997	Water consumption 1995 (mil gal/ day)
	117	118	119	120	121	122	123	124	125	126	127	128	129	130	131	132
KANSAS—Cont'd																
Osage	360	3.1	404	1	221	248	615	47	41	45 749	58.9	41.1	53.1	10.9	1.8	2.1
Osborne	505	-7.6	1 087	8	306	387	372	81	41	88 096	61.4	38.6	79.1	28.0	0.5	4.6
Ottawa	400	5.3	803	4	238	383	514	69	62	124 251	44.4	55.6	70.1	23.9	0.0	2.8
Pawnee	480	6.9	1 129	70	388	637	533	104	118	276 605	36.1	63.9	69.2	33.2	0.1	68.1
Phillips	555	-4.7	1 107	9	322	456	422	71	45	89 340	51.9	48.1	74.7	26.9	1.0	32.2
Pottawatomie	443	-1.8	563	13	199	390	686	50	52	65 834	33.4	66.6	57.2	13.0	1.6	39.7
Pratt	437	1.2	1 008	73	365	540	541	128	148	339 931	32.1	67.9	67.3	35.5	0.0	77.0
Rawlins	647	0.9	1 500	15	407	568	383	99	38	88 351	68.8	31.2	85.4	27.1	0.0	16.3
Reno	662	-5.6	486	28	500	361	728	58	134	98 303	44.0	56.0	59.6	19.4	0.7	58.2
Republic	428	-3.4	626	43	321	400	669	83	93	135 807	48.8	51.2	73.5	28.4	0.0	28.8
Rice	458	5.7	882	22	346	463	566	99	97	186 606	46.8	53.2	70.7	30.6	0.1	20.4
Riley	238	4.3	508	3	122	299	673	60	30	64 527	45.9	54.1	59.0	18.6	21.3	6.1
Rooks	570	-1.5	1 309	2	330	443	338	73	41	94 489	47.8	52.2	69.9	21.4	0.8	17.0
Rush	412	-3.4	848	6	329	370	421	73	30	60 746	72.5	27.5	70.6	19.5	0.0	10.1
Russell	429	-7.5	869	D	261	327	359	68	27	55 379	59.8	40.2	61.7	15.0	1.8	1.2
Saline	414	2.7	575	2	284	428	730	57	45	62 933	67.7	32.3	61.5	18.6	7.5	10.1
Scott	476	-1.6	1 422	46	394	694	510	147	451	1 347 057	9.5	90.5	84.2	51.6	0.0	63.6
Sedgwick	540	5.8	387	28	413	493	1 329	57	82	58 636	70.0	30.0	55.0	16.6	0.6	89.3
Seward	328	0.0	1 306	80	237	834	596	193	257	1 022 381	13.4	86.6	60.6	37.1	0.0	159.6
Shawnee	224	-1.3	272	12	148	280	1 084	39	29	35 362	73.7	26.3	42.0	9.7	0.6	42.9
Sheridan	507	-5.2	1 148	64	364	537	510	102	80	180 547	55.9	44.1	85.7	40.0	0.0	78.1
Sherman	653	5.3	1 365	98	527	684	493	116	83	173 565	64.5	35.5	79.1	35.1	0.0	89.8
Smith	492	-8.4	883	6	344	490	575	104	52	93 311	55.9	44.1	77.2	26.2	0.0	4.8
Stafford	435	-0.3	915	71	351	503	545	130	100	210 542	46.3	53.7	70.5	33.1	3.0	75.6
Stanton	400	-2.9	1 582	109	344	947	624	193	119	469 197	38.6	61.4	75.1	48.6	0.0	163.6
Stevens	512	13.5	1 684	162	408	908	525	250	154	507 326	44.4	55.6	71.7	43.8	0.2	189.1
Sumner	667	-3.0	627	5	555	412	603	74	89	83 744	80.1	19.9	68.8	25.9	0.0	6.9
Thomas	679	-3.4	1 229	88	584	705	595	116	118	212 719	53.4	46.6	82.5	34.5	0.0	91.0
Trego	462	-4.5	1 159	4	302	571	450	87	41	102 777	33.5	66.5	78.4	17.3	1.5	4.6
Wabaunsee	478	13.1	801	6	155	379	497	45	41	69 070	30.4	69.6	58.6	15.4	0.0	3.6
Wallace	480	1.7	1 733	42	266	614	376	106	36	130 115	60.7	39.3	66.1	30.3	0.0	62.2
Washington	536	2.9	688	7	348	444	683	80	85	108 655	42.6	57.4	71.9	26.4	0.0	5.6
Wichita	450	1.3	1 450	65	363	764	525	131	274	883 396	13.5	86.5	80.0	47.1	0.0	75.5
Wilson	301	-3.7	557	1	176	280	534	68	35	65 173	65.9	34.1	58.6	17.4	0.0	2.8
Woodson	254	-4.3	686	D	122	336	460	45	27	72 527	45.8	54.2	62.3	16.2	0.9	1.0
Wyandotte	22	-2.8	118	0	17	263	2 200	29	5	24 647	68.2	31.9	20.1	4.8	0.0	479.2
KENTUCKY	13 334	-2.4	162	58	8 549	230	1 450	33	3 064	37 247	51.5	48.5	44.0	6.8	4.6	4 420.2
Adair	160	-9.9	119	0	98	121	1 037	24	30	21 956	37.3	62.7	40.7	4.9	5.1	2.4
Allen	159	1.4	145	1	96	153	1 167	24	35	32 019	22.7	77.3	39.5	3.2	1.7	2.1
Anderson	84	-6.7	121	0	53	246	2 172	30	11	16 494	54.2	45.8	37.5	1.9	1.6	3.3
Ballard	119	5.9	246	0	96	322	1 380	58	35	71 998	62.8	37.2	49.6	14.7	0.0	23.5
Barren	250	0.3	125	1	185	180	1 455	31	60	29 894	42.6	57.4	47.6	6.6	2.4	7.7
Bath	129	-3.2	161	0	82	150	1 039	31	23	28 475	66.5	33.5	56.7	4.8	9.2	4.5
Bell	4	-26.3	68		2	104	1 524	14	0	2 352	24.4	75.6	1.9	0.0	3.7	7.6
Boone	80	-1.4	116	0	48	356	3 043	33	16	22 946	75.2	24.8	37.0	4.3	0.0	8.3
Bourbon	197	-5.1	216	1	141	522	2 385	42	90	98 757	31.8	68.2	69.9	17.8	0.0	3.0
Boyd	26	-6.8	126	0	11	182	1 480	24	2	10 969	20.3	79.7	13.5	2.4	0.0	80.0
Boyle	95	-12.1	141	0	66	228	1 609	31	27	40 178	38.9	61.1	46.4	8.2	0.0	4.8
Bracken	92	-7.4	140	1	54	160	1 117	29	18	26 888	80.0	20.0	57.5	5.2	0.0	1.6
Breathitt	47	8.5	242	0	6	217	827	17	1	7 351	83.9	16.1	23.3	0.0	0.0	1.1
Breckinridge	268	0.3	194	0	147	195	1 043	34	32	23 172	62.0	38.0	45.5	4.5	1.5	1.8
Bullitt	57	-7.3	100	0	32	306	2 937	36	8	13 445	50.6	49.4	25.5	2.1	18.6	3.9
Butler	151	7.4	216	0	79	192	922	29	22	30 766	39.9	60.1	29.1	5.9	0.0	1.5
Caldwell	148	14.7	243	D	99	204	812	34	23	37 221	70.2	29.7	33.7	7.4	0.0	1.3
Calloway	146	6.5	195	1	117	305	1 583	50	49	65 571	69.1	30.9	47.1	14.4	0.0	5.1
Campbell	45	4.9	90	0	25	274	2 890	27	5	10 817	59.1	40.9	21.7	2.0	0.0	31.8
Carlisle	90	14.3	279	0	74	285	1 006	46	25	77 243	65.7	34.3	46.7	14.6	0.0	2.6
Carroll	60	-1.7	185	1	29	209	1 313	32	9	26 829	77.8	22.2	54.6	4.9	0.0	43.5
Carter	109	-3.8	125	0	42	95	822	21	9	10 748	67.8	32.2	26.9	0.7	3.3	3.1
Casey	191	-0.7	143	0	95	114	884	22	29	21 625	51.2	48.8	43.9	4.1	0.0	1.9
Christian	310	3.6	267	2	230	370	1 393	60	83	71 293	76.5	23.5	52.3	14.9	2.9	10.4
Clark	147	1.3	173	1	102	318	1 951	29	35	41 879	45.2	54.8	51.0	9.1	0.0	108.5
Clay	57	-15.9	142	0	16	138	955	26	5	13 176	84.3	15.7	33.1	1.5	25.2	2.8
Clinton	78	4.1	122	0	44	163	1 383	23	11	17 179	43.1	56.9	39.9	2.2	5.3	1.3
Crittenden	142	13.2	236	0	85	180	775	27	10	16 502	50.3	49.7	28.7	3.7	0.0	1.0

Table B. States and Counties — Residential Construction, Wholesale and Retail Trade, and Real Estate

STATE County	Value of Residential Construction Authorized by Building Permits, 2000		Wholesale Trade, 1997				Retail Trade[1], 1997				Real Estate and Rental and Leasing, 1997			
	New Construction ($1,000)	Number of Housing Units	Number of Establishments	Number of Employees	Sales (mil dol)	Annual Payroll (mil dol)	Number of Establishments	Number of Employees	Sales (mil dol)	Annual Payroll (mil dol)	Number of Establishments	Number of Employees	Receipts (mil dol)	Annual Payroll (mil dol)
	133	134	135	136	137	138	139	140	141	142	143	144	145	146
KANSAS—Cont'd														
Osage	8 669	75	9	90	45.7	1.6	65	444	67.7	5.7	8	13	1.0	0.2
Osborne	595	3	13	156	65.9	2.8	45	244	34.2	2.8	1	D	D	D
Ottawa	857	5	12	92	72.1	2.6	24	132	16.8	1.7	NA	NA	NA	NA
Pawnee	180	3	11	92	43.1	2.3	42	298	40.8	4.2	3	7	0.2	0.0
Phillips	281	3	16	138	58.8	2.9	39	281	34.7	3.0	1	D	D	D
Pottawatomie	12 921	95	22	266	113.9	5.0	94	854	119.6	12.1	18	35	2.5	0.5
Pratt	1 945	26	30	357	258.0	8.7	62	632	88.0	9.5	10	D	D	D
Rawlins	280	2	12	77	47.0	2.0	23	114	13.8	1.2	1	D	D	D
Reno	14 432	128	94	1 239	474.6	36.3	327	3 961	667.0	65.7	55	185	54.9	2.4
Republic	45	1	24	153	85.8	2.3	51	255	34.5	3.6	3	4	0.3	0.0
Rice	393	5	19	116	47.7	3.1	50	337	40.1	4.1	5	D	D	D
Riley	20 200	169	42	493	140.7	12.1	305	3 331	442.9	43.6	73	245	18.4	2.8
Rooks	0	0	17	114	53.8	2.6	43	258	37.3	3.0	2	D	D	D
Rush	0	0	16	160	58.8	4.2	18	93	13.5	1.2	NA	NA	NA	NA
Russell	230	2	17	138	108.7	3.2	53	310	42.0	4.2	2	D	D	D
Saline	17 049	139	103	1 261	841.2	36.0	313	4 340	679.3	63.8	70	279	34.4	4.3
Scott	740	4	22	149	67.4	3.7	40	297	48.9	3.9	5	D	D	D
Sedgwick	183 499	1 949	798	9 903	5 875.1	336.3	1 804	25 223	4 265.4	423.1	541	2 663	340.6	54.2
Seward	1 543	15	48	299	133.3	9.2	135	1 394	249.1	21.5	31	112	12.1	2.3
Shawnee	83 668	591	204	2 298	947.1	65.9	768	10 625	1 619.6	166.7	199	1 216	88.8	22.4
Sheridan	NA	NA	9	109	56.6	3.1	22	110	15.9	1.4	NA	NA	NA	NA
Sherman	980	11	21	203	126.6	5.7	62	453	88.7	7.4	6	10	1.0	0.1
Smith	517	5	15	133	61.4	2.4	39	230	25.7	2.5	2	D	D	D
Stafford	0	0	15	157	57.1	3.4	21	108	12.0	1.1	1	D	D	D
Stanton	0	0	16	132	65.5	3.7	12	61	13.1	1.2	NA	NA	NA	NA
Stevens	918	11	19	181	113.9	4.9	23	138	26.4	2.1	2	D	D	D
Sumner	7 369	64	33	212	143.2	6.1	93	733	114.5	9.4	16	42	2.2	0.4
Thomas	411	3	28	255	207.8	6.5	70	606	81.5	8.0	9	35	2.3	0.4
Trego	210	1	11	52	38.6	1.1	29	177	21.4	2.0	2	D	D	D
Wabaunsee	2 610	32	5	21	6.7	0.2	30	139	18.4	1.9	2	D	D	D
Wallace	0	0	6	D	D	D	12	68	7.7	0.7	NA	NA	NA	NA
Washington	0	0	21	226	83.8	4.7	42	211	19.6	1.8	NA	NA	NA	NA
Wichita	140	2	8	43	31.7	1.2	22	104	19.1	1.7	2	D	D	D
Wilson	182	2	11	D	D	D	38	253	26.8	2.6	6	13	0.3	0.1
Woodson	400	7	9	D	D	D	25	101	11.7	1.2	3	6	0.1	0.0
Wyandotte	23 345	239	311	6 891	4 013.4	224.7	436	5 172	932.9	91.8	126	758	84.9	15.9
KENTUCKY	1 767 181	18 460	5 051	69 309	37 242.9	2 071.2	17 369	212 189	33 332.7	3 128.1	3 227	16 284	1 961.6	314.3
Adair	0	0	16	131	29.4	3.6	65	525	83.0	6.3	10	31	1.5	0.2
Allen	NA	NA	11	102	15.3	1.8	70	469	78.6	5.9	5	20	1.3	0.2
Anderson	5 460	167	10	D	D	D	54	528	92.7	8.0	7	D	D	D
Ballard	NA	NA	5	50	28.7	1.1	37	264	49.0	3.6	3	12	0.5	0.0
Barren	3 708	61	35	328	97.6	8.1	208	2 171	355.5	31.2	26	55	6.6	0.7
Bath	436	4	1	D	D	D	42	238	38.5	2.9	6	11	0.3	0.1
Bell	3 615	69	26	328	88.9	7.6	163	1 955	299.2	36.2	12	34	2.8	0.8
Boone	122 576	1 452	122	1 683	1 005.0	59.6	435	8 561	1 666.2	132.5	92	676	101.9	13.5
Bourbon	16 372	157	18	D	D	D	75	781	127.9	10.1	10	54	2.8	0.7
Boyd	1 842	18	94	1 435	515.3	38.7	345	4 313	641.6	60.8	63	215	25.8	4.4
Boyle	15 234	146	33	285	197.0	4.8	149	2 152	301.8	29.0	20	74	7.8	1.3
Bracken	NA	NA	4	47	18.2	1.0	27	127	19.7	1.5	3	14	0.5	0.1
Breathitt	0	0	5	75	40.1	1.7	52	715	102.8	8.7	5	15	1.6	0.3
Breckinridge	704	14	10	D	D	D	69	525	95.1	7.4	8	36	1.9	0.5
Bullitt	76 181	689	31	288	92.8	7.1	151	1 547	243.3	22.5	33	89	10.7	1.3
Butler	75	1	8	31	13.9	0.5	41	270	35.7	3.1	8	21	1.0	0.2
Caldwell	1 749	27	11	61	27.2	1.3	64	752	126.3	11.8	3	D	D	D
Calloway	3 582	65	53	D	D	D	192	2 020	336.5	28.4	25	94	7.6	1.1
Campbell	32 083	299	78	649	230.1	26.0	266	3 874	644.1	57.6	68	507	58.9	15.8
Carlisle	NA	NA	8	28	22.0	0.6	19	134	20.3	3.0	4	D	D	D
Carroll	294	4	13	234	63.4	3.6	59	549	121.8	8.7	3	D	D	D
Carter	508	15	12	D	D	D	130	1 071	179.2	14.8	14	D	D	D
Casey	219	2	17	87	18.2	1.4	53	310	44.2	4.2	3	11	0.4	0.1
Christian	15 512	329	79	1 281	682.5	39.9	301	2 836	464.9	43.7	74	266	26.6	4.0
Clark	38 267	390	34	D	D	D	147	1 922	348.2	30.3	24	60	6.0	0.5
Clay	0	0	14	70	13.4	1.1	78	812	110.2	9.4	11	35	1.2	0.2
Clinton	147	6	8	55	12.8	1.0	55	374	47.2	4.5	4	18	1.8	0.4
Crittenden	NA	NA	7	D	D	D	29	261	28.9	3.2	4	D	D	D

1. Establishments with payroll.

STATE County	Professional, Scientific, and Technical Services[1], 1997				Manufacturing, 1997				Accommodation and Foodservices, 1997			
	Number of Establishments	Number of Employees	Receipts (mil dol)	Annual Payroll (mil dol)	Number of Establishments	Number of Employees	Receipts (mil dol)	Annual Payroll (mil dol)	Number of Establishments	Number of Employees	Sales (mil dol)	Annual Payroll (mil dol)
	147	148	149	150	151	152	153	154	155	156	157	158
KANSAS—Cont'd												
Osage	13	52	2.4	0.9	NA	NA	NA	NA	32	189	5.2	1.1
Osborne	5	22	1.7	0.5	NA	NA	NA	NA	11	83	1.4	0.5
Ottawa	4	D	D	D	NA	NA	NA	NA	14	50	1.4	0.3
Pawnee	11	30	2.1	0.8	NA	NA	NA	NA	18	195	8.6	1.3
Phillips	14	51	3.4	1.5	NA	NA	NA	NA	18	150	3.1	0.8
Pottawatomie	27	83	4.9	1.4	22	720	134.2	25.8	32	320	7.3	1.9
Pratt	25	91	5.1	1.9	NA	NA	NA	NA	34	478	10.3	3.0
Rawlins	5	15	0.7	0.2	NA	NA	NA	NA	7	D	D	D
Reno	89	453	26.9	11.5	97	5 141	849.7	161.3	141	2 382	67.5	17.6
Republic	8	29	1.5	0.5	8	D	D	D	12	172	3.1	0.8
Rice	15	33	1.6	0.4	NA	NA	NA	NA	28	317	6.2	1.7
Riley	91	660	54.8	21.0	28	533	75.8	14.4	156	2 998	74.6	21.0
Rooks	7	18	1.3	0.5	NA	NA	NA	NA	19	79	1.6	0.4
Rush	7	15	0.9	0.4	NA	NA	NA	NA	8	D	D	D
Russell	14	57	2.5	0.8	NA	NA	NA	NA	21	288	6.2	1.6
Saline	84	702	52.1	20.4	87	6 434	1 212.2	193.2	136	2 464	68.9	21.0
Scott	14	36	1.8	0.5	NA	NA	NA	NA	12	148	3.3	0.8
Sedgwick	957	6 367	537.9	217.7	595	61 675	10 638.7	2 569.7	969	17 828	585.6	166.7
Seward	31	209	12.3	4.7	10	D	D	D	56	820	24.2	6.2
Shawnee	405	3 227	233.6	94.7	140	7 722	1 805.6	265.4	374	6 745	199.2	54.3
Sheridan	5	15	0.8	0.2	NA	NA	NA	NA	4	D	D	D
Sherman	18	57	2.6	0.7	NA	NA	NA	NA	20	246	6.6	1.7
Smith	9	22	0.7	0.2	NA	NA	NA	NA	14	81	2.3	0.6
Stafford	8	18	0.9	0.2	NA	NA	NA	NA	14	D	D	D
Stanton	5	13	0.6	0.2	NA	NA	NA	NA	6	D	D	D
Stevens	14	41	2.3	0.8	NA	NA	NA	NA	13	94	3.0	0.6
Sumner	27	70	3.4	1.1	44	1 262	194.6	45.1	36	444	10.7	3.2
Thomas	20	55	3.6	0.8	NA	NA	NA	NA	34	487	13.5	3.9
Trego	6	12	0.6	0.2	NA	NA	NA	NA	13	D	D	D
Wabaunsee	4	8	0.3	0.1	NA	NA	NA	NA	8	21	1.4	0.2
Wallace	1	D	D	D	NA	NA	NA	NA	2	D	D	D
Washington	10	28	1.4	0.3	NA	NA	NA	NA	17	159	2.8	0.7
Wichita	3	9	0.3	0.1	NA	NA	NA	NA	1	D	D	D
Wilson	12	29	1.8	0.3	29	1 256	261.5	35.0	13	D	D	D
Woodson	4	11	0.3	0.1	NA	NA	NA	NA	10	55	1.3	0.4
Wyandotte	157	1 127	88.8	33.4	262	15 083	7 678.2	638.9	230	3 191	109.3	30.3
KENTUCKY	6 189	41 991	3 820.3	1 260.1	4 218	288 405	86 636.1	9 198.1	6 546	129 442	4 056.1	1 140.6
Adair	16	28	1.9	0.6	20	533	30.8	8.3	19	221	7.3	2.0
Allen	8	38	1.5	0.5	12	1 858	285.1	41.6	20	232	6.3	1.7
Anderson	16	44	3.0	1.1	20	D	D	D	19	283	6.5	2.2
Ballard	7	54	2.0	1.1	12	D	D	D	6	D	D	D
Barren	44	204	13.5	4.5	55	5 672	796.0	154.5	85	1 338	44.6	11.9
Bath	12	25	1.1	0.3	NA	NA	NA	NA	11	105	2.7	0.7
Bell	36	157	9.4	4.1	22	858	125.8	18.6	50	766	26.0	6.5
Boone	125	857	117.1	35.9	134	9 050	1 857.4	305.7	171	4 381	156.0	43.2
Bourbon	23	58	2.6	0.8	19	D	D	D	27	308	9.9	2.6
Boyd	97	624	53.0	26.6	42	4 395	2 930.8	203.4	109	2 172	68.7	18.1
Boyle	46	208	16.9	5.9	33	4 604	778.3	130.5	54	1 088	32.5	8.8
Bracken	7	9	0.6	0.2	NA	NA	NA	NA	11	D	D	D
Breathitt	13	34	3.9	0.8	NA	NA	NA	NA	19	329	10.0	2.7
Breckinridge	11	41	1.4	0.4	NA	NA	NA	NA	22	188	4.7	1.5
Bullitt	45	143	8.5	2.6	49	2 959	344.8	85.6	56	1 169	36.0	10.4
Butler	6	21	0.7	0.2	15	1 886	355.1	37.6	12	134	3.0	0.9
Caldwell	16	38	2.0	0.5	19	659	121.6	18.7	24	283	7.2	2.0
Calloway	37	169	10.9	3.0	28	2 983	817.4	69.1	63	995	26.5	7.2
Campbell	101	387	30.0	9.8	83	3 043	726.1	105.0	169	D	D	D
Carlisle	4	12	0.4	0.1	NA	NA	NA	NA	7	D	D	D
Carroll	8	37	1.8	1.2	18	2 378	1 408.7	94.8	27	430	12.7	3.3
Carter	24	82	3.7	1.1	18	612	40.0	8.9	33	445	14.2	4.0
Casey	11	331	8.1	6.3	27	946	80.3	16.0	16	D	D	D
Christian	79	320	25.3	7.6	56	4 469	780.8	115.4	101	2 208	55.5	18.2
Clark	46	271	16.8	8.5	46	3 635	661.1	87.0	58	1 105	31.1	8.5
Clay	21	64	3.4	0.9	NA	NA	NA	NA	20	281	9.6	2.4
Clinton	12	21	1.3	0.2	15	671	45.7	9.9	16	155	6.5	1.8
Crittenden	9	29	1.3	0.5	NA	NA	NA	NA	12	D	D	D

1. Firms subject to federal tax.

STATE County	Health Care and Social Assistance[1], 1997				Other Services[1], 1997				Federal funds and grants, fiscal 2001[2]			
									Expenditures (mil dol)			
									Total	Direct payments for individuals[3]		
	Number of Establishments	Number of Employees	Receipts (mil dol)	Annual Payroll (mil dol)	Number of Establishments	Number of Employees	Receipts (mil dol)	Annual Payroll (mil dol)	Total	Social Security and government retirement	Medicare	Food stamps and Supplemental Security Income
	159	160	161	162	163	164	165	166	167	168	169	170
KANSAS—Cont'd												
Osage	22	317	9.0	4.2	21	38	3.6	0.6	85.8	43.7	13.3	1.7
Osborne	11	169	4.9	2.5	9	22	1.0	0.2	44.5	13.4	7.0	0.2
Ottawa	8	112	3.1	1.7	9	34	4.6	0.8	39.2	14.4	5.6	0.4
Pawnee	16	142	8.2	3.0	12	39	2.8	1.2	55.5	17.9	7.7	0.6
Phillips	15	50	2.6	0.7	15	42	2.5	0.6	52.2	16.7	8.3	0.6
Pottawatomie	27	322	10.2	5.2	27	73	4.9	1.1	75.2	37.1	14.9	1.4
Pratt	29	244	11.7	4.7	32	83	5.9	1.0	69.4	24.7	13.2	0.7
Rawlins	3	9	0.4	0.1	6	9	0.5	0.1	49.9	8.7	3.8	0.2
Reno	86	1 387	98.3	48.0	118	586	32.0	9.7	315.5	150.9	62.0	8.8
Republic	10	55	3.6	1.2	18	37	2.7	0.4	68.9	17.5	7.0	0.4
Rice	13	89	5.6	2.3	15	57	3.4	0.9	68.3	27.8	10.2	1.0
Riley	100	949	55.4	22.0	94	463	20.0	6.4	321.6	93.6	21.4	3.5
Rooks	7	41	1.4	0.6	12	33	2.0	0.6	45.8	15.9	9.1	0.5
Rush	4	15	1.1	0.7	5	11	0.6	0.2	35.8	11.4	6.2	0.4
Russell	14	170	6.8	2.7	18	46	4.5	0.7	54.4	23.2	11.4	0.9
Saline	125	1 149	91.8	36.6	110	697	49.0	15.8	239.9	117.1	43.0	6.1
Scott	7	44	3.4	1.6	19	37	3.0	0.5	41.1	6.4	4.1	0.2
Sedgwick	776	15 442	1 149.0	469.4	787	5 172	322.6	100.3	2 731.2	867.3	333.7	63.7
Seward	46	314	22.2	8.9	53	167	15.3	3.4	81.2	28.7	10.7	2.6
Shawnee	322	5 720	309.5	159.9	296	1 914	127.2	41.7	1 477.7	469.6	125.3	26.1
Sheridan	4	10	0.6	0.3	5	9	1.0	0.1	41.4	6.4	2.9	0.1
Sherman	12	144	5.9	2.3	23	151	5.8	1.7	80.6	16.4	8.2	0.7
Smith	11	160	4.2	2.0	11	29	1.6	0.3	49.2	14.4	6.1	0.2
Stafford	7	150	4.0	2.5	10	18	2.1	0.3	48.6	13.0	6.3	0.4
Stanton	4	31	0.5	0.2	3	D	D	D	35.8	4.4	1.5	0.1
Stevens	9	25	1.3	0.5	15	29	2.7	0.4	48.7	10.2	4.7	0.4
Sumner	44	444	15.2	6.6	33	101	7.0	1.6	151.3	67.9	24.8	1.7
Thomas	14	141	8.3	3.3	23	72	5.9	1.1	78.6	16.8	7.9	0.6
Trego	6	55	1.2	0.4	10	22	1.8	0.3	29.5	8.7	5.3	0.2
Wabaunsee	4	110	3.1	1.6	7	11	0.8	0.2	85.0	48.3	5.4	0.3
Wallace	1	D	D	D	4	7	0.6	0.1	27.8	4.4	2.5	0.1
Washington	14	116	3.3	1.3	16	29	1.8	0.4	62.0	19.2	8.1	0.5
Wichita	2	D	D	D	7	7	1.2	0.2	51.2	5.5	1.9	0.1
Wilson	19	229	8.3	3.7	17	37	2.8	0.6	66.2	26.2	11.2	1.8
Woodson	5	93	2.7	0.9	6	33	3.6	0.8	27.5	11.6	4.9	0.2
Wyandotte	223	4 049	301.9	108.6	231	1 379	78.5	25.1	1 031.6	319.0	171.8	35.8
KENTUCKY	6 805	94 720	5 936.2	2 620.3	5 383	31 164	1 870.3	551.4	25 835.1	8 794.1	3 291.4	1 284.9
Adair	23	353	14.7	7.6	13	31	2.3	0.6	94.3	33.4	19.0	6.9
Allen	13	55	2.7	1.1	9	27	2.0	0.3	81.1	33.4	15.1	5.0
Anderson	19	192	9.2	3.7	20	91	4.2	1.1	58.4	35.2	9.9	2.2
Ballard	5	154	3.7	1.7	9	43	2.4	0.7	58.8	24.7	12.2	1.8
Barren	75	1 002	53.7	26.1	40	198	12.3	3.0	171.0	76.4	28.6	8.7
Bath	10	102	2.6	1.2	13	20	1.3	0.2	56.1	22.9	6.6	6.3
Bell	61	557	28.5	11.7	39	184	9.3	2.9	60.2	81.4	35.2	25.3
Boone	142	1 452	94.8	38.1	132	1 244	68.7	19.5	309.2	139.9	38.5	7.9
Bourbon	32	274	21.4	6.9	23	94	4.0	1.1	130.9	41.6	16.2	4.3
Boyd	164	1 480	124.4	69.4	97	644	32.7	10.2	333.2	147.1	62.3	17.6
Boyle	76	724	49.1	24.4	41	195	7.9	2.4	126.5	61.0	22.4	6.6
Bracken	7	36	1.3	0.5	4	10	0.6	0.1	39.1	17.5	7.5	2.4
Breathitt	19	290	26.0	8.5	18	54	5.0	1.3	117.4	37.3	13.3	15.7
Breckinridge	18	144	6.7	2.0	20	80	4.5	1.1	95.8	44.2	15.4	4.4
Bullitt	47	537	21.8	10.3	69	285	18.2	4.6	266.6	88.0	26.0	7.9
Butler	10	78	2.9	1.4	12	62	7.6	0.9	61.1	24.0	11.8	3.8
Caldwell	18	93	8.1	1.9	17	55	3.7	0.7	72.7	35.3	13.1	3.4
Calloway	81	936	50.4	26.5	56	235	12.3	3.2	159.9	73.8	31.0	5.4
Campbell	117	1 487	84.5	41.8	116	640	41.1	12.2	347.7	179.8	74.1	16.1
Carlisle	4	70	2.6	1.0	5	11	0.6	0.1	33.7	13.9	6.7	1.2
Carroll	12	140	5.1	2.4	10	39	2.4	0.6	48.7	20.2	8.7	3.0
Carter	23	231	8.2	3.3	28	85	5.3	1.2	158.0	58.9	22.2	10.5
Casey	12	109	6.3	2.4	9	21	1.4	0.4	77.4	29.2	12.6	8.4
Christian	96	1 231	64.9	29.6	84	320	18.6	5.0	1 275.4	123.8	42.6	17.4
Clark	58	470	25.2	9.8	49	212	11.1	3.1	139.5	75.0	21.3	8.3
Clay	19	209	8.4	3.2	14	49	3.2	1.0	188.7	45.4	18.5	28.4
Clinton	13	200	9.0	4.2	4	9	0.7	0.1	65.8	21.2	15.7	3.2
Crittenden	9	153	5.2	3.0	13	30	2.2	0.4	51.9	23.9	11.4	2.3

1. Firms subject to federal tax.　　2. October 1, 2000 to September 30, 2001.　　3. State totals may include programs not allocated by county.

Table B. States and Counties — Federal Funds and Local Government Finances

STATE County	Federal funds and grants, fiscal 2001[1] (cont'd)							Local government finances, 1997				
	Expenditures (mil dol) (cont'd)							General revenue				
	Procurement contract awards		Grants[2]							Taxes		
											Per capita[3] (dollars)	
	Salaries and wages	Defense	Other	Medicaid and other health-related	Nutrition and family welfare	Education	Other	Total (mil dol)	Intergovern-mental (mil dol)	Total (mil dol)	Total	Property
	171	172	173	174	175	176	177	178	179	180	181	182
KANSAS—Cont'd												
Osage	4.0	0.0	0.8	5.0	1.1	0.3	4.7	32.5	17.8	8.9	519	496
Osborne	1.5	0.0	0.7	3.4	0.3	0.1	1.6	9.6	3.2	3.5	774	729
Ottawa	1.2	0.0	0.3	2.8	0.4	0.1	1.0	17.4	9.3	5.2	895	786
Pawnee	2.4	0.0	0.6	2.2	0.8	0.2	2.8	19.7	7.6	6.9	949	845
Phillips	2.2	0.0	0.6	4.1	0.4	0.2	4.6	18.9	10.3	5.5	904	879
Pottawatomie	3.2	0.0	0.8	5.0	1.1	0.3	1.6	57.4	17.4	25.8	1 414	1 339
Pratt	1.9	0.0	0.5	1.9	0.5	0.2	1.4	26.6	9.8	10.6	1 091	1 015
Rawlins	0.9	0.0	0.2	2.2	0.2	0.1	11.4	9.4	3.8	4.8	1 510	928
Reno	14.6	0.4	2.8	26.2	7.0	3.0	5.1	144.5	54.7	57.5	915	757
Republic	2.0	0.0	0.5	2.2	0.3	0.2	10.9	16.7	7.0	6.9	1 125	1 046
Rice	2.4	0.0	0.6	2.8	1.1	0.4	2.3	26.4	12.5	9.9	991	918
Riley	21.8	75.5	5.9	16.2	3.9	9.4	48.1	92.3	37.6	35.8	566	428
Rooks	1.2	0.0	0.3	2.2	0.4	0.2	1.5	20.8	6.8	6.7	1 168	1 144
Rush	1.4	0.0	0.3	1.6	0.3	0.1	0.3	12.7	4.1	5.1	1 494	1 482
Russell	1.9	0.0	0.5	2.8	0.6	0.2	0.9	27.1	8.3	8.4	1 103	1 042
Saline	18.6	3.4	3.3	19.5	5.9	1.4	2.9	110.8	41.7	40.6	787	553
Scott	1.1	0.0	0.3	1.6	0.3	0.1	1.3	12.8	5.5	5.9	1 192	1 065
Sedgwick	384.0	604.6	90.5	199.0	53.6	19.6	50.9	961.5	388.0	342.5	781	546
Seward	5.2	0.0	2.4	6.9	2.2	0.8	0.7	87.9	22.2	25.9	1 287	944
Shawnee	171.4	5.7	36.0	134.9	158.2	92.1	216.0	423.2	144.6	175.0	1 061	836
Sheridan	0.6	0.0	0.1	1.2	0.1	0.1	2.0	9.5	2.9	3.7	1 345	1 328
Sherman	3.1	0.0	0.3	2.5	0.6	0.2	14.0	20.3	6.0	6.5	990	857
Smith	2.1	0.0	0.4	1.9	0.3	0.1	3.4	11.1	5.0	4.4	942	912
Stafford	1.7	0.0	0.6	1.2	0.4	0.2	1.2	20.9	6.8	8.4	1 643	1 548
Stanton	0.4	0.0	0.1	0.3	0.2	0.1	0.9	12.6	1.0	8.5	3 660	3 603
Stevens	0.9	0.0	0.2	1.6	0.3	0.2	0.6	25.4	2.4	19.1	3 527	3 447
Sumner	5.1	1.1	1.2	9.0	2.0	2.1	2.4	62.1	24.4	18.3	679	614
Thomas	2.7	0.0	0.6	2.5	0.5	0.4	4.7	28.6	11.5	8.8	1 073	987
Trego	0.8	0.0	0.2	1.9	0.2	0.1	1.1	13.2	3.7	3.7	1 120	1 101
Wabaunsee	1.4	0.0	0.4	1.2	0.4	0.1	20.8	13.6	7.7	4.4	654	610
Wallace	0.5	0.0	0.3	0.6	0.2	0.1	1.4	5.7	2.5	2.4	1 351	1 332
Washington	2.8	0.0	0.7	3.7	0.4	0.2	2.7	26.6	9.7	9.5	1 440	1 373
Wichita	0.6	14.6	0.6	0.9	0.3	0.1	3.1	8.8	2.7	3.4	1 243	1 176
Wilson	2.3	0.0	0.5	9.0	1.2	0.4	3.9	28.1	12.5	7.4	715	677
Woodson	1.2	0.0	0.3	2.8	0.2	0.1	0.8	7.5	3.3	3.2	807	785
Wyandotte	142.4	4.6	47.9	206.5	41.6	12.3	16.2	494.3	168.7	168.0	1 101	788
KENTUCKY	2 804.7	1 133.8	1 625.4	2 737.0	722.4	474.6	1 166.1	X	X	X	X	X
Adair	2.2	0.0	0.5	21.3	1.9	1.0	1.8	22.8	12.7	4.5	273	197
Allen	1.9	0.0	0.5	18.0	1.3	1.0	1.9	23.5	12.8	6.1	374	209
Anderson	1.9	0.2	0.5	5.8	1.0	0.7	-0.2	24.1	12.5	7.6	422	308
Ballard	1.9	4.4	0.5	4.3	0.8	0.5	0.6	13.8	8.1	2.5	296	217
Barren	7.2	0.5	2.3	28.7	3.0	1.9	6.8	55.6	27.2	16.8	456	258
Bath	1.7	0.0	0.4	12.7	1.6	0.8	0.6	14.0	9.7	2.2	208	153
Bell	8.3	4.1	-158.6	44.1	7.6	2.8	4.5	46.6	29.9	11.2	376	211
Boone	48.5	31.5	5.0	9.2	3.4	2.1	15.8	135.2	37.3	65.0	854	462
Bourbon	2.3	8.2	35.6	10.7	2.6	1.6	2.1	29.9	15.2	10.1	520	262
Boyd	28.8	0.2	18.5	32.6	6.3	2.7	3.0	83.0	34.3	25.5	512	314
Boyle	4.8	0.6	1.0	18.4	2.2	1.8	3.5	42.3	18.4	15.5	571	304
Bracken	1.5	0.1	0.4	6.9	0.7	0.6	0.3	10.9	7.0	2.4	287	217
Breathitt	4.1	0.0	0.4	36.7	5.4	1.6	0.6	22.9	16.3	3.7	240	126
Breckinridge	3.6	0.5	0.7	14.6	2.5	1.2	0.7	23.6	15.0	4.4	257	193
Bullitt	3.7	106.6	1.0	11.5	4.0	2.5	13.0	64.1	41.0	17.7	305	236
Butler	1.8	0.0	0.4	12.1	1.2	0.8	0.3	20.1	12.1	5.0	423	150
Caldwell	2.6	0.0	0.5	9.1	1.2	0.9	0.2	30.5	9.5	4.4	330	132
Calloway	5.8	0.1	2.4	10.8	3.8	2.9	1.8	43.1	21.3	11.7	354	247
Campbell	16.0	3.7	3.6	27.7	7.6	4.9	0.2	118.2	46.8	52.6	602	351
Carlisle	1.0	0.0	0.2	2.9	0.5	0.4	1.0	6.1	4.1	1.2	218	157
Carroll	1.8	0.1	0.4	7.5	1.6	0.8	3.7	70.2	7.8	5.7	594	330
Carter	4.3	7.2	0.9	29.0	4.6	2.5	15.3	34.8	24.8	5.5	206	136
Casey	1.8	0.0	0.6	19.6	2.0	1.3	0.4	21.4	12.3	2.9	199	154
Christian	835.5	168.6	2.9	35.3	9.7	3.9	7.1	84.5	41.3	22.3	305	129
Clark	7.2	0.1	1.5	16.9	2.9	1.9	1.1	59.1	21.4	18.0	569	254
Clay	17.8	18.2	0.8	48.4	5.9	3.1	0.9	31.2	24.7	4.2	187	98
Clinton	1.7	0.0	0.3	19.3	1.6	1.6	0.2	12.1	9.6	1.6	175	126
Crittenden	2.0	-0.3	0.4	6.1	0.8	0.6	0.7	11.6	7.2	2.6	275	159

1. October 1, 2000 to September 30, 2001.   2. State totals may include programs not allocated by county.   3. Based on the resident population estimated as of July 1 of the year shown.

STATE County	Total (mil dol)	Per capita[1] (dollars)	Education	Health and hospitals	Police protection	Public welfare	Highways	Total (mil dol)	Per capita[1] (dollars)	Federal civilian	Federal military	State and local	Democratic	Republican	All other
	183	184	185	186	187	188	189	190	191	192	193	194	195	196	197
KANSAS—Cont'd															
Osage	31.0	1 812	62.0	1.7	3.9	0.0	9.1	17.7	1 035	94	82	1 189	38.3	57.0	4.7
Osborne	7.4	1 635	44.1	4.2	2.3	0.0	16.7	1.6	354	33	22	387	23.8	70.5	5.6
Ottawa	15.8	2 711	53.9	2.7	4.2	0.0	10.1	7.2	1 244	26	28	456	22.6	70.8	6.6
Pawnee	19.5	2 697	55.2	2.7	4.0	0.0	12.0	2.0	275	36	34	1 891	32.9	62.9	4.1
Phillips	19.3	3 187	55.9	4.0	3.0	3.8	8.1	8.7	1 433	37	28	785	21.9	73.7	4.4
Pottawatomie	55.4	3 044	53.5	11.2	2.7	0.0	8.3	73.9	4 062	59	91	1 339	26.3	64.5	9.2
Pratt	27.2	2 800	60.4	4.1	4.3	0.0	7.8	14.4	1 487	42	45	1 156	29.8	65.3	4.9
Rawlins	8.2	2 566	51.8	2.9	4.0	0.0	18.8	0.9	283	21	14	378	17.6	77.5	4.9
Reno	148.9	2 366	54.6	2.0	4.4	0.1	6.9	89.9	1 429	255	304	5 001	35.5	59.7	4.8
Republic	16.4	2 676	49.7	3.4	3.2	0.0	10.8	11.9	1 940	40	29	654	20.2	75.0	4.8
Rice	26.0	2 607	57.3	6.4	4.1	0.0	11.4	9.2	920	51	49	1 005	31.5	64.2	4.3
Riley	105.0	1 662	40.8	1.5	11.2	0.9	4.3	98.1	1 553	534	314	10 956	33.9	58.5	7.6
Rooks	21.9	3 824	35.1	15.3	3.3	5.9	10.6	5.9	1 028	29	27	730	21.5	72.6	5.8
Rush	12.6	3 676	40.4	20.7	2.8	0.0	12.2	1.3	366	29	16	385	27.2	66.6	6.1
Russell	30.0	3 928	32.4	21.7	1.4	0.0	9.8	5.1	662	39	36	676	25.4	69.9	4.7
Saline	112.3	2 176	44.7	1.1	4.4	0.0	6.9	138.0	2 673	314	246	3 818	34.8	57.7	7.6
Scott	12.9	2 587	51.1	3.8	4.2	0.1	6.8	8.7	1 743	17	24	497	18.2	78.6	3.2
Sedgwick	985.2	2 246	40.2	2.8	5.5	1.5	8.9	1 466.8	3 344	4 542	4 813	23 404	38.3	57.4	4.4
Seward	90.8	4 507	42.1	33.5	2.3	0.0	4.8	41.0	2 036	102	96	2 078	22.1	75.9	2.0
Shawnee	418.9	2 540	48.6	4.4	6.2	0.0	5.6	498.3	3 021	2 872	1 069	18 964	46.8	48.3	4.9
Sheridan	9.5	3 467	36.4	26.7	2.7	0.0	16.0	1.9	695	17	13	328	18.9	76.0	5.1
Sherman	19.9	3 015	37.3	26.3	3.6	0.2	7.9	2.3	342	59	31	719	25.4	70.6	4.0
Smith	10.4	2 230	52.4	3.9	2.7	0.0	11.2	2.8	594	39	22	328	24.5	70.2	5.3
Stafford	17.6	3 454	45.2	23.0	1.4	0.0	9.0	10.4	2 046	32	24	637	25.8	70.3	4.0
Stanton	11.5	4 932	38.5	21.2	5.4	3.8	8.0	2.3	998	0	11	309	20.9	76.3	2.8
Stevens	26.6	4 928	59.3	9.3	3.2	1.7	8.4	1.3	232	26	26	757	16.3	81.2	2.5
Sumner	59.6	2 209	44.4	15.2	3.5	3.5	9.4	40.0	1 483	96	130	1 960	34.7	60.4	5.0
Thomas	30.8	3 767	69.6	1.3	2.7	0.0	6.1	12.5	1 532	51	38	1 122	21.3	74.7	4.0
Trego	12.4	3 728	35.8	16.2	3.0	14.9	6.7	3.5	1 057	19	16	440	28.1	66.4	5.5
Wabaunsee	13.9	2 077	65.2	2.0	2.9	0.0	10.6	2.8	418	32	31	493	30.0	63.8	6.2
Wallace	5.6	3 084	58.8	3.0	2.4	0.0	10.1	3.0	1 658	10	0	186	12.0	85.6	2.4
Washington	26.9	4 075	36.2	12.4	2.4	0.0	11.3	1.8	272	53	31	820	21.0	74.9	4.1
Wichita	8.0	2 950	42.0	24.4	4.2	0.0	10.1	1.2	433	22	12	270	19.0	78.8	2.2
Wilson	27.3	2 648	50.1	23.8	3.3	0.1	6.3	7.5	730	47	49	901	29.0	67.1	3.9
Woodson	7.1	1 790	54.2	2.0	3.2	0.0	15.2	1.4	345	18	19	266	32.7	61.1	6.3
Wyandotte	480.2	3 146	43.2	2.2	7.2	0.0	2.9	1 698.0	11 125	2 418	724	15 189	67.1	29.1	3.8
KENTUCKY	X	X	X	X	X	X	X	X	X	35 989	48 044	250 501	41.4	56.5	2.1
Adair	21.6	1 309	63.3	13.1	2.2	0.0	5.4	21.6	1 309	50	56	772	24.3	74.5	1.3
Allen	21.2	1 306	59.2	8.5	4.9	0.2	8.0	35.0	2 157	40	57	707	30.3	68.7	1.0
Anderson	25.0	1 384	67.6	3.9	4.1	0.1	2.5	28.2	1 563	34	64	760	36.4	61.6	2.0
Ballard	13.7	1 644	50.8	1.1	1.9	0.0	6.7	119.5	14 315	36	29	439	49.9	48.4	1.7
Barren	56.2	1 528	62.3	0.8	3.2	0.0	5.8	101.2	2 753	127	126	1 973	35.6	63.1	1.3
Bath	13.1	1 265	74.6	1.6	2.2	0.0	6.0	8.7	836	32	36	552	46.7	51.5	1.9
Bell	49.7	1 669	68.2	1.4	3.4	0.0	3.4	18.8	632	153	98	1 760	45.1	52.6	2.3
Boone	145.5	1 910	40.8	1.0	4.8	0.5	3.9	328.8	4 317	817	283	3 613	28.9	68.8	2.2
Bourbon	30.4	1 571	65.4	4.1	3.8	0.0	4.1	24.3	1 254	47	65	941	42.9	54.6	2.5
Boyd	89.3	1 790	46.1	3.3	4.9	0.0	3.1	275.8	5 531	565	166	2 804	49.7	48.2	2.0
Boyle	40.3	1 487	55.5	5.5	4.5	0.1	5.3	67.2	2 484	80	92	1 795	38.4	59.3	2.3
Bracken	15.1	1 816	75.5	2.2	1.9	0.0	5.9	10.3	1 247	30	29	356	29.4	68.4	2.2
Breathitt	23.8	1 521	73.1	7.2	2.2	0.0	2.4	8.0	512	63	53	1 081	57.2	41.1	1.7
Breckinridge	23.7	1 370	72.1	0.1	2.5	0.0	5.9	36.1	2 087	75	60	770	34.8	63.9	1.2
Bullitt	72.6	1 252	73.4	3.0	4.9	0.0	2.9	30.5	525	58	206	2 029	36.1	62.0	1.9
Butler	24.1	2 051	58.9	2.6	1.7	0.0	6.9	36.6	3 117	35	41	683	25.9	72.9	1.1
Caldwell	27.9	2 091	37.9	35.7	2.7	0.0	4.4	39.5	2 960	55	45	816	40.6	57.7	1.8
Calloway	42.7	1 290	62.5	0.2	4.3	0.4	3.9	39.5	1 195	88	113	4 943	41.2	56.4	2.4
Campbell	115.7	1 324	55.5	0.4	8.6	0.4	3.7	130.8	1 496	241	295	5 087	35.6	61.5	2.9
Carlisle	6.4	1 193	64.5	3.6	1.6	0.0	16.8	1.4	252	23	18	219	44.3	54.2	1.5
Carroll	71.0	7 407	12.7	0.3	0.8	0.0	1.5	1 078.4	112 512	34	33	704	45.8	52.0	2.3
Carter	34.3	1 291	75.7	5.9	2.1	0.0	4.1	25.6	961	76	92	1 191	46.7	51.5	1.8
Casey	21.7	1 496	67.8	17.8	1.2	0.0	0.6	11.0	758	35	50	600	20.5	78.3	1.2
Christian	82.5	1 126	56.8	3.0	4.9	0.0	4.2	121.8	1 664	3 746	24 448	3 444	38.1	60.7	1.2
Clark	57.1	1 801	46.7	7.1	3.8	0.0	3.0	131.9	4 163	121	110	1 362	39.4	58.5	2.0
Clay	34.1	1 512	76.4	1.1	1.4	0.0	7.3	15.7	695	391	77	1 405	25.6	73.3	1.0
Clinton	12.3	1 325	82.5	0.0	1.6	0.0	6.4	8.1	871	34	32	531	24.0	74.9	1.2
Crittenden	12.1	1 276	64.6	0.5	2.5	0.0	9.8	14.1	1 485	37	32	370	38.8	59.4	1.8

1. Based on the resident population estimated as of July 1 of the year shown.   2. Data subject to copyright.

Table B. States and Counties — **Land Area and Population**

STATE/ County code	MSA/ PMSA/ NECMA code[1]	County Type[2]	STATE County	Land area,[3] (sq km) 2000	Total persons	Rank	Per square kilometer	White	Black	Am. Indian, Alaska Native	Asian and Pacific Islander	Percent Hispanic[4]	Under 5 years	5 to 17 years	18 to 24 years	25 to 34 years	35 to 44 years	45 to 54 years
				1	2	3	4	5	6	7	8	9	10	11	12	13	14	15
			KENTUCKY—Cont'd															
21 057	...	9	Cumberland	792	7 147	2 673	9.0	96.1	3.9	0.5	0.4	0.6	5.6	18.0	6.9	11.8	15.1	13.1
21 059	5990	3	Daviess	1 198	91 545	560	76.4	94.6	4.8	0.4	0.7	0.9	6.7	19.1	9.0	12.6	15.8	13.7
21 061	...	9	Edmonson	784	11 644	2 322	14.9	98.8	0.7	0.7	0.1	0.6	6.0	17.6	9.0	12.8	14.9	13.8
21 063	...	8	Elliott	606	6 748	2 715	11.1	99.9	0.1	0.6	0.2	0.6	6.5	18.9	9.1	12.7	14.8	14.3
21 065	...	6	Estill	658	15 307	2 070	23.3	99.6	0.2	0.5	0.1	0.5	6.0	18.1	9.1	14.1	15.1	13.6
21 067	4280	2	Fayette	737	260 512	211	353.5	82.4	14.1	0.6	2.9	3.3	6.2	15.1	14.6	17.1	16.1	13.2
21 069	...	7	Fleming	909	13 792	2 173	15.2	98.0	1.7	0.5	0.2	0.7	6.7	18.7	8.4	14.1	14.9	14.0
21 071	...	7	Floyd	1 021	42 441	1 047	41.6	98.1	1.4	0.4	0.4	0.6	5.9	17.7	9.4	14.3	16.0	14.9
21 073	...	4	Franklin	545	47 687	957	87.5	89.0	10.0	0.6	1.0	1.1	6.1	16.5	8.9	14.4	16.1	15.4
21 075	...	7	Fulton	541	7 752	2 629	14.3	76.0	23.6	0.4	0.4	0.7	6.5	18.4	8.9	11.5	14.0	13.3
21 077	1640	1	Gallatin	256	7 870	2 616	30.7	97.7	1.9	0.6	0.6	1.0	7.5	21.0	7.7	14.4	16.6	13.3
21 079	...	6	Garrard	599	14 792	2 104	24.7	96.3	3.4	0.3	0.1	1.3	6.1	18.2	8.1	13.9	17.0	13.6
21 081	1640	1	Grant	673	22 384	1 673	33.3	98.8	0.3	0.5	0.5	1.0	8.0	20.7	9.4	15.5	16.0	12.2
21 083	...	7	Graves	1 439	37 028	1 189	25.7	93.8	4.8	0.7	0.3	2.4	6.6	17.9	8.3	12.6	14.8	13.5
21 085	...	7	Grayson	1 305	24 053	1 591	18.4	98.9	0.7	0.6	0.2	0.8	6.3	18.2	9.0	13.0	15.0	13.8
21 087	...	9	Green	748	11 518	2 333	15.4	96.8	2.8	0.5	0.2	0.9	5.4	17.3	8.1	11.6	15.2	14.1
21 089	3400	2	Greenup	896	36 891	1 192	41.2	98.7	0.7	0.6	0.5	0.6	5.8	17.8	7.9	12.4	15.5	14.7
21 091	...	8	Hancock	489	8 392	2 574	17.2	98.5	1.0	0.5	0.3	0.8	7.1	19.6	8.5	13.5	15.5	14.6
21 093	...	4	Hardin	1 626	94 174	545	57.9	84.0	12.8	1.0	2.9	3.4	7.2	20.4	10.6	14.2	17.3	12.7
21 095	...	7	Harlan	1 210	33 202	1 307	27.4	96.5	2.9	1.0	0.4	0.7	6.1	18.9	8.5	12.5	15.0	15.3
21 097	...	6	Harrison	802	17 983	1 898	22.4	96.4	2.8	0.6	0.2	1.2	6.3	18.7	8.2	13.7	16.1	13.9
21 099	...	9	Hart	1 077	17 445	1 926	16.2	93.3	6.4	0.6	0.3	0.9	6.6	19.2	8.6	12.6	15.6	13.2
21 101	2440	2	Henderson	1 140	44 829	1 003	39.3	92.0	7.5	0.4	0.5	1.0	6.4	18.2	8.4	13.4	16.6	14.5
21 103	...	8	Henry	749	15 060	2 087	20.1	94.8	3.7	0.5	0.5	2.3	6.8	18.6	7.9	13.2	16.6	14.5
21 105	...	9	Hickman	633	5 262	2 834	8.3	89.6	10.4	0.9	0.1	1.0	5.4	16.7	6.9	11.9	14.7	13.8
21 107	...	7	Hopkins	1 426	46 519	972	32.6	92.8	6.6	0.5	0.4	0.9	6.1	18.0	8.3	12.8	15.4	14.4
21 109	...	8	Jackson	897	13 495	2 194	15.0	99.7	0.1	0.6	0.1	0.5	6.6	19.4	9.8	14.2	15.1	13.4
21 111	4520	2	Jefferson	997	693 604	73	695.7	78.6	19.5	0.6	1.8	1.8	6.7	17.5	8.9	14.1	16.3	14.1
21 113	4280	2	Jessamine	448	39 041	1 137	87.1	95.5	3.5	0.6	0.9	1.3	7.4	19.0	11.6	15.0	16.1	13.5
21 115	...	7	Johnson	677	23 445	1 620	34.6	99.2	0.3	0.5	0.4	0.6	6.1	17.9	8.8	13.4	15.4	15.4
21 117	1640	0	Kenton	419	151 464	354	361.5	94.9	4.3	0.5	0.9	1.1	7.3	19.0	9.2	15.3	16.7	13.5
21 119	...	9	Knott	912	17 649	1 919	19.4	98.8	0.9	0.5	0.2	0.6	6.0	18.5	10.8	13.1	16.0	14.8
21 121	...	7	Knox	1 004	31 795	1 350	31.7	98.6	0.9	0.8	0.4	0.6	7.1	19.1	9.7	13.7	14.4	13.3
21 123	...	7	Larue	682	13 373	2 199	19.6	95.7	4.0	0.8	0.3	1.0	6.3	18.7	7.7	12.2	16.1	13.6
21 125	...	7	Laurel	1 128	52 715	884	46.7	98.5	0.8	1.0	0.5	0.6	7.1	18.3	9.2	14.5	16.0	13.9
21 127	...	8	Lawrence	1 085	15 569	2 049	14.3	99.6	0.2	0.6	0.1	0.4	5.9	19.4	8.8	13.8	14.9	14.4
21 129	...	9	Lee	544	7 916	2 613	14.6	95.7	3.8	0.9	0.1	0.4	5.2	17.5	9.0	14.7	15.1	13.8
21 131	...	9	Leslie	1 046	12 401	2 272	11.9	99.6	0.2	0.4	0.2	0.6	6.1	18.5	9.2	13.9	17.0	14.5
21 133	...	7	Letcher	878	25 277	1 554	28.8	99.1	0.5	0.3	0.3	0.4	5.7	18.0	9.2	12.6	16.1	15.4
21 135	...	8	Lewis	1 255	14 092	2 154	11.2	99.5	0.3	0.5	0.1	0.4	6.4	19.0	9.1	14.0	15.4	13.7
21 137	...	7	Lincoln	871	23 361	1 625	26.8	96.8	2.7	0.5	0.2	0.9	6.8	18.9	8.4	14.2	15.6	12.9
21 139	...	9	Livingston	819	9 804	2 464	12.0	99.1	0.2	0.9	0.1	0.8	5.3	17.1	7.5	12.5	15.7	14.9
21 141	...	7	Logan	1 439	26 573	1 495	18.5	91.6	8.0	0.6	0.3	1.1	6.8	18.8	8.4	12.9	15.6	13.4
21 143	...	9	Lyon	559	8 080	2 599	14.5	92.4	6.8	0.6	0.3	0.7	3.8	12.0	7.5	14.8	18.1	14.4
21 145	...	5	McCracken	650	65 514	746	100.8	87.9	11.4	0.7	0.8	1.1	6.1	17.3	7.9	12.4	15.7	14.8
21 147	...	9	McCreary	1 108	17 080	1 949	15.4	98.7	0.7	1.0	0.1	0.6	6.7	20.9	9.8	13.9	14.4	13.7
21 149	...	8	McLean	659	9 938	2 452	15.1	99.1	0.4	0.6	0.1	0.8	6.6	17.6	8.3	13.0	14.6	14.1
21 151	4280	2	Madison	1 141	70 872	700	62.1	94.1	5.0	0.7	0.9	1.0	6.4	15.5	18.8	15.3	14.2	12.1
21 153	...	9	Magoffin	801	13 332	2 201	16.6	99.6	0.2	0.4	0.1	0.4	7.0	19.7	10.1	14.2	16.0	13.5
21 155	...	7	Marion	897	18 212	1 885	20.3	89.9	9.5	0.4	0.6	0.8	6.7	18.6	9.9	14.1	16.2	13.4
21 157	...	7	Marshall	790	30 125	1 393	38.1	99.3	0.2	0.8	0.2	0.8	5.1	16.7	7.5	11.7	15.3	14.2
21 159	...	9	Martin	598	12 578	2 259	21.0	99.8	0.1	0.5	0.2	0.6	7.0	21.1	9.5	13.5	15.8	14.8
21 161	...	6	Mason	624	16 800	1 969	26.9	91.7	7.6	0.4	0.4	1.0	6.3	17.8	8.0	13.0	15.4	14.6
21 163	...	6	Meade	799	26 349	1 506	33.0	93.6	4.5	1.1	1.2	2.2	8.7	21.0	9.1	15.4	17.3	12.3
21 165	...	9	Menifee	528	6 556	2 732	12.4	98.3	1.4	0.7	0.2	1.1	5.8	19.1	10.1	12.9	15.2	13.9
21 167	...	6	Mercer	650	20 817	1 746	32.0	94.9	4.2	0.5	0.7	1.3	6.4	18.0	7.4	13.2	15.9	14.1
21 169	...	9	Metcalfe	753	10 037	2 441	13.3	97.9	1.8	0.6	0.1	0.5	6.4	18.3	8.2	13.1	15.5	12.8
21 171	...	7	Monroe	857	11 756	2 313	13.7	96.1	3.0	0.4	0.0	1.4	6.3	17.6	8.9	12.5	15.2	13.2
21 173	...	6	Montgomery	514	22 554	1 667	43.9	95.8	3.7	0.5	0.4	1.1	7.0	17.9	8.7	14.7	15.4	14.2
21 175	...	9	Morgan	987	13 948	2 165	14.1	94.8	4.5	0.6	0.3	0.6	5.4	17.0	10.6	15.6	17.3	13.5
21 177	...	7	Muhlenberg	1 230	31 839	1 349	25.9	94.9	4.9	0.5	0.2	0.7	6.0	16.7	9.2	12.7	15.2	14.1
21 179	...	6	Nelson	1 095	37 477	1 178	34.2	93.4	5.8	0.4	0.6	1.1	7.4	20.3	8.7	13.8	17.0	13.8
21 181	...	8	Nicholas	509	6 813	2 710	13.4	98.5	0.9	0.4	0.3	0.5	6.2	17.4	8.3	13.2	15.1	14.0
21 183	...	6	Ohio	1 538	22 916	1 647	14.9	98.4	0.9	0.6	0.3	1.0	6.3	18.6	8.6	12.9	14.6	13.8
21 185	4520	2	Oldham	490	46 178	978	94.2	94.5	4.5	0.6	0.6	1.3	6.6	20.8	6.9	12.5	20.6	16.8
21 187	...	8	Owen	912	10 547	2 394	11.6	97.9	1.3	0.7	0.4	1.0	6.1	19.5	8.4	12.2	15.7	14.0

1. MSA = Metropolitan Statistical Area. PMSA = Primary MSA. NECMA = New England County Metropolitan Area. See Appendix A for explanation of these concepts. See Appendix B for list of metropolitan areas identified by type, with component counties.   2. County typology code from the Economic Research Service of USDA. See Appendix A for definition.   3. Dry land or land partially or temporarily covered by water.   4. Hispanic persons may be of any race.

STATE County	55 to 64 years	65 to 74 years	75 years and over	Percent female	Total persons 2001	Total persons 1990	Percent change 1990–2000	Percent change 2000–2001	Births	Deaths	Net migration	Number	Percent change, 1990–2000	Persons per house-hold	Female family house-holder[1]	One person
	16	17	18	19	20	21	22	23	24	25	26	27	28	29	30	31
KENTUCKY—Cont'd																
Cumberland	11.7	9.7	8.2	51.9	7 188	6 784	5.4	0.6	89	130	82	2 976	9.7	2.37	11.2	28.9
Daviess	9.2	7.3	6.5	51.9	91 793	87 189	5.0	0.3	1 709	1 092	-330	36 033	9.1	2.47	11.8	27.1
Edmonson	11.5	8.3	6.1	50.6	11 775	10 357	12.4	1.1	156	145	122	4 648	20.9	2.47	8.9	22.4
Elliott	10.5	7.1	6.2	51.2	6 777	6 455	4.5	0.4	78	74	27	2 638	13.5	2.54	9.7	24.7
Estill	10.6	7.4	6.1	51.6	15 407	14 614	4.7	0.7	267	209	48	6 108	14.0	2.48	12.9	24.6
Fayette	7.6	5.3	4.7	50.9	260 414	225 366	15.6	0.0	4 429	2 471	-2 027	108 288	21.0	2.29	11.5	31.7
Fleming	9.9	7.3	6.0	51.0	14 140	12 292	12.2	2.5	229	195	310	5 367	16.0	2.55	9.6	23.3
Floyd	9.6	6.8	5.4	50.8	42 350	43 586	-2.6	-0.2	648	584	-137	16 881	7.8	2.45	12.3	25.2
Franklin	9.6	6.7	5.7	51.6	48 210	44 143	8.0	1.1	808	548	281	19 907	14.5	2.30	12.2	30.4
Fulton	10.0	8.5	9.1	53.3	7 784	8 271	-6.3	0.4	148	161	45	3 237	-4.2	2.32	18.0	32.3
Gallatin	9.1	5.4	4.9	50.3	7 961	5 393	45.9	1.2	142	86	38	2 902	49.5	2.68	10.7	22.0
Garrard	10.0	7.4	5.7	50.8	15 260	11 579	27.7	3.2	221	188	428	5 741	29.4	2.56	9.4	21.1
Grant	8.7	5.2	4.4	50.7	23 237	15 737	42.2	3.8	453	216	605	8 175	46.4	2.72	11.1	19.8
Graves	10.3	7.7	8.3	51.3	36 900	33 550	10.4	-0.3	602	550	-169	14 841	10.9	2.44	10.0	26.2
Grayson	10.7	8.0	6.0	50.5	24 203	21 050	14.3	0.6	369	318	107	9 596	20.1	2.47	10.0	24.1
Green	11.3	8.7	8.2	50.8	11 627	10 371	11.1	0.9	135	155	131	4 706	15.1	2.41	8.5	25.4
Greenup	11.3	8.5	6.1	51.9	36 823	36 796	0.3	-0.2	478	479	-55	14 536	8.4	2.51	10.4	21.7
Hancock	10.2	6.1	4.9	50.6	8 434	7 864	6.7	0.5	132	75	-12	3 215	15.0	2.59	8.3	21.2
Hardin	7.9	5.6	4.0	49.5	95 070	89 240	5.5	1.0	1 875	792	-60	34 497	17.5	2.62	11.9	22.8
Harlan	9.8	7.4	6.6	52.1	32 683	36 574	-9.2	-1.6	541	505	-559	13 291	0.2	2.47	13.2	27.0
Harrison	9.7	7.0	6.4	51.3	18 048	16 248	10.7	0.4	311	256	17	7 012	15.2	2.53	10.3	24.0
Hart	10.3	7.7	6.2	50.8	17 383	14 890	17.2	-0.4	286	223	-128	6 769	17.9	2.54	10.4	25.3
Henderson	9.4	7.3	5.9	51.7	44 835	43 044	4.1	0.0	681	584	-68	18 095	9.3	2.43	11.6	26.4
Henry	10.2	6.6	5.7	50.2	15 178	12 823	17.4	0.8	254	203	72	5 844	19.4	2.57	10.4	22.0
Hickman	12.1	8.7	9.7	52.3	5 170	5 566	-5.5	-1.7	60	71	-79	2 188	0.0	2.34	10.8	27.6
Hopkins	10.2	7.5	7.2	52.4	46 327	46 126	0.9	-0.4	780	706	-253	18 820	6.0	2.43	11.9	25.8
Jackson	9.5	6.5	5.4	50.7	13 651	11 955	12.9	1.2	232	174	97	5 307	21.1	2.52	10.3	23.0
Jefferson	8.7	7.2	6.3	52.2	692 910	665 123	4.3	-0.1	12 805	9 001	-4 303	287 012	8.7	2.37	14.7	30.5
Jessamine	7.8	5.2	4.3	50.9	40 016	30 508	28.0	2.5	676	388	682	13 867	30.8	2.69	11.1	18.5
Johnson	10.3	7.1	5.5	51.8	23 471	23 248	0.8	0.1	397	316	-52	9 103	7.5	2.52	11.3	22.3
Kenton	7.9	5.9	5.1	51.0	151 366	142 005	6.7	-0.1	2 716	1 583	-1 195	59 444	12.8	2.52	12.1	27.8
Knott	9.5	6.2	5.2	50.7	17 653	17 906	-1.4	0.0	245	213	-21	6 717	10.4	2.54	12.6	23.6
Knox	9.9	6.5	6.2	51.8	31 717	29 676	7.1	-0.2	578	440	-209	12 416	15.8	2.51	13.6	25.7
Larue	10.4	7.9	7.1	51.2	13 395	11 679	14.5	0.2	192	179	13	5 275	17.1	2.49	10.5	23.7
Laurel	9.6	6.7	4.8	51.1	53 691	43 438	21.4	1.9	972	589	592	20 353	30.6	2.56	11.4	21.7
Lawrence	10.4	7.0	5.5	50.7	15 722	13 998	11.2	1.0	242	222	138	5 954	18.9	2.59	10.5	22.4
Lee	9.9	7.9	6.4	47.8	7 905	7 422	6.7	-0.1	103	126	16	2 985	8.2	2.41	12.8	26.6
Leslie	9.4	6.6	4.8	51.3	12 315	13 642	-9.1	-0.7	213	155	-144	4 885	3.7	2.52	12.9	22.4
Letcher	10.4	7.1	5.5	51.1	25 018	27 000	-6.4	-1.0	377	345	-289	10 085	3.6	2.48	11.5	24.1
Lewis	9.9	6.8	5.6	50.3	13 903	13 029	8.2	-1.3	165	192	-161	5 422	15.0	2.56	9.7	22.5
Lincoln	10.2	7.2	5.8	50.9	23 922	20 096	16.2	2.4	398	320	480	9 206	23.9	2.51	10.3	23.6
Livingston	12.1	8.2	6.7	50.6	9 769	9 062	8.2	-0.4	113	142	-3	3 996	11.2	2.42	7.9	24.4
Logan	10.2	7.2	6.6	51.8	26 586	24 416	8.8	0.0	424	383	-14	10 506	12.9	2.50	11.2	25.0
Lyon	12.5	9.4	7.4	42.8	8 216	6 624	22.0	1.7	81	107	162	2 898	23.1	2.26	8.1	26.8
McCracken	9.9	8.1	7.9	52.5	64 790	62 879	4.2	-1.1	1 053	945	-822	27 736	8.2	2.31	12.2	29.7
McCreary	10.0	6.1	4.5	50.8	17 057	15 603	9.5	-0.1	269	207	-79	6 520	19.0	2.55	13.8	24.7
McLean	11.2	7.5	7.0	50.9	9 949	9 628	3.2	0.1	164	141	-10	3 984	8.5	2.47	8.7	24.7
Madison	8.0	5.4	4.3	51.7	72 408	57 508	23.2	2.2	1 238	700	998	27 152	35.7	2.42	10.7	25.2
Magoffin	8.9	5.9	4.7	50.7	13 219	13 077	1.9	-0.8	228	152	-186	5 024	13.2	2.62	11.2	21.4
Marion	8.3	6.8	6.0	49.4	18 401	16 499	10.4	1.0	321	214	89	6 613	16.3	2.58	13.7	24.4
Marshall	12.1	9.4	8.1	51.0	30 308	27 205	10.7	0.6	385	433	239	12 412	15.0	2.38	7.9	25.0
Martin	8.5	5.8	3.9	50.5	12 596	12 526	0.4	0.1	239	160	-58	4 776	11.1	2.62	12.5	21.8
Mason	9.3	8.1	7.4	51.6	16 844	16 666	0.8	0.3	300	266	17	6 847	4.2	2.41	11.1	27.6
Meade	8.0	5.1	3.0	49.9	27 008	24 170	9.0	2.5	389	227	507	9 470	17.2	2.77	9.7	18.4
Menifee	11.2	7.1	4.7	49.6	6 642	5 092	28.8	1.3	112	82	53	2 537	37.7	2.49	8.8	22.1
Mercer	10.4	7.7	6.9	51.5	20 897	19 148	8.7	0.4	353	272	7	8 423	13.6	2.45	10.4	25.1
Metcalfe	10.7	8.5	6.5	51.2	10 119	8 963	12.0	0.8	171	147	59	4 016	17.0	2.47	10.0	25.2
Monroe	11.1	8.3	7.0	51.5	11 745	11 401	3.1	-0.1	208	185	-30	4 741	5.2	2.45	10.4	26.3
Montgomery	9.2	6.9	6.0	51.4	23 042	19 561	15.3	2.2	431	307	361	8 902	21.7	2.49	11.2	23.9
Morgan	8.8	6.6	5.2	44.8	14 168	11 648	19.7	1.6	208	162	176	4 752	16.2	2.55	9.2	22.6
Muhlenberg	10.7	8.1	7.4	50.5	31 813	31 318	1.7	-0.1	539	456	-96	12 357	5.8	2.45	10.4	24.3
Nelson	8.5	5.9	4.7	50.8	38 592	29 710	26.1	3.0	696	400	809	13 953	33.9	2.64	12.1	22.3
Nicholas	10.5	7.7	7.6	51.6	6 827	6 725	1.3	0.2	144	106	-23	2 710	3.4	2.48	10.0	24.6
Ohio	10.8	7.4	7.0	50.9	23 036	21 105	8.6	0.5	367	305	63	8 899	13.9	2.54	9.2	23.2
Oldham	8.7	4.2	2.9	46.7	48 000	33 263	38.8	3.9	663	276	1 408	14 856	39.2	2.85	7.8	14.9
Owen	10.1	7.5	6.5	49.9	10 766	9 035	16.7	2.1	160	144	200	4 086	19.8	2.55	8.0	23.1

1. No spouse present.

Table B. States and Counties — Vital Statistics, Health Resources, and Crime

	Births, average 1997–1999		Deaths, average 1997–1999				Physicians,[4] 2000		Hospitals,[4] 1998				Serious crimes known to police, 2000[6]	
			Number		Rate					Beds			Total	
STATE County												Medicare enrollees 2000		
	Total	Rate[1]	Total	Infant[2]	Total[1]	Infant[3]	Number	Rate[5]	Number	Number	Rate[5]		Number	Rate[7]
	32	33	34	35	36	37	38	39	40	41	42	43	44	45

KENTUCKY—Cont'd

STATE County	32	33	34	35	36	37	38	39	40	41	42	43	44	45
Cumberland	80	11.7	107	NA	15.6	NA	3	42	1	31	454	1 535	NA	NA
Daviess	1 287	14.1	871	NA	9.6	NA	145	158	2	526	577	15 005	3 368	3 679
Edmonson	131	11.5	112	NA	9.8	NA	3	26	0	0	0	1 640	NA	NA
Elliott	70	10.7	70	NA	10.7	NA	3	44	0	0	0	838	NA	NA
Estill	187	12.0	168	NA	10.9	NA	12	78	1	26	167	3 390	NA	NA
Fayette	3 423	14.1	1 931	27	8.0	7.9	1 297	498	5	1 906	788	30 002	13 657	5 242
Fleming	164	12.2	141	NA	10.5	NA	7	51	1	45	335	2 302	NA	NA
Floyd	576	13.3	450	NA	10.4	NA	56	132	3	295	681	8 047	NA	NA
Franklin	590	12.7	435	NA	9.4	NA	87	182	1	154	332	8 780	NA	NA
Fulton	99	13.1	112	NA	14.9	NA	20	258	1	65	862	1 859	NA	NA
Gallatin	109	15.3	69	NA	9.7	NA	3	38	0	0	0	920	NA	NA
Garrard	169	12.1	133	NA	9.5	NA	9	61	1	131	941	2 257	NA	NA
Grant	329	16.2	174	NA	8.5	NA	14	63	1	30	147	2 985	NA	NA
Graves	477	13.3	446	NA	12.4	NA	38	103	1	101	282	7 290	NA	NA
Grayson	293	12.4	249	NA	10.5	NA	23	96	1	71	299	4 279	NA	NA
Green	109	10.2	125	NA	11.8	NA	9	78	1	58	545	2 125	NA	NA
Greenup	394	10.7	377	NA	10.2	NA	44	119	0	0	0	6 393	NA	NA
Hancock	122	13.6	66	NA	7.4	NA	2	24	0	0	0	1 133	NA	NA
Hardin	1 511	16.6	623	15	6.8	10.2	174	185	1	296	324	11 200	NA	NA
Harlan	446	12.8	398	NA	11.4	NA	48	145	1	132	378	7 148	NA	NA
Harrison	224	12.8	200	NA	11.4	NA	14	78	1	81	461	2 854	NA	NA
Hart	218	13.0	193	NA	11.6	NA	14	80	1	36	215	2 776	NA	NA
Henderson	593	13.4	432	NA	9.7	NA	67	149	1	233	524	6 988	NA	NA
Henry	204	13.7	158	NA	10.7	NA	14	93	0	0	0	2 470	NA	NA
Hickman	53	10.2	71	NA	13.6	NA	3	57	0	0	0	864	NA	NA
Hopkins	593	12.8	521	NA	11.3	NA	103	221	1	429	925	8 441	NA	NA
Jackson	176	13.6	135	NA	10.5	NA	3	22	0	0	0	2 201	NA	NA
Jefferson	9 406	14.0	6 988	72	10.4	7.7	2 154	311	10	3 761	560	110 566	21 481	3 481
Jessamine	557	15.2	273	NA	7.4	NA	26	67	0	0	0	4 228	NA	NA
Johnson	290	12.0	248	NA	10.3	NA	30	128	1	78	325	4 397	NA	NA
Kenton	2 316	15.8	1 241	15	8.5	6.5	296	195	2	521	355	19 430	NA	NA
Knott	211	11.7	163	NA	9.1	NA	6	34	0	0	0	2 634	NA	NA
Knox	456	14.3	332	NA	10.5	NA	19	60	1	62	194	4 516	NA	NA
Larue	151	11.6	136	NA	10.4	NA	8	60	0	0	0	2 226	NA	NA
Laurel	718	14.1	424	NA	8.3	NA	47	89	1	80	158	7 365	NA	NA
Lawrence	176	11.3	171	NA	11.0	NA	17	109	1	106	677	2 670	NA	NA
Lee	93	11.7	96	NA	12.0	NA	4	51	0	0	0	1 502	NA	NA
Leslie	172	12.7	120	NA	8.8	NA	9	73	1	36	265	2 378	NA	NA
Letcher	306	11.7	273	NA	10.4	NA	35	138	2	149	569	4 921	NA	NA
Lewis	171	12.6	152	NA	11.2	NA	5	35	0	0	0	2 278	NA	NA
Lincoln	306	13.7	241	NA	10.8	NA	11	47	1	73	326	4 080	NA	NA
Livingston	99	10.5	115	NA	12.2	NA	8	82	1	26	276	1 926	NA	NA
Logan	340	13.0	296	NA	11.3	NA	19	72	1	106	405	4 480	NA	NA
Lyon	62	7.8	100	NA	12.4	NA	3	37	0	0	0	1 508	NA	NA
McCracken	809	12.5	758	NA	11.7	NA	178	272	2	769	1 193	11 885	NA	NA
McCreary	246	14.8	183	NA	11.0	NA	8	47	0	0	0	2 707	NA	NA
McLean	118	12.0	122	NA	12.4	NA	4	40	1	26	264	1 807	NA	NA
Madison	857	12.9	527	NA	7.9	NA	83	117	2	227	341	8 725	NA	NA
Magoffin	178	12.8	132	NA	9.5	NA	5	38	0	0	0	2 042	NA	NA
Marion	232	13.6	171	NA	10.0	NA	14	77	1	82	482	3 076	NA	NA
Marshall	311	10.3	341	NA	11.3	NA	18	60	1	41	135	5 990	NA	NA
Martin	181	15.0	121	NA	10.0	NA	7	56	0	0	0	2 090	NA	NA
Mason	228	13.5	202	NA	12.0	NA	27	161	1	117	687	2 910	NA	NA
Meade	399	14.0	174	NA	6.1	NA	13	49	0	0	0	2 302	NA	NA
Menifee	78	13.6	58	NA	10.1	NA	2	31	0	0	0	1 041	NA	NA
Mercer	257	12.4	219	NA	10.6	NA	14	67	1	59	285	3 585	NA	NA
Metcalfe	129	13.5	118	NA	12.3	NA	2	20	0	0	0	1 977	NA	NA
Monroe	146	13.0	152	NA	13.6	NA	7	60	1	49	437	2 487	NA	NA
Montgomery	291	13.8	224	NA	10.6	NA	20	89	1	97	463	3 547	NA	NA
Morgan	159	11.7	128	NA	9.4	NA	8	57	1	24	177	2 149	NA	NA
Muhlenberg	386	12.0	367	NA	11.4	NA	24	75	1	112	348	5 956	NA	NA
Nelson	550	15.3	296	NA	8.2	NA	28	75	1	47	131	5 283	NA	NA
Nicholas	87	12.4	80	NA	11.3	NA	8	117	1	73	1 043	1 305	NA	NA
Ohio	277	12.6	260	NA	11.8	NA	26	113	1	52	236	3 861	NA	NA
Oldham	529	11.9	229	NA	5.2	NA	42	91	1	123	277	3 515	NA	NA
Owen	125	12.2	105	NA	10.2	NA	8	76	1	50	487	1 263	NA	NA

1. Per 1,000 estimated resident population, average 1997–1999.   2. Deaths of infants under 1 year old.   3. Deaths of infants under 1 year old per 1,000 live births.   4. Data subject to copyright.   5. Per 100,000 resident population as of July 1 of the year shown.   6. Data for serious crimes have not been adjusted for underreporting; this may affect comparability between geographic areas and over time.   7. Per 100,000 population estimated by the FBI.

Table B. States and Counties — Crime, Education, Money Income, and Poverty

	Serious crimes known to police, 2000[1] (cont'd) Rate[2]		Education						Money income 1989				Income and poverty, 1998			
			School enrollment and attainment, 1990				Local government expenditures, fiscal 1999[5]			Households			Percent below poverty level			
			Enrollment[3]		Attainment[4] (percent)					Median						
STATE County	Violent	Property	Total	Percent private	High school graduate or more	Bachelor's degree or more	Total current expenditures (mil dol)	Current expenditures per student (dollars)	Per capita[6] (dollars)	Dollars	Percent change, 1979–1989 (constant 1989 dollars)	Percent with $100,000 or more	Median household income	All persons	Persons under 18	Persons 5–17 in families
	46	47	48	49	50	51	52	53	54	55	56	57	58	59	60	61

KENTUCKY—Cont'd

Cumberland	NA	NA	1 278	1.4	39.5	6.1	7.1	5 731	6 858	12 989	-8.4	0.1	19 395	25.9	36.4	34.7
Daviess	188	3 491	21 955	22.3	72.3	14.1	82.7	5 688	11 456	24 399	-8.5	1.9	36 162	12.7	18.7	15.6
Edmonson	NA	NA	2 509	1.3	48.6	5.4	9.9	5 053	7 181	15 134	-10.4	0.2	27 051	18.6	25.7	23.6
Elliott	NA	NA	1 597	0.5	44.0	5.6	7.5	6 002	6 823	13 890	-14.7	0.5	22 536	28.3	35.5	33.6
Estill	NA	NA	3 238	4.0	46.5	5.4	15.3	5 465	7 474	16 056	-10.6	0.5	25 910	22.4	31.1	27.7
Fayette	725	4 518	65 015	13.0	80.2	30.6	220.5	6 655	14 962	28 056	5.2	4.2	40 418	11.2	16.8	13.8
Fleming	NA	NA	2 823	1.1	53.8	8.7	14.1	5 785	8 950	18 014	-1.7	1.8	26 627	19.5	25.7	23.9
Floyd	NA	NA	10 744	4.5	50.8	7.4	40.4	5 294	7 922	15 661	-24.5	0.9	24 332	25.6	31.0	30.8
Franklin	NA	NA	10 592	9.8	76.0	21.3	35.9	5 179	13 383	27 484	0.7	1.9	38 955	10.3	15.8	13.8
Fulton	NA	NA	1 766	3.7	54.4	10.3	9.2	6 220	9 820	16 087	-11.8	1.7	25 393	23.2	34.3	31.6
Gallatin	NA	NA	1 240	10.4	59.8	5.0	6.6	4 415	9 717	21 454	-6.5	1.5	31 188	13.7	16.4	19.6
Garrard	NA	NA	2 395	6.9	54.3	6.3	11.7	4 837	10 011	21 057	9.1	1.4	31 860	15.2	22.6	19.1
Grant	NA	NA	3 940	4.7	61.6	7.2	20.5	4 818	10 356	24 502	-5.3	1.5	33 813	13.3	18.5	16.7
Graves	NA	NA	7 217	7.0	62.0	8.8	30.1	5 074	10 784	20 647	-9.7	1.3	31 226	14.4	21.3	18.4
Grayson	NA	NA	4 759	4.9	48.3	6.1	20.4	4 942	8 767	17 306	-3.9	1.0	26 532	18.1	22.9	22.8
Green	NA	NA	2 037	3.2	49.0	6.8	9.0	5 304	9 177	18 432	5.2	1.1	24 421	20.2	29.1	24.8
Greenup	NA	NA	8 921	5.0	64.7	11.1	34.0	5 239	11 165	24 527	-15.8	1.7	31 948	15.8	22.8	19.6
Hancock	NA	NA	1 987	6.9	69.3	6.9	8.8	5 762	10 891	26 080	-0.4	1.6	41 058	11.4	14.5	14.7
Hardin	NA	NA	22 617	7.9	75.3	12.9	83.1	5 272	10 624	24 431	6.1	1.6	37 054	12.4	17.9	14.3
Harlan	NA	NA	9 181	6.0	49.5	6.4	35.2	5 391	7 502	14 774	-21.1	0.7	22 203	27.7	32.2	33.0
Harrison	NA	NA	3 711	4.8	62.4	8.6	17.2	5 270	10 271	21 787	3.8	1.4	33 827	13.4	17.9	15.9
Hart	NA	NA	3 143	3.1	45.3	5.2	13.6	5 721	8 142	15 671	-3.3	0.8	24 591	22.2	28.6	27.8
Henderson	NA	NA	10 454	11.6	68.5	11.1	39.4	5 302	12 042	25 556	-7.5	1.8	36 197	13.2	19.0	16.4
Henry	NA	NA	2 646	3.7	60.9	8.2	14.7	5 454	10 344	22 528	6.2	1.1	33 761	14.2	20.3	18.7
Hickman	NA	NA	1 067	2.7	56.8	7.6	5.8	6 994	9 777	20 347	-7.2	0.3	30 297	16.2	22.4	24.0
Hopkins	NA	NA	10 894	7.3	62.5	9.6	42.7	5 297	10 751	22 155	-13.4	1.4	31 305	16.2	23.0	20.2
Jackson	NA	NA	2 812	3.9	38.3	4.9	14.4	5 880	7 097	11 885	-4.5	0.8	21 174	28.1	32.9	34.4
Jefferson	539	2 943	165 252	23.3	74.1	19.3	629.2	6 175	14 067	27 092	-3.0	3.3	39 756	12.0	19.6	14.7
Jessamine	NA	NA	8 578	25.0	69.0	19.1	33.7	5 209	11 733	27 059	9.0	2.5	38 565	12.0	16.5	14.5
Johnson	NA	NA	5 849	4.0	54.7	9.3	26.1	5 578	8 492	15 782	-21.2	1.1	25 168	24.3	30.0	29.7
Kenton	NA	NA	36 185	24.5	74.4	17.0	116.4	5 436	13 587	30 516	5.9	3.0	42 676	9.6	14.3	11.9
Knott	NA	NA	5 066	13.6	45.1	8.2	21.5	6 389	6 753	13 329	-24.5	0.6	25 133	26.2	29.3	31.0
Knox	NA	NA	7 439	11.8	46.6	8.0	32.6	5 780	7 776	12 697	-14.4	1.8	21 484	29.7	37.1	35.9
Larue	NA	NA	2 370	6.8	59.0	8.1	12.9	5 373	10 129	22 405	14.9	0.9	31 676	15.3	20.4	19.4
Laurel	NA	NA	10 549	7.8	52.7	8.2	46.5	5 204	8 879	18 584	-7.3	1.5	28 509	19.6	25.5	23.0
Lawrence	NA	NA	3 475	2.0	46.4	6.2	14.8	5 186	7 809	15 273	-3.2	1.7	23 991	25.7	30.9	32.1
Lee	NA	NA	1 729	4.7	43.4	5.8	7.8	5 545	6 869	12 461	-11.7	1.2	19 667	31.1	36.4	41.3
Leslie	NA	NA	3 464	4.7	40.4	6.6	15.3	6 115	7 190	13 692	-13.3	0.3	23 509	26.8	29.5	33.2
Letcher	NA	NA	6 971	5.5	45.6	6.7	26.7	5 809	7 340	15 112	-17.5	0.7	25 070	23.9	28.1	27.7
Lewis	NA	NA	3 235	2.3	45.4	6.7	13.6	5 423	7 477	15 775	-5.5	0.7	23 759	25.6	32.5	31.2
Lincoln	NA	NA	4 279	2.0	50.4	6.2	24.1	5 787	8 388	17 169	-2.2	0.7	27 717	18.7	24.4	23.4
Livingston	NA	NA	1 808	5.1	63.1	5.4	8.0	5 170	10 123	20 892	-5.6	1.2	32 531	13.8	19.9	18.5
Logan	NA	NA	5 306	5.5	57.7	8.1	23.8	4 875	9 907	21 279	3.9	1.2	31 776	14.5	20.1	17.3
Lyon	NA	NA	1 385	5.6	61.0	9.1	4.7	4 690	10 081	20 239	-14.1	0.8	30 821	13.4	19.7	17.6
McCracken	NA	NA	14 569	8.3	73.1	14.3	60.0	5 817	12 460	22 606	-11.1	2.1	35 805	14.3	22.1	18.6
McCreary	NA	NA	3 874	3.3	40.2	4.6	20.0	5 736	5 153	10 598	-16.1	0.0	18 615	32.1	36.0	39.5
McLean	NA	NA	2 179	4.6	58.6	6.6	8.6	5 095	9 599	20 474	-9.3	0.4	31 021	14.5	19.6	18.2
Madison	NA	NA	19 863	9.6	64.8	19.1	53.1	5 132	10 029	21 388	3.1	1.6	33 794	15.1	19.6	17.9
Magoffin	NA	NA	3 448	1.7	38.2	4.6	15.7	5 803	6 289	12 160	-20.2	0.5	21 240	29.6	31.0	35.6
Marion	NA	NA	3 791	17.7	58.9	6.4	16.7	5 524	9 121	18 181	-6.4	0.9	28 373	18.0	22.9	20.5
Marshall	NA	NA	5 709	7.0	67.6	9.6	24.6	4 983	11 374	22 413	-12.3	1.2	34 547	11.6	16.9	15.4
Martin	NA	NA	3 430	2.4	44.4	6.0	16.1	5 865	8 190	15 142	-34.0	0.9	23 479	28.8	32.7	35.1
Mason	NA	NA	3 942	9.0	60.7	10.2	16.6	6 004	9 888	20 582	-4.8	0.9	30 894	17.5	24.6	22.6
Meade	NA	NA	6 407	5.7	74.3	11.0	21.6	4 664	9 234	23 676	0.2	0.7	36 460	10.3	11.2	14.4
Menifee	NA	NA	1 152	1.2	46.0	4.9	6.5	5 815	6 911	14 650	-4.5	0.1	23 403	25.3	30.4	32.4
Mercer	NA	NA	4 037	5.0	62.8	8.9	18.3	5 188	10 821	22 774	-2.0	1.5	34 923	12.9	18.8	16.4
Metcalfe	NA	NA	1 732	2.2	45.2	5.0	9.0	5 351	7 542	14 815	-2.2	0.4	23 920	21.1	25.9	27.7
Monroe	NA	NA	2 314	2.3	47.1	6.9	12.5	5 917	8 347	15 214	1.4	0.9	24 984	20.7	26.1	26.8
Montgomery	NA	NA	4 544	3.4	56.1	9.2	22.0	5 568	9 636	20 025	-0.6	1.3	29 938	16.1	22.0	20.2
Morgan	NA	NA	2 704	3.3	44.1	6.7	13.9	5 809	6 871	13 229	-2.1	1.1	22 484	29.2	32.7	35.9
Muhlenberg	NA	NA	7 180	2.9	54.9	6.2	31.0	5 825	9 779	18 679	-23.3	1.5	28 384	16.5	22.8	20.4
Nelson	NA	NA	7 371	14.2	67.4	9.3	32.7	5 112	10 165	24 220	1.1	1.7	36 552	11.8	16.2	13.7
Nicholas	NA	NA	1 534	1.8	55.4	6.0	6.7	5 558	9 116	18 070	-3.5	0.6	26 703	17.7	21.4	24.9
Ohio	NA	NA	4 948	4.1	53.1	6.2	21.9	5 312	8 056	18 196	-21.4	0.6	28 069	18.1	24.0	21.9
Oldham	NA	NA	9 684	11.2	80.2	22.9	44.0	5 325	15 510	38 416	7.9	6.4	60 159	4.9	6.8	5.5
Owen	NA	NA	2 003	5.0	55.2	7.4	9.2	4 786	9 559	21 067	18.4	0.8	31 490	16.9	21.3	21.8

1. Data for serious crimes have not been adjusted for underreporting; this may affect comparability between geographic areas and over time. 2. Per 100,000 population estimated by the FBI. 3. All persons 3 years old and over enrolled in nursery school through college. 4. Persons 25 years old and over. 5. Elementary and secondary education expenditures, local government fiscal years ending between July 1, 1998 and June 30, 1999. 6. Based on population enumerated as of April 1, 1990.

Table B. States and Counties — **Personal Income**

STATE County	Personal income, 1999												
			Per capita[1]						Transfer payments				
										Government payments to individuals			
	Total (mil dol)	Percent change, 1998–1999	Dollars	Rank	Wages and salaries[2] (mil dol)	Proprietor's income (mil dol)	Dividends, interest, and rent (mil dol)	Total (mil dol)	Total (mil dol)	Social Security (mil dol)	Medical payments (mil dol)	Income mainte- nance (mil dol)	Unemploy- ment insurance (mil dol)
	62	63	64	65	66	67	68	69	70	71	72	73	74
KENTUCKY—Cont'd													
Cumberland	104	5.9	15 105	2 979	40	7	16	41	40	11	21	6	1
Daviess	2 132	4.5	23 383	990	1 271	130	443	354	337	151	130	29	8
Edmonson	174	5.1	15 034	2 985	39	7	27	42	40	17	15	5	1
Elliott	80	0.0	12 279	3 091	16	8	12	29	28	9	11	7	1
Estill	257	3.5	16 589	2 813	64	13	35	73	70	21	30	12	1
Fayette	7 719	6.3	31 663	161	5 995	758	1 598	719	674	296	244	60	8
Fleming	222	1.8	16 339	2 853	90	15	43	51	49	19	19	7	1
Floyd	738	2.8	17 058	2 724	346	62	111	244	236	77	93	39	3
Franklin	1 308	4.8	28 050	328	1 149	55	244	190	181	81	64	16	3
Fulton	152	0.7	20 412	1 860	82	12	31	41	40	15	15	6	1
Gallatin	127	4.9	17 101	2 717	68	8	12	25	23	8	11	2	0
Garrard	248	2.0	17 313	2 681	63	14	48	49	46	20	17	5	1
Grant	397	5.7	19 063	2 268	133	22	49	68	64	28	24	6	2
Graves	727	-0.4	20 060	1 976	351	60	141	159	152	68	61	13	2
Grayson	404	4.4	16 962	2 740	200	24	55	100	95	36	40	12	2
Green	167	-1.4	15 768	2 921	46	11	36	54	52	18	24	6	2
Greenup	723	2.6	19 681	2 091	261	32	94	169	162	54	54	14	4
Hancock	199	4.2	22 147	1 311	221	7	26	26	24	11	8	3	1
Hardin	1 952	4.6	21 317	1 565	1 663	102	362	286	271	95	108	26	6
Harlan	510	3.1	14 887	2 998	245	17	78	206	199	72	71	36	2
Harrison	351	0.8	19 847	2 036	161	9	63	60	56	26	20	6	1
Hart	273	1.9	16 211	2 874	100	24	42	67	64	23	27	10	1
Henderson	1 072	2.0	24 142	831	699	38	184	172	164	72	66	14	3
Henry	299	2.3	19 913	2 020	96	14	49	53	50	21	20	5	1
Hickman	151	35.2	29 283	244	31	60	18	24	23	10	10	2	0
Hopkins	953	2.9	20 638	1 796	535	66	201	201	193	84	69	20	3
Jackson	184	2.7	14 104	3 045	68	8	22	61	59	16	25	14	1
Jefferson	21 179	4.8	31 474	171	16 534	1 150	4 860	2 724	2 598	1 115	1 021	224	49
Jessamine	865	4.8	23 191	1 048	388	105	136	97	90	41	30	9	1
Johnson	400	3.0	16 680	2 796	174	27	55	128	123	39	51	20	2
Kenton	4 091	6.9	27 790	348	1 998	185	709	465	438	196	156	38	9
Knott	276	3.6	15 371	2 955	116	17	34	94	91	26	37	20	1
Knox	481	6.7	15 050	2 983	209	34	66	160	154	44	62	37	1
Larue	268	0.1	20 344	1 876	60	12	44	52	49	20	20	5	1
Laurel	987	7.2	18 969	2 288	591	69	145	203	193	72	73	30	3
Lawrence	234	4.7	14 789	3 006	86	14	28	77	74	24	29	14	1
Lee	115	4.8	14 441	3 025	42	9	15	45	43	12	19	9	0
Leslie	213	0.0	15 674	2 931	124	11	20	79	77	23	33	16	0
Letcher	405	3.7	15 528	2 942	175	22	51	147	142	48	56	26	1
Lewis	184	0.8	13 659	3 064	51	15	27	59	57	17	23	10	2
Lincoln	386	1.1	17 106	2 715	107	20	50	90	86	31	35	13	2
Livingston	217	4.6	22 835	1 128	72	15	32	43	41	19	17	3	1
Logan	511	3.9	19 456	2 156	300	39	85	102	97	39	43	10	2
Lyon	129	1.7	16 018	2 896	48	6	31	34	32	16	12	2	0
McCracken	1 778	4.0	27 602	362	1 235	115	401	283	271	118	102	24	4
McCreary	221	5.3	13 193	3 076	76	14	25	94	90	23	39	21	1
McLean	231	22.3	23 302	1 014	48	69	31	39	37	17	15	3	1
Madison	1 408	4.2	20 803	1 735	792	59	216	218	205	76	76	25	2
Magoffin	186	3.8	13 265	3 075	67	12	24	76	73	18	34	17	1
Marion	333	4.7	19 453	2 157	152	26	60	72	68	25	29	10	3
Marshall	660	5.0	21 828	1 405	396	52	129	128	122	62	45	7	2
Martin	192	1.9	16 112	2 884	100	11	29	73	71	24	26	16	1
Mason	345	0.5	20 498	1 834	264	17	71	65	61	26	24	8	1
Meade	512	3.6	17 553	2 640	111	16	73	68	62	26	21	6	1
Menifee	87	3.8	14 849	3 001	24	7	9	27	26	9	11	5	0
Mercer	452	3.8	21 722	1 442	228	25	77	73	69	33	24	7	1
Metcalfe	156	1.3	16 238	2 869	58	18	20	43	41	14	18	7	2
Monroe	215	2.4	19 304	2 208	92	18	30	61	59	18	28	8	2
Montgomery	440	5.0	20 335	1 879	251	28	74	84	80	31	32	11	2
Morgan	175	2.0	12 784	3 085	80	12	22	56	54	17	22	12	1
Muhlenberg	593	3.7	18 546	2 405	289	59	120	140	134	60	49	13	2
Nelson	819	6.8	22 162	1 306	373	47	140	119	112	49	42	11	5
Nicholas	116	0.1	16 295	2 860	40	4	14	29	28	10	12	3	0
Ohio	365	-3.5	16 514	2 825	147	15	66	97	93	39	36	11	3
Oldham	1 400	6.7	30 564	192	364	94	231	94	85	40	32	4	1
Owen	185	2.2	17 721	2 597	51	6	26	34	32	13	13	4	0

1. Based on the resident population estimated as of July 1 of the year shown. 2. Includes other labor income.

STATE County	Earnings, 1999									Social Security bene-ficiaries, December 2000			Housing units, 1990	
			Goods-related[1]		Service-related and other[2]							Supplemental Security Income recipients, December 2000		Percent change, 1980–1990
	Total (mil dol)	Farm	Total	Manu-facturing	Total	Retail trade	Finance, insur-ance, and real estate	Services	Govern-ment	Number	Rate[3]		Total	
	75	76	77	78	79	80	81	82	83	84	85	86	87	88
KENTUCKY—Cont'd														
Cumberland	46	3.1	D	15.0	D	11.4	5.0	30.2	25.3	1 759	246	700	3 051	-3.1
Daviess	1 400	-0.2	29.7	19.3	52.6	11.6	4.5	24.1	17.8	17 631	193	2 793	35 041	10.7
Edmonson	46	-3.4	D	D	D	8.3	4.3	26.1	48.4	2 467	212	525	5 009	18.7
Elliott	24	1.1	D	D	D	8.3	5.2	18.3	38.2	1 363	202	526	2 639	5.6
Estill	77	-2.0	D	13.4	D	15.5	3.5	15.8	28.4	3 028	198	1 253	5 863	11.7
Fayette	6 754	1.8	22.1	13.4	56.7	10.0	5.9	28.8	19.4	34 286	132	5 596	97 742	19.6
Fleming	105	-1.9	D	20.4	D	13.6	3.6	15.3	28.0	2 839	206	759	5 163	11.6
Floyd	408	0.1	24.0	3.4	56.5	9.7	2.5	27.1	19.6	10 484	247	3 837	17 169	-1.1
Franklin	1 203	0.0	D	11.7	D	6.3	4.4	14.7	55.9	9 930	208	2 541	18 543	9.3
Fulton	94	2.1	D	27.8	D	11.5	4.0	15.3	20.3	1 943	251	586	3 684	1.5
Gallatin	76	-0.4	D	50.4	D	6.8	1.6	9.4	13.4	1 090	139	238	2 290	28.7
Garrard	78	-3.1	34.5	13.3	40.0	8.5	5.9	17.6	28.6	2 868	194	561	4 929	13.8
Grant	155	-3.5	27.2	18.3	55.6	21.4	3.9	18.7	20.7	3 627	162	626	6 543	22.2
Graves	410	0.7	38.7	30.5	45.2	9.8	3.7	18.5	15.4	8 324	225	1 409	14 528	6.6
Grayson	225	0.8	D	31.5	D	10.1	2.9	13.4	18.9	5 087	211	1 307	10 446	9.4
Green	57	0.8	D	17.1	D	9.6	4.5	23.7	33.5	2 716	236	727	4 523	5.7
Greenup	293	0.8	D	21.1	D	8.6	3.1	18.8	14.6	6 580	178	1 452	14 657	5.8
Hancock	228	-0.5	84.5	80.6	D	1.9	0.8	3.3	5.7	1 429	170	224	3 080	9.6
Hardin	1 766	-0.3	21.0	16.6	30.8	8.3	2.4	14.5	48.5	13 088	139	2 503	32 375	19.1
Harlan	262	0.0	D	3.1	D	10.0	3.8	25.0	24.3	9 077	273	3 177	14 735	-0.5
Harrison	170	-2.9	47.7	39.9	38.8	9.9	3.3	18.7	16.4	3 492	194	655	6 488	8.4
Hart	124	4.2	D	33.3	D	10.1	3.7	16.9	19.1	3 460	198	1 096	6 501	1.1
Henderson	737	-0.5	46.4	38.1	42.9	8.2	3.6	22.3	11.2	8 283	185	1 368	17 932	15.5
Henry	110	2.0	D	27.1	D	9.7	5.4	19.3	20.8	2 722	181	521	5 447	6.7
Hickman	92	57.7	D	10.8	D	3.5	1.8	7.9	8.4	1 254	238	162	2 374	-1.3
Hopkins	601	2.3	29.6	17.7	51.5	10.6	3.7	26.5	16.6	9 819	211	1 799	19 325	9.3
Jackson	76	-2.8	D	31.0	D	7.6	2.2	14.1	27.3	2 664	197	1 510	4 895	12.1
Jefferson	17 685	0.0	24.5	18.7	64.5	10.0	7.8	28.2	11.0	123 765	178	18 983	282 578	6.3
Jessamine	493	10.0	D	20.2	D	11.8	2.2	15.6	12.8	5 400	138	876	11 209	23.8
Johnson	201	-0.4	16.7	5.6	D	15.9	D	23.6	24.4	5 200	222	1 849	9 381	6.4
Kenton	2 183	0.1	20.3	10.9	62.2	12.1	6.8	31.6	17.6	22 069	146	3 276	56 086	9.5
Knott	133	-0.2	45.0	1.8	32.8	5.5	1.8	13.5	22.4	3 670	208	1 832	6 718	14.5
Knox	242	0.1	23.0	15.3	52.1	14.1	3.5	19.9	24.9	6 687	210	3 786	11 731	8.4
Larue	72	-3.5	31.1	18.4	46.8	9.9	5.5	21.3	25.7	2 730	204	468	4 824	3.8
Laurel	660	-0.5	D	18.8	D	17.3	2.8	21.7	14.6	10 036	190	3 236	16 923	19.6
Lawrence	100	-1.4	D	D	D	14.5	2.1	25.9	21.7	3 257	209	1 369	5 684	8.8
Lee	51	0.0	18.9	7.3	D	13.0	3.4	25.2	27.1	1 758	222	921	3 025	8.1
Leslie	135	0.0	D	D	D	4.1	1.4	14.3	15.0	3 177	256	1 407	5 038	3.7
Letcher	197	0.0	29.6	2.8	50.1	9.8	2.2	28.2	20.3	6 346	251	2 337	10 808	1.4
Lewis	66	2.5	34.2	25.3	D	9.2	4.1	16.4	26.9	2 608	185	1 034	5 328	5.3
Lincoln	128	2.2	32.1	22.2	D	11.1	5.0	16.5	24.0	4 549	195	1 486	7 985	11.0
Livingston	87	0.9	D	5.0	D	11.2	1.6	D	17.5	2 285	233	304	4 177	8.7
Logan	339	-0.5	D	49.6	D	7.3	2.5	15.7	11.2	5 367	202	1 081	10 303	8.8
Lyon	54	-1.6	D	D	D	14.4	3.6	16.9	42.5	1 922	238	195	3 460	36.3
McCracken	1 350	0.4	D	15.4	D	12.6	3.8	30.5	12.7	13 656	208	2 557	27 581	11.2
McCreary	90	-1.1	D	23.9	D	11.8	2.8	16.5	32.9	3 435	201	1 529	6 039	16.7
McLean	117	51.2	14.2	5.1	22.4	6.3	1.9	8.6	12.2	2 066	208	1 111	4 042	4.9
Madison	851	-0.6	D	26.9	D	11.6	2.6	21.8	26.8	10 280	145	600	21 456	19.4
Magoffin	79	-0.5	29.1	10.3	D	8.6	D	18.0	25.9	2 629	197	1 373	4 800	7.0
Marion	178	3.2	43.3	36.6	D	8.6	2.8	22.8	14.7	3 465	190	669	6 115	3.3
Marshall	448	0.8	52.3	42.7	35.5	8.2	2.9	14.7	11.4	7 185	239	2 165	12 528	17.7
Martin	111	0.1	53.2	3.7	D	7.5	5.7	8.5	17.9	2 925	233	2 114	4 697	5.6
Mason	281	-1.0	39.9	36.9	48.6	12.0	3.0	19.0	12.5	3 410	203	300	7 089	4.9
Meade	128	-2.4	D	D	D	14.1	3.1	16.9	22.7	3 458	131	513	8 907	16.6
Menifee	31	-0.6	D	17.4	D	6.8	2.3	22.9	37.8	1 323	202	544	2 421	29.6
Mercer	253	-0.3	D	48.3	D	9.0	2.5	14.5	11.1	4 281	206	666	8 212	8.7
Metcalfe	76	11.0	D	37.0	D	7.5	3.6	8.3	18.6	2 310	230	737	3 793	6.4
Monroe	110	4.3	D	34.0	D	11.4	2.6	14.8	22.6	2 813	239	1 059	4 882	-5.1
Montgomery	279	-0.4	D	35.0	D	14.0	2.5	19.0	12.4	4 242	188	1 147	7 759	7.2
Morgan	92	-2.1	D	10.6	D	13.4	2.7	21.5	37.3	2 383	171	1 083	4 562	5.4
Muhlenberg	348	5.1	28.8	13.5	40.0	9.0	2.3	17.5	26.1	7 297	229	1 413	12 754	10.1
Nelson	420	-1.1	47.8	34.4	41.6	10.5	2.9	18.5	11.6	6 369	170	1 022	11 078	20.1
Nicholas	44	-4.1	D	D	D	6.9	3.0	20.8	23.0	1 489	219	398	2 930	5.7
Ohio	162	-2.7	D	29.4	D	11.4	2.5	16.6	25.1	4 808	210	989	8 680	7.5
Oldham	459	0.8	D	11.9	D	9.3	5.5	26.2	22.6	4 608	100	334	11 202	28.8
Owen	57	-4.2	D	D	D	8.7	4.9	22.5	25.8	1 725	164	355	4 723	18.9

1. Covers mining, construction, and manufacturing. 2. Covers private sector earnings in agricultural services, forestry, and fisheries; transportation and public utilities; wholesale trade; retail trade; finance, insurance, and real estate; and services. 3. Per 1,000 resident population estimated as of July 1 of the year shown.

Table B. States and Counties — **Housing, Labor Force, and Employment**

STATE County	Housing units, 1990 (cont'd)								Civilian labor force, 2001				Civilian employment, 1990[5]		
	Occupied units										Unemployment			Percent	
			Owner-occupied			Renter-occupied									
				Owner cost as a percent of income											
	Total	Percent	Median value[1]	With a mort-gage	Without a mort-gage	Median rent[2]	Rent as per-cent of income	Sub-stand-ard units[3] (percent)	Total	Percent change, 2000–2001	Total	Rate[4]	Total	Professional, managerial, and technical	Precision production, craft, and repair
	89	90	91	92	93	94	95	96	97	98	99	100	101	102	103
KENTUCKY—Cont'd															
Cumberland	2 714	75.0	27 700	22.2	12.9	181	24.2	8.7	2 963	-1.2	208	7.0	2 658	14.3	10.5
Daviess	33 036	68.8	48 000	16.3	11.8	286	24.9	2.7	49 525	-1.3	2 694	5.4	39 290	23.9	13.5
Edmonson	3 843	85.6	33 000	22.7	13.0	227	32.7	7.2	5 103	-0.2	315	6.2	3 711	16.3	17.1
Elliott	2 324	78.8	32 300	21.7	11.9	191	29.7	15.4	2 698	2.5	335	12.4	1 809	16.9	21.7
Estill	5 357	74.5	30 400	20.3	13.0	253	26.2	12.4	5 803	1.0	392	6.8	4 866	15.4	16.3
Fayette	89 529	53.0	73 900	18.4	11.7	394	24.9	2.5	144 218	-1.6	4 258	3.0	117 906	37.2	7.8
Fleming	4 626	76.2	36 500	17.0	12.1	209	26.1	10.1	6 356	-0.8	336	5.3	5 343	16.0	14.4
Floyd	15 664	74.6	37 800	22.7	12.7	266	27.5	6.1	13 195	-0.8	842	6.4	12 765	23.0	18.7
Franklin	17 385	64.0	60 200	17.1	11.6	351	23.4	2.5	24 708	-1.9	707	2.9	22 646	32.9	9.6
Fulton	3 378	66.5	33 900	20.3	13.6	253	29.0	4.2	3 408	2.7	244	7.2	2 890	20.9	10.6
Gallatin	1 941	75.6	45 300	17.3	12.0	266	23.2	6.7	3 787	-0.8	218	5.8	2 437	14.2	11.5
Garrard	4 435	74.5	45 800	20.5	12.8	248	24.2	6.2	7 906	-0.3	354	4.5	5 024	15.4	15.6
Grant	5 585	77.0	49 600	18.7	13.0	297	24.0	6.0	10 432	0.0	701	6.7	6 931	18.2	14.0
Graves	13 377	77.9	38 500	17.6	12.2	262	24.2	2.2	17 644	0.7	1 292	7.3	13 367	18.2	13.7
Grayson	7 991	79.6	35 700	20.4	12.3	245	24.6	6.6	13 034	2.9	1 147	8.8	8 176	14.0	15.4
Green	4 089	78.9	31 700	17.3	12.2	203	23.9	5.0	4 365	3.7	332	7.6	4 742	14.9	11.4
Greenup	13 414	81.6	44 100	16.7	12.3	319	23.4	3.9	16 211	-1.6	972	6.0	14 194	23.7	15.5
Hancock	2 795	80.5	43 600	15.2	11.7	271	20.3	4.4	4 100	-3.0	308	7.5	3 051	16.9	17.4
Hardin	29 358	63.5	58 300	20.3	11.8	353	23.7	3.9	37 654	0.7	2 423	6.4	30 858	26.0	11.3
Harlan	13 269	70.8	29 400	18.6	12.2	225	27.6	8.9	8 777	-3.8	767	8.7	9 932	20.9	23.3
Harrison	6 086	67.7	48 500	18.1	12.2	274	24.6	5.2	7 532	1.5	541	7.2	6 985	19.1	13.6
Hart	5 740	75.6	31 600	19.8	13.4	224	25.2	8.3	7 752	-1.1	445	5.7	5 922	14.2	13.6
Henderson	16 558	66.9	51 000	16.3	12.7	319	24.1	3.1	24 032	-0.4	1 374	5.7	19 857	22.4	14.5
Henry	4 896	76.2	41 100	16.9	12.6	268	25.0	7.0	7 312	1.7	320	4.4	5 851	18.3	10.6
Hickman	2 188	79.2	32 000	16.1	12.7	213	20.2	4.1	2 469	0.5	153	6.2	2 213	16.4	14.2
Hopkins	17 760	75.2	39 600	16.8	11.9	269	25.5	2.8	19 016	-2.5	1 335	7.0	18 634	22.8	15.8
Jackson	4 381	77.2	26 900	20.8	13.1	170	26.4	15.0	7 105	-2.8	494	7.0	3 666	13.4	20.2
Jefferson	264 138	64.5	57 000	17.0	12.2	346	24.7	2.4	378 510	-1.9	18 078	4.8	316 117	29.5	10.7
Jessamine	10 601	68.4	63 800	21.3	11.8	351	26.3	3.9	21 100	-1.5	590	2.8	15 287	25.7	11.8
Johnson	8 469	73.8	40 100	22.2	12.8	276	26.8	7.0	9 137	-0.6	568	6.2	7 565	22.5	14.3
Kenton	52 690	65.8	65 200	17.3	12.1	370	23.3	2.7	80 409	-1.0	3 700	4.6	69 688	28.9	11.5
Knott	6 086	78.4	27 700	20.4	13.1	199	28.7	10.7	5 645	-2.9	346	6.1	4 673	22.4	21.6
Knox	10 718	68.8	35 300	21.2	12.8	245	33.5	10.2	11 572	0.8	716	6.2	8 752	20.6	17.0
Larue	4 503	79.7	39 500	19.8	12.7	225	24.0	3.3	6 394	-0.1	320	5.0	4 848	16.6	17.4
Laurel	15 585	76.4	46 900	21.2	12.5	280	25.8	5.9	23 969	1.8	1 308	5.5	16 438	20.3	13.5
Lawrence	5 007	75.1	40 500	19.3	12.4	255	32.0	10.9	5 319	-3.5	536	10.1	3 835	20.5	20.1
Lee	2 760	75.1	28 400	19.2	13.7	177	27.5	15.2	2 530	-0.3	180	7.1	2 104	16.5	18.7
Leslie	4 711	77.6	24 400	18.2	12.1	192	26.4	13.9	4 309	-0.7	201	4.7	3 650	17.1	28.2
Letcher	9 731	78.6	27 300	21.2	12.6	226	26.9	8.9	7 844	-3.5	505	6.4	7 531	20.7	27.9
Lewis	4 713	78.8	31 400	18.9	12.7	207	24.9	14.0	4 235	-1.6	546	12.9	4 724	14.9	15.7
Lincoln	7 431	76.3	37 700	18.9	12.6	233	27.6	9.8	11 714	1.1	767	6.5	8 017	16.5	13.1
Livingston	3 593	84.8	36 500	20.1	13.8	310	21.2	4.1	4 958	-1.4	349	7.0	3 891	15.3	17.8
Logan	9 302	73.4	41 200	16.8	13.4	271	24.4	4.3	13 265	1.1	1 152	8.7	10 955	15.5	16.4
Lyon	2 355	79.8	46 300	17.5	11.9	255	24.6	3.8	3 331	-1.5	182	5.5	2 286	22.8	13.7
McCracken	25 625	68.2	48 500	15.8	12.2	291	24.7	1.8	33 488	-1.8	1 517	4.5	27 571	26.1	12.5
McCreary	5 479	74.7	26 300	24.5	11.7	217	32.2	13.5	6 898	7.4	815	11.8	3 918	16.5	16.4
McLean	3 672	80.1	36 200	15.9	12.4	222	22.0	3.8	4 306	-1.1	306	7.1	3 898	17.7	12.4
Madison	20 012	62.1	55 500	18.7	12.3	307	25.2	3.5	36 782	-1.0	1 595	4.3	27 242	27.8	10.3
Magoffin	4 440	78.0	35 500	24.1	12.8	197	35.1	10.9	5 043	-1.2	633	12.6	3 351	18.5	14.6
Marion	5 688	76.9	39 500	21.3	12.6	229	26.2	6.9	11 084	-0.9	620	5.6	6 808	13.4	13.5
Marshall	10 789	82.8	47 600	19.0	11.9	280	25.4	1.2	14 790	-0.1	1 096	7.4	10 878	20.3	16.1
Martin	4 300	78.7	37 500	16.9	12.9	256	29.8	7.2	3 252	4.7	209	6.4	3 272	17.4	28.2
Mason	6 537	64.9	43 800	17.5	12.3	244	22.6	6.1	8 342	-0.7	356	4.3	7 286	20.1	13.3
Meade	8 080	61.3	49 700	19.3	12.0	362	22.2	5.7	11 212	0.8	645	5.8	7 862	19.9	16.3
Menifee	1 842	81.8	32 600	26.7	12.1	214	26.7	8.3	3 064	1.3	242	7.9	1 814	15.4	17.3
Mercer	7 413	72.8	46 600	18.6	11.9	290	25.9	3.9	10 963	-2.5	577	5.3	8 870	18.3	13.1
Metcalfe	3 433	77.4	31 300	17.5	12.8	203	28.2	9.8	4 714	-1.7	238	5.7	3 837	10.8	12.0
Monroe	4 505	74.9	31 500	18.2	14.5	190	22.1	8.3	4 703	-7.3	608	12.9	4 948	14.7	12.0
Montgomery	7 312	70.2	43 600	19.2	12.1	285	26.6	4.4	13 428	2.0	863	6.4	8 409	17.0	15.0
Morgan	4 089	76.5	36 600	25.5	14.3	223	27.6	9.8	5 294	8.2	531	10.0	3 503	20.9	15.1
Muhlenberg	11 683	80.8	37 300	18.0	12.1	246	24.7	4.5	12 608	0.0	1 307	10.3	11 432	17.5	17.7
Nelson	10 417	78.0	45 800	17.7	12.0	292	24.2	5.3	19 518	0.3	1 360	7.0	13 289	16.8	15.7
Nicholas	2 621	71.9	38 200	17.7	11.8	217	24.6	9.6	2 487	-8.9	220	8.8	3 022	14.7	10.9
Ohio	7 816	79.1	34 300	17.3	12.5	265	23.8	5.7	9 647	-0.8	758	7.9	7 521	18.2	16.7
Oldham	10 673	83.1	86 500	19.7	11.7	367	24.3	2.1	25 209	-2.8	642	2.5	15 824	32.9	11.0
Owen	3 412	75.6	38 200	19.6	12.4	226	25.4	10.3	4 239	-1.6	180	4.2	3 984	17.9	12.5

1. Specified owner-occupied units. 2. Specified renter-occupied units. 3. Overcrowded or lacking complete plumbing facilities. 4. Percent of civilian labor force. 5. Persons 16 years and older.

STATE County	Private nonfarm establishments, employment and payroll, 1999									Agriculture, 1997			
		Employment						Annual payroll		Farms			Farm operators
											Percent with—		
	Number of establish-ments	Total	Health Care and Social Assistance	Manufac-turing	Retail trade	Finance and Insurance	Professional Scientific and Technical Services	Total (mil dol)	Average per employee (dollars)	Number	Less than 50 acres	500 acres and over	Whose principal occu-pation is farming (percent)
	104	105	106	107	108	109	110	111	112	113	114	115	116

KENTUCKY—Cont'd

Cumberland	116	1 059	265	203	220	67	11	19	18 010	524	28.6	9.7	45.4
Daviess	2 386	40 236	5 668	8 751	6 140	1 290	1 136	998	24 795	1 042	43.2	11.8	43.2
Edmonson	104	737	201	D	126	69	14	12	16 445	706	35.0	3.4	36.1
Elliott	57	401	100	D	62	D	D	6	15 761	439	28.0	3.0	39.0
Estill	229	2 022	260	371	418	94	17	31	15 249	432	27.8	4.4	32.4
Fayette	7 776	144 176	24 747	17 612	21 368	5 875	9 200	4 078	28 283	745	42.7	8.6	52.8
Fleming	274	2 604	569	663	578	137	48	52	19 949	1 132	27.7	6.4	51.0
Floyd	850	9 598	1 933	302	1 485	269	294	237	24 728	59	44.1	3.4	27.1
Franklin	1 151	15 687	1 812	3 036	2 991	798	996	375	23 933	675	35.0	2.5	38.2
Fulton	190	2 417	323	816	521	144	30	53	21 999	162	22.8	32.1	66.7
Gallatin	93	1 644	162	D	155	27	14	33	20 308	253	28.9	4.3	41.5
Garrard	243	1 944	331	398	241	39	52	36	18 630	880	32.6	5.0	51.5
Grant	440	4 276	394	753	1 209	174	74	89	20 821	936	30.7	2.6	35.3
Graves	691	10 423	1 920	3 364	1 588	361	227	248	23 795	1 371	35.8	8.2	37.7
Grayson	466	7 537	837	2 859	904	180	86	144	19 118	1 412	27.8	3.9	35.8
Green	180	1 413	423	324	269	85	D	25	17 462	1 059	31.2	2.6	46.6
Greenup	509	5 008	522	740	840	252	152	128	25 486	733	33.8	3.4	31.1
Hancock	134	2 960	109	2 073	183	54	21	102	34 310	449	30.5	3.8	30.7
Hardin	1 981	31 871	6 716	7 231	5 577	929	759	730	22 899	1 637	41.7	4.9	39.2
Harlan	542	6 105	1 134	285	1 243	194	209	142	23 281	27	48.1	0.0	14.8
Harrison	289	4 091	683	1 519	639	114	47	101	24 798	1 079	27.7	5.6	46.1
Hart	260	2 521	370	678	560	104	87	44	17 541	1 352	26.8	2.7	48.1
Henderson	1 080	18 640	2 265	7 237	2 236	450	316	485	26 004	526	37.3	18.3	45.1
Henry	250	2 449	178	715	490	152	48	56	22 846	955	28.8	5.2	46.5
Hickman	94	1 214	202	338	129	50	12	23	19 319	294	28.2	21.1	44.9
Hopkins	1 096	14 857	3 031	2 682	2 597	495	363	369	24 846	538	26.2	11.2	38.7
Jackson	142	1 930	269	790	179	53	9	36	18 580	689	38.8	2.2	36.7
Jefferson	19 751	406 891	50 958	56 602	47 150	27 260	18 470	12 745	31 322	475	61.5	1.7	38.3
Jessamine	870	11 979	414	2 593	2 148	169	204	277	23 108	754	47.9	4.5	41.1
Johnson	481	4 630	646	320	1 464	241	158	91	19 730	182	36.3	1.1	25.8
Kenton	3 242	60 989	7 503	7 777	6 122	1 370	2 662	1 848	30 293	442	45.9	0.9	31.2
Knott	229	2 558	415	11	317	45	48	70	27 451	21	23.8	9.5	19.0
Knox	435	5 784	996	1 045	1 421	145	182	109	18 871	322	33.2	4.0	31.1
Larue	237	1 869	260	653	217	104	43	34	17 963	806	35.2	5.1	42.8
Laurel	1 045	16 527	1 361	2 773	2 602	470	458	394	23 811	1 083	48.3	1.6	34.8
Lawrence	206	2 288	487	D	473	136	37	53	23 359	297	25.6	4.0	35.0
Lee	111	1 906	755	135	231	64	11	25	13 008	161	32.3	5.0	28.6
Leslie	134	1 527	460	D	193	D	D	35	22 981	17	41.2	5.9	11.8
Letcher	424	4 997	737	113	727	151	174	125	25 039	31	29.0	0.0	35.5
Lewis	130	1 477	169	730	239	96	30	28	18 959	774	26.1	7.1	44.6
Lincoln	290	2 828	494	805	485	282	91	53	18 853	1 258	40.5	5.3	44.2
Livingston	149	1 826	339	101	201	D	23	47	25 738	405	15.1	14.1	33.3
Logan	518	8 395	652	4 625	950	187	119	209	24 949	1 203	26.2	10.4	46.4
Lyon	181	1 504	236	D	423	40	22	21	13 718	249	22.1	7.6	34.9
McCracken	2 125	35 653	5 721	3 955	6 500	1 036	1 011	920	25 791	457	48.1	5.3	34.8
McCreary	180	2 215	291	981	368	96	56	31	13 849	108	38.9	0.9	14.8
McLean	180	1 376	127	170	267	112	22	30	21 497	422	32.2	17.5	53.6
Madison	1 430	22 124	2 813	6 331	3 859	463	366	497	22 449	1 444	40.4	6.0	43.4
Magoffin	209	1 905	350	D	282	70	91	37	19 476	373	42.1	2.1	31.1
Marion	329	5 210	880	1 861	662	135	104	103	19 769	983	27.4	5.3	41.2
Marshall	651	8 455	923	2 723	1 117	345	183	265	31 304	673	37.6	4.0	24.7
Martin	181	2 042	195	D	342	104	30	62	30 325	9	11.1	0.0	0.0
Mason	464	8 482	917	3 433	1 477	236	100	196	23 104	751	28.6	6.4	52.2
Meade	332	2 908	164	D	817	149	53	72	24 676	841	41.3	5.4	33.7
Menifee	72	564	186	205	72	D	10	10	17 590	346	34.1	2.6	37.0
Mercer	419	6 341	443	2 926	776	104	73	176	27 757	976	38.2	3.2	39.9
Metcalfe	133	2 455	D	1 769	277	78	14	52	21 073	950	28.2	3.5	45.2
Monroe	228	3 242	439	1 080	632	84	16	58	17 872	973	31.1	7.0	39.9
Montgomery	532	7 824	786	2 740	1 445	223	181	168	21 456	734	36.4	6.0	44.0
Morgan	181	1 979	374	368	420	81	25	41	20 937	698	30.1	5.9	34.8
Muhlenberg	593	7 023	1 291	1 318	1 382	243	146	151	21 461	559	25.9	8.9	39.5
Nelson	873	11 596	956	3 254	1 631	290	199	281	24 202	1 249	37.2	5.0	36.4
Nicholas	93	1 194	261	D	110	30	D	19	16 171	567	26.6	8.8	50.6
Ohio	352	4 774	787	1 807	636	150	99	92	19 237	943	38.5	5.5	35.9
Oldham	973	8 821	1 076	1 171	1 314	286	455	220	24 964	392	42.1	9.7	40.8
Owen	117	1 118	240	D	211	68	D	28	24 851	803	20.3	7.8	44.5

Table B. States and Counties — Agriculture, Land, and Water

STATE County	Agriculture, 1997 (cont'd)														Percent of land owned by fed. gov. 1997	Water consumption 1995 (mil gal/ day)
	Land in farms				Value of land and buildings		Value of machinery and equipment average per farm ($1,000)	Value of products sold				Percent of farms with sales of —			
		Acres								Percent from —				
	Acreage (1,000)	Percent change, 1992–1997	Average size of farm	Total irrigated (1,000)	Total cropland (1,000)	Average per farm ($1,000)	Average per acre (dollars)		Total (mil dol)	Average per farm (dollars)	Crops	Live-stock and poultry products	$10,000 or more	$100,000 or more		
	117	118	119	120	121	122	123	124	125	126	127	128	129	130	131	132

KENTUCKY—Cont'd

Cumberland	108	-0.5	207	D	40	132	670	21	8	14 525	62.1	37.9	40.3	1.1	1.3	0.8
Daviess	251	0.4	241	3	207	388	1 650	57	71	68 406	82.1	17.9	48.8	15.1	0.0	220.2
Edmonson	90	-2.6	127	0	53	134	1 305	23	11	15 175	40.9	59.1	30.7	2.7	23.7	1.2
Elliott	58	-3.9	131	D	21	102	816	19	4	9 205	81.5	18.5	31.9	0.2	4.6	0.4
Estill	62	-10.0	144	0	28	199	1 071	25	5	10 464	72.0	28.1	28.9	0.9	2.7	2.0
Fayette	136	-7.5	182	1	91	674	4 130	53	139	186 969	16.2	83.8	61.1	22.6	0.4	43.1
Fleming	189	-2.6	167	0	125	173	1 048	32	37	32 724	47.2	52.8	56.0	6.5	0.0	1.6
Floyd	7	-33.5	124	D	2	135	1 089	17	1	8 613	84.1	16.1	11.9	3.4	4.5	3.8
Franklin	83	-3.9	122	1	51	223	2 279	30	16	23 513	71.1	28.9	49.5	4.0	0.0	8.5
Fulton	94	-3.4	578	3	83	743	1 295	103	23	143 579	94.2	5.8	61.7	34.6	1.4	1.7
Gallatin	36	-11.2	144	0	21	197	1 364	31	7	26 662	78.3	21.7	45.1	7.1	0.0	0.8
Garrard	125	-9.6	142	0	86	199	1 357	29	30	33 923	49.7	50.3	57.8	7.2	0.0	1.7
Grant	115	-9.2	123	1	71	189	1 738	27	16	16 618	76.2	23.8	42.6	2.4	0.0	2.1
Graves	237	12.9	173	1	186	242	1 446	43	115	83 662	37.6	62.4	41.1	14.7	0.0	14.7
Grayson	209	1.4	148	0	130	155	1 066	26	33	23 260	36.7	63.3	38.7	4.0	2.2	3.4
Green	129	-4.4	122	0	85	127	1 096	28	24	22 529	53.9	46.1	49.0	3.8	0.0	1.6
Greenup	98	-2.0	134	0	37	140	1 209	22	8	11 327	64.4	35.6	27.6	1.2	0.0	16.4
Hancock	65	-7.1	145	0	37	177	1 300	30	12	26 923	69.7	30.3	41.0	4.5	0.0	250.9
Hardin	223	-1.3	136	0	158	235	1 689	31	39	23 792	58.8	41.2	37.4	5.1	14.8	13.4
Harlan	2	-53.5	86	D	1	142	1 650	17	0	6 817	35.9	64.1	18.5	0.0	1.0	4.8
Harrison	169	-4.8	157	3	113	226	1 427	30	29	26 862	72.1	27.9	54.1	5.7	0.0	3.4
Hart	186	-6.8	138	0	113	149	1 104	28	35	25 953	56.3	43.7	53.3	5.3	2.8	3.6
Henderson	196	-0.9	373	2	163	561	1 593	78	50	95 326	78.4	21.6	50.6	19.0	0.5	117.7
Henry	149	-6.8	156	3	101	243	1 714	37	37	38 571	69.9	30.1	62.0	8.1	0.0	3.0
Hickman	115	15.8	390	2	101	512	1 382	102	44	149 518	58.4	41.6	46.3	26.9	0.0	0.8
Hopkins	141	-2.6	263	0	105	279	1 077	44	27	50 950	62.9	37.1	34.2	10.4	0.0	18.1
Jackson	74	-9.0	107	0	34	106	966	21	9	13 536	62.3	37.7	30.6	1.0	26.2	1.2
Jefferson	34	-24.4	72	0	20	331	4 388	33	12	25 885	78.6	21.4	26.9	6.7	0.0	927.8
Jessamine	89	-10.6	117	1	61	329	2 663	31	66	88 133	22.0	78.0	50.9	9.5	0.0	3.9
Johnson	20	-11.4	112	0	5	139	1 191	20	1	6 918	81.1	18.9	20.3	0.0	4.1	2.0
Kenton	38	-14.1	85	0	23	271	2 394	25	5	11 524	61.7	38.3	23.1	0.0	0.0	8.5
Knott	4	23.7	177	0	1	159	902	21	0	3 037	18.8	81.2	14.3	0.0	1.3	0.9
Knox	46	1.0	144	0	19	166	946	25	3	9 855	64.8	35.2	17.4	0.0	0.0	1.0
Larue	117	-3.7	145	0	84	217	1 664	38	25	30 727	51.4	48.6	45.2	6.3	0.1	1.3
Laurel	96	-4.4	88	0	55	170	2 140	21	14	13 298	61.7	38.3	30.8	1.7	20.8	9.7
Lawrence	49	-0.1	165	0	12	119	899	24	2	6 763	75.3	24.6	18.9	0.0	6.5	15.9
Lee	24	14.1	149	0	9	93	666	18	2	11 052	67.1	32.9	27.3	0.6	5.7	0.7
Leslie	3	33.5	157	0	D	85	541	8	0	6 694	89.5	10.5	11.8	0.0	22.1	2.9
Letcher	3	-10.5	87	D	0	70	804	16	0	1 907	11.9	88.1	3.2	0.0	18.5	2.4
Lewis	143	-10.5	185	D	47	154	777	23	14	18 429	73.9	26.1	45.3	2.2	0.0	1.4
Lincoln	170	-2.1	135	0	110	163	1 186	24	39	30 662	44.0	56.0	45.7	7.0	0.0	2.3
Livingston	117	-1.4	290	D	74	210	768	31	10	24 539	39.7	60.3	31.9	4.7	0.5	23.8
Logan	273	-2.0	227	1	206	319	1 354	48	64	52 896	75.3	24.7	50.5	12.2	0.0	5.0
Lyon	48	-3.3	194	D	33	246	1 186	45	6	24 554	66.3	33.7	30.5	5.2	2.1	2.1
McCracken	67	5.6	146	0	55	195	1 406	33	16	36 035	69.7	30.3	32.6	7.9	2.0	1 005.5
McCreary	11	-22.1	101		5	96	1 078	22	1	4 767	25.4	74.6	13.0	0.0	61.3	1.1
McLean	134	-0.5	318	0	113	538	1 710	82	54	127 419	49.4	50.6	63.7	27.5	0.0	0.8
Madison	222	-10.3	153	0	140	270	1 811	26	44	30 670	48.2	51.8	52.8	5.3	5.1	11.8
Magoffin	41	-9.5	109	0	10	89	972	14	3	7 191	89.7	10.3	22.5	0.0	0.0	0.9
Marion	166	-5.6	169	1	101	188	1 147	40	34	34 171	43.4	56.6	57.0	9.2	0.0	2.9
Marshall	89	17.5	133	0	62	225	1 651	37	18	26 369	44.1	55.9	25.7	4.8	0.0	22.2
Martin	2	-55.4	248	D	D	288	1 164	31	0	5 550	14.0	86.0	0.0	0.0	0.0	5.8
Mason	131	-8.7	175	0	92	229	1 366	32	31	41 266	61.7	38.3	67.9	10.5	0.0	44.8
Meade	121	0.5	143	0	80	241	1 788	37	18	20 901	51.0	49.0	34.6	4.5	7.2	25.4
Menifee	38	-11.3	110	D	16	99	915	21	4	10 988	74.0	26.0	30.9	1.2	33.5	0.2
Mercer	126	-5.0	129	1	92	224	1 874	33	31	31 354	48.9	51.1	47.1	5.7	0.0	20.0
Metcalfe	134	-2.4	141	0	71	182	1 219	28	25	26 308	43.2	56.8	48.5	4.7	0.0	1.1
Monroe	167	0.7	172	0	91	169	1 013	28	26	26 312	36.4	63.6	43.4	6.5	0.0	1.9
Montgomery	112	-1.2	152	0	79	193	1 415	27	23	30 899	63.3	36.7	58.6	7.1	0.0	2.5
Morgan	111	6.0	159	0	41	94	629	20	10	13 995	76.5	23.5	36.1	1.1	7.0	1.4
Muhlenberg	115	-2.7	205	0	72	189	1 082	35	32	57 994	29.2	70.8	36.7	6.8	0.0	487.7
Nelson	176	-7.6	141	1	118	275	1 875	37	39	30 942	37.0	63.0	42.7	6.8	0.1	8.1
Nicholas	106	-5.1	187	1	67	181	1 023	32	16	28 261	69.3	30.7	55.7	4.4	0.0	2.5
Ohio	162	1.4	172	0	94	201	1 115	31	37	39 216	36.0	64.0	31.6	5.6	0.0	7.6
Oldham	71	-16.0	180	0	46	488	2 947	40	16	41 034	46.3	53.7	42.1	9.2	0.0	5.1
Owen	150	-15.0	187	2	85	230	1 189	41	22	27 817	74.0	26.0	54.5	5.7	0.0	2.3

STATE County	Value of Residential Construction Authorized by Building Permits, 2000		Wholesale Trade, 1997				Retail Trade[1], 1997				Real Estate and Rental and Leasing, 1997			
	New Construction ($1,000)	Number of Housing Units	Number of Establishments	Number of Employees	Sales (mil dol)	Annual Payroll (mil dol)	Number of Establishments	Number of Employees	Sales (mil dol)	Annual Payroll (mil dol)	Number of Establishments	Number of Employees	Receipts (mil dol)	Annual Payroll (mil dol)
	133	134	135	136	137	138	139	140	141	142	143	144	145	146
KENTUCKY—Cont'd														
Cumberland	141	3	2	D	D	D	34	231	35.1	3.1	6	17	2.2	0.7
Daviess	53 720	835	141	1 678	872.9	43.7	470	6 011	853.8	84.5	75	476	33.9	7.7
Edmonson	NA	NA	2	D	D	NA	22	140	18.9	1.5	2	D	D	D
Elliott	NA	NA	NA	NA	NA	NA	20	87	11.5	0.9	1	D	D	D
Estill	120	1	11	D	D	D	61	375	58.9	4.5	7	31	1.8	0.4
Fayette	243 912	2 544	492	6 529	4 181.5	203.8	1 251	20 363	3 133.1	308.7	368	2 018	289.5	40.7
Fleming	150	2	20	126	58.2	2.1	68	526	108.2	9.5	4	8	1.0	0.1
Floyd	268	6	55	771	312.6	19.7	185	1 568	259.4	22.9	30	156	17.1	2.7
Franklin	21 800	230	33	D	D	D	202	3 096	443.4	39.2	34	130	12.5	1.9
Fulton	283	5	12	D	D	D	61	498	70.5	7.0	5	9	0.8	0.1
Gallatin	0	0	6	D	D	D	19	179	21.6	2.0	5	D	D	D
Garrard	1 143	17	5	D	D	D	44	238	33.8	3.0	6	D	D	D
Grant	19 787	219	18	D	D	D	100	1 098	181.3	16.5	11	D	D	D
Graves	814	15	37	571	201.8	14.3	141	1 580	286.2	24.4	24	93	7.2	1.5
Grayson	150	3	17	D	D	D	103	942	131.4	12.0	13	70	3.2	1.0
Green	0	0	7	31	6.7	0.3	41	230	33.4	3.1	5	11	1.0	0.1
Greenup	6 587	52	18	D	D	D	111	788	119.7	11.2	15	33	3.2	0.4
Hancock	0	0	1	D	D	D	22	168	29.3	2.3	5	D	D	D
Hardin	42 316	440	68	596	134.7	13.1	422	5 431	897.0	82.9	83	241	23.6	3.6
Harlan	0	0	31	242	108.9	6.3	132	1 261	168.8	17.1	24	D	D	D
Harrison	4 544	73	11	D	D	D	64	695	106.6	9.0	9	46	2.8	0.5
Hart	1 992	37	10	D	D	D	90	589	76.7	7.3	7	D	D	D
Henderson	16 582	171	71	798	728.4	23.9	208	2 252	422.2	36.8	43	181	16.0	3.4
Henry	11 981	127	18	247	114.4	5.7	53	470	90.5	7.0	10	14	1.2	0.2
Hickman	NA	NA	6	97	40.4	2.3	19	93	13.5	1.4	5	31	0.5	0.2
Hopkins	3 822	40	57	435	190.0	10.5	246	2 805	409.0	39.9	37	114	8.6	1.3
Jackson	0	0	2	D	D	D	30	179	31.2	2.3	2	D	D	D
Jefferson	381 256	3 809	1 509	24 651	15 932.9	852.5	2 950	47 517	7 200.8	761.6	811	5 810	766.7	126.8
Jessamine	44 016	452	46	1 010	513.7	27.9	132	2 078	394.0	32.7	27	81	6.0	1.0
Johnson	609	4	24	187	60.1	5.4	127	1 606	229.2	20.7	10	32	1.6	0.3
Kenton	63 359	743	198	3 123	1 370.3	109.3	452	5 904	829.4	86.6	131	823	90.0	16.8
Knott	NA	NA	6	59	3.6	0.7	48	242	35.4	3.4	6	14	1.5	0.2
Knox	148	2	14	140	52.4	3.4	123	1 556	254.4	20.6	13	48	3.4	0.6
Larue	4 353	109	7	19	3.4	0.2	41	294	42.5	4.3	6	10	0.4	0.1
Laurel	1 266	17	67	1 239	520.2	28.3	230	2 827	499.8	40.6	31	108	10.2	2.2
Lawrence	0	0	9	D	D	D	51	440	63.7	5.5	4	16	0.7	0.2
Lee	NA	NA	6	50	16.3	2.0	27	179	25.8	2.8	5	D	D	D
Leslie	NA	NA	2	D	D	D	42	215	30.2	2.8	4	35	1.9	0.6
Letcher	0	0	14	374	111.3	5.1	92	837	110.2	10.8	3	16	1.0	0.2
Lewis	0	0	5	13	5.6	0.2	34	241	22.6	2.0	3	8	0.2	0.0
Lincoln	21 670	206	13	68	12.1	0.8	64	471	70.9	6.6	6	15	1.2	0.1
Livingston	NA	NA	4	39	4.4	0.4	33	188	22.7	2.7	3	13	1.1	0.2
Logan	2 210	50	27	203	79.8	3.5	106	975	147.8	13.8	13	34	6.1	0.3
Lyon	942	11	4	27	42.7	0.7	68	461	52.4	5.2	8	39	4.0	0.8
McCracken	21 194	171	136	2 700	1 557.0	72.3	515	6 266	1 012.0	91.1	79	418	62.7	11.3
McCreary	0	0	4	18	1.0	0.2	50	318	52.4	4.2	7	51	6.6	1.2
McLean	436	4	11	134	52.5	2.4	30	209	40.8	3.4	5	8	0.3	0.1
Madison	23 918	351	49	720	285.7	24.8	288	3 824	565.0	51.4	55	184	17.1	2.0
Magoffin	NA	NA	6	36	45.2	0.9	47	314	46.9	3.5	4	D	D	D
Marion	773	7	14	143	40.3	1.9	79	642	84.8	7.1	6	12	1.7	0.3
Marshall	13 106	130	38	292	124.2	7.6	128	1 054	179.2	16.4	16	110	11.7	2.3
Martin	NA	NA	8	48	73.9	2.1	51	344	58.0	5.3	4	D	D	D
Mason	2 304	17	31	394	93.7	7.4	109	1 467	246.3	20.2	12	28	3.7	0.6
Meade	2 119	27	12	51	59.0	1.5	85	570	122.8	9.4	14	35	2.6	0.3
Menifee	NA	NA	NA	NA	NA	NA	16	81	11.8	0.8	2	D	D	D
Mercer	9 915	117	18	67	23.7	1.2	84	637	125.6	10.1	11	100	2.6	0.5
Metcalfe	NA	NA	3	44	11.8	1.2	40	272	39.8	3.5	3	6	0.6	0.1
Monroe	NA	NA	12	D	D	D	64	405	63.7	5.3	6	7	1.2	0.1
Montgomery	10 757	134	31	243	126.7	5.2	117	1 479	225.2	18.1	25	75	6.0	1.0
Morgan	NA	NA	4	D	D	D	52	388	65.7	5.6	3	D	D	D
Muhlenberg	975	18	16	D	D	D	130	1 405	198.7	20.0	17	89	4.5	0.8
Nelson	40 516	468	41	448	133.3	12.8	178	1 445	218.8	19.5	27	80	7.9	1.1
Nicholas	327	3	1	D	D	D	14	114	18.5	1.6	5	11	0.5	0.0
Ohio	1 061	12	8	198	45.4	3.0	75	614	89.8	8.2	5	9	1.3	0.2
Oldham	114 370	626	58	451	272.6	15.0	113	1 209	192.1	19.1	23	108	12.2	1.5
Owen	269	8	6	17	3.0	0.2	23	220	50.4	2.9	4	14	0.5	0.1

1. Establishments with payroll.

STATE County	Professional, Scientific, and Technical Services[1], 1997				Manufacturing, 1997				Accommodation and Foodservices, 1997			
	Number of Establishments	Number of Employees	Receipts (mil dol)	Annual Payroll (mil dol)	Number of Establishments	Number of Employees	Receipts (mil dol)	Annual Payroll (mil dol)	Number of Establishments	Number of Employees	Sales (mil dol)	Annual Payroll (mil dol)
	147	148	149	150	151	152	153	154	155	156	157	158
KENTUCKY—Cont'd												
Cumberland	5	8	0.8	0.1	NA	NA	NA	NA	12	123	4.3	1.2
Daviess	145	857	56.4	23.3	114	8 011	2 938.2	276.8	150	3 331	100.6	26.6
Edmonson	4	D	D	D	NA	NA	NA	NA	11	179	6.1	1.9
Elliott	1	D	D	D	NA	NA	NA	NA	4	D	D	D
Estill	5	11	0.3	0.1	NA	NA	NA	NA	17	D	D	D
Fayette	765	8 482	1 043.1	292.0	283	17 403	4 313.9	654.0	610	15 216	508.1	146.9
Fleming	7	71	1.7	0.5	19	650	54.8	14.6	9	143	3.6	1.0
Floyd	56	300	21.7	8.5	NA	NA	NA	NA	43	608	19.3	5.4
Franklin	104	669	61.1	25.0	40	3 435	592.4	97.8	89	1 518	47.2	13.2
Fulton	9	15	0.9	0.2	14	1 087	194.1	23.4	15	D	D	D
Gallatin	3	6	0.4	0.1	NA	NA	NA	NA	9	103	4.7	0.7
Garrard	8	21	1.3	0.3	NA	NA	NA	NA	13	112	2.7	0.7
Grant	18	51	2.5	1.0	16	D	D	D	37	D	D	D
Graves	38	142	7.9	2.9	50	3 053	537.6	101.4	49	592	15.7	4.2
Grayson	19	57	2.7	0.9	31	2 462	382.5	47.8	36	370	12.9	3.0
Green	5	19	0.9	0.3	NA	NA	NA	NA	11	115	3.2	0.8
Greenup	29	130	6.5	2.0	13	600	108.6	23.4	33	789	20.3	5.6
Hancock	8	17	0.8	0.1	13	1 862	1 049.0	80.9	8	D	D	D
Hardin	109	509	34.2	13.0	68	7 162	1 633.9	216.8	141	2 975	85.7	24.3
Harlan	34	184	11.2	4.8	NA	NA	NA	NA	32	457	15.0	3.9
Harrison	13	36	1.7	0.6	19	1 730	353.3	54.9	18	D	D	D
Hart	13	38	2.4	0.6	10	D	D	D	17	189	5.5	1.5
Henderson	73	284	18.8	5.7	78	6 862	1 722.9	208.0	81	1 403	41.3	11.8
Henry	12	31	1.3	0.6	8	555	213.9	17.1	7	99	3.1	0.8
Hickman	4	14	0.9	0.4	NA	NA	NA	NA	3	D	D	D
Hopkins	69	334	23.3	7.7	55	2 606	572.8	89.7	74	982	30.4	8.3
Jackson	4	7	0.3	0.1	13	1 940	173.3	28.4	8	D	D	D
Jefferson	1 811	15 317	1 479.9	503.7	873	56 948	30 261.6	2 201.4	1 394	34 303	1 081.9	314.8
Jessamine	48	173	10.6	3.3	67	2 379	675.4	67.9	44	799	23.6	6.2
Johnson	34	189	14.2	3.6	NA	NA	NA	NA	28	470	15.3	4.3
Kenton	263	2 441	162.3	71.1	161	6 810	1 482.8	233.4	294	6 542	236.9	65.5
Knott	14	47	2.8	1.2	NA	NA	NA	NA	10	D	D	D
Knox	28	196	14.9	6.1	17	877	160.6	20.6	33	561	15.9	4.3
Larue	16	30	2.1	0.8	12	641	25.3	10.1	10	D	D	D
Laurel	60	246	18.6	4.7	44	2 595	319.1	57.4	64	1 698	50.9	14.4
Lawrence	10	34	2.5	0.8	NA	NA	NA	NA	18	280	8.3	2.2
Lee	5	8	0.3	0.1	NA	NA	NA	NA	8	D	D	D
Leslie	10	47	4.4	0.7	NA	NA	NA	NA	6	D	D	D
Letcher	27	169	9.5	3.2	NA	NA	NA	NA	19	314	9.5	2.7
Lewis	6	27	0.9	0.3	15	804	89.9	15.7	14	D	D	D
Lincoln	19	65	4.8	1.7	18	737	54.7	18.9	15	176	4.7	1.3
Livingston	9	31	1.3	0.4	NA	NA	NA	NA	11	249	8.7	3.1
Logan	23	83	5.1	1.8	41	4 650	781.7	126.0	29	479	11.6	2.6
Lyon	10	24	0.9	0.3	NA	NA	NA	NA	21	216	7.2	1.8
McCracken	133	947	67.3	21.8	58	4 081	978.9	155.2	184	4 116	125.1	35.3
McCreary	7	23	0.7	0.2	16	D	D	D	10	117	3.0	0.9
McLean	8	18	0.9	0.2	NA	NA	NA	NA	10	58	1.6	0.4
Madison	77	273	14.7	4.6	68	5 460	1 576.1	160.3	126	2 664	75.5	21.2
Magoffin	12	72	5.6	1.8	NA	NA	NA	NA	11	161	4.8	1.4
Marion	19	78	5.1	1.7	22	1 554	175.1	34.4	28	296	8.3	2.5
Marshall	37	224	12.8	6.4	35	2 881	1 715.5	141.0	72	774	24.0	6.3
Martin	13	31	2.5	0.6	NA	NA	NA	NA	15	235	7.6	2.1
Mason	20	72	4.2	1.4	19	3 167	545.5	85.6	42	526	20.2	4.9
Meade	10	36	1.6	0.5	NA	NA	NA	NA	24	284	9.4	2.7
Menifee	2	D	D	D	NA	NA	NA	NA	4	D	D	D
Mercer	24	52	3.7	1.0	16	3 053	888.7	94.9	36	403	14.0	3.7
Metcalfe	6	9	0.4	0.1	13	1 829	231.4	37.0	9	83	2.0	0.4
Monroe	7	14	0.8	0.1	32	1 966	160.9	35.8	21	D	D	D
Montgomery	23	101	5.9	1.6	32	2 124	281.4	45.4	38	785	20.5	5.5
Morgan	9	23	0.9	0.2	NA	NA	NA	NA	9	D	D	D
Muhlenberg	38	148	6.0	2.1	36	1 399	130.1	26.8	41	502	13.2	3.8
Nelson	46	181	11.5	3.2	56	3 616	960.2	99.0	55	863	27.2	7.5
Nicholas	4	6	0.3	0.1	5	D	D	D	4	59	0.8	0.2
Ohio	23	75	4.5	1.4	27	2 010	177.1	37.4	24	363	10.3	2.4
Oldham	78	261	23.2	9.3	41	1 004	252.5	37.5	51	957	29.2	8.4
Owen	5	25	2.4	1.4	NA	NA	NA	NA	6	75	1.8	0.5

1. Firms subject to federal tax.

STATE County	Health Care and Social Assistance[1], 1997				Other Services[1], 1997				Federal funds and grants, fiscal 2001[2] Expenditures (mil dol)			
										Direct payments for individuals[3]		
	Number of Establishments	Number of Employees	Receipts (mil dol)	Annual Payroll (mil dol)	Number of Establishments	Number of Employees	Receipts (mil dol)	Annual Payroll (mil dol)	Total	Social Security and government retirement	Medicare	Food stamps and Supplemental Security Income
	159	160	161	162	163	164	165	166	167	168	169	170
KENTUCKY—Cont'd												
Cumberland	10	165	8.3	3.7	4	7	0.8	0.1	52.0	15.4	10.2	4.5
Daviess	202	2 568	184.0	76.4	144	829	50.4	14.5	423.4	199.2	77.1	22.3
Edmonson	8	137	5.3	2.2	3	13	1.3	0.2	61.9	21.9	8.4	3.6
Elliott	5	76	2.5	0.8	4	18	0.6	0.1	50.0	10.4	3.1	3.9
Estill	11	126	6.5	2.2	13	26	3.0	0.8	95.1	43.2	17.6	6.3
Fayette	612	10 905	793.3	352.1	456	3 266	177.5	56.7	1 373.5	452.5	146.3	42.1
Fleming	14	195	8.4	3.9	26	43	2.8	0.5	66.0	26.2	10.2	5.0
Floyd	85	702	40.1	16.3	43	155	12.0	3.2	289.4	120.4	46.8	31.4
Franklin	88	1 258	87.8	36.3	69	408	22.4	9.1	1 102.7	176.1	46.7	16.2
Fulton	19	322	18.7	7.7	9	32	2.2	0.5	67.5	23.6	11.0	3.8
Gallatin	4	D	D	D	4	6	0.5	0.1	41.7	12.1	5.0	2.1
Garrard	10	61	2.6	1.2	7	22	1.4	0.4	63.1	30.5	9.4	2.7
Grant	22	316	12.5	6.7	19	65	2.6	0.7	84.3	41.9	13.9	4.0
Graves	50	898	53.3	21.8	33	293	10.3	3.5	201.1	90.3	41.6	9.0
Grayson	23	204	10.6	5.2	27	93	4.5	1.3	123.6	53.8	22.7	8.9
Green	16	267	11.0	4.9	9	17	1.3	0.2	54.1	23.5	12.7	4.4
Greenup	48	444	21.5	8.3	32	104	6.6	1.6	180.0	101.3	35.0	9.4
Hancock	6	74	2.8	0.9	9	13	0.8	0.2	31.6	15.5	4.9	0.9
Hardin	189	2 319	154.9	71.4	136	825	43.5	14.2	967.9	277.9	52.1	19.3
Harlan	26	429	22.7	13.7	32	132	8.3	1.9	386.0	107.2	32.6	130.6
Harrison	31	295	13.2	6.0	22	69	4.4	1.0	73.6	36.2	12.6	4.1
Hart	17	266	10.4	4.7	16	38	2.9	0.5	84.5	32.5	13.7	7.3
Henderson	92	687	48.5	19.4	68	503	32.0	10.4	204.1	95.0	43.0	10.2
Henry	14	150	6.2	3.3	16	44	3.5	0.8	64.3	27.0	13.5	3.2
Hickman	6	120	3.7	1.5	4	14	1.1	0.3	35.6	10.3	5.6	1.1
Hopkins	55	1 047	38.3	18.6	71	449	28.0	8.6	325.8	122.7	39.9	14.7
Jackson	5	160	6.5	2.9	7	22	1.4	0.3	78.4	26.0	11.4	7.2
Jefferson	1 622	27 669	1 872.1	835.3	1 317	9 422	586.0	187.4	4 086.2	1 587.3	664.8	56.1
Jessamine	37	286	10.8	3.8	51	227	13.6	4.1	125.3	63.9	16.6	5.5
Johnson	52	525	47.1	13.8	32	116	5.5	1.5	163.8	61.7	22.4	14.2
Kenton	219	2 729	173.5	89.7	221	1 586	103.2	31.0	714.0	280.8	112.0	28.3
Knott	8	142	7.5	3.1	9	30	2.3	0.5	104.3	36.5	13.2	15.4
Knox	33	269	14.1	6.1	20	86	5.7	1.3	184.9	56.9	23.3	26.5
Larue	11	86	3.4	1.5	11	34	2.4	0.6	66.2	30.4	12.8	3.0
Laurel	46	292	22.1	8.5	53	273	19.1	4.3	250.9	101.6	30.4	23.6
Lawrence	24	441	27.4	9.7	19	76	4.4	1.1	86.0	37.2	12.9	7.4
Lee	4	26	1.4	0.9	5	16	0.8	0.2	53.3	18.8	7.5	7.2
Leslie	9	154	6.6	2.8	5	15	1.5	0.5	88.6	34.7	13.2	10.9
Letcher	21	329	17.2	6.3	23	79	5.5	1.1	178.9	72.6	25.5	20.8
Lewis	7	161	7.0	3.4	4	7	0.6	0.1	70.9	27.4	10.9	7.7
Lincoln	13	217	9.3	4.1	16	31	3.0	0.7	120.4	47.5	18.4	10.6
Livingston	8	62	3.8	1.5	6	14	0.9	0.1	78.4	26.9	11.5	1.8
Logan	40	479	28.4	10.3	33	127	9.9	2.3	140.7	55.1	29.2	6.9
Lyon	9	207	7.3	3.3	6	14	1.0	0.2	40.5	22.2	7.5	1.5
McCracken	191	2 250	186.3	91.5	117	737	49.6	12.3	1 318.6	167.2	68.7	16.4
McCreary	12	271	11.3	5.2	6	14	1.1	0.3	107.8	37.7	16.4	14.9
McLean	13	143	5.4	2.3	12	38	3.7	0.8	54.8	23.3	10.3	2.1
Madison	116	1 034	52.1	23.6	63	316	13.3	3.9	324.8	122.8	40.6	18.4
Magoffin	11	237	9.2	3.4	6	24	3.7	0.4	86.0	25.6	11.5	12.5
Marion	27	519	31.3	12.0	14	56	3.9	0.9	85.6	33.6	14.1	7.2
Marshall	36	428	21.6	9.1	31	175	15.2	4.3	145.2	82.1	29.7	4.2
Martin	12	140	5.1	2.0	11	101	5.2	2.8	86.6	35.2	9.0	11.6
Mason	39	770	53.8	18.1	30	167	6.5	2.0	79.6	33.8	15.3	5.1
Meade	22	135	5.5	2.0	12	47	2.8	0.6	85.7	53.7	11.7	3.9
Menifee	3	D	D	D	3	D	D	D	43.3	13.4	4.1	5.7
Mercer	21	231	9.8	4.2	20	57	3.0	0.8	84.7	45.9	13.7	5.3
Metcalfe	6	59	3.0	1.1	6	9	0.6	0.1	54.4	20.5	9.2	5.9
Monroe	16	189	8.8	2.8	15	56	3.0	0.6	79.3	25.8	16.5	6.1
Montgomery	47	446	21.0	9.1	33	174	9.4	3.0	99.2	45.2	16.4	7.2
Morgan	11	122	5.6	2.0	15	38	2.3	0.4	78.9	24.8	9.5	9.4
Muhlenberg	37	532	25.4	11.7	35	136	9.3	2.1	287.6	86.9	31.9	10.6
Nelson	43	521	22.4	9.2	39	166	6.5	1.8	132.6	64.0	24.5	8.0
Nicholas	6	27	1.4	0.8	7	15	0.5	0.2	35.4	15.2	6.4	2.5
Ohio	31	619	28.7	11.5	22	107	15.2	2.3	110.4	52.3	19.9	8.5
Oldham	57	256	14.6	5.8	52	248	14.4	4.9	79.6	42.9	16.1	0.9
Owen	11	285	11.4	5.0	11	34	1.5	0.5	36.5	15.4	7.2	2.9

1. Firms subject to federal tax.   2. October 1, 2000 to September 30, 2001.   3. State totals may include programs not allocated by county.

STATE County	Federal funds and grants, fiscal 2001[1] (cont'd)							Local government finances, 1997				
	Expenditures (mil dol) (cont'd)							General revenue				
	Procurement contract awards			Grants[2]						Taxes		
											Per capita[3] (dollars)	
	Salaries and wages	Defense	Other	Medicaid and other health-related	Nutrition and family welfare	Education	Other	Total (mil dol)	Intergovern-mental (mil dol)	Total (mil dol)	Total	Property
	171	172	173	174	175	176	177	178	179	180	181	182
KENTUCKY—Cont'd												
Cumberland	1.0	5.6	0.2	12.5	1.2	0.6	-0.3	9.9	6.1	2.8	413	284
Daviess	17.8	5.6	4.9	35.3	16.2	5.0	9.3	189.8	66.1	43.6	479	299
Edmonson	7.7	0.5	1.1	8.8	1.2	1.0	6.3	11.6	8.6	2.0	182	134
Elliott	0.4	0.0	0.1	8.8	1.4	0.7	0.3	11.3	8.4	1.3	198	146
Estill	2.0	0.1	0.4	19.6	2.7	1.3	0.6	21.0	15.0	3.4	218	128
Fayette	191.8	116.0	42.4	153.0	20.7	20.5	75.2	487.9	102.9	218.7	912	394
Fleming	2.6	0.0	0.6	13.4	2.2	1.7	1.3	26.9	11.9	3.6	269	182
Floyd	8.9	5.8	9.1	46.8	6.7	3.6	2.2	60.6	39.4	11.6	268	197
Franklin	26.8	1.4	3.8	135.7	206.3	150.7	319.3	67.9	27.9	28.9	624	298
Fulton	2.4	0.0	0.7	10.2	1.6	1.7	2.6	16.9	9.3	3.4	447	257
Gallatin	1.5	0.3	0.3	3.5	0.7	0.4	15.6	18.6	4.8	2.2	329	240
Garrard	1.7	0.0	0.8	7.9	1.2	0.7	6.8	22.6	9.6	3.8	278	183
Grant	3.1	0.0	0.7	8.4	2.0	1.2	8.0	26.8	17.3	5.7	289	201
Graves	9.4	0.2	2.7	21.5	3.3	1.6	0.6	43.0	23.2	13.0	364	182
Grayson	3.4	0.2	0.8	22.0	3.5	1.4	1.4	31.5	18.4	7.4	320	156
Green	1.3	0.0	0.3	8.4	1.0	0.6	-0.3	19.3	8.4	2.4	228	157
Greenup	3.8	0.5	0.8	18.6	3.5	1.8	2.3	56.8	28.4	15.7	424	379
Hancock	1.2	0.0	0.3	4.6	0.6	0.5	0.2	17.2	6.4	6.2	696	220
Hardin	556.2	0.4	3.8	28.3	8.1	4.8	3.7	211.7	66.1	31.8	354	207
Harlan	6.8	0.6	52.6	39.6	7.4	4.4	0.9	63.0	37.7	9.2	261	197
Harrison	3.1	0.7	0.5	11.1	1.7	1.0	0.0	24.8	14.1	7.0	404	177
Hart	2.0	0.0	4.5	16.0	1.9	1.1	0.8	17.6	11.3	4.0	240	151
Henderson	6.3	0.0	1.2	17.1	3.8	2.6	2.7	84.5	33.7	19.7	441	253
Henry	3.0	0.0	0.7	9.8	1.7	0.8	2.4	19.6	11.3	5.7	388	275
Hickman	1.1	0.2	0.2	3.9	0.7	1.3	0.6	7.1	5.1	1.4	275	179
Hopkins	9.6	0.8	89.3	24.8	4.5	2.7	6.6	74.7	39.8	19.1	413	268
Jackson	2.0	0.0	0.4	22.4	2.8	1.7	3.0	16.6	13.7	2.2	169	112
Jefferson	376.4	572.4	106.7	327.3	85.5	52.4	106.9	1 438.0	409.4	609.2	908	432
Jessamine	4.5	0.0	10.6	10.5	2.3	1.8	6.3	53.8	23.4	21.0	582	350
Johnson	3.2	8.6	0.7	28.0	9.7	3.0	10.5	44.0	27.3	10.1	418	267
Kenton	155.9	2.1	16.6	46.3	13.3	6.9	31.3	330.3	104.3	106.0	725	412
Knott	2.6	0.1	1.1	26.7	3.9	1.9	0.6	26.4	18.6	5.0	280	238
Knox	8.7	0.0	0.7	47.8	12.4	3.6	0.2	43.2	29.9	6.3	201	143
Larue	2.3	0.0	0.5	8.4	1.3	0.8	2.6	15.8	10.9	3.3	257	203
Laurel	17.4	14.2	5.7	36.5	6.3	3.3	8.4	63.2	39.2	16.6	332	163
Lawrence	2.4	0.0	0.6	20.0	2.6	2.0	0.1	21.2	15.2	3.4	222	160
Lee	1.2	0.0	0.3	13.4	1.7	0.7	1.8	14.4	8.3	1.6	202	133
Leslie	1.9	0.0	0.5	22.3	3.1	1.7	0.0	20.4	16.0	3.7	271	220
Letcher	4.5	0.1	1.4	33.0	6.5	3.0	10.6	35.8	25.8	6.9	259	203
Lewis	1.2	0.0	0.3	17.1	2.1	1.0	1.8	16.8	13.0	2.3	167	124
Lincoln	6.8	0.0	0.7	25.6	3.3	1.7	2.6	27.3	20.4	4.4	199	146
Livingston	4.3	8.4	15.3	5.3	0.8	0.5	0.1	9.4	6.2	2.4	257	202
Logan	3.8	0.0	1.0	23.3	2.4	1.3	1.7	32.6	19.6	8.7	334	183
Lyon	1.5	0.0	0.3	3.2	0.4	0.3	0.9	7.4	3.7	2.3	283	206
McCracken	42.7	0.4	963.6	31.2	7.1	3.5	2.2	105.1	42.6	40.6	626	294
McCreary	4.3	2.8	1.8	21.5	4.2	3.0	0.6	24.8	20.3	2.1	124	90
McLean	1.7	0.0	0.4	4.6	0.9	0.6	0.1	15.2	8.1	2.7	275	172
Madison	27.5	10.4	1.8	37.5	7.2	5.8	29.6	100.2	48.9	30.4	465	203
Magoffin	1.4	0.0	0.4	25.9	3.5	1.7	2.6	21.5	16.8	2.8	201	143
Marion	2.8	0.0	0.8	16.1	5.2	1.3	0.6	25.4	15.1	6.5	382	203
Marshall	4.8	3.2	2.3	9.2	2.1	1.3	1.4	39.5	17.9	15.2	510	266
Martin	1.3	0.2	6.4	15.8	2.7	1.3	1.6	20.9	15.2	3.7	299	236
Mason	3.7	0.0	0.6	13.8	1.8	0.8	1.5	48.9	12.6	11.8	696	362
Meade	2.4	0.1	0.6	5.8	1.8	1.1	0.4	27.8	18.7	5.7	204	138
Menifee	9.3	0.1	0.4	7.2	0.9	0.4	1.5	7.9	5.3	1.5	262	183
Mercer	3.1	0.0	0.7	10.4	1.5	0.9	0.7	29.6	15.0	10.0	488	245
Metcalfe	1.6	0.0	0.4	11.8	1.2	1.4	1.2	11.9	8.4	2.8	298	146
Monroe	2.7	0.0	0.5	21.3	1.6	0.8	0.8	15.1	10.8	3.0	264	137
Montgomery	3.9	0.0	0.6	15.0	2.5	2.3	4.5	41.8	20.9	9.4	453	244
Morgan	1.8	0.0	0.5	18.9	4.2	2.4	7.1	18.4	13.9	2.4	180	106
Muhlenberg	35.2	0.4	95.3	18.6	3.3	1.6	-0.5	39.7	23.9	7.7	241	189
Nelson	5.9	0.5	1.2	15.3	3.2	1.5	3.0	50.2	22.3	12.6	360	263
Nicholas	1.4	0.0	0.2	6.8	0.8	0.5	0.5	9.6	5.9	2.7	381	235
Ohio	4.6	0.1	0.9	12.7	2.7	1.6	0.7	37.7	18.2	6.3	288	181
Oldham	4.6	0.1	1.2	4.9	1.7	1.3	4.1	50.3	25.2	20.5	473	381
Owen	1.3	0.0	0.3	6.2	1.1	0.7	0.7	12.1	8.5	2.8	275	217

1. October 1, 2000 to September 30, 2001.   2. State totals may include programs not allocated by county.   3. Based on the resident population estimated as of July 1 of the year shown.

Table B. States and Counties — Local Government Finances, Government Employment, and Elections

STATE County	Total (mil dol)	Per capita[1] (dollars)	Education	Health and hospitals	Police protection	Public welfare	Highways	Total (mil dol)	Per capita[1] (dollars)	Federal civilian	Federal military	State and local	Democratic	Republican	All other
	183	184	185	186	187	188	189	190	191	192	193	194	195	196	197
KENTUCKY—Cont'd															
Cumberland	9.7	1 408	62.8	12.0	2.6	0.0	8.6	5.6	813	19	23	373	24.5	73.9	1.6
Daviess	186.5	2 050	40.6	6.7	3.6	0.0	2.8	883.5	9 707	293	340	7 302	39.0	58.9	2.1
Edmonson	11.7	1 055	80.4	3.4	0.5	0.0	6.1	12.3	1 109	210	39	444	34.2	65.1	0.7
Elliott	11.9	1 812	72.3	0.8	0.1	0.0	5.9	6.2	947	0	22	296	64.0	34.7	1.2
Estill	24.9	1 609	75.2	5.1	1.7	0.0	3.2	16.5	1 066	26	52	714	33.8	64.4	1.8
Fayette	402.2	1 677	48.5	0.0	7.9	1.3	4.8	425.7	1 775	4 265	870	28 003	44.8	51.7	3.5
Fleming	26.0	1 967	46.8	41.6	1.6	0.0	2.7	10.3	783	51	46	846	35.0	63.4	1.6
Floyd	64.3	1 485	71.1	4.8	1.1	0.1	3.4	84.2	1 943	140	146	2 450	65.5	32.9	1.5
Franklin	62.0	1 341	51.7	2.3	5.4	0.0	3.9	48.0	1 039	464	182	15 658	50.1	47.1	2.8
Fulton	16.8	2 206	52.2	0.0	3.9	0.0	5.0	35.6	4 660	32	41	600	52.1	46.4	1.5
Gallatin	18.1	2 667	30.7	0.2	1.4	0.0	1.4	162.1	23 946	31	25	306	42.7	54.7	2.6
Garrard	23.9	1 749	51.1	31.9	1.3	0.0	3.7	11.6	846	28	48	766	29.4	69.4	1.1
Grant	27.1	1 366	70.2	0.9	2.2	0.0	7.1	22.9	1 157	59	70	935	36.2	62.0	1.9
Graves	44.9	1 263	62.9	0.2	3.0	0.1	7.9	159.7	4 488	178	123	1 634	42.8	55.2	2.0
Grayson	31.4	1 350	63.8	0.2	2.6	0.0	6.9	50.0	2 149	62	81	1 468	30.4	68.3	1.3
Green	17.7	1 674	44.0	41.8	1.4	0.0	5.7	7.7	726	30	36	643	22.8	76.0	1.2
Greenup	63.8	1 719	58.5	2.4	2.4	0.0	2.9	33.9	914	73	124	1 459	48.9	49.3	1.8
Hancock	15.5	1 757	51.8	2.1	1.9	0.2	1.8	695.4	78 610	25	30	411	41.8	56.3	2.0
Hardin	212.1	2 357	38.9	43.1	2.3	0.0	2.3	193.4	2 148	4 749	10 395	5 727	36.2	61.8	2.0
Harlan	62.0	1 754	58.1	23.7	2.1	0.0	4.0	14.9	420	104	116	2 211	50.9	47.3	1.8
Harrison	26.1	1 505	70.0	0.3	3.5	0.2	5.7	22.5	1 296	60	60	815	40.2	57.4	2.4
Hart	17.2	1 042	73.0	3.8	2.1	0.0	5.5	22.4	1 356	42	57	696	36.6	61.9	1.6
Henderson	81.2	1 819	45.7	0.3	4.5	0.5	1.8	539.6	12 094	137	150	2 369	50.2	48.0	1.8
Henry	20.4	1 384	69.6	4.2	3.1	0.2	4.1	12.4	842	62	51	631	38.7	59.3	2.0
Hickman	7.4	1 440	64.6	0.0	2.0	0.0	9.7	0.5	96	27	17	230	44.3	54.2	1.5
Hopkins	80.0	1 729	52.7	3.6	4.6	1.1	5.8	73.2	1 581	344	156	2 735	40.8	57.6	1.6
Jackson	15.7	1 228	81.8	0.0	0.6	0.0	5.4	13.7	1 067	37	44	731	14.4	84.0	1.5
Jefferson	1 533.9	2 287	35.1	2.3	5.9	1.7	2.3	3 266.0	4 870	7 050	2 482	39 917	49.6	48.0	2.5
Jessamine	56.8	1 577	59.6	1.7	4.1	0.0	3.4	71.9	1 995	72	126	1 922	30.8	66.9	2.4
Johnson	41.1	1 705	65.4	8.4	1.3	0.1	2.9	31.8	1 321	73	81	1 474	39.7	58.5	1.7
Kenton	366.4	2 506	28.2	2.5	5.2	0.0	4.0	674.1	4 610	3 637	499	6 106	34.0	62.9	3.1
Knott	27.1	1 501	75.2	1.8	1.8	0.0	5.0	5.2	291	51	61	899	67.3	31.4	1.3
Knox	38.8	1 232	73.7	9.7	2.1	0.0	1.0	8.3	262	176	109	1 765	37.2	61.1	1.6
Larue	15.2	1 179	69.7	0.1	1.6	0.0	5.9	9.7	753	48	44	564	33.3	65.3	1.3
Laurel	63.8	1 273	70.2	2.4	2.2	0.0	5.9	52.7	1 052	337	176	2 357	26.8	71.9	1.3
Lawrence	21.9	1 416	73.6	0.1	1.1	0.0	6.0	11.4	740	43	53	786	42.5	55.9	1.5
Lee	12.8	1 611	55.1	10.3	2.2	0.0	6.9	21.0	2 634	23	27	467	30.2	68.5	1.3
Leslie	18.4	1 359	76.8	0.2	1.0	2.3	6.1	6.2	457	35	46	638	27.3	71.2	1.4
Letcher	33.5	1 260	77.4	0.2	0.8	0.0	3.5	11.3	423	77	88	1 296	52.3	45.5	2.2
Lewis	23.5	1 733	56.4	1.2	1.6	0.1	3.7	114.4	8 435	20	46	557	28.3	70.4	1.3
Lincoln	30.3	1 374	79.0	2.0	1.7	0.1	3.7	16.1	731	54	76	933	35.3	63.1	1.6
Livingston	9.3	992	77.0	0.5	1.9	0.0	4.1	4.3	466	78	32	415	47.8	50.1	2.1
Logan	34.3	1 312	66.5	0.5	5.4	0.0	4.8	22.1	844	73	89	1 223	41.6	57.3	1.2
Lyon	8.9	1 105	48.2	2.0	3.3	0.4	7.2	6.3	786	33	27	702	49.1	49.4	1.5
McCracken	108.9	1 682	48.2	0.0	4.8	0.1	5.2	122.2	1 887	701	235	3 863	42.8	55.2	2.0
McCreary	26.9	1 624	78.2	0.9	0.3	0.0	5.4	13.3	803	120	57	794	29.5	69.2	1.3
McLean	13.9	1 437	54.7	20.0	1.7	0.0	1.7	26.7	2 748	40	33	470	43.4	55.2	1.4
Madison	98.0	1 499	59.0	8.4	2.8	0.0	3.2	113.8	1 742	594	238	5 773	39.3	57.8	2.8
Magoffin	20.3	1 469	77.0	4.4	0.7	0.0	4.7	6.2	446	22	47	774	47.7	51.1	1.2
Marion	24.4	1 435	62.6	1.0	3.7	0.0	7.7	28.7	1 688	53	58	789	45.0	52.8	2.2
Marshall	39.6	1 328	59.0	4.2	2.1	0.0	6.3	40.9	1 370	93	102	1 576	45.1	53.0	1.9
Martin	20.8	1 697	73.5	0.0	0.9	0.0	4.9	13.3	1 088	20	40	657	38.5	59.9	1.7
Mason	49.9	2 953	30.9	2.6	2.9	0.0	4.7	345.7	20 450	61	57	998	37.1	60.8	2.1
Meade	28.7	1 020	76.4	1.5	1.1	0.0	4.7	23.7	844	37	99	821	39.6	58.6	1.7
Menifee	7.6	1 345	77.6	0.1	0.8	0.0	9.8	5.7	1 015	61	20	338	46.2	52.0	1.8
Mercer	30.5	1 492	53.8	7.8	3.3	2.5	6.2	41.1	2 008	51	70	847	35.8	62.1	2.1
Metcalfe	10.7	1 133	75.4	0.8	3.2	0.0	6.8	7.4	780	28	32	562	34.2	64.3	1.5
Monroe	15.2	1 358	73.5	2.1	3.0	0.0	6.0	3.0	271	40	38	818	20.8	78.6	0.6
Montgomery	42.1	2 027	47.0	10.6	2.5	0.0	5.1	106.5	5 128	76	73	996	45.0	53.2	1.8
Morgan	17.5	1 302	72.1	2.7	2.4	0.0	9.4	13.7	1 016	34	46	1 118	44.2	54.1	1.6
Muhlenberg	39.2	1 226	69.9	3.7	2.1	0.0	4.0	56.6	1 770	574	108	1 640	52.7	46.2	1.2
Nelson	62.0	1 762	52.3	0.6	2.2	0.1	13.4	104.3	2 968	90	125	1 413	40.6	57.2	2.2
Nicholas	9.0	1 280	65.6	1.1	3.2	0.7	8.8	6.1	867	17	24	328	37.2	60.3	2.5
Ohio	36.6	1 668	49.1	0.3	2.0	0.1	4.2	163.4	7 444	91	75	1 493	37.2	60.9	1.9
Oldham	51.8	1 198	72.5	0.8	4.5	0.0	3.9	30.9	714	74	155	3 011	30.8	67.0	2.2
Owen	11.6	1 151	71.5	0.6	2.9	0.3	9.0	5.1	501	26	35	468	34.3	63.4	2.3

1. Based on the resident population estimated as of July 1 of the year shown. 2. Data subject to copyright.

Table B. States and Counties — **Land Area and Population**

STATE/County code	MSA/PMSA/NECMA code[1]	County Type[2]	STATE County	Land area,[3] (sq km) 2000	Population and population characteristics, 2000			Race alone or in combination (percent)				Percent Hispanic[4]	Age (percent)					
					Total persons	Rank	Per square kilometer	White	Black	Am. Indian, Alaska Native	Asian and Pacific Islander		Under 5 years	5 to 17 years	18 to 24 years	25 to 34 years	35 to 44 years	45 to 54 years
				1	2	3	4	5	6	7	8	9	10	11	12	13	14	15
			KENTUCKY—Cont'd															
21 189	...	9	Owsley	513	4 858	2 857	9.5	99.8	0.2	0.3	0.1	0.7	5.5	19.1	8.9	12.3	14.7	13.8
21 191	1640	1	Pendleton	727	14 390	2 133	19.8	98.8	0.5	0.4	0.2	0.7	6.7	21.6	8.5	13.9	17.3	12.6
21 193	...	7	Perry	886	29 390	1 417	33.2	97.7	1.8	0.3	0.5	0.5	5.8	18.5	9.1	14.4	16.3	15.0
21 195	...	7	Pike	2 040	68 736	716	33.7	98.9	0.5	0.4	0.6	0.7	6.1	17.6	9.2	14.0	16.0	15.1
21 197	...	6	Powell	467	13 237	2 210	28.3	99.1	0.7	0.5	0.2	0.7	6.8	19.8	9.5	14.2	15.9	13.7
21 199	...	7	Pulaski	1 714	56 217	841	32.8	98.1	1.2	0.6	0.4	0.8	5.9	17.5	8.0	13.2	15.4	14.1
21 201	...	9	Robertson	259	2 266	3 044	8.7	99.2	0.1	0.4	0.5	0.9	5.5	18.3	6.7	12.2	15.0	13.6
21 203	...	6	Rockcastle	822	16 582	1 984	20.2	99.4	0.2	0.8	0.2	0.6	6.0	18.5	8.8	14.7	15.3	13.4
21 205	...	7	Rowan	727	22 094	1 688	30.4	96.9	1.8	0.7	1.2	1.1	5.4	14.8	23.5	12.9	13.0	11.4
21 207	...	9	Russell	657	16 315	2 002	24.8	98.9	0.7	0.5	0.2	0.9	5.5	17.0	7.5	12.7	14.8	14.1
21 209	4280	2	Scott	737	33 061	1 317	44.9	93.0	5.7	0.6	0.7	1.6	7.6	18.7	11.8	16.0	16.6	12.9
21 211	...	6	Shelby	995	33 337	1 304	33.5	87.8	9.4	0.7	0.7	4.5	6.9	18.3	8.7	14.4	17.0	14.5
21 213	...	6	Simpson	612	16 405	1 997	26.8	88.7	10.7	0.4	0.7	0.9	7.5	18.8	8.5	13.7	15.4	13.4
21 215	...	8	Spencer	481	11 766	2 311	24.5	98.3	1.4	0.7	0.2	1.1	7.3	19.7	7.7	15.2	18.3	14.0
21 217	...	7	Taylor	699	22 927	1 646	32.8	94.2	5.4	0.4	0.2	0.8	6.0	17.4	10.4	11.5	15.0	13.6
21 219	...	8	Todd	975	11 971	2 296	12.3	89.9	9.0	0.4	0.5	1.7	7.5	19.1	8.7	13.3	15.1	12.6
21 221	...	8	Trigg	1 148	12 597	2 256	11.0	89.4	10.2	0.8	0.3	0.9	5.9	17.1	6.8	12.1	14.6	14.2
21 223	...	8	Trimble	386	8 125	2 596	21.0	98.5	0.4	0.8	0.2	1.4	6.7	19.7	7.7	14.8	16.1	14.4
21 225	...	6	Union	894	15 637	2 046	17.5	85.9	13.6	0.7	0.4	1.6	6.2	19.1	13.8	11.5	14.0	13.8
21 227	...	5	Warren	1 412	92 522	551	65.5	88.3	9.0	0.6	1.8	2.7	6.4	16.7	16.2	14.2	15.0	12.9
21 229	...	7	Washington	779	10 916	2 373	14.0	91.4	7.9	0.5	0.6	1.6	5.8	19.4	8.8	12.3	15.6	13.3
21 231	...	7	Wayne	1 190	19 923	1 796	16.7	97.7	1.7	0.7	0.1	1.5	6.7	18.6	8.9	13.5	14.6	13.5
21 233	...	6	Webster	867	14 120	2 152	16.3	94.2	4.9	0.4	0.2	1.9	6.0	18.1	8.9	12.9	15.0	14.0
21 235	...	7	Whitley	1 140	35 865	1 224	31.5	99.1	0.5	0.7	0.4	0.7	6.3	19.4	10.8	12.9	14.4	13.2
21 237	...	9	Wolfe	577	7 065	2 679	12.2	99.6	0.3	0.3	0.0	0.5	6.7	19.3	9.4	12.4	16.1	13.6
21 239	4280	2	Woodford	494	23 208	1 632	47.0	92.9	5.8	0.5	0.4	3.0	6.2	19.1	7.9	13.0	18.1	15.6
22 000	...	X	LOUISIANA	112 825	4 468 976	X	39.6	64.8	32.9	1.0	1.5	2.4	7.1	20.2	10.6	13.5	15.5	13.1
22 001	3880	2	Acadia	1 697	58 861	813	34.7	81.2	18.4	0.4	0.2	0.9	7.8	22.0	9.6	12.3	15.1	12.2
22 003	...	6	Allen	1 980	25 440	1 544	12.8	72.7	24.9	2.3	0.8	4.5	6.4	18.2	9.3	16.4	17.0	12.0
22 005	0760	2	Ascension	755	76 627	656	101.5	78.0	20.5	0.5	0.4	2.5	8.2	21.9	9.5	15.3	17.3	12.8
22 007	...	6	Assumption	877	23 388	1 624	26.7	67.7	31.7	0.5	0.3	1.2	7.0	21.5	9.8	13.0	15.7	13.2
22 009	...	6	Avoyelles	2 156	41 481	1 067	19.2	69.0	29.8	1.4	0.2	1.0	6.8	20.0	9.2	13.7	15.3	12.4
22 011	...	6	Beauregard	3 005	32 986	1 320	11.0	85.3	13.3	1.3	0.9	1.4	7.0	20.5	8.6	13.2	15.5	13.5
22 013	...	6	Bienville	2 100	15 752	2 036	7.5	55.3	44.0	0.5	0.3	0.9	6.5	20.8	8.0	10.8	13.9	12.4
22 015	7680	2	Bossier	2 174	98 310	530	45.2	76.1	21.3	1.1	1.8	3.1	7.6	20.4	9.7	14.0	16.6	12.7
22 017	7680	2	Caddo	2 284	252 161	224	110.4	53.6	45.0	0.8	1.0	1.5	6.9	19.9	10.2	12.9	14.5	13.3
22 019	3960	3	Calcasieu	2 774	183 577	297	66.2	74.5	24.4	0.7	0.9	1.3	7.2	20.2	10.3	13.0	15.7	13.2
22 021	...	8	Caldwell	1 371	10 560	2 393	7.7	81.0	18.0	0.8	0.2	1.5	6.1	18.6	9.6	13.3	15.2	13.3
22 023	...	8	Cameron	3 401	9 991	2 446	2.9	94.3	4.1	0.6	0.5	2.2	6.7	21.7	9.4	12.2	17.5	12.6
22 025	...	7	Catahoula	1 822	10 920	2 372	6.0	72.3	27.3	0.6	0.3	0.9	6.5	19.3	10.0	11.7	15.1	13.5
22 027	...	6	Claiborne	1 955	16 851	1 964	8.6	52.1	47.6	0.4	0.3	0.8	6.0	19.6	8.0	12.4	14.5	12.6
22 029	...	7	Concordia	1 802	20 247	1 777	11.2	61.2	38.0	0.4	0.5	1.5	7.3	20.5	8.9	10.7	15.0	13.3
22 031	...	6	De Soto	2 272	25 494	1 540	11.2	56.5	42.4	0.9	0.3	1.6	7.0	21.4	8.3	11.5	14.8	13.5
22 033	0760	2	East Baton Rouge	1 180	412 852	145	349.9	56.9	40.5	0.5	2.4	1.8	7.0	19.1	14.4	14.0	14.7	13.1
22 035	...	7	East Carroll	1 092	9 421	2 493	8.6	31.9	67.4	0.3	0.4	1.2	7.6	22.7	11.5	13.2	14.0	10.8
22 037	...	6	East Feliciana	1 174	21 360	1 720	18.2	52.2	47.3	0.4	0.4	0.7	6.5	19.2	9.3	13.8	16.9	14.4
22 039	...	7	Evangeline	1 720	35 434	1 237	20.6	70.8	28.8	0.4	0.2	1.0	7.9	21.6	9.6	12.6	15.0	11.8
22 041	...	7	Franklin	1 615	21 263	1 722	13.2	67.6	31.8	0.6	0.4	0.8	7.2	20.7	9.1	11.8	14.0	12.1
22 043	...	8	Grant	1 671	18 698	1 861	11.2	86.6	12.1	1.7	0.4	1.1	7.4	20.8	7.9	13.0	15.2	13.0
22 045	...	4	Iberia	1 490	73 266	684	49.2	66.0	31.3	0.7	2.3	1.5	8.0	22.0	9.6	12.8	15.6	12.3
22 047	...	6	Iberville	1 602	33 320	1 305	20.8	49.6	49.9	0.4	0.3	1.0	6.5	19.7	10.5	14.3	16.7	13.2
22 049	...	7	Jackson	1 476	15 397	2 059	10.4	71.4	28.0	0.4	0.3	0.6	6.5	18.8	9.3	11.7	13.9	13.0
22 051	5560	0	Jefferson	794	455 466	128	573.6	71.2	23.2	0.8	3.6	7.1	6.6	18.7	9.1	14.2	16.1	14.2
22 053	...	6	Jefferson Davis	1 689	31 435	1 362	18.6	81.3	18.2	0.6	0.3	1.0	7.6	21.7	9.1	12.2	15.0	11.9
22 055	3880	2	Lafayette	699	190 503	288	272.5	74.1	24.2	0.6	1.4	1.7	7.3	20.1	11.7	14.6	16.6	12.9
22 057	3350	3	Lafourche	2 809	89 974	574	32.0	83.7	12.8	2.9	0.9	1.4	6.9	20.4	10.5	13.7	16.0	12.7
22 059	...	7	La Salle	1 616	14 282	2 142	8.8	86.8	12.3	1.1	0.3	0.8	6.1	20.0	9.4	12.4	14.7	13.0
22 061	...	4	Lincoln	1 221	42 509	1 046	34.8	58.0	40.2	0.4	1.4	1.2	6.0	16.1	25.7	11.5	11.7	10.5
22 063	0760	2	Livingston	1 678	91 814	558	54.7	95.0	4.3	0.8	0.3	1.1	7.5	22.0	9.1	14.8	16.7	13.1
22 065	...	7	Madison	1 616	13 728	2 179	8.5	38.3	60.6	0.4	0.8	2.1	8.2	24.4	11.2	12.6	12.9	11.7
22 067	...	6	Morehouse	2 057	31 021	1 377	15.1	56.1	43.6	0.3	0.3	0.7	7.0	20.5	9.5	12.2	14.3	12.8
22 069	...	6	Natchitoches	3 252	39 080	1 135	12.0	58.8	38.9	1.6	0.6	1.4	7.1	18.9	17.9	11.6	12.7	11.7
22 071	5560	0	Orleans	468	484 674	117	1 035.6	28.9	67.9	0.5	2.6	3.1	6.9	19.8	11.4	14.5	14.8	13.1
22 073	5200	2	Ouachita	1 581	147 250	368	93.1	65.0	33.8	0.5	0.9	1.2	7.2	20.7	12.0	13.1	15.1	12.2
22 075	5560	1	Plaquemines	2 187	26 757	1 492	12.2	70.9	23.6	2.8	3.1	1.6	7.4	21.8	9.2	13.6	16.9	12.7

1. MSA = Metropolitan Statistical Area. PMSA = Primary MSA. NECMA = New England County Metropolitan Area. See Appendix A for explanation of these concepts. See Appendix B for list of metropolitan areas identified by type, with component counties.   2. County typology code from the Economic Research Service of USDA. See Appendix A for definition.   3. Dry land or land partially or temporarily covered by water.   4. Hispanic persons may be of any race.

STATE County	Age (percent) (cont'd)				Total persons		Percent change		Components of change, 2000–2001			Households, 2000			Percent	
	55 to 64 years	65 to 74 years	75 years and over	Percent female	2001	1990	1990–2000	2000–2001	Births	Deaths	Net migration	Number	Percent change, 1990–2000	Persons per household	Female family householder[1]	One person
	16	17	18	19	20	21	22	23	24	25	26	27	28	29	30	31
KENTUCKY—Cont'd																
Owsley	10.7	8.1	6.9	49.5	4 856	5 036	-3.5	0.0	81	92	11	1 894	2.5	2.51	12.7	24.5
Pendleton	8.8	6.0	4.5	49.9	14 611	12 062	19.3	1.5	218	161	165	5 170	19.3	2.75	9.6	20.1
Perry	9.7	6.4	4.8	51.4	29 279	30 283	-2.9	-0.4	502	377	-230	11 460	8.1	2.53	13.2	23.3
Pike	9.8	7.1	5.2	51.2	67 887	72 584	-5.3	-1.2	1 050	986	-908	27 612	5.6	2.46	11.4	24.1
Powell	9.6	6.3	4.3	50.2	13 294	11 686	13.3	0.4	258	162	-35	5 044	24.3	2.60	12.4	21.8
Pulaski	10.8	8.5	6.6	51.1	56 774	49 489	13.6	1.0	906	806	470	22 719	20.4	2.42	10.1	24.9
Robertson	11.9	8.5	8.4	51.3	2 294	2 124	6.7	1.2	33	37	32	866	5.6	2.54	9.1	24.7
Rockcastle	10.2	7.5	5.8	50.5	16 629	14 803	12.0	0.3	254	250	48	6 544	19.8	2.49	11.4	24.4
Rowan	8.6	5.9	4.5	51.4	22 174	20 353	8.6	0.4	306	226	6	7 927	17.4	2.39	10.2	27.0
Russell	11.8	9.1	7.3	51.6	16 492	14 716	10.9	1.1	226	263	215	6 941	17.7	2.33	10.2	28.0
Scott	7.5	4.8	4.0	51.1	34 519	23 867	38.5	4.4	595	340	1 177	12 110	42.5	2.61	11.5	21.0
Shelby	9.4	5.9	4.9	51.3	34 120	24 824	34.3	2.3	539	377	618	12 104	33.8	2.63	10.6	20.2
Simpson	9.5	6.6	6.6	51.2	16 460	15 145	8.3	0.3	275	197	-21	6 415	11.2	2.52	11.5	24.2
Spencer	8.7	5.2	3.9	49.5	13 039	6 801	73.0	10.8	207	107	1 136	4 251	73.4	2.74	7.6	17.1
Taylor	10.5	8.6	6.6	51.9	23 034	21 146	8.4	0.5	353	294	55	9 233	12.4	2.41	11.5	26.0
Todd	9.8	7.4	6.5	51.3	12 048	10 940	9.4	0.6	204	197	72	4 569	11.3	2.59	11.6	23.0
Trigg	12.8	9.7	6.9	50.8	12 828	10 361	21.6	1.8	174	174	225	5 215	27.1	2.39	8.4	25.0
Trimble	9.2	6.0	5.4	50.8	8 442	6 090	33.4	3.9	130	101	282	3 137	39.7	2.57	8.5	22.0
Union	8.7	6.8	6.0	49.6	15 488	16 557	-5.6	-1.0	231	207	-171	5 710	2.3	2.50	11.4	26.1
Warren	8.2	5.6	4.8	51.0	93 232	77 720	19.0	0.8	1 574	991	161	35 365	22.7	2.46	11.2	26.1
Washington	9.8	7.6	7.4	50.9	11 032	10 441	4.5	1.1	167	151	101	4 121	11.1	2.57	10.0	24.0
Wayne	10.5	7.8	5.9	50.6	19 950	17 468	14.1	0.1	319	270	-17	7 913	21.4	2.49	10.6	23.9
Webster	10.1	7.9	7.1	51.1	14 034	13 955	1.2	-0.6	223	223	-81	5 560	3.5	2.49	10.3	24.3
Whitley	10.0	7.0	6.0	51.7	36 466	33 326	7.6	1.7	591	509	523	13 780	13.4	2.52	13.0	25.2
Wolfe	9.9	6.8	5.9	50.4	6 953	6 503	8.6	-1.6	139	98	-156	2 816	14.9	2.45	12.5	27.0
Woodford	9.5	5.8	4.6	51.8	23 331	19 955	16.3	0.5	373	208	-35	8 893	23.1	2.57	9.7	21.0
LOUISIANA	8.5	6.3	5.2	51.6	4 465 430	4 221 826	5.9	-0.1	87 433	51 633	-39 132	1 656 053	10.5	2.62	16.6	25.3
Acadia	8.7	6.7	5.5	51.7	58 910	55 882	5.3	0.1	1 181	726	-386	21 142	9.6	2.74	14.9	22.6
Allen	8.8	6.8	5.0	44.2	25 342	21 226	19.9	-0.4	425	275	-244	8 102	14.4	2.62	15.2	24.3
Ascension	7.4	4.4	3.3	50.8	79 873	58 214	31.6	4.2	1 605	639	2 238	26 691	38.0	2.85	13.3	18.3
Assumption	9.0	6.0	4.9	51.6	23 257	22 753	2.8	-0.6	394	260	-263	8 239	11.4	2.81	14.9	20.3
Avoyelles	9.0	7.1	6.6	50.9	41 458	39 159	5.9	-0.1	749	597	-159	14 736	9.3	2.60	15.7	25.0
Beauregard	9.8	6.9	5.0	49.8	33 192	30 083	9.6	0.6	551	406	77	12 104	16.8	2.63	10.9	22.2
Bienville	10.1	8.7	8.9	52.3	15 563	16 232	-3.0	-1.2	251	280	-156	6 108	4.4	2.52	17.7	28.8
Bossier	8.6	6.1	4.3	51.0	99 285	86 088	14.2	1.0	1 812	996	219	36 628	19.2	2.63	14.1	22.9
Caddo	8.7	7.0	6.6	52.7	250 760	248 253	1.6	-0.6	4 796	3 222	-2 929	97 974	5.1	2.51	19.8	28.9
Calcasieu	8.6	6.8	5.1	51.3	182 842	168 134	9.2	-0.4	3 635	2 150	-2 195	68 613	13.7	2.61	14.7	24.0
Caldwell	10.0	7.5	6.4	49.3	10 549	9 806	7.7	-0.1	150	152	-4	3 941	10.2	2.50	12.6	25.4
Cameron	9.4	6.6	4.0	49.8	9 805	9 260	7.9	-1.9	143	99	-234	3 592	13.9	2.76	9.0	20.9
Catahoula	9.5	7.9	6.5	50.9	10 847	11 065	-1.3	-0.7	208	147	-131	4 082	3.9	2.55	14.5	24.3
Claiborne	9.7	8.7	8.6	50.1	16 629	17 405	-3.2	-1.3	274	242	-259	6 270	3.4	2.50	17.6	28.5
Concordia	9.7	8.3	6.3	51.2	20 090	20 828	-2.8	-0.8	411	261	-307	7 521	2.5	2.60	19.0	25.3
De Soto	9.5	7.5	6.6	52.4	25 742	25 668	-0.7	1.0	543	409	122	9 691	6.2	2.60	18.6	25.4
East Baton Rouge	7.7	5.3	4.6	52.1	409 667	380 105	8.6	-0.8	8 171	3 957	-7 446	156 365	12.8	2.55	16.8	26.9
East Carroll	7.7	6.8	5.7	48.9	9 224	9 709	-3.0	-2.1	213	124	-289	2 969	-5.1	2.82	27.7	25.6
East Feliciana	9.3	5.9	4.7	46.2	21 420	19 211	11.2	0.3	404	278	-57	6 699	19.9	2.76	18.0	22.5
Evangeline	8.6	7.0	5.8	50.1	35 546	33 274	6.5	0.3	754	451	-178	12 736	8.0	2.64	15.5	25.8
Franklin	9.8	7.9	7.4	52.3	21 018	22 387	-5.0	-1.2	434	382	-294	7 754	-0.3	2.64	16.5	23.9
Grant	10.0	7.0	5.7	51.0	18 717	17 526	6.7	0.1	350	257	-67	7 073	13.0	2.61	12.9	22.6
Iberia	8.2	6.1	5.3	51.9	73 530	68 297	7.3	0.4	1 637	771	-584	25 381	11.1	2.82	17.2	21.1
Iberville	8.3	6.0	4.8	50.1	33 261	31 049	7.3	-0.2	669	376	-345	10 674	8.1	2.81	20.4	21.9
Jackson	10.6	8.1	8.0	52.3	15 409	15 859	-2.9	0.1	244	228	2	6 086	4.6	2.48	14.4	27.0
Jefferson	9.1	6.6	5.3	52.0	451 459	448 306	1.6	-0.9	8 358	5 170	-7 218	176 234	5.9	2.56	15.4	26.7
Jefferson Davis	9.1	7.3	6.0	51.1	31 275	30 722	2.3	-0.5	623	464	-321	11 480	7.6	2.70	13.7	22.6
Lafayette	7.3	5.5	4.0	51.5	190 894	164 762	15.6	0.2	3 798	1 758	-1 622	72 372	19.8	2.57	14.0	25.4
Lafourche	8.6	6.4	4.8	51.2	90 273	85 860	4.8	0.3	1 608	837	-443	32 057	11.2	2.75	12.4	19.6
La Salle	9.6	8.0	6.8	49.9	14 245	13 662	4.5	-0.3	241	200	-73	5 291	4.0	2.52	9.8	25.7
Lincoln	7.1	5.6	5.7	51.5	42 173	41 745	1.8	-0.8	722	436	-621	15 235	11.5	2.44	15.3	27.0
Livingston	8.3	5.1	3.4	50.4	96 257	70 523	30.2	4.8	1 720	745	3 397	32 630	37.0	2.80	10.7	18.2
Madison	7.4	6.2	5.4	49.2	13 506	12 463	10.2	-1.6	320	195	-350	4 469	5.1	2.74	24.2	26.6
Morehouse	8.6	8.1	7.0	52.3	30 675	31 938	-2.9	-1.1	652	526	-469	11 382	3.8	2.64	19.8	24.4
Natchitoches	8.1	6.4	5.7	52.5	38 558	37 254	4.9	-1.3	756	464	-823	14 263	12.8	2.56	17.7	27.1
Orleans	7.8	6.0	5.7	53.1	476 492	496 938	-2.5	-1.7	10 611	6 560	-12 406	188 251	0.0	2.48	24.5	33.2
Ouachita	8.1	6.5	5.4	52.8	146 678	142 191	3.6	-0.4	2 926	1 683	-1 795	55 216	9.3	2.58	17.9	25.8
Plaquemines	8.6	6.1	3.7	50.2	27 004	25 575	4.6	0.9	512	251	-7	9 021	9.8	2.89	14.6	18.6

1. No spouse present.

Table B. States and Counties — **Vital Statistics, Health Resources, and Crime**

STATE County	Births, average 1997–1999 Total	Rate[1]	Deaths, average 1997–1999 Number Total	Number Infant[2]	Rate Total[1]	Rate Infant[3]	Physicians,[4] 2000 Number	Rate[5]	Hospitals,[4] 1998 Number	Beds Number	Beds Rate[5]	Medicare enrollees 2000	Serious crimes known to police, 2000[6] Total Number	Rate[7]
	32	33	34	35	36	37	38	39	40	41	42	43	44	45
KENTUCKY—Cont'd														
Owsley	66	12.2	73	NA	13.6	NA	2	41	0	0	0	1 084	NA	NA
Pendleton	201	14.5	128	NA	9.3	NA	2	14	0	0	0	1 792	NA	NA
Perry	410	13.2	307	NA	9.9	NA	75	255	1	295	950	5 767	NA	NA
Pike	864	12.0	750	NA	10.4	NA	113	164	2	354	491	13 239	NA	NA
Powell	195	15.1	123	NA	9.5	NA	4	30	0	0	0	1 288	NA	NA
Pulaski	688	12.2	575	NA	10.2	NA	82	146	1	248	441	11 355	NA	NA
Robertson	28	12.6	31	NA	13.8	NA	0	0	0	0	0	381	NA	NA
Rockcastle	196	12.4	180	NA	11.3	NA	10	60	1	28	176	2 516	NA	NA
Rowan	254	11.5	165	NA	7.5	NA	44	199	1	169	761	2 914	NA	NA
Russell	181	11.1	192	NA	11.8	NA	12	74	1	47	290	3 426	NA	NA
Scott	435	14.1	232	NA	7.5	NA	27	82	1	79	257	3 493	NA	NA
Shelby	417	14.0	278	NA	9.4	NA	32	96	1	78	264	3 834	NA	NA
Simpson	233	14.3	156	NA	9.6	NA	11	67	1	58	354	2 409	NA	NA
Spencer	138	14.1	84	NA	8.6	NA	2	17	0	0	0	1 284	NA	NA
Taylor	261	11.4	246	NA	10.7	NA	29	126	1	98	427	4 526	NA	NA
Todd	164	14.6	146	NA	13.0	NA	4	33	0	0	0	1 829	NA	NA
Trigg	140	11.3	132	NA	10.6	NA	5	40	1	42	339	2 519	NA	NA
Trimble	113	14.9	72	NA	9.4	NA	3	37	0	0	0	1 088	NA	NA
Union	189	11.4	160	NA	9.7	NA	8	51	1	42	253	2 482	NA	NA
Warren	1 177	13.5	737	NA	8.4	NA	176	190	2	623	713	12 399	NA	NA
Washington	134	12.3	116	NA	10.6	NA	7	64	0	0	0	1 896	NA	NA
Wayne	250	13.1	193	NA	10.1	NA	16	80	1	30	157	3 399	NA	NA
Webster	170	12.6	169	NA	12.5	NA	4	28	0	0	0	2 559	NA	NA
Whitley	466	13.0	404	NA	11.3	NA	57	159	1	286	796	8 138	NA	NA
Wolfe	97	13.1	89	NA	12.0	NA	2	28	0	0	0	1 336	NA	NA
Woodford	295	13.0	179	NA	7.9	NA	21	90	1	66	289	2 757	NA	NA
LOUISIANA	65 784	15.1	40 527	620	9.3	9.4	9 061	203	133	18 314	419	601 516	242 344	5 423
Acadia	940	16.3	577	NA	10.0	NA	45	76	2	217	376	8 652	2 019	3 430
Allen	322	13.4	230	NA	9.6	NA	17	67	2	87	364	3 310	468	1 840
Ascension	1 177	16.4	484	NA	6.7	NA	47	61	3	189	264	6 982	2 670	3 971
Assumption	317	13.8	201	NA	8.8	NA	11	47	1	38	165	3 013	402	1 719
Avoyelles	565	13.8	487	NA	11.9	NA	22	53	2	103	252	6 882	800	1 929
Beauregard	475	14.8	306	NA	9.6	NA	24	73	2	193	604	4 713	681	2 065
Bienville	210	13.3	220	NA	13.9	NA	5	32	0	0	0	3 084	135	857
Bossier	1 413	15.2	731	14	7.8	9.7	110	112	2	214	229	11 109	5 077	5 164
Caddo	3 612	14.9	2 593	49	10.7	13.5	888	352	7	1 611	664	38 501	18 712	7 421
Calcasieu	2 734	15.2	1 643	26	9.1	9.6	304	166	6	862	478	25 595	10 451	5 800
Caldwell	138	13.3	136	NA	13.1	NA	14	133	2	89	859	1 810	152	1 439
Cameron	114	12.7	73	NA	8.2	NA	3	30	1	27	298	852	252	2 522
Catahoula	155	14.1	119	NA	10.8	NA	6	55	0	0	0	2 002	191	1 749
Claiborne	203	12.0	203	NA	12.0	NA	13	77	1	40	236	2 888	293	1 739
Concordia	303	14.7	238	NA	11.5	NA	10	49	1	46	222	3 476	509	3 080
De Soto	374	14.9	309	NA	12.4	NA	9	35	1	35	140	4 264	890	3 491
East Baton Rouge	5 967	15.1	3 134	67	7.9	11.2	1 033	250	5	1 557	394	45 233	36 747	9 208
East Carroll	160	18.1	104	NA	11.7	NA	9	96	1	29	326	1 426	NA	NA
East Feliciana	298	14.2	218	NA	10.4	NA	9	42	0	0	0	2 763	697	3 263
Evangeline	570	16.7	358	NA	10.5	NA	42	119	2	311	912	5 910	640	2 008
Franklin	308	14.0	278	NA	12.6	NA	8	38	1	46	208	3 653	403	1 895
Grant	268	14.2	193	NA	10.2	NA	5	27	0	0	0	2 822	490	2 621
Iberia	1 243	17.0	638	13	8.7	10.5	78	106	2	156	213	9 964	NA	NA
Iberville	463	14.8	294	NA	9.4	NA	32	96	1	151	484	4 352	NA	NA
Jackson	201	12.9	199	NA	12.8	NA	11	71	1	66	424	2 905	117	760
Jefferson	6 335	14.1	4 028	50	8.9	7.9	1 456	320	7	1 772	393	62 311	28 277	6 208
Jefferson Davis	476	15.1	348	NA	11.0	NA	24	76	2	70	221	4 902	1 331	4 234
Lafayette	2 941	15.8	1 322	30	7.1	10.1	455	239	5	1 024	549	21 060	10 621	5 815
Lafourche	1 272	14.3	674	12	7.6	9.7	106	118	3	251	281	11 595	2 916	3 338
La Salle	181	13.2	163	NA	11.8	NA	14	98	2	114	834	2 500	119	1 052
Lincoln	521	12.5	334	NA	8.0	NA	55	129	1	107	257	5 319	2 008	5 425
Livingston	1 340	15.2	596	8	6.7	5.7	14	15	0	0	0	9 117	2 500	2 723
Madison	209	16.2	147	NA	11.4	NA	6	44	1	50	390	1 808	NA	NA
Morehouse	487	15.5	391	NA	12.4	NA	32	103	1	119	378	5 584	772	2 489
Natchitoches	579	15.5	383	NA	10.3	NA	35	90	1	196	529	5 447	1 917	4 905
Orleans	7 379	15.8	5 150	74	11.1	10.0	2 192	452	14	3 229	694	66 589	34 423	7 102
Ouachita	2 237	15.2	1 330	21	9.1	9.4	317	215	5	1 012	689	19 684	9 568	7 209
Plaquemines	399	15.3	195	NA	7.5	NA	15	56	0	0	0	3 115	440	1 644

1. Per 1,000 estimated resident population, average 1997–1999.   2. Deaths of infants under 1 year old.   3. Deaths of infants under 1 year old per 1,000 live births.   4. Data subject to copyright.   5. Per 100,000 resident population as of July 1 of the year shown.   6. Data for serious crimes have not been adjusted for underreporting; this may affect comparability between geographic areas and over time.   7. Per 100,000 population estimated by the FBI.

STATE County	Serious crimes known to police, 2000[1] (cont'd) Rate[2]		Education School enrollment and attainment, 1990				Local government expenditures, fiscal 1999[5]		Money income 1989				Income and poverty, 1998			
			Enrollment[3]		Attainment[4] (percent)					Households				Percent below poverty level		
											Median					
	Violent	Property	Total	Percent private	High school graduate or more	Bachelor's degree or more	Total current expenditures (mil dol)	Current expenditures per student (dollars)	Per capita[6] (dollars)	Dollars	Percent change, 1979–1989 (constant 1989 dollars)	Percent with $100,000 or more	Median household income	All persons	Persons under 18	Persons 5–17 in families
	46	47	48	49	50	51	52	53	54	55	56	57	58	59	60	61
KENTUCKY—Cont'd																
Owsley	NA	NA	1 170	1.0	35.5	9.8	6.4	7 122	5 791	8 595	-23.1	0.4	17 015	35.2	36.6	47.6
Pendleton	NA	NA	2 810	3.1	60.1	6.8	14.0	4 723	9 525	22 500	0.6	0.8	35 473	13.7	18.3	17.6
Perry	NA	NA	7 631	2.7	47.6	6.7	38.3	6 212	7 914	16 202	-19.7	1.0	25 012	25.8	30.7	31.0
Pike	NA	NA	18 222	5.6	50.2	7.7	69.4	5 601	8 674	17 468	-22.9	1.4	27 837	21.0	25.2	24.2
Powell	NA	NA	2 769	1.7	50.1	5.3	14.9	5 620	7 474	16 828	-9.8	0.6	25 176	21.7	26.5	26.9
Pulaski	NA	NA	11 064	4.3	56.2	9.2	51.9	5 348	9 209	18 198	3.4	1.5	26 823	18.1	24.6	22.5
Robertson	NA	NA	439	3.0	50.8	7.7	2.3	5 611	8 630	19 756	7.4	0.2	27 788	17.3	21.9	24.1
Rockcastle	NA	NA	3 335	2.2	44.9	5.9	16.8	5 545	7 630	14 967	0.8	0.4	24 962	22.3	28.4	28.5
Rowan	NA	NA	8 195	2.6	57.9	17.3	18.6	5 855	7 639	15 922	-10.1	1.0	27 696	20.9	25.4	25.4
Russell	NA	NA	2 956	4.4	50.2	6.2	14.5	5 108	8 967	16 788	15.8	1.4	22 338	22.0	29.2	29.0
Scott	NA	NA	6 629	19.8	69.1	15.2	31.6	5 572	12 314	27 563	7.9	2.5	44 984	10.4	14.4	13.4
Shelby	NA	NA	5 791	9.5	69.9	12.9	24.4	5 010	13 064	28 500	6.3	2.6	42 689	9.8	14.8	12.8
Simpson	NA	NA	3 369	5.6	58.9	8.8	15.8	5 262	10 635	21 793	-3.7	1.0	34 947	11.8	16.5	15.2
Spencer	NA	NA	1 635	6.1	57.5	9.9	10.1	5 074	10 502	22 680	-4.6	1.7	38 826	10.6	14.9	14.2
Taylor	NA	NA	4 965	15.7	57.4	10.1	21.2	5 424	9 848	21 083	-4.2	1.3	27 199	16.8	22.6	21.5
Todd	NA	NA	2 322	5.2	50.6	7.1	10.5	4 865	9 227	20 309	9.9	1.2	31 367	15.4	21.8	21.0
Trigg	NA	NA	2 056	1.3	58.9	11.4	10.5	5 293	10 124	19 860	-5.8	1.3	30 943	13.3	19.2	18.3
Trimble	NA	NA	1 360	6.0	61.6	7.3	7.2	5 208	10 128	22 372	-0.5	0.7	32 637	14.0	18.7	18.1
Union	NA	NA	4 295	14.3	68.1	8.9	16.1	6 211	11 080	23 798	-14.4	2.8	32 023	14.1	17.4	17.8
Warren	NA	NA	22 735	4.4	70.9	19.2	82.0	5 767	11 819	24 175	2.5	2.0	35 840	13.9	19.6	16.9
Washington	NA	NA	2 541	16.8	57.8	7.5	9.5	5 090	9 559	20 606	0.0	1.2	30 749	15.0	18.4	18.2
Wayne	NA	NA	3 901	1.6	44.6	5.5	21.2	5 867	6 550	12 560	-10.3	0.4	22 242	26.1	32.6	33.0
Webster	NA	NA	3 243	3.0	60.7	6.0	13.9	5 523	10 263	21 189	-2.1	0.9	31 878	14.8	20.9	18.0
Whitley	NA	NA	8 931	17.8	53.0	11.3	40.9	5 515	8 028	14 979	-9.0	1.2	22 462	25.7	31.5	32.4
Wolfe	NA	NA	1 711	7.8	42.8	7.7	8.9	6 507	5 998	11 000	-16.3	0.2	17 647	30.0	32.0	41.9
Woodford	NA	NA	4 975	15.5	73.5	19.5	20.3	5 306	14 151	32 858	13.1	2.9	48 273	7.6	11.1	9.7
LOUISIANA	681	4 742	1 185 759	17.4	68.3	16.1	4 265.0	5 548	10 635	21 949	-14.0	2.4	30 894	18.2	25.7	24.0
Acadia	438	2 992	15 299	17.7	54.6	8.4	52.9	5 040	7 952	16 022	-29.2	1.6	26 977	20.8	28.0	26.0
Allen	318	1 521	5 507	4.6	57.1	6.7	23.4	5 235	7 394	15 838	-22.6	0.6	27 326	22.1	27.4	26.5
Ascension	375	3 596	16 832	13.1	68.5	9.3	82.7	5 623	10 482	27 435	-14.7	1.5	41 731	11.7	16.7	15.3
Assumption	325	1 394	6 013	9.1	50.4	6.7	27.2	5 778	8 077	20 021	-19.7	1.5	32 346	18.9	27.7	24.7
Avoyelles	176	1 753	9 956	14.0	50.5	7.4	36.1	4 830	6 874	13 451	-19.5	1.0	23 463	25.3	32.4	31.4
Beauregard	343	1 722	7 533	4.1	70.6	13.0	33.2	5 406	10 096	22 442	-9.7	1.6	33 726	15.5	21.4	21.5
Bienville	184	673	3 780	5.1	62.6	9.3	17.5	6 131	8 194	16 043	-7.7	0.7	24 361	23.9	34.2	34.8
Bossier	620	4 544	23 528	8.5	78.9	15.5	99.1	5 307	11 317	26 058	-5.9	1.5	36 537	12.9	20.0	18.4
Caddo	823	6 598	68 907	10.8	73.4	18.2	268.8	5 708	11 604	22 395	-13.1	2.9	30 723	20.5	29.5	26.6
Calcasieu	649	5 152	47 034	12.1	70.3	14.7	176.3	5 323	11 233	24 375	-22.3	2.3	35 533	14.5	21.1	18.1
Caldwell	313	1 127	2 284	3.4	57.1	9.3	10.6	5 280	8 308	16 069	-6.0	1.6	25 071	19.9	26.5	28.0
Cameron	340	2 182	2 332	3.6	61.1	7.9	13.3	6 430	10 289	25 164	-18.6	1.8	37 502	11.9	15.7	17.4
Catahoula	412	1 337	2 818	3.1	53.9	8.7	11.8	5 673	7 862	14 956	-9.2	1.5	22 416	25.9	32.7	35.1
Claiborne	214	1 525	3 978	6.8	60.9	10.1	15.3	5 154	8 076	16 073	-12.2	0.7	25 223	24.6	33.6	34.4
Concordia	472	2 608	5 757	12.4	56.9	9.1	22.5	5 476	8 391	17 265	-15.4	1.3	23 595	24.9	33.7	33.9
De Soto	710	2 781	6 387	6.2	64.0	9.5	32.7	6 286	8 330	16 315	-15.1	1.0	26 755	22.2	30.8	30.5
East Baton Rouge	826	8 382	120 056	19.5	80.5	27.5	327.1	5 786	13 126	27 224	-10.0	3.8	36 732	15.7	23.2	20.2
East Carroll	NA	NA	2 841	10.8	49.1	10.3	10.8	5 354	6 059	9 791	-24.9	1.3	16 464	43.0	49.4	53.6
East Feliciana	1 297	1 966	4 919	16.9	58.2	8.9	14.3	5 009	7 746	20 139	-14.2	1.4	28 574	19.1	23.6	24.8
Evangeline	179	1 829	8 897	13.4	48.2	8.3	32.9	4 823	7 041	13 797	-18.1	0.9	24 548	24.6	30.8	32.3
Franklin	390	1 505	6 011	3.5	53.7	10.3	21.9	5 232	7 607	15 159	-5.6	1.6	21 250	27.4	34.9	35.5
Grant	540	2 080	4 399	5.6	62.8	9.6	18.9	5 108	8 330	17 711	-6.4	1.3	28 472	18.9	26.1	26.1
Iberia	NA	NA	18 628	12.6	59.3	9.0	84.7	5 618	9 466	20 838	-27.8	2.0	31 458	18.9	25.8	24.6
Iberville	NA	NA	8 383	20.7	59.0	8.9	33.3	6 296	9 449	20 371	-13.3	2.0	29 060	21.7	29.6	28.2
Jackson	117	643	4 109	4.4	63.9	9.2	15.4	5 617	9 960	18 804	1.7	1.3	28 264	19.4	32.3	25.7
Jefferson	724	5 484	119 881	35.9	76.0	18.8	315.9	5 892	12 845	27 916	-15.7	3.0	38 364	13.6	21.5	18.6
Jefferson Davis	964	3 270	8 274	7.1	59.9	8.0	32.5	5 308	8 486	18 467	-26.7	1.2	27 969	18.9	24.6	24.4
Lafayette	652	5 164	49 203	14.9	73.3	22.5	159.5	5 210	11 983	24 339	-21.9	3.4	37 387	14.4	20.3	18.5
Lafourche	282	3 057	24 080	12.7	56.2	10.0	86.8	5 517	9 250	21 416	-28.6	1.3	35 499	14.7	20.9	19.0
La Salle	256	796	3 277	2.7	61.0	7.9	14.6	4 812	9 015	18 597	-9.0	1.2	28 929	16.2	22.4	23.0
Lincoln	567	4 857	18 451	5.3	74.5	26.2	34.1	4 996	9 342	19 254	-9.4	2.4	29 861	17.6	22.2	23.2
Livingston	388	2 335	19 330	8.5	66.7	8.7	91.0	4 743	9 946	25 470	-12.1	1.0	38 514	11.4	16.2	14.7
Madison	NA	NA	3 789	7.5	53.3	9.2	15.1	4 659	6 723	12 792	-8.7	1.4	19 865	32.9	41.3	44.7
Morehouse	351	2 137	8 645	12.3	57.8	10.5	29.5	5 219	8 547	17 309	7.1	1.6	23 033	25.0	33.6	32.8
Natchitoches	885	4 020	12 336	7.2	65.0	16.4	39.5	5 500	8 112	15 778	-13.4	1.6	25 935	24.1	31.7	32.0
Orleans	1 068	6 035	146 515	28.9	68.1	22.4	434.0	5 281	11 372	18 477	-6.7	3.6	26 890	26.8	38.1	34.6
Ouachita	935	6 274	42 399	9.1	71.6	18.9	141.3	5 017	10 593	21 129	-9.2	2.3	29 671	19.9	28.3	26.7
Plaquemines	292	1 353	7 064	17.7	58.0	7.5	31.4	6 109	9 500	24 076	-18.5	1.1	32 623	16.6	23.0	22.5

1. Data for serious crimes have not been adjusted for underreporting; this may affect comparability between geographic areas and over time.   2. Per 100,000 population estimated by the FBI.   3. All persons 3 years old and over enrolled in nursery school through college.   4. Persons 25 years old and over.   5. Elementary and secondary education expenditures, local government fiscal years ending between July 1, 1998 and June 30, 1999.   6. Based on population enumerated as of April 1, 1990.

Table B. States and Counties — **Personal Income**

STATE County	Total (mil dol)	Percent change, 1998–1999	Per capita[1] Dollars	Per capita Rank	Wages and salaries[2] (mil dol)	Proprietor's income (mil dol)	Dividends, interest, and rent (mil dol)	Transfer payments Total (mil dol)	Government payments to individuals Total (mil dol)	Social Security (mil dol)	Medical payments (mil dol)	Income maintenance (mil dol)	Unemployment insurance (mil dol)
	62	63	64	65	66	67	68	69	70	71	72	73	74
KENTUCKY—Cont'd													
Owsley	73	7.0	13 663	3 063	18	5	7	37	36	7	17	9	0
Pendleton	256	4.4	18 327	2 463	74	14	39	43	40	17	15	4	1
Perry	560	5.1	18 191	2 502	369	38	78	179	173	52	71	32	2
Pike	1 367	3.4	19 105	2 256	769	112	215	373	359	134	132	52	5
Powell	190	4.1	14 325	3 029	71	15	20	50	47	18	17	9	1
Pulaski	1 088	4.2	19 043	2 273	621	78	179	267	256	96	110	31	3
Robertson	33	-3.6	14 508	3 021	8	1	4	9	8	3	4	1	0
Rockcastle	250	3.9	15 641	2 939	84	10	30	71	68	21	31	11	1
Rowan	352	4.7	15 883	2 908	229	23	53	76	72	26	26	10	1
Russell	265	3.3	16 406	2 843	126	28	39	85	82	28	34	12	4
Scott	823	4.4	25 514	581	1 025	79	109	80	74	32	28	7	1
Shelby	833	6.1	27 251	400	431	43	149	92	86	40	33	7	1
Simpson	329	5.9	19 862	2 032	242	22	63	54	51	23	20	5	1
Spencer	177	7.1	16 919	2 750	37	5	24	31	29	12	12	2	1
Taylor	389	-1.2	16 965	2 738	204	29	71	108	104	41	41	11	6
Todd	209	-2.0	18 498	2 413	84	20	37	42	40	16	17	5	1
Trigg	220	3.3	17 447	2 659	96	6	45	50	48	24	17	4	1
Trimble	121	0.6	15 210	2 968	27	5	17	27	26	10	11	2	0
Union	296	1.3	17 948	2 549	186	18	61	62	59	26	24	4	1
Warren	2 140	5.1	24 401	781	1 513	129	370	308	292	114	124	28	4
Washington	222	1.5	20 075	1 972	79	17	38	42	40	17	16	4	1
Wayne	285	-0.2	14 839	3 003	130	16	43	92	89	27	39	18	1
Webster	302	20.3	22 417	1 235	135	64	52	54	52	25	17	5	1
Whitley	599	5.5	16 589	2 813	338	37	95	207	200	55	86	31	2
Wolfe	102	5.1	13 575	3 067	32	9	10	43	41	11	19	10	0
Woodford	722	4.1	31 721	160	348	149	122	58	54	30	16	4	1
LOUISIANA	99 855	2.4	22 839	X	60 583	8 193	17 545	17 418	16 643	5 626	7 800	2 170	175
Acadia	1 019	0.1	17 591	2 628	374	72	180	257	247	76	126	34	3
Allen	410	6.5	16 923	2 749	225	34	50	98	94	31	45	12	1
Ascension	1 776	6.7	23 982	863	1 154	136	198	215	202	72	98	21	3
Assumption	427	-1.5	18 389	2 443	148	28	71	92	88	30	42	12	1
Avoyelles	694	6.8	17 036	2 728	250	64	99	198	191	53	98	31	1
Beauregard	600	3.1	18 583	2 402	263	53	89	116	111	40	50	12	2
Bienville	282	3.1	17 888	2 560	102	20	47	83	80	24	40	11	1
Bossier	2 144	5.7	22 958	1 098	1 281	123	323	317	302	106	139	28	4
Caddo	6 105	2.9	25 278	617	3 970	491	1 337	1 020	977	355	431	125	8
Calcasieu	4 116	2.0	22 792	1 144	2 761	289	722	692	659	257	299	57	8
Caldwell	176	4.6	16 792	2 782	64	17	28	56	54	14	32	6	1
Cameron	180	-1.5	20 099	1 965	140	15	32	28	26	11	11	2	0
Catahoula	184	9.2	16 867	2 762	56	29	25	55	53	16	26	8	1
Claiborne	295	3.2	17 549	2 644	109	30	62	79	76	26	36	11	1
Concordia	353	7.3	17 162	2 707	129	33	58	95	92	30	41	15	2
De Soto	521	4.9	20 709	1 773	199	56	75	108	104	37	44	17	1
East Baton Rouge	10 463	2.7	26 604	452	8 115	578	2 069	1 321	1 251	444	553	148	12
East Carroll	147	11.2	16 812	2 777	54	20	21	54	52	10	29	12	0
East Feliciana	416	5.5	19 696	2 086	137	49	54	91	88	22	51	9	1
Evangeline	564	1.7	16 440	2 836	194	46	88	188	182	48	95	32	1
Franklin	357	7.1	16 213	2 872	130	36	49	117	113	28	63	17	1
Grant	327	5.2	17 047	2 727	83	21	43	79	76	24	37	10	1
Iberia	1 503	-0.6	20 470	1 844	914	90	286	268	255	94	114	34	4
Iberville	649	3.6	20 695	1 777	636	38	104	134	128	40	64	19	1
Jackson	301	3.0	19 497	2 141	124	24	61	82	79	27	39	9	1
Jefferson	12 135	1.8	27 100	409	6 987	1 086	2 248	1 657	1 577	632	700	154	17
Jefferson Davis	512	0.8	16 280	2 863	174	42	97	128	122	45	56	14	2
Lafayette	4 849	-0.4	25 876	533	3 693	417	905	579	546	199	242	55	7
Lafourche	1 884	0.5	21 063	1 648	917	113	346	318	302	121	135	32	3
La Salle	231	1.3	16 858	2 764	96	21	37	68	65	23	32	7	1
Lincoln	847	3.8	20 593	1 814	529	55	156	166	159	42	70	17	1
Livingston	1 916	7.5	21 016	1 663	387	129	179	260	244	95	112	22	4
Madison	196	5.4	15 073	2 981	89	10	25	62	59	15	29	13	0
Morehouse	556	5.3	17 796	2 575	248	36	84	169	163	48	81	27	2
Natchitoches	689	6.7	18 524	2 410	352	82	111	152	145	42	65	26	1
Orleans	12 238	1.5	26 551	457	9 943	1 819	2 364	2 310	2 228	606	1 063	423	17
Ouachita	3 246	4.7	22 128	1 319	2 081	277	599	559	533	182	235	72	7
Plaquemines	566	-0.2	21 686	1 459	722	44	91	117	112	31	67	11	1

1. Based on the resident population estimated as of July 1 of the year shown.   2. Includes other labor income.

STATE County	Earnings, 1999								Social Security beneficiaries, December 2000			Housing units, 1990	
		Percent by selected industries											
		Goods-related[1]		Service-related and other[2]							Supplemental Security Income recipients, December 2000		
	Total (mil dol)	Farm	Total	Manufacturing	Total	Retail trade	Finance, insurance, and real estate	Services	Government	Number	Rate[3]		Total	Percent change, 1980–1990
	75	76	77	78	79	80	81	82	83	84	85	86	87	88
KENTUCKY—Cont'd														
Owsley	23	0.5	D	D	D	10.1	D	23.0	46.9	1 211	249	1 045	2 137	4.8
Pendleton	88	-2.2	D	15.3	D	7.0	4.3	13.7	21.9	2 281	159	418	4 782	14.1
Perry	407	0.0	D	5.0	D	11.8	3.1	27.9	18.7	7 123	242	3 146	11 565	2.6
Pike	881	0.0	33.9	2.7	51.8	11.6	3.4	23.7	14.3	16 955	247	5 165	28 760	2.0
Powell	87	1.1	D	27.0	D	10.4	2.8	12.9	27.3	2 651	200	970	4 458	16.6
Pulaski	699	0.2	26.9	20.0	55.9	13.3	4.0	23.3	16.9	13 478	240	4 037	22 328	14.3
Robertson	9	-11.8	D	D	D	9.5	1.5	D	48.3	436	192	110	955	5.6
Rockcastle	94	-2.6	D	17.7	D	10.0	3.5	30.3	24.5	3 182	192	1 224	5 958	18.3
Rowan	252	0.2	D	11.9	D	11.4	2.5	26.8	36.5	3 616	164	1 132	7 375	10.9
Russell	154	0.8	32.1	24.5	45.8	14.6	3.1	16.2	21.3	4 166	255	1 452	7 375	16.2
Scott	1 104	4.7	D	64.5	D	4.0	1.2	9.5	4.9	4 168	126	761	9 173	17.9
Shelby	473	0.9	48.8	43.6	40.1	9.6	3.2	18.2	10.2	4 969	149	627	9 617	11.5
Simpson	264	-1.0	D	53.0	D	12.7	2.2	13.6	10.4	2 932	179	480	6 172	8.0
Spencer	42	-4.1	25.6	4.8	46.3	10.4	5.3	21.4	32.3	1 684	143	228	2 640	21.1
Taylor	234	-0.9	D	21.4	D	13.9	4.1	19.8	20.7	5 425	237	1 428	8 798	7.1
Todd	104	9.0	D	37.5	D	7.1	2.4	10.4	15.1	2 247	188	451	4 415	-3.5
Trigg	103	-2.5	D	38.5	D	9.5	2.7	13.0	24.7	2 962	235	412	5 284	20.7
Trimble	32	-4.7	D	5.5	D	9.0	5.4	15.1	28.6	1 432	176	223	2 510	3.4
Union	203	-2.6	D	14.6	D	8.9	2.2	19.0	11.8	3 018	193	365	6 091	7.4
Warren	1 642	0.0	34.0	25.5	49.8	12.6	5.5	22.4	16.1	14 249	154	2 919	31 065	16.4
Washington	95	3.9	D	29.8	D	8.1	3.7	16.5	15.5	2 311	212	517	4 009	6.7
Wayne	146	3.0	D	35.0	D	11.1	3.0	17.5	21.0	4 338	218	1 994	7 791	8.7
Webster	199	25.1	D	10.7	D	5.0	2.2	7.0	10.7	3 019	214	492	5 914	2.1
Whitley	375	-0.6	19.8	13.6	64.1	12.1	4.7	27.7	16.7	7 265	203	3 223	13 399	8.2
Wolfe	41	1.4	D	21.5	D	12.5	1.4	17.1	33.8	1 860	263	1 279	2 779	8.1
Woodford	497	24.0	D	32.3	D	4.5	2.6	12.0	6.6	3 460	149	338	7 689	20.0
LOUISIANA	68 776	0.8	25.0	13.1	55.1	9.3	5.3	26.9	19.1	711 631	159	165 577	1 716 241	10.8
Acadia	446	3.6	26.2	12.1	50.3	10.8	3.9	21.0	19.8	10 692	182	2 942	21 441	11.3
Allen	259	2.1	D	5.9	D	6.2	D	43.6	31.0	4 204	165	942	8 275	5.5
Ascension	1 290	0.3	54.1	33.5	35.8	8.2	3.1	12.7	9.8	9 030	118	1 565	21 165	27.3
Assumption	176	5.3	45.8	38.1	30.0	7.0	3.5	11.5	18.9	3 914	167	1 026	8 644	14.4
Avoyelles	314	4.0	16.3	6.6	55.2	10.4	4.5	31.3	24.5	8 063	194	2 885	15 428	4.8
Beauregard	315	0.8	38.5	29.2	44.1	9.6	7.6	15.0	16.6	5 195	157	968	12 666	10.8
Bienville	122	2.7	38.0	30.1	40.2	7.8	4.0	14.4	19.1	3 337	212	869	7 085	1.9
Bossier	1 404	0.0	15.2	6.2	46.4	10.9	3.1	25.1	38.3	13 622	139	2 038	34 994	21.2
Caddo	4 461	0.1	23.8	15.2	56.3	8.5	4.3	29.4	19.7	43 219	171	9 653	107 615	10.3
Calcasieu	3 050	0.0	38.6	22.9	47.6	8.3	3.1	25.0	13.7	30 421	166	4 780	66 426	9.2
Caldwell	80	1.7	14.9	9.2	57.5	11.9	3.7	26.7	26.0	1 901	180	472	4 533	-2.0
Cameron	156	1.4	28.1	12.5	53.0	3.1	0.5	5.8	17.5	1 359	136	123	5 031	12.1
Catahoula	84	23.4	D	6.2	D	9.3	4.5	12.8	24.0	2 327	213	665	5 138	5.3
Claiborne	139	8.7	24.0	14.3	D	7.9	2.6	13.0	33.3	3 396	202	814	7 513	6.7
Concordia	162	10.4	D	D	D	11.7	4.7	17.6	27.3	3 984	197	1 166	9 043	1.4
De Soto	255	4.1	49.0	24.2	29.3	6.6	2.9	11.2	17.6	4 949	194	1 254	10 919	9.5
East Baton Rouge	8 693	0.0	22.6	9.4	57.3	9.1	7.4	28.6	20.1	53 084	129	10 262	156 760	17.3
East Carroll	75	28.1	9.2	7.3	32.9	4.6	2.1	9.3	29.8	1 533	163	766	3 563	-13.3
East Feliciana	186	1.7	21.6	16.2	28.8	4.0	2.9	14.5	47.9	2 984	140	884	6 476	10.5
Evangeline	240	6.3	22.4	16.9	51.5	10.1	3.8	28.5	19.8	6 967	197	2 916	13 311	8.1
Franklin	166	12.2	D	8.2	D	14.2	5.3	18.5	25.2	4 207	198	1 361	8 719	-1.9
Grant	104	1.4	D	24.2	D	5.5	3.5	11.3	29.3	3 382	181	689	7 494	10.5
Iberia	1 004	1.3	39.9	17.7	45.0	8.6	3.1	19.8	13.7	12 203	167	2 896	25 472	19.7
Iberville	674	1.3	D	43.8	D	4.1	1.4	10.0	15.6	5 159	155	1 450	11 352	3.4
Jackson	148	5.3	47.5	40.6	27.5	4.6	2.8	11.1	19.7	3 267	212	586	7 041	2.3
Jefferson	8 073	0.0	19.5	9.7	69.5	12.0	7.3	33.2	10.9	72 767	160	12 766	185 072	11.4
Jefferson Davis	217	5.1	20.3	11.1	51.7	14.6	4.9	21.1	22.9	5 866	187	1 172	11 963	8.4
Lafayette	4 110	0.1	30.0	7.1	58.6	10.7	4.1	29.6	11.3	25 078	132	4 764	67 431	26.9
Lafourche	1 030	0.7	24.7	14.9	52.7	8.3	2.7	17.3	21.9	15 020	167	2 527	31 332	15.9
La Salle	116	0.7	31.9	17.5	40.9	10.6	3.0	15.0	26.5	2 921	205	513	5 969	-9.7
Lincoln	584	1.6	28.0	17.0	42.2	9.0	6.0	17.1	28.2	5 632	132	1 217	15 286	14.5
Livingston	516	0.3	D	16.4	D	12.8	4.6	16.5	21.8	11 876	129	1 718	26 848	26.7
Madison	99	10.0	11.4	9.2	47.2	10.0	2.5	26.9	31.4	2 167	158	849	4 823	-19.9
Morehouse	283	5.8	D	23.1	D	10.3	3.1	18.5	16.7	6 106	197	1 843	12 314	-4.0
Natchitoches	434	4.3	D	22.0	D	9.7	3.3	15.7	28.0	6 042	155	1 988	15 210	2.1
Orleans	11 762	0.0	14.2	5.2	64.6	7.4	6.8	37.6	21.1	77 074	159	27 322	225 573	-0.4
Ouachita	2 358	0.3	22.0	16.2	62.0	10.5	10.4	26.4	15.6	22 543	153	4 876	56 300	9.4
Plaquemines	767	0.4	45.0	18.8	37.2	4.1	1.4	11.2	17.4	3 816	143	828	9 432	-1.2

1. Covers mining, construction, and manufacturing. finance, insurance, and real estate; and services.   2. Covers private sector earnings in agricultural services, forestry, and fisheries; transportation and public utilities; wholesale trade; retail trade;   3. Per 1,000 resident population estimated as of July 1 of the year shown.

Table B. States and Counties — Housing, Labor Force, and Employment

STATE County	Total	Percent	Median value[1]	With a mortgage	Without a mortgage	Median rent[2]	Rent as percent of income	Sub-standard units[3] (percent)	Total	Percent change, 2000–2001	Total	Rate[4]	Total	Professional, managerial, and technical	Precision production, craft, and repair
	89	90	91	92	93	94	95	96	97	98	99	100	101	102	103
KENTUCKY—Cont'd															
Owsley	1 848	74.7	24 400	27.9	14.9	140	31.5	18.0	1 793	2.3	103	5.7	1 176	24.9	13.3
Pendleton	4 332	75.1	43 700	21.3	13.2	274	24.5	6.9	6 751	-0.6	359	5.3	5 190	15.2	14.5
Perry	10 598	75.0	34 800	20.0	12.5	231	24.8	10.6	11 280	-0.6	685	6.1	9 198	20.4	16.6
Pike	26 148	76.9	41 300	21.6	12.2	301	26.8	4.6	26 525	-1.2	1 218	4.6	22 398	21.1	21.3
Powell	4 057	76.8	37 400	22.2	12.4	260	27.0	10.9	6 516	3.1	556	8.5	4 127	14.6	21.3
Pulaski	18 866	75.7	44 600	19.1	11.9	263	24.6	4.7	27 679	3.0	2 037	7.4	20 185	20.0	13.1
Robertson	820	72.7	33 700	17.8	11.6	161	21.1	12.3	1 016	-1.4	51	5.0	834	15.3	9.8
Rockcastle	5 464	78.2	31 100	22.1	13.4	197	24.9	11.6	6 330	1.1	505	8.0	5 180	14.2	14.7
Rowan	6 755	66.7	44 400	18.7	13.4	250	26.4	6.2	10 245	2.9	653	6.4	8 102	28.2	8.4
Russell	5 896	80.6	38 900	19.0	13.0	228	24.2	5.0	5 975	4.1	528	8.8	6 336	15.3	13.0
Scott	8 501	66.2	68 500	18.3	12.0	338	24.6	4.1	18 217	-1.5	600	3.3	11 881	23.3	12.4
Shelby	9 048	71.1	58 600	19.7	11.9	301	23.7	4.3	18 519	-0.4	789	4.3	12 565	23.6	10.9
Simpson	5 767	70.4	49 300	21.2	12.2	314	23.2	3.5	8 873	0.9	561	6.3	7 056	15.3	13.5
Spencer	2 451	74.4	49 300	20.5	12.1	282	23.9	3.9	5 766	1.0	302	5.2	3 116	17.8	13.6
Taylor	8 216	72.3	41 500	16.5	12.4	273	25.6	4.3	9 596	1.7	606	6.3	9 954	16.1	12.8
Todd	4 104	75.8	34 100	20.3	12.9	247	25.3	6.2	5 280	-0.3	495	9.4	4 702	12.4	11.6
Trigg	4 104	79.4	44 300	18.2	13.3	244	25.4	3.8	6 290	2.5	359	5.7	4 420	19.8	12.3
Trimble	2 246	81.5	43 800	19.9	11.9	268	23.9	6.5	3 265	1.1	259	7.9	2 611	15.7	18.7
Union	5 580	76.5	38 700	17.3	12.5	280	22.0	2.4	5 747	-4.3	401	7.0	6 310	18.1	18.8
Warren	28 819	65.0	57 600	18.6	12.2	337	27.1	2.6	50 566	-0.2	2 316	4.6	37 117	26.6	10.8
Washington	3 709	78.9	40 700	17.2	11.6	216	23.4	9.4	6 134	0.5	379	6.2	4 504	18.1	12.9
Wayne	6 517	76.0	30 200	21.8	12.9	216	28.3	12.7	8 433	0.4	754	8.9	6 184	15.1	13.6
Webster	5 372	78.0	29 000	16.2	13.5	253	22.3	5.2	5 252	-3.0	368	7.0	5 340	15.6	20.2
Whitley	12 153	70.8	36 600	21.2	12.4	270	31.4	9.6	14 791	1.9	910	6.2	11 121	23.0	13.8
Wolfe	2 451	74.4	28 200	30.3	14.6	162	31.4	15.6	3 040	-7.1	285	9.4	1 868	19.5	13.8
Woodford	7 223	71.1	73 800	18.2	12.7	369	23.1	2.9	13 615	-0.9	457	3.4	10 506	27.3	10.3
LOUISIANA	1 499 269	65.9	58 500	20.6	13.3	352	27.9	6.5	2 050 323	1.0	122 390	6.0	1 641 614	28.1	12.5
Acadia	19 285	71.3	40 600	21.8	13.9	246	30.5	8.5	24 065	2.7	1 465	6.1	18 641	19.8	17.5
Allen	7 080	77.7	35 400	22.4	13.5	232	31.7	6.5	9 283	-3.5	624	6.7	6 302	19.3	14.7
Ascension	19 337	78.3	61 000	17.0	12.3	325	25.0	5.7	36 904	1.2	2 412	6.5	23 556	21.7	20.4
Assumption	7 397	82.5	45 200	20.5	13.0	276	31.3	10.3	9 309	1.2	742	8.0	7 905	16.7	19.3
Avoyelles	13 480	74.8	34 900	23.9	14.1	215	29.4	7.4	16 363	-2.3	1 355	8.3	11 863	21.2	14.8
Beauregard	10 362	76.9	45 200	17.2	12.6	324	24.8	5.1	12 535	2.4	926	7.4	10 485	27.9	15.6
Bienville	5 852	78.6	33 600	20.1	15.1	235	25.4	10.0	5 475	-2.0	610	11.1	5 092	18.8	13.4
Bossier	30 718	66.7	61 000	20.5	12.5	378	26.4	5.6	47 025	1.9	2 609	5.5	35 082	28.1	12.0
Caddo	93 248	64.4	55 500	20.7	13.4	348	28.2	5.5	119 914	2.4	7 633	6.4	98 879	29.4	10.6
Calcasieu	60 328	70.4	54 700	17.6	12.8	338	26.3	4.5	90 247	0.5	5 465	6.1	67 327	26.2	17.1
Caldwell	3 575	80.2	34 900	22.8	13.2	238	28.7	5.8	4 403	-0.3	405	9.2	3 328	19.4	13.3
Cameron	3 153	85.1	44 500	19.2	12.8	275	18.7	8.2	3 791	-3.3	222	5.9	3 688	20.6	18.0
Catahoula	3 927	81.5	31 600	22.7	15.3	211	30.5	8.8	4 813	-4.4	532	11.1	3 619	19.3	12.5
Claiborne	6 065	75.4	35 800	22.5	14.2	224	26.9	7.9	5 883	4.3	478	8.1	5 390	22.4	10.6
Concordia	7 341	74.7	36 600	20.0	14.6	262	31.7	8.3	8 161	-0.5	1 047	12.8	6 931	22.0	14.0
De Soto	9 129	76.3	39 400	20.4	14.8	246	30.6	9.5	10 222	-9.4	969	9.5	8 533	19.0	15.4
East Baton Rouge	138 620	60.0	69 200	18.3	12.4	375	26.7	4.7	216 584	1.3	10 868	5.0	172 715	35.7	10.1
East Carroll	3 129	61.5	30 700	31.2	16.9	183	35.1	10.7	3 184	-1.7	591	18.6	2 471	22.0	8.4
East Feliciana	5 589	79.9	46 700	23.5	12.5	272	26.5	10.5	7 329	-1.5	487	6.6	6 234	21.7	12.7
Evangeline	11 795	69.5	32 700	23.6	14.7	224	32.2	9.3	11 407	-6.0	752	6.6	9 717	22.9	15.1
Franklin	7 776	75.6	34 100	22.1	13.8	235	29.0	7.8	10 045	-0.8	992	9.9	7 359	20.8	13.5
Grant	6 261	80.7	39 400	21.4	13.8	285	28.5	6.1	6 872	-0.8	648	9.4	6 117	21.7	14.1
Iberia	22 847	71.0	49 700	19.2	13.3	291	26.4	8.8	33 028	2.0	1 896	5.7	25 256	19.8	17.6
Iberville	9 875	74.8	50 800	19.1	14.8	280	30.8	9.0	12 595	-6.2	1 084	8.6	10 807	20.4	14.9
Jackson	5 817	77.7	37 900	19.5	13.5	228	27.4	6.2	5 950	-0.4	533	9.0	5 280	20.8	16.3
Jefferson	166 398	62.9	71 500	20.8	12.4	419	26.0	4.7	231 142	0.6	9 931	4.3	207 479	30.4	11.1
Jefferson Davis	10 669	74.7	40 700	20.5	14.5	268	27.0	5.7	11 463	-0.6	784	6.8	10 361	21.1	16.8
Lafayette	60 411	61.3	62 700	18.5	13.1	329	24.3	5.4	99 967	3.4	3 895	3.9	72 243	32.6	11.0
Lafourche	28 835	75.7	52 300	19.4	12.3	285	24.7	7.6	43 854	2.5	1 645	3.8	32 168	22.0	19.0
La Salle	5 086	82.1	34 300	21.1	14.2	272	22.6	5.0	5 423	2.7	390	7.2	4 953	21.9	15.6
Lincoln	13 669	62.1	56 200	20.1	12.9	326	33.6	4.4	19 089	-1.5	870	4.6	15 759	32.6	8.0
Livingston	23 814	82.2	56 900	18.8	12.9	353	25.9	6.2	45 636	0.6	2 801	6.1	28 780	22.0	21.5
Madison	4 252	64.3	30 100	24.6	16.7	224	32.0	10.6	5 939	6.1	684	11.5	3 791	18.6	10.6
Morehouse	10 961	73.8	36 100	20.6	14.0	278	31.2	8.1	12 052	-0.3	1 474	12.2	10 348	21.1	13.2
Natchitoches	12 644	67.0	46 600	23.6	15.0	300	35.1	6.7	18 823	2.3	1 270	6.7	12 617	25.4	12.9
Orleans	188 235	43.7	69 600	23.2	14.2	379	31.2	8.5	195 752	0.9	11 570	5.9	186 036	34.1	7.0
Ouachita	50 518	64.8	52 800	21.0	13.2	334	28.0	6.3	73 626	2.5	4 082	5.5	58 100	29.7	11.0
Plaquemines	8 213	75.9	62 200	20.5	13.2	396	23.6	9.0	10 578	0.0	538	5.1	9 219	22.5	16.7

1. Specified owner-occupied units. 2. Specified renter-occupied units. 3. Overcrowded or lacking complete plumbing facilities. 4. Percent of civilian labor force. 5. Persons 16 years and older.

	Private nonfarm establishments, employment and payroll, 1999								Agriculture, 1997			
		Employment						Annual payroll		Farms		Farm operators
STATE County											Percent with—	Whose principal occupation is farming (percent)
	Number of establishments	Total	Health Care and Social Assistance	Manufacturing	Retail trade	Finance and Insurance	Professional Scientific and Technical Services	Total (mil dol)	Average per employee (dollars)	Number	Less than 50 acres	500 acres and over	
	104	105	106	107	108	109	110	111	112	113	114	115	116
KENTUCKY—Cont'd													
Owsley	44	269	155	D	69	D	4	4	15 409	246	38.2	3.7	41.1
Pendleton	205	1 727	186	604	304	88	30	35	20 368	816	24.9	4.3	37.1
Perry	747	9 662	2 030	789	1 904	270	265	243	25 130	29	41.4	20.7	34.5
Pike	1 536	18 949	3 084	738	4 166	846	662	494	26 077	37	10.8	8.1	27.0
Powell	179	2 461	217	1 258	373	55	18	40	16 160	231	35.1	3.9	32.0
Pulaski	1 462	19 301	2 831	4 625	3 729	685	723	410	21 250	1 958	39.1	2.2	42.4
Robertson	28	155	D	D	17	D	D	2	12 342	272	18.8	5.5	48.5
Rockcastle	224	2 703	589	659	374	96	43	48	17 818	771	39.4	3.9	40.2
Rowan	449	6 064	1 616	1 055	1 220	157	71	113	18 562	413	44.3	2.2	32.7
Russell	347	3 922	425	1 226	741	122	57	75	19 215	943	46.7	2.3	38.8
Scott	672	19 351	847	10 318	1 607	229	283	758	39 189	851	35.5	8.2	49.9
Shelby	722	11 230	895	4 576	1 485	292	182	298	26 575	1 399	38.7	4.6	43.0
Simpson	382	7 316	340	3 211	906	144	72	187	25 580	582	35.2	8.2	47.6
Spencer	160	816	148	43	177	52	28	16	19 509	592	36.0	3.9	39.7
Taylor	670	6 892	1 004	1 444	1 717	213	81	142	20 660	971	39.8	2.6	40.3
Todd	202	2 392	149	1 389	271	81	40	47	19 624	679	21.2	15.3	49.9
Trigg	248	2 615	245	1 167	309	74	48	58	22 367	411	28.2	13.4	40.4
Trimble	78	503	121	D	82	59	7	12	23 175	526	35.7	2.3	37.3
Union	305	7 571	2 186	997	1 301	112	49	199	26 277	352	23.3	31.2	59.7
Warren	2 504	41 334	6 382	8 375	7 111	1 525	1 090	1 071	25 907	1 819	41.9	5.5	38.3
Washington	218	2 418	239	719	310	75	40	50	20 772	1 050	26.2	3.4	42.4
Wayne	308	4 360	433	2 057	675	130	D	76	17 526	803	36.6	6.7	44.8
Webster	258	2 957	223	852	427	142	33	74	25 091	455	25.3	14.9	46.4
Whitley	842	13 363	2 514	2 251	2 092	452	225	266	19 932	368	31.5	2.2	25.3
Wolfe	75	623	184	D	143	D	7	10	15 374	382	31.7	6.8	34.0
Woodford	500	7 989	644	3 733	905	199	230	228	28 577	678	36.9	8.8	51.2
LOUISIANA	101 020	1 579 949	231 349	165 079	230 720	68 566	75 438	41 488	26 259	23 823	34.1	17.3	47.4
Acadia	984	12 047	1 529	2 461	2 252	449	245	237	19 692	638	34.5	29.0	57.5
Allen	362	3 317	592	458	674	175	44	60	18 030	343	36.2	17.5	39.1
Ascension	1 489	24 001	1 781	5 609	4 168	735	426	752	31 320	279	53.8	8.6	37.6
Assumption	254	2 441	366	372	616	142	42	48	19 564	102	36.3	44.1	64.7
Avoyelles	724	8 099	1 812	558	1 508	359	152	137	16 885	827	31.9	17.9	48.7
Beauregard	616	6 694	1 087	1 114	1 276	758	182	170	25 440	676	32.8	10.7	38.5
Bienville	257	2 926	416	1 074	387	118	31	63	21 499	221	25.3	7.2	35.7
Bossier	1 951	30 736	3 790	2 563	4 963	942	634	620	20 187	372	35.2	18.8	39.5
Caddo	6 322	107 632	20 616	12 647	14 013	3 695	3 767	2 845	26 430	473	33.8	17.3	36.8
Calcasieu	4 272	70 100	10 422	11 083	10 653	2 005	2 901	1 832	26 129	749	35.6	17.5	34.6
Caldwell	206	1 707	486	D	249	108	40	33	19 217	217	28.6	14.7	45.2
Cameron	178	1 882	218	134	213	D	110	50	26 395	384	23.4	22.9	40.9
Catahoula	196	1 808	198	381	408	83	40	27	14 762	381	22.0	31.0	52.8
Claiborne	277	2 976	432	542	471	107	54	57	19 092	261	23.0	10.3	44.1
Concordia	355	3 473	586	D	702	158	87	63	18 147	292	17.5	50.7	72.6
De Soto	376	4 255	413	1 154	779	182	94	112	26 428	516	26.0	15.7	36.0
East Baton Rouge	11 475	210 595	27 804	11 574	28 792	11 535	15 105	5 869	27 869	441	44.4	7.5	31.5
East Carroll	140	907	129	86	221	52	24	18	20 338	244	15.6	50.8	79.1
East Feliciana	256	3 346	1 701	235	354	131	71	77	23 034	386	29.5	14.2	36.5
Evangeline	564	5 894	2 012	849	1 054	367	116	117	19 805	588	35.9	17.7	46.4
Franklin	415	4 355	961	322	1 008	234	521	68	15 591	732	24.7	21.7	59.3
Grant	191	1 496	179	503	176	D	D	31	20 516	186	32.8	13.4	36.6
Iberia	1 615	26 365	2 776	3 844	3 540	968	986	713	27 048	298	47.0	22.1	51.3
Iberville	542	10 704	887	4 295	1 228	258	164	399	37 277	161	21.1	35.4	55.9
Jackson	268	2 905	532	D	494	136	42	77	26 675	183	43.7	1.6	40.4
Jefferson	12 904	218 050	28 717	17 811	33 449	9 830	10 781	5 814	26 663	62	54.8	0.0	21.0
Jefferson Davis	615	6 426	924	708	1 426	327	161	111	17 207	576	26.2	34.9	55.4
Lafayette	6 652	99 423	14 347	5 896	14 757	3 119	6 810	2 589	26 041	577	62.4	7.3	40.4
Lafourche	1 820	24 558	3 106	3 050	3 968	696	1 752	606	24 675	398	33.7	17.6	42.7
La Salle	318	2 904	649	D	502	157	56	60	20 670	160	41.9	5.0	25.6
Lincoln	907	13 665	2 155	1 868	2 238	744	280	283	20 677	287	27.9	3.8	38.7
Livingston	1 235	11 582	1 037	1 473	2 486	378	332	227	19 574	345	58.3	2.3	38.0
Madison	214	2 339	671	87	522	60	68	37	15 673	279	11.5	53.4	72.4
Morehouse	525	6 032	1 388	1 231	1 052	212	104	147	24 293	402	18.2	40.3	61.2
Natchitoches	795	10 084	1 134	2 706	1 653	335	271	205	20 323	530	23.2	17.5	45.3
Orleans	10 666	209 735	31 147	9 366	20 824	11 889	13 308	6 173	29 431	10	100.0	0.0	50.0
Ouachita	4 093	62 353	9 902	7 692	9 348	5 525	3 482	1 548	24 827	377	37.9	11.9	42.4
Plaquemines	748	12 298	284	2 281	666	175	718	411	33 443	127	64.6	9.4	45.7

Table B. States and Counties — Agriculture, Land, and Water

	Agriculture, 1997 (cont'd)															
	Land in farms					Value of land and buildings		Value of machinery and equipment average per farm ($1,000)	Value of products sold				Percent of farms with sales of —		Percent of land owned by fed. gov. 1997	Water consumption 1995 (mil gal/day)
STATE County			Acres								Percent from —					
	Acreage (1,000)	Percent change, 1992–1997	Average size of farm	Total irrigated (1,000)	Total cropland (1,000)	Average per farm ($1,000)	Average per acre (dollars)		Total (mil dol)	Average per farm (dollars)	Crops	Live-stock and poultry products	$10,000 or more	$100,000 or more		
	117	118	119	120	121	122	123	124	125	126	127	128	129	130	131	132
KENTUCKY—Cont'd																
Owsley	32	-11.8	129	0	9	109	1 133	26	3	11 845	92.5	7.5	32.5	0.4	13.0	0.4
Pendleton	117	-8.1	143	1	67	182	1 338	32	15	18 129	72.8	27.2	36.0	3.2	0.0	1.5
Perry	7	69.6	234	D	3	238	1 016	37	0	15 752	51.4	48.6	37.9	3.4	1.8	6.1
Pike	6	-2.5	158	D	1	143	907	19	0	4 756	31.2	68.8	24.3	0.0	2.9	8.2
Powell	28	-13.7	123	0	12	130	982	24	3	11 071	70.6	29.4	30.7	1.7	12.2	0.4
Pulaski	215	-1.4	110	0	138	166	1 478	27	36	18 362	45.1	54.9	39.7	3.7	11.9	390.3
Robertson	48	-9.7	176	0	26	139	711	27	7	24 550	75.8	24.2	52.6	4.0	0.0	0.2
Rockcastle	94	0.7	121	D	45	130	1 138	23	10	13 512	58.6	41.4	35.7	1.7	7.2	1.5
Rowan	42	-15.1	103	0	21	129	1 179	20	4	10 727	75.6	24.4	27.4	0.7	32.7	3.5
Russell	95	4.2	101	0	64	152	1 606	20	28	29 634	32.9	67.1	43.3	6.2	9.4	3.0
Scott	146	-5.3	171	3	100	392	2 287	38	65	76 948	40.5	59.5	56.3	12.3	0.0	3.4
Shelby	199	-13.6	142	2	140	353	2 538	39	56	40 146	59.2	40.8	55.7	9.3	0.0	4.7
Simpson	115	-2.6	198	0	98	348	1 720	47	32	55 166	77.1	22.9	51.5	13.6	0.0	2.0
Spencer	81	-13.8	137	1	56	260	1 825	33	20	33 779	60.2	39.8	53.5	7.4	8.2	1.2
Taylor	112	-12.9	116	0	73	149	1 384	29	24	25 188	47.7	52.3	46.1	5.1	6.7	6.1
Todd	190	15.1	280	0	144	378	1 409	53	70	102 631	59.5	40.5	58.3	21.5	0.0	1.9
Trigg	117	4.4	285	0	81	369	1 293	74	27	64 563	67.4	32.6	49.1	10.7	8.0	2.2
Trimble	64	-9.7	122	1	34	171	1 358	24	11	20 555	83.5	16.5	50.0	2.7	0.0	0.7
Union	212	7.4	601	2	185	881	1 482	110	59	166 542	81.9	18.1	65.6	33.0	2.5	7.3
Warren	255	0.7	140	0	171	242	1 808	34	65	35 867	37.8	62.2	37.9	5.9	0.0	16.5
Washington	157	-4.6	150	1	107	185	1 242	25	33	31 033	52.1	47.9	53.6	5.2	0.0	2.0
Wayne	131	-3.4	164	0	60	142	860	28	50	62 260	18.5	81.5	39.4	6.2	4.6	2.4
Webster	136	-2.6	300	D	110	324	1 122	61	32	69 416	72.7	27.3	47.5	15.6	0.0	151.6
Whitley	44	-3.3	118	0	24	151	1 209	25	3	8 535	35.5	64.5	18.8	1.1	14.8	2.0
Wolfe	57	-7.0	148	D	14	131	734	21	4	10 146	84.5	15.5	28.5	0.0	11.1	0.6
Woodford	123	-0.9	181	2	79	548	2 649	49	115	170 208	18.6	81.4	63.1	19.5	0.0	16.6
LOUISIANA	7 877	0.5	331	943	5 331	381	1 206	59	2 031	85 265	69.5	30.5	40.2	17.6	4.2	9 847.8
Acadia	273	1.8	428	101	240	461	1 115	71	67	104 377	96.0	4.0	55.2	28.8	0.0	110.0
Allen	116	-2.0	337	20	58	417	1 225	43	11	33 452	84.5	15.5	27.7	10.2	0.0	24.1
Ascension	55	-12.3	198	0	32	418	2 047	49	15	54 757	90.1	9.9	22.6	7.2	0.0	226.8
Assumption	64	-5.8	628	D	53	868	1 362	205	32	314 372	93.4	6.6	66.7	54.9	0.0	29.0
Avoyelles	259	1.3	314	12	211	406	1 387	56	61	73 864	93.2	6.8	48.4	17.3	3.6	17.5
Beauregard	165	20.6	244	3	62	247	1 072	30	11	16 194	37.1	62.9	23.4	3.6	0.0	29.5
Bienville	47	-8.3	212	0	16	202	937	34	6	26 584	9.5	90.5	24.9	5.0	0.0	1.8
Bossier	111	0.4	300	0	56	398	1 436	43	9	23 949	42.9	57.1	32.3	7.0	8.7	12.2
Caddo	173	1.7	365	3	94	358	998	43	27	58 014	69.3	30.7	33.6	11.0	0.0	86.5
Calcasieu	312	-5.0	416	30	140	500	1 301	33	20	27 307	68.6	31.4	28.8	8.3	0.0	312.0
Caldwell	70	6.7	324	6	49	282	967	50	11	52 103	88.3	11.7	33.2	12.9	0.0	3.1
Cameron	245	-5.1	638	17	75	478	727	50	11	28 796	64.3	35.7	24.5	7.3	14.4	27.5
Catahoula	229	-8.9	600	8	171	409	763	85	43	112 731	90.8	9.2	56.4	26.0	0.3	17.3
Claiborne	58	-8.7	224	0	22	211	1 170	41	36	139 713	2.5	97.5	35.6	15.3	4.6	2.8
Concordia	253	11.1	867	12	221	706	862	118	61	208 371	88.2	11.8	71.6	44.5	3.7	31.5
De Soto	157	5.9	304	0	50	275	965	35	19	37 655	7.3	92.7	28.5	7.8	0.0	14.1
East Baton Rouge	66	-16.4	150	0	32	329	1 912	41	8	18 745	37.9	62.1	24.3	4.1	0.0	151.7
East Carroll	210	8.4	862	53	186	797	946	175	62	254 765	98.3	1.7	83.2	55.7	0.2	38.0
East Feliciana	115	-15.9	298	0	40	418	1 548	32	8	19 534	16.2	83.9	30.6	4.1	0.0	3.3
Evangeline	181	2.3	308	57	147	305	1 103	35	44	75 650	85.1	14.9	41.8	18.5	0.0	188.1
Franklin	269	1.8	367	74	220	328	951	62	88	120 255	77.1	22.9	57.9	25.7	0.5	27.4
Grant	49	10.5	261	0	28	318	1 161	35	6	32 456	85.9	14.1	26.3	5.4	35.2	4.4
Iberia	103	-6.7	344	1	90	578	1 698	119	50	167 106	98.1	1.9	47.0	28.2	0.0	30.7
Iberville	96	19.0	599	0	71	968	1 661	172	37	230 951	94.1	5.9	55.9	30.4	3.8	1 217.7
Jackson	16	-6.9	86	0	6	154	1 794	27	25	139 084	1.1	98.9	27.9	15.3	0.0	21.2
Jefferson	5	20.9	78	0	2	142	1 823	19	2	37 945	16.4	83.5	17.7	6.5	2.3	1 139.9
Jefferson Davis	304	4.0	527	100	252	449	1 009	71	52	90 902	93.1	6.9	54.0	30.0	0.0	151.5
Lafayette	88	-0.1	152	11	74	351	2 954	40	24	41 606	88.7	11.3	23.9	6.2	0.0	33.1
Lafourche	135	1.5	339	0	69	481	1 328	68	32	80 922	83.1	16.9	44.0	13.8	0.0	29.6
La Salle	27	0.9	170	D	11	189	1 122	24	1	7 161	40.3	59.6	13.1	0.6	1.7	2.1
Lincoln	41	-29.7	144	0	20	212	1 279	35	35	122 914	4.2	95.8	39.0	14.6	0.0	8.2
Livingston	40	12.4	117	1	19	333	2 695	23	9	24 911	19.2	80.8	17.4	4.3	0.0	16.0
Madison	266	7.9	955	21	237	777	828	160	63	227 439	99.2	0.8	78.5	53.0	9.5	18.6
Morehouse	258	6.7	642	119	224	626	1 050	139	78	195 044	97.1	2.9	67.7	44.0	0.1	72.8
Natchitoches	189	3.2	356	3	109	369	1 033	38	50	94 467	35.1	64.9	42.3	15.8	16.2	24.2
Orleans	0	0.0	4	0	0	85	20 710	11	0	2 058	D	D	0.0	0.0	8.8	635.5
Ouachita	89	19.0	236	11	60	277	1 239	68	26	68 248	64.5	35.5	35.0	13.3	2.1	111.9
Plaquemines	37	-20.1	289	0	5	341	1 219	38	5	36 640	71.9	28.1	41.7	11.0	3.6	115.7

Table B. States and Counties — **Residential Construction, Wholesale and Retail Trade, and Real Estate**

STATE County	Value of Residential Construction Authorized by Building Permits, 2000		Wholesale Trade, 1997				Retail Trade[1], 1997				Real Estate and Rental and Leasing, 1997			
	New Construction ($1,000)	Number of Housing Units	Number of Establishments	Number of Employees	Sales (mil dol)	Annual Payroll (mil dol)	Number of Establishments	Number of Employees	Sales (mil dol)	Annual Payroll (mil dol)	Number of Establishments	Number of Employees	Receipts (mil dol)	Annual Payroll (mil dol)
	133	134	135	136	137	138	139	140	141	142	143	144	145	146
KENTUCKY—Cont'd														
Owsley	NA	NA	NA	NA	NA	NA	16	99	25.9	1.0	2	D	D	D
Pendleton	0	0	10	D	D	D	40	287	35.5	2.9	6	D	D	D
Perry	1 630	20	50	467	233.7	14.4	183	1 917	294.6	25.7	17	78	17.7	1.5
Pike	2 645	38	78	711	318.4	21.3	347	4 618	664.7	61.2	42	140	21.7	3.3
Powell	NA	NA	8	115	23.2	2.2	39	297	38.1	3.0	6	20	0.8	0.2
Pulaski	3 570	34	76	1 068	318.4	21.1	336	3 508	543.3	48.7	57	203	16.3	3.3
Robertson	NA	NA	NA	NA	NA	NA	7	25	2.4	0.2	1	D	D	D
Rockcastle	NA	NA	9	62	11.4	0.9	54	365	44.3	4.3	4	33	1.5	0.2
Rowan	574	16	28	230	61.2	4.2	131	1 319	180.7	15.6	18	52	3.3	0.7
Russell	150	3	10	356	83.2	7.2	88	797	104.9	14.0	9	36	7.4	0.3
Scott	23 846	186	25	816	319.5	26.3	115	1 396	230.7	17.5	17	76	8.2	1.1
Shelby	50 436	422	46	375	140.4	11.2	111	1 338	253.0	19.6	32	108	10.7	1.5
Simpson	12 121	134	18	411	130.6	4.6	77	914	205.7	13.9	12	28	2.2	0.4
Spencer	31 039	317	7	D	D	D	23	147	16.9	2.5	2	D	D	D
Taylor	755	8	33	175	37.1	3.1	152	1 555	252.8	22.5	19	55	4.8	0.9
Todd	0	0	16	227	54.1	2.8	48	274	45.7	3.3	5	D	D	D
Trigg	1 175	12	10	66	18.3	1.8	52	324	51.8	4.1	8	36	3.4	0.5
Trimble	NA	NA	1	D	D	D	14	96	11.1	1.1	3	6	0.3	0.0
Union	4 540	42	21	226	66.8	4.4	77	623	91.4	7.7	5	16	0.6	0.1
Warren	75 112	801	155	2 029	1 367.4	57.4	525	7 144	1 108.8	102.5	100	407	38.9	6.0
Washington	621	5	10	D	D	D	41	301	44.6	3.9	5	11	0.9	0.1
Wayne	0	0	10	113	15.2	1.3	65	663	99.0	13.0	4	16	1.9	0.3
Webster	545	5	3	D	D	D	59	431	73.3	6.5	6	D	D	D
Whitley	1 278	25	28	D	D	D	164	1 609	275.6	23.5	29	99	8.1	1.4
Wolfe	NA	NA	3	15	3.9	0.1	27	161	25.7	1.7	1	D	D	D
Woodford	26 563	161	20	D	D	D	75	724	124.9	9.7	16	47	29.2	0.9
LOUISIANA	1 552 991	14 720	6 390	76 350	46 972.3	2 375.2	17 863	224 412	35 807.9	3 307.9	4 151	28 571	3 342.1	642.2
Acadia	14 320	152	61	598	280.7	12.9	199	2 093	278.0	27.9	34	96	8.1	1.6
Allen	1 234	17	16	113	37.7	2.0	93	672	99.1	7.8	13	37	1.9	0.4
Ascension	73 739	800	94	950	314.1	26.8	304	3 777	578.0	48.9	54	288	52.4	7.4
Assumption	8 706	81	15	114	32.5	2.7	59	599	75.1	7.5	8	D	D	D
Avoyelles	21 422	208	26	236	83.3	3.3	169	1 606	212.0	18.2	22	67	3.4	0.5
Beauregard	220	3	21	130	43.4	2.2	115	1 293	222.4	18.9	22	69	4.1	0.7
Bienville	0	0	10	76	188.8	2.2	65	414	57.3	5.0	10	51	5.6	1.3
Bossier	52 930	438	121	D	D	D	363	4 838	834.1	72.9	73	327	28.5	5.3
Caddo	76 969	505	451	5 864	2 586.1	176.2	1 053	13 945	2 338.2	221.5	247	1 185	120.6	22.9
Calcasieu	70 748	959	244	3 136	1 732.7	90.8	775	10 400	1 606.2	147.1	210	1 164	106.0	20.6
Caldwell	1 233	12	12	D	D	D	34	274	48.4	3.7	5	6	0.6	0.1
Cameron	3 054	42	19	115	416.8	4.7	34	240	29.1	2.4	4	11	1.5	0.2
Catahoula	1 813	24	15	193	111.8	3.0	52	407	62.2	4.9	3	D	D	D
Claiborne	0	0	20	173	121.7	4.2	63	486	63.7	6.3	7	17	1.0	0.2
Concordia	2 914	33	17	224	113.6	4.7	94	853	126.0	10.8	3	25	2.0	0.5
De Soto	0	0	17	D	D	D	83	748	116.3	9.6	48	129	9.6	1.7
East Baton Rouge	110 917	1 493	764	9 966	4 006.6	345.9	1 822	27 428	4 468.8	423.7	502	3 760	330.1	73.5
East Carroll	0	0	9	147	97.5	4.4	36	245	41.3	3.5	5	13	1.3	0.2
East Feliciana	50	1	11	D	D	D	45	373	45.0	4.3	13	38	2.2	0.7
Evangeline	6 871	112	17	122	30.4	2.3	129	1 012	144.5	13.4	21	73	4.0	0.7
Franklin	3 247	34	29	D	D	D	90	1 119	168.1	13.7	11	30	3.3	0.4
Grant	90	1	4	D	D	D	31	168	49.3	3.3	4	D	D	D
Iberia	22 456	181	118	1 447	359.2	44.4	282	3 354	613.9	54.1	82	1 274	218.2	47.5
Iberville	8 419	79	27	251	89.7	5.7	100	1 036	159.1	14.3	21	128	13.0	2.3
Jackson	212	2	8	36	28.0	1.1	53	521	59.8	5.6	10	28	2.1	0.4
Jefferson	102 487	817	1 168	15 313	10 041.1	500.0	2 038	32 403	5 787.0	535.8	533	5 485	627.9	121.6
Jefferson Davis	5 870	73	36	359	270.7	9.7	131	1 406	232.9	18.7	23	181	9.8	4.2
Lafayette	102 940	898	484	6 260	2 620.5	223.5	990	14 462	2 465.4	231.6	347	2 953	394.1	85.7
Lafourche	34 397	285	88	722	328.5	18.8	323	3 869	570.0	50.4	81	.426	56.1	9.4
La Salle	327	3	8	43	8.8	0.8	64	515	68.4	6.0	4	12	0.4	0.1
Lincoln	8 531	120	34	376	105.8	9.1	163	2 233	328.0	28.8	41	150	10.0	1.4
Livingston	98 367	843	55	502	140.1	12.8	213	2 403	368.9	32.4	39	214	14.2	2.2
Madison	2 427	20	14	D	D	D	53	512	83.8	6.5	14	50	1.9	0.8
Morehouse	1 931	45	15	143	45.8	4.0	126	1 263	216.2	16.3	14	27	4.3	0.4
Natchitoches	10 088	123	33	247	91.0	4.6	141	1 612	230.4	19.7	34	82	6.5	0.7
Orleans	93 433	679	484	6 086	2 450.5	210.2	1 871	20 405	2 771.3	315.6	481	3 538	407.4	72.3
Ouachita	48 742	395	248	2 912	1 257.2	82.4	753	9 649	1 483.5	134.0	176	805	79.7	12.7
Plaquemines	11 059	118	87	1 168	837.8	36.4	76	674	85.8	8.4	44	286	45.0	8.4

1. Establishments with payroll.

Table B. States and Counties — Professional, Manufacturing, and Accommodation and Foodservices

STATE County	Professional, Scientific, and Technical Services[1], 1997				Manufacturing, 1997				Accommodation and Foodservices, 1997			
	Number of Establishments	Number of Employees	Receipts (mil dol)	Annual Payroll (mil dol)	Number of Establishments	Number of Employees	Receipts (mil dol)	Annual Payroll (mil dol)	Number of Establishments	Number of Employees	Sales (mil dol)	Annual Payroll (mil dol)
	147	148	149	150	151	152	153	154	155	156	157	158
KENTUCKY—Cont'd												
Owsley	3	D	D	D	NA	NA	NA	NA	2	D	D	D
Pendleton	8	12	0.7	0.2	12	D	D	D	12	D	D	D
Perry	54	211	14.1	5.9	9	614	91.4	16.5	51	1 008	34.6	8.7
Pike	102	627	49.3	19.6	26	587	74.3	10.7	84	1 425	44.9	10.9
Powell	6	10	0.5	0.1	16	1 185	175.3	19.2	15	D	D	D
Pulaski	79	686	29.2	11.1	84	4 564	672.1	107.1	82	1 548	45.4	13.2
Robertson	1	D	D	D	NA	NA	NA	NA	3	12	0.1	0.0
Rockcastle	11	36	1.7	0.4	11	D	D	D	17	270	8.6	2.3
Rowan	18	70	2.9	1.1	13	647	111.6	10.5	43	899	24.0	6.8
Russell	16	40	2.7	0.6	24	2 098	348.9	40.5	29	324	9.8	2.7
Scott	44	182	52.5	4.7	45	D	D	D	51	1 209	43.2	12.2
Shelby	49	129	9.3	3.3	42	4 095	942.2	126.2	43	685	21.4	5.8
Simpson	16	63	3.5	1.0	34	3 390	549.4	107.2	37	697	23.7	6.3
Spencer	7	21	1.2	0.3	NA	NA	NA	NA	7	D	D	D
Taylor	40	62	5.7	1.7	38	4 088	599.8	96.6	45	685	18.8	5.0
Todd	10	34	1.3	0.5	19	1 299	147.3	25.7	10	75	2.0	0.5
Trigg	8	37	2.4	0.9	19	1 083	158.0	26.5	18	224	6.1	1.8
Trimble	3	5	0.6	0.1	NA	NA	NA	NA	7	30	0.6	0.2
Union	13	41	2.1	0.6	18	1 214	167.0	29.3	23	D	D	D
Warren	146	946	58.1	20.2	104	D	D	D	192	4 375	136.0	40.0
Washington	11	25	2.0	0.4	13	1 049	179.6	25.1	13	131	4.1	1.0
Wayne	20	44	2.9	0.7	33	1 877	190.0	33.4	20	D	D	D
Webster	10	28	1.3	0.3	19	798	82.5	16.4	15	138	3.1	0.9
Whitley	39	130	9.2	2.9	33	1 927	201.1	43.5	68	1 128	35.1	9.4
Wolfe	4	7	0.6	0.1	NA	NA	NA	NA	6	D	D	D
Woodford	37	124	9.9	2.9	22	D	D	D	41	529	14.9	4.3
LOUISIANA	9 077	63 642	5 754.6	2 159.0	3 545	165 777	80 424.0	6 054.5	7 151	147 016	5 259.9	1 408.9
Acadia	54	233	18.1	5.7	47	2 247	283.9	38.5	58	D	D	D
Allen	17	35	2.2	0.6	11	658	97.5	16.7	26	288	10.9	2.3
Ascension	80	820	34.7	15.5	86	5 577	7 012.9	300.0	103	1 729	58.8	15.9
Assumption	15	45	2.2	0.7	NA	NA	NA	NA	13	116	3.3	0.9
Avoyelles	46	132	9.6	2.5	20	622	92.8	11.4	37	1 931	131.2	34.6
Beauregard	28	68	4.0	1.1	26	1 413	627.1	63.0	32	449	15.7	3.2
Bienville	11	15	1.5	0.4	14	1 052	226.3	33.0	16	D	D	D
Bossier	95	440	29.0	10.4	76	2 578	376.5	65.4	173	5 610	300.8	69.8
Caddo	557	3 317	277.3	102.7	216	11 997	4 515.6	445.7	408	7 743	236.9	66.0
Calcasieu	348	2 432	183.4	69.2	134	11 274	10 153.5	542.4	294	8 019	306.4	75.4
Caldwell	12	38	3.3	0.6	NA	NA	NA	NA	8	D	D	D
Cameron	11	118	6.7	3.0	NA	NA	NA	NA	11	54	2.0	0.4
Catahoula	11	24	1.3	0.4	NA	NA	NA	NA	11	100	2.7	0.7
Claiborne	16	36	2.6	0.5	10	507	109.5	11.5	18	D	D	D
Concordia	21	59	3.7	0.9	NA	NA	NA	NA	27	D	D	D
De Soto	20	75	3.4	0.9	16	1 166	493.3	43.9	15	D	D	D
East Baton Rouge	1 376	12 183	1 200.8	452.8	354	12 159	9 831.6	570.1	754	16 452	504.7	138.3
East Carroll	11	20	1.9	0.9	NA	NA	NA	NA	6	D	D	D
East Feliciana	15	29	1.9	0.9	NA	NA	NA	NA	17	150	3.4	0.9
Evangeline	34	100	5.4	1.8	18	944	191.0	36.0	34	D	D	D
Franklin	24	494	7.5	4.8	13	506	36.1	6.9	18	D	D	D
Grant	5	D	D	D	NA	NA	NA	NA	3	D	D	D
Iberia	113	562	34.6	13.4	100	4 962	911.0	141.8	83	1 302	33.9	9.0
Iberville	36	158	11.7	4.4	39	4 360	4 176.1	270.0	31	478	13.0	3.5
Jackson	14	45	2.4	0.6	5	D	D	D	18	D	D	D
Jefferson	1 359	9 307	861.4	333.4	444	16 356	2 893.2	508.6	948	18 676	681.2	185.7
Jefferson Davis	35	119	10.4	2.6	21	598	110.2	13.9	44	684	20.4	5.4
Lafayette	786	5 714	535.5	207.1	215	5 419	868.5	150.1	382	9 058	270.1	78.8
Lafourche	139	1 486	123.5	41.5	66	2 464	424.2	72.9	129	1 554	48.6	10.9
La Salle	20	56	2.7	0.9	8	D	D	D	13	150	4.6	1.2
Lincoln	55	222	16.6	4.9	35	1 788	346.0	53.0	66	1 206	34.5	8.4
Livingston	76	255	17.1	5.1	54	1 342	227.4	39.6	84	1 282	37.1	9.5
Madison	15	65	2.2	0.7	NA	NA	NA	NA	15	D	D	D
Morehouse	18	65	4.5	1.9	14	D	D	D	28	D	D	D
Natchitoches	47	280	21.6	6.1	18	1 664	537.9	42.5	65	1 370	40.9	11.2
Orleans	1 420	12 469	1 401.8	551.5	261	10 453	2 305.0	362.2	1 105	32 081	1 371.8	377.5
Ouachita	358	2 042	145.3	50.7	152	8 235	1 983.4	287.6	265	5 360	170.1	42.6
Plaquemines	38	489	28.1	13.1	44	2 231	2 779.2	102.1	51	1 600	55.5	20.4

1. Firms subject to federal tax.

Table B. States and Counties — Health and Other Services and Federal Funds

STATE County	Health Care and Social Assistance[1], 1997				Other Services[1], 1997				Federal funds and grants, fiscal 2001[2] Expenditures (mil dol)			
										Direct payments for individuals[3]		
	Number of Establish-ments	Number of Employees	Receipts (mil dol)	Annual Payroll (mil dol)	Number of Establish-ments	Number of Employees	Receipts (mil dol)	Annual Payroll (mil dol)	Total	Social Security and government retirement	Medicare	Food stamps and Supplemental Security Income
	159	160	161	162	163	164	165	166	167	168	169	170
KENTUCKY—Cont'd												
Owsley	4	31	1.3	0.6	2	D	D	D	47.8	11.4	5.9	8.1
Pendleton	14	D	D	D	18	39	5.0	0.6	54.7	25.1	9.0	3.4
Perry	55	636	43.9	21.3	41	166	9.5	2.2	218.7	89.6	28.3	25.1
Pike	131	1 233	70.2	28.3	83	408	24.0	6.5	480.0	213.3	62.7	40.6
Powell	14	169	5.9	2.4	10	34	1.3	0.4	51.6	20.2	5.5	7.1
Pulaski	129	2 367	158.7	61.0	67	316	17.8	5.1	358.4	148.0	42.4	29.1
Robertson	4	D	D	D	1	D	D	D	10.5	4.2	2.2	0.7
Rockcastle	12	141	6.4	3.2	11	42	2.4	0.5	85.9	30.6	12.3	10.7
Rowan	29	540	28.3	15.3	19	91	4.6	1.0	109.3	37.5	12.7	8.3
Russell	18	233	9.9	3.9	15	56	3.0	0.9	98.9	39.0	15.6	10.0
Scott	42	634	34.9	14.3	45	276	12.2	4.5	96.0	48.2	17.1	5.7
Shelby	39	500	20.8	9.6	46	316	33.4	7.2	104.2	51.3	18.0	4.1
Simpson	27	232	11.2	4.3	28	180	11.5	3.1	73.0	30.0	15.5	3.1
Spencer	10	116	5.8	2.4	8	37	2.1	0.4	34.2	17.9	5.9	1.7
Taylor	59	421	22.6	10.3	41	134	7.7	1.6	129.7	56.2	23.3	11.7
Todd	11	147	5.3	2.1	12	41	2.2	0.7	62.5	22.2	11.6	2.9
Trigg	18	146	5.6	2.3	12	33	3.0	0.6	71.7	37.2	12.5	2.4
Trimble	4	86	2.9	1.3	6	17	0.7	0.3	29.5	15.2	6.1	1.6
Union	19	796	35.6	17.3	13	52	4.3	1.0	273.5	35.9	14.8	3.1
Warren	232	3 877	262.9	105.0	133	1 020	43.6	14.1	510.5	165.4	70.3	21.3
Washington	17	137	6.1	2.1	7	51	2.5	0.9	46.4	20.1	9.7	3.0
Wayne	27	310	13.0	6.6	21	50	3.8	0.8	112.5	37.3	18.5	13.8
Webster	11	191	6.2	2.9	18	71	5.4	1.3	80.1	34.9	12.7	3.2
Whitley	65	770	44.2	20.3	51	225	12.8	3.4	260.3	111.7	43.7	24.3
Wolfe	4	194	6.3	2.7	3	14	1.1	0.2	52.7	15.4	5.2	7.7
Woodford	28	124	9.0	3.0	34	142	7.5	2.0	68.5	41.6	9.8	2.6
LOUISIANA	8 580	129 773	7 967.6	3 341.5	5 998	39 764	2 595.2	767.2	27 816.4	8 229.3	4 585.4	1 344.7
Acadia	74	930	39.7	16.2	65	296	20.8	5.4	346.3	104.1	55.4	21.3
Allen	30	435	29.0	9.1	14	46	3.7	0.6	164.3	43.8	25.8	8.1
Ascension	92	1 542	68.9	30.3	92	571	37.7	12.0	235.9	102.4	57.7	13.6
Assumption	13	307	8.8	4.1	17	117	6.0	1.3	109.0	38.0	26.6	7.6
Avoyelles	55	954	39.7	16.3	44	121	7.7	1.9	262.2	77.3	47.8	18.6
Beauregard	42	349	21.5	9.1	39	117	7.0	1.6	152.1	75.5	28.6	7.1
Bienville	10	191	7.1	2.7	16	197	10.3	3.3	101.6	37.1	23.7	5.3
Bossier	112	1 773	93.6	37.7	154	830	48.5	13.8	743.6	237.4	62.1	56.2
Caddo	549	8 870	622.6	278.6	379	2 579	169.1	49.7	1 336.3	522.4	261.6	40.3
Calcasieu	405	4 756	319.7	131.7	262	1 914	122.2	35.7	803.7	355.8	175.5	38.8
Caldwell	22	532	25.4	10.0	9	26	2.3	0.5	68.9	21.9	17.5	3.3
Cameron	4	23	1.5	0.8	8	30	2.7	0.6	48.3	11.3	6.8	1.1
Catahoula	10	92	4.3	2.3	9	30	1.2	0.2	89.6	22.3	13.8	4.8
Claiborne	13	112	5.9	2.2	10	28	2.2	0.4	93.9	32.5	19.0	6.9
Concordia	32	372	20.2	8.4	20	74	4.0	1.3	143.1	41.2	22.6	7.9
De Soto	15	199	8.6	3.8	22	80	5.1	1.3	135.2	50.3	27.0	10.5
East Baton Rouge	983	14 707	973.8	426.5	724	5 646	355.3	111.1	2 850.3	700.7	350.9	97.8
East Carroll	8	138	2.3	1.3	11	28	1.3	0.4	95.9	13.0	14.2	6.6
East Feliciana	14	300	9.9	4.8	15	136	8.9	3.3	101.6	31.8	24.9	6.5
Evangeline	81	1 528	71.9	27.1	17	48	2.8	0.5	249.6	67.4	41.1	16.3
Franklin	40	767	26.9	11.7	28	114	5.6	1.3	164.9	37.3	31.5	9.8
Grant	13	111	4.4	1.6	7	30	2.2	0.6	121.0	41.7	20.8	5.3
Iberia	149	1 810	115.1	42.6	129	827	65.4	18.9	331.5	128.0	60.0	23.3
Iberville	50	989	54.2	21.8	25	194	11.2	4.5	186.3	55.0	44.2	11.5
Jackson	14	396	11.4	5.7	14	70	3.3	0.8	99.8	36.9	25.7	3.1
Jefferson	1 170	17 797	1 165.4	469.1	865	6 614	431.3	135.6	2 086.5	806.3	485.3	100.4
Jefferson Davis	51	471	20.9	6.9	35	118	5.6	1.6	206.3	61.2	29.6	7.2
Lafayette	616	7 560	589.9	228.8	359	2 443	160.6	49.2	726.7	280.1	131.4	35.3
Lafourche	144	1 330	85.6	41.3	95	1 011	79.9	23.4	384.5	152.4	81.8	21.2
La Salle	19	136	6.2	2.9	13	34	2.3	0.6	76.0	31.7	19.3	2.7
Lincoln	61	1 299	85.0	25.4	41	223	15.6	3.7	182.8	61.6	35.1	9.4
Livingston	71	1 458	41.3	18.7	62	346	19.9	6.0	282.5	132.5	67.9	14.4
Madison	26	458	17.1	8.3	12	30	1.8	0.4	132.1	19.6	18.2	6.6
Morehouse	66	688	33.6	15.2	35	105	6.5	1.5	245.9	63.6	45.0	14.1
Natchitoches	51	516	24.7	10.0	45	180	10.0	2.3	237.5	65.0	34.8	14.9
Orleans	1 022	19 447	1 245.4	530.6	605	4 684	257.7	77.8	5 039.8	957.1	670.7	266.9
Ouachita	355	5 465	339.6	153.9	224	1 332	74.1	22.2	680.3	250.9	150.6	42.6
Plaquemines	23	258	13.7	6.3	46	400	41.8	15.4	218.6	44.1	23.7	6.8

1. Firms subject to federal tax.   2. October 1, 2000 to September 30, 2001.   3. State totals may include programs not allocated by county.

STATE County	Federal funds and grants, fiscal 2001[1] (cont'd)							Local government finances, 1997				
	Expenditures (mil dol) (cont'd)							General revenue				
	Procurement contract awards			Grants[2]						Taxes		
								Total (mil dol)	Intergovernmental (mil dol)		Per capita[3] (dollars)	
	Salaries and wages	Defense	Other	Medicaid and other health-related	Nutrition and family welfare	Education	Other			Total (mil dol)	Total	Property
	171	172	173	174	175	176	177	178	179	180	181	182
KENTUCKY—Cont'd												
Owsley	1.0	0.0	0.3	14.3	2.1	1.0	3.3	7.8	6.6	0.7	133	109
Pendleton	1.6	0.0	0.4	6.2	1.3	0.7	5.9	18.2	12.4	3.1	226	169
Perry	8.8	0.1	8.9	36.7	5.5	4.0	9.8	58.6	35.7	11.4	366	242
Pike	15.4	2.0	4.5	50.3	8.2	5.1	69.2	111.6	66.8	27.8	383	210
Powell	1.8	0.0	0.8	12.0	2.2	1.0	0.3	18.8	14.2	2.6	209	88
Pulaski	10.9	0.3	2.0	51.7	6.3	3.8	59.5	77.7	43.8	21.7	389	216
Robertson	0.2	0.0	0.3	1.9	0.3	0.2	0.2	2.9	2.0	0.5	253	222
Rockcastle	1.9	0.0	0.5	20.5	2.4	1.5	2.9	19.0	14.8	2.5	160	115
Rowan	4.5	0.1	0.7	17.7	2.0	5.6	8.1	27.6	16.7	8.1	367	150
Russell	2.9	0.6	0.5	20.3	2.7	1.5	3.4	28.3	13.6	4.8	296	198
Scott	3.3	0.6	0.8	11.1	1.7	1.3	1.2	88.6	19.6	23.2	786	315
Shelby	5.1	0.0	3.2	12.2	3.3	2.3	0.0	40.4	16.4	16.9	586	392
Simpson	2.0	0.3	0.5	9.2	1.4	0.9	0.7	29.5	12.2	7.5	465	269
Spencer	1.6	0.3	0.4	3.6	0.9	0.5	0.0	11.6	8.2	2.5	273	213
Taylor	4.7	2.9	0.8	15.5	2.1	1.0	4.0	57.3	30.5	7.2	316	205
Todd	1.9	0.0	0.4	11.2	1.3	0.6	0.4	15.6	10.4	2.8	249	145
Trigg	4.2	0.0	0.8	7.2	1.0	0.9	0.1	17.7	7.9	4.1	338	235
Trimble	1.2	0.0	0.3	2.9	0.8	0.5	0.1	29.0	5.6	2.8	381	315
Union	2.7	0.0	187.4	6.1	1.4	1.1	4.7	22.4	13.8	5.4	327	223
Warren	44.4	4.0	10.5	38.9	13.6	9.2	101.4	146.5	55.9	54.7	632	301
Washington	2.2	0.0	0.4	7.8	1.3	0.7	-1.2	12.9	8.1	3.4	316	173
Wayne	2.3	0.0	0.5	33.0	3.2	1.6	0.5	24.5	18.6	3.8	204	143
Webster	2.3	0.0	6.1	7.3	1.5	0.7	0.3	35.3	21.3	7.0	515	409
Whitley	8.0	5.2	1.8	39.2	6.1	4.3	8.6	55.1	35.5	9.4	264	146
Wolfe	1.8	0.0	0.5	17.1	1.9	0.9	0.9	11.7	9.9	1.2	164	81
Woodford	2.6	0.0	1.2	5.9	1.3	0.9	0.7	36.1	12.8	16.6	744	352
LOUISIANA	2 309.9	1 473.7	1 151.6	3 404.6	846.5	582.4	1 339.2	X	X	X	X	X
Acadia	7.0	1.0	11.2	69.6	7.7	4.4	7.6	78.2	45.4	24.6	427	171
Allen	31.2	8.3	3.4	23.2	3.6	1.6	1.3	38.4	19.7	10.3	430	221
Ascension	8.6	1.9	3.1	26.9	6.3	3.5	2.7	169.6	57.8	75.8	1 083	402
Assumption	2.9	0.0	0.5	20.7	3.3	3.4	4.8	37.7	20.4	11.7	514	238
Avoyelles	6.0	2.1	5.4	65.3	6.6	3.3	4.3	60.1	41.7	14.5	354	90
Beauregard	6.5	0.3	1.1	20.4	2.5	1.9	4.2	75.6	23.2	24.8	779	401
Bienville	2.9	0.4	0.6	21.4	2.1	1.2	5.5	29.8	15.2	12.8	808	469
Bossier	265.7	43.9	2.7	33.6	9.0	5.0	13.4	235.4	79.6	75.8	817	245
Caddo	121.8	21.2	33.8	189.6	32.4	20.7	33.5	559.8	219.3	259.7	1 067	524
Calcasieu	36.4	8.5	15.8	84.5	16.1	11.6	15.9	480.0	111.0	238.5	1 334	449
Caldwell	1.6	0.0	0.4	11.7	1.4	1.0	4.3	14.2	9.1	4.3	416	184
Cameron	1.9	12.8	1.0	2.3	0.8	0.6	1.7	33.9	10.8	16.9	1 876	1 840
Catahoula	2.4	0.0	0.5	17.4	3.0	1.0	3.2	17.7	11.1	4.7	421	189
Claiborne	2.4	4.1	0.7	23.3	2.1	1.2	0.4	38.4	12.6	7.2	425	229
Concordia	3.9	3.0	0.5	28.6	4.0	3.4	7.3	28.1	18.1	7.9	383	120
De Soto	3.8	0.7	0.9	30.7	3.8	1.9	0.4	59.3	28.3	17.8	710	366
East Baton Rouge	134.0	202.8	27.8	221.1	287.4	205.8	516.6	794.9	243.5	391.9	994	318
East Carroll	1.3	4.3	0.4	21.0	3.8	1.4	3.5	21.1	9.4	8.2	907	591
East Feliciana	3.3	0.0	0.6	21.5	2.9	1.3	7.8	20.2	12.4	6.1	293	112
Evangeline	3.5	0.0	0.9	74.4	7.6	2.9	2.9	46.0	29.6	12.5	365	150
Franklin	4.0	0.0	0.7	38.4	4.0	2.1	10.6	26.3	17.7	6.9	314	79
Grant	18.1	2.0	5.4	17.5	2.4	1.3	2.8	22.7	17.3	3.7	197	109
Iberia	8.2	7.7	3.8	55.7	7.7	6.7	19.6	154.5	66.6	44.8	621	189
Iberville	6.1	3.0	3.2	37.2	7.4	2.4	13.2	84.5	22.6	51.7	1 662	522
Jackson	4.0	0.0	0.5	14.8	3.5	1.0	9.3	22.1	12.5	8.5	545	216
Jefferson	99.5	92.2	214.8	140.0	31.9	23.3	36.8	1 257.1	226.1	539.0	1 194	300
Jefferson Davis	4.5	0.0	1.9	23.9	4.0	2.6	25.4	60.1	30.0	19.0	600	277
Lafayette	56.4	10.8	24.5	87.1	15.8	12.7	29.0	266.9	99.7	121.6	660	150
Lafourche	10.3	20.8	16.1	38.8	10.9	7.6	4.6	217.2	74.7	51.0	579	220
La Salle	2.2	0.0	0.3	12.3	1.1	0.8	1.4	37.9	14.5	7.7	558	314
Lincoln	6.9	0.4	2.2	28.6	5.4	6.7	6.8	58.3	25.5	22.8	544	209
Livingston	7.8	0.0	1.8	26.7	5.7	3.8	14.3	107.2	66.4	30.0	351	120
Madison	2.3	6.5	0.3	24.9	4.3	1.6	16.2	21.1	13.4	5.4	416	159
Morehouse	4.0	0.9	0.8	49.4	6.4	2.8	6.2	70.8	22.5	19.3	608	250
Natchitoches	10.3	4.0	3.6	56.9	6.5	4.8	7.7	92.9	40.3	24.1	646	301
Orleans	727.3	675.8	535.2	647.7	109.2	69.2	190.2	1 235.2	447.5	510.8	1 089	441
Ouachita	29.0	3.0	7.8	102.8	16.6	11.0	17.5	289.6	116.9	136.3	927	353
Plaquemines	28.5	56.1	41.9	12.7	2.4	1.7	0.5	91.4	27.9	38.3	1 481	793

1. October 1, 2000 to September 30, 2001.   2. State totals may include programs not allocated by county.   3. Based on the resident population estimated as of July 1 of the year shown.

Table B. States and Counties — Local Government Finances, Government Employment, and Elections

	Local government finances, 1997 (cont'd)									Government employment, 1999			Presidential election, 2000[2]		
	Direct general expenditure							Debt outstanding					Percent of vote cast —		
STATE County	Total (mil dol)	Per capita[1] (dollars)	Educa-tion	Health and hospitals	Police protec-tion	Public welfare	High-ways	Total (mil dol)	Per capita[1] (dollars)	Federal civilian	Federal military	State and local	Demo-cratic	Republi-can	All other
	183	184	185	186	187	188	189	190	191	192	193	194	195	196	197
KENTUCKY—Cont'd															
Owsley	7.7	1 438	78.9	0.0	0.7	0.0	8.0	4.1	764	16	18	344	18.6	80.3	1.1
Pendleton	23.1	1 665	73.0	1.9	2.9	0.0	5.0	12.8	925	32	47	645	34.8	63.4	1.9
Perry	67.8	2 179	50.3	0.1	2.5	0.1	3.2	199.9	6 427	164	104	2 474	50.1	48.2	1.6
Pike	114.4	1 576	67.5	4.1	1.7	0.6	5.0	76.2	1 051	303	242	3 313	54.6	44.1	1.3
Powell	18.9	1 499	75.4	0.0	2.1	0.0	3.9	9.9	788	39	45	777	46.0	51.8	2.2
Pulaski	78.2	1 406	58.0	10.4	2.8	0.1	5.5	66.8	1 201	197	194	3 595	25.1	73.6	1.3
Robertson	3.0	1 394	62.7	2.5	3.4	0.0	17.7	1.2	557	0	0	181	34.2	63.1	2.7
Rockcastle	19.7	1 250	83.2	0.2	1.7	0.0	4.5	13.3	845	33	54	721	22.4	76.1	1.6
Rowan	26.5	1 203	59.6	1.2	3.7	0.1	7.9	16.6	752	93	79	2 861	48.5	49.1	2.4
Russell	27.7	1 698	49.7	28.3	1.9	0.0	3.4	23.0	1 407	61	55	1 065	24.2	74.5	1.4
Scott	110.8	3 763	40.8	0.7	3.8	0.9	1.8	641.1	21 773	65	109	1 636	39.7	57.7	2.7
Shelby	39.5	1 369	56.1	0.3	2.5	0.1	3.8	44.2	1 532	90	103	1 463	34.8	63.3	1.8
Simpson	28.2	1 746	50.4	20.6	4.2	0.1	4.1	24.3	1 500	38	56	1 005	44.4	54.4	1.3
Spencer	13.0	1 416	71.7	0.1	1.2	0.0	4.5	4.8	522	28	35	423	32.6	66.0	1.4
Taylor	54.9	2 397	36.1	48.8	1.9	0.0	2.6	77.4	3 377	90	78	1 435	30.8	68.0	1.2
Todd	14.9	1 332	59.8	3.9	3.3	0.0	5.4	13.2	1 180	40	38	511	35.7	63.2	1.0
Trigg	16.8	1 389	51.1	26.4	2.1	0.0	5.0	4.6	383	143	43	641	39.5	58.6	2.0
Trimble	32.5	4 457	19.8	0.0	0.1	0.0	1.7	304.0	41 673	16	27	256	38.3	59.6	2.0
Union	22.3	1 351	62.7	1.2	4.8	0.1	6.3	9.8	593	55	56	706	47.4	51.2	1.3
Warren	144.4	1 669	49.3	6.9	4.5	0.3	4.0	318.7	3 684	717	303	7 092	36.9	61.4	1.7
Washington	12.2	1 139	76.6	1.5	1.8	0.0	2.4	2.7	247	37	37	464	31.8	66.3	1.9
Wayne	22.7	1 214	82.8	0.2	1.8	0.1	1.6	11.8	632	38	65	969	35.7	62.9	1.4
Webster	33.0	2 442	39.9	1.3	2.1	0.1	0.8	38.6	2 855	45	45	672	47.1	51.2	1.7
Whitley	53.2	1 494	73.1	7.2	2.1	0.0	2.9	25.1	707	106	122	2 043	34.8	63.7	1.4
Wolfe	9.8	1 335	82.9	0.0	0.5	0.1	7.7	2.1	283	31	25	438	46.8	52.2	1.0
Woodford	36.5	1 633	54.7	12.3	5.7	0.1	5.5	17.3	772	45	77	1 043	39.4	58.1	2.5
LOUISIANA	X	X	X	X	X	X	X	X	X	34 892	42 395	330 492	44.9	52.6	2.6
Acadia	80.1	1 389	58.2	0.4	6.4	0.0	3.5	31.0	537	112	320	3 309	38.3	59.4	2.3
Allen	34.7	1 452	59.0	13.7	5.5	0.0	6.7	13.9	582	699	134	1 531	47.2	48.7	4.1
Ascension	157.8	2 255	48.3	21.2	6.0	0.4	6.4	130.7	1 868	122	409	3 481	43.4	54.5	2.1
Assumption	32.6	1 425	74.3	0.1	5.6	2.8	2.4	6.2	271	34	128	1 199	51.9	43.6	4.4
Avoyelles	57.5	1 411	57.0	0.6	13.3	0.0	8.5	10.0	246	94	225	3 049	45.7	50.0	4.3
Beauregard	76.8	2 415	43.1	30.1	4.9	0.2	9.0	33.0	1 036	117	178	1 660	32.4	64.4	3.2
Bienville	26.6	1 678	61.5	0.8	6.3	0.2	2.5	9.6	606	58	87	789	48.7	46.7	4.6
Bossier	213.7	2 304	46.0	24.3	5.6	2.3	4.0	108.5	1 169	1 903	5 890	6 106	33.2	64.7	2.1
Caddo	532.5	2 188	46.4	1.5	7.6	0.0	3.5	397.8	1 634	2 654	1 336	19 053	49.7	48.9	1.4
Calcasieu	455.7	2 548	39.3	7.7	8.3	0.4	7.4	617.0	3 450	644	1 007	12 597	46.1	51.7	2.2
Caldwell	13.0	1 260	74.5	0.5	1.3	0.0	6.3	3.3	316	38	58	834	31.4	65.1	3.6
Cameron	29.9	3 320	42.0	9.5	9.8	0.0	14.6	1.6	174	32	50	915	34.3	62.0	3.7
Catahoula	19.8	1 787	56.0	0.6	3.0	0.0	7.6	4.8	435	62	60	721	36.1	61.1	2.8
Claiborne	40.4	2 391	34.0	33.7	3.0	2.0	5.3	11.6	684	54	93	1 603	43.3	53.9	2.8
Concordia	30.9	1 490	69.9	0.9	4.0	0.5	10.0	6.8	327	81	114	1 584	42.0	54.4	3.5
De Soto	60.3	2 405	49.3	0.2	3.7	1.3	5.7	166.9	6 653	58	139	1 518	47.5	49.6	2.8
East Baton Rouge	812.7	2 061	37.3	1.2	8.1	0.2	6.2	852.7	2 163	2 312	2 261	49 934	45.3	52.7	1.9
East Carroll	19.4	2 157	50.3	10.7	9.2	3.3	4.3	0.6	64	24	48	910	57.8	39.4	2.7
East Feliciana	19.2	924	71.4	0.3	5.0	0.4	5.4	14.8	711	41	119	3 095	47.8	50.0	2.2
Evangeline	45.6	1 336	68.0	0.9	4.7	0.0	6.6	14.5	426	66	190	2 263	42.3	53.6	4.1
Franklin	25.4	1 149	79.4	0.2	1.4	0.0	10.1	3.7	169	62	121	1 413	33.4	64.2	2.4
Grant	20.7	1 114	82.0	0.3	1.9	0.0	4.8	4.3	232	96	114	1 041	29.8	67.8	2.4
Iberia	148.5	2 060	50.0	22.0	4.1	0.4	3.4	73.0	1 013	138	409	4 337	39.2	57.4	3.4
Iberville	72.2	2 319	45.8	0.1	11.4	3.3	6.4	105.5	3 391	188	175	3 295	57.6	38.4	4.0
Jackson	21.2	1 366	68.7	0.8	3.9	0.0	7.9	3.7	239	35	85	962	36.3	61.2	2.4
Jefferson	1 101.0	2 440	27.3	31.9	7.3	1.2	4.2	1 295.7	2 871	1 661	2 574	23 119	39.3	58.6	2.1
Jefferson Davis	61.7	1 949	48.6	5.3	4.7	3.9	7.7	19.0	599	76	174	1 638	41.1	55.4	3.5
Lafayette	250.2	1 359	60.6	0.3	4.7	0.0	4.7	527.0	2 863	1 013	1 050	11 388	34.7	61.9	3.3
Lafourche	195.0	2 215	42.3	36.1	3.8	0.2	2.4	82.4	936	153	516	7 207	42.5	53.9	3.6
La Salle	33.6	2 440	37.9	41.2	3.4	0.0	3.7	9.5	693	33	76	1 173	22.9	74.7	2.4
Lincoln	57.8	1 378	57.2	1.2	6.4	0.0	7.4	30.7	731	119	239	5 837	41.4	55.9	2.7
Livingston	108.5	1 269	78.0	0.2	2.5	0.3	3.7	40.5	474	125	504	3 903	29.9	67.5	2.6
Madison	19.9	1 529	69.1	1.4	2.8	0.0	5.8	3.8	291	50	72	1 044	52.5	44.8	2.7
Morehouse	68.8	2 167	37.9	30.0	7.4	0.0	2.3	78.9	2 488	74	173	1 629	42.9	53.9	3.1
Natchitoches	91.2	2 445	44.6	24.0	7.1	0.7	2.3	64.9	1 740	197	224	4 071	46.6	49.4	4.0
Orleans	1 121.7	2 391	36.0	2.4	6.2	0.3	1.7	1 648.7	3 515	12 810	6 107	44 260	75.9	21.7	2.3
Ouachita	299.4	2 036	48.8	0.7	7.9	0.3	7.7	168.6	1 147	494	815	12 005	36.9	60.3	2.8
Plaquemines	97.4	3 767	34.0	5.2	9.7	0.0	2.5	115.7	4 475	599	846	2 422	40.5	57.7	1.9

1. Based on the resident population estimated as of July 1 of the year shown.   2. Data subject to copyright.

Table B. States and Counties — Land Area and Population

STATE/ County code	MSA/ PMSA/ NECMA code[1]	County Type[2]	STATE County	Land area,[3] (sq km) 2000	Population and population characteristics, 2000 Total persons	Rank	Per square kilometer	White	Black	Am. Indian, Alaska Native	Asian and Pacific Islander	Percent Hispanic[4]	Under 5 years	5 to 17 years	18 to 24 years	25 to 34 years	35 to 44 years	45 to 54 years
				1	2	3	4	5	6	7	8	9	10	11	12	13	14	15
			LOUISIANA—Cont'd															
22 077	...	6	Pointe Coupee	1 444	22 763	1 658	15.8	61.3	38.1	0.4	0.3	1.1	6.9	20.4	8.8	11.5	15.5	13.8
22 079	0220	3	Rapides	3 425	126 337	430	36.9	67.3	30.8	1.2	1.1	1.4	7.1	20.2	9.5	12.6	15.3	13.2
22 081	...	8	Red River	1 008	9 622	2 477	9.5	58.3	41.2	0.5	0.4	1.0	7.5	22.6	9.3	11.1	13.7	12.3
22 083	...	6	Richland	1 446	20 981	1 737	14.5	61.3	38.2	0.4	0.3	1.1	7.4	19.9	9.9	11.8	14.9	12.1
22 085	...	7	Sabine	2 241	23 459	1 617	10.5	74.7	17.1	9.5	0.3	2.7	6.5	19.7	8.3	11.0	13.5	12.8
22 087	5560	0	St. Bernard	1 204	67 229	728	55.8	89.7	7.9	1.0	1.9	5.1	6.3	18.9	9.2	13.1	16.1	13.9
22 089	5560	0	St. Charles	735	48 072	951	65.4	73.2	25.5	0.6	0.7	2.8	7.3	23.0	8.3	12.7	18.7	13.7
22 091	...	8	St. Helena	1 058	10 525	2 395	9.9	47.0	52.7	0.4	0.4	1.0	7.5	21.5	9.1	11.9	14.3	13.9
22 093	5560	1	St. James	637	21 216	1 724	33.3	50.3	49.5	0.3	0.1	0.6	7.0	22.5	9.8	12.2	16.0	12.8
22 095	5560	1	St. John the Baptist	567	43 044	1 036	75.9	53.3	45.1	0.5	0.8	2.9	8.0	23.1	9.7	13.5	16.7	13.3
22 097	3880	2	St. Landry	2 405	87 700	597	36.5	57.0	42.5	0.4	0.3	0.9	7.8	21.7	9.2	11.8	14.6	12.3
22 099	3880	2	St. Martin	1 916	48 583	938	25.4	66.4	32.3	0.5	1.0	0.8	7.7	21.8	9.6	13.4	16.2	12.6
22 101	...	4	St. Mary	1 587	53 500	875	33.7	64.1	32.1	2.0	1.8	2.2	7.4	22.3	8.7	12.6	16.1	12.8
22 103	5560	0	St. Tammany	2 212	191 268	287	86.5	88.2	10.3	0.9	1.1	2.5	7.1	21.4	7.3	12.0	17.8	15.5
22 105	...	4	Tangipahoa	2 047	100 588	521	49.1	70.4	28.6	0.6	0.6	1.5	7.2	20.5	12.7	13.1	14.6	13.0
22 107	...	9	Tensas	1 560	6 618	2 725	4.2	43.7	55.9	0.4	0.3	1.3	6.6	19.9	10.0	10.2	14.8	14.2
22 109	3350	3	Terrebonne	3 250	104 503	506	32.2	75.3	18.1	6.2	1.1	1.6	7.4	21.8	10.1	13.7	16.2	12.7
22 111	...	6	Union	2 273	22 803	1 654	10.0	70.2	28.1	0.4	0.4	2.0	7.0	18.7	9.1	12.3	14.2	13.2
22 113	...	6	Vermilion	3 040	53 807	870	17.7	83.3	14.5	0.5	2.1	1.4	7.1	20.9	9.4	12.4	15.8	12.2
22 115	...	5	Vernon	3 441	52 531	888	15.3	76.5	18.1	2.8	3.0	5.9	9.5	19.7	14.7	17.9	13.6	9.8
22 117	...	6	Washington	1 734	43 926	1 019	25.3	67.8	31.7	0.5	0.3	0.8	7.2	19.6	9.5	12.2	14.5	13.0
22 119	7680	2	Webster	1 542	41 831	1 058	27.1	66.2	33.1	0.8	0.4	0.9	6.5	19.1	8.6	11.5	14.5	13.0
22 121	0760	2	West Baton Rouge	495	21 601	1 714	43.6	63.4	35.8	0.6	0.4	1.4	7.0	21.0	9.9	13.6	17.0	13.2
22 123	...	9	West Carroll	931	12 314	2 278	13.2	80.3	18.9	0.5	0.2	1.5	6.0	19.6	9.7	11.6	14.9	12.4
22 125	...	8	West Feliciana	1 052	15 111	2 083	14.4	49.0	50.6	0.4	0.3	1.0	4.6	15.7	8.7	17.6	22.4	14.6
22 127	...	7	Winn	2 462	16 894	1 961	6.9	67.0	32.4	0.9	0.4	0.9	6.3	18.5	9.6	13.6	15.3	13.3
23 000	...	X	MAINE	79 931	1 274 923	X	16.0	97.9	0.7	1.0	1.0	0.7	5.5	18.1	8.1	12.4	16.7	15.1
23 001	4243	3	Androscoggin	1 218	103 793	512	85.2	98.1	1.0	0.8	0.9	1.0	5.9	18.0	9.1	13.2	16.5	13.9
23 003	...	5	Aroostook	17 279	73 938	676	4.3	97.5	0.5	1.8	0.7	0.6	5.0	17.6	7.9	10.9	15.4	15.3
23 005	6403	3	Cumberland	2 164	265 612	207	122.7	96.7	1.4	0.7	1.8	1.0	5.8	17.5	8.4	13.9	17.5	14.9
23 007	...	6	Franklin	4 397	29 467	1 415	6.7	98.7	0.3	0.9	0.7	0.5	5.1	18.4	11.1	10.7	15.7	14.6
23 009	...	6	Hancock	4 112	51 791	895	12.6	98.7	0.4	1.0	0.7	0.6	4.9	17.4	7.4	11.3	16.2	16.3
23 011	...	4	Kennebec	2 247	117 114	462	52.1	98.4	0.5	0.9	0.8	0.7	5.5	18.4	8.5	11.9	16.7	15.2
23 013	...	7	Knox	947	39 618	1 123	41.8	99.0	0.4	0.7	0.5	0.6	5.3	17.1	6.3	11.7	15.7	16.2
23 015	...	9	Lincoln	1 181	33 616	1 296	28.5	99.1	0.3	0.7	0.5	0.5	4.8	17.9	5.5	10.1	15.5	16.1
23 017	...	6	Oxford	5 382	54 755	860	10.2	99.0	0.3	0.7	0.5	0.5	5.3	18.9	6.5	10.8	17.0	15.2
23 019	0733	3	Penobscot	8 795	144 919	377	16.5	97.5	0.7	1.4	1.0	0.6	5.4	17.5	11.3	12.5	16.5	14.6
23 021	...	6	Piscataquis	10 272	17 235	1 939	1.7	98.8	0.3	1.0	0.5	0.5	4.8	18.6	5.7	10.2	15.8	16.2
23 023	...	6	Sagadahoc	658	35 214	1 241	53.5	97.6	1.3	0.8	1.0	1.1	6.1	19.7	6.6	12.7	17.8	15.3
23 025	...	7	Somerset	10 170	50 888	911	5.0	98.8	0.4	0.9	0.5	0.5	5.7	19.0	7.0	12.3	16.4	15.0
23 027	...	6	Waldo	1 890	36 280	1 206	19.2	99.0	0.4	1.2	0.5	0.6	5.6	18.6	7.5	11.9	15.9	16.6
23 029	...	7	Washington	6 652	33 941	1 282	5.1	94.5	0.4	5.1	0.5	0.8	5.1	17.8	8.0	11.2	15.1	14.9
23 031	...	4	York	2 566	186 742	294	72.8	98.3	0.6	0.6	1.0	0.7	5.9	18.9	6.9	12.4	17.6	15.2
24 000	...	X	MARYLAND	25 314	5 296 486	X	209.2	65.4	28.8	0.7	4.6	4.3	6.7	18.9	8.5	14.1	17.3	14.3
24 001	1900	3	Allegany	1 102	74 930	666	68.0	93.7	5.7	0.4	0.8	0.8	5.0	15.5	11.2	12.4	14.4	13.2
24 003	0720	0	Anne Arundel	1 077	489 656	114	454.6	82.6	14.2	0.8	2.9	2.6	6.8	18.5	8.1	14.8	18.0	14.6
24 005	0720	0	Baltimore	1 550	754 292	63	486.6	75.4	20.8	0.6	3.7	1.8	6.0	17.6	8.5	13.4	16.4	14.4
24 009	8840	1	Calvert	557	74 563	671	133.9	85.1	13.6	0.8	1.3	1.5	6.8	22.8	6.4	12.2	19.5	14.9
24 011	...	6	Caroline	829	29 772	1 404	35.9	82.7	15.4	0.9	0.8	2.7	6.2	20.6	7.7	12.4	16.5	13.6
24 013	0720	1	Carroll	1 163	150 897	356	129.7	96.4	2.5	0.5	1.0	1.0	6.7	21.0	7.0	11.9	18.7	15.0
24 015	9160	2	Cecil	902	85 951	608	95.3	94.5	4.3	0.8	1.0	1.5	6.9	20.7	7.5	13.9	17.2	14.3
24 017	8840	1	Charles	1 194	120 546	451	101.0	70.2	27.1	1.4	2.5	2.3	7.1	21.6	7.6	14.4	18.8	14.0
24 019	...	7	Dorchester	1 444	30 674	1 382	21.2	70.0	28.9	0.5	0.8	1.3	5.4	17.9	6.7	11.3	15.5	14.2
24 021	8840	1	Frederick	1 717	195 277	283	113.7	90.6	7.0	0.6	2.2	2.4	7.2	20.4	7.4	13.8	18.9	14.6
24 023	...	8	Garrett	1 678	29 846	1 401	17.8	99.2	0.5	0.3	0.2	0.4	6.1	19.0	7.8	12.1	15.5	13.6
24 025	0720	0	Harford	1 140	218 590	258	191.7	88.0	9.9	0.6	2.0	1.9	7.2	20.7	6.8	13.1	18.4	15.5
24 027	0720	0	Howard	653	247 842	234	379.5	76.0	15.5	0.7	8.5	3.0	7.4	20.7	6.3	14.7	19.6	15.5
24 029	...	6	Kent	724	19 197	1 833	26.5	80.6	17.8	0.5	0.8	2.8	4.6	16.1	10.9	9.5	14.2	13.6
24 031	8840	0	Montgomery	1 283	873 341	49	680.7	67.3	16.3	0.8	12.5	11.5	6.9	18.5	6.9	14.5	17.8	15.2
24 033	8840	0	Prince George's	1 257	801 515	57	637.6	28.5	64.3	1.0	4.5	7.1	7.2	19.5	10.4	15.7	17.3	13.7
24 035	0720	1	Queen Anne's	964	40 563	1 099	42.1	89.8	9.1	0.5	0.9	1.1	6.4	19.0	5.8	11.6	18.4	14.9
24 037	...	4	St. Mary's	936	86 211	604	92.1	83.0	14.5	0.9	2.5	2.0	7.2	20.7	8.9	14.4	18.1	13.2
24 039	...	7	Somerset	847	24 747	1 566	29.2	57.2	41.7	0.9	0.7	1.3	4.8	13.7	15.7	13.4	16.1	12.9
24 041	...	6	Talbot	697	33 812	1 287	48.5	82.6	15.7	0.4	1.2	1.8	5.2	16.5	5.6	10.3	14.9	14.8

1. MSA = Metropolitan Statistical Area. PMSA = Primary MSA. NECMA = New England County Metropolitan Area. See Appendix A for explanation of these concepts. See Appendix B for list of metropolitan areas identified by type, with component counties. 2. County typology code from the Economic Research Service of USDA. See Appendix A for definition. 3. Dry land or land partially or temporarily covered by water. 4. Hispanic persons may be of any race.

	Population, 2000 (cont'd)				Population — change and components of change, 1990–2001							Households, 2000				
	Age (percent) (cont'd)				Total persons		Percent change		Components of change, 2000–2001						Percent	
STATE County	55 to 64 years	65 to 74 years	75 years and over	Percent female	2001	1990	1990–2000	2000–2001	Births	Deaths	Net migration	Number	Percent change, 1990–2000	Persons per house-hold	Female family house-holder[1]	One person
	16	17	18	19	20	21	22	23	24	25	26	27	28	29	30	31
LOUISIANA—Cont'd																
Pointe Coupee	9.3	7.7	6.2	51.4	22 619	22 540	1.0	-0.6	448	312	-277	8 397	8.5	2.67	15.3	23.4
Rapides	9.2	7.1	6.0	52.2	126 566	131 556	-4.0	0.2	2 493	1 667	-539	47 120	2.6	2.56	16.8	26.0
Red River	9.2	7.3	7.1	52.4	9 578	9 526	1.0	-0.5	167	141	-67	3 414	2.8	2.74	18.6	23.1
Richland	8.9	7.6	7.4	53.0	20 930	20 629	1.7	-0.2	482	330	-200	7 490	5.8	2.65	18.8	24.0
Sabine	11.6	9.2	7.3	51.1	23 460	22 646	3.6	0.0	411	344	-56	9 221	10.3	2.50	12.0	26.0
St. Bernard	8.7	7.9	5.9	51.7	66 486	66 631	0.9	-1.1	1 060	909	-890	25 123	8.5	2.64	14.6	22.9
St. Charles	7.3	5.4	3.6	51.2	48 548	42 437	13.3	1.0	886	400	7	16 422	14.6	2.90	14.7	16.7
St. Helena	9.4	7.0	5.5	52.0	10 360	9 874	6.6	-1.6	143	131	-180	3 873	16.4	2.70	18.4	25.4
St. James	8.6	6.4	4.8	51.8	21 224	20 879	1.6	0.0	416	214	-189	6 992	8.7	3.00	19.3	18.4
St. John the Baptist	7.8	4.5	3.3	51.5	43 798	39 996	7.6	1.8	931	381	216	14 283	12.4	2.98	18.1	17.5
St. Landry	9.1	7.4	6.0	52.2	88 186	80 312	9.2	0.6	1 894	1 158	-214	32 328	17.7	2.67	17.9	25.4
St. Martin	8.6	5.7	4.5	50.9	49 181	44 097	10.2	1.2	970	437	84	17 164	17.3	2.78	15.9	20.7
St. Mary	9.1	6.4	4.6	51.3	52 833	58 086	-7.9	-1.2	1 196	622	-1 256	19 317	-0.7	2.74	16.5	23.2
St. Tammany	8.8	5.7	4.3	51.0	197 683	144 500	32.4	3.4	3 287	1 742	4 800	69 253	37.6	2.73	11.0	19.7
Tangipahoa	8.2	6.0	4.6	51.8	101 930	85 709	17.4	1.3	2 089	1 194	485	36 558	23.2	2.66	16.2	24.0
Tensas	8.8	7.8	7.8	50.5	6 507	7 103	-6.8	-1.7	130	106	-135	2 416	-3.9	2.54	20.2	29.3
Terrebonne	8.4	5.7	4.1	50.9	105 123	96 982	7.8	0.6	2 167	1 035	-477	35 997	13.1	2.86	14.1	19.3
Union	10.6	8.1	6.8	51.4	22 869	20 796	9.7	0.3	430	330	-26	8 857	17.7	2.52	13.7	24.9
Vermilion	8.6	7.1	6.4	51.6	53 661	50 055	7.5	-0.3	1 042	626	-551	19 832	11.7	2.67	13.0	23.1
Vernon	7.0	4.8	3.2	47.8	51 273	61 961	-15.2	-2.4	1 222	426	-2 038	18 260	-4.5	2.69	10.7	22.0
Washington	9.6	7.6	6.7	51.2	44 072	43 185	1.7	0.3	888	668	-52	16 467	6.4	2.56	17.1	26.6
Webster	10.6	8.6	7.7	52.1	41 456	41 989	-0.4	-0.9	733	702	-396	16 501	4.1	2.48	16.3	27.0
West Baton Rouge	8.5	5.7	4.1	50.9	21 726	19 419	11.2	0.6	408	228	-49	7 663	16.0	2.74	18.2	21.5
West Carroll	10.2	7.9	7.6	49.5	12 160	12 093	1.8	-1.3	207	216	-143	4 458	1.5	2.59	12.3	24.8
West Feliciana	7.4	4.3	2.9	34.4	15 140	12 915	17.0	0.2	176	88	-56	3 645	33.0	2.73	15.6	23.1
Winn	9.4	7.1	6.9	47.4	16 636	16 498	2.4	-1.5	306	252	-313	5 930	2.5	2.55	15.3	26.2
MAINE	9.7	7.5	6.8	51.3	1 286 670	1 227 928	3.8	0.9	16 505	15 512	11 021	518 200	11.4	2.39	9.5	27.0
Androscoggin	9.0	7.1	7.3	51.5	104 131	105 259	-1.4	0.3	1 445	1 357	292	42 028	5.0	2.38	10.8	28.3
Aroostook	10.9	9.2	7.8	51.2	73 140	86 936	-15.0	-1.1	899	1 078	-586	30 356	-3.2	2.36	8.1	27.6
Cumberland	8.7	6.6	6.7	51.6	266 988	243 135	9.2	0.5	3 609	2 937	831	107 989	14.3	2.38	9.5	28.4
Franklin	10.2	7.8	6.4	51.7	29 586	29 008	1.6	0.4	357	346	119	11 806	9.5	2.40	9.2	25.8
Hancock	10.5	8.6	7.4	51.1	52 336	46 948	10.3	1.1	599	644	603	21 864	19.2	2.31	8.1	27.9
Kennebec	9.7	7.4	6.8	51.5	117 782	115 904	1.0	0.6	1 422	1 488	773	47 683	8.6	2.38	10.0	27.6
Knox	10.5	8.5	8.7	51.2	40 147	36 310	9.1	1.3	456	547	622	16 608	15.8	2.31	9.0	29.0
Lincoln	12.0	9.6	8.6	51.2	34 316	30 357	10.7	2.1	350	448	789	14 158	18.3	2.35	7.7	26.7
Oxford	10.3	8.6	7.5	51.2	55 378	52 602	4.1	1.1	648	775	754	22 314	11.2	2.42	9.5	25.6
Penobscot	9.2	7.2	5.8	51.2	145 385	146 601	-1.1	0.3	1 837	1 671	360	58 096	7.5	2.38	9.9	26.7
Piscataquis	11.3	9.0	8.4	50.9	17 177	18 653	-7.6	-0.3	178	265	39	7 278	1.2	2.34	8.4	27.8
Sagadahoc	9.6	6.4	5.9	50.9	35 761	33 535	5.0	1.6	531	353	375	14 117	12.2	2.47	9.6	25.2
Somerset	10.3	7.8	6.5	51.0	51 014	49 767	2.3	0.2	678	625	96	20 496	10.7	2.44	10.1	24.6
Waldo	10.2	7.6	6.0	50.9	37 252	33 018	9.9	2.7	488	404	873	14 726	18.6	2.43	9.0	24.9
Washington	10.7	9.1	8.2	51.2	33 573	35 308	-3.9	-1.1	458	545	-273	14 118	5.2	2.34	9.5	28.3
York	9.5	7.3	6.3	51.4	192 704	164 587	13.5	3.2	2 550	2 029	5 354	74 563	20.6	2.47	9.5	24.9
MARYLAND	8.9	6.1	5.2	51.7	5 375 156	4 780 753	10.8	1.5	94 603	54 845	39 542	1 980 859	13.3	2.61	14.1	25.0
Allegany	10.3	9.0	8.9	50.2	74 105	74 946	0.0	-1.1	917	1 229	-484	29 322	-1.1	2.35	10.3	30.1
Anne Arundel	9.3	5.7	4.3	50.2	497 893	427 239	14.6	1.7	8 638	4 316	4 128	178 670	19.8	2.65	11.1	21.3
Baltimore	9.0	7.4	7.3	52.6	762 378	692 134	9.0	1.1	11 759	9 437	6 049	299 877	11.8	2.46	12.8	27.3
Calvert	8.5	4.9	4.0	50.7	78 307	51 372	45.1	5.0	1 223	588	3 041	25 447	49.8	2.91	9.9	16.3
Caroline	9.5	7.1	6.4	51.1	30 049	27 035	10.1	0.9	459	444	271	11 097	11.2	2.64	13.6	21.5
Carroll	8.9	5.7	5.1	50.6	155 654	123 372	22.3	3.2	2 356	1 340	3 689	52 503	24.3	2.81	8.3	17.5
Cecil	9.0	6.0	4.5	50.4	88 850	71 347	20.5	3.4	1 454	877	2 287	31 223	26.3	2.71	11.1	19.9
Charles	8.7	4.5	3.3	51.2	125 371	101 154	19.2	4.0	2 160	886	3 506	41 668	26.5	2.86	14.5	17.2
Dorchester	11.3	9.4	8.3	52.7	30 612	30 236	1.4	-0.2	403	507	53	12 706	4.9	2.36	15.5	28.2
Frederick	8.1	5.2	4.5	50.8	203 789	150 208	30.0	4.4	3 402	1 573	6 566	70 060	33.3	2.72	9.4	20.1
Garrett	10.9	8.0	6.9	50.7	29 942	28 138	6.1	0.3	449	409	67	11 476	13.5	2.55	8.4	23.5
Harford	9.0	5.9	4.2	51.0	224 208	182 132	20.0	2.6	3 905	1 846	3 571	79 667	26.1	2.72	10.2	19.7
Howard	8.4	4.2	3.3	50.9	255 707	187 328	32.3	3.2	4 442	1 580	4 980	90 043	31.8	2.71	9.5	20.8
Kent	11.7	9.9	9.4	52.1	19 532	17 842	7.6	1.7	272	315	373	7 666	14.4	2.33	11.1	27.8
Montgomery	8.9	5.7	5.5	52.1	891 347	762 875	14.5	2.1	16 140	6 824	9 006	324 565	15.0	2.66	10.5	24.4
Prince George's	8.4	4.6	3.1	52.2	816 791	722 705	10.9	1.9	16 315	6 217	5 527	286 610	11.1	2.74	19.6	24.1
Queen Anne's	10.9	7.4	5.5	50.2	41 895	33 953	19.5	3.3	615	442	1 141	15 315	22.6	2.62	9.5	19.6
St. Mary's	8.3	5.0	4.0	49.5	87 721	75 974	13.5	1.8	1 623	715	641	30 642	20.2	2.72	10.6	21.3
Somerset	9.3	7.8	6.3	46.6	24 937	23 440	5.6	0.8	321	343	215	8 361	4.8	2.37	15.1	29.4
Talbot	12.3	10.5	9.9	52.3	34 151	30 549	10.7	1.0	415	545	474	14 307	12.9	2.32	9.8	27.8

1. No spouse present.

STATE County	Births, average 1997-1999 Total	Rate[1]	Deaths, average 1997-1999 Number Total	Infant[2]	Rate Total[1]	Infant[3]	Physicians,[4] 2000 Number	Rate[5]	Hospitals,[4] 1998 Number	Beds Number	Rate[5]	Medicare enrollees 2000	Serious crimes known to police, 2000[6] Total Number	Rate[7]
	32	33	34	35	36	37	38	39	40	41	42	43	44	45
LOUISIANA—Cont'd														
Pointe Coupee	328	13.9	237	NA	10.1	NA	20	88	1	32	136	3 331	528	2 967
Rapides	1 863	14.7	1 309	18	10.3	9.8	285	226	3	746	588	20 054	8 742	7 108
Red River	130	13.6	113	NA	11.8	NA	7	73	1	74	771	1 559	247	2 567
Richland	330	15.7	264	NA	12.5	NA	18	86	2	101	480	3 754	140	836
Sabine	324	13.6	271	NA	11.4	NA	12	51	2	104	437	4 221	420	1 790
St. Bernard	875	13.3	713	NA	10.8	NA	61	91	2	226	342	10 715	NA	NA
St. Charles	753	15.7	318	NA	6.6	NA	16	33	1	104	215	4 993	2 037	4 237
St. Helena	109	11.4	97	NA	10.1	NA	6	57	1	25	261	976	204	1 938
St. James	311	14.7	178	NA	8.4	NA	13	61	1	41	194	2 860	885	4 171
St. John the Baptist	706	16.7	302	NA	7.2	NA	46	107	1	102	241	4 191	1 564	3 633
St. Landry	1 354	16.1	882	15	10.5	11.3	109	124	3	274	327	14 239	3 817	4 543
St. Martin	760	16.0	368	NA	7.8	NA	16	33	1	12	25	5 756	599	1 235
St. Mary	914	16.1	489	NA	8.6	NA	62	116	2	147	257	7 561	3 073	6 025
St. Tammany	2 656	14.1	1 331	17	7.1	6.4	368	192	4	610	323	22 449	6 729	3 518
Tangipahoa	1 588	16.4	948	13	9.8	8.4	116	115	4	385	397	13 790	4 482	5 403
Tensas	95	14.3	81	NA	12.2	NA	3	45	0	0	0	1 173	NA	NA
Terrebonne	1 698	16.3	784	18	7.5	10.8	194	186	2	396	379	13 720	6 190	5 923
Union	316	14.4	268	NA	12.2	NA	8	35	2	60	273	3 766	639	2 802
Vermilion	757	14.6	499	NA	9.6	NA	41	76	2	150	288	8 181	1 263	2 347
Vernon	1 014	19.7	348	NA	6.8	NA	48	91	1	66	128	4 762	1 318	2 630
Washington	635	14.7	537	NA	12.4	NA	51	116	3	235	546	7 824	1 778	4 048
Webster	573	13.4	535	NA	12.5	NA	33	79	3	266	623	8 002	872	2 085
West Baton Rouge	333	16.2	182	NA	8.9	NA	7	32	0	0	0	2 528	1 408	6 518
West Carroll	148	12.1	161	NA	13.2	NA	7	57	1	50	409	2 296	246	1 998
West Feliciana	116	8.6	80	NA	5.9	NA	27	179	1	24	178	1 029	238	1 575
Winn	213	12.1	206	NA	11.7	NA	11	65	1	73	412	2 460	379	2 243
MAINE	13 614	10.9	12 130	74	9.7	5.5	2 816	221	40	4 371	351	216 459	33 400	2 620
Androscoggin	1 170	11.6	1 037	7	10.2	6.3	247	238	2	440	434	17 956	3 662	3 528
Aroostook	765	10.0	833	NA	10.9	NA	130	176	5	459	603	15 536	1 585	2 144
Cumberland	2 921	11.5	2 296	13	9.0	4.5	960	361	6	1 049	414	40 789	7 850	2 955
Franklin	295	10.2	270	NA	9.4	NA	44	149	1	70	242	5 005	928	3 149
Hancock	489	9.8	541	NA	10.9	NA	101	195	3	139	278	9 231	1 202	2 321
Kennebec	1 184	10.3	1 164	8	10.1	6.5	288	246	3	451	391	20 310	2 758	2 355
Knox	490	12.9	418	NA	11.0	NA	95	240	1	157	415	7 536	738	1 863
Lincoln	315	9.9	351	NA	11.0	NA	66	196	2	82	258	6 709	500	1 487
Oxford	576	10.7	590	NA	11.0	NA	65	119	2	99	184	10 162	1 203	2 197
Penobscot	1 536	10.7	1 328	12	9.3	7.8	353	244	4	633	445	23 855	4 230	2 930
Piscataquis	157	8.6	223	NA	12.2	NA	20	116	2	96	525	3 839	478	2 773
Sagadahoc	418	11.7	283	NA	7.9	NA	53	151	1	53	148	4 822	878	2 493
Somerset	579	11.0	483	NA	9.2	NA	63	124	2	100	191	8 827	1 537	3 020
Waldo	390	10.7	299	NA	8.2	NA	47	130	1	49	134	5 898	318	945
Washington	349	9.8	441	NA	12.4	NA	46	136	2	95	268	7 209	808	2 477
York	1 978	11.3	1 572	13	9.0	6.4	238	127	3	399	228	28 666	4 596	2 461
MARYLAND	70 680	13.8	42 314	611	8.2	8.6	16 561	313	48	13 611	265	645 450	255 085	4 816
Allegany	731	10.2	992	NA	13.9	NA	172	230	2	462	648	15 315	2 378	3 174
Anne Arundel	6 402	13.5	3 306	44	6.9	6.9	813	166	3	996	209	54 654	21 305	4 351
Baltimore	8 845	12.2	7 081	72	9.8	8.1	2 713	360	4	1 514	210	115 766	36 477	4 836
Calvert	969	13.5	440	NA	6.1	NA	98	131	1	157	218	7 276	1 652	2 216
Caroline	373	12.7	323	NA	11.0	NA	13	44	0	0	0	4 568	978	3 285
Carroll	1 998	13.3	1 066	12	7.1	6.0	192	127	1	158	106	19 836	3 505	2 323
Cecil	1 116	13.5	678	NA	8.2	NA	93	108	1	166	201	10 153	2 986	3 474
Charles	1 646	13.9	673	12	5.7	7.3	153	127	1	131	111	10 078	4 496	3 730
Dorchester	353	11.9	391	NA	13.2	NA	51	166	1	114	386	5 683	1 205	3 928
Frederick	2 548	13.6	1 189	13	6.4	5.1	277	142	1	248	133	19 580	4 948	2 534
Garrett	339	11.6	290	NA	9.9	NA	28	94	1	76	260	4 554	554	1 856
Harford	2 968	13.8	1 431	19	6.7	6.4	313	143	2	494	230	23 842	5 488	2 511
Howard	3 361	14.2	1 122	17	4.7	5.0	690	278	1	223	94	15 835	7 834	3 161
Kent	195	10.3	218	NA	11.5	NA	38	198	1	64	338	4 566	408	2 125
Montgomery	12 003	14.3	5 110	79	6.1	6.6	4 803	550	5	1 493	178	96 724	27 544	3 154
Prince George's	11 801	15.2	5 040	141	6.5	12.0	1 291	161	5	1 281	165	68 365	50 892	6 349
Queen Anne's	483	12.2	347	NA	8.7	NA	20	49	0	0	0	4 810	1 024	2 524
St. Mary's	1 332	15.3	556	NA	6.4	NA	71	82	1	107	122	8 232	2 175	2 523
Somerset	227	9.3	264	NA	10.9	NA	26	105	1	39	161	3 917	754	3 047
Talbot	337	10.2	382	NA	11.6	NA	138	408	1	191	578	7 212	1 052	3 111

1. Per 1,000 estimated resident population, average 1997-1999.   2. Deaths of infants under 1 year old.   3. Deaths of infants under 1 year old per 1,000 live births.   4. Data subject to copyright.   5. Per 100,000 resident population as of July 1 of the year shown.   6. Data for serious crimes have not been adjusted for underreporting; this may affect comparability between geographic areas and over time.   7. Per 100,000 population estimated by the FBI.

Table B. States and Counties — Crime, Education, Money Income, and Poverty

STATE County	Serious crimes known to police, 2000[1] (cont'd) Rate[2]		Education						Money income 1989				Income and poverty, 1998			
			School enrollment and attainment, 1990				Local government expenditures, fiscal 1999[5]		Per capita[6] (dollars)	Households		Percent with $100,000 or more	Median house-hold income	Percent below poverty level		
			Enrollment[3]		Attainment[4] (percent)					Median						
	Violent	Property	Total	Percent private	High school graduate or more	Bach-elor's degree or more	Total current expendi-tures (mil dol)	Current expendi-tures per student (dollars)		Dollars	Percent change, 1979–1989 (constant 1989 dollars)			All persons	Persons under 18	Persons 5–17 in families
	46	47	48	49	50	51	52	53	54	55	56	57	58	59	60	61
LOUISIANA—Cont'd																
Pointe Coupee	714	2 253	6 133	24.7	58.6	9.7	17.6	4 857	8 709	18 772	-10.6	1.3	29 433	19.2	25.2	25.7
Rapides	708	6 400	34 655	13.5	69.0	14.6	129.9	5 427	10 014	20 811	-7.3	2.1	28 424	20.1	28.9	26.4
Red River	395	2 172	2 410	10.4	57.4	8.7	12.3	5 966	7 213	14 831	-13.1	0.7	23 956	25.0	32.7	34.8
Richland	18	818	5 454	7.2	52.0	10.7	21.1	5 407	7 791	15 298	-4.4	0.6	20 955	27.2	34.4	36.1
Sabine	384	1 407	5 306	3.9	61.9	8.3	23.0	5 049	8 539	16 790	-11.7	1.2	27 889	18.5	25.0	26.2
St. Bernard	NA	NA	16 387	29.9	67.2	7.3	48.3	5 400	10 512	25 482	-19.5	1.2	32 878	13.2	21.2	19.4
St. Charles	803	3 434	11 898	18.2	74.0	14.8	77.3	7 630	11 901	31 777	-10.0	2.0	42 973	12.3	18.4	16.7
St. Helena	390	1 549	2 632	14.1	57.6	7.7	8.6	5 586	7 199	15 475	-4.3	0.4	24 951	27.3	42.6	35.9
St. James	980	3 191	5 860	16.8	61.1	8.1	28.0	6 111	8 959	23 105	-25.1	0.9	32 592	17.6	26.1	24.0
St. John the Baptist	207	3 427	11 725	32.2	71.5	11.4	39.2	5 914	10 454	29 035	-14.1	1.5	36 703	15.5	20.9	21.6
St. Landry	780	3 764	22 588	14.0	55.3	9.7	76.2	4 767	7 671	14 670	-22.5	1.5	24 831	24.4	30.9	30.7
St. Martin	278	956	11 958	9.9	53.7	6.7	46.4	5 339	7 990	19 116	-24.4	1.1	28 399	19.6	25.9	25.8
St. Mary	859	5 166	15 776	11.2	58.1	8.3	63.8	5 635	8 777	20 980	-32.1	1.3	31 097	19.7	25.8	26.2
St. Tammany	310	3 209	40 765	20.1	76.9	23.1	187.3	5 755	13 605	30 656	-7.6	4.8	45 966	10.2	14.4	12.7
Tangipahoa	882	4 521	24 866	10.5	60.7	12.9	88.5	4 726	8 150	16 849	-14.8	1.3	26 226	21.9	28.0	28.0
Tensas	NA	NA	1 942	18.4	58.1	11.7	8.0	6 213	7 896	11 931	-13.5	2.0	20 415	32.4	39.0	43.7
Terrebonne	766	5 157	27 274	12.0	59.6	9.4	109.7	5 320	9 505	21 765	-32.3	1.8	33 944	16.3	21.6	21.1
Union	338	2 465	4 870	4.7	64.3	11.0	16.3	4 358	8 903	18 083	-3.1	1.4	28 362	17.4	24.3	24.3
Vermilion	310	2 037	13 698	11.3	58.3	8.8	49.8	5 285	8 752	18 202	-24.1	1.4	30 031	17.7	24.0	22.9
Vernon	469	2 161	14 381	4.8	76.9	10.3	57.5	5 492	8 414	19 147	0.9	0.8	30 011	18.3	23.3	24.2
Washington	658	3 390	11 179	8.2	61.5	8.6	43.8	5 521	8 292	16 246	-12.6	1.3	24 238	25.6	35.2	34.8
Webster	543	1 542	10 156	6.5	63.9	10.0	39.3	4 939	9 191	18 716	-9.9	1.1	27 806	17.2	26.1	25.6
West Baton Rouge	620	5 898	5 078	21.4	66.0	9.9	19.3	4 898	10 255	24 852	-13.2	1.6	34 389	15.9	24.0	22.5
West Carroll	382	1 616	2 873	1.6	52.0	8.7	12.2	4 715	7 611	14 924	12.0	1.0	21 831	24.4	33.5	32.7
West Feliciana	185	1 390	2 637	11.9	57.2	7.8	17.7	7 450	6 796	19 402	-3.6	1.0	34 470	19.4	21.2	21.1
Winn	320	1 924	3 826	3.3	58.0	9.0	18.1	5 826	8 728	16 967	0.2	1.4	25 841	21.3	27.1	29.4
MAINE	110	2 510	304 868	12.3	78.8	18.8	1 510.0	7 155	12 957	27 854	20.3	2.4	35 560	10.3	14.2	12.3
Androscoggin	172	3 356	25 878	18.0	71.8	12.6	109.9	6 875	12 397	26 979	19.0	2.0	34 895	10.6	14.6	13.0
Aroostook	87	2 057	21 813	3.8	70.9	12.5	91.1	7 138	10 449	22 230	7.3	1.2	29 458	14.1	18.0	15.9
Cumberland	135	2 821	58 915	16.5	85.0	27.6	293.1	7 385	15 816	32 286	25.4	4.5	42 514	7.8	11.7	9.3
Franklin	51	3 098	8 106	5.0	79.7	17.7	37.4	6 994	10 830	24 432	8.0	0.9	31 674	12.1	15.7	14.4
Hancock	91	2 230	10 783	13.9	83.3	21.4	61.5	7 501	12 347	25 247	24.0	1.9	34 944	9.8	13.5	11.8
Kennebec	85	2 270	29 755	16.6	78.9	18.1	140.2	7 278	12 885	28 616	16.2	2.1	36 573	10.3	14.3	11.6
Knox	66	1 797	7 660	9.9	80.8	19.8	36.0	7 579	12 949	25 405	25.1	2.1	34 909	10.6	14.9	12.9
Lincoln	62	1 425	6 759	13.0	81.4	22.2	50.0	8 010	13 479	28 373	31.9	2.7	36 265	9.7	14.2	12.2
Oxford	79	2 119	12 130	8.4	76.9	12.7	75.7	7 093	11 373	24 535	12.4	1.6	31 012	12.0	16.4	14.6
Penobscot	107	2 824	41 743	9.7	79.1	17.7	157.7	6 873	12 231	26 631	12.0	2.3	34 966	11.8	16.1	13.4
Piscataquis	191	2 582	4 843	6.0	75.4	12.3	23.1	7 273	9 919	22 132	7.7	0.7	29 291	12.7	17.0	16.0
Sagadahoc	57	2 437	8 010	10.8	81.1	21.6	49.5	7 121	13 668	31 948	28.3	2.1	41 656	7.6	10.8	9.7
Somerset	90	2 930	12 262	6.7	71.9	10.5	80.3	6 967	10 471	22 829	15.1	1.2	29 195	13.7	16.8	16.4
Waldo	48	898	8 219	9.8	77.4	16.8	37.6	7 173	11 047	23 148	18.9	1.9	30 984	13.5	17.3	16.4
Washington	199	2 277	8 682	5.2	73.2	12.7	40.9	7 906	9 607	19 993	14.2	0.7	25 997	17.0	21.5	19.6
York	110	2 351	39 310	13.9	79.5	19.0	218.5	6 758	14 131	32 432	25.8	2.6	40 886	7.8	10.8	8.9
MARYLAND	787	4 030	1 212 333	19.0	78.4	26.5	6 165.9	7 326	17 730	39 386	15.9	6.9	47 492	8.8	12.6	12.2
Allegany	362	2 812	18 318	9.4	71.0	11.8	77.9	7 096	11 393	21 546	-7.4	1.7	29 945	15.1	21.1	21.4
Anne Arundel	697	3 654	108 751	16.7	81.1	24.6	490.8	6 625	18 509	45 147	18.8	7.6	57 408	5.5	8.7	8.0
Baltimore	822	4 014	164 527	22.6	78.4	25.0	759.6	7 172	18 658	38 837	7.1	6.4	46 577	7.3	11.5	10.1
Calvert	421	1 794	13 544	10.9	79.3	17.6	102.1	6 701	17 521	47 608	28.5	7.1	60 054	6.1	8.6	8.6
Caroline	729	2 556	5 886	7.6	66.8	10.8	37.1	6 523	11 926	27 758	14.6	1.8	34 211	12.0	16.5	17.6
Carroll	287	2 036	31 080	16.1	78.5	19.6	174.6	6 414	16 320	42 378	18.4	4.8	58 172	4.5	6.7	6.1
Cecil	529	2 945	17 521	12.8	72.2	12.1	100.3	6 448	14 314	36 019	17.3	3.2	46 984	8.0	11.4	11.7
Charles	572	3 157	27 744	16.4	81.0	16.2	146.6	6 585	16 555	46 415	14.3	5.6	55 584	6.9	9.6	9.8
Dorchester	593	3 335	6 171	7.2	64.7	10.9	36.2	7 047	12 437	24 922	8.0	2.0	30 247	15.0	21.0	22.9
Frederick	465	2 069	38 746	16.1	80.4	22.0	243.4	6 880	16 571	41 382	19.7	4.8	55 707	5.5	7.6	7.3
Garrett	154	1 702	6 779	5.4	68.4	9.5	36.5	7 175	10 124	22 733	3.8	1.2	30 771	15.2	19.5	21.1
Harford	283	2 227	47 534	15.4	81.6	21.5	237.6	6 106	16 612	41 680	15.2	4.9	54 852	5.9	8.2	7.9
Howard	203	2 958	52 053	18.8	91.1	46.9	315.0	7 526	22 704	54 348	17.4	11.9	72 187	3.9	5.6	5.4
Kent	302	1 823	4 193	28.3	71.4	16.9	21.9	7 570	15 488	30 104	28.5	4.8	37 981	10.4	15.9	15.8
Montgomery	214	2 939	193 806	24.7	90.6	49.9	1 100.8	8 604	25 591	54 089	11.3	16.2	65 091	5.3	7.9	7.2
Prince George's	924	5 425	202 502	17.5	83.2	25.5	909.1	6 979	17 391	43 127	14.9	5.5	50 050	8.7	12.7	11.4
Queen Anne's	279	2 246	7 643	12.4	76.8	19.9	49.7	7 218	17 489	39 190	35.0	5.9	51 651	6.7	8.9	10.0
St. Mary's	339	2 184	19 689	15.3	77.1	16.8	96.7	6 561	14 454	37 158	18.3	3.2	51 263	8.0	10.8	11.7
Somerset	501	2 546	5 775	9.9	61.2	9.6	24.0	7 699	10 232	23 379	16.5	1.2	27 412	19.8	22.8	25.6
Talbot	263	2 848	5 838	17.0	76.5	23.0	30.9	6 735	18 755	31 885	15.0	7.3	42 314	9.1	13.8	14.7

1. Data for serious crimes have not been adjusted for underreporting; this may affect comparability between geographic areas and over time. 2. Per 100,000 population estimated by the FBI. 3. All persons 3 years old and over enrolled in nursery school through college. 4. Persons 25 years old and over. 5. Elementary and secondary education expenditures, local government fiscal years ending between July 1, 1998 and June 30, 1999. 6. Based on population enumerated as of April 1, 1990.

Table B. States and Counties — Personal Income

STATE County	Personal income, 1999 Total (mil dol)	Percent change, 1998–1999	Per capita[1] Dollars	Per capita[1] Rank	Wages and salaries[2] (mil dol)	Proprietor's income (mil dol)	Dividends, interest, and rent (mil dol)	Transfer payments Total (mil dol)	Government payments to individuals Total (mil dol)	Social Security (mil dol)	Medical payments (mil dol)	Income maintenance (mil dol)	Unemployment insurance (mil dol)
	62	63	64	65	66	67	68	69	70	71	72	73	74
LOUISIANA—Cont'd													
Pointe Coupee	455	5.6	19 424	2 167	155	25	79	91	87	27	40	16	1
Rapides	2 918	3.3	23 020	1 086	1 640	256	552	660	637	167	359	69	4
Red River	169	4.1	17 839	2 570	61	19	22	44	42	13	19	7	0
Richland	352	5.6	16 681	2 795	151	24	55	112	108	29	58	17	1
Sabine	397	2.2	16 656	2 799	144	54	71	104	99	38	41	13	1
St. Bernard	1 389	1.5	21 239	1 586	472	73	199	282	271	108	128	20	3
St. Charles	1 187	3.0	24 407	780	921	38	157	139	130	53	55	14	2
St. Helena	179	3.0	18 584	2 401	42	17	17	44	42	15	17	8	0
St. James	434	3.5	20 497	1 835	307	15	69	81	78	28	36	9	2
St. John the Baptist	877	2.7	20 631	1 797	434	39	94	132	124	46	56	16	2
St. Landry	1 481	0.0	17 576	2 635	540	128	243	401	386	116	182	69	2
St. Martin	772	-0.2	16 200	2 875	278	38	109	164	156	55	70	23	4
St. Mary	1 092	-3.6	19 221	2 227	935	54	218	215	205	79	87	29	4
St. Tammany	5 064	4.8	26 245	489	1 560	256	854	573	539	231	235	41	5
Tangipahoa	1 776	2.4	18 072	2 528	833	122	242	450	433	111	234	62	4
Tensas	120	3.0	18 276	2 477	46	15	19	35	34	9	17	7	0
Terrebonne	2 114	-2.8	20 107	1 963	1 443	102	336	370	351	140	155	44	4
Union	430	3.7	19 394	2 184	141	44	59	96	92	33	43	10	1
Vermilion	948	-2.3	18 138	2 511	426	67	196	200	191	73	87	22	3
Vernon	1 012	4.1	19 629	2 103	743	42	126	141	134	40	61	18	2
Washington	800	2.4	18 534	2 407	323	57	118	243	235	70	121	33	1
Webster	836	3.3	19 529	2 134	344	57	135	208	200	73	93	22	2
West Baton Rouge	501	4.4	24 550	745	351	87	58	73	70	24	32	9	1
West Carroll	190	4.5	15 645	2 937	69	13	28	63	61	18	31	9	1
West Feliciana	220	5.3	15 876	2 911	258	11	38	32	30	10	14	5	0
Winn	270	1.0	15 431	2 948	137	17	36	76	73	22	36	10	1
MAINE	30 803	4.9	24 582	X	18 361	2 437	5 843	5 153	4 932	1 966	2 057	497	92
Androscoggin	2 388	3.0	23 570	947	1 403	144	346	459	441	166	199	47	9
Aroostook	1 468	4.0	19 352	2 196	808	132	210	374	361	128	156	42	8
Cumberland	8 074	6.1	31 484	169	5 999	547	1 690	976	931	385	393	88	9
Franklin	600	5.1	20 842	1 719	346	58	111	125	120	47	49	12	5
Hancock	1 279	3.8	25 749	549	640	154	351	201	192	86	75	16	5
Kennebec	2 819	3.8	24 468	763	1 828	193	483	490	470	184	189	50	9
Knox	993	4.7	25 989	518	469	122	285	157	150	69	59	14	2
Lincoln	835	4.2	26 149	497	276	86	262	132	127	63	46	10	2
Oxford	1 069	3.5	19 685	2 089	507	83	186	245	236	96	100	22	6
Penobscot	3 267	4.3	22 617	1 189	2 141	251	493	602	577	214	238	64	10
Piscataquis	329	3.3	18 225	2 488	154	34	58	84	81	30	31	8	2
Sagadahoc	883	4.7	24 335	797	603	53	165	114	108	48	41	9	2
Somerset	934	4.0	17 743	2 590	570	86	122	225	216	74	95	27	7
Waldo	737	6.4	19 933	2 015	265	77	133	143	137	53	56	17	4
Washington	675	3.7	19 098	2 258	327	72	105	190	183	59	84	22	5
York	4 453	6.6	25 078	656	2 023	344	841	636	604	266	247	51	8
MARYLAND	168 168	6.3	32 517	X	98 194	9 491	31 541	16 959	15 962	6 223	6 897	1 484	299
Allegany	1 527	3.0	21 453	1 533	898	79	291	412	398	139	178	28	11
Anne Arundel	15 667	6.0	32 607	137	9 325	677	2 906	1 309	1 219	538	483	77	29
Baltimore	24 784	4.6	34 236	103	14 143	993	5 772	2 800	2 659	1 257	1 079	151	56
Calvert	2 130	9.4	28 888	265	592	94	322	176	162	69	67	12	3
Caroline	577	4.8	19 431	2 165	260	39	100	107	101	45	44	9	0
Carroll	4 404	6.8	28 888	265	1 382	210	753	429	399	189	155	19	15
Cecil	2 134	7.7	25 333	607	801	132	316	249	233	101	96	17	3
Charles	3 350	7.8	27 701	357	1 182	136	495	284	261	94	116	24	5
Dorchester	651	3.6	21 916	1 385	314	55	142	139	133	55	57	13	4
Frederick	6 141	12.3	32 174	150	2 654	266	945	459	422	198	155	25	8
Garrett	569	4.1	19 360	2 193	253	106	103	120	115	44	47	11	4
Harford	6 081	6.4	27 907	339	2 488	251	946	573	531	238	203	36	10
Howard	9 290	7.9	38 212	57	5 261	471	1 516	448	401	192	143	22	6
Kent	538	4.0	28 165	310	201	47	198	92	88	46	33	5	1
Montgomery	38 855	6.8	45 595	18	21 856	2 765	8 747	2 073	1 909	862	768	115	18
Prince George's	23 099	6.1	29 547	226	13 230	805	3 232	1 899	1 748	578	790	166	29
Queen Anne's	1 219	7.6	29 952	214	285	87	230	108	100	50	36	7	1
St. Mary's	2 509	4.1	28 263	298	1 603	114	390	213	196	70	89	19	3
Somerset	421	6.8	17 360	2 674	207	29	71	96	92	35	38	9	2
Talbot	1 186	5.0	35 359	78	573	88	420	143	137	72	50	7	2

1. Based on the resident population estimated as of July 1 of the year shown.   2. Includes other labor income.

Table B. States and Counties — Earnings, Social Security, and Housing

STATE County	Earnings, 1999									Social Security beneficiaries, December 2000			Housing units, 1990	
			Goods-related[1]		Service-related and other[2]							Supplemental Security Income recipients, December 2000		
	Total (mil dol)	Farm	Total	Manufacturing	Total	Retail trade	Finance, insurance, and real estate	Services	Government	Number	Rate[3]		Total	Percent change, 1980–1990
	75	76	77	78	79	80	81	82	83	84	85	86	87	88
LOUISIANA—Cont'd														
Pointe Coupee	181	6.0	20.7	10.5	D	13.4	3.7	13.3	22.0	3 787	166	1 119	9 695	10.8
Rapides	1 897	0.5	18.6	10.9	56.1	10.0	4.6	28.9	24.7	22 863	181	6 121	51 239	6.2
Red River	80	5.8	28.5	13.8	44.2	7.6	4.1	21.4	21.5	1 837	191	527	3 839	-5.1
Richland	175	3.4	22.5	13.8	53.3	9.0	4.2	27.5	20.7	4 001	191	1 254	8 031	1.8
Sabine	198	10.4	33.8	28.5	38.2	10.9	4.1	12.8	17.6	5 052	215	1 013	12 789	5.7
St. Bernard	545	0.1	31.0	20.6	51.9	11.7	3.2	25.9	17.0	12 527	186	1 745	25 147	16.5
St. Charles	959	0.0	54.3	41.4	34.7	3.4	1.4	9.2	11.0	6 317	131	927	16 016	29.1
St. Helena	59	18.5	22.7	14.9	D	4.6	3.1	10.8	30.4	2 454	233	511	3 840	7.2
St. James	322	2.9	57.3	51.8	24.6	4.4	2.4	7.9	15.2	3 486	164	579	6 934	7.5
St. John the Baptist	473	0.4	44.4	30.1	42.2	8.0	2.7	13.0	13.0	5 726	133	1 328	14 255	35.5
St. Landry	668	2.1	23.6	17.5	50.4	11.5	4.8	24.4	23.8	16 780	191	6 231	31 137	5.6
St. Martin	315	3.6	37.9	25.6	37.2	10.5	3.6	15.3	21.4	7 883	162	1 912	17 592	28.4
St. Mary	989	0.8	40.3	15.5	46.2	6.6	2.2	16.5	12.7	9 862	184	2 309	21 884	1.6
St. Tammany	1 816	0.0	15.1	6.1	62.2	15.0	6.8	28.5	22.7	27 666	145	3 470	57 993	40.4
Tangipahoa	955	2.5	13.3	8.6	50.2	16.8	3.6	19.6	34.0	15 024	149	5 317	33 640	15.0
Tensas	61	20.8	D	D	D	4.6	D	16.5	21.9	1 256	190	494	3 334	-14.3
Terrebonne	1 545	0.2	33.5	11.0	53.9	10.8	3.5	23.6	12.3	17 553	168	3 908	35 416	14.9
Union	184	11.8	D	32.1	D	7.5	2.4	14.3	15.9	4 308	189	790	9 304	7.9
Vermilion	492	3.4	35.2	9.3	42.1	9.6	3.6	13.1	19.3	9 963	185	1 704	20 361	13.9
Vernon	785	0.1	6.0	3.2	19.6	4.8	2.0	8.5	74.2	5 794	110	1 093	21 622	19.2
Washington	380	2.7	27.1	20.7	44.0	9.6	3.4	20.3	26.2	9 274	211	2 852	17 617	5.1
Webster	401	0.4	40.6	28.3	43.1	11.2	3.4	19.1	16.0	8 921	213	1 646	18 365	3.1
West Baton Rouge	438	2.1	D	31.7	D	4.5	2.2	11.3	10.1	3 110	144	639	7 298	13.4
West Carroll	82	10.7	19.6	11.2	40.6	7.6	2.7	16.6	29.1	2 567	208	607	4 831	-4.8
West Feliciana	269	0.4	D	D	D	2.5	2.1	5.9	31.8	1 274	84	335	3 392	17.0
Winn	154	-0.2	39.1	35.8	42.7	8.6	2.4	20.8	18.4	3 038	180	663	7 006	-1.1
MAINE	20 798	0.7	23.5	16.5	57.7	11.7	6.8	27.5	18.1	250 724	197	29 727	587 045	17.2
Androscoggin	1 548	0.9	D	17.8	63.6	11.4	5.7	34.0	11.8	20 771	200	3 123	43 815	14.2
Aroostook	940	4.1	D	18.9	D	10.8	3.4	25.0	21.2	17 788	241	2 970	38 421	7.0
Cumberland	6 547	0.1	16.9	11.0	68.6	12.1	13.0	30.6	14.3	45 790	172	4 816	109 890	19.7
Franklin	404	0.2	D	33.7	D	11.8	3.4	20.6	15.1	6 043	205	704	17 280	24.2
Hancock	795	1.2	D	D	D	13.4	3.9	29.2	14.7	10 722	207	736	30 396	21.3
Kennebec	2 021	0.6	D	8.1	D	10.6	3.5	27.0	31.2	24 644	210	3 479	51 648	13.6
Knox	591	0.2	D	10.9	D	12.0	7.8	29.4	14.4	8 544	216	810	19 009	16.4
Lincoln	363	0.8	20.5	10.2	64.5	16.4	4.7	30.4	14.2	7 732	230	489	17 538	17.1
Oxford	590	1.0	36.2	27.3	47.0	11.1	2.7	26.0	15.7	12 111	221	1 264	29 689	24.8
Penobscot	2 392	0.4	21.0	15.2	58.5	11.8	4.0	28.5	20.1	27 597	190	4 137	61 359	14.9
Piscataquis	187	1.1	D	32.4	D	11.3	1.6	17.1	18.8	4 051	235	434	13 194	23.0
Sagadahoc	657	0.2	D	D	D	6.0	1.7	14.8	13.9	5 883	167	397	14 633	21.7
Somerset	656	1.4	D	31.1	D	8.6	1.9	20.1	14.0	9 922	195	1 685	24 927	19.3
Waldo	341	1.2	25.5	14.2	D	12.2	D	22.6	14.3	7 149	197	948	16 181	20.2
Washington	399	5.3	D	17.9	D	10.3	D	19.0	22.2	8 290	244	1 154	19 124	5.4
York	2 367	0.3	27.5	19.6	48.2	13.4	3.0	23.9	24.0	33 682	180	2 537	79 941	19.7
MARYLAND	107 685	0.3	15.1	8.1	61.3	8.9	8.2	32.5	23.3	724 544	137	88 138	1 891 917	20.4
Allegany	977	0.0	23.4	17.3	D	11.9	4.2	26.9	22.8	16 192	216	1 815	32 513	1.9
Anne Arundel	10 001	0.1	15.0	8.6	49.2	9.3	4.3	22.9	35.7	61 995	127	4 497	157 194	21.8
Baltimore	15 136	0.3	D	12.2	D	10.4	8.7	31.6	18.0	132 956	176	10 172	281 553	15.4
Calvert	686	0.0	18.8	4.6	D	11.4	4.0	D	17.8	8 501	114	667	18 974	48.4
Caroline	300	2.5	D	17.9	D	14.5	2.8	D	15.6	5 448	183	676	10 745	21.9
Carroll	1 592	1.1	D	14.2	D	11.7	5.1	22.6	15.8	21 395	142	1 097	43 553	35.6
Cecil	933	2.7	26.7	19.1	48.0	12.2	3.2	18.4	22.6	12 255	143	1 112	27 656	20.4
Charles	1 318	0.1	D	4.0	D	16.5	6.0	19.9	29.6	12 287	102	1 309	34 487	51.8
Dorchester	369	4.4	D	29.6	43.9	7.9	3.2	18.7	16.6	6 529	213	814	14 269	11.9
Frederick	2 920	1.1	22.2	10.7	57.0	10.6	9.7	26.7	19.7	23 884	122	1 334	54 872	38.3
Garrett	359	3.2	26.6	11.5	56.3	13.0	6.1	20.4	13.9	5 636	189	675	14 119	15.4
Harford	2 738	0.9	D	7.0	D	12.2	4.0	20.1	36.4	28 725	131	1 921	66 446	34.4
Howard	5 732	0.3	D	6.1	D	9.2	8.2	37.3	10.3	22 034	89	1 482	72 583	70.8
Kent	248	8.4	21.8	13.1	57.3	10.4	4.4	30.0	12.4	5 220	272	330	8 181	11.4
Montgomery	24 621	0.1	10.9	5.4	67.4	7.2	9.2	42.2	21.6	97 576	112	10 054	295 723	36.8
Prince George's	14 035	0.1	13.8	4.3	53.9	10.9	4.6	25.6	32.2	76 421	95	10 271	270 090	14.2
Queen Anne's	372	1.9	25.6	12.2	54.1	16.6	5.7	18.0	18.4	5 879	145	309	13 944	39.0
St. Mary's	1 717	0.0	5.4	1.2	46.0	6.0	2.1	29.0	48.6	9 312	108	1 060	27 863	30.9
Somerset	236	2.2	8.2	3.5	D	12.1	2.0	D	41.5	4 433	179	622	9 393	20.3
Talbot	661	1.3	D	13.6	D	12.9	6.2	34.8	13.3	7 987	236	522	14 697	30.9

1. Covers mining, construction, and manufacturing. 2. Covers private sector earnings in agricultural services, forestry, and fisheries; transportation and public utilities; wholesale trade; retail trade; finance, insurance, and real estate; and services. 3. Per 1,000 resident population estimated as of July 1 of the year shown.

STATE County	Housing units, 1990 (cont'd) Occupied units								Civilian labor force, 2001				Civilian employment, 1990[5]		
	Owner-occupied			Owner cost as a percent of income		Renter-occupied					Unemployment			Percent	
	Total	Percent	Median value[1]	With a mortgage	Without a mortgage	Median rent[2]	Rent as percent of income	Substandard units[3] (percent)	Total	Percent change, 2000–2001	Total	Rate[4]	Total	Professional, managerial, and technical	Precision production, craft, and repair
	89	90	91	92	93	94	95	96	97	98	99	100	101	102	103
LOUISIANA—Cont'd															
Pointe Coupee	7 736	74.1	48 300	21.6	13.2	237	33.0	8.8	9 369	-3.1	816	8.7	7 650	19.3	16.7
Rapides	45 941	66.5	52 600	19.6	13.4	338	27.6	5.2	59 746	-1.5	3 608	6.0	48 788	29.2	10.5
Red River	3 321	75.6	35 500	21.7	15.1	231	31.6	10.5	3 567	1.8	377	10.6	3 124	19.1	16.5
Richland	7 079	73.7	36 800	21.6	14.7	236	30.9	5.9	8 285	-2.9	873	10.5	7 019	20.2	13.2
Sabine	8 361	80.1	37 800	22.7	13.6	249	31.2	9.5	8 249	-2.6	593	7.2	7 517	20.7	15.0
St. Bernard	23 156	75.8	63 300	19.9	12.3	406	28.7	5.3	31 030	0.8	1 839	5.9	27 859	21.1	16.4
St. Charles	14 333	78.9	68 000	20.4	12.5	400	23.8	5.6	23 073	0.1	1 293	5.6	17 802	28.7	16.2
St. Helena	3 328	84.3	40 000	28.1	15.0	238	35.1	15.1	4 191	3.5	280	6.7	3 162	15.9	16.2
St. James	6 432	82.4	57 100	17.3	12.8	234	31.8	10.4	9 306	1.1	1 072	11.5	7 598	18.4	18.5
St. John the Baptist	12 710	79.7	62 200	20.8	13.4	368	25.8	6.9	19 667	0.6	1 603	8.2	15 928	25.9	15.7
St. Landry	27 477	71.8	40 500	22.6	14.0	234	32.9	9.0	33 143	3.1	2 482	7.5	25 000	24.0	14.6
St. Martin	14 634	79.9	44 400	21.7	13.8	266	28.8	11.5	22 496	5.2	1 804	8.0	16 380	17.3	16.5
St. Mary	19 456	68.6	49 200	20.2	13.3	291	24.2	10.7	23 796	0.6	2 032	8.5	20 980	21.9	14.1
St. Tammany	50 346	75.8	74 900	21.1	12.3	420	24.3	4.0	91 904	1.2	3 915	4.3	61 735	34.8	11.6
Tangipahoa	29 663	72.7	52 200	22.7	14.4	297	32.3	7.4	47 406	3.4	4 030	8.5	29 751	24.0	14.4
Tensas	2 515	71.7	34 100	26.5	15.4	179	35.1	8.4	2 852	-15.6	258	9.0	2 212	19.5	7.7
Terrebonne	31 837	73.2	52 900	20.4	12.9	347	27.1	8.8	50 157	2.6	1 893	3.8	35 356	22.5	16.3
Union	7 528	82.3	39 600	20.8	13.7	258	27.9	6.8	12 243	-2.8	726	5.9	7 459	21.4	16.4
Vermilion	17 762	75.7	43 800	21.6	13.4	263	30.2	8.3	21 915	-0.1	1 398	6.4	17 433	20.7	17.3
Vernon	19 111	50.4	47 800	21.9	13.5	351	24.5	6.0	17 108	0.8	1 058	6.2	14 599	25.3	13.0
Washington	15 475	76.4	37 900	23.1	14.5	243	31.7	6.1	16 672	4.4	1 394	8.4	14 061	19.8	14.3
Webster	15 849	74.1	40 600	21.2	13.8	276	28.6	5.0	19 582	2.7	1 643	8.4	15 078	21.8	15.0
West Baton Rouge	6 606	75.9	58 400	17.3	12.8	319	25.7	6.8	10 324	0.9	592	5.7	8 039	23.0	14.0
West Carroll	4 394	77.7	30 400	23.0	13.2	238	32.5	6.9	5 756	1.8	862	15.0	4 036	18.1	11.9
West Feliciana	2 741	68.2	61 300	20.7	14.2	248	22.6	9.9	3 488	-2.7	221	6.3	3 055	23.4	12.1
Winn	5 787	76.2	34 000	22.8	14.1	237	29.8	6.3	6 275	-0.1	451	7.2	5 562	18.6	14.1
MAINE	465 312	70.5	87 400	21.4	13.4	419	26.8	3.1	683 907	-0.7	27 143	4.0	571 842	27.8	13.4
Androscoggin	40 017	62.2	86 800	21.4	13.9	374	25.9	2.4	60 144	-2.2	2 444	4.1	50 588	23.4	14.5
Aroostook	31 366	69.5	45 900	18.5	14.0	332	27.6	2.8	37 313	-1.5	1 659	4.4	34 343	22.9	12.1
Cumberland	94 512	64.3	118 300	22.7	13.2	522	27.2	1.7	145 578	-0.7	3 379	2.3	123 322	33.9	10.2
Franklin	10 778	75.6	66 200	19.3	13.3	342	26.5	5.5	14 393	0.0	927	6.4	13 314	23.2	14.6
Hancock	18 342	75.7	85 200	20.9	13.6	403	25.9	4.9	29 110	-2.0	1 307	4.5	21 000	27.7	16.0
Kennebec	43 889	70.9	79 300	19.4	12.6	382	25.9	2.6	61 109	0.0	2 463	4.0	56 080	30.3	12.7
Knox	14 344	73.6	92 500	22.6	14.0	399	28.1	3.0	20 537	-1.0	587	2.9	16 200	26.9	14.2
Lincoln	11 968	83.2	103 000	22.1	13.5	438	26.0	4.4	18 134	-0.5	529	2.9	13 697	28.3	19.3
Oxford	20 064	76.1	69 900	19.7	12.6	333	25.9	4.6	26 485	-0.9	1 578	6.0	22 593	21.7	16.1
Penobscot	54 063	69.7	69 100	19.3	13.1	397	26.9	3.2	79 882	0.1	3 305	4.1	67 389	28.1	12.8
Piscataquis	7 194	78.6	46 800	17.6	14.0	324	27.9	5.8	8 223	-0.8	548	6.7	7 644	19.7	14.2
Sagadahoc	12 581	70.8	95 900	23.3	12.9	498	25.8	3.0	16 450	-1.9	520	3.2	15 810	29.1	16.7
Somerset	18 513	77.3	56 400	19.2	13.1	344	26.7	4.6	25 673	-1.8	1 945	7.6	21 652	20.8	14.7
Waldo	12 415	80.8	71 500	21.1	14.2	354	29.2	6.5	24 099	2.7	972	4.0	14 172	25.4	15.1
Washington	13 418	78.8	53 100	20.5	14.6	319	28.6	6.8	16 220	-0.9	1 315	8.1	13 271	24.4	13.1
York	61 848	71.6	115 200	23.2	13.3	498	26.4	2.1	100 557	-0.5	3 665	3.6	80 767	27.6	15.3
MARYLAND	1 748 991	65.0	116 500	21.1	12.4	548	25.4	3.3	2 837 433	1.2	115 709	4.1	2 481 342	37.0	10.3
Allegany	29 634	69.9	46 700	16.8	12.9	283	26.1	1.4	32 240	-0.6	2 447	7.6	29 731	26.5	11.5
Anne Arundel	149 114	72.9	127 900	21.3	12.4	616	25.0	2.0	262 096	1.4	8 331	3.2	224 381	36.4	11.7
Baltimore	268 280	66.3	99 900	19.7	12.1	529	23.6	1.6	403 022	1.2	17 771	4.4	366 276	36.4	10.9
Calvert	16 986	85.0	136 100	21.7	11.8	664	24.0	3.4	38 843	0.6	984	2.5	26 820	30.5	16.9
Caroline	9 983	73.5	75 000	21.2	13.4	348	25.6	4.2	16 562	3.3	838	5.1	13 229	20.2	16.0
Carroll	42 248	78.5	126 700	21.7	11.8	484	23.8	1.3	84 264	1.1	2 334	2.8	65 994	31.8	15.5
Cecil	24 725	75.0	97 000	20.7	12.6	471	22.9	3.1	42 304	0.6	2 403	5.7	35 227	24.1	16.5
Charles	32 950	75.7	122 300	21.9	12.4	690	26.1	4.0	63 470	0.7	1 622	2.6	52 605	32.3	14.9
Dorchester	12 117	67.6	68 600	19.5	13.3	330	23.6	5.1	14 836	0.0	1 373	9.3	14 379	20.3	15.2
Frederick	52 570	70.8	129 500	21.8	12.2	558	24.2	2.1	103 922	1.3	2 923	2.8	80 833	33.4	14.2
Garrett	10 110	79.1	60 200	20.9	12.4	310	24.9	4.3	13 495	0.4	1 036	7.7	11 748	19.7	18.3
Harford	63 193	73.9	114 700	20.9	11.7	481	23.4	2.2	117 031	1.5	4 535	3.9	93 500	34.8	12.9
Howard	68 337	72.2	166 500	22.5	11.7	680	24.7	1.4	147 206	1.8	3 767	2.6	109 907	52.6	6.6
Kent	6 702	71.6	87 700	20.7	12.0	406	25.5	4.3	10 080	0.1	412	4.1	8 822	23.9	13.6
Montgomery	282 228	67.9	200 800	22.1	11.5	740	26.5	3.4	489 166	1.2	11 465	2.3	431 572	53.0	6.3
Prince George's	258 011	58.9	122 600	21.7	11.8	642	25.6	5.5	454 011	0.9	18 510	4.1	412 742	35.9	9.0
Queen Anne's	12 489	81.0	118 000	21.9	12.4	471	24.4	3.0	21 810	1.4	713	3.3	17 506	30.6	13.9
St. Mary's	25 500	69.7	109 100	21.9	12.3	539	24.8	4.8	53 623	1.1	1 511	2.8	35 958	33.3	17.0
Somerset	7 977	72.2	55 600	21.3	13.4	302	26.5	6.4	11 526	0.4	867	7.5	8 962	19.5	11.3
Talbot	12 677	68.1	118 100	20.6	12.3	429	25.1	3.4	19 358	2.3	606	3.1	15 786	26.9	12.5

1. Specified owner-occupied units.   2. Specified renter-occupied units.   3. Overcrowded or lacking complete plumbing facilities.   4. Percent of civilian labor force.   5. Persons 16 years and older.

Table B. States and Counties — Nonfarm Employment and Agriculture

STATE / County	Private nonfarm establishments, employment and payroll, 1999									Agriculture, 1997			
	Number of establishments	Employment						Annual payroll		Farms			Farm operators
		Total	Health Care and Social Assistance	Manufacturing	Retail trade	Finance and Insurance	Professional Scientific and Technical Services	Total (mil dol)	Average per employee (dollars)	Number	Percent with—		Whose principal occupation is farming (percent)
											Less than 50 acres	500 acres and over	
	104	105	106	107	108	109	110	111	112	113	114	115	116
LOUISIANA—Cont'd													
Pointe Coupee	340	3 848	476	599	942	145	96	81	20 997	402	30.6	25.9	51.0
Rapides	3 122	45 955	12 171	2 890	7 677	1 756	1 846	1 062	23 108	817	39.4	11.9	46.5
Red River	158	1 672	384	D	331	93	23	35	20 679	218	23.9	20.2	46.3
Richland	405	4 795	1 566	567	787	202	87	89	18 492	483	19.0	35.0	65.2
Sabine	472	4 417	495	991	780	313	64	90	20 451	373	30.6	5.4	45.3
St. Bernard	1 183	14 156	2 377	1 795	3 411	386	354	324	22 891	27	59.3	7.4	40.7
St. Charles	847	16 711	1 048	4 767	1 534	233	421	655	39 184	71	32.4	11.3	45.1
St. Helena	92	893	259	166	99	73	50	16	18 166	333	30.6	4.5	46.8
St. James	309	5 966	384	2 481	671	226	67	211	35 291	65	38.5	46.2	81.5
St. John the Baptist	627	10 664	992	2 131	1 514	256	241	297	27 867	27	40.7	22.2	44.4
St. Landry	1 538	15 795	3 682	1 829	3 365	842	562	326	20 654	966	44.5	15.7	45.7
St. Martin	661	8 694	900	2 662	1 436	319	244	181	20 860	243	42.0	20.2	51.9
St. Mary	1 448	23 212	1 277	4 880	2 711	535	1 279	646	27 833	103	20.4	49.5	68.0
St. Tammany	4 510	50 285	9 560	2 655	10 144	1 840	2 472	1 103	21 940	451	64.7	2.9	40.4
Tangipahoa	1 967	24 589	4 675	2 845	5 568	866	729	478	19 430	923	41.4	3.5	50.1
Tensas	110	688	104	D	100	58	24	14	20 163	202	7.9	54.5	77.2
Terrebonne	2 679	39 186	4 659	4 415	6 533	1 111	1 155	1 038	26 483	137	38.0	21.2	39.4
Union	325	5 179	772	2 101	596	170	36	94	18 055	436	30.3	3.2	48.9
Vermilion	956	9 468	1 327	905	1 947	421	242	196	20 673	995	34.0	20.7	59.4
Vernon	635	7 218	1 699	117	1 608	325	566	142	19 614	387	40.1	3.1	41.6
Washington	728	8 443	1 765	1 567	1 623	340	168	186	22 005	814	37.7	3.1	45.1
Webster	863	10 881	1 992	2 340	1 903	405	312	230	21 145	341	35.5	5.0	39.9
West Baton Rouge	432	8 899	294	2 472	1 024	185	73	261	29 360	95	49.5	22.1	37.9
West Carroll	205	1 819	434	206	408	59	14	37	20 339	539	21.5	19.5	53.1
West Feliciana	161	2 776	244	D	262	58	D	116	41 809	148	21.6	27.7	30.4
Winn	347	4 100	627	1 048	656	100	D	96	23 391	147	37.4	3.4	43.5
MAINE	38 878	475 149	82 951	80 973	74 881	22 723	18 677	12 586	26 489	5 810	29.6	9.3	49.4
Androscoggin	2 732	43 092	7 404	8 387	6 387	2 197	2 034	1 054	24 461	288	27.4	9.7	52.1
Aroostook	2 307	24 338	5 526	4 539	4 172	736	375	517	21 226	889	12.8	21.0	59.6
Cumberland	10 057	145 538	22 969	15 486	20 799	12 375	8 081	4 311	29 621	455	47.3	3.5	47.3
Franklin	870	10 328	1 626	2 479	1 549	296	113	236	22 878	223	22.0	5.8	46.2
Hancock	2 123	16 480	2 741	2 037	2 869	572	1 378	437	26 488	310	41.9	4.2	38.1
Kennebec	3 206	40 793	10 145	4 491	7 290	1 215	1 243	1 023	25 089	455	27.7	7.7	52.1
Knox	1 517	13 904	2 400	1 685	2 303	378	349	343	24 666	194	35.6	1.5	46.4
Lincoln	1 294	7 921	1 426	D	1 658	261	268	182	23 035	210	37.6	4.3	49.0
Oxford	1 424	15 698	2 414	3 992	2 175	339	230	366	23 326	358	32.1	7.5	47.8
Penobscot	4 088	57 241	11 200	8 931	9 853	1 962	1 843	1 459	25 487	525	31.0	11.4	47.2
Piscataquis	457	5 075	969	1 880	1 026	89	90	115	22 710	141	22.0	13.5	48.2
Sagadahoc	783	14 265	923	D	1 392	249	827	449	31 458	118	34.7	5.9	46.6
Somerset	1 225	15 709	2 447	4 120	2 233	357	261	431	27 426	431	18.3	11.8	56.6
Waldo	841	8 371	1 262	1 360	1 287	116	161	196	23 450	315	23.8	9.5	54.9
Washington	933	8 388	1 951	1 664	1 691	272	89	183	21 826	399	37.8	7.5	36.3
York	5 021	48 008	7 548	10 986	8 197	1 309	1 335	1 284	26 739	499	40.3	2.8	44.5
MARYLAND	127 431	1 988 950	261 433	159 307	279 135	108 424	182 531	64 183	32 270	12 084	43.3	8.2	51.6
Allegany	1 854	24 365	4 865	4 229	4 550	908	673	561	23 035	239	21.8	8.4	43.1
Anne Arundel	11 981	171 047	17 749	13 109	28 731	6 641	13 151	5 312	31 057	412	60.0	3.4	48.1
Baltimore	19 189	307 955	46 111	29 243	51 697	22 224	20 747	9 455	30 703	781	60.2	2.9	44.9
Calvert	1 444	14 563	2 312	571	2 592	338	600	401	27 558	349	52.7	3.7	45.8
Caroline	584	6 276	513	1 631	961	D	D	143	22 793	525	38.5	11.2	61.9
Carroll	3 922	42 339	6 008	4 318	7 842	1 198	1 553	975	23 039	1 041	48.9	5.8	47.6
Cecil	1 617	18 597	3 299	2 534	3 587	499	538	506	27 222	464	43.5	9.1	51.3
Charles	2 432	28 261	3 294	937	8 025	874	1 256	655	23 162	410	43.4	5.4	48.0
Dorchester	724	9 572	1 596	3 354	1 278	265	172	232	24 223	297	26.6	27.9	63.3
Frederick	4 837	69 114	6 704	8 389	10 846	7 758	4 584	1 978	28 623	1 304	35.9	5.6	51.2
Garrett	867	9 133	1 236	1 305	1 476	369	170	172	18 865	649	19.7	4.6	47.3
Harford	4 784	56 618	6 033	6 484	10 802	2 139	3 308	1 491	26 334	651	48.2	5.7	48.1
Howard	7 171	133 647	10 946	7 329	13 402	5 851	24 438	5 122	38 323	318	58.2	6.3	39.9
Kent	667	6 577	1 122	1 026	965	220	339	147	22 360	314	21.0	20.4	61.5
Montgomery	25 149	387 064	42 146	15 110	46 980	21 582	57 065	15 072	38 940	526	56.5	6.5	42.0
Prince George's	13 893	246 457	22 539	11 572	37 950	9 321	25 314	7 697	31 230	473	59.2	3.0	41.9
Queen Anne's	1 150	8 999	677	916	1 818	260	411	198	21 986	419	28.2	27.4	64.0
St. Mary's	1 668	22 791	2 632	672	3 736	468	6 405	651	28 553	621	43.6	3.7	52.7
Somerset	415	3 183	714	458	487	209	58	62	19 341	288	43.4	8.7	57.3
Talbot	1 450	16 390	2 614	2 845	2 620	563	767	422	25 748	240	25.4	24.2	57.9

Table B. States and Counties — Agriculture, Land, and Water

STATE County	Land in farms Acreage (1,000) 117	Percent change, 1992–1997 118	Average size of farm 119	Total irrigated (1,000) 120	Total cropland (1,000) 121	Value of land and buildings Average per farm ($1,000) 122	Average per acre (dollars) 123	Value of machinery and equipment average per farm ($1,000) 124	Value of products sold Total (mil dol) 125	Average per farm (dollars) 126	Percent from — Crops 127	Livestock and poultry products 128	Percent of farms with sales of — $10,000 or more 129	$100,000 or more 130	Percent of land owned by fed. gov. 1997 131	Water consumption 1995 (mil gal/day) 132
LOUISIANA—Cont'd																
Pointe Coupee	201	4.2	500	3	160	582	1 131	89	54	133 487	90.3	9.7	49.5	23.1	3.7	290.1
Rapides	194	-7.8	238	7	122	333	1 464	56	55	67 534	88.5	11.5	39.8	16.4	11.6	497.7
Red River	113	15.5	519	D	51	420	931	51	11	50 114	68.3	31.7	36.2	11.0	0.0	1.6
Richland	237	-4.2	490	62	197	494	1 019	96	57	118 996	94.3	5.7	61.9	35.6	0.4	24.5
Sabine	57	-2.3	152	0	24	200	1 172	39	53	143 254	0.6	99.4	39.9	20.1	1.6	3.6
St. Bernard	3	-43.3	126	0	2	301	2 384	14	0	15 747	D	D	29.6	3.7	5.5	305.7
St. Charles	21	-7.2	301	D	9	484	1 610	44	5	71 337	87.5	12.5	39.4	7.0	2.8	1 953.5
St. Helena	66	31.5	197	0	24	251	1 251	38	30	90 762	1.6	98.4	32.7	12.0	0.0	6.3
St. James	45	5.5	698	D	40	1 050	1 506	249	27	410 626	99.8	0.2	72.3	52.3	0.0	246.7
St. John the Baptist	10	-43.9	353	D	6	777	2 200	104	4	131 351	98.4	1.7	48.1	22.2	0.0	731.5
St. Landry	265	-6.4	274	29	224	301	1 121	60	64	66 097	86.6	13.4	34.2	14.0	0.0	47.8
St. Martin	78	9.9	321	6	66	470	1 583	96	31	126 123	90.7	9.3	44.4	23.0	2.7	44.7
St. Mary	83	1.4	807	0	65	1 219	1 545	247	39	382 811	99.2	0.8	63.1	48.5	0.0	219.4
St. Tammany	42	4.7	93	1	17	305	3 530	49	12	27 504	66.6	33.4	26.8	6.7	3.9	23.9
Tangipahoa	120	-5.5	130	1	73	250	2 219	31	59	64 225	16.5	83.5	41.4	21.0	0.0	17.8
Tensas	241	-2.1	1 193	12	197	924	817	184	71	349 998	99.6	0.4	79.2	55.0	3.8	11.7
Terrebonne	53	20.2	386	0	31	676	1 650	75	14	103 506	85.6	14.4	41.6	14.6	0.0	33.1
Union	63	1.9	145	0	27	204	1 385	38	86	198 135	0.5	99.5	41.5	26.8	6.5	5.0
Vermilion	329	3.6	330	106	256	373	1 203	68	70	70 464	90.8	9.2	46.1	18.9	0.0	262.3
Vernon	44	-16.1	113	0	19	147	1 354	24	8	21 372	4.2	95.8	18.1	3.1	21.7	9.2
Washington	100	-13.8	123	1	60	233	1 922	41	45	55 427	26.1	73.9	33.4	16.6	0.2	31.6
Webster	50	-14.8	147	0	23	219	1 429	32	6	16 546	9.1	90.9	23.5	2.6	8.3	7.5
West Baton Rouge	29	-26.1	304	D	22	440	1 449	78	29	309 621	D	D	40.0	20.0	0.0	9.8
West Carroll	167	31.4	310	46	134	235	904	57	43	80 407	94.4	5.6	47.5	20.6	0.7	25.2
West Feliciana	76	-12.5	515	0	24	677	1 371	36	3	23 015	51.9	48.1	29.1	2.0	0.0	47.5
Winn	18	-22.3	122	D	8	111	953	25	3	20 925	6.2	93.8	21.8	2.0	21.9	3.0
MAINE	1 212	-3.7	209	22	540	251	1 190	49	439	75 503	48.4	51.6	41.2	13.2	1.0	221.0
Androscoggin	56	-9.8	194	1	23	304	1 715	71	62	216 587	12.7	87.3	47.9	19.4	0.0	14.0
Aroostook	325	-2.7	365	11	188	278	716	91	110	123 306	95.5	4.5	56.5	28.1	0.2	25.0
Cumberland	50	-7.7	110	1	26	322	2 600	35	17	38 061	64.5	35.5	38.9	10.5	0.6	36.9
Franklin	40	2.8	180	0	15	194	1 236	30	6	24 976	D	D	34.1	7.6	1.9	5.4
Hancock	43	-14.8	137	0	11	266	1 728	24	30	98 219	D	D	33.2	5.5	3.8	6.8
Kennebec	88	-7.2	194	0	45	258	1 509	52	45	99 299	13.7	86.3	41.3	14.5	0.1	29.8
Knox	25	-10.1	130	0	10	217	1 916	40	6	28 883	60.4	39.6	43.3	9.3	1.7	5.3
Lincoln	26	8.0	123	0	11	206	1 705	33	6	30 140	35.9	64.1	33.8	6.7	0.0	3.4
Oxford	64	1.5	179	1	21	293	1 417	45	20	54 607	53.2	46.8	33.8	8.4	3.8	10.5
Penobscot	117	-1.2	222	2	49	226	1 058	43	30	57 101	37.2	62.8	40.6	13.5	0.4	21.5
Piscataquis	34	-5.1	242	0	10	214	862	42	6	39 440	30.8	69.2	37.6	9.2	0.5	3.1
Sagadahoc	18	-6.0	151	0	7	288	1 893	35	3	25 993	46.0	54.0	28.8	5.9	0.1	4.6
Somerset	101	-5.4	235	0	36	219	921	57	25	57 371	19.8	80.2	45.9	13.5	0.3	8.3
Waldo	69	-4.8	218	0	28	222	952	34	15	46 884	17.2	82.8	42.2	12.7	0.2	3.8
Washington	98	3.5	246	4	36	215	885	35	43	107 956	61.1	38.9	35.6	5.3	1.7	5.0
York	58	-5.9	117	1	24	223	2 053	31	16	31 068	66.2	33.8	32.1	8.2	1.2	37.7
MARYLAND	2 155	-3.1	178	69	1 613	564	3 176	60	1 312	108 580	35.0	65.0	50.2	21.5	2.1	1 452.2
Allegany	42	10.3	175	0	20	263	1 625	31	3	13 899	34.6	65.4	24.3	2.5	2.8	45.1
Anne Arundel	35	-19.4	84	1	23	532	5 151	44	13	30 635	79.5	20.5	38.1	6.3	5.2	50.9
Baltimore	76	-8.7	97	1	54	457	4 742	49	51	65 530	68.3	31.7	37.6	11.3	0.4	282.9
Calvert	33	-9.6	96	0	18	375	3 584	32	8	22 075	89.1	10.9	39.8	4.6	0.2	7.4
Caroline	111	-12.3	212	16	95	500	2 297	95	95	181 181	30.2	69.8	69.1	38.7	0.0	17.0
Carroll	160	1.4	154	1	125	568	3 790	58	71	68 465	36.2	63.8	41.6	18.8	0.0	15.4
Cecil	86	7.1	185	1	63	683	3 628	56	59	127 267	38.8	61.2	43.5	15.1	0.6	9.0
Charles	56	-5.2	136	1	33	437	2 755	32	11	26 381	86.6	13.4	38.8	7.3	1.2	13.2
Dorchester	123	-0.9	414	15	99	862	2 018	102	82	277 411	41.9	58.1	79.5	51.2	2.3	18.6
Frederick	216	-3.2	166	1	171	626	3 769	60	102	77 960	17.2	82.8	47.1	18.8	1.9	39.0
Garrett	108	-3.0	166	0	54	249	1 578	46	21	32 353	11.5	88.5	38.4	10.2	0.2	9.1
Harford	94	-3.0	145	1	72	613	3 975	53	39	59 612	42.0	58.0	40.1	12.9	11.6	18.0
Howard	40	-11.5	125	1	31	691	5 490	51	20	61 667	61.6	38.4	34.3	11.0	0.1	3.6
Kent	118	-10.3	374	5	98	1 051	2 947	103	61	194 131	55.8	44.2	71.3	30.3	0.9	6.2
Montgomery	77	-5.8	147	1	61	659	4 396	55	29	54 303	69.4	30.6	34.6	11.8	3.3	728.5
Prince George's	48	-11.9	101	0	28	491	4 988	34	19	39 553	89.4	10.6	34.0	5.9	7.1	53.2
Queen Anne's	168	1.8	401	8	146	1 206	2 946	115	69	164 047	63.4	36.6	69.9	38.4	0.0	13.3
St. Mary's	72	-6.6	116	1	43	275	2 603	38	21	33 906	83.3	16.7	53.5	6.1	1.4	9.8
Somerset	55	-2.1	190	1	40	411	2 254	65	97	335 182	13.5	86.5	79.9	55.2	1.0	6.1
Talbot	110	0.5	457	2	93	1 414	3 157	118	49	202 208	50.0	50.0	73.3	40.8	0.0	7.0

Table B. States and Counties — **Residential Construction, Wholesale and Retail Trade, and Real Estate**

STATE County	Value of Residential Construction Authorized by Building Permits, 2000		Wholesale Trade, 1997				Retail Trade[1], 1997				Real Estate and Rental and Leasing, 1997			
	New Construction ($1,000)	Number of Housing Units	Number of Establishments	Number of Employees	Sales (mil dol)	Annual Payroll (mil dol)	Number of Establishments	Number of Employees	Sales (mil dol)	Annual Payroll (mil dol)	Number of Establishments	Number of Employees	Receipts (mil dol)	Annual Payroll (mil dol)
	133	134	135	136	137	138	139	140	141	142	143	144	145	146
LOUISIANA—Cont'd														
Pointe Coupee	8 924	101	13	D	D	D	84	807	159.0	11.6	8	17	0.6	0.2
Rapides	44 876	440	173	1 789	581.1	45.6	586	7 397	1 188.3	108.5	92	660	57.8	12.4
Red River	100	1	6	53	13.8	0.9	39	265	53.6	3.7	4	13	0.7	0.2
Richland	4 127	33	28	259	160.4	5.6	85	844	188.0	12.8	14	40	2.9	0.7
Sabine	0	0	13	D	D	D	93	840	120.2	11.2	8	19	1.5	0.2
St. Bernard	6 310	108	62	D	D	D	214	2 887	362.7	33.6	37	148	13.2	3.0
St. Charles	25 839	176	84	1 485	2 627.1	50.7	119	1 316	210.8	17.5	29	109	14.5	2.1
St. Helena	659	11	1	D	D	D	17	101	11.1	1.1	1	D	D	D
St. James	1 840	16	15	282	277.7	10.5	55	609	72.4	7.4	10	20	2.2	0.3
St. John the Baptist	28 804	250	30	D	D	D	119	1 643	231.5	19.9	30	365	45.0	9.8
St. Landry	24 692	237	85	948	415.1	21.5	327	3 522	515.8	43.9	48	146	12.7	1.9
St. Martin	16 267	171	36	332	116.5	8.2	121	1 260	192.4	17.2	27	224	24.1	4.7
St. Mary	9 461	102	124	1 384	705.3	46.9	256	2 829	396.1	38.3	80	522	178.5	16.7
St. Tammany	247 546	2 019	252	2 070	6 604.0	75.3	749	9 479	1 511.5	135.3	156	739	86.4	14.5
Tangipahoa	51 382	552	106	1 482	725.4	38.0	415	5 442	894.8	74.6	72	309	29.5	5.4
Tensas	3 036	28	8	103	50.5	3.3	22	114	27.5	1.5	3	11	0.7	0.2
Terrebonne	33 919	411	212	2 467	790.5	69.5	482	6 237	1 064.1	93.3	137	1 651	247.6	54.0
Union	200	2	11	75	9.0	1.3	73	578	92.3	7.8	9	22	1.8	0.3
Vermilion	13 436	125	66	738	361.9	19.6	198	1 836	277.5	23.7	27	129	10.9	1.4
Vernon	51	1	30	221	53.6	4.8	143	1 392	216.1	19.3	29	78	6.4	0.8
Washington	7 202	116	28	178	57.0	3.7	184	1 627	241.2	20.0	13	44	2.4	0.5
Webster	3 809	77	36	D	D	D	197	1 844	293.5	24.5	25	116	9.2	1.4
West Baton Rouge	10 529	86	38	575	444.2	19.1	63	843	124.3	11.9	11	68	7.4	1.1
West Carroll	70	2	9	19	8.9	0.4	37	426	54.0	4.6	8	20	1.0	0.2
West Feliciana	7 746	59	7	30	11.7	0.8	35	275	40.7	3.5	2	D	D	D
Winn	0	0	17	159	56.7	4.9	65	692	81.1	7.9	8	20	1.4	0.3
MAINE	722 979	6 177	1 726	19 932	7 305.6	616.2	7 074	72 897	12 737.1	1 164.2	1 343	5 929	601.7	114.2
Androscoggin	34 697	321	126	1 244	277.8	35.7	533	6 362	1 247.1	96.4	109	418	46.9	7.2
Aroostook	10 413	129	101	766	211.1	19.8	471	4 285	591.9	57.9	71	197	13.1	2.2
Cumberland	221 126	1 680	574	8 884	3 673.3	296.8	1 570	20 735	3 825.9	346.5	407	2 731	293.4	63.5
Franklin	13 914	109	16	91	26.8	2.7	179	1 537	245.5	22.4	37	130	6.8	1.4
Hancock	48 695	378	73	354	138.6	8.4	388	2 895	490.0	49.3	63	127	13.9	2.2
Kennebec	33 300	389	133	2 135	821.9	67.6	589	7 166	1 289.7	120.5	109	439	37.7	7.6
Knox	32 497	236	79	550	171.7	13.8	278	2 309	394.0	35.8	42	92	11.1	1.3
Lincoln	23 190	204	52	259	66.5	5.5	236	1 545	299.7	25.2	28	58	11.6	1.2
Oxford	23 041	272	36	366	122.2	9.8	280	2 104	320.4	30.6	48	127	16.0	2.4
Penobscot	38 476	482	196	2 786	938.0	85.6	796	9 433	1 654.6	148.0	146	620	66.9	9.5
Piscataquis	2 817	43	11	D	D	D	100	871	120.6	12.3	17	37	2.6	0.5
Sagadahoc	18 174	157	21	111	78.7	1.9	124	1 044	183.5	17.1	27	93	8.1	1.6
Somerset	6 211	82	30	473	120.9	18.9	260	2 234	356.5	35.1	32	124	5.8	1.8
Waldo	34 072	219	29	165	149.2	4.2	165	1 226	192.5	18.2	15	41	3.0	0.4
Washington	6 716	86	50	D	D	D	204	1 712	260.2	23.5	13	38	2.5	0.4
York	166 640	1 302	199	1 479	438.6	41.1	901	7 439	1 265.1	125.1	179	657	62.1	11.1
MARYLAND	3 232 127	30 358	6 283	92 458	54 906.6	3 656.3	19 798	274 260	46 428.2	4 914.0	5 065	39 502	4 764.7	971.3
Allegany	8 093	79	71	D	D	D	385	4 719	663.5	63.5	56	198	23.7	3.4
Anne Arundel	329 303	3 078	653	9 148	8 829.7	366.4	1 863	27 922	4 757.6	487.0	415	3 531	407.1	82.4
Baltimore	270 037	2 707	1 003	12 047	6 707.2	491.6	3 138	49 690	8 243.4	902.7	743	7 047	947.9	182.5
Calvert	108 425	931	29	202	61.7	4.8	190	2 566	404.0	42.7	60	151	19.3	2.7
Caroline	16 387	154	26	325	163.2	9.1	104	901	191.3	13.7	17	36	2.1	0.4
Carroll	169 731	1 459	146	966	292.9	27.8	604	7 366	1 160.6	116.5	121	395	56.1	6.8
Cecil	74 368	768	53	D	D	D	284	3 526	613.4	58.2	60	177	20.3	3.0
Charles	146 861	1 233	75	1 088	234.9	27.6	490	7 750	1 243.6	128.0	84	290	31.2	5.7
Dorchester	11 121	109	51	402	121.6	10.7	132	1 476	285.9	27.7	30	97	5.8	1.3
Frederick	306 995	2 747	212	2 783	847.7	94.0	741	10 644	1 839.3	186.8	185	862	88.0	18.2
Garrett	38 741	253	40	303	121.7	5.7	157	1 367	222.9	20.6	20	113	8.5	1.5
Harford	193 126	1 702	198	1 502	1 024.7	47.1	741	10 518	1 755.4	174.6	170	780	74.1	13.8
Howard	240 337	2 182	631	13 185	9 392.3	528.3	766	11 823	2 010.8	216.2	254	1 899	335.2	64.7
Kent	34 774	334	25	162	49.8	3.5	125	908	132.3	13.9	31	65	9.3	0.8
Montgomery	505 398	4 950	971	14 752	8 795.9	778.9	3 000	46 311	8 914.4	957.8	1 123	11 375	1 321.4	305.1
Prince George's	335 676	3 456	759	13 904	9 053.7	542.9	2 425	38 214	6 390.5	675.8	599	5 013	638.5	110.7
Queen Anne's	54 872	419	71	526	209.0	14.3	217	1 833	321.5	28.7	31	62	8.4	1.0
St. Mary's	111 987	1 163	27	D	D	D	278	3 615	553.2	55.4	55	241	27.0	3.6
Somerset	2 331	27	19	D	D	D	73	485	68.0	6.1	10	30	1.6	0.3
Talbot	47 181	339	69	527	243.4	15.5	262	2 621	457.5	47.0	71	179	20.8	3.4

1. Establishments with payroll.

STATE County	Professional, Scientific, and Technical Services[1], 1997				Manufacturing, 1997				Accommodation and Foodservices, 1997			
	Number of Establishments	Number of Employees	Receipts (mil dol)	Annual Payroll (mil dol)	Number of Establishments	Number of Employees	Receipts (mil dol)	Annual Payroll (mil dol)	Number of Establishments	Number of Employees	Sales (mil dol)	Annual Payroll (mil dol)
	147	148	149	150	151	152	153	154	155	156	157	158
LOUISIANA—Cont'd												
Pointe Coupee	23	79	5.4	1.7	11	539	146.1	12.9	26	D	D	D
Rapides	247	1 956	124.2	42.2	73	3 179	1 165.9	103.0	224	3 985	119.8	31.7
Red River	6	17	1.0	0.2	NA	NA	NA	NA	6	D	D	D
Richland	24	85	5.9	1.9	14	600	132.1	16.6	27	296	8.7	2.1
Sabine	24	74	3.6	1.3	19	1 121	253.1	28.8	24	217	7.6	2.2
St. Bernard	69	224	17.9	4.9	54	1 769	2 603.6	83.1	107	1 431	43.0	11.6
St. Charles	63	430	30.1	15.1	37	5 068	8 501.5	302.2	47	701	19.0	5.2
St. Helena	7	D	D	D	NA	NA	NA	NA	5	D	D	D
St. James	14	39	2.7	1.0	26	2 858	3 842.3	149.5	14	203	6.6	1.8
St. John the Baptist	42	194	11.6	3.4	29	2 304	3 057.5	104.2	36	783	21.8	5.7
St. Landry	113	490	35.1	12.3	57	1 919	904.7	50.8	76	1 034	32.2	8.6
St. Martin	42	170	12.3	4.4	44	3 501	1 259.8	69.7	52	D	D	D
St. Mary	94	1 044	139.2	32.8	67	5 098	944.4	163.6	91	1 385	41.3	10.3
St. Tammany	401	1 789	125.4	45.5	127	2 699	373.7	61.3	345	5 415	170.7	44.8
Tangipahoa	133	530	36.2	12.0	74	2 933	420.4	59.5	159	2 898	79.7	21.9
Tensas	9	15	1.6	0.3	NA	NA	NA	NA	8	25	1.6	0.2
Terrebonne	190	1 111	93.2	36.8	119	3 990	539.5	129.3	173	3 133	105.9	31.1
Union	12	29	1.7	0.4	NA	NA	NA	NA	19	D	D	D
Vermilion	64	225	12.1	5.1	27	1 348	203.9	28.6	64	775	22.6	5.5
Vernon	31	599	21.0	12.9	NA	NA	NA	NA	58	782	23.0	5.9
Washington	43	148	11.7	2.8	28	1 536	466.3	54.7	49	626	18.3	4.4
Webster	43	151	8.7	3.3	45	2 336	504.6	67.2	56	637	18.1	4.2
West Baton Rouge	16	79	10.7	2.4	39	2 452	1 376.7	84.0	31	591	18.1	4.5
West Carroll	6	D	D	D	NA	NA	NA	NA	7	D	D	D
West Feliciana	12	25	1.5	0.4	6	D	D	D	18	176	7.1	1.8
Winn	13	22	1.2	0.3	24	1 252	300.0	37.8	20	209	6.2	1.5
MAINE	2 552	13 747	1 215.6	474.8	1 812	82 288	14 097.6	2 591.1	3 714	39 624	1 509.3	428.8
Androscoggin	151	1 672	191.6	54.3	183	8 233	1 218.6	226.6	180	2 438	77.4	23.3
Aroostook	89	342	18.1	7.2	89	3 906	895.0	125.4	162	1 807	50.0	14.8
Cumberland	973	6 408	614.6	253.8	382	14 304	2 232.7	477.2	792	11 749	429.9	121.3
Franklin	36	95	5.0	2.0	53	3 457	867.8	110.3	94	1 328	33.6	11.0
Hancock	111	309	24.2	8.7	94	2 397	551.0	103.8	315	1 741	105.0	28.4
Kennebec	230	926	71.1	26.3	129	5 488	753.4	165.8	257	3 282	109.1	32.0
Knox	74	275	15.0	6.2	92	1 602	267.7	44.3	131	1 306	58.0	17.5
Lincoln	74	D	D	D	68	D	D	D	158	870	49.1	14.4
Oxford	56	149	8.9	3.6	84	4 038	758.5	118.7	140	1 203	44.2	12.2
Penobscot	271	1 388	102.7	45.9	155	8 897	1 658.6	285.9	344	4 778	151.3	45.8
Piscataquis	13	D	D	D	26	1 905	114.7	36.1	50	351	10.8	2.8
Sagadahoc	62	535	42.7	19.4	29	D	D	D	64	743	25.6	7.7
Somerset	58	221	16.6	6.1	76	4 441	1 239.9	143.7	105	778	26.0	6.8
Waldo	40	100	7.4	2.8	53	1 180	117.8	24.8	86	546	23.2	6.2
Washington	34	82	3.7	1.1	41	1 676	364.8	52.6	113	707	22.0	6.3
York	280	973	77.7	30.7	258	11 649	2 093.5	360.2	723	5 997	294.1	78.1
MARYLAND	14 115	146 814	15 940.2	6 483.8	3 996	163 992	36 505.9	5 840.5	9 049	161 273	5 972.5	1 644.7
Allegany	94	515	25.5	13.9	67	4 169	785.9	139.2	165	2 434	75.5	19.8
Anne Arundel	1 321	9 033	1 025.4	366.7	339	14 878	2 703.8	618.4	852	17 645	637.3	175.6
Baltimore	2 132	17 132	1 708.2	682.1	575	31 065	6 883.3	1 235.1	1 359	24 414	842.4	233.5
Calvert	105	516	38.9	17.2	NA	NA	NA	NA	94	1 859	56.9	15.5
Caroline	21	70	2.7	1.0	31	1 533	167.6	36.6	27	255	7.9	1.9
Carroll	289	1 073	67.4	27.5	144	4 330	716.9	131.1	214	3 906	110.3	31.4
Cecil	109	363	27.3	9.7	55	2 766	678.3	100.9	131	2 011	75.2	20.1
Charles	145	993	91.9	33.0	58	1 100	170.3	38.5	186	3 895	125.3	33.5
Dorchester	42	126	7.3	3.1	48	3 580	867.2	86.9	60	765	21.3	6.0
Frederick	449	3 821	296.2	130.2	162	7 795	1 509.1	268.5	304	6 028	193.2	54.5
Garrett	36	151	7.6	3.2	49	1 135	103.5	22.8	73	961	26.7	8.0
Harford	408	2 608	237.5	90.5	152	5 301	1 274.6	178.8	293	5 777	185.9	51.6
Howard	1 050	15 883	1 950.3	772.1	245	6 927	1 177.3	257.2	366	7 078	242.5	68.5
Kent	39	284	13.1	4.3	27	1 031	189.4	25.4	66	585	20.1	5.7
Montgomery	4 314	49 186	5 997.5	2 419.3	527	15 190	3 111.9	680.5	1 407	25 248	1 062.1	298.0
Prince George's	1 364	23 023	2 186.8	967.6	372	11 179	2 008.1	408.5	1 027	20 122	718.4	193.8
Queen Anne's	71	291	20.7	8.5	34	877	106.7	21.8	80	1 482	54.9	15.7
St. Mary's	166	4 226	364.8	177.5	NA	NA	NA	NA	111	2 017	62.6	17.5
Somerset	18	81	4.0	1.8	NA	NA	NA	NA	28	335	10.5	3.0
Talbot	112	604	58.9	27.6	54	3 035	836.1	69.1	96	1 639	69.8	20.0

1. Firms subject to federal tax.

Table B. States and Counties — **Health and Other Services and Federal Funds**

	Health Care and Social Assistance[1], 1997				Other Services[1], 1997				Federal funds and grants, fiscal 2001[2]			
									Expenditures (mil dol)			
										Direct payments for individuals[3]		
STATE County	Number of Establishments	Number of Employees	Receipts (mil dol)	Annual Payroll (mil dol)	Number of Establishments	Number of Employees	Receipts (mil dol)	Annual Payroll (mil dol)	Total	Social Security and government retirement	Medicare	Food stamps and Supplemental Security Income
	159	160	161	162	163	164	165	166	167	168	169	170
LOUISIANA—Cont'd												
Pointe Coupee	20	235	9.0	4.0	20	66	4.9	1.1	123.3	38.1	19.7	8.4
Rapides	335	5 666	306.0	129.1	170	984	55.3	16.7	813.0	292.4	142.6	41.1
Red River	13	294	17.3	6.4	7	32	2.5	0.9	62.7	18.1	11.9	3.7
Richland	52	908	32.1	13.7	20	103	5.4	1.7	155.6	38.7	29.4	8.5
Sabine	21	393	22.5	8.6	25	89	6.8	1.6	139.0	58.7	25.7	6.8
St. Bernard	111	2 263	135.1	53.5	93	459	31.3	9.6	313.5	147.1	94.4	15.0
St. Charles	58	771	39.0	14.3	32	314	40.7	7.6	212.0	72.0	36.7	7.9
St. Helena	7	39	2.4	0.7	2	D	D	D	43.8	11.2	10.2	3.0
St. James	23	289	14.6	6.5	8	91	3.6	1.2	111.7	37.9	24.9	5.3
St. John the Baptist	59	990	57.4	26.7	42	211	9.9	3.0	195.6	64.3	33.7	11.7
St. Landry	163	2 333	130.3	51.2	98	441	26.6	8.0	549.5	161.1	97.7	47.1
St. Martin	34	584	19.4	10.2	30	91	7.0	1.8	204.5	71.7	36.8	10.0
St. Mary	73	809	41.9	19.2	96	479	46.4	10.3	278.3	102.5	52.4	20.5
St. Tammany	444	5 248	345.0	141.4	239	1 263	81.4	21.6	687.8	361.5	145.9	25.5
Tangipahoa	158	1 778	95.5	42.6	121	704	49.7	12.3	519.8	169.3	117.2	40.0
Tensas	8	149	4.8	2.6	3	D	D	D	71.7	11.6	10.1	3.9
Terrebonne	175	2 234	145.0	69.3	172	1 457	132.1	35.6	431.0	192.4	91.7	32.7
Union	20	352	12.6	5.1	14	54	3.1	0.7	118.0	46.8	28.7	5.2
Vermilion	73	805	36.6	12.5	61	384	24.5	9.2	284.2	98.2	52.1	13.1
Vernon	34	531	51.6	14.3	48	196	12.0	3.1	683.8	107.2	35.8	8.4
Washington	72	1 369	62.2	29.3	33	201	9.0	2.5	294.9	99.1	84.1	22.5
Webster	59	1 449	82.0	34.8	41	183	8.8	2.6	247.1	105.4	56.3	12.0
West Baton Rouge	20	439	11.9	6.1	21	151	11.2	3.2	130.8	33.4	21.7	6.0
West Carroll	7	254	7.7	3.7	17	54	2.8	0.7	89.8	23.9	17.9	3.8
West Feliciana	12	137	4.6	2.1	4	24	2.4	0.7	38.6	12.6	7.8	2.5
Winn	24	388	26.3	10.0	14	47	3.2	0.8	87.5	30.6	21.9	6.0
MAINE	2 727	28 944	1 608.4	766.3	1 923	8 820	612.3	169.6	8 180.5	3 051.8	966.6	229.9
Androscoggin	221	2 542	149.6	68.4	191	714	46.2	12.9	536.8	234.0	90.2	24.4
Aroostook	140	1 681	78.7	34.0	108	448	32.3	5.6	528.9	202.7	68.3	19.6
Cumberland	764	9 092	602.3	303.5	503	3 458	226.7	71.3	1 488.8	566.2	191.2	36.9
Franklin	51	709	28.8	12.0	37	120	9.8	2.0	171.3	66.1	22.9	5.9
Hancock	79	888	42.5	20.5	75	256	22.8	8.4	320.2	127.6	40.7	6.6
Kennebec	316	2 870	143.3	68.7	170	655	43.2	10.7	1 063.9	303.0	80.8	25.5
Knox	95	747	41.2	18.0	78	324	22.4	6.5	206.6	98.5	33.9	5.9
Lincoln	49	361	20.5	10.2	50	160	11.7	2.9	167.0	92.0	28.0	4.0
Oxford	84	834	38.1	18.2	71	220	15.6	4.0	272.9	135.8	49.1	9.9
Penobscot	310	3 432	209.8	98.2	208	980	82.3	20.4	863.7	336.4	109.1	31.6
Piscataquis	36	310	12.7	5.7	13	47	2.9	0.7	101.9	52.8	15.8	3.4
Sagadahoc	68	589	25.4	11.7	48	176	11.1	2.6	400.0	86.4	17.5	3.5
Somerset	75	1 024	35.6	15.8	68	200	13.2	3.2	261.8	117.7	37.9	14.8
Waldo	49	448	21.3	7.9	43	115	10.1	2.0	223.3	79.6	22.4	8.1
Washington	53	721	23.9	10.4	41	132	10.1	1.9	259.6	93.0	32.5	8.7
York	337	2 696	134.8	63.0	219	815	51.8	14.4	1 004.1	446.3	126.2	21.1
MARYLAND	10 841	116 241	8 060.7	3 538.0	7 871	55 241	3 561.3	1 129.2	48 163.9	11 880.5	4 371.4	688.2
Allegany	170	1 348	98.4	47.9	135	790	39.2	11.7	507.9	210.3	117.9	13.9
Anne Arundel	864	8 875	598.3	264.2	771	5 428	360.2	103.3	3 730.9	1 239.4	343.8	34.5
Baltimore	2 003	25 262	1 700.4	764.7	1 244	8 780	510.4	177.5	4 444.9	1 710.5	779.4	85.7
Calvert	108	971	59.8	29.7	69	397	20.7	6.5	261.0	167.5	39.8	4.2
Caroline	22	154	6.5	2.4	31	143	11.6	3.4	148.8	63.1	27.5	4.5
Carroll	265	2 346	130.7	56.9	271	1 596	86.9	26.7	563.4	317.1	113.8	6.2
Cecil	97	1 047	59.1	27.8	107	495	31.4	9.3	390.3	177.3	61.6	7.7
Charles	209	1 836	101.8	46.6	174	1 111	77.1	22.3	626.9	296.7	62.4	10.8
Dorchester	57	715	35.9	14.7	48	176	9.0	2.4	216.6	73.2	39.1	5.4
Frederick	315	3 258	203.2	96.0	280	1 384	102.0	28.8	1 057.8	375.1	94.3	9.6
Garrett	42	436	21.6	9.7	45	313	17.2	5.1	140.6	63.9	26.7	5.1
Harford	354	3 253	197.9	84.0	322	1 824	96.7	31.8	1 420.6	470.2	135.7	15.7
Howard	486	7 205	525.2	216.7	328	2 830	228.5	66.1	909.3	368.9	81.3	11.0
Kent	37	319	17.0	6.4	35	128	7.7	2.1	140.5	63.3	25.2	2.1
Montgomery	2 438	19 961	1 704.3	701.7	1 398	9 308	650.5	221.9	10 626.6	1 962.9	553.6	71.9
Prince George's	1 396	13 111	939.8	408.1	1 025	9 635	647.1	207.1	7 960.2	1 818.0	458.1	78.0
Queen Anne's	42	430	16.7	7.3	58	221	15.2	4.3	167.3	83.4	24.6	2.0
St. Mary's	108	1 289	66.1	30.8	97	526	28.6	8.7	1 711.9	210.9	52.0	9.2
Somerset	19	251	13.0	5.9	16	67	6.8	0.8	140.8	50.2	21.9	3.6
Talbot	97	1 195	76.2	37.2	88	482	26.6	8.5	247.1	106.5	38.0	3.2

1. Firms subject to federal tax.   2. October 1, 2000 to September 30, 2001.   3. State totals may include programs not allocated by county.

Table B. States and Counties — Federal Funds and Local Government Finances

	Federal funds and grants, fiscal 2001[1] (cont'd)							Local government finances, 1997				
	Expenditures (mil dol) (cont'd)							General revenue				
	Procurement contract awards		Grants[2]							Taxes		
STATE County	Salaries and wages	Defense	Other	Medicaid and other health-related	Nutrition and family welfare	Education	Other	Total (mil dol)	Intergovernmental (mil dol)	Total (mil dol)	Per capita[3] (dollars) Total	Property
	171	172	173	174	175	176	177	178	179	180	181	182
LOUISIANA—Cont'd												
Pointe Coupee	3.3	0.6	0.6	32.0	4.0	1.8	1.5	45.2	15.2	13.5	573	331
Rapides	101.6	21.5	13.6	101.4	17.1	11.1	43.2	251.4	107.2	113.8	900	376
Red River	1.8	0.1	0.3	15.6	1.8	0.7	1.8	16.2	10.5	4.8	494	229
Richland	5.7	0.0	0.8	35.1	3.9	1.9	6.2	54.3	24.2	8.7	415	216
Sabine	3.0	0.6	0.7	30.1	3.1	1.9	4.6	35.1	21.4	11.0	465	216
St. Bernard	6.8	7.8	4.4	20.2	4.6	3.5	4.2	83.4	36.4	36.5	551	187
St. Charles	8.6	13.7	47.0	15.7	4.1	3.1	0.0	173.9	32.7	96.4	2 020	1 225
St. Helena	0.8	0.0	0.2	14.0	1.9	0.9	0.4	17.9	8.4	3.1	318	164
St. James	3.8	0.0	17.8	14.2	3.5	1.6	0.6	71.9	19.0	29.6	1 409	861
St. John the Baptist	4.7	0.3	45.7	13.7	5.3	2.3	10.7	68.1	25.7	32.9	783	357
St. Landry	11.2	0.0	2.3	151.3	17.0	9.1	16.8	157.5	75.6	34.6	415	157
St. Martin	5.3	8.5	4.8	47.1	5.1	4.1	3.7	68.9	38.7	18.9	403	216
St. Mary	9.9	17.7	1.8	38.0	9.1	5.4	15.1	153.2	50.1	53.7	943	327
St. Tammany	35.9	12.4	7.8	38.8	11.8	8.7	9.1	416.9	119.6	143.6	778	331
Tangipahoa	17.4	0.2	12.9	107.2	14.5	11.5	7.0	248.2	84.9	54.5	572	142
Tensas	0.9	0.0	0.3	15.1	2.2	1.0	3.0	11.2	7.2	3.1	457	213
Terrebonne	22.6	0.2	3.9	50.2	9.2	9.1	12.1	290.7	90.4	77.6	752	267
Union	5.1	0.0	0.8	23.2	2.3	1.3	1.7	29.9	17.1	8.4	385	156
Vermilion	8.0	5.3	2.6	35.9	5.7	3.5	6.9	130.0	40.1	33.5	649	325
Vernon	354.1	134.3	1.7	25.7	4.6	7.2	1.4	72.8	49.8	19.4	375	120
Washington	6.9	3.0	1.3	56.1	6.1	3.6	6.8	78.9	38.5	23.9	555	204
Webster	6.0	0.2	1.7	42.0	6.5	2.9	8.0	66.7	33.6	25.0	586	193
West Baton Rouge	3.1	46.0	0.9	13.5	2.2	1.1	0.3	58.0	15.9	26.2	1 278	584
West Carroll	2.4	0.0	0.4	20.4	1.9	0.9	2.5	16.4	11.2	4.3	356	134
West Feliciana	1.1	2.7	0.3	7.7	1.5	0.8	0.2	55.9	10.0	9.7	729	227
Winn	3.4	0.0	1.0	17.5	2.4	1.4	1.3	23.5	14.5	7.1	397	132
MAINE	807.6	503.4	170.9	1 073.5	261.7	149.9	419.6	X	X	X	X	X
Androscoggin	22.1	1.9	4.5	88.1	14.7	7.3	14.5	207.6	72.2	111.1	1 099	1 053
Aroostook	36.5	1.4	27.6	109.7	14.9	4.5	18.4	183.2	73.3	72.3	938	897
Cumberland	241.5	110.2	34.8	162.0	25.1	10.5	29.7	611.2	131.2	364.6	1 450	1 414
Franklin	5.0	0.0	31.7	19.0	5.6	1.5	4.9	72.9	18.2	40.9	1 410	1 391
Hancock	25.7	2.8	12.6	79.0	6.6	2.2	9.1	107.2	25.4	70.1	1 412	1 352
Kennebec	83.2	1.1	8.7	153.4	111.2	58.6	199.1	223.1	80.4	122.5	1 057	1 024
Knox	8.4	0.6	2.8	39.7	4.6	1.5	6.5	75.8	11.3	57.5	1 530	1 473
Lincoln	6.7	1.4	2.7	20.8	4.0	1.1	4.4	80.6	17.9	57.5	1 820	1 754
Oxford	9.6	1.1	2.7	41.7	8.8	2.2	5.4	129.2	39.1	79.8	1 483	1 435
Penobscot	93.5	23.4	15.2	122.5	18.4	13.8	58.4	315.8	121.4	137.6	960	908
Piscataquis	3.4	0.0	0.9	16.7	2.6	0.8	2.7	51.9	15.4	18.9	1 031	993
Sagadahoc	27.7	237.5	1.3	12.9	4.1	1.0	3.9	72.6	22.1	44.5	1 247	1 229
Somerset	10.1	1.4	2.3	51.5	7.7	2.8	10.6	119.7	42.8	65.3	1 251	1 212
Waldo	6.6	51.5	1.7	31.1	4.9	1.2	11.3	69.3	22.8	41.3	1 147	1 089
Washington	15.0	8.6	14.3	54.2	8.4	4.6	8.5	73.8	29.5	38.2	1 061	1 009
York	212.7	60.6	7.2	71.2	16.1	4.0	11.1	349.5	103.1	213.3	1 229	1 172
MARYLAND	8 921.4	4 909.1	5 827.2	3 975.0	827.0	492.9	2 291.6	X	X	X	X	X
Allegany	31.8	2.6	8.8	71.5	8.2	5.2	23.5	167.3	79.9	51.3	710	456
Anne Arundel	810.7	625.2	229.4	169.3	95.8	16.3	97.8	1 002.6	225.8	574.2	1 222	680
Baltimore	899.6	264.4	269.9	221.5	28.8	18.3	93.2	1 526.6	394.0	870.0	1 207	661
Calvert	6.6	2.2	4.3	22.9	2.8	1.8	5.7	163.0	49.0	88.1	1 269	880
Caroline	4.5	0.0	3.6	27.6	2.4	1.3	1.3	55.0	26.7	20.9	707	449
Carroll	18.2	33.3	10.1	37.1	3.2	3.0	3.8	288.7	95.2	152.6	1 038	611
Cecil	66.6	15.4	13.7	25.2	4.6	2.2	6.0	154.3	60.7	71.6	886	577
Charles	135.5	33.7	6.7	40.6	8.4	3.4	6.0	255.0	88.5	112.5	978	604
Dorchester	9.3	9.0	12.6	33.4	4.1	1.4	15.0	65.9	29.7	25.2	842	590
Frederick	194.1	166.5	104.9	58.2	6.5	3.7	24.9	391.4	123.8	193.2	1 055	668
Garrett	5.0	0.9	1.7	23.4	4.0	1.6	3.7	68.7	33.5	26.9	911	646
Harford	359.2	298.1	29.7	51.3	8.7	4.7	8.6	400.7	134.3	206.7	972	600
Howard	48.3	180.5	111.5	25.4	5.0	4.3	44.4	525.1	103.9	328.3	1 435	800
Kent	4.5	10.9	3.8	12.5	1.3	0.5	2.8	36.5	12.8	19.6	1 029	707
Montgomery	3 101.5	1 134.4	2 807.2	496.3	55.7	35.2	270.2	2 584.5	596.7	1 501.9	1 817	987
Prince George's	1 868.1	585.5	1 634.2	296.5	59.1	43.5	970.8	1 927.6	657.4	842.0	1 093	605
Queen Anne's	4.9	9.8	3.3	12.2	1.8	1.1	7.9	88.3	28.7	44.9	1 149	671
St. Mary's	509.2	841.9	14.0	40.3	4.5	4.4	16.9	163.0	60.2	70.4	822	433
Somerset	4.3	0.1	1.2	31.0	2.4	4.8	10.2	41.8	24.9	11.7	478	310
Talbot	16.4	37.9	8.2	19.2	1.6	1.4	2.4	64.3	11.8	39.0	1 180	627

1. October 1, 2000 to September 30, 2001.   2. State totals may include programs not allocated by county.   3. Based on the resident population estimated as of July 1 of the year shown.

Table B. States and Counties — Local Government Finances, Government Employment, and Elections

STATE County	Local government finances, 1997 (cont'd) Direct general expenditure Total (mil dol)	Per capita[1] (dollars)	Percent of total for — Education	Health and hospitals	Police protection	Public welfare	Highways	Debt outstanding Total (mil dol)	Per capita[1] (dollars)	Government employment, 1999 Federal civilian	Federal military	State and local	Presidential election, 2000[2] Percent of vote cast — Democratic	Republican	All other
	183	184	185	186	187	188	189	190	191	192	193	194	195	196	197
LOUISIANA—Cont'd															
Pointe Coupee	45.4	1 923	41.9	20.0	9.1	0.2	4.4	72.5	3 066	69	129	1 401	53.7	43.5	2.9
Rapides	250.5	1 981	51.6	0.1	7.9	0.0	4.4	201.5	1 593	2 143	706	11 473	38.5	58.8	2.6
Red River	17.1	1 763	62.5	0.3	6.3	0.2	2.6	0.5	55	37	52	632	48.1	48.7	3.2
Richland	49.4	2 370	41.2	37.6	5.4	0.3	6.2	5.3	252	117	116	1 301	38.7	57.7	3.6
Sabine	32.9	1 383	66.2	0.2	5.5	0.2	8.2	14.0	589	50	132	1 221	32.1	64.9	2.9
St. Bernard	92.5	1 396	48.8	3.2	4.5	0.6	5.1	123.9	1 870	124	361	3 057	40.8	56.8	2.4
St. Charles	160.9	3 374	47.7	12.2	8.4	0.4	2.8	268.6	5 630	165	269	2 886	41.5	55.7	2.8
St. Helena	18.0	1 840	42.3	35.5	3.8	1.8	6.1	3.1	316	11	57	742	58.2	37.4	4.3
St. James	68.4	3 257	43.8	10.8	6.1	2.0	3.8	178.3	8 495	64	117	1 549	60.9	35.6	3.5
St. John the Baptist	67.5	1 606	52.0	0.7	10.3	0.1	4.8	97.4	2 318	97	235	1 915	55.0	41.9	3.1
St. Landry	161.7	1 938	45.4	24.0	4.7	0.2	3.5	60.6	726	217	466	5 355	52.9	45.2	1.9
St. Martin	69.8	1 493	60.2	7.3	9.3	0.4	3.4	46.2	988	64	263	2 266	47.4	47.9	4.6
St. Mary	139.1	2 442	43.4	23.8	5.9	0.4	2.5	75.8	1 331	140	399	3 638	45.2	51.9	2.9
St. Tammany	418.6	2 268	43.8	29.5	6.0	0.2	4.7	293.1	1 588	588	1 069	10 961	27.1	70.7	2.1
Tangipahoa	259.7	2 726	32.0	45.9	5.4	0.2	3.1	137.2	1 441	268	545	10 219	42.6	55.0	2.4
Tensas	10.6	1 568	74.8	2.1	5.3	0.6	1.4	2.7	401	22	36	557	52.5	44.2	3.4
Terrebonne	270.6	2 623	35.3	37.5	4.4	0.7	4.8	128.6	1 246	283	608	6 233	39.3	58.1	2.5
Union	26.8	1 232	56.8	8.1	8.2	0.0	6.9	5.0	230	89	122	1 022	34.3	61.8	3.9
Vermilion	119.7	2 315	38.5	29.1	6.5	0.8	6.4	37.8	731	155	292	3 166	39.1	56.2	4.7
Vernon	80.6	1 555	65.3	0.4	4.6	2.8	8.7	30.1	582	2 640	8 474	2 831	33.7	63.6	2.7
Washington	75.5	1 753	55.4	13.4	6.3	0.5	4.4	10.7	249	106	238	3 362	43.8	53.2	2.9
Webster	71.8	1 686	50.8	0.1	5.3	1.3	5.6	28.9	679	117	236	1 928	42.1	55.1	2.8
West Baton Rouge	57.6	2 815	38.9	0.5	6.7	0.4	5.7	166.4	8 127	69	113	1 449	49.7	48.4	1.9
West Carroll	17.1	1 401	67.1	0.3	5.2	1.5	6.5	1.2	98	42	67	803	28.2	68.9	2.9
West Feliciana	56.0	4 220	25.5	6.9	1.9	0.1	2.8	471.7	35 535	16	76	2 702	45.0	51.7	3.3
Winn	25.9	1 459	67.2	2.0	7.0	0.1	5.1	4.4	249	71	97	928	34.1	63.3	2.6
MAINE	X	X	X	X	X	X	X	X	X	13 159	10 600	81 135	49.1	44.0	6.9
Androscoggin	206.5	2 044	54.0	0.1	3.8	0.4	5.8	144.9	1 434	376	499	4 768	53.3	40.5	6.1
Aroostook	181.3	2 352	52.7	13.0	2.0	0.6	6.7	66.6	864	760	434	4 956	48.9	47.1	4.0
Cumberland	569.7	2 266	44.4	0.4	4.8	3.3	5.1	420.3	1 671	3 112	4 162	17 185	52.0	41.0	6.9
Franklin	72.5	2 500	51.8	1.2	3.4	0.2	7.1	89.3	3 078	89	141	1 793	49.2	41.8	9.0
Hancock	110.4	2 224	52.8	0.4	2.2	0.2	6.6	50.3	1 014	410	675	2 809	45.4	44.6	10.0
Kennebec	218.0	1 881	62.0	0.3	3.6	0.5	6.8	164.3	1 418	1 593	567	14 191	53.0	40.7	6.3
Knox	72.9	1 941	60.2	0.3	3.4	0.3	6.7	30.7	819	123	262	2 339	46.1	43.7	10.1
Lincoln	73.8	2 335	63.3	1.1	2.5	0.6	7.8	17.6	557	100	180	1 561	43.9	48.1	8.0
Oxford	135.4	2 518	72.9	0.5	2.0	0.3	6.7	79.3	1 475	166	265	2 836	49.6	43.0	7.3
Penobscot	299.3	2 089	51.8	3.9	3.8	1.9	5.9	139.2	971	1 413	724	12 266	44.9	48.7	6.5
Piscataquis	52.9	2 889	51.8	29.3	2.1	0.3	5.6	19.7	1 077	58	88	1 079	40.5	52.3	7.2
Sagadahoc	74.6	2 093	69.7	0.5	3.7	0.1	4.4	35.7	1 001	361	481	1 480	48.0	43.7	8.2
Somerset	116.6	2 233	71.6	0.6	3.4	0.4	4.9	74.3	1 422	162	257	2 679	48.2	44.6	7.2
Waldo	64.3	1 786	65.8	0.8	2.9	0.4	7.0	25.3	702	114	180	1 458	44.3	45.4	10.3
Washington	70.3	1 954	58.1	0.4	2.6	0.3	7.5	41.5	1 154	303	308	2 303	42.7	50.7	6.7
York	344.3	1 984	60.8	0.6	5.2	1.4	5.4	201.4	1 161	4 019	1 377	7 432	49.3	44.7	6.0
MARYLAND	X	X	X	X	X	X	X	X	X	152 829	51 289	308 933	56.5	40.3	3.3
Allegany	178.3	2 467	52.9	0.9	3.1	3.4	6.2	99.2	1 372	584	263	5 514	41.3	55.6	3.1
Anne Arundel	1 031.4	2 194	51.7	1.5	6.1	0.7	4.3	1 399.8	2 978	33 323	15 584	24 903	44.7	51.9	3.4
Baltimore	1 505.5	2 089	52.6	2.2	5.7	0.5	3.4	1 367.8	1 898	15 483	2 679	39 151	52.8	43.7	3.4
Calvert	154.5	2 226	60.3	1.7	3.2	0.9	4.5	158.4	2 282	119	319	2 751	43.6	53.7	2.7
Caroline	53.6	1 816	60.4	2.7	4.0	0.1	4.9	23.6	801	83	109	1 240	37.9	59.2	2.8
Carroll	269.6	1 835	67.3	1.1	0.9	0.9	2.3	213.5	1 453	320	569	6 326	31.5	65.2	3.3
Cecil	160.1	1 983	65.5	1.0	3.9	0.5	5.3	96.9	1 199	1 652	310	3 083	42.7	53.7	3.6
Charles	254.9	2 215	65.0	0.8	5.8	0.4	2.1	158.6	1 378	2 404	711	4 942	49.1	48.8	2.1
Dorchester	71.2	2 381	52.4	1.0	4.5	0.4	7.4	28.2	942	131	120	1 503	45.9	51.3	2.7
Frederick	382.9	2 090	58.2	3.2	3.8	2.2	5.5	313.5	1 711	2 815	2 085	8 465	39.1	57.7	3.3
Garrett	66.7	2 259	57.8	0.5	1.5	0.0	21.8	25.4	861	78	108	1 399	27.0	70.5	2.5
Harford	421.3	1 982	60.9	0.7	4.5	2.1	6.1	184.7	869	7 659	3 850	8 534	39.0	57.8	3.2
Howard	548.9	2 399	61.2	1.3	4.4	0.6	3.3	735.2	3 213	715	897	13 459	51.9	44.2	3.9
Kent	36.5	1 913	52.9	1.1	4.4	0.3	7.4	14.2	745	72	71	811	44.9	51.4	3.7
Montgomery	2 544.2	3 077	46.9	3.7	4.1	1.1	4.1	3 287.2	3 976	41 044	7 200	38 056	62.5	33.5	4.0
Prince George's	1 861.8	2 416	46.0	2.2	5.9	0.2	3.3	2 153.3	2 794	25 568	9 235	51 747	79.1	18.7	2.2
Queen Anne's	89.9	2 299	65.7	1.2	2.1	0.1	4.1	42.9	1 098	86	150	1 789	37.3	59.5	3.2
St. Mary's	165.7	1 934	60.7	0.8	4.0	5.1	2.4	86.4	1 008	6 586	3 191	3 948	40.4	57.1	2.5
Somerset	43.7	1 785	53.9	1.0	2.9	0.1	4.6	12.3	501	67	117	2 787	49.8	47.5	2.8
Talbot	59.8	1 808	55.1	1.9	5.4	0.2	5.3	15.1	456	559	125	1 363	38.4	58.3	3.3

1. Based on the resident population estimated as of July 1 of the year shown.　2. Data subject to copyright.

Table B. States and Counties — Land Area and Population

STATE/County code	MSA/PMSA/NECMA code[1]	County Type[2]	STATE County	Land area,[3] (sq km) 2000	Total persons	Rank	Per square kilometer	White	Black	Am. Indian, Alaska Native	Asian and Pacific Islander	Percent Hispanic[4]	Under 5 years	5 to 17 years	18 to 24 years	25 to 34 years	35 to 44 years	45 to 54 years
				1	2	3	4	5	6	7	8	9	10	11	12	13	14	15
			MARYLAND—Cont'd															
24 043	3180	3	Washington	1 187	131 923	404	111.1	90.7	8.2	0.5	1.1	1.2	6.1	17.3	8.1	14.4	16.9	13.8
24 045	...	5	Wicomico	977	84 644	615	86.6	73.6	24.0	0.5	2.1	2.2	6.3	18.5	11.8	12.2	15.8	13.7
24 047	...	7	Worcester	1 226	46 543	970	38.0	82.0	17.1	0.5	0.9	1.3	4.9	15.7	6.2	11.1	15.3	13.9
24 510	0720	0	Baltimore city	209	651 154	82	3 115.6	32.6	65.2	0.8	1.9	1.7	6.4	18.4	10.9	14.3	15.6	12.8
25 000	...	X	**MASSACHUSETTS**	20 306	6 349 097	X	312.7	86.2	6.3	0.6	4.3	6.8	6.3	17.4	9.1	14.6	16.7	13.8
25 001	0743	3	Barnstable	1 024	222 230	256	217.0	95.6	2.4	1.0	0.9	1.3	4.8	15.7	5.2	9.7	15.3	14.8
25 003	6323	3	Berkshire	2 412	134 953	399	56.0	96.1	2.5	0.5	1.4	1.7	5.2	17.2	8.4	10.9	15.4	14.9
25 005	1123	2	Bristol	1 440	534 678	104	371.3	92.8	2.8	0.6	1.7	3.6	6.4	18.2	8.5	14.0	16.5	13.5
25 007	...	9	Dukes	269	14 987	2 091	55.7	93.5	3.3	2.7	0.9	1.0	5.5	17.2	5.5	11.6	18.0	18.6
25 009	1123	0	Essex	1 297	723 419	69	557.8	88.1	3.4	0.5	2.8	11.0	6.7	18.5	7.5	13.1	17.3	14.4
25 011	...	4	Franklin	1 818	71 535	691	39.3	96.8	1.4	1.0	1.5	2.0	5.2	18.3	7.8	11.8	16.7	16.9
25 013	8003	2	Hampden	1 602	456 228	127	284.8	80.8	9.0	0.7	1.8	15.2	6.5	19.5	9.2	12.6	15.7	13.4
25 015	8003	2	Hampshire	1 370	152 251	352	111.1	92.6	2.6	0.7	4.0	3.4	4.6	15.0	19.3	11.8	15.0	14.6
25 017	1123	0	Middlesex	2 133	1 465 396	19	687.0	87.6	4.0	0.4	7.0	4.6	6.3	16.2	9.0	16.1	17.3	13.8
25 019	...	7	Nantucket	124	9 520	2 488	76.8	88.9	9.0	0.3	1.0	2.2	5.5	13.7	7.4	19.6	20.9	14.1
25 021	1123	0	Norfolk	1 035	650 308	83	628.3	90.1	3.6	0.4	6.0	1.8	6.4	17.0	7.0	14.1	17.5	14.5
25 023	1123	1	Plymouth	1 712	472 822	121	276.2	90.1	6.0	0.6	1.3	2.4	7.0	19.8	7.2	12.9	17.5	14.7
25 025	1123	2	Suffolk	152	689 807	74	4 538.2	60.2	24.4	0.9	7.9	15.5	5.6	14.6	15.1	20.6	14.9	11.0
25 027	1123	2	Worcester	3 919	750 963	65	191.6	91.1	3.2	0.6	3.1	6.8	6.7	19.0	8.4	13.7	17.4	13.7
26 000	...	X	**MICHIGAN**	147 121	9 938 444	X	67.6	81.8	14.8	1.3	2.2	3.3	6.8	19.4	9.4	13.7	16.1	13.8
26 001	...	9	Alcona	1 747	11 719	2 317	6.7	98.9	0.2	1.3	0.3	0.7	4.3	14.7	4.6	7.9	13.0	14.1
26 003	...	7	Alger	2 377	9 862	2 460	4.1	89.8	6.2	5.1	0.4	1.0	4.6	16.0	7.3	12.4	16.3	15.3
26 005	3000	7	Allegan	2 143	105 665	503	49.3	94.7	1.6	1.1	0.8	5.7	7.2	21.6	8.0	12.9	17.2	13.6
26 007	...	7	Alpena	1 487	31 314	1 366	21.1	98.9	0.4	0.8	0.5	0.6	5.5	18.2	7.8	10.2	16.3	14.0
26 009	...	9	Antrim	1 235	23 110	1 637	18.7	98.2	0.4	1.7	0.4	1.2	5.7	18.6	6.3	10.3	15.0	13.7
26 011	...	8	Arenac	950	17 269	1 934	18.2	96.6	0.2	1.8	0.5	1.4	5.3	18.0	7.8	10.9	15.9	13.6
26 013	...	9	Baraga	2 341	8 746	2 550	3.7	82.1	5.4	15.1	0.5	0.9	5.6	17.4	7.3	13.7	14.7	14.5
26 015	...	6	Barry	1 440	56 755	834	39.4	98.5	0.4	1.1	0.4	1.5	6.6	20.5	7.5	12.2	16.8	14.6
26 017	6960	2	Bay	1 151	110 157	492	95.7	96.4	1.7	1.2	0.6	3.9	6.1	18.4	8.3	12.3	15.3	14.6
26 019	...	9	Benzie	832	15 998	2 024	19.2	97.6	0.4	2.4	0.2	1.5	5.9	17.5	6.2	11.3	15.7	14.2
26 021	0870	3	Berrien	1 479	162 453	330	109.8	81.0	16.7	1.0	1.5	3.0	6.5	19.5	8.3	12.1	15.4	14.1
26 023	...	6	Branch	1 314	45 787	987	34.8	94.9	2.9	1.2	0.6	3.0	6.3	19.2	8.4	13.3	16.5	13.6
26 025	3720	2	Calhoun	1 836	137 985	394	75.2	85.8	11.9	1.5	1.4	3.2	6.5	19.5	8.9	13.0	15.3	14.0
26 027	...	6	Cass	1 275	51 104	905	40.1	91.1	7.0	1.9	0.7	2.4	6.1	19.5	7.4	11.6	16.0	15.2
26 029	...	7	Charlevoix	1 080	26 090	1 512	24.2	97.5	0.4	2.4	0.4	1.0	6.5	19.4	6.5	11.5	16.0	14.2
26 031	...	7	Cheboygan	1 853	26 448	1 504	14.3	96.7	0.4	4.2	0.5	0.8	5.9	17.8	6.2	11.2	14.6	13.8
26 033	...	7	Chippewa	4 043	38 543	1 149	9.5	79.8	6.2	16.9	0.9	1.6	5.4	15.9	11.9	14.6	17.1	13.4
26 035	...	7	Clare	1 468	31 252	1 368	21.3	98.4	0.4	1.4	0.3	1.1	5.8	18.6	7.1	10.9	14.0	13.4
26 037	4040	2	Clinton	1 480	64 753	750	43.8	97.5	0.9	1.0	0.8	2.6	6.9	21.2	7.3	11.9	17.3	15.1
26 039	...	9	Crawford	1 446	14 273	2 143	9.9	97.4	1.7	1.3	0.4	1.0	5.4	19.1	6.3	10.8	15.9	13.9
26 041	...	7	Delta	3 030	38 520	1 150	12.7	97.2	0.2	3.4	0.4	0.5	5.5	18.4	7.9	10.4	15.6	15.1
26 043	...	7	Dickinson	1 985	27 472	1 468	13.8	98.2	0.2	0.9	0.7	0.7	5.5	19.6	6.3	10.8	14.6	14.3
26 045	4040	2	Eaton	1 493	103 655	513	69.4	91.8	5.8	1.1	1.4	3.2	6.4	19.8	9.1	12.6	16.2	15.4
26 047	...	7	Emmet	1 212	31 437	1 361	25.9	95.7	0.6	4.1	0.8	0.9	6.2	19.2	7.1	11.9	16.2	15.7
26 049	2640	2	Genesee	1 657	436 141	137	263.2	77.1	21.3	1.6	1.2	2.3	7.3	20.2	8.9	13.6	16.0	13.7
26 051	...	6	Gladwin	1 313	26 023	1 516	19.8	98.7	0.3	1.2	0.3	1.0	5.5	17.7	6.5	10.4	13.7	13.6
26 053	...	7	Gogebic	2 854	17 370	1 931	6.1	95.4	1.9	3.0	0.4	0.9	4.6	15.9	8.3	10.5	14.0	13.4
26 055	...	7	Grand Traverse	1 205	77 654	653	64.4	97.5	0.6	1.5	0.8	1.5	6.1	19.3	7.9	12.5	17.2	15.1
26 057	...	6	Gratiot	1 477	42 285	1 050	28.6	93.4	4.1	1.2	0.5	4.4	5.9	17.9	11.6	13.7	15.7	12.8
26 059	...	6	Hillsdale	1 551	46 527	971	30.0	98.5	0.5	0.9	0.5	1.2	6.5	19.9	10.0	11.5	15.3	13.6
26 061	...	7	Houghton	2 620	36 016	1 217	13.7	96.4	1.1	1.1	2.1	0.7	5.4	16.4	19.1	10.1	12.5	12.0
26 063	...	7	Huron	2 167	36 079	1 212	16.6	98.8	0.4	0.7	0.5	1.6	5.5	18.7	6.5	10.4	14.7	13.8
26 065	4040	2	Ingham	1 448	279 320	202	192.9	82.0	12.0	1.4	4.3	5.8	6.3	17.1	18.5	14.4	14.2	12.9
26 067	...	6	Ionia	1 485	61 518	791	41.4	93.2	5.0	1.4	0.7	2.8	6.9	20.0	11.5	14.7	16.3	12.8
26 069	...	7	Iosco	1 422	27 339	1 471	19.2	98.1	0.6	1.4	0.8	1.0	4.7	17.7	5.4	9.0	14.4	13.5
26 071	...	9	Iron	3 021	13 138	2 218	4.3	97.4	1.2	1.9	0.3	0.6	4.3	16.3	6.0	8.6	14.3	14.2
26 073	...	4	Isabella	1 487	63 351	765	42.6	93.0	2.4	3.6	1.7	2.2	5.2	15.1	29.4	11.5	12.2	10.7
26 075	3520	3	Jackson	1 830	158 422	335	86.6	90.1	8.7	1.1	0.8	2.2	6.6	19.1	8.1	13.6	16.8	14.2
26 077	3720	2	Kalamazoo	1 455	238 603	242	164.0	86.5	10.8	1.2	2.3	2.6	6.5	17.6	15.2	13.5	14.7	13.2
26 079	...	9	Kalkaska	1 453	16 571	1 986	11.4	98.6	0.4	1.5	0.5	0.9	6.4	19.1	7.6	12.1	16.5	13.6
26 081	3000	2	Kent	2 217	574 335	93	259.1	85.0	9.8	1.1	2.3	7.0	7.8	20.5	10.5	14.9	16.2	12.7
26 083	...	9	Keweenaw	1 401	2 301	3 038	1.6	95.9	3.7	0.8	0.3	0.8	4.5	18.0	6.4	8.1	13.3	16.1
26 085	...	9	Lake	1 470	11 333	2 347	7.7	86.8	12.3	2.3	0.4	1.7	5.2	16.7	8.0	9.2	13.5	13.5
26 087	2160	1	Lapeer	1 694	87 904	595	51.9	97.3	1.0	1.0	0.6	3.1	6.7	21.3	7.7	12.8	18.2	14.7

1. MSA = Metropolitan Statistical Area. PMSA = Primary MSA. NECMA = New England County Metropolitan Area. See Appendix A for explanation of these concepts. See Appendix B for list of metropolitan areas identified by type, with component counties.   2. County typology code from the Economic Research Service of USDA. See Appendix A for definition.   3. Dry land or land partially or temporarily covered by water.   4. Hispanic persons may be of any race.

Table B. States and Counties — **Population and Households**

STATE County	55 to 64 years	65 to 74 years	75 years and over	Percent female	2001	1990	1990–2000	2000–2001	Births	Deaths	Net migration	Number	Percent change, 1990–2000	Persons per house-hold	Female family house-holder[1]	One person
	16	17	18	19	20	21	22	23	24	25	26	27	28	29	30	31
MARYLAND—Cont'd																
Washington	9.2	7.4	6.7	48.9	133 197	121 393	8.7	1.0	2 074	1 613	863	49 726	11.1	2.46	10.7	26.0
Wicomico	8.9	7.0	5.8	52.3	85 426	74 339	13.9	0.9	1 436	990	368	32 218	16.0	2.53	14.1	24.8
Worcester	12.9	11.9	8.2	51.2	48 084	35 028	32.9	3.3	653	690	1 555	19 694	39.3	2.33	10.8	26.3
Baltimore city	8.4	6.9	6.3	53.4	635 210	736 014	-11.5	-2.4	13 172	11 119	-18 345	257 996	-6.7	2.42	25.0	34.9
MASSACHUSETTS	8.6	6.7	6.8	51.8	6 379 304	6 016 425	5.5	0.5	101 062	70 785	1 279	2 443 580	8.7	2.51	11.9	28.0
Barnstable	11.5	11.9	11.2	52.7	226 809	186 605	19.1	2.1	2 621	3 458	5 374	94 822	22.2	2.28	9.4	29.5
Berkshire	10.0	8.6	9.4	52.2	134 137	139 352	-3.2	-0.6	1 702	2 068	-391	56 006	3.1	2.30	11.0	31.6
Bristol	8.7	6.9	7.3	52.0	540 360	506 325	5.6	1.1	8 473	6 342	3 745	205 411	9.5	2.54	13.0	26.5
Dukes	9.2	7.6	6.8	51.1	15 402	11 639	28.8	2.8	226	182	367	6 421	28.3	2.30	9.8	32.0
Essex	8.7	6.8	7.0	52.1	730 296	670 080	8.0	1.0	12 034	8 125	3 327	275 419	9.6	2.57	12.4	27.1
Franklin	9.0	6.7	7.5	51.6	71 610	70 086	2.1	0.1	957	854	5	29 466	6.6	2.38	10.6	29.0
Hampden	8.5	7.0	7.5	52.1	455 862	456 310	0.0	-0.1	7 028	5 975	-1 241	175 288	3.2	2.52	15.9	28.4
Hampshire	7.6	5.7	6.3	53.4	152 876	146 568	3.9	0.4	1 693	1 474	465	55 991	11.9	2.39	9.8	28.6
Middlesex	8.6	6.5	6.2	51.6	1 463 454	1 398 468	4.8	-0.1	24 144	14 508	-11 405	561 220	8.0	2.52	9.9	27.1
Nantucket	8.3	5.7	4.8	48.7	9 938	6 012	58.3	4.4	156	101	355	3 699	42.4	2.37	8.0	29.8
Norfolk	9.1	7.2	7.2	52.2	653 232	616 087	5.6	0.4	10 719	7 381	-125	248 827	9.2	2.54	9.5	26.8
Plymouth	9.2	6.0	5.8	51.3	481 059	435 276	8.6	1.7	8 339	4 867	4 876	168 361	12.6	2.74	11.9	22.2
Suffolk	7.2	5.6	5.5	51.8	682 062	663 906	3.9	-1.1	10 564	6 932	-11 648	278 722	5.6	2.34	16.3	36.3
Worcester	8.1	6.3	6.8	51.1	762 207	709 711	5.8	1.5	12 406	8 518	7 575	283 927	9.1	2.56	11.4	26.2
MICHIGAN	8.7	6.5	5.8	51.0	9 990 817	9 295 287	6.9	0.5	169 278	109 292	-6 207	3 785 661	10.7	2.56	12.5	26.2
Alcona	16.9	14.0	10.4	49.4	11 651	10 145	15.5	-0.6	109	237	59	5 132	20.4	2.24	5.8	26.6
Alger	11.0	8.9	8.2	46.2	9 884	8 972	9.9	0.2	125	136	34	3 785	13.4	2.35	7.6	26.8
Allegan	8.4	5.8	5.3	50.1	108 225	90 509	16.7	2.4	1 797	1 062	1 821	38 165	20.4	2.72	9.1	20.7
Alpena	10.9	9.0	8.1	51.4	31 263	30 605	2.3	-0.2	402	422	-15	12 818	8.3	2.40	9.0	27.8
Antrim	12.8	10.2	7.3	50.0	23 610	18 185	27.1	2.2	316	323	495	9 222	32.1	2.47	7.9	23.4
Arenac	12.0	9.6	7.0	48.7	17 310	14 906	15.9	0.2	221	246	66	6 710	18.9	2.45	9.0	25.5
Baraga	10.7	7.1	9.2	47.4	8 735	7 954	10.0	-0.1	127	149	12	3 353	9.4	2.37	10.1	29.5
Barry	9.9	6.7	5.1	50.1	57 661	50 057	13.4	1.6	924	582	563	21 035	18.4	2.68	7.7	19.5
Bay	9.8	7.3	7.4	51.4	109 659	111 723	-1.4	-0.5	1 600	1 342	-720	43 930	4.1	2.47	10.9	27.2
Benzie	11.6	9.9	7.6	50.5	16 489	12 200	31.1	3.1	215	205	473	6 500	36.2	2.42	7.7	24.1
Berrien	9.6	7.5	6.9	51.5	161 820	161 378	0.7	-0.4	2 802	2 099	-1 293	63 569	4.2	2.49	13.2	27.1
Branch	9.5	7.0	6.1	49.4	45 726	41 502	10.3	-0.1	646	500	-193	16 349	9.6	2.61	9.9	24.2
Calhoun	9.2	7.2	6.5	51.4	138 031	135 982	1.5	0.0	2 348	1 770	-477	54 100	4.4	2.47	13.0	27.8
Cass	10.7	7.7	5.9	50.0	51 321	49 477	3.3	0.4	654	614	188	19 676	7.9	2.56	9.9	22.6
Charlevoix	11.1	8.2	6.8	50.5	26 458	21 468	21.5	1.4	401	303	270	10 400	26.2	2.48	8.1	25.2
Cheboygan	12.5	10.0	8.0	50.4	26 960	21 398	23.6	1.9	362	384	529	10 835	32.1	2.41	8.6	25.8
Chippewa	8.9	7.0	5.7	44.3	38 413	34 604	11.4	-0.3	512	412	-215	13 474	16.7	2.42	10.7	27.5
Clare	12.9	10.2	7.0	50.7	31 398	24 952	25.2	0.5	433	492	200	12 686	30.8	2.42	9.4	26.2
Clinton	9.5	6.0	4.9	50.3	65 883	57 893	11.8	1.7	968	566	736	23 653	17.0	2.70	8.4	19.8
Crawford	12.0	9.9	6.7	49.0	14 626	12 260	16.4	2.5	184	184	348	5 625	26.7	2.45	9.7	24.0
Delta	10.3	8.8	8.2	50.9	38 477	37 780	1.7	-0.1	513	503	-34	15 836	9.0	2.40	8.3	28.0
Dickinson	9.0	8.5	9.6	50.8	27 284	26 831	2.4	-0.7	333	393	-119	11 386	7.1	2.37	8.4	29.4
Eaton	9.2	6.0	5.3	51.4	104 837	92 879	11.6	1.1	1 454	1 019	774	40 167	18.0	2.54	10.3	24.5
Emmet	9.5	7.5	6.8	50.8	32 217	25 040	25.5	2.5	479	360	656	12 577	32.2	2.44	8.5	26.9
Genesee	8.7	6.6	5.0	51.9	439 117	430 459	1.3	0.7	8 113	4 796	-140	169 825	5.3	2.54	16.3	26.6
Gladwin	14.2	11.1	7.2	50.4	26 507	21 896	18.8	1.9	353	376	501	10 561	26.4	2.43	8.0	24.0
Gogebic	10.8	10.1	12.5	49.7	17 670	18 052	-3.8	1.7	178	339	449	7 425	-0.3	2.20	9.3	34.2
Grand Traverse	8.8	6.6	6.4	51.2	80 203	64 273	20.8	3.3	1 111	699	2 105	30 396	26.8	2.49	9.2	25.0
Gratiot	8.8	6.5	7.1	48.0	42 272	38 982	8.5	0.0	634	558	-80	14 501	6.2	2.57	10.2	23.7
Hillsdale	9.9	7.3	6.0	50.2	46 879	43 431	7.1	0.8	753	550	169	17 335	10.9	2.60	8.4	22.9
Houghton	8.9	7.0	8.5	46.8	35 698	35 446	1.6	-0.9	480	562	-222	13 793	4.7	2.39	8.0	32.6
Huron	11.0	9.9	9.6	50.5	35 688	34 951	3.2	-1.1	481	572	-287	14 597	10.0	2.42	7.4	27.3
Ingham	7.1	4.9	4.5	51.7	278 398	281 912	-0.9	-0.3	4 743	2 411	-3 260	108 593	5.8	2.42	12.1	30.2
Ionia	7.7	5.4	4.7	46.5	62 111	57 024	7.9	1.0	1 049	528	100	20 606	11.7	2.70	10.1	21.9
Iosco	13.8	12.4	9.1	51.0	27 162	30 209	-9.5	-0.6	327	422	-68	11 727	1.2	2.30	8.4	28.6
Iron	11.2	11.5	13.7	50.6	12 915	13 175	-0.3	-1.7	126	314	-30	5 748	1.6	2.19	8.4	33.7
Isabella	6.7	4.9	4.2	52.2	63 725	54 624	16.0	0.6	862	503	39	22 425	27.5	2.55	8.9	23.8
Jackson	8.8	6.6	6.2	49.0	159 665	149 756	5.8	0.8	2 530	1 772	546	58 168	8.4	2.55	12.0	24.6
Kalamazoo	7.9	5.8	5.5	51.6	238 544	223 411	6.8	0.0	3 991	2 324	-1 667	93 479	11.7	2.43	11.0	28.0
Kalkaska	10.9	8.1	5.6	49.7	16 827	13 497	22.8	1.5	263	179	169	6 428	30.3	2.55	9.0	22.3
Kent	7.1	5.3	5.1	50.8	580 331	500 631	14.7	1.0	11 626	5 112	-332	212 890	17.1	2.64	11.6	25.6
Keweenaw	13.3	11.6	8.7	46.2	2 257	1 701	35.3	-1.9	28	32	-41	998	28.4	2.13	5.7	35.8
Lake	14.1	12.0	7.7	47.8	11 630	8 583	32.0	2.6	150	186	323	4 704	33.0	2.28	8.7	29.6
Lapeer	9.2	5.5	4.1	49.4	89 728	74 768	17.6	2.1	1 364	761	1 223	30 729	24.6	2.80	8.1	18.5

1. No spouse present.

STATE County	Births, average 1997–1999 Total	Rate[1]	Deaths, average 1997–1999 Number Total	Infant[2]	Rate Total[1]	Infant[3]	Physicians,[4] 2000 Number	Rate[5]	Hospitals,[4] 1998 Number	Beds Number	Rate[5]	Medicare enrollees 2000	Serious crimes known to police, 2000[6] Total Number	Rate[7]
	32	33	34	35	36	37	38	39	40	41	42	43	44	45
MARYLAND—Cont'd														
Washington	1 528	12.0	1 239	8	9.7	5.2	254	193	1	320	251	20 200	3 600	2 729
Wicomico	1 039	13.1	775	NA	9.8	NA	218	258	1	400	504	11 805	4 455	5 263
Worcester	505	11.8	524	NA	12.2	NA	52	112	1	32	75	9 877	2 718	5 840
Baltimore city	9 579	14.8	8 875	135	13.7	14.1	4 044	621	12	4 945	766	102 463	67 859	10 421
MASSACHUSETTS	80 404	13.1	55 254	418	9.0	5.2	20 757	327	90	20 369	331	960 722	192 131	3 026
Barnstable	2 108	10.1	2 633	10	12.6	4.9	453	204	2	385	185	56 128	6 654	2 994
Berkshire	1 330	10.0	1 570	5	11.8	4.0	327	242	4	595	447	26 641	2 951	2 439
Bristol	6 566	12.7	4 859	38	9.4	5.8	704	132	5	1 232	238	87 777	16 753	3 133
Dukes	159	11.5	137	NA	9.9	NA	33	220	1	80	576	2 452	NA	NA
Essex	9 613	13.8	6 385	53	9.1	5.5	1 314	182	9	2 044	292	111 128	21 098	2 983
Franklin	761	10.8	673	NA	9.5	NA	106	148	1	128	181	11 445	1 912	2 773
Hampden	5 937	13.5	4 646	38	10.6	6.4	1 120	245	7	1 746	397	75 774	23 221	5 172
Hampshire	1 382	9.2	1 147	4	7.7	3.1	333	219	2	227	152	20 273	3 057	2 044
Middlesex	18 481	13.0	11 419	77	8.0	4.2	4 526	309	21	4 066	286	205 755	30 876	2 111
Nantucket	114	14.5	76	NA	9.7	NA	12	126	1	39	497	1 076	605	6 355
Norfolk	7 982	12.4	5 713	31	8.9	3.9	2 413	371	6	1 317	205	98 311	10 873	1 686
Plymouth	6 346	13.6	3 825	34	8.2	5.4	645	136	4	741	158	64 221	11 359	2 692
Suffolk	9 696	15.1	5 517	62	8.6	6.4	6 743	978	15	5 521	860	87 588	40 988	5 942
Worcester	9 929	13.6	6 654	57	9.1	5.7	2 028	270	12	2 248	307	111 988	21 269	2 927
MICHIGAN	132 550	13.5	85 231	1 089	8.7	8.2	21 114	212	167	31 719	323	1 403 325	408 456	4 110
Alcona	94	8.5	173	NA	15.7	NA	6	51	0	0	0	3 063	202	1 724
Alger	93	9.4	102	NA	10.2	NA	8	81	1	40	405	2 019	180	1 825
Allegan	1 434	14.1	820	11	8.1	7.7	121	115	2	106	104	11 624	2 060	1 961
Alpena	347	11.4	335	NA	11.0	NA	59	188	1	169	556	6 611	781	2 494
Antrim	243	11.3	245	NA	11.4	NA	16	69	0	0	0	4 207	282	1 220
Arenac	181	11.0	187	NA	11.4	NA	16	93	1	81	494	3 715	370	2 143
Baraga	99	11.7	123	NA	14.4	NA	8	91	1	61	725	1 641	66	994
Barry	677	12.4	449	7	8.2	10.3	41	72	1	91	167	6 579	1 124	2 128
Bay	1 348	12.3	1 054	7	9.6	5.4	143	130	1	341	310	18 056	3 657	3 320
Benzie	182	12.3	154	NA	10.4	NA	16	100	1	48	327	3 044	319	1 994
Berrien	2 123	13.2	1 596	22	10.0	10.2	268	165	4	733	457	28 205	6 207	3 835
Branch	541	12.4	409	NA	9.4	NA	42	92	1	130	298	6 672	1 195	2 711
Calhoun	1 859	13.2	1 464	15	10.4	7.9	211	153	4	527	374	22 429	8 495	6 156
Cass	576	11.6	467	NA	9.4	NA	14	27	1	57	115	6 823	1 403	2 745
Charlevoix	327	13.3	226	NA	9.2	NA	38	146	1	40	164	4 445	334	1 280
Cheboygan	286	12.0	293	NA	12.3	NA	38	144	1	129	543	4 777	545	2 061
Chippewa	404	10.7	307	NA	8.1	NA	37	96	1	137	361	5 709	730	1 894
Clare	368	12.5	379	NA	12.8	NA	30	96	1	64	216	6 817	788	2 521
Clinton	797	12.6	428	NA	6.8	NA	31	48	1	48	76	6 157	851	1 487
Crawford	155	11.0	144	NA	10.2	NA	26	182	1	130	919	2 324	342	2 396
Delta	411	10.6	405	NA	10.4	NA	56	145	1	66	169	7 665	NA	NA
Dickinson	301	11.1	324	NA	12.0	NA	66	240	2	126	465	5 427	602	2 191
Eaton	1 185	11.7	743	NA	7.4	NA	72	69	2	81	80	10 081	2 587	2 573
Emmet	362	12.6	263	NA	9.2	NA	131	417	1	249	868	5 126	727	2 313
Genesee	6 201	14.2	3 812	79	8.7	12.8	853	196	5	1 779	408	62 226	24 063	5 603
Gladwin	274	10.8	290	NA	11.5	NA	13	50	1	42	166	5 587	535	2 056
Gogebic	165	9.6	269	NA	15.6	NA	25	144	1	53	310	4 684	399	2 445
Grand Traverse	917	12.4	601	NA	8.1	NA	279	359	1	328	442	12 904	2 384	3 070
Gratiot	507	12.7	438	NA	10.9	NA	57	135	1	100	249	6 544	860	2 195
Hillsdale	585	12.5	435	NA	9.3	NA	47	101	1	68	146	6 960	1 103	2 611
Houghton	373	10.5	421	NA	11.8	NA	43	119	2	122	342	6 204	555	1 541
Huron	402	11.4	436	NA	12.4	NA	50	139	3	207	586	7 833	650	1 979
Ingham	3 864	13.5	1 839	25	6.4	6.6	900	322	4	1 503	527	36 476	12 795	4 581
Ionia	807	12.8	423	NA	6.7	NA	38	62	1	77	125	7 094	1 391	2 261
Iosco	307	12.1	342	NA	13.6	NA	25	91	1	69	275	6 811	718	2 626
Iron	112	8.7	228	NA	17.7	NA	13	99	2	71	551	3 696	255	1 941
Isabella	663	11.4	374	NA	6.4	NA	67	106	1	118	203	6 298	1 765	2 786
Jackson	2 039	13.0	1 405	22	9.0	11.0	220	139	2	507	325	23 820	6 426	4 243
Kalamazoo	3 074	13.4	1 805	24	7.9	7.9	758	318	2	817	356	31 061	11 728	5 015
Kalkaska	198	12.7	141	NA	9.0	NA	6	36	1	81	520	2 246	510	3 078
Kent	8 987	16.5	3 996	65	7.3	7.3	1 318	229	4	1 405	258	68 716	24 655	4 293
Keweenaw	22	10.7	30	NA	14.2	NA	4	174	0	0	0	505	65	2 825
Lake	118	11.3	141	NA	13.5	NA	3	26	0	0	0	2 478	613	5 409
Lapeer	1 092	12.4	587	10	6.7	8.9	81	92	1	182	206	8 995	1 243	1 553

1. Per 1,000 estimated resident population, average 1997–1999.   2. Deaths of infants under 1 year old.   3. Deaths of infants under 1 year old per 1,000 live births.   4. Data subject to copyright.   5. Per 100,000 resident population as of July 1 of the year shown.   6. Data for serious crimes have not been adjusted for underreporting; this may affect comparability between geographic areas and over time.   7. Per 100,000 population estimated by the FBI.

Table B. States and Counties — Crime, Education, Money Income, and Poverty

	Serious crimes known to police, 2000[1] (cont'd) Rate[2]		Education						Money income 1989				Income and poverty, 1998 Percent below poverty level			
			School enrollment and attainment, 1990				Local government expenditures, fiscal 1999[5]			Households						
			Enrollment[3]		Attainment[4] (percent)					Median						
STATE County	Violent	Property	Total	Percent private	High school graduate or more	Bachelor's degree or more	Total current expenditures (mil dol)	Current expenditures per student (dollars)	Per capita[6] (dollars)	Dollars	Percent change, 1979–1989 (constant 1989 dollars)	Percent with $100,000 or more	Median household income	All persons	Persons under 18	Persons 5–17 in families
	46	47	48	49	50	51	52	53	54	55	56	57	58	59	60	61

STATE County	46	47	48	49	50	51	52	53	54	55	56	57	58	59	60	61
MARYLAND—Cont'd																
Washington	333	2 396	25 860	10.8	69.3	11.4	126.8	6 290	12 970	29 632	6.4	2.0	39 106	9.7	14.0	13.7
Wicomico	912	4 351	19 738	11.6	72.1	18.5	94.5	6 593	13 425	28 512	7.5	3.0	35 623	13.0	18.3	19.0
Worcester	754	5 086	7 077	10.5	70.8	14.8	51.5	7 441	14 341	27 586	16.3	3.3	34 570	10.9	16.8	18.1
Baltimore city	2 469	7 953	181 558	21.5	60.7	15.5	775.8	7 282	11 994	24 045	12.0	2.4	28 398	21.8	28.5	29.8
MASSACHUSETTS	476	2 550	1 530 134	28.1	80.0	27.2	7 948.5	8 260	17 224	36 952	25.4	6.7	44 934	9.0	14.3	14.4
Barnstable	526	2 468	37 509	13.9	88.4	28.1	248.9	7 721	16 402	31 766	21.9	4.1	42 514	7.1	12.1	12.4
Berkshire	387	2 052	34 224	21.7	77.9	20.9	174.4	8 155	14 857	30 470	14.5	3.5	38 024	9.7	15.6	15.1
Bristol	558	2 575	123 204	17.9	65.0	15.9	632.5	7 394	13 853	31 520	21.5	3.0	40 862	10.2	15.8	15.7
Dukes	NA	NA	2 488	15.2	90.4	32.1	26.0	10 734	18 280	31 994	40.7	7.6	42 792	5.9	8.3	9.1
Essex	452	2 531	161 455	23.8	80.2	25.9	898.6	7 772	17 586	37 913	25.1	7.2	44 969	9.3	15.2	15.0
Franklin	761	2 011	17 354	12.9	82.4	24.2	100.5	8 443	13 944	30 350	18.7	2.3	39 466	8.9	13.5	14.9
Hampden	1 123	4 048	116 349	22.6	73.6	17.6	630.6	8 298	14 029	31 100	14.8	3.2	37 164	14.2	22.1	23.3
Hampshire	295	1 749	53 875	22.4	83.0	31.9	159.7	7 568	14 414	34 154	22.2	4.4	44 473	7.8	10.3	10.4
Middlesex	242	1 869	355 828	33.4	84.3	35.4	1 785.1	8 680	20 343	43 847	28.0	10.2	54 819	6.2	9.9	9.1
Nantucket	536	5 819	1 094	19.7	89.4	32.9	13.2	10 636	20 591	40 331	26.6	6.8	50 060	3.4	4.7	5.5
Norfolk	169	1 517	151 086	33.2	88.0	34.4	750.0	7 869	21 091	46 215	25.9	11.1	56 765	4.4	7.0	6.1
Plymouth	496	2 196	112 932	17.9	83.8	22.2	622.0	7 337	16 523	40 905	30.2	6.6	50 528	7.1	11.0	10.6
Suffolk	1 211	4 731	185 123	45.3	75.4	27.7	807.4	10 452	15 414	29 399	37.1	4.6	37 931	17.1	26.2	30.7
Worcester	577	2 350	177 613	23.5	77.4	22.2	951.5	7 495	15 500	35 774	24.2	4.5	41 142	9.3	14.0	14.0
MICHIGAN	555	3 555	2 581 042	13.1	76.8	17.4	12 785.5	7 432	14 154	31 020	-3.7	3.8	41 963	11.4	16.8	15.7
Alcona	68	1 655	2 013	3.0	68.6	9.0	6.9	6 615	9 466	18 013	0.2	0.7	27 860	14.5	24.5	23.2
Alger	335	1 491	2 058	5.4	73.0	11.5	10.1	6 280	9 669	21 569	-9.5	0.5	32 932	11.9	15.8	16.0
Allegan	236	1 725	23 805	13.1	74.4	12.0	117.8	6 474	12 498	30 596	2.0	2.3	45 003	8.5	11.9	11.0
Alpena	236	2 258	8 200	7.4	73.6	11.4	38.1	6 869	10 930	22 598	-11.1	1.4	33 329	13.4	19.1	18.2
Antrim	125	1 095	4 087	4.7	76.4	13.7	26.7	6 472	10 856	22 636	-3.7	1.4	35 748	10.3	16.5	15.0
Arenac	284	1 859	3 838	2.0	65.4	7.1	17.6	5 845	9 730	19 489	-11.8	1.1	28 865	17.3	25.8	25.1
Baraga	181	813	1 936	9.8	70.5	8.3	9.3	6 231	9 021	19 424	-3.5	0.6	30 733	13.6	19.6	19.6
Barry	203	1 925	13 088	8.0	78.3	10.8	51.0	6 215	12 417	30 516	-2.5	1.5	45 751	9.0	12.9	12.6
Bay	264	3 056	30 302	14.9	74.0	11.0	124.8	7 140	12 597	27 940	-12.5	2.1	37 524	12.2	18.4	17.4
Benzie	156	1 838	2 608	6.4	76.6	15.1	15.0	6 048	10 415	21 577	-4.0	1.0	33 000	10.4	17.5	16.1
Berrien	431	3 404	42 700	17.9	74.7	16.7	216.4	7 374	12 636	27 245	-0.1	2.4	36 552	14.4	21.7	20.2
Branch	306	2 404	10 467	6.8	73.8	10.3	55.6	7 076	11 033	25 332	-6.4	1.6	35 431	12.9	19.0	17.7
Calhoun	981	5 175	36 371	12.9	76.8	13.8	173.0	7 317	12 729	27 476	-6.9	1.9	38 041	13.4	19.9	19.4
Cass	194	2 552	12 605	8.1	72.3	9.2	47.6	6 321	12 167	28 002	1.3	1.8	38 362	12.6	18.2	17.8
Charlevoix	172	1 108	5 172	4.0	79.7	16.0	39.6	8 944	11 632	24 738	5.2	1.6	38 155	9.0	12.8	13.9
Cheboygan	151	1 909	5 056	6.5	73.5	10.0	30.8	7 651	9 568	21 006	-3.7	0.8	30 681	13.3	20.8	19.2
Chippewa	143	1 751	9 582	4.3	73.6	10.8	42.5	7 057	9 468	21 449	2.4	1.3	31 564	14.8	19.3	19.3
Clare	198	2 323	5 967	5.2	66.9	6.8	39.1	6 925	9 152	17 163	-9.8	0.9	26 801	17.8	27.7	26.3
Clinton	129	1 358	16 612	13.2	83.7	14.6	63.1	6 358	14 153	36 180	0.1	2.5	51 677	6.3	10.1	8.0
Crawford	161	2 235	2 966	4.2	73.2	12.6	12.8	5 633	9 610	21 497	8.4	0.8	30 332	14.6	21.9	22.5
Delta	NA	NA	10 107	5.1	76.9	11.3	51.7	7 152	10 810	22 791	-9.8	1.1	34 685	12.1	16.7	16.6
Dickinson	91	2 100	6 531	7.7	78.5	13.0	37.3	7 049	12 338	24 809	3.6	1.8	37 118	9.5	13.4	12.9
Eaton	211	2 362	26 580	11.7	85.5	18.5	110.7	6 597	14 896	35 734	-2.1	2.7	48 279	7.5	11.3	9.8
Emmet	156	2 157	5 905	10.0	81.5	19.2	33.4	6 406	12 606	26 015	2.8	3.2	38 139	8.6	11.9	12.4
Genesee	666	4 937	122 685	10.5	76.8	12.8	584.1	7 025	13 583	31 030	-11.8	2.5	40 296	14.6	22.8	20.4
Gladwin	265	1 791	5 140	8.1	64.8	6.5	24.8	6 283	9 482	18 587	-9.5	0.8	30 446	14.7	20.1	23.4
Gogebic	116	2 329	4 170	8.1	76.3	11.4	17.6	6 752	9 481	17 343	-5.7	0.8	27 186	15.1	21.4	22.1
Grand Traverse	187	2 883	17 423	9.7	84.9	22.1	108.8	7 975	13 289	29 034	3.8	3.1	41 264	7.7	11.3	10.6
Gratiot	128	2 067	11 017	14.3	77.1	10.9	58.6	7 132	10 673	24 530	-7.3	1.2	35 171	12.6	18.8	15.9
Hillsdale	230	2 381	11 461	16.1	75.2	11.3	52.3	6 727	11 198	26 019	0.8	1.1	37 329	11.0	14.9	15.0
Houghton	94	1 447	12 529	4.5	73.9	18.0	41.1	6 860	9 012	17 650	-8.1	1.1	29 540	15.0	19.1	19.4
Huron	125	1 854	8 370	11.4	68.0	8.9	50.1	6 888	10 089	21 852	-5.9	1.2	34 809	12.2	16.5	15.4
Ingham	567	4 014	105 724	7.8	83.9	29.2	382.9	7 973	13 740	30 162	-0.5	3.5	41 743	13.0	17.4	17.8
Ionia	260	2 001	15 466	11.9	77.2	8.9	78.4	6 301	10 896	29 430	0.7	1.4	40 687	10.5	12.9	13.2
Iosco	183	2 443	7 128	5.7	76.3	10.4	41.5	6 431	9 556	20 091	2.2	0.5	27 950	14.0	20.2	22.3
Iron	190	1 751	2 689	2.4	73.0	10.0	72.7	5 901	9 077	16 307	-14.1	0.4	26 737	14.2	20.3	20.3
Isabella	185	2 601	23 877	5.4	79.7	21.5	44.1	6 245	9 961	22 659	-9.9	1.8	35 537	13.8	16.9	16.7
Jackson	468	3 775	38 772	14.2	77.7	12.9	197.4	7 639	12 556	29 156	-6.1	2.3	39 781	11.7	16.9	15.8
Kalamazoo	487	4 528	70 282	11.2	83.4	27.1	249.8	7 369	14 548	31 060	-0.5	4.0	43 370	11.1	16.4	15.3
Kalkaska	223	2 854	3 516	4.8	69.6	7.1	11.5	5 574	9 502	22 078	-3.9	0.6	31 359	12.0	14.4	18.2
Kent	521	3 772	138 741	23.5	80.3	20.7	699.1	7 298	14 378	32 358	4.1	3.6	46 860	8.8	13.3	11.7
Keweenaw	391	2 434	334	5.1	64.3	11.1	0.1	11 167	8 620	13 871	-9.1	0.8	26 059	11.2	15.2	17.9
Lake	1 024	4 385	1 973	5.3	61.3	6.6	6.1	8 009	8 195	14 562	-4.9	0.5	23 379	20.4	28.6	32.3
Lapeer	102	1 451	21 293	8.3	77.6	9.3	94.5	6 275	13 313	35 874	0.0	2.6	50 835	6.9	9.9	8.8

1. Data for serious crimes have not been adjusted for underreporting; this may affect comparability between geographic areas and over time.   2. Per 100,000 population estimated by the FBI.   3. All persons 3 years old and over enrolled in nursery school through college.   4. Persons 25 years old and over.   5. Elementary and secondary education expenditures, local government fiscal years ending between July 1, 1998 and June 30, 1999.   6. Based on population enumerated as of April 1, 1990.

Table B. States and Counties — **Personal Income**

	Personal income, 1999												
			Per capita[1]					Transfer payments					
									Government payments to individuals				
STATE County	Total (mil dol)	Percent change, 1998–1999	Dollars	Rank	Wages and salaries[2] (mil dol)	Proprietor's income (mil dol)	Dividends, interest, and rent (mil dol)	Total (mil dol)	Total (mil dol)	Social Security (mil dol)	Medical payments (mil dol)	Income mainte- nance (mil dol)	Unemploy- ment insurance (mil dol)
	62	63	64	65	66	67	68	69	70	71	72	73	74
MARYLAND—Cont'd													
Washington	3 088	5.3	24 162	826	2 015	127	582	467	442	199	170	32	10
Wicomico	1 928	4.5	24 227	820	1 262	119	359	310	295	119	128	26	5
Worcester	1 156	5.6	26 471	469	556	124	329	203	195	100	67	12	8
Baltimore city	16 864	5.8	26 655	445	16 852	1 677	2 376	3 849	3 726	936	1 904	644	63
MASSACHUSETTS	219 386	6.9	35 527	X	148 510	17 531	39 568	27 328	26 204	9 230	12 974	2 133	832
Barnstable	7 326	7.7	34 470	92	3 020	647	2 108	1 163	1 124	552	441	48	38
Berkshire	3 848	3.8	29 103	253	2 129	319	883	710	686	266	331	48	19
Bristol	14 287	7.1	27 461	377	7 459	783	1 975	2 482	2 387	793	1 201	220	93
Dukes	495	6.1	35 211	80	222	71	162	55	52	25	20	2	3
Essex	24 235	7.3	34 405	96	12 472	1 500	4 325	3 093	2 965	1 079	1 425	256	104
Franklin	1 883	4.9	26 595	453	848	155	337	355	342	109	182	24	11
Hampden	11 992	4.3	27 361	387	7 248	669	1 978	2 610	2 530	718	1 398	271	64
Hampshire	4 003	5.3	26 531	460	1 910	315	771	462	434	192	153	26	16
Middlesex	61 060	7.1	42 801	30	44 419	4 822	11 757	5 237	4 978	2 035	2 248	322	161
Nantucket	380	7.8	46 354	16	210	65	102	26	24	12	10	1	1
Norfolk	27 087	7.0	42 089	33	14 309	2 030	5 223	2 358	2 240	995	968	108	68
Plymouth	14 385	7.6	30 410	197	6 281	1 039	2 197	1 828	1 742	633	842	127	63
Suffolk	26 148	6.7	40 748	41	35 532	3 705	4 531	3 883	3 767	721	2 369	442	92
Worcester	22 257	7.3	30 133	205	12 451	1 411	3 219	3 067	2 933	1 101	1 387	237	99
MICHIGAN	277 214	5.3	28 104	X	184 824	16 104	50 640	37 166	35 272	15 103	14 516	3 521	877
Alcona	214	4.1	19 215	2 229	49	18	66	64	62	33	20	4	2
Alger	178	3.6	17 613	2 622	85	17	33	44	42	20	16	3	1
Allegan	2 612	4.6	25 257	622	1 345	137	430	291	271	138	97	19	8
Alpena	701	2.8	22 913	1 108	415	48	142	146	140	66	53	11	5
Antrim	516	6.2	23 514	962	160	52	163	94	90	48	32	5	2
Arenac	316	4.5	19 075	2 264	113	29	65	83	80	35	34	7	2
Baraga	164	5.0	18 939	2 301	97	10	31	39	37	16	15	3	1
Barry	1 369	4.0	25 048	661	390	80	337	165	154	82	51	11	4
Bay	2 772	3.7	25 311	612	1 471	123	528	461	440	197	172	38	12
Benzie	333	6.5	21 801	1 412	100	23	101	68	65	31	25	3	2
Berrien	4 065	5.5	25 454	594	2 459	275	791	671	640	282	249	74	13
Branch	927	8.8	21 154	1 617	484	57	163	158	149	71	58	12	4
Calhoun	3 384	2.4	23 939	872	2 401	234	559	579	552	233	218	56	13
Cass	1 110	5.4	22 150	1 310	350	54	190	179	170	83	60	16	3
Charlevoix	629	7.2	25 124	650	369	54	143	95	90	45	34	5	3
Cheboygan	534	5.5	22 111	1 327	214	30	147	119	115	55	40	8	8
Chippewa	678	5.9	17 895	2 557	410	46	122	135	127	53	49	12	5
Clare	529	6.7	17 658	2 609	210	40	107	156	151	68	59	14	3
Clinton	1 635	5.9	25 526	579	464	82	317	164	152	85	50	9	3
Crawford	255	7.6	17 894	2 558	130	25	53	57	54	27	20	4	2
Delta	853	0.6	21 950	1 375	477	57	162	180	173	73	66	13	6
Dickinson	648	4.3	24 062	848	456	28	145	117	111	53	42	6	4
Eaton	2 509	3.9	24 691	716	1 189	116	459	286	266	146	86	17	6
Emmet	800	4.8	27 588	363	481	85	211	107	102	50	37	7	5
Genesee	10 677	3.3	24 412	779	7 136	414	1 882	1 860	1 776	695	744	225	61
Gladwin	493	6.4	19 194	2 233	137	30	86	132	127	60	50	10	3
Gogebic	350	5.5	20 524	1 828	161	24	72	98	95	42	38	7	2
Grand Traverse	2 125	6.1	28 195	309	1 509	199	497	262	248	122	95	13	7
Gratiot	839	6.8	20 962	1 676	417	70	157	157	149	65	64	12	4
Hillsdale	999	6.9	21 236	1 588	543	60	164	163	154	74	60	12	3
Houghton	706	5.7	19 904	2 022	386	36	143	156	149	61	63	11	3
Huron	913	7.8	25 863	534	428	110	213	167	160	77	65	10	4
Ingham	7 314	6.5	25 654	562	6 674	460	1 239	923	869	340	365	104	20
Ionia	1 212	8.0	18 055	2 529	541	65	162	167	154	74	57	15	4
Iosco	516	4.5	19 883	2 025	234	37	122	147	142	70	53	9	4
Iron	261	4.6	20 325	1 883	105	16	57	80	77	34	33	5	2
Isabella	1 227	6.5	20 748	1 756	775	75	214	206	195	70	91	15	4
Jackson	3 730	6.5	23 719	914	2 170	229	692	584	554	253	214	51	12
Kalamazoo	6 507	3.0	28 308	295	4 543	367	1 366	794	750	339	291	72	15
Kalkaska	279	3.8	17 651	2 611	150	22	38	63	59	27	24	5	2
Kent	16 307	5.5	29 628	225	13 146	1 024	3 051	1 699	1 593	716	601	153	48
Keweenaw	38	3.1	17 897	2 556	15	2	9	10	10	5	3	1	0
Lake	171	6.2	16 088	2 890	42	15	35	62	60	26	23	7	1
Lapeer	2 129	5.5	23 822	892	693	108	322	241	224	108	87	14	8

1. Based on the resident population estimated as of July 1 of the year shown. 2. Includes other labor income.

STATE County	Earnings, 1999 Total (mil dol)	Farm	Goods-related[1] Total	Manu-facturing	Service-related and other[2] Total	Retail trade	Finance, insurance, and real estate	Services	Govern-ment	Social Security beneficiaries, December 2000 Number	Rate[3]	Supplemental Security Income recipients, December 2000	Housing units, 1990 Total	Percent change, 1980–1990
	75	76	77	78	79	80	81	82	83	84	85	86	87	88
MARYLAND—Cont'd														
Washington	2 142	0.4	D	19.3	D	11.2	7.7	27.0	13.8	22 705	172	2 030	47 448	11.9
Wicomico	1 382	2.7	D	18.6	D	10.8	4.6	28.2	15.7	13 891	164	1 570	30 108	22.0
Worcester	680	4.0	D	8.6	D	23.4	7.3	27.3	15.4	11 724	252	698	41 800	40.0
Baltimore city	18 529	0.0	D	7.9	D	4.8	14.3	37.5	19.8	111 558	171	32 906	303 706	0.3
MASSACHUSETTS	166 041	0.1	20.6	15.4	67.2	8.3	11.3	35.5	12.1	1 060 613	167	167 559	2 472 711	12.0
Barnstable	3 666	0.1	D	9.4	D	16.9	7.2	31.1	16.7	61 851	278	3 625	135 192	35.3
Berkshire	2 448	0.1	25.4	19.0	62.1	12.0	7.1	33.6	12.4	30 012	222	3 609	64 324	8.6
Bristol	8 242	0.2	32.3	25.9	53.4	12.1	3.6	23.7	14.0	98 710	185	18 580	201 235	13.9
Dukes	294	0.2	18.6	1.2	66.1	20.5	9.3	24.7	15.1	2 751	184	161	11 604	31.6
Essex	13 972	0.1	31.6	26.0	56.2	9.6	6.2	29.0	12.1	123 086	170	20 692	271 977	11.3
Franklin	1 002	0.8	31.3	24.1	52.0	10.6	4.6	25.9	15.9	12 982	181	1 849	30 394	13.3
Hampden	7 917	0.1	24.2	18.5	57.3	9.7	8.8	28.5	18.4	85 826	188	20 497	180 025	7.7
Hampshire	2 226	0.5	17.3	10.3	54.0	10.7	3.3	31.3	28.3	22 732	149	2 153	53 068	13.8
Middlesex	49 242	0.1	23.1	18.5	68.7	7.1	5.5	42.5	8.1	222 488	152	24 874	543 796	10.3
Nantucket	275	0.0	16.3	1.3	71.5	23.1	10.0	26.6	12.2	1 241	130	38	7 021	46.8
Norfolk	16 339	0.0	19.6	12.8	71.6	11.4	13.6	31.5	8.8	107 504	165	8 430	236 816	11.3
Plymouth	7 320	0.1	19.1	10.0	62.5	14.1	5.9	27.1	18.3	74 042	157	8 862	168 555	11.4
Suffolk	39 236	0.0	D	5.2	D	4.0	25.5	39.9	12.8	90 287	131	35 181	289 276	4.5
Worcester	13 862	0.1	28.2	22.7	56.2	9.6	6.7	28.4	15.5	127 101	169	18 810	279 428	16.5
MICHIGAN	200 928	0.4	36.0	30.0	50.5	8.4	5.6	24.9	13.2	1 646 864	166	209 539	3 847 926	7.2
Alcona	67	0.3	35.3	26.4	44.2	12.6	4.0	20.9	20.3	3 879	331	235	10 414	11.1
Alger	103	0.4	D	38.3	D	8.3	5.9	14.2	21.3	2 271	230	213	5 775	14.0
Allegan	1 482	2.3	59.8	52.3	26.9	7.5	1.7	11.0	11.1	15 523	147	1 140	36 395	14.2
Alpena	463	-0.5	D	24.1	D	10.7	3.5	16.7	25.4	7 512	240	845	14 431	3.2
Antrim	212	3.1	D	26.5	D	9.7	4.9	20.8	18.7	5 524	239	318	13 145	21.9
Arenac	142	7.1	D	16.9	D	12.5	3.4	25.2	19.9	4 021	233	441	8 891	15.5
Baraga	106	0.1	33.9	29.4	40.1	6.7	2.7	22.9	25.9	1 900	217	208	4 684	9.7
Barry	470	1.1	D	30.7	D	9.4	6.9	19.3	16.0	9 227	163	514	20 887	9.1
Bay	1 594	0.9	D	29.9	D	11.0	4.1	22.2	16.0	21 657	197	2 233	44 234	1.9
Benzie	123	2.1	D	14.3	D	13.1	5.7	25.2	20.0	3 638	227	228	8 557	14.0
Berrien	2 733	0.8	40.6	35.5	47.1	8.4	3.2	23.4	11.6	31 371	193	4 662	69 532	1.1
Branch	541	1.8	D	27.7	D	12.4	3.2	13.9	26.4	8 222	180	637	18 449	2.5
Calhoun	2 635	0.1	42.4	37.8	38.8	9.4	4.8	18.4	18.8	26 367	191	3 742	55 619	2.6
Cass	404	0.0	42.4	35.1	38.1	8.5	4.7	14.8	19.4	9 464	185	827	22 644	4.9
Charlevoix	423	0.1	48.5	36.7	36.1	8.7	3.7	16.5	15.4	5 070	194	295	13 119	18.0
Cheboygan	244	0.4	25.9	12.0	55.9	19.9	3.9	25.3	17.9	6 390	242	456	14 090	12.8
Chippewa	456	0.3	13.8	8.3	46.8	10.0	2.7	27.0	39.1	6 631	172	718	18 023	9.8
Clare	250	1.3	27.0	18.4	50.6	17.7	3.6	20.0	21.1	8 001	256	1 059	19 135	3.2
Clinton	546	3.5	34.7	23.3	42.0	10.2	2.6	18.6	19.9	9 496	147	408	20 959	13.5
Crawford	155	0.0	31.1	25.7	D	11.1	D	25.7	22.9	3 106	218	254	8 727	16.5
Delta	534	0.6	D	29.5	D	10.7	3.6	20.1	16.3	8 645	224	785	17 928	6.1
Dickinson	484	0.1	38.1	26.1	38.5	9.2	2.2	14.7	23.3	6 326	230	421	12 902	14.7
Eaton	1 306	0.4	20.4	10.9	60.8	9.1	12.3	27.3	18.3	16 045	155	764	35 517	12.7
Emmet	566	0.1	D	14.0	D	15.0	4.8	32.4	11.6	5 612	179	548	14 731	17.8
Genesee	7 550	0.0	38.3	32.8	47.9	8.8	4.2	25.3	13.7	75 295	173	12 610	170 808	4.8
Gladwin	167	1.4	D	23.3	D	12.3	3.6	18.8	20.2	6 842	263	621	14 885	10.2
Gogebic	185	0.1	18.4	14.0	54.6	10.0	4.2	30.6	27.2	4 928	284	451	10 997	8.8
Grand Traverse	1 708	0.2	26.9	14.1	60.4	13.4	6.7	30.9	12.6	13 669	176	1 090	28 740	21.7
Gratiot	487	6.3	28.9	25.0	48.8	9.1	3.3	23.9	15.9	7 482	177	956	14 699	2.9
Hillsdale	602	1.7	52.5	48.6	30.9	6.9	2.2	14.0	14.9	8 485	182	799	18 547	8.5
Houghton	422	0.1	D	10.4	D	10.3	4.9	21.3	37.8	7 164	199	756	17 296	5.0
Huron	539	9.8	D	33.8	D	8.3	3.0	15.6	13.0	9 017	250	728	19 755	10.7
Ingham	7 133	0.1	23.3	18.4	48.3	8.1	7.7	25.2	28.3	37 038	133	6 500	108 542	9.1
Ionia	606	2.4	D	24.9	D	9.2	4.6	14.2	30.4	8 509	138	802	19 674	11.7
Iosco	271	0.8	D	14.9	50.3	12.5	4.3	23.2	23.8	8 199	300	581	19 517	8.4
Iron	122	0.3	D	12.3	D	13.0	4.0	20.3	32.6	4 016	306	297	9 039	16.8
Isabella	849	1.4	22.0	11.2	50.9	10.0	3.3	29.9	25.7	8 002	126	1 184	19 950	9.8
Jackson	2 400	0.2	33.5	26.9	49.6	9.8	3.3	21.7	16.7	27 742	175	3 339	57 979	4.0
Kalamazoo	4 910	0.5	37.3	31.4	48.0	8.3	6.8	24.6	14.3	36 547	153	4 432	88 955	11.5
Kalkaska	172	0.6	42.0	17.2	43.1	8.6	2.7	12.0	14.3	3 230	195	303	9 151	20.5
Kent	14 170	0.3	36.4	29.7	55.0	9.7	6.3	24.3	8.3	78 043	136	10 596	192 698	16.6
Keweenaw	17	0.0	D	10.5	D	10.1	1.1	37.2	35.6	597	259	32	2 257	5.0
Lake	57	0.5	27.0	19.3	D	13.6	3.8	19.4	27.4	3 208	283	505	12 114	15.2
Lapeer	801	0.9	37.3	26.8	40.0	11.8	4.0	16.5	21.9	11 986	136	674	26 445	14.8

1. Covers mining, construction, and manufacturing. 2. Covers private sector earnings in agricultural services, forestry, and fisheries; transportation and public utilities; wholesale trade; retail trade; finance, insurance, and real estate; and services. 3. Per 1,000 resident population estimated as of July 1 of the year shown.

Table B. States and Counties — Housing, Labor Force, and Employment

STATE County	Housing units, 1990 (cont'd) Occupied units — Owner-occupied Total	Percent	Median value[1]	Owner cost as a percent of income With a mortgage	Without a mortgage	Renter-occupied Median rent[2]	Rent as percent of income	Substandard units[3] (percent)	Civilian labor force, 2001 Total	Percent change, 2000–2001	Unemployment Total	Rate[4]	Civilian employment, 1990[5] Total	Percent Professional, managerial, and technical	Precision production, craft, and repair
	89	90	91	92	93	94	95	96	97	98	99	100	101	102	103
MARYLAND—Cont'd															
Washington	44 762	63.8	83 000	18.7	12.4	358	21.7	2.2	69 280	1.4	2 842	4.1	56 191	23.0	14.4
Wicomico	27 772	66.7	71 100	19.7	13.4	439	25.3	2.4	48 464	0.9	2 627	5.4	37 233	26.5	13.1
Worcester	14 142	69.3	83 500	20.3	13.1	398	24.6	4.2	25 520	2.8	2 517	9.9	17 322	22.8	13.6
Baltimore city	276 484	48.6	54 700	19.4	13.7	413	27.3	4.9	295 303	0.9	23 273	7.9	314 688	27.6	9.3
MASSACHUSETTS	2 247 110	59.3	162 800	22.3	13.8	580	26.8	2.7	3 283 709	1.5	120 605	3.7	3 027 950	36.2	10.0
Barnstable	77 586	72.4	162 800	25.1	14.4	646	30.6	1.4	107 916	1.8	4 250	3.9	82 526	31.0	12.4
Berkshire	54 315	65.2	114 900	21.0	13.3	437	26.2	1.0	63 369	1.3	2 324	3.7	65 136	32.0	12.7
Bristol	187 668	59.1	141 700	22.0	13.9	424	25.4	2.2	261 310	0.9	12 497	4.8	241 998	26.8	12.9
Dukes	5 003	71.3	195 800	26.4	15.0	647	31.2	1.9	9 214	-0.2	304	3.3	5 868	30.2	18.1
Essex	251 285	61.2	176 200	23.2	14.2	597	27.6	2.7	369 906	1.6	15 252	4.1	331 079	35.9	10.8
Franklin	27 640	65.6	114 100	22.4	13.9	478	27.0	2.2	37 376	0.0	1 187	3.2	35 245	33.1	13.1
Hampden	169 906	60.2	123 200	21.0	13.4	484	27.4	3.1	208 718	1.6	9 045	4.3	210 581	28.6	11.5
Hampshire	50 052	62.3	134 700	21.0	13.4	526	26.8	2.5	81 176	1.6	2 006	2.5	76 948	35.8	9.1
Middlesex	519 527	59.6	192 800	21.8	13.5	671	25.5	2.3	828 097	1.8	25 906	3.1	757 556	43.4	8.5
Nantucket	2 597	62.7	299 400	27.8	17.8	926	32.2	3.5	6 168	-3.2	90	1.5	3 569	30.8	19.8
Norfolk	227 798	67.7	182 900	21.9	13.4	674	25.3	1.4	359 555	1.2	10 226	2.8	328 006	41.0	8.5
Plymouth	149 519	73.0	156 400	23.4	14.8	620	28.2	2.1	244 185	0.8	8 541	3.5	215 264	31.5	11.7
Suffolk	264 061	32.5	162 100	22.9	14.4	625	28.5	6.7	340 532	1.5	13 956	4.1	331 135	35.8	6.9
Worcester	260 153	61.4	140 000	22.2	13.6	522	25.5	2.2	366 187	1.8	15 020	4.1	343 039	33.4	11.2
MICHIGAN	3 419 331	71.0	60 600	18.0	13.5	423	27.2	2.9	5 175 083	-0.5	274 360	5.3	4 166 196	28.3	12.0
Alcona	4 261	86.4	48 200	22.8	14.1	326	30.5	3.0	4 750	-4.5	483	10.2	3 256	20.8	14.0
Alger	3 337	80.0	39 200	17.4	14.0	296	26.5	3.9	4 458	-0.4	266	6.0	3 261	19.1	12.0
Allegan	31 709	80.7	59 300	18.5	12.9	377	24.6	3.0	58 767	-0.1	2 720	4.6	41 879	19.5	15.8
Alpena	11 838	78.1	41 600	18.0	14.1	307	28.7	1.7	16 362	0.7	1 430	8.7	12 439	23.9	12.3
Antrim	6 980	80.9	53 000	22.1	14.9	342	25.6	3.4	10 940	-0.1	816	7.5	7 332	20.2	16.3
Arenac	5 642	81.4	41 800	20.2	14.9	319	31.0	3.0	7 290	0.3	662	9.1	5 372	18.5	14.1
Baraga	3 065	73.9	37 900	18.0	13.4	235	25.0	4.0	4 352	-2.7	415	9.5	2 761	22.9	13.9
Barry	17 763	84.0	54 700	19.3	12.8	366	25.7	3.0	33 174	-1.4	1 425	4.3	22 709	20.1	16.2
Bay	42 188	76.9	44 100	16.8	13.5	344	28.5	1.9	56 066	-0.3	3 148	5.6	48 026	24.0	13.8
Benzie	4 772	81.9	50 200	22.7	14.1	337	27.5	3.5	8 059	-0.7	540	6.7	5 000	22.8	15.4
Berrien	61 025	69.6	52 800	16.9	13.2	368	26.9	2.9	84 313	-0.5	4 780	5.7	73 154	27.7	13.5
Branch	14 921	76.1	40 800	17.0	13.6	346	27.0	2.9	24 523	2.3	1 402	5.7	17 807	20.0	12.3
Calhoun	51 812	71.0	42 700	16.2	13.6	374	27.2	2.1	70 374	0.3	3 801	5.4	58 597	25.8	11.4
Cass	18 239	78.9	48 600	17.7	13.9	364	24.8	2.8	26 628	-0.8	1 378	5.2	22 870	19.9	15.8
Charlevoix	8 243	77.1	53 600	21.1	15.6	353	25.7	2.5	13 912	-2.3	943	6.8	9 635	21.6	17.0
Cheboygan	8 201	79.5	47 400	21.0	14.8	315	26.9	3.3	12 645	-1.7	1 421	11.2	8 164	19.3	13.7
Chippewa	11 541	73.4	37 500	18.4	13.9	323	24.8	3.7	17 891	-1.6	1 394	7.8	12 299	23.0	9.3
Clare	9 698	78.4	36 800	21.2	14.6	320	30.3	3.9	11 099	-0.9	983	8.9	7 986	19.6	14.7
Clinton	20 212	83.0	68 000	17.6	13.1	393	23.1	1.8	35 069	0.1	996	2.8	28 979	25.3	14.1
Crawford	4 441	80.3	44 500	21.2	14.1	350	28.3	3.6	5 681	-0.3	385	6.8	4 758	22.3	12.0
Delta	14 531	76.2	43 200	19.4	14.2	297	26.8	2.4	19 838	0.8	1 448	7.3	14 886	21.8	14.3
Dickinson	10 633	79.4	42 900	18.7	15.5	347	22.7	1.2	14 647	0.4	740	5.1	11 301	24.8	12.3
Eaton	34 027	72.9	68 200	18.0	12.7	436	23.1	1.8	57 322	0.3	1 860	3.2	47 712	28.3	12.0
Emmet	9 516	74.2	64 700	21.1	14.1	379	25.1	2.5	18 565	-0.3	1 311	7.1	11 822	27.3	14.1
Genesee	161 296	70.4	50 500	16.0	13.3	401	31.3	3.0	191 152	-0.5	14 554	7.6	179 087	24.6	13.6
Gladwin	8 357	81.6	42 700	19.4	14.1	307	29.6	4.8	9 289	2.2	799	8.6	6 892	17.6	18.0
Gogebic	7 449	78.2	23 300	16.7	14.8	257	28.7	3.0	8 323	2.2	607	7.3	6 494	21.8	11.6
Grand Traverse	23 965	74.8	66 700	21.0	13.5	446	25.5	2.2	46 519	-0.8	2 348	5.0	31 333	29.8	11.9
Gratiot	13 659	76.2	38 800	16.5	13.2	333	26.1	2.4	20 046	-1.6	1 098	5.5	16 362	21.0	11.9
Hillsdale	15 637	77.2	41 400	17.4	13.5	321	24.9	2.9	24 902	0.1	1 624	6.5	18 810	20.8	14.4
Houghton	13 172	69.5	28 300	18.8	14.5	281	29.0	4.0	17 302	-0.9	1 029	5.9	12 990	30.7	9.4
Huron	13 268	79.4	44 500	20.9	14.8	297	25.7	2.1	18 371	-0.6	1 503	8.2	13 660	18.9	13.0
Ingham	102 648	58.4	61 800	18.7	13.3	422	27.1	3.1	156 269	0.5	5 675	3.6	140 135	34.1	7.8
Ionia	18 447	77.3	47 700	16.5	12.9	341	25.1	3.5	28 440	1.1	1 609	5.7	23 420	19.2	13.1
Iosco	11 588	68.4	47 400	19.4	14.6	340	24.6	2.1	11 136	-4.9	1 179	10.6	9 728	23.6	11.9
Iron	5 655	80.1	30 100	20.1	16.2	269	29.5	2.8	5 462	0.0	356	6.5	4 552	21.8	12.1
Isabella	17 591	65.0	53 200	19.5	13.2	393	33.5	2.6	34 055	0.9	1 138	3.3	24 050	27.8	8.2
Jackson	53 660	73.7	47 900	16.1	12.7	376	25.0	2.1	80 869	1.2	4 309	5.3	64 317	24.7	12.5
Kalamazoo	83 702	64.4	62 800	17.2	13.1	417	27.4	2.3	130 143	0.5	5 426	4.2	110 927	33.0	9.1
Kalkaska	4 934	80.5	44 500	21.2	14.7	354	25.6	5.5	8 031	1.3	730	9.1	5 184	17.2	17.2
Kent	181 740	69.7	68 200	18.7	13.0	431	24.9	2.2	335 842	0.2	16 837	5.0	247 711	27.3	11.4
Keweenaw	777	86.5	19 200	20.7	17.1	231	25.0	1.5	873	0.2	86	9.9	499	27.3	8.4
Lake	3 536	80.8	29 800	23.6	16.1	303	33.0	4.5	3 741	2.0	344	9.2	2 291	17.8	14.0
Lapeer	24 659	81.0	62 300	18.9	12.9	407	27.3	2.9	45 993	-0.5	3 085	6.7	32 919	21.3	16.9

1. Specified owner-occupied units.   2. Specified renter-occupied units.   3. Overcrowded or lacking complete plumbing facilities.   4. Percent of civilian labor force.   5. Persons 16 years and older.

Table B. States and Counties — Nonfarm Employment and Agriculture

STATE County	Private nonfarm establishments, employment and payroll, 1999									Agriculture, 1997			
		Employment						Annual payroll		Farms			Farm operators
											Percent with—		
	Number of establishments	Total	Health Care and Social Assistance	Manufacturing	Retail trade	Finance and Insurance	Professional Scientific and Technical Services	Total (mil dol)	Average per employee (dollars)	Number	Less than 50 acres	500 acres and over	Whose principal occupation is farming (percent)
	104	105	106	107	108	109	110	111	112	113	114	115	116
MARYLAND—Cont'd													
Washington	3 246	53 662	7 947	9 821	8 385	4 563	1 182	1 397	26 040	768	34.1	4.7	54.9
Wicomico	2 515	35 774	6 136	5 748	6 503	1 215	1 113	898	25 101	580	56.2	9.1	60.5
Worcester	2 137	17 402	1 240	1 903	3 083	385	409	405	23 283	415	50.8	16.4	68.0
Baltimore city	13 706	297 169	63 000	25 803	20 819	20 041	18 187	10 144	34 134	NA	NA	NA	NA
MASSACHUSETTS	173 267	2 971 052	444 092	404 495	349 741	207 677	214 495	115 270	38 798	5 574	56.0	2.7	52.5
Barnstable	8 253	69 028	12 139	3 008	13 909	3 117	3 618	2 002	29 009	221	89.6	0.0	49.8
Berkshire	4 356	56 586	10 060	8 447	8 797	2 067	2 077	1 587	28 046	387	39.5	7.0	50.1
Bristol	12 977	198 280	29 976	47 389	34 323	5 648	4 635	5 409	27 282	555	58.7	1.3	55.9
Dukes	986	4 938	745	84	1 061	242	D	160	32 399	64	76.6	1.6	50.0
Essex	18 270	272 086	43 541	53 386	37 333	11 424	12 383	9 173	33 713	396	64.6	1.0	51.0
Franklin	1 754	22 871	3 553	6 108	3 073	747	388	589	25 756	543	35.0	4.4	50.6
Hampden	11 195	179 680	33 391	31 710	26 554	11 020	6 523	5 126	28 531	418	51.9	2.2	50.0
Hampshire	3 505	45 390	7 007	5 219	7 655	1 047	1 438	1 092	24 063	539	53.2	3.0	51.6
Middlesex	42 580	814 905	88 796	122 414	81 165	26 791	89 482	36 981	45 380	531	67.4	1.3	53.3
Nantucket	746	4 017	277	58	914	134	197	141	35 181	14	85.7	7.1	92.9
Norfolk	19 279	324 342	42 750	33 781	40 168	36 592	19 166	12 546	38 683	185	73.0	0.5	50.3
Plymouth	11 405	144 248	23 774	15 337	26 710	6 330	7 330	4 292	29 756	732	66.5	3.0	60.0
Suffolk	20 313	547 063	100 284	19 108	31 101	84 272	57 456	26 781	48 955	5	100.0	0.0	60.0
Worcester	17 622	287 137	47 799	58 446	36 978	18 176	9 503	9 364	32 611	984	45.3	2.4	49.4
MICHIGAN	236 456	3 996 300	492 761	816 625	541 841	169 065	202 469	138 301	34 607	46 027	31.9	10.7	47.9
Alcona	239	1 276	173	304	284	D	58	29	22 636	207	17.9	8.2	45.9
Alger	345	2 724	278	896	297	107	45	60	22 137	60	18.3	13.3	48.3
Allegan	2 140	36 970	2 845	17 959	3 714	507	446	1 135	30 697	1 337	40.6	8.3	48.4
Alpena	920	11 557	2 371	2 524	1 608	383	196	304	26 298	412	24.0	8.3	41.7
Antrim	638	5 017	514	1 428	661	119	598	113	22 448	261	26.4	8.4	46.0
Arenac	454	5 236	1 234	746	791	108	88	111	21 174	325	17.8	12.9	51.4
Baraga	234	2 245	372	768	352	69	9	51	22 753	54	16.7	25.9	51.9
Barry	993	11 472	1 108	3 547	1 903	664	256	288	25 125	881	27.1	8.3	38.5
Bay	2 603	34 739	5 378	5 876	6 901	1 248	974	995	28 630	730	28.2	14.2	56.0
Benzie	460	3 003	365	490	517	134	67	61	20 166	140	30.7	7.1	50.7
Berrien	4 021	61 186	7 534	16 121	8 274	1 438	1 570	1 795	29 340	1 182	49.1	5.8	54.2
Branch	936	12 758	1 615	3 822	1 998	408	289	320	25 108	980	26.2	11.9	45.6
Calhoun	3 062	60 866	8 563	15 940	7 928	3 282	1 065	1 828	30 039	1 085	24.4	11.0	45.4
Cass	821	8 864	741	3 787	995	221	199	232	26 145	700	29.0	14.3	52.0
Charlevoix	1 067	10 174	775	3 470	1 149	223	234	279	27 417	188	24.5	8.0	39.4
Cheboygan	932	6 231	1 074	691	1 340	200	234	149	23 865	210	21.0	11.9	39.0
Chippewa	940	9 267	1 203	692	1 661	254	228	189	20 367	319	11.3	20.4	43.6
Clare	640	6 338	970	1 286	1 413	206	112	137	21 565	350	24.0	9.4	50.3
Clinton	1 169	13 086	1 253	3 039	2 236	212	481	362	27 631	1 123	29.4	9.8	43.6
Crawford	305	3 035	798	478	518	100	78	65	21 366	27	48.1	3.7	48.1
Delta	1 206	13 440	1 609	2 789	2 477	534	734	342	25 480	253	14.6	15.8	49.0
Dickinson	965	12 758	1 522	2 457	2 363	364	232	356	27 918	116	26.7	11.2	42.2
Eaton	1 967	28 019	2 559	4 358	6 117	1 340	662	698	24 919	1 062	33.9	9.4	43.8
Emmet	1 370	13 819	2 756	1 663	2 419	336	411	360	26 016	207	23.2	8.2	42.0
Genesee	9 153	152 655	22 188	28 492	25 596	5 302	5 100	4 879	31 960	796	49.5	6.4	44.5
Gladwin	456	4 051	450	1 110	946	131	74	90	22 147	424	21.5	5.4	46.7
Gogebic	497	5 169	769	647	876	166	106	86	16 718	48	25.0	0.0	31.2
Grand Traverse	3 460	42 014	6 198	5 892	7 777	1 753	2 290	1 161	27 630	413	39.7	5.8	47.9
Gratiot	873	12 664	2 843	2 973	1 811	450	99	313	24 684	873	26.0	18.1	54.9
Hillsdale	922	15 077	1 211	6 910	1 687	368	180	387	25 697	1 236	29.6	9.9	40.0
Houghton	933	9 837	2 134	859	1 994	486	328	190	19 317	128	21.1	4.7	33.6
Huron	1 041	11 120	1 330	4 225	1 702	455	190	288	25 917	1 184	20.5	21.4	66.8
Ingham	7 168	127 870	18 389	18 759	18 381	9 395	6 292	4 071	31 839	827	42.1	10.5	45.2
Ionia	1 029	12 013	1 083	4 028	2 246	484	251	304	25 293	1 004	28.1	11.8	46.5
Iosco	680	5 760	616	840	1 261	322	114	126	21 907	238	30.7	8.4	47.9
Iron	419	3 063	677	332	556	153	99	62	20 192	86	17.4	14.0	43.0
Isabella	1 314	19 370	2 967	1 704	3 385	466	1 311	400	20 638	911	23.4	12.8	51.7
Jackson	3 439	53 997	7 555	11 974	8 388	1 446	1 477	1 558	28 849	987	34.7	8.0	38.0
Kalamazoo	5 968	111 230	14 678	20 619	15 111	4 959	4 912	3 403	30 598	696	44.0	12.8	48.3
Kalkaska	378	3 956	390	1 207	642	72	46	110	27 772	139	30.9	4.3	35.3
Kent	15 237	330 046	34 378	80 410	38 856	13 710	14 268	10 751	32 574	1 136	42.3	7.0	42.9
Keweenaw	62	385	D	D	17	D	D	7	16 938	5	60.0	0.0	40.0
Lake	184	1 151	215	142	250	52	12	20	17 253	126	24.6	6.3	29.4
Lapeer	1 755	21 229	2 281	6 420	4 054	512	528	575	27 102	1 020	37.8	7.9	47.8

Table B. States and Counties — **Agriculture, Land, and Water**

	Agriculture, 1997 (cont'd)														Percent of land owned by fed. gov. 1997	Water consumption 1995 (mil gal/day)
STATE County	Land in farms					Value of land and buildings		Value of machinery and equipment average per farm ($1,000)	Value of products sold				Percent of farms with sales of —			
			Acres								Percent from —					
	Acreage (1,000)	Percent change, 1992–1997	Average size of farm	Total irrigated (1,000)	Total cropland (1,000)	Average per farm ($1,000)	Average per acre (dollars)		Total (mil dol)	Average per farm (dollars)	Crops	Live-stock and poultry products	$10,000 or more	$100,000 or more		
	117	118	119	120	121	122	123	124	125	126	127	128	129	130	131	132
MARYLAND—Cont'd																
Washington	126	1.8	164	1	95	454	2 819	68	61	78 912	21.1	78.9	50.5	27.9	4.8	60.0
Wicomico	91	-0.4	156	6	71	406	2 686	61	186	321 197	16.0	84.0	81.0	53.3	0.0	19.8
Worcester	112	3.6	269	4	83	505	2 191	70	148	355 548	16.6	83.4	83.6	63.4	2.5	14.5
Baltimore city	NA	NA	NA	NA	NA	NA	NA	NA	NA	NA	NA	NA	NA	NA	0.2	4.8
MASSACHUSETTS	518	-1.5	93	25	224	455	5 207	40	454	81 522	78.6	21.4	46.4	15.4	1.8	1 145.7
Barnstable	5	-5.1	21	2	2	329	15 774	32	18	82 466	94.5	5.5	57.9	14.5	15.5	39.5
Berkshire	63	3.0	162	0	31	547	3 150	35	21	53 553	40.0	60.0	35.9	11.9	0.0	24.0
Bristol	37	9.3	67	2	18	456	7 625	31	34	61 444	73.6	26.4	47.0	13.5	0.1	114.6
Dukes	5	-18.4	77	0	1	661	8 640	22	1	19 524	78.9	21.1	28.1	9.4	0.8	2.8
Essex	26	2.2	65	1	12	527	8 602	54	25	63 361	79.2	20.8	45.2	13.9	1.4	115.0
Franklin	75	1.5	138	2	32	315	2 279	39	41	74 962	61.6	38.4	42.7	15.8	0.0	9.1
Hampden	37	1.1	90	1	16	358	4 617	29	29	69 633	85.8	14.2	37.6	13.4	2.0	232.0
Hampshire	52	-1.7	97	1	27	302	3 859	36	36	65 888	70.8	29.2	44.5	12.6	0.9	26.0
Middlesex	31	-4.0	58	2	15	503	9 762	41	58	108 421	86.5	13.5	45.4	14.1	2.0	108.3
Nantucket	1	0.0	75	0	D	680	9 077	66	3	210 821	100.0	0.0	71.4	21.4	0.3	1.6
Norfolk	10	-1.0	53	0	4	574	9 917	35	8	44 680	88.8	11.2	46.5	11.4	0.4	56.7
Plymouth	73	2.0	100	12	21	695	6 654	61	123	167 605	96.7	3.3	66.5	29.9	0.5	105.4
Suffolk	0	0.0	1	0	D	339	242 143	19	0	52 620	100.0	0.0	100.0	20.0	0.8	4.4
Worcester	103	-10.0	105	1	44	378	4 236	39	58	58 891	54.9	45.1	41.1	11.8	1.7	306.3
MICHIGAN	9 873	-2.1	215	393	7 892	358	1 671	66	3 568	77 516	61.7	38.3	49.1	15.8	8.8	12 059.3
Alcona	43	0.9	210	D	30	216	965	51	6	27 016	39.1	60.9	37.2	6.3	25.4	2.3
Alger	16	0.2	267	0	9	229	858	41	2	33 806	28.8	71.2	43.3	15.0	26.8	3.9
Allegan	237	-3.7	177	13	198	353	1 979	75	187	139 684	39.5	60.5	53.2	22.6	0.0	50.6
Alpena	78	1.4	189	1	56	228	1 172	46	11	27 078	39.4	60.6	33.3	7.3	0.0	409.3
Antrim	55	6.1	211	3	33	253	1 231	45	17	65 922	72.9	27.1	44.8	14.2	0.0	8.4
Arenac	86	5.2	265	1	69	326	1 286	87	23	71 133	71.1	28.9	48.0	18.8	0.0	52.9
Baraga	15	7.1	278	D	9	231	833	43	1	21 001	36.7	63.3	37.0	5.6	7.6	2.1
Barry	165	-0.1	187	2	126	319	1 813	45	48	54 258	30.2	69.8	31.6	9.3	0.0	8.6
Bay	176	-2.8	241	5	162	388	1 606	89	61	84 141	93.1	6.9	63.7	23.7	0.0	627.3
Benzie	23	12.8	161	0	12	297	2 026	41	7	47 400	71.2	28.8	40.7	16.4	4.9	3.5
Berrien	174	4.2	147	11	146	283	1 913	63	81	68 846	88.5	11.5	52.9	16.2	0.0	2 195.8
Branch	234	2.7	239	31	185	305	1 352	63	77	78 826	57.7	42.3	48.3	16.0	0.0	21.0
Calhoun	243	-0.8	224	9	188	301	1 333	53	61	56 208	57.3	42.7	50.4	11.5	0.5	60.7
Cass	177	-4.9	253	15	141	400	1 590	76	67	96 416	47.0	53.0	54.0	20.1	0.0	17.5
Charlevoix	31	-24.2	165	0	18	241	1 511	33	4	22 080	39.3	60.7	29.8	5.3	0.1	117.4
Cheboygan	51	23.4	241	0	28	249	1 052	43	6	27 847	20.7	79.3	28.6	8.6	0.0	4.1
Chippewa	99	6.4	310	0	68	265	881	40	7	23 043	39.3	60.7	36.1	6.0	27.2	10.4
Clare	63	-1.8	180	D	41	239	1 317	31	13	36 999	13.4	86.6	38.6	8.3	0.4	4.2
Clinton	244	-4.7	217	3	210	358	1 583	70	92	81 492	44.8	55.2	55.1	15.5	0.0	11.8
Crawford	3	156.8	95	D	1	158	1 662	25	0	4 326	34.2	65.8	14.8	0.0	10.7	2.7
Delta	70	-3.8	278	1	41	205	759	47	8	32 260	45.5	54.5	39.9	7.9	32.0	75.9
Dickinson	28	1.1	244	0	14	230	943	50	4	33 975	46.5	53.5	42.2	10.3	0.0	11.2
Eaton	232	-0.9	218	1	190	334	1 524	55	55	51 740	71.8	28.2	44.7	12.6	0.0	17.7
Emmet	40	0.3	194	0	25	352	1 820	44	5	26 321	35.9	64.1	40.1	6.3	0.0	6.1
Genesee	118	-13.9	148	1	99	301	2 106	52	28	35 169	73.2	26.8	36.2	7.8	0.0	54.5
Gladwin	68	9.7	160	0	49	173	1 204	31	10	22 539	41.9	58.1	36.8	4.7	0.0	3.3
Gogebic	4	-30.1	87	D	2	99	1 129	28	0	4 830	77.6	22.4	10.4	0.0	44.0	4.3
Grand Traverse	62	-7.8	150	2	42	330	2 051	42	17	41 537	79.9	20.1	47.7	11.1	0.0	17.6
Gratiot	277	0.0	317	2	245	454	1 401	90	102	117 342	63.9	36.1	59.8	25.0	0.0	9.2
Hillsdale	257	11.0	208	4	210	271	1 276	47	72	58 033	58.3	41.7	42.2	12.3	0.0	62.0
Houghton	23	-20.3	181	0	12	165	818	34	2	17 238	30.6	69.4	28.9	3.1	23.5	6.4
Huron	424	-3.4	358	2	384	606	1 681	116	211	178 559	47.5	52.5	72.4	33.9	0.0	53.3
Ingham	190	-1.9	230	2	159	390	1 680	71	53	64 564	60.8	39.2	47.6	15.1	0.0	163.3
Ionia	237	-7.2	236	2	197	334	1 439	65	87	86 846	40.2	59.8	51.9	17.1	0.0	12.8
Iosco	43	-9.2	179	1	29	206	1 235	42	7	28 442	23.8	76.2	35.3	7.1	35.7	5.5
Iron	24	-20.6	277	0	12	190	685	39	2	18 525	65.1	34.9	30.2	3.5	22.3	4.8
Isabella	217	8.3	238	1	176	290	1 217	55	57	62 377	47.3	52.7	51.9	15.9	0.0	10.4
Jackson	181	-14.1	184	3	138	272	1 600	51	44	44 895	53.7	46.3	41.7	9.1	0.0	37.3
Kalamazoo	147	-4.6	211	18	120	439	2 038	74	105	151 572	64.2	35.8	54.2	22.3	1.8	111.7
Kalkaska	21	33.6	154	4	13	171	1 111	40	5	36 405	78.0	22.0	28.1	6.5	4.7	4.5
Kent	186	-2.4	164	6	150	453	2 686	74	121	106 550	76.0	24.0	48.2	18.8	0.0	184.3
Keweenaw	D	D	D	0	0	80	1 249	18	0	994	0.0	100.0	0.0	0.0	36.5	0.3
Lake	23	27.6	182	0	14	190	992	44	2	16 454	48.3	51.7	25.4	3.2	30.5	1.2
Lapeer	178	-8.1	175	2	144	433	2 425	66	54	53 191	59.5	40.5	41.9	11.5	0.0	13.5

Table B. States and Counties — Residential Construction, Wholesale and Retail Trade, and Real Estate

STATE County	Value of Residential Construction Authorized by Building Permits, 2000		Wholesale Trade, 1997				Retail Trade[1], 1997				Real Estate and Rental and Leasing, 1997			
	New Construction ($1,000)	Number of Housing Units	Number of Establishments	Number of Employees	Sales (mil dol)	Annual Payroll (mil dol)	Number of Establishments	Number of Employees	Sales (mil dol)	Annual Payroll (mil dol)	Number of Establishments	Number of Employees	Receipts (mil dol)	Annual Payroll (mil dol)
	133	134	135	136	137	138	139	140	141	142	143	144	145	146
MARYLAND—Cont'd														
Washington	67 537	721	156	2 184	922.7	62.9	598	7 450	1 220.5	117.3	105	479	43.4	7.3
Wicomico	45 043	480	130	1 410	502.1	41.7	464	6 111	994.1	100.0	91	580	52.9	11.1
Worcester	92 581	810	76	1 181	476.0	39.1	505	3 285	546.0	59.1	137	1 095	53.9	16.5
Baltimore city	21 224	257	792	14 152	6 171.2	499.2	2 256	23 159	3 438.4	414.7	597	4 807	568.2	124.9
MASSACHUSETTS	2 741 243	18 000	9 993	146 827	112 792.4	6 484.8	26 209	335 736	58 578.0	5 894.8	5 834	41 233	5 925.4	1 214.1
Barnstable	363 416	1 882	259	1 361	462.8	45.5	1 592	13 675	2 518.8	256.5	286	917	138.1	21.4
Berkshire	50 246	314	136	D	D	D	832	8 513	1 280.7	137.7	122	410	43.9	7.5
Bristol	210 806	1 650	709	12 089	11 586.3	471.3	2 365	32 400	5 158.7	511.1	375	1 564	193.6	31.8
Dukes	33 350	246	22	D	D	D	222	931	207.6	24.3	45	112	19.3	2.9
Essex	288 443	1 937	1 071	14 836	9 270.7	671.4	2 703	34 590	6 156.2	585.5	563	2 555	319.4	58.2
Franklin	25 493	207	87	782	349.0	29.3	295	2 880	410.8	46.2	45	101	13.6	1.6
Hampden	108 644	750	573	7 696	4 481.2	285.4	1 862	24 675	3 919.9	384.7	373	1 852	238.0	40.2
Hampshire	51 886	370	109	D	D	D	604	6 976	964.6	107.5	128	500	61.1	8.7
Middlesex	561 730	3 617	2 914	49 166	33 893.5	2 386.3	5 701	78 812	14 462.1	1 491.7	1 412	9 998	1 669.0	305.0
Nantucket	63 581	217	13	D	D	D	178	799	195.7	23.0	37	124	27.3	6.5
Norfolk	278 322	1 542	1 451	23 872	21 949.4	1 128.8	2 599	38 832	7 332.9	715.5	687	5 682	981.6	196.0
Plymouth	243 874	1 815	700	9 214	5 772.6	361.1	1 917	27 147	4 895.9	472.3	337	1 399	243.6	31.3
Suffolk	79 148	652	923	11 910	10 935.6	523.8	2 543	30 091	4 842.5	532.2	887	13 000	1 585.4	432.5
Worcester	382 303	2 801	1 026	12 865	12 038.3	493.9	2 796	35 415	6 231.7	606.7	537	3 019	391.6	70.5
MICHIGAN	6 255 867	52 489	13 936	189 057	158 757.3	7 629.6	39 564	529 441	93 706.1	8 922.3	8 302	50 941	6 492.7	1 126.2
Alcona	13 423	135	1	D	D	D	40	290	49.7	3.9	2	D	D	D
Alger	3 960	91	7	D	D	D	55	294	37.1	3.3	9	24	11.0	0.8
Allegan	80 525	689	100	1 003	369.4	29.9	365	3 757	642.0	59.5	64	258	23.5	3.7
Alpena	8 328	90	45	396	143.3	10.3	162	1 719	288.5	25.0	23	127	9.1	2.0
Antrim	44 147	308	24	96	32.5	3.0	96	628	106.5	11.6	24	74	6.6	1.1
Arenac	6 341	81	27	227	74.6	5.3	79	758	127.8	10.6	19	31	4.1	0.4
Baraga	4 403	58	6	67	27.0	1.8	43	337	48.8	4.2	3	D	D	D
Barry	43 235	331	50	317	87.0	8.4	180	1 697	262.3	24.0	28	80	6.2	1.1
Bay	36 906	274	123	1 393	600.0	41.7	541	6 661	1 101.7	104.8	89	364	35.4	6.8
Benzie	27 157	250	9	48	4.6	0.7	78	532	104.8	10.0	16	27	3.3	0.8
Berrien	84 030	507	193	1 887	938.3	60.0	674	8 078	1 302.5	125.6	164	627	186.3	10.5
Branch	18 129	123	49	639	411.8	19.0	174	2 002	321.3	30.4	28	84	14.4	1.6
Calhoun	47 035	483	145	1 646	1 392.4	60.8	567	7 779	1 239.0	114.7	88	425	44.2	6.7
Cass	38 777	322	54	351	252.5	11.1	143	985	159.0	14.6	28	67	7.1	0.8
Charlevoix	55 298	371	14	113	33.9	3.4	172	1 288	202.8	19.3	29	96	9.1	1.3
Cheboygan	27 861	254	21	85	48.9	3.0	195	1 475	254.0	24.0	24	49	6.5	1.1
Chippewa	12 920	199	21	140	24.9	3.2	187	1 839	289.6	25.5	26	107	8.4	1.6
Clare	11 879	160	15	90	47.2	2.8	140	1 319	217.8	21.4	16	32	3.6	0.4
Clinton	77 309	680	56	685	522.2	23.2	207	2 378	426.2	40.1	38	152	17.8	3.3
Crawford	7 410	100	11	D	D	D	65	629	116.0	9.3	11	33	2.6	0.4
Delta	23 536	237	59	452	95.5	10.9	232	2 552	380.0	35.7	24	77	7.5	1.0
Dickinson	9 539	106	54	505	119.1	14.1	177	2 222	316.6	31.4	23	71	4.8	0.7
Eaton	74 361	649	86	774	673.9	25.1	342	5 587	898.7	82.4	77	342	40.7	6.4
Emmet	66 494	492	32	228	75.4	6.7	298	2 509	404.7	41.9	41	120	12.0	2.0
Genesee	268 677	2 324	422	5 884	1 899.4	217.2	1 809	25 369	4 521.3	409.3	350	1 613	193.6	28.7
Gladwin	28 368	266	15	40	11.2	1.1	90	895	152.8	14.2	22	36	4.2	0.6
Gogebic	5 368	46	16	115	35.4	2.6	102	920	135.0	11.4	17	160	3.1	0.9
Grand Traverse	83 764	979	167	1 580	729.9	51.9	634	7 300	1 232.7	117.5	113	441	52.7	9.7
Gratiot	9 061	112	37	493	196.0	14.1	200	1 891	295.8	26.9	20	55	5.5	0.7
Hillsdale	26 422	331	48	416	215.6	12.7	163	1 556	255.8	23.2	29	81	5.8	0.9
Houghton	11 269	122	27	179	33.7	5.3	181	2 052	262.3	25.4	24	80	5.9	0.7
Huron	24 799	206	51	536	194.5	14.0	211	1 800	262.6	23.3	22	41	3.6	0.7
Ingham	109 003	987	365	5 830	3 313.4	213.5	1 207	18 762	2 992.6	301.9	295	2 999	223.2	54.1
Ionia	39 514	424	42	325	143.5	11.1	184	2 189	331.2	32.1	17	109	6.2	1.9
Iosco	19 813	161	11	79	7.9	1.4	160	1 475	224.3	21.7	25	60	5.0	0.6
Iron	4 929	50	17	86	18.4	2.1	77	632	92.9	9.2	15	70	1.6	0.3
Isabella	61 345	1 210	69	817	327.9	23.7	220	3 187	458.6	44.0	46	581	21.3	7.0
Jackson	85 630	919	196	2 339	1 047.2	83.7	564	8 108	1 289.4	126.9	96	465	41.9	7.3
Kalamazoo	181 804	1 487	337	6 278	1 870.1	233.2	978	15 421	2 388.2	230.2	237	2 032	180.7	40.8
Kalkaska	11 252	132	27	225	76.2	8.2	70	660	144.3	11.6	15	56	5.3	1.1
Kent	376 702	3 050	1 314	28 386	15 882.3	1 043.6	2 194	38 200	6 491.8	658.0	567	4 030	493.9	88.5
Keweenaw	2 704	25	3	7	0.7	0.2	10	19	2.7	0.3	3	2	0.2	0.0
Lake	3 361	113	7	27	4.0	0.5	36	244	36.8	3.7	6	11	1.6	0.2
Lapeer	81 037	566	68	373	136.0	13.2	278	3 706	705.7	58.2	52	170	14.9	2.6

1. Establishments with payroll.

Table B. States and Counties — **Professional, Manufacturing, and Accommodation and Foodservices**

STATE County	Professional, Scientific, and Technical Services¹, 1997				Manufacturing, 1997				Accommodation and Foodservices, 1997			
	Number of Establishments	Number of Employees	Receipts (mil dol)	Annual Payroll (mil dol)	Number of Establishments	Number of Employees	Receipts (mil dol)	Annual Payroll (mil dol)	Number of Establishments	Number of Employees	Sales (mil dol)	Annual Payroll (mil dol)
	147	148	149	150	151	152	153	154	155	156	157	158
MARYLAND—Cont'd												
Washington	163	854	63.5	22.7	147	9 173	1 924.5	294.2	230	4 135	127.6	36.4
Wicomico	169	967	76.5	29.2	95	5 690	1 041.6	158.1	159	2 964	86.8	25.0
Worcester	103	319	23.1	8.7	38	1 754	275.4	30.9	393	5 697	309.7	77.8
Baltimore city	1 395	14 695	1 645.0	666.3	688	30 216	9 822.2	1 006.2	1 328	20 021	849.9	232.0
MASSACHUSETTS	18 086	177 345	22 744.1	9 261.4	9 554	417 135	77 876.6	16 379.0	14 800	227 476	9 269.9	2 575.6
Barnstable	571	1 919	173.7	63.9	226	2 561	349.4	82.4	1 144	11 852	624.3	177.3
Berkshire	247	1 420	129.3	50.6	207	9 176	1 423.0	344.7	485	7 060	247.3	75.6
Bristol	793	4 101	324.7	112.5	915	49 363	7 651.4	1 654.2	1 112	16 980	557.3	152.7
Dukes	44	109	10.3	4.3	NA	NA	NA	NA	139	888	87.9	25.3
Essex	1 735	9 589	1 058.1	377.4	1 200	57 660	13 728.1	2 362.4	1 573	22 544	872.0	238.5
Franklin	110	359	28.8	9.0	119	5 700	756.0	182.2	150	1 715	49.8	14.3
Hampden	738	5 108	398.3	173.7	802	33 350	5 953.5	1 204.0	931	13 492	430.3	119.7
Hampshire	265	1 411	93.8	34.2	180	5 760	1 048.3	192.3	332	4 816	147.8	42.8
Middlesex	5 744	73 319	9 250.9	4 134.1	2 437	118 002	22 587.1	5 216.5	3 045	48 816	2 055.4	558.2
Nantucket	44	133	14.3	6.0	NA	NA	NA	NA	106	899	69.1	20.1
Norfolk	2 286	16 489	1 983.8	768.5	863	36 648	6 528.4	1 515.2	1 299	21 115	802.5	222.0
Plymouth	937	5 219	530.4	228.1	613	16 063	2 210.8	534.4	887	14 410	482.0	135.0
Suffolk	3 140	50 260	7 923.2	2 969.3	624	21 366	4 317.9	745.4	2 075	41 647	2 129.0	598.5
Worcester	1 432	7 909	824.4	329.8	1 336	61 344	11 303.4	2 340.9	1 522	21 242	715.1	195.6
MICHIGAN	18 614	162 971	16 231.7	6 882.9	16 045	833 429	214 900.7	34 418.9	18 958	320 014	10 158.7	2 835.8
Alcona	10	94	3.4	1.7	NA	NA	NA	NA	38	194	5.5	1.3
Alger	8	13	1.1	0.3	13	873	195.8	29.7	57	392	12.6	3.1
Allegan	82	330	17.3	7.1	203	15 984	3 108.9	585.9	174	2 136	65.6	18.1
Alpena	33	127	8.6	3.5	58	2 445	480.1	90.8	74	1 130	27.2	7.4
Antrim	31	589	11.2	5.9	56	1 323	164.9	38.7	71	930	49.3	15.6
Arenac	20	54	4.4	1.5	37	732	91.8	18.9	51	499	14.7	3.8
Baraga	3	5	0.1	0.0	26	715	115.2	21.6	21	211	4.6	1.3
Barry	45	170	12.9	4.8	71	3 145	525.2	102.1	84	1 095	28.0	7.9
Bay	138	834	62.8	28.6	152	7 459	1 928.6	347.0	241	3 922	106.5	29.6
Benzie	19	49	2.6	0.9	23	657	70.1	12.3	60	819	28.7	8.0
Berrien	255	1 338	124.6	48.9	397	16 996	2 394.2	539.1	383	5 328	163.5	44.0
Branch	35	212	15.3	6.2	90	3 572	516.5	102.4	78	1 026	30.0	7.4
Calhoun	168	836	68.8	29.1	222	16 973	4 514.8	613.8	307	5 010	147.5	42.5
Cass	52	193	11.8	4.3	87	3 384	570.8	95.9	76	708	20.0	5.2
Charlevoix	57	191	14.1	5.4	69	3 624	724.1	116.9	84	1 384	45.0	16.4
Cheboygan	40	145	10.3	3.4	37	711	76.6	17.9	128	715	33.6	8.6
Chippewa	44	198	10.2	4.5	31	818	63.2	15.0	147	1 475	49.0	12.3
Clare	31	109	7.4	3.2	28	924	120.9	23.9	80	895	25.2	6.7
Clinton	84	410	39.2	13.6	62	2 586	450.3	100.3	83	1 213	32.4	9.2
Crawford	16	52	2.9	1.1	17	503	104.3	15.8	47	409	14.7	3.9
Delta	47	730	23.3	12.8	59	2 834	702.4	124.3	132	1 529	40.0	10.5
Dickinson	51	224	19.4	6.4	50	2 478	655.3	100.6	92	1 124	26.7	7.7
Eaton	133	580	38.1	17.3	94	D	D	D	156	3 008	88.4	25.4
Emmet	86	312	24.7	9.7	57	1 377	168.2	39.1	143	1 970	88.5	24.7
Genesee	660	4 149	274.3	125.2	355	34 414	11 240.3	1 744.6	794	13 618	403.9	111.2
Gladwin	22	64	5.3	1.2	46	1 406	206.8	42.1	42	475	11.7	3.4
Gogebic	25	103	4.9	2.2	27	709	62.5	14.8	70	1 175	40.0	10.5
Grand Traverse	284	1 990	133.7	58.1	190	5 867	875.9	177.1	233	3 895	134.2	37.3
Gratiot	38	94	5.7	1.9	51	2 282	265.7	77.0	67	1 009	29.8	7.6
Hillsdale	38	123	6.5	2.8	104	6 510	1 134.5	176.1	75	815	23.6	6.3
Houghton	48	266	15.4	7.1	43	698	72.1	16.3	118	1 272	30.3	8.3
Huron	38	150	7.1	3.2	67	4 216	612.8	126.9	103	719	23.2	6.1
Ingham	680	5 171	520.7	222.7	272	D	D	D	597	13 137	368.9	104.8
Ionia	56	205	12.3	4.5	80	4 308	852.8	138.0	85	893	26.0	6.5
Iosco	33	101	5.3	2.3	34	1 299	164.7	31.5	88	795	25.8	6.6
Iron	30	105	6.6	2.7	NA	NA	NA	NA	49	577	11.5	3.9
Isabella	86	457	39.4	16.2	58	2 221	402.5	61.2	103	2 498	68.5	19.5
Jackson	200	1 354	90.8	45.5	351	12 248	2 271.8	422.0	267	4 467	137.0	37.7
Kalamazoo	481	3 366	306.0	134.4	399	22 007	4 108.6	820.9	452	9 317	260.6	78.2
Kalkaska	13	42	3.5	1.3	19	1 187	178.2	34.5	29	296	9.0	2.4
Kent	1 303	11 722	1 113.1	457.4	1 205	80 020	14 765.5	3 189.9	954	20 741	617.5	181.6
Keweenaw	NA	NA	NA	NA	NA	NA	NA	NA	21	D	D	D
Lake	6	15	0.7	0.2	NA	NA	NA	NA	36	201	7.9	1.9
Lapeer	98	430	28.6	10.1	139	6 118	837.2	155.6	119	2 045	52.1	14.1

1. Firms subject to federal tax.

Table B. States and Counties — Health and Other Services and Federal Funds

STATE County	Health Care and Social Assistance[1], 1997				Other Services[1], 1997				Federal funds and grants, fiscal 2001[2] Expenditures (mil dol)			
									Total	Direct payments for individuals[3]		
	Number of Establishments	Number of Employees	Receipts (mil dol)	Annual Payroll (mil dol)	Number of Establishments	Number of Employees	Receipts (mil dol)	Annual Payroll (mil dol)		Social Security and government retirement	Medicare	Food stamps and Supplemental Security Income
	159	160	161	162	163	164	165	166	167	168	169	170
MARYLAND—Cont'd												
Washington	225	3 006	208.0	95.5	207	1 524	81.7	25.4	575.5	294.7	108.0	16.9
Wicomico	200	2 520	159.9	86.6	146	986	60.1	18.1	384.8	166.6	63.9	10.2
Worcester	67	597	27.2	11.1	85	364	19.7	6.0	364.1	154.8	45.3	5.1
Baltimore city	1 220	16 856	1 093.8	486.1	891	6 733	426.4	131.5	8 338.6	1 408.7	1 057.5	271.5
MASSACHUSETTS	11 887	182 902	11 361.4	5 310.5	10 806	61 557	4 359.8	1 338.6	44 178.6	12 515.6	7 097.7	985.5
Barnstable	482	5 989	336.5	163.8	439	1 819	124.6	36.0	1 559.8	757.8	339.6	19.4
Berkshire	268	4 334	254.6	113.7	231	1 074	62.7	18.7	952.7	331.3	186.0	19.7
Bristol	844	12 815	711.6	350.6	878	4 340	295.9	79.6	3 408.2	1 063.4	592.0	97.3
Dukes	33	D	D	D	36	D	D	D	63.0	32.3	15.5	0.8
Essex	1 317	19 159	1 104.7	558.8	1 181	6 614	441.3	149.5	4 534.1	1 432.1	787.7	125.6
Franklin	107	1 502	72.7	35.1	116	471	29.1	7.9	324.3	145.8	69.2	10.3
Hampden	806	13 261	794.1	367.4	742	4 092	278.1	85.2	2 804.5	961.3	483.9	134.1
Hampshire	225	2 407	143.5	65.9	195	818	56.7	16.1	679.6	266.5	112.3	10.9
Middlesex	2 991	42 136	2 707.8	1 227.3	2 661	16 875	1 307.7	428.7	10 578.9	2 658.2	1 572.0	129.6
Nantucket	20	D	D	D	20	D	D	D	33.4	15.3	7.7	0.1
Norfolk	1 672	25 589	1 542.9	714.3	1 266	7 302	501.0	159.0	3 118.8	1 055.2	767.0	33.8
Plymouth	811	13 663	737.4	372.8	702	3 550	243.6	70.3	1 997.9	896.9	444.4	51.1
Suffolk	1 067	20 943	1 517.1	737.0	1 157	8 142	558.9	160.9	8 630.7	1 445.0	907.8	241.2
Worcester	1 244	20 902	1 425.3	599.7	1 182	6 312	444.3	122.9	3 604.9	1 434.0	812.7	111.4
MICHIGAN	18 943	186 954	11 811.5	5 696.8	14 705	93 792	6 159.1	1 893.8	51 632.5	19 623.7	8 799.2	1 726.7
Alcona	7	153	5.4	2.6	8	19	1.7	0.2	84.2	45.2	15.0	1.5
Alger	12	147	4.8	1.9	13	31	1.9	0.4	56.8	27.7	10.9	1.2
Allegan	98	1 251	64.8	32.7	125	560	33.5	9.6	413.9	155.0	57.3	9.1
Alpena	72	661	33.8	15.2	61	393	18.3	6.8	188.6	88.2	34.9	9.2
Antrim	31	277	10.2	5.2	32	94	6.4	1.7	106.3	57.2	20.1	2.2
Arenac	39	938	21.1	9.2	28	107	6.8	1.7	108.7	49.6	19.7	3.7
Baraga	16	104	3.9	2.0	7	20	1.4	0.2	48.8	22.4	8.3	1.3
Barry	61	498	26.9	11.5	86	415	26.0	7.9	166.0	94.1	29.7	4.0
Bay	210	2 225	132.9	65.2	198	1 004	55.9	16.2	507.5	244.4	105.1	17.5
Benzie	22	146	7.0	3.2	19	48	2.7	0.7	77.4	42.5	11.9	1.5
Berrien	281	2 395	154.1	71.3	262	1 452	77.6	25.1	821.1	369.6	149.2	40.7
Branch	72	570	34.3	13.7	59	199	13.9	3.3	178.8	88.7	34.7	4.5
Calhoun	300	3 100	176.3	79.3	207	1 433	91.5	26.9	849.4	334.8	129.6	26.9
Cass	46	233	11.0	4.7	60	216	11.8	3.3	191.5	91.9	32.4	6.6
Charlevoix	48	216	12.2	4.5	59	208	15.3	4.0	106.7	58.9	18.6	1.9
Cheboygan	53	295	15.9	6.9	53	237	10.2	3.1	120.3	64.4	23.5	3.5
Chippewa	40	366	19.1	9.7	56	193	10.8	2.8	222.0	83.0	26.9	6.2
Clare	40	456	19.3	7.3	35	77	5.1	1.1	176.4	92.4	35.5	7.2
Clinton	65	666	30.8	13.3	71	268	17.6	5.2	180.1	88.3	29.9	3.3
Crawford	21	141	10.0	4.3	13	59	3.5	1.2	66.3	34.0	11.9	1.7
Delta	61	443	20.4	9.1	79	450	27.9	6.8	206.3	106.4	38.0	5.3
Dickinson	85	755	37.3	16.9	69	301	20.2	5.0	164.2	75.7	22.7	2.8
Eaton	158	1 269	59.5	26.2	103	592	32.4	9.3	469.4	143.3	52.1	4.3
Emmet	85	1 233	114.2	52.0	52	193	10.2	3.3	125.4	67.9	22.2	3.0
Genesee	1 037	9 466	610.5	310.7	627	4 165	255.2	74.4	2 077.5	893.1	440.8	114.5
Gladwin	22	191	7.3	3.3	23	81	5.0	1.3	137.3	76.6	29.6	5.1
Gogebic	26	364	14.3	9.2	31	113	6.8	1.7	119.3	59.2	23.8	2.6
Grand Traverse	272	2 175	157.5	72.2	187	1 045	70.5	22.1	360.5	177.5	55.5	6.0
Gratiot	76	885	44.7	21.8	63	234	17.2	4.4	203.3	84.0	35.9	7.0
Hillsdale	66	411	22.7	10.6	57	219	12.8	3.4	191.1	93.2	31.5	5.4
Houghton	60	650	26.5	12.7	54	175	12.9	3.1	188.3	79.6	32.9	5.1
Huron	88	566	27.3	12.9	53	190	12.1	2.8	199.1	94.5	38.5	4.4
Ingham	659	5 597	407.3	198.4	438	3 073	162.9	53.7	3 311.8	705.8	215.3	55.9
Ionia	78	747	34.4	14.9	75	354	21.5	6.2	195.1	93.1	37.2	5.5
Iosco	35	226	11.1	5.5	45	159	7.8	2.2	168.2	101.3	34.2	3.9
Iron	21	295	15.3	7.6	17	57	3.0	0.7	83.1	45.7	17.7	1.7
Isabella	101	1 005	50.8	23.8	80	414	22.7	5.6	195.2	84.0	29.1	7.4
Jackson	299	2 649	180.0	85.7	238	1 294	77.2	22.2	663.6	322.5	128.0	27.9
Kalamazoo	467	5 746	407.2	205.0	412	2 814	176.6	55.9	950.1	422.5	153.8	34.7
Kalkaska	14	73	4.3	2.1	26	174	10.8	3.6	58.4	30.2	11.6	2.8
Kent	1 075	12 469	832.0	420.3	975	7 146	503.4	149.3	2 166.9	923.2	327.8	79.5
Keweenaw	2	D	D	D	2	D	D	D	14.9	7.6	2.9	0.3
Lake	11	182	7.4	4.1	6	D	D	D	67.4	33.6	12.9	3.5
Lapeer	116	915	51.3	26.9	95	454	30.0	7.9	247.4	132.3	48.2	4.9

1. Firms subject to federal tax.   2. October 1, 2000 to September 30, 2001.   3. State totals may include programs not allocated by county.

	Federal funds and grants, fiscal 2001[1] (cont'd)							Local government finances, 1997				
	Expenditures (mil dol) (cont'd)							General revenue				
	Procurement contract awards		Grants[2]							Taxes		
STATE County											Per capita[3] (dollars)	
	Salaries and wages	Defense	Other	Medicaid and other health-related	Nutrition and family welfare	Education	Other	Total (mil dol)	Intergovern-mental (mil dol)	Total (mil dol)	Total	Property
	171	172	173	174	175	176	177	178	179	180	181	182

MARYLAND—Cont'd

County	171	172	173	174	175	176	177	178	179	180	181	182
Washington	29.0	4.2	11.7	66.7	10.0	3.8	11.8	237.6	87.8	104.0	811	520
Wicomico	19.2	15.9	7.7	53.4	8.7	4.1	15.4	160.1	60.8	70.8	892	544
Worcester	10.2	84.2	2.4	25.2	2.8	1.7	22.5	126.3	16.9	82.7	1 964	1 405
Baltimore city	764.9	552.3	526.5	2 114.4	476.3	213.2	566.2	2 137.2	1 192.6	698.2	1 062	719
MASSACHUSETTS	3 214.5	5 280.5	1 570.3	5 831.0	1 176.5	666.6	2 044.1	X	X	X	X	X
Barnstable	130.7	78.8	29.7	83.1	17.0	10.5	69.0	522.1	107.6	331.0	1 614	1 548
Berkshire	40.3	105.8	102.3	87.5	20.5	9.8	18.2	303.3	146.3	129.8	967	934
Bristol	97.5	763.7	23.8	456.9	83.5	37.5	57.0	1 091.3	577.8	400.1	776	763
Dukes	3.5	0.0	1.0	4.6	1.0	0.5	2.0	63.2	11.9	40.2	2 960	2 844
Essex	228.4	1 133.7	84.8	396.4	88.0	49.0	39.2	1 592.7	618.7	719.9	1 041	1 022
Franklin	13.2	2.9	3.9	36.0	14.2	5.6	5.9	168.4	82.1	69.9	980	965
Hampden	378.3	37.6	111.6	333.0	115.2	46.5	53.3	1 178.9	658.3	373.1	846	834
Hampshire	71.9	26.4	14.4	51.5	9.8	12.7	62.5	277.1	118.9	115.6	770	754
Middlesex	803.6	2 340.8	686.3	1 298.8	115.3	249.8	417.8	3 181.5	949.3	1 844.5	1 301	1 262
Nantucket	3.8	0.2	1.0	2.0	0.2	0.2	2.4	42.7	7.6	25.8	3 439	3 163
Norfolk	130.4	556.0	67.5	219.7	34.9	26.2	22.0	1 404.2	333.0	797.8	1 248	1 220
Plymouth	158.3	27.1	41.2	212.5	48.6	27.2	23.7	947.6	427.4	426.0	922	897
Suffolk	950.5	150.6	264.6	2 101.1	513.0	106.2	1 116.8	2 940.7	1 773.0	871.5	1 356	1 273
Worcester	204.0	57.0	138.1	514.1	89.3	51.0	68.8	1 569.7	789.0	602.0	830	811
MICHIGAN	3 150.0	2 262.6	1 115.7	5 182.0	2 042.9	1 094.3	2 567.5	X	X	X	X	X
Alcona	2.3	0.0	0.8	13.6	1.3	0.6	3.2	19.4	7.3	7.1	644	643
Alger	3.8	0.1	0.6	7.7	1.2	1.2	0.9	23.0	13.6	5.0	501	484
Allegan	10.4	1.1	2.8	30.1	8.3	117.3	6.6	211.8	124.8	49.3	490	479
Alpena	9.2	5.2	1.2	15.7	14.4	2.9	2.8	154.5	55.4	18.3	598	582
Antrim	3.5	4.6	3.5	10.0	1.9	1.1	0.9	59.1	27.0	20.4	974	949
Arenac	2.8	1.2	0.7	11.9	2.8	2.2	8.3	32.4	20.0	7.0	427	418
Baraga	2.1	0.0	0.6	6.4	1.9	1.2	3.4	32.3	13.2	3.7	436	429
Barry	6.0	1.0	1.9	13.9	4.3	1.4	1.1	94.4	57.1	19.1	357	350
Bay	16.8	1.5	5.1	48.2	16.6	8.3	16.7	334.9	155.4	85.0	769	752
Benzie	2.6	0.1	4.0	8.8	1.2	0.8	3.2	35.6	14.0	13.6	954	932
Berrien	24.7	2.6	12.9	115.4	26.8	13.5	35.6	404.7	221.7	101.0	629	610
Branch	5.4	0.0	1.4	16.9	5.5	2.8	2.5	149.2	65.5	20.1	462	444
Calhoun	144.4	20.9	27.7	88.4	27.8	11.4	11.5	416.5	226.4	100.4	708	605
Cass	5.2	0.2	1.4	19.9	5.3	3.1	4.9	94.6	53.4	21.2	425	417
Charlevoix	5.5	1.8	6.6	8.4	2.3	1.3	0.5	81.5	32.8	31.7	1 342	1 321
Cheboygan	6.7	0.0	1.4	13.1	2.9	1.3	2.2	63.1	30.5	17.9	759	748
Chippewa	19.3	11.1	2.9	28.1	12.2	5.4	13.0	88.8	47.3	17.2	455	447
Clare	3.6	0.0	1.0	16.5	7.1	2.3	5.4	75.5	45.5	17.1	588	577
Clinton	25.9	0.0	2.0	8.4	4.1	1.9	0.1	118.2	68.5	26.2	415	400
Crawford	8.8	1.3	0.5	4.0	2.0	0.8	0.7	27.4	13.4	9.4	679	665
Delta	11.8	2.2	2.1	21.0	7.7	4.1	3.0	101.0	58.7	20.4	526	523
Dickinson	30.5	11.7	5.0	8.9	2.9	1.0	1.0	106.5	35.8	20.3	749	721
Eaton	23.3	0.1	2.2	19.4	21.9	24.0	156.2	200.1	114.9	49.2	491	475
Emmet	5.7	0.0	1.4	13.2	2.5	1.7	1.9	97.4	38.4	30.1	1 063	1 037
Genesee	87.1	1.0	34.7	239.1	92.4	38.1	48.4	1 466.8	790.4	256.3	589	571
Gladwin	3.1	0.4	0.8	11.7	4.1	1.7	1.3	46.2	26.1	11.7	470	457
Gogebic	8.3	0.0	1.8	13.7	3.3	1.8	2.9	62.3	31.4	9.9	568	562
Grand Traverse	33.2	1.2	17.9	33.1	10.2	3.6	12.2	232.8	109.4	64.3	879	849
Gratiot	6.7	0.8	2.0	24.1	9.7	3.3	11.1	98.1	66.1	16.8	419	411
Hillsdale	6.3	0.2	1.6	20.5	5.5	2.7	5.3	104.1	55.0	17.8	385	373
Houghton	10.6	3.1	1.9	23.6	7.4	3.6	13.5	106.5	56.1	14.3	399	389
Huron	6.1	0.1	1.6	21.0	4.1	2.2	4.4	101.2	48.4	25.7	730	715
Ingham	119.4	64.4	29.3	332.8	580.7	257.8	818.8	880.5	450.2	237.6	836	734
Ionia	6.6	0.6	2.0	20.8	6.0	3.2	3.4	130.3	85.2	24.1	394	386
Iosco	6.1	1.8	2.0	7.9	3.9	2.5	2.4	79.6	44.8	18.4	732	719
Iron	3.0	0.0	0.6	9.6	1.6	0.8	1.1	45.4	26.7	8.2	629	620
Isabella	8.3	0.0	1.8	23.6	5.5	5.6	5.8	118.3	67.0	18.8	327	306
Jackson	27.5	11.2	7.2	64.4	21.5	9.0	15.1	370.0	218.4	75.9	489	432
Kalamazoo	75.5	5.5	18.8	107.7	28.0	18.0	29.6	582.0	292.0	158.5	692	669
Kalkaska	1.7	0.0	0.5	7.1	1.8	0.9	1.1	32.9	11.8	11.1	721	703
Kent	180.7	64.3	69.2	199.3	50.3	28.1	159.6	1 474.4	767.5	416.1	771	654
Keweenaw	0.5	0.0	0.1	0.9	0.3	0.2	1.2	4.8	1.9	0.8	397	383
Lake	2.7	0.0	0.6	9.2	2.5	0.9	0.1	14.8	5.0	6.4	633	598
Lapeer	9.8	0.5	2.5	27.0	6.7	3.2	1.6	169.5	100.2	34.1	392	357

1. October 1, 2000 to September 30, 2001.   2. State totals may include programs not allocated by county.   3. Based on the resident population estimated as of July 1 of the year shown.

Table B. States and Counties — Local Government Finances, Government Employment, and Elections

STATE County	Local government finances, 1997 (cont'd)									Government employment, 1999			Presidential election, 2000[2]		
	Direct general expenditure							Debt outstanding					Percent of vote cast —		
			Percent of total for —												
	Total (mil dol)	Per capita[1] (dollars)	Education	Health and hospitals	Police protection	Public welfare	Highways	Total (mil dol)	Per capita[1] (dollars)	Federal civilian	Federal military	State and local	Democratic	Republican	All other
	183	184	185	186	187	188	189	190	191	192	193	194	195	196	197
MARYLAND—Cont'd															
Washington	234.3	1 828	58.6	0.8	3.9	0.3	4.8	230.5	1 799	662	514	7 130	38.4	58.9	2.8
Wicomico	166.0	2 093	59.0	1.1	5.4	1.8	4.8	88.1	1 110	343	297	5 638	45.5	51.4	3.1
Worcester	129.5	3 075	39.3	1.3	7.6	0.3	6.3	112.1	2 662	232	191	2 760	45.2	51.8	3.0
Baltimore city	2 110.8	3 212	33.7	3.9	9.7	0.0	6.6	1 794.7	2 731	12 244	2 594	71 654	82.5	14.1	3.4
MASSACHUSETTS	X	X	X	X	X	X	X	X	X	55 138	23 619	368 598	59.8	32.5	7.7
Barnstable	579.2	2 823	47.9	0.9	5.6	0.5	6.2	414.6	2 021	1 832	1 302	11 272	51.5	41.0	7.5
Berkshire	324.7	2 418	55.8	0.6	3.7	0.1	6.8	145.7	1 085	461	421	7 361	63.9	26.6	9.5
Bristol	1 073.8	2 083	53.4	0.8	6.3	0.7	3.5	586.5	1 138	1 216	1 858	24 986	64.5	29.7	5.7
Dukes	71.9	5 298	46.0	1.4	5.0	0.0	4.4	61.9	4 561	42	44	1 100	61.8	26.1	12.0
Essex	1 648.9	2 385	50.5	2.4	5.0	0.6	3.3	1 251.5	1 810	4 352	2 297	33 936	57.5	35.4	7.1
Franklin	176.1	2 468	59.8	0.4	2.9	0.2	7.4	76.1	1 067	186	223	4 705	53.8	30.5	15.7
Hampden	1 169.2	2 651	52.3	1.6	5.6	1.2	3.1	1 756.6	3 983	5 445	1 472	27 834	58.2	34.6	7.2
Hampshire	285.1	1 899	55.0	0.7	4.2	2.2	5.6	131.1	873	1 250	492	14 764	56.2	28.0	15.9
Middlesex	3 110.1	2 194	52.9	0.7	5.8	0.2	4.3	1 247.5	880	13 377	6 329	65 859	61.5	30.3	8.2
Nantucket	42.3	5 631	25.8	1.6	5.0	5.2	4.3	21.8	2 903	53	57	589	58.3	33.0	8.7
Norfolk	1 381.6	2 161	48.9	7.7	6.3	0.1	4.6	535.6	838	1 379	2 053	29 434	59.4	33.7	6.8
Plymouth	1 001.0	2 166	55.6	1.5	5.4	0.2	4.5	344.0	744	4 612	1 548	23 463	54.5	39.1	6.3
Suffolk	1 994.5	3 102	34.1	4.9	11.0	5.3	3.5	4 668.6	7 262	17 957	3 118	76 816	71.4	20.5	8.1
Worcester	1 588.0	2 189	58.2	0.7	5.0	0.1	4.6	895.5	1 234	2 976	2 405	46 479	56.0	36.8	7.2
MICHIGAN	X	X	X	X	X	X	X	X	X	56 031	21 663	586 667	51.3	46.1	2.6
Alcona	17.8	1 625	37.9	1.8	5.8	1.0	26.4	4.3	392	48	22	375	45.0	52.6	2.5
Alger	22.8	2 289	45.4	1.3	1.8	0.6	21.6	17.8	1 785	87	20	530	47.4	49.1	3.5
Allegan	222.7	2 214	54.5	7.9	3.0	4.3	8.8	113.2	1 126	186	203	4 388	34.5	62.8	2.7
Alpena	153.2	5 001	31.5	45.5	1.6	0.4	4.5	72.9	2 378	106	61	3 137	49.9	47.9	2.2
Antrim	62.7	2 989	45.9	9.5	2.6	10.0	6.8	54.5	2 599	57	43	1 255	37.6	58.9	3.4
Arenac	33.3	2 027	52.0	1.9	3.2	1.0	12.1	13.4	815	55	33	763	50.7	47.1	2.2
Baraga	29.0	3 432	32.5	28.7	2.3	1.0	14.1	12.8	1 516	30	17	809	41.3	54.1	4.7
Barry	110.2	2 059	60.0	3.6	2.4	0.9	7.7	74.6	1 393	106	107	1 932	37.2	59.9	2.9
Bay	335.8	3 041	56.0	7.2	3.6	4.3	6.0	203.2	1 840	280	235	6 189	54.7	42.9	2.4
Benzie	34.8	2 438	41.7	0.7	2.5	0.9	12.1	11.3	791	38	44	674	43.9	51.7	4.4
Berrien	397.8	2 475	57.8	7.5	4.1	0.9	4.9	189.4	1 178	439	332	8 571	43.2	54.7	2.2
Branch	146.3	3 354	41.0	30.9	1.7	4.0	5.3	54.9	1 259	103	86	3 613	42.4	55.4	2.2
Calhoun	451.4	3 183	48.8	5.4	4.3	2.2	6.4	250.0	1 763	3 381	320	7 759	49.6	47.7	2.6
Cass	95.7	1 916	69.2	0.7	2.5	5.2	2.5	40.6	812	97	99	2 211	44.4	53.2	2.4
Charlevoix	88.3	3 738	49.0	8.9	2.0	4.8	6.0	25.3	1 072	65	114	1 673	39.7	56.2	4.1
Cheboygan	66.2	2 814	52.4	0.9	3.1	1.1	10.1	41.2	1 749	70	119	1 095	43.5	54.0	2.5
Chippewa	92.8	2 447	44.7	14.5	2.5	0.9	10.5	41.2	1 086	347	212	4 293	44.4	52.4	3.2
Clare	79.8	2 751	65.8	0.6	2.4	0.9	8.9	17.0	587	62	59	1 498	49.9	47.1	3.1
Clinton	133.4	2 114	63.5	0.4	3.2	0.5	9.2	164.9	2 614	309	414	1 857	41.6	56.1	2.4
Crawford	32.9	2 369	56.6	0.6	4.6	1.3	11.6	16.1	1 156	141	28	796	43.8	52.6	3.6
Delta	102.3	2 636	63.9	9.9	3.3	0.7	3.4	47.2	1 216	221	76	2 043	46.0	51.2	2.8
Dickinson	107.5	3 974	34.3	38.6	2.8	0.5	6.0	93.7	3 462	611	54	2 135	43.1	54.0	2.8
Eaton	244.4	2 439	65.3	2.4	3.1	1.8	5.6	162.5	1 623	253	206	5 638	47.1	50.3	2.5
Emmet	103.7	3 659	39.0	10.8	2.6	4.4	10.7	91.8	3 239	106	58	1 676	37.1	58.5	4.4
Genesee	1 443.2	3 315	47.5	22.9	4.3	1.2	3.6	652.5	1 499	1 478	863	23 553	62.8	34.9	2.3
Gladwin	51.9	2 085	51.9	1.6	2.4	0.6	13.2	29.7	1 193	59	51	980	47.9	49.4	2.7
Gogebic	62.9	3 609	43.3	11.7	3.2	8.0	9.8	14.1	808	162	34	1 365	48.8	47.1	4.1
Grand Traverse	260.6	3 562	55.0	6.4	3.1	7.2	4.1	281.3	3 845	477	280	4 939	37.6	58.5	3.9
Gratiot	99.4	2 483	63.5	4.5	2.5	0.6	7.3	54.6	1 365	120	79	2 053	43.1	54.8	2.1
Hillsdale	101.4	2 192	51.4	0.5	2.6	15.7	10.2	143.7	3 108	121	93	2 510	37.2	60.0	2.9
Houghton	114.7	3 203	42.8	18.9	1.4	8.4	7.9	80.5	2 247	147	102	4 382	40.0	55.5	4.4
Huron	101.9	2 889	42.3	9.1	2.5	5.4	14.8	54.0	1 532	107	74	2 062	42.9	55.4	1.7
Ingham	924.3	3 253	55.0	1.6	4.6	3.3	3.1	799.2	2 813	2 312	688	45 286	57.4	39.2	3.3
Ionia	147.2	2 408	64.3	5.0	2.3	0.5	6.6	141.1	2 309	123	132	4 347	39.6	58.1	2.4
Iosco	81.3	3 234	52.8	2.0	1.7	4.3	7.6	68.8	2 739	117	70	1 792	49.2	48.0	2.8
Iron	42.2	3 230	35.0	7.4	1.8	13.4	13.7	11.7	893	57	25	1 279	48.7	47.9	3.4
Isabella	128.4	2 228	43.1	19.9	2.2	0.9	8.1	66.3	1 151	148	124	6 539	48.5	47.7	3.8
Jackson	396.5	2 552	58.8	7.3	3.4	3.4	5.1	218.2	1 404	453	311	9 327	45.5	51.8	2.7
Kalamazoo	613.7	2 678	51.4	5.8	6.7	1.2	5.5	697.7	3 044	1 534	459	17 456	48.5	47.9	3.6
Kalkaska	35.1	2 274	35.4	25.4	4.9	2.8	8.4	22.3	1 440	30	31	737	40.5	56.1	3.4
Kent	1 561.1	2 894	56.7	6.9	4.2	0.8	4.6	1 688.3	3 130	3 071	1 112	23 680	38.1	59.4	2.5
Keweenaw	4.7	2 284	2.2	0.4	3.5	2.0	43.2	0.7	349	84	0	102	40.2	55.1	4.6
Lake	16.4	1 615	39.6	2.9	4.1	3.4	2.7	3.0	291	55	21	416	55.1	41.8	3.1
Lapeer	165.5	1 904	55.6	5.8	3.8	1.2	10.0	131.4	1 512	169	176	4 676	42.3	54.7	3.0

1. Based on the resident population estimated as of July 1 of the year shown.   2. Data subject to copyright.

Table B. States and Counties — **Land Area and Population**

					Population and population characteristics, 2000												
								Race alone or in combination (percent)				Age (percent)					
STATE/ County code	MSA/ PMSA/ NECMA code[1]	County Type[2]	STATE County	Land area,[3] (sq km) 2000	Total persons	Rank	Per square kilometer	White	Black	Am. Indian, Alaska Native	Asian and Pacific Islander	Percent Hispanic[4]	Under 5 years	5 to 17 years	18 to 24 years	25 to 34 years	35 to 44 years	45 to 54 years
					1	2	3	4	5	6	7	8	9	10	11	12	13	14	15

			MICHIGAN—Cont'd															
26 089	...	9	Leelanau	903	21 119	1 731	23.4	94.4	0.4	4.2	0.6	3.3	5.1	19.3	5.7	8.7	15.5	16.9
26 091	0440	1	Lenawee	1 944	98 890	526	50.9	93.9	2.5	0.9	0.6	7.0	6.3	19.6	9.1	12.8	15.8	14.5
26 093	0440	1	Livingston	1 472	156 951	339	106.6	98.1	0.6	1.1	0.9	1.2	7.2	21.5	6.6	12.4	19.2	15.7
26 095	...	9	Luce	2 339	7 024	2 682	3.0	85.3	8.1	7.8	0.9	1.8	5.0	16.4	8.6	14.5	16.0	13.6
26 097	...	7	Mackinac	2 646	11 943	2 298	4.5	84.9	0.3	18.9	0.4	0.9	4.7	17.5	6.0	10.2	14.9	15.3
26 099	2160	0	Macomb	1 244	788 149	60	633.6	94.3	3.1	0.9	2.6	1.6	6.5	17.6	8.0	14.7	16.8	13.7
26 101	...	7	Manistee	1 408	24 527	1 576	17.4	95.5	2.0	2.2	0.7	2.6	5.3	17.4	6.7	11.2	15.2	14.9
26 103	...	5	Marquette	4 717	64 634	752	13.7	96.4	1.5	2.4	0.7	0.7	5.1	16.3	13.6	11.5	15.4	15.5
26 105	...	7	Mason	1 282	28 274	1 438	22.1	97.3	1.0	1.7	0.4	3.0	5.4	18.8	7.1	10.8	15.4	14.7
26 107	...	7	Mecosta	1 439	40 553	1 101	28.2	94.3	4.3	1.5	1.2	1.3	6.0	16.5	19.8	10.8	12.2	11.7
26 109	...	7	Menominee	2 703	25 326	1 551	9.4	97.2	0.3	3.0	0.4	0.8	5.8	18.1	7.6	10.2	16.0	14.7
26 111	6960	2	Midland	1 350	82 874	626	61.4	96.5	1.3	0.9	1.8	1.6	6.5	20.4	8.7	12.5	16.7	14.2
26 113	...	9	Missaukee	1 468	14 478	2 124	9.9	98.7	0.3	1.3	0.3	1.2	6.4	20.7	7.5	11.3	15.9	12.8
26 115	2160	1	Monroe	1 427	145 945	375	102.3	96.7	2.3	0.9	0.6	2.1	6.6	20.8	8.1	12.8	17.0	14.6
26 117	...	6	Montcalm	1 834	61 266	795	33.4	96.1	2.5	1.4	0.6	2.3	6.5	20.5	8.3	13.7	16.5	13.0
26 119	...	9	Montmorency	1 418	10 315	2 413	7.3	99.2	0.3	1.0	0.2	0.6	4.4	15.9	5.9	8.0	12.8	14.4
26 121	3000	2	Muskegon	1 319	170 200	318	129.0	83.0	15.0	1.7	0.8	3.5	6.9	20.7	8.7	13.0	16.0	13.5
26 123	...	6	Newaygo	2 182	47 874	955	21.9	96.2	1.4	1.4	0.5	3.9	6.9	22.2	7.4	11.4	16.1	13.2
26 125	2160	0	Oakland	2 260	1 194 156	30	528.4	84.4	10.6	0.8	4.7	2.4	6.7	18.5	7.2	14.8	17.7	15.1
26 127	...	8	Oceana	1 400	26 873	1 489	19.2	92.1	0.5	1.9	0.5	11.6	6.4	21.7	7.9	11.1	15.2	13.5
26 129	...	7	Ogemaw	1 462	21 645	1 711	14.8	98.7	0.2	1.5	0.6	1.2	5.2	18.7	6.4	9.7	14.7	13.7
26 131	...	9	Ontonagon	3 397	7 818	2 622	2.3	98.5	0.1	2.0	0.3	0.7	4.4	15.8	4.7	8.7	14.6	15.7
26 133	...	9	Osceola	1 466	23 197	1 633	15.8	98.7	0.6	1.3	0.3	1.0	6.2	21.0	8.0	11.2	15.3	13.4
26 135	...	9	Oscoda	1 463	9 418	2 495	6.4	99.0	0.1	1.4	0.2	0.9	5.2	18.1	5.6	8.6	14.2	13.7
26 137	...	7	Otsego	1 333	23 301	1 629	17.5	98.6	0.3	1.5	0.5	0.8	6.2	20.6	7.0	12.1	16.5	13.7
26 139	3000	2	Ottawa	1 465	238 314	243	162.7	92.8	1.4	0.8	2.5	7.0	7.7	21.0	11.9	13.4	15.9	12.5
26 141	...	7	Presque Isle	1 710	14 411	2 130	8.4	98.8	0.4	1.1	0.2	0.5	4.8	16.1	6.5	8.4	14.0	14.8
26 143	...	7	Roscommon	1 350	25 469	1 542	18.9	98.7	0.4	1.1	0.4	0.8	4.3	15.7	5.5	8.1	13.3	13.8
26 145	6960	2	Saginaw	2 095	210 039	266	100.3	76.9	19.4	1.0	1.1	6.7	6.8	19.8	9.0	12.5	15.1	14.0
26 147	2160	0	St. Clair	1 876	164 235	328	87.5	96.3	2.6	1.1	0.6	2.2	6.7	20.1	7.9	13.1	16.9	14.1
26 149	...	6	St. Joseph	1 305	62 422	777	47.8	94.9	3.0	1.0	0.7	4.0	7.2	20.3	8.9	12.7	15.4	13.3
26 151	...	8	Sanilac	2 496	44 547	1 007	17.8	98.0	0.4	1.0	0.4	2.8	6.5	20.4	7.6	11.5	15.6	13.1
26 153	...	7	Schoolcraft	3 051	8 903	2 533	2.9	91.4	1.8	8.6	0.7	0.9	5.6	17.1	6.8	11.2	14.9	14.2
26 155	...	4	Shiawassee	1 395	71 687	689	51.4	98.5	0.4	1.2	0.4	1.8	6.8	20.1	8.3	12.6	16.7	14.2
26 157	...	6	Tuscola	2 104	58 266	821	27.7	97.2	1.2	1.3	0.5	2.3	6.0	20.7	8.2	12.0	16.1	14.1
26 159	3720	2	Van Buren	1 582	76 263	658	48.2	89.9	5.9	1.9	0.5	7.4	6.8	21.3	7.9	11.8	16.3	14.4
26 161	0440	0	Washtenaw	1 839	322 895	179	175.6	79.6	13.3	1.0	7.1	2.7	6.2	15.8	17.1	16.6	15.5	13.5
26 163	2160	0	Wayne	1 591	2 061 162	11	1 295.5	53.7	43.0	1.0	2.2	3.7	7.4	20.6	8.7	14.8	15.5	13.1
26 165	...	7	Wexford	1 465	30 484	1 386	20.8	98.3	0.4	1.3	0.6	1.0	6.4	20.5	7.7	11.8	16.2	13.6
27 000	...	X	MINNESOTA	206 189	4 919 479	X	23.9	90.8	4.1	1.6	3.4	2.9	6.7	19.5	9.6	13.7	16.8	13.5
27 001	...	9	Aitkin	4 712	15 301	2 072	3.2	97.1	0.4	2.8	0.3	0.6	4.5	16.4	5.5	7.9	13.7	14.0
27 003	5120	0	Anoka	1 097	298 084	189	271.7	95.2	2.1	1.3	2.2	1.7	7.6	21.3	8.3	15.0	19.1	13.7
27 005	...	6	Becker	3 394	30 000	1 396	8.8	91.3	0.3	9.5	0.6	0.8	6.3	20.4	7.1	10.0	14.9	14.4
27 007	...	7	Beltrami	6 489	39 650	1 122	6.1	78.4	0.6	21.8	0.9	1.0	7.1	21.6	13.9	11.3	14.0	12.5
27 009	6980	3	Benton	1 057	34 226	1 275	32.4	97.1	1.1	0.8	1.5	0.9	7.2	19.8	12.2	15.4	15.6	12.0
27 011	...	9	Big Stone	1 287	5 820	2 802	4.5	98.7	0.3	0.7	0.4	0.3	4.8	20.1	5.3	7.9	14.1	13.1
27 013	...	5	Blue Earth	1 949	55 941	844	28.7	95.8	1.5	0.6	2.2	1.8	5.6	15.8	22.1	12.4	13.2	11.8
27 015	...	7	Brown	1 582	26 911	1 487	17.0	98.4	0.2	0.3	0.5	2.0	5.4	19.9	9.7	10.2	15.4	13.0
27 017	...	6	Carlton	2 228	31 671	1 353	14.2	93.1	1.2	6.3	0.6	0.8	5.9	19.5	7.7	11.6	16.8	14.3
27 019	5120	1	Carver	925	70 205	707	75.9	96.7	0.9	0.4	1.8	2.6	8.8	22.7	6.9	13.9	20.8	13.1
27 021	...	9	Cass	5 226	27 150	1 477	5.2	87.9	0.3	12.6	0.4	0.8	5.1	19.9	6.1	8.8	14.2	14.2
27 023	...	7	Chippewa	1 509	13 088	2 223	8.7	97.5	0.4	1.5	0.6	1.9	5.9	19.5	7.1	9.9	14.7	13.6
27 025	5120	1	Chisago	1 082	41 101	1 078	38.0	97.9	0.7	0.8	1.0	1.2	7.6	22.6	7.1	13.9	18.3	12.9
27 027	2520	3	Clay	2 707	51 229	903	18.9	95.4	0.8	2.0	1.4	3.7	6.2	18.8	17.1	11.0	14.7	12.0
27 029	...	9	Clearwater	2 576	8 423	2 570	3.3	90.7	0.2	9.7	0.4	0.8	5.8	20.2	7.6	10.0	14.6	13.3
27 031	...	9	Cook	3 757	5 168	2 839	1.4	91.5	0.4	9.3	0.6	0.8	4.5	15.9	5.4	9.6	16.2	18.0
27 033	...	7	Cottonwood	1 658	12 167	2 286	7.3	95.9	0.4	0.5	2.3	2.2	5.8	19.2	6.5	9.6	13.6	13.3
27 035	...	7	Crow Wing	2 581	55 099	857	21.3	98.4	0.5	1.2	0.4	0.7	6.1	18.8	8.1	10.6	15.0	13.5
27 037	5120	0	Dakota	1 475	355 904	165	241.3	92.9	2.9	0.8	3.5	2.9	7.8	21.4	7.9	15.2	19.2	13.8
27 039	...	6	Dodge	1 138	17 731	1 915	15.6	97.3	0.3	0.4	0.6	3.0	7.6	22.6	7.6	12.6	17.3	12.4
27 041	...	7	Douglas	1 643	32 821	1 324	20.0	99.0	0.3	0.5	0.5	0.6	5.5	18.5	9.2	10.2	14.8	13.4
27 043	...	7	Faribault	1 848	16 181	2 010	8.8	97.7	0.4	0.4	0.6	3.5	5.2	19.2	6.7	8.7	14.5	13.3
27 045	...	8	Fillmore	2 231	21 122	1 730	9.5	99.3	0.3	0.3	0.3	0.5	5.7	20.4	7.0	10.2	14.9	13.0
27 047	...	7	Freeborn	1 833	32 584	1 329	17.8	96.0	0.4	0.4	0.7	6.3	5.7	18.2	7.5	10.5	15.0	13.6
27 049	...	6	Goodhue	1 964	44 127	1 014	22.5	97.2	0.8	1.3	0.8	1.1	6.1	20.4	7.4	11.1	16.7	14.3

1. MSA = Metropolitan Statistical Area. PMSA = Primary MSA. NECMA = New England County Metropolitan Area. See Appendix A for explanation of these concepts. See Appendix B for list of metropolitan areas identified by type, with component counties.   2. County typology code from the Economic Research Service of USDA. See Appendix A for definition.   3. Dry land or land partially or temporarily covered by water.   4. Hispanic persons may be of any race.

Table B. States and Counties — **Population and Households**

STATE County	Age (percent) (cont'd)				Population — change and components of change, 1990–2001							Households, 2000				
					Total persons		Percent change		Components of change, 2000–2001						Percent	
	55 to 64 years	65 to 74 years	75 years and over	Percent female	2001	1990	1990–2000	2000–2001	Births	Deaths	Net migration	Number	Percent change, 1990–2000	Persons per household	Female family householder[1]	One person
	16	17	18	19	20	21	22	23	24	25	26	27	28	29	30	31
MICHIGAN—Cont'd																
Leelanau	11.4	10.1	7.3	50.1	21 518	16 527	27.8	1.9	243	212	367	8 436	34.5	2.48	7.1	22.3
Lenawee	9.1	6.6	6.1	50.0	99 605	91 476	8.1	0.7	1 406	1 106	455	35 930	13.6	2.61	10.0	22.9
Livingston	8.9	4.7	3.6	49.5	164 678	115 645	35.7	4.9	2 379	1 180	6 377	55 384	42.4	2.80	6.8	17.1
Luce	10.5	8.2	7.2	44.5	6 991	5 763	21.9	-0.5	71	92	-14	2 481	15.2	2.40	8.5	26.3
Mackinac	13.1	10.5	7.8	50.1	11 782	10 674	11.9	-1.3	132	166	-128	5 067	19.5	2.32	8.1	28.0
Macomb	9.1	7.1	6.6	51.0	799 954	717 400	9.9	1.5	12 343	9 107	8 769	309 203	16.7	2.52	10.1	26.9
Manistee	11.4	9.8	8.3	49.2	24 857	21 265	15.3	1.3	296	356	394	9 860	14.9	2.37	9.1	27.3
Marquette	9.1	6.8	6.7	49.8	64 383	70 887	-8.8	-0.4	709	776	-151	25 767	1.3	2.35	8.9	28.9
Mason	11.1	8.3	8.5	50.6	28 508	25 537	10.7	0.8	378	423	285	11 406	14.2	2.43	9.2	26.5
Mecosta	9.8	7.6	5.6	49.3	41 011	37 308	8.7	1.1	608	422	278	14 915	21.7	2.49	9.3	24.5
Menominee	10.1	8.7	8.6	50.3	25 246	24 920	1.6	-0.3	366	392	-45	10 529	7.8	2.36	8.8	29.2
Midland	9.0	6.4	5.6	51.0	83 879	75 651	9.5	1.2	1 264	731	502	31 769	14.3	2.56	8.1	23.5
Missaukee	10.6	8.0	6.8	50.1	14 672	12 147	19.2	1.3	188	147	149	5 450	24.2	2.62	7.4	21.5
Monroe	8.9	6.2	4.9	50.4	147 946	133 600	9.2	1.4	2 005	1 285	1 315	53 772	15.6	2.69	10.1	21.7
Montcalm	9.3	6.7	5.5	48.7	61 828	53 059	15.5	0.9	1 013	690	262	22 079	18.9	2.65	9.7	21.9
Montmorency	14.7	13.9	10.0	50.9	10 494	8 936	15.4	1.7	115	197	254	4 455	23.8	2.29	7.1	27.5
Muskegon	8.4	6.6	6.2	50.4	171 361	158 983	7.1	0.7	2 976	2 006	271	63 330	9.6	2.59	13.9	25.2
Newaygo	9.9	7.2	5.6	50.1	48 875	38 206	25.3	2.1	792	513	723	17 599	27.8	2.68	9.0	22.2
Oakland	8.8	5.9	5.4	51.0	1 198 593	1 083 592	10.2	0.4	20 120	11 702	-3 702	471 115	14.8	2.51	9.5	27.3
Oceana	10.0	7.9	6.1	49.6	27 321	22 455	19.7	1.7	453	287	279	9 778	21.1	2.67	9.2	21.6
Ogemaw	13.3	10.9	7.8	50.4	21 810	18 681	15.9	0.8	301	328	198	8 842	23.0	2.41	8.8	25.7
Ontonagon	14.4	11.2	10.4	49.3	7 775	8 854	-11.7	-0.6	79	140	21	3 456	-5.1	2.21	6.3	31.5
Osceola	10.8	8.1	6.0	50.6	23 365	20 146	15.1	0.7	364	292	104	8 861	20.6	2.58	9.7	22.6
Oscoda	14.3	11.8	8.4	50.9	9 588	7 842	20.1	1.8	121	142	191	3 921	24.1	2.39	7.5	26.0
Otsego	10.3	8.1	5.7	50.4	23 818	17 957	29.8	2.2	346	243	410	8 995	37.9	2.61	8.3	22.5
Ottawa	7.5	5.1	5.0	50.8	243 571	187 768	26.9	2.2	4 450	1 846	2 695	81 662	30.3	2.81	7.5	19.6
Presque Isle	13.0	12.2	10.2	50.2	14 440	13 743	4.9	0.2	169	233	95	6 155	14.5	2.31	6.3	28.4
Roscommon	15.5	14.0	9.8	50.8	25 784	19 776	28.8	1.2	263	450	494	11 250	32.1	2.23	7.7	28.1
Saginaw	9.2	6.9	6.6	51.9	209 461	211 946	-0.9	-0.3	3 606	2 401	-1 731	80 430	2.8	2.54	15.4	26.0
St. Clair	9.1	6.4	5.8	50.7	166 541	145 607	12.8	1.4	2 611	1 866	1 592	62 072	17.4	2.62	10.4	23.4
St. Joseph	9.3	6.9	6.1	50.6	62 144	58 913	6.0	-0.4	1 108	786	-588	23 381	8.4	2.63	10.4	23.6
Sanilac	10.0	8.1	7.3	50.4	44 554	39 928	11.6	0.0	674	595	-56	16 871	15.1	2.60	8.6	24.3
Schoolcraft	11.6	9.7	8.9	50.0	8 859	8 302	7.2	-0.5	118	151	-9	3 606	9.5	2.36	8.1	27.4
Shiawassee	9.4	6.4	5.5	50.9	72 217	69 770	2.7	0.7	1 160	792	189	26 896	8.2	2.64	10.3	21.7
Tuscola	10.0	6.6	6.2	50.1	58 364	55 498	5.0	0.2	830	671	-36	21 454	10.2	2.65	9.2	21.9
Van Buren	9.3	6.7	5.6	50.4	76 880	70 060	8.9	0.8	1 298	872	220	27 982	10.2	2.66	11.2	22.5
Washtenaw	7.1	4.3	3.8	50.3	326 627	282 937	14.1	1.2	5 072	2 213	951	125 327	19.9	2.41	9.3	29.5
Wayne	7.8	6.3	5.8	52.0	2 045 473	2 111 687	-2.4	-0.8	41 242	25 831	-31 375	768 440	-1.5	2.64	20.6	28.3
Wexford	9.8	7.5	6.5	50.5	30 779	26 360	15.6	1.0	522	351	131	11 824	19.2	2.55	10.3	24.2
MINNESOTA	8.2	6.0	6.1	50.5	4 972 294	4 375 665	12.4	1.1	82 541	47 363	17 529	1 895 127	15.0	2.52	8.9	26.9
Aitkin	15.1	13.0	10.0	49.6	15 413	12 425	23.1	0.7	169	220	160	6 644	29.6	2.28	6.3	28.7
Anoka	7.9	4.2	2.8	49.7	305 681	243 641	22.3	2.5	5 232	1 611	3 992	106 428	29.1	2.77	9.8	19.3
Becker	10.6	8.6	7.8	50.1	30 537	27 881	7.6	1.8	460	387	460	11 844	13.0	2.49	7.9	26.9
Beltrami	7.9	6.0	5.6	50.7	40 399	34 384	15.3	1.9	755	399	398	14 337	20.8	2.63	13.6	24.8
Benton	6.7	5.1	5.9	50.1	35 421	30 185	13.4	3.5	614	382	948	13 065	19.5	2.56	8.8	25.8
Big Stone	10.9	11.0	13.0	51.5	5 737	6 285	-7.4	-1.4	71	120	-33	2 377	-3.5	2.38	5.3	30.2
Blue Earth	7.0	5.5	6.6	50.2	55 904	54 044	3.5	-0.1	816	542	-295	21 062	9.3	2.46	7.8	27.1
Brown	8.8	8.3	9.2	50.5	26 711	26 984	-0.3	-0.7	339	375	-153	10 598	2.7	2.43	6.9	29.0
Carlton	9.2	7.6	7.6	49.3	32 075	29 259	8.2	1.3	444	402	368	12 064	11.3	2.50	9.0	26.1
Carver	6.4	4.0	3.5	50.0	73 378	47 915	46.5	4.5	1 277	363	2 220	24 356	46.7	2.84	7.3	18.1
Cass	13.7	10.6	7.4	49.5	27 638	21 791	24.6	1.8	380	384	473	10 893	31.2	2.45	8.0	25.0
Chippewa	9.4	8.4	11.6	51.3	12 951	13 228	-1.1	-1.0	159	202	-89	5 361	2.2	2.39	6.6	29.5
Chisago	7.9	5.1	4.7	49.1	43 476	30 521	34.7	5.8	750	359	1 937	14 454	37.0	2.79	8.0	18.4
Clay	7.3	6.2	6.7	51.6	51 609	50 422	1.6	0.7	810	490	83	18 670	6.7	2.53	8.8	26.1
Clearwater	11.0	8.1	9.3	49.7	8 410	8 309	1.4	-0.2	104	128	12	3 330	8.7	2.48	7.5	27.9
Cook	13.3	9.4	7.8	50.1	5 170	3 868	33.6	0.0	58	56	-5	2 350	44.0	2.17	6.1	32.5
Cottonwood	9.8	9.6	12.5	51.4	11 958	12 694	-4.2	-1.7	159	217	-150	4 917	-2.8	2.39	6.9	28.9
Crow Wing	10.8	9.2	7.9	50.8	56 318	44 249	24.5	2.2	812	637	1 032	22 250	29.3	2.43	8.0	26.4
Dakota	7.3	4.2	3.2	50.6	363 866	275 210	29.3	2.2	6 634	1 883	3 297	131 151	33.4	2.70	9.1	21.7
Dodge	7.9	5.8	6.3	50.3	18 234	15 731	12.7	2.8	313	167	352	6 420	15.9	2.73	7.2	20.2
Douglas	10.5	8.8	9.1	50.3	33 378	28 674	14.5	1.7	450	428	536	13 276	20.8	2.42	6.4	26.5
Faribault	10.2	10.1	12.1	50.7	15 987	16 937	-4.5	-1.2	195	268	-117	6 652	-1.8	2.36	6.1	29.7
Fillmore	9.5	8.8	10.6	50.7	21 296	20 777	1.7	0.8	279	314	214	8 228	5.2	2.50	6.1	26.6
Freeborn	10.5	8.8	10.1	50.9	32 300	33 060	-1.4	-0.9	412	480	-206	13 356	2.5	2.40	7.5	28.2
Goodhue	9.0	7.1	7.9	50.5	44 655	40 690	8.4	1.2	622	571	485	16 983	11.7	2.53	7.2	25.2

1. No spouse present.

Table B. States and Counties — **Vital Statistics, Health Resources, and Crime**

STATE County	Births, average 1997–1999 Total	Rate[1]	Deaths, average 1997–1999 Number Total	Number Infant[2]	Rate Total[1]	Rate Infant[3]	Physicians,[4] 2000 Number	Rate[5]	Hospitals,[4] 1998 Number	Beds Number	Beds Rate[5]	Medicare enrollees 2000	Serious crimes known to police, 2000[6] Total Number	Rate[7]
	32	33	34	35	36	37	38	39	40	41	42	43	44	45
MICHIGAN—Cont'd														
Leelanau	209	11.0	164	NA	8.6	NA	23	109	1	90	470	3 134	244	1 155
Lenawee	1 248	12.7	845	NA	8.6	NA	118	119	4	317	322	15 059	2 276	2 302
Livingston	1 900	13.0	888	9	6.1	4.9	135	86	1	93	64	12 486	2 538	1 617
Luce	65	9.8	68	NA	10.3	NA	11	157	1	69	1 039	1 320	158	2 249
Mackinac	110	9.9	135	NA	12.2	NA	11	92	1	75	676	2 300	623	5 216
Macomb	9 658	12.3	6 932	65	8.8	6.7	1 225	155	7	1 466	186	118 812	22 283	2 827
Manistee	241	10.3	277	NA	11.9	NA	30	122	1	173	742	5 089	650	2 650
Marquette	664	10.7	627	NA	10.1	NA	166	257	2	376	611	10 083	1 674	2 630
Mason	309	11.1	310	NA	11.1	NA	49	173	1	85	304	5 237	935	3 307
Mecosta	467	11.7	322	NA	8.0	NA	38	94	1	74	185	5 973	1 447	3 568
Menominee	275	11.2	295	NA	12.1	NA	8	32	1	78	319	4 721	534	2 109
Midland	1 019	12.5	591	9	7.2	8.5	181	218	1	307	375	11 055	1 542	1 861
Missaukee	165	11.9	130	NA	9.4	NA	3	21	0	0	0	2 253	336	2 321
Monroe	1 874	13.1	1 149	9	8.0	5.0	114	78	1	173	121	18 711	4 359	3 013
Montcalm	845	14.0	539	NA	8.9	NA	83	135	4	300	495	9 579	1 484	2 565
Montmorency	101	10.1	153	NA	15.3	NA	5	48	0	0	0	3 211	154	1 493
Muskegon	2 366	14.2	1 578	23	9.5	9.9	296	174	3	618	371	27 078	8 158	4 793
Newaygo	649	14.2	430	NA	9.4	NA	31	65	1	73	159	6 597	1 520	3 175
Oakland	15 642	13.3	8 857	98	7.5	6.2	4 194	351	12	3 458	294	150 063	36 375	3 046
Oceana	345	13.9	234	NA	9.4	NA	16	60	1	35	141	4 685	521	1 973
Ogemaw	257	12.2	259	NA	12.3	NA	31	143	1	92	434	4 478	522	2 412
Ontonagon	64	8.1	121	NA	15.3	NA	7	90	1	87	1 104	1 959	94	1 202
Osceola	276	12.5	234	NA	10.6	NA	12	52	1	110	498	4 401	400	1 724
Oscoda	104	11.7	106	NA	12.0	NA	6	64	0	0	0	1 727	260	2 761
Otsego	284	12.8	182	NA	8.2	NA	38	163	1	111	502	3 860	575	2 468
Ottawa	3 426	15.2	1 408	22	6.3	6.4	205	86	3	336	150	27 281	5 486	2 302
Presque Isle	141	9.8	180	NA	12.4	NA	7	49	0	0	0	3 762	191	1 325
Roscommon	213	9.1	355	NA	15.2	NA	15	59	0	0	0	7 399	1 000	3 926
Saginaw	2 875	13.7	1 911	25	9.1	8.6	442	210	3	848	404	33 321	10 272	4 891
St. Clair	2 080	13.0	1 451	12	9.1	5.9	226	138	4	473	296	23 117	4 541	2 765
St. Joseph	849	13.9	602	NA	9.8	NA	56	90	2	117	191	9 240	2 124	3 403
Sanilac	558	13.0	481	NA	11.2	NA	31	70	3	144	335	7 638	737	1 654
Schoolcraft	87	9.9	124	NA	14.1	NA	9	101	1	47	534	1 966	NA	NA
Shiawassee	925	12.8	597	NA	8.2	NA	82	114	1	155	214	10 516	1 460	2 072
Tuscola	678	11.7	533	NA	9.2	NA	35	60	2	109	187	9 030	1 040	1 984
Van Buren	1 041	13.8	662	12	8.7	11.5	45	59	2	224	296	11 348	2 866	3 758
Washtenaw	3 980	13.1	1 717	24	5.7	6.0	2 127	659	5	1 637	540	30 381	11 938	3 697
Wayne	31 075	14.7	20 383	341	9.6	11.0	4 658	226	27	8 232	389	294 629	137 564	6 775
Wexford	381	13.0	299	NA	10.2	NA	51	167	1	154	528	5 273	1 382	4 534
MINNESOTA	64 544	13.6	37 548	392	7.9	6.1	10 124	206	142	17 140	363	654 405	171 611	3 488
Aitkin	131	9.3	181	NA	12.8	NA	8	52	1	84	594	3 753	488	3 189
Anoka	4 210	14.4	1 256	23	4.3	5.4	321	108	2	470	161	22 490	10 962	3 677
Becker	370	12.5	316	NA	10.7	NA	36	120	1	160	545	5 269	514	1 713
Beltrami	566	14.5	323	NA	8.3	NA	65	164	1	98	253	5 461	1 613	4 068
Benton	510	14.9	302	NA	8.8	NA	6	18	0	0	0	3 149	728	2 127
Big Stone	59	10.4	95	NA	16.9	NA	8	137	2	137	2 423	1 509	99	1 701
Blue Earth	600	11.1	438	NA	8.1	NA	123	220	1	153	285	8 580	2 159	3 859
Brown	278	10.3	289	NA	10.7	NA	29	108	3	126	466	5 324	446	1 657
Carlton	358	11.6	306	NA	9.9	NA	29	92	2	253	821	5 590	549	1 733
Carver	1 067	16.4	311	NA	4.8	NA	69	98	1	106	164	5 304	1 348	1 920
Cass	289	10.9	296	NA	11.2	NA	16	59	0	0	0	5 372	1 459	5 374
Chippewa	143	10.9	163	NA	12.5	NA	8	61	1	35	268	2 548	159	1 215
Chisago	578	14.1	282	NA	6.9	NA	33	80	2	115	282	5 200	1 102	2 681
Clay	632	12.2	390	NA	7.6	NA	21	41	0	0	0	7 116	1 199	2 340
Clearwater	87	10.5	111	NA	13.5	NA	7	83	1	18	217	1 558	174	2 066
Cook	49	10.3	40	NA	8.4	NA	10	193	1	63	1 315	910	161	3 115
Cottonwood	135	11.2	170	NA	14.1	NA	9	74	2	43	357	2 839	259	2 129
Crow Wing	613	11.8	503	NA	9.7	NA	87	158	2	322	623	10 701	2 344	4 254
Dakota	5 342	15.6	1 526	23	4.5	4.3	311	87	3	304	89	23 758	10 501	2 951
Dodge	248	14.4	131	NA	7.6	NA	7	39	0	0	0	2 265	186	1 049
Douglas	359	11.6	330	NA	10.6	NA	50	152	1	110	354	6 483	987	3 007
Faribault	156	9.6	219	NA	13.5	NA	14	87	1	43	265	3 870	240	1 483
Fillmore	241	11.6	257	NA	12.4	NA	14	66	2	129	620	4 512	171	810
Freeborn	342	10.8	380	NA	12.0	NA	36	110	1	115	364	6 535	744	2 283
Goodhue	506	11.8	450	NA	10.5	NA	53	120	3	124	287	6 965	1 447	3 279

1. Per 1,000 estimated resident population, average 1997–1999.   2. Deaths of infants under 1 year old.   3. Deaths of infants under 1 year old per 1,000 live births.   4. Data subject to copyright.   5. Per 100,000 resident population as of July 1 of the year shown.   6. Data for serious crimes have not been adjusted for underreporting; this may affect comparability between geographic areas and over time.   7. Per 100,000 population estimated by the FBI.

STATE County	Serious crimes known to police, 2000[1] (cont'd) Rate[2]		Education						Money income 1989					Income and poverty, 1998			
			School enrollment and attainment, 1990 Enrollment[3]		Attainment[4] (percent)		Local government expenditures, fiscal 1999[5]			Households Median					Percent below poverty level		
	Violent	Property	Total	Percent private	High school graduate or more	Bachelor's degree or more	Total current expenditures (mil dol)	Current expenditures per student (dollars)	Per capita[6] (dollars)	Dollars	Percent change, 1979-1989 (constant 1989 dollars)	Percent with $100,000 or more	Median household income	All persons	Persons under 18	Persons 5-17 in families
	46	47	48	49	50	51	52	53	54	55	56	57	58	59	60	61
MICHIGAN—Cont'd																
Leelanau	76	1 080	3 922	14.7	85.1	24.1	17.7	6 362	13 307	28 589	7.0	2.5	43 183	7.4	9.9	12.0
Lenawee	202	2 099	26 130	16.3	76.3	12.9	132.1	7 101	12 654	31 012	-0.2	1.9	42 864	9.0	12.6	12.0
Livingston	116	1 501	33 332	11.4	85.6	19.6	164.0	6 380	17 327	45 439	10.5	6.3	64 705	3.8	5.4	4.5
Luce	484	1 765	1 418	2.0	69.6	9.6	7.7	6 374	9 264	20 370	-8.3	0.7	29 338	16.7	21.5	24.5
Mackinac	310	4 907	2 360	3.1	71.4	10.4	12.9	6 960	9 751	19 397	-7.1	0.9	29 439	12.9	19.0	19.0
Macomb	332	2 495	186 105	12.9	76.9	13.5	918.0	7 411	16 187	38 931	-4.1	3.9	51 187	6.0	9.5	8.1
Manistee	298	2 353	4 785	8.9	73.3	10.5	27.1	7 639	10 118	19 977	-16.9	0.9	30 553	14.2	21.3	21.1
Marquette	173	2 457	21 668	4.4	81.8	20.3	76.6	7 138	11 025	25 137	-9.2	1.5	37 109	11.3	14.3	14.2
Mason	258	3 049	6 294	5.3	76.1	11.8	41.4	7 943	10 848	21 701	-10.1	1.5	32 748	13.1	18.9	19.2
Mecosta	358	3 211	15 778	4.9	77.7	17.9	56.0	7 098	9 271	20 784	-5.2	1.0	32 790	15.4	21.9	21.1
Menominee	158	1 951	6 022	8.4	74.3	9.3	27.0	6 569	10 336	21 586	-9.3	1.0	34 063	11.1	14.8	14.7
Midland	163	1 698	22 189	16.3	83.2	27.4	108.4	7 389	15 615	33 948	-5.9	5.5	50 536	8.8	12.7	12.3
Missaukee	145	2 176	3 020	12.2	69.4	8.0	13.0	5 409	9 139	20 932	1.4	0.8	32 041	14.4	19.5	20.7
Monroe	281	2 733	36 833	12.8	74.1	10.5	176.4	7 161	13 893	35 462	-0.9	2.8	50 505	7.6	11.3	10.4
Montcalm	290	2 275	14 100	6.4	73.4	8.2	90.5	6 585	10 081	23 880	-3.7	1.0	35 463	11.9	14.1	16.2
Montmorency	136	1 357	1 857	3.4	67.6	8.7	7.5	6 204	9 307	17 819	3.7	0.9	26 382	15.0	22.5	25.8
Muskegon	425	4 368	42 908	10.2	74.2	11.1	235.0	7 079	11 345	25 617	-5.5	1.6	36 648	14.0	20.1	19.3
Newaygo	299	2 876	10 046	7.7	71.1	10.5	69.1	6 915	10 307	23 468	-0.6	1.0	35 599	12.8	17.8	18.0
Oakland	312	2 734	286 218	16.0	84.6	30.2	1 580.2	8 267	21 125	43 407	2.3	10.1	62 538	6.2	9.9	8.3
Oceana	182	1 791	6 093	5.9	73.3	10.4	27.5	6 649	9 582	22 383	-5.7	1.0	32 798	15.1	18.9	22.9
Ogemaw	347	2 065	4 458	6.1	63.0	7.2	16.0	5 495	8 991	17 665	0.3	0.9	26 507	16.4	21.9	24.8
Ontonagon	141	1 062	1 866	1.7	74.6	9.2	11.9	9 288	10 939	21 147	-4.1	1.2	28 592	13.9	20.3	22.1
Osceola	233	1 492	5 400	5.8	72.1	8.7	33.2	5 728	9 258	20 880	-3.9	0.9	31 795	14.8	19.1	21.6
Oscoda	297	2 463	1 528	9.3	66.6	7.9	8.2	5 842	8 719	17 772	-5.1	0.7	26 599	15.9	21.1	27.0
Otsego	176	2 292	4 340	12.6	79.5	13.7	28.9	6 191	11 366	26 356	2.5	1.8	38 643	8.9	12.1	12.7
Ottawa	172	2 130	55 248	21.5	79.8	18.7	297.6	6 689	14 347	36 507	7.7	3.7	53 286	5.1	7.1	6.2
Presque Isle	167	1 159	3 187	16.4	65.7	8.7	12.4	5 774	9 654	20 941	0.0	0.3	29 755	11.8	16.1	17.6
Roscommon	302	3 624	3 969	5.9	69.4	7.9	33.2	7 767	9 709	17 047	-6.4	0.7	25 391	16.2	25.2	28.0
Saginaw	786	4 105	60 862	11.2	74.8	13.0	266.1	7 063	12 355	27 980	-15.4	2.0	37 297	15.3	23.1	21.9
St. Clair	256	2 509	38 403	8.2	74.8	10.7	185.8	6 631	13 257	30 692	-0.9	2.9	44 117	8.9	13.0	11.9
St. Joseph	335	3 068	15 261	10.7	73.8	10.9	78.5	6 508	12 039	27 510	2.0	2.1	37 675	11.3	15.4	15.7
Sanilac	159	1 495	10 303	5.0	72.1	8.4	54.3	6 134	10 330	23 107	-5.5	1.0	33 925	12.6	17.4	17.2
Schoolcraft	NA	NA	2 059	8.6	71.6	8.9	7.9	6 200	9 740	20 112	-3.6	0.6	30 237	15.3	21.5	22.9
Shiawassee	176	1 896	18 869	8.9	78.7	10.3	96.7	6 735	12 244	30 283	-8.4	1.5	39 898	9.5	12.7	13.1
Tuscola	158	1 826	14 722	9.5	73.0	8.1	86.7	7 029	11 543	27 374	-10.9	1.2	37 701	10.8	14.6	14.9
Van Buren	397	3 361	18 843	6.9	71.8	12.1	121.2	6 870	11 233	25 491	-1.2	1.7	35 586	13.9	17.9	20.4
Washtenaw	324	3 374	103 484	8.8	87.2	41.9	352.4	7 824	17 115	36 307	4.7	6.6	54 326	8.1	11.0	10.8
Wayne	1 293	5 482	569 252	15.7	70.0	13.7	2 737.4	7 714	13 016	27 997	-10.3	3.1	37 525	17.3	25.6	23.4
Wexford	371	4 163	6 764	6.7	74.6	12.6	41.3	7 146	10 952	22 915	2.1	1.4	32 931	13.7	19.0	19.9
MINNESOTA	281	3 208	1 175 027	14.4	82.4	21.8	5 816.3	6 791	14 389	30 909	3.8	3.6	45 311	8.9	12.6	10.9
Aitkin	144	3 046	2 629	2.3	70.5	9.5	15.2	6 427	9 281	17 564	-1.7	0.9	28 580	15.6	24.0	21.4
Anoka	191	3 486	67 791	10.0	86.7	15.5	374.4	5 905	14 554	40 076	2.2	2.7	55 398	5.3	8.1	6.7
Becker	63	1 650	7 079	5.5	72.9	12.0	31.3	6 355	9 889	20 920	-1.5	1.3	32 279	14.7	19.4	17.5
Beltrami	154	3 914	11 596	3.6	75.9	20.4	64.7	7 766	8 938	20 925	2.0	0.8	30 575	19.8	24.0	23.5
Benton	187	1 940	8 347	14.1	77.3	14.8	29.0	5 632	11 018	26 619	2.4	1.0	41 020	8.6	11.7	9.9
Big Stone	189	1 512	1 333	3.9	72.3	10.1	8.9	6 678	9 575	19 408	-6.0	0.9	28 715	15.2	21.7	19.3
Blue Earth	189	3 670	21 082	7.4	82.7	22.7	65.6	6 308	11 125	25 366	-3.0	1.6	38 723	10.7	13.5	11.5
Brown	74	1 583	6 678	30.6	71.7	12.3	27.2	6 050	11 244	25 032	-3.0	1.6	38 445	8.0	10.5	8.9
Carlton	104	1 629	7 616	6.2	75.1	12.2	42.6	6 496	10 878	24 900	-9.5	0.9	38 584	10.8	15.2	13.1
Carver	111	1 809	12 839	23.6	84.6	21.4	74.8	6 836	16 116	39 188	14.2	5.3	63 721	3.8	5.2	4.2
Cass	361	5 013	5 018	4.1	72.5	11.4	34.0	6 850	8 991	18 732	2.3	0.9	29 260	16.4	24.1	20.4
Chippewa	23	1 192	3 137	2.1	73.7	10.9	20.0	7 543	11 067	22 227	-0.8	1.5	36 461	10.4	14.6	12.2
Chisago	97	2 584	8 041	6.3	80.1	11.9	45.5	5 710	12 526	31 281	0.9	2.1	50 120	6.4	8.9	7.4
Clay	158	2 182	18 459	16.2	80.5	21.5	57.1	6 145	10 836	25 891	-6.8	1.5	39 498	11.8	15.8	14.4
Clearwater	249	1 816	2 076	2.0	64.9	9.8	12.1	6 730	8 359	17 752	4.9	0.7	27 856	19.5	25.2	24.0
Cook	77	3 038	798	8.8	84.9	20.7	5.1	6 874	12 067	22 908	-6.6	1.3	35 476	7.6	10.6	10.6
Cottonwood	107	2 022	2 874	7.4	71.7	12.3	14.4	7 226	10 335	21 661	-8.5	0.9	32 006	11.8	16.9	15.0
Crow Wing	212	4 042	11 049	5.1	75.7	13.5	61.6	6 075	10 911	22 250	4.7	1.1	34 540	11.8	16.0	14.9
Dakota	129	2 821	75 044	14.0	90.7	27.6	443.0	6 282	17 237	42 218	6.8	5.4	61 030	4.4	6.6	5.4
Dodge	73	976	4 164	3.8	78.7	11.7	21.8	5 509	11 932	29 071	3.2	1.7	46 218	6.9	9.4	7.8
Douglas	131	2 876	7 540	8.8	76.1	12.7	32.3	5 754	10 264	22 067	0.7	1.2	35 842	10.2	13.2	11.5
Faribault	93	1 391	4 121	7.3	74.4	12.0	16.0	5 911	11 276	22 421	-7.2	1.4	32 369	11.5	16.4	13.9
Fillmore	47	762	4 831	6.5	70.2	10.5	21.5	6 197	10 146	22 155	0.7	1.4	33 802	10.9	14.6	12.7
Freeborn	135	2 148	7 760	4.2	75.5	11.5	31.0	6 030	11 452	24 764	-10.3	1.3	35 243	10.6	15.3	13.5
Goodhue	190	3 089	10 269	7.3	78.0	14.1	55.6	5 966	12 892	29 237	2.4	2.3	44 863	6.5	8.9	7.6

1. Data for serious crimes have not been adjusted for underreporting; this may affect comparability between geographic areas and over time.   2. Per 100,000 population estimated by the FBI.   3. All persons 3 years old and over enrolled in nursery school through college.   4. Persons 25 years old and over.   5. Elementary and secondary education expenditures, local government fiscal years ending between July 1, 1998 and June 30, 1999.   6. Based on population enumerated as of April 1, 1990.

STATE County	Total (mil dol) 62	Percent change, 1998–1999 63	Dollars 64	Rank 65	Wages and salaries[2] (mil dol) 66	Proprietor's income (mil dol) 67	Dividends, interest, and rent (mil dol) 68	Total (mil dol) 69	Total (mil dol) 70	Social Security (mil dol) 71	Medical payments (mil dol) 72	Income maintenance (mil dol) 73	Unemployment insurance (mil dol) 74
MICHIGAN—Cont'd													
Leelanau	546	6.4	28 205	306	164	48	145	73	69	41	21	3	2
Lenawee	2 448	7.2	24 532	749	1 219	101	395	343	324	158	122	24	9
Livingston	4 963	7.7	32 763	133	1 666	227	778	331	302	170	99	14	8
Luce	123	-1.2	18 194	2 498	64	11	24	35	34	12	16	3	1
Mackinac	276	4.3	24 835	697	132	25	65	57	55	25	20	3	4
Macomb	23 122	4.8	29 192	251	15 535	892	4 270	2 770	2 618	1 316	1 043	127	70
Manistee	489	9.8	20 660	1 789	231	27	118	117	112	52	46	7	3
Marquette	1 394	5.8	22 207	1 297	874	63	258	255	243	101	94	17	8
Mason	604	5.1	21 608	1 484	337	36	126	121	116	53	40	10	4
Mecosta	723	4.6	17 758	2 585	344	52	146	143	136	63	45	13	3
Menominee	538	4.5	22 015	1 363	263	39	103	98	94	45	34	7	3
Midland	2 601	4.5	31 726	159	1 617	130	605	260	245	125	90	18	5
Missaukee	260	11.0	18 388	2 444	75	28	43	51	48	24	17	5	2
Monroe	3 942	7.5	27 203	401	1 713	249	599	475	448	220	166	32	10
Montcalm	1 055	5.8	17 184	2 703	599	86	147	212	200	91	77	19	5
Montmorency	177	5.5	17 716	2 598	53	15	47	63	61	31	21	4	2
Muskegon	3 693	5.3	21 977	1 372	2 258	164	615	671	638	284	238	78	17
Newaygo	876	6.8	18 894	2 320	344	68	151	170	162	76	57	15	7
Oakland	52 091	6.1	44 146	27	38 123	3 291	10 837	3 769	3 542	1 704	1 455	210	80
Oceana	486	5.8	19 532	2 131	183	36	90	105	100	45	36	11	5
Ogemaw	365	7.5	17 198	2 701	165	33	70	113	108	49	43	10	3
Ontonagon	154	4.1	20 141	1 956	70	13	29	45	44	20	17	3	2
Osceola	427	6.3	19 225	2 225	252	35	68	94	90	41	33	9	2
Oscoda	140	6.8	15 754	2 923	48	18	22	44	42	21	15	4	1
Otsego	519	4.5	22 829	1 131	344	59	97	82	77	40	27	5	3
Ottawa	6 443	4.7	27 983	335	4 193	382	1 206	556	512	286	164	27	16
Presque Isle	266	6.1	18 240	2 483	97	23	62	73	70	37	23	5	3
Roscommon	470	5.9	19 935	2 013	155	46	115	153	148	76	55	10	2
Saginaw	5 051	4.3	24 140	832	3 846	297	915	896	856	357	330	119	22
St. Clair	4 077	4.9	25 206	637	1 712	196	741	561	530	244	203	43	15
St. Joseph	1 405	6.5	22 864	1 121	862	73	240	219	207	100	79	17	5
Sanilac	973	6.4	22 400	1 242	359	78	184	187	179	79	76	12	6
Schoolcraft	185	7.3	21 023	1 662	84	17	34	47	45	19	18	4	2
Shiawassee	1 524	4.8	21 060	1 650	557	85	218	259	245	108	102	18	7
Tuscola	1 222	8.2	20 991	1 670	471	77	172	225	214	94	92	15	7
Van Buren	1 548	5.7	20 392	1 866	711	106	217	289	274	117	113	30	7
Washtenaw	11 400	8.2	37 244	68	8 652	633	2 117	803	744	332	300	58	12
Wayne	55 462	4.3	26 329	484	41 826	3 218	8 474	9 851	9 445	3 147	4 436	1 397	186
Wexford	651	10.9	22 014	1 364	503	46	113	119	114	52	43	10	4
MINNESOTA	146 810	5.4	30 742	X	98 294	9 707	30 777	15 951	14 978	6 273	6 082	1 342	359
Aitkin	290	5.4	20 296	1 890	93	27	77	79	76	35	28	6	2
Anoka	8 171	7.2	27 333	391	3 974	278	1 189	660	600	269	222	45	22
Becker	639	6.1	21 469	1 527	296	83	132	122	116	47	45	13	3
Beltrami	807	4.3	20 573	1 821	454	62	166	162	154	46	63	27	4
Benton	787	3.8	22 590	1 196	396	56	152	90	82	35	32	7	3
Big Stone	126	3.7	22 690	1 169	43	17	38	28	27	12	11	2	0
Blue Earth	1 450	5.2	26 918	422	982	123	360	172	161	72	58	13	3
Brown	679	5.5	25 248	625	399	61	177	101	96	48	36	5	2
Carlton	693	4.0	21 990	1 370	447	35	128	127	120	52	47	9	3
Carver	2 295	8.7	34 249	101	1 030	141	391	133	120	58	46	6	4
Cass	545	5.3	20 170	1 943	211	64	143	127	121	51	46	13	3
Chippewa	329	3.0	25 221	633	157	43	80	51	48	22	19	3	2
Chisago	1 087	7.6	25 693	557	354	62	193	118	110	49	43	7	4
Clay	1 122	3.8	21 702	1 452	476	79	229	174	164	65	63	16	2
Clearwater	153	5.4	18 824	2 340	72	16	29	38	37	12	16	5	2
Cook	125	3.8	26 226	491	63	18	33	19	18	9	6	1	1
Cottonwood	275	0.1	23 127	1 067	118	39	72	55	52	25	21	4	1
Crow Wing	1 242	5.7	23 606	941	732	96	277	227	216	97	79	17	5
Dakota	11 600	6.7	33 225	127	5 665	364	2 116	725	654	312	225	40	21
Dodge	428	2.2	24 593	731	138	40	79	50	47	21	20	3	1
Douglas	769	6.2	24 582	734	419	73	189	125	119	56	45	8	2
Faribault	364	0.8	22 431	1 232	154	41	98	73	70	33	29	5	1
Fillmore	464	4.1	22 435	1 231	174	54	109	85	81	36	36	5	1
Freeborn	719	3.1	22 835	1 128	379	44	165	132	126	64	46	8	1
Goodhue	1 197	4.0	27 611	361	670	91	269	144	135	67	52	7	3

1. Based on the resident population estimated as of July 1 of the year shown.　2. Includes other labor income.

Table B. States and Counties — Earnings, Social Security, and Housing

STATE County	Earnings, 1999									Social Security beneficiaries, December 2000			Housing units, 1990	
	Total (mil dol)	Percent by selected industries								Number	Rate[3]	Supplemental Security Income recipients, December 2000	Total	Percent change, 1980–1990
		Farm	Goods-related[1]		Service-related and other[2]				Govern-ment					
			Total	Manu-facturing	Total	Retail trade	Finance, insur-ance, and real estate	Services						
	75	76	77	78	79	80	81	82	83	84	85	86	87	88
MICHIGAN—Cont'd														
Leelanau	212	4.0	D	5.2	D	11.7	6.4	36.3	13.4	4 624	219	108	11 171	23.1
Lenawee	1 320	1.1	D	37.9	D	10.8	4.2	17.5	16.7	17 674	179	1 587	35 104	4.0
Livingston	1 892	0.2	36.8	25.0	52.8	10.9	9.6	20.5	10.3	18 434	117	580	41 863	19.8
Luce	74	1.9	18.1	13.6	33.4	11.5	2.4	8.9	46.6	1 462	208	220	3 594	0.6
Mackinac	156	0.0	D	5.9	D	16.8	2.6	32.7	22.5	3 008	252	211	9 254	21.4
Macomb	16 427	0.1	50.5	43.2	39.1	7.9	3.3	19.8	10.4	136 529	173	8 112	274 843	16.2
Manistee	258	0.7	35.7	27.7	42.3	11.1	2.9	18.1	21.3	6 067	247	466	13 330	8.9
Marquette	937	0.0	D	3.9	52.9	9.6	4.4	28.9	24.8	11 619	180	1 006	31 049	1.7
Mason	373	1.6	39.4	32.9	D	10.4	2.8	19.3	18.6	6 204	219	579	14 119	6.7
Mecosta	397	1.8	D	17.7	D	11.5	2.6	15.6	37.4	7 342	181	833	17 274	11.3
Menominee	301	2.1	36.4	32.0	44.7	7.9	2.6	18.4	16.8	5 393	213	393	12 509	8.3
Midland	1 747	0.1	57.6	48.9	33.8	6.1	2.7	21.1	8.5	13 821	167	1 051	29 343	11.3
Missaukee	104	8.7	36.2	26.0	38.5	9.8	2.7	10.5	16.7	2 980	206	219	7 112	16.3
Monroe	1 962	0.5	44.7	37.7	42.3	9.2	3.2	15.8	12.5	24 166	166	1 829	48 312	6.5
Montcalm	685	3.7	D	33.7	D	10.5	2.9	17.1	17.6	10 920	178	1 281	22 817	9.2
Montmorency	68	0.3	D	25.1	D	11.8	3.7	17.1	20.3	3 526	342	257	8 791	11.5
Muskegon	2 422	0.4	D	31.9	D	11.3	2.9	21.6	15.7	32 157	189	4 908	61 962	6.4
Newaygo	411	2.7	D	25.3	D	9.3	4.6	20.2	21.9	9 052	189	906	20 105	9.8
Oakland	41 414	0.0	29.0	23.4	64.8	7.8	8.6	35.2	6.2	171 148	143	14 155	432 684	15.9
Oceana	220	7.8	30.6	20.5	40.5	10.7	2.9	16.3	21.1	5 377	200	690	12 857	12.8
Ogemaw	198	2.2	24.9	18.0	51.4	19.1	4.0	16.0	21.5	5 808	268	593	13 977	7.7
Ontonagon	83	0.5	D	28.9	D	10.1	2.9	12.1	28.4	2 308	295	216	5 332	5.8
Osceola	288	1.3	D	44.8	D	7.7	1.3	12.1	14.2	5 005	216	672	11 444	15.3
Oscoda	66	0.5	38.3	32.5	38.7	13.9	3.7	15.3	22.5	2 545	270	189	8 112	11.0
Otsego	403	0.2	34.9	17.9	52.4	13.7	3.7	23.4	12.5	4 572	196	342	10 669	17.5
Ottawa	4 575	1.5	51.0	43.5	36.6	7.6	3.5	15.8	10.9	31 564	132	1 605	66 624	23.5
Presque Isle	120	3.7	D	9.8	D	13.9	3.4	18.0	19.8	4 205	292	322	8 917	6.6
Roscommon	201	0.0	D	6.2	D	22.4	4.3	20.3	25.5	8 505	334	608	19 881	10.9
Saginaw	4 143	0.6	42.7	37.1	45.6	9.2	4.1	22.6	11.1	39 103	186	6 778	81 931	3.0
St. Clair	1 908	0.3	32.0	24.4	53.3	10.7	4.0	23.3	14.4	27 015	164	2 464	57 494	10.8
St. Joseph	935	1.0	D	49.9	D	7.7	2.0	10.9	14.8	11 089	178	965	24 242	7.8
Sanilac	437	7.1	37.2	29.1	37.4	9.9	3.4	17.2	18.3	9 241	207	693	19 465	5.3
Schoolcraft	101	0.2	32.1	19.0	39.3	11.1	5.5	15.3	28.4	2 222	250	214	5 487	10.3
Shiawassee	641	1.4	28.5	21.3	50.7	12.8	4.4	23.0	19.5	12 080	169	1 255	25 833	5.6
Tuscola	548	5.6	25.3	18.6	44.5	9.2	11.6	13.6	24.6	10 730	184	1 040	21 231	5.9
Van Buren	818	3.1	D	26.3	D	9.8	D	14.0	22.0	13 541	178	1 860	31 530	9.5
Washtenaw	9 286	0.0	31.7	27.7	42.9	7.7	3.0	25.1	25.3	34 152	106	3 498	111 256	13.3
Wayne	45 044	0.0	36.4	32.5	50.3	6.8	5.6	23.2	13.2	339 671	165	76 657	832 710	-4.8
Wexford	549	0.2	D	37.2	D	11.1	2.4	21.2	13.3	6 106	200	712	12 862	11.1
MINNESOTA	108 000	1.0	26.2	19.6	59.8	9.3	8.8	27.1	13.0	739 824	150	64 059	1 848 445	14.6
Aitkin	120	-1.2	D	13.1	D	14.2	3.8	D	22.1	4 315	282	270	12 934	16.3
Anoka	4 252	0.0	42.0	31.8	45.2	10.7	2.9	20.3	12.8	30 737	103	1 625	85 519	36.0
Becker	379	4.9	D	14.6	D	10.8	D	24.5	18.7	6 232	208	533	15 563	0.9
Beltrami	516	0.2	16.0	6.3	56.6	13.6	3.6	26.3	27.3	6 305	159	988	14 670	12.0
Benton	453	2.7	43.0	30.3	44.3	12.7	2.4	16.2	9.9	4 593	134	264	11 521	30.7
Big Stone	60	15.0	D	2.1	D	9.7	5.4	16.4	26.5	1 645	283	99	3 192	-8.6
Blue Earth	1 105	2.5	D	13.9	D	11.2	5.1	26.3	17.7	8 550	153	840	20 358	5.0
Brown	461	4.9	D	32.8	D	8.3	D	19.6	11.2	5 753	214	236	10 814	3.3
Carlton	482	-0.2	43.3	24.9	36.4	7.3	2.9	17.0	20.5	6 193	196	451	12 342	4.8
Carver	1 172	1.2	D	36.7	D	6.4	6.0	20.3	12.8	6 756	96	185	17 449	38.6
Cass	276	-0.3	14.7	3.5	60.5	13.8	5.2	35.1	25.0	6 819	251	540	18 863	7.3
Chippewa	200	10.3	D	19.4	D	8.8	4.2	14.2	15.5	2 801	214	132	5 755	-6.0
Chisago	415	0.8	33.1	19.3	49.6	10.8	4.2	27.3	16.4	5 918	144	283	11 946	24.9
Clay	555	3.9	D	7.3	D	12.1	3.9	23.9	25.6	7 874	154	727	18 546	4.1
Clearwater	88	-0.7	D	16.3	D	7.9	2.5	13.2	26.7	1 744	207	228	4 008	4.8
Cook	81	0.0	D	D	D	13.1	2.6	36.9	25.1	1 055	204	34	4 312	24.8
Cottonwood	157	12.5	D	18.2	D	8.2	4.1	18.9	17.3	3 146	259	208	5 495	-5.3
Crow Wing	828	-0.4	D	15.7	D	13.8	6.6	24.3	19.4	11 757	213	893	29 916	16.5
Dakota	6 029	0.2	29.4	20.8	58.6	11.0	7.1	22.6	11.8	35 433	100	1 711	102 707	53.6
Dodge	179	8.1	D	24.6	D	7.2	4.4	13.5	17.7	2 569	145	132	5 771	4.3
Douglas	493	1.1	D	19.2	D	13.0	4.2	19.4	17.4	7 288	222	434	14 590	10.7
Faribault	194	3.9	34.0	24.6	46.1	7.2	5.0	16.9	16.0	4 123	255	215	7 416	-6.7
Fillmore	229	11.4	D	18.2	D	9.8	5.5	16.2	16.8	4 726	224	225	8 356	-1.1
Freeborn	423	1.7	D	27.9	D	12.3	4.4	22.9	12.3	7 587	233	412	13 783	-0.2
Goodhue	761	3.8	29.0	24.4	54.7	7.7	3.8	26.5	12.4	7 827	177	358	15 936	10.9

1. Covers mining, construction, and manufacturing. 2. Covers private sector earnings in agricultural services, forestry, and fisheries; transportation and public utilities; wholesale trade; retail trade; finance, insurance, and real estate; and services. 3. Per 1,000 resident population estimated as of July 1 of the year shown.

Table B. States and Counties — Housing, Labor Force, and Employment

	Housing units, 1990 (cont'd)								Civilian labor force, 2001				Civilian employment, 1990[5]		
	Occupied units										Unemployment			Percent	
	Owner-occupied					Renter-occupied										
				Owner cost as a percent of income											
STATE County	Total	Percent	Median value[1]	With a mortgage	Without a mortgage	Median rent[2]	Rent as percent of income	Substandard units[3] (percent)	Total	Percent change, 2000–2001	Total	Rate[4]	Total	Professional, managerial, and technical	Precision production, craft, and repair
	89	90	91	92	93	94	95	96	97	98	99	100	101	102	103
MICHIGAN—Cont'd															
Leelanau	6 274	81.5	73 100	21.6	13.7	414	24.2	2.7	11 237	-1.8	384	3.4	7 701	29.1	14.2
Lenawee	31 635	75.9	54 000	17.2	12.8	382	25.4	2.8	49 942	1.2	2 770	5.5	40 681	22.2	13.5
Livingston	38 887	84.5	97 300	20.0	13.5	521	24.3	1.9	84 182	0.5	2 620	3.1	58 567	30.8	14.9
Luce	2 154	79.1	30 800	18.6	12.1	306	29.5	3.4	2 654	2.0	184	6.9	2 073	22.9	9.5
Mackinac	4 240	76.0	43 900	19.4	13.6	297	25.9	3.8	7 451	-2.1	693	9.3	3 893	21.0	14.3
Macomb	264 991	77.2	76 800	18.4	13.4	493	24.5	2.0	450 513	-1.2	22 382	5.0	355 676	28.2	14.2
Manistee	8 580	78.2	40 400	18.8	14.0	287	29.3	2.1	11 464	0.8	813	7.1	7 967	20.8	13.9
Marquette	25 435	64.2	44 800	17.6	13.6	333	25.2	2.3	33 514	0.4	2 002	6.0	28 858	27.5	13.3
Mason	9 984	75.9	43 300	18.8	13.7	304	27.9	1.8	15 701	4.3	1 789	11.4	10 244	22.4	14.2
Mecosta	12 260	69.9	49 100	19.1	13.5	339	35.1	3.3	18 279	1.8	963	5.3	15 094	25.6	10.2
Menominee	9 766	78.9	37 900	19.5	15.2	293	24.8	3.0	12 643	-3.5	829	6.6	10 758	19.2	13.1
Midland	27 791	76.9	63 300	17.0	11.7	407	25.5	1.9	43 784	-0.8	1 765	4.0	34 488	37.2	12.3
Missaukee	4 389	83.0	40 500	19.7	13.6	340	30.9	3.7	6 865	-4.6	550	8.0	4 637	18.4	12.1
Monroe	46 508	77.8	67 200	16.1	13.3	423	26.3	2.1	75 230	-2.0	3 258	4.3	60 862	21.8	15.8
Montcalm	18 563	79.4	42 600	18.0	14.1	340	25.2	3.1	27 230	3.9	2 115	7.8	20 595	17.5	17.1
Montmorency	3 600	81.5	41 700	23.0	14.8	329	33.2	4.2	3 626	0.7	464	12.8	2 664	19.8	15.2
Muskegon	57 798	74.4	46 300	16.9	13.2	362	29.7	3.1	86 998	0.7	5 997	6.9	65 424	23.6	13.6
Newaygo	13 776	82.2	44 300	19.9	13.9	348	28.4	4.4	21 518	-0.4	1 757	8.2	15 139	20.9	15.5
Oakland	410 488	72.7	95 400	19.4	13.2	557	24.4	2.1	688 042	-1.5	26 616	3.9	557 134	39.0	10.0
Oceana	8 071	80.3	43 300	19.0	14.2	333	28.5	3.9	14 324	0.2	1 173	8.2	8 889	18.2	15.5
Ogemaw	7 190	81.4	39 500	22.7	15.0	327	31.4	4.1	9 575	0.9	799	8.3	6 029	18.8	14.1
Ontonagon	3 641	81.0	28 100	15.5	13.2	248	24.6	3.4	2 892	-4.2	267	9.2	3 464	18.9	18.5
Osceola	7 347	79.9	37 500	20.0	14.5	300	27.3	3.6	11 095	2.1	892	8.0	7 527	19.7	13.4
Oscoda	3 160	81.9	37 400	21.4	14.9	317	35.1	4.2	3 415	-2.8	376	11.0	2 490	19.2	12.3
Otsego	6 522	79.1	56 000	21.1	13.7	365	25.5	2.5	13 994	0.0	865	6.2	8 042	23.3	13.5
Ottawa	62 664	80.7	74 600	18.4	12.6	454	23.3	2.2	144 344	0.0	6 185	4.3	96 179	26.7	12.6
Presque Isle	5 376	83.7	44 000	20.7	13.7	276	28.1	3.5	6 479	-0.7	722	11.1	4 915	19.6	14.4
Roscommon	8 516	81.9	44 500	21.9	14.3	326	35.1	2.7	8 473	1.4	640	7.6	6 108	23.5	12.4
Saginaw	78 256	70.7	48 100	16.5	13.5	389	30.4	3.0	102 921	0.0	6 067	5.9	87 273	24.4	12.4
St. Clair	52 882	75.7	59 400	17.9	14.1	409	28.4	2.3	83 499	-0.3	5 770	6.9	64 179	22.9	16.3
St. Joseph	21 579	74.8	44 800	16.9	12.6	345	25.4	3.0	34 287	0.4	2 327	6.8	26 307	20.1	13.9
Sanilac	14 658	79.4	42 400	18.8	15.0	337	26.1	2.6	21 104	0.7	1 742	8.3	15 998	18.9	14.1
Schoolcraft	3 294	77.0	32 300	18.3	13.3	273	29.5	2.2	4 357	-2.2	394	9.0	2 862	21.8	10.2
Shiawassee	24 864	77.7	47 200	16.4	13.0	363	25.5	2.0	35 974	-1.2	2 170	6.0	31 533	20.9	15.0
Tuscola	19 469	81.2	46 000	17.7	13.1	358	28.7	2.7	27 903	1.2	2 203	7.9	22 632	18.5	14.8
Van Buren	25 402	76.7	48 000	19.3	13.9	343	27.7	3.7	37 784	0.8	2 265	6.0	29 997	22.8	13.4
Washtenaw	104 528	55.3	96 000	19.9	13.1	536	27.8	3.1	178 652	0.1	4 222	2.4	151 680	42.9	7.7
Wayne	780 535	63.9	48 500	17.4	13.9	406	29.8	4.1	974 264	-1.1	56 674	5.8	843 731	26.1	11.2
Wexford	9 923	74.7	41 200	17.2	13.2	356	28.1	3.1	15 396	-3.8	1 578	10.2	10 540	24.4	12.2
MINNESOTA	1 647 853	71.8	74 000	20.4	12.4	422	26.7	2.4	2 814 357	2.8	104 059	3.7	2 192 417	30.3	10.1
Aitkin	5 126	83.9	48 600	23.0	14.1	243	28.2	4.5	6 245	1.3	467	7.5	4 445	21.0	12.6
Anoka	82 437	81.2	83 500	21.1	11.5	498	27.0	1.9	187 438	3.0	6 274	3.3	132 961	26.2	13.8
Becker	10 477	77.8	49 000	19.6	13.2	269	28.2	3.9	15 140	3.1	931	6.1	11 354	21.7	12.4
Beltrami	11 870	73.1	49 200	21.1	13.1	320	30.9	6.1	20 841	1.9	1 019	4.9	13 931	29.7	8.9
Benton	10 935	67.0	60 800	19.3	12.9	395	26.0	2.7	21 617	2.6	946	4.4	14 938	21.8	12.2
Big Stone	2 463	80.9	27 000	17.1	12.7	227	27.6	1.5	2 733	-0.3	115	4.2	2 657	18.8	11.4
Blue Earth	19 277	64.0	59 500	18.3	12.3	374	29.0	2.3	34 825	2.4	924	2.7	27 709	24.9	10.3
Brown	10 321	77.3	48 900	16.3	12.0	283	24.6	2.0	15 265	1.8	657	4.3	12 798	20.9	12.3
Carlton	10 842	81.1	45 200	16.4	12.2	291	26.9	3.4	16 632	2.9	963	5.8	11 846	24.7	12.8
Carver	16 601	79.0	95 700	22.4	12.5	442	25.2	1.8	41 705	3.2	1 231	3.0	26 057	27.9	12.4
Cass	8 302	82.9	50 500	21.4	13.8	294	27.5	4.9	13 114	3.5	809	6.2	7 683	22.1	12.5
Chippewa	5 245	75.4	34 200	17.5	12.5	267	24.9	1.4	6 976	2.3	396	5.7	5 930	22.1	11.6
Chisago	10 551	85.0	72 600	22.3	12.6	375	28.9	1.8	22 608	3.1	1 073	4.7	13 992	23.1	14.7
Clay	17 490	68.3	58 600	18.1	12.2	335	31.7	3.0	30 783	3.1	824	2.7	24 274	27.2	8.2
Clearwater	3 064	81.6	29 400	20.1	14.8	240	28.5	7.4	4 278	0.0	495	11.6	2 909	22.1	11.6
Cook	1 632	76.6	55 600	20.6	12.6	316	21.8	8.4	3 131	5.4	144	4.6	1 782	27.1	10.7
Cottonwood	5 060	77.6	29 600	15.5	11.8	245	24.1	1.2	5 510	-3.2	213	3.9	5 527	20.7	8.7
Crow Wing	17 204	76.7	54 200	19.2	12.7	329	28.7	2.6	29 240	3.9	1 337	4.6	18 184	26.5	11.9
Dakota	98 293	73.9	95 900	21.9	11.9	542	25.3	1.8	222 432	2.9	6 155	2.8	153 515	34.2	9.6
Dodge	5 538	80.9	53 000	19.6	12.9	281	24.4	2.1	9 817	3.7	389	4.0	7 748	23.5	10.1
Douglas	10 988	74.2	56 400	20.7	12.7	297	28.2	2.3	17 657	3.6	645	3.7	12 805	23.6	11.5
Faribault	6 772	78.8	32 200	16.4	12.6	265	23.1	1.3	8 127	1.9	349	4.3	7 275	20.7	12.7
Fillmore	7 822	78.1	38 000	17.2	12.8	249	22.6	3.5	10 133	1.1	412	4.1	9 479	18.6	10.8
Freeborn	13 029	76.7	42 800	17.1	12.3	286	24.9	1.7	17 305	3.4	777	4.5	14 897	21.8	10.4
Goodhue	15 198	76.5	63 300	18.0	12.6	321	24.5	1.5	24 040	2.4	849	3.5	19 554	23.8	12.2

1. Specified owner-occupied units.   2. Specified renter-occupied units.   3. Overcrowded or lacking complete plumbing facilities.   4. Percent of civilian labor force.   5. Persons 16 years and older.

Table B. States and Counties — Nonfarm Employment and Agriculture

	Private nonfarm establishments, employment and payroll, 1999								Agriculture, 1997			
STATE County	Number of establish-ments	Employment					Annual payroll		Farms			Farm operators
		Total	Health Care and Social Assistance	Manufac-turing	Retail trade	Finance and Insurance	Professional Scientific and Technical Services	Total (mil dol)	Average per employee (dollars)	Number	Percent with—		Whose principal occu-pation is farming (percent)
											Less than 50 acres	500 acres and over	
	104	105	106	107	108	109	110	111	112	113	114	115	116

MICHIGAN—Cont'd													
Leelanau	686	4 214	356	262	648	98	121	100	23 629	369	26.3	4.9	61.0
Lenawee	2 131	30 515	3 588	9 597	4 958	933	546	845	27 689	1 317	30.1	14.7	45.0
Livingston	3 712	43 541	3 426	10 047	7 192	2 125	1 776	1 337	30 710	637	51.8	6.9	43.6
Luce	193	1 588	288	D	352	63	D	33	20 929	31	29.0	22.6	29.0
Mackinac	534	2 649	323	111	469	115	59	72	27 199	72	15.3	15.3	45.8
Macomb	18 732	319 239	29 160	90 091	49 225	7 135	15 256	12 385	38 794	523	49.5	5.5	52.2
Manistee	638	5 865	986	1 462	972	185	83	141	24 048	284	23.2	6.7	47.9
Marquette	1 682	20 901	4 881	788	3 684	911	540	545	26 080	108	33.3	11.1	30.6
Mason	842	9 223	1 081	2 676	1 568	242	260	236	25 639	413	30.0	8.7	46.0
Mecosta	917	9 695	1 362	2 026	1 970	283	178	201	20 708	597	17.9	8.0	43.7
Menominee	535	7 141	520	3 024	826	226	120	162	22 633	348	14.1	19.3	50.9
Midland	1 943	36 772	5 743	6 712	5 252	771	1 033	1 397	37 992	418	33.7	9.6	40.4
Missaukee	341	2 245	D	601	464	68	47	50	22 224	335	17.9	18.2	57.0
Monroe	2 514	37 729	4 084	10 124	5 649	953	669	1 284	34 024	1 058	44.0	11.2	44.4
Montcalm	1 072	14 991	1 720	5 748	2 719	438	168	361	24 090	954	25.3	12.8	48.2
Montmorency	253	1 721	184	404	300	59	D	39	22 512	103	15.5	13.6	42.7
Muskegon	3 632	56 293	7 807	16 132	9 004	1 373	1 350	1 601	28 447	410	44.6	7.1	44.9
Newaygo	782	9 033	1 097	2 178	1 557	286	247	248	27 437	670	27.6	8.7	47.3
Oakland	41 811	768 482	80 640	89 966	85 514	48 634	78 294	31 982	41 617	544	66.9	2.2	34.7
Oceana	598	4 152	416	1 129	775	118	82	93	22 337	573	28.1	11.0	51.5
Ogemaw	592	5 386	1 028	892	1 437	129	102	108	20 137	261	15.3	13.8	50.2
Ontonagon	229	1 609	205	D	361	82	D	38	23 463	92	5.4	20.7	56.5
Osceola	419	6 754	679	3 662	746	92	97	171	25 367	496	16.5	8.5	45.4
Oscoda	235	1 681	D	520	342	52	D	35	20 934	80	21.2	5.0	53.8
Otsego	894	10 202	1 190	1 704	1 690	197	231	253	24 751	139	17.3	13.7	36.0
Ottawa	5 783	103 389	8 886	41 072	12 851	2 181	2 992	3 083	29 817	1 292	48.4	5.4	50.9
Presque Isle	430	3 440	319	311	883	113	68	73	21 182	296	12.2	12.8	48.3
Roscommon	730	4 864	495	390	1 528	242	83	96	19 692	36	44.4	2.8	38.9
Saginaw	5 056	89 515	14 219	20 090	15 303	2 860	3 470	2 966	33 130	1 163	30.0	13.8	55.0
St. Clair	3 550	48 751	6 834	12 788	8 444	1 255	1 139	1 376	28 234	940	35.0	6.7	45.3
St. Joseph	1 311	20 414	1 736	9 350	2 497	508	243	576	28 211	791	28.2	15.8	52.2
Sanilac	998	11 013	1 503	4 667	1 710	355	192	245	22 266	1 448	21.5	16.2	62.0
Schoolcraft	281	1 972	322	279	464	134	36	49	24 986	45	22.2	22.2	44.4
Shiawassee	1 310	15 327	2 405	3 631	2 990	418	402	361	23 552	915	31.1	12.9	45.1
Tuscola	1 098	12 282	2 799	2 411	2 240	433	134	286	23 319	1 140	25.4	16.8	53.6
Van Buren	1 525	16 431	1 891	4 926	2 775	350	484	444	27 049	1 059	37.5	6.1	50.0
Washtenaw	8 188	154 719	28 105	30 461	18 808	3 789	10 958	6 015	38 876	1 030	39.9	8.8	46.4
Wayne	36 008	770 334	102 292	128 741	87 496	37 362	33 581	29 579	38 398	303	65.3	5.9	45.2
Wexford	848	14 125	1 747	4 493	2 726	270	307	349	24 736	251	21.9	5.6	41.0
MINNESOTA	137 305	2 338 642	313 049	378 953	297 066	140 283	115 887	75 338	32 214	73 367	18.0	20.8	60.0
Aitkin	403	3 096	580	466	550	88	44	58	18 628	587	13.3	14.8	40.2
Anoka	6 456	96 832	10 995	23 732	14 217	1 820	2 955	3 139	32 417	473	49.0	4.4	35.9
Becker	1 003	13 643	1 402	1 676	1 918	234	204	326	23 869	1 084	11.4	16.4	53.5
Beltrami	994	12 008	2 581	1 167	2 475	348	306	260	21 649	656	8.5	21.0	47.0
Benton	732	11 404	1 014	2 974	1 840	126	225	282	24 769	834	21.9	7.8	53.8
Big Stone	213	1 569	447	D	355	61	30	27	17 071	420	13.1	45.7	71.7
Blue Earth	1 677	26 729	4 678	4 287	5 531	865	798	613	22 924	1 037	19.1	29.4	67.0
Brown	724	12 432	1 855	3 861	1 699	390	344	285	22 915	1 054	13.1	20.2	75.0
Carlton	669	8 672	1 198	2 145	1 475	328	155	265	30 559	527	12.9	5.9	40.4
Carver	1 688	25 521	2 648	9 309	2 631	488	1 345	804	31 515	779	28.5	5.6	60.5
Cass	766	5 271	610	218	1 058	191	144	95	17 940	598	13.9	17.6	49.0
Chippewa	398	4 551	614	1 159	794	194	101	93	20 348	618	14.7	33.7	74.6
Chisago	1 058	10 148	2 520	2 222	1 531	278	293	240	23 678	762	30.8	5.8	37.1
Clay	1 132	15 131	1 907	1 021	2 848	412	366	291	19 218	887	14.0	39.8	69.6
Clearwater	207	1 828	487	384	294	74	75	38	20 587	570	6.3	19.6	50.4
Cook	267	1 863	145	D	308	35	D	35	19 053	11	9.1	9.1	18.2
Cottonwood	386	4 039	883	1 188	726	144	75	73	18 058	784	11.5	37.0	73.3
Crow Wing	1 883	20 026	3 563	2 814	3 850	724	1 040	493	24 634	593	20.9	10.6	42.7
Dakota	8 389	149 547	12 521	17 319	23 224	7 212	5 669	4 910	32 834	890	36.3	14.4	49.7
Dodge	404	3 570	161	1 107	574	134	67	97	27 215	674	24.6	22.0	60.7
Douglas	1 244	13 107	1 864	2 637	2 589	305	525	306	23 326	1 042	14.8	11.0	57.1
Faribault	484	4 998	829	1 543	655	225	130	99	19 723	878	13.4	35.0	76.5
Fillmore	656	5 593	1 110	1 210	894	226	107	106	19 014	1 546	19.2	16.2	62.5
Freeborn	979	12 179	2 037	3 297	2 177	364	265	276	22 630	1 151	25.0	24.0	63.6
Goodhue	1 271	19 064	2 678	4 907	2 473	546	403	477	25 041	1 489	25.5	14.4	57.0

Table B. States and Counties — **Agriculture, Land, and Water**

	Agriculture, 1997 (cont'd)															
STATE County	Land in farms					Value of land and buildings		Value of machinery and equipment average per farm ($1,000)	Value of products sold				Percent of farms with sales of —		Percent of land owned by fed. gov. 1997	Water consumption 1995 (mil gal/ day)
		Acres								Percent from —					
	Acreage (1,000)	Percent change, 1992–1997	Average size of farm	Total irrigated (1,000)	Total cropland (1,000)	Average per farm ($1,000)	Average per acre (dollars)		Total (mil dol)	Average per farm (dollars)	Crops	Livestock and poultry products	$10,000 or more	$100,000 or more		
	117	118	119	120	121	122	123	124	125	126	127	128	129	130	131	132
MICHIGAN—Cont'd																
Leelanau	62	-4.4	168	2	38	500	3 087	70	29	77 845	82.9	17.1	64.2	20.6	19.0	7.2
Lenawee	336	0.1	255	3	302	444	1 720	72	103	78 093	76.2	23.8	54.7	19.6	0.0	24.4
Livingston	98	-17.4	154	2	75	399	2 360	71	28	44 671	65.1	34.9	42.4	11.0	0.0	24.8
Luce	D	D	D	D	7	336	902	53	2	75 029	81.5	18.5	45.2	19.4	0.0	1.2
Mackinac	22	-2.2	299	D	14	196	657	34	3	35 373	13.5	86.5	36.1	4.2	22.3	14.7
Macomb	69	-1.7	132	2	59	430	3 446	61	45	85 534	92.3	7.7	54.1	16.4	0.9	80.0
Manistee	48	-1.0	167	3	28	239	1 368	47	9	32 030	89.2	10.8	33.8	7.7	24.3	37.2
Marquette	27	15.8	247	0	12	261	1 060	37	3	27 278	38.2	61.8	25.9	6.5	1.7	257.0
Mason	77	5.6	187	3	56	245	1 127	50	24	57 194	67.8	32.2	47.9	13.8	21.4	27.5
Mecosta	112	-7.5	188	7	82	217	1 270	50	25	41 651	40.4	59.6	37.9	8.9	0.7	15.9
Menominee	110	-0.3	315	0	63	226	728	60	18	52 592	13.3	86.7	46.0	16.7	0.0	7.6
Midland	80	-10.5	191	1	62	346	1 642	64	17	41 278	76.1	23.9	42.3	10.8	0.0	88.5
Missaukee	90	2.3	269	2	66	289	1 046	80	35	103 575	13.5	86.5	50.1	24.2	0.0	4.6
Monroe	210	-3.4	198	5	196	447	2 293	77	94	88 977	89.8	10.2	57.8	17.7	0.0	1 763.5
Montcalm	238	6.1	249	45	186	316	1 262	76	88	92 096	71.9	28.1	46.8	15.9	0.4	26.8
Montmorency	21	-4.4	204	D	14	200	993	46	3	31 755	36.7	63.3	39.8	8.7	0.0	2.8
Muskegon	73	-1.2	178	8	53	283	1 631	69	44	108 379	54.0	46.0	42.7	17.1	5.5	321.7
Newaygo	122	6.3	183	4	90	236	1 341	57	49	72 449	41.5	58.5	47.9	15.7	19.8	17.2
Oakland	45	-5.5	83	1	33	486	5 645	49	32	59 654	91.6	8.4	33.3	8.8	0.0	110.8
Oceana	128	-0.8	223	3	86	295	1 327	68	50	86 896	74.7	25.3	55.5	18.0	15.1	8.2
Ogemaw	73	-2.3	281	0	51	294	1 111	74	22	84 841	13.6	86.4	52.5	19.5	6.1	3.6
Ontonagon	33	-1.5	353	0	17	169	479	37	2	23 963	24.9	75.1	30.4	5.4	30.2	30.6
Osceola	108	-0.7	218	1	72	242	1 120	59	19	38 879	17.7	82.3	37.1	11.1	0.0	6.9
Oscoda	14	-0.7	174	0	8	195	1 121	25	2	23 494	19.1	80.9	43.8	3.8	41.5	1.5
Otsego	34	-4.3	248	1	19	343	1 300	62	4	27 407	65.7	34.3	30.2	7.2	0.0	4.2
Ottawa	171	-3.1	132	15	141	396	3 066	78	300	232 187	53.4	46.6	58.0	26.2	0.0	639.7
Presque Isle	82	3.1	279	3	54	204	878	37	13	44 206	59.7	40.3	41.2	11.8	0.3	6.3
Roscommon	4	3.5	115	0	3	149	1 299	23	1	14 255	73.1	26.9	41.7	0.0	0.0	3.6
Saginaw	298	-6.3	256	3	268	459	1 711	80	84	72 256	89.0	11.0	63.5	18.1	1.6	30.9
St. Clair	163	-10.5	173	1	141	416	2 517	56	36	38 378	76.7	23.3	43.7	8.2	0.0	1 562.5
St. Joseph	217	-7.5	275	91	185	504	1 762	95	81	102 533	77.1	22.9	59.2	20.0	0.0	58.1
Sanilac	430	-3.2	297	4	381	401	1 379	92	133	91 514	56.6	43.4	60.6	23.3	0.0	16.8
Schoolcraft	16	12.4	350	D	9	294	842	37	1	27 326	47.6	52.4	44.4	6.7	27.9	12.0
Shiawassee	214	-9.6	234	1	184	366	1 547	85	45	49 399	72.2	27.8	55.1	13.8	0.0	12.1
Tuscola	333	2.8	292	9	292	512	1 800	104	106	92 739	80.7	19.3	56.8	23.1	0.0	12.7
Van Buren	177	-14.3	167	20	136	322	1 789	67	101	95 034	86.6	13.4	51.9	17.0	0.0	102.1
Washtenaw	180	-4.6	175	5	153	507	2 892	56	57	54 874	61.1	38.9	47.7	12.9	0.1	54.6
Wayne	39	77.7	129	1	30	447	3 790	66	27	89 635	96.2	3.8	46.2	14.5	0.0	2 165.4
Wexford	43	39.7	173	0	29	200	1 171	36	9	34 621	63.8	36.2	32.3	7.2	30.9	8.7
MINNESOTA	25 995	1.3	354	380	21 492	408	1 164	85	8 290	112 997	50.7	49.3	64.4	28.1	6.2	3 391.5
Aitkin	164	-2.7	279	5	81	161	518	35	14	24 563	36.2	63.8	30.7	4.8	1.2	5.0
Anoka	57	-7.6	121	2	40	315	2 697	58	24	50 305	70.5	29.5	37.8	9.3	0.0	142.2
Becker	389	2.8	359	2	269	233	652	57	100	92 131	33.4	66.6	49.9	17.3	4.4	5.1
Beltrami	225	0.0	343	3	121	154	509	36	17	26 267	30.4	69.6	40.7	5.0	4.5	7.8
Benton	176	-4.2	211	11	131	212	986	71	90	107 446	21.8	78.2	59.7	21.3	0.0	18.3
Big Stone	254	-3.1	605	1	227	506	815	100	55	130 039	70.1	29.9	78.1	36.9	3.1	1.4
Blue Earth	403	5.3	389	1	370	738	1 941	113	221	213 568	44.8	55.2	79.3	43.1	0.0	32.1
Brown	350	1.0	332	3	321	588	1 778	103	182	172 526	42.8	57.2	89.2	41.5	0.0	3.7
Carlton	107	-5.2	203	0	56	142	590	38	8	16 035	19.6	80.4	25.6	2.7	0.0	22.4
Carver	153	-7.7	197	1	126	418	2 075	101	62	79 661	36.8	63.2	65.5	26.4	0.0	7.8
Cass	192	-4.1	321	3	95	178	574	31	21	34 514	12.2	87.8	42.5	6.0	17.3	4.0
Chippewa	318	-2.6	515	2	298	677	1 304	129	101	163 804	82.6	17.4	79.8	43.9	0.0	9.5
Chisago	122	-12.6	159	1	84	262	1 618	46	30	39 696	62.2	37.8	37.1	9.6	0.7	3.8
Clay	581	2.5	655	4	529	666	1 035	127	138	155 202	81.7	18.3	69.4	38.2	1.3	7.9
Clearwater	212	0.6	372	7	115	161	459	36	20	35 826	45.3	54.7	47.5	5.6	0.0	13.4
Cook	D	D	D	D	1	213	1 051	35	0	9 210	77.2	22.8	18.2	0.0	62.4	126.1
Cottonwood	368	-1.8	470	1	333	653	1 387	121	160	204 420	49.8	50.2	85.1	51.1	0.5	3.2
Crow Wing	135	3.3	228	1	69	186	846	34	14	23 978	27.1	72.9	36.6	5.4	0.1	9.0
Dakota	221	0.1	249	41	196	570	2 268	96	103	115 707	62.5	37.5	61.7	26.1	0.5	224.2
Dodge	247	2.4	366	D	224	579	1 599	104	105	155 481	55.8	44.2	70.2	36.1	0.0	2.0
Douglas	268	3.0	257	2	201	202	799	55	59	56 508	36.2	63.8	55.5	17.9	2.1	5.5
Faribault	413	-0.4	471	0	389	783	1 681	133	171	194 818	66.3	33.7	90.2	53.9	0.0	2.8
Fillmore	435	-1.9	281	0	327	297	1 048	77	148	95 900	41.3	58.7	68.1	26.8	0.0	14.7
Freeborn	380	3.4	330	1	351	523	1 603	95	163	141 674	61.6	38.4	73.5	38.8	0.2	6.6
Goodhue	385	1.2	258	2	315	384	1 537	76	161	107 886	40.3	59.7	69.0	31.1	0.3	599.8

STATE County	Value of Residential Construction Authorized by Building Permits, 2000		Wholesale Trade, 1997				Retail Trade[1], 1997				Real Estate and Rental and Leasing, 1997			
	New Construction ($1,000)	Number of Housing Units	Number of Establishments	Number of Employees	Sales (mil dol)	Annual Payroll (mil dol)	Number of Establishments	Number of Employees	Sales (mil dol)	Annual Payroll (mil dol)	Number of Establishments	Number of Employees	Receipts (mil dol)	Annual Payroll (mil dol)
	133	134	135	136	137	138	139	140	141	142	143	144	145	146
MICHIGAN—Cont'd														
Leelanau	42 004	329	18	90	20.0	1.7	143	661	92.0	10.5	23	59	4.6	1.0
Lenawee	55 863	498	92	685	429.5	22.6	375	4 859	826.3	75.8	80	270	31.5	4.1
Livingston	269 736	2 167	246	1 859	1 064.1	73.2	476	6 435	1 308.4	121.7	117	439	55.5	7.7
Luce	2 388	30	10	61	10.8	1.2	36	333	64.7	4.6	5	28	4.0	0.3
Mackinac	11 730	114	12	92	29.6	1.6	133	448	83.7	8.2	16	22	2.0	0.6
Macomb	725 964	5 963	1 040	12 592	6 608.7	521.7	2 901	47 125	9 010.8	859.9	625	3 058	456.3	64.0
Manistee	4 249	52	26	D	D	D	116	947	189.8	16.3	15	44	3.9	0.7
Marquette	21 419	267	68	545	159.1	15.4	331	3 822	522.7	51.1	66	286	21.8	4.2
Mason	15 848	191	25	118	41.0	3.2	159	1 470	223.0	21.0	19	62	7.4	0.8
Mecosta	17 926	263	31	187	43.0	4.9	175	1 925	301.1	25.6	46	115	10.2	1.7
Menominee	10 880	138	24	337	192.4	10.5	85	967	162.0	12.5	9	30	3.8	0.6
Midland	32 984	299	73	758	311.0	29.0	353	4 449	722.1	72.2	60	223	27.2	3.5
Missaukee	9 570	93	11	57	17.6	1.3	57	506	103.1	7.8	9	18	1.5	0.2
Monroe	115 785	1 202	96	1 213	731.5	46.2	448	5 489	1 035.0	91.1	74	278	30.0	4.4
Montcalm	20 947	272	48	287	158.7	7.1	217	2 613	403.7	36.5	20	64	7.2	1.0
Montmorency	10 063	99	3	D	D	D	48	312	49.9	4.1	10	47	1.6	0.3
Muskegon	103 755	836	162	1 852	891.4	57.6	591	8 672	1 365.4	132.3	112	469	55.5	7.2
Newaygo	18 390	210	27	323	56.0	9.4	156	1 394	244.2	22.8	21	54	4.5	0.7
Oakland	929 500	5 459	3 526	45 311	68 519.0	2 332.1	5 530	83 826	16 585.0	1 623.9	1 772	14 568	1 987.1	390.9
Oceana	15 594	153	11	72	14.6	2.3	110	786	124.3	10.7	13	24	2.3	0.4
Ogemaw	7 413	135	18	207	69.9	6.0	148	1 351	230.8	20.1	23	58	4.1	0.7
Ontonagon	1 200	18	2	D	D	D	51	388	60.4	5.2	3	2	0.1	0.0
Osceola	15 985	204	11	129	51.2	3.0	88	694	105.5	9.8	4	19	2.4	0.3
Oscoda	7 375	92	3	D	D	D	44	318	44.7	4.2	9	16	1.3	0.3
Otsego	39 230	317	38	387	207.8	11.3	163	1 903	334.8	29.9	31	184	12.1	1.9
Ottawa	239 684	2 039	326	3 471	2 213.3	110.2	828	12 375	1 920.7	193.1	168	774	93.6	15.9
Presque Isle	12 948	134	15	181	41.7	3.6	93	768	122.5	11.0	9	21	1.6	0.3
Roscommon	26 559	373	22	72	10.5	1.3	149	1 553	267.0	25.5	26	51	3.5	0.6
Saginaw	86 070	972	269	3 643	1 614.3	120.1	1 101	14 917	2 477.0	228.2	155	820	80.1	14.0
St. Clair	117 949	1 076	131	1 415	596.4	50.6	629	7 801	1 315.1	124.8	102	444	53.9	7.6
St. Joseph	26 150	240	59	680	252.1	27.8	230	2 627	399.3	37.4	52	199	19.7	3.0
Sanilac	15 247	226	37	238	99.5	5.2	183	1 707	287.6	25.7	29	105	9.3	2.2
Schoolcraft	2 854	59	12	D	D	D	56	410	78.6	6.2	8	17	0.9	0.2
Shiawassee	30 890	342	67	476	182.6	11.5	234	3 080	571.4	46.6	37	148	63.8	3.8
Tuscola	15 384	172	54	408	202.4	9.8	212	2 048	412.6	33.1	22	68	6.2	0.8
Van Buren	38 468	447	61	405	160.5	11.7	267	2 694	503.8	44.2	48	169	11.8	2.1
Washtenaw	319 642	1 980	435	4 778	3 338.4	182.3	1 204	18 464	3 371.9	329.6	315	2 147	184.5	47.9
Wayne	529 121	4 082	2 357	40 193	37 963.4	1 614.4	6 690	85 476	15 852.1	1 483.7	1 256	9 014	1 478.6	225.7
Wexford	19 587	226	29	334	83.5	9.0	174	2 127	359.1	33.1	28	156	12.7	2.2
MINNESOTA	4 203 928	32 814	9 348	131 787	99 444.5	5 024.0	20 883	282 282	48 077.7	4 525.7	5 051	30 172	3 886.4	687.2
Aitkin	17 985	183	16	D	D	D	60	490	77.7	6.5	9	26	1.3	0.2
Anoka	282 243	2 047	351	4 520	1 824.1	161.2	826	13 478	2 232.6	206.0	235	1 166	117.9	18.0
Becker	21 147	199	42	263	78.6	7.4	182	1 609	258.6	22.7	29	107	7.8	1.7
Beltrami	7 750	85	44	414	101.2	10.0	200	2 453	365.8	34.5	24	89	18.4	1.1
Benton	34 353	396	45	1 083	535.4	28.4	102	1 356	186.8	20.6	15	65	6.8	1.2
Big Stone	1 129	10	15	D	D	D	42	254	26.9	2.6	4	D	D	D
Blue Earth	36 824	331	108	1 520	558.0	39.0	325	5 166	744.4	70.4	62	344	29.2	6.2
Brown	4 394	39	41	438	417.7	9.8	152	1 850	234.7	22.2	23	84	9.2	1.4
Carlton	23 756	304	25	417	193.2	11.5	129	1 364	226.6	19.5	12	62	5.7	0.7
Carver	193 612	1 375	122	2 205	570.1	59.8	177	2 389	413.8	40.0	61	320	32.3	8.1
Cass	42 447	392	18	D	D	D	163	959	164.8	15.9	17	45	4.9	0.9
Chippewa	2 819	45	27	240	191.4	6.9	75	844	125.9	10.8	13	51	1.6	0.3
Chisago	72 369	659	33	D	D	D	148	1 421	221.9	20.0	39	171	7.4	1.5
Clay	22 383	225	67	765	410.6	17.8	193	2 828	458.0	37.8	38	127	10.1	1.4
Clearwater	470	5	10	75	17.7	1.4	40	260	34.5	3.0	3	8	0.3	0.1
Cook	11 457	117	2	D	D	D	48	271	44.0	4.5	19	30	3.9	0.5
Cottonwood	1 587	17	28	206	169.6	4.5	72	665	103.2	8.7	7	21	1.1	0.4
Crow Wing	87 242	817	79	713	178.7	16.4	376	3 749	708.3	61.9	76	220	28.3	3.5
Dakota	427 045	3 166	686	9 650	5 578.3	359.6	1 140	22 202	4 010.9	374.2	331	1 597	237.1	34.3
Dodge	18 231	181	22	321	156.1	10.1	68	448	70.5	6.5	6	23	16.6	0.5
Douglas	38 113	356	56	488	174.6	13.1	233	2 472	368.7	33.3	48	126	13.1	1.9
Faribault	1 820	18	40	D	D	D	84	634	80.5	7.7	6	7	0.9	0.1
Fillmore	13 868	128	35	319	240.8	8.4	135	810	149.2	12.7	9	11	1.7	0.1
Freeborn	11 703	106	68	646	522.1	19.1	183	1 965	310.8	29.5	21	61	6.6	0.6
Goodhue	39 679	307	63	1 051	680.4	31.3	244	2 390	337.0	32.7	43	107	10.9	1.6

1. Establishments with payroll.

Table B. States and Counties — Professional, Manufacturing, and Accommodation and Foodservices

STATE County	Professional, Scientific, and Technical Services[1], 1997				Manufacturing, 1997				Accommodation and Foodservices, 1997			
	Number of Establishments	Number of Employees	Receipts (mil dol)	Annual Payroll (mil dol)	Number of Establishments	Number of Employees	Receipts (mil dol)	Annual Payroll (mil dol)	Number of Establishments	Number of Employees	Sales (mil dol)	Annual Payroll (mil dol)
	147	148	149	150	151	152	153	154	155	156	157	158
MICHIGAN—Cont'd												
Leelanau	36	220	11.5	4.4	NA	NA	NA	NA	78	884	32.5	10.1
Lenawee	106	371	23.5	9.4	163	8 940	1 736.1	359.3	182	2 485	73.5	19.6
Livingston	288	1 629	103.7	50.5	264	10 560	2 782.8	374.1	193	3 494	116.1	29.9
Luce	7	16	0.7	0.2	NA	NA	NA	NA	33	275	7.3	2.0
Mackinac	21	109	10.2	4.9	NA	NA	NA	NA	129	723	50.4	13.3
Macomb	1 305	11 709	1 069.4	509.2	2 116	93 551	23 988.0	4 321.9	1 342	24 413	796.5	216.4
Manistee	28	77	4.7	2.0	31	1 300	244.6	48.4	73	671	18.5	5.2
Marquette	120	590	35.2	16.7	39	730	81.0	16.0	175	2 642	64.7	20.1
Mason	53	190	12.6	4.9	40	2 682	435.8	84.2	80	1 010	29.5	8.4
Mecosta	41	141	9.6	3.8	41	1 837	363.2	50.7	87	1 587	41.2	11.4
Menominee	26	92	5.0	2.5	56	2 901	425.2	78.0	51	D	D	D
Midland	142	697	71.5	23.4	71	5 613	1 690.8	285.4	132	2 688	78.1	22.9
Missaukee	9	32	2.4	0.8	23	548	73.0	17.5	25	179	4.6	1.2
Monroe	120	501	36.3	14.1	138	9 278	2 560.1	425.6	219	3 339	98.0	26.2
Montcalm	35	134	5.7	1.4	77	5 456	923.8	172.0	89	1 027	27.7	7.5
Montmorency	12	25	1.6	0.7	NA	NA	NA	NA	38	275	7.1	1.7
Muskegon	229	1 087	91.2	40.4	335	16 398	2 903.3	562.1	321	5 256	153.8	42.2
Newaygo	37	258	11.6	4.7	46	1 727	484.7	51.7	62	686	19.9	5.4
Oakland	5 522	60 999	6 922.0	2 990.6	2 366	90 481	27 172.7	3 747.5	2 453	48 174	1 668.0	478.6
Oceana	21	96	5.6	1.7	51	1 385	214.5	31.2	66	410	16.9	5.2
Ogemaw	24	78	7.4	2.1	29	872	85.9	23.3	69	654	20.8	5.7
Ontonagon	9	15	0.8	0.4	NA	NA	NA	NA	40	303	6.5	1.8
Osceola	20	58	3.9	1.8	36	3 582	661.3	99.2	43	334	10.6	2.6
Oscoda	6	27	0.8	0.3	NA	NA	NA	NA	24	210	5.6	1.7
Otsego	51	317	19.4	8.0	39	1 870	255.5	53.8	69	1 686	56.9	18.3
Ottawa	344	2 565	192.0	91.9	591	38 244	7 688.1	1 310.8	328	6 073	173.2	50.4
Presque Isle	14	59	2.2	1.3	NA	NA	NA	NA	57	295	9.1	2.5
Roscommon	28	61	3.8	1.5	NA	NA	NA	NA	79	994	26.5	7.5
Saginaw	320	2 908	195.1	86.5	239	20 681	5 172.2	1 148.6	408	9 236	270.5	78.9
St. Clair	176	851	56.8	25.2	294	14 162	2 667.6	431.5	290	4 520	138.3	38.4
St. Joseph	49	244	12.6	6.1	163	10 651	2 402.7	371.4	128	1 436	45.5	11.4
Sanilac	42	164	9.7	2.3	88	5 244	726.3	123.6	75	736	21.3	6.1
Schoolcraft	9	24	0.9	0.4	NA	NA	NA	NA	43	221	7.5	1.9
Shiawassee	70	334	26.5	11.9	86	4 139	453.8	99.6	110	1 467	41.1	11.0
Tuscola	43	127	9.0	3.0	65	2 818	486.4	96.9	84	1 101	29.0	8.2
Van Buren	77	439	37.2	13.7	127	4 879	1 007.8	152.1	146	1 677	51.6	15.1
Washtenaw	993	7 818	954.4	380.0	412	29 254	7 350.2	1 395.5	627	13 266	430.2	119.5
Wayne	2 512	29 950	3 133.0	1 233.0	2 390	133 703	54 375.0	6 514.3	3 313	58 336	2 023.7	542.5
Wexford	42	257	18.2	8.4	57	4 331	719.1	126.7	88	1 487	39.7	11.6
MINNESOTA	12 391	96 677	10 447.9	4 091.3	8 091	382 530	76 244.9	13 126.1	9 982	179 487	5 934.2	1 688.8
Aitkin	15	87	3.1	1.6	NA	NA	NA	NA	59	469	16.5	4.4
Anoka	533	2 440	167.8	68.0	614	24 754	3 860.7	908.7	351	7 744	215.4	62.3
Becker	45	157	9.9	4.2	42	1 320	193.0	35.7	104	973	33.3	8.4
Beltrami	47	208	13.3	6.0	43	1 112	175.9	32.0	100	1 339	40.9	11.4
Benton	25	179	12.9	5.4	53	2 797	300.2	71.4	53	962	26.8	7.5
Big Stone	8	28	1.5	0.8	NA	NA	NA	NA	21	155	3.3	0.8
Blue Earth	90	596	48.6	16.6	78	4 144	1 160.8	126.7	137	2 657	72.6	19.5
Brown	44	367	23.1	9.7	41	4 292	1 580.8	113.0	62	1 044	23.5	6.5
Carlton	33	133	7.2	3.1	30	2 131	425.0	89.8	74	808	23.4	6.4
Carver	140	1 096	75.2	31.5	143	10 470	1 920.0	391.7	109	1 566	43.6	12.8
Cass	34	100	6.6	2.5	NA	NA	NA	NA	121	669	26.8	6.0
Chippewa	13	61	3.4	1.5	24	1 498	116.3	34.5	30	329	7.6	2.0
Chisago	63	297	13.0	6.3	101	2 462	282.1	70.3	67	772	18.5	5.2
Clay	56	307	24.9	9.6	38	1 225	229.4	35.7	107	1 615	40.7	11.4
Clearwater	10	D	D	D	NA	NA	NA	NA	20	D	D	D
Cook	13	D	D	D	NA	NA	NA	NA	71	748	36.1	9.8
Cottonwood	18	66	3.4	1.7	16	930	486.9	20.5	24	258	6.0	1.6
Crow Wing	94	784	67.1	25.1	95	2 957	458.3	91.2	211	2 480	121.3	33.2
Dakota	854	4 016	399.0	151.1	439	17 957	5 922.4	636.3	488	11 244	344.9	100.8
Dodge	18	50	2.7	1.0	29	1 322	398.6	37.5	24	D	D	D
Douglas	54	270	15.7	7.8	72	2 806	448.4	76.0	106	1 258	42.2	11.1
Faribault	22	85	3.3	1.3	28	1 578	260.6	36.5	31	D	D	D
Fillmore	28	87	3.5	1.2	42	1 122	224.8	27.9	60	D	D	D
Freeborn	33	202	14.6	5.9	66	3 062	564.5	86.7	79	978	26.5	7.0
Goodhue	66	286	27.2	9.5	81	5 522	972.8	166.6	104	1 623	39.4	12.0

1. Firms subject to federal tax.

STATE County	Health Care and Social Assistance[1], 1997				Other Services[1], 1997				Federal funds and grants, fiscal 2001[2]			
									Expenditures (mil dol)			
										Direct payments for individuals[3]		
	Number of Establish-ments	Number of Employees	Receipts (mil dol)	Annual Payroll (mil dol)	Number of Establish-ments	Number of Employees	Receipts (mil dol)	Annual Payroll (mil dol)	Total	Social Security and government retirement	Medicare	Food stamps and Supplemental Security Income
	159	160	161	162	163	164	165	166	167	168	169	170
MICHIGAN—Cont'd												
Leelanau	34	147	8.8	3.7	26	145	11.3	2.7	75.5	42.7	12.8	0.9
Lenawee	183	1 335	71.3	33.2	134	605	38.8	12.0	400.5	201.6	80.9	10.8
Livingston	246	2 017	98.3	49.0	209	1 109	82.4	25.5	328.4	193.0	66.8	5.1
Luce	11	D	D	D	7	37	2.6	0.5	40.3	17.2	8.0	0.9
Mackinac	17	76	3.5	1.5	14	57	2.9	0.8	63.6	31.2	11.6	1.1
Macomb	1 492	14 800	995.8	477.1	1 366	8 618	573.3	184.6	4 889.3	1 628.9	811.3	60.3
Manistee	59	448	18.3	8.4	32	101	6.0	1.5	123.5	67.7	25.8	3.8
Marquette	137	1 582	98.4	56.2	99	485	29.1	7.9	302.5	156.4	54.8	7.1
Mason	74	509	27.3	12.9	36	166	9.6	2.9	137.4	71.0	24.8	4.8
Mecosta	68	612	27.1	13.5	61	276	14.2	4.1	156.7	80.3	24.8	8.0
Menominee	32	351	11.6	5.6	32	106	7.7	1.8	110.8	59.7	19.3	2.3
Midland	202	1 822	112.6	56.3	124	698	46.4	12.0	276.8	151.5	49.9	9.1
Missaukee	21	154	5.6	2.5	13	27	2.7	0.4	53.6	29.4	10.1	1.6
Monroe	171	1 480	90.2	41.9	141	892	60.7	22.4	506.4	272.2	113.8	13.6
Montcalm	73	596	31.7	13.9	76	350	22.4	6.5	253.8	125.8	49.1	10.0
Montmorency	13	179	6.2	3.1	11	30	2.4	0.5	70.4	41.7	15.7	2.2
Muskegon	272	2 682	157.8	82.2	234	1 299	67.2	21.8	837.0	365.0	133.2	39.0
Newaygo	43	542	26.3	12.3	53	187	12.4	2.7	171.7	91.0	31.1	4.5
Oakland	3 713	35 580	2 427.4	1 186.9	2 108	16 274	1 133.6	363.1	4 473.1	2 212.0	1 036.7	108.4
Oceana	31	192	7.4	3.9	41	107	6.0	1.4	121.0	60.3	20.8	5.3
Ogemaw	52	499	21.9	9.8	37	169	9.2	2.6	110.2	60.3	23.3	3.9
Ontonagon	10	120	3.9	2.0	8	32	2.8	0.4	62.9	26.4	10.0	1.2
Osceola	24	178	9.9	3.9	29	80	4.5	1.1	113.6	58.1	20.0	5.0
Oscoda	11	D	D	D	11	31	2.4	0.4	42.6	23.8	9.2	1.6
Otsego	66	499	28.1	12.1	55	250	20.9	4.9	101.6	53.1	15.2	2.1
Ottawa	332	4 128	213.1	105.4	346	2 032	141.6	40.5	707.3	371.2	102.2	10.8
Presque Isle	25	247	12.7	4.2	27	74	5.8	1.1	85.5	47.9	15.4	2.0
Roscommon	40	473	21.2	9.2	48	125	7.8	2.1	160.3	96.3	39.5	5.1
Saginaw	410	3 465	248.1	121.5	336	2 127	126.7	39.1	1 057.0	459.9	188.5	56.3
St. Clair	271	2 176	148.7	72.5	242	1 229	87.2	24.0	587.4	266.9	128.1	17.6
St. Joseph	98	805	36.6	15.3	97	578	40.2	13.8	246.4	122.2	47.8	6.2
Sanilac	82	527	25.2	10.5	59	189	15.2	2.8	219.8	96.7	44.5	5.1
Schoolcraft	8	136	5.7	3.5	19	55	3.6	0.8	59.7	25.9	10.8	1.6
Shiawassee	114	972	54.2	28.1	84	443	25.8	8.1	286.6	146.4	62.3	8.7
Tuscola	81	923	32.6	15.5	72	352	19.4	5.8	251.9	122.5	48.1	8.1
Van Buren	94	688	34.6	16.0	95	330	18.4	5.4	345.4	152.1	61.1	12.6
Washtenaw	703	6 534	525.1	228.3	392	2 628	158.7	53.6	1 665.6	450.7	184.6	27.1
Wayne	3 115	35 576	2 186.2	1 040.1	2 621	20 451	1 407.6	440.8	12 070.2	4 072.0	2 516.0	700.5
Wexford	67	477	33.2	15.5	51	304	17.4	5.0	195.2	70.6	24.0	5.4
MINNESOTA	8 033	106 839	5 864.5	2 946.0	7 614	55 723	3 394.6	1 103.6	24 935.4	8 614.4	3 066.3	527.8
Aitkin	12	264	7.3	3.6	11	30	3.0	0.6	99.1	47.5	14.7	2.2
Anoka	384	5 016	282.6	143.4	399	2 502	170.0	49.4	538.6	308.2	85.6	11.1
Becker	30	424	21.0	8.4	63	668	21.5	8.5	178.9	66.4	20.9	4.0
Beltrami	65	995	47.5	25.5	62	574	23.3	6.6	218.2	73.0	25.7	8.2
Benton	29	491	18.8	9.2	38	174	13.7	2.9	124.1	74.7	12.7	3.4
Big Stone	8	48	2.7	0.8	14	34	2.4	0.4	50.4	15.7	6.3	0.6
Blue Earth	118	2 027	103.3	53.6	101	662	36.1	10.6	260.2	104.5	30.8	5.8
Brown	35	414	18.1	9.9	47	190	12.4	3.3	144.3	59.3	19.9	1.5
Carlton	39	292	16.0	7.3	43	110	8.0	2.1	153.1	74.6	23.7	2.7
Carver	79	922	51.3	29.7	76	675	46.5	18.7	185.5	72.0	23.4	1.3
Cass	20	193	7.9	3.6	21	62	4.2	1.0	173.8	71.6	24.0	4.5
Chippewa	21	171	8.6	4.0	20	86	7.6	1.6	78.2	27.7	8.7	0.6
Chisago	49	1 150	47.6	27.8	50	192	11.8	2.6	129.8	73.2	23.2	2.2
Clay	56	496	24.9	11.6	76	299	17.9	4.9	239.2	93.6	30.3	7.5
Clearwater	12	71	3.6	2.0	8	21	2.2	0.2	54.1	17.4	7.6	1.5
Cook	2	D	D	D	4	8	0.7	0.2	30.6	12.3	3.1	0.2
Cottonwood	28	310	9.6	4.6	29	76	5.9	1.2	87.4	30.4	11.2	1.3
Crow Wing	99	1 353	63.0	35.8	84	352	21.1	5.2	271.0	143.7	44.8	6.4
Dakota	501	7 009	344.1	156.2	488	4 515	279.0	101.7	890.7	414.8	96.1	13.7
Dodge	16	66	3.3	1.5	34	173	14.3	4.7	79.9	26.4	11.3	1.2
Douglas	61	573	34.2	16.9	65	241	15.1	3.6	155.2	77.0	23.5	2.6
Faribault	33	150	7.0	2.8	27	55	5.3	0.9	117.9	42.4	15.4	1.3
Fillmore	27	263	10.5	4.7	32	74	7.0	1.2	125.5	47.5	20.4	1.5
Freeborn	47	447	33.3	14.2	50	225	9.8	2.4	194.6	80.3	27.8	3.2
Goodhue	65	764	39.2	14.2	74	383	29.0	6.3	177.2	86.2	29.0	2.0

1. Firms subject to federal tax.   2. October 1, 2000 to September 30, 2001.   3. State totals may include programs not allocated by county.

STATE County	Federal funds and grants, fiscal 2001[1] (cont'd) Expenditures (mil dol) (cont'd)							Local government finances, 1997 General revenue				
	Procurement contract awards			Grants[2]							Taxes	
												Per capita[3] (dollars)
	Salaries and wages	Defense	Other	Medicaid and other health-related	Nutrition and family welfare	Education	Other	Total (mil dol)	Intergovern-mental (mil dol)	Total (mil dol)	Total	Property
	171	172	173	174	175	176	177	178	179	180	181	182
MICHIGAN—Cont'd												
Leelanau	5.7	1.1	0.9	2.6	0.9	1.1	2.5	36.1	14.2	16.1	859	835
Lenawee	13.1	0.6	3.3	40.4	10.2	5.7	2.4	228.8	140.4	50.6	517	470
Livingston	16.1	3.1	4.5	19.3	6.1	3.8	4.1	309.9	156.2	73.7	520	495
Luce	1.1	0.3	0.3	8.3	1.1	0.7	1.8	41.8	13.8	2.8	429	423
Mackinac	4.5	1.7	0.9	5.7	1.5	1.1	3.7	41.3	13.8	12.8	1 153	1 118
Macomb	345.5	1 679.6	39.7	152.1	44.0	33.1	34.2	1 901.7	986.7	553.4	706	681
Manistee	5.8	0.4	1.5	7.9	3.0	4.9	0.6	86.2	39.9	14.6	631	616
Marquette	18.4	2.6	3.8	28.3	8.7	4.8	5.0	182.2	95.4	38.5	622	600
Mason	5.6	0.0	5.4	11.0	6.0	1.5	3.7	86.5	42.6	26.6	955	875
Mecosta	5.9	0.0	1.4	15.1	3.3	3.0	1.2	98.4	43.5	21.9	558	513
Menominee	4.4	0.0	1.1	10.7	2.8	1.7	2.9	52.7	32.8	11.5	470	463
Midland	10.0	0.2	2.6	22.0	7.5	3.8	8.7	227.3	101.3	77.1	950	935
Missaukee	1.8	0.4	0.6	5.2	1.6	1.1	0.1	27.5	17.4	5.9	428	406
Monroe	14.2	1.7	3.9	34.3	16.5	6.8	9.6	374.5	167.1	117.0	822	797
Montcalm	9.0	0.0	2.1	29.2	6.4	4.3	7.0	148.1	97.1	31.2	524	511
Montmorency	1.3	0.0	0.3	6.2	1.4	0.7	0.1	19.1	8.4	5.5	554	545
Muskegon	24.5	69.7	31.5	90.9	34.2	15.8	18.0	506.9	268.0	87.9	530	466
Newaygo	5.2	1.0	1.6	16.0	6.2	2.8	8.9	126.0	77.4	22.4	498	492
Oakland	296.2	58.5	118.5	286.2	74.9	47.5	127.8	3 356.3	1 516.9	1 217.3	1 044	994
Oceana	3.9	0.7	9.9	11.0	3.9	1.5	1.3	66.2	35.5	13.5	549	546
Ogemaw	3.2	0.0	0.7	10.7	2.9	1.1	2.0	39.3	21.8	9.1	437	412
Ontonagon	2.8	10.2	1.7	6.7	1.2	0.6	1.4	23.9	13.8	6.2	768	754
Osceola	3.4	0.6	0.9	15.8	3.3	2.0	2.1	53.2	35.1	11.0	499	490
Oscoda	2.1	0.0	0.4	2.4	1.1	0.7	0.8	16.9	11.3	4.5	511	500
Otsego	12.3	0.0	2.6	9.3	1.9	1.0	1.8	53.7	23.7	19.3	884	866
Ottawa	31.2	43.4	61.6	32.4	7.3	10.1	11.8	532.8	264.8	147.3	668	649
Presque Isle	2.9	0.0	1.1	9.5	1.4	1.0	2.0	28.2	14.9	10.4	720	713
Roscommon	2.1	0.0	0.6	10.0	3.5	1.5	0.1	68.0	29.1	23.5	1 015	994
Saginaw	79.0	4.8	18.8	123.0	47.5	17.7	21.2	547.4	319.8	107.1	507	421
St. Clair	28.8	14.3	7.4	56.9	21.6	8.5	18.4	411.8	201.6	117.9	747	694
St. Joseph	8.0	2.9	1.9	24.3	6.3	4.4	3.5	172.1	92.8	31.6	515	506
Sanilac	6.8	3.2	1.8	20.5	5.3	2.7	7.2	107.9	62.6	20.5	479	467
Schoolcraft	3.0	2.1	2.6	8.9	1.3	1.0	1.9	33.5	13.5	4.6	531	525
Shiawassee	8.8	1.0	2.0	25.8	8.7	4.2	2.6	164.4	106.5	25.7	356	344
Tuscola	8.1	4.1	2.2	26.0	8.0	4.3	1.8	152.4	102.0	24.0	413	399
Van Buren	9.8	0.2	20.4	55.1	15.4	5.7	4.0	232.7	128.1	50.6	669	654
Washtenaw	169.3	51.8	55.4	404.5	23.9	19.3	194.6	834.2	343.8	302.6	1 010	978
Wayne	984.2	40.9	411.7	1 720.4	568.2	190.9	511.3	7 365.7	4 120.9	1 847.0	868	666
Wexford	8.2	39.8	1.5	15.7	3.6	1.8	22.0	87.3	45.0	20.1	691	671
MINNESOTA	1 904.1	1 378.9	670.3	2 703.5	827.7	454.3	1 275.0	X	X	X	X	X
Aitkin	2.7	0.4	0.6	16.4	2.3	0.9	9.6	35.3	17.9	11.9	855	846
Anoka	14.1	0.4	6.4	42.7	21.7	10.7	24.2	769.2	368.8	225.2	785	758
Becker	11.3	0.2	2.4	29.2	10.9	2.2	4.4	68.6	39.0	16.2	555	545
Beltrami	16.6	0.2	2.4	41.0	12.1	11.6	8.2	107.5	69.2	20.7	534	526
Benton	3.9	0.1	0.4	12.3	2.8	1.0	2.4	63.4	37.4	17.6	523	515
Big Stone	2.2	0.0	0.4	4.6	0.9	0.3	0.3	38.2	19.1	4.6	810	802
Blue Earth	22.8	0.6	5.2	28.0	6.5	3.6	4.8	152.6	72.9	47.1	872	852
Brown	4.8	0.4	10.6	9.1	2.0	1.1	1.5	73.4	32.9	18.2	669	661
Carlton	5.3	0.1	1.5	21.7	5.9	3.6	7.0	93.6	54.2	22.4	731	721
Carver	14.2	1.5	38.4	7.3	7.1	1.6	1.9	229.6	65.8	75.6	1 197	1 150
Cass	10.4	0.7	0.9	35.8	8.8	5.3	3.3	75.7	37.1	27.4	1 065	1 060
Chippewa	2.9	0.3	0.5	5.9	3.0	0.7	0.4	43.7	22.9	10.5	807	798
Chisago	6.5	0.1	1.9	9.1	2.9	1.3	3.3	99.4	50.0	25.8	653	621
Clay	7.6	0.1	2.0	22.4	7.5	2.9	11.8	143.8	77.1	28.1	542	539
Clearwater	1.8	0.0	0.9	14.6	2.3	1.1	3.2	26.5	16.0	7.7	936	933
Cook	4.6	0.4	0.6	3.2	0.6	0.3	4.7	25.5	6.3	7.1	1 488	1 266
Cottonwood	3.1	0.0	0.8	5.5	1.3	0.8	0.6	42.1	19.1	10.3	843	840
Crow Wing	10.1	3.1	2.3	36.0	7.7	2.7	7.3	147.4	57.3	45.2	884	861
Dakota	116.9	105.9	24.8	30.6	14.9	10.2	8.5	900.5	380.4	306.5	916	885
Dodge	2.5	0.0	0.6	5.5	1.5	0.8	8.2	51.7	28.1	12.4	727	715
Douglas	7.0	0.6	1.7	21.1	3.4	1.4	1.7	108.7	38.3	23.9	779	766
Faribault	3.1	0.0	0.8	8.7	0.9	0.9	4.9	52.3	20.9	12.9	784	780
Fillmore	4.4	0.3	1.1	13.7	2.8	1.3	1.5	56.3	36.4	10.7	517	509
Freeborn	5.6	0.0	5.7	15.5	3.9	1.4	12.2	78.4	43.4	19.4	614	558
Goodhue	7.0	0.1	1.8	13.3	3.6	1.9	2.8	136.4	49.7	52.4	1 227	1 221

1. October 1, 2000 to September 30, 2001.   2. State totals may include programs not allocated by county.   3. Based on the resident population estimated as of July 1 of the year shown.

STATE County	Total (mil dol)	Per capita¹ (dollars)	Educa-tion	Health and hospitals	Police protec-tion	Public welfare	High-ways	Total (mil dol)	Per capita¹ (dollars)	Federal civilian	Federal military	State and local	Demo-cratic	Republi-can	All other
	183	184	185	186	187	188	189	190	191	192	193	194	195	196	197
MICHIGAN—Cont'd															
Leelanau	39.6	2 112	53.3	3.2	3.0	1.3	9.9	32.7	1 744	151	38	655	38.6	57.0	4.4
Lenawee	227.3	2 320	57.9	6.9	2.7	4.0	7.1	76.3	779	228	196	5 586	45.8	51.6	2.6
Livingston	306.3	2 158	54.9	5.2	3.5	0.3	5.4	495.8	3 493	256	298	5 025	38.1	59.1	2.7
Luce	42.2	6 410	17.4	64.4	0.6	0.6	5.7	5.3	804	20	13	972	37.7	58.4	3.9
Mackinac	45.0	4 045	37.3	17.9	2.2	0.6	9.7	27.7	2 490	63	63	950	42.4	54.8	2.8
Macomb	1 924.5	2 456	55.3	5.2	6.0	2.1	5.0	1 051.4	1 342	6 551	1 873	27 811	50.0	47.5	2.5
Manistee	83.7	3 611	32.4	31.6	1.9	6.8	7.7	11.5	498	102	52	1 493	49.3	47.3	3.4
Marquette	193.6	3 133	43.1	9.8	2.6	3.2	8.9	184.9	2 992	315	139	6 370	53.1	43.1	3.8
Mason	83.7	3 006	58.9	6.9	1.8	6.1	7.1	17.8	638	99	70	1 975	42.9	54.3	2.8
Mecosta	118.2	3 017	60.3	18.6	2.5	0.4	2.1	60.7	1 551	97	81	4 320	42.7	54.7	2.6
Menominee	51.6	2 109	53.1	7.2	3.8	0.7	10.7	35.9	1 468	76	48	1 456	44.1	53.0	3.0
Midland	220.2	2 710	49.0	7.5	3.8	1.2	6.6	301.4	3 710	184	162	3 543	41.0	56.3	2.6
Missaukee	29.6	2 161	43.8	8.8	1.0	0.7	15.7	22.4	1 639	31	28	525	31.7	65.8	2.5
Monroe	365.9	2 571	52.8	6.3	3.0	1.0	6.0	590.5	4 150	268	286	6 005	51.1	46.8	2.1
Montcalm	162.2	2 719	73.1	2.5	2.1	0.9	6.5	112.9	1 892	147	121	3 122	42.0	55.4	2.5
Montmorency	18.3	1 835	41.2	1.3	3.7	2.4	11.5	12.6	1 265	19	20	444	42.7	54.9	2.4
Muskegon	563.6	3 398	55.5	6.6	2.8	4.2	4.4	345.9	2 085	413	332	9 127	54.7	43.3	2.0
Newaygo	140.5	3 118	63.0	8.9	1.5	1.2	5.3	81.7	1 812	94	91	2 381	39.3	58.3	2.4
Oakland	3 498.2	2 999	52.5	4.8	5.5	0.1	5.6	2 263.7	1 941	5 407	2 335	50 925	49.3	48.1	2.6
Oceana	77.0	3 129	51.0	4.9	2.1	8.3	18.1	34.2	1 390	67	49	1 395	42.7	54.9	2.5
Ogemaw	38.4	1 832	42.2	10.6	3.3	1.9	13.7	12.6	602	62	42	1 278	49.7	47.8	2.5
Ontonagon	25.8	3 180	56.7	0.7	1.5	1.7	20.8	10.5	1 291	55	15	645	36.5	59.6	4.0
Osceola	59.1	2 683	69.5	1.8	1.7	0.6	6.9	30.5	1 384	64	44	1 208	40.3	57.2	2.5
Oscoda	14.3	1 621	52.4	1.7	3.6	0.4	19.8	2.8	315	44	18	400	42.0	55.3	2.7
Otsego	54.8	2 513	60.6	0.7	2.2	0.9	11.5	47.3	2 171	210	46	1 040	38.4	58.1	3.5
Ottawa	583.9	2 649	53.0	9.9	3.0	0.9	6.5	752.4	3 414	499	520	12 360	26.8	71.2	2.1
Presque Isle	28.3	1 969	45.1	1.1	2.7	1.0	14.4	14.2	988	51	29	700	45.8	51.7	2.5
Roscommon	67.0	2 892	64.5	2.2	2.2	1.4	7.2	31.6	1 366	37	46	1 455	49.8	47.9	2.4
Saginaw	546.0	2 584	47.6	11.0	4.5	1.0	4.5	351.4	1 663	1 338	433	10 140	54.2	43.9	1.9
St. Clair	419.2	2 658	49.7	8.3	3.8	1.0	6.7	241.3	1 530	470	385	6 333	48.2	49.0	2.9
St. Joseph	173.1	2 827	51.1	19.7	2.5	0.7	7.0	64.8	1 058	133	121	3 772	38.9	58.6	2.5
Sanilac	114.2	2 672	49.2	9.4	2.7	5.4	9.7	71.8	1 679	124	85	2 239	38.5	59.1	2.4
Schoolcraft	33.4	3 823	24.7	30.3	1.9	7.3	11.2	7.5	861	60	17	766	48.5	49.7	1.7
Shiawassee	169.2	2 343	56.7	5.1	3.4	5.1	8.8	90.4	1 252	141	142	3 634	48.2	49.1	2.8
Tuscola	149.2	2 569	60.3	8.2	2.4	3.7	9.5	55.0	947	155	115	3 550	44.0	53.6	2.4
Van Buren	241.6	3 192	54.7	18.4	2.3	1.0	5.8	135.3	1 787	163	149	4 872	46.8	50.2	3.0
Washtenaw	878.0	2 932	52.3	5.4	5.0	0.9	3.6	713.7	2 383	2 680	676	62 424	59.8	36.2	4.0
Wayne	7 119.6	3 347	39.4	6.7	6.9	1.5	5.0	5 738.0	2 698	16 991	4 735	111 610	69.0	29.0	2.0
Wexford	86.4	2 965	53.5	12.5	3.0	1.0	7.0	61.6	2 114	144	59	1 770	41.0	55.6	3.4
MINNESOTA	X	X	X	X	X	X	X	X	X	32 601	19 958	332 646	47.9	45.5	6.6
Aitkin	36.0	2 597	44.5	2.6	3.5	10.3	14.9	16.3	1 176	49	57	798	46.4	45.5	8.2
Anoka	796.9	2 780	58.9	0.6	3.7	6.5	4.7	867.9	3 028	243	1 195	13 423	46.7	47.6	5.7
Becker	86.8	2 967	53.0	0.2	2.3	10.0	13.0	52.2	1 787	212	119	1 828	36.6	56.9	6.5
Beltrami	117.3	3 029	61.4	0.1	2.6	11.6	5.5	72.1	1 863	311	157	3 756	42.4	48.5	9.1
Benton	63.9	1 897	46.4	0.9	3.3	8.8	13.3	71.8	2 131	53	140	1 266	40.3	51.4	8.3
Big Stone	32.4	5 687	29.5	19.3	2.2	4.4	13.0	287.9	50 604	32	22	563	48.0	46.0	6.1
Blue Earth	158.4	2 931	45.7	0.4	3.9	6.0	15.3	108.5	2 009	383	221	4 895	45.0	47.2	7.8
Brown	80.2	2 946	42.1	9.8	4.4	7.2	8.2	81.3	2 987	75	107	1 532	36.2	57.4	6.4
Carlton	98.4	3 205	47.2	1.7	3.1	9.0	9.0	157.8	5 141	86	126	2 890	57.2	37.0	5.9
Carver	249.7	3 950	32.4	18.8	1.2	4.2	8.9	293.7	4 648	214	267	4 068	35.6	59.4	5.0
Cass	75.9	2 948	45.5	2.4	3.5	9.3	14.0	40.0	1 554	250	108	1 753	40.7	52.5	6.8
Chippewa	52.6	4 038	49.6	0.3	3.0	12.2	13.1	36.8	2 824	44	52	954	46.5	46.9	6.6
Chisago	109.3	2 772	54.7	8.2	2.8	6.7	8.3	103.0	2 612	108	169	1 928	43.6	49.7	6.7
Clay	147.6	2 848	42.5	1.8	4.5	9.8	9.7	157.2	3 034	122	206	4 393	43.4	50.1	6.5
Clearwater	28.0	3 413	54.5	0.1	3.3	7.9	14.1	14.1	1 723	30	32	793	38.3	55.9	5.8
Cook	29.3	6 189	25.3	33.9	3.5	3.9	11.8	24.7	5 211	115	19	450	41.5	45.9	12.6
Cottonwood	44.3	3 617	39.2	13.1	2.7	8.0	14.3	19.8	1 611	60	47	853	40.5	54.5	5.0
Crow Wing	152.8	2 990	46.0	12.4	4.3	7.6	8.0	79.6	1 557	161	211	4 313	40.0	53.5	6.6
Dakota	945.1	2 825	53.8	0.6	4.3	5.7	7.6	1 419.1	4 241	1 572	1 395	15 381	46.9	47.9	5.3
Dodge	60.6	3 563	51.3	0.4	2.4	17.0	10.6	39.0	2 295	37	69	1 110	41.9	52.3	5.8
Douglas	103.5	3 367	33.7	28.4	2.8	6.0	9.3	52.0	1 692	116	125	2 568	36.9	57.0	6.0
Faribault	48.0	2 923	40.7	15.8	3.2	0.0	13.2	38.5	2 344	57	65	1 049	43.0	51.5	5.5
Fillmore	59.0	2 854	40.4	2.5	3.7	4.5	27.0	27.1	1 312	77	82	1 258	49.1	45.4	5.4
Freeborn	78.4	2 483	42.5	1.3	4.1	11.9	13.7	32.5	1 030	90	126	1 454	52.8	42.4	4.8
Goodhue	147.0	3 442	46.7	2.6	4.0	5.0	8.8	208.1	4 872	122	173	2 656	44.8	48.8	6.4

1. Based on the resident population estimated as of July 1 of the year shown.   2. Data subject to copyright.

STATE/ County code	MSA/ PMSA/ NECMA code[1]	County Type[2]	STATE County	Land area[3] (sq km) 2000	Total persons	Rank	Per square kilometer	White	Black	Am. Indian, Alaska Native	Asian and Pacific Islander	Percent Hispanic[4]	Under 5 years	5 to 17 years	18 to 24 years	25 to 34 years	35 to 44 years	45 to 54 years
					1	2	3	4	5	6	7	8	9	10	11	12	13	14
			MINNESOTA—Cont'd															
27 051	...	9	Grant	1 415	6 289	2 758	4.4	99.0	0.3	0.6	0.3	0.5	5.0	19.0	6.9	8.6	14.5	12.9
27 053	5120	0	Hennepin	1 442	1 116 200	32	774.1	82.4	10.3	1.6	5.6	4.1	6.6	17.4	9.7	16.5	17.2	14.0
27 055	3870	3	Houston	1 446	19 718	1 809	13.6	99.0	0.5	0.3	0.6	0.6	5.8	21.4	6.8	10.4	16.4	14.5
27 057	...	9	Hubbard	2 389	18 376	1 875	7.7	97.2	0.4	2.8	0.3	0.7	5.4	19.1	6.4	9.2	14.9	14.2
27 059	5120	1	Isanti	1 137	31 287	1 367	27.5	98.5	0.5	1.1	0.6	0.8	6.6	22.1	7.8	12.4	18.1	13.5
27 061	...	6	Itasca	6 902	43 992	1 016	6.4	95.9	0.3	4.5	0.4	0.6	5.3	19.1	7.6	9.3	15.1	15.6
27 063	...	7	Jackson	1 817	11 268	2 352	6.2	97.4	0.1	0.3	1.5	1.9	5.2	19.3	7.0	10.1	15.2	13.5
27 065	...	6	Kanabec	1 360	14 996	2 090	11.0	98.4	0.4	1.4	0.7	0.9	6.0	21.5	6.9	11.2	16.3	13.7
27 067	...	7	Kandiyohi	2 062	41 203	1 073	20.0	94.3	0.8	0.5	0.6	8.0	6.2	20.4	9.5	11.4	15.1	13.7
27 069	...	9	Kittson	2 841	5 285	2 830	1.9	98.8	0.3	0.6	0.5	1.3	6.4	18.7	5.5	9.0	14.6	14.4
27 071	...	7	Koochiching	8 035	14 355	2 136	1.8	97.3	0.3	3.0	0.4	0.6	5.4	18.4	6.4	10.4	15.4	15.2
27 073	...	9	Lac qui Parle	1 981	8 067	2 601	4.1	99.2	0.3	0.3	0.4	0.3	5.0	19.5	5.7	7.9	14.8	13.7
27 075	...	6	Lake	5 437	11 058	2 361	2.0	98.9	0.2	1.3	0.3	0.6	5.1	17.2	6.6	9.0	15.5	15.3
27 077	...	9	Lake of the Woods	3 358	4 522	2 877	1.3	98.2	0.6	1.9	0.4	0.6	4.2	20.6	5.7	8.9	16.3	15.3
27 079	...	6	Le Sueur	1 162	25 426	1 546	21.9	97.1	0.3	0.6	0.6	3.9	6.2	21.1	7.5	11.5	16.3	13.9
27 081	...	9	Lincoln	1 391	6 429	2 747	4.6	99.0	0.1	0.4	0.2	0.9	5.5	18.2	6.1	9.4	13.6	11.7
27 083	...	7	Lyon	1 850	25 425	1 547	13.7	94.4	1.8	0.6	2.0	4.0	6.6	19.6	13.3	11.9	14.6	11.9
27 085	...	6	McLeod	1 274	34 898	1 253	27.4	97.2	0.3	0.4	0.8	3.6	7.0	20.8	7.8	13.5	15.7	12.9
27 087	...	9	Mahnomen	1 440	5 190	2 837	3.6	70.6	0.3	36.5	0.2	0.9	7.1	22.1	7.2	9.4	14.1	12.9
27 089	...	8	Marshall	4 590	10 155	2 431	2.2	97.8	0.2	0.7	0.3	2.9	5.7	19.7	6.7	9.7	15.1	14.3
27 091	...	7	Martin	1 837	21 802	1 702	11.9	97.9	0.4	0.3	0.5	1.9	5.5	19.4	6.4	9.7	15.2	14.3
27 093	...	6	Meeker	1 576	22 644	1 663	14.4	97.8	0.3	0.3	0.5	2.2	6.4	20.5	7.4	10.9	15.4	13.7
27 095	...	6	Mille Lacs	1 488	22 330	1 678	15.0	94.5	0.5	5.2	0.4	1.0	6.2	20.8	7.5	11.0	15.8	12.7
27 097	...	6	Morrison	2 912	31 712	1 351	10.9	99.0	0.3	0.6	0.5	0.6	6.6	21.4	8.0	11.2	15.5	12.8
27 099	...	4	Mower	1 843	38 603	1 148	20.9	95.5	0.8	0.4	1.7	4.3	6.1	19.0	8.2	11.0	14.7	12.6
27 101	...	9	Murray	1 824	9 165	2 517	5.0	99.0	0.2	0.6	0.5	1.5	5.3	19.7	5.9	9.2	14.0	14.0
27 103	...	7	Nicollet	1 171	29 771	1 405	25.4	97.0	1.1	0.5	1.3	1.8	6.0	18.8	16.4	11.8	15.1	13.6
27 105	...	7	Nobles	1 853	20 832	1 742	11.2	87.6	1.3	0.6	4.6	11.2	6.9	19.6	8.2	11.8	14.8	12.4
27 107	...	8	Norman	2 270	7 442	2 645	3.3	96.7	0.2	2.8	0.4	3.1	6.1	19.6	6.2	9.3	14.8	12.8
27 109	6820	3	Olmsted	1 691	124 277	434	73.5	91.4	3.2	0.6	4.9	2.4	7.2	19.8	8.5	14.5	17.7	13.3
27 111	...	7	Otter Tail	5 127	57 159	833	11.1	97.8	0.4	0.8	0.7	1.7	5.5	19.4	7.2	9.3	14.9	13.8
27 113	...	7	Pennington	1 597	13 584	2 191	8.5	97.8	0.4	1.3	0.8	1.2	6.1	18.4	10.3	11.5	15.0	13.6
27 115	...	6	Pine	3 655	26 530	1 500	7.3	95.3	1.5	3.2	0.6	1.8	5.5	20.0	7.7	11.4	16.5	13.2
27 117	...	7	Pipestone	1 207	9 895	2 457	8.2	97.5	0.3	2.1	0.7	0.7	5.8	20.0	6.8	10.0	14.7	12.3
27 119	2985	3	Polk	5 103	31 369	1 363	6.1	95.4	0.5	2.0	0.5	4.8	6.0	20.0	9.7	10.0	14.8	13.2
27 121	...	6	Pope	1 736	11 236	2 354	6.5	99.2	0.4	0.4	0.2	0.5	4.9	19.9	6.7	8.7	14.3	13.7
27 123	5120	0	Ramsey	403	511 035	108	1 268.1	79.5	8.8	1.5	9.9	5.3	6.8	18.7	11.3	15.0	15.7	13.2
27 125	...	9	Red Lake	1 120	4 299	2 896	3.8	97.8	0.3	2.1	0.1	0.3	5.6	20.0	7.5	9.7	15.0	13.4
27 127	...	7	Redwood	2 278	16 815	1 966	7.4	95.7	0.3	3.8	0.5	1.1	6.1	20.4	6.6	10.5	14.3	12.9
27 129	...	7	Renville	2 546	17 154	1 945	6.7	96.4	0.1	0.8	0.4	5.1	6.0	20.5	6.6	10.3	15.0	12.7
27 131	...	4	Rice	1 289	56 665	836	44.0	94.7	1.6	0.8	1.9	5.5	6.1	19.1	15.8	11.7	15.7	12.3
27 133	...	6	Rock	1 250	9 721	2 468	7.8	97.8	0.7	0.7	0.7	1.3	5.9	20.4	7.2	10.0	14.1	13.2
27 135	...	9	Roseau	4 306	16 338	2 001	3.8	96.5	0.2	1.9	1.9	0.4	7.3	22.5	6.8	12.8	17.1	12.4
27 137	2240	3	St. Louis	16 123	200 528	275	12.4	96.1	1.2	2.8	1.0	0.8	5.2	17.1	11.4	10.8	15.2	15.1
27 139	5120	1	Scott	924	89 498	577	96.9	94.7	1.2	1.2	2.6	2.7	9.3	22.0	6.7	16.7	20.6	12.0
27 141	5120	1	Sherburne	1 130	64 417	756	57.0	97.6	1.1	0.9	0.9	1.1	8.4	22.5	9.6	15.5	18.4	12.0
27 143	...	8	Sibley	1 525	15 356	2 064	10.1	96.2	0.2	0.5	0.5	5.4	6.6	21.1	7.5	11.3	15.8	12.3
27 145	6980	3	Stearns	3 482	133 166	403	38.2	96.7	1.1	0.6	1.9	1.4	6.4	19.3	16.1	12.8	15.2	12.0
27 147	...	7	Steele	1 113	33 680	1 291	30.3	95.9	1.6	0.3	1.0	3.8	6.9	21.0	8.2	12.8	16.2	13.3
27 149	...	7	Stevens	1 456	10 053	2 439	6.9	97.1	1.1	1.2	0.9	0.9	5.3	16.3	20.8	8.6	13.0	11.8
27 151	...	7	Swift	1 926	11 956	2 297	6.2	91.9	2.8	0.8	5.0	2.7	5.4	17.7	7.3	12.7	16.9	12.9
27 153	...	6	Todd	2 440	24 426	1 578	10.0	98.4	0.2	0.8	0.5	1.9	5.9	21.4	8.1	9.6	15.1	13.5
27 155	...	9	Traverse	1 487	4 134	2 905	2.8	96.8	0.2	2.9	0.4	1.2	5.4	19.9	5.6	8.5	13.2	11.4
27 157	...	6	Wabasha	1 360	21 610	1 712	15.9	98.4	0.3	0.5	0.5	1.7	5.7	21.4	7.2	11.1	15.9	14.0
27 159	...	7	Wadena	1 386	13 713	2 182	9.9	98.4	0.6	0.9	0.3	0.9	6.4	19.5	8.1	9.5	14.1	12.5
27 161	...	7	Waseca	1 096	19 526	1 816	17.8	95.3	2.5	0.9	0.6	2.9	6.7	19.1	8.7	13.3	16.6	13.6
27 163	5120	0	Washington	1 015	201 130	272	198.2	94.9	2.3	0.8	2.6	1.9	7.6	21.8	6.8	13.6	19.3	15.0
27 165	...	7	Watonwan	1 125	11 876	2 300	10.6	89.5	0.6	0.4	1.2	15.2	7.2	20.4	7.8	10.4	13.9	12.3
27 167	...	6	Wilkin	1 946	7 138	2 675	3.7	98.8	0.3	0.9	0.4	1.5	6.3	21.5	7.0	10.6	17.1	12.5
27 169	...	4	Winona	1 622	49 985	915	30.8	96.5	0.9	0.5	2.2	1.4	5.6	17.2	18.6	11.1	13.9	12.7
27 171	5120	1	Wright	1 711	89 986	573	52.6	98.6	0.5	0.6	0.6	1.1	8.3	22.8	7.6	14.5	18.1	12.3
27 173	...	7	Yellow Medicine	1 963	11 080	2 360	5.6	96.7	0.2	2.5	0.3	1.8	5.7	20.0	7.4	9.1	15.1	12.3

1. MSA = Metropolitan Statistical Area. PMSA = Primary MSA. NECMA = New England County Metropolitan Area. See Appendix A for explanation of these concepts. See Appendix B for list of metropolitan areas identified by type, with component counties. 2. County typology code from the Economic Research Service of USDA. See Appendix A for definition. 3. Dry land or land partially or temporarily covered by water. 4. Hispanic persons may be of any race.

Table B. States and Counties — **Population and Households**

STATE County	Age (percent) (cont'd) 55 to 64 years	65 to 74 years	75 years and over	Percent female	Total persons 2001	1990	Percent change 1990–2000	2000–2001	Components of change, 2000–2001 Births	Deaths	Net migration	Households, 2000 Number	Percent change, 1990–2000	Persons per household	Percent Female family householder[1]	One person
	16	17	18	19	20	21	22	23	24	25	26	27	28	29	30	31
MINNESOTA—Cont'd																
Grant	10.2	10.2	12.7	51.4	6 238	6 246	0.7	-0.8	61	112	1	2 534	3.3	2.40	6.5	28.0
Hennepin	7.7	5.4	5.6	50.8	1 114 977	1 032 431	8.1	-0.1	20 567	10 251	-11 525	456 129	8.8	2.39	9.9	31.8
Houston	8.6	7.6	8.4	50.6	19 940	18 497	6.6	1.1	236	241	230	7 633	11.5	2.53	7.4	25.4
Hubbard	12.8	10.1	7.9	50.0	18 446	14 939	23.0	0.4	211	223	74	7 435	28.6	2.45	7.1	24.2
Isanti	8.7	5.3	5.5	49.9	32 767	25 921	20.7	4.7	456	290	1 286	11 236	27.5	2.74	8.4	20.1
Itasca	11.1	8.8	8.0	50.1	44 018	40 844	7.7	0.1	525	526	41	17 789	15.1	2.43	7.6	26.0
Jackson	9.2	9.1	11.3	49.8	11 160	11 677	-3.5	-1.0	146	160	-90	4 556	-0.1	2.40	5.4	28.5
Kanabec	10.2	7.9	6.2	49.5	15 346	12 802	17.1	2.3	204	156	301	5 759	21.2	2.58	8.4	23.8
Kandiyohi	8.8	7.1	7.8	50.5	41 106	38 761	6.3	-0.2	644	484	-244	15 936	11.5	2.53	7.5	25.7
Kittson	9.8	9.8	11.8	50.4	5 150	5 767	-8.4	-2.6	68	96	-107	2 167	-4.7	2.37	6.0	30.5
Koochiching	10.8	9.5	8.5	50.4	14 164	16 299	-11.9	-1.3	206	195	-202	6 040	0.2	2.33	8.5	30.4
Lac qui Parle	10.2	10.0	13.2	50.3	7 919	8 924	-9.6	-1.8	79	164	-61	3 316	-5.4	2.37	4.1	30.2
Lake	11.4	11.2	8.8	50.1	11 084	10 415	6.2	0.2	125	174	80	4 646	9.5	2.32	6.6	28.0
Lake of the Woods	11.9	8.6	8.6	49.8	4 443	4 076	10.9	-1.7	46	53	-72	1 903	20.7	2.35	5.3	29.7
Le Sueur	9.3	6.9	7.2	49.9	25 729	23 239	9.4	1.2	346	257	221	9 630	13.7	2.61	6.8	23.7
Lincoln	11.0	10.2	14.3	50.7	6 331	6 890	-6.7	-1.5	70	154	-14	2 653	-1.9	2.35	4.6	30.5
Lyon	7.7	6.3	8.3	51.1	25 231	24 789	2.6	-0.8	410	292	-309	9 715	7.1	2.49	7.1	27.9
McLeod	8.4	6.5	7.4	50.4	35 338	32 030	9.0	1.3	581	403	267	13 449	13.8	2.56	7.3	25.0
Mahnomen	10.5	8.2	8.5	49.3	5 215	5 044	2.9	0.5	102	72	-4	1 969	9.1	2.60	11.6	27.0
Marshall	10.4	9.0	9.5	49.2	10 025	10 993	-7.6	-1.3	139	122	-147	4 101	-2.2	2.45	5.4	28.7
Martin	9.7	8.9	11.0	51.2	21 536	22 914	-4.9	-1.2	277	362	-177	9 067	-0.7	2.35	7.2	30.0
Meeker	9.3	7.8	8.6	49.6	22 842	20 846	8.6	0.9	348	288	142	8 590	12.3	2.58	6.3	24.4
Mille Lacs	9.9	8.1	8.1	50.5	23 044	18 670	19.6	3.2	340	329	691	8 638	25.0	2.53	9.5	25.9
Morrison	8.9	7.8	7.8	49.7	32 216	29 604	7.1	1.6	500	364	373	11 816	13.6	2.64	7.8	24.9
Mower	8.8	9.0	10.6	50.8	38 631	37 385	3.3	0.1	553	565	60	15 582	3.7	2.42	8.0	29.1
Murray	10.7	10.3	10.9	50.4	9 003	9 660	-5.1	-1.8	98	135	-125	3 722	-1.0	2.42	4.6	27.1
Nicollet	7.6	5.7	5.2	50.2	30 106	28 076	6.0	1.1	384	230	186	10 642	12.3	2.56	7.9	24.0
Nobles	8.9	8.1	9.3	50.1	20 650	20 098	3.7	-0.9	370	250	-305	7 939	3.3	2.58	6.9	26.5
Norman	10.2	9.8	11.1	50.3	7 358	7 975	-6.7	-1.1	96	128	-51	3 010	-3.5	2.41	5.9	31.3
Olmsted	8.3	5.4	5.4	50.9	126 275	106 470	16.7	1.6	2 305	1 004	746	47 807	19.3	2.53	8.0	25.8
Otter Tail	10.9	9.5	9.5	49.9	57 797	50 714	12.7	1.1	745	835	739	22 671	16.2	2.46	6.1	26.6
Pennington	9.3	7.0	8.8	50.6	13 448	13 306	2.1	-1.0	213	207	-140	5 525	6.8	2.38	9.1	29.5
Pine	10.7	8.4	6.7	47.9	27 099	21 264	24.8	2.1	364	295	487	9 939	31.2	2.53	8.7	25.1
Pipestone	9.1	9.3	12.0	51.9	9 864	10 491	-5.7	-0.3	121	153	2	4 069	-0.2	2.38	6.5	30.1
Polk	9.0	7.7	9.7	50.5	31 160	32 589	-3.7	-0.7	424	443	-180	12 070	0.7	2.47	8.5	28.9
Pope	10.1	9.6	11.9	50.8	11 216	10 745	4.6	-0.2	128	185	42	4 513	9.1	2.42	5.9	28.7
Ramsey	7.6	5.6	6.0	51.8	508 667	485 760	5.2	-0.5	9 796	5 148	-7 083	201 236	5.6	2.45	11.9	32.0
Red Lake	9.8	9.0	10.0	49.8	4 295	4 525	-5.0	-0.1	59	62	-1	1 727	-0.2	2.39	6.8	30.5
Redwood	9.8	8.4	10.9	50.1	16 594	17 254	-2.5	-1.3	257	289	-187	6 674	1.8	2.44	7.1	28.8
Renville	9.0	9.1	10.7	50.2	16 961	17 673	-2.9	-1.1	252	261	-177	6 779	-0.2	2.48	5.6	28.5
Rice	7.8	5.6	5.8	49.6	57 683	49 183	15.2	1.8	829	510	711	18 888	15.5	2.65	8.6	23.9
Rock	8.9	8.8	11.6	50.6	9 698	9 806	-0.9	-0.2	144	142	-23	3 843	2.4	2.47	5.5	27.0
Roseau	8.5	5.6	7.0	48.8	16 172	15 026	8.7	-1.0	256	154	-269	6 190	14.3	2.60	6.8	24.6
St. Louis	9.2	7.6	8.5	50.8	199 460	198 232	1.2	-0.5	2 497	2 734	-749	82 619	4.7	2.32	9.4	31.2
Scott	6.5	3.4	2.8	49.5	98 100	57 846	54.7	9.6	1 881	494	7 013	30 692	58.5	2.89	7.4	16.0
Sherburne	6.5	3.6	3.5	48.9	68 621	41 945	53.6	6.5	1 220	436	3 335	21 581	58.2	2.91	7.5	15.7
Sibley	9.0	8.2	8.2	49.3	15 384	14 366	6.9	0.2	234	185	-18	5 772	8.4	2.60	5.8	25.4
Stearns	7.1	5.9	5.1	49.7	134 509	119 324	11.6	1.0	2 080	910	233	47 604	19.7	2.64	7.5	23.6
Steele	8.3	6.5	6.8	50.6	34 131	30 729	9.6	1.3	511	331	282	12 846	13.3	2.57	7.4	24.6
Stevens	7.2	7.7	9.3	51.6	9 845	10 634	-5.5	-2.1	141	111	-240	3 751	-1.9	2.43	5.1	29.1
Swift	8.7	7.8	10.7	45.3	11 645	10 724	11.5	-2.6	173	174	-314	4 353	2.0	2.39	6.1	30.9
Todd	10.3	8.3	7.9	49.5	24 569	23 363	4.5	0.6	327	266	83	9 342	8.8	2.58	6.1	26.3
Traverse	9.8	12.0	14.2	50.8	3 999	4 463	-7.4	-3.3	43	81	-99	1 717	-3.4	2.34	6.0	32.0
Wabasha	9.8	7.2	7.8	50.0	21 731	19 744	9.5	0.6	264	253	115	8 277	13.6	2.57	6.5	24.3
Wadena	10.0	9.5	10.4	50.5	13 646	13 154	4.2	-0.5	203	231	-33	5 426	9.0	2.45	7.6	29.2
Waseca	7.7	6.6	7.5	47.8	19 495	18 079	8.0	-0.2	327	219	-132	7 059	6.2	2.56	7.8	25.1
Washington	8.2	4.4	3.2	50.3	207 642	145 860	37.9	3.2	3 329	1 133	4 269	71 462	45.1	2.77	8.5	18.7
Watonwan	9.4	8.9	9.7	51.2	11 779	11 682	1.7	-0.8	203	163	-136	4 627	2.1	2.53	7.3	28.7
Wilkin	8.9	7.7	8.4	51.2	7 034	7 516	-5.0	-1.5	115	100	-118	2 752	-1.9	2.54	7.0	25.9
Winona	7.8	6.1	6.9	51.2	49 588	47 828	4.5	-0.8	698	552	-534	18 744	10.7	2.46	7.8	28.2
Wright	7.5	4.6	4.2	49.6	94 789	68 710	31.0	5.3	1 758	677	3 641	31 465	36.7	2.83	7.7	18.8
Yellow Medicine	9.8	8.9	11.6	50.5	10 883	11 684	-5.2	-1.8	142	164	-175	4 439	-3.6	2.42	5.7	29.3

1. No spouse present.

STATE County	Births, average 1997–1999 Total	Rate[1]	Deaths, average 1997–1999 Number Total	Number Infant[2]	Rate Total[1]	Rate Infant[3]	Physicians,[4] 2000 Number	Rate[5]	Hospitals,[4] 1998 Number	Beds Number	Beds Rate[5]	Medicare enrollees 2000	Serious crimes known to police, 2000[6] Total Number	Rate[7]
	32	33	34	35	36	37	38	39	40	41	42	43	44	45
MINNESOTA—Cont'd														
Grant	60	9.8	93	NA	15.1	NA	4	64	1	20	324	1 565	166	2 640
Hennepin	15 291	14.4	8 090	104	7.6	6.8	3 827	343	8	3 411	322	137 189	54 767	4 907
Houston	215	11.2	181	NA	9.4	NA	10	51	1	89	462	3 377	242	1 227
Hubbard	189	11.2	185	NA	10.9	NA	15	82	1	45	266	3 507	754	4 103
Isanti	375	12.4	231	NA	7.7	NA	43	137	1	86	286	3 434	679	2 170
Itasca	432	9.8	427	NA	9.7	NA	54	123	3	244	556	8 388	355	807
Jackson	119	10.4	126	NA	10.9	NA	9	80	1	41	356	2 142	171	1 518
Kanabec	172	12.2	139	NA	9.8	NA	6	40	1	49	346	2 275	411	2 741
Kandiyohi	534	13.0	365	NA	8.9	NA	106	257	1	122	297	6 745	1 201	2 915
Kittson	60	11.3	77	NA	14.6	NA	4	76	2	205	3 852	1 208	55	1 041
Koochiching	161	10.5	164	NA	10.7	NA	12	84	1	44	283	2 999	442	3 079
Lac qui Parle	81	10.1	129	NA	16.2	NA	7	87	2	106	1 321	1 861	92	1 140
Lake	103	9.7	131	NA	12.3	NA	13	118	1	80	757	2 238	176	1 592
Lake of the Woods	39	8.5	40	NA	8.8	NA	6	133	1	73	1 600	837	76	1 681
Le Sueur	311	12.3	211	NA	8.4	NA	8	31	2	131	517	4 389	276	1 086
Lincoln	58	8.9	101	NA	15.5	NA	8	124	3	231	3 576	1 556	8	124
Lyon	326	13.4	243	NA	10.0	NA	29	114	2	145	596	4 324	278	1 093
McLeod	473	13.9	300	NA	8.8	NA	34	97	2	215	632	5 280	1 099	3 149
Mahnomen	72	14.2	58	NA	11.4	NA	3	58	1	66	1 300	991	203	3 911
Marshall	107	10.3	106	NA	10.3	NA	1	10	1	18	175	2 064	183	1 802
Martin	237	10.8	266	NA	12.1	NA	23	105	1	108	491	4 680	342	1 569
Meeker	269	12.4	229	NA	10.6	NA	15	66	1	38	175	3 684	657	2 901
Mille Lacs	263	12.5	246	NA	11.7	NA	24	107	2	149	708	4 581	825	3 695
Morrison	392	12.9	303	NA	9.9	NA	24	76	1	55	180	5 402	766	2 415
Mower	432	11.6	428	NA	11.5	NA	71	184	1	94	254	8 337	1 381	3 577
Murray	97	10.2	101	NA	10.6	NA	4	44	1	32	336	1 952	105	1 146
Nicollet	340	11.5	179	NA	6.0	NA	36	121	1	121	409	2 741	765	2 570
Nobles	272	14.0	209	NA	10.8	NA	25	120	2	146	756	3 938	403	1 935
Norman	72	9.6	101	NA	13.3	NA	4	54	1	77	1 022	1 639	81	1 088
Olmsted	1 767	15.1	762	10	6.5	5.8	1 511	1 216	3	1 343	1 151	14 115	3 065	2 466
Otter Tail	602	11.0	637	NA	11.6	NA	67	117	2	267	486	11 140	1 172	2 050
Pennington	165	12.1	148	NA	10.9	NA	20	147	1	150	1 106	2 322	387	2 849
Pine	271	11.3	227	NA	9.4	NA	8	30	2	233	974	4 429	909	3 426
Pipestone	112	11.1	121	NA	12.0	NA	7	71	1	87	862	2 225	204	2 062
Polk	386	12.4	376	NA	12.0	NA	21	67	2	252	814	5 773	833	2 655
Pope	111	10.2	157	NA	14.4	NA	8	71	2	53	487	2 402	181	1 611
Ramsey	7 452	15.4	4 124	65	8.5	8.7	1 369	268	6	1 514	312	76 623	26 670	5 219
Red Lake	43	10.2	55	NA	12.8	NA	1	23	0	0	0	844	73	1 698
Redwood	195	11.8	219	NA	13.2	NA	10	59	1	35	212	3 509	296	1 760
Renville	200	11.8	221	NA	13.1	NA	8	47	1	30	177	3 448	358	2 087
Rice	663	12.2	406	NA	7.5	NA	69	122	2	114	211	6 932	1 919	3 387
Rock	112	11.5	109	NA	11.2	NA	6	62	1	38	390	2 039	81	833
Roseau	263	16.3	136	NA	8.4	NA	10	61	1	101	627	2 265	336	2 057
St. Louis	2 008	10.4	2 201	12	11.4	6.1	448	223	8	1 368	707	36 125	6 659	3 321
Scott	1 408	17.7	362	NA	4.6	NA	44	49	1	67	85	5 537	2 549	2 848
Sherburne	972	16.0	345	NA	5.7	NA	24	37	0	0	0	4 769	1 178	1 829
Sibley	191	13.0	152	NA	10.3	NA	3	20	1	17	117	2 621	52	339
Stearns	1 628	12.7	736	8	5.7	5.1	299	225	5	655	511	18 156	2 110	1 584
Steele	423	13.3	260	NA	8.2	NA	35	104	1	65	205	4 920	988	2 933
Stevens	99	9.8	95	NA	9.5	NA	9	90	1	38	375	1 815	171	1 701
Swift	125	11.4	139	NA	12.6	NA	7	59	2	138	1 277	2 400	145	1 213
Todd	270	11.2	221	NA	9.2	NA	6	25	2	262	1 091	4 133	523	2 141
Traverse	45	10.7	67	NA	15.8	NA	4	97	1	35	824	1 085	57	1 379
Wabasha	237	11.3	199	NA	9.5	NA	18	83	2	112	535	3 788	388	1 795
Wadena	156	11.9	175	NA	13.3	NA	12	88	1	48	365	3 020	383	2 793
Waseca	242	13.2	173	NA	9.5	NA	17	87	1	26	143	3 025	338	1 731
Washington	2 709	13.8	893	12	4.5	4.4	177	88	2	92	47	12 215	5 686	2 827
Watonwan	168	14.5	130	NA	11.2	NA	8	67	2	37	323	2 374	234	1 970
Wilkin	98	13.4	78	NA	10.7	NA	4	56	1	171	2 339	1 291	163	2 284
Winona	560	11.7	426	NA	8.9	NA	46	92	1	203	422	6 950	1 373	2 747
Wright	1 316	15.4	530	NA	6.2	NA	49	54	2	147	173	9 091	2 389	2 655
Yellow Medicine	121	10.5	142	NA	12.4	NA	4	36	2	193	1 691	2 581	97	875

1. Per 1,000 estimated resident population, average 1997–1999. 2. Deaths of infants under 1 year old. 3. Deaths of infants under 1 year old per 1,000 live births. 4. Data subject to copyright. 5. Per 100,000 resident population as of July 1 of the year shown. 6. Data for serious crimes have not been adjusted for underreporting; this may affect comparability between geographic areas and over time. 7. Per 100,000 population estimated by the FBI.

Table B. States and Counties — Crime, Education, Money Income, and Poverty

	Serious crimes known to police, 2000[1] (cont'd)		Education						Money income				Income and poverty, 1998			
	Rate[2]		School enrollment and attainment, 1990				Local government expenditures, fiscal 1999[5]		1989				Percent below poverty level			
			Enrollment[3]		Attainment[4] (percent)					Households							
											Median						
STATE County	Violent	Property	Total	Percent private	High school graduate or more	Bachelor's degree or more	Total current expenditures (mil dol)	Current expenditures per student (dollars)	Per capita[6] (dollars)	Dollars	Percent change, 1979–1989 (constant 1989 dollars)	Percent with $100,000 or more	Median household income	All persons	Persons under 18	Persons 5–17 in families
	46	47	48	49	50	51	52	53	54	55	56	57	58	59	60	61

MINNESOTA—Cont'd

STATE County	46	47	48	49	50	51	52	53	54	55	56	57	58	59	60	61
Grant	32	2 608	1 380	0.8	71.9	11.4	9.5	6 022	9 622	19 773	-2.0	0.9	32 010	13.2	17.7	16.5
Hennepin	533	4 374	258 020	16.8	88.2	31.6	1 221.3	7 854	18 496	35 659	6.0	6.3	49 449	9.3	14.7	12.3
Houston	76	1 151	4 620	14.4	75.9	14.4	21.4	5 849	11 587	25 846	2.8	1.8	40 275	8.1	10.7	9.7
Hubbard	185	3 918	3 615	4.4	76.4	14.7	18.5	6 284	9 527	20 151	3.2	0.9	30 440	14.5	18.8	18.3
Isanti	67	2 103	7 273	5.7	78.2	11.5	35.8	6 198	11 909	31 308	6.4	1.9	46 044	7.9	10.7	9.1
Itasca	59	748	11 081	6.5	77.5	12.5	56.9	7 010	10 541	22 442	-17.1	0.9	34 616	12.9	17.3	15.5
Jackson	98	1 420	2 831	5.9	74.2	10.0	11.8	6 074	11 287	23 157	-3.0	1.5	33 778	10.2	13.4	12.5
Kanabec	220	2 521	3 317	2.4	69.9	8.9	15.8	5 562	9 887	22 495	0.4	0.8	33 653	12.4	16.1	15.4
Kandiyohi	240	2 675	10 609	7.0	76.3	15.7	43.6	6 658	11 574	25 368	1.7	2.1	37 825	11.8	16.0	13.9
Kittson	38	1 003	1 291	3.2	71.0	12.5	8.0	7 248	11 050	23 518	6.4	1.1	33 640	12.6	17.2	15.8
Koochiching	237	2 842	4 100	10.4	73.0	10.4	17.9	7 072	11 732	23 411	-12.8	1.0	35 972	12.5	18.3	16.4
Lac qui Parle	62	1 078	2 012	2.8	72.2	10.9	13.0	6 271	10 368	21 646	1.9	0.9	32 589	10.7	14.0	12.5
Lake	99	1 492	2 299	5.5	80.2	12.2	13.7	6 427	11 415	23 478	-31.3	0.6	37 366	8.2	12.6	10.6
Lake of the Woods	44	1 636	933	2.3	75.2	11.0	5.2	5 973	10 623	24 383	23.8	0.3	33 608	10.0	12.8	14.0
Le Sueur	55	1 030	6 142	12.1	76.3	13.1	27.8	5 511	11 792	27 706	1.8	2.2	42 993	7.3	9.9	8.1
Lincoln	124	0	1 635	3.7	67.7	8.4	6.6	6 412	9 616	19 211	10.7	1.4	29 128	13.6	17.2	15.4
Lyon	83	1 011	7 542	9.1	75.9	16.8	38.4	7 959	11 121	24 689	-0.7	2.2	39 025	9.8	12.7	10.7
McLeod	232	2 917	8 036	16.6	75.5	11.7	36.1	5 731	12 689	29 549	4.4	2.0	44 052	6.9	9.2	8.0
Mahnomen	636	3 276	1 403	5.7	64.7	10.5	11.6	7 966	7 737	16 924	-3.7	0.4	25 513	22.0	28.3	26.8
Marshall	98	1 704	2 895	3.1	68.5	10.2	13.2	7 071	9 675	21 707	0.3	0.4	32 606	12.5	16.0	13.9
Martin	202	1 367	5 669	12.0	75.2	13.0	27.0	6 811	11 387	24 414	-4.8	1.9	35 356	11.2	15.6	13.6
Meeker	150	2 751	5 209	6.7	73.4	10.0	36.4	5 687	10 843	24 516	4.2	1.9	37 894	9.2	12.1	10.6
Mille Lacs	197	3 498	4 782	5.7	70.1	9.4	36.8	5 858	10 167	22 689	2.7	1.5	33 254	11.8	15.7	14.9
Morrison	145	2 270	7 841	9.6	67.7	9.0	41.4	6 635	9 666	22 102	9.2	1.3	33 060	12.9	16.1	14.3
Mower	272	3 305	9 073	10.5	75.8	12.9	38.8	6 351	11 599	23 763	-12.6	1.4	36 166	10.1	14.9	12.6
Murray	55	1 091	2 350	11.5	69.7	8.5	9.6	6 258	10 871	22 673	2.2	1.6	33 174	10.7	14.5	12.6
Nicollet	144	2 425	9 314	32.6	81.5	22.4	17.6	7 515	12 358	30 491	6.6	2.1	44 597	7.7	9.3	8.9
Nobles	134	1 800	4 981	7.8	70.4	11.1	23.7	6 509	10 860	22 942	-5.8	1.3	33 374	12.4	17.5	15.0
Norman	94	994	1 853	0.6	69.7	9.7	10.7	7 416	9 948	21 238	2.1	0.8	31 063	13.8	18.0	16.8
Olmsted	232	2 235	28 118	15.4	88.0	29.5	150.1	7 118	16 214	35 789	6.4	5.1	50 682	6.9	9.7	8.4
Otter Tail	86	1 965	11 799	8.6	71.6	13.0	82.5	8 803	10 467	21 909	4.0	1.1	33 279	11.9	16.0	13.7
Pennington	140	2 709	3 593	5.5	72.3	13.7	17.0	6 691	10 426	21 571	-12.0	1.1	33 529	12.3	16.2	14.9
Pine	162	3 264	5 461	4.7	69.2	9.5	27.7	6 070	9 538	21 191	3.2	1.1	32 448	13.2	16.7	16.0
Pipestone	101	1 961	2 575	13.7	70.4	9.9	13.6	6 203	10 050	20 737	5.9	1.5	32 098	12.1	15.4	14.7
Polk	214	2 442	8 740	8.5	73.0	12.9	40.0	6 566	10 199	22 559	-5.2	1.2	33 589	14.0	17.7	16.2
Pope	44	1 566	2 571	2.8	72.1	10.2	11.4	6 152	9 465	20 131	1.1	0.8	32 670	11.6	15.6	14.3
Ramsey	539	4 680	130 778	25.5	85.0	28.8	649.0	7 599	15 645	32 043	0.9	3.9	44 100	11.4	18.4	15.8
Red Lake	70	1 628	1 149	9.5	64.3	9.3	8.0	9 049	8 963	19 926	2.0	0.6	30 241	12.1	13.7	13.9
Redwood	202	1 558	3 948	10.4	71.3	11.1	21.2	6 032	10 489	22 827	0.4	1.4	35 258	9.9	13.1	11.5
Renville	239	1 848	4 323	10.7	71.7	10.2	17.7	6 315	10 795	23 278	-6.1	1.6	35 827	10.9	15.1	13.8
Rice	212	3 175	16 008	39.1	78.7	19.3	51.6	6 334	11 936	29 596	4.2	2.5	45 037	7.7	9.4	8.3
Rock	62	772	2 504	10.3	69.8	10.8	10.5	5 877	11 383	24 483	2.7	2.1	35 212	9.2	12.5	11.0
Roseau	73	1 983	3 518	3.4	71.8	10.2	23.7	6 117	10 280	25 910	16.0	0.9	38 291	8.2	10.5	9.6
St. Louis	234	3 086	53 991	8.5	80.3	17.3	213.3	6 863	11 833	24 093	-16.7	1.4	37 389	11.7	16.4	13.5
Scott	160	2 688	15 572	17.1	84.8	17.2	78.6	6 193	15 341	40 798	8.4	4.4	62 963	3.8	5.3	4.8
Sherburne	92	1 737	12 613	10.7	84.2	16.7	74.4	5 770	13 147	35 585	9.2	2.6	55 447	5.2	6.4	6.0
Sibley	0	339	3 574	11.2	68.2	8.9	16.7	6 973	10 899	24 957	1.1	1.6	35 364	9.3	12.2	12.0
Stearns	107	1 478	40 146	17.1	78.3	17.5	159.0	6 524	11 620	27 512	2.5	2.6	40 952	8.3	10.7	9.4
Steele	163	2 770	7 913	13.9	79.4	16.0	37.8	5 891	12 993	30 571	8.1	2.4	45 164	7.2	9.8	8.8
Stevens	99	1 602	3 873	5.1	77.0	17.0	11.4	6 725	9 814	21 921	4.2	0.8	37 913	10.3	12.8	11.8
Swift	50	1 163	2 493	7.3	68.2	11.2	10.6	5 513	9 222	18 740	-6.0	0.5	33 068	12.2	15.9	14.3
Todd	111	2 031	6 336	7.6	68.4	7.8	47.1	9 912	8 535	18 836	0.8	0.6	29 476	14.9	18.4	16.6
Traverse	97	1 282	968	2.7	71.2	9.8	5.0	6 984	9 882	20 746	2.0	1.0	29 858	14.7	19.9	19.9
Wabasha	97	1 698	4 948	9.5	76.4	12.4	22.6	5 430	11 862	26 998	6.7	2.0	40 092	7.8	10.3	9.3
Wadena	226	2 567	3 293	5.4	70.6	11.6	20.3	6 187	8 640	17 333	-7.2	0.7	28 331	16.5	19.3	20.0
Waseca	138	1 593	4 970	8.7	77.5	13.6	26.8	6 553	11 514	26 992	-0.9	1.2	39 521	8.8	11.7	10.7
Washington	122	2 705	42 488	13.6	90.0	26.2	207.2	6 035	17 435	44 122	8.5	6.4	65 748	3.8	5.3	4.4
Watonwan	118	1 852	2 782	10.5	72.2	10.1	14.0	6 391	10 658	22 496	-9.0	1.3	33 044	10.8	15.7	14.3
Wilkin	210	2 073	1 858	9.0	73.8	11.6	9.3	6 304	10 108	23 081	-10.9	1.1	36 142	11.1	14.7	13.7
Winona	138	2 609	16 128	19.2	77.7	19.7	42.0	6 345	11 323	25 937	2.2	1.8	38 496	9.9	12.5	11.0
Wright	93	2 562	18 754	9.8	80.1	12.1	109.1	5 988	12 687	33 456	7.0	2.6	50 181	5.8	7.4	6.6
Yellow Medicine	54	821	2 905	6.2	72.6	9.9	14.2	6 576	10 513	21 537	-0.1	1.4	33 426	10.5	12.5	12.5

1. Data for serious crimes have not been adjusted for underreporting; this may affect comparability between geographic areas and over time. 2. Per 100,000 population estimated by the FBI. 3. All persons 3 years old and over enrolled in nursery school through college. 4. Persons 25 years old and over. 5. Elementary and secondary education expenditures, local government fiscal years ending between July 1, 1998 and June 30, 1999. 6. Based on population enumerated as of April 1, 1990.

Table B. States and Counties — **Personal Income**

STATE County	Personal income, 1999 Total (mil dol)	Percent change, 1998–1999	Per capita[1] Dollars	Per capita[1] Rank	Wages and salaries[2] (mil dol)	Proprietor's income (mil dol)	Dividends, interest, and rent (mil dol)	Transfer payments Total (mil dol)	Government payments to individuals Total (mil dol)	Social Security (mil dol)	Medical payments (mil dol)	Income maintenance (mil dol)	Unemployment insurance (mil dol)
	62	63	64	65	66	67	68	69	70	71	72	73	74
MINNESOTA—Cont'd													
Grant	141	4.4	23 128	1 066	53	26	35	29	28	12	11	2	1
Hennepin	45 039	5.2	42 313	31	40 873	3 342	9 989	3 848	3 631	1 372	1 618	385	72
Houston	489	4.0	25 103	652	128	46	101	69	65	30	26	4	1
Hubbard	361	6.0	21 186	1 600	152	39	82	76	73	33	27	7	2
Isanti	723	6.5	23 416	983	261	65	113	89	83	37	32	6	3
Itasca	921	3.8	20 861	1 711	473	73	205	188	179	80	67	15	6
Jackson	252	-1.4	22 122	1 321	113	34	61	43	41	19	16	3	1
Kanabec	279	5.2	19 347	2 197	114	24	57	49	46	20	16	4	2
Kandiyohi	1 063	3.7	26 036	507	603	92	270	150	142	59	55	12	3
Kittson	134	8.3	25 843	536	44	25	33	24	23	10	10	2	0
Koochiching	339	2.4	22 753	1 153	197	18	72	66	63	28	24	5	2
Lac qui Parle	182	0.1	23 356	1 001	59	39	46	37	36	16	15	3	1
Lake	241	3.3	22 354	1 256	126	15	65	50	48	21	17	2	1
Lake of the Woods	94	1.2	20 333	1 881	42	5	23	17	16	7	7	1	0
Le Sueur	638	5.7	25 045	664	252	48	141	84	79	36	32	5	2
Lincoln	128	-1.6	19 935	2 013	41	22	32	29	28	12	12	2	1
Lyon	667	4.7	27 483	375	433	67	149	89	84	36	36	6	2
McLeod	931	4.1	26 944	420	635	72	202	107	100	48	39	6	3
Mahnomen	92	4.6	18 045	2 531	54	7	20	25	24	8	10	4	1
Marshall	211	-0.9	20 887	1 702	69	17	55	43	41	18	17	3	1
Martin	535	0.2	24 551	744	261	53	146	94	89	44	35	6	2
Meeker	491	6.1	22 558	1 203	178	50	110	75	71	33	27	5	2
Mille Lacs	446	7.6	20 900	1 695	243	42	80	98	93	39	40	8	3
Morrison	618	4.2	20 245	1 911	287	67	129	117	111	45	44	10	4
Mower	958	4.5	25 793	542	488	72	218	166	159	77	62	10	2
Murray	207	-1.4	21 719	1 444	67	42	53	39	37	18	14	3	1
Nicollet	745	3.4	25 464	592	403	51	146	74	68	34	23	5	2
Nobles	461	1.3	24 110	838	255	58	112	79	75	34	30	7	1
Norman	175	7.2	23 327	1 007	58	33	45	36	35	14	16	2	1
Olmsted	3 853	7.4	32 359	143	3 213	197	755	350	325	147	131	26	6
Otter Tail	1 226	5.0	22 050	1 348	555	135	309	232	221	100	86	16	5
Pennington	336	2.6	24 800	702	225	18	84	52	49	20	19	4	2
Pine	478	6.2	19 406	2 177	204	36	87	102	97	42	37	8	3
Pipestone	217	-0.8	21 729	1 440	97	36	54	41	39	17	16	3	1
Polk	720	3.6	23 376	992	332	62	145	132	125	49	54	12	2
Pope	243	4.6	22 324	1 269	97	25	60	48	46	21	18	3	1
Ramsey	16 707	4.3	34 360	97	14 128	697	3 893	1 948	1 849	644	835	226	32
Red Lake	80	0.3	18 941	2 300	30	11	15	19	18	7	8	2	1
Redwood	403	3.5	24 545	747	188	54	105	65	62	29	24	4	1
Renville	403	4.5	23 967	866	172	59	104	67	64	30	24	5	2
Rice	1 279	4.5	23 254	1 029	727	70	268	153	142	68	54	9	3
Rock	226	2.3	23 448	975	85	30	60	38	36	19	13	2	0
Roseau	349	-0.5	21 696	1 454	263	8	78	47	44	18	19	3	2
St. Louis	5 118	4.6	26 460	471	3 083	342	1 097	876	837	343	327	75	20
Scott	2 580	10.3	31 091	176	1 169	160	364	152	135	63	49	7	6
Sherburne	1 484	8.3	23 420	982	575	79	218	123	110	52	37	8	5
Sibley	302	4.5	20 426	1 859	92	32	69	52	49	23	20	3	1
Stearns	3 044	3.2	23 402	985	2 332	255	631	374	348	146	126	27	10
Steele	902	2.9	28 146	313	635	55	187	98	92	46	34	6	2
Stevens	246	4.1	24 678	717	136	34	62	37	35	15	14	3	0
Swift	247	1.2	21 780	1 422	111	33	55	47	45	19	20	4	1
Todd	421	4.2	17 369	2 673	172	40	86	93	88	34	34	10	2
Traverse	96	-0.8	22 987	1 092	30	15	32	21	21	10	8	2	0
Wabasha	534	4.4	25 274	619	209	59	114	73	68	33	27	4	1
Wadena	270	6.3	20 370	1 869	160	26	55	63	61	23	27	6	1
Waseca	429	1.3	23 140	1 062	240	34	101	60	56	28	19	4	1
Washington	6 594	8.9	32 547	138	2 330	212	1 252	387	346	181	110	20	11
Watonwan	261	1.8	22 617	1 189	126	36	58	47	45	21	18	3	1
Wilkin	164	8.0	22 478	1 219	61	21	37	28	27	11	12	2	0
Winona	1 186	4.0	24 823	698	723	90	277	155	145	67	57	10	3
Wright	2 250	7.8	25 604	571	830	154	332	211	193	90	73	12	8
Yellow Medicine	244	4.1	21 555	1 503	106	41	51	50	47	21	20	3	1

1. Based on the resident population estimated as of July 1 of the year shown.　2. Includes other labor income.

Table B. States and Counties — Earnings, Social Security, and Housing

STATE County	Earnings, 1999									Social Security beneficiaries, December 2000			Housing units, 1990	
	Total (mil dol)	Farm	Goods-related[1]		Service-related and other[2]							Supplemental Security Income recipients, December 2000		
			Total	Manufacturing	Total	Retail trade	Finance, insurance, and real estate	Services	Government	Number	Rate[3]		Total	Percent change, 1980–1990
	75	76	77	78	79	80	81	82	83	84	85	86	87	88

MINNESOTA—Cont'd

STATE County	75	76	77	78	79	80	81	82	83	84	85	86	87	88
Grant	79	15.4	D	10.8	D	6.5	4.8	24.2	14.5	1 664	265	72	3 178	-0.4
Hennepin	44 215	0.0	19.6	15.3	71.1	9.2	13.0	30.9	9.2	147 109	132	18 232	443 583	16.9
Houston	174	4.5	D	13.0	D	7.9	5.6	23.8	17.6	3 752	190	207	7 257	8.8
Hubbard	191	1.3	D	23.0	D	11.5	4.9	24.2	16.4	4 305	234	304	10 042	10.3
Isanti	326	-0.7	29.4	17.4	52.8	10.7	3.7	29.3	18.6	4 513	144	214	9 693	15.8
Itasca	547	-0.2	D	17.6	D	10.3	3.5	22.3	20.7	9 692	220	757	22 494	6.0
Jackson	147	11.5	23.0	16.9	D	6.1	4.2	17.6	16.4	2 410	214	112	5 121	-7.3
Kanabec	138	-1.5	D	16.6	D	19.2	5.2	17.5	21.4	2 692	180	184	6 098	11.2
Kandiyohi	695	3.3	D	15.2	D	10.3	4.1	21.3	22.0	7 523	183	609	16 669	10.4
Kittson	69	29.0	D	2.4	D	5.9	3.9	17.4	20.2	1 273	241	67	2 865	-5.1
Koochiching	215	-0.3	40.4	35.0	D	9.5	D	21.5	17.8	3 344	233	273	7 825	8.1
Lac qui Parle	98	24.3	D	12.3	D	8.0	4.1	13.8	20.2	2 088	259	93	3 955	-7.4
Lake	141	0.1	D	13.7	D	10.9	3.0	18.2	20.6	2 485	225	90	6 776	10.9
Lake of the Woods	47	-6.6	D	D	D	11.6	2.2	27.6	22.6	990	219	45	3 050	12.6
Le Sueur	301	3.2	47.5	35.1	36.4	8.1	3.6	16.2	13.0	4 466	176	231	9 785	2.9
Lincoln	63	17.4	11.5	3.4	54.5	6.8	3.2	26.6	16.6	1 753	273	86	3 050	-7.5
Lyon	500	5.3	D	30.3	D	7.9	6.0	13.7	18.3	4 534	178	315	9 675	5.2
McLeod	707	3.2	D	47.0	D	6.5	3.0	9.8	12.6	5 915	169	213	12 391	13.5
Mahnomen	62	0.1	10.9	1.7	D	7.3	8.2	D	19.5	1 111	214	131	2 505	3.9
Marshall	86	5.6	23.0	11.0	47.6	8.6	5.4	14.9	23.8	2 363	233	102	5 049	-3.9
Martin	314	6.7	28.1	22.0	51.6	9.1	5.1	20.7	13.6	5 311	244	332	9 847	0.6
Meeker	228	6.4	D	22.8	D	8.6	D	14.1	16.8	4 268	188	204	9 139	7.0
Mille Lacs	285	1.6	D	16.0	D	8.1	5.2	37.5	16.1	4 939	221	349	9 065	9.3
Morrison	353	4.1	25.2	15.5	49.5	10.3	3.7	22.6	21.1	6 446	203	491	12 434	7.0
Mower	560	2.7	D	35.4	D	9.2	3.4	20.0	14.4	8 980	233	613	15 831	1.0
Murray	108	21.8	D	D	D	6.5	4.6	15.1	15.5	2 344	256	97	4 611	-1.5
Nicollet	454	4.2	D	36.3	D	5.8	4.1	18.0	18.3	4 050	136	215	9 963	11.2
Nobles	313	5.3	D	24.0	D	11.2	4.1	15.2	17.6	4 333	208	307	8 094	-1.4
Norman	91	24.0	D	D	D	9.1	5.3	18.4	18.4	1 867	251	115	3 648	-9.2
Olmsted	3 409	0.6	D	21.7	D	7.2	3.6	46.4	8.8	17 035	137	1 355	41 603	21.1
Otter Tail	690	5.5	24.3	14.8	52.4	11.1	4.1	22.4	17.9	13 139	230	784	29 295	8.7
Pennington	243	-1.7	25.7	22.5	58.1	8.8	3.1	21.4	18.0	2 551	188	202	5 682	-5.0
Pine	239	1.2	D	5.5	D	12.0	2.9	33.0	25.8	5 440	205	424	12 738	23.7
Pipestone	133	5.4	D	16.9	D	12.6	5.2	15.8	18.7	2 321	235	151	4 387	-5.4
Polk	394	8.4	D	15.0	D	8.9	3.7	20.6	22.4	6 359	203	551	14 275	-3.3
Pope	122	10.1	D	14.7	D	10.1	D	15.2	19.0	2 705	241	107	5 836	3.1
Ramsey	14 825	0.0	29.3	24.2	54.2	7.0	9.4	27.2	16.5	70 654	138	11 863	201 016	13.6
Red Lake	41	10.5	D	7.8	D	8.5	3.5	16.6	21.0	907	211	55	1 899	-7.0
Redwood	241	10.7	D	17.7	D	8.2	4.0	21.0	15.7	3 838	228	192	7 144	-3.3
Renville	231	19.0	24.9	18.1	41.2	5.8	6.4	13.4	14.8	3 802	222	172	7 442	-5.9
Rice	797	0.5	33.9	25.7	48.4	8.6	3.1	26.7	17.2	8 001	141	506	17 520	11.8
Rock	115	15.9	D	8.6	D	9.2	10.5	18.6	20.9	2 387	246	80	3 963	-3.2
Roseau	271	-3.3	64.7	62.6	27.1	5.8	2.6	13.8	11.5	2 538	155	160	6 236	23.9
St. Louis	3 425	0.0	21.7	8.6	58.1	10.5	4.0	29.7	20.2	40 221	201	4 308	95 403	0.1
Scott	1 329	0.3	38.8	22.9	49.9	8.2	3.8	26.4	11.0	7 573	85	261	20 302	43.1
Sherburne	654	0.3	D	18.0	D	12.3	4.1	14.8	18.5	6 354	99	328	14 964	44.7
Sibley	124	11.3	25.4	12.7	43.2	7.1	4.1	16.4	20.0	3 066	200	109	5 625	-0.1
Stearns	2 587	2.1	24.6	17.8	57.3	14.3	5.1	25.2	16.0	19 004	143	1 440	43 806	21.8
Steele	690	1.7	D	38.1	D	8.6	13.7	14.8	9.2	5 547	165	270	11 840	5.2
Stevens	169	11.7	D	13.4	D	7.7	4.2	18.4	24.3	1 886	188	116	4 108	-2.7
Swift	144	10.5	D	21.3	D	7.7	3.5	18.1	18.7	2 523	211	161	4 795	-7.5
Todd	212	3.4	D	29.3	D	8.7	4.3	16.6	19.5	4 855	199	467	11 234	5.1
Traverse	45	18.4	D	6.2	D	7.4	6.6	12.6	25.2	1 284	311	41	2 220	-7.8
Wabasha	268	7.1	35.2	26.1	45.3	8.4	3.6	16.3	12.5	4 159	192	189	8 205	7.9
Wadena	187	1.6	24.3	18.0	52.3	9.6	3.3	22.9	21.9	3 251	237	356	5 801	6.7
Waseca	274	3.4	D	39.1	D	5.9	3.6	16.0	18.2	3 543	181	165	7 011	1.9
Washington	2 542	0.6	D	28.1	D	12.2	10.4	19.7	13.8	20 790	103	715	51 648	38.9
Watonwan	162	11.6	D	28.2	D	6.1	3.3	16.3	13.9	2 574	217	112	4 886	-1.3
Wilkin	82	19.9	D	4.3	D	6.3	5.1	22.3	16.8	1 395	195	70	3 140	-4.4
Winona	813	4.3	D	30.9	D	8.3	2.7	19.5	15.1	8 047	161	579	17 630	6.8
Wright	984	1.0	D	17.5	D	12.0	4.5	19.4	15.8	11 103	123	496	26 353	20.9
Yellow Medicine	147	14.4	D	12.1	D	6.3	3.5	23.3	21.9	2 706	244	138	4 983	-7.5

1. Covers mining, construction, and manufacturing. 2. Covers private sector earnings in agricultural services, forestry, and fisheries; transportation and public utilities; wholesale trade; retail trade; finance, insurance, and real estate; and services. 3. Per 1,000 resident population estimated as of July 1 of the year shown.

Table B. States and Counties — **Housing, Labor Force, and Employment**

STATE County	Housing units, 1990 (cont'd)								Civilian labor force, 2001				Civilian employment, 1990[5]		
	Occupied units										Unemployment			Percent	
		Owner-occupied				Renter-occupied									
				Owner cost as a percent of income			Rent as per-cent of income	Sub-stand-ard units[3] (percent)		Percent change, 2000–2001				Professional, managerial, and technical	Precision production, craft, and repair
	Total	Percent	Median value[1]	With a mort-gage	Without a mort-gage	Median rent[2]			Total		Total	Rate[4]	Total		
	89	90	91	92	93	94	95	96	97	98	99	100	101	102	103
MINNESOTA—Cont'd															
Grant	2 454	79.5	29 100	18.1	13.7	227	26.6	2.0	2 808	-0.8	191	6.8	2 628	21.1	11.3
Hennepin	419 060	63.4	91 000	21.0	12.1	487	27.0	2.3	676 171	3.0	21 967	3.2	571 425	37.1	7.6
Houston	6 844	79.6	52 400	18.2	12.2	300	24.7	2.1	11 494	2.7	440	3.8	9 042	23.7	11.4
Hubbard	5 781	83.1	48 700	19.5	12.5	275	27.7	3.0	8 838	2.3	489	5.5	5 869	25.0	11.1
Isanti	8 810	83.1	64 400	21.1	12.5	357	28.0	3.3	16 642	3.1	781	4.7	11 987	22.2	16.6
Itasca	15 461	83.1	44 300	17.8	12.5	297	27.9	3.6	20 480	3.8	1 453	7.1	15 202	24.2	13.1
Jackson	4 560	76.2	32 100	17.3	11.9	239	23.4	2.4	6 069	1.0	198	3.3	5 176	17.7	8.7
Kanabec	4 753	82.6	49 200	21.0	13.1	313	28.4	4.2	7 080	4.5	582	8.2	5 530	17.3	14.5
Kandiyohi	14 298	72.9	56 800	20.0	12.7	315	28.0	2.5	21 831	1.6	807	3.7	17 913	26.0	10.2
Kittson	2 274	81.8	28 000	14.5	13.2	253	24.6	2.1	2 274	-0.5	140	6.2	2 420	19.8	12.8
Koochiching	6 025	77.9	41 800	15.6	11.9	312	25.4	4.9	6 350	2.8	388	6.1	7 159	21.6	17.8
Lac qui Parle	3 505	78.9	26 000	16.2	12.1	235	25.7	2.1	3 730	1.5	161	4.3	3 723	20.0	10.7
Lake	4 242	82.9	39 400	15.0	11.5	271	25.4	3.7	5 815	6.6	302	5.2	4 303	21.4	16.2
Lake of the Woods	1 576	84.5	40 900	15.5	12.1	244	25.9	4.8	2 489	3.1	112	4.5	1 900	22.4	10.7
Le Sueur	8 468	82.0	57 800	19.2	13.0	315	23.5	2.4	15 433	3.1	722	4.7	10 939	21.3	15.1
Lincoln	2 704	79.9	22 900	19.1	13.4	209	23.2	1.6	3 035	-1.2	113	3.7	2 919	17.4	9.1
Lyon	9 073	68.4	48 200	16.5	12.4	300	23.9	1.9	15 287	3.2	560	3.7	11 940	24.5	10.0
McLeod	11 815	77.0	62 100	20.0	12.5	330	23.5	1.9	19 583	2.0	742	3.8	15 972	20.7	14.3
Mahnomen	1 805	79.4	33 900	20.1	14.8	246	24.7	5.2	2 180	-0.8	160	7.3	1 668	26.0	12.2
Marshall	4 194	82.1	34 600	17.1	12.7	217	24.3	3.2	4 505	-3.4	395	8.8	4 351	18.5	11.3
Martin	9 129	74.9	40 500	18.8	12.8	265	22.8	1.2	11 082	2.0	450	4.1	10 375	22.4	10.8
Meeker	7 651	79.6	49 100	18.1	12.8	301	26.6	2.9	9 931	1.6	659	6.6	9 299	20.9	13.8
Mille Lacs	6 911	79.7	50 800	19.9	13.9	308	27.9	4.3	10 047	2.7	704	7.0	7 960	19.1	13.5
Morrison	10 399	81.8	47 100	20.8	13.6	274	26.6	4.5	15 321	2.6	1 047	6.8	12 135	19.2	13.0
Mower	15 028	77.3	42 600	16.6	12.1	278	26.0	1.6	20 145	2.8	604	3.0	16 391	22.1	10.9
Murray	3 758	79.4	30 400	14.8	13.0	242	22.8	1.5	4 198	2.5	210	5.0	4 149	18.2	10.7
Nicollet	9 478	72.9	65 200	17.5	12.1	363	25.2	1.9	19 200	2.5	492	2.6	14 620	29.7	10.3
Nobles	7 683	75.4	39 600	15.8	12.4	299	22.8	2.4	9 683	1.2	350	3.6	9 219	20.7	13.0
Norman	3 118	80.1	30 200	15.6	13.1	231	21.9	1.8	3 290	0.0	153	4.7	3 183	21.2	12.1
Olmsted	40 058	72.4	72 300	18.6	11.8	410	23.4	2.1	78 135	4.3	1 955	2.5	57 318	40.1	7.6
Otter Tail	19 510	78.1	46 600	18.6	12.9	290	26.3	2.3	27 511	1.6	1 258	4.6	22 038	23.5	10.6
Pennington	5 173	74.0	41 400	17.0	13.5	242	25.7	2.0	8 039	1.0	412	5.1	5 691	23.9	11.2
Pine	7 577	82.5	44 900	19.5	13.3	287	27.6	5.4	11 785	4.1	937	8.0	8 030	20.0	12.3
Pipestone	4 078	76.7	31 700	15.7	12.5	237	24.7	2.1	5 247	2.0	181	3.4	4 491	19.5	10.8
Polk	11 984	74.7	47 200	19.8	12.6	293	27.6	2.1	17 032	1.8	726	4.3	13 789	22.8	10.0
Pope	4 135	78.7	39 200	18.5	13.2	243	24.9	2.1	5 416	0.3	216	4.0	4 480	20.3	9.2
Ramsey	190 500	62.2	83 600	20.9	12.7	450	27.4	3.2	289 988	2.8	9 573	3.3	252 277	36.1	7.8
Red Lake	1 730	78.8	28 200	16.3	12.4	199	24.6	3.1	1 857	-3.2	179	9.6	1 755	19.0	10.5
Redwood	6 554	77.1	32 800	17.0	12.5	250	23.1	1.9	9 052	1.2	375	4.1	7 573	20.5	10.0
Renville	6 790	79.2	31 600	15.8	12.5	261	22.6	2.6	8 315	0.6	503	6.0	7 445	20.4	10.0
Rice	16 347	75.5	67 800	19.7	12.6	370	26.7	2.1	29 294	3.5	1 089	3.7	25 025	27.3	11.3
Rock	3 754	75.3	36 600	15.8	12.1	248	22.2	1.8	4 613	0.7	112	2.4	4 488	17.9	9.2
Roseau	5 415	82.6	49 400	16.9	12.3	326	23.7	4.1	8 859	2.3	356	4.0	7 199	15.7	11.2
St. Louis	78 901	74.2	42 200	15.2	12.5	291	28.6	2.2	105 486	2.3	5 774	5.5	83 314	28.5	12.6
Scott	19 367	81.9	90 900	22.9	12.7	475	25.1	2.2	50 737	3.2	1 746	3.4	30 750	26.8	13.6
Sherburne	13 643	80.5	74 800	20.9	11.8	442	29.3	2.8	35 650	3.1	1 417	4.0	20 410	24.4	15.1
Sibley	5 323	81.5	44 400	18.4	12.7	253	21.6	2.3	6 780	1.7	344	5.1	6 741	15.6	13.2
Stearns	39 776	71.4	61 400	19.2	12.6	388	26.8	2.4	80 160	2.3	3 180	4.0	58 886	24.7	10.3
Steele	11 342	77.1	61 200	17.0	12.3	321	21.5	1.8	20 353	4.0	782	3.8	15 553	24.0	12.1
Stevens	3 823	67.2	37 700	15.8	12.9	286	24.8	3.3	5 614	1.0	159	2.8	4 703	25.5	8.5
Swift	4 268	77.5	27 500	15.9	12.6	206	23.8	1.8	5 504	1.3	243	4.4	4 464	20.2	10.0
Todd	8 589	80.8	35 000	18.1	14.1	235	25.8	3.3	9 699	2.2	591	6.1	9 445	17.1	11.7
Traverse	1 778	79.0	23 400	15.4	12.3	237	20.4	1.1	1 586	-2.2	84	5.3	1 770	19.8	9.8
Wabasha	7 286	81.7	51 900	17.0	13.2	301	23.3	2.6	12 473	1.6	427	3.4	9 236	22.7	11.9
Wadena	4 978	76.4	36 200	18.6	13.5	235	27.3	3.3	7 501	1.4	424	5.7	5 250	23.1	10.5
Waseca	6 649	77.3	53 500	18.1	12.6	310	24.0	1.4	9 697	2.9	387	4.0	8 627	22.0	13.0
Washington	49 246	83.9	94 200	21.5	12.2	489	26.2	1.5	121 422	2.8	3 187	2.6	76 652	34.4	10.6
Watonwan	4 530	74.8	35 500	16.1	11.7	252	21.5	1.8	5 683	1.8	205	3.6	5 343	17.7	12.9
Wilkin	2 805	77.6	38 400	17.1	12.2	260	26.3	2.5	3 787	-0.7	129	3.4	3 247	21.4	12.1
Winona	16 930	72.1	54 400	17.7	12.4	323	26.1	2.6	28 717	2.0	1 019	3.5	23 826	25.1	11.0
Wright	23 013	82.0	75 000	21.1	12.6	380	25.8	2.7	50 345	2.8	1 993	4.0	34 050	22.1	15.4
Yellow Medicine	4 607	77.9	31 100	16.7	13.1	242	24.1	1.8	5 440	2.3	332	6.1	4 904	22.0	12.5

1. Specified owner-occupied units.　2. Specified renter-occupied units.　3. Overcrowded or lacking complete plumbing facilities.　4. Percent of civilian labor force.　5. Persons 16 years and older.

STATE County	Number of establishments	Total	Health Care and Social Assistance	Manufacturing	Retail trade	Finance and Insurance	Professional Scientific and Technical Services	Total (mil dol)	Average per employee (dollars)	Number	Less than 50 acres	500 acres and over	Whose principal occupation is farming (percent)
	104	105	106	107	108	109	110	111	112	113	114	115	116
MINNESOTA—Cont'd													
Grant	224	1 672	357	197	318	85	50	30	17 923	468	13.5	36.1	67.7
Hennepin	38 873	854 534	90 680	105 415	82 567	77 571	66 172	32 701	38 268	574	56.3	5.1	41.6
Houston	412	4 261	1 053	668	481	166	85	84	19 657	954	11.4	17.7	61.5
Hubbard	547	4 923	817	1 055	1 010	149	71	103	20 933	431	10.4	14.2	37.8
Isanti	750	7 309	1 586	1 489	1 329	260	152	168	22 959	746	34.7	8.4	35.8
Itasca	1 227	13 738	2 098	2 608	2 492	353	535	343	25 003	415	14.9	11.1	36.6
Jackson	331	3 770	806	810	404	135	133	74	19 531	963	13.7	28.6	71.0
Kanabec	279	3 441	687	709	682	125	123	73	21 295	626	17.7	8.8	43.9
Kandiyohi	1 306	18 740	4 479	3 260	3 013	632	458	434	23 182	1 131	22.3	20.3	57.9
Kittson	162	1 124	338	30	215	75	D	20	18 164	558	5.4	52.9	61.6
Koochiching	454	4 767	626	1 302	803	D	71	127	26 665	213	4.2	25.8	38.5
Lac qui Parle	260	2 355	480	350	404	113	28	45	19 273	790	10.1	37.5	74.9
Lake	282	2 887	493	464	379	92	105	72	24 867	37	29.7	2.7	27.0
Lake of the Woods	159	1 243	D	251	236	D	D	25	20 163	196	11.2	34.2	41.8
Le Sueur	712	8 566	674	2 669	1 007	220	556	215	25 155	877	24.9	12.4	55.0
Lincoln	179	1 394	552	D	292	D	18	24	16 901	724	13.0	25.4	66.6
Lyon	777	14 958	1 608	2 318	1 973	792	211	339	22 668	931	15.5	33.1	71.1
McLeod	915	16 880	1 222	8 990	2 158	414	222	452	26 779	1 008	22.9	12.5	64.7
Mahnomen	129	1 864	182	D	229	D	D	30	16 025	341	8.5	36.4	72.4
Marshall	356	2 197	360	257	323	145	25	47	21 182	1 144	6.6	41.1	60.0
Martin	706	8 295	1 425	2 022	1 496	327	239	193	23 246	987	16.6	32.3	69.8
Meeker	601	5 645	850	1 524	774	171	138	131	23 207	1 016	21.8	15.8	61.7
Mille Lacs	614	9 392	1 483	1 143	1 098	203	65	186	19 855	711	21.9	7.3	48.5
Morrison	808	8 628	1 546	1 835	1 620	279	100	173	20 053	1 808	12.3	8.3	55.9
Mower	895	12 514	2 415	2 974	1 852	472	209	374	29 923	1 123	20.8	23.1	65.2
Murray	286	2 185	418	294	342	141	92	40	18 236	836	13.8	35.8	78.5
Nicollet	653	12 885	1 669	5 012	882	210	401	306	23 771	723	16.3	22.0	69.4
Nobles	652	8 334	1 286	2 278	1 359	308	158	173	20 768	1 021	14.1	24.2	74.4
Norman	213	1 385	350	D	323	89	53	26	18 686	670	10.6	45.4	68.2
Olmsted	2 926	70 786	26 415	10 786	9 486	1 564	2 492	2 490	35 174	1 317	28.3	10.9	51.3
Otter Tail	1 602	17 781	3 394	3 689	3 294	514	289	358	20 123	2 647	11.6	16.7	58.3
Pennington	334	6 274	1 046	1 548	954	123	77	137	21 784	528	7.0	32.4	57.0
Pine	618	4 983	894	422	1 068	215	68	90	18 064	950	12.4	11.6	45.7
Pipestone	311	3 701	639	627	557	138	D	68	18 306	690	18.7	23.3	71.9
Polk	848	9 180	2 280	1 359	1 360	323	231	177	19 306	1 366	8.6	45.0	66.8
Pope	323	3 284	673	530	375	110	189	72	21 794	825	12.8	22.3	62.1
Ramsey	13 526	302 522	40 191	37 459	32 478	22 339	15 127	10 737	35 490	59	74.6	1.7	45.8
Red Lake	111	1 347	240	D	128	65	4	29	21 285	376	7.4	33.8	52.1
Redwood	620	5 513	906	1 127	971	221	129	112	20 400	1 168	11.8	34.5	80.4
Renville	632	6 084	766	1 247	794	229	140	132	21 645	1 114	12.4	35.8	76.6
Rice	1 396	20 071	3 139	4 911	2 774	547	441	542	26 987	1 191	24.9	9.8	47.4
Rock	252	2 883	469	224	509	465	70	57	19 599	704	19.7	25.1	69.5
Roseau	393	7 838	710	4 688	785	163	80	185	23 597	1 051	9.2	31.6	47.7
St. Louis	5 516	78 600	16 793	5 129	12 549	3 071	2 702	1 999	25 431	713	19.5	8.4	31.7
Scott	2 132	29 070	2 558	4 603	2 344	510	612	931	32 040	805	46.5	6.0	40.4
Sherburne	1 224	13 702	1 649	3 237	2 358	380	289	365	26 615	512	36.5	9.4	42.2
Sibley	360	3 085	401	1 079	411	134	75	63	20 271	958	20.6	18.1	68.4
Stearns	3 904	66 828	9 412	13 170	11 916	2 435	1 685	1 729	25 866	2 982	16.8	6.5	66.5
Steele	939	20 141	1 473	8 309	2 527	2 469	173	592	29 410	774	23.5	15.9	61.9
Stevens	349	3 674	845	312	632	129	148	82	22 231	497	16.5	44.1	71.8
Swift	314	3 498	593	897	487	123	D	68	19 434	739	10.8	37.9	70.1
Todd	547	4 764	569	1 651	777	199	102	102	21 415	1 741	13.7	8.0	54.9
Traverse	132	932	D	92	227	D	D	14	15 392	385	7.3	56.9	79.0
Wabasha	614	7 180	995	2 348	975	170	105	165	22 945	963	16.0	12.0	63.0
Wadena	304	4 581	1 580	940	642	101	51	87	19 078	625	13.3	13.4	52.0
Waseca	464	7 324	1 160	2 904	741	176	96	194	26 555	709	19.2	22.7	63.9
Washington	4 373	54 919	5 159	11 034	10 354	1 995	1 885	1 729	31 481	653	49.0	6.3	43.6
Watonwan	333	3 655	558	1 170	394	137	56	72	19 802	576	12.5	31.1	75.0
Wilkin	180	1 766	475	30	236	73	D	33	18 793	441	8.8	54.9	80.7
Winona	1 311	22 515	2 707	6 915	2 550	503	773	535	23 758	1 044	14.7	14.6	66.3
Wright	2 204	23 261	3 356	4 693	4 126	625	931	596	25 609	1 422	31.6	7.5	49.9
Yellow Medicine	348	3 935	791	676	540	121	D	89	22 692	876	11.9	38.5	72.6

Table B. States and Counties — Agriculture, Land, and Water

STATE County	Agriculture, 1997 (cont'd)															
	Land in farms		Acres			Value of land and buildings		Value of machinery and equipment average per farm ($1,000)	Value of products sold		Percent from —		Percent of farms with sales of —		Percent of land owned by fed. gov. 1997	Water consumption 1995 (mil gal/day)
	Acreage (1,000)	Percent change, 1992–1997	Average size of farm	Total irrigated (1,000)	Total cropland (1,000)	Average per farm ($1,000)	Average per acre (dollars)		Total (mil dol)	Average per farm (dollars)	Crops	Livestock and poultry products	$10,000 or more	$100,000 or more		
	117	118	119	120	121	122	123	124	125	126	127	128	129	130	131	132
MINNESOTA—Cont'd																
Grant	278	3.5	595	3	251	584	1 000	124	61	129 757	81.7	18.3	68.4	36.3	2.3	1.7
Hennepin	69	-12.5	120	2	54	433	3 323	56	44	76 217	77.3	22.7	42.9	15.0	0.5	253.2
Houston	298	9.6	313	0	187	305	1 093	61	78	81 404	38.1	61.9	67.1	24.5	2.5	2.9
Hubbard	131	16.5	303	24	71	222	692	47	23	54 198	77.8	22.2	30.2	5.6	0.0	6.8
Isanti	139	5.6	187	1	99	273	1 584	38	25	33 408	65.8	34.2	35.3	8.8	0.0	3.0
Itasca	104	-4.0	250	0	55	168	591	35	5	11 958	34.0	66.0	30.1	1.0	16.5	174.6
Jackson	384	-4.3	398	0	355	642	1 651	96	150	156 169	59.1	40.9	85.8	42.4	0.8	1.7
Kanabec	139	-4.9	222	D	68	168	773	36	17	26 570	26.4	73.6	36.9	7.3	0.0	1.6
Kandiyohi	379	4.9	335	9	327	465	1 412	83	224	197 763	32.5	67.5	62.6	30.1	2.0	9.4
Kittson	501	3.8	899	D	431	536	585	127	56	99 626	90.7	9.3	58.4	30.6	0.0	0.7
Koochiching	77	11.1	360	D	42	135	435	29	4	16 519	29.9	70.1	33.3	2.3	0.6	42.9
Lac qui Parle	398	-1.8	503	3	362	519	1 059	104	113	143 139	62.4	37.6	82.7	38.4	2.3	3.5
Lake	4	-20.6	107	0	2	106	986	14	0	3 356	46.0	54.0	10.8	0.0	51.5	133.0
Lake of the Woods	118	13.1	600	D	78	297	452	61	8	39 886	81.5	18.5	48.0	11.7	4.0	1.2
Le Sueur	215	4.7	245	D	184	440	1 770	88	85	96 378	48.9	51.1	59.6	25.8	0.0	3.7
Lincoln	270	5.7	372	0	234	292	794	68	69	95 244	44.7	55.3	66.4	25.0	0.0	1.3
Lyon	403	2.0	433	0	366	503	1 180	86	147	158 058	49.7	50.3	77.6	45.4	0.0	5.8
McLeod	250	-0.3	248	0	223	362	1 566	91	83	82 130	55.4	44.6	73.0	24.8	0.2	7.4
Mahnomen	190	1.6	557	0	153	365	635	80	25	72 309	73.6	26.4	66.9	21.4	8.0	0.7
Marshall	774	3.9	677	1	691	381	563	110	91	79 624	89.7	10.3	56.6	23.0	3.9	1.0
Martin	421	1.8	426	1	398	839	1 933	130	254	257 064	43.2	56.8	89.5	53.3	0.0	45.1
Meeker	293	-2.6	289	3	249	335	1 217	93	139	137 190	34.2	65.8	66.8	25.4	1.2	4.3
Mille Lacs	135	-5.2	189	0	84	183	918	47	26	36 879	25.5	74.5	45.6	11.0	0.1	2.7
Morrison	430	1.8	238	14	250	175	731	67	157	86 708	16.2	83.8	59.5	21.3	0.2	9.6
Mower	404	2.9	360	2	375	567	1 596	103	163	144 955	62.0	38.0	77.8	39.3	0.0	7.3
Murray	384	2.1	459	D	355	546	1 159	108	126	151 214	54.6	45.4	87.0	48.9	0.0	2.1
Nicollet	249	3.0	345	0	233	595	1 746	123	172	238 322	35.2	64.8	86.9	46.1	0.0	6.3
Nobles	390	-6.4	382	0	366	561	1 462	107	159	155 287	48.5	51.5	89.1	41.7	0.0	5.0
Norman	483	5.5	721	1	435	521	780	106	75	112 303	91.2	8.8	67.2	34.6	0.0	0.8
Olmsted	304	-0.8	231	0	245	328	1 425	75	106	80 729	48.4	51.6	57.3	22.6	0.0	41.3
Otter Tail	840	2.4	317	48	595	226	723	70	201	76 098	40.1	59.9	56.6	19.4	1.3	77.5
Pennington	313	11.7	592	D	264	281	489	70	24	45 255	81.2	18.8	50.0	15.2	0.0	2.8
Pine	247	-6.2	260	3	129	213	769	37	38	39 848	26.0	74.0	42.6	9.2	0.8	2.7
Pipestone	244	-3.7	353	3	213	368	1 075	86	118	171 658	29.6	70.4	83.0	34.1	0.1	2.7
Polk	1 052	0.8	770	7	937	597	794	149	194	141 764	91.8	8.2	66.6	36.6	1.0	18.4
Pope	325	4.8	394	29	268	323	800	85	80	97 217	60.7	39.3	66.4	27.3	2.7	11.9
Ramsey	D	D	D	0	3	242	3 119	43	6	105 681	98.6	1.4	57.6	16.9	2.1	142.9
Red Lake	205	12.0	545	D	172	307	650	62	21	56 128	67.8	32.2	57.2	16.2	0.1	0.6
Redwood	508	3.3	435	D	473	689	1 593	120	210	179 558	55.8	44.2	89.1	52.6	0.0	2.8
Renville	601	0.2	540	2	567	913	1 703	165	301	269 849	56.1	43.9	87.7	51.3	0.0	3.0
Rice	251	10.1	211	1	209	404	1 976	72	127	106 977	36.2	63.8	56.1	19.9	0.0	6.9
Rock	281	4.0	399	D	260	543	1 400	100	135	191 537	40.7	59.3	83.8	43.5	0.0	3.3
Roseau	577	7.7	549	0	467	246	427	64	53	50 759	64.5	35.5	46.4	14.1	0.1	2.1
St. Louis	155	1.6	218	1	87	135	622	26	10	13 575	51.0	49.0	21.3	2.5	20.2	203.6
Scott	118	-10.7	146	0	100	416	2 969	62	46	57 329	46.8	53.2	46.1	16.6	1.4	9.7
Sherburne	105	-11.0	205	26	77	370	1 896	73	43	83 516	64.1	35.9	38.3	14.3	11.2	86.6
Sibley	310	-0.7	323	1	283	507	1 563	115	144	150 349	47.7	52.3	80.2	37.9	0.0	3.0
Stearns	646	0.3	217	30	492	227	1 099	72	302	101 356	18.1	81.9	69.1	31.2	0.6	27.7
Steele	227	-2.2	293	1	210	457	1 563	93	96	124 590	58.2	41.8	71.8	34.1	0.0	3.5
Stevens	299	4.7	602	13	284	648	1 098	137	107	214 580	55.8	44.2	78.3	47.7	2.2	3.8
Swift	388	-0.5	525	20	352	506	941	118	119	161 311	64.0	36.0	79.0	39.4	1.4	8.4
Todd	387	-1.9	223	8	248	155	687	49	113	64 641	22.7	77.3	53.1	15.5	0.1	7.3
Traverse	315	1.6	818	D	300	726	882	146	68	177 181	88.4	11.6	87.8	52.5	0.6	0.6
Wabasha	253	3.0	263	1	184	306	1 207	79	94	97 107	33.3	66.7	74.0	32.4	0.9	3.8
Wadena	175	2.2	280	14	100	162	636	47	53	84 717	22.9	77.1	45.8	10.9	0.0	7.6
Waseca	235	-0.7	332	D	213	586	1 777	101	118	166 811	51.2	48.8	81.0	38.2	0.0	2.9
Washington	90	-11.0	138	4	69	484	3 652	62	57	87 685	87.3	12.7	41.3	14.1	0.3	320.9
Watonwan	256	2.4	444	0	237	707	1 711	116	120	208 562	54.3	45.7	88.4	51.4	0.4	3.1
Wilkin	458	8.7	1 038	3	435	964	942	174	101	227 982	94.4	5.6	81.6	50.3	0.4	1.2
Winona	290	-0.4	277	0	191	307	1 084	86	122	116 920	21.3	78.7	70.3	30.3	0.7	12.0
Wright	252	-7.8	177	2	201	364	2 145	60	93	65 287	47.1	52.9	54.3	17.1	0.4	348.2
Yellow Medicine	415	1.8	474	1	380	504	1 102	117	125	142 838	66.0	34.0	81.1	45.3	0.2	1.5

Table B. States and Counties — **Residential Construction, Wholesale and Retail Trade, and Real Estate**

STATE County	Value of Residential Construction Authorized by Building Permits, 2000		Wholesale Trade, 1997				Retail Trade[1], 1997				Real Estate and Rental and Leasing, 1997			
	New Construction ($1,000)	Number of Housing Units	Number of Establish-ments	Number of Employees	Sales (mil dol)	Annual Payroll (mil dol)	Number of Establish-ments	Number of Employees	Sales (mil dol)	Annual Payroll (mil dol)	Number of Establish-ments	Number of Employees	Receipts (mil dol)	Annual Payroll (mil dol)
	133	134	135	136	137	138	139	140	141	142	143	144	145	146
MINNESOTA—Cont'd														
Grant	1 097	11	18	168	209.1	3.8	44	287	53.4	4.1	7	D	D	D
Hennepin	728 829	4 924	3 723	61 454	59 929.0	2 700.6	4 644	78 226	14 615.8	1 409.6	1 796	14 720	2 205.9	409.7
Houston	10 436	73	31	536	70.0	10.1	70	500	76.3	6.0	5	11	1.8	0.1
Hubbard	4 326	55	22	111	29.0	2.2	107	846	125.2	11.4	9	42	3.3	0.8
Isanti	34 011	330	19	D	D	D	103	1 195	193.6	15.7	18	54	3.7	0.5
Itasca	37 606	348	43	395	467.5	9.7	256	2 376	361.0	34.0	31	83	7.1	1.1
Jackson	1 805	26	23	254	131.3	6.9	55	478	57.6	5.6	3	7	0.5	0.1
Kanabec	8 271	85	9	D	D	D	75	665	114.0	9.5	7	D	D	D
Kandiyohi	22 443	212	73	1 071	548.8	31.5	267	3 022	447.6	44.2	52	189	31.4	3.0
Kittson	945	10	20	171	89.3	3.3	36	220	38.0	2.7	6	10	0.4	0.0
Koochiching	4 146	50	10	D	D	D	104	787	124.6	11.9	12	35	3.9	0.7
Lac qui Parle	1 431	12	21	207	124.6	5.2	56	355	50.1	3.8	7	12	0.6	0.1
Lake	13 819	131	9	D	D	D	53	407	121.4	9.3	2	D	D	D
Lake of the Woods	216	3	8	43	15.8	0.8	29	202	26.2	2.5	6	14	1.3	0.2
Le Sueur	16 854	204	30	415	154.0	11.6	117	955	150.1	13.1	19	35	2.8	0.4
Lincoln	843	13	15	99	40.2	1.9	34	228	35.9	4.2	5	9	0.5	0.0
Lyon	9 920	97	54	889	915.8	31.7	155	2 013	290.5	27.6	26	87	5.4	0.8
McLeod	22 926	190	43	413	239.0	13.6	188	2 079	286.6	27.7	28	72	8.7	1.0
Mahnomen	108	3	8	48	29.7	1.2	28	147	28.8	2.7	3	7	0.3	0.1
Marshall	534	6	32	D	D	D	45	293	72.0	5.6	2	D	D	D
Martin	8 573	92	53	377	419.4	12.6	131	1 552	250.4	21.3	18	47	4.2	0.7
Meeker	16 288	147	26	203	100.8	5.3	103	787	128.2	11.9	19	36	3.9	0.3
Mille Lacs	20 425	193	27	219	87.1	5.1	118	997	133.1	12.2	12	23	1.7	0.2
Morrison	29 403	296	31	282	161.5	5.3	141	1 468	247.8	20.1	13	42	4.3	0.5
Mower	15 457	120	44	279	443.3	9.8	191	1 957	269.0	26.0	21	112	4.2	1.0
Murray	3 780	44	15	124	78.6	3.0	53	335	54.0	4.3	3	D	D	D
Nicollet	14 365	139	41	492	207.3	21.1	80	756	121.7	10.3	19	72	3.8	0.7
Nobles	2 405	24	43	D	D	D	155	1 376	206.6	19.0	12	51	2.6	0.5
Norman	823	12	15	141	57.6	3.3	43	357	80.5	5.7	4	D	D	D
Olmsted	167 555	1 552	125	1 176	605.4	37.5	583	9 254	1 431.6	136.5	124	654	72.9	9.7
Otter Tail	12 815	127	73	602	233.4	10.2	317	2 922	474.8	43.3	47	113	10.4	1.4
Pennington	3 175	40	19	939	302.9	21.0	85	1 000	149.5	15.3	13	37	3.2	0.6
Pine	6 934	82	14	101	25.4	2.0	116	875	153.2	12.3	26	111	5.3	1.0
Pipestone	2 977	34	31	457	256.1	9.1	67	557	94.3	6.6	6	D	D	D
Polk	8 472	92	57	415	206.2	10.0	152	1 377	211.7	19.7	15	66	3.3	0.9
Pope	23 686	265	22	290	192.2	8.0	54	379	58.7	5.1	4	11	0.6	0.1
Ramsey	160 494	1 105	927	15 680	9 328.6	633.3	1 878	32 511	5 485.7	564.7	625	4 875	560.0	111.9
Red Lake	275	4	10	70	35.0	1.8	30	150	32.5	2.6	NA	NA	NA	NA
Redwood	3 520	36	51	478	400.0	16.1	87	927	126.9	11.7	26	40	2.3	0.2
Renville	3 318	29	31	478	364.7	13.3	104	681	111.7	9.8	9	29	1.4	0.3
Rice	55 847	427	63	1 009	543.5	32.2	242	2 788	416.8	40.5	37	130	11.7	1.5
Rock	2 634	30	22	126	108.5	3.2	50	517	85.6	7.2	8	16	0.9	0.1
Roseau	2 023	24	20	145	69.7	4.0	89	769	119.7	10.3	12	40	1.9	0.3
St. Louis	54 705	581	280	D	D	D	1 087	12 385	1 892.0	186.2	175	918	85.3	14.8
Scott	345 229	2 202	153	1 613	1 917.8	64.5	229	2 318	419.3	37.0	67	204	23.2	2.8
Sherburne	145 069	1 287	51	351	78.5	7.1	154	2 120	502.9	34.4	38	133	13.5	1.5
Sibley	7 194	64	13	110	146.7	3.6	62	497	63.1	5.3	8	14	1.0	0.2
Stearns	106 683	958	193	3 688	1 068.9	117.1	661	9 866	1 664.3	149.4	135	668	57.4	10.3
Steele	18 682	199	55	415	225.7	13.1	174	2 042	272.4	27.5	17	125	7.3	1.4
Stevens	2 424	28	22	379	151.6	11.0	64	569	119.4	8.5	12	17	1.6	0.2
Swift	2 340	22	21	266	180.6	6.5	65	486	68.5	6.7	7	39	1.2	0.3
Todd	15 410	146	32	217	49.3	4.1	112	780	124.1	10.1	13	28	1.8	0.2
Traverse	794	6	8	72	96.4	2.9	31	213	31.6	2.7	4	D	D	D
Wabasha	15 401	121	25	199	49.0	4.3	107	882	124.7	13.1	12	28	3.3	0.6
Wadena	4 540	65	17	D	D	D	66	589	104.8	9.0	7	18	1.7	0.2
Waseca	8 123	96	26	156	62.6	3.3	70	742	106.3	10.0	6	13	0.8	0.1
Washington	364 405	2 231	205	1 471	2 029.3	69.8	601	9 304	1 674.4	142.6	160	702	84.5	12.0
Watonwan	1 326	15	24	219	211.8	6.0	59	427	55.3	5.0	3	5	1.1	0.1
Wilkin	1 650	14	20	260	149.7	6.8	36	272	38.1	3.8	3	5	0.5	0.1
Winona	19 750	169	80	682	418.3	17.8	224	2 506	384.8	36.5	41	129	19.7	1.9
Wright	203 411	1 572	85	669	221.2	18.2	283	3 870	682.9	59.7	70	248	26.1	3.3
Yellow Medicine	2 830	26	24	124	91.7	2.7	66	514	79.7	6.5	6	18	1.0	0.1

1. Establishments with payroll.

STATE County	Professional, Scientific, and Technical Services[1], 1997				Manufacturing, 1997				Accommodation and Foodservices, 1997			
	Number of Establish-ments	Number of Employees	Receipts (mil dol)	Annual Payroll (mil dol)	Number of Establish-ments	Number of Employees	Receipts (mil dol)	Annual Payroll (mil dol)	Number of Establish-ments	Number of Employees	Sales (mil dol)	Annual Payroll (mil dol)
	147	148	149	150	151	152	153	154	155	156	157	158
MINNESOTA—Cont'd												
Grant	9	19	1.2	0.7	NA	NA	NA	NA	11	D	D	D
Hennepin	5 655	58 051	7 181.2	2 758.4	2 404	106 772	17 291.6	4 090.1	2 196	54 567	2 078.4	616.4
Houston	20	53	4.7	0.7	NA	NA	NA	NA	33	260	6.9	1.3
Hubbard	24	73	3.4	1.0	32	940	166.1	19.6	70	429	16.9	3.8
Isanti	41	149	10.7	4.1	59	1 330	153.5	35.6	43	570	14.5	4.1
Itasca	61	472	20.9	8.8	58	2 432	534.3	92.0	116	1 365	41.9	10.9
Jackson	12	122	15.9	3.4	18	D	D	D	16	D	D	D
Kanabec	13	46	2.7	0.8	17	803	96.7	19.4	23	D	D	D
Kandiyohi	74	381	27.4	9.7	66	3 265	605.5	84.0	88	1 551	41.5	11.0
Kittson	5	23	1.6	0.9	NA	NA	NA	NA	11	D	D	D
Koochiching	18	65	3.2	1.2	11	D	D	D	52	599	18.1	5.1
Lac qui Parle	10	D	D	D	NA	NA	NA	NA	17	D	D	D
Lake	10	27	1.4	0.3	12	507	84.4	18.6	49	481	15.6	3.9
Lake of the Woods	4	D	D	D	NA	NA	NA	NA	35	304	11.3	2.6
Le Sueur	31	575	40.4	24.6	51	2 751	728.9	79.5	47	D	D	D
Lincoln	5	D	D	D	NA	NA	NA	NA	15	83	2.3	0.4
Lyon	32	134	9.2	3.6	28	1 833	456.0	40.5	52	879	22.0	6.4
McLeod	49	195	9.1	3.5	67	9 080	1 670.5	291.0	67	1 040	26.9	7.1
Mahnomen	4	D	D	D	NA	NA	NA	NA	14	D	D	D
Marshall	9	28	1.5	0.6	NA	NA	NA	NA	27	D	D	D
Martin	31	207	13.6	5.7	44	2 111	294.1	61.6	52	775	18.1	5.2
Meeker	26	99	6.2	2.2	58	1 740	356.8	41.1	36	D	D	D
Mille Lacs	26	54	2.2	0.8	38	1 029	158.0	24.4	65	D	D	D
Morrison	21	67	4.0	1.3	44	1 883	256.3	47.3	91	804	22.4	5.6
Mower	38	191	13.3	5.1	37	D	D	D	87	1 211	31.5	8.5
Murray	14	89	5.2	2.0	NA	NA	NA	NA	22	D	D	D
Nicollet	34	207	12.4	4.7	34	3 748	868.2	79.9	44	826	22.9	6.1
Nobles	25	87	4.9	1.5	24	2 690	823.8	62.9	44	737	17.6	5.5
Norman	6	55	5.0	2.4	NA	NA	NA	NA	26	D	D	D
Olmsted	206	2 145	164.4	84.1	77	10 477	3 085.4	482.1	274	5 924	204.3	58.5
Otter Tail	65	199	12.0	4.0	91	3 732	661.7	82.1	138	1 354	37.9	9.7
Pennington	20	68	4.8	1.8	16	2 047	594.7	50.9	32	839	22.0	7.0
Pine	21	56	3.3	1.1	NA	NA	NA	NA	68	911	27.7	7.9
Pipestone	13	23	1.1	0.2	15	652	96.9	16.6	28	D	D	D
Polk	29	154	9.7	4.5	40	1 350	300.3	36.3	80	1 127	25.0	6.7
Pope	14	142	7.6	4.3	29	529	84.6	13.3	36	D	D	D
Ramsey	1 569	12 225	1 240.6	530.7	765	41 550	9 294.6	1 581.6	1 011	20 952	654.9	196.6
Red Lake	3	D	D	D	NA	NA	NA	NA	9	D	D	D
Redwood	23	94	4.7	1.8	21	1 250	165.9	34.9	41	397	10.5	2.9
Renville	26	104	8.7	3.5	34	884	155.7	21.5	33	1 068	39.9	12.5
Rice	81	254	23.0	7.6	86	4 838	954.9	161.3	110	1 825	55.0	15.5
Rock	12	21	1.6	0.3	NA	NA	NA	NA	20	D	D	D
Roseau	17	54	2.6	0.9	18	D	D	D	44	718	14.6	5.2
St. Louis	318	2 186	147.8	66.6	228	5 446	879.4	155.8	591	8 610	289.8	73.3
Scott	157	395	40.2	15.5	148	5 039	989.5	180.8	122	2 049	57.0	16.1
Sherburne	59	167	11.7	5.0	96	3 278	463.2	103.2	74	1 095	33.4	9.7
Sibley	17	42	3.2	1.1	25	1 054	352.1	28.7	18	180	4.2	0.8
Stearns	224	1 325	100.8	41.9	219	12 609	2 216.6	369.1	309	5 558	150.4	40.0
Steele	55	162	10.5	3.6	67	6 292	1 006.9	191.7	65	1 004	26.4	7.0
Stevens	17	131	9.0	4.0	NA	NA	NA	NA	24	D	D	D
Swift	16	58	3.0	1.3	13	829	56.5	19.3	28	219	6.6	1.5
Todd	16	76	3.4	1.4	47	1 519	278.2	46.4	49	D	D	D
Traverse	1	D	D	D	NA	NA	NA	NA	10	D	D	D
Wabasha	29	71	5.1	1.6	39	1 934	368.5	51.3	51	D	D	D
Wadena	14	52	2.4	0.7	21	784	74.4	19.8	22	D	D	D
Waseca	29	103	4.9	1.6	29	3 298	467.1	108.6	32	D	D	D
Washington	443	1 180	135.0	44.3	210	9 456	2 795.0	436.0	296	5 543	165.2	51.0
Watonwan	12	68	3.4	1.0	21	1 102	139.3	22.7	20	D	D	D
Wilkin	9	149	3.4	2.7	NA	NA	NA	NA	19	D	D	D
Winona	71	569	33.2	10.9	116	7 115	1 071.9	196.1	115	1 725	45.7	11.9
Wright	129	693	44.3	17.5	179	4 315	583.6	127.4	130	2 159	54.3	15.1
Yellow Medicine	13	47	4.3	1.1	NA	NA	NA	NA	21	D	D	D

1. Firms subject to federal tax.

STATE County	Health Care and Social Assistance[1], 1997				Other Services[1], 1997				Federal funds and grants, fiscal 2001[2] Expenditures (mil dol)			
										Direct payments for individuals[3]		
	Number of Establishments	Number of Employees	Receipts (mil dol)	Annual Payroll (mil dol)	Number of Establishments	Number of Employees	Receipts (mil dol)	Annual Payroll (mil dol)	Total	Social Security and government retirement	Medicare	Food stamps and Supplemental Security Income
	159	160	161	162	163	164	165	166	167	168	169	170
MINNESOTA—Cont'd												
Grant	13	221	5.3	2.9	11	33	2.3	0.4	56.2	16.9	6.8	0.5
Hennepin	2 292	32 525	2 031.0	1 019.3	1 929	23 352	1 348.6	514.2	6 546.8	1 896.9	796.0	169.7
Houston	17	174	7.5	3.3	33	77	6.5	1.3	88.2	40.2	12.7	1.3
Hubbard	26	238	14.5	5.0	19	48	3.5	0.7	90.8	44.7	15.8	2.2
Isanti	43	519	28.4	13.5	45	166	10.7	2.4	94.3	47.8	15.8	1.5
Itasca	75	855	39.9	18.9	61	216	14.4	3.4	234.1	111.7	34.7	6.2
Jackson	15	462	8.9	5.2	31	87	7.3	1.3	82.0	22.5	8.7	0.8
Kanabec	13	192	8.0	4.8	15	48	2.6	0.6	56.6	30.0	8.1	1.5
Kandiyohi	77	1 519	69.9	41.4	70	266	17.5	4.4	207.3	82.1	26.1	5.0
Kittson	10	157	4.7	1.7	7	18	1.5	0.3	67.8	13.0	5.9	0.3
Koochiching	21	230	9.5	5.0	17	67	4.1	0.8	85.3	39.4	11.6	1.9
Lac qui Parle	15	98	3.5	1.5	19	67	5.5	0.8	68.9	19.1	7.9	0.5
Lake	13	87	2.0	0.6	18	93	5.7	1.5	62.9	35.3	9.1	0.7
Lake of the Woods	5	10	0.6	0.1	7	12	1.1	0.2	25.5	10.6	3.5	0.2
Le Sueur	40	344	12.4	5.4	36	107	8.0	1.6	109.0	51.0	16.8	1.3
Lincoln	8	66	2.7	1.1	9	14	1.0	0.2	56.7	15.4	7.4	0.5
Lyon	50	707	27.0	14.0	56	168	11.9	2.2	144.4	49.2	17.1	2.2
McLeod	68	586	33.4	15.0	64	278	21.8	4.9	123.4	61.8	21.2	1.4
Mahnomen	7	29	1.2	0.4	5	D	D	D	41.3	11.4	3.7	1.2
Marshall	10	81	1.9	0.9	24	74	7.3	0.9	122.6	22.7	10.5	0.7
Martin	47	448	27.8	10.2	37	113	7.8	1.7	137.8	53.6	20.0	2.2
Meeker	23	215	10.2	5.7	19	56	3.1	0.9	100.4	42.9	14.7	1.3
Mille Lacs	28	285	11.7	6.1	38	121	10.1	2.3	136.1	57.3	22.3	2.7
Morrison	40	490	24.1	12.2	48	172	14.5	2.9	161.6	65.3	22.6	3.2
Mower	71	637	26.3	11.7	75	377	19.9	4.7	221.9	97.4	37.9	4.5
Murray	12	176	5.6	3.3	13	27	2.2	0.4	70.8	20.9	8.3	0.5
Nicollet	31	225	12.2	5.7	48	202	10.5	2.8	94.4	35.3	11.1	1.5
Nobles	28	455	21.2	9.5	43	149	8.7	2.1	118.6	41.9	15.2	2.0
Norman	10	42	1.9	0.8	10	37	1.9	0.3	78.4	18.4	7.5	0.8
Olmsted	168	2 241	102.8	50.7	180	1 363	69.8	20.4	544.4	185.1	67.1	10.6
Otter Tail	73	896	41.7	22.6	81	320	18.4	4.2	302.4	133.1	46.1	4.8
Pennington	15	183	12.9	3.8	29	92	5.4	1.5	88.7	28.0	9.7	1.4
Pine	34	587	25.8	10.7	22	51	3.2	0.7	130.7	57.9	17.5	3.0
Pipestone	16	88	4.1	1.8	20	72	4.9	1.0	71.9	22.7	9.1	0.9
Polk	49	475	16.0	7.0	55	237	12.7	3.1	234.1	67.1	28.0	5.5
Pope	15	77	3.6	1.3	24	50	3.7	0.7	70.4	27.0	11.1	0.9
Ramsey	1 030	15 342	939.0	502.5	826	6 378	401.6	124.5	3 694.5	1 066.9	428.1	107.5
Red Lake	2	D	D	D	2	D	D	D	34.7	8.6	4.2	0.3
Redwood	41	587	14.3	6.9	32	64	5.2	1.1	122.3	38.6	13.1	1.0
Renville	26	518	14.4	7.6	32	65	6.5	1.1	120.3	37.0	13.6	1.2
Rice	84	1 398	64.4	35.5	81	331	23.6	6.3	189.3	90.0	26.9	3.9
Rock	10	106	3.6	1.8	22	89	7.1	1.6	65.5	22.5	8.1	0.5
Roseau	19	134	5.5	1.6	17	66	4.2	1.1	89.7	25.0	10.5	0.9
St. Louis	376	5 334	240.6	125.7	327	1 807	124.4	35.9	1 158.2	490.0	170.8	34.2
Scott	99	1 131	53.9	25.5	120	607	51.1	12.6	161.7	82.2	20.7	2.1
Sherburne	77	665	30.5	15.1	59	302	14.8	4.5	138.0	73.4	16.4	2.2
Sibley	15	57	3.2	1.0	27	62	4.4	0.8	75.8	27.2	12.4	0.6
Stearns	238	3 178	239.5	121.3	243	1 493	89.0	24.7	508.9	202.7	66.6	9.4
Steele	46	667	33.2	17.2	55	223	18.0	4.1	129.2	58.5	19.9	2.2
Stevens	15	54	3.7	1.3	25	116	6.0	1.3	75.2	19.1	9.0	0.6
Swift	14	189	6.6	3.3	21	68	6.4	1.3	82.5	24.6	10.9	0.8
Todd	24	150	10.0	4.6	30	68	6.5	1.2	116.5	47.6	17.2	3.2
Traverse	7	55	2.7	1.2	8	14	1.4	0.3	47.4	11.5	4.9	0.5
Wabasha	27	316	15.6	6.0	34	90	6.1	1.3	109.8	45.4	16.5	1.2
Wadena	17	156	9.5	4.5	18	48	3.5	0.7	76.8	33.7	13.3	1.6
Waseca	42	585	18.7	8.5	37	98	6.7	1.2	107.4	34.2	11.3	1.3
Washington	265	3 251	177.8	89.2	219	1 700	99.3	29.4	312.3	178.3	50.7	5.8
Watonwan	20	216	8.9	3.6	17	49	4.5	0.7	77.8	26.9	9.1	0.8
Wilkin	6	52	1.3	0.5	6	8	1.0	0.2	56.5	15.2	4.9	0.7
Winona	71	705	38.2	17.1	67	296	16.9	4.3	182.9	86.8	29.7	4.0
Wright	126	1 244	56.2	26.7	124	482	29.2	7.4	245.3	122.8	38.9	4.4
Yellow Medicine	22	191	6.9	3.4	31	175	10.6	3.0	92.8	27.0	11.1	0.9

1. Firms subject to federal tax.　2. October 1, 2000 to September 30, 2001.　3. State totals may include programs not allocated by county.

Table B. States and Counties — Federal Funds and Local Government Finances

	Federal funds and grants, fiscal 2001[1] (cont'd)							Local government finances, 1997				
	Expenditures (mil dol) (cont'd)							General revenue				
	Procurement contract awards			Grants[2]							Taxes	
STATE County												Per capita[3] (dollars)
	Salaries and wages	Defense	Other	Medicaid and other health-related	Nutrition and family welfare	Education	Other	Total (mil dol)	Intergovern-mental (mil dol)	Total (mil dol)	Total	Property
	171	172	173	174	175	176	177	178	179	180	181	182
MINNESOTA—Cont'd												
Grant	1.5	0.0	0.4	5.0	2.1	0.4	0.5	21.5	11.6	6.1	989	977
Hennepin	737.8	972.1	299.1	879.5	141.8	72.1	338.6	3 868.0	1 284.4	1 435.9	1 363	1 263
Houston	3.4	4.2	0.7	9.1	1.5	0.8	1.2	44.8	27.4	9.4	491	480
Hubbard	2.3	0.0	1.6	14.6	3.1	1.1	2.1	44.6	21.0	12.4	742	730
Isanti	4.7	0.0	1.1	10.0	2.7	1.0	1.8	70.7	41.6	18.2	614	595
Itasca	18.0	0.7	3.1	31.5	9.7	3.7	10.4	170.3	62.0	43.2	991	986
Jackson	1.9	0.0	0.4	5.0	1.2	0.6	4.5	40.8	17.9	10.9	935	931
Kanabec	2.3	0.0	0.5	7.8	2.5	0.7	0.2	40.3	20.5	6.9	489	481
Kandiyohi	11.0	0.0	9.0	23.8	5.8	2.0	7.5	154.2	60.6	26.9	654	636
Kittson	3.0	0.0	0.5	5.0	0.8	0.4	1.8	22.0	10.2	7.8	1 455	1 443
Koochiching	5.8	0.0	2.0	11.4	3.1	1.0	5.0	45.7	24.7	11.2	714	701
Lac qui Parle	2.2	0.0	0.5	3.6	0.8	0.6	3.5	33.7	16.9	7.1	881	877
Lake	1.7	0.0	0.9	5.9	1.4	0.7	6.7	40.0	21.6	9.7	901	891
Lake of the Woods	1.3	0.0	0.4	4.1	0.5	0.2	1.3	17.0	8.2	3.4	738	729
Le Sueur	3.6	0.0	1.1	11.4	2.0	1.2	1.0	59.4	33.3	15.2	610	601
Lincoln	1.6	0.0	0.4	5.0	0.4	0.4	5.3	17.1	10.2	4.6	694	693
Lyon	7.7	5.8	5.2	10.9	4.7	1.8	3.3	93.8	38.7	20.6	840	827
McLeod	4.8	0.0	1.3	8.2	1.9	1.2	1.5	133.0	45.4	21.3	633	618
Mahnomen	1.1	0.0	0.7	7.3	1.8	2.3	1.4	26.6	20.0	4.8	944	942
Marshall	3.7	0.1	1.5	8.2	1.4	0.7	5.3	40.7	24.2	9.5	898	895
Martin	4.3	0.3	0.9	7.3	4.0	1.2	0.9	59.2	27.6	16.3	734	723
Meeker	4.5	0.1	0.8	8.7	2.5	1.3	0.9	72.0	38.0	15.8	735	727
Mille Lacs	3.6	0.0	1.1	16.1	4.5	1.9	17.5	61.9	37.4	16.3	788	777
Morrison	18.9	2.6	1.2	23.3	5.4	2.4	2.0	81.0	50.2	16.5	542	531
Mower	8.1	2.5	1.5	21.2	4.2	1.8	3.5	111.3	55.1	21.8	588	578
Murray	2.4	0.0	0.6	4.6	0.5	0.5	1.1	29.6	16.6	7.1	742	739
Nicollet	3.1	0.0	0.5	6.4	1.7	0.7	8.1	59.0	23.9	15.0	499	483
Nobles	5.3	0.0	0.9	12.3	2.6	1.1	1.4	74.3	31.4	13.6	689	674
Norman	2.3	0.1	0.6	5.5	0.9	0.5	4.0	31.1	15.6	7.0	909	897
Olmsted	50.2	6.2	8.6	154.2	8.8	6.0	11.3	326.5	131.8	102.9	898	812
Otter Tail	12.7	0.4	12.0	38.3	6.5	2.5	11.1	169.5	70.0	33.5	619	606
Pennington	4.0	0.0	0.8	15.0	2.2	2.3	3.3	43.7	23.5	9.9	730	708
Pine	16.2	0.0	1.3	18.2	3.7	1.6	5.4	60.1	34.9	15.2	645	636
Pipestone	3.1	0.0	0.5	7.8	1.4	0.7	8.0	26.8	15.5	7.4	734	725
Polk	7.2	6.1	2.5	25.3	9.6	3.2	7.7	109.7	64.9	23.8	742	715
Pope	2.1	0.1	0.5	5.9	1.4	0.6	0.9	33.3	17.0	7.2	663	655
Ramsey	312.8	237.5	88.6	347.6	267.9	173.6	466.8	2 041.7	784.1	603.4	1 246	1 154
Red Lake	1.2	0.0	0.3	3.2	1.8	0.3	1.2	15.3	9.3	2.6	602	594
Redwood	4.0	0.0	0.9	10.9	1.5	1.2	8.8	62.7	31.9	14.9	892	873
Renville	3.9	0.0	0.9	10.5	1.6	1.2	1.6	49.5	22.9	13.0	764	761
Rice	8.7	0.3	1.9	25.4	3.7	3.2	0.7	156.4	61.4	31.8	593	576
Rock	2.0	0.0	0.4	3.2	0.8	0.6	2.9	33.6	13.7	6.3	637	631
Roseau	3.5	0.0	0.7	9.6	2.2	1.3	2.4	61.3	27.5	9.6	591	587
St. Louis	122.8	3.9	25.3	160.2	41.0	15.0	48.4	710.7	335.6	160.2	822	749
Scott	15.8	0.4	5.1	6.9	3.6	2.3	6.5	178.4	71.7	67.6	889	834
Sherburne	11.0	0.3	1.7	9.1	3.2	1.8	12.0	145.0	58.0	51.3	887	867
Sibley	2.5	0.0	0.6	5.0	1.1	1.1	0.1	40.1	21.5	10.2	701	692
Stearns	73.8	0.2	18.8	49.9	12.0	8.1	14.4	382.6	184.1	100.0	784	738
Steele	4.6	1.5	6.1	8.7	1.9	1.4	0.2	84.2	44.2	20.1	638	620
Stevens	4.5	0.0	0.6	6.4	1.0	0.9	1.2	26.3	16.0	6.4	632	628
Swift	3.1	0.1	0.6	7.8	1.5	0.6	1.6	39.1	18.7	7.6	700	691
Todd	4.5	0.0	1.0	22.8	4.0	1.9	1.8	81.6	44.5	14.5	606	600
Traverse	1.1	0.8	0.3	2.3	0.6	0.5	1.2	17.2	7.8	4.0	928	873
Wabasha	3.7	0.0	15.5	8.7	1.6	1.0	0.8	60.5	28.4	14.0	674	664
Wadena	2.8	0.1	0.6	16.4	2.4	1.2	0.3	46.5	27.3	7.6	583	577
Waseca	13.4	11.9	1.1	6.4	1.7	1.0	0.3	53.6	27.6	14.2	781	762
Washington	17.4	3.1	4.9	19.3	8.1	5.2	2.1	448.3	179.8	156.2	816	777
Watonwan	3.2	0.0	9.1	2.3	0.7	0.7	1.9	30.4	16.8	8.7	739	735
Wilkin	1.7	0.5	0.4	4.1	0.9	0.5	1.0	25.9	14.1	6.2	836	828
Winona	8.0	1.0	1.8	18.9	4.0	2.6	5.3	102.8	57.2	27.2	563	528
Wright	12.9	0.0	3.1	18.8	6.1	2.9	16.8	219.3	100.5	68.3	821	797
Yellow Medicine	2.7	0.0	0.7	7.5	1.4	0.7	3.2	50.3	19.6	9.8	847	843

1. October 1, 2000 to September 30, 2001. 2. State totals may include programs not allocated by county. 3. Based on the resident population estimated as of July 1 of the year shown.

	Local government finances, 1997 (cont'd)									Government employment, 1999			Presidential election, 2000[2]		
	Direct general expenditure							Debt outstanding					Percent of vote cast —		
			Percent of total for —												
STATE County	Total (mil dol)	Per capita[1] (dollars)	Education	Health and hospitals	Police protection	Public welfare	Highways	Total (mil dol)	Per capita[1] (dollars)	Federal civilian	Federal military	State and local	Democratic	Republican	All other
	183	184	185	186	187	188	189	190	191	192	193	194	195	196	197
MINNESOTA—Cont'd															
Grant	22.4	3 649	49.5	3.5	3.1	7.5	16.8	10.5	1 702	25	24	365	41.6	49.8	8.6
Hennepin	3 978.8	3 778	35.1	12.1	4.9	4.7	4.8	5 234.9	4 971	13 198	4 871	81 500	53.6	39.3	7.1
Houston	45.9	2 388	50.8	0.4	3.0	6.4	16.4	14.8	770	74	78	968	44.3	49.9	5.7
Hubbard	44.4	2 649	43.4	0.2	2.5	19.6	14.2	26.5	1 581	40	68	1 027	37.8	55.2	7.0
Isanti	66.7	2 256	51.0	1.9	3.9	10.9	11.5	83.8	2 834	68	123	1 678	41.8	51.4	6.7
Itasca	173.8	3 990	35.3	17.6	2.4	11.1	12.0	178.2	4 092	193	176	3 184	48.7	44.0	7.3
Jackson	41.0	3 503	30.9	13.5	2.4	15.9	15.1	10.9	928	29	45	916	43.5	51.0	5.6
Kanabec	41.9	2 985	41.3	21.0	3.3	8.7	12.2	19.0	1 350	50	57	843	41.6	51.1	7.4
Kandiyohi	163.2	3 973	29.4	33.1	3.6	7.7	8.1	140.2	3 411	188	164	4 199	42.6	52.0	5.4
Kittson	21.4	3 999	41.6	5.2	3.1	6.7	20.6	16.7	3 109	52	21	372	42.0	51.3	6.7
Koochiching	52.9	3 374	45.7	1.4	4.3	13.0	10.1	56.2	3 586	128	59	993	42.2	51.2	6.6
Lac qui Parle	33.1	4 089	44.3	16.4	2.6	5.0	14.3	7.8	969	33	31	693	50.4	43.6	6.0
Lake	42.0	3 923	33.9	1.2	4.3	8.4	18.2	65.8	6 143	35	43	874	54.5	37.6	7.9
Lake of the Woods	13.9	3 051	39.7	0.6	5.7	6.2	21.1	360.1	79 325	21	22	293	38.8	55.6	5.6
Le Sueur	63.7	2 558	47.8	3.9	3.2	8.2	10.3	58.4	2 349	60	101	1 295	43.5	49.8	6.8
Lincoln	17.3	2 644	44.7	0.5	3.4	4.6	21.4	7.6	1 158	28	26	339	48.4	46.1	5.5
Lyon	99.6	4 061	44.7	18.2	3.1	4.3	8.7	65.2	2 659	129	97	2 729	41.2	53.0	5.8
McLeod	132.2	3 924	31.4	29.5	3.2	7.6	7.7	116.9	3 469	82	138	2 718	36.4	57.0	6.5
Mahnomen	27.3	5 363	44.6	0.3	4.2	23.7	8.0	8.2	1 610	20	20	384	41.4	50.4	8.1
Marshall	40.7	3 870	47.3	1.3	1.9	5.6	24.7	13.7	1 302	66	40	611	36.7	56.0	7.3
Martin	62.9	2 827	50.0	0.2	4.0	6.8	13.9	42.4	1 907	68	87	1 345	40.2	54.8	5.0
Meeker	79.0	3 670	52.5	10.4	2.8	8.8	8.1	57.7	2 683	70	87	1 261	41.2	51.7	7.0
Mille Lacs	61.8	2 990	63.6	1.0	3.0	9.1	6.9	48.5	2 348	63	85	1 343	42.7	50.9	6.4
Morrison	87.8	2 877	57.9	2.3	2.6	8.6	9.6	57.4	1 881	355	122	1 725	35.9	55.8	8.2
Mower	107.5	2 895	40.6	1.4	3.5	12.4	13.3	877.2	23 623	146	148	2 248	57.9	37.2	5.0
Murray	31.4	3 297	35.8	9.9	2.7	3.0	18.8	11.0	1 157	40	38	567	44.0	50.6	5.3
Nicollet	60.7	2 022	30.7	14.6	4.4	6.0	16.1	42.1	1 400	50	117	2 399	45.9	47.1	7.0
Nobles	74.7	3 787	35.0	22.4	3.1	7.8	11.5	29.1	1 476	92	76	1 743	42.4	53.7	3.9
Norman	30.6	3 971	39.9	14.6	1.8	5.6	18.8	9.4	1 213	39	30	551	43.3	49.7	7.1
Olmsted	335.5	2 927	51.7	1.4	4.4	7.7	6.8	254.0	2 216	908	478	6 530	43.5	51.6	4.9
Otter Tail	182.2	3 361	47.3	7.7	2.7	6.2	12.2	100.3	1 850	220	222	3 580	34.5	59.5	5.9
Pennington	43.3	3 195	40.0	0.1	4.4	11.7	13.7	34.5	2 547	81	54	1 304	38.9	53.5	7.6
Pine	66.5	2 819	53.9	5.8	3.9	8.8	10.1	46.2	1 959	312	98	1 432	47.0	44.8	8.1
Pipestone	29.9	2 964	48.3	0.5	2.9	7.2	11.6	11.6	1 151	51	40	841	40.3	55.0	4.8
Polk	122.6	3 821	40.1	0.2	3.8	12.0	12.3	72.1	2 247	122	123	2 716	40.8	53.8	5.4
Pope	32.4	2 968	38.9	14.1	3.2	4.2	17.3	23.1	2 115	35	43	706	46.3	46.9	6.8
Ramsey	2 130.7	4 399	31.3	1.8	3.8	7.8	4.9	2 838.1	5 860	5 091	2 090	50 653	56.7	35.9	7.5
Red Lake	19.2	4 409	58.1	0.4	3.8	5.4	11.2	12.8	2 946	22	17	272	39.7	52.2	8.2
Redwood	58.2	3 496	37.9	11.1	2.7	7.0	14.2	40.3	2 422	62	65	1 307	34.6	59.2	6.2
Renville	58.4	3 421	30.4	7.1	3.1	12.1	14.5	33.6	1 971	65	67	1 161	43.5	49.7	6.8
Rice	173.9	3 245	45.7	17.0	3.6	6.2	7.3	138.2	2 578	135	219	3 647	50.5	41.8	7.7
Rock	32.9	3 322	35.7	23.3	3.0	4.3	11.5	41.1	4 158	31	38	850	41.5	55.3	3.1
Roseau	62.5	3 835	35.6	19.7	2.5	3.5	11.7	61.5	3 771	64	64	909	29.7	65.5	4.8
St. Louis	710.1	3 642	32.6	7.3	4.9	9.5	11.8	540.8	2 774	1 988	884	16 909	59.8	33.0	7.3
Scott	207.6	2 728	45.9	0.9	4.3	4.9	11.6	217.2	2 855	255	331	3 454	40.0	54.7	5.4
Sherburne	148.9	2 572	52.8	0.7	3.0	5.6	6.4	316.9	5 476	174	253	2 948	39.3	54.5	6.2
Sibley	40.5	2 778	41.2	2.3	3.7	13.8	17.8	25.2	1 732	39	59	826	36.6	55.7	7.6
Stearns	380.7	2 985	44.7	4.2	3.6	6.9	9.9	587.2	4 604	1 491	523	9 479	39.7	51.9	8.4
Steele	85.5	2 711	46.0	0.9	4.0	9.9	12.9	87.3	2 768	75	128	1 649	42.9	51.2	5.8
Stevens	26.2	2 587	45.7	0.8	4.4	9.4	17.1	13.2	1 300	81	40	1 322	42.3	49.2	8.4
Swift	40.5	3 737	29.9	14.2	3.4	13.3	13.6	20.8	1 920	51	45	888	49.6	43.7	6.7
Todd	84.3	3 517	58.0	6.0	2.6	9.1	11.6	38.5	1 608	75	97	1 302	37.3	54.4	8.4
Traverse	19.8	4 630	27.7	18.2	3.2	8.1	15.1	7.1	1 658	23	17	420	42.0	51.0	7.0
Wabasha	59.0	2 842	42.6	7.5	3.1	13.7	9.0	32.5	1 565	63	84	969	42.9	49.8	7.2
Wadena	47.5	3 665	48.0	1.7	3.0	19.8	9.9	39.2	3 023	49	53	1 483	35.3	58.5	6.3
Waseca	59.4	3 267	57.6	0.6	3.4	11.1	9.3	39.2	2 156	273	74	1 229	41.7	52.0	6.4
Washington	471.0	2 459	47.6	1.4	5.8	4.5	7.8	595.8	3 111	253	807	8 534	46.4	48.1	5.5
Watonwan	31.4	2 676	47.2	1.2	5.2	10.6	14.7	10.2	866	47	46	716	44.0	49.9	6.1
Wilkin	29.5	4 006	43.4	2.0	3.7	7.3	23.3	32.7	4 434	27	29	403	31.6	61.5	6.8
Winona	104.3	2 162	47.3	2.0	5.0	9.0	11.3	65.5	1 356	145	191	3 577	46.3	45.0	8.7
Wright	237.9	2 861	53.3	6.2	3.1	7.2	7.9	283.5	3 410	185	350	4 374	38.7	55.0	6.4
Yellow Medicine	52.0	4 492	31.2	26.3	2.5	9.7	12.1	18.7	1 619	47	45	1 161	45.8	47.1	7.0

1. Based on the resident population estimated as of July 1 of the year shown.   2. Data subject to copyright.

Table B. States and Counties — Land Area and Population

STATE/County code	MSA/PMSA/NECMA code[1]	County Type[2]	STATE County	Land area,[3] (sq km) 2000	Population and population characteristics, 2000							Race alone or in combination (percent)				Age (percent)					
					Total persons	Rank	Per square kilometer	White	Black	Am. Indian, Alaska Native	Asian and Pacific Islander	Percent Hispanic[4]	Under 5 years	5 to 17 years	18 to 24 years	25 to 34 years	35 to 44 years	45 to 54 years
				1	2	3	4	5	6	7	8	9	10	11	12	13	14	15
28 000	...	X	MISSISSIPPI	121 488	2 844 658	X	23.4	61.9	36.6	0.7	0.9	1.4	7.2	20.1	10.9	13.4	15.0	12.7
28 001	...	7	Adams	1 192	34 340	1 269	28.8	46.4	53.1	0.4	0.5	0.8	6.8	20.0	8.6	10.6	15.0	13.9
28 003	...	7	Alcorn	1 036	34 558	1 263	33.4	87.9	11.3	0.4	0.4	1.3	6.5	17.4	9.1	13.4	14.5	13.6
28 005	...	9	Amite	1 890	13 599	2 190	7.2	56.8	42.8	0.5	0.1	0.8	5.9	20.1	8.5	11.2	14.3	13.7
28 007	...	6	Attala	1 904	19 661	1 814	10.3	58.8	40.2	0.5	0.3	1.4	6.4	19.5	9.2	12.1	13.1	12.5
28 009	...	8	Benton	1 054	8 026	2 602	7.6	62.2	36.9	0.9	0.1	1.0	7.4	19.5	10.0	12.2	13.6	12.1
28 011	...	5	Bolivar	2 270	40 633	1 096	17.9	33.6	65.4	0.2	0.7	1.2	7.4	22.2	14.0	12.9	12.8	12.2
28 013	...	9	Calhoun	1 519	15 069	2 086	9.9	69.9	28.9	0.4	0.3	2.1	6.5	18.7	8.4	13.4	13.6	13.0
28 015	...	9	Carroll	1 626	10 769	2 378	6.6	62.9	36.8	0.2	0.2	0.7	5.5	18.9	9.6	11.6	15.1	14.4
28 017	...	7	Chickasaw	1 299	19 440	1 821	15.0	57.3	41.4	0.4	0.4	2.3	7.6	21.0	9.3	12.9	14.7	12.0
28 019	...	9	Choctaw	1 085	9 758	2 465	9.0	68.3	30.9	0.5	0.3	0.8	6.8	21.0	8.8	10.7	14.2	13.7
28 021	...	8	Claiborne	1 261	11 831	2 302	9.4	15.4	84.4	0.2	0.2	0.8	6.8	19.5	23.1	9.9	12.3	11.1
28 023	...	7	Clarke	1 790	17 955	1 899	10.0	64.7	34.9	0.3	0.1	0.7	6.8	20.0	8.6	12.1	14.6	13.1
28 025	...	7	Clay	1 058	21 979	1 694	20.8	43.2	56.6	0.2	0.4	0.9	7.5	21.4	10.4	12.1	14.4	13.1
28 027	...	7	Coahoma	1 435	30 622	1 384	21.3	29.6	69.6	0.3	0.8	0.9	8.9	24.1	10.3	11.7	13.6	11.6
28 029	...	6	Copiah	2 011	28 757	1 429	14.3	48.2	51.2	0.3	0.3	1.2	6.6	20.3	12.5	11.6	15.1	12.7
28 031	...	7	Covington	1 072	19 407	1 823	18.1	63.8	35.9	0.4	0.4	0.8	7.5	21.3	9.6	13.2	14.2	11.9
28 033	4920	1	De Soto	1 238	107 199	498	86.6	86.4	11.6	0.5	0.9	2.3	7.8	20.4	8.2	15.8	16.9	13.1
28 035	3285	5	Forrest	1 208	72 604	686	60.1	65.0	33.9	0.5	1.0	1.3	6.9	17.6	18.2	14.3	13.4	11.0
28 037	...	9	Franklin	1 462	8 448	2 568	5.8	63.2	36.5	0.7	0.1	0.5	6.5	20.8	8.8	11.2	15.0	13.2
28 039	...	6	George	1 239	19 144	1 840	15.5	89.9	8.9	0.6	0.2	1.6	7.8	21.4	14.0	14.0	14.7	12.3
28 041	...	8	Greene	1 846	13 299	2 204	7.2	73.1	26.3	0.4	0.2	0.8	7.0	17.1	13.1	16.6	15.5	12.0
28 043	...	7	Grenada	1 092	23 263	1 630	21.3	58.3	41.1	0.3	0.6	0.6	6.9	20.3	9.0	12.8	14.7	12.8
28 045	0920	2	Hancock	1 235	42 967	1 037	34.8	91.2	7.1	1.2	1.2	1.8	6.3	18.8	7.3	12.2	15.8	14.4
28 047	0920	2	Harrison	1 505	189 601	290	126.0	74.6	21.6	1.0	3.3	2.6	7.1	18.9	11.1	14.5	16.1	12.8
28 049	3560	2	Hinds	2 251	250 800	229	111.4	37.7	61.5	0.3	0.8	0.8	7.4	20.5	12.1	13.9	15.0	12.6
28 051	...	6	Holmes	1 958	21 609	1 713	11.0	20.7	79.0	0.3	0.3	0.9	7.7	24.4	12.4	11.2	13.6	10.6
28 053	...	7	Humphreys	1 083	11 206	2 356	10.3	27.3	71.8	0.2	0.3	1.5	7.8	24.9	10.7	12.3	13.5	11.5
28 055	...	9	Issaquena	1 070	2 274	3 043	2.1	36.8	63.1	0.5	0.0	0.4	5.7	21.9	10.9	14.8	16.1	10.6
28 057	...	9	Itawamba	1 379	22 770	1 657	16.5	92.9	6.6	0.4	0.3	1.0	6.1	18.1	10.6	13.5	14.3	12.7
28 059	0920	2	Jackson	1 883	131 420	407	69.8	76.3	21.2	0.7	2.0	2.1	7.0	20.6	9.3	13.5	16.3	13.5
28 061	...	6	Jasper	1 751	18 149	1 890	10.4	46.8	53.1	0.3	0.2	0.6	6.9	21.0	9.6	12.3	14.4	12.6
28 063	...	9	Jefferson	1 345	9 740	2 467	7.2	13.2	86.7	0.2	0.2	0.7	7.3	21.5	12.1	12.3	16.2	12.0
28 065	...	9	Jefferson Davis	1 058	13 962	2 163	13.2	42.1	57.7	0.4	0.2	0.8	7.2	21.2	9.9	11.7	13.6	12.9
28 067	...	5	Jones	1 797	64 958	748	36.1	71.5	26.5	0.6	0.3	2.0	7.0	18.8	10.5	12.6	14.7	13.0
28 069	...	9	Kemper	1 984	10 453	2 401	5.3	39.4	58.5	2.3	0.3	0.7	6.7	18.8	12.5	11.8	13.4	12.6
28 071	...	7	Lafayette	1 635	38 744	1 146	23.7	72.5	25.2	0.4	2.1	1.1	5.4	14.2	27.1	13.8	12.5	10.2
28 073	3285	7	Lamar	1 287	39 070	1 136	30.4	85.9	13.1	0.5	0.8	1.1	7.4	20.6	10.9	14.5	15.9	12.9
28 075	...	5	Lauderdale	1 822	78 161	650	42.9	60.6	38.5	0.4	0.8	1.1	7.1	19.5	9.8	13.5	14.5	12.8
28 077	...	9	Lawrence	1 115	13 258	2 207	11.9	67.3	32.3	0.3	0.3	0.7	6.8	20.5	9.4	12.2	15.3	13.0
28 079	...	6	Leake	1 509	20 940	1 740	13.9	56.5	37.7	4.8	0.3	2.1	7.3	19.6	10.1	13.2	13.8	12.8
28 081	...	5	Lee	1 164	75 755	661	65.1	74.3	24.8	0.4	0.7	1.2	7.5	20.2	8.5	14.4	16.1	13.0
28 083	...	7	Leflore	1 533	37 947	1 167	24.8	30.2	68.0	0.3	0.9	1.9	7.8	21.9	13.1	13.4	13.6	11.1
28 085	...	7	Lincoln	1 517	33 166	1 310	21.9	69.7	29.8	0.4	0.3	0.7	7.1	19.6	9.5	12.7	14.9	13.3
28 087	...	5	Lowndes	1 301	61 586	790	47.3	57.1	41.9	0.5	0.9	1.1	7.7	20.9	10.6	13.9	15.3	12.4
28 089	3560	2	Madison	1 857	74 674	670	40.2	60.7	37.7	0.3	1.5	1.0	7.8	20.8	8.9	15.0	17.4	13.3
28 091	...	7	Marion	1 405	25 595	1 532	18.2	67.4	32.2	0.5	0.3	0.6	6.9	20.9	9.5	12.5	14.4	12.9
28 093	...	6	Marshall	1 829	34 993	1 249	19.1	48.8	50.6	0.4	0.2	1.2	7.0	19.5	11.8	13.2	15.4	12.9
28 095	...	7	Monroe	1 979	38 014	1 165	19.2	68.7	31.0	0.3	0.2	0.7	6.6	20.6	8.7	13.1	14.5	12.8
28 097	...	7	Montgomery	1 054	12 189	2 283	11.6	54.5	45.2	0.3	0.5	0.8	6.6	20.1	8.9	11.2	14.0	12.7
28 099	...	7	Neshoba	1 476	28 684	1 430	19.4	66.0	19.7	14.3	0.4	1.2	7.8	20.5	9.0	13.1	13.9	12.7
28 101	...	7	Newton	1 497	21 838	1 698	14.6	65.4	30.6	3.8	0.2	0.9	7.1	19.0	11.2	12.5	13.5	12.5
28 103	...	9	Noxubee	1 799	12 548	2 260	7.0	29.8	69.6	0.5	0.2	1.1	8.1	22.6	10.3	12.1	14.6	11.7
28 105	...	7	Oktibbeha	1 185	42 902	1 040	36.2	59.2	37.7	0.3	2.9	1.1	6.0	15.1	29.6	13.1	11.8	9.6
28 107	...	7	Panola	1 772	34 274	1 271	19.3	50.8	48.5	0.3	0.2	1.1	7.7	21.7	10.4	12.8	14.5	12.3
28 109	...	6	Pearl River	2 101	48 621	936	23.1	86.6	12.4	1.2	0.5	1.4	7.0	19.9	9.4	12.3	14.8	13.7
28 111	...	7	Perry	1 676	12 138	2 288	7.2	76.6	22.7	0.6	0.2	1.0	7.7	21.0	10.0	13.1	14.9	12.7
28 113	...	7	Pike	1 059	38 940	1 143	36.8	51.5	47.8	0.4	0.6	0.7	7.4	20.3	10.1	11.9	14.1	13.3
28 115	...	7	Pontotoc	1 288	26 726	1 494	20.8	84.8	14.1	0.5	0.2	1.8	7.2	20.4	8.7	14.0	15.5	12.8
28 117	...	7	Prentiss	1 075	25 556	1 537	23.8	86.5	13.2	0.6	0.3	0.7	6.8	18.2	11.6	13.4	13.8	12.5
28 119	...	9	Quitman	1 049	10 117	2 435	9.6	30.8	69.0	0.3	0.3	0.5	8.1	23.9	9.6	12.4	13.3	11.1
28 121	3560	2	Rankin	2 006	115 327	467	57.5	81.6	17.3	0.4	0.8	1.3	7.0	18.9	9.1	15.6	16.8	14.2
28 123	...	6	Scott	1 578	28 423	1 434	18.0	57.9	39.3	0.6	0.4	5.8	7.4	21.2	9.6	13.2	14.7	12.7
28 125	...	9	Sharkey	1 108	6 580	2 730	5.9	29.8	69.6	0.5	0.3	1.3	8.6	24.4	10.4	10.9	13.9	13.0
28 127	...	6	Simpson	1 525	27 639	1 460	18.1	64.9	34.5	0.4	0.2	1.2	7.1	20.8	9.4	12.7	14.8	13.0
28 129	...	8	Smith	1 647	16 182	2 009	9.8	76.4	23.3	0.3	0.2	0.6	7.0	20.5	8.7	12.9	14.4	12.6
28 131	...	6	Stone	1 153	13 622	2 189	11.8	80.1	19.3	0.6	0.2	1.2	6.9	19.9	12.2	12.6	14.8	13.0

1. MSA = Metropolitan Statistical Area. PMSA = Primary MSA. NECMA = New England County Metropolitan Area. See Appendix A for explanation of these concepts. See Appendix B for list of metropolitan areas identified by type, with component counties. 2. County typology code from the Economic Research Service of USDA. See Appendix A for definition. 3. Dry land or land partially or temporarily covered by water. 4. Hispanic persons may be of any race.

Table B. States and Counties — **Population and Households**

STATE County	55 to 64 years	65 to 74 years	75 years and over	Percent female	Total persons 2001	Total persons 1990	Percent change 1990–2000	Percent change 2000–2001	Births	Deaths	Net migration	Households 2000 Number	Percent change, 1990–2000	Persons per household	Female family householder[1]	One person
	16	17	18	19	20	21	22	23	24	25	26	27	28	29	30	31
MISSISSIPPI	8.6	6.5	5.5	51.7	2 858 029	2 575 475	10.5	0.5	56 970	35 931	-7 558	1 046 434	14.8	2.63	17.3	24.6
Adams	9.6	8.5	7.0	53.7	33 900	35 356	-2.9	-1.3	703	600	-545	13 677	3.1	2.48	21.5	28.0
Alcorn	10.7	7.8	7.1	51.6	34 612	31 722	8.9	0.2	532	546	87	14 224	14.3	2.39	11.5	27.6
Amite	10.9	8.4	7.0	51.7	13 509	13 328	2.0	-0.7	227	156	-160	5 271	9.1	2.58	16.3	24.5
Attala	9.9	9.0	8.3	52.2	19 655	18 481	6.4	0.0	361	375	17	7 567	9.0	2.55	16.7	26.4
Benton	9.9	8.5	6.8	51.4	7 950	8 046	-0.2	-0.9	154	137	-93	2 999	5.5	2.64	14.8	23.8
Bolivar	7.4	5.5	5.6	53.2	40 155	41 875	-3.0	-1.2	914	535	-866	13 776	3.6	2.79	27.3	25.3
Calhoun	9.7	8.4	8.2	52.4	14 901	14 908	1.1	-1.1	247	234	-180	6 019	6.3	2.46	15.4	27.1
Carroll	11.3	7.3	6.2	50.2	10 741	9 237	16.6	-0.3	150	134	-42	4 071	21.4	2.57	15.2	22.4
Chickasaw	9.0	6.9	6.6	51.9	19 400	18 085	7.5	-0.2	437	254	-222	7 253	11.9	2.65	18.0	24.9
Choctaw	9.8	7.8	7.1	52.1	9 663	9 071	7.6	-1.0	155	124	-127	3 686	14.6	2.56	14.6	25.0
Claiborne	6.8	5.0	5.5	53.9	11 823	11 370	4.1	-0.1	236	163	-76	3 685	10.3	2.72	26.9	28.0
Clarke	9.6	8.2	7.0	52.3	17 877	17 313	3.7	-0.4	314	244	-141	6 978	10.2	2.55	15.9	25.5
Clay	8.1	6.7	6.4	52.9	21 832	21 120	4.1	-0.7	483	313	-315	8 152	12.4	2.64	22.4	25.5
Coahoma	7.6	6.3	6.0	54.1	30 108	31 665	-3.3	-1.7	831	436	-924	10 553	0.2	2.83	28.7	26.2
Copiah	8.4	6.8	5.8	51.8	28 886	27 592	4.2	0.4	559	394	-23	10 142	9.0	2.71	20.1	23.6
Covington	9.3	6.9	6.1	51.9	19 527	16 527	17.4	0.6	394	272	6	7 126	23.2	2.68	17.2	23.6
De Soto	9.0	5.5	3.4	50.5	114 352	67 910	57.9	6.7	2 056	934	5 876	38 792	66.7	2.75	11.6	18.1
Forrest	7.3	5.9	5.4	52.8	72 890	68 314	6.3	0.4	1 389	952	-134	27 183	8.1	2.47	17.2	28.5
Franklin	9.4	8.2	7.0	52.0	8 377	8 377	0.8	-0.8	170	140	-99	3 211	4.1	2.60	14.6	25.6
George	9.6	6.2	4.7	49.8	19 582	16 673	14.8	2.3	475	213	178	6 742	16.7	2.78	10.4	19.1
Greene	8.6	5.5	4.6	43.5	13 376	10 220	30.1	0.6	225	107	-36	4 148	24.7	2.67	11.9	22.0
Grenada	9.1	7.4	7.0	53.2	22 938	21 555	7.9	-1.4	397	389	-332	8 820	14.5	2.58	18.6	25.3
Hancock	11.2	8.3	5.7	50.4	44 031	31 760	35.3	2.5	672	564	946	16 897	43.0	2.52	11.3	24.7
Harrison	8.5	6.5	4.6	50.2	189 409	165 365	14.7	-0.1	3 797	2 235	-1 660	71 538	20.1	2.55	15.1	25.8
Hinds	7.5	5.7	5.3	53.0	249 495	254 441	-1.4	-0.5	5 379	3 106	-3 579	91 030	0.0	2.64	22.7	26.7
Holmes	7.7	6.4	6.0	53.4	21 476	21 604	0.0	-0.6	598	353	-379	7 314	2.5	2.86	31.2	26.3
Humphreys	7.4	6.0	6.0	53.3	10 929	12 134	-7.6	-2.5	267	164	-387	3 765	-4.1	2.95	27.7	24.9
Issaquena	9.3	6.2	4.5	46.8	2 225	1 909	19.1	-2.2	28	17	-61	726	14.7	2.77	16.0	26.2
Itawamba	10.6	7.6	6.6	51.5	23 018	20 017	13.8	1.1	330	332	254	8 773	17.0	2.51	9.9	23.4
Jackson	9.4	6.1	4.2	50.4	132 823	115 243	14.0	1.1	2 406	1 454	508	47 676	17.9	2.72	14.5	20.8
Jasper	9.2	7.2	6.7	52.3	18 333	17 114	6.0	1.0	386	246	46	6 708	12.6	2.68	18.2	24.2
Jefferson	7.6	5.6	5.3	50.3	9 695	8 653	12.6	-0.5	171	109	-106	3 308	17.6	2.75	28.5	27.1
Jefferson Davis	9.6	7.1	6.7	52.7	13 855	14 051	-0.6	-0.8	280	184	-203	5 177	8.1	2.68	21.6	25.0
Jones	9.2	7.9	6.3	51.6	64 536	62 031	4.7	-1.2	1 250	816	-855	24 275	7.9	2.61	15.1	24.4
Kemper	9.2	7.4	7.7	52.0	10 464	10 356	0.9	0.1	209	123	-72	3 909	7.8	2.57	20.2	26.4
Lafayette	6.9	5.1	4.7	50.8	38 834	31 826	21.7	0.2	553	403	-50	14 373	29.6	2.36	11.4	29.1
Lamar	8.1	5.7	4.1	51.7	40 482	30 424	28.4	3.6	809	358	950	14 396	32.3	2.68	11.5	20.4
Lauderdale	8.6	7.1	7.0	52.5	77 414	75 555	3.4	-1.0	1 594	1 193	-1 129	29 990	6.2	2.49	18.3	28.0
Lawrence	9.6	7.5	5.8	52.0	13 379	12 458	6.4	0.9	238	177	64	5 040	11.9	2.61	14.4	24.1
Leake	8.9	7.8	6.5	50.5	21 145	18 436	13.6	1.0	427	312	94	7 611	12.1	2.65	16.5	24.3
Lee	8.8	6.0	5.4	52.0	76 680	65 579	15.5	1.2	1 594	911	274	29 200	19.4	2.55	14.6	25.0
Leflore	7.1	5.8	6.1	52.0	37 316	37 341	1.6	-1.7	855	513	-986	12 956	1.6	2.70	27.6	28.2
Lincoln	9.0	7.6	6.4	52.0	33 596	30 278	9.5	1.3	683	564	318	12 538	13.1	2.59	14.7	24.4
Lowndes	7.9	5.9	5.3	52.7	60 933	59 308	3.8	-1.1	1 300	646	-1 307	22 849	6.8	2.61	18.7	24.6
Madison	7.0	4.9	4.8	52.6	76 708	53 794	38.8	2.7	1 602	689	1 113	27 219	41.2	2.67	15.6	25.0
Marion	8.6	7.6	6.6	51.6	25 344	25 544	0.2	-1.0	507	430	-327	9 336	2.5	2.64	15.6	24.2
Marshall	9.1	6.5	4.6	50.5	35 329	30 361	15.3	1.0	684	440	103	12 163	20.7	2.74	20.1	22.0
Monroe	9.7	7.2	6.8	52.7	38 064	36 582	3.9	0.1	704	508	-131	14 603	9.4	2.57	17.2	24.7
Montgomery	9.7	8.6	8.0	53.6	12 056	12 387	-1.6	-1.1	224	181	-178	4 690	3.5	2.57	18.8	26.1
Neshoba	8.9	7.5	6.6	52.3	28 516	24 800	15.7	-0.6	639	382	-424	10 694	20.9	2.63	15.6	24.7
Newton	9.2	7.8	7.2	52.0	22 054	20 291	7.6	1.0	434	299	89	8 221	11.7	2.57	16.0	24.6
Noxubee	7.7	6.8	6.1	52.5	12 520	12 604	-0.4	-0.2	322	166	-185	4 470	8.0	2.77	24.7	25.9
Oktibbeha	6.5	4.6	4.0	50.0	42 286	38 375	11.8	-1.4	699	373	-952	15 945	23.5	2.42	14.8	27.7
Panola	8.5	6.6	5.5	52.1	34 697	29 996	14.3	1.2	789	456	106	12 232	20.8	2.75	19.9	23.2
Pearl River	10.2	7.5	5.1	51.4	49 969	38 714	25.6	2.8	839	533	1 034	18 078	31.4	2.65	12.5	21.7
Perry	9.5	6.4	4.6	51.1	12 273	10 865	11.7	1.1	263	139	15	4 420	16.3	2.72	13.2	21.9
Pike	8.8	7.3	6.8	53.2	38 956	36 882	5.6	0.0	871	573	-269	14 792	10.3	2.57	19.9	26.5
Pontotoc	8.5	6.8	6.1	51.4	27 053	22 237	20.2	1.2	470	301	165	10 097	21.0	2.62	11.9	22.7
Prentiss	9.9	7.3	6.6	51.5	25 480	23 278	9.8	-0.3	450	290	-234	9 821	13.6	2.52	12.6	24.9
Quitman	8.4	6.7	6.5	53.6	10 065	10 490	-3.6	-0.5	254	154	-153	3 565	1.2	2.80	26.8	26.9
Rankin	8.9	5.8	3.7	51.1	119 141	87 161	32.3	3.3	1 997	981	2 759	42 089	41.0	2.62	12.2	21.9
Scott	8.7	6.7	5.7	51.4	28 317	24 137	17.8	-0.4	570	403	-270	10 183	19.6	2.76	18.8	22.2
Sharkey	7.4	5.5	5.8	53.0	6 418	7 066	-6.9	-2.5	179	93	-255	2 163	3.8	2.99	26.8	23.5
Simpson	9.1	7.2	5.9	51.4	27 568	23 953	15.4	-0.3	531	364	-232	10 076	20.6	2.65	14.8	24.0
Smith	10.0	7.8	6.1	51.1	16 168	14 798	9.4	-0.1	289	225	-75	6 046	14.6	2.65	11.9	23.0
Stone	9.4	6.3	4.8	50.4	13 960	10 750	26.7	2.5	262	186	260	4 747	28.8	2.72	13.3	20.6

1. No spouse present.

STATE County	Births, average 1997–1999		Deaths, average 1997–1999				Physicians,[4] 2000		Hospitals,[4] 1998			Medicare enrollees 2000	Serious crimes known to police, 2000[6]	
			Number		Rate					Beds			Total	
	Total	Rate[1]	Total	Infant[2]	Total[1]	Infant[3]	Number	Rate[5]	Number	Number	Rate[5]		Number	Rate[7]
	32	33	34	35	36	37	38	39	40	41	42	43	44	45
MISSISSIPPI	41 978	15.3	27 845	437	10.1	10.4	4 116	145	104	12 563	456	418 527	113 911	4 004
Adams	487	14.2	441	8	12.9	15.8	65	189	2	238	695	6 294	2 143	6 241
Alcorn	445	13.5	410	NA	12.5	NA	35	101	1	150	458	6 618	NA	NA
Amite	176	12.8	129	NA	9.4	NA	5	37	0	0	0	2 283	10	74
Attala	249	13.5	274	NA	14.9	NA	13	66	1	72	391	3 917	364	1 851
Benton	105	13.0	99	NA	12.2	NA	3	37	0	0	0	1 527	NA	NA
Bolivar	682	16.9	436	8	10.8	11.2	18	44	1	119	295	6 089	NA	NA
Calhoun	214	14.3	189	NA	12.7	NA	5	33	2	77	519	2 962	NA	NA
Carroll	111	11.1	93	NA	9.4	NA	5	46	0	0	0	1 535	NA	NA
Chickasaw	303	16.7	202	NA	11.1	NA	10	51	2	160	888	3 684	134	818
Choctaw	123	13.1	96	NA	10.3	NA	6	61	1	88	938	1 362	NA	NA
Claiborne	172	14.8	114	NA	9.8	NA	4	34	1	27	232	1 463	188	1 589
Clarke	240	13.2	186	NA	10.2	NA	5	28	1	42	230	3 235	NA	NA
Clay	344	15.9	234	NA	10.8	NA	24	109	1	60	277	3 329	NA	NA
Coahoma	599	19.2	367	8	11.8	13.9	40	131	1	195	627	4 820	NA	NA
Copiah	416	14.4	302	NA	10.5	NA	14	49	1	49	169	5 262	NA	NA
Covington	294	16.5	211	NA	11.9	NA	12	62	1	82	461	3 136	289	1 489
De Soto	1 536	15.8	704	16	7.3	10.4	70	65	1	130	134	11 117	4 687	4 372
Forrest	1 119	15.0	740	NA	10.0	NA	151	208	2	672	904	11 508	NA	NA
Franklin	118	14.2	111	NA	13.4	NA	2	24	1	53	637	1 398	NA	NA
George	327	16.6	180	NA	9.2	NA	12	63	1	53	270	3 043	NA	NA
Greene	142	11.7	97	NA	8.1	NA	3	23	0	0	0	1 432	NA	NA
Grenada	339	15.1	289	NA	12.9	NA	33	142	1	118	526	4 003	1 072	4 608
Hancock	501	12.4	416	NA	10.3	NA	52	121	1	66	164	6 147	NA	NA
Harrison	2 852	16.1	1 744	25	9.8	8.6	447	236	4	722	406	26 176	13 281	7 005
Hinds	3 937	15.9	2 410	48	9.8	12.1	959	382	5	2 038	825	32 922	NA	NA
Holmes	380	17.7	254	NA	11.8	NA	13	60	2	113	525	3 826	152	814
Humphreys	191	16.9	123	NA	10.9	NA	12	107	1	28	247	1 759	NA	NA
Issaquena	26	16.0	16	NA	9.6	NA	0	0	0	0	0	157	0	0
Itawamba	268	12.7	254	NA	12.1	NA	6	26	0	0	0	3 183	NA	NA
Jackson	1 883	14.4	1 076	15	8.2	7.8	203	154	2	446	341	15 654	6 559	4 991
Jasper	283	15.9	182	NA	10.2	NA	5	28	1	114	645	3 147	NA	NA
Jefferson	127	15.1	97	NA	11.5	NA	4	41	1	30	356	1 378	NA	NA
Jefferson Davis	204	14.7	156	NA	11.3	NA	11	79	1	101	729	2 083	NA	NA
Jones	900	14.2	664	11	10.5	12.6	87	134	2	301	474	11 543	2 988	4 859
Kemper	138	13.1	100	NA	9.5	NA	5	48	1	24	227	1 741	8	84
Lafayette	416	12.0	295	NA	8.5	NA	63	163	1	150	434	3 857	NA	NA
Lamar	618	16.7	270	NA	7.3	NA	117	299	1	23	62	3 791	290	742
Lauderdale	1 177	15.4	873	15	11.4	12.7	225	288	3	619	813	12 829	2 724	3 485
Lawrence	174	13.4	137	NA	10.5	NA	9	68	1	53	406	2 912	NA	NA
Leake	310	15.9	254	NA	13.0	NA	13	62	1	76	392	3 806	NA	NA
Lee	1 185	15.9	700	13	9.4	11.0	185	244	1	607	813	11 631	3 293	4 430
Leflore	633	17.1	415	NA	11.2	NA	58	153	1	187	506	5 658	2 396	6 314
Lincoln	456	14.3	395	NA	12.4	NA	34	103	1	95	299	5 300	1 017	3 066
Lowndes	1 014	16.6	545	12	8.9	12.2	84	136	2	404	660	8 294	2 658	4 316
Madison	1 213	16.7	542	14	7.5	11.3	127	170	1	127	174	8 050	2 042	3 306
Marion	375	14.2	320	NA	12.1	NA	15	59	1	90	341	4 796	NA	NA
Marshall	505	15.6	337	NA	10.4	NA	14	40	1	40	124	5 023	NA	NA
Monroe	526	13.8	388	NA	10.2	NA	55	145	2	122	319	5 996	NA	NA
Montgomery	182	14.6	170	NA	13.7	NA	7	57	2	68	547	2 504	NA	NA
Neshoba	424	15.4	305	NA	11.1	NA	18	63	2	224	810	3 954	NA	NA
Newton	322	14.9	241	NA	11.2	NA	15	69	1	39	181	4 579	NA	NA
Noxubee	224	18.0	133	NA	10.7	NA	6	48	1	109	881	2 087	83	661
Oktibbeha	516	13.1	287	NA	7.3	NA	36	84	1	96	244	4 723	NA	NA
Panola	543	16.2	362	NA	10.8	NA	15	44	1	70	210	5 425	950	2 944
Pearl River	633	13.5	436	NA	9.3	NA	26	53	2	145	309	7 372	NA	NA
Perry	197	16.5	106	NA	8.9	NA	3	25	1	82	695	1 580	NA	NA
Pike	571	15.0	459	NA	12.1	NA	52	134	2	166	438	7 009	NA	NA
Pontotoc	363	14.3	241	NA	9.5	NA	11	41	1	61	240	3 867	239	894
Prentiss	331	13.6	231	NA	9.5	NA	25	98	1	78	321	4 939	478	2 020
Quitman	171	17.4	124	NA	12.6	NA	5	49	1	96	968	1 830	NA	NA
Rankin	1 548	14.1	765	10	7.0	6.5	185	160	3	233	213	12 928	2 229	1 974
Scott	426	17.0	292	NA	11.7	NA	12	42	2	104	416	4 460	NA	NA
Sharkey	123	18.7	74	NA	11.2	NA	2	30	1	29	436	980	NA	NA
Simpson	375	14.8	296	NA	11.7	NA	15	54	2	113	446	4 295	255	923
Smith	219	14.3	168	NA	11.0	NA	4	25	1	22	144	2 359	NA	NA
Stone	199	15.1	146	NA	11.1	NA	10	73	1	34	258	2 294	NA	NA

1. Per 1,000 estimated resident population, average 1997–1999.   2. Deaths of infants under 1 year old.   3. Deaths of infants under 1 year old per 1,000 live births.   4. Data subject to copyright.   5. Per 100,000 resident population as of July 1 of the year shown.   6. Data for serious crimes have not been adjusted for underreporting; this may affect comparability between geographic areas and over time.   7. Per 100,000 population estimated by the FBI.

STATE County	Serious crimes known to police, 2000[1] (cont'd) Rate[2] Violent	Serious crimes known to police, 2000[1] (cont'd) Rate[2] Property	Education School enrollment and attainment, 1990 Enrollment[3] Total	Enrollment[3] Percent private	Attainment[4] (percent) High school graduate or more	Attainment[4] (percent) Bach-elor's degree or more	Local government expenditures, fiscal 1999[5] Total current expenditures (mil dol)	Current expenditures per student (dollars)	Money income 1989 Per capita[6] (dollars)	Households Median Dollars	Households Median Percent change, 1979–1989 (constant 1989 dollars)	Percent with $100,000 or more	Income and poverty, 1998 Median house-hold income	Percent below poverty level All persons	Persons under 18	Persons 5–17 in families
	46	47	48	49	50	51	52	53	54	55	56	57	58	59	60	61
MISSISSIPPI	361	3 644	727 486	11.1	64.3	14.7	2 293.2	4 565	9 648	20 136	-0.7	1.7	28 925	17.6	23.9	21.3
Adams	312	5 929	9 515	17.8	67.3	14.8	25.4	4 718	9 469	17 214	-9.5	1.9	24 825	22.9	31.9	27.8
Alcorn	NA	NA	7 289	4.4	56.3	9.6	27.3	4 891	9 301	18 538	-8.2	0.5	29 917	15.5	23.2	19.1
Amite	59	15	3 338	18.9	57.1	8.7	8.7	5 047	8 268	15 669	-2.1	1.2	26 577	18.5	25.3	22.3
Attala	132	1 719	4 529	10.7	51.4	10.0	16.2	4 527	7 685	15 380	-1.4	1.0	23 448	21.4	31.6	25.7
Benton	NA	NA	2 053	4.3	46.4	7.8	6.0	4 648	6 982	15 794	-16.2	0.2	24 884	19.1	26.9	23.9
Bolivar	NA	NA	14 519	7.6	54.9	15.2	45.4	5 121	6 889	14 020	-8.4	1.3	22 956	28.3	33.2	31.2
Calhoun	NA	NA	3 296	8.0	52.8	8.2	12.1	4 691	8 806	18 182	8.2	0.6	26 633	17.5	26.6	22.3
Carroll	NA	NA	2 399	22.5	54.0	10.3	6.6	5 242	8 241	16 639	2.9	1.4	26 941	17.9	27.6	22.4
Chickasaw	195	623	4 446	7.4	52.9	9.5	15.5	4 427	8 725	18 259	-5.3	1.4	26 007	17.4	24.5	20.7
Choctaw	NA	NA	2 462	11.1	57.6	10.8	8.7	4 513	8 076	17 313	9.0	0.9	24 571	18.9	23.1	25.5
Claiborne	380	1 209	5 013	7.0	58.7	16.1	10.0	4 975	5 932	12 876	-21.6	0.1	22 369	26.9	30.8	28.7
Clarke	NA	NA	4 352	3.3	61.6	8.2	14.9	4 245	8 987	19 055	-3.3	0.8	27 030	15.8	24.1	18.5
Clay	NA	NA	6 109	15.2	60.4	12.9	17.3	4 125	9 224	18 337	-11.8	1.9	27 126	20.6	26.9	24.3
Coahoma	NA	NA	10 082	9.7	54.0	14.7	31.6	4 746	7 197	13 780	-7.9	1.3	21 072	28.7	34.5	31.1
Copiah	NA	NA	7 933	10.8	61.1	9.4	22.7	4 585	7 815	16 583	-1.7	1.1	24 730	20.2	28.7	24.9
Covington	278	1 211	4 453	4.5	55.5	8.6	16.4	4 541	7 847	17 589	7.3	0.8	25 089	19.7	26.0	23.3
De Soto	242	4 131	17 526	15.6	71.2	9.5	66.4	3 651	12 509	31 756	2.8	1.9	45 368	7.4	11.2	9.2
Forrest	NA	NA	23 219	7.4	72.1	19.8	58.2	4 900	9 765	17 986	-7.2	1.9	29 958	18.6	26.8	21.3
Franklin	NA	NA	2 196	8.8	58.1	7.4	9.1	5 124	7 426	14 341	-9.0	0.7	24 414	19.4	24.5	25.5
George	NA	NA	4 468	6.6	58.8	8.3	14.6	3 669	8 000	18 397	-19.0	0.4	32 556	14.7	20.2	17.4
Greene	NA	NA	2 704	3.9	62.4	6.0	9.1	4 812	6 882	17 958	3.9	0.3	26 347	20.3	22.8	22.3
Grenada	469	4 140	5 617	10.7	56.5	10.8	18.6	4 009	9 125	19 955	-2.3	1.3	27 991	17.6	24.5	21.3
Hancock	NA	NA	7 738	18.3	68.0	14.3	28.3	4 456	10 180	20 720	-5.9	1.9	31 865	14.9	21.3	19.7
Harrison	362	6 643	42 908	12.9	74.7	16.3	147.4	4 846	10 434	22 157	-1.4	1.6	32 255	14.8	21.2	18.3
Hinds	NA	NA	78 082	19.3	75.2	26.4	212.0	4 918	12 222	24 676	-1.7	3.4	32 477	18.0	26.0	21.0
Holmes	316	498	6 968	9.3	48.0	9.7	19.8	4 121	5 969	9 809	-16.7	1.3	17 031	33.0	36.4	36.9
Humphreys	NA	NA	3 716	18.9	46.4	10.4	11.0	4 453	7 201	12 696	-4.3	1.6	19 583	32.0	39.4	36.2
Issaquena	0	0	549	18.4	43.7	5.6	NA	NA	6 412	13 005	-15.4	0.5	20 715	31.3	39.0	41.6
Itawamba	NA	NA	4 855	2.8	49.0	6.7	15.9	4 170	9 476	20 770	1.5	0.4	32 139	12.4	18.8	15.0
Jackson	352	4 639	32 942	8.1	74.4	14.4	116.9	4 595	11 246	26 444	-7.1	1.7	36 143	13.0	18.3	15.5
Jasper	NA	NA	4 644	9.3	60.0	9.8	15.1	4 659	7 524	16 130	-5.6	0.6	24 173	18.4	22.8	21.2
Jefferson	NA	NA	2 746	6.5	53.0	10.3	9.1	5 223	5 349	10 267	-16.7	0.2	17 685	26.6	30.9	30.8
Jefferson Davis	NA	NA	3 895	7.3	57.4	8.9	12.2	4 962	7 303	15 442	-12.4	0.6	21 960	23.9	31.8	28.2
Jones	359	4 500	16 426	6.4	64.3	12.2	53.0	4 711	9 663	19 239	-7.6	1.7	28 280	16.1	21.7	18.6
Kemper	32	53	2 863	11.1	56.3	7.9	7.6	5 098	8 033	14 315	-4.6	1.1	23 733	20.7	28.3	24.5
Lafayette	NA	NA	14 147	6.1	70.2	29.2	24.4	4 750	9 196	18 186	-5.9	1.7	30 464	13.9	19.1	15.4
Lamar	28	714	8 907	8.6	73.3	20.9	29.5	3 951	10 619	23 263	-1.2	2.2	33 372	14.5	16.8	18.3
Lauderdale	292	3 193	19 601	7.8	69.7	13.3	65.0	4 636	10 649	20 414	-0.6	2.2	29 657	17.5	24.8	22.0
Lawrence	NA	NA	3 502	4.9	61.9	9.2	11.5	4 613	8 294	17 519	-15.5	0.8	26 328	18.4	26.1	21.5
Leake	NA	NA	4 649	14.5	54.3	9.2	13.6	4 241	7 279	15 975	4.5	0.4	25 154	19.6	26.9	23.3
Lee	295	4 136	16 256	6.1	67.8	15.0	69.0	4 665	11 702	24 647	7.7	2.5	34 642	12.5	18.8	15.2
Leflore	1 062	5 252	11 746	9.7	55.3	15.7	33.7	4 772	9 003	15 219	-4.9	2.0	22 134	27.2	33.0	30.7
Lincoln	416	2 650	7 818	9.2	63.0	11.6	26.8	4 370	9 134	18 193	-10.1	1.3	28 100	16.8	22.3	19.9
Lowndes	294	4 022	16 936	12.9	69.0	18.6	51.3	4 633	11 108	22 985	8.1	1.8	31 155	17.4	23.8	22.3
Madison	215	3 091	15 338	23.8	71.5	29.3	49.9	4 083	12 020	25 887	27.1	3.4	39 833	13.0	18.4	17.5
Marion	NA	NA	7 036	7.2	58.8	8.4	21.7	4 521	8 490	16 084	-10.8	1.0	24 034	22.6	30.3	26.4
Marshall	NA	NA	7 902	20.0	51.7	9.4	22.4	4 285	7 599	18 492	0.2	0.5	27 756	18.0	22.9	21.8
Monroe	NA	NA	9 135	5.1	55.6	8.4	28.5	4 306	8 979	20 047	2.1	1.0	29 205	15.5	22.1	18.8
Montgomery	NA	NA	3 328	7.4	56.6	9.5	11.2	5 099	7 660	15 396	-3.5	0.5	22 907	21.6	29.4	26.9
Neshoba	NA	NA	7 071	11.7	60.9	10.1	17.1	4 207	8 249	18 237	0.0	0.9	28 038	17.2	22.7	20.6
Newton	NA	NA	5 685	10.1	60.1	9.7	17.8	4 814	8 923	19 302	9.0	1.2	27 367	16.7	23.3	20.5
Noxubee	406	255	3 546	17.3	49.6	7.9	11.1	4 588	6 654	14 205	-2.2	1.0	21 585	27.5	33.6	33.0
Oktibbeha	NA	NA	17 325	7.2	73.0	31.7	29.4	5 275	9 166	18 507	0.8	1.4	29 087	18.1	22.6	21.5
Panola	310	2 634	8 085	6.8	54.3	8.7	27.9	4 153	7 537	17 686	9.3	0.8	24 513	20.7	26.6	24.0
Pearl River	NA	NA	10 674	7.7	68.4	11.4	35.1	4 153	9 418	20 133	-0.6	1.8	28 693	17.2	23.0	20.5
Perry	NA	NA	2 980	3.9	61.8	7.1	11.5	4 898	7 418	16 230	-12.1	0.9	25 747	18.7	23.6	23.1
Pike	NA	NA	10 425	6.8	60.6	12.8	34.5	4 738	8 119	15 149	-14.1	1.4	23 428	22.4	27.7	25.8
Pontotoc	217	677	5 157	2.9	57.4	8.1	20.8	4 054	9 143	20 223	6.5	0.5	31 019	11.8	15.2	15.1
Prentiss	165	1 855	6 024	2.4	52.9	8.4	22.2	4 525	8 947	17 736	-5.1	1.7	27 632	14.2	17.6	18.0
Quitman	NA	NA	2 974	13.0	45.5	9.0	7.4	4 311	6 450	13 730	0.4	0.6	18 804	28.6	33.5	33.7
Rankin	153	1 821	23 316	14.7	73.8	19.0	73.6	3 923	12 749	31 668	3.0	2.6	42 543	9.6	14.0	11.4
Scott	NA	NA	6 136	5.0	53.1	9.4	24.2	4 240	8 187	17 040	-5.4	1.4	25 301	18.8	24.9	22.7
Sharkey	NA	NA	2 329	11.1	51.3	12.4	8.1	4 956	6 032	13 304	-3.8	0.8	17 380	34.4	39.0	40.0
Simpson	54	868	6 122	10.4	58.0	8.7	18.7	4 234	8 284	19 053	-3.0	0.7	25 680	18.9	23.0	23.2
Smith	NA	NA	3 516	4.8	57.0	7.6	13.5	4 315	8 799	19 111	9.8	0.9	27 779	16.5	22.3	20.4
Stone	NA	NA	3 243	3.2	68.1	12.4	12.4	4 638	8 816	19 045	-13.3	1.4	26 705	17.1	18.9	23.8

1. Data for serious crimes have not been adjusted for underreporting; this may affect comparability between geographic areas and over time.   2. Per 100,000 population estimated by the FBI.   3. All persons 3 years old and over enrolled in nursery school through college.   4. Persons 25 years old and over.   5. Elementary and secondary education expenditures, local government fiscal years ending between July 1, 1998 and June 30, 1999.   6. Based on population enumerated as of April 1, 1990.

STATE County	Personal income, 1999												
			Per capita[1]					Transfer payments					
									Government payments to individuals				
	Total (mil dol)	Percent change, 1998–1999	Dollars	Rank	Wages and salaries[2] (mil dol)	Proprietor's income (mil dol)	Dividends, interest, and rent (mil dol)	Total (mil dol)	Total (mil dol)	Social Security (mil dol)	Medical payments (mil dol)	Income maintenance (mil dol)	Unemployment insurance (mil dol)
	62	63	64	65	66	67	68	69	70	71	72	73	74
MISSISSIPPI	57 272	4.2	20 686	X	33 773	4 459	9 498	10 630	10 075	3 863	4 102	1 381	118
Adams	697	3.4	20 705	1 774	403	68	145	159	152	62	56	24	3
Alcorn	669	3.8	20 212	1 925	397	48	108	148	141	62	56	16	1
Amite	212	3.1	15 260	2 964	64	24	37	54	51	20	19	9	1
Attala	328	3.1	17 878	2 562	145	25	63	89	85	34	34	13	1
Benton	123	2.6	15 236	2 967	43	5	16	33	31	12	13	5	0
Bolivar	686	0.7	17 219	2 698	358	31	114	178	169	49	67	42	2
Calhoun	289	5.8	19 437	2 162	103	37	51	69	66	27	27	9	0
Carroll	182	5.0	18 287	2 475	31	13	28	37	35	15	12	6	0
Chickasaw	345	6.2	19 029	2 274	189	36	58	81	77	32	32	10	1
Choctaw	142	5.6	15 163	2 974	51	14	19	36	34	12	13	6	0
Claiborne	176	3.2	15 199	2 970	180	10	28	45	43	13	18	9	1
Clarke	310	3.6	16 808	2 778	120	28	49	72	68	30	26	8	2
Clay	405	3.1	18 685	2 371	256	28	79	84	80	32	28	13	1
Coahoma	561	4.2	18 031	2 536	296	32	108	155	149	42	67	32	2
Copiah	471	3.7	16 294	2 862	180	42	71	119	113	42	46	18	1
Covington	315	4.2	17 603	2 625	111	50	44	74	71	27	28	11	1
De Soto	2 602	11.6	25 477	587	943	156	280	244	224	115	74	17	2
Forrest	1 544	3.8	20 601	1 810	1 094	126	347	293	278	98	117	31	2
Franklin	121	2.4	14 831	3 004	51	8	19	35	34	14	13	5	1
George	343	3.6	17 006	2 732	94	20	45	69	65	26	28	6	1
Greene	164	0.1	13 006	3 082	50	15	18	40	38	13	17	5	1
Grenada	448	3.3	19 965	1 999	319	31	87	103	99	36	46	12	1
Hancock	859	7.9	20 679	1 785	522	36	187	151	142	63	57	11	1
Harrison	4 331	6.2	24 257	815	3 243	263	776	673	640	235	282	63	5
Hinds	6 268	3.1	25 506	582	5 276	509	1 251	877	827	326	314	115	10
Holmes	294	0.4	13 617	3 066	114	19	46	112	107	25	48	27	2
Humphreys	191	-2.0	17 054	2 726	85	24	31	55	53	14	24	13	1
Issaquena	23	0.0	13 894	3 052	8	0	4	6	6	2	2	2	0
Itawamba	439	6.3	20 808	1 732	149	25	62	77	73	34	26	6	2
Jackson	2 830	0.8	21 259	1 580	1 953	107	438	416	390	178	147	33	5
Jasper	300	4.2	16 554	2 821	116	36	39	71	68	26	27	11	1
Jefferson	100	3.0	11 892	3 094	33	6	10	46	44	11	15	9	1
Jefferson Davis	214	1.7	15 516	2 943	59	20	31	57	54	21	21	9	1
Jones	1 374	3.3	21 792	1 415	798	134	223	306	293	107	144	27	2
Kemper	172	-0.7	16 422	2 840	39	16	28	44	42	15	16	7	1
Lafayette	721	6.5	20 643	1 793	450	51	133	121	114	39	57	9	0
Lamar	746	5.9	19 579	2 117	311	76	77	104	97	44	36	10	1
Lauderdale	1 726	2.4	22 722	1 157	1 153	103	322	312	297	113	121	39	4
Lawrence	234	2.7	17 917	2 555	106	29	33	64	62	27	24	7	1
Leake	374	0.2	19 054	2 270	140	64	50	90	86	32	38	12	1
Lee	1 860	4.3	24 734	711	1 654	103	334	257	242	111	92	24	6
Leflore	704	3.5	19 135	2 249	432	57	132	177	170	47	75	33	2
Lincoln	623	5.4	19 406	2 177	331	79	95	136	130	54	54	14	2
Lowndes	1 281	3.2	21 168	1 608	920	92	212	198	186	72	71	30	2
Madison	1 979	6.8	26 548	458	803	120	388	207	192	80	73	28	1
Marion	441	2.8	16 630	2 804	192	37	79	118	113	44	46	16	1
Marshall	588	4.4	18 191	2 502	182	47	58	120	113	42	44	19	1
Monroe	674	5.5	17 623	2 617	340	50	110	150	142	63	53	16	2
Montgomery	213	3.2	17 177	2 704	72	22	33	59	57	20	25	9	0
Neshoba	569	2.9	20 596	1 812	352	79	69	116	110	40	49	13	1
Newton	424	1.6	19 512	2 137	179	61	65	102	98	37	42	11	1
Noxubee	209	4.5	16 717	2 792	87	24	34	55	52	16	20	14	1
Oktibbeha	763	6.1	19 176	2 236	490	45	149	120	112	39	41	18	1
Panola	543	5.4	15 998	2 897	287	47	80	132	125	48	46	23	2
Pearl River	798	4.7	16 639	2 801	223	64	126	190	180	77	70	19	1
Perry	171	3.4	14 168	3 040	81	13	23	47	45	19	16	7	1
Pike	695	2.4	18 335	2 462	398	62	115	173	166	57	68	25	2
Pontotoc	474	8.1	18 440	2 430	272	57	84	79	35	31	8	1
Prentiss	397	3.3	16 187	2 877	216	22	60	94	89	37	35	10	2
Quitman	150	5.4	15 305	2 959	46	15	20	50	48	13	21	11	0
Rankin	2 876	6.8	25 597	574	1 535	211	374	340	318	136	140	21	2
Scott	501	2.8	20 105	1 964	272	109	63	104	99	35	44	14	1
Sharkey	86	-4.1	13 069	3 080	38	2	16	32	30	8	14	8	1
Simpson	473	0.7	18 631	2 383	151	68	57	121	116	37	61	12	1
Smith	305	1.5	19 738	2 078	107	77	32	63	60	28	22	8	0
Stone	221	3.9	16 386	2 846	99	19	27	58	55	20	23	5	0

1. Based on the resident population estimated as of July 1 of the year shown.   2. Includes other labor income.

STATE County	Total (mil dol)	Farm	Goods-related[1] Total	Manu- facturing	Service-related and other[2] Total	Retail trade	Finance, insur- ance, and real estate	Services	Govern- ment	Number	Rate[3]	Supple- mental Security Income recipients, December 2000	Total	Percent change, 1980– 1990
	75	76	77	78	79	80	81	82	83	84	85	86	87	88
MISSISSIPPI	38 233	2.3	27.0	20.1	49.3	10.1	4.5	23.0	21.5	514 300	181	128 910	1 010 423	10.8
Adams	471	0.3	38.5	17.8	46.8	11.4	3.3	24.1	14.4	7 624	222	1 999	14 715	8.4
Alcorn	444	0.0	D	39.9	D	13.7	3.1	13.5	16.7	8 256	239	1 904	13 704	7.0
Amite	87	14.0	D	34.8	D	6.7	D	12.9	15.9	2 774	204	757	5 695	7.9
Attala	171	0.6	32.5	21.5	49.9	14.6	5.6	16.8	17.1	4 633	236	1 207	7 674	0.7
Benton	47	0.5	38.7	32.4	D	D	1.2	16.4	17.4	1 556	194	563	3 379	10.5
Bolivar	389	3.6	23.4	19.7	47.0	9.9	2.9	15.6	26.0	7 033	173	3 676	14 514	-0.3
Calhoun	140	13.0	36.5	34.3	34.6	9.0	2.5	9.6	15.9	3 783	251	922	6 260	3.7
Carroll	44	3.8	D	16.2	D	10.6	D	18.9	22.2	2 192	204	535	3 948	10.2
Chickasaw	225	5.3	D	51.6	D	7.1	1.8	12.6	10.2	4 453	229	1 173	6 997	10.3
Choctaw	65	3.7	40.3	27.0	D	6.0	D	19.1	19.2	1 802	185	507	3 539	3.6
Claiborne	190	2.1	D	8.9	D	3.7	1.2	7.0	25.4	1 870	158	848	4 099	-6.8
Clarke	148	2.7	49.6	43.6	33.4	5.6	2.9	12.8	14.2	4 065	226	834	7 065	9.3
Clay	284	0.1	D	51.8	D	7.1	2.3	16.2	10.0	4 191	191	1 137	7 737	5.9
Coahoma	328	3.6	17.2	13.2	D	9.9	3.9	35.4	19.4	5 899	193	2 734	11 495	-11.1
Copiah	222	4.8	35.5	29.2	D	9.0	2.2	15.0	24.8	5 807	202	1 780	10 260	7.2
Covington	160	8.4	D	22.0	D	7.7	2.2	11.1	17.7	3 869	199	1 112	6 535	13.3
De Soto	1 098	0.1	D	26.3	D	14.6	3.6	21.5	10.0	14 091	131	1 495	24 472	42.7
Forrest	1 220	0.6	17.7	11.1	49.9	10.4	5.3	23.4	31.8	12 386	171	2 841	27 740	10.9
Franklin	59	0.8	D	20.0	D	6.3	3.7	14.7	28.1	1 736	205	398	3 555	4.3
George	114	3.5	D	12.3	D	14.6	3.9	14.7	30.2	3 616	189	596	6 663	16.4
Greene	66	8.8	D	16.5	D	7.2	2.2	10.4	43.7	1 613	121	459	3 864	13.0
Grenada	350	0.4	D	40.6	D	11.8	3.3	15.9	16.6	4 702	202	1 302	8 712	13.4
Hancock	558	0.1	D	13.3	D	6.8	1.8	32.2	34.6	7 931	185	1 086	16 561	32.1
Harrison	3 505	0.0	11.7	6.1	54.5	9.7	3.8	30.5	33.8	31 022	164	5 929	67 813	17.0
Hinds	5 784	0.3	12.4	7.0	63.1	9.9	9.9	28.5	24.2	39 917	159	10 250	99 860	9.0
Holmes	133	5.6	D	24.0	D	10.1	2.8	21.6	25.7	3 836	178	2 360	7 972	2.3
Humphreys	109	23.8	26.4	23.4	32.8	7.2	3.0	12.8	16.9	2 233	199	1 138	4 231	-10.7
Issaquena	8	18.8	D	D	D	D	D	11.0	32.8	306	135	96	698	-23.0
Itawamba	174	4.4	D	28.6	D	7.7	1.6	11.6	19.0	5 235	230	579	8 116	6.2
Jackson	2 061	0.0	D	42.0	D	7.4	2.2	15.8	20.1	21 605	164	2 461	45 542	6.8
Jasper	152	9.8	43.0	29.7	30.9	7.3	2.3	13.4	16.3	3 558	196	1 168	6 700	8.3
Jefferson	38	7.0	D	7.9	40.6	4.6	1.4	15.1	43.2	1 876	193	915	3 167	1.1
Jefferson Davis	79	9.8	D	13.0	D	11.4	2.7	15.4	24.3	3 028	217	824	5 336	8.8
Jones	932	5.1	38.7	25.6	36.6	8.5	2.3	15.3	19.6	13 602	209	3 130	25 044	4.7
Kemper	55	16.4	19.0	13.9	35.4	8.2	3.7	13.3	29.2	2 170	208	660	4 151	16.7
Lafayette	501	0.1	18.0	12.1	44.5	11.7	2.8	25.3	37.5	5 047	130	934	12 478	14.3
Lamar	387	2.7	19.5	10.3	67.9	20.5	4.1	32.5	9.8	5 721	146	882	11 849	37.8
Lauderdale	1 256	0.2	D	13.0	D	11.0	3.9	27.4	24.0	14 551	186	3 693	31 232	7.5
Lawrence	134	9.6	D	44.2	D	5.5	0.9	9.7	15.6	3 579	270	729	5 160	11.6
Leake	205	22.4	30.1	26.6	35.7	10.3	3.4	13.9	11.8	4 468	213	1 131	7 614	7.4
Lee	1 758	0.0	37.5	33.9	53.4	9.7	4.5	27.5	9.1	13 996	185	2 717	25 971	21.5
Leflore	489	2.4	25.1	20.7	47.8	9.6	3.4	19.0	24.7	6 524	172	3 002	13 799	0.4
Lincoln	410	3.1	27.8	17.6	58.1	19.5	3.2	18.6	11.0	7 054	213	1 435	12 133	10.0
Lowndes	1 012	1.5	32.8	23.7	43.5	10.5	2.5	19.2	22.1	9 409	153	2 559	23 117	16.3
Madison	923	0.2	19.9	10.6	67.3	15.1	11.4	25.2	12.7	10 339	138	2 285	20 761	48.4
Marion	229	6.6	30.3	12.3	44.4	13.4	3.8	14.7	18.8	5 930	232	1 446	10 132	7.0
Marshall	230	0.3	D	25.4	D	9.8	3.9	22.6	16.6	6 023	172	1 986	10 984	16.4
Monroe	390	0.7	47.9	39.4	37.5	9.8	2.1	16.5	13.9	8 436	222	1 528	14 285	7.8
Montgomery	94	2.7	D	15.8	D	13.4	3.6	22.7	21.3	2 906	238	843	4 987	0.0
Neshoba	430	8.4	34.1	18.0	44.9	7.9	2.4	29.2	12.6	5 538	193	1 245	9 770	9.9
Newton	240	16.1	D	25.9	D	8.3	2.4	14.0	22.5	5 198	238	1 171	8 095	4.3
Noxubee	111	9.8	D	36.5	D	7.8	2.2	11.9	19.0	2 596	207	1 287	4 645	6.1
Oktibbeha	535	0.3	17.7	14.4	D	9.4	3.6	12.7	53.3	5 152	120	1 729	13 861	17.6
Panola	334	1.0	34.4	25.6	45.0	11.8	2.8	17.3	19.7	6 977	204	2 108	11 482	11.5
Pearl River	287	-0.4	D	11.0	D	19.1	3.7	22.7	23.9	9 950	205	1 573	15 793	24.0
Perry	95	4.6	D	50.4	D	5.7	2.3	7.0	18.8	2 731	225	536	4 292	22.1
Pike	460	2.5	D	23.7	D	13.7	2.9	17.3	22.7	7 923	203	2 364	14 995	12.2
Pontotoc	304	1.4	D	59.2	D	6.2	2.0	11.0	9.7	4 866	182	839	9 001	10.5
Prentiss	238	-0.5	D	39.0	D	8.9	2.7	14.6	19.5	5 007	196	1 101	9 155	2.3
Quitman	61	8.9	D	14.4	53.7	8.7	14.2	21.7	19.1	2 032	201	1 094	3 880	-9.6
Rankin	1 746	1.3	23.8	15.0	58.9	9.1	5.7	19.7	16.0	16 841	146	2 140	31 872	32.8
Scott	381	20.7	D	33.3	D	7.2	D	10.5	10.6	4 945	174	1 499	9 488	6.3
Sharkey	40	6.9	D	D	D	10.0	3.7	22.8	32.5	1 142	174	577	2 290	-8.8
Simpson	218	19.1	D	6.1	D	11.7	3.0	20.7	21.3	5 021	182	1 286	9 374	7.4
Smith	184	33.5	D	32.5	D	3.2	1.0	7.5	9.9	3 988	246	681	5 850	2.4
Stone	118	0.7	D	24.4	D	8.6	3.0	20.2	27.3	2 758	202	506	4 148	19.6

1. Covers mining, construction, and manufacturing. 2. Covers private sector earnings in agricultural services, forestry, and fisheries; transportation and public utilities; wholesale trade; retail trade; finance, insurance, and real estate; and services. 3. Per 1,000 resident population estimated as of July 1 of the year shown.

Table B. States and Counties — Housing, Labor Force, and Employment

	Housing units, 1990 (cont'd)								Civilian labor force, 2001				Civilian employment, 1990[5]		
	Occupied units										Unemployment			Percent	
	Owner-occupied					Renter-occupied									
				Owner cost as a percent of income											
STATE County	Total	Percent	Median value[1]	With a mortgage	Without a mortgage	Median rent[2]	Rent as percent of income	Sub-standard units[3] (percent)	Total	Percent change, 2000–2001	Total	Rate[4]	Total	Professional, managerial, and technical	Precision production, craft, and repair
	89	90	91	92	93	94	95	96	97	98	99	100	101	102	103
MISSISSIPPI	911 374	71.5	45 600	20.8	13.5	309	27.1	7.2	1 296 193	-2.3	71 542	5.5	1 028 773	24.6	12.9
Adams	13 262	71.5	43 900	21.7	14.9	282	29.0	4.7	14 289	-2.4	982	6.9	12 895	27.0	11.5
Alcorn	12 449	75.7	38 800	19.3	13.1	240	26.7	3.1	15 584	-1.9	858	5.5	13 226	20.7	14.7
Amite	4 830	86.0	36 800	22.9	14.3	198	20.9	9.3	5 643	-4.4	232	4.1	4 426	19.3	11.9
Attala	6 945	78.2	36 500	21.8	13.9	231	25.9	10.4	7 653	-6.2	615	8.0	6 753	17.8	13.0
Benton	2 842	86.0	35 100	25.2	13.3	225	21.1	10.6	3 117	-4.9	195	6.3	2 804	14.2	13.4
Bolivar	13 292	59.4	39 200	21.0	15.5	258	31.5	13.0	17 208	-2.0	1 250	7.3	14 284	23.9	9.3
Calhoun	5 662	80.8	33 900	19.3	13.0	234	22.7	6.3	6 231	-2.1	649	10.4	6 275	14.7	14.4
Carroll	3 352	80.5	34 400	23.5	15.6	224	23.4	10.0	4 548	-2.4	313	6.9	3 543	18.8	15.5
Chickasaw	6 480	78.5	37 800	20.2	12.4	230	24.7	7.3	7 726	-4.4	1 121	14.5	7 816	15.8	16.8
Choctaw	3 217	85.6	36 000	22.5	12.8	235	23.6	7.4	3 458	-4.2	416	12.0	3 285	18.4	17.4
Claiborne	3 342	74.2	39 000	22.6	17.8	240	28.6	13.7	3 223	-5.0	304	9.4	3 078	28.3	9.5
Clarke	6 334	83.6	36 000	21.1	13.4	249	19.8	5.4	8 991	-1.8	843	9.4	7 209	19.3	16.4
Clay	7 251	74.4	41 500	20.4	12.6	262	26.7	9.9	9 559	3.3	984	10.3	8 297	19.8	11.9
Coahoma	10 530	56.7	36 700	21.3	15.5	247	30.0	13.0	11 661	-4.5	973	8.3	9 878	26.6	9.5
Copiah	9 304	79.7	35 600	22.7	14.8	243	28.8	9.2	11 160	-1.1	687	6.2	10 080	18.8	13.0
Covington	5 786	85.4	37 300	23.5	13.7	227	25.1	9.1	8 330	-4.4	371	4.5	6 238	21.1	16.1
De Soto	23 273	81.3	62 400	21.3	12.2	430	27.3	4.8	57 459	0.3	1 553	2.7	33 128	21.2	15.8
Forrest	25 150	60.9	45 200	21.4	12.8	299	28.2	5.1	34 806	-0.2	1 195	3.4	28 133	28.0	11.6
Franklin	3 086	85.0	35 900	22.8	13.4	201	27.7	8.8	2 998	-8.3	247	8.2	2 670	20.2	18.8
George	5 779	86.2	37 500	20.3	13.3	264	26.9	7.0	8 673	-5.0	799	9.2	6 033	18.5	21.7
Greene	3 327	86.4	33 800	21.9	13.8	228	26.2	10.0	3 897	-26.2	335	8.6	3 353	17.5	22.3
Grenada	7 701	70.1	44 300	18.7	13.4	295	24.9	6.6	10 060	-4.4	699	6.9	8 495	20.6	14.5
Hancock	11 817	79.0	52 800	21.1	13.0	331	27.1	5.5	18 224	-3.3	600	3.3	11 201	27.4	16.1
Harrison	59 557	61.4	55 100	20.9	12.4	345	25.5	4.6	85 746	-3.0	3 249	3.8	63 470	29.5	11.9
Hinds	91 023	61.6	57 500	21.4	13.7	390	28.5	6.5	132 070	0.4	5 608	4.2	114 761	31.7	9.0
Holmes	7 139	70.7	30 200	29.6	16.1	206	35.1	14.3	6 533	-8.2	1 176	18.0	5 611	19.4	12.9
Humphreys	3 926	58.7	36 600	24.8	16.2	235	31.2	14.1	4 811	-5.3	618	12.8	4 378	18.3	10.9
Issaquena	633	67.5	35 600	17.5	16.1	213	27.4	15.2	688	-2.0	122	17.7	674	14.5	8.0
Itawamba	7 497	85.3	35 500	19.8	12.4	249	20.8	3.6	11 442	-3.1	533	4.7	9 409	15.1	13.9
Jackson	40 454	73.5	50 900	18.9	13.0	348	25.4	4.8	70 603	-3.3	3 387	4.8	48 343	28.2	17.9
Jasper	5 956	88.3	36 000	22.4	13.7	193	27.0	10.4	8 362	-2.2	403	4.8	6 033	20.7	14.5
Jefferson	2 814	77.7	34 500	27.9	14.6	204	35.1	17.3	2 435	-11.7	421	17.3	2 312	21.5	13.5
Jefferson Davis	4 787	84.6	36 700	22.7	13.7	238	33.5	10.6	4 112	-7.5	436	10.6	4 659	18.0	15.7
Jones	22 506	76.4	41 500	20.3	13.4	269	25.6	5.3	31 781	-1.9	1 055	3.3	24 247	22.4	14.0
Kemper	3 626	80.4	36 600	22.9	13.1	201	25.0	13.0	4 303	-3.9	385	8.9	3 647	17.6	11.1
Lafayette	11 090	61.7	51 100	21.0	12.4	356	33.9	4.4	16 411	-2.3	356	2.2	13 606	34.8	9.2
Lamar	10 883	75.3	55 400	19.1	12.5	333	26.2	3.0	18 386	0.1	477	2.6	13 119	32.0	13.8
Lauderdale	28 232	66.4	47 300	19.1	12.8	297	25.4	5.7	34 249	-3.1	1 780	5.2	30 435	26.0	12.4
Lawrence	4 506	86.4	40 200	23.4	15.2	244	24.5	5.6	4 996	-12.3	464	9.3	4 488	17.2	16.6
Leake	6 788	84.8	34 700	22.3	13.2	211	26.4	9.2	10 056	2.9	538	5.4	6 875	16.4	16.2
Lee	24 450	69.0	54 000	18.8	12.9	319	23.7	3.3	41 193	-2.2	1 835	4.5	31 178	23.6	11.2
Leflore	12 749	52.3	42 700	21.7	13.0	245	30.0	12.0	15 876	-3.0	1 587	10.0	13 082	25.4	8.8
Lincoln	11 089	77.6	43 800	21.8	14.7	259	29.8	5.6	14 450	-2.3	706	4.9	11 433	22.0	12.6
Lowndes	21 402	63.6	49 500	18.9	13.2	322	24.5	6.1	26 695	-1.7	1 934	7.2	25 260	26.3	13.8
Madison	19 276	64.1	66 300	21.9	15.4	437	24.9	8.2	38 973	0.5	1 243	3.2	23 857	37.0	7.9
Marion	9 110	79.5	38 800	25.2	12.6	250	24.4	8.3	10 373	-4.2	549	5.3	8 678	19.7	16.2
Marshall	10 077	79.5	41 900	22.5	13.8	241	25.4	11.8	13 606	-2.9	1 041	7.7	11 389	16.1	18.2
Monroe	13 348	78.0	39 200	19.0	14.4	258	25.9	5.3	15 225	-3.2	1 632	10.7	15 923	15.8	13.8
Montgomery	4 532	74.2	35 400	22.7	16.2	224	27.4	8.3	5 553	-2.0	533	9.6	4 742	20.9	13.1
Neshoba	8 848	80.1	38 000	19.8	13.3	216	22.9	8.3	15 436	-2.1	746	4.8	10 060	18.2	13.8
Newton	7 358	81.5	37 600	20.6	12.1	204	23.8	6.7	8 041	-5.1	461	5.7	8 283	18.0	16.0
Noxubee	4 140	78.2	31 700	21.8	14.1	175	25.4	18.8	4 474	-3.5	506	11.3	4 166	12.7	13.8
Oktibbeha	12 916	59.0	51 200	18.4	13.4	330	33.7	7.2	21 704	0.6	681	3.1	16 243	35.5	8.9
Panola	10 130	76.1	39 300	20.6	13.9	249	24.5	12.4	13 013	-1.9	1 333	10.2	11 167	18.0	12.1
Pearl River	13 760	79.1	45 100	20.8	13.0	290	28.0	5.2	20 913	0.5	715	3.4	14 723	27.0	16.6
Perry	3 802	82.5	34 300	21.3	12.9	227	28.2	9.8	4 153	-3.6	284	6.8	3 801	18.5	16.3
Pike	13 408	74.8	41 000	23.5	14.5	243	28.5	6.7	16 659	-4.5	978	5.9	13 020	21.3	11.8
Pontotoc	8 346	80.5	41 200	19.3	13.1	255	24.1	3.9	13 986	-1.7	709	5.1	10 443	15.8	16.3
Prentiss	8 647	78.9	36 700	21.0	13.4	225	25.7	3.0	12 387	-2.4	583	4.7	10 190	19.0	14.9
Quitman	3 521	68.4	27 900	21.8	15.4	228	29.3	14.6	3 425	-3.5	396	11.6	3 306	19.3	10.4
Rankin	29 858	79.4	64 400	19.4	13.2	423	24.7	4.5	63 633	0.9	1 592	2.5	42 184	30.1	12.9
Scott	8 511	80.7	34 900	21.5	13.7	270	26.5	9.7	12 290	-3.1	558	4.5	9 810	17.5	17.0
Sharkey	2 084	61.2	40 800	22.0	14.5	223	28.4	17.2	2 448	-5.4	318	13.0	2 347	18.7	10.2
Simpson	8 357	81.0	38 900	22.3	12.6	246	27.4	9.4	10 650	-1.0	462	4.3	9 376	18.6	16.9
Smith	5 276	85.7	36 900	21.8	12.9	227	26.9	7.2	5 703	-5.2	304	5.3	5 955	15.1	15.1
Stone	3 685	79.8	39 100	20.7	13.1	263	32.0	5.6	5 156	-1.3	283	5.5	4 189	24.3	14.8

1. Specified owner-occupied units.   2. Specified renter-occupied units.   3. Overcrowded or lacking complete plumbing facilities.   4. Percent of civilian labor force.   5. Persons 16 years and older.

Table B. States and Counties — Nonfarm Employment and Agriculture

	Private nonfarm establishments, employment and payroll, 1999									Agriculture, 1997			
STATE County		Employment						Annual payroll		Farms			Farm operators
											Percent with—		
	Number of establishments	Total	Health Care and Social Assistance	Manufacturing	Retail trade	Finance and Insurance	Professional Scientific and Technical Services	Total (mil dol)	Average per employee (dollars)	Number	Less than 50 acres	500 acres and over	Whose principal occupation is farming (percent)
	104	105	106	107	108	109	110	111	112	113	114	115	116
MISSISSIPPI	59 834	948 883	124 477	223 302	138 089	34 574	26 586	22 172	23 367	31 318	22.3	14.5	40.7
Adams	1 033	11 547	1 845	1 938	2 338	401	231	249	21 529	132	26.5	21.2	37.1
Alcorn	862	13 667	1 673	4 647	2 177	327	193	320	23 411	449	28.5	8.0	26.7
Amite	177	1 600	D	695	230	37	24	35	21 683	471	15.1	9.6	38.2
Attala	406	6 065	693	1 189	1 134	236	71	124	20 514	385	12.7	14.3	34.3
Benton	69	1 049	154	284	136	D	D	21	20 068	213	15.5	17.4	33.8
Bolivar	781	9 865	1 737	2 591	1 746	427	157	208	21 099	394	11.7	57.4	79.7
Calhoun	323	3 425	204	1 854	449	90	44	64	18 735	427	11.5	18.5	44.3
Carroll	118	781	D	D	191	11	D	13	16 794	423	12.8	19.6	36.9
Chickasaw	427	6 988	362	4 310	729	101	59	150	21 398	447	17.4	15.0	36.5
Choctaw	145	1 468	187	558	187	D	7	31	21 345	217	11.1	7.4	33.6
Claiborne	155	2 553	238	651	260	58	D	90	35 344	170	13.5	25.3	40.6
Clarke	321	3 790	383	2 018	275	102	39	80	20 981	269	29.0	8.9	33.5
Clay	422	7 811	601	3 903	764	138	130	206	26 347	367	16.6	14.4	37.9
Coahoma	669	8 695	1 617	1 250	1 469	295	244	200	22 957	181	10.5	59.1	82.9
Copiah	459	5 850	574	2 558	775	150	40	115	19 664	510	18.2	11.6	38.6
Covington	312	4 032	553	1 513	429	99	65	78	19 300	475	22.3	7.4	40.8
De Soto	1 761	29 863	1 883	6 385	4 758	655	826	727	24 338	467	41.8	12.4	32.5
Forrest	2 134	33 173	7 179	4 883	5 660	1 302	998	755	22 754	291	36.8	5.2	39.2
Franklin	150	1 397	310	213	173	D	33	29	20 764	158	17.7	12.0	36.1
George	306	2 915	483	298	770	130	108	50	17 172	419	47.0	3.1	26.7
Greene	123	818	88	D	199	D	D	13	15 672	334	23.4	7.2	29.3
Grenada	627	10 510	1 158	4 321	1 424	268	154	233	22 133	211	13.3	19.9	41.2
Hancock	741	9 107	824	602	1 492	238	1 068	224	24 553	239	33.1	5.0	32.2
Harrison	4 394	79 823	12 715	4 435	10 968	2 702	2 231	1 863	23 338	275	60.0	0.7	25.8
Hinds	6 688	133 677	22 961	8 991	16 972	9 171	6 037	3 688	27 591	723	23.5	13.8	32.5
Holmes	284	3 661	345	1 893	668	97	52	60	16 364	352	11.1	25.0	42.0
Humphreys	178	3 005	203	1 515	340	109	33	49	16 240	240	15.8	45.4	77.1
Issaquena	16	64	D	0	D	D	0	1	16 625	82	7.3	54.9	72.0
Itawamba	337	5 164	301	1 731	640	74	26	107	20 654	387	19.4	9.8	36.4
Jackson	2 346	46 166	4 394	16 660	5 999	881	1 837	1 253	27 132	321	53.9	4.0	33.6
Jasper	273	3 738	276	1 643	451	111	110	76	20 463	367	15.5	7.6	42.5
Jefferson	80	795	180	D	D	D	D	15	18 935	158	12.7	23.4	48.7
Jefferson Davis	187	1 928	341	468	330	52	15	33	17 288	389	16.7	7.5	41.6
Jones	1 466	22 871	2 524	7 885	2 989	590	399	512	22 393	773	37.9	2.6	44.1
Kemper	113	946	129	263	200	51	14	16	17 303	382	17.5	13.6	37.7
Lafayette	887	11 557	2 015	2 120	1 895	263	960	226	19 555	372	12.6	11.3	29.8
Lamar	735	7 750	682	578	2 166	240	282	154	19 875	401	31.4	6.5	38.4
Lauderdale	2 110	32 883	6 470	5 235	5 708	1 232	595	775	23 565	356	25.6	9.6	27.8
Lawrence	223	2 628	284	D	317	51	D	69	26 182	308	16.9	7.5	41.6
Leake	345	6 175	715	3 363	827	171	44	99	16 068	583	22.5	6.2	42.4
Lee	2 308	46 924	6 294	17 184	6 383	1 686	1 335	1 240	26 434	488	27.7	11.9	34.2
Leflore	875	13 556	2 206	4 240	1 918	384	352	284	20 917	246	8.9	56.5	74.8
Lincoln	778	10 557	1 555	1 314	1 641	258	170	239	22 616	499	18.6	6.4	36.9
Lowndes	1 649	24 313	2 424	6 414	3 957	656	1 189	580	23 864	378	22.8	21.4	38.1
Madison	1 879	25 050	2 064	2 308	5 162	1 826	1 156	598	23 860	465	22.2	20.4	33.5
Marion	581	6 764	962	1 054	1 148	224	146	126	18 626	485	23.1	9.3	41.6
Marshall	442	7 101	1 067	1 417	871	210	33	126	17 743	469	21.7	16.6	34.5
Monroe	731	10 767	1 357	4 985	1 392	262	135	262	24 355	504	19.2	18.7	39.9
Montgomery	245	3 177	630	1 053	550	111	30	53	16 528	286	15.7	18.5	36.7
Neshoba	549	9 470	1 102	3 503	1 399	260	76	208	21 935	608	20.1	5.1	41.4
Newton	379	4 839	512	2 265	759	130	39	94	19 498	543	21.0	5.9	45.3
Noxubee	241	2 615	229	1 224	358	94	D	48	18 337	454	16.7	23.3	41.9
Oktibbeha	791	9 602	1 273	2 217	2 097	385	293	181	18 856	329	21.0	14.0	30.4
Panola	651	8 954	740	2 682	1 361	306	213	191	21 291	573	14.7	20.1	35.3
Pearl River	776	7 937	1 052	964	2 382	303	213	138	17 438	609	36.8	6.6	33.7
Perry	154	2 104	259	909	258	64	12	57	27 035	246	32.5	4.9	37.0
Pike	995	13 827	1 720	4 742	2 688	366	229	264	19 065	437	23.3	4.1	46.7
Pontotoc	469	9 420	445	6 455	715	159	215	204	21 635	552	25.0	9.8	29.9
Prentiss	528	7 278	831	3 363	835	180	138	153	21 024	412	20.9	8.3	32.3
Quitman	143	1 235	233	303	258	74	23	21	16 903	179	10.6	50.8	68.2
Rankin	2 541	40 400	6 226	6 120	4 818	2 246	1 047	1 012	25 048	558	26.9	10.6	36.2
Scott	525	9 750	614	5 444	1 082	218	70	175	17 960	674	29.1	5.0	49.0
Sharkey	130	823	228	D	176	D	21	14	17 339	110	9.1	65.5	80.9
Simpson	432	4 415	1 271	288	997	229	104	70	15 752	550	25.5	5.3	44.2
Smith	205	3 042	205	1 796	270	59	37	72	23 687	635	26.8	4.9	52.0
Stone	289	2 613	396	624	428	101	77	52	20 072	212	33.5	5.7	30.2

Table B. States and Counties — Agriculture, Land, and Water

STATE County	Land in farms — Acres — Acreage (1,000)	Percent change, 1992–1997	Average size of farm	Total irrigated (1,000)	Total cropland (1,000)	Value of land and buildings — Average per farm ($1,000)	Value of land and buildings — Average per acre (dollars)	Value of machinery and equipment average per farm ($1,000)	Value of products sold — Total (mil dol)	Value of products sold — Average per farm (dollars)	Percent from — Crops	Percent from — Livestock and poultry products	Percent of farms with sales of — $10,000 or more	Percent of farms with sales of — $100,000 or more	Percent of land owned by fed. gov. 1997	Water consumption 1995 (mil gal/day)
	117	118	119	120	121	122	123	124	125	126	127	128	129	130	131	132
MISSISSIPPI	10 125	-0.6	323	1 076	5 947	337	1 052	52	3 127	99 859	41.3	58.7	33.4	14.4	5.8	3 088.0
Adams	65	-19.3	489	0	29	295	702	39	6	43 844	79.4	20.6	26.5	6.1	9.1	51.2
Alcorn	81	2.0	180	D	43	189	1 205	29	8	16 875	67.1	32.9	19.2	3.3	0.0	3.2
Amite	118	4.5	251	D	43	379	1 699	36	28	59 599	1.8	98.2	27.2	8.9	7.4	2.3
Attala	129	19.2	334	0	43	266	819	35	13	34 164	61.5	38.5	21.6	5.7	0.5	3.9
Benton	81	-10.5	382	D	43	272	797	57	8	38 409	86.8	13.2	30.5	7.0	20.8	0.7
Bolivar	455	6.5	1 154	230	416	1 040	957	256	157	397 286	92.3	7.7	84.3	59.6	1.9	472.4
Calhoun	142	11.7	332	D	83	276	801	70	25	57 856	88.0	12.0	38.9	12.9	4.4	45.9
Carroll	143	-6.0	338	3	64	246	814	51	15	36 565	70.1	29.9	29.6	6.9	0.0	6.4
Chickasaw	138	-7.4	309	D	81	226	750	34	30	67 496	26.3	73.7	32.2	10.1	9.0	2.4
Choctaw	58	34.6	267	D	16	220	722	29	9	39 420	9.9	90.1	22.6	3.7	3.1	2.4
Claiborne	81	-8.7	478	D	29	343	800	41	6	36 493	42.5	57.5	29.4	5.3	1.1	34.4
Clarke	52	-24.6	193	0	19	160	930	22	5	17 796	6.2	93.8	21.9	1.9	0.0	2.9
Clay	132	4.5	359	D	61	250	689	28	11	30 857	38.6	61.4	31.3	7.9	0.7	6.6
Coahoma	273	-7.5	1 507	111	252	1 451	966	276	96	531 588	95.7	4.3	82.9	64.1	0.0	146.4
Copiah	121	-5.0	237	0	45	222	915	29	45	88 751	5.3	94.7	27.5	8.4	1.7	4.8
Covington	86	7.1	180	0	33	242	1 276	28	43	91 479	8.8	91.2	32.0	12.8	0.0	6.9
De Soto	149	6.7	320	7	103	539	1 913	39	27	57 680	87.5	12.5	22.9	8.4	5.6	16.7
Forrest	46	24.4	158	1	16	257	1 851	30	12	41 072	23.2	76.8	21.0	7.6	20.5	41.8
Franklin	42	-9.6	269	0	13	270	935	37	4	23 154	19.9	80.1	17.7	3.8	26.2	1.1
George	42	-2.9	100	1	19	167	1 528	29	9	21 730	67.8	32.2	22.7	6.0	2.8	1.9
Greene	59	20.2	176	0	17	153	1 063	24	12	35 419	7.8	92.2	25.4	5.7	7.2	1.4
Grenada	91	-9.0	431	3	45	313	757	45	10	45 985	73.6	26.4	26.5	8.5	17.8	20.8
Hancock	36	20.8	152	0	17	268	1 725	26	2	8 951	23.0	77.0	19.2	1.3	4.4	6.3
Harrison	18	5.1	65	0	8	223	3 316	32	3	9 354	59.1	40.9	15.6	2.9	16.7	153.4
Hinds	196	-15.0	272	0	89	334	1 226	51	52	71 239	21.7	78.3	23.5	4.6	0.6	48.3
Holmes	190	-14.9	539	36	119	452	915	78	37	105 359	93.9	6.1	33.8	17.0	4.1	47.6
Humphreys	198	10.1	826	43	145	816	1 063	168	124	516 587	40.0	60.0	78.3	62.5	3.0	158.0
Issaquena	113	-1.1	1 375	12	96	1 275	956	253	30	365 415	90.8	9.2	85.4	53.7	0.0	34.4
Itawamba	82	5.9	211	D	37	221	868	29	14	37 416	19.9	80.1	24.8	7.5	2.9	2.1
Jackson	33	30.4	102	0	15	251	2 499	22	5	14 927	54.9	45.1	17.4	1.6	9.8	68.2
Jasper	75	-16.1	204	D	25	240	1 152	35	28	77 577	0.6	99.4	29.4	12.0	3.1	3.1
Jefferson	64	-3.8	402	D	25	348	727	36	8	48 932	53.8	46.2	29.7	7.0	3.0	1.5
Jefferson Davis	79	-2.9	202	0	34	172	988	35	15	39 426	7.3	92.7	26.0	6.4	0.0	2.0
Jones	91	-6.1	118	0	39	230	1 628	36	99	128 511	1.5	98.5	38.7	21.0	7.4	16.6
Kemper	97	4.0	253		33	242	803	23	8	21 911	3.6	96.4	23.0	3.9	0.4	1.6
Lafayette	102	3.2	275	D	44	260	901	28	6	16 465	69.9	30.1	17.7	2.7	19.8	5.2
Lamar	74	39.9	185	0	25	368	1 669	28	34	84 052	6.0	94.0	32.4	9.2	0.0	8.7
Lauderdale	75	-7.7	210	0	22	165	825	23	5	13 295	44.6	55.4	18.0	1.1	1.6	14.7
Lawrence	55	-12.5	179	0	24	216	1 120	36	24	77 334	5.7	94.3	23.4	8.4	0.0	33.7
Leake	104	8.4	178	D	40	201	1 141	37	97	167 008	1.7	98.3	37.7	24.9	0.5	3.8
Lee	135	-3.6	277	D	93	283	1 074	44	21	42 669	60.0	40.0	31.1	9.6	1.0	12.5
Leflore	267	2.0	1 087	93	230	1 271	1 168	271	115	467 318	73.3	26.7	80.9	56.5	1.0	192.9
Lincoln	99	-0.1	198	0	44	240	1 180	32	31	63 091	4.6	95.4	30.5	9.4	2.1	13.3
Lowndes	145	15.2	384	1	71	347	970	41	45	119 865	21.2	78.8	31.0	10.8	2.6	14.9
Madison	182	-8.5	392	D	90	513	1 128	41	24	52 013	77.1	22.9	30.5	12.0	0.8	12.1
Marion	97	8.2	201	0	36	334	1 261	23	29	58 920	1.7	98.3	30.5	10.5	0.5	4.2
Marshall	181	-0.4	387	D	88	437	1 083	43	14	30 068	68.2	31.8	29.9	5.8	11.0	3.2
Monroe	162	-7.2	322	1	100	292	940	49	17	33 508	61.0	39.0	28.4	10.1	2.9	18.5
Montgomery	92	15.4	323	0	38	240	756	38	10	34 928	67.0	33.0	29.0	9.8	0.0	1.9
Neshoba	141	2.6	231	0	51	227	1 081	36	87	143 502	1.0	99.0	37.2	18.6	0.0	3.8
Newton	100	4.5	185	D	44	199	1 152	35	89	162 993	1.2	98.8	38.3	19.5	1.8	3.7
Noxubee	194	-4.2	426	2	100	363	794	54	44	95 942	33.8	66.2	46.7	20.5	3.0	4.1
Oktibbeha	85	5.3	259	0	42	280	1 118	28	9	26 713	17.4	82.6	21.9	4.9	5.7	8.3
Panola	238	9.4	416	10	151	386	956	51	31	54 140	88.1	11.9	33.7	9.4	1.4	14.8
Pearl River	103	10.9	169	0	44	240	1 381	23	9	14 513	26.7	73.3	25.0	3.8	2.5	5.8
Perry	32	-0.3	130	0	11	193	1 285	28	9	37 264	6.4	93.6	20.3	6.9	43.2	20.1
Pike	71	-11.9	161	0	35	253	1 629	22	50	113 449	1.4	98.6	30.0	12.1	0.0	7.2
Pontotoc	115	-7.5	208	0	65	194	886	33	9	15 616	61.9	38.1	19.4	3.1	0.4	2.8
Prentiss	88	2.4	214	D	51	189	921	31	8	18 391	70.0	30.0	21.8	4.4	1.2	2.1
Quitman	170	-8.8	947	29	156	747	786	139	46	257 976	98.0	2.0	74.3	48.0	1.6	111.8
Rankin	117	-1.4	210	0	50	298	1 467	32	51	91 945	8.0	92.0	35.1	13.3	2.0	12.7
Scott	107	-2.3	159	0	46	217	1 345	39	175	258 952	0.7	99.3	46.9	30.3	20.6	10.1
Sharkey	166	-9.0	1 505	22	153	1 266	845	265	59	537 224	81.9	18.1	88.2	72.7	23.3	64.1
Simpson	94	-3.4	170	D	39	227	1 335	33	103	187 502	1.2	98.8	40.2	21.8	0.0	4.0
Smith	95	-0.2	149	0	36	234	1 518	32	129	203 532	0.9	99.1	47.6	30.6	21.4	6.0
Stone	42	25.9	196	0	13	418	2 038	27	4	19 587	43.2	56.9	19.8	3.3	13.8	2.3

Table B. States and Counties — **Residential Construction, Wholesale and Retail Trade, and Real Estate**

STATE County	Value of Residential Construction Authorized by Building Permits, 2000		Wholesale Trade, 1997				Retail Trade[1], 1997				Real Estate and Rental and Leasing, 1997			
	New Construction ($1,000)	Number of Housing Units	Number of Establishments	Number of Employees	Sales (mil dol)	Annual Payroll (mil dol)	Number of Establishments	Number of Employees	Sales (mil dol)	Annual Payroll (mil dol)	Number of Establishments	Number of Employees	Receipts (mil dol)	Annual Payroll (mil dol)
	133	134	135	136	137	138	139	140	141	142	143	144	145	146
MISSISSIPPI	917 764	11 270	3 173	36 520	18 445.2	1 012.1	12 791	138 372	20 774.5	1 935.3	2 125	8 354	794.2	132.1
Adams	675	12	57	369	80.4	9.2	225	2 356	328.9	33.3	46	128	9.3	2.1
Alcorn	3 698	36	49	692	264.3	16.9	200	2 152	315.1	29.4	28	128	7.2	1.9
Amite	251	4	7	D	D	D	44	228	34.6	3.1	2	D	D	D
Attala	2 207	63	18	210	46.2	3.9	93	1 022	146.7	13.9	9	23	0.5	0.1
Benton	68	3	1	D	D	D	24	178	23.6	1.8	1	D	D	D
Bolivar	5 883	77	41	685	355.4	18.8	187	1 775	296.3	24.1	33	77	6.2	0.9
Calhoun	103	1	12	130	27.3	2.7	86	525	63.2	6.6	4	8	0.2	0.0
Carroll	NA	NA	9	32	17.3	0.9	24	161	15.5	1.9	NA	NA	NA	NA
Chickasaw	407	6	29	244	66.6	3.3	94	741	102.0	9.1	14	39	6.6	1.0
Choctaw	130	2	5	D	D	D	29	183	26.5	2.3	1	D	D	D
Claiborne	0	0	1	D	D	D	34	229	46.8	4.3	2	D	D	D
Clarke	466	7	14	142	33.1	2.3	63	325	38.3	3.7	7	13	0.7	0.1
Clay	2 288	25	18	217	561.8	14.1	94	771	109.5	9.4	12	26	2.9	0.4
Coahoma	1 495	22	37	529	203.2	14.3	160	1 613	250.4	22.2	39	100	11.1	1.4
Copiah	348	10	20	187	66.4	3.6	107	815	100.1	9.4	5	30	0.7	0.2
Covington	90	2	15	150	426.1	2.6	63	479	92.4	7.2	7	16	1.0	0.2
De Soto	200 907	2 475	78	D	D	D	278	4 248	663.2	58.5	69	205	31.8	4.1
Forrest	24 340	317	113	1 602	1 282.5	37.6	427	5 509	852.4	77.9	97	410	34.3	5.5
Franklin	450	2	5	D	D	D	37	198	25.4	2.2	4	14	1.4	0.3
George	162	2	12	D	D	D	70	706	92.4	8.0	5	10	0.5	0.1
Greene	0	0	5	92	18.6	1.9	36	203	28.2	2.1	2	D	D	D
Grenada	3 054	34	34	252	123.2	5.6	139	1 506	249.5	20.9	25	99	8.3	1.3
Hancock	45 527	620	30	251	68.8	7.6	128	1 583	214.2	19.9	34	124	9.1	1.7
Harrison	178 633	2 222	195	2 082	650.9	51.9	883	10 553	1 613.9	153.3	208	841	75.3	12.7
Hinds	75 054	873	454	6 671	2 600.7	206.0	1 092	17 356	2 760.8	280.3	295	1 560	152.6	24.6
Holmes	842	11	10	73	22.5	0.6	95	673	95.0	8.6	10	24	2.1	0.3
Humphreys	423	9	14	D	D	D	44	334	70.4	5.0	7	16	1.1	0.2
Issaquena	0	0	2	D	D	D	2	D	D	D	NA	NA	NA	NA
Itawamba	1 042	36	13	188	43.2	3.9	65	555	85.1	6.8	7	11	0.4	0.1
Jackson	66 490	977	70	576	272.6	16.7	512	6 119	948.6	82.3	100	367	29.4	5.6
Jasper	512	19	9	61	11.1	1.5	63	480	76.1	7.2	6	31	4.0	0.7
Jefferson	116	6	4	D	D	D	22	D	D	D	1	D	D	D
Jefferson Davis	0	0	4	17	2.0	0.2	51	357	45.5	4.6	4	8	0.7	0.1
Jones	2 473	12	102	764	211.8	20.8	303	3 059	467.1	43.3	49	275	19.1	6.0
Kemper	0	0	4	D	D	D	37	176	27.7	2.5	1	D	D	D
Lafayette	21 104	259	22	89	46.8	2.0	174	2 099	254.2	26.4	36	150	11.0	1.7
Lamar	570	9	29	D	D	D	170	2 250	283.4	28.0	22	67	7.2	1.3
Lauderdale	5 448	98	106	1 869	973.6	50.4	496	5 305	793.7	76.2	74	259	23.7	3.7
Lawrence	350	4	9	43	8.5	0.6	62	350	40.1	4.0	4	8	0.8	0.0
Leake	590	8	17	105	17.7	1.5	99	769	125.2	10.9	4	D	D	D
Lee	10 319	112	201	2 121	831.0	56.7	541	6 341	975.8	92.3	73	353	32.9	6.0
Leflore	2 330	20	56	803	905.1	23.4	222	2 033	277.8	26.4	40	95	9.7	1.3
Lincoln	770	8	37	762	415.6	17.9	164	1 809	315.2	24.7	20	75	7.2	1.5
Lowndes	16 817	170	93	1 098	333.5	30.0	367	3 856	601.2	54.3	58	332	27.5	5.2
Madison	84 353	606	118	1 565	1 180.0	45.4	377	4 987	679.8	69.6	72	235	28.6	4.5
Marion	265	3	29	D	D	D	130	1 154	167.4	15.0	14	41	4.2	0.6
Marshall	3 983	76	14	99	46.1	2.1	115	892	102.0	10.8	14	38	2.1	0.5
Monroe	1 243	19	33	200	104.5	5.4	169	1 525	228.1	21.3	18	50	3.1	0.5
Montgomery	2 182	84	10	57	20.7	1.0	68	507	63.1	5.5	2	D	D	D
Neshoba	1 383	14	32	297	85.3	5.9	117	1 384	226.0	18.4	9	150	17.5	3.0
Newton	860	16	8	D	D	D	91	829	116.0	10.6	9	18	1.1	0.4
Noxubee	200	3	9	57	21.2	0.9	62	378	50.9	4.3	4	4	0.3	0.1
Oktibbeha	14 846	356	11	63	25.3	1.5	172	2 029	241.4	23.5	37	109	12.7	2.0
Panola	1 058	18	37	465	248.0	14.6	186	1 525	239.7	20.8	14	32	2.3	0.4
Pearl River	29 109	340	34	276	58.0	3.8	178	2 086	336.3	30.2	26	83	9.5	1.1
Perry	465	4	3	D	D	D	36	253	29.4	2.7	4	7	0.7	0.1
Pike	1 089	12	64	527	164.0	11.9	252	2 339	343.0	33.2	34	130	9.6	1.6
Pontotoc	4 688	80	24	204	73.1	4.6	103	808	120.2	9.7	10	37	2.1	0.7
Prentiss	2 129	24	29	223	85.3	4.7	129	891	138.4	11.5	16	28	1.9	0.2
Quitman	41	1	4	D	D	D	35	249	44.4	3.9	4	4	0.8	0.1
Rankin	75 111	791	200	3 150	1 609.8	112.2	350	5 001	808.9	72.9	92	429	74.2	9.6
Scott	1 818	17	34	208	103.6	3.6	144	1 216	156.2	14.6	8	28	1.3	0.3
Sharkey	120	4	10	91	18.3	1.8	33	204	25.4	2.8	6	11	1.0	0.1
Simpson	2 684	32	13	76	31.3	1.6	103	1 039	147.9	13.3	13	33	1.9	0.3
Smith	352	4	7	D	D	D	49	279	35.5	3.4	5	16	2.3	0.3
Stone	605	10	17	76	17.0	1.3	59	425	63.6	6.7	7	26	1.8	0.3

1. Establishments with payroll.

STATE County	Professional, Scientific, and Technical Services[1], 1997				Manufacturing, 1997				Accommodation and Foodservices, 1997			
	Number of Establishments	Number of Employees	Receipts (mil dol)	Annual Payroll (mil dol)	Number of Establishments	Number of Employees	Receipts (mil dol)	Annual Payroll (mil dol)	Number of Establishments	Number of Employees	Sales (mil dol)	Annual Payroll (mil dol)
	147	148	149	150	151	152	153	154	155	156	157	158
MISSISSIPPI	3 627	21 671	1 761.6	662.1	3 008	227 800	39 658.3	5 599.4	4 050	84 834	3 064.8	814.5
Adams	66	234	14.9	3.9	38	2 299	550.0	76.0	88	1 189	37.7	10.3
Alcorn	43	191	10.7	3.6	58	4 918	955.6	150.8	66	913	26.9	6.8
Amite	11	22	4.2	0.3	10	691	97.3	17.2	4	D	D	D
Attala	17	39	8.5	2.2	22	1 267	119.9	21.8	28	373	10.8	2.3
Benton	3	D	D	D	NA	NA	NA	NA	1	D	D	D
Bolivar	42	139	10.2	3.6	22	2 724	417.8	67.0	49	626	17.9	4.3
Calhoun	15	47	4.0	1.1	34	1 874	296.2	35.4	16	D	D	D
Carroll	4	7	0.5	0.1	NA	NA	NA	NA	2	D	D	D
Chickasaw	16	62	2.2	0.7	80	4 896	420.8	93.4	27	D	D	D
Choctaw	3	D	D	D	10	598	105.0	13.9	5	D	D	D
Claiborne	7	15	1.1	0.2	10	629	88.6	13.9	6	46	1.5	0.4
Clarke	15	41	2.4	0.8	18	2 084	304.1	51.4	12	94	3.4	0.9
Clay	18	103	5.8	2.3	25	3 640	926.0	113.6	32	408	11.5	3.1
Coahoma	44	246	19.3	7.9	28	1 353	236.6	35.6	37	540	17.2	4.3
Copiah	15	50	3.5	0.8	32	2 735	407.7	52.6	30	425	12.6	3.0
Covington	12	37	2.5	0.7	17	1 950	194.2	32.2	15	D	D	D
De Soto	83	445	24.4	8.7	131	7 232	1 369.6	213.4	114	2 639	72.7	18.6
Forrest	166	799	61.1	19.8	84	5 170	1 037.1	116.3	163	D	D	D
Franklin	7	39	2.2	0.8	NA	NA	NA	NA	4	D	D	D
George	19	73	4.4	1.9	NA	NA	NA	NA	25	D	D	D
Greene	5	9	0.3	0.1	NA	NA	NA	NA	9	78	1.8	0.5
Grenada	29	127	8.8	4.1	24	4 194	571.8	109.5	46	806	24.4	5.9
Hancock	55	614	54.2	23.5	NA	NA	NA	NA	72	784	24.7	6.2
Harrison	335	2 049	152.0	55.6	139	4 498	1 079.7	133.6	377	9 573	323.4	87.8
Hinds	652	5 400	544.0	216.5	208	11 540	2 484.4	314.8	449	10 351	322.4	92.6
Holmes	7	27	3.2	0.5	14	1 674	214.5	31.4	18	113	3.1	0.8
Humphreys	7	21	1.4	0.4	4	D	D	D	9	D	D	D
Issaquena	NA	NA	NA	NA	NA	NA	NA	NA	NA	NA	NA	NA
Itawamba	10	31	1.3	0.5	40	1 366	371.6	30.1	29	341	6.9	1.5
Jackson	161	1 603	134.3	61.4	98	16 340	4 447.7	534.5	191	3 469	97.4	25.5
Jasper	16	150	6.8	3.3	15	1 720	151.3	30.0	12	D	D	D
Jefferson	4	12	1.3	0.1	NA	NA	NA	NA	5	131	2.3	0.5
Jefferson Davis	7	13	0.5	0.1	9	769	56.0	8.9	16	D	D	D
Jones	83	478	48.2	12.1	68	6 820	991.3	162.7	84	1 309	37.3	10.0
Kemper	2	D	D	D	NA	NA	NA	NA	4	30	0.6	0.2
Lafayette	70	422	27.6	14.1	29	2 017	304.5	43.2	109	1 665	43.2	11.5
Lamar	36	195	14.1	6.4	22	770	116.8	16.4	48	D	D	D
Lauderdale	117	483	33.9	10.6	83	6 076	916.6	164.2	147	2 855	87.4	23.9
Lawrence	4	10	0.6	0.1	9	D	D	D	15	126	2.9	0.7
Leake	16	36	1.5	0.3	18	2 481	242.0	29.8	20	D	D	D
Lee	140	865	64.0	26.6	191	17 717	2 708.4	472.9	158	3 037	84.7	23.2
Leflore	63	324	23.6	7.8	40	3 572	510.9	76.6	51	841	28.0	7.3
Lincoln	41	298	17.0	7.0	28	1 383	301.4	35.1	42	715	21.2	5.2
Lowndes	90	459	31.4	12.3	71	7 611	1 313.9	223.2	105	2 071	59.5	14.9
Madison	131	1 042	103.7	32.2	57	2 414	396.6	57.2	113	2 402	78.8	20.8
Marion	21	112	5.7	2.9	26	1 000	103.9	15.7	32	434	10.5	2.8
Marshall	20	32	4.3	0.6	29	1 777	201.3	41.2	19	322	7.7	1.9
Monroe	35	114	5.5	1.5	71	4 889	1 121.2	124.8	46	503	13.4	3.1
Montgomery	10	54	3.2	0.7	21	1 165	116.6	21.8	20	196	5.4	1.3
Neshoba	18	69	4.7	1.7	32	2 572	347.8	57.1	37	725	17.1	3.8
Newton	16	232	5.9	3.1	20	2 256	165.7	49.5	26	D	D	D
Noxubee	8	27	0.6	0.1	20	1 201	210.8	22.8	8	105	3.0	1.0
Oktibbeha	61	286	12.6	4.1	35	2 132	372.3	49.8	85	1 546	40.2	10.2
Panola	30	201	11.0	5.4	44	2 943	575.0	68.5	46	829	23.0	5.6
Pearl River	49	174	13.6	5.2	47	905	190.3	20.3	66	877	23.2	5.7
Perry	5	14	0.8	0.2	7	D	D	D	6	68	1.5	0.4
Pike	52	163	10.7	3.2	36	3 924	580.3	64.7	61	923	26.0	6.5
Pontotoc	19	75	4.3	1.1	92	5 549	720.2	116.5	25	340	8.0	1.9
Prentiss	21	87	7.5	2.0	46	4 507	702.2	86.1	34	425	10.9	2.8
Quitman	6	21	0.7	0.2	NA	NA	NA	NA	5	D	D	D
Rankin	129	740	73.8	24.4	127	5 763	1 088.2	150.3	127	2 286	78.1	20.7
Scott	19	66	2.9	1.1	28	5 487	607.4	95.8	36	448	13.0	3.4
Sharkey	7	22	1.4	0.6	NA	NA	NA	NA	3	D	D	D
Simpson	22	86	6.0	2.1	15	1 182	360.4	22.2	21	D	D	D
Smith	13	41	4.0	0.5	17	1 801	392.8	41.2	8	53	1.6	0.4
Stone	13	65	5.2	1.8	15	682	124.6	15.3	18	D	D	D

1. Firms subject to federal tax.

STATE County	Health Care and Social Assistance[1], 1997				Other Services[1], 1997				Federal funds and grants, fiscal 2001[2] Expenditures (mil dol)			
										Direct payments for individuals[3]		
	Number of Establishments	Number of Employees	Receipts (mil dol)	Annual Payroll (mil dol)	Number of Establishments	Number of Employees	Receipts (mil dol)	Annual Payroll (mil dol)	Total	Social Security and government retirement	Medicare	Food stamps and Supplemental Security Income
	159	160	161	162	163	164	165	166	167	168	169	170
MISSISSIPPI	4 139	55 529	3 632.3	1 547.0	3 491	17 449	1 057.1	299.6	20 211.6	5 997.6	2 441.3	878.2
Adams	82	1 136	74.8	29.7	55	260	13.0	4.0	202.0	82.7	30.1	14.6
Alcorn	73	540	32.5	11.9	55	163	9.2	2.5	173.8	83.4	34.9	10.5
Amite	5	20	1.5	0.7	5	42	1.3	0.4	73.6	29.5	13.6	5.4
Attala	21	309	15.3	6.6	29	132	12.2	2.3	117.1	48.0	22.9	8.4
Benton	6	112	3.8	1.9	3	3	0.2	0.0	55.7	18.2	8.5	6.1
Bolivar	48	735	38.7	15.2	49	167	12.9	2.7	306.1	66.9	35.4	26.6
Calhoun	19	153	8.2	2.6	12	55	2.5	0.6	93.3	34.8	17.5	5.1
Carroll	6	23	0.9	0.4	8	17	1.8	0.2	62.9	18.4	8.3	3.2
Chickasaw	27	396	20.7	8.0	22	64	3.2	0.8	113.5	44.6	20.0	6.5
Choctaw	8	37	2.7	0.8	7	18	1.6	0.3	44.5	17.1	6.8	5.0
Claiborne	12	149	5.8	2.9	7	14	0.6	0.1	60.5	18.9	10.6	6.9
Clarke	17	185	7.8	3.0	16	53	2.9	0.7	99.3	41.9	17.2	5.8
Clay	34	271	12.4	4.8	29	150	10.7	3.1	106.9	43.3	16.1	8.1
Coahoma	63	1 435	96.3	31.8	45	169	7.8	2.3	258.8	54.6	35.3	18.9
Copiah	26	431	16.0	6.5	27	109	8.1	1.7	169.3	69.1	31.1	10.8
Covington	13	130	5.7	2.3	16	66	6.0	1.3	95.6	42.4	17.8	6.6
De Soto	87	859	62.2	26.0	112	533	35.9	9.8	308.8	184.1	48.9	9.7
Forrest	122	2 562	159.7	91.3	101	753	45.2	12.9	452.1	174.5	68.3	22.3
Franklin	7	92	3.6	1.8	6	27	1.3	0.4	46.8	18.6	8.1	2.7
George	12	166	8.9	3.1	27	79	4.0	0.9	87.8	45.9	19.6	5.3
Greene	6	103	3.7	1.3	8	32	1.9	0.7	46.5	19.0	10.0	2.8
Grenada	59	652	39.1	14.4	29	133	10.6	2.3	142.5	51.7	29.8	9.0
Hancock	48	322	19.4	7.8	45	187	8.8	2.9	511.3	107.7	37.5	11.0
Harrison	372	5 503	407.7	157.6	284	1 663	89.6	28.6	1 610.1	534.8	170.0	48.3
Hinds	528	7 452	562.2	250.5	391	3 003	176.0	55.8	2 192.5	527.3	201.6	85.4
Holmes	20	267	14.0	6.0	15	43	2.0	0.4	179.1	40.1	30.0	16.6
Humphreys	14	159	6.7	3.0	15	36	2.9	0.5	103.4	18.7	15.7	7.4
Issaquena	NA	NA	NA	NA	NA	NA	NA	NA	30.7	2.0	1.3	0.7
Itawamba	19	309	9.6	4.2	19	60	2.7	0.6	93.0	39.8	17.9	3.0
Jackson	237	1 763	124.0	53.4	162	744	41.0	11.7	1 210.3	299.0	95.4	22.1
Jasper	14	64	2.5	1.0	16	82	5.5	1.4	95.5	39.0	17.0	7.4
Jefferson	3	15	0.8	0.1	4	9	0.4	0.1	72.5	16.9	8.6	6.0
Jefferson Davis	12	62	3.1	1.2	7	19	1.3	0.3	74.9	27.0	13.3	5.8
Jones	76	1 147	65.7	32.0	101	543	33.3	8.9	336.6	155.1	65.2	18.9
Kemper	4	140	3.7	1.9	6	11	0.7	0.2	65.1	20.9	8.8	4.0
Lafayette	72	713	58.8	25.9	40	238	10.1	3.3	158.1	54.7	16.6	3.0
Lamar	61	745	67.0	29.7	27	107	8.4	2.0	107.5	55.5	20.4	5.7
Lauderdale	149	2 063	164.4	82.5	136	690	36.6	10.7	541.3	188.3	76.5	24.8
Lawrence	11	120	4.3	1.4	7	27	2.5	0.5	85.9	40.5	16.9	4.7
Leake	25	775	37.9	18.5	18	44	3.8	0.8	132.6	47.6	25.9	4.6
Lee	161	2 064	168.4	92.8	127	859	52.7	21.9	340.6	160.2	55.6	13.9
Leflore	67	954	61.6	26.2	57	325	17.6	5.4	1 287.6	64.3	41.9	21.1
Lincoln	55	739	42.8	16.4	34	191	11.7	2.7	154.0	69.7	26.5	9.5
Lowndes	132	1 159	79.5	29.4	102	540	33.1	9.5	387.6	127.6	38.3	18.4
Madison	87	758	46.4	21.7	74	482	45.1	11.4	561.4	125.9	39.7	14.3
Marion	32	419	22.4	8.8	37	142	8.8	2.1	152.4	62.0	29.1	10.3
Marshall	19	332	17.2	5.9	16	86	3.8	1.1	181.2	63.4	25.8	12.7
Monroe	46	586	27.8	12.0	60	182	13.3	2.8	189.1	83.2	36.2	9.3
Montgomery	17	210	9.1	4.1	17	59	3.6	0.6	88.6	29.8	17.2	3.2
Neshoba	22	535	31.8	15.0	38	133	9.9	2.4	148.9	51.7	26.7	8.0
Newton	27	432	21.9	8.3	22	46	3.2	0.8	131.9	58.5	30.5	6.6
Noxubee	12	53	2.5	1.2	9	22	1.6	0.3	88.2	22.7	9.4	7.9
Oktibbeha	63	625	32.7	12.6	58	252	11.4	3.4	231.7	65.5	18.9	12.0
Panola	50	646	33.1	13.2	25	84	4.4	1.0	179.1	67.5	28.1	14.5
Pearl River	59	451	23.7	9.1	43	206	10.1	2.9	219.9	116.8	46.0	9.7
Perry	6	41	2.0	0.6	10	38	2.3	0.7	51.2	23.6	8.9	4.2
Pike	72	680	40.7	18.4	48	245	12.8	3.7	218.8	92.3	43.3	14.3
Pontotoc	28	285	10.6	4.1	32	104	5.2	1.3	105.1	49.1	20.3	4.2
Prentiss	37	331	14.7	6.3	37	148	10.1	2.8	126.0	58.6	22.7	6.2
Quitman	7	219	11.3	4.1	12	36	2.1	0.3	94.7	19.1	12.3	5.2
Rankin	154	3 534	269.9	104.4	143	744	55.9	13.4	350.6	200.1	58.9	11.5
Scott	25	290	15.0	6.2	32	173	10.1	2.9	141.0	56.2	29.6	8.7
Sharkey	11	138	6.3	2.5	10	19	1.0	0.2	64.8	11.1	7.4	5.5
Simpson	35	855	31.4	12.9	23	65	4.5	0.9	120.8	57.7	25.8	8.2
Smith	8	171	4.7	2.3	8	10	1.1	0.2	69.2	31.1	12.3	3.6
Stone	18	390	31.8	9.3	12	34	2.3	0.7	76.0	36.8	14.5	3.3

1. Firms subject to federal tax.   2. October 1, 2000 to September 30, 2001.   3. State totals may include programs not allocated by county.

	Federal funds and grants, fiscal 2001[1] (cont'd)							Local government finances, 1997				
	Expenditures (mil dol) (cont'd)							General revenue				
STATE County	Procurement contract awards			Grants[2]							Taxes	
											Per capita[3] (dollars)	
	Salaries and wages	Defense	Other	Medicaid and other health-related	Nutrition and family welfare	Education	Other	Total (mil dol)	Intergovern-mental (mil dol)	Total (mil dol)	Total	Property
	171	172	173	174	175	176	177	178	179	180	181	182
MISSISSIPPI	1 725.2	1 355.3	507.5	2 188.5	594.7	386.5	1 076.7	X	X	X	X	X
Adams	6.8	4.7	4.0	32.9	9.0	2.4	1.8	97.3	30.6	19.6	566	512
Alcorn	5.3	0.2	1.6	25.6	2.0	1.8	1.3	104.5	37.1	12.3	376	342
Amite	2.7	0.0	0.6	13.4	1.5	1.0	4.9	15.0	9.2	3.5	253	233
Attala	3.3	0.1	1.3	23.1	2.2	1.5	1.3	43.0	15.6	7.7	417	394
Benton	1.3	0.0	0.5	10.5	1.8	0.5	5.6	9.9	6.3	2.7	335	334
Bolivar	5.3	0.9	1.5	64.0	11.7	5.2	11.5	88.6	43.7	16.8	415	398
Calhoun	3.0	1.4	0.7	17.2	1.5	0.6	2.0	22.6	12.5	4.8	318	292
Carroll	1.3	0.1	0.3	9.6	1.0	0.6	13.1	11.5	5.9	3.2	318	314
Chickasaw	3.3	0.0	0.7	22.1	1.9	0.9	5.0	24.9	15.5	6.1	335	322
Choctaw	2.4	0.0	0.3	9.3	1.2	0.6	1.1	19.6	8.4	2.6	275	256
Claiborne	1.4	0.0	0.2	13.4	1.9	0.9	2.0	51.3	16.6	2.6	222	214
Clarke	2.1	0.0	0.5	17.5	1.8	1.0	10.5	26.5	13.2	7.2	400	362
Clay	4.6	0.0	1.2	18.9	3.1	3.1	1.7	29.9	18.1	8.4	391	340
Coahoma	5.4	1.4	0.8	50.4	10.6	5.1	21.4	64.7	39.3	13.7	437	423
Copiah	4.8	2.5	5.9	29.2	3.6	2.7	0.7	48.6	25.8	11.5	399	376
Covington	3.4	0.0	0.5	19.0	2.2	1.8	0.9	34.0	14.3	6.6	374	356
De Soto	8.3	0.5	2.6	24.0	3.6	1.5	11.0	110.6	53.7	42.4	461	427
Forrest	45.5	12.4	5.2	38.4	8.4	6.5	38.1	283.2	61.6	42.0	569	514
Franklin	2.8	0.0	2.0	7.5	1.1	0.6	2.8	14.5	9.8	3.1	374	370
George	2.6	0.1	0.6	6.6	1.8	0.9	2.4	20.6	13.5	5.3	282	255
Greene	1.0	0.1	0.3	8.4	1.2	2.4	0.6	12.9	8.6	3.2	269	248
Grenada	11.5	5.5	1.9	19.4	2.3	1.2	3.0	62.1	19.7	10.5	468	433
Hancock	111.3	63.8	147.9	7.7	2.8	1.6	15.6	80.6	23.2	19.2	488	453
Harrison	551.4	131.3	29.2	65.5	15.3	11.2	19.6	488.5	152.4	136.1	775	608
Hinds	245.4	22.9	44.8	259.2	218.4	139.9	330.5	527.0	243.2	185.2	748	702
Holmes	3.4	0.5	0.9	46.7	5.9	3.0	7.2	41.8	27.4	8.0	371	346
Humphreys	1.6	3.1	0.4	19.7	2.8	1.4	3.5	19.9	10.5	4.7	418	381
Issaquena	0.3	9.9	0.1	1.8	0.6	0.0	1.6	1.9	0.6	1.0	583	564
Itawamba	2.6	4.5	0.5	14.2	1.2	0.6	0.8	51.8	29.4	10.0	473	471
Jackson	95.7	634.4	4.4	21.6	11.8	6.2	8.2	379.4	89.6	90.9	707	648
Jasper	3.2	0.8	0.5	20.9	2.3	1.3	1.6	28.4	13.1	6.3	357	332
Jefferson	1.4	0.1	0.2	17.0	1.9	4.3	5.4	15.5	8.3	3.3	388	373
Jefferson Davis	1.6	0.0	0.3	16.6	6.7	1.1	1.6	16.9	10.7	4.0	288	282
Jones	13.2	0.2	11.3	43.6	5.7	4.1	3.9	169.4	66.4	27.7	437	401
Kemper	1.9	0.3	0.4	14.0	1.3	0.8	5.8	24.5	14.0	4.9	472	462
Lafayette	17.7	11.0	3.9	17.3	2.2	1.2	17.3	45.6	26.3	12.2	356	334
Lamar	3.0	0.0	0.6	11.7	2.2	2.0	4.9	48.7	24.2	13.2	368	357
Lauderdale	99.6	35.9	6.1	57.9	7.6	4.4	24.7	144.2	78.3	40.1	523	482
Lawrence	3.7	0.0	0.6	12.3	1.5	1.2	3.2	23.4	10.2	7.0	541	531
Leake	4.4	0.0	0.9	24.8	2.1	1.4	18.3	22.5	13.7	5.1	262	261
Lee	30.0	0.5	5.6	34.9	8.0	4.6	5.0	137.9	67.7	43.6	590	569
Leflore	10.6	2.1	0.9	48.4	7.1	7.7	12.5	106.9	34.7	18.1	488	468
Lincoln	5.7	0.0	0.9	21.1	3.1	1.8	12.1	44.5	23.6	12.1	383	364
Lowndes	76.8	53.3	4.8	38.9	5.5	3.6	2.9	103.5	57.6	30.8	504	464
Madison	11.0	204.1	59.5	37.0	6.2	4.6	39.6	124.4	55.6	32.8	462	434
Marion	3.7	6.0	1.2	25.6	9.0	1.8	1.2	48.8	24.1	8.2	308	289
Marshall	5.1	0.3	1.2	35.3	19.1	3.8	3.0	61.3	27.2	9.9	307	281
Monroe	5.8	0.1	1.9	28.4	3.4	1.9	4.6	61.0	28.8	12.0	314	307
Montgomery	4.2	1.8	0.5	19.6	6.6	1.0	2.0	24.8	10.1	4.4	356	325
Neshoba	5.5	0.0	1.1	23.1	5.3	3.8	5.1	28.3	17.4	6.8	252	222
Newton	5.2	0.0	0.8	20.7	1.9	0.9	0.6	43.9	23.9	6.9	322	296
Noxubee	2.2	0.4	0.6	23.3	2.8	1.2	8.4	23.8	10.7	4.3	352	321
Oktibbeha	17.3	5.1	10.8	26.7	3.9	7.1	43.8	77.9	28.0	15.6	399	363
Panola	5.9	0.2	0.8	33.5	4.5	2.4	4.0	51.5	27.8	12.7	387	358
Pearl River	7.9	2.6	1.5	17.9	3.6	2.2	2.4	72.7	43.5	17.2	378	362
Perry	1.5	0.0	0.3	8.6	1.4	0.8	0.4	63.6	11.3	4.7	397	374
Pike	10.4	0.1	2.2	34.2	5.0	3.0	1.9	113.3	39.1	15.8	415	398
Pontotoc	3.2	0.0	0.7	17.2	1.5	0.8	2.4	30.2	18.1	7.0	283	272
Prentiss	3.6	0.0	0.5	21.6	1.6	1.3	2.0	55.6	34.5	8.2	339	336
Quitman	1.5	0.0	0.4	20.8	3.0	1.5	5.4	19.7	8.7	4.1	422	370
Rankin	34.2	1.2	2.3	23.2	4.0	3.0	6.2	174.1	68.9	50.9	476	441
Scott	9.0	0.0	1.3	24.2	3.2	1.4	0.7	38.1	22.9	9.5	376	324
Sharkey	1.6	0.0	0.3	10.0	1.5	1.0	2.5	12.3	7.8	3.4	511	496
Simpson	3.1	0.0	1.1	18.4	2.3	1.6	0.5	38.9	18.8	8.4	332	304
Smith	3.1	0.0	0.3	14.9	1.3	0.8	1.2	19.9	12.0	4.7	310	283
Stone	3.9	0.0	0.8	4.8	1.1	1.1	0.5	73.0	38.3	15.7	1 220	1 209

1. October 1, 2000 to September 30, 2001.   2. State totals may include programs not allocated by county.   3. Based on the resident population estimated as of July 1 of the year shown.

Table B. States and Counties — Local Government Finances, Government Employment, and Elections

STATE County	Total (mil dol)	Per capita[1] (dollars)	Education	Health and hospitals	Police protection	Public welfare	Highways	Total (mil dol)	Per capita[1] (dollars)	Federal civilian	Federal military	State and local	Democratic	Republican	All other
	Direct general expenditure		Percent of total for —					Debt outstanding		Government employment, 1999			Percent of vote cast —		
	183	184	185	186	187	188	189	190	191	192	193	194	195	196	197
MISSISSIPPI	X	X	X	X	X	X	X	X	X	26 033	35 129	203 584	40.7	57.6	1.7
Adams	88.5	2 563	30.0	36.1	5.1	0.2	4.6	74.8	2 165	136	234	2 146	54.2	45.0	0.8
Alcorn	105.8	3 232	23.9	45.4	2.0	0.3	4.9	41.6	1 270	100	220	2 348	40.0	57.4	2.6
Amite	14.1	1 027	60.1	0.8	7.7	0.0	12.4	3.4	249	68	93	403	41.7	57.4	0.9
Attala	42.1	2 289	36.2	26.3	3.5	1.1	9.1	5.5	299	65	122	974	40.7	58.6	0.6
Benton	9.1	1 136	61.7	0.3	4.2	0.4	10.5	1.0	120	22	54	287	54.2	44.8	1.0
Bolivar	86.6	2 135	44.4	27.7	4.3	0.7	5.5	24.7	610	101	265	3 651	62.3	35.8	1.9
Calhoun	21.4	1 421	54.2	13.9	4.6	0.1	8.1	7.9	524	42	99	777	39.1	59.9	1.0
Carroll	10.1	1 000	61.8	0.7	3.5	0.7	15.2	2.3	227	29	66	329	35.1	64.3	0.7
Chickasaw	26.3	1 440	61.3	0.6	7.5	0.0	11.7	8.4	457	53	121	783	49.0	49.5	1.5
Choctaw	16.2	1 739	50.8	15.6	3.9	9.3	10.3	4.7	510	65	62	378	34.4	64.5	1.1
Claiborne	48.8	4 160	19.3	9.0	1.8	0.1	2.8	325.8	27 776	31	77	1 656	79.5	19.1	1.4
Clarke	23.2	1 288	59.6	1.0	5.7	0.7	11.0	11.7	649	39	123	756	34.2	65.1	0.6
Clay	32.9	1 526	55.1	2.5	3.8	0.8	1.2	15.7	726	85	144	889	55.3	43.7	1.0
Coahoma	65.8	2 101	61.1	0.3	6.1	0.3	5.1	44.2	1 412	92	207	2 246	59.3	38.7	2.0
Copiah	49.8	1 722	71.6	1.1	5.5	0.0	7.9	16.2	562	70	192	2 141	45.8	53.3	0.9
Covington	31.5	1 800	49.5	23.4	5.5	0.3	5.2	3.0	169	68	119	913	38.1	60.7	1.1
De Soto	116.7	1 268	58.6	1.6	6.5	0.0	9.2	111.4	1 211	140	680	3 498	27.4	71.2	1.4
Forrest	299.0	4 054	18.6	59.9	2.7	0.2	2.4	105.7	1 433	707	726	11 033	38.2	59.7	2.1
Franklin	12.7	1 541	68.1	1.7	3.4	0.6	10.5	1.8	223	66	54	515	37.6	61.4	1.0
George	20.3	1 072	65.1	1.0	6.1	0.0	15.5	7.6	405	47	134	1 141	27.1	70.6	2.2
Greene	12.8	1 080	64.0	1.4	3.8	0.5	10.1	6.2	527	17	84	1 095	29.7	69.5	0.8
Grenada	62.5	2 782	29.3	42.9	3.7	0.0	9.7	23.4	1 043	240	150	1 640	44.1	54.9	1.0
Hancock	75.8	1 931	34.6	25.3	4.6	0.2	5.9	53.0	1 349	1 674	543	1 980	33.0	64.1	2.9
Harrison	516.0	2 938	32.4	25.9	5.0	1.0	4.3	359.7	2 048	6 206	12 005	11 337	36.4	61.3	2.4
Hinds	532.3	2 151	51.0	1.1	7.3	1.0	5.6	399.6	1 615	4 601	1 847	33 331	53.3	43.0	3.7
Holmes	42.1	1 967	77.2	1.4	3.2	0.5	5.4	10.2	474	65	144	1 173	73.4	26.1	0.5
Humphreys	21.8	1 931	50.3	12.1	4.1	0.6	9.9	5.8	514	34	75	619	58.0	41.3	0.7
Issaquena	3.7	2 282	0.0	1.7	9.0	0.0	14.3	5.7	3 486	0	11	97	59.0	38.9	2.1
Itawamba	51.7	2 456	83.1	0.2	1.7	0.1	4.7	22.4	1 065	53	140	944	35.0	63.3	1.7
Jackson	418.2	3 253	29.6	36.3	3.0	0.2	4.8	685.6	5 333	843	2 788	8 751	31.5	66.7	1.9
Jasper	27.2	1 546	52.1	20.1	3.1	0.1	8.3	13.3	756	57	121	901	48.1	51.1	0.8
Jefferson	19.3	2 280	45.7	10.7	3.4	0.0	12.3	13.4	1 576	25	60	700	81.7	17.6	0.7
Jefferson Davis	16.4	1 175	69.7	0.7	4.0	0.4	8.0	0.9	66	29	92	748	53.3	45.8	0.8
Jones	174.1	2 745	45.3	30.5	2.5	0.3	3.8	158.5	2 500	253	420	6 320	31.7	67.1	1.2
Kemper	23.6	2 270	78.5	0.0	2.2	0.1	10.4	1.1	103	35	70	532	54.2	44.9	0.8
Lafayette	44.9	1 307	55.9	0.6	6.5	0.0	7.2	37.1	1 078	308	262	5 684	40.5	55.9	3.6
Lamar	50.3	1 405	56.9	4.2	3.5	0.3	8.7	55.5	1 550	49	254	1 407	20.9	77.1	2.0
Lauderdale	129.6	1 689	60.0	3.0	5.3	0.0	5.0	105.6	1 376	884	2 222	5 957	32.4	66.7	0.9
Lawrence	22.8	1 762	50.3	22.8	2.6	1.5	8.1	12.0	925	54	87	711	43.1	55.8	1.1
Leake	22.5	1 159	62.6	0.7	4.6	0.2	8.5	5.5	284	87	131	739	40.2	59.2	0.7
Lee	126.0	1 703	51.5	0.7	6.2	0.2	11.8	111.0	1 501	499	547	4 677	36.4	62.0	1.6
Leflore	104.6	2 814	31.1	41.8	4.5	0.9	4.2	34.2	921	176	250	3 772	56.8	41.0	2.2
Lincoln	44.2	1 394	60.7	0.8	4.9	0.7	8.1	35.4	1 117	102	214	1 550	33.5	65.7	0.8
Lowndes	111.6	1 823	44.9	0.9	4.6	0.5	8.5	168.5	2 753	895	1 803	3 534	39.2	59.3	1.5
Madison	116.5	1 644	40.9	10.9	6.2	0.2	8.1	122.9	1 734	193	497	3 377	34.9	64.0	1.1
Marion	44.4	1 679	49.8	26.4	4.3	0.0	5.2	8.6	325	64	177	1 455	37.4	61.8	0.8
Marshall	59.5	1 835	35.1	11.7	3.3	0.4	4.8	5.4	167	111	215	1 164	61.4	37.5	1.1
Monroe	61.6	1 615	44.8	19.4	5.2	0.4	8.6	16.1	421	156	255	1 657	43.3	55.4	1.3
Montgomery	25.1	2 022	42.1	31.6	2.2	0.5	5.2	4.0	323	35	83	748	45.1	54.2	0.7
Neshoba	27.0	994	63.6	1.8	5.9	0.0	7.8	13.1	481	519	184	1 252	28.3	70.7	1.1
Newton	43.5	2 035	70.4	8.4	3.0	0.1	7.4	14.2	663	85	145	1 864	27.7	71.6	0.7
Noxubee	22.2	1 794	47.1	21.9	3.9	0.6	11.9	7.1	571	46	83	710	68.3	30.9	0.8
Oktibbeha	81.8	2 088	42.5	29.5	3.9	0.1	3.9	34.7	887	358	274	8 363	43.5	53.8	2.7
Panola	51.7	1 573	51.9	14.7	9.0	0.2	7.0	19.0	578	122	226	2 103	51.6	47.6	0.8
Pearl River	70.9	1 555	73.8	0.8	4.9	0.0	4.8	23.2	509	110	319	2 536	28.0	70.2	1.7
Perry	62.2	5 278	19.2	5.4	1.6	0.0	1.8	577.6	48 993	25	80	734	29.5	69.4	1.1
Pike	111.7	2 941	35.8	37.8	2.5	0.1	3.5	69.2	1 821	143	252	3 341	46.2	52.7	1.1
Pontotoc	33.1	1 339	62.9	0.2	4.2	0.3	8.6	14.4	581	62	171	979	29.1	69.4	1.5
Prentiss	64.5	2 666	66.5	1.1	2.6	0.2	3.4	36.5	1 509	57	163	1 523	38.8	60.1	1.1
Quitman	21.0	2 142	39.0	30.6	4.8	0.0	5.7	5.4	546	31	65	412	61.6	37.5	0.8
Rankin	203.8	1 905	45.2	23.5	4.4	0.4	6.7	120.4	1 125	529	749	8 857	19.4	79.6	0.9
Scott	39.9	1 590	58.9	2.0	6.7	0.1	8.5	27.4	1 091	209	166	1 131	38.5	60.8	0.6
Sharkey	12.3	1 865	70.5	1.4	5.0	0.3	7.0	0.8	120	39	44	439	58.8	37.0	4.3
Simpson	41.1	1 631	45.2	22.6	4.2	1.3	7.4	12.2	483	51	169	1 685	33.7	65.3	1.0
Smith	18.8	1 241	69.1	1.5	5.3	1.0	9.8	3.2	213	62	103	582	24.8	74.1	1.1
Stone	71.4	5 545	86.3	5.7	1.2	0.1	2.6	8.7	674	84	90	1 020	30.4	67.0	2.6

1. Based on the resident population estimated as of July 1 of the year shown.   2. Data subject to copyright.

Table B. States and Counties — **Land Area and Population**

STATE/County code	MSA/PMSA/NECMA code[1]	County Type[2]	STATE County	Land area,[3] (sq km) 2000	Population and population characteristics, 2000			Race alone or in combination (percent)				Percent Hispanic[4]	Age (percent)					
					Total persons	Rank	Per square kilometer	White	Black	Am. Indian, Alaska Native	Asian and Pacific Islander		Under 5 years	5 to 17 years	18 to 24 years	25 to 34 years	35 to 44 years	45 to 54 years
				1	2	3	4	5	6	7	8	9	10	11	12	13	14	15
			MISSISSIPPI—Cont'd															
28 133	...	7	Sunflower	1 797	34 369	1 268	19.1	29.0	70.0	0.2	0.5	1.3	7.0	20.9	14.0	15.2	15.1	11.6
28 135	...	9	Tallahatchie	1 668	14 903	2 098	8.9	39.8	59.7	0.4	0.5	0.9	7.0	23.1	10.0	12.0	13.9	12.0
28 137	...	6	Tate	1 048	25 370	1 548	24.2	68.3	31.2	0.5	0.2	0.9	6.9	20.2	11.7	12.3	15.1	13.2
28 139	...	7	Tippah	1 186	20 826	1 743	17.6	82.4	16.1	0.5	0.2	2.1	6.3	18.6	10.1	13.6	14.4	12.6
28 141	...	6	Tishomingo	1 098	19 163	1 837	17.5	95.4	3.3	0.6	0.2	1.8	5.9	17.3	7.8	12.8	14.7	13.3
28 143	...	8	Tunica	1 178	9 227	2 510	7.8	27.9	70.5	0.5	0.9	2.5	8.4	23.1	10.9	13.0	14.4	12.4
28 145	...	7	Union	1 076	25 362	1 549	23.6	84.0	15.2	0.3	0.3	1.6	7.4	18.6	9.2	13.9	14.6	12.9
28 147	...	9	Walthall	1 046	15 156	2 080	14.5	55.1	44.3	0.4	0.4	1.3	7.1	21.3	9.9	11.6	13.8	12.6
28 149	...	4	Warren	1 519	49 644	923	32.7	55.4	43.5	0.5	0.8	1.0	7.6	21.0	9.1	12.7	15.7	13.7
28 151	...	5	Washington	1 875	62 977	771	33.6	34.3	64.9	0.3	0.8	0.8	8.4	23.1	10.1	12.6	13.9	12.6
28 153	...	7	Wayne	2 099	21 216	1 724	10.1	61.5	38.2	0.2	0.3	0.6	7.6	21.6	9.7	12.7	14.9	12.4
28 155	...	9	Webster	1 094	10 294	2 416	9.4	77.9	21.0	0.3	0.3	1.7	6.7	19.4	9.0	11.6	15.0	12.2
28 157	...	9	Wilkinson	1 753	10 312	2 414	5.9	31.5	68.5	0.2	0.2	0.4	5.8	20.0	10.7	13.5	15.5	12.2
28 159	...	7	Winston	1 572	20 160	1 784	12.8	55.6	43.5	0.8	0.2	1.2	6.7	20.0	9.2	12.2	13.8	13.2
28 161	...	7	Yalobusha	1 210	13 051	2 227	10.8	60.8	38.7	0.4	0.4	1.0	6.4	19.1	8.9	12.1	14.0	13.4
28 163	...	6	Yazoo	2 381	28 149	1 446	11.8	45.0	54.3	0.4	0.5	4.4	7.4	21.0	9.8	13.6	15.6	12.2
29 000	...	X	**MISSOURI**	178 414	5 595 211	X	31.4	86.1	11.7	1.1	1.5	2.1	6.6	18.9	9.6	13.2	15.9	13.3
29 001	...	7	Adair	1 469	24 977	1 560	17.0	96.6	1.4	0.6	1.8	1.3	5.3	13.9	27.4	10.9	11.9	10.8
29 003	7000	3	Andrew	1 127	16 492	1 989	14.6	98.8	0.5	0.7	0.2	0.8	6.3	20.0	7.9	11.6	16.1	14.4
29 005	...	9	Atchison	1 411	6 430	2 745	4.6	97.3	2.2	0.3	0.2	0.7	4.5	19.6	6.5	10.1	14.1	13.8
29 007	...	6	Audrain	1 795	25 853	1 523	14.4	91.9	7.6	0.6	0.6	0.7	6.4	18.2	7.9	12.7	15.5	13.3
29 009	...	7	Barry	2 018	34 010	1 280	16.9	95.5	0.2	1.9	0.4	5.0	6.7	19.4	7.8	11.3	14.8	12.7
29 011	...	6	Barton	1 539	12 541	2 261	8.1	98.3	0.4	1.8	0.5	0.9	7.7	19.8	8.3	11.1	15.0	12.9
29 013	...	6	Bates	2 198	16 653	1 981	7.6	98.2	0.7	1.3	0.2	1.1	6.1	20.4	7.5	11.0	15.0	12.6
29 015	...	9	Benton	1 827	17 180	1 942	9.4	99.0	0.2	1.3	0.3	0.9	4.8	15.7	5.7	8.3	13.5	14.1
29 017	...	9	Bollinger	1 608	12 029	2 293	7.5	98.7	0.3	1.5	0.3	0.6	6.1	20.1	7.8	11.9	14.9	13.8
29 019	1740	3	Boone	1 775	135 454	398	76.3	87.1	9.4	1.0	3.5	1.8	6.2	16.6	19.9	15.2	14.7	12.1
29 021	7000	3	Buchanan	1 061	85 998	606	81.1	94.0	4.9	0.9	0.7	2.4	6.3	18.1	11.0	13.1	15.5	12.6
29 023	...	7	Butler	1 807	40 867	1 087	22.6	93.4	5.6	1.3	0.6	1.0	6.4	17.8	8.4	12.1	14.5	13.6
29 025	...	8	Caldwell	1 112	8 969	2 529	8.1	98.0	0.3	0.7	0.2	0.7	6.3	20.8	7.1	10.5	14.6	13.3
29 027	...	6	Callaway	2 173	40 766	1 089	18.8	92.9	6.0	1.1	0.8	0.9	6.2	19.2	11.1	14.0	17.1	13.3
29 029	...	7	Camden	1 697	37 051	1 188	21.8	98.7	0.3	1.2	0.5	0.9	4.6	15.6	6.1	9.3	14.0	15.1
29 031	...	5	Cape Girardeau	1 499	68 693	717	45.8	93.2	5.7	0.9	1.0	0.9	6.0	17.5	13.4	12.9	14.8	13.2
29 033	...	6	Carroll	1 799	10 285	2 418	5.7	97.7	2.0	0.7	0.2	0.7	6.4	18.8	7.4	10.7	13.8	13.0
29 035	...	9	Carter	1 315	5 941	2 789	4.5	98.4	0.1	2.9	0.3	1.2	6.2	18.9	8.0	11.1	14.8	13.6
29 037	3760	1	Cass	1 810	82 092	632	45.4	96.9	1.7	1.3	0.8	2.2	7.4	21.0	7.3	12.9	17.3	13.1
29 039	...	7	Cedar	1 233	13 733	2 178	11.1	98.0	0.5	1.6	0.7	1.1	5.7	19.0	6.4	9.5	13.3	12.9
29 041	...	9	Chariton	1 958	8 438	2 569	4.3	96.4	3.3	0.4	0.2	0.6	5.1	18.6	6.5	9.1	14.6	13.2
29 043	7920	2	Christian	1 459	54 285	867	37.2	98.4	0.4	1.3	0.6	1.3	7.7	20.2	8.1	14.9	16.8	13.2
29 045	...	9	Clark	1 314	7 416	2 647	5.6	99.4	0.2	0.5	0.1	0.7	6.1	18.8	7.8	11.0	14.5	14.2
29 047	3760	3	Clay	1 027	184 006	296	179.2	94.1	3.1	1.1	1.9	3.6	7.2	18.6	8.7	15.4	17.0	13.7
29 049	3760	1	Clinton	1 085	18 979	1 847	17.5	97.7	1.8	1.0	0.2	1.1	6.6	20.2	7.4	11.6	16.6	13.5
29 051	...	4	Cole	1 014	71 397	693	70.4	88.0	10.5	0.8	1.3	1.3	6.5	17.7	9.8	15.2	17.1	14.4
29 053	...	6	Cooper	1 463	16 670	1 978	11.4	90.0	9.5	0.9	0.5	0.9	5.8	17.0	14.0	13.0	14.4	12.1
29 055	...	6	Crawford	1 923	22 804	1 653	11.9	99.1	0.2	1.1	0.3	0.8	6.5	19.8	7.9	11.4	15.6	12.7
29 057	...	8	Dade	1 270	7 923	2 612	6.2	98.6	0.3	1.7	0.4	0.8	5.8	18.5	6.8	9.6	14.6	13.0
29 059	...	8	Dallas	1 403	15 661	2 043	11.2	98.8	0.2	1.8	0.3	0.9	6.7	20.8	7.4	10.9	15.6	12.8
29 061	...	9	Daviess	1 468	8 016	2 603	5.5	99.1	0.2	0.5	0.3	0.7	7.0	20.0	7.6	10.7	13.4	12.9
29 063	...	8	De Kalb	1 099	11 597	2 325	10.6	89.9	9.0	1.2	0.5	1.1	5.2	15.5	8.2	15.4	20.8	12.3
29 065	...	7	Dent	1 952	14 927	2 097	7.6	98.4	0.5	1.8	0.3	0.8	6.4	18.5	7.6	10.8	14.8	12.9
29 067	...	6	Douglas	2 110	13 084	2 224	6.2	98.5	0.2	2.3	0.4	0.8	6.0	19.8	7.0	10.1	14.4	13.5
29 069	...	7	Dunklin	1 413	33 155	1 312	23.5	89.6	9.0	0.9	0.4	2.5	7.1	18.8	8.1	12.1	13.8	12.6
29 071	7040	1	Franklin	2 390	93 807	546	39.2	98.3	1.1	0.7	0.4	0.7	6.9	20.4	8.2	13.2	16.8	13.2
29 073	...	6	Gasconade	1 349	15 342	2 066	11.4	99.4	0.2	0.7	0.3	0.4	5.8	18.9	6.9	10.2	15.6	13.1
29 075	...	9	Gentry	1 273	6 861	2 702	5.4	99.1	0.3	0.7	0.5	0.6	6.2	19.8	7.0	9.7	14.0	11.2
29 077	7920	2	Greene	1 748	240 391	239	137.5	95.1	2.7	1.5	1.5	1.8	6.1	16.1	13.8	13.8	14.8	13.2
29 079	...	7	Grundy	1 129	10 432	2 403	9.2	98.5	0.5	0.9	0.3	1.6	6.1	17.1	8.3	10.2	13.5	12.9
29 081	...	7	Harrison	1 878	8 850	2 539	4.7	99.3	0.4	0.9	0.7	1.0	6.4	17.3	7.2	10.3	13.5	11.5
29 083	...	6	Henry	1 819	21 997	1 692	12.1	97.6	1.2	1.4	0.5	0.9	6.0	17.8	7.8	11.2	14.6	13.2
29 085	...	9	Hickory	1 032	8 940	2 531	8.7	98.9	0.3	1.7	0.2	0.8	4.3	15.6	5.3	7.5	11.5	13.7
29 087	...	8	Holt	1 196	5 351	2 825	4.5	99.1	0.3	1.1	0.1	0.4	4.8	19.0	6.5	10.0	14.3	13.8
29 089	...	6	Howard	1 206	10 212	2 426	8.5	92.2	7.2	0.9	0.3	0.9	5.6	18.4	13.3	10.6	14.6	12.5
29 091	...	7	Howell	2 403	37 238	1 184	15.5	98.0	0.4	2.1	0.7	1.2	6.7	19.3	7.8	11.8	14.4	12.7
29 093	...	9	Iron	1 428	10 697	2 384	7.5	97.7	1.7	1.1	0.3	0.6	5.9	19.1	7.8	10.9	14.4	13.5
29 095	3760	0	Jackson	1 567	654 880	81	417.9	71.9	24.2	1.3	1.9	5.4	7.0	18.8	9.1	14.8	16.2	13.2

1. MSA = Metropolitan Statistical Area. PMSA = Primary MSA. NECMA = New England County Metropolitan Area. See Appendix A for explanation of these concepts. See Appendix B for list of metropolitan areas identified by type, with component counties.   2. County typology code from the Economic Research Service of USDA. See Appendix A for definition.   3. Dry land or land partially or temporarily covered by water.   4. Hispanic persons may be of any race.

Table B. States and Counties — Population and Households

STATE County	Age (percent) (cont'd)				Population — change and components of change, 1990–2001							Households, 2000				
					Total persons		Percent change		Components of change, 2000–2001						Percent	
	55 to 64 years	65 to 74 years	75 years and over	Percent female	2001	1990	1990–2000	2000–2001	Births	Deaths	Net migration	Number	Percent change, 1990–2000	Persons per house-hold	Female family house-holder[1]	One person
	16	17	18	19	20	21	22	23	24	25	26	27	28	29	30	31
MISSISSIPPI—Cont'd																
Sunflower	6.5	4.9	4.8	46.3	33 930	35 129	-2.2	-1.3	761	414	-795	9 637	-0.1	3.01	28.4	21.2
Tallahatchie	8.8	6.8	6.4	53.3	14 640	15 210	-2.0	-1.8	294	199	-362	5 263	4.5	2.81	23.5	24.6
Tate	9.1	6.1	5.3	51.6	25 617	21 432	18.4	1.0	509	296	46	8 850	26.0	2.74	15.5	21.3
Tippah	9.9	7.4	7.1	51.6	20 928	19 523	6.7	0.5	428	340	21	8 108	13.3	2.52	11.8	24.9
Tishomingo	11.4	9.1	7.7	51.9	19 060	17 683	8.4	-0.5	308	342	-61	7 917	12.2	2.39	10.1	27.5
Tunica	7.8	5.4	4.7	52.3	9 365	8 164	13.0	1.5	236	111	16	3 258	29.0	2.80	26.9	26.9
Union	9.4	7.5	6.6	51.6	25 782	22 085	14.8	1.7	449	339	311	9 786	17.0	2.57	11.1	23.4
Walthall	9.7	7.4	6.7	52.2	15 380	14 352	5.6	1.5	307	223	138	5 571	13.0	2.69	16.9	24.0
Warren	8.6	6.0	5.6	53.1	49 343	47 880	3.7	-0.6	1 148	638	-812	18 756	7.7	2.61	19.1	25.8
Washington	7.8	6.0	5.5	53.3	61 827	67 935	-7.3	-1.8	1 626	857	-1 952	22 158	-1.9	2.80	26.0	24.6
Wayne	9.3	6.5	5.3	52.2	21 193	19 517	8.7	-0.1	473	288	-205	7 857	14.6	2.67	17.2	23.1
Webster	9.6	8.3	8.2	51.7	10 320	10 222	0.7	0.3	174	196	49	3 905	2.1	2.59	13.1	24.0
Wilkinson	8.4	6.9	6.9	48.1	10 334	9 678	6.6	0.2	192	141	-26	3 578	6.9	2.59	24.5	27.9
Winston	9.3	8.3	7.2	51.6	20 129	19 433	3.7	-0.2	367	293	-98	7 578	7.3	2.59	18.1	25.2
Yalobusha	10.4	8.2	7.5	52.3	13 308	12 033	8.5	2.0	250	224	230	5 260	14.0	2.46	17.6	28.7
Yazoo	7.9	6.5	5.9	49.1	27 809	25 506	10.4	-1.2	634	432	-546	9 178	4.1	2.81	23.7	24.5
MISSOURI	9.1	7.0	6.5	51.4	5 629 707	5 116 901	9.3	0.6	94 677	68 762	9 038	2 194 594	11.9	2.48	11.6	27.3
Adair	7.6	5.8	6.5	53.1	24 795	24 577	1.6	-0.7	367	288	-255	9 669	6.7	2.29	7.2	31.5
Andrew	9.3	6.9	7.5	51.3	16 694	14 632	12.7	1.2	215	204	191	6 273	15.5	2.59	7.4	22.3
Atchison	10.3	9.4	11.6	50.2	6 414	7 457	-13.8	-0.2	67	128	46	2 722	-8.1	2.25	6.1	31.5
Audrain	9.2	7.8	9.1	54.3	25 455	23 599	9.6	-1.5	396	427	-367	9 844	6.9	2.43	9.9	27.8
Barry	11.2	8.8	7.3	50.4	34 352	27 547	23.5	1.0	560	420	212	13 398	23.4	2.51	8.4	24.7
Barton	8.8	8.1	8.3	51.0	12 741	11 312	10.9	1.6	223	157	137	4 895	8.2	2.53	8.5	26.4
Bates	9.9	8.6	8.8	51.2	16 754	15 025	10.8	0.6	232	260	127	6 511	10.0	2.51	7.6	26.1
Benton	15.6	13.5	8.8	50.5	17 493	13 859	24.0	1.8	188	294	409	7 420	28.7	2.28	6.8	26.3
Bollinger	10.7	8.3	6.5	50.5	12 335	10 619	13.3	2.5	173	166	297	4 576	16.0	2.59	8.4	21.6
Boone	6.6	4.4	4.2	51.7	136 774	112 379	20.5	1.0	2 133	1 024	261	53 094	26.6	2.38	10.4	28.7
Buchanan	8.6	7.3	7.7	50.8	85 367	83 083	3.5	-0.7	1 400	1 221	-785	33 557	3.3	2.42	12.0	28.9
Butler	10.5	8.9	7.8	52.1	40 643	38 765	5.4	-0.5	678	650	-241	16 718	9.0	2.39	11.6	28.0
Caldwell	10.4	8.4	8.7	50.6	9 004	8 380	7.0	0.4	129	150	57	3 523	9.3	2.51	8.0	25.5
Callaway	8.2	6.0	5.0	48.2	41 590	32 809	24.3	2.0	580	397	638	14 416	24.8	2.56	10.4	23.0
Camden	16.2	12.2	8.0	50.0	37 588	27 495	34.8	1.4	440	486	550	15 779	39.6	2.31	6.6	23.3
Cape Girardeau	8.5	6.8	7.0	51.8	69 047	61 633	11.5	0.5	1 039	856	196	26 980	15.3	2.42	9.8	27.3
Carroll	9.9	9.0	11.0	51.5	10 242	10 748	-4.3	-0.4	162	160	-45	4 169	-3.8	2.42	8.0	27.8
Carter	11.4	9.4	6.5	50.9	5 930	5 515	7.7	-0.2	99	89	-19	2 378	11.7	2.46	8.9	26.7
Cass	9.2	6.4	5.4	51.0	85 630	63 808	28.7	4.3	1 384	786	2 882	30 168	31.8	2.69	9.1	20.0
Cedar	12.5	11.0	9.8	51.1	13 821	12 093	13.6	0.6	197	255	140	5 685	13.6	2.35	7.9	28.1
Chariton	10.5	10.6	11.7	52.1	8 297	9 202	-8.3	-1.7	101	164	-74	3 469	-5.2	2.38	6.5	29.8
Christian	8.6	5.9	4.7	51.4	57 270	32 644	66.3	5.5	944	455	2 435	20 425	71.1	2.63	9.3	19.1
Clark	10.8	8.2	8.5	50.6	7 504	7 547	-1.7	1.2	87	112	111	2 966	3.7	2.46	7.0	26.4
Clay	8.6	5.9	4.9	51.4	188 241	153 411	19.9	2.3	3 226	1 691	2 712	72 558	23.2	2.50	10.2	25.2
Clinton	10.0	6.8	7.3	51.0	19 530	16 595	14.4	2.9	293	235	487	7 152	17.0	2.59	8.8	22.0
Cole	8.0	5.8	5.5	48.6	71 540	63 579	12.3	0.2	1 141	795	-189	27 040	17.7	2.43	10.0	28.7
Cooper	8.5	7.0	8.2	46.0	16 659	14 835	12.4	-0.1	230	231	-3	5 932	10.7	2.46	9.0	26.1
Crawford	10.4	8.6	7.2	50.7	22 955	19 173	18.9	0.7	374	328	112	8 858	21.4	2.53	9.0	24.3
Dade	11.4	10.2	10.1	51.0	7 868	7 449	6.4	-0.7	96	139	-8	3 202	7.6	2.44	6.5	26.5
Dallas	10.7	8.3	6.8	50.4	15 784	12 646	23.8	0.8	250	197	72	6 030	23.1	2.57	8.4	23.7
Daviess	10.8	9.5	8.1	51.8	7 917	7 865	1.9	-1.2	146	113	-133	3 178	4.5	2.50	7.5	25.7
De Kalb	8.6	7.0	6.9	39.6	11 550	9 967	16.4	-0.4	137	165	-20	3 528	15.5	2.50	7.4	26.9
Dent	11.2	9.2	8.6	51.5	14 962	13 702	8.9	0.2	202	246	85	5 982	12.3	2.45	9.1	25.0
Douglas	12.0	9.5	7.6	50.9	13 220	11 876	10.2	1.0	153	185	169	5 201	13.4	2.49	7.6	26.1
Dunklin	10.9	8.1	8.4	52.7	33 017	33 112	0.1	-0.4	611	603	-134	13 411	2.2	2.42	13.2	28.1
Franklin	9.2	6.6	5.5	50.4	95 187	80 603	16.4	1.5	1 577	1 031	854	34 945	21.1	2.66	9.0	22.1
Gasconade	10.6	9.1	9.7	51.4	15 423	14 006	9.5	0.5	213	259	130	6 171	11.3	2.44	7.6	27.0
Gentry	10.4	9.7	11.9	51.2	6 763	6 854	0.1	-1.4	84	147	-33	2 747	-0.3	2.42	7.2	29.3
Greene	8.6	6.8	6.8	51.5	241 926	207 949	15.6	0.6	3 917	2 761	489	97 859	20.1	2.34	9.8	29.1
Grundy	11.3	9.7	10.9	52.5	10 281	10 536	-1.0	-1.4	172	167	-154	4 382	0.8	2.30	8.0	30.8
Harrison	11.6	10.4	11.6	51.5	8 756	8 469	4.5	-1.1	134	149	-78	3 658	2.4	2.36	7.7	28.8
Henry	11.2	9.0	9.2	51.2	22 302	20 044	9.7	1.4	304	380	379	9 133	11.5	2.37	9.3	27.7
Hickory	15.9	15.4	10.7	51.0	8 928	7 335	21.9	-0.1	85	159	61	3 911	22.9	2.26	6.7	26.5
Holt	10.1	9.5	12.0	50.6	5 268	6 034	-11.3	-1.6	62	109	-37	2 237	-8.3	2.35	6.1	29.7
Howard	8.9	7.3	8.8	51.6	10 034	9 631	6.0	-1.7	141	142	-177	3 836	7.4	2.46	9.5	27.3
Howell	10.5	8.8	7.9	51.7	37 209	31 447	18.4	-0.1	631	533	-109	14 762	20.2	2.47	9.9	25.0
Iron	11.3	8.9	8.2	51.3	10 546	10 726	-0.3	-1.4	166	243	-71	4 197	5.1	2.46	9.4	25.8
Jackson	8.3	6.5	6.0	51.8	655 855	633 234	3.4	0.1	12 913	7 811	-3 970	266 294	5.4	2.42	14.7	31.2

1. No spouse present.

STATE County	Births, average 1997–1999 Total	Rate[1]	Deaths, average 1997–1999 Number Total	Number Infant[2]	Rate Total[1]	Rate Infant[3]	Physicians,[4] 2000 Number	Rate[5]	Hospitals,[4] 1998 Number	Beds Number	Beds Rate[5]	Medicare enrollees 2000	Serious crimes known to police, 2000[6] Total Number	Rate[7]
	32	33	34	35	36	37	38	39	40	41	42	43	44	45
MISSISSIPPI—Cont'd														
Sunflower	523	15.3	343	NA	10.0	NA	18	52	2	155	448	4 039	NA	NA
Tallahatchie	234	15.8	156	NA	10.5	NA	5	34	1	77	517	2 392	NA	NA
Tate	361	15.0	224	NA	9.4	NA	12	47	1	52	217	3 585	NA	NA
Tippah	306	14.6	257	NA	12.2	NA	9	43	1	106	504	4 430	NA	NA
Tishomingo	227	12.2	262	NA	14.1	NA	9	47	1	88	472	4 476	NA	NA
Tunica	166	20.8	98	NA	12.2	NA	3	33	0	0	0	1 182	NA	NA
Union	347	14.5	239	NA	10.0	NA	23	91	1	153	642	4 287	480	1 893
Walthall	218	15.3	169	NA	11.8	NA	21	139	1	49	341	2 217	NA	NA
Warren	775	15.7	518	12	10.5	15.1	81	163	2	343	694	6 797	2 299	4 631
Washington	1 143	17.5	703	14	10.8	12.0	87	138	2	287	440	9 105	5 420	8 606
Wayne	334	16.4	208	NA	10.2	NA	14	66	1	77	378	2 785	141	880
Webster	139	13.1	137	NA	13.0	NA	6	58	1	76	721	2 032	NA	NA
Wilkinson	130	14.2	121	NA	13.3	NA	9	87	1	66	719	1 665	NA	NA
Winston	251	13.0	226	NA	11.7	NA	8	40	1	185	954	3 409	NA	NA
Yalobusha	182	14.6	161	NA	12.9	NA	5	38	1	85	687	3 019	NA	NA
Yazoo	445	17.5	319	NA	12.5	NA	21	75	1	34	133	4 189	NA	NA
MISSOURI	74 189	13.6	55 108	575	10.1	7.8	11 883	212	134	21 768	400	860 558	253 338	4 528
Adair	276	11.4	213	NA	8.8	NA	81	324	2	194	799	3 406	NA	NA
Andrew	180	11.6	157	NA	10.1	NA	5	30	1	205	1 317	2 044	NA	NA
Atchison	65	9.3	94	NA	13.3	NA	5	78	1	44	629	1 421	41	638
Audrain	313	13.3	321	NA	13.6	NA	47	182	1	165	700	4 595	466	1 802
Barry	442	13.4	371	NA	11.2	NA	23	68	2	71	214	6 792	NA	NA
Barton	165	13.6	143	NA	11.8	NA	8	64	1	44	364	2 167	267	2 129
Bates	193	12.2	214	NA	13.5	NA	5	30	1	33	209	3 178	NA	NA
Benton	153	9.0	237	NA	13.9	NA	7	41	0	0	0	4 487	313	1 822
Bollinger	133	11.5	123	NA	10.6	NA	2	17	0	0	0	1 976	NA	NA
Boone	1 773	13.7	785	10	6.1	5.8	775	572	3	931	721	14 050	4 809	3 550
Buchanan	1 124	13.7	980	8	12.0	7.4	162	188	1	277	339	15 149	3 927	5 307
Butler	517	12.8	528	NA	13.0	NA	92	225	2	376	927	8 153	1 551	3 795
Caldwell	103	11.6	120	NA	13.6	NA	2	22	0	0	0	1 739	54	602
Callaway	480	12.8	330	NA	8.8	NA	36	88	1	36	96	5 342	NA	NA
Camden	330	9.7	362	NA	10.7	NA	37	100	1	91	268	6 518	947	2 563
Cape Girardeau	796	12.0	666	NA	10.0	NA	182	265	2	510	769	10 229	3 159	4 599
Carroll	125	12.2	134	NA	13.1	NA	10	97	1	52	509	2 216	NA	NA
Carter	85	13.4	85	NA	13.5	NA	1	17	0	0	0	1 296	91	1 532
Cass	1 083	13.5	641	NA	8.0	NA	31	38	2	89	111	10 371	1 596	2 011
Cedar	155	11.7	209	NA	15.8	NA	11	80	1	34	257	3 280	194	1 413
Chariton	85	9.9	141	NA	16.3	NA	4	47	0	0	0	1 764	18	213
Christian	697	14.2	380	NA	7.7	NA	7	13	0	0	0	6 740	562	1 035
Clark	81	10.9	92	NA	12.3	NA	2	27	0	0	0	1 296	38	512
Clay	2 528	14.3	1 339	15	7.6	5.8	328	178	3	608	345	22 895	12 380	6 728
Clinton	241	12.6	197	NA	10.3	NA	7	37	1	38	199	3 028	306	1 612
Cole	906	13.1	622	NA	9.0	NA	178	249	3	290	418	9 450	2 221	3 111
Cooper	194	12.0	180	NA	11.2	NA	12	72	1	49	306	2 754	339	2 034
Crawford	301	13.5	248	NA	11.2	NA	16	70	0	0	0	3 883	329	1 443
Dade	88	11.1	115	NA	14.6	NA	2	25	0	0	0	1 793	NA	NA
Dallas	195	12.8	154	NA	10.1	NA	6	38	0	0	0	2 649	NA	NA
Daviess	107	13.6	108	NA	13.7	NA	3	37	0	0	0	1 540	89	1 110
De Kalb	106	9.5	128	NA	11.5	NA	2	17	0	0	0	1 430	157	1 354
Dent	170	12.0	192	NA	13.6	NA	12	80	1	46	326	3 088	NA	NA
Douglas	145	11.7	147	NA	11.9	NA	3	23	0	0	0	2 301	NA	NA
Dunklin	463	14.1	486	NA	14.9	NA	30	90	1	116	355	6 758	769	2 319
Franklin	1 270	13.8	852	NA	9.3	NA	84	90	2	194	211	14 020	2 402	2 561
Gasconade	182	12.2	199	NA	13.4	NA	13	85	1	41	275	3 249	NA	NA
Gentry	73	10.6	108	NA	15.6	NA	4	58	1	35	504	1 805	15	219
Greene	2 960	13.1	2 239	20	9.9	6.9	663	276	5	1 657	731	36 837	15 341	6 382
Grundy	121	11.8	145	NA	14.3	NA	10	96	1	48	472	2 352	254	2 435
Harrison	93	11.0	126	NA	14.9	NA	7	79	1	23	270	2 118	NA	NA
Henry	245	11.6	293	NA	13.8	NA	25	114	1	108	509	4 935	920	4 840
Hickory	69	8.0	142	NA	16.4	NA	0	0	0	0	0	2 313	43	481
Holt	55	9.8	75	NA	13.4	NA	3	56	0	0	0	1 239	NA	NA
Howard	108	11.1	116	NA	12.0	NA	5	49	0	0	0	1 741	112	1 097
Howell	475	13.3	444	NA	12.4	NA	37	99	2	140	391	7 628	994	2 669
Iron	128	11.7	186	NA	17.1	NA	11	103	1	50	460	2 287	75	750
Jackson	9 892	15.1	6 299	84	9.6	8.5	1 890	289	14	3 347	511	94 620	48 613	7 486

1. Per 1,000 estimated resident population, average 1997–1999. 2. Deaths of infants under 1 year old. 3. Deaths of infants under 1 year old per 1,000 live births. 4. Data subject to copyright. 5. Per 100,000 resident population as of July 1 of the year shown. 6. Data for serious crimes have not been adjusted for underreporting; this may affect comparability between geographic areas and over time. 7. Per 100,000 population estimated by the FBI.

	Serious crimes known to police, 2000[1] (cont'd)		Education						Money income				Income and poverty, 1998		
	Rate[2]		School enrollment and attainment, 1990				Local government expenditures, fiscal 1999[5]		1989				Percent below poverty level		
			Enrollment[3]		Attainment[4] (percent)					Households					
										Median					
STATE County	Violent	Property	Total	Percent private	High school graduate or more	Bachelor's degree or more	Total current expenditures (mil dol)	Current expenditures per student (dollars)	Per capita[6] (dollars)	Dollars	Percent change, 1979–1989 (constant 1989 dollars)	Percent with $100,000 or more	Median household income	All persons	Persons under 18	Persons 5–17 in families
	46	47	48	49	50	51	52	53	54	55	56	57	58	59	60	61

MISSISSIPPI—Cont'd

STATE County	46	47	48	49	50	51	52	53	54	55	56	57	58	59	60	61
Sunflower	NA	NA	10 209	10.9	49.2	12.4	27.8	4 317	7 067	14 431	-10.5	1.4	21 304	32.0	36.9	32.8
Tallahatchie	NA	NA	4 221	10.7	48.2	7.9	14.7	4 739	6 180	13 593	2.7	0.8	19 386	27.2	33.3	31.1
Tate	NA	NA	5 963	8.2	61.0	11.7	20.2	4 328	9 212	22 207	9.4	1.5	32 194	14.6	19.9	18.1
Tippah	NA	NA	4 654	5.8	54.4	9.0	18.0	4 397	8 747	17 991	3.8	0.8	28 532	14.0	19.2	17.6
Tishomingo	NA	NA	3 671	3.4	55.0	6.6	14.5	4 507	8 735	17 500	-17.6	0.8	27 794	13.6	19.9	18.2
Tunica	NA	NA	2 637	12.7	45.9	8.5	12.0	5 987	6 449	10 965	-1.2	1.9	23 318	26.1	30.2	29.7
Union	71	1 822	5 131	4.6	57.3	10.1	20.2	4 455	9 735	21 128	9.6	1.1	31 417	12.4	17.0	15.7
Walthall	NA	NA	4 017	4.6	55.0	10.1	12.7	4 584	7 263	14 135	-17.7	0.7	22 386	23.0	25.9	28.8
Warren	582	4 049	13 893	11.5	67.7	19.1	46.5	4 941	10 861	22 804	-14.3	1.6	32 827	16.9	24.1	19.8
Washington	686	7 920	20 778	15.0	58.8	14.3	59.0	4 549	8 704	17 492	-1.6	2.1	25 027	25.8	32.6	28.6
Wayne	44	837	5 389	6.7	56.1	8.9	18.2	4 333	7 545	16 095	-6.8	0.6	25 948	19.4	23.3	23.6
Webster	NA	NA	2 533	5.0	58.6	10.8	8.8	4 346	8 354	17 094	-9.8	0.8	25 063	17.7	26.4	22.0
Wilkinson	NA	NA	2 428	21.7	48.3	8.9	8.4	4 733	6 670	11 910	-22.1	0.7	20 710	27.3	31.1	31.6
Winston	NA	NA	5 227	8.7	59.1	10.8	15.9	4 629	8 907	18 320	2.3	1.7	27 031	18.8	25.4	24.1
Yalobusha	NA	NA	2 860	7.0	55.7	9.9	10.0	4 460	8 049	15 885	-7.9	0.9	24 378	18.9	23.2	26.2
Yazoo	NA	NA	7 116	16.8	53.4	12.0	23.2	4 747	7 786	14 234	-13.6	1.9	22 348	28.9	35.6	32.4
MISSOURI	490	4 038	1 292 623	17.9	73.9	17.8	5 348.4	5 855	12 989	26 362	1.0	2.8	37 186	11.7	16.8	15.0
Adair	NA	NA	9 691	7.6	74.3	22.7	15.6	5 283	9 197	17 285	-15.1	1.4	30 256	14.7	18.6	17.4
Andrew	NA	NA	3 534	6.0	78.6	13.5	13.9	4 838	10 984	26 103	1.6	1.6	40 010	9.0	13.7	10.6
Atchison	47	591	1 900	22.9	76.8	14.2	7.1	5 533	10 042	20 126	-7.8	1.6	32 288	12.5	16.6	15.7
Audrain	93	1 710	5 146	10.1	68.0	10.9	19.8	5 246	11 310	23 424	-9.9	1.5	33 919	12.6	19.3	16.5
Barry	NA	NA	5 625	3.7	67.4	8.5	33.1	4 994	9 465	19 169	2.8	1.3	28 095	15.3	22.5	19.7
Barton	263	1 866	2 502	5.1	68.2	8.2	11.3	5 181	10 229	19 951	6.0	1.9	29 396	13.3	18.6	16.4
Bates	NA	NA	3 274	5.2	64.9	8.4	14.5	4 857	9 598	20 085	1.1	0.6	29 005	14.3	20.6	18.0
Benton	52	1 769	2 692	4.7	64.5	7.7	12.9	4 650	9 112	16 925	-2.1	0.6	24 288	16.9	24.8	24.2
Bollinger	NA	NA	2 263	4.7	52.7	6.9	9.8	4 679	8 757	19 430	16.7	1.0	27 394	15.6	20.9	20.5
Boone	332	3 218	42 951	9.7	84.8	36.5	113.8	5 510	12 707	25 647	-1.4	2.6	40 448	10.8	14.3	12.9
Buchanan	303	5 005	20 161	9.4	72.1	13.5	76.0	5 292	11 193	23 019	-4.0	1.7	32 768	13.5	19.0	17.5
Butler	426	3 369	8 922	6.1	56.8	8.6	33.3	4 902	9 000	16 285	-2.6	1.4	26 280	19.0	26.6	24.8
Caldwell	67	535	1 905	4.3	75.4	8.1	11.1	5 828	9 491	19 448	-0.8	1.1	30 037	13.6	18.8	17.0
Callaway	NA	NA	8 652	23.0	70.1	13.9	29.2	5 490	11 024	26 663	-6.7	1.0	36 562	10.4	15.1	13.5
Camden	254	2 309	5 096	7.5	73.6	12.4	27.0	5 125	12 403	22 564	14.5	2.9	31 394	12.0	19.9	18.2
Cape Girardeau	239	4 360	17 779	11.5	74.4	19.2	46.2	4 797	11 858	24 510	-1.4	2.1	38 245	10.7	15.3	13.6
Carroll	NA	NA	2 447	3.3	70.3	11.7	10.9	5 678	10 102	19 697	-2.0	1.4	28 429	14.6	19.8	18.8
Carter	269	1 262	1 303	2.0	56.0	8.8	8.1	5 682	7 470	15 357	-2.8	0.5	21 448	22.7	29.4	31.0
Cass	189	1 822	16 185	11.4	80.0	13.0	76.2	4 934	12 991	31 373	-1.5	1.9	46 135	6.4	9.8	8.5
Cedar	51	1 362	2 387	6.8	63.9	7.6	11.6	4 733	8 864	16 939	2.7	0.8	24 197	17.6	24.9	24.0
Chariton	12	201	1 965	10.6	71.3	10.4	8.1	5 505	10 589	20 829	0.4	1.2	28 882	12.4	16.5	15.8
Christian	31	1 004	8 153	8.9	76.6	12.5	43.6	4 626	10 862	25 995	9.7	1.2	38 751	8.9	12.7	10.7
Clark	13	499	1 730	5.5	67.4	7.9	7.3	5 137	8 849	19 674	-4.5	0.5	30 188	14.2	19.4	18.5
Clay	862	5 866	38 853	16.0	84.7	20.0	165.4	5 270	15 369	34 370	-2.5	2.7	49 060	5.3	8.9	7.2
Clinton	374	1 238	3 996	4.9	77.1	10.3	18.8	5 462	11 492	26 306	-3.2	1.5	38 830	9.0	12.1	11.4
Cole	333	2 777	15 956	21.5	77.3	22.3	54.6	5 094	13 918	30 362	0.2	2.4	43 742	7.8	11.1	9.5
Cooper	102	1 932	3 462	18.5	70.9	11.5	15.4	5 961	10 006	22 785	-0.6	1.0	32 986	11.7	15.5	14.4
Crawford	149	1 294	4 432	4.5	58.6	7.1	16.4	4 723	9 284	19 711	-0.3	1.0	28 185	15.5	21.2	19.4
Dade	NA	NA	1 505	6.8	71.8	9.0	7.8	5 520	9 490	18 724	-0.4	1.4	27 535	14.9	20.5	20.0
Dallas	NA	NA	2 537	7.7	63.0	6.5	10.9	4 968	8 530	16 673	3.7	1.5	26 089	17.0	22.1	21.3
Daviess	150	961	1 658	10.8	70.6	8.9	9.3	6 769	9 008	18 351	-3.5	0.7	28 419	16.6	23.7	21.3
De Kalb	86	1 268	2 041	6.9	73.1	8.3	7.9	5 615	9 047	22 771	14.0	1.4	32 338	14.1	15.1	16.4
Dent	NA	NA	3 035	4.9	53.9	7.9	12.7	4 928	9 033	16 594	-8.3	1.4	26 036	17.9	23.1	23.6
Douglas	NA	NA	2 585	8.0	59.8	7.5	9.5	4 899	8 899	16 187	5.7	1.0	23 591	20.6	27.5	26.0
Dunklin	323	1 997	7 748	3.6	51.2	8.0	31.6	5 072	9 028	15 388	-6.1	1.3	24 085	23.3	31.0	30.5
Franklin	163	2 397	19 681	15.2	67.5	9.3	82.9	4 864	11 606	28 622	2.8	1.3	41 308	8.1	11.8	10.1
Gasconade	NA	NA	2 938	8.1	61.1	8.0	15.4	4 781	10 774	22 328	5.5	1.2	32 879	10.1	14.0	13.0
Gentry	0	219	1 437	3.4	71.0	10.3	8.1	5 707	9 535	17 594	-1.9	1.0	27 052	12.6	17.0	15.2
Greene	409	5 973	57 451	15.9	78.9	20.7	181.7	5 028	12 468	24 285	0.8	2.7	34 324	12.1	18.0	15.1
Grundy	393	2 042	2 357	3.4	71.3	10.1	9.7	5 394	9 858	18 084	-6.8	1.9	29 291	15.4	22.1	20.5
Harrison	NA	NA	1 675	3.1	71.6	8.3	10.2	6 335	10 118	17 460	2.6	1.5	25 964	15.4	21.4	21.0
Henry	289	4 551	4 197	4.7	67.6	10.3	18.4	5 508	9 835	18 476	-9.1	0.8	28 369	14.3	20.7	19.5
Hickory	101	380	1 137	5.0	60.4	6.4	10.1	5 243	8 583	16 010	11.0	0.4	21 343	18.6	27.3	27.5
Holt	NA	NA	1 328	2.2	75.4	12.2	5.4	5 417	9 757	18 729	-3.8	1.2	28 637	14.8	20.3	19.4
Howard	59	1 038	2 613	27.6	69.9	16.8	9.0	5 430	9 854	21 378	6.1	0.8	29 919	14.1	19.1	17.4
Howell	322	2 347	6 815	6.4	61.2	8.7	37.9	5 181	8 776	16 564	1.3	1.4	25 065	19.9	27.9	24.3
Iron	220	530	2 462	4.1	56.3	6.8	13.4	5 459	8 232	17 303	-12.2	0.5	24 355	19.9	26.7	25.2
Jackson	958	6 528	155 666	17.1	79.5	20.0	685.8	6 353	13 712	27 853	-1.6	2.6	39 895	11.3	17.3	14.4

1. Data for serious crimes have not been adjusted for underreporting; this may affect comparability between geographic areas and over time.   2. Per 100,000 population estimated by the FBI.   3. All persons 3 years old and over enrolled in nursery school through college.   4. Persons 25 years old and over.   5. Elementary and secondary education expenditures, local government fiscal years ending between July 1, 1998 and June 30, 1999.   6. Based on population enumerated as of April 1, 1990.

Table B. States and Counties — **Personal Income**

STATE County	Personal income, 1999												
			Per capita[1]					Transfer payments					
									Government payments to individuals				
	Total (mil dol)	Percent change, 1998–1999	Dollars	Rank	Wages and salaries[2] (mil dol)	Proprietor's income (mil dol)	Dividends, interest, and rent (mil dol)	Total (mil dol)	Total (mil dol)	Social Security (mil dol)	Medical payments (mil dol)	Income maintenance (mil dol)	Unemployment insurance (mil dol)
	62	63	64	65	66	67	68	69	70	71	72	73	74
MISSISSIPPI—Cont'd													
Sunflower	485	2.3	14 593	3 018	314	43	74	126	119	35	50	27	2
Tallahatchie	208	3.6	14 287	3 033	65	10	35	66	63	21	25	15	1
Tate	522	6.1	21 369	1 555	172	38	59	89	84	31	30	10	1
Tippah	381	4.5	18 090	2 523	207	25	60	94	89	34	40	11	1
Tishomingo	317	4.0	16 908	2 753	162	21	58	87	83	37	34	7	1
Tunica	160	5.3	20 203	1 929	470	8	32	34	32	9	14	8	1
Union	489	6.7	20 267	1 901	248	32	75	90	85	39	33	9	1
Walthall	228	3.2	16 044	2 895	78	32	30	60	57	20	24	10	1
Warren	1 236	2.1	25 140	648	829	78	215	186	176	61	78	23	2
Washington	1 184	0.0	18 421	2 438	693	89	200	263	250	84	95	60	4
Wayne	350	-0.2	16 941	2 745	154	47	56	75	71	28	26	13	1
Webster	183	4.4	17 237	2 695	77	15	33	50	48	21	20	5	0
Wilkinson	136	1.2	15 024	2 986	45	7	23	46	44	13	19	9	1
Winston	353	3.6	18 351	2 457	173	29	60	82	78	31	30	12	1
Yalobusha	219	4.2	17 333	2 675	86	15	36	64	62	23	27	9	1
Yazoo	478	1.9	18 956	2 292	210	53	91	117	112	38	46	22	1
MISSOURI	144 389	4.4	26 404	X	93 607	10 133	29 519	20 965	19 960	8 424	8 403	1 766	298
Adair	473	2.8	19 542	2 122	289	32	99	94	89	32	42	7	1
Andrew	354	4.2	22 718	1 164	60	27	81	49	46	21	18	3	1
Atchison	147	-0.3	20 895	1 696	48	27	36	29	28	13	10	2	0
Audrain	543	-1.3	23 175	1 052	299	37	122	105	101	46	43	7	1
Barry	622	4.1	18 739	2 358	383	65	133	136	130	56	54	11	2
Barton	240	3.4	19 759	2 066	142	11	49	48	45	20	19	4	1
Bates	303	4.6	18 888	2 323	88	31	65	74	71	31	31	5	1
Benton	283	3.9	16 338	2 854	73	29	63	95	92	42	36	7	1
Bollinger	181	5.2	15 311	2 958	42	16	27	46	44	18	17	6	1
Boone	3 459	4.1	26 568	456	2 397	230	689	364	340	138	148	29	2
Buchanan	1 956	5.2	23 964	867	1 325	136	358	360	345	143	146	28	4
Butler	872	4.2	21 590	1 490	489	89	139	223	216	72	100	26	2
Caldwell	155	1.9	17 394	2 666	37	15	33	35	34	15	14	3	0
Callaway	804	5.3	21 199	1 596	420	50	134	127	120	53	51	9	2
Camden	784	6.3	22 667	1 174	379	72	204	155	148	78	52	8	2
Cape Girardeau	1 672	6.3	24 886	688	1 183	110	356	235	222	99	86	17	3
Carroll	207	3.6	20 440	1 854	64	21	53	47	45	20	19	4	1
Carter	98	3.5	15 652	2 935	29	13	15	32	31	11	14	4	1
Cass	1 940	6.5	23 351	1 003	498	115	315	243	228	107	91	12	3
Cedar	224	1.2	16 712	2 793	69	19	56	68	66	29	28	5	1
Chariton	165	-0.6	19 297	2 211	51	21	41	40	39	17	17	3	1
Christian	1 043	8.0	20 309	1 888	304	109	183	145	136	64	53	9	2
Clark	120	-0.8	16 306	2 858	34	1	27	30	28	12	12	3	1
Clay	5 134	5.5	28 503	281	3 048	307	771	524	491	238	194	22	8
Clinton	453	6.2	23 210	1 041	108	30	73	62	59	26	25	4	1
Cole	1 938	4.7	27 884	341	1 682	100	393	219	207	94	84	13	3
Cooper	325	1.6	20 150	1 952	138	26	68	62	59	26	26	4	1
Crawford	412	4.4	18 373	2 450	139	27	69	97	93	40	38	9	2
Dade	148	3.2	18 703	2 366	46	12	29	35	34	16	13	2	0
Dallas	271	5.6	17 388	2 668	61	31	47	62	59	26	24	6	1
Daviess	148	-1.7	18 323	2 464	43	15	35	31	30	14	11	3	0
De Kalb	169	2.2	14 969	2 990	74	21	25	37	35	16	14	3	0
Dent	269	1.5	18 900	2 317	115	23	48	72	70	28	30	8	1
Douglas	191	2.6	15 393	2 952	60	18	38	54	52	22	20	7	1
Dunklin	618	3.7	19 007	2 276	255	46	96	191	185	57	91	29	2
Franklin	2 236	5.6	24 007	857	1 009	111	383	299	282	137	110	19	5
Gasconade	320	3.1	21 357	1 560	146	18	73	62	59	29	24	3	1
Gentry	130	-1.8	18 983	2 283	48	13	30	36	35	15	16	2	0
Greene	6 015	4.1	26 496	464	4 355	627	1 282	836	795	342	310	66	8
Grundy	211	3.2	20 802	1 737	93	15	45	50	48	20	19	4	1
Harrison	164	-0.5	19 502	2 140	62	12	38	43	42	17	19	4	0
Henry	428	4.3	20 120	1 959	200	27	104	105	102	44	44	8	1
Hickory	130	3.7	14 951	2 991	26	11	30	53	51	24	20	4	0
Holt	113	-1.6	20 370	1 869	36	15	26	26	25	12	10	2	0
Howard	194	1.3	20 114	1 960	61	15	45	41	39	15	18	3	0
Howell	664	4.0	18 420	2 439	347	62	131	175	168	69	71	18	2
Iron	182	2.6	16 619	2 808	98	12	33	59	57	22	25	6	1
Jackson	18 494	5.0	28 258	300	15 895	1 632	3 452	2 495	2 374	957	1 030	224	41

1. Based on the resident population estimated as of July 1 of the year shown.   2. Includes other labor income.

STATE County	Earnings, 1999									Social Security beneficiaries, December 2000			Housing units, 1990	
			Goods-related[1]		Service-related and other[2]							Supplemental Security Income recipients, December 2000		Percent change, 1980–1990
	Total (mil dol)	Farm	Total	Manufacturing	Total	Retail trade	Finance, insurance, and real estate	Services	Government	Number	Rate[3]		Total	
	75	76	77	78	79	80	81	82	83	84	85	86	87	88
MISSISSIPPI—Cont'd														
Sunflower	357	8.4	19.8	17.7	38.3	9.9	2.1	11.3	33.5	5 090	148	2 093	10 167	-1.0
Tallahatchie	75	5.5	D	11.4	D	9.9	2.8	16.6	30.5	3 298	221	1 403	5 492	-5.5
Tate	210	3.5	D	26.3	D	15.3	3.9	16.4	21.7	4 139	163	980	7 474	16.9
Tippah	232	1.5	D	49.5	D	8.3	2.6	9.7	12.6	4 971	239	1 362	7 846	10.1
Tishomingo	183	0.1	50.7	42.9	37.2	9.2	3.0	15.3	12.0	4 910	256	932	8 455	7.4
Tunica	477	1.2	4.6	2.5	90.3	1.9	0.5	86.1	3.9	1 442	156	666	2 990	-2.0
Union	280	0.4	43.2	39.2	45.2	17.2	2.3	15.2	11.2	5 368	212	881	9 104	10.2
Walthall	110	16.7	D	24.0	D	7.6	2.7	12.3	18.4	2 853	188	913	5 643	14.4
Warren	906	0.2	D	20.7	D	9.5	2.2	31.8	24.9	8 157	164	1 926	19 512	1.2
Washington	781	2.9	D	20.9	53.7	9.5	2.6	26.2	19.6	11 200	178	4 872	24 567	1.6
Wayne	201	11.4	35.9	19.2	36.4	11.8	3.4	11.6	16.4	4 063	192	1 253	7 723	12.8
Webster	92	2.6	45.9	39.7	37.9	8.6	2.0	17.0	13.6	3 014	293	590	4 326	10.4
Wilkinson	52	0.8	D	12.9	D	9.8	4.6	26.9	29.6	1 979	192	890	4 242	12.5
Winston	202	1.7	D	36.9	D	10.0	2.7	15.6	11.7	4 183	207	984	7 613	5.9
Yalobusha	101	-1.0	D	37.9	D	10.8	3.7	10.4	21.3	3 405	261	963	5 414	-3.8
Yazoo	263	7.5	D	28.0	35.8	8.6	3.4	14.0	24.0	5 310	189	1 832	9 549	0.2
MISSOURI	103 740	0.1	24.1	17.1	60.5	9.6	8.1	27.2	15.3	1 008 424	180	112 213	2 199 129	10.6
Adair	321	-0.7	20.4	15.9	54.8	13.4	3.7	31.1	25.4	4 150	166	533	10 097	2.7
Andrew	87	0.1	D	D	D	12.4	2.7	25.5	23.0	2 881	175	143	5 841	5.9
Atchison	75	11.3	D	1.9	D	11.6	5.2	23.6	16.9	1 568	244	97	3 298	-8.8
Audrain	336	-0.6	D	33.4	D	11.2	4.1	13.0	24.0	5 381	208	356	10 039	-4.8
Barry	448	3.5	D	41.4	D	8.5	2.7	17.1	12.0	7 461	219	728	12 908	15.5
Barton	153	-2.9	53.8	47.2	34.3	8.9	3.6	11.5	14.8	2 699	215	244	5 014	3.6
Bates	119	6.6	D	7.0	D	12.5	4.8	15.7	25.8	3 914	235	338	6 782	-3.2
Benton	102	-1.3	D	7.0	D	18.0	6.2	19.9	27.1	5 297	308	407	10 280	23.5
Bollinger	58	-1.6	D	12.1	D	11.1	3.7	16.9	22.9	2 659	221	355	4 542	6.7
Boone	2 628	-0.2	14.4	8.5	48.2	9.8	8.7	21.6	37.6	16 448	121	1 800	44 695	19.4
Buchanan	1 461	0.0	D	21.4	D	10.2	5.2	25.4	15.5	16 505	192	2 030	35 652	-1.5
Butler	578	2.6	D	16.8	D	11.8	3.1	27.9	19.4	9 799	240	2 221	17 046	7.2
Caldwell	52	-1.2	D	2.0	D	12.9	5.9	14.6	30.3	1 952	218	153	3 649	-5.3
Callaway	470	0.0	25.7	15.9	47.3	8.5	3.0	13.8	27.1	6 587	162	551	13 003	10.9
Camden	452	0.1	D	10.3	D	20.8	8.5	30.4	11.4	9 228	249	429	25 662	51.4
Cape Girardeau	1 293	-0.2	26.7	17.7	59.8	11.7	4.0	29.0	13.7	11 845	172	1 256	25 315	11.3
Carroll	85	9.3	D	13.5	D	10.7	5.9	18.4	20.8	2 434	237	230	5 001	-8.8
Carter	41	-2.4	17.1	12.2	D	13.0	5.1	16.1	34.6	1 534	258	325	2 693	18.8
Cass	613	-0.4	27.1	6.5	50.9	14.9	5.0	19.2	22.4	12 573	153	490	24 337	27.2
Cedar	88	-2.3	D	12.8	D	16.7	4.4	17.4	28.1	3 736	272	370	6 035	7.2
Chariton	71	7.4	D	12.8	D	9.5	5.9	15.9	18.5	2 112	250	132	4 479	-6.9
Christian	413	-0.5	D	17.5	D	15.8	6.5	16.5	14.2	8 448	156	661	12 812	48.5
Clark	36	-19.2	D	10.1	D	14.2	5.6	16.2	40.8	1 549	209	114	3 398	-2.8
Clay	3 355	0.1	31.9	25.3	56.2	11.9	3.9	24.0	12.0	26 367	143	1 318	63 000	20.4
Clinton	138	-2.4	D	5.0	D	16.0	11.8	26.9	20.3	3 090	163	245	6 559	7.1
Cole	1 783	-0.3	D	6.9	D	9.2	6.2	21.1	41.1	11 317	159	941	24 939	18.1
Cooper	165	-2.3	28.1	20.6	49.9	10.7	3.7	16.0	24.3	3 168	190	215	6 002	2.3
Crawford	165	-1.2	D	29.8	D	17.9	3.6	16.3	15.4	5 144	226	531	9 030	4.2
Dade	59	0.2	D	9.8	D	8.8	3.6	14.6	26.1	2 053	259	167	3 543	1.9
Dallas	91	-2.5	D	10.2	D	19.0	5.7	16.9	22.3	3 568	228	404	5 484	8.2
Daviess	58	-1.5	D	17.9	D	9.4	6.1	11.3	26.2	1 821	227	107	3 613	-5.5
De Kalb	95	4.0	D	3.2	D	11.1	3.4	11.2	46.9	2 117	183	92	3 358	-3.6
Dent	139	-0.2	D	12.3	D	14.2	3.9	13.5	20.1	3 748	251	547	6 115	-3.2
Douglas	78	3.4	D	28.8	D	11.9	2.7	15.0	20.3	3 133	239	423	5 105	9.5
Dunklin	301	1.9	D	19.5	D	14.6	4.7	22.7	17.4	8 048	243	2 347	14 102	-4.8
Franklin	1 120	-0.3	42.3	32.6	46.1	11.6	4.9	19.0	11.8	16 508	176	1 363	32 451	17.9
Gasconade	165	-1.3	D	34.9	D	11.9	3.2	14.4	15.8	3 545	231	197	7 158	8.1
Gentry	61	8.0	D	14.5	D	12.9	4.3	21.1	21.8	1 987	290	142	3 232	-9.6
Greene	4 983	0.0	20.5	15.2	67.0	12.7	7.0	30.0	12.5	42 178	175	4 980	87 910	17.3
Grundy	108	-1.6	D	24.8	D	11.6	3.5	21.6	23.6	2 591	248	241	5 113	-8.1
Harrison	74	-2.4	D	2.8	D	26.0	4.8	19.4	27.0	2 287	258	213	4 245	-12.5
Henry	227	-1.3	D	20.2	D	15.7	5.1	18.8	20.8	5 629	256	630	9 317	5.2
Hickory	37	-0.7	D	8.1	D	16.3	4.4	19.1	27.4	3 074	344	205	5 482	15.8
Holt	51	16.8	D	6.9	D	10.7	6.1	12.3	19.9	1 416	265	93	3 190	-14.0
Howard	76	0.1	D	24.2	D	8.5	3.8	24.6	18.4	1 947	191	215	4 025	-1.8
Howell	409	-0.2	26.5	21.4	57.4	15.0	3.4	24.9	16.3	9 588	257	1 358	13 326	12.3
Iron	110	0.1	51.0	20.4	D	7.9	2.5	17.8	15.0	2 791	261	475	4 700	7.1
Jackson	17 527	0.0	18.4	11.5	66.1	7.7	11.5	30.8	15.5	108 583	166	12 769	280 729	7.0

1. Covers mining, construction, and manufacturing.   2. Covers private sector earnings in agricultural services, forestry, and fisheries; transportation and public utilities; wholesale trade; retail trade; finance, insurance, and real estate; and services.   3. Per 1,000 resident population estimated as of July 1 of the year shown.

STATE County	Housing units, 1990 (cont'd)								Civilian labor force, 2001				Civilian employment, 1990[5]		
	Occupied units										Unemployment			Percent	
			Owner-occupied			Renter-occupied									
				Owner cost as a percent of income											
	Total	Percent	Median value[1]	With a mort-gage	Without a mort-gage	Median rent[2]	Rent as per-cent of income	Sub-stand-ard units[3] (percent)	Total	Percent change, 2000–2001	Total	Rate[4]	Total	Professional, managerial, and technical	Precision production, craft, and repair
	89	90	91	92	93	94	95	96	97	98	99	100	101	102	103
MISSISSIPPI—Cont'd															
Sunflower	9 650	60.1	37 800	22.1	15.6	253	29.4	13.2	9 458	-17.9	1 202	12.7	10 293	20.6	11.1
Tallahatchie	5 034	69.5	31 500	23.9	14.5	189	26.6	17.3	5 332	-9.6	650	12.2	4 896	15.0	12.9
Tate	7 024	75.6	49 500	20.4	13.7	293	26.3	10.7	10 404	-1.8	501	4.8	9 143	19.9	13.9
Tippah	7 158	79.4	35 200	20.6	12.4	241	22.7	6.1	9 808	-4.3	585	6.0	8 247	16.5	16.3
Tishomingo	7 059	79.4	38 700	20.6	12.5	212	21.8	2.7	9 010	-5.5	670	7.4	7 300	17.6	16.5
Tunica	2 526	53.8	35 400	26.5	14.3	222	35.1	21.2	5 924	11.0	323	5.5	2 360	16.4	9.1
Union	8 367	78.2	39 700	21.1	12.6	248	22.1	3.7	12 761	-2.2	538	4.2	10 168	16.2	15.6
Walthall	4 929	84.3	39 100	30.3	15.9	223	27.3	12.7	5 542	-7.2	370	6.7	4 653	16.9	14.3
Warren	17 407	68.9	50 600	18.7	13.4	332	28.5	5.8	26 399	-2.2	1 055	4.0	19 373	32.5	12.2
Washington	22 593	59.6	41 700	20.6	15.2	318	31.3	11.2	26 495	-4.4	2 964	11.2	24 131	24.3	10.4
Wayne	6 858	83.7	37 100	26.5	12.9	220	27.3	9.7	8 692	-2.3	659	7.6	7 091	18.7	17.1
Webster	3 826	78.5	36 000	21.2	12.4	205	24.7	6.7	4 501	-1.7	492	10.9	3 819	17.8	12.4
Wilkinson	3 347	81.4	35 700	25.7	19.0	207	24.2	10.2	2 992	-2.4	259	8.7	2 957	15.2	9.3
Winston	7 061	81.6	39 100	21.0	12.9	256	28.7	8.2	7 445	-7.6	984	13.2	7 523	18.4	14.2
Yalobusha	4 614	79.2	35 500	23.0	14.1	205	25.9	8.5	4 733	-3.5	356	7.5	4 549	16.8	13.7
Yazoo	8 813	66.3	38 400	21.1	14.8	234	30.1	10.9	9 199	-5.7	735	8.0	8 298	19.8	11.6
MISSOURI	1 961 206	68.8	59 800	18.4	12.3	368	25.2	3.0	2 970 118	1.4	139 715	4.7	2 367 395	27.8	11.1
Adair	9 060	59.4	41 900	17.8	13.0	307	33.3	2.2	13 665	0.1	484	3.5	11 011	29.9	8.7
Andrew	5 429	78.6	45 900	16.9	11.9	303	21.5	1.0	8 698	3.9	403	4.6	6 645	21.6	13.0
Atchison	2 961	65.9	28 800	18.9	12.2	243	21.0	1.1	3 021	2.3	93	3.1	3 258	21.7	11.3
Audrain	9 205	74.2	36 000	16.1	12.4	276	24.6	3.1	13 646	2.9	550	4.0	10 332	22.3	12.7
Barry	10 858	77.2	42 300	20.5	12.2	280	22.8	4.6	15 941	4.2	741	4.6	11 640	13.9	15.3
Barton	4 524	73.8	31 800	17.8	12.8	253	20.8	2.5	7 116	0.5	252	3.5	5 057	16.9	11.0
Bates	5 918	74.6	31 400	19.4	13.3	266	26.4	3.3	7 296	1.2	442	6.1	5 939	19.5	15.5
Benton	5 764	81.4	38 300	22.2	12.7	262	30.5	4.8	6 345	5.7	506	8.0	4 831	18.2	12.2
Bollinger	3 946	81.7	29 400	15.3	13.4	241	27.3	8.1	5 581	2.2	400	7.2	4 151	15.7	14.9
Boone	41 937	55.0	65 700	17.5	12.0	381	27.3	2.1	87 354	3.4	1 557	1.8	58 017	38.3	7.8
Buchanan	32 486	68.0	40 800	15.2	11.9	304	24.0	2.0	43 717	4.1	2 320	5.3	35 952	23.4	11.5
Butler	15 334	68.1	36 300	18.7	12.8	255	27.5	3.3	19 959	2.3	1 199	6.0	15 285	22.8	12.0
Caldwell	3 222	76.2	25 600	17.5	12.9	243	24.4	2.4	3 287	6.1	202	6.1	3 354	16.9	12.3
Callaway	11 552	76.9	48 900	17.2	12.2	313	22.1	2.9	22 554	3.8	790	3.5	15 556	23.4	11.8
Camden	11 305	80.7	71 700	22.3	11.6	346	24.5	2.9	17 933	3.1	1 073	6.0	11 544	26.0	13.2
Cape Girardeau	23 390	67.7	56 900	17.8	12.2	327	27.2	1.9	38 069	0.7	1 492	3.9	29 939	27.2	10.7
Carroll	4 332	73.4	26 900	16.7	12.4	231	24.2	2.4	5 121	6.4	250	4.9	4 206	19.1	8.8
Carter	2 128	73.8	29 900	19.2	13.6	241	27.9	7.8	2 756	2.4	179	6.5	1 917	21.6	10.4
Cass	22 892	76.4	64 600	20.1	12.5	404	24.4	2.3	47 407	1.6	1 694	3.6	31 131	24.1	16.0
Cedar	5 003	79.6	34 200	19.7	11.8	231	25.7	3.2	5 348	5.2	267	5.0	4 655	19.2	8.0
Chariton	3 661	77.9	26 100	17.6	13.1	222	20.4	3.7	4 516	6.4	304	6.7	4 012	15.6	11.2
Christian	11 937	79.6	58 500	19.9	12.0	340	23.0	2.7	29 247	-0.8	1 129	3.9	15 889	20.2	14.7
Clark	2 859	75.9	26 300	16.4	12.8	225	25.9	5.7	3 897	5.8	283	7.3	3 252	13.5	13.1
Clay	58 915	67.5	68 500	18.0	11.7	429	23.1	2.0	111 202	1.5	3 453	3.1	81 396	28.5	11.1
Clinton	6 112	77.6	47 900	18.0	13.0	312	24.0	2.2	10 231	1.4	378	3.7	7 428	20.7	14.8
Cole	22 976	67.6	60 200	17.3	11.8	334	22.0	1.6	41 940	3.5	1 208	2.9	30 764	33.2	9.4
Cooper	5 359	75.0	39 600	17.7	13.1	274	24.6	3.0	8 286	-0.1	396	4.8	6 419	21.5	13.9
Crawford	7 299	78.4	37 900	20.9	12.6	278	26.3	3.7	10 416	3.6	671	6.4	7 583	16.9	16.8
Dade	2 976	77.3	30 900	18.3	12.6	218	22.1	3.9	3 509	4.4	158	4.5	3 086	17.5	13.2
Dallas	4 899	78.8	33 000	23.2	13.1	233	26.7	4.7	6 183	8.3	432	7.0	4 947	15.6	16.6
Daviess	3 040	75.3	24 600	16.2	13.6	238	22.9	4.6	3 529	3.7	181	5.1	3 059	17.8	11.2
De Kalb	3 054	73.1	33 200	17.2	12.1	229	23.1	3.2	4 615	-0.2	174	3.8	3 416	21.8	12.0
Dent	5 327	73.9	34 800	19.6	12.7	258	28.8	4.5	5 988	-1.4	529	8.8	4 952	20.8	11.2
Douglas	4 587	77.6	34 000	18.5	12.8	247	23.0	6.2	5 542	2.8	558	10.1	4 756	13.1	14.4
Dunklin	13 128	66.8	30 000	18.3	13.2	229	28.4	3.7	14 238	2.0	1 034	7.3	11 883	20.0	13.3
Franklin	28 856	78.0	58 300	18.5	11.9	348	23.3	4.0	48 900	0.8	2 671	5.5	37 568	19.8	16.3
Gasconade	5 543	80.3	41 800	17.9	12.6	253	22.9	2.8	7 866	-0.4	420	5.3	6 288	16.9	14.9
Gentry	2 756	74.5	23 000	17.3	13.8	219	22.3	2.7	3 783	4.5	149	3.9	2 878	21.4	9.8
Greene	81 463	63.4	58 200	17.9	11.6	344	25.8	2.2	129 190	-1.3	4 238	3.3	101 750	27.5	10.1
Grundy	4 346	72.5	24 200	16.1	13.6	231	25.3	2.4	5 052	0.9	204	4.0	4 420	20.2	10.6
Harrison	3 574	73.9	20 200	16.3	13.1	201	23.4	3.8	4 151	-0.4	139	3.3	3 678	20.1	9.1
Henry	8 189	73.4	36 500	20.0	13.4	275	27.0	3.1	10 535	-0.6	608	5.8	8 179	20.3	14.1
Hickory	3 183	84.2	37 500	22.4	11.8	225	27.2	2.9	2 674	0.0	233	8.7	2 351	18.2	11.3
Holt	2 440	73.6	22 600	16.9	12.8	203	22.5	3.4	2 660	-0.5	114	4.3	2 449	19.8	10.7
Howard	3 571	75.0	31 400	15.8	13.0	263	23.7	2.5	4 552	1.9	222	4.9	4 319	21.8	10.8
Howell	12 283	73.8	36 800	18.9	13.0	243	26.6	6.0	17 666	2.4	842	4.8	12 712	17.6	13.4
Iron	3 995	75.9	34 900	17.8	12.8	256	28.2	6.7	4 850	7.9	386	8.0	3 716	20.2	14.5
Jackson	252 582	61.3	58 400	18.4	12.4	402	25.5	2.8	378 796	1.9	18 618	4.9	309 069	29.2	9.9

1. Specified owner-occupied units.   2. Specified renter-occupied units.   3. Overcrowded or lacking complete plumbing facilities.   4. Percent of civilian labor force.   5. Persons 16 years and older.

STATE County		Private nonfarm establishments, employment and payroll, 1999								Agriculture, 1997			
		Employment						Annual payroll		Farms			Farm operators
											Percent with—		
	Number of establishments	Total	Health Care and Social Assistance	Manufacturing	Retail trade	Finance and Insurance	Professional Scientific and Technical Services	Total (mil dol)	Average per employee (dollars)	Number	Less than 50 acres	500 acres and over	Whose principal occupation is farming (percent)
	104	105	106	107	108	109	110	111	112	113	114	115	116
MISSISSIPPI—Cont'd													
Sunflower	486	7 556	994	2 800	1 088	238	93	143	18 915	350	8.9	52.6	70.3
Tallahatchie	193	1 549	263	348	268	45	21	29	18 912	355	12.4	38.0	52.7
Tate	414	5 517	344	2 007	1 397	193	64	108	19 541	508	24.0	13.2	40.0
Tippah	394	6 771	529	3 099	774	173	88	141	20 781	501	18.4	7.8	33.9
Tishomingo	411	5 132	452	2 595	589	146	66	112	21 852	258	21.7	6.2	26.4
Tunica	188	18 356	202	587	302	59	19	396	21 575	95	1.1	74.7	88.4
Union	464	9 145	657	4 254	1 080	186	91	220	24 023	549	23.3	6.4	29.0
Walthall	220	2 575	372	894	363	69	36	46	17 880	538	21.4	6.7	47.2
Warren	1 194	20 850	2 059	5 369	3 011	394	791	500	23 978	159	17.0	32.7	49.7
Washington	1 499	20 694	2 927	5 062	3 428	447	449	462	22 322	283	8.8	60.4	76.7
Wayne	394	4 916	621	1 326	868	183	43	100	20 337	458	31.2	6.1	40.8
Webster	192	2 932	379	1 592	257	61	47	53	18 244	289	19.4	11.4	38.1
Wilkinson	171	1 673	356	215	240	57	D	32	18 956	196	19.9	26.5	40.8
Winston	399	5 303	388	2 099	792	135	77	122	22 948	458	19.9	7.2	34.3
Yalobusha	254	2 579	70	1 194	398	100	26	59	22 790	278	14.4	13.7	37.1
Yazoo	452	5 493	637	2 078	983	209	78	114	20 695	424	9.7	39.9	53.3
MISSOURI	144 874	2 350 965	319 287	372 771	308 065	128 811	112 157	68 536	29 152	98 860	20.1	15.5	45.3
Adair	625	8 721	1 761	1 414	1 664	236	117	178	20 462	861	14.4	18.2	43.3
Andrew	250	2 297	350	26	1 081	62	29	42	18 078	820	18.4	15.5	50.1
Atchison	212	1 666	616	32	330	87	17	25	15 182	471	11.9	46.5	72.0
Audrain	648	8 653	1 479	2 834	1 408	253	128	219	25 324	1 005	15.1	23.5	57.7
Barry	807	13 081	1 015	6 943	1 556	325	834	292	22 325	1 598	27.8	6.4	45.7
Barton	288	4 934	606	2 484	564	128	135	102	20 581	896	15.3	24.2	53.3
Bates	395	2 983	501	436	609	159	68	51	17 213	1 250	17.3	18.9	47.8
Benton	395	2 431	243	298	577	121	65	37	15 030	804	14.1	15.0	49.8
Bollinger	206	1 381	179	314	287	39	22	21	15 489	832	13.5	12.5	40.0
Boone	3 775	60 320	13 509	5 757	9 268	5 220	2 101	1 428	23 675	1 227	28.8	10.8	35.6
Buchanan	2 369	35 768	5 937	6 919	4 430	1 935	992	922	25 785	776	28.5	12.5	45.7
Butler	1 050	15 016	3 239	3 437	2 424	434	288	321	21 390	678	22.3	25.1	52.2
Caldwell	186	986	195	71	174	84	18	20	19 991	845	17.0	13.6	43.0
Callaway	703	10 134	2 077	1 785	1 206	268	99	268	26 470	1 338	19.7	10.3	37.5
Camden	1 603	12 543	1 351	1 402	2 881	477	344	257	20 455	257	14.0	15.6	36.6
Cape Girardeau	2 321	37 097	7 505	7 017	6 338	1 206	880	876	23 603	1 161	21.7	9.7	46.6
Carroll	247	1 855	208	436	279	125	21	33	17 829	952	15.7	25.8	55.9
Carter	140	718	124	181	145	34	14	10	14 538	202	15.3	15.3	33.2
Cass	1 697	14 305	2 103	1 330	3 274	461	304	297	20 756	1 519	31.4	8.7	41.2
Cedar	311	2 556	627	557	414	88	68	45	17 627	865	18.3	11.2	45.5
Chariton	203	1 327	134	321	269	100	23	23	17 552	1 071	14.5	23.4	54.2
Christian	1 147	10 506	912	2 780	1 981	346	199	205	19 481	1 209	34.7	5.0	41.4
Clark	151	844	82	72	280	69	14	14	16 156	634	9.5	24.3	55.0
Clay	4 613	83 071	9 072	14 322	12 360	1 808	5 070	2 514	30 258	634	34.7	9.8	35.0
Clinton	437	3 243	842	239	796	217	63	60	18 415	768	25.0	14.6	40.1
Cole	2 144	35 904	5 439	3 206	5 195	1 776	1 156	879	24 495	1 045	20.0	5.4	34.3
Cooper	410	3 936	716	650	717	135	77	69	17 522	879	15.1	20.7	51.3
Crawford	479	4 912	584	1 462	1 140	137	116	98	19 910	691	15.8	12.7	38.2
Dade	158	1 146	106	278	125	D	17	21	18 463	808	17.3	17.3	47.6
Dallas	264	2 779	899	551	440	129	40	35	12 546	1 130	23.3	8.2	44.8
Daviess	178	1 286	152	452	202	54	13	19	14 778	886	15.8	20.2	47.5
De Kalb	201	1 650	353	50	237	241	29	28	17 118	769	17.7	16.8	45.0
Dent	348	3 806	508	878	750	131	60	78	20 363	727	11.8	17.3	36.0
Douglas	206	1 976	268	532	379	69	22	31	15 482	1 206	16.7	12.1	47.3
Dunklin	760	7 670	1 978	1 138	1 648	388	114	139	18 107	473	16.5	43.3	70.2
Franklin	2 393	31 717	3 029	10 857	4 793	755	738	767	24 175	1 592	25.4	7.4	37.4
Gasconade	432	4 466	432	1 742	705	123	87	101	22 645	762	11.7	10.0	37.3
Gentry	207	1 755	517	367	290	57	24	30	17 232	667	13.5	22.0	43.8
Greene	7 598	131 014	21 767	18 128	19 118	5 805	4 969	3 256	24 852	1 997	40.7	5.0	36.8
Grundy	273	3 251	510	1 334	473	105	51	70	21 616	667	15.0	18.4	46.9
Harrison	250	2 275	512	D	665	102	23	36	15 645	901	13.2	25.7	48.3
Henry	640	6 956	1 306	1 993	1 318	230	132	145	20 868	938	17.9	19.0	46.7
Hickory	153	846	113	88	150	31	20	11	13 175	521	10.4	19.0	56.2
Holt	134	935	151	164	221	53	D	18	19 644	465	12.0	34.2	63.0
Howard	213	1 896	374	358	191	83	90	35	18 503	709	13.3	18.2	44.6
Howell	1 024	12 656	2 569	3 821	2 103	287	217	241	19 014	1 637	22.0	9.2	38.7
Iron	254	2 395	649	361	328	72	16	58	24 304	274	14.6	11.3	35.0
Jackson	18 084	366 617	47 441	36 320	38 243	28 910	23 813	12 092	32 982	765	45.0	7.2	36.7

Table B. States and Counties — Agriculture, Land, and Water

	Agriculture, 1997 (cont'd)															
	Land in farms					Value of land and buildings			Value of products sold					Percent of farms with sales of —			
		Acres						Value of machinery and equipment average per farm ($1,000)				Percent from —				Percent of land owned by fed. gov. 1997	Water consumption 1995 (mil gal/day)
STATE County	Acreage (1,000)	Percent change, 1992–1997	Average size of farm	Total irrigated (1,000)	Total cropland (1,000)	Average per farm ($1,000)	Average per acre (dollars)		Total (mil dol)	Average per farm (dollars)	Crops	Livestock and poultry products	$10,000 or more	$100,000 or more		
	117	118	119	120	121	122	123	124	125	126	127	128	129	130	131	132
MISSISSIPPI—Cont'd																
Sunflower	348	-3.5	995	156	296	1 160	1 147	239	164	469 528	61.7	38.3	81.1	61.4	0.6	352.8
Tallahatchie	297	8.7	836	95	250	743	947	131	83	232 887	96.9	3.1	49.6	34.6	5.0	107.4
Tate	135	-4.5	265	1	77	288	1 136	36	24	48 042	47.4	52.6	36.0	10.2	5.7	5.7
Tippah	114	5.4	227	D	47	181	799	22	9	18 921	65.1	34.9	20.8	3.2	5.2	2.5
Tishomingo	45	9.4	174	D	17	187	887	27	3	10 766	32.1	67.8	15.1	1.2	7.7	4.4
Tunica	202	-12.4	2 130	60	185	1 971	938	346	64	676 490	89.9	10.1	87.4	66.3	1.2	140.4
Union	102	2.2	186	0	50	142	756	24	10	17 971	46.0	54.0	19.3	4.0	4.0	3.0
Walthall	110	2.2	205	D	50	250	1 310	27	51	94 370	2.4	97.6	34.2	16.5	0.0	2.2
Warren	98	-14.2	615	D	51	547	902	71	12	77 345	92.5	7.5	34.0	15.1	0.8	81.8
Washington	343	0.2	1 211	137	308	1 285	1 095	271	146	517 598	78.6	21.4	85.5	64.7	3.1	302.9
Wayne	76	3.8	165	0	28	215	1 349	46	63	136 739	2.1	97.9	38.9	22.5	17.3	2.2
Webster	79	3.5	272	D	35	201	731	44	13	43 294	56.7	43.3	28.0	8.7	0.6	1.4
Wilkinson	109	21.4	557	D	38	573	1 052	37	5	27 020	28.8	71.2	27.0	4.6	6.1	2.5
Winston	88	6.1	192	D	36	155	1 008	25	8	18 082	14.4	85.6	19.7	3.3	13.9	3.3
Yalobusha	86	9.7	308	D	41	196	707	49	9	34 150	80.0	20.0	26.3	5.4	19.8	2.7
Yazoo	312	-13.7	737	15	209	548	746	89	75	176 468	78.5	21.5	51.4	29.2	5.2	29.9
MISSOURI	28 826	1.0	292	882	19 229	309	1 069	41	5 368	54 297	43.0	57.0	44.4	10.8	4.3	7 029.0
Adair	268	0.4	311	D	171	211	650	32	22	25 324	47.7	52.3	47.2	4.8	0.0	4.0
Andrew	227	-0.1	276	0	178	321	1 174	47	40	49 318	70.0	30.0	55.2	14.1	0.0	3.0
Atchison	294	-3.2	625	6	256	708	1 119	117	63	132 798	89.1	10.9	81.3	44.8	0.7	19.0
Audrain	382	1.5	381	16	316	481	1 193	73	82	81 576	63.0	37.0	63.9	23.1	0.0	10.0
Barry	285	-2.3	178	0	163	217	1 309	29	152	95 115	2.7	97.3	42.4	13.4	11.3	7.3
Barton	335	7.8	374	9	252	309	776	52	64	71 699	52.3	47.7	55.4	16.9	0.0	4.7
Bates	445	3.4	356	1	297	341	942	44	66	52 644	49.1	50.9	51.4	11.4	0.0	2.8
Benton	232	-2.8	289	0	124	249	918	39	31	38 143	20.6	79.4	43.9	6.8	6.6	1.9
Bollinger	209	5.7	251	7	117	222	1 008	25	19	22 908	42.7	57.3	36.1	4.2	0.4	9.7
Boone	250	-8.1	204	4	172	331	1 599	37	40	32 684	42.0	58.0	34.8	5.9	0.8	18.2
Buchanan	182	0.3	234	0	145	303	1 217	56	32	41 487	79.4	20.6	46.9	11.9	0.0	57.6
Butler	255	0.0	376	108	218	441	1 191	80	60	88 338	91.5	8.5	51.0	22.9	11.0	155.8
Caldwell	227	-2.1	269	D	164	217	886	29	26	30 232	52.6	47.4	40.8	5.8	0.0	1.2
Callaway	330	-2.5	247	4	210	309	1 217	39	54	40 658	40.1	59.9	35.5	7.1	2.2	26.6
Camden	172	5.7	295	0	71	227	782	23	16	26 736	3.2	96.8	30.3	5.0	0.0	3.7
Cape Girardeau	261	3.1	225	9	197	325	1 361	49	46	39 814	50.0	50.0	44.3	9.5	0.0	12.2
Carroll	396	4.9	416	2	324	392	967	65	59	61 938	75.5	24.5	56.2	17.8	0.0	2.7
Carter	63	14.4	311	D	20	244	790	28	3	15 193	7.5	92.5	27.7	3.5	32.7	0.7
Cass	310	-4.8	204	5	229	320	1 517	36	56	36 603	61.2	38.8	37.1	6.1	0.1	6.4
Cedar	204	8.3	235	0	111	204	890	24	21	24 127	12.4	87.6	38.4	3.9	3.5	2.1
Chariton	414	2.6	387	1	332	368	996	59	85	79 565	56.0	44.0	59.3	19.0	1.3	1.7
Christian	203	-3.9	168	0	115	304	1 760	26	26	21 290	7.9	92.1	31.2	3.7	14.3	4.7
Clark	248	1.4	392	2	184	325	813	52	36	56 079	81.8	18.2	57.1	15.9	0.3	1.7
Clay	134	3.2	212	0	93	421	1 825	42	26	41 512	43.6	56.4	36.4	8.2	2.6	25.7
Clinton	216	4.1	282	0	156	356	1 254	39	35	45 007	51.8	48.2	46.1	11.8	1.8	2.1
Cole	179	-4.3	171	0	98	185	1 154	26	26	25 324	18.8	81.2	30.6	3.8	0.0	9.3
Cooper	302	0.9	343	0	224	332	941	56	53	60 099	45.3	54.7	57.6	16.0	0.4	2.9
Crawford	182	-9.8	264	0	82	230	902	20	9	12 630	17.1	82.9	30.5	1.6	10.4	2.5
Dade	249	-1.5	308	4	159	283	903	34	31	37 882	32.0	68.0	48.1	8.0	5.7	3.8
Dallas	222	-2.8	196	0	127	202	1 152	21	28	25 093	4.7	95.3	36.4	5.8	0.0	2.1
Daviess	302	8.2	341	0	209	263	717	39	57	64 538	42.2	57.8	48.3	11.9	0.0	1.8
De Kalb	215	2.0	280	D	162	252	882	35	29	38 063	51.4	48.6	45.3	10.9	0.0	1.2
Dent	222	1.4	305	0	96	249	746	22	10	13 578	7.7	92.3	35.2	1.7	15.3	1.7
Douglas	302	0.2	250	0	135	200	781	17	30	24 487	4.5	95.5	35.2	6.5	7.8	2.7
Dunklin	313	8.4	662	87	303	970	1 486	149	110	232 604	98.7	1.3	79.1	46.9	0.0	45.4
Franklin	290	-2.2	182	1	180	301	1 624	31	47	29 293	31.7	68.3	30.0	5.3	0.0	966.6
Gasconade	188	-4.6	247	0	96	264	1 045	29	15	19 929	26.6	73.4	33.1	4.6	0.0	2.6
Gentry	249	1.1	373	D	191	283	776	46	54	81 109	33.4	66.6	51.7	14.1	0.0	1.3
Greene	277	-2.8	139	0	183	310	2 206	23	33	16 732	16.0	84.0	28.8	3.1	0.3	175.9
Grundy	222	-1.8	333	1	170	227	727	41	29	43 256	72.9	27.1	44.7	11.2	0.0	3.2
Harrison	387	-2.9	430		255	275	635	37	44	49 272	56.2	43.8	47.8	11.0	0.0	4.0
Henry	315	-1.7	336	1	235	267	831	36	43	45 461	40.8	59.2	50.5	9.2	9.6	358.0
Hickory	172	-1.3	330	1	85	229	696	27	15	27 985	8.5	91.5	45.5	4.4	4.7	1.1
Holt	231	-0.8	497	9	204	455	1 040	80	53	114 557	83.8	16.2	77.4	33.1	1.9	2.5
Howard	242	1.4	342	3	159	354	1 046	37	31	44 328	64.2	35.8	50.4	11.3	0.8	1.6
Howell	387	4.0	236	0	162	238	975	20	50	30 637	3.3	96.7	35.5	4.9	8.3	5.4
Iron	63	-9.4	228	0	29	208	936	16	6	23 277	D	D	23.0	1.5	27.2	5.1
Jackson	151	12.4	197	1	114	377	2 122	37	28	36 060	80.7	19.3	32.3	7.3	0.3	546.7

Table B. States and Counties — Residential Construction, Wholesale and Retail Trade, and Real Estate

STATE County	Value of Residential Construction Authorized by Building Permits, 2000		Wholesale Trade, 1997				Retail Trade[1], 1997				Real Estate and Rental and Leasing, 1997			
	New Construction ($1,000)	Number of Housing Units	Number of Establishments	Number of Employees	Sales (mil dol)	Annual Payroll (mil dol)	Number of Establishments	Number of Employees	Sales (mil dol)	Annual Payroll (mil dol)	Number of Establishments	Number of Employees	Receipts (mil dol)	Annual Payroll (mil dol)
	133	134	135	136	137	138	139	140	141	142	143	144	145	146
MISSISSIPPI—Cont'd														
Sunflower	1 971	35	31	D	D	D	144	1 250	212.3	16.8	13	49	2.8	0.6
Tallahatchie	179	3	10	59	24.2	1.5	45	276	35.3	3.3	5	16	6.3	1.5
Tate	13 902	157	15	151	34.2	2.1	93	1 182	220.4	17.0	13	31	2.1	0.3
Tippah	1 400	20	20	181	59.9	2.8	105	831	106.7	10.2	11	38	6.1	0.7
Tishomingo	220	3	31	288	82.7	6.3	98	635	91.1	8.7	9	52	1.3	0.3
Tunica	11 902	244	11	109	110.6	2.9	40	304	61.8	4.8	10	20	1.6	0.2
Union	1 379	16	21	217	334.5	9.2	107	1 084	138.3	12.8	11	34	3.3	0.4
Walthall	105	4	14	181	53.3	1.9	54	378	56.2	5.3	2	D	D	D
Warren	2 729	42	46	359	151.6	10.6	281	3 316	454.7	43.7	46	127	14.2	2.0
Washington	10 022	126	78	795	393.8	24.5	324	3 441	507.2	48.2	78	305	25.5	4.0
Wayne	364	4	25	159	174.4	7.6	99	868	124.1	12.7	8	21	1.9	0.2
Webster	485	7	6	D	D	D	45	329	42.4	3.9	3	5	0.3	0.1
Wilkinson	0	0	12	88	27.3	1.5	31	228	31.1	2.7	3	8	0.7	0.1
Winston	2 124	16	13	242	98.0	8.6	90	741	103.9	10.2	7	123	5.6	1.9
Yalobusha	643	19	11	36	48.9	1.1	50	372	41.0	4.2	6	17	0.8	0.1
Yazoo	134	2	28	224	93.5	6.1	121	1 043	196.5	16.0	17	45	3.3	0.5
MISSOURI	2 569 404	24 321	9 522	125 929	91 411.9	4 639.8	24 181	297 556	51 269.9	4 945.0	5 500	31 301	3 991.1	698.1
Adair	6 369	111	30	376	87.6	6.8	143	1 595	225.2	21.7	26	198	11.1	2.5
Andrew	3 030	39	9	D	D	D	47	513	86.8	7.1	9	21	1.5	0.2
Atchison	541	6	13	D	D	D	45	376	59.5	4.8	5	12	0.8	0.1
Audrain	1 584	20	46	356	125.1	7.4	122	1 108	166.5	16.8	16	33	2.9	0.7
Barry	6 340	83	39	252	98.1	5.3	160	1 383	255.3	19.8	26	85	4.9	0.8
Barton	656	13	17	D	D	D	58	546	78.4	6.7	6	18	1.8	0.4
Bates	0	0	23	183	72.0	3.7	82	636	81.4	7.8	4	12	0.8	0.1
Benton	423	5	13	131	29.6	1.9	82	587	99.3	8.2	18	40	4.9	0.9
Bollinger	217	2	16	135	56.6	3.4	41	274	40.5	3.8	3	5	0.5	0.1
Boone	118 678	1 263	138	1 651	684.7	49.9	602	8 880	1 469.7	135.3	173	642	75.2	11.0
Buchanan	25 286	247	153	D	D	D	399	4 841	797.9	73.4	86	433	32.3	5.8
Butler	1 860	22	66	523	170.0	12.2	248	2 419	425.7	35.9	25	122	8.1	1.9
Caldwell	71	2	14	57	22.9	0.9	31	175	25.4	2.2	4	D	D	D
Callaway	12 108	124	35	238	130.0	5.0	119	1 109	208.2	16.3	19	56	4.2	0.8
Camden	7 292	122	58	244	88.4	5.0	328	2 639	437.0	42.1	80	272	26.8	4.6
Cape Girardeau	29 083	330	144	1 585	647.2	42.0	473	5 997	959.5	88.0	87	273	27.7	4.9
Carroll	649	6	24	105	78.8	2.1	52	286	36.3	3.2	7	15	0.7	0.1
Carter	100	1	5	20	4.7	0.4	29	149	17.9	1.3	7	17	1.3	0.2
Cass	83 389	811	58	D	D	D	218	2 833	492.9	44.4	60	176	17.5	3.3
Cedar	1 147	12	12	40	11.4	0.6	67	416	70.0	5.5	8	D	D	D
Chariton	433	4	20	190	121.4	4.2	49	260	47.9	3.6	9	D	D	D
Christian	47 724	545	58	403	134.3	8.6	176	1 298	247.7	20.7	42	109	7.9	1.2
Clark	433	4	17	155	69.1	3.5	38	327	44.2	3.8	5	D	D	D
Clay	81 535	663	334	4 707	5 773.2	165.4	721	11 919	2 476.5	211.4	179	1 179	169.4	27.9
Clinton	17 407	180	14	D	D	D	72	787	129.3	11.5	14	29	3.5	0.4
Cole	76 948	631	100	3 286	897.5	65.9	349	4 884	764.1	72.0	74	194	23.5	3.7
Cooper	6 188	75	26	125	63.2	2.8	71	640	96.5	8.6	10	36	1.7	0.3
Crawford	1 462	19	19	117	46.3	3.8	83	1 014	224.5	14.2	23	39	4.2	0.7
Dade	0	0	8	328	104.6	8.0	27	156	20.9	1.7	3	5	0.2	0.0
Dallas	NA	NA	17	75	23.8	1.2	59	423	80.9	6.8	13	22	0.9	0.2
Daviess	180	2	13	119	41.6	2.1	45	203	24.8	2.3	2	D	D	D
De Kalb	0	0	12	77	29.6	2.2	28	232	44.9	3.1	2	D	D	D
Dent	220	3	11	D	D	D	77	675	105.5	9.1	19	34	2.9	0.7
Douglas	1 221	12	8	56	27.1	0.8	40	324	46.6	4.3	3	9	0.8	0.1
Dunklin	3 933	48	53	384	134.3	9.0	186	1 690	256.6	25.2	27	98	6.4	1.2
Franklin	91 833	579	104	753	185.3	19.5	398	4 495	803.1	74.5	86	254	20.8	3.8
Gasconade	787	11	26	D	D	D	84	605	91.2	9.8	13	102	6.8	2.3
Gentry	275	4	12	D	D	D	48	304	40.9	4.1	3	10	0.5	0.0
Greene	201 684	1 914	576	8 856	5 101.7	263.9	1 302	17 819	3 271.8	294.0	336	1 736	151.7	32.3
Grundy	1 592	20	13	136	59.1	2.6	54	451	65.7	6.5	11	21	1.2	0.2
Harrison	1 182	11	19	225	74.6	4.6	56	605	92.7	8.7	9	23	1.2	0.2
Henry	3 475	53	48	534	218.6	14.2	136	1 126	177.1	15.0	18	37	2.7	0.4
Hickory	0	0	4	3	2.0	0.2	28	141	22.5	1.7	6	D	D	D
Holt	378	4	6	34	45.7	1.2	28	191	39.4	2.9	2	D	D	D
Howard	260	3	13	129	48.4	3.1	41	199	24.8	2.1	3	9	0.3	0.1
Howell	5 676	63	55	418	273.4	10.5	213	2 123	351.7	30.1	38	155	9.4	2.2
Iron	280	2	5	D	D	D	53	317	56.1	4.3	9	20	0.9	0.3
Jackson	461 250	4 347	1 197	19 252	11 305.8	712.5	2 670	39 198	7 239.1	704.8	746	4 888	793.7	127.3

1. Establishments with payroll.

STATE County	Professional, Scientific, and Technical Services[1], 1997				Manufacturing, 1997				Accommodation and Foodservices, 1997			
	Number of Establishments	Number of Employees	Receipts (mil dol)	Annual Payroll (mil dol)	Number of Establishments	Number of Employees	Receipts (mil dol)	Annual Payroll (mil dol)	Number of Establishments	Number of Employees	Sales (mil dol)	Annual Payroll (mil dol)
	147	148	149	150	151	152	153	154	155	156	157	158
MISSISSIPPI—Cont'd												
Sunflower	27	90	6.5	1.7	22	2 654	508.3	48.3	27	299	9.8	2.5
Tallahatchie	10	19	1.6	0.5	7	500	41.2	5.6	11	56	1.1	0.3
Tate	21	54	2.8	0.8	16	2 047	199.9	45.3	25	357	10.4	2.4
Tippah	12	42	2.3	0.9	42	3 247	344.1	71.2	21	D	D	D
Tishomingo	16	43	3.1	1.5	46	3 361	321.6	70.8	21	D	D	D
Tunica	6	19	2.5	0.5	NA	NA	NA	NA	26	11 575	826.9	226.1
Union	27	75	4.8	1.4	39	4 204	445.8	97.2	38	D	D	D
Walthall	7	19	0.9	0.2	24	940	68.9	15.8	17	149	4.3	1.2
Warren	76	577	34.2	17.4	43	4 698	1 181.8	131.7	97	3 294	160.8	38.0
Washington	83	361	36.2	10.5	65	5 067	1 030.3	121.8	95	1 486	47.5	12.3
Wayne	15	37	1.7	0.4	16	1 323	294.9	28.7	20	D	D	D
Webster	11	52	3.2	1.1	17	1 567	149.8	25.2	5	D	D	D
Wilkinson	6	13	0.7	0.1	NA	NA	NA	NA	9	79	2.2	0.6
Winston	20	176	5.9	3.2	26	1 850	318.3	53.5	22	326	8.9	2.4
Yalobusha	10	54	2.4	0.9	17	1 576	224.2	33.4	10	D	D	D
Yazoo	19	67	9.4	1.3	21	1 987	236.1	52.1	24	340	9.9	2.5
MISSOURI	10 601	93 792	9 953.3	3 643.6	7 497	371 448	93 115.5	11 647.0	11 150	203 849	6 780.8	1 933.3
Adair	34	112	6.8	2.2	10	1 619	412.4	39.8	59	1 364	29.0	8.7
Andrew	10	18	0.9	0.4	NA	NA	NA	NA	14	149	3.5	1.0
Atchison	6	13	0.7	0.2	NA	NA	NA	NA	21	D	D	D
Audrain	24	137	7.7	4.2	38	2 721	531.3	79.7	46	626	17.1	4.2
Barry	39	D	D	D	61	7 537	1 096.2	154.3	66	667	17.9	4.6
Barton	19	122	6.4	2.8	19	2 080	269.6	52.0	25	324	7.2	2.0
Bates	16	56	2.4	0.8	NA	NA	NA	NA	23	282	7.1	1.8
Benton	16	49	2.0	0.6	NA	NA	NA	NA	43	427	9.6	2.5
Bollinger	10	16	0.7	0.2	NA	NA	NA	NA	10	61	1.5	0.3
Boone	272	1 588	112.4	39.1	87	5 703	1 595.0	165.3	312	5 983	180.1	48.4
Buchanan	133	779	64.4	21.7	96	7 365	2 293.8	235.1	196	3 208	96.2	26.7
Butler	44	245	14.8	5.5	53	3 010	494.5	66.7	76	1 210	36.4	9.3
Caldwell	6	13	0.4	0.1	NA	NA	NA	NA	9	58	1.0	0.4
Callaway	22	85	5.5	1.9	37	1 896	320.6	59.6	48	739	22.6	5.9
Camden	73	275	19.9	6.4	53	1 269	132.0	32.6	200	2 412	103.9	31.4
Cape Girardeau	119	731	48.4	16.3	93	5 912	1 569.7	163.3	137	3 017	89.4	24.9
Carroll	11	21	1.0	0.2	NA	NA	NA	NA	13	D	D	D
Carter	5	D	D	D	NA	NA	NA	NA	18	63	2.0	0.5
Cass	80	209	16.5	5.3	71	1 057	116.6	24.6	104	1 647	50.4	12.8
Cedar	12	40	2.5	0.4	15	505	76.5	9.9	33	291	6.4	1.7
Chariton	11	18	1.0	0.2	NA	NA	NA	NA	11	39	1.1	0.2
Christian	44	156	8.1	2.9	101	D	D	D	62	841	20.3	5.9
Clark	5	D	D	D	NA	NA	NA	NA	4	31	0.8	0.3
Clay	337	3 362	401.0	154.3	214	14 743	9 891.7	569.6	320	12 228	527.2	145.2
Clinton	17	48	2.2	0.7	NA	NA	NA	NA	22	D	D	D
Cole	173	910	75.1	29.8	53	D	D	D	134	2 751	84.5	24.6
Cooper	17	64	3.6	1.0	16	865	138.6	19.2	32	391	10.2	2.8
Crawford	23	63	3.8	0.9	52	1 639	142.9	33.8	47	447	11.6	3.1
Dade	6	17	0.6	0.2	NA	NA	NA	NA	11	D	D	D
Dallas	11	25	1.1	0.3	11	530	40.2	8.7	27	298	6.7	1.9
Daviess	7	13	0.8	0.2	NA	NA	NA	NA	10	79	2.2	0.5
De Kalb	11	28	0.9	0.3	NA	NA	NA	NA	27	415	10.3	2.9
Dent	18	51	2.0	0.7	27	951	84.3	17.3	22	300	8.3	2.2
Douglas	8	10	0.7	0.2	NA	NA	NA	NA	8	148	3.6	1.0
Dunklin	39	113	6.9	1.5	26	1 281	259.7	28.5	51	563	14.6	3.7
Franklin	125	578	39.4	15.8	210	10 641	1 836.3	284.4	160	2 514	70.9	20.2
Gasconade	26	67	5.2	1.0	38	1 643	161.8	41.9	36	357	7.4	2.0
Gentry	6	15	0.8	0.3	NA	NA	NA	NA	12	62	1.3	0.3
Greene	574	4 028	363.7	121.3	371	19 475	3 788.6	513.1	595	11 812	350.3	100.0
Grundy	10	40	2.1	0.4	11	798	242.4	20.7	17	238	5.0	1.5
Harrison	8	25	0.8	0.2	NA	NA	NA	NA	17	320	8.8	2.2
Henry	28	85	4.9	1.2	32	1 780	390.1	33.0	53	568	16.2	4.1
Hickory	6	16	0.6	0.2	NA	NA	NA	NA	20	121	3.5	0.8
Holt	3	8	0.2	0.1	NA	NA	NA	NA	12	99	2.7	0.7
Howard	8	19	1.2	0.4	NA	NA	NA	NA	12	152	2.9	0.8
Howell	41	160	9.2	4.1	70	3 690	485.6	72.5	76	1 093	29.3	8.0
Iron	8	17	0.6	0.2	NA	NA	NA	NA	18	151	3.8	1.0
Jackson	1 728	19 506	2 015.2	843.0	907	38 785	8 984.7	1 301.5	1 393	28 200	1 005.3	292.5

1. Firms subject to federal tax.

STATE County	Health Care and Social Assistance[1], 1997				Other Services[1], 1997				Federal funds and grants, fiscal 2001[2] Expenditures (mil dol)		Direct payments for individuals[3]	
	Number of Establishments	Number of Employees	Receipts (mil dol)	Annual Payroll (mil dol)	Number of Establishments	Number of Employees	Receipts (mil dol)	Annual Payroll (mil dol)	Total	Social Security and government retirement	Medicare	Food stamps and Supplemental Security Income
	159	160	161	162	163	164	165	166	167	168	169	170
MISSISSIPPI—Cont'd												
Sunflower	35	457	25.5	9.4	41	172	10.4	3.0	216.2	45.7	30.4	17.9
Tallahatchie	8	122	7.2	2.5	13	34	1.5	0.3	130.6	24.7	15.7	8.6
Tate	27	335	18.8	6.6	31	111	7.4	1.8	116.7	47.7	18.6	6.3
Tippah	20	253	9.6	4.7	12	34	1.8	0.5	119.0	51.5	24.6	7.6
Tishomingo	19	303	14.4	5.1	23	64	4.5	1.1	136.0	57.2	22.5	4.4
Tunica	7	166	5.9	2.9	12	34	1.3	0.4	77.2	14.2	7.9	2.0
Union	35	280	17.6	6.5	25	94	6.1	1.4	108.1	53.1	20.7	4.9
Walthall	18	230	11.3	4.8	11	41	2.3	0.5	77.9	27.2	15.4	6.5
Warren	66	1 867	143.5	54.9	69	278	15.5	4.5	426.7	114.2	54.1	15.0
Washington	125	1 267	84.3	32.9	111	508	27.8	7.9	508.4	116.3	55.7	36.9
Wayne	27	268	14.6	5.6	18	57	3.3	0.8	100.1	36.6	14.3	8.0
Webster	12	176	7.9	3.2	8	19	1.8	0.3	58.7	24.9	11.0	3.3
Wilkinson	13	200	9.1	4.3	10	43	5.6	0.6	54.6	18.7	9.6	5.8
Winston	21	205	9.2	4.6	20	67	3.5	0.8	98.4	42.6	17.4	6.5
Yalobusha	14	62	4.2	1.1	5	17	1.1	0.2	91.1	39.3	18.5	5.3
Yazoo	24	326	17.6	6.8	35	106	6.7	1.6	321.8	50.8	29.6	13.3
MISSOURI	10 213	131 485	7 885.4	3 596.7	9 427	52 060	3 203.3	963.1	39 190.9	12 211.6	5 075.9	978.1
Adair	77	2 068	114.5	51.6	45	211	9.9	2.5	113.9	40.8	23.4	3.7
Andrew	14	131	5.1	2.5	18	69	4.4	1.2	58.2	25.6	10.3	1.5
Atchison	10	412	17.1	7.5	17	25	2.3	0.3	54.6	16.9	7.2	0.6
Audrain	60	452	26.1	11.8	49	241	15.7	4.2	144.2	58.7	31.3	3.7
Barry	36	277	9.9	4.2	46	139	8.8	2.1	161.9	87.8	31.0	5.3
Barton	17	199	7.5	2.9	24	90	4.6	1.0	67.2	25.8	12.1	2.1
Bates	23	272	12.1	4.4	33	62	4.1	0.8	98.6	39.1	17.7	2.5
Benton	16	190	7.6	3.1	28	45	3.5	0.7	115.2	64.6	22.5	2.6
Bollinger	6	79	2.4	1.0	14	59	3.5	0.8	61.9	25.1	9.6	1.8
Boone	328	4 024	321.4	129.7	230	1 269	67.1	20.6	655.6	214.6	83.1	17.8
Buchanan	174	2 235	138.5	62.8	161	786	46.6	13.2	450.6	201.0	89.4	19.2
Butler	92	2 502	160.4	53.5	64	243	13.6	4.1	319.9	109.2	43.7	14.8
Caldwell	4	D	D	D	11	18	1.4	0.2	52.1	21.8	9.4	1.4
Callaway	34	395	14.9	5.9	46	267	13.6	4.1	171.1	72.8	31.0	5.2
Camden	61	569	32.8	13.3	82	293	14.3	4.0	173.2	98.4	35.0	3.7
Cape Girardeau	201	2 170	162.1	73.5	129	584	36.4	10.6	298.1	136.3	44.7	12.7
Carroll	16	136	6.4	2.3	16	45	2.8	1.0	76.9	25.9	12.7	1.9
Carter	8	98	2.9	1.4	3	15	2.1	0.3	54.6	17.9	6.1	2.6
Cass	83	713	31.4	14.9	115	487	27.9	8.2	379.8	173.6	49.6	5.7
Cedar	14	211	8.0	3.6	13	28	1.6	0.3	80.5	41.1	16.3	2.8
Chariton	8	151	4.3	1.9	14	31	1.6	0.4	64.2	20.6	10.6	0.8
Christian	49	672	22.6	8.7	67	256	18.2	3.9	162.1	102.0	26.2	4.3
Clark	5	33	2.0	0.6	10	19	1.5	0.2	49.4	15.7	7.3	1.1
Clay	382	4 689	308.2	148.7	317	1 839	115.9	35.2	505.4	237.8	130.1	7.4
Clinton	24	177	7.8	3.2	33	101	5.1	1.2	88.9	41.9	17.0	2.2
Cole	160	1 936	127.1	70.5	115	609	30.8	9.4	1 175.5	211.0	55.6	8.8
Cooper	22	199	7.9	3.2	34	151	8.3	2.5	88.5	35.8	15.8	1.7
Crawford	26	412	10.8	4.5	27	71	7.5	1.1	101.3	52.8	19.5	4.8
Dade	4	12	0.7	0.1	10	28	2.1	0.4	49.3	22.0	8.4	1.1
Dallas	18	176	4.7	1.9	17	38	2.7	0.5	73.2	34.7	12.8	3.2
Daviess	8	51	1.6	0.5	10	10	0.8	0.1	50.3	19.0	7.8	0.8
De Kalb	13	214	7.6	2.9	9	30	2.3	0.6	40.7	17.5	6.5	0.9
Dent	21	213	7.9	3.3	20	61	3.3	0.7	102.3	40.2	16.7	1.8
Douglas	11	150	6.2	2.3	10	33	1.6	0.5	66.0	27.4	10.6	3.6
Dunklin	57	1 841	75.0	29.9	45	129	8.6	1.8	266.5	79.5	39.9	15.1
Franklin	159	1 507	74.1	30.9	140	561	34.3	11.0	365.2	198.4	69.6	10.7
Gasconade	23	309	9.9	4.5	19	66	4.6	1.2	71.9	40.2	16.4	1.4
Gentry	22	216	7.1	3.2	9	32	1.8	0.4	57.7	19.5	11.1	0.5
Greene	457	7 245	532.1	253.3	514	3 519	184.4	56.9	1 125.5	519.4	176.2	40.9
Grundy	17	159	4.9	2.0	23	94	4.1	1.0	72.9	27.8	12.7	1.7
Harrison	16	133	5.0	1.9	24	63	4.3	0.8	65.1	23.5	12.6	1.5
Henry	35	581	30.9	14.1	37	156	7.7	2.0	132.6	64.6	27.3	4.5
Hickory	5	D	D	D	9	17	1.2	0.2	57.2	31.8	12.5	1.8
Holt	5	114	4.2	1.7	11	17	1.3	0.2	57.1	15.3	7.3	0.6
Howard	16	298	8.4	3.7	10	24	1.4	0.2	65.1	21.1	12.3	1.4
Howell	63	631	29.1	10.9	61	218	16.0	3.3	205.4	97.0	34.0	9.9
Iron	19	151	5.3	1.7	15	57	2.9	0.9	65.7	29.1	12.7	2.9
Jackson	1 334	18 242	1 254.8	614.8	1 265	8 921	539.1	170.9	4 859.5	1 586.2	672.5	78.3

1. Firms subject to federal tax.　2. October 1, 2000 to September 30, 2001.　3. State totals may include programs not allocated by county.

STATE County	Federal funds and grants, fiscal 2001[1] (cont'd) Expenditures (mil dol) (cont'd)							Local government finances, 1997 General revenue				
	Procurement contract awards			Grants[2]						Taxes		
	Salaries and wages	Defense	Other	Medicaid and other health-related	Nutrition and family welfare	Education	Other	Total (mil dol)	Intergovern-mental (mil dol)	Total (mil dol)	Per capita[3] (dollars) Total	Property
	171	172	173	174	175	176	177	178	179	180	181	182
MISSISSIPPI—Cont'd												
Sunflower	4.2	0.0	1.1	38.0	8.7	3.7	5.0	72.1	39.3	13.4	383	354
Tallahatchie	2.9	6.8	0.5	27.0	3.4	1.6	7.6	23.2	13.2	4.4	291	266
Tate	4.2	0.6	0.6	18.9	2.7	1.3	2.1	52.9	30.4	10.9	463	436
Tippah	3.5	0.0	0.8	22.0	1.6	1.0	2.8	36.4	18.1	6.0	286	278
Tishomingo	3.7	27.3	0.8	16.3	1.3	0.5	0.6	23.8	15.2	4.9	263	228
Tunica	1.1	0.0	0.2	14.0	2.5	1.4	9.4	43.3	32.1	6.2	772	674
Union	3.5	0.4	0.8	16.6	1.4	0.8	1.1	32.5	19.7	8.0	339	304
Walthall	1.7	0.0	0.3	19.5	2.3	1.1	1.9	26.6	12.5	4.3	301	277
Warren	86.9	87.1	9.2	31.1	5.3	2.3	7.1	99.7	47.8	38.3	778	711
Washington	24.7	3.0	4.2	70.3	14.7	8.5	116.0	167.1	71.9	33.0	501	462
Wayne	2.1	0.4	0.4	18.1	2.9	1.3	15.0	49.0	17.8	4.9	241	229
Webster	2.1	0.0	0.4	10.6	1.2	0.5	1.5	15.8	8.8	3.3	320	313
Wilkinson	0.6	0.0	0.2	15.0	1.8	0.8	0.5	15.6	9.5	3.8	418	397
Winston	2.6	0.0	0.7	21.5	2.7	1.4	0.9	36.2	18.2	5.5	286	246
Yalobusha	4.0	0.4	0.7	15.6	1.3	0.7	1.8	25.6	11.5	4.0	321	294
Yazoo	16.4	2.8	97.8	35.6	5.3	2.4	16.3	44.5	27.6	11.8	466	441
MISSOURI	3 463.0	5 021.1	1 719.5	3 804.4	882.1	535.3	1 643.5	X	X	X	X	X
Adair	4.7	1.0	1.4	23.6	2.1	1.8	1.2	38.8	11.5	12.6	518	264
Andrew	2.6	0.0	0.5	5.3	1.0	0.3	0.2	19.9	10.0	6.4	416	330
Atchison	2.0	0.1	0.5	3.0	0.5	0.2	0.2	14.5	6.4	6.2	870	717
Audrain	4.5	0.0	1.0	12.0	2.1	1.2	2.9	37.2	15.1	14.1	597	368
Barry	6.9	0.6	1.1	22.7	2.7	1.8	0.4	48.4	24.9	16.3	498	374
Barton	2.7	0.0	0.5	5.7	0.9	0.3	2.3	16.1	7.5	6.3	526	349
Bates	3.3	0.0	0.8	11.0	1.6	0.7	3.5	20.3	11.0	6.6	415	325
Benton	4.4	0.2	0.7	9.7	1.4	0.8	2.1	23.7	9.5	6.7	407	291
Bollinger	1.8	0.0	0.4	17.6	1.1	0.7	0.0	13.5	7.6	4.6	401	318
Boone	99.1	5.5	18.9	77.8	8.7	18.7	73.1	223.9	79.2	93.9	731	424
Buchanan	29.2	0.4	3.9	57.5	10.1	4.6	10.1	149.4	58.1	65.2	797	411
Butler	22.5	0.1	3.6	67.8	6.0	3.2	9.2	61.2	27.8	22.8	564	294
Caldwell	2.1	0.0	0.5	4.1	0.6	0.4	2.6	14.8	7.8	3.8	433	360
Callaway	23.9	0.0	3.4	17.1	2.1	1.2	1.6	56.5	19.7	26.2	709	359
Camden	3.7	0.1	1.3	12.3	1.7	2.0	13.7	55.5	16.5	25.7	773	400
Cape Girardeau	24.0	3.7	5.0	33.4	3.9	4.5	12.1	94.7	31.5	44.6	676	327
Carroll	2.9	0.0	0.6	6.9	1.1	0.7	1.3	16.7	8.2	6.0	593	465
Carter	2.8	0.0	0.9	8.0	1.3	0.5	14.3	8.9	6.1	2.0	318	268
Cass	42.3	13.7	2.7	12.1	3.2	3.6	35.0	145.1	57.4	49.9	641	470
Cedar	2.7	0.4	0.5	12.6	1.1	0.6	0.3	24.6	10.5	5.6	430	299
Chariton	2.7	0.0	0.6	7.8	0.6	0.5	0.6	12.3	4.9	4.6	526	421
Christian	6.7	0.0	1.6	14.7	2.1	2.2	1.2	58.3	30.8	20.5	437	320
Clark	1.9	0.0	0.4	3.2	0.8	0.5	4.6	16.2	6.5	4.1	540	452
Clay	42.6	0.3	19.7	27.5	5.1	5.3	20.6	529.7	94.2	161.7	929	622
Clinton	3.4	0.0	4.4	9.2	1.0	0.8	0.4	26.2	12.9	8.9	476	351
Cole	17.4	0.5	3.2	116.1	264.8	154.3	320.2	105.1	36.9	52.0	755	462
Cooper	3.0	1.0	0.7	11.7	1.2	0.7	4.0	25.3	11.7	7.8	483	300
Crawford	2.3	0.5	0.6	14.0	2.0	1.1	3.1	22.9	12.2	7.8	352	244
Dade	1.8	0.1	0.5	7.1	0.7	1.1	1.4	13.3	6.0	3.3	415	308
Dallas	2.0	0.0	0.5	15.6	1.1	0.6	0.5	15.1	8.4	4.6	306	182
Daviess	2.3	1.0	0.8	4.6	0.8	0.7	0.8	16.9	10.3	4.4	563	452
De Kalb	1.6	0.0	0.4	2.1	0.5	0.7	1.0	11.2	6.2	3.5	311	249
Dent	3.6	14.0	0.6	20.4	1.9	1.0	1.3	20.4	10.2	6.1	433	291
Douglas	2.2	0.0	0.5	17.5	1.4	0.8	1.1	11.8	7.9	3.1	255	195
Dunklin	5.7	0.6	1.1	79.7	7.7	3.1	4.6	47.5	26.6	14.4	440	341
Franklin	14.5	0.4	3.6	28.7	5.0	4.0	18.0	131.8	51.3	58.2	639	415
Gasconade	2.4	0.0	0.6	7.3	0.8	0.7	0.2	29.2	13.1	9.5	645	439
Gentry	2.8	0.4	0.6	6.4	0.8	0.5	2.5	42.6	36.9	4.0	583	492
Greene	130.7	3.2	35.7	107.7	22.7	11.9	30.6	384.5	131.0	161.1	714	398
Grundy	3.1	0.0	0.6	8.1	2.0	1.0	2.0	23.9	11.6	5.6	547	371
Harrison	2.9	0.0	1.0	6.9	0.9	0.8	1.0	22.0	8.4	5.9	707	541
Henry	4.7	0.1	1.1	14.6	1.6	1.0	3.2	33.8	15.8	13.1	624	414
Hickory	1.9	0.0	0.4	5.7	0.9	0.5	0.8	12.6	8.1	3.5	407	342
Holt	2.0	1.2	0.4	3.9	0.4	0.2	8.1	9.5	4.0	4.2	753	497
Howard	2.1	0.6	0.7	10.7	0.8	0.7	3.9	15.6	6.7	5.4	550	392
Howell	6.4	0.6	1.2	37.7	5.7	2.5	4.6	57.4	33.1	15.8	444	295
Iron	1.5	0.0	0.4	15.6	1.6	1.2	0.7	19.1	9.9	7.6	690	548
Jackson	850.5	137.6	674.9	377.9	74.9	44.8	131.1	1 962.8	630.3	904.0	1 395	665

1. October 1, 2000 to September 30, 2001. 2. State totals may include programs not allocated by county. 3. Based on the resident population estimated as of July 1 of the year shown.

STATE County	Total (mil dol)	Per capita[1] (dollars)	Education	Health and hospitals	Police protection	Public welfare	Highways	Total (mil dol)	Per capita[1] (dollars)	Federal civilian	Federal military	State and local	Democratic	Republican	All other
	183	184	185	186	187	188	189	190	191	192	193	194	195	196	197
MISSISSIPPI—Cont'd															
Sunflower	71.9	2 058	61.7	14.8	4.8	0.6	5.5	21.9	628	73	222	4 285	59.2	40.0	0.8
Tallahatchie	22.7	1 510	57.8	15.2	6.7	0.5	2.8	3.0	200	52	97	855	55.1	44.0	1.0
Tate	51.4	2 181	77.0	1.0	4.4	0.2	4.8	18.0	763	82	163	1 539	39.6	59.2	1.2
Tippah	36.9	1 764	47.0	25.4	2.7	1.5	6.8	6.1	293	61	140	1 018	34.6	64.0	1.3
Tishomingo	22.4	1 205	57.5	0.1	5.6	0.7	8.5	3.9	212	74	125	691	39.3	59.0	1.7
Tunica	31.7	3 921	44.3	0.3	7.6	0.3	27.7	6.2	770	21	53	638	65.0	33.5	1.5
Union	32.2	1 362	56.5	1.1	3.5	0.4	10.3	11.8	499	63	161	995	33.2	65.4	1.4
Walthall	28.4	1 982	43.1	27.5	5.9	0.5	3.8	1.5	107	28	95	719	40.0	59.0	1.1
Warren	93.3	1 895	45.9	1.9	6.7	0.8	6.5	59.7	1 213	2 189	359	2 648	40.2	58.5	1.3
Washington	159.4	2 422	36.5	24.1	5.6	0.7	4.5	53.0	805	499	444	4 175	56.8	40.2	3.1
Wayne	49.3	2 450	36.4	45.3	3.0	0.1	5.0	10.2	509	35	137	1 162	38.7	60.2	1.1
Webster	14.0	1 346	63.6	0.1	5.8	0.0	12.4	8.8	842	40	71	405	31.4	67.5	1.1
Wilkinson	15.2	1 652	60.2	2.3	3.7	0.0	16.2	6.0	650	12	60	553	62.2	34.7	3.0
Winston	38.9	2 018	39.9	2.8	3.8	0.1	15.7	9.9	514	48	128	778	43.9	55.5	0.6
Yalobusha	22.1	1 796	42.3	24.0	4.6	0.1	8.1	6.7	543	97	84	682	51.1	47.2	1.6
Yazoo	43.9	1 729	48.8	0.3	6.5	0.1	15.2	27.6	1 086	350	168	1 446	47.5	50.0	2.5
MISSOURI	X	X	X	X	X	X	X	X	X	59 186	40 460	357 264	47.1	50.4	2.5
Adair	38.7	1 591	42.0	26.0	4.0	0.0	5.6	21.8	895	88	118	2 678	38.9	57.3	3.8
Andrew	20.3	1 327	65.9	2.7	1.4	0.1	13.5	5.3	349	45	75	681	38.4	58.5	3.1
Atchison	14.1	1 978	52.5	4.6	3.1	0.0	21.9	2.5	350	39	34	421	35.3	62.6	2.1
Audrain	38.7	1 641	51.9	0.7	6.3	6.6	10.9	30.7	1 301	89	112	2 704	45.6	52.6	1.8
Barry	49.7	1 521	66.0	1.4	2.9	0.8	9.8	21.1	645	143	159	1 678	33.4	63.8	2.9
Barton	16.4	1 370	64.2	1.8	4.1	0.0	10.0	8.0	671	41	58	820	26.5	71.5	2.0
Bates	20.1	1 268	68.9	0.4	4.5	0.0	10.7	6.2	389	65	77	1 115	43.5	54.5	2.1
Benton	22.5	1 364	54.4	0.8	2.9	25.0	6.9	6.1	372	106	83	806	41.8	56.0	2.2
Bollinger	13.7	1 193	72.9	1.8	2.6	0.4	6.8	2.3	196	35	57	432	32.0	65.9	2.2
Boone	227.7	1 775	52.0	1.3	5.0	2.0	8.3	248.9	1 940	2 028	657	26 435	48.3	47.7	4.0
Buchanan	155.1	1 896	46.0	1.2	6.0	0.2	5.8	27.1	331	526	397	6 052	49.2	47.3	3.5
Butler	66.7	1 650	64.8	0.0	3.5	0.0	4.2	28.5	705	517	195	2 667	34.7	63.3	2.0
Caldwell	14.0	1 613	67.8	2.6	1.1	10.3	8.1	2.9	329	42	43	595	38.6	57.7	3.7
Callaway	57.7	1 563	53.7	3.8	4.8	0.0	5.8	26.6	721	193	200	4 062	43.8	53.8	2.3
Camden	57.7	1 735	49.5	2.1	3.5	8.4	12.7	26.4	793	67	166	1 677	37.0	60.6	2.4
Cape Girardeau	94.8	1 436	49.0	0.5	6.2	0.0	6.7	98.6	1 493	417	333	5 315	31.3	66.4	2.4
Carroll	17.4	1 710	59.9	4.1	4.0	0.0	12.3	6.0	591	56	48	633	35.4	62.9	1.8
Carter	9.1	1 440	83.5	1.8	1.7	0.0	3.7	0.3	55	70	30	396	35.5	61.6	2.9
Cass	146.6	1 882	62.0	8.5	4.5	0.1	5.2	98.9	1 269	255	842	3 282	41.6	56.1	2.3
Cedar	23.7	1 820	48.8	26.3	6.8	0.0	8.7	1.9	146	60	64	753	34.9	62.3	2.7
Chariton	12.7	1 441	62.0	3.2	3.3	0.0	15.1	2.1	236	53	41	455	43.1	55.4	1.5
Christian	59.4	1 264	70.6	0.8	4.3	0.0	6.9	32.7	696	113	246	1 724	34.0	63.8	2.2
Clark	16.4	2 180	52.7	3.4	1.4	18.1	13.4	4.2	564	37	35	565	47.7	49.9	2.4
Clay	498.1	2 862	36.5	39.8	2.5	0.3	3.3	212.3	1 220	350	1 309	10 725	48.7	48.7	2.5
Clinton	25.9	1 391	61.6	1.2	7.6	0.0	9.4	16.3	874	66	94	838	46.8	50.7	2.6
Cole	104.5	1 519	50.7	1.2	6.0	0.0	13.7	41.1	598	517	333	19 536	36.8	61.5	1.7
Cooper	25.5	1 587	62.0	1.1	4.1	5.2	9.1	5.6	348	53	83	1 401	37.8	60.0	2.2
Crawford	21.4	971	70.8	4.7	4.8	0.0	5.4	6.6	298	39	108	847	40.4	57.3	2.4
Dade	14.5	1 821	57.5	0.7	3.0	21.2	10.2	4.3	547	38	38	612	31.8	65.8	2.4
Dallas	16.4	1 086	73.5	0.0	4.2	0.0	9.5	1.2	81	37	75	631	37.2	59.9	3.0
Daviess	14.2	1 822	66.4	6.0	2.6	0.1	7.1	4.0	520	62	39	475	39.1	57.6	3.4
De Kalb	10.6	953	70.6	1.6	3.5	0.0	6.3	7.0	630	34	54	1 537	38.6	58.4	3.1
Dent	21.2	1 503	73.2	0.6	3.2	0.0	5.8	3.7	261	84	68	912	30.7	66.7	2.6
Douglas	11.3	916	77.7	0.5	5.0	0.0	6.8	0.0	2	57	60	474	29.3	68.2	2.6
Dunklin	47.7	1 453	67.3	0.3	5.9	0.0	5.8	13.6	416	107	156	1 600	47.0	51.6	1.4
Franklin	135.0	1 484	60.4	2.0	5.9	0.1	10.5	97.8	1 075	236	448	3 880	41.3	55.8	2.9
Gasconade	28.8	1 949	56.1	17.5	3.9	0.0	6.8	8.9	603	48	72	961	34.0	63.2	2.8
Gentry	11.4	1 661	65.0	4.1	3.4	0.0	11.6	1.2	176	45	33	431	40.9	57.0	2.1
Greene	373.7	1 657	51.0	1.6	4.8	1.1	8.7	405.8	1 799	2 213	1 127	14 292	39.9	57.5	2.6
Grundy	24.5	2 390	64.3	1.6	3.2	12.1	7.5	7.9	774	55	49	936	33.2	63.2	3.6
Harrison	20.8	2 481	47.2	22.8	2.3	0.0	10.8	4.3	511	50	40	720	33.3	63.9	2.8
Henry	33.7	1 601	50.7	14.5	3.6	0.0	11.0	11.5	547	89	102	1 501	45.6	52.4	2.1
Hickory	15.1	1 746	83.0	0.4	2.3	0.0	2.9	4.7	539	45	42	311	46.3	51.3	2.5
Holt	9.0	1 601	60.7	0.8	2.7	0.0	14.4	2.5	447	40	27	322	32.7	65.3	2.0
Howard	15.3	1 561	56.4	2.6	4.0	1.8	7.4	5.7	586	41	46	493	43.1	53.5	3.4
Howell	53.8	1 511	67.2	9.0	3.9	0.0	8.3	4.9	139	111	175	2 220	33.0	64.1	3.0
Iron	18.6	1 689	74.4	1.5	3.7	0.0	9.7	0.8	69	27	52	569	46.3	50.7	3.0
Jackson	1 993.4	3 076	42.9	3.9	7.4	0.3	3.8	1 825.1	2 817	17 060	3 389	44 006	59.0	38.4	2.7

1. Based on the resident population estimated as of July 1 of the year shown. 2. Data subject to copyright.

					Population and population characteristics, 2000												
								Race alone or in combination (percent)						Age (percent)				
STATE/ County code	MSA/ PMSA/ NECMA code[1]	County Type[2]	STATE County	Land area,[3] (sq km) 2000	Total persons	Rank	Per square kilometer	White	Black	Am. Indian, Alaska Native	Asian and Pacific Islander	Percent Hispanic[4]	Under 5 years	5 to 17 years	18 to 24 years	25 to 34 years	35 to 44 years	45 to 54 years
				1	2	3	4	5	6	7	8	9	10	11	12	13	14	15
			MISSOURI—Cont'd															
29 097	3710	3	Jasper	1 657	104 686	504	63.2	94.7	1.9	2.7	1.0	3.5	7.3	18.5	11.0	13.4	14.7	12.7
29 099	7040	1	Jefferson	1 701	198 099	279	116.5	98.4	0.9	0.8	0.5	1.0	7.2	20.7	8.5	13.8	18.1	13.8
29 101	...	6	Johnson	2 151	48 258	943	22.4	91.9	4.9	1.4	2.2	2.9	6.7	18.4	20.2	13.0	14.6	10.6
29 103	...	9	Knox	1 310	4 361	2 890	3.3	99.6	0.4	0.7	0.3	0.6	6.1	18.8	6.2	9.1	14.6	12.7
29 105	...	6	Laclede	1 984	32 513	1 330	16.4	98.4	0.6	1.3	0.6	1.2	6.9	19.8	8.4	12.3	15.5	13.0
29 107	3760	1	Lafayette	1 630	32 960	1 321	20.2	96.6	2.6	0.9	0.5	1.2	6.1	20.1	7.6	11.8	15.7	13.2
29 109	...	6	Lawrence	1 588	35 204	1 242	22.2	97.0	0.4	1.6	0.3	3.4	7.1	20.1	7.9	12.1	14.8	12.5
29 111	...	7	Lewis	1 308	10 494	2 399	8.0	96.6	2.9	0.3	0.4	0.7	7.2	17.8	12.9	10.7	13.9	11.7
29 113	7040	1	Lincoln	1 633	38 944	1 141	23.8	97.2	2.1	1.0	0.4	1.1	7.3	22.7	8.1	12.6	17.6	12.4
29 115	...	7	Linn	1 607	13 754	2 177	8.6	98.7	0.9	0.7	0.3	0.8	6.1	19.3	7.0	10.5	13.9	12.5
29 117	...	7	Livingston	1 384	14 558	2 117	10.5	96.7	2.7	0.7	0.5	0.6	6.1	18.3	7.4	11.4	14.9	13.4
29 119	...	8	McDonald	1 397	21 681	1 708	15.5	92.9	0.3	5.5	0.5	9.4	7.8	21.1	8.7	13.4	15.1	12.6
29 121	...	7	Macon	2 082	15 762	2 034	7.6	97.0	2.5	0.8	0.2	0.8	6.4	17.8	7.5	11.2	14.0	13.5
29 123	...	9	Madison	1 287	11 800	2 305	9.2	99.1	0.2	0.8	0.4	0.6	5.9	18.7	7.9	11.3	15.0	13.0
29 125	...	9	Maries	1 367	8 903	2 533	6.5	98.7	0.5	1.5	0.2	1.2	6.6	19.4	7.3	11.4	15.2	13.0
29 127	...	5	Marion	1 135	28 289	1 437	24.9	94.5	5.2	0.8	0.5	0.9	6.8	18.9	9.5	11.8	14.6	13.4
29 129	...	9	Mercer	1 176	3 757	2 934	3.2	99.2	0.2	1.0	0.1	0.3	5.6	17.4	6.7	9.3	15.0	12.7
29 131	...	7	Miller	1 534	23 564	1 610	15.4	98.8	0.4	1.1	0.2	1.0	6.8	19.5	8.4	12.2	15.2	12.8
29 133	...	7	Mississippi	1 070	13 427	2 198	12.5	78.7	20.8	0.7	0.2	1.0	7.2	19.2	8.8	11.8	13.6	12.9
29 135	...	6	Moniteau	1 079	14 827	2 102	13.7	93.8	4.0	1.2	0.6	2.9	6.7	19.2	8.2	14.3	16.8	12.7
29 137	...	9	Monroe	1 673	9 311	2 505	5.6	95.4	4.1	0.8	0.2	0.6	6.5	19.4	7.3	10.5	14.6	13.0
29 139	...	8	Montgomery	1 392	12 136	2 289	8.7	97.2	2.4	0.9	0.5	0.8	5.7	19.7	7.4	10.7	15.4	13.3
29 141	...	9	Morgan	1 547	19 309	1 827	12.5	98.5	0.6	1.4	0.3	0.8	6.0	17.8	6.2	9.9	13.2	13.4
29 143	...	7	New Madrid	1 756	19 760	1 805	11.3	83.9	15.6	0.6	0.3	0.9	6.6	19.8	8.5	11.9	14.5	13.0
29 145	3710	3	Newton	1 622	52 636	886	32.5	95.3	0.8	3.9	0.9	2.2	7.0	19.2	8.7	12.0	15.1	13.5
29 147	...	6	Nodaway	2 270	21 912	1 696	9.7	97.3	1.5	0.6	1.1	0.7	4.7	14.7	25.1	10.5	12.6	10.9
29 149	...	9	Oregon	2 050	10 344	2 409	5.0	96.7	0.1	4.9	0.2	1.1	5.9	18.4	7.0	10.5	13.6	14.0
29 151	...	9	Osage	1 570	13 062	2 225	8.3	99.4	0.3	0.9	0.2	0.6	6.7	19.6	9.5	12.5	15.2	12.3
29 153	...	9	Ozark	1 922	9 542	2 485	5.0	98.9	0.3	1.7	0.4	0.9	5.4	16.7	6.9	9.2	13.6	14.1
29 155	...	7	Pemiscot	1 277	20 047	1 791	15.7	72.5	26.6	0.6	0.4	1.6	8.1	21.9	9.1	11.7	13.3	12.2
29 157	...	7	Perry	1 229	18 132	1 891	14.8	98.8	0.2	0.6	0.8	0.5	6.8	19.3	8.6	12.5	15.4	12.9
29 159	...	7	Pettis	1 774	39 403	1 127	22.2	93.6	3.5	1.0	0.8	3.9	7.0	19.3	9.3	12.3	15.6	12.2
29 161	...	7	Phelps	1 743	39 825	1 117	22.8	94.9	1.8	1.4	2.8	1.2	5.7	18.0	14.5	11.9	14.2	12.4
29 163	...	6	Pike	1 743	18 351	1 876	10.5	89.3	9.7	0.6	0.4	1.6	5.4	18.0	9.1	13.3	16.5	13.0
29 165	3760	0	Platte	1 089	73 781	680	67.8	93.1	4.0	1.1	2.2	3.0	6.8	18.9	8.3	14.4	18.2	15.4
29 167	...	6	Polk	1 650	26 992	1 483	16.4	98.3	0.6	1.3	0.4	1.3	6.8	19.0	12.6	11.6	13.9	11.6
29 169	...	7	Pulaski	1 417	41 165	1 076	29.1	81.3	13.0	2.0	4.0	5.8	7.7	19.9	16.6	16.8	15.2	9.7
29 171	...	9	Putnam	1 341	5 223	2 836	3.9	99.6	0.1	0.4	0.2	0.6	6.5	17.5	6.2	10.4	13.6	12.8
29 173	...	9	Ralls	1 220	9 626	2 476	7.9	98.6	1.2	0.5	0.2	0.4	5.7	19.6	7.1	10.9	16.0	15.2
29 175	...	6	Randolph	1 249	24 663	1 568	19.7	91.7	7.4	1.1	0.7	1.1	6.4	17.5	9.6	13.4	15.9	13.7
29 177	3760	1	Ray	1 475	23 354	1 626	15.8	97.6	1.8	1.0	0.4	1.1	6.6	20.9	7.4	11.9	16.4	13.7
29 179	...	9	Reynolds	2 101	6 689	2 718	3.2	97.7	0.7	2.9	0.6	0.8	5.8	18.2	6.8	11.4	13.6	14.2
29 181	...	9	Ripley	1 630	13 509	2 193	8.3	98.3	0.1	2.2	0.3	1.0	6.0	18.8	7.9	11.0	14.2	13.0
29 183	7040	0	St. Charles	1 451	283 883	198	195.6	95.7	3.0	0.6	1.2	1.5	7.6	21.3	8.2	14.0	18.6	13.6
29 185	...	9	St. Clair	1 753	9 652	2 473	5.5	98.5	0.4	1.6	0.2	1.0	5.5	17.5	5.6	9.3	13.6	13.4
29 186	...	6	Ste. Genevieve	1 301	17 842	1 908	13.7	98.7	0.8	0.7	0.2	0.7	6.0	20.6	7.6	11.1	16.8	13.5
29 187	...	6	St. Francois	1 164	55 641	848	47.8	96.9	2.2	0.9	0.6	0.8	6.0	17.9	9.2	13.3	16.1	12.9
29 189	7040	0	St. Louis	1 315	1 016 315	34	772.9	77.8	19.6	0.5	2.7	1.4	6.3	18.9	8.3	12.6	16.3	14.4
29 195	...	7	Saline	1 957	23 756	1 600	12.1	91.5	6.1	0.8	0.8	4.4	6.1	18.2	12.0	10.8	14.4	13.0
29 197	...	9	Schuyler	797	4 170	2 901	5.2	99.3	0.2	0.9	0.2	0.6	6.0	18.6	6.7	10.5	14.3	12.3
29 199	...	9	Scotland	1 136	4 983	2 850	4.4	99.4	0.3	0.6	0.1	0.8	7.2	21.4	7.6	10.2	13.9	10.9
29 201	...	5	Scott	1 090	40 422	1 107	37.1	88.5	10.8	0.8	0.3	1.1	7.0	20.4	8.5	12.7	14.8	13.4
29 203	...	9	Shannon	2 600	8 324	2 579	3.2	97.6	0.3	4.2	0.3	0.9	6.2	20.3	7.2	11.1	15.0	13.4
29 205	...	9	Shelby	1 297	6 799	2 712	5.2	98.4	1.1	0.5	0.2	0.6	5.7	19.7	7.2	9.7	14.6	13.2
29 207	...	7	Stoddard	2 142	29 705	1 408	13.9	98.3	1.0	1.1	0.3	0.8	5.7	18.2	8.5	11.6	14.7	13.2
29 209	...	8	Stone	1 200	28 658	1 431	23.9	98.8	0.1	1.5	0.4	1.0	5.5	16.0	6.2	10.1	13.7	14.3
29 211	...	9	Sullivan	1 686	7 219	2 664	4.3	95.8	0.3	0.6	0.3	8.8	7.1	17.9	7.5	12.4	13.9	12.6
29 213	...	6	Taney	1 638	39 703	1 118	24.2	97.6	0.4	1.7	0.7	2.4	6.1	16.3	10.2	12.2	14.0	13.4
29 215	...	9	Texas	3 052	23 003	1 641	7.5	98.2	0.4	2.3	0.7	1.0	5.8	19.2	7.1	9.9	15.0	13.8
29 217	...	7	Vernon	2 160	20 454	1 762	9.5	97.9	0.7	1.4	0.5	0.8	6.7	19.9	9.2	11.4	14.0	13.2
29 219	7040	1	Warren	1 117	24 525	1 577	22.0	96.8	2.2	1.0	0.5	1.3	6.5	20.3	7.6	11.4	17.4	13.1
29 221	...	6	Washington	1 967	23 344	1 627	11.9	96.5	2.6	1.4	0.2	0.7	6.6	20.0	9.8	13.4	15.9	12.9
29 223	...	9	Wayne	1 971	13 259	2 206	6.7	99.0	0.2	1.7	0.2	0.5	5.3	17.9	6.7	9.7	13.8	13.1
29 225	7920	2	Webster	1 537	31 045	1 376	20.2	97.5	1.3	1.5	0.5	1.3	7.5	21.3	8.3	13.5	16.2	12.5
29 227	...	9	Worth	690	2 382	3 034	3.5	99.4	0.2	0.5	0.5	0.3	5.5	18.8	6.8	8.4	15.1	11.9
29 229	...	6	Wright	1 767	17 955	1 899	10.2	98.6	0.4	1.4	0.4	0.8	7.0	20.2	8.2	10.9	14.3	12.3

1. MSA = Metropolitan Statistical Area. PMSA = Primary MSA. NECMA = New England County Metropolitan Area. See Appendix A for explanation of these concepts. See Appendix B for list of metropolitan areas identified by type, with component counties. 2. County typology code from the Economic Research Service of USDA. See Appendix A for definition. 3. Dry land or land partially or temporarily covered by water. 4. Hispanic persons may be of any race.

STATE County	55 to 64 years	65 to 74 years	75 years and over	Percent female	2001	1990	1990–2000	2000–2001	Births	Deaths	Net migration	Number	Percent change, 1990–2000	Persons per house-hold	Female family house-holder[1]	One person
	16	17	18	19	20	21	22	23	24	25	26	27	28	29	30	31
MISSOURI—Cont'd																
Jasper	8.7	7.0	6.7	51.5	105 664	90 465	15.7	0.9	1 961	1 367	431	41 412	14.6	2.46	11.1	27.2
Jefferson	8.7	5.4	3.8	50.3	201 826	171 380	15.6	1.9	3 356	1 895	2 285	71 499	20.8	2.74	10.4	18.9
Johnson	7.2	5.1	4.2	49.5	48 888	42 514	13.5	1.3	846	428	239	17 410	19.4	2.58	8.5	22.7
Knox	11.2	10.9	10.4	51.8	4 294	4 482	-2.7	-1.5	77	77	-67	1 791	-1.5	2.38	6.9	29.3
Laclede	10.0	7.6	6.5	50.9	32 868	27 158	19.7	1.1	540	444	269	12 760	22.5	2.52	9.4	24.0
Lafayette	10.1	7.6	7.8	51.1	32 975	31 107	6.0	0.0	475	471	27	12 569	7.1	2.55	9.4	24.0
Lawrence	9.9	7.7	7.9	50.8	35 651	30 236	16.4	1.3	570	445	328	13 568	15.7	2.55	9.0	24.5
Lewis	9.7	7.7	8.4	51.0	10 375	10 233	2.6	-1.1	164	144	-139	3 956	5.6	2.46	8.3	27.4
Lincoln	8.5	5.8	5.0	50.4	41 010	28 892	34.8	5.3	646	401	1 781	13 851	34.3	2.77	10.1	19.7
Linn	10.2	9.2	11.4	52.8	13 628	13 885	-0.9	-0.9	214	260	-77	5 697	-0.1	2.37	8.9	30.3
Livingston	9.7	8.5	10.5	54.1	14 500	14 592	-0.2	-0.4	240	244	-52	5 736	1.6	2.38	8.4	30.5
McDonald	10.0	6.4	4.8	49.4	21 632	16 938	28.0	-0.2	426	239	-236	8 113	27.0	2.65	9.6	23.3
Macon	10.5	8.6	10.4	51.2	15 569	15 345	2.7	-1.2	226	262	-152	6 501	5.5	2.38	8.4	29.0
Madison	10.3	9.1	8.9	52.1	11 784	11 127	6.0	-0.1	173	206	21	4 711	8.4	2.46	10.1	25.9
Maries	11.5	8.9	6.7	49.7	8 690	7 976	11.6	-2.4	131	98	-253	3 519	16.2	2.51	7.7	25.7
Marion	8.3	7.7	9.0	52.8	28 086	27 682	2.2	-0.7	496	460	-237	11 066	3.2	2.44	11.4	28.1
Mercer	11.3	10.9	11.2	51.1	3 740	3 723	0.9	-0.5	63	67	-13	1 600	1.5	2.31	6.7	29.3
Miller	9.9	8.1	7.2	50.7	24 092	20 700	13.8	2.2	409	320	440	9 284	16.4	2.50	9.2	26.1
Mississippi	10.7	8.0	7.9	53.3	13 162	14 442	-7.0	-2.0	262	224	-306	5 383	-0.5	2.44	17.3	28.5
Moniteau	8.2	6.5	7.4	46.9	14 861	12 298	20.6	0.2	228	182	-7	5 259	14.8	2.56	8.6	25.6
Monroe	11.2	8.5	9.1	50.9	9 357	9 104	2.3	0.5	138	173	83	3 656	5.3	2.50	7.7	26.5
Montgomery	10.6	8.0	9.2	50.5	12 111	11 355	6.9	-0.2	167	213	26	4 775	10.0	2.47	8.6	26.3
Morgan	13.8	11.8	7.8	50.7	19 597	15 574	24.0	1.5	245	277	308	7 850	25.2	2.42	7.1	25.1
New Madrid	10.2	8.1	7.4	52.0	19 421	20 928	-5.6	-1.7	325	324	-340	7 824	0.4	2.48	14.6	26.5
Newton	10.3	7.6	6.5	51.1	52 852	44 445	18.4	0.4	888	669	20	20 140	19.3	2.57	8.8	22.7
Nodaway	7.7	6.5	7.4	50.1	21 714	21 709	0.9	-0.9	274	269	-197	8 138	6.8	2.33	6.2	30.0
Oregon	12.5	9.6	8.4	50.9	10 255	9 470	9.2	-0.9	145	162	-72	4 263	10.7	2.40	8.4	26.2
Osage	9.4	7.4	7.3	49.3	12 999	12 018	8.7	-0.5	211	167	-105	4 922	15.5	2.61	6.7	23.8
Ozark	14.6	11.5	8.0	50.5	9 488	8 598	11.0	-0.6	122	147	-26	3 950	13.3	2.40	6.9	24.4
Pemiscot	8.9	7.6	7.2	53.1	19 774	21 921	-8.5	-1.4	451	385	-338	7 855	-4.3	2.52	18.5	28.8
Perry	8.9	7.5	8.2	50.2	18 153	16 648	8.9	0.1	289	230	-29	6 904	13.0	2.57	7.4	24.5
Pettis	8.9	7.8	7.6	51.4	39 346	35 437	11.2	-0.1	687	540	-187	15 568	10.8	2.49	10.5	27.0
Phelps	9.3	7.1	6.8	49.2	40 206	35 248	13.0	1.0	589	538	340	15 683	18.1	2.38	9.5	28.6
Pike	9.8	7.4	7.5	45.6	18 285	15 969	14.9	-0.4	246	240	-68	6 451	6.0	2.50	9.6	26.7
Platte	9.1	4.7	4.2	50.5	76 223	57 867	27.5	3.3	1 255	509	1 676	29 278	32.2	2.49	8.8	24.9
Polk	9.2	8.0	7.3	51.3	27 458	21 826	23.7	1.7	433	357	392	9 917	23.5	2.56	8.2	23.2
Pulaski	6.2	4.7	3.2	47.2	41 470	41 307	-0.3	0.7	743	311	-100	13 433	8.4	2.68	9.7	21.6
Putnam	12.3	10.3	10.4	51.0	5 233	5 079	2.8	0.2	81	98	29	2 228	2.9	2.32	7.2	28.7
Ralls	11.3	7.5	6.8	49.8	9 609	8 476	13.6	-0.2	100	127	10	3 736	15.8	2.55	6.5	21.2
Randolph	8.7	7.4	7.5	48.2	24 635	24 370	1.2	-0.1	358	422	44	9 199	2.9	2.43	11.1	27.9
Ray	10.2	7.0	5.9	50.0	23 431	21 968	6.3	0.3	367	295	14	8 743	9.0	2.63	8.0	22.1
Reynolds	13.7	9.6	6.6	49.6	6 606	6 661	0.4	-1.2	92	97	-81	2 721	7.0	2.40	7.8	26.0
Ripley	11.8	9.6	7.7	51.5	13 504	12 303	9.8	0.0	220	213	-10	5 416	13.1	2.46	9.6	25.9
St. Charles	8.0	5.1	3.7	50.7	296 679	212 751	33.4	4.5	5 059	1 974	9 508	101 663	36.8	2.76	9.2	19.4
St. Clair	13.9	11.2	10.1	50.4	9 645	8 457	14.1	-0.1	110	168	55	4 040	15.5	2.34	7.7	27.4
Ste. Genevieve	9.8	7.9	6.6	49.7	18 005	16 037	11.3	0.9	231	214	150	6 586	15.4	2.66	7.6	21.8
St. Francois	9.6	7.9	7.0	49.2	56 147	48 904	13.8	0.9	824	816	512	20 793	17.7	2.48	11.3	24.9
St. Louis	9.1	7.2	6.8	52.6	1 015 417	993 508	2.3	-0.1	16 307	12 184	-4 664	404 312	6.4	2.47	12.7	28.0
Saline	9.3	7.4	8.8	51.0	23 334	23 523	1.0	-1.8	382	373	-432	9 015	1.3	2.45	10.3	28.2
Schuyler	11.7	9.2	10.6	51.8	4 162	4 236	-1.6	-0.2	57	100	37	1 725	-0.2	2.39	7.2	28.2
Scotland	9.9	8.1	10.9	51.5	4 940	4 822	3.3	-0.9	78	115	-3	1 902	-2.8	2.55	7.0	28.2
Scott	9.4	7.0	6.7	52.2	40 509	39 376	2.7	0.2	757	548	-105	15 626	5.9	2.55	13.4	25.0
Shannon	11.9	8.5	6.5	51.2	8 359	7 613	9.3	0.4	114	111	34	3 319	13.8	2.49	8.2	25.8
Shelby	10.1	8.7	11.0	52.2	6 758	6 942	-2.1	-0.6	81	134	13	2 745	-2.3	2.38	7.3	30.3
Stoddard	10.9	8.6	8.7	51.9	29 659	28 895	2.8	-0.2	402	481	49	12 064	6.0	2.39	9.4	26.6
Stone	15.4	11.5	6.8	51.0	28 919	19 078	50.2	0.9	366	326	208	11 822	49.9	2.40	7.2	21.4
Sullivan	10.1	8.3	10.2	50.0	7 168	6 326	14.1	-0.7	123	121	-50	2 925	11.9	2.42	9.1	29.1
Taney	11.5	9.3	6.9	51.6	40 224	25 561	55.3	1.3	623	487	393	16 158	56.6	2.37	8.6	25.7
Texas	11.5	9.7	8.1	51.7	23 109	21 476	7.1	0.5	343	334	105	9 378	11.1	2.42	8.9	26.0
Vernon	9.3	8.4	8.0	51.7	20 304	19 041	7.4	-0.7	317	284	-181	7 966	9.1	2.44	9.6	28.1
Warren	10.6	7.5	5.5	50.3	25 452	19 534	25.6	3.8	404	285	794	9 185	29.9	2.64	8.9	20.8
Washington	9.8	7.0	4.7	48.4	23 454	20 380	14.5	0.5	409	299	6	8 406	20.4	2.64	10.6	22.0
Wayne	13.7	11.7	8.1	50.4	13 215	11 543	14.9	-0.3	174	222	7	5 551	20.5	2.36	9.2	27.2
Webster	9.1	6.2	5.3	49.7	32 183	23 753	30.7	3.7	557	289	857	11 073	32.0	2.72	8.3	20.4
Worth	11.3	10.5	11.8	51.0	2 355	2 440	-2.4	-1.1	36	49	-15	1 009	-2.7	2.31	7.7	30.0
Wright	10.5	8.8	7.7	51.5	18 016	16 758	7.1	0.3	331	290	28	7 081	8.8	2.50	8.8	26.3

1. No spouse present.

Table B. States and Counties — Vital Statistics, Health Resources, and Crime

STATE County	Births, average 1997–1999 Total	Rate[1]	Deaths, average 1997–1999 Number Total	Number Infant[2]	Rate Total[1]	Rate Infant[3]	Physicians,[4] 2000 Number	Rate[5]	Hospitals,[4] 1998 Number	Beds Number	Beds Rate[5]	Medicare enrollees 2000	Serious crimes known to police, 2000[6] Total Number	Rate[7]
	32	33	34	35	36	37	38	39	40	41	42	43	44	45
MISSOURI—Cont'd														
Jasper	1 480	14.8	1 110	NA	11.1	NA	151	144	4	705	708	19 295	5 474	5 323
Jefferson	2 832	14.5	1 492	14	7.6	4.9	96	48	1	228	117	20 250	4 418	2 345
Johnson	680	14.3	326	NA	6.8	NA	41	85	1	70	147	4 926	NA	NA
Knox	52	12.0	65	NA	15.0	NA	2	46	0	0	0	983	0	0
Laclede	417	13.4	339	NA	10.9	NA	23	71	1	48	155	5 508	NA	NA
Lafayette	387	11.9	381	NA	11.7	NA	25	76	1	37	113	5 685	468	1 421
Lawrence	471	14.2	403	NA	12.2	NA	31	88	2	174	525	5 816	NA	NA
Lewis	136	13.3	128	NA	12.5	NA	4	38	0	0	0	1 893	NA	NA
Lincoln	508	13.9	288	NA	7.9	NA	33	85	1	36	98	4 634	NA	NA
Linn	180	13.0	210	NA	15.1	NA	10	73	1	34	246	3 228	177	1 287
Livingston	174	12.3	203	NA	14.3	NA	9	62	1	80	565	2 950	NA	NA
McDonald	342	17.2	199	NA	10.0	NA	1	5	0	0	0	2 873	17	78
Macon	189	12.3	212	NA	13.8	NA	12	76	1	38	249	3 282	NA	NA
Madison	142	12.3	162	NA	14.0	NA	13	110	1	147	1 280	2 464	NA	NA
Maries	98	11.7	88	NA	10.5	NA	2	22	0	0	0	1 272	NA	NA
Marion	386	13.9	372	NA	13.4	NA	50	177	1	105	378	5 439	901	3 185
Mercer	40	9.9	53	NA	13.4	NA	1	27	0	0	0	823	47	1 251
Miller	315	14.0	254	NA	11.2	NA	6	25	0	0	0	4 421	676	2 869
Mississippi	196	14.6	179	NA	13.4	NA	5	37	0	0	0	2 679	NA	NA
Moniteau	188	14.1	158	NA	11.9	NA	9	61	0	0	0	2 258	NA	NA
Monroe	110	12.2	117	NA	12.9	NA	4	43	0	0	0	1 817	47	505
Montgomery	141	11.8	167	NA	13.9	NA	10	82	0	0	0	2 374	187	1 541
Morgan	214	11.6	247	NA	13.4	NA	13	67	0	0	0	4 224	293	1 517
New Madrid	271	13.3	262	NA	12.9	NA	10	51	0	0	0	3 404	NA	NA
Newton	699	14.2	507	NA	10.3	NA	150	285	1	54	110	6 213	NA	NA
Nodaway	205	9.9	205	NA	9.9	NA	22	100	1	55	265	3 225	316	1 442
Oregon	118	11.6	129	NA	12.7	NA	1	10	0	0	0	2 219	NA	NA
Osage	163	13.0	137	NA	10.9	NA	4	31	0	0	0	1 835	NA	NA
Ozark	98	9.9	125	NA	12.7	NA	2	21	0	0	0	2 173	85	891
Pemiscot	370	17.3	303	NA	14.1	NA	18	90	1	209	971	3 746	191	953
Perry	229	13.1	186	NA	10.7	NA	13	72	1	55	316	2 904	103	568
Pettis	528	14.2	437	NA	11.8	NA	40	102	1	147	397	6 766	NA	NA
Phelps	455	11.8	405	NA	10.5	NA	75	188	1	227	588	6 604	1 024	2 571
Pike	206	12.6	196	NA	12.1	NA	14	76	1	25	153	3 038	NA	NA
Platte	956	13.6	410	NA	5.8	NA	67	91	1	55	78	7 010	4 651	6 446
Polk	330	12.9	300	NA	11.7	NA	26	96	1	74	290	5 005	627	2 323
Pulaski	644	16.8	253	NA	6.6	NA	47	114	0	0	0	4 350	NA	NA
Putnam	58	11.9	79	NA	16.0	NA	4	77	1	26	529	1 171	NA	NA
Ralls	93	10.4	93	NA	10.5	NA	1	10	0	0	0	1 147	NA	NA
Randolph	312	13.0	318	NA	13.3	NA	31	126	1	101	420	4 257	942	3 819
Ray	304	12.9	229	NA	9.7	NA	8	34	1	50	211	2 946	NA	NA
Reynolds	77	11.5	74	NA	11.1	NA	4	60	1	29	438	1 284	NA	NA
Ripley	164	11.6	174	NA	12.4	NA	8	59	1	26	185	2 924	86	637
St. Charles	4 165	15.3	1 581	24	5.8	5.8	284	100	4	659	242	28 288	7 597	2 676
St. Clair	94	10.2	143	NA	15.6	NA	8	83	2	72	793	2 138	NA	NA
Ste. Genevieve	193	11.1	159	NA	9.2	NA	14	78	1	34	194	2 791	224	1 255
St. Francois	666	12.0	656	NA	11.9	NA	82	147	2	210	378	10 467	NA	NA
St. Louis	12 741	12.8	9 726	106	9.7	8.3	3 188	314	12	3 981	399	158 731	37 902	3 874
Saline	272	11.9	295	NA	13.0	NA	24	101	1	56	247	4 526	452	1 903
Schuyler	60	13.5	67	NA	15.1	NA	2	48	0	0	0	1 061	40	959
Scotland	73	14.9	75	NA	15.4	NA	3	60	1	32	665	1 008	NA	NA
Scott	573	14.2	426	NA	10.5	NA	51	126	1	148	368	7 224	NA	NA
Shannon	108	13.1	77	NA	9.4	NA	1	12	0	0	0	1 391	57	685
Shelby	70	10.4	104	NA	15.5	NA	4	59	0	0	0	1 538	45	662
Stoddard	334	11.3	376	NA	12.7	NA	15	50	1	50	169	6 152	NA	NA
Stone	305	11.3	279	NA	10.3	NA	10	35	0	0	0	5 375	753	2 628
Sullivan	87	12.6	96	NA	13.9	NA	3	42	1	47	668	1 448	NA	NA
Taney	460	13.2	397	NA	11.4	NA	38	96	1	99	287	7 443	NA	NA
Texas	262	11.7	259	NA	11.6	NA	10	43	1	53	237	4 612	NA	NA
Vernon	262	13.5	249	NA	12.8	NA	27	132	1	97	499	3 747	801	3 916
Warren	325	13.3	208	NA	8.5	NA	6	24	0	0	0	3 462	597	2 434
Washington	309	13.4	227	NA	9.8	NA	11	47	1	42	183	3 128	413	1 769
Wayne	137	10.5	170	NA	13.1	NA	6	45	0	0	0	3 561	NA	NA
Webster	440	15.1	259	NA	8.9	NA	8	26	0	0	0	5 008	264	850
Worth	26	11.3	39	NA	16.8	NA	0	0	0	0	0	570	39	1 637
Wright	252	12.8	230	NA	11.7	NA	8	45	0	0	0	3 939	NA	NA

1. Per 1,000 estimated resident population, average 1997–1999.　2. Deaths of infants under 1 year old.　3. Deaths of infants under 1 year old per 1,000 live births.　4. Data subject to copyright.　5. Per 100,000 resident population as of July 1 of the year shown.　6. Data for serious crimes have not been adjusted for underreporting; this may affect comparability between geographic areas and over time.　7. Per 100,000 population estimated by the FBI.

Table B. States and Counties — **Crime, Education, Money Income, and Poverty**

STATE County	Serious crimes known to police, 2000[1] (cont'd) Rate[2]		Education						Money income 1989				Income and poverty, 1998			
			School enrollment and attainment, 1990				Local government expenditures, fiscal 1999[5]			Households			Percent below poverty level			
			Enrollment[3]		Attainment[4] (percent)						Median					
	Violent	Property	Total	Percent private	High school graduate or more	Bachelor's degree or more	Total current expenditures (mil dol)	Current expenditures per student (dollars)	Per capita[6] (dollars)	Dollars	Percent change, 1979–1989 (constant 1989 dollars)	Percent with $100,000 or more	Median household income	All persons	Persons under 18	Persons 5–17 in families
	46	47	48	49	50	51	52	53	54	55	56	57	58	59	60	61
MISSOURI—Cont'd																
Jasper	249	5 074	21 911	8.9	71.4	13.4	88.1	4 848	10 621	20 924	0.0	1.5	31 323	13.8	19.5	17.0
Jefferson	335	2 010	44 624	14.2	71.6	9.0	174.4	4 905	12 226	32 281	-1.7	1.4	44 924	7.4	10.7	9.1
Johnson	NA	NA	15 605	2.7	80.7	21.4	41.3	5 124	10 202	23 044	1.7	1.2	34 862	11.5	14.8	13.8
Knox	0	0	928	8.2	72.2	8.1	4.9	6 681	9 048	17 293	-8.0	0.7	22 841	18.9	25.9	24.2
Laclede	NA	NA	5 951	4.1	64.4	8.0	26.9	4 526	9 522	20 122	7.9	1.1	30 066	14.3	19.5	18.5
Lafayette	106	1 314	7 264	11.6	71.1	11.5	32.7	5 509	11 470	24 669	-5.9	1.2	34 792	10.2	14.6	13.6
Lawrence	NA	NA	6 607	7.1	68.9	9.7	29.5	5 012	9 672	20 643	6.8	0.8	29 352	13.9	18.1	17.5
Lewis	NA	NA	2 748	29.5	71.7	10.3	8.7	5 062	9 298	20 575	-10.4	0.7	30 242	14.2	19.5	17.8
Lincoln	NA	NA	7 019	14.2	66.8	8.0	30.3	4 402	11 123	28 054	7.6	0.9	40 133	10.0	14.1	12.9
Linn	109	1 178	2 835	3.1	70.8	10.6	17.1	5 761	9 391	17 367	-8.0	0.6	26 990	14.3	19.7	17.7
Livingston	NA	NA	3 318	8.9	71.7	12.5	14.7	5 866	11 316	21 647	-3.0	1.9	32 469	12.6	17.0	16.0
McDonald	23	55	3 582	5.8	61.1	6.6	13.2	3 704	8 409	17 312	-0.2	0.7	26 367	18.0	23.8	23.5
Macon	NA	NA	3 387	6.8	70.3	11.5	14.0	5 556	9 976	20 271	-4.1	0.9	28 494	12.4	17.7	15.7
Madison	NA	NA	2 449	1.4	54.4	6.7	11.1	5 092	8 560	17 100	6.1	0.7	25 598	17.0	23.7	22.6
Maries	NA	NA	1 755	8.7	61.2	8.3	7.8	5 171	9 426	19 041	-2.1	0.5	28 271	13.3	17.7	17.4
Marion	442	2 743	6 721	17.0	70.9	12.9	26.5	5 022	10 110	21 420	-8.2	1.3	31 637	13.9	19.2	17.5
Mercer	293	958	807	0.2	71.0	8.2	4.7	6 930	9 132	16 629	0.7	0.4	26 869	13.2	16.4	16.7
Miller	505	2 364	4 451	4.8	63.0	7.5	26.9	5 367	9 356	18 985	-4.5	0.8	27 674	14.5	19.5	19.0
Mississippi	NA	NA	3 646	3.9	49.2	7.2	13.9	5 153	8 945	16 159	-7.1	1.4	23 162	25.3	32.4	33.9
Moniteau	NA	NA	2 683	13.9	67.8	8.7	12.8	5 203	10 172	22 110	1.9	1.5	32 932	9.9	13.3	12.1
Monroe	118	387	2 170	12.9	69.8	8.1	10.0	5 263	9 444	19 804	-4.7	1.1	31 134	11.8	15.8	14.7
Montgomery	25	1 516	2 424	4.1	62.6	7.8	10.7	5 094	10 128	21 726	5.6	0.8	30 700	12.4	17.0	16.2
Morgan	124	1 393	2 764	10.0	64.3	7.2	10.6	4 734	9 867	19 158	10.1	1.3	26 711	15.1	22.4	22.3
New Madrid	NA	NA	5 199	4.5	52.0	6.7	20.3	5 485	9 034	17 491	3.9	1.6	25 762	21.2	27.6	26.9
Newton	NA	NA	10 467	7.5	72.8	12.1	36.5	4 358	11 136	22 263	6.0	1.8	32 395	12.7	17.4	16.2
Nodaway	196	1 246	8 413	4.8	80.7	17.5	20.4	6 520	9 268	20 347	-3.8	1.7	34 446	10.9	12.4	11.2
Oregon	NA	NA	1 979	4.9	59.3	7.8	9.8	5 005	7 622	13 705	3.0	0.4	20 916	23.0	29.4	30.6
Osage	NA	NA	2 888	19.8	65.0	7.1	10.0	5 859	10 032	24 983	4.9	0.5	37 264	8.3	10.9	10.2
Ozark	126	765	1 774	3.9	60.9	8.0	9.4	5 090	8 611	16 417	7.0	0.9	22 031	20.3	26.4	26.4
Pemiscot	140	813	5 570	2.2	49.5	6.8	25.9	5 644	7 709	13 911	-9.2	0.7	22 074	27.1	33.5	34.4
Perry	22	546	3 849	24.7	56.4	6.4	13.3	5 281	10 730	23 803	11.5	0.9	35 235	9.4	12.3	11.7
Pettis	NA	NA	8 450	9.6	72.2	12.5	31.9	5 099	11 010	22 101	-1.6	1.6	32 118	13.3	19.9	17.8
Phelps	171	2 401	11 050	8.9	70.1	18.3	35.7	5 351	10 531	20 885	0.8	1.5	31 372	14.3	20.4	18.4
Pike	NA	NA	3 622	11.2	67.5	10.6	15.7	5 112	9 887	21 178	-2.3	1.0	30 785	13.6	19.2	17.8
Platte	918	5 529	15 060	13.2	87.8	25.6	74.7	6 193	16 737	38 173	1.2	4.5	56 430	4.7	7.4	6.2
Polk	111	2 212	5 756	31.7	67.0	12.0	26.1	5 220	8 873	18 672	3.8	1.5	28 105	15.8	20.0	19.8
Pulaski	NA	NA	10 369	7.9	78.5	12.8	44.7	5 646	9 159	21 559	5.6	0.5	33 694	13.1	15.8	15.6
Putnam	NA	NA	980	3.0	64.5	8.7	4.9	5 692	9 025	15 549	-4.9	1.5	23 990	16.8	23.6	22.4
Ralls	NA	NA	1 951	10.1	70.2	7.8	4.4	4 581	10 554	22 070	-14.0	1.1	34 743	9.7	12.3	12.3
Randolph	235	3 584	6 038	7.0	68.4	10.8	20.6	5 372	10 855	21 425	-3.5	0.9	29 349	14.1	16.5	17.6
Ray	NA	NA	5 307	7.0	71.2	8.4	19.7	5 120	11 213	27 124	-3.2	1.3	38 720	8.9	11.4	12.0
Reynolds	NA	NA	1 465	0.5	53.1	6.5	8.5	6 458	8 667	17 008	-1.3	1.1	23 466	21.1	26.9	29.8
Ripley	141	496	2 704	4.9	48.5	6.1	12.6	5 354	7 295	13 740	2.4	0.4	20 792	23.5	29.6	31.5
St. Charles	176	2 500	59 400	25.2	83.3	21.2	271.4	5 765	15 366	40 307	7.3	3.1	57 182	4.3	6.6	5.4
St. Clair	NA	NA	1 596	5.8	60.8	7.9	8.9	5 347	9 097	17 265	9.7	0.3	24 076	18.4	25.5	25.8
Ste. Genevieve	34	1 222	3 608	25.1	62.8	7.4	10.8	4 877	10 775	26 712	-1.0	1.7	38 500	9.7	14.2	12.5
St. Francois	NA	NA	11 213	8.7	62.5	9.1	51.4	4 904	9 585	20 745	-6.1	1.0	29 893	14.9	20.4	19.2
St. Louis	256	3 618	259 500	31.5	82.3	29.2	1 113.4	7 165	18 625	38 127	2.8	7.0	49 412	7.3	12.2	9.1
Saline	38	1 865	6 057	21.9	67.3	11.9	22.9	5 708	10 624	21 685	-1.6	1.5	29 400	12.8	17.7	16.3
Schuyler	0	959	867	4.2	68.0	8.0	4.0	5 119	9 059	16 729	-6.2	1.4	24 148	15.9	19.1	21.1
Scotland	NA	NA	898	7.1	69.5	8.5	4.5	5 952	8 581	15 944	-4.5	0.4	25 018	17.4	23.9	23.8
Scott	NA	NA	9 513	8.4	62.4	9.5	37.2	4 717	9 907	20 764	-3.9	1.2	29 380	16.9	22.7	21.5
Shannon	168	517	1 660	8.1	54.0	6.2	5.1	5 604	7 720	14 910	-1.0	0.6	21 399	24.0	30.0	32.2
Shelby	15	647	1 443	3.6	74.2	8.0	7.4	5 783	9 545	18 316	-0.9	1.3	28 619	13.7	17.9	17.7
Stoddard	NA	NA	6 326	2.5	55.9	8.2	27.8	4 862	9 644	18 259	0.1	1.5	27 060	16.7	23.1	21.7
Stone	454	2 174	3 443	7.0	70.6	11.1	22.7	5 200	11 173	21 049	9.6	1.7	30 040	12.5	19.2	18.7
Sullivan	NA	NA	1 214	1.3	65.8	6.8	6.1	5 626	9 193	15 826	-2.2	0.5	26 169	16.0	21.0	20.2
Taney	NA	NA	5 591	23.5	70.8	14.3	30.4	5 235	11 198	20 260	2.0	1.8	27 943	13.1	20.3	17.9
Texas	NA	NA	4 861	6.6	60.9	7.0	23.1	5 218	8 507	16 757	1.9	1.3	23 806	18.9	23.7	24.7
Vernon	181	3 735	4 464	14.0	67.8	13.1	18.3	5 255	9 587	19 641	-2.3	1.0	26 436	16.5	21.4	20.9
Warren	114	2 320	4 498	22.6	68.0	9.1	16.8	4 432	11 640	28 944	7.2	1.7	39 739	8.5	12.0	12.4
Washington	287	1 482	5 094	6.7	50.8	5.7	21.3	5 195	7 650	17 117	-10.6	0.4	25 590	21.3	25.2	27.1
Wayne	NA	NA	2 391	5.2	48.9	5.9	11.1	5 125	8 434	13 815	-2.6	0.9	19 828	22.8	30.2	32.3
Webster	245	606	5 484	7.1	66.8	8.5	20.8	4 534	9 116	20 525	2.0	1.0	30 233	15.0	20.1	19.2
Worth	294	1 343	492	1.8	74.3	8.7	2.5	5 430	8 475	14 568	-7.0	0.3	24 876	15.9	19.7	19.8
Wright	NA	NA	3 839	4.7	59.7	7.4	22.6	5 595	7 692	15 770	-3.3	0.4	23 641	19.8	24.0	25.1

1. Data for serious crimes have not been adjusted for underreporting; this may affect comparability between geographic areas and over time.   2. Per 100,000 population estimated by the FBI.   3. All persons 3 years old and over enrolled in nursery school through college.   4. Persons 25 years old and over.   5. Elementary and secondary education expenditures, local government fiscal years ending between July 1, 1998 and June 30, 1999.   6. Based on population enumerated as of April 1, 1990.

Table B. States and Counties — **Personal Income**

STATE County	Personal income, 1999												
			Per capita[1]						Transfer payments				
										Government payments to individuals			
	Total (mil dol)	Percent change, 1998–1999	Dollars	Rank	Wages and salaries[2] (mil dol)	Proprietor's income (mil dol)	Dividends, interest, and rent (mil dol)	Total (mil dol)	Total (mil dol)	Social Security (mil dol)	Medical payments (mil dol)	Income mainte- nance (mil dol)	Unemploy- ment insurance (mil dol)
	62	63	64	65	66	67	68	69	70	71	72	73	74
MISSOURI—Cont'd													
Jasper	2 293	4.2	22 865	1 120	1 638	168	449	421	403	164	180	36	5
Jefferson	4 279	6.0	21 600	1 487	1 191	169	538	550	514	238	202	34	10
Johnson	931	6.7	19 365	2 191	567	41	172	128	120	49	47	10	1
Knox	74	-5.2	17 133	2 710	27	1	22	20	20	8	9	2	0
Laclede	612	4.0	19 473	2 148	338	62	121	117	111	47	44	12	2
Lafayette	736	3.1	22 445	1 230	225	61	134	146	140	57	70	7	2
Lawrence	599	3.6	17 882	2 561	206	53	100	134	127	58	49	11	2
Lewis	174	0.3	16 965	2 738	68	3	34	40	38	16	17	3	0
Lincoln	818	9.0	21 685	1 461	236	52	121	119	112	49	50	8	2
Linn	278	0.8	20 038	1 980	135	25	62	68	66	25	28	4	1
Livingston	337	1.6	24 013	855	164	32	92	64	61	26	27	5	1
McDonald	340	5.3	16 850	2 766	138	32	47	71	68	27	28	9	1
Macon	296	3.0	19 163	2 242	126	17	71	72	69	29	31	4	1
Madison	204	3.9	17 498	2 647	65	16	37	60	58	23	26	6	1
Maries	149	1.9	17 648	2 613	35	6	29	35	33	14	14	3	0
Marion	615	3.8	22 188	1 301	400	30	119	129	124	48	56	10	2
Mercer	62	-1.6	15 737	2 924	45	6	13	17	16	7	6	1	0
Miller	403	4.6	17 833	2 571	181	34	68	93	89	35	39	8	2
Mississippi	249	3.5	18 681	2 374	93	27	40	73	70	23	32	12	1
Moniteau	272	4.1	20 452	1 851	108	19	59	48	45	20	19	3	1
Monroe	173	-1.6	18 945	2 297	84	6	41	38	37	16	15	3	1
Montgomery	243	1.6	20 094	1 967	85	21	48	54	52	22	24	3	1
Morgan	342	3.3	18 091	2 522	95	38	85	88	84	40	33	7	1
New Madrid	356	5.2	17 862	2 567	247	28	53	100	96	30	46	15	1
Newton	1 073	4.7	21 587	1 493	547	94	172	177	168	76	66	13	3
Nodaway	410	1.6	19 958	2 003	230	28	88	67	63	28	24	5	0
Oregon	154	3.9	14 930	2 995	57	13	27	54	52	18	22	7	1
Osage	290	5.4	23 143	1 061	85	17	50	42	40	18	16	3	1
Ozark	145	3.8	14 563	3 019	34	12	31	48	46	20	17	5	1
Pemiscot	368	5.9	17 388	2 668	158	33	51	118	114	31	55	23	2
Perry	382	4.3	21 923	1 381	231	20	74	64	61	27	26	5	1
Pettis	854	5.0	23 018	1 087	549	51	165	156	150	62	64	12	2
Phelps	820	4.5	21 041	1 657	444	63	169	152	145	57	61	13	1
Pike	322	3.4	19 651	2 097	155	14	68	73	70	29	32	6	1
Platte	2 348	6.6	32 753	134	1 220	128	336	170	157	78	59	7	3
Polk	454	4.3	17 624	2 616	170	44	88	107	103	38	47	9	1
Pulaski	881	8.9	23 039	1 080	644	38	121	112	106	34	44	12	2
Putnam	83	1.8	16 976	2 736	22	6	21	24	23	10	10	2	0
Ralls	184	-1.3	20 047	1 979	76	7	37	33	31	14	12	2	1
Randolph	464	3.5	19 448	2 159	263	30	81	106	102	35	45	9	2
Ray	475	3.7	20 005	1 988	123	50	62	77	73	34	29	5	1
Reynolds	109	3.4	16 395	2 844	60	9	18	36	35	12	16	4	0
Ripley	201	4.1	14 199	3 038	56	20	33	76	73	26	33	11	1
St. Charles	7 736	7.7	27 586	364	3 115	210	1 074	657	606	311	229	27	10
St. Clair	154	2.2	16 615	2 809	45	10	36	47	46	21	17	4	1
Ste. Genevieve	369	4.0	21 152	1 618	168	20	73	62	59	28	23	4	1
St. Francois	1 016	4.0	18 215	2 491	514	62	166	258	248	100	109	23	4
St. Louis	38 737	3.4	38 886	52	27 138	2 457	10 170	3 563	3 379	1 690	1 320	194	51
Saline	514	1.6	22 556	1 204	261	40	100	130	126	40	73	7	1
Schuyler	65	0.4	14 773	3 008	17	5	15	20	19	7	9	2	0
Scotland	91	-0.2	18 429	2 435	29	13	22	22	22	8	10	2	0
Scott	844	5.3	20 813	1 730	412	73	139	191	183	65	84	21	3
Shannon	124	4.7	14 898	2 997	41	18	17	37	36	13	15	5	1
Shelby	129	-3.1	19 397	2 182	54	9	32	31	30	13	13	2	1
Stoddard	579	7.6	19 552	2 120	247	77	95	141	136	53	61	14	2
Stone	596	7.1	21 660	1 468	152	64	131	119	114	58	38	8	3
Sullivan	136	-2.4	19 856	2 034	81	13	21	34	33	11	18	3	0
Taney	782	6.0	22 035	1 352	537	82	169	161	155	71	59	9	5
Texas	341	3.5	15 166	2 973	137	32	64	97	93	34	39	11	2
Vernon	378	2.9	19 420	2 169	195	28	74	105	102	34	55	8	1
Warren	536	6.3	21 060	1 650	170	26	85	84	79	38	33	4	1
Washington	371	4.1	15 883	2 908	109	24	40	99	94	32	43	14	2
Wayne	197	5.9	15 137	2 977	53	17	30	80	77	29	34	9	1
Webster	504	5.2	16 822	2 774	163	42	69	99	94	40	39	9	1
Worth	39	0.2	16 911	2 752	11	5	10	10	9	4	4	1	0
Wright	287	2.7	14 410	3 028	111	35	55	84	81	31	34	10	1

1. Based on the resident population estimated as of July 1 of the year shown.   2. Includes other labor income.

Table B. States and Counties — **Earnings, Social Security, and Housing**

STATE County	Earnings, 1999									Social Security beneficiaries, December 2000			Housing units, 1990	
			Percent by selected industries											
			Goods-related[1]		Service-related and other[2]									
	Total (mil dol)	Farm	Total	Manufacturing	Total	Retail trade	Finance, insurance, and real estate	Services	Government	Number	Rate[3]	Supplemental Security Income recipients, December 2000	Total	Percent change, 1980–1990
	75	76	77	78	79	80	81	82	83	84	85	86	87	88

MISSOURI—Cont'd														
Jasper	1 807	0.3	29.4	24.2	59.5	11.7	3.6	20.9	10.8	20 310	194	2 852	39 554	9.2
Jefferson	1 360	-0.2	28.6	14.9	52.8	13.4	4.5	22.5	18.8	28 163	142	1 916	63 423	24.0
Johnson	608	-1.2	D	14.0	D	7.4	3.2	10.0	56.3	6 187	128	571	16 010	15.2
Knox	27	-15.9	D	8.5	D	13.4	6.2	23.1	36.6	1 145	263	127	2 254	-10.3
Laclede	400	-0.5	D	38.7	D	16.4	2.8	16.6	11.1	6 630	204	906	11 564	17.5
Lafayette	287	4.4	21.0	11.9	51.5	13.9	5.3	18.9	23.1	6 790	206	435	12 820	8.0
Lawrence	260	3.2	D	16.7	D	16.7	3.9	14.8	20.0	7 652	217	721	12 788	8.8
Lewis	71	-9.2	D	19.1	D	12.0	4.5	26.8	25.1	2 056	196	179	4 244	-3.1
Lincoln	288	1.0	35.6	17.9	43.6	12.8	4.3	13.1	19.8	5 961	153	433	12 284	27.2
Linn	160	0.3	D	31.3	D	11.1	3.2	17.6	16.6	3 282	239	301	6 566	-8.0
Livingston	196	0.8	26.0	16.6	54.7	13.1	6.1	21.5	18.5	3 316	228	348	6 294	-6.1
McDonald	170	7.3	D	40.2	D	9.3	2.6	7.6	14.6	3 757	173	487	7 327	14.4
Macon	144	-5.0	D	17.7	D	13.5	5.0	14.8	32.4	3 674	233	266	6 955	-3.6
Madison	81	-1.1	D	17.6	D	15.4	3.1	17.5	26.1	2 982	253	381	5 282	5.3
Maries	41	-11.7	D	20.8	D	12.7	6.9	19.5	22.3	1 691	190	151	3 715	8.7
Marion	430	-0.3	D	25.7	D	10.6	3.1	25.5	13.7	6 052	214	856	12 026	1.9
Mercer	51	51.5	D	3.1	D	3.8	2.3	7.5	14.8	982	261	74	2 225	-9.6
Miller	215	0.0	29.5	16.8	55.1	17.5	5.1	16.5	15.4	4 537	193	455	9 766	23.2
Mississippi	121	8.8	D	13.8	D	13.9	4.0	13.0	18.9	3 149	235	721	5 757	-4.6
Moniteau	127	1.7	D	27.2	D	9.8	3.5	11.6	24.7	2 561	173	142	5 043	8.8
Monroe	90	-4.2	D	44.0	D	7.0	3.0	11.6	23.1	2 067	222	146	4 114	0.5
Montgomery	106	-5.1	34.9	21.6	51.5	11.5	5.0	15.2	18.7	2 669	220	218	5 241	1.4
Morgan	133	6.6	D	15.4	D	19.3	5.2	15.8	18.3	5 079	263	395	12 642	21.4
New Madrid	274	6.5	45.2	43.5	36.3	9.6	1.9	7.8	12.0	4 212	213	1 079	8 557	-5.2
Newton	641	1.8	D	25.3	D	10.7	2.4	29.4	9.7	9 764	186	670	18 384	14.6
Nodaway	259	-1.5	34.5	26.8	38.5	9.6	3.6	16.0	28.5	3 561	163	279	8 349	-1.9
Oregon	70	-4.2	D	17.0	D	15.0	4.9	16.6	19.7	2 624	254	535	4 484	-0.3
Osage	102	-3.4	41.1	30.9	43.7	13.3	3.6	13.6	18.6	2 288	175	109	5 414	7.2
Ozark	46	-4.2	D	11.3	D	12.4	6.4	23.6	27.6	2 775	291	384	4 451	18.8
Pemiscot	191	8.3	D	15.2	D	9.8	3.0	15.6	29.5	4 640	231	1 759	8 806	-10.3
Perry	251	-1.2	D	39.5	D	9.4	3.2	13.1	11.6	3 373	186	255	6 867	6.4
Pettis	600	0.0	43.2	35.5	41.2	11.1	4.0	15.5	15.5	7 819	198	884	15 443	1.2
Phelps	507	-0.8	14.9	9.0	46.2	13.3	3.3	21.7	39.6	7 716	194	992	14 715	13.9
Pike	169	-2.0	29.8	21.6	43.1	11.2	3.6	16.4	29.1	3 597	196	335	7 128	-3.5
Platte	1 348	0.0	15.5	9.6	75.8	7.2	5.9	23.7	8.7	8 740	118	322	24 362	35.8
Polk	214	-0.8	D	6.6	D	14.7	4.1	28.6	21.9	5 233	194	652	8 979	15.9
Pulaski	683	-0.4	4.4	1.5	19.3	6.4	1.7	8.6	76.7	5 076	123	751	13 838	16.6
Putnam	28	-2.9	D	D	D	10.1	8.0	11.0	39.0	1 370	262	161	2 590	-10.3
Ralls	83	-4.3	47.8	42.5	D	7.6	4.4	12.1	15.3	1 757	183	104	3 766	10.4
Randolph	293	-0.5	D	13.9	D	14.7	6.1	17.7	19.8	4 404	179	646	10 131	0.0
Ray	172	0.7	D	16.8	D	9.6	6.7	18.1	21.1	4 061	174	215	8 611	4.6
Reynolds	69	-1.2	D	21.6	D	4.6	1.7	13.0	18.7	1 724	258	304	3 537	2.6
Ripley	76	2.0	D	18.0	D	14.3	4.0	18.9	27.5	3 598	266	771	5 597	4.9
St. Charles	3 325	0.2	33.6	21.2	53.6	13.2	4.6	24.4	12.6	35 290	124	1 418	79 113	58.1
St. Clair	55	-6.3	D	D	D	16.1	3.9	24.4	33.5	2 721	282	249	4 645	11.6
Ste. Genevieve	188	0.2	D	31.4	D	9.4	3.5	11.4	15.0	3 431	192	208	6 766	14.1
St. Francois	577	0.1	24.8	16.4	51.7	13.7	3.8	24.6	23.4	12 406	223	1 827	20 321	16.7
St. Louis	29 595	0.0	25.7	18.9	66.8	8.6	9.9	31.5	7.5	177 855	175	11 470	401 839	12.2
Saline	301	1.8	D	27.1	D	8.8	3.3	18.1	22.6	4 924	207	544	10 033	-2.6
Schuyler	21	-8.8	D	D	D	17.8	3.8	11.4	37.6	993	238	126	1 986	-5.7
Scotland	42	0.2	D	9.7	D	13.7	4.5	13.6	36.9	1 108	222	97	2 302	-2.3
Scott	485	0.8	20.9	14.0	62.0	12.1	4.6	23.9	16.3	8 424	208	1 610	15 881	4.4
Shannon	59	-1.1	D	33.5	D	8.3	3.5	13.7	25.4	1 957	235	350	3 312	2.2
Shelby	63	-4.3	39.0	27.5	41.6	7.1	4.3	12.4	23.8	1 671	246	138	3 277	-9.5
Stoddard	324	10.2	D	22.1	D	12.3	D	15.0	14.1	7 265	245	1 154	12 288	2.5
Stone	217	0.2	D	3.9	D	14.1	4.5	38.3	13.5	7 204	251	399	11 294	27.7
Sullivan	94	14.8	D	40.7	D	6.5	4.3	8.6	14.3	1 513	210	218	3 093	-11.7
Taney	619	0.0	D	3.3	D	21.1	11.3	39.8	8.6	8 998	227	598	13 273	29.2
Texas	170	-1.0	24.8	18.2	51.2	13.4	4.8	14.9	25.0	4 891	213	807	9 525	9.4
Vernon	223	-1.8	D	23.4	D	11.7	6.0	18.9	25.1	4 441	217	656	8 181	-1.9
Warren	196	-0.5	42.0	30.1	44.1	12.0	6.2	14.5	14.4	4 586	187	204	8 841	35.2
Washington	133	-0.6	D	9.5	D	12.0	2.6	21.6	35.6	4 363	187	972	8 075	13.6
Wayne	70	-0.3	25.9	15.4	D	14.7	4.5	18.7	27.6	4 041	305	763	6 406	13.1
Webster	206	-0.6	D	24.4	D	13.3	4.9	15.4	18.2	5 599	180	677	9 067	17.7
Worth	16	3.9	D	D	D	7.3	4.7	14.0	32.3	640	269	39	1 269	-13.0
Wright	146	2.7	D	17.8	D	19.4	3.6	13.7	21.9	4 648	259	823	7 214	7.6

1. Covers mining, construction, and manufacturing. 2. Covers private sector earnings in agricultural services, forestry, and fisheries; transportation and public utilities; wholesale trade; retail trade; finance, insurance, and real estate; and services. 3. Per 1,000 resident population estimated as of July 1 of the year shown.

Table B. States and Counties — Housing, Labor Force, and Employment

STATE County	Housing units, 1990 (cont'd)								Civilian labor force, 2001				Civilian employment, 1990[5]		
	Occupied units										Unemployment			Percent	
			Owner-occupied			Renter-occupied										
															Owner cost as a percent of income										
	Total	Percent	Median value[1]	With a mort-gage	Without a mort-gage	Median rent[2]	Rent as per-cent of income	Sub-stand-ard units[3] (percent)	Total	Percent change, 2000–2001	Total	Rate[4]	Total	Professional, managerial, and technical	Precision production, craft, and repair
	89	90	91	92	93	94	95	96	97	98	99	100	101	102	103
MISSOURI—Cont'd															
Jasper	36 134	69.3	38 300	16.9	12.0	301	24.8	2.4	56 050	1.7	2 283	4.1	41 148	22.7	12.3
Jefferson	59 199	81.2	65 300	18.4	12.1	418	25.4	2.9	106 512	0.7	5 126	4.8	82 349	20.5	17.5
Johnson	14 579	58.6	55 300	18.3	11.6	341	27.7	3.2	23 300	0.2	831	3.6	17 708	25.7	10.9
Knox	1 819	75.0	20 500	20.7	13.8	230	24.8	1.9	2 116	7.5	95	4.5	1 915	16.8	8.7
Laclede	10 420	73.5	42 100	20.7	12.9	271	23.2	3.6	16 798	1.2	1 099	6.5	11 591	17.9	15.0
Lafayette	11 732	74.1	45 300	18.9	11.8	307	24.3	2.7	17 230	1.5	758	4.4	13 851	20.1	13.6
Lawrence	11 724	74.4	37 900	17.9	12.1	267	23.7	3.2	16 608	4.5	811	4.9	13 157	19.3	12.1
Lewis	3 745	74.0	28 000	16.7	12.8	222	24.0	2.5	6 060	7.8	247	4.1	4 491	20.7	11.1
Lincoln	10 316	80.0	55 200	17.9	12.9	341	26.8	3.4	19 167	0.9	985	5.1	13 072	18.4	17.5
Linn	5 704	77.6	22 400	15.9	14.0	234	23.7	2.7	6 519	2.0	598	9.2	5 708	20.3	10.9
Livingston	5 645	70.9	35 800	16.7	12.6	269	26.1	2.5	7 508	2.4	273	3.6	6 163	22.6	10.9
McDonald	6 386	75.6	31 800	19.2	13.2	239	23.8	5.7	8 467	3.2	441	5.2	6 932	13.5	15.7
Macon	6 160	76.5	32 700	16.7	12.6	244	22.5	2.3	7 272	-1.0	747	10.3	6 370	20.1	14.5
Madison	4 344	76.7	33 100	20.3	12.4	261	26.4	4.0	4 593	2.6	379	8.3	4 154	16.6	15.6
Maries	3 028	82.2	35 000	22.1	13.4	224	25.3	4.1	4 685	3.9	237	5.1	3 418	18.4	11.7
Marion	10 728	69.1	36 000	14.3	12.1	256	22.8	2.7	15 684	0.8	861	5.5	11 999	23.5	11.1
Mercer	1 577	75.0	18 900	16.7	13.7	195	24.2	3.0	1 590	4.1	57	3.6	1 364	17.1	13.6
Miller	7 977	76.2	43 700	22.2	14.2	277	26.0	4.2	12 044	3.0	789	6.6	8 871	16.8	17.6
Mississippi	5 411	64.9	32 300	19.9	14.2	230	29.0	4.1	6 179	3.1	561	9.1	5 429	17.1	11.4
Moniteau	4 583	78.8	38 700	17.6	12.2	264	23.7	2.7	7 766	4.2	322	4.1	5 678	16.4	14.1
Monroe	3 471	77.5	31 800	18.4	13.5	240	22.4	4.0	4 202	-2.8	309	7.4	3 812	19.0	11.7
Montgomery	4 341	78.9	33 000	17.1	12.2	272	24.1	4.1	5 788	3.7	342	5.9	4 803	18.1	14.3
Morgan	6 269	80.7	45 300	21.1	12.2	273	28.3	3.4	8 663	1.8	609	7.0	6 435	16.0	17.3
New Madrid	7 795	64.0	32 800	18.4	13.6	266	27.1	5.5	8 805	2.4	698	7.9	7 596	18.2	12.3
Newton	16 886	76.9	42 900	18.2	12.1	292	23.5	3.0	28 389	1.9	1 462	5.1	20 419	22.0	14.5
Nodaway	7 620	65.4	37 100	17.8	12.5	277	29.4	2.2	13 316	3.2	248	1.9	10 298	22.9	10.0
Oregon	3 851	79.0	26 000	21.8	14.9	210	26.2	4.2	4 429	2.5	194	4.4	3 377	18.4	11.4
Osage	4 262	82.9	43 700	19.7	11.6	235	22.3	2.8	7 822	3.8	399	5.1	5 882	15.4	14.5
Ozark	3 486	82.0	36 500	21.7	12.1	241	23.9	6.7	4 306	6.3	254	5.9	3 277	19.0	11.2
Pemiscot	8 210	56.9	28 800	19.2	14.6	234	29.2	6.4	8 284	1.2	778	9.4	7 412	18.1	12.9
Perry	6 111	81.1	43 500	16.2	12.4	276	21.1	4.3	11 087	0.3	393	3.5	7 660	15.1	15.4
Pettis	14 056	74.5	40 100	18.7	13.1	319	26.0	2.7	22 574	3.5	1 408	6.2	15 835	22.2	12.5
Phelps	13 277	65.6	47 200	17.9	11.8	294	26.6	2.9	20 865	2.9	722	3.5	14 793	30.7	11.1
Pike	6 083	74.7	32 600	15.9	12.6	259	25.5	4.8	8 111	2.7	456	5.6	6 869	19.5	13.5
Platte	22 142	65.1	81 200	18.6	11.7	443	21.8	1.7	46 000	1.5	1 305	2.8	31 998	33.5	11.1
Polk	8 031	73.5	39 600	20.1	12.1	261	25.6	3.9	12 726	5.5	542	4.3	9 207	21.6	10.8
Pulaski	12 397	55.6	51 400	23.2	12.2	353	24.0	4.2	12 961	2.6	812	6.3	11 288	23.6	9.8
Putnam	2 166	77.0	21 300	20.7	13.0	205	24.0	3.1	2 019	5.3	80	4.0	1 966	16.8	10.2
Ralls	3 226	80.3	37 900	18.3	13.2	270	26.9	3.1	5 498	1.0	311	5.7	3 886	16.6	15.2
Randolph	8 943	73.0	33 200	17.8	13.3	276	25.3	2.4	11 060	1.0	660	6.0	9 868	21.9	12.6
Ray	8 020	79.0	46 400	18.0	12.5	331	25.0	2.7	11 891	0.8	516	4.3	9 328	18.6	14.7
Reynolds	2 542	76.5	29 300	22.4	13.5	224	26.0	6.9	2 325	-11.7	215	9.2	2 402	16.6	15.7
Ripley	4 788	75.3	29 200	20.7	13.2	241	31.6	6.0	5 571	3.2	412	7.4	3 800	19.2	11.2
St. Charles	74 331	76.4	83 600	20.0	11.5	485	23.0	2.0	163 230	0.3	5 440	3.3	112 393	32.5	13.0
St. Clair	3 499	75.2	28 400	22.2	13.2	217	24.0	4.2	4 134	4.4	232	5.6	3 188	19.6	14.8
Ste. Genevieve	5 707	82.7	53 800	18.7	12.1	295	24.9	4.2	9 004	0.9	471	5.2	7 189	16.9	16.4
St. Francois	17 670	74.0	40 200	17.9	12.3	307	27.1	3.8	24 729	1.9	1 797	7.3	17 811	21.8	13.7
St. Louis	380 110	73.9	83 500	18.1	11.8	482	24.1	1.6	563 721	0.2	21 744	3.9	507 521	38.0	8.5
Saline	8 903	70.6	37 600	19.0	12.7	308	23.4	2.6	11 985	0.5	626	5.2	10 528	19.0	12.4
Schuyler	1 729	75.4	20 400	18.7	14.8	203	24.6	3.3	2 368	0.0	125	5.3	1 770	17.1	10.8
Scotland	1 956	73.6	24 300	18.5	14.1	190	24.6	3.9	2 278	4.8	97	4.3	2 035	18.5	13.2
Scott	14 761	69.1	41 700	17.8	12.9	295	27.4	2.8	20 757	1.1	1 235	5.9	16 912	20.6	12.5
Shannon	2 917	78.7	25 900	21.0	12.5	194	26.5	8.6	4 051	3.0	269	6.6	3 007	12.7	13.7
Shelby	2 809	75.7	22 900	18.4	12.9	202	23.6	3.1	3 476	1.1	238	6.8	2 843	17.2	10.1
Stoddard	11 383	71.9	34 100	17.5	13.3	253	24.7	2.5	13 615	2.5	951	7.0	11 779	17.3	14.9
Stone	7 885	81.6	58 800	21.2	11.5	305	23.5	3.4	13 775	3.8	1 360	9.9	7 582	21.2	15.3
Sullivan	2 615	75.6	16 100	18.4	15.0	209	22.6	4.3	4 058	6.0	146	3.6	2 616	16.7	15.0
Taney	10 321	74.7	55 400	20.2	12.5	307	24.6	2.9	31 489	2.7	2 474	7.9	10 947	25.9	12.4
Texas	8 441	75.3	33 700	21.8	12.8	220	25.0	4.8	9 933	7.7	707	7.1	8 401	14.9	14.2
Vernon	7 301	72.5	32 100	18.4	13.7	272	24.2	3.2	8 939	1.1	336	3.8	8 000	23.6	10.0
Warren	7 070	80.8	63 600	20.0	12.2	341	24.9	3.1	13 100	1.0	669	5.1	8 964	18.6	15.1
Washington	6 982	78.5	34 200	19.4	13.4	292	30.4	9.5	9 666	2.4	840	8.7	6 824	16.5	13.7
Wayne	4 607	76.5	29 000	20.4	12.9	246	26.7	6.1	3 642	3.5	423	11.6	3 891	15.9	14.5
Webster	8 391	77.8	41 200	20.8	12.5	268	24.3	5.5	14 934	-1.0	650	4.4	10 061	15.6	16.3
Worth	1 037	75.9	14 999	18.3	13.3	183	22.4	2.0	827	7.5	41	5.0	938	16.5	12.3
Wright	6 510	73.7	31 100	20.0	13.9	219	27.0	3.9	7 062	1.2	657	9.3	6 543	13.9	11.8

1. Specified owner-occupied units.   2. Specified renter-occupied units.   3. Overcrowded or lacking complete plumbing facilities.   4. Percent of civilian labor force.   5. Persons 16 years and older.

STATE County	Number of establishments	Total	Health Care and Social Assistance	Manufacturing	Retail trade	Finance and Insurance	Professional Scientific and Technical Services	Total (mil dol)	Average per employee (dollars)	Number	Less than 50 acres	500 acres and over	Whose principal occupation is farming (percent)
	104	105	106	107	108	109	110	111	112	113	114	115	116
MISSOURI—Cont'd													
Jasper	3 042	53 906	6 851	11 858	7 968	1 233	1 097	1 260	23 382	1 355	30.0	8.5	39.3
Jefferson	3 458	34 709	4 920	5 461	6 240	814	743	821	23 655	659	31.1	5.8	33.8
Johnson	841	9 578	1 370	2 188	1 780	433	197	185	19 366	1 626	21.9	12.1	42.0
Knox	112	585	56	D	117	47	22	11	18 173	602	10.6	29.7	61.1
Laclede	814	11 710	705	5 223	2 060	296	114	234	20 006	1 300	18.1	12.5	41.1
Lafayette	845	7 147	882	1 351	1 552	291	136	122	17 061	1 215	25.3	16.8	52.0
Lawrence	649	6 831	1 107	1 496	1 159	146	90	147	21 457	1 733	28.7	8.3	42.5
Lewis	238	1 974	366	D	324	99	8	39	19 875	719	15.2	20.6	49.5
Lincoln	739	6 589	853	1 085	1 382	253	118	153	23 185	989	25.8	14.6	45.1
Linn	340	4 419	575	1 980	668	144	74	91	20 628	933	14.1	22.5	47.5
Livingston	460	5 028	845	790	1 072	175	135	103	20 530	738	15.4	20.5	47.3
McDonald	340	4 730	196	2 997	480	95	50	93	19 740	1 078	23.1	7.6	39.7
Macon	374	3 844	472	1 100	672	178	84	67	17 541	1 155	13.7	17.3	42.3
Madison	274	2 426	381	479	426	76	112	39	16 260	386	10.9	15.5	36.3
Maries	136	961	125	234	201	67	28	21	21 537	817	12.9	16.5	42.8
Marion	811	11 716	1 834	3 361	1 869	338	254	266	22 716	695	15.7	18.7	49.1
Mercer	78	412	65	D	78	41	4	8	18 711	539	12.1	24.9	45.8
Miller	593	6 084	384	1 379	1 076	155	186	133	21 877	1 067	12.7	9.5	41.3
Mississippi	291	2 825	352	525	597	101	23	50	17 577	267	10.5	57.3	77.5
Moniteau	339	3 068	328	1 032	494	111	52	58	18 893	1 024	17.5	9.7	40.5
Monroe	219	2 205	251	D	249	76	25	53	23 961	886	12.4	21.0	45.5
Montgomery	360	2 826	335	814	451	136	28	56	19 793	765	17.1	20.3	41.3
Morgan	489	3 244	135	875	903	107	106	55	16 922	869	19.4	10.8	47.4
New Madrid	366	6 261	636	2 748	1 012	190	47	150	24 021	429	7.7	55.5	76.0
Newton	1 018	15 557	3 512	4 102	1 713	404	197	339	21 818	1 622	31.3	6.0	39.3
Nodaway	533	6 618	995	1 837	1 021	211	112	138	20 809	1 257	14.3	26.1	57.9
Oregon	212	1 675	268	359	423	66	25	26	15 616	798	17.3	14.8	45.0
Osage	257	2 770	231	1 021	391	94	20	60	21 643	1 147	13.3	11.5	41.7
Ozark	175	927	93	160	259	79	24	16	14 707	781	12.5	14.7	47.5
Pemiscot	357	4 360	1 060	889	688	145	32	86	19 697	306	12.7	58.2	78.1
Perry	478	7 916	774	3 301	1 042	202	83	173	21 799	857	20.0	10.6	43.4
Pettis	1 053	16 797	2 240	5 544	2 326	420	250	378	22 515	1 249	20.7	16.1	50.2
Phelps	1 079	12 274	3 201	1 590	2 457	309	418	232	18 905	758	21.0	12.9	34.7
Pike	419	3 580	621	732	635	157	143	81	22 692	944	17.1	18.8	46.0
Platte	1 807	34 324	1 913	1 716	2 716	3 724	1 112	934	27 216	714	31.4	13.6	43.1
Polk	575	7 269	1 997	911	1 048	182	131	122	16 837	1 575	23.5	9.7	44.8
Pulaski	680	5 692	922	662	1 307	273	215	101	17 680	539	16.7	15.8	35.6
Putnam	101	652	116	66	147	63	23	10	14 781	615	12.7	24.7	50.6
Ralls	165	2 086	240	981	205	40	18	46	22 190	550	13.8	26.2	48.5
Randolph	579	7 307	1 164	1 243	1 228	565	124	160	21 914	801	16.0	14.2	42.8
Ray	404	3 525	558	544	648	119	131	74	20 882	1 075	23.7	12.3	40.6
Reynolds	168	1 781	246	589	124	D	14	45	25 107	302	10.9	19.9	34.1
Ripley	240	1 975	510	549	396	68	47	31	15 943	472	13.8	18.2	46.8
St. Charles	6 128	88 613	9 500	14 387	14 465	2 338	4 645	2 412	27 217	680	29.4	16.0	48.8
St. Clair	184	1 478	643	72	298	75	23	20	13 823	778	16.1	22.1	53.1
Ste. Genevieve	371	4 913	608	1 871	510	127	76	118	23 950	631	17.7	11.6	37.1
St. Francois	1 285	16 593	4 031	3 462	2 850	448	340	325	19 573	649	25.6	6.3	34.4
St. Louis	30 348	582 084	66 615	80 671	73 467	35 715	38 500	20 158	34 630	291	45.7	9.6	40.5
Saline	568	7 604	1 294	2 594	1 088	190	156	162	21 360	936	14.4	28.8	57.7
Schuyler	85	359	D	18	140	20	D	5	14 493	493	13.8	18.1	52.5
Scotland	138	871	D	157	181	68	17	14	15 629	600	12.3	22.2	52.3
Scott	1 135	13 011	2 006	2 628	1 983	459	261	281	21 605	541	21.8	26.1	53.0
Shannon	147	1 252	201	552	164	51	8	18	14 324	470	16.8	15.7	36.0
Shelby	194	1 492	86	466	219	82	53	31	20 527	644	12.3	27.3	59.9
Stoddard	734	8 074	1 216	2 405	1 315	248	83	153	18 987	941	22.6	27.1	59.1
Stone	631	4 613	247	268	806	172	70	107	23 104	684	23.4	9.4	39.9
Sullivan	118	2 450	225	D	167	36	23	50	20 545	791	9.2	25.7	49.9
Taney	1 765	18 989	1 481	716	3 425	388	630	410	21 576	459	17.0	17.4	40.3
Texas	482	4 958	653	1 412	878	201	67	97	19 599	1 478	16.6	13.3	47.2
Vernon	513	5 911	1 136	1 406	1 044	385	104	121	20 519	1 265	21.1	17.2	46.8
Warren	548	5 662	477	1 938	983	132	65	123	21 742	555	26.8	13.3	41.8
Washington	340	2 925	611	645	522	91	26	52	17 835	499	14.6	11.6	33.7
Wayne	243	1 941	328	603	448	84	55	30	15 545	380	10.3	12.4	36.6
Webster	616	5 332	494	1 404	981	273	117	99	18 660	1 691	31.3	6.9	40.0
Worth	67	312	33	94	D	14	D	4	12 205	356	12.4	26.1	50.0
Wright	393	3 753	361	922	912	171	91	71	18 899	1 331	19.8	12.1	51.3

							Agriculture, 1997 (cont'd)								
STATE County	Land in farms					Value of land and buildings		Value of machinery and equipment average per farm ($1,000)	Value of products sold		Percent from —		Percent of farms with sales of —		Percent of land owned by fed. gov. 1997	Water consumption 1995 (mil gal/day)
			Acres												
	Acreage (1,000)	Percent change, 1992–1997	Average size of farm	Total irrigated (1,000)	Total cropland (1,000)	Average per farm ($1,000)	Average per acre (dollars)		Total (mil dol)	Average per farm (dollars)	Crops	Live-stock and poultry products	$10,000 or more	$100,000 or more		
	117	118	119	120	121	122	123	124	125	126	127	128	129	130	131	132

MISSOURI—Cont'd

STATE County	117	118	119	120	121	122	123	124	125	126	127	128	129	130	131	132
Jasper	271	-3.5	200	6	180	230	1 196	29	76	56 399	36.7	63.3	35.9	7.8	0.0	25.9
Jefferson	109	-8.8	166	0	57	290	2 021	21	9	13 606	41.6	58.4	19.9	2.1	0.0	835.2
Johnson	400	7.7	246	1	279	275	1 112	40	54	33 082	38.4	61.6	39.8	6.3	0.7	5.5
Knox	281	4.7	466	0	207	382	796	64	37	60 814	59.5	40.5	58.5	16.3	0.0	0.8
Laclede	317	4.0	244	0	166	218	920	24	32	24 734	6.1	93.9	37.5	7.2	0.0	5.0
Lafayette	349	-1.9	287	2	286	389	1 421	56	108	88 799	53.4	46.6	57.0	19.3	0.2	4.4
Lawrence	338	1.5	195	1	223	248	1 277	32	122	70 304	7.8	92.2	40.2	9.1	0.0	5.3
Lewis	269	7.9	374	D	190	328	879	58	41	56 521	70.6	29.4	52.7	15.3	0.0	1.7
Lincoln	262	3.7	265	2	188	438	1 654	53	52	52 947	53.5	46.5	44.7	11.8	0.1	3.1
Linn	346	2.4	371	1	251	233	684	33	49	52 086	33.9	66.1	54.0	11.6	0.0	2.3
Livingston	273	0.7	370	1	213	325	876	52	37	50 378	78.7	21.3	48.8	11.7	0.0	2.5
McDonald	232	16.4	215	0	97	251	1 256	27	155	143 799	1.0	99.0	36.4	13.1	0.0	5.3
Macon	381	-0.4	329	0	249	216	676	38	35	30 230	55.0	45.0	45.2	7.1	1.0	2.8
Madison	110	-1.7	285	D	48	187	707	26	7	17 007	7.7	92.3	30.1	2.6	14.7	1.4
Maries	229	-1.8	280	0	105	231	735	36	19	23 557	8.4	91.6	41.1	5.0	0.0	3.3
Marion	221	0.6	318	4	164	339	1 025	53	40	57 489	62.2	37.8	53.5	15.7	0.0	7.6
Mercer	230	9.3	426	D	159	351	882	36	123	227 791	D	D	45.6	5.8	0.0	1.8
Miller	255	5.2	239	1	118	213	874	28	76	71 191	3.2	96.8	41.1	10.5	0.0	3.2
Mississippi	264	-0.5	987	70	255	1 596	1 591	200	80	299 051	99.1	0.9	91.8	60.7	0.0	19.2
Moniteau	223	2.7	218	0	147	195	931	37	53	51 629	17.7	82.3	46.6	8.0	0.0	2.8
Monroe	328	7.3	370	3	240	342	901	56	56	62 679	52.9	47.1	53.4	15.8	5.5	3.2
Montgomery	248	10.1	324	1	171	397	1 174	61	37	47 849	62.2	37.8	51.5	13.9	0.0	2.2
Morgan	202	0.2	233	0	112	221	1 001	32	91	104 835	6.1	93.9	48.4	15.1	0.0	2.2
New Madrid	386	4.5	899	150	375	1 304	1 462	203	109	255 031	97.0	3.0	89.7	58.7	0.0	848.7
Newton	256	-0.2	158	0	168	232	1 352	24	123	76 067	4.8	95.2	34.7	9.7	0.1	7.2
Nodaway	492	-3.2	391	0	396	327	845	50	84	66 707	63.5	36.5	65.9	19.6	0.0	3.9
Oregon	248	-1.6	311	0	100	253	816	30	20	25 470	5.9	94.1	40.0	4.9	20.9	4.0
Osage	305	-3.8	266	1	140	238	919	31	51	44 834	10.2	89.8	41.8	10.6	0.8	34.8
Ozark	253	1.1	324	0	85	247	724	27	21	26 932	2.9	97.1	41.5	7.4	11.2	5.2
Pemiscot	296	1.3	966	49	291	1 424	1 383	199	86	280 575	99.3	0.7	87.9	62.7	0.0	28.2
Perry	201	-3.6	235	0	131	253	1 083	45	32	37 589	48.9	51.1	46.7	9.2	0.0	2.7
Pettis	366	2.0	293	1	263	285	996	60	104	83 278	28.1	71.9	53.8	15.0	0.0	5.6
Phelps	196	-2.4	259	0	84	220	867	21	9	12 208	13.7	86.3	28.9	1.8	14.7	3.9
Pike	317	-1.9	336	1	218	397	1 184	51	55	57 810	63.5	36.5	53.2	15.1	0.8	9.8
Platte	180	-4.5	253	1	139	435	1 874	50	36	50 106	84.2	15.8	50.1	13.0	0.5	364.9
Polk	348	0.5	221	1	209	248	1 221	26	50	31 439	9.6	90.4	39.6	7.0	1.9	4.3
Pulaski	140	0.5	259	0	65	183	731	28	12	22 174	6.7	93.3	32.8	2.4	13.6	7.5
Putnam	261	2.9	425	D	154	242	599	37	27	43 740	27.8	72.2	58.2	11.2	0.0	2.2
Ralls	232	1.2	421	1	172	469	1 061	70	39	70 450	66.7	33.3	53.1	17.8	3.0	1.8
Randolph	230	4.0	287	1	143	236	887	35	27	33 364	40.7	59.3	36.3	7.0	1.1	877.3
Ray	274	-1.0	255	3	202	297	1 275	45	39	36 335	63.6	36.4	41.4	7.5	0.2	3.9
Reynolds	113	25.8	375	0	34	229	599	19	3	10 282	8.6	91.4	29.8	1.0	20.0	3.7
Ripley	152	-0.7	322	8	70	214	795	28	11	22 731	50.5	49.5	35.2	5.7	23.8	19.2
St. Charles	187	-8.3	275	2	148	728	2 664	62	42	62 436	79.9	20.1	51.9	15.1	0.0	446.4
St. Clair	263	2.3	338	0	162	240	724	32	25	31 638	36.2	63.8	46.8	8.1	7.1	1.5
Ste. Genevieve	168	-0.5	266	0	86	292	1 102	28	18	28 376	38.9	61.1	39.6	6.0	3.2	1.8
St. Francois	113	-3.6	174	1	61	263	1 254	33	13	20 492	46.3	53.7	29.6	2.3	0.3	306.5
St. Louis	45	-16.6	155	1	31	418	2 789	31	21	73 314	84.3	15.7	39.5	16.8	(1)0.0	176.4
Saline	430	3.8	459	2	347	543	1 214	74	103	109 651	66.6	33.4	69.9	27.1	1.5	5.1
Schuyler	160	-3.3	324	D	111	212	624	33	14	29 097	43.0	57.0	51.5	6.9	0.0	0.7
Scotland	225	3.5	374	D	165	288	769	60	34	56 797	60.6	39.4	57.7	17.3	0.0	0.9
Scott	241	9.9	445	66	223	578	1 337	101	77	141 644	77.7	22.3	60.8	29.0	0.0	19.5
Shannon	133	11.1	284	0	51	158	588	23	6	11 702	5.8	94.2	34.3	0.4	18.3	1.0
Shelby	272	-0.3	423	2	210	400	912	65	59	90 893	50.8	49.2	66.1	23.4	0.0	2.5
Stoddard	449	2.4	477	204	415	769	1 566	114	154	163 274	76.3	23.7	55.5	30.3	2.2	153.3
Stone	136	-1.5	199	0	62	219	1 273	20	16	23 228	4.8	95.2	33.0	5.1	8.4	3.8
Sullivan	326	-1.3	412	D	212	299	664	35	185	234 391	4.9	95.1	53.1	7.6	0.0	3.1
Taney	158	-1.6	345	0	40	389	1 148	38	10	21 650	5.3	94.7	35.1	1.7	19.5	9.5
Texas	430	-6.5	291	0	206	205	758	24	37	24 727	6.0	94.0	39.5	6.0	6.6	5.4
Vernon	389	-3.3	307	4	274	260	883	32	88	69 353	31.5	68.5	43.4	9.2	0.0	4.9
Warren	133	5.2	239	1	85	351	1 766	36	22	40 525	55.0	45.0	40.2	11.4	0.0	3.6
Washington	127	13.3	254	0	53	219	804	20	25	49 464	1.8	98.2	26.7	2.0	16.8	8.9
Wayne	98	5.0	257		38	182	780	29	4	11 066	27.5	72.5	22.4	1.3	26.8	1.8
Webster	297	2.4	176	0	166	210	1 192	23	46	27 408	5.0	95.0	36.0	6.3	0.0	4.2
Worth	150	12.1	422	D	105	253	552	29	13	36 642	53.1	46.9	53.9	9.3	0.0	0.5
Wright	312	-1.5	235	1	163	200	881	24	42	31 550	3.8	96.2	41.0	10.4	1.6	3.8

1. St. Louis City included with St. Louis County.

Table B. States and Counties — Residential Construction, Wholesale and Retail Trade, and Real Estate

STATE County	Value of Residential Construction Authorized by Building Permits, 2000		Wholesale Trade, 1997				Retail Trade[1], 1997				Real Estate and Rental and Leasing, 1997			
	New Construction ($1,000)	Number of Housing Units	Number of Establishments	Number of Employees	Sales (mil dol)	Annual Payroll (mil dol)	Number of Establishments	Number of Employees	Sales (mil dol)	Annual Payroll (mil dol)	Number of Establishments	Number of Employees	Receipts (mil dol)	Annual Payroll (mil dol)
	133	134	135	136	137	138	139	140	141	142	143	144	145	146
MISSOURI—Cont'd														
Jasper	36 559	444	198	2 164	897.0	54.3	597	7 658	1 153.1	108.8	115	455	39.7	7.5
Jefferson	137 783	1 272	158	1 115	352.6	35.7	549	6 265	1 110.0	99.9	134	460	42.5	8.4
Johnson	5 981	73	37	373	93.8	8.0	154	1 551	243.8	22.1	29	79	6.8	1.1
Knox	180	2	7	D	D	D	31	115	20.4	1.3	1	D	D	D
Laclede	8 042	106	44	337	126.4	7.3	191	1 964	318.9	28.1	35	89	7.0	1.3
Lafayette	2 042	16	48	362	220.3	9.1	185	1 516	201.4	19.3	16	49	7.8	0.5
Lawrence	2 898	43	26	108	205.6	2.2	120	1 202	270.8	21.4	17	36	4.6	0.3
Lewis	360	8	13	D	D	D	49	261	47.2	4.0	16	15	1.2	0.1
Lincoln	11 005	114	47	254	144.2	6.5	110	1 249	234.1	18.9	26	60	7.8	0.9
Linn	902	10	23	123	34.0	2.8	71	531	80.4	7.0	8	19	0.6	0.1
Livingston	2 789	34	36	591	196.3	12.6	83	987	150.4	14.8	12	32	5.2	0.6
McDonald	388	7	16	D	D	D	79	478	82.6	6.4	11	22	1.6	0.3
Macon	1 190	11	23	227	82.9	3.7	73	642	85.6	7.7	8	21	1.2	0.1
Madison	470	8	11	64	19.0	0.6	53	475	62.9	7.0	4	13	0.9	0.1
Maries	NA	NA	8	142	87.0	0.7	30	199	31.5	2.3	3	7	0.5	0.2
Marion	8 791	107	37	437	138.6	8.4	178	1 889	298.6	25.4	26	85	4.8	1.0
Mercer	0	0	4	33	11.8	0.6	16	78	17.5	1.1	NA	NA	NA	NA
Miller	3 114	55	22	182	62.8	2.9	130	1 004	208.1	17.8	33	73	8.0	1.4
Mississippi	1 136	23	22	236	313.2	6.2	67	588	94.7	7.6	6	10	0.7	0.1
Moniteau	517	4	19	D	D	D	59	447	108.9	7.2	10	19	0.8	0.1
Monroe	2 071	34	13	40	17.0	0.9	42	267	47.1	3.8	3	4	0.6	0.1
Montgomery	2 169	23	21	180	93.7	4.0	67	438	74.4	6.3	5	12	0.6	0.1
Morgan	NA	NA	23	129	31.1	2.0	112	921	146.0	12.8	20	D	D	D
New Madrid	1 185	15	31	482	310.5	11.2	95	741	145.0	10.4	11	53	1.6	0.4
Newton	3 300	37	52	411	195.1	10.0	193	1 644	291.2	24.8	36	130	10.6	1.8
Nodaway	4 824	59	29	266	240.0	5.0	100	1 029	128.1	12.5	20	51	3.3	0.4
Oregon	0	0	14	113	29.0	2.0	46	378	57.1	4.9	5	13	0.7	0.1
Osage	NA	NA	15	34	24.4	0.9	52	387	91.9	7.1	4	D	D	D
Ozark	188	5	8	D	D	D	37	249	39.6	3.2	4	16	0.7	0.1
Pemiscot	1 887	36	25	239	213.8	5.7	91	667	129.8	10.4	9	D	D	D
Perry	4 688	57	17	122	39.1	3.9	83	880	170.2	14.7	14	36	1.7	0.4
Pettis	1 505	16	67	765	211.6	18.3	204	2 230	355.7	33.5	40	142	12.0	2.4
Phelps	10 208	166	44	428	99.0	9.6	209	2 352	375.8	33.7	27	88	6.3	1.2
Pike	974	13	28	D	D	D	95	636	86.1	9.0	7	19	0.8	0.1
Platte	72 857	467	119	1 943	3 334.6	92.4	204	2 471	581.5	40.4	74	731	99.4	13.0
Polk	5 363	66	26	788	120.2	7.0	110	919	167.2	14.6	16	52	3.2	0.5
Pulaski	613	7	15	D	D	D	143	1 041	178.8	15.6	29	88	7.6	1.2
Putnam	330	4	10	D	D	D	18	116	17.7	1.4	5	D	D	D
Ralls	135	2	12	86	61.3	2.6	31	172	23.2	2.3	3	D	D	D
Randolph	2 348	21	26	188	76.9	4.7	110	1 384	211.7	19.1	16	98	13.9	1.4
Ray	10 094	99	19	D	D	D	72	608	109.9	8.9	13	34	1.9	0.3
Reynolds	NA	NA	7	59	8.3	0.7	27	123	19.1	1.5	2	D	D	D
Ripley	325	3	7	32	11.0	0.5	54	371	68.4	5.1	3	D	D	D
St. Charles	392 862	4 001	345	2 729	1 831.7	91.9	934	13 688	2 343.7	220.7	189	1 095	304.6	24.6
St. Clair	NA	NA	8	38	34.4	0.5	48	314	42.5	3.5	3	4	0.3	0.0
Ste. Genevieve	1 432	9	24	137	36.0	3.2	64	469	82.5	6.7	5	D	D	D
St. Francois	19 147	240	51	556	145.1	14.4	260	2 792	440.1	39.9	39	121	9.1	1.6
St. Louis	370 199	2 691	2 639	38 765	39 755.5	1 890.0	4 287	72 497	12 385.5	1 347.8	1 319	10 396	1 405.8	275.6
Saline	1 932	23	41	459	226.2	12.0	122	1 025	140.9	12.9	16	71	2.7	0.5
Schuyler	2 163	20	3	D	D	D	22	138	22.6	1.6	1	D	D	D
Scotland	423	6	9	56	25.3	0.7	33	170	24.2	2.1	3	D	D	D
Scott	5 473	59	80	1 142	629.5	30.8	243	2 248	355.1	34.3	33	81	5.7	1.0
Shannon	15	13	10	61	22.3	1.5	29	128	19.1	1.5	10	11	0.9	0.2
Shelby	0	0	20	98	32.3	1.9	45	233	28.0	2.8	4	D	D	D
Stoddard	2 483	33	52	355	177.2	8.1	152	1 292	245.1	18.7	24	41	3.9	0.6
Stone	1 881	24	17	51	28.0	1.2	131	828	134.0	13.1	32	61	6.4	0.9
Sullivan	643	6	2	D	D	D	31	191	34.4	2.7	4	5	0.2	0.0
Taney	34 918	475	40	302	73.0	6.9	391	2 976	442.6	47.3	78	831	66.0	18.1
Texas	620	9	26	184	66.7	3.0	105	916	136.7	11.9	11	50	3.5	0.9
Vernon	1 318	15	29	164	56.3	3.3	89	1 003	143.7	14.5	13	37	4.2	0.8
Warren	40 716	339	26	145	53.7	4.3	114	1 027	188.8	15.3	17	45	7.1	0.8
Washington	100	1	15	65	11.3	1.0	67	633	101.7	11.6	8	31	1.0	0.3
Wayne	NA	NA	5	18	3.6	0.2	53	457	57.5	5.2	4	7	0.4	0.1
Webster	6 567	99	23	120	25.8	2.2	114	876	146.3	11.9	19	46	2.5	0.6
Worth	0	0	7	D	D	D	14	58	6.1	0.6	3	D	D	D
Wright	1 243	15	20	147	94.8	2.4	94	795	130.4	10.7	14	39	2.3	0.4

1. Establishments with payroll.

Table B. States and Counties — Professional, Manufacturing, and Accommodation and Foodservices

STATE County	Professional, Scientific, and Technical Services[1], 1997				Manufacturing, 1997				Accommodation and Foodservices, 1997			
	Number of Establishments	Number of Employees	Receipts (mil dol)	Annual Payroll (mil dol)	Number of Establishments	Number of Employees	Receipts (mil dol)	Annual Payroll (mil dol)	Number of Establishments	Number of Employees	Sales (mil dol)	Annual Payroll (mil dol)
	147	148	149	150	151	152	153	154	155	156	157	158
MISSOURI—Cont'd												
Jasper	145	948	53.9	23.0	198	11 904	2 154.6	289.8	222	4 100	109.5	31.7
Jefferson	152	570	40.9	16.0	182	5 304	1 199.3	168.2	214	3 981	113.8	31.8
Johnson	42	108	15.2	2.5	31	1 856	183.2	46.7	83	1 144	31.5	8.2
Knox	6	15	0.7	0.2	NA	NA	NA	NA	4	24	0.7	0.2
Laclede	31	101	6.0	2.2	57	5 177	809.7	130.4	62	827	27.9	6.9
Lafayette	36	117	11.5	2.4	42	1 166	130.4	22.9	70	D	D	D
Lawrence	26	63	3.6	1.3	54	1 614	259.0	34.8	54	690	17.6	4.8
Lewis	6	D	D	D	NA	NA	NA	NA	18	66	2.1	0.4
Lincoln	27	296	4.2	1.4	43	1 078	176.8	29.0	48	700	19.4	5.1
Linn	11	52	2.2	1.0	24	1 739	137.8	45.0	26	241	6.6	1.7
Livingston	22	123	8.2	2.6	28	903	117.1	23.6	28	405	11.7	3.1
McDonald	11	29	3.2	0.7	34	3 052	469.8	52.5	34	218	7.2	2.0
Macon	16	76	3.6	1.4	15	D	D	D	26	355	9.8	3.0
Madison	8	77	2.8	0.8	16	553	28.7	8.3	23	278	5.7	1.6
Maries	5	D	D	D	NA	NA	NA	NA	9	D	D	D
Marion	44	226	15.0	5.5	46	3 179	1 707.1	87.5	69	1 053	28.9	8.2
Mercer	2	D	D	D	NA	NA	NA	NA	8	49	0.8	0.3
Miller	36	180	16.7	3.7	29	1 500	128.5	31.8	63	1 090	40.0	12.5
Mississippi	9	21	1.3	0.2	14	571	66.4	10.7	16	D	D	D
Moniteau	14	35	1.9	0.5	22	1 095	173.8	19.5	21	210	5.5	1.4
Monroe	7	14	0.8	0.1	7	1 047	74.8	27.9	22	160	3.4	0.9
Montgomery	9	16	0.7	0.1	32	811	82.1	16.6	17	240	4.7	1.2
Morgan	20	80	3.6	1.3	29	649	115.0	12.0	51	330	11.4	3.2
New Madrid	17	39	2.5	1.3	17	2 504	529.8	83.4	26	298	7.9	2.2
Newton	37	144	6.8	2.3	63	4 315	692.9	109.8	87	1 664	50.0	14.3
Nodaway	22	92	5.6	1.6	23	1 677	647.2	48.2	41	764	18.4	4.7
Oregon	9	17	0.7	0.2	NA	NA	NA	NA	18	139	4.2	1.1
Osage	7	11	0.6	0.2	24	914	169.8	20.3	21	D	D	D
Ozark	5	17	0.6	0.2	NA	NA	NA	NA	14	63	2.3	0.5
Pemiscot	13	28	1.9	0.5	12	893	131.1	19.8	36	404	10.6	3.0
Perry	14	75	4.1	1.8	31	2 855	609.3	61.9	39	469	12.5	3.5
Pettis	50	215	13.2	4.9	69	5 324	958.9	130.2	76	1 313	36.2	10.8
Phelps	64	282	18.0	7.0	55	1 132	218.2	29.6	103	1 346	45.1	12.1
Pike	16	87	6.0	2.2	27	771	277.4	25.7	25	304	8.7	2.3
Platte	138	830	105.3	34.1	47	1 599	344.7	52.4	157	3 218	139.2	38.3
Polk	27	93	4.2	1.6	34	859	81.1	13.9	40	462	12.0	3.3
Pulaski	27	144	9.8	3.0	18	682	36.4	9.4	77	914	29.5	10.7
Putnam	3	20	0.8	0.3	NA	NA	NA	NA	5	D	D	D
Ralls	3	17	1.3	0.4	10	913	253.9	21.6	17	239	6.1	2.1
Randolph	17	83	5.9	1.3	37	1 381	182.6	30.5	45	656	16.1	4.2
Ray	31	104	14.4	2.4	21	654	63.9	16.5	26	244	7.1	1.8
Reynolds	6	D	D	D	33	634	52.7	10.9	14	70	3.0	1.0
Ripley	5	14	0.6	0.2	42	629	42.8	10.0	16	156	4.1	1.0
St. Charles	446	2 971	208.6	71.0	279	12 160	4 432.9	431.9	418	8 656	245.2	71.3
St. Clair	6	13	0.8	0.2	NA	NA	NA	NA	14	D	D	D
Ste. Genevieve	17	73	3.9	1.2	32	1 752	208.2	47.8	32	399	9.5	2.6
St. Francois	73	330	16.5	5.7	66	3 797	394.6	80.3	100	1 602	45.1	13.1
St. Louis	3 296	35 334	4 078.7	1 437.2	1 272	78 218	25 347.9	3 359.8	2 030	46 507	1 579.7	465.7
Saline	23	56	3.1	0.8	24	2 530	647.5	55.4	50	603	15.3	4.0
Schuyler	1	D	D	D	NA	NA	NA	NA	8	51	0.8	0.2
Scotland	5	D	D	D	NA	NA	NA	NA	10	66	2.3	0.5
Scott	59	209	16.2	5.6	77	3 008	532.6	66.1	78	1 102	35.1	9.8
Shannon	3	D	D	D	22	710	40.9	8.1	16	44	2.1	0.5
Shelby	10	41	3.8	1.0	5	D	D	D	11	94	1.5	0.4
Stoddard	26	103	5.5	2.1	40	2 372	264.0	42.4	47	504	14.6	4.1
Stone	23	60	3.6	0.8	NA	NA	NA	NA	86	530	19.2	5.8
Sullivan	4	13	1.1	0.8	5	D	D	D	7	D	D	D
Taney	80	295	18.9	6.5	59	798	87.8	15.8	328	4 947	245.4	68.6
Texas	16	39	2.4	0.8	53	1 399	169.6	26.2	32	212	4.7	1.3
Vernon	25	89	4.9	1.6	21	1 561	425.8	44.0	41	520	13.8	3.6
Warren	19	49	2.8	0.8	37	2 042	242.7	50.1	34	503	14.3	4.1
Washington	13	30	1.0	0.4	NA	NA	NA	NA	17	D	D	D
Wayne	9	22	1.6	0.3	28	510	44.0	8.3	20	144	3.5	0.9
Webster	24	75	3.3	1.2	44	D	D	D	38	420	11.7	3.1
Worth	2	D	D	D	NA	NA	NA	NA	6	13	0.4	0.1
Wright	13	31	1.2	0.3	18	730	102.0	14.2	40	303	8.3	2.0

1. Firms subject to federal tax.

Table B. States and Counties — Health and Other Services and Federal Funds

STATE County	Health Care and Social Assistance[1], 1997				Other Services[1], 1997				Federal funds and grants, fiscal 2001[2] Expenditures (mil dol)			
									Total	Direct payments for individuals[3]		
	Number of Establishments	Number of Employees	Receipts (mil dol)	Annual Payroll (mil dol)	Number of Establishments	Number of Employees	Receipts (mil dol)	Annual Payroll (mil dol)	Total	Social Security and government retirement	Medicare	Food stamps and Supplemental Security Income
	159	160	161	162	163	164	165	166	167	168	169	170
MISSOURI—Cont'd												
Jasper	235	2 360	144.4	65.4	227	1 189	69.2	18.9	855.2	249.4	100.5	22.0
Jefferson	216	2 633	108.7	48.1	291	1 426	83.0	24.4	591.1	327.6	116.2	16.9
Johnson	59	650	26.9	11.0	55	212	10.9	2.8	356.7	88.9	24.7	5.5
Knox	7	53	1.6	0.8	11	51	11.7	0.7	38.6	10.7	7.2	0.7
Laclede	41	492	26.2	10.3	48	133	8.4	2.0	154.6	81.9	23.8	6.5
Lafayette	45	489	18.8	8.6	48	146	7.6	2.0	182.4	77.1	34.7	4.3
Lawrence	36	211	12.7	4.3	44	106	6.4	1.6	148.8	75.7	27.9	5.5
Lewis	8	120	3.3	1.8	19	52	3.7	0.8	60.4	22.3	10.0	1.2
Lincoln	39	376	12.6	4.6	53	155	9.6	2.5	141.4	66.5	26.0	3.7
Linn	24	476	13.8	5.9	31	86	6.0	1.1	93.7	39.2	20.7	2.2
Livingston	34	537	19.3	7.4	32	97	6.5	1.6	103.3	34.8	16.8	2.4
McDonald	15	148	6.1	2.8	18	64	1.6	0.6	91.5	39.2	14.2	4.9
Macon	20	226	7.2	3.0	29	73	4.5	1.0	94.6	40.5	20.5	1.9
Madison	16	150	4.5	1.5	11	24	2.3	0.4	66.9	31.8	13.0	3.4
Maries	9	145	5.1	1.9	10	28	1.8	0.4	36.7	17.8	8.3	1.3
Marion	61	798	39.7	19.7	43	216	15.0	3.8	170.9	65.9	30.9	6.5
Mercer	6	85	2.6	1.3	5	9	0.9	0.2	29.0	9.3	4.5	0.5
Miller	26	261	9.4	5.0	43	141	8.0	2.2	113.2	60.2	25.2	3.3
Mississippi	13	255	7.5	3.1	20	56	3.2	0.8	125.3	32.2	13.9	6.3
Moniteau	19	158	7.3	2.6	18	63	2.7	0.8	61.3	27.4	13.3	0.8
Monroe	14	78	2.8	1.2	12	25	1.7	0.4	65.1	22.7	11.3	1.2
Montgomery	19	268	8.9	4.1	25	245	8.4	3.2	78.8	29.6	13.8	1.8
Morgan	13	61	2.7	1.4	33	87	4.9	0.9	101.3	59.1	21.0	3.5
New Madrid	14	479	14.5	6.5	21	86	6.0	1.0	183.2	40.5	17.8	8.7
Newton	63	1 108	60.4	21.3	72	222	10.3	2.5	183.6	86.7	32.4	5.7
Nodaway	29	391	13.5	5.6	43	136	8.3	1.9	112.8	36.6	15.9	1.7
Oregon	8	203	7.2	3.2	14	28	2.1	0.5	68.8	29.2	10.1	3.2
Osage	10	229	6.6	2.4	15	33	2.7	0.4	49.2	22.4	12.0	0.7
Ozark	4	93	3.1	1.4	11	19	1.1	0.2	61.3	28.9	9.2	2.6
Pemiscot	26	361	11.3	4.5	21	102	5.8	1.4	205.1	42.5	23.9	13.6
Perry	29	255	8.8	3.2	31	106	10.2	2.1	77.2	35.0	15.6	2.0
Pettis	89	998	43.5	19.4	77	821	36.8	13.8	202.9	92.8	36.9	7.0
Phelps	88	1 529	56.6	27.3	66	306	16.7	4.4	249.3	105.9	32.6	8.0
Pike	24	273	9.1	4.0	23	68	6.9	1.3	101.3	38.7	18.2	2.5
Platte	101	1 309	60.2	28.5	106	604	59.2	11.3	249.6	53.6	33.7	62.5
Polk	32	626	15.1	6.8	41	111	7.1	1.2	135.0	64.8	24.6	4.6
Pulaski	26	300	9.1	3.4	54	204	11.1	2.9	716.9	102.4	20.6	5.1
Putnam	9	31	1.3	0.4	8	17	1.0	0.2	36.9	13.2	7.4	1.0
Ralls	8	260	8.2	3.7	9	34	1.8	0.4	49.5	17.2	7.4	0.9
Randolph	44	864	45.9	18.2	48	189	10.3	2.6	130.5	56.0	29.3	5.6
Ray	21	164	5.7	2.9	42	113	6.3	1.7	91.7	41.9	19.4	1.8
Reynolds	10	194	5.7	2.5	3	7	0.6	0.1	43.1	17.5	7.4	2.4
Ripley	15	251	9.3	3.9	13	23	1.7	0.4	99.9	37.9	14.2	6.0
St. Charles	417	5 042	344.0	161.4	425	2 506	145.7	48.2	858.0	468.7	135.5	15.1
St. Clair	8	213	5.9	2.8	5	11	1.8	0.2	74.2	27.5	10.9	1.7
Ste. Genevieve	26	189	7.0	2.9	21	75	4.5	1.2	70.0	37.8	13.6	1.9
St. Francois	123	1 649	68.7	33.9	83	271	15.1	3.9	288.4	141.4	58.5	13.2
St. Louis	2 719	29 766	2 077.0	972.8	1 877	12 884	819.2	270.5	4 837.5	2 306.3	970.4	117.8
Saline	44	499	18.7	7.7	43	141	9.0	2.3	146.0	54.3	26.6	3.7
Schuyler	6	22	1.0	0.5	6	11	0.8	0.1	32.7	12.3	6.0	1.6
Scotland	3	21	0.5	0.2	15	32	2.4	0.4	37.7	10.3	6.6	0.6
Scott	87	1 452	56.1	23.1	57	262	19.8	5.0	233.1	94.7	35.3	11.8
Shannon	4	9	0.5	0.3	7	13	1.1	0.2	45.3	18.2	6.7	2.7
Shelby	7	44	2.4	1.6	15	52	2.4	0.7	51.2	17.6	9.1	1.0
Stoddard	47	977	33.1	15.6	40	169	10.3	3.2	233.9	76.7	30.5	7.0
Stone	19	195	10.8	3.5	37	117	7.1	2.0	126.4	79.0	22.8	4.2
Sullivan	9	177	6.1	2.7	11	24	1.9	0.5	51.3	15.4	9.8	1.3
Taney	64	537	31.1	11.8	66	267	14.0	4.4	192.4	103.6	35.2	4.3
Texas	17	295	8.3	3.7	32	77	5.9	0.9	130.2	65.1	18.8	8.7
Vernon	48	639	24.7	9.7	27	77	4.3	1.1	117.5	46.0	18.9	4.5
Warren	27	210	7.2	2.6	29	81	5.4	2.1	93.8	50.0	19.8	2.1
Washington	18	83	4.8	2.0	17	37	2.0	0.5	103.8	42.9	16.4	8.2
Wayne	10	244	7.5	2.6	9	26	2.1	0.5	103.0	46.9	*16.7	4.8
Webster	22	150	4.4	2.0	36	112	6.8	1.6	128.6	66.4	22.1	4.5
Worth	6	27	1.0	0.3	4	10	0.7	0.1	18.7	6.0	2.4	0.3
Wright	23	351	13.7	6.1	29	72	5.4	1.1	114.2	47.7	19.4	5.7

1. Firms subject to federal tax.   2. October 1, 2000 to September 30, 2001.   3. State totals may include programs not allocated by county.

	Federal funds and grants, fiscal 2001[1] (cont'd)							Local government finances, 1997				
	Expenditures (mil dol) (cont'd)							General revenue				
	Procurement contract awards		Grants[2]								Taxes		
STATE County												Per capita[3] (dollars)	
	Salaries and wages	Defense	Other	Medicaid and other health-related	Nutrition and family welfare	Education	Other	Total (mil dol)	Intergovern-mental (mil dol)	Total (mil dol)	Total	Property
	171	172	173	174	175	176	177	178	179	180	181	182
MISSOURI—Cont'd												
Jasper	21.5	16.0	330.4	68.6	11.8	5.7	7.9	183.4	61.0	68.6	694	359
Jefferson	20.1	2.3	5.1	39.6	10.2	6.5	37.4	257.6	113.4	103.1	534	374
Johnson	148.0	44.5	1.6	11.2	2.9	7.0	2.0	66.3	32.2	21.3	449	289
Knox	1.9	0.0	0.4	3.7	0.4	0.3	0.6	10.8	7.0	2.8	635	466
Laclede	5.2	0.0	1.0	28.0	2.9	1.5	1.8	41.4	19.1	14.7	482	268
Lafayette	7.3	1.4	1.2	10.4	2.1	2.1	19.2	48.4	21.7	16.8	515	314
Lawrence	7.9	0.0	1.1	20.0	2.6	2.0	1.8	59.6	23.6	19.2	584	302
Lewis	2.9	0.0	1.0	7.1	0.9	0.6	0.2	17.0	7.5	4.3	427	330
Lincoln	5.3	0.0	1.1	14.3	1.6	0.7	6.4	75.7	22.4	16.9	479	321
Linn	3.5	0.0	1.3	11.2	1.4	0.8	1.5	28.2	15.6	8.2	590	361
Livingston	5.7	0.0	1.3	13.5	1.3	0.7	12.1	25.7	10.7	8.9	617	340
McDonald	5.5	0.0	0.7	18.5	1.9	1.1	4.5	21.1	12.6	5.4	272	192
Macon	4.8	0.0	1.2	10.7	1.1	0.8	0.9	38.1	11.6	8.7	571	369
Madison	1.4	0.0	0.6	11.5	1.5	0.7	2.6	24.2	9.2	4.1	350	281
Maries	0.8	0.0	0.2	6.2	0.5	0.4	0.3	10.3	5.6	3.5	417	334
Marion	3.4	1.2	0.4	25.7	5.5	1.6	14.0	51.0	20.2	18.0	646	394
Mercer	1.1	0.0	0.2	3.7	0.3	0.1	2.4	7.9	3.5	2.7	676	587
Miller	3.0	0.0	0.7	14.3	1.9	1.3	1.5	36.3	17.4	14.5	643	514
Mississippi	2.1	1.5	0.5	34.7	4.3	2.3	2.0	32.8	13.3	9.5	708	400
Moniteau	2.8	0.0	0.6	7.1	0.7	0.7	2.9	17.7	8.0	6.3	476	381
Monroe	3.1	0.8	0.6	8.2	0.6	0.7	0.8	21.3	12.4	5.6	621	449
Montgomery	2.8	0.5	0.8	9.2	0.9	0.8	6.3	16.1	7.2	5.7	485	297
Morgan	2.4	0.0	0.7	10.6	1.4	0.7	0.1	17.3	7.8	7.2	397	295
New Madrid	3.7	0.5	0.8	48.7	10.8	1.9	3.3	32.5	15.0	13.0	635	489
Newton	10.1	1.4	6.3	21.7	3.7	4.5	6.2	64.6	31.5	20.4	422	286
Nodaway	6.0	0.2	1.3	10.1	2.6	3.1	6.4	34.0	15.2	13.0	621	419
Oregon	1.9	0.0	0.5	18.3	1.6	0.8	2.5	12.1	7.8	3.2	321	231
Osage	2.1	0.0	0.5	7.1	0.3	0.4	0.7	13.1	6.8	4.5	358	298
Ozark	1.6	0.2	0.4	14.9	1.2	1.0	0.5	12.0	7.4	3.6	369	276
Pemiscot	3.3	2.0	0.7	69.0	7.7	5.3	5.2	37.1	22.2	9.7	449	301
Perry	3.0	0.7	1.9	9.9	1.3	0.6	0.1	33.9	9.9	8.8	503	346
Pettis	8.4	0.3	1.6	29.0	4.0	2.2	3.1	108.3	27.0	24.0	651	377
Phelps	34.0	3.5	3.5	27.6	3.1	3.0	19.0	123.2	41.1	18.9	490	257
Pike	3.8	2.5	0.8	12.6	1.7	1.5	4.0	31.4	11.2	9.1	563	402
Platte	45.3	0.5	16.9	7.1	4.0	2.5	2.6	104.0	38.2	48.4	705	542
Polk	4.4	0.1	1.1	21.3	1.8	2.7	5.6	63.7	20.5	9.2	363	251
Pulaski	429.2	112.8	1.6	20.1	6.5	14.0	0.4	55.9	37.7	11.9	311	223
Putnam	1.3	0.1	0.6	4.9	0.4	0.3	1.5	8.9	4.5	2.7	546	436
Ralls	3.9	0.0	1.1	3.4	0.5	0.3	0.9	8.6	4.3	3.2	359	228
Randolph	4.7	0.0	1.0	17.2	2.3	1.3	2.0	47.1	19.8	17.1	714	432
Ray	3.3	0.0	0.7	6.2	1.9	1.3	1.3	48.7	18.7	12.0	518	365
Reynolds	1.4	0.2	0.4	11.3	1.0	0.7	0.4	9.9	4.9	4.1	607	570
Ripley	2.4	3.6	0.5	25.8	2.8	1.1	1.4	18.9	10.9	5.7	409	371
St. Charles	36.4	20.3	85.0	34.2	9.6	6.4	21.0	481.6	153.7	246.6	933	623
St. Clair	1.7	0.0	0.4	8.0	3.6	0.7	12.5	22.6	10.4	3.2	351	294
Ste. Genevieve	1.8	1.9	0.4	6.2	1.0	0.6	0.1	30.8	7.8	9.1	530	362
St. Francois	7.6	0.5	2.2	40.9	9.1	4.4	1.1	83.2	44.8	25.0	458	284
St. Louis	352.1	75.0	69.5	553.9	48.6	39.1	198.6	2 001.6	563.8	1 188.8	1 185	772
Saline	5.0	0.0	0.9	19.5	2.1	1.3	0.7	42.0	20.6	13.3	582	369
Schuyler	2.6	0.0	0.4	3.9	0.5	0.3	0.9	7.7	3.5	2.1	476	397
Scotland	1.3	0.2	0.3	3.3	0.5	0.4	0.7	14.2	5.8	2.9	590	452
Scott	6.1	0.9	1.4	48.5	6.4	2.7	0.9	66.6	32.2	21.8	541	356
Shannon	2.8	0.0	0.3	11.0	2.5	0.3	0.3	6.8	4.4	1.6	200	143
Shelby	2.4	0.5	0.8	4.8	0.6	0.5	0.5	13.2	6.9	3.8	551	431
Stoddard	9.6	0.0	3.0	41.5	3.7	2.2	1.3	41.7	20.4	14.5	490	383
Stone	2.1	0.0	0.6	10.1	1.8	1.7	3.4	29.2	14.6	11.7	443	348
Sullivan	2.7	0.0	1.8	10.8	0.8	0.3	0.9	12.7	4.7	3.9	585	489
Taney	5.6	21.5	1.5	13.1	1.5	0.9	1.1	72.2	17.5	43.0	1 265	506
Texas	4.5	0.0	0.8	22.2	2.7	2.4	1.8	90.6	35.2	33.3	1 482	463
Vernon	5.2	0.1	1.0	13.3	2.0	1.1	3.4	46.6	15.4	11.0	576	346
Warren	3.8	0.1	1.0	6.2	1.1	0.8	3.0	25.9	9.6	12.9	547	345
Washington	3.2	0.0	0.6	23.6	3.8	1.7	2.6	36.0	17.6	7.4	326	216
Wayne	3.2	3.7	0.6	19.7	2.1	1.0	3.4	15.4	8.8	4.9	384	229
Webster	4.6	0.0	1.3	22.9	1.8	1.6	1.7	32.2	17.3	8.1	285	207
Worth	1.1	0.0	0.4	2.1	0.2	0.2	0.9	5.0	2.2	1.1	478	311
Wright	3.2	0.0	0.8	29.1	2.1	1.4	1.5	30.7	17.6	7.0	361	255

1. October 1, 2000 to September 30, 2001. 2. State totals may include programs not allocated by county. 3. Based on the resident population estimated as of July 1 of the year shown.

STATE County	Total (mil dol)	Per capita[1] (dollars)	Education	Health and hospitals	Police protection	Public welfare	Highways	Total (mil dol)	Per capita[1] (dollars)	Federal civilian	Federal military	State and local	Democratic	Republican	All other
	183	184	185	186	187	188	189	190	191	192	193	194	195	196	197
MISSOURI—Cont'd															
Jasper	191.9	1 942	48.0	9.4	4.8	0.5	8.7	54.5	551	363	483	5 906	31.3	66.4	2.2
Jefferson	258.9	1 340	69.2	2.0	4.5	0.0	5.9	95.3	493	335	950	7 228	50.0	47.6	2.3
Johnson	65.6	1 386	64.7	8.2	5.2	0.2	7.0	28.3	598	850	3 369	4 860	41.3	55.6	3.1
Knox	10.3	2 362	41.9	2.6	0.1	32.1	14.8	1.4	312	41	21	393	38.3	59.7	2.1
Laclede	39.8	1 308	66.4	1.0	2.5	0.4	15.7	8.2	271	86	151	1 378	32.1	65.6	2.4
Lafayette	50.5	1 554	63.4	0.1	4.2	0.0	10.3	30.5	937	117	164	2 142	43.7	54.1	2.2
Lawrence	59.3	1 805	50.6	17.3	6.1	4.7	7.7	8.7	265	83	161	1 734	32.8	64.4	2.8
Lewis	17.4	1 715	52.0	1.5	2.7	17.1	7.0	4.6	452	64	49	645	45.1	53.3	1.7
Lincoln	75.7	2 152	39.9	43.3	3.2	0.0	5.0	22.8	647	116	181	1 613	43.7	53.7	2.5
Linn	30.0	2 149	60.3	2.6	2.7	0.7	12.9	10.7	769	67	67	868	44.0	54.0	2.0
Livingston	26.0	1 812	54.9	3.6	3.0	5.7	9.3	5.0	348	102	67	1 062	38.6	59.1	2.3
McDonald	21.0	1 063	66.5	0.7	3.8	2.7	7.6	3.6	184	106	97	690	28.6	68.3	3.1
Macon	38.6	2 527	39.6	23.7	1.3	16.1	8.0	8.3	544	85	74	1 619	39.3	59.0	1.7
Madison	25.6	2 210	42.9	36.0	2.3	0.7	3.4	2.5	218	30	56	783	41.8	56.3	2.0
Maries	10.4	1 250	70.7	4.6	2.0	0.0	8.6	0.4	47	13	40	359	40.3	57.5	2.1
Marion	51.5	1 850	52.8	3.1	4.9	7.8	5.7	84.9	3 050	86	133	1 851	42.6	55.9	1.4
Mercer	8.4	2 102	63.7	3.3	2.4	0.0	14.0	1.7	420	23	19	259	30.1	67.9	2.0
Miller	40.4	1 786	73.1	1.9	2.3	4.2	4.2	21.7	961	53	109	1 063	34.4	63.5	2.1
Mississippi	27.7	2 056	48.0	4.4	4.7	0.6	9.4	14.1	1 046	46	64	752	52.8	45.9	1.3
Moniteau	18.1	1 368	67.8	5.0	5.6	0.0	7.7	6.7	507	52	64	1 048	35.9	62.1	2.1
Monroe	20.7	2 296	48.0	2.1	3.4	24.0	5.9	30.2	3 344	83	44	747	45.4	53.1	1.5
Montgomery	16.4	1 381	65.2	3.1	4.5	0.0	11.1	1.4	120	53	58	677	39.4	58.6	2.0
Morgan	17.4	961	59.8	0.9	3.9	8.2	8.9	1.2	65	48	91	894	41.0	56.6	2.4
New Madrid	33.6	1 637	66.2	2.6	4.8	0.2	7.9	14.5	706	66	96	1 065	51.4	47.0	1.5
Newton	59.3	1 227	71.3	3.3	4.8	0.0	5.0	5.6	116	139	238	1 970	30.5	67.3	2.2
Nodaway	34.4	1 646	60.8	1.7	4.8	0.0	12.7	21.8	1 041	101	98	2 610	39.3	57.0	3.7
Oregon	12.4	1 241	81.5	0.5	0.4	0.0	6.7	0.6	63	34	49	481	37.0	59.6	3.4
Osage	13.9	1 112	72.8	1.1	2.4	0.0	12.8	4.3	346	34	60	611	31.4	67.2	1.4
Ozark	12.3	1 279	75.2	2.9	2.4	0.0	7.2	6.4	664	27	48	478	33.4	62.0	4.5
Pemiscot	36.5	1 694	68.4	0.4	6.3	0.3	5.4	8.8	408	73	101	1 963	53.5	45.4	1.1
Perry	37.1	2 122	34.7	32.2	3.5	0.0	6.1	10.1	577	57	84	995	30.2	67.6	2.2
Pettis	110.2	2 996	39.0	41.1	2.8	0.0	4.0	42.0	1 141	156	178	2 806	37.2	60.5	2.3
Phelps	120.4	3 130	30.5	48.4	2.1	1.9	3.3	48.8	1 268	531	322	5 242	38.8	58.5	2.8
Pike	33.6	2 084	48.0	23.9	5.1	0.0	8.1	7.3	450	86	79	1 692	48.4	49.6	2.0
Platte	116.6	1 698	68.0	3.4	4.1	0.1	6.1	87.6	1 276	354	347	2 810	45.0	52.2	2.8
Polk	61.6	2 420	38.2	45.6	2.7	0.0	7.0	19.9	781	81	123	1 561	35.0	62.5	2.6
Pulaski	52.3	1 369	82.1	6.1	2.7	0.2	2.8	7.0	183	2 379	8 843	1 807	36.1	62.0	1.9
Putnam	9.3	1 876	54.8	1.7	3.2	12.9	15.0	3.7	753	27	23	408	30.3	68.3	1.4
Ralls	8.7	981	55.6	3.7	5.1	0.1	15.9	7.4	836	53	44	383	44.8	53.9	1.4
Randolph	54.9	2 299	61.4	1.2	3.4	0.0	5.7	28.1	1 175	83	114	1 933	44.8	52.7	2.4
Ray	46.6	2 005	42.3	21.1	1.7	9.4	11.2	24.7	1 062	63	114	1 203	51.0	46.3	2.7
Reynolds	11.5	1 718	74.5	3.9	2.6	0.0	7.2	0.5	68	23	32	474	41.5	56.3	2.2
Ripley	18.6	1 342	68.5	7.9	2.0	0.0	15.4	10.6	763	58	68	645	35.9	61.6	2.4
St. Charles	532.6	2 015	53.3	1.2	5.5	0.1	8.6	480.9	1 820	580	1 347	10 388	41.8	56.0	2.2
St. Clair	22.9	2 523	38.7	25.3	2.0	0.0	10.1	4.6	504	35	44	635	39.4	57.6	3.0
Ste. Genevieve	33.3	1 933	31.5	33.7	4.7	7.5	5.6	7.5	437	36	84	875	49.2	47.9	2.8
St. Francois	89.2	1 634	71.8	2.1	3.4	0.3	5.9	27.3	501	134	269	4 371	48.2	49.5	2.3
St. Louis	2 003.9	1 997	55.4	1.5	7.0	0.0	5.2	1 349.7	1 345	5 771	4 829	48 658	51.5	46.1	2.3
Saline	39.3	1 718	56.1	2.3	3.2	0.6	9.9	19.0	832	107	109	2 294	49.0	48.9	2.1
Schuyler	7.6	1 746	53.3	5.1	2.2	18.3	11.3	1.5	333	32	21	305	40.3	57.8	1.9
Scotland	12.5	2 593	36.1	18.2	2.5	25.6	9.0	1.1	222	30	24	576	36.3	61.3	2.5
Scott	61.4	1 523	58.3	2.5	6.5	0.0	5.6	257.4	6 384	117	195	2 274	41.1	57.3	1.6
Shannon	7.3	896	67.9	0.0	1.3	0.0	10.8	0.8	93	70	40	440	37.8	59.4	2.8
Shelby	12.8	1 884	57.5	4.9	2.5	13.0	12.5	2.4	350	47	32	576	38.7	59.4	1.8
Stoddard	42.3	1 431	65.3	2.8	4.1	0.0	10.6	8.6	290	191	142	1 311	35.9	62.0	2.0
Stone	31.0	1 171	82.7	0.0	1.9	0.3	2.1	18.9	715	37	132	940	33.4	64.1	2.5
Sullivan	12.9	1 942	43.3	27.2	3.8	0.0	14.1	2.9	441	53	33	456	36.8	61.3	2.0
Taney	80.1	2 357	37.5	1.4	4.0	0.0	8.6	127.5	3 755	105	170	1 559	33.7	63.8	2.4
Texas	122.5	5 457	19.5	9.9	0.6	0.0	66.5	35.0	1 558	91	108	1 352	35.1	61.8	3.1
Vernon	47.8	2 495	40.3	30.4	3.2	5.0	6.1	15.7	819	96	93	1 852	37.5	59.3	3.2
Warren	25.8	1 090	66.0	3.3	9.8	0.0	8.3	10.8	458	59	122	903	42.1	55.7	2.2
Washington	38.4	1 691	52.7	22.0	3.6	0.0	5.1	10.4	458	68	112	1 545	49.0	48.6	2.3
Wayne	14.9	1 158	73.3	1.9	3.1	0.9	4.7	2.2	171	90	63	599	40.8	57.2	1.9
Webster	30.8	1 084	66.5	0.0	3.1	11.1	8.9	3.2	113	80	144	1 144	35.1	61.9	3.0
Worth	5.0	2 132	51.1	1.7	2.2	23.4	10.3	0.5	196	22	11	199	40.5	56.2	3.3
Wright	29.9	1 538	73.3	0.8	3.2	7.2	4.7	1.6	80	61	96	1 017	28.7	68.8	2.6

1. Based on the resident population estimated as of July 1 of the year shown.   2. Data subject to copyright.

Table B. States and Counties — Land Area and Population

STATE/County code	MSA/PMSA/NECMA code[1]	County Type[2]	STATE County	Land area[3] (sq km) 2000	Total persons	Rank	Per square kilometer	White	Black	Am. Indian, Alaska Native	Asian and Pacific Islander	Percent Hispanic[4]	Under 5 years	5 to 17 years	18 to 24 years	25 to 34 years	35 to 44 years	45 to 54 years
				1	2	3	4	5	6	7	8	9	10	11	12	13	14	15
			MISSOURI—Cont'd															
29 510	7040	0	St. Louis city	160	348 189	168	2 176.2	45.2	52.1	0.8	2.4	2.0	6.7	19.0	10.6	15.6	15.3	11.8
30 000	...	X	MONTANA	376 979	902 195	X	2.4	92.2	0.5	7.4	0.9	2.0	6.1	19.4	9.5	11.4	15.7	15.0
30 001	...	7	Beaverhead	14 355	9 202	2 513	0.6	97.0	0.2	2.2	0.6	2.7	5.7	18.8	11.9	10.1	15.0	14.9
30 003	...	6	Big Horn	12 936	12 671	2 249	1.0	39.1	0.2	62.0	0.5	3.7	9.3	26.5	8.6	12.1	14.4	12.6
30 005	...	9	Blaine	10 946	7 009	2 685	0.6	53.9	0.3	46.7	0.2	1.0	8.1	24.5	8.0	10.2	14.6	12.9
30 007	...	9	Broadwater	3 086	4 385	2 887	1.4	98.0	0.3	2.0	0.2	1.3	5.3	19.9	4.8	9.3	16.9	15.9
30 009	...	8	Carbon	5 304	9 552	2 484	1.8	98.1	0.3	1.3	0.4	1.8	5.2	18.8	5.7	9.3	16.9	16.8
30 011	...	9	Carter	8 649	1 360	3 099	0.2	99.1	0.1	0.5	0.2	0.6	4.0	22.5	4.1	9.1	15.8	14.6
30 013	3040	3	Cascade	6 988	80 357	638	11.5	92.9	1.5	5.7	1.5	2.4	6.6	19.4	9.1	12.3	15.8	13.3
30 015	...	8	Chouteau	10 291	5 970	2 787	0.6	84.7	0.1	15.1	0.5	0.7	6.5	22.4	6.5	8.9	15.2	14.0
30 017	...	7	Custer	9 798	11 696	2 319	1.2	98.0	0.2	1.9	0.5	1.5	5.9	19.2	8.4	10.3	15.3	14.4
30 019	...	9	Daniels	3 694	2 017	3 064	0.5	97.7	0.3	2.6	0.3	1.6	4.3	17.8	4.9	6.8	13.1	16.6
30 021	...	7	Dawson	6 146	9 059	2 525	1.5	98.0	0.3	1.6	0.2	0.9	5.1	18.0	8.8	9.9	15.1	15.3
30 023	...	7	Deer Lodge	1 909	9 417	2 496	4.9	97.5	0.3	3.0	0.6	1.6	4.6	17.9	7.9	9.5	14.5	15.7
30 025	...	9	Fallon	4 197	2 837	3 003	0.7	99.0	0.2	0.6	0.5	0.4	4.9	20.7	6.2	9.3	16.2	15.3
30 027	...	7	Fergus	11 238	11 893	2 299	1.1	98.2	0.2	2.0	0.4	0.8	5.2	19.4	6.1	8.8	14.8	15.0
30 029	...	5	Flathead	13 205	74 471	672	5.6	97.7	0.3	2.1	0.9	1.4	5.9	20.0	7.4	10.8	16.6	16.5
30 031	...	5	Gallatin	6 749	67 831	723	10.1	97.3	0.4	1.4	1.4	1.5	5.8	16.2	18.5	14.8	15.6	13.7
30 033	...	9	Garfield	12 090	1 279	3 101	0.1	99.4	0.1	0.5	0.2	0.4	6.7	17.7	7.1	9.7	13.6	16.2
30 035	...	7	Glacier	7 756	13 247	2 209	1.7	37.2	0.7	63.9	0.3	1.2	8.1	26.8	9.1	11.0	15.3	12.1
30 037	...	8	Golden Valley	3 044	1 042	3 109	0.3	99.3	0.0	0.7	0.2	1.2	5.2	22.5	5.9	8.3	14.8	14.6
30 039	...	9	Granite	4 474	2 830	3 004	0.6	98.1	0.1	2.6	0.4	1.3	4.8	19.4	5.7	8.4	14.9	17.0
30 041	...	7	Hill	7 502	16 673	1 977	2.2	81.8	0.2	19.0	0.6	1.2	7.1	21.1	11.6	10.7	15.3	13.7
30 043	...	9	Jefferson	4 291	10 049	2 440	2.3	97.7	0.2	2.4	0.8	1.5	5.2	22.6	5.2	8.4	18.4	18.9
30 045	...	8	Judith Basin	4 843	2 329	3 036	0.5	99.5	0.0	1.0	0.3	0.6	5.2	21.6	4.6	7.5	15.8	16.2
30 047	...	7	Lake	3 869	26 507	1 502	6.9	74.9	0.2	26.8	0.6	2.5	6.7	21.4	8.0	9.9	14.6	14.6
30 049	...	5	Lewis and Clark	8 964	55 716	847	6.2	96.8	0.3	3.1	0.9	1.5	6.2	19.4	8.5	11.2	16.7	16.8
30 051	...	9	Liberty	3 703	2 158	3 054	0.6	99.5	0.1	0.2	0.4	0.2	5.1	20.8	5.8	8.9	15.8	14.3
30 053	...	7	Lincoln	9 357	18 837	1 851	2.0	97.9	0.3	2.5	0.6	1.4	5.0	20.4	5.5	8.7	15.5	16.7
30 055	...	9	McCone	6 844	1 977	3 065	0.3	98.3	0.5	2.0	0.5	1.0	5.4	19.4	5.4	8.0	16.3	15.5
30 057	...	9	Madison	9 289	6 851	2 705	0.7	98.3	0.1	1.6	0.4	1.9	4.7	18.2	4.9	9.2	15.8	17.0
30 059	...	8	Meagher	6 195	1 932	3 069	0.3	98.2	0.1	1.7	0.4	1.5	5.0	20.0	6.1	7.6	15.1	16.7
30 061	...	9	Mineral	3 159	3 884	2 924	1.2	97.0	0.5	3.6	0.9	1.6	5.0	19.3	6.4	9.8	15.6	16.3
30 063	5140	5	Missoula	6 729	95 802	540	14.2	95.8	0.5	3.4	1.6	1.6	5.7	17.2	15.4	14.0	15.1	14.6
30 065	...	8	Musselshell	4 836	4 497	2 880	0.9	98.0	0.2	2.1	0.5	1.6	4.9	18.4	5.7	8.8	15.2	18.4
30 067	...	7	Park	7 258	15 694	2 038	2.2	97.7	0.5	1.7	0.7	1.8	5.8	17.8	6.5	11.1	16.8	17.6
30 069	...	9	Petroleum	4 284	493	3 136	0.1	99.6	0.0	0.4	0.0	1.2	7.1	18.9	6.1	9.9	12.8	16.6
30 071	...	9	Phillips	13 311	4 601	2 872	0.3	91.4	0.2	9.6	0.3	1.2	4.9	22.4	5.5	8.0	16.5	14.5
30 073	...	7	Pondera	4 208	6 424	2 748	1.5	85.1	0.2	15.6	0.3	0.8	6.2	23.4	6.4	9.3	15.5	13.5
30 075	...	9	Powder River	8 540	1 858	3 075	0.2	97.9	0.0	2.2	0.2	0.6	5.9	20.7	4.8	8.1	15.2	16.4
30 077	...	7	Powell	6 024	7 180	2 668	1.2	94.7	0.6	5.3	0.9	1.9	4.6	16.6	7.8	12.4	18.4	15.7
30 079	...	9	Prairie	4 498	1 199	3 104	0.3	99.2	0.0	1.3	0.4	0.7	4.2	14.5	4.3	7.3	12.7	19.7
30 081	...	7	Ravalli	6 201	36 070	1 213	5.8	98.1	0.3	1.8	0.7	1.9	5.7	19.8	6.2	9.9	14.8	16.2
30 083	...	7	Richland	5 398	9 667	2 472	1.8	97.4	0.1	2.0	0.3	2.2	5.8	21.8	6.4	10.1	16.6	14.7
30 085	...	7	Roosevelt	6 101	10 620	2 389	1.7	43.3	0.1	57.8	0.7	1.2	8.1	26.5	7.9	10.4	15.4	12.8
30 087	...	7	Rosebud	12 982	9 383	2 499	0.7	66.2	0.4	34.1	0.5	2.3	7.7	25.8	7.2	9.9	15.8	15.9
30 089	...	9	Sanders	7 154	10 227	2 423	1.4	94.5	0.3	6.8	0.6	1.6	4.7	19.1	5.5	8.2	13.8	17.7
30 091	...	9	Sheridan	4 342	4 105	2 907	0.9	98.2	0.1	2.2	0.5	1.1	4.5	18.5	4.8	6.9	15.2	15.7
30 093	...	5	Silver Bow	1 860	34 606	1 262	18.6	96.7	0.3	3.0	0.8	2.7	5.8	17.9	9.6	11.2	15.4	14.2
30 095	...	8	Stillwater	4 649	8 195	2 594	1.8	97.9	0.3	1.4	0.6	2.0	5.5	19.8	5.7	10.1	16.8	16.7
30 097	...	9	Sweet Grass	4 805	3 609	2 943	0.8	98.3	0.1	1.4	0.6	1.5	5.8	20.1	5.3	10.4	14.3	15.5
30 099	...	8	Teton	5 886	6 445	2 743	1.1	97.7	0.3	2.7	0.2	1.1	6.2	21.1	6.1	9.2	15.4	14.3
30 101	...	7	Toole	4 949	5 267	2 833	1.1	95.8	0.3	4.9	0.7	1.2	5.4	20.2	6.8	11.3	16.9	14.7
30 103	...	8	Treasure	2 535	861	3 118	0.3	97.0	0.2	2.0	0.6	1.5	5.3	22.4	5.0	7.8	15.4	14.6
30 105	...	7	Valley	12 745	7 675	2 631	0.6	89.9	0.3	10.7	0.5	0.8	5.5	19.6	6.0	8.8	15.5	14.8
30 107	...	9	Wheatland	3 686	2 259	3 045	0.6	98.5	0.4	1.4	0.6	1.1	6.0	20.8	6.4	9.7	12.3	14.2
30 109	...	9	Wibaux	2 303	1 068	3 107	0.5	98.9	0.5	0.7	0.6	0.4	5.2	20.6	5.8	8.3	14.1	15.7
30 111	0880	3	Yellowstone	6 825	129 352	415	19.0	94.5	0.8	4.1	0.9	3.7	6.6	18.9	9.3	12.6	16.2	14.4
31 000	...	X	NEBRASKA	199 099	1 711 263	X	8.6	90.8	4.4	1.3	1.7	5.5	6.8	19.5	10.2	13.0	15.4	13.2
31 001	...	5	Adams	1 459	31 151	1 373	21.4	95.3	0.8	0.7	1.9	4.6	6.4	18.1	11.9	11.7	14.5	13.3
31 003	...	9	Antelope	2 220	7 452	2 644	3.4	99.3	0.1	0.5	0.1	0.7	6.0	21.5	6.2	8.2	15.1	13.5
31 005	...	9	Arthur	1 853	444	3 137	0.2	98.0	0.0	1.1	1.1	1.4	5.2	18.7	5.4	12.6	16.9	10.8
31 007	...	9	Banner	1 933	819	3 122	0.4	96.5	0.1	0.6	0.4	5.6	4.8	24.1	3.7	8.2	16.1	15.9

1. MSA = Metropolitan Statistical Area. PMSA = Primary MSA. NECMA = New England County Metropolitan Area. See Appendix A for explanation of these concepts. See Appendix B for list of metropolitan areas identified by type, with component counties.   2. County typology code from the Economic Research Service of USDA. See Appendix A for definition.   3. Dry land or land partially or temporarily covered by water.   4. Hispanic persons may be of any race.

Table B. States and Counties — **Population and Households**

STATE County	Age (percent) (cont'd)				Population — change and components of change, 1990–2001							Households, 2000				
	55 to 64 years	65 to 74 years	75 years and over	Percent female	Total persons		Percent change		Components of change, 2000–2001				Percent change, 1990–2000	Persons per house-hold	Female family house-holder[1]	One person
					2001	1990	1990–2000	2000–2001	Births	Deaths	Net migration	Number				
	16	17	18	19	20	21	22	23	24	25	26	27	28	29	30	31
MISSOURI—Cont'd																
St. Louis city	7.2	6.6	7.1	53.0	339 211	396 685	-12.2	-2.6	7 611	5 593	-11 276	147 076	-10.8	2.30	21.3	40.3
MONTANA	9.4	6.9	6.5	50.2	904 433	799 065	12.9	0.2	13 320	10 165	-907	358 667	17.1	2.45	8.9	27.4
Beaverhead	10.0	7.2	6.4	48.8	9 089	8 424	9.2	-1.2	129	96	-148	3 684	14.7	2.36	6.2	29.7
Big Horn	7.9	4.6	4.0	50.7	12 763	11 337	11.8	0.7	312	134	-83	3 924	13.8	3.17	17.6	19.3
Blaine	8.7	6.9	6.0	50.6	6 870	6 728	4.2	-2.0	151	87	-208	2 501	5.1	2.78	14.4	26.0
Broadwater	11.5	9.0	7.4	49.0	4 457	3 318	32.2	1.6	62	46	55	1 752	36.9	2.47	6.9	24.1
Carbon	10.5	8.7	8.1	49.9	9 696	8 080	18.2	1.5	106	127	161	4 065	24.3	2.32	6.7	28.8
Carter	11.9	8.5	9.4	51.3	1 375	1 503	-9.5	1.1	16	18	16	543	-7.8	2.47	7.0	27.1
Cascade	9.4	7.2	10.5	50.5	79 298	77 691	3.4	-1.3	1 353	936	-1 461	32 547	8.0	2.41	9.9	28.8
Chouteau	9.2	8.5	9.0	49.8	5 738	5 452	9.5	-3.9	48	62	-225	2 226	7.8	2.59	8.4	24.9
Custer	9.3	8.5	8.6	51.1	11 372	11 697	0.0	-2.8	168	196	-299	4 768	3.0	2.36	10.0	29.9
Daniels	12.9	10.9	12.6	51.0	1 998	2 266	-11.0	-0.9	20	39	-2	892	-2.9	2.22	5.5	33.6
Dawson	10.1	9.0	8.7	50.4	8 877	9 505	-4.7	-2.0	107	125	-164	3 625	-1.8	2.37	6.8	28.4
Deer Lodge	11.0	9.6	9.3	50.1	9 171	10 356	-9.1	-2.6	109	180	-178	3 995	-1.6	2.26	9.4	33.4
Fallon	9.6	9.9	8.0	49.5	2 761	3 103	-8.6	-2.7	30	47	-59	1 140	-2.2	2.45	6.0	26.6
Fergus	10.9	9.5	10.4	51.3	11 693	12 083	-1.6	-1.7	130	211	-117	4 860	5.6	2.33	6.7	30.5
Flathead	9.9	6.9	6.1	50.4	76 269	59 218	25.8	2.4	1 061	815	1 542	29 588	29.6	2.48	8.3	25.2
Gallatin	6.8	4.4	4.1	48.0	69 422	50 484	34.4	2.3	900	448	1 133	26 323	38.4	2.46	6.6	24.1
Garfield	9.6	8.4	10.9	48.4	1 243	1 589	-19.5	-2.8	16	22	-32	532	-7.8	2.38	4.5	28.2
Glacier	7.8	5.1	4.1	50.5	13 125	12 121	9.3	-0.9	318	146	-299	4 304	12.8	3.03	16.2	21.6
Golden Valley	12.4	10.6	6.0	48.3	1 019	912	14.3	-2.2	17	13	-28	365	10.6	2.41	3.3	24.4
Granite	13.9	8.5	7.4	48.8	2 899	2 548	11.1	2.4	22	42	87	1 200	14.2	2.33	7.4	30.1
Hill	7.7	6.6	6.2	50.2	16 467	17 654	-5.6	-1.2	366	185	-392	6 457	0.5	2.53	10.9	28.6
Jefferson	10.9	6.1	4.2	49.8	10 405	7 939	26.6	3.5	106	112	353	3 747	30.7	2.62	5.9	20.2
Judith Basin	12.0	9.1	8.1	48.1	2 280	2 282	2.1	-2.1	21	23	-49	951	4.7	2.45	4.3	27.5
Lake	10.4	7.9	6.6	50.9	26 904	21 041	26.0	1.5	464	310	247	10 192	30.4	2.54	11.5	24.5
Lewis and Clark	9.5	6.2	5.6	50.9	56 094	47 495	17.3	0.7	794	560	169	22 850	22.5	2.38	9.2	29.1
Liberty	9.8	9.1	10.6	50.7	2 096	2 295	-6.0	-2.9	23	31	-57	833	5.7	2.51	5.6	27.9
Lincoln	13.1	8.9	6.3	49.3	18 664	17 481	7.8	-0.9	214	255	-127	7 764	16.4	2.40	7.8	26.7
McCone	11.0	10.2	8.8	50.1	1 900	2 276	-13.1	-3.9	25	14	-89	810	-4.0	2.44	3.8	24.6
Madison	13.0	9.6	7.6	49.4	6 939	5 989	14.4	1.3	75	89	103	2 956	23.8	2.29	4.4	29.3
Meagher	11.3	9.7	8.5	49.9	1 938	1 819	6.2	0.3	32	28	3	803	13.3	2.37	6.1	31.0
Mineral	13.5	8.6	5.5	48.5	3 843	3 315	17.2	-1.1	56	35	-61	1 584	23.6	2.41	6.0	26.6
Missoula	7.9	5.0	5.0	50.0	96 303	78 687	21.8	0.5	1 328	844	51	38 439	24.9	2.40	9.2	28.0
Musselshell	11.1	8.5	9.0	51.2	4 450	4 106	9.5	-1.0	61	80	-28	1 878	13.1	2.33	6.6	30.1
Park	9.5	7.4	7.4	50.6	15 686	14 515	8.1	-0.1	193	188	-13	6 828	21.5	2.27	7.3	32.4
Petroleum	11.6	9.3	7.7	47.5	488	519	-5.0	-1.0	10	6	-9	211	1.0	2.34	5.7	31.3
Phillips	10.6	8.2	9.4	49.9	4 420	5 163	-10.9	-3.9	50	66	-166	1 848	-4.3	2.45	6.8	29.1
Pondera	9.5	8.3	7.9	50.7	6 345	6 433	-0.1	-1.2	98	81	-97	2 410	7.3	2.63	8.4	25.5
Powder River	10.4	10.1	8.4	50.7	1 824	2 090	-11.1	-1.8	23	15	-42	737	-8.4	2.48	4.1	24.8
Powell	10.5	7.2	6.7	41.1	7 076	6 620	8.5	-1.4	85	71	-118	2 422	8.4	2.39	7.7	28.6
Prairie	13.2	10.7	13.4	48.4	1 216	1 383	-13.3	1.4	14	22	24	537	-5.5	2.19	2.4	31.3
Ravalli	11.8	8.3	7.2	50.3	37 304	25 010	44.2	3.4	460	369	1 123	14 289	47.3	2.48	7.5	24.1
Richland	9.1	7.8	7.8	50.3	9 343	10 716	-9.8	-3.4	134	121	-343	3 878	-2.0	2.46	7.4	28.8
Roosevelt	7.4	5.8	5.8	50.4	10 561	10 999	-3.4	-0.6	301	116	-247	3 581	-3.1	2.89	18.9	23.6
Rosebud	8.8	5.1	3.8	49.8	9 282	10 505	-10.7	-1.1	194	90	-207	3 307	-4.9	2.81	11.8	24.3
Sanders	14.1	9.7	7.1	49.5	10 443	8 669	18.0	2.1	125	133	222	4 273	25.8	2.35	7.1	28.0
Sheridan	10.8	11.3	12.3	50.3	3 940	4 732	-13.3	-4.0	45	94	-116	1 741	-8.3	2.29	4.8	32.3
Silver Bow	9.8	7.7	8.3	50.6	33 604	33 941	2.0	-2.9	478	560	-932	14 432	3.8	2.32	10.5	32.8
Stillwater	10.9	7.9	6.6	49.0	8 433	6 536	25.4	2.9	78	105	261	3 234	28.2	2.48	5.0	24.1
Sweet Grass	10.9	8.1	9.4	50.1	3 585	3 154	14.4	-0.7	40	39	-26	1 476	15.2	2.41	4.5	28.9
Teton	11.1	7.8	8.8	50.8	6 387	6 271	2.8	-0.9	90	104	-42	2 538	9.0	2.51	5.9	27.3
Toole	8.9	7.8	8.1	48.4	5 151	5 046	4.4	-2.2	59	66	-112	1 962	2.1	2.47	6.5	30.2
Treasure	12.7	7.5	9.2	49.0	802	874	-1.5	-6.9	12	12	-62	357	5.3	2.41	4.2	30.0
Valley	10.8	9.5	9.5	50.5	7 524	8 239	-6.8	-1.0	95	143	-103	3 150	-3.6	2.38	8.2	29.3
Wheatland	11.3	8.9	10.4	50.5	2 153	2 246	0.6	-4.7	31	30	-110	853	0.5	2.24	4.9	34.5
Wibaux	8.6	10.6	11.0	52.0	1 050	1 191	-10.3	-1.7	17	21	-15	421	-7.3	2.45	5.9	29.0
Yellowstone	8.8	6.8	6.5	51.2	130 398	113 419	14.0	0.8	2 048	1 357	409	52 084	16.5	2.43	10.1	27.9
NEBRASKA	8.3	6.8	6.8	50.7	1 713 235	1 578 417	8.4	0.1	30 192	18 878	-9 047	666 184	10.6	2.49	9.1	27.6
Adams	8.4	7.2	8.7	51.0	30 917	29 625	5.2	-0.8	491	397	-322	12 141	4.7	2.43	8.3	28.6
Antelope	9.6	9.1	10.8	50.8	7 271	7 965	-6.4	-2.4	93	111	-164	2 953	-3.0	2.49	5.5	27.8
Arthur	14.0	9.7	6.8	49.5	411	462	-3.9	-7.4	4	5	-34	185	-1.1	2.40	7.6	21.6
Banner	11.4	10.9	5.1	48.0	802	852	-3.9	-2.1	5	4	-18	311	2.0	2.63	4.2	19.9

1. No spouse present.

Table B. States and Counties — Vital Statistics, Health Resources, and Crime

STATE County	Births, average 1997–1999 Total	Rate[1]	Deaths, average 1997–1999 Number Total	Number Infant[2]	Rate Total[1]	Rate Infant[3]	Physicians,[4] 2000 Number	Rate[5]	Hospitals,[4] 1998 Number	Beds Number	Beds Rate[5]	Medicare enrollees 2000	Serious crimes known to police, 2000[6] Total Number	Total Rate[7]
	32	33	34	35	36	37	38	39	40	41	42	43	44	45
MISSOURI—Cont'd														
St. Louis city	5 550	16.3	4 569	81	13.5	14.5	2 098	603	12	3 411	1 005	56 623	50 674	14 554
MONTANA	10 724	12.2	7 959	76	9.0	7.1	1 646	182	54	4 084	464	136 726	31 878	3 533
Beaverhead	101	11.4	82	NA	9.2	NA	17	185	1	31	350	1 366	119	1 293
Big Horn	249	19.7	111	NA	8.8	NA	12	95	1	54	428	1 176	0	0
Blaine	111	15.5	68	NA	9.5	NA	5	71	0	0	0	934	NA	NA
Broadwater	39	9.4	39	NA	9.4	NA	6	137	1	42	1 016	792	55	1 254
Carbon	86	9.1	98	NA	10.3	NA	12	126	1	46	487	1 683	49	664
Carter	14	9.1	14	NA	9.3	NA	1	74	1	10	651	262	NA	NA
Cascade	1 086	13.8	730	9	9.3	8.6	198	246	2	402	509	12 797	4 939	6 146
Chouteau	49	9.6	55	NA	10.7	NA	1	17	2	82	1 581	1 033	127	2 127
Custer	132	11.0	150	NA	12.5	NA	30	256	1	141	1 172	2 234	NA	NA
Daniels	16	8.1	26	NA	12.8	NA	2	99	1	54	2 699	503	NA	NA
Dawson	91	10.3	100	NA	11.3	NA	8	88	1	104	1 175	1 703	217	2 395
Deer Lodge	95	9.6	131	NA	13.2	NA	16	170	2	134	1 340	2 141	503	5 341
Fallon	32	11.0	32	NA	11.0	NA	1	35	1	52	1 768	543	NA	NA
Fergus	119	9.6	161	NA	13.1	NA	17	143	1	132	1 076	2 536	NA	NA
Flathead	868	12.0	633	7	8.8	7.7	144	193	2	249	347	11 711	NA	NA
Gallatin	747	11.9	330	NA	5.3	NA	121	178	1	86	138	6 387	NA	NA
Garfield	18	12.5	16	NA	11.0	NA	0	0	0	0	0	249	NA	NA
Glacier	237	18.8	116	NA	9.2	NA	12	91	1	59	470	1 347	286	2 159
Golden Valley	13	12.5	8	NA	8.0	NA	0	0	0	0	0	215	33	3 167
Granite	33	12.5	32	NA	12.2	NA	2	71	1	31	1 162	440	79	2 792
Hill	258	14.9	154	NA	8.9	NA	25	150	1	140	806	2 427	1 061	6 364
Jefferson	100	9.9	76	NA	7.5	NA	11	109	0	0	0	1 315	NA	NA
Judith Basin	19	8.2	23	NA	10.0	NA	0	0	0	0	0	415	NA	NA
Lake	336	13.1	246	NA	9.6	NA	36	136	2	121	472	4 063	472	2 101
Lewis and Clark	640	11.9	427	NA	7.9	NA	125	224	1	79	147	7 673	NA	NA
Liberty	22	9.4	26	NA	11.3	NA	1	46	1	67	2 884	641	NA	NA
Lincoln	188	10.0	185	NA	9.9	NA	16	85	1	26	139	3 525	325	1 927
McCone	19	9.5	17	NA	8.8	NA	1	51	0	0	0	367	NA	NA
Madison	60	8.7	67	NA	9.8	NA	7	102	2	23	335	1 207	42	613
Meagher	26	14.7	20	NA	11.3	NA	4	207	1	37	2 059	383	63	3 261
Mineral	37	9.7	33	NA	8.7	NA	2	51	1	30	800	788	12	309
Missoula	1 044	11.7	650	NA	7.3	NA	257	268	2	336	378	11 151	NA	NA
Musselshell	42	9.1	61	NA	13.3	NA	2	44	1	48	1 042	889	NA	NA
Park	171	10.7	147	NA	9.2	NA	14	89	1	35	221	2 555	NA	NA
Petroleum	8	15.8	NA	NA	NA	NA	0	0	0	0	0	81	NA	NA
Phillips	54	11.3	52	NA	10.9	NA	5	109	1	21	436	895	67	1 456
Pondera	79	12.5	71	NA	11.1	NA	6	93	1	94	1 468	1 187	90	1 401
Powder River	16	8.6	22	NA	12.2	NA	0	0	0	0	0	300	NA	NA
Powell	67	9.6	58	NA	8.3	NA	6	84	1	35	500	1 133	221	3 078
Prairie	11	7.9	17	NA	12.7	NA	0	0	1	21	1 575	302	NA	NA
Ravalli	365	10.4	310	NA	8.8	NA	36	100	1	48	137	6 332	512	1 582
Richland	121	11.9	106	NA	10.4	NA	12	124	1	49	485	1 680	NA	NA
Roosevelt	203	18.4	91	NA	8.3	NA	11	104	3	116	1 056	1 478	55	518
Rosebud	156	15.5	80	NA	7.9	NA	5	53	1	75	746	1 034	129	1 375
Sanders	100	9.8	111	NA	10.9	NA	11	108	1	44	432	2 049	250	2 445
Sheridan	37	8.7	71	NA	16.7	NA	3	73	1	103	2 413	1 043	NA	NA
Silver Bow	397	11.6	439	NA	12.8	NA	72	208	1	115	333	6 357	NA	NA
Stillwater	91	11.3	74	NA	9.2	NA	5	61	1	23	285	1 287	127	1 550
Sweet Grass	37	10.8	41	NA	11.8	NA	2	55	0	0	0	631	78	2 161
Teton	72	11.4	77	NA	12.0	NA	2	31	0	0	0	1 130	150	2 327
Toole	60	12.7	56	NA	11.9	NA	9	171	1	83	1 756	568	NA	NA
Treasure	8	9.7	7	NA	8.6	NA	0	0	0	0	0	175	NA	NA
Valley	89	10.8	101	NA	12.2	NA	10	130	1	42	513	1 661	NA	NA
Wheatland	26	11.1	26	NA	11.0	NA	3	133	1	44	1 854	471	28	1 239
Wibaux	11	9.4	17	NA	15.3	NA	0	0	0	0	0	229	NA	NA
Yellowstone	1 618	12.8	1 065	13	8.4	8.0	342	264	2	520	412	19 204	7 349	5 681
NEBRASKA	23 266	14.0	15 353	169	9.2	7.3	3 091	181	89	7 870	473	253 639	70 085	4 096
Adams	391	13.3	343	NA	11.6	NA	62	199	1	190	645	5 205	1 155	3 708
Antelope	88	12.2	82	NA	11.4	NA	7	94	1	49	682	1 441	66	886
Arthur	6	13.4	NA	NA	NA	NA	0	0	0	0	0	107	3	676
Banner	5	5.8	NA	NA	NA	NA	0	0	0	0	0	91	NA	NA

1. Per 1,000 estimated resident population, average 1997–1999.   2. Deaths of infants under 1 year old.   3. Deaths of infants under 1 year old per 1,000 live births.   4. Data subject to copyright.   5. Per 100,000 resident population as of July 1 of the year shown.   6. Data for serious crimes have not been adjusted for underreporting; this may affect comparability between geographic areas and over time.   7. Per 100,000 population estimated by the FBI.

STATE County	Serious crimes known to police, 2000[1] (cont'd) Rate[2]		Education						Money income 1989				Income and poverty, 1998			
			School enrollment and attainment, 1990				Local government expenditures, fiscal 1999[5]			Households				Percent below poverty level		
			Enrollment[3]		Attainment[4] (percent)						Median					
	Violent	Property	Total	Percent private	High school graduate or more	Bachelor's degree or more	Total current expenditures (mil dol)	Current expenditures per student (dollars)	Per capita[6] (dollars)	Dollars	Percent change, 1979–1989 (constant 1989 dollars)	Percent with $100,000 or more	Median household income	All persons	Persons under 18	Persons 5–17 in families
	46	47	48	49	50	51	52	53	54	55	56	57	58	59	60	61
MISSOURI—Cont'd																
St. Louis city	2 279	12 274	96 794	30.2	62.8	15.3	361.2	7 855	10 798	19 458	0.9	1.3	27 331	24.1	34.4	31.9
MONTANA	241	3 293	215 759	8.5	81.0	19.8	955.7	5 974	11 213	22 988	-11.1	1.7	31 271	15.7	21.9	19.5
Beaverhead	141	1 152	2 701	3.6	83.9	20.6	10.1	6 200	10 376	20 925	-2.5	0.8	29 231	17.6	22.9	21.2
Big Horn	0	0	3 571	11.2	69.2	12.8	21.1	8 435	7 148	19 101	-18.1	0.7	24 406	28.8	32.8	32.6
Blaine	NA	NA	1 995	3.1	70.4	14.4	12.3	7 792	8 290	18 512	-15.0	1.0	23 828	28.0	32.7	32.5
Broadwater	456	798	752	1.1	73.9	13.5	3.8	4 783	10 125	20 257	-11.2	1.3	29 725	16.3	21.6	20.1
Carbon	176	488	1 959	2.9	78.1	19.2	10.4	6 239	10 727	19 042	-7.1	1.5	29 995	13.4	17.1	15.6
Carter	NA	NA	296	7.4	76.0	10.8	1.7	7 639	10 670	16 458	-12.6	3.4	22 050	19.2	26.5	26.1
Cascade	815	5 331	18 971	12.3	82.9	18.4	72.8	5 060	12 011	23 700	-11.9	2.3	32 424	14.7	21.6	18.0
Chouteau	603	1 524	1 247	3.1	83.4	16.8	7.6	7 385	11 290	22 362	-11.8	2.5	30 644	13.5	18.2	16.7
Custer	NA	NA	3 087	5.8	77.1	16.0	11.0	5 276	10 310	21 348	-8.0	0.8	29 480	17.9	25.7	23.0
Daniels	NA	NA	517	1.4	74.4	11.5	3.4	8 569	9 963	21 433	-5.3	1.1	29 532	15.6	23.4	18.7
Dawson	375	2 020	2 531	5.1	74.5	13.2	10.8	6 633	10 629	23 414	-18.9	0.9	32 962	13.1	19.6	16.8
Deer Lodge	2 379	2 963	2 291	2.9	74.5	11.5	8.6	5 199	9 444	20 281	-23.9	0.5	27 811	18.2	26.2	24.9
Fallon	NA	NA	714	2.5	75.3	10.6	5.8	8 297	10 308	23 162	-14.6	1.4	32 597	13.6	17.1	15.5
Fergus	NA	NA	2 705	6.4	77.4	14.5	15.3	6 659	10 995	21 398	4.3	2.4	28 283	16.0	21.9	18.8
Flathead	NA	NA	14 832	9.0	82.1	17.2	69.4	5 109	11 718	24 145	-10.5	1.6	34 059	14.6	21.0	17.1
Gallatin	NA	NA	18 710	6.8	90.4	33.8	49.9	5 244	12 252	23 345	-9.1	2.2	36 569	12.1	15.6	13.4
Garfield	NA	NA	387	2.8	72.6	8.8	1.8	7 280	9 843	17 201	-13.8	3.4	25 551	13.7	17.7	17.4
Glacier	694	1 464	3 909	3.3	72.0	14.5	23.8	7 469	7 458	18 598	-17.2	0.2	21 758	35.6	38.9	38.2
Golden Valley	1 248	1 919	176	9.1	72.4	14.7	1.7	7 588	8 505	18 062	-4.4	0.6	19 018	23.2	21.8	24.9
Granite	883	1 908	529	2.6	75.9	16.9	3.5	6 883	10 049	18 278	-14.3	2.5	26 961	19.6	27.5	26.3
Hill	1 709	4 654	5 539	7.5	78.4	18.1	23.2	6 680	11 121	25 467	-8.2	1.8	31 180	19.8	25.6	23.7
Jefferson	NA	NA	2 287	11.4	81.3	20.8	10.1	5 043	13 233	31 400	11.7	3.5	43 074	10.1	14.0	12.1
Judith Basin	NA	NA	496	5.6	80.4	19.8	3.5	7 536	12 060	22 578	3.7	3.2	26 161	18.6	24.6	23.1
Lake	298	1 803	5 495	4.5	77.3	15.7	27.9	5 848	9 274	19 755	-3.9	1.3	27 473	21.1	26.7	26.1
Lewis and Clark	NA	NA	12 205	15.4	87.4	27.8	55.2	5 471	12 342	26 409	-7.1	1.3	38 091	12.3	18.5	15.7
Liberty	NA	NA	554	16.6	77.2	16.9	3.8	7 899	10 544	24 969	3.9	2.4	26 325	15.2	16.0	17.4
Lincoln	130	1 797	4 496	7.3	73.3	12.5	19.3	5 421	9 813	20 898	-20.3	1.1	28 463	19.0	26.0	24.3
McCone	NA	NA	589	2.5	79.5	14.3	2.3	7 420	9 347	20 487	2.0	0.9	29 745	15.5	19.9	19.4
Madison	58	555	1 405	5.8	85.0	19.7	7.7	6 788	10 718	22 066	8.5	0.6	29 741	12.6	17.5	16.5
Meagher	466	2 795	372	8.3	73.9	14.4	2.0	7 227	9 201	18 936	-13.2	0.4	22 084	22.6	26.9	27.1
Mineral	129	180	846	3.5	74.0	13.1	5.7	6 937	9 440	20 938	-22.2	0.5	25 782	20.7	30.1	28.1
Missoula	NA	NA	25 497	6.4	85.4	27.7	79.9	5 692	11 944	23 388	-14.2	2.1	34 897	14.7	20.0	17.3
Musselshell	NA	NA	974	8.0	70.9	11.4	5.0	6 286	8 941	16 661	-13.0	1.1	22 119	19.6	26.9	23.9
Park	NA	NA	3 063	18.3	81.7	19.3	14.5	5 966	11 378	22 658	-7.5	1.7	30 120	13.6	19.0	18.4
Petroleum	NA	NA	94	0.0	81.9	17.5	0.9	9 612	9 876	19 219	5.7	1.9	21 625	18.8	21.3	26.1
Phillips	261	1 195	1 245	9.0	74.1	13.1	8.2	7 847	10 793	22 245	11.3	2.1	26 164	21.4	27.2	25.5
Pondera	156	1 245	1 634	5.4	73.7	15.0	11.1	7 487	9 811	23 533	-12.9	1.3	26 820	22.1	27.1	25.1
Powder River	NA	NA	473	3.2	75.2	15.3	2.8	7 208	12 722	22 354	-11.5	3.7	27 248	16.6	22.2	21.9
Powell	682	2 396	1 500	4.0	76.5	16.6	7.3	6 504	9 978	21 621	-12.2	0.9	30 945	18.7	25.6	23.3
Prairie	NA	NA	299	2.0	71.1	13.2	1.6	7 154	8 497	16 694	5.4	0.9	24 982	13.5	17.4	16.3
Ravalli	445	1 137	6 025	9.8	79.1	18.2	32.1	5 138	10 130	21 113	-5.0	1.2	30 003	15.3	21.8	19.8
Richland	NA	NA	2 767	5.7	75.4	13.4	13.5	6 284	10 091	23 264	-21.2	1.3	31 710	15.3	20.1	18.1
Roosevelt	113	405	3 079	2.9	70.1	11.3	22.6	7 757	7 751	19 445	-21.7	0.7	23 779	31.7	38.5	39.0
Rosebud	576	799	3 303	10.1	78.3	13.4	19.7	8 590	10 415	27 192	-3.1	0.6	35 548	21.0	26.7	24.5
Sanders	714	1 731	2 083	5.6	75.2	14.8	12.2	6 239	9 459	18 616	-12.0	1.2	25 554	19.3	25.2	24.3
Sheridan	NA	NA	1 012	2.7	74.5	11.7	6.5	8 348	10 001	20 728	-17.3	0.6	29 662	13.7	19.5	17.1
Silver Bow	NA	NA	8 527	12.0	78.3	17.9	30.5	5 399	11 364	21 216	-13.2	1.6	31 262	16.3	24.6	21.5
Stillwater	244	1 306	1 520	2.1	78.2	16.9	9.7	6 252	10 975	23 582	6.3	1.3	36 425	10.6	14.3	13.2
Sweet Grass	360	1 801	674	2.2	78.9	20.0	3.6	6 063	10 838	20 867	9.0	1.8	29 814	13.3	18.3	17.3
Teton	171	2 157	1 488	9.6	76.8	17.8	8.4	5 948	10 772	22 072	-6.0	1.6	28 061	16.4	20.7	19.5
Toole	NA	NA	1 208	8.7	77.4	14.0	6.5	6 366	11 375	25 108	5.9	1.2	30 152	17.4	20.8	19.1
Treasure	NA	NA	217	1.8	85.1	13.2	1.4	7 885	10 244	18 152	-10.7	4.1	24 997	16.8	24.2	22.0
Valley	NA	NA	1 889	5.0	78.6	13.2	11.7	7 830	10 529	21 781	-10.7	0.9	29 836	18.1	25.4	22.9
Wheatland	266	974	519	8.3	72.2	10.6	3.1	8 023	8 656	16 946	-19.4	0.7	20 597	22.0	27.4	30.4
Wibaux	NA	NA	277	2.5	68.3	10.9	1.5	6 875	9 338	19 375	3.5	0.2	24 573	18.3	23.7	21.3
Yellowstone	302	5 379	30 202	11.0	83.7	21.5	120.7	5 462	12 416	25 942	-11.3	2.2	36 490	12.4	18.4	15.1
NEBRASKA	328	3 768	433 409	14.9	81.8	18.9	1 821.3	6 256	12 452	26 016	-2.5	2.2	37 233	10.3	13.8	11.7
Adams	61	3 647	7 591	20.2	81.2	15.6	32.7	6 525	12 650	24 399	-4.9	2.3	36 677	10.1	13.8	11.9
Antelope	13	872	2 014	11.7	77.5	9.9	10.7	8 737	9 221	18 447	3.8	1.2	30 827	15.1	18.4	16.5
Arthur	0	676	98	0.0	83.7	13.8	0.9	9 978	9 094	19 038	-5.9	0.0	18 400	12.1	17.8	14.4
Banner	NA	NA	213	2.3	87.7	12.0	1.4	7 151	9 120	22 176	11.3	0.6	29 179	12.3	13.5	14.0

1. Data for serious crimes have not been adjusted for underreporting; this may affect comparability between geographic areas and over time.   2. Per 100,000 population estimated by the FBI.   3. All persons 3 years old and over enrolled in nursery school through college.   4. Persons 25 years old and over.   5. Elementary and secondary education expenditures, local government fiscal years ending between July 1, 1998 and June 30, 1999.   6. Based on population enumerated as of April 1, 1990.

STATE County	Personal income, 1999 Total (mil dol)	Percent change, 1998–1999	Per capita[1] Dollars	Per capita[1] Rank	Wages and salaries[2] (mil dol)	Proprietor's income (mil dol)	Dividends, interest, and rent (mil dol)	Transfer payments Total (mil dol)	Government payments to individuals Total (mil dol)	Social Security (mil dol)	Medical payments (mil dol)	Income maintenance (mil dol)	Unemployment insurance (mil dol)
	62	63	64	65	66	67	68	69	70	71	72	73	74
MISSOURI—Cont'd													
St. Louis city	9 005	2.4	26 963	418	11 375	641	1 938	1 950	1 889	535	883	327	33
MONTANA	19 419	3.6	21 997	X	10 644	1 990	4 616	3 021	2 854	1 310	885	245	67
Beaverhead	184	3.7	20 943	1 683	92	20	48	32	31	13	11	2	1
Big Horn	168	0.7	13 386	3 072	126	10	30	37	35	10	13	7	1
Blaine	111	1.7	15 661	2 933	40	17	29	25	23	8	8	4	1
Broadwater	80	4.7	19 172	2 239	32	12	17	16	15	8	5	4	0
Carbon	199	4.6	20 889	1 699	54	21	73	32	30	16	10	2	1
Carter	25	29.2	17 261	2 691	6	5	9	5	4	2	1	1	0
Cascade	1 915	2.5	24 463	765	1 101	155	440	294	280	123	91	23	5
Chouteau	113	5.0	22 220	1 295	31	18	38	20	19	10	7	1	0
Custer	247	1.2	20 889	1 699	124	19	66	47	44	20	15	4	1
Daniels	58	16.2	29 731	219	20	17	15	9	8	5	2	0	0
Dawson	190	4.5	21 887	1 391	105	18	42	34	32	15	10	2	1
Deer Lodge	175	0.3	17 968	2 545	77	11	39	46	44	21	14	4	1
Fallon	62	0.7	21 607	1 485	31	12	12	11	10	5	3	1	0
Fergus	246	2.4	20 232	1 914	106	30	70	49	47	22	16	3	1
Flathead	1 620	0.2	22 265	1 282	870	181	418	242	228	112	67	14	7
Gallatin	1 534	5.4	24 017	853	890	195	389	139	127	64	31	8	2
Garfield	26	22.7	18 660	2 378	8	7	8	4	4	2	1	0	0
Glacier	192	-1.8	15 205	2 969	109	20	33	48	45	12	16	11	2
Golden Valley	17	3.0	16 134	2 881	4	1	6	4	3	2	1	0	0
Granite	51	2.1	19 127	2 251	19	8	14	10	10	5	3	1	0
Hill	364	1.5	21 365	1 558	188	44	82	67	64	20	20	7	2
Jefferson	240	6.6	23 111	1 068	73	20	43	29	27	13	7	1	1
Judith Basin	42	2.6	18 428	2 437	10	6	15	7	7	4	2	1	0
Lake	446	4.2	17 234	2 696	206	37	110	94	89	39	30	10	2
Lewis and Clark	1 315	4.5	24 325	799	889	97	300	174	164	79	47	12	3
Liberty	45	1.8	20 032	1 982	18	8	14	9	8	4	3	0	0
Lincoln	314	1.8	16 711	2 794	142	44	65	79	76	36	23	7	3
McCone	42	16.9	21 620	1 476	14	11	9	7	6	3	2	1	0
Madison	127	7.3	18 399	2 441	46	12	41	23	22	12	6	1	1
Meagher	40	9.2	22 465	1 225	13	10	10	8	7	4	2	0	0
Mineral	58	2.8	14 931	2 994	24	7	14	16	16	7	5	1	1
Missoula	2 187	4.9	24 476	760	1 402	232	466	267	250	108	77	23	5
Musselshell	67	1.2	14 645	3 013	21	7	19	19	18	9	6	2	0
Park	312	4.7	19 514	2 136	130	37	89	54	51	20	14	3	0
Petroleum	9	22.6	16 893	2 756	3	2	2	2	2	1	0	0	0
Phillips	82	0.7	17 387	2 670	35	10	22	18	17	8	6	2	0
Pondera	125	0.4	20 022	1 985	50	14	37	26	25	11	9	3	1
Powder River	33	14.6	18 683	2 372	10	6	10	5	5	3	2	0	0
Powell	126	2.7	18 213	2 494	64	13	30	23	22	10	6	2	0
Prairie	27	8.6	19 739	2 076	7	6	7	5	5	2	2	1	0
Ravalli	650	4.8	18 157	2 509	234	81	182	124	117	59	36	8	4
Richland	203	2.7	20 202	1 931	105	21	50	36	34	16	12	2	1
Roosevelt	182	4.7	16 678	2 797	85	29	35	45	42	14	15	9	1
Rosebud	185	2.4	18 733	2 359	144	9	30	27	25	10	7	4	1
Sanders	165	4.2	16 090	2 888	67	13	41	42	40	20	12	3	1
Sheridan	100	11.0	24 284	808	31	24	30	18	17	10	5	1	0
Silver Bow	763	0.1	22 474	1 222	439	60	160	149	142	66	47	13	2
Stillwater	182	13.2	21 827	1 407	104	13	47	26	25	12	8	2	1
Sweet Grass	71	7.7	19 810	2 059	24	8	27	11	11	6	3	1	0
Teton	123	1.6	19 090	2 260	43	19	37	23	21	12	7	1	1
Toole	114	6.9	24 568	739	56	21	27	17	17	8	5	1	0
Treasure	14	3.3	16 446	2 835	5	1	4	3	3	2	1	0	0
Valley	184	5.6	22 636	1 182	73	33	46	34	32	15	11	3	1
Wheatland	36	-0.7	15 819	2 919	13	2	11	10	9	4	4	1	0
Wibaux	19	3.0	16 793	2 780	5	4	4	4	4	2	1	0	0
Yellowstone	3 214	4.1	25 253	623	2 024	250	701	417	393	187	120	29	8
NEBRASKA	45 061	4.9	27 047	X	28 037	4 768	9 228	5 678	5 382	2 425	2 083	407	49
Adams	751	5.2	25 649	563	430	60	189	112	107	51	40	7	1
Antelope	169	-0.6	23 285	1 017	52	45	41	30	28	13	11	2	0
Arthur	4	45.9	10 655	3 104	2	-3	3	1	1	1	0	0	0
Banner	13	10.7	15 892	2 906	5	2	3	2	2	1	0	0	0

1. Based on the resident population estimated as of July 1 of the year shown. 2. Includes other labor income.

STATE County	Earnings, 1999									Social Security bene-ficiaries, December 2000			Housing units, 1990	
				Percent by selected industries										
		Goods-related[1]		Service-related and other[2]								Supple-mental Security Income recipients, December 2000		
	Total (mil dol)	Farm	Total	Manu-facturing	Total	Retail trade	Finance, insur-ance, and real estate	Services	Govern-ment	Number	Rate[3]		Total	Percent change, 1980–1990
	75	76	77	78	79	80	81	82	83	84	85	86	87	88
MISSOURI—Cont'd														
St. Louis city	12 016	0.0	D	16.0	D	5.7	10.0	30.2	17.5	63 973	184	18 257	194 919	-3.6
MONTANA	12 633	2.7	17.1	7.3	58.6	11.8	5.9	27.0	21.6	157 443	175	13 877	361 155	10.0
Beaverhead	113	10.8	D	1.9	D	10.6	8.6	19.6	26.4	1 581	172	116	4 128	10.3
Big Horn	136	3.5	27.2	0.8	35.0	6.1	3.1	20.5	34.3	1 534	121	314	4 304	11.3
Blaine	57	18.9	D	0.9	D	8.1	3.1	13.5	40.9	1 115	159	145	2 930	13.4
Broadwater	44	14.5	D	21.7	D	5.3	3.3	12.0	15.0	949	216	64	1 593	9.9
Carbon	75	5.2	15.3	3.7	58.8	15.1	7.3	26.5	20.7	1 955	205	97	4 828	10.7
Carter	12	34.5	D	D	D	4.8	2.9	D	23.4	290	213	13	816	2.6
Cascade	1 256	0.7	D	3.4	D	11.8	7.4	28.6	29.2	14 652	182	1 434	33 063	2.7
Chouteau	50	32.9	5.5	2.0	35.4	7.0	5.1	10.8	26.3	1 130	189	50	2 668	-0.8
Custer	142	0.5	8.5	2.9	61.7	15.1	6.4	27.3	29.3	2 475	212	229	5 405	-1.2
Daniels	36	35.3	D	D	D	5.0	2.2	10.8	15.2	561	278	22	1 220	-6.4
Dawson	123	8.5	D	1.1	D	10.0	3.8	18.5	20.8	1 771	195	84	4 487	-3.2
Deer Lodge	88	0.2	D	3.8	D	11.6	3.6	33.2	34.7	2 350	250	230	4 830	-7.1
Fallon	43	8.2	D	D	D	7.4	2.3	15.5	17.2	620	219	26	1 525	0.4
Fergus	136	4.7	20.6	5.8	51.7	11.9	4.5	23.1	23.1	2 776	233	188	5 732	6.3
Flathead	1 050	0.3	25.8	15.6	59.6	13.7	6.7	28.0	14.4	13 576	182	1 003	26 979	20.0
Gallatin	1 085	1.4	20.5	9.2	57.3	15.0	5.5	26.2	20.9	7 518	111	381	21 350	24.3
Garfield	15	40.2	D	D	D	7.0	D	D	22.4	278	217	7	924	6.5
Glacier	129	7.1	D	0.6	D	10.2	3.1	25.1	37.1	1 646	124	421	4 797	19.9
Golden Valley	5	20.0	D	D	D	D	0.0	D	41.1	218	209	9	432	-8.5
Granite	27	6.6	D	18.6	D	9.0	D	10.0	26.8	579	205	27	1 924	17.7
Hill	232	8.9	6.0	0.8	65.7	10.8	4.2	28.0	19.4	2 470	148	332	7 345	2.1
Jefferson	93	0.0	43.4	6.6	30.4	6.9	2.9	14.7	26.2	1 637	163	110	3 302	15.2
Judith Basin	16	29.3	D	D	D	4.7	D	7.5	32.9	472	203	14	1 346	-1.0
Lake	243	0.3	23.8	14.3	59.4	13.0	4.7	34.5	16.5	5 122	193	484	10 972	21.4
Lewis and Clark	987	0.2	10.1	3.9	54.7	10.0	8.1	27.8	35.0	9 302	167	818	21 412	15.3
Liberty	26	27.9	19.2	3.6	D	6.8	2.6	16.0	19.4	398	184	7	1 007	-12.7
Lincoln	186	0.1	32.0	24.8	40.2	10.0	3.9	16.3	27.7	4 366	232	452	8 002	14.0
McCone	25	38.4	D	0.0	D	4.9	2.0	9.2	16.1	373	189	39	1 161	3.6
Madison	58	1.8	D	4.6	D	13.2	6.3	19.2	24.1	1 460	213	18	3 902	42.4
Meagher	23	23.9	D	8.9	D	7.7	D	21.2	19.2	483	250	21	1 259	4.8
Mineral	31	0.6	23.0	18.2	D	19.3	D	17.2	33.1	876	226	84	1 635	-0.7
Missoula	1 634	-0.2	16.2	8.5	64.9	12.6	6.4	30.7	19.2	12 787	133	1 562	33 466	9.6
Musselshell	28	6.7	21.8	3.9	D	10.6	3.8	20.2	23.9	1 039	231	77	2 183	7.1
Park	166	4.5	18.2	9.1	63.1	13.2	7.3	32.0	14.2	2 478	158	202	6 926	16.1
Petroleum	5	44.5	D	0.0	D	D	0.0	D	28.1	89	181	4	293	-4.2
Phillips	45	9.3	15.9	3.4	48.4	10.0	5.1	16.4	26.4	1 002	218	116	2 765	10.0
Pondera	64	15.6	D	3.2	D	10.2	5.5	17.9	21.2	1 339	208	111	2 618	-3.1
Powder River	17	20.7	D	1.6	D	9.5	2.1	12.4	30.9	356	192	17	1 096	-2.4
Powell	77	6.2	D	20.4	D	6.8	2.6	12.7	43.6	1 215	169	96	2 835	0.2
Prairie	13	45.7	D	D	D	5.0	4.7	5.8	26.1	324	270	13	749	-7.3
Ravalli	315	0.3	D	13.8	D	12.7	5.3	23.5	19.7	7 584	210	450	11 099	21.5
Richland	125	9.2	D	9.5	D	11.0	3.3	19.3	16.4	1 947	201	125	4 825	2.9
Roosevelt	114	17.1	D	2.2	D	8.9	3.4	24.9	31.7	1 804	170	281	4 265	12.0
Rosebud	153	2.3	D	D	D	4.5	2.1	21.0	17.1	1 321	141	164	4 251	12.3
Sanders	79	-2.9	D	12.5	D	9.5	4.0	27.1	25.8	2 473	242	229	4 335	12.8
Sheridan	55	32.6	D	D	D	7.6	3.7	17.3	20.5	1 100	268	44	2 417	0.0
Silver Bow	499	0.2	14.7	5.2	67.2	13.0	4.6	30.6	18.0	7 238	209	817	15 474	-3.7
Stillwater	117	1.8	D	8.1	D	5.8	4.7	8.5	10.6	1 472	180	78	3 291	22.8
Sweet Grass	32	2.9	24.2	4.9	D	18.4	4.6	13.6	24.8	702	195	14	1 639	10.8
Teton	62	20.9	D	1.4	51.7	5.8	4.9	10.5	20.7	1 369	212	69	2 725	-0.8
Toole	77	14.6	D	1.0	D	7.0	3.4	12.7	23.8	957	182	71	2 354	-3.2
Treasure	6	23.3	D	D	D	4.6	D	7.5	30.1	189	220	8	448	-3.0
Valley	106	20.2	D	1.8	D	9.3	4.7	19.2	21.8	1 839	240	156	5 304	-5.5
Wheatland	15	8.2	D	2.9	D	13.2	5.4	21.4	34.4	460	204	27	1 129	-1.0
Wibaux	9	28.2	D	D	D	5.4	1.3	D	29.2	260	243	21	563	-17.2
Yellowstone	2 274	0.6	14.9	6.3	69.9	12.4	6.3	32.1	14.5	21 565	167	1 864	48 781	14.1
NEBRASKA	32 806	4.5	19.7	13.2	59.1	8.8	7.6	25.5	16.6	285 555	167	21 249	660 621	5.7
Adams	490	4.7	25.8	19.2	53.0	10.0	3.1	26.8	16.4	5 807	186	400	12 491	-1.3
Antelope	97	32.8	D	3.6	D	7.8	3.6	15.4	15.0	1 691	227	71	3 478	-5.7
Arthur	0	0.0	D	0.0	D	0.0	D	D	0.0	107	241	10	242	3.9
Banner	7	47.1	D	2.0	D	0.0	D	3.0	26.9	141	172	NA	366	-10.7

1. Covers mining, construction, and manufacturing. 2. Covers private sector earnings in agricultural services, forestry, and fisheries; transportation and public utilities; wholesale trade; retail trade; finance, insurance, and real estate; and services. 3. Per 1,000 resident population estimated as of July 1 of the year shown.

Table B. States and Counties — **Housing, Labor Force, and Employment**

STATE County	Housing units, 1990 (cont'd)								Civilian labor force, 2001				Civilian employment, 1990[5]		
	Occupied units							Substandard units[3] (percent)			Unemployment			Percent	
	Owner-occupied					Renter-occupied									
				Owner cost as a percent of income						Percent change, 2000–2001					
	Total	Percent	Median value[1]	With a mortgage	Without a mortgage	Median rent[2]	Rent as percent of income		Total		Total	Rate[4]	Total	Professional, managerial, and technical	Precision production, craft, and repair
	89	90	91	92	93	94	95	96	97	98	99	100	101	102	103
MISSOURI—Cont'd															
St. Louis city	164 931	45.1	50 700	19.1	13.6	342	27.9	5.8	157 690	0.8	12 944	8.2	161 434	27.3	7.7
MONTANA	306 163	67.3	56 600	20.2	12.5	311	25.0	3.2	465 223	-2.9	21 319	4.6	350 723	26.9	10.4
Beaverhead	3 211	61.5	55 500	15.7	13.9	262	20.4	3.9	4 798	-5.4	156	3.3	3 770	24.8	10.3
Big Horn	3 448	62.6	41 600	19.0	13.8	247	23.8	13.3	5 345	-7.8	896	16.8	3 595	25.8	7.4
Blaine	2 379	62.2	40 800	19.6	13.0	235	23.7	5.6	2 626	-9.8	147	5.6	2 706	20.2	9.4
Broadwater	1 280	74.9	46 800	21.0	11.4	287	20.2	2.3	2 064	-3.9	88	4.3	1 446	19.7	8.5
Carbon	3 269	73.1	45 700	21.5	14.2	287	19.3	2.2	4 580	-4.9	212	4.6	3 431	23.5	9.5
Carter	589	77.4	22 500	35.0	12.9	242	22.2	4.6	928	-13.4	21	2.3	827	9.3	3.7
Cascade	30 133	63.7	60 100	20.5	11.9	318	25.7	2.5	36 833	-1.7	1 663	4.5	31 669	27.9	10.2
Chouteau	2 064	69.3	41 900	17.8	12.6	272	25.3	1.2	2 652	-10.6	81	3.1	2 372	19.7	8.7
Custer	4 631	66.9	37 400	17.8	13.0	270	24.3	3.1	5 697	-6.0	210	3.7	5 351	25.5	7.6
Daniels	919	79.4	30 800	22.2	14.8	226	16.5	1.6	1 197	-9.2	33	2.8	1 035	18.8	10.5
Dawson	3 691	72.7	37 100	16.2	13.0	271	22.3	1.6	4 699	-6.2	127	2.7	4 416	22.1	11.9
Deer Lodge	4 060	72.9	34 000	16.4	12.5	199	21.5	2.1	3 965	-0.5	269	6.8	3 501	24.5	10.9
Fallon	1 166	77.0	36 700	18.5	11.5	249	17.5	1.3	1 548	-6.1	40	2.6	1 419	17.8	12.5
Fergus	4 603	71.5	40 800	18.8	12.1	269	25.1	2.7	6 031	-5.3	352	5.8	5 160	20.2	10.6
Flathead	22 834	70.6	64 200	21.4	12.3	332	25.7	3.4	39 943	0.8	2 358	5.9	25 607	24.2	11.8
Gallatin	19 015	58.5	70 200	21.3	11.8	342	27.9	2.9	44 240	-1.3	1 108	2.5	25 153	30.7	10.2
Garfield	577	70.9	32 000	16.8	15.2	280	23.5	5.2	906	-14.9	20	2.2	809	12.4	5.4
Glacier	3 816	60.9	43 800	17.6	12.8	257	23.4	10.7	5 272	-3.5	587	11.1	4 137	27.3	10.7
Golden Valley	330	79.1	30 800	17.9	13.1	243	19.3	4.4	511	-12.9	24	4.7	431	14.2	5.3
Granite	1 051	75.4	37 700	24.0	13.2	252	19.7	6.6	1 146	-6.1	88	7.7	1 001	18.0	10.4
Hill	6 426	63.1	53 200	17.5	13.0	292	22.9	3.8	8 672	-2.9	356	4.1	7 551	25.8	11.1
Jefferson	2 867	80.7	63 700	16.6	12.8	299	18.4	3.7	5 114	-2.6	226	4.4	3 680	33.3	11.1
Judith Basin	908	72.9	30 600	14.2	11.1	253	20.0	2.6	1 121	-8.8	42	3.7	1 065	18.8	5.1
Lake	7 814	70.2	61 300	20.5	12.8	263	24.7	5.5	11 852	-6.6	1 018	8.6	8 268	23.9	13.7
Lewis and Clark	18 649	68.5	61 800	20.3	12.3	329	25.1	2.0	27 889	-1.8	1 207	4.3	23 036	38.5	7.9
Liberty	788	71.7	41 300	16.0	12.6	267	21.8	4.5	1 052	-12.6	31	2.9	862	21.2	13.8
Lincoln	6 668	73.3	48 900	17.2	12.2	280	21.6	4.8	6 664	-4.2	753	11.3	6 500	24.4	11.8
McCone	844	78.2	32 300	18.5	14.1	297	16.8	1.6	1 175	-10.8	27	2.3	1 050	13.8	9.1
Madison	2 387	68.8	56 800	22.0	13.6	319	22.5	5.3	3 934	-1.0	133	3.4	2 802	18.8	12.0
Meagher	709	67.4	36 500	18.1	11.9	275	20.2	4.4	998	-11.2	59	5.9	851	14.8	8.9
Mineral	1 282	72.9	43 700	18.9	12.3	258	22.8	7.2	1 763	7.0	144	8.2	1 393	20.7	9.7
Missoula	30 782	60.1	66 200	20.3	12.2	334	28.0	3.3	54 198	-1.9	1 960	3.6	37 122	30.8	9.1
Musselshell	1 661	78.1	29 600	17.3	12.3	264	23.7	5.2	1 737	-6.8	115	6.6	1 597	16.8	11.0
Park	5 619	66.3	48 100	21.5	12.3	299	24.4	3.1	9 488	-7.7	448	4.7	6 389	22.3	16.0
Petroleum	209	76.1	15 500	27.5	15.2	291	18.6	7.1	297	-19.5	7	2.4	277	21.7	6.9
Phillips	1 931	69.8	41 500	19.0	13.1	273	21.0	4.0	2 108	-11.1	93	4.4	2 304	17.2	11.1
Pondera	2 246	69.5	42 100	18.4	12.0	271	22.7	5.5	3 173	-8.5	134	4.2	2 700	21.7	11.3
Powder River	805	73.4	43 800	18.8	12.3	305	16.9	5.3	1 173	-11.5	22	1.9	1 063	18.3	9.3
Powell	2 234	71.8	41 900	17.7	12.4	253	20.1	1.2	2 362	-7.8	113	4.8	2 411	29.4	9.6
Prairie	568	78.9	19 100	13.9	13.4	239	14.3	3.2	626	-10.4	29	4.6	607	17.6	7.7
Ravalli	9 698	75.1	61 500	21.5	12.1	313	25.7	4.3	18 163	-0.6	840	4.6	9 928	24.7	11.8
Richland	3 956	70.7	44 200	16.8	12.6	280	18.4	1.5	5 270	-7.1	260	4.9	4 537	19.8	14.6
Roosevelt	3 694	63.9	40 400	18.4	14.0	280	25.5	5.3	3 990	-7.1	288	7.2	3 866	22.8	11.2
Rosebud	3 479	68.8	51 800	13.7	12.9	285	17.6	8.5	4 594	-3.9	325	7.1	4 345	19.4	16.1
Sanders	3 397	75.1	42 000	20.4	13.9	243	18.5	5.5	4 219	-1.2	349	8.3	3 061	26.4	9.3
Sheridan	1 899	77.0	39 500	21.8	12.5	276	23.1	1.7	1 914	-10.6	61	3.2	1 858	20.6	12.8
Silver Bow	13 899	70.8	44 300	17.4	13.4	265	25.6	2.2	16 359	-5.2	839	5.1	13 935	29.6	10.6
Stillwater	2 523	73.6	56 200	16.1	13.0	303	20.6	2.8	5 401	7.2	166	3.1	2 982	17.9	17.8
Sweet Grass	1 281	72.1	48 000	17.4	12.3	252	24.8	1.8	1 838	1.0	47	2.6	1 368	18.4	9.7
Teton	2 329	73.4	44 900	20.2	12.0	271	22.6	2.9	3 141	-8.8	110	3.5	2 731	20.7	10.8
Toole	1 922	71.9	39 100	16.8	12.1	243	20.6	2.3	2 731	-8.6	74	2.7	2 387	23.9	8.4
Treasure	339	64.6	35 200	13.9	11.2	188	26.5	2.9	438	-14.1	14	3.2	421	18.3	7.8
Valley	3 268	71.4	36 800	16.2	12.8	272	24.7	2.9	3 948	-7.6	140	3.5	3 685	20.1	11.3
Wheatland	849	75.3	27 600	20.5	13.3	226	21.6	2.2	1 139	-9.4	40	3.5	978	14.5	8.7
Wibaux	454	72.5	28 900	21.4	14.1	214	16.5	1.9	543	-11.0	14	2.6	478	20.7	9.0
Yellowstone	44 689	65.7	62 800	21.4	12.0	343	25.5	1.6	71 160	-1.4	2 353	3.3	54 760	28.6	9.9
NEBRASKA	602 363	66.5	50 400	19.4	12.6	348	23.7	1.9	928 297	0.4	28 868	3.1	772 813	26.2	10.3
Adams	11 593	64.5	44 800	17.4	12.5	301	23.9	1.3	15 509	-0.1	430	2.8	14 314	25.0	11.5
Antelope	3 045	74.0	26 100	17.9	14.4	216	19.6	3.5	3 051	-0.5	117	3.8	3 258	17.2	8.9
Arthur	187	60.4	23 200	10.0	11.6	197	11.5	1.1	204	1.5	7	3.4	218	11.5	2.8
Banner	305	63.0	32 500	16.3	13.5	242	35.1	1.3	419	-1.9	7	1.7	395	17.2	9.1

1. Specified owner-occupied units. 2. Specified renter-occupied units. 3. Overcrowded or lacking complete plumbing facilities. 4. Percent of civilian labor force. 5. Persons 16 years and older.

Table B. States and Counties — Nonfarm Employment and Agriculture

| | Private nonfarm establishments, employment and payroll, 1999 | | | | | | | | | Agriculture, 1997 | | | |
| | Employment | | | | | | Annual payroll | | Farms | | | Farm operators |
STATE County	Number of establishments	Total	Health Care and Social Assistance	Manufacturing	Retail trade	Finance and Insurance	Professional Scientific and Technical Services	Total (mil dol)	Average per employee (dollars)	Number	Less than 50 acres	500 acres and over	Whose principal occupation is farming (percent)
	104	105	106	107	108	109	110	111	112	113	114	115	116
MISSOURI—Cont'd													
St. Louis city	9 729	268 736	37 131	30 792	15 530	20 258	16 141	9 870	36 727	NA	NA	NA	NA
MONTANA	31 365	288 358	46 901	20 631	51 148	13 877	13 502	6 441	22 338	24 279	18.4	53.0	64.7
Beaverhead	367	2 180	343	81	479	109	62	39	17 885	360	19.2	57.2	61.9
Big Horn	209	2 154	536	24	407	75	61	57	26 681	530	13.4	60.0	67.4
Blaine	167	1 023	314	D	210	56	13	21	20 964	541	6.3	68.8	74.9
Broadwater	105	770	92	223	89	30	20	16	20 261	219	13.2	51.1	68.9
Carbon	316	1 881	285	88	296	57	D	31	16 502	623	15.4	35.6	62.0
Carter	23	111	D	D	21	D	D	2	16 676	305	3.3	88.5	81.6
Cascade	2 534	27 093	5 515	926	5 352	1 940	1 197	573	21 140	903	20.3	44.3	57.5
Chouteau	154	761	248	40	149	53	D	11	14 686	750	2.8	84.0	83.1
Custer	399	3 858	1 032	114	817	179	113	78	20 230	405	18.8	53.3	63.2
Daniels	80	524	D	D	119	28	9	11	21 458	363	3.3	80.4	72.2
Dawson	314	2 382	634	D	507	93	51	39	16 574	502	8.2	72.5	70.9
Deer Lodge	250	2 431	900	107	268	67	32	48	19 645	83	24.1	44.6	53.0
Fallon	115	705	D	9	138	38	14	15	21 172	309	7.1	73.1	69.9
Fergus	434	2 998	665	264	477	157	94	60	19 984	898	11.0	67.2	70.0
Flathead	3 081	26 606	3 343	3 673	4 590	1 248	832	622	23 371	835	49.0	12.6	43.1
Gallatin	3 291	26 758	2 589	2 337	5 120	797	1 308	569	21 275	835	31.3	30.4	54.6
Garfield	23	138	D	D	40	D	D	2	13 232	244	3.3	90.2	91.4
Glacier	275	2 046	403	D	465	76	60	45	21 991	425	9.4	68.5	64.5
Golden Valley	15	63	D	D	D	D	0	1	8 508	118	7.6	72.9	76.3
Granite	89	489	60	D	79	D	9	9	17 865	117	8.5	67.5	77.8
Hill	518	4 772	1 186	67	900	175	157	87	18 190	692	4.2	73.4	71.7
Jefferson	194	1 453	165	D	143	33	18	38	26 048	266	28.2	36.5	48.1
Judith Basin	54	146	14	D	15	D	D	2	14 884	329	8.5	72.9	80.5
Lake	692	5 512	1 021	1 214	1 026	237	162	110	20 038	1 011	40.2	14.5	52.0
Lewis and Clark	1 943	20 861	3 942	721	3 294	1 716	1 448	473	22 689	502	43.6	25.5	42.0
Liberty	74	537	229	D	60	29	9	10	18 406	280	1.1	88.6	87.1
Lincoln	581	3 944	602	703	649	147	88	78	19 690	252	35.3	6.7	40.5
McCone	46	336	D	D	52	22	D	7	20 497	430	2.8	83.7	77.7
Madison	255	1 091	119	121	167	70	34	23	21 470	460	16.7	47.0	68.7
Meagher	63	273	106	0	42	D	8	4	14 238	142	9.9	65.5	76.1
Mineral	109	703	147	133	203	15	D	11	16 020	71	36.6	14.1	56.3
Missoula	3 576	39 548	5 939	2 969	7 517	1 610	1 982	905	22 884	482	53.1	13.9	35.5
Musselshell	134	572	129	19	117	25	D	9	15 785	232	9.1	63.8	64.2
Park	706	4 379	616	455	673	155	179	81	18 505	420	20.0	50.0	61.0
Petroleum	7	11	D	D	D	D	0	0	7 273	88	2.3	81.8	73.9
Phillips	144	840	205	25	188	50	28	13	15 512	489	8.2	71.0	75.5
Pondera	204	1 383	295	77	284	79	40	26	18 778	474	8.9	69.0	78.9
Powder River	71	224	D	D	68	D	8	2	10 103	297	4.7	81.5	82.2
Powell	142	1 160	262	D	130	38	15	23	19 893	230	13.9	57.4	59.6
Prairie	34	182	D	D	D	19	D	2	13 473	158	5.7	75.3	82.9
Ravalli	1 130	7 817	972	890	1 241	348	290	161	20 659	1 080	56.8	6.8	48.2
Richland	388	2 925	392	397	507	127	94	60	20 650	571	10.3	62.7	72.0
Roosevelt	237	1 800	391	104	451	77	44	28	15 529	609	4.9	71.8	68.3
Rosebud	192	2 672	170	D	356	44	25	83	31 108	362	7.5	68.8	73.2
Sanders	343	1 761	330	206	245	71	36	33	18 554	412	18.9	25.5	52.9
Sheridan	159	919	265	27	204	59	13	13	14 600	581	2.6	77.5	75.9
Silver Bow	1 151	12 470	2 239	497	2 176	287	1 012	298	23 909	116	17.2	32.8	44.0
Stillwater	212	2 381	200	335	318	53	D	80	33 444	473	18.6	53.1	63.4
Sweet Grass	122	644	13	54	146	23	31	11	17 661	301	12.3	57.1	70.1
Teton	187	1 041	178	49	211	85	24	19	18 560	557	10.2	58.2	72.9
Toole	207	1 253	199	69	166	55	34	28	22 058	382	2.6	80.9	74.6
Treasure	26	97	D	D	24	D	D	1	14 526	110	5.5	64.5	72.7
Valley	258	1 880	476	50	348	125	65	32	16 870	655	4.3	69.2	72.5
Wheatland	61	304	D	D	74	26	D	4	13 283	144	3.5	80.6	77.8
Wibaux	25	164	D	0	14	6	4	2	11 939	178	5.6	69.1	66.9
Yellowstone	4 857	56 986	8 557	2 955	9 483	2 935	3 618	1 418	24 890	1 097	32.5	32.0	53.5
NEBRASKA	48 968	733 905	98 651	108 807	104 595	52 533	31 144	19 436	26 483	51 454	14.2	42.2	69.5
Adams	977	14 192	2 782	3 724	2 099	321	268	307	21 611	623	15.2	44.6	74.5
Antelope	244	1 441	282	116	364	92	D	25	17 115	803	12.0	41.2	75.7
Arthur	12	40	0	D	D	D	D	1	14 500	83	4.8	88.0	85.5
Banner	5	D	0	0	0	0	0	D	D	220	3.6	77.3	69.5

Table B. States and Counties — Agriculture, Land, and Water

STATE County	Land in farms Acreage (1,000)	Percent change, 1992–1997	Acres Average size of farm	Total irrigated (1,000)	Total cropland (1,000)	Value of land and buildings Average per farm ($1,000)	Average per acre (dollars)	Value of machinery and equipment average per farm ($1,000)	Value of products sold Total (mil dol)	Average per farm (dollars)	Percent from — Crops	Live-stock and poultry products	Percent of farms with sales of — $10,000 or more	$100,000 or more	Percent of land owned by fed. gov. 1997	Water consumption 1995 (mil gal/day)
	117	118	119	120	121	122	123	124	125	126	127	128	129	130	131	132
MISSOURI—Cont'd																
St. Louis city	NA	NA	NA	NA	NA	NA	NA	NA	NA	NA	NA	NA	NA	NA	(1)NA	147.8
MONTANA	58 608	-1.7	2 414	1 994	17 629	699	294	78	1 871	77 051	48.3	51.7	61.6	22.1	28.8	8 847.2
Beaverhead	1 152	-14.2	3 200	225	203	1 359	401	101	55	153 815	18.4	81.6	66.9	30.3	58.8	570.7
Big Horn	2 770	-7.7	5 227	53	408	1 217	229	85	61	115 332	45.0	55.0	70.4	27.5	2.0	315.4
Blaine	2 258	-3.5	4 173	63	660	731	190	94	48	88 609	53.3	46.7	70.1	26.6	17.1	274.2
Broadwater	453	0.6	2 067	53	131	839	378	97	20	92 131	66.8	33.2	71.7	28.3	32.0	241.0
Carbon	736	22.9	1 181	82	172	564	459	61	44	70 257	35.5	64.5	64.2	17.8	42.9	448.8
Carter	1 589	-1.8	5 211	5	245	592	107	77	27	88 494	13.9	86.1	81.0	31.8	27.9	4.1
Cascade	1 441	1.2	1 596	33	508	620	373	61	67	73 899	48.0	52.0	55.6	16.1	12.5	153.2
Chouteau	2 212	-2.9	2 949	12	1 346	1 015	351	150	93	123 608	83.9	16.1	81.9	44.7	6.2	36.5
Custer	1 898	-9.0	4 685	28	170	919	187	70	33	80 459	21.8	78.2	66.2	24.0	16.3	74.9
Daniels	765	0.5	2 106	2	529	535	251	110	26	70 645	79.4	20.6	68.0	23.7	0.2	5.0
Dawson	1 417	6.2	2 823	18	466	452	166	88	35	69 220	59.3	40.7	69.1	24.5	4.2	72.4
Deer Lodge	102	-24.7	1 225	18	22	683	558	52	4	50 807	20.3	79.7	53.0	16.9	38.4	48.0
Fallon	953	0.9	3 084	1	232	630	200	75	20	66 042	27.3	72.7	67.3	21.7	11.7	6.6
Fergus	2 249	0.7	2 756	16	676	666	259	82	72	88 041	44.7	55.3	72.2	27.9	18.1	74.7
Flathead	216	-21.9	241	27	106	450	1 649	37	27	29 693	67.0	33.0	31.6	7.3	70.6	64.9
Gallatin	760	8.7	910	91	253	832	976	66	59	70 545	52.5	47.5	53.3	19.9	38.0	489.2
Garfield	2 163	8.2	8 866	5	302	952	111	95	32	131 271	30.5	69.5	82.0	40.6	23.8	12.4
Glacier	1 623	-6.3	3 818	24	497	842	224	77	45	106 867	62.6	37.4	68.5	28.5	20.2	86.9
Golden Valley	638	0.2	5 407	10	117	1 249	236	109	13	109 674	35.0	65.0	72.9	32.2	4.3	85.4
Granite	268	-23.3	2 294	36	45	951	449	74	10	82 412	15.0	85.0	72.6	33.3	63.6	103.5
Hill	1 643	0.0	2 374	5	1 080	709	294	126	67	96 907	82.6	17.4	71.5	36.7	1.8	18.4
Jefferson	364	-0.8	1 369	26	76	549	433	30	9	32 198	22.9	77.1	36.8	10.2	52.1	148.1
Judith Basin	835	-3.8	2 537	6	289	713	300	124	38	114 269	38.5	61.5	80.5	33.7	26.2	65.0
Lake	597	-5.4	590	100	150	443	816	40	38	37 134	42.8	57.2	49.3	7.5	16.0	308.5
Lewis and Clark	822	-6.9	1 638	40	97	709	447	42	19	37 842	35.4	64.6	34.5	8.2	47.4	183.4
Liberty	915	-3.8	3 269	8	631	981	298	169	38	137 423	76.1	23.9	84.3	41.1	2.1	22.4
Lincoln	46	-7.7	183	5	17	461	1 997	23	4	14 582	38.8	61.2	21.4	2.4	73.8	36.6
McCone	1 313	1.8	3 053	7	555	491	151	109	29	66 740	62.2	37.8	76.5	21.9	14.5	14.8
Madison	1 080	-15.1	2 347	108	154	1 109	501	65	35	77 079	27.9	72.1	59.6	21.3	46.2	540.4
Meagher	940	3.1	6 620	46	114	1 987	303	97	23	161 251	18.2	81.8	68.3	38.7	31.6	349.6
Mineral	16	-14.1	230	1	6	401	1 744	27	1	16 662	25.1	74.9	31.0	4.2	82.0	8.1
Missoula	262	5.8	544	22	47	494	993	34	8	16 643	27.4	72.6	28.2	3.1	42.1	113.6
Musselshell	953	-7.7	4 106	12	134	851	207	55	17	75 176	32.3	67.7	53.4	18.1	9.7	81.7
Park	749	-3.7	1 784	49	132	1 178	640	76	20	48 708	30.2	69.8	55.2	14.0	45.0	333.0
Petroleum	541	-19.2	6 152	11	64	1 110	188	77	9	106 484	23.8	76.2	78.4	33.0	36.3	56.7
Phillips	1 978	0.4	4 045	42	634	683	175	89	41	83 569	39.8	60.2	73.8	26.6	41.0	210.0
Pondera	878	-1.7	1 853	63	564	678	374	122	58	121 694	75.2	24.8	80.6	39.2	10.3	212.1
Powder River	1 559	-4.3	5 250	9	166	712	142	74	27	91 895	11.5	88.5	79.5	27.9	28.4	15.1
Powell	649	-3.9	2 824	63	75	1 290	451	51	18	77 423	12.7	87.3	61.7	23.0	48.7	211.2
Prairie	613	-10.3	3 879	11	123	600	158	108	20	128 428	30.9	69.1	80.4	36.7	40.1	74.4
Ravalli	184	-24.1	170	77	83	394	2 451	30	24	22 175	25.3	74.7	31.3	5.3	72.9	167.0
Richland	1 215	1.5	2 127	48	507	561	273	111	54	94 702	65.0	35.0	73.9	29.9	3.9	316.7
Roosevelt	1 430	1.1	2 348	10	784	479	216	112	39	63 731	77.4	22.6	68.0	22.0	0.4	44.5
Rosebud	2 681	3.7	7 406	31	207	919	127	78	38	104 049	23.1	76.9	71.5	29.0	10.3	165.3
Sanders	410	7.6	995	18	62	464	453	31	12	27 995	36.7	63.3	42.0	5.8	51.7	76.1
Sheridan	1 001	4.1	1 723	6	677	422	272	95	36	61 874	80.6	19.4	74.2	20.5	2.5	5.2
Silver Bow	100	0.2	864	8	15	446	587	30	3	27 910	7.0	93.0	37.1	7.8	51.3	39.3
Stillwater	897	0.9	1 896	26	250	682	384	53	29	61 313	28.1	71.9	63.4	15.6	17.5	113.6
Sweet Grass	839	0.2	2 789	45	101	1 199	423	73	21	70 914	9.4	90.6	66.4	21.3	24.9	323.6
Teton	1 117	-5.3	2 005	118	581	686	360	103	72	129 196	63.9	36.1	72.0	36.3	18.3	518.8
Toole	1 091	2.6	2 856	6	680	730	278	119	39	102 560	79.2	20.8	71.5	36.6	2.6	8.5
Treasure	606	1.1	5 505	17	47	905	175	124	18	159 700	35.5	64.5	72.7	28.2	2.0	117.2
Valley	1 787	5.8	2 728	50	740	535	199	95	48	72 954	54.0	46.0	70.2	19.4	35.3	153.4
Wheatland	834	-2.0	5 790	19	182	1 224	217	104	23	158 571	28.2	71.8	78.5	34.7	7.3	184.6
Wibaux	475	-3.2	2 671	0	139	449	170	72	11	59 337	40.0	60.0	69.7	21.9	4.7	2.5
Yellowstone	1 526	4.9	1 391	80	381	524	372	57	96	87 551	31.4	68.6	51.3	16.7	5.2	440.4
NEBRASKA	45 525	2.6	885	6 939	22 093	567	645	85	9 832	191 074	38.6	61.4	77.6	35.4	1.3	10 543.2
Adams	344	2.8	553	185	288	702	1 283	143	159	255 834	49.3	50.7	81.5	48.5	0.2	188.7
Antelope	492	0.6	613	184	378	500	842	90	156	194 496	49.2	50.8	80.9	44.8	0.0	130.0
Arthur	465	1.2	5 606	16	59	1 168	208	61	13	162 497	14.8	85.2	91.6	44.6	0.0	18.0
Banner	446	9.4	2 029	22	210	612	310	93	49	221 591	29.4	70.6	75.9	25.0	0.0	26.4

1. St. Louis City included with St. Louis County.

Table B. States and Counties — Residential Construction, Wholesale and Retail Trade, and Real Estate

STATE County	Value of Residential Construction Authorized by Building Permits, 2000		Wholesale Trade, 1997				Retail Trade[1], 1997				Real Estate and Rental and Leasing, 1997			
	New Construction ($1,000)	Number of Housing Units	Number of Establishments	Number of Employees	Sales (mil dol)	Annual Payroll (mil dol)	Number of Establishments	Number of Employees	Sales (mil dol)	Annual Payroll (mil dol)	Number of Establishments	Number of Employees	Receipts (mil dol)	Annual Payroll (mil dol)
	133	134	135	136	137	138	139	140	141	142	143	144	145	146
MISSOURI—Cont'd														
St. Louis city	37 265	397	902	16 599	10 582.9	646.4	1 241	14 511	2 361.7	282.4	401	3 520	402.9	76.7
MONTANA	235 126	2 572	1 577	14 381	7 709.5	372.3	5 042	48 337	7 779.1	746.5	1 186	4 265	353.4	58.1
Beaverhead	1 167	9	11	95	16.3	1.6	60	474	69.5	7.2	13	36	2.1	0.6
Big Horn	156	5	10	D	D	D	50	415	56.5	5.7	7	D	D	D
Blaine	175	2	13	81	58.2	1.2	36	204	30.5	2.7	3	4	0.4	0.0
Broadwater	345	6	8	61	37.1	1.8	17	103	12.7	1.1	3	5	0.1	0.0
Carbon	2 810	27	13	55	9.9	1.0	45	267	32.8	3.2	14	28	1.4	0.2
Carter	0	0	1	D	D	D	4	18	2.6	0.2	NA	NA	NA	NA
Cascade	11 989	99	141	1 231	1 114.8	32.6	427	5 049	803.0	81.8	100	395	30.4	4.6
Chouteau	170	2	14	89	108.7	2.1	34	169	33.5	2.4	6	D	D	D
Custer	676	8	20	147	94.3	2.6	72	770	113.5	10.7	13	19	1.1	0.1
Daniels	65	1	7	29	23.7	0.7	17	125	30.9	2.7	NA	NA	NA	NA
Dawson	220	1	22	117	39.7	2.6	61	522	69.6	6.9	9	30	9.4	0.9
Deer Lodge	793	11	2	D	D	D	42	259	49.5	3.8	7	21	1.0	0.2
Fallon	0	0	7	52	15.1	0.5	20	120	22.5	1.6	2	D	D	D
Fergus	464	5	27	199	187.8	4.4	80	581	89.6	7.2	11	54	2.5	0.4
Flathead	27 323	234	102	784	347.1	19.7	475	4 285	696.4	70.0	132	467	34.0	5.9
Gallatin	60 309	723	129	1 126	476.1	31.9	472	4 594	710.3	73.6	142	516	50.6	6.9
Garfield	0	0	1	D	D	D	5	35	4.4	0.4	NA	NA	NA	NA
Glacier	70	1	15	77	72.2	1.5	54	426	71.1	6.8	9	100	4.2	2.4
Golden Valley	0	0	2	D	D	D	2	D	D	D	NA	NA	NA	NA
Granite	0	0	3	12	3.6	0.3	11	73	13.2	0.9	1	D	D	D
Hill	592	5	28	218	145.2	4.9	90	907	140.7	13.0	22	69	4.6	0.7
Jefferson	105	3	10	18	6.9	0.5	25	148	17.8	1.9	10	D	D	D
Judith Basin	0	0	6	D	D	D	8	26	4.4	0.2	1	D	D	D
Lake	5 622	65	23	129	34.1	2.2	125	1 056	157.5	15.8	24	35	2.4	0.4
Lewis and Clark	8 078	99	76	772	217.0	18.2	304	3 196	529.4	49.7	80	377	27.1	5.1
Liberty	0	0	5	40	43.9	0.9	14	72	11.1	0.9	2	D	D	D
Lincoln	275	22	10	30	4.9	0.7	94	602	91.5	8.7	18	47	2.5	0.4
McCone	0	0	5	55	25.1	1.3	8	58	8.0	0.7	NA	NA	NA	NA
Madison	905	2	6	17	5.7	0.4	40	165	24.6	2.3	10	14	0.5	0.2
Meagher	0	0	1	D	D	D	12	43	8.2	0.6	NA	NA	NA	NA
Mineral	645	5	NA	NA	NA	NA	19	164	20.3	2.5	3	D	D	D
Missoula	40 177	571	183	1 991	775.9	50.0	540	6 800	1 069.0	105.7	138	593	46.2	8.2
Musselshell	77	1	7	28	7.8	0.6	22	134	15.6	1.6	4	11	1.6	0.1
Park	518	15	23	138	33.9	3.3	111	588	102.7	8.5	28	39	6.2	0.5
Petroleum	0	0	1	D	D	D	2	D	D	D	NA	NA	NA	NA
Phillips	84	1	5	37	15.7	0.8	29	209	31.1	2.8	2	D	D	D
Pondera	75	1	21	132	55.3	2.4	32	260	51.8	4.2	7	15	1.0	0.2
Powder River	0	0	NA	NA	NA	NA	14	78	9.0	0.9	1	D	D	D
Powell	0	0	6	D	D	D	24	131	15.8	1.9	5	5	0.6	0.1
Prairie	0	0	3	D	D	D	5	37	5.2	0.4	NA	NA	NA	NA
Ravalli	7 883	74	44	283	166.4	8.7	154	1 197	179.8	16.8	53	178	10.7	2.3
Richland	641	7	26	228	188.7	4.2	66	506	83.6	7.5	12	34	2.5	0.3
Roosevelt	64	1	10	42	57.5	1.1	53	367	53.0	5.2	7	16	1.0	0.1
Rosebud	350	2	NA	NA	NA	NA	39	392	42.4	4.6	6	66	2.3	1.2
Sanders	224	14	12	51	65.0	1.2	51	239	33.2	3.2	11	10	0.9	0.1
Sheridan	0	0	13	67	44.1	1.1	41	176	26.2	2.3	2	D	D	D
Silver Bow	3 195	31	55	534	192.0	10.7	220	2 147	333.1	32.0	39	134	11.3	2.0
Stillwater	2 304	24	6	14	6.1	0.3	37	339	47.7	4.0	4	1	0.7	0.1
Sweet Grass	1 822	25	2	D	D	D	26	177	36.4	2.9	6	11	0.5	0.1
Teton	211	4	10	66	31.2	1.6	33	247	50.1	3.6	7	13	0.5	0.1
Toole	165	2	18	99	71.5	2.8	30	181	24.2	2.5	8	32	1.4	0.2
Treasure	0	0	3	22	8.8	0.6	5	25	2.2	0.2	NA	NA	NA	NA
Valley	0	0	15	126	71.2	2.5	52	342	53.1	4.8	7	28	1.2	0.3
Wheatland	0	0	3	17	3.8	0.3	14	89	10.6	0.8	2	D	D	D
Wibaux	0	0	1	D	D	D	2	D	D	D	NA	NA	NA	NA
Yellowstone	54 381	464	389	4 915	2 648.9	143.4	717	8 736	1 575.6	144.9	195	770	85.9	12.3
NEBRASKA	830 393	9 105	3 157	41 002	38 015.4	1 170.2	8 295	102 684	16 529.3	1 554.6	1 587	8 240	891.1	160.8
Adams	8 399	85	60	D	D	D	180	2 204	289.5	30.4	39	97	10.9	1.3
Antelope	1 730	16	21	162	88.4	3.1	51	314	52.1	3.7	2	D	D	D
Arthur	NA	NA	NA	NA	NA	NA	3	5	0.3	0.0	NA	NA	NA	NA
Banner	NA	NA	1	D	D	D	NA	NA	NA	NA	NA	NA	NA	NA

1. Establishments with payroll.

STATE County	Professional, Scientific, and Technical Services[1], 1997				Manufacturing, 1997				Accommodation and Foodservices, 1997			
	Number of Establishments	Number of Employees	Receipts (mil dol)	Annual Payroll (mil dol)	Number of Establishments	Number of Employees	Receipts (mil dol)	Annual Payroll (mil dol)	Number of Establishments	Number of Employees	Sales (mil dol)	Annual Payroll (mil dol)
	147	148	149	150	151	152	153	154	155	156	157	158
MISSOURI—Cont'd												
St. Louis city	963	13 915	1 819.8	663.7	802	33 836	8 605.5	1 243.6	954	18 843	686.6	195.8
MONTANA	2 082	10 735	769.4	297.7	1 160	19 611	4 866.3	560.1	3 278	38 533	1 198.9	325.4
Beaverhead......................	22	51	2.9	0.9	NA	NA	NA	NA	47	337	11.1	2.4
Big Horn......................	13	50	2.3	1.0	NA	NA	NA	NA	35	241	8.1	2.0
Blaine......................	8	12	0.6	0.3	NA	NA	NA	NA	18	101	2.5	0.7
Broadwater......................	4	7	0.6	0.2	NA	NA	NA	NA	17	128	3.3	0.8
Carbon......................	14	51	2.1	0.7	NA	NA	NA	NA	52	417	14.3	4.4
Carter......................	1	D	D	D	NA	NA	NA	NA	5	17	0.4	0.1
Cascade......................	176	994	69.3	28.6	80	925	228.5	23.9	267	3 592	109.7	29.4
Chouteau......................	4	10	0.5	0.1	NA	NA	NA	NA	22	71	1.7	0.4
Custer......................	26	117	5.7	2.4	NA	NA	NA	NA	43	629	17.2	4.9
Daniels......................	3	9	0.4	0.1	NA	NA	NA	NA	10	D	D	D
Dawson......................	12	50	1.5	0.5	NA	NA	NA	NA	29	415	9.4	2.6
Deer Lodge......................	10	25	2.7	0.4	NA	NA	NA	NA	39	420	12.2	3.3
Fallon......................	5	11	0.3	0.1	NA	NA	NA	NA	12	88	2.9	0.5
Fergus......................	27	77	4.2	1.0	NA	NA	NA	NA	49	652	16.5	4.2
Flathead......................	187	659	44.8	16.0	124	3 887	790.5	121.5	319	3 940	132.1	35.9
Gallatin......................	259	1 031	87.6	33.3	148	1 992	273.8	48.3	285	4 694	154.0	44.1
Garfield......................	1	D	D	D	NA	NA	NA	NA	5	D	D	D
Glacier......................	16	46	2.8	1.2	NA	NA	NA	NA	52	403	18.5	4.4
Golden Valley......................	NA	NA	NA	NA	NA	NA	NA	NA	4	13	0.5	0.1
Granite......................	4	2	0.5	0.1	NA	NA	NA	NA	15	85	1.8	0.4
Hill......................	32	156	9.0	3.6	NA	NA	NA	NA	53	679	18.6	4.9
Jefferson......................	11	21	1.5	0.5	NA	NA	NA	NA	27	205	5.1	1.2
Judith Basin......................	1	D	D	D	NA	NA	NA	NA	13	D	D	D
Lake......................	37	127	7.1	2.7	30	840	115.3	19.5	86	594	20.5	5.3
Lewis and Clark......................	159	1 174	104.9	39.3	46	D	D	D	182	2 343	67.7	18.1
Liberty......................	5	14	0.8	0.2	NA	NA	NA	NA	4	16	0.5	0.1
Lincoln......................	23	56	3.1	1.0	33	657	125.4	21.3	68	439	16.7	3.8
McCone......................	1	D	D	D	NA	NA	NA	NA	5	D	D	D
Madison......................	8	16	1.0	0.4	NA	NA	NA	NA	44	117	7.7	1.9
Meagher......................	3	3	0.3	0.1	NA	NA	NA	NA	16	57	2.6	0.6
Mineral......................	3	4	0.4	0.0	NA	NA	NA	NA	24	178	4.8	1.5
Missoula......................	276	1 617	109.7	45.2	136	2 690	562.3	89.4	329	4 782	145.6	40.4
Musselshell......................	11	20	1.1	0.3	NA	NA	NA	NA	20	D	D	D
Park......................	46	138	7.4	2.6	36	535	63.3	13.3	111	1 043	34.0	9.7
Petroleum......................	NA	NA	NA	NA	NA	NA	NA	NA	3	D	D	D
Phillips......................	5	14	0.8	0.3	NA	NA	NA	NA	23	140	4.0	0.9
Pondera......................	10	45	1.8	0.8	NA	NA	NA	NA	18	D	D	D
Powder River......................	2	D	D	D	NA	NA	NA	NA	7	D	D	D
Powell......................	4	5	0.3	0.1	NA	NA	NA	NA	25	D	D	D
Prairie......................	2	D	D	D	NA	NA	NA	NA	5	D	D	D
Ravalli......................	52	223	11.9	6.4	66	870	95.2	21.3	92	793	21.1	6.0
Richland......................	25	95	6.1	2.3	NA	NA	NA	NA	40	401	10.3	2.7
Roosevelt......................	11	36	1.8	0.8	NA	NA	NA	NA	29	210	5.9	1.5
Rosebud......................	7	14	0.7	0.2	NA	NA	NA	NA	29	301	7.5	1.8
Sanders......................	11	38	1.1	0.5	NA	NA	NA	NA	27	189	4.9	1.2
Sheridan......................	8	30	1.3	0.4	NA	NA	NA	NA	26	D	D	D
Silver Bow......................	88	861	60.2	25.7	NA	NA	NA	NA	130	1 354	47.8	12.3
Stillwater......................	11	20	1.7	0.4	NA	NA	NA	NA	24	D	D	D
Sweet Grass......................	4	25	1.2	0.5	NA	NA	NA	NA	15	170	6.2	1.7
Teton......................	4	8	0.3	0.1	NA	NA	NA	NA	26	122	3.3	0.8
Toole......................	10	32	1.7	0.5	NA	NA	NA	NA	27	135	4.8	1.0
Treasure......................	2	D	D	D	NA	NA	NA	NA	4	D	D	D
Valley......................	9	44	2.9	1.0	NA	NA	NA	NA	33	261	7.6	1.8
Wheatland......................	2	D	D	D	NA	NA	NA	NA	14	77	1.8	0.4
Wibaux......................	3	6	0.2	0.1	NA	NA	NA	NA	9	D	D	D
Yellowstone......................	404	2 664	199.7	74.9	182	3 223	1 797.9	110.1	365	6 691	205.3	58.7
NEBRASKA......................	3 076	25 720	2 273.4	838.0	1 960	106 690	27 859.2	3 040.5	4 070	61 048	1 726.6	488.2
Adams......................	41	188	12.2	5.2	63	3 526	593.0	88.9	82	1 230	29.1	8.4
Antelope......................	11	19	0.9	0.3	NA	NA	NA	NA	17	146	2.8	0.7
Arthur......................	NA	NA	NA	NA	NA	NA	NA	NA	NA	NA	NA	NA
Banner......................	NA	NA	NA	NA	NA	NA	NA	NA	NA	NA	NA	NA

1. Firms subject to federal tax.

Table B. States and Counties — Health and Other Services and Federal Funds

STATE County	Health Care and Social Assistance[1], 1997				Other Services[1], 1997				Federal funds and grants, fiscal 2001[2] Expenditures (mil dol)			
									Total	Direct payments for individuals[3]		
	Number of Establishments	Number of Employees	Receipts (mil dol)	Annual Payroll (mil dol)	Number of Establishments	Number of Employees	Receipts (mil dol)	Annual Payroll (mil dol)		Social Security and government retirement	Medicare	Food stamps and Supplemental Security Income
	159	160	161	162	163	164	165	166	167	168	169	170
MISSOURI—Cont'd												
St. Louis city	581	9 806	612.5	263.9	673	4 693	334.1	101.2	8 500.5	766.7	528.6	174.3
MONTANA	2 034	15 673	928.6	412.6	1 612	6 986	449.1	117.0	6 617.9	2 062.9	603.7	125.2
Beaverhead	29	194	9.8	3.6	18	45	3.3	0.6	58.2	20.7	8.1	1.0
Big Horn	7	113	2.5	1.7	6	23	1.2	0.3	103.6	16.4	6.6	3.5
Blaine	5	25	1.2	0.4	8	17	1.3	0.3	80.3	12.5	3.8	1.1
Broadwater	6	20	0.6	0.2	9	8	1.2	0.1	31.0	11.4	3.1	0.5
Carbon	10	120	4.2	2.0	10	21	0.9	0.2	50.0	21.4	8.0	0.6
Carter	1	D	D	D	1	D	D	D	22.6	2.7	0.8	0.1
Cascade	205	1 729	104.2	40.5	153	690	43.3	11.4	689.5	220.1	62.8	11.5
Chouteau	6	44	1.1	0.5	6	8	0.7	0.1	99.2	12.8	4.4	0.3
Custer	38	273	13.7	7.7	17	80	5.6	1.4	92.5	32.1	9.0	0.7
Daniels	3	16	0.7	0.2	5	6	0.7	0.1	32.6	6.5	2.2	0.1
Dawson	20	92	4.1	1.4	22	81	5.1	1.3	60.5	23.0	7.2	0.6
Deer Lodge	30	153	9.2	3.1	9	23	1.8	0.4	60.6	29.5	10.7	2.0
Fallon	NA	NA	NA	NA	9	20	1.9	0.3	26.6	6.3	2.2	0.2
Fergus	36	239	11.1	3.9	21	64	4.3	0.7	95.5	31.8	12.5	1.2
Flathead	195	1 213	77.8	32.0	163	710	50.7	12.0	353.4	183.9	42.0	8.3
Gallatin	165	1 134	63.6	27.0	139	642	36.4	9.2	280.4	100.4	22.1	3.2
Garfield	NA	NA	NA	NA	1	D	D	D	20.4	2.7	1.0	0.1
Glacier	16	40	2.2	0.6	18	90	5.5	1.3	129.5	19.5	7.4	4.7
Golden Valley	1	D	D	D	NA	NA	NA	NA	11.7	2.5	0.8	0.1
Granite	2	D	D	D	NA	NA	NA	NA	13.9	6.6	2.0	0.2
Hill	25	107	6.3	3.0	52	167	8.8	2.2	178.7	37.5	12.7	3.4
Jefferson	18	129	5.2	2.8	7	21	1.2	0.3	49.3	23.3	4.6	0.7
Judith Basin	1	D	D	D	1	D	D	D	27.1	5.6	1.6	0.1
Lake	39	400	13.8	7.3	32	53	3.9	0.8	186.2	57.4	17.2	4.0
Lewis and Clark	159	1 257	70.4	27.3	88	412	24.0	6.5	654.6	144.3	33.3	14.6
Liberty	2	D	D	D	5	5	0.6	0.1	48.8	8.1	2.0	0.1
Lincoln	33	214	9.7	3.3	30	70	5.4	1.1	129.2	58.0	12.4	4.4
McCone	3	D	D	D	1	D	D	D	31.4	3.8	1.9	0.2
Madison	3	9	0.6	0.1	10	39	2.5	0.5	36.9	16.5	4.8	0.2
Meagher	4	18	0.5	0.1	1	D	D	D	13.8	4.7	1.5	0.3
Mineral	7	15	0.7	0.2	5	8	0.4	0.1	26.3	12.6	2.9	0.7
Missoula	285	2 305	151.7	70.7	184	956	61.9	17.0	465.6	177.4	49.1	13.4
Musselshell	3	9	0.4	0.1	4	9	0.8	0.2	35.4	11.8	4.2	0.6
Park	31	342	13.8	6.1	35	147	9.1	2.2	73.0	37.5	12.1	1.5
Petroleum	NA	NA	NA	NA	NA	NA	NA	NA	6.8	0.9	0.3	0.0
Phillips	6	19	0.7	0.4	11	31	2.6	0.4	52.7	10.9	4.6	0.7
Pondera	12	46	2.2	0.5	10	25	2.0	0.4	68.8	15.1	6.5	0.9
Powder River	1	D	D	D	5	6	0.5	0.1	38.0	3.2	1.0	0.1
Powell	9	96	1.9	1.0	6	9	0.5	0.1	37.6	15.5	4.6	0.9
Prairie	NA	NA	NA	NA	2	D	D	D	14.8	3.6	1.4	0.3
Ravalli	56	395	17.6	7.2	51	186	11.1	2.9	198.8	100.3	23.3	3.8
Richland	21	86	5.8	1.5	23	61	4.6	1.1	70.4	20.3	8.9	1.1
Roosevelt	10	214	6.9	4.4	11	19	1.2	0.2	106.3	19.6	8.2	3.5
Rosebud	11	40	2.0	0.5	6	22	2.0	0.4	73.4	15.5	4.5	1.9
Sanders	19	110	6.8	3.0	10	26	1.6	0.3	60.2	32.8	8.1	1.9
Sheridan	5	37	1.7	0.9	6	19	1.5	0.3	49.2	12.1	4.4	0.3
Silver Bow	114	1 055	53.4	24.7	71	282	16.6	4.3	231.5	90.7	35.5	7.1
Stillwater	7	128	4.0	1.9	11	26	2.3	0.4	41.5	17.8	5.3	0.4
Sweet Grass	2	D	D	D	3	5	0.5	0.1	14.9	7.4	2.3	0.2
Teton	9	76	7.0	1.6	5	4	0.5	0.2	67.5	15.9	5.6	0.6
Toole	13	47	3.8	1.6	3	6	0.5	0.1	96.0	8.4	4.9	0.5
Treasure	NA	NA	NA	NA	NA	NA	NA	NA	6.2	1.9	0.8	0.0
Valley	15	63	4.2	1.9	15	38	3.2	0.5	94.5	23.6	7.0	1.2
Wheatland	2	D	D	D	1	D	D	D	20.0	6.0	3.2	0.2
Wibaux	NA	NA	NA	NA	1	D	D	D	11.6	2.5	0.7	0.1
Yellowstone	334	2 942	228.1	114.5	291	1 788	114.1	34.1	687.9	275.7	85.7	15.3
NEBRASKA	3 057	34 763	2 027.7	970.3	3 288	16 940	1 039.2	297.1	10 771.4	3 575.5	1 120.2	171.5
Adams	71	598	49.0	23.2	50	229	16.4	4.3	174.7	69.5	21.6	3.1
Antelope	9	127	3.9	2.2	18	36	2.3	0.4	109.0	15.6	6.8	0.5
Arthur	NA	NA	NA	NA	1	D	D	D	2.8	1.3	0.3	0.1
Banner	NA	NA	NA	NA	NA	NA	NA	NA	11.4	1.1	0.3	0.0

1. Firms subject to federal tax.   2. October 1, 2000 to September 30, 2001.   3. State totals may include programs not allocated by county.

Table B. States and Counties — **Federal Funds and Local Government Finances**

	Federal funds and grants, fiscal 2001[1] (cont'd)							Local government finances, 1997				
	Expenditures (mil dol) (cont'd)							General revenue				
	Procurement contract awards			Grants[2]						Taxes		
											Per capita[3] (dollars)	
STATE County	Salaries and wages	Defense	Other	Medicaid and other health-related	Nutrition and family welfare	Education	Other	Total (mil dol)	Intergovern-mental (mil dol)	Total (mil dol)	Total	Property
	171	172	173	174	175	176	177	178	179	180	181	182

MISSOURI—Cont'd

St. Louis city	744.8	4 511.6	344.3	678.6	131.2	42.5	379.1	1 446.8	474.8	554.4	1 622	667
MONTANA	710.8	127.2	243.3	528.9	180.6	190.9	764.7	X	X	X	X	X
Beaverhead	9.0	0.0	1.4	4.7	1.0	1.2	5.8	33.4	6.9	9.8	1 091	1 075
Big Horn	20.1	0.0	3.8	9.5	3.4	10.6	13.7	28.8	15.5	9.0	713	699
Blaine	7.7	-0.4	2.8	7.7	2.6	8.2	7.3	20.0	12.0	4.9	697	681
Broadwater	1.9	0.0	1.1	1.8	0.4	0.1	4.5	7.3	2.9	3.2	784	763
Carbon	3.0	0.0	0.5	4.0	0.7	0.3	7.0	18.0	8.8	6.2	657	627
Carter	0.9	0.0	0.2	0.7	0.1	0.1	8.7	3.3	1.1	1.7	1 162	1 147
Cascade	169.2	60.9	8.0	66.8	11.6	5.1	31.8	135.2	61.8	42.8	541	514
Chouteau	1.7	0.0	1.4	1.1	0.4	0.2	10.1	21.8	4.7	7.9	1 515	1 473
Custer	11.0	0.0	2.8	9.9	1.6	0.9	15.6	28.0	11.4	6.9	572	551
Daniels	1.2	0.0	0.2	0.4	0.1	0.1	1.3	8.4	2.7	2.6	1 244	1 225
Dawson	2.5	0.0	0.5	4.1	1.6	1.0	4.1	23.9	10.4	7.2	795	778
Deer Lodge	3.9	0.0	0.5	7.7	3.0	0.7	1.4	15.8	7.7	4.9	491	467
Fallon	0.5	0.0	0.2	0.7	0.2	0.2	7.5	14.7	9.4	3.1	1 012	990
Fergus	7.4	0.1	1.9	7.7	1.2	0.9	7.0	23.3	10.7	8.5	677	659
Flathead	35.1	6.6	15.2	26.3	7.7	4.0	15.6	135.0	51.0	52.9	737	677
Gallatin	30.2	2.3	4.8	26.1	3.6	3.7	65.0	105.6	35.5	37.6	616	555
Garfield	0.8	0.0	0.6	0.4	0.0	0.1	2.7	3.4	1.4	1.4	965	947
Glacier	16.3	0.0	3.8	14.4	4.8	13.7	14.1	36.5	20.0	7.6	599	586
Golden Valley	0.3	0.0	0.1	0.0	0.1	0.0	2.1	3.1	1.2	1.4	1 370	1 341
Granite	1.4	0.0	0.6	1.1	0.4	0.2	0.8	8.3	2.4	3.1	1 161	1 141
Hill	6.4	0.0	2.0	12.7	4.7	10.6	25.1	39.2	21.0	11.9	678	660
Jefferson	10.4	-0.2	0.5	4.4	0.7	0.6	2.9	17.6	6.7	7.2	727	712
Judith Basin	1.4	0.0	0.4	1.1	0.1	0.1	3.8	5.9	2.2	2.9	1 254	1 234
Lake	6.2	30.6	9.5	17.6	3.8	10.9	12.4	42.8	20.6	13.0	513	503
Lewis and Clark	66.1	4.5	21.5	53.8	58.5	50.0	167.6	105.2	41.1	37.5	703	665
Liberty	1.3	0.1	0.9	0.4	0.1	0.1	4.9	10.1	2.9	3.1	1 304	1 288
Lincoln	16.9	2.3	12.3	8.7	4.0	2.2	7.0	32.1	17.6	8.3	442	429
McCone	1.0	0.2	0.2	1.1	0.2	0.1	2.5	4.6	1.6	2.4	1 174	1 156
Madison	3.0	0.0	0.9	1.8	0.2	0.2	7.1	19.4	4.6	7.7	1 117	953
Meagher	0.9	0.0	1.0	1.5	0.2	0.1	1.1	4.1	1.4	2.3	1 247	1 224
Mineral	2.1	0.2	1.0	1.1	0.6	0.5	4.6	12.1	6.7	3.8	1 008	990
Missoula	69.9	5.6	22.2	55.6	12.7	10.6	27.7	158.2	57.6	74.9	843	814
Musselshell	0.8	0.0	0.1	2.2	0.5	0.2	8.9	9.4	5.5	2.5	552	537
Park	4.0	0.1	0.9	7.5	1.6	1.2	3.1	27.2	10.2	9.0	566	542
Petroleum	0.2	0.1	0.0	0.0	0.0	0.0	1.2	2.3	1.3	0.5	967	936
Phillips	2.6	0.0	0.5	5.8	0.5	0.5	8.3	15.3	6.9	4.4	907	882
Pondera	2.2	0.0	0.4	4.3	0.5	3.1	3.5	15.8	9.0	4.7	723	699
Powder River	0.9	0.0	0.7	0.4	0.1	0.3	22.7	10.8	3.3	2.7	1 425	1 365
Powell	3.4	0.0	1.9	2.6	0.9	1.2	5.8	11.6	5.7	3.9	549	524
Prairie	0.4	0.0	0.1	0.7	0.0	0.1	1.7	6.5	1.9	1.5	1 159	1 138
Ravalli	21.9	0.7	11.8	12.0	3.2	2.0	16.9	46.7	23.5	16.7	482	465
Richland	4.1	0.0	7.1	4.8	1.2	0.6	2.2	24.4	12.2	6.7	655	639
Roosevelt	9.7	2.7	2.0	8.9	2.9	14.8	8.8	38.8	20.3	7.5	675	663
Rosebud	8.0	0.0	6.2	7.4	1.9	5.7	10.4	54.1	12.1	11.7	1 143	1 130
Sanders	4.7	0.0	1.1	5.8	1.2	1.5	2.3	20.6	9.1	8.2	801	782
Sheridan	2.9	0.0	0.8	2.9	0.3	0.3	2.5	11.6	5.9	3.6	838	822
Silver Bow	14.7	3.7	27.3	28.3	7.2	2.7	7.6	64.5	25.1	23.8	691	607
Stillwater	1.7	0.0	0.4	1.1	0.4	0.4	6.1	15.5	6.4	6.6	849	825
Sweet Grass	1.5	0.0	0.2	0.7	0.2	0.2	1.0	7.4	2.0	2.3	673	655
Teton	2.5	0.0	0.5	3.3	0.4	0.2	9.5	18.7	5.8	5.6	889	830
Toole	3.4	0.0	27.8	2.2	0.4	0.3	15.7	23.8	6.8	5.9	1 217	1 182
Treasure	0.3	0.0	0.1	0.0	0.1	0.0	1.1	2.2	0.7	1.1	1 347	1 327
Valley	7.1	5.4	3.1	5.4	0.8	1.8	9.5	21.6	9.5	8.0	963	946
Wheatland	1.5	0.0	0.2	1.1	0.2	0.1	2.1	5.2	2.0	2.7	1 145	1 123
Wibaux	0.3	0.0	0.1	1.1	0.1	0.0	1.3	3.6	1.7	1.5	1 350	1 333
Yellowstone	102.5	1.6	27.1	65.6	15.2	8.8	42.5	248.1	82.9	83.5	664	613
NEBRASKA	1 053.5	189.6	257.3	953.2	287.0	192.7	621.5	X	X	X	X	X
Adams	6.5	2.7	1.0	19.2	4.1	1.5	2.1	89.3	24.9	40.4	1 357	1 194
Antelope	1.9	0.3	2.5	4.5	0.7	0.3	41.8	17.3	6.6	8.6	1 175	1 067
Arthur	0.1	0.0	0.0	0.0	0.0	0.0	0.0	1.7	0.2	1.2	2 836	2 785
Banner	0.1	0.0	0.0	0.0	0.0	0.1	0.8	3.0	0.7	1.6	1 866	1 740

1. October 1, 2000 to September 30, 2001. 2. State totals may include programs not allocated by county. 3. Based on the resident population estimated as of July 1 of the year shown.

Table B. States and Counties — Local Government Finances, Government Employment, and Elections

	Local government finances, 1997 (cont'd)									Government employment, 1999			Presidential election, 2000[2]		
	Direct general expenditure							Debt outstanding					Percent of vote cast —		
			Percent of total for —												
STATE County	Total (mil dol)	Per capita[1] (dollars)	Education	Health and hospitals	Police protection	Public welfare	Highways	Total (mil dol)	Per capita[1] (dollars)	Federal civilian	Federal military	State and local	Democratic	Republican	All other
	183	184	185	186	187	188	189	190	191	192	193	194	195	196	197
MISSOURI—Cont'd															
St. Louis city	1 294.2	3 786	37.2	2.4	8.6	0.0	1.1	947.1	2 770	17 358	2 578	27 111	77.4	19.9	2.7
MONTANA	X	X	X	X	X	X	X	X	X	12 522	8 563	62 346	33.4	58.4	8.1
Beaverhead	27.1	3 008	41.3	34.2	3.2	0.5	3.8	7.6	841	194	49	768	19.0	74.2	6.8
Big Horn	31.1	2 464	69.5	1.2	3.0	1.5	6.7	2.3	179	434	71	774	56.4	39.7	3.9
Blaine	20.2	2 849	65.4	1.2	3.8	1.7	9.0	4.0	570	196	40	468	45.2	51.1	3.7
Broadwater	7.5	1 844	54.1	3.0	7.1	1.8	3.9	2.5	624	38	23	173	22.3	71.7	5.9
Carbon	19.0	2 019	57.8	1.6	4.6	1.6	6.5	7.6	811	73	54	475	29.9	62.8	7.2
Carter	3.6	2 406	53.6	6.7	3.0	2.4	12.6	0.5	319	21	0	122	8.2	88.8	3.0
Cascade	145.9	1 843	53.3	1.9	4.1	0.8	3.0	71.9	908	1 458	3 954	3 889	39.4	54.5	6.0
Chouteau	22.5	4 290	40.4	32.3	2.3	1.3	6.0	10.5	2 009	36	29	465	23.8	70.7	5.6
Custer	26.9	2 218	61.2	3.2	5.6	1.3	5.4	3.9	325	275	67	824	30.6	64.3	5.0
Daniels	9.1	4 401	46.8	25.2	2.5	1.1	3.5	4.4	2 140	30	11	175	27.3	67.6	5.1
Dawson	24.1	2 667	62.1	2.5	3.6	1.9	6.1	7.2	795	43	49	875	31.9	63.8	4.3
Deer Lodge	16.7	1 671	55.7	3.2	7.9	0.8	3.7	11.8	1 181	79	55	873	58.9	32.9	8.1
Fallon	13.7	4 505	49.8	8.4	3.5	2.4	8.2	0.5	162	13	16	258	18.7	77.5	3.8
Fergus	24.0	1 924	71.7	1.5	3.8	1.5	4.3	3.8	303	143	69	904	22.6	72.6	4.9
Flathead	130.6	1 821	62.7	2.9	5.4	0.7	3.9	46.7	651	824	411	3 338	24.6	66.5	8.8
Gallatin	108.3	1 772	49.5	1.0	3.4	4.6	4.0	82.9	1 357	540	379	7 676	31.2	58.8	9.9
Garfield	3.8	2 614	51.5	4.8	4.9	2.5	8.1	0.0	18	25	0	114	8.2	87.5	4.3
Glacier	41.0	3 233	65.5	12.8	2.3	1.8	3.6	3.9	309	434	71	815	53.6	41.4	5.0
Golden Valley	3.3	3 140	72.9	0.5	2.5	1.2	5.0	2.0	1 855	10	0	74	16.6	76.3	7.2
Granite	8.4	3 206	42.1	4.0	5.0	17.9	7.3	1.0	367	39	15	230	18.6	74.3	7.2
Hill	39.6	2 256	67.1	1.1	4.7	0.8	4.7	14.5	824	125	101	1 415	42.1	51.7	6.2
Jefferson	19.1	1 937	58.4	1.6	4.1	1.2	4.2	12.9	1 306	62	58	801	29.3	64.1	6.7
Judith Basin	5.6	2 410	66.0	1.7	2.2	1.2	8.8	0.0	17	35	13	171	19.9	75.8	4.2
Lake	44.7	1 765	67.2	5.9	4.3	0.6	4.4	7.3	290	131	146	1 161	33.9	56.3	9.9
Lewis and Clark	103.8	1 950	53.9	3.0	5.2	3.3	5.0	66.3	1 245	1 328	307	7 101	36.6	55.3	8.0
Liberty	9.9	4 155	44.5	32.0	2.8	1.5	5.5	1.4	568	24	13	166	23.3	72.0	4.7
Lincoln	35.4	1 886	64.7	1.9	6.0	0.2	8.8	4.7	252	496	106	890	20.8	71.1	8.1
McCone	5.1	2 522	56.5	3.9	3.8	2.4	6.0	0.0	3	22	11	139	23.4	72.4	4.2
Madison	19.6	2 845	42.3	13.8	3.7	12.6	6.0	1.5	210	72	39	424	20.7	72.6	6.6
Meagher	4.5	2 483	50.4	2.9	6.0	1.0	17.2	0.4	217	31	10	131	18.8	74.7	6.5
Mineral	12.5	3 352	55.3	0.6	3.9	0.3	2.8	5.6	1 505	62	22	256	23.3	65.8	10.9
Missoula	163.4	1 839	54.6	4.7	5.4	0.4	3.6	111.4	1 254	1 302	515	7 731	37.0	46.1	16.9
Musselshell	9.1	1 983	64.1	1.3	4.4	1.6	4.4	1.0	215	16	26	226	23.2	71.7	5.1
Park	28.6	1 800	58.8	2.6	4.8	0.1	3.6	8.0	502	85	90	634	29.1	61.1	9.8
Petroleum	3.0	5 882	32.7	0.3	0.9	3.5	4.3	1.1	2 195	0	0	62	11.8	83.0	5.3
Phillips	16.8	3 432	61.1	1.2	4.1	1.5	8.3	6.6	1 345	57	26	361	19.0	77.5	3.5
Pondera	16.7	2 591	72.7	2.0	4.0	0.9	5.7	4.6	716	46	35	434	27.3	67.3	5.4
Powder River	8.1	4 247	43.7	1.2	2.8	18.8	6.2	0.3	178	19	10	210	11.4	85.3	3.3
Powell	12.5	1 762	62.3	1.5	6.0	0.2	8.9	0.9	129	76	39	975	22.5	69.6	7.9
Prairie	6.4	4 790	29.2	38.3	2.4	1.9	3.2	1.8	1 379	15	0	158	22.0	72.5	5.5
Ravalli	49.8	1 441	68.0	0.9	4.6	2.1	4.1	15.1	437	464	202	1 276	25.8	65.2	8.9
Richland	23.9	2 348	65.0	1.1	5.1	1.0	7.9	12.3	1 210	80	57	608	25.2	70.9	3.9
Roosevelt	40.0	3 594	61.6	18.0	3.3	1.1	3.5	5.3	479	225	61	841	54.0	42.1	3.9
Rosebud	54.6	5 353	39.7	0.7	2.8	0.7	2.5	426.0	41 732	194	56	574	40.7	53.3	5.9
Sanders	21.6	2 104	61.8	0.8	4.2	0.9	7.5	7.7	750	133	58	543	24.7	66.6	8.8
Sheridan	12.0	2 765	63.2	0.7	5.1	2.5	8.4	1.5	337	72	23	283	35.7	59.8	4.5
Silver Bow	77.3	2 245	41.7	2.4	5.2	1.3	3.9	73.4	2 130	316	209	2 155	53.7	37.7	8.6
Stillwater	16.2	2 062	56.4	1.6	4.0	0.8	7.7	2.8	353	38	47	385	23.6	70.6	5.8
Sweet Grass	7.8	2 295	49.9	3.2	4.9	16.1	6.3	0.9	264	37	20	274	16.5	78.5	4.9
Teton	19.9	3 136	50.3	19.9	2.5	0.7	5.3	8.6	1 360	63	36	414	25.6	69.2	5.2
Toole	21.5	4 453	36.3	36.7	4.0	1.4	6.6	4.9	1 014	71	26	572	26.5	68.9	4.5
Treasure	2.5	2 920	63.2	1.3	3.7	0.9	7.7	0.5	580	0	0	75	22.1	71.8	6.0
Valley	23.4	2 815	56.4	1.0	3.5	3.3	5.2	6.8	818	135	46	574	32.1	63.1	4.8
Wheatland	5.6	2 387	67.8	1.9	5.4	0.7	7.1	0.4	150	40	13	150	24.3	70.9	4.8
Wibaux	4.1	3 727	39.6	3.3	7.6	2.6	13.4	0.2	201	11	0	93	23.4	71.2	5.4
Yellowstone	245.0	1 948	51.1	3.9	7.0	1.0	3.1	122.8	976	1 724	735	6 793	35.4	59.0	5.5
NEBRASKA	X	X	X	X	X	X	X	X	X	15 621	14 981	129 284	33.3	62.2	4.5
Adams	82.2	2 764	71.3	0.5	4.9	0.2	8.0	92.5	3 108	124	122	2 502	29.6	65.6	4.7
Antelope	18.7	2 537	65.0	0.2	0.7	0.0	14.5	2.0	278	42	30	528	20.1	76.1	3.8
Arthur	1.7	3 869	54.4	0.2	1.3	0.0	6.9	0.0	12	0	0	42	9.6	86.4	4.0
Banner	2.9	3 385	69.5	0.0	1.1	0.0	13.6	0.0	0	0	0	70	14.1	84.4	1.5

1. Based on the resident population estimated as of July 1 of the year shown.   2. Data subject to copyright.

Table B. States and Counties — Land Area and Population

					Population and population characteristics, 2000													
STATE/ County code	MSA/ PMSA/ NECMA code[1]	County Type[2]	STATE County	Land area,[3] (sq km) 2000				Race alone or in combination (percent)					Age (percent)					
					Total persons	Rank	Per square kilometer	White	Black	Am. Indian, Alaska Native	Asian and Pacific Islander	Percent Hispanic[4]	Under 5 years	5 to 17 years	18 to 24 years	25 to 34 years	35 to 44 years	45 to 54 years
				1	2	3	4	5	6	7	8	9	10	11	12	13	14	15

NEBRASKA—Cont'd

STATE/ County code	MSA code	Type	County	Land area	Total persons	Rank	Per sq km	White	Black	Am. Ind.	Asian	Hispanic	Under 5	5–17	18–24	25–34	35–44	45–54
31 009	...	9	Blaine	1 841	583	3 133	0.3	99.5	0.0	1.0	0.0	0.2	5.5	20.8	3.9	11.1	15.4	13.6
31 011	...	9	Boone	1 779	6 259	2 760	3.5	99.5	0.1	0.2	0.0	0.9	5.9	23.2	5.0	8.9	15.2	12.3
31 013	...	7	Box Butte	2 785	12 158	2 287	4.4	92.6	0.6	3.8	0.8	7.6	6.6	21.6	7.4	10.8	16.0	15.2
31 015	...	9	Boyd	1 399	2 438	3 027	1.7	99.3	0.0	0.9	0.2	0.1	5.0	19.9	5.4	6.8	14.4	13.5
31 017	...	9	Brown	3 163	3 525	2 952	1.1	99.2	0.2	0.5	0.5	0.8	5.3	19.5	5.2	9.0	13.9	13.8
31 019	...	5	Buffalo	2 507	42 259	1 052	16.9	96.1	0.8	0.6	1.0	4.7	6.6	18.4	17.8	13.1	13.6	12.1
31 021	...	8	Burt	1 276	7 791	2 626	6.1	98.3	0.2	1.5	0.4	1.3	5.7	20.0	5.4	8.5	14.9	13.5
31 023	...	6	Butler	1 511	8 767	2 548	5.8	98.7	0.2	0.4	0.2	1.7	6.8	21.0	6.6	10.3	15.1	13.1
31 025	5920	2	Cass	1 448	24 334	1 581	16.8	98.8	0.3	0.7	0.6	1.5	7.0	20.9	7.0	11.9	17.1	14.4
31 027	...	9	Cedar	1 917	9 615	2 478	5.0	99.5	0.1	0.4	0.3	0.4	6.1	23.4	6.0	9.7	14.6	12.0
31 029	...	9	Chase	2 317	4 068	2 914	1.8	98.1	0.2	0.2	0.2	3.4	5.6	19.6	5.9	9.3	14.6	13.6
31 031	...	7	Cherry	15 438	6 148	2 767	0.4	95.7	0.2	4.5	0.8	0.9	6.2	20.8	6.2	11.1	14.4	13.6
31 033	...	7	Cheyenne	3 099	9 830	2 463	3.2	97.3	0.2	0.9	0.6	4.5	6.4	19.9	7.0	11.4	15.3	13.8
31 035	...	9	Clay	1 484	7 039	2 680	4.7	98.0	0.2	0.5	0.3	3.5	5.8	21.5	5.9	9.7	15.6	13.8
31 037	...	7	Colfax	1 070	10 441	2 402	9.8	83.3	0.2	0.4	0.6	26.2	7.2	21.7	8.5	12.6	15.3	10.9
31 039	...	7	Cuming	1 481	10 203	2 428	6.9	96.7	0.2	0.4	0.4	5.5	6.5	20.7	6.5	10.5	14.7	12.2
31 041	...	7	Custer	6 671	11 793	2 307	1.8	99.2	0.1	0.7	0.2	0.9	5.7	20.6	5.5	9.2	14.3	13.5
31 043	7720	3	Dakota	683	20 253	1 776	29.7	81.1	1.0	2.6	3.6	22.6	8.7	21.7	10.1	14.4	15.0	12.3
31 045	...	7	Dawes	3 616	9 060	2 524	2.5	94.8	1.0	3.7	0.8	2.4	5.0	16.2	23.4	9.3	11.1	11.7
31 047	...	7	Dawson	2 623	24 365	1 580	9.3	83.7	0.4	1.1	0.8	25.4	8.4	20.8	8.4	13.4	14.2	12.6
31 049	...	9	Deuel	1 139	2 098	3 058	1.8	98.0	0.0	0.7	0.6	2.7	4.3	19.0	4.9	8.2	16.2	13.7
31 051	...	8	Dixon	1 234	6 339	2 752	5.1	95.4	0.1	0.7	0.4	5.5	6.4	21.1	7.1	10.7	14.2	13.7
31 053	...	4	Dodge	1 384	36 160	1 209	26.1	96.5	0.6	0.6	0.9	3.9	6.2	18.5	9.6	11.3	14.9	12.7
31 055	5920	2	Douglas	857	463 585	124	540.9	82.4	12.3	1.1	2.2	6.7	7.4	19.2	10.3	15.2	16.0	13.3
31 057	...	9	Dundy	2 382	2 292	3 040	1.0	97.8	0.2	1.4	0.6	3.2	5.3	18.0	5.7	9.1	14.4	15.7
31 059	...	9	Fillmore	1 493	6 634	2 722	4.4	98.4	0.3	1.0	0.1	1.7	5.8	20.5	5.1	9.6	14.4	13.3
31 061	...	9	Franklin	1 492	3 574	2 946	2.4	99.6	0.0	0.5	0.1	0.6	5.2	19.3	4.5	9.3	14.3	13.0
31 063	...	9	Frontier	2 524	3 099	2 985	1.2	99.0	0.1	0.7	0.5	1.0	5.5	20.5	11.3	8.6	14.2	12.9
31 065	...	9	Furnas	1 860	5 324	2 828	2.9	99.0	0.1	0.9	0.2	1.1	5.6	18.5	5.3	9.0	13.9	13.6
31 067	...	6	Gage	2 215	22 993	1 643	10.4	98.5	0.5	1.1	0.5	0.9	5.9	18.1	7.7	11.0	15.3	13.4
31 069	...	9	Garden	4 414	2 292	3 040	0.5	98.8	0.1	0.7	0.3	1.4	3.6	18.2	4.6	7.2	15.4	13.7
31 071	...	9	Garfield	1 476	1 902	3 073	1.3	99.3	0.1	0.6	0.2	1.0	4.8	18.7	4.4	7.0	13.5	14.1
31 073	...	9	Gosper	1 187	2 143	3 057	1.8	99.2	0.0	0.4	0.3	1.3	5.2	18.6	5.4	8.4	15.6	13.8
31 075	...	9	Grant	2 010	747	3 129	0.4	98.8	0.0	0.1	0.3	1.3	5.0	24.2	5.2	7.9	16.5	15.8
31 077	...	9	Greeley	1 476	2 714	3 013	1.8	98.4	0.8	0.3	0.1	0.8	5.7	21.3	5.9	8.7	13.0	12.8
31 079	...	5	Hall	1 415	53 534	874	37.8	89.8	0.5	0.6	1.5	14.0	7.6	19.5	8.9	13.2	15.2	13.3
31 081	...	7	Hamilton	1 408	9 403	2 497	6.7	99.0	0.3	0.3	0.3	1.1	6.7	22.4	5.9	10.6	15.9	14.2
31 083	...	9	Harlan	1 432	3 786	2 930	2.6	99.5	0.2	0.4	0.1	0.8	4.8	19.4	5.0	7.9	13.7	14.8
31 085	...	9	Hayes	1 847	1 068	3 107	0.6	97.8	0.4	0.2	0.5	2.5	4.4	22.2	5.5	6.3	15.3	15.8
31 087	...	9	Hitchcock	1 839	3 111	2 984	1.7	99.2	0.2	0.9	0.1	1.4	4.3	19.4	5.9	7.6	15.0	13.9
31 089	...	7	Holt	6 249	11 551	2 329	1.8	99.2	0.1	0.5	0.3	0.7	5.8	21.4	5.7	8.9	15.6	13.3
31 091	...	9	Hooker	1 868	783	3 126	0.4	99.4	0.0	1.0	0.1	1.0	4.1	19.9	4.1	7.0	14.6	13.8
31 093	...	9	Howard	1 475	6 567	2 731	4.5	99.0	0.3	0.4	0.1	1.0	6.0	22.3	6.6	10.5	14.8	13.1
31 095	...	7	Jefferson	1 484	8 333	2 578	5.6	98.8	0.1	0.7	0.3	1.3	5.3	18.0	6.1	9.6	14.1	14.3
31 097	...	8	Johnson	974	4 488	2 881	4.6	94.1	0.2	0.9	3.4	2.9	5.5	18.7	5.7	8.8	15.6	13.3
31 099	...	7	Kearney	1 337	6 882	2 698	5.1	98.4	0.2	0.5	0.3	2.3	6.2	20.6	6.4	11.2	16.3	13.4
31 101	...	7	Keith	2 749	8 875	2 535	3.2	97.5	0.2	1.0	0.4	4.2	5.7	19.5	5.7	9.9	15.4	13.8
31 103	...	9	Keya Paha	2 003	983	3 112	0.5	99.8	0.0	0.4	0.0	3.9	6.1	17.7	6.7	9.8	13.6	13.1
31 105	...	6	Kimball	2 465	4 089	2 910	1.7	98.3	0.4	1.4	0.1	3.3	5.4	19.3	5.9	8.4	14.7	13.5
31 107	...	9	Knox	2 870	9 374	2 500	3.3	92.2	0.1	7.5	0.3	0.9	5.7	19.8	5.5	8.1	13.8	13.6
31 109	4360	3	Lancaster	2 173	250 291	230	115.2	91.7	3.5	1.1	3.4	3.4	6.7	16.8	15.4	15.3	15.1	13.1
31 111	...	5	Lincoln	6 641	34 632	1 261	5.2	95.8	0.8	0.8	0.5	5.4	6.6	19.6	8.3	11.8	14.7	14.5
31 113	...	9	Logan	1 478	774	3 127	0.5	98.8	0.1	1.3	0.0	0.9	5.2	22.1	4.4	8.5	15.5	16.3
31 115	...	9	Loup	1 476	712	3 132	0.5	99.2	0.0	0.4	0.1	1.7	6.3	20.4	4.5	7.7	14.6	14.7
31 117	...	9	McPherson	2 225	533	3 135	0.2	97.9	0.0	0.0	0.4	1.5	7.3	20.3	5.3	10.5	15.6	13.7
31 119	...	5	Madison	1 483	35 226	1 240	23.8	92.3	1.2	1.5	0.6	8.6	6.9	19.9	11.6	11.6	15.5	12.4
31 121	...	7	Merrick	1 256	8 204	2 592	6.5	98.7	0.3	0.3	0.3	2.0	6.4	21.2	6.4	10.0	14.7	13.5
31 123	...	9	Morrill	3 687	5 440	2 821	1.5	94.9	0.2	1.0	0.2	10.1	5.9	21.3	7.2	9.6	14.8	13.5
31 125	...	9	Nance	1 143	4 038	2 919	3.5	99.1	0.0	0.8	0.1	1.1	6.2	21.7	6.8	7.9	15.7	13.3
31 127	...	7	Nemaha	1 060	7 576	2 638	7.1	98.2	0.5	0.7	0.8	1.0	4.6	18.5	11.9	8.8	15.1	14.0
31 129	...	9	Nuckolls	1 490	5 057	2 848	3.4	99.2	0.1	0.3	0.2	1.0	4.9	18.5	5.4	8.2	14.3	12.9
31 131	...	6	Otoe	1 595	15 396	2 060	9.7	98.1	0.3	0.6	0.4	2.4	6.4	19.9	6.4	10.6	15.5	13.4
31 133	...	9	Pawnee	1 118	3 087	2 986	2.8	99.5	0.0	0.5	0.3	0.7	4.9	17.8	5.1	8.0	13.0	13.0
31 135	...	9	Perkins	2 287	3 200	2 979	1.4	98.1	0.2	0.5	0.3	2.3	5.4	21.2	6.0	9.5	13.9	14.7
31 137	...	7	Phelps	1 399	9 747	2 466	7.0	98.4	0.3	0.5	0.6	2.3	6.2	20.3	6.1	10.7	15.1	13.9
31 139	...	9	Pierce	1 486	7 857	2 618	5.3	99.1	0.1	0.6	0.3	0.7	6.0	23.0	7.0	9.9	16.1	12.0

1. MSA = Metropolitan Statistical Area. PMSA = Primary MSA. NECMA = New England County Metropolitan Area. See Appendix A for explanation of these concepts. See Appendix B for list of metropolitan areas identified by type, with component counties.   2. County typology code from the Economic Research Service of USDA. See Appendix A for definition.   3. Dry land or land partially or temporarily covered by water.   4. Hispanic persons may be of any race.

STATE County	55 to 64 years	65 to 74 years	75 years and over	Percent female	2001	1990	1990–2000	2000–2001	Births	Deaths	Net migration	Number	Percent change, 1990–2000	Persons per household	Female family householder[1]	One person
	16	17	18	19	20	21	22	23	24	25	26	27	28	29	30	31
NEBRASKA—Cont'd																
Blaine	12.9	10.1	6.7	49.6	548	675	-13.6	-6.0	8	13	-30	238	-11.2	2.45	2.5	26.9
Boone	9.1	9.5	10.9	50.2	6 168	6 667	-6.1	-1.5	87	95	-84	2 454	-4.1	2.50	5.5	29.1
Box Butte	7.9	7.2	7.3	50.2	11 844	13 130	-7.4	-2.6	204	154	-369	4 780	-2.4	2.50	8.3	27.5
Boyd	10.6	11.0	13.3	51.7	2 394	2 835	-14.0	-1.8	32	49	-27	1 014	-11.7	2.36	3.7	32.0
Brown	10.8	10.2	12.3	50.9	3 542	3 657	-3.6	0.5	55	56	19	1 530	2.1	2.27	5.9	31.6
Buffalo	6.9	5.4	6.1	51.0	42 399	37 447	12.9	0.3	736	357	-226	15 930	16.0	2.48	8.3	26.1
Burt	10.2	11.0	10.8	51.6	7 696	7 868	-1.0	-1.2	99	145	-48	3 155	0.5	2.43	6.2	26.5
Butler	9.4	8.9	8.8	49.0	8 832	8 601	1.9	0.7	134	122	55	3 426	5.3	2.53	5.7	28.3
Cass	9.4	6.6	5.7	50.6	24 646	21 318	14.1	1.3	411	250	160	9 161	17.5	2.63	7.6	21.6
Cedar	8.4	9.3	10.8	50.0	9 472	10 131	-5.1	-1.5	147	137	-152	3 623	-0.8	2.60	4.3	27.0
Chase	10.1	10.1	11.0	50.9	3 974	4 381	-7.1	-2.3	64	81	-78	1 662	-2.5	2.39	5.5	27.3
Cherry	10.4	8.7	8.6	50.3	6 120	6 307	-2.5	-0.5	89	58	-58	2 508	2.9	2.42	6.9	28.9
Cheyenne	9.0	8.8	8.5	51.0	9 974	9 494	3.5	1.5	160	139	124	4 071	5.7	2.38	8.0	30.1
Clay	9.7	8.9	9.1	51.3	6 926	7 123	-1.2	-1.6	112	118	-108	2 756	0.5	2.52	5.5	25.7
Colfax	7.7	7.5	8.5	48.5	10 423	9 139	14.2	-0.2	184	135	-77	3 682	3.4	2.80	7.1	25.7
Cuming	8.7	9.3	10.9	49.5	10 093	10 117	0.9	-1.1	169	135	-144	3 945	2.4	2.53	5.3	27.1
Custer	10.2	9.7	11.3	51.0	11 621	12 270	-3.9	-1.5	147	224	-93	4 826	-2.6	2.39	5.4	28.9
Dakota	7.8	5.1	4.9	50.1	20 347	16 742	21.0	0.5	486	223	-174	7 095	17.6	2.81	11.9	22.9
Dawes	8.6	7.0	7.8	51.1	8 934	9 021	0.4	-1.4	129	115	-142	3 512	5.6	2.28	7.9	31.0
Dawson	8.1	6.8	7.3	49.6	24 432	19 940	22.2	0.3	488	306	-117	8 824	12.7	2.71	7.9	24.6
Deuel	10.8	10.0	12.9	51.3	2 073	2 237	-6.2	-1.2	20	30	-14	908	-0.8	2.29	5.9	31.2
Dixon	8.7	8.3	9.8	50.4	6 226	6 143	3.2	-1.8	115	59	-171	2 413	3.2	2.58	6.5	25.9
Dodge	9.2	8.6	9.0	51.8	35 931	34 500	4.8	-0.6	497	520	-197	14 433	7.3	2.42	8.5	27.6
Douglas	7.7	5.7	5.2	51.1	465 683	416 444	11.3	0.5	9 220	4 434	-2 574	182 194	13.1	2.48	12.1	29.8
Dundy	9.4	10.2	12.2	50.8	2 203	2 582	-11.2	-3.9	18	49	-61	961	-11.4	2.29	3.9	30.9
Fillmore	10.0	9.2	12.0	51.7	6 470	7 103	-6.6	-2.5	91	105	-151	2 689	-4.9	2.37	5.0	30.2
Franklin	10.5	10.9	13.0	51.9	3 495	3 938	-9.2	-2.2	38	79	-38	1 485	-10.3	2.34	6.0	29.2
Frontier	10.1	8.6	8.3	49.9	3 066	3 101	-0.1	-1.1	43	38	-39	1 192	-1.2	2.48	4.8	26.3
Furnas	10.3	10.9	12.8	52.0	5 182	5 553	-4.1	-2.7	69	125	-87	2 278	-2.4	2.28	5.9	32.5
Gage	9.5	8.9	10.3	51.5	23 053	22 794	0.9	0.3	336	321	51	9 316	3.3	2.36	7.1	29.2
Garden	13.3	11.8	12.2	51.3	2 220	2 460	-6.8	-3.1	20	51	-42	1 020	-1.9	2.19	6.0	32.5
Garfield	12.7	9.5	15.3	52.1	1 904	2 141	-11.2	0.1	28	41	14	813	-5.9	2.27	3.6	32.7
Gosper	12.3	10.1	10.7	49.5	2 049	1 928	11.2	-4.4	24	36	-83	863	13.0	2.42	3.9	22.8
Grant	11.8	8.6	5.1	46.7	741	769	-2.9	-0.8	13	4	-14	292	-3.6	2.56	6.5	22.3
Greeley	9.6	11.1	12.1	50.7	2 670	3 006	-9.7	-1.6	43	48	-39	1 077	-4.9	2.46	6.4	30.5
Hall	8.4	6.9	7.0	50.4	53 304	48 925	9.4	-0.4	1 089	639	-683	20 356	9.0	2.57	9.7	25.5
Hamilton	9.0	7.6	7.7	50.2	9 448	8 862	6.1	0.5	146	128	30	3 503	8.3	2.64	5.9	21.1
Harlan	11.4	11.2	11.8	50.5	3 759	3 810	-0.6	-0.7	40	67	1	1 597	0.8	2.34	4.3	30.8
Hayes	10.7	11.7	8.1	49.9	1 099	1 222	-12.6	2.9	6	7	31	430	-10.4	2.48	2.6	26.5
Hitchcock	11.5	10.7	11.6	51.3	3 082	3 750	-17.0	-0.9	42	68	0	1 287	-12.3	2.37	6.4	27.4
Holt	9.4	9.4	10.4	50.8	11 351	12 599	-8.3	-1.7	171	176	-196	4 608	-2.9	2.46	5.6	28.7
Hooker	9.6	10.3	16.6	54.5	749	793	-1.3	-4.3	9	20	-25	335	0.9	2.26	3.9	33.1
Howard	9.5	8.5	8.6	49.7	6 483	6 057	8.4	-1.3	94	100	-77	2 546	10.3	2.56	6.2	26.0
Jefferson	10.0	9.7	13.0	51.1	8 305	8 759	-4.9	-0.3	104	147	20	3 527	-2.9	2.32	5.8	29.6
Johnson	10.2	9.8	12.3	52.1	4 348	4 673	-4.0	-3.1	59	71	-131	1 887	-2.7	2.35	5.5	29.9
Kearney	9.3	7.9	8.8	50.4	6 871	6 629	3.8	-0.2	113	93	-29	2 643	4.8	2.50	6.4	24.3
Keith	11.6	9.9	8.4	50.9	8 839	8 584	3.4	-0.4	104	136	0	3 707	8.1	2.37	7.0	27.9
Keya Paha	12.3	10.5	10.2	49.6	948	1 029	-4.5	-3.6	5	18	-24	409	-2.4	2.40	4.4	26.2
Kimball	11.8	10.4	10.6	51.1	4 023	4 108	-0.5	-1.6	61	52	-75	1 727	4.7	2.33	6.7	30.5
Knox	10.3	10.5	12.6	50.8	9 167	9 564	-2.0	-2.2	144	171	-181	3 811	-0.2	2.40	6.0	29.9
Lancaster	7.2	5.3	5.1	50.0	252 090	213 641	17.2	0.7	4 448	1 988	-573	99 187	19.9	2.40	9.1	29.1
Lincoln	9.2	7.7	7.4	50.9	34 516	32 508	6.5	-0.3	545	425	-225	14 076	11.0	2.41	8.0	28.3
Logan	10.5	9.9	7.6	50.3	776	878	-11.8	0.3	6	11	7	316	-1.3	2.45	3.8	25.0
Loup	12.2	10.7	8.8	47.9	709	683	4.2	-0.4	12	6	-10	289	4.7	2.46	4.2	27.0
McPherson	9.2	8.8	9.4	50.1	536	546	-2.4	0.6	5	6	3	202	-4.7	2.64	3.5	19.8
Madison	7.7	6.6	7.8	50.4	35 549	32 655	7.9	0.9	622	398	108	13 436	9.4	2.52	8.4	27.9
Merrick	10.3	8.5	9.0	51.0	8 092	8 062	1.8	-1.4	131	114	-130	3 209	4.8	2.51	6.5	25.0
Morrill	10.7	8.8	8.2	50.5	5 363	5 423	0.3	-1.4	84	96	-65	2 138	2.6	2.49	6.5	26.9
Nance	8.6	10.3	9.4	49.0	3 969	4 275	-5.5	-1.7	62	65	-65	1 577	-0.5	2.49	5.6	27.6
Nemaha	8.8	8.1	10.3	51.7	7 456	7 980	-5.1	-1.6	87	134	-73	3 047	-1.0	2.32	7.2	30.5
Nuckolls	11.4	11.5	12.8	51.9	4 987	5 786	-12.6	-1.4	61	99	-28	2 218	-6.0	2.26	4.6	32.3
Otoe	9.6	8.4	10.0	51.0	15 505	14 252	8.0	0.7	242	225	98	6 060	7.1	2.48	7.2	26.4
Pawnee	11.1	12.0	15.1	52.0	3 015	3 317	-6.9	-2.3	37	59	-49	1 339	-4.9	2.27	5.6	32.9
Perkins	9.9	7.7	11.6	49.8	3 153	3 367	-5.0	-1.5	30	47	-28	1 275	-0.6	2.47	4.6	27.5
Phelps	9.6	8.6	9.5	51.0	9 704	9 715	0.3	-0.4	147	141	-46	3 844	2.0	2.47	5.8	26.7
Pierce	8.9	7.7	9.4	50.0	7 818	7 827	0.4	-0.5	105	108	-34	2 979	1.7	2.59	5.7	25.7

1. No spouse present.

STATE County	Births, average 1997–1999 Total	Rate[1]	Deaths, average 1997–1999 Number Total	Number Infant[2]	Rate Total[1]	Rate Infant[3]	Physicians,[4] 2000 Number	Rate[5]	Hospitals,[4] 1998 Number	Beds Number	Beds Rate[5]	Medicare enrollees 2000	Serious crimes known to police, 2000[6] Total Number	Rate[7]
	32	33	34	35	36	37	38	39	40	41	42	43	44	45
NEBRASKA—Cont'd														
Blaine	6	10.6	8	NA	12.9	NA	0	0	0	0	0	88	NA	NA
Boone	81	12.6	72	NA	11.3	NA	6	96	1	34	533	1 382	48	767
Box Butte	171	13.3	122	NA	9.5	NA	7	58	1	36	281	1 948	262	2 155
Boyd	26	10.2	37	NA	14.3	NA	4	164	1	29	1 131	686	20	820
Brown	39	10.9	48	NA	13.4	NA	5	142	1	23	647	843	49	1 390
Buffalo	565	14.0	305	NA	7.5	NA	113	267	1	183	451	5 412	1 975	4 674
Burt	81	10.2	122	NA	15.3	NA	6	77	1	23	288	1 841	114	1 463
Butler	98	11.3	100	NA	11.5	NA	4	46	1	34	392	1 693	84	958
Cass	330	13.5	204	NA	8.4	NA	6	25	0	0	0	3 284	467	1 919
Cedar	121	12.5	114	NA	11.8	NA	1	10	0	0	0	1 898	32	333
Chase	55	12.9	59	NA	13.9	NA	2	49	1	26	612	922	24	590
Cherry	80	12.5	57	NA	8.9	NA	4	65	1	36	569	1 247	181	2 944
Cheyenne	124	13.1	114	NA	12.0	NA	11	112	1	106	1 119	1 909	NA	NA
Clay	71	10.0	93	NA	13.0	NA	2	28	0	0	0	1 472	9	128
Colfax	150	14.1	109	NA	10.2	NA	5	48	1	49	457	3 691	172	1 647
Cuming	138	13.7	113	NA	11.3	NA	6	59	1	49	490	1 985	74	725
Custer	128	10.7	175	NA	14.6	NA	8	68	3	146	1 214	2 568	116	984
Dakota	361	19.1	165	NA	8.7	NA	6	30	0	0	0	2 391	470	2 321
Dawes	98	10.9	91	NA	10.2	NA	8	88	2	51	568	1 522	150	1 656
Dawson	382	16.4	247	NA	10.6	NA	16	66	3	118	509	3 608	791	3 246
Deuel	19	9.3	26	NA	12.9	NA	1	48	0	0	0	534	33	1 573
Dixon	84	13.3	62	NA	9.8	NA	1	16	0	0	0	1 214	74	1 167
Dodge	427	12.1	405	NA	11.5	NA	41	113	1	262	742	6 758	1 085	3 001
Douglas	6 950	15.6	3 596	58	8.1	8.3	1 609	347	8	2 604	587	59 090	28 305	6 106
Dundy	19	8.4	37	NA	16.5	NA	4	175	1	14	608	506	30	1 309
Fillmore	72	10.5	84	NA	12.1	NA	3	45	1	33	476	1 428	100	1 507
Franklin	33	8.7	59	NA	15.9	NA	4	112	1	20	536	912	41	1 147
Frontier	34	10.9	27	NA	8.5	NA	0	0	0	0	0	529	73	2 356
Furnas	54	10.0	100	NA	18.4	NA	4	75	1	65	1 208	1 484	80	1 503
Gage	262	11.5	290	NA	12.7	NA	28	122	1	143	631	4 989	633	2 753
Garden	18	8.3	46	NA	21.6	NA	4	175	1	56	2 619	628	43	1 876
Garfield	21	10.5	34	NA	16.7	NA	2	105	0	0	0	550	2	105
Gosper	22	9.6	27	NA	11.8	NA	0	0	0	0	0	502	24	1 120
Grant	9	12.1	NA	NA	NA	NA	1	134	0	0	0	148	18	2 410
Greeley	36	12.5	38	NA	13.3	NA	0	0	0	0	0	648	31	1 142
Hall	822	15.9	509	9	9.8	10.5	85	159	1	197	380	8 077	3 419	6 387
Hamilton	108	11.4	102	NA	10.7	NA	10	106	1	82	866	1 498	227	2 414
Harlan	37	10.0	58	NA	15.5	NA	2	53	1	25	667	845	NA	NA
Hayes	7	6.9	NA	NA	NA	NA	0	0	0	0	0	125	NA	NA
Hitchcock	38	11.2	50	NA	14.7	NA	0	0	0	0	0	761	19	611
Holt	154	12.8	134	NA	11.1	NA	11	95	2	47	390	2 411	140	1 212
Hooker	6	9.0	15	NA	20.8	NA	1	128	0	0	0	220	1	128
Howard	86	13.3	75	NA	11.6	NA	3	46	1	37	573	1 192	227	3 457
Jefferson	84	10.1	118	NA	14.2	NA	6	72	1	73	871	2 040	195	2 340
Johnson	46	10.1	58	NA	12.8	NA	3	67	1	30	657	1 065	NA	NA
Kearney	84	12.4	83	NA	12.2	NA	6	87	1	80	1 167	1 192	158	2 296
Keith	95	10.9	96	NA	11.0	NA	3	34	1	41	473	1 695	192	2 163
Keya Paha	9	9.0	11	NA	11.7	NA	0	0	0	0	0	198	1	102
Kimball	46	11.5	49	NA	12.2	NA	1	24	1	30	735	920	93	2 274
Knox	114	12.4	140	NA	15.2	NA	4	43	1	77	836	2 322	71	757
Lancaster	3 259	13.8	1 609	22	6.8	6.8	488	195	3	702	298	29 293	15 254	6 095
Lincoln	430	12.8	333	NA	9.9	NA	50	144	1	105	313	5 833	304	878
Logan	9	10.1	7	NA	7.5	NA	0	0	0	0	0	160	NA	NA
Loup	7	11.0	NA	NA	NA	NA	0	0	0	0	0	95	2	281
McPherson	5	9.6	NA	NA	NA	NA	0	0	0	0	0	124	3	563
Madison	534	15.5	343	NA	9.9	NA	67	190	3	199	575	5 878	1 134	3 451
Merrick	108	13.3	99	NA	12.3	NA	2	24	1	79	981	1 488	117	1 426
Morrill	61	11.4	76	NA	14.2	NA	4	74	1	20	367	1 033	104	1 912
Nance	50	12.1	55	NA	13.4	NA	1	25	1	20	488	833	32	792
Nemaha	79	10.3	103	NA	13.4	NA	5	66	1	39	507	1 453	114	1 505
Nuckolls	46	8.9	79	NA	15.2	NA	4	79	1	49	938	1 363	NA	NA
Otoe	180	12.2	199	NA	13.5	NA	7	45	2	67	453	2 880	362	2 351
Pawnee	26	8.4	55	NA	17.6	NA	3	97	1	17	543	875	19	615
Perkins	29	9.0	39	NA	12.2	NA	5	156	1	76	2 397	620	33	1 031
Phelps	126	12.8	119	NA	12.1	NA	8	82	1	55	555	1 801	246	2 524
Pierce	100	12.6	90	NA	11.4	NA	1	13	2	59	746	1 388	92	1 171

1. Per 1,000 estimated resident population, average 1997–1999. 2. Deaths of infants under 1 year old. 3. Deaths of infants under 1 year old per 1,000 live births. 4. Data subject to copyright. 5. Per 100,000 resident population as of July 1 of the year shown. 6. Data for serious crimes have not been adjusted for underreporting; this may affect comparability between geographic areas and over time. 7. Per 100,000 population estimated by the FBI.

Table B. States and Counties — Crime, Education, Money Income, and Poverty

STATE County	Serious crimes known to police, 2000[1] (cont'd) Rate[2] Violent	Property	Education School enrollment and attainment, 1990 Enrollment[3] Total	Percent private	Attainment[4] (percent) High school graduate or more	Bachelor's degree or more	Local government expenditures, fiscal 1999[5] Total current expenditures (mil dol)	Current expenditures per student (dollars)	Money income 1989 Per capita[6] (dollars)	Households Median Dollars	Percent change, 1979–1989 (constant 1989 dollars)	Percent with $100,000 or more	Income and poverty, 1998 Median household income	Percent below poverty level All persons	Persons under 18	Persons 5–17 in families
	46	47	48	49	50	51	52	53	54	55	56	57	58	59	60	61
NEBRASKA—Cont'd																
Blaine	NA	NA	167	4.8	85.3	15.8	1.5	9 882	9 681	19 716	12.4	1.5	21 337	22.5	31.3	29.3
Boone	48	719	1 612	15.1	76.1	9.4	8.1	6 174	10 062	21 653	18.5	2.0	31 459	13.6	16.8	15.0
Box Butte	189	1 966	3 465	6.8	84.0	13.0	14.9	5 442	11 880	26 493	-13.7	1.3	41 215	11.1	13.1	12.0
Boyd	205	615	619	1.6	72.1	9.9	4.0	6 889	8 979	16 329	4.2	0.9	22 452	17.9	21.0	19.9
Brown	57	1 333	790	3.8	79.8	11.3	5.1	7 887	9 209	17 067	-6.6	0.9	25 447	16.4	20.8	18.7
Buffalo	244	4 430	13 295	4.6	83.3	23.7	44.4	6 261	11 190	23 999	-5.8	2.0	38 025	10.8	13.3	11.6
Burt	77	1 386	1 748	5.0	77.6	13.5	9.4	5 630	10 030	21 061	-0.1	0.9	31 580	12.1	16.5	14.1
Butler	34	924	2 058	25.4	72.5	8.0	7.4	5 568	11 662	23 267	2.0	1.1	34 878	9.9	13.0	10.2
Cass	111	1 808	5 762	10.4	82.1	13.6	22.2	5 819	11 792	28 490	0.1	1.5	45 022	7.9	10.6	9.4
Cedar	0	333	2 613	26.5	75.2	10.3	10.5	6 094	8 978	21 014	8.5	1.0	32 816	11.5	15.4	12.3
Chase	98	492	1 080	3.3	79.0	15.1	6.5	6 400	10 011	21 488	4.4	1.1	33 729	12.5	14.9	13.9
Cherry	374	2 570	1 295	3.6	75.2	13.1	6.8	6 252	10 758	18 962	-18.4	3.0	27 372	17.0	22.0	20.5
Cheyenne	NA	NA	2 313	8.3	80.3	15.1	14.2	6 869	11 517	23 400	-7.4	1.5	35 016	11.4	15.4	13.5
Clay	14	114	1 752	6.1	76.9	11.7	10.6	6 992	10 511	22 949	-1.0	1.5	34 878	11.2	15.8	13.1
Colfax	48	1 599	2 051	10.2	70.4	8.5	11.6	5 357	10 180	22 140	1.7	1.2	31 839	10.4	16.8	11.9
Cuming	49	676	2 409	31.9	71.5	11.8	9.8	5 746	10 171	21 623	-10.9	1.1	33 976	10.7	14.0	11.6
Custer	0	984	2 740	5.0	80.5	10.8	14.9	6 607	11 116	21 440	3.7	2.0	29 702	15.9	20.1	17.3
Dakota	109	2 212	4 330	14.1	74.9	11.7	18.1	4 971	10 635	25 397	-10.7	0.7	35 917	11.7	16.3	13.9
Dawes	33	1 623	3 366	3.4	80.0	23.1	8.1	5 766	9 357	17 784	-17.7	1.2	27 289	18.6	21.4	20.5
Dawson	119	3 127	4 993	2.9	78.8	12.3	26.7	5 316	10 849	22 420	-18.4	1.6	33 833	11.4	16.0	12.7
Deuel	48	1 525	513	1.9	79.2	12.9	3.7	7 260	10 434	21 272	-7.9	1.2	32 348	10.4	13.2	12.3
Dixon	63	1 104	1 388	4.4	76.1	11.0	9.9	8 174	9 074	20 047	0.0	0.5	33 656	9.6	12.2	10.7
Dodge	86	2 915	8 608	18.7	78.3	13.5	37.9	5 958	11 638	24 817	-8.2	1.3	36 946	9.3	12.8	10.7
Douglas	712	5 394	116 102	22.0	84.5	24.9	452.3	5 898	14 644	29 857	0.5	3.8	43 748	10.1	14.9	11.8
Dundy	44	1 265	569	2.1	71.3	13.0	2.7	7 552	10 894	21 271	8.5	1.0	30 755	13.6	17.2	15.2
Fillmore	90	1 417	1 611	7.5	81.4	11.9	9.5	7 175	11 961	23 219	-0.2	1.4	36 146	10.8	14.8	13.3
Franklin	0	1 147	731	2.3	71.1	11.8	3.4	6 624	10 968	20 553	6.3	0.7	29 470	13.1	17.4	16.3
Frontier	97	2 259	819	3.1	81.0	10.5	6.3	7 225	9 611	20 364	-5.3	0.4	30 672	15.1	19.4	17.1
Furnas	94	1 409	1 225	4.5	75.3	12.0	9.1	7 149	9 432	17 949	-1.7	0.6	28 784	15.2	19.8	17.2
Gage	83	2 670	5 041	9.8	73.7	11.3	22.2	6 510	11 099	22 876	-1.9	1.1	33 201	10.6	14.2	12.1
Garden	87	1 789	508	4.3	76.4	13.9	3.5	8 517	10 135	18 614	-12.9	0.3	26 580	16.1	23.4	22.1
Garfield	53	53	447	4.3	73.8	12.9	2.5	6 159	9 043	17 308	-4.6	0.2	26 650	15.6	19.1	17.4
Gosper	0	1 120	425	3.1	79.1	13.9	1.7	5 870	11 738	25 669	16.6	1.1	34 764	8.8	13.5	10.7
Grant	535	1 874	166	1.2	89.5	14.6	2.0	8 135	10 273	19 063	-8.0	2.9	25 612	14.7	23.1	18.5
Greeley	37	1 105	825	18.2	78.9	11.5	4.6	7 112	8 595	18 248	16.8	0.4	25 148	16.3	19.9	16.5
Hall	325	6 062	12 047	9.5	79.3	14.6	51.6	5 481	11 526	25 546	-8.7	1.6	35 659	11.3	15.4	12.7
Hamilton	74	2 340	2 206	8.6	79.9	13.0	10.1	5 789	11 103	25 026	-5.3	2.1	39 248	8.3	11.5	9.8
Harlan	NA	NA	769	4.2	80.9	12.9	2.4	5 912	9 721	18 478	-5.2	0.8	28 344	13.0	17.5	16.1
Hayes	NA	NA	274	2.2	80.6	10.7	1.5	8 463	13 871	20 531	10.8	4.0	30 415	15.6	19.8	18.2
Hitchcock	64	546	918	6.1	80.4	12.1	5.9	11 974	10 689	19 735	-5.1	1.2	26 663	15.2	18.0	18.4
Holt	43	1 169	2 880	16.3	76.1	12.8	13.3	6 073	10 164	20 059	3.5	2.1	28 734	14.7	17.8	16.1
Hooker	0	128	173	4.0	79.5	13.5	1.7	8 444	9 381	18 682	1.9	0.0	22 568	15.8	23.5	19.4
Howard	183	3 274	1 436	6.4	75.2	8.6	9.1	5 673	9 551	21 688	-4.4	0.6	32 070	12.1	15.9	14.2
Jefferson	72	2 268	1 888	7.0	75.1	12.7	12.2	6 278	11 126	21 740	2.1	1.3	32 074	10.6	13.0	12.5
Johnson	NA	NA	1 009	4.7	73.6	8.5	6.1	6 542	11 229	19 925	3.2	1.3	29 910	12.2	16.0	14.7
Kearney	29	2 267	1 504	7.9	80.3	17.9	8.2	5 560	11 751	27 207	5.6	0.8	38 197	8.6	11.4	10.7
Keith	68	2 096	2 029	7.4	81.5	13.1	11.8	7 157	10 771	22 909	-13.7	0.8	31 914	11.5	14.0	13.1
Keya Paha	0	102	216	0.0	76.8	8.1	1.1	7 388	7 907	17 202	-7.4	0.0	20 197	20.6	26.1	23.2
Kimball	24	2 250	953	4.9	73.8	12.7	4.4	6 118	11 105	23 232	-7.9	0.2	31 051	13.1	17.2	16.8
Knox	75	683	2 139	11.2	71.1	8.8	13.5	6 648	9 881	17 877	-1.4	1.7	26 469	17.3	21.8	20.1
Lancaster	490	5 605	67 322	12.9	88.1	27.6	218.7	6 161	13 803	28 909	-1.0	2.5	40 865	9.0	11.9	9.7
Lincoln	84	794	8 459	9.6	81.4	14.2	33.8	5 569	12 091	25 915	-15.9	1.3	37 387	12.6	16.6	14.5
Logan	NA	NA	264	4.2	82.9	13.4	1.6	7 218	9 186	21 250	19.3	1.0	26 603	14.7	15.5	16.3
Loup	140	140	178	6.7	78.3	9.8	1.0	7 929	8 817	17 933	-13.5	0.7	16 642	19.1	23.1	22.6
McPherson	0	563	126	4.0	78.0	9.0	0.8	6 791	10 601	17 500	-18.8	2.3	17 391	20.6	27.6	28.0
Madison	143	3 308	8 863	20.0	78.3	13.2	36.2	5 540	11 054	24 461	-8.8	1.4	37 198	10.2	13.9	11.0
Merrick	73	1 353	1 918	8.5	77.0	11.7	9.2	5 900	10 194	22 518	-11.9	1.8	32 659	11.0	14.3	12.9
Morrill	110	1 801	1 290	3.4	74.1	12.7	7.1	6 318	10 102	19 398	5.2	1.1	28 468	15.4	18.8	18.5
Nance	50	743	1 002	5.2	71.0	10.7	4.7	5 736	8 936	20 742	11.5	0.6	29 449	14.5	18.6	16.6
Nemaha	40	1 465	2 486	2.9	77.2	18.5	10.1	7 830	11 343	22 383	-0.6	1.8	35 129	12.1	15.1	13.2
Nuckolls	NA	NA	1 277	13.5	74.2	10.1	5.8	6 714	9 862	20 250	-7.4	1.0	29 040	12.8	16.5	14.7
Otoe	65	2 286	3 285	8.9	77.4	13.1	15.9	5 874	10 990	23 189	-4.3	1.0	36 970	9.2	12.0	10.4
Pawnee	32	583	658	5.9	75.0	11.1	4.6	6 612	9 316	18 286	9.8	0.1	27 307	14.4	18.3	17.9
Perkins	63	969	857	3.9	79.0	16.7	4.7	7 835	9 933	23 132	1.2	0.5	33 625	11.4	14.2	13.6
Phelps	92	2 432	2 266	6.5	85.0	15.5	15.0	7 580	12 837	26 693	4.1	2.8	38 196	9.8	12.8	11.3
Pierce	51	1 120	1 954	21.9	73.8	9.1	8.8	5 573	10 430	22 293	2.5	1.4	34 665	10.2	12.2	11.5

1. Data for serious crimes have not been adjusted for underreporting; this may affect comparability between geographic areas and over time.   2. Per 100,000 population estimated by the FBI.   3. All persons 3 years old and over enrolled in nursery school through college.   4. Persons 25 years old and over.   5. Elementary and secondary education expenditures, local government fiscal years ending between July 1, 1998 and June 30, 1999.   6. Based on population enumerated as of April 1, 1990.

Table B. States and Counties — **Personal Income**

STATE County	Total (mil dol)	Percent change, 1998–1999	Per capita Dollars	Per capita Rank	Wages and salaries[2] (mil dol)	Proprietor's income (mil dol)	Dividends, interest, and rent (mil dol)	Transfer payments Total (mil dol)	Govt payments Total (mil dol)	Social Security (mil dol)	Medical payments (mil dol)	Income maintenance (mil dol)	Unemployment insurance (mil dol)
	62	63	64	65	66	67	68	69	70	71	72	73	74
NEBRASKA—Cont'd													
Blaine	7	18.7	11 576	3 095	5	-3	3	2	2	1	1	0	0
Boone	137	1.1	21 620	1 476	45	28	37	24	23	11	9	2	0
Box Butte	311	4.0	24 519	752	206	40	55	43	41	16	14	3	1
Boyd	43	-1.8	17 031	2 729	14	6	14	12	12	5	5	1	0
Brown	64	1.4	18 336	2 460	27	3	21	14	14	7	5	1	0
Buffalo	962	4.2	23 897	880	611	90	195	122	115	52	42	8	1
Burt	173	4.5	21 830	1 404	49	35	40	36	34	16	14	2	0
Butler	188	3.3	21 900	1 388	54	29	51	32	31	16	11	2	0
Cass	635	5.9	25 554	576	127	50	96	74	69	33	26	4	1
Cedar	209	2.0	21 769	1 425	62	49	52	32	31	16	11	2	0
Chase	115	0.2	26 932	421	39	33	30	18	17	9	6	1	0
Cherry	120	6.3	18 938	2 302	49	10	41	22	21	10	8	2	0
Cheyenne	245	8.1	26 017	513	147	28	47	38	36	18	13	2	0
Clay	164	3.1	23 140	1 062	77	29	40	28	26	13	10	2	0
Colfax	216	2.3	20 248	1 908	119	33	55	39	37	16	18	2	0
Cuming	304	6.1	30 414	196	99	117	59	36	35	19	12	2	0
Custer	264	0.6	22 344	1 263	91	53	70	49	47	23	18	3	0
Dakota	409	3.4	21 370	1 554	341	35	61	57	54	23	22	5	0
Dawes	162	5.4	18 384	2 445	80	10	38	34	32	14	10	3	0
Dawson	517	3.1	22 229	1 290	296	84	105	76	72	35	28	5	1
Deuel	51	3.3	25 704	555	13	12	16	9	9	5	3	0	0
Dixon	141	2.0	22 200	1 299	42	39	25	21	20	10	8	2	0
Dodge	861	4.6	24 457	768	431	69	192	140	134	68	51	7	1
Douglas	15 283	6.0	34 246	102	12 047	1 483	3 028	1 526	1 447	574	609	138	13
Dundy	66	2.5	30 240	202	19	16	21	11	10	5	4	1	0
Fillmore	184	1.8	26 663	443	57	47	55	26	25	14	8	1	0
Franklin	75	-0.8	20 496	1 836	18	13	24	17	16	9	6	1	0
Frontier	65	4.8	20 654	1 791	21	16	14	10	10	5	3	1	0
Furnas	122	5.9	22 498	1 216	44	18	34	28	27	13	11	2	0
Gage	567	3.6	24 979	676	239	67	117	135	131	46	73	5	1
Garden	49	6.7	23 740	910	17	4	17	11	11	6	4	0	0
Garfield	44	3.1	21 739	1 437	14	8	15	9	9	4	4	1	0
Gosper	52	5.7	23 259	1 027	11	9	16	9	9	5	3	0	0
Grant	11	21.8	14 874	2 999	5	-1	5	2	2	1	1	0	0
Greeley	55	-1.0	19 495	2 143	15	12	17	11	11	5	4	1	0
Hall	1 272	3.7	24 573	738	865	102	275	181	171	76	66	14	2
Hamilton	215	2.1	22 525	1 212	71	42	50	30	28	16	9	2	0
Harlan	78	4.7	21 181	1 602	22	17	19	16	16	8	5	1	0
Hayes	26	4.1	24 537	748	6	10	4	3	3	2	1	0	0
Hitchcock	63	9.7	18 634	2 382	17	9	17	14	13	7	4	1	0
Holt	256	4.3	21 502	1 521	99	57	62	47	44	20	18	4	0
Hooker	11	8.8	15 318	2 957	7	-4	6	4	4	2	1	0	0
Howard	124	2.5	18 996	2 280	32	20	29	21	20	10	7	1	0
Jefferson	188	3.6	22 700	1 168	77	27	49	35	34	17	12	2	0
Johnson	92	6.5	20 174	1 941	36	8	25	19	18	9	6	1	0
Kearney	180	3.7	26 176	496	55	43	40	30	28	12	15	1	0
Keith	192	6.4	21 633	1 475	85	30	46	33	32	17	11	2	0
Keya Paha	10	-9.8	9 993	3 106	3	-1	4	3	3	2	1	0	0
Kimball	89	0.7	22 224	1 293	37	12	25	17	16	9	5	1	0
Knox	187	2.8	20 631	1 797	58	28	50	44	42	18	19	3	0
Lancaster	6 772	5.2	28 493	284	4 726	451	1 367	694	651	292	240	47	5
Lincoln	792	1.5	23 400	986	487	59	157	133	127	46	43	10	1
Logan	14	-2.6	15 642	2 938	4	2	4	3	3	1	1	0	0
Loup	3	4.3	4 896	3 110	2	-5	3	2	2	1	1	0	0
McPherson	4	13.6	6 940	3 109	1	-3	3	2	2	1	1	0	0
Madison	821	1.3	24 030	851	550	88	169	118	112	53	43	8	2
Merrick	167	2.6	20 714	1 771	52	29	37	30	29	14	11	2	0
Morrill	93	-1.2	17 586	2 632	32	11	23	20	19	9	7	2	0
Nance	82	-1.6	20 295	1 892	20	19	18	19	18	8	9	1	0
Nemaha	196	0.2	25 708	554	125	17	43	31	30	14	12	2	0
Nuckolls	112	0.7	21 894	1 389	35	19	32	26	25	13	10	1	0
Otoe	325	3.1	21 940	1 378	148	28	84	58	56	28	21	3	1
Pawnee	71	2.3	22 983	1 095	17	12	19	15	15	7	6	1	0
Perkins	86	4.1	26 862	428	26	34	18	13	12	7	4	1	0
Phelps	276	3.0	28 075	327	129	70	58	40	39	19	15	2	0
Pierce	161	-0.7	20 202	1 931	46	29	36	26	25	13	9	1	0

1. Based on the resident population estimated as of July 1 of the year shown.   2. Includes other labor income.

STATE County	Earnings, 1999									Social Security bene-ficiaries, December 2000			Housing units, 1990	
			Percent by selected industries											
			Goods-related[1]		Service-related and other[2]							Supple-mental Security Income recipients, December 2000		
	Total (mil dol)	Farm	Total	Manu-facturing	Total	Retail trade	Finance, insur-ance, and real estate	Services	Govern-ment	Number	Rate[3]		Total	Percent change, 1980–1990
	75	76	77	78	79	80	81	82	83	84	85	86	87	88
NEBRASKA—Cont'd														
Blaine	2	-105.5	D	D	D	14.7	D	23.7	111.5	103	177	7	381	3.5
Boone	73	28.9	D	3.6	42.7	8.8	4.2	12.1	22.0	1 485	237	60	2 878	-6.1
Box Butte	245	11.6	D	D	D	5.3	2.7	D	12.0	1 923	158	140	5 534	-0.3
Boyd	20	-8.4	D	D	D	10.7	5.9	18.9	31.7	732	300	45	1 538	5.6
Brown	30	-4.2	D	D	D	11.9	6.8	17.6	37.5	937	266	41	1 950	-2.3
Buffalo	702	3.4	24.2	18.0	56.3	13.7	3.7	26.6	16.1	6 018	142	325	14 538	8.2
Burt	84	28.6	10.8	5.0	41.0	6.4	4.9	14.3	19.6	2 020	259	99	3 740	-1.7
Butler	83	26.1	18.5	14.5	36.6	7.4	3.1	15.6	18.7	1 922	219	75	3 801	-0.2
Cass	176	9.3	D	8.0	D	10.3	5.5	16.3	18.5	3 780	155	137	8 951	7.6
Cedar	111	30.3	D	7.6	D	6.1	D	13.1	18.1	2 165	225	64	4 149	1.3
Chase	71	35.7	4.5	1.8	41.5	9.2	4.1	10.4	18.3	1 012	249	42	2 011	-4.2
Cherry	59	-0.4	D	D	D	18.1	6.4	22.0	25.0	1 314	214	109	3 023	2.0
Cheyenne	175	4.2	15.8	9.1	D	33.4	3.1	D	12.8	2 079	211	128	4 345	-2.9
Clay	106	20.5	D	9.4	D	4.0	D	8.6	26.1	1 547	220	57	3 173	-5.4
Colfax	153	15.9	D	D	D	5.2	2.7	12.7	11.1	1 806	173	61	3 971	-1.8
Cuming	217	43.2	D	10.3	D	6.0	2.9	11.7	8.6	2 381	233	67	4 132	-4.4
Custer	145	26.5	14.2	10.2	42.1	8.7	3.0	17.9	17.3	2 925	248	139	5 728	-7.3
Dakota	376	2.7	D	D	D	6.3	7.4	11.0	7.9	2 845	140	280	6 486	5.8
Dawes	90	-7.0	D	1.0	D	17.7	4.6	23.3	39.5	1 711	189	120	3 909	-1.4
Dawson	379	15.9	D	33.1	D	8.3	2.6	10.9	14.7	4 113	169	249	9 021	-3.7
Deuel	25	29.4	D	D	D	10.0	6.3	11.3	18.6	568	271	17	1 075	-3.8
Dixon	81	36.8	D	D	D	2.6	1.8	8.6	13.5	1 282	202	55	2 613	-8.3
Dodge	500	3.7	D	21.7	D	13.6	4.2	19.7	17.1	7 780	215	347	14 601	2.5
Douglas	13 530	0.0	D	10.9	D	8.4	11.1	32.9	10.9	64 718	140	7 343	172 335	10.7
Dundy	35	40.0	D	D	38.7	3.6	2.1	11.7	18.2	597	260	27	1 326	-7.8
Fillmore	103	30.9	11.1	3.0	D	6.0	4.0	9.3	18.3	1 604	242	70	3 102	-5.3
Franklin	31	27.6	D	1.8	D	8.0	5.8	14.3	23.9	1 046	293	60	1 950	-5.1
Frontier	36	35.5	D	D	D	5.0	5.4	12.2	25.7	625	202	20	1 565	-12.6
Furnas	62	20.5	D	1.6	D	6.4	4.5	21.6	23.0	1 487	279	84	2 905	-5.7
Gage	306	10.2	D	20.3	D	9.3	3.2	20.6	22.4	5 564	242	426	9 735	-1.8
Garden	21	14.2	D	D	D	13.8	9.1	7.7	35.3	696	304	21	1 343	-4.1
Garfield	21	13.2	D	10.3	D	9.5	2.9	15.6	18.8	584	307	27	1 021	-5.0
Gosper	20	38.8	D	D	D	6.1	7.1	9.2	21.1	618	288	18	1 212	-3.0
Grant	3	-51.3	D	D	D	18.9	D	28.0	66.0	196	262	4	425	-1.2
Greeley	27	29.4	9.5	4.3	D	5.9	4.4	15.9	23.8	695	256	31	1 284	-9.8
Hall	967	1.7	D	23.8	D	11.9	5.4	21.4	15.6	8 933	167	757	19 528	4.0
Hamilton	113	25.6	D	12.5	45.4	6.0	3.8	19.1	14.4	1 826	194	59	3 589	-0.4
Harlan	39	26.7	D	D	D	8.8	3.6	9.5	18.7	958	253	40	2 409	13.2
Hayes	15	70.0	D	D	D	1.3	3.0	D	14.5	195	183	8	583	-13.1
Hitchcock	26	23.7	D	3.2	D	6.0	2.8	7.3	29.7	875	281	48	1 873	7.6
Holt	156	13.2	5.6	2.4	67.1	9.6	3.9	19.4	14.1	2 717	235	193	5 472	1.1
Hooker	3	-129.8	D	D	D	22.0	7.1	68.3	74.4	249	318	10	433	-3.6
Howard	52	29.0	D	D	D	10.8	4.2	11.0	28.0	1 325	202	63	2 598	-2.4
Jefferson	104	17.4	D	16.0	D	10.2	3.3	14.2	14.3	2 171	261	143	4 082	-4.4
Johnson	45	5.4	D	D	D	10.2	4.5	16.4	26.7	1 171	261	45	2 153	-2.2
Kearney	98	34.6	11.0	4.5	D	4.2	3.1	13.9	14.4	1 289	187	74	2 756	-2.5
Keith	115	14.5	D	10.7	D	15.2	5.8	20.9	15.7	2 028	229	103	4 938	3.2
Keya Paha	2	-81.4	D	D	D	21.8	0.0	26.8	70.2	262	267	12	584	3.2
Kimball	49	5.8	D	D	D	12.9	3.6	D	21.1	1 065	260	43	1 967	-3.2
Knox	87	15.5	D	D	D	10.3	3.9	18.2	28.0	2 468	263	183	4 799	-0.1
Lancaster	5 178	0.4	20.2	13.9	58.0	8.3	8.8	27.5	21.4	32 984	132	3 124	86 734	13.6
Lincoln	546	1.7	D	2.0	D	10.8	3.6	24.0	18.0	5 636	163	573	14 210	-3.7
Logan	6	22.0	D	D	D	5.1	D	D	31.5	187	242	8	387	-3.7
Loup	-3	0.0	0.0	0.0	D	0.0	D	D	0.0	168	236	7	399	8.7
McPherson	-2	0.0	D	0.0	D	0.0	0.0	D	0.0	109	205	12	257	-2.7
Madison	638	3.3	D	20.6	D	11.2	3.3	21.4	16.2	6 341	180	490	13 069	6.0
Merrick	81	25.7	D	3.2	D	6.7	5.8	12.1	20.0	1 880	229	100	3 533	-2.0
Morrill	43	16.0	D	D	D	8.3	D	12.1	30.4	1 142	210	88	2 530	-2.4
Nance	38	33.9	D	D	D	5.0	5.5	13.9	24.6	992	246	78	1 807	-8.6
Nemaha	142	4.7	12.5	9.5	26.0	5.1	2.7	11.9	56.7	1 662	219	117	3 432	-1.9
Nuckolls	54	13.5	D	0.8	D	10.5	4.6	27.7	18.8	1 500	297	63	2 699	-6.9
Otoe	176	4.0	D	23.5	D	9.9	4.8	18.6	21.1	3 344	217	142	6 137	-2.9
Pawnee	30	23.5	15.4	10.9	D	8.0	3.8	16.5	23.7	960	311	54	1 674	-6.9
Perkins	60	42.4	7.1	1.0	35.2	3.5	3.1	9.6	15.3	721	225	21	1 537	-1.4
Phelps	198	29.1	22.4	17.1	36.7	6.0	3.8	15.0	11.8	2 086	214	116	4 084	0.0
Pierce	75	19.6	12.5	1.6	D	9.1	4.1	20.2	17.8	1 580	201	50	3 177	-1.9

1. Covers mining, construction, and manufacturing.   2. Covers private sector earnings in agricultural services, forestry, and fisheries; transportation and public utilities; wholesale trade; retail trade; finance, insurance, and real estate; and services.   3. Per 1,000 resident population estimated as of July 1 of the year shown.

STATE County	Total	Percent	Median value[1]	With a mortgage	Without a mortgage	Median rent[2]	Rent as percent of income	Substandard units[3] (percent)	Total	Percent change, 2000–2001	Total	Rate[4]	Total	Professional, managerial, and technical	Precision production, craft, and repair
	89	90	91	92	93	94	95	96	97	98	99	100	101	102	103
NEBRASKA—Cont'd															
Blaine	268	64.6	22 300	16.7	14.7	150	10.0	2.3	385	0.8	6	1.6	358	16.8	6.7
Boone	2 560	73.1	30 500	16.6	13.0	226	17.2	0.9	2 832	0.4	99	3.5	2 897	16.4	11.2
Box Butte	4 898	67.9	44 000	16.3	12.6	283	21.9	2.9	6 414	0.9	284	4.4	5 869	16.6	14.0
Boyd	1 148	79.3	16 800	16.4	14.6	224	16.8	2.0	1 097	-0.5	42	3.8	1 108	17.9	6.9
Brown	1 499	73.6	29 400	21.8	13.7	263	23.0	1.5	1 759	-0.3	59	3.4	1 586	19.0	10.2
Buffalo	13 736	61.8	49 500	19.2	13.3	320	25.0	1.8	25 417	0.9	755	3.0	19 558	23.5	10.4
Burt	3 139	71.1	29 600	15.8	13.0	247	22.9	1.1	3 455	-1.4	148	4.3	3 301	18.7	12.5
Butler	3 253	75.2	30 200	19.2	12.3	279	20.2	2.6	4 423	1.6	153	3.5	3 813	18.1	11.1
Cass	7 797	76.7	48 200	21.5	12.6	345	21.8	1.6	13 152	0.7	412	3.1	9 877	21.4	13.4
Cedar	3 652	76.9	31 100	17.5	12.9	222	17.0	1.8	4 693	0.9	116	2.5	4 485	15.3	10.7
Chase	1 704	74.9	38 000	20.6	13.6	270	19.2	1.5	1 851	-1.4	41	2.2	1 880	18.1	10.1
Cherry	2 438	63.5	35 500	18.9	13.3	266	23.4	3.9	3 413	0.3	63	1.8	2 955	16.6	7.6
Cheyenne	3 851	70.4	35 700	15.8	12.0	277	21.1	2.2	6 601	0.8	137	2.1	4 616	20.8	10.9
Clay	2 741	75.8	28 100	15.5	12.6	254	20.0	1.0	3 420	-0.5	91	2.7	3 137	20.1	9.8
Colfax	3 562	75.9	34 300	15.8	13.2	258	18.8	2.3	5 093	3.0	128	2.5	4 193	15.8	15.7
Cuming	3 851	71.7	38 500	17.1	12.4	266	18.7	1.2	5 278	0.0	110	2.1	4 755	15.9	8.7
Custer	4 953	71.0	27 900	15.1	12.0	234	21.3	1.9	5 509	1.1	106	1.9	5 579	17.9	9.3
Dakota	6 035	68.3	43 700	17.9	12.9	348	23.1	4.0	10 225	0.4	287	2.8	8 147	18.9	16.8
Dawes	3 327	63.1	33 400	15.1	13.7	291	30.3	2.3	4 513	-3.1	174	3.9	3 913	26.9	8.8
Dawson	7 829	69.7	40 800	18.2	12.3	291	21.7	1.7	13 066	-1.0	423	3.2	9 672	18.5	11.3
Deuel	915	74.0	28 800	15.7	13.0	246	21.1	2.2	855	-3.3	24	2.8	986	16.7	12.0
Dixon	2 338	74.2	27 100	15.7	13.0	237	18.4	1.8	2 454	-2.3	70	2.9	2 798	16.9	12.5
Dodge	13 445	67.6	42 800	17.8	12.8	311	22.6	1.3	20 346	0.8	727	3.6	16 481	20.5	13.2
Douglas	161 113	62.7	59 900	20.4	12.7	393	24.8	2.0	260 359	0.8	8 911	3.4	211 964	32.5	8.9
Dundy	1 085	69.5	23 600	20.2	12.6	229	17.9	0.8	1 075	0.7	21	2.0	1 202	20.5	6.0
Fillmore	2 829	74.6	30 900	19.3	12.5	272	19.4	0.9	3 197	-1.0	87	2.7	3 187	18.6	11.2
Franklin	1 655	78.9	19 300	17.7	12.7	231	17.2	1.1	1 608	1.4	41	2.5	1 617	19.2	9.4
Frontier	1 206	71.8	25 500	14.8	13.2	231	19.3	1.2	1 546	0.3	33	2.1	1 489	17.0	5.3
Furnas	2 334	75.9	19 900	18.4	13.0	208	20.6	1.7	2 417	-1.4	46	1.9	2 352	19.0	9.1
Gage	9 019	70.7	36 600	17.1	12.0	280	21.5	1.4	12 575	1.9	337	2.7	10 837	19.7	12.3
Garden	1 040	68.7	30 700	18.0	12.7	230	18.8	1.1	929	-9.8	29	3.1	1 148	19.3	5.5
Garfield	864	71.6	24 000	19.6	12.5	212	19.3	2.2	1 033	1.2	19	1.8	1 003	16.1	10.7
Gosper	764	77.2	40 300	17.5	11.4	280	17.0	2.2	1 309	-1.1	29	2.2	977	18.0	9.5
Grant	303	63.4	25 900	19.2	12.9	245	22.2	0.6	356	1.1	6	1.7	372	17.2	7.5
Greeley	1 133	78.5	19 200	18.3	12.8	209	16.5	2.4	1 319	-1.8	39	3.0	1 370	18.8	9.3
Hall	18 678	63.6	48 200	17.7	12.6	319	22.6	2.0	30 928	-0.7	908	2.9	24 542	22.7	12.0
Hamilton	3 235	69.4	41 400	17.9	12.4	296	19.4	2.3	5 427	-0.9	102	1.9	4 267	20.6	11.6
Harlan	1 585	77.7	28 400	20.3	13.6	262	22.6	0.6	1 723	1.9	42	2.4	1 768	17.3	9.6
Hayes	480	70.4	19 600	13.2	13.4	235	17.5	1.1	460	-4.0	11	2.4	495	15.2	3.6
Hitchcock	1 467	75.5	22 700	18.1	12.2	250	15.9	1.5	1 613	-0.3	50	3.1	1 588	17.8	8.4
Holt	4 744	69.9	35 200	19.7	13.5	261	20.4	2.8	6 372	0.6	191	3.0	5 754	19.0	8.7
Hooker	332	76.8	26 300	18.5	13.0	223	16.1	1.7	455	3.6	14	3.1	358	20.1	7.8
Howard	2 309	74.4	31 600	15.9	12.9	236	17.3	2.2	3 505	-0.6	98	2.8	2 729	15.8	10.7
Jefferson	3 634	76.2	19 400	15.5	12.3	257	18.7	2.1	3 944	-1.5	185	4.7	4 140	19.5	12.4
Johnson	1 940	76.4	25 900	16.3	12.4	247	21.4	2.7	2 263	4.9	73	3.2	2 201	18.4	17.6
Kearney	2 523	72.2	42 500	17.5	12.6	307	20.0	1.1	3 863	1.3	90	2.3	3 107	23.8	9.3
Keith	3 430	69.7	41 500	21.7	12.7	285	21.9	1.3	4 663	1.5	136	2.9	4 311	19.1	10.2
Keya Paha	419	70.9	17 500	12.5	13.3	183	15.2	1.2	524	-1.9	7	1.3	493	8.9	5.7
Kimball	1 650	74.5	35 300	18.1	11.6	289	19.1	2.5	1 985	-0.3	43	2.2	1 881	18.3	14.8
Knox	3 817	73.4	24 900	18.5	14.1	202	20.2	2.1	4 373	-4.0	159	3.6	4 104	16.6	8.2
Lancaster	82 759	60.5	62 200	18.9	11.9	378	25.6	1.4	145 823	1.1	4 151	2.8	117 484	32.7	9.5
Lincoln	12 676	67.9	42 900	16.4	11.8	288	23.9	1.7	17 275	2.6	597	3.5	14 962	21.0	13.5
Logan	320	66.6	29 200	28.8	12.3	282	16.4	3.5	438	2.8	10	2.3	392	19.6	7.1
Loup	276	72.8	14 999	27.5	11.9	182	12.6	3.3	372	-6.5	7	1.9	329	13.4	5.5
McPherson	212	63.7	30 600	10.0	11.5	179	28.8	7.0	294	2.4	3	1.0	272	9.2	5.5
Madison	12 283	65.4	48 000	19.6	12.8	307	22.7	2.1	19 719	-1.1	714	3.6	16 235	21.0	13.0
Merrick	3 061	73.0	33 200	17.8	12.4	266	17.9	1.3	4 570	-0.8	114	2.5	3 853	17.1	11.2
Morrill	2 083	68.4	28 400	16.7	13.5	272	22.7	2.2	2 772	3.7	78	2.8	2 390	16.4	9.4
Nance	1 585	76.3	24 300	16.0	12.8	235	18.9	1.2	1 722	-0.5	71	4.1	1 914	16.8	8.8
Nemaha	3 079	69.3	33 500	16.8	13.1	255	21.1	1.6	4 078	-0.6	142	3.5	3 679	26.1	9.6
Nuckolls	2 359	78.7	22 200	16.0	12.8	219	22.0	2.2	2 166	-3.2	55	2.5	2 431	16.8	10.8
Otoe	5 657	71.5	38 800	15.3	12.7	296	21.6	2.2	7 825	1.0	268	3.4	6 735	20.5	12.1
Pawnee	1 408	80.8	14 999	17.9	13.3	190	23.9	3.1	1 699	2.2	49	2.9	1 491	17.4	11.2
Perkins	1 283	77.5	36 600	16.9	12.8	301	16.8	1.3	1 473	1.6	28	1.9	1 438	17.9	9.1
Phelps	3 769	71.9	39 700	16.3	11.4	284	19.6	1.2	5 146	2.2	119	2.3	4 881	19.8	11.6
Pierce	2 929	76.6	34 200	17.0	14.4	244	17.7	2.0	4 024	-0.9	119	3.0	3 440	17.7	13.0

1. Specified owner-occupied units. 2. Specified renter-occupied units. 3. Overcrowded or lacking complete plumbing facilities. 4. Percent of civilian labor force. 5. Persons 16 years and older.

Table B. States and Counties — Nonfarm Employment and Agriculture

STATE County	Number of establishments	Employment Total	Health Care and Social Assistance	Manufacturing	Retail trade	Finance and Insurance	Professional Scientific and Technical Services	Annual payroll Total (mil dol)	Average per employee (dollars)	Farms Number	Percent with— Less than 50 acres	500 acres and over	Farm operators Whose principal occupation is farming (percent)
	104	105	106	107	108	109	110	111	112	113	114	115	116
NEBRASKA—Cont'd													
Blaine	12	D	0	D	D	D	D	D	D	118	10.2	72.0	88.1
Boone	202	1 475	363	68	298	74	23	27	18 002	767	9.8	38.1	75.6
Box Butte	365	3 440	524	492	685	164	88	63	18 386	508	6.5	61.0	73.4
Boyd	80	406	135	D	71	37	12	6	15 034	361	9.7	54.3	70.9
Brown	150	848	176	25	241	66	15	12	14 492	349	14.3	56.7	63.9
Buffalo	1 286	19 513	3 165	4 161	3 798	690	435	434	22 257	1 081	16.1	39.0	67.9
Burt	227	1 240	222	93	241	107	56	23	18 497	580	14.7	35.5	70.9
Butler	174	1 678	307	462	221	80	37	33	19 524	804	13.4	32.6	68.7
Cass	502	3 821	388	276	679	181	58	80	21 035	694	22.6	28.2	62.7
Cedar	281	1 763	150	255	304	106	44	32	18 146	971	12.5	33.5	72.5
Chase	136	996	157	D	278	61	17	19	18 777	374	7.2	68.4	70.3
Cherry	231	1 552	244	D	434	82	45	25	16 226	672	9.2	75.7	79.8
Cheyenne	321	4 025	433	463	1 151	205	44	96	23 966	645	4.7	62.8	73.6
Clay	198	1 208	97	67	212	74	27	25	20 348	538	14.9	46.5	75.8
Colfax	266	3 862	333	D	380	111	D	80	20 586	604	20.4	28.3	69.2
Cuming	356	3 199	463	742	504	181	67	61	19 053	995	19.8	23.7	74.4
Custer	365	2 538	664	D	546	131	72	45	17 772	1 307	13.4	57.3	71.3
Dakota	443	12 248	410	5 338	839	640	D	334	27 282	289	13.8	27.7	57.8
Dawes	300	2 246	309	D	627	77	67	32	14 363	471	10.0	59.2	66.7
Dawson	712	9 694	946	4 084	1 484	301	180	210	21 640	858	16.2	45.1	73.8
Deuel	76	480	16	0	209	39	D	8	16 617	251	5.6	62.9	66.1
Dixon	132	637	216	D	98	57	3	10	15 295	583	14.9	27.8	67.2
Dodge	1 086	14 182	1 890	3 482	2 561	448	290	306	21 596	798	19.7	29.1	68.4
Douglas	13 867	298 720	37 545	28 565	33 361	28 561	15 495	9 510	31 837	368	37.0	19.3	51.4
Dundy	75	445	165	D	71	16	D	8	18 369	323	6.8	68.7	77.1
Fillmore	240	1 750	328	D	222	128	15	36	20 834	584	9.8	50.0	82.0
Franklin	106	566	186	D	90	47	30	9	15 210	430	10.5	48.8	74.0
Frontier	82	498	79	D	67	24	D	9	17 890	362	8.3	68.8	79.6
Furnas	179	1 304	360	D	313	79	48	26	19 742	432	10.6	55.3	74.8
Gage	684	7 608	1 500	1 863	1 279	234	122	144	18 892	1 144	16.3	34.4	65.1
Garden	64	368	D	0	76	36	7	6	15 383	308	7.1	61.0	72.1
Garfield	90	508	107	D	142	D	26	8	15 020	206	11.2	51.0	68.0
Gosper	53	166	D	D	D	30	D	3	16 012	252	6.7	58.3	83.3
Grant	23	91	0	0	26	D	D	1	14 813	88	14.8	76.1	77.3
Greeley	84	438	56	47	127	39	D	7	15 648	387	8.8	49.1	74.7
Hall	1 836	27 037	3 618	6 253	5 017	1 438	456	626	23 169	702	20.8	32.3	65.2
Hamilton	274	2 515	276	716	263	110	46	59	23 322	661	11.3	43.9	75.0
Harlan	93	577	149	D	110	39	D	8	14 047	371	11.9	52.3	70.1
Hayes	21	75	D	D	D	D	D	1	14 933	257	5.8	63.8	74.7
Hitchcock	64	294	D	0	92	D	D	5	18 058	339	8.6	65.2	77.0
Holt	424	2 875	578	151	639	154	67	47	16 342	1 291	12.3	54.0	68.3
Hooker	33	176	D	D	45	D	0	3	14 381	88	4.5	76.1	73.9
Howard	154	790	174	D	197	72	D	13	16 694	646	12.4	34.2	71.8
Jefferson	243	2 688	306	685	480	83	D	49	18 258	626	11.2	37.2	67.4
Johnson	137	1 032	190	D	186	67	D	17	16 852	491	9.8	29.7	62.9
Kearney	187	1 615	553	112	161	78	11	30	18 733	492	10.4	52.4	80.3
Keith	377	2 975	339	409	713	155	95	55	18 446	375	10.1	51.7	69.1
Keya Paha	19	41	0	D	D	0	D	1	12 439	225	3.1	79.6	85.8
Kimball	154	1 461	85	294	227	68	D	25	16 829	326	4.9	71.8	64.1
Knox	284	1 471	325	D	416	102	45	20	13 538	1 053	12.2	40.2	73.5
Lancaster	6 894	122 307	16 504	16 224	16 742	9 808	8 006	3 188	26 068	1 457	32.3	19.1	46.0
Lincoln	981	9 902	1 790	387	2 359	477	264	191	19 314	1 019	15.8	52.4	61.1
Logan	16	58	0	D	18	D	0	1	15 121	124	8.9	58.1	86.3
Loup	8	12	0	0	D	D	0	0	14 167	143	7.0	60.1	79.7
McPherson	7	14	0	0	D	0	0	0	10 286	112	7.1	80.4	81.2
Madison	1 298	18 495	2 846	4 259	3 324	479	380	429	23 181	782	19.8	30.7	65.5
Merrick	226	1 883	316	359	301	69	42	37	19 542	553	13.6	37.4	70.0
Morrill	122	737	127	16	175	46	D	13	17 476	474	12.0	53.2	71.7
Nance	115	480	126	0	98	54	16	7	14 148	419	13.6	41.5	76.6
Nemaha	202	1 652	346	339	326	95	40	31	18 844	483	9.7	36.9	67.9
Nuckolls	192	1 280	398	D	270	108	38	20	15 360	496	9.9	51.0	69.8
Otoe	445	4 640	726	1 266	800	211	75	93	20 136	821	19.2	29.2	67.6
Pawnee	79	446	138	D	50	41	27	7	16 363	444	8.3	33.6	61.3
Perkins	108	773	196	D	106	35	D	15	19 506	490	4.3	59.4	73.3
Phelps	325	3 792	788	921	526	193	90	87	22 814	552	11.8	50.5	82.8
Pierce	220	1 491	311	42	359	72	16	26	17 145	717	14.6	31.9	67.1

Table B. States and Counties — **Agriculture, Land, and Water**

	Agriculture, 1997 (cont'd)															
STATE County	Land in farms					Value of land and buildings		Value of machinery and equipment average per farm ($1,000)	Value of products sold				Percent of farms with sales of —		Percent of land owned by fed. gov. 1997	Water consumption 1995 (mil gal/day)
		Acres									Percent from —					
	Acreage (1,000)	Percent change, 1992–1997	Average size of farm	Total irrigated (1,000)	Total cropland (1,000)	Average per farm ($1,000)	Average per acre (dollars)		Total (mil dol)	Average per farm (dollars)	Crops	Live-stock and poultry products	$10,000 or more	$100,000 or more		
	117	118	119	120	121	122	123	124	125	126	127	128	129	130	131	132
NEBRASKA—Cont'd																
Blaine	452	-1.9	3 831	9	44	757	196	58	16	138 027	11.0	89.0	78.0	34.7	2.3	29.5
Boone	448	2.3	584	129	317	511	952	85	164	213 762	33.7	66.3	85.5	38.9	0.0	87.6
Box Butte	697	7.2	1 371	136	389	528	347	107	151	296 892	40.8	59.2	76.4	36.8	0.0	171.1
Boyd	297	0.2	822	5	113	272	307	62	31	85 106	33.5	66.5	80.9	21.9	0.0	4.4
Brown	701	7.8	2 008	52	133	726	364	68	87	250 341	18.1	81.9	75.4	32.1	0.2	19.4
Buffalo	621	5.7	575	208	380	535	941	83	159	146 671	51.7	48.3	76.1	36.3	0.0	207.5
Burt	292	8.3	504	38	264	646	1 371	88	113	194 000	53.7	46.3	79.0	44.1	0.0	46.3
Butler	354	5.2	440	95	307	476	1 178	82	102	127 451	65.8	34.2	75.9	34.5	0.0	100.6
Cass	301	1.5	433	D	255	663	1 576	74	67	96 772	83.8	16.2	70.5	30.7	0.0	16.2
Cedar	445	3.8	459	63	359	444	925	84	154	158 153	31.9	68.1	81.2	40.6	0.1	52.9
Chase	557	6.8	1 488	168	317	1 048	756	121	104	278 593	68.6	31.4	84.0	54.3	0.1	180.1
Cherry	3 882	-0.2	5 777	44	395	1 153	200	84	100	149 226	7.7	92.3	80.1	36.2	5.3	98.9
Cheyenne	779	1.0	1 208	48	559	541	434	92	111	172 597	34.1	65.9	79.8	23.3	0.0	66.2
Clay	365	2.1	678	182	288	831	1 229	111	171	317 096	43.8	56.2	83.8	54.3	11.1	198.3
Colfax	230	0.6	381	52	203	479	1 417	86	179	295 749	25.1	74.9	82.3	38.7	0.0	60.2
Cuming	360	3.9	361	32	313	549	1 571	73	507	509 501	11.8	88.2	86.3	43.8	0.0	43.8
Custer	1 552	8.9	1 188	199	486	547	444	67	289	220 766	26.4	73.6	78.3	33.7	0.0	241.2
Dakota	142	2.9	492	12	120	504	1 015	75	29	100 188	80.9	19.1	64.7	26.0	0.5	20.7
Dawes	822	-2.4	1 745	16	198	460	266	50	28	59 863	27.0	73.0	66.0	13.8	8.1	43.2
Dawson	650	-1.4	757	219	354	625	859	84	399	465 589	22.4	77.6	82.3	45.1	0.0	332.6
Deuel	282	6.2	1 122	16	231	538	497	88	21	83 956	73.9	26.1	79.7	24.3	0.0	43.1
Dixon	243	-0.2	416	16	194	352	868	59	117	200 988	24.0	76.0	74.1	29.3	0.0	42.6
Dodge	323	8.1	405	93	295	664	1 654	96	141	176 815	51.0	49.0	82.2	40.1	0.0	100.7
Douglas	113	17.5	306	16	92	676	2 261	93	44	119 956	56.4	43.6	57.3	23.9	0.3	363.9
Dundy	591	11.7	1 830	85	217	849	480	110	87	268 209	46.3	53.7	83.0	47.1	0.0	102.7
Fillmore	357	5.0	611	195	326	842	1 383	114	142	242 554	62.0	38.0	90.2	56.5	0.7	163.2
Franklin	351	8.6	816	87	192	632	812	90	56	129 496	66.9	33.1	80.5	39.5	0.5	99.6
Frontier	531	1.0	1 467	55	226	686	480	86	76	208 946	36.2	63.8	82.0	42.0	1.9	76.2
Furnas	450	4.5	1 042	54	279	514	539	89	77	177 901	50.1	49.9	83.8	39.8	0.2	73.6
Gage	519	2.0	454	48	410	394	899	71	115	100 326	55.1	44.9	75.1	29.1	0.0	42.2
Garden	1 078	0.7	3 499	38	197	890	252	76	58	186 855	24.4	75.6	78.2	33.1	4.0	58.0
Garfield	308	-8.9	1 495	13	67	446	326	51	29	140 121	14.4	85.6	76.7	26.2	0.1	103.3
Gosper	234	1.8	929	68	127	560	577	99	52	204 972	51.1	48.9	85.7	45.6	0.4	164.9
Grant	477	-12.7	5 419	1	41	1 087	201	67	11	127 084	5.6	94.4	77.3	40.9	0.0	3.7
Greeley	291	-4.3	752	58	124	483	646	77	46	119 946	40.4	59.6	80.6	35.9	0.5	44.5
Hall	342	8.0	488	175	258	733	1 449	106	146	208 512	47.1	52.9	74.9	38.7	3.4	169.6
Hamilton	344	7.0	520	238	310	869	1 626	127	149	225 844	64.4	35.6	88.2	58.1	0.6	224.9
Harlan	325	6.4	877	76	219	554	721	103	83	223 006	41.9	58.1	77.1	40.2	2.4	122.0
Hayes	426	6.1	1 659	35	173	926	591	77	68	265 256	26.9	73.1	82.1	38.5	0.0	61.5
Hitchcock	406	0.6	1 198	29	239	654	465	118	34	99 410	66.8	33.2	83.2	33.3	1.4	49.5
Holt	1 464	5.5	1 134	209	618	554	547	98	246	190 607	35.1	64.9	77.8	30.2	0.0	168.0
Hooker	371	-0.9	4 221	3	20	667	158	29	9	97 062	1.6	98.4	80.7	30.7	0.0	6.1
Howard	330	1.5	511	111	210	405	828	73	116	179 093	32.7	67.3	79.9	31.9	1.6	42.3
Jefferson	315	-3.6	503	55	238	457	916	72	77	122 997	54.5	45.5	75.7	30.4	0.0	41.2
Johnson	197	5.3	401	10	146	306	826	48	30	60 289	59.4	40.6	66.8	20.2	0.0	8.4
Kearney	320	3.2	650	189	267	852	1 366	148	197	399 506	43.2	56.8	85.2	57.7	0.8	167.7
Keith	607	-9.3	1 618	78	254	684	422	97	103	274 101	32.0	68.0	75.7	35.7	0.0	122.7
Keya Paha	500	12.0	2 221	11	104	596	275	58	27	120 633	16.1	83.9	86.2	27.1	0.0	9.1
Kimball	565	11.9	1 734	25	339	468	286	74	23	70 197	60.8	39.2	66.9	19.9	0.0	38.6
Knox	596	-2.8	566	38	327	294	497	70	165	156 379	17.1	82.9	78.5	27.0	0.2	51.3
Lancaster	421	1.5	289	13	344	400	1 410	51	82	56 545	72.4	27.6	51.6	17.4	1.4	21.0
Lincoln	1 420	-2.0	1 394	196	434	737	494	72	192	188 732	36.6	63.4	74.0	33.1	0.0	1 086.3
Logan	323	-3.9	2 605	15	58	646	250	74	19	154 087	33.9	66.1	83.9	43.5	0.0	19.9
Loup	339	2.8	2 372	11	39	639	254	56	15	104 425	17.2	82.8	82.5	25.9	0.0	35.9
McPherson	443	-4.7	3 958	7	36	705	178	41	14	124 563	7.2	92.8	80.4	31.2	0.0	8.9
Madison	329	2.3	421	79	275	467	1 082	92	116	148 042	44.9	55.1	72.6	30.6	0.0	68.7
Merrick	274	-5.9	495	163	220	603	1 255	94	163	295 044	36.0	64.0	82.6	43.4	0.0	125.2
Morrill	861	18.9	1 816	117	232	658	363	72	148	311 459	24.6	75.4	79.1	36.9	0.0	116.0
Nance	244	3.1	583	60	165	440	787	84	67	158 869	46.5	53.5	85.7	38.9	0.0	39.3
Nemaha	239	5.8	495	4	202	586	1 148	67	56	116 127	64.2	35.8	79.5	30.2	0.0	636.9
Nuckolls	327	-1.7	660	50	228	426	766	78	54	109 156	70.5	29.5	83.7	36.5	0.0	54.0
Otoe	354	8.7	432	4	276	400	973	70	71	86 677	67.7	32.3	72.1	26.4	0.0	308.3
Pawnee	230	2.5	517	D	145	328	685	43	28	63 133	50.9	49.1	63.3	18.0	0.0	2.4
Perkins	553	3.7	1 128	120	446	606	521	97	65	132 353	83.1	16.9	76.3	34.9	0.0	141.1
Phelps	379	0.7	686	224	302	876	1 376	165	336	609 402	25.5	74.5	89.7	63.2	1.2	337.6
Pierce	309	4.0	431	92	258	416	945	82	108	150 820	42.2	57.8	79.6	36.7	0.0	78.4

STATE County	Value of Residential Construction Authorized by Building Permits, 2000		Wholesale Trade, 1997				Retail Trade[1], 1997				Real Estate and Rental and Leasing, 1997			
	New Construction ($1,000)	Number of Housing Units	Number of Establish-ments	Number of Employees	Sales (mil dol)	Annual Payroll (mil dol)	Number of Establish-ments	Number of Employees	Sales (mil dol)	Annual Payroll (mil dol)	Number of Establish-ments	Number of Employees	Receipts (mil dol)	Annual Payroll (mil dol)
	133	134	135	136	137	138	139	140	141	142	143	144	145	146
NEBRASKA—Cont'd														
Blaine	NA	NA	3	D	D	D	4	7	0.9	0.1	NA	NA	NA	NA
Boone	305	3	21	200	164.8	4.2	49	334	60.5	5.2	4	8	0.6	0.1
Box Butte	154	2	24	250	84.0	6.1	72	698	107.3	9.7	16	31	1.4	0.3
Boyd	0	0	6	D	D	D	15	62	7.9	0.6	2	D	D	D
Brown	390	4	9	D	D	D	30	191	28.8	2.5	1	D	D	D
Buffalo	29 872	214	68	915	589.2	22.5	239	3 234	455.3	48.7	43	155	14.8	1.8
Burt	755	7	18	129	52.2	3.8	51	241	49.2	3.7	4	10	0.4	0.1
Butler	1 218	15	13	D	D	D	25	210	23.3	2.4	2	D	D	D
Cass	14 299	171	28	D	D	D	77	740	113.5	8.8	15	41	4.0	0.6
Cedar	2 774	23	24	154	79.8	3.2	51	308	62.9	4.3	6	15	0.7	0.2
Chase	1 098	12	19	222	118.5	5.4	35	240	44.8	3.7	1	D	D	D
Cherry	712	7	13	51	37.2	1.2	49	399	60.7	5.8	3	D	D	D
Cheyenne	3 212	36	18	D	D	D	61	964	649.8	22.2	7	34	0.9	0.2
Clay	1 609	19	19	185	100.2	4.1	40	202	43.9	2.9	4	8	0.2	0.1
Colfax	660	7	23	207	81.4	4.5	51	383	76.3	5.9	5	8	0.3	0.1
Cuming	2 150	21	24	D	D	D	60	466	97.8	6.7	7	17	1.8	0.2
Custer	754	6	19	142	74.3	2.7	83	534	81.2	6.7	8	16	1.6	0.1
Dakota	6 432	76	30	D	D	D	80	878	105.0	11.5	16	D	D	D
Dawes	304	7	16	D	D	D	61	663	81.4	6.7	12	26	1.2	0.1
Dawson	1 558	22	46	504	306.3	11.4	149	1 401	185.4	18.9	19	70	4.2	0.6
Deuel	310	3	5	D	D	D	15	136	24.6	1.6	1	D	D	D
Dixon	1 140	11	9	80	47.1	1.7	16	97	23.5	1.4	1	D	D	D
Dodge	12 076	141	71	748	587.7	21.1	185	2 313	479.8	37.8	37	172	13.5	2.4
Douglas	230 885	2 888	1 039	17 083	11 542.8	574.0	1 931	34 920	5 634.5	591.7	574	4 411	553.6	106.0
Dundy	0	0	5	D	D	D	17	84	15.7	1.4	3	5	0.3	0.0
Fillmore	1 133	10	21	170	83.0	4.5	38	229	30.5	2.5	4	9	0.2	0.1
Franklin	733	4	7	43	20.9	0.9	23	97	13.0	1.2	NA	NA	NA	NA
Frontier	70	2	7	D	D	D	17	78	6.3	0.6	NA	NA	NA	NA
Furnas	966	6	11	D	D	D	41	285	55.2	4.0	1	D	D	D
Gage	8 646	148	46	277	148.3	6.6	153	1 310	190.1	15.8	20	98	3.8	0.9
Garden	165	2	4	D	D	D	15	80	9.6	0.9	NA	NA	NA	NA
Garfield	234	3	3	D	D	D	26	135	33.0	1.8	2	D	D	D
Gosper	700	8	4	D	D	D	5	17	2.0	0.1	NA	NA	NA	NA
Grant	NA	NA	2	D	D	D	6	41	2.9	0.4	NA	NA	NA	NA
Greeley	0	0	7	D	D	D	19	111	32.8	1.9	1	D	D	D
Hall	15 190	147	116	1 534	690.4	41.5	347	4 646	722.1	69.2	61	178	22.4	3.3
Hamilton	2 836	33	26	376	208.8	8.1	35	302	39.9	4.2	10	21	0.9	0.3
Harlan	243	2	7	D	D	D	20	103	17.0	1.3	NA	NA	NA	NA
Hayes	110	2	2	D	D	D	1	D	D	D	1	D	D	D
Hitchcock	0	0	7	D	D	D	14	93	18.2	1.3	1	D	D	D
Holt	3 383	44	40	341	166.2	4.7	95	610	99.6	7.5	6	17	1.3	0.1
Hooker	0	0	1	D	D	D	8	43	4.1	0.5	NA	NA	NA	NA
Howard	3 999	56	7	54	30.7	1.7	38	210	25.1	2.8	2	D	D	D
Jefferson	620	5	22	246	144.3	5.7	51	448	60.6	6.1	7	34	0.8	0.2
Johnson	362	6	7	71	29.0	1.1	34	196	29.1	2.6	4	8	0.3	0.0
Kearney	540	7	11	131	135.3	3.8	28	166	24.2	2.1	3	5	0.2	0.0
Keith	4 733	140	24	213	190.6	4.8	75	669	97.8	9.6	8	11	0.9	0.2
Keya Paha	NA	NA	3	D	D	D	6	12	2.1	0.2	1	D	D	D
Kimball	0	0	10	D	D	D	30	183	21.1	2.1	2	D	D	D
Knox	618	6	17	D	D	D	73	373	61.3	4.5	4	12	0.3	0.1
Lancaster	187 802	1 697	304	D	D	D	996	15 734	2 270.4	232.0	267	1 480	150.3	25.4
Lincoln	12 640	161	56	461	259.7	11.9	198	2 107	314.5	28.9	31	100	7.7	1.3
Logan	NA	NA	NA	NA	NA	NA	2	D	D	D	NA	NA	NA	NA
Loup	0	0	NA	NA	NA	NA	3	D	D	D	NA	NA	NA	NA
McPherson	NA	NA	2	D	D	D	2	D	D	D	NA	NA	NA	NA
Madison	10 614	95	81	D	D	D	226	3 048	479.6	41.6	46	147	12.8	2.0
Merrick	1 542	18	20	137	109.4	3.7	39	250	31.5	3.2	4	5	0.2	0.1
Morrill	233	3	11	119	30.7	2.7	23	162	23.9	2.0	4	5	0.5	0.0
Nance	200	2	10	D	D	D	21	111	14.8	1.2	5	4	0.2	0.0
Nemaha	868	9	12	D	D	D	45	323	51.5	3.7	4	6	0.5	0.1
Nuckolls	290	3	13	109	44.9	1.7	40	284	43.2	3.7	2	D	D	D
Otoe	11 741	128	21	159	131.3	3.6	98	694	110.6	9.5	11	15	1.7	0.3
Pawnee	67	2	6	D	D	D	12	53	7.1	0.6	2	D	D	D
Perkins	85	1	20	125	136.7	2.8	18	92	12.4	1.2	2	D	D	D
Phelps	721	8	25	D	D	D	70	533	81.8	7.4	6	17	0.9	0.2
Pierce	1 960	20	18	97	40.0	1.9	51	312	45.1	3.6	2	D	D	D

1. Establishments with payroll.

Table B. States and Counties — Professional, Manufacturing, and Accommodation and Foodservices

STATE County	Professional, Scientific, and Technical Services[1], 1997				Manufacturing, 1997				Accommodation and Foodservices, 1997			
	Number of Establishments	Number of Employees	Receipts (mil dol)	Annual Payroll (mil dol)	Number of Establishments	Number of Employees	Receipts (mil dol)	Annual Payroll (mil dol)	Number of Establishments	Number of Employees	Sales (mil dol)	Annual Payroll (mil dol)
	147	148	149	150	151	152	153	154	155	156	157	158
NEBRASKA—Cont'd												
Blaine	1	D	D	D	NA	NA	NA	NA	1	D	D	D
Boone	2	D	D	D	NA	NA	NA	NA	14	60	1.8	0.4
Box Butte	21	63	3.7	1.3	NA	NA	NA	NA	35	441	10.3	3.1
Boyd	3	7	0.5	0.1	NA	NA	NA	NA	6	17	0.5	0.1
Brown	4	10	0.5	0.2	NA	NA	NA	NA	16	95	2.3	0.6
Buffalo	65	343	21.1	8.0	47	4 392	817.1	122.1	118	2 322	65.8	18.7
Burt	8	26	1.7	0.4	NA	NA	NA	NA	17	141	3.1	0.7
Butler	7	24	1.1	0.6	NA	NA	NA	NA	18	D	D	D
Cass	24	D	D	D	NA	NA	NA	NA	45	340	10.3	2.6
Cedar	9	17	1.0	0.3	NA	NA	NA	NA	21	D	D	D
Chase	3	7	0.3	0.1	NA	NA	NA	NA	12	75	1.8	0.5
Cherry	12	33	2.1	0.4	NA	NA	NA	NA	27	179	5.9	1.5
Cheyenne	15	50	2.3	0.8	NA	NA	NA	NA	37	456	12.5	3.4
Clay	10	22	0.9	0.2	NA	NA	NA	NA	21	D	D	D
Colfax	5	17	1.1	0.3	4	D	D	D	31	D	D	D
Cuming	16	57	2.7	0.8	30	803	522.2	18.0	33	265	6.2	1.5
Custer	15	42	2.5	0.5	NA	NA	NA	NA	32	206	5.0	1.0
Dakota	26	97	5.5	1.8	23	D	D	D	41	656	21.2	6.1
Dawes	14	46	2.5	1.0	NA	NA	NA	NA	37	398	9.4	2.5
Dawson	34	109	6.0	2.1	26	3 899	1 300.0	88.8	63	759	19.4	4.8
Deuel	2	D	D	D	NA	NA	NA	NA	10	50	1.1	0.4
Dixon	4	4	0.2	0.0	NA	NA	NA	NA	9	39	1.4	0.2
Dodge	48	285	13.2	5.8	67	3 437	1 009.7	87.5	99	1 490	41.3	10.2
Douglas	1 244	12 434	1 125.5	466.4	555	27 335	7 140.4	897.4	1 033	19 822	618.8	184.4
Dundy	8	8	0.6	0.1	NA	NA	NA	NA	8	D	D	D
Fillmore	5	13	0.9	0.3	NA	NA	NA	NA	23	121	3.7	0.7
Franklin	6	23	1.2	0.3	NA	NA	NA	NA	10	44	1.3	0.2
Frontier	2	D	D	D	NA	NA	NA	NA	4	D	D	D
Furnas	8	46	2.6	1.5	NA	NA	NA	NA	17	D	D	D
Gage	25	80	4.2	1.3	34	1 700	305.5	43.9	50	583	15.6	4.1
Garden	3	3	0.2	0.0	NA	NA	NA	NA	10	42	1.1	0.2
Garfield	2	D	D	D	NA	NA	NA	NA	8	61	0.9	0.2
Gosper	5	12	0.9	0.2	NA	NA	NA	NA	5	16	0.6	0.1
Grant	NA	NA	NA	NA	NA	NA	NA	NA	3	D	D	D
Greeley	1	D	D	D	NA	NA	NA	NA	6	25	0.9	0.1
Hall	99	427	32.4	11.9	81	5 791	1 823.3	156.3	155	2 833	71.5	21.0
Hamilton	14	37	2.6	0.7	21	691	332.7	19.9	12	129	2.9	0.9
Harlan	4	7	0.9	0.1	NA	NA	NA	NA	15	D	D	D
Hayes	NA	NA	NA	NA	NA	NA	NA	NA	1	D	D	D
Hitchcock	1	D	D	D	NA	NA	NA	NA	4	D	D	D
Holt	14	56	2.7	0.8	NA	NA	NA	NA	30	313	7.3	1.6
Hooker	NA	NA	NA	NA	NA	NA	NA	NA	4	19	0.5	0.1
Howard	7	13	0.5	0.1	NA	NA	NA	NA	17	107	1.9	0.5
Jefferson	13	27	1.3	0.4	11	649	67.5	11.8	19	D	D	D
Johnson	3	9	0.4	0.1	NA	NA	NA	NA	10	73	1.4	0.4
Kearney	8	17	1.0	0.2	NA	NA	NA	NA	15	D	D	D
Keith	15	70	4.3	1.5	NA	NA	NA	NA	57	584	20.0	4.7
Keya Paha	1	D	D	D	NA	NA	NA	NA	2	D	D	D
Kimball	12	28	1.3	0.3	NA	NA	NA	NA	18	205	6.3	1.7
Knox	14	19	1.2	0.2	NA	NA	NA	NA	30	122	3.4	0.6
Lancaster	483	7 161	688.0	211.6	267	15 322	3 855.1	502.3	545	11 230	318.5	91.8
Lincoln	53	269	17.0	6.2	NA	NA	NA	NA	96	1 645	44.8	13.1
Logan	NA	NA	NA	NA	NA	NA	NA	NA	2	D	D	D
Loup	NA	NA	NA	NA	NA	NA	NA	NA	1	D	D	D
McPherson	1	D	D	D	NA	NA	NA	NA	1	D	D	D
Madison	66	262	16.1	7.1	52	4 908	1 402.4	154.3	101	1 541	40.2	11.3
Merrick	6	16	0.6	0.3	NA	NA	NA	NA	17	168	3.4	0.9
Morrill	NA	NA	NA	NA	NA	NA	NA	NA	16	109	2.3	0.7
Nance	3	10	0.3	0.1	NA	NA	NA	NA	4	12	0.4	0.1
Nemaha	8	14	0.6	0.2	NA	NA	NA	NA	21	221	4.8	1.4
Nuckolls	8	29	0.8	0.3	NA	NA	NA	NA	14	D	D	D
Otoe	20	57	4.3	1.3	17	1 354	212.3	35.0	47	658	17.4	4.7
Pawnee	3	D	D	D	NA	NA	NA	NA	8	36	0.9	0.2
Perkins	5	12	0.6	0.2	NA	NA	NA	NA	9	D	D	D
Phelps	21	79	6.6	1.8	8	D	D	D	20	221	5.7	1.5
Pierce	8	29	1.2	0.4	NA	NA	NA	NA	14	58	1.7	0.3

1. Firms subject to federal tax.

Table B. States and Counties — Health and Other Services and Federal Funds

STATE County	Health Care and Social Assistance[1], 1997				Other Services[1], 1997				Federal funds and grants, fiscal 2001[2] Expenditures (mil dol)			
										Direct payments for individuals[3]		
	Number of Establishments	Number of Employees	Receipts (mil dol)	Annual Payroll (mil dol)	Number of Establishments	Number of Employees	Receipts (mil dol)	Annual Payroll (mil dol)	Total	Social Security and government retirement	Medicare	Food stamps and Supplemental Security Income
	159	160	161	162	163	164	165	166	167	168	169	170
NEBRASKA—Cont'd												
Blaine	NA	NA	NA	NA	NA	NA	NA	NA	3.1	1.1	0.4	0.0
Boone	9	90	2.6	1.2	13	22	2.1	0.4	60.9	14.5	5.6	0.4
Box Butte	20	180	8.1	3.1	25	117	6.1	1.5	69.1	27.8	6.7	1.2
Boyd	5	82	2.2	0.8	4	6	0.3	0.0	22.9	7.0	3.9	0.2
Brown	6	82	2.6	1.2	10	28	1.4	0.2	26.7	9.4	3.0	0.2
Buffalo	92	827	67.8	36.4	82	463	29.9	8.6	177.3	71.8	22.5	2.7
Burt	10	154	4.4	2.5	16	37	2.8	0.5	64.3	20.7	9.2	0.9
Butler	9	140	5.1	2.8	13	39	2.2	0.5	66.2	19.3	6.0	0.5
Cass	22	279	9.0	4.7	24	101	7.0	1.7	120.3	56.7	15.3	1.6
Cedar	13	165	5.4	2.7	17	58	3.6	0.9	65.6	19.6	7.0	0.3
Chase	7	77	2.4	1.1	8	23	2.2	0.4	50.3	10.5	4.1	0.2
Cherry	10	51	3.1	1.2	10	23	2.4	0.3	34.6	13.8	4.4	0.7
Cheyenne	17	146	6.3	3.1	21	71	4.4	1.1	72.0	24.4	8.9	1.1
Clay	7	130	3.1	1.9	12	23	1.6	0.2	72.9	18.7	5.4	0.4
Colfax	16	198	7.1	3.5	28	77	4.5	1.1	63.6	22.3	12.4	0.4
Cuming	12	126	4.6	1.9	30	104	9.3	1.6	68.4	21.7	8.3	0.5
Custer	17	245	10.4	4.8	24	58	3.7	0.7	104.3	29.6	10.7	1.1
Dakota	20	235	12.5	5.5	32	275	29.7	8.5	83.8	32.2	12.0	2.1
Dawes	19	131	6.5	3.0	22	41	2.5	0.5	51.4	21.0	5.5	1.2
Dawson	32	395	18.4	8.6	52	181	16.5	3.1	132.6	44.4	14.9	1.9
Deuel	3	10	0.7	0.1	5	22	0.7	0.2	25.1	6.5	2.2	0.1
Dixon	8	133	3.5	1.5	15	33	2.4	0.5	43.8	13.0	5.2	0.3
Dodge	77	852	42.7	19.4	96	360	19.3	5.1	182.7	86.9	30.9	3.1
Douglas	966	11 736	835.2	393.7	899	6 682	398.4	127.0	2 441.5	947.0	332.9	67.2
Dundy	3	9	0.6	0.1	3	6	0.5	0.1	32.5	6.0	3.1	0.1
Fillmore	12	152	5.1	2.7	20	53	2.6	0.6	76.0	17.3	5.7	0.5
Franklin	5	113	2.7	1.6	6	11	0.8	0.1	39.5	10.5	3.9	0.3
Frontier	2	D	D	D	9	28	1.5	0.4	37.2	6.5	2.3	0.1
Furnas	6	102	4.0	2.2	15	39	2.5	0.4	61.0	17.2	6.6	0.4
Gage	28	287	12.8	5.4	58	181	9.8	2.2	156.1	60.4	16.4	2.3
Garden	2	D	D	D	1	D	D	D	34.5	8.0	2.8	0.1
Garfield	2	D	D	D	3	5	0.4	0.1	13.6	5.8	2.3	0.2
Gosper	2	D	D	D	1	D	D	D	29.6	6.5	1.7	0.1
Grant	NA	NA	NA	NA	2	D	D	D	3.0	1.9	0.5	0.0
Greeley	3	D	D	D	7	16	1.4	0.3	28.8	6.9	2.3	0.1
Hall	109	1 263	75.6	38.6	118	858	50.2	15.6	297.6	113.1	34.3	6.3
Hamilton	14	84	4.0	1.6	19	53	4.3	0.9	76.6	19.2	5.8	0.4
Harlan	3	7	0.5	0.2	8	25	2.3	0.3	38.5	10.5	3.7	0.2
Hayes	NA	NA	NA	NA	1	D	D	D	17.8	1.6	0.9	0.1
Hitchcock	NA	NA	NA	NA	4	11	0.5	0.1	35.7	9.6	2.9	0.3
Holt	20	179	7.7	3.4	30	83	6.7	1.2	92.7	25.8	11.4	1.2
Hooker	2	D	D	D	3	5	0.2	0.0	4.3	2.4	0.8	0.1
Howard	6	74	2.5	1.3	9	21	1.6	0.3	48.7	14.6	5.7	0.3
Jefferson	9	136	4.8	2.5	16	35	1.9	0.4	73.3	23.5	7.1	0.8
Johnson	7	83	3.7	1.5	8	17	1.4	0.3	38.8	11.6	3.9	0.2
Kearney	10	30	1.6	0.4	14	43	3.2	0.6	62.4	14.7	5.9	0.3
Keith	15	130	6.1	2.5	28	112	6.7	1.5	58.8	21.8	5.9	0.3
Keya Paha	NA	NA	NA	NA	1	D	D	D	8.1	1.9	0.7	0.1
Kimball	6	23	1.4	0.4	10	34	2.1	0.3	44.3	12.4	2.9	0.3
Knox	12	97	4.1	1.8	15	29	2.4	0.4	80.8	23.7	10.0	1.0
Lancaster	548	6 380	376.7	184.1	418	2 512	134.2	42.0	1 436.7	461.4	116.4	25.1
Lincoln	80	813	49.0	18.5	70	335	19.7	5.6	229.0	87.9	23.8	5.1
Logan	NA	NA	NA	NA	1	D	D	D	9.0	2.2	0.7	0.1
Loup	1	D	D	D	2	D	D	D	4.3	1.2	0.7	0.0
McPherson	NA	NA	NA	NA	1	D	D	D	6.2	1.6	0.4	0.0
Madison	91	932	53.2	26.0	90	410	23.6	6.5	187.5	71.9	21.3	3.4
Merrick	12	164	4.6	2.5	19	41	2.8	0.6	60.6	18.6	7.2	0.6
Morrill	3	D	D	D	6	27	1.0	0.3	35.9	12.8	4.1	0.5
Nance	6	109	3.5	1.8	9	21	1.2	0.3	41.2	9.0	3.9	0.3
Nemaha	12	62	3.6	1.6	17	44	3.4	0.7	53.3	18.3	6.4	0.9
Nuckolls	9	65	3.5	1.5	12	32	2.6	0.5	55.9	15.5	5.5	0.4
Otoe	31	362	14.8	6.8	28	85	5.9	1.4	88.0	36.0	11.4	1.1
Pawnee	4	63	2.3	1.0	10	30	1.9	0.3	31.6	9.3	3.7	0.4
Perkins	4	24	1.0	0.3	10	24	3.3	0.6	52.1	8.2	3.1	0.2
Phelps	12	118	7.9	4.3	23	94	7.3	1.4	85.1	24.0	7.7	1.1
Pierce	8	104	3.2	1.2	14	38	6.1	0.6	55.2	15.4	5.9	0.5

1. Firms subject to federal tax.   2. October 1, 2000 to September 30, 2001.   3. State totals may include programs not allocated by county.

Table B. States and Counties — Federal Funds and Local Government Finances

	Federal funds and grants, fiscal 2001 [1] (cont'd)							Local government finances, 1997				
	Expenditures (mil dol) (cont'd)							General revenue				
	Procurement contract awards			Grants [2]						Taxes		
											Per capita [3] (dollars)	
STATE County	Salaries and wages	Defense	Other	Medicaid and other health-related	Nutrition and family welfare	Education	Other	Total (mil dol)	Intergovern-mental (mil dol)	Total (mil dol)	Total	Property
	171	172	173	174	175	176	177	178	179	180	181	182
NEBRASKA—Cont'd												
Blaine	0.3	0.0	0.1	0.4	0.1	0.0	0.0	2.0	0.4	1.4	2 180	2 055
Boone	1.9	0.0	0.4	3.0	0.5	0.3	2.5	21.1	4.0	8.7	1 360	1 233
Box Butte	3.4	0.0	0.9	4.1	1.1	0.7	3.8	35.2	11.5	12.2	941	776
Boyd	1.0	0.0	0.2	1.5	0.3	0.3	1.9	8.8	4.0	3.2	1 202	1 079
Brown	0.9	0.0	0.2	2.6	0.3	0.2	2.1	11.5	2.5	4.4	1 227	1 149
Buffalo	8.8	0.0	1.8	11.9	3.6	1.6	6.1	84.7	23.5	41.6	1 034	843
Burt	1.8	0.0	0.4	4.9	1.3	0.3	0.6	22.6	5.4	10.7	1 355	1 159
Butler	2.6	0.0	0.6	4.1	0.5	0.3	0.6	25.2	4.6	12.7	1 475	1 408
Cass	4.0	0.7	1.1	6.4	2.3	0.7	7.2	42.7	12.1	21.3	888	842
Cedar	3.8	0.1	0.6	4.1	0.8	0.5	2.6	21.5	8.1	8.9	904	801
Chase	1.2	0.0	0.7	1.5	0.4	0.2	1.1	16.9	3.2	8.0	1 887	1 740
Cherry	2.2	0.0	0.9	3.4	0.6	0.3	4.9	19.8	3.5	8.1	1 272	1 147
Cheyenne	3.2	0.7	0.7	5.2	0.7	0.4	3.5	32.0	7.7	16.3	1 706	1 366
Clay	9.1	0.0	1.4	1.9	0.5	0.5	0.6	20.6	5.7	12.2	1 699	1 595
Colfax	3.3	0.0	0.5	4.5	0.6	0.2	0.5	19.8	7.0	8.7	826	739
Cuming	2.5	0.1	0.5	2.6	1.7	0.5	2.0	21.8	5.5	11.1	1 112	1 021
Custer	3.2	0.0	0.7	8.2	1.1	0.5	6.5	31.1	9.5	17.1	1 414	1 311
Dakota	4.0	0.0	0.6	12.7	1.9	1.0	3.4	29.8	13.4	12.0	641	598
Dawes	6.0	0.0	0.7	4.9	2.3	0.7	1.5	17.5	6.6	7.9	870	671
Dawson	5.2	1.5	0.9	11.2	2.1	0.6	8.0	83.0	19.7	30.2	1 304	1 097
Deuel	0.5	0.0	0.1	1.9	0.2	0.1	2.5	8.8	1.5	4.6	2 269	2 024
Dixon	1.6	0.1	1.4	2.6	0.6	0.2	1.8	15.4	5.3	6.7	1 039	950
Dodge	8.6	0.4	3.1	13.5	3.2	1.2	2.0	112.1	25.6	35.0	997	852
Douglas	312.6	28.7	122.2	339.5	70.2	33.2	103.4	1 131.3	333.7	571.6	1 296	947
Dundy	0.7	0.0	0.2	1.5	0.2	0.0	1.5	10.1	1.2	3.9	1 669	1 514
Fillmore	1.9	0.0	0.5	3.4	0.5	0.1	7.2	20.6	4.4	10.3	1 496	1 445
Franklin	1.3	0.1	0.3	1.5	0.2	0.2	0.9	11.3	1.9	5.4	1 426	1 292
Frontier	1.0	0.0	0.2	1.5	0.2	0.2	4.2	8.9	2.7	5.0	1 558	1 465
Furnas	1.8	0.0	0.4	6.0	0.4	0.3	4.2	18.9	5.2	9.5	1 752	1 652
Gage	7.3	0.0	1.1	14.6	2.3	4.5	6.9	51.3	20.3	19.1	837	794
Garden	0.8	0.0	12.7	1.5	0.2	0.1	0.8	12.5	1.8	6.7	3 006	2 865
Garfield	0.4	0.0	0.1	1.1	0.1	0.1	0.7	5.3	2.1	1.9	914	828
Gosper	0.4	0.0	0.1	0.0	0.1	0.0	2.7	6.2	1.2	4.5	1 979	1 201
Grant	0.3	0.0	0.1	0.0	0.0	0.0	0.0	2.9	0.4	2.1	2 837	2 682
Greeley	1.0	0.0	0.2	1.1	0.3	0.2	1.5	10.5	3.9	4.3	1 454	1 376
Hall	32.1	1.5	12.7	27.4	6.0	2.8	16.6	118.2	34.3	53.6	1 038	823
Hamilton	1.7	0.0	0.4	4.5	0.6	0.3	0.6	23.8	8.7	11.7	1 239	1 212
Harlan	1.3	0.0	0.2	1.5	0.2	0.2	1.2	9.0	2.6	2.9	764	690
Hayes	0.2	0.0	0.0	0.4	0.0	0.0	1.1	3.0	0.7	2.0	1 833	1 782
Hitchcock	0.9	0.0	0.6	1.9	0.3	0.1	2.6	9.1	4.0	3.5	1 034	944
Holt	2.8	0.0	0.5	8.2	1.4	0.5	3.9	26.0	8.6	13.7	1 122	958
Hooker	0.2	0.0	0.0	0.4	0.1	0.0	0.0	3.3	0.4	1.8	2 459	2 240
Howard	1.4	0.0	0.3	2.6	0.5	0.3	3.4	17.5	5.9	7.1	1 094	983
Jefferson	2.1	0.0	0.5	6.0	2.1	1.0	5.4	20.8	6.5	10.9	1 304	1 157
Johnson	1.9	0.0	0.3	2.2	0.3	0.4	4.6	15.8	5.2	6.1	1 342	1 225
Kearney	1.4	0.4	0.4	1.9	0.3	0.2	0.4	22.0	2.8	10.9	1 626	1 465
Keith	1.9	0.1	0.4	3.0	0.6	0.3	7.7	22.5	6.4	12.8	1 490	1 045
Keya Paha	0.2	0.0	0.1	0.7	0.1	0.0	2.3	2.1	0.5	1.4	1 440	1 387
Kimball	0.8	0.0	0.8	1.5	0.3	0.1	9.5	13.0	1.7	5.1	1 271	1 111
Knox	2.7	0.0	1.2	11.3	1.7	1.8	3.9	24.2	10.6	10.2	1 083	965
Lancaster	148.9	27.9	26.4	162.5	116.7	75.7	191.1	605.8	149.9	273.2	1 171	924
Lincoln	12.9	17.5	2.1	18.4	3.5	1.7	15.3	97.2	27.5	48.5	1 446	1 202
Logan	0.1	0.0	0.0	0.7	0.1	0.1	0.9	2.6	0.7	1.4	1 532	1 427
Loup	0.1	0.0	0.0	0.0	0.0	0.0	0.5	1.8	0.6	1.1	1 632	1 552
McPherson	0.1	0.0	0.0	0.7	0.0	0.1	2.0	1.2	0.3	0.8	1 457	1 417
Madison	13.3	0.0	19.4	17.6	2.9	1.2	3.6	96.5	32.7	40.2	1 154	942
Merrick	1.8	0.0	0.5	3.7	0.6	0.5	1.2	27.3	6.5	11.4	1 398	1 240
Morrill	1.1	0.0	0.3	2.2	0.7	0.3	1.1	20.7	5.5	8.7	1 596	1 460
Nance	0.8	0.0	0.2	4.1	0.4	0.1	3.1	8.3	3.2	3.8	901	813
Nemaha	1.9	0.0	0.4	4.1	0.6	0.5	1.0	21.9	7.0	7.9	1 017	882
Nuckolls	1.5	0.0	0.3	3.7	0.4	0.2	5.4	12.6	5.1	5.4	1 003	897
Otoe	3.2	0.0	1.0	6.4	1.3	0.5	1.4	35.4	9.3	20.3	1 394	1 042
Pawnee	0.9	0.0	0.2	2.6	0.3	0.1	0.7	11.6	3.8	4.1	1 285	1 199
Perkins	0.8	0.0	0.2	0.0	0.2	0.2	4.4	17.9	1.8	5.8	1 750	1 708
Phelps	2.1	0.0	0.5	4.1	0.6	0.5	1.2	24.2	6.0	14.1	1 421	1 241
Pierce	1.5	0.0	0.4	2.2	0.5	0.3	2.0	22.1	5.6	9.8	1 238	977

1. October 1, 2000 to September 30, 2001. 2. State totals may include programs not allocated by county. 3. Based on the resident population estimated as of July 1 of the year shown.

Table B. States and Counties — Local Government Finances, Government Employment, and Elections

	Local government finances, 1997 (cont'd)									Government employment, 1999			Presidential election, 2000[2]		
	Direct general expenditure							Debt outstanding					Percent of vote cast —		
			Percent of total for —												
STATE County	Total (mil dol)	Per capita[1] (dollars)	Educa- tion	Health and hospitals	Police protec- tion	Public welfare	High- ways	Total (mil dol)	Per capita[1] (dollars)	Federal civilian	Federal military	State and local	Demo- cratic	Republi- can	All other
	183	184	185	186	187	188	189	190	191	192	193	194	195	196	197

NEBRASKA—Cont'd

Blaine	2.0	3 172	71.0	0.0	1.6	0.0	9.7	0.0	0	29	0	66	12.3	85.7	2.0
Boone	23.8	3 723	47.9	26.3	1.2	0.0	8.0	7.2	1 121	38	26	570	20.1	76.7	3.2
Box Butte	33.6	2 602	49.7	17.6	4.9	0.1	7.9	6.7	520	60	53	985	31.7	63.0	5.3
Boyd	8.1	3 080	60.3	0.4	1.3	0.0	7.1	7.1	2 698	19	10	277	21.3	75.0	3.7
Brown	12.0	3 336	44.1	16.6	3.1	0.0	10.2	11.0	3 050	22	15	398	14.8	81.7	3.5
Buffalo	94.3	2 345	52.6	0.2	4.1	0.1	8.7	51.2	1 274	164	167	3 372	23.9	72.5	3.6
Burt	21.8	2 763	45.4	9.6	2.9	6.2	12.4	5.9	746	38	33	606	36.1	60.6	3.4
Butler	27.3	3 175	33.2	15.2	3.4	0.0	11.1	18.1	2 104	56	36	540	26.9	68.9	4.2
Cass	45.4	1 891	60.8	3.4	3.2	0.1	8.4	39.7	1 656	80	103	1 073	35.6	59.8	4.7
Cedar	19.7	2 009	57.2	0.1	2.6	6.4	10.9	8.6	873	97	40	662	24.9	70.0	5.1
Chase	17.0	4 003	41.1	25.5	0.8	0.0	6.4	4.4	1 036	26	18	554	16.3	80.3	3.4
Cherry	20.4	3 183	32.1	28.5	2.7	0.2	14.7	2.4	379	50	26	495	15.7	81.6	2.8
Cheyenne	30.9	3 234	49.9	0.5	2.8	0.0	6.3	30.5	3 193	47	39	767	20.2	76.6	3.2
Clay	19.5	2 725	60.0	1.0	2.4	0.1	8.0	5.9	826	169	29	696	24.1	72.3	3.6
Colfax	20.0	1 895	56.9	0.1	2.8	0.1	13.0	3.0	280	75	44	579	26.0	70.5	3.5
Cuming	20.3	2 040	50.6	0.2	2.7	6.8	14.4	9.0	907	58	41	669	20.3	76.7	3.0
Custer	31.1	2 573	50.8	7.9	2.5	0.0	17.6	13.1	1 081	52	49	887	18.0	78.4	3.6
Dakota	28.7	1 531	57.5	0.6	7.1	0.0	5.9	9.4	500	83	79	876	44.5	51.5	4.0
Dawes	18.5	2 052	44.4	6.2	3.6	6.3	6.9	10.8	1 195	151	37	970	22.7	70.4	6.9
Dawson	79.8	3 452	44.0	18.0	4.4	0.0	9.3	36.2	1 563	102	97	1 795	23.2	73.4	3.4
Deuel	8.5	4 200	53.8	0.1	3.1	8.2	8.4	0.9	420	18	0	161	20.6	75.8	3.6
Dixon	19.6	3 055	57.6	8.8	2.7	0.0	10.3	1.7	271	39	26	407	29.4	65.7	4.9
Dodge	116.3	3 312	33.4	35.7	2.1	2.8	5.7	8.7	246	128	147	2 574	34.7	61.3	4.0
Douglas	1 031.1	2 338	48.1	3.0	5.5	0.6	5.6	1 499.9	3 401	5 623	2 382	28 917	40.0	55.2	4.8
Dundy	9.1	3 923	33.1	30.7	1.8	0.0	9.7	1.2	509	17	0	228	17.7	79.2	3.1
Fillmore	21.9	3 171	47.9	17.9	1.4	5.4	8.7	3.0	441	38	29	756	28.3	67.5	4.2
Franklin	10.4	2 720	41.4	21.3	2.4	0.0	13.7	1.4	354	32	15	280	25.2	71.7	3.2
Frontier	9.2	2 891	63.5	0.3	4.5	0.0	14.3	0.4	116	19	13	349	17.5	79.1	3.3
Furnas	17.3	3 185	54.4	0.3	2.5	0.0	7.8	24.4	4 495	40	22	578	22.0	76.1	2.0
Gage	52.8	2 306	53.4	1.5	3.9	0.0	9.7	36.6	1 601	112	94	2 258	37.0	58.3	4.7
Garden	12.3	5 519	32.3	18.4	1.5	7.6	5.8	0.5	230	23	0	315	16.7	79.0	4.3
Garfield	5.2	2 501	52.5	0.1	3.1	0.1	8.1	0.5	247	10	0	158	21.0	74.6	4.4
Gosper	5.8	2 542	29.8	0.1	3.3	0.0	13.5	1.0	447	17	0	160	22.5	74.7	2.9
Grant	3.1	4 201	64.6	0.2	2.3	0.1	13.4	1.2	1 566	0	0	94	12.7	84.2	3.1
Greeley	10.3	3 505	48.3	0.1	0.6	7.5	8.9	5.9	1 995	17	12	285	31.8	64.0	4.2
Hall	117.4	2 271	51.2	0.7	4.4	0.2	7.1	104.3	2 019	604	217	3 627	32.1	63.6	4.3
Hamilton	18.8	1 991	58.6	0.6	2.6	0.0	9.0	2.8	297	39	40	562	23.7	72.4	3.8
Harlan	9.4	2 500	27.8	24.2	2.0	0.0	11.3	1.9	509	38	15	264	23.7	73.3	3.0
Hayes	3.0	2 730	62.5	0.0	2.0	0.0	19.8	0.3	269	13	0	85	11.6	85.1	3.3
Hitchcock	10.4	3 041	71.7	0.1	1.9	0.0	7.6	8.5	2 491	19	14	324	21.1	76.1	2.8
Holt	26.0	2 131	55.4	0.4	2.5	0.1	13.1	9.4	772	60	49	841	17.1	79.7	3.2
Hooker	3.2	4 439	49.1	25.3	1.3	0.1	7.0	0.1	127	0	0	92	18.1	77.5	4.4
Howard	16.6	2 564	54.8	0.2	1.9	0.0	8.2	5.3	816	36	27	545	33.8	62.3	4.0
Jefferson	21.4	2 551	68.7	0.2	3.4	0.1	7.9	7.6	901	39	34	488	35.4	61.1	3.6
Johnson	15.5	3 387	47.0	14.2	1.3	0.0	13.7	4.1	887	42	19	423	37.6	57.3	5.1
Kearney	19.7	2 947	44.5	11.7	2.5	0.3	5.5	6.7	1 009	33	28	514	21.8	74.7	3.5
Keith	22.8	2 646	56.8	2.3	2.2	0.5	8.5	5.6	646	34	37	595	20.2	76.7	3.0
Keya Paha	2.1	2 123	56.0	0.2	1.0	0.0	23.5	0.0	4	0	0	69	15.2	82.3	2.6
Kimball	12.9	3 193	35.7	17.6	3.3	13.1	7.9	0.5	129	18	17	388	20.8	75.8	3.5
Knox	22.3	2 375	61.0	0.2	2.5	0.1	14.9	8.1	867	58	38	1 010	26.1	70.0	4.0
Lancaster	589.1	2 525	45.1	13.3	3.6	2.8	5.0	639.3	2 740	2 506	1 039	27 306	41.7	51.8	6.5
Lincoln	86.8	2 588	55.3	5.6	1.3	0.2	5.8	18.8	560	233	141	2 419	34.4	61.0	4.5
Logan	2.3	2 610	75.0	0.2	3.1	0.0	8.9	0.0	0	0	0	78	14.6	81.6	3.9
Loup	1.6	2 432	69.9	0.0	3.3	0.0	12.2	0.0	0	0	0	53	22.2	75.1	2.7
McPherson	1.2	2 121	71.4	0.0	1.7	0.0	11.0	0.1	167	0	0	39	15.9	81.1	3.0
Madison	106.3	3 049	55.0	1.2	3.4	1.8	6.8	58.9	1 691	227	143	3 251	21.6	75.0	3.5
Merrick	26.1	3 193	43.3	22.7	1.3	0.0	9.4	13.5	1 653	38	33	603	25.4	71.3	3.3
Morrill	18.3	3 371	39.6	11.8	2.0	8.1	7.3	6.6	1 213	24	22	481	21.5	74.7	3.8
Nance	10.4	2 467	67.2	0.5	2.5	0.0	10.9	2.6	617	20	17	374	29.8	66.4	3.8
Nemaha	21.2	2 709	54.1	16.0	0.8	0.1	10.2	7.2	925	39	32	1 603	31.6	64.6	3.8
Nuckolls	12.5	2 321	54.5	0.1	3.4	0.4	13.4	1.1	211	34	21	389	26.4	69.6	4.0
Otoe	32.3	2 218	50.2	1.9	4.8	0.1	12.1	22.6	1 548	64	61	1 078	33.1	62.7	4.2
Pawnee	10.9	3 442	43.5	20.9	1.2	0.0	8.6	1.4	446	25	13	256	34.4	61.7	3.9
Perkins	16.4	4 974	30.9	57.1	2.0	0.0	1.8	2.0	610	22	13	377	16.7	80.6	2.7
Phelps	24.8	2 506	66.0	0.0	2.4	0.1	9.5	7.3	732	44	41	781	20.2	77.3	2.6
Pierce	20.5	2 595	45.4	17.7	1.8	0.0	10.9	11.2	1 416	33	33	470	17.8	79.0	3.2

1. Based on the resident population estimated as of July 1 of the year shown.   2. Data subject to copyright.

Items 183—197

Table B. States and Counties — **Land Area and Population**

STATE/County code	MSA/PMSA/NECMA code[1]	County Type[2]	STATE County	Land area[3] (sq km) 2000	Total persons	Rank	Per square kilometer	White	Black	Am. Indian, Alaska Native	Asian and Pacific Islander	Percent Hispanic[4]	Under 5 years	5 to 17 years	18 to 24 years	25 to 34 years	35 to 44 years	45 to 54 years
					1	2	3	4	5	6	7	9	10	11	12	13	14	15
			NEBRASKA—Cont'd															
31 141	...	7	Platte	1 756	31 662	1 354	18.0	95.4	0.5	0.7	0.6	6.5	7.3	21.8	8.1	11.8	15.7	13.1
31 143	...	9	Polk	1 137	5 639	2 811	5.0	99.3	0.1	0.4	0.3	1.1	5.8	19.4	6.0	10.0	14.3	14.0
31 145	...	7	Red Willow	1 856	11 448	2 338	6.2	98.3	0.3	0.8	0.2	2.5	6.2	18.6	8.8	9.9	14.7	12.8
31 147	...	7	Richardson	1 433	9 531	2 487	6.7	97.1	0.4	3.3	0.2	1.0	5.2	20.3	5.9	8.9	14.8	12.9
31 149	...	9	Rock	2 612	1 756	3 082	0.7	99.2	0.0	0.7	0.3	0.5	5.5	17.5	6.5	8.3	15.3	14.7
31 151	...	6	Saline	1 490	13 843	2 170	9.3	94.1	0.6	0.6	2.0	6.6	6.2	18.9	12.3	10.7	14.3	12.2
31 153	5920	2	Sarpy	623	122 595	443	196.8	91.1	5.1	0.9	2.9	4.4	8.2	22.2	9.4	15.9	17.8	12.6
31 155	...	6	Saunders	1 953	19 830	1 799	10.2	99.0	0.2	0.6	0.3	1.0	6.4	21.5	6.3	10.8	16.8	13.7
31 157	...	5	Scotts Bluff	1 915	36 951	1 191	19.3	89.0	0.4	2.4	0.8	17.2	6.5	19.4	8.4	11.1	14.3	13.8
31 159	...	6	Seward	1 489	16 496	1 988	11.1	98.8	0.4	0.5	0.5	1.1	5.6	19.1	14.3	10.0	14.6	12.7
31 161	...	9	Sheridan	6 322	6 198	2 762	1.0	90.0	0.4	10.7	0.3	1.5	5.8	19.8	6.2	9.4	13.5	13.8
31 163	...	9	Sherman	1 466	3 318	2 972	2.3	98.9	0.1	0.6	0.5	1.0	5.2	19.3	4.5	9.9	13.8	13.4
31 165	...	9	Sioux	5 352	1 475	3 094	0.3	98.5	0.0	0.5	0.3	2.3	5.4	19.0	7.2	8.6	16.1	15.7
31 167	...	9	Stanton	1 113	6 455	2 742	5.8	97.6	0.6	0.9	0.2	2.3	6.7	23.1	7.6	11.3	16.1	12.8
31 169	...	9	Thayer	1 488	6 055	2 775	4.1	99.3	0.1	0.5	0.2	1.0	5.7	18.4	4.9	8.8	13.5	13.8
31 171	...	9	Thomas	1 846	729	3 130	0.4	99.7	0.0	0.4	0.0	0.8	5.9	17.7	4.4	10.3	13.6	17.4
31 173	...	8	Thurston	1 020	7 171	2 670	7.0	46.8	0.4	53.2	0.1	2.4	9.6	27.2	8.3	11.3	12.6	10.1
31 175	...	9	Valley	1 471	4 647	2 870	3.2	98.6	0.3	0.4	0.3	1.6	5.6	19.1	4.8	9.3	13.3	13.6
31 177	5920	2	Washington	1 011	18 780	1 856	18.6	98.7	0.5	0.5	0.5	1.1	6.4	20.7	9.3	10.4	16.3	15.2
31 179	...	7	Wayne	1 148	9 851	2 461	8.6	97.4	1.2	0.6	0.7	1.5	5.3	16.3	25.4	9.1	12.1	10.8
31 181	...	9	Webster	1 489	4 061	2 916	2.7	98.8	0.2	0.7	0.8	0.5	5.2	18.4	4.6	8.3	14.6	13.2
31 183	...	9	Wheeler	1 490	886	3 117	0.6	99.2	0.0	0.2	0.0	0.6	7.8	21.3	6.4	7.7	14.2	15.0
31 185	...	7	York	1 491	14 598	2 112	9.8	97.5	1.2	0.7	0.7	1.4	5.6	19.7	9.0	10.4	15.0	13.7
32 000	...	X	**NEVADA**	284 448	1 998 257	X	7.0	78.4	7.5	2.1	6.4	19.7	7.3	18.3	9.0	15.3	16.1	13.5
32 001	...	6	Churchill	12 766	23 982	1 594	1.9	87.1	1.9	6.0	4.2	8.7	8.0	20.9	8.1	13.4	15.3	12.9
32 003	4120	2	Clark	20 488	1 375 765	25	67.1	75.0	10.0	1.5	7.5	22.0	7.5	18.1	9.2	16.2	16.0	12.9
32 005	...	7	Douglas	1 839	41 259	1 072	22.4	93.9	0.5	2.5	2.3	7.4	5.2	18.9	5.5	9.6	16.8	16.8
32 007	...	5	Elko	44 493	45 291	993	1.0	84.6	0.8	6.3	1.2	19.7	8.5	24.0	8.8	14.5	17.1	13.5
32 009	...	9	Esmeralda	9 294	971	3 113	0.1	86.8	0.1	8.3	0.2	10.2	4.3	16.2	6.0	9.6	13.8	16.1
32 011	...	9	Eureka	10 815	1 651	3 087	0.2	92.7	0.5	4.1	0.9	9.6	5.9	21.9	5.2	11.3	17.3	14.5
32 013	...	7	Humboldt	24 988	16 106	2 015	0.6	86.1	0.7	5.1	1.0	18.9	8.0	23.4	7.5	13.3	17.8	14.2
32 015	...	7	Lander	14 228	5 794	2 804	0.4	86.7	0.4	4.8	0.5	18.5	7.5	24.7	6.8	12.3	16.7	15.1
32 017	...	8	Lincoln	27 541	4 165	2 902	0.2	93.3	2.1	2.6	0.8	5.3	6.3	23.8	6.0	9.1	12.8	12.9
32 019	...	6	Lyon	5 164	34 501	1 264	6.7	91.4	1.0	3.7	1.4	11.0	6.5	20.6	6.6	11.3	16.0	14.0
32 021	...	7	Mineral	9 729	5 071	2 847	0.5	76.1	5.3	16.5	1.1	8.4	5.3	19.1	6.2	9.2	13.2	14.3
32 023	4120	2	Nye	47 000	32 485	1 333	0.7	92.5	1.5	3.4	1.7	8.4	6.0	17.8	5.4	9.5	14.5	14.1
32 027	...	9	Pershing	15 635	6 693	2 717	0.4	80.7	5.6	4.9	1.4	19.3	6.5	19.2	8.5	17.0	19.0	12.5
32 029	...	8	Storey	682	3 399	2 963	5.0	95.3	0.4	2.8	1.8	5.1	4.4	15.3	4.7	8.6	18.2	20.6
32 031	6720	2	Washoe	16 426	339 486	172	20.7	83.2	2.6	2.7	5.9	16.6	7.0	17.9	9.8	14.5	16.5	14.7
32 033	...	7	White Pine	22 980	9 181	2 515	0.4	88.1	4.2	4.3	1.5	11.0	6.0	18.2	7.6	13.8	16.1	14.9
32 510	...	4	Carson City city	371	52 457	891	141.4	87.2	2.1	3.3	2.5	14.2	6.3	17.1	7.9	12.9	16.0	14.7
33 000	...	X	**NEW HAMPSHIRE**	23 227	1 235 786	X	53.2	97.0	1.0	0.6	1.7	1.7	6.1	18.9	8.4	13.0	17.9	14.9
33 001	...	6	Belknap	1 039	56 325	839	54.2	98.6	0.4	0.9	0.8	0.7	5.3	18.3	6.7	11.3	16.8	16.0
33 003	...	6	Carroll	2 419	43 666	1 023	18.1	99.0	0.3	0.7	0.5	0.5	4.8	17.8	5.3	10.2	16.3	16.1
33 005	...	4	Cheshire	1 832	73 825	678	40.3	98.6	0.6	0.7	0.8	0.7	5.2	18.1	11.7	11.1	15.9	14.9
33 007	...	7	Coos	4 663	33 111	1 315	7.1	99.0	0.2	0.8	0.5	0.6	5.1	17.8	6.3	10.9	15.8	15.1
33 009	...	5	Grafton	4 438	81 743	635	18.4	96.9	0.8	0.9	2.2	1.1	5.2	16.7	13.5	11.9	15.1	14.8
33 011	1123	2	Hillsborough	2 270	380 841	153	167.8	95.0	1.6	0.6	2.4	3.2	6.8	19.6	7.7	14.3	18.4	14.4
33 013	...	4	Merrimack	2 420	136 225	396	56.3	98.1	0.8	0.7	1.1	1.0	6.0	19.0	8.1	12.4	18.2	15.3
33 015	1123	2	Rockingham	1 800	277 359	204	154.1	97.6	0.8	0.5	1.5	1.2	6.5	19.9	6.2	13.1	19.7	15.6
33 017	1123	2	Strafford	955	112 233	479	117.5	97.3	0.9	0.6	1.8	1.0	5.9	17.7	13.6	13.6	17.0	13.1
33 019	...	7	Sullivan	1 392	40 458	1 105	29.1	98.9	0.4	0.9	0.5	0.5	5.6	18.3	6.4	11.9	16.2	15.6
34 000	...	X	**NEW JERSEY**	19 211	8 414 350	X	438.0	74.4	14.4	0.6	6.3	13.3	6.7	18.1	8.0	14.1	17.1	13.8
34 001	0560	2	Atlantic	1 453	252 552	223	173.8	70.2	18.6	0.8	5.7	12.2	6.5	18.8	8.1	13.3	17.3	13.4
34 003	0875	0	Bergen	607	884 118	46	1 456.5	80.2	5.8	0.4	11.4	10.3	6.3	16.7	6.6	13.3	17.3	14.6
34 005	6160	0	Burlington	2 084	423 394	142	203.2	80.0	16.2	0.7	3.4	4.2	6.4	18.7	7.5	13.6	17.9	14.2
34 007	6160	0	Camden	576	508 932	110	883.6	72.2	19.0	0.7	4.3	9.7	6.8	20.0	8.1	13.9	16.7	13.6
34 009	0560	2	Cape May	661	102 326	519	154.8	92.5	5.6	0.6	0.9	3.3	5.1	17.2	6.4	10.2	15.3	14.0
34 011	8760	3	Cumberland	1 267	146 438	373	115.6	67.9	21.5	1.7	1.4	19.0	6.3	19.1	8.5	15.1	16.1	13.2
34 013	5640	0	Essex	327	793 633	59	2 427.0	46.4	42.9	0.6	4.4	15.4	7.3	18.8	9.4	15.0	16.1	13.0
34 015	6160	0	Gloucester	841	254 673	221	302.8	88.1	9.7	0.5	1.9	2.6	6.6	19.8	8.9	12.8	17.6	14.1
34 017	3640	0	Hudson	121	608 975	88	5 032.9	59.9	14.7	0.8	10.5	39.8	6.4	16.2	10.4	19.6	16.0	11.9
34 019	5015	1	Hunterdon	1 114	121 989	445	109.5	94.8	2.5	0.4	2.3	2.8	6.6	19.1	5.8	11.4	19.9	17.3

1. MSA = Metropolitan Statistical Area. PMSA = Primary MSA. NECMA = New England County Metropolitan Area. See Appendix A for explanation of these concepts. See Appendix B for list of metropolitan areas identified by type, with component counties. 2. County typology code from the Economic Research Service of USDA. See Appendix A for definition. 3. Dry land or land partially or temporarily covered by water. 4. Hispanic persons may be of any race.

Table B. States and Counties — Population and Households

STATE County	55 to 64 years	65 to 74 years	75 years and over	Percent female	2001	1990	1990–2000	2000–2001	Births	Deaths	Net migration	Number	Percent change, 1990–2000	Persons per household	Female family householder[1]	One person
	16	17	18	19	20	21	22	23	24	25	26	27	28	29	30	31
NEBRASKA—Cont'd																
Platte	8.4	6.9	7.0	50.4	31 332	29 820	6.2	-1.0	560	315	-586	12 076	10.2	2.59	7.6	25.9
Polk	9.2	9.2	12.2	49.9	5 547	5 655	-0.3	-1.6	94	90	-96	2 259	1.6	2.43	4.1	27.6
Red Willow	9.8	9.4	9.6	51.6	11 410	11 705	-2.2	-0.3	166	157	-41	4 710	-0.3	2.37	7.2	28.6
Richardson	10.4	9.5	12.0	51.7	9 226	9 937	-4.1	-3.2	131	176	-263	3 993	-3.1	2.34	7.4	32.2
Rock	9.9	10.6	11.7	52.0	1 728	2 019	-13.0	-1.6	18	23	-23	763	-4.4	2.26	6.4	31.3
Saline	8.2	7.4	9.8	50.6	13 840	12 715	8.9	0.0	181	218	36	5 188	7.4	2.50	7.2	27.5
Sarpy	7.1	4.1	2.5	50.3	125 836	102 583	19.5	2.6	2 558	642	1 379	43 426	27.9	2.79	9.6	18.4
Saunders	9.2	8.0	7.3	50.2	20 096	18 285	8.4	1.3	306	259	223	7 498	10.1	2.61	6.7	23.6
Scotts Bluff	9.2	8.7	8.5	52.3	36 617	36 025	2.6	-0.9	657	500	-486	14 887	5.9	2.44	10.7	27.8
Seward	8.5	7.1	8.1	49.2	16 403	15 450	6.8	-0.6	239	213	-115	6 013	10.7	2.53	5.6	24.9
Sheridan	9.8	9.9	11.7	51.0	5 997	6 750	-8.2	-3.2	79	94	-189	2 549	-2.6	2.38	8.0	29.6
Sherman	10.7	11.3	11.8	50.8	3 253	3 718	-10.8	-2.0	51	51	-66	1 394	-2.6	2.34	5.7	30.4
Sioux	11.9	10.4	5.8	47.4	1 399	1 549	-4.8	-5.2	8	8	-79	605	-1.1	2.44	5.1	23.6
Stanton	9.0	6.7	6.8	50.4	6 425	6 244	3.4	-0.5	112	55	-87	2 297	6.0	2.76	7.2	19.2
Thayer	10.4	10.7	13.9	51.1	5 864	6 635	-8.7	-3.2	89	138	-143	2 541	-4.8	2.31	5.0	31.5
Thomas	10.4	9.9	10.4	50.1	705	851	-14.3	-3.3	15	10	-30	325	2.8	2.24	4.3	31.4
Thurston	7.6	7.4	5.8	50.1	7 094	6 936	3.4	-1.1	234	103	-212	2 255	-1.4	3.14	19.1	21.3
Valley	10.3	11.3	12.7	52.2	4 594	5 169	-10.1	-1.1	60	77	-36	1 965	-8.2	2.32	5.1	31.0
Washington	8.9	6.7	6.2	50.3	19 191	16 607	13.1	2.2	293	214	330	6 940	15.3	2.63	7.0	21.8
Wayne	7.2	6.9	6.8	52.0	9 668	9 364	5.2	-1.9	151	78	-261	3 437	6.3	2.51	5.4	25.1
Webster	11.4	10.6	13.7	51.9	4 015	4 279	-5.1	-1.1	50	76	-22	1 708	-2.7	2.28	5.0	32.6
Wheeler	10.7	10.0	6.8	51.0	858	948	-6.5	-3.2	13	15	-26	352	0.6	2.52	3.1	29.0
York	9.3	8.2	9.2	52.2	14 371	14 428	1.2	-1.6	207	182	-253	5 722	4.7	2.42	6.0	27.5
NEVADA	9.5	6.6	4.4	49.1	2 106 074	1 201 675	66.3	5.4	37 234	18 588	87 422	751 165	61.1	2.62	11.1	24.9
Churchill	9.4	6.7	5.3	49.8	24 044	17 938	33.7	0.3	472	245	-164	8 912	33.7	2.64	10.4	22.5
Clark	9.4	6.6	4.1	49.1	1 464 653	741 368	85.6	6.5	26 628	12 447	73 245	512 253	78.5	2.65	11.8	24.5
Douglas	12.1	9.3	5.9	49.5	42 658	27 637	49.3	3.4	378	351	1 352	16 401	55.2	2.50	8.0	20.7
Elko	7.8	3.5	2.4	47.9	45 275	33 463	35.3	0.0	846	264	-610	15 638	32.8	2.85	8.4	20.9
Esmeralda	16.9	10.3	6.9	44.7	978	1 344	-27.8	0.7	3	15	19	455	-22.6	2.12	6.4	36.0
Eureka	11.4	8.1	4.3	48.4	1 632	1 547	6.7	-1.2	24	9	-34	666	7.9	2.47	5.0	29.1
Humboldt	8.1	4.4	3.1	47.6	15 322	12 844	25.4	-4.9	407	128	-1 099	5 733	26.3	2.77	7.6	22.8
Lander	9.9	4.1	2.8	48.7	5 480	6 266	-7.5	-5.4	155	45	-435	2 093	-5.4	2.73	8.1	22.3
Lincoln	13.0	9.0	7.2	48.1	4 198	3 775	10.3	0.8	42	52	44	1 540	16.2	2.48	7.9	31.3
Lyon	11.2	8.5	5.3	49.4	36 783	20 001	72.5	6.6	513	375	2 093	13 007	69.4	2.61	9.1	21.4
Mineral	12.2	11.0	8.8	49.6	4 886	6 475	-21.7	-3.6	82	84	-187	2 197	-13.1	2.26	11.5	31.6
Nye	14.4	12.2	6.2	48.7	34 075	17 781	82.7	4.9	418	391	1 523	13 309	99.7	2.42	7.4	25.7
Pershing	9.5	4.3	3.5	38.6	6 598	4 336	54.4	-1.4	91	47	-141	1 962	21.6	2.69	7.3	24.3
Storey	15.1	8.4	4.7	48.2	3 467	2 526	34.6	2.0	15	24	73	1 462	45.3	2.32	7.5	25.6
Washoe	9.1	6.0	4.6	49.3	353 336	254 667	33.3	4.1	6 041	3 278	10 990	132 084	29.1	2.53	10.3	27.0
White Pine	9.9	7.4	6.1	43.8	8 766	9 264	-0.9	-4.5	125	107	-443	3 282	-0.4	2.42	9.3	29.6
Carson City city	10.2	7.8	7.1	48.3	53 923	40 443	29.7	2.8	994	726	1 196	20 171	26.9	2.44	11.0	27.8
NEW HAMPSHIRE	8.9	6.3	5.6	50.8	1 259 181	1 109 252	11.4	1.9	17 683	12 137	17 926	474 606	15.4	2.53	9.1	24.4
Belknap	10.5	8.0	7.1	50.7	58 384	49 216	14.4	3.7	689	690	2 022	22 459	19.2	2.45	9.2	24.4
Carroll	11.6	9.9	7.9	50.9	44 612	35 410	23.3	2.2	488	534	985	18 351	28.8	2.35	7.8	26.6
Cheshire	9.4	7.2	6.5	51.3	74 243	70 121	5.3	0.6	867	842	420	28 299	9.4	2.47	9.0	25.5
Coos	10.6	9.4	9.0	51.1	32 964	34 828	-4.9	-0.4	385	546	29	13 961	1.2	2.33	8.8	28.8
Grafton	9.4	7.0	6.4	50.8	82 254	74 929	9.1	0.6	1 043	843	345	31 598	14.7	2.38	8.3	27.4
Hillsborough	8.2	5.5	5.1	50.7	387 674	335 838	13.4	1.8	6 156	3 412	4 177	144 455	16.0	2.58	9.5	24.3
Merrimack	8.7	6.3	6.1	50.8	139 324	120 240	13.3	2.3	1 862	1 443	2 667	51 843	16.3	2.51	9.8	24.6
Rockingham	8.8	5.6	4.5	50.7	284 061	245 845	12.8	2.4	4 091	2 309	4 897	104 529	17.3	2.63	8.2	22.0
Strafford	7.8	6.0	5.2	51.5	114 632	104 233	7.7	2.1	1 557	1 022	1 860	42 581	12.8	2.50	10.0	24.8
Sullivan	10.3	8.5	7.3	50.7	41 033	38 592	4.8	1.4	545	496	524	16 530	11.1	2.41	8.6	25.7
NEW JERSEY	9.0	6.8	6.4	51.5	8 484 431	7 747 750	8.6	0.8	138 856	89 267	21 146	3 064 645	9.7	2.68	12.6	24.5
Atlantic	9.0	7.2	6.4	51.7	255 479	224 327	12.6	1.2	4 223	2 892	1 720	95 024	11.6	2.59	14.8	27.0
Bergen	9.9	7.8	7.5	51.9	886 680	825 380	7.1	0.3	12 756	10 127	150	330 817	7.1	2.64	9.7	24.7
Burlington	9.1	6.9	5.7	50.5	432 121	395 066	7.2	2.1	6 051	4 173	6 891	154 371	13.0	2.65	10.9	22.9
Camden	8.5	6.5	6.1	51.7	509 350	502 824	1.2	0.1	8 848	5 583	-2 714	185 744	3.9	2.68	15.4	25.1
Cape May	11.5	10.4	9.8	51.9	102 352	95 089	7.6	0.0	1 274	1 567	360	42 148	11.3	2.36	10.9	30.2
Cumberland	8.7	6.6	6.4	49.0	146 289	138 053	6.1	-0.1	2 441	1 749	-808	49 143	4.3	2.73	17.3	23.6
Essex	8.6	6.2	5.7	52.4	793 133	777 964	2.0	-0.1	15 698	8 793	-7 560	283 736	1.8	2.72	20.4	26.7
Gloucester	8.5	6.3	5.3	51.6	259 347	230 082	10.7	1.8	3 755	2 395	3 335	90 717	15.1	2.75	11.6	21.2
Hudson	8.2	6.0	5.3	50.9	607 554	553 099	10.1	-0.2	10 958	5 798	-6 871	230 546	10.4	2.60	16.6	29.5
Hunterdon	9.8	5.6	4.5	50.6	125 135	107 852	13.1	2.6	1 697	889	2 305	43 678	15.2	2.69	6.3	20.0

1. No spouse present.

Table B. States and Counties — Vital Statistics, Health Resources, and Crime

STATE County	Births, average 1997–1999 Total	Rate[1]	Deaths, average 1997–1999 Number Total	Number Infant[2]	Rate Total[1]	Rate Infant[3]	Physicians,[4] 2000 Number	Rate[5]	Hospitals,[4] 1998 Number	Beds Number	Rate[5]	Medicare enrollees 2000	Serious crimes known to police, 2000[6] Total Number	Rate[7]
	32	33	34	35	36	37	38	39	40	41	42	43	44	45
NEBRASKA—Cont'd														
Platte	473	15.5	250	NA	8.2	NA	23	73	1	81	264	3 044	1 058	3 342
Polk	57	10.2	77	NA	13.8	NA	1	18	1	21	373	1 126	78	1 383
Red Willow	141	12.5	129	NA	11.4	NA	14	122	1	44	391	2 433	347	3 031
Richardson	101	10.8	156	NA	16.6	NA	6	63	2	69	732	2 253	140	1 469
Rock	17	10.0	19	NA	10.8	NA	2	114	1	54	3 098	410	21	1 196
Saline	139	10.6	168	NA	12.9	NA	6	43	2	130	1 003	2 557	253	1 828
Sarpy	1 973	16.4	524	11	4.3	5.7	125	102	1	185	153	7 522	3 147	2 567
Saunders	234	12.2	189	NA	9.8	NA	5	25	1	30	156	3 169	228	1 150
Scotts Bluff	486	13.4	408	NA	11.3	NA	84	227	1	218	604	7 245	1 246	3 372
Seward	177	10.9	162	NA	9.9	NA	9	55	1	49	301	2 517	316	1 916
Sheridan	65	10.0	89	NA	13.7	NA	4	65	1	40	620	1 418	217	3 501
Sherman	38	10.9	48	NA	13.9	NA	3	90	0	0	0	793	54	1 627
Sioux	11	7.3	8	NA	5.7	NA	1	68	0	0	0	129	5	339
Stanton	97	15.7	48	NA	7.8	NA	0	0	0	0	0	609	66	1 022
Thayer	62	9.9	106	NA	17.0	NA	3	50	1	20	319	1 565	70	1 156
Thomas	8	10.0	NA	NA	NA	NA	0	0	0	0	0	144	NA	NA
Thurston	148	20.7	79	NA	11.1	NA	4	56	1	47	655	1 004	NA	NA
Valley	48	10.4	68	NA	14.6	NA	4	86	1	96	2 086	1 138	NA	NA
Washington	209	11.2	166	NA	8.9	NA	10	53	1	46	247	2 395	328	1 747
Wayne	103	11.1	65	NA	6.9	NA	5	51	1	31	330	1 385	118	1 198
Webster	43	10.7	75	NA	18.8	NA	2	49	1	16	398	1 081	69	1 699
Wheeler	13	14.3	9	NA	9.7	NA	0	0	0	0	0	152	18	2 032
York	180	12.5	156	NA	10.8	NA	9	62	2	108	744	2 665	365	2 500
NEVADA	28 009	16.0	14 309	189	8.2	6.8	2 983	149	23	3 716	213	239 746	85 297	4 269
Churchill	378	16.4	202	NA	8.7	NA	27	113	1	40	172	3 167	664	2 769
Clark	19 230	16.5	9 544	129	8.2	6.7	1 969	143	8	2 249	194	159 007	62 162	4 518
Douglas	390	10.6	288	NA	7.8	NA	46	111	0	0	0	5 793	871	2 111
Elko	835	18.3	197	NA	4.3	NA	37	82	1	50	108	2 999	1 470	3 246
Esmeralda	9	8.0	12	NA	10.6	NA	0	0	0	0	0	145	6	618
Eureka	24	12.6	12	NA	6.1	NA	1	61	0	0	0	232	29	1 757
Humboldt	317	17.8	101	NA	5.7	NA	11	68	1	30	165	1 501	370	2 297
Lander	129	18.5	37	NA	5.3	NA	3	52	1	6	86	466	121	2 088
Lincoln	57	13.5	42	NA	10.1	NA	4	96	1	19	450	781	52	1 248
Lyon	424	14.1	290	NA	9.6	NA	13	38	1	44	146	5 641	844	2 446
Mineral	72	13.3	67	NA	12.3	NA	2	39	1	35	641	1 118	136	2 682
Nye	328	11.5	306	NA	10.7	NA	10	31	1	45	156	6 862	1 001	3 081
Pershing	90	17.4	34	NA	6.5	NA	1	15	1	34	626	519	157	2 346
Storey	20	6.6	19	NA	6.5	NA	0	0	0	0	0	165	92	2 707
Washoe	4 864	15.5	2 522	36	8.1	7.5	735	217	4	1 009	322	40 054	15 335	4 517
White Pine	134	13.4	88	NA	8.8	NA	8	87	1	39	387	1 389	220	2 396
Carson City city	707	14.3	547	NA	11.1	NA	116	221	1	116	235	9 770	1 767	3 368
NEW HAMPSHIRE	14 389	12.1	9 497	69	8.0	4.8	2 603	211	26	3 179	268	170 070	30 068	2 433
Belknap	558	10.6	531	NA	10.1	NA	108	192	1	115	219	10 636	NA	NA
Carroll	400	10.1	427	NA	10.8	NA	59	135	2	128	325	8 569	917	2 495
Cheshire	753	10.5	654	NA	9.1	NA	113	153	1	177	246	11 322	1 287	2 061
Coos	314	9.5	425	NA	12.9	NA	62	187	3	172	523	7 275	474	1 730
Grafton	816	10.4	689	NA	8.8	NA	555	679	5	613	783	12 473	NA	NA
Hillsborough	4 869	13.4	2 635	22	7.3	4.4	732	192	5	938	258	46 302	NA	NA
Merrimack	1 465	11.5	1 125	7	8.8	4.8	318	233	3	347	272	19 055	NA	NA
Rockingham	3 444	12.7	1 797	13	6.6	3.9	405	146	3	405	149	32 723	NA	NA
Strafford	1 313	12.0	805	9	7.4	7.1	179	159	2	213	196	14 555	NA	NA
Sullivan	457	11.4	409	NA	10.2	NA	72	178	1	71	177	6 946	NA	NA
NEW JERSEY	111 957	13.8	72 576	740	8.9	6.6	20 834	248	94	30 258	373	1 203 231	265 935	3 161
Atlantic	3 455	14.5	2 412	26	10.1	7.5	493	195	4	1 043	438	37 842	14 128	5 594
Bergen	10 432	12.2	7 535	50	8.8	4.8	2 882	326	6	3 153	367	140 397	16 579	1 875
Burlington	5 203	12.4	3 369	28	8.0	5.4	891	210	3	922	219	57 683	10 488	2 477
Camden	7 339	14.6	4 648	67	9.2	9.1	1 529	300	8	2 067	409	72 524	20 363	4 001
Cape May	1 133	11.6	1 298	NA	13.3	NA	153	150	1	239	244	21 951	5 318	5 197
Cumberland	1 948	13.9	1 432	21	10.2	10.8	240	164	3	631	450	22 186	6 583	4 495
Essex	11 647	15.5	7 230	121	9.6	10.4	2 824	356	13	4 875	650	102 434	43 263	5 451
Gloucester	3 233	13.0	2 032	17	8.2	5.2	325	128	1	339	137	31 605	8 144	3 198
Hudson	8 518	15.3	4 789	68	8.6	7.9	1 206	198	9	2 435	437	72 248	23 990	3 939
Hunterdon	1 472	12.0	742	7	6.1	5.0	225	184	1	197	161	13 653	1 342	1 100

1. Per 1,000 estimated resident population, average 1997–1999. 2. Deaths of infants under 1 year old. 3. Deaths of infants under 1 year old per 1,000 live births. 4. Data subject to copyright. 5. Per 100,000 resident population as of July 1 of the year shown. 6. Data for serious crimes have not been adjusted for underreporting; this may affect comparability between geographic areas and over time. 7. Per 100,000 population estimated by the FBI.

STATE County	Serious crimes known to police, 2000[1] (cont'd) Rate[2]		Education						Money income 1989				Income and poverty, 1998			
			School enrollment and attainment, 1990				Local government expenditures, fiscal 1999[5]			Households				Percent below poverty level		
			Enrollment[3]		Attainment[4] (percent)						Median					
	Violent	Property	Total	Percent private	High school graduate or more	Bachelor's degree or more	Total current expenditures (mil dol)	Current expenditures per student (dollars)	Per capita[6] (dollars)	Dollars	Percent change, 1979–1989 (constant 1989 dollars)	Percent with $100,000 or more	Median household income	All persons	Persons under 18	Persons 5–17 in families
	46	47	48	49	50	51	52	53	54	55	56	57	58	59	60	61
NEBRASKA—Cont'd																
Platte	63	3 278	8 187	25.4	79.5	12.8	29.8	6 323	11 566	26 123	-9.9	1.8	39 798	8.9	11.6	10.2
Polk	53	1 330	1 364	7.5	81.0	12.4	7.0	5 978	11 377	25 959	12.6	1.1	37 039	8.5	11.3	10.4
Red Willow	227	2 804	3 025	7.0	82.2	14.9	13.5	6 235	11 146	22 336	-12.8	1.0	32 279	13.2	17.9	16.0
Richardson	52	1 416	2 137	13.9	73.3	11.7	10.3	5 693	9 943	19 521	0.2	0.2	29 083	13.9	16.9	15.8
Rock	57	1 139	489	0.0	79.4	10.1	2.3	7 335	9 396	18 974	-9.1	1.2	26 897	16.9	21.0	21.3
Saline	79	1 748	3 419	24.1	76.0	12.6	14.6	5 397	10 732	24 455	-4.1	0.6	36 926	9.1	11.6	10.1
Sarpy	60	2 507	33 538	16.1	91.0	25.4	107.6	5 533	13 284	35 575	3.8	1.9	52 368	4.6	6.1	5.4
Saunders	45	1 104	4 535	13.4	79.1	12.0	17.5	5 802	11 115	26 058	-0.3	1.3	38 578	8.0	9.9	9.0
Scotts Bluff	179	3 193	9 589	4.7	74.3	13.9	37.1	5 414	10 644	21 369	-11.9	1.6	30 645	15.9	20.5	18.6
Seward	24	1 891	4 701	31.4	80.5	14.8	19.0	6 816	11 154	27 200	2.4	1.0	41 728	7.3	9.4	8.1
Sheridan	355	3 146	1 656	2.8	74.4	15.5	8.0	6 449	10 891	19 237	-14.4	2.7	26 103	18.4	22.9	20.7
Sherman	30	1 597	908	1.9	72.2	11.4	4.2	7 082	8 176	17 025	-4.3	0.4	25 639	15.7	18.4	17.0
Sioux	0	339	356	2.2	77.1	17.8	1.4	8 994	11 001	18 810	-20.8	1.8	24 900	11.8	12.8	14.9
Stanton	15	1 007	1 720	11.2	79.4	7.6	2.9	5 552	9 861	24 375	-7.9	0.9	35 759	10.0	9.1	11.3
Thayer	50	1 107	1 482	10.7	72.7	10.2	8.3	7 145	10 172	20 298	-10.3	1.4	31 708	12.0	16.0	13.9
Thomas	NA	NA	226	1.3	78.8	11.4	1.1	8 398	7 865	17 273	-23.2	0.0	26 140	17.2	19.8	19.6
Thurston	NA	NA	1 949	6.5	70.6	8.8	11.5	7 029	7 940	18 588	-10.5	1.4	25 596	25.3	28.7	30.0
Valley	NA	NA	1 143	9.0	75.7	11.6	5.0	6 417	9 589	19 201	1.4	0.0	28 730	14.0	17.3	15.8
Washington	80	1 667	4 727	15.1	82.7	15.4	18.6	5 305	13 132	29 805	-1.0	2.7	47 386	5.6	7.3	5.9
Wayne	71	1 127	3 495	4.5	80.4	19.8	9.9	5 468	9 128	20 956	-9.5	1.0	35 342	10.5	11.7	11.4
Webster	74	1 625	891	2.5	74.0	10.3	4.4	6 288	9 339	18 349	-5.3	0.9	28 233	12.0	14.9	13.1
Wheeler	0	2 032	230	6.1	79.0	12.1	1.5	9 715	10 329	22 604	21.2	1.1	30 435	14.1	15.9	17.3
York	21	2 480	3 644	18.7	81.8	13.0	13.6	6 328	11 434	25 722	-2.6	1.9	38 940	8.4	10.8	9.6
NEVADA	524	3 744	280 411	8.7	78.8	15.3	1 738.0	5 587	15 214	31 011	1.6	3.8	39 867	10.5	15.0	13.9
Churchill	329	2 439	4 499	4.5	79.5	13.1	30.0	6 208	12 611	29 007	22.5	2.5	40 210	10.6	13.3	13.6
Clark	591	3 927	168 500	9.5	77.3	13.8	1 100.9	5 402	15 109	30 746	1.3	3.7	40 720	10.8	15.6	14.2
Douglas	170	1 941	6 731	8.0	87.3	20.0	44.9	6 127	17 620	35 209	-0.6	5.7	47 837	7.1	11.1	10.9
Elko	415	2 831	9 073	5.1	78.5	13.3	65.5	6 272	14 050	33 715	24.0	3.1	52 823	7.8	9.6	9.5
Esmeralda	103	515	274	10.9	71.5	11.1	1.5	12 772	12 776	25 577	-12.1	1.2	35 309	14.8	17.8	24.1
Eureka	606	1 151	307	2.3	75.2	13.6	5.2	14 447	14 474	31 047	40.5	3.7	49 626	8.9	10.5	12.3
Humboldt	329	1 968	3 403	4.4	75.5	12.2	26.1	6 081	13 544	33 269	36.0	2.1	50 762	9.0	11.6	11.7
Lander	621	1 467	1 574	2.0	73.2	10.8	10.7	6 275	13 167	33 988	12.6	2.9	52 942	9.0	10.5	11.4
Lincoln	96	1 152	1 066	2.7	77.6	13.1	9.7	9 249	9 074	20 872	-12.6	0.7	36 264	13.7	16.6	20.7
Lyon	281	2 165	4 659	5.2	75.2	9.4	38.3	6 034	11 704	25 065	-7.3	1.5	36 196	11.6	15.7	15.9
Mineral	197	2 485	1 516	6.9	73.1	9.1	7.5	7 193	11 785	26 278	6.8	0.2	34 237	16.6	22.5	25.2
Nye	329	2 752	3 369	3.5	75.1	9.5	35.0	6 640	15 454	30 211	8.9	2.6	37 926	12.9	19.1	20.2
Pershing	448	1 898	1 083	1.3	73.1	7.2	7.4	7 509	11 488	27 519	15.8	1.4	42 474	11.3	12.6	15.3
Storey	1 206	1 500	553	6.1	84.4	17.6	5.0	9 935	15 623	32 457	11.2	2.3	58 347	6.1	11.2	6.5
Washoe	413	4 104	61 679	8.9	82.5	20.7	283.8	5 374	16 365	31 891	-2.7	4.5	43 750	9.9	14.1	13.2
White Pine	120	2 276	2 600	6.7	73.1	11.4	12.6	6 798	12 317	27 427	2.0	2.3	41 954	12.4	14.9	16.3
Carson City city	395	2 974	9 525	7.0	82.7	16.3	50.4	6 035	15 131	31 570	0.9	2.8	42 380	10.2	14.7	14.1
NEW HAMPSHIRE	175	2 258	276 765	20.7	82.2	24.4	1 316.9	6 433	15 959	36 329	27.4	4.5	45 401	7.5	10.6	9.5
Belknap	NA	NA	11 408	13.6	80.4	20.5	66.6	6 572	14 439	31 474	23.3	3.2	40 292	8.8	13.0	11.6
Carroll	158	2 338	7 423	12.2	83.5	23.4	53.7	7 292	14 041	28 145	23.8	2.8	36 816	10.5	16.0	15.0
Cheshire	165	1 896	18 976	16.8	80.8	23.9	91.3	6 922	13 887	31 648	17.7	2.9	41 640	8.1	11.1	10.5
Coos	139	1 592	7 660	7.6	70.0	11.0	36.2	6 283	11 963	25 897	12.8	1.5	33 181	12.4	17.4	17.0
Grafton	NA	NA	21 591	26.0	81.4	26.4	113.5	7 629	13 611	30 065	23.5	3.6	40 676	9.3	12.7	11.7
Hillsborough	NA	NA	82 585	25.7	82.2	26.4	361.4	5 770	17 404	40 404	29.0	5.6	49 285	7.0	10.2	8.6
Merrimack	NA	NA	29 435	21.8	83.2	25.4	138.5	6 413	16 057	35 801	27.8	4.2	45 330	7.4	9.9	9.0
Rockingham	NA	NA	59 612	21.5	86.2	25.9	309.4	7 011	17 694	41 881	31.6	6.0	57 667	5.2	7.3	6.2
Strafford	NA	NA	29 658	14.1	79.8	21.7	98.5	6 031	13 999	32 812	21.5	2.7	41 413	9.5	13.4	12.8
Sullivan	NA	NA	8 417	9.3	75.0	16.5	35.6	6 815	12 935	29 053	13.3	1.7	38 668	9.8	14.6	14.2
NEW JERSEY	384	2 777	1 867 402	22.2	76.7	24.9	12 874.6	10 145	18 714	40 927	23.3	8.8	49 615	8.8	13.2	13.3
Atlantic	445	5 149	50 006	16.9	72.9	16.4	386.4	9 393	16 016	33 716	27.7	4.6	39 698	10.5	16.6	16.5
Bergen	127	1 748	186 843	28.0	81.6	31.7	1 308.9	11 203	24 080	49 249	22.2	14.6	60 760	5.3	7.9	7.2
Burlington	202	2 275	97 234	18.1	81.9	23.6	648.2	9 385	17 707	42 373	19.3	6.6	54 230	5.7	8.6	8.3
Camden	584	3 417	125 512	19.6	75.5	21.0	888.4	10 098	15 773	36 190	19.6	5.6	42 508	12.2	17.7	18.5
Cape May	371	4 826	19 171	15.6	74.0	17.2	157.3	10 348	15 536	30 435	29.3	4.2	36 930	10.7	15.8	17.4
Cumberland	717	3 778	33 115	13.3	63.4	10.8	265.3	10 531	12 560	29 985	16.3	2.6	36 545	14.8	20.8	22.7
Essex	1 049	4 402	197 601	22.4	70.1	24.0	1 378.0	11 608	17 574	34 518	27.2	9.1	40 595	16.0	23.3	24.1
Gloucester	221	2 977	61 760	15.9	77.5	18.1	402.9	9 179	15 207	39 387	18.5	3.9	50 868	7.0	9.6	9.6
Hudson	654	3 286	128 644	29.0	64.1	19.7	807.8	10 387	14 480	30 917	28.2	4.7	35 743	16.2	24.1	25.0
Hunterdon	57	1 044	26 315	16.9	85.9	34.6	217.1	10 543	23 236	54 628	35.2	15.2	74 457	2.8	3.9	3.8

1. Data for serious crimes have not been adjusted for underreporting; this may affect comparability between geographic areas and over time.   2. Per 100,000 population estimated by the FBI.   3. All persons 3 years old and over enrolled in nursery school through college.   4. Persons 25 years old and over.   5. Elementary and secondary education expenditures, local government fiscal years ending between July 1, 1998 and June 30, 1999.   6. Based on population enumerated as of April 1, 1990.

Table B. States and Counties — **Personal Income**

	Personal income, 1999												
			Per capita[1]					Transfer payments					
									Government payments to individuals				
STATE County	Total (mil dol)	Percent change, 1998–1999	Dollars	Rank	Wages and salaries[2] (mil dol)	Proprietor's income (mil dol)	Dividends, interest, and rent (mil dol)	Total (mil dol)	Total (mil dol)	Social Security (mil dol)	Medical payments (mil dol)	Income maintenance (mil dol)	Unemployment insurance (mil dol)
	62	63	64	65	66	67	68	69	70	71	72	73	74
NEBRASKA—Cont'd													
Platte	771	2.9	25 377	601	490	101	159	87	82	46	24	5	1
Polk	134	1.6	24 267	812	34	35	30	22	21	12	8	1	0
Red Willow	264	6.4	23 359	1 000	123	42	67	48	46	21	17	3	0
Richardson	210	1.4	22 537	1 209	67	43	51	45	44	20	17	3	0
Rock	33	-4.6	19 418	2 173	12	3	11	7	6	3	2	0	0
Saline	295	3.9	22 470	1 223	172	42	65	46	43	23	15	2	0
Sarpy	2 991	8.5	24 417	778	1 623	97	401	228	207	95	64	12	2
Saunders	425	3.4	22 061	1 345	110	64	77	63	59	29	23	3	1
Scotts Bluff	852	6.0	23 626	936	454	125	164	155	149	69	54	15	1
Seward	387	2.9	23 532	957	164	60	80	50	47	25	16	2	0
Sheridan	117	4.2	18 214	2 493	42	6	35	27	26	13	9	2	0
Sherman	59	-0.8	17 131	2 711	16	8	17	14	14	7	5	1	0
Sioux	16	6.8	11 147	3 099	5	-4	6	3	3	2	1	0	0
Stanton	127	1.0	20 852	1 714	54	26	17	16	15	7	5	1	0
Thayer	159	4.0	25 819	540	58	33	41	29	28	14	11	1	0
Thomas	12	6.4	14 755	3 009	7	-3	5	3	3	1	1	0	0
Thurston	124	2.1	17 535	2 645	64	19	19	32	30	9	14	6	0
Valley	97	-2.4	21 437	1 539	37	13	27	20	19	10	7	1	0
Washington	537	6.2	28 500	283	245	25	98	52	49	25	18	2	0
Wayne	208	3.4	22 589	1 197	100	37	37	29	28	13	10	2	0
Webster	83	0.6	21 041	1 657	25	13	23	18	18	9	7	1	0
Wheeler	21	-3.8	22 327	1 267	9	5	5	3	3	1	1	0	0
York	373	2.0	25 905	529	235	45	81	51	48	27	17	3	0
NEVADA	56 094	7.9	31 004	X	36 067	4 826	12 609	5 606	5 310	2 367	1 835	384	193
Churchill	544	4.1	23 262	1 025	324	50	108	74	70	28	25	7	3
Clark	37 278	8.9	30 628	190	24 833	3 214	7 675	3 814	3 616	1 592	1 280	263	130
Douglas	1 541	6.3	40 972	39	669	146	587	119	113	65	30	4	3
Elko	1 100	2.2	24 189	823	659	65	175	81	74	27	22	7	4
Esmeralda	20	1.8	17 563	2 638	15	0	4	3	3	2	1	0	0
Eureka	39	-6.4	20 885	1 704	249	3	7	5	4	2	1	1	0
Humboldt	417	1.5	23 332	1 005	295	40	73	36	33	14	9	4	2
Lander	149	-1.5	22 155	1 308	100	12	23	15	14	5	5	2	1
Lincoln	90	2.0	21 358	1 559	55	4	18	16	15	7	5	2	0
Lyon	726	8.7	23 071	1 075	271	32	161	113	107	55	31	6	6
Mineral	131	-0.8	25 327	609	71	8	24	25	24	9	9	3	1
Nye	733	11.3	24 668	721	361	43	160	130	126	69	38	7	3
Pershing	112	-2.9	23 363	997	81	2	21	14	14	5	5	2	0
Storey	85	5.4	28 403	288	34	5	17	8	8	5	1	1	0
Washoe	11 303	6.7	35 343	79	6 812	1 041	3 109	939	886	389	300	60	32
White Pine	214	2.0	21 771	1 423	135	15	40	32	30	13	10	4	1
Carson City city	1 612	5.8	32 206	148	1 103	145	409	181	173	80	62	11	5
NEW HAMPSHIRE	37 626	7.2	31 325	X	21 766	2 943	7 081	3 977	3 749	1 729	1 528	228	31
Belknap	1 561	5.2	29 082	257	788	141	374	216	206	104	78	12	1
Carroll	1 180	5.2	29 376	240	490	159	362	179	172	84	69	9	1
Cheshire	1 938	4.3	26 771	432	1 044	151	440	254	241	117	97	14	1
Coos	795	2.1	24 303	805	404	84	149	175	168	71	78	11	1
Grafton	2 446	5.5	31 125	175	1 688	273	632	299	284	126	125	15	2
Hillsborough	12 358	8.5	33 650	117	8 037	891	2 045	1 135	1 065	481	440	72	7
Merrimack	4 003	6.1	30 805	184	2 455	250	783	447	422	195	173	25	3
Rockingham	9 451	8.7	34 305	99	4 887	742	1 570	751	699	339	265	34	12
Strafford	2 874	6.9	25 972	521	1 531	168	491	359	338	142	139	25	2
Sullivan	1 020	3.4	25 345	605	442	85	236	163	155	72	65	10	1
NEW JERSEY	290 004	4.9	35 612	X	176 927	24 074	51 995	31 852	30 259	12 761	12 565	2 358	1 114
Atlantic	7 689	4.0	32 086	153	5 155	1 552	1 156	1 028	981	380	427	71	57
Bergen	41 153	5.8	48 017	12	22 953	5 605	8 764	3 106	2 938	1 558	1 055	106	83
Burlington	13 052	4.2	30 747	185	7 831	735	2 153	1 415	1 333	625	508	65	37
Camden	14 104	3.0	28 035	330	8 286	975	2 226	2 055	1 957	733	855	210	61
Cape May	2 887	2.2	29 455	234	1 150	250	643	537	518	228	208	23	35
Cumberland	3 208	3.1	22 894	1 111	2 021	248	494	651	624	225	271	64	39
Essex	26 026	3.5	34 824	88	18 309	2 107	4 825	3 770	3 623	1 062	1 718	570	125
Gloucester	6 783	4.8	27 077	412	3 129	423	864	834	785	354	306	43	32
Hudson	15 292	3.8	27 662	359	11 978	1 138	1 820	2 452	2 344	674	1 114	323	129
Hunterdon	5 584	6.4	44 833	22	2 351	449	923	310	286	155	99	9	7

1. Based on the resident population estimated as of July 1 of the year shown.   2. Includes other labor income.

Table B. States and Counties — Earnings, Social Security, and Housing

STATE County	Earnings, 1999									Social Security beneficiaries, December 2000		Supplemental Security Income recipients, December 2000	Housing units, 1990	
			Goods-related[1]		Service-related and other[2]									
	Total (mil dol)	Farm	Total	Manu-facturing	Total	Retail trade	Finance, insur-ance, and real estate	Services	Govern-ment	Number	Rate[3]		Total	Percent change, 1980–1990
	75	76	77	78	79	80	81	82	83	84	85	86	87	88
NEBRASKA—Cont'd														
Platte	590	8.0	D	32.9	D	7.8	3.5	15.8	15.1	5 489	173	253	11 716	7.1
Polk	69	41.0	D	2.2	D	5.6	3.3	12.7	16.0	1 307	232	32	2 742	6.5
Red Willow	165	13.3	14.4	8.5	54.7	13.8	5.0	18.2	17.6	2 564	224	157	5 279	-0.6
Richardson	110	18.2	D	7.9	D	9.6	3.9	18.0	15.6	2 442	256	168	4 704	-4.4
Rock	15	7.2	D	3.6	D	5.3	3.5	13.7	34.9	392	223	27	1 001	-3.8
Saline	214	10.6	D	39.9	D	7.1	2.9	13.3	14.9	2 730	197	104	5 299	-1.7
Sarpy	1 720	0.2	D	4.5	D	6.6	2.3	15.3	39.5	11 577	94	442	35 994	30.0
Saunders	174	21.3	D	5.0	D	8.9	4.9	15.4	19.7	3 487	176	139	7 594	0.1
Scotts Bluff	580	8.0	16.1	10.8	60.0	11.2	5.4	25.1	16.0	8 248	223	863	15 514	1.3
Seward	224	15.0	22.0	15.7	48.2	6.6	3.7	21.1	14.8	2 897	176	83	5 908	3.8
Sheridan	48	-8.9	D	D	D	14.8	7.0	16.2	37.5	1 552	250	79	3 211	1.1
Sherman	23	18.0	D	2.2	D	9.1	4.8	17.1	29.5	906	273	47	1 874	3.3
Sioux	2	-164.1	D	0.0	D	29.6	D	46.1	125.1	239	162	4	869	5.8
Stanton	80	23.0	D	D	D	1.8	1.6	7.7	9.9	959	149	35	2 355	2.9
Thayer	91	25.0	D	16.5	D	7.3	4.7	11.4	17.8	1 725	285	81	3 017	-5.2
Thomas	4	-63.3	D	D	D	25.4	D	18.7	49.3	211	289	7	404	-5.2
Thurston	84	14.3	D	9.7	D	5.3	3.5	25.9	27.4	1 185	165	186	2 548	-0.9
Valley	50	14.6	D	D	46.4	9.4	6.4	14.1	33.0	1 259	271	73	2 469	-2.9
Washington	270	4.6	D	15.8	D	10.3	2.7	19.4	25.4	2 916	155	76	6 378	12.1
Wayne	137	19.2	22.4	16.7	34.0	6.3	6.7	13.2	24.4	1 600	162	82	3 517	-1.5
Webster	38	20.8	D	D	D	9.2	4.4	14.3	20.5	1 173	289	68	2 048	-7.1
Wheeler	14	67.3	D	D	D	1.6	D	5.5	12.4	198	223	7	561	3.5
York	280	7.7	D	18.4	D	9.8	3.5	17.0	12.7	3 051	209	115	5 861	1.2
NEVADA	40 893	0.2	17.1	4.4	68.4	9.7	8.7	39.4	14.4	286 981	144	25 540	518 858	52.6
Churchill	374	2.4	D	6.0	D	9.7	3.8	25.6	37.0	3 791	158	313	7 290	26.3
Clark	28 047	0.0	15.0	2.9	72.1	9.9	9.7	42.4	12.9	191 281	139	18 674	317 188	66.4
Douglas	815	0.1	D	9.8	D	6.5	11.1	48.2	9.6	7 690	186	175	14 121	50.2
Elko	724	1.4	22.0	1.1	D	8.7	D	34.9	19.2	3 739	83	352	13 461	75.6
Esmeralda	15	0.7	D	1.5	D	2.7	0.0	D	20.3	246	253	17	966	162.5
Eureka	252	1.0	92.4	0.1	D	0.6	D	1.6	3.5	252	153	22	817	35.0
Humboldt	336	2.5	44.4	3.4	36.3	9.3	1.7	12.5	16.8	1 807	112	184	5 044	31.8
Lander	111	2.0	D	D	D	6.8	0.7	6.1	20.6	598	103	66	2 586	55.4
Lincoln	59	1.0	D	D	D	6.2	2.1	D	39.2	890	214	55	1 800	6.8
Lyon	304	2.5	31.5	18.3	47.9	12.9	3.4	19.1	18.1	6 953	202	393	8 722	50.0
Mineral	79	-0.2	D	D	D	5.6	1.9	38.3	27.1	1 256	248	110	2 994	-0.8
Nye	405	2.8	21.6	1.5	58.4	6.4	2.8	44.3	17.3	8 845	272	380	8 073	88.1
Pershing	83	2.2	48.0	1.6	D	7.8	D	4.0	30.9	661	99	47	1 908	34.9
Storey	39	0.0	D	D	D	9.6	D	14.7	18.4	674	198	16	1 085	49.4
Washoe	7 852	0.0	17.7	7.7	68.2	9.8	7.6	35.9	14.1	46 770	138	3 963	112 193	30.4
White Pine	150	0.9	28.7	0.5	D	8.2	4.6	13.9	37.6	1 644	179	131	3 982	8.7
Carson City city	1 248	0.0	D	13.1	D	9.8	6.7	21.5	36.3	9 883	188	579	16 628	24.4
NEW HAMPSHIRE	24 709	0.2	27.8	20.9	60.7	12.0	7.6	28.9	11.3	199 781	162	11 592	503 904	30.4
Belknap	929	0.1	29.9	19.7	57.8	17.9	3.6	27.2	12.2	12 095	215	669	30 306	26.3
Carroll	648	0.2	21.6	9.0	66.6	21.3	4.9	33.4	11.5	9 952	228	434	32 146	40.7
Cheshire	1 195	0.4	D	22.5	D	12.4	10.0	23.5	11.9	13 212	179	761	30 350	19.6
Coos	488	0.3	D	23.7	D	13.2	2.8	28.6	14.4	8 448	255	573	18 712	16.9
Grafton	1 961	0.1	23.9	19.4	65.2	11.4	5.2	41.2	10.7	14 459	177	747	42 206	30.9
Hillsborough	8 928	0.1	30.0	24.6	61.0	10.5	9.9	29.0	9.0	54 229	142	3 579	135 622	34.0
Merrimack	2 705	0.4	21.9	14.3	58.4	10.1	8.4	28.8	19.2	22 632	166	1 538	50 870	28.3
Rockingham	5 629	0.1	25.3	17.0	66.3	13.8	7.0	28.0	8.3	39 152	141	1 417	101 773	33.7
Strafford	1 698	0.1	32.1	25.9	48.4	10.9	2.8	22.3	19.4	17 255	154	1 217	42 387	30.6
Sullivan	528	0.7	D	32.3	D	12.4	3.7	21.4	13.3	8 345	206	647	19 532	18.5
NEW JERSEY	201 001	0.1	18.9	14.3	66.9	7.8	9.8	31.7	14.0	1 348 996	160	146 112	3 075 310	10.9
Atlantic	6 706	0.3	D	2.8	D	7.4	2.9	58.8	14.9	42 977	170	5 002	106 877	19.6
Bergen	28 558	0.0	D	14.9	D	7.6	8.4	35.8	7.2	152 081	172	8 528	324 817	5.9
Burlington	8 566	0.4	D	13.1	D	9.7	9.9	27.3	17.5	67 821	160	4 122	143 236	18.2
Camden	9 261	0.1	18.0	12.3	64.8	9.5	6.4	33.9	17.1	80 728	159	12 053	190 145	9.5
Cape May	1 399	0.2	11.2	2.1	D	18.3	7.8	27.4	26.1	25 108	245	1 562	85 537	18.6
Cumberland	2 269	1.5	26.9	20.8	47.6	9.1	4.6	20.2	24.0	25 658	175	4 400	50 294	6.2
Essex	20 416	0.0	D	9.5	D	5.5	13.2	33.3	18.7	114 419	144	25 518	298 710	-5.8
Gloucester	3 552	0.6	26.8	18.4	55.4	11.6	3.5	22.3	17.1	39 662	156	2 896	82 459	19.3
Hudson	13 116	0.0	D	8.8	D	6.8	21.5	22.9	16.8	77 741	128	21 467	229 682	3.8
Hunterdon	2 800	0.3	D	22.0	D	9.2	8.1	28.4	12.4	16 017	131	627	39 987	33.2

1. Covers mining, construction, and manufacturing.   2. Covers private sector earnings in agricultural services, forestry, and fisheries; transportation and public utilities; wholesale trade; retail trade; finance, insurance, and real estate; and services.   3. Per 1,000 resident population estimated as of July 1 of the year shown.

Table B. States and Counties — Housing, Labor Force, and Employment

STATE County	Housing units, 1990 (cont'd)								Civilian labor force, 2001				Civilian employment, 1990[5]		
	Occupied units										Unemployment			Percent	
			Owner-occupied	Owner cost as a percent of income		Renter-occupied		Sub-stand-ard units[3] (percent)		Percent change, 2000–2001				Professional, managerial, and technical	Precision production, craft, and repair
	Total	Percent	Median value[1]	With a mort-gage	Without a mort-gage	Median rent[2]	Rent as per-cent of income		Total		Total	Rate[4]	Total		
	89	90	91	92	93	94	95	96	97	98	99	100	101	102	103
NEBRASKA—Cont'd															
Platte	10 954	73.4	51 900	18.5	12.2	315	20.6	2.0	17 779	1.6	666	3.7	14 757	22.5	12.8
Polk	2 223	76.3	30 700	14.4	11.8	247	17.1	1.1	2 369	1.8	69	2.9	2 598	17.6	10.2
Red Willow	4 723	69.7	39 000	18.3	12.5	281	21.8	1.0	6 047	-1.5	134	2.2	5 582	21.9	11.4
Richardson	4 120	71.7	24 800	15.9	12.8	218	20.8	1.9	4 343	0.7	229	5.3	4 169	19.5	11.7
Rock	798	70.1	26 600	16.0	13.5	232	22.1	2.4	812	-4.1	31	3.8	974	13.7	6.6
Saline	4 829	73.3	37 500	15.9	12.4	296	18.5	1.2	7 002	2.8	194	2.8	6 020	20.9	12.5
Sarpy	33 960	63.0	66 900	21.8	12.1	473	23.5	2.2	62 227	0.7	1 585	2.5	45 877	30.9	8.6
Saunders	6 809	79.7	43 600	20.2	13.0	299	21.0	1.8	10 830	4.1	356	3.3	8 723	18.7	13.0
Scotts Bluff	14 056	64.3	40 400	19.8	13.3	306	25.8	3.3	18 287	-1.0	740	4.0	16 361	23.8	10.8
Seward	5 432	70.4	48 900	17.5	12.2	327	21.6	1.5	9 263	-4.0	292	3.2	7 841	21.2	11.5
Sheridan	2 618	69.3	28 800	16.3	14.1	269	25.5	3.3	2 739	-4.1	74	2.7	2 942	20.2	8.7
Sherman	1 431	75.6	16 400	19.9	14.3	231	19.7	1.8	1 424	0.4	39	2.7	1 613	15.5	9.1
Sioux	612	71.8	27 000	24.2	12.4	307	16.7	5.3	753	-0.4	10	1.3	755	19.1	4.6
Stanton	2 167	76.1	41 700	21.0	12.4	274	20.3	1.6	3 267	-1.3	96	2.9	2 903	17.3	11.9
Thayer	2 669	78.1	24 200	17.0	12.8	254	18.5	1.1	3 246	-4.1	86	2.6	3 019	18.7	9.2
Thomas	316	71.2	24 800	21.1	13.1	286	23.3	4.4	418	-2.8	24	5.7	374	13.9	8.6
Thurston	2 288	60.7	30 700	16.7	12.2	197	17.7	9.2	2 685	-4.9	201	7.5	2 349	22.3	10.2
Valley	2 141	71.8	23 800	16.2	13.2	228	23.2	1.4	2 369	-2.6	67	2.8	2 576	18.6	8.6
Washington	6 017	74.9	58 200	18.4	12.8	327	23.9	2.9	11 048	0.7	292	2.6	8 567	25.8	12.3
Wayne	3 232	64.8	44 100	17.4	12.7	262	24.3	1.3	6 126	-4.8	211	3.4	4 514	21.8	8.2
Webster	1 755	78.4	22 600	17.6	13.3	200	21.2	1.5	1 736	-0.3	44	2.5	1 728	18.3	11.2
Wheeler	350	66.0	18 800	11.4	13.1	227	16.8	4.5	380	-1.8	11	2.9	427	16.6	4.2
York	5 467	68.6	45 200	19.1	12.0	309	21.6	1.0	8 494	-1.8	169	2.0	6 813	20.2	11.4
NEVADA	466 297	54.8	95 700	22.4	11.9	509	26.8	6.4	1 023 488	3.8	54 729	5.3	607 437	24.8	11.4
Churchill	6 666	63.1	84 500	21.4	12.0	459	24.4	4.6	9 035	-2.1	782	8.7	7 273	24.5	16.5
Clark	287 025	51.9	93 300	22.4	11.6	516	27.3	6.8	719 872	4.6	39 750	5.5	370 583	23.7	10.9
Douglas	10 571	68.9	121 000	22.6	11.8	621	26.3	4.3	18 621	2.7	888	4.8	13 859	27.4	12.3
Elko	11 777	64.5	81 600	18.3	11.9	435	21.9	8.8	19 277	-3.3	1 149	6.0	16 587	22.5	19.4
Esmeralda	588	60.4	41 400	18.6	12.7	351	16.8	11.1	478	-0.8	39	8.2	673	18.0	19.5
Eureka	617	68.2	54 600	15.0	13.6	424	14.3	5.5	808	-3.8	29	3.6	808	18.1	21.0
Humboldt	4 538	67.3	74 000	18.9	11.6	449	18.4	8.7	6 962	-5.0	427	6.1	6 400	23.6	15.4
Lander	2 212	70.3	58 300	15.6	14.7	374	18.8	7.3	2 173	-5.5	208	9.6	2 918	18.6	22.3
Lincoln	1 325	73.5	50 900	16.1	11.7	264	21.7	7.4	1 057	3.3	76	7.2	1 371	23.0	9.7
Lyon	7 680	72.4	74 900	22.2	12.4	391	25.0	5.1	13 687	2.4	991	7.2	8 583	21.2	16.2
Mineral	2 529	66.5	56 900	16.4	14.6	432	20.8	7.8	1 830	-10.2	158	8.6	2 861	22.8	14.7
Nye	6 664	70.2	70 800	17.9	11.8	380	17.7	7.3	16 508	4.4	1 088	6.6	8 256	20.6	22.4
Pershing	1 614	60.7	66 500	21.2	12.7	389	21.1	7.7	2 029	-4.5	95	4.7	1 947	19.5	15.5
Storey	1 006	73.0	99 500	23.2	11.9	441	27.8	3.5	1 602	3.1	62	3.9	1 384	30.1	11.4
Washoe	102 294	54.1	111 200	23.4	12.2	509	26.6	5.7	183 058	2.7	7 561	4.1	140 734	27.7	9.5
White Pine	3 296	72.6	53 000	14.1	14.3	387	21.2	5.0	2 655	-6.4	119	4.5	3 840	25.1	17.2
Carson City city	15 895	60.3	99 300	20.9	10.6	480	27.4	3.0	23 838	4.4	1 308	5.5	19 360	30.6	12.4
NEW HAMPSHIRE	411 186	68.2	129 400	24.4	14.7	549	26.4	2.1	688 657	0.5	24 364	3.5	574 237	32.6	12.5
Belknap	18 839	71.5	114 000	24.0	14.5	510	27.4	2.2	29 056	-2.1	876	3.0	24 333	27.8	14.9
Carroll	14 253	75.3	119 000	25.7	14.7	521	27.9	2.7	21 630	-2.9	678	3.1	16 948	26.7	14.5
Cheshire	25 856	70.4	110 600	23.9	15.4	516	28.0	2.7	37 965	-1.6	1 202	3.2	36 083	28.8	13.5
Coos	13 799	70.3	71 600	20.5	14.6	340	27.1	2.3	16 589	-1.0	908	5.5	15 472	20.8	14.5
Grafton	27 542	67.2	105 700	23.4	15.2	479	27.1	3.3	43 795	1.2	933	2.1	37 497	31.5	11.0
Hillsborough	124 567	63.7	137 500	24.2	14.6	588	26.0	1.8	212 653	1.1	8 075	3.8	179 821	34.9	11.3
Merrimack	44 595	69.7	117 800	24.4	14.9	534	26.2	2.0	77 072	0.5	2 053	2.7	61 201	33.6	12.4
Rockingham	89 118	72.2	149 800	25.3	14.3	614	25.4	1.8	169 165	0.9	7 306	4.3	131 222	35.7	12.6
Strafford	37 744	64.8	116 400	24.8	14.5	522	27.3	1.9	60 098	1.1	1 878	3.1	53 105	29.5	13.9
Sullivan	14 873	70.7	90 900	23.8	15.9	440	27.1	2.8	20 635	-0.6	456	2.2	18 555	24.7	15.1
NEW JERSEY	2 794 711	64.9	162 300	23.4	15.1	592	26.3	4.1	4 179 451	-0.2	175 650	4.2	3 868 698	34.0	10.0
Atlantic	85 123	64.5	105 900	22.4	15.6	574	27.4	4.0	123 819	-0.6	6 628	5.4	113 910	25.6	10.0
Bergen	308 880	67.9	227 700	23.2	15.3	689	25.6	2.6	430 004	-1.3	15 678	3.6	436 439	39.4	8.9
Burlington	136 554	75.4	122 500	22.4	13.7	597	25.8	2.1	221 124	-0.7	7 041	3.2	197 588	34.1	10.3
Camden	178 758	69.8	99 300	22.2	15.0	507	27.3	3.8	251 306	-0.8	10 416	4.1	238 771	33.1	10.7
Cape May	37 856	72.0	112 800	23.7	15.6	565	28.1	2.2	44 107	-0.7	3 628	8.2	40 777	29.1	11.6
Cumberland	47 118	68.5	73 900	20.8	14.4	480	27.9	4.7	62 138	-1.7	4 660	7.5	60 937	22.8	12.6
Essex	278 752	45.3	196 100	22.9	15.0	528	26.8	8.1	363 600	-0.6	19 535	5.4	364 513	31.6	8.3
Gloucester	78 845	78.3	99 300	22.2	14.5	521	26.4	2.0	128 492	-0.9	4 966	3.9	112 523	30.7	13.7
Hudson	208 739	32.5	157 000	24.0	15.6	525	25.0	9.9	280 386	-0.4	17 482	6.2	268 816	27.2	8.8
Hunterdon	37 906	80.5	209 900	25.4	14.4	721	26.2	0.9	71 361	0.7	1 491	2.1	58 463	42.3	10.6

1. Specified owner-occupied units.   2. Specified renter-occupied units.   3. Overcrowded or lacking complete plumbing facilities.   4. Percent of civilian labor force.   5. Persons 16 years and older.

Table B. States and Counties — Nonfarm Employment and Agriculture

STATE County	Private nonfarm establishments, employment and payroll, 1999									Agriculture, 1997			
		Employment						Annual payroll		Farms			Farm operators
											Percent with—		
	Number of establishments	Total	Health Care and Social Assistance	Manufacturing	Retail trade	Finance and Insurance	Professional Scientific and Technical Services	Total (mil dol)	Average per employee (dollars)	Number	Less than 50 acres	500 acres and over	Whose principal occupation is farming (percent)
	104	105	106	107	108	109	110	111	112	113	114	115	116
NEBRASKA—Cont'd													
Platte	998	15 297	1 051	5 937	2 046	527	417	360	23 534	1 024	18.8	30.1	69.7
Polk	145	946	268	D	134	90	24	17	18 010	601	16.6	34.1	76.0
Red Willow	426	4 244	655	461	1 102	174	125	74	17 388	438	17.6	53.4	69.2
Richardson	286	2 125	447	296	364	119	64	36	17 120	717	12.1	29.4	55.9
Rock	63	432	D	D	63	18	D	6	12 752	316	8.2	64.6	75.0
Saline	319	5 084	483	2 385	595	147	50	118	23 206	727	14.7	31.9	66.6
Sarpy	2 129	27 401	2 294	1 798	4 985	1 562	1 678	702	25 606	367	30.8	19.9	57.8
Saunders	454	3 220	426	487	619	173	114	62	19 381	1 176	18.8	25.9	66.8
Scotts Bluff	1 213	12 925	2 350	1 256	2 470	519	419	285	22 084	789	14.6	26.5	68.1
Seward	411	5 576	605	1 021	566	207	52	112	20 139	833	22.2	30.1	60.5
Sheridan	195	1 156	262	D	313	103	36	18	15 335	656	10.8	60.4	71.6
Sherman	84	429	75	D	87	27	14	6	14 245	483	9.1	41.8	71.0
Sioux	16	34	0	D	D	D	D	0	11 882	343	8.2	65.0	74.9
Stanton	79	476	10	D	68	51	9	8	17 029	609	13.8	27.4	63.5
Thayer	214	1 799	403	437	278	140	23	36	19 897	569	8.6	45.2	76.8
Thomas	41	189	0	D	28	D	D	3	18 360	87	8.0	75.9	69.0
Thurston	131	1 460	382	303	240	40	18	30	20 578	379	13.2	33.8	62.8
Valley	176	1 152	321	42	235	66	51	20	16 968	445	11.9	48.3	76.4
Washington	472	5 728	674	1 051	762	173	140	145	25 385	692	25.6	20.8	58.5
Wayne	253	3 796	380	1 739	416	341	65	76	20 057	612	17.0	30.7	69.4
Webster	100	622	174	D	119	35	7	10	16 285	433	12.0	46.2	63.7
Wheeler	19	98	0	D	19	D	0	1	8 235	186	10.8	61.3	70.4
York	501	6 727	865	1 221	924	314	127	142	21 094	712	14.5	40.9	78.5
NEVADA	46 890	854 358	62 186	38 833	101 922	29 551	36 692	24 391	28 549	2 829	39.6	26.1	55.1
Churchill	504	4 855	741	251	1 094	125	183	109	22 444	511	50.1	9.8	56.2
Clark	28 523	597 099	39 658	18 430	68 529	21 509	25 716	17 019	28 503	209	70.3	3.8	40.2
Douglas	1 346	17 228	663	2 082	1 288	440	672	477	27 687	156	53.2	14.1	48.1
Elko	1 011	16 484	978	132	2 129	369	387	447	27 141	402	25.1	49.5	59.5
Esmeralda	15	190	0	D	D	D	0	8	41 763	20	10.0	35.0	85.0
Eureka	45	2 559	D	D	D	D	D	126	49 093	84	4.8	45.2	66.7
Humboldt	408	6 255	355	303	979	80	84	191	30 526	218	20.2	49.1	65.6
Lander	95	1 269	95	D	205	D	6	39	30 673	76	21.1	46.1	72.4
Lincoln	83	534	D	0	188	36	D	8	14 878	121	30.6	19.8	49.6
Lyon	529	6 091	438	1 497	905	55	283	146	23 997	305	42.6	22.0	59.7
Mineral	91	1 368	258	D	132	33	6	32	23 269	37	54.1	21.6	37.8
Nye	566	5 400	208	208	905	137	72	133	24 672	144	42.4	23.6	56.2
Pershing	94	1 578	101	35	239	D	D	45	28 303	120	15.8	35.0	62.5
Storey	79	335	D	D	100	D	D	6	17 191	8	62.5	0.0	50.0
Washoe	10 958	167 777	15 541	11 773	20 976	5 584	7 956	4 916	29 304	285	56.1	17.5	36.8
White Pine	215	2 331	371	D	399	52	30	64	27 646	115	24.3	35.7	61.7
Carson City city	2 311	22 846	2 713	3 960	3 791	1 088	1 258	619	27 101	18	33.3	27.8	55.6
NEW HAMPSHIRE	37 180	528 902	68 310	97 217	90 647	23 796	22 565	16 060	30 365	2 937	41.2	5.2	42.9
Belknap	1 858	21 347	2 933	4 445	5 075	599	554	546	25 590	184	41.8	3.8	37.0
Carroll	1 866	18 168	2 329	1 600	3 496	356	2 011	368	20 262	177	36.7	4.5	37.9
Cheshire	1 973	28 017	3 954	6 043	5 055	1 826	598	757	27 009	293	40.6	5.8	36.5
Coos	983	11 562	2 096	2 629	2 243	361	135	267	23 096	185	24.3	10.3	45.9
Grafton	2 918	48 004	7 856	7 015	6 472	909	1 147	1 432	29 824	406	27.8	8.4	44.3
Hillsborough	10 870	180 068	20 853	36 487	27 349	8 098	8 862	5 987	33 250	391	51.2	1.8	47.6
Merrimack	3 999	53 509	9 637	9 288	8 325	3 211	2 295	1 559	29 134	413	41.4	6.5	45.8
Rockingham	9 227	118 414	11 943	17 033	24 058	5 039	5 359	3 786	31 972	407	55.0	1.5	46.4
Strafford	2 417	37 370	5 229	8 155	6 179	3 000	1 358	1 042	27 886	235	45.5	3.0	42.1
Sullivan	1 069	12 443	1 480	4 522	2 395	397	246	316	25 421	246	35.8	8.1	36.6
NEW JERSEY	231 823	3 440 721	413 222	390 385	422 085	206 019	251 175	133 446	38 784	9 101	66.5	3.8	43.1
Atlantic	6 226	121 676	12 146	4 656	14 761	2 544	4 635	3 376	27 745	424	69.8	1.9	46.7
Bergen	33 045	454 885	46 986	55 157	53 312	22 135	28 551	18 995	41 758	121	92.6	0.8	52.1
Burlington	10 138	166 231	19 607	21 060	23 098	11 959	11 152	5 539	33 319	857	64.8	3.7	50.4
Camden	12 561	181 368	30 689	21 130	26 821	7 987	13 394	5 715	31 509	211	79.6	1.4	40.3
Cape May	3 984	24 960	3 770	710	5 533	867	1 005	671	26 865	149	70.5	2.0	38.3
Cumberland	3 030	44 706	6 620	11 955	7 065	1 508	1 479	1 291	28 872	573	61.8	4.7	53.1
Essex	19 944	334 015	54 352	34 015	27 242	34 423	24 083	13 104	39 232	21	90.5	0.0	47.6
Gloucester	5 569	77 793	8 278	10 169	14 633	1 893	2 697	2 234	28 714	652	66.3	3.2	48.5
Hudson	13 294	214 721	20 191	20 840	20 189	23 245	9 639	8 349	38 883				
Hunterdon	3 813	40 762	4 848	4 213	6 482	1 345	3 964	1 723	42 265	1 313	65.0	3.0	37.8

STATE County	Land in farms — Acreage (1,000)	Percent change, 1992–1997	Acres — Average size of farm	Total irrigated (1,000)	Total cropland (1,000)	Value of land and buildings — Average per farm ($1,000)	Average per acre (dollars)	Value of machinery and equipment average per farm ($1,000)	Value of products sold — Total (mil dol)	Average per farm (dollars)	Percent from — Crops	Live-stock and poultry products	Percent of farms with sales of — $10,000 or more	$100,000 or more	Percent of land owned by fed. gov. 1997	Water consumption 1995 (mil gal/day)
	117	118	119	120	121	122	123	124	125	126	127	128	129	130	131	132
NEBRASKA—Cont'd																
Platte	420	2.4	410	148	356	658	1 582	104	225	219 502	36.1	63.9	84.0	43.1	0.0	117.0
Polk	259	3.4	430	132	220	584	1 415	106	166	275 579	38.1	61.9	86.5	46.3	0.0	116.2
Red Willow	436	-0.6	996	54	262	578	562	95	92	211 040	41.0	59.0	74.2	36.1	0.3	62.2
Richardson	319	5.5	444	2	242	367	904	52	69	96 572	60.7	39.3	75.7	26.6	0.0	2.6
Rock	631	-4.1	1 997	41	169	581	281	66	56	176 043	26.7	73.3	74.1	33.9	0.0	25.7
Saline	318	1.8	437	75	265	396	975	76	77	105 298	67.9	32.1	77.9	31.6	0.0	66.3
Sarpy	102	-3.2	277	8	90	623	2 357	69	57	155 882	38.5	61.5	67.6	25.1	4.3	64.8
Saunders	436	-0.3	371	76	382	581	1 556	89	144	122 166	57.3	42.7	76.0	28.0	0.5	123.1
Scotts Bluff	443	6.0	561	173	227	373	619	78	232	293 785	24.6	75.4	77.4	32.3	1.1	371.3
Seward	321	1.8	385	108	279	606	1 521	89	147	176 233	46.8	53.2	71.3	34.1	0.3	99.4
Sheridan	1 487	0.3	2 267	56	335	555	232	60	66	100 779	29.1	70.9	70.6	26.2	0.0	81.5
Sherman	324	8.7	671	59	178	367	510	77	43	89 291	54.5	45.5	77.0	29.8	0.7	115.1
Sioux	1 115	10.8	3 250	41	97	744	249	56	71	205 982	13.0	87.0	81.6	35.3	7.0	30.0
Stanton	226	4.3	372	23	183	341	928	68	104	170 418	26.8	73.2	71.6	29.6	0.0	22.3
Thayer	368	5.9	648	116	288	674	979	109	107	188 864	59.0	41.0	83.1	42.4	0.0	111.5
Thomas	369	2.4	4 236	2	14	678	160	41	8	96 126	9.5	90.5	77.0	27.6	17.3	7.6
Thurston	189	-2.6	499	6	170	476	1 023	82	60	157 132	50.6	49.4	74.7	38.8	0.2	7.6
Valley	333	-1.9	747	72	154	468	691	77	90	202 807	29.7	70.3	83.8	35.3	0.9	45.7
Washington	219	-3.9	317	15	196	635	2 083	89	93	133 736	48.7	51.3	69.8	29.3	1.7	445.0
Wayne	257	3.3	420	18	233	431	1 013	79	92	151 118	41.4	58.6	75.5	37.3	0.0	21.0
Webster	314	1.9	725	37	183	442	569	51	114	262 592	23.2	76.8	73.0	27.9	0.0	116.6
Wheeler	293	10.9	1 574	49	122	582	343	133	127	681 953	10.6	89.4	79.6	41.9	0.0	30.4
York	353	2.0	496	228	320	888	1 788	142	178	250 437	56.5	43.5	88.1	56.7	0.1	232.1
NEVADA	6 409	-30.8	2 266	765	847	876	388	70	357	126 039	42.5	57.5	51.8	18.0	84.6	2 259.3
Churchill	129	-51.8	253	47	54	463	2 203	54	38	74 478	29.7	70.3	48.3	11.2	78.8	140.0
Clark	71	-13.7	338	6	9	814	1 610	47	19	90 557	33.4	66.6	28.7	7.2	88.3	412.7
Douglas	90	13.0	579	38	26	1 200	1 993	47	9	56 382	24.4	75.6	48.1	15.4	51.2	130.8
Elko	2 855	-9.4	7 103	205	237	933	132	57	49	122 458	8.6	91.4	60.4	22.1	71.9	358.6
Esmeralda	27	-98.6	1 373	16	12	1 264	921	164	4	200 822	83.8	16.2	90.0	45.0	97.6	35.9
Eureka	215	-8.9	2 559	49	41	881	344	118	13	156 344	52.8	47.2	75.0	42.9	79.3	99.0
Humboldt	733	-0.6	3 364	157	172	887	267	141	57	262 912	67.8	32.2	67.9	35.8	81.1	279.9
Lander	486	-1.6	6 395	26	32	1 477	231	109	13	168 342	42.1	57.9	72.4	40.8	84.8	95.3
Lincoln	49	-0.2	404	16	17	368	953	48	7	60 469	54.4	45.6	41.3	10.7	98.4	54.4
Lyon	174	-7.7	572	74	79	909	1 738	86	54	175 922	54.9	45.1	59.0	22.0	66.7	194.2
Mineral	D	D	D	10	11	3 171	D	88	2	48 881	40.5	59.5	45.9	13.5	86.4	23.0
Nye	86	-38.9	594	17	28	558	956	69	28	193 003	26.6	73.4	39.6	10.4	97.6	72.6
Pershing	119	-80.9	995	40	50	794	711	114	33	272 326	44.5	55.5	66.7	25.0	74.3	86.0
Storey	D	D	D	0	0	332	D	33	0	11 626	D	D	50.0	0.0	8.1	3.2
Washoe	772	8.6	2 709	35	42	1 326	498	32	23	79 012	67.4	32.6	34.4	7.0	68.9	153.2
White Pine	247	6.7	2 152	29	34	892	437	68	8	71 617	21.9	78.1	58.3	18.3	94.5	105.1
Carson City city	7	44.5	401	1	1	438	1 091	40	0	11 021	D	D	22.2	0.0	52.2	15.2
NEW HAMPSHIRE	415	7.5	141	3	133	324	2 250	38	149	50 891	49.3	50.7	33.0	9.4	12.8	445.5
Belknap	21	-1.8	112	0	5	228	2 020	29	4	19 924	65.2	34.8	29.3	3.3	0.5	6.7
Carroll	24	-3.4	136	0	6	278	2 096	27	4	20 089	63.7	36.3	26.6	4.5	24.1	8.1
Cheshire	42	22.5	142	0	12	367	2 234	45	28	93 972	11.5	88.5	29.0	10.6	0.5	9.2
Coos	43	-6.7	232	0	14	213	840	41	8	42 111	20.3	79.7	37.3	9.2	20.1	46.3
Grafton	76	-0.2	187	0	27	290	1 533	38	17	42 808	17.4	82.6	36.8	14.0	31.1	19.4
Hillsborough	38	-6.1	96	1	15	397	3 473	31	16	41 586	72.1	27.9	32.5	8.7	1.3	59.1
Merrimack	63	34.9	154	1	17	315	2 362	42	29	70 796	70.8	29.2	32.0	11.1	1.8	244.9
Rockingham	35	4.3	87	1	14	322	4 301	43	17	41 204	74.0	26.0	34.4	9.1	0.9	24.5
Strafford	26	4.3	111	0	9	357	2 932	37	9	38 865	64.0	36.0	38.3	6.0	0.0	21.7
Sullivan	47	24.4	192	0	13	382	1 999	39	18	73 739	58.7	41.3	31.7	10.2	0.1	5.6
NEW JERSEY	833	-1.8	91	93	595	594	6 642	48	697	76 627	85.0	15.0	39.0	12.8	2.8	2 137.5
Atlantic	31	3.5	73	12	19	363	5 251	69	63	149 690	99.0	1.0	46.2	19.8	5.3	46.2
Bergen	3	-12.2	22	0	1	554	21 468	31	9	74 444	96.0	4.0	57.0	15.7	0.0	121.9
Burlington	104	6.9	121	11	70	615	5 250	67	88	102 141	86.6	13.4	47.7	14.6	4.1	233.8
Camden	9	12.6	43	3	7	359	8 288	27	17	82 811	98.5	1.5	38.9	12.3	0.0	72.6
Cape May	10	-19.4	65	1	6	296	4 669	39	7	45 685	95.9	4.1	34.9	8.1	2.1	25.6
Cumberland	66	-3.9	116	19	51	421	3 738	77	94	164 315	96.0	4.0	53.8	27.9	0.0	87.4
Essex	D	D	D	0	0	500	29 020	64	1	58 235	99.3	0.7	71.4	19.0	0.1	31.8
Gloucester	58	-5.9	90	13	46	457	5 103	50	67	102 717	91.5	8.5	46.3	18.9	0.0	73.2
Hudson															1.5	0.2
Hunterdon	105	-0.7	80	1	78	582	7 346	35	36	27 461	78.1	21.9	28.1	5.0	0.0	73.2

STATE County	Value of Residential Construction Authorized by Building Permits, 2000		Wholesale Trade, 1997				Retail Trade[1], 1997				Real Estate and Rental and Leasing, 1997			
	New Construction ($1,000)	Number of Housing Units	Number of Establishments	Number of Employees	Sales (mil dol)	Annual Payroll (mil dol)	Number of Establishments	Number of Employees	Sales (mil dol)	Annual Payroll (mil dol)	Number of Establishments	Number of Employees	Receipts (mil dol)	Annual Payroll (mil dol)
	133	134	135	136	137	138	139	140	141	142	143	144	145	146
NEBRASKA—Cont'd														
Platte	12 225	116	55	680	324.8	14.8	176	1 984	293.7	27.9	23	90	7.1	1.0
Polk	739	10	11	141	117.1	4.0	24	126	23.8	1.7	1	D	D	D
Red Willow	2 058	32	20	D	D	D	109	1 124	176.3	15.7	14	51	3.3	0.5
Richardson	0	0	25	119	74.0	2.6	66	387	59.4	4.6	7	11	1.0	0.1
Rock	145	2	7	D	D	D	10	57	6.4	0.6	NA	NA	NA	NA
Saline	3 147	41	15	109	72.7	2.8	62	584	95.6	8.9	6	24	1.1	0.4
Sarpy	160 566	1 893	84	D	D	D	291	4 663	695.6	63.7	72	D	D	D
Saunders	11 383	105	21	150	72.1	2.7	79	602	92.8	7.5	8	14	1.2	0.2
Scotts Bluff	6 914	70	79	826	225.8	19.0	239	2 624	391.9	38.8	40	136	9.2	1.9
Seward	8 451	74	25	235	94.2	5.9	63	564	80.7	6.8	10	45	1.6	0.3
Sheridan	125	1	17	245	117.2	3.6	58	397	56.9	4.4	4	D	D	D
Sherman	111	2	4	D	D	D	18	84	17.8	1.2	1	D	D	D
Sioux	NA	NA	2	D	D	D	5	17	2.2	0.2	NA	NA	NA	NA
Stanton	1 708	15	5	D	D	D	13	59	8.2	0.8	4	11	0.3	0.1
Thayer	528	7	16	112	96.0	2.1	45	285	44.2	3.5	3	D	D	D
Thomas	NA	NA	1	D	D	D	6	27	4.2	0.3	1	D	D	D
Thurston	1 684	12	9	54	31.4	1.2	29	239	42.4	3.1	1	D	D	D
Valley	134	3	13	151	101.4	3.1	38	226	27.3	2.9	3	8	0.4	0.1
Washington	19 244	112	22	D	D	D	72	675	233.9	14.3	14	D	D	D
Wayne	1 834	13	11	D	D	D	46	386	47.0	4.5	7	D	D	D
Webster	175	2	13	103	48.4	2.0	22	143	21.3	2.0	NA	NA	NA	NA
Wheeler	0	0	1	D	D	D	4	16	1.7	0.1	NA	NA	NA	NA
York	2 383	21	38	363	207.4	10.2	98	1 027	160.2	13.9	12	24	1.9	0.3
NEVADA	3 312 242	32 285	2 253	27 251	12 806.9	918.5	6 222	89 452	18 220.8	1 798.2	2 460	16 890	2 276.5	381.5
Churchill	11 020	117	17	123	29.3	2.3	87	1 023	177.6	16.9	21	80	4.1	0.8
Clark	2 666 696	26 224	1 298	15 824	6 366.0	526.9	3 803	58 477	12 321.5	1 201.7	1 521	12 437	1 672.5	291.4
Douglas	97 909	646	46	205	67.6	6.8	141	1 143	203.3	23.5	95	506	61.1	8.8
Elko	13 338	144	61	636	268.9	24.2	171	2 226	426.8	39.1	34	237	22.3	4.2
Esmeralda	NA	NA	1	D	D	D	2	D	D	D	NA	NA	NA	NA
Eureka	NA	NA	3	4	3.4	0.1	7	D	D	D	1	D	D	D
Humboldt	3 274	48	29	161	64.2	4.4	79	967	193.7	15.7	11	23	2.1	0.2
Lander	337	4	7	46	19.8	1.0	20	311	36.6	4.0	3	12	2.3	0.1
Lincoln	805	12	1	D	D	D	15	141	12.5	1.5	5	14	0.6	0.1
Lyon	18 978	227	26	145	46.0	4.5	81	723	140.6	13.9	22	63	6.9	0.8
Mineral	104	3	2	D	D	D	23	172	32.1	2.7	2	D	D	D
Nye	0	0	19	D	D	D	107	777	140.4	13.0	20	62	4.3	0.7
Pershing	410	4	2	D	D	D	21	177	36.4	2.4	2	D	D	D
Storey	2 611	30	2	D	D	D	24	82	7.5	1.4	1	D	D	D
Washoe	463 001	4 544	639	9 339	5 663.6	324.9	1 328	19 418	3 751.1	389.5	614	3 058	444.5	66.1
White Pine	875	6	12	64	17.6	1.6	51	376	55.5	6.1	6	27	3.2	0.6
Carson City city	32 884	276	88	557	222.4	18.7	262	3 383	678.4	66.1	102	343	51.2	7.4
NEW HAMPSHIRE	936 623	6 680	2 033	22 631	11 371.1	875.0	6 645	84 170	15 890.1	1 428.2	1 399	6 639	719.4	151.1
Belknap	59 116	458	74	628	181.7	25.9	414	4 073	713.8	69.2	75	241	26.6	4.9
Carroll	63 659	418	61	371	80.8	10.6	428	3 267	551.1	55.4	73	314	33.6	6.5
Cheshire	29 780	284	92	1 187	403.5	37.6	402	5 097	1 155.4	92.0	68	312	26.2	5.9
Coos	8 065	77	27	308	81.0	6.6	229	1 959	423.8	32.8	23	111	6.2	1.1
Grafton	46 881	367	112	944	333.4	31.6	589	6 164	1 031.6	110.2	122	432	38.8	7.9
Hillsborough	273 662	1 843	721	8 588	4 792.9	366.4	1 692	25 208	4 927.0	455.6	436	2 269	233.8	53.1
Merrimack	99 115	692	189	2 328	799.5	78.0	628	7 629	1 500.7	127.7	139	882	116.2	20.2
Rockingham	257 668	1 729	605	6 504	4 328.9	271.2	1 617	22 905	4 218.8	356.8	331	1 702	192.0	45.2
Strafford	73 556	598	109	1 508	281.0	39.9	436	5 807	1 020.0	92.8	91	279	34.8	4.9
Sullivan	25 122	214	43	265	88.4	7.4	210	2 061	347.8	35.8	41	97	11.2	1.4
NEW JERSEY	3 375 977	34 585	17 812	266 944	227 366.7	11 886.1	34 837	420 724	79 914.9	7 926.0	8 292	47 558	8 881.9	1 376.5
Atlantic	119 766	1 625	234	2 312	831.5	81.0	1 258	14 308	2 513.2	253.8	236	1 424	203.3	27.0
Bergen	369 406	2 847	3 876	55 657	62 435.3	2 713.6	4 284	52 065	10 766.1	1 052.8	1 360	8 772	1 821.6	278.9
Burlington	240 292	2 775	769	13 262	16 206.9	547.1	1 570	22 857	4 410.8	426.6	322	2 872	788.8	85.9
Camden	64 545	796	922	10 789	6 139.0	400.0	2 052	26 577	4 612.4	481.0	376	3 159	432.5	92.7
Cape May	134 861	1 242	74	907	201.0	21.6	784	4 990	961.1	102.7	208	589	126.5	18.9
Cumberland	22 446	255	189	2 230	989.4	69.4	578	7 157	1 226.5	130.1	115	486	52.0	9.4
Essex	135 105	1 491	1 478	23 082	17 599.5	1 025.5	2 819	27 068	4 518.1	512.9	915	6 280	1 084.7	165.4
Gloucester	112 132	1 337	381	6 268	6 023.1	218.8	989	14 030	2 441.7	231.3	152	663	81.8	14.2
Hudson	83 481	1 338	1 065	21 629	11 271.5	864.6	2 327	22 670	3 842.9	384.9	542	3 070	628.1	96.1
Hunterdon	104 764	616	208	1 595	1 201.5	74.9	600	6 415	1 454.5	143.7	98	270	57.2	6.2

1. Establishments with payroll.

Table B. States and Counties — Professional, Manufacturing, and Accommodation and Foodservices

STATE County	Professional, Scientific, and Technical Services[1], 1997				Manufacturing, 1997				Accommodation and Foodservices, 1997			
	Number of Establishments	Number of Employees	Receipts (mil dol)	Annual Payroll (mil dol)	Number of Establishments	Number of Employees	Receipts (mil dol)	Annual Payroll (mil dol)	Number of Establishments	Number of Employees	Sales (mil dol)	Annual Payroll (mil dol)
	147	148	149	150	151	152	153	154	155	156	157	158
NEBRASKA—Cont'd												
Platte	54	307	23.1	8.4	74	6 120	1 217.2	164.1	75	1 130	29.7	8.3
Polk	9	18	1.1	0.2	NA	NA	NA	NA	12	56	1.5	0.3
Red Willow	29	119	6.1	2.3	NA	NA	NA	NA	39	536	12.7	3.5
Richardson	16	41	2.0	0.6	NA	NA	NA	NA	26	214	4.7	1.3
Rock	2	D	D	D	NA	NA	NA	NA	9	33	0.7	0.2
Saline	16	36	1.7	0.6	19	2 512	659.9	64.7	39	442	10.0	2.7
Sarpy	141	1 410	146.1	55.8	55	D	D	D	155	2 462	72.2	20.5
Saunders	21	95	5.6	2.8	NA	NA	NA	NA	39	D	D	D
Scotts Bluff	68	379	19.3	9.1	54	1 732	357.5	46.2	100	1 207	33.1	9.2
Seward	21	48	3.7	0.7	18	1 039	111.7	30.1	37	589	12.6	3.2
Sheridan	8	20	1.0	0.3	NA	NA	NA	NA	24	D	D	D
Sherman	4	D	D	D	NA	NA	NA	NA	9	D	D	D
Sioux	1	D	D	D	NA	NA	NA	NA	2	D	D	D
Stanton	3	D	D	D	NA	NA	NA	NA	6	D	D	D
Thayer	9	21	1.0	0.2	NA	NA	NA	NA	14	124	2.4	0.5
Thomas	NA	NA	NA	NA	NA	NA	NA	NA	4	43	1.0	0.3
Thurston	4	13	0.9	0.1	NA	NA	NA	NA	8	95	3.0	1.3
Valley	12	46	1.6	0.8	NA	NA	NA	NA	20	D	D	D
Washington	21	D	D	D	21	861	372.1	25.1	45	489	11.8	3.0
Wayne	13	28	1.6	0.4	15	1 473	221.3	28.6	26	411	7.6	2.0
Webster	3	D	D	D	NA	NA	NA	NA	9	40	1.3	0.3
Wheeler	NA	NA	NA	NA	NA	NA	NA	NA	5	D	D	D
York	22	117	6.4	2.4	33	1 207	214.6	32.8	43	804	22.1	6.3
NEVADA	4 171	28 963	2 974.4	1 171.1	1 615	37 849	6 361.8	1 178.0	3 632	241 672	15 322.7	4 665.3
Churchill	28	120	6.2	2.8	NA	NA	NA	NA	53	706	26.0	8.0
Clark	2 405	20 281	2 105.8	832.7	814	D	D	D	2 164	185 322	12 412.3	3 771.0
Douglas	149	526	47.0	20.9	65	1 897	241.8	66.3	92	8 414	523.9	151.1
Elko	68	353	27.4	10.9	NA	NA	NA	NA	134	6 268	301.0	78.6
Esmeralda	1	D	D	D	NA	NA	NA	NA	5	12	0.5	0.1
Eureka	NA	NA	NA	NA	NA	NA	NA	NA	6	55	2.0	0.4
Humboldt	18	80	4.9	2.3	NA	NA	NA	NA	53	1 125	46.4	15.2
Lander	1	D	D	D	NA	NA	NA	NA	19	160	5.8	1.3
Lincoln	2	D	D	D	NA	NA	NA	NA	18	100	2.5	0.7
Lyon	31	240	18.4	6.8	50	1 561	280.4	47.9	43	465	15.8	4.4
Mineral	3	8	0.1	0.1	NA	NA	NA	NA	12	258	9.7	3.2
Nye	17	73	13.6	2.4	NA	NA	NA	NA	54	1 035	40.5	12.8
Pershing	4	5	0.3	0.1	NA	NA	NA	NA	21	289	7.6	2.2
Storey	5	16	1.3	0.5	NA	NA	NA	NA	10	49	2.4	0.7
Washoe	1 193	6 422	659.7	259.7	418	11 522	1 931.3	361.9	778	34 517	1 815.8	583.1
White Pine	13	23	3.0	1.7	NA	NA	NA	NA	37	493	17.4	4.8
Carson City city	233	806	86.2	30.2	186	4 157	514.5	120.8	133	2 404	93.1	27.7
NEW HAMPSHIRE	3 341	18 268	1 626.6	713.1	2 328	98 934	19 813.1	3 361.4	3 029	43 942	1 543.5	449.8
Belknap	110	479	36.6	16.4	133	4 658	497.4	133.4	213	2 237	89.1	26.1
Carroll	108	1 906	43.0	23.2	93	1 634	180.7	45.9	269	3 810	143.2	42.4
Cheshire	144	553	41.1	16.7	168	6 212	787.3	196.4	133	2 178	68.9	21.2
Coos	43	142	10.0	4.8	50	3 051	494.3	94.0	121	1 572	56.2	18.2
Grafton	227	1 024	87.9	39.0	148	6 886	881.5	205.6	325	4 761	156.3	47.3
Hillsborough	1 210	7 164	741.2	330.5	737	36 656	6 260.7	1 397.9	702	12 020	412.7	120.6
Merrimack	392	1 938	196.2	85.9	224	9 674	1 314.4	304.9	261	3 807	126.1	36.2
Rockingham	873	3 862	386.0	161.0	500	16 582	6 596.5	573.3	727	9 947	384.2	109.3
Strafford	167	949	68.7	29.0	159	9 080	2 106.2	281.5	209	2 830	84.3	22.1
Sullivan	67	251	15.9	6.6	116	4 501	694.2	128.6	69	780	22.6	6.3
NEW JERSEY	25 849	220 238	25 943.8	10 441.0	11 812	409 788	97 060.8	15 430.2	16 974	251 872	13 407.4	3 608.2
Atlantic	513	3 885	380.8	157.4	160	4 927	600.3	143.0	766	55 638	5 015.2	1 328.3
Bergen	4 134	24 327	3 087.0	1 149.8	1 806	59 877	10 419.7	2 223.7	1 910	24 315	1 116.9	304.0
Burlington	1 048	10 752	1 204.1	466.6	464	18 766	3 945.9	740.7	711	11 085	391.4	109.3
Camden	1 464	11 673	1 073.7	485.3	677	21 055	3 617.6	729.5	881	11 826	440.4	120.2
Cape May	211	795	69.1	26.7	82	813	110.4	19.1	961	4 642	368.1	95.0
Cumberland	200	1 061	88.9	34.1	210	12 985	1 896.1	398.3	218	2 554	78.8	21.1
Essex	2 232	23 080	3 055.9	1 213.8	1 206	35 578	8 416.4	1 359.9	1 320	16 915	853.8	234.2
Gloucester	404	2 099	213.9	71.8	290	11 013	6 882.8	416.5	386	6 419	201.6	53.6
Hudson	977	7 208	931.6	342.8	979	26 470	4 220.8	787.8	1 127	10 056	466.5	119.6
Hunterdon	493	3 163	709.5	183.4	175	5 064	1 104.4	194.8	237	2 439	102.5	28.9

1. Firms subject to federal tax.

STATE County	Health Care and Social Assistance[1], 1997				Other Services[1], 1997				Federal funds and grants, fiscal 2001[2] Expenditures (mil dol)			
										Direct payments for individuals[3]		
	Number of Establishments	Number of Employees	Receipts (mil dol)	Annual Payroll (mil dol)	Number of Establishments	Number of Employees	Receipts (mil dol)	Annual Payroll (mil dol)	Total	Social Security and government retirement	Medicare	Food stamps and Supplemental Security Income
	159	160	161	162	163	164	165	166	167	168	169	170
NEBRASKA—Cont'd												
Platte	49	561	30.8	14.2	79	309	18.6	5.4	142.0	58.9	13.4	2.2
Polk	7	21	0.9	0.3	10	25	1.7	0.3	51.6	13.0	5.2	0.2
Red Willow	28	185	9.5	3.8	24	93	4.9	1.2	78.6	31.0	9.8	1.4
Richardson	20	248	8.8	3.9	17	57	3.2	0.7	73.1	27.1	10.5	1.0
Rock	3	D	D	D	7	19	1.1	0.3	15.6	4.0	1.3	0.1
Saline	25	237	9.3	4.2	20	67	3.8	0.9	87.3	31.2	9.1	0.7
Sarpy	121	1 820	71.1	37.9	142	753	44.7	14.1	715.5	192.8	23.6	3.1
Saunders	21	234	6.6	3.3	26	57	5.0	0.9	110.0	40.6	14.5	0.9
Scotts Bluff	91	886	58.3	30.2	91	460	25.6	7.4	206.5	94.2	26.5	7.2
Seward	22	262	10.4	5.9	37	117	9.0	2.1	85.2	33.1	8.2	0.7
Sheridan	7	34	2.9	1.0	16	23	1.8	0.3	39.6	16.7	5.5	0.7
Sherman	4	D	D	D	7	9	0.8	0.1	38.3	8.9	3.1	0.2
Sioux	NA	NA	NA	NA	2	D	D	D	6.1	1.7	0.4	0.0
Stanton	4	D	D	D	6	11	1.3	0.2	28.8	7.3	2.3	0.2
Thayer	6	82	3.1	1.7	17	31	3.0	0.4	65.9	17.9	5.5	0.5
Thomas	NA	NA	NA	NA	2	D	D	D	5.3	1.7	0.8	0.1
Thurston	4	D	D	D	7	19	1.5	0.3	86.7	12.4	6.6	1.6
Valley	9	75	3.2	1.5	12	35	3.3	0.5	45.7	13.1	4.8	0.4
Washington	14	108	6.4	2.6	27	74	3.8	1.0	75.4	33.0	10.8	0.6
Wayne	11	228	7.6	3.8	20	65	3.0	0.9	55.7	15.3	4.7	0.5
Webster	8	132	3.3	1.7	4	17	1.6	0.2	41.2	12.0	4.7	0.4
Wheeler	NA	NA	NA	NA	NA	NA	NA	NA	10.3	1.6	0.7	0.1
York	27	154	8.2	3.6	49	205	11.9	3.4	103.7	33.5	10.4	1.1
NEVADA	3 226	39 476	3 406.5	1 358.9	2 175	16 185	1 061.7	328.0	9 623.6	4 068.8	1 166.8	202.6
Churchill	24	234	8.4	4.4	30	102	6.5	1.9	244.1	63.4	16.6	2.2
Clark	2 053	29 105	2 567.0	988.7	1 324	11 045	707.8	221.1	5 901.3	2 738.2	808.3	151.0
Douglas	67	358	28.2	11.3	44	177	11.5	3.2	138.9	92.4	21.8	2.8
Elko	52	459	34.6	13.7	57	422	38.4	9.6	115.9	48.9	10.4	2.5
Esmeralda	NA	NA	NA	NA	1	D	D	D	15.4	12.4	0.5	0.1
Eureka	NA	NA	NA	NA	2	D	D	D	10.7	2.8	1.0	0.1
Humboldt	19	122	8.7	2.7	28	115	6.1	1.7	50.9	23.2	6.5	1.4
Lander	2	D	D	D	4	D	D	D	31.5	7.6	2.7	0.3
Lincoln	2	D	D	D	2	D	D	D	23.2	12.6	3.4	0.9
Lyon	16	100	3.9	1.7	25	256	15.3	5.4	143.4	90.3	21.5	2.5
Mineral	6	135	5.3	2.5	6	15	1.6	0.3	72.2	20.5	5.1	1.2
Nye	19	118	6.8	3.1	22	88	9.6	1.4	166.9	116.4	22.5	3.2
Pershing	3	16	0.3	0.1	1	D	D	D	27.1	7.5	2.4	0.3
Storey	1	D	D	D	NA	NA	NA	NA	6.4	4.4	0.6	0.1
Washoe	779	7 430	649.9	288.0	518	3 269	217.6	68.7	1 519.9	648.5	194.6	29.4
White Pine	11	109	5.6	2.8	7	30	2.1	0.6	54.3	20.3	5.0	1.3
Carson City city	172	1 274	86.7	39.8	104	634	42.2	13.5	558.6	152.8	43.8	3.3
NEW HAMPSHIRE	2 373	28 889	1 734.1	836.3	2 159	11 379	794.5	236.6	6 313.7	2 591.3	780.5	90.3
Belknap	116	1 145	69.8	32.6	108	437	27.6	7.6	283.7	152.7	48.2	5.3
Carroll	82	920	41.2	17.3	67	204	13.6	3.3	223.7	123.8	34.4	3.8
Cheshire	106	1 454	71.2	34.8	126	690	50.7	13.6	309.3	156.7	49.3	6.2
Coos	43	340	16.6	7.7	52	210	18.7	3.8	202.9	95.0	39.3	4.2
Grafton	148	1 312	107.0	64.7	153	753	45.4	13.5	484.6	181.2	57.8	4.8
Hillsborough	742	9 268	587.4	284.8	640	4 143	286.7	93.3	1 923.6	717.5	215.2	28.4
Merrimack	260	3 170	208.9	109.2	265	1 218	96.4	25.4	836.5	269.3	88.8	10.6
Rockingham	580	8 259	465.7	205.7	537	2 853	186.5	58.2	1 124.0	543.6	150.2	12.0
Strafford	230	2 534	136.7	67.4	144	701	50.9	14.5	515.6	245.5	65.1	9.7
Sullivan	66	487	29.7	12.0	67	170	18.0	3.3	211.7	100.1	32.1	5.3
NEW JERSEY	18 905	172 723	13 702.4	5 900.2	15 077	78 644	5 434.8	1 665.1	46 239.5	16 833.7	8 069.7	1 048.0
Atlantic	540	5 024	376.4	175.3	429	2 485	130.7	42.1	1 407.6	533.6	266.5	35.6
Bergen	2 738	24 529	2 115.1	914.8	2 088	11 009	807.5	256.1	3 842.9	1 934.4	868.0	51.5
Burlington	747	8 697	624.8	287.6	656	3 844	265.5	87.6	2 929.5	983.5	330.8	29.1
Camden	1 144	11 362	836.3	391.6	846	5 239	332.6	100.1	2 725.8	1 052.9	527.3	99.1
Cape May	208	1 289	94.5	43.3	168	803	42.6	14.7	621.9	303.2	156.1	8.7
Cumberland	238	2 191	161.8	74.8	243	1 156	65.2	20.6	776.1	292.3	162.3	30.8
Essex	1 966	17 414	1 352.7	619.9	1 371	8 525	595.8	191.2	5 072.7	1 353.4	849.3	215.9
Gloucester	385	4 443	272.5	134.0	424	2 172	141.1	40.0	1 012.8	484.6	214.2	19.5
Hudson	1 003	6 962	521.4	213.4	915	4 477	264.3	77.8	3 194.0	809.6	543.3	153.9
Hunterdon	224	1 932	132.7	62.1	200	956	65.3	20.3	360.5	208.5	74.8	2.4

1. Firms subject to federal tax.   2. October 1, 2000 to September 30, 2001.   3. State totals may include programs not allocated by county.

	Federal funds and grants, fiscal 2001[1] (cont'd)							Local government finances, 1997				
	Expenditures (mil dol) (cont'd)							General revenue				
	Procurement contract awards		Grants[2]							Taxes		
STATE County											Per capita[3] (dollars)	
	Salaries and wages	Defense	Other	Medicaid and other health-related	Nutrition and family welfare	Education	Other	Total (mil dol)	Intergovern-mental (mil dol)	Total (mil dol)	Total	Property
	171	172	173	174	175	176	177	178	179	180	181	182
NEBRASKA—Cont'd												
Platte	7.8	1.2	1.7	9.0	1.8	1.9	2.6	86.2	17.0	31.3	1 026	900
Polk	1.1	0.0	0.3	1.5	0.3	0.2	1.4	16.8	3.1	8.9	1 589	1 456
Red Willow	4.1	0.0	0.6	3.7	1.1	0.7	3.3	29.2	12.0	10.7	940	854
Richardson	2.3	0.0	0.5	6.4	1.7	0.4	2.8	17.5	6.7	8.5	889	814
Rock	0.4	0.0	0.1	0.7	0.2	0.1	1.1	7.3	1.1	3.5	1 999	1 898
Saline	3.9	0.1	4.6	4.9	0.7	0.9	2.4	39.0	10.2	14.0	1 075	921
Sarpy	330.3	98.7	1.9	12.7	4.6	17.5	12.0	204.2	77.1	89.1	752	619
Saunders	5.0	6.3	0.9	4.1	1.1	0.6	1.4	39.6	10.9	18.1	944	875
Scotts Bluff	9.9	0.0	5.2	27.4	8.7	2.9	4.3	106.5	36.9	39.3	1 084	920
Seward	3.2	0.0	0.9	3.0	0.8	0.7	1.7	36.9	9.5	20.3	1 249	1 169
Sheridan	1.2	0.0	0.3	2.6	0.9	0.4	0.8	21.9	6.1	6.9	1 044	839
Sherman	0.9	0.0	0.2	3.0	2.1	0.1	2.9	8.9	3.1	4.4	1 222	1 158
Sioux	0.5	0.0	0.0	0.4	0.0	0.1	0.3	2.9	1.0	1.7	1 151	1 098
Stanton	1.2	0.0	0.2	1.5	0.2	0.1	0.3	8.0	3.5	3.1	503	472
Thayer	1.8	0.0	0.6	3.7	0.5	0.1	4.8	20.1	4.1	9.3	1 477	1 416
Thomas	1.9	0.0	0.4	0.0	0.1	0.0	0.0	2.3	0.6	1.2	1 513	1 429
Thurston	6.3	0.3	5.6	20.0	4.5	8.4	3.7	21.7	11.1	4.1	565	531
Valley	1.6	0.0	0.4	6.4	0.4	0.2	2.4	21.5	3.4	6.8	1 428	1 244
Washington	2.6	0.3	0.7	5.2	0.6	0.6	2.9	39.2	12.7	20.7	1 121	979
Wayne	2.1	0.0	0.3	2.6	0.5	1.4	2.3	18.9	6.0	8.1	868	725
Webster	1.4	0.0	0.3	3.0	0.3	0.2	1.2	12.4	4.3	4.7	1 174	1 094
Wheeler	0.3	0.0	0.1	0.0	0.1	0.1	0.2	2.4	0.6	1.6	1 730	1 709
York	3.4	0.0	0.7	3.7	0.8	0.3	6.1	44.4	9.2	18.7	1 282	1 182
NEVADA	1 019.4	323.0	718.2	511.7	222.1	166.7	541.3	X	X	X	X	X
Churchill	47.3	79.9	4.9	13.7	1.8	2.7	9.7	65.3	33.1	11.6	511	416
Clark	708.2	153.3	644.5	291.3	98.8	51.2	133.1	3 420.1	1 268.5	1 030.0	931	516
Douglas	5.0	1.5	3.4	3.1	1.9	1.9	4.4	105.6	44.2	38.5	1 067	812
Elko	18.4	0.6	4.4	12.4	2.7	3.0	7.6	141.1	77.1	25.3	557	446
Esmeralda	0.4	0.0	0.1	0.3	0.6	0.1	0.2	4.6	2.6	1.5	1 275	1 235
Eureka	0.2	0.0	0.7	0.3	0.6	0.1	4.7	18.3	6.4	9.7	5 236	5 079
Humboldt	6.8	0.0	1.6	5.3	1.4	1.4	1.6	73.0	35.4	15.7	896	733
Lander	3.8	0.0	1.7	1.9	0.8	0.7	10.0	30.0	13.0	6.8	952	904
Lincoln	1.5	0.0	0.2	0.7	1.0	0.4	1.5	16.8	12.0	2.9	650	601
Lyon	4.2	0.3	1.4	7.0	2.2	1.6	10.5	67.2	41.8	16.9	585	467
Mineral	3.4	33.5	0.4	4.6	0.9	1.0	1.1	27.1	9.7	4.2	736	623
Nye	9.3	0.4	1.8	3.6	1.5	1.5	4.9	87.9	42.6	21.4	786	677
Pershing	0.6	0.0	0.3	1.6	0.8	0.1	11.7	24.5	9.7	6.0	1 115	961
Storey	0.2	0.0	0.0	0.0	0.6	0.2	0.2	12.4	6.2	5.1	1 693	1 323
Washoe	175.3	35.6	43.6	113.1	25.3	17.7	179.5	874.3	369.6	293.3	959	668
White Pine	7.4	0.1	4.5	4.2	1.1	1.2	2.9	32.8	16.2	7.3	718	644
Carson City city	27.4	17.8	4.6	48.6	58.4	72.5	115.7	168.6	56.2	26.7	551	399
NEW HAMPSHIRE	516.0	479.2	175.9	609.8	139.2	103.0	435.6	X	X	X	X	X
Belknap	13.8	6.7	3.5	33.9	4.9	3.2	5.6	138.3	17.8	99.5	1 908	1 899
Carroll	8.2	0.0	3.2	17.1	3.2	2.5	23.4	108.7	13.0	79.7	2 049	2 022
Cheshire	11.3	2.3	2.7	39.6	7.8	3.3	13.0	175.7	33.5	120.9	1 691	1 678
Coos	8.3	0.1	1.5	28.2	6.0	2.1	8.1	96.4	28.1	59.2	1 784	1 751
Grafton	28.2	33.4	20.4	101.4	6.4	4.8	31.3	204.9	30.1	149.8	1 918	1 895
Hillsborough	263.1	313.3	73.4	150.3	23.5	16.2	57.8	716.7	93.3	518.3	1 448	1 425
Merrimack	46.2	4.0	8.8	95.3	55.7	44.1	155.6	264.4	40.9	190.6	1 513	1 501
Rockingham	109.0	115.6	54.5	67.0	13.6	8.6	26.4	539.2	64.6	419.0	1 569	1 554
Strafford	21.8	3.9	5.9	50.2	10.8	8.1	72.6	213.5	41.2	148.5	1 374	1 354
Sullivan	6.1	0.0	2.1	26.8	5.1	2.2	20.9	82.0	20.5	51.3	1 289	1 265
NEW JERSEY	3 782.1	2 799.7	1 358.2	4 390.2	1 238.0	726.6	2 122.9	X	X	X	X	X
Atlantic	192.0	12.6	46.5	149.2	27.5	9.3	57.1	880.9	301.3	477.6	2 019	1 991
Bergen	191.2	186.4	133.3	207.2	20.5	15.1	108.7	2 628.6	520.4	1 691.6	1 987	1 966
Burlington	424.3	849.5	84.6	118.2	25.2	20.3	34.4	1 072.7	406.6	529.6	1 267	1 247
Camden	183.1	218.7	92.3	293.8	85.4	25.2	53.1	1 870.8	767.6	677.5	1 343	1 326
Cape May	48.6	21.8	21.0	33.2	6.9	4.4	8.4	428.4	95.2	252.1	2 569	2 516
Cumberland	40.1	22.7	8.7	126.1	29.7	10.4	10.9	463.2	280.5	121.7	864	853
Essex	425.6	60.7	102.4	846.6	217.8	33.9	576.1	2 458.7	908.0	1 243.5	1 656	1 591
Gloucester	75.3	27.0	44.3	72.9	16.3	6.4	13.5	669.6	282.4	293.1	1 191	1 173
Hudson	463.4	19.7	162.2	624.1	108.0	18.1	60.7	1 636.7	711.2	666.5	1 209	1 191
Hunterdon	20.3	2.5	6.8	22.5	1.7	1.1	11.6	345.8	68.3	230.2	1 909	1 886

1. October 1, 2000 to September 30, 2001.   2. State totals may include programs not allocated by county.   3. Based on the resident population estimated as of July 1 of the year shown.

Table B. States and Counties — Local Government Finances, Government Employment, and Elections

STATE County	Local government finances, 1997 (cont'd)									Government employment, 1999			Presidential election, 2000[2]		
	Direct general expenditure							Debt outstanding					Percent of vote cast —		
			Percent of total for —												
	Total (mil dol)	Per capita[1] (dollars)	Education	Health and hospitals	Police protection	Public welfare	Highways	Total (mil dol)	Per capita[1] (dollars)	Federal civilian	Federal military	State and local	Democratic	Republican	All other
	183	184	185	186	187	188	189	190	191	192	193	194	195	196	197
NEBRASKA—Cont'd															
Platte	57.3	1 877	60.4	0.2	4.3	0.4	8.6	1 463.2	47 954	126	126	2 413	20.3	76.7	3.0
Polk	17.2	3 058	47.3	19.6	1.9	0.1	10.8	5.1	906	27	23	454	23.3	73.7	3.0
Red Willow	23.8	2 095	62.8	0.4	2.8	0.0	5.4	15.9	1 397	71	47	1 001	23.6	73.2	3.1
Richardson	17.3	1 806	61.8	0.2	6.7	0.1	13.6	2.8	296	47	39	611	33.3	63.2	3.5
Rock	7.0	4 033	35.1	33.2	2.4	0.1	7.4	1.1	661	0	0	223	15.8	81.1	3.1
Saline	40.7	3 125	40.7	17.4	3.5	1.3	6.7	6.9	528	69	54	1 158	45.1	50.2	4.7
Sarpy	224.4	1 892	52.3	0.4	4.3	0.1	7.8	165.1	1 393	2 353	7 991	4 294	32.3	64.0	3.7
Saunders	39.4	2 059	47.7	15.1	2.3	0.7	11.2	15.1	788	104	80	1 178	32.0	63.8	4.2
Scotts Bluff	107.5	2 962	48.4	0.4	4.1	0.3	6.3	16.5	455	163	150	2 772	28.4	67.9	3.7
Seward	34.2	2 099	57.2	0.2	3.4	0.0	9.5	12.6	774	58	68	960	32.1	63.5	4.4
Sheridan	20.5	3 100	37.8	28.9	2.4	6.6	7.6	4.3	642	31	27	751	15.2	81.7	3.1
Sherman	9.0	2 500	55.6	0.1	2.0	0.1	17.0	7.7	2 164	19	14	279	33.1	62.9	4.0
Sioux	2.9	1 932	51.8	0.0	1.8	0.1	17.2	0.0	9	11	0	85	13.0	83.6	3.3
Stanton	8.3	1 335	40.0	0.1	4.5	0.2	19.7	25.8	4 169	26	25	308	20.1	76.2	3.6
Thayer	20.7	3 299	44.5	20.4	2.0	0.0	7.4	2.5	403	39	26	647	27.3	69.7	3.0
Thomas	2.1	2 680	60.8	0.0	1.4	0.0	9.6	0.0	16	15	0	88	13.9	83.3	2.8
Thurston	19.6	2 731	55.6	20.1	1.7	0.0	5.3	7.6	1 056	149	29	605	44.4	50.0	5.7
Valley	17.6	3 679	30.5	37.5	1.3	0.1	7.1	2.3	485	34	19	650	25.8	71.1	3.1
Washington	44.0	2 380	56.2	0.4	4.3	0.1	10.0	23.7	1 283	51	78	1 480	29.6	66.8	3.7
Wayne	19.5	2 092	51.1	0.1	2.3	0.1	10.5	4.0	435	39	38	1 055	25.4	70.4	4.2
Webster	13.1	3 258	40.0	12.9	2.3	0.4	15.9	5.3	1 327	30	16	307	30.0	66.9	3.1
Wheeler	2.5	2 639	58.4	0.0	1.6	0.8	22.0	0.1	110	0	0	70	18.8	77.5	3.7
York	35.7	2 447	40.0	0.6	3.6	0.0	10.3	26.0	1 777	60	60	1 011	21.8	74.6	3.7
NEVADA	X	X	X	X	X	X	X	X	X	14 276	11 363	99 598	46.0	49.5	4.5
Churchill	62.4	2 744	47.1	1.4	7.4	1.5	4.1	29.8	1 310	704	1 098	1 284	24.8	70.7	4.4
Clark	3 710.3	3 355	31.8	8.3	7.2	1.3	7.3	5 998.0	5 423	8 607	9 068	58 027	51.3	44.7	4.0
Douglas	96.4	2 672	45.8	2.8	7.6	1.2	3.1	63.3	1 755	102	76	1 785	32.5	62.3	5.3
Elko	142.2	3 131	48.6	12.5	5.9	0.6	6.9	37.0	814	365	91	3 012	17.9	77.8	4.4
Esmeralda	4.5	3 835	34.7	1.8	16.1	0.6	12.1	0.0	10	0	0	97	23.6	67.8	8.6
Eureka	22.3	11 985	35.8	2.9	4.7	1.2	12.3	2.5	1 346	0	0	228	17.9	75.5	6.6
Humboldt	64.6	3 695	38.1	17.2	4.4	1.1	6.0	128.7	7 363	143	36	1 190	22.4	72.3	5.2
Lander	32.8	4 611	29.9	28.3	4.6	1.1	4.1	12.1	1 701	80	13	482	18.6	76.4	4.9
Lincoln	15.8	3 555	60.9	0.7	6.1	1.4	7.0	6.3	1 425	35	0	564	23.6	70.1	6.2
Lyon	67.6	2 347	57.1	5.1	7.5	1.3	5.9	40.5	1 404	61	63	1 400	33.0	60.6	6.4
Mineral	27.2	4 756	30.2	39.6	5.8	1.2	1.9	7.2	1 248	92	13	431	39.9	53.5	6.5
Nye	84.6	3 113	36.0	22.1	8.0	0.8	6.4	32.1	1 182	182	71	1 429	37.1	56.7	6.1
Pershing	23.4	4 350	32.1	33.4	4.4	1.1	4.3	11.6	2 155	11	10	661	26.4	67.8	5.9
Storey	9.4	3 137	47.1	1.0	14.8	0.0	2.0	6.6	2 191	0	0	195	37.0	56.4	6.6
Washoe	877.3	2 869	32.5	2.5	7.8	2.5	5.9	985.2	3 222	3 156	676	18 547	42.6	52.0	5.3
White Pine	30.8	3 016	44.1	15.4	8.6	0.6	6.4	15.5	1 515	189	20	1 090	30.2	63.1	6.7
Carson City city	151.7	3 135	30.0	36.4	5.4	0.7	3.3	105.5	2 181	532	108	9 176	37.8	57.0	5.2
NEW HAMPSHIRE	X	X	X	X	X	X	X	X	X	7 803	4 374	70 040	46.8	48.1	5.1
Belknap	132.8	2 547	47.8	0.5	4.8	11.1	5.0	48.9	937	232	183	3 260	40.0	55.2	4.7
Carroll	104.4	2 684	50.3	1.2	4.1	7.6	6.6	57.2	1 470	134	136	2 309	41.3	52.8	5.9
Cheshire	167.5	2 341	51.3	0.7	3.6	8.4	6.2	46.6	652	202	247	4 545	52.0	41.3	6.6
Coos	84.3	2 538	41.0	1.2	2.8	15.2	5.7	34.7	1 046	156	111	2 331	45.0	50.2	4.8
Grafton	197.9	2 533	53.7	0.9	3.9	7.4	6.0	83.6	1 070	645	274	5 756	47.3	46.7	6.0
Hillsborough	703.2	1 965	51.9	0.8	5.4	5.6	5.5	405.3	1 133	3 792	1 277	14 821	46.8	48.7	4.5
Merrimack	283.2	2 248	55.2	0.4	4.5	8.2	5.2	161.6	1 283	868	447	13 981	48.1	47.2	4.8
Rockingham	578.5	2 166	58.4	1.1	5.5	5.2	4.1	247.4	926	1 314	1 168	11 183	45.9	49.1	5.0
Strafford	197.5	1 827	50.2	0.4	5.0	8.4	3.7	113.2	1 047	345	394	9 474	51.4	42.7	5.8
Sullivan	81.6	2 050	43.3	1.0	3.8	17.5	6.6	41.3	1 038	115	137	2 380	44.1	49.8	6.1
NEW JERSEY	X	X	X	X	X	X	X	X	X	65 375	30 600	497 045	56.1	40.3	3.6
Atlantic	1 007.3	4 258	42.2	1.0	7.7	4.3	3.6	690.7	2 919	2 506	780	17 648	58.0	39.1	2.9
Bergen	2 623.4	3 082	50.9	5.3	6.7	2.9	3.1	971.5	1 141	3 285	2 082	38 078	55.3	41.6	3.0
Burlington	1 126.3	2 695	57.5	2.7	4.2	3.2	7.8	637.0	1 524	5 772	6 340	21 645	56.0	40.7	3.3
Camden	1 800.1	3 568	47.3	2.8	5.3	7.1	5.7	1 923.9	3 813	3 347	1 222	30 740	64.6	31.7	3.7
Cape May	441.4	4 498	35.3	2.0	6.9	4.1	5.0	467.7	4 766	384	1 518	7 922	46.6	50.0	3.4
Cumberland	441.6	3 134	55.9	3.2	4.0	7.7	4.3	153.1	1 086	755	341	11 644	57.9	38.8	3.4
Essex	2 458.0	3 274	34.7	4.7	7.7	11.5	2.3	1 101.7	1 467	9 278	1 830	63 485	71.5	25.8	2.8
Gloucester	678.8	2 759	62.6	1.1	4.8	1.9	3.7	586.6	2 384	543	609	14 386	56.9	39.4	3.6
Hudson	1 555.6	2 821	28.9	5.2	7.7	7.3	2.3	1 414.7	2 565	7 842	1 458	33 814	70.6	26.2	3.2
Hunterdon	377.4	3 130	59.7	1.5	3.9	1.2	6.6	232.4	1 928	381	302	7 192	37.9	57.1	5.1

1. Based on the resident population estimated as of July 1 of the year shown.   2. Data subject to copyright.

STATE/ County code	MSA/ PMSA/ NECMA code[1]	County Type[2]	STATE County	Land area,[3] (sq km) 2000	Population and population characteristics, 2000													
								Race alone or in combination (percent)					Age (percent)					
					Total persons	Rank	Per square kilometer	White	Black	Am. Indian, Alaska Native	Asian and Pacific Islander	Percent Hispanic[4]	Under 5 years	5 to 17 years	18 to 24 years	25 to 34 years	35 to 44 years	45 to 54 years
				1	2	3	4	5	6	7	8	9	10	11	12	13	14	15
			NEW JERSEY—Cont'd															
34 021	8480	2	Mercer	585	350 761	167	599.6	70.0	20.7	0.5	5.7	9.7	6.3	17.7	10.2	14.0	16.5	14.0
34 023	5015	0	Middlesex	802	750 162	66	935.4	70.3	9.8	0.6	14.7	13.6	6.6	17.1	9.5	15.6	17.2	13.4
34 025	5190	0	Monmouth	1 222	615 301	87	503.5	85.7	8.7	0.5	4.5	6.2	6.9	19.2	6.9	12.2	18.2	15.0
34 027	5640	0	Morris	1 215	470 212	123	387.0	88.5	3.1	0.4	6.9	7.8	7.0	17.8	6.4	13.5	18.4	15.3
34 029	5190	0	Ocean	1 648	510 916	109	310.0	94.2	3.3	0.4	1.6	5.0	6.3	17.0	6.6	11.2	14.9	12.4
34 031	0875	0	Passaic	480	489 049	115	1 018.9	65.4	14.1	0.8	4.5	30.0	7.4	18.7	9.3	15.0	16.3	12.8
34 033	6160	1	Salem	875	64 285	758	73.5	82.3	15.5	0.9	0.8	3.9	6.1	19.5	7.8	11.9	16.0	14.6
34 035	5015	0	Somerset	789	297 490	190	377.0	80.8	8.0	0.4	9.1	8.7	7.5	18.1	5.9	14.2	19.6	14.7
34 037	5640	1	Sussex	1 350	144 166	379	106.8	96.8	1.3	0.4	1.6	3.3	6.8	21.1	6.2	12.1	19.3	16.2
34 039	5640	0	Union	268	522 541	106	1 949.8	67.8	21.9	0.6	4.3	19.7	7.0	17.9	7.9	14.4	16.9	13.3
34 041	5640	1	Warren	927	102 437	518	110.5	95.6	2.2	0.4	1.5	3.7	6.9	19.2	6.3	12.8	18.5	14.6
35 000	...	X	NEW MEXICO	314 309	1 819 046	X	5.8	69.9	2.3	10.5	1.7	42.1	7.2	20.8	9.8	12.9	15.5	13.5
35 001	0200	2	Bernalillo	3 020	556 678	100	184.3	74.4	3.4	5.2	2.7	42.0	6.9	18.4	10.3	14.3	16.1	14.0
35 003	...	9	Catron	17 943	3 543	2 951	0.2	91.1	0.5	3.7	1.0	19.2	4.2	16.9	4.2	6.7	12.8	18.6
35 005	...	5	Chaves	15 723	61 382	792	3.9	74.8	2.3	1.9	0.9	43.8	7.2	21.9	9.4	11.2	14.1	12.7
35 006	...	6	Cibola	11 757	25 595	1 532	2.2	42.2	1.3	41.8	0.6	33.4	7.9	22.7	9.6	12.1	15.4	12.6
35 007	...	7	Colfax	9 730	14 189	2 148	1.5	84.9	0.4	2.5	0.5	47.5	5.4	19.7	6.9	9.8	14.7	14.7
35 009	...	5	Curry	3 641	45 044	998	12.4	75.5	7.9	1.8	2.8	30.4	8.6	21.5	11.5	13.9	14.9	10.7
35 011	...	9	De Baca	6 021	2 240	3 048	0.4	86.2	0.1	1.7	0.4	35.3	5.1	19.0	5.7	8.6	13.1	12.6
35 013	4100	3	Dona Ana	9 861	174 682	313	17.7	71.0	2.0	2.2	1.3	63.4	7.8	21.9	13.3	12.9	14.1	11.5
35 015	...	5	Eddy	10 831	51 658	898	4.8	78.7	1.9	1.9	0.7	38.8	7.3	21.5	8.4	10.9	14.8	13.5
35 017	...	7	Grant	10 272	31 002	1 378	3.0	78.5	0.8	2.3	0.6	48.8	6.9	19.4	8.5	10.4	13.3	14.0
35 019	...	9	Guadalupe	7 849	4 680	2 868	0.6	57.6	1.3	1.5	0.9	81.2	5.3	19.0	9.2	11.8	18.9	12.5
35 021	...	9	Harding	5 505	810	3 123	0.1	87.3	0.4	3.1	0.0	44.9	3.1	17.2	4.6	7.4	11.4	17.3
35 023	...	7	Hidalgo	8 924	5 932	2 790	0.7	86.5	0.6	1.2	0.5	56.0	7.7	24.1	7.8	10.7	14.4	12.5
35 025	...	5	Lea	11 378	55 511	850	4.9	70.1	4.8	1.7	0.6	39.6	7.7	22.4	10.1	12.3	15.0	12.2
35 027	...	7	Lincoln	12 512	19 411	1 822	1.6	85.8	0.6	2.9	0.5	25.6	5.1	17.7	6.0	8.9	14.3	16.2
35 028	7490	3	Los Alamos	283	18 343	1 877	64.8	92.4	0.6	1.2	4.5	11.7	5.6	20.2	4.4	10.2	17.5	17.6
35 029	...	6	Luna	7 680	25 016	1 559	3.3	77.1	1.2	1.9	0.5	57.7	7.7	22.3	7.6	10.4	12.3	11.1
35 031	...	5	McKinley	14 112	74 798	667	5.3	18.2	0.7	76.4	0.7	12.4	9.1	28.8	9.7	13.1	14.7	10.9
35 033	...	8	Mora	5 002	5 180	2 838	1.0	61.3	0.3	1.6	0.2	81.6	6.1	20.6	7.5	9.5	14.8	15.0
35 035	...	4	Otero	17 163	62 298	781	3.6	76.9	4.5	6.6	2.1	32.2	7.4	22.0	9.3	12.9	15.7	12.0
35 037	...	7	Quay	7 446	10 155	2 431	1.4	84.4	1.0	2.1	1.2	38.0	5.5	19.5	6.7	9.6	13.7	14.1
35 039	...	6	Rio Arriba	15 171	41 190	1 074	2.7	59.5	0.5	14.7	0.5	72.9	7.0	21.6	8.9	13.2	15.6	13.9
35 041	...	7	Roosevelt	6 342	18 018	1 896	2.8	76.5	2.0	1.8	0.9	33.3	7.5	20.6	16.0	12.5	13.0	10.7
35 043	0200	2	Sandoval	9 607	89 908	575	9.4	68.1	2.2	17.2	1.7	29.4	7.3	22.2	7.5	12.7	17.4	14.1
35 045	...	5	San Juan	14 281	113 801	473	8.0	55.2	0.7	38.2	0.6	15.0	8.0	24.6	10.0	12.3	15.8	12.5
35 047	...	6	San Miguel	12 217	30 126	1 392	2.5	60.1	1.1	2.8	1.0	78.0	6.5	20.9	10.9	11.6	15.4	13.6
35 049	7490	3	Santa Fe	4 945	129 292	417	26.1	77.1	0.9	4.1	1.5	49.0	6.2	17.9	8.1	13.1	16.6	17.3
35 051	...	6	Sierra	10 827	13 270	2 205	1.2	89.4	0.6	2.5	0.6	26.3	4.8	15.3	5.4	7.6	11.9	13.4
35 053	...	7	Socorro	17 214	18 078	1 895	1.1	66.6	1.0	12.2	1.7	48.7	7.0	21.4	12.6	12.0	14.2	12.7
35 055	...	7	Taos	5 706	29 979	1 397	5.3	67.3	0.6	7.6	0.8	57.9	5.8	18.7	6.9	11.8	15.6	17.7
35 057	...	8	Torrance	8 663	16 911	1 958	2.0	77.6	2.0	3.4	0.8	37.2	6.9	23.4	7.5	12.5	16.7	14.1
35 059	...	9	Union	9 920	4 174	2 900	0.4	82.4	0.1	1.8	0.6	35.1	6.0	21.3	6.3	10.1	14.5	13.2
35 061	0200	2	Valencia	2 765	66 152	739	23.9	70.6	1.6	4.5	0.8	55.0	7.6	22.5	8.4	13.3	16.4	13.2
36 000	...	X	NEW YORK	122 283	18 976 457	X	155.2	70.0	17.0	0.9	6.4	15.1	6.5	18.2	9.3	14.5	16.2	13.5
36 001	0160	2	Albany	1 356	294 565	191	217.2	84.5	11.9	0.6	3.3	3.1	5.7	16.9	11.3	13.4	15.5	14.3
36 003	...	7	Allegany	2 668	49 927	917	18.7	97.8	1.0	0.7	0.9	0.9	5.6	18.8	15.5	10.1	13.8	13.0
36 005	5600	0	Bronx	109	1 332 650	27	12 226.1	33.1	38.3	1.5	3.9	48.4	8.2	21.6	10.6	15.6	15.0	11.2
36 007	0960	2	Broome	1 831	200 536	274	109.5	92.7	4.0	0.6	3.2	2.0	5.6	17.4	11.0	11.3	15.5	13.4
36 009	...	4	Cattaraugus	3 393	83 955	619	24.7	95.6	1.4	3.1	0.6	0.9	6.2	20.0	9.3	11.3	15.2	14.0
36 011	8160	2	Cayuga	1 795	81 963	633	45.7	94.3	4.5	0.7	0.7	2.0	5.9	19.2	8.2	12.9	16.8	13.9
36 013	3610	3	Chautauqua	2 751	139 750	391	50.8	95.2	2.6	0.8	0.6	4.2	5.8	18.7	10.3	11.3	15.0	13.6
36 015	2335	3	Chemung	1 057	91 070	565	86.2	92.3	6.7	0.6	1.0	1.8	6.0	18.4	8.8	12.3	16.0	13.9
36 017	...	6	Chenango	2 316	51 401	900	22.2	98.4	1.0	0.7	0.4	1.1	5.9	20.2	7.0	11.4	16.1	14.1
36 019	...	5	Clinton	2 691	79 894	643	29.7	94.2	3.9	0.7	1.0	2.5	5.1	17.8	12.4	13.4	17.1	13.4
36 021	...	6	Columbia	1 647	63 094	769	38.3	93.3	5.3	0.6	1.2	2.5	5.3	18.7	6.4	11.1	15.8	15.3
36 023	...	4	Cortland	1 294	48 599	937	37.6	98.1	1.2	0.8	0.7	1.2	5.9	17.8	15.5	11.8	14.7	13.0
36 025	...	6	Delaware	3 746	48 055	952	12.8	97.3	1.5	0.8	0.7	2.0	5.1	17.9	8.2	9.8	14.1	14.4
36 027	2281	2	Dutchess	2 076	280 150	201	134.9	85.1	10.2	0.7	3.0	6.4	6.2	18.8	9.4	12.5	17.7	14.2
36 029	1280	0	Erie	2 704	950 265	37	351.4	83.2	13.6	0.9	1.8	3.3	6.1	18.2	8.7	12.5	15.8	13.7
36 031	...	6	Essex	4 654	38 851	1 145	8.3	95.7	2.9	0.8	0.6	2.2	5.0	17.8	6.9	13.1	16.7	14.4
36 033	...	7	Franklin	4 226	51 134	904	12.1	84.7	6.8	6.6	0.5	4.0	4.9	17.8	9.5	15.2	17.9	13.3
36 035	...	4	Fulton	1 285	55 073	858	42.9	96.8	2.1	0.5	0.8	1.6	5.7	19.2	7.2	12.3	15.8	14.1

1. MSA = Metropolitan Statistical Area. PMSA = Primary MSA. NECMA = New England County Metropolitan Area. See Appendix A for explanation of these concepts. See Appendix B for list of metropolitan areas identified by type, with component counties. 2. County typology code from the Economic Research Service of USDA. See Appendix A for definition. 3. Dry land or land partially or temporarily covered by water. 4. Hispanic persons may be of any race.

Table B. States and Counties — **Population and Households**

STATE County	Population, 2000 (cont'd) Age (percent) (cont'd) 55 to 64 years	65 to 74 years	75 years and over	Percent female	Population — change and components of change, 1990–2001 Total persons 2001	1990	Percent change 1990–2000	2000–2001	Components of change, 2000–2001 Births	Deaths	Net migration	Households, 2000 Number	Percent change, 1990–2000	Persons per house-hold	Percent Female family house-holder[1]	One person
	16	17	18	19	20	21	22	23	24	25	26	27	28	29	30	31
NEW JERSEY—Cont'd																
Mercer	8.6	6.4	6.1	51.3	353 529	325 759	7.7	0.8	5 575	3 513	854	125 807	7.6	2.62	13.8	25.6
Middlesex	8.3	6.5	5.8	50.9	757 191	671 712	11.7	0.9	12 364	6 997	1 883	265 815	11.3	2.74	10.8	22.4
Monmouth	9.1	6.5	6.0	51.4	622 977	553 192	11.2	1.2	9 698	6 292	4 534	224 236	13.5	2.70	10.0	23.8
Morris	10.0	6.3	5.3	51.1	472 859	421 330	11.6	0.6	7 696	4 000	-928	169 711	14.1	2.72	7.9	21.5
Ocean	9.5	10.6	11.5	52.5	527 207	433 203	17.9	3.2	7 423	8 336	16 906	200 402	19.2	2.51	9.2	27.0
Passaic	8.5	6.2	5.9	51.5	491 077	470 872	3.9	0.4	9 529	5 025	-2 515	163 856	5.5	2.92	16.0	22.2
Salem	9.6	7.3	7.2	51.7	64 364	65 294	-1.5	0.1	944	827	-12	24 295	2.1	2.60	13.3	24.3
Somerset	8.8	6.0	5.2	51.2	301 955	240 222	23.8	1.5	5 238	2 349	1 677	108 984	23.4	2.69	8.2	22.8
Sussex	9.0	4.9	4.2	50.5	146 671	130 936	10.1	1.7	2 095	1 167	1 595	50 831	14.3	2.80	8.0	18.9
Union	8.8	6.8	7.0	51.9	523 396	493 819	5.8	0.2	9 128	5 852	-2 428	186 124	3.4	2.77	14.2	23.6
Warren	8.9	6.6	6.3	51.3	105 765	91 675	11.7	3.2	1 465	943	2 772	38 660	13.7	2.61	9.2	24.0
NEW MEXICO	8.7	6.5	5.2	50.8	1 829 146	1 515 069	20.1	0.6	33 732	16 862	-6 546	677 971	24.9	2.63	13.2	25.4
Bernalillo	8.4	6.1	5.4	51.2	562 458	480 577	15.8	1.0	10 018	5 248	1 263	220 936	19.1	2.47	12.9	28.5
Catron	17.8	11.8	7.0	48.9	3 512	2 563	38.2	-0.9	32	30	-36	1 584	56.8	2.23	7.6	30.1
Chaves	8.7	7.6	7.1	51.0	60 301	57 849	6.1	-1.8	1 138	811	-1 434	22 561	9.6	2.66	13.7	24.8
Cibola	8.9	6.7	4.0	51.1	25 888	23 794	7.6	1.1	622	246	-75	8 327	14.2	2.95	18.3	21.1
Colfax	11.8	8.9	8.0	49.3	14 140	12 925	9.8	-0.3	190	160	-77	5 821	17.4	2.37	10.3	27.7
Curry	7.5	6.1	5.3	50.6	44 229	42 207	6.7	-1.8	1 036	435	-1 428	16 766	10.9	2.62	12.8	25.5
De Baca	10.6	12.6	12.8	51.0	2 138	2 252	-0.5	-4.6	24	32	-96	922	1.0	2.35	7.3	30.8
Dona Ana	7.7	6.2	4.4	50.9	176 790	135 510	28.9	1.2	3 576	1 285	-142	59 556	32.2	2.85	14.7	21.3
Eddy	8.9	7.6	7.1	51.0	51 067	48 605	6.3	-1.1	961	677	-882	19 379	10.9	2.63	11.9	24.2
Grant	11.0	9.1	7.3	51.3	30 722	27 676	12.0	-0.9	542	371	-447	12 146	24.3	2.50	12.9	25.7
Guadalupe	9.4	7.8	6.0	45.1	4 602	4 156	12.6	-1.7	60	63	-78	1 655	8.9	2.51	14.3	27.9
Harding	10.9	15.9	12.3	49.4	772	987	-17.9	-4.7	3	6	-36	371	-6.3	2.18	7.5	35.3
Hidalgo	9.3	7.3	6.4	50.1	5 612	5 958	-0.4	-5.4	361	167	-530	2 152	7.4	2.72	13.6	25.3
Lea	8.1	7.0	5.2	49.9	55 149	55 765	-0.5	-0.7	1 164	552	-987	19 699	2.0	2.73	12.2	22.5
Lincoln	13.9	11.4	6.4	51.0	19 730	12 219	58.9	1.6	235	193	274	8 202	71.3	2.34	9.3	26.7
Los Alamos	12.4	6.7	5.4	49.6	17 798	18 115	1.3	-3.0	221	119	-663	7 497	3.9	2.43	5.7	24.9
Luna	10.4	10.7	7.5	51.2	25 002	18 110	38.1	-0.1	498	344	-168	9 397	38.3	2.64	12.4	26.4
McKinley	6.7	4.1	2.8	51.7	75 032	60 686	23.3	0.3	1 891	584	-1 078	21 476	29.5	3.44	22.7	19.5
Mora	11.1	9.0	6.4	49.5	5 236	4 264	21.5	1.1	61	62	56	2 017	32.8	2.54	11.9	26.9
Otero	9.0	7.2	4.5	50.2	60 747	51 928	20.0	-2.5	1 082	534	-2 115	22 984	26.6	2.66	11.8	23.3
Quay	12.0	10.1	8.9	51.4	9 829	10 823	-6.2	-3.2	138	152	-316	4 201	-0.9	2.37	12.0	28.9
Rio Arriba	8.9	6.4	4.5	50.5	40 772	34 365	19.9	-1.0	774	388	-811	15 044	31.3	2.71	15.9	23.5
Roosevelt	7.7	6.3	5.8	50.9	18 120	16 702	7.9	0.6	341	143	-91	6 639	10.8	2.60	11.7	24.7
Sandoval	8.1	5.7	5.0	51.2	93 883	63 319	42.0	4.4	2 053	770	2 644	31 411	50.5	2.84	12.2	19.9
San Juan	7.7	5.3	3.8	50.4	115 380	91 605	24.2	1.4	1 383	550	765	37 711	31.2	2.99	14.7	19.3
San Miguel	9.4	6.4	5.3	50.8	30 156	25 743	17.0	0.1	991	518	-447	11 134	28.0	2.58	16.4	26.6
Santa Fe	10.0	6.1	4.6	51.1	130 915	98 928	30.7	1.3	1 953	1 002	723	52 482	38.7	2.42	11.7	29.4
Sierra	13.9	14.9	12.8	50.0	13 188	9 912	33.9	-0.6	121	288	93	6 113	38.1	2.13	8.6	35.9
Socorro	9.3	6.2	4.7	49.2	17 856	14 764	22.4	-1.2	318	160	-385	6 675	27.9	2.62	13.3	26.8
Taos	11.1	7.0	5.4	51.0	30 353	23 118	29.7	1.2	438	247	193	12 675	44.8	2.34	12.7	32.1
Torrance	9.1	5.8	4.0	48.7	16 792	10 285	64.4	-0.7	265	130	-260	6 024	64.1	2.72	12.3	23.2
Union	10.9	9.7	8.1	50.8	4 022	4 124	1.2	-3.6	48	56	-148	1 733	7.3	2.40	9.1	30.0
Valencia	8.6	5.9	4.2	49.8	66 955	45 235	46.2	1.2	1 194	539	173	22 681	49.5	2.86	13.1	18.8
NEW YORK	8.9	6.7	6.2	51.8	19 011 378	17 990 778	5.5	0.2	323 772	197 846	-90 510	7 056 860	6.3	2.61	14.7	28.1
Albany	8.5	7.1	7.4	52.2	294 007	292 812	0.6	-0.2	4 052	3 616	-883	120 512	4.0	2.32	12.2	33.0
Allegany	9.1	7.5	6.5	50.0	49 881	50 470	-1.1	-0.1	690	622	-91	18 009	5.9	2.53	9.0	26.0
Bronx	7.7	5.3	4.7	53.5	1 337 928	1 203 789	10.7	0.4	29 684	13 199	-11 454	463 212	9.2	2.78	30.4	27.4
Broome	9.3	8.0	8.4	51.8	199 267	212 160	-5.5	-0.6	2 742	2 671	-1 279	80 749	-1.3	2.37	10.8	31.0
Cattaraugus	9.4	7.7	6.9	50.8	83 403	84 234	-0.3	-0.7	1 244	1 068	-707	32 023	5.1	2.52	10.8	26.8
Cayuga	8.8	7.1	7.3	49.5	81 401	82 313	-0.4	-0.7	1 069	918	-695	30 558	5.1	2.53	11.0	26.2
Chautauqua	9.3	8.0	8.0	51.2	138 662	141 895	-1.5	-0.8	1 865	1 815	-1 099	54 515	1.5	2.45	10.8	28.1
Chemung	9.0	7.8	7.8	50.6	90 675	95 195	-4.3	-0.4	1 273	1 225	-406	35 049	-0.6	2.44	12.4	27.9
Chenango	10.3	7.5	7.4	50.8	51 142	51 768	-0.7	-0.5	663	638	-264	19 926	4.1	2.52	9.8	26.1
Clinton	8.8	6.8	5.1	48.8	80 085	85 969	-7.1	0.2	940	816	116	29 423	1.0	2.47	10.2	26.3
Columbia	11.0	8.3	8.1	50.2	63 193	62 982	0.2	0.2	708	829	251	24 796	4.6	2.43	10.3	27.1
Cortland	8.7	6.2	6.3	51.7	48 463	48 963	-0.7	-0.3	710	567	-264	18 210	5.6	2.50	10.3	26.5
Delaware	11.7	9.7	8.9	50.8	47 520	47 352	1.5	-1.1	541	653	-416	19 270	9.2	2.39	9.0	28.3
Dutchess	9.0	6.5	5.5	50.0	284 447	259 462	8.0	1.5	4 058	2 625	2 943	99 536	11.1	2.63	10.3	24.6
Erie	9.1	8.0	7.9	52.2	944 408	968 584	-1.9	-0.6	14 162	12 614	-7 145	380 873	1.0	2.41	13.7	30.5
Essex	10.2	8.5	7.5	48.2	38 822	37 152	4.6	-0.1	436	518	67	15 028	9.5	2.39	8.9	28.3
Franklin	8.4	6.8	6.1	45.1	50 890	46 540	9.9	-0.5	576	513	-295	17 931	10.1	2.46	11.1	28.2
Fulton	9.5	7.9	8.4	50.7	54 996	54 191	1.6	-0.1	704	662	-95	21 884	4.2	2.43	11.3	27.7

1. No spouse present.

STATE County	Births, average 1997–1999 Total	Rate[1]	Deaths, average 1997–1999 Number Total	Number Infant[2]	Rate Total[1]	Rate Infant[3]	Physicians[4] 2000 Number	Rate[5]	Hospitals[4] 1998 Number	Beds Number	Beds Rate[5]	Medicare enrollees 2000	Serious crimes known to police, 2000[6] Total Number	Rate[7]
	32	33	34	35	36	37	38	39	40	41	42	43	44	45
NEW JERSEY—Cont'd														
Mercer	4 415	13.3	2 978	36	9.0	8.2	1 046	298	5	1 674	505	51 718	14 069	4 011
Middlesex	9 958	13.9	5 641	51	7.9	5.1	1 998	266	6	1 907	266	96 899	19 857	2 647
Monmouth	8 062	13.3	5 173	48	8.6	5.9	1 504	244	5	1 857	308	87 031	13 743	2 234
Morris	6 083	13.2	3 314	23	7.2	3.7	1 305	278	4	1 909	415	58 369	7 901	1 680
Ocean	6 228	12.7	6 636	32	13.5	5.2	726	142	5	1 433	293	118 579	12 538	2 454
Passaic	7 642	15.8	4 175	45	8.6	5.9	991	203	6	1 947	401	65 021	16 104	3 293
Salem	764	11.8	702	NA	10.8	NA	90	140	2	243	374	10 491	1 637	2 546
Somerset	4 183	14.8	1 928	20	6.8	4.8	822	276	1	374	132	32 411	5 215	1 753
Sussex	1 899	13.3	980	10	6.8	5.3	168	117	2	271	189	15 423	1 890	1 311
Union	7 047	14.1	4 701	48	9.4	6.9	1 280	245	7	2 422	484	79 107	19 911	3 810
Warren	1 297	13.1	862	NA	8.7	NA	136	133	2	320	325	15 467	1 635	1 596
NEW MEXICO	27 035	15.6	13 079	183	7.5	6.8	3 602	198	36	4 015	231	234 319	100 391	5 519
Bernalillo	7 848	14.9	3 976	54	7.6	6.9	1 987	357	8	1 619	308	70 607	44 962	8 077
Catron	22	7.9	25	NA	9.0	NA	2	56	0	0	0	683	20	564
Chaves	967	15.5	612	NA	9.8	NA	82	134	2	277	443	10 025	3 958	6 448
Cibola	NA	NA	NA	NA	NA	NA	18	70	1	43	164	2 423	856	3 344
Colfax	170	12.5	135	NA	9.9	NA	27	190	1	46	338	2 557	NA	NA
Curry	820	18.1	377	10	8.3	12.2	55	122	1	106	234	5 901	2 658	5 999
De Baca	23	9.6	29	NA	12.1	NA	1	45	1	25	1 046	571	493	22 009
Dona Ana	3 037	18.0	1 021	19	6.1	6.3	240	137	1	221	131	20 191	NA	NA
Eddy	795	14.9	546	8	10.2	9.6	58	112	2	174	325	8 628	2 865	5 546
Grant	462	14.7	307	NA	9.8	NA	50	161	1	68	215	5 531	189	700
Guadalupe	59	14.7	44	NA	11.0	NA	8	171	1	20	494	784	NA	NA
Harding	7	8.3	10	NA	11.0	NA	0	0	0	0	0	248	6	741
Hidalgo	90	14.6	50	NA	8.2	NA	2	34	0	0	0	834	NA	NA
Lea	902	16.2	488	NA	8.8	NA	39	70	2	278	496	7 702	2 021	4 660
Lincoln	196	12.0	150	NA	9.2	NA	23	118	1	38	232	3 472	641	3 567
Los Alamos	177	9.7	90	NA	4.9	NA	45	245	1	53	289	2 143	196	1 069
Luna	378	15.7	266	NA	11.0	NA	22	88	1	119	494	4 715	1 149	4 593
McKinley	1 402	20.8	422	13	6.3	9.0	121	162	1	70	104	5 900	3 771	5 042
Mora	56	11.6	39	NA	8.0	NA	0	0	0	0	0	912	18	347
Otero	896	16.4	408	NA	7.5	NA	54	87	1	67	123	7 516	1 638	2 629
Quay	119	11.9	134	NA	13.4	NA	7	69	1	37	369	2 117	NA	NA
Rio Arriba	663	17.5	308	NA	8.1	NA	42	102	1	80	212	5 366	NA	NA
Roosevelt	268	14.9	125	NA	6.9	NA	23	128	1	151	830	2 594	709	3 935
Sandoval	1 370	15.6	521	9	5.9	6.8	72	80	0	0	0	10 512	2 015	2 241
San Juan	1 832	17.2	670	10	6.3	5.6	152	134	1	126	119	11 779	3 983	3 500
San Miguel	416	14.5	244	NA	8.5	NA	42	139	1	56	193	4 353	1 143	3 985
Santa Fe	1 612	13.1	777	NA	6.3	NA	329	254	1	208	169	15 217	6 300	5 033
Sierra	115	10.5	228	NA	20.7	NA	15	113	1	47	426	3 541	NA	NA
Socorro	253	15.5	121	NA	7.4	NA	10	55	1	32	196	2 028	780	4 315
Taos	374	14.0	197	NA	7.4	NA	43	143	1	29	108	4 172	780	3 310
Torrance	217	14.0	94	NA	6.0	NA	4	24	0	0	0	1 777	NA	NA
Union	44	11.1	50	NA	12.6	NA	3	72	1	25	627	868	NA	NA
Valencia	1 441	17.7	547	7	6.0	4.6	26	39	0	0	0	8 467	1 817	2 868
NEW YORK	253 738	14.0	158 400	1 659	8.7	6.5	58 453	308	235	73 682	405	2 714 837	588 189	3 100
Albany	3 341	11.4	2 878	22	9.8	6.5	1 384	470	3	1 322	452	44 999	13 993	4 750
Allegany	573	11.3	493	NA	9.7	NA	39	78	2	177	347	7 941	872	1 825
Bronx	22 432	18.8	10 571	158	8.9	7.0	3 122	234	12	5 509	461	145 941	NA	NA
Broome	2 240	11.4	2 151	19	10.9	8.6	473	236	3	802	408	38 210	5 987	2 998
Cattaraugus	1 044	12.3	875	9	10.3	8.3	129	154	3	353	415	14 612	1 827	2 278
Cayuga	952	11.7	764	NA	9.4	NA	102	124	1	266	327	12 773	1 766	2 155
Chautauqua	1 608	11.6	1 476	11	10.7	6.8	181	130	4	687	497	25 825	3 800	2 719
Chemung	1 072	11.7	972	NA	10.6	NA	216	237	2	495	538	16 579	2 724	2 991
Chenango	625	12.2	520	NA	10.2	NA	59	115	1	132	259	8 906	1 160	2 271
Clinton	877	11.0	657	NA	8.2	NA	143	179	1	409	511	10 896	1 415	1 771
Columbia	677	10.7	699	NA	11.1	NA	98	155	1	194	307	11 191	1 124	1 824
Cortland	591	12.3	447	NA	9.3	NA	58	119	1	260	541	7 035	1 633	3 360
Delaware	502	10.9	549	NA	11.9	NA	35	73	4	214	464	9 111	709	1 502
Dutchess	3 383	12.7	2 172	18	8.2	5.2	576	206	3	686	259	40 269	5 905	2 169
Erie	11 553	12.4	10 055	93	10.8	8.1	2 870	302	12	4 100	439	168 918	33 515	4 074
Essex	403	10.7	430	NA	11.5	NA	25	64	3	95	253	7 387	649	1 670
Franklin	503	10.3	442	NA	9.1	NA	78	153	2	245	504	7 739	952	1 862
Fulton	632	11.9	553	NA	10.4	NA	65	118	1	208	393	9 241	1 264	2 329

1. Per 1,000 estimated resident population, average 1997–1999.   2. Deaths of infants under 1 year old.   3. Deaths of infants under 1 year old per 1,000 live births.   4. Data subject to copyright.   5. Per 100,000 resident population as of July 1 of the year shown.   6. Data for serious crimes have not been adjusted for underreporting; this may affect comparability between geographic areas and over time.   7. Per 100,000 population estimated by the FBI.

Table B. States and Counties — Crime, Education, Money Income, and Poverty

STATE County	Serious crimes known to police, 2000[1] (cont'd) Rate[2] Violent	Property	Education — School enrollment and attainment, 1990 — Enrollment[3] Total	Percent private	Attainment[4] (percent) High school graduate or more	Bachelor's degree or more	Local government expenditures, fiscal 1999[5] Total current expenditures (mil dol)	Current expenditures per student (dollars)	Money income 1989 Per capita[6] (dollars)	Households Median Dollars	Percent change, 1979–1989 (constant 1989 dollars)	Percent with $100,000 or more	Income and poverty, 1998 Median household income	Percent below poverty level All persons	Persons under 18	Persons 5–17 in families
	46	47	48	49	50	51	52	53	54	55	56	57	58	59	60	61
NEW JERSEY—Cont'd																
Mercer	517	3 494	86 125	29.5	77.1	29.5	581.4	11 078	18 936	41 227	25.1	9.0	50 863	9.2	13.9	14.3
Middlesex	244	2 403	167 895	18.2	79.4	26.5	1 026.5	10 019	18 714	45 623	19.3	8.2	54 070	6.5	9.8	9.5
Monmouth	197	2 036	135 897	23.9	82.8	28.4	968.7	9 816	20 565	45 912	30.1	11.2	60 447	6.1	8.8	8.6
Morris	119	1 561	104 706	25.3	87.0	36.7	755.3	10 869	25 177	56 273	26.1	17.4	69 490	3.3	4.9	4.4
Ocean	180	2 274	93 686	19.1	74.9	15.3	643.6	8 976	15 598	33 110	21.8	3.5	43 345	7.4	11.4	11.1
Passaic	504	2 789	109 773	22.1	68.8	18.7	753.9	10 444	16 048	37 596	25.3	6.7	40 923	12.2	17.8	18.7
Salem	272	2 274	16 232	12.1	72.6	11.8	113.7	9 567	13 961	33 155	9.8	2.2	43 386	10.0	14.8	15.5
Somerset	102	1 651	56 216	22.6	86.3	38.3	435.6	10 312	25 111	55 519	26.3	16.1	71 779	3.7	5.7	5.7
Sussex	83	1 228	34 646	17.3	85.1	24.9	269.2	10 046	18 566	48 823	33.2	7.5	62 626	4.1	5.3	5.5
Union	440	3 370	115 297	23.3	75.2	25.0	803.6	10 552	19 660	41 791	15.3	10.1	51 524	9.0	14.2	14.2
Warren	90	1 506	20 728	16.0	77.6	19.6	169.4	9 788	16 716	39 929	25.6	4.9	53 382	6.2	9.1	9.8
NEW MEXICO	758	4 761	435 989	8.2	75.1	20.4	1 788.4	5 440	11 246	24 087	-1.9	2.5	31 445	19.0	27.1	24.1
Bernalillo	1 075	7 002	133 386	11.2	82.1	26.7	445.6	5 190	13 594	27 382	0.6	3.4	38 731	14.2	21.9	18.1
Catron	141	423	613	3.1	73.3	18.7	4.0	8 286	8 537	18 460	7.3	0.0	23 613	23.9	30.7	33.9
Chaves	904	5 544	15 920	7.6	67.3	14.3	66.1	5 243	10 550	21 764	4.9	2.5	29 092	22.0	30.1	28.1
Cibola	738	2 606	7 281	8.2	66.7	8.8	20.7	5 498	6 803	16 848	NA	0.9	24 902	23.7	28.7	28.9
Colfax	NA	NA	3 388	5.2	71.1	14.7	16.6	6 148	10 076	20 800	0.2	1.1	27 717	19.3	27.8	26.9
Curry	1 095	4 904	12 521	5.0	75.8	13.7	48.9	5 036	9 843	21 303	-2.8	1.4	29 410	20.6	28.8	26.9
De Baca	6 295	15 714	444	0.9	63.0	11.4	3.2	7 249	8 896	15 686	-3.5	1.1	22 228	23.2	32.4	32.5
Dona Ana	NA	NA	46 488	4.4	70.4	21.9	196.2	5 370	9 374	21 859	5.5	1.4	27 565	25.6	34.6	31.2
Eddy	428	5 118	13 489	4.8	67.3	10.9	60.0	5 320	10 490	23 418	-5.1	2.3	31 792	18.7	26.3	23.2
Grant	130	570	8 301	3.3	70.5	16.4	35.1	5 901	9 381	21 350	-19.9	1.7	30 182	19.6	27.0	25.5
Guadalupe	NA	NA	1 047	3.0	57.8	6.1	7.7	7 693	6 529	13 350	-9.5	0.8	19 122	29.7	36.4	37.1
Harding	247	494	246	1.6	65.9	15.7	1.9	10 642	9 731	19 020	3.3	1.0	25 488	16.1	18.2	22.0
Hidalgo	NA	NA	1 549	2.4	71.6	11.7	10.0	6 810	10 092	23 504	4.3	0.9	27 884	22.4	27.9	28.0
Lea	736	3 924	16 457	4.2	63.8	11.5	65.5	5 073	10 025	23 352	-24.2	1.4	32 005	21.1	28.0	25.2
Lincoln	957	2 610	2 658	4.6	77.1	16.1	24.1	6 561	10 701	19 489	-13.4	1.5	26 997	18.3	28.0	26.2
Los Alamos	76	992	5 020	10.2	94.7	53.4	27.3	7 417	22 900	54 801	17.2	10.2	81 879	2.5	4.0	3.0
Luna	560	4 033	4 560	1.7	58.8	11.1	25.8	4 624	8 116	15 684	-5.0	0.8	19 073	30.5	43.4	38.0
McKinley	695	4 346	19 705	7.4	58.5	11.1	91.2	5 665	6 628	17 468	-14.0	1.1	21 936	37.4	48.8	38.5
Mora	193	154	1 161	0.9	59.7	14.2	7.3	8 146	7 021	12 993	2.0	0.7	17 979	29.4	36.6	38.7
Otero	395	2 234	14 677	7.5	81.6	15.0	47.5	4 832	10 053	22 624	0.6	1.0	30 861	17.4	25.0	23.5
Quay	NA	NA	2 497	1.0	70.3	9.9	13.6	6 285	9 461	18 711	-9.9	1.1	22 328	27.1	38.2	36.5
Rio Arriba	NA	NA	9 651	9.1	65.9	10.3	41.6	6 011	7 859	18 373	4.8	0.5	26 333	21.8	28.4	27.7
Roosevelt	272	3 663	6 019	4.2	66.1	18.1	19.7	5 559	9 254	18 699	10.5	1.7	25 316	26.0	34.3	33.1
Sandoval	331	1 910	17 097	8.3	79.3	19.1	80.7	5 487	10 849	28 950	18.8	1.8	41 096	12.7	17.5	16.9
San Juan	612	2 888	29 208	4.9	69.2	12.3	134.3	5 426	8 911	22 300	-20.3	1.4	30 512	21.9	29.1	23.1
San Miguel	739	3 246	8 384	6.7	68.4	16.2	34.1	5 935	8 149	17 885	17.8	1.2	23 361	26.7	33.0	34.6
Santa Fe	537	4 496	25 743	17.6	82.6	32.3	80.9	5 154	15 327	29 403	10.7	4.7	39 899	11.7	17.0	15.3
Sierra	NA	NA	1 586	5.2	63.7	8.5	10.2	5 437	10 124	15 612	17.0	1.4	22 038	22.9	39.2	36.3
Socorro	1 339	2 976	4 873	7.3	67.2	17.1	16.0	5 828	9 154	19 165	4.8	1.5	24 503	29.3	36.1	38.5
Taos	777	2 533	5 954	8.4	71.8	18.5	34.7	6 427	9 158	16 966	-5.5	1.7	24 679	24.0	31.7	30.5
Torrance	NA	NA	2 793	3.2	72.6	10.9	32.9	5 330	8 950	19 619	8.1	1.2	27 787	21.5	25.9	28.1
Union	NA	NA	830	5.5	63.6	12.0	6.8	7 439	10 603	18 227	-2.6	1.8	26 786	23.6	33.5	31.9
Valencia	431	2 437	12 443	7.2	73.3	12.1	70.7	5 261	10 244	24 312	NA	1.5	32 025	17.6	24.2	22.9
NEW YORK	554	2 546	4 656 218	24.0	74.8	23.1	26 885.4	9 344	16 501	32 965	18.2	6.8	38 290	15.4	23.3	22.7
Albany	460	4 291	77 425	25.1	80.9	28.3	364.4	8 834	16 363	33 358	17.0	4.6	41 604	11.2	18.2	17.3
Allegany	293	1 532	16 500	19.2	76.9	15.6	78.3	8 938	9 907	24 164	5.9	1.3	32 263	18.3	25.7	25.6
Bronx	NA	NA	342 170	22.0	58.5	12.2	[7]NA	[7]NA	10 535	21 944	19.6	2.3	25 750	29.2	38.2	40.6
Broome	207	2 791	55 776	11.2	78.9	20.7	275.7	8 240	13 626	28 743	5.5	2.5	35 866	13.8	21.8	20.7
Cattaraugus	233	2 044	23 035	18.5	74.5	12.8	142.7	8 261	10 595	23 421	-1.2	1.6	32 057	15.3	21.2	21.5
Cayuga	201	1 953	20 367	11.5	73.3	13.0	98.3	7 684	11 671	27 568	5.4	1.5	36 663	12.9	18.9	18.7
Chautauqua	205	2 514	37 059	7.9	74.4	14.2	214.8	8 510	11 287	24 183	-3.2	1.4	32 017	16.5	23.8	24.1
Chemung	284	2 707	23 886	17.8	77.2	15.4	114.4	8 165	12 069	26 135	2.5	2.0	35 101	13.9	20.6	20.5
Chenango	202	2 069	12 733	6.2	75.5	13.1	85.2	8 350	11 830	26 032	8.9	1.6	32 813	15.9	23.0	24.1
Clinton	299	1 472	24 367	10.2	74.2	16.5	120.8	8 884	11 444	26 903	13.2	1.9	36 913	15.0	20.2	21.0
Columbia	235	1 589	14 263	13.7	73.6	18.5	89.8	9 100	14 044	29 785	18.6	3.6	38 449	11.9	18.4	18.7
Cortland	216	3 144	15 358	6.3	76.8	18.2	64.7	8 104	11 228	26 791	12.2	1.7	35 166	14.0	19.0	19.4
Delaware	220	1 282	11 803	6.0	74.0	13.2	73.0	9 434	11 180	24 132	6.1	1.8	31 339	14.8	21.8	22.5
Dutchess	198	1 970	67 685	24.7	79.8	24.8	399.4	8 940	17 420	42 250	24.4	6.1	50 370	8.2	12.6	11.8
Erie	537	3 537	247 150	18.8	76.4	20.0	1 302.1	9 015	13 560	28 005	-2.4	2.9	37 641	14.0	22.3	20.5
Essex	239	1 431	8 326	14.6	74.2	15.8	49.6	9 906	11 354	25 002	8.8	1.5	33 136	13.9	19.5	21.0
Franklin	375	1 486	11 907	12.4	69.5	11.7	84.4	9 254	9 771	21 791	6.0	0.8	30 500	18.4	24.1	24.5
Fulton	245	2 084	13 102	6.8	70.5	11.4	81.5	8 142	11 330	23 862	2.4	1.2	31 525	15.4	23.4	24.1

1. Data for serious crimes have not been adjusted for underreporting; this may affect comparability between geographic areas and over time. 2. Per 100,000 population estimated by the FBI. 3. All persons 3 years old and over enrolled in nursery school through college. 4. Persons 25 years old and over. 5. Elementary and secondary education expenditures, local government fiscal years ending between July 1, 1998 and June 30, 1999. 6. Based on population enumerated as of April 1, 1990. 7. Bronx, Kings, Queens, and Richmond Counties included with New York County.

	Personal income, 1999												
			Per capita[1]						Transfer payments				
										Government payments to individuals			
STATE County	Total (mil dol)	Percent change, 1998–1999	Dollars	Rank	Wages and salaries[2] (mil dol)	Proprietor's income (mil dol)	Dividends, interest, and rent (mil dol)	Total (mil dol)	Total (mil dol)	Social Security (mil dol)	Medical payments (mil dol)	Income mainte-nance (mil dol)	Unemploy-ment insurance (mil dol)
	62	63	64	65	66	67	68	69	70	71	72	73	74
NEW JERSEY—Cont'd													
Mercer	13 230	6.3	39 626	45	9 556	875	2 507	1 404	1 339	535	586	113	36
Middlesex	24 602	4.4	34 267	100	20 049	1 395	3 895	2 458	2 318	1 072	900	118	92
Monmouth	22 841	6.0	37 356	65	10 575	1 419	4 385	2 127	2 008	915	805	105	78
Morris	23 157	6.0	49 957	9	15 928	1 640	4 321	1 327	1 236	637	459	40	35
Ocean	13 779	3.2	27 694	358	4 430	905	3 197	2 552	2 455	1 266	956	77	55
Passaic	13 368	5.5	27 559	367	7 578	932	2 214	1 963	1 868	675	830	206	90
Salem	1 754	3.0	27 178	404	956	121	272	285	273	115	120	19	8
Somerset	15 003	6.4	52 078	6	10 211	1 636	2 440	789	732	380	264	26	21
Sussex	4 380	5.0	30 270	201	1 320	284	642	381	353	169	135	16	13
Union	19 196	5.3	38 487	54	11 807	1 204	3 790	2 047	1 949	843	810	139	70
Warren	2 917	5.2	29 079	259	1 355	181	465	360	340	159	139	16	10
NEW MEXICO	37 991	3.5	21 836	X	23 173	2 987	7 366	5 892	5 570	2 164	2 026	766	92
Bernalillo	14 284	3.3	27 287	395	10 648	847	2 872	1 740	1 643	675	590	192	26
Catron	46	4.7	15 972	2 900	17	4	14	13	12	6	3	2	0
Chaves	1 208	1.7	19 356	2 194	542	230	238	232	221	94	80	32	3
Cibola	363	0.7	13 501	3 070	153	19	41	97	92	28	35	14	2
Colfax	272	3.9	19 925	2 017	139	25	65	57	55	24	19	6	1
Curry	938	4.2	21 537	1 513	518	127	158	163	156	50	58	25	1
De Baca	41	5.9	17 268	2 688	15	6	9	11	11	5	4	1	0
Dona Ana	2 897	3.8	17 003	2 733	1 574	252	549	519	488	170	183	84	8
Eddy	1 054	0.9	19 843	2 039	589	110	189	205	195	88	72	22	4
Grant	547	-0.9	17 465	2 654	286	35	118	136	130	56	49	15	2
Guadalupe	61	5.9	15 152	2 976	35	4	10	19	18	6	7	3	0
Harding	15	0.1	17 214	2 700	5	2	3	4	3	2	1	0	0
Hidalgo	103	-5.5	17 019	2 730	62	7	14	25	24	8	8	3	0
Lea	1 043	-1.1	18 948	2 295	588	110	158	202	192	81	75	26	4
Lincoln	330	4.6	19 678	2 092	139	33	104	70	66	34	22	6	1
Los Alamos	720	3.3	39 387	46	957	25	197	35	32	18	10	1	0
Luna	345	2.9	14 158	3 042	151	32	68	98	94	42	30	12	4
McKinley	980	7.1	14 643	3 015	595	51	117	244	232	43	93	58	3
Mora	63	3.6	12 763	3 086	21	1	10	23	22	7	7	5	1
Otero	1 027	3.3	18 945	2 297	667	64	193	171	162	68	54	18	2
Quay	185	5.2	18 699	2 369	81	26	38	48	47	18	18	7	0
Rio Arriba	583	6.3	15 272	2 962	246	32	93	151	144	47	56	26	3
Roosevelt	339	6.0	19 486	2 144	130	81	51	70	67	22	24	11	0
Sandoval	1 873	4.0	20 747	1 758	823	68	296	244	228	100	78	23	4
San Juan	1 993	3.8	18 131	2 514	1 346	167	290	327	306	113	112	42	8
San Miguel	459	2.4	16 110	2 885	201	32	72	134	128	34	54	26	1
Santa Fe	3 646	4.2	29 346	241	1 791	359	992	344	321	149	108	31	5
Sierra	212	0.2	19 265	2 218	66	23	57	71	69	32	24	7	0
Socorro	262	3.1	15 866	2 912	134	21	44	62	59	17	21	13	1
Taos	500	3.1	18 430	2 433	229	71	109	102	97	36	35	16	3
Torrance	273	6.5	16 629	2 806	75	21	28	49	46	17	16	8	1
Union	97	2.5	24 862	693	32	34	16	18	17	8	6	2	0
Valencia	1 234	8.8	18 961	2 290	316	71	153	206	194	66	75	27	3
NEW YORK	616 878	5.3	33 901	X	400 330	60 988	111 933	96 863	93 031	27 279	47 585	12 104	1 624
Albany	9 459	4.0	32 392	142	9 105	707	1 944	1 465	1 404	479	513	132	16
Allegany	899	2.4	17 775	2 581	414	68	159	214	203	81	78	27	6
Bronx	24 263	3.7	20 319	1 884	8 127	889	2 780	7 923	7 671	1 314	4 597	1 445	134
Broome	4 919	4.2	25 196	639	3 290	332	971	914	873	389	339	91	14
Cattaraugus	1 657	3.5	19 620	2 105	931	122	273	367	349	140	136	41	10
Cayuga	1 724	2.6	21 096	1 639	770	118	286	324	307	129	122	31	7
Chautauqua	2 869	1.8	20 877	1 707	1 627	194	515	652	623	258	249	74	12
Chemung	2 162	4.0	23 563	949	1 309	113	375	440	420	170	175	42	7
Chenango	1 054	4.6	20 787	1 741	500	87	189	214	203	88	78	21	5
Clinton	1 734	4.2	21 744	1 434	1 057	135	271	321	304	111	129	35	9
Columbia	1 691	4.3	26 840	429	611	155	368	286	273	116	114	24	4
Cortland	979	3.5	20 402	1 862	533	92	164	189	179	71	73	22	5
Delaware	952	4.7	20 533	1 826	515	93	217	219	209	94	84	18	4
Dutchess	8 268	7.0	30 822	182	4 374	446	1 520	1 062	1 006	430	420	79	15
Erie	25 245	3.5	27 263	398	16 339	1 550	4 571	4 630	4 434	1 740	1 792	562	84
Essex	812	4.1	21 661	1 467	422	73	161	174	166	67	69	15	5
Franklin	922	4.2	19 013	2 275	497	78	147	208	198	76	83	23	6
Fulton	1 217	4.2	23 024	1 083	532	112	224	266	255	97	115	24	5

1. Based on the resident population estimated as of July 1 of the year shown.   2. Includes other labor income.

STATE County	Total (mil dol)	Farm	Goods-related[1] Total	Manu- facturing	Service-related and other[2] Total	Retail trade	Finance, insur- ance, and real estate	Services	Govern- ment	Number	Rate[3]	Supple- mental Security Income recipients, December 2000	Total	Percent change, 1980– 1990
	75	76	77	78	79	80	81	82	83	84	85	86	87	88
NEW JERSEY—Cont'd														
Mercer	10 431	0.0	D	11.9	D	5.8	8.6	35.9	25.7	56 901	162	8 000	123 666	10.8
Middlesex	21 444	0.0	22.2	18.8	65.9	6.8	10.0	30.4	11.8	109 486	146	9 415	250 174	23.0
Monmouth	11 994	0.2	D	5.1	D	9.3	9.4	36.4	17.7	96 502	157	6 743	218 408	17.6
Morris	17 568	0.1	D	19.2	D	7.0	11.5	30.3	8.3	64 573	137	3 284	155 745	12.9
Ocean	5 335	0.1	15.5	5.0	63.5	15.3	5.7	31.4	20.9	134 065	262	4 655	219 863	26.7
Passaic	8 510	0.0	27.9	21.2	56.9	10.1	7.8	24.7	15.2	73 213	150	13 578	162 512	1.8
Salem	1 077	1.0	D	25.4	D	6.7	2.7	19.2	15.5	12 553	195	1 160	25 349	4.9
Somerset	11 847	0.0	D	15.8	D	5.9	10.7	28.7	6.5	38 988	131	1 794	92 653	32.8
Sussex	1 604	0.0	17.0	8.0	63.1	10.5	7.9	32.3	19.8	18 446	128	1 353	51 574	17.6
Union	13 011	0.0	28.9	23.7	60.0	6.9	7.3	28.1	11.1	84 860	162	8 703	187 033	2.3
Warren	1 536	0.0	35.2	28.3	49.8	10.6	3.2	21.1	14.9	17 195	168	1 093	36 589	16.2
NEW MEXICO	26 159	2.6	15.8	6.6	54.4	10.7	5.4	27.7	27.2	277 262	152	46 660	632 058	24.5
Bernalillo	11 495	0.1	13.7	7.1	63.8	10.5	6.9	34.5	22.4	82 161	148	11 475	201 235	24.1
Catron	21	-4.8	11.2	3.2	D	7.3	D	16.4	56.3	871	246	70	1 552	11.2
Chaves	772	18.9	19.5	9.6	42.0	10.1	3.4	19.2	19.6	11 704	191	2 002	23 386	12.3
Cibola	172	0.8	D	5.7	D	14.1	D	27.2	34.9	3 690	144	636	9 692	NA
Colfax	164	1.7	D	5.6	D	13.6	4.8	D	28.6	2 991	211	383	8 265	19.9
Curry	644	13.4	5.9	1.6	40.7	10.0	2.9	13.6	40.0	6 631	147	1 363	16 906	4.3
De Baca	21	24.2	D	D	D	12.8	2.4	9.7	31.0	610	272	83	1 329	-1.6
Dona Ana	1 826	7.1	10.9	5.1	45.7	9.7	3.8	23.2	36.3	23 611	135	4 969	49 148	NA
Eddy	700	3.8	33.1	6.2	45.8	9.5	3.0	18.4	17.3	10 188	197	1 383	20 134	10.9
Grant	321	-0.6	31.4	5.0	38.0	11.3	4.0	14.8	31.2	6 673	215	738	11 349	17.8
Guadalupe	39	-3.8	D	D	D	19.6	0.6	16.9	30.0	919	196	245	2 149	0.3
Harding	7	18.6	D	D	D	6.9	D	D	40.2	255	315	26	614	11.0
Hidalgo	68	6.4	D	D	D	11.3	1.6	10.5	24.8	967	163	166	2 413	3.7
Lea	698	5.4	29.3	1.7	50.1	9.6	3.3	21.7	15.2	9 329	168	1 451	23 333	10.7
Lincoln	172	0.1	D	2.2	D	19.3	7.2	29.4	23.9	4 158	214	303	12 622	29.6
Los Alamos	982	0.0	1.9	0.3	D	2.2	2.0	23.7	69.3	2 236	122	43	7 565	14.9
Luna	182	9.6	13.3	8.4	46.8	13.3	2.3	18.0	30.3	5 642	226	842	7 766	23.5
McKinley	647	0.1	D	2.8	D	16.2	2.9	19.3	37.6	7 189	96	3 741	20 933	15.5
Mora	22	-9.3	D	D	D	5.9	D	24.8	46.6	1 117	216	350	2 486	18.1
Otero	731	0.7	D	2.3	D	8.0	3.1	20.0	51.8	9 406	151	1 058	23 177	29.0
Quay	107	9.5	D	D	D	13.5	3.2	18.8	29.7	2 447	241	404	5 576	13.5
Rio Arriba	278	0.1	11.6	5.5	56.8	13.6	2.8	32.0	31.4	7 059	171	1 752	14 357	29.3
Roosevelt	211	35.7	7.3	3.1	32.1	8.7	1.6	11.1	24.9	3 017	167	549	6 902	6.0
Sandoval	891	0.2	D	D	D	9.0	3.7	13.8	13.5	12 729	142	1 439	23 667	92.6
San Juan	1 513	4.0	27.4	2.6	50.0	11.2	3.0	21.2	18.6	14 764	130	3 288	34 248	15.2
San Miguel	233	0.3	D	2.1	D	12.3	3.2	21.6	50.0	4 892	162	1 832	11 066	11.7
Santa Fe	2 150	0.2	11.3	3.0	62.7	13.9	9.6	33.4	25.8	18 054	140	1 795	41 464	46.4
Sierra	90	6.5	D	D	D	13.6	4.3	25.0	31.5	3 934	296	471	6 457	19.8
Socorro	155	6.3	D	2.8	D	8.8	2.0	28.2	44.0	2 490	138	693	6 289	35.7
Taos	300	0.4	D	1.7	63.0	17.5	5.7	33.7	19.9	5 128	171	1 033	12 020	28.7
Torrance	95	7.2	9.8	3.0	D	12.9	D	17.5	37.4	2 317	137	383	4 878	47.4
Union	66	48.2	D	D	D	6.9	4.9	10.6	16.3	998	239	103	2 299	1.2
Valencia	387	2.8	D	8.6	D	15.2	3.8	14.4	31.7	9 074	137	1 553	16 781	-24.9
NEW YORK	461 318	0.1	14.7	10.9	70.8	6.6	21.4	31.3	14.3	3 007 120	158	616 502	7 226 891	5.2
Albany	9 812	0.0	D	6.0	D	7.6	9.1	28.7	32.1	52 376	178	6 219	124 255	7.4
Allegany	482	2.8	28.8	23.4	40.4	9.8	1.8	22.4	28.0	9 588	192	1 477	21 951	5.9
Bronx	9 016	0.0	D	4.4	D	7.5	6.4	47.8	14.3	160 250	120	84 243	440 955	-2.3
Broome	3 622	0.2	D	24.0	D	8.9	4.4	26.7	19.2	43 318	216	5 211	87 969	7.3
Cattaraugus	1 054	0.7	D	22.9	D	10.1	2.8	20.6	24.7	16 724	199	2 634	36 839	5.7
Cayuga	888	2.9	D	17.9	D	9.4	2.7	24.3	24.6	14 588	178	1 883	33 280	7.5
Chautauqua	1 821	1.5	33.4	28.9	45.3	10.6	2.7	21.8	19.9	29 535	211	3 970	62 682	2.9
Chemung	1 422	0.3	31.1	25.0	49.8	10.6	3.9	24.5	18.8	19 272	212	2 787	37 290	1.6
Chenango	588	1.4	35.0	29.8	41.8	9.1	7.1	16.7	21.8	10 612	206	1 528	22 164	17.5
Clinton	1 192	1.5	D	18.3	D	10.7	2.4	19.8	28.4	14 093	176	2 479	32 190	14.6
Columbia	766	4.1	D	15.0	D	9.9	4.9	26.3	20.8	13 169	209	1 672	29 139	12.3
Cortland	625	0.8	D	22.1	D	13.3	3.0	26.3	22.4	8 418	173	1 234	18 681	5.6
Delaware	609	1.7	38.4	32.8	35.2	10.1	3.6	13.8	24.7	10 974	228	1 231	27 361	20.3
Dutchess	4 820	0.2	32.7	27.4	48.9	8.2	4.8	28.8	18.2	46 909	167	4 927	97 632	12.4
Erie	17 889	0.1	24.4	19.6	57.8	9.1	7.9	28.5	17.8	190 325	200	25 213	402 131	3.4
Essex	494	0.5	21.0	12.2	47.7	13.3	2.5	25.6	30.8	7 865	202	1 043	21 493	12.4
Franklin	574	1.4	D	5.2	D	10.6	2.8	29.9	39.9	9 848	193	1 702	21 962	8.0
Fulton	644	0.7	D	25.1	D	10.1	3.8	20.3	23.4	11 767	214	1 633	26 260	3.0

1. Covers mining, construction, and manufacturing.   2. Covers private sector earnings in agricultural services, forestry, and fisheries; transportation and public utilities; wholesale trade; retail trade; finance, insurance, and real estate; and services.   3. Per 1,000 resident population estimated as of July 1 of the year shown.

Table B. States and Counties — Housing, Labor Force, and Employment

STATE County	Housing units, 1990 (cont'd)								Civilian labor force, 2001				Civilian employment, 1990[5]		
	Occupied units							Sub-standard units[3] (percent)	Total	Percent change, 2000–2001	Unemployment		Percent		
	Owner-occupied					Renter-occupied									
				Owner cost as a percent of income			Rent as per-cent of income							Professional, managerial, and technical	Precision production, craft, and repair
	Total	Percent	Median value[1]	With a mort-gage	Without a mort-gage	Median rent[2]					Total	Rate[4]	Total		
	89	90	91	92	93	94	95	96	97	98	99	100	101	102	103
NEW JERSEY—Cont'd															
Mercer	116 941	66.5	137 900	22.2	14.4	570	25.7	3.1	178 173	2.2	6 035	3.4	166 432	38.8	8.0
Middlesex	238 833	67.4	164 700	23.4	15.1	667	25.2	3.5	413 674	0.9	15 156	3.7	360 509	35.1	9.8
Monmouth	197 570	72.6	180 400	24.5	15.6	634	28.0	2.0	313 950	1.2	11 365	3.6	275 140	38.0	9.9
Morris	148 751	74.0	217 300	23.3	14.0	724	24.8	1.9	261 198	-0.7	7 481	2.9	234 721	41.6	9.1
Ocean	168 147	82.9	126 000	26.1	16.7	681	31.7	1.8	216 040	1.0	8 769	4.1	181 415	29.0	13.5
Passaic	155 269	55.8	185 500	24.4	15.2	583	27.0	7.1	225 180	-1.2	12 747	5.7	225 555	27.2	11.5
Salem	23 794	72.3	82 700	20.3	13.6	452	26.9	2.5	31 097	-0.8	1 432	4.6	29 766	25.7	14.2
Somerset	88 346	75.3	196 300	23.7	14.3	719	25.5	1.8	174 362	0.9	4 725	2.7	136 761	45.1	8.1
Sussex	44 456	82.3	156 300	25.8	15.4	697	28.9	1.5	76 098	-0.6	2 722	3.6	67 578	34.8	12.6
Union	180 076	62.5	180 500	23.2	15.1	596	25.7	4.7	262 173	-0.7	11 877	4.5	252 215	32.5	9.6
Warren	33 997	69.5	143 900	25.1	15.2	552	27.1	1.7	51 170	-0.8	1 818	3.6	45 869	28.3	14.0
NEW MEXICO	542 709	67.4	70 100	21.6	12.5	372	26.5	8.8	837 780	0.6	39 802	4.8	629 272	31.6	12.0
Bernalillo	185 582	60.7	85 300	22.3	12.3	402	27.4	5.4	295 300	0.9	10 469	3.5	227 463	36.3	10.0
Catron	1 010	76.3	39 700	35.1	12.8	249	19.7	11.2	1 104	-1.4	75	6.8	901	24.9	9.1
Chaves	20 589	69.9	44 600	19.4	12.7	335	27.9	7.3	24 665	0.2	1 435	5.8	22 913	24.8	11.5
Cibola	7 292	73.8	37 500	18.3	13.0	245	21.3	16.7	11 672	1.2	658	5.6	7 473	24.3	13.3
Colfax	4 959	70.6	46 700	20.7	13.4	266	26.5	4.5	6 602	-1.7	335	5.1	5 143	24.2	10.1
Curry	15 113	61.6	51 300	20.9	12.8	349	25.5	5.5	19 308	-0.7	626	3.2	15 267	24.9	13.3
De Baca	913	74.5	33 000	23.9	13.3	245	28.9	5.0	1 011	1.0	48	4.7	855	18.7	9.5
Dona Ana	45 029	64.6	67 300	20.7	12.3	347	28.2	9.7	71 301	0.5	4 785	6.7	53 059	32.1	10.5
Eddy	17 472	72.9	44 800	17.3	11.7	304	23.4	6.8	22 739	-1.3	1 153	5.1	18 649	23.9	17.8
Grant	9 773	70.3	50 900	19.4	11.9	302	23.6	7.8	12 944	2.6	876	6.8	10 034	22.5	16.5
Guadalupe	1 520	70.9	33 100	28.9	15.5	229	33.3	7.6	1 609	-9.4	140	8.7	1 487	19.4	10.1
Harding	396	77.8	16 000	13.1	14.2	229	17.7	4.3	418	-2.3	14	3.3	400	17.8	11.5
Hidalgo	2 004	61.2	36 700	20.2	13.3	191	15.6	7.2	1 801	-8.7	156	8.7	2 421	15.7	18.9
Lea	19 306	71.5	39 600	17.6	12.1	312	24.5	7.7	25 707	4.2	828	3.2	21 346	22.1	20.0
Lincoln	4 789	72.4	67 400	25.8	14.7	348	26.8	5.4	7 579	-0.8	312	4.1	5 182	24.5	10.7
Los Alamos	7 213	74.4	126 100	17.3	10.5	467	18.1	2.6	10 274	-1.1	107	1.0	9 942	64.5	6.5
Luna	6 797	71.1	47 200	23.6	12.1	252	27.8	10.4	10 994	-1.5	2 606	23.7	5 419	22.2	12.3
McKinley	16 588	71.1	42 800	19.6	12.8	294	19.6	41.2	24 499	-0.6	1 489	6.1	19 765	27.1	17.2
Mora	1 519	81.2	30 200	13.8	14.7	235	29.5	15.2	1 709	-1.9	208	12.2	1 129	19.8	12.1
Otero	18 155	62.3	58 000	21.3	11.7	355	24.7	5.7	19 860	-0.7	1 078	5.4	17 904	28.0	15.0
Quay	4 238	72.2	37 600	20.2	13.4	279	27.1	3.1	4 207	-6.5	187	4.4	4 359	20.1	8.9
Rio Arriba	11 461	80.4	58 800	21.0	13.8	285	27.0	13.3	19 974	1.0	1 316	6.6	12 695	25.9	13.9
Roosevelt	5 991	64.4	44 000	20.0	12.5	268	28.0	5.4	7 631	3.5	217	2.8	6 864	25.2	9.6
Sandoval	20 867	82.8	69 600	23.5	12.0	468	26.1	10.6	45 179	1.2	1 754	3.9	26 501	30.7	12.7
San Juan	28 740	72.0	58 400	19.7	12.5	345	24.3	19.6	49 784	1.9	3 026	6.1	32 280	26.8	16.6
San Miguel	8 701	72.0	47 500	24.8	14.3	270	26.5	11.9	12 407	1.8	793	6.4	9 152	32.6	9.4
Santa Fe	37 840	67.7	103 300	22.6	12.0	489	27.7	6.4	64 628	-0.2	1 698	2.6	49 452	38.3	9.8
Sierra	4 428	73.3	49 500	23.3	12.3	226	26.9	4.4	4 093	-0.8	156	3.8	3 017	22.1	13.6
Socorro	5 217	68.7	52 500	21.1	13.1	305	28.4	9.8	6 600	1.5	401	6.1	5 867	30.5	12.3
Taos	8 752	74.8	71 700	23.5	14.1	369	32.5	9.8	12 700	-0.1	1 234	9.7	9 128	25.5	15.3
Torrance	3 670	82.0	46 500	24.5	14.5	318	27.0	9.2	7 118	1.7	328	4.6	3 931	20.8	14.6
Union	1 615	72.4	36 200	22.5	13.6	284	27.9	5.2	1 999	-0.8	50	2.5	1 671	16.3	11.8
Valencia	15 170	83.4	72 100	22.8	13.0	344	27.9	7.4	30 366	0.7	1 245	4.1	17 603	25.1	14.3
NEW YORK	6 639 322	52.2	131 600	21.5	14.4	486	26.3	6.8	8 831 770	-1.2	429 339	4.9	8 370 718	33.5	9.4
Albany	115 824	57.0	110 900	19.9	12.8	481	24.9	1.7	153 538	-1.1	4 051	2.6	149 954	37.5	7.3
Allegany	17 011	73.1	37 600	16.5	13.3	318	27.2	2.7	22 285	-1.5	1 274	5.7	21 003	27.3	12.8
Bronx	424 112	17.9	173 900	22.7	14.5	443	27.0	17.3	471 143	-1.5	35 094	7.4	441 957	24.1	8.8
Broome	81 843	65.4	79 000	19.7	12.9	388	26.6	1.5	95 258	-0.7	3 977	4.2	98 783	34.9	10.1
Cattaraugus	30 456	73.2	42 100	17.7	13.3	314	25.9	2.8	39 414	-0.9	2 631	6.7	35 967	23.6	12.1
Cayuga	29 075	70.9	59 800	20.1	14.5	391	28.0	2.4	36 784	-1.2	1 820	4.9	35 840	23.8	13.0
Chautauqua	53 696	68.6	47 800	18.0	13.5	326	28.6	1.6	64 029	-2.3	3 466	5.4	62 263	24.1	12.0
Chemung	35 275	68.3	53 600	17.5	14.6	361	27.3	1.6	42 027	-1.7	2 217	5.3	41 063	28.5	11.8
Chenango	19 141	74.4	55 900	19.3	13.5	344	24.6	2.6	23 520	-0.9	1 193	5.1	23 540	25.1	13.2
Clinton	29 123	63.9	65 000	18.7	13.0	385	25.8	2.6	38 783	-0.7	1 617	4.2	35 380	26.5	9.9
Columbia	23 696	69.5	103 100	20.3	13.9	437	27.2	2.3	33 259	-2.9	888	2.7	29 520	28.8	12.4
Cortland	17 247	64.4	66 200	19.3	14.0	396	27.6	1.5	22 242	0.3	1 336	6.0	22 941	28.9	10.8
Delaware	17 646	74.1	67 000	20.8	14.0	361	28.3	2.1	20 210	-1.4	875	4.3	20 169	24.4	14.7
Dutchess	89 567	69.1	149 200	22.3	14.1	600	25.8	2.0	120 387	0.6	3 904	3.2	127 925	39.1	10.6
Erie	376 994	63.7	74 000	19.1	13.9	384	28.5	1.7	442 320	-2.0	22 581	5.1	442 126	30.5	10.4
Essex	13 721	72.1	62 200	20.0	13.6	368	26.2	3.0	17 881	0.0	953	5.3	15 289	26.8	12.5
Franklin	16 284	68.9	48 900	18.4	14.2	324	27.6	3.7	21 399	-3.2	1 500	7.0	18 281	25.3	10.4
Fulton	20 995	71.4	56 000	19.9	14.3	348	28.1	2.4	25 878	-0.9	1 253	4.8	23 909	23.8	12.7

1. Specified owner-occupied units.   2. Specified renter-occupied units.   3. Overcrowded or lacking complete plumbing facilities.   4. Percent of civilian labor force.   5. Persons 16 years and older.

Table B. States and Counties — Nonfarm Employment and Agriculture

STATE County	Private nonfarm establishments, employment and payroll, 1999									Agriculture, 1997			
		Employment						Annual payroll		Farms			Farm operators
											Percent with—		
	Number of establishments	Total	Health Care and Social Assistance	Manufacturing	Retail trade	Finance and Insurance	Professional Scientific and Technical Services	Total (mil dol)	Average per employee (dollars)	Number	Less than 50 acres	500 acres and over	Whose principal occupation is farming (percent)
	104	105	106	107	108	109	110	111	112	113	114	115	116
NEW JERSEY—Cont'd													
Mercer	9 435	165 029	21 421	9 805	18 088	9 921	15 821	6 349	38 471	285	64.9	4.6	42.5
Middlesex	20 421	381 140	32 374	50 359	39 919	22 030	41 051	15 894	41 702	275	73.5	5.5	44.7
Monmouth	18 456	204 186	31 090	11 280	35 054	8 855	16 754	7 231	35 412	874	80.0	3.5	45.5
Morris	17 309	288 017	25 064	30 031	29 459	18 193	31 598	14 072	48 858	383	73.6	1.8	40.2
Ocean	10 796	106 721	22 771	6 648	24 561	3 493	5 515	2 857	26 766	235	83.4	2.1	41.7
Passaic	11 930	162 851	20 815	31 029	23 624	9 167	8 038	5 555	34 112	55	80.0	0.0	36.4
Salem	1 318	17 672	D	3 997	2 630	601	298	648	36 679	660	50.8	6.5	44.8
Somerset	9 680	167 745	14 979	16 445	15 483	15 705	16 376	8 579	51 141	437	66.4	4.8	35.5
Sussex	3 471	27 998	5 073	2 162	5 224	1 841	1 430	792	28 297	827	62.2	3.4	33.6
Union	14 663	227 087	25 327	37 648	23 284	7 545	12 296	9 410	41 437	19	94.7	0.0	57.9
Warren	2 710	30 606	4 238	7 076	5 623	689	1 231	1 039	33 949	730	54.4	4.7	41.8
NEW MEXICO	42 918	541 386	73 922	38 541	91 627	23 408	36 214	13 639	25 192	14 094	37.0	35.5	51.1
Bernalillo	15 715	248 391	31 864	18 175	35 906	13 128	24 501	6 897	27 767	468	76.9	7.3	32.3
Catron	64	243	D	D	35	D	D	3	12 597	217	9.7	59.9	65.0
Chaves	1 517	14 899	2 237	2 115	2 993	633	497	318	21 329	562	29.9	44.1	61.4
Cibola	353	5 330	675	487	1 049	129	107	110	20 557	166	24.7	59.0	57.8
Colfax	501	4 102	519	286	697	166	107	73	17 907	322	14.3	51.9	64.6
Curry	1 076	10 920	2 207	219	2 625	522	300	205	18 740	655	13.4	51.0	56.6
De Baca	62	348	86	D	68	D	D	5	15 514	191	24.1	52.9	65.4
Dona Ana	3 260	35 749	5 863	2 303	6 608	1 324	2 634	724	20 252	1 290	75.7	7.8	40.4
Eddy	1 272	16 127	2 134	1 562	2 767	614	264	426	26 402	467	34.3	34.5	53.5
Grant	686	7 393	1 107	274	1 373	246	201	168	22 766	286	19.6	52.4	53.8
Guadalupe	113	1 096	108	0	377	D	D	16	14 676	236	15.7	64.8	58.9
Harding	19	49	D	D	19	D	D	1	19 694	172	3.5	78.5	70.3
Hidalgo	107	1 461	133	D	271	D	D	33	22 376	146	10.3	65.1	58.2
Lea	1 423	13 820	1 685	688	2 284	477	354	323	23 404	528	19.1	47.0	51.7
Lincoln	709	4 489	494	60	1 031	239	188	84	18 663	337	21.4	57.0	63.5
Los Alamos	444	6 233	1 023	65	517	290	954	184	29 536	4	100.0	0.0	0.0
Luna	410	3 235	460	279	924	152	72	59	18 320	192	17.7	48.4	69.3
McKinley	1 047	14 562	2 916	629	3 673	354	276	304	20 853	224	21.4	47.8	39.3
Mora	60	389	180	D	57	D	D	7	16 946	398	19.1	34.9	46.0
Otero	1 050	11 636	1 834	534	2 522	453	731	212	18 213	417	48.9	21.3	48.0
Quay	297	2 110	328	142	554	132	53	34	16 268	583	9.4	60.4	65.7
Rio Arriba	640	6 654	1 276	259	1 589	152	D	133	19 931	940	56.6	16.5	43.5
Roosevelt	351	2 755	307	202	694	124	D	46	16 817	738	15.2	49.1	57.0
Sandoval	1 226	19 941	1 043	5 473	2 606	453	457	643	32 253	353	48.4	22.4	43.6
San Juan	2 493	34 410	4 132	1 260	5 743	876	851	917	26 651	666	64.3	7.5	44.7
San Miguel	512	4 874	1 534	142	1 163	178	116	92	18 883	643	18.5	46.3	45.9
Santa Fe	4 589	43 308	5 751	1 287	8 421	1 811	2 425	1 087	25 101	336	53.9	23.2	37.8
Sierra	293	1 921	271	D	408	73	52	30	15 482	180	24.4	49.4	65.6
Socorro	266	2 486	390	114	380	96	323	51	20 558	395	41.5	32.4	56.5
Taos	1 109	8 403	1 164	238	1 620	225	217	141	16 795	422	53.1	11.1	38.9
Torrance	236	2 014	106	D	495	43	D	35	17 353	473	15.2	51.2	54.1
Union	121	719	117	D	115	107	D	12	17 318	448	7.8	70.8	67.6
Valencia	837	8 727	1 946	1 108	2 043	301	229	165	18 863	639	80.8	4.2	38.8
NEW YORK	485 954	7 135 960	1 149 524	728 532	813 025	585 006	514 993	294 641	41 290	31 757	24.3	10.7	58.0
Albany	8 901	166 714	26 441	9 278	22 850	16 839	11 518	5 160	30 954	396	35.6	3.8	45.7
Allegany	837	11 599	1 829	2 787	1 524	201	180	252	21 685	724	14.0	8.6	47.5
Bronx	14 147	198 751	78 921	11 675	20 763	2 900	3 925	6 094	30 662				
Broome	4 307	80 696	11 965	18 378	11 641	3 219	3 396	2 266	28 083	511	26.6	4.9	47.2
Cattaraugus	1 805	25 116	3 365	5 094	4 107	670	382	628	24 998	946	17.0	7.2	52.6
Cayuga	1 546	18 864	3 493	4 104	3 101	697	612	442	23 439	846	17.3	15.7	59.3
Chautauqua	3 129	47 379	7 224	13 795	6 791	956	1 141	1 091	23 024	1 557	33.2	5.3	56.0
Chemung	1 899	35 641	6 100	9 014	5 807	849	969	908	25 479	313	23.3	8.0	39.0
Chenango	1 022	12 021	1 707	3 615	1 846	971	336	304	25 285	801	18.6	10.2	60.5
Clinton	1 890	23 528	3 863	4 142	4 636	484	511	560	23 800	488	15.6	16.0	55.3
Columbia	1 666	15 359	3 597	2 261	2 547	577	705	365	23 737	464	31.0	13.4	62.5
Cortland	1 031	16 095	3 480	3 844	2 528	410	673	351	21 828	452	15.3	14.4	54.2
Delaware	1 118	12 557	2 135	4 166	1 731	441	264	324	25 767	717	15.9	12.3	59.7
Dutchess	6 634	85 854	15 780	13 491	13 485	3 336	4 623	2 541	29 599	539	33.0	9.8	54.7
Erie	22 413	394 894	54 610	62 301	52 683	23 692	21 594	11 166	28 277	973	37.2	5.4	53.2
Essex	1 181	9 863	1 619	1 384	1 699	223	344	227	22 982	197	22.8	14.2	42.1
Franklin	1 084	10 157	2 642	1 300	1 822	337	196	213	20 974	476	9.9	14.3	68.5
Fulton	1 088	13 015	2 308	3 408	1 976	321	218	313	24 067	176	18.8	5.1	62.5

Table B. States and Counties — Agriculture, Land, and Water

STATE County	Land in farms — Acreage (1,000)	Percent change, 1992–1997	Acres — Average size of farm	Total irrigated (1,000)	Total cropland (1,000)	Value of land and buildings — Average per farm ($1,000)	Average per acre (dollars)	Value of machinery and equipment average per farm ($1,000)	Value of products sold — Total (mil dol)	Average per farm (dollars)	Percent from — Crops	Live-stock and poultry products	Percent of farms with sales of — $10,000 or more	$100,000 or more	Percent of land owned by fed. gov. 1997	Water con-sumption 1995 (mil gal/day)
	117	118	119	120	121	122	123	124	125	126	127	128	129	130	131	132
NEW JERSEY—Cont'd																
Mercer	28	-21.1	100	1	23	1 359	13 871	44	13	46 510	92.5	7.5	38.2	10.5	0.0	506.1
Middlesex	28	12.4	102	2	22	756	8 225	50	34	124 927	96.7	3.3	50.2	16.7	0.0	49.2
Monmouth	59	0.7	68	6	46	676	9 710	54	68	77 772	92.2	7.8	41.3	12.2	3.9	79.4
Morris	22	-6.9	58	1	14	710	13 552	38	30	78 215	96.0	4.0	31.6	10.4	4.6	101.6
Ocean	11	13.8	48	1	6	349	6 791	19	8	34 767	68.1	31.9	32.3	8.9	6.8	59.7
Passaic	2	11.6	41	0	0	576	14 201	24	4	70 232	93.9	6.1	40.0	10.9	0.0	300.2
Salem	92	-6.1	139	18	75	537	3 887	66	68	102 892	64.2	35.8	45.8	15.9	2.4	33.1
Somerset	46	5.1	106	1	31	796	8 454	49	14	32 096	71.0	29.0	34.3	8.0	0.9	127.0
Sussex	73	-3.9	88	1	41	477	5 493	25	19	23 201	58.7	41.3	25.6	6.4	6.9	20.1
Union	D	D	D	0	0	1 085	80 852	49	10	525 587	99.8	0.2	78.9	31.6	0.0	26.7
Warren	83	-5.8	114	2	58	737	6 502	41	46	63 021	42.8	57.2	32.7	12.7	3.8	68.8
NEW MEXICO	45 787	-2.3	3 249	805	2 179	625	195	44	1 618	114 780	28.6	71.4	38.9	12.2	34.0	3 505.3
Bernalillo	465	12.0	993	11	18	403	436	23	31	66 298	17.9	82.1	15.8	4.1	16.0	189.9
Catron	1 795	15.6	8 274	2	12	928	112	26	14	66 793	0.5	99.5	48.4	10.1	62.7	17.3
Chaves	2 944	-5.4	5 239	66	D	1 075	194	71	220	391 684	15.4	84.6	62.6	29.9	31.8	289.6
Cibola	1 699	-18.3	10 237	2	21	1 231	123	26	6	34 290	3.7	96.3	33.7	5.4	28.5	8.8
Colfax	2 227	6.8	6 917	27	46	1 348	187	40	40	124 955	3.5	96.5	57.1	18.6	3.2	47.5
Curry	948	2.5	1 447	93	444	588	434	90	195	298 378	24.4	75.6	57.4	29.2	0.4	229.9
De Baca	1 442	7.3	7 548	8	18	873	120	55	25	131 798	18.1	81.9	55.5	23.0	2.4	52.6
Dona Ana	581	10.5	451	82	91	541	1 305	65	235	182 546	54.5	45.5	32.7	13.3	76.1	441.4
Eddy	1 276	12.0	2 731	46	65	578	203	60	85	181 127	29.7	70.3	52.2	18.4	60.3	237.8
Grant	1 174	-2.9	4 103	3	13	558	133	33	7	25 590	3.0	97.0	38.1	7.3	48.7	60.8
Guadalupe	1 419	-7.4	6 013	2	7	722	121	25	12	52 645	2.1	97.9	38.1	10.2	3.3	19.3
Harding	1 255	-2.7	7 296	D	20	D	D	26	14	79 845	0.2	99.8	58.7	14.5	5.1	4.1
Hidalgo	1 105	31.1	7 567	10	23	1 125	153	49	18	125 417	69.2	30.8	64.4	21.9	42.4	40.6
Lea	2 002	-6.8	3 792	41	104	563	161	52	60	114 379	25.6	74.4	47.7	15.3	15.1	157.5
Lincoln	1 975	4.9	5 861	3	9	858	139	36	14	41 620	0.8	99.2	48.4	12.5	35.1	34.7
Los Alamos	D	D	D	D	D	D	D	9	2	D	0.0	D	0.0	0.0	48.4	5.3
Luna	603	-24.3	3 143	31	D	738	243	103	49	255 557	78.3	21.7	65.1	35.4	40.0	131.5
McKinley	3 157	-2.1	14 094	4	D	1 396	99	34	9	41 651	0.8	99.2	21.9	3.6	17.9	18.2
Mora	975	7.7	2 449	13	41	634	261	27	11	27 787	3.9	96.1	21.4	5.3	8.8	33.3
Otero	1 081	-7.3	2 592	6	D	605	241	21	10	23 247	35.7	64.3	26.6	5.3	69.5	46.6
Quay	1 856	4.9	3 183	41	245	514	167	58	41	69 691	32.9	67.1	61.4	16.1	0.1	134.3
Rio Arriba	1 463	-5.8	1 557	24	65	370	250	25	10	11 101	19.7	80.3	22.2	1.2	52.4	85.1
Roosevelt	1 419	-13.8	1 923	68	349	521	275	65	128	173 839	30.3	69.7	55.0	21.3	5.3	143.7
Sandoval	780	1.3	2 209	11	32	374	178	26	10	28 291	21.4	78.6	23.2	3.1	40.5	67.5
San Juan	D	D	D	69	84	314	D	31	D	D	D	D	22.7	2.4	25.3	345.0
San Miguel	2 557	-0.9	3 976	12	50	762	189	24	21	32 121	5.3	94.7	21.5	5.1	12.7	30.9
Santa Fe	652	25.9	1 940	11	23	685	312	29	13	37 223	52.6	47.4	20.2	4.8	27.4	45.7
Sierra	1 287	4.3	7 149	6	D	1 467	215	33	16	87 589	27.7	72.3	53.9	13.9	61.9	42.3
Socorro	1 651	-11.6	4 180	15	20	652	165	39	25	63 872	18.6	81.4	45.3	10.9	52.5	147.1
Taos	310	-4.2	735	14	27	390	554	21	4	8 882	35.1	64.9	14.2	1.2	53.6	98.3
Torrance	1 477	-17.8	3 123	20	65	498	175	45	31	65 215	38.2	61.8	35.9	9.9	8.0	42.3
Union	2 227	-5.8	4 972	47	90	682	141	58	130	291 281	10.3	89.7	71.4	28.3	2.4	76.5
Valencia	384	9.9	600	17	17	295	494	24	27	41 625	23.6	76.4	21.9	4.1	7.3	179.9
NEW YORK	7 254	-2.7	228	69	4 722	287	1 284	60	2 835	89 256	35.3	64.7	54.0	21.6	0.7	10 277.6
Albany	57	-2.1	143	0	36	236	1 878	40	16	39 823	42.7	57.3	43.9	7.6	0.0	566.1
Allegany	158	-2.6	218	1	90	163	801	33	35	48 138	11.8	88.2	39.5	12.0	0.0	9.5
Bronx															0.0	7.5
Broome	86	-12.4	168	0	47	155	1 025	39	24	46 997	19.4	80.6	32.3	11.5	0.1	132.6
Cattaraugus	192	-5.9	203	0	105	192	986	46	53	56 526	19.5	80.5	46.6	15.1	0.0	15.8
Cayuga	252	-0.9	298	1	193	318	1 092	76	115	136 452	32.6	67.4	63.8	28.3	0.0	17.2
Chautauqua	245	-5.8	157	1	145	172	1 145	46	89	56 951	32.9	67.1	52.0	15.5	0.0	1 204.1
Chemung	59	0.5	189	0	36	186	983	41	13	41 209	31.1	68.9	33.9	12.1	0.0	18.2
Chenango	183	-2.5	229	0	104	195	857	53	53	66 359	7.3	92.7	54.2	22.0	0.0	9.2
Clinton	149	-5.9	305	4	77	275	946	72	69	142 066	23.0	77.0	54.7	28.9	0.4	15.6
Columbia	115	2.6	248	3	79	627	2 586	86	73	156 627	26.0	74.0	62.3	23.5	0.0	8.7
Cortland	121	-13.1	267	0	67	270	977	64	37	82 848	8.2	91.8	53.5	26.1	0.0	11.3
Delaware	184	-4.3	256	0	95	246	1 044	46	43	60 666	11.1	88.9	53.1	21.8	0.0	490.2
Dutchess	107	-3.0	198	1	63	791	4 619	53	34	63 013	48.5	51.5	53.6	15.2	0.0	39.2
Erie	143	-1.9	147	2	103	249	1 698	58	78	79 990	39.9	60.1	47.1	18.4	0.0	1 094.9
Essex	48	-12.4	245	0	25	316	1 338	51	8	40 639	31.6	68.4	42.1	9.6	0.0	10.9
Franklin	163	18.1	342	D	78	217	640	65	44	93 037	12.6	87.4	66.4	32.8	0.0	10.3
Fulton	34	-2.0	195	0	22	232	1 215	62	10	54 686	13.2	86.8	51.1	22.2	0.0	7.6

STATE County	Value of Residential Construction Authorized by Building Permits, 2000		Wholesale Trade, 1997				Retail Trade[1], 1997				Real Estate and Rental and Leasing, 1997			
	New Construction ($1,000)	Number of Housing Units	Number of Establishments	Number of Employees	Sales (mil dol)	Annual Payroll (mil dol)	Number of Establishments	Number of Employees	Sales (mil dol)	Annual Payroll (mil dol)	Number of Establishments	Number of Employees	Receipts (mil dol)	Annual Payroll (mil dol)
	133	134	135	136	137	138	139	140	141	142	143	144	145	146
NEW JERSEY—Cont'd														
Mercer	135 034	1 283	472	8 480	4 403.0	291.5	1 442	18 217	3 183.1	326.1	289	1 685	256.7	43.1
Middlesex	227 026	2 460	1 866	36 168	24 256.4	1 554.4	2 785	39 421	7 364.0	720.8	616	4 098	743.5	129.7
Monmouth	322 127	2 912	1 197	9 577	6 298.1	410.3	2 870	34 839	6 400.5	627.7	599	2 795	444.5	74.8
Morris	277 074	2 684	1 397	20 533	20 939.4	1 027.2	2 241	30 767	6 499.9	635.5	536	2 920	620.8	109.8
Ocean	494 013	5 633	429	2 903	937.2	95.4	1 923	23 431	4 728.3	431.5	386	1 345	190.3	30.2
Passaic	50 368	457	1 006	13 154	9 085.0	601.8	1 843	25 468	4 659.9	469.0	415	1 710	251.4	45.8
Salem	17 249	161	45	517	440.3	19.3	226	2 682	401.3	41.5	52	183	20.5	3.6
Somerset	229 836	2 282	672	12 018	18 285.3	643.4	1 178	15 351	3 305.8	306.7	271	1 555	249.8	45.8
Sussex	98 247	719	181	D	D	D	502	4 689	953.9	92.7	82	256	36.5	5.6
Union	54 487	776	1 222	22 744	15 712.5	1 085.7	2 100	22 616	4 809.2	464.9	648	3 184	756.1	88.6
Warren	83 718	896	129	D	D	D	466	5 106	862.2	90.1	74	242	35.2	4.7
NEW MEXICO	1 072 810	8 869	2 182	21 344	7 397.6	601.1	7 421	86 300	14 984.5	1 455.5	1 887	8 844	893.9	165.2
Bernalillo	389 116	3 847	1 037	12 824	4 594.3	388.2	2 307	34 361	6 497.7	623.6	751	4 519	504.2	85.0
Catron	NA	NA	NA	NA	NA	NA	12	37	3.1	0.3	3	22	1.6	0.4
Chaves	3 682	30	74	599	231.3	13.8	269	2 702	411.0	40.5	74	198	18.6	3.1
Cibola	NA	NA	17	82	21.8	1.4	77	809	149.3	11.3	13	80	4.0	1.2
Colfax	NA	NA	13	D	D	D	95	606	104.6	9.1	16	49	3.0	0.5
Curry	4 261	39	44	342	120.5	7.3	235	2 455	342.6	34.6	53	177	9.8	1.8
De Baca	NA	NA	1	D	D	D	13	59	8.7	0.8	2	D	D	D
Dona Ana	95 920	982	122	978	283.6	25.0	511	6 266	1 059.1	98.1	175	530	44.8	7.4
Eddy	3 745	31	69	384	274.7	10.3	232	2 312	372.7	38.9	58	217	15.6	3.8
Grant	NA	NA	32	198	56.6	4.1	125	1 165	190.4	17.9	31	89	6.7	1.2
Guadalupe	NA	NA	5	7	9.8	0.2	27	333	32.0	3.5	2	D	D	D
Harding	NA	NA	NA	NA	NA	NA	3	13	8.1	0.5	NA	NA	NA	NA
Hidalgo	NA	NA	3	D	D	D	36	238	49.3	3.7	1	D	D	D
Lea	312	2	121	964	308.7	27.2	248	2 375	405.3	42.6	58	360	43.0	10.5
Lincoln	27 523	180	16	35	7.7	0.6	148	1 079	149.1	15.1	53	129	11.4	1.7
Los Alamos	28 405	196	9	75	41.4	4.1	59	555	74.1	8.0	16	D	D	D
Luna	2 187	25	22	233	49.3	3.1	95	950	177.5	12.3	13	38	2.7	0.5
McKinley	11 591	144	74	761	191.9	13.5	269	3 670	585.5	59.6	36	156	11.7	2.1
Mora	NA	NA	NA	NA	NA	NA	12	57	7.3	0.7	2	D	D	D
Otero	14 948	144	22	121	29.7	2.5	215	2 281	326.5	32.3	47	170	11.8	2.1
Quay	NA	NA	10	33	4.5	0.4	71	594	99.6	8.5	12	44	1.7	0.4
Rio Arriba	1 573	9	19	84	40.2	1.6	104	1 149	189.0	18.2	15	33	2.4	0.4
Roosevelt	1 317	15	17	103	33.7	2.0	71	626	121.2	10.6	11	18	1.0	0.1
Sandoval	50 634	576	48	456	248.3	11.2	155	1 902	274.0	31.0	42	193	18.0	3.1
San Juan	23 418	172	158	1 278	381.9	35.7	494	5 896	990.8	96.7	87	495	35.1	15.3
San Miguel	NA	NA	16	62	19.4	1.3	114	1 087	168.4	15.1	14	53	2.8	0.5
Santa Fe	49 056	395	167	1 260	340.2	39.3	846	7 868	1 422.9	149.4	200	D	D	D
Sierra	NA	NA	7	21	7.5	0.8	60	379	62.6	5.2	15	47	1.8	0.4
Socorro	1 265	8	6	102	12.3	1.4	57	385	70.6	6.3	10	26	1.5	0.2
Taos	24 186	234	16	59	11.8	1.0	259	1 554	206.8	23.7	39	145	7.3	1.4
Torrance	NA	NA	10	57	10.4	1.2	44	441	73.2	5.6	6	6	0.5	0.1
Union	NA	NA	2	D	D	D	27	103	15.3	1.3	2	D	D	D
Valencia	34 240	350	25	104	38.1	1.7	131	1 993	336.2	30.4	30	96	8.5	1.2
NEW YORK	4 991 529	44 105	37 499	414 249	319 697.6	17 185.8	75 241	805 208	139 303.9	14 329.8	27 214	145 326	27 770.1	4 447.8
Albany	99 605	735	581	8 866	4 335.8	322.3	1 483	21 444	3 567.2	348.1	343	2 535	383.6	57.6
Allegany	6 801	99	26	235	54.8	3.9	181	1 646	210.6	20.4	18	57	3.4	0.6
Bronx	110 146	1 646	755	10 728	5 373.6	389.9	3 110	21 641	3 434.9	352.5	2 171	7 435	1 212.8	182.5
Broome	22 604	158	261	D	D	D	829	11 881	1 763.3	164.2	128	613	82.3	10.1
Cattaraugus	10 427	162	86	979	409.1	28.0	380	4 190	570.7	56.1	52	182	16.1	2.8
Cayuga	13 970	148	78	746	201.3	20.7	265	3 250	516.8	50.5	42	187	18.7	3.1
Chautauqua	28 983	236	159	2 171	748.6	57.6	591	7 096	1 011.1	96.6	86	395	41.9	7.0
Chemung	22 604	178	107	1 667	447.2	49.2	412	5 963	875.9	82.9	66	345	47.9	7.4
Chenango	4 174	81	30	332	64.3	6.7	204	1 793	293.8	27.3	32	66	7.4	1.1
Clinton	24 905	241	115	1 515	407.0	29.6	445	4 967	756.6	70.8	65	219	18.2	2.5
Columbia	29 782	190	81	686	250.6	20.2	260	2 647	424.1	42.0	49	128	11.6	2.4
Cortland	5 506	63	35	401	195.7	11.8	200	2 658	423.9	38.5	24	90	11.1	1.3
Delaware	12 575	135	40	278	150.8	7.4	243	1 810	307.8	29.2	38	118	13.1	1.6
Dutchess	172 169	1 003	274	D	D	D	1 097	13 506	2 259.5	225.7	256	1 502	165.9	28.5
Erie	255 671	2 183	1 680	25 712	14 962.5	884.6	3 628	55 286	8 036.3	797.2	738	5 325	719.1	126.1
Essex	18 509	148	22	178	49.7	5.2	251	1 611	283.8	25.9	34	89	10.1	2.2
Franklin	7 195	93	37	310	126.7	6.8	215	1 834	283.9	26.0	25	71	6.6	1.3
Fulton	10 652	114	78	763	336.1	22.7	195	2 019	331.8	30.1	26	72	7.8	1.1

1. Establishments with payroll.

STATE County	Professional, Scientific, and Technical Services[1], 1997				Manufacturing, 1997				Accommodation and Foodservices, 1997			
	Number of Establish-ments	Number of Employees	Receipts (mil dol)	Annual Payroll (mil dol)	Number of Establish-ments	Number of Employees	Receipts (mil dol)	Annual Payroll (mil dol)	Number of Establish-ments	Number of Employees	Sales (mil dol)	Annual Payroll (mil dol)
	147	148	149	150	151	152	153	154	155	156	157	158
NEW JERSEY—Cont'd												
Mercer	1 223	10 930	1 407.3	586.2	352	13 537	2 413.6	579.7	703	9 870	394.0	109.9
Middlesex	2 682	33 101	3 953.4	1 790.4	977	49 983	13 688.0	1 950.6	1 318	17 941	761.8	201.0
Monmouth	2 195	13 292	1 460.2	617.6	587	12 820	2 318.3	402.7	1 377	18 131	689.8	194.5
Morris	2 452	26 674	3 528.4	1 443.6	749	24 461	7 531.5	979.6	1 080	14 790	665.8	184.0
Ocean	831	4 325	347.8	151.1	309	7 174	939.8	201.1	946	10 569	420.2	108.7
Passaic	1 083	7 338	817.1	256.0	1 059	34 589	6 464.2	1 237.6	764	8 212	338.9	91.0
Salem	86	301	22.3	9.1	48	4 188	1 156.2	207.5	109	1 246	45.1	12.5
Somerset	1 501	23 781	2 218.9	898.2	376	16 289	5 148.4	856.7	618	8 092	356.6	102.2
Sussex	329	1 059	109.1	40.6	146	2 854	320.8	87.2	254	3 006	106.2	31.4
Union	1 554	10 502	1 178.1	480.0	996	40 157	13 883.3	1 619.7	1 064	11 982	513.2	138.3
Warren	237	892	86.8	36.4	164	7 188	1 982.3	294.4	224	2 144	80.6	20.8
NEW MEXICO	3 702	31 535	3 243.4	1 307.3	1 593	39 664	17 906.1	1 135.8	3 825	67 134	2 144.9	599.1
Bernalillo	1 881	23 092	2 578.3	1 040.4	703	D	D	D	1 202	26 744	878.1	248.1
Catron	2	D	D	D	NA	NA	NA	NA	11	45	1.7	0.4
Chaves	87	458	37.5	13.6	51	D	D	D	115	1 970	54.8	14.7
Cibola	18	62	3.1	1.1	NA	NA	NA	NA	46	642	21.4	5.3
Colfax	31	77	5.0	2.0	NA	NA	NA	NA	79	1 205	34.6	12.7
Curry	66	249	13.5	5.3	NA	NA	NA	NA	83	1 631	45.9	13.1
De Baca	2	D	D	D	NA	NA	NA	NA	8	44	1.2	0.3
Dona Ana	222	1 334	107.3	45.7	111	2 290	395.5	46.9	253	4 278	121.7	32.6
Eddy	53	231	20.3	9.0	41	1 057	641.4	43.9	102	1 761	52.5	14.3
Grant	37	173	8.7	3.3	NA	NA	NA	NA	72	823	25.1	6.2
Guadalupe	2	D	D	D	NA	NA	NA	NA	33	317	10.1	2.4
Harding	2	D	D	D	NA	NA	NA	NA	3	10	0.1	0.0
Hidalgo	2	D	D	D	2	D	D	D	24	301	7.9	2.6
Lea	67	338	19.9	8.4	45	524	379.7	14.8	109	1 510	42.0	11.3
Lincoln	53	154	10.4	3.8	NA	NA	NA	NA	99	866	30.1	7.6
Los Alamos	67	728	76.2	32.1	NA	NA	NA	NA	42	696	20.5	6.3
Luna	20	68	2.7	1.1	16	776	49.5	10.7	51	595	16.0	4.4
McKinley	38	219	10.6	3.7	NA	NA	NA	NA	133	2 061	69.3	17.5
Mora	3	D	D	D	NA	NA	NA	NA	4	12	0.2	0.1
Otero	53	240	12.3	5.3	26	593	93.8	10.5	99	1 324	37.0	9.9
Quay	12	48	1.8	0.8	NA	NA	NA	NA	46	526	16.2	3.9
Rio Arriba	35	87	5.9	1.6	NA	NA	NA	NA	89	1 059	33.9	9.5
Roosevelt	12	37	2.2	0.6	NA	NA	NA	NA	30	581	12.4	3.3
Sandoval	97	396	28.0	10.7	57	D	D	D	92	1 501	46.0	12.1
San Juan	166	919	50.9	19.9	71	1 147	257.8	30.3	173	3 478	100.0	27.3
San Miguel	30	87	4.0	1.3	NA	NA	NA	NA	69	796	24.0	5.8
Santa Fe	464	1 964	205.9	85.1	162	1 436	124.8	31.7	361	7 498	304.8	89.1
Sierra	18	41	1.9	0.6	NA	NA	NA	NA	47	437	13.0	3.2
Socorro	20	102	7.6	2.8	NA	NA	NA	NA	51	658	18.7	5.2
Taos	71	181	11.8	4.0	NA	NA	NA	NA	167	2 232	63.7	19.1
Torrance	10	24	1.6	0.4	NA	NA	NA	NA	32	361	8.9	2.5
Union	7	17	1.0	0.3	NA	NA	NA	NA	20	226	4.8	1.2
Valencia	54	180	12.7	3.8	40	967	110.3	22.3	80	946	28.3	7.0
NEW YORK	45 619	416 892	57 475.0	21 773.1	23 908	785 891	146 720.2	26 515.8	38 045	473 327	21 671.1	6 101.1
Albany	860	8 250	848.7	330.0	272	9 065	2 182.4	335.9	841	12 586	449.2	125.0
Allegany	49	148	11.4	3.7	57	2 919	542.8	102.4	87	961	29.1	7.8
Bronx	391	1 980	158.6	50.7	527	12 941	1 252.3	319.6	1 067	8 264	371.6	95.7
Broome	316	2 334	183.7	68.6	242	20 429	3 147.6	787.8	476	6 940	204.2	58.1
Cattaraugus	79	357	31.5	7.8	95	5 341	930.5	162.9	227	3 309	79.5	23.4
Cayuga	90	532	36.1	15.0	100	3 859	618.6	110.4	172	1 688	52.5	14.2
Chautauqua	168	815	48.5	19.2	222	13 084	2 973.6	409.1	368	4 323	124.9	35.4
Chemung	104	827	56.5	18.3	94	9 098	1 357.3	278.1	213	2 965	86.2	24.4
Chenango	65	267	19.9	6.7	86	3 829	790.4	120.3	97	848	24.0	6.0
Clinton	92	328	20.9	8.1	82	4 188	777.9	131.8	189	2 243	64.7	20.0
Columbia	132	538	43.8	16.1	86	2 531	331.1	62.2	142	1 130	41.9	11.1
Cortland	62	457	36.4	13.8	70	4 521	736.1	123.5	125	1 845	53.0	13.7
Delaware	75	224	10.1	3.6	60	4 386	783.7	147.9	124	740	31.1	7.3
Dutchess	591	3 149	284.3	113.6	210	11 848	3 032.9	521.3	558	6 243	252.1	64.4
Erie	1 790	15 551	1 413.9	527.1	1 251	63 234	14 054.5	2 422.1	2 143	31 916	935.4	271.6
Essex	59	145	11.9	3.5	40	1 474	285.2	50.4	219	1 942	86.9	28.1
Franklin	53	170	10.8	4.0	26	1 165	144.4	24.9	127	899	30.6	7.9
Fulton	59	183	12.4	4.0	116	3 548	443.6	86.6	112	957	28.2	7.3

1. Firms subject to federal tax.

Table B. States and Counties — Health and Other Services and Federal Funds

STATE County	Health Care and Social Assistance[1], 1997				Other Services[1], 1997				Federal funds and grants, fiscal 2001[2] Expenditures (mil dol)			
									Total	Direct payments for individuals[3]		
	Number of Establishments	Number of Employees	Receipts (mil dol)	Annual Payroll (mil dol)	Number of Establishments	Number of Employees	Receipts (mil dol)	Annual Payroll (mil dol)	Total	Social Security and government retirement	Medicare	Food stamps and Supplemental Security Income
	159	160	161	162	163	164	165	166	167	168	169	170
NEW JERSEY—Cont'd												
Mercer	792	6 837	576.4	260.0	538	2 985	210.3	62.1	3 441.0	815.5	388.8	52.0
Middlesex	1 429	13 628	1 231.2	469.8	1 261	6 628	511.4	145.4	3 173.7	1 284.7	633.8	59.8
Monmouth	1 695	13 866	1 057.5	462.7	1 177	5 961	382.6	119.5	3 644.0	1 316.5	574.4	43.6
Morris	1 330	11 147	930.5	387.8	1 031	5 308	403.3	119.0	1 729.5	850.0	331.3	18.4
Ocean	984	12 337	855.6	362.5	767	3 074	185.1	50.9	2 852.3	1 634.5	726.0	29.5
Passaic	1 033	8 552	840.7	306.5	823	3 926	287.8	89.5	2 261.6	818.4	442.1	99.0
Salem	108	744	56.1	22.9	102	285	20.0	4.5	311.6	142.6	76.4	8.5
Somerset	706	7 075	613.1	252.4	498	2 331	175.9	54.8	950.4	500.6	169.8	9.9
Sussex	244	2 849	151.9	67.9	250	886	61.8	16.6	443.5	238.0	94.2	7.9
Union	1 194	10 405	800.1	348.7	1 100	5 844	432.1	137.8	2 374.3	1 047.4	534.7	66.3
Warren	197	1 440	101.0	42.3	190	750	53.8	14.5	425.7	215.5	105.6	6.8
NEW MEXICO	2 923	32 824	2 057.3	864.3	2 318	13 448	759.1	227.2	16 586.9	3 812.4	1 027.4	376.5
Bernalillo	1 152	16 080	1 115.2	463.3	896	6 596	374.4	121.2	5 675.3	1 303.1	337.3	94.9
Catron	NA	NA	NA	NA	2	D	D	D	23.9	11.3	1.7	0.5
Chaves	121	826	48.5	22.8	79	335	19.5	5.0	335.3	137.8	40.5	16.2
Cibola	20	203	10.3	4.2	28	72	3.7	0.9	129.5	40.1	0.0	4.7
Colfax	18	154	8.0	3.3	22	54	2.8	0.8	74.5	36.9	11.7	2.7
Curry	96	738	41.0	16.5	76	334	17.7	4.7	400.6	105.4	27.4	4.6
De Baca	3	D	D	D	3	7	0.4	0.1	17.7	6.5	2.4	0.6
Dona Ana	272	3 149	177.9	75.3	169	1 025	43.9	13.2	1 088.9	321.3	82.3	49.9
Eddy	84	1 101	70.4	26.4	84	353	25.1	5.5	419.2	118.9	43.8	11.4
Grant	46	298	18.7	8.4	46	149	6.9	1.7	171.0	80.9	22.2	6.7
Guadalupe	4	37	0.9	0.6	5	22	1.4	0.3	49.0	8.7	4.0	1.6
Harding	1	D	D	D	1	D	D	D	6.3	2.6	0.8	0.1
Hidalgo	5	D	D	D	4	5	0.6	0.1	32.7	13.8	4.1	1.4
Lea	86	1 121	70.6	23.1	100	722	43.4	12.7	248.5	101.0	45.3	14.9
Lincoln	35	214	9.3	5.6	23	96	5.4	1.3	90.1	52.2	11.5	2.1
Los Alamos	48	352	20.1	10.0	16	68	4.3	1.5	2 137.9	27.6	8.5	0.3
Luna	34	155	8.3	3.1	18	78	4.3	1.0	135.1	61.9	17.7	7.6
McKinley	41	391	15.1	5.9	69	332	16.1	4.5	494.7	90.8	26.9	33.8
Mora	3	72	1.4	0.9	1	D	D	D	42.3	11.0	3.1	2.1
Otero	61	491	27.0	11.6	59	284	13.8	4.2	587.8	168.1	27.0	8.9
Quay	19	123	4.7	2.1	19	79	4.4	0.9	77.6	27.5	9.5	3.1
Rio Arriba	46	545	30.4	13.0	27	68	4.4	0.9	256.2	71.9	22.4	11.5
Roosevelt	12	44	2.9	1.4	27	82	5.2	1.1	121.9	33.8	14.6	2.5
Sandoval	57	610	37.7	15.5	55	302	13.7	4.0	332.6	165.0	40.3	13.5
San Juan	169	1 379	85.8	39.6	176	1 076	66.4	18.7	592.2	176.9	52.3	24.4
San Miguel	55	523	21.5	9.8	29	88	4.5	1.1	210.4	54.1	19.9	12.3
Santa Fe	298	2 831	164.1	74.0	170	854	54.5	15.8	982.7	261.5	60.2	11.7
Sierra	9	54	1.6	0.7	16	62	2.3	0.7	98.3	50.9	16.4	3.9
Socorro	12	81	5.5	2.2	12	24	2.1	0.4	114.9	29.9	8.0	6.1
Taos	53	397	23.0	8.4	31	86	5.5	1.2	159.5	58.4	15.3	6.5
Torrance	7	29	1.7	0.8	10	21	1.1	0.2	86.4	28.5	5.9	3.9
Union	4	57	3.3	1.0	5	16	1.0	0.2	33.5	10.8	4.0	0.8
Valencia	52	628	28.4	12.4	40	151	9.3	3.1	262.7	140.1	40.6	11.3
NEW YORK	36 054	358 075	26 008.3	10 970.9	30 104	146 365	10 014.6	2 858.7	116 366.1	35 486.0	19 011.7	4 651.3
Albany	601	7 195	516.5	239.9	513	3 599	270.1	79.1	5 235.2	904.8	233.7	43.9
Allegany	66	1 028	34.0	14.3	49	181	10.5	2.2	228.5	104.2	38.5	10.6
Bronx	1 050	15 530	1 014.2	448.1	1 254	4 612	319.1	93.3	(4)	(4)	(4)	(4)
Broome	343	3 912	286.7	131.3	296	1 407	93.2	24.7	1 037.8	486.0	184.6	37.5
Cattaraugus	112	1 266	87.1	25.9	94	400	27.0	6.1	518.9	187.8	69.0	15.9
Cayuga	136	969	60.5	25.6	85	411	31.5	7.1	372.2	166.0	65.7	12.1
Chautauqua	243	2 304	109.8	49.9	178	721	45.2	11.3	750.1	323.1	121.2	27.2
Chemung	162	1 675	123.1	60.7	108	553	36.1	9.8	519.7	219.9	79.3	18.6
Chenango	62	417	22.8	9.8	59	164	12.2	2.7	234.5	115.5	34.8	9.1
Clinton	146	1 302	79.3	33.9	115	466	29.7	8.3	368.7	165.2	52.9	16.2
Columbia	106	1 196	63.4	26.8	94	308	27.3	6.1	312.8	145.8	52.8	7.6
Cortland	82	967	44.5	20.5	71	484	45.9	15.9	196.0	92.6	31.6	8.4
Delaware	54	243	15.8	5.1	60	162	12.1	2.5	261.6	116.5	43.2	7.3
Dutchess	583	4 980	347.7	145.8	448	1 802	125.0	33.3	1 160.3	566.3	201.7	28.3
Erie	1 916	25 392	1 397.0	624.4	1 603	9 094	585.9	169.4	5 539.9	2 265.5	893.6	191.4
Essex	39	288	14.5	7.2	43	148	9.7	2.0	229.3	99.7	34.8	6.4
Franklin	71	354	30.1	11.0	49	129	7.0	1.6	245.5	98.4	36.2	9.2
Fulton	70	430	26.6	9.7	59	343	19.6	6.6	241.0	118.6	43.2	10.4

1. Firms subject to federal tax. included with New York County. 2. October 1, 2000 to September 30, 2001. 3. State totals may include programs not allocated by county. 4. Bronx, Kings, Queens, and Richmond Counties

Table B. States and Counties — Federal Funds and Local Government Finances

STATE County	Federal funds and grants, fiscal 2001[1] (cont'd)							Local government finances, 1997				
	Expenditures (mil dol) (cont'd)							General revenue				
	Procurement contract awards			Grants[2]						Taxes		
											Per capita[3] (dollars)	
	Salaries and wages	Defense	Other	Medicaid and other health-related	Nutrition and family welfare	Education	Other	Total (mil dol)	Intergovernmental (mil dol)	Total (mil dol)	Total	Property
	171	172	173	174	175	176	177	178	179	180	181	182
NEW JERSEY—Cont'd												
Mercer	179.5	146.6	126.2	419.9	362.0	219.4	592.5	1 212.4	434.8	560.9	1 701	1 678
Middlesex	236.8	68.2	227.3	297.3	37.7	21.5	185.9	1 989.8	532.9	1 136.3	1 605	1 576
Monmouth	467.6	726.6	80.4	240.5	37.5	18.2	54.0	1 901.5	504.4	1 053.5	1 767	1 727
Morris	232.1	122.0	38.3	80.1	8.3	5.9	6.4	1 449.5	291.0	922.2	2 030	2 012
Ocean	179.0	39.6	19.9	119.9	31.5	14.7	12.6	1 213.5	365.3	699.3	1 455	1 438
Passaic	105.7	171.4	41.6	334.7	73.5	11.2	58.9	1 224.9	436.1	624.7	1 291	1 275
Salem	12.9	6.4	2.4	35.4	7.4	2.9	3.9	239.0	105.9	83.4	1 263	1 234
Somerset	96.5	35.6	33.0	51.0	7.9	3.5	27.9	779.7	132.4	527.7	1 906	1 882
Sussex	21.6	5.1	16.9	30.5	3.8	2.5	16.4	411.4	137.9	229.5	1 615	1 602
Union	169.3	40.1	62.8	257.3	48.4	18.5	38.5	1 626.8	571.6	831.7	1 670	1 647
Warren	17.2	16.4	4.6	29.7	6.7	2.6	5.2	313.5	99.9	162.5	1 653	1 638
NEW MEXICO	1 747.4	760.6	4 361.0	1 501.5	421.2	460.1	1 203.4	X	X	X	X	X
Bernalillo	822.1	377.3	1 856.4	389.2	77.1	43.9	266.1	1 290.2	662.0	345.2	656	395
Catron	3.8	0.0	0.3	2.3	0.3	0.1	2.9	7.1	5.6	1.0	368	348
Chaves	20.3	13.3	10.5	56.8	10.0	7.4	6.8	167.8	72.4	25.7	409	160
Cibola	16.6	11.9	18.9	1.2	9.2	4.2	8.2	43.5	32.6	6.7	259	111
Colfax	3.2	0.5	0.6	11.3	2.2	1.1	3.1	39.7	24.6	9.1	667	349
Curry	131.9	31.2	1.7	36.7	9.9	3.8	6.5	87.7	59.6	16.7	358	152
De Baca	0.6	0.0	0.1	2.3	0.5	0.1	3.2	6.1	4.6	0.8	325	220
Dona Ana	143.6	160.4	63.2	110.9	26.9	18.8	71.6	371.2	203.5	61.6	365	198
Eddy	26.8	3.9	150.0	41.1	8.6	2.7	3.1	116.9	63.9	30.1	566	272
Grant	10.2	0.0	1.7	26.8	4.6	2.4	8.4	84.6	41.2	12.0	382	203
Guadalupe	1.5	0.2	0.2	14.7	1.1	0.4	14.0	13.3	10.3	2.2	532	312
Harding	0.5	0.0	0.1	0.6	0.1	0.1	0.1	4.2	3.3	0.5	555	377
Hidalgo	2.8	0.0	0.6	4.3	1.5	0.4	-0.2	20.0	11.0	3.1	483	350
Lea	6.3	0.0	1.4	37.6	7.9	4.8	10.5	139.3	79.3	37.9	673	342
Lincoln	4.6	0.3	1.1	8.2	2.1	1.4	5.5	49.0	25.3	14.2	884	557
Los Alamos	11.3	5.1	2 060.4	15.0	0.2	0.5	9.2	62.1	41.4	11.6	635	259
Luna	9.1	0.1	0.7	18.0	4.4	2.0	6.1	43.7	30.1	7.1	296	160
McKinley	103.0	0.1	12.9	114.6	24.4	66.9	13.3	135.2	96.0	24.3	359	193
Mora	1.9	0.0	1.9	15.8	2.5	0.8	2.4	13.2	10.0	1.7	355	207
Otero	196.2	111.8	9.9	27.4	6.6	6.4	19.0	85.5	57.5	17.0	305	159
Quay	2.7	0.0	0.5	11.3	2.7	0.6	6.9	23.5	16.3	4.9	482	217
Rio Arriba	15.6	1.0	6.0	83.6	11.5	10.4	14.5	72.6	52.0	13.6	360	191
Roosevelt	3.1	0.0	0.7	18.4	3.5	3.0	12.9	29.4	20.8	4.5	241	117
Sandoval	13.8	1.2	2.6	46.1	10.9	12.9	20.8	121.4	71.9	31.0	361	194
San Juan	79.3	2.3	45.8	78.6	15.4	36.3	33.9	281.4	146.4	67.4	651	394
San Miguel	7.7	0.5	2.7	73.8	9.4	8.5	13.3	70.7	47.2	13.4	465	298
Santa Fe	70.2	8.1	95.9	123.1	117.8	78.8	123.1	232.7	112.8	75.0	616	244
Sierra	5.1	0.4	1.0	13.2	1.5	0.9	2.6	19.7	13.4	3.5	314	231
Socorro	9.1	4.7	5.2	19.7	3.9	2.6	19.1	26.8	19.0	4.0	245	135
Taos	12.8	0.1	4.6	45.9	6.2	2.2	3.7	58.3	39.3	12.9	484	229
Torrance	2.7	25.0	0.5	12.1	2.2	1.0	1.8	40.1	30.7	6.8	465	365
Union	2.5	0.0	1.7	5.2	0.6	0.2	1.2	12.7	8.8	1.9	454	225
Valencia	6.6	1.3	1.5	35.9	9.0	4.0	8.7	80.8	60.4	13.8	219	143
NEW YORK	8 121.9	3 245.6	2 922.3	19 938.6	5 446.2	2 259.3	5 252.6	X	X	X	X	X
Albany	325.0	24.9	93.3	409.6	834.4	632.8	1 509.3	1 003.4	251.1	540.9	1 838	1 228
Allegany	7.6	5.1	2.1	31.6	11.3	3.4	7.4	162.2	87.4	57.5	1 113	873
Bronx	(4)	(4)	(4)	(4)	(4)	(4)	(4)	(4)	(4)	(4)	(4)	(4)
Broome	48.3	53.2	15.2	118.0	26.3	14.9	28.5	679.9	250.3	314.4	1 582	1 170
Cattaraugus	16.8	0.4	17.4	57.1	17.2	79.7	14.3	303.8	144.5	112.9	1 324	932
Cayuga	11.2	3.5	2.9	54.8	11.6	7.9	19.8	239.4	101.6	93.9	1 141	819
Chautauqua	26.3	22.4	46.1	96.2	27.1	13.3	24.0	483.0	200.9	189.6	1 354	1 078
Chemung	27.7	1.3	33.5	72.2	16.6	7.0	25.0	284.8	128.5	107.2	1 151	822
Chenango	7.0	2.4	1.9	35.3	7.9	4.3	7.9	176.0	79.5	74.1	1 416	1 234
Clinton	28.3	7.6	5.7	54.7	10.8	6.2	9.1	255.3	118.4	93.7	1 162	837
Columbia	10.9	1.6	8.1	60.1	7.4	3.3	3.4	202.3	67.1	102.9	1 606	1 259
Cortland	7.5	1.9	2.3	26.6	8.5	3.8	7.4	158.4	69.7	63.7	1 303	859
Delaware	19.4	8.8	5.3	38.2	7.0	3.1	7.5	197.1	76.0	76.5	1 644	1 475
Dutchess	66.1	6.7	12.6	184.0	21.4	12.4	16.4	866.8	254.0	462.0	1 745	1 391
Erie	473.6	185.6	128.3	779.9	200.9	70.9	140.0	3 231.0	1 155.0	1 413.2	1 496	1 047
Essex	19.5	7.2	4.1	33.6	6.2	1.6	12.9	144.6	41.3	75.0	1 955	1 617
Franklin	9.4	0.0	2.7	56.0	9.1	4.6	11.3	167.8	77.3	58.8	1 202	998
Fulton	6.1	2.6	1.4	37.6	7.2	3.8	5.1	201.8	87.2	71.3	1 339	1 096

1. October 1, 2000 to September 30, 2001.   2. State totals may include programs not allocated by county.   3. Based on the resident population estimated as of July 1 of the year shown.   4. Bronx, Kings, Queens, and Richmond Counties included with New York County.

STATE County	Total (mil dol) 183	Per capita[1] (dollars) 184	Education 185	Health and hospitals 186	Police protection 187	Public welfare 188	Highways 189	Total (mil dol) 190	Per capita[1] (dollars) 191	Federal civilian 192	Federal military 193	State and local 194	Democratic 195	Republican 196	All other 197
NEW JERSEY—Cont'd															
Mercer	1 200.7	3 641	49.0	2.4	5.9	5.8	3.0	1 028.7	3 119	2 978	854	48 436	61.4	34.4	4.2
Middlesex	2 003.7	2 830	52.9	3.5	6.5	3.7	2.3	1 370.5	1 935	3 827	1 884	48 028	59.9	36.1	4.0
Monmouth	1 898.0	3 183	52.8	1.8	6.0	4.0	2.8	1 326.5	2 225	8 596	4 539	30 391	50.2	45.5	4.4
Morris	1 469.8	3 236	53.3	2.2	5.6	2.9	4.1	921.9	2 030	5 142	1 200	22 794	42.6	53.8	3.6
Ocean	1 228.4	2 555	53.9	1.5	5.7	2.5	4.2	1 088.4	2 264	3 018	1 797	20 536	47.2	48.8	4.0
Passaic	1 181.5	2 441	39.2	0.8	7.3	10.7	3.3	769.7	1 590	1 953	1 179	24 413	57.7	39.0	3.3
Salem	239.5	3 627	49.7	2.1	3.8	6.8	3.9	338.5	5 126	188	157	3 947	50.9	45.4	3.6
Somerset	778.0	2 811	56.2	3.5	4.5	2.0	4.5	507.6	1 834	2 667	700	12 686	46.7	49.6	3.6
Sussex	398.8	2 807	64.0	2.8	4.6	2.7	4.2	239.2	1 684	373	352	6 695	37.1	57.9	5.0
Union	1 640.0	3 292	47.5	3.3	6.5	3.8	4.2	813.2	1 632	2 251	1 213	27 440	60.1	36.8	3.2
Warren	327.9	3 336	54.8	2.8	3.4	4.6	5.9	168.6	1 716	289	243	5 125	40.5	54.3	5.1
NEW MEXICO	X	X	X	X	X	X	X	X	X	29 123	17 711	141 439	47.9	47.8	4.3
Bernalillo	1 330.4	2 529	41.1	2.5	7.4	0.4	5.4	1 311.5	2 493	13 109	6 093	44 221	48.7	46.6	4.7
Catron	8.1	2 886	47.4	1.1	5.8	0.0	16.1	0.5	166	126	10	214	20.6	74.4	4.9
Chaves	159.1	2 525	41.8	28.5	4.0	2.5	3.8	116.1	1 843	374	233	4 284	34.9	62.7	2.4
Cibola	41.7	1 608	51.4	0.4	3.3	0.7	3.7	12.9	497	387	96	1 533	58.2	38.8	2.9
Colfax	38.4	2 801	46.2	6.4	5.5	0.8	9.1	18.5	1 349	55	49	1 443	48.6	47.6	3.8
Curry	91.6	1 959	66.2	1.4	5.9	0.8	5.3	29.4	629	954	3 244	2 352	29.0	69.4	1.6
De Baca	6.2	2 675	50.9	1.6	6.8	0.9	9.6	3.5	1 506	14	0	234	35.5	62.3	2.1
Dona Ana	387.8	2 302	48.7	22.3	3.4	1.1	3.6	251.1	1 490	3 440	672	14 713	51.3	45.6	3.2
Eddy	118.9	2 233	50.9	7.6	6.8	1.4	5.6	35.5	666	493	189	2 913	40.0	58.1	1.9
Grant	81.0	2 583	38.6	33.5	4.8	0.0	3.1	36.2	1 156	243	111	3 099	50.5	44.1	5.4
Guadalupe	13.3	3 251	55.0	0.3	6.0	0.0	3.4	1.9	467	28	14	374	65.2	33.2	1.7
Harding	4.1	4 551	51.2	0.1	2.7	0.0	17.4	1.1	1 177	16	0	92	36.1	61.7	2.2
Hidalgo	20.1	3 161	50.1	1.3	3.9	1.6	5.6	56.1	8 835	57	21	465	45.7	52.0	2.2
Lea	132.1	2 342	56.5	4.6	9.9	1.0	6.8	23.5	416	123	196	3 347	27.0	71.2	1.7
Lincoln	46.7	2 920	45.2	0.6	7.2	0.0	6.6	32.6	2 037	122	60	1 065	29.9	65.8	4.3
Los Alamos	61.0	3 337	42.1	1.0	6.5	0.9	8.3	109.9	6 014	201	68	9 960	40.6	55.0	4.3
Luna	42.8	1 788	51.9	1.6	7.9	6.2	8.5	4.7	196	181	87	1 408	45.0	51.3	3.6
McKinley	155.3	2 297	59.2	0.6	4.9	0.8	3.6	51.0	754	2 274	238	4 102	64.7	31.9	3.4
Mora	13.0	2 715	56.0	0.1	2.5	0.0	16.6	1.7	365	43	18	291	66.5	30.5	3.0
Otero	86.1	1 544	52.2	0.7	7.6	0.7	6.7	31.7	568	2 011	4 305	2 867	33.7	63.3	3.0
Quay	24.2	2 398	54.7	1.7	7.8	0.6	6.0	6.0	597	79	35	1 010	38.3	59.6	2.1
Rio Arriba	72.5	1 919	56.6	0.7	3.7	1.5	5.1	16.6	439	391	136	2 593	67.5	28.9	3.6
Roosevelt	28.6	1 543	65.3	0.0	6.7	0.6	3.9	8.8	477	62	62	1 887	31.2	66.6	2.2
Sandoval	132.0	1 538	55.0	0.6	9.5	2.0	7.6	152.1	1 772	356	321	3 220	46.9	48.6	4.5
San Juan	308.1	2 976	56.5	0.3	3.9	0.9	4.0	1 075.2	10 387	1 705	393	5 957	34.6	61.8	3.6
San Miguel	73.4	2 537	61.6	0.8	4.8	0.2	4.2	23.9	828	165	101	4 006	71.4	24.2	4.5
Santa Fe	256.5	2 106	40.2	1.2	6.2	3.9	8.7	349.9	2 873	1 229	450	14 011	64.7	28.2	7.0
Sierra	22.7	2 066	40.3	1.7	5.2	1.4	10.4	10.2	925	108	39	760	36.8	59.3	3.9
Socorro	27.7	1 704	54.1	0.0	3.0	0.1	11.7	5.8	359	223	59	2 057	48.3	46.5	5.3
Taos	63.0	2 374	60.8	0.6	3.6	0.9	7.7	37.4	1 409	280	96	1 604	64.6	25.2	10.2
Torrance	41.5	2 824	77.1	1.2	3.3	1.6	4.1	14.9	1 016	82	58	1 036	37.7	58.3	4.1
Union	12.1	2 932	54.0	1.0	5.5	2.0	11.7	0.6	147	57	14	325	25.8	72.3	2.0
Valencia	89.6	1 424	73.4	0.1	4.4	1.2	2.9	44.7	711	135	232	3 996	45.9	50.5	3.6
NEW YORK	X	X	X	X	X	X	X	X	X	138 446	57 225	1 260 309	60.2	35.2	4.6
Albany	1 001.7	3 404	39.5	2.8	4.7	15.2	3.9	1 036.5	3 522	6 236	965	64 455	60.3	33.5	6.1
Allegany	178.0	3 448	54.4	2.8	1.2	12.0	9.0	89.8	1 740	145	101	3 686	33.9	61.2	4.9
Bronx	(3)	(3)	(3)	(3)	(3)	(3)	(3)	(3)	(3)	8 274	2 448	15 656	86.3	11.8	1.9
Broome	677.0	3 406	46.0	2.3	2.9	14.0	4.7	285.2	1 435	831	402	17 533	52.1	42.4	5.4
Cattaraugus	311.5	3 654	50.0	3.6	2.0	12.8	8.8	123.2	1 445	233	177	7 400	40.6	54.5	4.9
Cayuga	257.6	3 130	48.1	3.2	2.3	10.7	7.2	156.8	1 905	190	164	5 510	50.1	44.1	5.8
Chautauqua	511.1	3 650	49.3	1.7	2.8	13.4	7.8	276.8	1 977	414	278	9 491	46.0	49.5	4.5
Chemung	297.6	3 197	43.8	2.8	2.8	17.0	5.2	123.1	1 322	447	195	6 992	46.2	49.8	4.0
Chenango	175.7	3 356	50.4	2.5	0.9	8.5	8.5	59.7	1 140	123	101	3 843	45.0	49.5	5.5
Clinton	255.6	3 169	51.5	3.8	1.6	11.6	6.7	101.4	1 257	508	160	7 582	50.9	43.4	5.7
Columbia	218.4	3 409	54.2	4.0	1.7	11.6	7.5	98.6	1 538	188	126	4 075	47.0	45.8	7.1
Cortland	157.4	3 223	45.1	3.9	2.5	11.0	7.8	72.5	1 485	102	97	3 506	46.8	47.6	5.7
Delaware	207.3	4 453	42.3	8.6	1.4	11.6	11.5	72.7	1 562	157	93	4 220	41.9	52.8	5.3
Dutchess	889.0	3 359	48.6	5.3	4.1	9.0	4.7	485.9	1 836	1 364	536	20 490	46.9	47.1	6.0
Erie	3 346.2	3 543	41.2	6.8	4.2	14.6	3.9	1 675.1	1 774	8 933	2 254	63 873	56.6	37.7	5.7
Essex	148.4	3 868	36.3	4.2	1.1	12.5	9.9	54.6	1 424	383	75	3 866	44.2	49.2	6.6
Franklin	175.6	3 588	50.8	3.0	1.5	11.6	5.4	82.9	1 694	149	97	6 047	50.8	43.8	5.4
Fulton	225.9	4 239	48.5	1.1	2.2	13.9	4.5	215.9	4 051	110	106	4 068	43.0	52.8	4.3

1. Based on the resident population estimated as of July 1 of the year shown.   2. Data subject to copyright.   3. Bronx, Kings, Queens, and Richmond Counties included with New York County.

Table B. States and Counties — Land Area and Population

STATE/ County code	MSA/ PMSA/ NECMA code[1]	County Type[2]	STATE County	Land area,[3] (sq km) 2000	Population and population characteristics, 2000 — Total persons	Rank	Per square kilometer	Race alone or in combination (percent) — White	Black	Am. Indian, Alaska Native	Asian and Pacific Islander	Percent Hispanic[4]	Age (percent) — Under 5 years	5 to 17 years	18 to 24 years	25 to 34 years	35 to 44 years	45 to 54 years
				1	2	3	4	5	6	7	8	9	10	11	12	13	14	15
			NEW YORK—Cont'd															
36 037	6840	1	Genesee	1 280	60 370	802	47.2	95.7	2.7	1.2	0.6	1.5	6.1	20.0	7.5	12.5	17.0	13.4
36 039	...	6	Greene	1 678	48 195	944	28.7	92.0	6.0	0.7	0.9	4.3	5.4	17.6	9.5	11.4	15.6	14.2
36 041	...	8	Hamilton	4 456	5 379	2 822	1.2	98.4	0.6	0.7	0.3	1.1	4.3	15.4	5.2	9.8	14.4	16.4
36 043	8680	2	Herkimer	3 655	64 427	755	17.6	98.6	0.7	0.6	0.5	0.9	5.6	18.8	8.3	11.3	15.2	14.0
36 045	...	5	Jefferson	3 295	111 738	482	33.9	90.2	6.6	1.1	1.6	4.2	7.3	19.1	11.8	15.5	15.9	11.7
36 047	5600	0	Kings	183	2 465 326	7	13 471.7	43.7	38.1	0.8	8.6	19.8	7.4	19.5	10.3	15.8	15.0	12.5
36 049	...	6	Lewis	3 303	26 944	1 485	8.2	98.7	0.5	0.6	0.4	0.6	6.1	21.7	7.7	11.6	16.5	13.4
36 051	6840	1	Livingston	1 637	64 328	757	39.3	95.0	3.4	0.7	1.0	2.3	5.4	18.0	14.2	12.0	16.9	13.9
36 053	8160	2	Madison	1 699	69 441	713	40.9	97.2	1.6	0.9	0.7	1.1	5.9	19.0	12.0	11.5	16.1	13.7
36 055	6840	0	Monroe	1 708	735 343	68	430.5	80.6	14.7	0.7	2.9	5.3	6.4	19.2	9.5	13.3	16.1	14.0
36 057	0160	2	Montgomery	1 048	49 708	921	47.4	96.0	1.5	0.6	0.7	6.9	5.9	18.6	7.2	11.6	14.7	13.8
36 059	5380	0	Nassau	743	1 334 544	26	1 796.2	80.8	10.8	0.4	5.4	10.0	6.5	18.2	7.3	12.2	16.7	14.6
36 061	5600	0	New York	59	1 537 195	17	26 054.2	57.1	19.0	1.0	10.4	27.2	4.9	11.8	10.2	21.5	16.7	13.4
36 063	1280	2	Niagara	1 354	219 846	257	162.4	91.8	6.7	1.4	0.7	1.3	6.0	18.7	8.5	11.9	16.5	14.0
36 065	8680	2	Oneida	3 141	235 469	246	75.0	91.6	6.3	0.5	1.5	3.2	5.7	18.2	8.6	12.5	15.6	13.6
36 067	8160	2	Onondaga	2 021	458 336	126	226.8	86.4	10.3	1.5	2.5	2.4	6.5	19.2	9.5	12.8	16.1	13.6
36 069	6840	2	Ontario	1 669	100 224	524	60.1	96.2	2.6	0.6	1.0	2.1	6.0	19.4	8.3	11.6	16.8	15.2
36 071	5660	2	Orange	2 114	341 367	171	161.5	85.5	9.1	0.8	2.0	11.6	7.6	21.4	8.7	12.7	17.3	13.8
36 073	6840	1	Orleans	1 014	44 171	1 013	43.6	90.2	7.9	0.9	0.6	3.9	6.2	19.9	8.2	13.6	17.8	13.3
36 075	8160	2	Oswego	2 469	122 377	444	49.6	98.0	0.8	0.8	0.6	1.3	6.2	20.6	10.9	12.3	16.6	13.5
36 077	...	6	Otsego	2 597	61 676	788	23.7	96.7	2.1	0.6	0.9	1.9	4.8	17.9	14.4	10.2	14.1	13.9
36 079	5600	1	Putnam	599	95 745	541	159.8	95.2	2.0	0.5	1.6	6.2	6.9	19.6	6.3	12.4	19.7	16.0
36 081	5600	0	Queens	283	2 229 379	9	7 877.7	47.4	21.8	1.2	19.6	25.0	6.4	16.4	9.6	16.8	16.3	12.9
36 083	0160	2	Rensselaer	1 694	152 538	349	90.0	92.3	5.3	0.6	2.0	2.1	6.1	18.2	10.1	12.9	16.2	14.2
36 085	5600	0	Richmond	151	443 728	134	2 938.6	79.5	10.5	0.6	6.4	12.1	6.7	18.8	8.5	14.3	16.6	14.3
36 087	5600	0	Rockland	451	286 753	195	635.8	78.4	12.2	0.6	6.2	10.2	7.6	20.4	7.9	12.2	15.8	14.3
36 089	...	5	St. Lawrence	6 956	111 931	481	16.1	95.2	2.6	1.3	1.0	1.8	5.4	18.0	13.8	12.2	15.2	13.4
36 091	0160	2	Saratoga	2 103	200 635	273	95.4	96.9	1.7	0.6	1.3	1.4	6.5	18.6	7.8	13.8	17.7	15.0
36 093	0160	2	Schenectady	534	146 555	372	274.4	89.4	7.8	0.7	2.5	3.2	6.1	18.2	7.9	12.1	16.1	14.1
36 095	0160	2	Schoharie	1 611	31 582	1 359	19.6	97.5	1.6	0.8	0.6	1.9	5.6	18.4	10.6	11.0	15.2	14.6
36 097	...	8	Schuyler	851	19 224	1 831	22.6	97.4	1.7	1.0	0.3	1.2	5.8	19.5	7.9	11.2	15.4	15.2
36 099	...	6	Seneca	842	33 342	1 303	39.6	96.0	2.6	0.7	1.0	2.0	5.6	19.2	7.5	12.9	15.8	14.2
36 101	...	4	Steuben	3 607	98 726	528	27.4	97.2	1.6	0.6	1.0	0.8	6.1	19.9	7.4	11.6	15.5	14.4
36 103	5380	0	Suffolk	2 363	1 419 369	22	600.7	86.1	7.7	0.6	3.0	10.5	7.1	19.0	7.6	13.5	17.7	13.9
36 105	...	6	Sullivan	2 512	73 966	675	29.4	86.8	9.3	0.7	1.5	9.2	5.9	19.1	7.3	11.7	16.4	14.8
36 107	0960	2	Tioga	1 343	51 784	896	38.6	98.3	0.8	0.7	0.7	1.0	6.3	20.7	7.0	11.0	17.8	14.1
36 109	...	5	Tompkins	1 233	96 501	535	78.3	87.3	4.4	0.8	8.3	3.1	4.4	14.5	26.0	13.4	12.8	12.5
36 111	...	4	Ulster	2 918	177 749	310	60.9	90.6	6.3	0.9	1.6	6.2	5.5	18.0	8.7	12.4	17.3	15.2
36 113	2975	3	Warren	2 251	63 303	766	28.1	98.3	0.9	0.6	0.7	1.0	5.4	18.6	7.5	12.0	16.3	14.8
36 115	2975	3	Washington	2 164	61 042	798	28.2	95.7	3.1	0.6	0.5	2.0	5.6	19.0	8.3	13.0	16.3	14.0
36 117	6840	1	Wayne	1 565	93 765	547	59.9	94.3	3.8	0.8	0.6	2.4	6.6	20.8	6.8	12.6	17.5	14.3
36 119	5600	0	Westchester	1 121	923 459	40	823.8	73.6	15.2	0.6	5.2	15.6	7.0	18.0	7.2	13.4	17.0	14.1
36 121	...	6	Wyoming	1 536	43 424	1 030	28.3	92.4	5.6	0.5	0.6	2.9	5.3	18.8	8.2	14.6	18.2	14.1
36 123	...	6	Yates	876	24 621	1 570	28.1	98.6	0.8	0.5	0.5	0.9	6.6	20.0	9.3	10.0	14.6	13.5
37 000	...	X	**NORTH CAROLINA**	126 161	8 049 313	X	63.8	73.1	22.1	1.6	1.8	4.7	6.7	17.7	10.0	15.1	16.0	13.5
37 001	3120	3	Alamance	1 114	130 800	410	117.4	76.5	19.2	0.7	1.2	6.8	6.4	17.4	9.9	14.3	15.6	13.2
37 003	3290	2	Alexander	674	33 603	1 297	49.9	92.7	4.9	0.5	1.2	2.5	6.9	17.6	7.9	14.9	16.1	14.2
37 005	...	9	Alleghany	608	10 677	2 387	17.6	96.5	1.4	0.8	0.2	5.0	5.2	14.2	7.4	12.2	14.0	14.7
37 007	...	6	Anson	1 377	25 275	1 555	18.4	49.9	48.8	0.7	0.7	0.8	6.5	18.7	8.6	13.8	15.2	13.5
37 009	...	9	Ashe	1 104	24 384	1 579	22.1	97.7	0.8	0.6	0.3	2.4	5.3	14.5	7.5	12.1	14.9	15.3
37 011	...	9	Avery	640	17 167	1 943	26.8	94.6	3.6	0.8	0.4	2.4	4.8	14.6	10.3	14.8	15.3	13.7
37 013	...	6	Beaufort	2 144	44 958	1 000	21.0	69.0	29.3	0.4	0.3	3.2	6.0	17.4	7.7	11.7	14.4	15.4
37 015	...	9	Bertie	1 811	19 773	1 803	10.9	36.6	62.6	0.5	0.2	1.0	6.4	19.7	7.7	11.1	15.3	13.8
37 017	...	6	Bladen	2 266	32 278	1 340	14.2	57.8	38.2	2.4	0.3	3.7	6.6	18.0	8.7	12.6	14.6	14.7
37 019	9200	3	Brunswick	2 214	73 143	685	33.0	83.2	14.7	1.2	0.5	2.7	5.5	15.7	7.0	11.6	14.1	14.5
37 021	0480	3	Buncombe	1 699	206 330	269	121.4	90.2	7.9	0.9	1.0	2.8	5.6	16.2	8.6	13.6	15.7	14.9
37 023	3290	2	Burke	1 312	89 148	582	67.9	86.7	7.0	0.7	4.2	3.6	6.2	17.8	8.9	14.1	15.6	13.8
37 025	1520	0	Cabarrus	944	131 063	408	138.8	84.1	12.5	0.6	1.2	5.1	7.1	18.7	8.1	15.5	17.0	13.4
37 027	3290	2	Caldwell	1 221	77 415	655	63.4	92.4	5.7	0.5	0.5	2.5	6.4	17.0	7.8	14.7	15.8	14.4
37 029	...	8	Camden	623	6 885	2 696	11.1	81.6	17.5	1.0	0.7	0.7	5.6	18.9	6.3	12.2	18.3	13.9
37 031	...	6	Carteret	1 346	59 383	809	44.1	91.2	7.3	0.9	1.0	1.7	4.9	15.8	6.4	11.5	15.7	15.7
37 033	...	6	Caswell	1 100	23 501	1 615	21.4	61.7	37.0	0.5	0.4	1.8	5.7	17.5	7.7	13.8	16.4	15.2
37 035	3290	2	Catawba	1 036	141 685	386	136.8	85.9	8.7	0.5	3.3	5.6	6.5	17.7	8.8	15.1	16.0	14.0
37 037	6640	2	Chatham	1 769	49 329	927	27.9	75.9	17.5	0.8	0.8	9.6	6.3	16.2	7.3	14.3	16.1	14.9
37 039	...	7	Cherokee	1 179	24 298	1 584	20.6	96.0	1.8	2.5	0.4	1.2	5.4	15.1	6.5	11.4	13.0	14.9

1. MSA = Metropolitan Statistical Area. PMSA = Primary MSA. NECMA = New England County Metropolitan Area. See Appendix A for explanation of these concepts. See Appendix B for list of metropolitan areas identified by type, with component counties. 2. County typology code from the Economic Research Service of USDA. See Appendix A for definition. 3. Dry land or land partially or temporarily covered by water. 4. Hispanic persons may be of any race.

Table B. States and Counties — **Population and Households**

	Population, 2000 (cont'd)				Population — change and components of change, 1990–2001							Households, 2000				
	Age (percent) (cont'd)				Total persons		Percent change		Components of change, 2000–2001						Percent	
STATE County	55 to 64 years	65 to 74 years	75 years and over	Percent female	2001	1990	1990–2000	2000–2001	Births	Deaths	Net migration	Number	Percent change, 1990–2000	Persons per house-hold	Female family house-holder[1]	One person
	16	17	18	19	20	21	22	23	24	25	26	27	28	29	30	31
NEW YORK—Cont'd																
Genesee	9.1	7.1	7.3	50.8	59 995	60 060	0.5	-0.6	881	699	-545	22 770	5.3	2.59	9.8	24.8
Greene	10.6	8.4	7.3	48.4	48 347	44 739	7.7	0.3	550	641	255	18 256	10.0	2.42	10.3	27.9
Hamilton	14.5	11.1	8.9	50.0	5 307	5 279	1.9	-1.3	34	82	-28	2 362	9.7	2.24	6.7	29.6
Herkimer	9.9	7.9	8.9	51.5	64 066	65 809	-2.1	-0.6	832	876	-294	25 734	3.2	2.46	10.3	27.6
Jefferson	7.4	5.8	5.5	48.2	109 535	110 943	0.7	-2.0	2 143	1 058	-3 311	40 068	5.9	2.58	10.4	24.4
Kings	8.2	6.1	5.4	53.1	2 465 286	2 300 664	7.2	0.0	51 743	23 774	-29 288	880 727	6.3	2.75	22.3	27.8
Lewis	9.2	7.7	6.1	50.3	26 820	26 796	0.6	-0.5	398	284	-233	10 040	8.5	2.66	8.4	22.6
Livingston	8.3	6.1	5.3	49.8	64 498	62 372	3.1	0.3	802	605	5	22 150	4.5	2.60	10.0	23.1
Madison	9.4	6.6	5.8	50.9	69 714	69 166	0.4	0.4	967	710	45	25 368	7.6	2.55	9.7	24.5
Monroe	8.6	6.3	6.7	51.8	733 607	713 968	3.0	-0.2	11 850	7 851	-5 610	286 512	5.4	2.47	13.4	28.6
Montgomery	9.0	8.5	10.7	52.2	49 318	51 981	-4.4	-0.8	697	746	-322	20 038	-0.7	2.42	11.6	29.5
Nassau	9.4	7.9	7.1	51.9	1 334 648	1 287 873	3.6	0.0	21 325	13 952	-7 028	447 387	3.7	2.93	10.9	18.8
New York	9.2	6.4	5.7	52.5	1 541 150	1 487 536	3.3	0.3	25 112	15 171	-5 997	738 644	3.1	2.00	12.6	48.0
Niagara	9.1	7.8	7.6	51.7	218 509	220 756	-0.4	-0.6	3 216	2 987	-1 498	87 846	3.6	2.45	12.3	28.6
Oneida	9.2	7.8	8.7	50.3	233 659	250 836	-6.1	-0.8	3 169	3 154	-1 759	90 496	-2.2	2.43	12.0	29.5
Onondaga	8.4	7.0	6.8	52.2	457 866	468 973	-2.3	-0.1	7 472	5 030	-2 778	181 153	1.8	2.46	12.9	29.4
Ontario	9.5	6.6	6.5	51.1	100 888	95 101	5.4	0.7	1 302	1 098	498	38 370	9.9	2.53	9.9	24.7
Orange	8.1	5.3	5.0	49.9	348 783	307 571	11.0	2.2	5 823	3 074	4 734	114 788	13.1	2.85	11.4	21.5
Orleans	8.6	6.2	6.2	50.4	43 853	41 846	5.6	-0.7	633	495	-448	15 363	6.5	2.65	11.2	23.7
Oswego	8.6	6.0	5.3	50.6	122 271	121 785	0.5	-0.1	1 788	1 240	-611	45 522	7.3	2.60	10.8	24.3
Otsego	9.7	7.5	7.5	51.8	61 452	60 390	2.1	-0.4	683	743	-137	23 291	7.2	2.43	9.5	27.0
Putnam	9.5	5.4	4.1	50.1	97 163	83 941	14.1	1.5	1 448	709	688	32 703	16.4	2.86	8.3	18.1
Queens	8.8	6.6	6.1	51.8	2 224 516	1 951 598	14.2	-0.2	41 603	20 968	-26 721	782 664	8.7	2.81	16.0	25.6
Rensselaer	8.8	6.9	6.6	51.0	152 582	154 429	-1.2	0.0	2 101	1 819	-165	59 894	4.0	2.46	12.0	27.9
Richmond	9.2	6.3	5.3	51.7	450 153	378 977	17.1	1.4	7 212	4 323	3 728	156 341	19.8	2.78	13.9	23.2
Rockland	10.1	6.7	5.1	51.2	288 567	265 475	8.0	0.6	5 524	2 604	-1 057	92 675	9.2	3.01	10.3	19.3
St. Lawrence	9.0	7.1	5.9	49.2	111 173	111 974	0.0	-0.7	1 414	1 238	-905	40 506	6.7	2.49	10.3	26.5
Saratoga	9.2	6.1	5.3	50.7	204 485	181 276	10.7	1.9	2 984	1 716	2 600	78 165	17.7	2.51	9.0	24.1
Schenectady	8.9	7.8	8.9	51.9	146 014	149 285	-1.8	-0.4	2 129	2 019	-596	59 684	0.8	2.38	12.3	30.6
Schoharie	9.8	7.9	7.0	50.2	31 489	31 840	-0.8	-0.3	375	348	-110	11 991	6.5	2.49	9.3	25.8
Schuyler	10.3	7.6	7.0	49.9	19 269	18 662	3.0	0.2	266	236	22	7 374	8.2	2.52	9.7	23.6
Seneca	9.6	7.9	7.2	50.0	33 486	33 683	-1.0	0.4	456	367	60	12 630	2.8	2.51	10.3	25.3
Steuben	9.8	7.9	7.2	51.0	99 171	99 088	-0.4	0.5	1 386	1 260	344	39 071	4.8	2.49	10.6	27.2
Suffolk	9.4	6.5	5.3	51.0	1 438 973	1 321 339	7.4	1.4	24 484	13 570	9 295	469 299	10.5	2.96	10.8	18.3
Sullivan	10.6	7.9	6.4	49.1	74 107	69 277	6.8	0.2	996	928	100	27 661	12.6	2.50	11.4	27.9
Tioga	9.9	7.4	5.7	50.6	51 620	52 337	-1.1	-0.3	714	456	-412	19 725	4.7	2.60	9.8	22.4
Tompkins	6.9	4.8	4.8	50.4	96 500	94 097	2.6	0.0	1 078	801	-263	36 420	9.2	2.32	8.2	32.5
Ulster	9.5	7.1	6.3	50.2	178 028	165 380	7.5	0.2	2 145	1 972	181	67 499	11.0	2.47	10.9	27.9
Warren	10.2	8.1	7.1	51.5	63 924	59 209	6.9	1.0	847	720	515	25 726	14.0	2.41	10.4	27.3
Washington	9.7	7.5	6.5	48.7	61 072	59 330	2.9	0.0	702	721	71	22 458	10.9	2.55	10.4	24.0
Wayne	9.2	6.5	5.7	50.5	93 900	89 123	5.2	0.1	1 496	933	-394	34 908	9.2	2.64	10.3	22.4
Westchester	9.4	7.2	6.7	52.2	928 888	874 866	5.6	0.6	15 962	9 463	-859	337 142	5.3	2.67	12.2	25.7
Wyoming	8.7	6.2	6.0	45.8	42 975	42 507	2.2	-1.0	524	493	-472	14 906	7.3	2.62	9.2	23.2
Yates	10.4	8.3	7.2	51.2	24 561	22 810	7.9	-0.2	389	343	-94	9 029	7.2	2.59	9.4	24.6
NORTH CAROLINA	9.0	6.6	5.4	51.0	8 186 268	6 632 448	21.4	1.7	150 843	89 957	76 874	3 132 013	24.4	2.49	12.5	25.4
Alamance	9.1	7.4	6.7	52.0	133 323	108 213	20.9	1.9	2 298	1 681	1 925	51 584	20.9	2.46	12.7	26.0
Alexander	10.5	7.0	4.9	50.2	34 034	27 544	22.0	1.3	561	367	246	13 137	27.2	2.54	9.4	21.9
Alleghany	13.0	10.8	8.4	50.7	10 763	9 590	11.3	0.8	139	182	131	4 593	18.0	2.28	7.5	27.8
Anson	9.3	7.2	7.2	50.9	25 335	23 474	7.7	0.2	494	364	-59	9 204	7.9	2.59	19.8	25.1
Ashe	12.4	9.5	8.4	50.7	24 715	22 209	9.8	1.4	361	398	370	10 411	17.7	2.31	8.4	25.8
Avery	10.7	8.7	7.1	47.2	17 395	14 867	15.5	1.3	223	268	274	6 532	18.3	2.34	9.1	26.6
Beaufort	11.6	8.9	6.9	52.3	45 224	42 283	6.3	0.6	803	698	180	18 319	13.4	2.42	13.3	25.7
Bertie	10.0	8.7	7.3	53.3	19 803	20 388	-3.0	0.2	349	351	38	7 743	4.5	2.53	20.1	27.0
Bladen	10.5	8.0	6.3	51.9	32 491	28 663	12.6	0.7	616	507	111	12 897	19.9	2.45	15.7	27.7
Brunswick	14.7	11.1	5.8	50.8	77 058	50 985	43.5	5.4	1 052	876	3 655	30 438	51.7	2.38	10.2	22.9
Buncombe	9.9	7.9	7.5	52.0	208 850	174 357	18.3	1.2	3 264	2 877	2 176	85 776	21.1	2.33	10.8	28.9
Burke	10.2	7.5	5.9	50.0	89 359	75 740	17.7	0.2	1 450	1 091	-112	34 528	18.3	2.48	11.0	25.5
Cabarrus	8.7	6.2	5.4	50.8	136 418	98 935	32.5	4.1	2 421	1 430	4 298	49 519	32.0	2.60	10.5	21.8
Caldwell	10.7	7.5	5.8	50.6	78 109	70 709	9.5	0.9	1 387	926	258	30 768	13.2	2.48	11.0	23.1
Camden	11.3	8.0	5.5	50.4	7 097	5 904	16.6	3.1	78	103	232	2 662	22.1	2.58	9.4	20.7
Carteret	12.7	10.1	7.1	50.9	59 901	52 407	13.3	0.9	782	835	591	25 204	18.7	2.31	9.6	26.1
Caswell	10.7	7.1	5.9	49.4	23 693	20 662	13.7	0.2	385	342	155	8 670	16.1	2.56	14.2	23.2
Catawba	9.5	6.8	5.7	50.7	145 071	118 412	19.7	2.4	2 506	1 583	2 470	55 533	21.5	2.51	10.9	24.6
Chatham	9.8	8.0	7.3	50.8	51 645	38 979	26.6	4.7	881	627	2 027	19 741	29.1	2.47	10.0	24.5
Cherokee	13.9	10.7	9.0	51.5	24 643	20 170	20.5	1.4	320	366	388	10 336	29.8	2.32	9.3	25.7

1. No spouse present.

Table B. States and Counties — **Vital Statistics, Health Resources, and Crime**

STATE County	Births, average 1997–1999 Total	Rate[1]	Deaths, average 1997–1999 Number Total	Infant[2]	Rate Total[1]	Infant[3]	Physicians,[4] 2000 Number	Rate[5]	Hospitals,[4] 1998 Number	Beds Number	Rate[5]	Medicare enrollees 2000	Serious crimes known to police, 2000[6] Total Number	Rate[7]
	32	33	34	35	36	37	38	39	40	41	42	43	44	45
NEW YORK—Cont'd														
Genesee	722	11.9	572	NA	9.4	NA	74	123	2	166	274	9 913	1 384	2 323
Greene	506	10.6	506	NA	10.6	NA	29	60	1	195	408	8 607	874	2 089
Hamilton	42	8.0	64	NA	12.3	NA	2	37	0	0	0	1 245	123	2 287
Herkimer	699	10.9	709	NA	11.1	NA	50	78	2	320	500	11 892	1 343	2 174
Jefferson	1 749	15.7	870	7	7.8	4.2	195	175	3	391	352	15 230	2 134	1 923
Kings	38 433	16.9	19 006	311	8.4	8.1	5 659	230	19	9 324	411	292 825	NA	NA
Lewis	360	13.1	223	NA	8.1	NA	24	89	1	189	687	4 064	262	972
Livingston	712	10.8	495	NA	7.5	NA	46	72	1	72	109	8 922	1 550	2 410
Madison	848	11.9	559	NA	7.9	NA	85	122	2	334	470	10 190	1 293	1 875
Monroe	9 809	13.7	6 189	68	8.7	7.0	2 493	339	7	2 481	346	108 967	31 856	4 372
Montgomery	612	12.1	602	NA	11.9	NA	79	159	2	381	751	11 382	841	1 692
Nassau	16 296	12.5	11 128	89	8.5	5.4	5 602	420	15	5 925	455	221 523	NA	NA
New York	19 066	12.3	12 143	112	7.8	5.9	14 006	911	18	11 672	753	211 719	288 311	3 600
Niagara	2 658	12.2	2 345	18	10.8	6.8	283	129	5	974	447	39 624	6 354	3 216
Oneida	2 707	11.7	2 534	20	11.0	7.4	485	206	4	959	416	44 932	6 399	2 718
Onondaga	6 018	13.1	4 115	46	9.0	7.6	1 583	345	4	1 674	365	72 345	16 126	3 528
Ontario	1 199	12.0	886	NA	8.9	NA	210	210	3	667	669	15 215	1 975	2 000
Orange	4 988	15.1	2 474	31	7.5	6.2	595	174	6	1 054	320	41 757	8 515	2 616
Orleans	551	12.3	391	NA	8.7	NA	40	91	1	101	227	6 189	665	1 570
Oswego	1 554	12.5	1 026	9	8.3	5.6	109	89	2	271	219	17 601	1 991	1 801
Otsego	596	9.8	597	NA	9.8	NA	220	357	2	438	721	10 622	1 032	1 730
Putnam	1 270	13.6	588	NA	6.3	NA	148	155	1	188	201	10 364	1 046	1 092
Queens	30 319	15.2	16 614	196	8.3	6.5	5 170	232	13	4 681	234	283 513	NA	NA
Rensselaer	1 813	11.9	1 454	15	9.5	8.3	242	159	3	616	403	23 785	4 874	3 195
Richmond	5 829	14.3	3 487	36	8.6	6.2	1 223	276	5	1 387	341	58 591	NA	NA
Rockland	4 200	14.9	2 028	20	7.2	4.8	866	302	2	745	265	39 662	5 936	2 070
St. Lawrence	1 228	10.8	1 045	8	9.2	6.2	148	132	5	372	327	18 177	2 625	2 345
Saratoga	2 551	12.9	1 376	10	7.0	3.9	217	108	1	227	115	26 640	3 025	1 508
Schenectady	1 790	12.3	1 610	13	11.1	7.3	371	253	2	619	425	29 110	5 240	3 575
Schoharie	320	9.9	300	NA	9.3	NA	26	82	1	70	216	5 223	555	1 757
Schuyler	217	11.4	189	NA	9.9	NA	19	99	1	173	905	3 008	420	2 185
Seneca	386	12.1	299	NA	9.4	NA	20	60	0	0	0	5 499	361	1 105
Steuben	1 209	12.3	990	8	10.1	6.9	137	139	3	651	665	17 227	1 992	2 089
Suffolk	19 310	14.1	10 849	110	7.9	5.7	3 324	234	13	4 236	309	197 592	NA	NA
Sullivan	872	12.6	761	NA	11.0	NA	92	124	2	295	427	12 715	2 221	3 003
Tioga	627	12.0	428	NA	8.2	NA	24	46	0	0	0	7 501	505	975
Tompkins	900	9.3	616	NA	6.4	NA	183	190	1	204	212	10 586	2 483	2 616
Ulster	1 954	11.7	1 585	9	9.5	4.6	300	169	3	413	248	27 036	3 847	2 164
Warren	689	11.2	592	NA	9.7	NA	166	262	1	440	718	11 190	1 772	2 896
Washington	662	11.0	559	NA	9.3	NA	52	85	1	113	187	9 581	1 054	1 866
Wayne	1 289	13.6	758	NA	8.0	NA	82	87	2	336	354	15 054	2 143	2 328
Westchester	12 366	13.7	7 505	62	8.3	5.0	4 057	439	14	3 695	412	139 369	20 490	2 416
Wyoming	477	10.8	360	NA	8.2	NA	37	85	1	262	595	6 152	1 112	2 561
Yates	329	13.5	269	NA	11.1	NA	27	110	1	217	897	4 535	283	1 149
NORTH CAROLINA	109 174	14.5	67 872	1 020	9.0	9.3	16 441	204	121	21 735	288	1 133 419	395 972	4 919
Alamance	1 647	13.8	1 241	18	10.4	11.1	172	131	1	220	184	21 754	5 496	4 264
Alexander	422	13.5	272	NA	8.7	NA	18	54	1	44	141	4 501	911	2 711
Alleghany	106	10.8	129	NA	13.1	NA	13	122	1	46	467	2 447	107	1 002
Anson	327	13.5	276	NA	11.3	NA	11	44	1	125	513	4 295	1 056	4 583
Ashe	250	10.4	287	NA	11.9	NA	21	86	1	115	479	4 978	363	1 581
Avery	176	11.2	180	NA	11.5	NA	11	64	2	115	731	3 346	125	770
Beaufort	566	12.7	524	NA	11.7	NA	64	142	2	146	328	8 601	1 559	3 468
Bertie	251	12.3	260	NA	12.7	NA	10	51	1	16	78	4 275	530	2 680
Bladen	438	14.2	372	NA	12.1	NA	19	59	1	62	202	5 422	1 479	4 582
Brunswick	801	11.7	667	NA	9.7	NA	53	72	2	100	146	13 941	2 969	4 185
Buncombe	2 395	12.3	2 126	22	10.9	9.3	620	300	2	714	366	36 463	8 485	4 125
Burke	1 087	13.2	807	10	9.8	9.5	131	147	2	228	276	13 312	2 477	2 789
Cabarrus	1 753	14.6	1 066	12	8.9	6.8	207	158	1	331	276	19 513	2 988	2 280
Caldwell	1 024	13.5	708	NA	9.3	NA	75	97	1	81	106	11 847	2 548	3 293
Camden	55	8.1	66	NA	9.8	NA	1	15	0	0	0	1 051	54	784
Carteret	674	11.3	632	NA	10.6	NA	92	155	1	117	195	10 317	2 069	3 484
Caswell	244	11.0	244	NA	11.0	NA	4	17	0	0	0	3 297	453	2 116
Catawba	1 801	13.6	1 228	14	9.3	8.0	274	193	2	459	346	20 598	6 737	4 770
Chatham	634	13.9	454	NA	10.0	NA	56	114	1	50	110	6 761	1 513	3 067
Cherokee	253	11.1	284	NA	12.5	NA	41	169	2	222	975	5 622	301	1 239

1. Per 1,000 estimated resident population, average 1997–1999. 2. Deaths of infants under 1 year old. 3. Deaths of infants under 1 year old per 1,000 live births. 4. Data subject to copyright. 5. Per 100,000 resident population as of July 1 of the year shown. 6. Data for serious crimes have not been adjusted for underreporting; this may affect comparability between geographic areas and over time. 7. Per 100,000 population estimated by the FBI.

Table B. States and Counties — Crime, Education, Money Income, and Poverty

STATE County	Serious crimes known to police, 2000[1] (cont'd) Rate[2] Violent	Rate[2] Property	Education — School enrollment and attainment, 1990 — Enrollment[3] Total	Percent private	Attainment[4] (percent) High school graduate or more	Bachelor's degree or more	Local government expenditures, fiscal 1999[5] Total current expenditures (mil dol)	Current expenditures per student (dollars)	Money income — 1989 Per capita[6] (dollars)	Households Median Dollars	Percent change, 1979–1989 (constant 1989 dollars)	Percent with $100,000 or more	Income and poverty, 1998 Median household income	Percent below poverty level All persons	Persons under 18	Persons 5–17 in families
	46	47	48	49	50	51	52	53	54	55	56	57	58	59	60	61
NEW YORK—Cont'd																
Genesee	128	2 196	15 324	12.1	77.4	14.0	96.3	8 556	12 705	30 955	4.9	1.6	39 004	10.2	15.6	15.0
Greene	366	1 723	10 571	12.3	72.8	13.4	66.4	8 775	12 722	27 469	19.8	2.4	35 287	13.5	19.3	20.9
Hamilton	130	2 157	1 121	7.1	77.3	15.1	11.1	15 511	11 682	23 195	12.7	1.6	32 165	11.4	17.6	19.9
Herkimer	261	1 914	16 331	7.8	72.6	12.9	99.1	8 189	10 543	23 075	-1.9	1.0	31 390	14.1	20.8	21.2
Jefferson	141	1 781	25 873	10.3	76.4	13.6	160.0	8 361	11 160	25 929	14.2	1.7	32 381	16.3	22.4	22.7
Kings	NA	NA	643 175	25.4	63.7	16.6	[7]NA	[7]NA	12 388	25 684	28.6	3.7	27 556	25.7	35.8	35.1
Lewis	52	920	6 648	5.9	73.6	10.5	43.3	8 486	10 455	25 599	5.5	1.4	33 767	14.3	18.7	20.8
Livingston	134	2 276	18 902	11.2	77.5	18.1	88.7	8 490	12 585	30 981	8.8	2.4	41 004	10.9	15.2	14.9
Madison	126	1 749	20 667	21.9	79.2	18.2	103.8	8 136	12 334	29 547	9.6	2.5	39 845	11.2	15.9	15.5
Monroe	284	4 088	188 654	25.9	80.1	26.3	1 109.5	8 985	16 162	35 337	4.4	4.8	41 945	12.0	20.7	19.3
Montgomery	201	1 491	11 785	11.0	70.1	10.8	70.3	8 683	11 640	24 068	2.4	1.4	31 309	15.2	24.1	24.3
Nassau	NA	NA	317 875	28.8	84.2	30.0	2 388.5	12 042	23 352	54 283	24.1	17.0	61 096	6.2	10.6	8.4
New York	945	2 655	332 012	38.6	75.3	42.2	[7]9 458.8	[7]8 818	27 862	32 262	38.4	12.9	41 590	20.0	33.6	37.7
Niagara	331	2 885	54 566	15.4	75.8	13.6	329.0	9 013	12 710	28 408	-5.0	1.6	36 599	12.5	20.1	18.8
Oneida	242	2 475	63 045	15.4	75.1	16.7	326.8	8 455	12 227	26 710	4.4	2.1	35 422	15.2	23.3	22.9
Onondaga	438	3 091	128 198	26.6	80.7	24.4	668.2	8 391	14 703	31 783	7.9	3.6	39 947	12.8	19.6	18.5
Ontario	107	1 893	24 035	18.9	81.0	19.5	156.4	8 547	14 601	33 133	9.6	3.1	42 806	9.5	14.8	14.2
Orange	304	2 313	84 728	19.6	77.2	19.5	554.8	9 068	15 198	39 198	29.8	5.2	49 401	11.6	16.6	15.9
Orleans	127	1 442	10 575	7.7	71.5	10.7	64.3	7 533	11 776	28 359	-1.9	1.5	36 566	12.3	18.1	19.1
Oswego	79	1 723	34 681	6.9	74.7	12.9	218.3	8 470	11 792	29 083	7.4	1.7	37 194	13.7	19.1	19.4
Otsego	225	1 506	18 563	14.3	77.7	19.9	85.4	8 393	11 657	25 099	14.5	2.2	33 434	13.8	19.0	19.5
Putnam	49	1 043	20 679	22.3	86.5	27.8	164.7	10 958	20 536	53 634	32.8	12.6	65 568	4.3	6.2	6.0
Queens	NA	NA	468 837	27.7	71.1	20.6	[7]NA	[7]NA	15 348	34 186	19.8	4.9	36 480	17.2	27.2	25.0
Rensselaer	313	2 882	41 951	29.9	77.7	19.5	210.8	8 942	14 031	31 958	19.4	2.8	40 584	11.6	18.3	18.2
Richmond	NA	NA	99 464	31.6	78.6	20.7	[7]NA	[7]NA	17 507	43 861	23.4	8.3	51 977	9.5	15.4	14.7
Rockland	217	1 853	75 625	34.2	83.3	33.0	495.3	12 398	20 195	52 731	22.7	15.1	59 898	10.3	17.7	16.3
St. Lawrence	203	2 142	34 891	19.9	73.1	15.1	165.2	8 759	10 346	23 799	3.9	1.3	32 418	17.5	23.1	22.8
Saratoga	131	1 377	46 244	19.2	83.0	25.2	297.5	8 542	15 644	36 635	19.3	4.1	48 375	7.3	10.9	10.3
Schenectady	379	3 196	35 063	22.5	80.7	23.0	191.6	8 675	15 378	31 569	11.3	3.6	41 992	11.0	18.5	18.6
Schoharie	82	1 675	8 954	4.9	73.7	14.4	51.4	8 892	11 333	26 077	13.2	1.5	34 777	13.0	17.9	20.1
Schuyler	104	2 081	4 350	9.0	74.2	13.6	22.2	9 373	10 825	25 712	6.0	1.1	33 543	13.3	19.4	21.1
Seneca	58	1 047	7 738	15.4	76.2	14.2	44.2	8 149	12 408	28 604	4.1	1.4	36 049	12.3	18.9	19.3
Steuben	135	1 953	24 272	9.2	75.0	14.4	170.6	8 748	11 933	25 312	0.8	1.8	35 003	15.3	22.0	22.2
Suffolk	NA	NA	347 688	17.7	82.2	23.0	2 745.8	11 532	18 481	49 128	31.1	10.8	54 008	7.6	11.9	10.1
Sullivan	411	2 592	16 233	10.0	71.2	14.4	120.7	10 722	12 567	27 582	26.7	2.6	33 958	16.5	24.5	25.0
Tioga	66	910	13 564	9.9	80.6	18.0	74.7	7 566	13 064	31 497	8.5	2.4	40 155	10.9	16.5	16.6
Tompkins	118	2 498	40 342	51.6	87.2	41.7	121.5	9 095	13 171	27 742	14.9	4.6	38 797	13.1	15.5	17.4
Ulster	209	1 955	40 410	13.7	76.6	21.6	275.0	9 614	14 921	34 033	29.4	3.6	40 425	11.6	17.3	17.4
Warren	180	2 716	14 438	14.4	78.3	19.4	96.6	8 574	14 378	30 434	24.2	3.2	37 812	12.0	18.5	17.9
Washington	359	1 507	14 495	8.9	74.0	11.6	90.7	8 351	12 221	28 660	15.9	1.4	34 441	12.9	17.8	18.8
Wayne	131	2 197	21 576	10.2	74.3	14.0	163.8	8 625	13 313	32 469	9.3	2.2	40 842	10.8	15.6	15.4
Westchester	297	2 120	213 279	32.3	81.0	35.3	1 653.0	12 200	25 584	48 405	27.1	17.8	56 865	9.1	15.2	13.9
Wyoming	260	2 301	10 427	8.1	70.3	9.7	48.8	8 099	10 552	27 515	2.5	1.3	37 453	10.5	13.5	14.1
Yates	81	1 068	5 457	20.1	73.7	15.0	25.1	7 771	11 065	24 874	9.0	1.5	33 522	14.3	20.4	23.0
NORTH CAROLINA	498	4 422	1 624 913	11.1	70.0	17.4	7 097.9	5 656	12 885	26 647	9.8	2.6	35 982	13.0	19.4	18.2
Alamance	355	3 909	23 920	18.2	67.9	14.6	101.9	5 153	13 290	27 231	3.7	2.2	36 965	9.8	16.7	13.5
Alexander	182	2 530	6 005	4.9	59.0	7.9	27.6	5 214	11 624	26 539	5.5	1.3	36 869	11.0	17.1	15.9
Alleghany	103	899	1 881	1.6	52.6	9.0	10.4	6 952	10 237	18 476	3.0	2.5	29 960	15.5	23.6	23.4
Anson	395	4 188	5 574	5.3	60.8	7.3	26.3	5 791	9 402	21 836	6.0	0.8	28 153	19.2	27.5	25.4
Ashe	91	1 489	4 420	3.5	55.6	8.1	19.9	6 033	9 545	18 951	9.0	1.3	28 407	16.3	22.5	22.8
Avery	43	727	3 648	19.8	62.2	12.4	16.9	6 634	9 729	20 403	9.3	1.5	30 005	16.3	22.6	22.9
Beaufort	454	3 014	10 145	7.3	65.9	10.8	43.9	5 753	10 722	21 738	8.2	1.9	29 535	18.9	27.9	25.4
Bertie	344	2 337	4 839	5.8	54.9	8.0	23.7	6 132	8 392	17 795	8.1	0.9	24 163	23.4	32.6	32.2
Bladen	864	3 718	7 310	4.1	56.4	7.7	34.6	5 861	9 497	19 015	4.8	0.9	27 440	21.3	32.8	27.1
Brunswick	302	3 883	10 890	4.3	69.2	10.7	60.3	6 013	11 688	23 480	8.7	1.8	36 786	14.3	21.7	21.8
Buncombe	393	3 732	38 449	13.3	74.5	19.1	173.8	5 964	13 211	25 847	9.9	2.4	36 786	12.9	20.1	18.1
Burke	135	2 654	16 414	7.1	60.1	10.6	74.2	5 212	11 604	25 879	7.8	1.4	33 631	12.4	19.6	17.2
Cabarrus	181	2 099	21 672	9.7	67.4	12.3	113.5	5 211	13 552	30 133	13.2	2.6	43 813	8.6	14.7	11.8
Caldwell	322	2 971	14 987	6.0	56.8	8.9	64.9	5 310	11 522	25 691	5.3	1.5	34 604	11.7	18.1	17.2
Camden	58	726	1 396	9.0	66.2	10.1	7.7	5 978	10 465	26 699	6.2	0.4	36 276	13.6	21.8	19.3
Carteret	226	3 259	11 371	9.9	75.5	16.2	55.3	6 531	13 227	25 811	9.9	2.4	35 359	12.4	19.2	18.8
Caswell	313	1 803	4 613	6.0	55.0	6.6	21.2	5 962	9 817	22 736	7.0	1.1	32 872	14.8	23.4	19.9
Catawba	320	4 450	27 090	10.5	66.7	14.2	123.4	5 469	13 764	29 228	7.4	2.6	40 481	9.8	16.6	13.6
Chatham	231	2 836	8 101	6.5	70.0	19.5	40.1	5 931	13 321	28 539	10.7	2.2	44 824	8.9	17.0	13.1
Cherokee	74	1 165	4 239	4.4	59.9	8.0	21.8	6 093	9 258	19 625	20.5	0.7	27 165	16.6	23.5	23.9

1. Data for serious crimes have not been adjusted for underreporting; this may affect comparability between geographic areas and over time.   2. Per 100,000 population estimated by the FBI.   3. All persons 3 years old and over enrolled in nursery school through college.   4. Persons 25 years old and over.   5. Elementary and secondary education expenditures, local government fiscal years ending between July 1, 1998 and June 30, 1999.   6. Based on population enumerated as of April 1, 1990.   7. Bronx, Kings, Queens, and Richmond Counties included with New York County.

STATE County	Total (mil dol)	Percent change, 1998–1999	Per capita[1] Dollars	Per capita[1] Rank	Wages and salaries[2] (mil dol)	Proprietor's income (mil dol)	Dividends, interest, and rent (mil dol)	Transfer payments Total (mil dol)	Government payments to individuals Total (mil dol)	Social Security (mil dol)	Medical payments (mil dol)	Income maintenance (mil dol)	Unemployment insurance (mil dol)
	62	63	64	65	66	67	68	69	70	71	72	73	74
NEW YORK—Cont'd													
Genesee	1 383	2.4	22 868	1 119	660	92	241	243	230	102	88	18	6
Greene	1 076	5.4	22 251	1 284	380	65	209	210	199	88	77	19	4
Hamilton	118	3.6	22 821	1 134	38	13	33	27	26	13	10	2	1
Herkimer	1 314	2.3	20 740	1 763	484	80	230	291	277	119	112	25	6
Jefferson	2 401	3.2	21 843	1 401	1 655	137	374	415	394	146	155	52	14
Kings	55 791	3.6	24 596	730	15 371	2 437	7 129	14 851	14 373	2 469	8 689	2 609	271
Lewis	472	2.4	17 314	2 679	187	47	85	104	98	40	38	10	4
Livingston	1 437	3.0	21 828	1 405	569	75	246	228	214	93	82	22	6
Madison	1 649	3.6	23 186	1 050	633	136	286	253	238	101	96	20	5
Monroe	21 799	3.2	30 599	191	15 877	1 259	4 346	3 363	3 213	1 180	1 365	467	55
Montgomery	1 175	3.4	23 325	1 008	525	71	219	274	263	111	114	21	5
Nassau	57 419	4.1	43 997	28	26 342	4 520	14 261	6 039	5 764	2 468	2 611	302	73
New York	126 732	9.0	81 665	1	175 032	31 972	22 658	10 771	10 444	1 995	5 940	1 539	171
Niagara	5 261	3.6	24 339	796	2 726	241	840	1 018	972	422	379	99	24
Oneida	5 492	4.2	23 910	876	3 408	324	1 052	1 145	1 096	427	464	125	16
Onondaga	12 362	3.7	27 097	410	9 225	793	2 244	1 993	1 897	762	773	217	27
Ontario	2 652	2.9	26 573	455	1 438	157	467	376	355	157	135	29	8
Orange	8 681	5.1	25 977	520	4 108	445	1 464	1 269	1 200	434	550	132	20
Orleans	859	3.7	19 090	2 260	352	61	137	165	156	68	58	18	4
Oswego	2 601	3.3	20 993	1 669	1 189	145	346	469	443	186	169	50	12
Otsego	1 334	4.4	22 011	1 366	672	126	277	254	241	101	99	20	5
Putnam	3 310	5.7	34 902	86	799	184	572	305	285	120	123	15	6
Queens	58 209	5.6	29 095	256	19 131	2 175	9 099	12 981	12 559	2 719	7 526	1 768	211
Rensselaer	3 892	3.6	25 697	556	1 695	164	695	666	635	241	278	60	11
Richmond	13 076	4.6	31 639	163	3 195	529	1 955	2 746	2 660	629	1 581	328	40
Rockland	10 573	6.4	37 227	69	4 347	912	1 974	1 195	1 136	426	543	89	19
St. Lawrence	2 140	2.5	18 967	2 289	1 225	184	349	473	449	174	178	58	14
Saratoga	5 622	5.5	28 150	312	2 112	374	946	649	607	277	232	42	12
Schenectady	4 312	3.1	29 971	212	2 475	262	973	692	662	277	285	59	9
Schoharie	676	6.8	21 105	1 638	265	48	113	129	122	50	51	11	3
Schuyler	358	5.0	18 593	2 398	121	26	59	82	78	33	32	7	2
Seneca	725	2.4	22 704	1 167	310	50	125	137	130	57	53	11	3
Steuben	2 370	6.4	24 256	816	1 574	160	380	443	423	171	160	48	10
Suffolk	46 778	4.7	33 803	115	23 486	2 655	8 902	5 613	5 322	2 163	2 340	422	91
Sullivan	1 728	4.1	24 922	682	701	189	351	384	370	131	185	34	6
Tioga	1 154	4.4	22 094	1 338	520	70	180	192	181	82	68	18	3
Tompkins	2 299	6.7	23 542	954	1 667	160	495	294	273	111	98	32	4
Ulster	4 244	5.3	25 367	602	1 841	281	872	742	707	287	311	68	11
Warren	1 636	3.3	26 623	448	1 006	163	384	263	250	115	94	22	6
Washington	1 153	3.0	19 176	2 236	518	95	201	244	231	94	97	23	5
Wayne	2 258	4.0	23 641	929	921	138	331	364	344	152	133	32	9
Westchester	46 214	5.2	51 033	7	20 039	3 495	10 462	4 393	4 202	1 530	1 955	430	55
Wyoming	831	4.5	18 807	2 343	403	65	136	152	143	63	55	12	6
Yates	485	4.2	19 750	2 070	157	46	99	99	94	44	34	9	2
NORTH CAROLINA	202 109	5.2	26 417	X	133 032	13 902	38 001	27 201	25 828	10 942	10 427	2 654	455
Alamance	3 231	7.1	26 679	442	1 943	187	654	460	438	216	170	28	9
Alexander	719	5.6	22 478	1 219	282	64	113	98	92	42	38	7	2
Alleghany	256	7.2	26 021	512	107	44	54	47	45	19	19	4	1
Anson	521	3.7	21 511	1 520	233	51	85	115	111	39	53	13	2
Ashe	520	5.6	21 423	1 543	199	88	99	111	106	41	46	13	2
Avery	379	6.1	23 946	869	162	76	72	74	72	27	34	6	1
Beaufort	942	1.7	20 859	1 712	516	59	188	206	198	79	80	26	5
Bertie	393	0.9	19 283	2 214	174	57	47	107	103	35	47	18	1
Bladen	608	-0.5	19 656	2 095	334	24	76	156	150	49	68	24	3
Brunswick	1 437	4.1	20 178	1 940	635	101	289	311	298	143	114	25	5
Buncombe	5 376	4.1	27 393	383	3 299	361	1 326	805	770	347	305	63	9
Burke	1 835	4.6	22 085	1 341	1 097	118	335	309	294	130	125	23	4
Cabarrus	3 505	8.7	28 071	329	1 785	197	618	422	399	183	171	25	5
Caldwell	1 796	6.2	23 497	964	952	131	278	276	262	118	109	20	5
Camden	145	4.0	21 115	1 631	41	9	33	25	24	10	9	2	0
Carteret	1 448	3.9	24 128	834	524	107	368	234	223	103	85	16	3
Caswell	425	2.8	18 951	2 294	107	15	69	85	81	32	34	11	1
Catawba	3 795	5.0	28 253	301	3 077	264	782	446	422	217	156	28	6
Chatham	1 397	4.7	30 046	211	453	142	401	162	154	78	60	9	2
Cherokee	426	6.3	18 384	2 445	226	35	82	123	119	49	47	11	5

1. Based on the resident population estimated as of July 1 of the year shown.   2. Includes other labor income.

Table B. States and Counties — Earnings, Social Security, and Housing

| | Earnings, 1999 | | | | | | | | | Social Security beneficiaries, December 2000 | | | Housing units, 1990 | |
STATE County	Total (mil dol)	Farm	Goods-related[1] Total	Manu-facturing	Service-related and other[2] Total	Retail trade	Finance, insur-ance, and real estate	Services	Govern-ment	Number	Rate[3]	Supple-mental Security Income recipients, December 2000	Total	Percent change, 1980–1990
	75	76	77	78	79	80	81	82	83	84	85	86	87	88
NEW YORK—Cont'd														
Genesee	752	3.4	26.2	20.4	45.3	9.7	2.5	20.9	25.2	11 446	190	1 000	22 596	6.3
Greene	445	0.4	D	9.5	D	11.6	4.0	21.9	35.1	10 156	211	1 088	25 000	17.1
Hamilton	52	0.0	17.4	4.3	44.0	15.2	2.5	20.9	38.7	1 413	263	114	8 234	16.6
Herkimer	564	1.8	D	25.0	D	11.8	3.2	19.0	25.6	13 849	215	1 703	30 799	8.0
Jefferson	1 792	0.5	D	8.9	D	9.4	2.8	17.5	48.7	17 764	159	2 802	50 519	20.2
Kings	17 808	0.0	D	7.5	D	8.4	11.9	39.9	11.0	293 440	119	144 036	873 671	-0.9
Lewis	234	2.5	D	25.9	D	9.4	1.9	12.1	30.8	4 995	185	674	13 182	13.6
Livingston	644	1.4	19.8	13.9	38.9	12.8	2.5	15.3	39.9	10 549	164	1 027	23 084	13.7
Madison	768	1.4	20.0	13.8	58.4	11.4	5.7	30.3	20.2	11 606	167	1 253	26 641	11.4
Monroe	17 136	0.1	35.6	31.5	53.4	8.0	5.8	28.5	10.9	126 414	172	17 410	285 524	8.0
Montgomery	597	1.1	D	24.4	D	10.1	4.1	28.1	17.1	12 924	260	1 448	21 851	3.1
Nassau	30 861	0.0	D	7.1	D	10.2	13.6	36.1	13.7	242 129	181	16 540	446 292	2.8
New York	207 004	0.0	7.7	6.4	81.1	3.5	37.3	31.5	11.2	214 661	140	77 914	785 127	4.0
Niagara	2 966	0.6	D	33.6	D	10.1	3.0	19.9	18.1	45 982	209	4 860	90 385	6.1
Oneida	3 732	0.4	18.2	14.5	56.9	10.5	8.0	29.1	24.4	50 834	216	7 426	101 251	5.7
Onondaga	10 019	0.1	24.5	19.4	60.7	8.6	8.4	27.4	14.7	83 434	182	11 128	190 878	7.8
Ontario	1 594	0.8	30.2	21.1	48.6	13.2	3.7	21.8	20.3	18 091	181	1 665	38 947	14.3
Orange	4 553	0.5	14.6	9.6	56.6	11.8	5.2	24.6	28.3	49 656	145	6 266	110 814	18.8
Orleans	413	5.6	19.5	14.0	34.5	8.2	2.3	16.3	40.3	7 661	173	907	16 345	8.7
Oswego	1 334	0.7	D	21.5	D	9.8	2.2	16.6	28.0	21 694	177	2 897	48 548	13.2
Otsego	799	0.8	D	10.3	D	11.8	7.5	35.9	19.5	12 114	196	1 463	26 385	10.5
Putnam	983	0.1	D	12.3	D	8.6	7.5	32.2	17.8	12 622	132	744	31 898	14.5
Queens	21 306	0.0	D	8.6	D	8.5	6.9	31.2	9.0	296 122	133	74 094	752 690	1.7
Rensselaer	1 859	0.2	19.1	10.8	58.7	9.9	4.7	34.7	22.1	27 257	179	3 167	62 591	9.1
Richmond	3 724	0.0	11.8	2.6	78.1	10.7	8.5	44.3	10.1	68 492	154	10 950	139 726	17.4
Rockland	5 259	0.0	D	12.6	D	8.8	9.6	30.9	17.1	44 794	156	5 120	88 264	10.1
St. Lawrence	1 409	1.1	27.2	21.0	41.4	10.2	2.4	20.7	30.4	20 911	187	3 745	47 521	8.8
Saratoga	2 487	0.4	D	15.3	D	11.9	8.1	27.6	20.2	30 877	154	2 568	75 105	24.4
Schenectady	2 737	0.1	28.8	22.9	56.8	9.5	4.1	35.4	14.3	30 628	209	3 777	62 769	5.4
Schoharie	312	2.3	D	8.1	D	15.1	5.9	15.0	36.0	6 014	190	744	14 431	14.1
Schuyler	147	0.8	23.2	17.9	49.2	13.1	2.1	25.1	26.8	3 945	205	494	8 472	12.1
Seneca	360	1.5	29.8	25.0	44.5	11.8	2.7	17.4	24.1	6 782	203	739	14 314	7.2
Steuben	1 734	0.7	D	44.8	D	7.3	4.1	18.3	16.9	19 928	202	2 881	43 019	6.2
Suffolk	26 141	0.2	19.7	13.1	60.8	9.4	8.3	29.0	19.3	232 533	164	21 670	481 317	11.5
Sullivan	890	0.1	8.1	2.9	65.3	9.6	10.0	28.6	26.5	15 414	208	2 731	41 814	-8.8
Tioga	590	1.2	D	52.2	D	6.7	2.0	11.8	15.5	9 521	184	964	20 254	12.6
Tompkins	1 827	0.5	13.8	10.6	72.8	7.6	3.2	55.2	12.9	12 301	127	1 544	35 338	14.0
Ulster	2 122	0.9	18.1	13.1	56.2	11.7	5.6	29.0	24.9	32 257	181	4 274	71 716	3.5
Warren	1 169	0.0	D	15.5	D	13.5	7.6	35.0	13.5	13 211	209	1 521	31 737	18.3
Washington	613	2.8	32.3	25.8	32.9	8.2	1.8	15.4	31.9	10 952	179	1 469	24 216	10.5
Wayne	1 059	3.6	36.8	31.2	36.2	9.3	2.2	16.9	23.4	17 656	188	2 034	35 188	9.6
Westchester	23 534	0.0	20.0	13.7	65.9	7.3	12.6	32.8	14.1	151 967	165	14 742	336 727	6.3
Wyoming	468	6.9	23.2	18.2	35.0	9.3	3.7	13.0	34.9	7 330	169	671	15 848	5.1
Yates	202	3.1	D	15.4	D	12.5	3.2	25.2	19.5	5 160	210	567	11 629	8.1
NORTH CAROLINA	146 934	1.4	28.4	21.4	52.5	9.4	7.1	23.5	17.7	1 351 121	168	191 137	2 818 193	23.9
Alamance	2 130	0.3	D	29.2	D	10.6	5.6	28.3	9.2	24 910	190	2 317	45 312	18.7
Alexander	346	6.9	54.5	49.1	27.1	7.4	1.9	12.2	11.6	5 418	161	527	11 197	19.3
Alleghany	150	19.1	D	27.4	D	6.9	2.8	16.3	11.5	2 649	248	359	5 344	14.4
Anson	284	10.1	34.9	29.2	31.2	6.9	1.5	11.6	23.8	5 105	202	1 018	9 255	2.0
Ashe	287	14.0	D	28.9	D	9.2	3.2	14.3	11.7	5 825	239	999	11 119	16.7
Avery	238	13.5	D	14.9	D	10.4	4.2	26.3	13.6	3 568	208	514	8 923	26.1
Beaufort	575	-0.3	36.6	28.7	47.2	9.8	2.9	20.6	16.5	10 373	231	1 898	19 598	14.1
Bertie	231	21.3	35.8	33.3	26.5	4.6	1.3	11.1	16.4	5 224	264	1 533	8 331	5.4
Bladen	358	1.2	48.0	44.1	30.1	6.7	1.6	12.2	20.6	7 078	219	1 910	12 685	11.0
Brunswick	737	0.1	D	16.6	D	10.6	6.5	19.3	17.4	17 615	241	1 872	37 114	72.2
Buncombe	3 660	1.1	24.5	17.1	58.7	11.2	4.8	31.5	15.7	42 039	204	4 433	77 951	17.9
Burke	1 214	3.0	D	41.2	D	7.8	1.9	16.9	21.3	15 976	179	1 812	31 575	14.7
Cabarrus	1 982	0.4	36.2	26.5	47.2	11.1	4.3	20.7	16.3	21 061	161	1 781	39 713	22.3
Caldwell	1 083	2.9	52.0	45.5	34.1	8.3	1.8	15.3	11.0	14 525	188	1 352	29 454	15.2
Camden	51	1.5	25.0	3.2	D	10.0	D	24.5	21.6	1 400	203	134	2 466	14.8
Carteret	632	0.2	D	7.1	D	17.8	7.1	22.8	24.2	12 894	217	1 100	34 576	45.6
Caswell	121	1.8	D	20.5	D	5.7	1.9	17.1	39.9	4 390	187	790	8 254	7.8
Catawba	3 341	0.4	D	42.2	D	9.4	2.7	9.1	9.1	25 111	177	2 012	49 192	20.8
Chatham	595	10.0	43.7	34.9	35.3	7.3	2.3	18.3	11.0	9 801	199	706	16 642	29.0
Cherokee	260	1.6	D	25.6	D	13.0	3.7	24.8	17.1	6 546	269	968	10 319	20.9

1. Covers mining, construction, and manufacturing. 2. Covers private sector earnings in agricultural services, forestry, and fisheries; transportation and public utilities; wholesale trade; retail trade; finance, insurance, and real estate; and services. 3. Per 1,000 resident population estimated as of July 1 of the year shown.

Table B. States and Counties — **Housing, Labor Force, and Employment**

STATE County	Housing units, 1990 (cont'd)								Civilian labor force, 2001				Civilian employment, 1990[5]		
	Occupied units										Unemployment			Percent	
			Owner-occupied			Renter-occupied									
				Owner cost as a percent of income											
	Total	Percent	Median value[1]	With a mortgage	Without a mortgage	Median rent[2]	Rent as percent of income	Sub-standard units[3] (percent)	Total	Percent change, 2000–2001	Total	Rate[4]	Total	Professional, managerial, and technical	Precision production, craft, and repair
	89	90	91	92	93	94	95	96	97	98	99	100	101	102	103
NEW YORK—Cont'd															
Genesee	21 614	72.8	65 800	20.5	13.6	402	24.5	1.8	30 708	-1.9	1 544	5.0	28 880	24.6	13.4
Greene	16 596	72.9	91 700	22.2	14.5	421	27.1	2.0	20 765	-1.9	914	4.4	18 756	25.3	13.7
Hamilton	2 153	77.5	71 800	20.1	13.2	351	23.5	3.4	2 378	-3.8	128	5.4	2 230	26.5	17.4
Herkimer	24 936	71.4	54 400	17.2	14.4	316	26.7	2.1	29 778	-3.1	1 404	4.7	27 558	23.3	13.3
Jefferson	37 851	59.3	59 400	20.0	14.1	400	26.3	2.6	42 044	-2.3	3 413	8.1	40 821	26.3	12.5
Kings	828 199	25.9	196 100	21.8	14.4	477	26.8	14.0	977 247	-1.7	65 898	6.7	929 335	28.8	8.3
Lewis	9 253	76.3	49 800	17.3	13.2	358	28.4	3.2	11 734	-2.8	1 009	8.6	11 035	21.1	12.6
Livingston	21 197	73.3	72 800	20.7	14.0	412	25.7	1.6	33 220	-2.0	1 513	4.6	29 942	27.2	13.4
Madison	23 567	74.3	69 300	20.5	14.5	398	26.9	2.2	34 711	-1.0	1 735	5.0	32 626	27.6	13.2
Monroe	271 944	65.1	90 700	21.1	13.7	478	28.4	1.6	370 369	-1.4	16 193	4.4	353 883	36.0	10.3
Montgomery	20 185	66.3	61 600	19.6	14.4	341	24.7	2.4	22 869	-0.9	1 304	5.7	22 264	22.8	12.2
Nassau	431 515	80.4	209 500	23.1	16.0	749	27.7	2.8	681 139	-0.8	20 925	3.1	661 486	37.6	8.7
New York	716 422	17.9	487 300	19.7	12.8	513	24.0	10.8	849 675	-0.8	50 606	6.0	770 084	50.6	3.4
Niagara	84 809	68.1	62 700	19.2	14.2	362	27.6	1.5	104 680	-1.6	6 894	6.6	100 560	24.8	13.3
Oneida	92 562	65.2	72 300	18.7	13.7	373	27.0	2.0	108 992	-2.1	4 982	4.6	106 191	29.3	11.0
Onondaga	177 898	63.5	81 000	20.6	13.8	440	26.9	1.8	227 641	-1.1	9 474	4.2	228 180	34.5	9.4
Ontario	34 929	73.3	78 300	21.1	13.2	437	25.8	1.7	51 908	-1.7	2 209	4.3	47 221	30.3	12.4
Orange	101 506	67.5	141 700	23.3	15.5	595	29.0	3.5	156 899	-0.2	5 711	3.6	141 415	31.1	12.1
Orleans	14 428	74.4	56 900	20.4	13.7	388	26.1	2.6	20 409	-1.8	1 126	5.5	17 869	20.8	14.5
Oswego	42 434	73.0	65 100	17.7	13.4	392	28.0	2.7	55 451	-1.4	3 585	6.5	51 881	24.0	15.6
Otsego	21 725	73.0	67 800	20.6	14.3	380	29.3	2.1	30 965	-1.0	1 320	4.3	27 007	29.8	10.5
Putnam	28 094	81.9	195 000	24.0	14.7	765	27.7	1.5	54 785	2.0	1 465	2.7	45 002	35.8	12.2
Queens	720 149	42.4	191 000	21.8	14.0	560	25.3	11.7	1 008 464	-1.8	51 031	5.1	938 996	29.3	9.1
Rensselaer	57 612	63.9	93 200	20.3	13.1	421	24.0	2.1	77 786	-0.9	2 927	3.8	76 367	30.9	10.8
Richmond	130 519	63.7	186 300	21.6	13.7	578	26.0	3.9	201 965	-1.7	9 691	4.8	177 265	32.6	9.6
Rockland	84 874	72.1	217 100	22.9	15.0	708	28.0	4.7	143 229	-0.8	4 480	3.1	136 170	40.4	9.1
St. Lawrence	37 964	68.8	44 100	16.5	13.1	331	28.2	2.5	49 284	-2.2	3 732	7.6	44 157	26.9	11.2
Saratoga	66 425	72.3	107 500	20.6	12.9	501	25.3	1.6	102 991	-1.2	3 106	3.0	90 694	35.1	10.3
Schenectady	59 181	65.7	94 000	20.6	13.6	452	27.1	1.3	70 260	-1.3	2 128	3.0	70 726	34.1	10.0
Schoharie	11 257	74.1	73 600	20.3	14.4	392	26.2	3.4	14 697	-1.5	621	4.2	13 998	25.7	12.8
Schuyler	6 818	77.3	48 500	19.6	13.5	344	26.4	3.7	8 641	-1.0	576	6.7	8 177	24.0	12.8
Seneca	12 285	74.3	57 500	19.5	13.9	396	26.4	2.2	14 924	-2.6	657	4.4	15 205	27.1	14.5
Steuben	37 299	73.1	46 200	17.4	13.0	341	26.1	2.5	48 972	0.8	2 814	5.7	43 056	26.9	13.2
Suffolk	424 719	80.1	165 900	23.9	16.7	802	30.4	2.5	710 574	-0.8	24 872	3.5	665 182	32.5	12.0
Sullivan	24 576	68.7	93 400	22.6	15.4	459	29.6	4.4	30 240	-1.7	1 484	4.9	29 816	27.2	12.3
Tioga	18 838	78.8	72 800	19.9	12.9	382	27.4	1.9	25 762	-0.7	1 082	4.2	24 636	33.2	14.1
Tompkins	33 338	55.3	94 700	21.3	12.9	489	33.6	2.8	51 137	0.3	1 344	2.6	46 056	44.4	8.0
Ulster	60 807	69.2	114 300	21.5	14.0	529	27.4	2.5	80 479	-1.6	2 831	3.5	80 213	34.7	11.8
Warren	22 559	69.3	91 200	20.7	13.7	452	26.6	1.6	30 488	-1.9	1 461	4.8	27 380	30.3	11.9
Washington	20 256	73.8	70 200	20.3	13.7	407	28.3	2.6	27 472	-1.8	1 074	3.9	25 490	21.5	13.1
Wayne	31 977	76.7	70 700	20.4	14.3	410	27.0	1.8	48 427	-1.1	2 553	5.3	42 674	25.4	15.2
Westchester	320 030	59.7	283 500	23.0	15.5	600	25.8	4.4	443 595	-0.5	15 336	3.5	445 942	42.0	8.2
Wyoming	13 897	75.1	52 500	19.5	13.9	354	25.3	1.6	20 055	-1.6	1 085	5.4	18 167	20.7	14.7
Yates	8 419	76.5	55 500	20.8	14.1	333	27.4	3.0	13 605	0.1	474	3.5	10 215	24.5	14.3
NORTH CAROLINA	2 517 026	68.0	65 800	20.5	12.9	382	24.4	3.9	3 994 789	0.9	221 300	5.5	3 238 414	25.7	13.3
Alamance	42 652	71.8	65 300	19.3	12.6	381	23.9	2.8	66 498	0.0	3 795	5.7	57 514	22.9	15.0
Alexander	10 331	82.3	58 100	18.6	11.7	312	22.4	4.5	17 961	2.9	1 115	6.2	15 084	14.9	16.8
Alleghany	3 894	80.0	48 300	21.9	12.3	275	25.5	3.5	5 891	2.3	503	8.5	4 510	17.7	13.1
Anson	8 531	75.5	41 600	18.6	14.4	296	23.3	8.1	10 567	3.1	1 104	10.4	10 801	14.2	14.1
Ashe	8 848	82.7	57 600	21.8	12.4	265	24.2	4.9	11 886	3.6	1 102	9.3	10 341	14.9	16.8
Avery	5 520	81.0	55 100	18.7	12.8	293	22.4	4.0	8 066	-0.1	368	4.6	6 629	21.4	14.7
Beaufort	16 157	74.1	52 600	19.9	13.6	289	28.3	6.1	19 595	0.9	1 883	9.6	19 187	21.0	15.2
Bertie	7 412	74.2	39 100	20.2	14.0	229	24.0	13.1	8 809	2.1	756	8.6	8 269	15.0	15.3
Bladen	10 760	77.5	41 000	21.8	15.0	245	24.2	6.1	20 021	3.1	1 479	7.4	12 109	17.7	15.2
Brunswick	20 069	81.5	70 600	22.0	12.7	378	26.6	3.7	34 350	0.6	1 844	5.4	22 310	20.4	16.6
Buncombe	70 802	70.3	64 400	20.3	13.0	372	24.9	2.4	101 947	-0.4	3 698	3.6	85 640	28.0	13.1
Burke	29 184	74.8	52 800	18.3	12.1	326	20.1	3.4	44 462	2.4	2 949	6.6	39 339	21.5	16.8
Cabarrus	37 515	73.7	65 500	18.4	12.6	370	22.3	3.0	70 047	1.2	3 359	4.8	51 808	23.7	15.2
Caldwell	27 172	74.8	51 600	18.5	12.3	320	21.9	3.7	42 119	3.4	2 820	6.7	37 802	17.0	16.8
Camden	2 180	80.9	59 400	23.2	12.6	242	22.2	8.2	3 240	-0.6	108	3.3	2 655	21.2	20.9
Carteret	21 238	74.2	73 100	22.7	12.3	385	25.3	2.1	29 099	0.2	1 423	4.9	23 837	26.8	14.3
Caswell	7 468	78.5	47 300	18.4	13.3	250	23.5	6.0	12 839	0.3	694	5.4	9 633	13.8	15.9
Catawba	45 700	72.8	62 400	18.5	11.8	371	20.9	2.5	78 050	3.6	5 212	6.7	66 768	19.7	14.0
Chatham	15 293	77.1	63 600	20.6	12.3	399	24.8	4.1	27 024	1.4	864	3.2	20 878	24.6	14.8
Cherokee	7 966	81.0	52 900	20.8	13.0	266	26.7	3.9	11 511	-0.2	937	8.1	8 317	18.2	17.7

1. Specified owner-occupied units.　2. Specified renter-occupied units.　3. Overcrowded or lacking complete plumbing facilities.　4. Percent of civilian labor force.　5. Persons 16 years and older.

Table B. States and Counties — Nonfarm Employment and Agriculture

	Private nonfarm establishments, employment and payroll, 1999									Agriculture, 1997			
	Employment						Annual payroll		Farms			Farm operators
											Percent with—		
STATE County	Number of establishments	Total	Health Care and Social Assistance	Manufacturing	Retail trade	Finance and Insurance	Professional Scientific and Technical Services	Total (mil dol)	Average per employee (dollars)	Number	Less than 50 acres	500 acres and over	Whose principal occupation is farming (percent)
	104	105	106	107	108	109	110	111	112	113	114	115	116
NEW YORK—Cont'd													
Genesee	1 350	16 618	2 564	3 907	2 453	367	349	413	24 823	516	28.7	15.5	58.1
Greene	1 117	9 791	784	749	2 334	413	381	188	19 211	244	24.2	10.7	46.7
Hamilton	204	691	51	24	D	D	4	15	21 593	13	61.5	0.0	30.8
Herkimer	1 197	13 508	2 210	4 415	2 122	385	209	310	22 925	583	15.6	11.8	67.6
Jefferson	2 323	26 297	5 295	3 713	5 567	845	668	641	24 357	916	12.9	17.4	62.2
Kings	37 436	421 678	132 027	44 679	47 496	13 718	11 701	12 089	28 668	8	100.0	0.0	25.0
Lewis	544	4 781	778	1 598	752	105	99	114	23 800	623	9.5	12.8	72.4
Livingston	1 217	12 335	1 475	2 346	2 687	319	370	267	21 607	625	21.8	17.9	54.9
Madison	1 354	19 365	2 849	2 900	2 768	476	662	455	23 496	692	16.8	14.2	67.6
Monroe	16 666	367 103	50 770	72 961	42 561	13 846	17 853	12 660	34 487	480	46.7	12.3	52.5
Montgomery	1 156	15 527	3 594	4 775	2 297	598	279	364	23 421	542	18.1	11.8	67.5
Nassau	46 686	543 465	89 819	36 787	82 278	45 980	39 095	19 590	36 046	55	83.6	0.0	49.1
New York	105 670	2 001 945	203 027	70 559	108 137	341 464	271 645	133 503	66 687	2	100.0	0.0	100.0
Niagara	4 547	65 542	9 506	17 223	10 863	1 368	2 293	1 869	28 517	687	39.9	7.7	49.5
Oneida	4 969	85 608	15 672	14 861	12 951	7 608	2 822	2 083	24 332	928	18.8	11.2	63.8
Onondaga	11 652	227 818	30 556	33 015	29 497	12 912	12 022	6 939	30 458	602	33.1	12.6	58.6
Ontario	2 551	38 556	5 974	7 622	7 659	923	1 191	1 041	27 012	692	28.6	16.2	56.5
Orange	7 922	91 214	14 526	9 373	18 031	4 220	3 830	2 475	27 139	624	38.5	5.0	69.7
Orleans	701	7 189	1 446	1 837	1 327	231	65	149	20 783	456	29.6	15.4	58.3
Oswego	2 025	24 585	3 698	5 279	4 477	688	573	672	27 319	605	25.1	4.8	52.1
Otsego	1 361	17 698	4 477	1 357	3 087	1 217	524	414	23 381	865	13.9	11.8	63.6
Putnam	2 548	17 985	3 357	1 481	2 972	525	966	544	30 221	48	54.2	0.0	33.3
Queens	35 765	454 941	84 391	47 671	49 019	11 797	11 160	14 550	31 983	2	100.0	0.0	0.0
Rensselaer	2 721	42 024	8 218	4 872	5 728	1 400	2 984	1 115	26 525	459	26.8	9.8	50.5
Richmond	7 211	82 844	25 263	2 140	14 072	2 772	3 530	2 360	28 493	7	100.0	0.0	42.9
Rockland	8 419	99 685	18 585	9 731	13 785	4 267	5 242	3 186	31 965	21	81.0	0.0	42.9
St. Lawrence	2 126	29 202	5 430	5 045	5 030	811	646	709	24 292	1 363	10.3	14.9	59.9
Saratoga	4 042	53 131	5 816	7 198	9 881	4 769	2 349	1 392	26 209	472	36.9	6.6	49.8
Schenectady	2 977	48 873	10 406	5 209	7 611	1 686	3 781	1 565	32 029	151	33.1	1.3	39.1
Schoharie	573	5 703	821	993	1 305	278	208	127	22 263	518	21.2	9.5	60.0
Schuyler	341	2 981	733	661	494	78	59	70	23 405	318	19.5	6.3	50.9
Seneca	666	7 356	940	1 864	1 656	164	91	189	25 698	413	24.0	16.0	62.5
Steuben	1 784	30 352	5 091	7 467	3 998	945	1 164	1 133	37 344	1 295	14.1	13.7	53.9
Suffolk	42 477	499 811	73 178	67 237	70 418	21 973	34 020	16 969	33 950	606	71.6	2.3	67.0
Sullivan	1 922	17 489	3 671	597	2 821	1 858	486	432	24 715	311	24.8	8.4	62.4
Tioga	809	11 163	858	5 471	1 262	219	518	372	33 293	497	18.7	9.7	60.8
Tompkins	2 106	42 141	3 477	4 186	4 530	912	1 875	1 076	25 524	447	30.0	11.4	51.7
Ulster	4 320	45 534	7 636	6 414	8 694	2 996	2 303	1 091	23 957	409	38.4	5.1	57.2
Warren	2 313	31 855	4 700	3 856	5 455	1 509	987	854	26 816	58	37.9	5.2	41.4
Washington	1 062	9 945	1 403	3 660	1 753	202	170	252	25 359	738	18.0	14.8	64.8
Wayne	1 648	22 568	2 637	7 186	3 325	473	512	565	25 027	840	31.2	8.8	59.3
Westchester	30 452	375 959	68 362	18 355	45 828	20 027	23 257	16 299	43 353	91	60.4	3.3	47.3
Wyoming	783	8 578	1 386	2 495	1 553	361	254	188	21 907	702	19.8	13.4	63.7
Yates	508	5 168	988	726	810	91	136	100	19 440	657	19.8	4.3	64.5
NORTH CAROLINA	201 706	3 324 155	383 050	754 669	435 977	138 834	137 948	92 842	27 929	49 406	39.6	8.2	49.3
Alamance	3 284	57 465	5 864	20 486	7 686	1 345	1 203	1 458	25 378	731	34.3	4.5	45.6
Alexander	590	8 934	525	5 331	1 042	127	137	195	21 860	565	41.9	2.8	48.5
Alleghany	284	3 261	491	1 400	333	54	D	63	19 368	545	38.3	7.2	42.0
Anson	454	5 989	313	2 631	707	86	91	142	23 765	442	26.0	8.4	50.0
Ashe	524	5 949	815	2 159	868	126	57	120	20 111	1 043	48.7	3.0	40.7
Avery	576	6 197	1 351	859	817	60	106	121	19 557	429	59.0	0.7	42.2
Beaufort	1 134	15 051	1 924	4 713	2 457	400	621	338	22 475	385	27.3	23.4	66.8
Bertie	384	5 608	888	2 772	461	75	55	106	18 821	371	25.9	19.9	70.6
Bladen	528	10 551	1 074	6 315	928	125	137	214	20 250	553	34.7	13.4	54.6
Brunswick	1 691	16 996	1 551	2 620	2 672	347	438	421	24 774	213	44.6	7.0	53.1
Buncombe	6 311	94 730	16 446	17 624	14 332	2 682	2 978	2 347	24 773	1 009	59.3	2.3	39.6
Burke	1 564	32 780	3 555	16 800	3 572	373	504	780	23 803	354	55.6	1.7	35.6
Cabarrus	3 075	48 901	5 916	12 972	7 573	1 031	1 336	1 365	27 908	481	34.1	4.4	38.3
Caldwell	1 543	29 324	2 375	14 689	3 210	430	343	715	24 377	331	42.9	3.6	34.7
Camden	111	557	D	D	D	11	D	9	16 223	76	27.6	39.5	69.7
Carteret	1 912	17 300	2 532	1 554	3 775	448	511	324	18 716	101	47.5	7.9	58.4
Caswell	230	1 604	295	315	276	D	D	28	17 691	564	24.6	13.8	51.2
Catawba	4 390	93 103	7 498	42 179	10 135	1 675	1 406	2 490	26 741	596	40.6	3.7	39.8
Chatham	958	13 284	1 453	6 700	1 422	185	246	304	22 858	956	39.0	2.5	44.0
Cherokee	585	9 488	1 147	4 697	1 313	195	232	200	21 107	243	50.6	3.7	41.6

STATE County	Agriculture, 1997 (cont'd)															
	Land in farms					Value of land and buildings			Value of products sold				Percent of farms with sales of —			
			Acres								Percent from —					
	Acreage (1,000)	Percent change, 1992–1997	Average size of farm	Total irrigated (1,000)	Total cropland (1,000)	Average per farm ($1,000)	Average per acre (dollars)	Value of machinery and equipment average per farm ($1,000)	Total (mil dol)	Average per farm (dollars)	Crops	Livestock and poultry products	$10,000 or more	$100,000 or more	Percent of land owned by fed. gov. 1997	Water consumption 1995 (mil gal/day)
	117	118	119	120	121	122	123	124	125	126	127	128	129	130	131	132
NEW YORK—Cont'd																
Genesee	171	-0.7	331	5	143	342	1 085	103	110	212 430	43.9	56.1	58.5	26.2	1.6	11.2
Greene	49	6.0	200	0	25	282	1 352	46	9	35 988	36.4	63.6	40.6	9.8	0.0	9.5
Hamilton	1	0.0	61	0	D	126	2 083	34	0	6 065	89.9	10.1	15.4	0.0	0.0	1.0
Herkimer	142	-13.0	243	0	90	207	876	59	46	78 600	7.9	92.1	61.9	27.8	0.0	16.3
Jefferson	291	-3.3	318	0	194	219	711	66	77	84 144	9.2	90.8	57.2	25.3	10.9	30.1
Kings	0	0.0	1	0	0	102	102 188	16	0	46 719	100.0	0.0	62.5	12.5	5.4	25.0
Lewis	180	6.0	288	0	102	187	646	68	62	99 015	5.1	94.9	73.5	41.9	2.3	7.4
Livingston	197	-3.7	316	1	154	334	1 091	95	73	116 698	36.9	63.1	49.0	21.9	0.0	12.7
Madison	186	-5.1	269	0	121	238	953	64	66	94 928	13.4	86.6	64.3	31.1	0.1	11.4
Monroe	103	-6.3	215	3	90	402	1 998	61	48	99 904	79.8	20.2	53.5	22.7	0.0	344.2
Montgomery	135	-2.9	249	0	105	215	832	64	49	89 894	16.0	84.0	62.0	28.0	0.0	15.3
Nassau	1	-30.5	25	0	1	994	39 340	47	3	56 716	91.7	8.3	60.0	14.5	0.3	216.0
New York	D	D	D	D	D	D	D	D	D	D	100.0	100.0	100.0	100.0	1.0	81.8
Niagara	127	-5.7	185	2	112	226	1 222	69	58	84 026	66.1	33.9	49.1	15.1	0.4	434.2
Oneida	216	-11.1	233	0	139	239	1 032	54	74	79 802	21.5	78.5	60.6	27.3	0.6	39.0
Onondaga	147	1.5	244	1	112	297	1 243	74	71	117 859	29.4	70.6	55.3	22.8	0.3	169.5
Ontario	186	2.2	269	1	154	388	1 441	83	78	112 692	48.4	51.6	58.1	21.4	0.0	17.9
Orange	95	-8.0	152	5	66	576	3 819	76	70	111 934	63.6	36.4	69.9	29.6	3.3	1 368.8
Orleans	143	7.0	314	2	122	326	1 076	91	62	136 246	85.5	14.5	53.1	25.4	2.1	4.4
Oswego	103	-8.4	169	1	59	186	1 174	52	31	51 991	56.6	43.4	44.6	13.9	0.0	1 171.4
Otsego	207	-5.1	239	0	116	232	923	51	52	59 667	8.6	91.4	50.6	21.5	0.0	9.7
Putnam	3	-14.2	72	0	2	478	6 682	35	3	60 997	96.9	3.1	47.9	12.5	0.1	131.2
Queens	D	D	D	D	D	D	D	D	D	D	D	D	50.0	0.0	4.0	44.5
Rensselaer	99	6.4	216	1	59	407	1 813	51	29	62 528	33.5	66.5	45.3	15.5	0.0	37.7
Richmond	0	0.0	4	0	D	625	150 764	43	0	67 486	D	D	71.4	28.6	3.3	2.8
Rockland	1	-44.0	27	0	0	1 392	52 106	56	2	112 448	D	D	47.6	28.6	0.0	46.7
St. Lawrence	396	-0.1	291	0	220	192	666	48	89	65 354	7.5	92.5	54.4	19.4	0.0	21.0
Saratoga	73	4.2	155	0	46	368	2 429	52	30	63 252	29.6	70.4	44.3	11.7	1.2	20.4
Schenectady	18	-4.4	120	0	11	272	2 369	35	6	40 447	71.8	28.2	27.2	7.3	0.9	31.1
Schoharie	111	-6.1	214	1	70	231	1 089	40	27	52 071	21.7	78.3	48.5	18.0	0.0	130.6
Schuyler	65	0.4	205	0	37	203	1 056	42	14	44 133	24.8	75.2	40.9	11.0	4.9	4.1
Seneca	117	2.1	284	0	97	314	1 326	60	41	99 440	49.4	50.6	66.6	28.1	8.0	4.8
Steuben	349	-3.9	269	3	217	200	762	50	79	60 745	30.2	69.8	48.7	16.7	0.1	65.1
Suffolk	36	2.5	59	16	30	642	10 648	72	168	276 993	92.8	7.2	71.9	35.5	1.0	174.1
Sullivan	58	3.7	187	0	35	380	1 861	62	23	75 126	9.1	90.9	49.8	16.7	0.1	150.8
Tioga	109	-4.9	220	1	63	182	854	43	28	55 405	11.7	88.3	46.5	17.1	0.0	8.9
Tompkins	95	3.8	214	0	64	348	1 419	69	48	106 372	16.2	83.8	50.1	19.2	0.0	260.2
Ulster	69	-1.4	169	5	38	536	3 136	53	42	103 368	87.5	12.5	47.9	15.9	0.1	481.9
Warren	9	53.1	158	0	2	299	1 887	45	2	37 581	61.1	38.9	36.2	12.1	0.0	13.8
Washington	195	-5.4	264	1	123	320	1 234	62	78	105 073	13.1	86.9	60.4	27.8	0.0	10.5
Wayne	167	-4.5	199	2	125	311	1 595	74	108	128 055	66.0	34.0	58.8	26.7	0.0	483.3
Westchester	8	25.5	83	0	3	690	8 342	60	11	116 135	69.6	30.4	59.3	20.9	0.0	365.6
Wyoming	195	-7.2	278	2	136	292	1 099	93	135	191 835	10.0	90.0	59.0	34.6	0.0	10.6
Yates	105	2.7	159	1	77	246	1 477	54	40	61 277	48.1	51.9	64.7	19.0	0.0	112.4
NORTH CAROLINA	9 122	2.1	185	156	5 608	376	2 081	49	7 677	155 376	33.8	66.2	46.2	20.5	7.4	7 730.2
Alamance	108	6.7	147	2	59	340	2 402	42	35	47 337	37.7	62.3	38.0	12.7	0.0	27.6
Alexander	60	12.9	106	0	35	218	2 322	26	47	82 817	9.9	90.1	43.9	20.0	0.0	5.0
Alleghany	86	17.8	158	0	42	357	2 035	34	25	46 496	43.8	56.2	40.6	9.5	5.2	2.9
Anson	82	15.5	185	0	35	341	1 791	41	99	222 973	5.2	94.8	47.3	30.3	2.3	13.4
Ashe	105	0.9	101	0	47	238	2 213	28	22	21 246	74.9	25.1	33.7	2.7	0.1	3.6
Avery	27	35.2	63	1	14	201	3 568	29	17	39 411	98.1	1.9	46.9	9.1	18.7	8.7
Beaufort	155	7.2	404	2	136	577	1 430	103	82	212 196	68.2	31.8	69.6	38.2	0.5	16.6
Bertie	154	-9.2	416	9	97	468	1 216	100	111	298 986	59.8	40.2	79.8	44.7	1.3	8.1
Bladen	128	0.2	232	3	75	346	1 586	56	239	431 696	15.2	84.8	58.6	31.3	0.0	8.7
Brunswick	37	-8.1	173	1	24	454	2 449	35	30	142 283	41.9	58.1	46.9	18.8	1.3	11.9
Buncombe	87	-7.0	87	1	36	323	3 603	23	34	34 106	73.0	27.0	20.3	3.4	10.2	37.8
Burke	29	-8.2	83	1	14	255	3 337	36	28	79 779	34.1	65.9	30.8	11.9	14.8	29.0
Cabarrus	63	0.2	131	0	40	464	3 520	22	21	43 368	24.8	75.2	28.5	6.0	0.0	30.8
Caldwell	37	19.5	112	0	18	236	2 216	31	24	71 638	58.1	41.9	27.8	11.5	16.3	13.4
Camden	52	20.2	680	D	48	1 053	1 549	173	20	259 827	93.7	6.3	67.1	42.1	4.3	0.9
Carteret	60	-6.5	593	0	46	980	1 646	62	19	187 703	96.0	4.0	55.4	27.7	16.7	8.4
Caswell	138	10.3	244	3	54	371	1 542	40	28	50 327	77.1	22.9	54.3	13.1	0.0	3.6
Catawba	72	14.7	121	1	48	336	2 809	32	24	40 933	27.1	72.9	25.5	7.0	0.0	806.0
Chatham	113	4.6	118	1	54	293	2 248	30	121	126 261	3.8	96.2	41.8	20.0	3.2	396.5
Cherokee	25	2.2	101	0	10	241	2 687	27	13	51 899	11.3	88.7	18.5	4.1	44.7	7.6

Table B. States and Counties — Residential Construction, Wholesale and Retail Trade, and Real Estate

STATE County	Value of Residential Construction Authorized by Building Permits, 2000		Wholesale Trade, 1997				Retail Trade[1], 1997				Real Estate and Rental and Leasing, 1997			
	New Construction ($1,000)	Number of Housing Units	Number of Establishments	Number of Employees	Sales (mil dol)	Annual Payroll (mil dol)	Number of Establishments	Number of Employees	Sales (mil dol)	Annual Payroll (mil dol)	Number of Establishments	Number of Employees	Receipts (mil dol)	Annual Payroll (mil dol)
	133	134	135	136	137	138	139	140	141	142	143	144	145	146
NEW YORK—Cont'd														
Genesee	12 182	106	99	1 140	385.6	31.5	231	2 649	366.4	35.6	42	136	15.3	2.5
Greene	20 975	185	39	516	222.6	14.8	230	1 673	278.3	27.1	33	122	12.2	1.8
Hamilton	4 103	52	2	D	D	D	35	140	23.7	2.6	3	D	D	D
Herkimer	12 591	124	33	D	D	D	254	2 183	313.4	29.7	45	96	9.8	1.1
Jefferson	15 323	164	93	958	280.7	26.0	514	5 679	1 016.3	90.8	94	407	56.9	7.5
Kings	198 210	2 904	2 953	25 838	11 371.6	742.8	6 994	45 941	7 983.6	821.8	3 230	10 872	1 924.2	256.5
Lewis	7 328	150	25	186	68.8	3.7	99	743	134.0	11.1	10	D	D	D
Livingston	21 736	293	68	633	212.6	18.7	245	2 676	411.3	38.4	34	132	13.0	2.3
Madison	14 114	127	63	473	159.8	13.4	260	2 935	463.3	43.2	48	134	10.4	2.1
Monroe	283 998	2 160	1 113	15 298	9 311.1	634.8	2 546	43 294	6 513.2	634.1	614	5 984	684.3	127.4
Montgomery	4 415	53	54	561	148.6	14.7	222	2 381	378.4	34.0	21	100	7.5	1.9
Nassau	270 131	1 506	4 124	36 401	23 793.6	1 597.9	6 751	81 902	16 483.6	1 615.9	2 157	9 913	1 894.6	287.4
New York	310 901	5 110	11 629	119 913	151 792.8	6 473.4	11 222	102 965	19 502.4	2 447.2	8 510	59 793	14 318.2	2 331.7
Niagara	56 328	489	237	2 573	656.6	64.4	886	11 500	1 607.6	159.9	111	509	50.8	8.1
Oneida	29 036	281	245	D	D	D	971	12 664	1 846.1	180.5	163	652	79.1	11.5
Onondaga	149 628	1 223	992	13 949	11 159.8	526.1	1 974	30 203	4 372.3	443.4	403	4 020	364.9	88.9
Ontario	61 735	447	152	1 092	471.6	36.4	520	7 791	1 118.6	106.3	62	226	22.5	4.3
Orange	227 118	2 000	448	D	D	D	1 438	17 131	3 047.7	290.4	278	1 075	156.1	22.6
Orleans	6 361	65	26	205	36.3	3.9	139	1 371	191.5	18.1	17	52	3.9	0.7
Oswego	19 248	241	73	443	140.0	11.0	396	4 609	747.1	69.5	60	264	34.2	6.3
Otsego	14 983	577	50	427	99.4	9.8	298	3 064	539.3	47.4	36	135	11.7	2.0
Putnam	67 412	359	126	729	278.2	27.0	320	2 707	497.6	49.9	107	251	37.8	6.8
Queens	184 381	2 723	2 787	27 165	12 942.0	952.6	5 933	48 425	8 756.0	890.1	2 385	11 853	1 919.0	297.2
Rensselaer	42 877	380	131	1 066	780.5	33.5	440	5 814	854.3	86.0	75	300	43.7	7.0
Richmond	260 142	2 667	358	1 763	627.1	55.5	1 197	13 522	2 235.3	219.4	234	842	152.1	18.8
Rockland	67 365	547	662	5 606	5 826.0	221.0	1 114	11 601	2 229.9	228.2	338	1 260	231.7	44.8
St. Lawrence	17 140	242	74	665	316.4	18.3	483	5 161	791.8	73.6	70	203	18.8	3.5
Saratoga	152 718	1 152	195	2 324	1 539.6	74.8	721	9 063	1 509.8	139.0	137	666	95.1	13.5
Schenectady	30 248	250	121	1 733	618.3	60.0	582	7 606	1 174.0	119.1	76	461	45.2	10.7
Schoharie	7 101	80	12	89	24.4	1.9	134	1 364	190.1	18.4	17	54	5.2	0.8
Schuyler	3 592	38	14	D	D	D	72	713	119.5	11.7	11	D	D	D
Seneca	5 121	46	28	311	53.9	6.0	174	1 560	250.3	22.6	17	D	D	D
Steuben	27 069	245	46	366	89.9	8.1	403	4 526	663.4	63.8	59	261	22.1	4.1
Suffolk	843 105	4 932	3 400	42 107	21 953.6	1 616.1	6 393	68 059	13 509.7	1 352.7	1 281	5 853	1 009.5	166.2
Sullivan	27 236	283	82	688	235.8	16.7	344	2 842	485.9	49.0	82	231	26.1	3.9
Tioga	8 459	95	31	D	D	D	145	1 205	218.1	20.0	13	55	4.1	0.6
Tompkins	52 291	556	71	432	239.6	13.8	373	4 367	616.3	65.7	81	450	42.1	8.2
Ulster	72 667	548	183	2 163	522.0	59.5	771	8 107	1 278.3	132.1	135	418	54.6	7.9
Warren	51 225	378	93	D	D	D	466	5 236	850.6	83.9	63	265	39.2	5.2
Washington	19 292	172	44	D	D	D	209	1 693	265.2	25.9	24	76	6.1	0.9
Wayne	32 726	320	78	745	327.1	26.0	296	3 569	576.4	54.2	46	148	15.2	2.3
Westchester	438 763	2 126	1 947	31 486	23 918.0	1 313.0	4 191	46 984	9 189.0	958.6	1 760	7 321	1 533.8	235.8
Wyoming	8 599	92	32	202	107.4	4.7	159	1 609	247.0	23.8	16	89	3.6	1.0
Yates	5 582	66	21	D	D	D	107	739	105.4	10.6	23	105	6.1	1.4
NORTH CAROLINA	8 643 193	78 376	12 284	157 774	98 080.1	5 574.1	35 563	416 287	72 356.8	6 697.4	7 346	39 349	5 026.0	900.6
Alamance	101 108	945	172	1 756	550.7	53.7	643	7 630	1 245.1	117.8	97	397	69.3	7.3
Alexander	29 875	166	24	91	23.1	1.9	100	900	142.5	11.6	8	21	1.2	0.2
Alleghany	14 815	151	3	D	D	D	53	317	59.0	4.7	7	13	0.8	0.1
Anson	3 371	31	17	208	86.2	6.5	96	771	105.4	9.8	11	26	1.8	0.4
Ashe	29 162	239	24	69	44.2	1.3	103	830	163.0	13.2	19	37	4.1	0.7
Avery	40 537	148	19	98	35.1	2.6	108	822	130.9	11.9	38	187	11.0	2.7
Beaufort	30 608	190	77	683	245.4	16.6	234	2 398	386.0	33.1	30	118	8.4	1.3
Bertie	1 093	28	21	268	158.6	4.8	69	458	70.8	6.5	7	14	1.1	0.2
Bladen	7 582	63	29	298	144.7	7.5	111	895	129.4	11.9	12	56	9.8	1.1
Brunswick	161 461	1 449	57	367	77.0	8.6	276	2 490	441.9	38.1	86	949	64.7	15.0
Buncombe	158 997	1 327	340	D	D	D	1 136	13 179	2 193.4	210.4	221	1 037	131.9	21.8
Burke	34 532	302	78	583	248.4	16.0	315	3 079	557.8	46.2	43	103	10.3	1.6
Cabarrus	156 062	1 724	157	1 480	953.9	45.4	468	6 467	1 131.8	103.6	98	497	60.0	11.1
Caldwell	51 410	442	77	842	791.3	31.6	330	3 329	515.1	45.8	39	116	11.3	1.9
Camden	7 515	63	5	D	D	D	24	128	14.9	1.6	1	D	D	D
Carteret	72 742	459	61	623	141.3	13.5	406	3 510	598.7	53.4	112	478	46.8	7.1
Caswell	10 250	89	5	75	4.5	1.1	49	267	44.0	3.9	3	4	0.5	0.0
Catawba	152 036	1 280	308	5 844	2 543.2	177.7	779	10 011	1 719.8	161.1	146	643	80.5	13.2
Chatham	83 820	418	58	523	262.9	12.8	177	1 451	226.1	21.3	20	61	3.6	0.6
Cherokee	23 102	271	24	186	51.1	3.1	139	1 266	217.0	18.3	17	89	11.2	2.0

1. Establishments with payroll.

STATE County	Professional, Scientific, and Technical Services[1], 1997				Manufacturing, 1997				Accommodation and Foodservices, 1997			
	Number of Establishments	Number of Employees	Receipts (mil dol)	Annual Payroll (mil dol)	Number of Establishments	Number of Employees	Receipts (mil dol)	Annual Payroll (mil dol)	Number of Establishments	Number of Employees	Sales (mil dol)	Annual Payroll (mil dol)
	147	148	149	150	151	152	153	154	155	156	157	158
NEW YORK—Cont'd												
Genesee	67	715	25.7	10.4	107	3 979	778.1	127.0	131	1 770	51.7	14.5
Greene	58	283	25.1	6.1	37	740	118.4	22.4	207	1 508	62.6	16.4
Hamilton	3	6	0.7	0.1	NA	NA	NA	NA	59	140	10.4	2.8
Herkimer	58	192	8.7	2.9	71	4 971	662.4	135.8	153	1 225	40.6	10.6
Jefferson	98	591	36.8	16.0	84	3 896	812.6	132.0	295	2 835	102.5	28.1
Kings	1 906	7 731	790.0	250.4	2 672	48 589	5 725.5	1 139.9	2 221	15 748	734.5	188.1
Lewis	20	58	3.1	1.0	24	1 560	505.3	53.1	67	314	10.9	2.4
Livingston	77	344	20.4	8.0	48	2 196	500.5	59.5	138	1 399	39.3	10.3
Madison	89	495	41.7	12.0	69	2 526	506.7	69.3	171	1 948	59.9	17.5
Monroe	1 623	15 316	1 643.0	622.2	1 007	82 459	21 774.7	3 521.8	1 439	22 914	760.6	219.4
Montgomery	55	237	21.1	7.0	84	4 790	637.7	123.6	115	910	36.9	8.5
Nassau	5 784	34 253	3 832.4	1 425.5	1 653	42 717	7 117.3	1 550.8	2 881	35 707	1 544.2	431.3
New York	15 163	230 278	38 237.5	14 755.2	5 165	93 784	14 028.9	2 551.8	7 219	127 621	8 318.2	2 423.4
Niagara	253	1 269	128.7	36.2	310	18 164	4 403.5	836.5	592	6 876	207.6	58.3
Oneida	344	2 312	177.2	62.8	280	15 079	2 485.3	447.1	528	5 931	180.1	50.8
Onondaga	1 057	10 334	935.4	370.6	510	33 289	6 614.4	1 296.3	1 062	16 009	509.8	151.5
Ontario	171	946	108.6	34.5	161	7 196	999.1	226.4	262	3 516	110.7	31.5
Orange	605	2 643	269.0	96.7	346	D	D	D	687	6 763	256.5	67.0
Orleans	27	66	5.5	1.1	48	2 269	496.0	71.2	66	598	15.2	4.1
Oswego	108	436	31.0	12.8	108	5 082	2 210.7	204.9	262	3 128	87.0	25.4
Otsego	84	299	27.5	8.1	68	1 481	225.0	38.0	165	1 675	62.8	16.7
Putnam	248	853	73.2	28.6	74	1 595	258.9	60.3	144	1 207	45.7	12.0
Queens	1 756	7 829	678.8	231.1	2 043	50 505	6 412.8	1 433.2	2 666	25 321	1 336.5	357.1
Rensselaer	226	1 546	125.6	53.3	110	5 023	767.2	169.1	269	3 092	92.0	25.8
Richmond	574	2 143	210.4	68.0	162	2 156	316.2	59.6	553	5 427	239.6	55.3
Rockland	923	4 197	526.9	177.3	309	10 739	3 649.8	413.3	558	5 553	246.6	64.4
St. Lawrence	109	445	26.2	10.5	85	5 311	1 602.2	201.4	259	2 497	74.9	20.3
Saratoga	369	2 011	132.0	47.3	139	6 400	1 513.9	263.2	380	5 431	197.3	58.4
Schenectady	227	3 994	484.7	196.4	119	5 134	1 687.8	212.2	313	3 126	106.6	29.8
Schoharie	31	116	5.5	2.1	28	1 024	180.8	24.0	51	547	14.4	4.1
Schuyler	21	38	3.2	0.6	17	574	88.8	18.3	49	281	11.4	3.1
Seneca	33	97	9.2	3.1	31	2 037	457.2	71.2	72	646	23.3	7.0
Steuben	113	550	35.4	13.2	74	8 070	1 338.5	264.2	211	2 332	74.7	21.4
Suffolk	3 680	21 383	2 149.9	773.5	2 535	70 317	12 009.2	2 433.5	2 795	29 208	1 266.9	336.3
Sullivan	140	407	33.4	9.1	54	D	D	D	246	3 607	148.1	43.4
Tioga	53	417	60.8	14.2	48	5 055	1 569.6	239.8	84	749	24.2	6.7
Tompkins	188	1 411	135.8	49.5	94	3 613	667.1	123.6	312	3 477	113.2	31.7
Ulster	321	2 013	183.7	69.3	215	6 449	785.0	183.7	468	5 662	215.7	63.1
Warren	151	1 114	127.8	40.2	84	4 014	820.7	144.0	407	4 078	179.5	51.6
Washington	59	125	8.5	2.5	99	3 852	642.0	122.7	100	584	19.8	4.8
Wayne	98	386	23.0	8.5	145	8 041	1 435.2	221.8	140	1 473	46.2	12.4
Westchester	3 550	20 530	2 818.2	1 016.6	869	18 797	3 012.0	626.3	1 833	19 829	1 018.1	285.1
Wyoming	37	143	8.0	3.0	55	3 011	371.9	79.1	73	544	16.4	4.1
Yates	27	85	6.1	2.3	27	522	225.2	15.6	55	322	13.0	3.1
NORTH CAROLINA	14 351	101 610	9 760.9	3 693.5	11 306	773 548	161 900.5	21 297.9	14 579	262 848	8 625.0	2 393.2
Alamance	173	878	66.5	29.8	282	21 490	3 324.8	588.2	246	5 028	145.1	39.9
Alexander	31	106	5.4	2.0	99	5 512	635.0	129.2	38	575	15.5	4.5
Alleghany	15	27	1.3	0.4	22	1 422	245.3	27.2	25	246	6.2	1.8
Anson	19	73	4.0	1.4	37	3 426	364.8	74.3	30	406	12.1	3.3
Ashe	17	46	2.8	0.8	37	2 093	242.1	42.2	43	464	12.5	3.8
Avery	20	59	8.2	1.5	11	802	85.4	14.6	47	468	22.1	5.6
Beaufort	60	569	24.3	9.7	65	5 772	927.8	139.8	68	924	29.1	7.2
Bertie	5	40	2.3	0.8	16	D	D	D	15	162	4.4	1.1
Bladen	25	147	10.1	3.0	36	6 559	1 040.9	127.4	50	544	17.9	4.7
Brunswick	89	281	20.8	6.4	57	2 340	1 013.3	86.9	155	1 843	67.4	16.7
Buncombe	466	2 386	174.1	77.3	332	D	D	D	506	9 130	334.3	98.9
Burke	91	447	25.9	10.3	171	17 279	2 126.9	416.7	118	2 451	63.1	16.7
Cabarrus	158	808	59.2	24.6	166	13 099	7 991.8	409.7	155	3 317	123.7	31.7
Caldwell	55	259	17.6	7.2	167	15 254	1 633.1	344.4	102	1 332	40.9	10.8
Camden	4	18	0.8	0.4	NA	NA	NA	NA	3	D	D	D
Carteret	93	319	30.8	9.0	69	1 576	173.1	29.4	202	3 010	106.0	28.7
Caswell	13	29	2.8	0.8	NA	NA	NA	NA	14	88	2.7	0.7
Catawba	238	1 109	86.6	30.8	575	40 469	5 512.8	1 035.2	315	6 274	179.7	52.0
Chatham	63	170	12.3	4.8	76	7 109	1 014.3	158.2	51	D	D	D
Cherokee	34	178	8.0	4.0	27	2 776	315.0	56.3	47	525	15.4	4.0

1. Firms subject to federal tax.

Table B. States and Counties — **Health and Other Services and Federal Funds**

	Health Care and Social Assistance[1], 1997				Other Services[1], 1997				Federal funds and grants, fiscal 2001[2]			
									Expenditures (mil dol)			
										Direct payments for individuals[3]		
STATE County	Number of Establishments	Number of Employees	Receipts (mil dol)	Annual Payroll (mil dol)	Number of Establishments	Number of Employees	Receipts (mil dol)	Annual Payroll (mil dol)	Total	Social Security and government retirement	Medicare	Food stamps and Supplemental Security Income
	159	160	161	162	163	164	165	166	167	168	169	170
NEW YORK—Cont'd												
Genesee	90	912	44.9	18.3	90	559	31.0	8.5	287.8	135.1	50.7	5.7
Greene	63	444	25.2	9.9	61	191	16.7	3.8	224.1	115.5	40.7	8.6
Hamilton	1	D	D	D	9	17	1.6	0.3	28.5	16.5	5.8	0.6
Herkimer	63	454	24.5	9.9	86	512	61.8	15.2	306.3	147.9	60.4	10.4
Jefferson	157	1 324	89.2	47.9	129	482	33.6	9.0	957.1	220.8	65.5	19.1
Kings	3 102	28 475	2 029.6	781.4	2 747	10 809	715.0	212.2	(4)	(4)	(4)	(4)
Lewis	26	D	D	D	30	50	5.5	0.9	114.0	53.6	16.4	4.5
Livingston	79	449	26.6	10.3	75	300	16.3	4.1	234.6	121.3	43.6	7.8
Madison	87	669	46.2	19.8	81	206	17.2	3.7	265.2	141.0	42.6	6.5
Monroe	1 299	14 414	951.7	402.5	1 048	6 001	401.6	118.8	3 910.4	1 457.8	632.1	135.5
Montgomery	103	992	56.7	24.9	86	323	18.2	4.4	277.4	137.8	61.5	8.9
Nassau	4 486	45 327	3 665.3	1 504.1	3 201	17 088	1 105.6	342.1	6 921.1	3 124.2	1 578.7	96.1
New York	5 360	39 451	3 780.3	1 523.5	4 188	26 361	1 825.5	505.9	(4)48 976.1	(4)11 467.0	(4)9 190.8	(4)3 137.1
Niagara	359	3 906	182.8	78.7	305	1 279	78.8	20.4	1 143.4	536.6	206.6	34.6
Oneida	421	4 299	287.8	133.6	328	1 733	112.9	29.0	1 524.0	623.1	219.6	50.5
Onondaga	894	9 567	722.2	341.2	762	5 753	413.2	119.8	2 591.8	991.6	357.4	84.8
Ontario	142	1 391	86.3	33.6	133	495	31.5	8.5	459.2	224.4	74.4	9.6
Orange	651	5 619	366.9	158.9	548	2 588	189.5	50.7	1 783.7	627.1	248.8	44.5
Orleans	62	417	25.5	9.9	50	108	8.6	2.0	185.4	83.2	31.3	5.9
Oswego	119	1 103	58.1	25.8	133	426	32.8	7.6	510.7	249.3	79.6	20.5
Otsego	75	536	35.2	15.5	84	298	22.6	5.9	298.3	137.4	50.6	7.8
Putnam	189	1 999	132.1	58.2	168	670	50.3	12.6	278.2	158.7	65.7	5.3
Queens	2 966	32 874	2 271.0	935.6	2 834	12 307	766.9	235.7	(4)	(4)	(4)	(4)
Rensselaer	244	2 820	150.8	67.9	187	755	51.1	13.2	1 677.7	336.9	126.4	23.1
Richmond	732	8 746	651.7	299.6	600	2 398	153.3	41.5	(4)	(4)	(4)	(4)
Rockland	761	6 753	508.3	227.1	527	1 985	147.2	38.2	1 452.4	545.4	260.8	30.9
St. Lawrence	158	1 295	76.0	31.2	113	475	25.6	6.4	567.6	240.3	81.0	24.8
Saratoga	286	2 050	132.7	51.6	203	1 027	63.3	17.9	714.2	391.9	111.4	15.1
Schenectady	311	4 202	274.7	126.0	196	1 239	84.3	22.9	1 229.4	382.5	143.4	26.3
Schoharie	33	297	14.5	5.2	43	103	7.3	1.6	140.6	69.3	24.1	3.9
Schuyler	18	181	8.0	3.6	15	38	2.9	0.5	83.7	41.2	12.3	3.0
Seneca	38	372	19.7	7.5	31	96	7.1	1.3	151.0	79.5	24.8	4.2
Steuben	139	1 282	75.5	33.7	106	371	24.2	5.9	509.8	239.3	80.5	20.4
Suffolk	3 042	33 419	2 448.6	1 030.0	2 986	12 507	944.8	266.3	7 328.8	2 894.2	1 278.6	134.6
Sullivan	130	1 001	58.9	22.9	112	563	29.0	7.5	434.5	169.1	82.6	15.8
Tioga	46	322	14.1	6.0	50	166	10.7	2.8	553.3	99.5	29.4	6.9
Tompkins	157	1 307	85.1	35.3	108	555	32.4	8.8	515.2	145.2	42.8	10.9
Ulster	343	3 292	191.7	75.6	243	938	55.6	15.1	761.2	365.5	134.5	26.2
Warren	146	1 371	104.1	52.7	107	511	39.9	12.1	298.4	150.8	48.8	8.5
Washington	45	614	25.9	11.6	62	157	11.4	2.6	247.9	128.8	43.7	8.5
Wayne	99	761	40.6	17.2	106	317	24.3	5.9	395.9	196.0	70.0	12.1
Westchester	2 629	23 146	1 909.4	815.9	1 883	8 331	617.8	180.7	4 627.3	1 909.9	1 029.4	104.3
Wyoming	40	513	22.7	11.5	47	180	10.3	2.7	167.7	80.7	28.8	4.0
Yates	21	D	D	D	25	113	8.2	1.8	116.4	60.5	19.0	3.6
NORTH CAROLINA	12 582	173 770	10 708.8	4 859.6	11 483	64 802	4 060.6	1 204.0	44 557.1	16 594.1	5 409.5	1 344.9
Alamance	212	3 555	289.1	106.9	202	1 339	80.3	23.2	527.7	281.7	100.5	14.3
Alexander	31	317	14.0	7.1	41	176	10.9	2.7	103.2	57.8	20.8	3.6
Alleghany	12	200	5.7	2.5	11	20	1.6	0.2	62.5	29.2	10.7	2.1
Anson	23	261	10.8	5.5	28	106	6.8	1.8	144.7	53.2	25.6	5.9
Ashe	27	244	11.7	5.6	25	70	5.1	1.1	138.3	57.9	21.3	5.7
Avery	26	342	12.6	6.6	25	77	5.2	1.4	92.1	42.0	17.7	3.8
Beaufort	63	893	45.4	20.6	91	387	24.1	7.2	253.6	117.8	35.8	12.7
Bertie	20	355	13.7	5.0	20	76	5.0	1.0	145.9	49.8	20.5	7.3
Bladen	54	719	27.4	12.4	23	81	4.0	1.1	189.9	74.5	26.9	12.0
Brunswick	94	1 170	67.3	26.0	68	239	16.7	3.8	429.0	224.2	58.5	11.8
Buncombe	459	6 057	428.7	214.9	347	1 834	104.9	33.0	1 121.2	526.8	170.7	35.0
Burke	122	1 068	69.6	35.7	81	468	27.4	8.9	344.7	172.1	61.4	11.6
Cabarrus	163	2 348	148.2	73.7	216	965	57.8	17.5	483.2	266.0	106.1	12.0
Caldwell	94	1 492	62.5	28.6	98	433	26.8	7.2	282.5	156.1	56.0	9.2
Camden	2	D	D	D	5	25	2.2	0.8	44.0	21.5	5.4	0.9
Carteret	95	1 123	51.2	24.0	103	409	20.0	5.1	339.3	197.7	44.8	8.1
Caswell	20	303	8.7	3.8	10	18	0.9	0.2	102.5	41.2	15.2	5.0
Catawba	251	4 733	345.0	149.4	239	1 385	82.6	26.1	503.8	280.3	85.8	13.3
Chatham	43	525	25.3	9.4	56	209	12.9	4.3	176.5	94.0	34.0	4.4
Cherokee	43	285	16.7	6.6	19	63	5.3	1.2	153.5	73.3	22.0	5.5

1. Firms subject to federal tax. 2. October 1, 2000 to September 30, 2001. 3. State totals may include programs not allocated by county. 4. Bronx, Kings, Queens, and Richmond Counties included with New York County.

Table B. States and Counties — Federal Funds and Local Government Finances

STATE County	Federal funds and grants, fiscal 2001[1] (cont'd)							Local government finances, 1997				
	Expenditures (mil dol) (cont'd)							General revenue				
	Procurement contract awards			Grants[2]							Taxes	
											Per capita[3] (dollars)	
	Salaries and wages	Defense	Other	Medicaid and other health-related	Nutrition and family welfare	Education	Other	Total (mil dol)	Intergovern-mental (mil dol)	Total (mil dol)	Total	Property
	171	172	173	174	175	176	177	178	179	180	181	182
NEW YORK—Cont'd												
Genesee	25.0	0.2	11.3	29.5	5.4	5.0	6.6	260.1	85.4	82.5	1 335	966
Greene	7.2	3.2	1.9	25.3	6.0	3.3	7.1	154.2	56.6	83.4	1 743	1 418
Hamilton	1.3	0.0	0.4	1.5	0.5	0.9	0.8	29.9	4.1	22.5	4 318	3 966
Herkimer	7.9	2.9	5.4	41.2	7.9	5.1	7.5	204.9	93.8	79.9	1 217	958
Jefferson	435.3	59.5	6.0	70.8	18.1	17.9	24.1	362.1	171.4	125.0	1 105	827
Kings	[4]	[4]	[4]	[4]	[4]	[4]	[4]					[4]
Lewis	4.2	0.5	1.2	21.0	3.8	1.5	2.1	106.8	42.3	30.7	1 089	925
Livingston	9.1	0.3	2.3	26.6	5.6	3.4	4.5	189.8	79.6	74.2	1 116	897
Madison	9.5	0.2	2.7	35.3	6.8	4.4	7.9	204.7	92.8	85.0	1 187	1 028
Monroe	216.6	135.3	80.9	540.7	134.1	86.3	165.1	2 629.4	938.4	1 206.5	1 681	1 220
Montgomery	7.4	3.2	3.7	32.8	6.2	3.1	3.0	176.4	71.2	61.6	1 197	936
Nassau	454.0	573.2	123.2	598.3	69.4	55.6	52.1	5 981.3	1 189.9	4 027.2	3 089	2 527
New York	[4]3 392.3	[4]285.9	[4]1 028.6	[4]12 631.0	[4]2 536.1	[4]260.6	[4]1 925.4	[4]45 887.1	[4]16 661.7	[4]19 368.2	[4]2 638	[4]1 006
Niagara	83.9	26.4	8.8	128.7	39.2	13.7	23.9	807.0	303.7	323.9	1 471	1 125
Oneida	130.3	101.9	30.0	206.9	31.7	17.3	45.3	827.8	337.3	325.9	1 398	1 017
Onondaga	250.1	271.9	60.9	280.4	67.1	32.4	100.4	1 571.2	614.0	706.1	1 530	1 145
Ontario	50.3	4.5	5.7	41.7	8.1	5.9	17.4	342.9	125.9	157.9	1 579	1 177
Orange	400.4	145.8	29.0	171.7	37.0	20.2	18.4	1 503.0	395.0	553.4	1 691	1 355
Orleans	5.3	0.0	14.4	19.3	6.8	3.1	8.1	129.0	61.3	48.3	1 079	830
Oswego	17.0	11.5	6.8	68.5	17.5	9.1	16.8	452.0	179.9	213.6	1 705	1 584
Otsego	10.4	1.4	19.9	48.7	7.1	3.5	6.0	172.2	73.4	71.8	1 168	967
Putnam	12.8	1.5	3.5	19.4	2.4	5.0	2.1	294.9	58.2	204.2	2 211	1 960
Queens	[4]	[4]	[4]	[4]	[4]	[4]	[4]	[4]	[4]	[4]	[4]	[4]
Rensselaer	30.7	3.4	9.2	383.0	653.0	8.6	49.0	531.7	218.2	208.5	1 351	1 061
Richmond	[4]	[4]	[4]	[4]	[4]	[4]	[4]	[4]	[4]	[4]	[4]	[4]
Rockland	41.7	249.6	20.2	179.4	28.0	14.2	14.9	1 184.5	247.5	761.3	2 720	2 185
St. Lawrence	28.3	1.8	7.8	102.4	22.8	9.4	33.7	368.5	167.6	124.5	1 090	837
Saratoga	75.6	1.3	8.6	52.2	12.0	6.3	25.6	534.7	177.4	285.2	1 451	1 107
Schenectady	65.5	189.2	247.5	89.3	18.4	10.5	23.0	471.9	164.1	229.7	1 561	1 221
Schoharie	5.5	0.0	1.4	23.3	4.3	2.1	2.7	101.5	48.6	43.1	1 325	1 099
Schuyler	3.3	0.0	0.8	13.9	2.1	1.4	3.6	51.4	24.0	19.4	1 014	821
Seneca	6.0	1.6	1.6	19.4	2.3	1.6	4.0	99.3	48.3	39.2	1 193	906
Steuben	44.7	6.3	10.3	61.6	12.4	8.5	8.0	368.7	173.9	128.4	1 296	952
Suffolk	732.2	391.6	621.6	765.8	144.8	70.2	140.8	5 486.0	1 485.4	3 377.9	2 479	1 995
Sullivan	14.4	0.1	9.2	103.4	9.2	5.6	6.5	312.2	96.2	156.8	2 229	1 928
Tioga	9.9	359.5	3.4	16.6	6.9	3.1	15.2	150.1	74.6	54.4	1 028	841
Tompkins	20.5	7.8	10.5	93.3	10.9	9.1	134.7	293.8	104.5	136.1	1 408	1 028
Ulster	30.6	3.3	8.9	132.1	19.5	10.6	7.3	596.9	179.9	335.1	2 007	1 643
Warren	16.5	0.2	3.8	40.2	7.3	3.8	7.4	219.5	69.3	117.9	1 905	1 398
Washington	8.9	1.6	2.2	33.9	8.0	4.4	1.3	197.6	85.3	74.6	1 229	1 036
Wayne	12.3	6.6	6.1	57.6	10.7	6.2	4.6	315.9	136.5	126.2	1 325	1 087
Westchester	322.3	56.7	96.6	558.3	109.3	52.0	156.0	4 215.4	872.0	2 548.0	2 843	2 351
Wyoming	6.6	0.3	18.8	16.0	2.9	1.9	3.1	133.8	45.8	43.0	965	731
Yates	5.2	0.1	2.6	12.1	2.2	1.9	2.9	66.2	23.6	35.1	1 455	1 249
NORTH CAROLINA	5 502.0	1 555.8	1 597.8	5 145.0	1 270.8	735.1	1 971.5	X	X	X	X	X
Alamance	15.1	8.7	4.9	58.0	8.9	5.4	7.6	226.3	114.5	61.3	520	387
Alexander	2.9	0.0	0.8	11.0	1.9	1.6	0.5	41.1	23.9	11.1	364	232
Alleghany	2.4	0.0	1.9	12.6	0.9	0.6	0.2	17.7	9.4	5.4	553	406
Anson	3.3	15.1	0.8	27.4	4.3	2.0	1.1	85.5	31.6	11.4	470	358
Ashe	4.2	0.8	1.5	31.7	2.2	1.4	5.4	31.4	17.6	10.3	428	290
Avery	2.8	0.0	0.7	15.4	1.9	1.2	5.2	29.2	14.9	11.5	734	551
Beaufort	6.5	0.1	1.6	43.3	5.7	4.2	5.0	116.0	51.3	24.1	545	396
Bertie	4.2	5.7	0.9	39.1	4.9	1.9	1.0	39.1	28.0	7.7	377	280
Bladen	6.0	0.0	6.0	41.6	6.2	3.8	2.4	85.9	38.1	16.8	548	419
Brunswick	16.3	65.9	2.2	33.4	5.7	2.7	2.9	149.7	56.0	63.1	957	762
Buncombe	131.8	14.7	34.8	104.8	17.6	12.3	39.2	427.7	186.5	144.1	748	554
Burke	7.5	11.2	2.1	41.6	6.3	8.8	14.2	144.5	78.8	35.8	438	377
Cabarrus	17.4	0.6	3.9	41.3	7.4	7.1	7.1	227.4	103.6	76.3	658	513
Caldwell	7.3	0.0	2.2	30.5	6.0	4.3	4.1	130.4	77.2	30.9	408	295
Camden	1.9	0.0	0.2	3.6	0.7	0.3	0.1	12.0	8.2	3.2	485	357
Carteret	22.9	3.5	12.5	21.2	5.1	3.1	12.6	146.5	53.3	41.4	693	485
Caswell	2.6	0.0	0.6	25.3	3.0	1.3	4.7	32.4	20.6	8.3	381	257
Catawba	33.1	2.6	9.6	34.7	8.3	6.1	18.0	358.8	139.7	83.4	640	473
Chatham	6.8	0.2	1.3	19.9	2.9	1.6	8.0	74.4	33.8	27.4	611	469
Cherokee	6.7	10.8	1.5	23.3	3.0	1.9	1.7	40.7	24.0	10.3	460	282

1. October 1, 2000 to September 30, 2001.   2. State totals may include programs not allocated by county.   3. Based on the resident population estimated as of July 1 of the year shown.   4. Bronx, Kings, Queens, and Richmond Counties included with New York County.

Table B. States and Counties — Local Government Finances, Government Employment, and Elections

STATE County	Local government finances, 1997 (cont'd)									Government employment, 1999			Presidential election, 2000[2]		
	Direct general expenditure							Debt outstanding					Percent of vote cast —		
			Percent of total for —												
	Total (mil dol)	Per capita[1] (dollars)	Educa-tion	Health and hospitals	Police protec-tion	Public welfare	High-ways	Total (mil dol)	Per capita[1] (dollars)	Federal civilian	Federal military	State and local	Demo-cratic	Republi-can	All other
	183	184	185	186	187	188	189	190	191	192	193	194	195	196	197
NEW YORK—Cont'd															
Genesee	254.4	4 116	46.5	2.6	2.1	11.1	5.0	100.0	1 617	585	121	4 710	39.1	55.5	5.4
Greene	146.3	3 057	50.1	3.1	1.7	10.4	8.9	39.0	815	111	96	3 876	40.2	53.7	6.1
Hamilton	30.1	5 766	39.2	5.2	1.4	3.4	17.1	6.4	1 237	15	10	636	30.3	64.9	4.9
Herkimer	221.6	3 373	57.9	3.4	1.8	8.4	8.4	92.4	1 406	136	131	4 594	44.1	51.1	4.8
Jefferson	370.0	3 271	47.6	3.9	2.2	11.0	7.5	297.2	2 627	2 711	10 929	7 975	46.1	50.0	3.9
Kings	(3)	(3)	(3)	(3)	(3)	(3)	(3)	(3)	(3)	8 784	4 923	23 812	80.6	15.7	3.7
Lewis	108.3	3 840	39.8	23.0	0.8	8.1	8.2	44.6	1 581	63	54	2 082	39.7	55.9	4.5
Livingston	190.4	2 863	47.5	3.6	2.2	20.9	7.9	84.2	1 266	165	131	6 572	38.5	56.0	5.5
Madison	222.9	3 111	58.9	3.0	1.7	6.2	8.1	127.2	1 776	157	142	4 204	42.4	52.5	5.2
Monroe	2 740.4	3 818	44.1	4.2	3.9	15.5	3.2	1 861.9	2 594	3 116	1 518	43 952	50.9	44.5	4.6
Montgomery	192.7	3 745	45.3	2.1	2.5	12.0	5.2	110.5	2 148	122	100	3 121	49.3	46.9	3.8
Nassau	6 346.0	4 868	40.8	6.3	8.6	7.1	3.3	4 870.5	3 736	7 029	2 996	73 632	57.9	38.5	3.6
New York	(3)42 603.8	(3)5 802	(3)22.2	(3)9.5	(3)6.8	(3)17.5	(3)2.5	(3)52 567.4	(3)7 159	32 623	3 310	427 040	79.8	14.2	6.0
Niagara	814.2	3 697	48.1	2.5	3.4	11.4	4.4	661.7	3 004	1 163	447	11 441	51.2	43.9	4.9
Oneida	834.9	3 580	42.9	2.1	2.8	11.9	4.8	421.4	1 807	2 185	575	20 450	45.8	49.6	4.6
Onondaga	1 676.2	3 632	43.9	2.4	3.6	14.1	4.7	1 078.8	2 338	4 387	1 227	34 823	54.0	41.1	4.9
Ontario	343.9	3 440	52.8	3.4	2.6	8.5	6.0	288.2	2 883	1 202	200	6 914	43.0	52.0	5.0
Orange	1 533.0	4 686	38.2	1.9	2.9	10.3	3.1	658.7	2 013	5 412	6 352	20 139	46.0	49.7	4.4
Orleans	127.3	2 846	52.0	3.7	2.5	14.6	6.4	53.0	1 185	94	90	4 393	37.8	58.1	4.1
Oswego	448.8	3 581	49.2	2.4	2.9	11.5	6.9	231.3	1 846	243	266	8 994	47.2	48.0	4.9
Otsego	177.4	2 885	50.5	3.4	1.5	13.9	10.2	88.4	1 438	168	122	4 466	45.2	48.2	6.6
Putnam	293.1	3 173	56.0	3.1	4.2	4.5	6.5	127.3	1 378	205	189	3 718	43.5	51.4	5.1
Queens	(3)	(3)	(3)	(3)	(3)	(3)	(3)	(3)	(3)	12 064	4 064	20 197	75.0	22.0	3.0
Rensselaer	572.3	3 708	53.0	2.3	2.4	11.9	3.7	318.2	2 061	393	329	9 986	50.9	43.2	5.9
Richmond	(3)	(3)	(3)	(3)	(3)	(3)	(3)	(3)	(3)	1 251	1 139	5 487	51.9	45.0	3.1
Rockland	1 152.2	4 117	45.2	7.9	4.8	8.3	3.9	557.8	1 993	667	567	18 603	56.7	39.5	3.8
St. Lawrence	369.2	3 234	43.9	9.7	1.8	10.9	7.4	187.3	1 641	489	249	10 219	53.8	41.4	4.9
Saratoga	519.4	2 642	57.8	2.5	2.3	9.4	5.7	256.2	1 303	389	1 657	10 863	45.6	49.0	5.3
Schenectady	491.9	3 341	44.2	1.8	3.6	19.0	4.4	226.4	1 538	728	336	9 218	53.1	41.8	5.2
Schoharie	107.1	3 298	58.1	3.0	1.0	8.5	9.9	53.4	1 645	94	64	2 647	39.8	55.1	5.2
Schuyler	49.7	2 592	44.7	6.9	1.5	10.5	10.7	20.7	1 080	58	38	1 068	40.5	53.7	5.8
Seneca	97.3	2 965	55.6	3.4	2.5	9.3	6.0	60.6	1 847	188	69	2 246	47.7	47.0	5.3
Steuben	381.9	3 855	58.2	3.3	1.4	10.7	8.5	165.2	1 668	926	196	6 931	36.0	59.7	4.3
Suffolk	5 546.5	4 070	52.2	2.6	6.8	6.7	2.9	3 577.2	2 625	13 008	3 006	85 336	53.4	42.0	4.6
Sullivan	320.4	4 554	41.1	5.5	2.1	13.4	9.0	217.9	3 097	224	138	5 799	50.3	44.5	5.2
Tioga	145.1	2 739	54.5	4.2	2.2	9.7	6.2	45.2	853	180	110	2 485	40.8	54.5	4.7
Tompkins	289.6	2 996	47.8	4.5	2.9	9.3	5.6	195.3	2 021	319	220	5 882	54.4	33.3	12.2
Ulster	600.5	3 597	48.4	3.0	2.6	15.1	5.8	270.1	1 618	471	350	12 861	48.8	42.8	8.5
Warren	220.3	3 560	46.0	4.7	3.0	9.7	7.6	126.6	2 045	275	131	4 127	42.6	52.4	5.0
Washington	197.5	3 255	55.0	2.4	1.7	12.9	7.5	115.5	1 904	138	120	4 986	40.9	53.5	5.6
Wayne	314.7	3 302	54.0	5.5	1.9	12.0	5.4	159.2	1 671	200	192	6 808	39.1	56.6	4.3
Westchester	4 269.8	4 764	38.4	10.1	4.6	10.7	2.7	2 024.3	2 259	5 926	1 809	55 456	58.6	37.5	3.9
Wyoming	136.4	3 060	37.5	23.7	2.4	8.9	10.5	39.6	887	115	88	4 205	33.7	61.3	5.0
Yates	60.1	2 492	43.6	2.9	3.1	9.1	13.2	22.4	927	77	49	1 062	39.4	55.4	5.2
NORTH CAROLINA	X	X	X	X	X	X	X	X	X	60 796	118 700	546 285	43.1	56.0	0.9
Alamance	228.8	1 940	47.0	10.3	5.2	5.4	2.0	169.1	1 434	273	364	5 993	37.1	62.2	0.7
Alexander	37.9	1 236	64.0	5.8	4.1	8.1	0.8	3.4	111	53	96	1 278	30.9	68.5	0.6
Alleghany	17.0	1 741	58.3	4.1	3.4	6.3	0.4	7.0	720	51	30	515	39.8	58.7	1.6
Anson	85.4	3 510	38.0	20.6	2.4	4.6	0.8	25.9	1 064	61	73	2 275	60.0	39.6	0.4
Ashe	30.1	1 257	63.7	2.4	3.3	10.9	1.5	4.7	198	77	73	1 081	38.9	60.4	0.8
Avery	28.5	1 822	55.8	3.3	3.9	5.7	1.9	2.3	147	50	48	1 054	25.2	74.0	0.8
Beaufort	119.3	2 698	44.0	23.0	3.2	6.2	0.6	57.6	1 302	131	136	2 929	38.3	60.8	0.9
Bertie	35.8	1 752	62.8	4.5	3.9	11.5	1.6	2.1	103	103	61	1 101	64.9	34.7	0.4
Bladen	89.7	2 932	43.4	22.4	3.2	7.2	1.1	81.3	2 658	121	93	2 285	54.0	45.6	0.4
Brunswick	142.6	2 163	45.0	11.2	5.1	5.7	1.8	50.9	772	341	264	3 482	45.5	53.5	1.0
Buncombe	434.7	2 255	44.2	9.6	5.4	5.6	2.4	326.5	1 694	2 482	675	12 596	45.1	53.9	1.0
Burke	140.1	1 714	58.0	3.3	6.0	6.6	1.6	69.8	854	149	249	7 946	38.9	60.2	0.9
Cabarrus	224.2	1 933	46.4	5.2	6.0	7.0	2.1	223.2	1 924	266	375	9 274	32.9	66.0	1.1
Caldwell	134.2	1 775	57.0	5.8	4.5	9.2	1.8	26.8	355	129	229	3 924	32.9	66.4	0.7
Camden	11.7	1 744	66.7	0.4	2.5	9.5	0.0	1.5	219	16	21	349	41.9	57.5	0.6
Carteret	163.1	2 731	37.7	29.8	5.1	4.9	1.2	60.1	1 006	259	414	4 040	33.3	65.4	1.4
Caswell	32.3	1 491	58.5	8.6	3.6	9.0	0.1	7.8	357	52	67	1 598	48.6	50.7	0.7
Catawba	351.0	2 693	37.2	26.3	3.6	6.8	3.7	162.0	1 242	557	404	8 353	32.0	67.4	0.7
Chatham	85.1	1 897	58.9	7.1	4.3	6.7	1.0	49.9	1 112	129	140	1 942	50.0	49.0	1.1
Cherokee	44.4	1 991	65.5	4.7	3.1	6.6	1.1	15.5	694	152	70	1 235	33.5	65.2	1.3

1. Based on the resident population estimated as of July 1 of the year shown.   2. Data subject to copyright.   3. Bronx, Kings, Queens, and Richmond Counties included with New York County.

Table B. States and Counties — **Land Area and Population**

STATE/ County code	MSA/ PMSA/ NECMA code[1]	County Type[2]	STATE County	Land area[3] (sq km) 2000	Total persons	Rank	Per square kilometer	White	Black	Am. Indian, Alaska Native	Asian and Pacific Islander	Percent Hispanic[4]	Under 5 years	5 to 17 years	18 to 24 years	25 to 34 years	35 to 44 years	45 to 54 years
					1	2	3	4	5	6	7	8	9	10	11	12	13
			NORTH CAROLINA— Cont'd															
37 041	...	7	Chowan	447	14 526	2 120	32.5	61.1	37.9	0.6	0.4	1.5	5.9	18.1	9.6	9.9	14.3	13.7
37 043	...	9	Clay	556	8 775	2 547	15.8	98.6	0.9	0.7	0.3	0.8	4.2	14.3	6.2	9.4	13.4	16.3
37 045	...	4	Cleveland	1 203	96 287	538	80.0	77.4	21.2	0.4	0.9	1.5	6.7	18.5	8.8	13.6	15.2	13.8
37 047	...	6	Columbus	2 426	54 749	861	22.6	64.0	31.3	3.5	0.4	2.3	6.6	19.1	8.7	12.6	14.8	14.1
37 049	...	5	Craven	1 835	91 436	561	49.8	71.2	25.8	0.9	1.6	4.0	7.3	17.3	12.8	13.3	14.6	12.4
37 051	2560	2	Cumberland	1 691	302 963	187	179.2	57.4	36.3	2.4	3.2	6.9	8.2	19.7	13.7	17.3	15.6	10.9
37 053	5720	1	Currituck	678	18 190	1 888	26.8	91.3	7.5	0.9	0.7	1.4	6.1	19.3	6.7	12.3	18.3	14.4
37 055	...	7	Dare	993	29 967	1 398	30.2	95.7	2.9	0.7	0.6	2.2	5.2	16.2	6.3	12.9	17.8	16.1
37 057	3120	2	Davidson	1 430	147 246	369	103.0	87.8	9.4	0.7	1.0	3.2	6.5	17.8	7.6	14.6	16.6	14.1
37 059	3120	2	Davie	687	34 835	1 257	50.7	91.2	7.2	0.5	0.6	3.5	6.5	17.8	7.1	13.2	16.2	14.9
37 061	...	6	Duplin	2 118	49 063	929	23.2	59.4	29.3	0.5	0.3	15.1	7.4	18.7	9.6	14.4	14.9	12.8
37 063	6640	2	Durham	752	223 314	254	297.0	52.2	40.2	0.8	3.8	7.6	6.9	16.0	12.8	19.0	15.8	12.7
37 065	6895	3	Edgecombe	1 308	55 606	849	42.5	40.4	57.8	0.4	0.2	2.8	6.8	20.3	8.6	12.6	15.8	14.3
37 067	3120	2	Forsyth	1 061	306 067	186	288.5	69.5	26.2	0.6	1.4	6.4	6.7	17.2	9.6	14.9	16.2	13.9
37 069	6640	2	Franklin	1 274	47 260	963	37.1	66.7	30.4	0.8	0.6	4.4	7.0	18.3	8.4	14.9	17.5	13.9
37 071	1520	0	Gaston	923	190 365	289	206.2	83.7	14.2	0.6	1.2	3.0	6.7	18.0	8.2	15.2	15.9	14.2
37 073	...	8	Gates	882	10 516	2 396	11.9	59.8	39.5	0.8	0.6	0.8	5.8	20.9	6.1	11.7	17.4	13.2
37 075	...	9	Graham	756	7 993	2 607	10.6	92.6	0.3	7.5	0.3	0.8	5.8	16.1	7.3	11.7	13.5	14.7
37 077	...	6	Granville	1 376	48 498	941	35.2	61.5	35.5	0.9	0.7	4.0	6.2	17.7	8.5	15.5	17.8	13.7
37 079	...	8	Greene	687	18 974	1 848	27.6	52.5	41.5	0.5	0.3	8.0	7.0	18.3	9.4	14.6	16.3	13.4
37 081	3120	2	Guilford	1 682	421 048	143	250.3	65.5	29.9	0.8	2.9	3.8	6.6	17.1	11.0	15.5	15.9	13.6
37 083	...	4	Halifax	1 879	57 370	832	30.5	43.0	53.0	3.5	0.7	1.0	6.2	19.9	8.0	12.5	15.2	13.6
37 085	...	6	Harnett	1 541	91 025	566	59.1	72.3	23.1	1.4	1.1	5.9	7.6	19.3	10.6	16.6	15.5	12.0
37 087	...	6	Haywood	1 434	54 033	868	37.7	97.5	1.4	0.9	0.4	1.4	5.3	15.5	6.2	12.4	14.5	14.4
37 089	...	6	Henderson	969	89 173	581	92.0	93.4	3.3	0.7	0.9	5.5	5.6	15.2	6.4	12.0	14.1	13.5
37 091	...	6	Hertford	915	22 601	1 666	24.7	38.0	60.1	1.5	0.6	1.6	5.5	19.9	7.8	11.0	15.3	14.5
37 093	...	6	Hoke	1 013	33 646	1 293	33.2	46.1	38.4	12.3	1.6	7.2	9.2	20.6	10.7	18.2	15.9	10.9
37 095	...	9	Hyde	1 587	5 826	2 801	3.7	63.2	35.4	0.6	0.5	2.2	4.5	15.9	7.9	14.2	16.6	14.2
37 097	...	4	Iredell	1 491	122 660	442	82.3	82.9	14.0	0.5	1.5	3.4	6.9	18.7	7.5	14.4	16.9	13.8
37 099	...	7	Jackson	1 271	33 121	1 314	26.1	86.9	1.8	11.2	0.6	1.7	5.1	13.9	17.9	11.6	12.8	13.9
37 101	6640	2	Johnston	2 051	121 965	446	59.5	78.9	15.9	0.7	0.5	7.7	7.8	18.2	8.1	17.2	17.0	13.1
37 103	...	8	Jones	1 222	10 381	2 404	8.5	61.6	36.3	0.7	0.6	2.7	6.0	19.6	6.8	11.1	15.8	14.8
37 105	...	6	Lee	666	49 040	930	73.6	70.8	20.8	0.7	1.0	11.7	6.9	18.7	9.0	13.9	15.8	13.5
37 107	...	4	Lenoir	1 036	59 648	805	57.6	57.0	40.7	0.4	0.6	3.2	6.6	18.7	7.9	12.2	15.4	14.5
37 109	1520	1	Lincoln	774	63 780	761	82.4	91.2	6.7	0.5	0.4	5.7	6.4	18.5	7.7	14.9	16.8	14.3
37 111	...	6	McDowell	1 144	42 151	1 055	36.8	92.9	4.4	0.6	1.1	2.9	6.1	16.7	8.2	14.6	15.3	14.1
37 113	...	7	Macon	1 338	29 811	1 403	22.3	97.7	1.3	0.7	0.5	1.5	5.0	15.4	6.1	9.9	13.3	14.5
37 115	0480	3	Madison	1 164	19 635	1 815	16.9	98.2	0.9	0.6	0.3	1.4	5.9	15.4	10.3	12.4	14.1	14.8
37 117	...	6	Martin	1 194	25 593	1 534	21.4	52.9	45.7	0.5	0.4	2.1	6.2	19.3	7.5	11.7	15.0	14.7
37 119	1520	0	Mecklenburg	1 363	695 454	72	510.2	65.2	28.4	0.7	3.6	6.5	7.0	18.7	9.7	18.7	17.6	13.1
37 121	...	9	Mitchell	573	15 687	2 039	27.4	98.4	0.3	0.9	0.3	2.0	5.1	16.1	6.8	12.0	14.4	14.6
37 123	...	7	Montgomery	1 273	26 822	1 490	21.1	70.1	22.1	0.9	2.0	10.4	6.8	18.1	9.0	13.8	14.7	13.7
37 125	...	6	Moore	1 807	74 769	668	41.4	81.0	15.8	1.0	0.7	4.0	5.6	16.5	6.6	11.6	14.2	12.5
37 127	6895	3	Nash	1 399	87 420	599	62.5	62.7	34.4	0.8	0.9	3.4	6.6	18.8	8.5	13.8	16.3	14.6
37 129	9200	3	New Hanover	515	160 307	332	311.3	80.8	17.3	0.7	1.1	2.0	5.7	15.2	12.0	15.1	15.3	14.1
37 131	...	9	Northampton	1 389	22 086	1 689	15.9	39.5	59.8	0.7	0.2	0.7	5.7	16.9	6.9	11.4	15.1	13.8
37 133	3605	3	Onslow	1 986	150 355	358	75.7	74.6	19.7	1.6	3.0	7.2	8.8	17.3	23.8	15.8	13.4	8.6
37 135	6640	2	Orange	1 036	118 227	457	114.1	79.4	14.4	0.9	4.7	4.5	5.0	15.3	21.0	15.1	14.8	13.5
37 137	...	9	Pamlico	873	12 934	2 238	14.8	73.8	24.8	0.9	0.5	1.3	5.0	16.1	6.4	10.8	15.0	15.2
37 139	...	7	Pasquotank	588	34 897	1 254	59.3	57.9	40.6	0.9	1.2	1.2	6.2	18.6	11.3	12.4	16.0	12.6
37 141	...	8	Pender	2 255	41 082	1 080	18.2	73.5	23.9	0.9	0.4	3.6	5.9	17.3	7.4	13.1	16.4	14.5
37 143	...	9	Perquimans	640	11 368	2 344	17.8	71.4	28.3	0.5	0.3	0.6	5.2	17.8	6.8	10.2	14.2	13.6
37 145	...	6	Person	1 016	35 623	1 228	35.1	69.5	28.7	0.9	0.2	2.1	6.3	17.7	7.4	13.6	17.0	14.4
37 147	3150	3	Pitt	1 688	133 798	401	79.3	62.9	34.1	0.6	1.4	3.2	6.5	17.1	17.5	15.4	14.5	12.3
37 149	...	8	Polk	616	18 324	1 879	29.7	93.0	6.1	0.5	0.3	3.0	5.2	14.9	5.8	10.7	13.5	14.6
37 151	3120	2	Randolph	2 039	130 454	411	64.0	90.1	5.9	0.8	0.9	6.6	6.8	18.2	8.0	15.0	16.3	13.9
37 153	...	7	Richmond	1 228	46 564	969	37.9	65.7	31.0	2.3	0.9	2.8	6.8	19.0	10.1	13.3	14.4	13.3
37 155	...	4	Robeson	2 457	123 339	437	50.2	33.7	25.5	39.0	0.6	4.9	8.0	21.1	10.6	14.5	14.8	12.8
37 157	...	4	Rockingham	1 467	91 928	556	62.7	78.0	19.9	0.6	0.5	3.1	6.2	17.7	7.6	13.7	15.7	14.6
37 159	1520	1	Rowan	1 324	130 340	413	98.4	80.8	16.1	0.7	1.1	4.1	6.6	18.1	9.1	13.8	15.9	13.3
37 161	...	6	Rutherford	1 461	62 899	773	43.1	87.5	11.5	0.5	0.5	1.8	6.2	17.6	8.0	13.3	14.6	13.8
37 163	...	6	Sampson	2 449	60 161	804	24.6	60.5	30.4	2.1	0.7	10.8	7.3	18.5	9.4	14.8	14.9	12.9
37 165	...	7	Scotland	827	35 998	1 218	43.5	52.5	37.7	9.8	0.6	1.2	7.3	20.8	9.5	12.8	14.8	14.2
37 167	...	6	Stanly	1 023	58 100	823	56.8	85.3	11.7	0.5	2.0	2.1	6.2	18.8	8.4	13.5	15.5	13.7
37 169	3120	2	Stokes	1 170	44 711	1 004	38.2	93.9	4.8	0.5	0.3	1.9	6.6	17.9	7.3	14.3	17.0	14.6
37 171	...	6	Surry	1 390	71 219	697	51.2	91.4	4.4	0.5	0.7	6.5	6.3	17.2	7.9	14.0	15.1	13.6

1. MSA = Metropolitan Statistical Area. PMSA = Primary MSA. NECMA = New England County Metropolitan Area. See Appendix A for explanation of these concepts. See Appendix B for list of metropolitan areas identified by type, with component counties. 2. County typology code from the Economic Research Service of USDA. See Appendix A for definition. 3. Dry land or land partially or temporarily covered by water. 4. Hispanic persons may be of any race.

Table B. States and Counties — **Population and Households**

STATE County	55 to 64 years (16)	65 to 74 years (17)	75 years and over (18)	Percent female (19)	2001 (20)	1990 (21)	1990–2000 (22)	2000–2001 (23)	Births (24)	Deaths (25)	Net migration (26)	Number (27)	Percent change, 1990–2000 (28)	Persons per household (29)	Female family householder[1] (30)	One person (31)
NORTH CAROLINA—Cont'd																
Chowan	10.7	9.4	8.5	53.2	14 554	13 506	7.6	0.2	286	238	-13	5 580	9.1	2.48	15.7	25.3
Clay	13.5	12.1	10.6	51.3	9 086	7 155	22.6	3.5	86	136	354	3 847	31.4	2.25	7.5	26.3
Cleveland	9.9	7.3	6.2	51.9	97 432	84 958	13.3	1.2	1 697	1 219	700	37 046	15.6	2.53	13.7	23.6
Columbus	10.3	7.8	6.0	51.9	54 905	49 587	10.4	0.3	1 109	794	-133	21 308	15.4	2.50	15.8	26.5
Craven	8.8	8.0	5.4	49.5	91 316	81 812	11.8	-0.1	2 196	1 048	-1 217	34 582	17.1	2.50	12.5	23.4
Cumberland	6.8	4.8	2.9	49.4	299 203	274 713	10.3	-1.2	7 561	2 392	-8 835	107 358	17.3	2.65	15.5	22.4
Currituck	11.0	7.2	4.8	50.3	19 018	13 736	32.4	4.6	257	238	789	6 902	37.0	2.61	9.2	19.4
Dare	11.7	8.7	5.1	49.6	31 168	22 746	31.7	4.0	419	284	1 043	12 690	35.7	2.34	8.1	25.0
Davidson	10.0	7.1	5.6	51.0	149 690	126 688	16.2	1.7	2 483	1 562	1 561	58 156	18.8	2.50	10.8	22.9
Davie	10.5	7.4	6.4	50.8	36 193	27 859	25.0	3.9	541	444	1 235	13 750	27.5	2.51	9.2	22.2
Duplin	9.3	7.1	5.7	50.4	49 446	39 995	22.7	0.8	1 007	707	107	18 267	22.4	2.63	14.2	24.5
Durham	7.1	4.9	4.8	51.8	227 034	181 844	22.8	1.7	4 619	2 292	1 487	89 015	23.1	2.40	14.8	30.0
Edgecombe	9.1	6.9	5.6	53.5	54 754	56 692	-1.9	-1.5	1 105	796	-1 180	20 392	0.4	2.67	21.5	24.0
Forsyth	8.9	6.9	5.7	52.2	310 187	265 855	15.1	1.3	5 813	3 561	1 997	123 851	15.3	2.39	13.5	28.9
Franklin	8.9	6.0	5.0	50.7	49 065	36 414	29.8	3.8	791	534	1 519	17 843	32.1	2.58	13.1	23.5
Gaston	9.3	7.1	5.5	51.6	191 952	174 769	8.9	0.8	3 497	2 403	589	73 936	13.1	2.53	13.2	23.3
Gates	10.5	7.8	6.6	51.0	10 592	9 305	13.0	0.7	147	145	73	3 901	16.4	2.66	13.3	21.7
Graham	12.8	9.9	8.0	51.2	8 017	7 196	11.1	0.3	128	130	25	3 354	21.0	2.35	8.4	26.0
Granville	9.1	6.5	4.9	47.5	50 183	38 341	26.5	3.5	799	588	1 451	16 654	26.8	2.58	15.0	23.9
Greene	9.0	6.6	5.4	48.6	19 193	15 384	23.3	1.2	350	208	77	6 696	24.1	2.65	17.3	22.6
Guilford	8.5	6.3	5.4	52.1	425 382	347 431	21.2	1.0	7 614	4 367	1 303	168 667	22.5	2.41	13.4	27.9
Halifax	9.6	8.1	6.8	52.4	56 703	55 516	3.3	-1.2	1 023	852	-832	22 122	8.8	2.51	20.4	27.7
Harnett	8.0	5.9	4.5	50.6	93 602	67 833	34.2	2.8	1 846	926	1 663	33 800	34.4	2.61	13.5	23.3
Haywood	12.7	10.4	8.6	52.1	54 623	46 948	15.1	1.1	709	817	697	23 100	20.2	2.30	9.5	26.7
Henderson	11.6	11.2	10.5	51.6	91 267	69 747	27.9	2.3	1 301	1 291	2 076	37 414	30.3	2.33	8.4	25.7
Hertford	10.3	8.5	7.3	54.1	22 099	22 317	1.3	-2.2	404	357	-556	8 953	9.9	2.48	19.5	26.9
Hoke	6.7	4.7	3.0	49.5	34 906	22 856	47.2	3.7	901	280	635	11 373	53.6	2.86	18.2	19.0
Hyde	10.4	8.5	7.9	47.1	5 703	5 411	7.7	-2.1	71	77	-119	2 185	4.3	2.36	13.1	30.6
Iredell	9.5	6.8	5.5	51.0	127 409	93 205	31.6	3.9	2 244	1 372	3 816	47 360	33.1	2.56	11.3	22.7
Jackson	11.0	7.9	5.9	51.2	33 566	26 835	23.4	1.3	438	398	405	13 191	36.2	2.30	10.0	27.0
Johnston	8.6	5.5	4.3	50.3	128 248	81 306	50.0	5.2	2 463	1 255	4 976	46 595	47.6	2.58	10.6	23.1
Jones	10.4	8.4	7.1	51.8	10 392	9 361	10.9	0.1	173	152	-7	4 061	16.3	2.53	15.2	24.5
Lee	9.2	7.2	5.7	50.6	49 279	41 370	18.5	0.5	1 147	640	-263	18 466	17.7	2.61	13.4	23.5
Lenoir	10.1	8.2	6.4	52.5	59 310	57 274	4.1	-0.6	1 145	911	-564	23 862	8.8	2.43	17.3	28.4
Lincoln	10.0	6.5	5.0	50.3	64 999	50 319	26.8	1.9	1 083	701	843	24 041	28.1	2.62	10.0	20.1
McDowell	10.7	7.9	6.4	50.2	42 796	35 681	18.1	1.5	686	556	523	16 604	21.4	2.45	10.2	24.3
Macon	13.4	12.1	10.2	52.1	30 533	23 504	26.8	2.4	388	491	816	12 828	30.4	2.28	8.0	27.0
Madison	11.2	8.3	7.7	50.7	19 970	16 953	15.8	1.7	305	293	322	8 000	23.3	2.34	8.9	26.3
Martin	10.3	8.2	7.0	53.6	25 374	25 078	2.1	-0.9	500	404	-312	10 020	7.5	2.53	17.6	25.7
Mecklenburg	7.2	4.7	3.9	50.9	716 407	511 211	36.0	3.0	14 410	5 670	12 243	273 416	36.6	2.49	12.4	27.6
Mitchell	12.4	10.3	8.3	51.1	15 869	14 433	8.7	1.2	211	233	202	6 551	13.4	2.53	12.4	25.2
Montgomery	10.0	7.5	6.5	49.4	26 898	23 359	14.8	0.3	568	339	-148	9 848	18.8	2.61	12.4	24.1
Moore	11.2	11.5	10.3	51.8	77 163	59 000	26.7	3.2	1 266	1 116	2 217	30 713	28.9	2.38	10.2	24.9
Nash	8.9	6.8	5.6	51.9	88 443	76 677	14.0	1.2	1 668	1 047	418	33 644	15.9	2.54	14.5	25.0
New Hanover	9.6	7.2	5.7	51.7	163 455	120 284	33.3	2.0	2 584	1 711	2 292	68 183	41.6	2.29	11.5	28.9
Northampton	11.1	9.2	8.2	52.1	21 980	21 004	5.2	-0.5	382	369	-112	8 691	14.5	2.44	18.3	28.4
Onslow	5.8	4.0	2.3	44.8	145 988	149 838	0.3	-2.9	4 168	979	-7 451	48 122	18.4	2.72	11.6	18.6
Orange	6.9	4.5	3.9	52.6	119 894	93 662	26.2	1.4	1 538	922	1 084	45 863	27.0	2.36	9.4	28.1
Pamlico	12.8	11.2	7.5	49.6	12 929	11 368	13.8	0.0	147	204	56	5 178	14.5	2.38	11.5	25.0
Pasquotank	8.8	7.3	6.8	51.6	34 947	31 298	11.5	0.1	599	494	-38	12 907	13.4	2.52	16.3	25.4
Pender	11.4	8.5	5.5	49.7	42 007	28 855	42.4	2.3	586	500	836	16 054	44.5	2.49	11.2	22.9
Perquimans	13.0	10.6	8.7	52.3	11 487	10 447	8.8	1.0	141	174	154	4 645	16.5	2.42	12.6	24.1
Person	9.8	7.5	6.2	51.8	36 114	30 180	18.0	1.4	586	444	356	14 085	23.3	2.50	13.8	24.2
Pitt	7.1	5.2	4.3	52.6	134 977	108 480	23.3	0.9	2 613	1 269	-110	52 539	29.8	2.43	14.4	28.3
Polk	11.7	10.7	12.9	52.6	18 741	14 458	26.7	2.3	231	331	509	7 908	29.4	2.28	7.9	28.9
Randolph	9.7	6.7	5.4	50.6	131 790	106 546	22.4	1.0	2 407	1 340	320	50 659	23.3	2.55	10.2	22.5
Richmond	9.5	7.4	6.2	50.9	46 677	44 511	4.6	0.2	921	661	-128	17 873	6.4	2.51	17.0	26.3
Robeson	8.2	5.6	4.3	51.4	123 891	105 170	17.3	0.4	2 963	1 574	-808	43 677	20.8	2.75	20.6	22.7
Rockingham	10.2	7.9	6.9	51.7	92 123	86 064	6.8	0.2	1 629	1 296	-94	36 989	10.6	2.45	12.8	25.7
Rowan	9.1	7.2	6.8	50.6	132 233	110 605	17.8	1.5	2 231	1 804	1 495	49 940	17.5	2.52	11.9	24.7
Rutherford	10.5	8.4	7.7	51.8	63 332	56 956	10.4	0.7	1 078	955	333	25 191	13.5	2.44	11.7	25.5
Sampson	9.4	7.0	5.8	50.5	60 683	47 297	27.2	0.9	1 215	830	167	22 273	27.1	2.64	14.3	23.7
Scotland	9.2	6.3	5.1	53.1	35 889	33 763	6.6	-0.3	734	409	-431	13 399	13.2	2.61	20.4	24.4
Stanly	9.7	7.6	6.6	50.7	58 622	51 765	12.2	0.9	936	752	360	22 223	12.5	2.53	10.5	24.3
Stokes	10.4	6.5	5.3	51.0	45 179	37 224	20.1	1.0	677	514	314	17 579	24.5	2.51	9.7	22.8
Surry	10.5	8.1	7.3	51.1	71 600	61 704	15.4	0.5	1 231	987	174	28 408	17.1	2.46	9.7	25.0

1. No spouse present.

Items 16—31

STATE County	Births, average 1997–1999 Total	Rate[1]	Deaths, average 1997–1999 Number Total	Number Infant[2]	Rate Total[1]	Rate Infant[3]	Physicians,[4] 2000 Number	Rate[5]	Hospitals,[4] 1998 Number	Beds Number	Beds Rate[5]	Medicare enrollees 2000	Serious crimes known to police, 2000[6] Total Number	Rate[7]
	32	33	34	35	36	37	38	39	40	41	42	43	44	45
NORTH CAROLINA—Cont'd														
Chowan	199	13.9	178	NA	12.5	NA	27	186	1	111	782	2 937	510	3 511
Clay	73	8.5	98	NA	11.5	NA	2	23	0	0	0	2 184	104	1 185
Cleveland	1 303	14.0	952	16	10.3	12.0	116	120	3	421	454	16 348	5 201	5 517
Columbus	755	14.3	600	NA	11.4	NA	33	60	1	136	258	10 071	2 991	5 660
Craven	1 618	18.3	794	14	9.0	8.4	168	184	1	276	313	14 924	2 764	3 023
Cumberland	5 600	19.7	1 843	64	6.5	11.4	543	179	2	515	181	29 240	18 375	6 065
Currituck	209	11.8	164	NA	9.2	NA	9	49	0	0	0	2 465	459	2 523
Dare	354	12.3	218	NA	7.6	NA	20	67	0	0	0	4 361	1 908	6 367
Davidson	1 826	12.9	1 216	15	8.6	8.2	99	67	2	195	138	19 484	3 909	2 681
Davie	386	12.1	330	NA	10.3	NA	36	103	1	46	143	5 338	723	2 075
Duplin	691	16.0	526	NA	12.2	NA	31	63	1	80	186	7 189	1 721	3 537
Durham	3 191	15.8	1 737	35	8.6	11.1	1 736	777	2	1 187	586	25 274	18 572	8 317
Edgecombe	817	14.8	617	NA	11.2	NA	42	76	1	127	230	9 488	3 068	5 561
Forsyth	4 182	14.5	2 659	51	9.2	12.2	1 102	360	3	1 648	573	45 624	21 891	7 152
Franklin	586	13.1	398	NA	8.9	NA	32	68	1	67	150	5 712	1 361	2 902
Gaston	2 632	14.3	1 834	23	10.0	8.9	234	123	1	404	219	28 754	NA	NA
Gates	125	12.4	115	NA	11.4	NA	0	0	0	0	0	1 779	144	1 369
Graham	92	12.1	102	NA	13.3	NA	4	50	0	0	0	1 629	114	1 426
Granville	571	13.2	421	NA	9.8	NA	58	120	1	66	154	6 703	1 944	4 008
Greene	245	13.4	163	NA	8.9	NA	3	16	0	0	0	2 274	686	3 615
Guilford	5 390	13.9	3 361	51	8.7	9.5	857	204	3	1 155	298	56 496	25 059	5 952
Halifax	763	13.6	642	10	11.4	12.7	54	94	2	262	464	11 713	2 715	4 732
Harnett	1 421	17.2	704	12	8.5	8.7	53	58	2	134	163	9 846	3 840	4 383
Haywood	545	10.6	623	NA	12.1	NA	77	143	1	141	274	11 539	1 507	2 789
Henderson	958	11.8	1 019	NA	12.6	NA	179	201	2	281	348	21 108	2 401	2 693
Hertford	271	12.2	261	NA	11.8	NA	30	133	1	124	556	4 228	1 147	5 075
Hoke	575	18.9	212	NA	7.0	NA	11	33	0	0	0	2 533	1 372	4 078
Hyde	57	10.0	67	NA	11.8	NA	2	34	0	0	0	988	44	755
Iredell	1 630	14.4	1 032	14	9.1	8.4	186	152	3	442	390	17 388	4 789	3 904
Jackson	318	10.6	294	NA	9.8	NA	73	220	1	186	616	4 978	552	1 667
Johnston	1 746	16.4	939	14	8.8	7.8	63	52	1	127	119	14 205	5 621	4 609
Jones	117	12.4	109	NA	11.6	NA	5	48	0	0	0	1 808	112	1 079
Lee	765	15.6	458	8	9.3	10.5	85	173	1	137	278	8 540	2 196	4 573
Lenoir	798	13.5	691	12	11.7	15.4	109	183	1	252	427	11 448	3 095	5 234
Lincoln	797	13.7	502	NA	8.6	NA	53	83	1	75	129	8 884	2 125	3 332
McDowell	444	11.1	338	NA	8.5	NA	32	76	1	65	162	7 224	992	2 353
Macon	294	10.4	370	NA	13.1	NA	41	138	2	105	371	7 171	604	2 026
Madison	222	11.9	211	NA	11.2	NA	9	46	0	0	0	3 613	70	427
Martin	411	15.6	356	NA	13.5	NA	33	129	1	49	187	4 798	1 241	4 849
Mecklenburg	10 065	15.9	4 255	71	6.7	7.1	1 648	237	6	1 895	300	69 100	52 354	7 528
Mitchell	155	10.5	194	NA	13.1	NA	21	134	1	40	270	3 324	NA	NA
Montgomery	406	16.8	249	NA	10.3	NA	15	56	1	86	357	4 256	897	3 450
Moore	894	12.5	816	10	11.4	11.6	194	259	1	359	503	17 709	2 268	3 088
Nash	1 181	13.0	825	13	9.1	11.0	148	169	2	285	313	13 109	5 088	5 901
New Hanover	1 890	12.7	1 300	13	8.7	6.9	405	253	2	611	408	24 130	11 246	7 082
Northampton	250	11.8	283	NA	13.3	NA	7	32	0	0	0	4 586	468	2 119
Onslow	3 196	22.4	736	23	5.2	7.3	175	116	1	133	93	11 871	5 840	3 884
Orange	1 234	11.2	676	12	6.1	9.5	988	836	1	648	588	11 553	5 394	4 562
Pamlico	124	10.1	155	NA	12.6	NA	4	31	0	0	0	2 442	210	1 624
Pasquotank	472	13.3	351	NA	9.9	NA	81	232	1	130	366	5 544	1 272	3 645
Pender	483	12.3	357	NA	9.1	NA	18	44	1	66	167	6 291	859	2 091
Perquimans	117	10.5	139	NA	12.4	NA	2	18	0	0	0	2 452	252	2 217
Person	447	13.3	330	NA	9.8	NA	18	51	1	93	276	5 519	1 079	3 029
Pitt	1 866	14.8	1 010	22	8.0	11.8	511	382	1	571	451	16 086	9 302	6 952
Polk	163	9.7	254	NA	15.1	NA	31	169	1	26	154	4 532	294	1 604
Randolph	1 734	14.3	1 025	13	8.4	7.3	91	70	1	105	87	18 398	5 105	3 921
Richmond	655	14.2	513	NA	11.2	NA	37	79	2	193	418	8 484	2 609	5 603
Robeson	2 007	17.4	1 157	29	10.0	14.3	92	75	1	280	242	17 490	8 856	7 205
Rockingham	1 152	12.8	992	11	11.0	9.6	95	103	2	372	413	16 182	3 553	3 908
Rowan	1 686	13.5	1 355	13	10.8	7.5	178	137	1	238	190	18 396	4 469	3 429
Rutherford	792	13.0	708	NA	11.6	NA	68	108	1	114	187	11 398	2 209	3 556
Sampson	784	15.0	604	7	11.5	9.3	48	80	1	146	278	8 665	2 316	3 964
Scotland	550	15.4	355	9	9.9	16.4	49	136	1	174	486	5 246	1 912	5 399
Stanly	748	13.4	605	NA	10.8	NA	59	102	1	119	212	9 884	2 466	4 244
Stokes	535	12.4	381	NA	8.8	NA	20	45	1	93	215	5 568	995	2 301
Surry	920	13.7	748	8	11.1	8.7	75	105	2	253	377	13 375	2 629	3 691

1. Per 1,000 estimated resident population, average 1997–1999.   2. Deaths of infants under 1 year old.   3. Deaths of infants under 1 year old per 1,000 live births.   4. Data subject to copyright.   5. Per 100,000 resident population as of July 1 of the year shown.   6. Data for serious crimes have not been adjusted for underreporting; this may affect comparability between geographic areas and over time.   7. Per 100,000 population estimated by the FBI.

STATE County	Serious crimes known to police, 2000[1] (cont'd) Rate[2]		Education						Money income 1989				Income and poverty, 1998			
			School enrollment and attainment, 1990				Local government expenditures, fiscal 1999[5]							Percent below poverty level		
			Enrollment[3]		Attainment[4] (percent)					Households						
										Median						
	Violent	Property	Total	Percent private	High school graduate or more	Bachelor's degree or more	Total current expenditures (mil dol)	Current expenditures per student (dollars)	Per capita[6] (dollars)	Dollars	Percent change, 1979–1989 (constant 1989 dollars)	Percent with $100,000 or more	Median household income	All persons	Persons under 18	Persons 5–17 in families
	46	47	48	49	50	51	52	53	54	55	56	57	58	59	60	61
NORTH CAROLINA—Cont'd																
Chowan	282	3 229	3 168	4.6	63.3	12.2	15.7	6 027	10 606	20 397	6.0	1.9	28 390	18.4	26.1	27.3
Clay	125	1 060	1 615	3.0	62.9	12.6	8.2	6 305	9 456	18 532	7.9	0.9	28 614	15.1	20.9	22.8
Cleveland	487	5 030	19 330	8.5	63.5	11.1	97.4	5 645	11 875	26 476	4.2	1.8	34 996	14.1	22.2	19.2
Columbus	522	5 138	12 617	5.0	59.4	9.1	58.2	5 668	9 134	18 468	1.1	1.2	26 160	21.1	27.8	27.1
Craven	330	2 693	20 091	9.5	75.9	15.1	81.6	5 505	11 619	25 619	17.0	1.7	34 357	14.4	21.3	21.0
Cumberland	544	5 521	73 885	9.7	80.3	16.6	264.8	5 163	11 100	25 462	13.1	1.6	35 272	16.3	22.8	20.9
Currituck	308	2 216	3 078	5.4	67.7	8.2	20.3	6 503	12 630	27 905	30.2	1.2	38 184	11.0	15.8	17.5
Dare	200	6 167	4 547	12.2	81.0	21.4	27.9	6 145	15 107	29 322	29.1	3.8	36 440	8.8	12.9	13.5
Davidson	216	2 465	27 585	6.9	64.2	10.0	127.8	5 278	12 597	27 913	9.3	2.0	38 569	11.1	18.2	15.2
Davie	126	1 949	6 323	6.7	69.6	14.7	29.4	5 492	14 648	29 659	12.4	3.8	43 273	8.7	13.2	12.1
Duplin	399	3 139	9 603	4.5	56.4	6.6	43.7	5 131	9 406	19 695	5.6	0.8	26 980	19.7	27.3	24.1
Durham	879	7 437	51 606	26.7	78.9	33.4	192.3	6 622	15 030	30 526	18.3	3.3	41 970	12.6	20.5	18.6
Edgecombe	555	5 007	14 587	6.4	58.5	8.1	45.9	5 737	9 530	21 390	-2.3	0.8	27 614	22.8	32.7	29.3
Forsyth	930	6 222	64 607	21.1	77.6	24.1	261.2	6 096	16 151	30 449	9.4	4.5	41 114	11.4	18.3	16.2
Franklin	115	2 787	8 429	16.2	62.4	9.2	38.2	5 192	10 959	25 049	27.1	1.3	35 915	13.7	21.2	19.0
Gaston	NA	NA	40 639	10.4	60.9	10.8	160.2	5 278	12 447	28 126	5.6	1.8	38 293	12.5	19.3	17.4
Gates	162	1 208	2 202	5.0	60.8	7.4	13.3	6 427	11 561	23 408	7.0	1.9	31 553	15.3	23.3	24.0
Graham	263	1 164	1 624	1.7	56.9	10.0	8.8	7 112	8 877	16 754	-11.1	1.3	26 461	17.9	25.3	27.2
Granville	417	3 592	8 398	5.6	62.0	9.6	42.5	5 433	10 939	26 488	16.4	1.2	36 073	12.5	18.5	17.4
Greene	348	3 268	3 799	8.7	59.2	8.9	18.4	6 193	9 567	22 703	11.7	0.9	30 307	17.5	27.6	23.3
Guilford	681	5 271	88 607	13.4	76.1	24.8	370.0	6 050	15 373	30 148	9.2	4.3	41 315	11.4	18.3	15.6
Halifax	465	4 267	13 501	6.9	53.9	8.6	65.3	6 063	8 980	18 932	8.0	1.1	26 255	23.5	32.3	30.9
Harnett	506	3 878	16 468	15.9	64.0	9.5	79.7	5 111	10 053	21 743	7.1	1.3	33 702	15.7	23.3	21.2
Haywood	246	2 543	9 656	5.0	68.0	12.8	45.2	5 858	11 731	22 462	3.3	1.5	32 200	14.0	22.1	20.9
Henderson	173	2 520	13 784	9.7	76.2	19.5	63.3	5 511	13 702	26 967	13.5	2.1	36 716	11.8	18.5	18.2
Hertford	522	4 553	6 125	13.7	58.1	10.7	23.5	5 509	9 016	18 180	-9.3	0.9	24 984	22.8	32.3	31.7
Hoke	285	3 792	6 430	5.0	55.7	8.4	31.5	5 078	8 688	22 770	6.1	0.7	28 237	18.6	25.5	23.8
Hyde	17	738	1 188	11.4	60.0	7.7	7.5	9 419	9 434	17 665	8.3	2.3	24 488	24.4	31.8	36.5
Iredell	388	3 516	20 320	6.8	66.5	11.8	105.2	5 301	13 000	28 627	13.0	2.1	40 389	9.4	14.2	12.6
Jackson	133	1 534	8 915	4.3	68.7	19.7	21.3	5 924	10 326	21 520	12.8	1.5	31 486	15.5	20.1	21.1
Johnston	412	4 196	18 463	6.6	64.6	11.1	102.5	5 308	11 839	25 169	21.9	1.6	39 844	12.7	18.8	16.6
Jones	116	963	2 135	7.6	62.4	8.1	11.2	6 741	8 832	19 392	3.5	0.5	27 356	18.7	28.5	27.8
Lee	325	4 248	9 869	6.7	72.4	14.3	47.6	5 435	12 042	26 419	6.6	1.5	36 612	13.2	20.2	19.1
Lenoir	619	4 615	14 394	6.0	62.9	11.5	58.1	5 597	10 647	21 207	-1.7	1.5	28 554	19.4	28.2	26.4
Lincoln	160	3 172	11 002	6.7	62.0	10.5	51.4	5 037	12 440	28 662	7.8	1.9	37 077	9.8	12.0	15.9
McDowell	142	2 211	7 920	3.9	58.5	8.1	34.1	5 330	10 516	22 562	0.1	1.1	32 864	12.1	17.0	16.1
Macon	97	1 929	4 334	5.1	66.7	13.2	23.9	5 993	11 017	20 450	9.5	1.1	30 487	13.7	21.3	24.2
Madison	37	391	4 027	23.1	56.4	11.3	15.9	6 140	9 149	18 956	18.8	0.7	29 551	17.1	22.4	23.7
Martin	516	4 333	6 221	4.2	58.3	9.5	30.5	6 069	9 486	19 995	1.2	0.8	26 618	20.4	27.9	27.9
Mecklenburg	1 104	6 424	129 647	16.5	81.6	28.3	611.6	6 193	16 910	33 830	13.2	5.1	46 033	9.9	15.7	13.8
Mitchell	NA	NA	2 835	5.3	55.3	9.2	13.8	5 760	10 219	20 554	2.0	1.1	31 235	13.9	20.8	20.8
Montgomery	219	3 231	5 579	5.7	55.3	7.8	25.7	5 882	10 695	22 682	5.5	1.7	30 575	15.8	23.4	22.1
Moore	219	2 869	12 901	8.1	74.3	19.9	61.6	5 678	14 934	28 053	15.6	3.9	38 703	11.1	18.5	18.1
Nash	554	5 347	18 427	11.6	65.1	13.7	99.2	5 492	12 684	25 834	13.1	2.7	35 576	14.1	21.0	19.3
New Hanover	585	6 497	31 336	10.0	78.1	21.2	129.4	6 019	13 863	27 320	6.3	2.9	39 546	13.2	20.0	18.8
Northampton	308	1 811	5 042	6.8	52.8	8.8	22.9	5 743	8 244	18 029	4.0	0.9	26 433	22.1	32.2	31.7
Onslow	297	3 587	33 122	8.6	83.0	13.4	107.2	5 025	10 713	23 386	13.1	1.0	31 532	16.1	20.2	20.3
Orange	321	4 242	35 128	9.3	83.6	46.1	103.6	7 067	15 776	29 968	19.7	6.0	42 202	9.9	11.7	12.7
Pamlico	131	1 492	2 635	2.7	65.9	11.6	12.5	6 752	10 665	21 060	6.8	1.2	30 041	18.0	26.1	27.3
Pasquotank	510	3 135	8 699	6.1	67.4	14.4	35.2	5 627	10 718	21 816	5.9	2.3	30 655	18.6	24.8	26.4
Pender	144	1 947	6 367	5.2	64.6	11.6	34.6	5 446	11 460	23 270	16.9	1.7	31 621	15.0	21.2	22.4
Perquimans	194	2 023	2 194	7.5	61.2	8.8	12.5	6 530	9 821	20 022	9.5	1.5	28 100	19.6	28.5	30.3
Person	413	2 616	6 770	6.1	63.2	7.6	32.3	5 568	11 158	25 625	12.0	1.0	34 251	11.6	16.9	17.6
Pitt	655	6 297	35 790	6.7	71.0	21.9	108.7	5 428	11 642	23 324	7.8	2.3	33 195	17.8	23.2	23.1
Polk	175	1 430	2 558	11.6	69.6	20.1	14.9	6 301	14 213	26 801	19.1	3.5	37 262	10.4	18.1	16.1
Randolph	141	3 779	22 444	8.8	62.0	9.1	105.4	5 110	12 102	27 130	4.3	1.7	37 254	9.0	13.4	12.8
Richmond	427	5 176	10 872	6.7	60.4	7.9	45.9	5 503	9 841	21 953	-2.4	1.0	27 904	18.9	26.5	25.7
Robeson	674	6 532	29 676	3.7	57.0	11.0	123.4	5 125	8 878	19 716	2.3	1.5	25 946	23.7	29.0	28.6
Rockingham	316	3 592	18 946	5.4	59.2	8.8	81.0	5 500	11 546	25 402	3.8	1.2	33 300	12.4	17.7	17.7
Rowan	366	3 063	25 239	12.9	66.0	11.7	107.0	5 387	12 018	26 354	2.9	1.5	36 409	11.7	16.7	17.0
Rutherford	295	3 261	12 624	6.3	59.4	9.8	57.9	5 627	11 287	23 828	6.8	1.3	31 944	13.9	19.5	20.0
Sampson	264	3 700	11 810	5.1	61.3	8.1	56.1	5 525	9 480	19 709	2.3	1.3	28 588	17.6	23.5	23.1
Scotland	438	4 961	9 478	11.6	60.7	13.6	43.5	6 075	9 768	22 561	-3.2	1.2	29 762	19.4	26.3	25.3
Stanly	227	4 017	11 585	10.1	62.1	9.4	52.6	5 206	11 265	25 374	4.3	1.3	36 322	11.1	16.8	16.4
Stokes	173	2 127	8 407	6.3	62.8	7.3	40.5	5 669	12 181	27 945	9.1	1.5	37 991	10.8	16.7	14.5
Surry	598	3 093	13 340	4.5	57.3	9.4	66.4	5 865	11 342	23 444	5.2	1.7	32 266	12.4	17.3	17.6

1. Data for serious crimes have not been adjusted for underreporting; this may affect comparability between geographic areas and over time.   2. Per 100,000 population estimated by the FBI.   3. All persons 3 years old and over enrolled in nursery school through college.   4. Persons 25 years old and over.   5. Elementary and secondary education expenditures, local government fiscal years ending between July 1, 1998 and June 30, 1999.   6. Based on population enumerated as of April 1, 1990.

Table B. States and Counties — Personal Income

STATE County	Personal income, 1999												
			Per capita[1]					Transfer payments					
									Government payments to individuals				
	Total (mil dol)	Percent change, 1998–1999	Dollars	Rank	Wages and salaries[2] (mil dol)	Proprietor's income (mil dol)	Dividends, interest, and rent (mil dol)	Total (mil dol)	Total (mil dol)	Social Security (mil dol)	Medical payments (mil dol)	Income mainte-nance (mil dol)	Unemploy-ment insurance (mil dol)
	62	63	64	65	66	67	68	69	70	71	72	73	74
NORTH CAROLINA—Cont'd													
Chowan	311	3.6	21 711	1 448	144	32	66	69	66	26	27	9	0
Clay	177	5.8	20 252	1 905	43	21	42	42	41	19	16	4	0
Cleveland	2 035	2.6	21 647	1 472	1 122	110	359	379	362	160	142	36	12
Columbus	1 049	-0.8	19 815	2 054	495	111	132	290	281	88	134	42	6
Craven	2 173	3.5	24 312	801	1 647	105	459	335	321	131	128	37	4
Cumberland	7 172	4.3	25 285	616	5 401	324	1 072	888	845	267	306	128	14
Currituck	427	8.0	23 319	1 010	98	25	70	56	53	23	20	5	1
Dare	728	7.1	24 566	741	403	99	181	94	89	45	33	4	3
Davidson	3 481	4.7	24 365	788	1 508	219	704	472	446	217	169	35	8
Davie	964	5.9	29 473	231	301	70	219	116	110	54	43	8	2
Duplin	830	-3.6	19 133	2 250	450	73	104	191	183	63	79	26	4
Durham	6 057	3.1	29 677	220	8 278	297	1 247	675	637	255	261	68	9
Edgecombe	938	-14.8	17 153	2 709	747	65	39	264	254	82	117	41	5
Forsyth	9 466	5.2	32 775	132	6 621	694	2 143	1 028	976	455	379	85	14
Franklin	1 034	5.5	22 667	1 174	302	83	144	156	148	53	68	19	2
Gaston	4 527	3.9	24 449	769	2 521	293	751	698	665	293	273	62	14
Gates	189	1.7	18 586	2 400	46	15	33	41	39	16	16	5	0
Graham	138	5.4	18 116	2 518	58	18	23	39	38	14	17	4	1
Granville	985	5.3	22 102	1 332	606	46	173	152	144	61	59	16	2
Greene	328	-3.2	17 698	2 601	110	24	35	68	65	22	29	10	1
Guilford	12 299	4.3	31 425	172	10 197	778	2 750	1 349	1 278	581	494	116	23
Halifax	1 082	1.6	19 377	2 188	533	90	170	300	289	100	118	57	4
Harnett	1 665	4.2	19 705	2 083	615	122	286	280	265	93	117	33	5
Haywood	1 160	3.4	22 301	1 274	476	106	259	244	234	114	87	20	4
Henderson	2 285	6.4	27 782	350	1 068	207	683	400	385	204	142	22	3
Hertford	398	0.0	18 161	2 507	224	15	58	114	110	38	49	18	1
Hoke	425	3.3	13 560	3 068	198	19	61	95	90	31	37	14	3
Hyde	103	-7.4	17 613	2 622	49	13	13	27	26	8	12	4	1
Iredell	2 965	6.8	25 233	627	1 755	190	533	398	377	174	160	25	6
Jackson	669	5.8	22 097	1 336	350	57	135	120	115	46	45	11	2
Johnston	2 670	8.2	24 085	846	995	211	375	365	345	133	152	40	4
Jones	170	-6.7	18 194	2 498	49	13	15	45	44	15	20	5	1
Lee	1 273	4.6	25 740	550	856	83	239	189	180	79	75	16	3
Lenoir	1 250	-2.7	21 244	1 585	869	60	207	292	281	98	129	37	5
Lincoln	1 283	4.3	21 781	1 421	561	87	156	188	177	83	71	14	4
McDowell	831	3.7	20 491	1 839	525	72	120	151	143	68	53	12	3
Macon	652	6.3	22 559	1 202	271	64	172	138	133	66	49	10	2
Madison	370	4.7	19 582	2 114	116	32	58	82	78	28	33	11	1
Martin	491	-0.4	18 770	2 353	304	23	82	124	120	40	51	17	4
Mecklenburg	24 199	8.5	37 321	66	22 091	1 980	4 385	1 721	1 604	717	620	163	28
Mitchell	303	4.4	20 519	1 831	156	21	53	70	67	28	27	7	2
Montgomery	521	6.3	21 440	1 537	309	62	82	97	92	35	42	9	2
Moore	2 173	5.3	29 820	218	892	190	774	341	327	174	116	20	3
Nash	2 225	2.0	24 088	845	1 322	172	323	315	298	116	116	39	6
New Hanover	4 184	6.7	27 731	354	2 798	301	1 033	580	553	244	215	52	9
Northampton	415	0.1	19 539	2 123	142	65	57	114	110	40	47	19	1
Onslow	3 299	4.1	23 157	1 058	2 502	135	449	334	315	104	125	41	5
Orange	3 290	5.0	29 500	228	2 091	163	760	277	257	116	106	18	2
Pamlico	270	2.9	21 919	1 384	71	14	61	56	54	24	21	6	1
Pasquotank	741	3.5	20 791	1 738	440	43	147	142	135	48	59	17	2
Pender	709	-1.6	17 605	2 624	215	50	93	155	148	61	63	15	2
Perquimans	214	3.5	18 938	2 302	45	25	42	51	49	22	19	6	0
Person	739	4.2	21 835	1 403	376	29	114	133	127	53	54	12	3
Pitt	2 974	1.4	23 239	1 032	2 003	113	480	439	416	145	180	62	9
Polk	519	4.2	30 729	186	106	43	217	83	80	45	27	4	1
Randolph	2 927	5.0	23 721	913	1 435	276	402	397	374	184	145	22	8
Richmond	916	4.6	20 032	1 982	455	88	133	230	222	75	94	26	4
Robeson	2 028	2.0	17 391	2 667	1 123	73	265	533	512	145	245	89	12
Rockingham	1 952	4.0	21 616	1 480	980	102	336	384	367	157	155	34	9
Rowan	2 889	4.3	22 820	1 136	1 636	146	545	455	432	198	161	34	8
Rutherford	1 276	3.2	20 751	1 755	713	90	205	256	244	109	91	23	10
Sampson	1 046	0.1	19 815	2 054	470	95	146	231	221	82	99	29	3
Scotland	724	4.9	20 182	1 937	547	20	111	160	153	54	67	23	3
Stanly	1 290	5.7	22 816	1 139	630	100	231	213	203	96	82	15	4
Stokes	929	4.5	21 170	1 605	209	47	142	131	123	57	48	11	2
Surry	1 594	4.2	23 465	968	962	177	266	281	269	116	116	21	6

1. Based on the resident population estimated as of July 1 of the year shown.   2. Includes other labor income.

STATE County	Earnings, 1999									Social Security beneficiaries, December 2000		Supplemental Security Income recipients, December 2000	Housing units, 1990	
			Goods-related[1]		Service-related and other[2]									
	Total (mil dol)	Farm	Total	Manu-facturing	Total	Retail trade	Finance, insurance, and real estate	Services	Govern-ment	Number	Rate[3]		Total	Percent change, 1980–1990
	75	76	77	78	79	80	81	82	83	84	85	86	87	88
NORTH CAROLINA—Cont'd														
Chowan	176	11.1	D	22.0	D	9.2	3.5	21.2	16.0	3 432	236	533	5 910	12.3
Clay	64	4.6	D	6.4	D	13.4	5.6	23.2	20.2	2 539	289	285	4 158	23.4
Cleveland	1 232	1.3	D	37.4	D	9.0	3.0	20.1	13.0	19 604	204	2 567	34 232	12.6
Columbus	605	7.3	D	28.9	D	9.9	1.7	20.3	18.0	12 371	226	3 775	20 513	7.6
Craven	1 752	-0.3	D	10.1	D	6.6	2.6	16.1	53.3	16 970	186	2 472	32 293	26.4
Cumberland	5 726	0.1	D	8.8	D	8.5	2.7	13.3	57.1	36 219	120	7 460	98 360	20.9
Currituck	122	0.7	19.5	3.7	D	19.6	6.3	17.9	27.4	2 980	164	255	7 367	36.3
Dare	502	0.0	18.4	6.0	64.5	22.8	12.0	21.0	17.1	5 272	176	264	21 567	96.0
Davidson	1 727	0.4	D	39.9	D	9.4	3.0	17.3	11.8	25 825	175	2 250	53 266	20.3
Davie	371	0.2	D	35.0	D	10.0	3.7	18.8	12.4	6 464	186	536	11 496	21.3
Duplin	523	9.9	D	33.7	D	7.7	D	12.8	18.1	9 208	188	2 086	16 395	5.2
Durham	8 575	0.1	D	39.4	D	4.9	4.5	32.9	9.0	29 299	131	4 187	77 710	33.2
Edgecombe	812	4.0	D	20.8	D	5.5	D	15.6	20.6	11 238	202	3 072	21 827	7.6
Forsyth	7 315	0.0	D	21.7	D	9.9	10.5	31.7	8.4	50 997	167	5 275	115 715	20.7
Franklin	385	7.9	D	23.1	D	10.4	D	18.0	18.1	7 278	154	1 608	14 957	34.1
Gaston	2 814	0.4	44.6	38.1	43.9	10.0	3.4	20.8	11.1	34 534	181	3 940	69 133	16.8
Gates	61	15.9	D	D	36.0	5.6	2.4	14.8	34.6	2 168	206	331	3 696	14.6
Graham	76	5.0	D	D	D	6.8	2.0	13.9	21.0	1 957	245	340	4 132	15.5
Granville	652	0.8	D	34.1	D	5.9	1.7	9.2	38.4	8 311	171	1 475	14 164	22.5
Greene	134	10.0	25.8	17.2	31.6	5.8	1.3	14.1	32.5	3 076	162	717	5 944	6.4
Guilford	10 975	0.3	29.8	23.4	59.6	9.6	7.9	24.6	10.4	65 289	155	7 082	146 812	21.9
Halifax	623	5.5	27.2	22.3	41.4	11.4	2.9	14.9	25.9	13 997	244	4 531	22 480	10.8
Harnett	737	2.8	D	22.0	D	10.6	3.2	21.8	20.1	12 348	136	2 259	27 896	25.8
Haywood	582	2.8	D	21.3	D	15.1	3.7	21.7	19.5	13 706	254	1 471	23 975	17.7
Henderson	1 275	6.4	D	26.2	D	10.8	D	22.1	12.2	23 319	262	1 651	34 131	25.5
Hertford	239	1.0	27.4	21.2	49.8	11.7	2.1	27.3	21.8	5 047	223	1 530	8 870	7.4
Hoke	217	2.0	D	34.4	D	4.6	D	11.9	30.4	4 378	130	943	7 999	23.5
Hyde	62	6.0	16.1	8.3	41.1	10.0	4.7	11.1	36.9	1 164	200	258	2 905	2.4
Iredell	1 945	2.2	38.4	30.6	47.9	11.9	2.5	23.3	11.6	20 762	169	1 923	39 191	21.1
Jackson	407	3.5	15.5	7.8	52.7	11.0	4.1	32.2	28.4	5 949	180	746	14 052	17.5
Johnston	1 207	4.3	D	25.9	D	12.4	4.5	16.2	16.1	18 121	149	3 551	34 172	22.2
Jones	62	7.8	14.4	6.7	51.8	7.8	1.5	26.3	26.0	2 248	217	413	3 829	4.8
Lee	938	1.5	50.4	44.1	38.1	10.1	2.4	15.8	10.0	9 373	191	1 202	16 954	21.1
Lenoir	928	0.2	D	23.9	D	8.8	3.2	21.3	24.1	13 006	218	2 901	23 739	5.2
Lincoln	648	2.3	D	35.5	D	9.3	4.5	14.1	15.4	10 060	158	984	20 189	24.9
McDowell	596	4.9	D	50.0	D	7.5	1.5	12.6	12.4	8 561	203	1 118	15 091	8.2
Macon	335	1.7	D	11.5	D	15.4	5.4	27.5	14.6	8 365	281	777	17 174	28.6
Madison	148	6.0	35.9	18.0	D	5.3	2.4	20.3	19.0	4 212	215	876	7 667	7.0
Martin	327	1.2	48.2	42.6	33.9	8.2	1.7	13.5	16.7	5 576	218	1 425	10 104	8.4
Mecklenburg	24 071	0.5	16.8	10.2	74.0	8.2	17.7	26.6	8.7	80 008	115	9 111	216 416	38.6
Mitchell	178	3.3	39.3	23.6	D	8.3	2.4	20.8	18.1	3 684	235	644	6 983	15.3
Montgomery	371	7.3	D	46.2	D	6.4	2.1	10.1	14.2	4 537	169	806	10 421	9.5
Moore	1 082	6.4	20.0	12.8	61.7	9.9	4.6	40.2	11.9	19 971	267	1 423	27 358	30.0
Nash	1 494	3.7	D	27.1	D	11.3	6.9	19.6	13.1	15 530	178	3 128	31 024	20.6
New Hanover	3 100	0.2	25.1	16.4	56.8	13.8	6.8	25.8	17.9	27 983	175	3 617	57 076	31.8
Northampton	207	27.5	D	16.0	D	4.9	D	12.4	21.9	5 619	254	1 447	8 974	2.9
Onslow	2 637	0.3	D	2.8	D	6.6	1.6	8.2	73.2	14 565	97	2 313	47 526	34.1
Orange	2 254	0.6	8.9	4.6	41.0	9.0	7.0	20.6	49.6	12 748	108	1 175	38 683	34.7
Pamlico	86	1.1	18.3	7.7	53.9	12.0	2.1	26.4	26.7	3 137	243	351	6 050	20.7
Pasquotank	482	0.9	10.1	4.8	45.2	12.6	4.3	18.1	43.8	6 459	185	1 202	12 298	17.1
Pender	265	4.0	D	14.8	D	8.8	D	16.1	26.8	8 141	198	1 124	15 437	50.0
Perquimans	70	16.1	11.6	3.5	D	7.9	D	15.0	27.7	2 961	260	402	4 972	19.2
Person	405	-1.7	47.1	39.3	38.8	10.2	2.4	14.5	15.7	6 854	192	1 008	12 548	17.4
Pitt	2 116	-0.8	D	18.7	D	10.0	4.4	21.3	32.0	19 446	145	4 702	43 070	30.6
Polk	148	3.1	28.2	18.5	D	9.6	4.5	31.8	16.7	5 149	281	273	7 273	22.7
Randolph	1 711	6.4	45.9	36.8	37.1	8.5	2.1	16.8	10.5	22 368	171	1 854	43 634	23.8
Richmond	542	8.5	29.9	23.9	43.9	10.6	2.9	18.7	17.6	9 903	213	2 031	18 218	6.9
Robeson	1 197	-0.9	36.7	29.1	D	10.9	2.7	20.8	21.4	21 115	171	7 388	39 045	17.2
Rockingham	1 082	0.0	48.7	40.3	37.8	9.8	2.3	17.7	13.5	19 165	208	2 758	35 657	10.5
Rowan	1 782	1.3	38.9	32.3	43.2	12.7	2.4	18.2	16.6	23 811	183	2 181	46 264	18.5
Rutherford	803	0.1	D	40.0	D	9.5	2.3	14.1	12.9	13 475	214	1 674	25 220	15.7
Sampson	565	10.3	28.1	21.6	40.4	10.9	2.2	15.1	21.1	11 849	197	2 240	19 183	5.2
Scotland	567	0.1	50.6	47.4	37.6	7.1	1.9	22.2	11.7	7 179	199	1 680	12 759	14.8
Stanly	730	2.9	45.3	36.2	37.8	10.4	2.7	17.8	14.0	11 559	199	1 006	21 808	13.7
Stokes	256	2.4	34.4	16.6	D	10.2	2.6	19.0	22.3	7 486	167	832	15 160	19.3
Surry	1 140	6.9	D	30.6	D	10.1	2.3	12.8	12.4	15 037	211	1 927	26 022	11.8

1. Covers mining, construction, and manufacturing.   2. Covers private sector earnings in agricultural services, forestry, and fisheries; transportation and public utilities; wholesale trade; retail trade; finance, insurance, and real estate; and services.   3. Per 1,000 resident population estimated as of July 1 of the year shown.

STATE County	Total	Percent	Median value[1]	With a mortgage	Without a mortgage	Median rent[2]	Rent as percent of income	Sub-standard units[3] (percent)	Total	Percent change, 2000–2001	Total	Rate[4]	Total	Professional, managerial, and technical	Precision production, craft, and repair
	89	90	91	92	93	94	95	96	97	98	99	100	101	102	103
NORTH CAROLINA—Cont'd															
Chowan	5 113	70.6	60 700	22.0	13.7	279	24.4	5.5	6 747	1.6	342	5.1	5 736	19.6	13.1
Clay	2 928	84.4	56 500	21.3	12.2	262	29.2	4.0	4 150	-1.1	168	4.0	2 944	17.7	17.1
Cleveland	32 037	72.8	53 400	18.6	12.4	327	23.8	3.7	45 744	4.0	5 231	11.4	42 546	19.8	15.8
Columbus	18 459	75.8	45 800	21.2	15.0	275	30.4	6.8	22 319	-1.7	2 129	9.5	20 348	19.7	15.0
Craven	29 542	63.3	65 900	21.8	12.7	374	24.2	4.3	36 783	0.7	1 932	5.3	31 305	24.5	14.5
Cumberland	91 500	57.7	63 500	23.1	13.9	406	26.1	4.3	120 051	-0.2	6 514	5.4	96 204	26.5	11.8
Currituck	5 038	80.3	79 200	22.6	14.4	423	22.7	4.0	9 103	0.1	251	2.8	6 357	19.8	22.3
Dare	9 349	71.1	108 100	24.3	12.5	516	27.6	2.2	18 222	-1.4	1 160	6.4	12 199	26.3	16.4
Davidson	48 944	73.6	60 800	18.0	12.2	351	22.9	2.9	80 163	0.7	5 080	6.3	68 344	18.9	17.2
Davie	10 785	82.1	68 000	17.8	12.3	362	22.9	2.8	17 609	-2.2	892	5.1	14 623	21.5	15.8
Duplin	14 925	75.9	42 600	18.9	14.0	267	24.4	6.2	22 200	1.4	1 387	6.2	18 301	16.2	15.1
Durham	72 297	53.0	85 500	21.8	13.2	444	24.6	2.6	117 745	1.6	4 454	3.8	96 658	40.7	8.8
Edgecombe	20 319	61.8	47 100	20.1	14.8	304	25.8	8.2	24 326	0.6	2 331	9.6	26 297	17.4	12.7
Forsyth	107 419	63.5	75 700	18.9	12.4	384	24.0	1.9	150 509	-1.5	6 269	4.2	136 304	32.7	10.6
Franklin	13 503	75.5	55 500	21.4	14.9	312	24.5	9.2	23 958	1.9	1 064	4.4	17 501	19.1	14.9
Gaston	65 347	69.3	57 700	18.6	13.0	360	22.0	3.8	104 809	1.0	8 495	8.1	89 280	20.0	15.8
Gates	3 352	81.1	49 700	19.5	13.3	237	17.4	11.7	4 676	1.9	164	3.5	3 898	14.2	16.0
Graham	2 772	81.7	47 400	18.4	12.2	226	27.1	4.5	4 285	-0.2	398	9.3	2 823	20.8	18.3
Granville	13 134	73.4	59 100	20.0	13.5	323	22.9	8.8	23 088	1.5	1 381	6.0	18 113	22.2	14.0
Greene	5 395	70.3	48 600	21.2	12.6	288	22.7	8.6	9 138	1.6	574	6.3	6 993	17.6	14.2
Guilford	137 706	61.3	79 400	20.8	12.8	428	24.4	2.4	217 328	-1.0	10 529	4.8	188 433	29.2	10.4
Halifax	20 335	65.3	44 800	19.5	14.7	287	26.8	10.6	22 853	3.5	2 547	11.1	21 954	18.1	13.8
Harnett	25 150	68.4	50 800	21.4	14.5	326	26.0	5.0	36 835	3.2	2 536	6.9	29 629	19.8	16.5
Haywood	19 211	77.1	59 600	20.4	12.8	305	24.4	3.0	23 997	0.4	1 368	5.7	20 763	22.4	15.3
Henderson	28 709	76.7	78 400	20.1	11.5	372	24.1	2.3	38 593	1.1	1 300	3.4	30 618	24.0	14.7
Hertford	8 150	68.6	44 900	21.8	14.0	275	25.3	9.4	10 975	1.3	774	7.1	9 519	19.4	14.0
Hoke	7 405	75.3	44 800	20.5	14.1	322	25.7	8.8	12 016	-0.4	968	8.1	9 117	16.7	16.2
Hyde	2 094	77.0	43 700	24.6	13.9	263	25.6	11.2	3 181	3.6	216	6.8	2 160	17.0	11.8
Iredell	35 573	75.1	63 300	18.5	12.5	360	22.3	3.5	65 605	2.7	3 771	5.7	48 907	20.1	15.1
Jackson	9 683	75.6	63 000	19.2	12.1	300	25.1	2.7	15 872	-0.6	616	3.9	12 346	27.3	13.3
Johnston	31 566	69.9	59 400	21.8	14.4	322	25.1	4.0	61 415	1.5	2 172	3.5	41 608	22.1	18.1
Jones	3 492	78.1	43 700	22.0	14.7	287	28.5	6.5	4 377	0.0	242	5.5	4 109	15.3	14.4
Lee	15 689	72.6	61 100	21.1	13.2	350	25.6	3.3	26 004	0.4	1 591	6.1	19 590	24.2	17.1
Lenoir	21 938	63.1	52 400	20.6	14.7	287	26.4	5.2	29 805	2.4	2 407	8.1	26 237	23.8	13.9
Lincoln	18 764	78.9	60 500	19.2	12.0	338	23.3	3.7	33 797	2.6	2 578	7.6	26 148	19.4	17.8
McDowell	13 680	77.1	45 100	16.7	12.0	296	21.4	3.5	19 765	2.1	1 584	8.0	17 266	17.8	16.8
Macon	9 834	82.8	62 500	21.8	12.7	318	23.9	2.8	13 858	-1.4	528	3.8	10 077	20.4	18.9
Madison	6 488	77.8	47 800	20.1	12.2	234	24.4	6.6	9 117	0.6	472	5.2	7 586	20.0	15.9
Martin	9 317	68.8	46 600	20.5	13.4	268	23.5	8.1	10 459	-1.1	857	8.2	11 079	18.0	15.2
Mecklenburg	200 219	59.7	86 900	20.4	12.4	467	24.1	3.0	379 224	0.6	15 589	4.1	281 201	33.0	9.2
Mitchell	5 779	82.5	44 700	21.5	12.7	282	21.6	4.0	7 830	5.2	796	10.2	6 253	17.1	17.7
Montgomery	8 290	77.1	43 900	19.7	12.9	287	22.6	7.6	12 227	3.1	882	7.2	11 205	14.8	16.0
Moore	23 827	77.6	80 300	20.9	12.1	356	24.7	3.7	30 299	0.8	1 527	5.0	26 342	24.2	13.6
Nash	29 041	64.4	63 200	18.7	13.5	345	22.9	6.3	43 135	-0.3	2 866	6.6	38 532	24.3	13.1
New Hanover	48 139	62.7	72 000	20.7	13.0	417	27.4	2.1	82 640	1.0	3 889	4.7	60 179	29.9	12.3
Northampton	7 591	76.6	38 100	21.5	14.7	231	23.9	8.9	8 372	2.7	795	9.5	8 069	16.3	13.0
Onslow	40 658	53.7	62 200	23.4	13.2	398	25.3	4.8	48 654	-0.9	2 199	4.5	38 674	24.0	13.8
Orange	36 104	55.3	101 500	22.0	12.5	472	28.9	2.2	64 302	1.0	1 413	2.2	50 671	44.4	9.0
Pamlico	4 523	81.1	54 300	21.2	13.1	328	30.6	3.4	5 441	0.5	246	4.5	4 718	20.3	16.2
Pasquotank	11 384	65.2	59 300	23.0	14.2	359	29.2	4.6	15 326	-0.4	694	4.5	12 673	24.6	16.7
Pender	11 112	82.6	60 200	20.4	13.4	350	24.8	6.1	17 097	0.7	1 039	6.1	12 868	21.7	16.6
Perquimans	3 988	76.8	53 200	22.4	12.8	306	26.4	4.7	4 863	0.0	236	4.9	4 220	17.9	13.5
Person	11 423	72.5	55 700	19.5	13.2	309	23.8	7.0	17 040	0.8	1 350	7.9	15 576	19.4	16.8
Pitt	40 491	58.1	65 300	20.3	13.5	350	28.2	5.4	69 128	0.1	4 184	6.1	53 492	30.0	10.5
Polk	6 110	79.9	60 200	19.9	12.2	332	21.9	2.8	8 014	-0.1	277	3.5	6 511	23.7	15.2
Randolph	41 096	77.0	60 200	18.6	12.3	341	23.0	3.1	70 928	-0.6	3 830	5.4	59 463	17.7	17.5
Richmond	16 793	72.3	40 000	19.4	14.6	301	22.9	4.6	19 686	3.1	1 900	9.7	20 375	16.9	14.6
Robeson	36 154	70.1	44 200	21.0	14.6	273	27.1	8.0	53 140	2.3	6 127	11.5	44 412	18.4	16.5
Rockingham	33 446	74.3	48 800	17.8	12.8	307	22.1	4.7	44 505	0.8	3 290	7.4	42 607	17.5	15.4
Rowan	42 512	73.6	54 600	18.2	12.4	347	22.8	2.8	68 407	0.7	4 512	6.6	54 730	20.3	15.4
Rutherford	22 198	73.0	46 300	18.1	13.1	310	22.7	3.3	28 640	-0.9	2 408	8.4	27 581	17.8	15.3
Sampson	17 526	72.9	46 500	19.9	13.8	283	26.6	6.2	24 303	5.3	1 759	7.2	21 789	16.9	16.2
Scotland	11 837	69.4	48 000	20.0	14.0	312	28.8	6.0	17 542	2.4	1 769	10.1	14 777	21.6	11.0
Stanly	19 747	76.6	52 800	19.6	12.6	329	21.3	3.3	27 037	2.5	2 237	8.3	26 260	18.5	17.3
Stokes	14 123	81.0	59 100	17.0	12.4	319	20.8	4.9	23 056	-1.1	1 154	5.0	19 065	17.2	17.9
Surry	24 252	76.6	48 600	17.5	12.7	292	23.0	3.3	34 410	1.6	2 251	6.5	31 213	18.0	17.1

1. Specified owner-occupied units.   2. Specified renter-occupied units.   3. Overcrowded or lacking complete plumbing facilities.   4. Percent of civilian labor force.   5. Persons 16 years and older.

Table B. States and Counties — Nonfarm Employment and Agriculture

	Private nonfarm establishments, employment and payroll, 1999									Agriculture, 1997			Farm operators
	Employment							Annual payroll		Farms			
											Percent with—		Whose principal occupation is farming (percent)
STATE County	Number of establishments	Total	Health Care and Social Assistance	Manufacturing	Retail trade	Finance and Insurance	Professional Scientific and Technical Services	Total (mil dol)	Average per employee (dollars)	Number	Less than 50 acres	500 acres and over	
	104	105	106	107	108	109	110	111	112	113	114	115	116
NORTH CAROLINA—Cont'd													
Chowan	342	4 555	956	1 283	738	125	88	93	20 335	151	26.5	27.2	71.5
Clay	212	1 454	253	216	320	D	D	31	21 065	166	41.0	4.8	45.2
Cleveland	2 187	33 701	4 000	13 609	4 832	632	470	858	25 468	864	33.9	3.1	34.1
Columbus	1 202	14 607	2 297	4 269	2 563	654	222	316	21 640	884	35.9	11.2	49.4
Craven	2 167	27 911	4 684	4 861	4 648	743	1 213	679	24 331	277	34.3	18.4	61.0
Cumberland	5 340	89 199	13 328	13 252	15 699	3 040	2 833	2 020	22 648	433	37.9	12.9	43.0
Currituck	447	2 731	180	129	830	49	57	54	19 642	86	40.7	29.1	62.8
Dare	1 648	11 695	443	323	2 829	313	674	254	21 759	9	55.6	33.3	66.7
Davidson	2 693	44 537	3 916	19 650	5 161	915	630	1 062	23 851	929	40.7	3.3	40.5
Davie	690	8 821	764	3 123	1 022	147	133	194	22 047	557	35.7	3.8	43.4
Duplin	979	11 943	1 506	4 042	1 862	225	243	230	19 270	1 224	40.1	10.0	61.7
Durham	5 828	159 441	18 762	30 780	14 249	5 137	13 883	6 146	38 547	159	40.3	8.2	46.5
Edgecombe	996	17 088	2 032	5 804	1 571	285	287	455	26 634	315	29.2	33.0	66.7
Forsyth	8 380	174 616	23 230	26 819	20 968	13 384	7 831	5 360	30 696	621	56.2	2.3	45.7
Franklin	724	7 790	1 139	2 032	1 172	115	200	189	24 261	524	23.1	13.9	50.6
Gaston	4 195	73 309	7 073	29 154	10 439	1 608	1 465	1 888	25 748	333	41.7	1.8	40.5
Gates	133	971	111	190	230	33	D	17	17 435	147	21.1	26.5	68.0
Graham	187	1 830	175	D	260	D	D	39	21 106	110	60.9	0.9	35.5
Granville	797	14 138	2 492	6 525	1 365	156	127	359	25 405	637	22.8	11.5	51.8
Greene	199	1 859	587	307	282	D	D	33	17 711	313	26.2	20.8	70.3
Guilford	13 569	263 287	23 337	49 985	31 272	16 433	10 444	8 019	30 456	920	43.9	4.6	47.6
Halifax	1 144	14 549	2 769	2 912	3 088	416	247	322	22 122	339	26.0	28.0	66.4
Harnett	1 476	21 125	2 024	5 559	2 672	399	386	431	20 412	626	40.9	9.6	53.7
Haywood	1 394	14 219	2 465	2 539	2 921	337	347	336	23 601	776	56.6	2.2	38.8
Henderson	2 183	29 066	3 893	8 000	4 342	741	639	771	26 520	488	56.8	2.9	52.9
Hertford	569	7 211	1 381	1 442	1 305	153	102	143	19 856	169	16.0	26.0	72.8
Hoke	300	5 363	555	3 054	501	82	D	114	21 234	162	37.0	20.4	55.6
Hyde	168	938	35	143	158	D	D	18	18 873	100	17.0	53.0	74.0
Iredell	3 253	49 021	5 729	16 667	6 395	941	1 005	1 293	26 373	1 189	39.4	5.1	46.1
Jackson	913	7 781	1 970	737	1 473	191	255	165	21 198	217	56.7	2.8	40.6
Johnston	2 531	29 230	2 935	7 165	4 905	674	781	667	22 833	1 216	40.1	8.0	54.9
Jones	165	1 163	323	176	168	D	D	26	22 408	154	24.7	26.6	70.1
Lee	1 405	25 609	2 136	11 883	3 113	379	364	639	24 943	311	43.1	4.5	44.7
Lenoir	1 508	26 313	5 586	6 460	3 561	655	522	646	24 551	447	30.9	20.4	67.8
Lincoln	1 324	18 921	1 463	7 787	2 696	353	427	468	24 760	497	39.0	3.8	36.6
McDowell	769	15 885	1 207	9 057	1 608	215	163	338	21 305	223	43.9	3.1	40.4
Macon	1 060	9 088	1 394	1 660	1 903	299	169	203	22 389	309	50.8	0.0	35.6
Madison	318	3 111	380	911	377	D	D	61	19 706	907	49.4	1.5	45.5
Martin	548	6 445	731	1 764	1 287	154	98	119	18 512	389	25.7	19.0	71.0
Mecklenburg	23 779	481 787	40 566	37 623	49 335	41 237	34 074	16 995	35 274	295	47.8	2.4	45.1
Mitchell	366	4 538	571	1 687	538	87	65	97	21 284	306	58.8	2.0	30.1
Montgomery	539	10 101	345	6 151	968	204	65	214	21 148	256	35.2	6.2	44.9
Moore	2 039	26 949	6 697	4 744	4 004	610	741	649	24 090	683	41.6	6.0	48.0
Nash	2 279	39 744	4 600	9 899	5 876	1 891	1 168	1 022	25 716	472	32.8	16.1	61.7
New Hanover	6 021	75 263	10 539	7 742	13 125	2 599	4 861	1 922	25 533	62	67.7	4.8	27.4
Northampton	317	2 877	444	675	545	D	50	63	22 035	342	24.6	31.3	68.7
Onslow	2 610	28 213	4 464	1 835	6 479	941	846	505	17 915	369	40.7	8.4	56.9
Orange	2 827	33 324	7 826	1 255	6 025	2 130	2 265	917	27 519	485	32.6	6.0	50.1
Pamlico	230	1 849	180	102	369	D	D	37	20 043	67	25.4	38.8	67.2
Pasquotank	928	10 337	2 172	732	2 682	340	265	210	20 289	174	25.9	29.9	70.7
Pender	726	5 603	984	1 214	874	89	114	105	18 724	283	31.4	13.4	58.3
Perquimans	189	1 283	152	125	239	D	D	21	16 390	202	21.8	25.7	71.3
Person	742	10 786	910	4 805	1 551	203	182	265	24 571	401	27.9	15.2	56.9
Pitt	3 148	51 832	9 760	9 262	8 061	1 764	1 518	1 224	23 613	474	26.8	23.0	67.1
Polk	443	3 685	995	884	458	74	93	72	19 464	188	38.3	4.3	36.2
Randolph	2 757	47 028	3 000	23 899	5 164	815	563	1 088	23 130	1 366	39.5	2.7	46.1
Richmond	987	14 023	2 297	4 800	2 266	335	231	290	20 658	251	29.5	9.2	51.4
Robeson	2 000	33 294	4 678	11 925	5 220	943	610	699	20 983	1 004	35.8	14.8	53.8
Rockingham	1 810	30 921	4 077	13 164	3 729	581	340	729	23 563	780	32.2	6.8	49.4
Rowan	2 469	45 249	5 862	14 801	4 717	850	715	1 197	26 447	779	35.4	4.7	40.3
Rutherford	1 312	21 519	2 166	10 322	2 789	330	234	480	22 296	505	32.5	3.4	34.9
Sampson	1 090	13 062	1 957	3 777	2 516	318	182	284	21 711	1 186	36.6	9.9	58.9
Scotland	735	16 993	1 663	7 960	1 876	271	D	411	24 174	123	28.5	24.4	51.2
Stanly	1 422	19 309	2 225	8 135	2 806	354	255	448	23 199	558	34.8	5.7	38.9
Stokes	575	5 199	896	1 263	714	101	120	120	23 170	926	38.0	3.0	48.3
Surry	1 833	35 459	2 858	13 856	4 538	668	415	801	22 586	1 194	42.3	2.8	47.0

Table B. States and Counties — Agriculture, Land, and Water

STATE County	Agriculture, 1997 (cont'd)														Percent of land owned by fed. gov. 1997	Water consumption 1995 (mil gal/day)
	Land in farms					Value of land and buildings		Value of machinery and equipment average per farm ($1,000)	Value of products sold				Percent of farms with sales of —			
			Acres								Percent from —					
	Acreage (1,000)	Percent change, 1992–1997	Average size of farm	Total irrigated (1,000)	Total cropland (1,000)	Average per farm ($1,000)	Average per acre (dollars)		Total (mil dol)	Average per farm (dollars)	Crops	Livestock and poultry products	$10,000 or more	$100,000 or more		
	117	118	119	120	121	122	123	124	125	126	127	128	129	130	131	132
NORTH CAROLINA—Cont'd																
Chowan	51	-4.9	340	3	38	519	1 611	119	34	225 181	76.7	23.3	70.9	43.0	0.0	3.3
Clay	18	14.3	110	0	9	309	3 377	29	5	28 181	14.4	85.6	27.7	5.4	55.7	4.7
Cleveland	104	10.7	120	0	62	328	2 667	25	34	38 990	27.0	73.0	24.4	6.8	0.0	39.3
Columbus	170	4.3	192	1	116	275	1 508	53	140	158 273	48.0	52.0	58.9	23.4	0.0	7.4
Craven	84	-4.7	303	1	62	356	1 302	84	67	241 636	52.9	47.1	63.5	36.1	15.1	14.2
Cumberland	103	4.2	238	2	57	461	2 205	66	68	156 313	32.8	67.2	45.7	18.9	10.4	35.7
Currituck	40	-5.8	460	0	34	836	1 816	103	15	174 005	93.1	6.9	58.1	36.0	3.4	2.2
Dare	5	-29.1	551	0	4	555	1 007	76	1	92 923	D	D	66.7	33.3	25.1	4.6
Davidson	99	7.6	107	1	56	392	3 690	30	24	25 452	44.9	55.1	28.5	6.5	0.3	22.0
Davie	71	2.3	127	0	42	372	2 814	36	16	28 099	38.1	61.9	29.6	7.9	0.0	5.6
Duplin	238	-4.3	195	6	157	457	2 321	68	746	609 844	9.5	90.5	72.7	51.5	0.0	29.1
Durham	22	11.2	140	1	11	555	4 228	46	7	45 576	85.6	14.4	43.4	17.6	2.2	31.4
Edgecombe	172	-4.7	545	5	116	723	1 408	113	149	472 312	43.5	56.5	71.1	49.8	0.0	12.3
Forsyth	51	6.4	82	1	30	269	3 561	29	16	26 187	83.8	16.2	29.5	6.3	0.0	61.5
Franklin	137	16.1	261	5	72	480	1 947	49	61	116 015	66.0	34.0	49.4	20.2	0.0	9.1
Gaston	35	-0.4	105	0	20	324	3 207	26	10	29 872	33.4	66.6	21.6	4.2	0.0	399.1
Gates	62	-4.6	422	0	49	630	1 469	145	45	305 737	38.3	61.7	71.4	40.8	5.2	2.4
Graham	7	-20.1	65	D	3	119	2 335	18	1	9 946	21.7	78.3	18.2	0.9	67.2	42.3
Granville	162	3.7	254	5	59	385	1 650	40	37	58 102	85.9	14.1	55.6	17.3	2.1	7.4
Greene	103	-7.9	330	2	80	680	2 110	137	181	578 160	29.1	70.9	84.7	56.9	0.0	5.0
Guilford	112	-1.9	122	3	60	356	3 063	34	49	53 121	68.2	31.8	38.7	12.5	0.2	95.3
Halifax	185	-9.1	547	3	128	679	1 314	110	97	286 794	54.7	45.3	64.3	43.1	0.0	13.2
Harnett	116	-9.4	185	3	73	426	2 512	58	94	150 292	47.1	52.9	50.0	27.2	2.2	96.9
Haywood	65	-6.8	84	0	28	262	3 057	24	15	18 874	37.3	62.7	26.4	3.9	43.3	84.7
Henderson	45	-14.4	91	2	28	394	4 808	41	47	95 785	85.9	14.1	44.5	11.9	8.3	14.4
Hertford	76	1.9	452	4	53	594	1 283	116	61	358 317	44.4	55.6	86.4	44.4	0.0	5.0
Hoke	67	17.4	413	0	42	594	1 500	92	66	407 919	27.5	72.5	54.3	27.8	35.5	4.5
Hyde	95	1.4	953	D	83	1 150	1 171	153	33	329 965	91.1	8.9	83.0	54.0	8.9	0.5
Iredell	157	5.9	132	1	98	376	2 553	38	100	83 780	9.6	90.4	36.6	14.1	0.0	23.6
Jackson	19	45.2	87	0	6	296	3 856	27	6	28 735	89.3	10.7	33.6	5.1	34.6	4.5
Johnston	211	-8.3	174	3	138	419	2 490	52	179	147 557	53.9	46.1	54.7	22.5	0.0	13.5
Jones	72	4.0	466	0	50	647	1 362	98	108	698 891	24.2	75.8	73.4	48.7	13.4	5.1
Lee	45	22.2	145	1	22	370	2 942	36	26	83 853	59.2	40.8	41.8	16.1	0.0	8.6
Lenoir	150	5.4	335	1	110	703	2 020	107	200	446 473	36.5	63.5	77.2	51.2	0.0	11.5
Lincoln	63	8.9	127	0	39	287	2 273	25	19	38 660	16.3	83.7	25.6	7.0	0.0	10.6
McDowell	21	-1.5	93	1	9	208	2 463	22	13	60 418	61.7	38.3	25.6	8.1	28.2	10.5
Macon	23	3.6	74	0	11	261	4 286	18	3	11 157	46.4	53.6	21.0	1.6	56.4	17.0
Madison	80	-13.9	88	0	27	196	2 385	16	10	11 158	77.6	22.4	27.6	0.7	23.0	4.2
Martin	115	-12.7	296	1	81	356	1 286	78	63	161 846	85.6	14.4	80.7	39.3	0.0	5.9
Mecklenburg	29	3.6	98	0	16	604	5 456	67	43	145 769	79.4	20.6	28.8	7.1	0.0	2 749.0
Mitchell	25	9.4	82	0	11	147	1 984	26	4	12 394	80.0	20.0	28.8	0.7	18.8	6.6
Montgomery	42	13.0	163	1	15	305	1 510	34	46	180 312	7.8	92.2	37.5	25.0	11.8	6.8
Moore	101	15.7	147	5	37	306	2 116	44	113	165 771	18.2	81.8	45.1	29.3	0.6	26.6
Nash	175	-2.1	371	14	110	794	2 076	123	168	355 426	50.8	49.2	67.6	39.2	0.0	24.0
New Hanover	5	81.2	88	0	4	300	3 422	54	4	69 753	D	D	43.5	9.7	1.1	66.6
Northampton	160	3.5	469	2	104	597	1 260	108	92	269 673	45.1	54.9	78.4	45.3	0.0	4.8
Onslow	63	-0.9	172	0	42	291	1 729	48	102	275 201	21.6	78.4	55.6	31.4	15.4	14.8
Orange	73	8.2	150	1	41	446	3 226	46	26	53 268	46.6	53.4	39.6	12.4	0.0	16.0
Pamlico	50	14.2	750	1	43	980	1 307	217	23	341 358	90.5	9.5	64.2	49.3	0.0	3.0
Pasquotank	86	4.0	496	D	79	731	1 545	114	33	190 271	96.7	3.3	76.4	38.5	2.6	5.3
Pender	69	5.9	243	1	42	434	2 043	55	110	387 196	20.7	79.3	60.8	33.9	0.0	4.1
Perquimans	77	11.9	382	0	70	603	1 660	106	38	188 338	58.4	41.6	77.2	44.1	0.6	2.1
Person	120	3.9	300	3	56	504	1 694	50	29	72 423	85.9	14.1	58.4	22.7	0.0	678.3
Pitt	193	-0.3	408	2	144	767	1 865	112	196	413 795	49.8	50.2	76.8	49.6	0.8	26.0
Polk	31	33.5	163	D	10	373	2 268	34	3	17 631	50.6	49.4	22.3	5.3	0.0	2.7
Randolph	148	2.3	109	1	78	282	2 530	38	147	107 855	10.3	89.7	39.3	22.3	1.8	23.7
Richmond	54	4.8	217	1	26	336	1 360	37	66	263 348	16.6	83.4	53.4	39.0	1.3	11.9
Robeson	285	-2.3	284	2	214	377	1 378	60	221	220 562	45.8	54.2	60.1	27.2	0.0	37.8
Rockingham	134	2.2	172	4	55	260	1 611	34	37	47 657	81.1	18.9	49.2	12.3	0.0	68.8
Rowan	108	2.4	138	1	71	322	2 341	42	32	40 858	41.2	58.8	31.2	6.8	0.0	71.9
Rutherford	61	11.2	121	0	30	220	1 850	22	5	10 768	23.7	76.3	19.8	1.8	0.0	32.9
Sampson	271	1.8	228	9	183	464	1 971	72	733	617 925	13.7	86.3	70.0	42.1	0.0	20.6
Scotland	54	-0.9	435	1	36	459	1 201	80	55	447 609	23.0	77.0	60.2	41.5	2.1	8.9
Stanly	95	6.4	170	0	67	289	1 808	46	68	121 307	20.4	79.6	38.9	15.9	0.1	13.3
Stokes	110	4.8	119	1	50	205	2 030	29	34	36 486	68.9	31.1	50.4	7.9	0.0	898.3
Surry	130	7.3	109	2	70	221	2 154	34	98	82 382	32.4	67.6	44.9	15.4	0.2	25.5

STATE County	Value of Residential Construction Authorized by Building Permits, 2000		Wholesale Trade, 1997				Retail Trade[1], 1997				Real Estate and Rental and Leasing, 1997			
	New Construction ($1,000)	Number of Housing Units	Number of Establishments	Number of Employees	Sales (mil dol)	Annual Payroll (mil dol)	Number of Establishments	Number of Employees	Sales (mil dol)	Annual Payroll (mil dol)	Number of Establishments	Number of Employees	Receipts (mil dol)	Annual Payroll (mil dol)
	133	134	135	136	137	138	139	140	141	142	143	144	145	146
NORTH CAROLINA—Cont'd														
Chowan	5 356	42	14	207	72.1	5.7	67	730	109.6	9.8	9	14	1.5	0.1
Clay	18 488	151	1	D	D	D	38	324	52.2	3.8	9	20	1.4	0.3
Cleveland	42 346	370	126	1 434	1 355.9	39.1	431	4 707	707.4	68.9	76	354	45.8	6.6
Columbus	9 483	99	62	463	241.3	10.6	296	2 565	387.7	37.4	28	97	8.7	1.4
Craven	52 808	490	76	746	307.6	23.2	443	4 560	772.6	71.3	74	325	28.1	5.2
Cumberland	104 664	1 544	205	2 454	845.3	66.5	1 061	14 929	2 563.3	239.3	272	1 182	137.5	23.4
Currituck	67 464	340	20	D	D	D	81	541	98.6	10.2	20	110	11.0	3.4
Dare	182 289	920	41	374	103.9	7.1	389	2 494	442.4	43.4	106	872	61.8	16.8
Davidson	88 063	893	193	1 972	791.9	67.8	494	5 131	892.0	88.7	100	371	29.4	7.2
Davie	45 564	328	33	406	109.2	8.3	107	902	166.2	14.4	10	15	2.6	0.4
Duplin	14 690	167	44	D	D	D	226	1 879	280.4	25.2	18	65	7.5	0.9
Durham	296 014	2 863	249	4 343	2 306.3	158.4	1 010	13 322	2 032.6	213.2	246	1 301	160.8	30.6
Edgecombe	7 486	95	47	602	454.3	19.9	196	1 631	214.2	21.5	43	354	45.6	7.8
Forsyth	285 217	2 875	478	6 706	3 625.1	219.9	1 489	20 888	3 731.2	344.9	350	1 819	276.6	38.7
Franklin	42 631	374	34	481	166.1	13.8	127	1 057	176.2	15.0	19	60	5.3	0.9
Gaston	118 555	1 213	269	2 047	958.5	67.6	767	9 662	1 587.9	146.5	119	423	37.0	6.8
Gates	3 382	18	6	51	16.7	1.1	29	248	41.8	3.1	3	10	0.5	0.1
Graham	4 489	58	2	D	D	D	36	278	44.6	3.5	5	5	0.7	0.1
Granville	46 818	414	32	222	219.0	8.2	151	1 334	217.1	19.9	24	60	4.2	0.6
Greene	5 844	31	13	122	34.8	2.7	38	302	47.7	4.2	4	8	0.5	0.1
Guilford	373 766	3 529	1 347	21 568	13 448.1	882.9	2 059	29 817	5 179.3	530.8	529	3 704	441.0	82.9
Halifax	10 515	94	36	424	101.7	11.1	306	3 255	462.0	43.7	29	210	17.6	3.7
Harnett	49 281	692	62	756	257.7	18.5	284	2 713	443.2	37.0	45	154	10.7	2.0
Haywood	54 792	393	49	349	127.3	9.4	266	2 847	569.8	46.5	48	119	11.3	1.8
Henderson	120 851	720	91	613	228.0	15.8	386	4 192	901.3	75.2	66	252	28.1	4.9
Hertford	2 317	31	27	264	126.0	5.7	134	1 313	176.9	17.7	14	51	2.7	1.0
Hoke	27 950	261	7	102	30.3	2.8	74	486	67.5	5.9	11	24	1.4	0.3
Hyde	2 209	20	9	61	21.8	1.3	36	164	26.8	2.5	5	D	D	D
Iredell	235 947	1 830	196	2 443	1 373.6	76.5	510	5 993	1 065.8	93.2	95	341	33.8	6.4
Jackson	92 495	745	16	66	18.2	1.6	178	1 472	220.6	20.1	44	112	9.8	2.2
Johnston	142 853	1 635	117	1 269	836.8	26.3	486	4 580	857.9	71.5	65	221	20.4	3.3
Jones	545	5	7	60	12.9	1.2	30	142	33.7	2.2	1	D	D	D
Lee	24 996	231	75	1 159	517.1	32.2	292	3 109	591.9	51.0	59	196	18.2	3.3
Lenoir	21 731	242	80	1 382	486.7	28.2	352	3 597	565.6	51.2	45	170	14.1	2.5
Lincoln	88 508	833	73	1 035	629.9	29.4	212	2 346	406.2	36.6	40	151	13.0	2.5
McDowell	13 586	132	30	293	59.0	6.1	167	1 557	273.4	22.0	22	50	5.0	0.8
Macon	69 833	359	30	101	16.5	1.7	241	1 750	308.1	27.5	38	80	10.6	1.5
Madison	15 667	143	9	D	D	D	51	327	49.0	4.0	8	16	0.6	0.1
Martin	5 691	50	32	220	76.1	5.3	117	1 263	195.1	17.1	10	33	1.7	0.4
Mecklenburg	1 402 702	13 960	2 638	38 333	35 019.8	1 574.3	2 971	44 557	8 517.2	815.7	994	9 430	1 449.2	292.7
Mitchell	7 530	70	11	D	D	D	81	486	97.3	7.3	15	38	3.2	0.6
Montgomery	18 843	102	22	110	58.6	3.0	100	825	137.0	11.7	10	150	5.2	3.1
Moore	105 806	672	92	579	297.6	16.5	360	4 003	616.7	60.5	70	240	19.8	4.7
Nash	52 840	695	125	2 204	1 038.8	67.9	524	5 885	1 035.5	93.0	80	404	50.2	7.3
New Hanover	207 885	1 860	324	3 528	1 216.9	95.4	1 026	12 352	2 461.1	210.9	252	1 140	117.7	22.4
Northampton	4 767	45	22	243	214.8	6.1	66	532	85.4	8.9	4	D	D	D
Onslow	67 461	915	69	D	D	D	564	6 542	1 090.1	96.7	129	497	53.0	7.5
Orange	169 135	1 070	78	428	312.3	12.0	387	5 549	837.2	95.0	126	414	60.0	9.3
Pamlico	9 191	56	12	144	19.0	2.4	49	364	53.8	5.0	9	16	2.4	0.2
Pasquotank	9 807	108	46	606	150.7	12.8	201	2 548	405.0	37.6	37	133	10.1	1.9
Pender	53 955	348	33	326	99.1	8.0	131	906	153.9	13.5	28	94	9.9	1.7
Perquimans	11 909	63	9	87	32.6	1.7	38	274	31.7	3.0	3	D	D	D
Person	31 209	180	30	273	81.1	6.4	160	1 556	250.2	22.7	13	76	4.3	0.9
Pitt	123 846	1 766	181	2 153	1 246.8	66.4	643	7 956	1 384.8	124.8	121	495	51.4	7.9
Polk	15 002	121	14	39	19.7	0.8	61	417	63.3	5.9	21	34	3.7	0.5
Randolph	67 232	915	174	1 637	582.0	44.5	457	4 821	845.0	77.1	58	211	22.3	3.2
Richmond	14 734	274	38	368	96.9	8.9	229	2 165	368.2	32.8	34	139	8.8	1.5
Robeson	48 780	413	82	843	349.6	22.0	450	4 844	1 011.7	79.8	46	260	14.0	4.5
Rockingham	34 679	342	59	394	177.6	10.0	421	3 974	619.8	55.4	59	224	17.6	2.8
Rowan	91 828	764	117	1 392	548.3	39.7	450	4 820	799.2	74.3	69	236	25.3	5.0
Rutherford	29 818	290	66	525	334.9	15.0	286	2 861	443.5	41.1	51	164	12.8	3.0
Sampson	14 688	134	52	587	231.1	17.6	246	2 125	373.8	31.1	25	85	5.3	1.2
Scotland	11 771	144	29	212	75.0	6.1	178	1 856	255.3	26.1	27	113	7.3	1.4
Stanly	29 268	287	61	474	228.3	15.8	265	2 722	472.3	44.5	32	123	12.2	1.9
Stokes	21 659	183	18	D	D	D	118	774	135.5	11.7	12	63	2.2	0.4
Surry	26 828	222	90	1 147	646.3	24.8	381	5 594	780.0	75.6	60	183	20.0	2.5

1. Establishments with payroll.

STATE County	Professional, Scientific, and Technical Services[1], 1997				Manufacturing, 1997				Accommodation and Foodservices, 1997			
	Number of Establishments	Number of Employees	Receipts (mil dol)	Annual Payroll (mil dol)	Number of Establishments	Number of Employees	Receipts (mil dol)	Annual Payroll (mil dol)	Number of Establishments	Number of Employees	Sales (mil dol)	Annual Payroll (mil dol)
	147	148	149	150	151	152	153	154	155	156	157	158
NORTH CAROLINA—Cont'd												
Chowan	13	65	4.7	1.9	18	1 061	114.2	23.8	27	364	10.1	2.5
Clay	12	25	2.1	0.7	NA	NA	NA	NA	13	D	D	D
Cleveland	110	425	26.4	9.9	173	14 655	2 497.0	399.9	131	2 422	60.5	17.6
Columbus	46	129	10.0	2.2	46	4 767	895.5	129.9	75	1 058	26.7	6.7
Craven	145	1 022	71.2	32.1	86	4 344	796.4	118.5	159	3 004	87.1	24.8
Cumberland	329	2 084	142.1	47.7	121	12 282	2 766.9	384.6	495	10 654	318.4	91.2
Currituck	19	36	2.7	0.8	NA	NA	NA	NA	45	339	13.7	4.0
Dare	76	345	20.7	7.7	NA	NA	NA	NA	274	2 854	140.0	37.6
Davidson	129	438	31.4	10.5	326	21 576	2 249.4	521.7	177	2 802	87.4	24.8
Davie	28	91	5.2	2.0	45	2 886	406.9	76.4	41	D	D	D
Duplin	47	121	7.2	2.4	48	4 688	675.9	95.2	65	976	28.6	7.6
Durham	614	7 922	1 119.6	369.6	181	31 489	11 223.8	1 027.2	468	9 414	378.5	105.7
Edgecombe	42	301	17.0	5.0	50	7 720	1 606.6	234.0	52	747	22.1	6.2
Forsyth	781	5 462	536.2	203.9	399	26 545	9 676.3	908.6	632	12 945	408.0	116.2
Franklin	35	131	8.9	3.4	55	2 259	444.6	67.3	37	D	D	D
Gaston	231	1 157	80.5	29.7	492	31 175	5 772.7	863.2	297	5 315	158.7	42.3
Gates	4	10	0.5	0.1	NA	NA	NA	NA	4	53	1.2	0.4
Graham	3	D	D	D	3	D	D	D	17	160	7.7	2.4
Granville	38	117	8.7	2.7	57	6 990	1 534.2	185.2	52	680	23.3	5.9
Greene	10	23	1.5	0.5	NA	NA	NA	NA	10	117	2.9	0.8
Guilford	1 155	8 157	762.2	273.6	862	47 158	10 546.4	1 431.2	924	19 991	637.5	185.4
Halifax	51	229	9.6	3.4	59	4 136	567.7	113.7	76	1 531	51.7	13.4
Harnett	90	292	23.9	8.5	82	5 959	633.7	149.2	88	1 289	37.1	10.0
Haywood	58	250	14.1	6.5	49	3 321	726.3	130.2	151	2 038	65.9	17.5
Henderson	120	429	28.8	11.6	132	8 361	1 745.8	260.1	167	3 146	97.2	28.6
Hertford	16	74	6.0	2.2	30	1 695	459.2	37.2	39	632	16.8	4.6
Hoke	13	30	1.9	0.5	11	3 151	414.8	72.8	19	189	5.4	1.3
Hyde	5	13	0.7	0.2	NA	NA	NA	NA	33	158	10.2	2.4
Iredell	176	872	88.0	26.3	263	16 978	3 172.6	476.5	195	3 470	117.5	31.9
Jackson	49	194	14.6	4.7	36	699	76.3	15.9	102	942	32.9	8.6
Johnston	133	506	33.9	13.2	114	6 588	1 622.3	192.1	151	2 548	90.9	23.7
Jones	4	7	0.4	0.1	NA	NA	NA	NA	6	41	1.3	0.3
Lee	63	271	17.5	6.5	108	12 130	2 167.9	319.4	83	1 390	40.5	11.4
Lenoir	65	424	28.5	13.9	82	7 120	1 596.1	201.4	95	1 678	51.5	14.6
Lincoln	69	236	14.0	5.9	112	8 047	990.9	196.4	73	962	26.8	7.1
McDowell	28	126	7.0	3.0	63	6 084	866.3	140.9	64	861	26.7	7.0
Macon	38	142	7.2	3.2	34	1 358	174.7	32.5	92	943	30.0	8.2
Madison	11	23	0.8	0.3	NA	NA	NA	NA	24	230	6.1	1.9
Martin	21	73	4.5	2.0	22	1 902	307.9	40.6	43	659	17.5	4.8
Mecklenburg	2 315	27 365	2 902.6	1 123.7	1 001	42 494	8 831.4	1 429.8	1 553	33 351	1 194.2	330.2
Mitchell	10	38	1.9	0.8	32	1 868	151.4	37.1	25	324	8.9	2.6
Montgomery	14	60	2.7	0.9	78	5 292	666.7	112.1	28	D	D	D
Moore	130	562	42.8	16.8	105	5 943	903.7	129.8	154	3 202	133.0	34.6
Nash	113	688	60.8	22.2	104	9 879	1 721.8	267.8	168	3 481	111.6	30.2
New Hanover	497	3 123	251.6	103.9	203	8 378	2 698.2	338.8	455	8 834	281.4	76.7
Northampton	18	42	2.4	0.6	13	749	233.0	20.5	12	D	D	D
Onslow	137	725	34.9	11.9	37	1 829	346.4	37.7	249	4 420	127.9	34.5
Orange	349	1 746	149.0	63.4	78	1 209	142.1	34.0	283	4 443	154.1	44.3
Pamlico	12	28	1.9	0.4	NA	NA	NA	NA	18	293	13.6	4.4
Pasquotank	52	231	15.8	5.1	31	884	148.6	18.5	74	1 183	31.7	9.3
Pender	36	65	4.7	1.3	39	1 123	135.8	24.3	48	499	15.2	4.5
Perquimans	8	28	1.6	0.5	NA	NA	NA	NA	11	D	D	D
Person	34	125	8.3	2.8	39	5 138	1 084.8	135.5	45	716	20.8	5.4
Pitt	219	1 303	88.0	35.3	119	9 305	2 741.9	280.8	237	5 342	153.5	41.8
Polk	28	65	4.4	1.4	25	904	150.9	19.9	36	431	10.9	3.3
Randolph	127	464	42.9	12.9	411	24 954	3 612.7	559.8	150	2 433	75.9	21.0
Richmond	47	186	11.1	3.8	58	4 814	719.7	114.5	69	1 140	28.6	7.1
Robeson	93	534	29.0	7.9	96	11 890	2 407.9	264.0	171	2 685	85.3	22.4
Rockingham	79	327	16.4	5.6	124	13 958	3 214.4	387.0	124	1 913	60.2	16.5
Rowan	120	451	45.0	15.0	201	14 324	3 677.9	413.8	158	2 891	82.4	22.4
Rutherford	52	177	12.7	3.3	97	11 480	1 514.2	278.6	93	1 280	37.4	10.2
Sampson	48	162	9.8	3.6	61	4 202	768.5	102.4	66	903	26.6	7.3
Scotland	27	86	6.7	2.9	59	8 534	1 533.3	234.0	52	1 134	28.9	7.0
Stanly	50	187	11.3	4.0	124	8 086	1 167.5	210.3	92	1 338	34.1	9.1
Stokes	29	72	4.3	1.3	33	1 218	167.7	37.0	39	D	D	D
Surry	101	371	23.5	7.4	149	14 915	1 697.3	300.1	149	1 899	56.6	15.4

1. Firms subject to federal tax.

STATE County	Health Care and Social Assistance[1], 1997				Other Services[1], 1997				Federal funds and grants, fiscal 2001[2] Expenditures (mil dol)			
										Direct payments for individuals[3]		
	Number of Establishments	Number of Employees	Receipts (mil dol)	Annual Payroll (mil dol)	Number of Establishments	Number of Employees	Receipts (mil dol)	Annual Payroll (mil dol)	Total	Social Security and government retirement	Medicare	Food stamps and Supplemental Security Income
	159	160	161	162	163	164	165	166	167	168	169	170
NORTH CAROLINA—Cont'd												
Chowan	29	419	17.5	8.5	17	68	4.2	1.0	83.4	41.1	12.4	4.1
Clay	7	125	5.0	2.0	10	22	1.0	0.3	52.4	29.0	8.4	1.6
Cleveland	158	1 782	102.2	51.5	133	466	30.8	8.6	457.2	214.9	71.3	18.6
Columbus	89	1 544	62.7	32.4	77	310	18.8	4.7	360.4	130.7	63.4	22.8
Craven	158	1 872	128.5	55.6	124	679	35.1	10.6	1 035.3	278.7	64.1	17.9
Cumberland	407	6 135	366.5	159.9	402	2 631	145.7	45.1	3 426.3	786.5	124.1	65.2
Currituck	16	67	3.5	1.0	20	56	4.3	1.0	81.0	50.1	11.7	2.2
Dare	33	474	20.9	8.9	46	184	10.9	3.3	164.0	80.6	17.9	1.9
Davidson	136	1 834	87.1	41.6	147	603	38.3	10.6	593.5	256.7	93.4	17.0
Davie	33	521	21.9	8.7	27	102	4.9	1.5	129.4	74.1	24.2	3.2
Duplin	69	815	29.0	11.9	63	273	16.5	4.5	256.0	100.2	39.0	12.1
Durham	387	5 893	338.6	159.6	333	2 215	121.0	43.2	1 791.0	374.2	140.4	34.4
Edgecombe	55	1 370	75.8	32.7	75	340	16.9	4.8	323.5	83.5	63.9	21.4
Forsyth	538	7 866	624.0	257.2	511	3 492	188.9	65.2	1 379.9	636.7	221.0	43.5
Franklin	44	1 217	46.3	18.9	37	132	8.4	2.2	182.6	77.0	33.4	8.6
Gaston	268	3 601	222.2	106.3	293	1 736	108.7	31.1	739.3	393.2	150.7	30.6
Gates	4	D	D	D	8	44	2.8	0.6	56.2	26.3	8.7	2.7
Graham	3	106	4.1	1.8	11	25	1.7	0.4	43.4	20.7	7.1	1.6
Granville	53	782	26.6	11.7	39	138	9.2	2.6	245.8	86.5	32.3	9.2
Greene	15	271	10.0	4.7	10	37	3.3	0.9	78.2	28.6	12.9	4.5
Guilford	816	11 217	822.5	392.9	768	5 117	346.8	101.1	2 059.5	827.8	272.2	56.3
Halifax	73	1 286	57.4	27.3	93	442	23.0	6.7	387.4	147.0	56.7	32.3
Harnett	95	908	41.9	17.2	88	370	18.5	4.8	337.7	147.7	58.6	16.3
Haywood	97	1 131	55.1	24.3	85	391	16.8	5.4	302.0	159.4	46.5	9.9
Henderson	158	1 545	103.1	44.9	122	489	30.9	9.0	456.0	286.1	87.9	8.8
Hertford	52	569	21.7	9.4	48	225	12.4	3.0	227.9	52.7	19.1	10.0
Hoke	23	302	10.8	4.6	17	51	2.9	0.7	112.6	47.7	13.6	7.4
Hyde	4	18	1.0	0.2	3	15	0.8	0.2	44.6	12.1	5.4	1.8
Iredell	254	3 584	223.7	87.6	169	939	54.8	16.6	438.5	236.9	96.5	12.1
Jackson	55	560	41.8	19.2	48	189	10.6	2.5	135.1	67.1	20.6	5.8
Johnston	126	1 766	77.5	34.3	138	513	33.4	9.1	453.2	195.9	82.6	20.7
Jones	12	222	13.8	6.3	4	8	0.4	0.1	67.2	27.9	10.4	2.5
Lee	95	1 679	97.1	48.2	83	358	21.0	6.0	235.5	125.4	41.5	7.7
Lenoir	138	1 891	100.5	43.4	88	613	28.6	8.8	388.7	150.1	71.9	19.2
Lincoln	80	793	42.8	21.7	80	332	17.0	5.0	206.9	121.3	39.0	7.1
McDowell	47	615	27.5	13.0	35	148	8.1	2.3	183.5	94.1	26.8	6.9
Macon	52	509	27.1	12.5	61	218	12.7	3.5	174.8	95.1	29.3	4.8
Madison	19	253	12.2	5.6	14	39	3.4	0.9	154.1	42.3	16.1	5.0
Martin	35	435	17.9	8.0	28	99	4.4	1.3	156.6	63.1	23.8	9.6
Mecklenburg	1 223	17 239	1 346.8	597.4	1 297	10 102	675.5	215.0	2 797.1	1 021.5	326.6	82.7
Mitchell	22	216	10.5	4.5	19	82	6.2	1.5	92.6	40.1	14.2	3.3
Montgomery	31	333	11.9	5.6	33	91	3.9	1.1	123.6	53.8	21.2	5.4
Moore	136	2 037	147.2	78.6	98	393	27.4	7.7	421.2	271.5	69.5	9.4
Nash	150	3 089	204.2	82.6	136	907	57.7	16.0	407.6	214.0	50.5	19.4
New Hanover	402	5 653	372.8	157.1	331	1 889	116.3	35.2	822.4	378.1	112.2	30.1
Northampton	16	243	9.9	4.6	20	45	2.6	0.5	149.6	58.6	20.4	8.5
Onslow	188	2 489	127.1	57.5	195	914	45.5	13.4	1 624.5	328.2	48.3	18.8
Orange	217	2 446	122.8	60.3	144	738	40.4	13.0	701.4	173.3	62.3	8.2
Pamlico	15	183	7.4	3.1	15	54	3.9	1.0	72.1	40.9	8.9	2.4
Pasquotank	77	803	49.5	24.4	59	277	15.0	4.3	261.3	84.9	29.4	9.1
Pender	35	432	21.8	8.4	41	147	8.9	2.4	183.9	96.0	28.0	6.7
Perquimans	11	169	5.7	2.5	11	44	1.6	0.4	73.2	37.9	9.9	3.1
Person	42	344	16.4	7.7	53	147	10.2	2.2	149.7	68.7	26.4	7.6
Pitt	205	3 334	216.7	115.5	158	875	49.1	13.7	549.6	218.7	82.4	35.9
Polk	30	401	15.8	6.8	17	47	3.7	1.0	102.4	60.6	15.9	1.6
Randolph	144	1 747	87.5	39.0	188	1 064	70.9	15.7	389.8	213.3	77.7	10.8
Richmond	80	1 051	55.8	22.1	66	279	16.9	4.5	256.7	120.9	43.9	14.2
Robeson	154	2 076	95.9	47.2	120	437	27.6	7.2	644.2	236.2	97.4	49.2
Rockingham	141	1 697	84.6	36.4	126	480	26.9	8.0	434.4	206.8	84.5	17.6
Rowan	186	2 571	128.8	58.8	150	645	38.9	12.3	574.7	271.3	92.8	17.2
Rutherford	93	1 060	47.1	22.6	81	269	16.1	4.2	280.4	147.7	44.5	11.0
Sampson	66	758	34.7	17.2	70	332	22.7	6.2	282.1	113.4	44.9	15.6
Scotland	70	715	42.3	20.2	47	189	10.5	2.9	188.1	75.4	25.1	13.2
Stanly	98	1 115	44.2	21.9	81	410	34.5	11.9	230.7	128.4	44.9	7.3
Stokes	30	488	21.2	8.8	38	157	9.6	3.0	136.0	76.4	23.0	3.3
Surry	108	1 278	71.4	34.7	93	407	25.2	6.5	324.5	160.4	65.7	10.9

1. Firms subject to federal tax.   2. October 1, 2000 to September 30, 2001.   3. State totals may include programs not allocated by county.

Table B. States and Counties — **Federal Funds and Local Government Finances**

	Federal funds and grants, fiscal 2001[1] (cont'd)							Local government finances, 1997				
	Expenditures (mil dol) (cont'd)							General revenue				
	Procurement contract awards			Grants[2]							Taxes	
											Per capita[3] (dollars)	
STATE County	Salaries and wages	Defense	Other	Medicaid and other health-related	Nutrition and family welfare	Education	Other	Total (mil dol)	Intergovern-mental (mil dol)	Total (mil dol)	Total	Property
	171	172	173	174	175	176	177	178	179	180	181	182
NORTH CAROLINA—Cont'd												
Chowan	2.6	0.0	0.5	11.9	3.1	1.0	0.6	27.5	16.2	7.7	544	394
Clay	1.4	0.0	0.4	9.5	0.7	0.5	0.1	12.8	8.1	3.8	462	313
Cleveland	11.6	31.3	3.0	64.3	12.0	5.9	7.7	239.4	98.2	46.0	500	378
Columbus	7.8	2.4	2.3	78.8	11.4	4.7	14.6	109.6	72.1	23.8	453	335
Craven	444.2	122.6	3.6	60.4	9.2	7.2	7.2	267.0	91.9	42.5	487	341
Cumberland	1 722.7	398.4	35.5	136.7	47.0	25.7	29.4	709.7	294.8	158.4	558	407
Currituck	2.5	0.0	1.8	5.8	1.2	0.9	1.7	40.7	15.9	19.9	1 164	856
Dare	14.5	8.8	2.8	4.3	1.2	0.7	30.1	84.3	22.9	44.6	1 599	1 127
Davidson	10.8	109.7	21.5	42.2	9.3	6.5	15.2	214.6	126.4	59.3	426	298
Davie	3.6	0.7	1.2	13.8	1.7	1.6	0.3	58.4	24.5	15.0	480	354
Duplin	8.1	3.2	2.6	50.2	8.1	4.0	12.1	93.6	57.6	21.2	491	364
Durham	256.6	49.0	294.8	420.4	21.7	21.8	136.9	634.3	189.7	202.0	1 012	827
Edgecombe	35.9	0.5	12.1	61.7	14.1	4.2	4.9	104.3	59.5	26.9	485	380
Forsyth	68.2	12.8	28.2	231.0	30.3	19.8	39.9	895.3	329.0	400.2	1 400	1 100
Franklin	4.5	0.5	1.3	39.5	4.7	2.5	3.3	71.2	37.0	22.1	507	379
Gaston	22.5	1.8	5.8	77.8	20.0	10.3	10.4	382.4	193.2	108.2	590	469
Gates	1.6	0.0	0.4	10.3	1.7	0.6	0.1	16.6	11.1	4.1	413	306
Graham	2.0	0.0	1.0	8.7	1.0	0.9	0.2	14.6	9.6	3.3	453	311
Granville	46.3	3.3	10.8	32.3	4.9	2.9	11.2	90.9	42.4	19.3	457	325
Greene	2.2	0.0	1.4	14.0	3.9	1.5	1.4	28.4	18.1	6.6	364	253
Guilford	251.5	163.9	81.8	148.9	40.4	34.3	109.1	940.2	391.5	346.5	907	734
Halifax	7.4	0.2	2.0	90.2	17.7	9.4	4.3	133.8	78.7	30.5	538	411
Harnett	7.5	10.4	8.4	57.5	10.5	4.4	1.1	169.5	92.0	31.7	393	272
Haywood	8.1	16.8	1.8	36.7	5.0	2.5	8.9	158.3	55.7	32.4	633	474
Henderson	12.7	0.2	3.2	31.7	6.1	3.7	4.2	204.4	67.3	45.1	568	409
Hertford	4.6	0.0	92.6	30.9	5.3	2.7	1.4	50.9	33.3	11.9	530	387
Hoke	3.2	0.3	3.5	20.1	5.5	2.1	4.6	47.8	31.1	11.2	381	276
Hyde	1.9	1.3	0.6	8.1	1.1	0.5	2.8	13.8	7.6	4.3	803	618
Iredell	15.0	0.3	4.1	40.8	8.1	4.4	10.3	186.6	96.0	57.0	524	369
Jackson	3.6	0.0	0.9	22.1	2.4	5.0	0.6	52.1	29.3	17.7	597	400
Johnston	11.9	3.4	3.2	86.4	9.0	4.7	12.4	227.5	104.6	56.0	549	389
Jones	1.2	0.0	0.5	12.1	2.1	0.8	2.4	17.0	11.4	4.1	456	345
Lee	10.2	0.4	1.7	30.1	4.8	3.1	3.3	104.1	56.2	29.9	616	483
Lenoir	21.3	1.8	6.6	65.7	10.1	5.6	12.9	140.4	79.2	32.2	540	397
Lincoln	6.9	0.0	1.8	17.0	4.0	2.5	3.5	92.6	46.2	30.4	531	391
McDowell	4.7	0.0	1.1	25.5	3.5	4.3	14.3	61.5	37.6	17.0	436	292
Macon	9.8	1.1	6.4	19.7	3.7	1.4	1.8	47.1	20.2	18.9	686	498
Madison	2.8	0.0	9.3	29.4	2.4	1.9	39.7	27.5	17.6	7.3	396	293
Martin	4.4	0.0	0.9	30.1	8.0	1.7	2.0	88.9	35.1	15.9	605	464
Mecklenburg	314.6	42.8	536.7	197.7	56.7	37.6	82.1	2 651.2	669.9	668.8	1 090	824
Mitchell	2.5	0.0	0.5	20.8	3.5	4.6	1.5	30.0	19.9	6.9	466	319
Montgomery	3.0	12.2	0.8	19.2	3.1	1.4	1.1	49.3	28.9	12.5	513	401
Moore	10.0	0.0	2.5	35.5	5.3	4.5	1.1	144.4	79.6	43.3	617	450
Nash	4.3	2.2	1.7	63.3	14.9	6.9	8.7	280.2	116.1	47.0	523	398
New Hanover	50.1	73.2	25.7	81.1	15.9	7.5	14.6	543.3	166.8	117.5	796	559
Northampton	2.5	0.0	0.6	37.9	8.1	2.3	1.0	41.3	25.7	10.5	496	403
Onslow	928.6	209.9	5.1	40.9	11.2	7.5	6.4	222.6	130.6	48.8	341	218
Orange	23.2	1.3	40.6	287.3	11.9	14.6	63.2	213.3	85.1	95.0	875	727
Pamlico	2.3	0.0	0.8	9.2	1.5	0.7	1.0	28.3	17.6	7.0	574	441
Pasquotank	54.3	0.3	10.7	18.8	5.9	6.1	21.4	130.8	48.1	17.3	507	351
Pender	4.6	0.8	4.6	25.6	5.3	2.3	5.3	61.5	31.5	21.8	573	428
Perquimans	1.7	0.0	0.4	10.4	2.1	1.3	0.3	22.1	12.0	5.6	507	398
Person	3.4	0.0	0.8	30.0	4.3	2.6	0.3	75.3	35.5	21.7	653	504
Pitt	22.5	14.4	7.4	102.8	17.8	9.2	10.9	615.5	129.6	64.9	536	396
Polk	2.8	5.9	0.7	8.1	1.0	0.7	4.1	23.7	12.8	8.1	490	382
Randolph	13.6	1.6	5.3	35.0	5.7	5.4	8.9	188.0	105.1	54.2	454	330
Richmond	6.8	0.0	1.2	42.6	6.6	3.6	8.4	89.0	53.0	21.5	467	340
Robeson	15.7	0.0	3.6	149.0	28.8	13.0	14.4	224.3	138.8	47.1	412	287
Rockingham	10.0	0.5	22.5	64.6	9.0	5.5	1.0	168.9	89.0	48.2	535	413
Rowan	71.8	0.4	12.2	38.6	13.4	8.0	32.3	213.5	118.7	61.6	499	378
Rutherford	7.3	0.1	1.8	46.8	6.3	4.5	5.5	115.9	63.9	28.3	471	334
Sampson	8.9	0.0	5.2	58.3	8.6	4.3	4.3	101.5	65.3	23.9	462	344
Scotland	3.6	0.0	0.9	41.6	11.9	5.5	0.4	73.8	43.6	20.0	561	416
Stanly	10.1	0.1	1.7	20.7	3.6	2.9	3.0	106.4	61.8	26.7	481	359
Stokes	4.3	0.0	5.5	18.0	2.4	1.8	0.3	59.6	33.8	17.2	404	282
Surry	9.3	0.0	2.3	50.8	4.5	3.6	11.8	125.8	69.8	33.6	505	343

1. October 1, 2000 to September 30, 2001.   2. State totals may include programs not allocated by county.   3. Based on the resident population estimated as of July 1 of the year shown.

STATE County	Local government finances, 1997 (cont'd)									Government employment, 1999			Presidential election, 2000[2]		
	Direct general expenditure							Debt outstanding					Percent of vote cast —		
			Percent of total for —												
	Total (mil dol)	Per capita[1] (dollars)	Education	Health and hospitals	Police protection	Public welfare	Highways	Total (mil dol)	Per capita[1] (dollars)	Federal civilian	Federal military	State and local	Democratic	Republican	All other
	183	184	185	186	187	188	189	190	191	192	193	194	195	196	197
NORTH CAROLINA—Cont'd															
Chowan	30.2	2 132	48.7	3.7	4.5	10.5	1.5	15.1	1 066	48	43	851	49.7	49.4	0.9
Clay	12.7	1 529	58.6	7.9	5.0	2.8	0.3	2.0	238	24	26	424	35.3	62.7	1.9
Cleveland	238.4	2 594	41.0	32.3	3.6	6.6	1.0	177.9	1 935	201	282	5 102	41.1	58.2	0.7
Columbus	109.9	2 093	60.4	5.3	3.6	7.7	1.5	57.5	1 096	153	159	3 422	54.2	45.3	0.5
Craven	281.6	3 223	35.5	35.5	3.4	4.5	1.2	115.2	1 319	5 859	8 626	7 621	38.2	60.9	0.9
Cumberland	746.1	2 627	37.7	26.6	5.8	5.7	1.4	475.3	1 673	10 028	44 938	20 376	50.1	49.4	0.5
Currituck	41.0	2 396	55.8	1.4	3.7	4.1	0.1	25.5	1 492	47	55	956	38.5	60.8	0.7
Dare	82.8	2 969	30.9	8.8	8.5	3.4	2.7	42.6	1 529	213	235	2 229	43.0	56.2	0.9
Davidson	221.3	1 591	60.3	7.2	5.0	5.4	1.4	69.4	499	188	429	6 135	31.1	68.0	0.9
Davie	62.4	2 001	51.3	23.8	3.0	4.2	0.6	16.6	532	64	98	1 291	26.1	72.8	1.2
Duplin	87.1	2 017	55.1	2.6	3.9	8.4	3.3	36.3	841	154	132	3 136	45.0	54.5	0.5
Durham	620.3	3 107	31.1	26.7	5.4	5.7	2.3	541.5	2 712	4 559	662	12 354	63.3	35.4	1.3
Edgecombe	98.8	1 776	52.8	8.6	4.3	13.7	1.0	9.0	162	500	165	4 367	62.2	37.6	0.3
Forsyth	738.9	2 585	38.2	3.7	5.8	4.8	2.7	558.8	1 955	1 198	875	15 791	43.4	56.0	0.6
Franklin	74.2	1 704	52.2	5.9	4.0	9.4	0.7	39.2	900	78	137	2 126	46.4	53.0	0.6
Gaston	404.7	2 207	42.2	8.5	5.4	6.7	4.3	256.6	1 400	392	556	8 758	32.6	66.7	0.8
Gates	16.7	1 665	76.9	0.8	1.2	7.4	0.3	0.1	14	33	31	627	56.4	42.9	0.6
Graham	13.6	1 773	61.2	3.7	3.1	6.6	1.2	4.8	628	70	23	475	29.9	68.6	1.5
Granville	83.7	1 985	47.0	20.0	3.9	5.9	1.8	40.5	961	726	134	6 290	50.9	48.5	0.6
Greene	28.4	1 576	57.6	3.5	4.8	10.1	0.6	10.9	605	59	56	1 316	42.2	57.1	0.7
Guilford	932.9	2 443	41.3	8.4	6.7	6.5	3.0	575.4	1 507	4 309	1 237	27 107	48.6	50.8	0.7
Halifax	143.0	2 521	53.2	10.2	3.9	8.6	1.6	45.6	804	139	168	5 000	60.2	39.5	0.3
Harnett	154.9	1 921	47.3	21.1	4.1	6.3	2.5	61.3	760	119	265	4 435	37.9	61.1	1.0
Haywood	163.8	3 202	31.9	42.3	3.1	4.3	1.4	75.8	1 481	143	156	3 428	41.0	50.8	8.2
Henderson	191.8	2 417	35.4	38.5	3.8	4.9	0.8	30.7	386	226	247	4 528	32.5	66.5	0.9
Hertford	50.7	2 267	58.3	6.1	3.8	10.3	1.7	5.7	255	71	66	1 761	69.4	30.2	0.4
Hoke	46.2	1 572	62.4	2.6	4.1	8.8	0.8	15.5	527	52	94	2 078	58.5	40.1	1.5
Hyde	13.0	2 423	54.4	8.6	3.1	9.3	0.2	4.0	736	41	19	752	48.6	50.6	0.8
Iredell	181.2	1 664	59.6	3.6	5.3	5.9	1.2	77.2	709	264	354	6 496	33.9	65.5	0.7
Jackson	48.7	1 644	57.1	6.1	3.4	8.2	0.9	19.6	663	69	92	3 697	47.2	51.5	1.3
Johnston	235.9	2 315	47.7	20.4	3.9	4.8	1.3	76.1	747	203	333	5 758	33.3	66.1	0.6
Jones	16.8	1 867	62.0	4.2	3.5	12.4	0.7	1.2	135	26	28	516	46.0	53.3	0.7
Lee	107.3	2 214	58.2	2.8	5.6	5.5	1.7	74.1	1 529	162	148	2 717	41.7	57.8	0.6
Lenoir	163.2	2 736	59.8	5.7	2.4	6.2	1.1	105.5	1 769	335	177	6 597	45.0	54.4	0.6
Lincoln	88.4	1 546	58.3	4.5	4.7	6.9	0.4	102.9	1 798	105	177	2 949	34.3	65.0	0.7
McDowell	58.4	1 495	63.3	3.6	4.4	8.8	1.4	6.5	167	98	122	2 448	33.9	65.0	1.1
Macon	43.0	1 558	49.2	6.0	5.2	6.8	2.5	8.0	289	234	87	1 299	35.4	63.5	1.1
Madison	27.1	1 466	56.9	5.2	3.6	12.4	1.7	2.3	125	70	57	873	42.1	56.2	1.7
Martin	86.4	3 281	40.2	19.6	2.9	5.2	0.7	242.9	9 228	85	78	1 789	52.6	47.2	0.2
Mecklenburg	2 495.5	4 069	26.2	35.3	4.6	5.1	2.1	2 850.3	4 647	5 000	2 038	46 239	48.2	51.0	0.8
Mitchell	29.6	2 000	71.0	1.9	2.8	7.4	1.4	2.8	189	61	44	1 175	23.3	75.5	1.2
Montgomery	49.6	2 042	61.8	4.4	5.0	6.3	1.6	20.3	835	77	73	1 617	44.3	55.1	0.5
Moore	151.0	2 152	47.8	19.5	5.1	3.7	1.8	49.5	705	164	219	4 051	35.9	63.5	0.6
Nash	287.3	3 194	39.0	35.7	3.9	4.1	2.0	41.6	463	82	277	5 656	40.6	59.0	0.5
New Hanover	559.6	3 790	25.9	42.7	3.3	4.6	1.0	311.4	2 109	858	633	13 912	44.2	55.0	0.8
Northampton	40.3	1 900	55.1	7.5	3.5	12.2	1.5	14.1	665	58	64	1 526	67.2	32.5	0.2
Onslow	245.6	1 717	54.8	7.5	4.2	4.9	1.4	93.6	655	5 284	37 114	7 289	34.0	65.1	1.0
Orange	207.1	1 909	49.3	2.1	6.5	4.8	1.3	147.3	1 358	347	403	26 954	62.7	36.3	1.0
Pamlico	26.9	2 208	60.9	3.2	2.6	8.0	1.0	13.3	1 090	33	57	780	41.7	57.2	1.0
Pasquotank	139.1	4 065	39.3	40.0	2.4	3.4	0.5	67.2	1 964	632	686	4 810	53.9	45.3	0.8
Pender	62.1	1 635	54.6	5.0	3.7	7.6	0.5	28.8	758	83	121	2 216	45.3	54.1	0.6
Perquimans	23.1	2 074	52.5	1.3	3.0	7.4	1.0	7.3	653	39	34	623	47.2	51.8	1.0
Person	74.2	2 233	53.2	5.1	3.5	7.2	0.9	101.5	3 054	66	102	2 073	42.6	56.8	0.6
Pitt	538.9	4 452	21.3	56.9	2.9	3.2	1.0	243.6	2 012	390	400	17 176	45.7	53.8	0.5
Polk	23.5	1 422	56.5	2.7	7.8	6.8	1.9	11.3	686	44	51	760	37.5	61.1	1.4
Randolph	200.1	1 674	61.5	7.6	3.9	4.7	1.3	107.0	895	210	370	5 640	26.6	72.5	0.9
Richmond	85.9	1 862	57.5	3.1	4.2	8.0	1.4	38.6	836	128	137	3 088	55.6	43.9	0.5
Robeson	227.7	1 993	56.0	8.5	4.5	10.0	1.3	82.6	722	486	353	7 490	60.0	39.4	0.6
Rockingham	162.5	1 803	53.4	7.4	6.3	5.7	2.7	82.6	917	177	271	4 368	40.8	58.3	0.9
Rowan	220.0	1 781	58.7	2.6	4.5	6.0	2.5	88.2	714	1 638	381	5 835	33.7	65.5	0.7
Rutherford	115.5	1 920	53.0	10.0	4.6	6.4	1.6	56.8	944	127	185	3 392	35.4	63.3	1.2
Sampson	102.1	1 971	58.7	9.0	4.3	7.3	1.4	36.4	703	141	159	3 762	45.6	54.1	0.3
Scotland	75.2	2 112	53.2	6.7	4.4	8.8	1.0	16.0	449	59	108	1 999	59.8	39.8	0.4
Stanly	104.5	1 881	57.4	3.4	4.1	5.9	2.2	32.7	588	159	171	3 037	31.0	68.1	0.9
Stokes	59.4	1 390	62.1	7.2	3.7	7.3	0.4	21.4	501	82	132	1 632	29.3	70.0	0.7
Surry	129.3	1 944	61.5	7.0	3.9	5.6	1.5	60.4	908	171	204	4 519	33.2	65.9	0.9

1. Based on the resident population estimated as of July 1 of the year shown. 2. Data subject to copyright.

Table B. States and Counties — **Land Area and Population**

					Population and population characteristics, 2000											
STATE/ County code	MSA/ PMSA/ NECMA code[1]	County Type[2]	STATE County	Land area,[3] (sq km) 2000			Race alone or in combination (percent)					Age (percent)					
					Total persons	Rank	Per square kilometer	White	Black	Am. Indian, Alaska Native	Asian and Pacific Islander	Percent Hispanic[4]	Under 5 years	5 to 17 years	18 to 24 years	25 to 34 years	35 to 44 years	45 to 54 years
				1	2	3	4	5	6	7	8	9	10	11	12	13	14	15
			NORTH CAROLINA— Cont'd															
37 173	...	9	Swain	1 368	12 968	2 235	9.5	68.4	1.8	31.0	0.3	1.5	6.1	18.1	8.3	12.2	14.5	14.1
37 175	...	6	Transylvania	980	29 334	1 418	29.9	94.7	4.7	0.8	0.6	1.0	4.9	15.5	8.2	9.9	13.2	13.6
37 177	...	9	Tyrrell	1 010	4 149	2 903	4.1	57.0	39.8	0.5	1.3	3.6	4.9	17.7	8.2	13.0	17.3	13.3
37 179	1520	1	Union	1 651	123 677	435	74.9	83.7	12.8	0.7	0.8	6.2	8.1	20.0	8.2	15.5	17.7	13.1
37 181	...	6	Vance	657	42 954	1 038	65.4	48.8	48.7	0.4	0.6	4.6	7.0	20.0	8.9	14.1	14.7	13.6
37 183	6640	2	Wake	2 155	627 846	85	291.3	73.7	20.3	0.7	3.9	5.4	7.2	17.9	10.7	18.1	18.4	13.4
37 185	...	8	Warren	1 110	19 972	1 794	18.0	39.3	55.1	5.4	0.3	1.6	5.4	18.2	8.0	11.4	14.9	13.9
37 187	...	7	Washington	903	13 723	2 180	15.2	48.8	49.3	0.3	0.6	2.3	6.6	19.4	7.7	11.0	14.0	14.8
37 189	...	7	Watauga	809	42 695	1 044	52.8	97.0	1.7	0.5	0.8	1.5	3.9	12.4	27.8	11.0	12.4	12.8
37 191	2980	3	Wayne	1 431	113 329	475	79.2	62.2	33.6	0.7	1.4	4.9	7.0	19.2	9.9	14.2	16.3	13.0
37 193	...	7	Wilkes	1 961	65 632	743	33.5	93.6	4.4	0.4	0.5	3.4	6.2	16.4	7.9	14.0	15.7	14.6
37 195	...	4	Wilson	961	73 814	679	76.8	56.5	39.7	0.5	0.7	6.0	6.9	18.7	9.1	13.5	15.3	14.2
37 197	3120	2	Yadkin	869	36 348	1 204	41.8	93.2	3.6	0.5	0.4	6.5	6.6	17.3	7.5	14.1	16.0	13.7
37 199	...	8	Yancey	809	17 774	1 911	22.0	98.5	0.7	0.6	0.2	2.7	5.5	15.7	7.0	12.2	14.2	15.3
38 000	...	X	**NORTH DAKOTA**	178 647	642 200	X	3.6	93.4	0.8	5.5	0.9	1.2	6.1	18.9	11.4	12.0	15.3	13.3
38 001	...	9	Adams	2 559	2 593	3 021	1.0	98.8	0.5	0.6	0.2	0.3	4.5	18.7	4.1	7.6	14.0	15.7
38 003	...	7	Barnes	3 863	11 775	2 309	3.0	98.5	0.6	1.1	0.3	0.5	5.3	17.0	11.3	9.3	13.7	13.9
38 005	...	9	Benson	3 576	6 964	2 689	1.9	51.6	0.2	48.8	0.0	0.8	8.9	27.2	7.8	10.4	12.9	11.1
38 007	...	9	Billings	2 982	888	3 115	0.3	99.7	0.0	0.9	0.2	0.3	3.5	21.4	4.5	7.5	19.0	17.7
38 009	...	7	Bottineau	4 322	7 149	2 672	1.7	98.0	0.3	2.0	0.3	0.5	3.9	18.3	8.0	7.9	14.4	15.5
38 011	...	9	Bowman	3 010	3 242	2 977	1.1	99.6	0.1	0.4	0.3	0.7	4.6	19.5	5.3	8.7	15.9	14.4
38 013	...	9	Burke	2 858	2 242	3 047	0.8	99.4	0.2	0.2	0.3	0.4	3.7	17.2	3.5	7.5	14.8	16.7
38 015	1010	3	Burleigh	4 230	69 416	715	16.4	95.8	0.4	3.8	0.6	0.7	6.2	18.5	11.0	13.0	16.3	14.3
38 017	2520	3	Cass	4 572	123 138	438	26.9	96.2	1.1	1.5	1.7	1.2	6.6	16.8	16.0	15.9	15.4	12.9
38 019	...	9	Cavalier	3 855	4 831	2 858	1.3	99.1	0.4	1.2	0.2	0.6	4.3	20.3	3.7	7.0	14.3	15.4
38 021	...	9	Dickey	2 929	5 757	2 805	2.0	98.5	0.3	0.7	0.8	1.4	5.7	18.1	10.2	9.5	12.9	12.1
38 023	...	9	Divide	3 262	2 283	3 042	0.7	99.2	0.1	0.2	0.5	0.6	3.1	17.2	3.6	6.0	14.1	14.7
38 025	...	9	Dunn	5 205	3 600	2 944	0.7	87.4	0.1	13.1	0.1	0.8	5.7	21.7	5.8	8.5	15.0	15.4
38 027	...	9	Eddy	1 632	2 757	3 008	1.7	97.1	0.2	3.0	0.2	0.6	5.0	18.6	6.1	7.6	14.8	13.5
38 029	...	8	Emmons	3 911	4 331	2 894	1.1	99.1	0.1	0.2	0.4	1.2	5.3	19.5	3.7	7.8	14.5	12.2
38 031	...	9	Foster	1 645	3 759	2 933	2.3	99.4	0.3	0.5	0.0	0.2	5.3	20.9	5.5	9.9	16.0	11.8
38 033	...	9	Golden Valley	2 595	1 924	3 070	0.7	98.7	0.2	1.7	0.2	1.0	5.5	22.9	5.1	8.3	13.9	13.3
38 035	2985	3	Grand Forks	3 724	66 109	740	17.8	94.4	1.8	3.0	1.5	2.1	6.4	17.4	19.6	14.2	14.5	11.7
38 037	...	8	Grant	4 298	2 841	3 002	0.7	97.6	0.0	2.2	0.5	0.6	4.3	19.1	4.3	7.9	12.6	15.0
38 039	...	9	Griggs	1 835	2 754	3 009	1.5	99.5	0.1	0.3	0.1	0.4	4.7	17.8	4.9	7.7	13.3	16.3
38 041	...	9	Hettinger	2 933	2 715	3 012	0.9	99.3	0.1	0.6	0.2	0.2	4.4	18.9	3.9	7.3	13.3	15.1
38 043	...	8	Kidder	3 499	2 753	3 010	0.8	99.6	0.2	0.1	0.2	0.6	5.0	18.2	5.0	7.5	15.4	14.1
38 045	...	9	La Moure	2 971	4 701	2 867	1.6	99.6	0.2	0.3	0.1	0.6	4.4	19.8	5.4	7.8	15.1	13.3
38 047	...	9	Logan	2 571	2 308	3 037	0.9	99.5	0.1	0.2	0.3	0.7	5.5	17.1	3.6	8.1	13.6	11.7
38 049	...	9	McHenry	4 854	5 987	2 782	1.2	99.4	0.2	0.9	0.2	0.4	4.9	19.0	5.9	8.8	14.4	14.3
38 051	...	9	McIntosh	2 526	3 390	2 964	1.3	99.4	0.0	0.5	0.5	0.8	4.2	15.2	4.6	6.5	12.9	10.6
38 053	...	9	McKenzie	7 102	5 737	2 808	0.8	78.5	0.2	22.0	0.2	1.0	6.3	24.4	5.5	7.8	15.5	14.9
38 055	...	8	McLean	5 465	9 311	2 505	1.7	93.6	0.1	6.9	0.2	0.9	4.7	19.1	5.1	8.1	14.6	16.5
38 057	...	7	Mercer	2 708	8 644	2 555	3.2	97.2	0.1	2.6	0.8	0.4	4.6	24.5	4.2	7.6	20.0	16.0
38 059	1010	3	Morton	4 989	25 303	1 553	5.1	96.9	0.3	3.1	0.5	0.6	6.5	20.5	7.8	11.7	16.5	14.1
38 061	...	9	Mountrail	4 724	6 631	2 723	1.4	69.3	0.1	31.0	0.3	1.3	6.5	21.6	6.8	9.5	13.7	14.5
38 063	...	8	Nelson	2 542	3 715	2 941	1.5	99.2	0.1	0.6	0.4	0.2	3.7	18.4	4.0	7.0	13.4	14.5
38 065	...	8	Oliver	1 874	2 065	3 062	1.1	98.4	0.2	2.1	0.1	0.6	4.5	22.9	4.7	7.9	15.6	19.8
38 067	...	9	Pembina	2 898	8 585	2 558	3.0	96.9	0.2	2.6	0.3	3.1	5.0	19.9	6.2	9.2	15.4	13.5
38 069	...	7	Pierce	2 636	4 675	2 869	1.8	98.9	0.1	0.9	0.4	0.6	5.3	18.6	5.5	9.1	14.8	12.5
38 071	...	7	Ramsey	3 069	12 066	2 291	3.9	93.9	0.3	6.8	0.3	0.5	5.7	19.4	8.0	10.2	15.7	13.2
38 073	...	8	Ransom	2 235	5 890	2 794	2.6	98.9	0.4	0.8	0.4	0.8	5.9	19.1	5.9	10.8	14.6	13.3
38 075	...	9	Renville	2 266	2 610	3 019	1.2	98.5	0.3	1.2	0.6	0.7	4.3	19.0	4.9	9.2	15.3	14.8
38 077	...	6	Richland	3 721	17 998	1 897	4.8	97.5	0.4	2.1	0.5	0.7	6.0	18.7	14.5	10.4	15.3	12.4
38 079	...	9	Rolette	2 337	13 674	2 186	5.9	26.6	0.2	74.5	0.1	0.8	8.8	27.6	9.5	11.2	14.6	10.9
38 081	...	9	Sargent	2 224	4 366	2 889	2.0	98.9	0.1	0.9	0.2	0.7	5.7	20.8	5.3	10.7	15.0	14.7
38 083	...	9	Sheridan	2 517	1 710	3 084	0.7	99.4	0.1	0.5	0.1	0.4	3.8	18.2	3.8	6.4	13.5	14.8
38 085	...	9	Sioux	2 834	4 044	2 917	1.4	15.0	0.1	85.3	0.2	1.6	10.5	29.8	11.1	13.5	13.4	9.8
38 087	...	9	Slope	3 154	767	3 128	0.2	99.9	0.0	0.3	0.0	0.1	4.7	20.6	4.2	8.1	16.9	17.6
38 089	...	7	Stark	3 466	22 636	1 664	6.5	98.3	0.4	1.4	0.4	1.0	5.8	19.8	11.6	10.4	15.6	13.1
38 091	...	8	Steele	1 845	2 258	3 046	1.2	99.1	0.3	1.2	0.0	0.2	5.6	22.0	4.7	8.2	14.8	13.4
38 093	...	7	Stutsman	5 753	21 908	1 697	3.8	98.1	0.4	1.3	0.6	0.9	5.4	17.5	10.5	10.1	15.7	14.1
38 095	...	9	Towner	2 654	2 876	3 001	1.1	97.8	0.1	2.5	0.1	0.2	4.8	19.9	3.6	7.6	16.4	14.6
38 097	...	8	Traill	2 232	8 477	2 567	3.8	97.7	0.2	1.2	0.2	2.2	6.0	18.8	9.7	9.9	14.9	12.7
38 099	...	6	Walsh	3 320	12 389	2 273	3.7	95.8	0.5	1.5	0.5	5.7	5.7	19.2	6.5	9.6	15.4	14.4

1. MSA = Metropolitan Statistical Area. PMSA = Primary MSA. NECMA = New England County Metropolitan Area. See Appendix A for explanation of these concepts. See Appendix B for list of metropolitan areas identified by type, with component counties. 2. County typology code from the Economic Research Service of USDA. See Appendix A for definition. 3. Dry land or land partially or temporarily covered by water. 4. Hispanic persons may be of any race.

Table B. States and Counties — **Population and Households**

| | Population, 2000 (cont'd) | | | | Population — change and components of change, 1990–2001 | | | | | | | Households, 2000 | | | | |
| | Age (percent) (cont'd) | | | | Total persons | | Percent change | | Components of change, 2000–2001 | | | | | | Percent | |
STATE County	55 to 64 years	65 to 74 years	75 years and over	Percent female	2001	1990	1990–2000	2000–2001	Births	Deaths	Net migration	Number	Percent change, 1990–2000	Persons per house-hold	Female family house-holder[1]	One person
	16	17	18	19	20	21	22	23	24	25	26	27	28	29	30	31
NORTH CAROLINA—Cont'd																
Swain	11.3	8.4	6.9	51.4	13 061	11 268	15.1	0.7	234	167	27	5 137	23.1	2.44	13.9	25.8
Transylvania	13.3	11.7	9.7	51.9	29 487	25 520	14.9	0.5	357	445	252	12 320	24.1	2.30	8.7	26.1
Tyrrell	9.5	8.3	7.8	46.7	4 031	3 856	7.6	-2.8	54	58	-114	1 537	4.5	2.42	16.6	28.2
Union	8.4	5.3	3.7	50.1	132 676	84 210	46.9	7.3	2 594	1 000	7 225	43 390	48.1	2.81	9.8	17.0
Vance	9.0	7.0	5.6	52.7	43 622	38 892	10.4	1.6	912	636	403	16 199	14.4	2.60	20.4	24.2
Wake	7.0	4.1	3.2	50.4	655 642	426 311	47.3	4.4	12 441	4 164	19 257	242 040	46.0	2.51	9.8	25.7
Warren	10.9	9.6	7.8	50.9	19 904	17 265	15.7	-0.3	305	315	-54	7 708	22.3	2.48	17.3	26.2
Washington	11.0	8.3	7.2	52.7	13 597	13 997	-2.0	-0.9	210	194	-140	5 367	6.2	2.52	18.8	24.7
Watauga	8.7	6.1	4.9	50.2	42 909	36 952	15.5	0.5	445	395	181	16 540	20.8	2.26	6.8	28.6
Wayne	8.9	6.8	4.8	50.7	112 736	104 666	8.3	-0.5	2 357	1 416	-1 489	42 612	15.5	2.55	15.4	24.5
Wilkes	11.1	7.9	6.2	50.7	66 166	59 393	10.5	0.8	1 094	829	289	26 650	15.8	2.43	9.4	24.5
Wilson	9.4	7.1	5.8	52.3	74 310	66 061	11.7	0.7	1 529	988	-14	28 613	14.0	2.51	16.5	26.4
Yadkin	10.6	7.9	6.3	50.9	36 859	30 488	19.2	1.4	646	469	344	14 505	20.2	2.47	9.0	24.0
Yancey	11.8	9.7	8.5	51.1	17 874	15 419	15.3	0.6	243	226	92	7 472	22.0	2.36	7.8	25.4
NORTH DAKOTA	8.3	7.1	7.6	50.1	634 448	638 800	0.5	-1.2	9 452	7 379	-9 822	257 152	6.8	2.41	7.8	29.3
Adams	11.3	10.8	13.3	52.2	2 523	3 174	-18.3	-2.7	17	53	-35	1 121	-11.5	2.24	5.5	32.6
Barnes	9.8	8.5	11.3	50.8	11 463	12 545	-6.1	-2.6	147	179	-282	4 884	-1.8	2.29	4.8	31.5
Benson	8.3	7.0	6.5	49.5	6 879	7 198	-3.3	-1.2	178	93	-173	2 328	-3.6	2.97	16.6	24.5
Billings	10.4	8.2	7.8	47.0	857	1 108	-19.9	-3.5	8	5	-34	366	-5.4	2.43	4.4	26.8
Bottineau	10.7	9.7	11.6	49.6	6 975	8 011	-10.8	-2.4	58	135	-96	2 962	-4.6	2.30	4.3	31.5
Bowman	9.8	10.4	11.4	51.4	3 124	3 596	-9.8	-3.6	30	64	-84	1 358	-4.4	2.32	4.1	31.5
Burke	11.6	13.4	11.7	49.6	2 191	3 002	-25.3	-2.3	19	33	-38	1 013	-19.1	2.21	5.3	31.6
Burleigh	8.2	6.5	5.9	51.1	70 069	60 131	15.4	0.9	983	571	270	27 670	22.0	2.42	8.7	28.1
Cass	6.7	4.9	4.7	49.9	124 021	102 874	19.7	0.7	1 956	920	-99	51 315	27.4	2.32	7.6	31.2
Cavalier	12.1	11.3	11.7	50.3	4 655	6 064	-20.3	-3.6	41	83	-135	2 017	-15.1	2.34	3.8	30.8
Dickey	10.1	9.3	12.0	50.7	5 612	6 107	-5.7	-2.5	64	122	-90	2 283	-0.7	2.36	4.9	32.0
Divide	11.9	12.2	17.3	49.8	2 203	2 899	-21.2	-3.5	13	49	-45	1 005	-15.8	2.18	4.2	33.4
Dunn	10.6	8.4	8.9	49.0	3 563	4 005	-10.1	-1.0	32	64	-3	1 378	-3.8	2.57	7.2	25.3
Eddy	9.6	11.3	13.4	51.1	2 691	2 951	-6.6	-2.4	34	68	-34	1 164	-2.5	2.30	5.0	34.2
Emmons	11.4	12.7	12.8	49.6	4 209	4 830	-10.3	-2.8	39	79	-84	1 786	-3.4	2.38	4.4	28.4
Foster	9.2	10.9	12.5	50.3	3 624	3 983	-5.6	-3.6	48	79	-106	1 540	-0.1	2.39	6.4	30.6
Golden Valley	9.7	9.0	12.3	51.9	1 845	2 108	-8.7	-4.1	14	15	-79	761	-6.2	2.38	4.9	31.5
Grand Forks	6.4	4.7	4.9	49.1	64 390	70 683	-6.5	-2.6	1 076	498	-2 322	25 435	0.4	2.43	8.8	28.3
Grant	12.1	11.6	13.2	49.0	2 775	3 549	-19.9	-2.3	28	43	-53	1 195	-13.0	2.30	3.8	31.8
Griggs	9.5	10.9	14.8	50.1	2 628	3 303	-16.6	-4.6	25	58	-95	1 178	-9.0	2.29	4.7	31.6
Hettinger	11.9	12.3	12.9	49.9	2 650	3 445	-21.2	-2.4	32	43	-54	1 152	-14.1	2.30	3.8	31.2
Kidder	10.9	12.1	12.0	49.2	2 666	3 332	-17.4	-3.2	34	52	-69	1 158	-7.1	2.34	4.1	29.9
La Moure	10.7	11.5	11.9	49.4	4 616	5 383	-12.7	-1.8	37	68	-56	1 942	-6.4	2.38	4.0	30.8
Logan	13.3	13.6	13.4	50.4	2 221	2 847	-18.9	-3.8	28	35	-81	963	-12.1	2.32	3.1	29.2
McHenry	10.8	10.8	11.0	49.0	5 742	6 528	-8.3	-4.1	73	85	-238	2 526	-1.0	2.35	5.6	29.8
McIntosh	11.8	14.9	19.4	52.2	3 306	4 021	-15.7	-2.5	24	81	-25	1 467	-13.0	2.19	3.5	32.0
McKenzie	10.0	7.4	8.3	49.8	5 705	6 383	-10.1	-0.6	81	71	-43	2 151	-6.5	2.64	9.3	25.8
McLean	11.5	9.4	11.0	50.4	9 144	10 457	-11.0	-1.8	118	158	-125	3 815	-3.0	2.40	5.6	26.6
Mercer	8.8	6.9	7.4	49.7	8 531	9 808	-11.9	-1.3	85	104	-92	3 346	-6.0	2.55	5.1	24.8
Morton	8.3	7.6	7.0	50.2	25 194	23 700	6.8	-0.6	363	275	-239	9 889	14.0	2.51	8.5	25.7
Mountrail	9.7	8.0	9.7	50.8	6 553	7 021	-5.6	-1.2	117	108	-88	2 560	-1.0	2.53	11.8	28.5
Nelson	11.7	12.1	15.4	51.1	3 563	4 410	-15.8	-4.1	25	92	-85	1 628	-11.1	2.18	5.2	36.3
Oliver	10.4	7.8	6.4	48.2	1 960	2 381	-13.3	-5.1	20	18	-112	791	-2.2	2.61	3.9	21.0
Pembina	9.4	9.2	10.3	49.9	8 408	9 238	-7.1	-2.1	95	131	-140	3 535	-0.6	2.38	5.3	30.5
Pierce	10.2	10.7	13.5	50.9	4 597	5 052	-7.5	-1.7	52	99	-30	1 964	-0.5	2.31	6.3	32.0
Ramsey	9.1	8.4	10.4	50.7	11 833	12 681	-4.8	-1.9	189	195	-228	4 957	-0.4	2.34	8.5	31.1
Ransom	9.2	9.8	11.4	48.5	5 841	5 921	-0.5	-0.8	65	118	6	2 350	2.9	2.39	5.1	30.7
Renville	10.5	10.5	11.6	49.9	2 542	3 160	-17.4	-2.6	25	38	-55	1 085	-10.3	2.35	5.6	29.4
Richland	7.6	7.0	8.2	48.1	17 701	18 148	-0.8	-1.7	248	226	-320	6 885	5.6	2.43	6.5	29.4
Rolette	7.6	5.2	4.5	50.7	13 745	12 772	7.1	0.5	364	154	-139	4 556	9.8	2.97	22.7	22.6
Sargent	11.0	8.1	8.8	47.5	4 296	4 549	-4.0	-1.6	54	52	-73	1 786	1.3	2.43	3.9	27.7
Sheridan	13.5	13.7	12.9	48.6	1 605	2 148	-20.4	-6.1	12	14	-107	731	-14.8	2.31	4.4	27.5
Sioux	6.4	3.7	1.9	49.0	4 066	3 761	7.5	0.5	138	26	-91	1 095	7.1	3.63	29.1	16.6
Slope	10.0	11.3	6.5	46.2	754	907	-15.4	-1.7	11	5	-20	313	-6.0	2.45	3.8	27.2
Stark	8.3	7.5	8.0	50.8	22 213	22 832	-0.9	-1.9	322	245	-506	8 932	5.3	2.44	7.9	29.1
Steele	11.3	10.8	8.8	48.3	2 191	2 420	-6.7	-3.0	19	25	-61	923	-6.9	2.45	4.4	28.3
Stutsman	9.1	8.6	9.1	50.9	21 575	22 241	-1.5	-1.5	260	315	-274	8 954	3.4	2.28	7.5	32.7
Towner	9.9	9.8	13.5	50.8	2 770	3 627	-20.7	-3.7	20	55	-71	1 218	-15.0	2.31	4.6	33.6
Traill	8.8	8.4	10.7	49.8	8 392	8 752	-3.1	-1.0	110	127	-67	3 341	0.4	2.41	5.4	29.3
Walsh	9.8	8.9	10.3	50.0	12 081	13 840	-10.5	-2.5	179	202	-288	5 029	-3.8	2.39	7.5	31.3

1. No spouse present.

Table B. States and Counties — **Vital Statistics, Health Resources, and Crime**

STATE County	Births, average 1997–1999 Total	Rate[1]	Deaths, average 1997–1999 Number Total	Number Infant[2]	Rate Total[1]	Rate Infant[3]	Physicians,[4] 2000 Number	Rate[5]	Hospitals,[4] 1998 Number	Beds Number	Beds Rate[5]	Medicare enrollees 2000	Serious crimes known to police, 2000[6] Total Number	Rate[7]
	32	33	34	35	36	37	38	39	40	41	42	43	44	45
NORTH CAROLINA—Cont'd														
Swain	169	13.8	140	NA	11.4	NA	16	123	1	24	195	2 442	NA	NA
Transylvania	286	10.1	334	NA	11.8	NA	49	167	1	90	316	6 853	618	2 107
Tyrrell	40	10.4	47	NA	12.2	NA	1	24	0	0	0	731	58	1 398
Union	1 905	17.2	793	16	7.2	8.6	78	63	1	226	205	11 470	4 217	3 484
Vance	641	15.2	464	NA	11.0	NA	44	102	1	87	206	7 311	3 047	7 094
Wake	8 874	15.6	3 151	72	5.5	8.2	1 235	197	7	1 295	227	56 678	28 897	4 728
Warren	214	11.6	227	NA	12.3	NA	11	55	0	0	0	3 458	489	2 552
Washington	177	13.0	155	NA	11.4	NA	8	58	1	49	360	2 576	354	2 580
Watauga	356	8.7	286	NA	7.0	NA	96	225	2	205	500	5 013	1 526	3 574
Wayne	1 689	15.1	1 028	20	9.2	11.6	152	134	1	267	238	16 859	5 842	5 155
Wilkes	761	12.1	631	NA	10.0	NA	55	84	1	130	207	10 453	1 775	2 704
Wilson	1 031	15.1	759	11	11.1	11.0	98	133	1	277	406	11 536	4 128	5 749
Yadkin	459	13.1	335	NA	9.6	NA	15	41	1	50	143	6 029	836	2 477
Yancey	181	10.9	171	NA	10.3	NA	10	56	0	0	0	3 674	89	551
NORTH DAKOTA	7 992	12.5	5 972	57	9.4	7.2	1 355	211	46	4 304	674	103 196	14 694	2 288
Adams	24	8.9	41	NA	15.2	NA	15	578	1	45	1 658	578	23	887
Barnes	127	10.6	155	NA	13.0	NA	7	59	1	50	418	2 552	157	1 333
Benson	129	18.9	73	NA	10.7	NA	1	14	0	0	0	1 033	NA	NA
Billings	10	9.3	NA	NA	NA	NA	0	0	0	0	0	77	NA	NA
Bottineau	60	8.2	103	NA	14.1	NA	3	42	1	67	927	1 592	32	448
Bowman	36	10.9	49	NA	15.0	NA	6	185	1	36	1 085	762	NA	NA
Burke	13	5.6	29	NA	12.8	NA	0	0	0	0	0	639	9	466
Burleigh	824	12.3	464	9	6.9	10.5	257	370	2	513	767	9 686	1 983	2 857
Cass	1 569	13.4	764	10	6.5	6.6	425	345	3	667	571	13 584	3 574	2 902
Cavalier	50	10.1	65	NA	13.1	NA	3	62	1	28	559	1 146	82	1 697
Dickey	50	8.8	79	NA	13.9	NA	6	104	1	30	532	1 209	44	764
Divide	16	6.8	46	NA	19.5	NA	0	0	1	25	1 057	563	NA	NA
Dunn	34	9.7	48	NA	13.6	NA	0	0	0	0	0	575	0	0
Eddy	24	8.5	46	NA	16.3	NA	0	0	0	0	0	697	24	871
Emmons	44	10.1	56	NA	12.9	NA	1	23	1	25	580	1 116	31	716
Foster	39	10.3	64	NA	16.8	NA	4	106	1	70	1 841	855	NA	NA
Golden Valley	17	9.0	15	NA	8.1	NA	2	104	0	0	0	455	NA	NA
Grand Forks	982	14.7	409	NA	6.1	NA	188	284	2	413	618	7 068	2 522	3 904
Grant	27	9.2	38	NA	12.9	NA	1	35	1	50	1 684	707	8	282
Griggs	21	7.5	45	NA	15.9	NA	3	109	1	69	2 428	689	NA	NA
Hettinger	23	7.9	39	NA	13.4	NA	0	0	0	0	0	764	2	74
Kidder	23	8.1	40	NA	14.1	NA	0	0	0	0	0	641	23	835
La Moure	43	8.9	60	NA	12.5	NA	0	0	0	0	0	1 170	NA	NA
Logan	23	10.0	32	NA	13.8	NA	0	0	0	0	0	596	NA	NA
McHenry	59	9.7	71	NA	11.6	NA	2	33	0	0	0	1 509	51	852
McIntosh	26	7.4	72	NA	20.8	NA	5	147	2	94	2 731	1 197	16	485
McKenzie	77	13.6	61	NA	10.7	NA	0	0	1	26	458	816	47	819
McLean	90	9.3	127	NA	13.2	NA	8	86	2	84	866	2 154	139	1 493
Mercer	90	9.6	79	NA	8.5	NA	7	81	1	32	340	1 368	NA	NA
Morton	294	12.0	217	NA	8.8	NA	12	47	1	36	146	4 225	645	2 549
Mountrail	84	12.7	85	NA	12.9	NA	5	75	1	25	377	1 293	37	558
Nelson	29	7.8	74	NA	19.7	NA	3	81	1	14	377	1 100	NA	NA
Oliver	17	7.8	14	NA	6.4	NA	0	0	0	0	0	233	13	630
Pembina	83	9.8	107	NA	12.7	NA	2	23	1	90	1 061	1 773	88	1 025
Pierce	48	10.5	69	NA	15.0	NA	11	235	1	220	4 759	1 058	72	1 540
Ramsey	150	12.4	158	NA	13.0	NA	28	232	1	55	454	2 510	NA	NA
Ransom	57	9.8	98	NA	17.0	NA	4	68	1	70	1 212	1 219	NA	NA
Renville	25	8.7	32	NA	11.2	NA	2	77	0	0	0	571	29	1 111
Richland	211	11.6	176	NA	9.7	NA	10	56	0	0	0	2 774	476	2 645
Rolette	289	20.4	117	NA	8.3	NA	13	95	1	101	710	1 562	68	497
Sargent	44	10.0	45	NA	10.2	NA	0	0	0	0	0	824	64	1 466
Sheridan	13	7.8	18	NA	10.4	NA	1	58	0	0	0	455	32	1 871
Sioux	98	23.6	28	NA	6.8	NA	1	25	0	0	0	277	NA	NA
Slope	9	10.4	NA	NA	NA	NA	0	0	0	0	0	92	NA	NA
Stark	269	11.9	205	NA	9.1	NA	38	168	2	135	593	4 022	440	1 971
Steele	19	8.3	23	NA	10.4	NA	0	0	0	0	0	451	NA	NA
Stutsman	209	9.9	240	NA	11.4	NA	42	192	1	56	267	4 333	446	2 036
Towner	27	8.8	49	NA	16.1	NA	0	0	1	32	1 060	672	NA	NA
Traill	95	11.1	109	NA	12.7	NA	3	35	2	52	609	1 672	64	926
Walsh	148	10.9	170	NA	12.6	NA	16	129	2	49	362	2 686	295	2 381

1. Per 1,000 estimated resident population, average 1997–1999. 2. Deaths of infants under 1 year old. 3. Deaths of infants under 1 year old per 1,000 live births. 4. Data subject to copyright. 5. Per 100,000 resident population as of July 1 of the year shown. 6. Data for serious crimes have not been adjusted for underreporting; this may affect comparability between geographic areas and over time. 7. Per 100,000 population estimated by the FBI.

Table B. States and Counties — Crime, Education, Money Income, and Poverty

STATE County	Serious crimes known to police, 2000 (cont'd) Rate² Violent	Property	Education — School enrollment and attainment, 1990 — Enrollment³ Total	Percent private	Attainment⁴ (percent) High school graduate or more	Bachelor's degree or more	Local government expenditures, fiscal 1999⁵ Total current expenditures (mil dol)	Current expenditures per student (dollars)	Money income 1989 Per capita⁶ (dollars)	Households Median Dollars	Percent change, 1979–1989 (constant 1989 dollars)	Percent with $100,000 or more	Income and poverty, 1998 Median household income	Percent below poverty level All persons	Persons under 18	Persons 5–17 in families
	46	47	48	49	50	51	52	53	54	55	56	57	58	59	60	61
NORTH CAROLINA—Cont'd																
Swain	NA	NA	2 526	6.3	59.0	9.9	11.2	6 612	8 922	16 068	-2.8	0.9	23 701	21.4	31.3	29.4
Transylvania	123	1 984	5 724	19.7	72.1	17.9	22.4	5 732	12 737	25 179	-6.4	2.1	36 527	12.5	20.4	20.7
Tyrrell	169	1 229	887	8.5	58.0	7.6	6.5	8 083	7 884	16 363	-8.4	0.0	22 070	26.7	34.3	35.7
Union	279	3 204	21 170	14.8	69.0	13.2	106.3	5 106	13 135	30 957	11.1	3.2	44 382	8.9	13.1	12.7
Vance	759	6 335	9 756	7.8	57.1	9.5	45.2	5 516	10 457	21 555	7.8	2.2	27 033	19.7	27.4	27.9
Wake	415	4 312	114 706	16.1	85.4	35.3	516.0	5 593	17 195	36 222	15.9	5.2	55 169	7.5	11.6	10.4
Warren	172	2 380	3 857	6.4	53.7	7.1	19.5	6 024	8 502	16 937	-0.2	0.9	24 569	21.8	27.9	31.7
Washington	386	2 193	3 637	5.8	60.6	8.7	16.3	6 207	9 827	21 840	-2.2	1.2	27 377	21.8	30.7	31.2
Watauga	145	3 429	14 404	2.8	72.0	27.4	27.8	5 792	10 628	20 252	9.5	2.3	33 295	13.9	15.4	15.6
Wayne	592	4 563	27 469	11.4	71.2	12.7	101.4	5 271	10 843	23 560	8.7	1.2	32 023	16.9	23.0	22.5
Wilkes	245	2 459	12 767	3.9	54.1	8.8	56.7	5 678	10 816	22 261	-2.0	1.8	32 759	13.2	18.3	17.4
Wilson	630	5 120	17 118	13.3	62.2	14.4	68.4	5 675	11 641	24 021	5.9	2.1	31 012	18.4	26.3	25.3
Yadkin	196	2 281	6 340	4.4	58.9	7.1	31.3	5 487	11 843	25 062	9.7	1.5	35 971	10.9	16.4	15.9
Yancey	68	483	3 045	3.8	60.7	10.0	15.6	6 160	9 462	19 401	7.3	1.1	29 580	16.6	23.7	24.8
NORTH DAKOTA	81	2 207	177 543	7.5	76.7	18.1	625.4	5 442	11 051	23 213	-9.4	1.6	32 430	12.9	17.3	14.9
Adams	39	848	661	0.0	72.5	11.2	2.7	5 499	10 382	20 722	-11.3	2.1	28 009	14.1	18.1	15.4
Barnes	8	1 325	3 396	3.9	75.4	15.4	11.6	5 913	10 102	20 419	-13.0	0.9	31 557	14.3	20.2	16.9
Benson	NA	NA	2 010	1.8	65.4	9.2	7.2	6 746	6 983	16 917	-21.3	0.6	22 758	29.4	34.3	33.0
Billings	NA	NA	282	11.7	71.5	12.6	1.6	14 551	9 172	22 639	-33.3	0.5	30 089	16.0	18.4	19.8
Bottineau	0	448	1 984	2.9	74.9	14.3	7.6	6 005	10 557	22 294	1.0	1.8	29 632	14.0	17.9	15.9
Bowman	NA	NA	834	3.1	74.3	13.9	4.6	5 871	10 060	21 478	-7.2	0.3	31 627	13.6	18.4	15.7
Burke	0	466	653	2.3	66.9	8.7	2.9	7 148	9 176	19 160	-5.0	0.3	28 386	15.8	22.5	18.1
Burleigh	58	2 799	16 359	16.1	83.0	25.1	54.9	4 949	13 018	28 450	-11.1	2.5	40 985	8.9	12.7	9.7
Cass	107	2 795	31 588	7.3	87.1	26.5	101.7	5 277	13 240	26 806	-9.2	2.8	39 924	9.0	12.0	9.3
Cavalier	0	1 697	1 330	8.5	68.4	12.6	5.6	6 341	10 653	21 250	-13.0	1.7	33 132	14.0	20.4	16.4
Dickey	17	747	1 620	26.7	68.8	16.0	4.9	5 081	9 747	20 248	1.2	1.1	29 933	15.9	21.5	18.2
Divide	NA	NA	563	2.5	69.4	12.8	2.4	6 038	10 603	21 507	-8.7	0.5	28 781	14.6	21.8	19.0
Dunn	0	0	972	8.8	70.5	10.1	3.3	5 932	8 689	19 824	-6.7	0.9	25 855	18.3	23.2	20.3
Eddy	0	871	635	0.0	66.5	11.0	3.5	5 940	9 398	19 310	-9.5	0.5	27 429	14.3	18.6	16.4
Emmons	0	716	1 022	0.6	57.3	9.0	4.7	5 661	8 421	16 892	-8.2	0.3	26 044	16.2	22.9	18.5
Foster	NA	NA	947	6.0	69.4	12.1	3.2	4 155	9 393	20 760	-13.0	0.8	33 299	12.8	17.3	15.1
Golden Valley	NA	NA	568	2.5	74.6	15.7	3.0	6 565	9 290	20 281	-14.9	0.2	25 590	18.4	25.6	22.3
Grand Forks	156	3 748	24 841	5.0	85.6	25.8	56.8	5 162	11 414	25 162	-3.0	1.8	37 854	12.0	15.8	13.6
Grant	35	246	770	0.9	62.6	8.9	3.1	7 032	8 511	17 368	10.2	0.6	21 463	25.0	34.0	30.3
Griggs	NA	NA	729	2.3	67.9	12.1	3.9	6 200	8 816	19 417	-12.7	0.8	29 788	15.0	21.8	18.4
Hettinger	0	74	685	15.6	69.5	12.2	4.1	6 459	9 203	19 601	-0.7	1.0	30 153	14.2	20.5	17.2
Kidder	36	799	796	5.0	60.5	11.3	3.5	6 487	8 700	17 378	-0.8	0.4	25 942	17.7	23.9	20.3
La Moure	NA	NA	1 215	7.5	66.4	12.4	6.5	6 132	9 271	19 710	-3.7	1.0	30 090	12.9	17.4	14.7
Logan	NA	NA	552	2.9	51.9	9.3	2.8	5 931	10 304	19 490	11.6	1.9	25 150	20.2	27.3	24.3
McHenry	0	852	1 508	1.1	66.7	9.7	6.6	5 455	8 871	18 275	-5.0	0.6	25 179	18.1	23.7	19.8
McIntosh	0	485	1 067	0.5	48.8	9.5	3.2	5 644	9 133	17 798	4.8	0.3	24 638	16.9	25.8	21.2
McKenzie	105	715	1 684	3.9	72.4	14.2	9.5	8 199	9 832	24 662	-4.6	1.0	32 096	20.8	23.9	25.4
McLean	0	1 493	2 551	4.2	68.2	11.9	11.5	5 334	9 733	21 853	-14.1	0.6	32 626	14.2	17.9	14.4
Mercer	NA	NA	2 468	2.1	71.2	11.2	11.6	5 418	12 195	31 969	2.1	1.0	48 482	8.5	9.8	8.3
Morton	130	2 419	6 351	9.6	70.4	13.8	23.5	4 761	10 534	23 685	-14.0	1.1	33 964	13.1	17.9	14.7
Mountrail	15	543	1 866	2.7	73.0	12.9	8.8	5 452	9 265	19 399	-10.1	0.6	28 536	19.6	25.7	21.6
Nelson	NA	NA	902	2.7	69.4	10.6	4.3	5 705	9 590	19 360	-1.7	0.4	27 677	12.0	16.8	13.8
Oliver	0	630	635	8.2	68.2	10.8	1.8	5 476	9 749	23 000	-18.3	0.0	34 795	14.3	17.5	15.7
Pembina	82	944	2 186	1.6	73.1	13.1	11.4	6 078	11 308	23 256	-0.8	1.6	36 848	11.6	16.2	13.3
Pierce	43	1 497	1 059	7.5	65.9	13.4	4.0	4 953	8 993	20 216	-0.7	0.0	27 069	15.8	22.3	17.7
Ramsey	NA	NA	3 311	6.1	74.5	16.3	13.2	5 688	11 125	21 780	-14.7	1.3	31 881	15.3	21.8	18.5
Ransom	NA	NA	1 217	1.5	73.1	11.1	5.6	4 668	11 297	23 017	0.6	1.3	35 546	9.6	12.7	10.5
Renville	115	996	725	1.1	74.2	9.8	4.2	5 465	10 759	22 659	0.2	1.5	30 629	12.7	16.9	14.8
Richland	72	2 573	5 540	6.6	75.9	13.0	17.6	5 620	10 562	24 248	-7.2	1.9	37 147	11.7	15.5	13.0
Rolette	15	483	4 011	2.6	59.4	11.7	21.0	6 274	6 773	15 163	-19.1	0.4	23 182	30.9	32.4	33.2
Sargent	23	1 443	1 040	1.5	72.7	9.7	4.2	4 819	10 867	23 838	0.2	0.7	39 305	9.6	13.1	10.6
Sheridan	0	1 871	388	0.3	49.5	8.2	1.6	7 363	8 152	17 145	-11.7	0.0	24 994	23.1	33.5	28.8
Sioux	NA	NA	1 399	7.2	68.3	9.9	5.4	9 608	5 185	14 838	-22.8	0.5	19 845	35.3	31.8	37.9
Slope	NA	NA	231	17.3	71.5	10.4	0.3	6 854	8 234	18 355	-9.8	0.6	23 406	17.4	18.9	18.0
Stark	85	1 885	6 335	17.6	73.1	14.8	19.1	4 706	10 136	22 048	-21.0	0.8	33 069	14.2	17.7	14.6
Steele	NA	NA	527	1.3	71.9	13.7	2.4	6 492	11 586	23 307	-13.7	1.3	35 901	12.9	20.5	16.1
Stutsman	64	1 972	5 644	20.4	73.5	16.7	17.6	5 108	11 369	22 415	-11.2	1.7	33 777	12.7	17.7	14.5
Towner	NA	NA	733	0.5	71.9	12.7	3.2	5 555	9 481	18 608	-23.2	1.0	29 310	16.4	22.8	19.8
Traill	101	824	2 477	3.5	76.6	17.7	10.2	5 617	10 509	22 050	-14.6	1.1	37 171	11.1	14.5	12.9
Walsh	129	2 252	3 159	2.3	68.0	13.0	14.4	5 985	10 766	21 973	4.5	1.5	31 375	13.3	18.1	15.9

1. Data for serious crimes have not been adjusted for underreporting; this may affect comparability between geographic areas and over time. 2. Per 100,000 population estimated by the FBI. 3. All persons 3 years old and over enrolled in nursery school through college. 4. Persons 25 years old and over. 5. Elementary and secondary education expenditures, local government fiscal years ending between July 1, 1998 and June 30, 1999. 6. Based on population enumerated as of April 1, 1990.

Table B. States and Counties — **Personal Income**

STATE County	Total (mil dol)	Percent change, 1998–1999	Per capita[1] Dollars	Per capita[1] Rank	Wages and salaries[2] (mil dol)	Proprietor's income (mil dol)	Dividends, interest, and rent (mil dol)	Transfer payments Total (mil dol)	Government payments to individuals Total (mil dol)	Social Security (mil dol)	Medical payments (mil dol)	Income maintenance (mil dol)	Unemployment insurance (mil dol)
	62	63	64	65	66	67	68	69	70	71	72	73	74
NORTH CAROLINA—Cont'd													
Swain	211	6.5	17 104	2 716	140	12	36	59	57	21	24	7	2
Transylvania	706	4.6	24 473	762	336	59	237	135	130	70	46	8	1
Tyrrell	65	0.2	16 581	2 815	23	5	10	18	17	6	7	3	0
Union	2 708	7.5	23 522	960	1 405	168	386	292	271	129	102	22	4
Vance	857	5.5	20 168	1 945	500	46	148	187	179	67	73	29	4
Wake	20 988	9.6	35 759	75	14 270	1 290	3 596	1 357	1 251	561	489	106	19
Warren	320	3.8	16 991	2 735	105	36	46	84	81	28	34	14	1
Washington	254	1.5	18 906	2 314	86	13	48	67	64	25	25	11	1
Watauga	916	4.9	22 122	1 321	511	107	208	121	114	49	41	10	1
Wayne	2 240	1.2	20 050	1 978	1 463	127	378	419	399	148	167	53	6
Wilkes	1 493	6.3	23 455	971	801	150	258	249	238	97	103	23	4
Wilson	1 689	3.4	24 550	745	1 225	70	276	300	287	110	121	36	7
Yadkin	783	4.2	22 222	1 294	270	63	122	127	120	56	49	10	2
Yancey	325	6.0	19 277	2 215	120	38	60	78	75	32	29	9	1
NORTH DAKOTA	14 747	1.7	23 273	X	9 025	1 198	3 242	2 333	2 220	938	823	155	34
Adams	50	-0.9	18 982	2 284	24	1	15	13	13	6	6	1	0
Barnes	233	-3.1	19 632	2 099	108	11	70	50	48	23	17	3	1
Benson	94	-11.4	13 846	3 054	46	-1	24	32	30	9	11	5	0
Billings	15	0.5	14 166	3 041	8	1	5	2	2	1	0	0	0
Bottineau	125	-16.9	17 261	2 691	50	-5	48	33	31	14	12	2	0
Bowman	72	-2.7	22 029	1 356	28	10	23	15	15	7	6	1	0
Burke	48	-4.2	22 074	1 342	17	3	17	12	11	5	4	1	0
Burleigh	1 751	4.4	25 993	516	1 208	110	340	231	219	93	83	12	3
Cass	3 327	6.6	28 100	323	2 521	273	649	330	309	133	102	17	5
Cavalier	132	9.3	27 292	394	42	29	39	21	20	10	8	1	0
Dickey	111	-8.1	19 625	2 104	48	12	28	26	25	10	11	2	0
Divide	50	-4.8	21 879	1 395	14	5	22	11	10	6	4	1	0
Dunn	50	0.2	14 444	3 024	20	0	17	13	13	5	6	1	0
Eddy	51	-2.1	18 106	2 519	20	4	13	14	14	6	6	1	0
Emmons	76	-6.2	17 601	2 626	27	8	22	20	19	9	7	1	0
Foster	85	-3.6	22 452	1 228	46	9	21	17	16	8	7	1	0
Golden Valley	29	-6.2	16 089	2 889	14	-3	11	7	7	4	2	0	0
Grand Forks	1 559	0.0	24 105	841	1 141	85	299	187	176	69	57	12	3
Grant	39	-5.0	13 774	3 060	14	0	13	13	13	6	5	1	0
Griggs	59	-10.8	21 306	1 568	23	9	18	13	13	6	5	1	0
Hettinger	59	-2.3	20 892	1 697	17	11	18	14	14	6	6	1	0
Kidder	48	-8.0	17 290	2 685	14	7	15	13	12	5	5	1	0
La Moure	87	-9.8	18 444	2 428	28	8	28	21	20	10	8	1	0
Logan	45	-2.6	19 969	1 998	12	7	15	12	11	5	5	1	0
McHenry	92	-12.5	15 414	2 949	28	0	28	27	26	12	10	2	1
McIntosh	72	-1.6	21 188	1 598	24	8	22	22	21	9	10	1	0
McKenzie	111	4.5	19 955	2 004	61	12	28	21	20	8	7	3	0
McLean	194	-3.7	20 229	1 916	94	9	55	44	42	19	17	2	1
Mercer	212	1.9	23 021	1 084	170	9	37	30	28	13	11	1	1
Morton	516	4.1	21 004	1 666	244	28	97	94	90	36	36	6	2
Mountrail	131	-1.0	20 139	1 958	55	13	33	32	31	11	13	3	1
Nelson	77	-9.2	21 059	1 652	24	5	26	22	22	9	10	1	0
Oliver	38	-0.3	17 778	2 579	29	-1	8	6	6	3	2	0	0
Pembina	245	1.8	29 339	242	126	55	59	34	32	16	11	2	1
Pierce	89	-7.6	19 284	2 213	44	2	24	22	21	10	9	1	0
Ramsey	273	-2.5	22 878	1 117	137	15	74	54	52	23	21	3	1
Ransom	128	7.0	22 398	1 244	51	15	27	26	25	10	10	1	0
Renville	46	-24.2	16 533	2 823	17	-2	16	12	11	5	5	1	0
Richland	414	8.9	23 091	1 072	231	73	86	60	56	26	18	3	1
Rolette	212	-0.3	14 916	2 996	124	3	27	70	68	13	26	18	2
Sargent	122	17.5	28 435	287	90	22	27	15	14	7	5	1	0
Sheridan	30	-11.7	18 276	2 477	9	2	10	9	9	4	4	1	0
Sioux	46	5.5	11 023	3 100	39	-1	4	16	15	2	6	4	0
Slope	11	-10.6	12 097	3 092	2	1	4	3	2	1	1	0	0
Stark	481	3.0	21 402	1 549	261	52	102	87	83	34	34	5	2
Steele	45	-16.4	20 440	1 854	15	5	16	8	8	5	2	1	0
Stutsman	494	-1.6	23 434	979	266	51	113	89	85	37	32	5	1
Towner	55	-18.4	18 602	2 394	23	-3	24	14	13	6	6	1	0
Traill	189	0.9	22 095	1 337	81	32	42	34	32	16	12	1	0
Walsh	287	1.3	21 498	1 522	124	53	70	53	51	24	19	3	1

1. Based on the resident population estimated as of July 1 of the year shown. 2. Includes other labor income.

Table B. States and Counties — Earnings, Social Security, and Housing

STATE County	Earnings, 1999									Social Security beneficiaries, December 2000		Supplemental Security Income recipients, December 2000	Housing units, 1990	
			Percent by selected industries											
			Goods-related[1]		Service-related and other[2]									
	Total (mil dol)	Farm	Total	Manu-facturing	Total	Retail trade	Finance, insurance, and real estate	Services	Govern-ment	Number	Rate[3]		Total	Percent change, 1980–1990
	75	76	77	78	79	80	81	82	83	84	85	86	87	88
NORTH CAROLINA—Cont'd														
Swain	152	0.4	D	6.5	D	16.1	1.9	44.0	23.9	3 086	238	392	5 664	16.7
Transylvania	395	1.9	D	36.5	D	8.6	4.5	21.7	11.3	7 937	271	576	12 893	26.0
Tyrrell	28	5.0	12.4	8.5	40.6	11.2	3.2	13.7	42.0	891	215	209	1 907	8.0
Union	1 573	3.9	D	28.8	D	9.5	D	13.3	11.8	15 817	128	1 364	30 760	27.8
Vance	546	0.5	D	27.1	D	16.3	3.2	19.8	18.3	8 996	209	2 271	15 743	14.0
Wake	15 560	0.2	D	8.5	D	9.9	8.2	31.4	17.5	65 343	104	7 629	177 146	56.3
Warren	141	14.8	22.2	16.5	34.2	6.1	2.3	19.8	28.9	4 057	203	1 103	8 714	24.3
Washington	99	1.3	17.2	11.1	44.2	11.9	3.1	16.6	37.3	3 083	225	689	5 644	3.9
Watauga	618	2.5	D	7.0	D	15.7	5.3	26.0	27.3	6 247	146	669	19 538	33.3
Wayne	1 590	2.1	D	14.5	D	9.4	4.7	18.7	33.1	19 960	176	4 460	39 483	12.7
Wilkes	950	7.0	D	25.5	D	22.8	5.2	12.1	14.1	13 150	200	1 939	24 960	12.9
Wilson	1 295	0.7	D	29.4	D	8.7	7.8	16.8	15.5	14 488	196	2 918	26 662	13.7
Yadkin	333	6.1	41.4	31.9	37.6	11.0	2.0	15.7	14.9	7 208	198	699	12 921	16.4
Yancey	158	11.3	D	27.4	D	10.6	2.9	15.1	16.6	4 387	247	734	7 994	16.2
NORTH DAKOTA	10 223	2.0	17.3	8.1	59.2	9.9	5.9	26.2	21.4	114 627	178	8 166	276 340	6.8
Adams	24	-15.3	D	2.0	D	16.2	3.8	51.6	17.8	699	270	31	1 504	-3.8
Barnes	119	-4.6	D	8.0	D	11.2	6.3	25.9	24.2	2 809	239	158	5 801	-2.9
Benson	45	-17.3	D	11.3	D	5.5	6.2	45.6	31.4	1 248	179	191	3 163	2.6
Billings	9	4.6	D	D	D	D	0.0	D	40.9	149	168	4	533	3.1
Bottineau	44	-39.2	D	4.3	D	16.8	7.3	35.3	35.6	1 758	246	58	4 661	-0.4
Bowman	38	0.0	D	2.4	D	12.0	5.4	29.7	16.5	809	250	32	1 691	-1.8
Burke	20	-3.7	D	D	D	8.8	6.1	6.8	35.2	699	312	25	1 691	-6.9
Burleigh	1 318	0.2	13.9	5.9	63.8	10.4	6.3	32.1	22.2	11 109	160	898	23 803	14.2
Cass	2 794	1.6	D	8.9	D	9.7	9.1	29.5	13.2	15 181	123	1 223	42 407	20.4
Cavalier	71	26.5	11.4	1.1	D	D	6.8	17.0	12.8	1 309	271	44	3 038	-2.7
Dickey	60	9.3	15.9	11.6	61.4	9.7	3.3	26.7	13.4	1 339	233	86	2 763	-2.6
Divide	19	6.5	D	D	D	9.4	6.3	31.8	24.8	634	278	18	1 667	-6.5
Dunn	20	-13.9	D	D	D	9.6	3.9	D	32.3	732	203	48	2 057	11.2
Eddy	24	3.4	D	D	D	8.3	6.0	26.3	21.4	750	272	35	1 470	-4.6
Emmons	35	4.3	10.9	1.9	D	10.2	D	24.9	20.5	1 223	282	52	2 200	-5.3
Foster	54	3.9	D	D	D	9.2	3.8	22.9	13.4	915	243	26	1 876	2.7
Golden Valley	11	-43.5	D	D	D	13.6	7.6	37.9	34.6	475	247	11	1 035	0.2
Grand Forks	1 226	0.8	D	4.5	D	11.0	3.5	24.2	34.5	7 819	118	544	27 085	10.3
Grant	14	-29.1	D	5.8	D	8.8	9.3	38.2	34.5	794	279	68	2 011	2.1
Griggs	32	12.8	11.3	8.1	60.4	8.4	5.7	18.3	15.6	759	276	37	1 660	-4.5
Hettinger	28	23.9	D	3.4	D	4.9	4.7	15.9	21.1	846	312	26	1 637	-1.9
Kidder	20	14.4	D	1.6	D	8.6	6.0	14.1	24.2	706	256	35	1 672	-3.9
La Moure	36	6.2	D	5.7	D	7.7	8.2	12.3	24.4	1 290	274	56	2 434	-3.7
Logan	19	19.2	D	D	D	7.9	7.0	18.7	21.8	707	306	41	1 335	-6.1
McHenry	28	-23.7	D	D	D	8.3	5.6	19.2	39.6	1 552	259	77	3 320	-3.4
McIntosh	32	11.2	9.1	6.1	63.8	9.4	6.8	34.4	15.9	1 274	376	55	2 031	-7.6
McKenzie	73	7.3	19.5	2.9	53.6	3.7	4.2	32.9	19.6	967	169	78	3 178	7.9
McLean	103	-0.7	D	D	D	5.1	3.8	15.1	21.5	2 298	247	113	5 515	-4.2
Mercer	179	-1.9	30.3	0.5	62.4	5.0	1.6	9.8	9.3	1 549	179	56	4 496	13.0
Morton	273	-0.7	D	13.2	D	11.9	4.1	22.7	15.7	4 618	183	338	9 467	0.9
Mountrail	68	8.7	D	D	D	8.1	7.7	20.0	23.7	1 466	221	130	3 675	14.8
Nelson	29	-1.9	D	D	D	9.2	10.9	28.8	25.1	1 085	292	29	2 261	-7.4
Oliver	27	-7.9	D	D	D	2.7	D	5.3	12.4	387	187	9	968	0.8
Pembina	181	22.7	D	22.6	D	6.1	D	10.5	13.1	1 921	224	93	4 294	-3.2
Pierce	46	-15.2	D	8.8	D	11.8	7.3	39.1	14.9	1 204	258	63	2 355	-0.9
Ramsey	153	-5.5	D	3.8	D	17.5	6.2	27.8	26.3	2 698	224	218	5 616	6.8
Ransom	67	14.7	17.2	10.1	51.5	8.5	4.5	18.8	16.7	1 291	219	51	2 569	-5.3
Renville	16	-37.3	20.8	8.1	D	13.5	5.4	38.1	36.4	634	243	13	1 558	1.8
Richland	304	17.1	D	25.7	D	6.5	D	17.2	12.7	3 127	174	138	7 394	3.0
Rolette	127	-8.3	D	7.1	D	11.1	4.6	34.4	39.9	1 966	144	624	4 742	20.9
Sargent	112	16.2	D	D	D	2.9	1.7	3.2	6.0	885	203	30	2 057	-6.9
Sheridan	11	0.0	D	D	D	5.9	6.3	9.2	25.2	513	300	40	1 061	-10.1
Sioux	38	-7.3	2.9	0.0	D	3.4	D	57.7	36.9	371	92	189	1 175	10.6
Slope	3	32.7	D	0.0	D	D	0.0	D	21.6	166	216	7	481	-6.2
Stark	313	0.3	24.6	9.4	57.7	12.1	4.4	27.4	17.3	4 515	199	359	9 585	12.9
Steele	19	11.1	D	8.5	D	8.4	8.6	9.4	20.5	552	244	19	1 311	-9.4
Stutsman	317	-1.8	D	15.4	D	11.3	5.1	23.8	19.0	4 588	209	447	9 770	1.1
Towner	20	-42.1	D	22.4	D	13.3	10.3	D	24.8	739	257	23	1 770	4.6
Traill	113	23.4	D	D	D	6.5	4.6	14.7	16.4	1 817	214	40	3 770	-4.0
Walsh	177	23.6	D	7.0	44.8	6.8	4.0	16.8	20.3	2 956	239	111	6 093	-1.0

1. Covers mining, construction, and manufacturing.   2. Covers private sector earnings in agricultural services, forestry, and fisheries; transportation and public utilities; wholesale trade; retail trade; finance, insurance, and real estate; and services.   3. Per 1,000 resident population estimated as of July 1 of the year shown.

Table B. States and Counties — **Housing, Labor Force, and Employment**

STATE County	Housing units, 1990 (cont'd) Occupied units Owner-occupied Total	Percent	Median value[1]	With a mortgage	Without a mortgage	Median rent[2]	Rent as percent of income	Substandard units[3] (percent)	Civilian labor force, 2001 Total	Percent change, 2000–2001	Unemployment Total	Rate[4]	Civilian employment, 1990[5] Total	Percent Professional, managerial, and technical	Precision production, craft, and repair
	89	90	91	92	93	94	95	96	97	98	99	100	101	102	103
NORTH CAROLINA—Cont'd															
Swain	4 173	76.3	49 100	14.9	12.7	235	24.1	5.0	5 950	2.9	664	11.2	4 450	21.1	14.5
Transylvania	9 924	78.9	72 200	17.4	11.5	345	27.1	3.0	11 193	-0.1	527	4.7	10 835	24.3	16.0
Tyrrell	1 471	76.4	37 400	23.1	14.2	270	24.4	8.3	1 843	-3.4	163	8.8	1 532	14.4	12.1
Union	29 307	75.9	70 600	19.3	12.7	406	24.5	4.4	63 349	0.5	2 418	3.8	43 685	22.5	16.5
Vance	14 166	65.3	53 100	18.6	13.5	301	26.6	7.9	19 892	1.4	2 046	10.3	18 184	20.2	12.8
Wake	165 743	60.9	97 200	22.0	12.6	480	24.1	2.6	357 865	1.9	11 779	3.3	240 692	40.6	8.7
Warren	6 305	76.4	48 200	22.4	14.2	246	26.6	12.1	7 397	2.7	759	10.3	6 770	15.7	12.6
Washington	5 052	73.6	45 500	15.6	14.4	266	26.1	5.5	6 256	3.8	447	7.1	5 736	13.5	14.9
Watauga	13 693	64.2	73 200	20.3	12.6	374	35.1	3.6	24 340	2.6	503	2.1	18 198	31.3	10.7
Wayne	36 889	62.7	58 000	21.1	13.8	322	24.1	4.1	49 593	0.8	2 663	5.4	44 564	23.2	13.1
Wilkes	23 021	79.4	52 800	21.5	12.4	299	22.9	3.7	33 743	3.7	1 928	5.7	29 920	16.7	13.6
Wilson	25 093	59.3	59 600	20.7	13.9	321	26.4	4.4	37 350	1.5	3 111	8.3	31 193	23.0	12.1
Yadkin	12 068	81.2	52 900	17.8	12.6	294	22.0	4.2	18 115	-1.4	883	4.9	15 301	19.5	16.7
Yancey	6 124	80.8	51 300	21.9	13.2	259	26.1	5.4	7 215	9.0	918	12.7	6 547	18.1	17.3
NORTH DAKOTA	240 878	65.6	50 800	20.3	13.0	313	23.9	2.5	338 768	0.0	9 550	2.8	287 558	26.4	9.8
Adams	1 266	70.4	34 000	20.9	14.4	242	20.2	2.5	1 222	-8.9	24	2.0	1 504	22.5	6.3
Barnes	4 975	68.5	38 400	16.7	12.1	251	23.9	1.2	5 484	-2.3	141	2.6	5 346	22.0	10.0
Benson	2 415	68.2	18 900	17.1	14.2	243	24.8	11.1	2 655	-1.2	198	7.5	2 372	15.9	8.2
Billings	387	77.5	50 800	21.7	11.8	294	13.5	6.8	462	-3.1	18	3.9	472	14.4	11.4
Bottineau	3 105	78.3	37 400	21.7	12.8	274	24.3	2.2	3 268	-0.5	101	3.1	3 173	25.3	11.0
Bowman	1 420	78.9	44 000	21.8	12.8	240	20.9	1.3	1 772	-1.4	34	1.9	1 786	21.1	10.9
Burke	1 252	81.8	19 900	16.6	13.1	233	21.6	2.0	857	-8.2	21	2.5	1 176	21.3	9.5
Burleigh	22 684	64.8	67 500	20.7	12.2	348	23.3	2.0	40 312	1.1	906	2.2	30 963	34.8	8.1
Cass	40 281	54.8	67 900	20.8	12.5	350	24.8	1.8	74 144	1.1	1 145	1.5	54 931	30.7	8.7
Cavalier	2 375	79.7	39 300	21.0	13.5	276	22.4	1.4	2 398	-2.6	70	2.9	2 346	22.5	10.2
Dickey	2 299	70.1	32 900	17.2	12.4	243	23.1	2.1	2 865	-1.9	63	2.2	2 750	20.4	7.5
Divide	1 193	79.6	27 600	21.0	11.8	220	19.3	4.0	1 018	-4.9	19	1.9	1 115	20.2	6.3
Dunn	1 433	78.4	27 300	21.1	13.5	233	23.4	4.2	1 913	-2.3	69	3.6	1 773	14.7	9.2
Eddy	1 194	71.5	27 400	18.5	13.2	267	23.0	1.6	1 221	1.3	58	4.8	1 182	25.5	9.1
Emmons	1 849	82.2	31 500	22.6	14.3	193	25.4	3.3	1 940	-4.3	90	4.6	1 819	18.0	8.6
Foster	1 541	74.0	36 500	20.0	13.1	254	20.1	0.9	2 029	-5.4	57	2.8	1 759	20.0	9.8
Golden Valley	811	75.6	31 800	20.3	14.3	264	18.9	1.9	847	-2.0	18	2.1	964	19.0	9.8
Grand Forks	25 340	48.7	62 700	20.6	12.2	367	25.1	2.3	35 606	0.2	946	2.7	31 544	31.8	8.3
Grant	1 374	81.4	24 100	24.8	14.7	187	18.5	1.9	1 499	-0.5	41	2.7	1 508	13.4	5.6
Griggs	1 294	75.9	29 500	20.9	13.2	230	20.5	0.9	1 555	-0.8	26	1.7	1 396	18.3	10.2
Hettinger	1 341	82.0	24 900	20.1	14.2	197	18.7	2.5	1 249	-2.6	27	2.2	1 429	18.6	8.4
Kidder	1 247	83.8	22 600	20.6	12.8	210	22.8	1.6	1 386	-2.6	74	5.3	1 386	12.4	7.9
La Moure	2 075	79.1	22 300	18.5	12.9	222	23.3	2.6	2 244	-0.4	65	2.9	2 167	14.9	8.9
Logan	1 096	86.6	20 900	21.0	14.4	222	21.3	2.6	1 119	-1.3	25	2.2	1 193	16.8	5.9
McHenry	2 551	80.6	22 600	17.1	13.2	207	21.7	2.0	2 775	0.0	139	5.0	2 454	18.5	10.0
McIntosh	1 687	81.9	20 300	18.1	13.3	211	22.5	1.7	1 614	-3.3	35	2.2	1 756	17.4	9.0
McKenzie	2 301	74.3	43 900	19.6	11.4	233	16.7	5.5	3 160	0.7	83	2.6	2 666	17.4	12.7
McLean	3 933	79.0	40 100	16.5	13.3	250	25.7	2.6	4 196	-3.1	249	5.9	4 189	21.4	13.9
Mercer	3 560	80.4	52 200	16.4	13.7	278	18.2	1.7	4 569	-0.5	232	5.1	4 293	21.6	19.6
Morton	8 677	73.1	51 100	20.4	12.9	315	26.1	1.9	13 733	1.1	457	3.3	11 274	22.6	12.3
Mountrail	2 587	75.4	31 400	18.2	14.0	240	22.4	5.5	3 002	-2.7	140	4.7	2 747	22.9	13.0
Nelson	1 831	76.0	23 900	22.2	12.0	214	20.3	0.7	1 546	-0.3	62	4.0	1 635	21.2	11.4
Oliver	809	85.4	47 300	15.0	11.7	255	17.2	4.5	1 051	-2.2	51	4.9	1 073	13.1	14.6
Pembina	3 555	77.4	41 700	18.8	12.8	268	20.7	2.5	4 809	0.3	244	5.1	4 006	17.0	11.4
Pierce	1 974	73.9	35 400	19.2	15.7	271	24.8	1.2	2 262	-12.6	75	3.3	2 103	22.2	7.9
Ramsey	4 977	64.1	45 700	20.8	12.6	288	23.4	2.6	6 334	1.2	206	3.3	5 717	27.6	10.1
Ransom	2 284	74.9	32 200	15.7	13.6	245	21.4	0.7	2 695	-1.2	56	2.1	2 470	21.3	8.5
Renville	1 209	78.5	35 000	22.0	12.4	273	22.6	2.6	1 353	-0.1	26	1.9	1 273	19.8	13.4
Richland	6 518	68.9	43 800	19.8	12.9	281	23.6	1.6	8 842	-3.2	252	2.9	7 800	21.4	10.7
Rolette	4 150	64.9	39 400	16.3	14.7	189	23.9	13.4	5 968	7.0	640	10.7	3 725	28.3	10.7
Sargent	1 763	79.4	25 000	13.5	12.1	223	18.2	1.9	2 495	-3.1	69	2.8	2 055	13.0	10.4
Sheridan	858	85.1	14 999	17.3	13.6	219	24.6	2.8	712	2.3	44	6.2	719	19.5	10.4
Sioux	1 022	43.6	20 700	21.0	12.6	147	16.1	22.2	1 701	3.8	92	5.4	1 015	27.8	5.3
Slope	333	82.0	14 999	23.8	11.8	233	28.3	1.2	369	-4.9	8	2.2	428	7.7	8.4
Stark	8 479	68.7	42 800	20.9	14.1	266	24.0	2.7	12 255	0.4	340	2.8	10 541	24.2	12.3
Steele	991	75.6	24 800	19.1	12.8	214	17.8	1.2	1 070	-3.8	13	1.2	979	20.9	15.8
Stutsman	8 661	65.7	45 400	19.0	12.7	285	24.4	1.4	11 373	-0.6	239	2.1	10 292	28.0	10.3
Towner	1 433	70.8	30 900	20.3	13.3	265	22.8	1.5	1 247	-6.1	34	2.7	1 439	19.0	10.8
Traill	3 327	71.0	40 200	19.8	13.1	270	24.0	2.2	3 637	-0.3	116	3.2	3 476	21.7	11.8
Walsh	5 229	75.0	41 900	20.8	13.2	281	22.7	2.5	6 166	-1.6	222	3.6	6 066	25.2	9.6

1. Specified owner-occupied units.   2. Specified renter-occupied units.   3. Overcrowded or lacking complete plumbing facilities.   4. Percent of civilian labor force.   5. Persons 16 years and older.

	Private nonfarm establishments, employment and payroll, 1999								Agriculture, 1997			
		Employment					Annual payroll		Farms			Farm operators
										Percent with—		
STATE County	Number of establishments	Total	Health Care and Social Assistance	Manufacturing	Retail trade	Finance and Insurance	Professional Scientific and Technical Services	Total (mil dol)	Average per employee (dollars)	Number	Less than 50 acres	500 acres and over	Whose principal occupation is farming (percent)
	104	105	106	107	108	109	110	111	112	113	114	115	116
NORTH CAROLINA—Cont'd													
Swain	398	5 287	545	413	491	61	56	103	19 478	77	46.8	3.9	42.9
Transylvania	735	9 669	1 212	3 039	1 368	437	242	255	26 362	174	60.9	1.7	35.6
Tyrrell	74	328	D	D	105	21	D	6	18 851	83	25.3	28.9	67.5
Union	2 817	37 741	2 250	13 239	4 552	639	656	1 002	26 553	1 142	48.9	5.7	48.7
Vance	953	14 725	1 721	4 411	2 774	258	217	321	21 779	232	17.2	16.8	53.0
Wake	19 899	317 994	33 473	23 983	41 791	15 350	25 575	10 300	32 391	772	43.0	5.8	54.5
Warren	263	2 513	218	856	345	41	82	42	16 848	282	19.1	14.9	53.2
Washington	268	3 832	327	D	490	83	D	123	31 991	203	35.5	27.1	62.1
Watauga	1 531	15 623	2 387	1 078	3 348	274	516	288	18 422	674	57.7	2.1	38.0
Wayne	2 364	37 017	6 884	8 837	6 046	1 215	728	824	22 255	827	39.5	13.1	62.8
Wilkes	1 334	22 489	2 081	8 479	3 183	366	373	598	26 605	1 170	45.6	2.3	47.9
Wilson	1 814	33 191	3 386	9 141	4 103	1 965	1 616	849	25 565	385	33.8	22.6	67.8
Yadkin	642	8 728	1 009	3 502	879	102	446	185	21 177	884	42.2	3.8	46.8
Yancey	342	3 623	349	1 388	569	148	184	81	22 242	604	63.9	1.3	31.5
NORTH DAKOTA	20 380	250 292	46 407	22 935	41 644	13 388	8 681	5 789	23 129	30 504	6.4	63.9	74.3
Adams	107	751	318	D	169	D	21	15	19 779	367	4.4	72.8	69.5
Barnes	382	3 803	945	313	556	114	79	66	17 290	772	7.5	60.0	75.6
Benson	113	1 143	D	141	77	30	3	21	18 384	604	4.6	64.2	75.8
Billings	33	153	0	0	6	0	D	5	31 366	237	5.5	67.5	73.8
Bottineau	270	1 633	372	69	339	84	43	27	16 524	808	4.8	61.5	70.5
Bowman	166	986	226	29	206	58	40	17	17 318	358	6.1	65.1	69.6
Burke	93	310	0	0	56	37	6	6	18 529	479	2.3	71.2	72.4
Burleigh	2 309	33 808	7 489	1 251	5 441	1 819	2 146	803	23 757	867	12.8	50.4	54.9
Cass	4 174	72 540	10 405	6 745	10 595	5 685	2 728	1 907	26 288	919	10.8	61.8	81.8
Cavalier	181	1 316	326	29	216	100	15	25	18 912	682	2.9	74.6	84.2
Dickey	199	1 742	446	101	305	71	34	28	15 876	517	7.0	58.6	78.7
Divide	85	576	D	D	72	33	13	7	12 757	535	4.3	76.1	78.1
Dunn	84	612	D	D	115	D	3	12	19 299	618	8.1	72.3	74.1
Eddy	85	512	173	D	66	23	9	8	16 242	288	3.8	74.0	77.8
Emmons	153	1 219	253	D	203	81	22	28	23 036	744	3.2	65.1	71.0
Foster	153	1 586	368	D	254	37	13	29	18 576	282	5.7	65.6	83.0
Golden Valley	78	451	D	D	92	27	14	7	15 501	244	4.9	71.3	76.2
Grand Forks	1 798	27 334	5 655	1 875	5 682	884	851	630	23 056	768	8.1	55.1	71.7
Grant	84	454	182	D	71	29	4	7	15 141	596	6.5	71.1	77.7
Griggs	114	951	D	109	149	D	97	18	18 448	357	7.0	58.5	72.0
Hettinger	93	414	91	D	82	38	4	7	17 754	436	3.9	71.3	78.0
Kidder	65	337	D	D	68	33	19	6	17 344	513	3.7	71.5	72.1
La Moure	143	897	127	79	124	90	9	14	15 452	616	5.8	62.8	78.6
Logan	75	422	114	D	50	29	D	5	12 341	401	3.5	73.3	80.5
McHenry	143	663	108	D	103	49	10	12	17 804	905	5.2	61.7	70.2
McIntosh	119	915	354	D	149	58	5	15	16 123	505	4.8	60.4	70.3
McKenzie	156	1 139	148	141	154	88	16	21	18 198	668	6.0	67.2	74.4
McLean	257	1 924	401	D	296	133	19	54	27 825	969	5.1	63.1	72.9
Mercer	260	3 436	413	65	423	84	33	127	36 934	473	7.0	53.9	61.7
Morton	646	6 977	1 355	887	969	280	294	155	22 175	907	9.0	62.1	69.9
Mountrail	195	1 518	386	D	270	71	45	26	17 375	755	2.8	70.3	73.0
Nelson	142	847	282	D	113	72	7	14	15 978	471	3.8	62.6	74.3
Oliver	41	397	D	D	D	D	5	19	48 690	327	6.1	59.0	69.4
Pembina	339	3 371	333	1 281	576	135	21	84	25 056	615	7.3	57.9	82.6
Pierce	157	1 495	436	D	262	89	30	26	17 561	491	5.1	69.2	77.0
Ramsey	437	4 463	1 111	184	878	240	92	78	17 382	525	7.0	66.3	74.3
Ransom	209	1 471	339	223	250	57	43	27	18 570	485	10.3	52.6	72.6
Renville	90	544	D	D	115	27	D	9	16 202	390	1.8	74.1	80.5
Richland	554	6 646	668	2 344	799	146	115	156	23 446	874	10.2	55.6	70.5
Rolette	210	2 908	548	374	449	72	8	58	19 844	511	7.6	58.5	70.5
Sargent	126	1 931	D	D	148	41	6	70	36 106	449	8.0	60.8	77.3
Sheridan	48	183	D	D	32	17	6	4	23 399	380	3.2	71.3	76.3
Sioux	31	851	D	0	46	0	D	19	22 120	193	3.6	76.7	81.9
Slope	10	44	0	0	D	0	0	1	18 955	263	4.2	72.6	82.5
Stark	846	8 164	1 531	874	1 575	276	247	163	20 025	802	12.8	56.1	68.0
Steele	77	328	D	57	D	32	2	7	22 162	290	5.5	75.2	84.5
Stutsman	685	9 046	2 113	1 545	1 440	413	134	190	21 021	979	6.8	64.9	74.0
Towner	96	762	D	197	74	60	22	13	16 900	428	6.5	72.0	79.7
Traill	298	2 420	576	341	297	166	48	47	19 547	471	8.5	67.1	83.2
Walsh	448	3 779	683	428	810	164	90	70	18 653	755	5.7	57.9	78.3

Table B. States and Counties — Agriculture, Land, and Water

STATE County	Land in farms Acreage (1,000)	Percent change, 1992–1997	Average size of farm	Acres Total irrigated (1,000)	Acres Total cropland (1,000)	Value of land and buildings Average per farm ($1,000)	Value of land and buildings Average per acre (dollars)	Value of machinery and equipment average per farm ($1,000)	Value of products sold Total (mil dol)	Value of products sold Average per farm (dollars)	Percent from Crops	Percent from Live-stock and poultry products	Percent of farms with sales of $10,000 or more	$100,000 or more	Percent of land owned by fed. gov. 1997	Water consumption 1995 (mil gal/day)
	117	118	119	120	121	122	123	124	125	126	127	128	129	130	131	132
NORTH CAROLINA—Cont'd																
Swain	7	10.4	86	0	2	192	2 228	24	2	30 158	31.8	68.2	20.8	7.8	69.3	22.7
Transylvania	13	5.6	73	0	6	318	4 382	31	10	59 279	33.3	66.7	31.6	6.3	30.8	29.5
Tyrrell	55	-19.4	661	0	51	850	1 287	150	36	429 966	54.6	45.4	73.5	41.0	15.5	0.5
Union	178	6.7	156	0	131	428	2 790	45	284	248 304	10.9	89.1	47.2	31.6	0.0	27.5
Vance	67	-2.1	287	3	27	396	1 558	86	20	84 341	97.4	2.6	58.2	24.6	3.9	22.0
Wake	113	-5.7	147	6	60	508	3 886	45	71	91 720	80.3	19.7	48.3	20.9	0.7	78.8
Warren	80	-7.9	284	2	35	309	1 237	50	38	133 356	35.8	64.2	51.1	24.5	0.0	2.9
Washington	107	4.2	528	2	92	658	1 302	132	68	332 784	62.2	37.8	66.0	40.9	6.2	5.6
Watauga	57	20.2	84	0	24	260	2 854	24	12	17 272	58.9	41.1	36.1	3.3	6.5	6.3
Wayne	229	27.5	277	2	147	542	2 025	83	337	407 604	21.4	78.6	71.0	41.8	0.8	32.0
Wilkes	127	10.8	109	0	59	258	2 178	31	215	183 665	4.1	95.9	44.3	28.4	1.4	18.5
Wilson	128	-9.8	333	2	91	613	2 021	114	120	312 840	70.1	29.9	68.6	42.6	0.0	16.8
Yadkin	102	-2.1	115	1	67	269	2 359	39	50	56 742	44.7	55.3	41.4	14.7	0.0	6.3
Yancey	40	5.4	66	0	14	142	2 316	17	5	8 853	80.0	20.0	20.4	0.8	18.9	2.3
NORTH DAKOTA	39 359	-0.2	1 290	180	27 025	513	401	112	2 869	94 064	76.5	23.5	75.1	28.4	3.9	1 122.4
Adams	630	5.8	1 716		375	399	228	101	28	75 871	53.9	46.1	76.0	28.6	0.0	0.8
Barnes	870	1.4	1 127	2	767	537	485	137	80	103 586	87.7	12.3	80.8	36.4	0.6	2.3
Benson	758	-2.5	1 255	2	610	412	320	116	50	82 735	78.5	21.5	78.8	28.1	1.3	2.7
Billings	794	-3.1	3 350	0	124	797	247	81	12	51 435	30.0	70.0	75.9	14.8	49.6	1.4
Bottineau	960	1.0	1 188	D	811	460	417	104	61	75 398	90.5	9.5	72.9	26.7	1.8	1.9
Bowman	715	5.5	1 998	1	335	422	223	78	26	73 205	49.1	50.9	72.6	19.8	4.0	2.9
Burke	615	10.1	1 285		455	390	325	106	29	60 100	86.6	13.4	71.8	18.8	4.2	0.8
Burleigh	896	2.1	1 033	3	480	322	331	54	36	41 567	52.3	47.7	58.2	10.6	1.7	12.2
Cass	1 068	-0.3	1 162	8	1 013	942	826	164	169	183 941	91.7	8.3	82.4	53.1	0.2	18.8
Cavalier	875	2.4	1 284	D	812	636	499	163	72	105 924	97.6	2.4	88.1	41.2	1.0	0.9
Dickey	580	-7.6	1 122	10	454	511	459	140	64	123 022	68.3	31.7	75.0	33.1	0.9	7.1
Divide	733	1.0	1 371	3	555	404	316	111	35	65 446	84.9	15.1	76.8	25.2	1.4	2.3
Dunn	1 336	-1.3	2 161	2	429	517	238	73	39	63 774	29.9	70.1	80.3	19.1	2.5	3.4
Eddy	344	-6.8	1 195	2	258	466	355	94	23	78 200	66.1	33.9	77.8	29.5	1.0	1.5
Emmons	824	-1.2	1 107	4	509	293	266	85	51	68 902	50.1	49.9	75.8	19.8	0.8	6.4
Foster	370	1.2	1 313	3	312	603	476	129	36	127 502	69.3	30.7	80.1	36.5	0.2	2.2
Golden Valley	579	14.6	2 372	1	221	565	224	96	18	74 860	56.5	43.5	73.8	24.6	15.4	3.0
Grand Forks	775	0.7	1 009	15	719	777	762	155	130	168 764	91.5	8.5	68.8	39.6	1.4	15.6
Grant	970	-4.9	1 627	2	448	400	252	74	35	58 553	37.6	62.4	74.7	16.1	0.9	7.9
Griggs	390	-1.5	1 092	4	318	422	375	109	28	78 767	83.7	16.3	70.6	27.2	0.4	1.6
Hettinger	707	2.8	1 622	D	578	520	328	115	44	101 926	81.1	18.9	77.8	33.7	0.1	0.6
Kidder	725	0.1	1 413	7	416	307	221	75	34	66 159	46.8	53.2	76.6	18.1	1.7	6.1
La Moure	671	0.3	1 089	7	570	457	427	133	73	118 228	74.1	25.9	80.2	35.7	0.7	5.1
Logan	531	-11.3	1 325	2	287	349	254	110	32	80 612	35.2	64.8	79.3	24.4	1.4	2.0
McHenry	1 067	1.7	1 179	8	683	382	333	66	57	62 476	63.4	36.6	70.9	17.3	2.9	18.6
McIntosh	508	-6.8	1 006		348	315	321	73	35	69 873	43.8	56.2	70.1	19.2	2.1	1.1
McKenzie	1 170	0.3	1 751	23	522	464	263	90	46	69 610	54.9	45.1	76.0	24.0	29.7	13.0
McLean	1 143	1.3	1 179	5	866	450	360	98	74	76 650	82.8	17.2	73.7	24.9	1.7	161.0
Mercer	551	3.6	1 165	2	284	322	280	67	23	48 708	53.5	46.5	67.7	11.8	0.5	277.9
Morton	1 229	-0.4	1 355	4	565	452	296	75	60	66 496	30.3	69.7	69.8	20.0	0.5	37.5
Mountrail	997	-0.4	1 321	D	650	404	318	105	49	65 130	78.0	22.0	74.0	21.2	0.7	1.5
Nelson	535	-3.2	1 136	D	441	506	476	108	37	77 838	84.6	15.4	68.6	26.8	0.8	1.1
Oliver	400	4.2	1 224	4	186	271	240	62	19	58 368	38.8	61.2	73.4	20.5	0.0	434.5
Pembina	633	5.4	1 030	D	587	1 006	1 008	203	128	207 327	96.7	3.3	78.5	45.4	0.3	2.1
Pierce	567	-3.2	1 155	0	444	427	363	102	36	73 840	75.4	24.6	77.8	24.8	1.3	1.7
Ramsey	658	2.8	1 254	0	597	504	391	188	45	85 590	93.9	6.1	72.6	29.3	1.6	0.6
Ransom	515	6.2	1 062	17	360	586	511	123	61	126 570	76.7	23.3	70.7	34.6	8.4	13.2
Renville	516	2.3	1 322	D	456	605	494	146	38	96 901	92.1	7.9	87.9	32.6	3.0	0.3
Richland	809	1.2	926	2	748	836	901	162	166	189 914	82.1	17.9	83.4	47.4	4.0	3.8
Rolette	493	-5.7	965		356	318	345	85	30	57 933	73.4	26.6	65.8	18.4	0.7	2.0
Sargent	477	-3.9	1 062	6	403	589	550	121	65	143 729	74.2	25.8	80.4	45.2	2.1	6.3
Sheridan	492	-5.6	1 295		340	456	372	91	27	72 075	63.8	36.2	76.8	24.5	0.8	0.5
Sioux	705	-5.5	3 652	D	D	813	216	80	15	75 273	22.8	77.2	80.8	22.8	1.2	0.9
Slope	757	-3.7	2 879	0	D	559	199	93	21	81 490	57.3	42.7	81.7	21.3	21.8	1.0
Stark	806	-4.3	1 005	1	536	320	349	64	46	57 088	47.6	52.4	68.3	17.3	0.1	1.7
Steele	413	-6.2	1 423	4	377	685	496	201	47	161 097	95.9	4.1	85.9	52.8	0.6	0.9
Stutsman	1 265	-0.4	1 292	7	985	471	380	115	93	94 528	72.6	27.4	73.1	32.4	2.2	6.3
Towner	570	-3.5	1 332	D	499	524	376	124	42	99 052	93.1	6.9	76.2	35.3	0.8	0.7
Traill	494	-1.3	1 050		480	847	815	193	85	179 445	97.3	2.7	87.9	58.2	0.1	1.4
Walsh	718	-2.6	950	1	642	734	783	151	122	162 111	96.0	4.0	72.5	35.1	0.2	2.2

Table B. States and Counties — Residential Construction, Wholesale and Retail Trade, and Real Estate

STATE County	Value of Residential Construction Authorized by Building Permits, 2000		Wholesale Trade, 1997				Retail Trade[1], 1997				Real Estate and Rental and Leasing, 1997			
	New Construction ($1,000)	Number of Housing Units	Number of Establishments	Number of Employees	Sales (mil dol)	Annual Payroll (mil dol)	Number of Establishments	Number of Employees	Sales (mil dol)	Annual Payroll (mil dol)	Number of Establishments	Number of Employees	Receipts (mil dol)	Annual Payroll (mil dol)
	133	134	135	136	137	138	139	140	141	142	143	144	145	146
NORTH CAROLINA—Cont'd														
Swain	11 601	155	9	109	27.3	2.7	118	472	62.1	6.3	7	12	0.5	0.1
Transylvania	55 863	238	16	68	20.9	1.8	110	1 127	158.2	14.9	32	73	7.9	1.4
Tyrrell	2 382	9	4	14	16.0	0.3	19	107	18.1	1.4	1	D	D	D
Union	286 646	2 457	241	2 214	813.4	75.6	383	4 245	753.0	69.2	67	222	25.9	4.4
Vance	14 732	138	33	489	274.0	13.2	251	2 763	454.0	42.1	46	146	17.2	2.6
Wake	1 368 381	12 193	1 249	18 833	13 259.1	826.0	2 719	38 755	7 391.9	664.3	792	4 777	862.5	130.1
Warren	11 064	89	9	22	5.6	0.6	55	369	44.1	5.3	6	D	D	D
Washington	2 226	17	15	91	36.4	2.5	65	446	71.0	6.4	7	32	2.0	0.5
Watauga	101 199	573	47	422	166.1	12.0	342	3 207	519.8	44.3	69	231	18.4	3.1
Wayne	40 778	428	151	2 217	891.1	59.4	523	6 169	1 033.0	88.1	81	263	21.0	4.5
Wilkes	32 464	242	66	818	431.1	22.8	259	2 906	458.6	41.3	38	127	16.7	2.3
Wilson	44 460	598	121	1 264	471.1	33.6	393	4 416	735.4	66.2	63	192	19.3	3.0
Yadkin	18 053	138	32	D	D	D	144	851	167.9	13.6	15	46	5.1	0.5
Yancey	4 911	87	5	15	1.5	0.2	66	541	112.6	8.8	13	28	2.1	0.3
NORTH DAKOTA	190 196	2 128	1 604	16 992	8 618.4	454.4	3 569	40 685	6 702.1	616.1	657	3 325	287.0	46.3
Adams	333	10	10	67	51.0	1.4	21	169	34.3	2.7	2	D	D	D
Barnes	727	11	35	281	150.2	6.3	76	602	81.1	7.4	3	2	0.3	0.0
Benson	0	0	10	36	31.8	1.3	18	76	14.7	0.7	4	D	D	D
Billings	0	0	1	D	D	D	6	10	1.4	0.2	NA	NA	NA	NA
Bottineau	124	1	13	71	84.2	2.4	54	325	57.3	4.7	9	D	D	D
Bowman	480	4	5	97	56.1	2.2	27	196	43.5	2.8	2	D	D	D
Burke	173	3	7	41	33.4	0.7	16	89	14.5	0.9	4	6	0.1	0.0
Burleigh	54 026	409	143	1 574	619.8	43.5	366	5 114	814.6	82.5	92	563	48.9	6.9
Cass	77 640	1 079	366	5 945	2 755.5	182.6	572	9 697	1 669.2	161.3	163	1 067	111.5	17.3
Cavalier	0	0	20	113	93.6	3.2	33	241	48.7	3.4	2	D	D	D
Dickey	75	1	22	153	93.2	3.5	41	297	46.9	4.3	3	4	0.2	0.0
Divide	0	0	8	45	59.8	1.2	15	70	9.0	1.0	4	7	0.4	0.0
Dunn	180	2	9	35	9.5	0.8	19	110	29.3	1.6	2	D	D	D
Eddy	415	3	7	42	23.1	0.9	11	59	9.9	0.7	2	D	D	D
Emmons	854	12	9	64	34.3	0.8	34	174	35.1	2.4	2	D	D	D
Foster	310	3	17	109	68.0	2.7	30	222	38.7	3.2	5	D	D	D
Golden Valley	0	0	4	58	32.8	1.3	17	88	17.7	1.2	NA	NA	NA	NA
Grand Forks	8 529	63	130	1 511	552.4	41.3	351	5 596	934.7	81.4	70	524	33.9	7.0
Grant	130	1	10	51	19.4	0.9	15	77	14.0	1.1	2	D	D	D
Griggs	0	0	15	83	36.7	2.1	22	133	22.6	1.9	3	D	D	D
Hettinger	0	0	9	54	27.3	1.2	13	79	16.9	1.1	3	D	D	D
Kidder	210	4	5	23	9.8	0.4	11	62	13.9	0.6	1	D	D	D
La Moure	550	6	17	155	88.6	2.9	22	105	18.7	1.6	3	3	0.1	0.0
Logan	0	0	8	111	96.9	1.2	12	52	11.8	0.8	1	D	D	D
McHenry	420	5	19	92	64.7	2.3	23	109	14.3	1.1	7	13	0.5	0.0
McIntosh	357	5	8	43	22.2	0.9	27	146	29.0	2.1	2	D	D	D
McKenzie	0	0	11	62	18.3	1.6	27	179	23.8	2.2	2	D	D	D
McLean	650	9	22	124	114.3	3.2	46	343	47.0	3.9	4	13	0.4	0.1
Mercer	612	8	12	58	22.8	1.1	46	440	56.2	5.2	5	6	0.3	0.0
Morton	9 661	93	49	409	193.4	9.2	101	944	196.0	18.4	21	53	3.9	0.5
Mountrail	609	8	13	D	D	D	46	299	47.0	3.7	4	D	D	D
Nelson	465	4	20	188	92.1	3.4	22	114	15.5	1.2	5	11	0.2	0.0
Oliver	70	1	2	D	D	D	3	23	4.0	0.2	NA	NA	NA	NA
Pembina	543	5	28	211	113.7	4.4	77	620	103.0	8.4	4	9	0.2	0.0
Pierce	550	5	13	183	90.1	3.5	30	252	42.5	3.0	4	3	0.3	0.0
Ramsey	1 927	18	35	374	170.5	9.3	92	1 014	141.2	14.0	11	161	5.2	1.1
Ransom	3 076	46	9	154	130.2	4.6	39	275	39.4	3.3	4	8	0.4	0.0
Renville	100	4	15	56	57.8	1.4	14	105	27.7	1.9	1	D	D	D
Richland	1 801	23	54	479	208.3	8.7	91	797	137.9	11.9	18	73	5.7	0.7
Rolette	260	3	10	71	79.4	1.5	49	486	79.7	6.5	4	D	D	D
Sargent	663	6	11	80	48.5	1.6	28	161	25.5	2.0	3	7	0.2	0.0
Sheridan	0	0	5	25	7.5	0.4	8	33	6.1	0.5	3	7	0.1	0.0
Sioux	0	0	2	D	D	D	11	60	14.0	0.7	1	D	D	D
Slope	0	0	NA	NA	NA	NA	NA	NA	NA	NA	1	D	D	D
Stark	4 655	34	57	434	276.6	9.8	166	1 591	255.9	23.5	30	74	6.3	1.1
Steele	0	0	7	42	47.1	1.4	8	51	12.3	0.7	1	D	D	D
Stutsman	4 692	51	37	300	235.0	8.0	137	1 419	207.8	19.4	24	95	6.9	1.1
Towner	0	0	11	D	D	D	19	87	10.4	0.8	4	23	1.0	0.1
Traill	721	7	30	293	184.0	6.6	47	314	49.2	4.4	8	D	D	D
Walsh	1 026	8	42	383	151.7	8.2	91	706	116.1	10.2	10	18	0.5	0.2

1. Establishments with payroll.

STATE County	Professional, Scientific, and Technical Services[1], 1997				Manufacturing, 1997				Accommodation and Foodservices, 1997			
	Number of Establish-ments	Number of Employees	Receipts (mil dol)	Annual Payroll (mil dol)	Number of Establish-ments	Number of Employees	Receipts (mil dol)	Annual Payroll (mil dol)	Number of Establish-ments	Number of Employees	Sales (mil dol)	Annual Payroll (mil dol)
	147	148	149	150	151	152	153	154	155	156	157	158
NORTH CAROLINA—Cont'd												
Swain	6	46	2.1	1.1	NA	NA	NA	NA	79	796	38.1	10.4
Transylvania	50	150	11.6	3.9	28	3 071	715.1	119.3	72	798	34.0	10.7
Tyrrell	3	D	D	D	NA	NA	NA	NA	8	D	D	D
Union	141	744	65.2	19.9	228	13 113	2 543.5	356.9	151	2 618	73.0	18.6
Vance	34	208	10.2	4.1	53	5 085	1 218.0	119.2	66	1 532	38.6	10.7
Wake	2 366	18 158	2 000.3	798.8	639	23 789	10 420.0	784.7	1 229	24 776	896.6	251.0
Warren	15	36	2.1	0.7	13	813	95.5	15.3	13	D	D	D
Washington	8	20	0.8	0.3	15	D	D	D	22	334	9.6	2.5
Watauga	97	331	21.0	7.2	56	1 223	97.4	24.8	165	2 847	91.3	25.0
Wayne	129	596	43.4	16.0	101	9 495	1 417.5	231.1	158	2 953	84.4	23.1
Wilkes	73	336	19.9	6.5	108	8 082	1 081.2	168.1	97	1 436	42.9	10.8
Wilson	90	1 238	61.9	27.5	96	8 954	4 980.3	288.1	138	2 771	85.4	23.1
Yadkin	27	198	7.0	3.5	43	3 616	787.3	94.5	70	922	26.2	7.7
Yancey	21	115	4.3	1.8	21	1 645	373.4	39.3	26	268	7.4	2.2
NORTH DAKOTA	1 077	7 076	418.0	175.7	704	21 956	5 115.9	604.8	1 827	26 330	684.9	189.0
Adams	6	13	0.5	0.2	NA	NA	NA	NA	9	54	1.2	0.4
Barnes	15	58	4.3	1.5	NA	NA	NA	NA	36	318	8.1	2.1
Benson	3	2	0.3	0.1	NA	NA	NA	NA	12	D	D	D
Billings	NA	NA	NA	NA	NA	NA	NA	NA	8	92	6.7	1.9
Bottineau	12	33	2.4	0.9	NA	NA	NA	NA	30	151	4.8	1.3
Bowman	8	29	1.9	0.9	NA	NA	NA	NA	18	128	3.2	0.7
Burke	3	6	0.3	0.0	NA	NA	NA	NA	18	D	D	D
Burleigh	176	1 604	87.5	37.2	54	1 310	99.7	47.3	156	3 485	96.8	27.8
Cass	272	2 318	164.1	65.9	183	6 757	1 512.2	173.5	294	7 184	195.0	55.2
Cavalier	10	17	0.7	0.2	NA	NA	NA	NA	23	D	D	D
Dickey	8	22	0.9	0.4	NA	NA	NA	NA	20	177	3.2	0.8
Divide	4	13	0.5	0.2	NA	NA	NA	NA	8	52	1.4	0.2
Dunn	2	D	D	D	NA	NA	NA	NA	10	D	D	D
Eddy	1	D	D	D	NA	NA	NA	NA	13	55	1.9	0.4
Emmons	7	11	0.5	0.1	NA	NA	NA	NA	15	D	D	D
Foster	7	13	0.7	0.2	NA	NA	NA	NA	14	D	D	D
Golden Valley	5	10	0.9	0.3	NA	NA	NA	NA	7	57	1.3	0.3
Grand Forks	109	771	51.3	24.1	52	1 737	251.5	39.0	180	4 126	93.8	27.1
Grant	3	4	0.2	0.0	NA	NA	NA	NA	8	37	1.0	0.2
Griggs	3	D	D	D	NA	NA	NA	NA	12	71	1.7	0.5
Hettinger	3	8	0.2	0.1	NA	NA	NA	NA	9	34	0.9	0.2
Kidder	2	D	D	D	NA	NA	NA	NA	5	49	1.3	0.4
La Moure	3	7	0.2	0.0	NA	NA	NA	NA	16	D	D	D
Logan	2	D	D	D	NA	NA	NA	NA	8	33	0.9	0.2
McHenry	5	10	0.7	0.1	NA	NA	NA	NA	14	D	D	D
McIntosh	2	D	D	D	NA	NA	NA	NA	16	67	1.5	0.3
McKenzie	5	23	0.7	0.4	NA	NA	NA	NA	21	75	2.3	0.5
McLean	7	14	0.8	0.2	NA	NA	NA	NA	35	155	4.2	0.9
Mercer	10	33	1.7	0.5	NA	NA	NA	NA	32	276	6.3	1.9
Morton	30	286	8.6	3.6	27	883	573.4	27.2	49	580	15.7	4.1
Mountrail	4	22	0.5	0.3	NA	NA	NA	NA	30	158	4.1	1.0
Nelson	5	14	0.3	0.1	NA	NA	NA	NA	17	68	2.0	0.5
Oliver	2	D	D	D	NA	NA	NA	NA	5	D	D	D
Pembina	13	25	1.8	0.7	16	D	D	D	29	244	5.5	1.3
Pierce	8	27	1.1	0.3	NA	NA	NA	NA	17	104	3.2	0.9
Ramsey	19	51	3.3	1.1	NA	NA	NA	NA	43	551	15.2	4.2
Ransom	8	15	0.6	0.2	NA	NA	NA	NA	25	176	4.2	0.9
Renville	4	5	0.1	0.0	NA	NA	NA	NA	12	D	D	D
Richland	29	112	6.6	2.5	34	2 261	373.0	69.2	44	384	11.3	2.6
Rolette	4	8	0.4	0.1	NA	NA	NA	NA	21	109	3.6	0.7
Sargent	5	8	0.3	0.1	5	D	D	D	17	D	D	D
Sheridan	3	3	0.1	0.0	NA	NA	NA	NA	5	46	1.6	0.3
Sioux	NA	NA	NA	NA	NA	NA	NA	NA	3	23	0.9	0.2
Slope	NA	NA	NA	NA	NA	NA	NA	NA	2	D	D	D
Stark	46	214	12.0	6.0	30	718	75.8	17.6	64	1 059	26.6	7.2
Steele	2	D	D	D	NA	NA	NA	NA	8	21	0.8	0.1
Stutsman	26	119	6.4	3.4	28	1 446	250.3	41.0	61	850	22.1	6.3
Towner	5	12	0.7	0.3	NA	NA	NA	NA	9	40	1.5	0.3
Traill	12	31	1.8	0.8	NA	NA	NA	NA	36	363	6.9	1.8
Walsh	17	57	3.2	0.9	NA	NA	NA	NA	41	271	7.4	1.7

1. Firms subject to federal tax.

Table B. States and Counties — Health and Other Services and Federal Funds

STATE County	Health Care and Social Assistance[1], 1997				Other Services[1], 1997				Federal funds and grants, fiscal 2001[2] Expenditures (mil dol)			
									Total	Direct payments for individuals[3]		
	Number of Establishments	Number of Employees	Receipts (mil dol)	Annual Payroll (mil dol)	Number of Establishments	Number of Employees	Receipts (mil dol)	Annual Payroll (mil dol)		Social Security and government retirement	Medicare	Food stamps and Supplemental Security Income
	159	160	161	162	163	164	165	166	167	168	169	170
NORTH CAROLINA—Cont'd												
Swain	17	430	14.8	7.5	18	70	3.5	1.0	104.0	34.0	11.1	3.2
Transylvania	51	543	25.7	11.5	33	85	5.2	1.3	158.0	98.0	25.8	4.2
Tyrrell	2	D	D	D	5	10	1.2	0.2	28.1	8.7	3.1	1.2
Union	114	1 263	75.0	36.2	158	788	46.4	12.8	309.9	165.9	49.4	11.3
Vance	69	1 252	49.6	24.2	41	147	9.4	2.4	225.6	93.1	32.2	15.6
Wake	1 202	16 538	1 124.1	514.0	1 005	7 036	559.0	152.3	3 644.4	963.5	277.5	54.9
Warren	13	237	8.3	4.0	15	53	2.5	0.5	106.6	41.7	15.1	6.6
Washington	15	147	4.1	1.8	18	61	4.5	0.9	83.1	34.5	11.8	4.5
Watauga	98	1 386	70.3	35.3	61	288	13.4	3.9	136.9	67.0	22.5	4.2
Wayne	181	2 357	114.4	56.0	151	998	58.5	18.5	805.6	273.3	83.5	27.0
Wilkes	81	966	48.9	21.7	66	302	18.9	5.5	275.8	129.3	46.8	10.7
Wilson	133	1 903	100.6	48.5	108	776	39.2	12.7	356.8	150.9	61.6	18.8
Yadkin	33	471	19.7	9.0	40	248	11.2	3.8	151.2	74.0	26.3	4.1
Yancey	16	243	8.5	3.5	14	30	1.9	0.6	93.7	43.7	13.5	4.6
NORTH DAKOTA	1 013	13 181	904.1	386.4	1 281	6 294	364.3	101.3	5 948.3	1 316.0	483.4	63.6
Adams	7	104	5.2	3.0	8	14	1.2	0.2	32.5	7.0	3.0	0.1
Barnes	17	106	4.2	2.3	28	99	5.8	1.5	127.2	29.7	10.4	1.1
Benson	2	D	D	D	3	D	D	D	118.9	12.5	5.8	1.9
Billings	NA	NA	NA	NA	2	D	D	D	12.4	1.1	0.4	0.0
Bottineau	6	15	1.1	0.2	12	29	2.0	0.4	94.1	18.8	8.3	0.6
Bowman	7	82	4.0	1.3	15	25	2.9	0.4	30.1	8.2	3.9	0.1
Burke	NA	NA	NA	NA	5	5	0.4	0.0	38.5	7.3	3.6	0.2
Burleigh	137	1 456	121.5	55.6	135	811	44.5	13.6	625.7	142.2	42.7	6.7
Cass	244	5 939	474.2	191.5	261	2 059	115.5	36.1	613.0	198.5	53.5	9.3
Cavalier	8	26	2.6	1.0	12	31	1.7	0.4	104.4	13.0	5.4	0.3
Dickey	10	43	3.8	2.2	13	32	1.8	0.4	64.9	13.0	6.4	0.6
Divide	3	8	0.8	0.4	6	12	1.1	0.1	39.3	6.8	3.2	0.2
Dunn	1	D	D	D	3	5	0.2	0.0	27.4	5.9	3.1	0.3
Eddy	2	D	D	D	8	15	1.3	0.2	32.9	7.7	3.6	0.2
Emmons	5	8	0.5	0.2	7	11	0.7	0.2	50.1	10.7	5.0	0.3
Foster	9	94	3.0	1.2	14	55	2.9	0.8	55.7	9.5	4.0	0.2
Golden Valley	4	D	D	D	6	13	0.9	0.2	24.6	5.2	2.2	0.1
Grand Forks	84	1 492	65.4	44.1	113	731	36.6	11.3	494.8	94.6	33.4	4.4
Grant	4	17	0.6	0.2	6	9	0.7	0.1	31.9	6.5	4.7	0.4
Griggs	3	D	D	D	5	15	0.7	0.2	37.1	7.5	3.4	0.3
Hettinger	4	D	D	D	6	11	1.0	0.2	42.6	8.2	4.0	0.2
Kidder	2	D	D	D	2	D	D	D	31.1	6.2	3.7	0.2
La Moure	4	16	0.6	0.3	9	13	0.9	0.1	64.0	12.5	5.4	0.3
Logan	5	53	1.1	0.5	4	9	0.7	0.1	28.1	5.3	3.0	0.2
McHenry	6	17	0.6	0.2	7	12	1.4	0.1	71.2	16.8	7.6	0.5
McIntosh	4	30	1.5	0.9	8	14	1.0	0.2	41.6	10.7	6.9	0.3
McKenzie	3	D	D	D	9	28	1.4	0.4	44.2	10.0	3.7	0.8
McLean	10	136	3.6	1.9	19	48	3.0	0.7	120.7	26.0	10.8	0.7
Mercer	10	57	3.5	1.3	15	59	2.7	0.6	41.7	16.0	7.1	0.4
Morton	24	133	7.1	3.7	49	219	15.2	4.3	153.2	51.9	20.2	2.6
Mountrail	7	12	0.6	0.1	10	16	1.2	0.3	84.4	15.8	6.8	0.9
Nelson	8	118	2.0	0.9	11	12	1.2	0.2	65.7	12.2	6.3	0.2
Oliver	2	D	D	D	1	D	D	D	13.5	2.8	1.4	0.1
Pembina	10	53	2.6	1.3	16	43	2.5	0.4	106.9	21.2	8.7	0.5
Pierce	8	80	4.9	2.2	9	31	1.1	0.4	49.6	11.3	5.4	0.3
Ramsey	24	209	11.7	5.4	22	91	5.1	1.4	160.7	30.8	12.3	1.2
Ransom	15	60	2.3	0.8	13	24	2.1	0.4	56.3	13.8	6.2	0.3
Renville	3	2	0.3	0.0	6	41	3.6	0.7	54.3	7.7	3.2	0.1
Richland	21	181	10.2	4.2	27	89	5.3	1.2	153.9	33.8	11.5	1.3
Rolette	9	52	3.4	1.7	9	26	1.3	0.3	177.2	22.0	8.6	7.1
Sargent	4	D	D	D	7	12	0.4	0.1	51.5	9.2	4.0	0.2
Sheridan	NA	NA	NA	NA	4	13	0.3	0.0	29.5	4.6	2.6	0.3
Sioux	1	D	D	D	NA	NA	NA	NA	52.3	4.4	1.9	2.0
Slope	NA	NA	NA	NA	1	D	D	D	13.9	1.1	0.4	0.0
Stark	43	284	15.7	7.3	64	257	18.4	4.4	119.7	46.2	19.1	3.0
Steele	1	D	D	D	8	16	1.0	0.2	38.6	5.5	2.5	0.2
Stutsman	39	509	21.0	7.4	44	192	10.7	2.6	199.6	50.9	16.9	3.0
Towner	3	D	D	D	6	11	1.2	0.2	66.9	7.6	3.8	0.2
Traill	11	73	4.0	2.5	20	39	4.2	0.7	83.0	20.7	8.1	0.5
Walsh	19	99	4.2	2.1	38	123	6.7	1.5	127.3	30.7	13.4	1.0

1. Firms subject to federal tax.   2. October 1, 2000 to September 30, 2001.   3. State totals may include programs not allocated by county.

	Federal funds and grants, fiscal 2001[1] (cont'd)							Local government finances, 1997				
	Expenditures (mil dol) (cont'd)							General revenue				
	Procurement contract awards		Grants[2]							Taxes		
											Per capita[3] (dollars)	
STATE County	Salaries and wages	Defense	Other	Medicaid and other health-related	Nutrition and family welfare	Education	Other	Total (mil dol)	Intergovern-mental (mil dol)	Total (mil dol)	Total	Property
	171	172	173	174	175	176	177	178	179	180	181	182
NORTH CAROLINA—Cont'd												
Swain	13.1	0.1	2.0	16.5	3.2	3.0	6.8	18.2	12.8	3.7	307	173
Transylvania	7.2	0.1	4.6	11.7	2.0	1.4	1.0	45.6	21.4	18.8	674	507
Tyrrell	0.5	0.0	0.1	5.6	1.1	0.4	0.5	9.5	6.2	2.3	618	495
Union	12.7	10.8	3.0	26.3	9.1	4.8	2.0	191.0	90.3	59.4	559	425
Vance	5.6	0.0	6.6	47.0	8.9	4.1	0.8	106.3	68.6	21.3	512	367
Wake	281.7	54.7	102.9	322.2	411.4	233.8	729.9	1 333.0	472.2	477.3	865	639
Warren	2.1	0.0	0.5	30.3	4.7	1.3	2.3	35.6	20.4	9.7	533	414
Washington	2.3	0.0	0.6	14.6	3.7	1.6	0.6	33.3	17.8	6.2	451	340
Watauga	5.8	0.4	1.7	18.5	2.4	3.5	4.1	82.5	28.1	24.8	610	429
Wayne	192.4	34.4	13.2	93.4	22.2	9.7	20.7	200.0	123.1	47.0	420	291
Wilkes	10.4	0.8	2.5	56.6	5.2	3.4	4.8	120.4	69.1	28.6	458	305
Wilson	9.6	3.9	4.9	66.2	13.6	5.5	7.8	167.4	85.4	43.8	646	493
Yadkin	4.1	0.1	1.0	20.9	2.7	1.5	12.2	55.7	26.8	14.9	431	299
Yancey	2.5	0.0	0.7	22.2	2.0	1.0	1.1	26.1	15.1	6.9	421	283
NORTH DAKOTA	634.1	158.8	121.2	371.1	133.3	133.1	646.7	X	X	X	X	X
Adams	0.9	0.0	0.2	2.4	0.3	0.1	6.5	6.3	2.3	2.4	881	863
Barnes	4.9	2.3	1.2	6.2	1.4	0.9	15.5	23.9	10.1	8.7	724	708
Benson	5.8	1.7	1.1	9.9	3.7	4.4	26.7	14.1	7.7	4.0	590	579
Billings	1.5	0.0	2.2	0.0	0.0	0.1	4.3	5.3	3.1	0.9	770	736
Bottineau	3.3	0.8	0.6	3.4	1.0	0.3	8.4	17.3	6.4	6.5	873	853
Bowman	1.0	0.1	0.2	1.0	0.4	0.1	3.6	8.1	4.6	2.4	730	717
Burke	2.3	0.0	0.4	1.4	0.3	0.1	3.0	7.0	2.4	3.3	1 416	1 373
Burleigh	56.9	1.4	7.4	41.5	46.5	45.8	183.2	127.7	39.8	50.2	753	623
Cass	111.2	15.3	19.0	43.8	9.1	3.9	60.3	238.0	72.1	97.6	852	711
Cavalier	1.8	0.0	0.4	2.7	0.7	0.2	7.5	16.1	3.8	8.3	1 604	1 565
Dickey	1.7	0.0	0.4	3.8	0.8	0.2	4.5	10.4	3.9	4.6	820	814
Divide	1.1	0.0	0.2	2.7	0.2	0.1	4.5	7.2	2.2	3.4	1 408	1 378
Dunn	1.1	0.4	0.2	1.7	0.5	0.6	1.3	8.4	4.2	2.9	787	779
Eddy	1.2	0.0	0.2	1.7	0.4	0.4	2.4	10.7	2.5	4.4	1 521	1 501
Emmons	1.2	0.0	0.2	3.8	0.7	0.2	4.2	15.1	4.2	6.1	1 398	1 390
Foster	1.5	0.1	5.4	1.0	0.4	0.1	11.8	10.6	3.3	4.7	1 257	1 243
Golden Valley	0.5	0.0	0.1	1.0	0.2	0.2	6.4	6.6	2.3	2.6	1 342	1 315
Grand Forks	131.0	41.0	10.2	31.9	7.1	14.7	37.4	139.4	49.2	54.9	789	622
Grant	1.2	0.0	0.2	3.4	0.5	0.1	0.2	5.5	2.2	2.5	823	815
Griggs	1.3	0.0	0.3	1.0	0.4	1.0	2.0	10.2	2.4	5.9	2 065	2 045
Hettinger	1.2	0.0	0.2	4.4	0.4	0.1	0.6	7.3	2.8	3.2	1 095	1 091
Kidder	1.2	0.0	0.2	2.1	0.4	0.2	2.7	13.5	3.6	6.1	2 098	2 097
La Moure	2.0	0.0	0.7	3.4	0.6	0.3	2.2	24.3	13.4	7.7	1 564	1 545
Logan	0.8	0.0	0.2	2.4	0.3	0.1	1.5	5.0	2.2	2.0	841	835
McHenry	3.1	0.0	0.6	4.1	2.3	0.3	8.3	11.9	5.9	4.4	708	679
McIntosh	1.2	0.0	0.2	3.1	0.4	0.2	1.6	7.3	2.5	2.8	798	793
McKenzie	2.4	0.2	2.1	1.4	0.9	0.4	7.1	17.6	10.5	4.2	736	718
McLean	5.2	8.9	1.0	10.9	1.1	0.6	9.5	20.9	12.1	4.8	496	488
Mercer	2.2	0.0	0.4	4.1	0.6	0.2	1.1	31.8	12.2	8.4	895	881
Morton	5.6	24.9	6.3	10.9	3.4	0.9	1.9	49.9	21.3	17.1	701	689
Mountrail	4.8	0.1	1.3	6.4	2.9	3.4	9.5	18.7	9.6	5.4	808	791
Nelson	1.5	0.0	0.4	3.4	0.4	0.2	7.3	10.4	3.6	5.5	1 442	1 432
Oliver	0.2	0.0	0.0	1.4	0.1	0.1	0.7	12.8	2.5	1.0	473	429
Pembina	7.5	3.9	2.0	6.2	0.8	0.2	4.2	20.0	7.3	8.1	942	908
Pierce	1.6	0.0	0.4	4.1	0.6	0.2	2.7	8.7	3.4	4.1	887	821
Ramsey	10.4	1.5	3.7	8.6	1.7	1.0	26.5	27.1	10.5	10.0	810	726
Ransom	1.8	0.0	1.5	2.4	0.6	0.1	2.7	12.4	5.1	5.0	866	818
Renville	1.0	0.0	0.4	1.0	0.2	0.3	7.9	7.9	3.5	3.1	1 084	1 046
Richland	3.8	0.3	1.0	6.8	1.5	0.5	21.2	36.0	14.8	13.1	716	708
Rolette	26.8	2.4	26.2	24.2	8.8	9.2	14.6	27.7	19.8	4.4	313	291
Sargent	2.1	0.0	0.4	2.7	0.7	0.1	3.0	9.6	3.2	4.1	929	923
Sheridan	0.5	0.0	0.1	3.4	0.3	0.1	2.5	3.6	1.4	1.3	742	736
Sioux	7.3	0.2	0.8	5.3	5.6	4.8	4.8	6.8	5.2	1.2	293	292
Slope	0.1	0.0	0.0	0.3	0.0	0.0	1.5	3.8	1.0	0.6	704	647
Stark	7.6	0.0	1.1	10.9	3.5	1.1	3.1	41.7	18.0	14.0	618	527
Steele	0.8	0.0	1.1	0.3	0.2	0.1	2.1	5.1	1.6	2.8	1 247	1 228
Stutsman	11.1	0.1	2.5	22.9	3.8	0.6	25.1	41.5	16.2	16.1	763	677
Towner	1.1	0.0	0.6	1.4	0.5	0.1	9.5	7.3	2.5	3.2	1 051	1 041
Traill	2.3	0.0	0.6	3.1	1.2	0.2	5.8	22.4	7.4	8.3	963	939
Walsh	3.7	2.9	1.2	5.8	1.5	0.5	10.8	28.9	11.2	12.0	877	840

1. October 1, 2000 to September 30, 2001.   2. State totals may include programs not allocated by county.   3. Based on the resident population estimated as of July 1 of the year shown.

STATE County	Total (mil dol) [183]	Per capita[1] (dollars) [184]	Education [185]	Health and hospitals [186]	Police protection [187]	Public welfare [188]	Highways [189]	Total (mil dol) [190]	Per capita[1] (dollars) [191]	Federal civilian [192]	Federal military [193]	State and local [194]	Democratic [195]	Republican [196]	All other [197]
NORTH CAROLINA—Cont'd															
Swain	19.2	1 575	54.2	7.3	4.7	8.8	0.5	8.2	672	335	37	808	48.0	50.9	1.1
Transylvania	45.1	1 619	47.7	5.2	6.7	10.5	1.1	9.2	331	164	87	1 205	35.5	63.3	1.2
Tyrrell	10.3	2 725	58.6	1.5	4.1	7.2	0.5	2.1	562	14	12	381	54.2	45.1	0.7
Union	169.7	1 596	55.0	3.9	6.4	7.2	1.0	189.1	1 778	210	346	5 495	31.5	67.4	1.1
Vance	109.4	2 630	48.9	16.6	3.9	7.2	1.5	28.5	684	102	128	3 332	55.8	43.8	0.4
Wake	1 231.5	2 233	46.8	5.4	4.7	3.9	2.5	7 733.2	14 020	4 371	2 467	63 924	45.8	52.9	1.3
Warren	35.7	1 963	54.1	7.3	3.4	10.7	0.4	22.5	1 238	44	57	1 336	67.3	32.4	0.3
Washington	33.1	2 409	44.7	17.7	3.6	9.3	1.3	11.6	845	51	40	1 223	55.3	44.4	0.3
Watauga	73.0	1 793	35.7	5.5	5.3	6.9	2.8	35.0	860	108	131	4 955	42.5	55.7	1.7
Wayne	192.4	1 718	54.5	4.8	4.1	6.9	3.0	104.1	929	1 443	4 604	8 277	38.4	61.3	0.4
Wilkes	122.4	1 960	56.8	17.4	2.9	6.6	1.0	29.9	479	194	191	4 305	29.7	69.2	1.1
Wilson	166.6	2 458	45.9	7.5	5.4	8.7	1.6	45.3	668	211	207	5 912	45.4	54.2	0.4
Yadkin	54.1	1 565	54.1	17.9	4.2	7.4	1.3	6.9	198	81	106	1 584	22.9	76.3	0.9
Yancey	26.3	1 602	55.2	15.2	2.3	7.2	0.6	3.8	233	75	51	804	42.4	56.7	0.9
NORTH DAKOTA	X	X	X	X	X	X	X	X	X	8 985	12 501	50 192	33.1	60.7	6.3
Adams	6.3	2 302	43.4	0.4	3.1	4.2	20.6	1.7	635	17	21	162	24.7	71.2	4.1
Barnes	22.9	1 894	51.4	2.3	2.9	3.3	11.9	3.4	284	93	95	996	33.6	60.1	6.3
Benson	13.0	1 909	52.7	1.6	1.6	6.7	14.7	0.7	100	121	54	331	44.2	49.0	6.8
Billings	4.8	4 348	32.1	0.9	3.7	2.3	42.3	0.0	0	36	0	84	15.6	75.0	9.3
Bottineau	17.4	2 331	48.1	0.0	1.8	3.4	15.9	1.5	201	64	58	520	31.8	63.7	4.6
Bowman	8.3	2 512	56.4	0.4	2.9	3.3	18.5	0.0	10	23	26	229	22.4	73.4	4.1
Burke	7.0	3 002	43.1	0.4	1.9	2.5	13.4	0.2	65	56	17	180	28.5	67.2	4.3
Burleigh	119.6	1 794	45.0	0.7	5.9	3.6	9.0	100.5	1 508	918	541	7 513	28.5	65.2	6.3
Cass	237.8	2 075	42.3	1.2	3.9	2.4	4.5	326.6	2 851	2 044	986	8 449	36.4	56.8	6.8
Cavalier	17.1	3 316	32.3	0.0	2.4	4.0	15.2	6.2	1 203	41	38	294	26.1	63.8	10.1
Dickey	11.6	2 060	62.4	0.5	2.2	4.4	11.1	4.8	848	35	45	292	28.9	66.5	4.6
Divide	8.8	3 625	27.7	24.2	2.4	2.3	25.3	1.9	773	31	18	133	38.5	55.8	5.7
Dunn	7.8	2 149	58.8	0.0	2.8	1.5	21.4	0.1	23	29	28	230	27.4	65.0	7.5
Eddy	9.1	3 182	35.8	0.0	3.2	1.2	6.8	0.5	160	32	22	172	36.1	55.4	8.4
Emmons	15.3	3 491	31.6	0.9	0.7	1.8	9.6	4.7	1 080	33	34	244	20.3	71.8	7.9
Foster	9.3	2 472	52.4	0.5	1.8	3.7	10.2	2.7	705	29	30	233	27.2	67.2	5.6
Golden Valley	7.0	3 681	41.7	3.8	3.6	4.7	11.3	0.0	25	14	14	165	19.2	75.2	5.5
Grand Forks	138.0	1 982	41.5	3.1	4.1	1.5	5.3	117.6	1 689	1 262	3 333	8 141	37.3	55.9	6.8
Grant	5.8	1 919	56.3	1.2	0.9	6.7	20.3	1.9	614	33	23	167	16.5	75.4	8.1
Griggs	10.5	3 698	21.2	0.9	1.4	2.9	9.3	1.4	509	25	22	156	32.9	62.6	4.4
Hettinger	7.7	2 608	57.1	0.0	2.1	6.2	10.8	0.8	270	29	23	200	23.2	69.6	7.2
Kidder	12.0	4 096	30.6	3.2	1.0	2.1	9.0	2.1	720	30	22	161	22.2	65.6	12.2
La Moure	28.9	5 888	23.8	0.0	0.9	2.2	6.5	8.9	1 808	45	37	284	27.9	64.4	7.7
Logan	4.8	1 993	66.9	0.6	2.1	2.6	13.3	0.3	136	23	18	139	19.5	70.9	9.6
McHenry	11.8	1 908	57.7	0.0	2.2	4.5	17.0	1.9	308	70	47	387	32.4	61.5	6.1
McIntosh	7.1	2 002	51.5	0.0	2.3	2.1	18.0	0.7	188	24	27	191	21.5	72.4	6.0
McKenzie	18.1	3 140	53.9	1.4	2.2	2.4	15.0	0.2	43	73	44	377	27.6	69.1	3.3
McLean	20.4	2 093	57.4	0.5	4.6	1.7	7.9	1.6	167	132	76	679	31.5	62.2	6.2
Mercer	33.3	3 530	35.9	0.4	3.2	1.9	8.1	107.7	11 407	41	73	586	23.2	68.6	8.2
Morton	49.5	2 029	46.9	2.0	3.1	4.1	7.8	27.5	1 128	114	196	1 385	30.6	62.3	7.0
Mountrail	17.6	2 647	54.0	2.0	2.0	3.0	6.1	1.3	190	115	52	435	43.4	50.6	6.0
Nelson	10.0	2 623	46.9	0.4	2.2	3.9	17.2	3.7	962	37	29	226	37.3	56.0	6.6
Oliver	13.1	5 919	14.6	1.5	1.6	0.5	7.6	160.7	72 492	12	17	123	23.2	67.5	9.3
Pembina	19.3	2 245	58.3	0.6	3.0	2.5	7.6	3.8	442	127	95	537	28.9	64.3	6.8
Pierce	7.6	1 675	55.4	4.4	3.2	5.3	11.8	0.7	164	35	37	215	25.4	68.4	6.2
Ramsey	24.9	2 009	55.5	0.0	3.0	6.4	10.6	9.1	735	189	95	1 235	33.3	60.4	6.3
Ransom	10.5	1 806	54.8	1.7	3.7	4.8	12.0	5.4	922	43	46	437	39.7	54.7	5.6
Renville	9.3	3 248	46.9	0.7	2.1	1.9	21.5	1.1	369	25	22	188	33.3	61.6	5.2
Richland	38.1	2 093	52.0	1.7	2.8	2.8	13.2	11.2	615	83	143	1 347	31.1	62.4	6.6
Rolette	26.9	1 902	76.5	0.3	1.9	3.4	5.1	6.0	427	565	113	720	61.0	32.2	6.8
Sargent	9.0	2 028	46.8	2.3	2.8	3.6	14.0	4.4	984	49	34	211	43.9	50.5	5.6
Sheridan	3.2	1 776	50.6	0.7	2.8	6.3	17.2	0.3	173	18	13	108	17.3	-76.2	6.5
Sioux	5.4	1 331	81.4	0.1	0.8	0.6	7.5	0.0	2	174	33	194	69.5	25.8	4.6
Slope	2.7	3 135	10.3	0.0	1.4	2.2	24.5	0.2	178	0	0	40	19.2	71.5	9.3
Stark	40.3	1 775	52.4	0.2	4.9	5.6	8.7	8.2	361	174	179	1 783	28.5	65.3	6.2
Steele	5.0	2 226	47.1	0.9	2.7	5.0	22.7	0.3	112	26	17	129	39.3	54.1	6.6
Stutsman	44.0	2 083	40.1	0.6	4.6	4.4	14.7	5.7	272	207	168	1 654	33.6	60.2	6.2
Towner	7.5	2 443	48.9	9.3	2.1	4.2	11.7	4.4	1 418	24	24	153	34.5	58.4	7.1
Traill	22.1	2 561	48.8	0.6	1.6	3.2	13.8	6.4	740	44	68	671	36.8	58.2	5.1
Walsh	28.6	2 090	51.7	0.3	2.3	1.4	12.5	3.9	288	75	106	1 363	33.6	59.8	6.6

1. Based on the resident population estimated as of July 1 of the year shown.   2. Data subject to copyright.

Table B. States and Counties — Land Area and Population

STATE/ County code	MSA/ PMSA/ NECMA code[1]	County Type[2]	STATE County	Land area,[3] (sq km) 2000	Population and population characteristics, 2000													
								Race alone or in combination (percent)					Age (percent)					
					Total persons	Rank	Per square kilometer	White	Black	Am. Indian, Alaska Native	Asian and Pacific Islander	Percent Hispanic[4]	Under 5 years	5 to 17 years	18 to 24 years	25 to 34 years	35 to 44 years	45 to 54 years
				1	2	3	4	5	6	7	8	9	10	11	12	13	14	15
			NORTH DAKOTA—Cont'd															
38 101	...	5	Ward	5 213	58 795	815	11.3	93.9	2.8	2.8	1.4	1.9	7.4	18.8	13.0	14.1	15.0	11.7
38 103	...	9	Wells	3 293	5 102	2 843	1.5	99.4	0.2	0.4	0.3	0.3	4.4	18.1	4.6	7.5	15.2	13.1
38 105	...	7	Williams	5 362	19 761	1 804	3.7	95.1	0.3	6.3	0.3	0.9	5.7	20.4	7.8	9.4	16.2	14.7
39 000	...	X	**OHIO**	106 056	11 353 140	X	107.0	86.1	12.1	0.7	1.5	1.9	6.6	18.8	9.3	13.4	15.9	13.8
39 001	...	6	Adams	1 512	27 330	1 472	18.1	98.8	0.3	1.6	0.2	0.6	6.4	19.9	8.7	13.1	15.1	13.2
39 003	4320	3	Allen	1 047	108 473	497	103.6	86.3	13.0	0.6	0.7	1.4	6.7	19.2	9.9	12.3	15.3	13.7
39 005	...	4	Ashland	1 099	52 523	889	47.8	98.3	1.0	0.5	0.8	0.6	6.6	19.1	10.8	11.8	14.7	13.5
39 007	1680	1	Ashtabula	1 819	102 728	517	56.5	95.4	3.7	0.7	0.6	2.2	6.5	19.6	7.6	12.4	15.6	14.0
39 009	...	4	Athens	1 312	62 223	782	47.4	94.9	2.9	1.0	2.3	1.0	4.8	13.6	30.7	12.0	11.6	11.0
39 011	4320	3	Auglaize	1 039	46 611	968	44.9	98.9	0.5	0.6	0.5	0.7	6.8	20.8	7.8	12.4	15.8	13.6
39 013	9000	3	Belmont	1 392	70 226	706	50.4	95.7	4.0	0.4	0.4	0.4	5.0	16.7	7.7	11.9	15.5	15.0
39 015	1640	1	Brown	1 274	42 285	1 050	33.2	98.7	1.1	0.5	0.2	0.4	7.0	20.5	8.1	13.7	16.6	13.2
39 017	3200	0	Butler	1 210	332 807	175	275.0	92.2	5.7	0.6	1.9	1.4	6.9	19.0	11.9	13.4	16.4	13.6
39 019	1320	2	Carroll	1 022	28 836	1 425	28.2	98.9	0.7	0.7	0.2	0.5	6.0	19.1	7.5	11.6	15.9	15.1
39 021	...	6	Champaign	1 110	38 890	1 144	35.0	96.7	2.9	0.8	0.4	0.7	6.5	19.6	7.9	13.0	15.8	14.2
39 023	2000	2	Clark	1 036	144 742	378	139.7	89.5	9.7	0.9	0.8	1.2	6.5	18.6	9.1	12.2	14.6	14.3
39 025	1640	0	Clermont	1 171	177 977	309	152.0	97.9	1.1	0.6	0.8	0.9	7.6	20.3	8.4	14.1	17.6	14.2
39 027	...	6	Clinton	1 064	40 543	1 102	38.1	96.9	2.6	0.7	0.5	0.7	7.1	19.3	10.2	12.9	16.2	13.5
39 029	9320	2	Columbiana	1 379	112 075	480	81.3	97.2	2.5	0.5	0.3	1.2	5.9	18.4	7.8	12.7	15.3	14.5
39 031	...	6	Coshocton	1 461	36 655	1 197	25.1	98.2	1.4	0.6	0.4	0.6	6.4	19.8	7.8	11.9	15.4	13.8
39 033	4800	3	Crawford	1 041	46 966	964	45.1	98.6	0.8	0.5	0.4	0.8	6.6	18.4	8.0	12.5	15.1	13.9
39 035	1680	0	Cuyahoga	1 187	1 393 978	23	1 174.4	68.7	28.2	0.6	2.2	3.4	6.5	18.4	8.0	13.5	15.7	13.5
39 037	...	6	Darke	1 553	53 309	877	34.3	98.8	0.7	0.5	0.4	0.9	6.7	19.6	7.8	12.3	15.2	13.4
39 039	...	4	Defiance	1 065	39 500	1 126	37.1	93.9	2.1	0.6	0.4	7.2	7.0	19.6	9.2	12.2	15.2	14.6
39 041	1840	1	Delaware	1 146	109 989	494	96.0	95.3	2.9	0.6	1.9	1.0	7.9	20.3	7.6	13.6	19.0	15.2
39 043	...	4	Erie	660	79 551	645	120.5	90.1	9.5	0.7	0.5	2.1	6.0	18.7	7.2	11.4	15.6	15.2
39 045	1840	1	Fairfield	1 308	122 759	441	93.9	96.1	3.0	0.7	1.0	0.8	7.0	19.8	8.0	13.3	16.9	14.6
39 047	...	6	Fayette	1 053	28 433	1 433	27.0	96.7	2.6	0.6	0.7	1.2	6.7	18.6	8.0	13.1	15.3	14.2
39 049	1840	0	Franklin	1 398	1 068 978	33	764.6	77.1	19.1	0.9	3.6	2.3	7.2	17.9	11.7	17.1	16.2	12.8
39 051	8400	2	Fulton	1 054	42 084	1 056	39.9	96.6	0.4	0.6	0.6	5.8	7.2	21.1	7.7	12.4	15.3	14.3
39 053	...	6	Gallia	1 214	31 069	1 375	25.6	96.3	3.1	1.0	0.4	0.6	6.3	18.7	9.7	11.8	15.7	13.7
39 055	1680	1	Geauga	1 045	90 895	568	87.0	98.1	1.4	0.4	0.7	0.6	6.8	21.6	6.4	9.9	16.7	16.1
39 057	2000	2	Greene	1 075	147 886	367	137.6	90.7	7.1	0.9	2.6	1.2	5.9	18.0	13.7	11.6	15.5	14.4
39 059	...	7	Guernsey	1 352	40 792	1 088	30.2	97.6	2.1	1.0	0.4	0.6	6.7	19.4	7.9	12.1	15.3	13.8
39 061	1640	0	Hamilton	1 055	845 303	52	801.2	74.0	24.1	0.6	2.0	1.1	6.7	19.1	9.6	13.9	15.7	13.3
39 063	...	4	Hancock	1 376	71 295	696	51.8	96.2	1.4	0.5	1.4	3.1	6.8	19.0	9.7	13.0	15.7	13.7
39 065	...	6	Hardin	1 218	31 945	1 347	26.2	98.4	0.9	0.7	0.6	0.8	6.4	17.9	15.4	12.3	13.7	12.5
39 067	...	6	Harrison	1 045	15 856	2 029	15.2	97.5	2.8	0.4	0.2	0.4	5.8	17.2	6.9	11.1	15.5	14.9
39 069	...	6	Henry	1 079	29 210	1 422	27.1	96.1	0.7	0.5	0.5	5.4	6.7	20.9	8.2	12.1	15.9	13.2
39 071	...	6	Highland	1 433	40 875	1 086	28.5	97.7	1.8	0.7	0.5	0.5	7.1	19.9	8.5	13.0	14.9	13.2
39 073	...	6	Hocking	1 095	28 241	1 441	25.8	98.6	1.1	1.0	0.2	0.4	6.7	18.8	8.1	12.3	16.6	14.3
39 075	...	7	Holmes	1 096	38 943	1 142	35.5	99.4	0.4	0.3	0.1	0.7	10.3	25.3	10.4	12.7	12.9	10.6
39 077	...	4	Huron	1 276	59 487	807	46.6	96.9	1.3	0.5	0.3	3.6	7.5	20.8	8.5	13.3	15.6	13.3
39 079	...	7	Jackson	1 089	32 641	1 327	30.0	98.7	0.8	0.8	0.3	0.6	6.6	19.4	8.7	13.4	15.3	13.7
39 081	8080	3	Jefferson	1 061	73 894	677	69.6	93.4	6.2	0.6	0.5	0.6	5.2	16.2	8.5	10.9	14.6	15.2
39 083	...	6	Knox	1 365	54 500	864	39.9	98.5	0.9	0.7	0.4	0.7	6.2	18.6	11.7	11.4	15.3	13.5
39 085	1680	0	Lake	591	227 511	250	385.0	96.3	2.3	0.4	1.1	1.7	6.1	18.1	7.3	12.9	16.9	14.8
39 087	3400	2	Lawrence	1 178	62 319	779	52.9	97.4	2.5	0.6	0.3	0.6	6.2	18.3	8.6	13.1	14.9	13.9
39 089	1840	0	Licking	1 778	145 491	376	81.8	96.7	2.5	0.7	0.9	0.8	6.9	19.1	8.8	12.6	16.8	14.2
39 091	...	6	Logan	1 187	46 005	983	38.8	97.3	2.3	0.6	0.7	0.7	6.9	19.8	8.2	12.3	15.6	13.8
39 093	1680	0	Lorain	1 276	284 664	197	223.1	87.5	9.4	0.9	0.9	6.9	6.9	19.3	8.7	12.8	16.6	14.3
39 095	8400	2	Lucas	882	455 054	129	515.9	79.4	17.9	0.8	1.6	4.5	6.9	19.4	9.8	13.9	15.3	13.5
39 097	1840	1	Madison	1 205	40 213	1 110	33.4	92.7	6.7	0.5	0.7	0.7	6.2	18.4	9.1	14.8	18.0	13.7
39 099	9320	2	Mahoning	1 075	257 555	218	239.6	82.2	16.6	0.6	0.6	3.0	6.0	17.8	8.4	11.5	14.4	14.4
39 101	...	4	Marion	1 046	66 217	737	63.3	92.9	6.1	0.5	0.7	1.1	6.0	18.4	8.3	13.7	16.6	14.3
39 103	1680	1	Medina	1 092	151 095	355	138.4	98.0	1.1	0.4	0.8	0.9	7.0	20.5	7.0	12.7	17.9	15.2
39 105	...	6	Meigs	1 112	23 072	1 640	20.7	98.7	1.0	0.9	0.2	0.6	5.7	18.2	8.4	12.4	15.3	14.6
39 107	...	7	Mercer	1 200	40 924	1 083	34.1	99.0	0.2	0.6	0.3	1.1	7.3	22.3	7.9	11.5	15.4	13.0
39 109	2000	2	Miami	1 054	98 868	527	93.8	96.7	2.4	0.5	0.9	0.7	6.4	19.5	7.6	12.5	15.9	14.6
39 111	...	6	Monroe	1 180	15 180	2 078	12.9	99.3	0.3	0.6	0.2	0.4	5.3	18.3	7.1	11.3	14.7	15.1
39 113	2000	2	Montgomery	1 196	559 062	99	467.4	77.8	20.6	0.7	1.8	1.3	6.6	18.1	9.7	13.6	15.4	13.7
39 115	...	8	Morgan	1 082	14 897	2 099	13.8	95.6	5.0	1.7	0.2	0.4	6.1	19.2	7.8	11.2	15.1	14.1
39 117	...	6	Morrow	1 052	31 628	1 355	30.1	99.1	0.4	0.8	0.2	0.6	6.8	20.8	7.6	12.8	16.5	14.4
39 119	...	4	Muskingum	1 721	84 585	616	49.1	95.2	4.9	0.7	0.4	0.5	6.7	19.3	9.4	12.5	15.2	13.3
39 121	...	8	Noble	1 033	14 058	2 159	13.6	92.9	6.8	0.5	0.1	0.4	5.0	17.6	11.7	14.9	16.9	12.2

1. MSA = Metropolitan Statistical Area. PMSA = Primary MSA. NECMA = New England County Metropolitan Area. See Appendix A for explanation of these concepts. See Appendix B for list of metropolitan areas identified by type, with component counties.   2. County typology code from the Economic Research Service of USDA. See Appendix A for definition.   3. Dry land or land partially or temporarily covered by water.   4. Hispanic persons may be of any race.

Table B. States and Counties — **Population and Households**

STATE County	Population, 2000 (cont'd) Age (percent) (cont'd)				Population — change and components of change, 1990–2001							Households, 2000				
					Total persons		Percent change		Components of change, 2000–2001						Percent	
	55 to 64 years	65 to 74 years	75 years and over	Percent female	2001	1990	1990–2000	2000–2001	Births	Deaths	Net migration	Number	Percent change, 1990–2000	Persons per house-hold	Female family house-holder[1]	One person
	16	17	18	19	20	21	22	23	24	25	26	27	28	29	30	31
NORTH DAKOTA—Cont'd																
Ward	7.4	6.2	6.3	50.2	57 247	57 921	1.5	-2.6	1 084	579	-2 071	23 041	7.2	2.46	8.4	27.2
Wells	11.2	12.2	13.8	50.9	4 882	5 864	-13.0	-4.3	46	99	-170	2 215	-7.9	2.25	4.8	32.6
Williams	9.3	7.9	8.6	51.0	19 606	21 129	-6.5	-0.8	312	273	-193	8 095	0.7	2.38	8.8	30.9
OHIO	8.9	7.0	6.3	51.4	11 373 541	10 847 115	4.7	0.2	195 720	136 432	-37 015	4 445 773	8.8	2.49	12.1	27.3
Adams	10.2	7.4	5.9	51.0	27 566	25 371	7.7	0.9	483	379	140	10 501	14.2	2.57	10.4	24.0
Allen	8.7	7.3	6.9	50.0	108 276	109 755	-1.2	-0.2	2 011	1 422	-750	40 646	3.1	2.52	12.4	26.3
Ashland	9.5	7.1	6.8	50.9	52 754	47 507	10.6	0.4	878	647	29	19 524	14.2	2.58	8.5	24.0
Ashtabula	9.6	7.6	7.0	51.3	102 514	99 880	2.9	-0.2	1 634	1 420	-383	39 397	7.2	2.56	11.4	24.8
Athens	7.0	4.9	4.4	51.1	62 235	59 549	4.5	0.0	719	580	-106	22 501	11.7	2.40	9.2	28.3
Auglaize	8.4	7.0	7.4	50.9	46 797	44 585	4.5	0.4	775	590	16	17 376	8.8	2.62	7.8	23.3
Belmont	9.9	9.0	9.2	50.9	69 451	71 074	-1.2	-1.1	907	1 189	-467	28 309	0.5	2.37	11.2	28.7
Brown	9.3	6.6	5.0	50.8	42 890	34 966	20.9	1.4	723	504	390	15 555	25.7	2.69	10.0	20.2
Butler	8.1	6.1	4.6	51.2	337 013	291 479	14.2	1.3	5 901	3 220	1 648	123 082	17.7	2.61	10.7	22.7
Carroll	10.6	8.0	6.2	50.5	29 086	26 521	8.7	0.9	372	337	223	11 126	15.1	2.56	7.7	22.9
Champaign	10.4	6.5	6.1	51.0	39 182	36 019	8.0	0.8	672	439	76	14 952	12.8	2.56	9.2	23.5
Clark	10.1	7.5	7.2	51.9	144 076	147 538	-1.9	-0.5	2 538	2 176	-990	56 648	2.6	2.49	12.8	26.0
Clermont	8.4	5.4	4.0	50.9	181 673	150 094	18.6	2.1	3 373	1 543	1 892	66 013	25.2	2.67	10.0	21.0
Clinton	8.6	6.4	5.8	51.0	40 987	35 444	14.4	1.1	741	454	169	15 416	18.2	2.56	10.1	23.7
Columbiana	9.7	8.0	7.1	50.3	111 678	108 276	3.5	-0.4	1 616	1 499	-474	42 973	5.4	2.52	10.3	24.8
Coshocton	10.2	7.8	6.9	51.2	36 779	35 427	3.5	0.3	550	555	144	14 356	6.9	2.52	9.2	25.4
Crawford	10.4	7.9	7.3	51.7	46 594	47 870	-1.9	-0.8	761	671	-454	18 957	3.1	2.45	10.5	26.3
Cuyahoga	8.7	7.7	7.9	52.8	1 380 421	1 412 140	-1.3	-1.0	24 532	19 173	-18 889	571 457	1.5	2.39	15.7	32.8
Darke	9.8	7.5	7.8	51.0	53 078	53 617	-0.6	-0.4	882	654	-445	20 419	4.9	2.56	8.0	23.5
Defiance	9.4	6.8	6.1	50.7	39 360	39 350	0.4	-0.4	704	417	-421	15 138	7.6	2.57	9.6	23.0
Delaware	8.1	4.8	3.4	50.5	119 752	66 929	64.3	8.9	1 818	685	8 388	39 674	71.6	2.70	6.7	18.1
Erie	10.3	8.1	7.5	51.3	79 312	76 781	3.6	-0.3	1 126	1 049	-297	31 727	9.7	2.45	11.2	27.0
Fairfield	9.2	6.1	5.0	50.2	127 395	103 468	18.6	3.8	2 177	1 186	3 592	45 425	23.4	2.65	9.1	20.7
Fayette	9.8	7.6	6.8	50.7	28 241	27 466	3.5	-0.7	493	432	-247	11 054	8.1	2.51	11.5	24.5
Franklin	7.3	5.3	4.5	51.4	1 071 524	961 437	11.2	0.2	21 363	10 391	-8 210	438 778	15.9	2.39	13.0	30.9
Fulton	8.6	6.4	6.3	51.1	42 205	38 498	9.3	0.3	710	465	-106	15 480	14.6	2.69	8.2	21.1
Gallia	10.5	7.6	5.9	51.2	31 183	30 954	0.4	0.4	513	383	-2	12 060	6.1	2.50	11.0	25.2
Geauga	10.6	6.5	5.5	50.8	92 180	81 087	12.1	1.4	1 462	824	664	31 630	17.6	2.84	7.2	17.6
Greene	9.2	6.7	5.2	51.3	148 426	136 731	8.2	0.4	2 248	1 470	-176	55 312	14.4	2.53	9.6	23.0
Guernsey	10.2	7.9	6.5	51.4	40 959	39 024	4.5	0.4	702	571	54	16 094	8.1	2.50	11.4	26.1
Hamilton	8.2	6.9	6.6	52.3	835 362	866 228	-2.4	-1.2	15 892	10 689	-15 233	346 790	2.3	2.38	14.3	32.9
Hancock	8.9	6.5	6.7	51.5	72 046	65 536	8.8	1.1	1 216	764	326	27 898	13.2	2.49	8.7	26.0
Hardin	8.8	6.6	6.3	51.0	31 762	31 111	2.7	-0.6	545	416	-307	11 963	6.3	2.51	8.9	26.5
Harrison	10.9	9.1	8.6	51.5	15 886	16 085	-1.4	0.2	205	243	75	6 398	4.7	2.44	8.8	25.6
Henry	8.9	7.0	7.0	50.6	29 310	29 108	0.4	0.3	500	329	-57	10 935	5.1	2.62	8.1	23.5
Highland	9.7	7.5	6.3	51.2	41 439	35 728	14.4	1.4	740	573	407	15 587	17.8	2.60	10.3	23.2
Hocking	10.7	7.5	5.6	50.2	28 436	25 533	10.6	0.7	432	359	121	10 843	16.0	2.54	9.5	23.7
Holmes	7.2	5.6	4.9	50.1	39 854	32 849	18.6	2.3	1 070	345	197	11 337	21.7	3.35	6.5	16.1
Huron	8.6	6.7	5.6	51.0	59 437	56 238	5.8	-0.1	1 113	672	-478	22 307	10.2	2.64	10.4	23.1
Jackson	9.3	7.2	6.4	51.7	32 668	30 230	8.0	0.1	564	463	-58	12 619	12.1	2.55	12.0	24.0
Jefferson	10.7	9.6	9.0	52.3	72 855	80 298	-8.0	-1.4	909	1 251	-680	30 417	-2.9	2.36	11.6	28.5
Knox	9.5	7.3	6.5	51.4	55 521	47 473	14.8	1.9	854	702	869	19 975	15.9	2.56	8.5	23.9
Lake	9.9	7.5	6.6	51.4	228 100	215 500	5.6	0.3	3 294	2 591	-13	89 700	11.5	2.50	10.0	25.6
Lawrence	10.6	8.1	6.3	52.0	62 009	61 834	0.8	-0.5	925	906	-306	24 732	8.0	2.49	11.9	24.9
Licking	9.7	6.6	5.3	51.3	147 723	128 300	13.4	1.5	2 483	1 573	1 351	55 609	17.7	2.56	10.0	23.1
Logan	9.5	7.6	6.3	51.0	46 023	42 310	8.7	0.0	912	596	-281	17 956	12.6	2.53	9.5	24.8
Lorain	9.0	6.6	5.9	50.9	286 768	271 126	5.0	0.7	4 808	3 025	464	105 836	10.2	2.61	12.6	23.6
Lucas	8.2	6.7	6.4	51.9	453 348	462 361	-1.6	-0.4	8 371	5 621	-4 373	182 847	3.0	2.44	14.7	30.1
Madison	8.8	6.0	4.9	46.1	40 217	37 078	8.5	0.0	671	428	-227	13 672	14.0	2.62	9.9	22.3
Mahoning	9.3	8.8	8.9	52.2	254 958	264 806	-2.7	-1.0	3 883	3 987	-2 428	102 587	1.4	2.44	14.1	29.1
Marion	9.2	7.2	6.2	48.3	66 014	64 274	3.0	-0.3	1 034	866	-348	24 578	4.7	2.50	11.4	25.1
Medina	9.2	5.7	4.8	50.7	155 698	122 354	23.5	3.0	2 453	1 330	3 435	54 542	30.5	2.74	7.8	18.9
Meigs	10.6	7.9	6.8	51.4	22 987	22 987	0.4	-0.4	358	315	-120	9 234	6.6	2.47	10.0	25.0
Mercer	8.2	7.5	7.0	50.1	40 899	39 443	3.8	-0.1	750	431	-333	14 756	10.1	2.74	7.4	22.7
Miami	10.2	7.1	6.2	51.0	99 351	93 184	6.1	0.5	1 588	1 137	84	38 437	11.2	2.54	9.7	23.2
Monroe	12.0	8.8	7.5	50.6	15 163	15 497	-2.0	-0.1	194	262	56	6 021	4.6	2.50	8.1	24.0
Montgomery	9.2	7.3	6.4	52.0	554 232	573 809	-2.6	-0.9	10 086	7 159	-7 708	229 229	1.3	2.37	13.8	30.4
Morgan	10.9	8.6	7.0	50.9	14 891	14 194	5.0	0.0	222	221	-4	5 890	13.9	2.50	9.9	25.5
Morrow	9.8	6.6	4.9	50.2	32 674	27 749	14.0	3.3	500	316	849	11 499	19.1	2.72	8.1	19.0
Muskingum	9.3	7.5	6.8	52.1	84 900	82 068	3.1	0.4	1 430	1 155	73	32 518	5.7	2.53	12.0	24.9
Noble	8.6	7.3	5.7	43.3	14 038	11 336	24.0	-0.1	163	122	-56	4 546	9.9	2.61	7.7	24.3

1. No spouse present.

STATE County	Births, average 1997–1999 Total	Rate[1]	Deaths, average 1997–1999 Number Total	Infant[2]	Rate Total[1]	Infant[3]	Physicians,[4] 2000 Number	Rate[5]	Hospitals,[4] 1998 Number	Beds Number	Rate[5]	Medicare enrollees 2000	Serious crimes known to police, 2000[6] Total Number	Rate[7]
	32	33	34	35	36	37	38	39	40	41	42	43	44	45
NORTH DAKOTA—Cont'd														
Ward	956	16.3	455	NA	7.8	NA	172	293	3	768	1 309	8 291	1 444	2 456
Wells	40	7.7	91	NA	17.6	NA	5	98	1	149	2 865	1 421	31	692
Williams	230	11.4	212	NA	10.6	NA	43	218	2	128	635	3 769	328	1 660
OHIO	151 021	13.5	106 584	1 218	9.5	8.1	23 939	211	188	39 924	356	1 701 227	458 874	4 042
Adams	375	13.1	302	NA	10.6	NA	18	66	1	64	224	4 969	NA	NA
Allen	1 489	13.9	1 074	11	10.0	7.2	203	187	3	581	542	16 941	5 056	4 827
Ashland	647	12.4	503	NA	9.7	NA	49	93	1	65	124	7 562	110	221
Ashtabula	1 329	12.9	1 089	9	10.6	7.0	99	96	3	280	271	17 324	NA	NA
Athens	618	10.1	473	NA	7.7	NA	89	143	2	150	244	7 458	NA	NA
Auglaize	605	12.9	454	NA	9.6	NA	32	69	1	122	259	8 150	NA	NA
Belmont	724	10.3	929	6	13.3	8.7	82	117	3	391	565	14 081	456	724
Brown	540	13.2	393	NA	9.6	NA	37	88	1	58	142	5 569	NA	NA
Butler	4 510	13.7	2 550	41	7.7	9.0	381	114	5	792	240	41 185	14 557	4 589
Carroll	325	11.2	259	NA	8.9	NA	18	62	0	0	0	3 350	513	2 000
Champaign	489	12.8	349	NA	9.1	NA	17	44	1	73	191	5 446	1 033	2 781
Clark	1 884	12.9	1 618	17	11.1	9.2	202	140	2	464	319	24 239	7 538	5 218
Clermont	2 629	14.9	1 249	22	7.1	8.4	134	75	1	151	86	16 179	4 446	2 568
Clinton	549	13.7	355	NA	8.9	NA	56	138	1	81	203	6 017	992	2 447
Columbiana	1 380	12.4	1 164	12	10.5	8.7	118	105	2	361	324	19 685	NA	NA
Coshocton	435	12.0	421	NA	11.7	NA	30	82	1	151	418	6 032	845	2 305
Crawford	602	12.8	518	NA	11.0	NA	53	113	3	242	513	8 320	NA	NA
Cuyahoga	18 923	13.7	15 076	185	10.9	9.8	5 559	399	23	7 398	536	237 427	46 840	4 480
Darke	678	12.5	536	NA	9.9	NA	31	58	1	92	170	8 486	852	1 691
Defiance	549	13.8	333	NA	8.4	NA	60	152	2	111	279	5 778	NA	NA
Delaware	1 315	13.9	555	10	5.9	7.3	124	113	1	110	119	8 769	2 369	2 154
Erie	952	12.2	808	7	10.3	7.4	157	197	2	444	567	13 493	3 466	4 357
Fairfield	1 612	13.0	932	8	7.5	5.2	158	129	1	219	177	15 289	NA	NA
Fayette	378	13.3	345	NA	12.1	NA	22	77	1	44	154	4 325	1 216	4 277
Franklin	15 914	15.6	8 017	147	7.8	9.2	2 891	270	11	3 872	379	122 467	77 670	7 364
Fulton	575	13.7	360	NA	8.6	NA	24	57	1	86	205	6 497	754	1 792
Gallia	392	11.8	319	NA	9.6	NA	86	277	1	269	805	5 344	NA	NA
Geauga	1 188	13.4	620	NA	7.0	NA	137	151	1	122	137	9 563	NA	NA
Greene	1 676	11.4	1 128	8	7.6	4.6	293	198	1	210	143	15 079	5 769	3 901
Guernsey	530	12.9	448	NA	11.0	NA	64	157	1	141	344	7 243	NA	NA
Hamilton	12 054	14.2	8 391	122	9.9	10.1	3 066	363	12	4 114	485	134 453	37 331	4 770
Hancock	934	13.5	613	NA	8.9	NA	109	153	1	150	218	9 339	NA	NA
Hardin	408	12.9	312	NA	9.8	NA	19	59	1	51	161	4 753	NA	NA
Harrison	183	11.4	195	NA	12.1	NA	13	82	1	48	298	3 261	153	965
Henry	384	12.9	271	NA	9.1	NA	15	51	1	44	147	4 612	810	3 045
Highland	568	14.0	420	NA	10.4	NA	35	86	2	95	235	6 516	NA	NA
Hocking	349	12.0	276	NA	9.5	NA	20	71	1	91	314	4 058	551	1 951
Holmes	851	22.5	257	NA	6.8	NA	25	64	1	55	145	2 998	259	728
Huron	905	15.0	508	NA	8.4	NA	60	101	3	212	352	9 732	1 223	2 086
Jackson	435	13.3	346	NA	10.6	NA	25	77	1	49	150	5 220	NA	NA
Jefferson	776	10.4	1 000	9	13.4	12.0	95	129	2	374	502	16 165	NA	NA
Knox	617	11.6	536	NA	10.1	NA	45	83	1	117	219	8 365	NA	NA
Lake	2 705	12.0	2 008	17	8.9	6.2	347	153	2	339	151	35 715	NA	NA
Lawrence	795	12.4	702	NA	10.9	NA	41	66	1	183	284	11 206	NA	NA
Licking	1 807	13.2	1 234	13	9.0	7.0	138	95	1	185	135	18 847	3 923	3 019
Logan	631	13.6	457	NA	9.9	NA	47	102	1	87	188	7 225	968	2 104
Lorain	3 800	13.5	2 435	31	8.6	8.2	392	138	5	970	344	39 407	NA	NA
Lucas	6 580	14.7	4 495	47	10.0	7.2	1 455	320	8	2 676	597	67 425	28 635	6 511
Madison	514	12.4	342	NA	8.3	NA	23	57	1	107	257	5 460	NA	NA
Mahoning	3 031	11.9	3 162	39	12.4	12.9	598	232	4	1 284	503	51 620	NA	NA
Marion	837	12.8	673	NA	10.3	NA	126	190	2	233	360	10 645	2 712	4 096
Medina	1 863	12.9	1 026	8	7.1	4.5	157	104	3	198	137	17 484	NA	NA
Meigs	280	11.7	280	NA	11.7	NA	15	65	1	69	287	3 778	NA	NA
Mercer	612	14.9	349	NA	8.5	NA	53	130	1	87	211	6 556	NA	NA
Miami	1 240	12.6	874	NA	8.9	NA	138	140	2	287	292	15 005	1 795	2 297
Monroe	150	9.8	188	NA	12.2	NA	6	40	0	0	0	2 746	NA	NA
Montgomery	7 731	13.8	5 542	60	9.9	7.8	1 548	277	8	2 957	530	93 099	27 941	6 246
Morgan	173	11.9	168	NA	11.6	NA	3	20	0	0	0	2 270	205	1 376
Morrow	402	12.7	236	NA	7.5	NA	8	25	1	66	210	3 523	165	623
Muskingum	1 155	13.7	892	8	10.5	6.6	141	167	2	511	605	14 654	NA	NA
Noble	135	10.3	107	NA	8.1	NA	4	28	0	0	0	1 697	72	512

1. Per 1,000 estimated resident population, average 1997–1999.   2. Deaths of infants under 1 year old.   3. Deaths of infants under 1 year old per 1,000 live births.   4. Data subject to copyright.   5. Per 100,000 resident population as of July 1 of the year shown.   6. Data for serious crimes have not been adjusted for underreporting; this may affect comparability between geographic areas and over time.   7. Per 100,000 population estimated by the FBI.

Table B. States and Counties — Crime, Education, Money Income, and Poverty

	Serious crimes known to police, 2000[1] (cont'd) Rate[2]		Education						Money income 1989				Income and poverty, 1998 Percent below poverty level			
			School enrollment and attainment, 1990				Local government expenditures, fiscal 1999[5]			Households						
			Enrollment[3]		Attainment[4] (percent)						Median					
STATE County	Violent	Property	Total	Percent private	High school graduate or more	Bachelor's degree or more	Total current expenditures (mil dol)	Current expenditures per student (dollars)	Per capita[6] (dollars)	Dollars	Percent change, 1979–1989 (constant 1989 dollars)	Percent with $100,000 or more	Median household income	All persons	Persons under 18	Persons 5–17 in families
	46	47	48	49	50	51	52	53	54	55	56	57	58	59	60	61
NORTH DAKOTA—Cont'd																
Ward	97	2 359	16 826	6.6	82.8	19.0	51.6	5 032	10 708	22 996	-11.6	1.4	34 219	12.0	16.7	14.2
Wells	67	625	1 200	2.8	63.2	11.3	6.1	5 871	9 957	18 568	-9.0	1.1	29 554	14.6	20.5	17.2
Williams	71	1 589	5 491	5.4	76.8	14.3	22.2	5 625	11 165	23 249	-26.1	1.5	32 806	14.2	18.9	15.8
OHIO	334	3 708	2 798 226	16.4	75.7	17.0	12 207.1	6 627	13 461	28 706	-3.5	2.9	38 726	10.7	16.4	14.4
Adams	NA	NA	6 283	3.0	58.4	5.2	29.5	5 450	8 407	16 318	-8.1	0.9	26 372	19.1	26.2	24.4
Allen	432	4 394	28 723	17.2	76.1	11.4	112.4	6 019	11 830	27 166	-6.8	1.9	36 857	11.5	17.0	14.9
Ashland	12	209	12 557	22.7	76.0	13.0	48.5	6 170	11 623	26 668	-4.6	1.8	38 438	8.2	13.0	10.9
Ashtabula	NA	NA	23 643	10.4	72.4	9.0	111.3	6 027	10 672	24 126	-16.0	1.2	33 669	13.2	20.0	17.7
Athens	NA	NA	26 587	2.2	74.6	23.4	63.2	6 954	9 170	19 169	-3.4	1.5	31 125	18.4	23.5	22.7
Auglaize	NA	NA	11 176	10.0	76.5	9.8	50.3	5 405	12 398	30 090	2.8	1.8	41 533	6.0	8.6	7.5
Belmont	49	675	16 446	9.8	72.3	9.0	60.6	6 063	10 329	20 987	-24.3	0.9	28 631	15.9	24.2	21.2
Brown	NA	NA	8 495	6.8	64.9	7.4	46.8	5 528	10 498	25 286	0.6	1.3	34 815	11.1	15.5	14.8
Butler	329	4 260	81 500	12.7	76.0	18.7	321.3	5 949	13 947	32 440	-1.2	3.3	45 339	7.7	11.3	9.2
Carroll	113	1 887	6 398	8.7	71.5	7.9	19.1	4 682	10 693	25 787	-6.4	0.9	36 143	10.9	16.3	14.6
Champaign	245	2 536	8 821	10.1	75.4	9.7	44.7	5 823	12 539	31 198	12.9	1.2	42 582	7.9	12.8	10.3
Clark	615	4 603	37 618	14.6	73.4	12.2	155.0	6 191	12 348	27 743	-1.7	1.7	37 252	12.1	19.2	17.6
Clermont	144	2 424	38 213	12.8	72.8	14.5	167.4	5 807	13 338	32 465	-3.6	2.5	46 632	6.8	11.1	8.8
Clinton	111	2 336	9 126	11.8	74.3	11.6	46.9	5 577	11 736	27 157	4.8	1.8	39 149	8.9	13.6	11.4
Columbiana	NA	NA	25 882	7.5	71.8	8.5	110.7	6 063	10 567	23 368	-16.6	1.2	32 984	13.0	19.3	17.5
Coshocton	52	2 253	7 948	8.4	71.3	8.1	36.9	5 713	10 685	23 617	-11.1	1.5	33 347	11.8	18.7	15.7
Crawford	NA	NA	11 499	11.8	73.8	9.3	48.6	5 894	11 401	24 981	-7.7	1.2	34 542	10.4	16.7	14.1
Cuyahoga	666	3 814	344 407	25.7	74.0	20.1	1 611.6	8 023	14 912	28 595	-5.3	4.0	38 522	13.5	22.2	18.8
Darke	141	1 550	12 837	6.7	73.5	8.8	52.2	5 563	11 693	27 640	1.6	1.5	38 270	7.7	11.2	9.8
Defiance	NA	NA	10 477	14.2	76.8	12.5	39.0	5 319	12 545	31 505	-3.7	1.6	42 751	7.2	11.1	9.7
Delaware	87	2 067	18 442	23.4	84.4	26.4	87.1	6 266	17 437	37 896	13.1	8.0	60 634	4.6	7.8	5.4
Erie	308	4 049	18 429	15.2	76.2	13.8	111.3	7 759	13 833	30 470	-5.0	2.7	39 787	9.0	14.6	12.5
Fairfield	NA	NA	25 629	11.1	78.8	15.5	122.9	5 288	13 609	31 284	1.6	3.1	44 396	6.7	11.0	8.9
Fayette	130	4 147	6 080	6.0	65.3	8.5	27.2	5 127	10 300	22 704	-3.1	1.0	34 412	11.5	16.8	16.0
Franklin	636	6 728	263 166	15.2	81.0	26.6	1 154.2	6 907	14 907	30 375	6.1	3.5	41 267	11.0	17.1	15.2
Fulton	71	1 720	10 059	9.2	78.3	10.3	65.6	6 952	12 467	31 890	2.0	1.6	42 710	6.0	8.7	7.7
Gallia	NA	NA	8 017	8.9	64.2	10.9	35.4	6 478	9 711	20 972	-13.2	1.3	29 503	18.1	25.2	25.1
Geauga	NA	NA	21 009	26.2	82.0	25.9	83.4	6 468	17 587	41 113	0.7	9.4	54 104	5.0	8.4	6.8
Greene	131	3 770	42 519	18.1	82.4	26.0	151.1	6 358	14 384	35 116	3.2	3.3	48 664	7.2	11.2	9.7
Guernsey	NA	NA	9 358	6.6	71.4	9.2	37.5	5 834	9 929	21 143	-11.5	0.9	28 982	15.3	22.7	20.9
Hamilton	459	4 311	225 274	24.8	75.6	23.7	915.0	7 156	15 354	29 498	0.9	4.7	40 141	11.3	17.4	14.7
Hancock	NA	NA	16 673	17.4	82.9	18.7	73.1	6 161	14 239	31 897	4.0	2.5	42 305	7.5	10.8	9.6
Hardin	NA	NA	9 170	26.6	74.0	11.6	36.3	5 804	10 957	24 589	-7.6	1.3	35 542	10.8	15.5	14.4
Harrison	44	921	3 959	4.9	69.8	7.0	15.1	5 263	9 146	19 943	-22.4	0.6	28 858	14.3	21.5	20.2
Henry	143	2 902	7 223	12.3	75.4	10.3	38.0	7 037	12 115	31 032	0.9	1.1	41 524	6.3	9.2	8.6
Highland	NA	NA	8 717	4.6	66.5	8.2	41.1	4 977	9 848	21 505	-1.6	1.5	31 482	11.4	14.9	15.0
Hocking	81	1 870	5 737	4.9	67.8	8.1	21.5	5 039	10 265	22 727	-4.9	1.1	32 422	12.5	17.9	17.7
Holmes	65	664	7 224	23.2	46.9	6.6	23.4	5 026	9 191	25 448	1.3	2.1	34 794	10.5	13.7	13.8
Huron	49	2 036	13 876	13.4	74.1	9.4	64.5	5 483	11 552	27 401	-7.0	1.5	38 242	8.9	13.5	11.8
Jackson	NA	NA	7 474	5.4	60.9	7.9	31.3	5 219	9 228	18 298	-12.5	0.9	30 110	16.2	22.5	21.7
Jefferson	NA	NA	19 180	19.1	71.9	8.8	75.1	6 386	11 001	22 142	-27.3	1.1	30 507	14.8	22.7	21.1
Knox	NA	NA	12 476	25.5	75.2	12.8	51.5	6 114	10 688	24 701	-0.4	1.5	36 850	10.1	15.6	13.5
Lake	NA	NA	53 639	20.1	81.1	17.5	254.9	7 288	15 465	35 605	-5.0	3.2	45 871	5.7	9.2	7.7
Lawrence	NA	NA	15 207	4.2	65.9	8.2	68.5	5 956	9 336	19 454	-22.5	0.9	27 329	19.6	27.1	27.0
Licking	129	2 890	31 787	16.0	76.4	13.0	142.3	5 910	12 864	29 606	-0.3	2.3	40 896	8.9	14.0	12.2
Logan	187	1 917	9 826	5.5	74.5	8.9	49.5	6 226	11 741	26 857	8.3	1.4	39 105	9.1	13.0	12.3
Lorain	NA	NA	73 473	16.7	75.3	12.3	294.1	6 478	12 733	31 098	-8.9	2.0	41 518	10.4	16.1	14.0
Lucas	577	5 934	124 450	20.1	76.2	17.0	491.1	7 050	13 778	28 245	-4.9	3.3	38 833	13.4	20.5	17.9
Madison	NA	NA	8 756	10.4	69.5	9.0	45.1	6 360	12 053	29 935	2.2	1.6	41 616	8.0	11.4	10.7
Mahoning	NA	NA	66 139	13.7	74.6	14.0	255.1	6 511	11 668	24 062	-17.9	1.9	32 821	14.1	21.5	18.9
Marion	104	3 991	15 485	9.7	73.8	9.9	76.8	6 381	11 547	26 330	-7.4	1.6	36 250	11.7	17.4	15.8
Medina	NA	NA	33 184	13.0	82.4	18.0	171.7	6 212	14 852	38 083	-0.4	3.7	50 869	4.9	7.3	6.1
Meigs	NA	NA	5 587	5.0	64.0	7.3	22.4	5 638	8 644	17 707	-17.1	0.7	26 798	19.3	24.6	27.4
Mercer	NA	NA	9 731	5.8	75.5	8.6	56.5	5 627	11 673	29 618	-3.5	1.6	39 894	6.6	9.2	8.3
Miami	99	2 199	23 538	11.7	76.6	14.1	112.2	6 366	13 896	31 425	5.0	2.7	42 640	7.0	11.1	9.5
Monroe	NA	NA	3 685	8.7	69.4	6.8	17.7	5 971	9 101	20 413	-23.2	0.4	29 516	16.5	23.5	22.6
Montgomery	600	5 646	149 601	20.1	77.8	20.0	616.8	7 279	14 495	30 111	1.9	3.0	38 726	10.9	17.5	14.5
Morgan	107	1 269	3 450	3.7	71.6	7.4	14.9	5 936	9 373	21 396	-6.7	0.6	30 886	16.2	24.6	21.9
Morrow	42	581	7 188	6.3	71.3	7.2	28.7	5 131	10 581	27 318	-0.2	1.1	37 895	9.0	11.9	13.0
Muskingum	NA	NA	20 345	13.4	71.1	10.1	98.9	5 962	10 844	23 967	-2.8	1.4	32 207	14.1	21.0	19.8
Noble	21	491	2 537	1.2	69.9	5.6	12.3	4 910	9 028	21 617	-10.7	0.5	30 442	13.7	14.7	18.1

1. Data for serious crimes have not been adjusted for underreporting; this may affect comparability between geographic areas and over time. 2. Per 100,000 population estimated by the FBI. 3. All persons 3 years old and over enrolled in nursery school through college. 4. Persons 25 years old and over. 5. Elementary and secondary education expenditures, local government fiscal years ending between July 1, 1998 and June 30, 1999. 6. Based on population enumerated as of April 1, 1990.

Table B. States and Counties — **Personal Income**

STATE County	Personal income, 1999												
			Per capita[1]					Transfer payments					
									Government payments to individuals				
	Total (mil dol)	Percent change, 1998–1999	Dollars	Rank	Wages and salaries[2] (mil dol)	Proprietor's income (mil dol)	Dividends, interest, and rent (mil dol)	Total (mil dol)	Total (mil dol)	Social Security (mil dol)	Medical payments (mil dol)	Income mainte- nance (mil dol)	Unemploy- ment insurance (mil dol)
	62	63	64	65	66	67	68	69	70	71	72	73	74
NORTH DAKOTA—Cont'd													
Ward	1 400	2.3	23 989	860	911	95	271	200	191	75	68	13	3
Wells	111	-2.4	21 766	1 426	44	7	38	26	25	12	10	1	0
Williams	430	1.7	21 736	1 438	212	42	105	83	79	37	27	5	2
OHIO	305 855	3.9	27 171	X	198 097	18 618	60 181	42 788	40 367	16 976	15 657	3 592	665
Adams	467	3.0	16 278	2 864	181	40	88	122	116	39	49	19	3
Allen	2 526	4.9	23 631	934	1 909	110	547	406	383	177	135	34	6
Ashland	1 078	1.9	20 739	1 764	593	49	240	163	152	77	50	8	3
Ashtabula	2 241	5.0	21 685	1 461	1 037	120	362	460	438	164	193	31	8
Athens	1 121	1.1	18 202	2 497	619	60	226	203	190	59	73	28	3
Auglaize	1 183	3.9	25 071	658	646	70	265	156	146	69	56	7	2
Belmont	1 465	4.4	20 560	1 822	608	85	320	346	330	144	128	28	5
Brown	861	5.3	20 699	1 776	212	58	127	145	136	54	57	11	3
Butler	8 823	5.1	26 456	472	4 450	375	1 619	1 042	970	438	354	72	14
Carroll	634	3.4	21 652	1 471	182	65	105	101	95	45	34	7	2
Champaign	917	2.0	23 769	904	333	57	158	132	123	56	46	8	2
Clark	3 594	2.8	24 791	705	1 984	138	647	617	586	229	244	53	8
Clermont	4 708	7.1	26 340	483	1 704	224	645	523	485	227	167	32	11
Clinton	1 056	4.3	25 949	523	862	51	181	137	128	58	46	9	2
Columbiana	2 355	4.2	21 159	1 614	1 001	170	404	460	436	194	171	34	7
Coshocton	765	2.9	21 130	1 621	420	56	157	143	135	61	52	10	3
Crawford	1 031	1.2	21 924	1 379	515	50	219	189	179	83	63	14	4
Cuyahoga	44 226	3.1	32 241	145	33 491	3 819	9 817	6 415	6 119	2 383	2 554	659	86
Darke	1 280	2.6	23 678	921	560	105	243	182	170	86	58	10	3
Defiance	983	3.2	24 793	704	722	58	175	128	120	61	38	8	2
Delaware	3 633	9.6	35 042	81	1 096	168	849	241	219	104	71	11	3
Erie	2 197	4.3	28 210	305	1 346	145	461	307	290	136	106	17	5
Fairfield	3 384	6.5	26 704	440	1 009	145	579	368	341	159	122	22	5
Fayette	585	2.2	20 597	1 811	288	16	111	106	100	40	43	9	2
Franklin	31 677	4.9	30 820	183	27 242	2 087	5 256	3 353	3 132	1 150	1 262	336	42
Fulton	1 063	3.5	25 191	640	654	79	209	135	126	63	45	7	2
Gallia	646	4.1	19 438	2 161	366	30	124	172	164	47	83	20	3
Geauga	3 049	5.3	34 027	106	1 081	174	668	249	230	122	70	8	4
Greene	4 044	4.1	27 114	408	2 619	156	830	427	396	172	125	29	5
Guernsey	763	2.5	18 641	2 380	398	52	149	178	169	67	71	15	5
Hamilton	28 535	3.5	33 953	109	24 049	2 163	7 085	3 337	3 155	1 277	1 256	299	39
Hancock	1 950	5.9	28 091	324	1 429	81	406	212	197	103	62	11	3
Hardin	631	2.8	19 950	2 006	277	49	106	107	100	46	37	8	1
Harrison	300	3.1	18 669	2 376	106	22	61	72	69	30	26	6	1
Henry	712	2.9	23 833	889	361	48	132	102	96	46	36	4	2
Highland	774	2.7	18 847	2 333	319	59	130	150	142	60	55	12	2
Hocking	559	5.0	19 174	2 238	206	27	85	109	102	40	42	9	2
Holmes	674	4.9	17 591	2 628	416	100	118	85	77	30	33	7	1
Huron	1 375	2.9	22 720	1 160	874	79	248	207	194	84	65	12	6
Jackson	608	4.5	18 628	2 386	307	50	100	134	127	48	46	17	3
Jefferson	1 526	1.8	20 720	1 768	791	77	333	389	373	161	144	34	5
Knox	1 124	1.3	20 850	1 716	546	83	219	214	202	82	92	13	3
Lake	6 650	3.9	29 276	245	3 526	271	1 231	820	771	379	280	29	14
Lawrence	1 138	3.0	17 691	2 602	345	57	172	308	294	103	116	44	4
Licking	3 670	7.7	26 891	425	1 725	197	624	458	428	193	153	31	8
Logan	1 170	5.2	24 988	673	736	78	170	161	150	67	57	11	2
Lorain	7 253	4.3	25 712	552	3 787	298	1 255	1 010	949	417	352	78	21
Lucas	12 216	3.8	27 361	387	8 855	704	2 325	1 948	1 852	680	775	213	32
Madison	901	2.8	21 782	1 419	417	56	146	121	112	48	45	8	1
Mahoning	6 086	2.6	24 095	843	3 412	311	1 281	1 253	1 199	508	475	114	19
Marion	1 480	2.4	22 136	1 313	905	64	263	253	238	100	86	23	3
Medina	4 264	6.4	28 954	262	1 733	181	733	433	401	187	150	17	8
Meigs	394	2.7	16 426	2 838	159	41	57	103	98	35	38	15	3
Mercer	959	-1.3	23 376	992	434	121	201	135	126	65	41	6	4
Miami	2 692	4.0	27 271	397	1 422	113	486	330	309	154	106	17	5
Monroe	274	2.6	17 702	2 600	170	15	51	63	60	26	22	6	2
Montgomery	15 908	3.0	28 113	319	12 064	688	3 405	2 185	2 064	869	799	194	26
Morgan	258	-0.9	17 794	2 577	122	16	49	61	58	23	22	6	2
Morrow	571	4.3	17 776	2 580	162	42	84	91	84	40	28	7	2
Muskingum	1 870	4.3	22 055	1 347	1 116	106	328	335	317	138	114	35	7
Noble	208	2.5	14 028	3 048	99	14	39	44	41	18	15	4	2

1. Based on the resident population estimated as of July 1 of the year shown.   2. Includes other labor income.

Table B. States and Counties — Earnings, Social Security, and Housing

STATE County	Earnings, 1999									Social Security beneficiaries, December 2000		Supplemental Security Income recipients, December 2000	Housing units, 1990	
	Total (mil dol)	Farm	Goods-related[1]		Service-related and other[2]				Govern-ment	Number	Rate[3]		Total	Percent change, 1980–1990
			Total	Manu-facturing	Total	Retail trade	Finance, insur-ance, and real estate	Services						
	75	76	77	78	79	80	81	82	83	84	85	86	87	88

NORTH DAKOTA—Cont'd

STATE County	75	76	77	78	79	80	81	82	83	84	85	86	87	88
Ward	1 007	-0.7	9.7	2.1	54.2	10.8	4.6	25.9	36.8	9 026	154	676	23 585	9.6
Wells	50	-1.1	D	0.7	D	13.5	5.8	27.4	17.1	1 436	281	94	2 869	-0.6
Williams	254	4.2	19.6	2.2	59.0	11.8	4.3	28.7	17.2	4 267	216	290	10 180	13.7
OHIO	216 714	0.3	30.8	24.7	54.3	9.4	6.9	25.3	14.6	1 912 006	168	240 002	4 371 945	6.4
Adams	222	1.1	D	18.9	D	13.0	3.3	14.4	21.8	5 500	201	1 731	10 237	12.3
Allen	2 019	-0.3	35.1	29.1	50.5	9.5	3.0	25.6	14.7	19 685	181	2 444	42 758	2.1
Ashland	642	-0.2	D	38.3	D	9.7	2.4	22.2	16.3	8 833	168	479	18 139	6.2
Ashtabula	1 157	0.2	41.6	34.4	42.4	9.9	2.8	19.6	15.8	18 779	183	2 372	41 214	1.7
Athens	680	0.2	7.7	3.6	38.2	11.5	3.2	17.9	54.0	7 905	127	2 086	21 737	9.4
Auglaize	716	1.3	55.8	48.2	29.8	7.7	2.7	11.3	13.1	7 780	167	368	16 907	9.1
Belmont	693	-0.3	23.7	10.4	56.1	17.8	4.5	22.6	20.5	16 254	231	1 962	30 575	-4.0
Brown	270	-0.3	31.0	23.1	43.7	10.2	2.9	19.9	25.6	6 891	163	847	13 720	15.8
Butler	4 825	0.1	33.8	24.9	51.9	9.6	7.8	19.9	14.4	49 035	147	5 208	110 353	19.3
Carroll	247	13.7	38.7	31.7	34.7	9.8	2.7	12.1	12.9	5 218	181	310	11 536	11.8
Champaign	389	2.2	D	42.2	D	9.2	3.6	15.4	16.1	6 485	167	488	14 030	12.2
Clark	2 123	0.1	D	34.1	D	11.1	3.5	21.2	14.0	26 815	185	3 584	58 377	3.5
Clermont	1 928	-0.2	D	20.1	D	12.3	7.2	25.6	13.4	26 177	147	2 100	55 315	23.6
Clinton	913	-0.3	D	19.8	D	7.5	4.0	10.7	11.7	7 200	178	659	13 740	6.8
Columbiana	1 171	1.4	34.7	26.6	47.8	10.3	3.4	20.6	16.1	21 824	195	2 652	44 035	2.3
Coshocton	476	1.6	41.6	35.4	44.9	7.5	2.5	18.7	11.8	7 147	195	719	14 964	5.2
Crawford	565	0.1	D	43.8	D	8.6	4.6	15.9	13.4	9 328	199	897	19 514	-0.1
Cuyahoga	37 310	0.0	24.4	20.0	63.0	7.3	9.7	32.4	12.5	256 176	184	39 700	604 538	1.3
Darke	665	2.2	D	34.5	D	8.8	3.9	17.4	11.3	9 926	186	650	20 338	1.6
Defiance	780	0.5	58.7	53.2	D	8.5	3.2	12.8	9.1	6 726	170	596	14 737	3.4
Delaware	1 264	0.4	27.3	16.3	57.9	12.1	8.9	25.3	14.4	12 361	112	566	24 377	29.6
Erie	1 491	0.4	41.8	36.1	44.5	9.5	2.7	24.3	13.4	14 891	187	1 179	32 827	4.8
Fairfield	1 154	-0.3	27.8	19.5	49.7	13.1	6.4	21.7	22.7	18 614	152	1 676	39 014	15.1
Fayette	304	-3.0	D	33.8	D	19.9	3.4	14.0	17.6	4 850	171	732	10 816	4.2
Franklin	29 329	0.0	17.1	11.9	65.8	12.2	12.1	28.3	17.1	132 780	124	22 709	405 418	16.8
Fulton	733	2.1	D	48.6	D	7.0	2.6	13.2	10.7	6 906	164	349	14 095	5.7
Gallia	397	-0.2	14.9	10.6	D	12.3	3.4	12.1	18.7	6 174	199	1 724	12 564	9.8
Geauga	1 254	0.1	43.3	32.9	46.1	7.6	3.7	22.5	10.5	13 181	145	438	27 922	15.0
Greene	2 775	0.0	11.0	7.5	37.4	9.0	3.1	20.1	51.5	21 300	144	1 693	50 238	11.5
Guernsey	450	-0.4	28.0	20.8	49.3	11.7	3.5	22.2	23.0	8 347	205	1 262	17 262	3.7
Hamilton	26 212	0.0	27.5	22.0	61.8	7.5	8.8	29.3	10.7	140 422	166	20 890	361 421	5.3
Hancock	1 510	0.2	49.3	37.4	42.3	10.8	3.7	18.5	8.1	11 450	161	705	26 107	6.1
Hardin	325	5.1	D	36.1	D	8.5	2.6	19.6	15.4	5 369	168	528	11 976	-0.2
Harrison	128	-0.2	D	17.7	D	7.6	4.8	15.9	19.4	3 513	222	405	7 301	3.3
Henry	409	0.9	D	37.2	D	8.0	2.7	12.8	17.4	5 255	180	298	11 000	1.8
Highland	379	-1.1	41.8	31.5	40.7	11.8	4.7	14.9	18.6	7 658	187	1 007	14 842	6.8
Hocking	233	-1.6	D	31.6	D	9.6	2.3	13.8	25.5	4 987	177	768	10 481	9.4
Holmes	516	3.2	D	39.0	D	10.3	2.7	14.2	9.3	3 715	95	261	10 007	13.9
Huron	953	1.6	50.7	40.9	37.3	8.2	2.2	13.3	10.4	9 554	161	906	21 382	5.9
Jackson	358	2.8	D	36.2	D	12.6	3.6	12.2	14.3	6 102	187	1 489	12 452	6.8
Jefferson	867	0.1	D	23.9	D	10.7	2.9	26.0	15.3	17 584	238	2 463	33 911	-4.9
Knox	629	2.5	39.7	27.3	42.0	9.0	3.1	22.4	15.8	9 693	178	868	18 508	7.2
Lake	3 797	1.8	D	34.2	D	10.4	4.2	19.6	12.2	39 976	176	1 685	83 194	10.7
Lawrence	402	-0.2	D	17.2	D	13.5	3.2	17.8	29.3	12 796	205	3 787	24 788	5.2
Licking	1 922	1.3	32.5	23.8	51.7	13.2	7.5	20.4	14.5	22 789	157	2 221	50 032	11.2
Logan	815	2.0	49.7	43.5	38.9	7.6	3.0	17.6	9.4	7 715	168	596	19 473	5.0
Lorain	4 086	0.7	D	37.7	D	8.6	3.1	18.9	15.6	46 069	162	4 601	99 937	4.2
Lucas	9 559	0.3	29.8	23.0	55.7	9.4	4.8	28.8	14.2	75 412	166	14 150	191 388	3.5
Madison	472	-1.3	D	28.5	D	8.4	2.5	16.9	27.3	5 730	142	470	12 621	11.1
Mahoning	3 723	0.3	20.5	12.7	63.0	13.4	6.2	29.9	16.3	56 511	219	7 352	107 915	-0.6
Marion	968	0.0	34.2	29.0	43.3	9.6	3.3	17.0	22.4	11 736	177	1 839	25 149	-0.6
Medina	1 914	0.6	33.8	25.1	53.2	11.2	5.9	23.6	12.4	20 807	138	850	43 330	14.0
Meigs	200	8.7	D	2.7	D	11.4	2.5	13.0	17.0	4 344	188	1 006	9 795	5.4
Mercer	554	11.3	D	25.3	D	9.5	4.4	12.3	15.1	7 518	184	359	14 969	5.2
Miami	1 534	0.1	D	41.3	D	10.9	3.1	17.1	11.8	17 217	174	1 207	35 985	6.8
Monroe	184	-1.3	D	57.5	D	4.9	1.7	D	15.2	3 223	212	445	6 567	1.2
Montgomery	12 752	0.1	32.2	27.1	53.6	7.7	5.2	28.7	14.1	98 895	177	13 378	240 820	5.8
Morgan	138	1.3	D	D	D	6.4	2.6	D	16.4	2 887	194	440	6 681	8.9
Morrow	204	3.0	38.2	28.9	36.6	9.3	3.0	14.4	22.2	4 890	155	405	10 312	8.6
Muskingum	1 222	-0.2	31.9	24.0	54.3	13.8	3.1	23.3	14.0	16 541	196	2 551	33 029	3.5
Noble	113	-2.7	D	D	D	9.0	3.6	12.2	35.7	2 294	163	237	4 998	4.3

1. Covers mining, construction, and manufacturing.   2. Covers private sector earnings in agricultural services, forestry, and fisheries; transportation and public utilities; wholesale trade; retail trade; finance, insurance, and real estate; and services.   3. Per 1,000 resident population estimated as of July 1 of the year shown.

Table B. States and Counties — Housing, Labor Force, and Employment

STATE County	Housing units, 1990 (cont'd) Occupied units Owner-occupied Total	Percent	Median value[1]	Owner cost as a percent of income With a mort-gage	Without a mort-gage	Renter-occupied Median rent[2]	Rent as per-cent of income	Sub-stand-ard units[3] (percent)	Civilian labor force, 2001 Total	Percent change, 2000-2001	Unemployment Total	Rate[4]	Civilian employment, 1990[5] Total	Percent Professional, managerial, and technical	Precision production, craft, and repair
	89	90	91	92	93	94	95	96	97	98	99	100	101	102	103
NORTH DAKOTA—Cont'd															
Ward	21 485	59.7	54 200	21.0	12.9	322	24.8	1.9	28 781	0.1	849	2.9	23 571	26.2	9.4
Wells	2 406	74.7	29 100	17.5	14.3	229	24.4	2.0	2 377	-3.8	82	3.4	2 332	21.4	8.6
Williams	8 041	70.7	43 100	19.1	12.8	266	20.8	2.4	9 615	2.5	260	2.7	9 410	23.4	12.7
OHIO	4 087 546	67.5	63 500	18.2	12.5	379	25.3	2.2	5 857 254	1.3	251 321	4.3	4 931 357	28.5	11.6
Adams	9 192	73.2	36 900	19.9	13.3	275	33.3	8.3	11 547	0.1	1 079	9.3	8 699	17.6	15.3
Allen	39 408	71.7	52 100	15.7	11.9	346	24.8	2.1	51 541	-0.5	2 640	5.1	46 585	23.3	12.9
Ashland	17 101	74.0	53 600	16.6	12.0	337	23.7	2.8	26 435	2.0	1 208	4.6	22 062	22.5	12.7
Ashtabula	36 760	71.9	45 800	17.5	12.9	335	26.4	2.5	47 899	1.4	3 135	6.5	40 782	20.7	15.9
Athens	20 139	62.0	47 600	18.2	12.6	355	35.1	4.4	28 358	3.5	1 084	3.8	23 672	32.9	9.4
Auglaize	15 976	76.9	58 500	16.2	11.7	347	21.1	2.1	24 908	0.3	1 101	4.4	20 880	21.9	13.3
Belmont	28 161	73.8	42 100	17.8	12.3	285	26.9	2.4	32 545	0.7	1 326	4.1	26 979	23.6	14.3
Brown	12 379	76.0	49 200	18.0	13.3	303	23.9	6.0	20 704	1.9	1 316	6.4	15 042	18.0	17.1
Butler	104 535	69.2	73 000	18.9	12.3	415	25.8	2.0	196 184	3.1	6 341	3.2	137 316	30.0	11.4
Carroll	9 667	78.5	46 600	18.0	11.7	288	19.8	2.2	13 926	1.6	648	4.7	10 888	17.3	15.0
Champaign	13 253	73.9	55 400	15.7	12.5	348	20.9	2.5	20 205	2.2	926	4.6	17 277	19.8	14.5
Clark	55 198	69.1	54 900	16.9	12.6	361	26.3	2.2	70 161	2.0	3 699	5.3	65 055	25.8	12.5
Clermont	52 726	72.1	71 200	20.0	12.4	407	24.2	2.4	97 954	1.8	3 776	3.9	72 989	26.0	15.0
Clinton	13 038	67.7	52 200	16.9	12.6	350	24.9	2.8	26 140	1.4	749	2.9	16 268	21.8	13.3
Columbiana	40 775	75.0	42 600	18.0	12.5	306	26.4	2.0	51 543	-0.6	2 853	5.5	44 381	20.3	14.8
Coshocton	13 433	75.7	44 500	15.7	11.8	292	24.9	2.8	17 185	-1.3	1 035	6.0	14 824	18.3	12.4
Crawford	18 383	71.1	43 100	15.7	12.2	303	24.0	2.3	22 177	2.8	1 520	6.9	20 781	20.5	15.1
Cuyahoga	563 243	62.0	72 100	19.5	13.0	397	26.7	1.9	679 469	0.3	31 146	4.6	629 512	32.1	9.6
Darke	19 459	76.4	52 300	15.7	11.9	327	22.4	2.2	29 459	1.0	1 228	4.2	24 783	18.9	14.0
Defiance	14 070	78.4	53 300	16.4	11.8	364	23.2	2.1	21 504	1.6	1 099	5.1	18 586	20.3	14.8
Delaware	23 116	78.1	95 900	21.0	12.6	426	23.6	1.3	61 156	2.5	1 315	2.2	33 902	33.4	10.4
Erie	28 932	71.3	65 100	17.1	12.4	361	23.6	1.9	43 318	1.8	2 043	4.7	35 398	25.1	13.1
Fairfield	36 813	74.7	68 900	18.8	12.2	375	23.5	1.7	69 844	2.4	1 957	2.8	48 647	27.8	12.9
Fayette	10 221	64.9	43 800	17.4	12.6	316	25.5	3.0	16 586	8.1	604	3.6	11 906	17.0	11.5
Franklin	378 723	54.9	73 800	19.7	12.2	430	24.7	2.1	621 978	2.5	17 143	2.8	496 524	34.8	7.8
Fulton	13 504	78.5	59 700	17.0	12.3	387	22.3	2.0	23 765	0.8	1 019	4.3	18 618	20.5	15.1
Gallia	11 367	73.8	48 400	19.6	13.5	307	32.4	4.5	15 302	0.9	855	5.6	11 526	24.7	14.8
Geauga	26 906	85.7	107 700	20.4	12.5	453	23.1	3.1	48 142	0.5	1 523	3.2	39 815	34.4	13.6
Greene	48 351	69.4	78 200	18.5	11.7	434	25.4	2.1	73 797	1.3	2 530	3.4	62 830	37.3	10.2
Guernsey	14 894	73.0	38 600	18.0	12.6	279	26.9	3.0	18 869	-0.5	1 111	5.9	15 617	23.3	14.8
Hamilton	338 881	58.3	72 200	18.6	12.3	355	24.9	2.8	444 117	1.6	16 095	3.6	406 974	34.6	8.9
Hancock	24 642	74.2	63 300	16.5	11.7	366	22.6	1.6	43 207	1.1	1 366	3.2	31 675	27.5	12.6
Hardin	11 250	71.7	42 100	15.6	12.6	289	25.5	2.7	15 403	0.2	707	4.6	13 135	21.6	11.5
Harrison	6 111	75.7	33 300	19.2	12.3	277	28.7	3.8	6 700	1.4	312	4.7	5 727	18.3	15.2
Henry	10 401	78.4	55 200	16.1	12.8	336	19.8	1.7	15 973	1.0	822	5.1	13 445	20.1	15.5
Highland	13 230	72.9	42 200	19.9	13.3	306	26.1	5.2	18 714	0.1	994	5.3	14 491	18.4	14.5
Hocking	9 351	75.8	43 400	16.7	12.6	311	27.0	4.9	11 551	-1.8	768	6.6	10 328	18.4	16.5
Holmes	9 315	77.2	63 400	18.9	11.7	297	18.9	7.7	19 681	3.3	510	2.6	13 643	12.8	14.9
Huron	20 239	71.6	56 700	16.8	11.9	362	23.4	2.4	29 780	0.0	2 147	7.2	25 225	19.6	14.5
Jackson	11 260	73.4	39 400	20.4	13.6	283	30.3	5.6	14 411	0.2	1 044	7.2	10 408	21.9	13.3
Jefferson	31 311	73.5	42 900	15.8	12.6	289	26.6	2.1	29 239	1.1	1 559	5.3	29 528	20.8	16.5
Knox	17 230	72.2	49 100	19.0	12.5	321	24.0	2.3	26 613	2.4	997	3.7	21 118	24.0	11.4
Lake	80 421	75.8	74 200	18.6	12.4	475	24.1	1.1	127 485	0.9	5 360	4.2	109 281	29.7	14.1
Lawrence	22 899	72.2	43 700	17.0	12.7	299	31.3	4.4	26 737	-0.7	1 395	5.2	22 263	21.5	15.0
Licking	47 254	72.0	61 600	17.9	11.8	357	25.6	1.8	75 096	2.3	2 738	3.6	59 694	26.2	13.1
Logan	15 952	73.3	53 000	16.1	12.6	339	23.1	2.3	28 342	1.4	858	3.0	18 919	18.5	14.8
Lorain	96 064	71.9	66 100	18.5	12.3	378	24.6	2.4	143 003	0.9	8 051	5.6	122 333	25.4	13.8
Lucas	177 500	65.0	57 300	17.4	13.6	390	26.3	1.9	232 045	0.7	11 535	5.0	204 890	29.0	10.7
Madison	11 990	70.2	62 300	19.3	12.5	377	22.2	2.5	21 559	2.5	559	2.6	16 522	20.1	13.2
Mahoning	101 136	71.7	47 900	18.6	13.4	342	27.9	1.7	115 158	-0.7	6 801	5.9	106 433	25.7	12.0
Marion	23 484	70.9	42 500	16.1	12.4	343	24.7	2.3	31 903	1.5	1 397	4.4	27 324	22.4	14.5
Medina	41 792	79.3	83 700	20.2	12.2	441	23.6	1.7	80 254	0.7	3 119	3.9	60 441	28.0	14.4
Meigs	8 662	78.7	35 700	20.1	13.8	264	33.6	5.4	8 161	-1.7	706	8.7	7 677	20.6	19.3
Mercer	13 398	79.8	61 100	17.8	11.5	324	21.8	2.6	19 498	2.0	1 123	5.8	18 263	18.2	12.9
Miami	34 559	72.7	65 000	16.4	12.1	382	23.5	1.6	51 783	2.3	2 215	4.3	44 993	26.3	13.3
Monroe	5 754	79.9	39 600	15.6	12.8	274	27.9	6.5	5 344	-6.9	354	6.6	5 414	18.2	18.0
Montgomery	226 192	62.9	65 000	17.7	12.6	403	25.1	2.1	284 937	1.8	12 216	4.3	265 950	33.1	10.0
Morgan	5 170	77.2	39 900	15.5	12.3	262	27.9	6.4	4 433	0.5	665	15.0	5 036	17.9	15.3
Morrow	9 656	81.0	47 600	18.3	12.8	336	22.8	2.5	14 859	3.4	893	6.0	12 536	17.4	17.1
Muskingum	30 753	73.0	47 100	16.8	12.2	301	26.1	2.7	45 688	2.1	2 680	5.9	34 894	22.2	12.9
Noble	4 137	80.0	37 200	18.2	12.4	290	24.5	6.1	5 568	-0.1	314	5.6	4 291	14.3	17.1

1. Specified owner-occupied units.   2. Specified renter-occupied units.   3. Overcrowded or lacking complete plumbing facilities.   4. Percent of civilian labor force.   5. Persons 16 years and older.

Table B. States and Counties — Nonfarm Employment and Agriculture

	Private nonfarm establishments, employment and payroll, 1999									Agriculture, 1997			
STATE County	Employment						Annual payroll		Farms			Farm operators
											Percent with—		
	Number of establishments	Total	Health Care and Social Assistance	Manufacturing	Retail trade	Finance and Insurance	Professional Scientific and Technical Services	Total (mil dol)	Average per employee (dollars)	Number	Less than 50 acres	500 acres and over	Whose principal occupation is farming (percent)
	104	105	106	107	108	109	110	111	112	113	114	115	116
NORTH DAKOTA—Cont'd													
Ward	1 657	21 619	4 230	759	4 695	719	993	461	21 303	1 172	8.1	57.8	69.0
Wells	207	1 359	408	21	264	89	33	22	16 121	593	4.9	65.3	77.9
Williams	831	6 554	1 265	141	1 386	309	174	123	18 801	850	6.0	67.3	72.9
OHIO	270 766	4 867 368	636 776	982 853	628 586	257 448	217 328	148 513	30 512	68 591	30.7	10.0	45.2
Adams	425	4 663	783	1 047	1 001	157	90	97	20 862	1 315	30.5	4.9	41.8
Allen	2 836	51 005	9 207	10 330	7 670	1 365	981	1 405	27 537	918	27.7	12.0	46.7
Ashland	1 053	18 339	1 814	7 294	2 125	374	483	449	24 476	929	26.9	7.8	47.4
Ashtabula	2 279	30 418	4 402	10 819	4 720	626	442	744	24 474	993	28.9	4.4	46.5
Athens	1 181	12 659	2 091	1 490	2 712	523	412	240	18 920	481	18.5	4.4	37.2
Auglaize	1 047	17 628	1 693	7 711	2 056	425	259	505	28 636	1 001	27.3	10.8	49.1
Belmont	1 628	19 465	3 737	1 803	5 277	873	380	404	20 759	622	16.7	9.5	44.1
Brown	594	6 413	1 283	1 240	1 041	218	112	147	22 876	1 378	36.3	5.2	42.2
Butler	6 228	108 389	14 256	20 908	13 243	6 996	4 379	3 279	30 255	849	40.8	6.6	43.7
Carroll	470	5 057	418	1 655	703	D	90	119	23 447	683	21.5	4.2	42.9
Champaign	721	10 239	1 071	4 465	1 208	282	118	243	23 702	836	35.8	16.6	46.8
Clark	2 752	50 386	7 482	13 276	7 107	1 446	742	1 364	27 069	671	42.0	14.8	43.5
Clermont	3 232	45 735	4 309	7 261	8 995	2 293	2 250	1 396	30 534	744	50.0	5.1	32.8
Clinton	800	23 470	1 628	4 893	2 175	691	201	664	28 280	761	28.3	19.6	54.0
Columbiana	2 423	29 423	4 424	8 624	4 859	941	760	671	22 801	980	36.2	4.4	41.8
Coshocton	737	15 288	1 664	4 701	1 490	276	357	493	32 260	864	20.1	8.0	43.6
Crawford	994	15 259	1 818	6 614	1 621	463	528	411	26 950	712	25.3	17.6	51.8
Cuyahoga	38 447	757 284	110 460	114 898	77 726	54 453	47 763	25 805	34 076	118	78.8	0.0	53.4
Darke	1 275	16 791	1 993	5 402	2 337	612	224	417	24 855	1 726	33.8	10.0	44.7
Defiance	874	16 976	1 444	6 897	2 577	509	232	578	34 049	861	25.7	10.6	41.9
Delaware	2 359	39 946	3 054	6 388	4 597	6 743	1 611	1 248	31 241	627	41.8	14.2	49.3
Erie	2 093	31 648	3 736	9 778	4 566	704	605	968	30 598	380	36.1	15.0	48.7
Fairfield	2 523	30 456	4 522	5 971	5 529	768	869	676	22 200	1 024	37.5	9.2	47.9
Fayette	714	9 255	854	2 893	2 661	180	82	213	23 009	520	26.5	32.5	62.7
Franklin	27 827	615 487	67 018	51 013	80 508	65 298	36 158	19 883	32 304	407	46.4	11.5	44.5
Fulton	1 096	19 298	1 743	10 170	1 825	395	385	533	27 605	794	30.4	14.0	48.0
Gallia	664	9 557	2 398	944	1 995	331	319	249	26 059	776	24.7	3.4	35.4
Geauga	2 616	29 714	2 985	11 018	3 513	580	1 342	839	28 248	661	44.9	2.1	43.1
Greene	2 894	44 369	4 835	4 777	8 810	1 192	5 914	1 127	25 403	764	40.8	13.5	45.7
Guernsey	954	12 236	2 145	2 987	1 683	326	180	301	24 618	802	20.6	5.0	42.5
Hamilton	24 835	540 671	75 544	71 679	58 842	31 427	35 744	18 339	33 919	302	59.9	3.6	43.4
Hancock	1 797	39 865	3 563	12 215	5 014	907	672	1 156	29 008	979	25.4	18.1	46.6
Hardin	523	8 449	831	2 797	1 100	203	79	200	23 685	837	23.2	17.9	52.2
Harrison	329	3 101	517	775	368	D	40	66	21 338	423	15.6	11.6	44.2
Henry	642	8 799	1 180	3 526	1 045	273	89	251	28 546	872	22.7	16.6	50.0
Highland	752	10 680	1 498	3 991	1 675	363	138	233	21 836	1 239	28.2	10.0	42.3
Hocking	552	5 632	958	1 510	850	157	159	124	21 952	353	24.4	1.4	31.4
Holmes	966	12 867	1 306	5 224	1 635	310	268	291	22 630	1 404	24.6	2.5	60.4
Huron	1 255	23 194	2 001	10 384	2 645	523	332	632	27 240	782	24.9	16.0	46.8
Jackson	648	10 610	962	3 743	1 664	1 560	174	219	20 602	408	17.4	6.4	33.6
Jefferson	1 607	22 384	4 056	3 973	3 715	687	359	540	24 128	410	16.8	6.6	38.8
Knox	1 110	17 032	1 999	4 456	2 154	456	289	441	25 894	1 103	28.6	8.4	45.7
Lake	6 415	96 526	9 090	26 938	16 370	2 320	3 230	2 782	28 825	274	68.6	2.2	54.4
Lawrence	915	10 353	2 081	1 964	2 430	354	151	229	22 082	490	28.6	2.4	34.7
Licking	2 839	45 663	4 661	9 406	6 576	3 865	1 267	1 249	27 348	1 218	35.0	8.3	42.2
Logan	949	19 221	1 536	6 575	1 983	339	696	561	29 194	895	30.5	12.7	39.4
Lorain	5 750	93 973	11 300	26 239	13 189	2 826	2 295	2 725	28 995	778	43.7	6.8	44.1
Lucas	11 225	216 082	40 165	30 757	29 406	7 586	10 340	6 684	30 933	385	53.0	14.3	45.5
Madison	701	10 709	885	3 702	1 349	182	359	269	25 093	667	28.5	24.7	57.3
Mahoning	6 451	95 110	17 221	12 941	14 247	4 024	3 134	2 406	25 293	542	39.5	3.7	45.4
Marion	1 378	24 739	3 617	6 956	3 583	718	470	629	25 415	543	28.2	22.7	52.3
Medina	3 881	51 014	5 930	11 317	8 268	2 508	1 409	1 392	27 287	851	47.9	4.6	42.9
Meigs	356	3 410	648	D	650	141	73	98	28 727	491	17.7	4.7	39.5
Mercer	972	12 796	1 444	3 449	1 911	615	254	288	22 537	1 255	26.6	10.4	50.6
Miami	2 264	38 549	3 753	13 990	5 477	867	671	1 031	26 754	983	42.6	11.5	43.9
Monroe	292	3 981	192	D	418	115	D	130	32 744	589	12.4	4.9	43.5
Montgomery	13 324	281 373	40 920	53 791	33 443	10 434	13 784	9 174	32 604	760	50.7	6.4	39.9
Morgan	202	2 135	334	720	314	106	41	52	24 485	500	12.2	6.8	40.4
Morrow	400	4 593	664	1 683	613	D	151	104	22 653	759	31.2	9.4	43.1
Muskingum	2 042	34 057	5 372	9 986	4 850	875	560	803	23 578	1 018	22.7	7.1	43.6
Noble	200	2 420	420	752	332	79	21	56	23 149	519	15.0	4.6	32.8

STATE County	Acreage (1,000)	Percent change, 1992–1997	Average size of farm	Total irrigated (1,000)	Total cropland (1,000)	Average per farm ($1,000)	Average per acre (dollars)	Value of machinery and equipment average per farm ($1,000)	Total (mil dol)	Average per farm (dollars)	Crops	Live-stock and poultry products	$10,000 or more	$100,000 or more	Percent of land owned by fed. gov. 1997	Water consumption 1995 (mil gal/day)
	117	118	119	120	121	122	123	124	125	126	127	128	129	130	131	132
NORTH DAKOTA—Cont'd																
Ward	1 208	4.0	1 030	1	949	555	529	96	83	70 742	82.8	17.2	75.1	24.2	1.5	9.3
Wells	744	-0.9	1 255	D	617	509	422	146	62	103 856	83.8	16.2	74.7	35.6	1.8	0.9
Williams	1 205	1.9	1 418	14	829	426	312	97	53	62 379	80.5	19.5	72.1	19.2	2.2	11.0
OHIO	14 103	-1.0	206	34	11 341	415	2 039	58	4 684	68 293	60.4	39.6	52.3	15.7	1.4	10 523.3
Adams	195	-0.7	148	0	110	209	1 476	35	27	20 744	58.6	41.4	42.1	4.5	0.0	735.0
Allen	190	-2.1	207	D	173	446	2 112	72	59	64 678	76.6	23.4	68.4	19.4	0.2	39.9
Ashland	164	-4.1	176	0	128	383	2 135	64	49	52 672	38.4	61.6	53.7	15.2	0.2	6.4
Ashtabula	149	-4.3	150	0	103	242	1 637	50	35	35 153	43.7	56.3	39.1	8.2	0.0	211.0
Athens	83	2.3	172	0	39	230	1 241	30	6	12 906	33.9	66.1	24.5	3.7	5.0	7.0
Auglaize	213	4.0	213	D	195	464	2 109	75	86	85 472	55.3	44.7	71.4	24.7	0.0	14.5
Belmont	148	17.7	238	0	65	213	936	41	12	19 788	18.7	81.3	30.2	5.3	0.0	239.6
Brown	196	-3.1	142	0	144	269	1 827	42	38	27 412	81.8	18.2	48.4	5.9	0.0	3.8
Butler	135	-2.5	158	0	108	517	3 024	50	35	41 262	61.4	38.6	43.0	11.7	0.3	73.9
Carroll	113	-7.1	166	0	68	236	1 508	43	21	31 153	45.2	54.8	36.7	7.0	2.2	3.6
Champaign	222	2.6	265	D	196	561	2 110	75	71	85 265	76.0	24.0	58.4	22.6	0.0	5.1
Clark	172	-3.9	256	2	154	595	2 278	72	73	109 416	86.7	13.3	55.0	20.0	0.0	25.4
Clermont	88	-10.8	119	0	66	322	2 906	38	17	22 399	84.2	15.8	33.7	5.8	2.2	547.4
Clinton	223	-1.8	293	0	201	606	2 211	67	66	86 502	84.4	15.6	64.9	24.7	0.0	2.3
Columbiana	138	-4.0	141	1	99	267	2 113	48	47	47 880	36.1	63.9	40.4	13.2	0.0	14.2
Coshocton	170	5.0	197	D	104	293	1 391	57	37	42 968	39.6	60.4	40.9	10.4	1.7	238.4
Crawford	227	1.6	318	0	207	578	1 792	84	75	105 623	71.1	28.9	72.8	24.9	0.0	5.7
Cuyahoga	4	6.7	36	0	3	435	13 094	60	17	145 310	97.0	3.0	44.9	21.2	1.0	429.1
Darke	329	-1.9	191	0	302	460	2 439	67	247	143 147	30.1	69.9	68.1	25.6	0.0	7.6
Defiance	186	-5.4	216	0	166	382	1 757	57	45	52 553	74.2	25.8	59.8	14.3	0.0	6.3
Delaware	161	-4.9	256	0	145	721	3 019	53	54	85 814	85.8	14.2	54.1	17.5	2.0	16.8
Erie	90	1.0	237	0	81	483	2 168	82	35	93 321	83.1	16.9	63.7	22.6	3.3	22.1
Fairfield	197	-0.5	192	0	162	482	2 439	54	51	50 103	74.0	26.0	50.1	14.4	0.0	13.1
Fayette	243	2.8	466	0	224	914	1 913	100	72	138 805	89.5	10.5	72.7	37.3	0.9	3.5
Franklin	80	-17.9	196	0	69	588	3 041	64	41	101 143	92.3	7.7	52.6	17.0	1.2	162.3
Fulton	197	-4.2	249	0	185	554	2 268	72	88	110 639	64.5	35.5	74.7	28.5	0.0	5.8
Gallia	117	6.5	151	0	53	200	1 243	34	15	19 529	41.2	58.8	33.2	3.6	5.9	1 285.3
Geauga	59	-8.9	90	0	38	348	3 985	29	18	27 658	49.0	51.0	38.4	7.1	0.0	7.8
Greene	178	-3.1	233	1	155	549	2 474	68	59	76 695	82.8	17.2	54.1	19.5	2.9	18.2
Guernsey	138	7.5	172	0	70	167	989	27	11	13 408	22.4	77.6	23.2	2.5	0.0	7.0
Hamilton	29	0.5	97	1	21	384	4 819	35	17	57 289	83.2	16.8	35.1	14.2	0.3	310.9
Hancock	277	0.4	283	0	259	651	2 237	76	82	83 620	82.3	17.7	76.1	24.4	0.0	18.2
Hardin	247	-0.5	295	D	225	483	1 612	61	115	137 360	47.4	52.6	68.7	23.2	0.0	3.7
Harrison	110	-2.9	259	0	53	234	964	44	10	23 664	23.6	76.4	30.0	4.0	3.6	2.2
Henry	244	-0.3	280	1	230	596	2 114	78	75	86 114	89.5	10.5	79.5	25.9	0.0	9.4
Highland	242	5.0	196	0	190	354	1 807	48	46	37 271	73.8	26.2	47.1	9.3	1.7	4.3
Hocking	48	-0.1	136	0	23	220	1 422	32	3	9 724	68.5	31.5	18.4	2.0	8.2	4.6
Holmes	172	-3.0	122	0	113	349	2 744	44	88	62 546	8.9	91.1	65.0	17.5	0.0	5.3
Huron	232	5.7	296	3	203	454	1 711	91	78	99 154	82.3	17.7	64.1	20.1	0.0	10.9
Jackson	74	0.0	181	0	43	222	1 173	51	18	42 928	75.1	24.9	28.9	3.7	0.6	2.4
Jefferson	71	4.9	174	D	40	156	1 052	26	7	16 348	29.1	70.9	23.4	3.2	0.0	2 146.8
Knox	206	-2.2	187	0	159	364	1 915	50	62	56 111	45.5	54.5	49.6	14.1	0.7	7.4
Lake	19	12.1	70	4	13	388	6 196	60	74	268 510	99.3	0.7	47.4	17.2	0.0	803.9
Lawrence	59	-4.1	121	0	23	126	1 030	22	4	8 070	56.3	43.7	17.3	1.2	24.1	8.7
Licking	237	4.4	195	0	184	466	2 497	56	129	105 813	32.7	67.3	43.2	11.0	0.1	18.2
Logan	219	7.9	245	D	188	383	1 624	57	89	99 528	45.9	54.1	50.6	15.6	0.0	6.2
Lorain	131	-8.6	168	1	110	477	2 926	84	83	106 647	83.1	16.9	50.6	13.9	0.0	544.5
Lucas	80	7.5	207	1	75	628	2 768	85	61	158 117	75.1	24.9	60.8	26.0	1.6	753.7
Madison	262	0.5	393	0	238	810	2 033	94	80	120 355	83.9	16.1	69.1	34.0	0.0	4.1
Mahoning	73	0.6	135	1	56	322	2 650	48	32	59 035	56.1	43.9	44.8	12.0	0.1	7.9
Marion	221	1.7	406	0	207	701	1 654	111	64	118 347	81.3	18.7	68.3	26.2	0.5	9.1
Medina	104	0.0	122	0	81	433	3 950	50	34	40 047	52.7	47.3	39.4	8.8	0.0	16.8
Meigs	85	-2.6	173	1	39	201	1 138	28	13	26 439	69.8	30.2	28.7	4.9	0.0	8.5
Mercer	261	-3.0	208	D	237	582	2 812	81	288	229 213	19.1	80.9	80.6	39.5	0.0	6.9
Miami	192	-3.8	196	1	174	562	2 814	56	64	65 206	77.8	22.2	57.7	18.9	0.0	42.1
Monroe	110	-0.3	186	0	48	161	871	38	7	12 560	13.7	86.3	21.6	3.1	7.6	3.7
Montgomery	106	-1.0	139	0	93	410	2 956	56	36	47 603	81.8	18.2	47.8	11.2	0.6	178.9
Morgan	98	-13.8	197	0	42	186	1 100	25	8	16 804	19.8	80.2	27.2	2.8	1.1	3.8
Morrow	161	-2.3	212	0	132	380	1 804	46	42	54 855	66.7	33.3	46.8	11.7	0.2	2.6
Muskingum	180	-4.2	177	0	103	204	1 266	41	26	25 320	38.6	61.4	34.2	5.6	2.3	19.5
Noble	99	-4.8	191	D	51	156	772	25	4	7 366	16.9	83.1	16.6	1.0	0.2	1.4

STATE County	Value of Residential Construction Authorized by Building Permits, 2000		Wholesale Trade, 1997				Retail Trade[1], 1997				Real Estate and Rental and Leasing, 1997			
	New Construction ($1,000)	Number of Housing Units	Number of Establishments	Number of Employees	Sales (mil dol)	Annual Payroll (mil dol)	Number of Establishments	Number of Employees	Sales (mil dol)	Annual Payroll (mil dol)	Number of Establishments	Number of Employees	Receipts (mil dol)	Annual Payroll (mil dol)
	133	134	135	136	137	138	139	140	141	142	143	144	145	146
NORTH DAKOTA—Cont'd														
Ward	10 737	149	95	1 203	701.6	32.9	339	4 819	753.7	74.3	60	234	27.1	3.6
Wells	108	1	18	148	91.2	3.7	42	238	41.4	3.4	7	12	0.7	0.1
Williams	1 924	25	89	693	331.0	17.4	138	1 417	207.5	19.7	27	109	12.9	3.0
OHIO	6 153 624	49 745	17 322	254 226	158 310.2	9 192.2	44 521	630 098	102 938.8	9 924.5	9 692	62 628	7 243.7	1 334.6
Adams	50	1	9	50	32.1	1.2	105	913	134.5	12.0	9	25	1.3	0.3
Allen	32 684	231	190	D	D	D	542	7 908	1 291.4	116.0	107	454	37.7	6.8
Ashland	19 579	185	47	282	121.3	7.3	183	2 242	311.1	33.0	34	124	10.0	2.0
Ashtabula	47 650	449	86	572	152.0	12.9	429	4 962	711.1	68.9	78	249	22.9	3.9
Athens	2 983	41	37	298	72.5	7.7	232	2 609	345.7	36.3	61	252	16.6	3.4
Auglaize	21 183	164	46	D	D	D	192	2 114	341.5	30.1	32	97	10.0	1.3
Belmont	2 595	25	58	D	D	D	383	5 359	737.6	68.3	48	226	11.5	2.8
Brown	11 622	111	15	239	73.7	5.6	114	922	141.7	12.4	18	56	3.2	0.5
Butler	253 380	2 385	454	D	D	D	922	13 529	2 188.6	208.5	235	1 324	149.7	25.7
Carroll	2 407	24	25	180	83.6	5.2	79	819	129.6	11.3	7	23	1.5	0.1
Champaign	19 112	175	31	427	160.8	11.4	124	1 254	204.1	18.3	27	83	6.2	0.8
Clark	29 932	284	124	1 704	1 035.2	49.6	528	7 439	1 102.9	107.9	82	317	32.4	5.0
Clermont	184 620	1 657	186	2 602	1 935.9	96.5	540	8 901	1 656.2	141.0	112	525	62.7	8.8
Clinton	25 458	206	39	360	192.2	11.1	154	2 101	434.7	33.4	23	200	56.1	5.7
Columbiana	11 693	140	111	866	278.0	24.5	468	4 934	823.4	68.7	65	303	22.5	4.7
Coshocton	1 085	8	31	203	70.5	4.7	146	1 538	209.8	20.1	13	73	7.1	2.3
Crawford	11 291	93	52	520	175.4	13.3	173	1 726	251.8	23.6	27	83	6.6	1.1
Cuyahoga	365 738	2 209	3 292	52 577	31 169.4	2 131.0	5 700	78 658	12 662.9	1 310.3	1 516	16 216	1 939.1	351.0
Darke	19 531	177	65	985	491.2	30.1	206	2 398	385.4	37.4	30	133	15.5	3.6
Defiance	14 075	142	46	568	306.7	16.4	195	2 580	424.8	39.7	24	123	11.0	2.2
Delaware	421 394	3 093	173	1 596	828.4	62.2	258	4 080	792.9	70.2	86	230	29.0	4.5
Erie	40 028	309	94	1 123	397.0	31.0	382	4 784	732.0	71.4	77	292	27.2	5.1
Fairfield	138 298	914	104	649	209.1	18.6	405	5 430	841.7	81.9	87	418	38.6	7.2
Fayette	13 210	105	44	329	749.2	10.8	246	2 154	329.8	30.6	14	48	7.0	0.9
Franklin	964 305	9 321	1 843	36 442	22 320.0	1 411.7	4 276	76 175	13 622.2	1 355.4	1 262	10 255	1 089.3	237.6
Fulton	21 068	163	68	603	365.4	16.9	179	1 715	294.2	26.3	32	171	15.6	2.5
Gallia	465	7	27	187	45.2	2.6	172	1 665	281.5	24.0	25	74	4.4	0.9
Geauga	106 308	519	194	1 425	691.5	53.9	317	3 311	565.0	55.6	68	194	30.0	3.8
Greene	96 110	860	110	1 316	1 540.4	47.0	564	8 922	1 321.9	125.0	104	386	52.6	6.9
Guernsey	5 868	84	42	390	97.3	10.8	167	1 722	294.0	24.9	30	160	11.3	1.8
Hamilton	299 984	1 940	2 047	37 207	32 788.6	1 413.1	3 774	59 154	9 310.4	938.2	1 076	7 783	1 197.0	207.2
Hancock	40 241	305	103	1 053	507.6	30.5	323	4 557	767.9	67.6	63	389	39.4	7.4
Hardin	5 210	67	19	D	D	D	111	1 089	160.7	14.5	13	47	2.9	0.4
Harrison	0	0	18	185	63.1	6.0	60	379	55.2	5.0	8	103	2.9	0.9
Henry	8 988	72	43	283	216.7	7.8	106	1 060	191.5	16.3	15	74	7.4	1.3
Highland	4 702	59	45	424	218.2	7.8	160	1 698	258.5	22.9	24	112	7.5	1.1
Hocking	415	4	14	D	D	D	92	880	145.1	14.3	16	45	3.5	0.4
Holmes	964	19	38	418	92.5	9.4	159	1 495	242.0	24.0	11	28	1.9	0.5
Huron	16 272	160	54	573	204.4	16.0	234	2 616	445.0	38.1	45	144	12.8	2.6
Jackson	16 161	186	27	304	72.5	7.2	162	1 542	234.8	21.5	13	42	2.9	0.5
Jefferson	5 994	112	69	D	D	D	335	3 969	531.4	52.9	50	198	15.9	3.2
Knox	32 220	325	58	362	168.3	9.0	183	2 076	313.4	28.8	39	147	9.8	1.5
Lake	119 799	761	425	4 392	1 590.9	148.8	975	15 509	2 831.2	260.7	180	801	87.0	13.9
Lawrence	5 832	103	37	D	D	D	206	2 503	360.7	31.7	24	D	D	D
Licking	156 165	1 135	144	1 600	623.1	45.1	502	6 392	1 105.2	104.2	100	493	37.4	8.4
Logan	25 957	260	45	1 671	844.2	47.2	187	1 919	309.0	26.9	29	79	6.9	1.2
Lorain	268 252	1 784	245	2 627	997.6	74.8	929	13 595	2 379.8	210.1	204	868	76.6	13.7
Lucas	156 915	1 227	751	10 580	6 302.2	377.3	1 860	29 585	4 842.2	473.7	403	2 530	289.8	55.5
Madison	20 963	185	38	904	355.4	26.2	122	1 423	276.8	22.5	19	75	5.5	0.8
Mahoning	91 391	716	407	5 559	2 132.4	177.3	1 187	16 420	2 547.9	235.5	173	1 028	102.8	19.4
Marion	12 536	134	61	559	219.3	17.5	237	3 549	548.9	53.8	55	202	17.5	3.9
Medina	251 521	1 681	295	2 724	1 155.8	93.5	524	7 764	1 346.0	123.4	99	378	46.0	7.0
Meigs	764	12	12	70	21.7	1.5	98	798	113.9	11.0	8	26	1.6	0.3
Mercer	19 041	159	57	952	384.7	24.1	192	2 151	330.0	32.3	29	116	16.4	3.0
Miami	43 250	265	110	1 832	3 072.8	56.2	371	5 018	845.4	72.4	82	332	33.2	5.5
Monroe	0	0	8	D	D	D	58	445	50.5	5.3	7	D	D	D
Montgomery	177 309	1 384	888	12 913	7 638.5	508.0	2 143	35 936	5 603.5	549.9	533	3 336	393.4	75.4
Morgan	104	1	10	D	D	D	35	345	45.4	3.8	4	D	D	D
Morrow	4 955	51	8	D	D	D	65	670	113.5	8.6	18	43	2.6	0.3
Muskingum	8 480	186	79	1 114	415.6	30.0	428	4 690	787.9	68.1	67	214	23.1	4.4
Noble	2 546	32	8	109	28.2	2.1	47	393	54.0	4.9	3	D	D	D

1. Establishments with payroll.

STATE County	Professional, Scientific, and Technical Services[1], 1997				Manufacturing, 1997				Accommodation and Foodservices, 1997			
	Number of Establishments	Number of Employees	Receipts (mil dol)	Annual Payroll (mil dol)	Number of Establishments	Number of Employees	Receipts (mil dol)	Annual Payroll (mil dol)	Number of Establishments	Number of Employees	Sales (mil dol)	Annual Payroll (mil dol)
	147	148	149	150	151	152	153	154	155	156	157	158
NORTH DAKOTA—Cont'd												
Ward	86	818	38.0	17.4	58	770	281.6	18.0	158	2 896	72.1	20.9
Wells	14	31	1.1	0.3	NA	NA	NA	NA	21	164	2.9	0.7
Williams	42	171	8.5	4.0	NA	NA	NA	NA	63	819	20.8	6.0
OHIO	21 182	182 805	18 294.7	6 948.0	17 974	984 201	241 902.9	35 950.5	22 631	401 206	12 411.0	3 444.2
Adams	23	82	4.9	1.1	31	D	D	D	37	508	13.9	3.7
Allen	171	951	59.8	21.9	132	9 529	6 631.7	407.8	231	4 260	127.5	33.1
Ashland	48	396	28.5	10.2	98	7 135	1 157.5	215.7	102	1 440	40.7	11.4
Ashtabula	105	340	23.8	7.8	175	9 984	1 794.3	302.6	235	2 759	83.8	21.7
Athens	61	333	18.7	8.1	43	1 351	222.1	32.5	141	2 364	57.4	16.2
Auglaize	46	207	18.1	4.7	93	8 236	1 737.6	288.7	102	1 533	37.9	10.4
Belmont	81	327	23.7	7.3	55	1 523	272.5	36.9	152	2 281	67.6	18.0
Brown	28	84	5.4	1.7	25	1 110	280.8	33.4	60	531	15.6	3.8
Butler	444	3 148	291.9	89.2	396	20 391	6 567.8	819.2	519	9 919	286.3	79.6
Carroll	20	52	3.8	1.1	40	1 782	302.3	56.7	45	459	10.5	2.7
Champaign	26	93	5.4	1.5	55	3 452	946.8	101.3	64	776	20.0	5.2
Clark	146	738	43.5	16.7	230	13 231	4 071.5	520.0	248	4 662	132.8	36.6
Clermont	258	1 541	183.0	58.8	167	7 892	1 544.3	305.5	224	4 370	133.9	37.7
Clinton	34	166	8.5	3.8	50	4 969	809.6	135.5	74	1 268	36.3	10.1
Columbiana	127	850	51.5	22.3	209	8 616	1 109.3	246.3	210	2 526	70.1	19.2
Coshocton	31	321	26.5	6.4	55	4 814	1 191.3	162.9	52	719	19.2	5.7
Crawford	41	159	9.2	3.1	90	6 575	1 194.7	211.6	94	1 160	30.5	7.8
Cuyahoga	3 936	40 008	4 384.1	1 769.9	2 712	116 680	23 382.3	4 640.6	3 031	55 025	1 846.3	493.4
Darke	50	166	11.7	4.7	92	5 811	1 147.4	172.4	91	1 143	32.4	8.5
Defiance	42	221	19.2	5.9	48	7 150	1 338.9	329.2	72	1 281	33.4	8.9
Delaware	211	1 435	304.2	79.3	117	5 131	1 285.7	187.6	160	2 623	79.3	23.9
Erie	107	470	38.4	17.2	117	9 176	2 251.5	409.2	248	4 622	167.9	46.6
Fairfield	159	587	45.5	17.0	154	6 251	833.7	188.2	185	3 478	106.8	30.4
Fayette	26	75	5.7	1.5	45	2 959	572.8	83.5	56	1 002	32.4	9.2
Franklin	2 934	30 270	3 163.8	1 195.7	1 061	48 265	11 837.7	1 754.6	2 330	49 486	1 669.9	483.2
Fulton	43	204	17.9	5.2	110	9 108	1 673.4	276.5	78	1 002	27.8	7.3
Gallia	31	314	12.4	7.0	18	948	117.6	26.9	59	970	30.9	7.9
Geauga	236	716	66.9	24.6	233	9 851	1 380.2	306.2	146	1 977	58.6	16.8
Greene	328	5 471	628.3	231.4	141	4 952	738.0	166.2	248	5 129	157.3	44.3
Guernsey	49	203	17.2	5.3	59	3 773	899.9	113.7	91	1 459	49.3	14.1
Hamilton	2 527	29 765	3 162.6	1 244.3	1 450	76 053	20 077.9	3 027.9	1 967	40 513	1 365.9	387.4
Hancock	104	508	35.5	14.2	97	11 964	2 792.4	422.5	172	3 184	87.5	25.8
Hardin	22	61	3.3	0.8	38	2 412	484.3	84.6	58	647	17.2	5.0
Harrison	19	72	2.0	0.6	24	678	105.8	14.2	37	225	5.7	1.4
Henry	26	87	4.7	1.4	54	3 947	1 721.1	148.6	60	D	D	D
Highland	38	107	5.2	1.4	41	3 851	653.8	94.4	58	743	22.9	5.8
Hocking	22	142	6.1	2.8	26	2 102	341.2	60.4	51	619	20.4	5.5
Holmes	32	180	10.1	3.7	164	4 621	710.1	100.2	58	845	26.0	7.5
Huron	61	488	24.6	10.0	110	11 114	2 152.7	326.0	110	1 696	43.6	12.5
Jackson	29	139	9.4	2.3	37	3 631	780.5	83.4	49	694	21.7	5.6
Jefferson	88	352	17.6	6.9	45	2 244	463.3	78.7	166	1 724	48.6	13.6
Knox	46	211	14.2	5.1	72	4 924	972.3	174.4	96	1 418	36.9	10.5
Lake	499	3 214	235.8	103.3	769	25 423	4 661.0	893.2	482	9 435	257.2	68.6
Lawrence	40	140	8.4	3.2	44	1 969	998.1	65.0	73	1 078	32.1	8.3
Licking	162	1 433	76.2	32.9	150	9 489	2 455.1	321.1	266	4 206	124.4	35.8
Logan	54	658	38.6	13.9	58	6 295	3 766.0	238.9	101	1 502	37.0	10.5
Lorain	329	1 766	119.0	53.4	437	27 252	11 225.5	1 054.4	489	7 639	215.9	56.2
Lucas	932	9 186	895.0	329.7	652	33 116	12 071.0	1 404.8	1 034	18 683	602.0	161.6
Madison	35	264	19.3	7.2	51	3 401	606.5	102.8	61	1 219	39.6	11.0
Mahoning	426	2 485	189.4	76.5	405	13 001	2 110.0	398.6	536	8 653	255.8	69.3
Marion	81	399	23.0	8.2	86	6 842	1 924.7	229.8	116	1 947	57.7	15.4
Medina	276	1 157	89.1	33.2	306	10 672	1 744.7	346.7	229	4 400	117.6	33.6
Meigs	21	63	2.9	0.9	NA	NA	NA	NA	26	313	10.1	2.3
Mercer	27	179	14.9	4.8	62	4 473	775.7	130.8	79	1 027	27.5	7.4
Miami	135	534	36.5	16.6	265	13 848	2 611.8	454.9	178	3 231	91.4	26.2
Monroe	16	54	2.6	0.7	21	D	D	D	18	D	D	D
Montgomery	1 206	12 424	1 232.1	442.6	927	56 299	15 734.7	2 337.3	1 129	23 022	717.5	202.7
Morgan	13	53	3.5	0.6	10	921	135.5	27.5	15	178	4.2	1.2
Morrow	13	46	1.8	0.6	27	1 778	366.2	57.5	39	370	10.2	2.5
Muskingum	79	397	31.4	11.0	113	10 096	1 214.6	248.8	189	3 177	91.6	25.2
Noble	6	22	1.1	0.4	12	D	D	D	18	204	6.1	1.7

1. Firms subject to federal tax.

STATE County	Health Care and Social Assistance[1], 1997				Other Services[1], 1997				Federal funds and grants, fiscal 2001[2] Expenditures (mil dol)	Direct payments for individuals[3]		
	Number of Establishments	Number of Employees	Receipts (mil dol)	Annual Payroll (mil dol)	Number of Establishments	Number of Employees	Receipts (mil dol)	Annual Payroll (mil dol)	Total	Social Security and government retirement	Medicare	Food stamps and Supplemental Security Income
	159	160	161	162	163	164	165	166	167	168	169	170
NORTH DAKOTA—Cont'd												
Ward	105	1 081	92.6	29.7	110	592	28.7	8.7	527.6	129.4	38.8	5.2
Wells	6	29	1.8	0.6	13	23	2.0	0.4	76.2	15.5	6.4	0.3
Williams	49	251	14.3	5.2	52	234	16.4	3.9	124.3	49.0	17.2	2.4
OHIO	20 399	261 520	15 440.1	7 477.0	17 314	116 165	7 087.5	2 165.7	61 704.8	22 840.7	9 860.7	1 994.0
Adams	31	393	15.2	6.1	18	47	2.3	0.4	178.4	59.8	24.5	11.0
Allen	201	2 625	161.8	86.0	182	1 071	61.2	17.0	645.0	364.3	87.7	24.3
Ashland	83	851	37.4	18.6	75	350	19.7	5.8	180.0	96.1	31.6	3.8
Ashtabula	149	2 319	122.5	53.6	140	585	27.0	7.6	480.7	228.6	110.5	19.1
Athens	77	891	49.5	21.9	53	266	10.7	3.4	307.4	88.0	41.1	17.3
Auglaize	67	815	41.3	17.8	74	431	25.4	8.7	174.6	82.9	41.9	2.5
Belmont	121	1 643	66.0	29.6	93	418	21.5	6.3	387.3	191.7	83.4	15.8
Brown	28	646	22.5	10.8	37	106	7.4	1.5	170.3	73.5	29.3	8.6
Butler	464	5 629	329.1	164.6	422	2 924	192.6	59.6	1 151.4	565.3	208.4	40.9
Carroll	24	277	13.4	5.5	25	152	8.9	3.0	88.4	45.8	15.7	3.6
Champaign	37	328	16.7	6.4	59	236	13.9	3.6	167.8	76.1	25.3	3.4
Clark	240	2 758	159.6	78.1	202	1 384	72.8	21.4	806.5	364.3	137.4	29.5
Clermont	187	2 554	127.9	62.1	220	1 177	71.5	21.9	455.7	243.4	77.5	15.2
Clinton	52	634	35.3	16.7	55	266	12.0	4.6	190.0	84.2	31.7	5.4
Columbiana	182	2 229	106.7	49.7	164	737	37.8	12.9	508.7	254.9	111.0	22.0
Coshocton	52	679	30.1	13.1	46	178	9.5	2.5	152.5	75.3	28.1	5.1
Crawford	77	810	36.0	16.2	53	326	19.8	6.1	218.3	107.0	46.3	7.6
Cuyahoga	3 042	36 747	2 409.7	1 137.5	2 511	19 147	1 466.9	396.0	8 778.7	3 040.9	1 735.3	356.1
Darke	61	729	32.3	15.6	88	348	21.4	5.6	224.9	105.1	40.0	4.5
Defiance	59	736	47.0	18.9	59	275	16.5	4.5	156.9	75.4	27.6	4.8
Delaware	132	1 349	71.2	30.6	98	459	29.9	7.9	493.9	133.6	37.6	4.7
Erie	168	1 369	87.3	45.4	123	647	29.0	9.2	392.8	181.4	77.5	9.5
Fairfield	226	2 544	137.0	62.5	157	811	44.3	14.5	398.3	218.3	75.8	11.5
Fayette	41	547	22.6	10.5	37	159	6.8	1.8	147.5	52.8	21.2	4.5
Franklin	2 171	28 471	1 920.5	962.2	1 579	12 799	783.6	249.5	6 713.3	1 802.5	687.8	196.1
Fulton	62	717	37.4	15.7	63	258	16.1	4.3	159.3	81.9	34.5	1.6
Gallia	45	885	62.1	30.0	34	127	6.6	1.8	171.6	67.0	29.2	12.6
Geauga	158	1 490	73.1	33.8	140	695	44.3	13.5	210.1	129.1	43.4	2.5
Greene	212	2 290	138.0	67.2	217	1 318	69.4	24.8	2 166.5	295.0	65.4	14.1
Guernsey	81	946	44.5	21.9	65	293	12.8	3.8	195.1	91.2	38.6	8.9
Hamilton	1 956	27 934	1 781.5	898.4	1 591	11 379	724.4	232.3	6 311.0	1 775.3	832.9	174.8
Hancock	130	1 505	90.6	45.0	107	656	36.8	11.6	229.2	112.4	40.1	5.1
Hardin	28	383	14.0	5.5	32	111	6.0	1.7	124.1	37.7	26.0	3.1
Harrison	14	280	10.5	4.7	19	42	2.4	0.6	86.9	42.9	17.0	3.6
Henry	30	451	17.0	7.9	37	165	12.6	3.1	120.2	58.5	22.1	2.2
Highland	49	624	25.4	11.9	39	240	15.0	4.4	196.3	83.3	32.8	6.0
Hocking	38	442	19.8	8.4	37	130	6.0	1.5	115.1	53.6	22.0	5.8
Holmes	41	1 047	45.7	20.1	34	120	10.6	2.2	70.1	36.3	9.9	1.5
Huron	77	997	52.7	25.2	67	388	20.2	5.8	247.1	132.9	47.5	7.8
Jackson	28	415	17.8	6.9	44	168	10.3	2.1	174.9	68.2	24.2	10.3
Jefferson	135	1 788	87.0	39.1	121	820	38.7	12.4	462.7	219.9	105.9	20.1
Knox	98	1 237	56.2	23.2	60	511	17.2	5.5	215.7	106.2	43.1	5.9
Lake	429	4 882	258.6	119.2	464	2 577	166.6	52.4	823.6	473.8	194.4	13.5
Lawrence	54	1 013	36.8	16.6	63	217	11.9	3.4	351.2	155.9	59.1	23.0
Licking	185	3 415	147.2	75.7	176	1 191	62.0	24.2	645.7	286.0	89.9	17.1
Logan	73	605	32.5	14.1	55	394	29.3	6.6	210.5	91.9	39.6	4.9
Lorain	444	5 189	310.7	162.5	379	2 474	131.6	40.4	1 149.9	533.6	235.6	41.0
Lucas	944	13 899	900.9	461.4	798	5 289	332.8	100.2	2 317.9	873.7	486.2	124.2
Madison	54	457	25.9	9.4	31	159	9.9	2.5	160.8	70.9	29.1	3.5
Mahoning	629	7 696	434.1	203.3	415	2 852	162.8	49.9	1 450.9	645.6	317.4	65.1
Marion	116	1 754	99.9	50.3	95	389	20.5	6.0	297.1	137.9	57.3	14.8
Medina	265	3 147	151.0	71.5	239	1 347	75.0	22.7	435.1	248.4	89.6	6.7
Meigs	16	336	13.0	4.7	19	45	3.1	0.7	121.1	49.7	19.8	8.6
Mercer	63	816	36.1	16.7	71	298	22.3	5.6	104.9	24.6	30.4	1.0
Miami	151	1 606	99.0	45.2	154	824	44.1	13.5	532.3	204.8	72.0	9.3
Monroe	9	140	5.1	1.7	21	60	2.9	0.6	77.9	34.7	14.3	2.6
Montgomery	1 167	15 974	1 017.3	491.6	914	9 895	499.5	183.9	3 576.7	1 414.5	525.7	106.5
Morgan	10	129	5.4	2.6	13	33	2.1	0.6	66.8	29.9	11.4	3.2
Morrow	28	368	12.6	5.9	20	61	3.1	0.7	89.6	46.9	12.9	2.7
Muskingum	159	1 935	124.7	58.6	141	999	56.4	17.8	400.0	188.0	68.1	20.1
Noble	17	353	10.7	5.0	14	28	1.7	0.4	42.9	20.7	7.8	2.0

1. Firms subject to federal tax.   2. October 1, 2000 to September 30, 2001.   3. State totals may include programs not allocated by county.

	Federal funds and grants, fiscal 2001[1] (cont'd)							Local government finances, 1997				
	Expenditures (mil dol) (cont'd)							General revenue				
	Procurement contract awards		Grants[2]							Taxes		
STATE County											Per capita[3] (dollars)	
	Salaries and wages	Defense	Other	Medicaid and other health-related	Nutrition and family welfare	Education	Other	Total (mil dol)	Intergovern-mental (mil dol)	Total (mil dol)	Total	Property
	171	172	173	174	175	176	177	178	179	180	181	182
NORTH DAKOTA—Cont'd												
Ward	174.8	50.1	11.7	21.7	8.1	12.3	13.7	98.9	45.5	33.7	573	490
Wells	1.6	0.0	0.4	3.8	0.5	0.2	6.9	10.9	4.3	4.4	841	810
Williams	5.3	0.1	1.9	9.3	2.6	0.9	5.6	40.2	16.9	16.4	805	743
OHIO	4 850.6	3 311.9	1 812.0	6 246.7	2 176.3	1 066.9	2 271.7	X	X	X	X	X
Adams	4.4	0.4	1.3	57.9	6.7	2.7	2.2	71.9	26.7	26.5	930	774
Allen	27.4	11.5	8.6	49.5	16.2	7.0	10.2	223.2	93.9	88.2	817	535
Ashland	6.3	0.8	1.5	10.8	3.6	2.2	11.2	99.4	40.0	41.5	799	567
Ashtabula	14.5	6.9	20.0	38.3	15.2	6.6	7.1	225.3	115.7	74.7	725	550
Athens	21.7	13.6	6.3	52.3	11.2	6.5	22.7	132.6	76.6	39.4	643	488
Auglaize	5.9	1.7	1.4	9.1	3.0	1.7	6.5	96.6	40.3	35.6	758	508
Belmont	11.3	0.2	3.9	38.3	12.5	4.4	12.7	131.6	65.4	42.8	616	427
Brown	5.0	0.0	1.5	23.1	6.6	2.2	5.5	105.9	54.9	21.4	531	423
Butler	34.4	40.8	11.0	115.5	28.4	12.9	53.4	673.7	251.8	283.0	866	645
Carroll	2.8	0.0	0.7	12.6	2.9	1.2	0.1	38.1	21.4	10.8	372	316
Champaign	4.6	12.0	2.0	15.7	3.1	1.8	1.5	86.3	34.8	29.1	762	500
Clark	45.9	24.5	28.1	86.6	20.4	12.1	17.6	307.5	139.9	118.4	810	551
Clermont	18.1	0.1	4.8	48.4	14.5	6.7	1.5	375.5	149.5	144.7	836	699
Clinton	8.7	0.3	1.6	19.7	3.5	3.5	3.4	122.5	42.5	30.8	782	564
Columbiana	25.0	3.7	4.4	49.3	16.5	6.7	3.7	212.6	113.6	67.8	608	471
Coshocton	5.6	0.0	1.1	15.2	4.9	1.9	6.6	77.3	27.7	35.9	992	768
Crawford	4.4	0.2	1.2	18.0	5.7	2.8	1.0	94.5	39.9	36.0	764	586
Cuyahoga	930.9	176.7	357.4	1 152.5	258.4	102.7	260.2	4 906.0	1 641.5	2 262.7	1 632	962
Darke	6.4	0.5	2.1	16.6	11.6	2.3	6.9	96.2	44.4	36.5	671	457
Defiance	5.7	0.7	3.6	11.4	5.2	1.8	2.5	115.4	53.5	38.5	965	709
Delaware	13.1	4.6	4.1	13.2	2.7	2.6	257.6	178.1	52.5	88.6	1 013	833
Erie	12.9	8.1	12.5	21.7	8.5	4.1	40.4	223.6	75.5	96.3	1 223	924
Fairfield	15.1	0.1	3.8	29.9	8.2	4.2	7.2	231.4	97.6	90.9	749	530
Fayette	3.5	0.0	1.1	18.5	4.4	2.2	15.5	61.1	23.4	17.4	608	433
Franklin	681.6	261.0	228.5	821.6	790.9	410.9	536.7	3 051.9	952.6	1 557.1	1 531	946
Fulton	5.5	1.6	2.0	7.0	2.3	1.7	1.5	89.7	30.1	44.9	1 085	724
Gallia	4.5	0.0	1.2	38.5	7.7	2.6	2.2	74.5	28.0	20.6	624	564
Geauga	7.2	5.7	2.4	7.9	2.2	2.8	4.1	181.1	57.3	97.1	1 105	956
Greene	874.1	761.1	34.1	49.3	10.2	10.3	6.7	319.0	115.1	130.0	930	697
Guernsey	6.5	0.2	1.6	30.4	6.1	2.4	2.0	80.6	34.9	31.0	761	546
Hamilton	602.4	1 041.8	475.7	691.1	128.4	58.0	163.9	2 694.5	846.9	1 282.5	1 506	974
Hancock	9.9	0.2	2.2	17.5	5.4	3.5	6.1	146.1	55.7	63.4	921	659
Hardin	6.3	5.8	1.6	10.0	3.6	3.7	0.6	55.6	29.0	19.6	617	367
Harrison	3.7	1.7	0.8	8.4	2.9	1.3	2.2	38.1	17.5	15.4	955	523
Henry	5.4	0.0	1.4	6.8	1.8	1.8	0.1	74.5	36.6	26.7	892	691
Highland	5.9	0.0	1.4	30.4	6.2	2.2	5.5	88.1	41.5	19.1	479	320
Hocking	3.0	0.0	0.9	14.2	3.9	1.3	6.7	65.6	26.0	15.9	553	376
Holmes	4.0	0.3	3.1	7.5	1.3	1.9	0.7	54.2	23.6	22.2	595	555
Huron	8.7	0.2	2.2	17.5	5.3	3.2	1.9	146.7	59.2	64.3	1 071	502
Jackson	3.9	0.0	1.2	42.7	6.9	2.3	10.9	54.8	33.4	11.9	367	305
Jefferson	15.2	1.1	4.2	53.3	14.1	6.0	6.9	140.4	66.4	52.4	689	591
Knox	6.7	0.1	1.9	24.2	4.7	3.7	2.0	96.7	45.2	37.0	704	522
Lake	28.4	8.0	11.8	35.4	12.1	9.0	21.2	621.7	166.6	336.2	1 503	1 097
Lawrence	7.8	0.4	5.7	68.1	17.5	7.0	2.0	112.5	76.3	22.9	355	249
Licking	28.2	113.6	4.4	49.6	13.5	6.2	8.9	302.5	133.6	126.1	904	639
Logan	12.0	1.4	4.8	18.7	4.2	2.0	7.8	100.0	41.5	40.2	875	716
Lorain	102.0	8.0	10.3	97.0	34.3	18.5	18.5	679.1	261.1	292.7	1 036	706
Lucas	136.5	52.7	30.2	301.1	78.6	31.8	91.9	1 329.5	486.9	587.8	1 302	767
Madison	4.7	0.2	1.2	18.0	2.8	1.8	6.9	90.0	42.3	33.8	815	627
Mahoning	80.9	2.7	26.4	181.7	47.3	19.5	22.6	554.5	258.4	215.5	837	593
Marion	9.2	2.4	2.1	29.7	10.8	3.2	4.3	147.0	64.6	50.7	778	547
Medina	19.2	8.7	5.8	18.0	5.2	5.3	15.8	318.4	122.1	135.7	956	813
Meigs	3.8	0.2	1.1	22.0	5.3	2.0	5.5	41.5	28.4	9.2	384	309
Mercer	6.0	0.0	1.7	7.7	3.4	1.8	5.4	102.0	43.9	31.7	774	553
Miami	13.3	142.4	4.6	27.3	6.9	3.8	17.9	222.6	79.7	92.9	951	655
Monroe	3.1	0.2	0.7	14.5	2.5	1.5	2.8	30.5	15.3	12.4	812	707
Montgomery	297.6	335.4	210.5	321.9	92.4	41.2	97.6	1 745.3	605.7	741.8	1 321	795
Morgan	4.7	0.7	0.5	10.0	2.6	1.1	0.8	26.5	16.4	7.5	515	405
Morrow	3.1	0.0	0.8	7.9	3.0	1.6	0.1	51.0	27.6	15.3	492	392
Muskingum	18.0	3.9	4.0	56.5	11.2	6.7	10.5	192.6	93.8	66.9	792	525
Noble	1.7	0.0	0.5	6.8	2.0	0.9	0.1	23.8	13.9	6.6	539	454

1. October 1, 2000 to September 30, 2001.   2. State totals may include programs not allocated by county.   3. Based on the resident population estimated as of July 1 of the year shown.

STATE County	Direct general expenditure Total (mil dol) [183]	Per capita[1] (dollars) [184]	Education [185]	Health and hospitals [186]	Police protection [187]	Public welfare [188]	Highways [189]	Debt outstanding Total (mil dol) [190]	Per capita[1] (dollars) [191]	Government employment, 1999 Federal civilian [192]	Federal military [193]	State and local [194]	Presidential election, 2000[2] Democratic [195]	Republican [196]	All other [197]
NORTH DAKOTA—Cont'd															
Ward	89.3	1 520	55.8	2.4	5.5	3.9	5.9	44.7	760	1 293	5 029	3 603	33.5	62.3	4.2
Wells	10.0	1 895	61.4	0.0	1.7	5.6	14.1	0.8	159	37	41	298	27.4	66.8	5.8
Williams	42.0	2 058	55.3	0.5	4.1	3.2	8.1	16.3	800	107	157	1 442	29.8	66.4	3.7
OHIO	X	X	X	X	X	X	X	X	X	82 916	36 228	682 730	46.4	50.0	3.6
Adams	96.4	3 386	62.7	12.9	2.2	4.3	5.0	45.3	1 591	79	73	1 513	35.0	62.3	2.7
Allen	219.4	2 032	51.1	3.1	5.1	4.8	3.9	89.0	824	478	278	7 041	32.0	65.4	2.6
Ashland	97.3	1 871	58.9	2.4	4.8	4.4	8.8	13.3	256	114	132	2 799	31.4	63.7	4.8
Ashtabula	217.2	2 106	49.5	5.9	4.6	10.1	6.0	33.3	323	263	273	5 094	50.2	45.4	4.3
Athens	127.8	2 085	57.2	3.0	3.7	12.0	6.9	37.4	611	247	174	9 726	51.7	38.1	10.1
Auglaize	90.2	1 920	55.8	1.7	3.2	7.8	6.6	49.4	1 051	98	120	2 747	28.0	69.2	2.8
Belmont	127.7	1 835	48.9	9.6	4.5	7.1	6.3	43.4	624	172	181	4 026	53.0	41.9	5.1
Brown	95.1	2 362	54.1	21.3	1.9	4.0	4.7	24.8	616	98	106	1 945	36.4	61.0	2.6
Butler	685.0	2 096	52.2	5.4	5.7	5.0	5.6	758.6	2 322	568	874	18 391	33.9	63.3	2.8
Carroll	37.1	1 283	48.6	6.2	5.1	8.7	13.0	4.5	155	52	74	936	40.5	54.9	4.6
Champaign	90.0	2 354	47.7	12.1	3.9	5.3	6.8	20.0	523	81	98	1 755	38.0	58.8	3.2
Clark	304.7	2 084	49.2	8.9	5.5	10.3	4.2	106.5	728	635	373	7 271	48.6	48.1	3.3
Clermont	369.9	2 136	50.0	2.7	4.3	4.5	3.8	608.4	3 514	320	454	6 462	29.9	67.4	2.6
Clinton	115.9	2 947	41.4	31.3	3.5	2.0	4.6	44.8	1 139	151	103	2 946	31.8	65.2	3.1
Columbiana	200.7	1 797	55.4	3.7	4.3	8.2	5.3	72.1	646	570	284	4 736	46.5	49.1	4.4
Coshocton	74.8	2 069	49.4	2.5	4.1	8.7	7.0	9.2	255	104	92	1 639	39.2	57.8	3.1
Crawford	98.7	2 095	46.3	4.7	5.3	6.7	8.0	28.8	613	88	119	2 065	35.0	60.8	4.1
Cuyahoga	4 613.2	3 326	38.3	12.5	6.4	5.0	3.8	4 727.5	3 409	17 638	4 091	83 694	62.5	33.5	4.0
Darke	91.7	1 688	54.5	1.3	5.7	9.2	8.9	10.5	193	127	137	2 142	33.3	63.7	3.0
Defiance	95.6	2 395	42.5	8.2	5.1	6.5	16.4	4.9	122	110	101	1 937	38.0	58.7	3.2
Delaware	196.0	2 243	57.0	4.1	4.3	2.4	5.2	175.0	2 002	230	264	4 293	30.9	66.1	3.0
Erie	218.1	2 770	50.1	2.1	4.4	6.7	4.1	75.7	962	201	206	5 116	50.6	46.0	3.4
Fairfield	227.9	1 877	54.0	4.6	4.7	3.1	7.5	99.3	817	262	323	6 841	35.2	62.0	2.8
Fayette	62.2	2 173	44.1	22.8	4.1	4.7	7.0	22.7	794	57	72	1 495	36.2	61.3	2.5
Franklin	2 999.8	2 949	38.5	8.1	7.2	5.0	4.9	2 872.2	2 823	12 907	3 282	101 779	48.8	47.8	3.4
Fulton	90.5	2 189	60.8	1.0	4.2	2.7	12.3	46.8	1 133	109	107	2 195	36.0	61.1	2.9
Gallia	72.3	2 185	50.1	21.9	3.5	2.9	8.3	11.9	360	86	85	1 928	38.1	58.8	3.1
Geauga	182.2	2 073	51.4	6.0	4.6	2.6	8.4	73.9	841	142	228	3 518	36.0	59.7	4.4
Greene	313.8	2 246	47.8	2.7	7.7	5.3	4.7	233.8	1 674	11 497	3 282	9 888	38.4	58.2	3.3
Guernsey	72.7	1 782	48.9	1.6	4.7	10.1	8.3	37.5	918	117	104	2 632	43.1	53.0	3.9
Hamilton	2 677.2	3 144	34.2	8.5	6.3	5.6	4.8	1 063.9	1 249	10 182	2 251	52 654	42.8	54.0	3.2
Hancock	153.0	2 223	46.9	7.7	5.7	7.0	7.4	79.9	1 161	181	177	3 058	28.7	68.5	2.7
Hardin	54.5	1 719	65.4	2.3	5.4	3.3	8.7	6.2	195	88	80	1 614	37.8	59.0	3.2
Harrison	36.2	2 242	42.3	1.3	7.2	11.9	14.0	3.4	208	64	41	866	46.8	47.7	5.5
Henry	73.5	2 460	57.5	0.6	3.2	9.5	10.9	23.0	768	78	76	2 068	33.0	64.4	2.6
Highland	84.5	2 122	45.7	21.6	3.1	3.5	4.5	17.9	450	111	104	2 019	34.5	63.0	2.5
Hocking	63.0	2 192	32.9	32.8	2.8	5.9	7.3	17.1	593	53	74	1 597	41.6	53.0	5.4
Holmes	49.0	1 312	50.1	0.5	4.9	11.7	13.6	18.4	492	79	97	1 418	22.6	73.9	3.6
Huron	126.4	2 105	54.6	1.7	6.6	5.1	7.2	35.3	589	141	155	2 653	38.3	57.5	4.1
Jackson	53.2	1 643	54.6	2.9	3.7	7.6	8.0	28.1	868	73	83	1 398	41.1	55.7	3.2
Jefferson	137.2	1 805	51.7	1.1	4.9	12.6	6.1	34.5	453	264	188	3 726	50.5	43.4	6.1
Knox	92.9	1 769	52.7	2.2	4.4	6.5	7.7	61.6	1 174	111	137	2 665	33.5	63.0	3.5
Lake	570.3	2 549	50.2	7.7	5.6	2.0	5.1	248.1	1 109	527	595	11 146	45.3	50.5	4.2
Lawrence	115.5	1 791	60.4	3.2	2.2	7.4	4.5	29.6	459	148	164	3 596	46.2	51.2	2.5
Licking	286.8	2 057	51.4	7.1	2.8	6.6	4.9	64.2	460	519	361	6 637	37.1	59.5	3.3
Logan	97.0	2 111	55.9	1.3	5.8	5.2	6.7	46.8	1 019	149	122	2 162	32.2	64.2	3.5
Lorain	651.2	2 305	52.1	5.8	5.5	4.2	4.1	243.7	863	1 214	727	13 341	53.3	42.8	3.9
Lucas	1 375.4	3 047	35.1	7.9	5.8	5.1	3.5	906.1	2 008	2 138	1 206	29 505	57.8	39.1	3.1
Madison	78.9	1 901	56.6	3.0	4.0	9.0	7.7	9.1	220	92	105	3 022	36.0	60.6	3.3
Mahoning	532.3	2 067	48.8	6.1	5.4	5.3	4.6	269.2	1 046	1 576	664	15 740	60.6	35.5	3.9
Marion	140.4	2 156	50.2	4.5	5.6	9.0	4.8	129.2	1 984	172	171	5 734	41.8	54.9	3.4
Medina	307.5	2 166	53.4	4.5	5.2	2.4	4.4	124.3	875	312	375	5 948	39.8	55.8	4.3
Meigs	43.2	1 800	53.6	0.9	3.2	12.9	13.3	6.8	285	76	61	1 140	37.5	58.7	3.8
Mercer	102.9	2 511	54.0	12.0	3.3	5.0	6.8	41.5	1 014	101	104	2 543	28.5	68.2	3.2
Miami	218.1	2 232	50.7	3.7	5.6	3.2	5.9	75.6	773	231	252	4 516	36.4	60.8	2.9
Monroe	31.4	2 047	59.8	1.5	3.9	4.5	13.2	13.8	897	63	39	891	50.7	44.2	5.1
Montgomery	1 649.0	2 938	41.0	4.2	6.5	6.4	4.7	990.2	1 764	6 457	4 428	29 646	49.6	47.5	2.8
Morgan	26.1	1 786	54.5	1.0	3.8	10.5	9.1	1.9	127	47	37	683	37.7	57.6	4.7
Morrow	47.1	1 515	56.9	5.1	3.2	5.4	11.8	13.7	439	58	82	1 392	35.3	61.1	3.7
Muskingum	178.6	2 113	53.7	3.6	5.7	6.9	5.2	84.1	995	304	217	4 659	41.1	55.2	3.7
Noble	21.2	1 723	55.1	2.8	2.6	7.2	14.5	6.2	501	28	38	1 061	38.3	57.4	4.3

1. Based on the resident population estimated as of July 1 of the year shown.   2. Data subject to copyright.

Table B. States and Counties — **Land Area and Population**

STATE/ County code	MSA/ PMSA/ NECMA code[1]	County Type[2]	STATE County	Land area,[3] (sq km) 2000	Total persons	Rank	Per square kilometer	White	Black	Am. Indian, Alaska Native	Asian and Pacific Islander	Percent Hispanic[4]	Under 5 years	5 to 17 years	18 to 24 years	25 to 34 years	35 to 44 years	45 to 54 years
				1	2	3	4	5	6	7	8	9	10	11	12	13	14	15
			OHIO—Cont'd															
39 123	...	6	Ottawa	660	40 985	1 081	62.1	97.4	0.9	0.5	0.4	3.7	5.2	18.0	6.7	10.8	16.1	15.4
39 125	...	6	Paulding	1 078	20 293	1 774	18.8	97.1	1.3	0.8	0.2	3.0	6.6	20.2	8.6	12.3	15.7	14.2
39 127	...	6	Perry	1 061	34 078	1 278	32.1	99.3	0.4	0.7	0.3	0.4	7.4	20.8	8.5	13.4	15.7	13.5
39 129	1840	1	Pickaway	1 300	52 727	883	40.6	92.8	6.7	0.8	0.4	0.6	5.9	18.3	9.0	14.9	17.7	13.9
39 131	...	7	Pike	1 143	27 695	1 459	24.2	98.1	1.2	1.7	0.4	0.6	6.9	20.3	8.9	13.5	15.4	12.3
39 133	0080	2	Portage	1 275	152 061	353	119.3	95.5	3.6	0.7	1.0	0.7	6.1	17.6	14.3	12.7	15.9	13.7
39 135	...	6	Preble	1 100	42 337	1 049	38.5	99.1	0.5	0.6	0.3	0.4	6.3	19.7	7.7	12.4	16.3	14.5
39 137	...	6	Putnam	1 253	34 726	1 260	27.7	97.0	0.3	0.3	0.2	4.4	7.3	22.4	8.3	11.9	16.2	12.6
39 139	4800	3	Richland	1 287	128 852	419	100.1	89.3	10.1	0.7	0.8	0.9	6.4	18.4	8.4	12.9	15.7	14.2
39 141	...	4	Ross	1 783	73 345	682	41.1	92.9	6.7	0.9	0.6	0.6	6.2	17.8	8.6	14.4	17.2	14.1
39 143	...	4	Sandusky	1 060	61 792	785	58.3	93.7	3.3	0.4	0.4	7.0	6.5	19.7	8.1	12.4	15.9	13.9
39 145	...	4	Scioto	1 586	79 195	648	49.9	96.1	3.0	1.5	0.5	0.6	6.3	18.1	9.6	13.6	14.7	13.0
39 147	...	5	Seneca	1 426	58 683	817	41.2	96.2	2.3	0.5	0.5	3.4	6.2	19.7	10.4	11.7	15.5	13.9
39 149	...	6	Shelby	1 060	47 910	954	45.2	97.0	2.0	0.5	1.3	0.8	7.6	21.0	8.2	13.5	15.8	13.2
39 151	1320	2	Stark	1 492	378 098	155	253.4	91.6	0.8	0.7	0.7	0.9	6.4	18.5	8.3	12.2	15.6	14.4
39 153	0080	2	Summit	1 069	542 899	103	507.9	84.7	13.9	0.7	1.8	0.9	6.6	18.4	8.2	13.4	16.2	14.3
39 155	9320	2	Trumbull	1 597	225 116	252	141.0	91.2	8.4	0.5	0.6	0.8	6.1	18.2	7.7	12.2	15.1	14.7
39 157	...	4	Tuscarawas	1 470	90 914	567	61.8	98.6	1.0	0.5	0.4	0.7	6.6	18.8	8.0	12.4	15.7	14.1
39 159	...	6	Union	1 131	40 909	1 084	36.2	96.2	3.1	0.6	0.7	0.8	7.6	20.0	7.5	15.7	18.3	13.3
39 161	...	6	Van Wert	1 062	29 659	1 410	27.9	98.2	1.0	0.3	0.3	1.6	6.4	19.7	8.3	11.9	15.3	13.6
39 163	...	9	Vinton	1 072	12 806	2 246	11.9	99.0	0.4	1.2	0.2	0.5	7.2	19.7	8.8	13.5	15.5	13.4
39 165	1640	1	Warren	1 035	158 383	336	153.0	95.4	3.0	0.5	1.6	1.0	7.8	19.9	7.1	14.8	19.2	13.8
39 167	6020	3	Washington	1 645	63 251	767	38.5	98.2	1.3	0.7	0.7	0.5	5.8	17.7	8.8	11.7	15.8	14.7
39 169	...	4	Wayne	1 438	111 564	483	77.6	97.3	1.9	0.5	0.8	0.8	7.0	20.4	9.8	12.2	15.7	13.7
39 171	...	7	Williams	1 092	39 188	1 133	35.9	97.3	0.9	0.6	0.6	2.7	6.4	19.8	8.3	12.6	16.1	13.4
39 173	8400	2	Wood	1 599	121 065	448	75.7	95.9	1.5	0.6	1.4	3.3	5.8	17.9	17.2	12.0	14.9	13.5
39 175	...	7	Wyandot	1 051	22 908	1 648	21.8	98.5	0.2	0.3	0.7	1.5	6.5	19.4	8.2	12.5	15.4	13.4
40 000	...	X	OKLAHOMA	177 847	3 450 654	X	19.4	80.3	8.3	11.4	1.8	5.2	6.8	19.0	10.3	13.1	15.2	13.1
40 001	...	6	Adair	1 491	21 038	1 733	14.1	55.6	0.3	49.6	0.3	3.1	7.5	22.7	8.9	13.3	13.9	12.3
40 003	...	8	Alfalfa	2 245	6 105	2 769	2.7	91.3	4.5	4.5	0.3	2.9	4.5	14.9	6.4	10.9	17.8	13.3
40 005	...	7	Atoka	2 534	13 879	2 168	5.5	81.7	6.2	16.9	0.4	1.4	5.9	17.7	8.2	13.1	16.0	13.8
40 007	...	9	Beaver	4 699	5 857	2 798	1.2	94.5	0.4	2.4	0.2	10.8	5.7	21.1	6.5	10.2	15.5	13.7
40 009	...	7	Beckham	2 336	19 799	1 800	8.5	89.1	5.9	4.1	0.6	5.4	6.2	17.9	9.8	13.7	15.9	12.7
40 011	...	6	Blaine	2 405	11 976	2 295	5.0	79.1	7.5	11.0	3.3	6.6	5.7	18.3	9.1	13.1	15.5	12.2
40 013	...	6	Bryan	2 354	36 534	1 201	15.5	84.7	1.7	16.5	0.7	2.6	6.5	18.3	11.7	12.4	13.2	12.6
40 015	...	6	Caddo	3 311	30 150	1 391	9.1	69.2	3.8	27.8	0.5	6.3	6.6	21.9	8.5	11.5	14.5	12.4
40 017	5880	2	Canadian	2 330	87 697	598	37.6	89.6	2.5	6.2	2.8	3.9	6.8	21.3	8.2	13.1	17.6	14.6
40 019	...	5	Carter	2 134	45 621	989	21.4	81.7	4.5	12.1	0.9	2.8	6.9	19.3	7.9	11.7	15.1	13.6
40 021	...	6	Cherokee	1 945	42 521	1 045	21.9	63.6	1.6	39.4	0.6	4.1	7.0	19.3	14.6	12.2	13.6	12.2
40 023	...	7	Choctaw	2 004	15 342	2 066	7.7	72.7	11.7	19.4	0.4	1.6	6.4	19.6	7.8	11.4	13.3	13.1
40 025	...	9	Cimarron	4 753	3 148	2 982	0.7	88.3	0.7	2.1	0.2	15.4	6.6	21.0	6.4	10.1	13.3	13.2
40 027	5880	2	Cleveland	1 389	208 016	267	149.8	87.5	4.2	7.2	3.5	4.0	6.3	18.2	14.7	14.6	16.2	13.6
40 029	...	9	Coal	1 342	6 031	2 777	4.5	81.0	0.6	22.9	0.5	2.1	6.6	20.0	7.7	11.5	13.8	12.7
40 031	4200	3	Comanche	2 770	114 996	471	41.5	69.0	20.6	7.0	3.9	8.4	7.9	19.8	13.9	15.5	15.2	10.7
40 033	...	6	Cotton	1 649	6 614	2 726	4.0	87.4	3.1	9.7	0.5	4.9	6.6	18.8	7.4	12.1	14.6	12.3
40 035	...	6	Craig	1 971	14 950	2 095	7.6	79.4	3.9	27.0	0.5	1.2	6.0	17.9	7.8	11.6	16.3	13.3
40 037	8560	2	Creek	2 475	67 367	727	27.2	87.2	3.0	13.6	0.5	1.9	6.8	20.6	8.0	12.0	15.3	14.1
40 039	...	7	Custer	2 555	26 142	1 511	10.2	84.1	3.5	7.8	1.2	9.0	6.1	18.2	17.4	10.8	13.7	11.7
40 041	...	6	Delaware	1 918	37 077	1 187	19.3	76.6	0.3	28.5	0.4	1.8	6.1	18.3	6.9	10.8	13.5	13.5
40 043	...	9	Dewey	2 590	4 743	2 864	1.8	94.3	0.3	6.5	0.1	2.7	4.8	18.5	7.1	8.5	14.5	13.6
40 045	...	9	Ellis	3 183	4 075	2 912	1.3	97.9	0.3	2.2	0.2	2.6	4.9	16.8	6.0	8.8	12.9	16.6
40 047	2340	3	Garfield	2 741	57 813	826	21.1	91.0	3.8	3.6	1.8	4.1	6.7	18.3	9.1	12.1	15.3	13.0
40 049	...	6	Garvin	2 091	27 210	1 475	13.0	88.0	2.9	10.2	0.5	3.4	6.5	18.4	8.1	11.7	14.3	12.6
40 051	...	6	Grady	2 851	45 516	991	16.0	90.4	3.4	7.4	0.7	2.9	6.8	19.8	9.3	11.8	15.9	13.3
40 053	...	8	Grant	2 591	5 144	2 841	2.0	96.5	0.2	3.4	0.4	1.8	5.1	20.1	6.5	9.3	14.8	12.7
40 055	...	7	Greer	1 656	6 061	2 774	3.7	84.0	9.4	4.5	0.4	7.4	4.7	15.3	9.1	13.5	15.0	12.8
40 057	...	7	Harmon	1 393	3 283	2 974	2.4	74.4	10.0	1.9	0.4	22.8	6.1	19.8	7.9	10.1	14.0	12.3
40 059	...	9	Harper	2 691	3 562	2 948	1.3	96.5	0.0	1.3	0.2	5.6	4.7	18.6	6.4	8.5	14.9	14.3
40 061	...	6	Haskell	1 495	11 792	2 308	7.9	83.7	1.0	20.1	0.6	1.5	6.8	19.2	8.1	11.3	13.1	13.0
40 063	...	7	Hughes	2 089	14 154	2 150	6.8	77.8	4.8	21.2	0.5	2.5	5.8	17.4	8.0	12.6	14.5	13.1
40 065	...	5	Jackson	2 079	28 439	1 432	13.7	79.0	8.8	3.0	2.0	15.6	8.2	21.0	10.3	13.7	15.3	11.6
40 067	...	9	Jefferson	1 965	6 818	2 709	3.5	89.8	0.8	7.7	1.3	7.0	6.1	17.8	7.2	11.7	13.6	12.7
40 069	...	7	Johnston	1 669	10 513	2 397	6.3	81.3	2.1	20.1	0.5	2.5	6.3	19.2	9.7	10.9	14.2	13.6
40 071	...	5	Kay	2 379	48 080	949	20.2	87.9	2.1	10.8	0.9	4.3	6.8	19.6	8.8	10.6	14.4	13.3
40 073	...	6	Kingfisher	2 339	13 926	2 166	6.0	90.7	1.9	5.1	0.3	6.9	6.2	21.0	8.2	10.4	16.5	13.1

1. MSA = Metropolitan Statistical Area. PMSA = Primary MSA. NECMA = New England County Metropolitan Area. See Appendix A for explanation of these concepts. See Appendix B for list of metropolitan areas identified by type, with component counties. 2. County typology code from the Economic Research Service of USDA. See Appendix A for definition. 3. Dry land or land partially or temporarily covered by water. 4. Hispanic persons may be of any race.

STATE County	55 to 64 years	65 to 74 years	75 years and over	Percent female	Total persons 2001	Total persons 1990	Percent change 1990–2000	Percent change 2000–2001	Births	Deaths	Net migration	Number	Percent change, 1990–2000	Persons per household	Female family householder[1]	One person
	16	17	18	19	20	21	22	23	24	25	26	27	28	29	30	31
OHIO—Cont'd																
Ottawa	11.4	8.8	7.6	50.6	41 029	40 029	2.4	0.1	544	550	62	16 474	8.6	2.45	8.5	25.0
Paulding	9.8	6.7	5.9	50.8	20 081	20 488	-1.0	-1.0	289	241	-259	7 773	7.2	2.59	8.1	23.0
Perry	8.9	6.6	5.5	50.3	34 380	31 557	8.0	0.9	660	433	90	12 500	11.0	2.70	9.8	21.4
Pickaway	9.5	6.2	4.7	45.0	52 986	48 248	9.3	0.5	801	568	48	17 599	12.8	2.63	9.8	20.6
Pike	9.2	7.1	6.4	51.2	27 841	24 249	14.2	0.5	465	380	74	10 444	18.6	2.61	11.9	22.8
Portage	8.7	6.2	4.7	51.2	152 743	142 585	6.6	0.4	2 211	1 385	-74	56 449	14.7	2.56	10.1	23.3
Preble	10.0	7.2	5.9	50.2	42 520	40 113	5.5	0.4	650	445	-9	16 001	11.5	2.62	8.5	20.6
Putnam	8.0	6.7	6.6	50.4	34 808	33 819	2.7	0.2	622	369	-162	12 200	10.1	2.81	7.4	21.3
Richland	9.9	7.7	6.4	49.7	128 051	126 137	2.2	-0.6	2 138	1 677	-1 230	49 534	4.1	2.47	11.4	26.5
Ross	9.5	6.7	5.5	48.0	74 061	69 330	5.8	1.0	1 134	871	478	27 136	11.6	2.50	11.1	24.9
Sandusky	9.1	7.4	7.0	51.1	61 673	61 963	-0.3	-0.2	1 015	814	-296	23 717	5.6	2.56	10.5	24.1
Scioto	9.7	8.0	6.9	51.2	78 435	80 327	-1.4	-1.0	1 361	1 263	-841	30 871	3.6	2.45	13.1	26.9
Seneca	8.5	7.5	6.6	50.5	58 314	59 733	-1.8	-0.6	912	718	-547	22 292	4.8	2.56	10.2	24.7
Shelby	8.5	6.2	6.0	50.4	48 183	44 915	6.7	0.6	900	519	-86	17 636	12.9	2.68	9.3	22.0
Stark	9.5	7.7	7.4	52.0	377 438	367 585	2.9	-0.2	6 141	4 855	-1 799	148 316	6.3	2.49	11.5	26.1
Summit	8.7	7.3	6.8	51.8	544 217	514 990	5.4	0.2	9 206	6 658	-1 004	217 788	8.9	2.45	12.6	28.0
Trumbull	10.1	8.2	7.6	51.6	223 982	227 795	-1.2	-0.5	3 514	3 107	-1 462	89 020	3.4	2.48	12.5	26.9
Tuscarawas	9.5	7.7	7.2	51.3	91 066	84 090	8.1	0.2	1 499	1 166	-138	35 653	11.5	2.52	9.3	24.9
Union	7.9	5.3	4.3	52.2	42 793	31 969	28.0	4.6	760	350	1 445	14 346	30.0	2.70	8.0	19.9
Van Wert	9.3	7.8	7.7	51.2	29 440	30 464	-2.6	-0.7	446	393	-265	11 587	2.8	2.52	8.5	24.7
Vinton	9.7	7.1	5.0	50.2	13 150	11 098	15.4	2.7	214	171	297	4 892	20.2	2.59	10.2	23.6
Warren	8.0	5.4	4.0	49.4	169 025	113 973	39.0	6.7	2 936	1 322	8 792	55 966	43.0	2.72	8.0	18.9
Washington	10.5	8.0	6.9	51.4	62 991	62 254	1.6	-0.4	955	877	-320	25 137	6.4	2.45	9.1	25.4
Wayne	9.0	6.5	5.7	50.6	112 193	101 461	10.0	0.6	2 079	1 247	-165	40 445	13.5	2.68	8.7	22.7
Williams	9.5	6.8	7.0	50.3	39 211	36 956	6.0	0.1	629	470	-123	15 105	9.4	2.52	9.0	24.9
Wood	7.7	5.8	5.3	51.6	122 001	113 269	6.9	0.8	1 720	1 119	381	45 172	13.8	2.51	8.5	25.8
Wyandot	9.3	7.9	7.6	51.3	22 773	22 254	2.9	-0.6	370	292	-207	8 882	8.7	2.53	9.2	25.4
OKLAHOMA	9.2	7.0	6.2	50.9	3 460 097	3 145 576	9.7	0.3	60 327	43 267	-7 177	1 342 293	11.3	2.49	11.4	26.7
Adair	9.3	6.7	5.3	50.7	21 118	18 421	14.2	0.4	430	279	-64	7 471	17.0	2.76	12.9	22.8
Alfalfa	11.8	9.9	10.5	43.3	6 005	6 416	-4.8	-1.6	61	120	-40	2 199	-10.9	2.29	5.7	31.0
Atoka	10.5	7.8	6.9	45.9	14 011	12 778	8.6	1.0	206	173	97	4 964	10.4	2.48	10.2	27.1
Beaver	10.4	8.7	8.2	49.5	5 640	6 023	-2.8	-3.7	86	68	-242	2 245	-3.5	2.57	6.1	22.0
Beckham	8.3	7.6	7.8	47.7	19 846	18 812	5.2	0.2	331	369	86	7 356	0.1	2.44	10.4	28.5
Blaine	9.2	8.0	8.8	45.6	11 920	11 470	4.4	-0.5	203	224	-31	4 159	-5.9	2.50	8.6	29.0
Bryan	9.7	8.0	7.4	51.3	36 477	32 089	13.9	-0.2	578	445	-182	14 422	15.2	2.47	10.8	26.6
Caddo	9.6	7.8	7.2	50.4	29 966	29 550	2.0	-0.6	524	500	-198	10 957	0.7	2.62	13.0	24.8
Canadian	8.9	5.5	4.1	50.1	89 978	74 409	17.9	2.6	1 243	770	1 791	31 484	23.0	2.71	9.7	19.2
Carter	9.6	8.4	7.6	51.9	45 909	42 919	6.3	0.6	868	700	133	17 992	8.4	2.47	12.0	26.6
Cherokee	9.3	6.8	5.2	50.9	42 697	34 049	24.9	0.4	740	490	-62	16 175	27.8	2.52	11.9	25.3
Choctaw	11.0	8.7	8.7	52.5	15 169	15 302	0.3	-1.1	241	237	-178	6 220	4.5	2.43	14.4	28.3
Cimarron	10.8	8.4	10.2	50.7	3 023	3 301	-4.6	-4.0	33	39	-122	1 257	-3.3	2.47	6.0	29.3
Cleveland	8.1	4.9	3.5	49.8	211 908	174 253	19.4	1.9	2 919	1 482	2 484	79 186	23.7	2.51	10.0	24.4
Coal	9.8	9.5	8.4	50.9	6 074	5 780	4.3	0.7	102	79	21	2 373	4.1	2.51	10.6	27.3
Comanche	7.2	5.6	4.1	48.2	112 466	111 486	3.1	-2.2	2 535	1 062	-3 987	39 808	6.0	2.63	14.1	23.4
Cotton	10.5	8.3	9.4	50.4	6 528	6 651	-0.6	-1.3	96	104	-81	2 614	0.2	2.46	9.7	27.3
Craig	11.0	8.5	7.7	49.7	14 757	14 104	6.0	-1.3	223	246	-167	5 620	6.6	2.46	9.7	27.0
Creek	10.4	7.2	5.7	51.0	68 488	60 915	10.6	1.7	1 018	839	938	25 289	12.5	2.64	10.9	21.6
Custer	8.4	6.8	7.0	51.3	25 358	26 897	-2.8	-3.0	468	366	-903	10 136	2.2	2.45	9.5	27.8
Delaware	13.2	10.1	7.4	50.9	37 699	28 070	32.1	1.7	504	572	669	14 838	34.9	2.46	8.9	24.0
Dewey	12.1	9.4	12.1	51.3	4 672	5 551	-14.6	-1.5	66	100	-38	1 962	-11.7	2.35	5.0	30.0
Ellis	12.0	9.7	12.3	50.6	3 952	4 497	-9.4	-3.0	52	70	-107	1 769	-3.1	2.27	6.0	29.2
Garfield	9.4	7.9	8.1	51.6	57 114	56 735	1.9	-1.2	997	828	-863	23 175	3.2	2.42	10.5	27.7
Garvin	10.5	8.9	9.0	51.9	27 105	26 605	2.3	-0.4	444	481	-58	10 865	4.3	2.45	10.1	26.9
Grady	9.9	7.0	6.1	51.2	46 139	41 747	9.0	1.4	731	585	478	17 341	11.6	2.58	9.7	22.9
Grant	10.1	10.8	10.7	51.4	5 091	5 689	-9.6	-1.0	62	102	-12	2 089	-10.2	2.42	6.3	28.4
Greer	9.6	9.3	10.8	44.7	5 883	6 559	-7.6	-2.9	81	123	-138	2 237	-12.3	2.27	9.6	33.4
Harmon	8.8	8.9	12.1	51.5	3 155	3 793	-13.4	-3.9	48	82	-97	1 266	-14.8	2.47	9.2	29.0
Harper	10.9	11.5	10.2	50.9	3 464	4 063	-12.3	-2.8	56	56	-100	1 509	-8.3	2.33	6.5	29.2
Haskell	11.3	9.0	8.2	51.1	11 763	10 940	7.8	-0.2	158	196	13	4 624	7.1	2.52	9.1	24.7
Hughes	10.1	9.3	9.3	48.6	13 927	13 014	8.8	-1.6	215	254	-187	5 319	1.8	2.42	11.3	28.6
Jackson	8.0	6.2	5.7	50.2	27 661	28 764	-1.1	-2.7	592	338	-1 037	10 590	1.3	2.61	10.7	24.2
Jefferson	10.6	10.0	10.2	51.4	6 623	7 010	-2.7	-2.9	93	151	-138	2 716	-4.5	2.38	9.2	28.8
Johnston	10.7	8.2	7.2	50.8	10 569	10 032	4.8	0.5	175	161	45	4 057	7.2	2.53	10.7	25.2
Kay	9.5	8.4	8.6	51.6	47 541	48 056	0.0	-1.1	887	801	-617	19 157	0.4	2.45	10.2	27.9
Kingfisher	9.3	7.8	7.5	51.3	13 854	13 212	5.4	-0.5	243	198	-115	5 247	6.4	2.60	8.0	23.5

1. No spouse present.

STATE County	Births, average 1997–1999 Total	Rate[1]	Deaths, average 1997–1999 Number Total	Number Infant[2]	Rate Total[1]	Rate Infant[3]	Physicians,[4] 2000 Number	Rate[5]	Hospitals,[4] 1998 Number	Beds Number	Beds Rate[5]	Medicare enrollees 2000	Serious crimes known to police, 2000[6] Total Number	Rate[7]
	32	33	34	35	36	37	38	39	40	41	42	43	44	45
OHIO—Cont'd														
Ottawa	421	10.3	417	NA	10.2	NA	37	90	1	41	100	7 914	NA	NA
Paulding	274	13.6	183	NA	9.1	NA	5	25	1	51	254	2 866	NA	NA
Perry	478	13.9	339	NA	9.9	NA	6	18	0	0	0	5 326	706	2 235
Pickaway	619	11.6	437	NA	8.2	NA	28	53	2	131	244	6 373	NA	NA
Pike	373	13.4	304	NA	10.9	NA	25	90	1	40	144	4 265	NA	NA
Portage	1 822	12.1	1 078	10	7.1	5.5	145	95	1	285	188	18 447	2 642	1 737
Preble	509	11.8	355	NA	8.2	NA	16	38	0	0	0	6 204	975	2 303
Putnam	512	14.6	297	NA	8.5	NA	14	40	0	0	0	5 076	NA	NA
Richland	1 632	12.7	1 280	13	10.0	7.8	185	144	3	411	323	21 206	5 548	4 339
Ross	908	12.0	704	NA	9.3	NA	117	160	1	212	281	10 907	3 251	4 432
Sandusky	844	13.6	611	NA	9.8	NA	65	105	1	130	209	8 823	NA	NA
Scioto	1 047	13.0	983	11	12.2	10.2	93	117	2	281	350	14 861	3 764	4 898
Seneca	756	12.6	545	NA	9.1	NA	44	75	2	134	223	11 006	828	1 411
Shelby	709	14.9	393	NA	8.3	NA	37	77	1	106	223	6 234	NA	NA
Stark	4 750	12.7	3 797	32	10.2	6.7	734	194	5	1 710	458	66 414	NA	NA
Summit	7 136	13.3	5 212	53	9.7	7.5	1 339	247	6	1 936	360	84 143	14 899	2 895
Trumbull	2 716	12.0	2 387	24	10.6	9.0	369	164	2	660	293	38 591	NA	NA
Tuscarawas	1 148	13.0	931	8	10.5	7.0	99	109	2	273	308	15 052	747	822
Union	542	13.7	280	NA	7.1	NA	42	103	1	56	142	3 876	NA	NA
Van Wert	362	12.0	312	NA	10.3	NA	26	88	1	99	328	4 456	663	2 235
Vinton	169	13.8	140	NA	11.5	NA	1	8	0	0	0	1 778	NA	NA
Warren	2 138	14.6	1 012	11	6.9	5.1	122	77	0	0	0	15 998	1 555	1 077
Washington	724	11.4	672	NA	10.6	NA	97	153	2	250	394	10 885	1 200	1 956
Wayne	1 582	14.3	960	17	8.7	10.7	126	113	2	128	116	15 799	NA	NA
Williams	496	13.1	360	NA	9.5	NA	30	77	1	78	205	6 072	370	1 199
Wood	1 358	11.4	898	8	7.5	6.1	134	111	1	98	82	14 474	NA	NA
Wyandot	280	12.3	229	NA	10.0	NA	12	52	1	31	136	3 905	351	1 847
OKLAHOMA	48 572	14.5	34 191	399	10.2	8.2	5 448	158	110	11 495	343	507 849	157 302	4 559
Adair	353	17.3	220	NA	10.8	NA	8	38	1	34	167	3 154	565	2 686
Alfalfa	56	9.3	85	NA	14.1	NA	2	33	0	0	0	1 351	76	1 245
Atoka	162	12.2	156	NA	11.7	NA	6	43	1	45	340	2 160	295	2 126
Beaver	62	10.3	64	NA	10.6	NA	2	34	1	24	396	1 007	97	1 656
Beckham	292	14.9	279	NA	14.2	NA	27	136	2	128	654	3 246	615	3 106
Blaine	142	13.6	176	NA	16.8	NA	8	67	2	97	923	2 042	243	2 029
Bryan	462	13.3	418	NA	12.1	NA	30	82	1	103	297	6 553	1 197	3 276
Caddo	413	13.4	385	NA	12.5	NA	15	50	2	87	281	5 368	674	2 235
Canadian	1 130	13.2	576	11	6.8	10.0	36	41	1	54	63	8 503	4 271	4 870
Carter	635	14.3	555	NA	12.5	NA	70	153	2	206	463	8 814	2 281	5 000
Cherokee	583	14.9	392	NA	10.0	NA	40	94	1	61	156	5 523	1 212	2 850
Choctaw	223	14.8	212	NA	14.0	NA	12	78	1	66	438	3 297	476	3 103
Cimarron	42	14.0	39	NA	13.1	NA	3	95	1	20	676	621	17	540
Cleveland	2 575	12.8	1 151	14	5.7	5.3	239	115	1	236	117	16 701	10 671	5 130
Coal	83	13.6	73	NA	11.9	NA	2	33	1	20	333	1 203	180	2 985
Comanche	2 049	18.4	855	20	7.7	9.9	186	162	2	339	299	12 555	5 563	4 838
Cotton	90	13.4	90	NA	13.4	NA	2	30	0	0	0	1 229	116	1 754
Craig	171	11.8	198	NA	13.7	NA	21	140	1	28	194	3 220	337	2 254
Creek	911	13.6	670	8	10.0	8.4	30	45	3	220	328	9 088	1 738	2 580
Custer	370	14.5	291	NA	11.4	NA	29	111	2	96	377	3 785	852	3 259
Delaware	416	12.1	445	NA	13.0	NA	20	54	1	62	182	5 832	754	2 034
Dewey	47	9.5	92	NA	18.8	NA	2	42	1	18	365	1 071	104	2 193
Ellis	48	11.3	58	NA	13.8	NA	7	172	1	59	1 375	946	33	810
Garfield	796	14.0	669	7	11.7	8.8	115	199	2	298	524	10 245	2 925	5 059
Garvin	334	12.4	392	NA	14.6	NA	24	88	2	75	277	5 951	857	3 150
Grady	604	13.2	463	NA	10.1	NA	45	99	1	156	340	6 169	1 449	3 183
Grant	56	10.5	78	NA	14.7	NA	1	19	0	0	0	1 149	85	1 652
Greer	57	8.9	100	NA	15.7	NA	10	165	1	40	628	1 405	142	2 343
Harmon	46	13.3	56	NA	16.3	NA	2	61	1	24	690	720	147	4 478
Harper	33	9.1	50	NA	14.0	NA	2	56	1	25	695	864	50	1 404
Haskell	141	12.4	162	NA	14.2	NA	6	51	1	41	361	2 492	209	1 772
Hughes	166	11.8	206	NA	14.6	NA	14	99	2	72	511	3 054	409	2 890
Jackson	543	19.0	275	NA	9.6	NA	47	165	1	103	358	3 724	1 391	4 891
Jefferson	65	9.9	118	NA	17.9	NA	5	73	1	41	623	1 620	112	1 643
Johnston	132	12.8	137	NA	13.3	NA	5	48	1	36	348	1 941	162	1 541
Kay	682	14.6	634	NA	13.6	NA	57	119	2	168	360	9 235	2 219	4 615
Kingfisher	185	13.7	156	NA	11.5	NA	9	65	1	28	207	2 334	247	1 774

1. Per 1,000 estimated resident population, average 1997–1999.   2. Deaths of infants under 1 year old.   3. Deaths of infants under 1 year old per 1,000 live births.   4. Data subject to copyright.   5. Per 100,000 resident population as of July 1 of the year shown.   6. Data for serious crimes have not been adjusted for underreporting; this may affect comparability between geographic areas and over time.   7. Per 100,000 population estimated by the FBI.

Table B. States and Counties — Crime, Education, Money Income, and Poverty

STATE County	Serious crimes known to police, 2000[1] (cont'd) Rate[2] Violent	Property	Education — Enrollment[3] Total	Percent private	Attainment[4] (percent) High school graduate or more	Bachelor's degree or more	Local government expenditures, fiscal 1999[5] Total current expenditures (mil dol)	Current expenditures per student (dollars)	Money income 1989 Per capita[6] (dollars)	Households Median Dollars	Percent change, 1979–1989 (constant 1989 dollars)	Percent with $100,000 or more	Income and poverty, 1998 Median household income	Percent below poverty level All persons	Persons under 18	Persons 5–17 in families
	46	47	48	49	50	51	52	53	54	55	56	57	58	59	60	61
OHIO—Cont'd																
Ottawa	NA	NA	9 302	11.3	75.9	13.5	45.9	6 923	14 144	31 360	0.8	2.2	41 242	7.0	10.9	9.8
Paulding	NA	NA	5 226	6.7	72.2	6.9	26.8	6 558	11 254	28 345	-10.4	0.9	38 702	7.5	10.4	10.0
Perry	70	2 165	7 878	8.8	68.6	5.8	37.0	5 587	9 247	21 517	-9.0	0.8	30 992	13.9	17.6	19.7
Pickaway	NA	NA	10 829	9.7	69.7	9.0	52.2	5 373	11 490	28 403	-0.2	1.1	40 265	10.2	14.8	14.6
Pike	NA	NA	5 966	4.7	60.8	8.0	35.2	6 003	8 958	19 486	-1.5	0.7	29 473	19.2	28.9	25.9
Portage	81	1 657	47 037	9.0	79.3	17.6	154.6	6 337	12 509	30 253	-3.9	2.8	41 542	8.2	12.3	10.9
Preble	158	2 145	9 843	4.8	72.5	7.0	46.3	5 869	11 466	27 582	-4.2	1.2	39 109	7.8	11.6	10.9
Putnam	NA	NA	9 150	12.3	77.5	8.8	42.8	5 673	11 943	32 492	1.9	1.1	43 284	5.7	7.9	7.1
Richland	181	4 159	29 632	12.6	73.5	11.6	150.0	6 787	12 514	27 329	-5.0	1.8	35 730	11.0	15.9	15.2
Ross	101	4 332	16 760	6.9	67.6	9.2	78.7	6 328	10 758	24 286	-9.2	1.7	36 015	13.7	18.6	18.5
Sandusky	NA	NA	15 840	13.6	76.6	10.7	75.7	6 622	12 230	29 060	-5.7	1.9	38 381	8.5	12.1	11.1
Scioto	260	4 637	20 304	4.6	63.8	8.5	90.7	6 371	9 253	17 595	-15.7	1.4	27 247	20.0	25.3	27.7
Seneca	26	1 385	16 634	20.5	75.3	10.1	60.5	6 162	11 226	26 988	-8.1	1.3	35 301	9.3	12.9	12.0
Shelby	NA	NA	11 431	8.9	72.9	11.2	50.2	5 547	13 150	30 929	5.5	2.4	41 662	7.2	10.3	9.4
Stark	NA	NA	88 455	16.0	76.0	14.3	393.5	6 053	13 003	27 852	-10.8	2.3	39 701	10.2	16.5	13.8
Summit	200	2 695	130 885	13.9	78.3	19.7	568.5	6 681	14 409	28 996	-5.9	3.5	40 102	10.7	17.3	14.5
Trumbull	NA	NA	54 893	13.3	75.2	11.4	237.7	6 413	12 899	28 186	-13.9	2.0	37 463	11.0	17.9	15.4
Tuscarawas	33	789	18 700	9.5	71.9	9.0	89.6	5 731	11 141	24 773	-8.0	1.4	34 541	10.1	15.2	13.6
Union	NA	NA	7 918	12.0	76.2	12.0	35.2	5 729	13 644	33 244	13.6	2.8	47 018	6.0	7.9	8.1
Van Wert	128	2 107	7 423	12.7	79.2	9.3	28.4	6 477	11 913	28 642	-4.7	1.6	38 637	6.5	9.1	8.4
Vinton	NA	NA	2 670	3.1	58.7	4.8	12.4	4 883	8 826	19 066	-4.1	1.2	28 120	17.7	23.1	26.5
Warren	59	1 018	28 785	14.6	75.5	18.0	145.4	5 790	14 615	36 728	5.5	3.9	52 526	5.2	7.5	6.8
Washington	121	1 836	15 478	15.3	77.5	13.2	63.1	5 833	11 438	24 456	-9.9	1.6	34 666	12.7	18.2	17.5
Wayne	NA	NA	26 038	17.3	73.6	13.9	124.6	6 496	12 237	29 190	-3.3	2.4	39 783	8.8	13.6	11.9
Williams	39	1 160	9 085	7.3	76.1	8.9	39.9	5 541	12 473	28 451	-3.4	2.0	38 654	6.7	9.7	8.7
Wood	NA	NA	40 718	8.3	83.8	21.9	134.5	7 172	13 853	31 197	-1.3	4.3	44 500	7.0	9.2	7.8
Wyandot	47	1 799	5 411	10.0	76.5	8.7	20.7	5 171	11 279	27 454	0.7	1.3	36 571	6.7	8.8	8.6
OKLAHOMA	498	4 061	838 811	10.0	74.6	17.8	3 332.7	5 303	11 893	23 577	-4.6	2.3	32 373	16.1	23.2	21.5
Adair	566	2 120	4 936	6.4	56.1	9.6	31.2	6 209	7 378	16 886	10.5	0.5	24 840	24.9	33.8	31.7
Alfalfa	82	1 163	1 416	6.9	77.3	17.3	6.1	6 286	9 999	18 407	-21.8	1.9	26 259	17.3	22.6	22.5
Atoka	324	1 801	3 085	4.2	59.8	10.2	13.4	5 840	8 308	13 898	-7.1	0.7	22 777	27.0	33.9	34.6
Beaver	68	1 588	1 470	2.6	75.3	15.4	9.0	6 932	11 910	27 372	-1.1	0.8	35 350	11.0	14.8	14.4
Beckham	192	2 914	4 911	4.0	66.5	12.3	20.4	5 311	10 400	19 154	-12.5	2.2	27 750	20.0	24.4	25.8
Blaine	443	1 587	2 716	4.1	71.2	12.4	13.7	6 150	9 787	20 395	-10.9	1.5	27 972	21.2	29.7	28.5
Bryan	309	2 967	8 532	3.1	67.3	16.9	36.1	5 204	9 082	16 610	-2.3	0.9	25 805	20.6	27.7	27.7
Caddo	255	1 980	7 355	1.6	66.2	11.6	39.2	5 878	8 735	17 857	-12.4	1.4	26 561	24.3	32.6	31.4
Canadian	439	4 431	21 552	8.3	82.3	16.7	82.4	4 651	13 077	33 855	-2.7	2.1	46 563	9.0	13.0	11.2
Carter	625	4 375	10 656	6.7	70.3	13.4	49.7	5 459	11 266	21 800	-4.7	2.1	28 850	19.6	27.6	26.6
Cherokee	473	2 378	10 522	5.9	69.9	21.1	40.1	5 609	9 446	17 513	-0.5	1.4	25 478	22.4	30.9	30.5
Choctaw	717	2 386	3 646	4.3	57.9	7.1	17.3	5 782	7 548	12 451	-17.1	0.4	20 077	29.9	38.7	41.0
Cimarron	222	318	839	4.2	71.0	15.1	4.9	7 839	9 929	19 173	-10.5	2.0	28 658	17.1	23.7	24.0
Cleveland	376	4 753	59 525	8.0	83.9	25.9	169.6	4 695	13 182	29 975	-1.8	2.5	42 978	10.5	14.6	12.9
Coal	746	2 238	1 370	3.0	60.4	9.1	7.9	6 283	7 695	14 177	-3.9	0.5	21 175	23.6	30.2	33.9
Comanche	573	4 264	30 373	6.9	81.1	18.4	121.7	5 275	10 602	24 378	5.5	1.5	32 876	18.3	26.0	24.5
Cotton	529	1 225	1 644	7.1	62.8	8.9	6.6	5 260	9 147	18 978	1.6	0.5	28 173	17.7	24.0	25.4
Craig	201	2 054	3 143	4.9	66.8	10.0	16.4	5 221	9 886	18 986	-7.1	1.2	26 555	16.6	23.9	22.8
Creek	315	2 265	15 474	7.7	68.9	10.6	66.1	4 918	10 608	23 795	-7.4	1.2	33 411	13.7	20.9	18.7
Custer	302	2 957	8 929	2.3	75.1	20.4	29.2	5 500	10 461	22 592	-5.5	1.3	30 914	17.3	22.9	22.6
Delaware	289	1 745	5 999	4.6	66.2	10.8	33.2	5 018	9 572	18 681	10.1	2.0	27 040	18.1	26.8	26.6
Dewey	232	1 961	1 287	3.8	68.2	12.1	8.3	7 336	9 726	18 968	-15.1	1.3	27 254	16.8	22.5	21.7
Ellis	0	810	1 043	1.4	73.8	14.0	5.7	7 272	10 082	20 017	-10.6	1.0	27 767	15.0	19.6	20.2
Garfield	391	4 669	13 899	14.1	76.5	17.3	56.3	5 371	11 564	23 243	-16.4	2.1	31 988	14.9	22.2	20.1
Garvin	375	2 775	5 996	4.7	63.4	10.1	28.7	5 144	9 548	18 659	-9.9	1.4	25 712	19.3	28.0	25.0
Grady	598	2 586	11 023	4.9	69.0	13.2	41.7	4 854	10 420	21 885	-5.6	1.4	32 964	16.2	22.1	21.3
Grant	19	1 633	1 239	5.6	77.9	15.6	7.0	6 404	11 255	21 659	-7.9	2.3	30 026	14.4	19.3	19.8
Greer	66	2 277	1 204	6.0	64.7	10.0	6.0	5 926	9 089	17 010	4.5	1.4	25 943	25.1	34.2	34.5
Harmon	366	4 112	877	1.4	58.0	10.5	4.2	6 078	7 817	13 880	-10.8	0.6	22 262	31.8	40.6	47.6
Harper	84	1 319	895	2.1	76.1	13.6	5.3	7 102	11 752	22 813	-17.9	2.0	33 396	11.1	17.2	15.2
Haskell	136	1 637	2 638	2.1	56.4	7.7	12.6	5 230	8 320	15 592	-4.0	1.3	23 031	23.9	32.2	32.2
Hughes	283	2 607	2 946	3.5	58.7	7.7	15.9	6 169	8 849	15 168	1.2	0.7	21 696	24.8	33.5	32.4
Jackson	369	4 522	7 871	2.7	74.1	16.5	31.3	5 100	10 224	21 715	8.8	1.5	32 645	17.3	24.1	24.8
Jefferson	293	1 349	1 485	2.1	58.7	6.6	8.1	5 697	8 430	15 553	-8.9	0.7	22 792	23.8	32.4	31.8
Johnston	428	1 113	2 915	2.2	61.0	9.3	11.7	5 674	7 821	15 264	12.6	1.0	23 626	23.3	30.7	31.8
Kay	483	4 133	11 494	7.9	76.8	18.5	45.9	4 838	12 394	24 295	-6.4	2.0	32 554	15.7	24.4	21.7
Kingfisher	50	1 723	3 355	7.8	76.2	13.4	17.9	5 489	11 141	25 367	-10.5	1.3	35 458	12.0	16.3	15.4

1. Data for serious crimes have not been adjusted for underreporting; this may affect comparability between geographic areas and over time. 2. Per 100,000 population estimated by the FBI. 3. All persons 3 years old and over enrolled in nursery school through college. 4. Persons 25 years old and over. 5. Elementary and secondary education expenditures, local government fiscal years ending between July 1, 1998 and June 30, 1999. 6. Based on population enumerated as of April 1, 1990.

Table B. States and Counties — **Personal Income**

STATE County	Personal income, 1999							Transfer payments					
	Total (mil dol)	Percent change, 1998–1999	Per capita[1]		Wages and salaries[2] (mil dol)	Proprietor's income (mil dol)	Dividends, interest, and rent (mil dol)	Total (mil dol)	Government payments to individuals				
			Dollars	Rank					Total (mil dol)	Social Security (mil dol)	Medical payments (mil dol)	Income mainte-nance (mil dol)	Unemploy-ment insurance (mil dol)
	62	63	64	65	66	67	68	69	70	71	72	73	74

OHIO—Cont'd													
Ottawa	1 130	3.7	27 370	386	473	56	238	176	167	79	66	6	4
Paulding	401	1.6	19 961	2 001	147	19	68	63	59	31	18	4	1
Perry	559	2.8	16 313	2 857	196	35	75	129	121	49	48	12	3
Pickaway	1 088	2.7	20 364	1 872	574	41	178	152	141	63	49	14	2
Pike	514	2.4	18 353	2 456	373	35	96	126	120	41	51	17	4
Portage	3 660	4.0	24 146	829	1 816	196	628	466	434	194	157	27	9
Preble	968	3.5	22 272	1 280	323	54	151	142	132	64	48	8	2
Putnam	868	4.7	24 643	725	352	62	169	107	99	50	34	5	2
Richland	2 945	3.6	22 721	1 158	1 987	163	536	495	467	212	167	37	11
Ross	1 537	3.6	20 291	1 896	952	76	249	261	244	97	91	29	5
Sandusky	1 441	3.4	23 315	1 012	886	70	253	221	208	100	74	12	5
Scioto	1 525	2.7	18 978	2 285	702	94	246	424	407	127	174	61	8
Seneca	1 297	2.7	21 695	1 455	684	73	238	246	233	97	103	13	4
Shelby	1 224	2.6	25 520	580	1 047	62	213	147	136	67	46	9	3
Stark	9 409	2.4	25 214	634	5 635	465	1 900	1 494	1 414	648	524	108	23
Summit	15 698	3.8	29 187	252	9 720	706	3 135	2 182	2 066	881	805	188	33
Trumbull	5 638	2.9	25 022	667	3 575	309	1 074	973	924	423	353	72	16
Tuscarawas	1 927	3.1	21 708	1 450	1 014	175	370	324	305	147	103	21	7
Union	969	5.2	23 776	901	1 137	54	140	101	92	43	33	6	1
Van Wert	690	5.4	22 916	1 106	369	39	130	99	93	52	27	5	1
Vinton	203	4.1	16 423	2 839	64	10	36	49	47	15	19	7	1
Warren	4 354	9.6	28 402	289	1 868	196	607	412	379	175	137	19	7
Washington	1 405	2.1	22 298	1 276	759	111	257	250	236	105	89	19	5
Wayne	2 640	2.9	23 776	901	1 544	240	537	355	331	155	124	22	5
Williams	952	3.4	25 226	630	599	64	185	129	121	58	43	6	2
Wood	3 216	3.9	26 737	436	2 020	155	671	350	324	147	111	16	5
Wyandot	508	2.4	22 183	1 303	282	38	95	81	76	36	28	4	2
OKLAHOMA	77 093	4.0	22 958	X	44 741	8 805	13 911	11 975	11 370	4 891	4 194	1 125	141
Adair	336	5.3	16 374	2 849	119	49	42	73	70	25	24	12	1
Alfalfa	115	5.2	19 611	2 109	35	30	28	23	22	12	8	1	0
Atoka	202	8.4	15 134	2 978	79	37	31	50	47	19	17	8	0
Beaver	138	14.5	23 000	1 089	38	39	29	19	18	9	6	2	0
Beckham	342	3.8	17 256	2 694	159	41	83	73	69	30	26	8	1
Blaine	217	7.1	21 083	1 643	80	43	50	43	41	19	14	5	0
Bryan	662	5.6	18 958	2 291	286	63	99	153	147	57	58	16	1
Caddo	524	4.9	17 092	2 719	222	70	108	114	109	46	36	17	1
Canadian	1 974	5.3	22 821	1 134	733	134	291	209	193	87	55	12	3
Carter	984	2.7	22 104	1 331	564	144	199	194	186	80	72	20	3
Cherokee	665	4.9	16 825	2 772	298	60	104	149	142	50	50	18	1
Choctaw	247	8.0	16 472	2 832	91	29	37	74	72	26	26	13	1
Cimarron	78	26.9	26 534	459	24	26	17	11	10	6	3	1	0
Cleveland	4 550	5.2	22 362	1 255	1 633	270	650	456	419	191	130	33	5
Coal	86	9.1	13 960	3 050	29	7	14	26	25	10	9	3	0
Comanche	2 360	2.6	22 134	1 316	1 650	135	352	341	324	114	98	47	2
Cotton	124	4.1	18 826	2 339	26	19	23	25	24	11	8	3	0
Craig	268	5.0	18 511	2 411	169	13	49	71	69	26	32	5	0
Creek	1 232	2.5	18 076	2 526	486	93	195	238	225	101	84	18	3
Custer	511	2.3	19 960	2 002	269	59	121	91	87	36	32	9	1
Delaware	642	5.3	18 366	2 453	174	80	118	135	129	61	43	13	1
Dewey	94	-2.1	19 347	2 197	30	16	26	20	19	9	7	2	0
Ellis	86	5.6	20 580	1 819	24	18	24	17	17	8	6	1	0
Garfield	1 342	1.1	23 559	950	732	129	287	253	243	102	108	16	2
Garvin	531	2.9	19 871	2 030	211	61	107	155	150	54	77	11	2
Grady	802	2.9	17 411	2 664	322	73	142	139	130	62	39	16	2
Grant	116	-1.9	22 181	1 304	35	23	32	23	22	11	8	1	0
Greer	130	4.3	20 361	1 873	46	16	22	30	29	12	11	3	0
Harmon	67	8.4	20 083	1 969	19	17	11	17	16	6	7	2	0
Harper	89	5.3	24 972	677	26	21	24	16	15	9	5	1	0
Haskell	200	8.4	17 487	2 650	67	21	36	58	56	21	22	6	1
Hughes	213	3.6	15 180	2 972	61	28	41	64	61	25	22	7	1
Jackson	576	2.1	19 276	1 900	397	40	105	95	90	33	34	12	1
Jefferson	125	6.8	19 115	2 255	43	22	23	32	31	14	11	3	0
Johnston	156	8.1	15 101	2 980	71	18	23	43	42	17	13	6	0
Kay	1 026	-0.4	22 091	1 339	597	107	234	178	170	92	51	12	3
Kingfisher	287	-2.4	21 234	1 590	153	24	69	49	46	22	18	3	0

1. Based on the resident population estimated as of July 1 of the year shown. 2. Includes other labor income.

Table B. States and Counties — Earnings, Social Security, and Housing

STATE County	Earnings, 1999 Total (mil dol)	Farm	Goods-related[1] Total	Manu-facturing	Service-related and other[2] Total	Retail trade	Finance, insurance, and real estate	Services	Govern-ment	Social Security beneficiaries, December 2000 Number	Rate[3]	Supplemental Security Income recipients, December 2000	Housing units, 1990 Total	Percent change, 1980–1990
	75	76	77	78	79	80	81	82	83	84	85	86	87	88
OHIO—Cont'd														
Ottawa	529	-0.9	31.9	24.8	52.7	12.4	3.9	16.7	16.3	8 736	213	291	23 340	1.2
Paulding	166	-1.0	D	34.8	D	9.2	2.7	11.7	23.4	3 529	174	279	7 951	4.2
Perry	231	1.1	40.0	22.9	37.4	8.7	2.8	14.9	21.4	5 957	175	849	12 260	6.9
Pickaway	615	-1.6	D	36.9	D	7.9	3.2	10.7	29.0	7 617	144	908	16 385	8.3
Pike	409	-0.8	D	57.1	D	7.7	1.5	10.4	13.2	5 346	193	1 466	9 722	11.6
Portage	2 012	0.5	36.9	29.7	36.7	9.0	2.7	14.0	26.0	21 709	143	1 821	52 299	10.0
Preble	376	-1.1	D	38.3	D	10.0	3.3	13.1	17.5	7 376	174	421	15 174	8.7
Putnam	414	2.2	D	42.4	D	8.2	D	10.7	13.7	5 681	164	279	11 600	5.5
Richland	2 150	0.4	38.9	33.9	44.8	10.4	3.6	19.4	15.9	23 744	184	2 616	50 350	2.4
Ross	1 028	-0.6	D	27.8	D	10.6	2.4	17.9	27.6	12 089	165	2 526	26 173	10.2
Sandusky	955	0.6	50.5	45.0	D	8.0	2.9	18.4	12.8	11 117	180	816	23 753	2.4
Scioto	796	-0.3	20.6	13.8	54.0	13.6	3.4	27.1	25.7	15 953	201	5 568	32 408	2.3
Seneca	757	-1.0	D	37.7	D	9.1	3.6	18.3	14.7	10 981	187	900	22 473	1.0
Shelby	1 109	0.7	D	59.3	D	4.6	1.4	10.4	8.6	7 524	157	528	16 509	7.9
Stark	6 100	0.3	38.3	30.8	49.6	10.3	4.5	23.6	11.8	71 154	188	6 558	146 910	2.6
Summit	10 426	0.0	30.8	25.1	56.5	10.0	5.8	25.8	12.6	95 393	176	10 826	211 477	5.5
Trumbull	3 884	0.0	53.2	49.1	36.5	9.0	3.3	16.3	10.4	45 712	203	4 510	90 533	2.6
Tuscarawas	1 188	2.0	38.5	29.7	45.7	12.2	3.6	18.1	13.7	16 809	185	1 433	33 982	5.4
Union	1 191	0.0	D	65.6	D	4.2	D	8.5	8.8	5 054	124	316	11 599	9.2
Van Wert	408	-1.5	D	47.4	D	8.8	6.6	15.6	11.1	5 813	196	295	11 998	3.2
Vinton	74	-0.3	D	27.5	D	7.3	5.9	12.3	30.3	2 070	162	505	4 856	10.3
Warren	2 064	0.1	32.2	25.3	54.4	15.0	7.7	20.2	13.4	19 844	125	1 159	40 636	22.1
Washington	871	0.4	38.2	28.0	47.7	10.1	3.6	22.6	13.7	12 363	195	1 626	25 752	7.5
Wayne	1 784	3.1	45.9	36.8	36.6	8.8	4.6	14.0	14.3	17 390	156	1 375	37 036	7.9
Williams	663	0.7	D	51.3	D	6.6	2.8	14.7	10.7	6 658	170	376	14 745	5.7
Wood	2 175	0.8	42.2	33.7	38.3	7.8	3.0	15.0	18.7	16 437	136	929	41 760	10.7
Wyandot	320	0.7	56.5	44.4	30.1	7.2	2.9	10.8	12.7	4 209	184	230	8 596	3.6
OKLAHOMA	53 546	1.8	25.6	15.6	52.1	9.6	5.2	24.2	20.5	594 155	172	72 204	1 406 499	13.7
Adair	168	18.8	D	27.5	D	8.0	1.8	12.6	21.3	3 736	178	890	7 124	7.5
Alfalfa	65	35.8	D	2.0	D	8.2	3.2	10.4	21.9	1 417	232	57	3 357	3.2
Atoka	116	6.4	D	14.0	D	13.6	2.1	12.0	33.7	2 746	198	582	5 110	10.5
Beaver	77	38.1	D	D	D	3.7	2.2	6.9	18.8	1 116	191	42	2 923	5.5
Beckham	200	3.1	23.2	4.1	58.0	17.0	4.5	27.4	15.7	3 811	192	532	9 117	11.0
Blaine	123	24.0	24.8	17.9	30.6	6.9	3.4	12.6	20.6	2 398	200	216	5 729	-2.4
Bryan	349	3.0	D	11.9	D	10.9	3.6	32.8	21.5	7 459	204	1 318	14 875	11.6
Caddo	293	13.2	D	2.9	D	7.6	3.8	20.2	25.1	6 092	202	893	13 191	6.2
Canadian	867	1.3	41.9	31.3	36.4	10.0	3.6	15.1	20.5	10 758	123	522	28 560	38.1
Carter	708	-0.2	38.5	18.0	49.2	13.2	3.1	21.2	12.4	9 529	209	1 445	19 201	7.6
Cherokee	358	6.7	D	1.1	D	12.1	3.2	29.5	35.3	6 797	160	1 115	15 935	24.9
Choctaw	121	9.9	D	1.2	50.2	13.5	2.5	18.6	26.2	3 700	241	1 015	6 844	-5.2
Cimarron	50	53.5	D	D	D	8.8	2.8	5.4	19.3	739	235	40	1 690	6.2
Cleveland	1 902	0.1	16.6	8.1	49.7	13.9	5.1	23.3	33.8	23 432	113	1 902	71 038	43.4
Coal	36	1.7	D	D	D	9.9	D	22.1	30.6	1 322	219	269	2 725	8.2
Comanche	1 784	0.5	D	9.9	D	7.7	2.8	14.4	55.9	15 021	131	2 197	43 589	9.1
Cotton	45	27.4	D	1.7	D	8.3	4.3	12.1	26.3	1 385	209	129	3 152	-0.3
Craig	182	0.8	D	18.1	D	9.0	3.9	14.2	33.9	3 347	224	456	6 041	-0.5
Creek	579	-0.6	38.8	27.4	46.1	9.5	3.5	18.8	15.6	12 092	179	1 018	25 143	11.0
Custer	328	3.2	22.2	14.0	48.9	12.1	4.2	20.2	25.7	4 335	166	543	11 636	11.5
Delaware	254	14.9	D	11.7	D	12.3	7.2	23.1	17.4	7 750	209	817	16 808	57.8
Dewey	45	13.3	D	4.9	D	8.3	4.9	14.2	32.2	1 147	242	89	2 733	1.9
Ellis	43	28.0	D	D	D	10.8	2.6	11.6	29.3	1 046	257	57	2 449	-0.6
Garfield	861	1.9	19.6	8.7	54.1	10.4	4.1	23.3	24.5	11 528	199	1 160	26 502	3.6
Garvin	272	1.9	30.0	11.8	42.7	13.7	4.0	12.5	25.4	6 687	246	908	11 932	4.9
Grady	395	4.3	34.3	24.4	41.0	10.8	3.5	17.7	20.3	7 850	172	934	17 788	12.9
Grant	58	30.0	D	D	D	4.4	6.1	D	18.9	1 274	248	62	2 955	-0.9
Greer	63	20.6	D	3.1	D	5.5	2.4	6.9	43.6	1 558	257	186	3 126	-5.4
Harmon	36	38.0	D	D	D	7.5	4.7	7.2	26.7	814	248	152	1 793	-8.2
Harper	48	33.5	D	D	D	8.2	4.0	10.3	25.5	1 015	285	40	2 077	-2.9
Haskell	87	9.7	18.4	5.6	44.4	12.7	2.3	20.4	27.5	2 893	245	506	5 138	8.2
Hughes	88	13.7	D	1.3	D	13.6	3.4	17.7	30.3	3 383	239	503	6 021	-4.5
Jackson	437	4.6	D	7.3	D	8.8	2.7	11.2	56.2	4 327	152	667	12 125	3.3
Jefferson	65	18.4	D	16.2	37.4	13.2	4.5	10.3	21.9	1 763	259	219	3 522	-4.4
Johnston	90	9.6	D	D	D	7.6	0.9	12.5	26.1	2 403	229	404	4 478	3.3
Kay	704	1.1	D	23.4	D	11.3	3.5	D	12.8	10 408	216	800	22 456	5.6
Kingfisher	177	3.1	25.3	7.6	D	9.6	D	14.6	13.8	2 631	189	151	5 791	2.2

1. Covers mining, construction, and manufacturing. finance, insurance, and real estate; and services.   2. Covers private sector earnings in agricultural services, forestry, and fisheries; transportation and public utilities; wholesale trade; retail trade;   3. Per 1,000 resident population estimated as of July 1 of the year shown.

Table B. States and Counties — Housing, Labor Force, and Employment

STATE County	Housing units, 1990 (cont'd) Occupied units — Owner-occupied Total	Percent	Median value[1]	Owner cost as a percent of income With a mortgage	Without a mortgage	Renter-occupied Median rent[2]	Rent as percent of income	Sub-standard units[3] (percent)	Civilian labor force, 2001 Total	Percent change, 2000–2001	Unemployment Total	Rate[4]	Civilian employment, 1990[5] Total	Percent Professional, managerial, and technical	Precision production, craft, and repair
	89	90	91	92	93	94	95	96	97	98	99	100	101	102	103
OHIO—Cont'd															
Ottawa	15 170	78.3	68 600	16.8	12.5	379	22.8	1.9	21 747	3.4	1 248	5.7	18 274	24.7	15.3
Paulding	7 252	83.2	42 500	15.1	12.3	295	20.2	3.0	10 058	1.6	519	5.2	8 936	16.0	13.7
Perry	11 264	78.1	36 900	17.9	12.7	290	25.7	4.5	14 493	1.4	1 047	7.2	12 179	17.7	15.3
Pickaway	15 602	71.7	62 200	17.4	11.9	357	23.4	2.8	25 882	2.6	912	3.5	19 787	20.9	15.0
Pike	8 805	69.4	42 300	17.5	12.9	297	30.9	7.6	11 707	0.3	931	8.0	8 019	22.5	15.6
Portage	49 229	70.1	69 000	19.1	12.1	407	27.7	2.1	83 722	0.3	3 414	4.1	68 974	25.7	13.5
Preble	14 347	77.1	52 700	18.2	12.6	329	21.6	2.1	21 931	1.4	966	4.4	17 968	18.5	16.4
Putnam	11 082	84.3	58 000	15.6	11.9	326	18.5	1.9	20 734	-0.5	820	4.0	15 648	19.2	16.5
Richland	47 573	70.8	52 200	16.5	12.3	343	24.0	1.9	61 688	0.6	3 230	5.2	56 207	22.6	14.6
Ross	24 325	70.5	49 200	17.7	12.7	317	25.5	4.3	34 936	0.1	1 766	5.1	26 080	23.1	12.8
Sandusky	22 464	74.5	57 200	16.2	12.3	365	23.1	1.9	31 173	1.2	1 602	5.1	27 857	19.7	17.0
Scioto	29 786	69.7	37 100	17.8	13.1	281	30.1	4.1	33 559	1.6	2 337	7.0	25 320	26.4	12.3
Seneca	21 277	74.0	47 700	16.3	11.8	322	22.9	2.1	28 986	2.9	1 687	5.8	26 213	20.4	14.4
Shelby	15 626	74.3	59 900	16.6	11.8	369	22.6	2.6	28 972	1.9	1 185	4.1	21 474	22.6	14.0
Stark	139 573	70.1	57 700	16.9	12.1	356	24.5	1.5	192 110	1.2	7 738	4.0	164 452	27.0	11.2
Summit	199 998	68.7	61 900	18.8	12.7	394	26.5	1.4	282 851	0.4	12 169	4.3	236 637	30.9	11.2
Trumbull	86 056	73.1	53 300	16.6	12.3	346	24.4	1.7	111 271	0.1	6 960	6.3	98 808	22.8	13.4
Tuscarawas	31 971	75.0	49 900	17.9	12.0	311	24.7	1.7	45 036	1.4	2 130	4.7	35 842	19.9	13.0
Union	11 037	74.4	67 400	18.4	12.8	395	23.6	1.9	19 573	6.3	536	2.7	15 129	23.0	13.3
Van Wert	11 266	80.6	46 000	15.8	11.6	325	21.1	1.4	16 597	-1.0	935	5.6	14 390	19.1	12.4
Vinton	4 069	80.4	34 900	19.2	13.2	267	26.7	9.7	3 790	0.8	443	11.7	3 820	15.2	14.8
Warren	39 150	74.7	77 600	19.1	11.8	434	23.7	2.2	83 000	1.9	2 733	3.3	55 033	29.2	12.3
Washington	23 636	74.5	51 900	16.8	11.9	300	24.2	2.4	32 282	-0.5	1 233	3.8	27 251	27.0	12.7
Wayne	35 619	71.2	65 700	18.9	11.6	367	23.4	2.8	59 034	3.1	2 290	3.9	47 862	22.5	12.6
Williams	13 807	77.0	48 200	16.2	11.8	327	22.5	1.7	20 675	-1.1	1 197	5.8	18 115	17.1	16.7
Wood	39 677	69.9	72 200	17.7	12.2	395	25.3	1.9	68 361	0.9	2 414	3.5	55 716	30.6	10.9
Wyandot	8 168	75.7	46 600	16.7	11.8	293	20.6	1.7	13 250	6.4	577	4.4	10 371	19.3	14.9
OKLAHOMA	1 206 135	68.1	48 100	20.0	12.8	340	25.4	3.7	1 665 427	1.1	63 506	3.8	1 369 138	27.9	12.0
Adair	6 386	73.0	30 200	18.7	13.0	226	26.2	7.8	9 215	-1.7	440	4.8	7 030	17.6	13.5
Alfalfa	2 469	81.1	23 900	18.4	13.1	239	16.7	1.3	2 512	-1.4	36	1.4	2 649	18.5	7.9
Atoka	4 495	75.0	30 300	21.2	13.9	230	29.7	4.8	5 006	2.4	201	4.0	4 332	19.1	8.7
Beaver	2 327	77.7	47 800	18.7	11.6	288	18.5	3.6	2 633	1.9	70	2.7	2 857	21.8	14.4
Beckham	7 351	69.8	31 200	19.3	13.8	272	22.8	3.5	10 471	3.0	279	2.7	7 571	25.1	12.9
Blaine	4 418	76.1	34 000	20.3	13.4	272	22.2	3.8	4 673	-0.4	218	4.7	4 732	18.1	13.1
Bryan	12 524	69.7	36 000	19.9	12.7	278	29.3	3.8	18 231	7.3	525	2.9	12 530	24.8	11.3
Caddo	10 879	72.6	31 400	20.6	14.1	259	25.5	4.2	11 936	-1.8	639	5.4	10 629	21.1	11.8
Canadian	25 597	76.5	58 100	20.3	12.4	415	24.0	3.0	47 076	0.5	1 473	3.1	36 215	28.2	11.9
Carter	16 601	72.4	38 100	19.8	13.0	311	24.7	3.2	20 828	2.6	874	4.2	17 541	24.8	12.5
Cherokee	12 657	68.2	43 300	20.5	13.5	291	32.1	5.5	19 739	5.3	614	3.1	13 245	27.9	10.7
Choctaw	5 952	72.3	30 900	22.0	14.4	197	26.4	4.9	5 798	6.7	388	6.7	5 086	17.7	12.1
Cimarron	1 300	74.5	29 000	15.0	12.8	226	20.9	2.9	1 775	2.5	41	2.3	1 566	14.0	5.7
Cleveland	63 991	63.1	61 800	20.5	12.2	383	26.5	2.9	113 956	0.7	3 613	3.2	87 247	33.5	10.9
Coal	2 279	73.7	25 100	23.1	14.1	226	27.0	5.9	2 344	-0.2	160	6.8	2 114	20.8	14.0
Comanche	37 569	60.2	54 000	21.3	12.3	377	25.7	4.8	40 669	-0.6	1 352	3.3	37 640	31.0	8.9
Cotton	2 609	77.0	32 800	18.4	12.5	279	24.6	3.9	2 115	-0.8	86	4.1	2 465	19.2	14.5
Craig	5 272	75.5	33 000	20.2	12.2	288	27.0	3.5	6 529	-1.6	232	3.6	5 830	19.6	12.8
Creek	22 470	77.6	44 500	20.8	12.7	320	25.8	3.7	33 643	0.1	1 229	3.7	26 546	21.6	16.0
Custer	9 918	63.5	46 900	17.4	12.6	307	26.0	3.7	11 984	1.8	408	3.4	12 369	25.7	12.1
Delaware	11 003	79.1	44 500	22.5	12.7	302	27.2	5.0	17 295	-0.1	628	3.6	10 664	21.9	14.2
Dewey	2 221	80.9	27 900	15.6	13.0	229	22.2	2.3	1 978	4.3	54	2.7	2 180	17.8	12.6
Ellis	1 826	80.3	29 100	17.5	12.6	291	16.3	3.0	1 593	1.3	49	3.1	2 034	20.4	12.9
Garfield	22 460	69.1	38 000	19.9	12.3	339	24.0	2.0	26 014	-1.9	744	2.9	24 402	24.7	12.5
Garvin	10 417	74.4	32 800	20.9	13.4	300	25.6	3.4	12 060	9.6	489	4.1	10 349	19.6	15.9
Grady	15 544	75.8	42 000	20.2	12.7	309	26.1	2.8	20 321	4.3	741	3.6	17 571	21.8	13.9
Grant	2 327	80.2	26 100	16.9	12.4	280	19.7	1.7	2 120	-2.3	58	2.7	2 384	21.4	11.4
Greer	2 551	75.6	21 800	21.6	13.6	238	28.2	3.9	2 403	0.2	75	3.1	2 224	20.5	9.1
Harmon	1 486	75.2	22 800	23.9	14.9	176	22.4	5.8	1 294	3.3	51	3.9	1 266	18.5	10.6
Harper	1 645	79.0	29 100	16.0	12.7	274	17.5	1.9	2 026	0.5	56	2.8	1 890	21.1	13.3
Haskell	4 319	78.0	31 300	18.4	13.1	247	27.2	6.4	5 448	10.6	254	4.7	3 652	17.7	14.8
Hughes	5 224	77.1	21 000	21.9	14.4	245	29.9	4.5	5 977	-1.6	300	5.0	4 496	18.3	14.3
Jackson	10 455	60.8	43 800	20.5	12.7	357	23.9	4.9	13 007	1.6	366	2.8	9 572	28.5	9.1
Jefferson	2 843	73.4	22 800	21.0	14.3	209	24.1	3.7	2 716	-8.6	101	3.7	2 612	17.1	14.7
Johnston	3 783	73.1	28 600	21.5	14.1	247	30.8	5.0	5 162	4.4	260	5.0	3 526	20.3	11.9
Kay	19 083	72.9	42 600	17.5	12.2	327	24.4	2.4	22 034	2.8	1 103	5.0	21 246	28.1	13.6
Kingfisher	4 932	79.2	47 900	21.2	13.1	319	21.5	4.5	6 843	4.8	176	2.6	5 967	22.5	14.0

1. Specified owner-occupied units.   2. Specified renter-occupied units.   3. Overcrowded or lacking complete plumbing facilities.   4. Percent of civilian labor force.   5. Persons 16 years and older.

	Private nonfarm establishments, employment and payroll, 1999									Agriculture, 1997			Farm operators
	Employment						Annual payroll		Farms			
											Percent with—		Whose principal occupation is farming (percent)
STATE County	Number of establishments	Total	Health Care and Social Assistance	Manufacturing	Retail trade	Finance and Insurance	Professional Scientific and Technical Services	Total (mil dol)	Average per employee (dollars)	Number	Less than 50 acres	500 acres and over	
	104	105	106	107	108	109	110	111	112	113	114	115	116
OHIO—Cont'd													
Ottawa	1 147	11 915	1 110	2 846	1 719	324	205	328	27 497	474	31.4	12.4	38.6
Paulding	339	4 232	443	1 750	563	125	54	97	22 912	542	21.2	26.6	49.8
Perry	495	4 868	825	1 581	734	178	138	110	22 694	606	25.1	5.0	38.1
Pickaway	807	11 772	1 575	4 235	1 611	347	292	330	28 030	703	31.4	21.5	56.5
Pike	474	9 620	1 131	5 225	1 168	196	63	288	29 922	435	19.8	6.2	38.6
Portage	3 113	44 927	4 449	13 775	6 115	1 160	897	1 207	26 859	719	45.9	4.0	42.6
Preble	718	9 247	708	3 477	1 466	232	173	232	25 071	977	35.9	10.4	44.7
Putnam	735	9 871	828	4 146	1 263	309	130	243	24 633	1 352	23.1	10.3	40.3
Richland	3 062	54 261	6 717	15 685	8 222	1 263	984	1 399	25 785	908	28.6	7.0	48.3
Ross	1 359	21 972	4 084	5 353	3 614	445	307	625	28 450	885	25.2	13.1	42.1
Sandusky	1 456	24 364	2 714	10 254	2 923	552	470	644	26 437	795	30.3	14.1	46.9
Scioto	1 474	18 129	4 862	2 160	3 698	833	319	368	20 323	630	28.4	5.6	35.1
Seneca	1 369	20 401	2 258	6 690	2 469	542	249	503	24 651	1 210	24.0	13.7	45.3
Shelby	1 063	24 164	1 596	12 915	1 960	350	393	812	33 595	991	27.7	10.3	43.6
Stark	9 432	158 015	23 121	39 969	22 356	5 599	4 454	4 212	26 654	1 086	45.5	4.7	43.8
Summit	14 490	245 134	32 460	41 784	32 196	9 367	11 104	7 972	32 520	251	64.5	1.2	41.0
Trumbull	4 785	84 059	10 165	29 285	12 324	2 219	2 130	2 802	33 332	788	33.0	4.2	45.1
Tuscarawas	2 373	32 691	3 799	9 368	5 199	825	654	782	23 927	920	28.2	5.3	46.8
Union	797	20 712	1 255	9 080	1 421	210	1 288	916	44 235	811	31.8	14.5	46.1
Van Wert	634	11 302	1 548	4 720	1 478	679	142	278	24 578	707	21.9	23.9	57.1
Vinton	150	1 637	265	D	177	D	D	40	24 682	202	19.3	4.5	30.2
Warren	2 894	56 543	3 765	13 018	6 726	2 762	3 375	1 765	31 213	741	49.7	6.7	39.3
Washington	1 552	22 025	3 049	5 366	2 981	704	561	574	26 078	900	19.6	4.0	38.8
Wayne	2 579	43 920	3 940	16 818	5 370	1 464	791	1 215	27 665	1 601	35.5	5.8	58.7
Williams	925	17 354	1 774	8 837	1 567	430	214	458	26 405	908	25.7	10.9	39.4
Wood	2 643	46 916	3 642	14 581	6 030	831	2 133	1 422	30 302	1 015	27.1	19.8	51.0
Wyandot	558	8 974	778	4 455	790	259	106	217	24 233	608	24.2	22.0	52.1
OKLAHOMA	84 854	1 171 356	166 399	167 321	167 595	56 419	49 496	29 888	25 515	74 214	20.5	21.6	44.5
Adair	210	3 069	419	1 486	512	108	38	63	20 638	1 090	26.0	8.4	43.7
Alfalfa	153	901	223	D	129	68	26	14	15 479	709	8.9	43.4	62.1
Atoka	227	2 184	595	355	471	74	45	35	16 110	1 087	16.7	15.5	42.2
Beaver	173	819	75	58	103	54	30	18	21 560	738	3.9	56.9	56.1
Beckham	641	5 459	1 152	118	1 165	234	120	98	17 900	825	14.4	34.8	46.5
Blaine	295	2 684	674	634	338	128	54	52	19 243	841	8.2	39.4	52.6
Bryan	600	9 798	1 479	1 242	1 428	323	349	191	19 518	1 516	20.0	14.2	39.9
Caddo	544	4 648	764	581	940	235	135	97	20 955	1 496	11.8	29.4	53.5
Canadian	1 640	15 833	1 418	2 657	2 811	480	396	338	21 374	1 165	25.2	26.0	50.0
Carter	1 346	15 702	2 570	2 824	2 682	514	330	385	24 521	1 165	22.1	15.0	33.6
Cherokee	679	8 532	1 688	244	1 801	245	182	157	18 417	1 154	27.5	7.5	39.0
Choctaw	273	3 082	804	134	548	94	49	43	14 048	991	17.7	18.9	44.2
Cimarron	97	497	D	0	104	40	17	8	15 924	481	3.1	66.3	66.5
Cleveland	4 174	46 048	6 909	3 943	9 056	1 354	2 073	987	21 440	1 017	42.4	7.4	35.0
Coal	65	903	215	D	100	D	D	15	16 093	586	13.0	26.8	48.0
Comanche	2 199	27 491	4 994	3 662	5 119	1 068	1 168	598	21 752	1 030	18.2	25.2	44.3
Cotton	99	535	147	39	110	46	D	6	11 811	512	8.8	36.5	54.7
Craig	370	5 305	1 510	953	613	158	117	115	21 585	1 120	18.3	17.3	42.2
Creek	1 251	15 451	2 084	4 135	2 148	546	285	347	22 444	1 475	32.7	10.4	30.6
Custer	827	8 004	1 343	1 363	1 523	336	355	153	19 093	788	10.3	41.9	58.8
Delaware	621	5 734	1 316	661	1 211	292	224	94	16 419	1 303	24.2	8.6	45.0
Dewey	134	735	83	D	184	70	D	19	26 235	713	6.2	43.3	54.1
Ellis	116	732	224	9	182	44	25	13	17 212	622	5.1	50.0	52.1
Garfield	1 655	18 913	3 812	1 429	3 448	653	507	403	21 287	1 069	13.5	35.3	55.1
Garvin	612	6 119	1 103	1 208	1 129	211	97	129	21 052	1 380	19.9	18.3	45.4
Grady	919	10 382	1 451	2 780	1 390	387	235	223	21 455	1 625	20.6	19.5	46.6
Grant	144	796	118	D	102	72	23	18	22 241	688	4.5	50.9	63.8
Greer	113	819	186	D	134	54	11	15	18 009	478	7.3	38.3	53.6
Harmon	76	478	D	D	154	55	16	7	14 688	338	5.6	48.5	55.0
Harper	114	576	135	D	93	36	25	10	18 127	443	5.6	56.7	55.8
Haskell	206	2 041	582	98	421	50	30	36	17 512	872	17.3	15.7	44.0
Hughes	243	1 889	347	D	407	71	D	29	15 223	897	11.5	17.9	44.0
Jackson	559	7 448	1 492	1 056	1 433	318	394	142	19 126	723	16.0	34.3	50.1
Jefferson	139	956	85	285	128	78	23	15	15 544	499	11.4	36.9	54.3
Johnston	148	2 155	400	927	195	30	11	44	20 354	624	20.0	21.3	38.0
Kay	1 271	17 824	1 947	3 760	2 738	559	961	448	25 143	929	18.5	32.2	55.8
Kingfisher	428	4 510	541	391	594	353	85	104	23 143	998	12.0	34.7	55.1

Table B. States and Counties — Agriculture, Land, and Water

STATE County	Acreage (1,000) 117	Percent change, 1992–1997 118	Average size of farm 119	Total irrigated (1,000) 120	Total cropland (1,000) 121	Average per farm ($1,000) 122	Average per acre (dollars) 123	Value of machinery and equipment average per farm ($1,000) 124	Total (mil dol) 125	Average per farm (dollars) 126	Crops 127	Live-stock and poultry products 128	$10,000 or more 129	$100,000 or more 130	Percent of land owned by fed. gov. 1997 131	Water consumption 1995 (mil gal/day) 132
OHIO—Cont'd																
Ottawa	106	-1.1	223	1	97	470	2 212	72	29	60 427	93.1	6.9	62.7	14.8	1.9	50.9
Paulding	210	-4.1	387		196	615	1 639	84	54	99 897	82.8	17.2	69.0	27.5	0.0	3.2
Perry	97	0.6	159	0	63	217	1 409	33	15	25 331	62.0	37.9	35.5	5.9	7.2	3.5
Pickaway	267	3.2	380	1	241	784	2 046	79	79	112 857	83.1	16.9	62.2	25.7	0.3	37.4
Pike	78	-11.0	180	0	44	230	1 208	44	8	17 281	52.1	47.9	26.4	3.9	1.3	4.2
Portage	87	-8.9	122	1	62	372	3 138	40	24	33 071	55.7	44.3	36.3	7.6	6.9	17.1
Preble	197	-3.4	202	0	172	424	2 195	55	68	69 531	64.5	35.5	56.0	19.3	0.0	4.5
Putnam	292	1.9	216	0	275	452	2 107	71	103	76 097	68.0	32.0	77.4	19.3	0.0	4.8
Richland	156	-3.4	171	0	120	329	2 045	54	47	51 922	49.0	51.0	50.4	16.0	0.0	16.3
Ross	252	-0.5	284	D	184	432	1 551	48	46	51 758	80.4	19.6	43.4	12.1	0.6	41.9
Sandusky	199	-1.3	251	0	186	439	1 824	73	66	83 018	85.7	14.3	70.1	22.6	0.0	19.8
Scioto	103	7.3	163	0	59	218	1 318	34	14	22 123	61.9	38.1	29.2	4.6	3.1	11.7
Seneca	293	-1.1	242	D	261	430	1 720	67	84	69 166	73.2	26.8	71.8	19.0	0.0	5.1
Shelby	202	-0.5	204	0	181	491	2 328	61	72	72 451	57.4	42.6	69.5	22.8	0.0	13.4
Stark	137	-0.2	126	1	107	347	3 091	44	73	67 217	39.0	61.0	46.3	13.6	0.2	44.5
Summit	17	-9.3	69	0	11	341	5 553	31	9	35 586	84.7	15.3	41.0	9.2	5.6	82.7
Trumbull	112	-7.0	143	0	82	283	1 815	53	25	32 319	53.7	46.3	42.1	8.0	2.9	231.2
Tuscarawas	141	-4.5	154	0	90	308	1 939	45	56	61 119	20.5	79.5	40.9	14.6	0.7	40.1
Union	205	-8.2	252	0	185	531	2 271	72	70	85 851	61.7	38.3	55.6	18.7	0.0	5.8
Van Wert	237	-2.0	336	D	225	719	2 093	103	73	102 619	86.7	13.3	80.9	31.0	0.0	4.8
Vinton	37	-11.6	184	D	20	185	942	22	2	8 437	40.2	59.8	19.3	1.0	0.6	1.2
Warren	118	-8.2	160	0	94	554	3 858	51	34	45 589	84.0	16.0	38.2	9.9	2.0	21.5
Washington	147	4.6	163	0	72	214	1 406	38	20	22 698	36.8	63.2	29.4	4.8	7.9	690.5
Wayne	241	-2.5	150	1	195	402	2 807	63	156	97 287	22.1	77.9	65.0	24.9	0.0	19.2
Williams	203	8.7	224	D	175	342	1 560	50	51	56 590	69.0	31.0	51.1	13.3	0.0	5.2
Wood	304	0.7	299	0	288	633	2 151	89	96	95 027	90.8	9.2	75.2	26.9	0.0	11.8
Wyandot	209	-3.2	344	0	191	566	1 638	93	64	104 753	71.9	28.1	70.2	28.3	0.0	7.1
OKLAHOMA	33 219	3.3	448	506	14 844	272	610	37	4 146	55 870	21.9	78.1	40.0	8.5	2.6	1 781.3
Adair	225	8.9	207	1	100	206	913	31	74	68 183	1.6	98.4	33.4	10.8	0.0	9.6
Alfalfa	502	2.9	708	3	376	485	713	71	90	126 777	35.3	64.7	76.0	24.5	4.5	3.3
Atoka	421	11.9	387	1	128	173	430	25	20	18 808	7.7	92.3	33.5	2.2	1.3	55.5
Beaver	1 048	6.2	1 420	22	397	476	325	71	89	120 056	16.0	84.0	58.0	14.9	0.0	33.6
Beckham	499	1.1	605	2	222	281	475	39	25	30 007	33.2	66.8	44.7	6.4	0.0	7.9
Blaine	547	6.4	650	3	304	363	549	62	77	91 994	22.7	77.3	64.1	11.8	0.4	5.2
Bryan	420	1.7	277	6	192	186	684	26	33	21 469	27.6	72.4	31.9	3.4	1.7	16.0
Caddo	727	0.0	486	45	403	331	670	52	91	60 919	47.9	52.1	55.9	14.7	0.2	47.6
Canadian	467	-6.6	401	4	280	397	978	59	67	57 156	29.1	70.9	51.8	13.9	1.9	9.9
Carter	382	2.5	328	1	118	220	709	23	22	18 850	9.5	90.5	24.8	3.3	0.0	4.2
Cherokee	238	8.5	206	1	91	186	951	28	66	56 916	58.9	41.1	28.4	5.5	3.2	23.0
Choctaw	338	12.3	341	0	132	172	507	19	24	24 429	12.9	87.1	34.9	3.6	3.5	12.7
Cimarron	1 077	4.1	2 239	69	454	705	320	102	181	375 359	16.8	83.2	65.7	29.5	9.9	216.9
Cleveland	162	3.4	160	1	84	251	1 577	24	12	11 969	32.3	67.7	22.0	1.9	1.7	25.4
Coal	273	3.0	466	0	90	229	457	25	18	30 477	4.2	95.8	45.1	3.9	0.0	6.7
Comanche	435	7.0	422	1	194	309	720	39	32	31 380	35.0	65.0	42.1	7.2	23.4	21.1
Cotton	350	-2.2	684	0	194	286	485	38	36	71 092	29.5	70.5	61.9	13.9	0.9	2.4
Craig	418	-6.4	374	1	166	236	659	36	62	55 057	10.1	89.9	42.0	6.9	0.0	3.1
Creek	351	4.6	238	0	122	168	724	19	15	9 893	14.6	85.4	19.4	1.1	2.7	7.1
Custer	625	-1.5	793	3	312	465	602	80	65	82 151	31.5	68.5	66.0	19.3	1.2	13.3
Delaware	265	9.3	203	0	129	219	1 114	28	94	72 441	3.1	96.9	38.5	13.6	0.0	5.9
Dewey	619	6.2	869	2	227	352	385	52	34	48 051	31.5	68.5	58.1	9.8	0.9	4.2
Ellis	670	-4.3	1 077	13	194	296	285	43	35	56 762	24.5	75.5	55.3	10.1	0.0	45.0
Garfield	615	-7.1	575	0	459	384	693	59	83	77 621	46.5	53.5	66.5	19.0	0.3	6.1
Garvin	449	6.8	325	2	196	201	672	35	34	24 815	25.4	74.6	36.3	4.8	0.0	5.5
Grady	609	7.6	375	7	278	253	656	38	89	54 936	15.5	84.5	42.4	8.7	0.0	17.5
Grant	585	-2.6	850	D	431	559	664	90	61	88 888	64.1	35.9	78.1	23.1	0.0	2.9
Greer	314	-7.3	658	9	173	238	395	44	17	36 108	52.7	47.3	50.6	10.5	0.2	4.7
Harmon	304	6.4	900	21	161	371	402	56	22	64 315	56.1	43.9	61.8	18.0	0.0	16.4
Harper	580	-4.5	1 308	7	201	369	291	50	100	225 782	8.7	91.3	65.2	19.4	0.9	15.6
Haskell	268	-0.1	307	1	116	226	670	32	33	38 193	3.3	96.7	38.4	8.0	2.3	4.1
Hughes	355	2.4	396	4	116	190	473	30	41	45 177	10.2	89.8	34.0	5.4	0.0	16.9
Jackson	477	1.4	659	50	333	379	609	68	69	95 000	61.2	38.8	55.0	20.1	0.5	46.1
Jefferson	441	9.0	884	0	135	385	421	33	51	101 823	8.9	91.1	53.1	14.6	0.5	7.1
Johnston	334	3.1	535	1	92	300	557	30	28	44 165	6.9	93.1	37.3	5.1	3.2	5.6
Kay	469	-1.8	505	0	331	351	695	59	56	60 803	65.8	34.2	58.8	18.1	4.0	25.2
Kingfisher	555	6.3	556	5	367	431	768	68	99	99 669	21.5	78.5	66.7	20.1	0.0	8.8

Table B. States and Counties — Residential Construction, Wholesale and Retail Trade, and Real Estate

STATE County	Value of Residential Construction Authorized by Building Permits, 2000		Wholesale Trade, 1997				Retail Trade[1], 1997				Real Estate and Rental and Leasing, 1997			
	New Construction ($1,000)	Number of Housing Units	Number of Establishments	Number of Employees	Sales (mil dol)	Annual Payroll (mil dol)	Number of Establishments	Number of Employees	Sales (mil dol)	Annual Payroll (mil dol)	Number of Establishments	Number of Employees	Receipts (mil dol)	Annual Payroll (mil dol)
	133	134	135	136	137	138	139	140	141	142	143	144	145	146
OHIO—Cont'd														
Ottawa	20 302	243	42	184	85.8	5.1	171	1 648	353.3	29.3	60	364	21.4	4.1
Paulding	10 727	143	19	155	69.8	4.0	62	638	102.4	8.9	6	32	1.8	0.3
Perry	3 699	34	15	D	D	D	83	648	105.2	8.9	14	44	2.7	1.7
Pickaway	28 715	205	38	326	141.8	9.1	147	1 630	284.0	23.8	34	82	7.8	1.0
Pike	5 206	96	16	103	26.1	2.8	98	1 105	153.5	12.9	8	52	3.8	0.4
Portage	133 868	737	183	2 648	1 180.5	96.5	465	5 828	1 117.9	92.8	104	409	39.4	6.3
Preble	16 756	176	32	586	249.6	20.2	112	1 334	218.3	18.7	17	83	5.0	1.0
Putnam	11 121	92	51	330	162.0	7.7	115	1 344	181.2	17.2	14	103	4.4	1.1
Richland	52 003	538	157	1 902	633.2	53.8	590	8 848	1 297.7	127.7	98	407	43.3	6.3
Ross	6 911	68	63	531	147.5	12.8	279	3 882	581.9	52.7	51	167	22.4	3.9
Sandusky	16 710	149	64	880	213.7	24.2	241	2 945	470.3	43.2	32	129	9.8	2.0
Scioto	265	6	68	550	219.3	12.3	321	3 629	543.0	53.4	40	185	17.5	2.6
Seneca	11 991	203	63	756	359.2	20.7	231	2 447	407.9	38.9	39	101	7.9	1.1
Shelby	27 791	210	51	666	276.3	18.6	167	2 126	309.4	28.4	32	186	16.9	4.1
Stark	188 773	1 255	517	8 242	4 151.7	275.8	1 618	23 170	3 671.2	357.2	274	1 273	126.1	22.9
Summit	325 318	2 605	1 070	13 375	8 443.7	501.6	2 172	32 463	5 515.7	546.7	476	2 994	373.8	68.4
Trumbull	49 913	468	231	2 867	1 212.0	80.4	913	12 617	1 943.2	192.9	175	1 139	123.5	21.8
Tuscarawas	21 632	173	109	1 096	300.2	26.4	439	5 240	758.8	75.6	73	285	29.8	5.1
Union	67 599	450	38	280	165.6	11.5	103	1 291	279.1	22.0	28	105	16.1	2.7
Van Wert	7 882	84	40	D	D	D	110	1 279	207.6	17.9	14	34	10.0	0.9
Vinton	0	0	4	D	D	D	28	201	27.1	2.3	4	D	D	D
Warren	307 381	2 906	181	2 324	6 034.5	91.2	455	6 709	1 111.7	106.3	95	414	48.4	8.0
Washington	2 868	19	74	826	166.6	19.3	279	3 063	501.0	45.8	48	146	17.7	2.7
Wayne	55 808	497	144	1 489	654.1	41.5	393	5 250	801.4	79.5	80	345	26.7	6.1
Williams	18 559	170	49	557	344.7	17.4	153	1 573	227.7	21.4	25	80	6.5	1.1
Wood	74 891	754	169	2 731	1 496.8	82.5	436	5 864	947.2	83.4	97	597	77.3	14.3
Wyandot	7 768	68	28	296	129.6	7.4	94	842	109.4	11.2	11	44	2.3	0.5
OKLAHOMA	1 204 003	11 148	5 191	59 641	32 132.3	1 756.1	14 352	161 613	27 065.6	2 406.9	3 344	15 354	1 576.0	284.5
Adair	680	10	4	31	5.6	0.4	54	482	67.0	5.1	5	11	0.6	0.1
Alfalfa	0	0	19	129	52.0	2.1	25	136	18.4	1.5	4	5	0.3	0.1
Atoka	140	1	19	124	48.8	2.2	49	530	71.9	6.2	4	6	0.4	0.1
Beaver	80	1	10	30	10.3	0.7	25	116	14.4	1.1	2	D	D	D
Beckham	5 326	96	31	163	58.0	3.5	130	1 036	204.1	13.6	24	151	15.1	3.4
Blaine	65	1	17	D	D	D	69	357	42.6	3.7	6	6	0.2	0.0
Bryan	1 738	21	44	597	287.4	12.3	127	1 243	206.8	17.6	27	83	4.4	0.9
Caddo	1 266	28	26	284	111.4	5.8	142	998	128.7	11.7	10	D	D	D
Canadian	28 827	259	87	670	819.0	17.5	212	2 957	620.1	46.6	69	309	29.7	5.6
Carter	12 030	148	78	835	244.7	23.7	275	2 594	413.3	35.5	50	166	13.5	2.4
Cherokee	4 004	158	21	201	44.5	2.7	144	1 843	235.0	20.2	26	62	6.7	1.3
Choctaw	385	7	14	D	D	D	71	551	75.4	5.9	5	D	D	D
Cimarron	0	0	7	36	13.7	0.6	19	116	24.4	1.5	2	D	D	D
Cleveland	94 055	811	159	1 462	528.6	37.2	616	7 679	1 318.6	115.2	205	764	68.7	11.6
Coal	100	1	2	D	D	D	18	150	17.1	1.4	NA	NA	NA	NA
Comanche	15 161	138	84	766	200.6	16.4	436	5 216	691.8	67.8	133	523	48.7	8.1
Cotton	132	2	7	40	10.7	0.6	20	114	21.7	1.3	3	3	0.2	0.0
Craig	140	2	24	208	74.9	3.7	67	571	99.2	8.6	10	34	3.7	0.5
Creek	12 308	103	77	914	255.9	25.4	186	1 854	284.4	23.7	28	87	6.2	1.1
Custer	4 201	45	45	367	211.8	9.9	172	1 472	235.0	18.9	38	111	11.3	2.1
Delaware	14 096	115	15	82	27.1	1.1	132	1 067	148.9	13.8	24	67	4.9	0.9
Dewey	0	0	7	D	D	D	32	174	20.8	1.8	5	19	2.0	0.6
Ellis	175	2	7	34	14.9	0.8	28	143	20.1	1.7	2	D	D	D
Garfield	9 770	59	122	1 967	570.1	48.9	302	3 423	501.7	47.8	70	287	24.6	4.8
Garvin	752	8	26	287	67.8	5.3	127	1 097	172.0	13.4	18	48	6.4	1.3
Grady	8 467	65	63	576	173.4	14.7	162	1 512	241.3	19.7	32	93	8.8	1.7
Grant	34	1	18	D	D	D	18	92	12.8	0.9	1	D	D	D
Greer	80	1	5	49	13.4	0.4	26	129	15.4	1.5	3	6	0.5	0.0
Harmon	NA	NA	3	D	D	D	25	154	20.2	1.9	3	6	0.5	0.1
Harper	211	2	9	42	13.4	0.9	17	90	10.8	0.9	3	4	0.1	0.0
Haskell	182	3	7	90	41.5	1.2	42	395	57.9	5.2	7	12	0.6	0.1
Hughes	524	9	14	222	35.7	2.8	64	431	58.6	4.8	3	6	0.2	0.0
Jackson	1 551	14	34	161	66.7	3.9	125	1 420	241.2	19.8	23	57	4.4	0.7
Jefferson	192	1	5	D	D	D	30	164	25.5	1.8	6	17	0.9	0.2
Johnston	1 294	27	7	54	14.4	1.1	37	167	22.1	1.9	5	D	D	D
Kay	9 025	78	61	444	210.2	12.0	263	2 718	397.6	36.5	53	134	11.5	1.7
Kingfisher	3 697	27	33	234	159.3	7.3	60	576	90.0	7.3	10	22	1.2	0.2

1. Establishments with payroll.

Items 133—146

Table B. States and Counties — Professional, Manufacturing, and Accommodation and Foodservices

STATE County	Professional, Scientific, and Technical Services[1], 1997				Manufacturing, 1997				Accommodation and Foodservices, 1997			
	Number of Establishments	Number of Employees	Receipts (mil dol)	Annual Payroll (mil dol)	Number of Establishments	Number of Employees	Receipts (mil dol)	Annual Payroll (mil dol)	Number of Establishments	Number of Employees	Sales (mil dol)	Annual Payroll (mil dol)
	147	148	149	150	151	152	153	154	155	156	157	158
OHIO—Cont'd												
Ottawa	51	156	11.7	4.1	56	2 886	634.2	100.8	168	1 346	62.6	15.7
Paulding	13	62	3.9	1.5	39	1 628	256.5	46.4	32	332	10.1	2.6
Perry	20	107	5.1	2.2	35	1 763	238.9	50.8	38	294	8.3	2.0
Pickaway	51	168	10.4	4.0	44	4 726	1 134.4	188.6	72	1 069	31.7	9.2
Pike	13	44	2.3	0.5	28	4 953	1 202.3	190.2	51	643	21.2	5.6
Portage	194	635	55.4	18.9	298	12 984	2 154.2	417.8	267	4 761	124.6	35.1
Preble	42	158	7.7	2.3	61	3 274	698.0	109.2	67	689	22.1	6.0
Putnam	25	89	5.2	1.5	42	4 005	1 237.1	129.9	54	D	D	D
Richland	168	933	73.3	23.5	220	15 212	2 444.7	567.1	272	4 613	140.1	38.6
Ross	66	263	22.8	7.1	48	D	D	D	119	2 225	61.3	16.8
Sandusky	80	383	23.8	8.9	124	10 156	2 533.6	307.1	110	1 699	50.0	12.9
Scioto	68	368	19.3	7.4	63	1 942	290.8	55.0	151	2 199	65.4	17.9
Seneca	63	234	13.2	4.1	101	6 882	1 124.6	231.2	128	1 325	33.9	9.7
Shelby	55	363	22.9	13.4	136	13 278	5 129.2	470.5	95	1 554	48.6	12.4
Stark	640	3 610	312.3	109.0	629	39 352	8 222.5	1 324.1	761	14 302	389.8	107.6
Summit	1 305	9 742	996.9	382.8	1 091	42 312	6 846.7	1 506.1	1 156	20 197	612.2	173.1
Trumbull	278	2 058	129.6	58.2	282	34 101	11 235.6	1 622.1	449	7 323	203.5	55.7
Tuscarawas	113	1 212	46.0	27.1	226	9 823	2 054.6	304.1	212	3 365	90.6	25.7
Union	45	1 079	231.5	69.4	40	8 462	7 467.2	370.7	57	766	23.1	6.8
Van Wert	30	102	7.5	2.5	50	4 553	942.1	140.8	58	878	21.9	5.6
Vinton	6	21	1.1	0.3	17	624	91.2	15.4	15	D	D	D
Warren	215	1 557	180.8	56.4	198	12 145	2 186.4	407.3	243	4 694	154.7	44.6
Washington	77	385	29.8	10.9	104	5 242	1 900.9	187.8	122	2 023	65.4	18.6
Wayne	126	671	43.9	14.7	252	16 172	3 105.0	521.5	178	3 206	79.0	23.9
Williams	30	136	9.2	2.4	131	9 132	1 831.5	267.1	84	1 197	30.3	9.1
Wood	177	1 674	187.3	50.2	192	13 357	2 602.3	512.7	270	4 905	134.4	37.0
Wyandot	25	81	4.3	1.1	53	4 188	573.1	112.1	57	656	16.3	4.5
OKLAHOMA	7 009	40 633	3 543.0	1 323.7	4 087	164 060	37 453.2	4 963.2	6 534	105 934	3 151.3	856.8
Adair	13	39	1.6	0.5	14	1 626	312.6	33.9	15	D	D	D
Alfalfa	8	18	1.0	0.2	NA	NA	NA	NA	6	D	D	D
Atoka	13	32	1.5	0.4	NA	NA	NA	NA	15	D	D	D
Beaver	10	28	1.8	0.3	NA	NA	NA	NA	8	D	D	D
Beckham	30	127	6.7	1.6	NA	NA	NA	NA	56	721	19.7	5.1
Blaine	18	55	2.5	0.8	15	622	98.0	17.1	24	236	5.0	1.5
Bryan	35	128	6.0	2.3	31	949	122.5	19.3	50	733	23.5	5.8
Caddo	26	92	3.7	1.3	NA	NA	NA	NA	48	277	8.0	2.0
Canadian	139	336	24.0	7.3	64	3 003	1 024.4	82.3	122	1 704	49.4	12.7
Carter	86	288	16.9	5.8	45	2 801	1 012.6	105.4	97	1 466	44.3	12.5
Cherokee	39	146	6.7	2.1	NA	NA	NA	NA	78	930	26.6	7.0
Choctaw	14	29	2.0	0.4	NA	NA	NA	NA	25	D	D	D
Cimarron	5	11	0.4	0.1	NA	NA	NA	NA	11	91	1.8	0.4
Cleveland	395	1 656	138.9	47.5	151	4 287	902.3	116.4	330	6 474	188.1	51.6
Coal	2	D	D	D	NA	NA	NA	NA	3	D	D	D
Comanche	127	1 062	63.0	30.5	51	3 325	900.8	119.8	203	3 660	96.9	28.9
Cotton	7	14	0.5	0.2	NA	NA	NA	NA	7	D	D	D
Craig	13	41	3.6	0.7	18	978	128.1	21.7	39	409	14.1	3.9
Creek	78	246	19.0	6.3	96	4 032	703.3	116.4	86	991	31.2	7.8
Custer	53	259	14.2	4.6	23	D	D	116.4	65	1 110	27.7	7.8
Delaware	38	115	7.1	2.8	30	673	45.2	12.1	67	808	24.1	6.7
Dewey	6	13	0.8	0.3	NA	NA	NA	NA	5	D	D	D
Ellis	9	19	0.7	0.3	NA	NA	NA	NA	7	D	D	D
Garfield	92	432	33.6	12.1	66	2 389	506.2	62.7	123	1 896	51.9	14.7
Garvin	35	94	4.8	1.4	26	1 153	615.4	29.4	44	458	13.3	3.5
Grady	69	202	16.6	4.9	64	2 792	747.0	70.0	63	983	24.5	6.5
Grant	6	14	0.9	0.2	NA	NA	NA	NA	7	30	0.8	0.2
Greer	6	7	0.3	0.1	NA	NA	NA	NA	8	55	1.4	0.4
Harmon	3	7	0.3	0.1	NA	NA	NA	NA	3	D	D	D
Harper	7	19	0.7	0.2	NA	NA	NA	NA	8	34	0.7	0.2
Haskell	11	29	1.3	0.4	NA	NA	NA	NA	16	D	D	D
Hughes	11	33	1.6	0.5	NA	NA	NA	NA	21	D	D	D
Jackson	29	404	15.3	6.5	12	896	205.1	16.3	56	841	24.2	6.3
Jefferson	8	16	0.5	0.1	NA	NA	NA	NA	13	D	D	D
Johnston	6	10	0.6	0.2	10	678	98.4	17.1	12	142	2.8	0.9
Kay	73	829	36.4	14.9	74	4 019	2 001.2	126.5	102	1 446	40.3	10.8
Kingfisher	18	77	3.1	1.3	NA	NA	NA	NA	27	D	D	D

1. Firms subject to federal tax.

Table B. States and Counties — Health and Other Services and Federal Funds

STATE County	Health Care and Social Assistance[1], 1997				Other Services[1], 1997				Federal funds and grants, fiscal 2001[2] Expenditures (mil dol)			
										Direct payments for individuals[3]		
	Number of Establishments	Number of Employees	Receipts (mil dol)	Annual Payroll (mil dol)	Number of Establishments	Number of Employees	Receipts (mil dol)	Annual Payroll (mil dol)	Total	Social Security and government retirement	Medicare	Food stamps and Supplemental Security Income
	159	160	161	162	163	164	165	166	167	168	169	170
OHIO—Cont'd												
Ottawa	48	538	26.8	13.5	67	344	18.7	5.4	192.0	107.3	41.8	3.0
Paulding	23	193	6.8	2.9	16	96	4.2	1.3	72.0	25.7	14.0	1.6
Perry	24	400	13.4	6.7	22	64	4.0	0.8	150.4	70.6	28.3	8.0
Pickaway	52	953	37.2	19.2	50	175	10.9	2.9	219.8	55.3	19.6	11.4
Pike	30	522	18.9	8.4	20	61	4.0	1.0	219.8	55.3	19.6	11.4
Portage	174	1 715	100.7	46.4	182	984	49.4	16.3	508.8	242.8	96.2	14.7
Preble	39	585	23.1	9.0	57	262	13.5	4.0	170.9	83.8	30.2	3.0
Putnam	34	516	17.9	8.0	36	137	8.6	2.5	102.4	37.5	22.4	2.7
Richland	256	2 797	156.8	72.6	199	1 512	81.1	31.0	586.8	272.3	104.5	19.9
Ross	107	1 218	60.6	28.6	92	554	26.4	8.4	402.7	154.2	48.9	18.6
Sandusky	116	966	50.8	22.5	96	620	30.8	10.6	238.7	113.9	50.4	6.9
Scioto	151	2 448	105.9	52.2	82	347	17.8	4.4	509.1	189.1	85.5	48.0
Seneca	108	927	50.5	22.4	80	382	17.4	5.2	265.7	135.5	54.0	6.8
Shelby	62	643	36.7	17.1	52	249	19.0	4.8	158.7	76.5	31.6	4.8
Stark	732	9 505	603.8	291.3	685	4 541	265.0	82.0	1 697.2	854.9	341.4	56.5
Summit	1 130	14 026	863.9	438.0	977	6 761	368.7	117.2	2 675.7	1 075.2	553.9	96.1
Trumbull	476	5 373	297.3	135.8	310	1 805	98.9	26.8	1 051.8	526.9	247.1	42.6
Tuscarawas	159	2 663	103.8	48.7	161	917	66.3	18.5	356.7	191.2	65.9	10.3
Union	47	435	26.2	12.5	51	226	11.6	4.0	113.3	50.7	20.4	2.0
Van Wert	51	529	30.2	13.2	38	233	10.2	3.0	116.6	48.3	20.1	2.0
Vinton	6	179	4.2	2.3	4	13	1.8	0.2	58.3	22.8	8.4	4.8
Warren	156	2 400	94.2	43.0	161	1 201	72.7	28.1	401.1	234.3	66.5	8.1
Washington	101	1 419	81.8	36.0	113	509	31.8	8.3	298.2	142.1	55.5	12.8
Wayne	135	1 906	93.7	44.8	141	665	50.2	10.9	373.1	199.0	68.6	9.9
Williams	48	762	46.3	17.6	51	291	22.7	4.7	145.5	76.0	31.4	2.8
Wood	143	1 915	83.5	37.8	169	1 187	70.3	21.3	394.6	178.0	75.6	6.7
Wyandot	24	269	11.4	5.1	43	177	12.1	3.5	104.5	47.4	18.5	1.5
OKLAHOMA	6 991	91 803	5 061.4	2 244.0	4 572	26 308	1 599.4	458.5	22 671.6	7 832.2	2 933.8	604.9
Adair	21	373	11.1	5.3	9	23	1.2	0.2	135.2	39.4	20.4	5.5
Alfalfa	8	55	1.7	0.8	10	18	1.1	0.2	50.0	16.4	7.6	0.4
Atoka	19	257	6.9	3.1	16	42	2.8	0.5	82.0	27.9	14.1	3.7
Beaver	6	26	1.3	0.5	9	33	1.8	0.3	40.8	11.7	4.0	0.3
Beckham	62	589	23.3	10.6	29	121	15.8	2.0	98.8	39.1	19.4	4.5
Blaine	16	237	7.9	3.4	14	36	1.7	0.4	84.5	25.6	13.3	2.0
Bryan	54	1 038	61.3	23.5	30	176	9.4	3.0	274.7	87.7	38.9	8.6
Caddo	44	420	12.1	5.6	29	79	4.9	1.0	220.7	75.3	30.8	7.5
Canadian	93	1 101	39.9	16.5	84	384	21.8	6.4	316.3	164.6	41.1	6.7
Carter	128	1 418	76.0	35.2	70	325	17.2	4.5	232.6	112.2	50.8	9.9
Cherokee	54	535	22.3	8.0	30	115	6.7	1.7	254.9	83.3	32.9	9.7
Choctaw	22	289	10.7	5.3	15	66	2.7	0.7	131.7	40.5	21.3	5.6
Cimarron	3	D	D	D	10	30	1.3	0.2	35.2	7.9	2.6	0.3
Cleveland	361	3 856	203.4	91.1	198	1 123	60.7	16.7	835.6	383.7	85.1	79.2
Coal	6	31	1.4	0.6	2	D	D	D	40.9	15.6	7.3	1.2
Comanche	208	2 349	141.5	52.8	146	778	36.3	10.9	1 224.2	323.2	59.6	21.6
Cotton	8	122	3.4	1.7	8	26	1.8	0.4	54.3	18.0	8.0	0.8
Craig	21	102	5.2	1.8	18	44	3.7	1.0	88.7	40.9	16.6	1.5
Creek	86	1 358	49.0	22.6	70	301	22.8	6.6	262.5	138.1	47.4	11.1
Custer	64	632	26.6	10.9	38	201	11.8	3.0	124.8	32.7	26.8	2.6
Delaware	46	555	21.6	8.6	25	94	4.5	1.2	166.9	83.2	33.3	6.6
Dewey	5	24	0.9	0.3	4	16	1.0	0.2	38.1	12.6	7.5	0.6
Ellis	8	96	3.0	1.5	8	22	1.0	0.2	32.6	11.5	6.2	0.3
Garfield	145	1 487	90.8	40.6	104	476	26.0	7.0	418.3	147.7	56.7	10.1
Garvin	42	842	28.5	14.9	24	117	7.7	1.7	226.1	77.5	42.2	5.6
Grady	67	997	45.4	22.2	49	213	13.9	3.8	186.7	90.9	31.3	8.7
Grant	3	D	D	D	9	12	1.4	0.2	58.9	14.1	7.7	0.3
Greer	12	188	7.8	4.1	4	13	0.7	0.2	52.9	17.6	11.5	1.2
Harmon	3	D	D	D	4	15	0.7	0.1	42.9	7.9	6.5	1.2
Harper	8	74	2.0	0.8	10	17	1.5	0.3	28.8	10.4	4.7	0.2
Haskell	20	256	9.6	4.5	13	49	2.5	0.7	83.9	35.3	15.3	3.2
Hughes	18	271	9.0	4.4	5	19	1.4	0.2	96.2	39.3	18.7	3.4
Jackson	48	489	19.0	7.8	26	131	9.3	2.3	328.5	77.1	27.4	5.6
Jefferson	13	273	7.5	4.3	9	23	1.5	0.3	55.4	20.2	10.0	1.3
Johnston	15	232	7.0	3.7	7	14	0.9	0.2	74.3	25.6	10.6	2.7
Kay	110	864	44.9	19.0	80	304	18.5	4.8	349.9	126.0	42.3	6.8
Kingfisher	14	224	7.7	3.1	26	95	6.1	1.4	115.8	30.1	12.8	1.4

1. Firms subject to federal tax.　2. October 1, 2000 to September 30, 2001.　3. State totals may include programs not allocated by county.

Table B. States and Counties — **Federal Funds and Local Government Finances**

STATE County	Federal funds and grants, fiscal 2001[1] (cont'd)							Local government finances, 1997				
	Expenditures (mil dol) (cont'd)							General revenue				
	Procurement contract awards			Grants[2]						Taxes		
											Per capita[3] (dollars)	
	Salaries and wages	Defense	Other	Medicaid and other health-related	Nutrition and family welfare	Education	Other	Total (mil dol)	Intergovern-mental (mil dol)	Total (mil dol)	Total	Property
	171	172	173	174	175	176	177	178	179	180	181	182
OHIO—Cont'd												
Ottawa	12.1	1.2	3.1	5.8	2.4	1.5	4.3	108.8	32.4	52.6	1 294	1 082
Paulding	2.9	0.4	0.8	6.1	1.7	1.0	1.0	47.4	19.9	11.7	582	450
Perry	4.2	0.0	1.2	22.2	5.3	2.3	2.4	60.0	39.7	12.2	357	289
Pickaway	5.7	0.0	1.6	25.5	6.0	2.3	5.4	124.5	54.7	37.0	696	516
Pike	3.9	0.6	74.2	32.5	8.3	2.6	4.1	66.4	46.4	12.6	458	392
Portage	18.7	8.1	4.3	35.9	13.4	11.5	19.2	395.7	115.2	138.7	920	643
Preble	5.8	0.0	1.5	10.7	3.8	2.5	11.8	120.1	36.8	32.7	762	466
Putnam	4.4	0.1	2.5	7.5	1.9	1.9	1.7	78.0	38.3	23.2	660	437
Richland	49.9	10.8	7.0	54.7	14.5	8.7	25.7	303.0	140.9	120.7	945	634
Ross	63.8	0.1	8.1	54.7	10.0	4.3	18.5	139.6	69.3	51.0	678	423
Sandusky	6.8	0.0	4.0	17.0	9.8	3.6	6.3	141.4	55.9	56.8	911	598
Scioto	11.3	0.0	3.3	108.9	21.9	16.9	5.1	170.5	104.3	35.7	442	321
Seneca	8.3	0.1	2.9	18.7	5.3	5.1	2.6	114.0	52.9	43.5	724	463
Shelby	5.3	0.1	1.4	12.4	4.2	1.9	3.8	112.8	38.7	47.8	1 009	622
Stark	78.8	15.6	30.2	150.3	42.2	24.4	40.6	799.1	335.4	328.9	880	612
Summit	167.0	182.9	53.5	246.4	74.3	32.3	89.8	1 507.5	496.2	727.6	1 369	853
Trumbull	41.4	9.8	8.4	78.5	31.2	15.4	18.3	485.5	209.1	193.4	855	593
Tuscarawas	13.0	2.8	3.0	33.2	9.6	6.7	11.7	189.0	77.9	77.1	874	577
Union	4.2	0.1	1.2	9.6	2.2	1.3	4.1	103.6	21.2	36.3	938	807
Van Wert	3.9	0.1	1.3	7.0	2.0	1.0	11.4	59.9	26.2	22.6	747	540
Vinton	1.7	0.1	0.8	11.4	2.5	1.7	2.6	24.8	16.5	5.2	431	373
Warren	18.0	4.4	4.7	32.3	7.7	3.6	5.7	293.9	89.4	143.4	1 024	782
Washington	11.5	1.2	5.5	34.1	8.3	6.3	9.0	123.0	51.0	54.5	857	591
Wayne	15.4	3.2	3.1	30.8	9.2	5.7	10.4	318.8	110.1	98.7	901	653
Williams	5.5	0.0	1.3	7.7	2.2	1.6	0.5	85.9	34.3	35.0	923	603
Wood	15.3	1.3	4.8	23.8	5.4	10.2	21.2	281.3	91.2	138.1	1 159	738
Wyandot	3.7	0.1	0.9	8.6	1.4	0.9	3.8	62.2	19 3	16.3	718	536
OKLAHOMA	3 050.4	1 567.5	645.0	1 896.8	650.7	477.5	1 094.1	X	X	X	X	X
Adair	2.7	9.3	0.6	41.7	4.9	8.1	1.0	34.2	24.8	4.9	245	213
Alfalfa	2.4	0.0	0.8	2.4	0.3	0.2	1.3	9.0	4.6	2.9	484	356
Atoka	3.3	0.0	0.4	17.8	2.5	1.5	8.5	19.6	11.3	4.5	334	230
Beaver	1.5	0.1	0.4	0.8	0.4	0.2	4.5	19.9	8.8	3.7	1 289	1 113
Beckham	2.8	0.0	0.7	13.7	2.1	1.7	2.2	36.2	15.6	15.5	837	519
Blaine	3.7	0.2	0.6	6.2	2.8	1.6	12.4	25.4	13.0	4.4	417	308
Bryan	7.3	17.8	30.2	37.7	10.3	11.7	5.8	47.8	28.4	11.9	347	174
Caddo	19.8	0.1	4.0	26.7	8.3	6.8	14.9	59.7	36.2	12.9	417	268
Canadian	53.7	0.2	4.9	10.8	5.7	4.5	3.4	130.1	57.5	41.5	491	335
Carter	7.8	0.6	1.5	31.7	5.8	4.1	2.3	78.3	38.0	27.3	618	331
Cherokee	23.3	0.0	4.3	41.8	25.8	10.9	8.4	80.6	34.9	10.1	262	109
Choctaw	3.1	3.9	0.6	35.0	5.7	3.1	7.1	24.5	16.2	4.4	291	118
Cimarron	0.9	0.0	0.1	1.2	0.2	0.2	1.5	13.3	5.8	2.3	759	582
Cleveland	47.1	89.2	22.4	33.8	11.8	16.4	38.3	376.5	129.3	97.9	497	300
Coal	1.0	0.0	0.3	10.5	1.1	2.3	0.5	12.7	6.0	4.6	754	651
Comanche	577.9	119.9	10.7	41.0	15.7	13.6	15.7	265.5	104.9	49.1	431	208
Cotton	1.5	0.0	0.3	5.6	0.8	0.4	2.6	9.4	6.2	1.8	275	166
Craig	3.2	0.0	0.7	15.6	1.4	2.2	2.0	25.4	11.0	8.3	577	268
Creek	7.4	0.8	1.7	28.3	7.0	3.9	12.3	100.0	55.7	27.4	414	261
Custer	8.7	0.0	1.0	9.1	2.7	2.3	15.4	61.2	20.6	19.0	739	456
Delaware	4.0	0.3	0.8	25.6	5.4	5.0	1.2	41.1	23.7	13.3	392	248
Dewey	1.9	0.0	0.5	2.5	0.3	0.4	0.8	17.8	8.5	3.1	622	439
Ellis	1.3	0.0	0.3	1.2	0.2	0.3	2.8	11.8	6.3	4.1	964	791
Garfield	66.8	71.2	2.9	18.4	4.6	3.7	3.3	99.4	42.6	35.9	633	324
Garvin	5.2	55.5	1.0	24.9	2.8	3.0	2.6	55.9	25.4	12.1	447	265
Grady	6.1	0.5	1.2	24.9	5.0	3.1	1.4	87.6	33.3	16.9	371	232
Grant	1.8	0.0	0.4	1.7	0.3	0.2	4.0	12.3	6.4	4.5	842	767
Greer	1.4	0.0	0.3	7.9	0.6	0.3	1.9	15.6	6.6	2.4	369	268
Harmon	1.0	0.0	0.2	4.6	0.7	0.3	3.4	6.4	4.1	1.2	356	243
Harper	1.2	0.0	0.3	0.8	0.1	0.1	0.9	9.6	4.9	2.7	757	601
Haskell	2.8	0.1	0.5	16.4	5.3	1.5	2.7	18.6	12.0	3.0	266	115
Hughes	2.8	0.0	0.6	21.3	2.0	1.8	2.2	44.8	15.8	5.3	401	247
Jackson	109.4	32.3	9.9	19.5	5.4	3.7	4.3	88.6	33.2	13.1	458	239
Jefferson	1.8	0.3	0.4	9.8	0.5	0.5	5.2	16.7	8.5	3.9	592	491
Johnston	2.9	6.5	0.7	14.9	3.0	1.5	1.9	17.2	12.1	3.3	325	258
Kay	8.7	87.8	1.9	18.3	4.7	3.8	18.5	81.1	33.2	29.2	624	408
Kingfisher	3.3	1.6	45.3	2.2	1.0	1.4	0.9	26.9	12.8	9.7	717	467

1. October 1, 2000 to September 30, 2001.   2. State totals may include programs not allocated by county.   3. Based on the resident population estimated as of July 1 of the year shown.

STATE County	Total (mil dol)	Per capita[1] (dollars)	Education	Health and hospitals	Police protection	Public welfare	Highways	Total (mil dol)	Per capita[1] (dollars)	Federal civilian	Federal military	State and local	Democratic	Republican	All other
	183	184	185	186	187	188	189	190	191	192	193	194	195	196	197
OHIO—Cont'd															
Ottawa	107.5	2 644	47.3	8.7	4.8	5.9	7.0	39.5	971	165	138	2 072	47.5	49.7	2.9
Paulding	43.7	2 166	50.6	22.8	3.5	3.0	8.7	10.5	520	57	51	1 173	37.8	58.2	3.9
Perry	56.2	1 647	62.3	3.3	2.3	7.6	6.8	10.5	307	72	87	1 659	46.0	50.2	3.8
Pickaway	120.3	2 261	41.0	30.7	2.6	3.5	4.9	23.5	442	94	136	4 220	37.2	60.4	2.4
Pike	63.6	2 306	63.2	3.1	2.5	7.0	6.2	3.7	133	68	71	1 596	46.6	50.5	2.9
Portage	394.3	2 615	40.7	29.3	3.5	4.0	5.0	138.4	918	313	403	13 735	50.0	44.9	5.0
Preble	111.3	2 597	40.4	36.5	3.0	2.0	5.7	16.6	388	97	111	1 971	35.1	61.5	3.4
Putnam	74.5	2 124	54.6	4.4	4.0	8.9	9.6	20.1	572	86	89	1 835	23.4	74.0	2.6
Richland	297.1	2 326	49.2	7.6	5.0	4.7	5.9	60.8	476	698	331	8 245	39.0	57.1	3.9
Ross	137.9	1 834	55.7	3.8	5.4	5.6	7.8	38.6	513	1 398	195	4 892	44.8	52.7	2.5
Sandusky	132.3	2 124	55.5	1.3	6.3	10.0	6.8	46.9	753	125	157	3 313	43.3	53.2	3.5
Scioto	162.1	2 008	61.2	1.5	2.5	11.2	4.5	55.0	682	194	205	5 398	46.7	50.2	3.1
Seneca	111.6	1 860	52.9	5.5	6.2	5.1	7.0	37.2	619	145	153	3 069	39.1	56.9	4.0
Shelby	96.5	2 035	50.5	2.7	4.8	1.4	8.3	25.6	540	99	122	2 535	33.5	63.4	3.1
Stark	779.9	2 087	51.0	6.6	5.7	5.5	4.7	297.2	795	1 261	952	17 962	47.1	48.9	4.0
Summit	1 433.3	2 696	39.5	8.7	6.0	4.9	5.9	968.9	1 822	2 684	1 395	29 390	53.3	43.0	3.7
Trumbull	486.4	2 151	47.8	5.5	7.6	6.0	4.4	162.7	720	512	577	10 629	59.9	36.0	4.1
Tuscarawas	181.5	2 057	51.5	4.2	4.3	3.8	5.9	73.8	836	220	227	4 687	42.8	52.7	4.6
Union	92.7	2 400	39.9	34.7	3.3	1.4	2.1	59.7	1 545	76	104	2 739	29.6	67.6	2.9
Van Wert	58.9	1 944	53.1	1.0	5.8	9.7	7.8	10.5	346	72	76	1 342	31.9	65.7	2.5
Vinton	24.4	2 023	53.5	4.3	3.0	8.6	6.2	0.7	57	25	31	802	41.2	55.0	3.8
Warren	290.3	2 072	54.2	3.5	6.4	3.0	6.3	228.2	1 629	281	390	6 617	27.7	69.9	2.3
Washington	120.7	1 897	51.7	8.2	5.1	5.6	10.5	23.5	370	258	160	3 141	39.2	57.9	3.0
Wayne	287.4	2 623	44.5	25.2	3.3	4.3	4.8	117.9	1 076	273	283	6 866	34.8	61.0	4.2
Williams	79.1	2 090	50.7	5.4	3.8	7.7	8.6	13.3	352	96	96	2 107	34.3	62.4	3.3
Wood	269.8	2 264	47.2	7.7	5.1	5.1	5.6	97.7	820	240	329	11 826	43.5	52.7	3.8
Wyandot	58.2	2 561	36.3	33.6	3.6	5.8	6.7	8.6	378	69	58	1 261	34.6	62.2	3.2
OKLAHOMA	X	X	X	X	X	X	X	X	X	44 571	41 370	229 881	38.4	60.3	1.3
Adair	33.4	1 659	79.9	1.6	2.5	0.0	4.8	5.5	273	43	102	1 165	39.5	58.6	1.9
Alfalfa	9.6	1 581	55.6	0.6	3.5	0.1	16.4	1.9	317	47	29	462	23.3	75.2	1.5
Atoka	20.4	1 528	60.0	11.8	3.1	0.1	8.2	5.9	440	71	67	1 175	44.1	54.9	1.0
Beaver	16.8	2 814	48.5	12.0	2.6	0.0	27.3	1.8	299	34	30	505	13.8	85.2	1.0
Beckham	33.8	1 821	57.9	1.7	5.9	0.0	17.7	7.6	409	56	99	981	36.9	62.3	0.9
Blaine	26.4	2 492	47.3	22.0	1.5	1.8	9.1	4.2	392	73	51	862	34.2	64.3	1.4
Bryan	48.8	1 427	66.6	1.4	4.2	0.1	7.6	26.0	762	129	176	2 546	47.3	51.8	0.9
Caddo	57.2	1 848	71.8	5.6	1.7	0.0	4.8	12.5	405	403	153	1 841	46.4	52.5	1.1
Canadian	136.5	1 612	61.9	9.5	3.4	0.0	4.7	56.1	662	605	858	3 952	26.7	72.3	1.0
Carter	88.7	2 011	57.7	2.1	5.5	0.4	9.1	25.9	587	125	223	2 772	40.5	58.7	0.8
Cherokee	77.5	2 024	46.3	38.9	1.8	0.0	3.9	12.5	325	485	197	3 763	50.2	47.8	2.0
Choctaw	24.6	1 614	66.2	5.1	3.4	0.6	8.0	8.2	535	68	75	998	52.7	46.3	1.0
Cimarron	13.7	4 452	32.4	34.4	2.4	0.0	17.1	0.9	308	18	19	358	15.3	82.9	1.8
Cleveland	369.2	1 872	46.5	24.5	5.4	0.1	3.9	204.1	1 035	743	1 118	19 068	36.5	62.2	1.3
Coal	11.0	1 823	69.1	5.9	1.1	0.0	12.1	3.4	562	22	31	388	48.6	50.6	0.8
Comanche	259.6	2 278	44.8	33.8	3.9	0.0	2.7	87.0	763	3 672	13 949	7 930	40.8	58.3	0.9
Cotton	10.2	1 519	59.3	0.7	1.3	0.1	13.5	2.8	422	34	33	400	43.0	55.9	1.0
Craig	25.2	1 743	61.1	13.0	3.7	0.0	8.4	9.0	625	61	72	1 856	46.8	51.3	1.8
Creek	91.4	1 383	70.8	2.4	4.9	0.1	6.5	67.2	1 016	125	341	2 810	41.1	57.2	1.7
Custer	57.6	2 234	49.1	18.3	4.0	0.3	8.2	23.9	926	166	128	2 787	32.0	67.0	1.0
Delaware	42.5	1 256	72.5	2.0	4.4	0.0	6.1	13.3	393	71	174	1 320	41.3	57.1	1.7
Dewey	16.3	3 229	47.3	23.6	0.8	0.0	14.7	3.5	693	40	24	516	27.0	72.4	0.6
Ellis	9.8	2 332	56.0	1.6	2.7	0.0	21.7	0.4	94	26	21	413	23.2	75.2	1.6
Garfield	99.7	1 758	54.5	0.6	4.7	0.0	6.7	128.6	2 268	393	1 485	3 633	30.2	68.7	1.1
Garvin	55.4	2 051	47.6	22.9	3.3	0.1	7.2	23.2	860	93	133	2 214	42.6	56.2	1.2
Grady	87.5	1 927	43.8	33.3	3.4	0.0	6.3	24.9	549	103	230	2 549	37.1	61.7	1.2
Grant	13.9	2 579	56.1	0.9	3.6	0.6	25.1	2.8	518	39	26	353	28.3	70.4	1.3
Greer	16.2	2 533	36.5	27.8	4.0	0.0	8.7	0.3	49	29	32	891	39.0	59.8	1.2
Harmon	6.8	1 960	62.9	2.8	5.4	0.0	14.1	0.1	40	24	17	346	42.1	57.4	0.5
Harper	8.7	2 416	58.8	1.8	3.3	0.1	18.1	0.0	0	28	18	421	22.2	77.0	0.8
Haskell	17.6	1 549	61.7	11.4	3.8	0.3	9.5	1.6	141	64	57	814	54.2	44.1	1.7
Hughes	42.0	3 207	37.2	14.3	1.4	0.0	4.9	43.9	3 351	46	70	914	50.9	47.9	1.2
Jackson	87.1	3 033	36.8	29.2	3.5	9.1	4.9	60.5	2 108	1 577	2 169	2 368	30.8	68.5	0.6
Jefferson	15.4	2 307	46.7	1.2	2.1	0.0	11.5	46.1	6 917	44	33	482	48.0	50.9	1.1
Johnston	17.5	1 701	65.7	1.1	2.8	0.0	17.2	3.1	300	49	51	787	46.0	52.7	1.2
Kay	86.4	1 844	53.8	1.2	6.2	0.0	6.0	70.6	1 507	188	232	2 879	33.7	64.8	1.5
Kingfisher	24.8	1 838	65.5	0.3	3.8	0.0	9.9	6.4	471	60	67	777	21.5	77.5	1.0

1. Based on the resident population estimated as of July 1 of the year shown. 2. Data subject to copyright.

Table B. States and Counties — **Land Area and Population**

STATE/ County code	MSA/ PMSA/ NECMA code[1]	County Type[2]	STATE County	Land area,[3] (sq km) 2000	Population and population characteristics, 2000													
								Race alone or in combination (percent)					Age (percent)					
					Total persons	Rank	Per square kilometer	White	Black	Am. Indian, Alaska Native	Asian and Pacific Islander	Percent Hispanic[4]	Under 5 years	5 to 17 years	18 to 24 years	25 to 34 years	35 to 44 years	45 to 54 years
				1	2	3	4	5	6	7	8	9	10	11	12	13	14	15
			OKLAHOMA—Cont'd															
40 075	...	6	Kiowa	2 628	10 227	2 423	3.9	85.8	5.1	7.9	0.7	6.7	5.6	18.5	7.5	9.7	14.9	12.7
40 077	...	7	Latimer	1 870	10 692	2 385	5.7	78.7	1.3	25.0	0.3	1.5	6.8	19.0	11.4	10.4	13.8	11.8
40 079	...	6	Le Flore	4 107	48 109	947	11.7	85.2	2.5	15.2	0.5	3.8	6.8	19.3	9.7	12.6	14.4	13.2
40 081	...	6	Lincoln	2 481	32 080	1 343	12.9	90.1	2.8	9.8	0.5	1.5	6.5	20.9	7.8	11.2	15.5	13.6
40 083	5880	2	Logan	1 928	33 924	1 283	17.6	84.2	11.6	5.0	0.6	2.9	6.1	19.3	12.0	11.0	15.5	14.1
40 085	...	9	Love	1 335	8 831	2 542	6.6	87.5	2.5	8.8	0.6	7.0	6.1	19.6	7.0	11.2	14.3	13.8
40 087	5880	2	McClain	1 475	27 740	1 457	18.8	91.1	0.9	8.9	0.5	4.9	6.6	20.2	8.1	12.1	17.0	13.4
40 089	...	7	McCurtain	4 797	34 402	1 267	7.2	75.1	10.0	18.0	0.3	3.1	7.3	20.9	8.3	12.2	14.0	13.1
40 091	...	7	McIntosh	1 606	19 456	1 820	12.1	78.5	5.0	22.3	0.4	1.3	5.4	17.2	6.4	9.3	13.0	13.2
40 093	...	6	Major	2 478	7 545	2 639	3.0	96.3	0.3	2.0	0.2	4.0	5.7	18.9	6.7	9.2	15.2	13.4
40 095	...	6	Marshall	961	13 184	2 211	13.7	82.4	2.1	13.0	0.4	8.6	6.2	17.3	7.5	10.5	13.6	13.0
40 097	...	6	Mayes	1 699	38 369	1 155	22.6	79.6	0.5	26.3	0.5	1.9	6.8	19.8	8.6	11.8	14.4	13.3
40 099	...	7	Murray	1 083	12 623	2 254	11.7	84.9	2.2	15.4	0.4	3.1	6.6	17.6	8.0	11.2	13.9	13.3
40 101	...	4	Muskogee	2 108	69 451	712	32.9	69.4	14.3	20.7	0.9	2.7	7.0	18.9	9.5	11.9	14.8	13.2
40 103	...	7	Noble	1 896	11 411	2 340	6.0	89.7	1.8	10.5	0.4	1.8	6.4	19.1	7.9	11.9	15.6	13.2
40 105	...	6	Nowata	1 463	10 569	2 392	7.2	80.3	3.0	24.1	0.4	1.2	6.5	19.6	7.6	10.6	14.7	13.1
40 107	...	6	Okfuskee	1 618	11 814	2 304	7.3	70.3	11.1	23.0	0.2	1.6	6.2	18.5	8.2	11.6	15.0	13.1
40 109	5880	2	Oklahoma	1 837	660 448	80	359.5	73.7	16.1	5.7	3.5	8.7	7.3	18.3	10.9	14.6	15.3	13.1
40 111	...	6	Okmulgee	1 805	39 685	1 119	22.0	75.4	11.2	18.5	0.5	1.9	6.8	20.1	9.5	11.1	14.1	13.0
40 113	8560	2	Osage	5 830	44 437	1 009	7.6	73.4	11.6	20.7	0.5	2.1	6.2	20.2	7.7	11.1	16.4	14.9
40 115	...	6	Ottawa	1 221	33 194	1 309	27.2	80.8	0.8	22.8	0.7	3.2	6.6	19.1	9.7	11.7	13.1	12.6
40 117	...	6	Pawnee	1 475	16 612	1 983	11.3	86.6	1.0	16.2	0.3	1.2	6.3	20.3	7.3	11.3	14.9	14.0
40 119	...	4	Payne	1 778	68 190	722	38.4	87.7	4.2	7.1	3.6	2.1	5.4	14.1	25.9	13.5	12.6	10.6
40 121	...	7	Pittsburg	3 382	43 953	1 017	13.0	82.0	4.6	17.0	0.5	2.1	5.6	17.9	7.8	12.1	14.9	13.7
40 123	...	6	Pontotoc	1 864	35 143	1 243	18.9	80.6	2.9	20.3	0.6	2.3	6.3	18.4	12.5	12.0	14.0	12.2
40 125	5880	2	Pottawatomie	2 040	65 521	745	32.1	84.2	3.5	15.1	1.1	2.4	6.8	19.0	11.2	12.2	14.7	12.9
40 127	...	7	Pushmataha	3 619	11 667	2 320	3.2	82.9	1.1	20.4	0.3	1.6	6.2	19.7	6.6	10.4	13.6	13.0
40 129	...	9	Roger Mills	2 957	3 436	2 960	1.2	93.4	0.4	7.1	0.1	2.6	5.5	18.3	6.7	9.3	15.4	13.9
40 131	8560	2	Rogers	1 748	70 641	703	40.4	86.2	0.9	17.9	0.6	1.8	6.9	21.7	7.4	12.0	16.6	14.0
40 133	...	6	Seminole	1 638	24 894	1 561	15.2	75.3	6.6	22.0	0.5	2.2	6.7	19.6	9.0	10.6	13.8	13.0
40 135	2720	3	Sequoyah	1 745	38 972	1 139	22.3	77.2	2.3	28.5	0.5	2.0	7.1	20.4	8.2	12.3	14.6	13.2
40 137	...	4	Stephens	2 264	43 182	1 033	19.1	91.0	2.4	7.1	0.6	4.0	6.3	18.3	7.8	10.3	14.9	13.8
40 139	...	7	Texas	5 276	20 107	1 789	3.8	79.1	0.9	2.1	0.8	29.9	8.5	20.3	12.7	14.7	14.4	11.5
40 141	...	6	Tillman	2 258	9 287	2 507	4.1	76.9	9.8	4.2	0.6	17.7	6.2	20.5	7.2	10.8	13.2	12.0
40 143	8560	2	Tulsa	1 477	563 299	98	381.4	78.9	11.8	8.3	2.1	6.0	7.4	18.9	10.0	14.7	15.7	13.4
40 145	8560	2	Wagoner	1 458	57 491	830	39.4	85.2	4.3	14.1	0.8	2.5	7.1	21.1	7.9	12.3	16.2	14.8
40 147	...	4	Washington	1 080	48 996	933	45.4	87.1	3.0	13.9	1.0	2.6	6.0	19.1	7.7	10.6	14.4	14.1
40 149	...	7	Washita	2 599	11 508	2 334	4.4	94.1	0.6	4.2	0.4	4.5	6.1	20.1	7.6	10.3	15.0	12.3
40 151	...	7	Woods	3 332	9 089	2 522	2.7	94.8	2.6	2.6	0.7	2.4	4.4	14.7	16.8	10.8	12.4	11.2
40 153	...	7	Woodward	3 218	18 486	1 870	5.7	93.6	1.2	3.2	0.6	4.8	6.6	19.2	9.3	11.5	16.1	13.2
41 000	...	X	OREGON	248 631	3 421 399	X	13.8	89.3	2.1	2.5	4.2	8.0	6.5	18.2	9.6	13.8	15.4	14.8
41 001	...	7	Baker	7 946	16 741	1 973	2.1	97.3	0.4	2.0	0.7	2.3	5.3	18.9	5.8	9.1	14.6	15.2
41 003	1890	4	Benton	1 752	78 153	651	44.6	91.5	1.2	1.7	5.9	4.7	5.1	16.2	20.2	12.9	13.8	14.2
41 005	6440	0	Clackamas	4 839	338 391	173	69.9	93.5	1.0	1.6	3.6	4.9	6.5	19.7	8.0	12.1	16.6	16.6
41 007	...	6	Clatsop	2 143	35 630	1 227	16.6	95.2	0.7	2.2	2.2	4.5	5.6	18.0	8.9	10.5	14.7	16.4
41 009	6440	1	Columbia	1 701	43 560	1 028	25.6	96.9	0.4	2.8	1.3	2.5	6.4	20.9	7.0	11.6	16.4	16.0
41 011	...	7	Coos	4 145	62 779	775	15.1	95.0	0.6	4.7	1.6	3.4	4.9	17.1	7.1	9.6	14.4	15.8
41 013	...	7	Crook	7 717	19 182	1 834	2.5	94.4	0.1	2.1	0.8	5.6	6.5	20.1	7.5	11.3	14.2	14.6
41 015	...	7	Curry	4 215	21 137	1 728	5.0	95.7	0.3	4.1	1.1	3.6	4.1	15.1	4.8	7.3	12.7	15.2
41 017	...	5	Deschutes	7 817	115 367	466	14.8	96.7	0.4	1.8	1.4	3.7	6.1	18.6	7.8	12.7	15.9	15.7
41 019	...	4	Douglas	13 045	100 399	523	7.7	96.5	0.4	3.4	1.2	3.3	5.6	18.4	7.5	10.1	14.1	15.2
41 021	...	9	Gilliam	3 119	1 915	3 071	0.6	97.7	0.2	1.6	0.3	1.8	4.5	18.7	5.4	9.6	16.0	15.4
41 023	...	9	Grant	11 729	7 935	2 611	0.7	97.4	0.2	2.7	0.4	2.1	5.7	20.1	5.6	9.3	14.7	15.9
41 025	...	7	Harney	26 248	7 609	2 635	0.3	94.0	0.2	5.1	1.0	4.2	5.7	20.3	6.4	10.3	16.2	15.1
41 027	...	6	Hood River	1 353	20 411	1 765	15.1	81.2	0.8	1.7	2.2	25.0	7.4	20.6	8.2	13.4	16.1	13.7
41 029	4890	3	Jackson	7 214	181 269	304	25.1	94.4	0.7	2.4	1.8	6.7	6.0	18.4	8.7	11.2	14.3	15.4
41 031	...	7	Jefferson	4 612	19 009	1 845	4.1	71.7	0.5	17.5	1.0	17.7	7.7	22.1	7.7	12.8	14.1	12.8
41 033	...	4	Josephine	4 247	75 726	662	17.8	96.5	0.5	2.9	1.3	4.3	5.3	17.7	6.5	9.6	13.6	15.3
41 035	...	5	Klamath	15 395	63 775	762	4.1	90.6	1.0	6.1	1.6	7.8	6.4	19.4	8.6	11.4	14.1	15.0
41 037	...	7	Lake	21 072	7 422	2 646	0.4	93.4	0.3	4.0	1.0	5.4	5.0	19.9	5.1	9.5	14.7	16.0
41 039	2400	2	Lane	11 795	322 959	178	27.4	93.7	1.3	2.6	3.2	4.6	5.8	17.1	12.0	13.0	14.5	15.3
41 041	...	7	Lincoln	2 537	44 479	1 008	17.5	93.6	0.6	5.3	1.8	4.8	4.9	16.6	6.5	9.4	14.1	16.7
41 043	...	4	Linn	5 937	103 069	515	17.4	95.5	0.5	2.6	1.5	4.4	6.8	19.2	8.4	12.3	14.7	14.3
41 045	...	7	Malheur	25 607	31 615	1 356	1.2	78.1	1.4	1.9	2.6	25.6	7.6	20.1	10.6	13.1	14.1	12.5
41 047	7080	2	Marion	3 066	284 834	196	92.9	84.6	1.3	2.6	3.0	17.1	7.7	19.7	10.3	14.1	14.6	13.2

1. MSA = Metropolitan Statistical Area. PMSA = Primary MSA. NECMA = New England County Metropolitan Area. See Appendix A for explanation of these concepts. See Appendix B for list of metropolitan areas identified by type, with component counties. 2. County typology code from the Economic Research Service of USDA. See Appendix A for definition. 3. Dry land or land partially or temporarily covered by water. 4. Hispanic persons may be of any race.

STATE County	Population, 2000 (cont'd) Age (percent) (cont'd)				Population — change and components of change, 1990–2001							Households, 2000				
					Total persons		Percent change		Components of change, 2000–2001						Percent	
	55 to 64 years	65 to 74 years	75 years and over	Percent female	2001	1990	1990– 2000	2000– 2001	Births	Deaths	Net migration	Number	Percent change, 1990– 2000	Persons per house- hold	Female family house- holder[1]	One person
	16	17	18	19	20	21	22	23	24	25	26	27	28	29	30	31
OKLAHOMA—Cont'd																
Kiowa	10.7	9.7	10.6	51.1	9 945	11 347	-9.9	-2.8	143	237	-191	4 208	-7.5	2.35	10.4	30.6
Latimer	10.7	8.6	7.5	50.6	10 634	10 333	3.5	-0.5	165	149	-72	3 951	7.0	2.54	11.5	24.9
Le Flore	10.2	7.3	6.4	50.2	48 041	43 270	11.2	-0.1	712	620	-143	17 861	12.1	2.61	11.0	23.1
Lincoln	10.6	7.6	6.3	50.7	32 154	29 216	9.8	0.2	473	403	11	12 178	12.4	2.59	9.2	22.4
Logan	9.6	6.7	5.6	50.6	34 209	29 011	16.9	0.8	418	396	264	12 389	21.7	2.57	9.8	23.7
Love	11.9	8.6	7.6	50.5	8 863	7 788	13.4	0.4	130	120	24	3 442	15.0	2.54	10.0	22.9
McClain	10.6	6.9	5.1	50.3	27 825	22 795	21.7	0.3	403	317	9	10 331	24.0	2.66	9.0	19.4
McCurtain	10.3	7.6	6.4	51.9	34 194	33 433	2.9	-0.6	622	447	-376	13 216	8.0	2.56	14.6	25.4
McIntosh	13.7	12.3	9.5	52.2	19 522	16 779	16.0	0.3	234	364	198	8 085	19.1	2.37	10.4	26.7
Major	11.5	9.5	9.9	51.2	7 528	8 055	-6.3	-0.2	99	113	-1	3 046	-2.4	2.44	6.0	25.2
Marshall	12.5	10.8	8.7	50.9	13 433	10 829	21.7	1.9	229	204	223	5 371	23.5	2.40	8.8	26.4
Mayes	10.5	8.2	6.7	50.4	38 697	33 366	15.0	0.9	688	514	170	14 823	17.0	2.55	9.0	23.8
Murray	11.0	9.5	9.0	50.7	12 721	12 042	4.8	0.8	205	260	155	5 003	7.6	2.45	10.2	25.2
Muskogee	9.4	7.6	7.7	51.7	69 887	68 078	2.0	0.6	1 354	1 078	195	26 458	5.1	2.51	13.3	26.7
Noble	10.7	8.1	7.1	50.7	11 388	11 045	3.3	-0.2	168	161	-25	4 504	6.6	2.47	8.4	25.5
Nowata	10.6	9.1	8.2	50.8	10 634	9 992	5.8	0.6	171	145	43	4 147	3.8	2.50	9.8	25.5
Okfuskee	11.1	8.3	8.0	48.4	11 781	11 551	2.3	-0.3	191	197	-25	4 270	2.5	2.52	11.2	27.8
Oklahoma	8.3	6.5	5.8	51.5	662 153	599 611	10.1	0.3	13 374	8 213	-3 298	266 834	12.2	2.41	13.5	30.2
Okmulgee	10.2	7.8	7.3	51.2	39 715	36 490	8.8	0.1	661	632	17	15 300	8.9	2.53	13.1	27.1
Osage	10.6	7.5	5.6	49.5	45 034	41 645	6.7	1.3	530	504	569	16 617	8.0	2.58	10.3	23.3
Ottawa	10.3	8.9	8.0	51.5	33 046	30 561	8.6	-0.4	559	510	-187	12 984	7.1	2.48	10.7	26.6
Pawnee	11.2	7.9	6.9	50.7	16 845	15 575	6.7	1.4	250	247	230	6 383	6.3	2.58	9.0	22.8
Payne	7.0	5.2	5.5	49.2	67 830	61 507	10.9	-0.5	986	660	-687	26 680	11.9	2.29	8.3	30.1
Pittsburg	10.9	9.0	8.2	49.6	43 779	40 950	7.3	-0.4	618	693	-80	17 157	7.8	2.40	11.2	27.7
Pontotoc	9.7	7.7	7.2	51.7	34 611	34 119	3.0	-1.5	581	588	-523	13 978	5.0	2.44	10.8	28.1
Pottawatomie	9.5	7.5	6.3	51.7	66 269	58 760	11.5	1.1	1 098	905	572	24 540	12.6	2.55	11.8	24.0
Pushmataha	12.2	9.9	8.4	51.9	11 706	10 997	6.1	0.3	163	197	71	4 739	8.4	2.42	10.8	27.9
Roger Mills	12.1	9.4	9.3	49.9	3 331	4 147	-17.1	-3.1	51	43	-115	1 428	-10.0	2.38	6.8	28.6
Rogers	10.0	6.6	4.7	50.8	74 066	55 170	28.0	4.8	1 013	689	3 025	25 724	29.5	2.71	8.9	19.0
Seminole	10.4	8.7	8.1	51.8	24 652	25 412	-2.0	-1.0	456	456	-238	9 575	-0.9	2.54	13.3	25.9
Sequoyah	10.8	7.8	5.7	50.7	39 262	33 828	15.2	0.7	541	445	211	14 761	19.7	2.61	11.9	22.4
Stephens	10.2	9.8	8.6	51.6	42 970	42 299	2.1	-0.5	659	706	-147	17 463	4.2	2.44	9.2	25.3
Texas	7.7	5.5	4.7	48.6	19 754	16 419	22.5	-1.8	438	176	-635	7 153	15.1	2.75	7.5	21.2
Tillman	10.8	9.0	10.4	51.0	9 146	10 384	-10.6	-1.5	141	169	-113	3 594	-8.6	2.48	10.7	28.8
Tulsa	8.1	6.2	5.6	51.5	564 079	503 341	11.9	0.1	11 386	6 266	-4 236	226 892	12.0	2.43	12.1	29.6
Wagoner	10.6	6.2	3.9	50.6	59 059	47 883	20.1	2.7	828	436	1 167	21 010	24.0	2.73	9.8	17.7
Washington	10.4	9.1	8.6	52.0	49 087	48 066	1.9	0.2	702	741	152	20 179	4.9	2.40	9.3	27.5
Washita	9.8	8.9	9.9	51.6	11 473	11 441	0.6	-0.3	165	195	-1	4 506	1.9	2.50	8.5	25.3
Woods	9.7	8.8	11.1	49.0	8 832	9 103	-0.2	-2.8	110	174	-195	3 684	-3.1	2.20	7.3	33.4
Woodward	9.9	7.5	6.7	50.0	18 392	18 976	-2.6	-0.5	303	207	-186	7 141	0.8	2.48	8.4	25.4
OREGON	8.9	6.4	6.4	50.4	3 472 867	2 842 337	20.4	1.5	55 999	36 994	32 923	1 333 723	20.9	2.51	9.8	26.1
Baker	12.1	9.7	9.3	50.5	16 743	15 317	9.3	0.0	216	272	64	6 883	12.5	2.37	8.6	27.8
Benton	7.2	5.1	5.2	50.2	77 926	70 811	10.4	-0.3	1 037	591	-674	30 145	15.4	2.43	7.2	26.1
Clackamas	9.5	5.6	5.5	50.6	346 558	278 850	21.4	2.4	5 122	3 080	6 113	128 201	23.8	2.62	9.0	22.0
Clatsop	10.3	8.0	7.6	50.5	35 586	33 301	7.0	-0.1	460	466	-21	14 703	9.9	2.35	9.7	29.5
Columbia	10.0	6.2	5.4	50.0	44 547	37 557	16.0	2.3	689	444	741	16 375	17.7	2.65	8.7	21.1
Coos	12.1	10.0	9.1	51.0	62 459	60 273	4.2	-0.5	800	1 014	-72	26 213	8.6	2.34	9.9	27.2
Crook	11.1	8.2	6.5	50.1	20 062	14 111	35.9	4.6	264	229	826	7 354	34.8	2.57	8.2	21.3
Curry	14.2	14.2	12.4	50.9	21 118	19 327	9.4	-0.1	192	401	183	9 543	14.8	2.19	7.2	29.7
Deschutes	10.0	7.2	5.9	50.3	121 949	74 976	53.9	5.7	1 690	1 093	5 840	45 595	56.1	2.50	8.5	22.0
Douglas	11.2	9.6	8.2	50.8	100 866	94 649	6.1	0.5	1 405	1 458	561	39 821	11.0	2.48	9.6	23.9
Gilliam	11.3	9.6	9.5	49.5	1 851	1 717	11.5	-3.3	25	25	-65	819	17.7	2.31	5.9	29.5
Grant	12.0	8.6	8.1	50.2	7 566	7 853	1.0	-4.7	94	107	-364	3 246	5.0	2.39	7.9	27.1
Harney	11.0	8.3	6.7	49.3	7 404	7 060	7.8	-2.7	113	111	-211	3 036	10.0	2.45	6.8	25.9
Hood River	7.8	6.3	6.6	50.3	20 439	16 903	20.8	0.1	369	208	-134	7 248	12.8	2.70	8.8	22.7
Jackson	10.0	7.9	8.1	51.4	184 963	146 387	23.8	2.0	2 592	2 273	3 372	71 532	25.0	2.48	10.5	25.1
Jefferson	10.4	7.6	4.9	49.5	19 425	13 676	39.0	2.2	349	184	255	6 727	41.8	2.80	10.4	18.6
Josephine	11.9	10.2	9.9	51.4	77 123	62 649	20.9	1.8	1 028	1 221	1 586	31 000	23.6	2.41	10.4	25.4
Klamath	10.2	8.1	6.8	50.0	64 116	57 702	10.5	0.5	1 024	836	181	25 205	12.8	2.49	10.0	25.3
Lake	12.1	9.8	7.9	49.9	7 470	7 186	3.3	0.6	82	92	52	3 084	11.5	2.39	7.5	26.2
Lane	9.0	6.6	6.7	50.8	324 316	282 912	14.2	0.4	4 655	3 511	376	130 453	17.7	2.42	10.0	26.6
Lincoln	12.3	10.7	8.8	51.5	44 264	38 889	14.4	-0.5	529	683	-64	19 296	17.3	2.27	10.0	29.3
Linn	9.8	7.2	7.3	50.6	103 974	91 227	13.0	0.9	1 786	1 263	413	39 541	13.9	2.58	10.0	23.0
Malheur	8.5	6.8	6.9	46.3	31 456	26 038	21.4	-0.5	657	327	-495	10 221	8.1	2.77	10.4	23.7
Marion	8.1	6.0	6.3	49.7	288 269	228 483	24.7	1.2	5 529	3 072	1 100	101 641	21.7	2.70	11.0	24.0

1. No spouse present.

STATE County	Births, average 1997–1999 Total	Births Rate[1]	Deaths, average 1997–1999 Number Total	Deaths Number Infant[2]	Deaths Rate Total[1]	Deaths Rate Infant[3]	Physicians,[4] 2000 Number	Physicians Rate[5]	Hospitals,[4] 1998 Number	Hospitals Beds Number	Hospitals Beds Rate[5]	Medicare enrollees 2000	Serious crimes known to police, 2000[6] Total Number	Total Rate[7]
	32	33	34	35	36	37	38	39	40	41	42	43	44	45
OKLAHOMA—Cont'd														
Kiowa	143	13.4	181	NA	17.0	NA	5	49	1	50	471	2 282	275	2 689
Latimer	133	13.0	124	NA	12.1	NA	2	19	1	33	320	1 449	174	1 627
Le Flore	681	14.6	537	NA	11.5	NA	37	77	1	84	180	8 320	911	1 894
Lincoln	404	12.8	332	NA	10.6	NA	9	28	2	44	140	4 781	480	1 496
Logan	387	12.6	302	NA	9.8	NA	20	59	1	32	103	3 807	749	2 208
Love	110	12.8	100	NA	11.6	NA	1	11	1	40	469	1 539	190	2 152
McClain	327	12.4	240	NA	9.1	NA	11	40	1	32	122	3 903	739	2 664
McCurtain	543	15.6	400	NA	11.5	NA	17	49	1	89	256	5 810	1 156	3 360
McIntosh	216	11.3	279	NA	14.6	NA	8	41	1	33	173	4 738	797	4 096
Major	88	11.4	91	NA	11.8	NA	5	66	1	24	307	1 454	138	1 829
Marshall	165	13.4	160	NA	13.0	NA	5	38	1	25	203	2 775	272	2 063
Mayes	508	13.5	406	NA	10.8	NA	17	44	1	43	114	6 107	1 009	2 630
Murray	157	12.6	194	NA	15.6	NA	11	87	1	48	389	2 414	267	2 115
Muskogee	1 008	14.4	856	10	12.2	9.9	116	167	1	225	321	12 541	3 188	4 590
Noble	143	12.6	136	NA	12.0	NA	5	44	1	42	368	1 892	135	1 183
Nowata	128	12.8	120	NA	12.1	NA	8	76	1	32	321	2 071	333	3 151
Okfuskee	132	11.7	151	NA	13.3	NA	7	59	1	20	175	2 259	380	3 217
Oklahoma	10 439	16.5	6 332	107	10.0	10.3	1 929	292	13	3 325	525	90 514	49 341	7 471
Okmulgee	525	13.6	494	NA	12.8	NA	34	86	2	118	304	6 789	1 494	3 765
Osage	452	10.6	384	NA	9.0	NA	16	36	3	411	959	3 721	1 334	3 002
Ottawa	430	13.9	430	NA	13.9	NA	25	75	1	119	385	7 207	1 368	4 121
Pawnee	217	13.2	189	NA	11.5	NA	8	48	2	43	262	2 760	414	2 492
Payne	805	12.3	492	NA	7.5	NA	85	125	2	177	272	8 077	2 070	3 036
Pittsburg	495	11.5	531	NA	12.3	NA	49	111	1	171	400	7 951	1 552	3 531
Pontotoc	473	13.6	435	NA	12.5	NA	51	145	1	144	416	6 324	1 092	3 107
Pottawatomie	842	13.5	715	NA	11.5	NA	62	95	2	160	257	9 867	2 510	3 831
Pushmataha	130	11.3	178	NA	15.4	NA	5	43	1	46	397	2 448	278	2 383
Roger Mills	36	10.2	38	NA	10.6	NA	3	87	1	15	419	711	16	466
Rogers	879	12.9	529	NA	7.8	NA	65	92	1	86	126	7 839	1 332	1 886
Seminole	350	14.1	355	NA	14.3	NA	16	64	1	39	157	4 932	696	2 796
Sequoyah	536	14.3	390	NA	10.4	NA	14	36	1	41	109	6 380	1 425	3 656
Stephens	555	12.8	548	NA	12.7	NA	31	72	1	100	230	8 214	1 443	3 342
Texas	305	16.6	149	NA	8.1	NA	12	60	1	49	263	2 189	549	2 730
Tillman	116	12.2	133	NA	14.0	NA	6	65	1	58	610	1 903	219	2 358
Tulsa	8 813	16.2	4 909	64	9.0	7.2	1 493	265	6	1 898	349	82 230	31 919	5 666
Wagoner	702	12.7	347	NA	6.3	NA	25	43	1	100	181	4 633	1 308	2 275
Washington	557	11.7	554	NA	11.6	NA	69	141	1	233	490	9 744	1 849	3 774
Washita	144	12.3	161	NA	13.7	NA	2	17	1	38	322	2 321	119	1 034
Woods	90	10.8	136	NA	16.4	NA	3	33	1	50	598	1 836	271	2 982
Woodward	255	13.7	174	NA	9.4	NA	22	119	1	68	367	2 880	738	3 992
OREGON	44 443	13.5	29 192	254	8.9	5.7	7 338	214	62	7 352	224	489 312	165 780	4 845
Baker	188	11.5	216	NA	13.2	NA	22	131	1	129	784	3 501	618	3 692
Benton	829	10.7	452	NA	5.8	NA	179	229	1	124	159	8 138	3 601	4 608
Clackamas	4 164	12.5	2 505	23	7.5	5.5	597	176	3	339	101	39 578	15 122	4 469
Clatsop	418	11.8	372	NA	10.5	NA	57	160	2	69	195	6 219	1 715	4 813
Columbia	553	12.5	358	NA	8.1	NA	14	32	0	0	0	5 971	1 218	2 796
Coos	664	10.7	825	NA	13.3	NA	117	186	3	178	286	13 331	1 800	2 901
Crook	240	13.9	169	NA	9.8	NA	15	78	1	35	203	3 141	519	2 706
Curry	189	9.0	317	NA	15.0	NA	21	99	1	24	113	6 235	410	1 940
Deschutes	1 340	12.6	826	8	7.8	5.7	208	180	2	223	211	16 856	4 795	4 156
Douglas	1 171	11.5	1 168	10	11.5	8.5	181	180	3	284	279	20 367	3 215	3 202
Gilliam	20	9.7	16	NA	8.1	NA	1	52	0	0	0	406	25	1 305
Grant	93	11.7	90	NA	11.2	NA	5	63	1	75	929	1 490	118	1 487
Harney	85	11.8	83	NA	11.6	NA	8	105	1	52	722	1 273	213	2 799
Hood River	300	15.3	162	NA	8.3	NA	43	211	1	54	276	2 779	541	2 651
Jackson	2 120	12.2	1 755	11	10.1	5.3	400	221	3	471	272	32 010	8 137	4 489
Jefferson	306	18.3	150	NA	9.0	NA	16	84	1	109	656	3 014	614	3 230
Josephine	797	10.8	958	NA	12.9	NA	111	147	2	146	196	17 187	2 975	3 929
Klamath	828	13.1	666	7	10.5	8.5	109	171	1	256	405	10 661	1 981	3 106
Lake	77	10.7	77	NA	10.7	NA	8	108	1	67	937	1 535	181	2 439
Lane	3 709	11.8	2 806	22	9.0	5.8	636	197	4	620	197	48 362	18 224	5 643
Lincoln	463	10.2	530	NA	11.7	NA	71	160	2	75	165	9 744	2 317	5 209
Linn	1 441	13.8	1 003	9	9.6	6.0	129	125	2	120	115	17 163	5 066	4 915
Malheur	498	17.5	277	NA	9.7	NA	45	142	1	74	259	4 746	1 188	3 758
Marion	4 370	16.2	2 419	27	9.0	6.1	498	175	3	466	174	40 278	15 721	5 519

1. Per 1,000 estimated resident population, average 1997–1999.   2. Deaths of infants under 1 year old.   3. Deaths of infants under 1 year old per 1,000 live births.   4. Data subject to copyright.   5. Per 100,000 resident population as of July 1 of the year shown.   6. Data for serious crimes have not been adjusted for underreporting; this may affect comparability between geographic areas and over time.   7. Per 100,000 population estimated by the FBI.

Table B. States and Counties — **Crime, Education, Money Income, and Poverty**

	Serious crimes known to police, 2000[1] (cont'd) Rate[2]		Education						Money income 1989				Income and poverty, 1998		
			School enrollment and attainment, 1990				Local government expenditures, fiscal 1999[5]						Percent below poverty level		
			Enrollment[3]		Attainment[4] (percent)					Households					
										Median					
STATE County	Violent	Property	Total	Percent private	High school graduate or more	Bach-elor's degree or more	Total current expendi-tures (mil dol)	Current expendi-tures per student (dollars)	Per capita[6] (dollars)	Dollars	Percent change, 1979–1989 (constant 1989 dollars)	Percent with $100,000 or more	Median house-hold income	All persons	Persons under 18	Persons 5–17 in families
	46	47	48	49	50	51	52	53	54	55	56	57	58	59	60	61

OKLAHOMA—Cont'd																
Kiowa	372	2 317	2 622	3.1	65.0	11.1	12.0	5 889	9 213	16 322	0.5	1.1	23 118	23.4	28.9	32.4
Latimer	393	1 235	2 990	3.1	63.1	11.0	16.4	8 496	9 427	17 477	9.8	0.7	24 881	25.4	36.9	33.3
Le Flore	254	1 640	10 631	3.2	61.2	9.6	52.9	5 374	8 752	18 832	4.2	1.2	27 139	21.2	28.9	28.3
Lincoln	218	1 278	7 301	4.2	68.8	10.1	27.5	4 633	9 952	21 515	-1.5	1.1	32 855	15.4	23.7	20.1
Logan	321	1 887	8 398	6.5	72.0	14.8	23.0	5 133	10 946	24 050	1.7	1.9	37 716	14.8	23.2	19.1
Love	226	1 925	1 889	3.2	66.5	9.3	8.3	5 066	9 960	20 320	-7.3	1.9	29 488	15.9	22.5	23.4
McClain	371	2 293	6 015	5.1	72.2	13.3	27.7	5 102	11 114	25 437	-4.7	2.2	35 701	12.8	17.4	17.4
McCurtain	628	2 732	8 607	1.8	59.2	9.6	43.7	5 747	8 291	16 413	-4.4	1.0	24 718	26.2	33.9	34.3
McIntosh	298	3 798	3 616	2.2	61.5	10.7	18.3	5 501	9 403	17 738	7.3	0.8	23 542	21.9	34.2	33.3
Major	80	1 750	1 960	5.4	70.9	13.1	8.2	5 899	10 745	23 568	-7.6	2.1	32 022	14.1	18.6	18.9
Marshall	258	1 805	2 162	4.0	60.7	9.7	11.9	5 049	9 889	16 292	-2.5	2.0	24 352	19.5	29.6	28.8
Mayes	305	2 325	7 937	5.8	67.9	10.8	36.4	4 987	10 049	21 209	0.2	1.7	31 576	17.0	25.6	23.4
Murray	325	1 790	2 839	5.0	64.0	13.5	11.6	5 079	9 439	18 321	-13.7	0.9	26 331	19.1	26.9	28.1
Muskogee	661	3 929	17 050	7.5	68.3	14.1	77.3	5 469	9 756	20 407	-1.6	1.2	28 860	19.8	27.8	25.7
Noble	149	1 034	2 648	2.5	72.8	12.7	14.2	6 206	10 969	23 227	-0.7	1.7	33 446	15.0	21.0	20.9
Nowata	312	2 838	2 385	3.6	67.4	7.4	10.6	5 411	9 339	18 274	-18.0	0.6	27 252	17.1	25.5	24.5
Okfuskee	305	2 912	2 784	4.8	60.7	8.2	13.5	5 745	8 471	15 738	2.9	1.8	22 403	26.8	35.1	35.5
Oklahoma	611	6 860	157 291	14.4	79.1	22.6	574.5	5 313	13 794	26 129	-5.3	3.1	36 401	15.5	23.5	20.5
Okmulgee	509	3 256	9 541	5.2	66.3	8.8	38.5	5 095	8 799	17 368	-5.6	0.9	25 337	21.8	29.9	29.6
Osage	329	2 673	10 652	7.7	73.0	13.1	27.6	5 932	11 123	24 617	-6.8	1.1	33 669	15.9	24.3	20.7
Ottawa	322	3 799	7 848	3.0	67.8	10.4	36.4	5 731	9 057	17 716	-11.7	1.1	25 782	19.9	30.5	28.0
Pawnee	114	2 378	3 696	6.3	73.0	10.4	12.9	4 635	10 416	21 199	-9.7	1.4	31 975	15.8	22.1	22.3
Payne	334	2 701	26 011	3.1	82.2	30.1	56.2	5 560	10 907	19 591	-2.1	1.8	32 027	16.1	20.2	19.5
Pittsburg	284	3 247	9 422	3.7	64.3	10.3	45.6	5 426	9 832	18 906	-0.9	1.2	28 111	19.4	28.2	26.5
Pontotoc	427	2 680	9 151	2.3	69.3	18.0	37.9	5 427	10 005	17 945	-11.2	1.7	26 931	20.4	29.1	28.4
Pottawatomie	295	3 536	15 912	16.6	70.3	12.2	64.6	5 238	10 391	21 914	-2.4	1.2	31 611	19.2	26.9	25.8
Pushmataha	506	1 877	2 352	2.6	57.8	7.8	14.8	5 979	13 613	—	-7.5	0.3	20 618	26.4	35.6	37.4
Roger Mills	116	349	1 007	1.8	72.1	9.5	3.6	9 035	9 886	20 106	-6.8	2.3	28 204	17.2	21.1	22.4
Rogers	160	1 726	14 798	9.8	78.1	13.0	60.1	4 535	12 235	29 389	-5.4	1.9	43 950	8.8	15.2	12.5
Seminole	394	2 402	6 423	3.9	62.1	9.6	28.9	5 616	9 044	17 007	-11.2	1.2	22 954	26.4	37.1	36.1
Sequoyah	721	2 935	8 466	3.3	59.6	8.8	43.5	5 210	9 074	18 441	-1.2	0.9	26 940	21.3	29.5	28.4
Stephens	201	3 140	10 064	4.0	70.8	14.7	42.4	5 040	10 839	22 647	-9.7	1.3	30 870	17.1	24.2	22.7
Texas	358	2 372	4 577	4.4	75.5	15.1	21.6	5 680	11 096	23 587	-15.1	1.5	37 655	11.6	16.7	15.3
Tillman	258	2 100	2 624	2.9	61.7	11.4	11.6	5 880	8 597	17 799	-2.4	1.1	24 291	23.3	30.1	32.5
Tulsa	853	4 814	133 622	20.3	81.7	23.7	528.7	5 075	14 742	27 228	-6.9	4.0	37 125	12.9	19.8	17.5
Wagoner	137	2 138	13 136	11.3	74.7	12.0	27.6	4 660	11 839	28 544	-2.5	1.5	40 562	11.8	16.4	15.5
Washington	414	3 359	11 909	10.6	79.6	25.8	46.3	5 118	15 086	28 857	-9.7	3.9	39 514	12.2	19.6	17.5
Washita	61	973	2 590	3.6	66.6	11.0	14.2	6 212	9 642	18 385	-27.0	2.1	26 195	19.0	25.1	25.8
Woods	429	2 553	2 707	2.7	76.1	23.5	10.6	7 237	12 261	19 762	-13.0	2.8	29 272	16.2	22.9	21.8
Woodward	492	3 500	4 718	6.5	73.4	13.0	20.4	5 541	11 000	23 796	-21.9	2.1	33 431	15.0	20.2	20.0
OREGON	351	4 495	724 233	11.7	81.5	20.6	3 706.0	6 828	13 418	27 250	-3.1	2.8	38 773	12.1	16.9	14.9
Baker	203	3 488	3 275	6.0	75.0	13.3	21.2	7 329	10 802	22 150	-0.8	1.7	29 616	17.1	22.7	21.8
Benton	243	4 365	29 624	5.8	89.3	41.3	76.6	7 498	12 994	27 295	0.6	3.3	45 181	10.1	12.5	10.7
Clackamas	151	4 318	71 771	12.4	85.7	23.6	344.9	6 392	16 360	35 419	-0.2	5.2	50 999	7.3	10.8	8.1
Clatsop	269	4 544	8 040	7.9	81.8	16.7	34.4	6 721	12 568	25 115	-1.7	1.7	34 716	13.4	18.1	18.1
Columbia	69	2 727	9 429	8.8	78.0	11.0	56.8	6 214	12 798	29 507	-5.2	1.9	45 597	9.0	12.4	11.4
Coos	77	2 824	14 061	5.9	75.5	12.3	76.6	7 635	11 088	22 146	-17.9	1.6	30 766	17.5	24.2	23.4
Crook	297	2 409	3 108	6.7	71.8	10.1	18.9	6 045	11 017	24 275	-6.6	1.4	34 438	13.3	17.5	17.7
Curry	123	1 817	3 227	4.2	78.1	12.8	20.5	6 226	12 475	22 579	-8.0	2.4	29 180	15.0	24.8	23.8
Deschutes	170	3 986	18 147	8.5	83.2	18.9	117.5	6 194	13 401	27 317	-1.7	3.2	38 777	11.2	15.6	14.0
Douglas	103	3 100	22 054	7.0	74.5	11.0	120.4	6 986	10 809	23 693	-15.3	1.2	33 178	15.3	21.1	19.1
Gilliam	52	1 253	423	7.3	85.4	18.7	5.8	15 151	12 137	24 020	-6.5	2.4	36 772	8.8	12.3	12.8
Grant	113	1 374	1 772	2.8	77.2	12.5	12.5	8 357	11 310	24 640	-3.3	1.2	33 098	16.0	21.4	21.0
Harney	289	2 510	1 620	2.6	78.0	14.1	13.2	8 883	10 990	22 334	-21.3	1.4	30 395	15.6	20.6	20.3
Hood River	88	2 562	3 894	9.6	71.3	18.0	25.8	6 819	11 421	25 242	-6.6	1.7	35 227	13.9	20.3	18.2
Jackson	245	4 244	34 192	9.6	80.1	17.6	187.8	6 517	12 492	25 069	-3.3	2.1	34 295	14.7	20.5	17.8
Jefferson	100	3 130	3 368	5.7	73.9	12.2	26.9	7 618	9 863	23 532	-9.2	2.0	32 893	17.2	23.7	24.1
Josephine	151	3 778	13 135	11.9	75.2	12.0	71.9	6 103	10 809	20 936	-4.5	1.6	28 041	19.0	26.8	25.3
Klamath	365	2 741	14 456	5.9	76.2	12.4	75.1	6 774	11 138	23 054	-10.7	1.6	31 793	16.9	23.1	21.8
Lake	364	2 075	1 649	4.9	75.0	14.5	11.5	7 904	11 231	24 659	-5.0	2.3	29 894	17.2	22.3	22.3
Lane	314	5 329	80 983	8.3	83.0	22.2	350.9	7 147	12 570	25 268	-7.3	2.4	35 935	13.7	18.3	16.2
Lincoln	335	4 874	8 225	7.7	80.5	16.7	45.5	6 461	12 058	22 883	-6.9	1.5	31 466	15.8	23.0	23.1
Linn	186	4 729	22 122	9.2	76.2	11.0	110.9	6 208	11 443	25 209	-6.2	1.4	37 123	12.4	17.5	15.5
Malheur	250	3 508	7 341	6.6	69.9	11.1	42.2	7 174	9 949	20 242	-7.1	2.0	29 585	20.4	25.3	24.8
Marion	289	5 230	57 717	14.3	78.7	17.5	331.5	6 562	12 228	26 876	-0.4	2.2	38 149	14.1	19.9	17.2

1. Data for serious crimes have not been adjusted for underreporting; this may affect comparability between geographic areas and over time. 2. Per 100,000 population estimated by the FBI. 3. All persons 3 years old and over enrolled in nursery school through college. 4. Persons 25 years old and over. 5. Elementary and secondary education expenditures, local government fiscal years ending between July 1, 1998 and June 30, 1999. 6. Based on population enumerated as of April 1, 1990.

STATE County	Total (mil dol)	Percent change, 1998–1999	Per capita[1] Dollars	Per capita[1] Rank	Wages and salaries[2] (mil dol)	Proprietor's income (mil dol)	Dividends, interest, and rent (mil dol)	Transfer payments Total (mil dol)	Government payments to individuals Total (mil dol)	Social Security (mil dol)	Medical payments (mil dol)	Income mainte-nance (mil dol)	Unemploy-ment insurance (mil dol)
	62	63	64	65	66	67	68	69	70	71	72	73	74
OKLAHOMA—Cont'd													
Kiowa	195	4.0	18 601	2 396	68	31	40	52	50	20	19	7	0
Latimer	192	6.4	18 769	2 354	112	12	34	46	45	19	12	6	1
Le Flore	830	4.9	17 741	2 591	277	126	124	194	186	69	69	25	1
Lincoln	578	5.7	18 157	2 509	157	46	97	98	92	46	27	10	1
Logan	656	7.2	21 560	1 501	157	59	97	94	89	42	28	8	1
Love	145	6.5	16 918	2 751	47	12	24	31	29	14	10	3	0
McClain	504	6.2	18 885	2 325	159	44	72	76	72	35	22	6	1
McCurtain	620	4.9	17 822	2 573	303	138	79	132	125	49	43	22	2
McIntosh	312	7.3	16 216	2 871	93	29	60	94	91	40	32	9	1
Major	152	1.3	19 817	2 052	58	25	36	30	29	14	11	2	0
Marshall	226	7.0	18 297	2 473	97	13	41	73	70	26	35	5	0
Mayes	721	3.4	18 835	2 336	333	68	119	135	128	65	38	13	2
Murray	210	3.4	16 825	2 772	86	21	37	53	51	23	17	5	1
Muskogee	1 365	5.8	19 474	2 147	889	97	234	301	289	111	108	32	4
Noble	232	3.8	20 465	1 846	138	13	55	40	38	18	15	3	0
Nowata	162	0.7	16 093	2 887	44	10	31	41	40	20	14	3	0
Okfuskee	177	4.2	15 708	2 927	61	20	27	52	50	19	21	7	0
Oklahoma	16 739	4.3	26 297	486	14 002	1 526	3 203	2 235	2 121	850	853	229	27
Okmulgee	624	3.1	16 076	2 891	247	49	103	167	160	64	55	19	2
Osage	758	0.9	17 634	2 615	215	31	133	119	111	66	23	10	2
Ottawa	601	6.1	19 466	2 150	233	73	105	153	147	65	57	13	1
Pawnee	312	3.8	18 878	2 328	80	26	53	60	57	29	19	4	1
Payne	1 348	5.5	20 610	1 806	850	88	257	192	180	78	62	15	1
Pittsburg	799	5.4	18 381	2 447	399	82	168	179	171	73	60	19	3
Pontotoc	701	5.5	20 218	1 922	370	66	134	159	152	60	62	16	1
Pottawatomie	1 145	3.9	18 274	2 480	503	88	209	206	195	88	59	24	2
Pushmataha	164	4.8	14 175	3 039	58	14	29	57	55	20	22	8	1
Roger Mills	71	7.5	19 839	2 044	21	12	25	13	12	6	4	1	0
Rogers	1 454	3.9	20 610	1 806	567	97	223	192	179	92	54	10	3
Seminole	403	4.2	16 416	2 841	170	29	81	117	112	44	43	15	2
Sequoyah	671	5.1	17 722	2 595	190	84	84	151	145	58	55	19	1
Stephens	856	2.9	19 874	2 029	377	128	180	179	171	86	53	13	4
Texas	608	21.7	33 146	129	264	222	75	50	47	24	16	3	0
Tillman	161	5.3	17 109	2 714	60	28	28	40	38	17	14	5	0
Tulsa	17 262	2.8	31 483	170	11 952	3 054	3 089	1 936	1 837	785	758	140	27
Wagoner	1 033	3.0	18 410	2 440	163	76	134	140	130	70	33	12	2
Washington	1 286	2.2	26 979	417	615	92	383	188	179	101	56	10	2
Washita	180	1.3	15 410	2 951	56	21	42	45	43	20	15	4	0
Woods	188	0.4	22 972	1 096	72	32	50	37	35	17	11	2	0
Woodward	353	-1.4	19 002	2 277	200	46	71	62	59	29	20	5	1
OREGON	89 398	4.8	26 958	X	56 206	6 947	20 136	12 038	11 443	4 956	3 976	994	450
Baker	328	2.6	20 168	1 945	145	25	92	75	72	33	24	7	3
Benton	2 184	1.8	28 291	296	1 344	121	594	203	190	90	47	15	3
Clackamas	10 904	4.9	32 237	146	4 761	714	2 437	954	894	445	263	50	35
Clatsop	841	4.2	23 800	896	449	78	203	143	136	64	46	11	5
Columbia	1 084	5.8	23 889	882	332	75	189	151	142	66	47	11	7
Coos	1 359	2.7	22 031	1 354	618	102	344	323	312	136	109	31	13
Crook	374	5.8	21 168	1 608	196	25	99	72	69	32	24	5	3
Curry	481	4.0	22 726	1 156	162	32	173	119	116	64	35	7	3
Deschutes	2 890	8.0	26 077	504	1 451	349	799	387	367	176	117	26	18
Douglas	2 188	4.3	21 488	1 525	1 150	158	516	465	446	205	146	37	21
Gilliam	24	-21.2	11 518	3 096	25	-14	13	7	6	4	1	0	0
Grant	164	1.0	20 819	1 726	80	9	43	35	33	14	12	3	3
Harney	154	1.8	21 173	1 603	86	9	34	30	29	13	9	3	2
Hood River	444	4.6	22 314	1 271	254	50	114	62	58	28	18	4	4
Jackson	4 220	6.0	24 004	858	2 146	388	1 128	708	677	323	216	56	26
Jefferson	317	4.1	18 806	2 344	189	12	69	64	61	25	24	6	2
Josephine	1 548	5.6	20 666	1 788	596	154	430	398	385	168	141	41	11
Klamath	1 325	4.7	20 886	1 703	694	112	292	278	266	106	95	26	10
Lake	146	0.9	20 285	1 898	72	8	37	33	32	15	10	3	2
Lane	7 972	4.7	25 315	611	4 425	698	1 899	1 226	1 170	493	409	110	40
Lincoln	1 022	2.9	22 728	1 155	450	99	294	218	210	99	72	16	8
Linn	2 287	2.9	21 709	1 449	1 344	168	447	423	404	172	143	40	18
Malheur	556	-2.3	19 530	2 133	360	35	141	113	108	44	41	13	4
Marion	6 499	5.4	23 828	890	4 004	466	1 439	1 050	1 001	396	392	94	36

1. Based on the resident population estimated as of July 1 of the year shown.   2. Includes other labor income.

Table B. States and Counties — Earnings, Social Security, and Housing

STATE County	Earnings, 1999									Social Security beneficiaries, December 2000		Supplemental Security Income recipients, December 2000	Housing units, 1990	
	Total (mil dol)	Farm	Goods-related[1]		Service-related and other[2]					Number	Rate[3]		Total	Percent change, 1980–1990
			Total	Manufacturing	Total	Retail trade	Finance, insurance, and real estate	Services	Government					
	75	76	77	78	79	80	81	82	83	84	85	86	87	88

OKLAHOMA—Cont'd

STATE County	75	76	77	78	79	80	81	82	83	84	85	86	87	88
Kiowa	99	19.1	D	D	D	8.4	3.7	16.4	26.7	2 585	253	370	5 645	-3.3
Latimer	124	0.0	D	8.1	D	5.0	1.8	12.8	36.0	2 613	244	291	4 303	8.0
Le Flore	404	13.7	D	16.0	D	10.6	3.4	12.8	24.2	9 539	198	2 030	18 029	15.1
Lincoln	203	0.3	20.3	8.0	59.4	10.5	10.2	17.1	20.0	5 979	186	596	12 302	15.7
Logan	217	0.5	20.2	4.6	52.2	11.8	4.9	25.2	27.2	5 241	154	378	12 277	16.2
Love	59	-0.5	D	30.1	D	14.8	3.2	15.3	20.2	1 840	208	176	3 583	11.8
McClain	203	3.9	31.3	8.6	43.0	16.0	5.1	12.4	21.8	4 481	162	320	9 300	20.6
McCurtain	441	13.3	D	33.8	D	8.0	1.8	14.6	16.7	6 836	199	1 682	13 828	0.7
McIntosh	122	0.5	14.2	8.3	61.6	18.2	5.1	26.8	23.7	5 310	273	657	10 708	28.6
Major	83	12.1	D	7.4	D	8.9	3.8	15.5	16.6	1 778	236	76	3 855	8.1
Marshall	110	-1.9	D	32.0	D	12.0	4.0	14.2	19.8	3 278	249	362	7 389	43.2
Mayes	401	1.7	21.0	34.7	D	10.3	2.5	14.4	19.4	7 924	207	804	15 470	11.4
Murray	108	4.0	21.0	6.8	39.7	12.4	3.8	14.7	35.3	2 871	227	292	5 742	11.5
Muskogee	986	0.2	27.7	20.5	45.8	9.8	3.7	17.4	26.2	13 976	201	2 267	28 882	5.1
Noble	151	1.9	D	D	D	7.4	3.3	10.1	16.4	2 267	199	178	4 894	0.5
Nowata	54	0.9	D	19.1	D	7.7	5.2	23.7	26.7	2 471	234	199	4 534	-6.6
Okfuskee	81	4.8	26.1	7.3	36.7	9.8	2.7	19.6	32.4	2 543	215	583	4 894	2.5
Oklahoma	15 528	0.0	19.3	10.8	56.9	9.0	6.3	28.8	23.8	100 514	152	13 614	279 340	15.5
Okmulgee	297	1.4	28.1	22.4	45.0	11.8	4.1	20.7	25.5	8 121	205	1 308	16 431	5.2
Osage	245	-2.6	46.1	9.7	30.8	6.5	3.1	16.0	25.7	7 822	176	453	18 196	11.6
Ottawa	306	6.0	D	19.5	D	10.5	3.4	24.2	19.5	8 034	242	983	14 064	0.8
Pawnee	107	-1.2	D	3.5	D	13.4	4.3	27.5	28.9	3 573	215	272	7 407	15.1
Payne	938	0.0	16.2	9.7	41.0	10.3	3.4	20.2	42.8	9 272	136	1 006	27 381	12.9
Pittsburg	481	0.5	18.2	11.0	45.3	11.5	3.2	19.9	35.9	9 821	223	1 471	19 433	8.2
Pontotoc	435	0.6	21.1	14.3	58.2	11.5	6.3	31.9	20.2	7 418	211	1 127	15 094	13.5
Pottawatomie	590	0.9	29.9	22.6	52.4	13.6	3.7	27.9	16.8	11 774	180	1 523	24 528	11.5
Pushmataha	72	-3.2	14.8	6.8	50.9	12.5	3.5	26.1	37.5	2 888	248	609	5 190	3.8
Roger Mills	33	18.0	D	D	D	8.1	3.8	11.7	35.8	820	239	61	2 048	2.1
Rogers	664	0.1	41.5	31.1	41.2	8.5	3.3	15.6	17.3	10 854	154	593	21 455	26.5
Seminole	198	0.1	33.6	20.8	D	11.7	3.0	19.8	23.8	5 614	226	911	11 404	1.3
Sequoyah	274	0.0	16.8	10.4	59.7	14.0	4.0	33.4	23.6	7 932	204	1 529	14 314	20.4
Stephens	505	0.6	41.3	22.5	44.7	12.0	4.8	21.5	13.4	10 218	237	800	19 675	9.5
Texas	486	42.2	D	D	D	5.2	1.7	9.4	10.0	2 649	132	178	7 328	3.5
Tillman	88	25.6	D	D	32.7	6.1	3.3	10.6	23.1	2 193	236	178	4 704	-10.5
Tulsa	15 006	0.0	32.0	21.1	60.2	8.6	6.1	27.1	7.7	85 719	152	9 392	227 834	16.6
Wagoner	238	1.6	30.3	16.0	49.2	11.2	5.0	25.2	18.9	8 563	149	636	19 262	22.7
Washington	707	0.8	D	8.6	D	10.5	4.9	D	10.2	11 029	225	723	21 707	7.2
Washita	77	11.7	D	5.4	D	8.8	4.2	17.9	29.7	2 655	231	210	6 101	2.7
Woods	104	17.8	10.0	4.7	42.5	11.7	6.8	12.7	29.7	1 948	214	93	4 782	-2.8
Woodward	247	5.3	20.7	4.1	50.4	13.2	8.5	14.5	23.7	3 483	188	260	8 512	4.2
OREGON	63 154	1.0	25.5	18.0	57.6	10.7	6.8	25.5	15.9	562 381	164	52 046	1 193 567	10.2
Baker	169	-0.6	D	11.6	53.7	12.0	5.2	23.1	29.1	4 004	239	333	7 525	3.0
Benton	1 465	1.6	D	31.2	D	6.9	3.3	22.7	24.5	9 926	127	610	27 024	7.3
Clackamas	5 475	2.0	24.8	15.4	61.2	12.4	8.3	24.5	12.0	48 451	143	2 564	109 003	20.8
Clatsop	526	0.2	29.0	21.3	50.1	15.1	3.3	23.6	20.6	7 140	200	607	17 367	4.5
Columbia	407	2.3	D	24.3	D	10.2	3.6	13.4	18.3	7 385	170	422	14 576	6.9
Coos	720	0.6	18.3	12.1	53.2	13.2	4.3	21.7	27.8	15 720	250	1 572	26 668	3.8
Crook	222	-1.1	D	26.3	D	7.5	3.0	14.0	21.4	3 797	198	235	6 066	7.7
Curry	194	-1.7	D	15.6	D	18.2	5.1	21.2	22.7	7 263	344	387	9 885	32.0
Deschutes	1 800	-0.4	24.0	11.7	61.5	13.4	10.3	26.6	14.9	20 795	180	1 185	35 928	27.8
Douglas	1 308	0.1	31.4	25.2	46.8	10.1	3.5	21.3	21.9	23 948	239	1 835	38 298	7.4
Gilliam	12	-105.9	D	D	D	17.4	4.7	15.6	54.5	464	242	29	932	-11.2
Grant	89	-3.2	D	15.3	D	8.7	4.1	13.7	43.8	1 696	214	133	3 774	-1.0
Harney	95	-0.2	27.3	21.4	38.3	11.3	2.3	15.4	34.7	1 512	199	133	3 305	-2.1
Hood River	304	10.3	19.4	11.7	54.2	12.2	2.3	24.7	16.1	3 187	156	176	7 569	5.8
Jackson	2 534	0.2	22.5	14.4	61.0	16.5	5.9	26.3	16.3	37 469	207	2 746	60 376	15.5
Jefferson	200	-0.2	35.5	32.1	40.9	8.4	1.9	18.7	23.8	3 332	175	288	6 311	21.4
Josephine	749	0.1	23.6	14.6	57.6	15.9	5.2	25.9	18.9	19 729	261	1 646	26 912	15.4
Klamath	806	1.9	D	16.3	D	11.1	4.5	24.1	22.4	12 704	199	1 314	25 954	2.3
Lake	81	0.4	D	11.3	39.9	10.4	3.7	11.9	42.4	1 791	241	146	3 434	3.2
Lane	5 123	0.2	D	18.5	D	12.1	5.6	26.5	17.6	55 706	172	5 095	116 676	5.0
Lincoln	549	-0.4	D	10.6	D	17.3	4.9	26.6	23.0	11 239	253	731	22 389	6.9
Linn	1 511	2.1	40.7	32.0	43.2	9.8	3.2	16.8	14.0	19 878	193	1 882	36 482	3.8
Malheur	395	5.9	D	10.9	50.1	12.4	3.8	19.3	28.6	5 477	173	654	10 649	0.1
Marion	4 470	3.8	D	11.4	D	10.8	5.9	21.8	29.4	45 531	160	4 699	86 869	9.1

1. Covers mining, construction, and manufacturing. 2. Covers private sector earnings in agricultural services, forestry, and fisheries; transportation and public utilities; wholesale trade; retail trade; finance, insurance, and real estate; and services. 3. Per 1,000 resident population estimated as of July 1 of the year shown.

Table B. States and Counties — Housing, Labor Force, and Employment

STATE County	Housing units, 1990 (cont'd) Occupied units — Owner-occupied			Owner cost as a percent of income		Renter-occupied		Substandard units[3] (percent)	Civilian labor force, 2001		Unemployment		Civilian employment, 1990[5]	Percent	
	Total	Percent	Median value[1]	With a mortgage	Without a mortgage	Median rent[2]	Rent as percent of income		Total	Percent change, 2000–2001	Total	Rate[4]	Total	Professional, managerial, and technical	Precision production, craft, and repair
	89	90	91	92	93	94	95	96	97	98	99	100	101	102	103
OKLAHOMA—Cont'd															
Kiowa	4 551	74.2	27 000	20.7	13.4	229	24.5	4.1	4 924	1.9	153	3.1	4 339	19.9	8.1
Latimer	3 693	74.9	33 900	20.6	13.9	261	24.2	7.7	5 068	6.3	258	5.1	3 474	24.5	14.3
Le Flore	15 938	75.3	34 900	20.3	14.1	277	27.6	4.5	19 393	2.7	1 120	5.8	16 317	20.7	15.4
Lincoln	10 839	80.5	35 100	19.3	13.3	296	26.4	4.1	14 571	4.7	637	4.4	11 673	20.9	16.0
Logan	10 180	77.4	46 200	18.5	14.0	306	25.1	3.4	14 583	0.0	457	3.1	12 430	24.4	13.5
Love	2 992	78.7	35 900	22.3	12.5	270	26.4	4.3	3 962	3.1	185	4.7	3 275	19.0	13.1
McClain	8 332	80.2	46 500	20.4	13.6	348	26.1	2.7	13 528	1.1	533	3.9	10 240	24.3	15.1
McCurtain	12 234	73.1	29 200	17.9	13.5	238	26.9	8.6	16 733	9.7	1 056	6.3	12 085	18.7	13.5
McIntosh	6 786	77.8	38 700	20.2	13.1	256	29.0	4.9	7 728	0.2	450	5.8	5 844	23.4	12.9
Major	3 121	80.8	37 700	20.4	12.0	281	19.8	1.7	3 735	-1.3	97	2.6	3 430	19.2	13.4
Marshall	4 350	78.5	37 000	20.3	12.6	284	28.3	4.0	5 107	-3.7	212	4.2	3 999	22.8	9.4
Mayes	12 672	76.8	42 400	19.6	12.2	299	26.4	4.9	17 036	2.6	838	4.9	13 207	20.1	17.6
Murray	4 651	72.5	33 700	17.7	12.7	246	22.1	4.2	5 427	0.7	268	4.9	4 739	21.8	13.0
Muskogee	25 174	69.9	40 900	19.3	13.5	295	28.1	4.1	30 772	-0.3	1 320	4.3	26 378	24.2	12.2
Noble	4 225	75.0	33 500	17.3	12.7	285	22.7	3.5	5 665	-1.4	253	4.5	4 854	21.3	13.7
Nowata	3 994	78.1	27 900	20.4	13.1	267	23.7	3.8	3 825	4.8	222	5.8	4 033	21.0	13.2
Okfuskee	4 164	76.5	25 700	21.7	13.3	219	26.3	6.8	4 032	6.0	189	4.7	3 795	17.7	13.1
Oklahoma	237 879	61.3	53 300	19.9	12.3	368	25.4	4.1	336 502	0.9	13 923	4.1	280 519	31.3	10.1
Okmulgee	14 044	72.6	30 900	20.3	12.7	273	29.8	4.1	14 187	0.1	961	6.8	13 449	22.5	14.6
Osage	15 383	78.6	43 300	19.8	12.9	266	26.4	3.9	20 272	-0.1	705	3.5	17 380	24.0	16.9
Ottawa	12 124	73.9	30 200	17.9	12.3	250	26.2	2.9	14 698	4.5	1 071	7.3	11 958	22.5	11.5
Pawnee	6 006	79.0	39 200	21.0	13.6	308	26.6	3.9	7 020	3.3	344	4.9	6 642	22.6	14.4
Payne	23 834	54.5	50 700	20.4	12.1	343	32.9	2.2	36 359	-3.2	548	1.5	28 234	33.6	9.3
Pittsburg	15 911	75.4	34 700	20.8	13.1	286	24.8	2.7	17 256	-0.3	724	4.2	14 934	25.1	13.8
Pontotoc	13 310	69.0	39 900	20.1	13.6	283	26.1	2.8	17 406	0.8	671	3.9	14 237	26.6	12.4
Pottawatomie	21 796	73.9	42 400	19.6	13.1	325	27.7	3.1	29 284	1.2	1 512	5.2	24 045	25.3	13.9
Pushmataha	4 370	76.6	27 700	22.7	11.9	205	28.1	8.4	5 343	6.6	353	6.6	3 775	22.3	10.5
Roger Mills	1 586	79.1	25 900	25.8	15.2	197	19.6	3.6	1 984	0.1	38	1.9	1 811	16.3	10.8
Rogers	19 866	79.4	63 700	20.6	12.5	358	24.8	4.0	36 752	0.2	1 096	3.0	25 548	24.4	17.8
Seminole	9 665	73.0	27 300	20.9	14.1	246	27.0	4.6	10 415	2.7	591	5.7	9 082	23.5	14.4
Sequoyah	12 335	73.8	37 800	19.4	14.1	288	27.5	5.5	17 109	-0.8	903	5.3	13 610	18.1	14.5
Stephens	16 764	74.7	39 000	18.5	13.0	294	26.3	3.1	18 209	0.4	628	3.4	16 581	27.0	15.1
Texas	6 214	71.6	44 500	17.2	12.4	287	21.1	3.4	15 350	2.3	314	2.0	7 779	19.4	12.9
Tillman	3 933	75.0	22 700	21.1	13.6	258	21.0	4.7	3 533	0.5	167	4.7	3 854	22.7	9.7
Tulsa	202 537	60.7	60 700	20.1	12.7	366	24.4	2.9	301 421	0.4	10 325	3.4	244 911	32.9	11.0
Wagoner	16 946	79.0	58 300	19.2	12.1	347	24.7	3.5	29 081	0.3	872	3.0	22 060	23.4	16.5
Washington	19 242	74.5	51 900	16.4	11.6	358	24.4	1.8	19 268	3.1	635	3.3	21 213	36.4	11.5
Washita	4 421	76.5	28 400	17.1	12.9	287	20.4	3.8	4 878	1.3	146	3.0	4 705	19.6	15.0
Woods	3 803	73.0	32 700	16.5	12.8	254	22.7	2.0	4 614	2.7	71	1.5	4 099	25.3	10.0
Woodward	7 087	72.5	40 300	19.1	11.7	295	21.0	3.1	8 975	3.9	278	3.1	8 371	21.1	14.5
OREGON	1 103 313	63.1	67 100	20.4	13.4	408	25.5	3.9	1 793 724	-0.5	113 855	6.3	1 319 960	28.8	10.7
Baker	6 118	68.8	42 100	20.6	14.6	289	22.4	3.6	7 306	-1.6	646	8.8	6 154	19.9	9.3
Benton	26 126	55.1	72 900	20.1	12.2	387	29.4	3.7	40 034	-0.1	1 185	3.0	32 984	41.2	6.8
Clackamas	103 530	71.7	85 100	20.4	12.9	472	24.0	2.9	198 188	-0.4	9 016	4.5	141 004	31.0	11.2
Clatsop	13 374	63.2	62 500	19.6	14.1	352	24.4	3.7	17 313	-1.2	902	5.2	14 788	23.4	12.5
Columbia	13 910	74.1	62 800	17.7	12.4	350	22.2	4.0	23 707	1.0	1 838	7.8	16 369	21.6	16.4
Coos	24 134	66.5	49 800	20.0	14.0	331	25.6	4.1	26 865	-2.5	2 193	8.2	23 384	23.6	11.1
Crook	5 455	71.4	50 300	15.8	12.4	335	21.2	3.8	7 760	-2.1	752	9.7	5 968	16.5	9.8
Curry	8 311	72.5	83 400	22.1	13.1	387	22.7	4.3	8 247	-1.8	493	6.0	7 352	19.7	13.5
Deschutes	29 217	71.0	74 500	21.0	13.4	438	25.9	3.6	61 638	0.2	3 969	6.4	35 860	26.9	12.2
Douglas	35 872	68.9	56 000	21.2	13.3	350	23.8	4.5	44 327	-2.4	3 968	9.0	37 639	21.4	10.7
Gilliam	696	66.7	31 600	15.8	13.9	363	18.9	1.3	1 172	-1.8	68	5.8	785	22.9	6.4
Grant	3 092	70.8	46 900	17.2	12.8	310	18.9	4.2	3 774	-5.1	389	10.3	3 302	24.7	9.2
Harney	2 760	70.3	37 800	18.0	13.2	290	19.7	4.0	3 869	-4.0	546	14.1	3 051	20.1	11.6
Hood River	6 425	62.1	77 200	20.2	12.4	393	24.4	9.4	11 013	-1.4	1 012	9.2	7 720	25.0	9.0
Jackson	57 238	66.2	74 900	22.0	13.3	413	27.6	4.4	91 923	0.0	5 757	6.3	62 704	25.1	10.7
Jefferson	4 744	64.9	53 700	19.1	13.1	346	21.4	9.3	8 463	-3.8	647	7.6	5 598	18.8	9.7
Josephine	25 081	70.4	74 700	22.7	13.7	391	28.8	5.4	29 583	-0.2	2 505	8.5	23 039	22.9	12.2
Klamath	22 341	65.2	52 700	19.3	13.0	329	24.6	4.8	27 975	-3.2	2 662	9.5	23 638	21.7	11.3
Lake	2 765	67.8	41 900	16.9	14.1	299	20.4	5.0	3 293	-1.6	342	10.4	3 182	22.4	10.3
Lane	110 799	60.8	65 800	20.2	13.3	418	28.5	3.7	165 257	-0.9	11 182	6.8	129 698	28.3	10.4
Lincoln	16 455	66.0	69 400	22.2	12.8	376	25.7	3.7	20 649	-2.3	1 434	6.9	16 352	26.1	9.6
Linn	34 716	65.6	51 300	18.8	13.6	376	24.3	3.3	51 569	-0.5	4 264	8.3	39 402	20.4	13.7
Malheur	9 457	64.1	46 300	20.8	14.4	289	25.9	7.6	13 875	-3.9	1 242	9.0	10 794	20.0	8.4
Marion	83 494	62.9	59 900	20.8	13.0	401	25.4	4.6	141 336	-1.7	9 094	6.4	101 478	28.2	10.4

1. Specified owner-occupied units. 2. Specified renter-occupied units. 3. Overcrowded or lacking complete plumbing facilities. 4. Percent of civilian labor force. 5. Persons 16 years and older.

Table B. States and Counties — Nonfarm Employment and Agriculture

	Private nonfarm establishments, employment and payroll, 1999									Agriculture, 1997			Farm operators
		Employment						Annual payroll		Farms			
											Percent with—		
STATE County	Number of establishments	Total	Health Care and Social Assistance	Manufacturing	Retail trade	Finance and Insurance	Professional Scientific and Technical Services	Total (mil dol)	Average per employee (dollars)	Number	Less than 50 acres	500 acres and over	Whose principal occupation is farming (percent)
	104	105	106	107	108	109	110	111	112	113	114	115	116

OKLAHOMA—Cont'd

Kiowa	241	2 068	736	D	317	90	48	35	16 882	702	9.5	46.4	57.8
Latimer	161	1 498	356	D	211	63	22	30	19 705	643	20.2	14.5	41.4
Le Flore	753	8 081	1 851	1 056	1 872	369	371	153	18 933	1 744	29.0	9.9	40.8
Lincoln	534	5 036	633	570	948	626	125	91	18 151	1 916	19.0	9.9	35.4
Logan	549	4 577	1 159	338	784	169	149	79	17 170	983	20.7	20.8	42.2
Love	149	1 527	128	469	287	40	18	30	19 356	629	16.2	18.6	40.9
McClain	548	4 663	529	519	1 026	245	132	97	20 817	1 046	30.1	13.5	39.1
McCurtain	594	8 498	1 123	3 112	1 122	236	383	178	20 892	1 573	28.0	8.0	42.7
McIntosh	394	3 229	901	319	737	129	107	48	14 906	906	20.2	10.9	44.8
Major	211	1 776	272	201	377	82	30	34	19 206	877	11.1	35.5	51.8
Marshall	275	3 685	536	1 500	485	88	43	70	18 917	414	18.6	17.9	39.9
Mayes	728	9 731	928	3 222	1 577	263	171	227	23 357	1 406	29.9	8.6	39.7
Murray	243	2 334	369	101	560	98	52	43	18 236	454	18.5	19.6	41.6
Muskogee	1 585	24 288	4 755	5 426	3 427	690	454	551	22 697	1 468	28.3	8.7	40.8
Noble	230	3 498	455	D	559	125	32	101	28 844	739	11.1	31.9	48.8
Nowata	175	1 406	252	268	252	67	29	24	17 388	764	18.5	17.9	43.1
Okfuskee	162	2 060	790	271	302	66	20	39	18 779	784	14.5	17.5	40.4
Oklahoma	21 186	336 586	45 411	39 367	41 402	18 783	17 628	9 097	27 027	996	46.0	7.0	33.4
Okmulgee	671	6 594	1 497	1 038	1 433	266	176	131	19 904	1 107	23.6	11.5	40.7
Osage	531	4 247	585	837	858	183	101	84	19 701	1 196	20.7	29.3	42.6
Ottawa	725	7 319	1 451	1 692	1 116	278	161	137	18 656	972	31.4	9.1	39.8
Pawnee	303	2 616	569	227	580	124	72	51	19 380	671	18.0	23.0	42.0
Payne	1 575	20 086	2 976	2 831	3 586	657	894	388	19 336	1 281	26.9	14.0	34.1
Pittsburg	898	9 718	2 207	802	1 972	423	223	183	18 802	1 586	21.7	14.6	39.6
Pontotoc	896	11 549	2 254	2 257	1 899	837	397	238	20 606	1 133	22.9	13.9	39.3
Pottawatomie	1 315	18 249	2 450	4 039	3 028	559	341	357	19 540	1 448	22.5	10.4	39.3
Pushmataha	201	1 669	539	252	327	49	38	26	15 824	776	19.2	14.4	43.8
Roger Mills	85	497	106	0	110	D	10	8	16 553	680	3.5	52.1	59.4
Rogers	1 263	15 377	1 790	5 016	2 080	458	279	389	25 329	1 408	38.2	9.3	34.9
Seminole	519	5 664	1 002	1 510	900	178	98	105	18 477	1 018	20.2	11.3	35.9
Sequoyah	613	6 108	1 726	451	1 190	267	145	98	16 104	1 125	30.0	7.7	36.5
Stephens	1 058	11 290	1 618	1 596	2 146	623	246	237	21 033	1 165	20.5	17.4	44.7
Texas	542	6 606	668	2 416	906	196	122	147	22 236	785	6.5	58.2	55.5
Tillman	177	1 581	319	D	223	72	31	29	18 560	638	7.5	42.0	57.5
Tulsa	18 235	319 780	35 277	41 647	37 625	17 867	16 428	9 751	30 492	954	50.3	6.6	30.1
Wagoner	734	6 863	872	1 487	1 015	173	163	140	20 463	973	32.2	10.1	36.3
Washington	1 188	17 119	2 457	1 400	2 692	653	948	600	35 058	768	32.8	10.8	40.8
Washita	243	1 645	340	220	306	94	53	26	16 027	994	9.7	38.7	60.8
Woods	272	2 176	346	59	529	207	49	34	15 672	705	7.2	51.9	60.6
Woodward	656	5 971	1 050	511	1 185	543	130	129	21 543	800	12.1	16.0	50.6
OREGON	99 945	1 332 403	150 646	210 330	186 360	66 661	64 913	39 707	29 801	34 030	56.3	12.9	46.0
Baker	535	3 851	641	591	816	184	128	75	19 361	704	27.0	35.9	62.6
Benton	1 931	28 396	3 819	8 712	3 203	565	1 585	840	29 595	726	65.4	7.4	41.5
Clackamas	9 401	110 646	10 466	17 333	16 995	4 405	4 841	3 342	30 200	3 745	78.9	1.0	35.9
Clatsop	1 346	11 032	1 440	985	2 351	252	279	228	20 648	229	49.8	3.1	40.2
Columbia	861	8 975	826	2 835	1 275	234	259	285	31 791	686	63.4	2.3	34.3
Coos	1 730	17 160	3 048	1 577	3 082	534	505	395	22 990	675	42.1	9.6	54.7
Crook	416	4 821	388	1 393	514	87	76	126	26 086	521	46.1	26.9	44.7
Curry	697	4 934	595	782	1 074	186	145	100	20 325	168	33.9	26.8	60.1
Deschutes	4 343	41 919	4 230	5 072	8 051	1 453	1 627	1 041	24 826	1 235	74.7	3.5	35.5
Douglas	2 666	30 942	4 589	6 349	4 519	683	778	755	24 415	1 908	49.5	9.1	45.0
Gilliam	61	579	68	3	71	D	D	14	23 869	166	2.4	81.3	75.9
Grant	296	1 681	256	D	303	78	61	35	20 815	407	23.8	49.6	58.2
Harney	210	1 842	202	D	309	59	46	38	20 580	504	17.9	52.6	64.1
Hood River	776	7 606	996	976	1 409	117	237	159	20 918	537	67.2	0.7	56.8
Jackson	5 248	60 898	8 433	7 349	10 268	2 214	1 892	1 517	24 913	1 623	66.7	4.7	41.0
Jefferson	286	4 271	292	1 981	633	106	44	111	25 957	399	30.8	26.3	57.9
Josephine	1 861	17 326	2 972	3 074	3 439	613	437	383	22 103	616	74.0	1.1	46.8
Klamath	1 606	17 212	2 457	2 861	3 318	651	908	421	24 444	1 066	35.2	22.6	57.6
Lake	205	1 362	293	343	239	D	30	29	21 034	418	17.0	39.7	61.5
Lane	9 698	119 071	15 634	21 187	18 915	4 125	6 281	3 072	25 799	2 104	65.3	4.2	37.2
Lincoln	1 663	13 598	1 656	982	2 751	349	328	278	20 466	306	54.9	3.9	42.2
Linn	2 565	33 588	3 107	9 430	4 595	956	1 070	910	27 084	2 009	57.4	9.2	45.1
Malheur	769	8 795	1 169	1 361	2 105	231	230	176	20 037	1 207	28.7	22.5	66.5
Marion	7 452	91 770	13 031	11 228	14 773	7 222	3 176	2 331	25 401	2 546	65.0	5.8	47.5

Table B. States and Counties — Agriculture, Land, and Water

STATE County	Agriculture, 1997 (cont'd)															Percent of land owned by fed. gov. 1997	Water consumption 1995 (mil gal/day)
	Land in farms				Value of land and buildings		Value of machinery and equipment average per farm ($1,000)	Value of products sold				Percent of farms with sales of —				
		Acres								Percent from —						
	Acreage (1,000)	Percent change, 1992–1997	Average size of farm	Total irrigated (1,000)	Total cropland (1,000)	Average per farm ($1,000)	Average per acre (dollars)		Total (mil dol)	Average per farm (dollars)	Crops	Live-stock and poultry products	$10,000 or more	$100,000 or more		
	117	118	119	120	121	122	123	124	125	126	127	128	129	130	131	132
OKLAHOMA—Cont'd																
Kiowa	595	6.7	848	1	362	380	448	60	52	73 826	36.8	63.2	65.8	17.0	0.4	11.5
Latimer	202	4.2	314	2	63	205	579	32	11	16 659	5.7	94.3	26.1	2.5	0.6	2.2
Le Flore	407	6.9	234	4	189	211	902	27	119	68 066	6.5	93.5	34.1	12.8	23.4	14.2
Lincoln	431	8.4	225	0	181	189	838	23	24	12 271	12.8	87.2	23.2	2.2	0.0	8.4
Logan	381	10.6	387	1	183	315	837	32	39	40 084	27.3	72.7	39.6	6.2	0.0	6.3
Love	266	4.0	423	4	87	231	533	30	16	24 723	22.1	77.9	38.5	5.6	4.1	2.6
McClain	268	5.5	256	2	121	242	947	36	31	30 083	21.5	78.5	34.3	5.4	0.0	4.9
McCurtain	328	4.0	208	1	135	180	745	30	137	87 146	3.0	97.0	35.7	14.7	7.7	11.3
McIntosh	254	7.0	280	0	105	199	644	24	16	17 535	16.5	83.5	31.1	2.5	3.8	4.8
Major	491	-0.6	560	5	244	337	583	47	55	62 489	27.0	73.0	55.3	13.5	0.0	11.0
Marshall	164	0.4	395	1	42	218	558	30	6	14 677	19.5	80.5	26.6	2.4	11.7	2.5
Mayes	284	2.0	202	0	147	225	1 080	27	33	23 771	13.5	86.5	33.5	5.9	2.9	84.5
Murray	203	-11.9	448	D	49	289	615	31	20	45 064	3.0	97.0	36.6	6.6	3.5	14.4
Muskogee	333	-4.2	227	7	183	179	768	27	32	21 565	39.6	60.4	29.1	3.9	2.7	83.5
Noble	413	5.6	559	0	222	313	573	44	40	53 690	45.3	54.7	55.1	14.9	0.0	3.2
Nowata	309	9.3	405	D	99	240	596	23	29	37 325	6.6	93.4	36.6	4.1	2.2	1.7
Okfuskee	282	9.4	360	0	101	214	587	23	18	22 384	11.9	88.1	32.1	4.0	0.0	2.2
Oklahoma	160	2.2	161	1	78	272	1 688	24	15	15 003	56.7	43.3	23.6	2.5	1.3	77.4
Okmulgee	302	7.5	273	0	123	200	732	28	19	17 000	22.3	77.7	27.1	2.9	0.7	8.2
Osage	1 207	8.2	1 010	0	158	430	436	30	103	86 022	5.5	94.5	42.6	9.4	2.1	19.4
Ottawa	215	3.8	221	0	130	204	977	30	53	54 294	53.4	46.6	32.6	7.1	0.0	5.0
Pawnee	263	-6.6	393	0	93	194	521	28	18	26 640	19.9	80.1	37.7	6.3	1.1	25.3
Payne	339	3.1	265	0	142	212	777	22	22	17 467	17.4	82.6	28.3	2.8	0.0	6.1
Pittsburg	491	2.2	310	2	148	188	631	20	25	15 530	13.0	87.0	30.5	2.0	7.5	10.4
Pontotoc	335	-5.0	296	2	130	181	593	22	23	20 604	8.0	92.0	28.3	2.3	0.0	6.7
Pottawatomie	336	12.5	232	1	155	175	809	23	33	22 790	13.7	86.3	24.5	2.8	0.0	11.4
Pushmataha	256	6.8	330	0	71	178	570	27	8	9 928	4.7	95.3	24.7	1.3	1.6	2.7
Roger Mills	691	4.6	1 016	5	162	375	381	40	28	40 458	16.6	83.4	59.3	11.8	4.2	6.9
Rogers	313	0.9	222	1	125	236	1 004	23	27	19 268	21.9	78.1	23.9	3.1	2.2	79.0
Seminole	278	10.6	273	1	109	155	557	21	14	14 172	16.2	83.8	22.7	2.1	0.0	17.3
Sequoyah	293	36.4	261	2	95	190	762	30	39	34 760	12.1	87.9	24.2	2.8	1.5	14.1
Stephens	427	1.4	366	3	171	192	542	29	24	20 848	13.0	87.0	31.7	4.5	0.5	7.1
Texas	1 087	3.4	1 384	138	632	718	511	130	668	850 985	7.8	92.2	61.7	23.9	0.4	375.0
Tillman	466	-3.2	730	14	322	385	551	58	41	64 457	59.2	40.8	60.0	17.1	0.6	7.0
Tulsa	143	6.7	150	3	72	264	1 790	22	20	20 676	65.8	34.2	22.1	3.6	0.1	17.2
Wagoner	241	10.9	247	1	139	266	1 100	29	29	29 657	64.5	35.5	30.1	5.2	6.3	20.3
Washington	238	10.0	309	0	74	202	752	20	16	21 382	26.2	73.8	27.9	4.3	4.0	4.1
Washita	586	1.4	589	3	399	334	558	66	69	69 161	36.3	63.7	66.2	17.4	0.0	7.1
Woods	805	8.2	1 141	3	290	668	587	59	81	115 461	27.3	72.7	69.1	20.7	0.0	6.4
Woodward	722	5.1	902	6	214	329	358	37	50	62 121	17.7	82.3	50.9	11.9	1.0	16.3
OREGON	17 449	-0.9	513	1 949	5 286	479	960	55	2 969	87 252	71.2	28.8	38.2	13.4	50.3	7 906.0
Baker	1 008	23.0	1 431	143	161	727	504	62	54	76 528	25.3	74.7	56.4	17.6	50.9	462.8
Benton	131	9.9	180	20	92	413	2 527	55	70	96 697	87.3	12.7	31.5	11.3	17.6	80.9
Clackamas	180	20.6	48	24	107	367	7 447	37	276	73 765	78.4	21.6	31.4	8.4	46.1	228.5
Clatsop	23	-8.9	99	0	13	372	3 112	27	5	23 253	13.4	86.6	24.9	6.1	0.6	126.7
Columbia	66	-8.9	96	1	23	335	4 004	26	25	36 225	81.4	18.6	15.0	1.5	2.5	99.6
Coos	163	-6.8	242	11	43	345	1 450	30	31	45 225	46.7	53.3	42.7	12.4	21.5	36.6
Crook	916	2.4	1 759	72	77	608	359	67	31	60 338	42.5	57.5	42.4	14.8	49.6	226.2
Curry	85	14.6	505	3	17	754	2 017	41	13	77 743	67.1	32.9	42.9	12.5	59.8	19.8
Deschutes	124	-10.5	101	40	44	368	2 715	37	21	17 405	45.9	54.1	22.3	2.9	74.7	180.8
Douglas	402	0.0	211	17	118	324	1 814	27	35	18 521	27.8	72.2	27.0	3.4	48.0	189.7
Gilliam	743	-3.0	4 474	4	298	1 180	265	172	25	147 746	81.0	19.0	75.3	40.4	7.0	31.1
Grant	1 081	-6.3	2 655	48	87	938	339	50	17	41 998	14.5	85.5	50.4	12.3	60.6	223.5
Harney	1 359	-6.7	2 696	152	215	795	294	59	39	77 150	19.3	80.7	59.7	20.8	71.9	549.1
Hood River	28	5.0	53	19	21	436	6 681	60	63	117 888	98.6	1.4	57.5	31.7	62.3	117.5
Jackson	246	-6.1	152	53	70	353	1 784	32	51	31 396	74.5	25.5	22.1	3.4	47.7	363.6
Jefferson	783	47.5	1 964	52	100	766	384	105	43	108 150	81.2	18.8	57.9	25.1	27.5	163.7
Josephine	35	11.5	56	12	17	219	4 177	27	16	26 305	54.0	46.0	20.1	3.1	56.8	59.6
Klamath	714	-0.9	669	243	235	507	872	72	101	94 392	51.0	49.0	54.0	18.8	54.4	694.8
Lake	737	-11.6	1 762	200	187	775	529	72	43	102 294	47.3	52.7	64.6	25.4	67.1	686.0
Lane	224	-7.6	106	23	120	336	3 428	34	87	41 430	62.2	37.8	24.3	6.7	53.5	350.1
Lincoln	32	-6.1	104	1	10	278	3 285	24	4	13 488	61.8	38.2	19.9	2.0	29.4	41.8
Linn	393	3.5	196	30	305	456	2 552	62	174	86 717	78.5	21.5	33.7	14.2	37.3	184.0
Malheur	1 257	-4.6	1 042	239	279	655	587	104	208	172 509	58.7	41.3	67.2	28.5	74.2	610.2
Marion	306	1.4	120	92	251	500	4 248	88	438	172 179	83.6	16.4	45.3	19.9	29.4	265.7

Table B. States and Counties — **Residential Construction, Wholesale and Retail Trade, and Real Estate**

STATE County	Value of Residential Construction Authorized by Building Permits, 2000 New Construction ($1,000)	Number of Housing Units	Wholesale Trade, 1997 Number of Establishments	Number of Employees	Sales (mil dol)	Annual Payroll (mil dol)	Retail Trade[1], 1997 Number of Establishments	Number of Employees	Sales (mil dol)	Annual Payroll (mil dol)	Real Estate and Rental and Leasing, 1997 Number of Establishments	Number of Employees	Receipts (mil dol)	Annual Payroll (mil dol)
	133	134	135	136	137	138	139	140	141	142	143	144	145	146
OKLAHOMA—Cont'd														
Kiowa	186	3	18	123	44.7	2.4	56	353	37.5	3.3	8	13	1.6	0.3
Latimer	224	7	6	D	D	D	31	237	26.1	2.9	4	29	2.5	0.8
Le Flore	3 214	46	27	120	42.4	2.3	162	1 578	247.2	20.0	25	55	3.6	0.5
Lincoln	2 315	24	21	D	D	D	154	1 011	136.3	12.6	11	13	0.7	0.1
Logan	1 631	16	18	D	D	D	96	816	133.3	10.5	21	37	3.4	0.5
Love	0	0	6	79	28.7	1.9	35	290	51.7	3.5	1	D	D	D
McClain	12 128	123	19	D	D	D	96	940	192.0	14.6	13	27	2.2	0.5
McCurtain	1 631	28	30	239	69.8	4.8	138	1 119	167.2	15.1	11	46	2.1	0.5
McIntosh	2 215	67	10	17	6.7	0.3	94	650	140.1	9.2	11	22	1.4	0.2
Major	155	2	17	151	69.4	2.3	48	323	59.6	4.1	3	7	0.6	0.1
Marshall	76	1	12	124	48.7	3.5	56	416	56.6	5.3	11	26	1.0	0.2
Mayes	3 370	39	36	216	71.5	5.2	135	1 313	191.8	16.5	15	69	3.4	0.5
Murray	1 268	15	10	73	25.5	1.1	49	492	93.1	7.3	3	17	1.2	0.2
Muskogee	7 719	76	91	1 185	313.2	30.4	349	3 613	561.7	52.8	56	218	16.7	3.3
Noble	785	10	9	50	17.2	0.9	57	478	72.3	6.4	10	22	2.1	0.2
Nowata	440	6	9	107	28.4	1.6	33	180	27.3	2.1	7	22	1.6	0.6
Okfuskee	25	1	2	D	D	D	33	235	37.5	2.7	3	6	0.5	0.1
Oklahoma	428 842	4 092	1 517	21 108	15 144.3	638.9	3 098	41 034	7 479.8	681.3	913	5 379	612.2	107.7
Okmulgee	2 531	35	30	150	42.7	3.2	142	1 324	207.3	17.8	14	36	2.0	0.4
Osage	4 252	46	23	147	29.5	3.2	112	748	95.8	8.8	13	35	1.9	0.4
Ottawa	1 140	15	30	D	D	D	138	1 136	180.8	15.2	23	67	5.9	0.7
Pawnee	0	0	9	D	D	D	55	484	69.9	6.2	10	17	0.8	0.2
Payne	17 293	220	62	664	211.2	13.1	299	3 336	466.1	43.4	70	278	16.2	3.3
Pittsburg	4 536	43	51	333	114.2	8.2	185	2 059	326.3	26.7	39	150	8.3	1.9
Pontotoc	1 978	32	53	492	257.6	10.4	180	1 859	266.9	23.5	27	73	7.2	1.2
Pottawatomie	10 663	100	44	D	D	D	276	2 847	397.8	37.0	55	200	18.5	2.5
Pushmataha	43	1	10	130	11.1	1.4	56	294	42.0	3.3	5	3	0.4	0.0
Roger Mills	0	0	3	6	4.6	0.1	22	110	14.8	1.4	1	D	D	D
Rogers	49 649	448	65	518	357.8	16.7	192	1 994	353.2	28.6	38	243	15.8	3.2
Seminole	581	6	28	169	53.8	4.6	104	813	116.1	10.6	17	73	4.2	0.7
Sequoyah	6 235	96	15	110	47.6	1.4	159	1 387	218.9	17.0	16	44	2.1	0.5
Stephens	4 148	43	53	441	90.6	10.0	221	2 074	314.1	27.7	29	115	11.3	2.5
Texas	5 161	75	40	D	D	D	99	936	130.2	11.6	21	57	3.9	0.6
Tillman	0	0	13	155	33.4	3.0	43	346	31.4	2.6	2	7	0.3	0.1
Tulsa	349 144	2 715	1 438	18 675	9 427.0	658.2	2 440	35 520	6 410.4	590.8	802	4 358	506.2	92.5
Wagoner	41 456	428	34	209	98.3	4.3	109	971	149.2	12.0	33	113	10.1	2.0
Washington	6 663	37	34	284	52.0	7.1	216	2 613	425.8	38.7	42	161	10.2	2.5
Washita	80	1	16	118	33.2	2.0	51	310	46.2	3.8	12	46	2.0	0.5
Woods	620	5	21	170	48.0	3.2	58	533	65.4	6.8	8	10	0.6	0.2
Woodward	1 315	6	50	342	68.9	6.7	128	1 074	179.2	15.3	22	107	10.6	2.6
OREGON	2 533 332	19 877	5 943	74 790	53 679.1	2 578.7	14 467	178 349	33 396.8	3 308.8	4 556	23 058	2 704.0	470.9
Baker	3 155	28	19	90	13.2	2.0	93	805	121.3	11.7	23	55	5.0	0.6
Benton	43 104	264	63	681	112.6	15.9	294	3 175	473.9	53.2	111	379	38.9	5.5
Clackamas	388 547	2 311	685	8 723	6 383.3	314.7	1 092	16 098	3 448.3	312.3	422	2 231	240.5	44.9
Clatsop	22 468	154	39	383	88.4	7.0	274	2 173	332.4	36.8	57	181	14.3	2.1
Columbia	36 152	278	26	161	61.5	4.4	137	1 360	199.8	22.1	28	83	7.6	1.2
Coos	4 145	36	60	496	233.2	14.6	289	3 040	505.2	52.1	64	208	18.5	3.4
Crook	24 926	205	16	72	21.5	1.5	57	494	89.3	8.4	14	24	3.6	0.4
Curry	16 500	122	20	62	14.2	1.1	121	1 041	148.4	16.8	31	76	8.3	1.4
Deschutes	325 687	2 099	191	1 303	571.0	39.7	687	7 130	1 297.1	128.7	198	1 028	140.5	16.9
Douglas	46 311	363	84	1 152	404.1	27.0	457	4 416	669.0	71.2	126	391	34.9	5.1
Gilliam	67	1	3	D	D	D	13	72	8.7	1.1	NA	NA	NA	NA
Grant	NA	NA	4	28	5.9	0.8	45	316	42.4	4.4	7	7	0.6	0.1
Harney	987	11	6	31	9.7	0.7	41	299	51.5	5.4	7	15	1.1	0.2
Hood River	15 137	109	27	181	92.2	9.9	129	1 286	170.3	19.8	23	72	7.2	0.8
Jackson	160 010	1 351	284	2 678	1 022.7	69.8	835	9 564	2 075.3	172.2	248	1 003	95.9	15.2
Jefferson	14 457	209	18	221	78.0	5.3	57	647	109.9	11.4	17	34	2.8	0.4
Josephine	46 705	424	59	441	175.6	9.2	326	3 322	590.3	57.9	71	313	20.6	3.6
Klamath	26 029	150	66	954	293.1	22.1	290	3 116	544.8	55.5	67	200	20.7	2.8
Lake	2 020	16	7	D	D	D	48	266	39.4	4.3	9	D	D	D
Lane	183 158	1 330	535	6 144	2 498.6	179.6	1 462	18 145	3 322.6	328.3	463	2 042	226.5	35.0
Lincoln	33 233	314	39	296	72.5	7.0	372	2 794	415.2	43.8	77	183	22.7	2.6
Linn	55 155	512	131	1 534	766.0	44.5	391	4 662	800.9	78.7	97	361	31.5	5.2
Malheur	6 227	56	50	951	171.0	18.0	163	1 903	302.9	30.7	26	68	6.0	1.0
Marion	160 443	1 424	326	3 247	1 184.0	91.9	1 081	14 637	2 672.5	266.3	380	1 748	194.5	36.3

1. Establishments with payroll.

Items 133—146

STATE County	Professional, Scientific, and Technical Services[1], 1997				Manufacturing, 1997				Accommodation and Foodservices, 1997			
	Number of Establishments	Number of Employees	Receipts (mil dol)	Annual Payroll (mil dol)	Number of Establishments	Number of Employees	Receipts (mil dol)	Annual Payroll (mil dol)	Number of Establishments	Number of Employees	Sales (mil dol)	Annual Payroll (mil dol)
	147	148	149	150	151	152	153	154	155	156	157	158
OKLAHOMA—Cont'd												
Kiowa	14	41	1.6	0.4	NA	NA	NA	NA	15	D	D	D
Latimer	5	14	0.5	0.1	NA	NA	NA	NA	14	107	2.8	0.8
Le Flore	48	314	13.4	6.8	32	1 104	137.0	24.4	55	616	18.2	4.7
Lincoln	35	123	5.5	1.5	21	737	132.0	14.1	46	570	12.4	3.3
Logan	30	101	7.4	2.6	NA	NA	NA	NA	43	D	D	D
Love	7	21	0.7	0.2	NA	NA	NA	NA	17	157	5.3	1.3
McClain	34	81	3.8	1.3	19	D	D	D	38	D	D	D
McCurtain	29	388	10.7	6.0	25	2 758	794.7	79.6	51	537	14.9	3.7
McIntosh	19	84	4.5	1.7	NA	NA	NA	NA	46	439	12.6	3.4
Major	9	20	1.5	0.3	NA	NA	NA	NA	16	D	D	D
Marshall	15	43	2.1	0.6	20	1 196	130.5	24.3	27	222	7.3	1.8
Mayes	30	97	5.8	2.7	68	3 357	731.5	102.4	72	755	19.7	5.0
Murray	18	64	4.5	1.1	NA	NA	NA	NA	24	266	8.4	2.3
Muskogee	72	363	25.4	8.1	87	4 780	990.3	155.3	135	2 097	58.8	15.2
Noble	12	22	1.7	0.6	13	D	D	D	20	316	7.2	2.0
Nowata	11	20	1.2	0.3	NA	NA	NA	NA	12	139	3.1	0.9
Okfuskee	7	17	1.1	0.3	NA	NA	NA	NA	12	96	2.9	0.7
Oklahoma	2 262	14 060	1 266.2	502.1	851	39 462	9 922.1	1 281.5	1 493	29 780	918.6	255.9
Okmulgee	30	114	5.8	2.2	35	1 120	295.4	38.5	59	664	20.7	5.5
Osage	34	116	4.1	1.1	21	939	137.1	31.2	42	389	9.5	2.5
Ottawa	35	104	5.5	1.9	67	1 819	276.4	41.4	59	676	18.1	5.1
Pawnee	22	74	22.7	2.0	NA	NA	NA	NA	28	199	5.7	1.4
Payne	116	694	59.3	20.6	60	2 584	846.8	76.5	149	2 867	66.5	18.3
Pittsburg	61	203	14.1	4.0	27	875	217.1	20.7	75	1 275	37.3	10.2
Pontotoc	61	293	20.1	7.3	47	1 743	209.7	36.6	59	1 151	29.3	8.2
Pottawatomie	72	288	22.2	6.5	72	3 673	654.9	119.7	135	2 726	76.3	21.1
Pushmataha	14	36	2.6	0.6	NA	NA	NA	NA	17	96	3.3	0.8
Roger Mills	4	D	D	D	NA	NA	NA	NA	9	57	1.3	0.3
Rogers	67	237	16.8	6.3	122	4 562	822.9	147.4	89	1 324	38.0	10.0
Seminole	26	77	4.0	1.2	30	1 689	252.3	33.4	33	413	11.7	2.9
Sequoyah	31	93	7.5	2.4	NA	NA	NA	NA	74	900	24.0	6.3
Stephens	56	216	15.3	4.6	58	1 941	470.4	49.8	85	1 159	30.9	8.3
Texas	25	112	6.5	2.7	13	D	D	D	55	617	16.7	4.4
Tillman	13	38	1.8	0.7	NA	NA	NA	NA	14	D	D	D
Tulsa	1 953	13 985	1 437.7	533.5	1 136	39 402	7 858.1	1 310.7	1 316	23 663	771.3	207.7
Wagoner	45	104	11.5	2.5	66	1 924	432.7	50.8	60	786	23.1	5.1
Washington	76	827	76.2	24.4	48	1 327	183.8	50.0	92	1 595	51.6	14.0
Washita	16	51	2.7	0.8	NA	NA	NA	NA	9	37	0.9	0.1
Woods	21	45	2.9	0.5	NA	NA	NA	NA	23	317	6.3	1.8
Woodward	36	116	6.8	2.1	30	591	260.5	21.5	46	613	18.3	4.6
OREGON	8 117	52 514	4 734.6	1 925.0	5 768	213 111	47 666.0	7 095.3	8 363	124 425	4 385.7	1 236.6
Baker	27	105	7.4	2.4	NA	NA	NA	NA	62	540	19.0	4.7
Benton	210	1 367	116.7	50.1	106	8 547	1 391.9	494.5	205	2 807	85.9	24.0
Clackamas	745	3 526	348.4	129.8	589	18 655	3 667.4	632.2	571	10 002	331.1	94.6
Clatsop	60	212	12.6	4.0	49	858	142.4	21.2	200	2 250	89.4	25.5
Columbia	36	208	10.2	3.6	57	3 079	1 008.5	128.4	75	782	24.3	7.2
Coos	96	377	26.8	9.2	104	1 937	391.2	57.6	186	2 004	61.4	17.0
Crook	18	62	3.7	1.3	21	1 506	225.3	39.4	34	383	12.7	3.4
Curry	38	94	6.1	2.0	32	727	116.2	26.2	112	785	30.5	8.1
Deschutes	295	1 206	105.1	37.4	202	4 884	698.6	129.5	305	4 722	194.2	55.6
Douglas	140	550	30.9	13.2	157	7 141	1 494.7	226.4	274	3 635	138.1	37.9
Gilliam	4	D	D	D	NA	NA	NA	NA	8	67	1.7	0.4
Grant	16	49	2.4	1.1	NA	NA	NA	NA	32	179	5.8	1.4
Harney	7	25	1.7	0.5	NA	NA	NA	NA	25	170	5.2	1.5
Hood River	53	180	12.4	5.2	58	1 128	157.5	27.2	76	1 107	36.2	10.8
Jackson	341	1 917	99.5	35.4	301	7 428	1 424.0	201.7	474	6 253	205.3	60.3
Jefferson	12	35	3.0	0.7	21	1 793	351.3	52.2	31	371	11.9	3.2
Josephine	106	280	17.0	5.2	117	2 812	439.6	76.8	168	1 928	66.9	18.0
Klamath	88	775	35.2	13.7	72	3 013	562.6	86.1	156	1 899	73.1	17.2
Lake	7	20	1.2	0.4	NA	NA	NA	NA	26	196	6.1	1.5
Lane	797	4 682	374.3	138.8	624	19 262	3 881.8	589.8	809	12 022	387.8	110.5
Lincoln	74	297	21.2	7.0	59	1 060	255.2	34.4	274	3 644	134.7	37.8
Linn	142	861	48.9	21.5	184	9 794	1 918.8	347.8	183	2 400	73.1	20.3
Malheur	38	171	10.4	3.5	28	D	D	D	73	947	33.3	9.1
Marion	519	2 708	210.3	82.7	402	12 651	2 232.8	354.4	529	8 872	281.6	78.1

1. Firms subject to federal tax.

Table B. States and Counties — Health and Other Services and Federal Funds

STATE County	Health Care and Social Assistance[1], 1997				Other Services[1], 1997				Federal funds and grants, fiscal 2001[2] Expenditures (mil dol)			
										Direct payments for individuals[3]		
	Number of Establishments	Number of Employees	Receipts (mil dol)	Annual Payroll (mil dol)	Number of Establishments	Number of Employees	Receipts (mil dol)	Annual Payroll (mil dol)	Total	Social Security and government retirement	Medicare	Food stamps and Supplemental Security Income
	159	160	161	162	163	164	165	166	167	168	169	170
OKLAHOMA—Cont'd												
Kiowa	19	200	6.2	2.6	12	39	2.2	0.5	98.9	30.6	15.7	2.6
Latimer	24	426	12.5	7.6	9	26	1.3	0.3	64.7	23.4	11.7	2.6
Le Flore	63	1 000	32.2	16.2	39	117	9.9	1.9	298.0	117.9	52.4	14.7
Lincoln	36	510	14.3	6.0	15	56	2.4	0.9	145.3	80.1	23.5	4.5
Logan	40	1 045	22.9	11.2	28	99	5.5	1.7	151.4	60.3	23.9	4.3
Love	9	152	4.7	2.3	3	D	D	D	58.5	21.1	9.1	1.4
McClain	32	365	11.8	5.1	25	83	5.6	1.4	109.1	58.5	20.9	2.4
McCurtain	47	669	19.1	9.0	32	140	8.1	1.5	233.4	74.9	43.4	12.9
McIntosh	39	908	29.1	14.3	19	46	3.0	0.7	134.9	68.7	25.4	4.5
Major	6	28	1.5	0.5	3	D	D	D	48.5	18.0	7.5	0.4
Marshall	18	265	10.3	5.1	14	33	3.1	0.6	74.4	38.7	16.6	2.4
Mayes	48	462	15.9	6.4	39	117	7.3	1.7	167.8	86.7	32.1	7.2
Murray	22	341	11.2	5.2	13	33	2.3	0.4	75.5	34.8	14.2	2.6
Muskogee	175	2 633	111.4	49.5	76	399	24.2	7.3	486.3	190.5	74.6	17.8
Noble	17	327	9.5	4.6	9	12	1.3	0.3	65.5	25.0	10.6	1.5
Nowata	13	212	4.7	2.7	11	29	2.0	0.5	54.3	26.9	10.2	1.5
Okfuskee	17	435	10.5	4.5	3	11	0.5	0.1	82.9	32.5	14.3	3.5
Oklahoma	1 916	25 018	1 706.7	750.5	1 209	9 534	541.1	166.5	6 252.3	1 595.3	547.6	66.9
Okmulgee	63	921	33.0	15.5	37	108	7.3	1.5	242.4	94.2	44.2	10.9
Osage	41	471	14.9	7.1	21	44	2.5	0.5	149.5	59.5	23.2	6.0
Ottawa	57	695	22.7	11.7	34	118	7.1	1.9	217.2	95.0	45.0	8.6
Pawnee	23	262	8.9	4.2	16	35	2.8	0.6	86.4	39.5	16.4	2.4
Payne	113	1 283	60.8	28.2	92	441	19.6	5.6	322.9	116.2	47.4	7.9
Pittsburg	71	1 391	62.8	31.6	38	190	10.8	2.9	306.5	127.8	46.0	11.3
Pontotoc	82	1 037	48.4	22.0	57	325	18.3	5.7	232.9	88.8	38.5	8.8
Pottawatomie	105	1 694	74.2	32.8	65	272	15.7	4.1	338.0	169.8	46.7	14.3
Pushmataha	19	339	12.0	5.1	11	29	1.8	0.3	80.5	32.5	16.7	3.6
Roger Mills	3	D	D	D	3	D	D	D	25.9	7.7	4.8	0.4
Rogers	83	1 388	69.8	26.3	63	307	21.0	6.9	237.6	126.1	37.9	3.5
Seminole	33	792	22.9	10.8	21	43	3.9	0.7	169.7	67.9	30.9	7.4
Sequoyah	52	812	30.5	12.6	34	107	5.8	1.4	215.4	88.5	35.6	10.4
Stephens	83	979	44.1	19.4	56	214	12.4	2.8	244.0	124.5	44.6	6.8
Texas	34	192	13.4	4.2	32	103	6.5	1.3	118.9	29.1	14.6	1.6
Tillman	10	182	3.5	1.8	9	25	1.3	0.3	94.2	24.0	12.7	2.5
Tulsa	1 489	20 172	1 369.8	608.8	1 006	6 871	473.8	138.7	2 614.3	1 145.2	467.1	85.0
Wagoner	48	877	34.1	16.3	42	103	6.4	1.4	170.4	74.7	29.6	4.9
Washington	108	947	63.5	31.7	68	369	20.5	6.8	216.7	130.5	44.7	7.6
Washita	10	68	2.9	1.2	16	49	3.4	0.9	86.0	29.2	14.3	2.0
Woods	21	200	6.6	2.6	16	56	2.6	0.6	65.1	22.8	10.4	0.7
Woodward	41	357	16.1	6.4	34	134	10.0	2.3	83.0	38.8	15.9	2.5
OREGON	7 328	68 285	4 431.4	1 899.6	4 794	28 185	1 897.5	561.9	18 401.2	7 158.1	2 247.5	530.8
Baker	31	124	7.8	2.3	33	148	6.7	1.4	118.8	49.1	12.9	3.3
Benton	148	1 994	140.5	52.6	88	461	26.3	7.9	352.9	125.4	33.4	6.3
Clackamas	638	5 206	377.7	161.5	417	2 263	158.1	44.8	1 260.5	555.5	181.2	105.4
Clatsop	79	685	39.6	15.1	44	175	11.9	3.5	203.2	90.7	29.9	5.4
Columbia	59	340	20.0	8.6	33	119	6.3	1.8	158.9	88.2	29.5	4.4
Coos	156	1 328	85.3	30.9	79	298	23.2	5.9	379.8	195.5	56.3	15.6
Crook	36	202	9.3	3.1	14	49	3.2	0.9	96.1	47.7	14.2	2.5
Curry	45	237	11.9	3.8	28	65	4.3	0.8	162.3	90.7	26.6	4.5
Deschutes	253	2 073	147.7	57.1	159	904	56.1	18.4	481.4	269.7	63.2	12.5
Douglas	233	1 999	126.3	60.1	132	669	38.5	11.0	618.2	304.7	80.7	20.0
Gilliam	3	27	0.7	0.3	1	D	D	D	22.5	5.6	1.5	0.2
Grant	13	72	3.1	1.1	8	16	1.9	0.3	52.4	21.9	6.0	1.3
Harney	16	111	4.2	2.0	13	48	2.1	0.6	50.4	18.4	4.7	1.2
Hood River	55	367	18.2	7.0	24	160	6.5	1.6	111.7	37.8	10.9	2.0
Jackson	384	3 810	244.3	110.5	222	1 192	80.6	21.6	927.4	467.4	122.0	29.7
Jefferson	15	76	4.6	2.0	17	69	3.1	0.8	93.8	41.9	10.2	3.2
Josephine	164	1 555	81.9	30.7	94	369	23.7	5.6	427.0	242.5	63.1	20.5
Klamath	158	881	58.3	25.3	83	343	25.1	6.5	374.7	166.0	48.0	14.4
Lake	9	42	2.6	1.1	10	9	1.5	0.2	69.0	22.8	5.9	1.4
Lane	751	7 176	492.8	217.7	473	3 210	194.0	57.1	1 550.8	703.3	211.8	58.4
Lincoln	99	677	37.9	15.2	53	251	16.1	4.2	267.8	140.0	42.7	7.6
Linn	154	1 466	89.1	44.8	123	611	37.6	11.6	466.5	245.4	72.4	19.0
Malheur	70	381	23.5	8.3	52	188	13.6	3.4	147.9	59.3	18.2	7.2
Marion	629	5 965	354.9	156.3	373	2 003	116.9	37.4	1 984.4	644.1	178.7	48.7

1. Firms subject to federal tax.   2. October 1, 2000 to September 30, 2001.   3. State totals may include programs not allocated by county.

	Federal funds and grants, fiscal 2001[1] (cont'd)							Local government finances, 1997				
	Expenditures (mil dol) (cont'd)							General revenue				
	Procurement contract awards			Grants[2]						Taxes		
STATE County	Salaries and wages	Defense	Other	Medicaid and other health-related	Nutrition and family welfare	Education	Other	Total (mil dol)	Intergovern-mental (mil dol)	Total (mil dol)	Per capita[3] (dollars) Total	Property
	171	172	173	174	175	176	177	178	179	180	181	182
OKLAHOMA—Cont'd												
Kiowa	3.3	1.9	0.6	12.3	1.9	1.4	5.3	19.7	12.0	4.4	410	241
Latimer	1.2	0.0	4.5	8.0	1.7	2.0	3.9	31.1	16.9	11.2	1 089	986
Le Flore	9.7	1.5	2.6	52.6	9.6	7.8	23.7	73.2	42.8	15.3	329	198
Lincoln	5.6	0.0	1.0	17.1	3.1	1.4	4.5	43.0	24.0	10.6	342	188
Logan	4.4	0.9	5.2	12.6	3.0	5.4	18.7	45.5	20.3	9.0	295	189
Love	1.2	0.0	0.3	7.1	0.6	0.5	15.2	10.6	7.2	2.3	266	166
McClain	3.6	0.0	1.1	9.7	1.6	1.7	6.0	55.7	23.8	18.2	705	493
McCurtain	6.9	0.3	1.3	59.3	7.0	16.8	1.7	56.9	37.9	12.4	360	244
McIntosh	2.5	2.2	0.5	22.9	2.6	2.7	1.9	27.0	16.0	7.3	389	181
Major	1.9	0.0	4.0	2.0	0.5	1.6	1.2	14.8	7.8	3.4	431	305
Marshall	1.7	0.0	0.3	9.3	1.2	2.3	0.4	21.1	10.2	5.5	461	292
Mayes	4.3	0.1	1.2	21.7	3.1	5.3	2.3	45.5	25.8	14.1	382	186
Murray	4.4	0.0	1.8	12.4	1.5	0.9	2.0	22.2	12.6	4.9	400	230
Muskogee	64.8	3.9	7.3	75.2	10.5	9.4	3.0	194.4	56.5	50.8	732	411
Noble	2.6	0.0	0.5	4.1	1.5	2.0	5.7	21.4	9.2	8.6	766	682
Nowata	1.9	0.4	0.4	7.3	0.9	0.9	0.5	14.3	9.8	2.9	293	180
Okfuskee	2.3	0.0	0.4	17.3	3.0	1.7	5.8	18.4	12.0	4.4	392	299
Oklahoma	1 491.4	838.1	321.5	349.5	255.4	141.4	508.0	1 385.1	405.6	562.2	892	382
Okmulgee	7.0	0.7	1.3	40.8	14.9	6.3	5.1	64.1	33.9	12.7	334	147
Osage	23.1	0.0	5.0	13.5	5.5	5.6	3.5	44.0	27.0	9.1	214	127
Ottawa	7.3	5.7	5.2	21.8	7.3	6.1	5.7	54.6	28.4	17.4	570	412
Pawnee	5.0	0.0	2.4	7.6	6.4	1.1	2.7	22.6	12.0	5.1	312	178
Payne	21.1	9.8	11.9	17.2	4.0	28.8	35.9	155.2	47.9	34.2	533	298
Pittsburg	44.8	10.3	7.4	38.7	5.2	6.8	2.5	101.0	40.9	20.8	482	169
Pontotoc	13.8	1.8	5.1	29.1	9.1	9.7	11.3	102.3	32.3	19.7	566	234
Pottawatomie	22.1	2.7	2.6	38.9	14.4	7.6	5.8	122.5	56.9	28.4	460	234
Pushmataha	2.0	0.0	0.4	19.2	1.9	1.5	1.4	19.3	14.6	2.9	250	129
Roger Mills	1.9	0.0	0.4	2.7	0.4	0.2	1.1	5.9	3.3	1.7	477	394
Rogers	20.1	0.1	2.0	17.8	7.4	5.4	10.7	79.8	40.2	29.8	453	292
Seminole	7.0	0.1	0.8	30.5	7.2	5.8	5.4	49.0	23.8	9.8	391	256
Sequoyah	8.7	8.4	1.1	41.8	5.1	5.7	6.4	52.0	36.7	8.6	232	126
Stephens	6.3	0.3	1.5	21.9	4.6	2.6	23.0	62.9	37.1	17.0	390	222
Texas	3.4	0.0	3.8	4.0	1.2	1.8	13.8	35.3	17.0	11.1	616	371
Tillman	2.5	0.2	0.5	10.8	3.4	1.1	5.3	18.3	11.9	3.7	382	260
Tulsa	222.6	171.0	81.8	171.2	51.9	37.8	77.5	1 254.5	357.4	493.4	921	470
Wagoner	4.1	0.0	0.8	19.2	3.8	2.9	19.3	40.3	23.1	10.7	197	101
Washington	2.1	0.2	1.5	12.2	2.8	3.5	2.2	83.0	31.4	32.9	695	412
Washita	2.4	8.5	0.6	4.4	1.0	1.5	1.6	25.9	13.3	7.0	600	486
Woods	2.4	0.0	0.5	2.0	0.5	2.1	6.3	17.9	8.8	7.3	884	678
Woodward	5.5	0.1	1.0	4.6	1.2	1.2	3.0	36.9	18.2	11.8	633	321
OREGON	1 592.3	388.8	570.6	2 174.9	591.7	360.3	1 180.8	X	X	X	X	X
Baker	13.6	2.6	5.1	20.9	1.7	1.0	6.7	36.7	19.9	9.7	588	515
Benton	37.7	2.7	8.8	35.5	5.3	4.4	76.1	158.2	62.1	64.3	841	723
Clackamas	80.9	3.9	25.8	166.6	38.4	14.4	65.5	760.2	290.8	280.6	848	770
Clatsop	22.4	7.6	6.0	21.8	3.3	3.0	8.9	115.1	48.7	43.8	1 233	1 029
Columbia	5.1	2.1	1.3	16.3	5.1	2.1	3.5	117.7	46.1	39.5	902	770
Coos	29.5	5.5	7.1	40.7	9.0	5.1	6.2	230.4	81.8	46.6	745	656
Crook	14.1	0.0	3.8	8.0	1.5	1.2	1.0	43.8	24.4	10.2	601	551
Curry	6.6	0.0	1.1	8.8	1.9	1.1	20.1	63.1	32.6	14.7	690	600
Deschutes	38.1	1.1	30.2	30.8	7.6	5.6	14.8	259.4	94.0	107.5	1 061	873
Douglas	69.1	5.4	23.7	59.9	14.2	7.8	21.0	251.4	139.7	62.5	614	539
Gilliam	0.4	0.0	0.1	0.4	0.3	0.1	1.3	11.5	4.2	2.8	1 426	1 400
Grant	11.1	0.5	4.0	3.8	0.9	0.5	1.8	53.5	37.5	6.7	842	582
Harney	9.7	0.0	4.2	3.9	1.0	0.4	5.6	29.7	14.4	4.6	661	593
Hood River	6.1	10.2	5.5	9.1	5.1	1.5	21.4	51.1	21.2	11.9	608	557
Jackson	83.7	0.9	45.2	90.5	20.8	9.8	31.9	386.3	176.3	123.7	724	630
Jefferson	7.0	0.1	1.7	7.8	3.8	3.7	8.8	51.6	21.5	11.2	676	598
Josephine	15.4	0.3	7.0	51.4	9.9	5.1	1.4	159.4	89.6	37.5	510	450
Klamath	51.7	0.8	12.4	35.8	8.3	6.3	14.3	262.4	83.1	41.9	666	580
Lake	12.1	0.0	15.1	3.4	0.9	0.6	5.6	25.4	11.1	6.2	848	765
Lane	101.6	9.7	32.3	234.2	44.0	41.8	56.2	846.7	365.1	256.5	824	689
Lincoln	15.0	7.2	5.9	23.9	5.4	2.8	9.9	175.7	44.2	64.2	1 408	1 174
Linn	22.8	1.4	3.8	64.3	15.5	6.8	4.9	257.9	128.6	78.5	759	679
Malheur	9.9	0.0	2.7	20.1	4.2	3.0	11.4	85.9	49.5	16.4	575	497
Marion	84.7	2.9	17.8	218.1	194.5	117.6	410.9	666.4	314.9	198.5	749	673

1. October 1, 2000 to September 30, 2001.   2. State totals may include programs not allocated by county.   3. Based on the resident population estimated as of July 1 of the year shown.

STATE County	Local government finances, 1997 (cont'd)							Debt outstanding		Government employment, 1999			Presidential election, 2000[2]		
	Direct general expenditure												Percent of vote cast —		
			Percent of total for —												
	Total (mil dol)	Per capita[1] (dollars)	Education	Health and hospitals	Police protection	Public welfare	Highways	Total (mil dol)	Per capita[1] (dollars)	Federal civilian	Federal military	State and local	Democratic	Republican	All other
	183	184	185	186	187	188	189	190	191	192	193	194	195	196	197
OKLAHOMA—Cont'd															
Kiowa	20.9	1 926	61.5	1.0	4.0	0.0	16.0	22.5	2 079	62	52	906	41.2	57.9	0.9
Latimer	30.3	2 948	82.1	0.1	0.9	0.0	9.7	2.9	280	24	51	1 639	50.8	47.4	1.8
Le Flore	71.4	1 536	65.3	8.9	3.8	0.2	7.9	10.6	228	215	233	3 068	43.6	54.8	1.6
Lincoln	41.9	1 349	63.6	9.4	4.2	0.0	6.9	19.6	632	87	162	1 239	35.4	63.1	1.5
Logan	47.9	1 565	53.2	20.6	3.6	0.0	6.6	26.4	864	77	152	1 884	35.0	63.6	1.3
Love	10.8	1 255	75.3	0.8	2.8	0.0	10.0	2.2	255	26	43	382	45.4	53.6	1.0
McClain	52.5	2 035	64.0	14.7	3.8	0.0	5.6	22.7	878	68	133	1 359	34.9	64.0	1.0
McCurtain	57.2	1 660	72.6	2.2	3.7	0.7	5.0	14.9	433	149	174	2 272	35.8	63.0	1.2
McIntosh	26.2	1 394	65.6	1.3	4.8	0.2	12.5	10.9	580	38	96	963	54.1	44.3	1.7
Major	14.9	1 915	46.6	15.5	3.2	0.0	24.1	3.5	450	39	38	443	18.9	79.7	1.3
Marshall	23.0	1 911	54.9	18.9	4.6	0.0	6.2	6.7	557	27	62	723	45.1	53.9	1.0
Mayes	45.4	1 223	71.5	1.2	4.8	0.0	6.2	13.8	373	75	191	2 119	47.3	50.9	1.8
Murray	21.1	1 703	53.5	1.7	4.9	0.0	19.4	10.2	827	79	62	1 178	46.0	53.0	1.0
Muskogee	192.7	2 777	42.8	28.7	3.1	0.0	4.5	186.3	2 686	1 422	351	5 407	50.7	47.9	1.4
Noble	21.2	1 883	63.1	1.7	4.3	0.2	11.4	10.8	961	50	57	815	30.1	68.8	1.1
Nowata	13.7	1 381	74.3	0.0	2.2	0.0	10.3	6.8	691	33	50	456	44.2	53.8	2.0
Okfuskee	18.8	1 668	65.7	5.6	3.7	0.0	11.3	4.2	376	35	56	826	47.9	50.4	1.7
Oklahoma	1 319.5	2 093	41.9	6.2	8.8	0.3	4.4	1 664.9	2 641	23 927	10 514	48 686	36.6	62.3	1.1
Okmulgee	62.5	1 638	57.2	12.6	3.8	0.0	1.4	20.5	536	143	193	2 210	54.5	44.0	1.5
Osage	44.6	1 050	58.2	7.2	4.1	0.1	10.8	10.7	253	215	237	1 831	47.4	51.2	1.5
Ottawa	54.8	1 791	71.6	0.7	4.3	0.0	4.4	9.1	299	138	154	2 031	49.5	49.3	1.2
Pawnee	22.9	1 412	51.5	15.2	2.4	0.0	13.6	13.0	800	184	83	725	41.1	57.1	1.8
Payne	153.1	2 381	41.2	30.6	4.7	0.1	4.3	113.6	1 767	303	350	14 389	37.4	61.2	1.5
Pittsburg	102.2	2 366	42.7	34.1	2.7	0.1	4.5	50.4	1 166	1 258	223	3 267	46.6	52.1	1.3
Pontotoc	98.1	2 819	37.8	41.7	2.3	0.0	3.8	36.0	1 033	253	173	2 556	42.0	56.9	1.2
Pottawatomie	119.0	1 925	54.8	18.6	3.3	0.1	5.8	51.3	829	185	313	2 865	39.3	59.3	1.4
Pushmataha	17.7	1 536	73.9	1.6	3.0	0.0	11.6	1.4	124	39	58	953	45.3	53.6	1.1
Roger Mills	5.8	1 621	65.8	2.5	1.5	0.0	13.3	1.8	504	39	18	364	26.1	73.1	0.7
Rogers	78.1	1 189	69.6	0.8	3.6	0.0	8.9	43.1	657	456	352	2 894	37.3	61.2	1.5
Seminole	49.1	1 961	53.8	19.9	2.7	0.0	4.3	17.8	711	126	122	1 462	48.1	51.0	0.9
Sequoyah	52.8	1 432	73.7	0.4	3.7	0.0	6.0	27.0	732	142	206	2 018	44.3	54.0	1.8
Stephens	70.6	1 618	62.5	0.4	4.3	0.3	7.4	35.8	820	111	215	2 032	37.0	62.1	0.9
Texas	35.5	1 962	54.8	1.1	3.8	0.0	12.4	15.2	843	78	91	1 669	17.8	81.5	0.7
Tillman	18.6	1 930	56.4	4.0	4.4	0.1	14.0	8.1	843	49	47	639	41.8	57.3	0.9
Tulsa	1 268.3	2 367	41.2	2.4	6.3	0.0	2.5	2 209.9	4 124	4 156	2 758	28 295	37.3	61.3	1.3
Wagoner	40.1	739	62.9	2.4	4.8	0.0	11.0	33.7	622	81	280	1 286	38.3	60.3	1.4
Washington	74.2	1 566	59.1	0.5	5.8	0.0	5.5	34.8	734	117	238	2 066	32.0	66.5	1.5
Washita	25.8	2 208	62.8	5.8	2.8	0.0	14.5	5.1	439	54	58	757	35.0	63.8	1.2
Woods	16.6	2 014	67.9	1.6	3.4	0.0	6.6	1.6	193	44	41	1 182	30.5	68.6	0.9
Woodward	36.0	1 929	61.5	5.9	4.7	0.5	8.7	18.4	986	113	93	1 729	27.5	71.4	1.2
OREGON	X	X	X	X	X	X	X	X	X	29 822	12 605	220 234	47.0	46.5	6.5
Baker	36.6	2 229	58.2	2.9	5.7	1.6	7.6	8.1	495	300	54	999	26.6	68.0	5.4
Benton	139.9	1 828	45.9	8.3	9.3	1.7	5.9	27.2	355	659	331	9 857	50.9	41.4	7.7
Clackamas	804.6	2 430	46.3	2.9	4.5	1.5	5.1	543.7	1 642	1 981	1 303	13 789	47.1	47.8	5.1
Clatsop	112.7	3 172	47.1	5.9	5.5	0.0	4.9	60.4	1 699	184	467	2 476	50.4	42.2	7.5
Columbia	112.3	2 566	51.6	3.6	3.5	0.9	8.3	102.7	2 347	84	151	1 886	48.7	44.2	7.1
Coos	230.1	3 680	42.8	29.1	3.9	0.5	3.5	45.5	727	407	407	4 865	39.5	53.2	7.3
Crook	54.4	3 209	42.6	3.6	3.1	0.7	7.1	31.8	1 873	333	59	843	29.9	64.8	5.3
Curry	62.1	2 919	38.9	10.8	3.9	0.2	14.6	12.1	569	128	102	1 073	35.5	56.9	7.5
Deschutes	252.5	2 491	52.1	5.2	7.8	0.5	5.4	195.3	1 927	824	371	6 086	38.1	55.5	6.3
Douglas	256.0	2 515	51.7	8.9	4.8	0.0	7.9	37.0	364	1 579	402	5 682	30.1	64.2	5.7
Gilliam	10.4	5 340	43.9	4.3	4.7	0.0	12.1	1.4	719	0	0	213	32.9	62.3	4.8
Grant	52.5	6 563	29.2	12.0	1.2	2.7	41.2	2.2	279	320	26	750	15.3	80.0	4.6
Harney	27.8	3 948	41.9	28.9	2.3	0.2	12.5	0.7	99	227	24	704	20.5	75.0	4.5
Hood River	47.5	2 422	54.5	1.3	2.9	0.0	9.2	38.1	1 944	158	66	1 248	47.6	43.5	8.8
Jackson	398.8	2 333	49.9	8.6	6.6	0.0	5.7	125.9	736	1 722	593	8 984	39.1	54.3	6.6
Jefferson	56.9	3 433	53.9	23.3	2.3	0.3	3.6	43.9	2 649	156	56	1 228	38.9	55.6	5.5
Josephine	170.1	2 316	60.3	5.5	6.0	1.4	0.7	54.0	735	330	249	3 575	32.3	60.4	7.4
Klamath	242.1	3 842	34.6	38.4	2.6	0.2	5.0	290.0	4 603	904	218	3 787	27.1	67.7	5.2
Lake	25.8	3 522	43.0	22.0	4.1	0.0	11.4	4.7	644	282	24	636	19.0	75.9	5.2
Lane	874.9	2 810	47.8	3.5	4.9	1.1	7.3	757.5	2 433	2 004	1 079	23 532	51.6	40.5	7.9
Lincoln	175.2	3 842	34.5	26.3	4.0	2.5	6.0	109.1	2 392	244	211	3 034	51.4	40.0	8.6
Linn	280.1	2 708	54.0	2.5	4.2	1.5	8.4	102.2	988	336	352	5 946	37.6	57.1	5.2
Malheur	89.4	3 136	62.8	4.1	3.2	0.0	4.9	57.0	2 001	213	96	3 117	22.5	73.3	4.3
Marion	685.0	2 584	53.8	5.5	4.8	0.0	5.7	401.2	1 513	1 426	918	30 793	43.6	50.7	5.7

1. Based on the resident population estimated as of July 1 of the year shown.   2. Data subject to copyright.

STATE/County code	MSA/PMSA/NECMA code[1]	County Type[2]	STATE County	Land area,[3] (sq km) 2000	Population and population characteristics, 2000													
								Race alone or in combination (percent)					Age (percent)					
					Total persons	Rank	Per square kilometer	White	Black	Am. Indian, Alaska Native	Asian and Pacific Islander	Percent Hispanic[4]	Under 5 years	5 to 17 years	18 to 24 years	25 to 34 years	35 to 44 years	45 to 54 years
					1	3	4	5	6	7	8	9	10	11	12	13	14	15
			OREGON—Cont'd															
41 049	...	9	Morrow	5 264	10 995	2 367	2.1	78.0	0.3	2.4	0.9	24.4	8.5	22.2	8.9	12.3	15.0	13.4
41 051	6440	0	Multnomah	1 127	660 486	79	586.1	82.6	6.8	2.2	7.5	7.5	6.4	15.9	10.3	17.5	16.3	14.8
41 053	7080	2	Polk	1 919	62 380	778	32.5	91.8	0.7	3.1	2.0	8.8	6.3	19.1	11.7	11.0	13.7	14.6
41 055	...	9	Sherman	2 132	1 934	3 068	0.9	95.1	0.5	2.2	0.8	4.9	5.1	21.4	5.8	7.6	15.8	15.0
41 057	...	6	Tillamook	2 855	24 262	1 585	8.5	95.8	0.4	2.4	1.3	5.1	4.8	17.4	6.5	9.5	14.0	15.7
41 059	...	4	Umatilla	8 327	70 548	704	8.5	84.0	1.1	4.2	1.4	16.1	7.5	20.3	9.4	13.3	14.9	13.6
41 061	...	7	Union	5 275	24 530	1 575	4.7	95.9	0.7	1.6	2.0	2.4	5.9	18.7	12.1	10.2	13.3	15.4
41 063	...	9	Wallowa	8 146	7 226	2 663	0.9	98.0	0.2	1.7	0.5	1.7	4.9	19.4	4.9	7.5	14.4	18.0
41 065	...	7	Wasco	6 167	23 791	1 599	3.9	88.8	0.6	4.7	1.9	9.3	6.5	18.8	7.4	10.7	14.5	15.2
41 067	6440	0	Washington	1 874	445 342	133	237.6	84.9	1.6	1.4	8.5	11.2	7.9	19.0	9.3	17.1	16.9	13.8
41 069	...	9	Wheeler	4 442	1 547	3 092	0.3	95.3	0.3	2.3	0.6	5.1	4.7	18.0	3.4	8.0	11.3	14.8
41 071	6440	0	Yamhill	1 853	84 992	612	45.9	91.2	1.1	2.5	1.9	10.6	7.0	19.9	11.4	12.9	15.6	13.4
42 000		X	PENNSYLVANIA	116 074	12 281 054	X	105.8	86.3	10.5	0.4	2.1	3.2	5.9	17.9	8.9	12.7	15.9	13.9
42 001	...	6	Adams	1 347	91 292	563	67.8	96.3	1.5	0.4	0.7	3.6	5.9	19.0	9.2	12.5	16.4	13.8
42 003	6280	0	Allegheny	1 891	1 281 666	28	677.8	85.2	13.0	0.4	2.0	0.9	5.5	16.4	8.5	12.6	15.8	14.2
42 005	...	6	Armstrong	1 694	72 392	687	42.7	98.8	1.0	0.3	0.2	0.4	5.4	17.5	7.2	11.6	16.1	14.4
42 007	6280	0	Beaver	1 125	181 412	303	161.3	93.4	6.5	0.4	0.3	0.7	5.4	17.2	7.4	11.1	16.2	14.3
42 009	...	6	Bedford	2 628	49 984	916	19.0	99.1	0.5	0.4	0.4	0.5	6.0	17.5	7.2	12.6	15.5	13.6
42 011	6680	2	Berks	2 224	373 638	157	168.0	89.4	4.3	0.4	1.3	9.7	6.2	18.4	8.8	12.7	16.3	13.7
42 013	0280	3	Blair	1 362	129 144	418	94.8	98.2	1.4	0.3	0.5	0.5	5.6	17.1	8.9	12.0	15.0	14.3
42 015	...	6	Bradford	2 980	62 761	776	21.1	98.6	0.5	0.7	0.6	0.6	6.1	19.5	6.8	11.8	15.4	14.2
42 017	6160	2	Bucks	1 573	597 635	91	379.9	93.3	3.6	0.4	2.7	2.3	6.4	19.3	7.0	12.6	18.0	15.1
42 019	6280	1	Butler	2 042	174 083	314	85.3	98.3	1.0	0.3	0.8	0.6	6.4	18.2	8.8	12.4	16.9	14.2
42 021	3680	3	Cambria	1 782	152 598	348	85.6	96.4	3.2	0.3	0.6	0.9	5.0	16.0	9.0	11.4	14.7	14.5
42 023	...	7	Cameron	1 029	5 974	2 784	5.8	99.2	0.5	0.4	0.2	0.6	4.8	19.7	6.0	10.9	14.0	14.2
42 025	0240	2	Carbon	987	58 802	814	59.6	98.5	0.8	0.5	0.4	1.5	5.1	17.0	6.9	12.2	16.1	14.0
42 027	8050	3	Centre	2 868	135 758	397	47.3	92.3	2.9	0.4	4.6	1.7	4.6	13.4	26.8	13.4	13.1	11.1
42 029	6160	0	Chester	1 958	433 501	138	221.4	90.1	6.7	0.4	2.3	3.7	6.8	19.4	7.9	12.6	17.7	14.9
42 031	...	7	Clarion	1 560	41 765	1 060	26.8	98.6	0.9	0.3	0.5	0.4	5.4	16.2	15.4	11.4	13.8	12.9
42 033	...	6	Clearfield	2 972	83 382	624	28.1	97.8	1.6	0.3	0.3	0.6	5.5	17.2	7.7	12.9	15.9	13.8
42 035	...	6	Clinton	2 307	37 914	1 168	16.4	98.8	0.6	0.3	0.6	0.5	5.4	16.1	13.6	11.4	14.1	12.9
42 037	7560	2	Columbia	1 258	64 151	760	51.0	98.1	1.0	0.4	0.7	0.9	4.9	15.9	14.3	11.5	14.4	13.5
42 039	...	4	Crawford	2 623	90 366	571	34.5	97.7	1.9	0.5	0.4	0.6	5.9	18.8	9.2	11.8	14.8	14.1
42 041	3240	2	Cumberland	1 425	213 674	261	149.9	95.3	2.7	0.4	2.1	1.3	5.5	16.5	10.6	12.6	15.9	14.7
42 043	3240	2	Dauphin	1 360	251 798	226	185.1	78.6	18.1	0.5	2.4	4.1	6.2	18.1	7.6	13.6	16.5	14.9
42 045	6160	0	Delaware	477	550 864	102	1 154.9	81.2	15.1	0.4	3.7	1.5	6.2	18.6	8.9	12.5	16.2	13.4
42 047	...	7	Elk	2 146	35 112	1 246	16.4	99.2	0.2	0.3	0.5	0.4	5.7	18.3	6.8	12.5	16.1	13.6
42 049	2360	2	Erie	2 077	280 843	199	135.2	90.2	6.7	0.5	1.0	2.2	6.2	18.8	10.8	12.5	15.1	13.6
42 051	6280	1	Fayette	2 046	148 644	364	72.7	96.0	3.9	0.3	0.3	0.4	5.7	17.0	7.7	12.2	15.0	14.4
42 053	...	9	Forest	1 109	4 946	2 851	4.5	96.5	2.3	0.8	0.2	1.2	3.6	19.1	5.9	9.0	13.7	13.9
42 055	...	4	Franklin	1 999	129 313	416	64.7	96.7	2.1	0.4	0.8	1.8	6.3	17.8	7.9	13.0	15.2	13.7
42 057	...	8	Fulton	1 133	14 261	2 144	12.6	98.9	0.8	0.6	0.3	0.4	6.3	18.3	7.6	13.1	15.3	13.4
42 059	...	6	Greene	1 491	40 672	1 093	27.3	95.6	4.0	0.5	0.4	0.9	5.2	16.9	9.7	13.8	15.2	15.0
42 061	...	6	Huntingdon	2 264	45 586	990	20.1	94.1	5.4	0.3	0.3	1.1	5.4	16.3	10.1	13.9	15.5	14.0
42 063	...	6	Indiana	2 148	89 605	576	41.7	97.4	1.8	0.3	0.9	0.5	4.9	16.1	16.6	10.9	14.0	13.6
42 065	...	7	Jefferson	1 698	45 932	985	27.1	99.4	0.2	0.4	0.3	0.4	5.5	18.0	7.7	11.6	15.6	13.6
42 067	...	8	Juniata	1 014	22 821	1 652	22.5	98.5	0.5	0.3	0.6	1.6	6.5	18.5	8.0	12.8	15.2	13.6
42 069	7560	2	Lackawanna	1 188	213 295	263	179.5	97.2	1.6	0.2	0.9	1.4	5.3	16.5	8.9	11.7	14.7	13.8
42 071	4000	2	Lancaster	2 458	470 658	122	191.5	92.5	3.3	0.4	1.7	5.7	6.9	19.7	9.2	12.6	15.7	13.2
42 073	...	2	Lawrence	934	94 643	543	101.3	95.8	4.1	0.3	0.4	0.6	5.6	17.5	8.3	10.9	14.8	14.0
42 075	3240	2	Lebanon	937	120 327	452	128.4	95.3	1.6	0.3	1.1	5.0	6.1	17.6	8.2	12.4	15.6	14.1
42 077	0240	2	Lehigh	898	312 090	183	347.5	88.6	4.2	0.4	2.5	10.2	6.0	17.9	8.1	12.7	16.4	14.0
42 079	7560	2	Luzerne	2 307	319 250	181	138.4	97.1	1.9	0.2	0.7	1.2	5.0	16.1	8.1	12.2	15.0	14.0
42 081	9140	3	Lycoming	3 198	120 044	454	37.5	94.7	4.8	0.5	0.7	0.7	5.5	17.8	9.7	12.0	15.6	14.1
42 083	...	7	McKean	2 542	45 936	984	18.1	97.0	2.0	0.6	0.5	1.1	5.7	18.0	7.9	13.1	15.4	13.5
42 085	7610	3	Mercer	1 740	120 293	453	69.1	94.0	5.7	0.4	0.5	0.7	5.7	17.7	8.9	11.2	14.8	13.7
42 087	...	6	Mifflin	1 067	46 486	973	43.6	98.9	0.6	0.2	0.4	0.6	6.3	18.3	7.0	12.7	14.7	13.3
42 089	...	6	Monroe	1 576	138 687	393	88.0	89.7	6.9	0.7	1.5	6.6	6.0	20.8	8.6	10.9	17.9	14.3
42 091	6160	0	Montgomery	1 251	750 097	67	599.6	87.4	8.0	0.4	4.5	2.0	6.3	17.8	7.1	13.5	17.1	14.2
42 093	...	2	Montour	339	18 236	1 884	53.8	97.2	1.2	0.2	1.4	0.9	5.7	18.7	6.4	11.8	16.3	14.1
42 095	0240	2	Northampton	968	267 066	206	275.9	92.4	3.3	0.4	1.7	6.7	5.6	17.8	9.2	12.0	16.3	14.2
42 097	...	4	Northumberland	1 191	94 556	544	79.4	97.6	1.7	0.3	0.3	1.1	5.1	16.8	7.0	12.3	15.3	14.1
42 099	3240	2	Perry	1 434	43 602	1 027	30.4	99.1	0.6	0.3	0.2	0.7	6.1	19.4	7.4	13.1	16.3	15.5
42 101	6160	0	Philadelphia	350	1 517 550	18	4 335.9	46.4	44.3	0.7	5.1	8.5	6.5	18.8	11.1	14.8	14.5	12.0
42 103	5660	1	Pike	1 416	46 302	976	32.7	94.4	3.7	0.8	0.8	5.0	5.9	20.8	5.3	10.0	17.7	14.2

1. MSA = Metropolitan Statistical Area. PMSA = Primary MSA. NECMA = New England County Metropolitan Area. See Appendix A for explanation of these concepts. See Appendix B for list of metropolitan areas identified by type, with component counties. 2. County typology code from the Economic Research Service of USDA. See Appendix A for definition. 3. Dry land or land partially or temporarily covered by water. 4. Hispanic persons may be of any race.

Table B. States and Counties — **Population and Households**

STATE County	Population, 2000 (cont'd) Age (percent) (cont'd) 55 to 64 years	65 to 74 years	75 years and over	Percent female	Total persons 2001	1990	Percent change 1990–2000	2000–2001	Components of change, 2000–2001 Births	Deaths	Net migration	Households, 2000 Number	Percent change, 1990–2000	Persons per household	Female family householder[1]	One person
	16	17	18	19	20	21	22	23	24	25	26	27	28	29	30	31
OREGON—Cont'd																
Morrow	9.0	6.3	4.3	48.4	11 339	7 625	44.2	3.1	218	103	229	3 776	34.7	2.90	8.8	18.1
Multnomah	7.6	5.2	5.9	50.5	665 810	583 887	13.1	0.8	11 524	7 279	1 327	272 098	12.4	2.37	10.8	32.5
Polk	8.9	6.8	8.0	51.5	63 679	49 541	25.9	2.1	839	643	1 100	23 058	26.9	2.62	9.2	22.3
Sherman	11.1	10.1	8.1	49.3	1 827	1 918	0.8	-5.5	20	29	-100	797	1.7	2.43	6.5	28.7
Tillamook	12.3	11.2	8.5	49.9	24 308	21 570	12.5	0.2	283	365	129	10 200	15.3	2.33	7.7	27.9
Umatilla	8.6	6.2	6.1	48.8	70 751	59 249	19.1	0.3	1 351	716	-422	25 195	14.4	2.67	10.6	23.7
Union	9.7	7.3	7.4	51.3	24 327	23 598	3.9	-0.8	395	307	-293	9 740	7.8	2.45	8.5	26.1
Wallowa	12.1	10.0	8.8	50.0	7 207	6 911	4.6	-0.3	71	119	31	3 029	8.3	2.35	6.9	27.1
Wasco	10.2	8.2	8.5	50.5	23 895	21 683	9.7	0.4	392	361	80	9 401	9.2	2.47	9.9	26.1
Washington	7.2	4.3	4.5	50.2	461 119	311 554	42.9	3.5	8 678	3 264	10 315	169 162	42.2	2.61	9.0	24.7
Wheeler	16.5	13.8	9.4	49.5	1 513	1 396	10.8	-2.2	16	21	-30	653	11.8	2.32	4.0	27.4
Yamhill	8.0	5.8	6.0	49.5	86 642	65 551	29.7	1.9	1 505	826	994	28 732	28.1	2.78	9.9	19.7
PENNSYLVANIA	9.2	7.9	7.7	51.7	12 287 150	11 882 842	3.4	0.0	180 121	163 050	-8 095	4 777 003	6.3	2.48	11.6	27.7
Adams	9.2	7.3	6.6	50.9	92 997	78 274	16.6	1.9	1 194	1 035	1 543	33 652	19.9	2.61	8.5	21.3
Allegheny	9.2	8.8	9.0	52.6	1 270 612	1 336 449	-4.1	-0.9	18 034	19 532	-9 185	537 150	-0.8	2.31	12.4	32.7
Armstrong	9.8	9.1	8.9	51.4	72 101	73 478	-1.5	-0.4	949	1 102	-107	29 005	2.5	2.46	9.0	25.9
Beaver	9.9	9.6	8.8	52.1	179 871	186 093	-2.5	-0.8	2 271	2 711	-1 032	72 576	0.9	2.44	11.4	26.9
Bedford	11.0	9.1	7.4	50.7	49 899	47 919	4.3	-0.2	717	611	-171	19 768	9.6	2.50	7.7	23.5
Berks	8.9	7.7	7.3	51.0	377 679	336 523	11.0	1.1	5 526	4 608	3 250	141 570	10.9	2.55	9.9	24.6
Blair	9.7	8.6	8.8	52.1	128 391	130 542	-1.1	-0.6	1 797	2 051	-456	51 518	2.4	2.43	11.2	27.8
Bradford	10.5	8.1	7.6	51.3	62 859	60 967	2.9	0.2	850	789	68	24 453	8.7	2.52	8.9	24.7
Bucks	9.2	6.7	5.7	50.9	605 379	541 174	10.4	1.3	8 968	6 184	5 123	218 725	14.8	2.69	8.8	21.5
Butler	8.8	6.9	7.3	51.2	176 593	152 013	14.5	1.4	2 616	2 069	1 984	65 862	19.0	2.55	8.1	24.2
Cambria	9.6	9.6	10.1	51.5	150 726	163 062	-6.4	-1.2	1 793	2 438	-1 177	60 531	-2.4	2.38	10.4	29.8
Cameron	10.6	9.5	10.2	50.9	5 866	5 913	1.0	-1.8	70	102	-76	2 465	2.9	2.39	9.2	30.1
Carbon	10.2	9.6	8.9	51.3	59 506	56 803	3.5	1.2	698	936	947	23 701	7.8	2.44	9.9	26.0
Centre	7.2	5.6	4.8	48.9	135 940	124 812	8.8	0.1	1 509	1 002	-273	49 323	15.6	2.45	6.1	26.6
Chester	8.9	6.3	5.4	50.9	443 346	376 389	15.2	2.3	6 896	3 942	6 907	157 905	18.5	2.65	8.1	22.6
Clarion	9.8	8.0	7.2	51.7	41 478	41 699	0.2	-0.7	496	545	-224	16 052	7.1	2.46	8.4	26.0
Clearfield	10.1	8.5	8.4	50.1	83 167	78 097	6.8	-0.3	1 014	1 137	-62	32 785	10.0	2.44	9.3	26.3
Clinton	9.8	8.8	8.0	51.5	37 753	37 182	2.0	-0.4	530	503	-173	14 773	6.7	2.42	9.4	26.6
Columbia	9.6	8.0	7.9	52.4	64 152	63 202	1.5	0.0	719	849	159	24 915	6.1	2.42	8.7	26.6
Crawford	9.8	7.9	7.6	51.3	90 046	86 166	4.9	-0.4	1 344	1 204	-425	34 678	7.7	2.50	9.2	26.2
Cumberland	9.4	7.6	7.2	51.2	215 695	195 257	9.4	0.9	2 699	2 574	1 951	83 015	13.0	2.41	8.0	26.7
Dauphin	9.0	7.4	6.8	52.0	251 316	237 813	5.9	-0.2	3 899	3 130	-1 167	102 670	7.8	2.39	12.9	30.0
Delaware	8.5	7.4	7.9	52.3	551 158	547 658	0.6	0.1	8 729	7 336	-856	206 320	2.5	2.56	12.9	27.6
Elk	9.7	9.1	8.2	50.5	34 666	34 878	0.7	-1.3	444	482	-402	14 124	7.6	2.45	8.7	27.3
Erie	8.6	7.1	7.2	51.2	279 636	275 575	1.9	-0.4	4 277	3 443	-1 966	106 507	4.9	2.51	11.0	27.6
Fayette	9.8	9.0	9.1	52.1	147 367	145 351	2.3	-0.9	1 946	2 366	-794	59 969	6.9	2.43	12.4	28.0
Forest	14.9	11.0	8.9	47.4	4 910	4 802	3.0	-0.7	44	111	32	2 000	4.8	2.29	6.7	29.1
Franklin	10.0	8.3	7.7	51.3	130 506	121 082	6.8	0.9	2 108	1 572	708	50 633	10.9	2.49	8.2	23.7
Fulton	11.6	8.4	6.1	50.0	14 314	13 837	3.1	0.4	219	155	-4	5 660	10.1	2.50	8.2	24.0
Greene	9.0	7.5	7.7	48.5	40 492	39 550	2.8	-0.4	492	565	-86	15 060	3.0	2.48	10.9	25.7
Huntingdon	10.0	8.3	6.5	47.7	45 632	44 164	3.2	0.1	607	508	-33	16 759	7.9	2.44	8.3	25.8
Indiana	9.1	7.4	7.5	51.5	89 108	89 994	-0.4	-0.6	1 074	1 150	-384	34 123	7.6	2.47	8.2	26.5
Jefferson	10.0	8.9	9.0	51.1	45 712	46 083	-0.3	-0.5	577	697	-77	18 375	4.4	2.45	9.1	26.6
Juniata	10.2	8.2	7.0	50.3	22 877	20 625	10.6	0.2	353	291	4	8 584	13.0	2.60	6.3	21.1
Lackawanna	9.7	9.3	10.2	52.8	211 829	219 097	-2.6	-0.7	2 592	3 535	-414	86 218	2.0	2.38	11.8	31.3
Lancaster	8.6	6.9	7.1	51.2	474 601	422 822	11.3	0.8	8 045	5 250	1 322	172 560	14.3	2.64	8.6	23.1
Lawrence	9.6	9.3	9.9	52.5	94 160	96 246	-1.7	-0.5	1 241	1 429	-251	37 091	2.0	2.47	11.5	27.0
Lebanon	9.7	8.3	8.1	51.3	120 963	113 744	5.8	0.5	1 736	1 545	501	46 551	9.0	2.49	9.2	25.2
Lehigh	9.0	7.8	8.0	51.8	314 204	291 130	7.2	0.7	4 605	3 888	1 550	121 906	8.0	2.48	10.5	27.1
Luzerne	10.0	9.4	10.2	51.8	315 754	328 149	-2.7	-1.1	3 792	5 540	-1 625	130 687	1.7	2.34	11.5	31.3
Lycoming	9.4	8.2	7.8	51.1	118 977	118 710	1.1	-0.9	1 658	1 515	-1 184	47 003	4.6	2.44	10.3	26.9
McKean	9.7	8.4	8.3	49.9	45 440	47 131	-2.5	-1.1	620	735	-370	18 024	1.0	2.40	10.1	28.3
Mercer	9.7	9.1	9.0	51.3	119 682	121 003	-0.6	-0.5	1 624	1 856	-319	46 712	2.5	2.44	10.9	27.0
Mifflin	10.6	8.8	8.2	51.8	46 554	46 197	0.6	0.1	708	591	-25	18 413	4.0	2.49	8.5	26.0
Monroe	9.2	7.1	5.1	50.6	144 676	95 681	44.9	4.3	1 691	1 280	5 472	49 454	44.6	2.73	8.8	20.2
Montgomery	9.1	7.4	7.5	51.7	759 953	678 193	10.6	1.3	11 617	8 729	7 193	286 098	12.2	2.54	8.8	25.6
Montour	9.8	8.2	8.9	52.5	18 281	17 735	2.8	0.2	240	277	90	7 085	8.3	2.43	8.9	28.0
Northampton	9.1	7.8	7.9	51.3	269 779	247 110	8.1	1.0	3 417	2 961	2 350	101 541	11.6	2.53	9.8	24.7
Northumberland	10.3	9.3	9.7	51.0	93 662	96 771	-2.3	-0.9	1 164	1 554	-463	38 835	0.3	2.34	9.6	30.2
Perry	9.5	6.9	5.3	50.4	43 787	41 172	5.9	0.4	654	502	50	16 695	11.7	2.58	7.8	21.7
Philadelphia	8.3	7.1	7.0	53.5	1 491 812	1 585 577	-4.3	-1.7	29 037	22 659	-32 685	590 071	-2.2	2.48	22.3	33.8
Pike	11.0	9.6	5.6	50.2	48 507	28 032	65.2	4.8	438	364	2 077	17 433	65.5	2.63	7.6	20.7

1. No spouse present.

STATE County	Births, average 1997-1999 Total	Rate[1]	Deaths, average 1997-1999 Number Total	Number Infant[2]	Rate Total[1]	Rate Infant[3]	Physicians[4] 2000 Number	Rate[5]	Hospitals[4] 1998 Number	Beds Number	Beds Rate[5]	Medicare enrollees 2000	Serious crimes known to police, 2000[6] Total Number	Rate[7]
	32	33	34	35	36	37	38	39	40	41	42	43	44	45
OREGON—Cont'd														
Morrow	159	15.9	77	NA	7.7	NA	3	27	1	44	441	1 273	357	3 247
Multnomah	9 075	14.4	5 703	44	9.0	4.9	2 595	393	8	2 130	338	88 681	48 492	7 342
Polk	717	11.7	495	NA	8.1	NA	65	104	1	51	83	8 832	2 558	4 101
Sherman	20	11.4	20	NA	11.2	NA	0	0	0	0	0	407	55	2 844
Tillamook	241	9.9	291	NA	12.0	NA	35	144	1	45	185	5 354	716	2 951
Umatilla	1 023	15.6	585	NA	8.9	NA	88	125	2	98	150	9 823	2 638	3 739
Union	292	11.7	245	NA	9.8	NA	48	196	1	69	278	4 138	517	2 287
Wallowa	64	8.7	88	NA	12.0	NA	4	55	1	32	434	1 515	NA	NA
Wasco	298	12.9	274	NA	11.8	NA	40	168	1	49	212	4 390	927	3 896
Washington	6 532	16.3	2 518	35	6.3	5.3	856	192	4	742	186	39 421	14 171	3 194
Wheeler	13	8.3	18	NA	11.2	NA	0	0	0	0	0	375	21	1 357
Yamhill	1 146	14.0	679	8	8.3	7.3	113	133	2	102	124	11 002	3 014	3 609
PENNSYLVANIA	143 889	12.0	128 303	1 066	10.7	7.4	31 671	258	214	46 466	387	2 095 479	367 858	2 995
Adams	1 028	11.9	821	NA	9.5	NA	75	82	1	102	118	12 877	1 034	1 224
Allegheny	14 283	11.3	15 210	108	12.0	7.6	5 380	420	22	7 470	589	243 406	37 892	3 172
Armstrong	774	10.6	854	NA	11.7	NA	57	79	1	187	256	15 791	653	1 095
Beaver	1 940	10.5	2 082	11	11.3	5.5	241	133	2	558	303	35 945	2 205	1 491
Bedford	564	11.4	489	NA	9.9	NA	39	78	1	78	158	9 133	914	1 916
Berks	4 423	12.4	3 675	33	10.3	7.5	637	170	3	874	246	60 597	11 263	3 381
Blair	1 386	10.6	1 573	10	12.1	7.0	271	210	4	593	454	24 871	3 539	2 740
Bradford	722	11.6	645	NA	10.4	NA	185	295	3	404	647	11 258	784	1 359
Bucks	7 322	12.5	4 842	41	8.2	5.6	1 215	203	7	1 254	213	79 891	13 542	2 279
Butler	2 063	12.1	1 632	15	9.6	7.1	191	110	1	286	167	27 001	3 311	1 997
Cambria	1 493	9.6	1 904	9	12.2	6.3	342	224	4	872	559	33 646	2 508	1 833
Cameron	61	10.8	73	NA	12.9	NA	5	84	0	0	0	1 303	120	2 009
Carbon	591	10.1	719	NA	12.2	NA	52	88	2	270	459	12 194	1 237	2 397
Centre	1 290	9.7	802	6	6.1	4.4	244	180	2	232	175	15 420	3 476	2 560
Chester	5 478	13.0	3 041	30	7.2	5.4	942	217	5	745	177	51 060	8 378	1 962
Clarion	416	10.0	418	NA	10.0	NA	51	122	1	88	210	6 885	603	1 525
Clearfield	844	10.4	889	NA	11.0	NA	118	142	2	286	354	15 026	1 481	1 965
Clinton	405	11.0	412	NA	11.1	NA	48	127	2	315	851	6 781	985	3 296
Columbia	625	9.8	681	NA	10.7	NA	88	137	2	391	610	11 837	1 190	2 389
Crawford	1 061	11.9	971	9	10.9	8.5	126	139	2	248	277	15 884	1 719	1 925
Cumberland	2 161	10.3	1 921	14	9.2	6.5	486	227	3	552	265	34 773	4 449	2 082
Dauphin	3 174	12.9	2 451	21	10.0	6.5	998	396	4	1 435	584	38 639	7 429	3 038
Delaware	6 889	12.7	5 708	40	10.5	5.9	1 636	297	9	2 112	389	91 429	14 506	2 697
Elk	392	11.3	376	NA	10.9	NA	51	145	2	304	880	6 593	831	2 367
Erie	3 507	12.7	2 730	28	9.9	7.9	616	219	6	1 167	422	45 194	7 534	2 683
Fayette	1 600	11.1	1 836	12	12.7	7.7	146	98	3	440	304	31 184	2 723	2 149
Forest	38	7.6	84	NA	16.9	NA	1	20	0	0	0	1 341	210	4 246
Franklin	1 594	12.4	1 223	11	9.5	6.7	157	121	2	297	232	21 274	2 887	2 233
Fulton	168	11.6	119	NA	8.2	NA	7	49	1	96	662	2 300	212	1 487
Greene	422	10.2	464	NA	11.3	NA	37	91	1	107	263	7 193	644	1 919
Huntingdon	476	10.6	410	NA	9.2	NA	44	97	1	104	233	7 531	600	1 316
Indiana	862	9.7	882	11	10.0	12.8	108	121	1	150	169	14 807	1 264	1 481
Jefferson	493	10.7	532	NA	11.5	NA	64	139	2	127	275	9 177	624	1 616
Juniata	278	12.6	232	NA	10.5	NA	6	26	0	0	0	3 515	172	806
Lackawanna	2 142	10.3	2 848	11	13.7	5.1	498	233	5	1 143	548	44 804	2 220	1 140
Lancaster	6 577	14.4	4 103	46	9.0	7.0	756	161	5	1 118	245	69 680	11 989	2 554
Lawrence	1 034	10.9	1 137	10	12.0	9.7	114	120	3	526	554	21 552	2 347	2 529
Lebanon	1 431	12.2	1 205	7	10.3	4.7	208	173	2	216	184	20 911	2 958	2 458
Lehigh	3 668	12.3	3 055	30	10.2	8.3	1 006	322	4	1 077	360	52 341	10 844	3 475
Luzerne	3 095	9.8	4 411	18	14.0	5.8	717	225	6	1 337	426	68 574	NA	NA
Lycoming	1 332	11.3	1 197	10	10.2	7.8	248	207	4	612	522	21 426	1 726	1 576
McKean	492	10.6	594	NA	12.8	NA	58	126	2	269	578	8 630	773	1 745
Mercer	1 339	11.0	1 439	8	11.8	6.2	245	204	4	638	523	24 156	2 311	1 949
Mifflin	582	12.4	494	NA	10.5	NA	73	157	1	232	494	8 392	918	2 343
Monroe	1 522	12.1	1 023	8	8.2	5.3	163	118	1	228	182	19 390	3 810	2 762
Montgomery	8 964	12.5	6 824	52	9.5	5.8	3 182	424	9	2 062	287	125 202	18 162	2 421
Montour	215	12.1	229	NA	12.9	NA	310	1 700	1	460	2 594	3 477	232	1 272
Northampton	2 902	11.2	2 406	19	9.3	6.7	397	149	3	880	340	46 814	5 591	2 553
Northumberland	933	9.9	1 253	NA	13.3	NA	75	79	2	193	205	20 034	1 680	2 134
Perry	542	12.3	384	NA	8.7	NA	24	55	0	0	0	6 088	607	1 526
Philadelphia	21 296	14.8	17 937	272	12.5	12.8	6 593	434	31	8 778	611	238 470	98 004	6 458
Pike	477	11.9	345	NA	8.6	NA	17	37	0	0	0	6 183	956	2 124

1. Per 1,000 estimated resident population, average 1997-1999.   2. Deaths of infants under 1 year old.   3. Deaths of infants under 1 year old per 1,000 live births.   4. Data subject to copyright.   5. Per 100,000 resident population as of July 1 of the year shown.   6. Data for serious crimes have not been adjusted for underreporting; this may affect comparability between geographic areas and over time.   7. Per 100,000 population estimated by the FBI.

Table B. States and Counties — Crime, Education, Money Income, and Poverty

STATE County	Serious crimes known to police, 2000[1] (cont'd) Rate[2]		Education School enrollment and attainment, 1990 Enrollment[3]		Attainment[4] (percent)		Local government expenditures, fiscal 1999[5]		Money income 1989	Households Median			Income and poverty, 1998 Percent below poverty level			
	Violent	Property	Total	Percent private	High school graduate or more	Bachelor's degree or more	Total current expenditures (mil dol)	Current expenditures per student (dollars)	Per capita[6] (dollars)	Dollars	Percent change, 1979–1989 (constant 1989 dollars)	Percent with $100,000 or more	Median household income	All persons	Persons under 18	Persons 5–17 in families
	46	47	48	49	50	51	52	53	54	55	56	57	58	59	60	61
OREGON—Cont'd																
Morrow	437	2 810	1 909	5.4	73.9	11.8	14.9	6 674	10 412	23 969	-19.7	1.1	34 709	10.2	13.6	12.7
Multnomah	933	6 409	140 543	16.9	82.9	23.7	707.8	7 606	14 462	26 928	-0.1	3.0	40 038	12.3	17.8	15.4
Polk	196	3 905	14 360	8.9	80.0	21.2	39.5	6 200	12 405	26 292	-6.1	2.4	40 581	11.0	15.5	13.8
Sherman	52	2 792	436	0.5	83.1	18.9	3.6	9 149	13 242	25 030	6.5	3.4	31 625	14.3	17.4	20.0
Tillamook	99	2 852	4 478	9.0	76.3	13.1	27.0	7 056	11 550	21 965	-8.1	1.7	30 975	14.3	21.0	20.5
Umatilla	139	3 600	14 893	5.7	75.1	13.3	87.8	6 775	11 178	22 791	-13.6	1.6	33 298	15.8	21.5	19.1
Union	119	2 168	6 995	7.0	80.2	17.0	37.0	8 476	10 698	22 484	-10.3	1.4	33 692	14.6	18.1	17.1
Wallowa	NA	NA	1 541	4.6	81.2	15.7	11.3	8 575	10 811	21 300	-6.8	1.0	30 362	14.6	19.2	18.8
Wasco	198	3 699	5 345	9.3	77.4	14.5	29.5	7 782	12 542	24 908	-12.7	2.1	35 532	13.4	18.9	17.9
Washington	159	3 035	81 871	15.6	88.2	29.8	436.6	6 298	16 351	35 554	-1.7	4.4	51 775	6.9	9.9	8.3
Wheeler	452	905	287	2.1	69.4	10.7	3.3	12 243	9 299	15 224	-10.4	1.0	23 642	9.8	14.9	13.5
Yamhill	251	3 358	18 012	20.4	79.1	17.1	98.5	6 433	12 990	28 303	0.1	2.7	41 961	10.8	14.5	13.5
PENNSYLVANIA	420	2 575	2 829 553	23.6	74.7	17.9	13 532.2	7 450	14 068	29 069	2.8	3.6	39 116	10.7	16.5	15.4
Adams	117	1 107	17 801	22.6	70.0	13.2	135.9	9 339	13 018	30 304	8.4	2.1	43 085	6.8	11.1	9.7
Allegheny	456	2 715	311 846	24.9	79.0	22.6	1 545.3	8 907	15 115	28 136	-6.4	4.1	39 887	10.8	18.3	15.9
Armstrong	112	983	15 880	7.2	71.1	8.1	89.9	7 800	10 565	22 554	-13.0	0.9	32 309	12.6	19.4	17.7
Beaver	266	1 224	42 110	15.1	74.9	11.9	206.0	7 158	11 683	24 276	-27.7	1.5	34 755	11.0	17.1	16.0
Bedford	107	1 809	10 101	6.6	68.5	7.8	53.8	6 312	9 954	21 622	-2.0	1.1	31 958	11.8	17.7	17.1
Berks	413	2 968	75 295	18.3	70.0	15.1	450.7	7 130	14 604	32 048	9.1	3.1	41 460	8.9	14.8	13.0
Blair	245	2 496	29 518	13.6	75.0	10.5	130.9	6 299	11 233	23 271	-6.0	1.3	31 823	13.1	18.6	18.2
Bradford	97	1 262	14 009	8.2	75.7	12.9	82.5	6 889	10 810	23 970	-0.8	1.7	33 723	12.6	17.5	17.4
Bucks	142	2 137	136 047	27.1	82.9	24.8	780.6	8 785	18 292	43 347	17.5	7.6	55 244	4.9	7.5	6.2
Butler	106	1 891	39 210	10.7	78.6	15.6	172.1	6 203	12 747	29 358	-5.1	2.1	41 654	8.1	12.0	11.2
Cambria	248	1 584	38 054	19.2	71.2	10.8	168.8	8 265	10 460	21 462	-18.8	1.2	29 755	12.9	19.2	17.8
Cameron	167	1 841	1 158	3.2	73.1	9.8	6.5	5 429	10 190	20 839	-11.6	1.8	33 526	11.1	17.8	19.3
Carbon	186	2 211	11 659	15.0	69.4	8.4	60.3	7 250	11 729	25 501	-1.0	1.5	34 889	9.2	14.9	14.5
Centre	134	2 426	50 857	5.9	83.6	32.3	118.0	8 181	11 854	26 060	4.6	2.9	40 336	9.6	12.0	11.7
Chester	228	1 734	97 407	27.5	84.9	34.7	534.1	8 527	20 601	45 642	22.6	10.8	60 489	4.9	7.7	6.5
Clarion	94	1 432	12 677	5.2	73.1	11.7	64.4	8 283	9 698	21 602	-17.7	1.1	32 150	13.8	18.1	18.9
Clearfield	223	1 742	17 185	9.4	70.2	8.6	98.9	6 247	10 430	21 773	-12.8	1.3	31 366	13.4	19.1	19.0
Clinton	141	3 156	9 725	6.6	72.5	11.7	41.4	7 851	10 287	22 128	-11.1	1.4	31 490	13.4	20.3	20.3
Columbia	102	2 286	16 898	6.8	73.1	12.5	74.1	6 786	10 959	24 211	2.1	1.3	34 738	10.6	16.0	14.9
Crawford	114	1 811	21 135	16.6	74.1	11.8	80.4	6 577	10 833	23 083	-9.3	1.7	33 289	13.0	19.2	18.3
Cumberland	133	1 949	49 188	20.1	81.0	22.9	270.1	7 450	15 796	34 493	6.8	3.7	47 576	5.2	8.5	7.2
Dauphin	321	2 718	52 439	15.7	77.6	18.6	271.6	7 198	14 890	30 985	7.9	2.9	42 327	9.8	16.8	15.3
Delaware	477	2 219	137 289	40.5	81.4	24.8	599.0	8 546	17 210	37 337	11.7	6.5	47 029	8.6	13.8	12.7
Elk	259	2 108	7 546	24.8	74.9	9.5	31.1	6 617	10 775	24 866	-10.9	0.8	38 663	8.0	11.9	11.7
Erie	261	2 422	74 816	25.9	77.5	16.2	304.5	7 137	12 317	26 581	-5.4	2.3	35 871	12.4	18.2	17.3
Fayette	214	1 935	31 668	11.1	67.8	9.3	137.3	6 371	9 791	19 195	-19.8	1.0	27 612	18.8	27.9	26.6
Forest	182	4 064	983	16.8	70.5	7.9	6.4	8 112	9 349	19 170	-9.6	0.3	26 700	13.8	20.9	23.5
Franklin	334	1 898	26 020	12.6	69.4	12.4	111.5	6 207	13 060	28 806	1.6	2.3	39 387	8.0	12.7	12.0
Fulton	112	1 374	2 958	3.9	64.0	7.4	17.0	6 756	10 267	23 736	4.3	1.0	35 658	10.3	14.8	16.2
Greene	209	1 711	9 684	11.8	68.0	11.3	51.0	7 687	10 005	19 903	-20.7	1.1	28 549	17.8	23.3	25.1
Huntingdon	237	1 079	10 103	16.8	71.2	9.4	41.9	6 397	10 471	23 067	6.3	1.3	33 669	12.3	17.5	18.2
Indiana	155	1 327	28 253	6.6	74.0	14.4	104.8	7 931	10 260	22 966	-14.1	1.6	32 790	15.4	20.9	20.4
Jefferson	194	1 422	10 364	5.7	72.6	8.9	48.0	7 246	10 580	22 063	-12.0	1.3	31 730	12.7	18.2	18.3
Juniata	127	680	4 162	7.7	65.2	7.3	15.7	4 567	10 759	25 359	9.0	0.9	35 400	8.4	12.8	12.3
Lackawanna	127	1 012	49 554	31.0	73.3	14.8	219.3	7 917	12 358	24 816	3.8	2.3	32 894	11.0	17.1	15.5
Lancaster	238	2 316	97 202	22.1	70.5	16.7	487.6	7 160	14 235	33 255	10.6	3.4	44 812	7.6	12.1	10.9
Lawrence	356	2 174	21 996	14.1	73.0	11.8	96.1	6 234	10 830	22 317	-19.7	1.4	31 367	13.6	21.4	20.7
Lebanon	230	2 228	24 342	17.3	70.0	11.8	114.8	6 368	13 209	29 469	-0.5	2.2	40 319	8.1	12.6	11.9
Lehigh	331	3 144	64 915	22.7	74.6	19.6	332.4	7 461	15 458	32 455	3.1	3.6	42 307	8.7	14.8	13.4
Luzerne	NA	NA	71 492	24.2	72.0	13.1	302.8	7 504	12 002	23 600	0.7	1.8	32 929	10.7	16.6	14.8
Lycoming	106	1 470	27 909	12.3	74.5	12.3	139.5	7 055	11 714	25 552	1.5	1.8	33 937	11.6	17.7	16.9
McKean	133	1 612	10 551	10.3	75.4	12.2	67.4	8 667	10 817	23 106	-6.7	1.4	33 669	13.7	19.4	19.8
Mercer	156	1 793	28 594	20.5	75.1	13.6	159.9	8 284	11 336	24 599	-14.5	1.6	33 177	13.0	19.9	19.4
Mifflin	240	2 103	9 266	11.9	68.2	8.7	52.0	8 239	10 609	22 778	-2.6	1.1	32 081	12.5	19.4	19.8
Monroe	233	2 529	23 230	12.3	78.0	17.6	167.7	6 397	13 630	32 465	21.1	2.8	42 667	8.4	12.5	11.8
Montgomery	196	2 226	160 332	36.5	83.8	32.1	913.5	9 434	21 990	43 720	15.9	10.9	57 837	4.7	7.3	6.4
Montour	137	1 135	3 826	16.7	75.2	18.7	18.4	6 461	13 769	27 260	1.3	3.5	36 996	9.4	13.1	15.3
Northampton	246	2 307	61 028	28.1	73.1	16.7	306.4	7 442	14 562	32 890	6.2	3.3	45 055	7.0	11.8	10.9
Northumberland	343	1 791	19 007	16.2	68.5	8.6	86.3	5 988	10 819	22 124	2.1	1.1	32 455	11.1	16.5	16.2
Perry	186	1 340	8 994	8.8	72.3	8.9	45.6	6 012	11 941	29 539	8.3	1.2	41 480	7.6	11.4	11.5
Philadelphia	1 503	4 955	395 033	36.2	64.3	15.2	1 527.4	7 362	12 091	24 603	11.5	2.2	29 560	21.1	31.0	30.0
Pike	133	1 991	5 636	10.3	79.2	14.7	29.6	6 415	13 785	30 314	22.8	2.9	42 831	7.7	12.1	12.1

1. Data for serious crimes have not been adjusted for underreporting; this may affect comparability between geographic areas and over time. 2. Per 100,000 population estimated by the FBI. 3. All persons 3 years old and over enrolled in nursery school through college. 4. Persons 25 years old and over. 5. Elementary and secondary education expenditures, local government fiscal years ending between July 1, 1998 and June 30, 1999. 6. Based on population enumerated as of April 1, 1990.

Table B. States and Counties — Personal Income

STATE County	Personal income, 1999												
			Per capita[1]					Transfer payments					
									Government payments to individuals				
	Total (mil dol)	Percent change, 1998–1999	Dollars	Rank	Wages and salaries[2] (mil dol)	Proprietor's income (mil dol)	Dividends, interest, and rent (mil dol)	Total (mil dol)	Total (mil dol)	Social Security (mil dol)	Medical payments (mil dol)	Income mainte- nance (mil dol)	Unemploy- ment insurance (mil dol)
	62	63	64	65	66	67	68	69	70	71	72	73	74
OREGON—Cont'd													
Morrow	177	5.3	16 841	2 768	114	1	36	28	26	13	6	2	2
Multnomah	20 324	4.4	32 095	151	18 008	1 804	4 419	2 394	2 280	830	903	238	88
Polk	1 474	5.3	23 617	939	454	112	349	197	186	96	53	12	6
Sherman	21	-19.2	12 035	3 093	20	-11	10	8	8	3	3	1	0
Tillamook	525	5.0	21 492	1 523	220	61	144	112	108	56	34	7	3
Umatilla	1 471	6.3	22 024	1 360	883	87	279	255	243	94	92	25	10
Union	527	2.5	21 239	1 586	287	38	116	104	99	39	34	9	4
Wallowa	145	0.0	19 973	1 997	63	11	44	30	29	15	8	2	2
Wasco	548	3.9	23 454	972	287	35	131	97	93	43	30	8	4
Washington	12 908	5.8	31 537	168	9 650	793	2 377	1 015	942	440	288	58	44
Wheeler	26	-3.1	16 750	2 790	7	2	10	7	6	4	2	0	0
Yamhill	1 942	4.9	23 280	1 019	882	145	393	255	240	113	81	17	8
PENNSYLVANIA	343 263	4.5	28 619	X	207 046	29 634	64 246	55 093	52 674	21 154	22 598	4 711	1 474
Adams	2 105	5.2	24 004	858	864	164	418	276	258	134	92	15	6
Allegheny	42 070	4.9	33 474	122	29 490	4 753	8 126	6 532	6 278	2 487	2 811	496	157
Armstrong	1 632	6.6	22 353	1 258	578	144	295	350	335	144	134	27	12
Beaver	4 405	4.9	24 111	837	1 924	268	632	900	863	383	348	61	27
Bedford	973	5.1	19 575	2 118	460	110	162	199	189	86	66	16	9
Berks	10 002	3.8	27 921	337	6 000	724	1 898	1 472	1 400	631	583	95	38
Blair	3 034	4.8	23 352	1 002	1 827	322	495	633	606	203	250	55	16
Bradford	1 279	3.9	20 577	1 820	699	121	238	243	230	107	82	24	4
Bucks	20 184	5.0	33 978	107	9 195	1 115	3 682	1 999	1 879	895	740	96	62
Butler	4 423	6.5	25 637	566	2 266	311	736	647	612	278	243	39	22
Cambria	3 392	5.1	22 060	1 346	1 737	277	581	942	911	319	442	60	21
Cameron	142	6.0	25 412	598	82	9	28	30	29	13	11	2	2
Carbon	1 349	6.0	22 951	1 101	415	89	246	283	271	119	105	14	11
Centre	3 187	4.4	24 107	839	2 187	326	591	367	341	154	106	24	9
Chester	19 014	6.1	44 219	26	10 114	1 708	3 594	1 403	1 317	594	555	63	34
Clarion	892	4.5	21 422	1 544	426	139	158	182	173	73	70	15	5
Clearfield	1 694	3.4	20 987	1 673	885	191	294	375	359	150	136	30	19
Clinton	765	4.6	20 803	1 735	375	58	127	168	161	67	65	13	6
Columbia	1 382	4.4	21 705	1 451	764	113	270	261	248	111	97	17	11
Crawford	1 900	3.5	21 318	1 564	974	225	321	391	373	156	148	35	11
Cumberland	6 334	3.1	30 065	210	4 919	434	1 315	693	651	320	234	27	14
Dauphin	7 471	4.9	30 421	195	6 605	395	1 275	977	928	378	375	80	27
Delaware	18 367	3.0	33 919	110	8 867	1 708	4 003	2 365	2 256	977	949	155	60
Elk	856	2.1	24 917	683	535	64	165	155	148	71	57	8	7
Erie	6 768	4.0	24 433	775	4 258	544	1 254	1 144	1 089	461	418	115	35
Fayette	3 044	4.6	21 172	1 604	1 021	263	525	817	788	288	321	102	23
Forest	94	5.9	19 050	2 271	41	10	19	28	27	13	10	2	1
Franklin	3 077	3.3	23 886	884	1 553	232	629	527	501	202	239	27	11
Fulton	315	7.9	21 559	1 515	177	52	50	47	45	21	16	5	1
Greene	763	2.9	18 135	2 513	423	56	116	197	188	71	75	23	6
Huntingdon	805	4.5	17 982	2 543	379	67	127	167	158	69	55	14	10
Indiana	1 946	3.6	22 151	1 309	948	332	347	373	355	147	127	33	15
Jefferson	1 004	3.7	21 782	1 419	443	142	186	215	206	85	78	16	10
Juniata	449	4.9	20 230	1 915	162	49	88	79	75	33	28	5	4
Lackawanna	5 260	3.2	25 471	590	2 997	446	1 062	1 150	1 108	427	499	71	29
Lancaster	12 563	4.6	27 309	392	7 413	1 390	2 439	1 464	1 372	725	470	94	27
Lawrence	2 056	3.4	21 754	1 433	984	180	355	495	476	202	195	42	13
Lebanon	2 997	3.6	25 428	596	1 313	205	545	446	422	212	152	26	11
Lehigh	9 106	4.8	30 368	200	6 712	756	1 751	1 281	1 221	558	501	80	38
Luzerne	7 760	3.2	24 873	690	4 483	570	1 505	1 741	1 678	659	722	104	54
Lycoming	2 659	4.0	22 784	1 146	1 612	228	520	484	461	209	166	41	20
McKean	1 057	4.1	22 987	1 092	542	127	194	212	202	90	78	20	7
Mercer	2 656	3.5	21 864	1 397	1 449	217	483	578	553	248	221	46	13
Mifflin	910	3.7	19 437	2 162	483	93	143	198	189	85	73	17	7
Monroe	3 037	7.5	23 627	935	1 442	208	523	435	409	212	137	25	15
Montgomery	32 183	4.2	44 446	25	22 638	3 139	7 504	2 869	2 724	1 317	1 121	108	74
Montour	555	6.2	31 576	166	547	24	70	121	118	32	78	4	1
Northampton	7 158	5.3	27 559	367	3 014	410	1 356	1 057	1 005	477	402	59	26
Northumberland	2 084	3.6	22 372	1 252	919	135	387	453	434	189	175	29	11
Perry	979	3.2	22 107	1 329	204	76	142	135	126	53	43	9	4
Philadelphia	36 059	4.1	25 436	595	30 062	2 580	5 421	9 299	9 012	2 253	4 548	1 689	206
Pike	915	7.5	22 126	1 320	219	59	195	138	130	81	33	7	2

1. Based on the resident population estimated as of July 1 of the year shown.   2. Includes other labor income.

Table B. States and Counties — Earnings, Social Security, and Housing

STATE County	Earnings, 1999 Total (mil dol)	Farm	Goods-related[1] Total	Manu- facturing	Service-related and other[2] Total	Retail trade	Finance, insur- ance, and real estate	Services	Govern- ment	Social Security bene- ficiaries, December 2000 Number	Rate[3]	Supple- mental Security Income recipients, December 2000	Housing units, 1990 Total	Percent change, 1980– 1990
	75	76	77	78	79	80	81	82	83	84	85	86	87	88
OREGON—Cont'd														
Morrow	114	7.6	28.6	22.8	40.2	5.0	2.5	9.8	23.6	1 579	144	123	3 412	6.2
Multnomah	19 812	0.1	18.5	12.4	66.6	9.2	9.3	30.0	14.8	90 815	137	14 767	255 751	3.9
Polk	566	6.9	30.4	19.7	45.8	7.5	2.7	26.2	16.9	10 992	176	757	18 978	8.1
Sherman	8	-167.5	D	D	D	65.6	D	32.6	126.5	384	199	22	900	-8.4
Tillamook	282	7.4	24.5	17.2	45.6	11.3	3.8	21.2	22.5	6 317	260	355	13 324	4.6
Umatilla	970	2.7	D	14.3	D	13.5	3.0	17.4	22.4	11 104	157	1 139	24 333	3.5
Union	325	0.0	D	18.7	D	12.3	3.4	19.4	25.2	4 660	190	447	9 974	2.9
Wallowa	74	-12.0	25.5	15.9	53.4	15.2	5.2	16.9	33.1	1 796	249	112	3 755	3.3
Wasco	322	3.3	D	15.7	D	14.4	3.1	24.7	24.1	5 055	212	410	10 476	5.9
Washington	10 443	0.7	38.0	30.6	55.2	9.1	5.8	23.7	6.1	48 257	108	3 595	124 716	28.5
Wheeler	9	1.6	D	0.0	D	14.3	D	13.8	51.6	453	293	17	782	0.9
Yamhill	1 026	7.9	32.2	23.0	44.4	10.3	5.1	20.7	15.5	12 823	151	819	23 194	14.6
PENNSYLVANIA	236 680	0.3	26.5	20.1	60.1	8.9	8.1	30.1	13.1	2 356 051	192	283 785	4 938 140	7.4
Adams	1 028	3.4	35.3	26.0	45.8	9.9	3.2	21.3	15.6	16 092	176	816	30 141	23.0
Allegheny	34 243	0.0	22.7	16.3	66.9	7.7	9.6	35.8	10.4	266 702	208	29 845	580 738	1.7
Armstrong	722	1.9	30.4	15.4	51.8	12.3	3.2	21.2	16.0	16 624	230	2 092	31 757	2.3
Beaver	2 192	0.1	28.7	22.1	57.4	9.3	3.7	25.0	13.8	41 773	230	3 771	76 336	1.7
Bedford	570	1.9	D	26.4	D	16.1	2.6	14.1	14.2	10 484	210	1 029	21 738	9.7
Berks	6 723	0.9	34.6	28.4	53.5	9.7	6.6	24.5	11.1	68 831	184	5 615	134 482	12.1
Blair	2 148	0.5	D	17.5	D	14.6	3.4	26.3	14.7	24 572	190	4 125	54 349	4.4
Bradford	820	1.8	36.1	32.1	48.2	9.5	3.0	25.5	14.0	13 002	207	1 810	27 058	7.4
Bucks	10 310	0.2	29.8	20.2	60.4	11.6	6.4	29.1	9.6	94 550	158	5 245	199 934	20.9
Butler	2 577	0.1	36.9	28.3	49.0	9.6	3.6	19.3	14.0	31 268	180	3 085	59 061	11.4
Cambria	2 014	0.1	22.7	13.5	58.6	10.6	6.4	29.5	18.6	36 809	241	4 375	67 374	0.4
Cameron	91	0.0	64.0	61.1	D	6.4	1.2	7.8	15.3	1 468	246	125	4 399	-0.7
Carbon	504	0.2	D	23.0	D	11.8	4.5	26.3	18.8	13 693	233	930	27 380	18.1
Centre	2 513	0.4	18.1	13.0	41.6	7.7	4.1	22.1	40.0	17 568	129	1 534	46 195	16.8
Chester	11 822	0.9	26.3	20.7	65.8	8.4	13.5	30.6	7.0	62 331	144	3 107	139 597	26.7
Clarion	565	0.7	31.6	20.3	45.0	12.3	2.8	15.7	22.7	8 509	204	1 106	18 022	4.8
Clearfield	1 076	0.1	27.2	17.9	56.7	17.8	3.4	22.0	16.0	17 654	212	2 144	34 300	3.3
Clinton	433	0.7	37.6	33.0	39.4	12.3	2.9	15.0	22.2	7 828	206	852	16 478	2.7
Columbia	877	0.2	D	30.1	D	10.3	3.2	19.0	17.8	13 047	203	1 225	25 598	7.2
Crawford	1 198	0.6	43.0	36.8	42.6	9.9	2.8	22.3	13.7	18 153	201	2 473	40 462	2.7
Cumberland	5 354	0.2	15.7	10.9	67.0	10.0	10.8	26.1	17.1	36 052	169	1 611	77 108	17.4
Dauphin	7 000	0.1	20.0	15.1	53.9	6.4	8.5	24.4	26.0	43 310	172	4 991	102 684	7.3
Delaware	10 575	0.0	23.9	18.0	66.5	10.1	9.6	35.2	9.5	101 434	184	8 009	211 024	4.7
Elk	599	0.0	62.6	57.1	29.0	5.9	2.1	13.9	8.4	7 675	219	537	17 249	5.5
Erie	4 802	0.4	37.4	31.6	48.9	10.0	5.8	23.9	13.2	51 507	183	7 486	108 585	4.7
Fayette	1 285	0.2	23.5	14.0	59.1	15.0	3.0	25.8	17.2	34 010	229	7 960	61 406	0.6
Forest	51	0.1	D	D	D	8.8	1.1	31.4	29.6	1 569	317	154	8 445	-2.2
Franklin	1 785	1.8	D	28.3	D	11.4	3.6	20.2	18.5	24 808	192	1 912	48 629	14.1
Fulton	229	0.6	D	54.6	D	6.1	1.7	9.5	11.3	2 734	192	321	6 184	16.7
Greene	480	0.1	45.5	5.5	33.5	7.4	2.2	13.7	20.9	8 306	204	1 687	15 982	6.1
Huntingdon	446	2.6	D	21.2	D	9.1	4.0	20.4	26.1	8 540	187	1 077	19 286	14.1
Indiana	1 280	0.7	36.2	11.4	42.3	9.7	4.6	14.7	20.9	17 136	191	2 438	34 770	7.1
Jefferson	585	0.7	43.6	32.5	43.6	8.5	2.9	18.7	12.0	10 149	221	1 263	21 242	2.8
Juniata	211	3.8	34.0	33.6	42.9	11.0	3.7	12.2	10.2	4 164	182	370	8 505	9.2
Lackawanna	3 442	0.1	25.8	20.7	61.0	10.3	7.3	30.4	13.2	49 820	234	5 309	91 707	2.4
Lancaster	8 802	1.0	39.6	29.2	50.9	10.4	5.9	21.5	8.5	79 045	168	6 357	156 462	20.9
Lawrence	1 164	0.0	29.9	20.3	54.8	11.1	7.7	23.5	15.2	22 680	240	2 818	38 844	-1.9
Lebanon	1 518	0.9	D	25.4	D	11.9	3.3	22.3	17.8	23 944	199	1 596	44 634	11.3
Lehigh	7 468	0.0	D	26.3	D	8.2	6.4	29.0	8.4	60 338	193	5 805	118 335	11.6
Luzerne	5 053	0.1	24.1	18.1	60.3	10.0	6.4	25.5	15.5	76 985	241	7 538	138 724	1.9
Lycoming	1 840	0.4	30.8	25.2	54.8	9.9	6.1	24.9	14.1	23 950	200	3 010	49 580	4.3
McKean	669	0.3	44.8	36.3	38.5	8.4	2.3	18.5	16.4	10 134	221	1 525	21 454	-0.5
Mercer	1 666	0.4	35.3	28.9	52.0	11.5	4.0	25.9	12.3	27 438	228	3 233	48 689	2.2
Mifflin	576	1.0	41.4	35.8	46.7	10.8	3.4	19.9	10.9	9 946	214	1 320	19 641	5.8
Monroe	1 650	0.1	D	14.6	D	11.8	6.1	25.5	24.9	24 288	175	1 566	54 823	47.3
Montgomery	25 778	0.0	29.1	23.1	64.5	7.1	12.4	32.2	6.4	130 788	174	5 964	265 856	14.3
Montour	572	1.2	D	6.5	D	3.2	2.4	68.9	9.2	3 822	210	386	6 885	15.2
Northampton	3 424	0.1	30.3	22.1	55.3	10.3	6.5	26.8	14.3	52 147	195	3 905	95 345	13.1
Northumberland	1 054	0.2	39.7	32.5	45.2	13.3	3.1	16.1	14.9	22 755	241	2 335	41 900	2.5
Perry	280	4.4	D	10.4	D	13.5	3.8	15.7	23.4	6 559	150	529	17 063	15.4
Philadelphia	32 642	0.0	D	9.3	D	6.1	10.4	42.6	18.6	263 158	173	84 346	674 899	-1.6
Pike	278	0.1	16.5	6.1	58.2	13.6	8.1	29.2	25.2	9 100	197	398	30 852	74.0

1. Covers mining, construction, and manufacturing. 2. Covers private sector earnings in agricultural services, forestry, and fisheries; transportation and public utilities; wholesale trade; retail trade; finance, insurance, and real estate; and services. 3. Per 1,000 resident population estimated as of July 1 of the year shown.

STATE County	Total	Percent	Median value[1]	With a mortgage	Without a mortgage	Median rent[2]	Rent as percent of income	Substandard units[3] (percent)	Total	Percent change, 2000–2001	Total	Rate[4]	Total	Professional, managerial, and technical	Precision production, craft, and repair
	89	90	91	92	93	94	95	96	97	98	99	100	101	102	103
OREGON—Cont'd															
Morrow	2 803	68.0	43 500	17.8	12.4	332	23.7	6.7	4 277	1.0	463	10.8	3 238	16.1	11.8
Multnomah	242 140	55.3	61 800	20.3	14.1	407	25.6	3.6	374 677	0.3	23 660	6.3	292 646	30.9	10.1
Polk	18 167	66.4	63 600	20.1	13.2	360	27.6	3.3	31 087	-1.7	1 781	5.7	21 315	31.6	9.3
Sherman	784	66.1	30 600	21.8	12.9	295	21.6	1.1	1 045	-0.3	115	11.0	774	18.9	8.1
Tillamook	8 846	71.3	61 300	20.6	12.6	341	25.6	2.2	11 166	-1.1	614	5.5	8 344	22.3	11.8
Umatilla	22 020	62.0	47 800	19.2	13.7	313	23.0	5.8	37 451	-0.3	2 715	7.2	25 612	20.8	10.8
Union	9 035	64.4	43 900	18.4	13.8	309	24.9	4.0	12 352	-2.1	722	5.8	9 920	26.2	10.6
Wallowa	2 796	69.2	47 400	18.0	13.8	287	18.7	2.4	3 359	-3.3	362	10.8	2 892	23.9	10.1
Wasco	8 607	65.1	50 000	17.0	13.0	324	23.7	3.8	12 498	-0.1	1 267	10.1	8 811	24.7	11.4
Washington	118 997	60.8	85 500	20.5	12.8	489	24.1	3.0	252 752	0.4	13 460	5.3	164 686	36.4	10.2
Wheeler	584	70.7	30 400	18.6	13.4	247	22.1	3.6	601	-2.4	56	9.3	499	16.2	12.2
Yamhill	22 424	67.6	62 300	20.6	13.1	389	25.0	4.5	43 325	-0.4	2 537	5.9	28 978	25.4	13.1
PENNSYLVANIA	4 495 966	70.6	69 700	20.2	13.3	404	26.1	2.3	6 072 613	1.7	286 934	4.7	5 434 532	28.9	11.6
Adams	28 067	73.3	79 600	21.6	11.9	386	21.8	2.4	44 830	3.5	1 852	4.1	40 056	20.4	14.3
Allegheny	541 261	66.2	57 100	19.7	13.7	389	26.6	1.3	656 820	1.6	24 961	3.8	604 923	34.8	9.1
Armstrong	28 309	76.4	44 300	18.7	12.8	290	26.7	2.0	31 893	1.4	2 334	7.3	28 624	18.1	16.2
Beaver	71 939	73.3	50 500	19.8	13.7	321	26.8	1.6	87 053	2.2	4 291	4.9	75 901	24.8	12.5
Bedford	18 038	79.1	46 800	20.1	12.6	280	24.7	3.2	25 988	-0.5	1 912	7.4	20 013	16.7	14.5
Berks	127 649	73.9	81 800	19.7	12.5	413	24.7	2.2	186 241	1.3	9 166	4.9	166 292	25.2	13.1
Blair	50 332	72.6	41 100	17.0	13.2	299	26.8	1.6	63 742	1.7	3 737	5.9	55 022	23.0	13.2
Bradford	22 492	75.3	50 900	18.6	13.5	317	25.5	2.8	29 290	5.0	1 683	5.7	26 226	23.0	13.2
Bucks	190 507	75.7	140 000	23.1	13.5	604	26.1	1.5	333 191	2.0	12 808	3.8	283 836	33.7	12.2
Butler	55 325	76.6	62 900	18.1	12.0	352	24.7	1.5	90 619	2.0	3 921	4.3	68 777	25.9	13.6
Cambria	62 004	73.3	39 900	18.8	13.3	276	25.0	1.9	65 467	-0.1	4 436	6.8	60 374	24.7	12.7
Cameron	2 395	73.2	39 800	17.1	13.4	266	22.0	2.1	2 775	-3.2	280	10.1	2 318	18.7	15.2
Carbon	21 989	77.9	62 900	20.3	13.0	335	26.0	1.3	27 941	2.6	1 708	6.1	24 290	19.2	15.6
Centre	42 683	59.8	74 700	20.3	11.8	448	31.3	4.4	67 355	3.2	1 958	2.9	57 809	35.9	8.1
Chester	133 257	74.5	155 900	22.2	13.0	581	24.6	1.4	240 415	1.7	7 134	3.0	198 581	38.7	9.4
Clarion	14 990	72.5	46 200	18.1	12.4	298	28.4	2.2	19 435	1.9	908	4.7	16 296	22.0	13.4
Clearfield	29 808	78.5	40 000	19.7	13.6	295	26.3	2.7	37 368	1.7	3 110	8.3	30 777	21.1	15.0
Clinton	13 844	72.8	46 300	18.5	13.9	295	26.4	2.0	18 172	0.2	1 192	6.6	15 342	22.4	12.1
Columbia	23 478	73.5	54 800	17.8	13.2	337	24.4	2.1	33 359	0.5	1 834	5.5	28 882	21.2	13.0
Crawford	32 185	73.4	43 200	17.8	13.0	305	26.9	3.1	42 357	1.8	2 999	7.1	35 834	23.4	13.5
Cumberland	73 452	71.8	85 000	19.2	11.7	457	23.1	1.4	122 658	2.0	3 783	3.1	101 690	31.6	9.2
Dauphin	95 264	63.7	71 300	18.6	12.2	428	23.9	2.1	139 766	2.0	5 224	3.7	120 247	31.1	9.8
Delaware	201 374	72.6	113 200	21.4	14.1	526	26.5	2.0	281 551	1.7	11 020	3.9	266 074	35.5	11.1
Elk	13 131	79.7	49 900	16.6	12.9	290	25.8	1.4	17 491	0.3	1 569	9.0	14 961	18.2	13.9
Erie	101 564	68.6	54 000	17.5	12.7	329	25.5	1.9	140 711	0.3	8 228	5.8	122 635	26.8	12.4
Fayette	56 110	72.3	39 700	20.0	12.9	281	30.0	2.7	58 101	1.8	4 023	6.9	49 221	22.5	14.4
Forest	1 908	81.0	35 700	17.5	12.9	290	22.7	3.9	2 120	12.3	323	15.2	1 802	20.6	11.9
Franklin	45 675	72.7	70 500	18.2	11.8	344	21.3	2.3	62 938	-1.2	3 017	4.8	59 552	23.9	13.8
Fulton	5 139	78.8	50 700	17.7	12.7	295	22.6	4.1	6 613	1.5	492	7.4	6 127	17.1	16.3
Greene	14 624	72.5	38 400	18.0	13.0	270	27.9	3.8	16 515	3.5	935	5.7	13 506	23.8	18.1
Huntingdon	15 527	76.3	43 100	18.7	13.4	279	24.5	3.0	19 312	4.2	1 796	9.3	17 482	20.5	13.6
Indiana	31 710	73.5	50 500	20.9	13.0	334	29.7	3.6	36 286	2.1	2 190	6.0	35 222	24.8	14.8
Jefferson	17 608	77.2	42 500	20.0	12.5	285	27.0	1.9	21 247	1.2	1 519	7.1	18 320	19.9	14.7
Juniata	7 598	77.5	51 700	18.6	11.7	280	18.8	3.5	10 656	2.2	551	5.2	9 530	16.7	15.3
Lackawanna	84 528	67.0	68 900	19.0	14.0	323	24.8	1.5	105 139	1.7	5 667	5.4	97 407	25.9	11.9
Lancaster	150 956	69.4	89 400	20.7	11.9	441	23.8	2.9	249 866	1.6	7 984	3.2	215 292	24.0	13.6
Lawrence	36 350	76.1	41 500	18.2	13.6	298	28.6	2.2	40 052	-1.9	2 481	6.2	37 804	24.4	12.3
Lebanon	42 688	71.0	71 000	19.8	12.1	355	22.2	1.7	65 702	1.6	2 029	3.1	56 716	21.9	14.1
Lehigh	112 887	69.3	97 800	21.4	13.0	461	26.0	2.0	162 358	3.0	6 773	4.2	144 250	29.8	11.5
Luzerne	128 483	69.4	56 000	18.1	14.0	319	25.2	1.4	155 956	0.8	8 608	5.5	143 046	24.5	12.2
Lycoming	44 949	69.7	54 900	18.9	12.9	334	25.3	2.2	57 977	2.3	3 381	5.8	52 566	22.6	12.3
McKean	17 837	74.0	37 400	15.9	12.8	292	25.4	1.1	21 487	2.1	1 268	5.9	19 317	23.2	13.2
Mercer	45 591	75.0	41 900	17.1	13.0	321	26.4	2.3	58 621	0.9	2 998	5.1	50 027	23.3	11.8
Mifflin	17 697	72.8	44 800	19.3	12.7	286	23.4	3.2	21 139	-0.5	1 473	7.0	19 831	17.5	14.0
Monroe	34 206	75.7	116 500	23.4	13.1	517	26.8	1.8	57 511	4.9	3 367	5.9	45 021	24.7	14.3
Montgomery	254 995	72.3	143 400	21.6	13.1	593	24.8	1.3	407 836	2.0	14 177	3.5	358 563	39.4	9.6
Montour	6 543	71.6	62 200	16.8	11.9	329	22.2	2.6	8 678	-0.5	306	3.5	8 248	31.2	9.7
Northampton	90 955	73.6	105 400	21.7	12.4	452	25.9	1.7	135 433	2.8	5 589	4.1	117 962	27.4	12.4
Northumberland	38 736	73.3	39 500	17.8	13.0	284	24.6	1.6	43 416	-0.4	2 401	5.5	41 584	19.4	12.7
Perry	14 949	79.5	64 400	20.5	12.2	342	21.6	3.6	24 395	2.0	1 000	4.1	20 076	19.3	15.1
Philadelphia	603 075	61.9	49 400	19.3	14.8	452	29.8	5.1	639 775	1.6	40 703	6.4	651 621	28.6	9.0
Pike	10 536	83.3	117 700	26.0	14.1	548	26.6	2.0	19 478	3.8	930	4.8	12 528	24.4	16.8

1. Specified owner-occupied units.   2. Specified renter-occupied units.   3. Overcrowded or lacking complete plumbing facilities.   4. Percent of civilian labor force.   5. Persons 16 years and older.

Table B. States and Counties — Nonfarm Employment and Agriculture

STATE County	Number of establishments	Total	Health Care and Social Assistance	Manufacturing	Retail trade	Finance and Insurance	Professional Scientific and Technical Services	Total (mil dol)	Average per employee (dollars)	Number	Less than 50 acres	500 acres and over	Whose principal occupation is farming (percent)
	104	105	106	107	108	109	110	111	112	113	114	115	116
OREGON—Cont'd													
Morrow	149	1 682	107	620	237	79	14	46	27 090	420	24.8	52.6	59.3
Multnomah	23 479	400 511	44 603	48 456	41 090	27 605	26 556	13 377	33 401	577	82.1	1.6	35.2
Polk	1 139	12 667	1 421	2 535	1 481	244	299	288	22 762	1 147	60.0	6.8	43.6
Sherman	40	247	13	0	77	D	0	4	14 506	168	9.5	76.8	73.8
Tillamook	706	6 437	728	1 239	966	134	119	136	21 202	313	37.4	2.6	63.9
Umatilla	1 595	19 861	2 592	4 320	3 838	567	596	444	22 375	1 488	48.6	27.8	51.7
Union	726	7 106	1 129	1 403	1 351	191	210	156	21 985	832	39.7	25.1	43.9
Wallowa	315	1 558	273	229	293	82	42	33	21 237	459	29.0	38.6	55.6
Wasco	700	7 566	1 298	763	1 482	228	176	173	22 884	470	32.3	36.2	55.7
Washington	12 418	207 419	14 935	37 147	27 075	11 445	11 362	7 776	37 491	1 681	72.5	3.3	39.3
Wheeler	41	112	6	D	22	D	0	2	14 125	157	7.6	54.8	65.0
Yamhill	1 996	24 766	2 933	6 383	3 440	677	544	601	24 272	1 813	67.1	4.9	36.8
PENNSYLVANIA	293 491	4 986 591	733 507	809 825	653 260	278 808	284 105	154 388	30 961	45 457	29.2	5.4	56.4
Adams	1 823	27 617	3 518	7 816	3 082	674	419	643	23 295	984	36.8	7.7	55.5
Allegheny	34 967	683 062	103 627	55 384	78 376	47 511	53 965	23 223	33 999	334	52.1	1.2	34.7
Armstrong	1 507	16 462	2 567	3 016	3 650	539	667	371	22 553	654	18.8	6.4	45.4
Beaver	3 487	48 723	8 369	10 185	8 153	1 498	1 966	1 269	26 047	499	35.1	1.6	40.7
Bedford	1 114	13 988	1 349	4 195	2 816	360	169	311	22 249	943	17.4	8.4	57.9
Berks	8 079	145 991	16 011	39 884	20 146	5 585	6 452	4 331	29 665	1 586	39.0	5.0	63.0
Blair	3 264	50 331	8 647	9 177	8 078	1 897	2 176	1 223	24 297	422	20.6	10.2	68.5
Bradford	1 330	18 648	4 094	6 066	3 036	534	408	472	25 298	1 279	15.1	11.1	64.4
Bucks	17 582	240 779	28 110	40 425	39 174	9 298	14 397	7 436	30 883	739	58.9	5.4	47.5
Butler	4 292	60 989	7 849	15 905	9 910	1 399	1 821	1 755	28 779	972	30.7	2.8	46.9
Cambria	3 530	51 103	9 420	7 937	8 225	3 369	2 362	1 157	22 644	525	26.1	7.6	47.4
Cameron	143	1 973	D	1 184	263	D	D	51	25 637	26	30.8	3.8	38.5
Carbon	1 125	13 645	1 828	3 175	1 984	438	219	278	20 395	167	40.1	3.6	44.3
Centre	3 090	44 897	5 425	8 227	7 741	1 761	2 844	1 063	23 671	788	26.8	6.1	57.0
Chester	11 901	183 156	24 406	20 789	22 934	8 929	21 847	7 174	39 171	1 424	45.6	4.8	64.0
Clarion	1 058	12 804	1 653	2 624	2 263	920	253	300	23 426	457	15.8	9.4	43.3
Clearfield	1 903	26 928	4 780	4 715	4 524	824	505	584	21 693	339	25.1	4.4	44.2
Clinton	738	10 238	1 148	3 493	2 040	228	149	229	22 333	266	24.1	6.0	60.2
Columbia	1 526	23 370	3 067	7 915	3 638	600	742	566	24 212	702	24.5	4.8	52.1
Crawford	2 127	27 936	4 096	8 618	4 267	640	619	668	23 927	1 069	19.5	6.9	55.2
Cumberland	5 483	113 279	13 337	13 598	14 749	11 045	5 643	3 316	29 274	970	31.6	4.9	60.8
Dauphin	6 546	134 739	21 508	13 208	15 263	10 271	6 250	4 115	30 538	625	34.2	4.2	50.2
Delaware	13 242	216 717	34 723	19 613	28 594	12 038	15 706	8 055	37 156	63	68.3	3.2	42.9
Elk	996	15 278	2 038	8 115	1 547	262	215	421	27 585	145	25.5	1.4	34.5
Erie	6 824	120 101	17 574	34 253	15 694	4 790	3 473	3 233	26 918	1 123	31.7	4.2	55.8
Fayette	2 827	32 737	6 479	3 764	6 710	827	806	665	20 310	747	28.8	4.7	41.4
Forest	144	1 093	D	205	D	D	5	21	19 459	34	17.6	5.9	44.1
Franklin	2 760	42 935	5 578	12 053	6 502	1 300	1 280	1 029	23 965	1 304	27.7	6.1	65.1
Fulton	299	5 052	498	2 813	392	124	D	126	24 942	449	12.0	6.7	44.8
Greene	688	8 244	1 284	573	1 244	239	141	256	31 043	666	17.4	7.8	38.3
Huntingdon	829	9 721	1 454	2 380	1 520	398	266	210	21 640	586	15.7	7.5	53.2
Indiana	2 028	24 698	3 403	2 976	4 753	1 275	947	563	22 798	767	22.0	6.4	54.0
Jefferson	1 199	13 672	1 936	4 825	1 742	371	298	312	22 847	436	19.3	4.8	45.2
Juniata	481	5 800	622	2 480	732	243	52	128	21 997	611	27.7	2.6	63.2
Lackawanna	5 393	89 771	16 231	15 753	12 891	4 236	2 683	2 181	24 293	238	30.3	2.5	54.2
Lancaster	11 289	204 872	24 445	52 670	30 475	6 683	6 909	5 582	27 247	4 556	39.6	1.3	74.2
Lawrence	2 158	28 718	4 933	5 778	4 134	1 350	656	689	23 984	621	26.4	3.5	54.9
Lebanon	2 537	36 987	6 119	9 559	6 336	773	834	901	24 349	885	36.4	2.5	63.6
Lehigh	8 127	161 481	24 229	22 722	19 121	7 735	5 502	5 438	33 673	425	42.6	10.6	62.6
Luzerne	7 606	122 554	20 674	22 159	17 925	5 855	3 806	2 998	24 464	451	35.3	3.5	48.1
Lycoming	2 849	47 149	7 667	12 792	7 264	1 965	1 094	1 109	23 531	841	19.9	4.8	52.3
McKean	1 165	15 401	2 381	5 369	1 980	414	273	360	23 366	209	17.7	7.2	38.3
Mercer	2 951	44 414	8 413	10 883	7 341	1 228	788	1 060	23 864	1 030	20.4	4.7	51.7
Mifflin	938	14 476	2 367	5 633	2 342	326	202	355	24 522	619	25.5	1.8	69.6
Monroe	3 180	37 512	3 864	5 173	7 736	890	1 382	857	22 850	176	34.7	5.1	42.0
Montgomery	25 606	491 629	55 399	61 279	56 730	47 717	37 391	18 790	38 220	462	55.4	2.2	48.3
Montour	368	12 104	4 295	1 734	729	733	212	412	34 007	259	23.2	5.8	56.0
Northampton	5 631	77 935	8 716	16 996	10 344	5 180	2 200	2 239	28 727	396	44.4	11.1	56.1
Northumberland	1 822	24 893	2 936	7 652	3 974	685	482	576	23 152	596	30.4	7.6	56.2
Perry	730	5 789	639	863	1 248	202	155	108	18 708	618	21.8	6.1	52.1
Philadelphia	26 027	599 648	120 884	44 023	50 681	47 757	58 543	21 322	35 558	9	66.7	0.0	77.8
Pike	696	5 280	459	304	1 195	97	173	105	19 930	40	45.0	7.5	45.0

STATE County	Land in farms — Acreage (1,000) [117]	Percent change, 1992–1997 [118]	Acres — Average size of farm [119]	Total irrigated (1,000) [120]	Total cropland (1,000) [121]	Value of land and buildings — Average per farm ($1,000) [122]	Average per acre (dollars) [123]	Value of machinery and equipment average per farm ($1,000) [124]	Value of products sold — Total (mil dol) [125]	Average per farm (dollars) [126]	Percent from — Crops [127]	Livestock and poultry products [128]	Percent of farms with sales of — $10,000 or more [129]	$100,000 or more [130]	Percent of land owned by fed. gov. 1997 [131]	Water consumption 1995 (mil gal/day) [132]
OREGON—Cont'd																
Morrow	1 118	0.0	2 662	95	486	909	338	164	142	336 979	77.0	23.0	60.2	31.7	16.1	347.5
Multnomah	34	11.2	60	8	19	374	7 030	36	41	71 621	96.2	3.8	31.9	10.2	25.8	197.8
Polk	171	2.0	149	14	128	498	3 214	48	91	79 420	77.3	22.7	32.0	11.5	9.3	68.3
Sherman	425	-12.9	2 530	2	278	852	326	168	24	142 484	82.8	17.2	71.4	44.6	10.0	21.9
Tillamook	36	-11.1	114	6	20	387	4 082	66	63	199 693	0.6	99.4	54.0	43.8	19.2	85.3
Umatilla	1 345	-8.3	904	129	707	611	759	89	249	167 474	76.2	23.8	47.6	22.2	20.8	378.1
Union	532	12.5	639	62	176	471	823	55	48	57 369	70.7	29.3	42.9	10.8	47.5	202.8
Wallowa	621	-10.5	1 353	49	109	625	537	49	27	59 774	35.5	64.5	56.0	15.5	57.2	168.1
Wasco	1 135	-1.5	2 415	27	214	825	353	87	57	121 249	82.8	17.2	53.6	27.2	15.2	130.2
Washington	131	-6.5	78	26	100	458	6 045	46	186	110 675	90.6	9.4	37.2	12.7	2.6	106.9
Wheeler	680	-6.6	4 331	9	35	1 246	298	50	7	42 053	9.5	90.5	54.1	10.2	24.4	51.3
Yamhill	186	3.5	103	21	128	457	4 459	45	163	89 817	79.2	20.8	32.5	11.1	14.6	155.6
PENNSYLVANIA	7 168	-0.3	158	36	5 032	372	2 390	53	3 998	87 942	32.1	67.9	54.1	21.1	2.5	9 684.9
Adams	179	3.9	182	3	138	495	2 911	68	150	152 480	40.1	59.9	53.8	21.3	1.7	26.9
Allegheny	27	-18.4	81	0	18	256	3 403	35	9	27 058	76.3	23.7	34.1	8.4	0.1	904.2
Armstrong	120	-0.3	183	0	80	279	1 642	47	41	62 344	69.8	30.2	37.0	7.8	0.9	144.6
Beaver	54	-7.3	108	0	34	246	2 553	36	12	24 886	40.5	59.5	33.3	5.8	0.0	695.9
Bedford	199	0.0	211	0	125	321	1 568	52	58	61 575	16.9	83.1	48.6	22.1	0.0	12.0
Berks	222	-0.2	140	1	188	547	3 673	71	248	156 235	47.7	52.3	65.0	29.4	1.0	85.1
Blair	84	10.3	199	0	60	379	2 008	57	51	120 855	13.9	86.1	65.2	38.2	0.1	35.7
Bradford	307	-1.4	240	0	192	288	1 219	51	97	75 816	9.6	90.4	59.4	26.9	0.0	13.7
Bucks	84	8.5	113	1	71	710	5 713	54	70	94 339	79.1	20.9	49.7	16.6	0.2	94.9
Butler	119	-8.1	122	0	83	333	2 674	47	28	28 468	46.5	53.5	39.5	7.8	0.0	30.9
Cambria	88	14.0	167	0	59	233	1 322	48	22	41 921	53.8	46.2	39.2	10.5	0.1	22.6
Cameron	4	0.0	159		2	175	1 105	27	0	8 759	D	D	19.2	0.0	0.0	0.8
Carbon	20	4.0	119	0	14	388	3 194	48	8	45 745	83.7	16.3	46.1	7.8	1.1	37.4
Centre	136	-2.9	173	0	93	522	2 761	51	51	64 109	26.3	73.7	58.8	23.2	0.0	33.6
Chester	175	-0.9	123	1	139	670	5 658	67	343	240 778	77.5	22.5	62.7	32.2	0.1	274.1
Clarion	94	-1.0	206	0	63	233	1 139	52	17	36 164	25.3	74.7	39.6	10.9	0.0	4.5
Clearfield	53	-4.3	155	0	35	222	1 429	40	9	25 500	38.1	61.9	37.5	8.0	0.0	319.7
Clinton	41	5.9	155	1	30	315	1 940	60	21	77 991	32.4	67.6	54.1	25.9	0.0	35.7
Columbia	110	8.2	157	1	83	301	1 995	55	38	54 471	58.8	41.2	45.6	11.1	0.0	9.3
Crawford	207	-1.8	194	1	135	188	1 088	51	58	54 656	17.2	82.8	51.8	16.5	0.8	16.9
Cumberland	143	0.8	148	1	122	460	3 098	57	85	87 133	24.1	75.9	61.8	24.9	0.3	54.6
Dauphin	87	-3.9	138	1	70	445	3 264	58	54	85 747	22.7	77.3	55.4	19.2	1.7	123.0
Delaware	5	-3.2	77	0	3	693	9 013	46	7	111 874	90.5	9.5	42.9	19.0	0.7	828.2
Elk	17	6.8	118	0	11	242	2 192	51	2	14 223	30.1	69.9	26.2	4.1	24.5	17.5
Erie	168	-0.2	149	1	114	290	1 892	63	69	61 366	63.4	36.6	51.0	14.4	0.0	97.2
Fayette	109	2.5	145	0	70	223	1 620	50	20	26 781	42.5	57.5	33.5	5.9	0.4	43.0
Forest	5	7.2	158	D	3	206	1 305	51	1	29 743	18.5	81.5	41.2	11.8	50.1	0.5
Franklin	238	1.6	182	3	191	484	2 595	74	195	149 527	10.9	89.1	66.9	40.6	4.1	20.8
Fulton	94	5.9	210	0	51	294	1 266	66	21	47 183	16.4	83.6	41.2	15.4	0.0	2.0
Greene	131	3.9	197	0	67	174	991	34	7	10 654	24.5	75.5	18.2	2.0	0.0	43.9
Huntingdon	125	-4.0	213	0	76	362	1 722	54	41	70 184	12.5	87.5	50.0	19.5	4.4	9.3
Indiana	139	-3.1	181	1	90	262	1 484	50	46	60 065	56.0	44.0	48.4	12.1	1.3	239.6
Jefferson	80	1.2	183	0	52	184	1 073	40	16	36 285	43.6	56.4	34.6	10.6	0.0	6.8
Juniata	87	2.0	142	0	58	295	1 981	50	64	104 441	10.1	89.9	64.3	27.2	0.0	4.2
Lackawanna	30	-20.2	124	0	20	328	2 702	49	11	46 736	50.1	49.9	47.9	13.4	0.0	51.5
Lancaster	392	1.0	86	5	331	472	5 578	52	767	168 293	13.3	86.7	82.1	43.5	0.0	165.7
Lawrence	87	1.4	140	0	63	225	1 595	54	25	40 895	25.5	74.5	46.1	10.6	0.0	154.1
Lebanon	111	5.4	125	1	96	500	4 093	69	171	193 376	10.8	89.2	72.7	43.3	0.5	24.0
Lehigh	92	10.4	216	0	81	750	3 705	66	57	133 456	69.4	30.6	57.9	18.8	0.0	49.1
Luzerne	57	14.6	127	0	37	308	2 564	48	18	40 613	66.9	33.1	42.6	10.6	0.1	104.9
Lycoming	136	1.9	161	2	87	283	1 873	50	43	51 357	36.9	63.1	50.7	15.2	0.3	16.3
McKean	39	-2.4	187	0	18	185	1 056	24	4	20 483	24.7	75.3	33.5	6.7	25.5	15.2
Mercer	167	3.5	162	0	113	248	1 595	45	46	44 753	39.0	61.0	48.8	11.5	0.3	85.4
Mifflin	79	-2.0	128	0	53	261	2 068	58	52	83 751	9.3	90.7	66.4	26.8	0.0	15.5
Monroe	26	24.5	149	0	14	410	2 987	56	5	30 120	56.3	43.7	41.5	8.0	2.2	15.4
Montgomery	42	-5.6	90	0	34	500	4 667	51	29	63 625	56.9	43.1	52.2	15.8	1.1	141.6
Montour	40	-2.5	154	0	30	344	2 084	57	26	101 890	68.2	31.8	52.5	15.8	0.0	21.2
Northampton	78	-3.3	198	0	69	642	3 288	69	29	72 204	68.0	32.0	56.6	21.0	0.5	471.6
Northumberland	115	5.4	193	1	91	376	2 068	50	59	99 613	36.8	63.2	58.9	19.8	0.0	30.6
Perry	115	10.5	186	0	79	347	1 902	48	59	94 898	15.6	84.4	53.2	22.7	0.0	3.9
Philadelphia	0	0.0	32	0	D	709	22 395	78	1	85 864	D	D	77.8	22.2	1.5	574.5
Pike	6	-7.0	139	0	D	523	3 761	39	1	34 625	83.6	16.4	42.5	5.0	5.3	4.1

Table B. States and Counties — Residential Construction, Wholesale and Retail Trade, and Real Estate

STATE County	New Construction ($1,000)	Number of Housing Units	Number of Establish-ments	Number of Employees	Sales (mil dol)	Annual Payroll (mil dol)	Number of Establish-ments	Number of Employees	Sales (mil dol)	Annual Payroll (mil dol)	Number of Establish-ments	Number of Employees	Receipts (mil dol)	Annual Payroll (mil dol)
	133	134	135	136	137	138	139	140	141	142	143	144	145	146
OREGON—Cont'd														
Morrow	NA	NA	12	73	103.1	2.1	30	217	38.8	3.2	4	D	D	D
Multnomah	266 445	2 591	1 850	28 384	25 188.5	1 017.7	3 025	39 841	7 334.5	791.4	1 118	8 335	1 053.2	208.9
Polk	29 099	260	41	425	87.3	8.7	143	1 592	232.4	24.3	54	145	14.5	1.9
Sherman	600	4	2	D	D	D	13	91	12.9	1.3	NA	NA	NA	NA
Tillamook	25 128	179	22	114	18.8	2.0	123	1 044	144.1	15.0	28	104	6.7	1.3
Umatilla	16 027	144	75	954	331.6	22.8	290	3 188	567.2	53.7	61	164	14.5	2.2
Union	5 118	46	34	301	96.2	7.4	129	1 355	227.7	23.5	22	61	6.2	0.7
Wallowa	NA	NA	4	11	5.1	0.2	52	336	61.8	6.2	13	29	2.6	0.4
Wasco	4 265	31	36	550	115.7	11.3	134	1 468	256.9	26.1	28	81	7.0	1.3
Washington	466 146	3 827	1 035	13 622	13 153.8	603.2	1 499	25 124	5 453.5	512.3	579	3 098	418.9	64.6
Wheeler	536	4	1	D	D	D	6	19	8.5	0.5	1	D	D	D
Yamhill	82 566	750	73	485	259.1	14.8	269	3 313	627.2	58.4	82	306	36.1	4.6
PENNSYLVANIA	4 616 181	41 076	17 138	237 567	159 354.2	8 588.2	50 208	650 144	109 948.5	10 561.9	8 684	57 519	7 668.6	1 360.5
Adams	67 123	639	88	1 211	909.7	33.2	330	3 072	472.7	45.6	45	139	12.6	1.8
Allegheny	329 953	2 706	2 490	33 034	28 256.0	1 269.4	5 353	78 841	12 929.7	1 218.0	1 274	9 616	1 645.6	239.8
Armstrong	12 169	151	48	285	65.1	5.9	310	3 255	487.1	43.3	31	116	12.1	2.7
Beaver	49 594	467	148	1 515	570.5	46.5	668	8 513	1 180.5	113.7	80	374	35.1	7.2
Bedford	15 884	175	44	451	207.7	11.7	216	2 298	438.9	35.6	18	41	4.1	0.5
Berks	192 359	1 809	439	7 051	3 121.7	253.0	1 468	19 302	3 330.7	326.2	215	1 324	191.3	28.1
Blair	20 947	226	160	2 836	1 641.3	82.3	639	8 310	1 331.2	117.7	90	419	34.8	6.9
Bradford	12 757	159	55	512	175.1	10.7	296	3 315	521.2	46.4	31	92	10.0	1.5
Bucks	354 826	2 768	1 433	16 257	8 415.9	684.2	2 549	36 195	7 217.4	701.3	506	3 166	420.4	82.5
Butler	131 656	1 030	272	4 732	4 540.8	140.5	709	9 317	1 480.2	137.0	112	492	76.0	10.6
Cambria	19 450	220	144	2 115	580.7	57.5	693	8 555	1 244.8	111.5	77	347	32.4	5.1
Cameron	1 075	9	2	D	D	D	27	287	31.0	3.8	NA	NA	NA	NA
Carbon	26 576	207	34	240	91.4	7.0	219	2 102	316.7	30.9	27	81	5.5	1.3
Centre	67 780	653	100	D	D	D	617	7 861	1 153.9	108.7	111	704	83.1	14.0
Chester	431 764	3 051	1 013	10 955	15 420.9	459.6	1 517	22 625	5 879.6	490.8	328	2 052	319.1	55.0
Clarion	9 186	120	47	470	568.5	13.8	226	2 100	330.5	32.3	17	74	5.9	1.7
Clearfield	15 118	186	80	713	280.5	17.7	397	4 935	768.4	68.8	42	294	23.9	6.0
Clinton	11 131	137	28	D	D	D	176	1 877	296.2	24.6	19	74	7.9	1.1
Columbia	19 565	259	50	D	D	D	317	3 462	533.9	45.1	46	178	18.6	3.3
Crawford	18 658	240	81	652	175.5	14.6	360	3 970	628.8	58.6	49	165	15.3	1.9
Cumberland	121 075	1 008	260	3 589	2 439.6	122.7	955	15 697	2 759.5	268.2	177	1 390	195.7	35.7
Dauphin	76 674	780	341	9 844	8 700.1	320.2	1 125	15 204	2 532.8	246.1	196	1 369	198.2	29.3
Delaware	154 677	1 142	807	9 947	9 506.8	438.9	2 080	28 710	5 003.6	516.4	411	4 236	574.0	100.6
Elk	9 517	99	40	335	89.7	8.7	163	1 668	219.9	20.4	15	49	6.1	0.9
Erie	72 802	704	334	4 069	1 277.8	131.9	1 225	16 323	2 562.1	239.0	180	834	75.5	13.8
Fayette	22 041	352	123	1 566	406.8	29.3	599	7 056	1 110.2	96.3	77	296	28.4	4.7
Forest	2 992	47	4	D	D	D	35	162	28.6	2.3	5	6	0.4	0.2
Franklin	67 235	714	102	1 862	610.3	49.0	566	6 249	1 035.7	94.4	77	296	29.3	4.6
Fulton	4 010	49	7	32	6.6	0.5	55	402	70.7	5.3	5	37	2.8	0.7
Greene	7 139	106	34	364	78.9	6.9	136	1 240	259.2	18.4	15	40	4.1	0.4
Huntingdon	15 493	180	24	D	D	D	169	1 495	252.8	22.5	17	36	3.2	0.5
Indiana	21 129	335	80	870	418.8	19.6	391	4 986	723.6	64.3	58	223	15.7	2.8
Jefferson	9 496	143	62	515	121.4	12.0	209	1 828	299.2	24.6	26	87	5.1	1.0
Juniata	4 334	49	24	D	D	D	71	649	123.6	9.0	12	15	1.3	0.2
Lackawanna	55 179	520	286	3 636	1 126.0	95.7	1 039	13 167	1 966.3	189.8	145	747	72.7	12.8
Lancaster	250 470	2 016	663	11 020	10 936.6	341.6	2 012	29 237	4 671.7	480.8	281	1 906	247.2	41.9
Lawrence	26 889	270	90	1 070	430.2	29.0	370	4 286	627.1	61.4	58	264	27.6	5.2
Lebanon	51 505	514	118	D	D	D	490	6 480	1 209.1	106.8	59	270	29.2	4.0
Lehigh	165 633	1 344	560	7 469	4 668.7	255.6	1 376	18 976	3 509.2	333.2	264	1 659	207.1	33.1
Luzerne	67 490	603	388	5 697	2 149.6	152.3	1 406	18 945	2 856.4	269.2	208	1 240	113.0	26.5
Lycoming	31 726	313	137	2 195	481.9	51.4	605	7 600	1 149.3	108.4	78	299	32.2	4.7
McKean	7 062	88	44	426	229.2	12.7	200	1 969	280.5	26.8	21	58	4.5	0.5
Mercer	38 372	432	124	1 692	656.3	41.9	618	7 852	1 285.0	112.8	84	281	29.6	5.0
Mifflin	9 759	120	53	552	111.7	12.4	195	2 427	368.4	34.8	27	88	8.7	1.3
Monroe	220 699	1 630	93	1 012	345.3	28.5	658	7 621	1 160.6	111.7	111	808	60.9	12.4
Montgomery	324 100	3 058	2 004	29 378	22 878.2	1 395.6	3 689	54 728	9 607.4	1 025.8	876	6 649	1 019.2	199.7
Montour	8 607	62	15	209	65.8	5.2	76	797	131.3	10.0	10	24	2.7	0.3
Northampton	143 960	1 312	312	4 465	2 066.2	167.7	832	10 051	1 831.8	168.1	115	648	79.3	16.6
Northumberland	15 558	169	72	1 016	582.6	26.5	367	3 689	658.7	58.9	58	231	15.5	3.5
Perry	16 331	165	17	D	D	D	141	1 280	205.3	17.5	7	D	D	D
Philadelphia	87 571	1 333	1 403	22 298	12 004.0	848.4	4 782	51 398	8 118.2	887.1	964	9 550	1 158.1	253.5
Pike	64 093	475	23	D	D	D	107	1 203	182.6	16.9	27	274	40.9	3.0

1. Establishments with payroll.

STATE County	Professional, Scientific, and Technical Services[1], 1997				Manufacturing, 1997				Accommodation and Foodservices, 1997			
	Number of Establishments	Number of Employees	Receipts (mil dol)	Annual Payroll (mil dol)	Number of Establishments	Number of Employees	Receipts (mil dol)	Annual Payroll (mil dol)	Number of Establishments	Number of Employees	Sales (mil dol)	Annual Payroll (mil dol)
	147	148	149	150	151	152	153	154	155	156	157	158
OREGON—Cont'd												
Morrow	3	D	D	D	10	741	183.4	20.9	18	123	4.2	0.9
Multnomah	2 682	23 427	2 336.0	967.7	1 309	47 763	8 715.4	1 600.4	1 937	33 949	1 315.1	373.6
Polk	63	200	14.2	5.6	63	2 358	357.4	63.4	77	997	30.7	7.8
Sherman	NA	NA	NA	NA	NA	NA	NA	NA	9	D	D	D
Tillamook	32	96	5.8	2.4	31	1 227	317.8	32.5	128	1 086	35.5	10.1
Umatilla	67	235	16.7	5.4	75	4 623	790.6	107.2	159	1 950	66.4	17.2
Union	35	163	10.4	3.8	28	1 250	273.9	37.2	77	773	23.6	6.3
Wallowa	14	31	1.8	0.6	NA	NA	NA	NA	47	198	5.8	1.4
Wasco	38	154	9.7	4.0	26	751	374.7	28.1	73	925	34.3	11.8
Washington	1 203	8 082	800.5	354.2	828	38 997	14 360.2	1 413.2	798	14 299	495.8	140.6
Wheeler	NA	NA	NA	NA	NA	NA	NA	NA	6	D	D	D
Yamhill	111	408	32.6	12.4	159	6 092	1 268.3	194.9	146	1 997	58.3	17.0
PENNSYLVANIA	23 184	235 025	26 240.3	10 448.3	17 128	826 521	172 193.2	27 641.3	24 465	365 158	12 227.2	3 364.1
Adams	81	341	22.2	7.6	127	8 209	1 401.3	214.1	190	2 789	89.3	25.5
Allegheny	3 432	44 926	5 155.6	1 988.1	1 500	55 620	10 576.1	2 130.8	2 912	52 581	1 711.4	477.5
Armstrong	77	421	28.6	8.5	92	3 617	409.2	94.9	135	1 133	32.8	8.2
Beaver	208	1 760	108.0	45.3	221	10 311	3 161.9	383.1	307	3 796	108.3	28.1
Bedford	34	123	6.6	2.2	61	3 231	472.8	76.6	108	1 674	49.5	14.4
Berks	546	5 520	476.6	215.2	587	41 614	7 729.4	1 510.7	706	10 091	330.4	90.9
Blair	181	1 838	151.6	53.5	157	8 966	1 592.4	251.7	254	4 003	108.8	29.6
Bradford	67	318	17.9	5.2	73	6 405	1 273.7	191.5	117	1 185	35.3	9.7
Bucks	1 729	11 075	1 155.1	489.6	1 236	41 592	7 593.0	1 518.9	1 047	15 741	569.3	147.8
Butler	262	1 519	132.2	51.3	276	14 891	2 990.0	533.0	317	5 439	156.6	42.8
Cambria	184	1 619	98.6	42.3	153	7 403	1 349.5	186.3	314	4 143	111.4	30.6
Cameron	7	27	1.4	0.4	20	1 259	151.4	34.6	14	106	2.6	0.7
Carbon	63	182	11.2	3.9	63	3 646	311.9	76.2	97	1 200	41.8	11.3
Centre	211	2 332	167.5	85.9	159	8 546	1 409.3	255.4	287	5 241	154.8	41.2
Chester	1 567	18 172	2 446.6	972.8	629	20 791	4 332.2	771.1	642	10 790	365.4	102.7
Clarion	42	180	17.7	6.8	49	2 711	441.7	76.4	108	1 331	38.7	9.9
Clearfield	91	428	26.1	8.2	107	4 864	791.0	120.2	153	1 840	56.1	14.5
Clinton	30	139	8.3	2.5	54	3 212	677.1	89.2	79	932	28.6	6.9
Columbia	67	629	29.4	14.1	100	D	D	D	154	2 218	59.3	15.9
Crawford	97	442	31.2	11.0	301	8 714	1 263.4	289.4	180	2 357	67.3	19.0
Cumberland	404	3 989	326.3	155.4	221	13 804	3 307.3	444.8	415	7 623	235.2	65.6
Dauphin	560	5 277	559.2	198.0	222	14 871	3 590.9	522.4	611	10 456	394.4	107.3
Delaware	1 417	13 750	1 876.1	669.2	522	19 341	7 315.2	867.0	1 025	13 991	514.1	134.1
Elk	41	130	7.2	2.2	130	8 338	1 393.3	288.0	82	617	18.5	4.4
Erie	379	2 330	177.7	62.4	570	32 813	5 779.3	1 142.3	614	9 599	265.2	73.3
Fayette	115	700	49.4	14.7	128	3 842	656.7	106.0	278	4 886	157.3	47.7
Forest	3	D	D	D	NA	NA	NA	NA	20	142	4.9	1.2
Franklin	158	948	61.7	25.2	191	12 763	2 212.0	379.5	217	3 274	105.8	28.1
Fulton	12	31	1.6	0.4	22	D	D	D	24	278	10.0	2.7
Greene	27	99	5.9	1.9	27	630	81.5	15.1	56	620	19.4	4.7
Huntingdon	36	233	10.2	4.4	44	2 300	493.0	59.5	84	778	22.9	6.3
Indiana	89	601	62.6	20.2	88	3 175	344.1	98.9	167	2 707	64.8	17.5
Jefferson	56	253	14.4	5.5	88	4 634	680.9	132.0	89	928	23.9	6.4
Juniata	18	34	2.2	0.5	57	2 443	290.6	61.1	33	312	8.5	2.0
Lackawanna	358	2 585	230.1	88.2	306	16 052	2 562.7	463.0	520	7 421	219.3	59.4
Lancaster	639	5 130	439.8	165.6	918	52 908	10 585.4	1 752.0	877	15 724	506.4	145.6
Lawrence	103	553	37.7	14.8	169	5 092	1 076.6	156.4	196	2 488	67.3	17.2
Lebanon	113	608	42.2	17.9	199	9 376	1 710.3	254.3	209	2 687	76.0	22.3
Lehigh	651	4 837	410.7	164.1	504	23 277	7 690.1	877.2	648	11 892	412.7	114.7
Luzerne	466	3 666	251.7	98.7	408	24 362	4 501.1	700.8	694	9 780	292.7	79.8
Lycoming	137	1 014	68.8	27.1	208	12 982	2 460.4	370.2	283	3 571	106.1	28.5
McKean	57	226	11.4	3.3	67	5 346	875.7	158.7	118	1 057	30.0	7.8
Mercer	130	679	49.4	22.0	198	10 457	2 440.8	326.8	270	3 953	113.3	32.6
Mifflin	24	117	7.0	2.2	72	5 373	922.7	163.1	83	989	26.0	7.0
Monroe	235	1 110	77.4	31.5	113	4 744	812.9	171.1	345	6 179	241.8	67.7
Montgomery	2 934	29 664	3 693.5	1 488.4	1 398	67 234	20 666.6	2 649.5	1 504	23 896	915.4	254.0
Montour	17	D	D	D	22	1 530	820.4	65.8	39	586	15.8	4.5
Northampton	422	2 211	255.1	80.9	353	18 244	2 638.4	546.1	513	5 497	195.0	50.0
Northumberland	79	351	25.4	6.9	115	7 812	1 526.7	217.3	180	1 641	43.7	11.7
Perry	29	92	6.6	1.5	32	845	82.7	19.1	61	467	14.8	3.4
Philadelphia	2 444	49 894	6 317.4	2 690.5	1 342	47 928	11 098.1	1 582.4	2 989	38 521	1 691.6	461.1
Pike	53	137	11.9	3.7	NA	NA	NA	NA	91	1 221	49.0	15.2

1. Firms subject to federal tax.

Table B. States and Counties — **Health and Other Services and Federal Funds**

STATE County	Health Care and Social Assistance[1], 1997				Other Services[1], 1997				Federal funds and grants, fiscal 2001[2] — Expenditures (mil dol)			
										Direct payments for individuals[3]		
	Number of Establishments	Number of Employees	Receipts (mil dol)	Annual Payroll (mil dol)	Number of Establishments	Number of Employees	Receipts (mil dol)	Annual Payroll (mil dol)	Total	Social Security and government retirement	Medicare	Food stamps and Supplemental Security Income
	159	160	161	162	163	164	165	166	167	168	169	170
OREGON—Cont'd												
Morrow	4	20	0.6	0.3	8	29	1.6	0.5	70.3	19.5	6.6	0.9
Multnomah	1 649	17 599	1 221.2	535.8	1 268	9 706	688.9	211.7	4 299.4	1 382.2	522.7	64.7
Polk	92	510	24.7	10.2	58	229	14.3	3.6	224.6	86.9	33.2	5.9
Sherman	1	D	D	D	2	D	D	D	34.5	5.5	2.1	0.3
Tillamook	32	252	12.1	5.2	26	102	7.7	1.8	139.8	76.9	23.9	3.7
Umatilla	141	1 047	56.9	21.7	87	303	21.1	5.9	503.6	142.8	44.5	13.3
Union	71	517	26.4	10.0	34	112	7.9	2.0	131.9	59.8	20.1	4.5
Wallowa	14	85	4.3	1.6	18	41	3.3	0.7	50.4	21.3	6.2	0.8
Wasco	58	387	27.9	11.3	32	95	7.0	1.6	154.9	62.9	17.2	3.8
Washington	915	9 348	572.9	246.9	593	3 512	257.1	78.3	994.8	492.7	190.2	28.5
Wheeler	2	D	D	D	3	D	D	D	14.1	5.1	1.8	0.0
Yamhill	151	1 716	102.3	39.4	92	429	30.6	8.3	324.8	152.1	55.2	9.3
PENNSYLVANIA	24 888	262 603	17 633.5	7 994.9	19 754	107 502	7 085.7	2 049.0	79 310.1	28 793.8	14 571.8	2 231.5
Adams	109	807	44.7	22.0	106	496	33.0	9.6	377.6	200.4	57.9	5.0
Allegheny	3 230	39 435	2 895.2	1 276.4	2 570	15 947	1 084.0	308.5	10 164.0	3 299.2	2 009.6	236.6
Armstrong	125	1 089	50.7	21.4	97	307	20.0	4.4	445.3	207.2	104.1	14.9
Beaver	310	2 700	186.7	87.5	255	1 360	67.6	20.3	952.5	476.7	243.1	32.6
Bedford	88	465	27.8	11.1	73	195	12.4	2.8	272.1	119.0	50.0	7.3
Berks	601	6 387	412.6	200.5	559	3 102	183.2	56.4	1 528.4	782.9	322.6	42.9
Blair	284	2 816	200.5	83.6	251	1 319	72.7	18.9	745.2	343.0	149.6	28.5
Bradford	81	1 044	40.3	21.6	68	225	14.1	3.4	304.9	143.8	50.4	12.2
Bucks	1 329	13 239	859.9	379.8	1 132	6 494	450.6	145.0	2 250.6	1 208.3	523.5	34.6
Butler	311	2 751	160.1	71.3	296	1 456	95.1	28.2	968.4	384.3	183.8	20.4
Cambria	351	2 749	180.8	92.5	220	1 097	69.8	19.0	1 083.6	434.2	229.2	35.6
Cameron	10	40	2.0	1.0	9	12	1.2	0.2	35.3	16.6	7.3	0.7
Carbon	101	616	37.2	14.4	59	183	13.4	3.0	304.6	166.3	80.2	6.5
Centre	212	2 520	169.1	72.4	159	958	52.2	14.5	799.9	211.1	77.6	10.3
Chester	893	10 268	660.5	321.3	672	4 641	414.5	117.1	1 908.1	774.0	308.6	22.3
Clarion	71	685	38.0	18.2	58	252	20.5	4.5	217.5	93.6	52.8	7.7
Clearfield	159	1 397	81.0	30.1	103	509	34.9	8.6	419.7	200.4	96.6	16.1
Clinton	49	254	15.5	5.7	42	136	9.8	2.1	180.9	86.1	37.9	6.2
Columbia	113	1 185	57.7	24.3	89	320	18.8	4.2	278.9	149.6	66.2	7.6
Crawford	167	1 530	85.4	40.1	126	527	38.1	10.1	427.5	211.3	92.5	17.4
Cumberland	425	5 511	392.2	192.7	389	2 333	136.9	44.6	1 232.2	583.3	165.9	10.3
Dauphin	545	5 434	343.1	155.6	417	2 535	171.0	52.1	3 856.7	759.7	231.4	38.5
Delaware	1 280	14 634	995.3	454.5	985	5 017	332.8	104.5	2 728.1	1 306.0	712.3	65.6
Elk	66	329	21.1	10.0	49	192	11.8	2.9	156.5	86.4	39.5	3.2
Erie	560	5 498	423.4	190.6	476	2 174	135.0	39.6	1 324.6	596.3	258.9	61.5
Fayette	269	3 290	153.4	65.3	209	867	47.7	11.7	1 026.0	416.9	250.3	63.1
Forest	6	105	7.1	3.5	6	27	0.9	0.3	38.5	19.3	8.7	0.7
Franklin	181	1 666	109.9	50.1	219	938	52.9	14.4	652.9	354.4	95.5	12.6
Fulton	15	98	4.1	1.3	21	53	4.2	0.7	72.5	34.2	11.3	2.0
Greene	61	450	24.9	10.9	46	190	12.3	3.5	286.3	99.6	55.7	12.2
Huntingdon	65	325	19.5	8.0	55	130	8.6	1.8	208.7	100.8	41.4	8.2
Indiana	200	1 402	77.0	30.2	126	573	42.3	9.2	488.6	199.5	101.3	17.3
Jefferson	112	663	43.9	14.9	81	290	20.5	4.4	246.0	121.7	57.4	8.5
Juniata	22	208	9.5	3.7	22	72	5.6	1.1	87.5	46.7	18.8	2.1
Lackawanna	536	5 276	351.1	158.7	349	2 096	109.4	33.1	1 400.2	589.4	323.8	35.2
Lancaster	710	8 212	523.8	252.0	808	4 429	276.4	81.6	1 796.5	921.2	317.8	43.8
Lawrence	183	1 709	100.0	45.6	139	648	32.5	8.6	577.9	277.2	142.4	21.6
Lebanon	194	1 655	107.1	49.7	192	785	52.1	13.6	630.4	298.6	97.4	10.5
Lehigh	845	8 416	625.6	307.6	583	4 350	295.2	91.8	1 406.1	561.2	323.6	54.0
Luzerne	736	8 132	501.2	218.3	499	2 288	136.0	34.6	2 018.3	911.5	469.5	51.9
Lycoming	218	2 050	134.4	58.6	176	887	57.5	15.2	593.9	274.6	113.1	22.7
McKean	89	598	37.3	15.0	69	222	12.2	3.1	252.5	112.9	50.0	10.9
Mercer	303	2 686	162.7	72.5	203	876	44.3	12.9	660.6	330.0	160.1	25.7
Mifflin	79	550	40.2	19.3	53	198	14.2	3.0	227.8	104.7	52.0	8.2
Monroe	226	1 759	108.5	48.9	191	733	54.3	12.8	625.5	296.7	109.9	10.0
Montgomery	2 171	27 990	2 082.6	949.7	1 524	9 822	622.2	209.1	3 700.7	1 760.8	796.2	40.0
Montour	26	573	31.5	10.6	20	55	3.9	0.8	85.6	43.8	21.5	2.4
Northampton	515	4 607	284.1	115.7	409	2 186	139.2	42.8	1 314.8	663.5	317.0	15.5
Northumberland	147	1 673	68.6	28.3	121	553	34.3	8.5	532.1	253.6	119.2	15.6
Perry	45	326	13.5	5.4	42	93	5.8	1.1	185.3	92.9	34.0	3.6
Philadelphia	2 574	27 295	1 931.1	899.0	1 913	10 971	737.4	199.6	14 496.4	3 165.3	2 537.4	767.5
Pike	46	307	16.4	5.6	29	91	6.9	1.4	147.4	93.8	28.0	2.6

1. Firms subject to federal tax.   2. October 1, 2000 to September 30, 2001.   3. State totals may include programs not allocated by county.

STATE County	Federal funds and grants, fiscal 2001[1] (cont'd)							Local government finances, 1997				
	Expenditures (mil dol) (cont'd)							General revenue				
	Procurement contract awards			Grants[2]						Taxes		
											Per capita[3] (dollars)	
	Salaries and wages	Defense	Other	Medicaid and other health-related	Nutrition and family welfare	Education	Other	Total (mil dol)	Intergovern-mental (mil dol)	Total (mil dol)	Total	Property
	171	172	173	174	175	176	177	178	179	180	181	182
OREGON—Cont'd												
Morrow	2.6	3.9	0.4	1.7	0.8	0.5	5.2	39.8	11.7	13.5	1 402	1 266
Multnomah	658.5	147.8	240.2	755.0	94.2	52.7	234.2	2 776.0	1 020.6	1 000.1	1 601	1 091
Polk	6.8	0.1	2.9	39.0	5.0	8.3	15.1	77.2	43.4	21.5	358	330
Sherman	3.6	2.3	0.2	1.2	0.1	0.1	4.6	8.7	4.7	2.3	1 260	1 225
Tillamook	7.7	0.0	3.7	11.2	2.2	1.8	5.0	75.2	38.2	21.9	899	816
Umatilla	35.3	129.9	14.9	40.7	13.3	5.0	10.5	167.4	92.6	42.3	654	589
Union	9.8	0.1	5.3	13.0	3.8	1.9	1.3	57.1	31.2	14.6	582	522
Wallowa	4.5	0.0	4.1	6.7	0.7	0.4	1.0	28.0	14.2	7.9	1 064	1 012
Wasco	16.9	15.1	1.2	11.6	2.7	1.6	5.7	79.2	39.4	21.4	921	839
Washington	69.1	18.7	18.8	87.1	18.1	13.9	30.4	935.0	299.4	377.5	965	838
Wheeler	0.4	0.0	0.1	0.4	0.1	0.1	5.7	5.9	3.3	1.7	1 039	898
Yamhill	28.9	6.2	8.9	30.6	10.4	4.6	3.1	179.1	84.5	55.3	689	605
PENNSYLVANIA	5 762.8	4 214.2	2 573.8	8 100.5	2 170.7	1 136.5	3 439.7	X	X	X	X	X
Adams	30.1	1.1	18.1	40.7	4.5	1.9	5.3	175.1	77.6	69.1	805	565
Allegheny	901.8	738.5	717.5	1 175.0	173.3	47.1	403.7	4 249.4	1 711.3	1 679.0	1 311	973
Armstrong	13.2	5.2	3.3	45.8	7.8	2.2	35.9	141.8	69.6	54.8	745	618
Beaver	22.6	1.9	6.2	85.7	25.3	6.3	21.4	466.9	204.0	148.2	798	644
Bedford	8.3	1.5	2.8	32.5	4.5	1.7	38.2	86.7	45.4	28.8	584	460
Berks	72.5	25.5	21.5	118.0	26.5	10.9	60.6	888.2	318.7	394.0	1 113	880
Blair	49.5	0.3	8.4	87.9	20.4	5.8	30.2	243.5	120.0	78.2	598	430
Bradford	13.2	0.7	15.1	41.4	7.9	2.4	11.1	158.2	80.2	40.5	650	483
Bucks	83.6	107.3	52.8	106.2	24.7	7.1	49.0	1 386.5	370.1	708.6	1 216	1 025
Butler	67.4	4.9	191.9	71.8	12.6	3.8	7.2	331.8	133.8	131.7	778	600
Cambria	78.4	101.8	23.0	93.2	17.7	7.3	36.1	375.6	173.7	96.1	610	473
Cameron	1.0	0.0	0.3	4.8	1.8	0.2	-0.5	13.2	5.8	4.7	819	691
Carbon	7.4	2.5	2.6	21.4	4.0	1.3	6.1	119.8	47.8	49.8	846	651
Centre	37.7	72.0	14.5	74.7	8.0	13.9	222.4	229.7	80.9	92.8	698	468
Chester	176.8	54.6	349.3	90.6	18.9	7.6	63.3	920.8	250.5	491.5	1 180	961
Clarion	6.9	1.3	3.1	23.6	4.5	2.9	9.6	91.8	53.8	24.9	596	456
Clearfield	16.3	2.2	3.9	45.9	9.1	4.5	17.6	155.2	84.8	53.0	657	516
Clinton	9.6	0.1	2.0	19.5	4.7	2.9	2.4	89.0	36.8	29.5	800	621
Columbia	10.5	0.0	2.4	26.2	5.3	1.8	2.4	115.1	51.3	45.5	709	492
Crawford	14.5	0.1	9.5	43.8	13.2	3.0	10.7	166.8	78.8	54.8	614	491
Cumberland	316.1	47.6	21.2	39.1	6.0	5.2	8.1	429.4	127.2	209.5	1 008	686
Dauphin	193.9	127.4	47.0	353.7	715.6	359.7	909.8	717.3	261.3	267.3	1 087	776
Delaware	135.9	101.4	32.0	209.5	42.3	18.4	26.5	1 290.2	354.4	614.0	1 131	1 023
Elk	6.1	0.2	1.7	10.5	2.8	1.3	1.9	64.2	24.5	26.2	750	527
Erie	84.6	37.5	16.1	137.7	39.7	11.3	30.1	628.4	305.3	212.1	759	598
Fayette	27.2	2.5	7.5	176.3	27.7	8.4	17.5	223.0	136.0	60.7	418	316
Forest	2.3	0.0	0.6	3.7	0.6	0.2	2.3	11.4	4.3	5.9	1 205	899
Franklin	64.2	37.5	6.8	45.4	7.3	2.5	15.5	198.8	81.0	80.1	628	466
Fulton	1.9	1.9	1.1	10.0	1.6	0.4	5.8	26.8	14.7	9.3	647	525
Greene	8.8	0.3	42.1	44.8	5.9	3.1	5.1	83.2	35.2	35.5	840	717
Huntingdon	7.0	0.6	2.5	28.7	5.6	1.4	6.2	67.4	36.5	22.7	502	392
Indiana	17.0	6.0	3.8	66.8	9.4	3.9	37.7	157.5	84.9	52.6	590	452
Jefferson	8.8	0.5	1.9	26.4	4.7	1.5	10.2	77.4	40.0	26.4	568	427
Juniata	4.1	0.0	0.9	9.6	2.0	0.4	0.2	24.2	12.5	7.8	356	227
Lackawanna	62.8	124.2	17.4	128.5	24.3	5.7	41.2	452.9	170.2	182.8	868	612
Lancaster	100.0	86.2	54.0	124.0	28.3	12.4	60.6	904.6	306.8	395.6	871	677
Lawrence	27.1	0.9	8.8	56.6	13.7	4.0	6.0	179.8	94.2	59.8	627	478
Lebanon	98.3	16.6	16.7	31.7	5.8	2.2	35.2	231.1	93.0	94.3	804	608
Lehigh	58.8	155.9	19.2	102.4	19.8	7.7	62.9	818.9	272.3	322.8	1 084	851
Luzerne	166.0	30.9	40.6	178.6	35.1	11.4	45.3	626.7	245.8	254.8	802	592
Lycoming	36.1	19.7	14.9	55.8	13.7	4.1	14.9	254.6	105.3	97.0	819	555
McKean	25.5	0.0	4.1	27.3	6.1	2.0	6.4	116.0	59.0	33.0	705	545
Mercer	18.7	0.5	4.1	58.8	15.9	4.2	19.6	237.6	127.1	74.1	607	449
Mifflin	7.2	0.1	1.4	31.4	4.6	1.5	12.5	80.8	39.7	26.1	554	409
Monroe	96.8	35.4	30.6	20.5	6.4	3.2	6.2	267.8	69.1	167.2	1 365	1 215
Montgomery	262.7	293.6	194.9	159.7	24.9	10.0	93.6	1 819.3	435.4	980.0	1 375	1 133
Montour	2.2	0.2	1.1	9.9	1.1	0.4	0.5	40.2	11.4	14.0	778	507
Northampton	78.4	6.8	23.3	93.4	20.2	6.2	47.6	652.1	222.4	284.9	1 107	869
Northumberland	13.7	1.4	5.3	63.1	7.5	3.4	30.8	188.7	94.3	51.3	539	328
Perry	5.3	0.1	1.4	14.4	2.5	0.9	26.6	72.2	33.2	30.4	689	447
Philadelphia	1 793.8	1 366.1	398.7	2 825.3	494.7	131.1	523.5	6 608.1	3 309.2	2 309.6	1 591	575
Pike	11.5	0.0	2.1	3.7	1.1	0.6	3.1	59.7	13.8	37.7	964	918

1. October 1, 2000 to September 30, 2001.   2. State totals may include programs not allocated by county.   3. Based on the resident population estimated as of July 1 of the year shown.

Table B. States and Counties — Local Government Finances, Government Employment, and Elections

STATE County	Total (mil dol)	Per capita[1] (dollars)	Education	Health and hospitals	Police protection	Public welfare	Highways	Total (mil dol)	Per capita[1] (dollars)	Federal civilian	Federal military	State and local	Democratic	Republican	All other
	183	184	185	186	187	188	189	190	191	192	193	194	195	196	197
OREGON—Cont'd															
Morrow	45.8	4 760	45.8	16.7	2.9	0.0	6.7	29.7	3 080	64	45	720	33.2	61.6	5.2
Multnomah	2 594.4	4 154	34.1	6.1	5.3	0.0	5.0	2 960.6	4 740	11 690	2 597	51 916	63.5	28.2	8.3
Polk	86.4	1 437	52.0	10.5	6.1	0.0	5.5	47.7	792	119	208	3 114	41.9	52.7	5.4
Sherman	8.8	4 861	55.9	1.1	5.5	0.0	10.4	1.0	532	83	0	176	30.7	63.9	5.4
Tillamook	75.4	3 091	40.7	3.7	2.8	0.4	15.8	47.4	1 946	136	116	1 617	46.6	46.7	6.8
Umatilla	175.5	2 710	58.9	5.0	5.2	1.1	4.3	90.8	1 403	805	229	4 774	33.9	61.3	4.8
Union	54.7	2 182	55.7	0.6	5.0	0.0	7.9	14.8	590	225	87	2 383	29.6	64.9	5.5
Wallowa	25.1	3 380	45.0	27.3	3.5	0.0	6.6	7.4	996	130	24	613	19.5	76.4	4.2
Wasco	76.8	3 302	42.0	6.9	3.9	6.0	8.7	79.7	3 426	345	78	1 669	43.3	50.2	6.5
Washington	949.0	2 425	46.3	2.6	6.1	0.0	6.7	752.9	1 924	848	1 366	14 575	48.7	46.3	5.0
Wheeler	5.2	3 215	57.5	3.8	2.5	0.0	12.9	0.4	228	0	0	155	24.0	69.4	6.5
Yamhill	179.5	2 238	50.8	4.7	3.4	0.6	6.0	167.1	2 084	561	278	3 419	40.1	54.0	5.9
PENNSYLVANIA	X	X	X	X	X	X	X	X	X	108 996	44 758	611 006	50.6	46.4	3.0
Adams	213.8	2 493	71.4	0.2	1.4	3.2	3.3	174.2	2 031	444	294	4 024	34.9	62.4	2.7
Allegheny	4 129.5	3 225	42.9	7.1	4.4	3.0	3.4	6 637.9	5 183	15 040	4 909	60 153	56.6	40.4	2.9
Armstrong	133.8	1 818	66.3	0.2	1.2	6.4	5.5	87.2	1 185	247	245	2 953	40.6	56.6	2.9
Beaver	472.0	2 542	48.5	4.0	3.0	5.8	3.9	1 106.6	5 960	409	613	8 185	52.9	44.1	3.0
Bedford	94.6	1 920	68.8	3.8	0.6	0.4	4.8	76.7	1 556	138	167	2 192	28.2	70.0	1.9
Berks	906.5	2 560	55.6	3.1	2.9	6.8	2.9	1 461.7	4 129	1 168	1 220	18 012	43.8	52.7	3.5
Blair	242.1	1 849	59.3	0.3	2.9	5.5	3.7	328.0	2 505	962	437	7 463	34.9	62.9	2.2
Bradford	156.0	2 504	55.0	4.2	1.3	7.3	4.7	445.6	7 154	200	209	3 037	33.9	62.8	3.3
Bucks	1 463.3	2 512	58.9	3.0	4.0	2.7	4.7	1 563.1	2 683	1 510	1 997	19 566	50.5	46.3	3.3
Butler	341.1	2 016	60.0	3.5	1.5	3.7	3.9	575.4	3 401	1 391	580	7 487	35.4	62.1	2.5
Cambria	377.0	2 395	46.9	3.7	1.6	9.3	3.1	813.4	5 167	1 247	656	8 565	50.3	46.4	3.3
Cameron	13.3	2 324	50.0	0.4	1.2	3.5	7.5	9.6	1 683	17	19	382	34.7	61.6	3.7
Carbon	116.2	1 976	52.3	0.3	2.2	8.0	3.4	123.7	2 103	133	198	2 608	50.1	45.7	4.2
Centre	225.8	1 698	54.9	3.5	2.9	3.9	3.7	243.4	1 830	495	532	32 822	43.2	52.8	4.0
Chester	991.7	2 381	57.1	5.8	3.0	3.2	3.2	1 377.1	3 306	1 968	1 444	16 963	43.7	53.4	2.9
Clarion	105.2	2 517	73.6	0.7	0.8	0.2	4.1	101.8	2 434	113	140	3 452	35.4	61.8	2.7
Clearfield	147.1	1 824	70.9	1.1	1.3	1.3	5.0	146.0	1 810	262	273	4 442	38.3	58.9	2.9
Clinton	84.1	2 281	53.2	0.5	1.3	2.3	4.0	88.5	2 400	139	123	2 558	46.0	50.6	3.5
Columbia	120.1	1 869	66.3	0.0	2.4	0.4	4.4	76.1	1 185	161	215	4 286	41.0	55.2	3.7
Crawford	171.9	1 925	51.4	5.2	1.7	5.5	5.2	139.6	1 563	282	300	4 202	39.8	56.6	3.7
Cumberland	449.5	2 163	64.1	2.8	2.6	3.3	3.3	443.8	2 135	6 714	1 491	10 827	35.3	62.2	2.5
Dauphin	762.3	3 101	46.8	5.0	3.1	7.4	3.2	1 236.1	5 029	2 868	894	39 082	44.1	53.3	2.6
Delaware	1 385.4	2 551	46.6	3.9	4.5	5.5	2.4	2 533.1	4 665	2 241	1 864	20 972	54.4	42.7	3.0
Elk	63.5	1 819	52.7	5.6	2.3	2.6	6.5	69.6	1 994	107	115	1 320	42.4	54.1	3.5
Erie	657.1	2 352	51.9	5.6	3.9	5.4	3.4	883.8	3 163	1 639	982	14 240	52.9	43.6	3.5
Fayette	217.8	1 501	63.7	6.1	1.4	1.3	4.4	157.1	1 083	501	486	5 188	56.8	40.4	2.7
Forest	10.5	2 141	57.5	0.2	1.0	1.5	8.6	4.4	888	70	17	345	36.9	60.1	3.0
Franklin	194.0	1 523	57.6	4.4	2.2	5.9	4.3	186.0	1 460	2 151	437	5 402	30.5	67.5	2.1
Fulton	24.4	1 690	70.1	0.1	0.5	0.6	7.3	28.0	1 939	35	49	708	27.0	71.0	2.1
Greene	89.4	2 119	66.0	0.4	0.6	0.3	5.7	151.5	3 590	131	141	2 564	53.0	43.2	3.8
Huntingdon	69.4	1 537	64.7	0.6	1.4	1.6	5.4	78.1	1 729	130	150	2 869	31.8	65.2	3.0
Indiana	159.9	1 793	65.8	0.1	1.1	5.1	4.3	220.0	2 467	274	313	6 932	43.5	53.5	3.0
Jefferson	85.3	1 831	68.5	0.1	2.1	0.0	5.2	45.6	980	125	155	1 938	31.7	65.3	3.0
Juniata	22.6	1 031	67.4	2.4	0.8	2.0	8.4	3.1	143	79	74	580	30.6	66.9	2.5
Lackawanna	490.1	2 329	47.8	0.2	3.3	3.9	3.6	688.0	3 269	1 154	703	9 775	59.6	36.4	3.9
Lancaster	1 006.5	2 217	55.1	2.5	3.2	4.2	3.5	1 478.9	3 257	1 606	1 545	16 971	31.4	66.1	2.5
Lawrence	176.2	1 846	55.7	5.5	2.3	5.0	3.8	156.4	1 638	478	318	4 081	52.0	45.6	2.4
Lebanon	238.6	2 036	58.0	3.5	2.7	7.4	3.6	313.5	2 675	1 986	417	4 740	35.1	62.2	2.7
Lehigh	847.0	2 845	44.3	2.6	2.5	10.2	3.1	1 952.1	6 557	1 379	1 036	14 258	48.7	47.7	3.5
Luzerne	657.1	2 069	59.9	0.3	3.0	5.7	3.7	886.8	2 792	3 452	1 088	14 807	52.0	43.8	4.2
Lycoming	245.0	2 070	56.5	0.1	2.3	3.2	4.7	326.2	2 755	646	394	5 572	34.0	62.8	3.2
McKean	131.3	2 805	61.0	0.2	1.3	5.9	3.9	133.1	2 843	579	154	2 296	34.9	61.1	4.1
Mercer	253.9	2 080	63.9	4.1	2.4	1.8	4.2	227.7	1 866	299	408	5 396	48.9	47.5	3.6
Mifflin	78.3	1 659	64.9	1.0	2.3	0.3	3.9	67.6	1 433	108	158	1 635	33.1	64.3	2.6
Monroe	292.3	2 386	68.9	0.1	2.1	3.5	3.6	406.6	3 318	3 201	443	6 707	46.8	49.6	3.6
Montgomery	1 837.6	2 579	54.2	3.8	4.4	2.0	2.9	2 865.2	4 021	4 571	3 688	28 760	53.5	43.8	2.7
Montour	41.9	2 333	48.3	0.5	2.3	0.8	4.0	201.9	11 234	38	59	1 346	36.3	61.0	2.7
Northampton	704.9	2 740	52.8	2.5	3.1	6.3	2.5	1 078.2	4 191	1 335	872	11 208	50.7	45.3	4.0
Northumberland	190.3	2 001	51.3	5.1	2.2	7.8	4.5	192.1	2 020	215	312	4 409	41.1	54.6	4.4
Perry	65.7	1 488	67.3	0.2	1.0	0.1	6.8	58.9	1 333	95	149	1 774	27.7	69.6	2.6
Philadelphia	5 669.8	3 906	29.4	8.6	7.2	5.3	1.8	7 942.6	5 472	35 306	5 492	81 463	80.0	18.0	2.0
Pike	62.0	1 587	57.9	0.2	2.0	1.3	4.4	62.2	1 590	124	139	1 715	42.2	53.8	4.0

1. Based on the resident population estimated as of July 1 of the year shown. 2. Data subject to copyright.

Table B. States and Counties — **Land Area and Population**

STATE/ County code	MSA/ PMSA/ NECMA code[1]	County Type[2]	STATE County	Land area,[3] (sq km) 2000	Population and population characteristics, 2000												
					Total persons	Rank	Per square kilometer	White	Black	Am. Indian, Alaska Native	Asian and Pacific Islander	Percent Hispanic[4]	Under 5 years	5 to 17 years	18 to 24 years	25 to 34 years	35 to 44 years	45 to 54 years
				1	2	3	4	5	6	7	8	9	10	11	12	13	14	15
			PENNSYLVANIA—Cont'd															
42 105	...	7	Potter	2 800	18 080	1 894	6.5	98.7	0.4	0.6	0.6	0.6	6.2	19.8	6.9	11.4	14.7	13.8
42 107	...	4	Schuylkill	2 016	150 336	359	74.6	97.0	2.2	0.2	0.5	1.1	4.9	16.0	7.2	13.0	15.3	14.1
42 109	...	7	Snyder	858	37 546	1 175	43.8	98.4	0.9	0.2	0.6	1.0	5.6	18.4	11.2	12.2	15.2	13.5
42 111	3680	3	Somerset	2 783	80 023	641	28.8	97.8	1.7	0.2	0.3	0.7	5.2	17.0	7.6	12.4	15.4	14.3
42 113	...	8	Sullivan	1 165	6 556	2 732	5.6	96.3	2.4	1.2	0.3	1.1	4.3	16.5	7.9	9.4	14.7	13.1
42 115	...	8	Susquehanna	2 131	42 238	1 053	19.8	99.1	0.4	0.5	0.3	0.7	5.7	19.8	6.7	10.9	16.2	14.3
42 117	...	6	Tioga	2 936	41 373	1 069	14.1	98.7	0.8	0.6	0.4	0.5	5.4	18.3	10.6	10.9	14.5	13.4
42 119	...	6	Union	820	41 624	1 065	50.8	91.2	7.3	0.5	1.6	3.9	4.8	15.3	13.9	14.7	16.2	12.9
42 121	...	4	Venango	1 748	57 565	829	32.9	98.3	1.4	0.5	0.3	0.5	5.7	18.6	7.2	11.0	15.6	14.8
42 123	...	6	Warren	2 288	43 863	1 020	19.2	99.2	0.3	0.5	0.4	0.3	5.7	18.5	6.4	11.3	15.7	14.8
42 125	6280	0	Washington	2 220	202 897	271	91.4	96.0	3.7	0.3	0.6	0.6	5.5	16.6	7.7	11.4	15.7	15.0
42 127	...	6	Wayne	1 889	47 722	956	25.3	97.3	1.8	0.5	0.4	1.7	5.6	18.4	6.1	11.0	15.9	14.4
42 129	6280	0	Westmoreland	2 656	369 993	158	139.3	97.2	2.3	0.3	0.6	0.5	5.2	16.8	6.8	11.4	16.1	15.1
42 131	7560	2	Wyoming	1 029	28 080	1 449	27.3	98.9	0.7	0.4	0.4	0.7	5.8	19.7	8.0	12.3	15.7	15.0
42 133	9280	2	York	2 343	381 751	152	162.9	93.7	4.2	0.4	1.1	3.0	6.1	18.5	7.5	13.1	17.2	14.6
44 000	...	X	RHODE ISLAND	2 706	1 048 319	X	387.4	86.9	5.5	1.0	2.9	8.7	6.1	17.5	10.2	13.4	16.2	13.5
44 001	6483	2	Bristol	64	50 648	913	791.4	97.7	1.0	0.4	1.4	1.1	5.4	17.5	9.5	10.7	16.7	14.3
44 003	6483	2	Kent	441	167 090	323	378.9	96.7	1.3	0.7	1.7	1.7	5.9	17.3	7.0	13.0	17.5	14.9
44 005	...	4	Newport	269	85 433	611	317.6	93.0	4.7	1.0	1.9	2.8	5.8	16.7	8.4	12.9	17.0	15.2
44 007	6483	2	Providence	1 070	621 602	86	580.9	80.7	8.0	1.1	3.6	13.4	6.3	17.7	11.1	14.1	15.6	12.5
44 009	6483	2	Washington	862	123 546	436	143.3	95.9	1.5	1.5	1.9	1.4	5.9	17.5	11.2	11.5	16.9	15.1
45 000	...	X	SOUTH CAROLINA	77 983	4 012 012	X	51.4	68.0	29.9	0.7	1.2	2.4	6.6	18.6	10.2	14.0	15.6	13.7
45 001	...	6	Abbeville	1 316	26 167	1 510	19.9	68.9	30.6	0.4	0.3	0.8	6.7	18.6	9.5	12.3	14.4	14.1
45 003	0600	2	Aiken	2 778	142 552	382	51.3	72.3	26.0	0.9	0.9	2.1	6.7	19.5	8.8	12.8	16.1	14.0
45 005	...	7	Allendale	1 057	11 211	2 355	10.6	27.6	71.3	0.3	0.4	1.6	6.9	19.7	9.8	13.5	14.7	14.3
45 007	3160	2	Anderson	1 860	165 740	325	89.1	82.3	16.9	0.5	0.7	1.1	6.7	17.9	8.4	13.5	15.5	14.0
45 009	...	7	Bamberg	1 019	16 658	1 979	16.3	36.8	62.8	0.4	0.4	0.7	6.2	19.2	12.9	11.5	13.1	13.8
45 011	...	6	Barnwell	1 420	23 478	1 616	16.5	55.8	43.0	0.7	0.6	1.4	7.1	21.0	8.7	12.4	15.5	13.9
45 013	...	5	Beaufort	1 520	120 937	449	79.6	71.8	24.5	0.6	1.3	6.8	6.7	16.6	12.0	13.6	13.6	11.6
45 015	1440	2	Berkeley	2 843	142 651	381	50.2	69.4	27.2	1.0	2.6	2.8	7.2	20.8	11.7	14.7	16.5	12.9
45 017	...	8	Calhoun	985	15 185	2 076	15.4	50.6	48.9	0.4	0.4	1.4	6.3	18.7	7.4	11.9	15.1	15.8
45 019	1440	2	Charleston	2 379	309 969	184	130.3	62.8	35.0	0.6	1.5	2.4	6.4	17.3	12.0	14.9	15.4	13.3
45 021	3160	2	Cherokee	1 017	52 537	887	51.7	77.6	20.8	0.5	0.6	2.1	7.2	18.7	9.0	14.6	14.9	13.8
45 023	...	6	Chester	1 504	34 068	1 279	22.7	60.4	38.9	0.6	0.4	0.7	6.7	20.2	8.4	13.1	15.1	14.0
45 025	...	6	Chesterfield	2 068	42 768	1 041	20.7	65.0	33.6	0.7	0.5	2.3	6.8	19.9	8.5	13.7	15.3	14.3
45 027	...	6	Clarendon	1 573	32 502	1 331	20.7	45.2	53.4	0.4	0.5	1.7	6.1	19.7	10.5	11.2	14.0	14.0
45 029	...	6	Colleton	2 736	38 264	1 158	14.0	56.1	42.5	1.0	0.5	1.4	6.9	20.6	8.0	12.2	14.7	14.3
45 031	...	4	Darlington	1 453	67 394	726	46.4	57.4	42.0	0.4	0.3	1.0	6.9	19.4	9.0	13.2	15.0	14.7
45 033	...	6	Dillon	1 049	30 722	1 379	29.3	50.9	45.7	2.6	0.6	1.8	7.4	21.7	9.5	12.6	14.9	13.6
45 035	1440	2	Dorchester	1 489	96 413	537	64.8	72.1	25.6	1.2	1.7	1.8	6.7	22.2	7.7	14.0	17.7	14.4
45 037	0600	2	Edgefield	1 300	24 595	1 571	18.9	57.3	41.8	0.6	0.5	2.0	6.0	18.1	9.8	15.0	17.1	14.4
45 039	...	6	Fairfield	1 778	23 454	1 619	13.2	40.0	59.4	0.4	0.3	1.1	6.7	19.4	8.6	12.6	15.2	14.9
45 041	2655	3	Florence	2 072	125 761	432	60.7	59.2	39.6	0.5	1.0	1.1	6.5	19.4	9.7	13.6	15.3	14.4
45 043	...	6	Georgetown	2 110	55 797	846	26.4	60.0	38.8	0.3	0.5	1.6	6.2	18.9	7.7	11.6	14.3	14.5
45 045	3160	2	Greenville	2 046	379 616	154	185.5	78.5	18.7	0.5	1.7	3.8	6.8	17.8	9.6	15.0	16.2	13.8
45 047	...	5	Greenwood	1 180	66 271	736	56.2	66.1	32.0	0.4	1.0	2.9	6.9	18.6	10.4	13.8	14.4	13.0
45 049	...	7	Hampton	1 450	21 386	1 719	14.7	42.3	55.9	0.4	0.2	2.6	6.7	20.9	8.5	14.3	15.4	13.7
45 051	5330	3	Horry	2 936	196 629	281	67.0	82.0	15.9	0.8	1.1	2.6	5.7	15.6	9.4	14.2	15.1	13.7
45 053	...	8	Jasper	1 699	20 678	1 752	12.2	42.8	53.0	0.6	0.7	5.8	7.2	19.5	10.3	14.8	15.9	12.3
45 055	...	6	Kershaw	1 881	52 647	885	28.0	72.3	26.6	0.7	0.5	1.7	6.6	19.6	7.6	12.5	16.3	14.7
45 057	...	6	Lancaster	1 422	61 351	793	43.1	71.6	27.2	0.5	0.5	1.6	6.5	18.9	8.6	14.5	15.7	13.9
45 059	...	6	Laurens	1 852	69 567	710	37.6	72.2	26.4	0.6	0.4	1.9	6.6	18.7	9.2	13.6	14.9	13.8
45 061	...	6	Lee	1 063	20 119	1 787	18.9	35.3	63.8	0.4	0.4	1.3	6.3	19.4	10.0	13.2	16.0	14.4
45 063	1760	2	Lexington	1 811	216 014	260	119.3	85.0	12.9	0.7	1.3	1.9	6.8	19.2	8.3	14.4	17.2	14.7
45 065	...	8	McCormick	931	9 958	2 450	10.7	45.1	54.3	0.4	0.7	0.9	4.2	15.3	8.3	12.9	14.7	14.6
45 067	...	6	Marion	1 267	35 466	1 235	28.0	42.0	56.7	0.5	0.4	1.8	7.0	20.7	9.7	12.6	14.2	14.6
45 069	...	7	Marlboro	1 242	28 818	1 426	23.2	45.2	51.1	3.9	0.4	0.7	6.6	19.5	9.3	13.9	15.5	13.8
45 071	...	6	Newberry	1 634	36 108	1 210	22.1	64.7	33.4	0.6	0.5	4.2	6.4	17.7	9.8	12.9	14.7	13.8
45 073	...	6	Oconee	1 620	66 215	738	40.9	89.9	8.6	0.6	0.6	2.4	6.0	16.8	8.0	12.8	14.5	14.1
45 075	...	4	Orangeburg	2 865	91 582	559	32.0	37.6	61.3	0.8	0.6	1.0	6.5	19.4	11.9	11.7	14.4	13.4
45 077	3160	2	Pickens	1 287	110 757	490	86.1	91.0	7.1	0.5	1.4	1.7	6.1	16.2	17.5	13.3	14.3	12.4
45 079	1760	2	Richland	1 959	320 677	180	163.7	51.2	45.8	0.6	2.3	2.7	6.3	17.9	13.8	15.6	16.0	13.2
45 081	...	6	Saluda	1 172	19 181	1 835	16.4	66.3	30.3	0.4	0.1	7.3	6.5	18.4	9.2	13.0	14.6	13.5
45 083	3160	2	Spartanburg	2 100	253 791	222	120.9	75.9	21.1	0.6	1.8	2.8	6.6	18.2	9.2	14.3	15.6	14.0

1. MSA = Metropolitan Statistical Area. PMSA = Primary MSA. NECMA = New England County Metropolitan Area. See Appendix A for explanation of these concepts. See Appendix B for list of metropolitan areas identified by type, with component counties.   2. County typology code from the Economic Research Service of USDA. See Appendix A for definition.   3. Dry land or land partially or temporarily covered by water.   4. Hispanic persons may be of any race.

Table B. States and Counties — Population and Households

STATE County	55 to 64 years	65 to 74 years	75 years and over	Percent female	2001	1990	1990–2000	2000–2001	Births	Deaths	Net migration	Number	Percent change, 1990–2000	Persons per house-hold	Female family house-holder[1]	One person
	16	17	18	19	20	21	22	23	24	25	26	27	28	29	30	31
PENNSYLVANIA—Cont'd																
Potter	10.6	8.6	8.1	50.7	18 154	16 717	8.2	0.4	278	232	33	7 005	12.2	2.54	7.6	24.7
Schuylkill	9.7	9.7	10.2	50.2	149 176	152 585	-1.5	-0.8	1 673	2 595	-153	60 530	-0.4	2.36	10.2	29.9
Snyder	9.8	7.7	6.4	51.1	37 720	36 680	2.4	0.5	514	376	42	13 654	7.0	2.58	7.4	22.4
Somerset	10.0	8.9	9.1	50.1	79 553	78 218	2.3	-0.6	1 003	1 170	-267	31 222	5.6	2.45	8.5	26.1
Sullivan	12.2	11.3	10.6	49.5	6 532	6 104	7.4	-0.4	64	125	39	2 660	16.7	2.30	6.8	29.3
Susquehanna	11.0	8.2	7.3	50.3	42 165	40 380	4.6	-0.2	541	551	-46	16 529	10.9	2.53	8.6	24.3
Tioga	10.9	8.4	7.5	51.0	41 621	41 126	0.6	0.6	505	563	320	15 925	6.4	2.48	8.6	24.4
Union	8.7	6.6	6.8	44.7	41 701	36 176	15.1	0.2	457	413	52	13 178	12.7	2.50	6.9	25.3
Venango	10.3	9.2	7.6	51.2	57 098	59 381	-3.1	-0.8	798	822	-427	22 747	1.5	2.45	9.9	26.2
Warren	11.0	8.8	7.8	51.0	43 593	45 050	-2.6	-0.6	585	644	-193	17 696	2.6	2.42	8.4	27.2
Washington	10.0	8.9	9.1	52.0	203 737	204 584	-0.8	0.4	2 542	3 037	1 411	81 130	3.3	2.44	10.3	27.0
Wayne	11.1	9.5	8.0	49.8	48 392	39 944	19.5	1.4	618	693	748	18 350	25.4	2.50	8.9	25.2
Westmoreland	10.3	9.3	9.0	51.8	368 983	370 321	-0.1	-0.3	4 421	5 516	297	149 813	4.0	2.41	9.6	26.9
Wyoming	10.3	7.0	6.2	50.4	28 055	28 076	0.0	-0.1	385	341	-58	10 762	7.6	2.55	9.3	24.1
York	9.4	7.1	6.4	50.8	386 299	339 574	12.4	1.2	5 399	4 032	3 292	148 219	15.2	2.52	9.0	23.3
RHODE ISLAND	8.5	7.0	7.5	52.0	1 058 920	1 003 464	4.5	1.0	15 375	12 571	8 167	408 424	8.1	2.47	12.9	28.6
Bristol	9.1	8.1	8.6	51.8	51 173	48 859	3.7	1.0	616	641	560	19 033	8.4	2.52	9.9	25.1
Kent	9.2	7.5	7.5	52.0	169 224	161 143	3.7	1.3	2 330	2 127	1 960	67 320	8.5	2.45	10.5	27.6
Newport	9.6	7.3	7.1	51.4	85 218	87 194	-2.0	-0.3	1 136	911	-415	35 228	7.8	2.35	10.3	29.9
Providence	7.9	6.9	7.7	52.1	627 314	596 270	4.2	0.9	9 575	7 608	4 054	239 936	6.0	2.48	14.9	29.8
Washington	9.2	6.5	6.2	51.5	125 991	109 998	12.3	2.0	1 718	1 284	2 008	46 907	19.3	2.52	9.4	24.1
SOUTH CAROLINA	9.3	6.7	5.4	51.4	4 063 011	3 486 310	15.1	1.3	71 330	46 194	26 787	1 533 854	21.9	2.53	14.8	25.0
Abbeville	9.6	7.9	6.8	52.1	26 314	23 862	9.7	0.6	454	302	1	10 131	15.4	2.51	15.3	25.3
Aiken	9.4	7.3	5.6	51.8	143 905	120 991	17.8	0.9	2 333	1 642	716	55 587	23.8	2.53	13.8	25.2
Allendale	8.5	6.4	6.3	47.9	11 045	11 727	-4.4	-1.5	252	165	-258	3 915	3.3	2.56	25.8	30.0
Anderson	10.3	7.4	6.2	51.7	168 985	145 177	14.2	2.0	2 819	2 141	2 573	65 649	18.3	2.48	12.8	24.3
Bamberg	9.4	7.3	6.6	53.0	16 393	16 902	-1.4	-1.6	306	259	-313	6 123	9.6	2.55	21.3	27.8
Barnwell	8.8	6.9	5.7	51.9	23 525	20 293	15.7	0.2	456	351	-55	9 021	27.1	2.57	19.3	25.6
Beaufort	10.5	9.4	6.1	49.4	125 212	86 425	39.9	3.5	2 293	1 122	3 106	45 532	48.3	2.51	11.0	21.5
Berkeley	8.2	4.9	3.0	49.2	144 078	128 658	10.9	1.0	2 755	1 100	-169	49 922	17.8	2.75	14.2	19.4
Calhoun	11.0	7.6	6.2	52.6	15 351	12 753	19.1	1.1	223	201	145	5 917	31.9	2.54	15.8	24.5
Charleston	8.7	6.5	5.4	51.7	312 007	295 159	5.0	0.7	5 933	3 293	-415	123 326	15.2	2.42	15.9	28.3
Cherokee	9.4	6.8	5.6	51.6	53 161	44 506	18.0	1.2	896	650	395	20 495	24.5	2.53	15.4	25.0
Chester	9.8	6.9	5.7	52.0	34 055	32 170	5.9	0.0	628	401	-237	12 880	12.5	2.62	18.6	24.2
Chesterfield	9.6	6.8	5.2	51.8	43 014	38 575	10.9	0.6	715	580	123	16 557	17.9	2.54	16.3	25.9
Clarendon	10.7	8.2	5.8	50.9	32 789	28 450	14.2	0.9	539	415	170	11 812	23.8	2.62	19.8	24.6
Colleton	10.4	7.3	5.6	52.1	38 546	34 377	11.3	0.7	697	518	111	14 470	20.2	2.62	16.8	24.0
Darlington	9.7	6.6	5.5	52.7	67 812	61 851	9.0	0.6	1 273	951	127	25 793	17.2	2.57	18.7	25.1
Dillon	8.8	6.3	5.2	53.4	30 927	29 114	5.5	0.7	648	402	-29	11 199	13.3	2.71	22.3	25.1
Dorchester	8.6	5.2	3.9	51.1	98 746	83 060	16.1	2.4	1 493	946	1 787	34 709	23.0	2.72	14.6	20.2
Edgefield	8.8	6.0	4.9	47.0	24 470	18 360	34.0	-0.5	362	265	-217	8 270	28.7	2.66	15.5	22.4
Fairfield	9.4	7.2	6.0	52.4	23 703	22 295	5.2	1.1	433	318	139	8 774	17.5	2.63	20.0	24.4
Florence	9.2	6.3	5.5	53.0	126 607	114 344	10.0	0.7	2 503	1 638	35	47 147	17.2	2.59	18.1	24.5
Georgetown	11.7	8.7	6.2	52.1	57 189	46 302	20.5	2.5	1 015	682	1 053	21 659	33.1	2.55	15.1	23.3
Greenville	9.1	6.3	5.5	51.3	386 693	320 127	18.6	1.9	6 777	4 149	4 525	149 556	21.7	2.47	12.3	26.8
Greenwood	9.2	7.3	6.4	53.1	66 746	59 567	11.3	0.7	1 211	869	159	25 729	13.2	2.49	16.1	26.3
Hampton	8.4	6.8	5.4	49.1	21 411	18 186	17.6	0.1	406	254	-120	7 444	17.7	2.64	18.8	25.8
Horry	11.3	9.4	5.6	50.9	202 425	144 053	36.5	2.9	3 041	2 274	4 994	81 800	46.7	2.37	11.5	25.8
Jasper	9.0	6.2	4.8	47.4	20 818	15 487	33.5	0.7	382	257	24	7 042	32.9	2.75	18.2	23.2
Kershaw	9.8	7.3	5.6	51.7	53 409	43 599	20.8	1.4	876	595	480	20 188	27.7	2.58	13.6	22.6
Lancaster	9.7	6.7	5.3	50.5	61 509	54 516	12.5	0.3	1 010	739	-84	23 178	17.2	2.56	15.5	23.7
Laurens	10.0	7.1	6.0	51.6	70 138	58 132	19.7	0.8	1 115	929	402	26 290	27.3	2.55	15.6	24.6
Lee	8.2	6.6	5.8	49.7	20 090	18 437	9.1	-0.1	379	297	-105	6 886	13.7	2.68	23.8	25.9
Lexington	9.1	5.7	4.5	51.4	220 240	167 526	28.9	2.0	3 818	2 082	2 510	83 240	35.1	2.56	11.6	22.5
McCormick	13.5	9.7	6.8	46.8	10 121	8 868	12.3	1.6	114	167	214	3 558	30.3	2.39	17.6	24.4
Marion	9.2	6.6	5.5	53.8	35 191	33 899	4.6	-0.8	683	534	-422	13 301	13.0	2.64	23.6	25.4
Marlboro	9.0	6.8	5.5	50.9	28 653	29 716	-3.0	-0.6	563	463	-257	10 478	3.1	2.59	22.2	26.9
Newberry	9.9	7.4	7.4	51.8	36 344	33 172	8.9	0.7	650	463	68	14 026	13.9	2.50	16.1	26.5
Oconee	12.2	9.4	6.2	50.8	67 407	57 494	15.2	1.8	976	805	1 027	27 283	22.0	2.40	10.1	24.7
Orangeburg	9.5	7.2	6.0	53.5	91 337	84 804	8.0	-0.3	1 797	1 236	-787	34 118	18.0	2.58	20.3	26.0
Pickens	8.8	6.1	5.3	50.1	112 112	93 896	18.0	1.2	1 708	1 175	852	41 306	23.6	2.50	9.4	23.3
Richland	7.3	5.3	4.5	51.7	323 303	286 321	12.0	0.8	5 891	3 204	126	120 101	18.2	2.44	16.3	29.1
Saluda	10.3	7.7	6.8	50.4	19 114	16 441	16.7	-0.3	337	261	-141	7 127	22.4	2.65	14.5	22.5
Spartanburg	9.5	6.7	5.8	51.4	257 262	226 793	11.9	1.4	4 268	3 200	2 468	97 735	15.7	2.52	13.8	24.8

1. No spouse present.

Table B. States and Counties — Vital Statistics, Health Resources, and Crime

STATE County	Births, average 1997–1999		Deaths, average 1997–1999				Physicians,[4] 2000		Hospitals,[4] 1998			Medicare enrollees 2000	Serious crimes known to police, 2000[6]	
			Number		Rate					Beds			Total	
	Total	Rate[1]	Total	Infant[2]	Total[1]	Infant[3]	Number	Rate[5]	Number	Number	Rate[5]		Number	Rate[7]
	32	33	34	35	36	37	38	39	40	41	42	43	44	45
PENNSYLVANIA—Cont'd														
Potter	210	12.2	198	NA	11.5	NA	29	160	1	120	698	3 371	321	2 276
Schuylkill	1 432	9.6	2 049	11	13.8	7.7	188	125	4	605	408	32 426	2 406	1 796
Snyder	427	11.2	303	NA	8.0	NA	34	91	0	0	0	6 037	654	1 808
Somerset	829	10.3	922	NA	11.5	NA	86	107	3	230	287	15 658	1 006	1 312
Sullivan	50	8.2	106	NA	17.4	NA	3	46	0	0	0	1 497	127	1 937
Susquehanna	462	11.0	462	NA	11.0	NA	33	78	2	139	330	7 406	613	1 715
Tioga	421	10.1	444	NA	10.7	NA	49	118	1	103	248	7 570	523	1 321
Union	381	9.3	337	NA	8.2	NA	86	207	1	135	330	5 927	314	826
Venango	627	10.8	658	NA	11.4	NA	100	174	2	308	532	11 146	1 333	2 316
Warren	486	11.1	509	NA	11.6	NA	73	166	1	105	239	8 069	674	1 655
Washington	2 129	10.4	2 412	12	11.7	5.5	292	144	3	713	347	41 010	3 676	1 945
Wayne	513	11.3	544	NA	12.0	NA	63	132	1	95	210	11 200	977	2 120
Westmoreland	3 704	9.9	4 330	20	11.6	5.4	621	168	6	1 169	314	71 995	5 751	1 567
Wyoming	349	11.9	272	NA	9.3	NA	25	89	1	63	216	4 516	418	1 603
York	4 505	12.1	3 174	19	8.5	4.3	641	168	3	768	206	55 531	7 790	2 393
RHODE ISLAND	12 473	12.6	9 711	82	9.8	6.6	2 859	273	10	2 814	285	171 595	36 444	3 476
Bristol	520	10.6	481	NA	9.8	NA	74	146	0	0	0	8 932	1 011	1 996
Kent	1 811	11.2	1 629	10	10.1	5.5	334	200	1	359	222	29 122	4 566	2 733
Newport	984	11.9	737	NA	8.9	NA	153	179	1	200	241	13 701	2 844	3 329
Providence	7 762	13.5	5 889	61	10.3	7.9	2 078	334	6	2 030	354	102 535	25 102	4 038
Washington	1 396	11.6	975	5	8.1	3.6	220	178	2	225	186	17 226	2 827	2 288
SOUTH CAROLINA	52 747	13.7	34 857	526	9.1	10.0	6 704	167	64	11 249	293	567 854	209 482	5 221
Abbeville	343	13.9	229	NA	9.3	NA	20	76	0	0	0	3 874	1 005	3 841
Aiken	1 816	13.5	1 235	16	9.2	8.6	132	93	2	273	204	20 556	5 582	3 916
Allendale	160	13.9	122	NA	10.6	NA	18	161	1	78	681	1 601	356	3 175
Anderson	2 088	13.0	1 624	26	10.1	12.3	256	154	1	445	277	26 925	7 461	4 526
Bamberg	213	12.9	186	NA	11.3	NA	13	78	1	84	509	2 527	608	3 650
Barnwell	340	15.6	240	NA	11.0	NA	14	60	1	35	161	3 488	907	3 863
Beaufort	1 693	15.5	864	11	7.9	6.7	233	193	3	234	215	19 040	6 211	5 136
Berkeley	2 175	15.8	840	18	6.1	8.4	40	28	0	0	0	11 824	6 344	4 447
Calhoun	174	12.4	147	NA	10.5	NA	2	13	0	0	0	1 794	416	2 740
Charleston	4 487	14.2	2 491	54	7.9	12.0	1 414	456	7	1 760	556	42 929	22 335	7 206
Cherokee	690	14.0	487	7	9.9	9.7	42	80	1	125	254	7 420	2 418	4 602
Chester	475	13.8	326	NA	9.5	NA	20	59	1	163	474	5 499	1 763	5 175
Chesterfield	549	13.3	445	NA	10.8	NA	26	61	1	66	161	6 320	1 756	4 106
Clarendon	389	12.6	319	NA	10.4	NA	17	52	1	56	182	5 013	1 239	3 812
Colleton	510	13.6	372	NA	10.0	NA	34	89	1	116	310	5 840	2 120	5 540
Darlington	908	13.7	730	12	11.0	13.2	59	88	2	150	226	9 585	3 818	5 665
Dillon	467	15.7	319	NA	10.7	NA	22	72	1	90	303	4 555	2 236	7 278
Dorchester	1 260	14.3	696	11	7.9	9.0	66	68	1	111	126	10 944	3 903	4 048
Edgefield	268	13.4	200	NA	10.0	NA	5	20	0	0	0	2 557	604	2 456
Fairfield	314	14.0	267	NA	11.9	NA	10	43	1	41	183	3 525	1 211	5 163
Florence	1 748	14.0	1 286	20	10.3	11.6	290	231	4	765	612	18 720	8 887	7 120
Georgetown	724	13.5	526	9	9.8	12.4	72	129	1	141	262	11 983	2 827	5 067
Greenville	4 959	14.0	3 079	36	8.7	7.3	817	215	4	1 314	371	53 501	18 946	4 991
Greenwood	895	14.1	678	12	10.7	13.4	161	243	1	355	558	11 090	3 847	5 805
Hampton	299	15.6	187	NA	9.8	NA	10	47	1	36	188	3 679	744	3 479
Horry	2 206	12.7	1 685	19	9.7	8.5	272	138	3	480	275	29 998	16 129	8 203
Jasper	277	16.2	168	NA	9.8	NA	20	97	0	0	0	2 283	1 700	8 221
Kershaw	643	13.2	464	NA	9.5	NA	52	99	1	198	407	8 299	1 944	3 693
Lancaster	783	13.8	588	NA	10.0	NA	51	83	1	166	282	8 633	3 633	5 922
Laurens	845	13.4	704	9	11.2	10.3	42	60	1	80	126	10 010	3 377	4 854
Lee	242	11.9	206	NA	10.1	NA	3	15	0	0	0	2 805	776	3 857
Lexington	2 897	14.1	1 545	23	7.5	7.9	221	102	1	287	140	24 587	8 999	4 166
McCormick	84	8.7	116	NA	12.1	NA	8	80	0	0	0	1 897	240	2 410
Marion	463	13.3	393	NA	11.3	NA	32	90	2	190	549	5 756	1 719	4 885
Marlboro	410	13.8	359	NA	12.1	NA	19	66	1	108	365	4 753	2 144	7 440
Newberry	461	13.4	357	NA	10.4	NA	32	89	1	64	186	6 377	807	2 235
Oconee	771	12.0	598	NA	9.3	NA	66	100	1	195	304	12 289	1 908	2 882
Orangeburg	1 172	13.4	946	17	10.8	14.8	125	136	1	292	332	14 551	6 632	7 332
Pickens	1 315	12.3	865	12	8.1	9.1	91	82	2	132	123	15 706	3 174	2 866
Richland	4 131	13.5	2 454	46	8.0	11.1	1 099	343	4	1 267	413	37 714	19 176	5 980
Saluda	237	13.9	194	NA	11.4	NA	8	42	0	0	0	2 492	480	2 502
Spartanburg	3 206	13.0	2 415	24	9.8	7.6	418	165	3	681	275	39 231	14 486	5 708

1. Per 1,000 estimated resident population, average 1997–1999.   2. Deaths of infants under 1 year old.   3. Deaths of infants under 1 year old per 1,000 live births.   4. Data subject to copyright.   5. Per 100,000 resident population as of July 1 of the year shown.   6. Data for serious crimes have not been adjusted for underreporting; this may affect comparability between geographic areas and over time.   7. Per 100,000 population estimated by the FBI.

Table B. States and Counties — Crime, Education, Money Income, and Poverty

	Serious crimes known to police, 2000[1] (cont'd)		Education						Money income				Income and poverty, 1998			
	Rate[2]		School enrollment and attainment, 1990				Local government expenditures, fiscal 1999[5]		1989				Percent below poverty level			
			Enrollment[3]		Attainment[4] (percent)					Households							
										Median							
STATE County	Violent	Property	Total	Percent private	High school graduate or more	Bachelor's degree or more	Total current expenditures (mil dol)	Current expenditures per student (dollars)	Per capita[6] (dollars)	Dollars	Percent change, 1979–1989 (constant 1989 dollars)	Percent with $100,000 or more	Median household income	All persons	Persons under 18	Persons 5–17 in families
	46	47	48	49	50	51	52	53	54	55	56	57	58	59	60	61

PENNSYLVANIA—Cont'd

Potter	227	2 049	3 821	5.8	73.8	9.8	20.2	6 052	9 905	21 377	-1.8	1.2	32 747	13.8	19.9	20.7
Schuylkill	250	1 546	30 220	16.4	68.4	8.1	149.3	7 241	11 193	23 028	3.0	1.2	33 053	10.4	15.9	14.8
Snyder	218	1 590	8 384	27.6	64.4	10.6	34.7	6 097	10 859	25 864	-0.7	2.0	33 534	9.9	14.1	15.1
Somerset	106	1 206	16 854	8.3	68.9	8.9	81.6	6 374	10 422	21 674	-12.1	1.5	29 982	13.4	18.7	18.9
Sullivan	76	1 861	1 205	6.2	70.2	8.6	7.7	8 322	9 839	20 107	-4.2	1.0	29 657	12.7	16.3	20.9
Susquehanna	145	1 569	9 366	7.0	76.0	11.1	57.1	6 538	10 907	24 736	4.1	1.3	33 684	11.9	17.1	17.1
Tioga	109	1 212	10 837	5.9	72.9	12.6	45.7	6 436	10 290	22 571	-2.3	1.4	32 424	13.1	18.6	18.7
Union	53	773	10 400	40.9	73.1	17.5	65.1	14 510	11 679	27 622	3.9	2.8	38 836	10.5	14.4	14.3
Venango	134	2 182	13 511	10.5	74.2	10.8	71.3	6 556	10 696	22 593	-19.7	1.3	30 149	13.5	19.5	19.8
Warren	91	1 564	9 866	9.0	76.6	10.7	43.0	6 163	12 350	26 351	-4.5	2.1	34 977	10.7	15.8	16.1
Washington	184	1 761	46 605	13.3	73.2	13.6	240.9	7 838	12 744	25 469	-14.0	2.4	36 611	11.2	16.8	16.1
Wayne	226	1 894	8 747	9.9	74.2	13.1	69.9	7 409	11 257	24 912	12.7	1.9	32 539	11.8	17.3	18.0
Westmoreland	153	1 414	83 126	16.1	77.7	15.4	391.7	6 820	12 612	25 736	-13.7	2.1	35 215	10.0	15.3	13.6
Wyoming	119	1 484	7 273	17.5	77.6	13.2	35.0	7 125	11 628	27 207	6.1	1.8	36 826	11.0	15.3	16.8
York	174	2 219	72 386	15.9	72.8	13.9	342.0	6 129	14 544	32 605	5.8	2.7	45 685	6.8	10.8	9.6
RHODE ISLAND	298	3 179	254 635	24.7	72.0	21.3	1 283.9	8 294	14 981	32 181	19.3	4.1	39 907	10.6	16.3	15.6
Bristol	126	1 870	12 290	34.2	73.9	27.4	57.5	8 197	17 897	37 539	20.7	8.0	49 826	6.5	9.4	9.1
Kent	181	2 551	37 497	19.5	76.8	20.5	202.6	8 604	16 390	36 070	16.6	4.7	46 364	6.6	10.6	9.6
Newport	265	3 064	21 798	25.2	82.8	30.1	98.9	8 384	16 819	35 829	26.9	5.2	46 186	7.4	11.7	11.5
Providence	375	3 663	149 473	27.8	67.0	18.3	696.3	7 653	13 871	29 580	19.0	3.2	34 766	13.6	20.8	20.1
Washington	137	2 151	33 577	12.5	82.8	29.1	164.1	8 053	16 182	36 948	21.8	5.2	50 467	6.1	8.3	8.1
SOUTH CAROLINA	805	4 417	913 010	11.6	68.3	16.6	3 759.0	5 656	11 897	26 256	6.5	2.3	33 465	14.3	21.5	20.2
Abbeville	627	3 214	6 030	10.7	58.9	10.8	21.5	5 580	10 214	23 170	0.7	0.6	31 591	13.6	20.9	19.4
Aiken	555	3 361	31 894	11.4	70.7	17.2	121.5	4 969	13 127	29 994	11.8	2.9	39 209	13.8	23.2	19.1
Allendale	1 106	2 069	3 245	5.6	52.3	9.5	14.5	6 861	7 458	15 013	-7.1	1.2	22 731	32.3	40.2	42.7
Anderson	568	3 957	33 898	12.0	64.0	12.9	145.8	5 523	12 027	25 748	-0.5	1.7	35 866	11.0	17.6	14.8
Bamberg	810	2 839	5 435	10.7	59.2	11.2	19.5	6 598	8 438	17 496	-0.4	1.8	25 041	24.2	32.7	33.9
Barnwell	728	3 135	5 341	4.3	59.9	11.9	29.1	5 873	10 611	23 501	10.9	1.9	29 990	19.9	27.2	28.5
Beaufort	781	4 354	19 811	14.8	83.4	26.5	102.3	6 584	15 213	30 450	17.3	5.7	40 220	12.3	20.6	20.4
Berkeley	693	3 755	36 362	10.3	75.4	11.6	139.2	5 277	10 942	29 106	7.2	1.0	37 245	13.3	18.2	18.0
Calhoun	678	2 061	3 068	13.9	61.9	11.7	14.3	6 847	9 983	23 750	13.1	1.2	30 560	17.0	25.7	25.9
Charleston	854	6 352	76 617	16.2	75.5	22.4	243.2	5 536	13 068	26 875	8.2	3.0	36 313	15.4	23.8	23.6
Cherokee	841	3 761	10 400	6.8	57.2	9.3	47.8	5 572	10 406	24 655	-0.6	1.1	32 881	14.1	22.1	20.2
Chester	1 051	4 124	7 895	4.0	56.9	9.1	37.4	5 563	9 806	23 054	-1.2	1.2	30 335	15.7	23.4	22.3
Chesterfield	790	3 316	9 907	5.1	53.9	7.7	44.0	5 469	9 455	21 069	2.4	1.1	28 909	18.0	26.4	24.6
Clarendon	831	2 981	7 371	7.1	54.9	10.2	33.1	5 428	8 181	17 645	-5.2	1.4	25 191	24.3	34.3	32.4
Colleton	1 103	4 438	8 973	8.9	61.7	9.6	40.0	5 740	9 193	20 617	5.4	1.4	26 239	21.8	30.6	29.9
Darlington	662	5 003	15 789	7.6	62.3	12.4	64.2	5 880	10 510	22 642	4.0	1.9	29 027	20.2	29.7	27.6
Dillon	1 149	6 129	7 947	2.9	52.5	8.5	32.3	5 161	8 077	18 365	0.4	1.0	23 794	24.9	34.1	32.7
Dorchester	569	3 479	21 910	13.7	76.7	17.3	98.4	5 183	11 884	30 764	6.9	1.7	37 822	12.0	16.9	17.2
Edgefield	468	1 988	4 803	9.4	62.6	12.2	23.5	5 677	10 651	23 021	13.5	1.3	29 954	17.4	22.6	25.7
Fairfield	1 407	3 756	5 789	7.4	58.1	9.6	30.0	8 160	9 011	21 484	2.0	1.0	28 617	18.1	26.3	24.8
Florence	989	6 130	32 153	8.9	64.3	14.8	121.6	5 415	11 007	24 264	4.0	2.4	30 932	18.7	26.6	24.7
Georgetown	862	4 205	13 007	5.6	63.9	15.6	68.0	6 527	11 084	23 981	-0.1	2.9	31 483	17.5	27.0	25.9
Greenville	791	4 200	79 865	22.0	71.6	21.0	309.7	5 350	13 918	29 088	8.5	3.2	33 882	13.8	21.8	19.8
Greenwood	1 311	4 494	15 478	8.0	64.1	16.0	63.9	5 638	11 429	23 584	-3.7	1.7	33 882	14.3	21.8	19.8
Hampton	814	2 665	5 215	4.3	58.9	8.8	26.7	6 229	8 578	18 615	2.3	0.9	26 278	22.8	32.5	31.6
Horry	1 007	7 195	33 637	7.7	74.3	16.0	170.2	6 342	12 385	24 959	10.4	2.4	31 814	13.7	21.4	21.0
Jasper	1 272	6 949	4 340	18.7	54.5	4.8	16.0	5 598	7 984	18 071	-0.2	0.7	26 406	21.0	22.4	30.9
Kershaw	621	3 071	10 842	9.1	67.8	12.5	52.9	5 566	11 937	28 282	11.9	1.8	35 258	12.6	20.6	17.9
Lancaster	861	5 061	12 893	5.0	60.0	9.6	56.9	5 206	11 041	25 320	-4.1	1.6	33 614	14.0	21.7	21.0
Laurens	1 011	3 844	14 061	13.4	57.4	11.3	51.1	5 449	10 739	24 905	-1.1	1.2	30 265	14.0	22.0	20.1
Lee	1 128	2 729	5 292	9.4	53.5	7.5	18.5	5 762	7 569	18 174	-4.2	0.3	23 364	26.9	37.0	34.8
Lexington	536	3 630	43 506	8.7	77.3	21.0	262.6	5 903	14 259	32 914	7.6	2.9	44 291	9.4	15.3	13.0
McCormick	673	1 737	2 005	17.1	52.5	7.1	8.2	6 659	7 929	19 226	-2.4	1.3	28 452	17.8	27.6	27.5
Marion	816	4 069	9 695	3.9	55.3	9.1	38.0	5 609	8 185	17 825	-6.3	0.8	23 391	23.1	30.7	30.3
Marlboro	1 686	5 753	7 533	3.5	50.9	7.9	29.6	5 444	7 948	18 068	-8.2	0.8	24 171	23.1	31.4	29.9
Newberry	565	1 670	8 270	13.1	62.1	12.5	35.1	5 997	10 487	23 405	-2.9	1.5	31 283	14.4	23.0	21.5
Oconee	458	2 424	13 156	6.5	63.4	13.3	64.7	6 455	12 352	25 723	12.6	1.9	35 881	10.8	17.1	16.0
Orangeburg	1 530	5 802	26 054	11.6	62.4	13.7	100.5	6 189	9 004	20 216	4.7	1.5	27 611	22.1	30.3	27.6
Pickens	291	2 575	30 836	7.7	65.4	16.9	80.7	5 117	11 427	26 336	0.8	1.6	37 025	10.1	14.2	13.4
Richland	870	5 110	83 610	13.6	79.4	28.0	284.4	6 675	13 243	28 848	9.7	3.2	36 884	13.6	20.3	18.5
Saluda	506	1 997	3 983	6.1	59.8	8.0	12.6	5 816	9 814	22 176	9.3	0.8	30 300	15.9	24.4	24.2
Spartanburg	940	4 768	53 949	12.6	63.0	14.3	250.0	6 135	12 218	26 941	6.5	2.1	37 263	11.2	17.4	15.3

1. Data for serious crimes have not been adjusted for underreporting; this may affect comparability between geographic areas and over time.   2. Per 100,000 population estimated by the FBI.   3. All persons 3 years old and over enrolled in nursery school through college.   4. Persons 25 years old and over.   5. Elementary and secondary education expenditures, local government fiscal years ending between July 1, 1998 and June 30, 1999.   6. Based on population enumerated as of April 1, 1990.

Table B. States and Counties — **Personal Income**

STATE County	Personal income, 1999 Total (mil dol)	Percent change, 1998–1999	Per capita[1] Dollars	Per capita[1] Rank	Wages and salaries[2] (mil dol)	Proprietor's income (mil dol)	Dividends, interest, and rent (mil dol)	Transfer payments Total (mil dol)	Government payments to individuals Total (mil dol)	Social Security (mil dol)	Medical payments (mil dol)	Income mainte-nance (mil dol)	Unemploy-ment insurance (mil dol)
	62	63	64	65	66	67	68	69	70	71	72	73	74
PENNSYLVANIA—Cont'd													
Potter	401	8.5	23 458	970	212	65	56	77	73	33	27	7	3
Schuylkill	3 327	3.5	22 363	1 253	1 497	237	601	733	703	309	257	42	31
Snyder	999	7.1	26 367	478	453	95	163	311	303	58	228	8	4
Somerset	1 649	3.5	20 611	1 804	712	226	277	373	357	146	145	27	13
Sullivan	128	2.9	21 163	1 612	42	19	30	32	31	17	10	2	1
Susquehanna	891	4.0	21 108	1 635	220	121	158	161	153	74	51	14	5
Tioga	801	4.4	19 229	2 224	365	83	141	165	156	76	54	15	4
Union	905	5.0	22 325	1 268	548	78	190	172	164	57	91	7	3
Venango	1 452	4.2	25 224	631	642	109	229	486	475	117	314	25	8
Warren	1 012	2.6	23 250	1 030	509	85	177	230	221	87	111	12	5
Washington	5 485	4.4	26 772	431	2 416	396	893	1 071	1 030	427	455	69	28
Wayne	996	5.7	21 610	1 482	372	107	213	208	199	102	68	13	7
Westmoreland	9 550	5.1	25 766	545	4 330	699	1 627	1 807	1 732	755	725	106	60
Wyoming	628	4.2	21 438	1 538	342	77	96	105	99	44	39	8	5
York	9 931	3.9	26 370	477	5 758	881	1 810	1 166	1 091	587	346	76	33
RHODE ISLAND	29 066	5.0	29 335	X	16 771	1 854	5 780	4 813	4 626	1 659	2 096	438	155
Bristol	1 665	4.8	33 901	111	419	70	457	197	188	92	67	9	6
Kent	4 779	4.8	29 476	230	2 518	193	887	737	706	292	284	45	38
Newport	2 740	6.6	33 001	131	1 645	143	698	330	315	126	130	25	10
Providence	16 090	4.5	28 025	331	10 691	1 232	2 933	3 105	2 996	971	1 448	333	84
Washington	3 793	6.8	30 975	178	1 498	215	806	443	420	178	166	25	18
SOUTH CAROLINA	91 463	5.7	23 538	X	58 071	5 706	16 733	13 777	13 075	5 550	5 076	1 409	204
Abbeville	459	-1.6	18 598	2 397	209	28	82	91	87	42	26	9	2
Aiken	3 301	4.4	24 377	784	2 272	167	629	479	454	213	165	45	5
Allendale	196	7.5	17 321	2 677	125	7	27	52	50	14	22	11	1
Anderson	3 733	5.2	22 930	1 103	1 907	251	633	567	537	280	177	41	6
Bamberg	303	5.4	18 606	2 391	124	20	42	76	73	23	29	12	2
Barnwell	520	1.2	23 858	885	413	22	63	99	96	30	45	14	3
Beaufort	3 694	7.0	32 699	136	2 038	228	1 261	391	373	204	117	28	3
Berkeley	2 419	7.5	17 001	2 734	1 071	103	349	326	300	131	94	41	5
Calhoun	294	5.8	20 643	1 793	139	17	47	45	42	19	13	7	1
Charleston	8 345	7.6	26 085	502	6 468	700	1 806	1 037	981	379	399	121	13
Cherokee	995	7.6	19 861	2 033	639	42	154	174	165	79	60	15	2
Chester	636	6.0	18 215	2 491	375	29	87	130	124	54	48	13	3
Chesterfield	795	7.3	19 146	2 246	461	58	110	163	155	61	62	22	3
Clarendon	535	5.2	17 298	2 683	189	46	93	139	133	46	55	24	3
Colleton	685	5.9	18 182	2 504	292	57	103	166	159	56	70	23	2
Darlington	1 345	2.9	20 223	1 921	770	56	226	291	279	98	122	41	6
Dillon	510	1.8	17 174	2 705	240	34	67	144	138	39	66	26	3
Dorchester	1 919	7.2	21 187	1 599	758	81	277	328	312	101	160	27	3
Edgefield	395	7.1	19 751	2 069	179	17	57	73	69	27	27	11	1
Fairfield	472	5.8	20 888	1 701	296	21	66	101	97	32	47	12	2
Florence	2 925	4.9	23 360	999	2 033	177	446	555	532	160	257	72	9
Georgetown	1 203	5.5	21 892	1 390	587	75	324	240	230	100	91	24	6
Greenville	10 356	5.4	28 852	267	8 289	743	2 029	1 125	1 059	531	371	90	11
Greenwood	1 504	3.8	23 601	942	1 046	115	265	233	221	109	70	21	4
Hampton	394	6.6	20 613	1 803	194	30	63	88	85	29	37	13	2
Horry	4 373	7.7	24 492	759	2 589	463	937	657	624	327	200	55	12
Jasper	323	5.5	18 719	2 363	113	26	37	62	59	18	27	10	1
Kershaw	1 043	4.5	21 169	1 607	551	54	203	176	167	80	59	16	2
Lancaster	1 200	5.7	20 150	1 952	596	59	165	206	195	89	77	18	3
Laurens	1 369	3.2	21 607	1 485	593	55	217	380	368	107	229	20	3
Lee	279	2.1	13 725	3 062	98	16	43	78	74	25	29	15	1
Lexington	5 568	6.3	26 643	447	2 586	336	916	553	514	258	168	41	7
McCormick	155	2.8	16 098	2 886	62	10	33	40	38	18	12	5	1
Marion	616	4.7	17 867	2 566	328	30	84	165	159	46	75	24	4
Marlboro	467	4.2	15 837	2 918	234	23	66	131	126	42	55	21	2
Newberry	721	5.6	20 958	1 680	361	47	124	132	126	60	46	12	2
Oconee	1 569	6.0	24 104	842	853	79	348	242	231	123	78	16	3
Orangeburg	1 740	4.8	19 884	2 024	977	105	286	383	367	130	134	63	10
Pickens	2 251	5.4	20 816	1 729	1 067	120	363	308	289	152	97	19	3
Richland	8 600	5.6	27 988	334	7 660	474	1 518	1 115	1 061	356	472	98	9
Saluda	354	5.1	20 847	1 718	112	38	52	65	61	25	24	8	1
Spartanburg	5 783	4.8	23 165	1 054	4 191	320	942	842	796	390	266	71	16

1. Based on the resident population estimated as of July 1 of the year shown.   2. Includes other labor income.

Table B. States and Counties — Earnings, Social Security, and Housing

STATE County	Earnings, 1999									Social Security beneficiaries, December 2000			Housing units, 1990	
			Percent by selected industries									Supplemental Security Income recipients, December 2000		
			Goods-related[1]		Service-related and other[2]									
	Total (mil dol)	Farm	Total	Manufacturing	Total	Retail trade	Finance, insurance, and real estate	Services	Government	Number	Rate[3]		Total	Percent change, 1980–1990
	75	76	77	78	79	80	81	82	83	84	85	86	87	88
PENNSYLVANIA—Cont'd														
Potter	277	2.9	19.1	13.2	65.2	6.7	1.9	18.3	12.8	3 946	218	462	11 334	4.4
Schuylkill	1 734	0.3	38.3	30.0	45.6	11.0	3.4	20.8	15.8	36 348	242	2 949	66 457	2.5
Snyder	548	1.6	D	34.5	D	13.2	2.7	12.4	17.9	6 962	185	499	13 629	16.7
Somerset	939	1.6	32.1	19.0	49.5	11.9	3.6	20.4	16.9	17 652	221	2 062	35 713	6.9
Sullivan	61	1.6	D	D	D	11.0	3.7	23.7	20.6	1 967	300	103	5 458	12.4
Susquehanna	341	3.0	30.4	13.1	47.3	11.8	3.5	19.2	19.3	9 012	213	821	20 308	18.1
Tioga	448	2.2	30.6	25.8	44.0	10.9	3.3	17.4	23.2	9 050	219	1 153	18 202	7.1
Union	626	0.7	D	17.5	D	7.3	2.4	31.2	26.8	6 675	160	426	12 886	15.1
Venango	750	0.0	33.7	28.9	46.8	10.9	3.2	20.2	19.5	13 377	232	1 920	26 961	1.2
Warren	594	0.4	37.1	31.4	45.7	18.0	3.2	16.4	16.7	9 619	219	767	22 236	1.6
Washington	2 812	0.1	32.9	19.2	53.8	10.7	3.7	26.5	13.3	46 839	231	5 034	84 113	3.7
Wayne	478	1.7	21.2	8.2	56.8	12.3	5.6	27.3	20.3	11 901	249	815	28 480	45.3
Westmoreland	5 028	0.1	32.7	24.3	54.4	11.5	4.1	22.8	12.8	83 144	225	7 662	153 554	3.7
Wyoming	418	1.8	D	D	D	7.7	2.6	13.1	10.0	5 279	188	470	11 857	11.2
York	6 639	0.1	41.9	34.0	47.5	10.6	4.5	20.9	10.5	65 031	170	5 274	134 761	14.6
RHODE ISLAND	18 624	0.1	22.0	16.5	59.9	9.5	7.9	31.6	18.0	192 680	184	27 729	414 572	11.2
Bristol	489	0.1	D	23.0	D	10.0	4.1	29.7	16.9	10 282	203	403	18 567	13.4
Kent	2 712	0.0	D	18.8	D	13.3	9.4	28.6	13.8	33 226	199	2 906	65 450	14.8
Newport	1 788	0.4	D	9.9	D	9.1	3.2	28.6	39.9	15 211	178	1 371	37 475	13.9
Providence	11 924	0.0	22.0	16.3	63.0	8.2	9.0	34.0	14.9	113 826	183	21 803	243 224	7.9
Washington	1 713	0.4	25.2	19.5	51.0	13.0	4.1	23.6	23.4	20 123	163	1 218	49 856	21.9
SOUTH CAROLINA	63 777	0.6	28.1	21.0	51.3	10.9	6.1	22.3	19.9	688 569	172	107 558	1 424 155	23.4
Abbeville	237	1.8	49.0	43.1	31.2	7.6	2.0	13.2	18.0	5 152	197	614	9 846	15.2
Aiken	2 439	0.4	26.3	15.9	61.1	7.3	3.3	17.8	12.1	25 303	178	3 652	49 266	23.8
Allendale	132	2.5	32.2	29.6	D	5.4	D	10.2	35.0	1 960	175	802	4 242	6.8
Anderson	2 158	0.5	40.2	32.8	42.4	13.4	3.5	16.9	16.9	33 728	203	3 225	60 745	18.3
Bamberg	144	5.2	D	23.7	D	11.6	3.2	17.0	26.9	3 124	188	836	6 408	0.4
Barnwell	435	0.7	28.5	24.2	D	4.5	1.2	D	11.0	3 887	166	1 167	7 854	7.9
Beaufort	2 266	0.1	12.3	2.3	54.7	12.6	10.8	24.2	32.8	23 338	193	1 861	45 981	68.4
Berkeley	1 174	0.7	D	31.4	D	8.9	2.4	11.9	22.3	18 124	127	2 756	45 697	43.8
Calhoun	156	2.4	56.0	49.3	D	3.8	D	11.1	16.1	2 564	169	505	5 225	20.8
Charleston	7 168	0.1	12.5	6.0	58.3	11.1	7.0	29.5	29.2	47 567	153	8 328	123 550	23.7
Cherokee	682	0.3	D	45.2	D	9.4	1.8	12.5	10.8	9 909	189	1 159	17 610	17.8
Chester	405	1.3	47.1	42.0	32.9	7.6	1.4	8.8	18.7	6 746	198	926	12 293	14.5
Chesterfield	520	3.6	50.8	46.4	33.4	10.4	3.2	13.9	12.2	8 029	188	1 721	15 101	8.4
Clarendon	235	5.3	26.3	19.8	43.4	12.5	3.1	19.5	25.0	6 411	197	1 747	12 101	9.2
Colleton	349	1.6	30.0	20.5	49.6	11.6	4.1	18.7	18.7	7 822	204	1 906	14 926	22.9
Darlington	826	1.5	48.1	40.3	38.9	8.5	2.6	16.8	11.5	12 335	183	2 838	23 601	9.8
Dillon	274	3.8	35.5	33.6	42.7	15.2	2.2	18.1	18.0	5 615	183	2 107	10 590	4.3
Dorchester	840	0.7	33.3	24.4	47.5	11.7	3.2	19.2	18.4	13 661	142	2 174	30 632	51.5
Edgefield	196	1.9	36.5	33.1	29.9	7.5	1.9	13.2	31.7	3 639	148	726	7 290	17.4
Fairfield	317	1.5	D	39.5	D	4.5	1.3	8.7	15.5	4 257	182	900	8 730	17.1
Florence	2 210	0.5	D	19.3	D	10.6	8.4	25.2	18.9	20 989	167	5 880	43 209	10.3
Georgetown	662	0.7	D	20.3	D	14.5	5.6	24.1	20.0	12 244	219	1 679	21 134	28.7
Greenville	9 032	0.1	31.8	24.5	57.8	11.2	5.8	25.2	10.2	61 801	163	7 213	131 645	21.7
Greenwood	1 161	0.8	D	37.7	D	10.2	4.4	17.0	18.2	12 851	194	1 609	24 735	13.9
Hampton	223	1.5	29.7	24.8	43.5	10.5	2.8	18.1	25.3	4 034	189	1 086	7 058	6.3
Horry	3 051	0.6	D	8.3	D	20.1	9.9	32.3	12.3	40 118	204	4 260	89 960	63.6
Jasper	138	2.9	27.6	11.2	45.9	10.7	1.9	20.9	23.6	2 523	122	638	6 070	14.7
Kershaw	605	1.0	D	34.9	D	9.6	4.3	14.1	18.0	9 860	187	1 357	17 479	14.7
Lancaster	655	0.3	45.6	39.0	40.4	10.3	6.1	18.7	13.7	10 735	175	1 334	20 929	8.9
Laurens	648	1.1	D	33.0	D	15.9	3.0	15.9	20.0	13 329	192	1 862	23 201	18.2
Lee	114	5.6	D	19.1	D	10.9	2.7	18.7	24.5	3 608	179	1 080	6 537	6.5
Lexington	2 922	0.6	29.8	20.1	54.9	11.6	5.6	19.5	14.7	30 718	142	3 001	67 556	28.3
McCormick	72	3.3	D	20.8	D	4.5	3.3	15.1	43.9	2 385	240	356	3 347	12.4
Marion	358	2.0	D	38.6	D	9.1	3.1	15.0	22.4	6 476	183	1 950	12 777	7.0
Marlboro	257	1.5	D	37.3	D	7.9	1.7	16.3	22.6	5 837	203	1 830	10 955	2.5
Newberry	408	4.1	45.0	38.2	34.3	8.1	2.1	14.7	16.6	7 308	202	1 004	14 455	17.6
Oconee	932	1.9	46.3	37.8	D	7.7	2.5	D	13.2	14 896	225	1 164	25 983	28.5
Orangeburg	1 082	1.9	33.7	28.6	41.5	12.2	3.5	17.8	22.9	17 275	189	4 673	32 340	11.1
Pickens	1 188	0.4	D	23.2	D	12.5	5.4	17.8	25.7	18 230	165	1 485	35 865	26.0
Richland	8 134	0.1	11.5	6.8	56.4	8.7	11.6	25.6	32.1	43 618	136	7 268	109 564	19.2
Saluda	150	13.8	39.9	35.2	28.5	7.2	3.8	9.6	17.7	3 413	178	604	6 792	13.6
Spartanburg	4 511	0.3	41.2	34.4	45.3	11.2	3.7	18.4	13.2	46 658	184	6 099	89 927	19.3

1. Covers mining, construction, and manufacturing. 2. Covers private sector earnings in agricultural services, forestry, and fisheries; transportation and public utilities; wholesale trade; retail trade; finance, insurance, and real estate; and services. 3. Per 1,000 resident population estimated as of July 1 of the year shown.

Table B. States and Counties — Housing, Labor Force, and Employment

STATE County	Housing units, 1990 (cont'd) Occupied units Owner-occupied Total	Percent	Median value[1]	Owner cost as a percent of income With a mort-gage	Without a mort-gage	Renter-occupied Median rent[2]	Rent as per-cent of income	Sub-stand-ard units[3] (percent)	Civilian labor force, 2001 Total	Percent change, 2000–2001	Unemployment Total	Rate[4]	Civilian employment, 1990[5] Total	Percent Professional, managerial, and technical	Precision production, craft, and repair
	89	90	91	92	93	94	95	96	97	98	99	100	101	102	103
PENNSYLVANIA—Cont'd															
Potter	6 246	75.4	40 900	18.3	13.6	299	26.4	2.9	10 518	7.4	482	4.6	6 778	20.7	13.2
Schuylkill	60 773	78.1	38 200	17.3	13.7	284	24.3	1.6	66 987	1.1	4 703	7.0	64 562	19.1	15.4
Snyder	12 764	77.2	56 700	20.0	11.9	324	22.6	4.2	18 807	-0.5	714	3.8	17 103	16.9	12.8
Somerset	29 574	77.4	43 400	20.0	13.4	283	24.6	2.4	37 013	0.5	2 361	6.4	31 594	20.9	14.3
Sullivan	2 280	78.6	47 000	20.8	14.6	259	24.2	3.3	2 394	1.2	148	6.2	2 376	19.4	15.5
Susquehanna	14 898	79.2	64 200	20.1	13.8	342	25.7	2.3	19 405	3.7	1 348	6.9	17 444	21.9	15.6
Tioga	14 974	75.5	43 900	18.2	12.6	286	26.6	2.4	20 325	1.6	1 394	6.9	17 188	23.3	13.1
Union	11 689	74.6	66 800	19.2	12.6	351	23.6	1.8	18 607	-0.3	660	3.5	15 630	26.2	10.7
Venango	22 408	74.5	38 600	17.0	12.5	305	26.1	1.7	26 269	0.5	1 412	5.4	23 858	24.4	12.5
Warren	17 244	77.2	43 900	17.3	12.4	304	23.5	2.0	20 638	4.0	1 047	5.1	20 229	21.5	13.4
Washington	78 533	75.6	53 600	17.9	12.6	320	27.0	1.9	97 966	1.9	4 889	5.0	83 675	25.6	13.9
Wayne	14 638	79.2	89 800	22.3	13.9	386	26.0	1.6	19 946	0.9	1 103	5.5	17 487	21.6	16.2
Westmoreland	144 080	76.3	56 800	19.2	12.6	321	25.2	1.4	185 310	1.8	9 024	4.9	158 570	28.9	12.6
Wyoming	10 002	76.9	67 600	18.9	13.1	360	24.0	2.6	15 092	0.8	701	4.6	12 729	25.3	14.6
York	128 666	74.4	79 700	19.2	11.9	409	23.4	1.7	198 245	1.4	8 920	4.5	176 908	24.0	14.2
RHODE ISLAND	377 977	59.5	133 500	22.7	13.9	489	27.5	2.6	503 566	-0.2	23 736	4.7	487 913	30.1	12.0
Bristol	17 559	71.3	162 100	23.5	14.1	511	27.3	1.7	25 198	-0.9	856	3.4	24 539	33.9	10.9
Kent	62 058	72.0	122 500	22.8	14.0	526	27.1	1.6	86 112	-0.6	3 688	4.3	82 956	30.2	12.7
Newport	32 687	59.4	160 900	23.3	14.2	627	27.7	1.7	41 256	0.6	1 558	3.8	40 271	36.8	10.4
Providence	226 362	53.5	127 400	22.5	14.0	465	27.5	3.3	286 560	-0.1	15 476	5.4	284 662	27.9	12.1
Washington	39 311	68.9	152 700	22.7	12.9	580	27.6	1.7	64 442	-0.6	2 158	3.3	55 485	34.5	11.7
SOUTH CAROLINA	1 258 044	69.8	61 100	19.8	13.0	376	24.4	5.0	1 949 210	-1.8	105 817	5.4	1 603 425	25.4	13.8
Abbeville	8 780	80.1	43 600	16.5	12.8	242	23.5	5.0	12 136	0.1	966	8.0	10 713	18.8	14.8
Aiken	44 883	74.6	61 700	17.3	13.0	375	23.2	4.3	62 725	-2.0	3 629	5.8	55 268	28.4	16.6
Allendale	3 791	68.2	39 100	21.3	14.8	232	30.0	9.7	4 511	-3.1	206	4.6	3 952	19.2	12.9
Anderson	55 481	75.2	53 700	18.8	12.5	326	23.6	3.3	86 099	0.2	4 798	5.6	70 331	22.8	15.7
Bamberg	5 587	72.5	43 100	21.1	14.6	225	26.9	9.6	7 710	-1.9	466	6.0	6 469	18.5	12.5
Barnwell	7 100	73.2	44 900	18.0	14.2	279	22.6	7.7	10 755	-4.3	860	8.0	8 609	24.2	14.0
Beaufort	30 712	64.9	112 100	23.2	12.8	500	24.6	3.9	53 968	-0.4	1 395	2.6	33 743	29.6	11.9
Berkeley	42 386	69.7	68 500	21.6	13.2	424	23.2	5.3	65 394	-1.6	2 600	4.0	52 228	23.2	18.7
Calhoun	4 487	81.9	45 000	18.4	13.2	224	22.4	11.6	6 675	-5.8	485	7.3	5 573	18.9	15.8
Charleston	107 069	57.6	73 800	21.7	13.5	437	26.5	4.2	162 092	-2.0	5 762	3.6	132 506	31.0	13.5
Cherokee	16 456	75.2	46 900	17.4	12.9	290	23.3	4.9	26 548	0.1	2 046	7.7	21 125	16.8	17.3
Chester	11 448	76.4	40 700	17.7	13.4	282	22.9	7.9	15 790	-1.6	1 632	10.3	14 313	16.3	15.2
Chesterfield	14 047	75.4	42 200	16.9	12.9	266	22.7	6.9	19 878	-3.3	1 742	8.8	17 334	15.5	14.8
Clarendon	9 544	77.4	45 900	21.5	15.1	237	27.0	12.3	13 163	-3.3	1 165	8.9	11 109	18.8	14.4
Colleton	12 040	79.4	47 400	22.1	14.6	289	26.4	8.3	15 024	-2.0	773	5.1	14 161	18.2	15.5
Darlington	21 999	74.6	49 000	19.1	13.8	294	27.5	7.2	29 615	-3.2	2 204	7.4	27 574	20.3	13.7
Dillon	9 887	67.0	40 800	17.2	13.6	255	26.3	11.7	13 032	-6.4	1 628	12.5	11 789	18.2	11.8
Dorchester	28 213	71.0	73 600	22.0	13.0	428	24.0	4.5	44 765	-1.4	1 825	4.1	36 188	27.8	16.0
Edgefield	6 424	76.3	52 100	20.8	14.4	268	24.9	6.9	9 099	-2.0	440	4.8	8 324	20.7	14.2
Fairfield	7 467	78.1	47 500	18.2	13.3	262	23.9	11.1	10 292	-3.7	1 295	12.6	9 570	16.9	12.7
Florence	40 217	70.5	54 900	18.6	13.7	342	25.0	6.6	62 274	-2.6	3 640	5.8	51 984	24.7	13.4
Georgetown	16 275	79.4	63 800	22.1	13.8	351	24.4	7.7	26 075	1.1	2 529	9.7	19 699	21.2	14.6
Greenville	122 878	66.2	66 300	18.6	12.6	383	23.0	2.6	193 352	-1.6	6 246	3.2	161 895	29.9	11.8
Greenwood	22 730	69.1	50 100	18.3	12.6	308	24.1	4.6	32 664	-0.6	2 675	8.2	27 811	24.0	14.7
Hampton	6 322	74.4	43 700	21.5	14.1	240	24.1	8.0	8 142	-5.0	553	6.8	7 133	17.8	14.0
Horry	55 764	68.5	75 600	23.0	12.8	425	25.5	4.2	103 361	-2.7	4 903	4.7	66 730	24.8	13.6
Jasper	5 298	78.0	44 400	21.8	14.3	265	24.8	7.2	8 482	-0.5	333	3.9	6 145	15.4	14.4
Kershaw	15 810	81.4	60 200	17.3	13.0	321	23.4	5.0	22 983	-2.7	1 477	6.4	20 663	21.8	15.6
Lancaster	19 778	74.8	49 400	17.6	12.7	316	23.8	5.4	29 132	-1.3	1 776	6.1	25 854	17.8	17.2
Laurens	20 660	75.9	44 700	16.4	12.6	296	23.1	5.1	28 749	1.4	2 430	8.5	26 860	18.7	14.9
Lee	6 054	78.7	42 000	21.0	13.9	235	21.0	13.7	8 491	-2.0	697	8.2	7 245	14.5	12.6
Lexington	61 633	76.1	74 900	19.8	12.2	425	23.2	3.1	117 058	-2.8	3 260	2.8	89 550	30.4	13.4
McCormick	2 731	77.3	39 200	18.4	12.6	217	23.2	8.6	3 966	-0.5	433	10.9	3 236	17.3	14.9
Marion	11 766	71.3	42 600	20.6	14.3	273	27.9	9.4	14 768	-9.0	2 548	17.3	14 096	17.2	11.7
Marlboro	10 163	68.9	37 100	19.8	13.8	271	26.6	11.2	11 634	0.4	1 555	13.4	11 847	15.7	13.6
Newberry	12 314	76.1	49 200	17.4	13.0	276	23.5	5.6	17 973	-1.4	1 214	6.8	15 100	20.1	13.1
Oconee	22 358	76.9	56 900	17.5	11.9	305	21.5	3.2	28 593	-0.6	1 783	6.2	27 173	20.7	17.6
Orangeburg	28 909	73.2	50 500	19.6	13.6	269	25.6	8.8	40 564	-5.0	4 510	11.1	35 112	20.2	13.7
Pickens	33 422	73.2	59 800	17.4	11.9	344	24.7	2.7	56 935	-0.3	2 825	5.0	45 581	26.0	15.3
Richland	101 590	59.2	71 200	20.7	14.0	429	25.5	4.0	155 342	-2.9	5 368	3.5	137 105	36.2	8.4
Saluda	5 824	81.6	46 600	20.5	12.4	229	21.3	8.5	9 164	0.7	488	5.3	7 362	16.2	16.5
Spartanburg	84 503	69.8	54 200	17.7	12.7	353	23.2	4.0	133 175	-1.0	6 911	5.2	111 272	23.3	14.2

1. Specified owner-occupied units.   2. Specified renter-occupied units.   3. Overcrowded or lacking complete plumbing facilities.   4. Percent of civilian labor force.   5. Persons 16 years and older.

Table B. States and Counties — **Nonfarm Employment and Agriculture**

| | Private nonfarm establishments, employment and payroll, 1999 | | | | | | | | | Agriculture, 1997 | | | |
| | Employment | | | | | | Annual payroll | | Farms | | | Farm operators |
STATE County	Number of establishments	Total	Health Care and Social Assistance	Manufacturing	Retail trade	Finance and Insurance	Professional Scientific and Technical Services	Total (mil dol)	Average per employee (dollars)	Number	Percent with— Less than 50 acres	Percent with— 500 acres and over	Whose principal occupation is farming (percent)
	104	105	106	107	108	109	110	111	112	113	114	115	116
PENNSYLVANIA—Cont'd													
Potter	431	5 614	916	1 134	563	87	71	128	22 781	292	14.4	13.7	55.5
Schuylkill	3 125	43 609	6 528	14 907	7 012	1 432	794	1 049	24 054	605	32.9	6.8	50.1
Snyder	817	12 725	749	3 941	2 892	344	214	263	20 633	671	27.6	3.3	62.0
Somerset	1 943	21 173	3 054	5 282	3 205	782	504	465	21 962	958	15.9	8.2	62.2
Sullivan	185	1 262	352	254	181	D	14	25	19 626	123	10.6	8.1	52.0
Susquehanna	782	6 429	1 115	1 201	1 144	246	208	125	19 410	703	13.2	10.1	62.9
Tioga	852	10 105	1 511	2 912	1 846	344	207	206	20 378	823	13.7	11.2	58.2
Union	842	15 356	2 623	3 741	1 503	336	181	346	22 507	498	28.9	2.6	63.7
Venango	1 310	17 000	2 942	4 399	2 858	539	220	413	24 299	351	21.9	1.4	40.7
Warren	999	15 560	2 373	4 509	2 511	453	224	410	26 372	390	21.0	3.1	49.0
Washington	4 865	70 506	8 658	11 955	9 401	1 623	2 337	2 038	28 910	1 307	23.1	3.1	45.7
Wayne	1 423	13 029	2 045	1 010	2 603	512	385	260	19 968	564	14.7	6.0	58.2
Westmoreland	9 031	126 630	17 939	24 461	19 102	3 715	4 137	3 379	26 686	1 035	27.6	4.6	48.3
Wyoming	627	8 646	927	2 970	1 204	208	152	261	30 187	307	16.6	7.5	58.3
York	8 206	149 398	16 226	44 221	20 897	4 017	4 031	4 287	28 697	1 698	43.9	6.8	50.7
RHODE ISLAND	28 240	405 445	64 633	71 636	47 791	23 739	16 762	11 843	29 209	735	59.6	2.0	50.3
Bristol	1 113	12 391	1 559	2 795	1 346	303	220	264	21 301	37	62.2	0.0	62.2
Kent	4 918	69 472	9 098	11 320	12 439	5 607	2 265	1 947	28 020	74	64.9	2.7	43.2
Newport	2 706	28 076	4 753	2 504	3 971	1 015	2 188	745	26 530	139	56.1	2.2	62.6
Providence	16 040	260 953	43 356	48 213	23 635	15 792	9 863	7 962	30 512	255	63.1	0.4	46.3
Washington	3 463	34 553	5 867	6 804	6 400	1 022	2 226	925	26 771	230	55.7	3.9	47.8
SOUTH CAROLINA	96 440	1 561 727	168 527	336 776	217 761	59 535	58 207	40 900	26 189	20 189	34.4	10.6	39.4
Abbeville	333	6 300	598	3 733	482	127	72	160	25 440	471	25.7	6.2	32.5
Aiken	2 610	51 542	4 117	21 108	6 307	992	3 693	1 779	34 513	729	37.6	7.4	37.6
Allendale	158	2 394	218	1 495	226	D	D	54	22 568	131	21.4	31.3	39.7
Anderson	3 703	57 295	6 813	19 177	9 227	1 368	992	1 432	24 991	1 271	38.9	4.4	33.9
Bamberg	308	3 654	693	1 216	545	101	D	75	20 576	254	21.3	25.6	46.1
Barnwell	393	6 562	350	3 777	908	116	D	179	27 232	325	28.3	15.4	36.3
Beaufort	4 107	44 078	4 545	1 520	8 397	1 197	2 549	1 089	24 716	99	56.6	18.2	42.4
Berkeley	1 783	23 733	1 627	6 761	3 524	419	1 034	617	26 006	292	47.9	7.2	36.6
Calhoun	190	2 314	328	1 003	185	D	D	51	21 916	293	21.5	21.2	40.3
Charleston	10 371	169 180	26 063	10 646	23 148	5 510	9 497	4 303	25 436	266	53.4	8.6	43.2
Cherokee	1 049	20 266	1 151	8 922	2 658	297	182	503	24 803	412	32.3	4.9	26.7
Chester	567	10 007	760	5 097	1 039	164	82	255	25 493	340	21.8	11.2	42.6
Chesterfield	728	13 535	1 038	6 186	1 971	210	67	325	24 029	537	23.1	10.2	38.0
Clarendon	528	6 302	1 055	1 456	1 312	187	D	115	18 295	304	30.3	27.0	56.2
Colleton	815	8 589	890	1 696	1 892	346	251	176	20 505	416	33.4	15.1	40.1
Darlington	1 301	21 908	1 913	6 485	2 884	402	301	604	27 564	346	32.4	23.7	51.7
Dillon	527	8 781	1 281	3 636	1 596	161	84	174	19 759	199	21.6	26.6	58.3
Dorchester	1 696	21 685	1 995	4 137	3 636	559	699	505	23 299	314	41.7	9.6	40.1
Edgefield	358	4 721	421	2 154	474	65	59	102	21 690	271	29.5	13.3	36.9
Fairfield	328	6 587	590	2 442	705	89	74	234	35 583	172	27.9	16.3	29.7
Florence	3 329	55 933	10 617	10 808	9 556	4 307	1 510	1 405	25 111	615	33.3	15.4	52.7
Georgetown	1 768	19 989	2 285	4 748	3 113	409	422	458	22 929	206	41.7	15.0	38.3
Greenville	11 591	248 756	18 584	43 731	26 057	8 463	12 428	7 433	29 879	761	50.3	2.5	33.6
Greenwood	1 564	30 412	3 701	11 201	4 159	698	569	740	24 333	377	37.9	8.2	32.1
Hampton	443	4 712	308	1 345	997	140	79	108	22 923	207	25.1	24.2	40.6
Horry	7 152	82 166	6 435	6 084	15 198	3 239	2 278	1 732	21 082	896	31.1	9.8	54.9
Jasper	403	3 631	218	168	563	149	D	59	16 292	123	35.8	13.8	33.3
Kershaw	1 173	15 453	1 469	4 699	2 082	557	377	375	24 235	324	35.2	9.6	38.0
Lancaster	1 180	16 806	2 062	4 756	2 674	676	185	431	25 637	500	32.6	5.6	35.2
Laurens	928	16 746	1 723	5 926	2 033	549	288	386	23 062	686	30.2	9.2	33.5
Lee	253	2 510	301	612	475	73	54	55	21 765	222	18.5	30.6	48.6
Lexington	4 934	65 025	6 311	9 284	10 762	2 255	1 967	1 614	24 814	799	44.1	3.8	40.9
McCormick	132	1 105	80	342	153	D	16	22	19 560	92	28.3	12.0	28.3
Marion	672	10 284	1 092	4 924	1 489	268	107	210	20 391	200	25.0	23.0	53.5
Marlboro	426	6 244	797	2 804	1 030	149	50	143	22 855	180	22.8	33.9	54.4
Newberry	726	11 566	1 318	4 913	1 441	211	143	259	22 379	499	24.2	8.2	38.7
Oconee	1 482	21 426	2 048	7 392	2 778	363	402	550	25 647	611	40.4	3.1	33.1
Orangeburg	1 929	27 929	3 515	8 755	4 864	874	496	617	22 107	965	25.9	14.9	41.6
Pickens	2 196	30 267	2 723	10 909	4 392	625	572	669	22 102	532	53.2	1.9	32.0
Richland	9 071	172 133	22 923	14 683	22 429	17 758	9 997	4 758	27 642	350	42.6	6.6	42.0
Saluda	251	4 246	440	2 494	362	52	110	85	20 056	556	26.3	8.8	45.1
Spartanburg	6 270	120 724	13 224	32 947	14 469	2 658	3 466	3 410	28 249	1 067	48.0	2.7	32.5

Table B. States and Counties — Agriculture, Land, and Water

STATE County	Agriculture, 1997 (cont'd)															
	Land in farms					Value of land and buildings		Value of machinery and equipment average per farm ($1,000)	Value of products sold				Percent of farms with sales of —		Percent of land owned by fed. gov. 1997	Water con-sump-tion 1995 (mil gal/day)
		Acres									Percent from —					
	Acreage (1,000)	Percent change, 1992–1997	Average size of farm	Total irrigated (1,000)	Total cropland (1,000)	Average per farm ($1,000)	Average per acre (dollars)		Total (mil dol)	Average per farm (dollars)	Crops	Live-stock and poultry products	$10,000 or more	$100,000 or more		
	117	118	119	120	121	122	123	124	125	126	127	128	129	130	131	132
PENNSYLVANIA—Cont'd																
Potter	83	-7.3	286	0	44	247	938	43	20	67 738	24.7	75.3	44.9	19.9	0.0	4.1
Schuylkill	90	1.5	149	1	70	359	2 561	63	67	110 609	31.0	69.0	53.7	19.8	0.0	55.5
Snyder	93	6.6	138	1	68	269	2 250	41	75	111 575	12.5	87.5	67.2	25.5	0.0	299.3
Somerset	206	-6.2	215	1	128	274	1 226	59	60	62 541	12.7	87.3	56.7	18.4	0.2	40.1
Sullivan	27	-11.9	222	0	17	296	1 471	57	7	57 424	5.8	94.2	50.4	20.3	0.0	3.4
Susquehanna	169	-4.8	240	0	95	329	1 437	48	43	61 190	7.3	92.7	55.3	23.3	0.0	5.5
Tioga	202	-4.6	246	0	124	260	1 057	46	47	57 493	12.7	87.3	54.3	19.7	1.3	6.2
Union	63	0.4	127	0	54	363	2 660	51	49	99 208	16.8	83.2	68.5	32.1	1.5	7.5
Venango	46	-12.9	132	0	28	162	1 195	29	7	18 560	27.0	73.0	31.1	4.8	0.0	12.9
Warren	64	-3.7	165	D	32	164	1 002	36	15	37 516	14.3	85.7	36.2	11.0	25.6	72.2
Washington	186	-8.3	142	1	115	266	1 802	39	27	20 357	38.5	61.5	30.3	4.1	0.0	451.6
Wayne	110	-10.2	194	0	60	331	1 746	47	25	44 580	11.1	88.9	49.1	17.6	0.0	5.4
Westmoreland	148	-4.0	143	0	101	363	2 481	47	36	35 226	45.0	55.0	41.0	8.7	0.7	120.0
Wyoming	61	-3.2	199	0	37	282	1 395	49	30	97 856	13.3	86.7	48.9	15.6	0.0	17.6
York	261	3.6	154	1	217	472	3 187	57	129	75 748	39.9	60.1	50.0	17.3	0.2	2 350.0
RHODE ISLAND	55	10.5	75	3	26	442	5 885	39	48	65 578	81.8	18.2	46.7	13.2	0.5	136.2
Bristol	2	71.0	46	0	1	594	12 845	27	3	75 400	92.9	7.1	48.6	8.1	0.0	5.4
Kent	6	7.3	87	0	2	381	4 383	28	3	36 283	85.3	14.7	43.2	8.1	0.1	7.4
Newport	10	4.1	75	0	7	580	7 742	46	15	104 402	81.0	19.0	57.6	21.6	1.6	10.1
Providence	15	22.8	58	0	6	334	5 781	29	10	37 928	64.7	35.2	42.0	9.8	0.0	96.8
Washington	22	9.8	95	2	10	475	4 972	51	19	80 617	89.1	10.9	46.1	14.3	0.4	16.6
SOUTH CAROLINA	4 593	2.7	228	86	2 463	325	1 482	45	1 588	78 665	49.8	50.2	31.0	11.3	5.2	6 202.9
Abbeville	81	-9.7	172	0	36	213	1 531	22	8	17 599	17.4	82.6	21.0	1.7	7.6	4.4
Aiken	134	-2.1	184	2	62	254	1 315	39	59	80 595	24.5	75.5	27.4	10.4	9.6	303.1
Allendale	92	13.4	701	5	55	778	1 095	63	14	105 526	92.3	7.7	37.4	14.5	1.6	11.0
Anderson	166	3.0	131	1	90	308	2 761	28	35	27 174	41.7	58.3	18.9	3.1	1.4	81.7
Bamberg	101	16.0	397	4	53	352	936	49	21	81 554	67.1	32.9	44.1	20.1	0.0	2.6
Barnwell	97	29.4	299	6	48	323	1 045	32	15	44 970	78.1	21.9	33.2	8.9	33.1	3.6
Beaufort	39	-13.0	395	2	11	674	1 772	40	8	84 377	90.6	9.4	33.3	9.1	3.1	29.8
Berkeley	51	0.8	176	1	18	277	1 856	35	22	75 765	92.5	7.5	31.2	3.8	26.4	490.7
Calhoun	102	12.4	349	7	62	369	1 150	72	26	89 837	83.8	16.2	40.3	18.1	0.0	125.4
Charleston	44	37.8	166	2	17	437	2 658	46	27	100 974	85.3	14.7	39.1	15.4	14.8	147.7
Cherokee	65	-1.9	157	D	31	206	1 512	20	13	32 023	23.0	77.0	16.5	2.4	0.9	8.8
Chester	81	-14.2	237	0	33	319	1 179	34	12	34 338	11.4	88.6	23.8	6.5	3.4	3.8
Chesterfield	124	13.0	231	1	55	245	1 062	36	72	133 811	12.3	87.7	27.7	12.3	8.9	9.6
Clarendon	142	4.6	468	2	112	395	912	94	77	252 123	56.7	43.3	55.6	38.2	1.0	3.9
Colleton	155	22.9	372	1	50	396	1 122	41	15	36 516	75.7	24.3	30.5	7.5	0.0	8.3
Darlington	158	0.7	457	1	115	397	909	102	61	177 045	77.2	22.8	47.1	27.5	0.0	37.7
Dillon	91	-16.4	458	D	69	487	1 054	143	66	331 251	52.0	48.0	70.9	38.7	0.0	5.4
Dorchester	65	5.4	208	D	38	208	1 246	41	22	68 490	48.7	51.3	33.4	10.2	0.0	6.7
Edgefield	71	3.5	264	3	28	304	1 219	36	15	56 235	65.6	34.4	31.4	10.7	9.6	3.3
Fairfield	47	-16.8	271	0	15	286	1 116	28	14	78 512	2.3	97.7	19.8	5.2	2.4	860.8
Florence	169	-13.5	274	2	114	337	1 230	67	69	112 367	89.4	10.6	53.2	21.5	0.0	50.0
Georgetown	53	43.7	258	1	15	562	2 238	48	15	72 277	87.4	12.6	32.0	11.7	0.0	45.9
Greenville	70	5.0	92	2	38	299	3 413	30	18	23 012	75.4	24.6	16.0	2.8	0.0	176.9
Greenwood	68	-2.8	181	D	28	253	1 381	23	12	32 603	D	D	19.9	1.9	3.8	12.8
Hampton	117	21.0	567	1	58	572	1 065	73	16	76 204	91.7	8.3	41.1	16.9	0.1	4.1
Horry	184	-6.3	205	1	117	384	1 943	72	83	92 397	86.8	13.2	55.6	24.0	0.5	94.1
Jasper	68	-6.6	554	1	16	549	896	58	5	38 320	93.9	6.2	23.6	5.7	3.7	2.0
Kershaw	73	37.0	224	0	24	343	1 454	40	60	184 408	4.3	95.7	32.1	13.6	0.0	19.4
Lancaster	75	29.6	150	0	31	229	1 638	25	41	81 359	4.7	95.3	22.6	7.6	0.0	18.6
Laurens	127	-1.0	185	1	62	369	1 992	34	19	27 063	40.5	59.5	24.2	2.6	4.5	6.6
Lee	120	-12.0	539	0	89	507	914	87	45	204 427	61.6	38.4	54.5	32.9	0.0	3.4
Lexington	93	12.5	117	6	49	238	2 280	38	108	135 706	20.9	79.1	34.2	15.4	0.0	188.8
McCormick	20	6.9	221	0	7	360	1 632	32	7	75 688	D	D	15.2	2.2	20.7	2.9
Marion	80	2.8	401	1	53	534	1 259	97	33	163 593	94.8	5.2	53.5	26.5	0.0	11.6
Marlboro	117	11.0	647	1	84	603	979	132	36	202 605	79.1	20.9	48.3	34.4	0.0	10.2
Newberry	95	0.6	190	0	49	259	1 496	36	43	85 639	7.5	92.5	24.4	9.8	13.7	6.3
Oconee	66	-5.0	109	1	31	331	2 721	32	44	72 517	8.7	91.3	22.7	9.7	20.1	2 533.6
Orangeburg	272	3.7	282	15	164	319	1 169	56	88	91 088	55.7	44.3	38.8	14.2	0.2	24.9
Pickens	47	6.5	88	0	25	264	3 191	24	6	11 105	61.3	38.7	14.3	1.9	0.0	17.9
Richland	57	-14.3	162	1	28	341	2 549	28	11	30 943	43.4	56.6	26.0	6.6	14.2	495.0
Saluda	111	0.3	200	2	54	274	1 432	43	56	100 606	10.4	89.6	33.1	12.1	1.5	4.0
Spartanburg	107	0.0	100	1	64	256	2 767	30	23	21 663	57.6	42.4	18.0	2.3	0.0	65.6

Table B. States and Counties — Residential Construction, Wholesale and Retail Trade, and Real Estate

STATE County	Value of Residential Construction Authorized by Building Permits, 2000		Wholesale Trade, 1997				Retail Trade[1], 1997				Real Estate and Rental and Leasing, 1997			
	New Construction ($1,000)	Number of Housing Units	Number of Establishments	Number of Employees	Sales (mil dol)	Annual Payroll (mil dol)	Number of Establishments	Number of Employees	Sales (mil dol)	Annual Payroll (mil dol)	Number of Establishments	Number of Employees	Receipts (mil dol)	Annual Payroll (mil dol)
	133	134	135	136	137	138	139	140	141	142	143	144	145	146
PENNSYLVANIA—Cont'd														
Potter	9 778	105	13	58	17.4	1.0	77	611	88.3	8.3	5	45	1.6	0.3
Schuylkill	32 630	352	134	1 798	632.2	42.0	659	7 129	1 062.5	106.3	76	255	21.9	5.4
Snyder	11 050	121	29	444	160.4	11.8	190	2 558	365.6	33.5	16	59	6.4	0.9
Somerset	21 895	240	87	840	274.5	21.8	367	3 361	543.1	46.2	38	136	16.0	2.3
Sullivan	2 360	25	5	D	D	D	29	186	24.7	2.3	5	15	2.9	0.1
Susquehanna	10 966	130	34	D	D	D	161	1 221	217.8	17.3	10	26	5.6	0.5
Tioga	14 542	196	28	293	93.3	6.8	170	1 924	287.9	26.3	18	43	3.2	0.5
Union	10 796	111	33	313	89.9	10.0	140	1 492	225.3	19.6	29	149	19.7	2.8
Venango	9 532	129	53	530	128.3	12.1	247	2 792	417.4	37.8	37	119	14.9	1.6
Warren	6 120	88	36	285	67.1	8.4	185	2 742	718.6	52.9	18	91	4.8	1.2
Washington	127 621	876	305	3 803	1 481.0	132.5	778	9 187	1 531.6	152.6	129	551	72.1	9.9
Wayne	25 184	253	35	262	67.5	5.9	246	2 444	397.0	38.4	37	150	10.6	1.8
Westmoreland	127 228	999	473	6 482	3 967.1	221.0	1 557	19 333	3 230.2	280.5	237	1 015	114.5	20.2
Wyoming	8 815	98	23	D	D	D	126	1 241	214.3	17.4	11	32	1.8	0.4
York	216 475	2 009	450	9 498	3 428.1	275.9	1 447	20 356	3 250.6	315.4	236	1 138	128.3	21.5
RHODE ISLAND	296 393	2 596	1 590	18 762	7 602.7	635.2	4 169	45 747	7 505.8	752.1	922	4 649	573.4	105.4
Bristol	10 428	85	55	324	108.4	9.4	168	1 311	211.6	20.6	43	77	13.2	1.7
Kent	47 543	453	312	3 491	1 778.6	128.9	804	11 839	1 985.9	187.9	164	1 228	179.9	31.2
Newport	41 966	307	102	561	242.3	18.6	485	3 844	626.2	66.1	97	351	47.3	9.9
Providence	97 013	1 002	1 003	13 417	5 094.4	450.9	2 163	22 850	3 663.7	374.6	510	2 765	291.3	57.1
Washington	99 442	749	118	969	378.9	27.2	549	5 903	1 018.3	103.0	108	228	41.7	5.6
SOUTH CAROLINA	3 532 667	32 812	5 035	58 910	34 179.8	1 866.8	18 481	209 256	33 634.3	3 107.2	3 541	18 760	2 012.6	377.1
Abbeville	4 361	48	10	36	12.1	0.9	65	469	58.6	5.2	5	16	0.6	0.2
Aiken	74 145	678	97	D	D	D	533	6 455	936.6	87.1	101	277	28.2	4.8
Allendale	1 001	20	11	44	17.9	0.9	46	311	53.6	3.8	7	15	0.7	0.2
Anderson	112 512	1 110	186	1 704	873.0	46.4	743	8 860	1 349.1	124.7	113	418	50.3	6.6
Bamberg	1 485	21	10	D	D	D	78	524	68.4	6.4	6	24	1.0	0.2
Barnwell	546	4	8	D	D	D	107	1 020	116.2	11.6	12	27	2.9	0.3
Beaufort	438 370	2 689	118	548	169.4	15.2	751	7 444	1 340.9	129.2	273	1 886	231.0	44.3
Berkeley	56 001	556	75	926	577.6	25.7	292	3 347	537.5	47.1	67	547	66.2	10.2
Calhoun	4 725	84	10	114	24.1	2.9	37	267	31.1	2.9	2	D	D	D
Charleston	608 562	4 086	472	5 296	3 727.1	175.5	1 850	22 298	3 483.7	347.7	466	2 618	269.0	48.9
Cherokee	11 281	151	42	D	D	D	232	2 137	366.7	30.3	35	107	12.3	1.5
Chester	9 750	88	27	905	331.5	24.2	129	1 142	186.1	14.4	12	38	5.6	0.9
Chesterfield	22 529	268	33	330	91.8	8.6	182	1 632	240.9	21.4	19	45	2.1	0.6
Clarendon	10 389	109	22	187	56.2	4.2	130	1 120	165.6	14.9	9	30	1.8	0.4
Colleton	17 633	130	44	487	212.5	11.9	188	1 890	259.4	23.5	36	152	14.3	2.7
Darlington	15 327	169	81	858	728.0	19.1	310	2 715	423.4	36.3	29	93	7.4	1.2
Dillon	4 108	42	29	292	177.3	9.4	151	1 612	196.0	19.6	22	59	5.9	0.7
Dorchester	79 608	745	59	422	97.3	7.9	282	3 450	516.9	46.3	57	187	31.1	3.5
Edgefield	7 255	76	10	D	D	D	79	455	78.8	6.5	11	31	1.4	0.3
Fairfield	8 297	71	8	94	29.5	2.6	70	764	82.8	7.1	7	24	1.0	0.3
Florence	50 243	645	206	2 847	1 017.6	81.6	759	8 935	1 467.3	138.4	114	387	40.7	7.3
Georgetown	106 296	647	56	363	119.6	9.6	346	3 178	481.9	47.6	55	220	16.5	5.0
Greenville	281 807	3 411	930	12 025	10 685.9	451.4	1 852	24 775	4 496.4	380.2	415	2 158	288.9	48.3
Greenwood	24 509	384	52	760	148.1	13.6	339	4 601	606.1	60.7	56	206	22.0	3.5
Hampton	2 223	22	11	D	D	D	131	952	114.1	10.8	9	22	1.7	0.4
Horry	406 482	4 492	230	1 824	481.5	49.5	1 522	14 457	2 505.2	230.7	360	3 026	259.6	59.7
Jasper	7 589	72	12	177	65.5	4.7	79	531	76.9	6.8	9	37	2.9	0.7
Kershaw	33 217	314	24	113	36.9	3.1	221	2 150	296.5	27.2	29	83	6.8	1.0
Lancaster	46 653	367	48	353	136.3	9.2	264	2 608	401.3	36.3	35	108	9.3	1.9
Laurens	29 828	326	40	351	86.5	9.5	200	1 743	296.2	24.4	33	101	6.3	1.3
Lee	3 552	51	15	124	38.5	2.7	74	576	72.4	6.6	5	D	D	D
Lexington	146 110	1 383	301	4 749	2 282.6	152.0	803	10 332	1 803.7	156.6	141	684	86.4	13.6
McCormick	15 643	91	5	D	D	D	41	204	23.5	2.0	2	D	D	D
Marion	4 888	77	31	235	91.6	5.3	178	1 609	215.7	20.9	13	39	3.5	0.8
Marlboro	1 985	21	16	133	54.3	3.8	115	796	122.3	10.6	13	37	2.6	0.5
Newberry	15 651	128	22	D	D	D	152	1 388	198.1	19.4	12	64	3.2	0.9
Oconee	83 041	473	57	D	D	D	276	2 738	403.9	35.1	41	143	12.8	3.1
Orangeburg	18 849	234	103	933	380.9	25.4	461	4 793	704.3	65.2	46	224	15.1	2.9
Pickens	92 489	611	86	D	D	D	372	4 237	655.2	58.1	53	237	22.4	3.9
Richland	227 627	2 936	540	7 346	2 989.4	251.7	1 558	22 311	3 475.6	350.7	392	2 614	310.4	61.3
Saluda	5 169	47	11	102	38.7	1.7	67	415	76.4	5.4	4	12	0.7	0.2
Spartanburg	133 817	1 567	484	6 234	3 965.3	214.8	1 117	13 785	2 311.6	213.5	198	898	90.4	17.9

1. Establishments with payroll.

Table B. States and Counties — Professional, Manufacturing, and Accommodation and Foodservices

STATE County	Professional, Scientific, and Technical Services[1], 1997				Manufacturing, 1997				Accommodation and Foodservices, 1997			
	Number of Establishments	Number of Employees	Receipts (mil dol)	Annual Payroll (mil dol)	Number of Establishments	Number of Employees	Receipts (mil dol)	Annual Payroll (mil dol)	Number of Establishments	Number of Employees	Sales (mil dol)	Annual Payroll (mil dol)
	147	148	149	150	151	152	153	154	155	156	157	158
PENNSYLVANIA—Cont'd												
Potter	23	51	4.6	1.0	29	1 166	117.6	28.8	49	270	9.1	1.8
Schuylkill	127	628	44.5	15.6	226	14 370	2 625.1	393.7	297	2 931	85.2	22.8
Snyder	31	130	8.4	3.0	65	4 413	414.2	111.3	78	1 218	36.9	10.3
Somerset	85	471	27.0	8.9	118	4 828	644.1	117.1	168	1 902	54.4	15.4
Sullivan	6	D	D	D	NA	NA	NA	NA	24	105	3.9	0.9
Susquehanna	35	167	8.1	2.6	51	1 160	132.6	22.1	79	693	22.2	5.3
Tioga	45	170	8.6	3.9	46	2 930	415.9	69.4	89	1 091	31.8	7.9
Union	40	146	10.3	4.0	36	3 394	434.5	86.0	90	1 501	46.3	12.1
Venango	45	185	9.3	2.8	89	3 950	1 084.6	137.8	99	1 143	31.5	9.2
Warren	45	162	10.3	4.0	81	4 670	1 116.3	147.8	112	984	27.9	6.7
Washington	297	1 729	197.2	68.1	278	11 725	2 788.4	402.3	351	4 812	133.0	38.8
Wayne	78	329	21.7	8.5	68	1 039	182.3	24.5	172	2 459	106.7	32.2
Westmoreland	611	3 878	398.3	129.6	597	24 404	4 000.2	800.2	710	12 235	320.9	93.5
Wyoming	32	105	8.0	3.3	35	D	D	D	56	722	19.0	4.9
York	502	3 457	268.4	105.2	661	45 754	8 156.9	1 557.5	635	10 721	318.7	91.1
RHODE ISLAND	2 349	14 866	1 418.1	541.5	2 535	75 599	10 482.0	2 288.6	2 617	34 162	1 220.9	340.6
Bristol	59	141	13.5	3.5	100	2 634	267.0	73.0	104	1 386	38.9	10.7
Kent	392	1 573	151.5	52.3	411	12 933	2 115.3	417.1	409	6 904	221.4	61.5
Newport	235	2 401	256.1	92.4	98	2 304	296.1	100.0	328	4 643	207.1	59.8
Providence	1 419	8 957	888.0	345.9	1 774	49 910	6 435.0	1 440.9	1 338	17 307	581.4	162.6
Washington	244	1 794	109.0	47.4	152	7 818	1 368.6	257.6	438	3 922	172.1	45.9
SOUTH CAROLINA	6 576	47 679	6 820.9	1 850.5	4 450	346 142	70 797.0	10 369.4	7 775	150 621	4 835.8	1 313.8
Abbeville	10	30	2.5	1.0	36	3 978	607.5	101.4	26	368	8.3	2.5
Aiken	176	3 782	439.6	166.2	99	19 999	4 256.3	896.7	212	3 618	99.4	26.3
Allendale	7	24	2.3	0.7	14	1 440	310.3	33.6	6	50	1.7	0.4
Anderson	199	777	55.2	16.2	240	20 589	4 180.1	611.4	283	4 919	144.6	37.1
Bamberg	10	35	2.2	0.6	24	1 175	180.4	28.5	24	310	6.5	1.7
Barnwell	19	256	30.9	15.0	22	3 376	450.3	75.9	33	327	10.6	2.6
Beaufort	367	2 006	193.0	85.2	94	1 087	137.5	28.7	353	7 838	337.6	93.2
Berkeley	79	365	24.0	10.2	75	6 396	2 811.2	210.6	135	2 304	63.8	17.4
Calhoun	16	24	2.0	0.5	18	809	97.6	22.9	7	D	D	D
Charleston	950	7 688	732.4	293.3	261	10 530	3 039.4	366.3	847	19 759	710.6	198.0
Cherokee	40	158	9.1	4.0	76	8 195	1 767.1	231.4	85	1 771	40.6	10.8
Chester	22	60	3.4	1.2	54	5 260	964.1	145.8	46	660	19.2	5.0
Chesterfield	29	78	3.6	0.8	58	7 450	1 408.2	196.4	65	882	23.3	6.4
Clarendon	20	89	5.7	3.1	24	1 396	122.4	26.1	50	617	16.2	4.3
Colleton	57	245	18.2	4.4	26	1 779	196.0	46.9	57	856	26.2	7.6
Darlington	60	300	22.1	6.2	63	6 002	2 054.6	185.9	91	964	31.4	8.3
Dillon	21	86	4.8	1.7	25	3 613	394.3	62.9	54	929	26.0	7.1
Dorchester	81	486	27.6	11.1	79	3 669	738.3	110.6	115	2 188	61.8	17.4
Edgefield	17	37	2.0	0.5	28	2 041	333.3	44.6	23	289	6.0	1.7
Fairfield	21	69	3.4	1.2	20	2 239	1 001.9	79.8	21	297	7.8	1.8
Florence	179	1 194	83.8	33.0	139	11 011	2 114.2	328.2	245	4 857	147.1	40.5
Georgetown	103	362	40.3	14.9	78	4 974	1 057.6	141.6	151	2 804	86.9	25.8
Greenville	1 040	11 157	3 374.0	547.5	672	45 372	9 507.5	1 431.8	818	17 006	506.6	141.8
Greenwood	87	467	34.0	12.2	93	11 612	1 875.1	339.6	122	2 320	64.5	17.5
Hampton	18	88	15.5	1.9	20	1 307	196.7	44.2	30	393	10.4	2.9
Horry	400	1 766	135.5	53.8	160	6 687	927.8	173.4	1 044	20 246	881.7	228.5
Jasper	20	55	3.5	0.9	NA	NA	NA	NA	35	769	21.7	5.8
Kershaw	69	266	17.2	5.2	62	4 916	1 637.9	151.8	80	1 197	31.0	8.0
Lancaster	42	128	7.2	2.6	54	5 341	1 561.6	145.5	76	1 112	33.2	8.2
Laurens	33	128	7.8	2.0	72	6 447	834.1	171.7	68	1 218	31.3	8.6
Lee	10	42	2.0	0.9	9	641	172.4	18.3	14	D	D	D
Lexington	330	1 535	115.6	47.2	225	9 964	2 080.7	324.2	338	7 502	203.3	55.4
McCormick	5	12	0.3	0.2	NA	NA	NA	NA	8	127	2.2	0.6
Marion	25	64	4.1	1.5	32	5 007	727.0	112.5	45	610	14.2	3.6
Marlboro	21	58	3.2	0.9	22	2 935	755.2	82.1	36	403	10.5	2.6
Newberry	36	132	8.5	2.0	49	5 553	735.4	130.5	43	697	16.7	4.2
Oconee	77	299	29.0	7.7	80	7 487	1 136.0	202.8	101	1 845	42.2	11.0
Orangeburg	84	459	29.9	12.2	90	9 370	1 700.3	222.9	149	2 583	72.1	18.6
Pickens	110	466	24.5	9.1	134	11 790	1 916.3	305.7	193	3 985	97.9	27.3
Richland	913	7 920	944.2	323.7	235	13 558	3 220.7	460.8	695	13 674	418.6	117.0
Saluda	11	27	0.8	0.3	14	2 565	375.2	46.9	18	D	D	D
Spartanburg	330	2 445	215.8	95.7	481	35 102	7 534.6	1 108.6	465	9 520	244.2	68.7

1. Firms subject to federal tax.

STATE County	Health Care and Social Assistance[1], 1997				Other Services[1], 1997				Federal funds and grants, fiscal 2001[2] Expenditures (mil dol)			
										Direct payments for individuals[3]		
	Number of Establishments	Number of Employees	Receipts (mil dol)	Annual Payroll (mil dol)	Number of Establishments	Number of Employees	Receipts (mil dol)	Annual Payroll (mil dol)	Total	Social Security and government retirement	Medicare	Food stamps and Supplemental Security Income
	159	160	161	162	163	164	165	166	167	168	169	170
PENNSYLVANIA—Cont'd												
Potter	27	242	13.3	4.8	18	74	5.1	1.0	89.6	42.9	15.7	3.4
Schuylkill	234	3 154	170.2	76.2	203	797	47.0	11.4	834.3	426.6	210.0	20.2
Snyder	51	308	18.2	7.5	50	200	14.2	3.2	135.7	74.6	29.1	3.2
Somerset	133	983	52.9	22.2	125	395	26.3	5.7	419.2	196.2	99.7	13.6
Sullivan	6	116	7.4	3.1	5	8	0.5	0.1	36.8	19.4	6.9	0.6
Susquehanna	47	564	25.1	9.7	53	109	10.7	2.1	185.9	97.7	36.8	6.6
Tioga	70	408	21.2	9.3	48	142	12.8	3.0	202.6	98.4	37.5	7.1
Union	84	704	47.1	20.2	38	105	6.4	1.5	246.3	80.5	26.8	2.9
Venango	112	730	49.0	23.7	94	442	41.1	12.1	306.7	148.5	68.4	14.1
Warren	61	641	37.9	18.5	69	207	12.5	2.6	219.7	106.6	46.2	8.6
Washington	462	4 547	285.1	130.5	331	2 213	167.2	44.3	1 172.9	554.0	313.7	38.5
Wayne	74	710	39.0	17.3	85	260	16.7	4.4	263.3	153.6	51.7	5.6
Westmoreland	851	6 910	432.2	183.6	642	3 158	191.3	52.4	2 006.1	955.0	542.0	55.0
Wyoming	46	340	15.9	7.1	43	124	9.6	2.3	120.3	61.8	25.7	4.1
York	586	6 842	469.4	214.2	585	3 058	202.4	58.0	1 948.2	780.7	256.4	35.3
RHODE ISLAND	2 074	25 368	1 459.3	647.4	1 949	8 602	546.2	167.8	6 988.6	2 319.8	1 028.4	194.8
Bristol	76	977	49.7	26.1	72	257	15.2	4.0	224.6	119.9	48.0	3.8
Kent	375	4 650	285.3	112.5	341	1 447	87.5	25.8	854.5	415.3	173.5	23.0
Newport	151	1 726	79.3	33.8	156	782	46.1	17.5	1 023.4	238.4	71.8	10.9
Providence	1 223	15 312	909.9	414.2	1 157	5 106	345.3	103.1	3 947.0	1 278.6	641.5	145.8
Washington	249	2 703	135.1	60.8	223	1 010	52.2	17.3	595.0	264.1	93.6	11.3
SOUTH CAROLINA	6 261	78 888	5 318.5	2 361.3	5 672	32 166	1 901.0	563.8	24 674.8	8 970.4	2 707.5	800.5
Abbeville	29	223	8.8	4.3	19	64	3.7	0.9	106.2	53.2	14.1	4.4
Aiken	201	3 163	222.5	87.8	160	937	45.7	12.3	2 236.7	322.8	103.7	27.6
Allendale	5	44	3.6	1.0	10	25	1.2	0.3	75.6	19.8	9.8	6.7
Anderson	244	2 970	183.4	95.2	220	1 123	65.4	22.4	707.4	379.9	119.0	20.9
Bamberg	28	268	13.6	6.0	17	51	3.1	0.9	105.3	32.4	15.2	5.9
Barnwell	36	285	13.1	5.4	28	60	4.8	1.0	130.7	44.9	21.1	9.1
Beaufort	206	1 814	134.8	50.4	181	1 060	58.9	18.3	854.4	343.7	76.0	15.0
Berkeley	87	986	39.6	16.3	111	473	23.6	5.8	507.2	273.5	50.3	19.3
Calhoun	10	138	4.6	2.2	13	56	2.4	0.8	61.3	23.9	7.2	3.9
Charleston	841	9 962	678.6	280.8	628	4 622	268.8	88.5	3 036.6	840.1	245.4	72.4
Cherokee	59	688	50.2	19.6	64	325	18.8	6.3	211.7	101.8	34.4	7.0
Chester	34	187	12.8	6.2	36	154	8.0	1.9	161.4	75.8	29.8	8.0
Chesterfield	46	709	39.8	15.7	35	135	7.6	2.1	205.2	83.1	31.1	11.9
Clarendon	36	468	19.5	8.6	29	135	9.6	2.1	187.7	68.8	25.6	12.8
Colleton	48	829	57.2	19.8	39	201	12.5	3.2	228.8	93.5	39.2	13.3
Darlington	75	1 008	66.8	27.0	80	351	22.7	5.7	319.7	132.9	49.6	17.5
Dillon	56	784	38.4	15.9	36	158	8.2	2.1	181.6	57.9	29.7	16.5
Dorchester	122	1 530	93.9	32.5	124	541	28.6	8.6	395.8	245.2	49.0	12.5
Edgefield	21	206	7.7	3.2	16	46	2.4	0.6	107.3	34.5	12.3	5.1
Fairfield	16	292	9.9	4.5	14	50	2.9	0.8	118.5	47.8	19.1	7.6
Florence	276	5 558	399.9	193.5	191	1 268	73.1	21.7	665.2	261.1	105.3	44.5
Georgetown	125	991	67.4	28.4	97	386	24.0	6.6	330.2	184.4	61.0	12.6
Greenville	673	7 746	575.5	285.4	674	4 537	290.3	86.2	1 594.4	750.7	248.2	53.1
Greenwood	105	1 370	88.1	44.1	96	431	23.8	7.3	304.9	155.1	43.9	11.5
Hampton	22	210	14.4	3.5	25	154	7.0	2.1	150.8	49.1	18.8	8.2
Horry	326	4 036	295.9	117.8	336	1 477	91.5	25.5	877.5	475.0	127.6	31.7
Jasper	21	123	5.8	2.5	22	130	6.0	1.3	94.9	31.6	12.3	5.2
Kershaw	55	588	40.9	18.4	87	308	16.1	4.7	232.4	124.3	37.3	9.4
Lancaster	90	1 530	109.5	40.0	87	344	23.5	4.8	244.0	127.5	45.4	10.7
Laurens	54	532	27.2	13.0	58	217	12.3	3.2	287.4	162.4	42.2	14.1
Lee	14	93	3.0	1.6	16	70	2.8	0.6	110.6	35.1	14.3	8.2
Lexington	281	3 405	193.8	89.3	346	2 257	145.4	41.8	797.0	427.2	105.8	20.6
McCormick	5	47	3.2	1.6	6	20	0.7	0.1	59.8	29.5	6.4	2.4
Marion	65	564	27.6	13.8	38	134	6.9	1.8	270.2	76.3	39.4	14.0
Marlboro	33	507	38.1	13.8	20	73	2.9	0.7	177.9	60.1	28.9	12.1
Newberry	41	441	17.1	8.2	55	252	17.8	4.7	178.9	88.5	28.0	8.1
Oconee	99	777	48.8	24.1	84	362	18.2	5.3	290.2	174.6	51.0	6.4
Orangeburg	146	1 161	73.0	31.2	135	603	27.6	8.7	526.5	197.0	71.7	34.4
Pickens	133	2 019	117.3	61.0	114	441	26.1	7.2	438.6	227.6	62.8	12.7
Richland	686	9 381	723.4	331.4	509	3 641	199.5	62.5	3 059.2	761.7	184.5	60.7
Saluda	17	220	5.7	2.6	14	53	3.5	0.7	73.2	32.8	9.3	3.6
Spartanburg	377	4 899	364.5	167.8	377	2 038	153.4	41.2	1 017.4	551.5	166.7	41.7

1. Firms subject to federal tax.   2. October 1, 2000 to September 30, 2001.   3. State totals may include programs not allocated by county.

Table B. States and Counties — **Federal Funds and Local Government Finances**

STATE County	Federal funds and grants, fiscal 2001[1] (cont'd) Expenditures (mil dol) (cont'd)							Local government finances, 1997 General revenue				
	Procurement contract awards			Grants[2]							Taxes	
												Per capita[3] (dollars)	
	Salaries and wages	Defense	Other	Medicaid and other health-related	Nutrition and family welfare	Education	Other	Total (mil dol)	Intergovern-mental (mil dol)	Total (mil dol)	Total	Property
	171	172	173	174	175	176	177	178	179	180	181	182
PENNSYLVANIA—Cont'd												
Potter	3.2	0.5	0.9	13.2	2.2	0.7	4.3	40.5	16.3	13.3	778	642
Schuylkill	40.0	2.5	11.7	75.7	11.5	3.9	11.1	285.4	139.2	89.4	591	415
Snyder	5.0	0.2	1.5	12.7	1.9	1.1	1.2	57.2	24.1	24.3	635	384
Somerset	13.4	8.3	3.3	52.8	8.7	3.0	7.9	138.8	66.0	47.9	597	470
Sullivan	1.7	0.0	0.5	3.7	0.5	0.2	2.3	12.9	5.0	6.6	1 089	958
Susquehanna	7.9	0.1	1.9	17.8	3.7	1.6	7.6	81.0	44.5	28.8	683	616
Tioga	9.5	1.1	2.0	27.5	6.8	1.4	5.2	86.3	44.7	27.5	661	519
Union	74.0	0.6	10.6	11.1	5.4	0.8	24.7	79.0	37.5	25.4	608	394
Venango	9.0	0.3	2.3	38.3	7.7	2.9	5.1	136.9	71.0	40.7	701	546
Warren	10.6	6.4	3.2	18.0	4.1	2.0	10.2	88.7	44.2	31.9	720	514
Washington	35.9	7.8	11.1	120.8	23.6	9.4	31.5	404.5	180.0	160.3	779	615
Wayne	8.7	2.2	6.7	16.2	3.8	1.5	4.5	103.2	33.4	54.6	1 203	1 148
Westmoreland	64.6	14.8	19.1	176.4	38.4	11.4	75.9	773.5	317.1	299.8	800	637
Wyoming	4.3	0.6	1.1	10.9	3.1	0.9	5.8	54.8	25.0	23.2	788	630
York	111.1	545.6	26.4	109.5	19.2	6.6	28.5	735.0	264.7	307.6	830	614
RHODE ISLAND	747.4	283.1	109.1	845.3	220.6	120.6	421.0	X	X	X	X	X
Bristol	9.3	2.6	1.8	20.7	3.4	2.3	5.9	103.3	36.6	55.4	1 131	1 116
Kent	49.1	7.9	10.2	67.6	15.8	10.6	33.5	345.5	90.9	225.1	1 392	1 368
Newport	363.8	247.9	7.9	40.2	8.9	9.3	2.9	190.1	46.4	117.1	1 418	1 369
Providence	274.3	11.8	79.5	673.4	179.8	90.9	273.7	1 241.1	445.5	676.3	1 177	1 167
Washington	50.9	12.8	9.7	42.8	9.2	6.3	61.0	250.8	66.2	160.6	1 342	1 319
SOUTH CAROLINA	2 525.5	1 063.7	2 091.5	2 644.5	576.7	433.4	1 075.4	X	X	X	X	X
Abbeville	2.8	0.3	0.6	19.2	2.3	1.3	4.1	32.8	16.2	11.7	478	422
Aiken	59.4	3.1	1 591.5	81.2	10.9	6.9	9.8	216.3	98.6	70.7	528	477
Allendale	1.6	0.0	0.3	23.4	2.9	1.6	2.3	21.4	11.1	8.0	695	596
Anderson	24.4	1.5	4.9	73.2	9.1	13.3	31.9	224.3	105.7	84.7	535	466
Bamberg	2.4	0.1	5.2	22.5	3.5	5.6	1.4	27.0	15.3	8.6	518	443
Barnwell	2.6	3.2	0.6	29.0	3.4	2.0	8.3	55.8	31.3	10.1	465	408
Beaufort	281.3	63.8	4.0	38.7	8.9	7.5	5.4	239.9	65.6	101.8	955	864
Berkeley	24.1	21.4	2.6	44.0	17.8	12.7	23.5	183.1	103.7	51.8	385	360
Calhoun	1.6	0.0	0.3	13.1	1.8	1.0	0.8	21.5	9.5	9.5	689	673
Charleston	666.2	559.6	129.4	259.3	31.5	19.9	151.5	762.7	236.2	298.6	1 048	747
Cherokee	5.4	0.0	2.1	27.2	4.2	3.0	19.2	117.1	35.5	30.0	620	551
Chester	4.1	0.0	0.9	22.7	4.1	2.9	9.1	63.2	30.4	23.0	681	592
Chesterfield	5.6	0.0	1.5	54.6	5.7	2.7	2.3	60.3	34.3	19.1	476	428
Clarendon	3.7	0.0	0.8	48.6	5.5	4.3	2.9	63.3	28.7	12.4	404	366
Colleton	6.2	1.7	1.1	43.3	7.4	2.8	12.5	60.2	30.5	23.7	639	555
Darlington	6.9	0.1	2.2	70.0	9.5	5.8	7.9	99.5	49.9	36.0	547	512
Dillon	4.2	0.0	0.8	46.9	5.4	2.9	3.6	46.2	28.3	9.9	334	232
Dorchester	11.6	1.5	2.9	45.7	6.4	4.4	4.8	133.8	70.8	41.4	456	410
Edgefield	21.0	5.6	1.9	18.3	2.2	1.5	1.1	34.4	19.2	11.2	569	513
Fairfield	3.0	4.1	1.5	22.0	3.1	1.9	4.7	52.9	16.8	30.2	1 352	1 333
Florence	41.0	2.0	8.3	134.4	18.5	9.9	10.5	208.8	107.8	62.9	505	339
Georgetown	7.3	4.6	1.7	37.2	6.0	3.6	6.1	122.9	49.3	45.4	868	812
Greenville	105.0	101.4	58.5	143.2	27.6	20.5	25.8	1 037.3	236.3	250.7	719	631
Greenwood	10.9	2.8	2.0	37.7	11.3	4.7	9.9	206.2	45.9	35.7	563	524
Hampton	16.9	0.2	6.1	34.2	3.5	1.7	2.6	42.6	25.4	12.9	680	584
Horry	27.6	4.7	7.7	83.0	15.5	9.6	67.0	409.2	115.7	165.7	980	789
Jasper	2.1	6.5	0.7	24.6	2.7	1.6	5.6	27.2	13.5	10.5	619	503
Kershaw	6.7	0.1	1.4	33.9	3.9	2.7	7.5	128.1	37.5	26.6	557	517
Lancaster	6.6	0.0	5.8	32.8	5.5	4.1	0.3	82.3	44.5	28.1	485	378
Laurens	6.6	0.0	1.4	38.5	4.8	2.9	3.8	107.4	43.1	23.9	386	357
Lee	2.0	0.0	0.5	28.2	3.8	1.8	3.9	27.4	16.8	8.2	407	350
Lexington	33.1	3.1	8.7	52.3	9.2	9.9	112.7	576.2	214.9	134.9	673	636
McCormick	3.8	0.6	0.4	11.6	1.2	2.4	0.3	14.4	7.7	4.5	474	421
Marion	5.5	66.9	1.0	49.2	5.8	3.1	2.3	110.6	36.7	17.2	494	387
Marlboro	4.4	0.8	1.2	47.0	4.9	2.3	7.0	46.2	28.9	12.0	407	307
Newberry	7.8	0.1	1.3	27.6	3.0	2.2	5.4	54.2	26.9	19.4	566	537
Oconee	9.3	0.2	2.1	31.9	2.9	3.2	2.4	96.5	35.7	49.8	785	754
Orangeburg	12.5	0.2	3.0	112.3	18.8	16.6	25.6	220.1	80.0	51.7	591	538
Pickens	15.2	7.7	2.9	32.1	4.3	5.7	55.1	124.7	60.1	43.6	417	337
Richland	791.6	164.5	88.5	275.9	183.5	145.8	279.4	766.6	215.4	160.9	530	444
Saluda	3.1	0.0	0.7	15.0	1.4	1.1	2.2	20.3	12.3	5.7	338	293
Spartanburg	32.3	0.7	11.4	130.0	18.5	14.2	20.3	412.8	192.6	162.1	662	603

1. October 1, 2000 to September 30, 2001.   2. State totals may include programs not allocated by county.   3. Based on the resident population estimated as of July 1 of the year shown.

STATE County	Total (mil dol) [183]	Per capita[1] (dollars) [184]	Education [185]	Health and hospitals [186]	Police protection [187]	Public welfare [188]	Highways [189]	Total (mil dol) [190]	Per capita[1] (dollars) [191]	Federal civilian [192]	Federal military [193]	State and local [194]	Democratic [195]	Republican [196]	All other [197]
PENNSYLVANIA—Cont'd															
Potter	35.8	2 088	56.8	0.0	0.8	6.8	8.8	35.0	2 041	49	57	1 018	28.7	68.5	2.8
Schuylkill	291.3	1 926	53.9	4.8	2.1	6.7	4.8	320.3	2 118	707	500	6 500	45.0	51.2	3.8
Snyder	62.5	1 632	69.8	0.1	1.0	0.8	5.9	26.8	700	90	127	2 498	27.5	69.8	2.7
Somerset	154.5	1 925	62.8	2.9	1.8	0.1	5.5	159.1	1 982	222	268	4 170	36.5	61.3	2.3
Sullivan	12.5	2 053	65.2	0.1	0.6	0.1	9.9	3.7	611	27	20	343	34.3	62.1	3.5
Susquehanna	87.2	2 073	73.9	0.2	0.5	2.4	5.7	61.6	1 463	121	143	1 828	37.5	59.2	3.3
Tioga	87.4	2 101	58.1	5.0	1.2	8.8	6.1	73.0	1 754	166	141	2 953	31.3	65.2	3.5
Union	86.1	2 062	65.9	2.5	1.2	2.3	3.5	106.9	2 559	1 595	142	1 910	31.9	64.7	3.3
Venango	137.3	2 364	54.3	6.4	1.6	2.9	3.4	217.7	3 750	171	193	3 734	39.9	56.7	3.4
Warren	89.3	2 020	48.1	8.4	1.9	13.1	5.9	45.7	1 033	255	146	2 445	43.0	53.0	4.1
Washington	447.1	2 172	60.5	0.2	2.3	4.9	3.9	640.0	3 110	632	700	9 202	53.2	44.2	2.5
Wayne	98.0	2 158	66.1	1.0	0.9	2.7	4.1	142.8	3 145	128	155	2 324	36.5	59.2	4.3
Westmoreland	774.5	2 067	57.6	3.3	2.4	6.6	4.0	1 082.5	2 889	1 117	1 247	15 115	45.8	51.6	2.6
Wyoming	53.1	1 806	65.0	0.1	1.4	0.1	6.5	25.7	875	74	98	1 083	37.3	59.2	3.4
York	690.5	1 864	50.9	3.9	3.7	4.5	3.5	964.9	2 604	3 679	1 707	12 651	36.0	60.8	3.2
RHODE ISLAND	X	X	X	X	X	X	X	X	X	10 334	9 337	55 455	61.0	31.9	7.1
Bristol	105.1	2 147	70.9	0.2	4.7	0.0	5.2	62.1	1 269	116	303	1 687	57.7	36.0	6.3
Kent	316.6	1 958	58.2	0.2	6.7	0.7	3.1	148.0	915	644	918	8 177	58.9	34.4	6.7
Newport	174.7	2 115	54.1	0.4	7.5	0.3	2.2	77.5	939	4 150	4 040	3 232	54.9	37.7	7.4
Providence	1 157.0	2 014	52.2	0.1	7.5	0.5	2.7	653.8	1 138	4 861	3 332	31 688	65.3	28.1	6.7
Washington	277.9	2 322	64.7	0.4	6.2	0.0	3.1	171.1	1 430	563	744	10 671	52.6	37.8	9.6
SOUTH CAROLINA	X	X	X	X	X	X	X	X	X	28 683	57 898	285 424	40.9	56.8	2.3
Abbeville	32.9	1 347	62.2	0.6	6.4	0.0	2.8	17.6	720	47	132	1 380	45.0	53.1	1.9
Aiken	207.3	1 547	59.9	4.1	3.1	0.2	2.8	104.5	780	899	724	6 320	32.3	65.4	2.3
Allendale	21.0	1 812	62.1	4.6	4.3	0.5	2.1	17.9	1 548	26	61	1 544	70.0	29.0	1.0
Anderson	226.9	1 434	66.6	0.9	5.0	0.3	4.7	141.6	895	397	872	10 415	34.6	63.2	2.2
Bamberg	25.3	1 520	69.2	1.2	5.4	0.2	1.8	11.2	675	39	87	1 244	62.2	36.9	1.0
Barnwell	49.9	2 285	54.7	14.8	4.2	0.1	1.9	41.6	1 907	51	117	1 720	44.2	54.6	1.1
Beaufort	254.8	2 391	40.8	20.7	4.9	0.1	2.0	258.6	2 426	2 120	11 614	5 888	39.6	57.9	2.5
Berkeley	188.6	1 404	67.7	1.7	4.3	0.3	1.8	264.3	1 968	389	770	6 574	40.9	57.2	1.9
Calhoun	20.4	1 479	75.7	2.7	4.1	0.2	0.0	4.0	290	34	76	934	48.1	50.5	1.5
Charleston	707.7	2 485	35.5	2.6	7.4	0.4	2.3	1 140.0	4 003	7 857	12 552	32 236	44.4	52.2	3.3
Cherokee	83.0	1 716	67.4	1.4	4.6	0.2	2.2	1 403.9	29 033	93	268	2 127	37.6	60.7	1.7
Chester	60.3	1 789	64.7	2.8	4.4	0.3	1.8	82.8	2 455	69	187	2 515	50.2	47.8	2.0
Chesterfield	61.0	1 524	70.8	1.1	5.7	0.4	2.8	23.5	586	97	222	1 981	48.8	50.0	1.2
Clarendon	56.1	1 830	57.9	23.6	3.5	0.1	1.9	21.8	710	66	165	1 976	53.1	45.9	0.9
Colleton	62.2	1 679	61.5	3.4	6.3	0.9	2.3	15.5	419	111	201	2 193	48.2	50.5	1.3
Darlington	93.8	1 426	67.6	1.3	5.1	0.3	2.4	48.8	743	112	356	2 917	46.9	51.6	1.5
Dillon	49.7	1 673	64.2	1.0	4.9	0.2	2.9	15.6	524	89	159	1 482	54.8	44.2	0.9
Dorchester	145.0	1 598	72.9	1.0	3.4	0.4	2.9	106.5	1 174	181	484	4 750	36.2	61.6	2.2
Edgefield	34.5	1 748	64.4	2.7	4.2	0.2	5.4	20.7	1 048	488	107	1 059	44.7	53.9	1.4
Fairfield	53.7	2 398	62.8	2.0	4.5	0.4	1.9	38.4	1 717	47	121	1 504	62.7	35.9	1.5
Florence	195.4	1 571	63.5	1.1	5.0	0.6	1.8	270.0	2 171	702	673	11 384	41.4	57.1	1.5
Georgetown	114.8	2 194	57.4	1.6	5.0	0.2	2.5	181.2	3 462	101	325	3 802	46.4	51.8	1.8
Greenville	1 006.4	2 888	29.9	41.5	3.0	0.0	0.7	631.8	1 813	1 726	1 959	22 798	31.2	66.1	2.7
Greenwood	177.7	2 806	34.3	47.8	2.8	0.1	1.6	87.8	1 386	201	341	6 469	39.0	58.5	2.5
Hampton	42.5	2 231	60.1	3.7	4.6	0.4	2.3	8.7	456	381	102	1 209	63.1	36.1	0.8
Horry	446.4	2 639	45.2	9.2	4.8	0.3	4.0	435.0	2 571	446	957	9 788	40.9	56.5	2.6
Jasper	29.2	1 724	51.1	4.0	7.5	0.4	2.6	18.3	1 079	40	92	1 046	56.4	37.3	6.3
Kershaw	127.5	2 671	38.8	38.8	2.1	1.2	0.8	62.9	1 317	113	264	3 354	37.7	60.5	1.7
Lancaster	77.5	1 339	66.7	2.5	6.4	0.2	2.1	72.0	1 244	108	322	2 702	42.4	56.4	1.2
Laurens	107.8	1 741	42.0	27.5	3.7	0.2	2.9	73.3	1 185	105	346	4 230	38.8	59.3	1.9
Lee	24.8	1 226	69.9	0.5	3.2	0.0	1.8	4.9	244	45	109	879	58.7	40.3	1.0
Lexington	576.5	2 877	43.0	38.0	2.9	0.1	0.8	336.6	1 680	514	1 119	12 240	27.5	69.9	2.6
McCormick	15.2	1 600	52.8	2.4	3.8	0.1	2.3	20.4	2 136	88	51	937	51.8	46.5	1.7
Marion	102.0	2 922	36.2	43.1	3.3	0.1	2.6	64.6	1 851	83	186	2 613	60.6	38.6	0.9
Marlboro	50.8	1 717	57.5	0.5	5.2	0.2	1.1	31.8	1 075	85	158	1 748	64.2	34.2	1.6
Newberry	52.0	1 520	69.6	0.7	4.6	0.4	2.3	28.0	818	143	184	2 021	35.8	60.6	3.7
Oconee	103.9	1 637	70.8	0.5	4.5	0.2	4.4	83.0	1 309	165	348	3 477	32.1	65.2	2.7
Orangeburg	232.1	2 653	46.6	33.1	1.7	0.1	1.2	101.2	1 156	226	482	7 325	60.5	38.7	0.8
Pickens	127.5	1 219	64.8	1.2	5.2	0.3	3.3	79.7	762	241	591	8 029	25.8	71.4	2.8
Richland	815.1	2 685	33.6	32.3	4.1	0.2	1.1	676.5	2 228	7 687	11 866	52 895	54.3	43.0	2.6
Saluda	18.7	1 115	63.3	0.7	5.3	0.3	2.5	6.1	363	47	91	846	38.9	59.5	1.6
Spartanburg	407.0	1 662	62.5	1.9	5.1	0.3	2.4	1 121.9	4 579	518	1 344	15 518	35.4	62.4	2.3

1. Based on the resident population estimated as of July 1 of the year shown.   2. Data subject to copyright.

Table B. States and Counties — **Land Area and Population**

| | | | | | Population and population characteristics, 2000 | | | | | | | | | | | | |
| | | | | | | | | Race alone or in combination (percent) | | | | | Age (percent) | | | | | |
STATE/ County code	MSA/ PMSA/ NECMA code[1]	County Type[2]	STATE County	Land area,[3] (sq km) 2000	Total persons	Rank	Per square kilometer	White	Black	Am. Indian, Alaska Native	Asian and Pacific Islander	Percent Hispanic[4]	Under 5 years	5 to 17 years	18 to 24 years	25 to 34 years	35 to 44 years	45 to 54 years
				1	2	3	4	5	6	7	8	9	10	11	12	13	14	15
			SOUTH CAROLINA— Cont'd															
45 085	8140	3	Sumter	1 723	104 646	505	60.7	51.0	47.2	0.6	1.3	1.8	7.5	20.6	10.5	13.7	15.7	12.4
45 087	...	6	Union	1 332	29 881	1 399	22.4	68.3	31.4	0.4	0.4	0.7	6.3	17.5	8.2	12.8	15.1	14.1
45 089	...	6	Williamsburg	2 419	37 217	1 185	15.4	33.0	66.6	0.4	0.3	0.7	6.9	21.7	9.0	11.7	14.0	14.4
45 091	1520	2	York	1 768	164 614	327	93.1	78.0	19.4	1.2	1.1	2.0	6.8	19.5	9.5	14.4	16.7	13.9
46 000	...	X	SOUTH DAKOTA	196 540	754 844	X	3.8	89.9	0.9	9.0	0.9	1.4	6.8	20.1	10.3	12.1	15.3	12.9
46 003	...	9	Aurora	1 834	3 058	2 988	1.7	96.2	0.4	2.1	0.3	2.1	5.7	21.9	6.5	8.5	13.5	12.6
46 005	...	7	Beadle	3 260	17 023	1 951	5.2	97.8	1.0	1.3	0.5	0.9	5.7	19.0	8.3	9.6	15.1	13.8
46 007	...	9	Bennett	3 070	3 574	2 946	1.2	47.1	0.5	58.1	0.4	2.0	8.9	27.4	9.2	11.0	14.3	10.5
46 009	...	9	Bon Homme	1 459	7 260	2 658	5.0	96.0	0.9	3.3	0.1	0.6	4.9	18.1	7.6	10.9	16.0	12.6
46 011	...	7	Brookings	2 058	28 220	1 444	13.7	97.1	0.5	1.2	1.6	0.9	5.7	15.1	26.8	12.0	12.3	10.7
46 013	...	5	Brown	4 437	35 460	1 236	8.0	96.3	0.4	3.3	0.6	0.7	6.4	17.2	11.6	11.9	14.8	13.2
46 015	...	9	Brule	2 121	5 364	2 824	2.5	90.9	0.4	9.1	0.6	0.5	5.7	24.8	6.8	10.1	14.6	12.4
46 017	...	9	Buffalo	1 219	2 032	3 063	1.7	17.8	0.1	83.3	0.1	0.9	10.6	30.7	11.0	12.2	12.9	9.0
46 019	...	6	Butte	5 824	9 094	2 521	1.6	96.9	0.2	2.7	0.4	2.9	6.1	22.2	7.2	10.1	15.8	14.4
46 021	...	9	Campbell	1 906	1 782	3 080	0.9	99.6	0.0	0.6	0.1	0.2	5.5	21.2	3.5	8.1	16.4	11.7
46 023	...	9	Charles Mix	2 843	9 350	2 502	3.3	70.7	0.3	29.5	0.3	1.9	8.6	23.4	7.1	10.1	13.1	11.1
46 025	...	9	Clark	2 481	4 143	2 904	1.7	99.0	0.1	0.7	0.2	0.5	5.4	21.6	5.8	8.3	13.7	13.3
46 027	...	7	Clay	1 066	13 537	2 192	12.7	94.0	1.3	3.4	2.3	0.9	5.4	13.4	31.5	13.3	10.6	9.9
46 029	...	7	Codington	1 781	25 897	1 521	14.5	97.5	0.3	1.9	0.4	1.1	7.1	19.7	10.4	12.4	15.7	12.8
46 031	...	9	Corson	6 405	4 181	2 899	0.7	38.7	0.2	62.3	0.1	2.1	9.1	27.9	9.8	10.4	13.9	10.7
46 033	...	8	Custer	4 034	7 275	2 657	1.8	96.0	0.5	4.5	0.6	1.5	4.6	19.4	6.3	8.4	14.0	17.4
46 035	...	7	Davison	1 128	18 741	1 857	16.6	96.9	0.4	2.4	0.7	0.7	6.5	18.8	12.0	11.3	14.6	12.5
46 037	...	9	Day	2 664	6 267	2 759	2.4	92.1	0.2	8.2	0.2	0.4	5.5	20.4	5.2	8.3	14.2	13.7
46 039	...	9	Deuel	1 615	4 498	2 879	2.8	99.2	0.1	0.7	0.4	0.8	5.5	19.9	5.9	10.2	15.2	12.5
46 041	...	9	Dewey	5 964	5 972	2 786	1.0	25.5	0.1	75.4	0.3	0.9	9.2	29.7	9.0	12.1	15.1	9.7
46 043	...	9	Douglas	1 123	3 458	2 957	3.1	98.6	0.2	1.4	0.1	0.4	5.8	21.9	4.9	8.6	13.8	13.1
46 045	...	9	Edmunds	2 967	4 367	2 888	1.5	99.5	0.1	0.3	0.2	0.5	5.7	21.0	5.1	8.5	14.8	12.1
46 047	...	7	Fall River	4 506	7 453	2 643	1.7	92.9	0.4	8.1	0.5	1.7	4.8	18.0	5.8	7.2	13.4	16.2
46 049	...	9	Faulk	2 590	2 640	3 018	1.0	99.7	0.1	0.4	0.0	0.2	5.5	21.1	5.4	8.4	14.7	12.0
46 051	...	7	Grant	1 768	7 847	2 619	4.4	98.9	0.0	0.6	0.3	0.5	5.9	20.7	5.7	9.3	15.8	14.0
46 053	...	9	Gregory	2 631	4 792	2 860	1.8	93.9	0.1	6.2	0.5	0.9	4.9	19.4	5.1	7.8	14.3	13.3
46 055	...	9	Haakon	4 696	2 196	3 051	0.5	97.4	0.0	3.4	0.2	0.6	5.3	20.4	7.0	8.7	16.5	14.5
46 057	...	9	Hamlin	1 313	5 540	2 813	4.2	99.0	0.2	0.9	0.3	0.6	6.5	22.9	6.9	10.0	14.1	11.6
46 059	...	9	Hand	3 721	3 741	2 938	1.0	99.6	0.1	0.3	0.2	0.3	5.2	19.4	5.1	7.6	14.8	13.3
46 061	...	9	Hanson	1 126	3 139	2 983	2.8	99.7	0.0	0.2	0.3	0.1	7.5	22.0	7.7	11.7	14.4	12.0
46 063	...	9	Harding	6 917	1 353	3 100	0.2	98.0	0.3	1.1	0.6	1.6	4.2	28.3	4.4	8.8	16.0	16.0
46 065	...	7	Hughes	1 919	16 481	1 990	8.6	90.3	0.3	9.9	0.6	1.2	6.6	21.2	6.2	12.2	16.5	14.9
46 067	...	9	Hutchinson	2 105	8 075	2 600	3.8	99.2	0.2	0.8	0.1	0.5	5.9	18.9	5.6	9.2	12.8	12.1
46 069	...	9	Hyde	2 230	1 671	3 086	0.7	91.7	0.2	8.4	0.1	0.5	7.6	18.0	5.8	8.8	14.7	11.7
46 071	...	9	Jackson	4 841	2 930	2 997	0.6	51.7	0.1	49.6	0.2	0.4	8.3	28.2	8.0	10.4	13.2	12.1
46 073	...	9	Jerauld	1 372	2 295	3 039	1.7	99.3	0.1	0.8	0.1	0.3	3.7	17.7	6.9	7.9	11.9	15.1
46 075	...	9	Jones	2 514	1 193	3 105	0.5	97.3	0.3	3.9	0.1	0.3	4.9	21.4	6.2	9.2	16.3	13.7
46 077	...	9	Kingsbury	2 171	5 815	2 803	2.7	99.0	0.1	0.6	0.5	0.7	5.4	19.1	6.1	8.1	14.8	13.2
46 079	...	6	Lake	1 459	11 276	2 351	7.7	98.2	0.3	0.9	0.6	0.8	5.5	18.2	15.0	9.2	14.2	13.1
46 081	...	6	Lawrence	2 072	21 802	1 702	10.5	96.8	0.4	2.9	0.6	1.8	4.8	18.3	13.7	10.5	14.9	14.4
46 083	7760	3	Lincoln	1 497	24 131	1 589	16.1	98.3	0.6	0.8	0.7	0.7	8.0	21.6	7.6	14.4	17.6	13.5
46 085	...	9	Lyman	4 247	3 895	2 923	0.9	66.2	0.1	34.7	0.5	0.5	8.6	23.5	7.6	10.9	14.9	12.0
46 087	...	8	McCook	1 488	5 832	2 800	3.9	99.2	0.1	0.6	0.3	0.8	6.7	21.7	6.2	10.5	15.0	11.7
46 089	...	9	McPherson	2 945	2 904	2 998	1.0	99.6	0.0	0.4	0.2	0.2	5.5	16.7	4.5	8.3	11.7	11.7
46 091	...	9	Marshall	2 170	4 576	2 873	2.1	93.2	0.2	6.8	0.3	0.8	5.9	21.1	5.1	9.1	13.7	13.4
46 093	...	6	Meade	8 989	24 253	1 586	2.7	95.0	1.9	3.4	1.3	2.1	7.7	20.7	10.6	13.2	16.4	13.5
46 095	...	9	Mellette	3 384	2 083	3 060	0.6	47.1	0.0	54.9	0.2	1.7	9.0	26.3	7.5	11.3	13.3	12.0
46 097	...	9	Miner	1 477	2 884	3 000	2.0	99.0	0.6	0.4	0.1	0.6	5.1	20.4	5.6	8.5	14.2	13.1
46 099	7760	3	Minnehaha	2 097	148 281	365	70.7	94.3	2.0	2.3	1.4	2.1	7.3	18.9	10.8	15.3	16.7	12.8
46 101	...	8	Moody	1 346	6 595	2 727	4.9	87.0	0.5	13.8	0.8	0.8	6.2	22.9	7.2	11.1	15.4	13.5
46 103	6660	3	Pennington	7 190	88 565	589	12.3	89.2	1.4	9.9	1.4	2.6	7.1	19.5	10.5	12.9	16.3	13.7
46 105	...	9	Perkins	7 437	3 363	2 966	0.5	97.5	0.3	2.2	0.3	0.7	5.8	18.3	5.6	8.7	14.7	13.6
46 107	...	9	Potter	2 244	2 693	3 015	1.2	98.9	0.0	1.2	0.6	0.2	4.5	18.5	3.9	7.2	15.1	14.3
46 109	...	9	Roberts	2 852	10 016	2 444	3.5	69.7	0.2	31.2	0.3	0.6	6.7	23.3	7.2	10.0	13.5	12.7
46 111	...	9	Sanborn	1 474	2 675	3 016	1.8	99.1	0.1	0.4	0.5	1.0	5.8	19.9	7.7	8.6	15.1	14.0
46 113	...	7	Shannon	5 423	12 466	2 268	2.3	5.2	0.1	95.1	0.2	1.4	10.9	34.4	10.6	13.3	12.4	8.5
46 115	...	7	Spink	3 895	7 454	2 642	1.9	98.1	0.3	1.8	0.2	0.4	5.6	19.9	6.7	10.3	15.8	13.5
46 117	...	9	Stanley	3 738	2 772	3 006	0.7	94.4	0.4	6.2	0.3	0.4	5.6	21.5	7.1	11.8	16.5	15.4
46 119	...	9	Sully	2 608	1 556	3 091	0.6	99.0	0.2	1.3	0.3	0.8	5.7	19.9	6.1	10.2	16.4	12.9
46 121	...	9	Todd	3 595	9 050	2 526	2.5	13.7	0.2	86.9	0.2	1.5	12.0	31.9	10.4	12.5	12.6	9.5

1. MSA = Metropolitan Statistical Area. PMSA = Primary MSA. NECMA = New England County Metropolitan Area. See Appendix A for explanation of these concepts. See Appendix B for list of metropolitan areas identified by type, with component counties. 2. County typology code from the Economic Research Service of USDA. See Appendix A for definition. 3. Dry land or land partially or temporarily covered by water. 4. Hispanic persons may be of any race.

STATE County	Population, 2000 (cont'd) Age (percent) (cont'd)				Population — change and components of change, 1990–2001 Total persons		Percent change		Components of change, 2000–2001			Households, 2000			Percent	
	55 to 64 years	65 to 74 years	75 years and over	Percent female	2001	1990	1990–2000	2000–2001	Births	Deaths	Net migration	Number	Percent change, 1990–2000	Persons per house-hold	Female family house-holder[1]	One person
	16	17	18	19	20	21	22	23	24	25	26	27	28	29	30	31
SOUTH CAROLINA—Cont'd																
Sumter	8.3	6.1	5.1	51.6	104 237	101 276	3.3	-0.4	2 287	1 205	-1 449	37 728	15.3	2.68	18.3	23.2
Union	10.3	8.3	7.3	52.9	29 548	30 337	-1.5	-1.1	506	500	-336	12 087	6.0	2.44	16.8	26.8
Williamsburg	9.2	7.3	5.7	53.2	36 810	36 815	1.1	-1.1	754	535	-628	13 714	13.3	2.69	22.4	24.9
York	8.9	5.8	4.6	51.6	170 259	131 497	25.2	3.4	2 755	1 659	4 479	61 051	29.9	2.63	13.3	21.3
SOUTH DAKOTA	8.3	7.0	7.3	50.4	756 600	696 004	8.5	0.2	12 866	8 822	-2 240	290 245	12.0	2.50	9.0	27.6
Aurora	9.6	10.0	11.6	49.0	3 015	3 135	-2.5	-1.4	31	47	-27	1 165	1.7	2.45	5.0	28.2
Beadle	9.2	9.1	10.2	50.9	16 785	18 253	-6.7	-1.4	239	224	-253	7 210	-1.8	2.30	7.4	33.1
Bennett	7.6	6.0	5.1	50.4	3 554	3 206	11.5	-0.6	92	45	-68	1 123	9.0	3.14	17.5	23.3
Bon Homme	9.0	9.4	11.5	44.8	7 193	7 089	2.4	-0.9	89	100	-53	2 635	-0.5	2.38	5.1	29.5
Brookings	6.6	4.9	5.9	49.5	28 016	25 207	12.0	-0.7	376	214	-363	10 665	19.7	2.38	6.6	29.6
Brown	8.7	7.6	8.6	51.7	35 074	35 580	-0.3	-1.1	572	464	-493	14 638	5.6	2.32	7.9	30.8
Brule	8.8	7.6	9.3	51.8	5 262	5 485	-2.2	-1.9	98	62	-139	1 998	0.1	2.49	7.2	29.9
Buffalo	7.1	3.5	3.0	48.7	2 014	1 759	15.5	-0.9	56	30	-45	526	17.9	3.83	31.4	16.0
Butte	9.0	7.9	7.3	50.8	9 059	7 914	14.9	-0.4	142	120	-53	3 516	15.9	2.55	9.0	25.6
Campbell	11.7	11.2	10.9	49.8	1 761	1 965	-9.3	-1.2	23	22	-20	725	-5.5	2.43	2.6	28.6
Charles Mix	9.4	8.3	9.0	50.9	9 202	9 131	2.4	-1.6	208	161	-196	3 343	3.4	2.74	11.7	28.1
Clark	9.7	10.5	11.7	50.7	4 120	4 403	-5.9	-0.6	61	64	-19	1 598	-6.0	2.54	4.7	28.1
Clay	5.9	4.7	5.4	51.5	13 266	13 186	2.7	-2.0	199	123	-352	4 878	10.0	2.32	8.1	31.0
Codington	7.9	6.7	7.4	50.4	25 782	22 698	14.1	-0.4	434	309	-237	10 357	18.5	2.46	8.1	27.9
Corson	7.7	6.4	4.1	49.5	4 221	4 195	-0.3	1.0	111	40	-32	1 271	-2.5	3.29	19.7	22.1
Custer	13.7	8.9	7.1	48.9	7 370	6 179	17.7	1.3	73	81	100	2 970	26.3	2.35	6.6	25.9
Davison	8.0	7.5	8.7	51.5	18 556	17 503	7.1	-1.0	289	238	-234	7 585	9.2	2.38	8.2	30.8
Day	9.7	10.8	12.7	50.9	6 141	6 978	-10.2	-2.0	92	136	-83	2 586	-5.3	2.36	6.8	31.8
Deuel	10.1	10.5	10.1	50.1	4 465	4 522	-0.5	-0.7	63	70	-24	1 843	4.3	2.40	4.9	28.6
Dewey	6.9	5.2	3.0	51.1	6 049	5 523	8.1	1.3	176	68	-31	1 863	8.3	3.15	22.3	22.1
Douglas	9.3	9.9	12.6	51.2	3 421	3 746	-7.7	-1.1	43	54	-24	1 321	-2.3	2.54	3.6	26.8
Edmunds	10.6	10.6	11.6	50.7	4 331	4 356	0.3	-0.8	53	62	-27	1 681	0.7	2.52	4.8	25.6
Fall River	12.1	11.5	11.0	47.7	7 392	7 353	1.4	-0.8	86	144	0	3 127	9.2	2.23	8.5	32.7
Faulk	10.0	11.9	10.9	50.0	2 543	2 744	-3.8	-3.7	38	43	-94	1 014	-4.1	2.56	3.4	29.1
Grant	9.6	8.5	10.6	50.6	7 741	8 372	-6.3	-1.4	117	123	-98	3 116	-1.2	2.44	5.2	28.6
Gregory	10.5	10.3	14.5	51.4	4 607	5 359	-10.6	-3.9	49	110	-126	2 022	-5.5	2.32	5.7	33.9
Haakon	9.6	7.5	10.5	50.9	2 099	2 624	-16.3	-4.4	26	33	-93	870	-6.0	2.47	4.8	26.0
Hamlin	8.9	8.3	10.8	50.3	5 549	4 974	11.4	0.2	97	93	8	2 048	10.5	2.62	4.8	27.0
Hand	10.5	12.2	12.0	51.0	3 665	4 272	-12.4	-2.0	46	52	-70	1 543	-5.0	2.38	4.4	30.2
Hanson	9.8	8.4	6.5	49.9	3 294	2 994	4.8	4.9	58	19	114	1 115	4.0	2.82	3.7	21.7
Harding	8.8	6.5	6.9	48.9	1 292	1 669	-18.9	-4.5	14	15	-62	525	-11.3	2.50	5.3	31.0
Hughes	8.8	6.7	7.0	51.9	16 487	14 817	11.2	0.0	285	138	-141	6 512	12.7	2.41	8.9	29.8
Hutchinson	9.2	11.1	15.2	51.3	7 995	8 262	-2.3	-1.0	113	175	-15	3 190	-1.0	2.43	4.4	29.6
Hyde	11.1	10.4	11.9	49.5	1 600	1 696	-1.5	-4.2	22	26	-70	679	-0.1	2.41	6.0	30.3
Jackson	8.2	6.0	5.6	50.3	2 846	2 811	4.2	-2.9	78	36	-128	945	4.7	3.08	14.7	25.2
Jerauld	11.1	11.0	14.6	50.4	2 275	2 425	-5.4	-0.9	23	34	-8	987	2.2	2.28	6.3	31.3
Jones	10.1	10.1	8.1	49.0	1 118	1 324	-9.9	-6.3	20	18	-80	509	-1.9	2.34	7.5	33.2
Kingsbury	9.2	11.0	13.2	51.0	5 695	5 925	-1.9	-2.1	79	128	-73	2 406	2.1	2.34	4.4	31.5
Lake	8.3	7.7	8.6	50.1	11 257	10 550	6.9	-0.2	144	140	-19	4 372	8.5	2.41	5.9	29.2
Lawrence	8.8	7.4	7.3	50.8	21 638	20 655	5.6	-0.8	247	216	-188	8 881	12.0	2.33	8.5	29.6
Lincoln	6.9	5.0	5.4	50.1	26 322	15 427	56.4	9.1	420	202	1 920	8 782	60.8	2.72	6.7	19.5
Lyman	8.9	7.5	6.1	48.9	3 969	3 638	7.1	1.9	97	43	21	1 400	10.4	2.77	13.8	24.6
McCook	8.7	8.7	10.8	50.1	5 860	5 688	2.5	0.5	90	89	28	2 204	2.8	2.58	5.1	26.8
McPherson	11.8	14.0	15.5	51.6	2 805	3 228	-10.0	-3.4	29	50	-80	1 227	-7.9	2.31	2.7	31.1
Marshall	10.4	9.6	11.6	50.0	4 442	4 844	-5.5	-2.9	46	69	-113	1 844	-3.9	2.43	6.5	30.1
Meade	7.5	5.6	4.8	49.5	24 233	21 878	10.9	-0.1	484	191	-306	8 805	24.3	2.66	8.3	24.9
Mellette	7.5	7.2	6.0	49.7	2 082	2 137	-2.5	0.0	53	31	-23	694	1.9	2.94	16.7	24.2
Miner	9.2	10.4	13.5	50.1	2 839	3 272	-11.9	-1.6	36	48	-31	1 212	-5.0	2.33	5.4	32.3
Minnehaha	7.2	5.6	5.4	50.5	150 327	123 809	19.8	1.4	2 666	1 397	820	57 996	21.6	2.46	9.5	27.8
Moody	8.7	6.2	8.7	50.0	6 552	6 507	1.4	-0.7	91	88	-45	2 526	5.3	2.58	8.5	26.4
Pennington	8.2	6.4	5.4	50.4	89 829	81 343	8.9	1.4	1 656	876	526	34 641	13.4	2.49	11.7	26.1
Perkins	9.6	11.1	12.6	50.9	3 284	3 932	-14.5	-2.3	47	58	-68	1 429	-9.9	2.31	5.2	32.9
Potter	11.5	11.6	13.4	50.8	2 544	3 190	-15.6	-5.5	30	52	-130	1 145	-8.3	2.29	4.9	31.3
Roberts	9.5	8.5	8.5	50.3	10 010	9 914	1.0	-0.1	176	173	-10	3 683	1.8	2.66	11.8	26.8
Sanborn	9.5	10.5	9.0	48.3	2 617	2 833	-5.6	-2.2	39	31	-68	1 043	-1.5	2.53	4.9	25.4
Shannon	5.3	3.2	1.6	50.1	12 783	9 902	25.9	2.5	478	162	5	2 785	26.3	4.36	36.4	13.2
Spink	9.1	9.5	9.5	48.3	7 178	7 981	-6.6	-3.7	92	112	-262	2 847	-5.8	2.45	6.1	29.3
Stanley	11.2	6.5	4.5	49.6	2 754	2 453	13.0	-0.6	27	21	-23	1 111	20.6	2.49	10.1	25.2
Sully	11.5	9.8	7.6	48.7	1 514	1 589	-2.1	-2.7	21	14	-52	630	1.4	2.47	4.3	25.7
Todd	5.3	3.8	2.0	50.5	9 269	8 352	8.4	2.4	328	89	-16	2 462	11.4	3.62	31.8	18.9

1. No spouse present.

Table B. States and Counties — Vital Statistics, Health Resources, and Crime

STATE County	Births, average 1997–1999 Total	Rate[1]	Deaths, average 1997–1999 Number Total	Number Infant[2]	Rate Total[1]	Rate Infant[3]	Physicians,[4] 2000 Number	Rate[5]	Hospitals,[4] 1998 Number	Beds Number	Beds Rate[5]	Medicare enrollees 2000	Serious crimes known to police, 2000[6] Total Number	Rate[7]
	32	33	34	35	36	37	38	39	40	41	42	43	44	45
SOUTH CAROLINA—Cont'd														
Sumter	1 682	15.5	875	18	8.0	10.7	127	121	1	230	215	13 606	5 793	5 589
Union	362	11.9	380	NA	12.5	NA	26	87	2	117	384	5 855	1 130	3 782
Williamsburg	497	13.4	393	NA	10.6	NA	18	48	1	48	129	5 652	931	2 502
York	2 122	13.7	1 260	22	8.2	10.2	181	110	1	276	179	20 463	8 268	5 023
SOUTH DAKOTA	10 146	13.8	6 895	89	9.4	8.7	1 307	173	51	4 195	568	119 437	17 511	2 320
Aurora	28	9.2	39	NA	13.1	NA	0	0	0	0	0	637	1	33
Beadle	191	11.1	195	NA	11.3	NA	30	176	1	95	553	3 625	425	2 497
Bennett	65	19.6	37	NA	11.2	NA	3	84	1	68	2 006	430	NA	NA
Bon Homme	70	9.3	82	NA	10.9	NA	5	69	2	47	611	1 590	6	83
Brookings	298	11.5	183	NA	7.0	NA	16	57	1	140	539	3 211	489	1 733
Brown	444	12.5	366	NA	10.3	NA	68	192	1	203	573	6 320	661	1 864
Brule	70	12.7	55	NA	10.0	NA	9	168	1	54	972	996	NA	NA
Buffalo	43	24.5	21	NA	12.2	NA	1	49	0	0	0	129	NA	NA
Butte	125	14.1	95	NA	10.6	NA	9	99	1	128	1 419	1 607	90	990
Campbell	17	8.7	15	NA	7.9	NA	0	0	0	0	0	697	NA	NA
Charles Mix	156	16.7	109	NA	11.6	NA	5	53	2	87	932	1 696	141	1 508
Clark	45	10.5	55	NA	12.8	NA	0	0	0	0	0	973	NA	NA
Clay	152	10.5	99	NA	6.8	NA	7	52	1	95	626	1 489	351	2 593
Codington	360	14.1	240	NA	9.4	NA	51	197	1	119	467	4 163	756	3 736
Corson	71	16.8	36	NA	8.7	NA	0	0	0	0	0	943	24	574
Custer	62	8.9	71	NA	10.2	NA	6	82	1	11	159	1 348	NA	NA
Davison	240	13.2	192	NA	10.5	NA	37	197	1	99	550	3 485	574	3 063
Day	70	11.0	102	NA	16.0	NA	1	16	1	28	438	1 581	NA	NA
Deuel	48	10.6	52	NA	11.6	NA	2	44	1	20	443	971	61	1 356
Dewey	133	22.7	44	NA	7.6	NA	3	50	0	0	0	611	34	569
Douglas	38	10.8	46	NA	13.0	NA	2	58	1	9	253	804	3	87
Edmunds	46	10.9	53	NA	12.6	NA	2	46	1	58	1 375	978	5	114
Fall River	67	9.6	109	NA	15.6	NA	20	268	1	74	1 037	1 953	NA	NA
Faulk	33	12.9	28	NA	11.1	NA	0	0	1	12	476	706	11	417
Grant	91	11.4	93	NA	11.6	NA	2	25	1	115	1 426	1 627	NA	NA
Gregory	47	9.5	72	NA	14.5	NA	2	42	2	113	2 284	1 311	NA	NA
Haakon	27	11.4	24	NA	10.3	NA	1	46	1	50	2 125	420	NA	NA
Hamlin	70	13.1	74	NA	13.7	NA	0	0	0	0	0	1 089	NA	NA
Hand	45	10.8	43	NA	10.5	NA	3	80	1	30	724	796	47	1 256
Hanson	45	15.3	18	NA	5.9	NA	0	0	0	0	0	480	NA	NA
Harding	20	13.6	12	NA	8.2	NA	0	0	0	0	0	202	0	0
Hughes	223	14.5	123	NA	8.0	NA	24	146	1	86	559	2 330	519	3 149
Hutchinson	87	10.8	134	NA	16.5	NA	12	149	2	210	2 610	2 113	23	285
Hyde	19	11.8	25	NA	15.4	NA	0	0	0	0	0	372	1	60
Jackson	55	19.0	27	NA	9.4	NA	2	68	0	0	0	275	NA	NA
Jerauld	18	8.2	34	NA	15.5	NA	3	131	1	28	1 260	598	0	0
Jones	14	11.4	12	NA	9.8	NA	0	0	0	0	0	225	NA	NA
Kingsbury	67	11.6	85	NA	14.8	NA	4	69	1	17	298	1 566	NA	NA
Lake	118	10.9	110	NA	10.2	NA	7	62	1	49	440	2 017	NA	NA
Lawrence	219	10.0	185	NA	8.4	NA	30	138	2	64	284	3 520	559	2 564
Lincoln	287	14.0	151	NA	7.4	NA	13	54	1	28	137	1 905	NA	NA
Lyman	62	16.3	36	NA	9.5	NA	2	51	0	0	0	576	19	488
McCook	75	13.4	81	NA	14.4	NA	1	17	0	0	0	1 164	43	737
McPherson	21	7.5	43	NA	15.7	NA	2	69	1	25	913	599	NA	NA
Marshall	46	10.0	50	NA	11.0	NA	2	44	1	25	548	1 039	40	874
Meade	372	17.1	165	NA	7.6	NA	35	144	1	114	520	3 247	438	1 806
Mellette	43	21.1	21	NA	10.5	NA	0	0	0	0	0	261	NA	NA
Miner	22	8.0	43	NA	15.3	NA	1	35	0	0	0	701	39	1 352
Minnehaha	2 069	14.5	1 043	20	7.3	9.7	500	337	3	821	574	19 344	4 431	3 012
Moody	76	11.8	69	NA	10.7	NA	4	61	1	20	307	940	NA	NA
Pennington	1 362	15.6	663	10	7.6	7.1	241	272	1	328	374	12 170	4 359	4 922
Perkins	38	10.7	47	NA	13.5	NA	0	0	1	56	1 598	861	42	1 249
Potter	24	8.4	47	NA	16.5	NA	5	186	2	104	3 640	757	37	1 374
Roberts	156	15.9	127	NA	12.9	NA	4	40	1	31	317	1 783	NA	NA
Sanborn	30	11.0	29	NA	10.6	NA	0	0	0	0	0	629	46	1 720
Shannon	322	26.3	116	7	9.5	22.8	8	64	0	0	0	797	NA	NA
Spink	86	11.4	90	NA	11.9	NA	8	107	1	35	462	1 739	30	402
Stanley	33	11.5	22	NA	7.7	NA	2	72	0	0	0	386	48	1 732
Sully	19	12.5	11	NA	7.4	NA	0	0	0	0	0	246	2	129
Todd	256	27.5	70	NA	7.5	NA	6	66	0	0	0	536	NA	NA

1. Per 1,000 estimated resident population, average 1997–1999.   2. Deaths of infants under 1 year old.   3. Deaths of infants under 1 year old per 1,000 live births.   4. Data subject to copyright.   5. Per 100,000 resident population as of July 1 of the year shown.   6. Data for serious crimes have not been adjusted for underreporting; this may affect comparability between geographic areas and over time.   7. Per 100,000 population estimated by the FBI.

STATE County	Serious crimes known to police, 2000[1] (cont'd) Rate[2]		Education						Money income 1989				Income and poverty, 1998			
			School enrollment and attainment, 1990				Local government expenditures, fiscal 1999[5]		Households					Percent below poverty level		
			Enrollment[3]		Attainment[4] (percent)					Median						
	Violent	Property	Total	Percent private	High school graduate or more	Bachelor's degree or more	Total current expenditures (mil dol)	Current expenditures per student (dollars)	Per capita[6] (dollars)	Dollars	Percent change, 1979–1989 (constant 1989 dollars)	Percent with $100,000 or more	Median household income	All persons	Persons under 18	Persons 5–17 in families
	46	47	48	49	50	51	52	53	54	55	56	57	58	59	60	61
SOUTH CAROLINA—Cont'd																
Sumter	964	4 625	28 487	12.2	69.8	15.0	100.1	5 284	9 997	22 387	9.6	1.4	30 068	18.3	24.6	24.4
Union	733	3 049	7 089	3.6	55.0	7.2	29.7	6 105	9 669	21 526	-9.4	0.6	29 650	14.0	21.5	20.6
Williamsburg	575	1 927	11 058	9.5	55.6	9.9	38.8	5 861	7 632	18 409	-6.6	1.0	22 962	26.4	33.8	33.5
York	812	4 211	34 511	9.2	67.5	16.9	161.1	5 719	13 306	31 288	9.3	3.0	40 365	10.6	16.4	14.8
SOUTH DAKOTA	167	2 153	185 246	10.4	77.1	17.2	696.8	5 259	10 661	22 503	2.1	1.7	33 267	13.0	17.6	15.0
Aurora	33	0	782	3.3	70.2	11.0	3.5	5 753	8 129	16 497	-5.1	1.0	28 252	16.5	23.0	18.2
Beadle	59	2 438	4 250	14.1	75.7	15.1	15.4	5 274	10 373	22 425	-0.1	0.9	33 582	11.7	16.5	13.3
Bennett	NA	NA	891	2.0	67.7	10.4	3.7	6 318	7 841	16 864	1.6	1.8	22 610	32.9	36.4	37.0
Bon Homme	14	69	1 438	12.2	68.0	11.3	7.6	5 253	8 208	17 778	-0.6	0.7	30 372	13.2	16.6	13.6
Brookings	57	1 676	10 655	2.7	82.2	27.3	21.1	4 908	9 926	21 807	-4.3	1.1	38 126	10.3	12.3	9.2
Brown	104	1 760	9 663	10.5	77.9	20.7	26.7	5 055	11 579	22 967	-2.4	1.6	36 452	9.9	13.2	10.0
Brule	NA	NA	1 478	21.4	73.4	14.9	6.8	5 470	9 681	21 184	11.2	1.3	31 764	12.9	17.2	15.8
Buffalo	NA	NA	645	8.2	61.2	4.2	NA	NA	5 067	14 566	-4.4	1.4	16 793	39.0	39.4	39.9
Butte	99	891	1 937	3.2	74.5	12.3	9.5	5 036	9 843	19 811	-8.9	1.3	28 738	17.1	23.4	19.4
Campbell	NA	NA	323	0.0	65.5	10.7	1.9	5 879	8 678	17 202	13.6	1.6	26 431	16.7	27.8	20.1
Charles Mix	374	1 134	2 282	15.6	67.5	9.9	9.8	5 279	7 475	16 541	-2.5	0.8	27 823	23.8	30.0	26.9
Clark	NA	NA	972	10.5	70.4	9.8	4.2	4 753	9 280	19 035	12.2	0.9	29 372	14.3	20.0	16.8
Clay	126	2 467	6 596	3.7	84.4	36.3	8.4	5 131	9 160	19 392	-2.1	0.8	32 563	17.3	20.8	16.9
Codington	163	3 573	5 633	6.7	76.0	12.9	21.3	4 485	10 508	21 816	-4.0	1.5	36 456	10.0	13.4	10.3
Corson	167	407	1 267	0.2	63.3	10.5	5.2	6 844	6 299	14 324	-10.4	0.3	19 342	35.3	38.3	37.7
Custer	NA	NA	1 485	5.5	80.4	17.5	6.2	5 499	10 942	22 662	-10.8	1.5	31 779	12.5	16.6	14.7
Davison	101	2 961	4 616	19.6	75.9	14.8	16.9	5 258	10 105	20 733	-0.2	1.1	34 547	11.8	17.2	13.9
Day	NA	NA	1 568	7.4	69.2	11.3	6.7	5 511	9 191	18 760	4.9	1.1	27 544	17.2	23.0	19.9
Deuel	89	1 267	988	4.7	69.2	9.7	2.9	4 809	9 117	17 784	4.0	1.1	31 661	11.9	16.4	12.5
Dewey	184	385	1 780	2.2	67.1	10.4	5.5	7 028	6 515	14 599	-18.1	1.3	22 618	31.9	33.1	31.6
Douglas	0	87	892	20.9	58.0	11.2	2.5	5 046	7 869	17 067	9.2	0.7	30 907	14.4	19.8	16.1
Edmunds	0	114	894	9.6	64.2	11.3	4.2	5 238	8 792	20 569	19.8	0.8	32 320	12.2	16.5	13.7
Fall River	NA	NA	1 765	3.9	74.1	16.3	7.3	5 621	10 944	20 483	-14.4	1.5	28 515	16.2	22.5	17.5
Faulk	0	417	558	9.1	67.1	10.6	2.7	5 211	8 653	18 709	17.6	0.5	30 173	12.9	17.7	15.0
Grant	NA	NA	2 053	12.8	74.0	9.3	8.2	5 300	10 394	23 431	10.8	1.4	35 039	9.9	13.0	10.3
Gregory	NA	NA	1 275	0.8	70.3	11.8	5.4	5 281	8 906	16 848	13.0	1.2	24 862	20.8	27.1	22.4
Haakon	NA	NA	736	0.5	83.6	12.7	2.7	4 945	10 117	21 166	4.6	3.5	31 642	14.6	17.6	14.7
Hamlin	NA	NA	1 183	6.5	69.5	11.2	6.1	4 668	9 086	19 949	20.2	1.0	33 140	11.8	16.3	12.8
Hand	53	1 203	940	16.9	73.4	12.8	3.6	5 667	9 305	19 310	11.3	1.0	29 657	14.3	19.6	17.0
Hanson	NA	NA	659	8.6	73.1	15.3	2.9	5 218	9 846	21 920	30.7	0.6	35 419	12.0	16.2	13.2
Harding	0	0	406	3.9	82.8	16.2	1.9	5 802	8 555	20 217	-2.6	1.0	24 596	15.4	19.7	16.7
Hughes	152	2 997	3 750	10.4	84.5	25.6	14.7	4 796	12 263	27 058	-7.5	1.2	41 365	9.9	14.8	11.5
Hutchinson	37	248	1 722	7.3	62.6	11.3	9.3	5 153	9 514	18 832	9.4	1.2	31 493	12.7	16.7	13.6
Hyde	0	60	366	0.5	71.2	14.5	1.8	5 492	9 648	19 907	0.6	1.0	30 699	15.9	22.8	19.0
Jackson	NA	NA	767	1.7	68.9	10.9	2.2	4 993	6 947	17 246	-15.5	0.6	22 276	30.9	33.4	33.8
Jerauld	0	0	509	3.1	68.0	11.3	2.9	6 023	9 867	18 588	4.6	1.0	29 434	12.8	17.9	15.2
Jones	NA	NA	277	2.5	75.7	14.4	1.3	4 649	9 592	21 202	6.9	0.8	29 040	13.9	18.7	17.0
Kingsbury	NA	NA	1 250	3.6	74.0	11.6	6.8	5 449	9 857	20 290	13.5	1.0	32 345	10.4	13.9	11.7
Lake	NA	NA	2 933	5.8	79.6	18.5	11.1	4 966	11 388	23 674	17.4	1.4	35 288	10.3	13.7	10.9
Lawrence	225	2 339	6 024	4.9	81.7	19.2	18.8	5 443	11 378	24 815	8.9	1.4	31 879	11.9	15.1	12.0
Lincoln	NA	NA	4 083	7.9	79.5	16.4	15.4	4 609	12 246	28 543	11.9	3.1	48 386	5.1	7.2	5.5
Lyman	51	436	992	11.6	71.0	10.5	2.6	5 998	9 724	21 993	16.7	2.9	27 683	22.1	27.1	26.0
McCook	17	720	1 314	11.0	71.6	11.9	5.8	5 276	9 542	20 764	10.1	1.1	34 180	11.3	15.2	11.9
McPherson	NA	NA	571	2.1	46.0	10.0	2.9	5 433	8 790	15 345	2.0	2.1	25 528	14.0	17.0	15.6
Marshall	0	874	942	2.1	65.7	10.2	4.6	5 165	8 799	18 305	6.4	1.0	30 385	14.0	20.0	16.1
Meade	95	1 711	6 198	5.5	81.8	16.4	15.7	4 847	9 725	24 672	-0.9	0.6	36 203	11.7	16.3	11.6
Mellette	NA	NA	641	6.1	68.0	12.3	3.2	6 316	6 964	14 539	-10.3	1.3	20 319	33.1	34.4	35.7
Miner	139	1 214	686	2.0	71.3	10.3	2.7	4 880	9 711	18 750	32.7	1.7	28 963	14.1	18.6	16.5
Minnehaha	276	2 736	31 148	22.4	83.1	21.3	123.2	5 043	13 345	27 764	-1.9	2.6	41 984	7.8	11.3	8.2
Moody	NA	NA	1 589	4.0	74.6	13.9	6.1	4 893	10 169	23 926	12.5	1.2	36 574	11.0	15.3	12.6
Pennington	351	4 571	21 946	9.7	84.8	21.2	90.4	5 140	12 031	25 340	1.5	2.4	34 924	13.1	18.2	15.5
Perkins	0	1 249	804	2.1	72.5	12.7	4.2	5 950	10 982	19 862	-2.9	2.0	25 943	17.5	24.7	19.3
Potter	74	1 300	730	14.4	71.1	12.3	3.2	5 842	10 177	20 674	9.5	1.7	31 615	13.5	18.9	14.7
Roberts	NA	NA	2 427	7.5	63.5	10.4	10.4	5 392	7 981	17 480	1.2	0.9	26 347	20.5	27.1	23.8
Sanborn	262	1 458	661	3.6	73.9	16.4	3.0	5 463	8 956	19 818	48.3	1.2	29 462	13.3	17.0	15.5
Shannon	NA	NA	3 534	12.7	59.4	10.7	10.5	9 500	3 417	11 105	-33.4	0.0	20 353	37.1	35.6	36.5
Spink	40	362	1 678	4.7	72.8	12.7	8.7	5 463	9 674	19 398	-4.2	1.6	28 190	14.6	19.2	16.0
Stanley	72	1 659	661	5.3	77.5	14.6	2.9	4 694	10 759	22 321	-10.1	2.9	35 972	10.8	13.8	12.1
Sully	0	129	383	2.9	78.9	12.9	2.5	6 504	11 559	23 601	18.6	3.8	36 425	10.0	14.1	11.6
Todd	NA	NA	3 124	5.2	67.2	11.8	16.6	7 759	5 043	13 327	-17.7	0.5	18 810	38.8	34.1	39.9

1. Data for serious crimes have not been adjusted for underreporting; this may affect comparability between geographic areas and over time. 2. Per 100,000 population estimated by the FBI. 3. All persons 3 years old and over enrolled in nursery school through college. 4. Persons 25 years old and over. 5. Elementary and secondary education expenditures, local government fiscal years ending between July 1, 1998 and June 30, 1999. 6. Based on population enumerated as of April 1, 1990.

Table B. States and Counties — **Personal Income**

STATE County	Personal income, 1999												
			Per capita[1]					Transfer payments					
									Government payments to individuals				
	Total (mil dol)	Percent change, 1998–1999	Dollars	Rank	Wages and salaries[2] (mil dol)	Proprietor's income (mil dol)	Dividends, interest, and rent (mil dol)	Total (mil dol)	Total (mil dol)	Social Security (mil dol)	Medical payments (mil dol)	Income mainte-nance (mil dol)	Unemploy-ment insurance (mil dol)
	62	63	64	65	66	67	68	69	70	71	72	73	74
SOUTH CAROLINA—Cont'd													
Sumter	2 050	4.3	18 238	2 484	1 372	101	343	377	358	125	137	59	5
Union	581	4.8	19 125	2 254	293	24	88	128	122	58	45	11	3
Williamsburg	603	5.9	16 373	2 850	265	40	82	165	159	49	70	30	4
York	3 887	5.3	24 574	737	2 054	163	581	459	430	216	147	34	10
SOUTH DAKOTA	18 358	5.6	25 041	X	10 213	2 483	4 190	2 477	2 356	1 076	878	187	15
Aurora	63	3.5	21 091	1 641	20	14	19	12	11	5	5	1	0
Beadle	435	6.4	26 141	498	209	66	112	71	68	32	28	4	0
Bennett	55	12.0	16 630	2 804	20	9	12	14	13	4	5	3	0
Bon Homme	145	-0.3	20 168	1 945	50	26	44	27	26	13	10	2	0
Brookings	639	6.6	24 645	724	407	56	142	67	63	30	21	3	0
Brown	965	5.8	27 387	384	527	136	241	127	121	57	46	6	1
Brule	119	2.3	21 587	1 493	44	23	33	20	19	9	7	1	0
Buffalo	25	19.8	14 271	3 035	15	4	3	9	9	1	4	2	0
Butte	157	4.3	17 926	2 552	55	22	45	30	29	15	9	2	0
Campbell	43	8.7	23 139	1 064	11	14	11	8	7	4	3	1	0
Charles Mix	194	0.5	21 065	1 647	73	46	49	41	39	14	16	5	0
Clark	101	10.8	23 559	950	22	38	24	16	15	8	5	1	0
Clay	309	14.6	23 576	945	167	34	59	36	34	14	12	3	0
Codington	649	3.4	25 600	572	389	85	152	77	72	37	26	4	1
Corson	59	9.1	14 297	3 031	19	9	12	19	18	4	8	4	0
Custer	139	7.9	19 739	2 076	54	13	39	26	24	13	7	1	0
Davison	485	5.5	27 144	405	282	51	129	69	66	30	28	4	0
Day	133	5.9	21 579	1 496	43	30	35	27	26	13	10	2	0
Deuel	105	4.3	23 642	927	35	27	23	16	16	8	6	1	0
Dewey	87	6.4	14 430	3 026	50	6	14	22	21	5	7	5	0
Douglas	75	-2.8	21 258	1 581	23	21	17	14	13	6	6	1	0
Edmunds	107	3.4	25 471	590	23	30	29	17	17	8	7	1	0
Fall River	156	7.5	22 830	1 130	77	14	40	36	35	15	11	2	0
Faulk	59	-3.4	23 506	963	14	16	17	12	11	5	5	1	0
Grant	197	3.6	24 804	701	89	47	43	29	27	14	10	1	0
Gregory	102	-1.1	20 876	1 708	31	21	30	22	21	10	8	2	0
Haakon	61	5.3	26 366	479	19	21	16	7	7	4	2	1	0
Hamlin	112	3.8	20 693	1 778	30	25	26	19	18	9	7	1	0
Hand	96	9.0	23 245	1 031	26	28	29	14	14	8	4	1	0
Hanson	59	-0.4	19 465	2 151	12	16	15	8	7	4	2	1	0
Harding	21	20.4	14 781	3 007	9	1	8	3	3	2	1	0	0
Hughes	429	3.6	27 760	351	276	37	106	48	45	22	17	3	0
Hutchinson	184	-3.1	22 845	1 125	57	38	58	34	33	17	12	2	0
Hyde	39	9.7	24 912	685	12	10	12	7	6	3	2	0	0
Jackson	40	3.1	13 560	3 068	14	5	11	11	11	3	4	2	0
Jerauld	58	8.4	27 421	380	18	19	13	10	10	5	4	1	0
Jones	31	7.0	25 463	593	11	9	7	4	4	2	1	0	0
Kingsbury	141	2.6	24 634	727	41	39	34	25	24	13	10	1	0
Lake	261	1.8	24 443	771	118	42	55	38	36	18	13	2	0
Lawrence	443	1.5	20 748	1 756	235	42	126	73	70	35	24	4	1
Lincoln	512	3.9	23 653	924	137	60	88	45	42	25	12	2	0
Lyman	77	-1.6	20 226	1 919	29	13	17	14	14	5	5	2	0
McCook	127	0.1	22 825	1 132	34	33	29	20	20	10	8	1	0
McPherson	57	1.2	20 999	1 668	14	13	17	11	11	7	3	1	0
Marshall	121	12.8	26 659	444	35	40	30	17	17	9	6	1	0
Meade	548	8.8	25 614	568	179	73	108	62	59	26	19	4	0
Mellette	28	4.4	13 755	3 061	7	3	7	9	9	2	4	2	0
Miner	66	6.7	24 560	742	20	17	14	12	11	5	4	1	0
Minnehaha	4 478	7.4	31 355	174	3 291	407	872	403	379	186	145	19	2
Moody	157	1.6	24 431	776	58	36	30	19	18	9	6	1	0
Pennington	2 211	6.6	25 088	654	1 476	177	548	283	269	119	95	21	2
Perkins	76	5.7	21 987	1 371	28	13	24	15	15	8	5	1	0
Potter	83	5.8	29 207	249	21	25	27	12	12	6	4	1	0
Roberts	181	5.1	18 510	2 412	62	43	39	38	36	15	13	4	0
Sanborn	67	2.4	25 048	661	15	15	22	10	10	4	4	1	0
Shannon	141	4.8	11 280	3 098	91	8	9	52	50	5	19	17	1
Spink	207	12.4	27 867	343	57	66	43	47	46	15	28	2	0
Stanley	68	6.8	23 527	958	23	8	18	7	7	4	2	0	0
Sully	58	9.0	39 079	49	11	28	11	5	4	3	1	0	0
Todd	104	3.9	10 920	3 101	65	2	8	38	36	4	14	11	0

1. Based on the resident population estimated as of July 1 of the year shown.   2. Includes other labor income.

Table B. States and Counties — Earnings, Social Security, and Housing

STATE County	Earnings, 1999									Social Security beneficiaries, December 2000		Supplemental Security Income recipients, December 2000	Housing units, 1990	
			Goods-related[1]		Service-related and other[2]									
	Total (mil dol)	Farm	Total	Manufacturing	Total	Retail trade	Finance, insurance, and real estate	Services	Government	Number	Rate[3]		Total	Percent change, 1980–1990
	75	76	77	78	79	80	81	82	83	84	85	86	87	88
SOUTH CAROLINA—Cont'd														
Sumter	1 472	0.5	D	24.1	D	8.6	3.4	17.4	32.0	16 819	161	4 267	35 016	18.4
Union	317	0.6	D	43.8	D	8.3	2.9	13.0	23.1	7 211	241	933	12 230	7.4
Williamsburg	305	4.5	36.5	31.1	37.4	8.0	3.7	13.3	21.6	7 220	194	2 343	13 265	6.1
York	2 217	0.5	29.8	23.4	55.9	11.4	5.0	22.6	13.8	25 241	153	2 526	50 438	36.4
SOUTH DAKOTA	12 696	7.9	20.2	13.7	55.1	10.0	7.2	24.5	16.8	136 227	180	12 648	292 436	5.6
Aurora	33	24.1	4.1	1.4	D	7.8	4.1	17.4	29.2	744	243	36	1 342	-7.4
Beadle	276	11.6	D	10.6	D	8.5	4.4	24.0	18.5	3 923	230	347	8 093	-1.7
Bennett	29	24.2	D	D	D	11.2	2.1	6.7	36.3	551	154	167	1 292	12.7
Bon Homme	76	18.7	18.1	13.5	D	9.6	D	18.0	20.2	1 772	244	85	3 087	-4.7
Brookings	464	5.9	D	28.0	D	8.0	3.6	11.8	28.2	3 685	131	221	9 824	8.3
Brown	663	6.2	18.0	11.7	60.9	11.2	5.9	30.1	15.0	6 925	195	521	15 101	2.9
Brule	67	13.5	D	D	D	14.3	3.6	30.3	15.7	1 113	207	76	2 275	4.8
Buffalo	20	21.1	0.0	0.0	D	D	D	34.0	36.9	236	116	101	535	7.2
Butte	77	1.9	D	2.7	D	15.2	5.0	19.8	19.9	1 872	206	153	3 502	2.9
Campbell	25	43.9	D	D	D	4.7	D	4.1	11.0	500	281	26	944	-1.7
Charles Mix	119	21.6	5.8	1.4	52.9	8.5	3.9	25.6	19.6	1 877	201	258	3 751	-1.3
Clark	61	53.5	D	D	D	5.3	2.1	7.1	10.5	1 081	261	68	2 026	-6.9
Clay	202	3.9	D	D	D	6.9	2.1	13.0	39.0	1 672	124	99	4 892	-0.6
Codington	474	5.0	32.6	26.0	50.7	13.3	4.3	19.7	11.7	4 735	183	354	9 539	12.1
Corson	28	22.6	D	D	D	3.4	1.2	19.5	39.0	630	151	212	1 557	-7.5
Custer	68	-2.7	15.4	3.5	51.1	13.7	3.1	23.8	36.2	1 654	227	97	3 003	7.8
Davison	333	3.4	D	19.0	D	15.6	4.4	29.9	10.9	3 836	205	356	7 490	3.6
Day	73	28.6	D	9.0	D	7.3	5.4	14.7	15.4	1 745	278	123	3 914	-3.0
Deuel	63	32.2	18.2	12.7	D	5.6	3.5	10.3	10.3	1 093	243	55	2 208	-5.2
Dewey	56	-0.5	7.9	0.9	D	6.2	4.1	D	40.0	762	128	307	2 123	13.5
Douglas	44	28.4	D	5.3	D	5.9	3.0	19.6	11.1	873	252	52	1 517	-4.9
Edmunds	53	40.0	6.7	1.1	37.0	8.5	3.2	10.1	16.3	1 065	244	41	2 004	-5.1
Fall River	91	1.5	D	1.3	D	12.2	2.3	13.9	44.4	2 084	280	174	3 692	-7.6
Faulk	30	44.8	D	D	D	10.4	2.4	9.9	14.2	702	266	46	1 286	-9.8
Grant	136	23.2	D	10.5	D	7.5	7.8	15.9	8.7	1 762	225	98	3 549	-0.5
Gregory	52	14.7	D	1.5	D	13.0	5.6	23.0	15.5	1 391	290	128	2 595	-0.6
Haakon	40	35.6	D	9.6	D	8.6	4.0	18.0	11.0	457	208	21	1 071	-5.1
Hamlin	55	31.2	D	9.6	D	6.9	3.4	9.4	20.7	1 199	216	67	2 500	-2.1
Hand	54	43.3	D	2.3	D	7.1	4.0	14.6	12.7	990	265	46	2 053	1.7
Hanson	28	41.7	D	9.7	D	5.3	4.3	5.4	13.2	598	191	22	1 232	-1.7
Harding	11	-7.4	D	D	D	10.8	D	29.2	32.4	240	177	8	776	-3.4
Hughes	313	2.3	D	1.1	D	10.7	6.4	25.3	43.0	2 726	165	253	6 255	11.6
Hutchinson	95	27.9	13.3	8.3	46.1	8.1	4.9	21.0	12.8	2 304	285	95	3 657	-5.4
Hyde	22	34.4	D	D	D	11.4	3.0	12.4	11.4	428	256	26	816	-5.4
Jackson	19	12.3	5.5	0.7	D	15.9	D	16.2	37.2	466	159	27	1 147	-11.5
Jerauld	37	22.3	D	D	D	5.8	3.3	28.9	12.0	676	295	31	1 182	-2.3
Jones	20	26.9	D	D	D	23.1	3.3	12.9	14.1	254	213	7	699	-3.6
Kingsbury	79	36.4	16.4	11.0	36.9	6.2	5.3	12.5	10.4	1 584	272	71	2 765	-9.1
Lake	160	11.3	D	18.2	D	9.8	3.0	18.0	16.7	2 268	201	155	5 148	1.3
Lawrence	277	0.3	26.7	9.1	53.3	12.8	3.3	31.9	19.6	4 114	189	260	9 092	14.3
Lincoln	197	14.1	23.4	13.0	51.7	11.1	2.8	19.8	10.8	3 217	133	89	5 823	8.9
Lyman	42	19.3	D	D	D	10.7	4.3	29.4	17.3	719	185	88	1 523	-3.5
McCook	66	36.6	12.6	9.9	38.3	8.8	2.7	13.0	12.4	1 279	219	64	2 371	-8.3
McPherson	27	30.3	12.7	6.4	D	6.2	6.0	19.0	15.2	942	324	44	1 566	-7.8
Marshall	75	42.1	D	16.5	D	3.9	3.6	9.2	11.4	1 136	248	56	2 640	-4.5
Meade	252	3.4	D	5.5	D	8.5	3.8	21.9	34.5	3 477	143	257	7 592	7.0
Mellette	10	23.0	D	D	D	8.6	D	D	37.9	319	153	111	910	4.8
Miner	37	34.6	D	D	D	6.8	3.4	30.9	12.5	734	255	34	1 474	-11.0
Minnehaha	3 698	0.8	D	13.3	D	10.2	13.3	29.7	9.3	21 597	146	1 894	49 780	16.6
Moody	94	28.6	D	D	D	4.1	2.2	21.0	16.2	1 133	172	62	2 666	-2.3
Pennington	1 653	0.4	16.2	8.1	60.0	13.1	6.9	28.4	23.4	14 822	167	1 621	33 741	19.6
Perkins	40	12.4	D	11.0	D	8.7	5.2	15.5	18.3	950	282	63	2 007	-3.6
Potter	46	45.8	D	4.1	D	5.2	4.1	13.6	12.2	803	298	30	1 664	8.5
Roberts	105	29.2	D	4.0	D	7.0	4.8	23.5	18.8	2 087	208	255	4 728	-0.8
Sanborn	30	39.2	D	D	D	6.2	2.1	9.8	13.4	620	232	35	1 326	-7.8
Shannon	99	4.1	D	D	D	3.7	D	43.1	38.8	1 157	93	981	2 699	1.2
Spink	123	45.1	3.2	0.4	29.8	5.6	2.9	9.8	22.0	1 832	246	158	3 545	-6.7
Stanley	32	13.0	38.6	1.6	D	8.2	D	10.3	14.2	449	162	18	1 056	9.1
Sully	39	69.3	D	D	D	6.8	2.8	2.8	8.1	328	211	11	811	-2.4
Todd	67	-1.1	D	D	D	5.1	D	38.7	45.5	717	79	553	2 572	8.7

1. Covers mining, construction, and manufacturing. 2. Covers private sector earnings in agricultural services, forestry, and fisheries; transportation and public utilities; wholesale trade; retail trade; finance, insurance, and real estate; and services. 3. Per 1,000 resident population estimated as of July 1 of the year shown.

Table B. States and Counties — Housing, Labor Force, and Employment

	Housing units, 1990 (cont'd)								Civilian labor force, 2001				Civilian employment, 1990[5]		
	Occupied units										Unemployment			Percent	
		Owner-occupied				Renter-occupied									
				Owner cost as a percent of income											
STATE County	Total	Percent	Median value[1]	With a mortgage	Without a mortgage	Median rent[2]	Rent as percent of income	Substandard units[3] (percent)	Total	Percent change, 2000–2001	Total	Rate[4]	Total	Professional, managerial, and technical	Precision production, craft, and repair
	89	90	91	92	93	94	95	96	97	98	99	100	101	102	103
SOUTH CAROLINA—Cont'd															
Sumter	32 723	65.2	56 900	21.0	14.3	356	25.7	7.0	46 785	-2.6	3 372	7.2	37 746	21.8	14.9
Union	11 407	76.9	38 000	16.4	12.7	270	23.4	5.3	14 525	-1.2	1 587	10.9	13 728	15.6	15.2
Williamsburg	12 108	79.2	42 600	19.7	13.5	236	24.5	10.5	14 345	-2.6	2 089	14.6	14 580	16.0	12.3
York	47 006	71.9	71 300	19.3	12.9	417	24.3	4.2	91 413	-0.5	4 700	5.1	67 039	24.5	14.9
SOUTH DAKOTA	259 034	66.1	45 200	19.8	13.3	306	24.6	3.4	405 088	1.0	13 463	3.3	321 891	24.5	10.4
Aurora	1 146	76.7	15 500	19.6	13.7	200	20.8	1.2	1 233	-3.3	30	2.4	1 253	20.1	11.5
Beadle	7 341	65.8	34 200	16.3	12.7	279	24.4	1.7	8 714	2.0	319	3.7	8 553	21.7	13.4
Bennett	1 030	65.0	29 500	20.5	13.8	263	26.1	13.7	1 059	-2.8	62	5.9	1 090	17.7	9.9
Bon Homme	2 647	75.8	25 100	17.4	14.2	217	19.2	2.5	3 018	-1.9	92	3.0	2 866	18.8	7.7
Brookings	8 910	58.6	51 200	17.5	12.4	293	28.1	2.0	16 962	-2.2	324	1.9	12 705	27.4	7.0
Brown	13 867	62.9	46 600	17.5	13.0	292	23.8	1.4	21 079	1.5	621	2.9	18 016	27.7	10.1
Brule	1 996	72.5	41 300	19.6	14.1	245	22.7	3.4	2 512	0.8	82	3.3	2 637	22.3	7.5
Buffalo	446	42.4	14 999	13.9	14.4	235	21.5	22.6	906	2.3	76	8.4	512	18.8	6.8
Butte	3 033	68.0	38 700	22.4	14.8	277	23.5	2.3	3 713	-1.3	148	4.0	3 404	20.4	12.1
Campbell	767	82.5	16 400	15.5	14.9	227	20.0	2.2	839	-5.9	57	6.8	903	13.8	7.1
Charles Mix	3 232	67.9	27 200	18.0	13.9	199	21.7	5.9	4 554	2.4	150	3.3	3 532	18.9	9.3
Clark	1 700	78.4	18 700	18.9	13.9	221	22.8	3.1	1 843	-1.0	134	7.3	1 843	14.8	9.5
Clay	4 433	52.9	47 800	20.7	13.2	291	32.9	1.8	7 673	-2.8	100	1.3	6 384	33.9	6.4
Codington	8 739	67.6	50 600	20.3	12.5	281	25.9	1.2	14 925	1.2	680	4.6	11 079	22.2	12.1
Corson	1 303	59.2	18 100	16.6	14.7	145	17.6	15.3	1 457	-2.7	121	8.3	1 254	19.7	3.7
Custer	2 352	71.9	45 200	21.4	12.6	315	24.2	3.3	3 529	0.3	135	3.8	2 841	27.5	11.1
Davison	6 948	60.5	38 400	18.3	13.7	275	25.0	2.1	10 777	5.3	250	2.3	8 367	25.4	9.8
Day	2 732	73.8	22 500	16.6	13.3	239	23.0	3.9	2 944	2.5	190	6.5	2 761	20.6	9.7
Deuel	1 767	78.5	23 100	20.0	13.2	241	24.1	2.8	2 422	1.0	123	5.1	1 986	14.8	9.0
Dewey	1 721	49.2	23 700	13.2	14.0	271	29.5	21.6	2 479	3.1	398	16.1	1 815	28.4	7.4
Douglas	1 352	78.6	19 600	17.9	15.4	211	23.0	2.8	1 521	-0.9	36	2.4	1 472	17.8	9.0
Edmunds	1 669	79.4	22 700	17.6	14.8	216	21.0	2.4	2 225	1.1	49	2.2	1 972	16.7	11.2
Fall River	2 864	65.6	34 100	19.8	13.0	273	23.8	3.2	3 327	-0.9	136	4.1	3 044	27.5	8.3
Faulk	1 057	80.1	17 900	14.4	13.1	201	21.6	3.7	1 050	-3.8	28	2.7	1 199	18.6	4.3
Grant	3 154	73.2	36 600	17.0	13.8	247	22.0	1.8	4 261	2.0	193	4.5	3 821	17.5	11.1
Gregory	2 139	73.0	26 300	19.2	13.7	208	24.8	3.8	2 429	-0.5	91	3.7	2 299	18.1	9.4
Haakon	926	73.2	33 800	22.5	13.8	244	18.8	3.4	1 063	-2.5	28	2.6	1 089	17.4	10.7
Hamlin	1 854	77.8	22 800	15.7	15.5	215	20.2	3.4	2 630	0.9	111	4.2	2 010	17.7	9.8
Hand	1 625	71.1	32 600	14.2	13.0	213	23.9	2.5	1 958	-0.9	43	2.2	1 920	16.6	8.7
Hanson	1 072	74.8	19 900	17.8	14.5	295	17.7	2.9	1 845	5.7	43	2.3	1 451	17.6	10.8
Harding	592	73.3	33 300	20.8	13.2	214	22.8	4.2	750	-0.4	24	3.2	800	17.9	5.5
Hughes	5 780	63.2	58 700	16.9	12.2	315	22.7	1.8	9 782	-0.1	229	2.3	7 875	36.1	7.6
Hutchinson	3 221	79.1	25 000	20.0	14.5	220	22.6	0.8	3 689	-0.9	110	3.0	3 675	17.2	7.2
Hyde	680	72.2	21 900	15.0	12.7	230	18.2	4.2	839	0.7	22	2.6	781	18.6	10.5
Jackson	903	63.7	22 100	14.0	12.8	256	22.3	13.6	1 088	2.5	76	7.0	1 001	19.1	7.5
Jerauld	966	72.8	18 200	14.9	12.2	186	20.4	2.1	1 614	8.9	39	2.4	1 045	16.8	8.4
Jones	519	76.9	23 400	20.0	13.3	232	23.1	4.2	721	-6.1	11	1.5	623	19.3	10.6
Kingsbury	2 357	73.8	22 800	14.9	13.8	205	20.5	1.1	2 541	3.9	100	3.9	2 549	18.9	8.6
Lake	4 030	67.5	37 600	17.1	11.9	238	20.8	1.6	6 260	2.5	206	3.3	5 091	24.4	9.7
Lawrence	7 926	64.2	52 300	18.2	12.1	306	25.9	2.5	10 614	0.7	325	3.1	9 879	23.8	16.7
Lincoln	5 461	79.3	49 100	20.3	13.2	284	20.3	1.8	13 357	1.7	248	1.9	7 909	22.3	11.9
Lyman	1 268	73.3	30 200	17.0	12.3	235	19.9	7.1	2 347	2.7	114	4.9	1 643	19.8	6.9
McCook	2 145	77.0	22 500	16.6	14.3	222	22.2	2.1	2 331	-3.4	89	3.8	2 555	19.3	10.3
McPherson	1 332	81.3	14 999	21.6	17.3	177	22.1	3.0	1 280	-4.2	30	2.3	1 371	15.9	11.4
Marshall	1 919	73.0	22 900	15.7	13.1	219	24.6	2.2	2 002	-4.2	146	7.3	2 012	18.3	9.8
Meade	7 084	66.8	50 600	23.1	13.2	315	24.6	2.8	13 443	0.0	425	3.2	8 552	22.4	14.4
Mellette	681	65.9	14 999	21.6	15.2	227	27.0	16.5	722	6.5	47	6.5	723	19.6	7.3
Miner	1 276	74.8	19 600	17.6	12.2	200	22.6	2.7	1 219	-11.7	71	5.8	1 439	13.8	7.9
Minnehaha	47 681	62.3	58 400	20.0	12.8	377	24.5	1.8	92 478	1.8	2 169	2.3	66 313	27.8	10.0
Moody	2 398	71.2	33 100	15.0	13.1	243	22.4	3.6	3 627	5.3	249	6.9	3 003	18.3	11.0
Pennington	30 553	61.4	56 600	22.3	13.1	386	26.1	2.9	48 315	1.7	1 483	3.1	36 145	27.9	13.0
Perkins	1 586	76.3	25 700	20.4	12.9	199	20.4	1.8	1 861	-1.7	50	2.7	2 068	16.9	8.1
Potter	1 249	75.3	29 300	20.5	13.2	264	23.0	2.3	1 389	-0.4	50	3.6	1 442	19.5	8.5
Roberts	3 619	66.5	24 100	18.8	14.4	215	24.3	5.1	4 708	-0.5	261	5.5	3 976	18.8	10.7
Sanborn	1 059	77.2	14 999	14.6	13.4	206	19.6	3.6	1 455	0.4	50	3.4	1 187	16.6	9.4
Shannon	2 205	44.9	14 999	12.4	16.5	248	26.4	49.8	3 677	18.6	464	12.6	1 977	32.8	10.6
Spink	3 022	70.9	20 300	20.6	13.5	251	21.5	2.8	3 100	-8.7	112	3.6	3 412	19.5	7.2
Stanley	921	73.6	48 300	20.5	15.5	325	30.4	2.5	1 844	0.2	52	2.8	1 306	23.8	8.7
Sully	621	72.6	28 400	20.8	12.4	250	21.6	2.4	818	-4.0	20	2.4	823	14.7	9.7
Todd	2 210	46.4	14 999	17.8	13.7	243	31.3	24.5	3 112	3.4	258	8.3	2 138	30.5	8.0

1. Specified owner-occupied units.   2. Specified renter-occupied units.   3. Overcrowded or lacking complete plumbing facilities.   4. Percent of civilian labor force.   5. Persons 16 years and older.

STATE County	Private nonfarm establishments, employment and payroll, 1999									Agriculture, 1997			Farm operators
		Employment						Annual payroll		Farms			
											Percent with—		
	Number of establishments	Total	Health Care and Social Assistance	Manufacturing	Retail trade	Finance and Insurance	Professional Scientific and Technical Services	Total (mil dol)	Average per employee (dollars)	Number	Less than 50 acres	500 acres and over	Whose principal occupation is farming (percent)
	104	105	106	107	108	109	110	111	112	113	114	115	116
SOUTH CAROLINA—Cont'd													
Sumter	1 900	34 751	3 639	12 483	4 944	908	570	800	23 020	396	35.9	16.7	46.2
Union	541	8 037	847	3 393	1 480	195	90	161	20 081	255	23.5	7.5	31.0
Williamsburg	541	8 144	333	3 133	993	272	177	170	20 828	602	28.1	19.8	40.7
York	3 708	51 800	5 088	11 595	8 152	1 240	1 760	1 478	28 531	726	31.8	6.3	34.8
SOUTH DAKOTA	23 693	295 139	49 613	47 793	47 090	20 883	7 606	6 857	23 235	31 284	11.5	52.2	72.6
Aurora	93	429	D	D	101	29	12	7	17 219	421	11.4	54.4	75.3
Beadle	609	6 719	1 232	1 307	992	264	99	150	22 374	731	13.1	52.9	68.0
Bennett	69	595	129	D	137	17	7	10	16 679	258	5.8	69.8	75.6
Bon Homme	206	1 633	450	358	230	71	11	28	17 041	672	10.4	34.4	78.3
Brookings	726	10 904	1 133	3 986	1 543	413	256	234	21 493	886	19.4	31.5	59.9
Brown	1 331	16 097	2 707	2 382	3 106	665	424	348	21 625	1 006	15.7	52.0	68.4
Brule	219	1 801	485	27	305	65	43	30	16 436	382	7.6	65.4	82.2
Buffalo	7	57	D	0	D	0	D	1	17 351	77	3.9	79.2	80.5
Butte	269	1 937	233	202	498	73	73	34	17 402	547	14.1	45.7	59.2
Campbell	53	330	D	D	28	D	D	6	18 000	286	4.5	69.9	75.5
Charles Mix	294	2 547	520	D	452	88	35	41	15 915	735	10.2	57.7	81.6
Clark	125	749	110	181	86	43	13	12	16 063	563	8.2	54.5	75.0
Clay	311	2 728	533	151	668	104	30	41	15 115	397	9.8	43.1	77.1
Codington	983	13 100	1 652	4 073	2 416	358	219	283	21 597	619	19.4	38.8	64.3
Corson	44	250	29	D	67	D	D	3	10 616	425	6.1	74.1	79.8
Custer	214	973	109	28	220	36	23	20	20 753	326	12.9	46.9	63.5
Davison	743	9 150	1 432	1 868	1 509	299	320	208	22 718	429	21.4	37.8	60.1
Day	203	1 362	355	165	227	73	19	25	18 125	693	8.2	49.1	74.6
Deuel	127	897	204	172	121	66	20	19	20 758	564	9.8	38.5	68.4
Dewey	103	1 290	606	D	207	D	16	26	19 811	375	6.1	72.5	66.4
Douglas	121	912	230	115	147	34	7	13	14 046	392	11.5	49.2	80.9
Edmunds	119	734	140	D	178	50	7	13	18 042	449	7.3	69.0	76.4
Fall River	222	2 446	D	D	365	69	48	68	27 637	309	7.4	69.6	69.6
Faulk	74	446	D	7	98	D	8	6	14 025	316	7.9	71.8	83.5
Grant	264	2 963	367	437	408	250	65	62	20 890	534	10.1	42.9	73.0
Gregory	178	1 048	235	D	237	81	32	17	16 672	570	11.1	56.8	78.1
Haakon	100	647	D	D	91	D	D	11	17 091	309	4.9	79.6	80.9
Hamlin	152	802	149	113	190	56	5	15	18 600	413	15.0	44.8	75.8
Hand	133	987	213	37	146	62	33	16	16 010	488	6.6	69.3	80.9
Hanson	48	275	D	D	62	33	D	5	18 356	326	10.7	47.5	77.0
Harding	35	175	D	0	D	D	3	2	13 606	275	7.3	82.9	83.3
Hughes	638	6 157	1 140	94	1 524	389	204	122	19 759	287	11.8	55.1	70.4
Hutchinson	247	2 268	620	425	412	101	31	41	17 960	804	9.5	45.9	80.0
Hyde	49	574	D	D	32	D	8	9	16 399	229	9.2	68.6	79.5
Jackson	62	279	D	D	111	D	D	4	14 086	295	4.7	80.0	82.0
Jerauld	77	494	105	D	128	D	18	8	17 053	276	9.8	56.2	73.9
Jones	57	291	D	D	107	22	8	6	20 330	203	4.4	70.9	76.4
Kingsbury	208	1 400	276	289	248	111	26	25	17 904	580	12.1	49.5	75.9
Lake	360	3 619	596	1 043	539	100	49	74	20 337	500	15.6	45.4	70.8
Lawrence	833	8 311	971	610	1 244	173	161	161	19 423	270	19.3	31.1	55.9
Lincoln	542	4 866	639	797	859	222	82	113	23 193	806	17.4	28.5	65.5
Lyman	75	602	D	0	308	32	10	8	13 399	414	5.6	74.2	71.7
McCook	174	1 251	287	229	282	44	45	21	17 070	544	13.1	43.4	77.8
McPherson	93	450	139	33	73	55	15	7	14 751	397	3.8	70.5	80.6
Marshall	145	1 237	245	317	149	51	33	25	20 255	490	8.4	57.8	77.8
Meade	494	4 489	1 385	316	683	169	97	103	22 992	829	11.0	62.2	70.0
Mellette	32	188	D	0	50	D	6	2	12 255	217	3.2	82.5	80.6
Miner	73	720	164	D	84	D	D	14	19 383	369	9.2	46.9	74.0
Minnehaha	5 095	96 935	15 932	12 725	12 814	12 371	2 899	2 492	25 707	1 125	26.3	24.6	56.8
Moody	182	1 524	115	D	188	46	71	32	21 283	549	12.6	35.7	71.9
Pennington	3 216	38 420	6 765	4 239	6 670	1 728	1 325	897	23 338	637	16.2	46.8	64.1
Perkins	133	894	162	175	152	63	11	14	15 310	520	6.2	76.3	80.4
Potter	126	882	184	D	274	66	10	15	16 893	285	8.4	67.0	78.6
Roberts	267	1 863	531	68	369	92	23	27	14 557	803	10.8	46.8	73.5
Sanborn	62	516	D	D	42	24	30	8	16 382	382	11.0	51.6	69.9
Shannon	58	1 504	274	D	247	D	D	30	19 916	175	8.0	62.9	70.3
Spink	180	1 236	283	D	268	85	21	21	17 307	647	7.0	66.3	78.1
Stanley	84	740	0	D	133	D	19	16	21 680	194	6.7	78.4	71.1
Sully	55	240	D	D	91	27	3	4	17 842	261	4.6	72.8	80.5
Todd	65	1 072	255	0	193	D	D	23	21 466	210	2.9	78.1	85.7

Table B. States and Counties — Agriculture, Land, and Water

STATE County	\[117\] Acreage (1,000)	\[118\] Percent change, 1992–1997	\[119\] Average size of farm	\[120\] Total irrigated (1,000)	\[121\] Total cropland (1,000)	\[122\] Avg per farm ($1,000)	\[123\] Avg per acre (dollars)	\[124\] Value of machinery and equipment avg per farm ($1,000)	\[125\] Total (mil dol)	\[126\] Avg per farm (dollars)	\[127\] Crops	\[128\] Livestock and poultry products	\[129\] $10,000 or more	\[130\] $100,000 or more	\[131\] Percent of land owned by fed. gov. 1997	\[132\] Water consumption 1995 (mil gal/day)
SOUTH CAROLINA—Cont'd																
Sumter	139	0.3	352	5	95	362	994	66	60	151 951	52.0	48.0	38.4	20.2	0.9	32.1
Union	53	-5.1	208	D	22	157	967	29	2	7 125	21.1	78.9	16.5	0.4	18.1	7.2
Williamsburg	189	9.5	315	1	93	364	1 161	61	48	79 522	87.0	13.0	43.4	19.1	0.0	4.6
York	115	-4.6	159	0	56	328	2 365	29	41	56 710	37.3	62.7	22.6	5.0	0.4	216.1
SOUTH DAKOTA	44 355	-1.1	1 418	344	19 355	487	348	91	3 570	114 114	46.3	53.7	76.9	30.2	6.3	460.0
Aurora	343	-9.8	814	D	226	455	472	69	55	130 547	34.1	65.9	79.8	29.9	1.0	0.8
Beadle	707	-2.4	968	8	493	436	434	97	96	131 603	45.4	54.6	75.5	35.8	1.1	9.3
Bennett	797	1.2	3 090	5	234	697	247	125	29	111 521	34.7	65.3	78.7	34.5	2.1	7.1
Bon Homme	311	-3.5	462	6	247	348	723	92	66	97 480	42.1	57.9	81.5	27.7	2.8	4.4
Brookings	408	-8.2	460	13	331	295	703	75	88	98 903	44.0	56.0	67.4	24.6	1.1	6.7
Brown	1 070	4.2	1 063	5	818	586	563	119	146	145 130	63.2	36.8	72.3	34.7	2.3	8.4
Brule	461	-7.3	1 206	2	272	464	380	78	46	119 856	39.3	60.7	83.8	34.6	1.5	4.0
Buffalo	302	8.3	3 923	11	85	904	231	124	22	281 127	37.2	62.8	81.8	42.9	2.6	3.2
Butte	1 166	-6.2	2 132	42	162	454	219	60	41	75 171	13.8	86.2	65.6	17.7	11.1	88.6
Campbell	396	-5.4	1 383	4	212	395	296	82	31	106 695	39.2	60.8	83.9	28.0	2.2	2.7
Charles Mix	680	-1.2	925	15	496	438	486	115	111	151 493	44.6	55.4	85.2	37.1	2.6	10.6
Clark	514	-3.9	913	5	359	333	391	90	73	129 111	43.0	57.0	77.1	29.5	0.9	2.9
Clay	226	-4.7	569	8	208	488	910	122	46	116 222	81.3	18.7	86.6	40.6	0.2	4.5
Codington	385	-2.2	621	4	286	340	550	84	65	104 421	42.1	57.9	71.2	24.6	1.3	11.1
Corson	1 605	-5.7	3 775	3	336	657	171	85	31	71 901	32.1	67.9	80.5	20.9	3.0	2.0
Custer	476	3.1	1 462	6	71	498	345	46	11	34 982	10.4	89.6	54.9	8.6	40.4	4.2
Davison	274	1.3	640	2	215	365	570	79	39	91 464	60.5	39.5	71.8	25.9	0.0	4.0
Day	536	-4.4	774	1	385	335	416	76	49	70 967	61.1	38.9	71.7	19.5	1.5	1.2
Deuel	311	-8.9	551	2	216	300	527	76	47	84 096	41.9	58.1	75.5	23.8	0.7	1.1
Dewey	1 851	-0.4	4 935	D	240	880	177	76	26	70 283	22.9	77.1	74.7	22.1	2.5	1.8
Douglas	247	-2.0	630	1	197	340	560	93	55	139 817	35.6	64.4	88.5	41.6	1.5	1.7
Edmunds	635	-1.0	1 415	1	431	427	327	110	62	137 237	44.3	55.7	77.5	30.7	1.2	1.7
Fall River	978	0.3	3 165	16	119	530	177	43	60	195 411	4.2	95.8	68.3	17.5	26.6	37.6
Faulk	571	2.0	1 808	D	344	603	333	149	53	168 635	53.0	47.0	84.2	41.8	0.3	0.7
Grant	359	-4.0	672	2	271	344	548	95	78	145 766	46.6	53.4	78.7	36.0	1.2	5.6
Gregory	566	-5.9	992	1	264	342	381	63	43	75 621	39.4	60.6	81.8	22.1	1.9	2.1
Haakon	1 325	10.1	4 288	D	428	683	167	95	41	131 994	34.4	65.6	84.1	39.2	0.3	2.1
Hamlin	279	0.6	675	5	232	459	664	120	49	117 660	56.1	43.9	79.4	34.4	0.9	2.7
Hand	811	-5.8	1 662	0	472	468	316	110	66	135 200	44.4	55.6	84.8	35.2	0.3	1.7
Hanson	231	-5.5	710	1	183	359	557	108	43	132 963	49.3	50.7	81.6	36.2	0.2	0.9
Harding	1 702	2.7	6 190	1	193	1 065	169	105	28	101 567	11.0	89.0	83.6	37.1	6.0	1.2
Hughes	391	0.0	1 364	12	237	524	374	105	37	128 599	56.8	43.2	73.2	33.4	2.5	21.7
Hutchinson	479	-4.5	596	2	404	382	653	107	103	128 073	47.4	52.6	84.8	37.8	0.1	2.7
Hyde	532	-2.3	2 324	1	214	590	257	103	30	132 541	40.8	59.2	84.7	36.7	0.1	1.4
Jackson	1 354	-0.5	4 591	1	267	877	188	92	28	95 841	31.7	68.3	77.3	23.1	10.2	2.0
Jerauld	346	3.7	1 255	1	184	359	291	92	37	134 731	30.9	69.1	79.3	27.5	0.4	1.2
Jones	589	0.8	2 900	D	214	626	215	85	19	91 546	28.8	71.2	76.4	25.1	3.2	1.0
Kingsbury	481	4.5	828	2	386	419	503	99	73	126 052	59.0	41.0	79.8	36.7	1.0	3.2
Lake	307	3.1	614	2	260	478	770	107	68	135 773	55.8	44.2	79.6	34.0	1.4	3.4
Lawrence	171	-12.1	635	2	48	454	724	39	9	35 139	12.6	87.4	53.0	7.8	53.5	14.8
Lincoln	319	-1.3	395	1	291	469	1 227	85	100	124 261	61.1	38.9	81.4	35.1	0.1	2.8
Lyman	944	11.5	2 279	8	418	701	333	77	40	97 675	48.8	51.2	77.1	30.7	9.7	5.0
McCook	312	-4.1	574	D	254	378	601	97	64	116 961	60.3	39.7	79.6	39.3	0.9	1.5
McPherson	569	-13.9	1 433	1	311	415	296	142	56	142 123	18.2	81.8	76.3	23.9	2.8	1.9
Marshall	505	3.9	1 030	1	325	454	433	112	80	162 441	37.4	62.6	74.7	31.8	1.9	1.6
Meade	2 074	0.0	2 502	10	432	564	230	55	52	62 803	19.4	80.6	68.3	18.2	3.7	5.2
Mellette	655	-6.6	3 017	0	161	591	201	68	18	81 746	19.9	80.1	82.0	28.6	0.0	1.1
Miner	280	-10.5	760	D	199	399	506	67	40	108 524	48.9	51.1	74.8	30.1	0.4	0.7
Minnehaha	406	-4.4	361	1	352	412	1 149	88	104	92 390	59.6	40.4	68.8	28.4	1.0	24.9
Moody	284	-0.4	517	2	237	507	984	85	68	123 439	56.9	43.1	81.2	33.9	0.7	2.2
Pennington	1 044	-2.1	1 639	9	288	512	325	49	40	62 288	29.2	70.7	61.2	14.1	43.1	30.2
Perkins	1 705	-1.2	3 279	1	454	510	161	77	42	81 322	22.5	77.5	77.3	26.0	7.8	1.5
Potter	530	4.5	1 860	4	352	670	380	128	45	156 802	57.2	42.8	75.8	41.4	0.8	3.8
Roberts	571	-5.5	711	2	441	378	533	85	87	107 883	63.3	36.7	76.2	33.3	0.7	1.6
Sanborn	347	7.3	907	D	220	313	382	76	41	108 247	35.7	64.3	79.3	27.0	0.0	0.8
Shannon	1 474	4.0	8 423	1	102	2 084	251	55	13	72 515	25.6	74.4	68.0	24.0	10.4	1.2
Spink	849	-4.7	1 313	14	686	583	430	143	117	180 290	63.9	36.1	83.9	46.2	0.3	8.5
Stanley	896	-0.9	4 617	1	243	902	192	113	23	118 250	46.1	53.9	73.2	30.9	7.9	2.5
Sully	599	-2.6	2 295	20	470	1 016	428	180	53	202 026	76.8	23.2	87.0	49.8	5.8	12.9
Todd	1 084	0.5	5 164	15	173	932	173	79	25	119 666	29.4	70.6	81.4	29.5	0.1	8.3

Table B. States and Counties — Residential Construction, Wholesale and Retail Trade, and Real Estate

STATE County	Value of Residential Construction Authorized by Building Permits, 2000 New Construction ($1,000)	Number of Housing Units	Wholesale Trade, 1997 Number of Establishments	Number of Employees	Sales (mil dol)	Annual Payroll (mil dol)	Retail Trade¹, 1997 Number of Establishments	Number of Employees	Sales (mil dol)	Annual Payroll (mil dol)	Real Estate and Rental and Leasing, 1997 Number of Establishments	Number of Employees	Receipts (mil dol)	Annual Payroll (mil dol)
	133	134	135	136	137	138	139	140	141	142	143	144	145	146
SOUTH CAROLINA—Cont'd														
Sumter	28 197	294	84	671	208.6	18.1	425	4 841	782.0	72.8	74	277	26.6	4.3
Union	4 916	47	13	38	14.2	1.1	113	1 228	155.2	15.0	17	51	3.1	0.7
Williamsburg	717	50	39	367	98.0	7.0	146	1 006	155.6	13.3	6	31	1.0	0.3
York	273 284	2 977	267	3 598	3 001.9	124.2	615	7 155	1 244.4	112.7	120	486	46.0	9.8
SOUTH DAKOTA	369 135	4 196	1 402	15 509	7 874.2	389.8	4 311	45 867	11 707.1	689.6	719	2 951	245.7	45.1
Aurora	93	2	4	38	13.4	1.1	18	D	D	D	3	3	0.1	0.0
Beadle	2 994	29	27	279	183.9	5.8	120	1 082	152.9	15.5	24	99	4.0	1.0
Bennett	50	1	4	59	44.9	0.5	21	D	D	D	1	D	D	D
Bon Homme	472	5	17	129	51.4	1.8	43	D	D	D	5	17	0.6	0.0
Brookings	7 904	101	29	505	265.8	8.3	139	1 513	169.2	17.5	28	80	5.7	0.8
Brown	6 240	111	83	897	637.3	21.5	237	3 128	497.4	47.9	50	123	11.6	2.0
Brule	911	13	9	94	36.5	1.7	51	D	D	D	2	D	D	D
Buffalo	NA	NA	NA	NA	NA	NA	2	D	D	D	2	D	D	D
Butte	665	12	19	139	83.1	2.4	59	402	66.7	6.5	10	D	D	D
Campbell	0	0	6	D	D	D	10	D	D	D	1	D	D	D
Charles Mix	662	7	16	120	63.6	2.3	73	497	63.9	5.7	4	5	0.4	0.0
Clark	136	2	7	76	80.6	1.4	16	D	D	D	3	4	0.1	0.0
Clay	5 090	49	9	44	18.3	1.2	52	493	75.4	6.8	12	24	2.0	0.3
Codington	10 873	109	74	560	320.7	15.8	191	2 382	347.2	32.8	33	94	7.5	1.3
Corson	0	0	5	D	D	D	14	D	D	D	NA	NA	NA	NA
Custer	5 265	70	2	D	D	D	32	D	D	D	9	19	2.6	0.5
Davison	5 147	70	36	504	216.7	12.6	153	1 747	230.7	21.8	27	64	4.0	0.5
Day	1 444	21	7	85	53.2	1.8	42	D	D	D	5	9	0.7	0.1
Deuel	2 120	22	6	19	7.6	0.2	26	D	D	D	1	D	D	D
Dewey	1 066	16	6	33	12.6	0.7	27	D	D	D	2	D	D	D
Douglas	145	5	9	60	17.4	1.2	18	D	D	D	1	D	D	D
Edmunds	503	6	11	147	101.5	3.3	21	D	D	D	4	8	0.3	0.1
Fall River	371	5	6	31	5.5	0.5	45	D	D	D	5	6	0.9	0.1
Faulk	270	4	6	25	10.6	0.4	11	D	D	D	1	D	D	D
Grant	2 092	19	18	413	106.2	7.4	55	451	68.1	5.3	2	D	D	D
Gregory	0	0	14	88	39.2	1.3	44	D	D	D	3	6	0.2	0.1
Haakon	0	0	10	124	62.4	1.6	20	D	D	D	1	D	D	D
Hamlin	2 229	23	10	60	38.3	1.4	29	D	D	D	3	3	0.1	0.0
Hand	410	3	12	156	58.5	3.0	22	D	D	D	2	D	D	D
Hanson	NA	NA	9	30	34.3	0.5	10	D	D	D	1	D	D	D
Harding	0	0	2	D	D	D	6	28	4.9	0.5	NA	NA	NA	NA
Hughes	6 055	49	22	159	85.8	4.2	121	1 221	194.7	17.4	19	102	4.0	0.9
Hutchinson	1 802	22	23	245	147.3	5.3	53	D	D	D	2	D	D	D
Hyde	0	0	3	D	D	D	11	D	D	D	NA	NA	NA	NA
Jackson	0	0	2	D	D	D	17	D	D	D	1	D	D	D
Jerauld	106	3	6	D	D	D	16	D	D	D	2	D	D	D
Jones	320	4	3	9	7.5	0.3	13	D	D	D	1	D	D	D
Kingsbury	2 218	21	10	94	69.3	2.4	40	D	D	D	3	7	0.3	0.0
Lake	5 698	81	12	125	81.0	3.5	67	581	115.0	10.4	14	25	1.8	0.3
Lawrence	16 183	136	21	59	12.1	0.9	147	1 334	226.1	18.6	35	134	8.9	1.2
Lincoln	19 032	168	39	305	200.4	8.0	72	625	150.5	11.1	7	65	2.8	1.6
Lyman	300	5	5	D	D	D	18	D	D	D	NA	NA	NA	NA
McCook	4 389	45	13	53	33.5	1.0	31	D	D	D	2	D	D	D
McPherson	0	0	2	D	D	D	16	D	D	D	3	4	0.2	0.0
Marshall	1 253	24	10	82	43.0	1.2	23	D	D	D	NA	NA	NA	NA
Meade	12 549	101	22	134	94.8	2.4	81	630	115.9	9.8	16	77	4.1	0.8
Mellette	0	0	NA	NA	NA	NA	9	58	5.1	0.5	1	D	D	D
Miner	260	2	8	39	19.9	0.7	15	D	D	D	NA	NA	NA	NA
Minnehaha	168 099	2 137	356	5 412	2 145.1	163.3	770	12 238	1 999.4	191.7	185	947	97.5	17.4
Moody	162	2	6	32	13.1	0.8	23	D	D	D	5	D	D	D
Pennington	44 883	427	173	2 027	675.7	57.8	581	6 870	1 132.0	112.2	126	530	52.7	9.0
Perkins	0	0	8	62	49.4	1.8	26	159	15.8	1.8	1	D	D	D
Potter	270	4	11	98	57.3	2.3	28	D	D	D	2	D	D	D
Roberts	4 097	38	19	144	202.6	2.6	49	D	D	D	1	D	D	D
Sanborn	348	6	9	39	15.6	0.7	8	D	D	D	1	D	D	D
Shannon	NA	NA	NA	NA	NA	NA	15	D	D	D	1	D	D	D
Spink	402	8	16	146	133.0	3.8	39	261	51.7	4.0	3	6	0.2	0.0
Stanley	1 853	18	5	D	D	D	19	D	D	D	1	D	D	D
Sully	645	7	4	D	D	D	14	D	D	D	1	D	D	D
Todd	0	0	1	D	D	D	17	D	D	D	1	D	D	D

1. Establishments with payroll.

STATE County	Professional, Scientific, and Technical Services[1], 1997				Manufacturing, 1997				Accommodation and Foodservices, 1997			
	Number of Establishments	Number of Employees	Receipts (mil dol)	Annual Payroll (mil dol)	Number of Establishments	Number of Employees	Receipts (mil dol)	Annual Payroll (mil dol)	Number of Establishments	Number of Employees	Sales (mil dol)	Annual Payroll (mil dol)
	147	148	149	150	151	152	153	154	155	156	157	158
SOUTH CAROLINA—Cont'd												
Sumter	116	471	29.1	8.9	84	12 655	2 050.4	303.0	133	2 311	70.0	19.1
Union	21	50	3.3	1.2	43	5 355	679.6	129.2	36	646	13.5	3.6
Williamsburg	27	131	10.1	2.6	34	3 392	533.4	86.8	35	334	10.1	3.1
York	268	1 362	97.5	39.5	222	11 731	2 325.7	391.8	264	5 073	152.9	39.0
SOUTH DAKOTA	1 282	6 228	450.4	161.7	888	46 539	12 305.5	1 162.6	2 258	30 131	888.0	234.4
Aurora	3	10	0.2	0.1	NA	NA	NA	NA	15	49	1.3	0.3
Beadle	25	85	6.0	1.6	21	1 134	263.5	25.7	66	671	17.2	4.8
Bennett	4	5	0.1	0.0	NA	NA	NA	NA	6	47	1.3	0.2
Bon Homme	5	22	5.2	0.7	NA	NA	NA	NA	22	D	D	D
Brookings	41	173	11.3	4.1	31	3 449	902.0	92.4	62	1 236	26.9	7.2
Brown	72	374	22.4	8.0	38	2 492	397.5	61.0	105	1 616	47.4	13.3
Brule	13	31	1.2	0.4	NA	NA	NA	NA	30	276	10.2	2.8
Buffalo	NA	NA	NA	NA	NA	NA	NA	NA	NA	NA	NA	NA
Butte	14	59	4.4	1.1	NA	NA	NA	NA	23	D	D	D
Campbell	2	D	D	D	NA	NA	NA	NA	8	20	0.7	0.1
Charles Mix	12	31	1.7	0.6	NA	NA	NA	NA	27	592	38.8	6.8
Clark	4	7	0.3	0.1	NA	NA	NA	NA	11	56	1.4	0.3
Clay	12	31	1.6	0.3	NA	NA	NA	NA	46	812	15.5	3.8
Codington	53	261	13.7	6.4	63	4 115	395.8	102.6	78	1 185	33.1	9.1
Corson	2	D	D	D	NA	NA	NA	NA	3	5	0.2	0.0
Custer	17	33	1.6	0.6	NA	NA	NA	NA	46	243	14.8	3.9
Davison	33	294	21.3	6.9	36	1 719	365.9	47.2	79	1 190	33.2	9.4
Day	5	17	1.2	0.4	NA	NA	NA	NA	20	125	2.7	0.7
Deuel	4	18	0.7	0.2	NA	NA	NA	NA	12	65	1.6	0.3
Dewey	3	9	0.4	0.1	NA	NA	NA	NA	7	64	1.7	0.5
Douglas	3	2	0.3	0.0	NA	NA	NA	NA	9	28	0.6	0.1
Edmunds	4	2	0.2	0.1	NA	NA	NA	NA	10	61	1.4	0.3
Fall River	11	27	1.2	0.3	NA	NA	NA	NA	35	278	12.4	1.7
Faulk	3	6	0.2	0.1	NA	NA	NA	NA	6	14	0.5	0.1
Grant	12	37	1.6	0.6	6	D	D	D	21	216	5.6	1.5
Gregory	6	20	1.5	0.3	NA	NA	NA	NA	19	91	2.3	0.5
Haakon	3	6	0.3	0.1	NA	NA	NA	NA	9	44	1.3	0.3
Hamlin	5	4	0.3	0.1	NA	NA	NA	NA	13	D	D	D
Hand	5	11	0.5	0.1	NA	NA	NA	NA	9	46	1.2	0.2
Hanson	3	3	0.1	0.0	NA	NA	NA	NA	4	25	0.5	0.1
Harding	2	D	D	D	NA	NA	NA	NA	7	77	1.0	0.2
Hughes	39	197	15.5	5.2	NA	NA	NA	NA	55	894	25.7	7.7
Hutchinson	10	25	1.3	0.5	NA	NA	NA	NA	16	D	D	D
Hyde	2	D	D	D	NA	NA	NA	NA	4	D	D	D
Jackson	NA	NA	NA	NA	NA	NA	NA	NA	17	66	3.8	0.8
Jerauld	3	3	0.2	0.0	NA	NA	NA	NA	7	38	0.8	0.2
Jones	2	D	D	D	NA	NA	NA	NA	12	41	2.4	0.7
Kingsbury	4	12	0.7	0.2	NA	NA	NA	NA	22	98	3.3	0.5
Lake	15	51	3.1	0.8	23	950	167.2	19.7	34	353	8.1	2.2
Lawrence	42	145	8.8	3.5	30	502	88.2	13.1	111	1 728	59.2	15.7
Lincoln	15	56	3.9	1.8	30	D	D	D	33	344	7.8	2.0
Lyman	1	D	D	D	NA	NA	NA	NA	15	96	3.2	0.7
McCook	6	15	0.7	0.3	NA	NA	NA	NA	23	132	2.7	0.6
McPherson	3	8	0.1	0.1	NA	NA	NA	NA	10	D	D	D
Marshall	9	25	1.2	0.4	NA	NA	NA	NA	18	71	1.9	0.5
Meade	21	57	4.9	1.1	NA	NA	NA	NA	54	517	15.7	4.1
Mellette	2	D	D	D	NA	NA	NA	NA	4	14	0.6	0.1
Miner	3	9	0.3	0.1	NA	NA	NA	NA	8	43	1.0	0.2
Minnehaha	366	2 381	182.7	72.6	168	D	D	D	386	8 074	223.4	64.0
Moody	7	54	3.3	1.2	NA	NA	NA	NA	17	D	D	D
Pennington	207	1 119	91.0	30.6	134	4 263	867.3	100.8	326	5 125	163.7	44.3
Perkins	3	10	0.3	0.1	NA	NA	NA	NA	15	91	1.6	0.4
Potter	5	D	D	D	NA	NA	NA	NA	12	79	3.2	0.6
Roberts	10	16	0.6	0.3	NA	NA	NA	NA	29	187	4.6	1.1
Sanborn	6	10	0.6	0.2	NA	NA	NA	NA	6	D	D	D
Shannon	2	D	D	D	NA	NA	NA	NA	6	39	1.2	0.4
Spink	6	17	1.2	0.2	NA	NA	NA	NA	18	191	4.2	1.0
Stanley	4	4	0.4	0.1	NA	NA	NA	NA	8	55	1.5	0.4
Sully	3	2	0.3	0.1	NA	NA	NA	NA	6	87	1.9	0.3
Todd	1	D	D	D	NA	NA	NA	NA	5	40	1.2	0.3

1. Firms subject to federal tax.

Table B. States and Counties — Health and Other Services and Federal Funds

STATE County	Health Care and Social Assistance[1], 1997				Other Services[1], 1997				Federal funds and grants, fiscal 2001[2] Expenditures (mil dol)		Direct payments for individuals[3]	
	Number of Establishments	Number of Employees	Receipts (mil dol)	Annual Payroll (mil dol)	Number of Establishments	Number of Employees	Receipts (mil dol)	Annual Payroll (mil dol)	Total	Social Security and government retirement	Medicare	Food stamps and Supplemental Security Income
	159	160	161	162	163	164	165	166	167	168	169	170
SOUTH CAROLINA—Cont'd												
Sumter	128	1 347	81.0	40.6	123	827	47.5	14.1	752.4	254.5	62.6	33.6
Union	35	325	17.0	7.4	34	130	5.7	1.5	147.9	77.7	26.7	6.9
Williamsburg	42	342	18.6	7.7	45	220	10.1	3.2	320.1	70.5	29.3	18.0
York	212	4 122	263.1	110.3	223	1 226	66.6	21.9	542.6	299.7	96.2	18.7
SOUTH DAKOTA	1 314	14 080	881.6	414.3	1 356	5 828	344.7	90.7	5 807.0	1 594.3	523.2	101.8
Aurora	4	D	D	D	5	15	1.2	0.1	29.1	6.9	3.1	0.2
Beadle	40	394	19.8	7.9	35	148	6.6	1.9	150.0	44.8	16.9	2.0
Bennett	2	D	D	D	3	7	0.4	0.1	28.8	5.5	2.0	1.8
Bon Homme	7	35	2.0	1.1	7	17	1.4	0.3	51.1	16.6	7.9	0.5
Brookings	37	274	15.8	7.4	40	171	8.2	2.3	130.4	42.1	14.2	1.7
Brown	105	749	54.0	20.8	79	383	21.6	5.5	305.7	79.0	31.4	3.4
Brule	22	239	10.1	3.9	12	36	4.3	0.6	46.0	11.6	5.3	0.6
Buffalo	1	D	D	D	NA	NA	NA	NA	29.4	1.8	1.2	0.8
Butte	17	80	3.3	1.1	20	65	4.0	0.8	47.2	22.1	5.2	1.2
Campbell	1	D	D	D	2	D	D	D	23.2	6.5	2.7	0.1
Charles Mix	15	117	3.3	1.2	22	51	5.0	0.7	102.4	19.4	8.9	2.1
Clark	5	95	2.7	1.4	9	14	0.9	0.1	46.7	10.3	4.0	0.4
Clay	14	120	4.9	2.2	18	70	2.8	0.7	79.4	19.5	6.9	1.2
Codington	46	408	26.0	12.6	63	265	13.9	3.4	127.4	51.8	14.0	2.5
Corson	2	D	D	D	1	D	D	D	43.3	10.3	4.4	1.9
Custer	9	21	1.2	0.3	7	7	0.4	0.1	49.7	22.7	4.1	0.7
Davison	58	507	29.6	12.5	44	158	10.3	2.3	110.4	40.1	18.0	2.4
Day	11	80	3.7	1.1	12	21	2.0	0.4	69.1	16.9	7.7	0.8
Deuel	2	D	D	D	7	11	1.4	0.2	37.6	10.1	4.1	0.4
Dewey	3	D	D	D	1	D	D	D	70.2	8.2	2.6	3.7
Douglas	2	D	D	D	7	38	1.8	0.4	27.6	8.0	3.7	0.2
Edmunds	4	86	2.7	1.5	7	11	0.9	0.1	41.1	9.7	4.9	0.2
Fall River	11	44	1.8	0.7	11	28	2.2	0.3	77.7	34.0	6.4	1.3
Faulk	1	D	D	D	7	14	2.1	0.2	29.3	7.1	3.1	0.4
Grant	13	149	6.5	2.9	19	51	4.0	0.8	52.7	18.6	7.3	0.7
Gregory	8	29	2.1	1.1	9	20	1.4	0.2	43.9	13.5	5.8	0.8
Haakon	2	D	D	D	6	14	1.4	0.2	27.7	5.0	1.8	0.1
Hamlin	5	153	3.5	1.9	7	8	1.0	0.2	38.2	11.6	3.8	0.4
Hand	5	33	2.0	1.0	13	18	1.0	0.2	51.4	8.2	3.6	0.3
Hanson	NA	NA	NA	NA	NA	NA	NA	NA	22.2	6.1	1.6	0.2
Harding	1	D	D	D	NA	NA	NA	NA	11.7	2.4	0.8	0.1
Hughes	41	485	23.9	7.2	33	140	7.8	2.0	274.2	40.7	9.4	1.4
Hutchinson	12	77	3.7	1.3	16	41	3.1	0.6	71.7	20.6	8.9	0.5
Hyde	3	D	D	D	3	6	0.4	0.0	21.1	3.9	1.5	0.2
Jackson	2	D	D	D	NA	NA	NA	NA	20.9	4.4	1.0	1.0
Jerauld	3	5	0.3	0.0	7	9	1.2	0.1	23.6	6.0	3.3	0.2
Jones	1	D	D	D	NA	NA	NA	NA	18.7	2.6	1.1	0.1
Kingsbury	11	172	5.0	2.3	11	44	2.5	0.5	55.7	16.9	7.0	0.5
Lake	12	156	6.3	3.1	19	50	3.5	0.7	69.6	24.3	9.8	1.0
Lawrence	49	255	16.4	5.8	50	154	9.4	2.5	114.4	53.7	14.2	1.3
Lincoln	19	300	17.6	6.2	33	135	10.9	2.5	72.6	26.2	8.1	0.7
Lyman	3	8	0.5	0.3	2	D	D	D	67.9	7.5	2.5	1.4
McCook	14	202	6.0	3.2	9	30	2.2	0.4	44.3	12.7	5.5	0.4
McPherson	5	13	0.6	0.1	4	7	0.7	0.1	23.2	5.5	2.7	0.3
Marshall	7	176	4.3	2.2	11	38	2.5	0.6	43.9	11.1	4.8	0.4
Meade	19	134	6.2	1.8	34	65	5.5	1.1	164.8	53.1	12.8	1.4
Mellette	1	D	D	D	2	D	D	D	15.2	2.7	1.6	0.9
Miner	1	D	D	D	8	22	2.3	0.4	28.6	6.8	3.9	0.3
Minnehaha	284	4 344	347.2	194.3	283	1 858	101.3	31.5	810.1	281.2	79.4	14.6
Moody	7	46	1.2	0.5	8	27	1.7	0.3	53.2	12.3	5.3	0.4
Pennington	226	2 315	163.6	65.6	191	1 049	55.5	17.4	612.1	224.5	48.0	14.0
Perkins	6	8	0.6	0.2	11	22	2.2	0.4	31.9	8.9	4.0	0.3
Potter	5	19	0.6	0.3	6	17	1.9	0.2	40.8	8.1	3.8	0.1
Roberts	11	157	4.9	1.9	15	28	1.8	0.3	84.7	20.2	8.0	2.0
Sanborn	2	D	D	D	7	11	1.1	0.1	31.1	6.3	3.2	0.2
Shannon	1	D	D	D	1	D	D	D	169.5	12.8	5.3	10.9
Spink	8	111	4.1	1.8	9	20	1.8	0.5	85.7	19.3	9.2	0.6
Stanley	NA	NA	NA	NA	6	14	0.7	0.2	21.3	5.2	1.4	0.1
Sully	NA	NA	NA	NA	1	D	D	D	35.3	2.8	1.1	0.0
Todd	2	D	D	D	1	D	D	D	95.2	8.7	3.9	6.6

1. Firms subject to federal tax. 2. October 1, 2000 to September 30, 2001. 3. State totals may include programs not allocated by county.

	Federal funds and grants, fiscal 2001[1] (cont'd)							Local government finances, 1997				
	Expenditures (mil dol) (cont'd)							General revenue				
		Procurement contract awards		Grants[2]							Taxes	
STATE County												Per capita[3] (dollars)
	Salaries and wages	Defense	Other	Medicaid and other health-related	Nutrition and family welfare	Education	Other	Total (mil dol)	Intergovern-mental (mil dol)	Total (mil dol)	Total	Property
	171	172	173	174	175	176	177	178	179	180	181	182
SOUTH CAROLINA—Cont'd												
Sumter	203.8	29.7	4.9	100.1	19.3	11.9	6.4	163.3	93.2	51.4	482	399
Union	4.7	0.0	1.0	20.5	3.2	1.6	2.4	74.1	25.2	16.1	527	494
Williamsburg	5.5	0.1	110.4	60.1	6.9	4.4	0.1	62.2	35.0	13.1	351	330
York	22.1	0.9	5.0	48.2	13.1	8.0	13.1	266.5	98.7	124.6	828	781
SOUTH DAKOTA	600.4	116.8	184.3	424.8	149.7	163.2	516.7	X	X	X	X	X
Aurora	1.0	0.0	0.2	0.9	0.2	0.1	1.9	5.9	2.2	2.6	875	763
Beadle	21.6	0.0	2.5	13.9	1.1	0.5	9.0	34.9	12.1	16.0	891	668
Bennett	1.0	0.0	1.0	3.0	0.5	2.5	3.8	9.2	2.7	2.4	739	608
Bon Homme	1.7	0.0	0.5	3.6	0.5	0.3	4.3	15.7	4.7	6.7	869	754
Brookings	8.1	0.1	1.3	7.8	1.3	0.6	21.5	62.2	11.2	21.4	817	668
Brown	29.5	0.1	15.3	19.0	2.5	2.9	43.7	63.5	19.0	34.0	952	688
Brule	1.8	0.1	0.7	3.8	0.4	0.8	4.5	11.4	4.4	5.6	1 011	842
Buffalo	5.3	0.7	1.6	3.1	1.5	0.1	2.5	0.4	0.1	0.3	151	145
Butte	2.5	0.0	0.4	3.3	1.3	0.3	5.7	17.8	7.1	6.4	716	568
Campbell	0.6	0.0	0.2	2.1	0.1	0.1	0.4	3.6	1.4	1.7	851	782
Charles Mix	8.3	0.7	1.3	8.5	5.3	5.3	10.1	16.8	7.7	7.2	762	679
Clark	1.4	0.0	0.7	3.3	0.3	0.2	4.1	7.3	2.5	4.0	908	824
Clay	3.3	0.2	0.6	12.6	1.9	1.6	6.2	18.4	4.7	10.1	657	516
Codington	11.6	0.0	6.7	10.7	1.5	0.7	5.3	48.1	10.6	25.7	1 010	680
Corson	3.8	0.5	1.3	4.4	1.1	4.7	2.1	7.8	5.3	1.9	449	365
Custer	8.1	0.0	5.8	2.7	0.4	0.1	4.1	12.8	4.0	6.6	953	787
Davison	5.9	0.0	8.9	10.4	1.5	0.7	5.0	33.0	11.3	16.6	885	577
Day	3.1	0.0	1.0	6.5	0.7	0.4	6.5	13.3	6.1	5.5	856	773
Deuel	1.6	0.2	0.4	2.7	0.3	0.1	2.2	6.6	2.0	3.6	780	674
Dewey	14.3	0.0	8.1	9.1	4.1	6.0	5.0	8.1	5.4	2.2	387	311
Douglas	1.3	0.0	0.3	1.2	0.2	0.1	0.6	5.3	2.0	2.7	757	603
Edmunds	1.0	0.0	0.2	2.1	0.2	0.2	3.7	11.9	2.8	4.3	1 017	947
Fall River	21.3	0.2	1.9	4.7	0.8	0.7	3.4	15.8	5.6	7.2	1 011	846
Faulk	1.0	0.0	0.2	1.2	0.1	0.1	1.0	4.9	1.8	2.6	1 026	958
Grant	2.4	0.0	0.5	4.4	0.5	0.1	0.4	17.4	4.6	8.9	1 106	1 001
Gregory	1.9	0.9	0.6	3.3	0.6	3.0	3.4	10.8	5.0	4.7	930	777
Haakon	0.8	0.0	0.1	0.0	0.2	0.1	4.8	7.5	1.6	2.8	1 151	956
Hamlin	1.5	0.0	0.4	1.8	0.4	0.2	1.0	13.5	4.0	5.8	1 084	977
Hand	1.0	0.0	0.2	1.8	0.2	0.1	12.8	7.8	2.4	4.8	1 157	1 030
Hanson	0.7	0.0	0.2	0.6	0.2	0.1	0.4	4.6	2.0	2.2	769	682
Harding	1.1	0.0	0.1	0.0	0.1	0.0	3.0	3.6	1.1	1.9	1 242	1 018
Hughes	11.7	1.6	5.6	27.6	39.2	41.8	72.0	27.6	7.9	14.4	937	738
Hutchinson	2.4	0.0	0.6	4.7	0.5	0.3	6.7	16.5	6.0	8.2	1 011	907
Hyde	0.2	0.0	0.0	0.6	0.1	0.0	4.7	3.4	1.1	1.9	1 162	988
Jackson	3.1	0.0	0.5	0.6	0.3	0.6	0.7	3.6	1.7	1.6	553	434
Jerauld	0.7	0.0	0.2	0.9	0.2	0.1	1.9	5.0	2.2	2.2	986	888
Jones	0.3	0.0	0.1	0.6	0.0	0.0	5.9	2.9	0.8	1.6	1 267	1 049
Kingsbury	2.1	0.0	0.5	1.8	0.4	0.2	2.4	11.5	4.4	5.6	954	860
Lake	3.3	0.0	1.8	4.4	2.7	0.5	0.7	21.5	7.7	9.7	911	797
Lawrence	7.9	0.1	2.4	8.9	1.6	0.9	17.1	53.4	17.0	25.4	1 149	913
Lincoln	2.4	0.0	0.6	3.8	0.6	0.2	6.7	29.0	12.1	14.2	705	633
Lyman	3.1	1.3	0.9	3.9	1.0	0.9	21.5	5.6	1.6	2.9	739	631
McCook	2.1	0.0	0.4	2.4	0.4	0.1	2.1	11.2	4.4	5.7	1 002	862
McPherson	0.7	0.0	0.2	2.4	0.2	0.1	0.8	5.6	1.8	3.3	1 182	1 097
Marshall	1.4	0.0	0.3	3.0	0.4	0.2	1.7	8.4	2.8	4.5	974	814
Meade	29.4	32.7	3.9	5.3	1.2	6.9	8.2	27.1	9.6	13.5	612	495
Mellette	0.5	0.0	0.1	3.0	0.6	1.7	0.3	5.3	2.9	1.4	685	576
Miner	1.0	0.0	0.2	3.2	0.2	0.1	0.7	6.5	2.2	3.5	1 210	1 042
Minnehaha	116.9	6.8	47.6	58.1	7.4	2.9	41.1	276.2	55.1	166.5	1 185	798
Moody	5.9	0.0	1.1	4.3	0.7	2.5	1.4	13.1	3.9	5.7	874	775
Pennington	170.2	5.1	26.6	35.3	12.6	10.2	29.1	192.8	68.0	91.5	1 050	748
Perkins	1.5	0.0	0.5	3.6	0.3	0.2	2.4	9.0	4.1	3.7	1 056	950
Potter	0.9	0.0	0.7	1.5	0.2	0.1	3.5	8.8	2.7	4.0	1 352	1 237
Roberts	6.0	0.0	0.6	11.9	2.7	3.5	1.9	16.8	8.0	6.7	671	597
Sanborn	0.9	0.0	0.2	1.5	0.2	0.1	5.6	4.6	2.3	1.9	689	593
Shannon	23.8	1.9	5.7	24.4	13.2	14.0	35.5	10.3	9.2	0.6	49	29
Spink	2.9	0.0	0.6	4.7	0.4	0.3	3.4	18.9	5.4	8.3	1 079	932
Stanley	0.1	0.2	0.0	0.3	0.2	0.3	1.2	5.8	2.0	3.1	1 064	868
Sully	0.3	0.0	0.1	0.0	0.1	0.1	0.5	3.8	0.9	2.6	1 701	1 508
Todd	12.3	0.0	1.1	16.1	6.5	15.1	12.8	16.1	13.6	1.7	184	127

1. October 1, 2000 to September 30, 2001.   2. State totals may include programs not allocated by county.   3. Based on the resident population estimated as of July 1 of the year shown.

Table B. States and Counties — Local Government Finances, Government Employment, and Elections

STATE County	Direct general expenditure — Total (mil dol)	Per capita¹ (dollars)	Education	Health and hospitals	Police protection	Public welfare	Highways	Debt outstanding — Total (mil dol)	Per capita¹ (dollars)	Federal civilian	Federal military	State and local	Democratic	Republican	All other
	183	184	185	186	187	188	189	190	191	192	193	194	195	196	197
SOUTH CAROLINA—Cont'd															
Sumter	160.6	1 507	63.3	2.3	6.3	0.5	1.9	82.5	774	1 165	5 507	5 668	46.8	51.9	1.3
Union	69.8	2 286	40.3	35.9	2.0	0.0	1.3	36.5	1 194	95	162	2 304	44.0	54.5	1.5
Williamsburg	64.6	1 731	58.2	17.6	2.8	0.7	2.0	21.3	571	91	197	2 192	59.3	39.9	0.7
York	253.6	1 685	59.4	0.6	5.0	0.3	1.4	439.0	2 917	355	847	9 191	35.4	62.1	2.4
SOUTH DAKOTA	X	X	X	X	X	X	X	X	X	10 675	8 368	50 350	37.6	60.3	2.1
Aurora	5.5	1 834	59.1	0.4	3.4	0.9	19.0	0.0	0	26	22	343	36.3	59.9	3.8
Beadle	36.9	2 054	48.7	0.2	3.9	0.7	8.8	21.1	1 175	377	120	975	41.6	56.2	2.3
Bennett	9.0	2 741	39.3	32.8	4.2	0.6	5.8	0.7	204	31	24	357	33.8	63.8	2.4
Bon Homme	14.1	1 836	51.8	0.9	2.0	0.0	12.4	13.5	1 760	37	52	566	37.0	60.6	2.4
Brookings	63.9	2 442	35.5	19.7	3.1	3.0	7.0	19.7	751	144	198	4 803	41.4	56.6	2.1
Brown	64.6	1 811	44.3	0.6	4.8	1.8	14.5	11.3	318	539	255	2 463	43.3	54.7	2.0
Brule	10.7	1 924	64.0	1.7	4.0	0.5	8.4	3.5	626	42	40	355	37.7	58.5	3.7
Buffalo	0.4	202	0.0	0.0	9.8	0.6	56.0	0.0	0	127	13	0	62.7	34.3	2.9
Butte	17.5	1 960	49.5	0.7	3.0	0.1	7.5	5.2	580	48	63	514	22.8	74.8	2.4
Campbell	3.3	1 676	53.8	0.1	1.5	0.5	18.2	0.3	153	12	13	111	16.0	80.6	3.4
Charles Mix	15.9	1 671	56.8	0.4	3.5	0.6	17.0	7.8	825	187	66	524	36.3	61.6	2.1
Clark	7.1	1 636	57.0	1.4	1.9	0.7	17.9	0.6	145	31	31	238	37.5	60.3	2.1
Clay	19.8	1 287	44.0	0.6	7.2	0.5	18.1	9.7	631	56	99	2 841	51.7	46.3	2.0
Codington	52.9	2 080	41.7	0.2	4.1	0.5	8.0	27.3	1 072	174	183	1 486	37.6	60.3	2.0
Corson	6.9	1 606	75.8	0.0	3.7	0.0	9.9	0.0	0	104	30	262	44.2	50.6	5.2
Custer	12.4	1 786	51.2	5.0	7.6	0.5	13.6	6.5	929	189	51	546	26.7	69.8	3.4
Davison	34.6	1 840	48.0	0.8	4.6	0.6	7.5	15.5	824	116	129	1 104	39.0	59.0	2.0
Day	12.9	2 002	55.2	1.5	2.2	0.1	20.3	2.7	422	68	44	381	46.7	50.8	2.6
Deuel	6.3	1 375	47.7	3.7	4.1	1.9	23.7	0.4	95	37	32	242	41.6	56.0	2.4
Dewey	7.4	1 307	75.7	1.1	2.6	0.1	9.0	0.1	21	318	43	256	52.3	45.3	2.4
Douglas	4.9	1 383	52.2	2.5	4.6	1.0	19.4	0.3	89	31	25	169	21.2	76.7	2.0
Edmunds	11.2	2 637	34.4	18.3	3.0	15.1	16.3	0.5	114	27	30	367	34.0	63.3	2.7
Fall River	14.0	1 962	50.4	0.8	3.8	0.3	14.9	1.6	224	523	49	516	33.0	63.7	3.2
Faulk	4.4	1 752	57.5	0.9	1.8	0.9	23.5	0.0	14	22	18	161	29.2	68.0	2.8
Grant	17.2	2 143	46.8	0.8	3.0	0.5	11.1	33.3	4 134	45	57	381	38.5	58.4	3.1
Gregory	10.4	2 059	53.2	0.3	3.3	0.5	13.9	0.5	107	41	35	299	31.8	65.9	2.3
Haakon	7.5	3 025	39.9	0.0	1.8	1.0	13.3	1.0	411	17	17	143	14.5	83.1	2.4
Hamlin	17.4	3 282	67.1	2.2	0.9	10.0	10.7	9.8	1 850	35	39	465	33.9	63.6	2.5
Hand	7.6	1 825	49.5	1.0	3.5	0.3	23.7	2.6	620	26	30	219	27.8	69.9	2.3
Hanson	4.4	1 508	62.5	1.1	2.3	0.5	19.6	0.6	193	11	22	139	32.2	66.4	1.4
Harding	3.5	2 318	53.6	0.3	5.0	0.6	22.2	0.1	69	24	10	114	8.8	88.9	2.3
Hughes	29.5	1 912	54.1	0.5	6.1	0.3	5.9	10.5	684	269	112	3 361	29.4	68.9	1.8
Hutchinson	15.1	1 861	58.7	1.7	2.5	0.7	21.2	3.8	475	48	58	468	29.0	68.9	2.1
Hyde	3.2	1 951	51.5	0.3	3.9	0.2	20.7	0.0	1	0	11	102	26.1	70.9	3.0
Jackson	3.5	1 197	66.2	0.0	2.7	0.8	10.6	0.1	34	90	21	134	30.7	66.1	3.3
Jerauld	5.1	2 256	56.5	0.9	1.8	0.9	13.0	0.4	185	23	15	171	41.7	55.6	2.7
Jones	2.6	2 009	50.4	0.9	4.3	0.0	19.9	0.3	217	12	0	106	20.6	76.7	2.7
Kingsbury	11.1	1 896	60.9	1.3	2.4	0.3	14.6	4.5	764	47	41	266	38.5	59.1	2.4
Lake	19.5	1 830	55.8	0.4	4.0	0.7	12.5	68.5	6 430	62	77	968	45.2	52.9	1.9
Lawrence	51.7	2 334	34.4	0.5	5.9	0.1	8.4	46.0	2 077	209	154	1 627	29.7	67.3	3.0
Lincoln	27.9	1 385	54.5	2.0	2.8	0.0	20.8	17.1	848	53	156	739	36.4	62.0	1.6
Lyman	5.6	1 414	44.7	1.1	5.5	0.2	18.0	0.7	166	70	27	178	34.8	63.1	2.1
McCook	10.8	1 907	51.5	1.3	2.4	0.9	20.5	1.6	275	36	40	283	36.7	61.2	2.1
McPherson	5.7	2 049	50.4	0.9	2.9	0.8	27.3	0.8	274	23	19	158	20.8	75.7	3.5
Marshall	8.1	1 759	55.9	2.0	5.1	0.7	19.8	0.7	143	31	33	322	45.2	52.8	2.1
Meade	27.2	1 237	54.7	0.8	4.0	0.6	9.6	10.2	463	1 212	154	856	24.2	73.4	2.4
Mellette	4.8	2 417	59.1	0.7	3.0	0.2	5.1	0.2	99	16	15	156	30.3	67.5	2.2
Miner	6.0	2 051	45.8	0.8	4.6	0.4	24.2	1.4	467	24	19	170	41.3	57.2	1.5
Minnehaha	259.7	1 848	46.6	1.1	5.3	1.3	9.3	277.8	1 977	2 085	1 073	6 459	44.1	54.5	1.5
Moody	12.6	1 928	46.9	18.2	4.7	0.4	16.6	0.7	110	145	46	292	48.2	49.8	2.0
Pennington	193.4	2 218	44.5	0.9	5.1	0.5	4.9	108.9	1 249	1 296	3 660	5 309	30.4	67.6	2.0
Perkins	8.7	2 457	54.4	0.7	2.5	0.0	17.1	2.1	584	35	25	286	18.4	76.6	5.0
Potter	8.3	2 835	40.0	0.2	3.0	0.5	20.0	1.2	412	31	20	177	23.8	74.4	1.7
Roberts	16.8	1 684	64.3	3.9	2.9	1.0	12.5	1.6	164	142	71	531	41.7	54.9	3.4
Sanborn	4.2	1 504	70.1	0.7	1.5	0.1	13.3	0.3	95	18	19	164	36.9	60.5	2.6
Shannon	9.0	752	95.7	0.1	0.2	0.0	1.8	0.0	0	511	90	367	85.4	12.9	1.7
Spink	18.3	2 376	46.2	21.1	3.7	0.5	11.3	1.8	236	54	54	976	38.8	59.6	1.6
Stanley	5.6	1 922	49.1	0.9	5.4	0.1	19.9	1.6	543	0	21	154	29.1	69.2	1.7
Sully	3.5	2 282	79.1	0.0	1.7	0.5	8.1	0.0	0	11	11	120	24.0	72.7	3.3
Todd	15.2	1 630	91.5	0.0	0.6	0.1	4.3	0.4	48	269	68	607	66.5	32.0	1.5

1. Based on the resident population estimated as of July 1 of the year shown.   2. Data subject to copyright.

Table B. States and Counties — Land Area and Population

STATE/ County code	MSA/ PMSA/ NECMA code[1]	County Type[2]	STATE County	Land area,[3] (sq km) 2000	Total persons	Rank	Per square kilometer	White	Black	Am. Indian, Alaska Native	Asian and Pacific Islander	Percent Hispanic[4]	Under 5 years	5 to 17 years	18 to 24 years	25 to 34 years	35 to 44 years	45 to 54 years
				1	2	3	4	5	6	7	8	9	10	11	12	13	14	15
			SOUTH DAKOTA—Cont'd															
46 123	...	7	Tripp	4 179	6 430	2 745	1.5	88.6	0.2	12.2	0.1	0.9	6.3	21.4	6.2	9.4	15.0	12.5
46 125	...	8	Turner	1 598	8 849	2 540	5.5	99.3	0.3	0.5	0.3	0.4	5.7	20.1	6.2	9.9	14.9	13.6
46 127	...	8	Union	1 192	12 584	2 257	10.6	97.7	0.5	0.7	1.6	1.3	6.9	20.1	7.3	12.7	15.7	15.0
46 129	...	7	Walworth	1 833	5 974	2 784	3.3	87.9	0.2	13.0	0.2	0.6	6.3	17.8	6.5	9.0	13.4	13.5
46 135	...	7	Yankton	1 351	21 652	1 710	16.0	95.9	1.5	2.2	0.6	1.8	6.3	19.4	8.7	12.5	16.6	13.6
46 137	...	9	Ziebach	5 082	2 519	3 025	0.5	27.4	0.0	73.2	0.1	1.0	10.8	29.9	10.8	11.1	13.6	9.5
47 000	...	X	**TENNESSEE**	106 752	5 689 283	X	53.3	81.2	16.8	0.7	1.3	2.2	6.6	18.0	9.6	14.3	15.4	13.8
47 001	3840	2	Anderson	874	71 330	694	81.6	94.5	4.3	0.9	1.0	1.1	5.6	17.6	7.5	12.1	15.2	14.9
47 003	...	6	Bedford	1 227	37 586	1 174	30.6	87.9	8.9	0.7	0.7	7.5	7.4	18.4	9.9	14.5	15.2	12.7
47 005	...	7	Benton	1 023	16 537	1 987	16.2	97.1	2.2	0.7	0.4	0.9	5.2	16.8	7.0	11.6	14.6	14.4
47 007	...	8	Bledsoe	1 052	12 367	2 276	11.8	95.5	3.9	1.1	0.3	1.1	5.9	17.2	8.4	14.3	17.0	15.0
47 009	3840	2	Blount	1 447	105 823	502	73.1	95.7	3.1	0.8	0.9	1.1	5.8	17.0	8.3	13.4	15.9	14.8
47 011	...	4	Bradley	851	87 965	594	103.4	94.1	4.3	0.9	0.8	2.1	6.6	17.1	11.3	14.2	15.0	13.5
47 013	...	6	Campbell	1 243	39 854	1 116	32.1	99.0	0.4	1.0	0.3	0.7	5.9	17.0	8.5	13.7	14.3	13.9
47 015	...	8	Cannon	688	12 826	2 245	18.6	97.6	1.6	0.9	0.2	1.2	6.7	18.7	8.3	13.4	15.5	13.1
47 017	...	6	Carroll	1 551	29 475	1 414	19.0	88.7	10.8	0.7	0.4	1.3	5.9	17.3	8.4	12.5	14.2	13.4
47 019	3660	2	Carter	883	56 742	835	64.3	98.2	1.2	0.6	0.4	0.9	5.6	15.8	9.2	14.1	15.0	14.2
47 021	5360	2	Cheatham	784	35 912	1 221	45.8	97.5	1.6	0.8	0.4	1.2	7.1	20.5	7.3	14.5	19.0	14.4
47 023	3580	6	Chester	747	15 540	2 051	20.8	89.1	10.2	0.7	0.5	1.0	6.7	17.5	14.4	12.4	14.0	12.5
47 025	...	6	Claiborne	1 125	29 862	1 400	26.5	98.5	0.8	0.6	0.5	0.6	5.7	17.9	8.9	13.7	15.0	14.6
47 027	...	9	Clay	612	7 976	2 608	13.0	97.5	1.7	0.9	0.3	1.4	5.1	16.4	7.9	12.5	14.9	14.6
47 029	...	7	Cocke	1 125	33 565	1 298	29.8	97.1	2.2	1.0	0.3	1.1	5.9	16.9	8.3	13.4	15.4	15.0
47 031	...	5	Coffee	1 111	48 014	953	43.2	94.4	4.0	0.7	1.0	2.2	6.6	18.5	8.3	12.8	15.6	13.1
47 033	...	8	Crockett	687	14 532	2 119	21.2	82.6	14.5	0.5	0.1	5.5	6.4	18.7	8.1	13.0	15.3	12.4
47 035	...	7	Cumberland	1 765	46 802	965	26.5	98.9	0.2	0.8	0.4	1.2	5.5	15.9	6.7	11.5	13.6	12.7
47 037	5360	2	Davidson	1 301	569 891	95	438.0	68.5	26.6	0.7	2.9	4.6	6.6	15.6	11.6	17.6	16.4	13.2
47 039	...	9	Decatur	865	11 731	2 315	13.6	94.8	3.7	0.7	0.4	2.0	5.6	16.1	7.9	12.1	13.8	13.9
47 041	...	6	De Kalb	789	17 423	1 927	22.1	96.5	1.6	0.8	0.3	3.6	6.1	17.2	8.5	13.8	15.6	13.9
47 043	5360	2	Dickson	1 269	43 156	1 034	34.0	94.2	4.9	0.9	0.4	1.1	6.9	19.7	8.1	14.2	16.5	13.4
47 045	...	7	Dyer	1 322	37 279	1 183	28.2	86.0	13.2	0.5	0.4	1.2	6.6	19.1	8.7	13.3	15.4	13.9
47 047	4920	1	Fayette	1 825	28 806	1 431	15.8	63.2	36.1	0.7	0.3	1.0	6.7	19.0	8.2	11.3	16.1	14.9
47 049	...	9	Fentress	1 291	16 625	1 982	12.9	99.6	0.1	0.4	0.1	0.5	6.2	18.0	8.0	13.4	14.7	14.4
47 051	...	7	Franklin	1 436	39 270	1 131	27.3	93.2	5.8	0.7	0.6	1.6	6.0	17.1	10.9	11.6	14.9	13.8
47 053	...	4	Gibson	1 561	48 152	945	30.8	79.4	19.9	0.6	0.2	1.1	6.2	17.7	8.1	12.2	14.7	13.3
47 055	...	6	Giles	1 582	29 447	1 416	18.6	87.3	12.1	0.7	0.5	0.9	6.2	18.4	8.3	12.4	15.3	13.9
47 057	...	8	Grainger	726	20 659	1 754	28.5	99.0	0.4	0.6	0.1	1.1	6.1	16.8	8.2	14.8	15.7	14.5
47 059	...	6	Greene	1 610	62 909	772	39.1	97.0	2.2	0.5	0.3	1.0	5.8	16.5	8.1	13.6	15.1	14.5
47 061	...	6	Grundy	934	14 332	2 138	15.3	99.0	0.2	0.9	0.2	1.0	6.8	18.3	9.0	13.5	14.3	13.0
47 063	...	5	Hamblen	417	58 128	822	139.4	91.6	4.5	0.6	0.8	5.7	6.6	16.7	8.9	14.5	15.1	13.8
47 065	1560	2	Hamilton	1 405	307 896	185	219.1	77.3	20.6	0.7	1.6	1.8	6.0	17.2	9.6	13.6	15.5	14.8
47 067	...	9	Hancock	576	6 786	2 713	11.8	98.8	0.6	0.9	0.1	0.4	5.3	17.8	8.8	12.2	14.8	14.5
47 069	...	6	Hardeman	1 729	28 105	1 448	16.3	57.9	41.3	0.7	0.5	1.0	5.9	18.0	9.8	14.6	16.7	13.6
47 071	...	6	Hardin	1 497	25 578	1 536	17.1	95.5	3.9	0.6	0.2	1.0	5.9	17.2	7.9	12.4	14.2	14.5
47 073	3660	2	Hawkins	1 260	53 563	873	42.5	97.8	1.7	0.5	0.3	0.8	6.2	17.1	7.5	14.7	15.3	14.5
47 075	...	6	Haywood	1 381	19 797	1 802	14.3	47.2	51.3	0.3	0.3	2.6	7.2	20.0	9.8	12.7	14.6	13.6
47 077	...	6	Henderson	1 347	25 522	1 539	18.9	91.4	8.4	0.6	0.2	1.0	6.5	17.9	8.7	13.3	15.5	13.9
47 079	...	7	Henry	1 455	31 115	1 374	21.4	90.1	9.3	0.6	0.4	1.0	5.7	16.5	7.6	11.6	14.6	13.9
47 081	...	6	Hickman	1 586	22 295	1 680	14.1	94.6	4.7	1.1	0.2	1.0	6.5	18.1	8.5	14.6	16.5	13.8
47 083	...	8	Houston	519	8 088	2 598	15.6	95.5	3.6	0.7	0.3	1.2	6.7	17.7	7.3	12.4	13.6	13.8
47 085	...	6	Humphreys	1 378	17 929	1 904	13.0	96.3	3.1	0.7	0.5	0.8	6.0	17.9	7.6	12.5	15.0	14.4
47 087	...	9	Jackson	800	10 984	2 368	13.7	99.3	0.2	0.8	0.2	0.8	5.7	16.5	7.8	12.9	15.2	15.0
47 089	...	6	Jefferson	709	44 294	1 011	62.5	96.4	2.6	0.7	0.4	1.3	6.1	16.7	10.6	13.9	15.2	14.3
47 091	...	8	Johnson	773	17 499	1 923	22.6	96.8	2.4	0.6	0.3	0.9	4.9	14.8	7.4	14.6	16.2	14.7
47 093	3840	2	Knox	1 317	382 032	151	290.1	89.2	9.0	0.7	1.6	1.3	6.1	16.2	11.6	14.4	15.9	14.1
47 095	...	9	Lake	423	7 954	2 610	18.8	67.3	31.6	0.9	0.5	1.4	5.0	12.7	13.7	17.2	16.6	12.5
47 097	...	6	Lauderdale	1 218	27 101	1 478	22.3	64.4	34.5	0.4	0.2	1.2	6.8	18.0	10.3	15.1	16.0	12.8
47 099	...	6	Lawrence	1 598	39 926	1 114	25.0	97.5	1.7	0.7	0.4	1.0	6.7	19.5	8.4	13.5	14.5	12.8
47 101	...	7	Lewis	731	11 367	2 345	15.5	97.8	1.6	0.6	0.3	1.2	6.5	19.3	8.3	12.2	15.2	14.3
47 103	...	6	Lincoln	1 477	31 340	1 364	21.2	91.4	7.8	1.2	0.5	1.0	6.1	17.8	8.0	12.1	15.6	14.0
47 105	3840	2	Loudon	593	39 086	1 134	65.9	96.8	1.3	0.9	0.4	2.3	5.8	16.1	6.7	12.6	14.9	14.6
47 107	...	7	McMinn	1 114	49 015	932	44.0	93.7	4.8	0.8	0.9	1.8	6.3	17.6	8.4	13.3	15.3	13.9
47 109	...	7	McNairy	1 451	24 653	1 569	17.0	93.1	6.5	0.7	0.3	0.9	6.2	17.5	8.1	12.3	14.4	13.9
47 111	...	6	Macon	795	20 386	1 769	25.6	98.3	0.3	0.7	0.4	1.7	7.1	19.0	8.5	14.6	14.8	13.4
47 113	3580	3	Madison	1 443	91 837	557	63.6	65.9	32.8	0.5	0.8	1.7	6.9	18.9	11.0	13.5	15.6	13.5
47 115	1560	2	Marion	1 291	27 776	1 456	21.5	95.1	4.3	0.7	0.3	0.7	5.9	17.8	8.5	13.0	15.6	15.1

1. MSA = Metropolitan Statistical Area. PMSA = Primary MSA. NECMA = New England County Metropolitan Area. See Appendix A for explanation of these concepts. See Appendix B for list of metropolitan areas identified by type, with component counties. 2. County typology code from the Economic Research Service of USDA. See Appendix A for definition. 3. Dry land or land partially or temporarily covered by water. 4. Hispanic persons may be of any race.

STATE County	55 to 64 years	65 to 74 years	75 years and over	Percent female	2001	1990	1990–2000	2000–2001	Births	Deaths	Net migration	Number	Percent change, 1990–2000	Persons per house-hold	Female family house-holder[1]	One person
	16	17	18	19	20	21	22	23	24	25	26	27	28	29	30	31
SOUTH DAKOTA—Cont'd																
Tripp	9.4	9.2	10.5	50.7	6 278	6 924	-7.1	-2.4	98	84	-169	2 550	-0.9	2.48	6.6	29.6
Turner	9.2	9.1	11.4	50.7	8 737	8 576	3.2	-1.3	100	163	-47	3 510	5.3	2.46	5.6	26.5
Union	8.7	6.8	6.7	50.2	12 713	10 189	23.5	1.0	204	125	55	4 927	27.7	2.53	6.3	24.2
Walworth	11.5	11.0	10.9	51.5	5 806	6 087	-1.9	-2.8	104	114	-161	2 506	2.4	2.31	8.9	31.4
Yankton	8.4	7.0	7.6	49.5	21 586	19 252	12.5	-0.3	345	243	-163	8 187	15.2	2.43	8.3	29.3
Ziebach	6.9	4.7	2.7	50.8	2 517	2 220	13.5	-0.1	47	20	-32	741	17.6	3.40	23.8	17.4
TENNESSEE	9.4	6.7	5.6	51.3	5 740 021	4 877 203	16.7	0.9	99 246	68 953	20 833	2 232 905	20.5	2.48	12.9	25.8
Anderson	10.6	8.4	8.2	52.3	71 457	68 250	4.5	0.2	982	966	140	29 780	8.7	2.37	11.5	27.7
Bedford	9.3	6.8	5.9	50.4	38 327	30 411	23.6	2.0	697	448	501	13 905	19.8	2.67	11.9	21.5
Benton	12.7	9.7	8.0	51.6	16 616	14 524	13.9	0.5	210	277	148	6 863	18.7	2.37	9.5	25.7
Bledsoe	10.7	6.8	4.6	45.2	12 516	9 669	27.9	1.2	157	157	150	4 430	35.8	2.53	9.1	22.1
Blount	10.6	7.4	6.7	51.6	108 270	85 962	23.1	2.3	1 539	1 242	2 136	42 667	26.9	2.43	10.0	24.4
Bradley	10.1	6.8	5.0	51.2	88 850	73 712	19.3	1.0	1 455	1 014	477	34 281	24.2	2.50	10.9	23.4
Campbell	11.6	8.5	6.6	51.8	40 048	35 079	13.6	0.5	618	606	196	16 125	22.6	2.44	12.6	25.4
Cannon	10.6	7.7	6.0	51.0	12 946	10 467	22.5	0.9	180	178	118	4 998	25.6	2.53	9.9	24.3
Carroll	10.9	8.8	8.5	52.0	29 538	27 514	7.1	0.2	467	531	140	11 779	9.8	2.42	11.5	26.8
Carter	11.2	8.0	7.0	51.4	56 927	51 505	10.2	0.3	751	812	266	23 486	16.3	2.35	11.0	26.5
Cheatham	8.6	5.1	3.5	49.9	36 552	27 140	32.3	1.8	650	310	307	12 878	35.3	2.76	9.6	16.9
Chester	8.9	7.2	6.4	51.4	15 711	12 819	21.2	1.1	224	201	151	5 660	24.2	2.55	11.5	22.6
Claiborne	10.8	7.5	6.0	51.7	30 146	26 137	14.3	1.0	433	383	243	11 799	22.5	2.48	11.0	23.4
Clay	12.9	8.6	7.0	51.4	7 918	7 238	10.2	-0.7	101	116	-42	3 379	18.4	2.33	9.7	27.6
Cocke	11.4	8.1	5.5	51.4	33 884	29 141	15.2	1.0	501	445	272	13 762	23.0	2.41	13.0	25.7
Coffee	10.4	8.2	6.4	51.3	48 667	40 343	19.0	1.4	788	621	498	18 885	21.8	2.50	11.1	24.3
Crockett	10.3	7.4	8.4	51.7	14 547	13 378	8.6	0.1	224	214	8	5 632	8.7	2.53	11.8	25.3
Cumberland	13.5	12.7	7.9	51.4	48 058	34 736	34.7	2.7	626	595	1 210	19 508	45.3	2.37	9.6	22.4
Davidson	7.9	5.9	5.3	51.6	565 352	510 786	11.6	-0.8	11 078	6 509	-9 182	237 405	14.4	2.30	14.3	33.4
Decatur	12.5	9.6	8.6	51.4	11 697	10 472	12.0	-0.3	172	216	10	4 908	16.4	2.34	9.0	27.6
De Kalb	10.7	7.8	6.5	50.6	17 552	14 360	21.3	0.7	271	270	133	6 984	22.6	2.45	11.1	25.5
Dickson	9.5	6.5	5.2	51.0	43 843	35 061	23.1	1.6	741	496	446	16 473	26.5	2.59	11.5	22.3
Dyer	9.6	6.9	6.5	52.1	37 121	34 854	7.0	-0.4	625	583	-191	14 751	8.3	2.49	13.6	25.3
Fayette	10.7	7.3	5.7	50.9	30 536	25 559	12.7	6.0	559	342	1 471	10 467	23.8	2.71	14.0	20.5
Fentress	11.7	7.6	6.0	51.0	16 805	14 669	13.3	1.1	293	259	149	6 693	21.4	2.46	11.3	25.5
Franklin	10.6	8.6	6.6	51.3	39 770	34 923	12.4	1.3	616	554	447	15 003	18.5	2.51	10.4	22.6
Gibson	10.0	8.8	8.9	52.8	48 031	46 315	4.0	-0.3	788	903	21	19 518	6.3	2.41	13.6	27.4
Giles	11.0	7.3	7.1	51.4	29 675	25 741	14.4	0.8	506	466	198	11 713	19.1	2.47	11.9	25.7
Grainger	11.4	7.6	4.9	50.2	20 934	17 095	20.8	1.3	296	269	249	8 270	29.3	2.48	8.8	22.5
Greene	11.6	8.5	6.3	51.3	63 388	55 832	12.7	0.8	937	851	409	25 756	19.9	2.38	10.8	25.8
Grundy	11.1	7.3	6.7	50.9	14 288	13 362	7.3	-0.3	250	211	-77	5 562	16.3	2.54	12.0	24.0
Hamblen	11.1	7.7	5.6	50.7	58 337	50 480	15.2	0.4	963	734	6	23 211	19.5	2.47	11.3	24.7
Hamilton	9.6	7.4	6.5	52.2	307 377	285 536	7.8	-0.2	4 921	4 087	-1 239	124 444	11.3	2.41	13.5	27.9
Hancock	11.0	8.6	7.1	51.3	6 768	6 739	0.7	-0.3	75	105	11	2 769	11.5	2.39	11.0	27.7
Hardeman	8.7	6.8	5.8	46.1	28 361	23 377	20.2	0.9	438	389	214	9 412	13.7	2.56	17.6	25.1
Hardin	11.9	9.0	7.1	50.8	25 791	22 633	13.0	0.8	341	400	277	10 426	19.5	2.41	10.1	25.5
Hawkins	11.4	7.4	5.8	51.4	54 370	44 565	20.2	1.5	840	646	619	21 936	27.8	2.42	9.8	24.4
Haywood	8.3	7.2	6.6	53.3	19 761	19 437	1.9	-0.2	390	319	-99	7 558	7.8	2.59	22.0	25.4
Henderson	10.0	7.9	6.3	51.8	25 732	21 844	16.8	0.8	431	419	202	10 306	20.9	2.44	11.7	24.9
Henry	11.8	9.8	8.4	51.7	31 083	27 888	11.6	-0.1	483	560	58	13 019	14.6	2.35	11.2	27.0
Hickman	10.1	6.6	5.4	47.1	22 740	16 754	33.1	2.0	342	271	369	8 081	35.2	2.59	9.6	22.6
Houston	11.8	9.0	7.7	50.6	7 916	7 018	15.2	-2.1	131	116	-191	3 216	19.9	2.46	10.4	25.3
Humphreys	11.8	8.5	6.3	50.8	18 114	15 813	13.4	1.0	269	258	177	7 238	19.4	2.44	10.2	25.0
Jackson	11.8	8.3	6.6	50.6	11 162	9 297	18.1	1.6	121	195	250	4 466	22.6	2.43	10.3	25.5
Jefferson	11.2	7.5	5.4	50.6	45 070	33 016	34.2	1.8	614	521	684	17 155	39.1	2.49	9.8	22.5
Johnson	12.4	8.1	6.9	46.6	17 638	13 766	27.1	0.8	233	231	138	6 827	26.3	2.35	10.0	26.4
Knox	9.0	6.8	5.9	51.7	385 572	335 749	13.8	0.9	6 014	4 484	2 149	157 872	18.1	2.34	10.0	29.6
Lake	9.0	6.7	6.6	39.8	7 764	7 129	11.6	-2.4	101	150	-141	2 410	-0.3	2.36	16.3	30.0
Lauderdale	9.0	6.0	6.0	48.1	27 021	23 491	15.4	-0.3	546	412	-207	9 567	13.6	2.55	17.6	25.6
Lawrence	10.2	7.7	6.6	51.5	40 003	35 303	13.1	0.2	662	556	-9	15 480	16.1	2.56	10.6	23.7
Lewis	10.5	7.5	6.1	50.8	11 437	9 247	22.9	0.6	172	156	57	4 381	24.0	2.54	10.7	23.5
Lincoln	10.9	8.4	7.2	51.6	31 616	28 157	11.3	0.9	452	459	292	12 503	14.9	2.47	10.9	24.6
Loudon	13.1	9.5	6.7	51.3	40 240	31 255	25.1	3.0	598	534	1 074	15 944	31.2	2.42	8.9	22.8
McMinn	10.9	7.8	6.5	51.7	49 857	42 383	15.6	1.7	718	657	781	19 721	20.6	2.45	10.6	24.4
McNairy	11.6	8.8	7.2	51.5	24 644	22 422	10.0	0.0	382	383	3	9 980	13.0	2.42	9.9	25.9
Macon	10.0	6.8	5.9	50.6	20 873	15 906	28.2	2.4	350	276	412	7 916	28.5	2.55	8.8	23.8
Madison	8.3	6.3	6.0	52.1	92 389	77 982	17.8	0.6	1 728	1 172	36	35 552	20.1	2.49	15.9	26.2
Marion	11.2	7.6	5.3	51.1	27 750	24 683	12.5	-0.1	407	415	-6	11 037	19.8	2.49	11.6	23.6

1. No spouse present.

Table B. States and Counties — Vital Statistics, Health Resources, and Crime

STATE County	Births, average 1997–1999		Deaths, average 1997–1999				Physicians,[4] 2000		Hospitals,[4] 1998			Medicare enrollees 2000	Serious crimes known to police, 2000[6]	
			Number		Rate					Beds			Total	
	Total	Rate[1]	Total	Infant[2]	Total[1]	Infant[3]	Number	Rate[5]	Number	Number	Rate[5]		Number	Rate[7]
	32	33	34	35	36	37	38	39	40	41	42	43	44	45

SOUTH DAKOTA—Cont'd

STATE County	Total	Rate[1]	Total	Infant[2]	Total[1]	Infant[3]	Number	Rate[5]	Number	Number	Rate[5]	Medicare	Number	Rate[7]
Tripp	88	13.0	65	NA	9.6	NA	6	93	1	116	1 722	1 314	NA	NA
Turner	86	10.0	113	NA	13.1	NA	5	57	1	77	892	1 844	NA	NA
Union	153	12.6	104	NA	8.5	NA	12	95	0	0	0	2 073	NA	NA
Walworth	73	12.9	91	NA	16.2	NA	5	84	1	35	627	907	249	4 754
Yankton	265	12.6	191	NA	9.0	NA	78	360	1	271	1 287	3 472	492	2 272
Ziebach	42	19.4	9	NA	4.3	NA	0	0	0	0	0	150	17	675
TENNESSEE	75 695	13.9	53 282	624	9.8	8.2	11 281	198	135	21 953	404	829 246	278 218	4 890
Anderson	818	11.5	767	NA	10.8	NA	182	255	1	305	429	13 314	2 804	3 931
Bedford	518	15.0	374	NA	10.8	NA	24	64	1	182	527	5 523	1 082	2 879
Benton	171	10.5	210	NA	12.8	NA	13	79	1	47	288	3 431	284	1 717
Bledsoe	127	11.8	118	NA	10.9	NA	2	16	1	26	241	1 436	154	1 245
Blount	1 227	12.1	1 025	NA	10.1	NA	145	137	1	203	200	16 665	3 332	3 175
Bradley	1 107	13.4	766	NA	9.2	NA	126	143	2	266	319	12 192	3 279	3 728
Campbell	460	12.1	445	NA	11.6	NA	25	63	2	200	523	8 081	1 163	2 918
Cannon	152	12.5	134	NA	11.1	NA	7	55	1	55	453	1 992	213	1 661
Carroll	357	12.2	395	NA	13.5	NA	23	78	2	92	316	6 398	624	2 117
Carter	568	10.7	604	NA	11.3	NA	46	81	1	100	188	8 684	1 953	3 442
Cheatham	516	14.6	244	NA	6.9	NA	9	25	1	19	54	3 456	781	2 175
Chester	188	12.8	149	NA	10.2	NA	3	19	0	0	0	2 090	338	2 175
Claiborne	353	12.0	307	NA	10.4	NA	18	60	1	110	373	5 876	658	2 203
Clay	75	10.3	100	NA	13.7	NA	5	63	1	28	386	1 182	128	1 605
Cocke	396	12.4	367	NA	11.5	NA	20	60	1	109	341	5 980	1 537	4 579
Coffee	643	14.0	483	NA	10.5	NA	81	169	3	286	625	8 407	1 689	3 518
Crockett	177	12.7	181	NA	13.0	NA	5	34	0	0	0	2 719	240	1 652
Cumberland	508	11.5	476	NA	10.8	NA	65	139	1	160	361	10 408	1 481	3 164
Davidson	8 276	15.5	5 013	73	9.4	8.8	2 499	439	10	3 405	638	72 848	51 502	9 037
Decatur	128	11.9	167	NA	15.4	NA	7	60	1	40	370	2 132	195	1 662
De Kalb	205	12.8	203	NA	12.7	NA	13	75	1	58	364	3 027	588	3 375
Dickson	608	14.5	390	NA	9.3	NA	35	81	1	114	270	6 081	1 384	3 207
Dyer	507	13.8	437	NA	11.9	NA	56	150	1	125	340	6 159	1 457	3 908
Fayette	388	12.8	275	NA	9.0	NA	12	42	1	38	125	3 291	837	2 906
Fentress	203	12.5	199	NA	12.3	NA	9	54	1	71	439	3 257	388	2 334
Franklin	448	12.0	398	NA	10.6	NA	56	143	2	72	192	6 510	1 260	3 209
Gibson	546	11.4	695	NA	14.5	NA	29	60	3	218	452	9 840	1 601	3 325
Giles	375	13.0	336	NA	11.7	NA	20	68	1	109	377	4 947	777	2 639
Grainger	246	12.4	201	NA	10.1	NA	5	24	0	0	0	3 558	491	2 377
Greene	725	12.0	681	NA	11.3	NA	77	122	2	285	471	11 787	2 167	3 445
Grundy	192	13.7	162	NA	11.5	NA	4	28	0	0	0	2 647	367	2 561
Hamblen	733	13.6	565	NA	10.5	NA	78	134	2	302	559	9 037	2 413	4 151
Hamilton	3 850	13.1	3 102	28	10.5	7.4	927	301	8	1 589	539	49 410	23 177	7 528
Hancock	70	10.3	79	NA	11.6	NA	4	59	0	0	0	1 150	127	1 872
Hardeman	339	13.7	291	NA	11.8	NA	22	78	1	48	193	4 494	912	3 245
Hardin	300	12.0	299	NA	11.9	NA	17	66	1	121	485	4 580	600	2 346
Hawkins	592	11.9	512	NA	10.3	NA	30	56	1	50	101	8 365	1 111	2 074
Haywood	282	14.4	223	NA	11.4	NA	11	56	1	54	277	2 883	1 151	5 814
Henderson	331	13.5	283	NA	11.6	NA	11	43	1	25	102	4 589	834	3 268
Henry	346	11.5	428	NA	14.2	NA	32	103	1	101	336	6 545	1 119	3 596
Hickman	269	13.1	216	NA	10.5	NA	10	45	1	18	88	3 256	356	1 597
Houston	97	12.3	95	NA	12.1	NA	8	99	1	35	446	1 505	149	1 842
Humphreys	211	12.4	189	NA	11.1	NA	12	67	1	42	246	3 093	321	1 790
Jackson	115	12.0	141	NA	14.7	NA	6	55	1	32	332	1 610	146	1 329
Jefferson	477	10.9	411	NA	9.4	NA	29	65	1	67	153	8 159	1 743	3 935
Johnson	162	9.7	197	NA	11.8	NA	12	69	1	51	304	3 429	228	1 303
Knox	4 768	12.9	3 518	28	9.5	5.9	1 215	318	6	1 897	517	56 499	17 196	4 501
Lake	87	10.6	104	NA	12.7	NA	4	50	0	0	0	1 269	63	792
Lauderdale	370	15.3	311	NA	12.8	NA	10	37	1	70	289	4 275	1 199	4 424
Lawrence	564	14.3	435	NA	11.1	NA	23	58	1	83	211	7 418	1 422	3 562
Lewis	131	12.0	115	NA	10.5	NA	5	44	0	0	0	1 718	223	1 962
Lincoln	375	12.7	365	NA	12.3	NA	18	57	1	63	212	5 450	818	2 610
Loudon	447	11.4	414	NA	10.6	NA	38	97	1	30	77	7 954	1 370	3 505
McMinn	565	12.2	505	NA	10.9	NA	50	102	2	169	365	8 189	2 269	4 629
McNairy	291	12.1	295	NA	12.3	NA	10	41	1	48	200	5 264	737	3 085
Macon	257	14.1	197	NA	10.8	NA	12	59	1	43	237	2 876	348	1 707
Madison	1 225	14.3	874	11	10.2	9.0	288	314	2	710	826	13 202	5 765	6 277
Marion	352	13.1	301	NA	11.2	NA	26	94	2	92	343	4 224	881	3 172

1. Per 1,000 estimated resident population, average 1997–1999.   2. Deaths of infants under 1 year old.   3. Deaths of infants under 1 year old per 1,000 live births.   4. Data subject to copyright.   5. Per 100,000 resident population as of July 1 of the year shown.   6. Data for serious crimes have not been adjusted for underreporting; this may affect comparability between geographic areas and over time.   7. Per 100,000 population estimated by the FBI.

STATE County	Serious crimes known to police, 2000[1] (cont'd) Rate[2] Violent	Property	Education — School enrollment and attainment, 1990 Enrollment[3] Total	Percent private	Attainment[4] (percent) High school graduate or more	Bachelor's degree or more	Local government expenditures, fiscal 1999[5] Total current expenditures (mil dol)	Current expenditures per student (dollars)	Money income — 1989 Per capita[6] (dollars)	Households Median Dollars	Percent change, 1979–1989 (constant 1989 dollars)	Percent with $100,000 or more	Income and poverty, 1998 Median house-hold income	Percent below poverty level All persons	Persons under 18	Persons 5–17 in families
	46	47	48	49	50	51	52	53	54	55	56	57	58	59	60	61
SOUTH DAKOTA—Cont'd																
Tripp	NA	NA	1 627	2.8	71.5	9.6	6.1	4 691	10 340	20 082	8.2	1.7	28 942	18.8	23.8	21.3
Turner	NA	NA	1 926	4.5	72.8	12.5	7.9	5 057	9 355	19 926	4.6	0.7	34 270	10.4	14.7	11.2
Union	NA	NA	2 546	7.7	74.2	13.9	13.7	5 208	9 997	22 274	-3.6	0.9	43 757	8.0	10.9	8.9
Walworth	57	4 696	1 275	6.0	71.5	14.5	5.4	5 220	10 518	19 513	-3.1	2.3	28 554	17.8	26.3	21.6
Yankton	139	2 134	4 787	15.0	77.2	18.6	16.4	4 416	10 305	21 798	-9.3	1.4	34 811	10.7	15.0	12.1
Ziebach	278	397	765	0.7	62.5	8.5	2.0	7 712	6 132	14 129	-9.0	2.2	17 786	37.6	31.2	42.5
TENNESSEE	707	4 183	1 171 640	12.6	67.1	16.0	4 638.9	5 123	12 255	24 807	4.7	2.6	34 188	13.1	18.5	15.8
Anderson	357	3 574	15 418	5.9	72.4	18.6	77.3	6 111	13 182	26 496	-1.7	1.9	37 317	13.1	20.4	16.6
Bedford	415	2 464	6 666	3.8	57.6	10.5	25.7	4 288	11 311	23 613	2.4	2.1	33 573	12.1	17.3	14.6
Benton	151	1 566	2 888	6.3	56.3	7.4	12.3	4 800	10 046	20 382	0.9	1.2	27 385	16.6	23.9	22.3
Bledsoe	97	1 148	1 988	6.2	52.1	5.4	8.2	4 694	8 053	18 250	2.5	0.6	28 758	17.7	21.5	22.3
Blount	462	2 713	18 929	8.5	68.5	14.3	85.9	5 346	12 674	25 575	1.3	2.1	37 600	10.5	15.9	13.4
Bradley	444	3 283	17 848	15.9	64.4	11.9	66.0	4 939	11 768	25 678	4.6	1.8	35 902	11.8	16.5	14.0
Campbell	391	2 527	7 499	5.1	47.5	6.6	30.0	4 708	8 098	16 450	-4.5	0.9	24 337	20.2	25.9	25.5
Cannon	249	1 411	2 223	3.9	54.6	6.9	8.9	4 326	9 863	22 847	16.7	0.4	31 067	13.8	19.9	16.8
Carroll	214	1 903	5 985	7.6	55.3	7.3	24.3	4 682	10 121	20 763	5.3	1.2	30 810	14.0	22.3	16.8
Carter	280	3 162	10 892	10.0	57.5	10.8	42.8	5 423	9 809	19 140	-0.1	1.0	27 899	16.0	22.2	19.6
Cheatham	231	1 944	6 121	11.1	65.0	10.5	29.4	4 355	11 868	30 778	12.7	1.4	42 689	8.6	12.0	10.6
Chester	367	1 808	3 427	34.2	54.6	8.7	10.1	4 091	8 281	19 413	-1.0	0.3	31 367	14.4	19.6	16.8
Claiborne	208	1 996	6 178	13.4	50.8	8.0	24.0	5 067	8 371	17 132	9.2	0.8	25 293	20.3	25.5	24.5
Clay	313	1 291	1 562	3.6	48.5	7.8	6.2	5 017	8 753	17 799	19.6	0.5	22 774	20.2	26.7	25.2
Cocke	658	3 921	5 892	3.1	50.4	5.5	25.1	4 626	8 574	16 818	-3.0	1.1	24 876	20.3	28.4	25.6
Coffee	171	3 347	9 120	5.7	65.1	15.3	46.3	5 310	11 416	24 802	3.3	1.7	34 004	12.8	18.2	15.9
Crockett	282	1 369	2 633	2.9	57.2	6.4	12.2	4 651	10 636	20 296	5.8	1.6	29 405	15.4	22.1	18.5
Cumberland	175	2 989	7 127	5.4	59.8	10.2	28.8	4 301	9 782	20 474	5.5	0.9	28 756	14.7	22.3	19.5
Davidson	1 615	7 422	121 420	28.6	75.9	24.4	442.8	6 608	15 195	28 377	3.2	3.8	41 166	11.9	18.4	15.0
Decatur	188	1 475	2 006	4.3	52.9	4.8	8.3	4 467	9 345	17 925	-1.3	0.7	27 772	15.4	22.2	19.2
De Kalb	672	2 703	2 988	4.0	50.3	8.4	10.8	4 085	9 570	19 388	6.6	1.4	29 394	15.3	22.6	19.7
Dickson	366	2 841	7 792	5.4	61.5	9.2	36.4	4 628	11 162	24 419	2.1	1.6	36 059	11.6	15.6	14.4
Dyer	563	3 345	7 961	3.9	55.3	9.4	36.7	5 331	11 270	22 105	9.0	2.2	32 562	14.7	20.2	17.7
Fayette	542	2 364	6 344	16.8	55.5	8.0	19.5	5 113	9 627	22 199	16.0	1.7	35 504	13.2	18.9	15.2
Fentress	319	2 015	3 319	2.2	44.9	6.6	11.2	4 764	6 927	13 924	0.8	0.4	21 798	23.2	29.8	27.7
Franklin	346	2 862	8 622	18.7	63.5	13.1	28.2	4 798	10 513	23 438	3.7	1.3	33 023	12.6	17.1	15.3
Gibson	519	2 806	9 752	5.5	57.5	8.0	38.8	4 524	10 277	20 938	3.1	0.8	30 657	13.8	20.3	17.0
Giles	462	2 177	5 765	10.1	60.1	8.9	22.1	4 678	10 983	22 078	2.6	1.1	33 918	12.5	17.7	15.0
Grainger	397	1 980	3 465	2.1	46.3	4.8	14.2	4 434	8 415	19 097	4.1	0.6	28 473	16.3	21.4	21.2
Greene	307	3 138	11 364	7.4	58.1	10.3	47.5	5 011	10 161	21 513	5.3	1.1	28 810	14.5	20.7	17.7
Grundy	537	2 023	3 115	5.2	44.7	5.4	11.9	5 019	7 227	16 425	-7.0	0.5	23 656	22.9	28.0	26.9
Hamblen	514	3 637	10 900	7.8	61.6	11.2	47.1	5 280	11 127	23 853	6.7	1.5	33 594	12.8	19.5	16.3
Hamilton	1 067	6 461	69 981	18.7	72.5	19.7	232.8	5 505	13 619	26 523	0.8	3.5	35 930	12.6	18.7	14.6
Hancock	162	1 709	1 396	1.6	42.4	5.1	6.1	5 321	6 266	11 822	5.4	0.6	20 555	25.9	29.1	32.9
Hardeman	619	2 626	5 578	4.9	53.0	7.6	20.7	4 363	8 650	19 128	5.1	1.0	26 112	18.0	22.7	20.9
Hardin	137	2 209	4 599	4.0	54.8	6.1	18.9	4 762	9 654	17 719	-9.3	1.5	27 470	17.5	23.5	22.0
Hawkins	241	1 833	9 231	5.0	58.0	8.4	36.6	4 795	10 358	21 960	1.5	0.8	32 490	14.3	20.7	18.4
Haywood	1 460	4 354	4 919	2.9	53.0	8.7	19.2	5 243	8 696	17 376	6.0	1.4	26 576	19.4	24.3	22.1
Henderson	451	2 817	4 702	3.6	55.2	6.8	19.5	4 517	9 564	21 099	4.1	0.8	32 339	13.2	17.4	16.3
Henry	553	3 044	5 651	5.9	60.0	8.5	23.1	4 797	10 423	18 891	-5.4	1.3	28 629	14.9	21.4	18.8
Hickman	323	1 274	3 333	6.2	55.6	7.2	15.8	4 435	9 723	21 567	-1.5	1.8	31 980	14.2	18.9	17.9
Houston	309	1 533	1 444	4.0	52.8	6.3	6.1	4 444	9 060	20 112	1.1	0.7	27 659	14.4	19.9	17.4
Humphreys	251	1 539	3 550	5.9	63.5	9.2	14.3	4 681	10 614	22 256	-15.9	1.3	31 185	12.9	18.0	16.3
Jackson	118	1 211	1 949	2.2	45.2	6.8	7.5	4 663	9 159	18 081	8.7	1.5	26 895	17.2	25.7	20.3
Jefferson	391	3 544	7 735	22.2	60.5	11.7	29.2	4 569	10 562	22 219	9.2	1.9	30 640	13.5	20.3	16.9
Johnson	309	994	2 676	3.9	47.2	5.0	12.2	5 243	7 531	14 967	-9.4	0.7	23 424	21.0	26.3	26.4
Knox	667	3 834	86 906	9.7	74.6	23.9	279.8	5 415	14 007	26 010	5.0	3.5	37 857	11.2	16.0	13.5
Lake	151	641	1 545	2.8	49.6	5.0	4.8	5 324	8 285	16 804	0.7	1.2	21 513	27.9	32.1	31.5
Lauderdale	815	3 609	5 304	2.0	52.1	6.0	22.4	4 752	8 607	18 972	3.0	1.1	27 113	18.1	22.4	21.0
Lawrence	461	3 101	7 665	7.9	53.7	6.7	31.2	4 503	10 094	20 842	-3.8	0.9	30 457	13.9	18.4	17.0
Lewis	211	1 751	2 113	7.0	51.5	5.0	7.8	4 064	8 180	17 362	-3.1	0.6	26 372	16.7	20.5	19.7
Lincoln	396	2 214	6 038	4.2	57.5	9.1	23.4	4 401	10 704	21 996	7.9	1.5	32 504	13.4	18.1	16.4
Loudon	356	3 149	6 261	7.0	63.8	9.6	31.5	4 254	12 006	24 258	4.4	2.0	36 750	10.8	16.3	14.5
McMinn	504	4 125	8 816	6.8	57.1	10.5	37.4	4 756	10 508	21 901	-5.0	1.4	32 023	13.7	19.6	16.6
McNairy	381	2 704	4 667	4.6	57.4	5.2	18.2	4 389	9 185	18 715	-1.1	1.0	28 590	16.5	22.3	20.4
Macon	211	1 496	3 246	2.2	49.2	5.5	15.5	4 425	10 158	19 147	-8.3	1.2	28 955	16.3	22.5	20.7
Madison	1 154	5 123	20 069	19.4	68.3	16.6	80.2	5 862	11 655	23 716	3.3	2.4	34 206	13.9	18.6	16.5
Marion	612	2 560	5 613	3.9	51.9	6.4	21.4	4 678	9 274	20 045	-6.4	0.7	30 518	14.8	19.9	18.5

1. Data for serious crimes have not been adjusted for underreporting; this may affect comparability between geographic areas and over time. 2. Per 100,000 population estimated by the FBI. 3. All persons 3 years old and over enrolled in nursery school through college. 4. Persons 25 years old and over. 5. Elementary and secondary education expenditures, local government fiscal years ending between July 1, 1998 and June 30, 1999. 6. Based on population enumerated as of April 1, 1990.

Table B. States and Counties — **Personal Income**

	Personal income, 1999												
			Per capita[1]						Transfer payments				
										Government payments to individuals			
STATE County	Total (mil dol)	Percent change, 1998–1999	Dollars	Rank	Wages and salaries[2] (mil dol)	Proprietor's income (mil dol)	Dividends, interest, and rent (mil dol)	Total (mil dol)	Total (mil dol)	Social Security (mil dol)	Medical payments (mil dol)	Income mainte-nance (mil dol)	Unemploy-ment insurance (mil dol)
	62	63	64	65	66	67	68	69	70	71	72	73	74
SOUTH DAKOTA—Cont'd													
Tripp	137	2.3	20 684	1 782	53	26	38	26	25	11	10	2	0
Turner	201	-2.6	23 233	1 034	46	46	43	30	29	16	10	1	0
Union	404	2.9	32 352	144	457	43	103	36	34	18	12	2	0
Walworth	134	6.5	23 907	877	52	26	37	24	23	12	7	2	0
Yankton	515	3.8	24 309	803	318	67	119	68	64	32	25	3	0
Ziebach	22	9.7	10 390	3 105	7	2	3	8	8	1	3	2	0
TENNESSEE	140 094	4.8	25 548	X	89 896	13 487	22 630	21 510	20 577	8 024	9 131	1 997	359
Anderson	1 788	2.9	25 181	644	1 516	117	388	318	306	139	122	27	4
Bedford	766	5.7	21 945	1 377	418	79	131	128	122	52	52	9	3
Benton	320	4.5	19 409	2 174	115	34	56	82	79	33	34	6	2
Bledsoe	201	6.6	18 396	2 442	71	34	19	44	42	14	21	5	0
Blount	2 407	4.2	23 416	983	1 245	176	420	378	361	171	141	27	6
Bradley	2 090	6.0	24 839	696	1 214	279	307	303	289	122	127	23	4
Campbell	637	2.8	16 556	2 820	242	41	94	224	218	72	97	28	4
Cannon	249	5.2	20 315	1 885	45	18	39	55	53	19	27	4	1
Carroll	599	3.1	20 330	1 882	223	53	104	150	145	57	65	12	5
Carter	962	2.8	18 046	2 530	299	58	141	237	228	93	94	22	4
Cheatham	804	7.0	22 258	1 283	203	78	87	96	89	38	40	6	2
Chester	275	5.9	18 531	2 409	99	20	39	56	53	22	22	5	1
Claiborne	549	6.4	18 471	2 420	221	50	86	157	152	49	71	21	1
Clay	128	4.4	17 663	2 608	48	12	20	39	38	12	19	5	1
Cocke	578	4.4	17 891	2 559	227	43	74	159	153	52	68	21	5
Coffee	1 056	3.8	22 778	1 148	751	103	179	200	192	80	87	15	3
Crockett	293	2.3	20 817	1 728	113	23	51	67	64	24	31	6	2
Cumberland	914	5.2	20 154	1 950	397	115	193	227	220	107	86	16	3
Davidson	18 253	3.7	34 437	94	16 542	2 376	3 318	2 019	1 929	729	898	175	36
Decatur	217	2.9	20 156	1 949	97	17	29	64	62	22	32	5	1
De Kalb	326	2.9	20 179	1 939	124	42	59	76	73	26	36	5	2
Dickson	972	5.4	22 602	1 194	479	105	121	154	146	59	67	8	3
Dyer	810	3.5	22 046	1 349	526	68	132	158	152	60	69	16	3
Fayette	654	6.0	20 790	1 739	179	42	101	105	100	40	42	14	1
Fentress	292	4.2	17 869	2 565	91	52	33	98	95	26	48	12	2
Franklin	799	3.2	21 114	1 633	259	101	133	162	155	67	67	12	3
Gibson	1 024	2.4	21 321	1 563	526	82	165	242	234	92	109	20	5
Giles	653	5.1	22 502	1 215	339	49	102	116	111	46	49	9	2
Grainger	341	4.0	16 874	2 759	99	34	42	86	83	28	40	10	1
Greene	1 364	7.2	22 403	1 240	782	68	205	349	338	106	190	25	6
Grundy	249	6.2	17 758	2 585	45	36	24	78	76	23	38	10	1
Hamblen	1 319	6.1	24 344	795	1 050	119	199	229	219	95	91	21	4
Hamilton	8 745	5.2	29 671	221	6 624	782	1 640	1 266	1 216	502	524	103	15
Hancock	90	3.0	13 370	3 073	26	6	11	36	35	8	18	7	0
Hardeman	411	2.5	16 805	2 779	183	29	64	122	117	38	57	16	2
Hardin	511	3.9	20 246	1 910	245	51	78	128	124	45	59	12	3
Hawkins	974	4.3	19 434	2 164	403	44	148	210	202	84	86	21	3
Haywood	375	1.8	19 306	2 206	181	34	53	88	85	26	41	13	2
Henderson	512	3.7	20 682	1 784	266	47	72	107	103	37	50	9	3
Henry	653	2.4	21 690	1 457	341	70	128	147	142	63	59	10	3
Hickman	388	6.4	18 237	2 485	95	35	47	78	74	30	34	6	2
Houston	131	3.4	16 595	2 812	35	10	21	40	39	14	20	3	1
Humphreys	333	5.1	19 365	2 191	212	16	59	76	73	31	32	5	2
Jackson	191	3.2	19 847	2 036	50	15	33	51	49	17	24	5	1
Jefferson	841	5.6	18 649	2 379	327	64	133	178	170	68	76	14	4
Johnson	245	4.7	14 666	3 012	94	19	41	83	80	27	36	10	3
Knox	10 294	4.6	27 376	385	7 023	1 012	1 835	1 368	1 304	558	538	112	17
Lake	102	7.6	12 556	3 089	40	6	16	37	36	11	19	5	1
Lauderdale	442	3.3	18 234	2 487	252	41	57	113	109	36	54	14	3
Lawrence	782	2.5	19 745	2 073	358	71	113	177	170	65	73	15	11
Lewis	178	2.7	15 997	2 898	62	17	23	51	49	17	25	4	1
Lincoln	622	5.0	20 878	1 706	221	69	100	120	115	48	50	11	2
Loudon	967	7.0	24 247	817	315	83	164	171	164	76	71	10	2
McMinn	946	5.4	20 395	1 865	595	76	148	200	192	79	82	16	4
McNairy	480	4.2	19 729	2 081	228	46	57	124	120	42	59	12	2
Macon	323	3.9	17 441	2 661	101	27	49	78	75	26	37	7	2
Madison	2 249	5.1	25 921	528	1 792	194	332	346	331	125	149	33	5
Marion	559	6.3	20 783	1 743	173	50	60	126	122	43	58	11	2

1. Based on the resident population estimated as of July 1 of the year shown. 2. Includes other labor income.

Table B. States and Counties — Earnings, Social Security, and Housing

STATE County	Earnings, 1999 Total (mil dol)	Farm	Goods-related[1] Total	Manu-facturing	Service-related and other[2] Total	Retail trade	Finance, insurance, and real estate	Services	Government	Social Security beneficiaries, December 2000 Number	Rate[3]	Supplemental Security Income recipients, December 2000	Housing units, 1990 Total	Percent change, 1980-1990
	75	76	77	78	79	80	81	82	83	84	85	86	87	88
SOUTH DAKOTA—Cont'd														
Tripp	79	16.8	D	1.6	D	11.5	4.8	28.9	14.4	1 484	231	152	3 023	-0.4
Turner	92	30.0	D	5.4	D	6.6	5.4	15.3	13.0	2 033	230	91	3 800	-5.5
Union	500	4.8	66.5	63.9	D	3.1	3.3	14.5	3.7	2 148	171	90	4 286	-3.7
Walworth	77	13.9	D	1.3	D	13.3	3.9	30.5	14.8	1 524	255	149	2 928	-1.2
Yankton	385	4.6	D	23.1	D	11.6	6.5	23.9	14.6	3 961	183	281	7 571	5.6
Ziebach	9	28.1	D	D	D	D	10.8	D	31.1	172	68	85	800	2.4
TENNESSEE	103 383	0.0	26.3	19.7	60.1	10.6	6.9	27.8	13.6	991 029	174	164 288	2 026 067	15.9
Anderson	1 633	0.0	D	34.9	D	6.5	2.2	32.6	13.3	15 912	223	2 324	29 323	13.4
Bedford	497	0.7	50.4	43.0	37.0	9.3	3.9	13.7	11.9	6 566	175	805	12 638	16.9
Benton	149	-1.2	D	23.4	D	12.1	3.1	16.0	16.2	4 139	250	495	7 107	8.9
Bledsoe	106	18.1	D	20.0	D	5.4	2.9	D	28.1	1 999	162	390	3 771	10.7
Blount	1 421	-0.2	40.7	32.2	46.7	13.3	5.4	17.8	12.8	20 160	191	2 335	36 532	18.5
Bradley	1 493	0.1	D	33.6	D	9.4	6.0	26.5	10.9	15 171	172	2 240	29 562	19.7
Campbell	283	-0.5	30.1	18.1	47.2	14.3	7.2	18.2	23.2	9 826	247	2 964	14 817	11.8
Cannon	62	-5.1	D	16.2	D	14.4	3.9	29.9	20.4	2 570	200	299	4 368	9.1
Carroll	276	-1.0	37.4	30.7	47.7	11.7	4.7	21.5	15.8	7 240	246	939	11 783	4.2
Carter	357	0.0	D	17.2	D	14.5	6.3	25.0	18.6	12 171	214	1 898	21 779	12.8
Cheatham	280	-0.3	D	27.1	D	7.6	4.0	18.0	15.5	4 702	131	376	10 297	37.6
Chester	119	-2.5	27.5	20.8	D	13.3	D	23.2	17.9	2 963	191	374	4 944	10.6
Claiborne	270	0.7	D	32.2	D	11.6	4.1	17.5	17.7	7 148	239	2 137	10 711	14.1
Clay	60	0.0	D	32.3	D	15.4	2.5	16.9	18.6	1 853	232	432	3 340	10.8
Cocke	270	0.7	D	35.0	D	12.8	2.6	20.7	17.1	7 301	218	1 922	12 282	8.6
Coffee	854	0.2	D	22.2	D	11.8	3.1	37.5	13.6	9 755	203	1 336	16 786	12.0
Crockett	136	-2.8	46.2	38.2	42.9	7.2	3.6	14.2	13.6	3 254	224	521	5 521	-2.4
Cumberland	512	2.5	D	19.8	D	15.2	9.3	25.1	10.4	13 236	283	1 343	15 864	44.2
Davidson	18 918	0.0	16.0	10.0	73.5	10.9	9.6	38.7	10.5	81 758	143	12 024	229 064	22.2
Decatur	114	-2.3	D	26.1	D	9.3	4.0	19.0	16.3	3 037	259	376	5 346	9.6
De Kalb	166	1.4	D	28.1	D	8.9	2.5	29.2	12.7	3 531	203	646	6 694	10.1
Dickson	584	-0.7	D	36.2	D	13.2	3.8	19.8	12.1	7 315	170	949	14 149	27.0
Dyer	595	-0.8	42.0	35.2	46.0	10.3	5.1	21.0	12.7	7 515	202	1 436	14 384	7.9
Fayette	221	-2.2	42.2	30.7	41.6	8.8	10.5	14.2	18.4	5 474	190	1 123	9 115	11.8
Fentress	143	2.0	D	15.6	D	14.2	3.9	27.0	15.3	3 982	240	1 185	6 120	9.2
Franklin	360	3.9	D	20.8	D	13.8	3.5	30.6	13.3	8 200	209	959	13 717	18.4
Gibson	608	-1.1	49.3	42.3	38.4	9.7	3.7	16.4	13.4	11 393	237	1 542	19 635	0.3
Giles	388	-0.9	D	48.4	D	11.3	3.9	14.9	10.5	5 898	200	792	10 828	13.3
Grainger	133	1.1	D	42.3	D	8.1	D	11.5	15.6	3 915	190	1 006	7 501	5.9
Greene	850	-0.4	D	35.5	D	12.0	3.3	21.3	12.8	14 257	227	2 581	23 270	10.1
Grundy	80	7.4	D	11.0	D	16.0	2.6	16.9	20.6	3 254	227	882	5 155	0.4
Hamblen	1 169	0.1	D	45.9	D	9.3	4.2	15.3	9.1	11 721	202	1 840	20 514	11.1
Hamilton	7 406	0.0	D	17.2	D	10.7	9.1	25.5	15.4	56 359	183	7 703	122 588	11.1
Hancock	31	1.0	32.7	23.1	D	15.2	D	14.9	29.9	1 347	198	661	2 890	7.6
Hardeman	212	-2.2	38.1	30.7	36.8	10.1	4.0	15.3	27.2	5 176	184	1 634	9 174	9.1
Hardin	296	-1.0	D	38.3	D	10.8	2.8	12.0	15.4	6 080	238	1 135	10 275	14.8
Hawkins	447	-1.1	D	51.6	D	8.4	1.7	11.7	15.8	10 953	204	1 840	18 779	10.4
Haywood	215	-1.7	41.0	34.0	44.8	8.9	8.2	15.3	15.9	3 702	187	1 131	7 475	6.1
Henderson	313	-1.5	52.4	45.9	38.4	10.2	3.4	15.4	10.8	4 902	192	774	9 278	11.8
Henry	411	-0.5	D	31.6	D	13.3	3.2	17.9	16.0	7 808	251	923	13 774	2.1
Hickman	130	-2.7	34.9	24.3	D	11.0	2.2	19.2	28.5	3 992	179	525	6 662	18.2
Houston	45	-2.8	20.1	10.8	D	13.6	D	38.6	23.5	1 725	213	301	3 085	10.2
Humphreys	228	-2.0	D	42.2	D	7.8	2.7	9.7	22.1	3 786	211	447	7 136	9.6
Jackson	65	-2.8	34.9	26.5	D	8.3	5.4	19.4	17.5	2 472	225	516	4 219	13.9
Jefferson	391	-0.2	D	23.2	D	10.2	2.7	20.5	12.7	8 711	197	1 255	14 170	15.9
Johnson	113	0.1	D	27.9	D	14.8	4.0	15.4	15.7	3 977	227	928	6 090	13.1
Knox	8 036	0.0	17.6	10.3	66.1	12.4	6.5	32.1	16.3	64 826	170	9 787	143 582	14.1
Lake	46	3.2	12.9	10.6	D	13.9	2.4	18.4	42.1	1 455	183	406	2 610	-13.0
Lauderdale	294	0.2	D	44.6	D	10.0	3.5	11.6	16.8	4 862	179	1 326	9 343	0.8
Lawrence	429	-1.5	D	33.0	D	13.8	3.9	17.5	13.7	8 465	212	1 366	14 229	13.5
Lewis	78	-1.5	D	28.1	D	14.1	3.2	16.5	17.8	2 315	204	325	3 943	21.4
Lincoln	290	0.2	D	29.8	D	12.5	4.6	14.4	20.1	6 426	205	854	11 902	15.6
Loudon	398	5.0	D	30.0	D	10.4	5.0	18.0	15.2	9 147	234	885	12 995	19.9
McMinn	671	0.0	D	48.8	D	9.4	3.5	13.8	10.8	10 075	206	1 542	17 616	11.5
McNairy	273	-1.6	D	33.4	D	8.5	2.5	29.9	11.4	5 860	238	1 279	9 734	8.0
Macon	128	-1.0	D	24.7	D	14.0	5.9	16.3	17.8	3 880	190	659	6 879	12.8
Madison	1 987	0.1	D	26.0	D	9.8	3.8	23.7	17.9	15 314	167	2 890	31 809	10.3
Marion	223	-0.5	D	25.4	D	18.4	4.2	17.8	14.8	5 437	196	977	10 011	10.9

1. Covers mining, construction, and manufacturing. 2. Covers private sector earnings in agricultural services, forestry, and fisheries; transportation and public utilities; wholesale trade; retail trade; finance, insurance, and real estate; and services. 3. Per 1,000 resident population estimated as of July 1 of the year shown.

Table B. States and Counties — Housing, Labor Force, and Employment

STATE County	Housing units, 1990 (cont'd) Occupied units								Civilian labor force, 2001				Civilian employment, 1990[5]		
	Owner-occupied					Renter-occupied					Unemployment			Percent	
				Owner cost as a percent of income											
	Total	Percent	Median value[1]	With a mortgage	Without a mortgage	Median rent[2]	Rent as percent of income	Substandard units[3] (percent)	Total	Percent change, 2000–2001	Total	Rate[4]	Total	Professional, managerial, and technical	Precision production, craft, and repair
	89	90	91	92	93	94	95	96	97	98	99	100	101	102	103
SOUTH DAKOTA—Cont'd															
Tripp	2 573	73.6	35 600	20.2	13.5	253	25.1	5.6	3 230	-1.6	99	3.1	3 033	18.5	9.8
Turner	3 332	76.1	22 800	17.2	14.5	240	20.6	1.8	3 900	-3.4	128	3.3	3 810	18.4	10.8
Union	3 859	72.7	37 600	18.0	12.9	266	22.6	2.0	6 901	-0.5	280	4.1	4 724	20.3	11.3
Walworth	2 447	71.5	27 600	16.7	14.1	298	24.6	2.8	3 052	-0.5	105	3.4	2 795	22.3	8.9
Yankton	7 107	66.0	48 500	20.6	13.9	286	23.7	1.9	11 410	1.6	379	3.3	9 488	24.9	10.9
Ziebach	630	58.3	14 999	12.7	16.1	251	35.1	25.1	672	-1.0	97	14.4	650	21.7	4.6
TENNESSEE	1 853 725	68.0	58 400	20.1	12.6	357	25.0	3.8	2 817 654	0.7	125 978	4.5	2 250 842	26.1	12.2
Anderson	27 384	70.8	55 100	16.7	11.7	342	24.5	3.0	36 371	2.3	1 454	4.0	30 758	32.1	14.2
Bedford	11 608	71.8	48 400	19.5	13.0	307	24.5	3.9	18 291	2.0	1 059	5.8	14 679	18.3	16.2
Benton	5 784	80.2	39 700	18.6	12.4	270	22.6	3.9	7 321	-3.3	534	7.3	6 159	19.9	15.1
Bledsoe	3 261	78.7	36 000	19.0	12.4	232	23.0	4.8	3 686	-2.7	187	5.1	3 662	14.9	15.5
Blount	33 624	74.6	60 200	18.1	11.9	321	23.9	2.2	52 772	2.8	2 101	4.0	38 840	25.9	14.6
Bradley	27 604	68.8	55 000	19.7	12.3	329	24.0	2.8	41 490	-1.7	1 592	3.8	36 565	22.2	15.1
Campbell	13 150	73.8	37 900	23.0	12.6	250	27.0	6.9	16 916	-0.5	974	5.8	12 298	18.2	18.7
Cannon	3 980	79.3	41 500	17.7	12.7	238	21.1	4.9	5 154	2.3	251	4.9	4 978	14.7	17.4
Carroll	10 727	79.0	35 700	16.8	13.5	262	23.7	3.1	11 778	-2.5	1 121	9.5	12 066	16.3	13.4
Carter	20 189	76.3	43 800	19.4	13.3	282	24.7	3.2	25 213	0.2	1 214	4.8	22 520	21.7	15.0
Cheatham	9 515	83.1	64 000	22.0	13.8	387	24.7	5.3	20 030	1.4	561	2.8	13 449	22.3	17.0
Chester	4 558	77.4	40 200	21.1	13.6	241	23.6	3.5	8 305	-1.6	338	4.1	5 615	19.6	13.1
Claiborne	9 629	78.3	41 400	21.7	13.5	248	25.5	7.7	12 537	-1.8	624	5.0	10 158	18.8	16.9
Clay	2 855	81.4	37 100	18.6	13.3	215	24.7	8.9	2 561	-4.0	256	10.0	3 183	16.1	14.8
Cocke	11 191	72.7	40 300	17.7	12.6	213	25.3	8.6	16 285	-1.3	1 206	7.4	12 474	14.4	13.5
Coffee	15 500	70.1	52 800	18.6	12.9	319	23.5	3.6	23 139	2.5	1 013	4.4	18 010	23.7	13.5
Crockett	5 183	76.4	38 600	19.7	13.3	258	23.8	3.7	7 084	0.1	398	5.6	5 787	17.5	14.1
Cumberland	13 426	78.4	49 100	22.2	11.7	296	24.3	4.0	21 772	1.0	1 391	6.4	14 009	19.1	14.5
Davidson	207 530	53.8	76 000	20.9	12.6	433	25.3	2.6	308 184	1.1	9 498	3.1	264 680	33.4	8.6
Decatur	4 216	80.5	34 700	21.8	13.6	253	23.6	3.9	5 198	-2.7	418	8.0	4 351	14.5	13.5
De Kalb	5 696	76.4	44 200	17.4	13.4	261	24.7	3.8	8 102	0.0	439	5.4	6 571	17.5	14.8
Dickson	13 019	75.7	54 100	20.9	12.5	337	27.0	3.5	22 352	1.5	939	4.2	16 049	21.1	15.5
Dyer	13 617	65.8	44 100	17.3	13.3	310	24.6	3.2	17 904	-1.7	1 290	7.2	15 652	20.1	13.6
Fayette	8 453	74.8	51 400	22.5	12.5	241	23.4	13.5	14 787	1.3	819	5.5	10 569	16.2	15.9
Fentress	5 511	78.6	32 300	23.2	13.2	212	23.1	7.9	5 970	-3.7	656	11.0	5 717	17.1	16.6
Franklin	12 660	77.7	48 700	17.6	12.0	296	22.7	2.9	18 535	2.2	709	3.8	15 307	22.7	15.0
Gibson	18 361	72.6	39 200	16.5	13.3	271	23.7	2.8	20 467	-3.1	1 966	9.6	19 830	16.7	14.4
Giles	9 832	73.0	44 600	18.8	12.1	272	25.9	5.0	16 260	-0.5	995	6.1	11 449	17.6	12.9
Grainger	6 394	82.4	40 300	20.4	12.0	246	21.1	9.8	10 133	-0.7	574	5.7	7 408	11.0	17.3
Greene	21 482	77.0	44 500	18.0	12.1	272	22.9	4.6	35 572	-2.2	2 566	7.2	26 279	20.2	17.1
Grundy	4 784	81.4	29 800	23.3	13.7	211	30.3	7.2	5 063	-3.0	297	5.9	4 946	14.3	15.4
Hamblen	19 429	72.1	51 300	18.0	12.4	291	22.7	3.0	30 047	0.4	1 858	6.2	24 066	19.2	14.4
Hamilton	111 799	64.1	62 000	18.1	12.9	373	24.9	2.8	151 587	0.4	4 620	3.0	134 440	29.8	10.7
Hancock	2 484	78.3	32 200	24.1	11.8	145	28.3	19.2	2 525	-2.5	188	7.4	2 022	12.8	17.3
Hardeman	8 276	73.6	39 200	19.9	13.2	258	24.9	8.3	9 352	0.3	832	8.9	8 962	16.5	13.6
Hardin	8 726	77.4	39 100	20.2	12.4	252	23.5	5.3	12 369	2.5	744	6.0	9 602	15.4	14.7
Hawkins	17 167	77.1	48 600	16.6	12.0	295	22.7	5.5	23 712	1.6	1 324	5.6	19 335	19.1	16.7
Haywood	7 014	66.4	40 400	21.8	14.3	257	26.0	8.5	8 707	4.4	810	9.3	7 725	17.7	12.4
Henderson	8 527	79.7	42 200	16.4	12.9	266	25.1	3.2	13 771	-3.1	942	6.8	10 228	17.4	14.8
Henry	11 362	76.5	41 700	20.9	13.0	270	25.2	3.0	14 328	-0.5	913	6.4	11 422	19.0	13.7
Hickman	5 976	80.8	43 200	18.3	13.0	285	23.7	5.2	7 979	3.8	445	5.6	6 957	19.4	16.7
Houston	2 683	78.7	35 300	18.7	13.4	264	25.5	4.0	2 611	-2.1	272	10.4	2 672	17.3	22.0
Humphreys	6 063	77.3	43 700	19.6	12.7	288	22.9	3.5	8 052	-1.7	604	7.5	6 613	18.9	17.5
Jackson	3 642	81.6	38 000	17.9	13.1	229	27.4	7.2	4 429	-2.1	287	6.5	3 873	14.7	16.3
Jefferson	12 329	77.2	47 900	18.9	11.9	275	25.5	3.9	23 825	-1.0	1 177	4.9	15 196	19.8	14.8
Johnson	5 406	80.7	41 300	24.8	12.7	211	25.9	7.1	6 309	-4.1	541	8.6	5 537	13.6	17.3
Knox	133 639	63.9	63 900	19.1	12.8	351	25.5	2.0	205 118	2.1	5 197	2.5	163 586	33.6	9.8
Lake	2 418	58.4	35 100	19.4	13.6	215	27.7	5.0	2 435	2.1	136	5.6	2 484	12.8	9.7
Lauderdale	8 423	66.9	38 700	20.8	14.1	273	24.0	6.8	10 049	1.1	996	9.9	9 071	14.5	14.6
Lawrence	13 338	76.6	43 300	18.0	12.3	255	23.7	3.8	18 963	-3.1	2 087	11.0	15 410	16.6	14.3
Lewis	3 533	75.8	37 200	21.0	12.3	222	26.3	5.1	4 064	0.8	386	9.5	3 893	16.2	14.5
Lincoln	10 881	73.4	47 100	20.3	12.7	281	24.3	3.5	14 432	1.2	657	4.6	13 260	17.7	14.8
Loudon	12 155	77.6	51 000	20.2	12.2	280	22.8	2.2	21 284	2.6	743	3.5	14 749	21.9	14.5
McMinn	16 351	76.1	45 600	18.7	12.5	269	25.4	3.1	21 274	0.8	1 640	7.7	18 760	18.6	16.1
McNairy	8 834	79.2	36 400	21.2	13.3	238	24.5	3.8	11 108	6.8	711	6.4	9 509	15.1	17.7
Macon	6 159	78.8	36 600	19.4	13.8	244	22.4	6.5	8 939	1.5	640	7.2	7 369	13.1	17.0
Madison	29 609	65.4	53 500	20.4	12.9	337	24.3	2.8	50 773	-0.5	2 380	4.7	35 540	27.9	10.7
Marion	9 215	79.0	42 600	20.7	13.1	263	23.8	3.8	12 806	0.8	651	5.1	10 603	16.2	17.9

1. Specified owner-occupied units.   2. Specified renter-occupied units.   3. Overcrowded or lacking complete plumbing facilities.   4. Percent of civilian labor force.   5. Persons 16 years and older.

Table B. States and Counties — Nonfarm Employment and Agriculture

	Private nonfarm establishments, employment and payroll, 1999									Agriculture, 1997			
STATE County	Number of establishments	Employment						Annual payroll		Farms			Farm operators
		Total	Health Care and Social Assistance	Manufacturing	Retail trade	Finance and Insurance	Professional Scientific and Technical Services	Total (mil dol)	Average per employee (dollars)	Number	Percent with—		Whose principal occupation is farming (percent)
											Less than 50 acres	500 acres and over	
	104	105	106	107	108	109	110	111	112	113	114	115	116
SOUTH DAKOTA—Cont'd													
Tripp	229	1 723	378	D	363	84	51	30	17 607	654	7.0	62.5	72.9
Turner	269	1 713	398	124	300	105	D	34	19 818	832	15.3	31.9	71.0
Union	388	11 301	443	6 852	984	390	108	471	41 696	494	15.0	38.3	69.4
Walworth	233	1 819	388	12	404	76	89	29	15 975	338	10.9	61.8	73.4
Yankton	692	10 301	1 663	2 557	1 873	697	223	210	20 413	636	16.7	32.4	68.6
Ziebach	19	219	D	0	13	D	0	4	18 950	259	4.6	81.9	76.4
TENNESSEE	131 116	2 338 780	278 089	475 774	310 229	113 293	94 209	65 964	28 204	76 818	39.5	5.0	36.0
Anderson	1 698	39 105	3 495	11 435	3 792	776	10 060	1 441	36 847	462	47.8	1.9	27.7
Bedford	726	12 927	965	5 938	1 282	260	166	312	24 102	1 408	33.3	5.3	39.3
Benton	359	3 487	418	869	734	127	D	70	20 114	433	27.9	4.8	27.0
Bledsoe	137	1 423	227	658	136	31	D	30	21 330	525	24.4	6.7	37.7
Blount	2 159	36 712	3 866	8 175	5 877	1 531	806	1 077	29 342	1 053	52.9	2.6	32.4
Bradley	1 906	39 620	5 173	13 155	4 659	1 229	743	1 027	25 922	781	44.6	4.1	37.3
Campbell	653	7 790	1 331	1 960	1 539	295	119	153	19 704	398	45.2	1.3	36.4
Cannon	166	1 402	276	305	212	59	54	25	18 098	754	33.7	2.9	34.2
Carroll	537	7 646	970	2 959	946	278	92	150	19 643	851	25.5	8.0	32.5
Carter	749	9 336	1 217	2 160	1 621	336	D	210	22 527	622	64.6	0.8	29.1
Cheatham	513	6 358	380	2 774	806	37	178	155	24 454	556	35.3	3.8	33.6
Chester	237	3 472	294	806	493	73	51	66	19 047	410	24.6	7.3	33.7
Claiborne	471	8 030	852	3 612	725	238	98	167	20 753	1 397	43.7	2.1	41.9
Clay	121	1 463	321	631	196	34	D	30	20 489	503	30.4	3.8	35.8
Cocke	514	6 851	837	2 505	1 175	180	73	142	20 768	886	45.5	1.0	34.5
Coffee	1 239	21 758	2 036	5 682	3 212	626	2 561	608	27 961	968	41.5	5.6	35.6
Crockett	297	3 264	334	1 159	361	141	D	75	23 051	380	34.2	22.6	52.6
Cumberland	958	12 085	1 876	2 530	2 517	380	238	263	21 777	726	40.8	5.8	31.4
Davidson	18 747	390 210	49 432	30 161	44 846	24 125	18 845	12 593	32 273	533	47.1	2.4	30.0
Decatur	254	3 385	709	1 245	413	92	66	70	20 701	437	19.7	8.7	30.0
De Kalb	305	4 961	478	2 620	422	133	62	116	23 375	806	40.0	3.5	30.8
Dickson	890	13 050	1 369	4 276	2 276	434	152	296	22 651	1 106	32.8	3.8	35.4
Dyer	948	15 688	1 465	6 473	2 003	542	287	390	24 855	526	30.2	25.5	49.8
Fayette	423	4 151	391	1 436	411	174	66	114	27 569	716	28.4	15.6	39.1
Fentress	293	3 582	926	1 151	636	132	D	63	17 600	504	35.9	4.8	40.1
Franklin	692	8 073	1 054	2 132	1 536	224	204	178	22 032	985	45.1	6.1	42.9
Gibson	1 092	15 858	1 471	7 803	2 075	463	202	376	23 709	874	36.5	17.4	45.8
Giles	575	9 914	850	4 378	1 331	296	218	235	23 708	1 570	26.0	5.2	33.8
Grainger	256	2 949	174	1 552	486	D	D	59	19 925	1 095	45.5	1.3	37.1
Greene	1 195	22 059	2 603	7 948	2 856	566	285	514	23 310	3 086	56.3	1.1	38.2
Grundy	187	1 415	281	239	454	56	D	20	14 327	337	49.6	3.9	46.9
Hamblen	1 397	31 544	3 057	14 757	3 668	545	335	759	24 076	667	57.9	1.9	35.2
Hamilton	8 987	171 283	18 966	33 332	20 269	14 921	6 690	4 771	27 853	604	49.2	2.5	29.3
Hancock	60	770	98	D	110	D	D	11	14 605	633	39.5	1.7	43.0
Hardeman	433	6 178	1 142	1 804	733	206	54	136	22 011	559	22.4	15.2	36.3
Hardin	516	6 303	640	2 496	1 038	171	119	142	22 475	594	28.1	7.6	34.7
Hawkins	623	11 225	878	6 021	1 438	230	112	297	26 464	1 813	48.5	0.7	35.7
Haywood	377	4 370	368	1 763	724	258	D	106	24 162	360	24.2	31.1	59.4
Henderson	544	8 732	502	4 101	1 122	247	163	196	22 405	858	21.4	7.1	29.8
Henry	770	9 791	1 242	3 118	1 535	330	213	218	22 272	831	25.5	8.7	36.6
Hickman	301	2 342	407	726	335	85	D	48	20 468	678	21.7	7.2	36.1
Houston	115	1 058	288	330	161	28	D	19	18 256	289	23.9	5.2	26.3
Humphreys	310	4 506	354	2 000	707	63	56	143	31 671	577	24.6	9.9	32.4
Jackson	105	1 635	154	978	129	D	D	35	21 253	605	31.7	3.8	37.5
Jefferson	642	9 643	756	2 515	1 459	182	128	205	21 283	1 147	50.2	1.0	38.6
Johnson	247	3 216	192	1 377	475	83	D	71	21 964	679	58.2	1.2	37.4
Knox	11 204	185 975	28 139	17 654	29 205	7 801	10 872	5 033	27 061	1 193	58.1	1.3	33.6
Lake	95	725	204	D	164	D	D	13	17 921	80	15.0	51.2	71.2
Lauderdale	381	6 801	524	3 300	742	219	D	151	22 150	505	28.3	18.8	47.3
Lawrence	799	11 417	899	5 148	1 759	289	143	244	21 414	1 617	33.0	3.8	31.2
Lewis	215	2 027	373	604	385	56	D	40	19 958	222	23.0	3.6	32.0
Lincoln	634	7 195	834	2 864	1 439	200	156	160	22 304	1 661	31.7	6.6	37.1
Loudon	733	9 750	1 048	3 133	1 612	271	176	239	24 532	763	51.6	2.4	37.1
McMinn	939	17 260	1 580	8 568	2 102	545	216	460	26 634	1 074	39.9	4.0	35.3
McNairy	467	8 990	696	2 652	875	152	D	189	21 030	720	22.1	7.1	29.7
Macon	314	3 709	449	1 483	679	174	D	68	18 370	1 238	40.0	1.9	33.6
Madison	2 651	49 585	7 808	12 734	7 201	1 227	1 055	1 331	26 838	571	30.8	11.2	38.7
Marion	442	5 504	617	1 541	1 228	192	102	111	20 220	294	37.1	6.5	33.3

Table B. States and Counties — Agriculture, Land, and Water

STATE County	Agriculture, 1997 (cont'd)															
	Land in farms				Value of land and buildings			Value of products sold				Percent of farms with sales of —			
			Acres				Value of machinery and equipment average per farm ($1,000)		Percent from —					Percent of land owned by fed. gov. 1997	Water consumption 1995 (mil gal/day)
	Acreage (1,000)	Percent change, 1992–1997	Average size of farm	Total irrigated (1,000)	Total cropland (1,000)	Average per farm ($1,000)	Average per acre (dollars)		Total (mil dol)	Average per farm (dollars)	Crops	Livestock and poultry products	$10,000 or more	$100,000 or more		
	117	118	119	120	121	122	123	124	125	126	127	128	129	130	131	132
SOUTH DAKOTA—Cont'd																
Tripp	930	-7.6	1 423	2	454	444	330	79	66	100 485	30.8	69.2	79.2	26.8	0.0	5.1
Turner	352	-4.0	424	17	312	383	926	107	97	116 883	53.0	47.0	81.9	34.6	0.2	15.1
Union	254	-2.3	514	31	236	608	1 101	98	86	174 768	58.6	41.4	82.2	43.7	0.3	16.0
Walworth	437	-2.6	1 294	2	246	347	308	88	31	92 349	46.9	53.1	73.4	26.0	1.6	6.5
Yankton	261	-3.7	410	6	219	378	960	71	60	94 970	57.6	42.4	78.9	24.4	0.8	10.5
Ziebach	1 499	6.6	5 788	D	240	912	154	75	23	88 517	41.9	58.1	77.6	25.9	0.2	0.8
TENNESSEE	11 122	-0.4	145	46	7 069	261	1 808	33	2 178	28 358	52.5	47.5	27.7	5.1	4.6	10 076.2
Anderson	41	-2.6	89	0	21	353	3 378	29	5	11 849	49.7	50.3	14.7	1.9	5.1	507.7
Bedford	207	-3.1	147	0	125	225	1 693	34	69	49 041	7.4	92.6	32.3	9.7	0.0	6.5
Benton	69	9.4	159	0	36	189	1 162	27	4	10 079	41.1	58.9	19.9	1.6	2.0	4.2
Bledsoe	96	3.1	183	0	57	239	1 377	37	41	79 044	10.6	89.4	37.1	5.9	0.0	1.7
Blount	93	-2.9	89	0	64	341	3 812	30	19	17 634	45.2	54.8	20.1	2.6	26.7	14.1
Bradley	90	-2.1	115	0	51	300	2 827	35	55	70 283	4.7	95.3	27.8	12.2	0.0	18.7
Campbell	31	2.3	77	D	19	129	1 826	27	3	6 885	48.7	51.3	18.1	0.5	0.0	4.1
Cannon	103	5.9	136	0	53	195	1 533	29	12	16 070	36.0	63.9	21.9	3.7	0.0	1.3
Carroll	172	3.4	202	0	108	245	1 202	35	22	26 126	78.4	21.6	24.9	5.8	3.2	5.0
Carter	39	5.1	63	0	22	149	2 385	22	7	11 730	42.6	57.4	19.0	1.8	36.1	19.8
Cheatham	68	17.5	123	0	38	293	2 469	25	9	15 918	70.5	29.4	32.4	3.8	0.4	2.4
Chester	73	1.5	178	D	42	153	925	25	6	14 302	69.8	30.1	21.7	3.9	0.0	1.6
Claiborne	144	0.7	103	0	73	134	1 372	23	20	14 459	40.6	59.4	31.2	1.5	0.8	2.6
Clay	72	2.3	142	0	34	169	1 181	19	6	12 510	56.4	43.6	33.6	0.6	0.3	1.6
Cocke	75	-10.5	85	1	41	193	2 349	24	14	15 956	46.4	53.6	19.1	2.4	23.2	7.4
Coffee	136	2.7	140	1	89	268	1 837	33	30	30 846	38.0	62.0	30.2	8.0	8.9	5.6
Crockett	151	3.9	396	D	135	567	1 460	99	48	126 462	97.1	2.9	50.8	26.1	0.0	3.4
Cumberland	100	3.5	138	0	57	255	1 818	33	37	51 280	21.4	78.6	22.9	4.5	0.6	7.6
Davidson	52	11.2	98	0	27	371	3 757	31	11	19 974	76.0	24.0	17.3	1.9	0.2	148.4
Decatur	88	1.6	202	D	42	196	960	27	4	9 774	30.6	69.4	24.0	0.7	0.8	6.9
De Kalb	99	3.3	123	0	56	212	1 629	25	26	32 371	80.7	19.3	26.4	2.7	0.6	1.6
Dickson	149	3.2	134	0	77	255	1 788	34	12	10 911	41.5	58.5	26.8	1.3	0.0	4.4
Dyer	234	1.4	445	3	217	570	1 256	90	56	105 750	94.3	5.7	54.6	24.0	0.0	7.1
Fayette	271	4.9	378	1	180	553	1 476	62	51	71 771	70.8	29.2	34.6	12.2	0.0	5.9
Fentress	70	0.2	139	0	34	220	1 572	28	22	43 301	13.9	86.1	35.1	8.7	8.0	19.9
Franklin	132	-2.2	134	1	94	259	1 984	37	63	63 492	27.8	72.2	38.2	14.2	0.3	4.8
Gibson	278	2.2	318	1	249	404	1 250	83	68	78 346	87.0	13.0	41.9	16.5	3.2	8.3
Giles	249	-2.6	159	2	139	199	1 284	27	30	19 287	16.6	83.4	23.5	3.5	0.0	4.8
Grainger	97	-6.9	88	1	52	162	2 046	25	16	14 843	62.3	37.7	27.3	1.7	0.0	1.7
Greene	226	-4.8	73	0	153	177	2 369	28	51	16 595	36.8	63.2	26.2	2.9	9.5	10.4
Grundy	36	-15.6	108	0	18	177	1 454	25	31	91 371	17.2	82.8	43.3	23.4	0.0	1.8
Hamblen	52	-8.8	78	1	37	261	3 165	35	14	20 576	41.3	58.7	19.9	3.3	0.0	8.3
Hamilton	57	-9.8	94	0	30	318	2 710	27	8	13 712	21.8	78.3	17.5	2.6	2.3	1 533.3
Hancock	68	-15.2	107	0	32	117	1 243	19	8	11 947	44.8	55.2	26.4	1.1	0.0	0.6
Hardeman	166	3.9	297	1	91	287	981	32	19	33 490	72.7	27.3	23.4	7.0	0.0	3.2
Hardin	116	5.1	195	0	65	242	1 244	27	10	16 243	65.3	34.7	22.2	4.2	0.9	28.8
Hawkins	147	-5.8	81	0	76	166	1 973	25	16	8 812	54.4	45.6	21.4	0.7	1.8	552.7
Haywood	212	-5.4	589	2	186	684	1 214	116	63	175 142	97.4	2.6	58.1	28.9	2.9	2.9
Henderson	152	3.4	177	0	89	228	1 128	32	18	21 159	33.6	66.4	26.3	4.2	0.0	3.0
Henry	185	-3.0	223	0	118	265	1 103	46	38	45 433	58.0	42.0	40.3	9.1	1.8	4.2
Hickman	128	-1.7	189	0	64	233	1 273	26	9	12 753	22.8	77.2	26.1	1.9	0.6	3.3
Houston	49	10.8	169	0	24	222	1 293	37	4	13 916	22.0	78.0	27.7	2.1	0.0	1.3
Humphreys	122	2.5	211	0	56	250	1 206	36	8	14 152	44.0	56.0	25.0	2.9	1.8	1 220.6
Jackson	83	-4.3	138	0	34	145	1 161	19	5	8 402	50.2	49.8	22.8	0.5	0.1	1.3
Jefferson	98	-0.9	85	1	68	241	3 183	29	20	17 454	30.2	69.8	24.8	2.2	0.0	7.4
Johnson	49	-10.0	73	0	26	174	2 299	23	8	11 205	56.6	43.4	27.8	0.9	26.5	2.7
Knox	88	-6.6	74	0	53	279	3 831	28	15	12 978	57.6	42.4	15.3	1.5	1.4	63.3
Lake	90	-1.5	1 120	3	86	1 655	1 477	227	23	292 546	99.5	0.5	86.2	53.8	1.4	2.1
Lauderdale	192	4.9	380	2	161	439	1 083	85	47	93 649	94.0	6.0	45.1	19.2	5.9	5.0
Lawrence	214	8.6	132	0	134	199	1 535	32	27	16 662	29.2	70.8	24.2	3.4	0.1	6.1
Lewis	37	-0.5	166	D	16	229	1 395	32	2	10 774	37.7	62.3	18.9	0.9	1.5	1.6
Lincoln	276	0.4	166	1	158	228	1 423	34	49	29 737	32.1	67.9	28.6	5.5	0.1	4.5
Loudon	74	0.0	97	0	48	329	2 820	44	45	59 065	D	D	21.1	4.2	0.0	16.6
McMinn	127	2.7	119	0	79	238	2 052	29	34	31 816	10.5	89.5	24.0	6.9	0.8	85.4
McNairy	130	6.7	181	D	70	149	845	30	11	15 439	60.4	39.6	20.0	4.4	0.0	4.3
Macon	135	-2.9	109	0	74	171	1 543	23	20	16 250	71.0	29.0	36.3	2.4	0.0	1.8
Madison	146	3.3	255	D	104	283	1 148	58	29	50 607	79.4	20.6	31.0	10.0	0.0	18.6
Marion	51	0.1	174	D	30	254	1 491	36	11	36 343	15.3	84.7	26.5	7.5	0.0	3.1

STATE County	Value of Residential Construction Authorized by Building Permits, 2000		Wholesale Trade, 1997				Retail Trade[1], 1997				Real Estate and Rental and Leasing, 1997			
	New Construction ($1,000)	Number of Housing Units	Number of Establishments	Number of Employees	Sales (mil dol)	Annual Payroll (mil dol)	Number of Establishments	Number of Employees	Sales (mil dol)	Annual Payroll (mil dol)	Number of Establishments	Number of Employees	Receipts (mil dol)	Annual Payroll (mil dol)
	133	134	135	136	137	138	139	140	141	142	143	144	145	146
SOUTH DAKOTA—Cont'd														
Tripp	642	13	17	175	82.4	3.1	52	364	52.1	4.5	3	11	0.3	0.1
Turner	2 616	25	14	76	99.5	1.8	42	D	D	D	5	D	D	D
Union	10 672	71	26	210	225.0	6.1	45	D	D	D	7	15	1.6	0.1
Walworth	236	2	11	69	34.2	1.5	61	398	54.3	4.9	6	8	0.4	0.1
Yankton	7 653	79	50	428	290.1	8.6	162	1 988	229.6	25.2	19	72	6.4	1.2
Ziebach	NA	NA	2	D	D	D	3	D	D	D	NA	NA	NA	NA
TENNESSEE	3 377 629	32 203	8 234	120 228	82 626.4	3 975.4	24 808	304 452	50 813.2	4 810.3	4 999	29 626	3 732.0	667.3
Anderson	25 841	212	51	342	105.9	9.9	331	3 923	700.9	60.8	74	336	39.2	6.4
Bedford	3 722	61	43	284	72.3	7.7	145	1 298	207.4	18.1	29	70	9.7	1.3
Benton	656	5	14	99	35.2	2.5	78	746	92.5	9.4	11	28	2.1	0.3
Bledsoe	NA	NA	2	D	D	D	31	162	23.6	1.8	2	D	D	D
Blount	20 685	188	97	1 347	655.2	38.2	385	5 590	1 189.1	99.3	80	443	48.3	7.4
Bradley	37 192	510	93	2 328	1 651.3	51.0	392	4 103	745.7	66.1	72	278	29.4	4.9
Campbell	2 028	46	26	477	117.6	15.0	159	1 551	228.9	21.3	18	106	8.9	1.5
Cannon	850	8	8	D	D	D	30	213	33.3	2.9	4	D	D	D
Carroll	1 040	13	26	210	48.2	4.6	121	950	127.4	11.6	14	30	3.1	0.2
Carter	1 951	17	28	D	D	D	156	1 602	265.1	23.2	19	71	5.8	0.8
Cheatham	20 098	236	20	119	29.3	3.1	75	729	130.0	10.5	14	D	D	D
Chester	5 040	63	10	62	34.4	1.3	65	481	99.8	7.8	5	20	0.8	0.3
Claiborne	15 558	254	17	D	D	D	97	736	111.5	10.2	15	78	5.5	0.9
Clay	NA	NA	2	D	D	D	23	127	19.0	1.7	2	D	D	D
Cocke	385	6	19	167	68.9	5.3	126	1 361	191.3	16.3	22	96	4.1	0.9
Coffee	12 673	224	50	482	127.4	10.7	283	3 127	490.6	43.8	46	134	13.0	2.2
Crockett	590	7	15	D	D	D	58	339	58.4	4.4	3	3	0.5	0.0
Cumberland	7 759	101	35	276	130.5	7.7	222	2 171	368.6	32.4	44	512	43.9	11.2
Davidson	469 117	3 087	1 445	26 012	17 005.2	962.7	3 017	44 452	7 737.6	782.7	866	6 603	1 119.8	173.2
Decatur	238	6	7	36	3.3	0.5	50	371	65.1	5.2	4	7	0.6	0.1
De Kalb	645	10	8	271	96.3	6.6	65	419	67.3	5.7	14	26	1.4	0.3
Dickson	36 339	314	27	471	274.7	11.5	185	2 158	412.9	35.2	32	D	D	D
Dyer	14 003	274	47	572	221.2	15.7	220	2 237	362.4	30.4	33	92	8.0	1.9
Fayette	22 563	162	21	163	102.8	5.1	69	459	77.4	7.0	10	26	2.1	0.4
Fentress	50	4	8	20	4.3	0.4	64	570	77.2	7.1	5	54	3.3	0.8
Franklin	24 147	306	23	145	46.9	3.4	164	1 555	231.0	21.9	20	73	4.2	0.7
Gibson	14 037	151	51	520	333.2	14.4	248	2 221	358.4	33.0	30	76	5.4	0.8
Giles	1 147	49	34	302	93.1	9.5	137	1 218	201.7	16.9	16	78	3.0	0.8
Grainger	0	0	9	46	18.6	1.0	59	385	57.2	4.5	4	11	0.4	0.1
Greene	22 948	282	44	679	283.5	12.4	253	2 871	440.2	39.9	35	97	11.2	1.6
Grundy	NA	NA	4	20	2.1	0.4	57	414	51.5	5.4	8	33	1.1	0.2
Hamblen	24 232	308	70	1 199	460.2	35.1	323	3 595	645.9	54.7	52	184	29.4	3.2
Hamilton	174 580	1 426	694	D	D	D	1 531	20 122	3 269.6	325.8	347	2 045	236.7	58.5
Hancock	93	3	4	25	3.2	0.2	20	100	13.4	1.4	NA	NA	NA	NA
Hardeman	9 826	97	22	D	D	D	103	860	120.7	11.2	10	32	2.6	0.3
Hardin	440	10	18	92	35.9	3.0	131	1 079	183.3	15.4	18	50	3.4	0.6
Hawkins	10 033	138	11	D	D	D	138	1 230	194.9	16.0	19	56	4.0	0.7
Haywood	3 707	59	12	135	114.6	3.4	100	830	146.4	12.0	13	33	2.3	0.4
Henderson	2 633	27	20	150	44.1	3.1	124	1 090	177.7	16.0	8	22	1.4	0.2
Henry	1 876	17	41	625	198.0	16.1	167	1 608	244.6	21.9	20	55	5.0	0.5
Hickman	0	0	8	35	9.2	0.5	66	360	48.8	4.5	8	18	1.0	0.2
Houston	139	2	4	D	D	D	29	164	23.7	2.0	2	D	D	D
Humphreys	1 770	20	11	142	52.0	3.0	77	657	110.8	9.5	3	16	0.7	0.2
Jackson	0	0	1	D	D	D	27	145	20.5	1.4	3	5	0.3	0.1
Jefferson	30 125	320	42	246	73.8	6.2	120	1 415	249.5	21.1	18	53	2.6	0.6
Johnson	3 679	82	3	D	D	D	57	417	67.5	6.3	8	D	D	D
Knox	259 943	2 814	950	12 580	7 507.7	449.4	1 946	28 344	5 029.7	478.9	464	2 822	326.5	65.7
Lake	410	7	9	D	D	D	26	172	20.1	2.0	4	13	1.0	0.1
Lauderdale	7 392	104	26	548	364.9	18.4	100	867	123.9	11.4	10	21	2.6	0.5
Lawrence	524	15	42	296	174.6	8.7	200	1 822	315.2	27.1	22	77	8.6	1.2
Lewis	454	9	8	67	11.6	1.3	59	367	66.3	5.4	6	5	0.4	0.1
Lincoln	670	6	29	211	102.6	3.9	138	1 360	205.6	18.0	25	92	9.8	1.6
Loudon	20 975	197	41	232	93.1	6.0	137	1 407	271.7	21.0	23	46	7.5	1.2
McMinn	4 700	65	32	D	D	D	209	2 119	361.7	30.3	35	120	12.5	2.2
McNairy	1 066	23	21	D	D	D	100	728	117.2	9.9	14	69	6.8	1.1
Macon	748	18	12	84	19.2	1.2	81	582	89.3	7.8	9	37	1.8	0.4
Madison	61 300	593	161	2 186	756.4	60.5	582	8 169	1 196.5	114.9	90	423	43.2	7.4
Marion	21 109	241	15	D	D	D	111	1 232	186.5	15.2	13	68	3.3	0.7

1. Establishments with payroll.

STATE County	Professional, Scientific, and Technical Services[1], 1997				Manufacturing, 1997				Accommodation and Foodservices, 1997			
	Number of Establishments	Number of Employees	Receipts (mil dol)	Annual Payroll (mil dol)	Number of Establishments	Number of Employees	Receipts (mil dol)	Annual Payroll (mil dol)	Number of Establishments	Number of Employees	Sales (mil dol)	Annual Payroll (mil dol)
	147	148	149	150	151	152	153	154	155	156	157	158
SOUTH DAKOTA—Cont'd												
Tripp	12	29	1.9	0.5	NA	NA	NA	NA	19	184	4.9	1.4
Turner	10	22	1.2	0.3	NA	NA	NA	NA	17	92	2.2	0.4
Union	31	80	5.7	2.1	26	D	D	D	37	473	15.7	3.8
Walworth	10	63	3.4	1.1	NA	NA	NA	NA	31	218	6.4	1.5
Yankton	41	203	12.9	4.7	30	2 517	452.2	62.3	67	989	23.6	6.2
Ziebach	NA	NA	NA	NA	NA	NA	NA	NA	2	D	D	D
TENNESSEE	8 812	72 225	6 911.8	2 686.6	7 407	483 823	98 503.1	14 351.9	9 604	197 881	6 790.2	1 880.3
Anderson	180	7 960	934.5	384.6	107	8 559	1 336.2	328.0	129	2 384	71.6	19.9
Bedford	36	233	10.9	3.2	64	5 582	1 302.7	146.6	49	727	19.8	4.9
Benton	11	44	2.0	0.5	17	1 150	97.5	23.7	39	339	10.7	2.1
Bledsoe	5	D	D	D	NA	NA	NA	NA	8	82	1.8	0.5
Blount	122	646	55.4	22.5	126	7 027	2 806.9	251.9	167	3 223	97.3	26.5
Bradley	116	699	48.8	17.8	142	12 974	2 931.7	363.8	138	2 533	81.8	21.8
Campbell	27	108	7.6	2.1	53	1 945	243.7	49.1	60	910	26.6	6.7
Cannon	7	19	2.5	0.2	NA	NA	NA	NA	10	119	2.9	0.8
Carroll	24	66	3.8	1.1	50	3 103	456.7	64.1	45	532	12.0	2.9
Carter	36	130	6.8	2.0	48	1 960	273.4	50.7	47	846	21.9	5.8
Cheatham	20	104	23.2	4.1	42	3 060	579.7	81.9	29	348	11.0	2.8
Chester	6	16	1.3	0.2	24	853	76.0	18.7	19	306	6.6	2.1
Claiborne	23	81	3.0	1.2	34	3 584	317.1	67.1	22	412	12.1	3.2
Clay	4	D	D	D	8	771	85.7	13.7	20	73	3.4	0.8
Cocke	20	43	2.7	0.7	40	2 627	382.8	64.6	52	978	30.5	8.3
Coffee	59	D	D	D	67	5 595	1 082.9	178.4	106	1 949	56.5	15.7
Crockett	10	D	D	D	16	1 241	160.8	26.6	16	82	4.8	0.7
Cumberland	42	168	9.7	3.8	47	2 437	442.9	58.9	75	1 300	39.6	11.4
Davidson	1 694	15 055	1 636.8	605.8	752	31 716	6 721.8	1 100.0	1 407	37 523	1 511.7	426.3
Decatur	11	D	D	D	35	1 113	137.0	21.8	21	175	3.9	0.9
De Kalb	14	54	2.4	0.7	28	2 740	333.9	65.7	22	317	6.6	1.7
Dickson	37	120	8.4	2.9	51	3 574	710.3	102.5	70	1 116	37.7	10.6
Dyer	45	179	12.2	3.2	42	6 404	1 121.4	183.5	67	998	30.2	7.6
Fayette	21	50	4.9	1.4	39	1 193	271.6	33.3	18	196	5.0	1.5
Fentress	12	64	3.7	2.1	31	1 471	141.4	22.5	18	225	6.0	1.5
Franklin	38	142	10.7	3.5	43	1 872	438.2	53.1	50	592	16.9	4.4
Gibson	41	176	9.2	2.9	90	7 607	1 085.6	200.7	62	815	22.1	5.9
Giles	28	127	11.5	5.1	48	3 515	679.7	104.6	38	615	14.7	3.7
Grainger	5	D	D	D	35	1 321	180.9	30.6	10	D	D	D
Greene	49	171	13.4	5.5	107	7 990	1 296.7	198.0	102	1 622	42.1	11.9
Grundy	3	D	D	D	NA	NA	NA	NA	8	60	1.9	0.5
Hamblen	68	309	20.2	7.1	129	14 586	2 039.2	369.6	100	2 269	58.3	15.6
Hamilton	664	4 570	401.5	162.7	515	32 559	5 493.2	991.4	711	13 376	453.2	128.2
Hancock	2	D	D	D	NA	NA	NA	NA	2	D	D	D
Hardeman	11	40	2.2	0.7	37	1 957	274.7	51.4	30	291	8.2	1.8
Hardin	26	78	3.5	1.1	52	2 628	530.2	70.0	49	576	17.2	4.4
Hawkins	32	123	7.1	1.9	50	6 534	1 040.9	219.4	45	788	18.0	4.9
Haywood	12	22	1.8	0.6	23	2 477	425.5	64.1	26	350	11.4	2.9
Henderson	24	48	4.2	0.9	47	4 302	710.9	101.6	36	568	13.5	3.7
Henry	32	191	14.5	4.9	66	3 483	506.1	79.7	61	890	22.1	6.0
Hickman	12	66	3.0	1.3	31	1 017	139.5	22.2	23	D	D	D
Houston	4	D	D	D	NA	NA	NA	NA	12	59	1.9	0.4
Humphreys	11	42	2.1	0.8	29	1 976	854.1	75.4	35	358	13.4	3.2
Jackson	5	D	D	D	8	681	104.9	11.8	7	41	1.4	0.3
Jefferson	31	79	5.1	1.3	56	2 880	434.0	59.7	51	790	24.6	6.4
Johnson	7	D	D	D	19	1 392	206.4	29.2	16	197	5.3	1.5
Knox	937	8 000	724.2	280.7	493	20 782	3 245.5	550.3	769	17 252	550.9	157.6
Lake	4	D	D	D	NA	NA	NA	NA	15	140	3.9	1.2
Lauderdale	15	57	2.1	0.6	22	3 525	353.8	74.4	22	283	7.5	1.8
Lawrence	36	110	6.2	1.9	56	5 501	1 063.8	145.8	45	740	21.6	5.8
Lewis	8	27	2.5	0.5	22	600	101.1	16.4	19	D	D	D
Lincoln	34	92	9.4	2.2	43	2 381	455.0	62.9	44	D	D	D
Loudon	43	132	10.2	2.8	45	3 150	806.7	93.0	56	825	26.3	7.3
McMinn	40	160	11.5	3.9	74	8 791	1 572.2	279.4	84	1 303	41.6	10.2
McNairy	14	29	2.1	0.7	48	2 632	328.1	58.2	28	360	6.8	1.7
Macon	12	26	2.6	0.3	38	1 403	80.1	25.9	19	253	6.2	1.5
Madison	142	993	77.8	36.9	138	12 429	3 473.4	382.5	183	4 110	137.7	37.1
Marion	22	53	2.9	0.8	29	1 726	212.8	38.5	41	673	20.4	5.4

1. Firms subject to federal tax.

Table B. States and Counties — **Health and Other Services and Federal Funds**

STATE County	Health Care and Social Assistance[1], 1997				Other Services[1], 1997				Federal funds and grants, fiscal 2001[2]			
									Expenditures (mil dol)			
										Direct payments for individuals[3]		
	Number of Establishments	Number of Employees	Receipts (mil dol)	Annual Payroll (mil dol)	Number of Establishments	Number of Employees	Receipts (mil dol)	Annual Payroll (mil dol)	Total	Social Security and government retirement	Medicare	Food stamps and Supplemental Security Income
	159	160	161	162	163	164	165	166	167	168	169	170
SOUTH DAKOTA—Cont'd												
Tripp	19	86	4.6	1.9	11	27	1.8	0.4	57.1	14.5	5.3	1.2
Turner	12	84	2.3	1.3	13	24	1.3	0.2	62.6	19.9	7.4	0.6
Union	17	191	9.9	3.3	19	60	4.9	1.3	156.0	25.1	10.6	0.7
Walworth	12	194	7.6	3.9	15	68	4.0	1.1	35.8	11.3	4.1	1.0
Yankton	46	530	37.7	17.8	43	200	11.2	2.8	111.6	41.5	16.8	2.1
Ziebach	NA	NA	NA	NA	1	D	D	D	16.9	1.9	0.7	1.1
TENNESSEE	10 113	155 667	10 753.0	4 659.9	7 767	49 204	2 996.7	918.7	36 757.8	12 131.2	4 942.6	1 277.2
Anderson	156	1 801	117.4	61.3	104	530	26.9	9.4	2 658.7	202.5	72.4	16.7
Bedford	50	439	21.5	8.2	40	378	18.1	5.4	142.9	73.4	27.0	6.3
Benton	20	270	10.7	4.1	15	53	3.4	0.9	97.8	52.1	20.3	3.9
Bledsoe	9	394	19.0	9.3	4	10	0.4	0.1	52.3	19.3	11.0	3.2
Blount	140	1 604	94.2	43.5	140	703	38.6	12.8	464.1	251.2	81.7	17.4
Bradley	201	10 357	442.3	201.0	101	1 304	69.6	26.1	337.3	169.6	71.3	15.7
Campbell	53	590	28.7	11.4	41	144	9.6	2.3	282.9	110.9	48.6	20.9
Cannon	10	192	15.7	6.0	12	33	1.8	0.7	62.3	27.7	17.1	2.0
Carroll	44	687	30.9	12.6	36	112	5.9	1.4	226.5	81.6	38.0	7.0
Carter	68	1 103	58.0	21.4	55	236	14.7	3.4	246.6	124.8	43.5	8.7
Cheatham	26	401	16.0	6.2	17	43	2.9	0.8	100.4	55.2	19.6	2.4
Chester	9	162	6.5	2.7	12	44	2.8	0.6	65.4	26.3	12.0	2.9
Claiborne	30	474	21.5	8.8	27	98	6.1	1.4	179.2	77.1	33.2	13.6
Clay	9	D	D	D	6	18	1.3	0.3	49.7	14.6	9.6	2.4
Cocke	26	324	20.7	6.8	30	103	5.2	1.4	185.9	76.3	31.8	12.9
Coffee	124	2 058	116.4	46.0	83	666	52.0	14.4	590.2	119.6	49.0	10.2
Crockett	15	284	10.2	5.1	22	59	5.4	1.0	89.9	32.4	17.1	2.6
Cumberland	87	764	45.6	18.0	49	179	8.8	2.4	177.0	148.0	47.2	9.2
Davidson	1 462	27 389	2 174.0	925.5	1 092	8 627	530.2	163.9	4 301.0	1 131.7	500.8	113.8
Decatur	18	527	22.5	10.3	20	98	6.5	1.7	69.2	26.2	20.5	3.8
De Kalb	33	426	24.6	10.8	15	60	3.4	1.0	106.9	38.1	21.9	4.3
Dickson	47	1 305	72.4	29.1	51	233	17.5	4.9	174.1	89.3	35.2	7.3
Dyer	85	746	49.5	19.6	64	324	14.1	4.4	209.5	81.0	37.9	10.0
Fayette	15	222	10.6	4.8	17	63	5.7	1.1	142.0	46.0	20.5	7.6
Fentress	26	886	45.8	17.7	20	52	3.5	0.7	109.2	41.7	25.8	7.4
Franklin	53	911	66.7	22.4	38	121	8.3	1.9	204.3	98.6	42.0	5.8
Gibson	81	1 068	45.6	19.4	64	313	15.6	4.9	310.1	122.0	64.3	9.4
Giles	38	561	27.0	10.6	35	115	8.4	1.6	153.6	66.8	30.4	5.2
Grainger	13	345	9.0	3.5	12	30	2.8	0.6	105.4	45.5	20.3	6.8
Greene	93	996	63.5	24.4	75	271	15.3	4.7	355.2	149.9	52.0	16.7
Grundy	10	44	1.9	0.6	9	20	1.8	0.3	80.7	33.6	17.3	6.7
Hamblen	129	1 760	108.8	41.2	76	429	24.3	8.1	269.9	123.0	51.0	13.3
Hamilton	756	10 787	832.6	371.4	546	3 752	221.0	68.0	2 459.2	765.8	322.5	65.9
Hancock	6	106	3.4	1.6	4	9	0.9	0.2	49.0	11.9	8.4	4.6
Hardeman	23	359	15.7	6.5	26	80	6.4	0.9	174.8	56.1	29.5	11.8
Hardin	35	280	14.7	4.7	29	75	6.0	1.3	150.0	59.0	28.9	7.8
Hawkins	38	402	18.2	7.9	36	120	7.7	2.1	258.3	118.5	40.9	11.5
Haywood	18	245	14.8	5.4	23	140	8.7	2.6	134.5	32.8	23.1	7.9
Henderson	30	375	16.9	6.7	38	102	7.5	1.6	159.5	57.7	29.8	5.3
Henry	62	779	36.8	17.2	46	215	10.7	3.1	207.1	89.9	35.5	6.3
Hickman	13	440	15.2	7.9	20	82	6.7	2.0	86.8	44.1	17.1	3.7
Houston	8	281	14.8	5.6	5	7	0.5	0.1	45.5	22.8	8.9	1.8
Humphreys	18	297	14.6	5.7	16	54	4.0	1.0	341.7	43.8	18.1	2.6
Jackson	8	172	7.4	3.0	5	18	1.2	0.3	55.4	20.0	12.8	3.0
Jefferson	39	581	22.5	9.1	39	119	7.5	1.8	210.0	115.0	38.7	7.7
Johnson	15	139	4.1	1.9	14	47	3.0	0.8	108.1	44.0	19.5	11.3
Knox	925	10 391	963.0	451.7	669	4 539	241.1	76.1	2 336.3	860.0	316.6	80.2
Lake	6	D	D	D	4	D	D	D	51.7	14.8	9.4	2.1
Lauderdale	13	209	11.0	4.1	24	78	6.6	1.6	156.9	51.9	28.4	8.6
Lawrence	59	889	48.9	17.4	36	122	7.6	1.8	208.7	97.3	41.9	9.3
Lewis	15	402	13.7	7.1	9	17	1.9	0.5	51.5	22.1	12.9	2.5
Lincoln	41	369	19.6	7.6	38	126	8.7	1.8	150.7	75.1	25.7	6.8
Loudon	43	622	29.5	12.2	41	211	11.9	3.4	214.6	119.3	40.4	6.6
McMinn	77	1 080	61.3	24.7	48	200	10.0	2.9	220.6	111.9	45.9	10.9
McNairy	34	516	23.4	9.4	33	89	6.4	1.4	170.6	63.9	32.1	8.1
Macon	17	221	11.9	3.9	13	34	2.8	0.6	91.7	33.6	20.2	3.8
Madison	205	3 755	293.3	150.0	170	1 062	57.5	18.4	450.2	179.8	80.0	21.4
Marion	33	658	35.8	13.3	21	101	5.9	1.6	137.8	62.4	34.4	7.3

1. Firms subject to federal tax.   2. October 1, 2000 to September 30, 2001.   3. State totals may include programs not allocated by county.

Table B. States and Counties — Federal Funds and Local Government Finances

	Federal funds and grants, fiscal 2001[1] (cont'd)							Local government finances, 1997				
	Expenditures (mil dol) (cont'd)							General revenue				
	Procurement contract awards			Grants[2]						Taxes		
STATE County	Salaries and wages	Defense	Other	Medicaid and other health-related	Nutrition and family welfare	Education	Other	Total (mil dol)	Intergovern-mental (mil dol)	Total (mil dol)	Per capita[3] (dollars) Total	Property
	171	172	173	174	175	176	177	178	179	180	181	182
SOUTH DAKOTA—Cont'd												
Tripp	2.0	0.0	0.6	4.1	0.6	0.6	9.2	11.3	4.3	5.5	805	689
Turner	2.0	0.0	0.5	4.1	0.5	0.3	1.1	13.7	5.0	7.1	823	732
Union	2.6	61.4	14.7	4.7	0.9	0.2	11.9	25.8	7.4	13.6	1 141	961
Walworth	1.8	0.1	0.4	3.8	0.6	0.2	0.5	10.9	4.7	4.7	844	690
Yankton	9.8	1.7	1.7	11.0	1.3	0.4	6.7	34.4	8.8	18.7	889	661
Ziebach	0.3	0.0	0.0	2.1	0.6	1.4	0.7	2.9	1.8	0.9	402	324
TENNESSEE	2 935.1	1 028.4	4 782.5	4 178.5	853.7	547.8	1 446.8	X	X	X	X	X
Anderson	77.3	17.8	2 192.5	51.8	7.5	4.2	6.9	118.4	53.6	38.5	539	413
Bedford	5.2	0.0	0.9	19.7	2.6	2.1	1.8	67.8	22.9	16.9	493	359
Benton	2.6	0.0	0.9	12.8	1.6	1.2	0.1	22.6	12.7	6.2	382	208
Bledsoe	1.0	0.1	0.2	11.0	3.3	0.8	0.8	15.5	10.7	2.9	276	181
Blount	17.2	7.8	7.1	46.1	6.3	5.7	5.9	222.1	55.3	63.0	628	376
Bradley	14.0	0.0	2.9	38.0	7.6	5.4	1.8	190.1	52.9	47.6	594	294
Campbell	5.1	32.2	1.4	43.5	5.8	3.3	3.7	76.2	30.1	17.5	462	261
Cannon	1.6	0.3	0.4	9.0	0.9	0.7	1.3	16.3	9.6	3.8	316	221
Carroll	5.4	41.2	2.8	31.4	2.9	1.7	4.1	42.9	22.5	12.1	418	247
Carter	5.7	0.0	2.2	41.7	4.9	3.4	4.4	73.1	34.4	26.6	501	311
Cheatham	4.7	2.3	1.1	9.3	1.8	1.4	1.7	47.9	21.9	14.8	429	272
Chester	2.3	0.0	0.4	12.5	2.2	0.7	0.4	18.5	10.2	5.3	366	207
Claiborne	3.5	0.0	1.0	36.5	6.2	4.1	1.1	48.7	22.7	9.2	319	194
Clay	1.9	0.8	0.3	14.4	0.9	0.6	2.3	12.3	7.7	2.7	371	305
Cocke	4.1	0.0	1.2	46.5	4.9	2.4	0.9	43.5	24.9	10.9	344	215
Coffee	30.5	304.1	20.7	26.5	3.3	3.1	11.7	76.5	31.3	22.9	503	299
Crockett	2.6	0.6	0.5	17.8	1.8	0.9	0.6	21.4	12.2	6.2	452	262
Cumberland	5.6	0.0	-70.6	25.5	3.4	2.1	3.4	59.7	28.4	20.6	478	224
Davidson	451.1	33.6	307.9	579.4	278.4	216.2	507.8	1 487.5	340.7	693.4	1 299	682
Decatur	2.2	0.0	0.5	11.2	0.9	0.7	1.6	17.4	11.5	3.7	341	172
De Kalb	2.5	2.2	0.7	15.0	1.4	1.1	17.2	20.0	11.8	4.9	308	215
Dickson	6.3	0.1	1.6	20.7	3.3	2.2	0.7	67.1	30.0	24.7	603	327
Dyer	7.3	0.2	1.0	39.0	3.5	4.2	3.4	65.1	28.7	20.8	570	293
Fayette	3.5	0.0	0.8	40.8	5.4	1.9	0.7	36.1	20.5	10.7	363	263
Fentress	2.6	0.2	0.6	25.2	2.3	1.1	1.1	20.5	12.7	5.7	359	183
Franklin	8.9	6.8	2.3	24.3	2.9	2.3	2.8	51.3	23.4	20.0	538	340
Gibson	9.9	9.6	1.7	47.6	5.5	3.1	10.9	93.2	42.7	31.4	652	405
Giles	4.3	0.0	1.3	26.4	2.3	1.5	8.1	40.8	19.3	13.8	484	338
Grainger	3.1	0.0	0.7	24.4	1.9	1.4	0.5	22.7	14.6	4.7	243	151
Greene	10.5	19.4	33.0	49.0	4.9	5.2	3.9	86.6	35.9	34.9	587	279
Grundy	1.7	0.1	0.4	13.3	2.0	1.2	3.1	20.0	12.8	4.2	301	222
Hamblen	10.1	2.9	1.4	41.2	7.4	4.7	4.1	90.2	31.4	40.4	753	379
Hamilton	440.1	12.6	503.9	186.2	33.2	27.9	49.1	976.3	233.3	264.1	896	639
Hancock	0.6	0.0	0.4	18.2	1.6	0.7	0.9	11.3	9.0	1.3	195	165
Hardeman	3.6	14.4	0.9	41.0	5.0	1.9	3.9	38.7	21.6	9.2	381	227
Hardin	6.3	-0.4	1.9	33.0	2.4	1.9	3.9	47.4	20.5	9.5	383	242
Hawkins	16.1	0.1	12.8	47.0	4.2	2.8	1.8	69.2	28.2	23.1	474	310
Haywood	3.2	0.0	1.1	37.7	4.7	1.7	4.0	33.9	18.3	10.0	506	319
Henderson	3.6	11.7	0.7	25.1	1.9	1.5	16.2	34.1	18.2	9.3	389	161
Henry	9.2	9.1	1.3	24.5	2.7	2.2	14.5	77.8	22.6	15.7	530	276
Hickman	4.1	0.0	0.8	13.0	1.4	1.0	0.1	32.2	15.8	6.6	333	225
Houston	1.4	0.0	0.7	7.4	1.4	0.4	0.2	11.1	7.2	2.6	336	210
Humphreys	23.6	2.8	231.2	13.7	1.5	1.1	0.7	32.8	12.2	10.3	613	369
Jackson	1.4	0.0	0.4	14.1	1.0	0.6	1.0	13.1	8.3	3.3	348	241
Jefferson	7.1	0.0	1.6	26.2	3.0	2.0	4.4	56.0	23.1	16.9	402	242
Johnson	2.4	0.0	3.7	21.7	2.1	1.1	0.9	21.4	12.1	5.2	317	230
Knox	228.7	9.9	316.5	215.9	35.6	34.1	103.7	691.5	192.8	368.3	1 007	536
Lake	1.4	0.3	0.6	11.8	1.5	0.6	0.5	10.2	6.3	2.4	297	186
Lauderdale	3.6	0.8	1.0	38.5	4.7	2.0	1.8	41.7	22.2	8.7	361	271
Lawrence	6.4	0.0	1.3	32.4	3.0	2.2	8.3	57.7	28.1	20.4	522	273
Lewis	1.5	0.0	0.2	9.1	1.0	0.7	0.3	15.4	9.3	3.5	324	186
Lincoln	4.1	0.4	1.0	25.4	4.3	1.8	0.8	62.7	21.6	13.2	453	259
Loudon	9.4	0.3	1.5	21.8	2.8	1.8	6.8	54.3	24.5	17.7	464	340
McMinn	6.4	0.0	1.3	30.9	2.6	3.0	0.2	90.9	28.5	24.3	530	354
McNairy	4.9	0.0	1.1	40.0	6.4	1.9	7.2	36.5	18.8	6.6	277	207
Macon	2.3	0.0	0.5	16.5	4.6	1.3	2.9	26.4	14.8	7.6	429	228
Madison	30.1	0.6	6.5	76.3	5.6	6.9	10.3	365.3	62.6	72.3	852	485
Marion	4.4	0.1	0.9	19.9	3.9	2.0	0.7	37.4	19.9	11.6	436	234

1. October 1, 2000 to September 30, 2001.   2. State totals may include programs not allocated by county.   3. Based on the resident population estimated as of July 1 of the year shown.

Table B. States and Counties — Local Government Finances, Government Employment, and Elections

	Local government finances, 1997 (cont'd)									Government employment, 1999			Presidential election, 2000[2]		
	Direct general expenditure							Debt outstanding					Percent of vote cast —		
STATE County	Total (mil dol)	Per capita[1] (dollars)	Percent of total for —					Total (mil dol)	Per capita[1] (dollars)	Federal civilian	Federal military	State and local	Demo-cratic	Republi-can	All other
			Educa-tion	Health and hospitals	Police protec-tion	Public welfare	High-ways								
	183	184	185	186	187	188	189	190	191	192	193	194	195	196	197
SOUTH DAKOTA—Cont'd															
Tripp	12.8	1 858	59.1	0.6	3.4	0.4	14.5	9.6	1 393	43	48	401	28.9	69.0	2.1
Turner	14.2	1 647	62.1	0.8	3.5	1.0	16.6	6.7	779	43	62	444	35.3	62.8	1.9
Union	29.4	2 461	63.9	0.3	3.8	0.2	11.3	17.7	1 483	48	90	606	40.9	56.6	2.6
Walworth	9.8	1 741	53.5	0.3	6.2	1.0	12.3	1.8	328	43	40	407	28.2	68.9	2.9
Yankton	36.0	1 714	53.6	0.8	4.8	0.9	10.7	39.0	1 857	190	153	1 526	41.1	56.1	2.7
Ziebach	2.9	1 285	70.6	0.6	2.5	0.2	12.1	0.0	0	0	16	111	43.6	53.3	3.2
TENNESSEE	X	X	X	X	X	X	X	X	X	50 746	23 702	335 379	47.3	51.1	1.6
Anderson	140.1	1 962	56.9	1.5	4.7	0.1	5.0	180.0	2 519	1 160	274	3 660	47.1	51.0	1.9
Bedford	78.3	2 291	47.5	19.5	3.1	3.9	5.7	41.5	1 215	96	134	2 098	50.3	48.4	1.4
Benton	21.6	1 326	55.6	1.3	5.7	0.0	10.0	12.7	776	77	63	752	58.6	39.4	2.0
Bledsoe	14.2	1 343	58.2	1.2	3.0	1.1	11.2	3.5	326	19	42	1 097	41.8	56.7	1.4
Blount	207.2	2 065	39.4	34.0	4.0	0.2	4.5	112.4	1 120	260	408	5 236	36.1	62.2	1.7
Bradley	187.8	2 341	32.3	35.6	3.6	3.9	3.4	78.5	978	259	326	4 788	29.8	68.5	1.7
Campbell	73.3	1 936	41.6	26.5	2.3	0.1	4.6	33.0	870	86	148	2 080	52.3	46.6	1.2
Cannon	14.7	1 217	56.7	2.5	5.4	0.1	9.9	8.7	726	35	47	421	57.4	41.0	1.7
Carroll	52.8	1 827	69.6	0.2	3.7	0.1	6.7	31.3	1 084	87	113	1 406	48.4	50.5	1.1
Carter	69.5	1 308	58.7	0.8	5.9	0.0	6.3	28.7	541	113	205	2 137	35.2	63.4	1.4
Cheatham	44.5	1 294	62.7	10.3	4.2	0.0	6.3	40.4	1 174	88	139	1 375	48.1	50.4	1.4
Chester	16.7	1 147	58.7	1.8	6.7	0.3	12.3	15.9	1 092	32	57	810	38.3	60.9	0.8
Claiborne	47.3	1 631	48.7	28.9	3.0	0.1	7.9	15.1	522	67	114	1 917	42.7	55.8	1.5
Clay	14.3	1 951	42.8	8.2	12.9	0.1	12.0	5.5	753	48	28	393	56.1	42.6	1.3
Cocke	48.8	1 545	51.2	0.7	4.3	0.0	8.7	21.9	693	73	124	1 467	37.8	60.4	1.8
Coffee	84.4	1 853	56.0	9.4	4.7	0.1	5.2	54.1	1 188	385	292	2 820	49.1	49.4	1.4
Crockett	20.2	1 466	58.3	2.5	3.6	1.3	9.8	19.2	1 390	48	54	617	49.7	49.2	1.1
Cumberland	54.9	1 274	50.6	2.0	5.2	0.5	6.6	32.2	746	96	174	1 676	40.2	57.8	2.0
Davidson	1 604.0	3 005	27.5	7.2	6.0	1.1	2.5	3 185.5	5 969	8 290	2 643	38 591	57.8	40.3	1.9
Decatur	14.3	1 329	58.7	0.3	4.4	0.2	12.0	5.5	512	36	41	698	52.1	46.8	1.0
De Kalb	17.2	1 090	63.0	2.0	6.0	2.5	8.8	15.6	990	42	62	713	60.1	38.5	1.4
Dickson	67.0	1 633	51.1	1.7	5.9	3.3	7.3	74.3	1 811	105	165	2 304	53.6	45.1	1.4
Dyer	79.2	2 172	54.2	1.1	6.3	0.3	9.8	37.0	1 014	113	141	2 403	45.8	53.1	1.1
Fayette	34.2	1 157	58.4	4.6	5.6	0.0	11.2	5.7	192	61	121	1 443	43.7	55.5	0.8
Fentress	20.5	1 291	62.7	2.2	3.1	0.0	11.0	10.9	687	41	63	808	41.9	56.7	1.4
Franklin	46.4	1 249	57.3	0.6	5.5	0.0	8.8	34.5	927	153	145	1 605	53.3	44.7	2.1
Gibson	97.2	2 021	56.2	1.5	5.1	0.1	6.7	52.9	1 100	163	187	2 435	50.6	48.4	1.1
Giles	41.6	1 460	50.8	2.6	5.0	0.1	11.9	24.9	874	81	112	1 323	54.9	43.5	1.6
Grainger	20.2	1 040	68.8	2.2	3.4	0.8	9.0	5.0	255	55	78	692	38.1	60.5	1.4
Greene	85.6	1 440	57.9	2.4	4.1	0.3	11.7	31.6	532	237	234	3 416	38.0	60.2	1.8
Grundy	19.4	1 386	59.6	1.1	3.3	0.2	14.0	18.7	1 341	22	54	633	64.6	33.8	1.6
Hamblen	93.1	1 733	47.9	13.3	5.6	0.2	5.9	41.3	769	179	209	3 236	38.4	60.0	1.6
Hamilton	1 000.3	3 394	23.3	31.0	4.8	4.4	3.3	981.9	3 332	6 268	1 180	19 428	43.0	55.3	1.7
Hancock	11.3	1 655	60.9	3.3	2.6	0.2	14.0	2.6	385	10	26	420	33.3	64.7	2.0
Hardeman	37.8	1 565	54.1	2.8	6.6	0.2	8.8	17.1	709	61	94	1 951	56.3	42.4	1.3
Hardin	43.3	1 748	51.4	20.9	3.4	0.1	5.7	4.6	186	123	97	1 465	42.5	56.4	1.1
Hawkins	64.1	1 315	53.4	13.8	3.9	0.0	8.5	35.3	723	258	193	1 991	39.5	58.9	1.6
Haywood	34.5	1 744	52.5	3.3	4.8	0.0	11.4	8.0	402	54	75	1 105	60.0	39.4	0.6
Henderson	29.6	1 234	60.2	0.3	4.7	0.0	10.7	26.8	1 115	59	95	1 025	37.7	61.4	0.9
Henry	76.3	2 570	35.6	34.7	3.9	0.0	7.4	23.7	798	123	133	2 034	49.5	48.3	2.2
Hickman	30.3	1 524	48.2	21.3	3.7	0.0	8.5	15.2	764	67	82	1 213	58.4	40.1	1.5
Houston	11.1	1 426	57.1	0.2	1.8	0.0	15.1	3.6	464	16	30	449	66.5	31.8	1.7
Humphreys	29.1	1 730	47.4	0.7	3.9	0.0	8.7	84.4	5 027	386	66	833	62.9	35.7	1.4
Jackson	13.3	1 390	55.5	2.9	4.6	0.0	13.7	3.6	372	28	37	393	69.5	29.1	1.4
Jefferson	54.0	1 284	49.3	19.4	4.9	0.6	5.8	28.7	683	126	173	1 762	37.1	61.5	1.5
Johnson	19.7	1 191	43.8	0.8	3.3	0.0	8.3	7.4	445	43	64	682	32.0	66.1	1.9
Knox	771.7	2 111	40.6	2.9	5.2	1.4	6.2	720.8	1 971	3 804	1 552	31 521	40.5	57.7	1.9
Lake	10.9	1 333	43.1	5.9	6.6	0.0	12.4	4.5	553	19	31	654	63.8	35.1	1.1
Lauderdale	40.4	1 672	64.3	0.6	5.2	0.4	7.7	30.0	1 243	66	93	1 726	55.4	43.7	0.9
Lawrence	58.0	1 483	48.7	1.8	6.7	0.1	15.1	60.3	1 543	118	152	1 859	45.9	52.6	1.5
Lewis	13.7	1 275	55.2	0.2	3.6	0.0	4.2	10.0	932	24	43	554	51.6	46.1	2.3
Lincoln	65.0	2 224	36.8	35.2	3.0	0.0	5.4	49.3	1 687	69	115	2 342	47.5	51.0	1.6
Loudon	51.4	1 345	55.0	0.3	6.7	0.0	5.4	96.6	2 526	160	153	1 562	36.0	62.6	1.4
McMinn	88.9	1 937	39.4	22.5	3.1	3.6	6.1	71.2	1 552	137	178	2 180	37.0	61.2	1.9
McNairy	34.9	1 473	48.8	20.9	3.9	0.0	6.9	26.2	1 108	91	94	1 064	44.5	54.5	1.0
Macon	29.8	1 677	63.6	2.8	4.7	0.0	6.2	19.8	1 116	38	71	885	47.1	51.9	1.1
Madison	398.3	4 697	18.5	50.1	2.6	0.0	2.5	226.4	2 670	546	337	9 913	46.5	52.6	0.8
Marion	34.6	1 293	60.0	3.0	6.7	0.0	6.9	10.5	394	83	103	1 065	53.1	45.4	1.5

1. Based on the resident population estimated as of July 1 of the year shown.   2. Data subject to copyright.

Table B. States and Counties — **Land Area and Population**

STATE/ County code	MSA/ PMSA/ NECMA code[1]	County Type[2]	STATE County	Land area,[3] (sq km) 2000	Total persons	Rank	Per square kilometer	White	Black	Am. Indian, Alaska Native	Asian and Pacific Islander	Percent Hispanic[4]	Under 5 years	5 to 17 years	18 to 24 years	25 to 34 years	35 to 44 years	45 to 54 years
								Race alone or in combination (percent)					Age (percent)					
				1	2	3	4	5	6	7	8	9	10	11	12	13	14	15
			TENNESSEE—Cont'd															
47 117	...	6	Marshall	972	26 767	1 491	27.5	90.1	8.1	0.6	0.4	2.9	6.5	19.0	8.7	13.7	16.3	14.1
47 119	...	4	Maury	1 587	69 498	711	43.8	83.5	14.7	0.7	0.6	3.3	6.9	19.4	8.7	12.9	16.9	14.5
47 121	...	8	Meigs	505	11 086	2 358	22.0	98.2	1.3	0.6	0.3	0.6	6.9	18.2	8.1	14.1	14.8	14.6
47 123	...	6	Monroe	1 644	38 961	1 140	23.7	96.5	2.5	1.1	0.5	1.8	6.4	18.4	8.7	13.9	14.7	13.7
47 125	1660	3	Montgomery	1 397	134 768	400	96.5	75.5	20.4	1.2	3.1	5.2	8.5	19.9	12.3	18.0	16.3	10.7
47 127	...	9	Moore	335	5 740	2 807	17.1	96.4	2.9	0.5	0.2	0.8	5.8	17.6	8.4	11.9	14.5	14.6
47 129	...	8	Morgan	1 352	19 757	1 806	14.6	97.3	2.2	0.6	0.2	0.6	5.8	17.4	8.8	15.3	16.6	14.5
47 131	...	7	Obion	1 411	32 450	1 335	23.0	88.8	10.1	0.4	0.4	1.9	6.4	17.0	8.4	13.1	14.5	14.6
47 133	...	7	Overton	1 122	20 118	1 788	17.9	99.1	0.3	0.7	0.2	0.7	6.2	16.9	8.4	13.3	14.5	14.1
47 135	...	9	Perry	1 075	7 631	2 634	7.1	97.4	1.8	1.0	0.2	0.8	6.1	18.3	7.5	11.9	13.5	14.5
47 137	...	9	Pickett	422	4 945	2 852	11.7	99.6	0.2	0.5	0.0	0.8	5.8	15.6	8.6	11.2	13.4	14.3
47 139	...	9	Polk	1 127	16 050	2 018	14.2	99.4	0.2	1.1	0.2	0.7	6.4	16.2	8.2	13.7	14.8	14.3
47 141	...	5	Putnam	1 039	62 315	780	60.0	95.4	1.9	0.6	1.2	3.0	6.0	16.2	14.7	13.8	14.0	12.5
47 143	...	6	Rhea	818	28 400	1 435	34.7	96.4	2.3	1.0	0.5	1.7	6.2	17.6	10.0	12.8	14.7	13.9
47 145	...	4	Roane	935	51 910	894	55.5	96.4	3.0	1.0	0.6	0.7	5.9	16.5	7.5	12.1	14.8	15.5
47 147	5360	2	Robertson	1 234	54 433	866	44.1	89.9	8.8	0.7	0.4	2.7	6.8	20.0	8.5	14.1	17.3	13.7
47 149	5360	2	Rutherford	1 603	182 023	302	113.6	86.7	9.9	0.6	2.3	2.8	7.5	18.9	13.2	16.4	17.1	12.4
47 151	...	6	Scott	1 378	21 127	1 729	15.3	99.4	0.1	1.0	0.2	0.6	7.0	19.1	10.3	14.1	14.6	13.6
47 153	...	6	Sequatchie	689	11 370	2 343	16.5	99.1	0.2	0.7	0.2	0.8	6.9	17.7	8.4	14.5	15.4	14.0
47 155	3840	2	Sevier	1 534	71 170	698	46.4	98.1	0.7	0.9	0.7	1.2	6.0	17.0	8.3	13.6	16.2	15.0
47 157	4920	0	Shelby	1 954	897 472	44	459.3	48.1	49.0	0.5	2.0	2.6	7.6	20.6	9.7	15.1	16.0	13.5
47 159	...	8	Smith	814	17 712	1 916	21.8	96.3	2.7	0.9	0.3	1.1	6.5	19.0	8.0	13.2	16.8	13.7
47 161	...	8	Stewart	1 187	12 370	2 274	10.4	96.3	1.4	1.3	1.8	1.0	5.9	18.1	7.5	12.5	15.3	14.1
47 163	3660	2	Sullivan	1 070	153 048	347	143.0	97.2	2.1	0.6	0.5	0.7	5.6	16.2	7.3	13.1	15.3	14.9
47 165	5360	2	Sumner	1 371	130 449	412	95.1	92.4	6.1	0.7	0.9	1.8	6.8	19.6	8.0	13.7	17.0	14.5
47 167	4920	1	Tipton	1 190	51 271	902	43.1	78.8	20.2	0.9	0.7	1.2	7.0	22.3	8.6	13.0	17.4	13.0
47 169	...	6	Trousdale	296	7 259	2 660	24.5	87.3	11.6	0.6	0.1	1.5	6.0	18.2	8.5	12.5	15.5	14.3
47 171	3660	2	Unicoi	482	17 667	1 918	36.7	98.6	0.2	0.6	0.2	1.9	5.5	15.0	7.5	12.5	15.0	14.8
47 173	3840	2	Union	579	17 808	1 909	30.8	99.3	0.1	0.9	0.3	0.8	6.7	19.0	8.9	14.0	17.0	13.5
47 175	...	9	Van Buren	708	5 508	2 817	7.8	99.5	0.1	0.6	0.1	0.3	5.9	17.0	9.2	12.3	15.2	15.1
47 177	...	7	Warren	1 121	38 276	1 157	34.1	92.5	3.4	0.6	0.6	4.9	6.6	17.7	9.1	14.2	15.2	13.6
47 179	3660	2	Washington	845	107 198	499	126.9	94.6	4.2	0.6	0.9	1.4	5.9	15.4	10.8	14.6	15.4	14.0
47 181	...	8	Wayne	1 901	16 842	1 965	8.9	92.5	6.9	0.6	0.3	0.8	5.1	16.3	9.1	15.6	16.1	13.5
47 183	...	7	Weakley	1 503	34 895	1 255	23.2	91.0	7.2	0.5	1.5	1.2	5.8	15.9	15.9	12.8	13.3	12.6
47 185	...	7	White	975	23 102	1 638	23.7	97.4	1.8	0.6	0.5	1.0	6.0	17.5	7.9	12.8	15.0	14.0
47 187	5360	2	Williamson	1 509	126 638	427	83.9	92.3	5.4	0.4	1.5	2.5	7.2	22.3	6.2	12.2	19.4	16.8
47 189	5360	2	Wilson	1 478	88 809	586	60.1	92.4	6.6	0.7	0.7	1.3	6.8	19.4	7.7	13.7	18.0	14.9
48 000	...	X	**TEXAS**	678 051	20 851 820	X	30.8	73.1	12.0	1.0	3.2	32.0	7.8	20.4	10.5	15.2	15.9	12.5
48 001	...	6	Anderson	2 773	55 109	856	19.9	67.3	23.8	1.0	0.7	12.2	5.5	15.2	9.3	18.5	19.2	12.8
48 003	...	6	Andrews	3 887	13 004	2 233	3.3	79.8	1.9	1.4	0.9	40.0	7.4	24.2	8.1	11.3	16.0	12.0
48 005	...	5	Angelina	2 076	80 130	640	38.6	76.4	15.0	0.7	0.8	14.3	7.7	20.0	9.7	13.8	14.8	12.6
48 007	...	6	Aransas	652	22 497	1 671	34.5	89.6	1.7	1.4	3.2	20.3	5.5	18.3	6.2	9.5	13.7	14.0
48 009	9080	3	Archer	2 356	8 854	2 538	3.8	96.8	0.2	1.4	0.3	4.9	6.3	21.9	7.0	10.0	17.4	13.5
48 011	...	8	Armstrong	2 366	2 148	3 056	0.9	96.3	0.3	1.1	0.0	5.4	5.6	20.4	6.1	10.2	14.6	13.3
48 013	...	6	Atascosa	3 191	38 628	1 147	12.1	76.5	0.7	1.2	0.6	58.6	8.3	23.5	8.9	12.9	14.7	12.6
48 015	...	6	Austin	1 690	23 590	1 606	14.0	81.6	11.1	0.7	0.4	16.1	6.6	20.4	8.1	11.1	15.2	14.1
48 017	...	7	Bailey	2 141	6 594	2 728	3.1	69.1	1.5	1.2	0.3	47.3	8.1	22.2	8.6	11.3	13.5	12.0
48 019	...	8	Bandera	2 051	17 645	1 920	8.6	95.8	0.5	1.7	0.6	13.5	5.5	19.1	5.8	9.6	15.1	16.3
48 021	0640	2	Bastrop	2 301	57 733	827	25.1	82.1	9.2	1.4	0.8	24.0	7.6	20.4	7.6	13.8	17.5	14.5
48 023	...	7	Baylor	2 255	4 093	2 909	1.8	92.1	3.5	1.0	0.8	9.3	4.9	18.5	5.5	8.3	13.1	13.5
48 025	...	6	Bee	2 280	32 359	1 338	14.2	69.7	10.1	0.7	0.9	53.9	6.1	17.3	13.3	19.6	15.7	10.8
48 027	3810	2	Bell	2 745	237 974	244	86.7	66.3	21.9	1.5	4.4	16.7	8.9	20.0	13.4	17.1	14.9	10.6
48 029	7240	0	Bexar	3 229	1 392 931	24	431.4	72.0	7.7	1.3	2.4	54.3	7.9	20.6	10.7	15.1	15.5	12.4
48 031	...	8	Blanco	1 842	8 418	2 572	4.6	92.6	0.9	1.5	0.3	15.3	6.2	18.2	6.2	10.5	15.1	15.8
48 033	...	9	Borden	2 328	729	3 130	0.3	93.3	0.1	1.2	0.3	11.9	3.7	20.9	6.7	9.6	17.8	11.8
48 035	...	6	Bosque	2 562	17 204	1 940	6.7	92.1	2.1	1.3	0.3	12.2	5.7	18.7	6.2	9.9	13.9	13.2
48 037	8360	3	Bowie	2 300	89 306	578	38.8	74.2	23.8	1.2	0.7	4.5	6.4	18.4	9.4	13.8	15.7	13.5
48 039	1145	1	Brazoria	3 591	241 767	238	67.3	79.1	8.8	1.0	2.4	22.8	7.7	20.8	8.6	14.4	18.0	13.6
48 041	1260	3	Brazos	1 517	152 415	350	100.5	76.2	11.0	0.8	4.5	17.9	6.2	15.3	32.0	14.5	11.4	8.6
48 043	...	7	Brewster	16 039	8 866	2 536	0.6	83.8	1.6	1.7	0.8	43.6	5.4	16.7	14.8	11.9	12.6	14.0
48 045	...	9	Briscoe	2 332	1 790	3 079	0.8	85.7	0.7	0.4	0.4	22.7	6.4	20.7	6.8	9.2	12.8	14.3
48 047	...	7	Brooks	2 443	7 976	2 608	3.3	77.4	0.3	0.6	0.2	91.6	8.3	23.3	8.9	10.3	13.1	11.9
48 049	...	7	Brown	2 445	37 674	1 170	15.4	88.9	4.3	1.1	0.6	15.4	6.2	19.6	10.1	11.0	13.7	12.9
48 051	...	6	Burleson	1 724	16 470	1 991	9.6	75.9	15.4	0.9	0.4	14.6	6.7	20.2	8.0	11.2	14.6	13.5
48 053	...	6	Burnet	2 580	34 147	1 277	13.2	91.1	1.7	1.3	0.6	14.8	6.5	18.0	7.0	10.7	15.3	13.3

1. MSA = Metropolitan Statistical Area. PMSA = Primary MSA. NECMA = New England County Metropolitan Area. See Appendix A for explanation of these concepts. See Appendix B for list of metropolitan areas identified by type, with component counties. 2. County typology code from the Economic Research Service of USDA. See Appendix A for definition. 3. Dry land or land partially or temporarily covered by water. 4. Hispanic persons may be of any race.

Table B. States and Counties — **Population and Households**

STATE County	55 to 64 years	65 to 74 years	75 years and over	Percent female	2001	1990	1990–2000	2000–2001	Births	Deaths	Net migration	Number	Percent change, 1990–2000	Persons per household	Female family householder[1]	One person
	16	17	18	19	20	21	22	23	24	25	26	27	28	29	30	31
TENNESSEE—Cont'd																
Marshall	9.1	6.5	6.1	51.2	27 106	21 539	24.3	1.3	425	315	231	10 307	24.7	2.56	11.6	23.9
Maury	8.7	6.5	5.5	51.4	70 376	54 812	26.8	1.3	1 222	906	576	26 444	28.3	2.58	12.9	23.2
Meigs	11.7	6.8	4.7	50.0	11 194	8 033	38.0	1.0	188	114	35	4 304	43.7	2.55	9.9	20.8
Monroe	11.1	7.2	6.0	50.7	39 846	30 541	27.6	2.3	649	489	722	15 329	34.9	2.51	10.0	23.3
Montgomery	6.5	4.6	3.2	49.7	135 023	100 498	34.1	0.2	3 129	1 037	-1 806	48 330	40.7	2.70	12.2	20.2
Moore	11.8	8.5	7.0	50.5	5 887	4 696	22.2	2.6	70	58	131	2 211	27.5	2.55	7.6	21.4
Morgan	10.0	6.5	5.0	46.7	20 003	17 300	14.2	1.2	266	270	251	6 990	19.7	2.58	10.3	22.1
Obion	10.8	7.8	7.4	51.7	32 346	31 717	2.3	-0.3	516	494	-114	13 182	6.2	2.42	11.1	25.7
Overton	11.8	8.3	6.7	51.0	20 186	17 636	14.1	0.3	267	316	121	8 110	20.4	2.46	9.9	24.1
Perry	11.8	9.5	6.9	50.2	7 504	6 612	15.4	-1.7	132	117	-145	3 023	20.3	2.48	8.8	25.2
Pickett	13.3	10.2	7.5	50.8	5 048	4 548	8.7	2.1	82	71	90	2 091	17.1	2.33	7.8	27.2
Polk	12.1	8.2	6.2	50.4	16 226	13 643	17.6	1.1	247	270	199	6 448	26.6	2.46	9.0	23.3
Putnam	9.4	7.2	6.1	50.4	63 188	51 373	21.3	1.4	1 010	777	654	24 865	25.9	2.40	9.8	27.1
Rhea	11.1	7.4	6.4	51.5	28 608	24 344	16.7	0.7	499	354	74	11 184	21.8	2.46	11.2	23.8
Roane	11.7	8.9	7.2	51.6	52 033	47 227	9.9	0.2	705	726	168	21 200	14.9	2.42	10.1	25.0
Robertson	8.8	6.2	4.6	50.3	56 083	41 492	31.2	3.0	982	586	1 241	19 906	34.5	2.71	11.2	18.6
Rutherford	7.0	4.3	3.2	50.2	190 143	118 570	53.5	4.5	3 379	1 303	5 931	66 443	57.8	2.65	11.2	20.8
Scott	10.0	6.2	5.1	50.7	21 548	18 358	15.1	2.0	386	252	288	8 203	25.5	2.55	11.8	24.3
Sequatchie	10.8	7.0	5.2	50.4	11 616	8 863	28.3	2.2	185	138	196	4 463	35.8	2.52	11.2	22.4
Sevier	11.3	7.5	5.1	51.0	73 703	51 050	39.4	3.6	1 080	765	2 178	28 467	45.8	2.48	10.1	22.0
Shelby	7.5	5.3	4.6	52.2	896 013	826 330	8.6	-0.2	20 086	10 005	-11 485	338 366	11.5	2.60	20.1	27.0
Smith	9.4	7.0	6.4	50.8	17 988	14 143	25.2	1.6	270	262	267	6 878	28.4	2.55	9.8	23.4
Stewart	11.2	8.5	6.4	50.2	12 650	9 479	30.5	2.3	185	183	275	4 930	34.0	2.49	8.1	23.1
Sullivan	11.7	8.7	7.2	51.7	152 787	143 596	6.6	-0.2	2 163	2 055	-294	63 556	12.0	2.36	10.2	26.4
Sumner	9.7	5.9	4.8	51.0	134 336	103 281	26.3	3.0	2 179	1 307	2 976	48 941	32.8	2.64	10.8	20.3
Tipton	8.8	5.6	4.3	50.8	52 956	37 568	36.5	3.3	893	480	1 251	18 106	38.9	2.78	13.9	18.7
Trousdale	10.6	7.3	7.0	50.8	7 345	5 920	22.6	1.2	122	111	71	2 780	23.0	2.55	11.3	23.0
Unicoi	11.7	9.4	8.7	51.2	17 713	16 549	6.8	0.3	255	277	75	7 516	13.5	2.31	9.5	27.5
Union	10.0	6.5	4.3	50.3	18 414	13 694	30.0	3.4	285	193	506	6 742	36.7	2.62	10.5	19.8
Van Buren	11.2	8.3	5.7	50.2	5 477	4 846	13.7	-0.6	73	92	-9	2 180	21.2	2.49	11.0	21.9
Warren	9.8	7.6	6.3	50.9	38 565	32 992	16.0	0.8	649	513	169	15 181	19.7	2.47	11.2	25.0
Washington	10.0	7.3	6.6	51.3	108 380	92 336	16.1	1.1	1 635	1 370	943	44 195	23.4	2.33	10.5	27.8
Wayne	10.7	7.5	6.1	45.1	16 845	13 935	20.9	0.0	203	226	28	5 936	14.7	2.47	10.1	24.4
Weakley	9.3	7.1	7.3	51.5	34 644	31 972	9.1	-0.7	490	495	-235	13 599	13.4	2.38	9.5	27.0
White	11.4	8.5	6.8	51.0	23 364	20 090	15.0	1.1	344	372	291	9 229	19.5	2.47	10.8	23.4
Williamson	8.2	4.5	3.3	50.8	133 883	81 021	56.3	5.7	2 064	869	5 845	44 725	60.1	2.81	7.8	16.6
Wilson	9.8	5.5	4.2	50.6	91 696	67 675	31.2	3.3	1 474	835	2 219	32 798	36.3	2.67	10.1	18.1
TEXAS	7.7	5.5	4.5	50.4	21 325 018	16 986 335	22.8	2.3	447 418	185 621	209 561	7 393 354	21.8	2.74	12.7	23.7
Anderson	7.8	6.1	5.6	39.1	55 329	48 024	14.8	0.4	888	719	77	15 678	10.2	2.58	13.2	24.8
Andrews	8.5	7.2	5.3	50.9	12 795	14 338	-9.3	-1.6	270	147	-339	4 601	-3.3	2.81	9.5	21.8
Angelina	8.9	6.7	5.9	50.3	80 513	69 884	14.7	0.5	1 673	1 029	-240	28 685	14.7	2.70	12.3	22.8
Aransas	13.1	11.8	7.9	50.3	22 695	17 892	25.7	0.9	286	342	260	9 132	31.6	2.43	9.4	25.3
Archer	9.9	7.9	6.0	50.0	8 926	7 973	11.0	0.8	153	95	9	3 345	13.1	2.63	7.2	21.9
Armstrong	10.5	8.8	10.4	51.8	2 129	2 021	6.3	-0.9	26	29	-17	802	4.4	2.58	6.1	21.4
Atascosa	8.3	6.0	4.8	50.9	40 264	30 533	26.5	4.2	712	394	1 294	12 816	28.9	2.99	13.0	18.9
Austin	9.7	7.4	7.4	50.9	24 454	19 832	18.9	3.7	469	304	689	8 747	17.0	2.67	9.6	22.8
Bailey	9.2	8.2	7.0	51.0	6 571	7 064	-6.7	-0.3	153	70	-108	2 348	-4.3	2.78	7.5	22.3
Bandera	12.3	9.9	6.2	50.2	18 553	10 562	67.1	5.1	226	189	850	7 010	67.7	2.49	7.3	23.2
Bastrop	8.3	5.8	4.5	48.7	62 059	38 263	50.9	7.5	1 046	514	3 704	20 097	50.2	2.77	10.5	21.5
Baylor	12.1	11.5	12.5	52.8	3 986	4 385	-6.7	-2.6	49	81	-77	1 791	-6.0	2.26	8.2	33.3
Bee	7.0	5.6	4.5	40.3	32 314	25 135	28.7	-0.1	527	263	-298	9 061	5.5	2.74	14.8	23.7
Bell	6.4	4.7	4.1	49.8	239 551	191 073	24.5	0.7	6 683	1 873	-3 113	85 507	27.2	2.68	12.3	22.3
Bexar	7.5	5.6	4.8	51.4	1 417 501	1 185 394	17.5	1.8	30 036	12 655	8 049	488 942	19.5	2.78	15.5	24.0
Blanco	11.3	8.2	8.5	50.0	8 767	5 972	41.0	4.1	111	106	338	3 303	41.3	2.50	7.2	24.0
Borden	13.2	10.7	5.6	49.2	677	799	-8.8	-7.1	5	7	-52	292	-0.7	2.50	6.2	22.6
Bosque	11.8	9.6	10.9	51.1	17 624	15 125	13.7	2.4	266	321	471	6 726	12.3	2.48	8.2	25.4
Bowie	9.0	7.1	6.7	49.6	89 961	81 665	9.4	0.7	1 562	1 219	342	33 058	8.1	2.50	15.0	26.0
Brazoria	7.9	5.3	3.6	48.4	249 832	191 707	26.1	3.3	4 762	1 925	5 197	81 954	28.0	2.82	10.4	19.1
Brazos	5.2	3.5	3.2	49.5	151 660	121 862	25.1	-0.5	2 751	826	-2 730	55 202	26.2	2.52	10.0	25.5
Brewster	9.8	8.1	6.5	50.2	8 859	8 653	2.5	-0.1	147	98	-55	3 669	9.5	2.31	10.0	32.8
Briscoe	10.7	10.1	9.2	51.3	1 710	1 971	-9.2	-4.5	32	23	-93	724	-8.2	2.47	7.6	27.9
Brooks	9.8	8.3	6.1	51.5	7 683	8 204	-2.8	-3.7	159	131	-327	2 711	1.4	2.92	19.1	21.4
Brown	10.0	8.4	8.1	50.7	37 774	34 371	9.6	0.3	602	558	71	14 306	9.2	2.48	10.9	26.5
Burleson	9.7	8.9	7.2	51.4	16 628	13 625	20.9	1.0	311	176	26	6 363	22.9	2.57	11.4	24.9
Burnet	11.2	10.0	7.9	51.6	36 151	22 677	50.6	5.9	542	438	1 860	13 133	45.0	2.53	8.6	22.5

1. No spouse present.

Table B. States and Counties — Vital Statistics, Health Resources, and Crime

STATE County	Births, average 1997-1999 Total	Rate[1]	Deaths, average 1997-1999 Number Total	Number Infant[2]	Rate Total[1]	Rate Infant[3]	Physicians,[4] 2000 Number	Rate[5]	Hospitals,[4] 1998 Number	Beds Number	Beds Rate[5]	Medicare enrollees 2000	Serious crimes known to police, 2000[6] Total Number	Rate[7]
	32	33	34	35	36	37	38	39	40	41	42	43	44	45
TENNESSEE—Cont'd														
Marshall	346	13.2	268	NA	10.3	NA	13	49	1	96	365	3 854	801	2 992
Maury	952	13.7	652	NA	9.4	NA	132	190	1	302	434	10 186	3 517	5 061
Meigs	129	12.9	90	NA	9.1	NA	3	27	0	0	0	1 720	215	1 939
Monroe	468	13.4	383	NA	11.0	NA	25	64	1	59	169	6 238	1 385	3 555
Montgomery	2 485	19.6	791	19	6.2	7.5	169	125	1	164	129	11 870	5 676	4 212
Moore	54	10.4	50	NA	9.7	NA	0	0	0	0	0	565	104	1 812
Morgan	219	11.8	191	NA	10.3	NA	5	25	0	0	0	2 502	164	830
Obion	392	12.2	395	NA	12.3	NA	42	129	1	133	413	6 125	1 175	3 621
Overton	231	11.9	236	NA	12.1	NA	13	65	1	79	404	3 541	232	1 153
Perry	100	13.3	97	NA	13.0	NA	4	52	1	74	986	1 443	124	1 625
Pickett	53	11.4	53	NA	11.3	NA	2	40	0	0	0	827	11	222
Polk	186	12.5	190	NA	12.8	NA	11	69	1	40	269	3 152	201	1 252
Putnam	790	13.4	591	NA	10.0	NA	108	173	1	116	196	11 223	2 227	3 574
Rhea	367	13.1	286	NA	10.2	NA	10	35	1	131	471	4 970	730	2 570
Roane	567	11.3	568	NA	11.4	NA	39	75	2	165	330	10 342	1 535	2 957
Robertson	780	14.7	457	NA	8.6	NA	37	68	1	115	217	7 104	2 289	4 205
Rutherford	2 608	15.7	1 014	18	6.1	6.9	226	124	1	221	133	15 447	7 518	4 130
Scott	305	15.2	207	NA	10.3	NA	16	76	1	97	484	3 458	496	2 348
Sequatchie	143	13.6	105	NA	10.0	NA	8	70	0	0	0	1 487	310	2 726
Sevier	829	12.9	586	NA	9.1	NA	61	86	1	46	71	10 855	3 257	4 576
Shelby	14 548	16.7	7 882	188	9.1	12.9	2 290	255	13	4 940	569	105 795	67 712	7 545
Smith	215	13.1	194	NA	11.8	NA	17	96	2	78	477	2 823	336	1 897
Stewart	131	11.4	135	NA	11.7	NA	4	32	0	0	0	2 245	132	1 067
Sullivan	1 727	11.5	1 621	15	10.8	8.7	469	306	3	802	532	29 517	5 039	3 292
Sumner	1 685	13.6	1 003	9	8.1	5.1	126	97	3	242	195	15 404	4 158	3 187
Tipton	727	15.4	405	7	8.6	10.1	32	62	1	100	211	5 992	1 841	3 591
Trousdale	80	11.7	79	NA	11.6	NA	8	110	1	26	380	1 063	222	3 058
Unicoi	205	11.8	212	NA	12.3	NA	16	91	1	48	279	3 941	381	2 157
Union	220	13.5	155	NA	9.5	NA	1	6	0	0	0	2 153	324	2 022
Van Buren	55	10.8	58	NA	11.4	NA	1	18	0	0	0	707	73	1 325
Warren	475	13.1	383	NA	10.6	NA	37	97	1	142	393	6 631	1 391	3 634
Washington	1 269	12.4	1 070	9	10.5	6.8	448	418	3	591	578	18 432	5 029	4 691
Wayne	185	11.2	168	NA	10.2	NA	10	59	1	54	327	2 505	192	1 140
Weakley	393	11.9	372	NA	11.3	NA	31	89	1	65	197	5 418	873	2 502
White	281	12.4	267	NA	11.8	NA	15	65	1	60	264	4 467	858	3 714
Williamson	1 558	13.2	626	NA	5.3	NA	237	187	1	109	93	11 324	2 793	2 205
Wilson	1 125	13.4	669	NA	8.0	NA	86	97	2	395	471	9 445	3 353	3 776
TEXAS	336 492	17.0	144 080	2 166	7.3	6.4	35 952	172	406	55 695	282	2 265 325	1 033 311	4 956
Anderson	631	12.1	578	NA	11.0	NA	61	111	2	225	430	7 506	1 592	2 889
Andrews	233	16.8	112	NA	8.1	NA	10	77	1	72	515	1 792	394	3 030
Angelina	1 202	15.5	760	NA	9.8	NA	111	139	3	346	447	12 185	3 651	4 556
Aransas	241	10.6	258	NA	11.3	NA	21	93	0	0	0	4 005	1 286	5 716
Archer	110	13.3	66	NA	8.0	NA	0	0	0	0	0	1 061	116	1 310
Armstrong	24	11.1	28	NA	12.7	NA	0	0	0	0	0	379	29	1 350
Atascosa	587	16.1	285	NA	7.8	NA	21	54	1	30	82	4 279	649	1 680
Austin	331	14.1	233	NA	10.0	NA	16	68	1	30	128	3 947	610	2 586
Bailey	117	17.2	62	NA	9.2	NA	3	45	1	31	449	1 105	115	1 744
Bandera	183	11.6	135	NA	8.5	NA	7	40	0	0	0	2 781	416	2 358
Bastrop	781	15.4	381	NA	7.5	NA	21	36	1	28	56	6 635	1 645	2 849
Baylor	43	10.4	71	NA	17.3	NA	2	49	1	39	939	1 086	103	2 516
Bee	439	15.9	225	NA	8.1	NA	17	53	1	59	213	3 462	640	1 978
Bell	4 928	22.1	1 453	36	6.5	7.3	665	279	4	755	338	22 289	10 394	4 388
Bexar	23 430	17.3	9 719	163	7.2	7.0	3 899	280	16	4 128	305	161 366	96 061	6 971
Blanco	92	11.0	85	NA	10.2	NA	3	36	0	0	0	3 513	132	1 568
Borden	6	7.5	NA	NA	NA	NA	0	0	0	0	0	47	12	1 646
Bosque	217	13.0	264	NA	15.9	NA	24	140	1	72	435	3 653	212	1 232
Bowie	1 115	13.3	929	NA	11.1	NA	193	216	4	711	851	13 888	3 493	3 911
Brazoria	3 580	15.6	1 520	21	6.6	5.9	179	74	4	310	135	23 809	6 832	2 835
Brazos	1 998	15.0	643	12	4.8	6.0	254	167	2	256	192	11 044	8 277	5 431
Brewster	110	12.4	84	NA	9.4	NA	9	102	1	34	382	1 377	158	1 782
Briscoe	26	14.0	23	NA	12.1	NA	0	0	0	0	0	392	13	726
Brooks	150	17.8	92	NA	10.9	NA	3	38	0	0	0	1 341	306	3 837
Brown	494	13.4	449	NA	12.2	NA	51	135	1	164	443	6 847	2 001	5 311
Burleson	213	13.7	157	NA	10.1	NA	6	36	1	33	211	2 864	389	2 362
Burnet	437	13.5	340	NA	10.5	NA	29	85	1	42	130	4 953	693	2 315

1. Per 1,000 estimated resident population, average 1997–1999.   2. Deaths of infants under 1 year old.   3. Deaths of infants under 1 year old per 1,000 live births.   4. Data subject to copyright.   5. Per 100,000 resident population as of July 1 of the year shown.   6. Data for serious crimes have not been adjusted for underreporting; this may affect comparability between geographic areas and over time.   7. Per 100,000 population estimated by the FBI.

Table B. States and Counties — **Crime, Education, Money Income, and Poverty**

STATE County	Serious crimes known to police, 2000[1] (cont'd) Rate[2] Violent	Serious crimes known to police, 2000[1] (cont'd) Rate[2] Property	Enrollment[3] Total	Enrollment[3] Percent private	Attainment[4] (percent) High school graduate or more	Attainment[4] (percent) Bachelor's degree or more	Local government expenditures, fiscal 1999[5] Total current expenditures (mil dol)	Local government expenditures, fiscal 1999[5] Current expenditures per student (dollars)	1989 Per capita[6] (dollars)	1989 Households Median Dollars	1989 Households Median Percent change, 1979–1989 (constant 1989 dollars)	1989 Households Percent with $100,000 or more	Income and poverty, 1998 Median household income	Income and poverty, 1998 Percent below poverty level All persons	Income and poverty, 1998 Percent below poverty level Persons under 18	Income and poverty, 1998 Percent below poverty level Persons 5–17 in families
	46	47	48	49	50	51	52	53	54	55	56	57	58	59	60	61
TENNESSEE—Cont'd																
Marshall	519	2 473	4 725	2.8	60.0	7.7	23.8	5 034	11 248	23 855	5.3	1.1	35 586	10.9	14.9	13.1
Maury	809	4 252	12 583	8.2	65.2	12.1	57.1	4 889	11 942	26 238	6.3	1.7	38 616	10.4	14.8	12.6
Meigs	90	1 849	1 774	4.4	52.7	6.6	7.9	4 616	9 237	20 181	-14.4	0.6	28 661	17.1	21.8	22.7
Monroe	601	2 954	7 034	8.2	49.9	7.6	28.1	4 506	9 080	19 932	0.9	0.8	28 958	16.6	22.4	20.4
Montgomery	513	3 699	26 250	7.1	77.9	16.5	107.4	4 601	11 056	25 568	8.1	1.2	37 022	11.2	15.1	13.4
Moore	192	1 620	1 152	3.6	66.7	11.7	4.8	4 997	11 545	28 056	14.2	1.6	37 734	9.1	10.9	12.1
Morgan	116	714	4 270	6.7	56.7	3.7	15.4	4 695	7 722	19 280	5.9	0.3	27 136	19.2	25.7	21.7
Obion	336	3 285	7 151	2.7	61.3	8.5	27.9	5 001	11 096	22 344	1.8	1.4	33 722	12.8	17.9	15.9
Overton	164	989	3 670	4.5	44.1	6.9	14.1	4 469	8 622	18 293	6.2	0.9	26 907	15.7	21.8	19.2
Perry	66	1 559	1 322	4.7	52.7	6.9	6.3	5 356	9 260	19 039	-0.5	1.3	27 756	16.0	21.7	21.8
Pickett	162	61	918	1.5	45.8	9.1	4.6	5 961	9 564	14 993	-0.7	1.4	24 167	18.8	22.8	25.1
Polk	137	1 115	2 866	4.2	51.3	5.8	11.2	4 837	9 311	21 663	7.0	0.8	29 032	14.1	19.5	18.3
Putnam	339	3 235	14 821	3.6	63.2	16.8	44.4	4 679	11 004	21 693	5.4	2.0	32 055	13.2	17.7	16.1
Rhea	187	2 384	5 657	12.3	56.0	8.5	20.6	4 408	9 333	19 915	-5.1	0.8	29 086	15.8	21.4	19.8
Roane	272	2 685	10 820	6.2	66.7	13.2	38.6	5 255	12 015	24 210	-4.8	2.2	32 578	13.8	18.9	17.9
Robertson	709	3 496	9 291	8.0	65.5	9.6	44.4	4 558	12 077	28 687	12.7	2.3	40 202	9.5	13.7	11.4
Rutherford	500	3 630	34 747	6.3	73.9	18.7	143.3	4 725	12 536	30 878	15.7	1.8	44 803	7.6	10.4	8.6
Scott	327	2 021	4 705	3.2	51.2	6.6	20.7	5 186	7 803	15 858	-3.8	1.0	22 872	21.8	25.5	26.2
Sequatchie	352	2 375	1 904	7.2	51.4	7.6	8.2	4 575	9 377	19 223	4.5	1.7	28 835	16.0	20.6	20.9
Sevier	243	4 333	10 640	6.3	63.0	10.8	58.9	4 947	10 848	23 042	5.1	1.6	31 291	13.2	18.0	16.9
Shelby	1 145	6 399	220 341	16.4	75.1	20.8	859.3	5 375	13 330	27 132	5.9	4.0	36 610	15.6	22.4	17.6
Smith	243	1 654	2 990	2.6	54.2	6.1	12.0	3 817	10 950	23 255	-0.5	1.6	33 163	12.2	16.1	15.6
Stewart	243	825	1 880	2.0	58.9	7.7	9.3	4 613	9 935	20 802	7.7	0.7	30 577	13.1	19.0	17.2
Sullivan	475	2 817	30 972	10.2	66.8	15.6	144.7	6 246	12 725	25 089	-3.6	2.4	34 362	12.7	19.6	16.1
Sumner	410	2 777	25 351	10.3	70.6	14.4	109.7	4 947	13 497	31 795	6.3	3.0	43 606	8.5	11.1	9.8
Tipton	433	3 158	9 449	5.6	61.8	6.7	47.1	4 433	9 796	23 860	8.2	0.9	34 881	12.9	16.3	15.8
Trousdale	455	2 604	1 239	5.2	47.7	7.0	5.4	4 375	9 618	20 127	-19.6	0.7	28 779	14.4	18.7	18.3
Unicoi	232	1 924	3 374	1.6	59.6	9.5	12.5	5 038	10 727	20 536	-0.8	1.5	30 165	14.0	20.4	18.7
Union	306	1 716	2 998	4.3	45.6	4.5	14.3	4 661	8 351	19 595	5.6	0.2	28 452	16.9	21.8	20.9
Van Buren	182	1 144	1 006	4.3	48.0	4.1	3.8	4 803	8 186	20 676	8.4	0.0	29 954	14.3	18.1	19.3
Warren	329	3 305	6 907	5.9	57.0	8.1	28.8	4 554	10 472	21 019	5.2	1.8	31 109	14.7	19.3	17.8
Washington	493	4 198	23 223	5.8	68.4	18.9	77.0	5 158	11 949	23 698	0.2	2.3	33 965	12.5	17.4	15.2
Wayne	143	998	2 799	2.4	51.0	5.0	12.5	4 667	8 240	18 429	-6.1	0.6	25 795	18.2	21.9	22.4
Weakley	241	2 261	8 923	3.0	56.9	10.3	22.6	4 416	9 857	21 004	8.7	0.9	31 622	13.2	17.8	15.9
White	234	3 480	3 974	4.2	53.2	7.6	15.5	4 002	9 299	19 874	3.6	0.7	28 299	14.8	18.5	18.5
Williamson	193	2 013	21 381	23.1	81.8	34.2	120.8	5 495	19 339	43 615	19.7	10.2	66 335	4.2	5.5	4.6
Wilson	470	3 306	16 337	14.6	71.4	15.6	67.5	4 676	13 681	32 852	7.1	2.8	46 849	7.4	10.4	8.8
TEXAS	545	4 410	4 805 895	10.2	72.1	20.3	22 430.2	5 685	12 904	27 016	-3.5	3.7	35 449	15.6	22.4	20.4
Anderson	443	2 446	11 242	8.4	67.7	9.5	47.5	5 391	9 384	22 737	-0.3	1.5	30 638	18.6	23.5	22.4
Andrews	92	2 938	4 261	4.2	61.2	9.8	24.0	6 926	10 361	26 434	-13.5	1.4	34 897	15.2	19.9	21.1
Angelina	673	3 884	18 706	6.5	65.3	13.2	85.0	5 317	11 248	22 986	-12.3	2.1	31 314	16.7	24.1	22.1
Aransas	173	5 543	4 147	8.6	67.2	14.5	21.9	6 304	11 394	21 315	-9.6	2.8	29 928	20.6	30.5	34.0
Archer	169	1 141	2 027	4.1	72.5	12.3	12.3	6 004	11 719	25 131	-6.1	2.5	38 687	10.2	15.6	14.3
Armstrong	0	1 350	468	0.6	77.4	14.1	2.6	6 749	11 212	23 081	-11.5	1.2	31 801	10.6	13.7	14.3
Atascosa	189	1 491	8 533	3.2	58.8	8.4	49.6	6 040	8 447	20 048	-6.8	1.3	28 053	22.2	30.8	30.0
Austin	343	2 242	4 836	6.3	62.6	13.8	28.4	5 431	11 837	25 043	3.9	2.2	35 350	11.7	16.6	15.9
Bailey	106	1 638	1 793	0.7	55.4	7.4	10.7	7 182	10 043	19 873	-5.3	4.2	27 522	23.2	31.2	32.8
Bandera	136	2 222	2 199	7.5	76.7	16.9	16.2	5 800	12 798	24 671	10.1	2.2	36 135	12.5	20.6	20.3
Bastrop	282	2 567	9 588	4.9	68.3	13.3	60.6	5 769	10 300	23 967	15.0	1.0	36 048	13.0	18.8	18.5
Baylor	366	2 150	720	3.5	63.6	10.3	4.8	6 430	11 040	17 228	-11.4	1.6	24 218	20.5	30.4	32.8
Bee	164	1 814	7 916	7.0	65.0	12.2	31.9	5 862	8 619	20 614	-3.1	0.9	27 982	24.1	30.1	32.1
Bell	410	3 979	49 611	9.3	79.1	17.2	264.7	5 428	10 908	23 755	8.4	1.9	33 034	14.5	22.0	19.9
Bexar	631	6 339	345 381	13.0	72.7	19.7	1 517.4	5 986	11 827	25 926	2.5	3.0	34 210	17.8	25.6	22.5
Blanco	166	1 402	1 244	7.8	68.9	13.0	10.0	6 483	12 388	22 297	7.0	2.4	29 691	9.1	14.3	13.3
Borden	137	1 509	183	2.7	71.2	17.3	2.8	13 493	17 533	29 375	17.3	11.6	34 150	11.5	17.1	21.6
Bosque	134	1 099	3 006	4.4	64.0	10.8	19.5	6 164	10 992	21 411	9.3	2.1	30 430	14.9	23.2	22.4
Bowie	488	3 423	20 935	4.8	72.1	14.3	86.8	5 254	11 846	24 237	2.2	2.2	32 561	16.7	25.8	23.0
Brazoria	257	2 578	55 183	8.0	75.5	15.1	253.1	5 339	13 468	34 418	-12.0	2.9	45 926	10.3	14.8	13.0
Brazos	400	5 030	58 837	5.3	79.8	35.8	120.3	5 769	10 987	20 411	-1.0	2.6	33 917	16.3	21.4	20.5
Brewster	259	1 523	2 825	2.8	73.2	28.0	11.0	6 971	10 730	17 586	-2.9	3.0	27 549	20.4	28.9	31.1
Briscoe	0	726	454	0.7	63.0	11.6	2.0	7 182	10 058	17 696	-3.4	2.0	25 010	21.5	30.1	33.1
Brooks	288	3 548	2 434	3.3	45.6	6.6	11.9	6 212	6 623	13 509	-23.6	1.6	18 768	35.4	43.4	50.2
Brown	653	4 658	8 560	15.1	67.1	13.7	41.5	5 759	9 797	19 291	-8.3	1.6	28 324	18.6	25.7	26.2
Burleson	383	1 979	3 070	6.5	58.2	9.5	19.9	6 155	9 354	19 785	-9.0	1.1	28 452	16.2	23.5	22.3
Burnet	247	2 068	4 711	6.7	69.1	14.0	34.5	5 536	11 530	21 420	5.3	2.0	34 638	11.8	17.5	16.7

1. Data for serious crimes have not been adjusted for underreporting; this may affect comparability between geographic areas and over time. 2. Per 100,000 population estimated by the FBI. 3. All persons 3 years old and over enrolled in nursery school through college. 4. Persons 25 years old and over. 5. Elementary and secondary education expenditures, local government fiscal years ending between July 1, 1998 and June 30, 1999. 6. Based on population enumerated as of April 1, 1990.

STATE County	Personal income, 1999 Total (mil dol)	Percent change, 1998–1999	Per capita[1] Dollars	Per capita[1] Rank	Wages and salaries[2] (mil dol)	Proprietor's income (mil dol)	Dividends, interest, and rent (mil dol)	Transfer payments Total (mil dol)	Government payments to individuals Total (mil dol)	Social Security (mil dol)	Medical payments (mil dol)	Income maintenance (mil dol)	Unemployment insurance (mil dol)
	62	63	64	65	66	67	68	69	70	71	72	73	74
TENNESSEE—Cont'd													
Marshall	615	7.6	23 274	1 020	382	57	95	95	90	38	41	7	1
Maury	1 528	5.8	21 693	1 456	1 409	146	246	252	240	96	110	21	4
Meigs	168	4.5	16 541	2 822	41	16	22	46	44	16	19	4	1
Monroe	652	5.3	18 314	2 466	332	50	91	156	150	60	64	16	3
Montgomery	3 034	8.5	23 442	976	1 119	190	421	354	332	115	128	30	5
Moore	102	1.7	19 842	2 043	45	2	16	18	17	7	7	1	0
Morgan	283	2.8	15 153	2 975	94	29	36	84	81	34	32	9	1
Obion	742	3.8	23 010	1 088	504	68	137	136	131	54	56	11	3
Overton	338	2.9	17 193	2 702	117	34	49	94	91	31	43	10	2
Perry	146	4.8	19 336	2 200	83	11	20	40	38	14	20	2	1
Pickett	86	4.0	18 349	2 458	26	11	12	26	25	9	12	3	0
Polk	288	5.6	19 055	2 269	68	21	39	77	75	30	34	6	2
Putnam	1 396	5.5	23 372	995	927	153	250	244	234	94	105	19	4
Rhea	504	7.1	17 935	2 551	346	38	74	129	124	46	57	13	2
Roane	1 087	3.6	21 728	1 441	736	69	148	244	236	97	105	20	3
Robertson	1 252	7.3	22 818	1 138	421	95	153	178	169	71	75	12	3
Rutherford	4 353	7.7	25 397	599	2 758	531	525	411	381	158	163	26	9
Scott	329	7.5	16 253	2 867	158	26	44	111	107	31	51	17	2
Sequatchie	200	9.3	18 430	2 433	68	16	23	47	45	15	22	5	1
Sevier	1 492	5.4	22 679	1 172	803	190	251	243	231	102	96	17	7
Shelby	26 647	4.3	30 524	193	20 279	2 638	4 210	3 172	3 024	1 017	1 354	445	43
Smith	339	3.8	20 207	1 927	158	23	56	73	70	24	36	5	2
Stewart	201	5.9	17 099	2 718	77	18	34	52	50	20	21	4	1
Sullivan	3 620	3.1	24 095	843	2 472	250	692	660	635	296	254	49	7
Sumner	3 155	5.7	25 034	666	1 210	263	428	392	370	163	161	24	7
Tipton	927	5.3	19 167	2 240	323	76	107	164	155	58	71	16	2
Trousdale	121	5.9	17 323	2 676	42	15	20	31	30	10	16	2	0
Unicoi	360	3.4	20 785	1 742	158	19	53	91	88	30	37	7	1
Union	259	5.4	15 610	2 940	67	16	29	64	62	25	25	8	1
Van Buren	84	4.7	16 779	2 784	32	5	10	21	20	7	10	2	0
Warren	809	4.5	22 225	1 292	498	94	127	170	163	58	83	14	3
Washington	2 452	3.4	23 849	887	1 692	185	411	422	404	164	172	30	5
Wayne	258	3.8	15 737	2 924	98	13	38	71	68	24	31	7	3
Weakley	659	1.9	19 993	1 993	315	61	111	138	132	54	58	10	3
White	413	3.9	18 045	2 531	193	47	56	102	99	39	45	9	2
Williamson	4 733	9.6	38 236	56	2 163	378	716	255	234	117	91	10	4
Wilson	2 228	6.8	25 755	548	858	200	307	271	256	106	113	14	5
TEXAS	537 857	5.8	26 834	X	346 880	71 402	82 928	61 386	57 931	21 512	25 264	6 430	1 255
Anderson	921	3.3	17 636	2 614	539	84	154	197	188	64	84	18	4
Andrews	240	-1.9	17 455	2 658	127	20	46	48	46	19	19	5	2
Angelina	1 681	3.3	21 667	1 463	1 014	146	314	328	315	119	146	29	5
Aransas	528	4.3	22 812	1 141	139	37	135	99	95	43	37	9	2
Archer	190	2.7	22 959	1 097	43	32	35	26	25	13	8	2	0
Armstrong	44	8.8	19 999	1 990	13	5	12	9	9	4	4	0	0
Atascosa	664	6.6	17 737	2 592	233	60	88	126	120	40	54	17	2
Austin	563	4.7	23 620	938	270	48	115	87	83	34	37	6	1
Bailey	162	11.4	24 157	827	58	47	26	28	27	10	12	4	0
Bandera	397	9.4	23 920	873	55	31	84	56	53	26	18	3	1
Bastrop	1 056	9.0	20 089	1 968	274	73	154	144	135	52	58	14	2
Baylor	79	-3.2	19 245	2 221	29	8	19	24	23	10	10	2	0
Bee	458	4.0	16 639	2 801	230	46	70	107	102	30	48	16	2
Bell	5 519	6.2	24 784	708	4 474	309	799	638	609	194	220	70	14
Bexar	34 026	4.8	24 785	707	23 117	4 295	5 772	4 452	4 220	1 352	1 851	573	56
Blanco	183	6.1	21 464	1 530	61	23	39	47	46	24	19	1	0
Borden	10	16.7	12 945	3 083	5	-2	4	2	2	1	0	0	0
Bosque	338	5.0	20 229	1 916	96	35	78	76	73	33	28	5	1
Bowie	1 920	3.9	22 992	1 091	1 152	192	371	346	331	114	151	38	6
Brazoria	5 559	4.1	23 724	912	2 822	353	786	624	584	242	254	44	21
Brazos	2 846	3.9	21 206	1 594	1 998	230	499	292	268	110	102	31	2
Brewster	177	4.4	20 111	1 961	97	12	43	31	30	12	9	4	0
Briscoe	37	2.4	20 170	1 943	13	6	8	9	9	3	4	1	0
Brooks	119	2.7	14 123	3 043	48	5	18	43	41	10	20	10	1
Brown	724	3.3	19 654	2 096	406	70	117	179	173	62	83	14	2
Burleson	284	5.3	18 221	2 490	87	22	66	65	63	27	24	6	1
Burnet	718	7.6	21 057	1 653	243	77	215	129	123	63	42	9	1

1. Based on the resident population estimated as of July 1 of the year shown. 2. Includes other labor income.

Table B. States and Counties — **Earnings, Social Security, and Housing**

STATE County	Earnings, 1999									Social Security beneficiaries, December 2000			Housing units, 1990	
			Goods-related[1]		Service-related and other[2]							Supplemental Security Income recipients, December 2000		Percent change, 1980–1990
	Total (mil dol)	Farm	Total	Manufacturing	Total	Retail trade	Finance, insurance, and real estate	Services	Government	Number	Rate[3]		Total	
	75	76	77	78	79	80	81	82	83	84	85	86	87	88
TENNESSEE—Cont'd														
Marshall	439	-0.6	D	56.8	D	7.6	2.7	9.9	10.1	4 700	176	519	8 909	16.5
Maury	1 555	-0.3	D	48.1	D	6.7	4.3	17.5	11.6	11 716	169	1 671	22 286	14.1
Meigs	57	-1.1	D	26.5	D	8.8	6.7	15.3	19.0	2 231	201	435	3 689	23.1
Monroe	381	-0.2	D	48.2	D	12.5	4.2	12.8	11.1	8 221	211	1 603	12 803	16.4
Montgomery	1 309	-0.2	D	20.3	D	15.5	4.5	23.7	19.2	15 122	112	2 215	37 233	25.3
Moore	47	0.2	D	15.7	D	4.1	D	7.5	37.9	909	158	85	1 912	14.6
Morgan	123	-0.7	D	29.2	D	5.9	2.4	12.2	33.9	4 612	233	616	6 378	7.7
Obion	572	-0.2	54.0	48.4	D	9.8	2.6	13.5	8.8	6 824	210	1 027	13 359	2.3
Overton	151	0.1	D	29.0	D	11.7	4.8	17.9	18.8	4 547	226	891	7 388	13.2
Perry	93	-1.8	D	56.7	D	5.5	3.4	17.4	10.9	1 863	244	237	3 225	13.5
Pickett	37	4.4	D	D	D	17.3	6.1	16.9	17.9	1 343	272	227	2 253	20.7
Polk	89	3.8	D	17.9	D	10.0	5.8	23.4	23.2	3 760	234	537	5 659	11.2
Putnam	1 081	-0.3	D	27.2	D	11.6	4.2	18.5	18.8	12 101	194	1 870	21 417	20.3
Rhea	384	0.0	43.1	38.2	25.4	7.6	2.2	12.4	31.5	5 782	204	1 123	10 361	10.4
Roane	805	-0.4	D	8.3	D	7.1	1.6	48.2	16.6	11 564	223	1 856	20 334	8.6
Robertson	515	-0.3	D	35.8	D	12.7	2.1	13.6	15.9	8 841	162	954	15 823	18.9
Rutherford	3 289	0.1	D	31.3	D	8.0	4.8	24.6	13.1	19 644	108	2 145	45 755	49.8
Scott	184	0.1	D	35.4	D	10.7	3.0	17.4	17.8	4 433	210	1 654	7 122	7.8
Sequatchie	84	-0.5	D	30.6	D	11.3	4.7	15.5	16.4	2 068	182	345	3 570	12.9
Sevier	993	-0.4	D	8.0	D	27.2	6.3	34.3	12.0	13 309	187	1 365	24 166	38.1
Shelby	22 917	0.0	16.1	10.5	70.3	9.3	8.2	28.4	13.6	122 880	137	31 189	327 796	14.5
Smith	180	-1.0	D	33.3	D	12.7	4.8	16.4	12.6	3 288	186	543	6 049	0.0
Stewart	95	-1.2	15.5	8.0	31.6	11.3	4.2	11.9	54.0	2 761	223	407	4 384	22.4
Sullivan	2 722	0.1	40.9	33.3	50.3	10.2	4.0	25.1	9.0	34 627	226	4 454	60 623	10.3
Sumner	1 473	0.1	37.6	27.2	49.5	10.4	4.7	23.5	13.0	19 666	151	2 099	39 807	32.0
Tipton	399	0.2	D	30.1	D	10.6	4.2	17.4	16.2	7 806	152	1 357	14 071	21.6
Trousdale	57	-1.4	41.8	30.5	D	10.1	6.4	13.0	21.9	1 451	200	252	2 537	1.6
Unicoi	176	0.0	D	42.3	D	5.0	2.1	11.8	16.6	3 980	225	660	7 076	10.6
Union	83	0.0	D	33.1	D	8.3	2.8	15.3	20.7	3 719	209	663	5 696	22.7
Van Buren	36	0.2	D	D	D	3.4	2.2	D	18.6	1 008	183	185	2 001	14.1
Warren	592	4.8	D	45.6	D	8.2	D	13.9	9.1	7 738	202	1 424	13 802	6.4
Washington	1 877	0.2	24.7	18.6	55.3	11.9	5.9	29.1	19.8	20 592	192	2 951	38 378	14.0
Wayne	111	-1.8	D	21.9	D	9.8	3.9	29.8	25.5	3 323	197	520	5 741	10.9
Weakley	376	-0.7	30.4	23.5	45.4	9.6	3.6	16.0	25.0	6 730	193	737	12 857	3.2
White	240	-1.0	D	43.8	D	14.4	2.9	14.0	11.4	5 300	229	899	8 369	10.3
Williamson	2 541	0.1	19.3	9.0	72.9	11.1	15.6	33.9	7.9	13 541	107	698	29 875	51.5
Wilson	1 058	-0.4	D	20.6	D	16.2	4.1	24.9	9.5	12 760	144	1 191	26 198	30.1
TEXAS	418 282	1.0	24.2	13.3	60.2	9.2	7.6	26.7	14.5	2 634 620	126	409 502	7 008 999	26.3
Anderson	623	0.7	11.8	4.7	57.4	18.9	3.7	21.2	30.1	7 867	143	1 177	16 909	21.4
Andrews	147	0.1	37.6	8.0	37.6	7.9	3.5	12.8	24.9	2 182	168	265	5 462	17.1
Angelina	1 160	0.5	30.4	25.0	52.4	13.3	3.9	24.0	16.7	14 123	176	2 240	28 796	16.8
Aransas	176	0.0	23.8	4.5	58.6	17.5	5.5	20.3	17.6	5 123	228	386	10 889	37.0
Archer	74	23.7	19.3	0.8	37.3	8.0	2.6	11.3	19.8	1 529	173	90	3 680	10.1
Armstrong	18	12.1	D	D	D	7.8	5.8	20.8	21.8	438	204	17	916	2.2
Atascosa	292	4.1	16.8	4.3	58.0	12.2	3.8	24.2	21.1	5 920	153	856	11 614	24.9
Austin	318	1.2	32.6	20.0	52.2	8.4	5.0	20.1	13.9	4 279	181	369	8 885	13.3
Bailey	106	36.5	8.3	4.2	39.1	6.9	3.7	7.0	16.1	1 234	187	153	3 109	-1.3
Bandera	86	-0.6	D	2.7	D	12.6	7.0	26.0	23.3	3 391	192	197	6 485	36.3
Bastrop	347	1.9	D	6.3	D	15.6	5.6	18.5	33.2	6 716	116	866	16 301	52.5
Baylor	36	-1.3	D	D	D	12.0	4.3	31.4	23.3	1 214	297	114	3 006	-4.3
Bee	276	3.3	14.8	3.9	41.0	8.9	3.9	20.9	40.9	4 177	129	909	10 208	14.0
Bell	4 783	0.3	12.0	7.3	32.1	7.5	2.8	15.5	55.7	25 919	109	3 583	75 957	27.3
Bexar	27 412	0.2	14.0	6.1	61.1	10.3	9.2	25.8	24.7	185 095	133	35 711	455 832	32.0
Blanco	84	8.5	D	2.3	D	10.1	8.5	16.2	18.6	1 584	188	100	3 135	28.3
Borden	3	-61.5	D	0.0	D	D	D	13.6	93.0	95	130	2	478	-14.5
Bosque	132	9.2	21.4	13.2	49.6	11.9	4.2	20.1	19.8	3 991	232	269	8 074	8.5
Bowie	1 344	1.8	D	8.6	D	13.5	4.6	28.3	26.1	15 351	172	2 577	34 234	14.8
Brazoria	3 175	0.4	48.4	32.0	36.6	8.7	2.9	16.1	14.6	27 007	112	2 785	74 504	23.2
Brazos	2 228	0.4	15.4	7.0	46.8	11.3	5.8	23.9	37.4	12 969	85	1 686	48 799	36.7
Brewster	109	-4.1	D	2.1	D	14.6	3.3	17.7	41.0	1 535	173	182	4 486	38.2
Briscoe	19	19.5	10.4	4.2	D	9.0	5.9	D	19.0	418	234	41	1 074	-6.3
Brooks	54	1.9	D	0.8	D	14.9	3.6	24.2	40.2	1 576	198	623	3 104	6.3
Brown	476	0.9	31.6	27.2	49.7	11.9	3.3	25.2	17.8	7 676	204	1 012	16 909	12.6
Burleson	110	4.6	24.7	4.9	47.5	13.4	4.7	13.6	23.1	3 303	201	402	7 044	12.8
Burnet	320	-0.5	22.5	9.7	59.2	17.3	8.0	21.4	18.7	7 705	226	457	12 801	29.2

1. Covers mining, construction, and manufacturing.   2. Covers private sector earnings in agricultural services, forestry, and fisheries; transportation and public utilities; wholesale trade; retail trade; finance, insurance, and real estate; and services.   3. Per 1,000 resident population estimated as of July 1 of the year shown.

STATE County	Housing units, 1990 (cont'd)								Civilian labor force, 2001				Civilian employment, 1990[5]		
	Occupied units										Unemployment			Percent	
			Owner-occupied			Renter-occupied									
				Owner cost as a percent of income											
	Total	Percent	Median value[1]	With a mortgage	Without a mortgage	Median rent[2]	Rent as percent of income	Substandard units[3] (percent)	Total	Percent change, 2000–2001	Total	Rate[4]	Total	Professional, managerial, and technical	Precision production, craft, and repair
	89	90	91	92	93	94	95	96	97	98	99	100	101	102	103
TENNESSEE—Cont'd															
Marshall	8 268	70.8	47 900	17.7	12.7	317	22.9	3.2	12 311	-1.3	750	6.1	10 632	17.5	14.0
Maury	20 608	69.0	60 700	18.7	12.4	366	22.8	3.3	37 052	-0.1	1 446	3.9	25 741	21.8	14.2
Meigs	2 996	79.9	44 200	19.5	12.0	268	27.2	8.1	4 462	0.0	326	7.3	3 429	15.0	17.4
Monroe	11 363	79.7	40 200	18.3	12.0	265	22.3	5.0	18 318	-2.5	1 311	7.2	13 059	14.7	16.3
Montgomery	34 345	61.1	58 100	21.3	12.2	373	24.2	3.7	60 226	1.4	2 242	3.7	37 778	25.6	12.1
Moore	1 734	83.7	50 400	16.8	12.9	295	17.5	2.5	2 959	2.9	95	3.2	2 461	19.1	12.1
Morgan	5 841	82.9	37 800	21.7	13.3	261	26.5	6.3	7 138	1.5	439	6.2	6 129	15.8	18.7
Obion	12 412	70.6	43 500	17.4	13.1	282	23.3	2.8	15 960	2.7	692	4.3	14 176	16.8	11.8
Overton	6 734	80.3	36 700	17.5	12.3	235	23.6	7.4	9 596	0.1	610	6.4	7 820	14.4	15.8
Perry	2 512	83.9	35 600	22.1	12.1	237	22.1	7.0	3 501	-3.6	251	7.2	2 776	16.9	12.2
Pickett	1 786	78.8	34 200	19.6	12.8	148	21.3	7.2	2 215	4.2	201	9.1	1 885	14.4	15.1
Polk	5 092	82.9	37 800	20.6	12.2	258	22.6	6.4	6 557	-2.2	325	5.0	5 891	14.1	17.5
Putnam	19 753	66.8	55 000	19.5	12.1	306	25.2	2.9	30 593	-0.5	1 368	4.5	24 376	24.8	12.1
Rhea	9 185	74.5	45 300	19.8	12.2	282	23.9	2.8	11 760	-5.0	702	6.0	10 324	18.8	16.2
Roane	18 453	76.4	48 700	17.4	12.9	287	22.8	3.2	23 147	-1.3	1 035	4.5	20 183	25.8	15.4
Robertson	14 801	74.9	61 300	20.8	12.8	337	26.1	3.4	29 887	1.5	1 236	4.1	19 926	20.2	15.6
Rutherford	42 118	66.1	71 800	21.5	12.4	403	26.2	3.2	99 417	1.6	3 545	3.6	60 987	25.7	12.1
Scott	6 534	75.4	33 600	23.9	12.7	230	26.6	8.6	8 922	-0.6	650	7.3	6 422	16.9	16.2
Sequatchie	3 287	77.6	39 000	24.1	12.8	288	25.8	5.6	4 653	-2.4	234	5.0	3 954	18.1	14.9
Sevier	19 520	75.8	62 400	20.7	11.6	347	24.5	4.9	36 342	1.8	2 156	5.9	24 309	23.0	15.5
Shelby	303 571	59.5	66 500	20.8	13.1	394	26.3	4.8	446 557	0.7	18 766	4.2	376 899	31.0	8.7
Smith	5 358	78.8	45 900	17.4	13.6	258	20.9	5.8	9 360	-0.9	455	4.9	6 398	17.5	16.7
Stewart	3 678	82.4	43 700	19.2	12.9	244	21.7	4.1	3 770	3.9	273	7.2	3 952	16.1	16.4
Sullivan	56 729	75.0	55 600	17.7	12.1	308	23.5	2.3	73 392	0.9	2 829	3.9	65 494	26.3	14.0
Sumner	36 850	75.0	73 400	20.7	12.8	418	24.6	2.6	71 475	2.4	3 202	4.5	51 458	26.4	13.6
Tipton	13 033	71.9	56 100	22.8	12.6	323	25.9	6.9	22 965	1.7	1 152	5.0	15 776	17.1	17.0
Trousdale	2 261	74.7	41 900	20.6	14.3	277	27.0	6.8	2 053	0.6	205	10.0	2 804	13.9	13.2
Unicoi	6 621	77.2	48 100	17.1	12.7	274	25.0	3.4	7 850	-1.7	464	5.9	6 857	21.2	14.2
Union	4 932	79.8	45 500	21.0	11.6	265	25.0	9.1	8 060	2.4	306	3.8	5 868	10.6	18.6
Van Buren	1 799	83.8	33 000	21.5	11.9	174	20.4	7.1	2 323	-1.5	176	7.6	2 016	10.1	16.2
Warren	12 681	73.2	42 200	18.1	12.7	279	25.0	3.7	19 148	-0.7	1 373	7.2	15 619	16.5	15.5
Washington	35 823	67.4	57 300	18.1	12.1	313	25.4	1.9	51 823	1.3	2 360	4.6	43 126	27.9	11.5
Wayne	5 174	83.6	32 800	17.8	12.3	245	22.2	6.8	7 131	0.9	697	9.8	6 257	12.2	14.7
Weakley	11 992	70.5	39 800	17.0	12.3	258	23.4	2.8	16 758	1.2	997	5.9	14 890	20.6	11.8
White	7 722	81.5	40 300	18.4	13.1	264	24.2	4.8	10 813	-2.8	612	5.7	8 988	14.8	18.5
Williamson	27 928	79.5	131 100	21.8	12.0	480	22.9	2.7	70 010	1.2	1 542	2.2	41 207	38.8	9.2
Wilson	24 070	80.5	82 000	21.6	12.4	401	24.6	3.1	49 079	1.4	1 735	3.5	34 063	25.9	14.9
TEXAS	6 070 937	60.9	59 600	20.9	13.1	395	24.6	8.4	10 462 712	1.3	507 442	4.9	7 634 279	30.0	11.7
Anderson	14 223	72.8	42 800	19.4	14.1	368	26.6	5.1	19 308	-0.1	775	4.0	15 905	22.1	12.0
Andrews	4 758	76.2	39 200	16.8	11.8	314	21.5	9.3	4 899	-2.0	190	3.9	5 775	23.6	21.5
Angelina	25 004	71.6	43 600	18.7	13.0	338	25.7	6.6	35 945	0.8	2 090	5.8	28 686	23.8	12.4
Aransas	6 938	73.1	56 700	22.0	13.2	360	23.3	9.9	10 233	5.3	597	5.8	6 772	26.0	15.7
Archer	2 957	80.4	45 200	21.9	14.0	328	22.7	2.2	4 023	0.8	96	2.4	3 553	22.0	14.8
Armstrong	768	80.7	43 700	17.7	13.0	289	21.7	3.7	1 137	-0.2	15	1.3	842	19.1	10.3
Atascosa	9 940	75.6	37 800	18.8	13.5	280	24.5	15.9	18 320	2.4	774	4.2	11 306	18.6	17.9
Austin	7 478	74.4	57 400	21.1	13.7	326	22.8	7.9	13 548	4.7	376	2.8	8 489	23.8	14.9
Bailey	2 454	69.7	35 300	19.3	14.0	275	20.3	7.5	3 460	-3.1	175	5.1	3 209	12.0	13.5
Bandera	4 180	79.6	61 900	20.9	11.3	348	26.9	5.5	7 351	1.8	196	2.7	4 583	25.1	14.8
Bastrop	13 379	77.6	53 900	22.4	14.6	355	24.5	9.5	29 949	1.9	1 190	4.0	16 870	23.1	15.5
Baylor	1 906	70.3	34 000	17.1	16.5	213	20.6	3.5	1 629	0.6	69	4.2	1 860	18.2	12.6
Bee	8 592	63.8	39 400	22.4	13.1	322	24.8	10.4	10 395	-0.4	524	5.0	8 666	25.7	16.0
Bell	67 240	52.1	59 000	21.5	12.9	374	25.0	5.8	94 826	0.8	3 987	4.2	67 891	28.8	11.7
Bexar	409 043	57.8	56 300	21.4	12.6	379	25.1	9.5	687 547	1.7	27 967	4.1	497 202	30.7	10.6
Blanco	2 338	72.8	56 400	24.1	12.3	296	25.4	5.8	3 762	-4.0	100	2.7	2 697	20.4	13.9
Borden	294	69.0	22 800	20.0	11.3	238	14.4	6.2	405	3.6	8	2.0	376	18.1	13.8
Bosque	5 990	75.8	42 000	17.9	12.6	309	24.0	4.3	6 636	-0.1	295	4.4	5 902	21.9	13.6
Bowie	30 595	70.8	48 100	18.0	12.9	354	25.3	4.0	38 469	-0.2	1 780	4.6	34 219	27.0	13.4
Brazoria	64 019	69.2	61 800	18.2	12.3	401	21.6	6.8	106 660	0.3	6 324	5.9	86 663	28.9	18.1
Brazos	43 725	41.9	66 600	20.1	13.0	411	34.0	6.6	77 554	1.1	1 269	1.6	56 368	38.9	8.2
Brewster	3 350	59.6	45 500	17.2	12.6	277	24.4	10.4	5 602	3.0	125	2.2	3 841	27.6	12.4
Briscoe	789	76.4	22 400	17.3	14.1	271	25.8	5.4	807	-10.3	22	2.7	805	18.4	8.9
Brooks	2 673	71.7	26 700	19.7	12.8	141	24.3	16.7	3 444	9.8	198	5.7	2 706	15.2	12.7
Brown	13 097	71.8	36 500	19.8	13.7	310	26.7	5.2	17 269	1.4	643	3.7	13 564	20.3	11.6
Burleson	5 176	78.8	41 600	24.1	14.4	322	26.4	7.2	7 062	2.9	207	2.9	5 461	18.7	14.7
Burnet	9 055	75.7	58 400	25.7	13.4	350	29.7	4.8	14 860	4.0	544	3.7	8 717	24.3	15.1

1. Specified owner-occupied units.   2. Specified renter-occupied units.   3. Overcrowded or lacking complete plumbing facilities.   4. Percent of civilian labor force.   5. Persons 16 years and older.

STATE County		Private nonfarm establishments, employment and payroll, 1999								Agriculture, 1997			
		Employment						Annual payroll		Farms			Farm operators
											Percent with—		
	Number of establish-ments	Total	Health Care and Social Assistance	Manufac-turing	Retail trade	Finance and Insurance	Professional Scientific and Technical Services	Total (mil dol)	Average per employee (dollars)	Number	Less than 50 acres	500 acres and over	Whose principal occu-pation is farming (percent)
	104	105	106	107	108	109	110	111	112	113	114	115	116

TENNESSEE—Cont'd

Marshall	508	12 893	593	6 915	1 125	203	94	327	25 374	1 097	32.1	4.7	33.4
Maury	1 516	29 663	3 857	11 355	3 490	1 409	885	1 078	36 351	1 532	31.1	5.5	36.9
Meigs	101	1 253	118	591	207	D	D	29	22 821	339	32.2	3.8	33.6
Monroe	659	10 810	913	5 530	1 540	234	191	257	23 789	855	39.8	2.8	33.5
Montgomery	2 297	32 721	3 574	7 401	7 270	1 012	1 010	710	21 709	988	35.1	8.4	41.4
Moore	57	737	D	D	D	D	0	20	27 047	371	30.2	3.2	36.4
Morgan	157	1 868	262	833	195	54	D	36	19 109	328	29.6	3.0	32.3
Obion	758	14 154	1 081	6 523	1 851	401	102	400	28 286	705	26.1	18.2	43.5
Overton	296	3 182	584	1 209	459	141	59	70	21 934	889	36.4	4.0	34.1
Perry	117	2 391	336	1 621	122	46	D	71	29 500	235	21.3	9.4	38.7
Pickett	79	1 208	99	622	86	32	D	22	17 934	374	43.3	1.6	34.8
Polk	266	2 152	310	585	333	154	D	41	19 082	255	47.1	1.6	34.9
Putnam	1 676	27 272	2 938	8 624	4 236	688	772	624	22 874	1 120	42.9	2.6	32.8
Rhea	482	8 646	647	4 704	948	135	81	175	20 232	404	31.4	3.7	35.6
Roane	723	8 816	1 377	2 358	1 804	272	176	173	19 671	539	39.5	1.3	33.6
Robertson	946	13 546	1 285	5 090	1 912	238	266	315	23 257	1 474	40.3	6.2	44.9
Rutherford	3 436	68 642	7 545	19 240	9 784	3 110	1 310	1 989	28 974	1 591	39.8	3.6	32.6
Scott	336	6 345	589	3 405	639	162	53	123	19 354	228	34.2	2.6	24.6
Sequatchie	176	2 224	293	822	324	96	D	40	18 027	169	34.9	6.5	40.8
Sevier	2 502	26 143	1 409	2 429	5 954	670	475	535	20 474	801	46.1	1.2	35.7
Shelby	21 403	463 516	54 876	40 387	54 886	21 640	21 155	14 431	31 134	683	53.1	8.8	32.1
Smith	308	5 000	673	2 054	610	148	D	118	23 537	1 045	25.8	3.6	31.8
Stewart	155	984	169	194	237	48	D	18	18 545	350	25.4	4.6	34.9
Sullivan	3 670	64 052	8 892	17 568	8 868	1 730	1 545	1 911	29 838	1 315	62.4	1.5	33.8
Sumner	2 571	33 228	3 738	10 447	4 198	850	780	863	25 970	1 703	47.7	2.6	33.7
Tipton	728	9 630	1 008	2 954	1 491	318	169	221	22 928	592	43.6	13.5	43.9
Trousdale	117	1 542	220	712	167	49	D	29	18 804	405	35.6	4.2	40.5
Unicoi	258	4 104	484	1 789	349	86	D	99	24 112	155	60.6	0.6	33.5
Union	179	1 916	108	997	218	67	D	40	20 650	544	44.9	1.8	33.3
Van Buren	51	609	D	D	D	D	D	17	27 750	228	34.2	6.1	37.7
Warren	772	13 082	1 062	6 184	1 769	317	130	309	23 653	1 347	45.1	3.5	41.8
Washington	2 757	55 342	8 730	9 934	8 116	6 212	1 266	1 211	21 888	1 807	62.3	1.2	36.0
Wayne	244	2 714	250	1 018	352	136	D	45	16 695	700	21.7	5.9	29.9
Weakley	648	10 141	1 444	3 389	1 189	269	152	210	20 697	1 010	29.4	10.7	31.8
White	400	6 623	539	3 468	861	88	72	146	22 117	1 034	43.3	3.6	34.3
Williamson	4 218	68 319	7 588	4 922	9 349	8 955	5 494	2 301	33 678	1 410	40.6	4.8	34.0
Wilson	1 926	22 922	2 030	4 905	3 886	685	586	716	31 247	1 676	33.5	2.9	36.0
TEXAS	467 087	7 763 815	916 646	955 235	1 006 271	378 075	439 664	245 163	31 578	194 301	27.6	21.4	42.9
Anderson	929	10 913	2 193	1 010	1 830	424	247	253	23 204	1 542	30.2	8.9	35.7
Andrews	281	2 739	371	402	364	103	39	63	23 135	142	28.9	43.7	46.5
Angelina	1 842	29 572	4 953	6 444	4 601	819	655	739	24 974	790	41.1	4.8	31.8
Aransas	479	3 544	343	102	866	96	148	62	17 493	54	37.0	18.5	24.1
Archer	149	644	76	16	117	D	12	13	19 884	496	11.5	40.1	51.2
Armstrong	38	D	D	D	D	D	D	D	D	235	3.4	59.1	55.3
Atascosa	529	5 664	958	499	1 309	158	278	111	19 532	1 322	21.9	23.2	42.8
Austin	555	5 198	652	817	1 139	325	221	115	22 095	1 820	33.0	8.3	34.8
Bailey	182	1 446	205	130	245	61	56	26	18 259	441	12.0	49.0	67.8
Bandera	310	1 723	95	83	366	57	47	31	17 778	650	22.2	27.5	43.5
Bastrop	757	6 630	1 147	800	1 531	303	281	132	19 911	1 765	33.1	9.3	39.8
Baylor	139	1 214	645	D	139	D	21	14	11 598	270	13.3	46.3	53.7
Bee	443	4 388	910	438	944	205	121	86	19 665	686	18.1	26.8	44.5
Bell	4 040	74 732	18 445	7 945	10 622	3 109	2 949	1 742	23 311	1 741	36.2	10.9	36.4
Bexar	29 712	546 098	77 699	39 612	69 905	36 530	33 421	14 653	26 833	1 964	46.1	7.8	37.4
Blanco	205	1 863	149	77	305	86	59	42	22 647	617	18.3	30.5	45.4
Borden	3	D	0	0	D	0	0	D	D	107	4.7	72.9	66.4
Bosque	316	2 478	632	503	463	128	53	50	20 160	1 077	16.2	21.7	41.3
Bowie	2 137	31 190	7 207	4 069	5 632	935	628	744	23 842	1 138	31.7	10.5	36.2
Brazoria	3 796	58 119	4 868	14 415	9 079	1 436	1 526	1 934	33 273	1 783	45.4	13.8	33.6
Brazos	3 177	45 391	5 647	4 801	8 251	1 867	3 259	1 015	22 353	1 084	35.4	11.5	35.1
Brewster	286	1 994	298	31	483	88	43	31	15 635	129	13.2	73.6	51.9
Briscoe	50	186	D	D	D	D	3	3	18 720	232	8.6	50.0	56.0
Brooks	147	1 317	286	4	350	84	18	17	13 263	283	13.4	23.7	40.6
Brown	878	12 256	2 682	3 326	1 957	372	137	268	21 855	1 228	19.5	23.1	42.5
Burleson	300	2 294	220	300	461	153	47	45	19 611	1 337	27.3	11.0	42.0
Burnet	841	6 329	684	711	1 623	230	201	134	21 141	1 110	25.4	24.1	40.2

Table B. States and Counties — **Agriculture, Land, and Water**

STATE County	Agriculture, 1997 (cont'd)															
	Land in farms					Value of land and buildings		Value of machinery and equipment average per farm ($1,000)	Value of products sold		Percent from —		Percent of farms with sales of —		Percent of land owned by fed. gov. 1997	Water consumption 1995 (mil gal/day)
			Acres													
	Acreage (1,000)	Percent change, 1992–1997	Average size of farm	Total irrigated (1,000)	Total cropland (1,000)	Average per farm ($1,000)	Average per acre (dollars)		Total (mil dol)	Average per farm (dollars)	Crops	Live-stock and poultry products	$10,000 or more	$100,000 or more		
	117	118	119	120	121	122	123	124	125	126	127	128	129	130	131	132

STATE County	117	118	119	120	121	122	123	124	125	126	127	128	129	130	131	132
TENNESSEE—Cont'd																
Marshall	167	3.0	152	0	96	244	1 571	28	22	19 710	15.7	84.3	29.1	4.2	0.0	3.5
Maury	243	-1.4	158	0	145	295	1 813	27	27	17 913	29.6	70.4	27.7	3.1	0.3	18.8
Meigs	49	-12.5	144	0	27	206	1 536	27	5	14 110	15.9	84.1	23.0	2.9	0.0	1.4
Monroe	97	-3.1	113	D	66	279	2 333	33	19	22 083	17.2	82.8	23.9	4.4	34.6	4.9
Montgomery	165	-6.0	167	0	109	318	2 033	32	31	31 185	73.4	26.6	38.6	8.5	12.4	25.0
Moore	52	8.5	140	0	29	230	1 563	31	9	25 092	9.8	90.2	25.3	4.6	0.0	0.8
Morgan	46	7.0	140	0	22	266	1 699	35	5	15 997	13.3	86.7	22.6	4.9	2.4	1.4
Obion	242	-5.7	344	1	209	487	1 479	78	64	90 427	78.5	21.5	50.2	19.3	1.7	6.0
Overton	109	3.2	123	0	63	171	1 368	21	12	13 166	30.1	69.9	27.6	1.9	0.0	1.2
Perry	54	2.6	231	0	21	254	1 059	29	4	15 843	41.7	58.3	23.4	2.6	0.0	1.1
Pickett	37	-1.3	100	0	21	184	2 554	17	5	12 564	55.9	44.1	35.0	1.6	3.2	0.6
Polk	32	3.6	126	D	20	362	2 385	44	22	86 858	9.5	90.5	28.2	20.0	52.7	33.3
Putnam	112	-4.2	100	0	59	232	2 259	23	12	10 635	32.9	67.1	19.6	1.2	0.0	10.9
Rhea	56	7.8	139	0	35	223	1 532	31	8	18 751	51.3	48.7	26.2	5.0	0.0	4.1
Roane	53	2.1	99	0	28	255	2 378	28	6	10 707	36.2	63.8	14.7	1.5	9.2	1 254.3
Robertson	236	1.5	160	1	183	340	2 077	45	72	48 781	69.3	30.7	46.7	8.8	0.0	5.8
Rutherford	195	-2.4	123	0	115	294	2 435	24	20	12 471	23.3	76.7	19.5	2.6	0.4	24.5
Scott	30	-9.9	130	D	13	183	1 170	23	5	21 379	D	D	16.2	5.3	17.0	2.5
Sequatchie	26	2.2	151	0	14	251	1 683	28	5	28 781	15.2	84.8	26.6	8.3	0.0	1.0
Sevier	72	-3.1	89	0	41	355	4 230	26	9	11 805	25.0	75.0	18.7	1.4	31.8	9.6
Shelby	128	-11.6	188	5	98	621	3 374	42	29	42 611	91.6	8.4	22.7	7.5	0.7	638.1
Smith	138	-7.8	132	0	73	215	1 543	24	13	12 287	47.8	52.2	26.8	2.1	1.9	3.2
Stewart	57	4.7	161	0	26	231	1 440	23	5	15 137	70.1	29.9	29.7	3.4	8.9	2 196.7
Sullivan	86	-7.1	66	0	55	240	3 142	24	18	13 880	39.1	60.9	22.2	2.0	13.6	543.8
Sumner	182	2.0	107	0	120	280	2 678	31	34	20 166	61.3	38.7	27.4	3.3	1.1	791.8
Tipton	170	-7.2	287	2	149	374	1 386	69	39	65 137	95.2	4.8	35.3	13.0	0.0	5.6
Trousdale	52	-6.1	128	0	31	240	1 687	40	7	17 138	68.1	31.9	42.2	3.2	7.4	0.8
Unicoi	8	-31.8	48	0	4	186	4 517	19	1	6 463	57.3	42.6	10.3	0.6	45.8	2.3
Union	51	4.7	94	0	27	164	2 139	20	4	7 063	43.9	56.2	17.6	0.4	0.0	2.6
Van Buren	32	-4.0	139	0	18	194	1 339	23	3	12 488	21.8	78.2	29.8	1.3	0.0	0.6
Warren	162	-1.8	120	3	112	227	1 796	39	83	61 622	84.7	15.3	42.0	10.2	0.0	6.0
Washington	120	1.4	66	1	88	278	4 159	30	45	24 760	55.1	44.9	27.6	3.4	8.2	21.6
Wayne	130	4.0	186	0	60	178	1 001	21	8	11 724	25.6	74.4	22.3	1.1	0.6	4.5
Weakley	223	9.1	220	0	178	272	1 256	52	55	54 097	63.4	36.6	35.5	12.7	0.0	3.6
White	119	-4.0	115	0	74	217	2 007	27	17	16 332	20.1	79.9	26.8	2.9	0.0	3.2
Williamson	198	-3.0	140	0	110	476	3 641	30	29	20 347	31.8	68.2	26.5	3.8	0.6	4.5
Wilson	211	-1.6	126	0	118	294	2 392	24	17	10 328	17.6	82.4	21.5	1.1	2.1	9.6
TEXAS	131 308	0.3	676	5 485	37 662	398	593	40	13 767	70 852	31.2	68.8	33.4	8.7	1.7	24 332.9
Anderson	354	0.6	230	1	138	205	929	25	24	15 732	14.1	85.9	25.6	1.6	0.0	11.5
Andrews	829	-13.9	5 837	5	70	603	104	51	9	65 340	59.6	40.4	38.7	18.3	0.0	24.3
Angelina	118	14.5	149	0	48	321	1 597	29	16	20 144	4.2	95.8	16.5	2.2	11.0	41.4
Aransas	19	-1.3	347	0	4	326	D	14	0	5 624	13.2	86.5	9.3	0.0	17.5	0.6
Archer	611	-0.3	1 232	0	123	583	505	50	63	127 810	7.8	92.2	61.1	23.8	0.0	22.0
Armstrong	560	11.9	2 385	8	D	729	299	77	28	118 728	19.9	80.1	59.6	19.1	0.0	10.6
Atascosa	708	-7.4	536	29	215	361	675	37	46	34 924	48.9	51.1	29.3	5.7	0.0	55.0
Austin	367	9.0	202	5	161	346	1 730	27	25	13 489	29.3	70.7	22.5	2.3	0.0	12.2
Bailey	409	-5.6	927	70	275	373	367	92	172	389 286	21.3	78.7	62.4	33.8	1.1	173.1
Bandera	364	-8.3	560	1	48	581	1 049	28	5	7 251	16.9	83.1	15.5	0.9	0.0	2.4
Bastrop	392	-0.7	222	3	141	305	1 422	23	28	15 833	26.0	74.0	20.9	2.1	2.1	11.5
Baylor	378	5.6	1 400	2	156	599	401	66	38	140 767	22.2	77.8	61.9	20.7	0.0	3.6
Bee	421	-4.7	614	2	128	357	654	34	28	40 361	36.7	63.3	28.6	6.3	0.3	3.9
Bell	407	-2.5	234	1	214	304	1 102	30	51	29 572	35.7	64.3	24.8	3.9	11.0	48.0
Bexar	448	9.5	228	13	177	297	1 395	28	68	34 767	67.4	32.6	17.4	2.9	6.1	837.5
Blanco	381	2.8	618	0	56	744	1 211	17	13	21 081	D	D	25.3	1.9	0.0	1.8
Borden	515	-18.3	4 810	1	70	1 210	252	80	12	116 226	49.9	50.1	70.1	33.6	0.0	2.2
Bosque	548	0.0	509	3	138	461	873	30	41	38 397	22.1	77.9	28.6	3.2	1.4	5.9
Bowie	281	6.8	247	3	135	308	1 478	30	40	35 288	19.7	80.3	28.0	6.3	6.3	57.6
Brazoria	567	0.5	318	30	203	403	1 293	38	43	23 904	58.9	41.1	22.5	5.0	2.7	286.0
Brazos	265	-10.4	245	6	104	402	1 517	34	41	37 992	18.9	81.1	26.8	3.5	0.0	33.5
Brewster	2 397	-0.3	18 581	D	6	3 130	170	31	9	69 835	D	D	51.9	12.4	19.3	3.7
Briscoe	533	30.3	2 298	28	154	650	282	90	23	97 468	74.4	25.6	57.3	27.6	0.0	26.9
Brooks	458	-19.0	1 620	1	64	723	428	37	9	30 607	13.1	86.9	22.6	5.3	0.0	2.3
Brown	516	0.4	420	6	141	261	643	26	33	26 759	12.3	87.7	30.0	3.0	0.0	19.1
Burleson	322	1.5	241	15	144	341	1 159	28	27	20 485	45.7	54.3	28.0	2.9	2.3	10.8
Burnet	537	-2.0	484	1	95	464	1 054	30	10	9 341	7.7	92.3	22.2	0.9	0.2	134.2

Table B. States and Counties — **Residential Construction, Wholesale and Retail Trade, and Real Estate**

STATE County	Value of Residential Construction Authorized by Building Permits, 2000		Wholesale Trade, 1997				Retail Trade[1], 1997				Real Estate and Rental and Leasing, 1997			
	New Construction ($1,000)	Number of Housing Units	Number of Establishments	Number of Employees	Sales (mil dol)	Annual Payroll (mil dol)	Number of Establishments	Number of Employees	Sales (mil dol)	Annual Payroll (mil dol)	Number of Establishments	Number of Employees	Receipts (mil dol)	Annual Payroll (mil dol)
	133	134	135	136	137	138	139	140	141	142	143	144	145	146
TENNESSEE—Cont'd														
Marshall	10 442	152	17	104	21.4	2.4	122	1 153	180.9	16.7	17	46	3.9	0.7
Maury	60 497	754	54	631	251.3	17.9	306	3 451	572.9	55.7	70	301	31.2	5.9
Meigs	505	7	3	D	D	D	21	163	24.2	2.3	1	D	D	D
Monroe	7 231	136	22	171	48.3	2.8	165	1 505	234.5	19.9	17	38	2.7	0.4
Montgomery	81 818	1 343	93	716	281.8	19.0	523	6 895	1 175.8	108.1	105	378	49.8	5.9
Moore	5 911	70	1	D	D	D	12	51	5.6	0.5	NA	NA	NA	NA
Morgan	55	1	9	D	D	D	41	209	31.2	2.8	2	D	D	D
Obion	8 075	87	43	768	243.7	19.1	183	1 834	296.5	26.8	32	107	6.2	1.5
Overton	410	3	10	D	D	D	64	439	77.1	5.9	8	38	3.2	0.9
Perry	100	1	2	D	D	D	27	145	21.5	1.7	7	10	0.6	0.1
Pickett	NA	NA	2	D	D	D	20	109	17.0	1.3	4	47	1.9	0.5
Polk	0	0	9	D	D	D	53	366	47.0	4.4	6	34	2.0	0.5
Putnam	16 266	243	88	1 188	425.9	31.6	379	3 925	648.6	60.2	56	180	20.7	3.2
Rhea	12 929	122	15	98	26.8	2.7	100	903	137.8	12.3	16	44	3.8	0.4
Roane	2 645	34	22	345	139.8	10.2	176	1 832	308.9	25.9	29	62	5.6	1.2
Robertson	56 893	610	68	785	233.0	19.0	178	1 823	331.4	29.1	28	78	9.2	1.3
Rutherford	248 436	3 486	189	3 908	2 177.0	129.4	594	8 766	1 515.6	144.4	142	725	142.4	17.0
Scott	270	4	20	158	50.1	2.9	74	555	88.0	7.3	7	22	1.4	0.2
Sequatchie	1 522	23	10	D	D	D	42	288	56.1	4.2	7	13	1.2	0.1
Sevier	42 847	485	50	D	D	D	683	5 554	857.5	86.3	140	727	70.0	14.1
Shelby	791 643	6 734	1 851	34 481	35 419.2	1 214.8	3 574	56 612	8 959.2	891.3	813	7 077	853.1	168.9
Smith	5 873	55	15	105	55.7	2.4	62	642	100.8	8.9	14	34	4.1	0.4
Stewart	240	3	NA	NA	NA	NA	35	260	43.5	3.4	5	26	2.4	0.2
Sullivan	46 030	457	236	2 971	1 268.6	78.9	754	8 945	1 515.6	141.2	127	555	62.5	9.3
Sumner	75 710	878	141	1 369	500.2	37.9	403	4 252	665.2	64.4	100	552	60.0	11.9
Tipton	44 979	483	36	229	101.7	4.2	169	1 571	279.7	23.0	21	59	5.1	0.7
Trousdale	1 486	19	8	224	38.6	3.3	28	190	23.4	2.3	2	D	D	D
Unicoi	1 013	8	9	121	70.3	5.0	50	342	59.1	4.9	11	35	2.1	0.4
Union	9 398	111	9	D	D	D	36	204	28.2	2.3	7	16	0.6	0.1
Van Buren	NA	NA	2	D	D	D	10	30	7.4	0.4	2	D	D	D
Warren	2 689	59	45	339	101.5	8.6	177	1 803	267.0	26.2	28	102	8.1	1.3
Washington	40 802	483	162	2 131	1 192.8	55.5	540	6 873	1 123.1	103.1	118	510	48.3	8.6
Wayne	170	2	8	D	D	D	67	370	45.8	4.2	4	D	D	D
Weakley	8 474	136	49	680	320.2	19.9	153	1 211	171.8	16.1	21	76	5.0	1.0
White	1 879	38	22	190	62.8	4.3	90	856	183.5	13.2	11	20	3.2	0.2
Williamson	287 028	1 205	228	1 749	2 559.9	95.7	540	7 729	1 421.4	142.1	156	1 505	168.7	35.8
Wilson	104 305	824	95	1 075	605.8	29.4	290	3 216	566.5	49.6	70	243	42.1	4.5
TEXAS	15 418 411	141 231	33 346	425 744	323 111.7	15 504.9	74 105	950 848	182 516.1	16 197.1	20 753	128 915	15 957.4	3 119.2
Anderson	4 039	68	46	338	166.1	9.7	194	1 877	316.1	27.2	28	111	13.3	2.2
Andrews	1 669	24	20	103	24.6	2.3	52	356	59.7	5.7	10	33	1.9	0.5
Angelina	14 638	141	81	1 237	288.2	31.1	343	4 238	688.8	62.7	77	275	20.7	4.8
Aransas	18 742	213	16	63	24.8	1.7	90	771	124.8	11.8	28	67	7.6	1.1
Archer	1 245	10	18	142	41.5	2.3	27	111	23.4	2.0	1	D	D	D
Armstrong	162	2	2	D	D	D	6	19	2.9	0.2	1	D	D	D
Atascosa	4 247	66	30	227	89.6	6.6	108	1 246	177.2	16.3	15	61	4.1	0.9
Austin	6 200	114	22	390	212.8	11.3	123	1 114	211.4	16.7	19	53	5.9	0.6
Bailey	305	1	20	203	112.1	4.3	36	271	33.9	3.1	2	D	D	D
Bandera	181	3	5	7	0.9	0.1	54	275	50.9	3.9	13	28	2.7	0.4
Bastrop	11 349	148	28	205	69.0	3.4	135	1 450	397.0	20.8	27	64	6.1	1.0
Baylor	0	0	14	D	D	D	21	126	21.4	1.5	2	D	D	D
Bee	145	4	18	128	92.3	3.2	92	1 008	141.8	15.5	22	60	7.0	1.1
Bell	165 675	1 795	150	D	D	D	829	10 409	1 733.5	163.4	240	1 089	93.2	15.9
Bexar	683 593	8 978	1 829	25 191	12 639.2	810.7	4 505	64 928	11 657.5	1 111.1	1 342	8 770	1 115.1	203.5
Blanco	1 150	12	9	D	D	D	46	231	35.2	3.4	9	25	1.8	0.3
Borden	NA	NA	1	D	D	D	1	D	D	D	NA	NA	NA	NA
Bosque	420	6	11	105	63.3	1.6	73	443	73.2	6.0	10	16	2.2	0.4
Bowie	12 274	258	134	D	D	D	445	5 222	940.7	83.0	88	510	60.2	8.5
Brazoria	292 168	2 085	220	2 524	840.2	102.1	629	8 945	1 534.4	136.0	196	1 231	142.8	29.3
Brazos	101 964	1 372	130	1 655	426.5	41.9	569	7 994	1 336.2	122.2	181	1 090	78.5	17.2
Brewster	2 216	35	12	62	18.3	1.1	56	460	58.1	6.1	10	26	1.3	0.2
Briscoe	NA	NA	6	D	D	D	9	29	4.3	0.3	1	D	D	D
Brooks	111	3	5	14	3.8	0.2	32	287	38.4	3.8	NA	NA	NA	NA
Brown	3 112	33	42	337	95.7	8.5	194	1 843	302.0	24.6	32	73	7.8	1.2
Burleson	158	2	26	136	133.1	4.3	66	477	81.4	6.5	5	8	1.1	0.1
Burnet	51 445	449	27	163	34.9	4.2	159	1 534	281.0	24.6	52	90	8.6	1.0

1. Establishments with payroll.

STATE County	Professional, Scientific, and Technical Services[1], 1997				Manufacturing, 1997				Accommodation and Foodservices, 1997			
	Number of Establish-ments	Number of Employees	Receipts (mil dol)	Annual Payroll (mil dol)	Number of Establish-ments	Number of Employees	Receipts (mil dol)	Annual Payroll (mil dol)	Number of Establish-ments	Number of Employees	Sales (mil dol)	Annual Payroll (mil dol)
	147	148	149	150	151	152	153	154	155	156	157	158
TENNESSEE—Cont'd												
Marshall	23	72	3.9	1.2	45	7 552	1 349.1	169.4	34	446	12.9	3.2
Maury	87	396	33.4	11.5	75	11 361	4 431.7	532.6	96	2 152	58.3	16.5
Meigs	6	D	D	D	13	764	125.1	14.2	7	83	1.9	0.6
Monroe	26	72	4.0	1.0	84	5 488	834.9	144.8	55	770	27.7	7.0
Montgomery	120	756	41.0	12.3	83	6 519	1 271.6	182.7	237	4 699	132.3	37.3
Moore	1	D	D	D	NA	NA	NA	NA	5	D	D	D
Morgan	5	D	D	D	24	925	98.8	20.1	8	289	3.8	1.1
Obion	25	74	7.0	1.5	46	5 656	.1 140.0	195.5	51	927	19.9	5.3
Overton	21	34	2.4	0.7	29	1 249	126.4	23.7	21	263	7.6	1.9
Perry	5	D	D	D	15	1 689	169.8	34.9	6	19	0.7	0.1
Pickett	2	D	D	D	NA	NA	NA	NA	7	D	D	D
Polk	6	D	D	D	22	1 061	72.1	18.3	18	160	4.8	1.2
Putnam	104	554	43.9	14.4	141	9 927	1 757.7	232.3	119	2 960	82.2	22.6
Rhea	18	46	4.6	1.0	40	4 674	434.7	105.6	46	531	17.3	4.3
Roane	34	87	9.2	1.9	42	2 075	256.0	47.1	60	1 083	27.2	7.6
Robertson	48	140	9.2	2.8	74	5 019	730.9	127.2	54	1 213	28.4	7.4
Rutherford	211	888	70.9	24.6	191	19 096	8 851.9	754.7	244	6 157	191.5	56.0
Scott	15	48	3.1	1.5	40	2 915	330.0	56.5	22	292	9.3	2.7
Sequatchie	6	D	D	D	11	948	223.8	18.3	16	D	D	D
Sevier	108	392	25.5	9.1	103	2 611	272.4	64.5	453	8 176	384.1	105.5
Shelby	1 675	15 189	1 503.4	565.4	902	44 145	11 758.7	1 476.9	1 429	35 241	1 362.6	371.5
Smith	11	33	2.1	0.6	23	1 710	396.6	44.9	19	D	D	D
Stewart	4	D	D	D	NA	NA	NA	NA	12	97	3.2	0.7
Sullivan	232	1 319	123.9	59.0	182	18 602	4 245.2	816.7	266	5 599	169.5	48.7
Sumner	157	1 200	54.3	21.3	205	11 852	1 932.0	333.8	144	2 207	67.1	18.6
Tipton	35	160	8.8	2.8	39	3 327	604.8	88.6	44	581	18.2	4.6
Trousdale	5	D	D	D	12	693	63.8	14.4	10	115	2.2	0.6
Unicoi	12	21	1.3	0.4	22	1 518	202.5	36.3	19	337	7.1	1.8
Union	7	18	0.6	0.1	20	1 099	141.1	23.6	10	101	3.0	0.8
Van Buren	2	D	D	D	NA	NA	NA	NA	2	D	D	D
Warren	32	105	7.3	1.9	73	6 610	1 133.3	192.5	56	880	24.0	6.6
Washington	196	1 340	75.9	26.0	151	10 370	1 300.9	257.6	190	4 858	140.6	41.1
Wayne	11	D	D	D	28	1 487	99.6	23.0	19	D	D	D
Weakley	30	73	4.0	1.1	45	3 287	574.0	74.9	55	797	18.7	4.7
White	23	72	5.6	1.5	49	3 442	457.3	81.0	17	D	D	D
Williamson	411	3 425	387.2	161.1	115	4 723	846.6	130.7	189	4 711	160.6	44.9
Wilson	104	346	29.5	9.3	114	5 533	1 122.9	161.1	111	2 225	68.7	19.8
TEXAS	42 492	351 422	42 044.1	15 906.7	21 808	959 665	297 657.0	32 760.8	34 160	638 333	22 698.8	6 175.4
Anderson	61	240	19.4	7.6	41	1 419	287.4	36.1	58	1 031	29.7	8.1
Andrews	14	37	3.0	0.8	NA	NA	NA	NA	20	D	D	D
Angelina	108	508	44.1	14.6	88	7 536	1 363.6	212.8	119	1 908	60.7	17.4
Aransas	32	436	17.6	12.2	NA	NA	NA	NA	72	823	24.9	6.8
Archer	5	16	0.6	0.2	NA	NA	NA	NA	5	31	1.0	0.2
Armstrong	NA	NA	NA	NA	NA	NA	NA	NA	4	21	0.4	0.1
Atascosa	30	312	13.2	4.1	NA	NA	NA	NA	44	450	13.4	3.6
Austin	37	145	8.3	3.4	32	947	153.6	26.8	46	425	15.4	3.8
Bailey	14	31	1.6	0.3	NA	NA	NA	NA	17	D	D	D
Bandera	17	30	4.0	1.0	NA	NA	NA	NA	36	288	10.0	3.0
Bastrop	48	146	10.8	4.1	52	801	78.3	18.5	68	889	25.7	7.3
Baylor	8	22	0.9	0.3	NA	NA	NA	NA	9	74	1.9	0.4
Bee	32	112	6.0	1.7	NA	NA	NA	NA	47	503	14.1	3.7
Bell	193	1 901	166.5	48.2	135	7 365	1 351.3	224.5	376	6 673	202.9	53.5
Bexar	2 841	21 741	2 052.4	805.6	1 101	35 919	5 565.5	986.5	2 558	56 118	2 027.8	563.1
Blanco	11	35	3.1	1.2	NA	NA	NA	NA	22	239	6.2	1.9
Borden	NA	NA	NA	NA	NA	NA	NA	NA	NA	NA	NA	NA
Bosque	15	28	1.6	0.6	18	548	74.9	13.4	19	99	2.8	0.7
Bowie	124	566	53.3	16.0	75	4 056	975.5	128.0	142	2 456	82.9	20.0
Brazoria	246	1 212	93.4	38.8	199	14 149	10 761.0	682.9	295	4 787	148.4	41.8
Brazos	279	2 086	200.9	74.8	101	3 126	382.2	79.6	275	5 668	170.7	48.2
Brewster	17	30	2.0	0.4	NA	NA	NA	NA	45	579	15.1	4.0
Briscoe	4	7	0.2	0.1	NA	NA	NA	NA	2	D	D	D
Brooks	8	25	2.2	0.3	NA	NA	NA	NA	21	201	7.2	2.0
Brown	38	130	7.7	1.8	39	3 055	848.5	98.7	77	1 048	31.7	8.3
Burleson	11	38	1.5	0.4	NA	NA	NA	NA	25	234	6.2	1.6
Burnet	49	125	7.8	3.0	42	714	72.5	16.7	63	878	33.9	10.5

1. Firms subject to federal tax.

Table B. States and Counties — Health and Other Services and Federal Funds

	Health Care and Social Assistance[1], 1997				Other Services[1], 1997				Federal funds and grants, fiscal 2001[2]			
									Expenditures (mil dol)			
										Direct payments for individuals[3]		
STATE County	Number of Establishments	Number of Employees	Receipts (mil dol)	Annual Payroll (mil dol)	Number of Establishments	Number of Employees	Receipts (mil dol)	Annual Payroll (mil dol)	Total	Social Security and government retirement	Medicare	Food stamps and Supplemental Security Income
	159	160	161	162	163	164	165	166	167	168	169	170
TENNESSEE—Cont'd												
Marshall	38	368	16.0	6.4	27	82	5.2	1.3	114.4	51.0	25.7	2.4
Maury	132	1 526	107.5	38.9	98	579	34.1	10.8	284.7	137.3	58.8	13.1
Meigs	5	148	4.2	1.6	4	4	0.7	0.1	54.7	26.7	8.7	3.0
Monroe	42	508	20.8	8.5	33	116	6.0	1.9	180.1	86.2	30.1	11.0
Montgomery	153	2 191	123.6	51.0	172	821	43.1	11.7	570.5	311.7	57.5	18.6
Moore	4	D	D	D	4	2	0.3	0.0	17.0	8.1	4.2	0.4
Morgan	5	38	2.3	0.9	4	D	D	D	85.4	37.6	16.1	5.5
Obion	55	593	34.6	13.8	46	375	18.5	6.2	192.8	80.2	34.9	7.7
Overton	22	524	33.0	13.1	17	71	4.3	0.8	110.1	43.3	26.7	4.6
Perry	12	287	15.3	5.7	6	10	0.7	0.2	44.3	18.9	11.8	1.3
Pickett	4	76	3.6	1.1	4	5	0.4	0.1	32.3	10.1	6.8	1.2
Polk	18	69	6.1	2.2	10	37	2.1	0.5	101.4	44.3	20.6	3.5
Putnam	134	1 325	84.4	34.9	107	451	29.4	7.3	338.3	149.1	60.8	12.9
Rhea	34	208	11.3	5.0	29	90	4.5	1.3	218.4	71.1	29.3	8.9
Roane	65	577	32.7	12.1	40	149	10.3	2.9	354.0	143.4	59.0	12.0
Robertson	60	639	31.8	13.0	69	219	15.1	3.1	209.0	101.5	40.2	8.5
Rutherford	250	3 668	197.6	93.2	203	1 001	67.1	19.6	869.8	263.8	80.4	15.5
Scott	30	637	30.1	14.1	17	408	12.4	6.3	235.9	46.0	26.0	12.4
Sequatchie	16	179	7.6	3.4	11	30	1.6	0.3	81.5	21.0	9.8	2.8
Sevier	76	674	34.7	13.7	110	415	25.4	7.3	283.1	158.4	42.6	11.3
Shelby	1 739	22 689	1 984.1	837.5	1 362	10 783	684.5	219.4	5 594.9	1 606.6	679.0	291.0
Smith	29	568	27.0	9.5	21	61	3.7	1.0	85.0	34.3	24.2	3.2
Stewart	7	115	5.4	2.0	7	29	2.2	0.6	112.3	40.4	10.8	2.6
Sullivan	352	5 392	403.3	190.0	239	1 608	88.0	26.9	785.1	416.0	144.2	35.2
Sumner	210	2 658	162.7	63.9	169	774	39.2	11.6	531.6	229.8	92.5	15.8
Tipton	53	618	28.3	11.9	44	190	12.0	2.6	232.4	104.0	34.7	11.5
Trousdale	14	143	6.4	2.2	5	15	1.2	0.2	35.1	12.7	9.9	1.5
Unicoi	21	259	11.9	5.1	16	55	3.7	0.7	148.5	54.7	20.6	3.3
Union	8	90	3.1	0.9	7	39	2.9	0.6	62.2	29.0	9.9	4.3
Van Buren	5	88	2.6	1.1	NA	NA	NA	NA	20.8	8.3	5.2	0.7
Warren	63	920	67.1	23.7	42	137	10.1	2.5	191.6	82.2	52.5	9.0
Washington	240	3 536	262.5	121.0	178	1 217	54.7	21.5	635.4	274.6	96.8	21.1
Wayne	15	323	13.5	5.6	12	16	1.9	0.3	73.4	32.0	15.0	3.7
Weakley	41	995	60.6	23.1	40	155	11.9	3.7	177.8	68.6	35.4	5.2
White	31	486	28.3	10.3	22	65	4.0	1.1	118.0	56.2	24.8	5.5
Williamson	268	5 184	312.7	154.3	158	1 806	188.3	57.2	308.1	183.8	55.4	4.9
Wilson	145	3 170	205.2	85.3	99	504	22.2	6.5	299.1	151.0	69.5	7.2
TEXAS	37 974	557 007	35 620.9	14 725.4	29 162	197 113	12 477.7	3 785.0	112 530.4	34 240.5	14 160.1	3 261.9
Anderson	112	1 568	90.0	39.4	55	209	14.1	3.6	252.5	105.8	54.5	7.4
Andrews	15	124	9.9	2.5	29	174	11.1	3.1	50.6	23.9	11.0	2.3
Angelina	187	3 211	176.1	76.9	141	692	46.9	13.1	360.8	165.9	81.5	14.4
Aransas	31	362	17.2	6.4	21	76	4.0	1.0	108.7	62.0	20.1	3.4
Archer	5	D	D	D	10	34	2.4	0.5	54.3	17.3	5.7	10.8
Armstrong	1	D	D	D	1	D	D	D	27.3	5.0	2.2	0.0
Atascosa	37	733	34.8	14.9	34	152	7.5	2.2	144.3	69.5	25.6	7.7
Austin	30	484	16.1	8.4	33	84	4.8	1.1	574.9	49.5	24.3	2.3
Bailey	6	27	1.3	0.4	20	78	3.6	0.9	59.5	12.3	7.5	0.8
Bandera	12	144	4.1	2.0	13	33	1.7	0.4	75.3	54.0	10.2	1.5
Bastrop	33	383	15.1	6.1	45	183	12.4	3.7	210.1	104.7	33.5	5.3
Baylor	8	794	6.5	3.6	16	27	3.3	0.3	39.3	13.1	7.3	0.7
Bee	46	493	23.0	10.5	38	164	8.0	2.2	134.6	50.0	28.5	6.8
Bell	292	5 985	414.0	140.2	323	1 765	82.8	26.7	2 804.0	563.5	112.4	28.4
Bexar	2 900	51 908	3 052.9	1 251.8	2 167	15 346	841.4	272.7	10 617.8	3 379.8	1 046.1	280.8
Blanco	10	158	4.6	3.0	10	30	2.5	0.5	69.4	45.5	14.0	1.1
Borden	NA	NA	NA	NA	NA	NA	NA	NA	9.4	0.6	0.4	0.0
Bosque	11	164	8.4	3.7	12	29	1.9	0.4	88.4	49.2	19.4	2.0
Bowie	233	3 731	231.1	110.2	138	872	55.1	15.5	640.0	248.8	95.4	18.0
Brazoria	306	2 905	155.5	65.8	298	1 312	88.5	24.1	703.4	353.6	136.0	22.0
Brazos	263	2 838	212.1	84.9	196	1 244	64.8	18.4	639.2	171.6	52.7	11.1
Brewster	10	42	2.4	0.9	12	35	1.8	0.3	48.5	19.5	6.0	0.9
Briscoe	NA	NA	NA	NA	3	9	0.2	0.0	24.6	4.7	3.3	0.2
Brooks	9	389	6.0	2.4	10	60	3.1	0.8	61.2	13.9	9.4	4.4
Brown	96	2 526	115.5	44.1	63	292	14.5	4.2	199.0	91.3	49.2	6.5
Burleson	10	136	5.5	2.3	21	90	5.2	1.3	84.8	37.9	14.7	2.9
Burnet	61	454	20.4	7.3	51	126	9.5	2.2	139.1	87.6	24.7	2.5

1. Firms subject to federal tax.   2. October 1, 2000 to September 30, 2001.   3. State totals may include programs not allocated by county.

Table B. States and Counties — Federal Funds and Local Government Finances

	Federal funds and grants, fiscal 2001[1] (cont'd)							Local government finances, 1997				
	Expenditures (mil dol) (cont'd)							General revenue				
	Procurement contract awards		Grants[2]							Taxes		
STATE County	Salaries and wages	Defense	Other	Medicaid and other health-related	Nutrition and family welfare	Education	Other	Total (mil dol)	Intergovern-mental (mil dol)	Total (mil dol)	Per capita[3] (dollars) Total	Property
	171	172	173	174	175	176	177	178	179	180	181	182

TENNESSEE—Cont'd

Marshall	3.9	2.1	1.3	16.2	1.3	2.0	5.0	40.3	16.5	17.0	662	430
Maury	11.7	0.1	6.9	38.3	4.1	3.7	1.6	211.4	44.8	36.4	535	331
Meigs	2.1	0.0	0.3	7.4	3.0	0.6	2.1	12.6	8.7	2.3	242	165
Monroe	5.0	0.0	1.9	32.1	2.2	2.9	5.7	46.5	25.1	13.9	409	209
Montgomery	79.7	0.6	5.6	41.1	9.6	8.4	8.7	266.3	86.5	76.8	618	330
Moore	0.3	0.0	0.1	1.2	1.7	0.3	0.4	5.4	3.5	0.6	112	69
Morgan	2.1	0.0	0.5	16.7	2.8	1.1	2.4	24.0	14.9	6.4	344	280
Obion	7.3	0.1	1.4	25.4	3.2	2.2	6.4	55.5	22.2	21.5	670	328
Overton	3.2	0.0	0.7	26.4	1.8	1.3	0.5	27.9	16.1	5.9	308	186
Perry	1.2	0.0	0.3	8.1	0.6	0.4	0.2	11.9	6.7	3.5	471	341
Pickett	0.6	0.0	0.2	8.3	0.5	0.3	3.2	8.5	5.5	1.7	376	248
Polk	4.5	1.7	4.2	15.9	1.2	1.0	2.9	19.2	11.5	5.9	404	266
Putnam	14.0	3.6	30.2	42.2	5.9	3.7	6.4	147.7	34.1	30.6	525	310
Rhea	60.6	0.0	4.4	24.0	3.0	1.9	12.4	51.4	22.5	10.6	385	233
Roane	28.6	0.0	45.0	40.9	5.8	3.1	4.4	98.7	35.8	26.5	531	332
Robertson	5.8	0.0	3.3	24.0	3.7	2.3	3.1	76.8	33.9	28.0	544	327
Rutherford	95.6	6.0	284.9	45.0	7.3	11.4	19.9	283.8	101.9	121.0	758	456
Scott	4.6	77.7	24.9	33.6	3.7	1.7	3.5	35.3	23.5	7.7	391	237
Sequatchie	0.9	0.0	19.9	7.1	1.2	0.7	17.3	14.5	8.6	4.0	396	259
Sevier	17.1	0.5	10.5	27.1	4.1	3.0	6.2	162.1	41.6	79.0	1 262	302
Shelby	801.9	373.8	512.1	758.4	157.2	58.5	149.6	2 121.2	671.8	804.3	929	552
Smith	4.7	0.1	0.7	13.0	1.2	0.7	0.3	21.7	12.1	5.6	348	207
Stewart	28.7	1.9	13.4	9.8	0.9	0.6	2.2	15.6	10.9	2.8	253	177
Sullivan	28.6	1.9	6.0	95.3	16.8	9.0	12.5	247.2	80.6	120.1	797	518
Sumner	25.9	0.3	96.5	43.4	5.4	4.8	6.4	200.0	75.1	75.7	621	382
Tipton	6.7	7.5	1.7	37.2	5.9	2.9	4.8	70.2	39.5	20.5	445	291
Trousdale	2.7	0.0	0.3	5.4	0.6	0.3	0.5	10.9	6.1	3.0	439	318
Unicoi	4.4	1.7	43.8	16.3	1.6	1.0	0.4	41.8	12.3	7.2	415	270
Union	1.2	0.0	0.3	13.1	1.8	0.9	1.4	19.4	13.6	3.9	245	176
Van Buren	0.3	0.0	0.1	4.2	0.5	0.3	0.7	8.2	5.6	1.9	377	243
Warren	6.7	0.6	1.3	27.2	2.7	2.2	0.7	52.9	24.7	18.4	515	302
Washington	90.3	1.1	36.7	65.3	7.7	7.8	6.0	160.0	57.6	69.0	679	414
Wayne	1.8	0.1	0.4	16.8	1.3	0.9	0.6	25.0	13.4	5.2	315	198
Weakley	8.6	0.0	1.7	19.4	6.0	2.1	11.1	46.4	22.2	13.6	415	245
White	3.4	0.1	0.8	21.2	1.6	1.3	0.6	27.7	15.2	7.6	342	225
Williamson	18.7	2.2	5.0	22.8	3.4	3.4	5.4	268.9	64.0	119.8	1 076	702
Wilson	11.7	0.0	2.1	29.7	9.0	3.2	10.8	112.1	45.0	46.6	574	319
TEXAS	12 104.2	9 460.4	6 188.4	9 950.1	3 101.7	2 848.1	5 775.3	X	X	X	X	X
Anderson	8.0	0.0	12.6	42.0	2.5	1.5	8.4	72.1	29.3	32.5	618	493
Andrews	1.2	0.0	0.2	4.5	0.7	0.6	1.2	49.5	2.9	31.0	2 204	2 091
Angelina	21.6	0.2	4.1	51.1	6.1	2.8	3.9	172.8	83.2	53.6	698	499
Aransas	1.4	0.2	0.7	6.4	1.6	0.9	10.5	34.4	8.3	19.7	870	734
Archer	10.3	0.0	0.2	3.2	0.2	0.2	1.0	16.4	7.6	7.0	846	665
Armstrong	0.3	0.0	0.1	1.3	0.1	0.1	11.1	3.7	1.7	1.6	721	594
Atascosa	3.0	-0.2	0.8	26.9	3.8	2.1	0.7	70.0	39.2	20.5	582	471
Austin	5.5	461.6	8.7	13.8	1.2	0.7	2.9	43.4	15.1	19.9	868	710
Bailey	1.4	0.0	0.3	4.7	0.8	0.4	6.3	22.3	8.4	5.8	843	726
Bandera	3.5	0.0	0.3	3.5	0.4	0.4	1.2	20.2	6.9	10.6	708	618
Bastrop	18.2	0.2	1.9	29.5	4.0	1.6	6.8	97.8	40.7	29.1	593	503
Baylor	0.9	0.0	0.2	4.1	0.5	0.2	3.0	8.7	4.0	3.2	775	668
Bee	2.4	0.1	1.8	23.7	4.9	2.8	1.0	66.9	34.5	14.7	525	406
Bell	1 572.7	257.9	36.0	63.2	15.1	44.3	23.0	537.2	269.8	150.4	676	492
Bexar	2 187.0	1 507.6	529.0	882.3	170.8	102.8	295.9	3 094.4	1 211.1	1 152.0	864	714
Blanco	3.3	0.0	0.9	2.1	0.1	0.5	1.3	13.7	5.8	6.0	725	615
Borden	0.1	0.0	0.2	0.0	0.1	0.0	1.0	5.7	0.2	4.6	6 210	6 148
Bosque	3.4	0.7	0.8	9.4	0.7	0.6	0.4	32.0	16.7	9.6	573	488
Bowie	95.8	48.1	7.3	64.2	9.8	3.5	27.3	170.6	82.0	58.5	699	485
Brazoria	28.0	11.8	8.5	45.7	6.0	5.8	26.3	460.1	111.3	246.4	1 093	978
Brazos	54.5	12.0	22.6	80.7	9.9	9.1	160.3	246.1	60.9	125.8	946	712
Brewster	8.3	0.0	1.0	4.7	0.7	1.6	1.7	30.6	9.3	6.1	675	520
Briscoe	0.5	0.0	0.1	2.7	0.1	0.1	2.5	3.4	1.4	1.6	808	705
Brooks	4.6	0.0	0.2	20.2	1.9	1.0	0.7	17.2	7.3	7.6	895	809
Brown	6.7	7.0	1.1	23.8	3.0	1.5	1.8	75.9	38.9	24.8	673	513
Burleson	2.5	0.6	0.5	15.2	1.5	0.5	2.1	28.0	10.2	14.1	916	775
Burnet	4.1	0.4	1.2	10.9	0.7	0.9	2.7	65.7	16.5	27.1	882	725

1. October 1, 2000 to September 30, 2001. 2. State totals may include programs not allocated by county. 3. Based on the resident population estimated as of July 1 of the year shown.

STATE County	Total (mil dol)	Per capita¹ (dollars)	Education	Health and hospitals	Police protection	Public welfare	Highways	Total (mil dol)	Per capita¹ (dollars)	Federal civilian	Federal military	State and local	Democratic	Republican	All other
	183	184	185	186	187	188	189	190	191	192	193	194	195	196	197
TENNESSEE—Cont'd															
Marshall	37.7	1 468	54.5	2.7	6.3	0.2	9.1	34.1	1 328	66	102	1 360	54.6	43.9	1.6
Maury	224.4	3 296	22.7	43.8	2.8	0.0	3.2	192.8	2 831	211	271	5 210	47.6	51.0	1.5
Meigs	15.6	1 608	70.2	1.1	2.7	0.0	8.7	6.4	656	22	39	397	45.9	53.0	1.2
Monroe	48.4	1 426	63.6	2.3	4.0	0.1	6.0	23.8	702	106	137	1 346	41.0	57.8	1.2
Montgomery	260.4	2 096	45.8	27.3	4.1	1.2	3.7	215.6	1 736	784	506	7 239	48.2	50.3	1.5
Moore	6.9	1 328	65.8	0.0	8.1	0.0	3.3	0.0	0	0	20	687	48.1	49.8	2.2
Morgan	21.4	1 159	69.5	2.1	2.1	0.0	9.8	6.4	346	41	72	1 507	47.4	51.0	1.5
Obion	52.5	1 635	53.2	0.3	5.9	3.2	8.6	16.3	508	128	124	1 539	48.7	49.6	1.7
Overton	24.9	1 304	55.6	2.4	4.0	0.0	9.3	17.4	907	52	76	1 005	60.1	38.4	1.5
Perry	10.8	1 448	52.9	3.6	4.3	0.0	15.0	4.0	540	19	29	339	57.6	40.6	1.8
Pickett	8.1	1 768	52.6	4.1	3.1	0.0	14.1	4.1	888	0	18	250	41.9	57.2	0.8
Polk	16.6	1 127	63.8	2.7	4.6	0.0	10.7	6.1	416	73	58	691	46.0	52.0	2.0
Putnam	159.3	2 735	29.4	35.1	4.2	0.0	4.3	96.7	1 660	254	237	6 356	48.1	50.1	1.8
Rhea	50.2	1 818	38.8	26.0	3.2	0.0	5.7	25.1	908	880	108	1 450	38.1	60.4	1.6
Roane	89.4	1 791	44.7	27.1	3.6	0.1	5.2	60.4	1 211	490	192	3 573	44.9	53.2	1.9
Robertson	77.2	1 500	52.6	1.5	12.6	0.0	7.3	75.0	1 457	96	211	2 543	50.8	48.0	1.2
Rutherford	268.4	1 682	47.5	3.1	10.2	0.0	5.0	314.1	1 969	1 886	668	9 942	44.0	53.8	2.2
Scott	31.4	1 585	61.8	1.9	4.3	0.0	10.7	38.2	1 929	90	78	1 186	44.9	54.1	1.1
Sequatchie	16.1	1 594	60.7	1.3	3.6	0.0	11.9	15.6	1 541	11	42	482	42.4	55.8	1.8
Sevier	147.0	2 348	40.8	1.3	5.9	0.1	7.3	152.0	2 428	369	253	3 576	32.4	66.0	1.6
Shelby	2 268.1	2 619	36.3	13.0	8.0	0.3	3.2	2 816.8	3 253	15 269	5 017	57 043	56.5	42.1	1.3
Smith	21.7	1 348	53.0	3.5	6.2	0.0	10.6	10.0	623	110	64	679	66.5	32.4	1.1
Stewart	17.0	1 513	69.3	1.8	4.1	0.1	9.7	10.8	958	486	45	599	60.0	38.2	1.8
Sullivan	246.3	1 635	56.1	1.5	5.5	0.2	5.9	255.8	1 698	515	580	6 999	38.3	60.1	1.6
Sumner	174.9	1 436	55.9	1.4	6.2	0.2	5.4	117.3	963	447	485	5 371	43.8	54.7	1.5
Tipton	69.7	1 515	62.3	0.5	9.2	0.0	7.1	63.5	1 380	109	186	2 051	38.1	60.8	1.1
Trousdale	9.6	1 414	51.0	1.1	9.8	0.0	13.0	7.7	1 132	47	27	374	66.8	32.3	1.0
Unicoi	41.8	2 423	27.9	47.5	3.4	0.2	4.4	15.9	924	90	67	943	39.9	58.8	1.3
Union	26.5	1 664	82.2	0.9	2.4	0.0	1.6	10.8	679	23	64	570	44.0	55.0	1.0
Van Buren	8.7	1 743	55.6	2.3	2.4	0.0	16.2	6.6	1 318	0	19	239	58.9	39.7	1.5
Warren	49.5	1 385	57.4	2.7	5.1	0.1	6.2	59.7	1 668	117	140	1 819	56.2	42.3	1.5
Washington	173.7	1 710	50.5	0.8	5.3	0.8	9.1	191.2	1 882	1 870	411	9 016	38.9	59.5	1.6
Wayne	22.6	1 368	52.2	2.1	3.7	12.1	12.8	5.8	353	28	63	1 097	35.0	63.5	1.4
Weakley	46.6	1 420	46.7	0.5	6.5	8.0	11.6	48.8	1 487	136	132	3 190	47.0	51.6	1.5
White	33.7	1 521	64.6	1.4	3.8	0.3	7.1	20.3	914	58	88	973	53.2	45.3	1.4
Williamson	260.2	2 336	45.6	18.5	3.7	0.1	7.4	285.0	2 559	292	476	5 552	32.1	66.6	1.3
Wilson	107.9	1 330	60.3	1.0	6.0	0.0	5.2	108.8	1 341	167	333	3 060	46.1	52.5	1.5
TEXAS	X	X	X	X	X	X	X	X	X	181 100	165 644	1 335 709	38.0	59.3	2.8
Anderson	68.3	1 301	65.4	0.3	5.3	0.0	5.2	36.0	686	128	137	5 759	33.4	65.2	1.4
Andrews	45.1	3 204	49.0	27.7	2.8	0.1	5.4	0.1	11	26	36	1 114	21.8	76.8	1.4
Angelina	181.2	2 360	59.2	14.0	3.5	0.4	4.4	130.4	1 698	381	205	5 949	36.9	61.7	1.4
Aransas	31.8	1 406	61.6	2.8	7.4	0.2	7.5	10.2	451	28	61	988	32.0	65.4	2.7
Archer	15.2	1 832	74.6	0.1	1.2	0.7	7.5	1.1	128	23	23	483	24.8	73.8	1.3
Armstrong	3.7	1 689	69.7	0.3	3.8	0.1	7.5	0.1	55	0	0	130	16.0	82.3	1.7
Atascosa	72.4	2 053	76.6	0.3	2.6	0.8	4.0	13.4	381	52	98	2 050	40.2	58.0	1.8
Austin	50.0	2 185	69.2	0.6	4.9	0.1	4.9	34.2	1 495	105	64	1 286	26.1	72.2	1.7
Bailey	22.2	3 250	46.4	21.5	3.3	6.1	2.8	1.8	257	32	18	576	23.3	76.0	0.6
Bandera	18.8	1 256	71.9	0.9	4.0	0.4	4.4	6.0	400	18	44	681	19.6	77.2	3.3
Bastrop	84.8	1 730	66.2	8.2	3.7	0.6	4.8	82.9	1 692	362	138	3 084	38.1	56.3	5.6
Baylor	8.1	1 954	57.2	2.8	6.0	0.0	9.2	4.4	1 047	19	11	264	33.4	64.8	1.8
Bee	67.9	2 422	72.0	0.5	2.7	0.0	2.9	27.2	969	49	72	3 819	45.6	53.2	1.3
Bell	508.0	2 285	65.0	3.7	3.8	0.5	2.4	618.6	2 783	7 785	42 646	14 643	33.2	65.1	1.7
Bexar	3 120.5	2 342	48.5	11.6	5.8	2.6	3.2	6 604.3	4 956	33 104	35 772	88 505	44.9	52.2	2.9
Blanco	12.0	1 463	71.0	0.2	5.4	0.7	4.2	5.9	719	84	22	395	21.5	73.7	4.7
Borden	4.9	6 505	79.1	0.1	1.5	0.0	9.2	0.0	0	0	0	90	17.6	80.2	2.2
Bosque	30.3	1 816	68.4	11.7	3.1	0.2	3.5	16.0	959	71	44	867	28.5	70.1	1.4
Bowie	166.2	1 987	62.4	3.4	4.5	0.5	2.8	101.4	1 212	3 290	233	5 803	38.5	60.4	1.1
Brazoria	453.6	2 012	61.7	6.0	4.8	0.5	5.1	409.3	1 816	462	657	14 007	31.1	66.8	2.1
Brazos	273.9	2 060	49.1	3.1	4.8	0.3	3.9	325.7	2 448	967	462	26 801	26.3	70.0	3.7
Brewster	30.0	3 317	37.9	41.0	2.3	0.0	2.6	6.7	741	165	23	1 356	37.7	52.2	10.1
Briscoe	2.6	1 334	67.6	0.1	2.2	0.0	7.3	10.5	5 300	13	0	124	29.0	70.5	0.5
Brooks	16.8	1 986	65.5	3.1	4.0	2.2	0.4	0.1	9	83	22	578	76.3	22.9	0.9
Brown	73.9	2 002	59.2	10.2	3.9	0.7	4.4	45.9	1 244	109	98	2 762	24.3	74.4	1.4
Burleson	28.7	1 871	64.8	3.1	4.7	0.1	10.0	6.9	449	58	41	820	38.1	60.4	1.5
Burnet	66.1	2 150	51.8	15.6	4.8	0.3	3.4	71.9	2 338	71	90	1 829	26.9	70.2	2.9

1. Based on the resident population estimated as of July 1 of the year shown.   2. Data subject to copyright.

Table B. States and Counties — **Land Area and Population**

STATE/ County code	MSA/ PMSA/ NECMA code[1]	County Type[2]	STATE County	Land area,[3] (sq km) 2000	Total persons	Rank	Per square kilometer	White	Black	Am. Indian, Alaska Native	Asian and Pacific Islander	Percent Hispanic[4]	Under 5 years	5 to 17 years	18 to 24 years	25 to 34 years	35 to 44 years	45 to 54 years
				1	2	3	4	5	6	7	8	9	10	11	12	13	14	15
			TEXAS—Cont'd															
48 055	0640	2	Caldwell	1 413	32 194	1 342	22.8	72.6	8.9	1.1	0.7	40.4	7.4	21.0	8.5	14.1	15.7	13.0
48 057	...	6	Calhoun	1 327	20 647	1 755	15.6	80.1	2.9	0.9	3.6	40.9	7.8	20.7	8.7	12.4	14.9	12.6
48 059	...	6	Callahan	2 327	12 905	2 240	5.5	96.0	0.4	1.1	0.7	6.3	5.5	20.7	6.6	9.8	15.1	13.9
48 061	1240	2	Cameron	2 346	335 227	174	142.9	82.4	0.6	0.6	0.7	84.3	9.5	24.3	10.5	13.8	12.9	10.7
48 063	...	6	Camp	512	11 549	2 330	22.6	70.5	19.5	0.8	0.3	14.8	7.3	19.5	8.5	12.0	13.6	12.7
48 065	...	8	Carson	2 391	6 516	2 738	2.7	95.1	0.8	1.6	0.3	7.0	6.1	21.7	6.2	9.8	16.5	13.6
48 067	...	6	Cass	2 428	30 438	1 387	12.5	79.1	19.8	1.0	0.2	1.7	6.0	18.9	7.6	10.6	13.9	13.9
48 069	...	7	Castro	2 327	8 285	2 582	3.6	77.1	2.6	1.6	0.0	51.6	8.5	24.6	9.0	10.9	13.4	12.4
48 071	3360	1	Chambers	1 552	26 031	1 515	16.8	82.9	10.0	0.9	0.8	10.8	6.9	22.0	8.2	12.7	17.2	15.3
48 073	...	6	Cherokee	2 725	46 659	967	17.1	75.5	16.3	0.9	0.6	13.2	7.0	19.3	9.3	12.9	14.5	12.5
48 075	...	7	Childress	1 840	7 688	2 630	4.2	69.4	14.5	0.8	0.5	20.5	5.7	16.4	12.1	13.8	16.9	10.8
48 077	...	6	Clay	2 843	11 006	2 365	3.9	96.8	0.5	2.0	0.2	3.7	5.8	19.0	6.8	10.1	16.3	14.3
48 079	...	7	Cochran	2 008	3 730	2 940	1.9	66.5	5.1	1.0	0.3	44.1	6.5	25.0	8.0	10.4	14.1	10.9
48 081	...	8	Coke	2 328	3 864	2 925	1.7	90.1	2.0	1.2	0.3	16.9	4.3	20.1	7.5	8.0	12.5	11.7
48 083	...	6	Coleman	3 264	9 235	2 509	2.8	90.2	2.4	1.2	0.4	14.0	5.8	17.9	6.6	9.4	13.3	12.3
48 085	1920	0	Collin	2 195	491 675	113	224.0	83.2	5.2	1.0	7.7	10.3	8.6	20.1	7.4	17.8	20.1	13.7
48 087	...	9	Collingsworth	2 380	3 206	2 978	1.3	82.0	5.5	2.6	0.3	20.4	5.9	20.5	6.6	9.4	13.2	12.8
48 089	...	7	Colorado	2 494	20 390	1 768	8.2	74.3	15.1	0.7	0.5	19.7	6.0	19.6	8.9	10.0	13.8	13.0
48 091	7240	1	Comal	1 454	78 021	652	53.7	90.9	1.2	1.0	0.8	22.6	6.2	19.3	7.0	11.4	16.1	14.9
48 093	...	7	Comanche	2 429	14 026	2 161	5.8	88.9	0.6	1.3	0.2	20.9	6.3	19.0	7.1	10.7	12.6	12.0
48 095	...	8	Concho	2 568	3 966	2 921	1.5	89.3	1.1	0.8	0.2	41.3	3.7	12.4	10.4	21.2	17.0	12.2
48 097	...	6	Cooke	2 263	36 363	1 203	16.1	90.3	3.3	1.6	0.6	10.0	6.7	20.6	8.7	11.6	14.5	13.1
48 099	3810	2	Coryell	2 724	74 978	665	27.5	68.0	23.2	1.6	3.5	12.6	7.8	18.4	17.9	19.8	16.5	8.6
48 101	...	9	Cottle	2 334	1 904	3 072	0.8	82.8	10.5	0.9	0.0	18.9	5.1	18.9	5.7	7.9	13.6	12.5
48 103	...	6	Crane	2 035	3 996	2 920	2.0	76.1	3.2	1.1	0.4	43.9	7.7	24.2	7.7	11.5	15.3	13.5
48 105	...	7	Crockett	7 271	4 099	2 908	0.6	78.5	0.9	1.0	0.3	54.7	6.7	22.2	7.1	10.8	15.6	14.2
48 107	...	8	Crosby	2 330	7 072	2 678	3.0	65.2	4.1	0.9	0.3	48.9	7.8	22.9	8.5	11.6	12.4	11.1
48 109	...	7	Culberson	9 874	2 975	2 993	0.3	70.9	0.7	0.8	0.7	72.2	7.5	24.6	7.8	12.8	13.0	12.5
48 111	...	7	Dallam	3 897	6 222	2 761	1.6	84.6	1.9	1.6	0.5	28.4	8.6	23.2	8.6	14.7	14.1	12.5
48 113	1920	0	Dallas	2 278	2 218 899	10	974.1	60.6	20.8	1.0	4.5	29.9	8.2	19.7	10.7	18.0	16.4	12.0
48 115	...	7	Dawson	2 336	14 985	2 092	6.4	74.1	8.8	0.6	0.3	48.2	6.3	19.3	8.9	14.6	16.2	12.6
48 117	...	6	Deaf Smith	3 878	18 561	1 868	4.8	74.1	1.7	1.1	0.6	57.4	9.0	24.3	9.6	12.5	13.0	11.4
48 119	...	8	Delta	718	5 327	2 827	7.4	89.4	8.8	1.8	0.2	3.1	5.6	20.0	7.5	11.2	14.3	12.0
48 121	1920	0	Denton	2 301	432 976	139	188.2	83.6	6.3	1.2	4.6	12.2	8.2	19.6	11.3	18.0	18.9	12.8
48 123	...	6	De Witt	2 355	20 013	1 793	8.5	77.9	11.3	0.9	0.4	27.2	5.5	18.3	7.0	10.9	16.1	13.6
48 125	...	9	Dickens	2 342	2 762	3 007	1.2	78.6	8.4	0.9	0.4	23.9	4.2	14.3	10.4	14.9	14.8	11.9
48 127	...	7	Dimmit	3 447	10 248	2 422	3.0	79.2	1.1	0.9	0.9	85.0	8.3	24.9	8.8	12.0	12.7	12.5
48 129	...	9	Donley	2 408	3 828	2 926	1.6	92.3	4.4	1.1	0.2	6.3	4.7	17.6	9.8	8.6	12.0	12.5
48 131	...	7	Duval	4 643	13 120	2 220	2.8	83.2	0.6	0.8	0.3	88.0	7.4	22.1	9.5	12.3	14.1	11.7
48 133	...	7	Eastland	2 398	18 297	1 880	7.6	92.2	2.3	0.9	0.2	10.8	5.9	17.4	9.8	9.2	13.1	12.6
48 135	5800	3	Ector	2 334	121 123	447	51.9	76.3	4.9	1.4	0.9	42.4	8.0	22.4	10.5	12.8	15.2	12.4
48 137	...	9	Edwards	5 490	2 162	3 053	0.4	85.0	1.4	1.2	0.2	45.1	5.8	22.7	6.5	8.4	14.8	13.2
48 139	1920	1	Ellis	2 434	111 360	486	45.8	82.3	8.9	1.1	0.5	18.4	7.6	22.6	9.3	13.1	16.7	13.5
48 141	2320	2	El Paso	2 624	679 622	75	259.0	76.8	3.5	1.1	1.5	78.2	8.7	23.3	10.6	14.5	14.8	11.3
48 143	...	6	Erath	2 814	33 001	1 319	11.7	91.0	1.0	1.2	0.8	15.0	6.5	18.1	17.0	12.7	13.2	11.2
48 145	...	6	Falls	1 992	18 576	1 866	9.3	62.9	27.7	0.8	0.2	15.8	6.0	21.7	7.8	12.7	14.3	11.6
48 147	...	6	Fannin	2 309	31 242	1 369	13.5	87.9	8.2	1.8	0.5	5.6	5.8	17.4	8.9	13.0	15.7	13.0
48 149	...	7	Fayette	2 461	21 804	1 701	8.9	85.6	7.2	0.6	0.4	12.8	5.4	17.8	7.0	9.1	14.5	13.8
48 151	...	9	Fisher	2 334	4 344	2 892	1.9	85.1	2.9	0.8	0.2	21.4	5.7	18.2	6.3	9.0	14.0	12.5
48 153	...	7	Floyd	2 570	7 771	2 628	3.0	75.8	3.6	1.1	0.3	45.9	8.2	23.2	7.4	11.5	12.9	11.5
48 155	...	9	Foard	1 830	1 622	3 088	0.9	85.6	3.5	1.4	0.2	16.3	5.7	20.1	5.8	10.0	12.3	11.9
48 157	3360	0	Fort Bend	2 265	354 452	166	156.5	58.9	20.4	0.6	12.1	21.1	7.7	24.3	7.6	12.9	19.3	15.6
48 159	...	9	Franklin	740	9 458	2 490	12.8	90.0	4.1	1.1	0.2	8.9	5.7	18.6	7.3	10.9	13.9	13.3
48 161	...	7	Freestone	2 273	17 867	1 907	7.9	76.5	19.1	0.6	0.4	8.2	5.6	18.1	8.9	13.1	14.9	13.0
48 163	...	7	Frio	2 935	16 252	2 004	5.5	74.2	5.0	0.8	0.6	73.8	7.7	21.0	11.2	16.8	14.0	11.3
48 165	...	7	Gaines	3 891	14 467	2 125	3.7	82.4	2.4	1.3	0.3	35.8	8.4	26.7	9.5	11.7	15.0	10.8
48 167	2920	0	Galveston	1 032	250 158	231	242.4	74.5	15.8	0.9	2.6	18.0	7.0	19.7	8.7	13.2	17.0	14.4
48 169	...	6	Garza	2 319	4 872	2 856	2.1	77.3	5.4	1.1	0.3	37.2	6.5	21.6	7.9	13.9	14.7	12.0
48 171	...	7	Gillespie	2 748	20 814	1 747	7.6	93.9	0.3	0.7	0.3	15.9	5.0	16.5	5.5	8.5	12.6	13.7
48 173	...	8	Glasscock	2 333	1 406	3 097	0.6	80.0	0.6	0.3	0.2	29.9	8.0	25.5	7.1	11.5	17.0	12.5
48 175	...	8	Goliad	2 211	6 928	2 693	3.1	84.2	5.0	1.0	0.2	35.2	5.8	20.1	6.5	10.0	15.1	14.4
48 177	...	6	Gonzales	2 765	18 628	1 865	6.7	73.9	8.8	0.8	0.6	39.6	7.0	21.0	8.7	11.6	14.0	11.8
48 179	...	7	Gray	2 404	22 744	1 661	9.5	84.3	6.2	2.3	0.6	13.0	5.9	18.2	8.4	12.2	15.0	13.2
48 181	7640	3	Grayson	2 418	110 595	491	45.7	89.1	6.3	2.4	0.9	6.8	6.5	18.8	9.3	12.1	15.4	13.2
48 183	4420	3	Gregg	710	111 379	490	156.9	74.2	20.3	1.1	0.9	9.1	7.0	19.7	10.3	13.0	15.2	12.9
48 185	...	6	Grimes	2 055	23 552	1 612	11.5	73.3	20.2	0.7	0.5	16.1	6.1	18.6	7.7	12.5	17.3	14.5

1. MSA = Metropolitan Statistical Area. PMSA = Primary MSA. NECMA = New England County Metropolitan Area. See Appendix A for explanation of these concepts. See Appendix B for list of metropolitan areas identified by type, with component counties. 2. County typology code from the Economic Research Service of USDA. See Appendix A for definition. 3. Dry land or land partially or temporarily covered by water. 4. Hispanic persons may be of any race.

Table B. States and Counties — **Population and Households**

STATE County	Age (percent) (cont'd)				Population — change and components of change, 1990–2001							Households, 2000				
					Total persons		Percent change		Components of change, 2000–2001						Percent	
	55 to 64 years	65 to 74 years	75 years and over	Percent female	2001	1990	1990–2000	2000–2001	Births	Deaths	Net migration	Number	Percent change, 1990–2000	Persons per house-hold	Female family house-holder[1]	One person
	16	17	18	19	20	21	22	23	24	25	26	27	28	29	30	31
TEXAS—Cont'd																
Caldwell	7.8	6.4	6.1	50.6	34 193	26 392	22.0	6.2	653	350	1 661	10 816	23.7	2.82	13.3	21.2
Calhoun	9.7	8.3	5.0	49.8	20 600	19 053	8.4	-0.2	443	195	-296	7 442	9.8	2.75	11.0	21.3
Callahan	11.4	9.3	7.7	51.4	12 863	11 859	8.8	-0.3	183	172	-51	5 061	10.9	2.53	9.3	23.3
Cameron	7.1	6.3	4.8	52.1	344 782	260 120	28.9	2.9	10 262	2 275	1 695	97 267	32.7	3.40	17.4	15.4
Camp	10.1	8.9	7.3	51.0	11 507	9 904	16.6	-0.4	248	178	-113	4 336	14.9	2.62	12.5	24.2
Carson	10.3	8.3	7.4	51.1	6 474	6 576	-0.9	-0.6	97	82	-56	2 470	2.8	2.60	8.1	22.3
Cass	11.5	8.9	8.6	52.0	30 471	29 982	1.5	0.1	487	512	74	12 190	7.7	2.46	12.2	26.4
Castro	8.5	7.6	5.1	49.9	8 129	9 070	-8.7	-1.9	187	78	-273	2 761	-4.0	2.98	8.7	20.5
Chambers	8.7	5.4	3.6	49.8	26 859	20 088	29.6	3.2	406	217	630	9 139	31.9	2.82	9.0	17.8
Cherokee	9.4	7.6	7.5	49.7	47 231	41 049	13.7	1.2	934	657	313	16 651	11.1	2.63	12.8	24.2
Childress	8.6	8.5	7.3	41.2	7 651	5 953	29.1	-0.5	121	106	-50	2 474	1.6	2.40	11.4	30.8
Clay	11.6	9.3	6.8	51.5	11 179	10 024	9.8	1.6	116	164	213	4 323	13.5	2.52	7.3	23.5
Cochran	10.3	8.0	6.5	52.1	3 689	4 377	-14.8	-1.1	81	45	-81	1 309	-8.5	2.79	9.9	20.9
Coke	11.9	13.3	10.8	50.0	3 873	3 424	12.9	0.2	39	89	59	1 544	12.4	2.31	8.1	29.0
Coleman	11.7	11.1	12.0	52.0	9 033	9 710	-4.9	-2.2	149	224	-126	3 889	-3.4	2.33	9.3	30.2
Collin	7.0	3.1	2.2	50.0	541 403	264 036	86.2	10.1	9 940	2 050	40 735	181 970	89.9	2.68	7.5	22.1
Collingsworth	9.6	10.3	11.7	51.8	3 135	3 573	-10.3	-2.2	43	68	-47	1 294	-10.6	2.44	9.8	27.8
Colorado	10.2	9.4	9.2	51.2	20 230	18 383	10.9	-0.8	349	383	-119	7 641	8.8	2.56	10.9	26.2
Comal	10.3	8.0	6.9	51.0	82 563	51 832	50.5	5.8	1 294	796	3 954	29 066	50.5	2.64	9.0	20.6
Comanche	12.0	10.0	10.3	51.1	13 751	13 381	4.8	-2.0	236	249	-266	5 522	3.8	2.48	8.1	26.3
Concho	9.3	6.4	7.4	35.6	3 917	3 044	30.3	-1.2	28	35	-43	1 058	-0.5	2.45	9.7	26.6
Cooke	9.9	7.7	7.2	50.7	37 193	30 777	18.1	2.3	567	456	718	13 643	18.2	2.60	9.9	23.3
Coryell	5.2	3.3	2.4	48.7	74 426	64 226	16.7	-0.2	1 263	420	-1 315	19 950	9.6	2.91	11.0	16.9
Cottle	10.8	11.1	14.4	53.4	1 805	2 247	-15.3	-5.2	25	33	-94	820	-10.4	2.28	10.6	32.0
Crane	9.2	5.7	5.2	51.3	3 919	4 652	-14.1	-1.9	89	59	-111	1 360	-11.5	2.91	7.9	18.8
Crockett	10.5	7.0	5.9	50.5	3 919	4 078	0.5	-4.4	77	62	-198	1 524	5.2	2.65	9.3	24.7
Crosby	10.0	8.2	7.5	52.3	6 899	7 304	-3.2	-2.4	137	115	-197	2 512	-0.2	2.78	11.4	23.8
Culberson	10.2	7.5	3.8	49.3	2 774	3 407	-12.7	-6.8	27	27	-207	1 052	-2.2	2.82	13.5	21.5
Dallam	8.0	5.8	4.4	49.5	6 157	5 461	13.9	-1.0	135	76	-126	2 317	9.2	2.68	9.7	26.2
Dallas	6.9	4.4	3.6	50.1	2 245 398	1 852 691	19.8	1.2	52 937	17 157	-9 360	807 621	15.1	2.71	14.1	27.3
Dawson	7.9	7.3	6.9	44.6	14 838	14 349	4.4	-1.0	278	182	-243	4 726	-7.0	2.69	11.0	23.9
Deaf Smith	8.1	6.4	5.7	51.1	18 235	19 153	-3.1	-1.8	472	199	-614	6 180	0.0	2.96	12.6	19.7
Delta	11.8	8.1	9.6	51.4	5 379	4 857	9.7	1.0	98	98	52	2 094	10.2	2.49	10.0	27.5
Denton	6.2	2.9	2.1	50.3	466 240	273 644	58.2	7.7	8 516	2 084	26 174	158 903	55.8	2.67	8.6	22.2
De Witt	9.6	9.4	9.5	48.7	20 114	18 840	6.2	0.5	296	368	179	7 207	0.2	2.53	11.8	26.4
Dickens	10.5	8.3	10.7	43.3	2 705	2 571	7.4	-2.1	30	42	-48	980	-8.7	2.29	7.9	32.4
Dimmit	8.1	6.5	6.2	51.5	10 170	10 433	-1.8	-0.8	192	123	-148	3 308	7.7	3.06	17.2	18.0
Donley	13.0	11.2	10.5	51.4	3 836	3 696	3.6	0.2	46	73	35	1 578	4.2	2.30	7.5	31.4
Duval	8.9	7.5	6.5	49.8	12 996	12 918	1.6	-0.9	263	129	-261	4 350	4.6	2.88	16.8	22.9
Eastland	11.3	10.4	10.4	51.5	18 158	18 488	-1.0	-0.8	288	392	-29	7 321	-0.4	2.39	9.5	28.6
Ector	7.8	6.4	4.5	51.4	121 298	118 934	1.8	0.1	2 944	1 233	-1 541	43 846	3.6	2.72	13.7	24.0
Edwards	12.4	9.9	6.2	49.4	2 044	2 266	-4.6	-5.5	26	25	-123	801	0.8	2.66	8.9	24.7
Ellis	8.0	5.1	4.2	50.4	116 555	85 167	30.8	4.7	2 177	1 046	3 995	37 020	29.5	2.96	11.0	16.6
El Paso	7.1	5.7	4.0	51.8	688 039	591 610	14.9	1.2	18 056	4 976	-4 616	210 022	17.7	3.18	18.0	17.8
Erath	7.9	6.6	6.8	50.6	32 989	27 991	17.9	0.0	555	385	-185	12 568	15.5	2.48	7.2	27.7
Falls	9.1	8.3	8.6	53.8	18 352	17 712	4.9	-1.2	289	318	-192	6 496	0.1	2.54	15.6	29.4
Fannin	10.2	8.1	8.0	46.8	31 556	24 804	26.0	1.0	422	511	405	11 105	14.6	2.51	10.3	25.2
Fayette	10.4	9.2	12.3	51.6	22 150	20 095	8.5	1.6	280	411	475	8 722	7.7	2.44	7.8	28.0
Fisher	11.6	11.6	11.1	51.8	4 278	4 842	-10.3	-1.5	62	65	-64	1 785	-5.7	2.39	8.1	28.3
Floyd	9.2	8.2	8.0	51.6	7 563	8 497	-8.5	-2.7	171	112	-271	2 730	-4.8	2.79	9.7	21.3
Foard	11.0	9.7	13.4	53.6	1 621	1 794	-9.6	-0.1	21	30	9	664	-10.1	2.38	9.5	31.8
Fort Bend	6.8	3.4	2.2	50.2	381 200	225 421	57.2	7.5	6 279	1 671	21 628	110 915	57.5	3.14	11.4	13.5
Franklin	11.7	10.5	8.0	51.5	9 727	7 802	21.2	2.8	112	150	302	3 754	24.4	2.48	8.4	24.6
Freestone	10.1	8.3	8.1	47.5	18 226	15 818	13.0	2.0	284	252	325	6 588	8.7	2.48	10.7	26.4
Frio	7.5	5.9	4.7	45.2	16 392	13 472	20.6	0.9	342	164	-34	4 743	14.9	2.98	16.0	20.6
Gaines	7.6	6.1	4.2	50.8	14 368	14 123	2.4	-0.7	301	117	-289	4 681	4.0	3.07	8.8	18.2
Galveston	8.9	6.3	4.8	51.0	255 865	217 396	15.1	2.3	4 768	2 649	3 625	94 782	16.4	2.60	13.1	25.1
Garza	9.3	6.9	7.2	47.1	5 011	5 143	-5.3	2.9	91	66	112	1 663	-8.7	2.65	11.2	23.8
Gillespie	12.6	12.7	12.8	52.7	21 280	17 204	21.0	2.2	249	329	541	8 521	27.0	2.38	7.0	25.8
Glasscock	9.5	6.0	3.0	47.9	1 371	1 447	-2.8	-2.5	21	6	-51	483	5.9	2.91	2.9	23.8
Goliad	10.8	9.0	8.0	50.3	7 074	5 980	15.9	2.1	102	87	129	2 644	19.7	2.57	8.7	22.8
Gonzales	9.1	8.5	8.2	50.4	18 745	17 205	8.3	0.6	372	300	56	6 782	8.8	2.69	12.3	25.2
Gray	9.8	9.1	9.0	49.0	22 083	23 967	-5.1	-2.9	372	357	-690	8 793	-7.9	2.39	9.0	28.7
Grayson	9.5	7.7	7.4	51.6	113 184	95 019	16.4	2.3	1 858	1 606	2 322	42 849	16.3	2.51	11.4	25.5
Gregg	8.6	7.0	6.2	51.6	112 397	104 948	6.1	0.9	2 317	1 433	172	42 687	6.6	2.54	13.5	26.1
Grimes	9.5	7.6	6.1	46.0	24 398	18 843	25.0	3.6	388	310	759	7 753	28.4	2.69	12.6	23.8

1. No spouse present.

Table B. States and Counties — **Vital Statistics, Health Resources, and Crime**

STATE County	Births, average 1997–1999 Total	Rate[1]	Deaths, average 1997–1999 Number Total	Number Infant[2]	Rate Total[1]	Rate Infant[3]	Physicians,[4] 2000 Number	Rate[5]	Hospitals,[4] 1998 Number	Beds Number	Beds Rate[5]	Medicare enrollees 2000	Serious crimes known to police, 2000[6] Total Number	Rate[7]
	32	33	34	35	36	37	38	39	40	41	42	43	44	45
TEXAS—Cont'd														
Caldwell	469	14.5	271	NA	8.4	NA	11	34	1	21	65	4 183	722	2 243
Calhoun	333	16.2	166	NA	8.1	NA	15	73	1	75	364	2 937	806	3 904
Callahan	146	11.4	138	NA	10.7	NA	1	8	0	0	0	2 287	81	628
Cameron	7 453	22.9	1 841	33	5.7	4.4	385	115	5	951	291	36 076	20 720	6 181
Camp	169	15.4	149	NA	13.6	NA	2	17	1	41	374	2 279	287	2 485
Carson	79	11.8	67	NA	10.0	NA	0	0	0	0	0	1 042	31	476
Cass	374	12.2	398	NA	12.9	NA	12	39	3	114	370	6 108	640	2 103
Castro	142	17.1	61	NA	7.4	NA	4	48	1	30	359	1 049	156	1 883
Chambers	305	12.9	169	NA	7.1	NA	13	50	2	60	253	2 077	896	3 442
Cherokee	655	15.1	522	NA	12.1	NA	66	141	2	148	345	6 732	1 489	3 194
Childress	85	11.2	95	NA	12.5	NA	6	78	1	35	465	1 243	228	2 966
Clay	111	10.6	117	NA	11.2	NA	2	18	1	32	303	1 522	181	1 645
Cochran	54	13.9	39	NA	10.0	NA	2	54	1	30	759	593	71	1 903
Coke	33	9.9	68	NA	20.3	NA	2	52	0	0	0	799	52	1 346
Coleman	118	12.3	168	NA	17.6	NA	8	87	1	25	262	2 340	132	1 429
Collin	7 201	16.8	1 568	30	3.7	4.1	565	115	4	498	116	24 558	17 341	3 527
Collingsworth	39	12.0	51	NA	15.8	NA	3	94	1	20	608	701	84	2 620
Colorado	243	12.8	269	NA	14.1	NA	22	108	3	98	515	3 765	550	2 697
Comal	1 002	13.6	636	NA	8.6	NA	93	119	1	77	105	12 722	3 778	4 842
Comanche	174	12.8	199	NA	14.7	NA	9	64	2	35	258	2 835	218	1 554
Concho	29	9.5	38	NA	12.5	NA	3	76	1	20	641	569	46	1 160
Cooke	469	14.2	365	NA	11.0	NA	19	52	2	80	244	5 427	1 040	2 860
Coryell	1 045	13.7	331	8	4.3	8.0	65	87	1	48	62	4 881	1 518	2 025
Cottle	16	8.2	32	NA	16.5	NA	1	53	0	0	0	493	32	1 681
Crane	66	15.0	39	NA	8.8	NA	4	100	1	28	621	478	74	1 852
Crockett	66	14.6	42	NA	9.2	NA	2	49	1	20	435	536	53	1 293
Crosby	115	16.0	90	NA	12.5	NA	1	14	1	35	485	1 138	28	396
Culberson	43	14.3	20	NA	6.5	NA	1	34	1	25	820	314	37	1 244
Dallam	114	17.5	62	NA	9.6	NA	1	16	1	130	1 969	1 227	133	2 138
Dallas	37 942	18.5	13 441	254	6.6	6.7	5 076	229	27	6 052	295	205 286	146 910	6 621
Dawson	201	13.8	145	NA	9.9	NA	8	53	1	40	272	2 318	424	2 829
Deaf Smith	386	20.3	164	NA	8.6	NA	12	65	1	39	205	2 385	586	3 157
Delta	62	12.5	82	NA	16.5	NA	1	19	0	0	0	1 005	89	1 671
Denton	6 457	16.8	1 559	33	4.1	5.1	386	89	4	605	158	21 628	14 525	3 382
De Witt	224	11.5	281	NA	14.4	NA	14	70	1	49	249	3 453	391	1 954
Dickens	25	11.4	42	NA	19.0	NA	0	0	0	0	0	600	20	724
Dimmit	191	18.5	91	NA	8.7	NA	7	68	1	26	251	1 489	239	2 332
Donley	38	9.9	63	NA	16.6	NA	0	0	0	0	0	858	88	2 299
Duval	217	16.0	106	NA	7.8	NA	0	0	0	0	0	2 050	261	1 989
Eastland	204	11.6	296	NA	16.7	NA	4	22	1	36	205	4 239	445	2 432
Ector	2 278	18.3	963	15	7.8	6.7	189	156	2	401	319	15 296	6 463	5 336
Edwards	27	7.4	21	NA	5.7	NA	2	93	0	0	0	1 825	55	2 544
Ellis	1 648	15.9	804	13	7.7	7.7	63	57	2	65	63	12 123	3 794	3 407
El Paso	14 379	20.6	3 853	75	5.5	5.2	1 047	154	6	1 829	260	74 371	37 913	5 579
Erath	432	13.8	314	NA	10.0	NA	35	106	1	75	238	4 890	819	2 482
Falls	225	12.8	246	NA	14.0	NA	24	129	1	29	166	2 981	525	2 826
Fannin	332	11.8	402	NA	14.3	NA	18	58	1	65	231	5 431	687	2 199
Fayette	237	11.1	296	NA	13.9	NA	27	124	1	43	201	5 047	227	1 041
Fisher	48	11.2	62	NA	14.7	NA	1	23	1	23	542	955	71	1 634
Floyd	138	17.0	80	NA	9.8	NA	4	51	1	27	330	1 278	NA	NA
Foard	21	12.5	23	NA	13.7	NA	0	0	0	0	0	380	12	740
Fort Bend	5 017	14.9	1 312	24	3.9	4.7	362	102	2	209	62	18 450	11 043	3 116
Franklin	102	10.5	107	NA	11.0	NA	6	63	1	30	310	1 379	199	2 104
Freestone	196	11.1	193	NA	11.0	NA	10	56	1	16	91	2 913	296	1 657
Frio	284	18.0	123	NA	7.8	NA	10	62	2	40	254	1 771	424	2 609
Gaines	252	17.1	99	NA	6.7	NA	6	41	1	33	220	1 543	215	1 486
Galveston	3 640	14.8	2 020	23	8.2	6.2	914	365	2	927	378	31 039	12 907	5 160
Garza	76	16.6	55	NA	12.0	NA	3	62	1	13	282	769	34	698
Gillespie	203	10.1	269	NA	13.4	NA	48	231	1	58	289	5 027	305	1 465
Glasscock	18	13.0	NA	NA	NA	NA	0	0	0	0	0	96	10	711
Goliad	79	11.4	64	NA	9.2	NA	4	58	0	0	0	1 124	54	779
Gonzales	263	15.0	208	NA	11.8	NA	17	91	1	34	194	3 353	335	1 798
Gray	289	12.3	274	NA	11.6	NA	32	141	1	92	390	4 357	934	4 107
Grayson	1 408	13.7	1 227	10	11.9	7.3	190	172	3	540	525	18 569	4 663	4 216
Gregg	1 718	15.2	1 155	17	10.2	9.7	207	186	3	460	406	19 280	6 965	6 253
Grimes	309	13.2	223	NA	9.5	NA	8	34	1	18	77	3 168	649	2 756

1. Per 1,000 estimated resident population, average 1997–1999.   2. Deaths of infants under 1 year old.   3. Deaths of infants under 1 year old per 1,000 live births.   4. Data subject to copyright.   5. Per 100,000 resident population as of July 1 of the year shown.   6. Data for serious crimes have not been adjusted for underreporting; this may affect comparability between geographic areas and over time.   7. Per 100,000 population estimated by the FBI.

STATE County	Serious crimes known to police, 2000[1] (cont'd) Rate[2]		Education						Money income				Income and poverty, 1998			
			School enrollment and attainment, 1990				Local government expenditures, fiscal 1999[5]		1989					Percent below poverty level		
			Enrollment[3]		Attainment[4] (percent)					Households						
										Median						
	Violent	Property	Total	Percent private	High school graduate or more	Bachelor's degree or more	Total current expenditures (mil dol)	Current expenditures per student (dollars)	Per capita[6] (dollars)	Dollars	Percent change, 1979–1989 (constant 1989 dollars)	Percent with $100,000 or more	Median household income	All persons	Persons under 18	Persons 5–17 in families
	46	47	48	49	50	51	52	53	54	55	56	57	58	59	60	61
TEXAS—Cont'd																
Caldwell	298	1 944	6 947	5.4	60.3	10.9	32.3	5 330	9 242	20 169	1.8	2.1	29 961	17.9	23.6	25.9
Calhoun	421	3 482	5 130	4.3	64.2	10.1	24.4	5 649	10 374	22 706	-25.1	1.3	33 160	18.0	26.0	25.9
Callahan	23	604	2 779	5.2	68.7	9.8	17.8	5 940	10 353	20 712	-10.7	0.9	29 638	16.7	23.1	23.2
Cameron	470	5 711	89 414	5.4	50.0	12.0	485.4	5 909	7 125	17 336	-11.8	1.5	22 959	33.2	39.5	38.3
Camp	260	2 225	2 302	5.2	63.8	10.0	12.3	5 897	9 936	19 673	-15.1	1.2	29 170	19.1	32.4	27.4
Carson	77	399	1 805	4.5	76.2	13.9	9.8	6 934	11 710	26 765	-8.9	1.6	39 775	8.5	12.0	11.2
Cass	276	1 827	7 312	4.6	66.5	9.0	36.5	5 889	9 391	19 886	-12.2	0.9	28 483	19.0	28.2	25.2
Castro	290	1 593	2 726	2.5	58.2	10.5	13.8	6 562	7 510	17 838	-17.6	1.5	29 737	25.7	31.4	35.2
Chambers	165	3 277	5 745	5.6	68.1	11.5	32.5	6 426	12 218	31 671	-5.0	2.5	44 177	11.5	20.9	13.7
Cherokee	547	2 647	9 912	11.0	62.7	10.2	43.5	5 500	9 195	19 296	-5.5	1.1	28 329	20.0	29.2	26.7
Childress	299	2 666	1 515	0.5	61.1	10.5	7.6	6 136	9 888	16 091	-12.0	2.3	26 067	22.9	28.8	30.7
Clay	164	1 481	2 328	3.8	68.9	11.1	12.6	6 187	10 978	23 721	-3.5	1.4	33 873	10.9	13.4	15.2
Cochran	161	1 743	1 219	1.1	57.3	10.6	9.7	8 529	8 533	19 301	-9.0	1.5	26 598	23.8	32.2	36.7
Coke	52	1 294	707	2.3	64.6	11.7	6.1	8 383	10 220	19 220	-10.4	1.0	26 975	16.5	25.1	24.7
Coleman	87	1 343	1 884	2.9	59.0	9.6	12.3	7 055	9 353	15 519	-14.7	0.6	22 257	23.4	33.5	36.1
Collin	344	3 183	74 317	13.0	88.3	39.1	454.6	5 638	20 503	46 020	13.5	10.9	71 423	4.0	6.4	5.2
Collingsworth	94	2 527	817	3.8	62.0	12.0	5.0	6 607	9 425	15 421	-13.6	1.7	23 361	24.9	34.1	35.5
Colorado	373	2 325	4 281	11.7	57.9	10.6	21.9	5 725	10 379	20 795	-4.1	2.0	30 077	17.1	25.3	23.5
Comal	354	4 489	12 127	11.0	75.7	20.3	87.1	5 422	13 400	29 457	6.8	3.3	41 720	9.5	15.0	13.5
Comanche	114	1 440	2 475	3.3	57.8	9.2	13.7	5 392	9 679	17 504	-1.1	1.6	24 807	21.3	33.1	30.8
Concho	151	1 009	625	7.5	54.2	10.3	4.0	7 443	8 126	15 942	-17.6	0.6	22 852	21.2	27.0	29.2
Cooke	118	2 742	7 811	9.3	71.5	11.9	35.0	5 753	11 594	24 525	-6.6	2.1	34 499	14.0	21.3	19.6
Coryell	245	1 779	17 275	6.1	80.3	11.0	58.9	5 649	8 924	23 504	12.0	0.9	35 134	14.0	16.7	16.7
Cottle	105	1 576	501	0.0	51.8	10.7	3.2	8 303	10 289	15 583	-17.4	1.3	22 026	27.5	40.4	41.5
Crane	175	1 677	1 478	0.3	71.5	9.4	9.2	8 351	10 751	30 659	5.0	2.5	37 537	12.2	16.5	17.2
Crockett	220	1 073	995	2.3	57.8	15.2	7.6	7 773	10 232	19 087	-30.2	2.0	29 957	17.4	23.9	26.4
Crosby	71	325	1 985	3.7	53.1	10.0	12.7	7 831	8 598	17 162	-12.6	1.2	22 951	27.9	37.8	40.2
Culberson	269	975	926	0.3	53.3	12.1	5.4	6 738	7 632	16 559	-13.2	1.6	21 246	30.3	38.7	42.7
Dallam	257	1 880	1 265	5.0	66.0	7.2	10.9	6 192	9 250	19 764	1.1	0.5	30 802	16.9	24.4	25.0
Dallas	843	5 778	479 675	15.2	77.1	26.3	2 106.6	5 426	16 243	31 605	1.5	5.6	42 736	12.6	19.9	16.5
Dawson	427	2 402	3 823	4.0	54.0	9.0	18.8	5 831	9 535	18 920	-20.7	2.0	26 097	26.3	33.4	34.9
Deaf Smith	636	2 521	5 650	9.0	57.5	11.0	29.1	6 554	9 296	21 177	-14.5	3.2	29 444	23.7	30.0	31.6
Delta	357	1 314	1 015	7.0	64.2	12.5	7.0	5 851	9 859	20 208	22.3	1.0	28 040	19.6	28.0	29.1
Denton	262	3 121	84 893	10.1	86.8	32.3	351.8	5 524	16 105	36 914	5.6	4.4	56 386	5.4	7.7	6.5
De Witt	255	1 699	4 394	8.2	55.2	9.2	29.7	6 364	9 564	18 041	-2.4	1.4	27 347	20.5	27.4	27.1
Dickens	145	579	557	2.7	60.3	11.2	4.2	9 154	8 465	14 484	-3.1	0.2	22 258	24.1	33.6	35.3
Dimmit	361	1 971	3 333	2.3	39.8	7.8	16.9	6 451	5 386	12 222	-29.9	0.5	18 213	38.5	45.1	49.2
Donley	209	2 090	926	1.7	67.8	11.1	5.1	7 383	9 388	16 747	-13.0	1.1	23 808	20.3	28.0	29.3
Duval	434	1 555	3 995	1.5	47.9	6.4	20.0	6 113	7 126	13 602	-27.8	1.2	20 861	29.3	35.8	40.4
Eastland	98	2 334	4 198	2.4	63.1	11.0	20.2	6 129	8 729	15 774	-11.9	0.8	24 372	21.0	29.4	28.3
Ector	512	4 824	34 687	5.9	66.9	11.4	142.0	5 002	10 897	23 801	-24.3	2.2	32 109	18.3	25.0	24.0
Edwards	185	2 359	667	0.4	58.3	13.8	6.3	7 666	7 537	19 432	-15.4	1.6	18 618	27.6	49.5	53.2
Ellis	274	3 133	22 695	12.4	71.7	13.4	122.0	5 233	12 199	30 553	7.4	2.9	41 578	10.4	15.1	13.6
El Paso	705	4 874	199 118	7.1	63.7	15.2	863.0	5 626	9 150	22 644	-3.5	2.2	26 318	26.8	35.6	31.8
Erath	106	2 376	9 066	2.8	71.3	20.3	29.3	5 235	10 832	19 881	-1.1	1.9	29 767	15.6	21.9	21.2
Falls	458	2 369	4 328	8.8	58.9	8.5	19.3	6 012	8 600	17 227	8.7	1.0	25 143	22.8	31.4	31.9
Fannin	288	1 911	5 125	3.3	64.6	11.2	31.1	5 930	10 298	20 669	2.4	0.9	30 229	15.2	20.8	20.3
Fayette	73	968	4 222	7.5	57.6	9.1	20.8	5 574	10 769	19 963	4.2	1.6	30 724	13.6	19.5	18.4
Fisher	161	1 473	1 123	1.8	63.0	11.5	5.5	7 567	9 760	19 368	-20.8	1.9	26 461	19.0	26.7	27.7
Floyd	NA	NA	2 000	1.3	60.7	11.2	13.2	6 725	9 564	19 186	-10.5	2.0	27 834	24.2	32.6	36.4
Foard	62	678	360	1.7	62.2	11.2	2.5	7 340	9 228	18 713	0.3	0.7	23 927	21.6	31.2	32.1
Fort Bend	381	2 734	70 286	11.9	80.9	30.2	374.4	5 283	16 056	42 809	-0.2	7.5	57 196	6.9	9.9	8.6
Franklin	307	1 797	1 759	4.7	64.9	11.3	8.0	5 176	12 370	23 103	6.9	3.2	30 825	14.5	22.5	20.3
Freestone	134	1 522	3 829	6.9	65.5	9.2	19.5	6 204	10 735	21 561	9.0	1.2	30 324	17.4	22.7	22.7
Frio	283	2 326	4 032	4.2	50.1	7.5	21.7	6 492	6 629	14 059	-22.2	1.7	21 729	32.5	36.9	41.7
Gaines	69	1 417	4 000	11.2	53.2	9.9	24.2	7 385	9 204	22 335	-6.1	1.9	29 423	21.0	26.7	27.6
Galveston	494	4 665	61 025	8.5	75.8	19.3	352.2	5 416	13 993	29 466	-9.7	3.6	41 666	12.2	19.0	16.7
Garza	62	636	1 240	3.9	57.6	9.8	7.8	6 611	9 112	18 994	-15.6	2.3	25 688	22.9	28.2	33.9
Gillespie	43	1 422	3 401	15.9	68.6	17.1	18.5	5 701	12 046	23 722	10.9	2.3	32 861	11.6	18.3	18.0
Glasscock	0	711	467	2.4	64.8	9.8	3.4	8 619	16 219	29 306	13.3	8.4	35 678	16.5	26.5	23.9
Goliad	43	736	1 561	9.2	62.6	9.9	9.5	6 765	10 875	21 411	-2.7	2.3	31 146	16.5	23.5	24.7
Gonzales	505	1 294	4 134	3.3	55.5	8.5	21.9	5 691	9 252	17 500	-3.3	1.5	25 802	24.1	32.9	33.9
Gray	453	3 654	5 760	8.0	71.1	11.9	23.3	5 511	12 771	24 118	-13.6	2.0	34 288	14.5	21.4	20.8
Grayson	307	3 910	23 758	10.3	72.1	14.0	112.8	5 665	12 201	25 241	-1.3	2.3	34 634	13.2	19.8	17.8
Gregg	540	5 713	27 844	12.1	75.8	17.7	131.0	5 544	12 457	25 484	-9.4	2.8	34 513	15.5	20.6	20.6
Grimes	289	2 467	4 687	8.0	59.6	8.6	24.7	5 673	8 920	20 623	8.1	2.2	29 508	17.8	20.7	22.9

1. Data for serious crimes have not been adjusted for underreporting; this may affect comparability between geographic areas and over time. 2. Per 100,000 population estimated by the FBI. 3. All persons 3 years old and over enrolled in nursery school through college. 4. Persons 25 years old and over. 5. Elementary and secondary education expenditures, local government fiscal years ending between July 1, 1998 and June 30, 1999. 6. Based on population enumerated as of April 1, 1990.

Table B. States and Counties — **Personal Income**

STATE County	Personal income, 1999 Total (mil dol)	Percent change, 1998–1999	Per capita[1] Dollars	Per capita[1] Rank	Wages and salaries[2] (mil dol)	Proprietor's income (mil dol)	Dividends, interest, and rent (mil dol)	Transfer payments Total (mil dol)	Government payments to individuals Total (mil dol)	Social Security (mil dol)	Medical payments (mil dol)	Income mainte- nance (mil dol)	Unemploy- ment insurance (mil dol)
	62	63	64	65	66	67	68	69	70	71	72	73	74
TEXAS—Cont'd													
Caldwell	579	5.7	17 653	2 610	162	40	91	111	106	37	47	13	1
Calhoun	431	5.5	21 121	1 625	476	46	73	74	71	30	29	8	1
Callahan	252	5.6	19 537	2 124	55	24	39	53	51	23	20	4	1
Cameron	4 700	4.0	14 280	3 034	2 609	405	702	1 171	1 114	271	536	237	21
Camp	287	7.4	26 184	495	92	73	51	52	50	20	22	5	1
Carson	186	10.0	27 586	364	219	42	27	22	21	10	8	1	0
Cass	650	4.4	21 219	1 591	252	97	104	150	144	55	64	15	3
Castro	241	2.2	29 103	253	78	111	23	30	28	10	12	6	0
Chambers	600	3.7	25 012	669	282	33	95	72	68	30	28	7	1
Cherokee	989	3.7	22 659	1 178	429	192	167	197	189	71	88	18	2
Childress	125	7.1	16 599	2 811	60	17	25	29	28	10	12	3	0
Clay	217	4.5	20 620	1 801	59	28	38	37	35	18	13	3	0
Cochran	86	21.4	22 667	1 174	28	27	16	16	16	6	7	3	0
Coke	66	4.2	19 839	2 044	26	3	16	17	16	8	7	1	0
Coleman	181	2.2	19 127	2 251	50	27	27	59	57	22	27	5	1
Collin	18 296	12.6	40 068	44	6 903	1 253	2 146	661	583	289	219	31	18
Collingsworth	67	8.9	21 013	1 664	24	11	14	17	17	6	8	3	0
Colorado	448	4.1	23 539	955	162	65	120	91	87	38	36	9	1
Comal	2 138	8.5	27 844	345	773	192	419	251	238	115	94	11	3
Comanche	287	6.6	21 157	1 615	95	42	61	70	67	28	30	5	1
Concho	56	21.0	18 818	2 342	23	10	13	14	13	5	7	1	0
Cooke	789	6.6	23 639	930	343	88	173	128	122	54	49	9	1
Coryell	1 194	4.3	16 212	2 873	327	60	177	130	117	44	50	15	3
Cottle	42	11.8	22 000	1 367	15	6	9	11	10	4	4	1	0
Crane	74	-0.7	17 233	2 697	51	6	12	13	12	5	5	1	0
Crockett	66	0.8	14 986	2 988	36	1	17	13	12	5	5	1	0
Crosby	129	0.6	18 346	2 459	43	19	24	38	37	11	19	6	0
Culberson	45	6.7	14 803	3 005	30	3	6	10	10	3	4	2	0
Dallam	196	10.0	29 646	223	94	87	26	25	24	8	11	3	0
Dallas	75 112	5.6	36 425	70	71 516	13 772	11 737	5 527	5 169	2 028	2 245	518	141
Dawson	305	13.7	21 132	1 620	126	60	61	69	66	22	34	8	1
Deaf Smith	489	12.5	25 986	519	162	190	69	67	64	21	30	11	1
Delta	111	8.5	22 226	1 291	33	10	15	25	24	9	10	3	0
Denton	11 908	10.5	29 471	232	3 719	534	1 191	661	592	254	250	27	15
De Witt	394	4.0	20 430	1 858	169	36	84	95	91	33	43	11	1
Dickens	45	3.4	20 822	1 725	15	7	8	16	16	5	8	2	0
Dimmit	132	4.7	12 789	3 084	65	10	16	48	46	11	21	12	1
Donley	71	5.5	18 627	2 387	23	10	15	19	18	8	7	2	0
Duval	180	0.5	13 184	3 078	83	9	24	70	68	16	37	12	2
Eastland	360	5.8	20 603	1 808	164	38	67	101	98	37	43	8	1
Ector	2 420	-3.8	19 558	2 119	1 451	197	409	430	408	156	175	44	21
Edwards	33	4.0	8 996	3 107	10	2	11	10	9	4	3	2	0
Ellis	2 644	8.5	24 577	736	973	253	316	332	313	116	123	23	33
El Paso	12 084	3.7	17 216	2 699	7 649	1 245	1 928	2 134	2 014	566	851	365	14
Erath	707	4.9	22 455	1 226	335	137	123	118	113	41	51	8	1
Falls	308	8.9	17 844	2 569	113	34	52	80	77	25	34	11	1
Fannin	590	6.5	20 584	1 818	241	67	86	133	128	50	58	10	2
Fayette	516	6.7	24 143	830	218	64	137	107	103	46	44	8	1
Fisher	92	20.6	21 920	1 382	27	12	18	22	22	9	9	2	0
Floyd	205	14.1	25 248	625	57	84	29	35	33	12	14	6	0
Foard	39	18.9	23 817	894	9	9	8	10	9	4	5	1	0
Fort Bend	9 372	6.4	26 496	464	3 363	555	1 345	549	488	218	197	34	16
Franklin	206	7.8	20 744	1 760	64	31	42	40	38	18	15	2	0
Freestone	313	6.4	17 747	2 589	135	25	62	69	66	28	25	7	1
Frio	227	2.7	14 263	3 036	97	33	31	58	55	14	27	11	1
Gaines	295	8.6	19 999	1 990	126	87	40	46	44	15	21	6	1
Galveston	6 285	2.3	25 296	614	2 943	370	1 072	837	794	314	354	68	22
Garza	87	6.0	19 373	2 190	31	18	18	22	21	7	11	2	0
Gillespie	496	5.3	24 326	798	171	51	176	94	91	45	38	4	1
Glasscock	26	41.4	18 130	2 515	12	6	5	2	2	1	1	1	0
Goliad	120	7.7	16 840	2 769	36	9	27	29	27	11	12	3	0
Gonzales	410	7.8	23 350	1 004	136	125	68	80	77	28	33	11	1
Gray	571	-0.7	24 493	758	272	81	112	110	106	46	46	8	3
Grayson	2 440	5.4	23 521	961	1 424	173	407	440	422	173	179	28	7
Gregg	2 898	2.4	25 613	569	1 861	328	576	479	460	180	204	41	12
Grimes	379	2.3	15 771	2 920	211	36	64	74	70	25	30	10	2

1. Based on the resident population estimated as of July 1 of the year shown. 2. Includes other labor income.

Table B. States and Counties — Earnings, Social Security, and Housing

STATE County	Earnings, 1999									Social Security beneficiaries, December 2000			Housing units, 1990	
			Percent by selected industries											
			Goods-related[1]		Service-related and other[2]							Supplemental Security Income recipients, December 2000		
	Total (mil dol)	Farm	Total	Manufacturing	Total	Retail trade	Finance, insurance, and real estate	Services	Government	Number	Rate[3]		Total	Percent change, 1980–1990
	75	76	77	78	79	80	81	82	83	84	85	86	87	88

TEXAS—Cont'd

Caldwell	201	2.5	D	5.5	D	12.3	4.1	32.5	23.2	4 878	152	778	10 123	23.1
Calhoun	523	2.7	70.1	49.4	18.4	5.0	1.9	6.2	8.8	3 514	170	399	9 559	14.1
Callahan	79	3.5	26.2	3.0	44.2	11.4	4.6	14.2	26.1	2 850	221	235	5 503	13.3
Cameron	3 014	2.4	14.5	11.1	56.0	12.7	5.3	26.3	27.1	41 810	125	15 977	88 759	34.5
Camp	165	34.1	D	8.7	D	8.5	3.7	13.2	9.4	2 385	207	400	4 530	18.9
Carson	261	12.3	D	D	D	2.2	D	3.0	11.5	1 146	176	72	2 856	8.4
Cass	349	7.2	36.1	27.9	39.3	10.7	3.1	12.6	17.4	7 038	231	995	13 191	12.3
Castro	189	60.3	6.3	4.3	22.4	4.1	1.2	5.3	11.1	1 313	158	162	3 357	-9.0
Chambers	315	3.9	52.5	37.2	28.5	5.2	1.6	9.2	15.1	3 426	132	314	8 061	10.6
Cherokee	621	21.8	19.7	15.5	39.0	12.3	3.3	14.6	19.5	8 951	192	1 092	17 629	12.9
Childress	77	9.7	D	2.5	D	13.3	3.1	13.8	44.6	1 312	171	141	3 046	-0.5
Clay	87	10.4	D	12.0	D	10.8	2.9	21.8	17.8	2 182	198	118	4 708	7.3
Cochran	56	42.1	D	0.7	D	3.6	1.9	7.4	21.8	698	187	120	1 763	-7.0
Coke	29	-11.3	D	2.7	D	17.4	7.0	23.0	35.8	921	238	59	2 793	33.1
Coleman	78	1.4	D	1.5	D	15.4	4.5	20.5	28.6	2 751	298	289	5 382	2.7
Collin	8 156	0.2	27.6	20.3	62.9	10.8	7.5	34.4	9.2	33 759	69	2 402	103 827	102.9
Collingsworth	35	24.0	3.8	0.9	46.3	7.7	5.2	15.5	25.9	769	240	98	1 952	-9.8
Colorado	227	6.6	23.8	12.8	55.4	14.5	7.9	17.6	14.2	4 345	213	432	8 537	-0.4
Comal	964	0.1	33.0	17.9	53.9	17.2	4.1	21.3	13.1	14 030	180	779	22 987	47.4
Comanche	137	18.7	11.9	6.1	D	11.3	3.4	D	19.2	3 530	252	304	6 724	9.9
Concho	34	24.3	D	D	D	5.7	3.7	28.8	20.9	603	152	87	1 514	6.3
Cooke	431	1.0	31.0	20.9	49.3	13.7	3.7	18.4	18.8	6 429	177	433	13 315	15.6
Coryell	386	0.2	D	4.2	D	11.4	4.6	16.6	48.4	6 068	81	536	18 970	18.3
Cottle	21	19.4	D	5.1	D	9.4	4.5	17.9	23.4	548	288	68	1 286	-6.3
Crane	57	-2.8	D	1.1	D	5.5	2.1	10.7	20.8	583	146	63	1 795	6.4
Crockett	37	-12.4	D	D	D	13.7	D	13.9	30.3	643	157	92	1 897	-4.3
Crosby	61	23.4	D	3.1	D	6.1	4.6	12.1	24.9	1 363	193	192	3 312	-5.6
Culberson	33	0.8	D	D	D	21.0	D	10.5	36.2	445	150	85	1 286	9.2
Dallam	181	38.8	6.6	2.8	43.4	5.5	2.7	10.2	11.2	912	147	121	2 577	-8.1
Dallas	85 287	0.0	21.3	12.7	71.3	7.6	11.8	31.0	7.4	227 190	102	32 391	795 513	27.3
Dawson	186	19.9	10.5	3.3	47.7	8.8	4.2	10.6	21.9	2 717	181	512	5 969	-3.5
Deaf Smith	352	49.3	11.2	8.2	28.0	4.4	2.3	7.7	11.5	2 739	148	524	7 152	-2.0
Delta	43	11.1	D	D	D	5.7	5.8	20.7	22.0	1 194	224	185	2 305	1.3
Denton	4 254	0.2	26.7	16.9	55.2	13.8	4.6	21.4	17.9	29 932	69	2 021	112 263	104.8
De Witt	205	1.1	22.7	15.6	44.4	11.5	6.2	17.9	31.9	4 385	219	629	8 568	4.1
Dickens	22	20.3	D	D	D	9.2	4.5	8.4	24.1	657	238	102	1 564	-3.1
Dimmit	75	3.9	D	D	D	11.1	2.6	15.5	44.6	1 799	176	694	3 991	9.5
Donley	33	17.5	D	1.3	D	13.4	4.3	14.2	35.1	969	253	82	2 304	9.1
Duval	92	-1.8	D	D	D	5.4	D	15.2	37.5	2 415	184	845	5 127	19.0
Eastland	202	2.0	40.6	18.1	38.1	10.5	3.7	13.2	19.3	4 612	252	481	9 768	4.3
Ector	1 648	-0.2	29.1	11.9	52.6	12.6	3.6	21.9	18.5	18 109	150	2 845	48 789	14.5
Edwards	13	-11.3	D	D	D	12.0	5.9	13.2	42.2	401	185	96	1 550	22.7
Ellis	1 226	0.9	44.0	36.4	42.1	9.3	3.8	17.3	13.0	14 005	126	21 639	31 314	46.9
El Paso	8 893	0.4	17.9	13.0	54.2	10.5	8.4	21.1	27.5	83 893	123	1 549	187 473	26.7
Erath	472	18.4	22.6	16.9	42.0	9.6	3.2	19.4	17.0	5 025	152	421	12 758	25.7
Falls	147	8.5	D	6.7	D	9.0	2.4	14.3	41.4	3 470	187	679	7 733	-2.6
Fannin	308	3.7	D	18.7	D	14.1	5.3	12.6	28.4	6 187	198	672	11 504	10.7
Fayette	282	4.1	20.4	9.3	56.4	12.4	6.4	20.6	19.1	5 905	271	447	10 756	12.9
Fisher	39	19.7	D	D	D	7.1	4.9	11.7	26.3	1 108	255	101	2 413	-8.7
Floyd	142	51.6	4.8	1.9	30.2	4.0	3.4	7.4	13.4	1 453	187	189	3 535	-8.4
Foard	19	38.6	D	D	D	4.0	D	12.8	19.2	447	276	43	890	-18.4
Fort Bend	3 918	2.0	35.8	16.9	47.2	9.4	6.1	20.7	15.0	26 169	74	2 657	77 075	78.6
Franklin	94	21.7	D	5.2	D	21.7	4.8	18.7	12.0	2 232	236	131	4 219	32.6
Freestone	159	-1.7	25.4	4.0	53.9	16.5	3.1	15.0	22.4	3 586	201	354	7 812	14.2
Frio	130	18.6	9.1	1.8	43.5	9.5	3.0	17.5	28.8	2 252	139	576	4 879	0.4
Gaines	214	36.6	14.0	0.7	33.5	5.7	2.5	6.4	15.9	1 894	131	297	5 221	11.8
Galveston	3 313	0.0	22.4	14.6	46.3	10.9	7.0	19.6	31.4	35 301	141	3 974	99 451	19.9
Garza	49	1.1	37.9	1.5	40.6	9.3	4.9	17.1	20.5	909	187	115	2 184	7.1
Gillespie	222	1.8	21.5	8.7	62.4	18.1	5.6	29.1	14.3	5 802	279	206	8 265	32.8
Glasscock	18	38.1	D	0.0	D	2.9	1.3	4.5	23.2	137	97	12	600	4.3
Goliad	46	6.5	D	D	D	11.5	D	12.1	32.8	1 395	201	192	2 835	33.8
Gonzales	261	40.8	D	6.3	D	6.6	3.5	12.3	14.0	3 831	206	678	7 810	7.1
Gray	352	6.7	37.8	22.3	41.6	9.9	2.9	17.0	13.8	4 908	216	402	11 532	2.7
Grayson	1 597	0.6	37.5	29.1	50.2	11.7	6.5	23.8	11.6	20 736	187	1 944	44 223	12.0
Gregg	2 189	0.0	31.4	17.0	58.3	13.6	4.2	25.7	10.4	20 593	185	2 970	44 689	13.1
Grimes	247	2.7	41.0	28.4	31.4	7.5	2.6	14.3	24.9	3 397	144	592	7 744	21.3

1. Covers mining, construction, and manufacturing.   2. Covers private sector earnings in agricultural services, forestry, and fisheries; transportation and public utilities; wholesale trade; retail trade; finance, insurance, and real estate; and services.   3. Per 1,000 resident population estimated as of July 1 of the year shown.

Table B. States and Counties — Housing, Labor Force, and Employment

	Housing units, 1990 (cont'd)								Civilian labor force, 2001				Civilian employment, 1990[5]		
	Occupied units										Unemployment			Percent	
	Owner-occupied					Renter-occupied									
				Owner cost as a percent of income											
STATE County	Total	Percent	Median value[1]	With a mortgage	Without a mortgage	Median rent[2]	Rent as percent of income	Substandard units[3] (percent)	Total	Percent change, 2000–2001	Total	Rate[4]	Total	Professional, managerial, and technical	Precision production, craft, and repair
	89	90	91	92	93	94	95	96	97	98	99	100	101	102	103
TEXAS—Cont'd															
Caldwell	8 745	68.4	44 200	22.8	13.9	303	29.3	11.3	17 106	1.1	716	4.2	10 620	21.5	16.3
Calhoun	6 777	71.0	45 000	18.8	11.9	333	28.4	7.6	9 610	-3.8	762	7.9	7 766	20.8	17.8
Callahan	4 565	81.0	35 500	20.8	13.6	292	25.9	5.1	6 310	4.4	236	3.7	4 832	20.1	14.6
Cameron	73 278	64.4	38 400	20.7	12.6	295	27.6	25.1	133 165	2.1	12 269	9.2	86 302	25.4	10.5
Camp	3 773	74.3	42 200	20.4	15.0	324	28.8	7.4	5 438	1.8	284	5.2	4 058	19.4	17.6
Carson	2 402	81.2	40 200	14.9	12.1	329	19.3	3.5	3 092	0.7	88	2.8	2 775	22.0	16.1
Cass	11 320	77.8	38 700	18.6	13.2	286	25.6	6.5	14 505	-2.5	871	6.0	11 628	20.0	17.2
Castro	2 877	66.6	39 900	18.4	13.0	286	24.2	13.9	3 411	-5.4	140	4.1	3 549	15.9	9.9
Chambers	6 930	80.9	57 000	16.7	13.4	391	20.1	7.0	12 086	1.4	546	4.5	8 924	23.5	17.2
Cherokee	14 981	72.7	39 500	21.6	13.9	291	24.6	7.4	19 421	-2.6	828	4.3	16 020	21.6	12.0
Childress	2 435	73.9	31 100	23.8	14.0	271	33.3	5.1	3 118	-9.4	91	2.9	2 284	21.0	11.7
Clay	3 808	82.7	37 500	21.1	14.5	317	22.8	3.2	5 610	-2.1	135	2.4	4 330	20.9	15.1
Cochran	1 430	72.7	22 400	18.7	13.1	231	20.9	10.0	1 260	-6.4	82	6.5	1 683	18.1	10.3
Coke	1 374	76.9	37 300	17.9	13.7	238	25.1	3.7	1 566	-5.0	30	1.9	1 338	20.2	18.1
Coleman	4 026	73.1	26 300	20.3	14.6	230	27.5	4.7	3 056	-3.7	147	4.8	3 636	19.5	11.5
Collin	95 805	66.6	106 600	22.9	13.3	526	23.4	3.3	294 277	2.6	11 969	4.1	145 946	43.1	8.2
Collingsworth	1 447	78.9	25 100	19.3	15.9	257	29.6	3.7	1 619	6.4	18	1.1	1 522	18.5	8.3
Colorado	7 024	75.8	45 300	19.5	13.0	277	23.9	7.2	8 103	-1.0	306	3.8	7 472	19.2	13.1
Comal	19 315	74.0	76 500	21.5	12.3	420	26.3	6.9	40 795	2.2	1 437	3.5	23 199	30.5	12.7
Comanche	5 318	77.3	31 700	20.1	14.1	251	26.8	6.2	6 419	-0.7	174	2.7	5 434	20.9	9.8
Concho	1 063	70.6	34 300	24.6	15.5	255	27.1	5.6	1 522	-0.1	29	1.9	1 246	15.8	9.2
Cooke	11 545	71.4	47 700	21.3	13.3	325	24.1	3.7	17 917	3.1	840	4.7	13 474	21.7	14.6
Coryell	16 687	51.7	51 200	21.8	13.2	402	25.9	4.1	21 683	0.6	1 059	4.9	15 670	24.2	10.7
Cottle	915	72.1	25 700	19.7	14.8	208	25.0	8.6	846	5.8	42	5.0	915	20.0	9.6
Crane	1 537	80.2	37 500	13.9	11.9	317	19.3	9.3	1 570	-12.6	94	6.0	1 946	24.3	19.9
Crockett	1 449	67.2	43 100	22.7	13.1	259	20.0	7.8	1 788	-2.2	47	2.6	1 674	20.3	15.1
Crosby	2 516	70.9	29 700	19.6	15.1	233	21.1	10.3	2 823	4.8	160	5.7	2 704	16.9	9.6
Culberson	1 076	65.0	27 500	21.4	12.3	267	23.4	15.5	1 045	-3.1	79	7.6	1 419	20.8	7.3
Dallam	2 122	68.7	28 100	18.1	12.3	305	23.7	3.5	3 598	-1.0	78	2.2	2 404	12.9	12.4
Dallas	701 686	51.7	79 200	21.3	12.8	448	24.3	8.3	1 265 215	2.4	67 174	5.3	962 376	32.0	9.7
Dawson	5 084	73.4	34 200	18.9	13.2	289	26.7	11.2	6 298	-0.5	294	4.7	5 019	19.5	13.3
Deaf Smith	6 182	66.3	41 700	18.5	12.9	310	24.1	12.2	7 322	-3.6	368	5.0	7 669	18.3	12.2
Delta	1 901	76.0	30 300	19.2	15.1	256	29.0	4.9	2 882	-11.0	134	4.6	1 925	20.8	10.1
Denton	101 984	57.4	89 100	23.4	13.1	477	25.6	3.6	261 347	1.5	7 916	3.0	153 373	37.2	9.1
De Witt	7 195	73.9	35 500	22.1	13.6	264	25.3	8.1	8 532	2.1	303	3.6	7 040	18.9	16.4
Dickens	1 073	75.8	19 100	15.5	17.3	223	23.9	6.2	763	-8.1	24	3.1	993	19.3	12.9
Dimmit	3 072	74.3	21 600	19.5	14.8	253	27.0	21.0	3 550	-2.5	346	9.7	3 075	22.4	13.2
Donley	1 515	72.9	31 000	18.3	15.1	268	33.5	2.7	1 581	-2.7	41	2.6	1 508	18.8	10.1
Duval	4 159	79.4	23 400	22.0	13.4	238	29.3	17.1	4 971	3.6	359	7.2	3 771	18.8	16.6
Eastland	7 354	74.3	27 800	20.5	13.9	255	23.4	4.2	9 311	1.4	334	3.6	6 970	21.2	14.2
Ector	42 322	65.8	44 800	18.9	12.7	314	22.8	9.1	59 112	1.3	3 072	5.2	49 951	23.7	17.0
Edwards	795	72.2	30 900	21.9	14.3	225	20.0	14.4	801	3.4	37	4.6	873	12.4	8.8
Ellis	28 588	72.5	67 900	21.2	14.1	420	25.5	6.2	58 098	1.5	2 461	4.2	39 378	22.8	14.6
El Paso	178 366	58.7	57 300	20.6	12.0	347	26.0	15.3	284 190	-0.4	23 266	8.2	216 790	27.7	11.0
Erath	10 877	62.7	48 600	20.7	14.4	328	28.1	4.2	16 650	-0.1	383	2.3	12 635	24.6	10.4
Falls	6 492	70.2	31 400	22.5	14.6	227	25.0	7.9	7 606	-0.6	298	3.9	6 408	19.3	13.1
Fannin	9 691	75.9	35 100	19.8	15.1	302	28.2	4.1	12 919	1.8	828	6.4	9 852	21.2	13.3
Fayette	8 101	75.1	53 100	22.2	13.1	301	23.9	5.3	11 038	2.4	256	2.3	8 800	18.2	14.1
Fisher	1 892	76.4	26 500	17.5	13.2	206	21.6	4.8	1 761	6.7	56	3.2	1 931	17.2	10.9
Floyd	2 982	69.8	29 200	18.5	12.9	269	24.6	8.8	3 015	-1.8	218	7.2	3 334	13.3	11.6
Foard	739	72.0	20 700	16.7	13.4	254	23.7	4.6	759	-11.2	21	2.8	762	22.8	9.4
Fort Bend	70 424	75.4	71 600	22.1	12.8	524	23.1	7.6	192 818	1.8	5 904	3.1	110 035	38.7	10.3
Franklin	3 017	76.2	46 800	20.8	13.3	324	29.9	5.1	4 604	1.3	129	2.8	3 054	20.2	16.3
Freestone	6 063	79.5	44 700	17.8	15.6	286	22.8	4.6	8 121	11.7	295	3.6	6 352	20.3	14.7
Frio	4 129	67.6	26 800	23.7	15.4	242	25.6	20.0	5 720	-3.0	404	7.1	4 955	15.9	16.8
Gaines	4 502	72.1	39 800	16.7	12.3	288	21.9	11.4	6 511	2.1	291	4.5	5 487	20.8	13.4
Galveston	81 451	62.0	59 700	19.6	13.4	401	25.4	5.7	117 791	-0.5	7 039	6.0	99 670	33.1	13.5
Garza	1 822	71.4	31 300	18.6	12.6	237	22.9	9.4	2 451	11.2	62	2.5	2 018	13.7	14.4
Gillespie	6 711	79.3	63 900	23.4	12.2	376	26.7	5.9	10 275	0.4	194	1.9	7 330	22.5	13.7
Glasscock	456	60.1	47 500	20.0	10.4	150	10.0	10.2	672	-1.5	20	3.0	570	14.9	4.4
Goliad	2 208	78.0	39 900	18.8	12.2	275	23.8	9.0	2 700	1.1	102	3.8	2 389	19.0	15.8
Gonzales	6 231	68.2	36 800	19.1	14.3	246	26.9	10.4	7 573	-0.2	236	3.1	7 058	16.0	11.6
Gray	9 548	75.6	35 500	18.0	12.5	337	25.2	3.9	8 949	-1.8	316	3.5	10 055	21.8	15.8
Grayson	36 847	69.3	46 600	18.3	13.5	368	23.8	3.4	50 095	-0.6	2 709	5.4	42 133	26.1	13.8
Gregg	40 027	63.2	56 000	18.4	13.3	348	23.6	4.9	58 204	-0.4	3 155	5.4	46 855	26.2	13.5
Grimes	6 040	74.0	39 300	21.2	15.1	286	25.6	10.6	8 286	-2.4	440	5.3	6 695	18.6	13.0

1. Specified owner-occupied units.   2. Specified renter-occupied units.   3. Overcrowded or lacking complete plumbing facilities.   4. Percent of civilian labor force.   5. Persons 16 years and older.

Table B. States and Counties — Nonfarm Employment and Agriculture

| | Private nonfarm establishments, employment and payroll, 1999 | | | | | | | | Agriculture, 1997 | | | |
| | Employment | | | | | | Annual payroll | | Farms | | | Farm operators |
STATE County	Number of establish-ments	Total	Health Care and Social Assistance	Manufac-turing	Retail trade	Finance and Insurance	Professional Scientific and Technical Services	Total (mil dol)	Average per employee (dollars)	Number	Percent with— Less than 50 acres	Percent with— 500 acres and over	Whose principal occu-pation is farming (percent)
	104	105	106	107	108	109	110	111	112	113	114	115	116
TEXAS—Cont'd													
Caldwell	500	4 039	720	466	757	168	87	73	17 968	1 068	26.1	11.8	41.9
Calhoun	414	7 989	602	3 855	770	187	286	303	37 870	257	23.0	36.6	50.2
Callahan	190	930	109	56	239	80	24	18	19 299	849	23.4	22.3	38.2
Cameron	5 751	83 540	18 924	12 106	13 406	2 635	2 058	1 554	18 605	902	55.0	16.9	48.1
Camp	266	2 811	434	382	457	152	40	74	26 405	427	32.6	5.4	42.9
Carson	120	835	172	D	134	58	D	16	19 246	348	10.6	60.6	63.5
Cass	607	5 565	1 239	502	1 051	221	112	102	18 393	852	25.1	7.7	37.1
Castro	197	1 419	278	166	243	91	22	28	19 706	489	5.1	59.3	75.9
Chambers	391	5 828	412	1 806	623	152	112	217	37 210	421	33.5	25.4	43.9
Cherokee	838	13 134	3 050	3 321	1 744	297	155	248	18 886	1 429	28.7	7.2	40.6
Childress	166	1 247	298	D	284	50	29	22	17 646	284	7.7	43.3	51.8
Clay	124	976	70	D	225	D	26	20	20 625	818	16.4	28.7	47.1
Cochran	64	421	137	D	73	D	D	8	18 382	276	4.0	63.8	66.7
Coke	77	614	0	13	100	D	D	13	21 140	336	6.5	54.5	46.1
Coleman	216	1 516	427	71	323	88	34	25	16 582	837	10.5	41.3	46.5
Collin	10 230	170 369	11 794	24 208	24 292	9 629	8 466	7 003	41 104	1 407	49.0	8.3	34.5
Collingsworth	68	459	144	D	104	D	22	8	18 390	547	21.0	32.5	44.6
Colorado	545	5 423	878	732	1 040	142	63	113	20 885	1 562	21.3	15.4	42.8
Comal	1 971	23 924	2 851	4 427	3 716	467	639	535	22 381	657	31.1	16.4	40.2
Comanche	316	2 840	599	276	524	134	54	54	18 883	1 438	19.8	18.4	50.3
Concho	59	602	146	D	80	D	D	10	16 942	380	4.5	56.1	63.9
Cooke	852	10 625	1 072	3 044	2 107	267	167	232	21 839	1 487	29.5	14.2	37.4
Coryell	733	7 493	819	580	1 686	443	341	131	17 510	1 075	17.3	26.2	43.5
Cottle	51	391	77	D	D	D	D	0	16 156	225	3.1	57.8	56.4
Crane	82	864	176	D	118	D	D	27	31 226	53	15.1	66.0	47.2
Crockett	131	894	D	D	196	D	32	18	20 246	170	6.5	83.5	69.4
Crosby	129	844	200	68	198	D	D	18	21 476	385	5.5	57.9	71.2
Culberson	70	616	106	D	169	D	D	10	15 768	92	6.5	76.1	47.8
Dallam	246	1 750	35	64	277	88	84	34	19 363	414	7.2	69.6	71.3
Dallas	63 830	1 442 288	112 364	153 069	124 208	102 225	114 276	56 927	39 470	768	54.6	8.7	31.9
Dawson	361	2 524	372	192	543	142	71	47	18 571	583	7.7	59.3	69.0
Deaf Smith	436	4 420	569	1 112	642	127	85	91	20 640	647	11.7	62.8	67.1
Delta	75	810	207	D	78	D	D	11	14 173	419	26.3	13.4	37.5
Denton	7 501	101 478	9 395	13 277	18 957	4 095	4 226	2 887	28 446	1 782	52.6	8.6	30.3
De Witt	379	3 517	860	689	587	155	103	67	18 945	1 502	18.7	16.6	43.9
Dickens	55	378	D	0	D	D	D	8	22 140	366	6.6	39.9	47.8
Dimmit	182	1 287	307	13	307	61	D	23	17 883	218	13.8	48.6	46.3
Donley	92	392	D	D	141	D	18	5	13 431	393	6.1	40.2	50.1
Duval	145	1 306	266	D	230	94	25	23	17 760	880	6.7	32.7	38.2
Eastland	480	4 503	649	761	735	150	68	94	20 882	1 137	12.8	20.9	42.5
Ector	3 078	38 814	6 551	3 082	6 590	1 003	1 239	899	23 152	208	63.9	19.7	36.5
Edwards	37	129	D	D	0	D	D	2	18 915	283	6.4	68.6	53.4
Ellis	1 988	27 173	2 311	9 854	3 521	725	472	698	25 695	1 713	38.1	10.9	33.9
El Paso	12 379	195 303	25 446	34 141	28 747	5 887	6 782	4 285	21 939	415	67.7	11.6	40.7
Erath	829	9 414	1 474	1 721	1 927	262	456	181	19 184	1 787	21.8	18.1	47.1
Falls	280	2 563	864	303	462	121	34	52	20 141	1 027	19.9	17.8	47.0
Fannin	508	5 851	1 157	1 773	941	409	87	145	24 704	1 604	25.7	13.2	39.0
Fayette	709	6 043	879	1 023	1 079	268	137	120	19 812	2 659	27.0	7.7	38.7
Fisher	86	746	158	D	111	50	11	17	23 231	603	9.1	40.5	52.4
Floyd	183	1 154	239	49	203	75	28	22	19 207	517	4.6	57.3	67.5
Foard	38	303	56	D	D	D	7	4	12 825	238	7.1	42.9	42.9
Fort Bend	5 730	76 134	6 071	11 091	13 756	2 197	7 415	2 437	32 013	1 295	40.1	15.1	43.6
Franklin	191	5 655	3 721	D	270	77	36	62	10 937	510	24.5	12.7	45.1
Freestone	335	3 580	491	142	501	107	91	109	30 397	1 205	26.1	14.8	38.5
Frio	266	2 017	457	59	455	104	31	37	18 428	485	9.7	43.5	50.3
Gaines	328	2 573	355	53	451	126	D	57	21 991	712	7.3	59.8	67.3
Galveston	4 791	69 272	13 462	6 952	11 301	3 904	1 910	1 791	25 857	519	59.3	8.3	30.8
Garza	122	711	93	31	113	D	D	14	19 433	259	9.3	56.4	57.9
Gillespie	800	6 461	1 178	701	1 453	228	308	127	19 697	1 462	21.3	26.4	44.4
Glasscock	19	126	0	0	D	D	D	3	26 254	200	3.0	76.0	67.5
Goliad	101	705	88	6	111	D	23	13	18 394	786	17.9	20.5	42.0
Gonzales	396	4 001	714	837	683	162	91	80	20 099	1 629	20.5	19.8	48.4
Gray	686	6 327	1 050	914	1 135	213	201	163	25 826	341	10.6	50.7	57.2
Grayson	2 540	38 147	6 762	9 952	6 115	2 264	872	1 013	26 566	2 080	39.6	8.7	36.6
Gregg	3 915	57 430	7 932	12 760	8 845	1 705	1 879	1 441	25 097	363	42.4	4.4	24.5
Grimes	347	4 615	317	1 897	780	146	144	136	29 506	1 423	30.7	12.2	37.2

Table B. States and Counties — **Agriculture, Land, and Water**

STATE County	Land in farms — Acreage (1,000)	Percent change, 1992–1997	Acres — Average size of farm	Acres — Total irrigated (1,000)	Acres — Total cropland (1,000)	Value of land and buildings — Average per farm ($1,000)	Value of land and buildings — Average per acre (dollars)	Value of machinery and equipment average per farm ($1,000)	Value of products sold — Total (mil dol)	Value of products sold — Average per farm (dollars)	Percent from — Crops	Percent from — Livestock and poultry products	Percent of farms with sales of — $10,000 or more	Percent of farms with sales of — $100,000 or more	Percent of land owned by fed. gov. 1997	Water consumption 1995 (mil gal/day)
	117	118	119	120	121	122	123	124	125	126	127	128	129	130	131	132
TEXAS—Cont'd																
Caldwell	265	0.5	248	1	105	299	1 303	25	32	30 322	14.5	85.5	25.0	3.6	0.1	5.8
Calhoun	213	2.6	830	3	76	611	732	60	21	79 775	75.4	24.6	55.3	20.6	5.4	85.4
Callahan	489	-0.5	576	1	133	252	417	25	21	24 700	13.6	86.4	32.4	4.4	0.0	3.3
Cameron	369	12.0	409	109	230	446	1 143	62	79	88 042	87.7	12.3	40.7	18.1	4.4	456.5
Camp	63	-7.3	148	0	34	278	1 558	33	151	353 008	0.8	99.2	37.7	15.7	0.0	2.9
Carson	468	-24.8	1 344	74	272	429	317	87	72	208 251	31.1	68.9	64.9	26.7	1.6	71.9
Cass	171	2.2	200	0	72	183	863	28	23	26 662	10.0	90.0	26.6	4.2	1.4	79.9
Castro	559	7.8	1 142	227	409	676	578	160	668	1 366 952	13.4	86.6	80.6	55.8	0.0	400.6
Chambers	242	-3.6	575	25	118	335	642	37	16	37 296	73.9	26.1	39.2	11.9	4.9	123.7
Cherokee	283	5.3	198	1	140	251	1 296	33	103	72 095	58.3	41.7	35.7	7.1	0.0	347.1
Childress	393	-12.6	1 384	6	D	429	312	54	19	67 802	71.2	28.8	50.0	16.9	0.0	6.6
Clay	604	-9.9	738	1	160	429	566	36	38	45 956	13.1	86.9	48.5	10.5	0.0	16.3
Cochran	402	8.4	1 457	69	283	477	318	111	51	185 809	72.2	27.8	57.2	38.4	0.0	54.1
Coke	482	-7.7	1 436	0	55	497	321	26	8	23 781	8.3	91.7	43.8	3.6	0.0	32.0
Coleman	737	8.2	880	2	199	376	470	31	21	24 828	18.4	81.6	47.2	4.9	0.3	3.8
Collin	270	-2.0	192	0	190	447	2 440	34	34	24 162	66.0	34.0	20.3	4.1	0.4	339.1
Collingsworth	488	5.5	893	22	177	443	453	59	31	55 909	65.1	34.9	43.0	13.3	0.0	28.1
Colorado	521	-5.2	333	46	222	399	1 314	32	53	34 106	63.7	36.3	30.2	7.7	1.2	230.8
Comal	183	-11.5	279	0	42	517	1 559	19	5	7 863	32.4	67.6	16.9	1.1	1.1	28.2
Comanche	535	-1.6	372	24	225	292	765	47	94	65 524	18.7	81.3	46.2	9.4	0.7	46.2
Concho	636	11.1	1 673	4	129	666	393	53	20	52 016	36.7	63.3	60.8	12.4	0.0	6.9
Cooke	479	11.4	322	2	188	310	955	32	37	25 075	16.7	83.3	35.1	5.0	1.4	8.1
Coryell	646	6.8	601	1	156	370	569	29	28	26 074	15.9	84.1	32.2	4.3	22.6	1.9
Cottle	507	7.6	2 253	2	127	424	191	48	15	65 567	32.0	68.0	52.9	13.3	0.0	2.8
Crane	491	24.3	9 266	0	28	1 107	119	31	2	38 854	0.0	100.0	54.7	13.2	0.0	3.7
Crockett	1 935	-3.3	11 383	D	D	2 004	177	46	15	89 385	0.5	99.5	72.9	25.3	0.0	5.1
Crosby	563	24.5	1 462	162	368	669	439	134	74	192 877	95.6	4.4	73.0	45.5	0.0	91.5
Culberson	1 569	-0.9	17 057	3	27	1 955	115	43	6	65 497	38.2	61.8	58.7	19.6	2.4	7.9
Dallam	932	19.3	2 250	246	D	1 181	516	153	357	862 291	29.6	70.4	76.6	52.7	10.8	329.2
Dallas	149	20.0	194	1	75	461	2 288	24	22	29 009	73.1	26.9	21.7	4.8	2.3	728.7
Dawson	605	9.5	1 038	65	504	609	529	124	90	153 691	96.9	3.1	68.6	46.1	0.0	45.7
Deaf Smith	880	2.6	1 360	169	572	611	430	136	657	1 014 894	8.2	91.8	71.3	43.4	0.0	278.6
Delta	120	11.2	287	D	82	187	730	28	12	27 647	53.4	46.6	30.3	4.3	3.8	0.8
Denton	363	-0.9	204	1	198	486	2 252	39	54	30 049	24.1	75.9	24.7	3.8	3.4	166.0
De Witt	560	-1.6	373	1	150	289	760	23	23	15 473	9.5	90.5	29.1	2.5	0.0	5.3
Dickens	533	-5.2	1 456	8	140	426	281	46	14	38 645	46.4	53.6	34.4	7.7	0.0	5.1
Dimmit	518	-23.5	2 375	6	44	963	416	54	20	91 295	13.1	86.9	37.2	8.3	0.0	13.5
Donley	643	7.2	1 637	12	93	482	276	42	92	234 013	7.6	92.4	49.9	13.7	0.0	15.5
Duval	844	5.4	959	4	131	459	460	28	13	14 704	35.4	64.6	20.8	2.5	0.0	16.5
Eastland	497	0.8	437	9	172	228	529	28	26	22 763	29.1	70.9	34.4	2.6	0.0	15.4
Ector	462	-10.9	2 223	2	D	300	136	20	3	16 346	5.3	94.7	18.3	3.4	0.0	17.9
Edwards	1 142	2.2	4 035	2	17	1 198	302	23	9	32 103	2.0	98.0	48.1	9.5	0.0	1.0
Ellis	426	0.0	249	1	255	338	1 253	34	40	23 602	61.1	38.9	23.2	4.6	0.4	15.8
El Paso	244	0.0	587	41	47	404	720	72	77	184 754	48.0	52.0	37.6	19.5	13.7	392.6
Erath	613	5.0	343	11	218	353	1 057	41	233	130 339	3.6	96.4	39.6	11.0	0.0	25.1
Falls	362	-4.2	353	3	223	278	798	46	52	50 969	37.4	62.6	43.5	9.7	0.0	8.8
Fannin	445	7.7	277	2	264	296	1 083	27	39	24 451	43.5	56.5	31.3	3.6	3.1	477.5
Fayette	515	3.6	194	1	222	261	1 371	23	60	22 444	9.1	90.9	23.0	2.4	0.0	17.4
Fisher	575	5.3	954	2	222	339	388	68	31	51 157	59.0	41.0	47.8	12.1	0.0	2.8
Floyd	556	-11.6	1 075	170	409	508	460	127	131	252 822	53.6	46.4	63.4	44.7	0.0	226.3
Foard	308	-4.4	1 293	1	128	382	297	56	11	46 674	46.1	53.9	42.4	8.8	0.0	4.7
Fort Bend	432	2.3	333	17	193	503	1 494	51	76	58 994	84.1	15.9	36.7	10.3	0.3	214.9
Franklin	135	4.6	265	0	55	258	995	42	49	96 441	2.5	97.5	40.4	15.9	0.0	4.6
Freestone	423	14.2	351	0	133	313	914	25	20	16 305	7.3	92.7	27.6	1.9	0.0	868.0
Frio	662	-11.7	1 365	47	149	720	531	80	68	140 378	58.3	41.7	41.9	14.8	0.0	100.0
Gaines	772	12.4	1 085	234	591	570	501	134	218	306 599	D	D	63.2	48.0	0.0	549.7
Galveston	105	2.9	202	1	30	251	1 053	28	7	13 112	31.4	68.6	18.3	1.9	0.1	61.1
Garza	514	-10.4	1 986	11	D	426	204	57	15	57 219	67.7	32.3	54.4	18.9	0.0	5.3
Gillespie	694	-0.9	475	3	118	630	1 277	25	29	20 014	16.4	83.6	29.8	2.1	0.1	7.3
Glasscock	437	-8.7	2 183	52	132	1 001	439	112	24	118 702	87.9	12.1	71.0	41.5	0.0	52.1
Goliad	434	-6.8	552	0	76	359	665	26	12	15 715	15.7	84.3	28.6	3.1	0.2	8.2
Gonzales	710	6.7	436	3	178	381	797	44	294	180 725	4.7	95.3	40.3	12.3	0.0	8.8
Gray	561	-2.6	1 645	24	D	666	426	69	85	249 747	11.2	88.8	53.4	15.8	0.1	25.2
Grayson	417	1.8	201	2	245	293	1 508	29	35	17 056	44.2	55.8	23.4	3.0	2.9	27.3
Gregg	51	9.3	142	0	26	271	1 377	30	3	7 605	17.5	82.5	17.9	0.6	0.0	24.5
Grimes	370	4.9	260	1	132	299	1 369	29	23	16 406	13.2	86.8	26.9	3.0	0.0	9.1

Table B. States and Counties — **Residential Construction, Wholesale and Retail Trade, and Real Estate**

STATE County	Value of Residential Construction Authorized by Building Permits, 2000		Wholesale Trade, 1997				Retail Trade[1], 1997				Real Estate and Rental and Leasing, 1997			
	New Construction ($1,000)	Number of Housing Units	Number of Establishments	Number of Employees	Sales (mil dol)	Annual Payroll (mil dol)	Number of Establishments	Number of Employees	Sales (mil dol)	Annual Payroll (mil dol)	Number of Establishments	Number of Employees	Receipts (mil dol)	Annual Payroll (mil dol)
	133	134	135	136	137	138	139	140	141	142	143	144	145	146
TEXAS—Cont'd														
Caldwell	2 826	57	25	166	63.1	2.9	92	806	128.4	10.1	19	55	4.9	0.7
Calhoun	5 856	68	29	135	51.9	3.7	77	725	111.1	10.3	16	81	12.7	1.9
Callahan	655	7	8	38	7.2	0.8	36	266	65.4	4.3	3	11	0.5	0.1
Cameron	194 470	3 111	387	3 772	1 218.9	81.6	1 117	13 089	1 904.0	179.3	283	1 208	98.5	18.1
Camp	192	3	11	80	13.2	0.9	58	532	109.6	9.1	7	19	2.2	0.2
Carson	291	1	6	37	20.4	0.8	29	233	25.2	2.3	4	28	0.3	0.1
Cass	1 108	15	30	222	106.8	6.1	137	1 261	161.5	16.8	18	64	3.5	0.5
Castro	0	0	20	D	D	D	41	208	47.7	3.2	5	D	D	D
Chambers	28 788	309	22	D	D	D	83	648	133.8	9.4	15	84	9.8	2.1
Cherokee	3 780	45	39	250	75.5	8.4	146	1 542	262.6	21.5	32	94	8.2	1.5
Childress	34	1	14	101	51.7	2.3	38	309	43.7	3.8	3	7	0.2	0.1
Clay	886	12	7	51	17.3	1.2	34	267	53.3	4.1	2	D	D	D
Cochran	0	0	7	26	7.9	0.5	15	87	15.6	1.5	NA	NA	NA	NA
Coke	0	0	3	D	D	D	21	98	24.2	1.3	1	D	D	D
Coleman	60	2	18	102	29.9	1.2	53	324	57.1	4.2	8	15	2.0	0.2
Collin	1 723 896	10 111	737	7 373	7 169.8	326.9	1 301	20 311	4 220.4	407.2	430	1 982	349.3	58.0
Collingsworth	0	0	5	18	7.4	0.4	17	113	17.4	2.1	1	D	D	D
Colorado	1 320	12	40	235	84.9	4.3	113	879	163.3	13.3	12	D	D	D
Comal	126 862	1 132	99	653	320.1	20.0	317	3 242	633.3	55.7	84	339	28.7	5.0
Comanche	46	1	29	370	124.5	8.5	77	456	79.6	6.4	4	D	D	D
Concho	NA	NA	4	20	2.7	0.4	14	82	14.1	1.2	NA	NA	NA	NA
Cooke	4 805	50	45	354	102.5	6.6	240	2 013	355.6	28.9	18	68	11.7	1.1
Coryell	10 396	90	17	D	D	D	144	1 781	268.7	22.0	44	139	7.4	1.6
Cottle	0	0	1	D	D	D	10	40	10.3	0.6	1	D	D	D
Crane	0	0	6	D	D	D	17	129	21.7	1.8	2	D	D	D
Crockett	NA	NA	6	15	6.7	0.4	31	263	26.6	3.2	2	D	D	D
Crosby	91	2	12	171	65.4	4.8	33	226	41.8	3.2	3	6	0.4	0.1
Culberson	0	0	1	D	D	D	25	162	28.2	1.7	NA	NA	NA	NA
Dallam	1 710	30	22	275	191.7	10.0	43	250	65.3	4.3	7	11	1.3	0.1
Dallas	1 794 051	13 745	6 054	108 131	100 787.3	4 621.7	7 878	117 812	24 538.2	2 400.4	3 352	30 049	4 268.4	932.5
Dawson	359	4	25	122	91.4	2.8	68	553	95.8	8.6	10	39	1.8	0.5
Deaf Smith	360	3	46	368	120.8	10.0	88	595	113.9	8.9	14	37	3.6	0.6
Delta	218	2	2	D	D	D	19	94	16.2	1.2	1	D	D	D
Denton	903 577	5 789	423	3 935	2 762.2	141.4	1 143	16 966	3 180.1	284.9	324	1 540	177.5	29.7
De Witt	498	10	22	155	86.4	2.6	81	663	93.0	9.1	14	73	5.0	1.4
Dickens	NA	NA	1	D	D	D	12	54	7.4	0.5	NA	NA	NA	NA
Dimmit	0	0	7	17	6.2	0.4	34	328	50.3	4.5	3	D	D	D
Donley	0	0	2	D	D	D	20	114	23.6	1.7	3	6	0.7	0.1
Duval	NA	NA	6	D	D	D	36	203	35.2	2.6	5	11	1.0	0.2
Eastland	55	1	29	368	255.7	9.1	113	682	116.5	8.8	10	22	3.4	0.4
Ector	20 621	238	355	3 518	1 047.6	117.9	538	6 060	1 139.9	104.4	136	D	D	D
Edwards	NA	NA	2	D	D	D	9	47	5.8	0.4	1	D	D	D
Ellis	93 905	976	94	751	375.7	19.6	310	3 054	572.7	47.5	86	321	35.2	5.5
El Paso	166 593	3 203	1 000	11 129	6 089.3	309.6	2 134	28 986	4 698.9	430.5	550	2 458	285.3	48.1
Erath	1 782	23	43	378	118.9	6.8	157	1 674	274.1	24.6	26	80	7.8	1.0
Falls	394	9	14	D	D	D	68	435	65.4	5.4	9	31	1.3	0.3
Fannin	3 088	50	26	321	187.8	7.7	101	929	193.8	14.8	15	29	2.4	0.3
Fayette	1 484	15	39	411	318.6	10.6	141	1 063	185.9	15.2	17	63	3.7	0.7
Fisher	0	0	3	D	D	D	17	96	12.4	1.3	2	D	D	D
Floyd	406	3	19	181	58.0	2.7	32	206	47.7	3.2	6	12	0.4	0.1
Foard	0	0	2	D	D	D	6	22	4.3	0.3	1	D	D	D
Fort Bend	144 963	1 313	405	3 793	2 972.1	143.0	825	11 992	2 229.9	196.4	220	763	93.3	17.7
Franklin	149	3	5	19	2.6	0.4	32	220	37.2	3.3	7	18	1.1	0.3
Freestone	3 065	49	15	61	26.4	1.2	63	481	105.9	7.7	6	21	0.9	0.2
Frio	418	15	23	D	D	D	52	461	82.1	6.2	7	10	0.8	0.1
Gaines	250	1	22	182	135.6	5.2	62	470	88.9	7.4	10	24	1.3	0.4
Galveston	338 069	2 931	198	1 522	561.3	46.6	921	10 591	1 786.9	165.8	224	1 160	128.5	25.4
Garza	150	3	8	32	18.7	0.8	29	123	18.3	1.5	3	20	0.8	0.1
Gillespie	8 568	61	36	334	89.8	5.8	153	1 361	172.9	18.6	25	82	5.5	1.0
Glasscock	NA	NA	1	D	D	D	5	D	D	D	NA	NA	NA	NA
Goliad	NA	NA	4	12	2.8	0.2	20	100	17.4	1.3	2	D	D	D
Gonzales	484	3	38	353	153.3	6.0	82	728	99.2	8.4	14	41	2.1	0.3
Gray	0	0	42	309	178.7	9.6	130	1 068	169.1	16.0	24	98	18.2	4.2
Grayson	20 604	200	132	958	406.1	25.1	474	6 213	1 092.0	98.5	104	351	32.0	5.8
Gregg	20 798	160	342	3 564	1 863.5	114.0	734	8 825	1 549.7	145.1	134	649	74.8	17.0
Grimes	941	13	19	187	137.0	4.1	73	663	120.5	9.9	12	93	5.7	1.0

1. Establishments with payroll.

STATE County	Professional, Scientific, and Technical Services[1], 1997				Manufacturing, 1997				Accommodation and Foodservices, 1997			
	Number of Establishments	Number of Employees	Receipts (mil dol)	Annual Payroll (mil dol)	Number of Establishments	Number of Employees	Receipts (mil dol)	Annual Payroll (mil dol)	Number of Establishments	Number of Employees	Sales (mil dol)	Annual Payroll (mil dol)
	147	148	149	150	151	152	153	154	155	156	157	158
TEXAS—Cont'd												
Caldwell	28	68	4.3	1.2	18	556	39.2	9.7	36	370	14.1	3.7
Calhoun	30	270	16.6	9.2	20	3 815	2 689.3	208.8	53	524	15.2	4.2
Callahan	9	18	1.5	0.4	NA	NA	NA	NA	15	130	2.9	0.8
Cameron	339	2 278	126.5	42.7	235	12 694	1 732.8	242.4	513	8 349	278.2	71.7
Camp	14	27	3.7	1.2	NA	NA	NA	NA	17	96	D	0.9
Carson	3	9	0.6	0.1	NA	NA	NA	NA	10	D	D	D
Cass	26	86	4.8	1.5	26	546	63.9	11.4	47	548	14.7	4.0
Castro	9	28	1.9	0.7	NA	NA	NA	NA	14	D	D	D
Chambers	20	80	6.3	1.9	15	1 499	1 989.7	83.5	31	577	14.9	3.9
Cherokee	47	153	9.5	2.6	91	3 178	327.4	67.0	47	632	20.3	4.9
Childress	9	32	1.6	0.4	NA	NA	NA	NA	24	256	7.2	1.8
Clay	8	12	1.0	0.2	NA	NA	NA	NA	11	61	1.5	0.4
Cochran	4	8	0.3	0.1	NA	NA	NA	NA	5	16	0.5	0.1
Coke	2	D	D	D	NA	NA	NA	NA	7	D	D	D
Coleman	13	34	1.4	0.4	NA	NA	NA	NA	21	173	4.2	1.2
Collin	1 161	6 165	783.9	285.6	318	21 326	6 235.9	972.3	563	11 830	430.9	119.6
Collingsworth	5	25	1.6	0.9	NA	NA	NA	NA	7	43	1.0	0.2
Colorado	28	65	4.0	1.3	29	825	76.0	17.4	48	569	15.3	3.7
Comal	121	382	30.6	11.3	84	4 016	558.6	101.2	172	2 468	80.4	22.8
Comanche	12	28	2.6	0.7	NA	NA	NA	NA	22	165	4.8	1.3
Concho	3	5	0.3	0.1	NA	NA	NA	NA	9	81	2.8	0.6
Cooke	37	112	7.4	2.7	68	3 318	437.7	88.2	64	965	29.0	7.6
Coryell	35	265	16.0	8.2	25	556	52.3	12.0	60	1 201	30.4	9.9
Cottle	NA	NA	NA	NA	NA	NA	NA	NA	5	D	D	D
Crane	4	3	0.4	0.0	NA	NA	NA	NA	7	83	1.9	0.5
Crockett	8	32	2.3	0.8	NA	NA	NA	NA	24	218	6.4	1.7
Crosby	4	6	0.4	0.1	NA	NA	NA	NA	5	34	1.1	0.3
Culberson	2	D	D	D	NA	NA	NA	NA	21	224	6.0	1.5
Dallam	14	D	D	D	NA	NA	NA	NA	27	264	8.7	1.9
Dallas	8 030	90 234	11 406.1	4 676.3	3 383	151 686	29 962.5	5 499.4	4 194	98 652	4 045.9	1 102.7
Dawson	15	60	4.2	1.2	NA	NA	NA	NA	30	283	9.8	2.7
Deaf Smith	16	60	3.5	1.4	32	1 128	376.7	28.9	29	D	D	D
Delta	4	4	0.2	0.1	NA	NA	NA	NA	2	D	D	D
Denton	624	5 359	319.1	237.8	305	13 556	2 741.8	459.8	488	9 742	325.0	90.4
De Witt	20	71	3.8	1.2	24	721	87.9	16.4	37	290	8.9	2.6
Dickens	2	D	D	D	NA	NA	NA	NA	7	38	1.5	0.3
Dimmit	10	24	1.7	0.8	NA	NA	NA	NA	12	125	4.0	1.0
Donley	7	11	0.6	0.1	NA	NA	NA	NA	14	79	2.2	0.5
Duval	4	10	0.4	0.1	NA	NA	NA	NA	16	88	2.8	0.7
Eastland	30	86	3.7	1.1	25	713	98.3	17.4	43	382	9.3	2.6
Ector	192	1 005	69.1	26.5	203	3 526	1 286.2	115.6	234	3 806	119.9	32.9
Edwards	2	D	D	D	NA	NA	NA	NA	3	D	D	D
Ellis	96	298	25.2	8.6	174	9 635	2 397.9	285.0	113	1 652	52.5	14.7
El Paso	927	5 777	398.1	161.7	652	36 723	7 966.5	773.9	1 094	19 292	703.3	194.0
Erath	42	320	16.8	7.2	37	2 186	387.7	53.3	68	1 029	30.2	7.9
Falls	10	28	1.4	0.6	NA	NA	NA	NA	20	92	3.7	0.9
Fannin	27	70	4.6	1.8	40	1 784	340.6	43.6	33	281	9.9	2.7
Fayette	34	127	7.1	2.3	39	1 056	148.6	23.2	55	780	20.9	6.0
Fisher	6	8	0.4	0.1	NA	NA	NA	NA	6	D	D	D
Floyd	8	21	1.3	0.3	NA	NA	NA	NA	16	75	2.0	0.6
Foard	3	8	0.2	0.1	NA	NA	NA	NA	3	8	0.2	0.1
Fort Bend	517	4 843	1 024.3	303.6	270	11 923	2 704.9	452.7	319	5 889	205.4	56.2
Franklin	11	31	1.8	0.6	NA	NA	NA	NA	18	198	5.1	1.3
Freestone	23	87	4.8	1.6	NA	NA	NA	NA	24	297	9.2	2.6
Frio	8	28	0.8	0.2	NA	NA	NA	NA	23	168	5.7	1.5
Gaines	9	33	1.9	1.1	NA	NA	NA	NA	21	D	D	D
Galveston	333	1 375	131.6	52.5	160	7 279	9 182.6	392.5	485	9 156	301.5	82.4
Garza	1	D	D	D	NA	NA	NA	NA	13	115	2.7	0.7
Gillespie	48	125	8.2	2.8	45	721	70.7	13.1	67	815	25.9	7.6
Glasscock	1	D	D	D	NA	NA	NA	NA	1	D	D	D
Goliad	7	16	0.9	0.3	NA	NA	NA	NA	13	114	2.6	0.7
Gonzales	26	69	4.3	1.2	19	747	173.6	16.8	26	242	7.1	1.9
Gray	41	181	11.9	3.9	20	1 082	419.9	53.2	55	658	19.0	5.0
Grayson	162	715	52.6	19.6	140	10 223	3 557.3	365.4	200	3 312	104.8	30.7
Gregg	277	1 516	113.5	44.0	205	13 008	3 408.6	447.6	274	4 575	146.3	41.5
Grimes	22	52	4.3	1.1	21	1 910	386.9	63.3	25	D	D	D

1. Firms subject to federal tax.

Table B. States and Counties — Health and Other Services and Federal Funds

STATE County	Health Care and Social Assistance[1], 1997				Other Services[1], 1997				Federal funds and grants, fiscal 2001[2] Expenditures (mil dol)			
									Total	Direct payments for individuals[3]		
	Number of Establishments	Number of Employees	Receipts (mil dol)	Annual Payroll (mil dol)	Number of Establishments	Number of Employees	Receipts (mil dol)	Annual Payroll (mil dol)		Social Security and government retirement	Medicare	Food stamps and Supplemental Security Income
	159	160	161	162	163	164	165	166	167	168	169	170
TEXAS—Cont'd												
Caldwell	33	506	19.2	8.2	29	88	4.9	1.1	130.7	57.7	27.1	6.3
Calhoun	25	288	11.9	4.9	31	106	5.7	1.6	93.8	39.7	14.9	3.1
Callahan	8	108	3.6	1.6	8	17	1.4	0.3	69.6	33.3	12.2	1.5
Cameron	509	11 065	498.3	216.2	338	2 279	96.3	30.0	1 467.0	389.7	216.4	123.7
Camp	19	174	6.9	2.9	10	28	1.9	0.4	67.2	31.1	15.6	2.6
Carson	2	D	D	D	9	22	2.0	0.3	65.9	13.9	6.8	0.4
Cass	39	723	28.5	11.6	33	144	10.6	3.5	184.2	87.7	37.9	6.6
Castro	6	58	1.8	0.6	18	55	4.7	1.0	73.1	11.7	6.3	0.9
Chambers	13	135	3.5	1.5	20	78	6.8	2.2	104.7	30.0	19.6	2.4
Cherokee	81	1 155	43.3	20.0	51	105	8.1	1.7	209.2	88.0	49.5	7.0
Childress	10	149	6.5	2.9	5	26	1.1	0.3	49.5	15.3	7.5	1.0
Clay	6	114	4.1	1.8	5	19	1.9	0.3	47.6	22.4	9.2	0.8
Cochran	1	D	D	D	1	D	D	D	43.4	7.3	3.8	1.0
Coke	NA	NA	NA	NA	5	14	0.8	0.1	19.0	9.7	4.0	0.3
Coleman	17	193	7.9	3.0	14	40	5.5	0.5	72.8	28.0	19.2	1.7
Collin	903	9 790	793.9	309.0	480	2 868	169.6	54.3	1 105.3	459.1	126.5	17.9
Collingsworth	5	133	3.8	2.2	3	7	0.7	0.1	58.6	8.0	5.2	0.7
Colorado	28	349	16.4	6.7	31	91	5.4	1.4	132.8	44.9	22.1	2.6
Comal	151	1 335	69.3	28.7	126	645	37.9	11.5	321.1	210.5	54.2	5.7
Comanche	25	357	13.2	6.0	11	53	3.0	0.8	86.9	34.3	21.5	1.8
Concho	4	D	D	D	2	D	D	D	30.8	6.5	4.3	0.4
Cooke	51	553	24.5	9.7	45	220	11.4	2.9	149.4	74.8	32.1	2.6
Coryell	33	439	18.3	7.9	55	200	11.3	2.9	223.6	147.3	24.1	2.8
Cottle	4	58	1.4	0.6	3	D	D	D	22.5	5.4	2.8	0.4
Crane	8	133	7.0	4.1	4	10	1.1	0.1	13.2	6.8	4.2	0.6
Crockett	2	D	D	D	7	66	2.9	1.0	15.6	6.8	2.4	0.6
Crosby	6	D	D	D	7	11	1.2	0.1	71.3	13.1	12.3	1.3
Culberson	1	D	D	D	1	D	D	D	12.8	3.6	2.8	0.6
Dallam	5	18	1.3	0.6	14	D	D	D	66.3	15.8	7.4	0.9
Dallas	5 123	69 423	5 748.0	2 306.3	3 683	30 022	2 019.0	651.6	9 359.7	2 911.2	1 367.9	290.9
Dawson	20	169	7.6	2.8	27	116	5.3	1.4	160.7	26.1	24.0	3.7
Deaf Smith	17	245	9.5	3.9	36	141	9.5	2.3	114.9	26.8	14.4	4.1
Delta	6	172	5.5	2.5	4	D	D	D	35.5	13.1	7.5	1.1
Denton	599	7 690	531.4	215.6	421	2 850	212.3	58.0	778.9	376.4	123.7	15.1
De Witt	26	407	19.0	6.9	28	83	5.3	1.3	104.3	39.6	24.3	3.9
Dickens	4	54	1.1	0.4	3	5	0.7	0.1	25.5	6.6	7.2	0.5
Dimmit	19	141	6.5	2.6	12	95	5.2	1.4	65.9	13.9	9.7	3.3
Donley	2	D	D	D	4	9	0.7	0.2	25.7	10.4	5.1	0.3
Duval	10	498	21.9	11.3	8	63	2.9	0.9	95.0	22.7	20.3	5.6
Eastland	39	447	19.3	8.5	33	111	6.7	1.7	145.6	53.2	28.1	2.7
Ector	227	3 674	163.7	68.9	233	1 777	194.4	40.8	429.1	202.4	101.0	24.0
Edwards	1	D	D	D	4	D	D	D	15.8	4.7	6.0	0.7
Ellis	113	1 385	73.2	31.0	108	488	31.1	7.9	345.3	174.8	77.0	11.2
El Paso	984	16 524	1 165.3	455.8	824	5 779	265.7	87.6	3 580.5	1 127.6	409.9	184.8
Erath	56	911	46.3	19.3	61	300	14.0	4.1	133.5	65.6	29.2	2.9
Falls	19	395	14.0	6.3	25	61	3.6	0.8	138.6	41.0	19.4	4.7
Fannin	34	699	24.5	12.4	24	82	5.9	1.2	184.7	75.9	34.2	3.7
Fayette	44	589	25.4	9.8	49	168	8.4	2.3	129.2	59.4	28.6	2.2
Fisher	5	57	2.3	0.9	6	16	1.1	0.2	55.9	11.1	6.6	0.5
Floyd	11	103	4.5	1.6	12	44	3.5	0.9	83.4	14.8	9.0	1.6
Foard	3	49	1.7	0.9	2	D	D	D	24.0	4.8	2.6	0.3
Fort Bend	441	4 969	297.4	122.0	337	2 296	141.9	44.5	970.2	303.1	84.1	24.1
Franklin	13	2 632	29.5	18.5	14	31	2.5	0.7	38.7	20.7	9.7	0.9
Freestone	26	310	11.3	4.6	20	83	5.4	1.2	82.6	39.0	14.1	2.7
Frio	22	288	12.7	4.6	13	54	1.9	0.6	77.5	20.1	11.2	5.1
Gaines	11	111	7.5	2.4	31	115	9.1	2.1	142.1	18.4	12.7	1.9
Galveston	360	4 424	215.2	97.2	358	2 159	134.4	39.7	1 295.4	460.5	220.2	36.8
Garza	3	84	2.3	1.1	4	12	0.9	0.2	32.2	9.2	7.2	0.9
Gillespie	56	587	29.5	10.2	47	144	9.7	2.2	109.7	71.3	23.0	1.1
Glasscock	NA	NA	NA	NA	2	D	D	D	32.1	1.6	0.5	0.1
Goliad	5	110	4.7	2.0	4	8	0.4	0.1	33.3	14.6	7.4	1.2
Gonzales	20	202	7.6	3.1	26	119	5.0	1.4	106.2	43.1	18.5	4.6
Gray	47	1 147	58.5	24.1	44	160	10.4	2.7	119.4	55.2	36.1	2.8
Grayson	278	4 362	225.0	104.6	123	649	32.9	9.6	532.3	282.7	109.7	14.6
Gregg	330	5 135	305.2	129.6	232	1 637	105.3	29.9	522.7	266.3	114.4	20.9
Grimes	17	363	13.4	5.8	16	46	3.6	0.7	98.3	40.8	19.2	4.1

1. Firms subject to federal tax.   2. October 1, 2000 to September 30, 2001.   3. State totals may include programs not allocated by county.

Table B. States and Counties — **Federal Funds and Local Government Finances**

STATE County	Federal funds and grants, fiscal 2001[1] (cont'd)							Local government finances, 1997				
	Expenditures (mil dol) (cont'd)							General revenue				
	Procurement contract awards			Grants[2]						Taxes		
											Per capita[3] (dollars)	
	Salaries and wages	Defense	Other	Medicaid and other health-related	Nutrition and family welfare	Education	Other	Total (mil dol)	Intergovern-mental (mil dol)	Total (mil dol)	Total	Property
	171	172	173	174	175	176	177	178	179	180	181	182
TEXAS—Cont'd												
Caldwell	3.3	0.1	1.0	26.3	1.6	2.4	1.9	53.4	26.3	12.9	407	329
Calhoun	3.5	6.1	0.5	9.7	1.8	0.8	3.3	72.9	6.4	33.3	1 601	1 419
Callahan	1.6	0.2	0.4	6.0	0.6	0.5	9.4	22.5	13.4	7.1	552	459
Cameron	108.3	3.7	16.3	314.8	68.6	39.3	99.9	726.9	441.5	157.7	492	367
Camp	1.8	0.0	0.4	13.6	0.7	0.5	0.3	19.7	7.4	8.5	777	663
Carson	0.9	0.2	0.2	1.5	0.2	0.1	18.6	14.3	2.2	10.1	1 510	1 401
Cass	4.3	1.0	1.1	30.1	5.9	1.4	5.1	79.0	27.4	24.7	808	697
Castro	0.9	0.0	0.2	3.5	1.7	0.6	3.4	19.6	10.4	6.3	753	619
Chambers	2.6	1.2	1.7	6.8	1.3	0.5	17.7	69.2	10.8	50.0	2 122	2 002
Cherokee	5.1	0.1	1.4	33.8	3.7	1.6	13.1	64.5	33.2	22.0	514	412
Childress	1.7	0.0	0.6	4.7	0.7	0.4	5.3	18.5	2.4	3.6	477	352
Clay	1.4	0.0	0.4	3.3	0.4	0.2	4.2	36.9	9.5	6.6	636	588
Cochran	0.7	0.0	0.2	2.5	0.3	0.4	6.0	16.3	4.6	8.9	2 241	2 114
Coke	0.8	0.0	0.2	1.1	0.2	0.1	0.9	11.9	3.9	4.1	1 190	1 090
Coleman	2.3	0.1	0.5	9.1	3.6	0.5	2.2	22.9	11.7	5.4	559	432
Collin	56.6	283.1	63.4	39.4	7.9	6.0	23.4	849.2	110.5	539.4	1 344	1 145
Collingsworth	1.2	0.0	0.3	3.5	0.3	0.2	7.7	10.5	5.0	2.4	717	606
Colorado	3.2	0.7	1.5	18.5	1.8	0.7	4.1	41.4	13.6	16.1	854	727
Comal	22.5	1.6	2.5	15.5	2.7	1.6	0.5	134.4	37.2	71.5	1 012	837
Comanche	2.4	0.0	0.6	11.4	0.7	0.5	7.2	34.9	11.3	7.4	545	470
Concho	0.9	0.0	0.2	2.8	0.3	0.1	4.3	15.9	2.6	3.3	1 056	885
Cooke	4.3	3.2	1.3	9.4	1.5	1.3	6.8	93.3	30.4	25.8	782	602
Coryell	10.6	2.6	2.7	12.8	3.0	10.4	1.6	104.4	58.5	24.5	317	235
Cottle	0.5	0.0	0.1	2.1	0.2	0.1	2.2	4.9	2.6	1.8	902	729
Crane	0.3	0.0	0.1	0.8	0.1	0.2	0.0	30.6	0.9	26.9	5 899	5 742
Crockett	0.3	0.0	0.1	2.5	0.4	0.3	0.0	18.7	1.9	12.6	2 799	2 724
Crosby	0.9	0.0	0.2	5.4	0.9	0.5	6.4	17.5	10.3	5.2	707	605
Culberson	2.3	0.0	0.0	1.6	0.1	0.2	0.0	8.8	2.7	4.2	1 330	1 154
Dallam	1.2	0.0	0.2	1.6	0.5	0.4	6.7	15.7	5.9	7.4	1 158	925
Dallas	1 473.5	1 405.7	430.8	781.6	147.9	71.1	250.7	5 985.1	1 174.8	3 078.1	1 521	1 100
Dawson	2.6	0.0	0.5	11.1	4.8	1.1	17.1	38.1	11.2	15.3	1 032	898
Deaf Smith	2.1	0.0	1.4	10.1	2.7	1.3	5.1	36.1	18.4	11.3	580	490
Delta	1.2	0.1	0.3	6.8	0.6	0.3	0.9	11.9	7.1	3.4	688	583
Denton	62.4	43.2	20.9	30.9	6.1	11.4	47.3	536.0	119.8	308.6	845	709
De Witt	2.7	0.0	0.6	22.2	2.7	1.2	4.6	54.5	32.6	11.9	606	522
Dickens	0.7	0.0	0.2	2.7	0.3	0.1	1.0	7.0	3.7	2.5	1 129	786
Dimmit	7.0	0.0	0.3	18.4	6.4	1.4	2.2	32.2	15.7	7.3	697	552
Donley	0.7	0.0	0.1	2.3	0.3	0.1	1.1	16.0	6.3	2.9	769	613
Duval	3.4	0.0	0.2	31.1	2.6	1.3	1.3	40.7	16.7	13.8	1 014	885
Eastland	3.5	0.3	0.9	14.4	0.9	0.7	4.2	49.9	22.2	9.9	555	436
Ector	11.5	1.3	3.0	38.7	11.9	10.8	6.9	415.2	109.5	115.8	929	699
Edwards	0.7	0.0	0.1	1.6	0.3	0.3	0.1	9.1	4.1	3.9	1 039	952
Ellis	12.0	0.1	3.9	35.0	3.7	2.7	3.7	180.3	70.6	82.4	819	679
El Paso	645.5	369.9	74.1	370.0	82.6	54.5	120.1	1 582.9	756.8	507.8	724	557
Erath	4.4	0.1	1.1	13.4	1.3	1.3	4.2	55.0	23.8	22.1	707	523
Falls	9.9	0.0	0.8	27.6	2.0	0.9	18.2	26.9	15.7	7.8	438	336
Fannin	21.8	0.1	1.5	27.6	2.5	0.7	3.0	44.1	24.6	13.5	488	402
Fayette	4.2	0.4	1.3	21.2	1.1	0.5	7.4	37.3	8.4	21.5	1 020	896
Fisher	1.1	0.0	0.3	4.1	0.3	0.2	7.2	14.3	4.7	4.3	991	902
Floyd	1.6	0.0	0.9	6.8	1.4	0.6	8.5	20.9	10.5	5.4	656	565
Foard	0.3	0.2	0.1	1.9	1.5	0.1	2.7	8.4	4.5	1.7	960	852
Fort Bend	31.8	2.9	8.0	32.8	8.9	6.6	22.2	586.7	161.4	339.4	1 057	945
Franklin	1.0	0.0	0.3	3.9	0.3	0.3	0.9	22.5	3.6	7.8	808	694
Freestone	2.2	0.1	0.6	14.2	1.2	0.5	6.3	33.4	6.2	17.5	998	885
Frio	1.3	0.0	0.3	18.2	3.8	1.2	6.6	46.9	16.6	9.0	568	464
Gaines	1.3	0.0	0.3	4.9	1.2	1.0	20.6	57.3	6.0	35.7	2 384	2 311
Galveston	58.6	173.6	49.6	160.2	18.5	9.7	29.0	701.8	155.0	395.5	1 628	1 437
Garza	0.8	0.0	0.3	2.9	0.7	0.3	1.8	13.1	3.8	7.2	1 551	1 386
Gillespie	3.9	0.6	0.7	3.5	0.9	0.5	2.4	32.5	7.7	17.8	895	700
Glasscock	0.2	0.0	0.0	0.6	0.1	0.1	4.4	6.9	0.7	5.8	3 964	3 847
Goliad	0.8	0.0	0.2	6.6	0.6	0.3	0.0	13.9	3.1	8.8	1 294	1 209
Gonzales	8.6	0.0	0.7	22.8	2.4	1.2	2.3	43.1	17.3	10.9	621	544
Gray	3.4	0.2	0.7	10.4	0.8	0.7	1.1	41.9	10.0	23.8	1 004	874
Grayson	17.1	1.6	6.0	50.7	7.0	2.7	20.7	217.3	82.9	85.6	843	680
Gregg	20.1	1.8	-0.3	60.2	7.9	3.9	11.9	256.6	84.5	130.5	1 153	878
Grimes	2.9	0.0	0.9	21.8	2.1	0.9	0.1	33.3	13.9	15.4	676	569

1. October 1, 2000 to September 30, 2001.   2. State totals may include programs not allocated by county.   3. Based on the resident population estimated as of July 1 of the year shown.

Table B. States and Counties — Local Government Finances, Government Employment, and Elections

STATE County	Local government finances, 1997 (cont'd)									Government employment, 1999			Presidential election, 2000[2]		
	Direct general expenditure							Debt outstanding					Percent of vote cast —		
			Percent of total for —												
	Total (mil dol)	Per capita[1] (dollars)	Education	Health and hospitals	Police protection	Public welfare	Highways	Total (mil dol)	Per capita[1] (dollars)	Federal civilian	Federal military	State and local	Democratic	Republican	All other
	183	184	185	186	187	188	189	190	191	192	193	194	195	196	197
TEXAS—Cont'd															
Caldwell	57.2	1 809	50.8	13.4	3.0	0.3	2.9	22.9	725	60	86	1 534	41.1	55.3	3.6
Calhoun	71.0	3 415	37.1	23.6	3.3	1.4	3.4	78.2	3 759	45	94	1 387	42.1	56.7	1.2
Callahan	21.9	1 711	80.1	0.2	2.9	0.2	1.2	5.0	393	31	34	657	24.0	74.7	1.4
Cameron	693.3	2 161	66.3	1.4	3.8	0.7	2.6	787.6	2 455	2 121	958	21 836	53.5	44.8	1.7
Camp	19.1	1 744	72.4	0.3	3.3	0.0	4.8	14.6	1 329	30	29	496	42.9	56.1	1.0
Carson	14.5	2 165	67.6	0.2	4.0	0.2	10.0	0.0	2	193	18	427	17.5	80.8	1.7
Cass	71.7	2 348	50.7	22.5	3.6	0.2	3.6	27.0	885	75	80	2 029	41.9	57.1	0.9
Castro	18.0	2 168	72.5	1.1	5.4	0.0	5.0	8.5	1 022	26	22	737	30.9	68.3	0.9
Chambers	68.9	2 924	62.0	5.3	4.8	0.5	5.2	37.0	1 569	55	63	1 403	29.5	69.0	1.5
Cherokee	64.6	1 510	66.7	1.3	4.4	0.9	4.9	33.5	783	82	115	3 984	32.7	66.0	1.2
Childress	19.4	2 538	40.6	42.4	4.0	0.0	2.1	0.7	89	37	20	1 097	28.3	70.8	0.8
Clay	37.0	3 552	35.9	0.6	2.0	0.2	4.0	289.0	27 772	28	28	517	31.5	67.1	1.4
Cochran	16.2	4 078	63.7	12.9	2.6	0.7	4.7	1.0	243	18	10	387	29.4	68.9	1.7
Coke	11.4	3 313	52.8	0.1	2.1	25.9	3.9	1.1	332	16	0	416	23.4	75.0	1.5
Coleman	23.7	2 472	59.5	16.9	3.0	0.0	3.3	9.0	939	45	25	778	23.8	75.1	1.1
Collin	891.8	2 222	58.3	2.4	4.0	0.0	4.6	1 401.9	3 493	864	1 200	20 014	24.4	73.1	2.5
Collingsworth	10.7	3 222	49.9	24.5	3.1	0.0	5.5	2.1	629	21	0	313	30.3	68.8	0.8
Colorado	38.3	2 027	59.7	14.7	3.6	0.8	5.4	10.1	532	64	50	1 050	30.7	67.8	1.5
Comal	140.1	1 982	67.5	1.3	4.8	0.3	2.6	136.2	1 927	175	202	3 768	21.8	75.1	3.1
Comanche	30.5	2 246	42.0	37.7	1.4	0.6	4.5	4.2	308	53	36	892	32.6	66.4	1.1
Concho	7.7	2 489	53.5	0.7	2.0	0.5	3.7	15.1	4 854	23	0	252	24.3	74.2	1.5
Cooke	89.2	2 702	56.6	21.3	3.4	0.1	3.3	24.1	731	75	88	2 557	23.4	75.2	1.4
Coryell	88.8	1 146	66.0	11.2	3.6	0.0	2.6	86.5	1 117	294	193	5 752	29.8	68.4	1.8
Cottle	4.8	2 472	67.9	0.9	1.8	0.5	4.3	1.0	501	17	0	160	31.8	66.3	1.9
Crane	19.7	4 313	48.6	13.3	4.8	3.2	2.6	4.4	959	0	11	384	23.4	75.3	1.3
Crockett	18.2	4 029	51.4	14.1	1.8	0.3	6.0	1.7	374	0	12	401	33.4	66.1	0.5
Crosby	17.2	2 338	75.5	1.5	3.0	0.0	5.5	1.2	156	23	19	520	35.2	63.4	1.3
Culberson	8.3	2 636	64.2	0.1	2.8	0.1	3.7	6.2	1 971	55	0	319	57.0	40.8	2.2
Dallam	15.1	2 372	67.0	1.7	6.1	0.1	7.2	1.0	159	27	17	659	19.6	79.4	1.0
Dallas	5 588.5	2 762	41.5	12.0	6.3	0.3	3.5	7 659.5	3 786	28 015	7 096	116 030	44.9	52.6	2.5
Dawson	36.9	2 492	54.1	20.4	3.6	0.5	5.3	76.6	5 176	67	38	1 317	30.2	69.0	0.9
Deaf Smith	35.9	1 845	63.3	9.9	6.6	0.2	3.9	3.2	166	51	49	1 334	24.9	74.0	1.1
Delta	15.0	3 035	79.5	0.0	1.1	0.1	3.7	11.4	2 305	24	13	310	38.2	60.2	1.6
Denton	573.3	1 570	61.9	0.7	5.4	0.3	3.2	938.6	2 571	1 196	1 069	22 080	27.3	69.6	3.0
De Witt	53.6	2 723	52.2	32.3	2.6	0.0	3.2	11.5	582	50	51	2 214	25.4	73.4	1.2
Dickens	8.3	3 678	69.8	0.0	2.7	0.4	3.7	0.4	182	17	0	180	32.2	66.9	0.9
Dimmit	27.8	2 649	60.2	18.3	2.0	0.1	3.2	4.9	464	114	27	958	71.4	27.5	1.1
Donley	16.1	4 228	60.1	0.4	1.6	23.6	3.1	15.2	3 993	19	10	434	20.9	77.5	1.5
Duval	44.1	3 244	51.8	20.0	3.8	1.2	3.7	5.0	366	62	36	1 190	79.3	20.1	0.6
Eastland	47.6	2 664	70.6	12.4	2.0	0.1	2.6	12.1	675	63	46	1 391	27.7	70.6	1.7
Ector	407.7	3 269	39.7	37.2	4.0	0.1	2.1	246.1	1 973	214	327	9 158	28.6	69.6	1.7
Edwards	8.0	2 144	68.4	0.0	4.7	0.8	0.4	3.3	873	18	10	179	27.9	70.8	1.3
Ellis	183.5	1 823	71.1	0.0	4.6	0.3	4.4	174.6	1 735	209	283	4 775	28.5	69.9	1.6
El Paso	1 543.2	2 200	60.6	10.3	5.7	0.6	1.6	1 258.7	1 794	8 493	11 588	45 063	57.8	39.7	2.5
Erath	54.5	1 743	51.1	14.8	6.3	0.0	5.1	24.9	796	84	83	2 937	25.2	73.1	1.7
Falls	27.4	1 543	76.4	0.1	3.2	0.1	2.9	5.2	293	385	45	1 565	42.3	56.7	1.1
Fannin	47.2	1 707	73.7	0.4	4.0	0.0	4.9	23.9	864	552	75	1 822	39.7	58.7	1.6
Fayette	35.2	1 668	58.3	1.6	5.0	0.3	9.8	12.8	608	78	56	1 420	27.1	70.9	2.0
Fisher	14.0	3 221	39.8	31.6	0.0	0.1	5.8	4.5	1 033	27	11	347	47.2	51.7	1.1
Floyd	20.5	2 497	65.8	21.9	2.6	0.0	3.3	0.3	33	38	21	618	24.0	75.6	0.4
Foard	4.9	2 839	52.1	2.5	1.7	0.1	5.2	3.6	2 094	11	0	120	47.3	51.4	1.3
Fort Bend	617.7	1 923	62.7	0.5	5.2	1.0	3.8	706.2	2 199	526	929	16 950	38.5	59.6	1.9
Franklin	20.6	2 146	33.4	29.5	4.3	0.4	7.3	51.7	5 391	16	26	359	29.3	69.7	0.9
Freestone	33.9	1 933	57.5	16.8	3.9	0.0	4.4	4.1	233	36	46	1 154	34.9	64.0	1.2
Frio	49.5	3 119	57.6	1.5	2.8	0.3	3.5	177.1	11 155	26	42	1 268	56.1	43.0	0.9
Gaines	58.4	3 894	56.4	24.8	2.5	0.1	6.7	0.9	63	32	39	1 169	20.9	77.8	1.3
Galveston	704.7	2 900	54.3	7.1	5.3	0.3	3.4	794.6	3 270	923	1 013	28 066	43.0	54.2	2.7
Garza	12.1	2 606	65.1	9.5	6.3	0.3	1.2	0.1	13	18	12	324	25.6	73.6	0.8
Gillespie	30.4	1 529	56.0	1.5	5.7	0.3	4.1	24.9	1 250	77	54	928	15.2	81.6	3.1
Glasscock	5.5	3 770	61.5	0.0	2.1	0.0	14.6	0.0	0	0	0	147	6.8	92.5	0.7
Goliad	13.3	1 962	61.6	2.0	9.7	0.0	9.3	5.6	821	19	19	435	36.4	62.1	1.5
Gonzales	37.7	2 147	55.5	16.4	4.2	0.0	4.9	6.6	378	70	46	1 223	30.9	67.4	1.7
Gray	48.4	2 039	62.9	0.4	4.2	0.2	6.8	19.6	824	70	61	1 517	16.8	82.2	1.0
Grayson	230.0	2 265	63.1	3.3	4.9	1.3	3.6	313.4	3 086	347	273	5 369	34.2	64.1	1.7
Gregg	265.9	2 350	54.8	9.5	6.3	0.9	5.1	206.1	1 821	335	298	6 848	29.3	69.6	1.1
Grimes	36.5	1 596	71.1	1.0	6.7	0.0	5.2	25.0	1 093	43	63	1 848	36.0	61.7	2.2

1. Based on the resident population estimated as of July 1 of the year shown.   2. Data subject to copyright.

STATE/ County code	MSA/ PMSA/ NECMA code[1]	County Type[2]	STATE County	Land area,[3] (sq km) 2000	Total persons	Rank	Per square kilometer	White	Black	Am. Indian, Alaska Native	Asian and Pacific Islander	Percent Hispanic[4]	Under 5 years	5 to 17 years	18 to 24 years	25 to 34 years	35 to 44 years	45 to 54 years
					1	2	3	4	5	6	7	8	9	10	11	12	13	14	15
			TEXAS—Cont'd															
48 187	7240	1	Guadalupe	1 842	89 023	584	48.3	80.5	5.4	1.1	1.5	33.2	7.3	21.2	9.0	12.7	16.4	13.4
48 189	...	4	Hale	2 602	36 602	1 199	14.1	68.9	6.1	1.4	0.5	47.9	8.3	21.9	11.4	12.9	14.3	10.4
48 191	...	9	Hall	2 339	3 782	2 931	1.6	73.1	8.5	0.9	0.3	27.5	7.3	19.9	6.8	9.5	12.6	11.3
48 193	...	6	Hamilton	2 164	8 229	2 589	3.8	94.8	0.2	1.0	0.4	7.4	5.6	18.2	6.0	9.7	13.1	11.8
48 195	...	7	Hansford	2 382	5 369	2 823	2.3	81.3	0.3	1.2	0.4	31.5	6.8	22.5	6.8	11.7	14.6	12.5
48 197	...	7	Hardeman	1 801	4 724	2 866	2.6	87.0	5.0	1.4	0.3	14.5	6.5	18.8	7.5	10.2	12.4	13.5
48 199	0840	2	Hardin	2 316	48 073	950	20.8	91.8	7.0	0.8	0.3	2.5	6.9	20.8	8.5	12.3	15.9	13.7
48 201	3360	0	Harris	4 478	3 400 578	3	759.4	61.2	19.0	0.8	5.8	32.9	8.3	20.7	10.3	16.9	16.5	12.8
48 203	4420	3	Harrison	2 328	62 110	783	26.7	72.2	24.3	0.8	0.6	5.3	6.5	20.4	10.0	11.5	15.5	13.7
48 205	...	7	Hartley	3 787	5 537	2 814	1.5	82.4	8.3	0.8	0.6	13.7	5.7	15.1	4.7	15.1	20.7	16.4
48 207	...	7	Haskell	2 339	6 093	2 771	2.6	84.7	3.1	1.1	0.2	20.5	5.0	18.8	5.7	8.3	13.9	12.4
48 209	0640	2	Hays	1 756	97 589	531	55.6	81.1	4.0	1.3	1.3	29.6	6.3	18.2	20.5	13.3	15.0	12.4
48 211	...	9	Hemphill	2 356	3 351	2 968	1.4	88.9	1.6	1.3	0.4	15.6	5.7	22.3	6.5	10.3	15.1	15.1
48 213	1920	1	Henderson	2 264	73 277	683	32.4	89.7	6.8	1.1	0.5	6.9	6.4	17.9	7.6	11.1	13.9	13.0
48 215	4880	2	Hidalgo	4 066	569 463	96	140.1	79.7	0.6	0.6	0.7	88.3	10.2	25.1	11.3	14.9	12.8	9.8
48 217	...	6	Hill	2 493	32 321	1 339	13.0	85.8	7.7	1.2	0.5	13.5	6.9	19.0	8.5	11.3	13.6	12.8
48 219	...	6	Hockley	2 352	22 716	1 662	9.7	76.4	4.0	1.3	0.3	37.2	7.2	21.9	11.8	11.1	14.8	12.0
48 221	2800	1	Hood	1 092	41 100	1 079	37.6	96.0	0.5	1.5	0.5	7.2	5.8	17.8	6.7	10.2	15.0	13.9
48 223	...	6	Hopkins	2 026	31 960	1 346	15.8	86.4	8.2	1.2	0.4	9.3	6.5	19.6	8.4	12.8	14.4	13.1
48 225	...	7	Houston	3 188	23 185	1 634	7.3	69.2	28.2	0.6	0.4	7.5	5.2	18.0	6.8	11.4	16.3	14.0
48 227	...	5	Howard	2 338	33 627	1 294	14.4	82.0	4.4	1.1	0.9	37.5	5.9	18.3	9.0	14.6	16.3	12.8
48 229	...	8	Hudspeth	11 839	3 344	2 969	0.3	89.3	0.4	1.9	0.2	75.0	8.6	25.5	8.9	13.5	13.2	11.3
48 231	1920	1	Hunt	2 179	76 596	657	35.2	85.1	9.9	1.5	0.8	8.3	6.7	19.8	10.0	12.7	15.3	12.9
48 233	...	6	Hutchinson	2 298	23 857	1 596	10.4	89.1	2.6	2.4	0.6	14.7	6.9	20.6	8.7	10.6	14.9	13.8
48 235	...	8	Irion	2 723	1 771	3 081	0.7	92.3	0.4	1.3	0.0	24.6	5.7	21.0	4.7	9.9	16.9	14.1
48 237	...	6	Jack	2 374	8 763	2 549	3.7	89.6	5.6	1.1	0.3	7.9	5.7	17.7	10.0	13.1	16.7	12.2
48 239	...	6	Jackson	2 148	14 391	2 132	6.7	78.6	8.1	0.8	0.7	24.7	7.1	20.3	8.2	11.3	14.8	13.4
48 241	...	6	Jasper	2 428	35 604	1 229	14.7	79.2	18.1	1.0	0.6	3.9	6.8	19.7	8.0	12.2	14.6	13.0
48 243	...	9	Jeff Davis	5 865	2 207	3 050	0.4	93.2	1.2	1.0	0.1	35.5	4.1	20.3	5.3	9.0	15.1	16.9
48 245	0840	2	Jefferson	2 340	252 051	225	107.7	58.4	34.2	0.7	3.2	10.5	6.7	19.2	10.0	13.6	15.8	12.9
48 247	...	6	Jim Hogg	2 943	5 281	2 832	1.8	82.7	0.5	1.0	0.2	90.0	7.9	23.7	8.1	11.8	12.8	11.7
48 249	...	4	Jim Wells	2 239	39 326	1 128	17.6	80.2	0.7	0.9	0.6	75.7	8.2	23.2	9.0	12.3	14.2	12.1
48 251	2800	1	Johnson	1 889	126 811	424	67.1	91.5	2.7	1.3	0.9	12.1	7.4	21.4	8.8	13.5	16.7	13.5
48 253	...	6	Jones	2 411	20 785	1 749	8.6	80.0	11.7	0.9	0.5	20.9	4.9	17.6	11.1	14.6	16.9	11.9
48 255	...	6	Karnes	1 943	15 446	2 056	7.9	70.5	11.1	1.1	0.7	47.4	5.4	16.4	11.5	18.3	15.9	10.8
48 257	1920	1	Kaufman	2 036	71 313	695	35.0	82.6	10.9	1.2	0.7	11.1	7.2	22.0	8.2	12.8	16.7	13.5
48 259	...	6	Kendall	1 716	23 743	1 601	13.8	94.3	0.5	1.2	0.5	17.9	6.3	20.9	6.1	10.0	16.4	15.7
48 261	...	9	Kenedy	3 773	414	3 138	0.1	65.9	0.7	0.7	0.7	79.0	8.9	20.3	9.7	12.3	14.0	13.3
48 263	...	9	Kent	2 337	859	3 119	0.4	95.7	0.2	0.5	0.0	9.1	3.5	17.1	5.4	6.5	15.3	12.6
48 265	...	7	Kerr	2 865	43 653	1 025	15.2	90.4	1.9	1.2	0.8	19.1	5.3	17.3	6.7	9.2	13.0	12.2
48 267	...	7	Kimble	3 239	4 468	2 884	1.4	91.5	0.2	0.9	0.5	20.7	6.1	17.6	6.0	9.7	12.9	14.4
48 269	...	9	King	2 363	356	3 139	0.2	95.8	0.0	1.7	0.0	9.6	6.7	27.0	3.7	9.6	19.9	15.2
48 271	...	9	Kinney	3 531	3 379	2 965	1.0	79.0	2.0	1.1	0.2	50.5	6.2	19.5	5.3	10.0	11.6	11.6
48 273	...	4	Kleberg	2 256	31 549	1 360	14.0	74.8	4.0	1.1	2.0	65.4	7.6	19.7	15.7	14.9	12.6	10.9
48 275	...	9	Knox	2 199	4 253	2 898	1.9	76.8	7.3	1.4	0.6	25.1	6.4	21.3	5.6	9.2	13.8	10.9
48 277	...	5	Lamar	2 375	48 499	940	20.4	83.7	13.9	1.8	0.5	3.3	7.1	19.1	8.6	12.6	14.2	12.6
48 279	...	6	Lamb	2 632	14 709	2 106	5.6	77.7	4.7	1.1	0.4	43.5	7.4	22.2	8.1	10.8	13.4	11.3
48 281	...	6	Lampasas	1 844	17 762	1 914	9.6	88.7	3.5	1.4	1.4	15.1	6.8	20.8	7.7	12.0	15.2	13.0
48 283	...	6	La Salle	3 856	5 866	2 797	1.5	83.6	3.6	0.6	0.4	77.1	7.3	22.0	10.0	13.9	13.9	12.1
48 285	...	6	Lavaca	2 512	19 210	1 832	7.6	87.9	7.1	0.4	0.2	11.4	5.9	18.3	6.9	9.5	14.0	13.0
48 287	...	6	Lee	1 628	15 657	2 044	9.6	78.3	12.4	0.9	0.5	18.2	6.9	21.9	9.2	11.2	15.1	12.5
48 289	...	8	Leon	2 777	15 335	2 069	5.5	84.5	10.6	0.7	0.5	7.9	5.6	18.7	6.7	9.4	14.1	13.2
48 291	3360	1	Liberty	3 004	70 154	708	23.4	80.2	13.1	1.0	0.6	10.9	7.1	20.5	9.2	14.7	16.8	13.1
48 293	...	6	Limestone	2 354	22 051	1 690	9.4	72.1	19.5	0.9	0.2	13.0	6.4	18.9	9.1	12.3	14.1	12.9
48 295	...	9	Lipscomb	2 414	3 057	2 989	1.3	84.9	0.6	2.1	0.1	20.7	6.1	21.3	5.9	9.5	15.2	13.1
48 297	...	6	Live Oak	2 684	12 309	2 279	4.6	89.0	2.5	0.8	0.4	38.0	4.9	17.3	9.5	12.2	14.9	14.3
48 299	...	7	Llano	2 421	17 044	1 950	7.0	97.1	0.4	1.0	0.4	5.1	3.8	12.1	4.5	6.9	11.5	14.1
48 301	...	9	Loving	1 743	67	3 141	0.0	91.0	0.0	0.0	0.0	10.4	3.0	16.4	1.5	3.0	23.9	22.4
48 303	4600	3	Lubbock	2 330	242 628	237	104.1	76.0	8.0	1.0	1.7	27.5	7.2	18.5	16.3	13.8	14.0	11.7
48 305	...	6	Lynn	2 310	6 550	2 735	2.8	77.6	3.1	1.4	0.4	44.6	7.3	23.9	7.8	10.7	15.3	11.2
48 307	...	7	McCulloch	2 769	8 205	2 591	3.0	86.2	1.7	0.6	0.2	27.0	6.8	19.9	6.6	10.1	12.8	13.7
48 309	8800	3	McLennan	2 698	213 517	262	79.1	73.7	15.6	0.9	1.4	17.9	7.1	19.5	14.6	12.4	14.0	11.8
48 311	...	9	McMullen	2 883	851	3 120	0.3	89.4	1.2	0.2	0.2	33.1	4.0	19.4	6.3	7.2	16.6	14.6
48 313	...	6	Madison	1 216	12 940	2 236	10.6	68.4	23.2	0.7	0.5	15.8	5.4	15.7	13.0	18.2	13.7	11.0
48 315	...	8	Marion	987	10 941	2 371	11.1	74.0	24.4	1.8	0.4	2.4	5.6	16.8	6.4	9.7	13.9	14.6
48 317	...	6	Martin	2 369	4 746	2 863	2.0	81.1	1.9	1.3	0.3	40.6	8.6	25.3	6.7	12.6	13.8	11.0

1. MSA = Metropolitan Statistical Area. PMSA = Primary MSA. NECMA = New England County Metropolitan Area. See Appendix A for explanation of these concepts. See Appendix B for list of metropolitan areas identified by type, with component counties. 2. County typology code from the Economic Research Service of USDA. See Appendix A for definition. 3. Dry land or land partially or temporarily covered by water. 4. Hispanic persons may be of any race.

Table B. States and Counties — **Population and Households**

STATE County	55 to 64 years	65 to 74 years	75 years and over	Percent female	2001	1990	1990–2000	2000–2001	Births	Deaths	Net migration	Number	Percent change, 1990–2000	Persons per house-hold	Female family house-holder[1]	One person
	16	17	18	19	20	21	22	23	24	25	26	27	28	29	30	31
TEXAS—Cont'd																
Guadalupe	8.7	6.3	5.0	50.8	92 753	64 873	37.2	4.2	1 511	764	2 929	30 900	36.3	2.83	11.2	18.9
Hale	7.9	6.9	6.0	49.4	36 061	34 671	5.6	-1.5	833	364	-1 026	11 975	2.3	2.86	11.6	21.0
Hall	11.0	10.3	11.2	52.2	3 848	3 905	-3.1	1.7	80	90	77	1 548	-7.2	2.42	9.0	32.4
Hamilton	11.9	11.0	12.6	51.7	8 029	7 733	6.4	-2.4	100	191	-111	3 374	3.8	2.37	7.7	28.4
Hansford	9.9	8.0	7.3	50.9	5 278	5 848	-8.2	-1.7	107	79	-119	2 005	-5.1	2.63	5.9	24.0
Hardeman	10.8	9.4	10.8	52.8	4 596	5 283	-10.6	-2.7	87	95	-120	1 943	-7.5	2.40	10.4	29.5
Hardin	9.5	7.0	5.2	50.8	48 730	41 320	16.3	1.4	801	643	507	17 805	21.2	2.68	10.2	20.7
Harris	7.0	4.3	3.1	50.2	3 460 589	2 818 101	20.7	1.8	79 319	24 369	5 831	1 205 516	17.4	2.79	13.7	25.1
Harrison	9.3	7.1	6.0	51.5	62 143	57 483	8.0	0.1	1 067	826	-186	23 087	11.5	2.62	13.6	23.7
Hartley	10.5	6.3	5.6	39.4	5 481	3 634	52.4	-1.0	116	51	-126	1 604	20.4	2.56	4.7	21.6
Haskell	10.5	12.7	12.8	52.9	5 951	6 820	-10.7	-2.3	91	117	-114	2 569	-6.7	2.33	8.8	29.4
Hays	6.6	4.2	3.4	49.7	105 115	65 614	48.7	7.7	1 684	627	6 302	33 410	50.4	2.69	9.0	21.0
Hemphill	10.3	7.5	7.2	49.7	3 346	3 720	-9.9	-0.1	56	55	-7	1 280	-5.0	2.50	5.9	24.4
Henderson	11.8	10.5	7.7	51.0	74 868	58 543	25.2	2.2	1 272	1 150	1 459	28 804	25.5	2.50	10.4	23.7
Hidalgo	6.2	5.5	4.2	51.4	590 285	383 545	48.5	3.7	17 678	3 364	6 772	156 824	51.6	3.60	15.7	13.1
Hill	10.6	9.0	8.3	50.8	33 077	27 146	19.1	2.3	521	551	779	12 204	18.9	2.58	10.1	24.8
Hockley	8.6	6.8	5.8	50.9	22 661	24 199	-6.1	-0.2	492	267	-278	7 994	0.1	2.77	11.5	21.2
Hood	12.7	10.6	7.3	51.0	43 181	28 981	41.8	5.1	562	571	2 045	16 176	45.2	2.50	7.8	21.6
Hopkins	9.9	7.6	7.6	51.0	32 191	28 833	10.8	0.7	531	469	182	12 286	12.0	2.56	10.0	24.1
Houston	10.4	9.0	8.9	46.7	23 195	21 375	8.5	0.0	340	407	90	8 259	6.0	2.44	14.2	27.9
Howard	8.5	7.9	6.7	45.9	33 180	32 343	4.0	-1.3	549	444	-556	11 389	-0.8	2.53	12.2	26.8
Hudspeth	9.1	6.7	3.2	49.3	3 318	2 915	14.7	-0.8	37	21	-44	1 092	15.4	3.03	11.4	21.1
Hunt	10.0	6.8	5.8	50.5	77 960	64 343	19.0	1.8	1 337	985	1 008	28 742	19.4	2.60	11.0	24.1
Hutchinson	8.9	8.4	7.2	50.8	23 332	25 689	-7.1	-2.2	415	315	-635	9 283	-3.7	2.54	9.1	23.9
Irion	12.1	9.4	6.2	49.9	1 751	1 629	8.7	-1.1	20	20	-20	694	15.5	2.55	6.6	21.8
Jack	9.4	8.3	6.9	45.4	8 785	6 981	25.5	0.3	118	120	28	3 047	11.8	2.52	9.2	24.5
Jackson	9.0	8.3	7.7	50.8	14 291	13 039	10.4	-0.7	255	233	-121	5 336	10.4	2.65	10.5	24.2
Jasper	10.4	8.7	6.7	51.4	35 731	31 102	14.5	0.4	653	520	8	13 450	17.7	2.58	12.5	23.3
Jeff Davis	13.0	8.6	7.7	48.9	2 211	1 946	13.4	0.2	29	26	-1	896	15.0	2.39	6.9	26.3
Jefferson	8.2	7.1	6.5	49.7	249 640	239 389	5.3	-1.0	4 742	3 269	-3 899	92 880	2.6	2.55	16.2	27.3
Jim Hogg	9.4	7.8	6.8	50.8	5 161	5 109	3.4	-2.3	105	54	-172	1 815	8.4	2.89	14.6	23.4
Jim Wells	8.6	6.8	5.6	51.2	39 950	37 679	4.4	1.6	826	424	234	12 961	8.2	2.99	15.2	19.7
Johnson	8.8	5.7	4.2	50.1	132 247	97 165	30.5	4.3	2 177	1 239	4 414	43 636	30.4	2.85	10.0	17.3
Jones	9.1	7.2	6.7	40.0	20 435	16 490	26.0	-1.7	219	287	-284	6 140	-0.6	2.58	10.1	24.1
Karnes	7.4	7.1	7.3	40.6	15 428	12 455	24.0	-0.1	216	211	-19	4 454	2.7	2.66	13.7	24.4
Kaufman	9.0	5.8	4.8	50.7	75 810	52 220	36.6	6.3	1 195	772	3 982	24 367	36.7	2.87	11.3	17.8
Kendall	10.7	7.2	6.6	51.3	24 869	14 589	62.7	4.7	388	252	973	8 613	61.2	2.70	7.9	19.2
Kenedy	10.9	7.0	3.6	47.6	413	460	-10.0	-0.2	7	3	-5	138	-4.8	2.97	10.9	18.8
Kent	14.2	12.6	12.9	52.2	812	1 010	-15.0	-5.5	5	18	-36	353	-11.5	2.33	5.9	28.0
Kerr	11.3	12.3	12.6	52.1	44 558	36 304	20.2	2.1	621	746	1 026	17 813	23.8	2.35	9.2	27.5
Kimble	12.4	11.2	9.6	51.9	4 520	4 122	8.4	1.2	71	70	53	1 866	14.9	2.37	8.6	28.6
King	7.6	7.9	2.5	51.1	319	354	0.6	-10.4	0	2	-36	108	-12.9	2.77	1.9	16.7
Kinney	11.5	14.7	9.6	50.0	3 430	3 119	8.3	1.5	55	45	41	1 314	10.7	2.55	6.4	26.6
Kleberg	8.0	5.9	4.7	49.8	31 015	30 274	4.2	-1.7	655	270	-931	10 896	8.3	2.78	13.9	22.3
Knox	10.1	10.5	12.1	52.8	4 039	4 837	-12.1	-5.0	61	73	-209	1 690	-10.4	2.44	9.9	29.6
Lamar	10.2	7.6	8.0	52.3	48 666	43 949	10.4	0.3	904	787	65	19 077	13.6	2.48	13.2	26.1
Lamb	9.5	8.7	8.6	51.5	14 572	15 072	-2.4	-0.9	298	228	-208	5 360	-2.3	2.69	10.2	23.7
Lampasas	10.1	7.7	6.8	50.9	18 502	13 521	31.4	4.2	298	187	622	6 554	29.6	2.66	9.5	21.9
La Salle	9.2	6.6	5.1	46.8	5 849	5 254	11.6	-0.3	132	72	-78	1 819	6.9	2.89	15.4	22.9
Lavaca	10.6	9.5	12.3	51.8	19 061	18 690	2.8	-0.8	292	321	-113	7 669	4.4	2.44	9.3	27.6
Lee	8.8	7.5	6.9	49.6	16 163	12 854	21.8	3.2	270	219	449	5 663	20.3	2.65	8.8	23.8
Leon	12.4	11.9	8.2	50.9	15 625	12 665	21.1	1.9	232	276	333	6 189	23.6	2.46	9.2	24.8
Liberty	8.3	5.9	4.3	51.1	72 620	52 726	33.1	3.5	1 371	799	1 873	23 242	25.4	2.80	11.4	20.4
Limestone	9.8	8.4	8.0	49.2	22 229	20 946	5.3	0.8	364	396	217	7 906	2.4	2.55	13.5	25.6
Lipscomb	10.3	9.2	9.2	51.4	3 034	3 143	-2.7	-0.8	47	51	-21	1 205	-2.0	2.50	5.9	28.0
Live Oak	10.9	8.8	7.1	45.0	12 177	9 556	28.8	-1.1	144	130	-145	4 230	19.2	2.53	8.7	23.9
Llano	16.4	17.0	13.7	51.4	17 561	11 631	46.5	3.0	157	314	657	7 879	49.3	2.13	5.9	28.3
Loving	13.4	13.4	3.0	46.3	70	107	-37.4	4.5	0	0	3	31	-26.2	2.16	6.5	32.3
Lubbock	7.5	6.0	5.1	51.1	243 999	222 636	9.0	0.6	4 729	2 427	-850	92 516	13.5	2.52	12.6	26.9
Lynn	9.8	7.8	6.2	50.1	6 433	6 758	-3.1	-1.8	126	78	-169	2 354	-1.2	2.76	11.1	23.1
McCulloch	10.6	9.7	9.8	52.6	8 046	8 778	-6.5	-1.9	151	174	-140	3 277	-3.9	2.47	10.2	28.2
McLennan	7.8	6.5	6.3	51.5	215 104	189 123	12.9	0.7	4 182	2 567	58	78 859	12.3	2.59	13.6	26.0
McMullen	14.1	10.5	7.4	49.7	849	817	4.2	-0.2	5	8	1	355	11.3	2.40	5.6	30.7
Madison	9.0	6.8	7.1	41.2	12 996	10 931	18.4	0.4	222	166	3	3 914	16.9	2.57	11.7	24.5
Marion	13.8	10.9	8.3	51.2	11 198	9 984	9.6	2.3	194	198	254	4 610	13.9	2.35	11.9	28.8
Martin	8.7	7.2	6.1	51.1	4 726	4 956	-4.2	-0.4	93	60	-54	1 624	-0.5	2.87	9.5	21.7

1. No spouse present.

STATE County	Births, average 1997–1999 Total	Rate[1]	Deaths, average 1997–1999 Number Total	Infant[2]	Rate Total[1]	Infant[3]	Physicians,[4] 2000 Number	Rate[5]	Hospitals,[4] 1998 Number	Beds Number	Rate[5]	Medicare enrollees 2000	Serious crimes known to police, 2000[6] Total Number	Rate[7]
	32	33	34	35	36	37	38	39	40	41	42	43	44	45
TEXAS—Cont'd														
Guadalupe	1 143	14.2	616	NA	7.7	NA	61	69	1	77	96	9 956	3 294	3 700
Hale	657	18.0	292	NA	8.0	NA	38	104	2	174	474	5 304	1 832	5 005
Hall	59	16.3	67	NA	18.4	NA	4	106	1	28	768	839	49	1 296
Hamilton	96	12.6	152	NA	20.0	NA	7	85	1	28	368	1 649	82	996
Hansford	82	15.3	57	NA	10.6	NA	1	19	1	113	2 113	855	81	1 509
Hardeman	61	13.4	77	NA	17.0	NA	9	191	2	44	958	1 019	54	1 143
Hardin	634	13.0	471	NA	9.6	NA	19	40	1	57	117	6 631	997	2 074
Harris	58 861	18.4	19 054	370	5.9	6.3	8 070	237	43	10 917	341	280 082	185 386	5 452
Harrison	770	12.9	620	8	10.4	10.0	42	68	1	108	181	8 090	2 122	3 417
Hartley	61	11.7	35	NA	6.8	NA	6	108	0	0	0	151	96	1 734
Haskell	70	11.5	92	NA	15.1	NA	6	98	1	32	520	1 579	65	1 205
Hays	1 270	14.3	466	NA	5.2	NA	107	110	1	113	128	8 340	3 725	3 817
Hemphill	39	11.0	41	NA	11.6	NA	4	119	1	19	538	477	55	1 641
Henderson	909	13.2	859	NA	12.4	NA	52	71	1	102	148	10 027	2 487	3 394
Hidalgo	12 762	24.4	2 667	61	5.1	4.8	513	90	5	1 036	198	53 630	32 306	5 673
Hill	396	12.9	419	NA	13.7	NA	17	53	2	140	459	6 064	927	2 868
Hockley	359	15.2	213	NA	9.0	NA	12	53	1	44	185	3 071	537	2 364
Hood	424	11.4	438	NA	11.7	NA	43	105	1	55	148	8 121	1 129	2 747
Hopkins	400	13.1	378	NA	12.4	NA	27	84	1	77	252	5 249	719	2 250
Houston	262	11.9	328	NA	14.9	NA	12	52	1	50	228	4 524	522	2 251
Howard	465	14.5	365	NA	11.4	NA	67	199	1	153	477	5 315	1 378	4 098
Hudspeth	37	11.5	18	NA	5.6	NA	0	0	0	0	0	341	33	987
Hunt	1 007	14.3	741	NA	10.5	NA	65	85	2	138	195	10 831	3 689	4 816
Hutchinson	338	14.1	245	NA	10.2	NA	22	92	1	40	166	4 114	1 002	4 571
Irion	18	10.4	12	NA	7.3	NA	0	0	0	0	0	266	37	2 089
Jack	93	12.5	91	NA	12.3	NA	4	46	1	18	242	1 284	151	1 723
Jackson	184	13.4	163	NA	11.9	NA	14	97	1	31	227	2 285	224	1 795
Jasper	460	13.7	406	NA	12.1	NA	31	87	2	96	287	5 716	1 054	2 960
Jeff Davis	22	9.6	20	NA	8.5	NA	1	45	0	0	0	370	20	906
Jefferson	3 343	13.8	2 563	30	10.6	8.9	526	209	7	1 589	657	38 258	13 914	5 520
Jim Hogg	87	17.5	45	NA	9.1	NA	1	19	0	0	0	817	95	1 799
Jim Wells	676	16.9	323	NA	8.1	NA	25	64	1	123	307	5 875	1 803	4 585
Johnson	1 688	14.3	956	11	8.1	6.3	75	59	1	102	86	15 372	4 304	3 394
Jones	187	10.0	211	NA	11.3	NA	11	53	3	85	455	2 826	463	2 228
Karnes	192	14.5	165	NA	12.4	NA	6	39	1	34	275	2 524	NA	NA
Kaufman	890	13.5	595	NA	9.0	NA	52	73	2	173	263	12 787	2 742	3 845
Kendall	300	14.2	203	NA	9.6	NA	28	118	0	0	0	3 977	375	1 579
Kenedy	8	17.6	NA	NA	NA	NA	0	0	0	0	0	55	5	1 208
Kent	8	8.8	14	NA	15.7	NA	0	0	0	0	0	212	4	466
Kerr	488	11.4	582	NA	13.6	NA	137	314	1	123	284	11 318	1 256	2 877
Kimble	56	13.3	54	NA	12.9	NA	4	90	1	18	436	871	85	1 902
King	2	6.8	NA	NA	NA	NA	0	0	0	0	0	37	0	0
Kinney	42	12.1	36	NA	10.4	NA	2	59	0	0	0	742	7	207
Kleberg	526	17.5	217	NA	7.2	NA	27	86	1	90	298	3 566	1 592	5 046
Knox	56	13.4	63	NA	14.9	NA	2	47	1	14	329	976	79	1 858
Lamar	623	13.6	599	NA	13.0	NA	99	204	2	355	771	8 412	3 512	7 241
Lamb	232	15.7	176	NA	11.9	NA	14	95	1	42	285	2 680	268	1 971
Lampasas	236	13.4	175	NA	9.9	NA	8	45	1	22	124	2 753	302	1 700
La Salle	97	16.2	53	NA	8.9	NA	1	17	0	0	0	774	101	1 722
Lavaca	226	12.0	269	NA	14.3	NA	21	109	2	56	298	4 969	223	1 161
Lee	205	13.8	169	NA	11.4	NA	4	26	0	0	0	2 111	239	1 526
Leon	175	12.0	210	NA	14.4	NA	5	33	0	0	0	3 802	229	1 493
Liberty	980	15.0	618	10	9.4	10.5	39	56	2	133	204	9 138	1 929	2 750
Limestone	276	13.3	312	NA	15.0	NA	12	54	2	74	354	4 174	703	3 188
Lipscomb	42	14.0	35	NA	11.6	NA	0	0	0	0	0	617	18	589
Live Oak	119	11.7	105	NA	10.4	NA	2	16	0	0	0	1 357	85	691
Llano	124	9.2	247	NA	18.3	NA	13	76	1	27	200	4 524	359	2 197
Loving	1	6.0	NA	NA	NA	NA	0	0	0	0	0	19	4	5 970
Lubbock	3 688	16.1	1 881	32	8.2	8.6	746	307	6	1 551	676	29 534	16 057	6 618
Lynn	103	15.5	63	NA	9.5	NA	3	46	1	24	358	999	92	1 405
McCulloch	127	14.5	137	NA	15.6	NA	8	98	1	27	309	1 793	326	3 973
McLennan	3 124	15.3	1 953	21	9.6	6.7	359	168	3	638	314	30 365	12 883	6 034
McMullen	10	12.2	8	NA	10.5	NA	0	0	0	0	0	135	6	705
Madison	147	12.3	130	NA	10.9	NA	14	108	1	28	236	1 738	233	1 801
Marion	134	12.4	156	NA	14.3	NA	4	37	0	0	0	1 811	306	2 797
Martin	80	16.1	48	NA	9.5	NA	4	84	1	26	516	650	57	1 201

1. Per 1,000 estimated resident population, average 1997–1999. 2. Deaths of infants under 1 year old. 3. Deaths of infants under 1 year old per 1,000 live births. 4. Data subject to copyright. 5. Per 100,000 resident population as of July 1 of the year shown. 6. Data for serious crimes have not been adjusted for underreporting; this may affect comparability between geographic areas and over time. 7. Per 100,000 population estimated by the FBI.

Table B. States and Counties — Crime, Education, Money Income, and Poverty

STATE County	Serious crimes known to police, 2000[1] (cont'd) Rate[2] Violent	Serious crimes known to police, 2000[1] (cont'd) Rate[2] Property	Education — Enrollment[3] Total	Education — Enrollment[3] Percent private	Education — Attainment[4] (percent) High school graduate or more	Education — Attainment[4] (percent) Bachelor's degree or more	Local government expenditures, fiscal 1999[5] Total current expenditures (mil dol)	Local government expenditures, fiscal 1999[5] Current expenditures per student (dollars)	Money income 1989 Per capita[6] (dollars)	Money income 1989 Households Median Dollars	Money income 1989 Households Median Percent change, 1979–1989 (constant 1989 dollars)	Money income 1989 Households Percent with $100,000 or more	Income and poverty, 1998 Median household income	Income and poverty, 1998 Percent below poverty level All persons	Income and poverty, 1998 Percent below poverty level Persons under 18	Income and poverty, 1998 Percent below poverty level Persons 5–17 in families
	46	47	48	49	50	51	52	53	54	55	56	57	58	59	60	61
TEXAS—Cont'd																
Guadalupe	275	3 425	17 398	12.6	69.8	13.9	82.6	5 331	11 330	26 801	2.1	1.8	36 172	14.3	20.5	20.4
Hale	295	4 710	9 705	12.5	61.1	12.7	49.8	5 864	9 932	21 183	-6.5	2.3	29 783	20.5	27.1	27.6
Hall	132	1 163	737	0.3	61.3	8.7	6.2	7 236	9 376	13 987	-17.1	1.2	20 718	26.0	40.1	42.1
Hamilton	109	887	1 522	7.6	62.9	12.4	10.8	6 867	11 193	18 161	6.9	1.9	26 579	18.5	24.3	27.6
Hansford	168	1 341	1 582	2.4	71.7	15.3	9.9	7 442	12 136	25 787	-13.6	3.1	37 866	11.3	16.1	16.0
Hardeman	191	953	1 220	1.8	62.8	11.0	7.3	7 916	10 502	18 657	-11.8	4.0	26 961	19.7	28.1	29.6
Hardin	198	1 876	11 165	6.6	70.6	9.7	62.6	5 700	11 178	25 289	-21.1	1.2	37 553	12.3	17.5	16.3
Harris	798	4 653	796 212	11.6	74.9	25.4	3 525.8	5 590	15 202	30 970	-11.2	5.5	40 690	13.9	20.2	16.7
Harrison	213	3 204	16 113	10.3	70.4	12.7	68.6	5 107	10 173	22 625	-9.7	1.5	30 726	17.1	23.0	22.6
Hartley	199	1 535	933	7.8	84.6	19.7	2.8	8 415	14 254	28 826	-9.4	4.0	47 541	5.7	6.5	6.8
Haskell	130	1 075	1 396	4.9	58.4	9.0	9.6	7 950	10 099	19 386	-2.3	1.5	23 189	24.1	35.1	35.9
Hays	406	3 411	26 265	6.6	76.9	26.4	99.8	5 582	11 422	25 492	17.3	2.2	39 273	11.5	15.5	15.3
Hemphill	209	1 432	902	1.4	72.9	12.3	6.7	8 161	14 244	28 697	-10.8	4.3	43 228	8.7	11.1	12.0
Henderson	393	3 001	12 997	5.4	64.7	10.3	54.1	5 403	10 692	20 747	-8.8	1.4	29 828	15.8	25.0	22.2
Hidalgo	483	5 191	134 820	4.4	46.6	11.5	805.3	5 937	6 630	16 703	-11.3	1.7	20 856	35.3	40.9	39.1
Hill	111	2 757	6 034	5.4	61.5	10.7	36.2	6 130	10 703	20 067	5.3	1.5	28 679	17.3	25.3	25.1
Hockley	361	2 003	7 763	2.5	64.0	12.4	35.3	6 588	10 648	23 713	-9.3	2.3	31 100	18.7	24.0	25.5
Hood	136	2 611	6 812	10.0	74.7	15.2	35.0	5 054	14 961	31 627	4.2	4.2	40 162	10.1	16.6	15.5
Hopkins	275	1 974	6 524	3.4	62.9	11.2	33.7	5 637	11 049	20 771	-3.3	2.4	30 384	15.0	21.6	20.1
Houston	272	1 980	4 835	7.1	64.0	10.1	24.1	5 935	9 965	18 138	9.7	2.4	26 418	22.4	30.7	30.9
Howard	330	3 768	8 162	4.0	65.2	11.8	34.1	5 683	10 644	23 145	-8.1	1.4	29 877	19.3	27.7	27.5
Hudspeth	269	718	831	1.8	48.1	8.0	5.7	7 050	7 994	15 401	-12.6	3.8	20 414	34.1	46.6	46.4
Hunt	547	4 269	16 680	7.3	69.1	15.9	77.6	5 601	11 845	25 317	8.9	1.8	33 193	14.4	22.1	20.0
Hutchinson	233	4 338	7 083	5.8	71.9	13.0	29.9	5 804	11 677	26 717	-15.6	1.6	38 894	11.7	17.3	16.2
Irion	56	2 033	391	6.1	70.5	13.8	3.3	9 578	11 659	24 280	-4.7	1.8	32 912	10.7	15.3	17.8
Jack	80	1 643	1 584	5.3	62.2	11.0	11.0	6 029	11 010	21 627	-5.2	2.1	29 462	16.5	22.2	23.1
Jackson	104	1 691	3 023	5.3	56.6	10.2	20.8	6 217	10 225	20 687	-15.5	2.0	31 817	15.7	23.2	22.0
Jasper	393	2 567	7 854	4.2	64.4	8.3	44.2	5 908	9 659	20 451	-14.6	1.1	30 157	18.5	27.3	24.6
Jeff Davis	136	770	486	4.3	69.5	25.1	3.4	8 111	9 975	18 995	7.8	1.4	26 550	15.9	21.4	25.6
Jefferson	630	4 890	64 519	11.0	74.4	15.5	268.9	5 963	12 348	25 132	-18.6	2.6	33 766	17.6	26.7	22.8
Jim Hogg	379	1 420	1 610	3.5	48.9	11.2	8.4	6 768	6 852	14 704	-23.9	0.5	23 332	29.1	39.2	42.9
Jim Wells	397	4 188	11 238	4.8	55.3	9.4	51.5	5 792	8 080	18 315	-24.4	1.9	25 515	25.6	32.5	33.2
Johnson	226	3 168	25 483	10.6	71.9	11.5	125.0	5 218	12 054	30 612	0.1	2.4	39 687	10.3	15.2	13.7
Jones	245	1 982	4 004	5.2	60.8	10.9	22.8	7 023	9 910	19 270	-8.9	1.5	25 616	21.8	26.8	27.0
Karnes	NA	NA	3 343	2.4	51.3	8.9	17.3	6 366	8 229	16 155	-21.4	1.5	24 301	27.2	30.8	34.1
Kaufman	494	3 351	13 616	8.3	67.9	10.9	85.9	5 196	11 567	27 280	4.4	2.5	37 408	12.4	17.5	16.5
Kendall	76	1 504	3 614	8.1	80.2	19.9	28.4	4 900	13 426	27 433	0.4	2.7	42 508	9.7	15.2	14.7
Kenedy	0	1 208	129	7.0	43.1	7.8	0.9	15 500	9 212	16 500	-13.2	6.0	23 693	16.1	20.8	25.0
Kent	116	349	212	5.7	63.4	10.3	2.3	12 357	10 087	19 508	-3.5	1.0	28 800	13.0	21.5	18.5
Kerr	206	2 671	7 700	15.4	75.9	20.2	39.7	5 658	12 899	23 205	-5.8	3.7	31 941	14.3	23.4	24.0
Kimble	179	1 723	862	3.8	64.7	12.4	5.0	6 624	11 372	17 553	-15.0	3.5	24 225	19.5	28.3	29.2
King	0	0	104	1.9	78.2	24.5	1.4	15 778	12 027	27 625	31.2	1.6	33 051	7.4	9.4	9.1
Kinney	89	118	729	1.1	56.2	11.0	4.3	6 711	7 931	15 750	-7.8	0.6	23 815	25.4	39.3	45.8
Kleberg	428	4 618	10 824	5.4	63.3	18.9	39.8	6 179	9 580	21 887	-4.4	1.9	28 516	24.2	32.7	34.3
Knox	259	1 599	1 032	2.9	58.6	10.9	7.7	7 804	9 241	17 730	-9.4	1.1	25 133	24.9	35.6	38.4
Lamar	1 198	6 043	10 887	3.7	67.3	13.0	50.9	5 618	10 511	21 551	7.4	1.7	30 546	18.9	28.1	26.2
Lamb	346	1 625	4 040	2.8	56.7	11.1	23.0	6 637	9 362	19 000	-9.4	1.9	27 573	21.6	29.5	30.7
Lampasas	62	1 638	3 134	6.0	70.7	12.8	19.2	5 410	10 586	22 572	10.1	1.8	29 688	15.8	21.1	23.7
La Salle	273	1 449	1 489	6.1	45.3	10.8	8.9	6 216	8 130	15 615	5.2	1.9	20 996	33.5	39.2	45.1
Lavaca	94	1 067	3 978	17.7	55.7	8.4	12.7	5 633	10 294	19 945	0.3	1.2	29 019	14.3	20.8	19.8
Lee	236	1 290	3 231	9.8	61.1	11.3	17.1	5 833	10 252	21 553	3.5	1.5	32 372	13.1	18.2	19.5
Leon	267	1 226	2 750	2.6	67.4	10.2	18.2	6 154	10 385	20 152	21.1	1.5	28 715	16.3	22.5	23.0
Liberty	221	2 529	13 631	5.4	62.4	7.9	70.6	5 170	9 928	22 637	-19.6	1.5	33 429	15.5	21.3	20.0
Limestone	435	2 753	4 769	3.7	60.2	10.6	27.3	6 744	9 745	19 620	17.2	1.2	25 830	20.5	28.8	28.9
Lipscomb	33	556	726	2.5	73.8	14.9	6.1	8 538	11 997	24 648	-3.9	2.8	34 249	12.8	18.2	18.8
Live Oak	49	642	2 485	3.5	60.9	12.0	13.7	6 705	10 055	20 898	-20.4	1.5	30 714	17.7	25.8	25.8
Llano	129	2 069	1 573	6.5	71.6	13.3	11.7	7 431	12 448	19 042	-8.0	2.2	28 610	13.3	24.4	24.0
Loving	0	5 970	24	0.0	56.0	4.0	NA	NA	12 482	26 563	-10.1	0.0	38 988	15.2	17.7	21.3
Lubbock	1 067	5 550	74 111	7.6	74.2	23.4	247.9	5 876	12 008	24 328	-7.6	2.9	32 894	17.8	25.2	23.7
Lynn	76	1 328	1 695	5.7	54.2	7.5	11.5	6 819	9 909	17 823	-9.6	3.5	25 663	22.8	30.8	33.5
McCulloch	695	3 278	1 991	2.1	62.5	13.8	11.9	6 941	8 847	16 544	-0.1	1.5	23 947	22.9	30.0	33.4
McLennan	565	5 469	57 779	25.3	71.6	16.6	225.1	5 775	11 185	22 665	-0.5	2.0	33 258	17.0	25.0	22.7
McMullen	118	588	167	0.0	64.6	14.6	1.9	9 899	13 485	29 205	4.6	5.3	35 078	14.8	25.0	27.3
Madison	185	1 615	2 726	13.6	58.8	10.1	13.3	8 767		17 838	-3.0	1.6	22 539	23.4	30.8	30.8
Marion	466	2 331	2 139	5.8	60.2	7.6	9.2	6 017	9 197	15 288	-14.3	1.2	22 539	22.6	28.5	37.6
Martin	42	1 159	1 413	2.3	54.3	6.7	8.0	7 604	9 867	20 596	-24.5	3.4	28 909	17.3	23.0	26.6

1. Data for serious crimes have not been adjusted for underreporting; this may affect comparability between geographic areas and over time. 2. Per 100,000 population estimated by the FBI. 3. All persons 3 years old and over enrolled in nursery school through college. 4. Persons 25 years old and over. 5. Elementary and secondary education expenditures, local government fiscal years ending between July 1, 1998 and June 30, 1999. 6. Based on population enumerated as of April 1, 1990.

Table B. States and Counties — **Personal Income**

	Personal income, 1999												
			Per capita[1]						Transfer payments				
										Government payments to individuals			
STATE County	Total (mil dol)	Percent change, 1998–1999	Dollars	Rank	Wages and salaries[2] (mil dol)	Proprietor's income (mil dol)	Dividends, interest, and rent (mil dol)	Total (mil dol)	Total (mil dol)	Social Security (mil dol)	Medical payments (mil dol)	Income mainte-nance (mil dol)	Unemploy-ment insurance (mil dol)
	62	63	64	65	66	67	68	69	70	71	72	73	74
TEXAS—Cont'd													
Guadalupe	1 830	7.0	22 100	1 333	651	142	272	250	235	99	89	22	2
Hale	794	6.4	21 758	1 431	388	175	125	143	137	48	61	20	2
Hall	70	21.6	19 457	2 154	24	15	15	21	20	8	8	3	0
Hamilton	180	5.2	23 636	933	58	34	41	44	42	17	19	4	0
Hansford	209	14.6	38 649	53	63	102	29	18	17	9	7	1	0
Hardeman	98	4.2	22 306	1 273	38	13	22	24	23	10	10	2	0
Hardin	1 043	3.0	20 990	1 671	278	63	149	191	183	71	83	14	5
Harris	110 071	4.8	33 864	112	80 826	22 483	14 858	8 498	7 934	2 816	3 694	844	245
Harrison	1 202	2.6	20 095	1 966	729	106	207	220	210	81	82	25	5
Hartley	174	14.1	33 021	130	28	89	22	8	7	5	1	1	0
Haskell	126	12.2	21 119	1 628	43	19	26	34	33	14	14	4	0
Hays	2 019	8.1	21 766	1 426	886	160	322	214	198	81	75	16	3
Hemphill	112	3.5	32 213	147	41	37	27	11	11	5	4	1	0
Henderson	1 480	6.2	20 937	1 687	402	148	259	301	289	140	111	18	3
Hidalgo	7 135	5.8	13 339	3 074	3 831	813	988	1 768	1 675	380	811	384	39
Hill	615	7.8	19 799	2 060	222	51	111	142	137	56	57	11	2
Hockley	463	4.3	19 821	2 051	215	70	76	93	89	31	39	11	2
Hood	1 091	9.2	28 151	311	238	58	214	165	159	82	59	5	2
Hopkins	673	1.2	21 999	1 368	319	116	119	126	121	51	53	10	2
Houston	485	8.5	21 845	1 400	231	62	82	113	109	41	49	14	1
Howard	678	2.5	21 404	1 547	356	70	135	144	138	49	63	15	2
Hudspeth	45	14.6	13 803	3 057	25	5	6	10	9	3	3	2	0
Hunt	1 514	6.7	21 117	1 630	801	105	228	277	265	110	108	25	4
Hutchinson	531	2.3	22 382	1 250	328	50	95	92	88	44	32	6	2
Irion	32	3.1	18 663	2 377	12	1	8	6	5	3	2	0	0
Jack	147	2.9	19 677	2 093	49	20	32	31	30	14	13	2	0
Jackson	327	9.7	23 944	870	151	40	63	59	57	22	27	5	1
Jasper	721	2.0	21 519	1 515	325	87	116	167	162	61	75	16	5
Jeff Davis	35	4.8	14 534	3 020	19	1	9	7	7	3	2	1	0
Jefferson	5 894	0.5	24 423	777	4 334	447	1 106	1 129	1 087	397	509	113	26
Jim Hogg	85	1.3	17 113	2 713	36	6	20	24	23	6	11	4	1
Jim Wells	691	1.7	17 172	2 706	323	61	101	187	180	50	95	26	4
Johnson	2 611	7.0	21 299	1 571	895	240	338	376	355	138	155	20	6
Jones	316	6.0	16 768	2 785	135	36	56	79	76	29	36	7	1
Karnes	227	3.1	15 054	2 982	100	16	42	61	59	20	28	9	1
Kaufman	1 546	8.2	22 720	1 160	568	119	197	250	238	90	115	18	4
Kendall	602	7.8	27 555	369	193	60	144	76	72	35	28	4	1
Kenedy	12	35.8	27 548	370	14	0	4	1	1	0	0	0	0
Kent	18	3.8	20 961	1 678	7	1	6	5	5	2	2	0	0
Kerr	1 119	3.7	25 887	532	408	115	421	206	198	105	67	10	1
Kimble	75	3.4	17 618	2 620	38	6	20	19	18	8	7	2	0
King	7	22.1	20 588	1 815	4	1	1	1	1	0	0	0	0
Kinney	50	6.6	14 292	3 032	17	1	15	15	15	7	5	2	0
Kleberg	560	2.8	18 882	2 326	308	51	87	124	119	30	47	19	2
Knox	87	3.4	21 290	1 574	33	16	16	24	24	8	11	3	0
Lamar	1 050	5.5	22 798	1 143	586	163	170	206	198	78	85	24	0
Lamb	325	3.8	22 029	1 356	120	94	46	74	71	24	31	9	5
Lampasas	315	7.6	17 805	2 574	98	27	68	75	72	23	32	6	1
La Salle	83	5.1	13 801	3 058	32	10	12	25	24	6	9	6	1
Lavaca	423	5.5	22 349	1 261	138	47	96	100	96	40	44	8	1
Lee	289	5.3	19 442	2 160	135	30	61	52	50	22	21	4	1
Leon	301	10.5	20 215	1 923	160	32	68	75	72	31	29	7	1
Liberty	1 261	4.5	18 778	2 351	451	102	158	262	251	86	128	23	7
Limestone	426	6.6	20 655	1 790	195	42	65	107	104	38	47	11	1
Lipscomb	78	1.3	21 999	558	28	16	20	11	11	5	4	1	0
Live Oak	197	3.8	19 459	2 153	89	17	41	40	38	15	17	4	1
Llano	349	10.0	25 214	634	101	33	104	89	87	47	31	3	0
Loving	4	-0.6	33 566	119	2	1	2	0	0	0	0	0	0
Lubbock	5 574	2.9	24 459	767	3 280	719	961	858	818	286	397	79	7
Lynn	135	17.4	20 313	1 886	45	32	21	28	27	10	12	5	0
McCulloch	166	3.3	18 891	2 321	64	19	43	44	43	16	20	5	1
McLennan	4 755	5.7	23 281	1 018	2 969	513	819	723	687	278	248	77	8
McMullen	21	7.3	26 030	509	8	3	9	3	3	1	1	0	0
Madison	228	2.4	19 213	2 231	95	44	40	47	45	19	19	5	0
Marion	174	3.5	15 840	2 917	47	21	28	53	51	20	18	8	1
Martin	84	19.5	16 857	2 765	38	14	17	18	17	6	8	2	0

1. Based on the resident population estimated as of July 1 of the year shown. 2. Includes other labor income.

Table B. States and Counties — Earnings, Social Security, and Housing

STATE County	Earnings, 1999									Social Security beneficiaries, December 2000		Housing units, 1990		
			Goods-related[1]		Service-related and other[2]							Supplemental Security Income recipients, December 2000		
	Total (mil dol)	Farm	Total	Manu-facturing	Total	Retail trade	Finance, insurance, and real estate	Services	Govern-ment	Number	Rate[3]		Total	Percent change, 1980–1990
	75	76	77	78	79	80	81	82	83	84	85	86	87	88

STATE County	75	76	77	78	79	80	81	82	83	84	85	86	87	88
TEXAS—Cont'd														
Guadalupe	793	1.1	40.4	31.6	41.1	11.3	5.1	16.8	17.4	13 225	149	1 401	25 592	42.1
Hale	564	20.4	17.5	13.7	47.9	18.0	2.8	15.5	14.2	5 844	160	877	13 168	-6.2
Hall	39	26.1	10.0	6.8	D	9.0	5.4	D	24.0	970	256	130	2 189	-16.8
Hamilton	92	15.6	D	6.6	D	13.0	D	18.1	18.1	2 176	264	169	4 266	-2.5
Hansford	165	60.2	10.3	1.0	19.5	3.3	2.4	3.6	10.0	958	178	64	2 525	-0.4
Hardeman	51	9.2	D	23.4	40.4	10.4	4.0	11.4	24.2	1 158	245	134	2 678	-6.3
Hardin	341	0.0	30.8	13.4	49.2	14.1	3.6	18.3	20.0	7 904	164	785	16 486	7.3
Harris	103 309	0.0	28.0	11.5	63.2	7.3	7.6	30.1	8.8	321 222	94	59 233	1 173 808	19.2
Harrison	836	1.1	46.8	35.0	41.0	7.7	4.5	19.2	11.1	9 942	160	1 645	23 481	15.9
Hartley	117	70.0	D	D	D	2.6	D	5.6	10.6	539	97	15	1 541	0.1
Haskell	62	17.2	9.2	0.7	50.1	13.6	5.5	16.0	23.5	1 754	288	161	3 843	5.0
Hays	1 046	-0.3	26.9	15.0	49.2	16.8	4.2	20.3	24.2	10 032	103	1 138	25 247	74.5
Hemphill	78	35.3	D	1.3	D	4.4	4.2	7.3	14.1	569	170	21	1 712	-15.4
Henderson	550	1.6	25.0	12.6	57.7	16.1	8.1	23.6	15.7	16 030	219	1 139	31 779	35.8
Hidalgo	4 644	2.3	15.2	7.4	55.3	15.4	4.1	22.9	27.2	63 055	111	26 057	128 241	44.0
Hill	274	6.0	26.4	15.9	46.7	18.9	4.7	15.2	20.9	7 000	217	634	12 899	8.0
Hockley	285	14.6	30.9	2.0	36.3	7.3	3.6	15.7	18.2	3 751	165	459	9 279	10.3
Hood	296	3.5	15.8	3.9	63.9	19.9	8.6	26.5	16.8	9 414	229	415	14 958	67.7
Hopkins	435	12.9	D	16.0	D	12.6	3.7	12.1	14.3	6 154	193	668	12 676	18.3
Houston	294	5.0	19.7	14.4	53.7	8.9	4.5	22.2	21.6	5 133	221	866	10 265	10.9
Howard	426	2.9	23.8	11.2	42.5	11.1	4.2	18.2	30.8	5 968	177	892	13 651	-1.6
Hudspeth	29	20.9	D	D	D	7.3	D	6.0	44.8	464	139	79	1 288	12.5
Hunt	907	0.4	40.1	35.1	38.1	10.8	3.4	14.4	21.3	13 409	175	1 660	28 959	20.2
Hutchinson	377	2.4	57.3	30.7	26.4	7.8	2.2	9.8	13.9	4 781	200	339	11 419	4.8
Irion	13	-17.7	D	D	D	10.0	D	15.5	26.6	320	181	31	842	19.9
Jack	69	-1.4	30.2	2.9	48.0	9.3	5.5	21.4	23.1	1 642	187	97	3 497	3.7
Jackson	191	11.0	D	D	D	7.6	D	10.3	15.6	2 632	183	284	5 841	8.5
Jasper	412	0.1	37.4	31.3	46.9	12.6	3.0	20.0	15.7	7 339	206	1 060	13 824	7.3
Jeff Davis	20	-9.9	D	D	D	8.8	6.3	35.5	38.2	398	180	52	1 348	40.0
Jefferson	4 781	0.2	31.4	20.8	53.6	10.0	3.7	28.8	14.9	44 387	176	6 467	101 289	3.6
Jim Hogg	42	0.8	20.8	1.4	D	13.7	D	10.0	37.6	976	185	278	2 103	19.1
Jim Wells	384	2.6	25.9	1.7	53.1	12.2	4.6	25.3	18.4	6 774	172	1 861	13 948	14.7
Johnson	1 136	1.0	32.1	23.4	52.5	13.2	3.8	20.4	14.4	16 755	132	1 534	37 029	49.4
Jones	171	4.8	9.9	3.6	39.3	6.9	4.9	14.1	46.0	3 486	168	357	7 639	2.4
Karnes	116	0.7	15.4	7.0	41.8	9.7	4.3	17.6	42.0	2 858	185	621	5 117	-3.1
Kaufman	687	0.7	D	22.5	D	13.8	4.7	20.8	19.9	11 642	163	1 473	20 097	40.6
Kendall	253	-1.2	24.4	10.0	61.1	17.2	10.6	23.7	15.7	4 423	186	153	6 137	30.3
Kenedy	14	8.7	D	0.0	D	D	1.7	6.0	12.9	52	126	6	213	3.9
Kent	8	3.7	D	0.0	D	8.5	D	9.2	56.1	241	281	12	603	9.8
Kerr	523	0.1	18.2	7.7	59.2	14.0	5.7	32.0	22.6	12 061	276	625	17 161	30.6
Kimble	44	-6.0	D	17.2	D	17.1	4.4	23.7	23.0	1 034	231	109	2 593	7.4
King	5	33.9	D	1.1	D	1.4	0.0	D	38.0	38	107	2	191	-11.2
Kinney	18	-3.9	D	D	D	4.9	D	13.2	63.6	866	256	141	1 821	65.4
Kleberg	359	3.7	9.1	1.6	40.5	12.0	3.0	19.5	46.7	4 222	134	867	12 008	7.1
Knox	49	21.1	D	D	D	5.8	3.7	14.9	26.6	1 080	254	155	2 459	0.9
Lamar	749	1.5	D	27.8	D	11.0	3.3	23.3	12.9	9 850	203	1 642	18 964	7.6
Lamb	214	39.2	D	D	35.5	6.5	2.3	8.3	14.7	3 070	209	400	6 531	-6.6
Lampasas	125	-0.7	24.6	9.7	53.7	15.2	5.4	23.0	22.4	3 246	183	333	6 193	21.6
La Salle	41	13.9	D	0.0	37.1	7.9	2.8	17.4	37.8	1 019	174	293	2 244	3.3
Lavaca	185	3.0	35.1	27.6	48.0	14.6	3.0	19.1	13.9	5 215	271	536	9 549	9.2
Lee	165	1.6	30.1	8.2	46.5	10.5	4.1	14.7	21.8	2 762	176	227	5 773	32.0
Leon	192	1.0	D	19.8	D	8.6	3.5	D	11.5	3 816	249	440	7 019	43.6
Liberty	553	1.4	26.3	15.6	50.5	14.1	4.1	19.5	21.9	10 183	145	1 518	22 243	12.3
Limestone	237	3.4	13.8	7.3	50.3	11.2	2.7	18.0	32.5	4 893	222	735	9 922	11.4
Lipscomb	44	19.2	D	D	D	5.4	4.2	5.8	20.3	651	213	25	1 683	8.0
Live Oak	106	-2.2	D	D	D	11.8	3.4	14.3	36.2	1 981	161	261	5 519	12.7
Llano	134	-0.8	D	2.3	D	12.5	9.4	28.7	22.5	5 327	313	194	9 773	29.1
Loving	3	4.5	D	0.0	D	D	D	D	12.9	18	269	0	59	18.0
Lubbock	3 998	1.0	12.8	6.9	65.4	14.6	6.3	29.1	20.8	34 088	140	4 712	91 770	14.0
Lynn	77	38.2	D	1.1	41.0	2.9	4.5	6.2	18.1	1 279	195	169	2 978	-6.1
McCulloch	82	4.0	D	11.1	D	14.6	4.9	19.4	23.7	2 042	249	285	4 424	8.7
McLennan	3 482	0.7	25.1	18.6	58.2	10.2	11.7	25.0	16.0	34 507	162	4 568	78 857	19.6
McMullen	10	13.2	D	0.0	D	3.5	D	11.0	32.0	162	190	13	565	10.8
Madison	139	29.0	D	0.6	D	10.6	3.9	18.1	26.0	2 235	173	251	4 326	10.9
Marion	68	1.9	D	15.5	D	13.5	2.7	20.3	20.1	2 524	231	375	5 729	1.7
Martin	52	17.6	9.4	1.8	49.2	11.9	2.5	11.7	23.8	784	165	111	2 039	11.1

1. Covers mining, construction, and manufacturing. 2. Covers private sector earnings in agricultural services, forestry, and fisheries; transportation and public utilities; wholesale trade; retail trade; finance, insurance, and real estate; and services. 3. Per 1,000 resident population estimated as of July 1 of the year shown.

Table B. States and Counties — Housing, Labor Force, and Employment

STATE County	Housing units, 1990 (cont'd)								Civilian labor force, 2001				Civilian employment, 1990[5]		
	Occupied units										Unemployment			Percent	
	Owner-occupied					Renter-occupied									
				Owner cost as a percent of income											
	Total	Percent	Median value[1]	With a mortgage	Without a mortgage	Median rent[2]	Rent as percent of income	Substandard units[3] (percent)	Total	Percent change, 2000–2001	Total	Rate[4]	Total	Professional, managerial, and technical	Precision production, craft, and repair
	89	90	91	92	93	94	95	96	97	98	99	100	101	102	103

TEXAS—Cont'd

STATE County	89	90	91	92	93	94	95	96	97	98	99	100	101	102	103
Guadalupe	22 663	72.4	60 100	20.4	12.6	369	25.9	7.7	44 145	1.6	1 314	3.0	29 294	23.7	14.6
Hale	11 703	62.4	39 000	18.4	13.0	314	23.9	10.8	16 809	-0.2	800	4.8	14 396	20.1	12.8
Hall	1 669	74.7	21 400	20.5	14.2	214	25.7	4.4	1 794	5.0	75	4.2	1 540	17.1	9.0
Hamilton	3 250	77.2	33 300	17.3	15.9	262	24.3	3.5	4 245	5.9	100	2.4	3 144	19.4	8.6
Hansford	2 112	74.1	43 800	16.7	12.4	325	19.4	7.0	2 439	-0.2	53	2.2	2 515	20.6	13.1
Hardeman	2 101	75.3	25 500	17.1	14.2	240	28.5	4.9	1 845	-0.8	64	3.5	1 981	18.2	8.4
Hardin	14 693	80.5	48 300	16.7	13.4	358	24.8	5.1	22 957	-1.2	1 566	6.8	16 863	22.2	20.1
Harris	1 026 448	52.0	63 500	20.1	13.0	405	23.2	9.8	1 805 965	1.8	80 493	4.5	1 381 829	33.2	11.4
Harrison	20 705	75.3	46 000	18.7	13.8	334	26.7	6.2	27 428	0.0	1 538	5.6	22 840	22.0	16.3
Hartley	1 332	77.3	60 600	18.3	12.5	300	18.8	1.6	2 970	-0.5	35	1.2	1 676	26.4	7.4
Haskell	2 753	76.2	28 200	17.2	13.8	234	27.1	6.1	2 992	15.6	88	2.9	2 640	18.9	12.8
Hays	22 218	58.2	81 300	23.5	13.0	407	34.5	7.5	55 744	1.1	1 821	3.3	30 737	33.8	9.5
Hemphill	1 348	73.5	47 500	14.3	12.9	341	18.7	5.7	1 865	6.3	31	1.7	1 667	15.0	16.7
Henderson	22 947	79.1	53 600	20.8	14.3	347	26.4	5.4	31 344	0.8	1 201	3.8	22 324	21.8	15.6
Hidalgo	103 479	70.3	35 900	21.5	12.7	282	26.5	28.4	208 182	2.1	27 277	13.1	122 112	23.3	10.5
Hill	10 268	74.3	37 200	18.6	15.4	309	24.9	5.5	15 657	-4.2	795	5.1	10 557	19.0	15.1
Hockley	7 988	72.6	41 900	18.7	12.8	308	25.8	8.5	11 161	3.2	376	3.4	9 881	21.9	15.8
Hood	11 137	79.1	73 800	19.4	11.8	455	22.5	3.8	17 878	1.3	745	4.2	11 757	29.7	15.3
Hopkins	10 965	70.8	43 600	20.7	14.7	332	25.1	5.2	14 528	-2.5	605	4.2	12 530	17.1	12.8
Houston	7 792	74.4	40 000	22.5	14.9	278	29.3	8.3	9 762	6.1	360	3.7	7 699	21.2	12.6
Howard	11 477	70.7	34 900	16.9	12.2	336	23.4	5.2	13 869	2.3	542	3.9	12 392	25.8	15.2
Hudspeth	946	68.8	23 100	21.3	13.0	391	19.9	17.8	1 457	-0.8	62	4.3	1 173	19.3	8.2
Hunt	24 075	70.0	47 300	19.1	14.1	378	27.8	5.0	37 802	1.1	1 834	4.9	28 850	24.7	15.4
Hutchinson	9 642	77.5	38 200	16.7	12.2	333	25.7	4.0	8 982	1.1	377	4.2	9 903	23.6	20.5
Irion	601	74.0	44 600	19.2	11.3	308	17.2	5.5	725	8.0	17	2.3	708	18.6	15.0
Jack	2 725	76.9	33 800	20.5	13.0	265	23.9	4.0	3 267	-4.6	104	3.2	2 804	20.5	17.3
Jackson	4 833	75.2	42 000	22.1	14.1	314	22.9	6.9	8 260	1.2	272	3.3	5 079	20.6	19.6
Jasper	11 427	79.1	40 300	18.8	13.6	322	29.9	5.9	14 155	0.0	1 615	11.4	10 766	19.2	17.6
Jeff Davis	779	67.1	43 800	25.0	12.3	292	16.3	5.9	1 348	1.7	24	1.8	826	28.9	6.4
Jefferson	90 520	66.0	41 800	17.3	13.0	363	25.8	5.2	114 082	-1.4	9 023	7.9	98 779	28.0	13.4
Jim Hogg	1 675	78.1	28 300	21.9	12.8	199	31.8	11.8	2 053	-5.1	93	4.5	1 834	21.3	13.1
Jim Wells	11 979	74.3	33 700	22.2	14.1	294	24.8	14.6	17 408	4.0	995	5.7	13 286	20.3	18.8
Johnson	33 462	76.2	61 100	20.8	13.3	411	25.5	5.3	64 262	1.2	2 655	4.1	44 802	23.5	16.2
Jones	6 180	78.1	29 600	20.1	14.3	275	24.0	4.5	9 303	-3.8	261	2.8	6 608	21.9	13.9
Karnes	4 337	74.5	29 600	22.2	13.9	229	24.8	13.0	5 902	0.9	226	3.8	4 508	20.3	13.7
Kaufman	17 827	76.3	56 000	22.3	14.2	378	28.6	6.3	35 003	1.9	1 951	5.6	22 670	23.6	15.4
Kendall	5 342	74.5	79 000	23.0	13.5	423	27.5	5.5	15 223	6.5	345	2.3	6 851	30.6	13.5
Kenedy	145	20.0	22 500	35.1	10.0	225	14.0	14.9	220	0.9	4	1.8	216	18.1	3.2
Kent	399	74.4	28 100	22.7	13.2	242	16.7	4.5	391	-6.0	8	2.0	429	20.3	8.9
Kerr	14 384	69.5	67 300	22.4	12.9	387	27.1	6.1	17 969	2.5	462	2.6	14 342	29.6	11.4
Kimble	1 624	73.8	38 900	21.0	14.0	270	26.7	4.2	2 320	2.0	39	1.7	1 860	12.7	11.5
King	124	35.5	17 500	26.7	15.0	313	15.0	1.6	159	10.4	6	3.8	192	17.7	3.1
Kinney	1 187	68.6	32 400	21.5	13.9	276	23.3	10.5	1 128	-1.6	71	6.3	961	17.4	7.8
Kleberg	10 058	59.7	40 800	17.9	13.2	341	27.2	10.7	12 386	0.1	597	4.8	11 416	29.8	13.1
Knox	1 887	76.0	27 600	21.8	15.2	213	25.5	6.2	1 844	-2.3	60	3.3	1 843	21.1	13.8
Lamar	16 798	68.9	39 000	17.7	13.7	338	28.5	4.0	21 671	-0.6	1 438	6.6	17 945	23.2	12.1
Lamb	5 488	73.5	28 900	16.8	13.1	274	24.8	9.0	6 587	2.3	444	6.7	5 595	20.6	12.4
Lampasas	5 058	72.7	49 600	21.6	12.7	330	27.5	6.5	9 293	8.7	288	3.1	5 583	21.7	17.4
La Salle	1 701	67.7	18 300	21.1	13.3	218	29.2	19.8	2 720	-2.3	168	6.2	1 932	17.8	13.5
Lavaca	7 349	78.7	40 700	20.3	13.0	252	21.7	7.2	8 680	-5.0	141	1.6	8 005	17.3	16.9
Lee	4 706	77.5	47 800	21.2	12.5	331	24.6	8.0	6 650	-2.1	252	3.8	5 481	21.8	17.2
Leon	5 006	81.1	43 500	23.9	14.8	319	27.0	6.7	6 699	-0.5	314	4.7	4 056	20.1	17.1
Liberty	18 538	75.5	42 100	20.1	14.2	352	26.1	7.6	29 924	1.3	1 918	6.4	20 309	19.5	19.4
Limestone	7 722	73.1	36 900	21.4	15.0	301	28.6	6.0	9 631	4.3	341	3.5	8 190	23.9	14.7
Lipscomb	1 230	77.2	35 500	20.9	13.3	317	17.6	4.1	1 483	-0.8	30	2.0	1 361	20.4	17.9
Live Oak	3 550	79.9	42 000	18.9	12.3	272	26.5	9.3	4 487	4.0	113	2.5	3 740	21.5	17.7
Llano	5 278	79.3	66 700	26.1	13.8	361	27.2	2.7	5 536	0.5	177	3.2	3 558	20.8	15.3
Loving	42	73.8	14 999	0.0	10.0	213	2.4	4.7	63	18.9	5	7.9	59	25.4	8.5
Lubbock	81 534	58.2	54 500	20.0	12.6	377	29.5	6.6	126 786	2.4	3 239	2.6	102 790	30.9	9.9
Lynn	2 383	71.0	31 900	21.4	12.9	244	24.7	9.1	2 658	-3.7	134	5.0	2 519	14.2	8.1
McCulloch	3 409	71.8	33 900	22.3	15.1	289	26.4	7.1	3 504	-2.7	203	5.8	3 135	21.4	7.6
McLennan	70 208	58.9	50 300	18.6	12.8	360	27.9	5.3	100 901	-0.4	3 938	3.9	82 485	27.5	11.6
McMullen	319	75.9	40 000	25.0	11.1	225	12.9	11.6	291	1.4	9	3.1	389	23.4	13.1
Madison	3 349	75.5	41 900	22.9	16.2	351	30.1	8.8	4 286	1.5	115	2.7	3 387	18.8	9.9
Marion	4 048	81.0	34 500	23.6	14.3	255	29.9	12.0	3 415	-3.7	270	7.9	3 443	17.7	12.8
Martin	1 632	72.4	40 500	18.0	12.9	233	26.0	9.5	1 903	9.0	78	4.1	1 786	17.0	12.3

1. Specified owner-occupied units.   2. Specified renter-occupied units.   3. Overcrowded or lacking complete plumbing facilities.   4. Percent of civilian labor force.   5. Persons 16 years and older.

Table B. States and Counties — **Nonfarm Employment and Agriculture**

STATE County	Private nonfarm establishments, employment and payroll, 1999									Agriculture, 1997			
	Number of establishments	Employment						Annual payroll		Farms			Farm operators
		Total	Health Care and Social Assistance	Manufacturing	Retail trade	Finance and Insurance	Professional Scientific and Technical Services	Total (mil dol)	Average per employee (dollars)	Number	Percent with—		Whose principal occupation is farming (percent)
											Less than 50 acres	500 acres and over	
	104	105	106	107	108	109	110	111	112	113	114	115	116
TEXAS—Cont'd													
Guadalupe	1 309	18 362	1 976	5 787	2 870	454	233	428	23 326	1 841	37.9	7.3	40.0
Hale	830	11 832	1 278	2 632	1 567	340	173	250	21 114	840	7.7	50.0	68.7
Hall	96	693	128	81	145	D	3	12	17 003	311	2.3	52.7	61.7
Hamilton	219	1 698	386	221	313	54	44	33	19 708	966	11.5	26.4	45.7
Hansford	189	1 169	D	3	242	99	37	25	21 607	279	5.4	76.3	73.1
Hardeman	100	822	167	D	117	47	16	18	22 365	342	6.1	44.4	50.9
Hardin	733	8 125	1 511	953	1 593	188	275	169	20 764	354	61.0	5.4	35.3
Harris	84 106	1 623 424	153 810	154 264	171 534	74 894	120 438	60 023	36 973	1 727	55.8	7.7	34.7
Harrison	1 220	15 961	1 544	3 881	2 312	984	534	369	23 106	1 107	36.3	10.1	34.1
Hartley	74	761	313	D	142	0	16	14	18 055	245	5.7	69.4	70.2
Haskell	155	963	209	32	224	76	27	16	16 852	611	11.0	40.6	56.8
Hays	2 074	23 045	3 822	3 291	4 482	478	606	501	21 723	816	33.6	16.1	38.1
Hemphill	137	960	151	19	135	70	15	20	20 812	230	8.3	62.2	66.1
Henderson	1 160	12 107	1 812	1 987	2 678	389	298	243	20 071	1 630	34.8	8.4	39.3
Hidalgo	8 187	108 951	19 533	11 865	22 671	4 252	3 218	2 061	18 914	1 373	49.5	18.9	45.4
Hill	705	6 463	877	1 225	1 816	198	93	124	19 248	1 563	25.6	14.3	42.7
Hockley	483	5 008	1 506	182	753	196	167	93	18 549	675	15.6	47.7	62.8
Hood	925	7 734	1 182	378	1 847	370	243	158	20 458	799	41.2	12.4	35.8
Hopkins	754	9 947	1 050	1 620	1 735	394	190	218	21 947	1 758	25.3	9.8	47.5
Houston	404	3 861	1 029	571	802	163	99	71	18 377	1 369	21.4	15.6	43.5
Howard	769	9 452	2 233	1 181	1 507	297	168	224	23 652	436	20.0	45.0	50.2
Hudspeth	49	250	D	0	57	D	D	4	17 644	147	7.5	61.9	75.5
Hunt	1 318	20 433	2 848	7 116	3 078	521	537	541	26 462	2 049	38.8	6.4	33.4
Hutchinson	537	7 526	1 440	1 720	939	148	125	230	30 576	190	13.7	53.7	56.3
Irion	38	214	0	D	D	D	D	6	26 374	146	21.9	54.8	50.0
Jack	174	1 281	192	D	167	80	30	25	19 512	730	9.7	31.8	37.8
Jackson	292	4 509	585	D	537	88	61	106	23 425	790	20.5	30.4	50.8
Jasper	736	8 912	1 906	1 863	1 688	273	155	197	22 102	639	55.6	2.0	31.6
Jeff Davis	58	405	87	D	D	D	D	7	16 247	83	7.2	77.1	71.1
Jefferson	5 957	102 551	16 224	14 540	15 262	3 081	4 256	3 053	29 766	562	39.1	25.6	40.0
Jim Hogg	108	782	98	13	221	54	D	13	17 215	188	7.4	61.2	46.8
Jim Wells	790	9 532	3 098	246	1 547	348	202	175	18 396	738	22.6	24.4	43.9
Johnson	2 105	25 568	2 396	6 437	4 151	963	597	586	22 921	2 062	48.6	6.1	33.1
Jones	330	3 069	589	76	479	114	54	57	18 730	867	17.2	27.5	44.6
Karnes	270	2 027	408	160	397	105	63	37	18 067	1 051	12.7	20.3	39.0
Kaufman	1 456	19 343	2 669	4 740	2 615	542	328	443	22 918	1 883	44.6	7.7	33.1
Kendall	689	6 074	517	582	1 109	510	254	133	21 973	730	25.5	22.2	38.8
Kenedy	3	D	0	0	0	0	0	D	D	31	3.2	71.0	80.6
Kent	19	118	0	0	D	D	0	5	38 593	171	5.8	51.5	52.6
Kerr	1 297	14 787	4 059	978	2 328	321	556	320	21 621	778	23.3	26.9	38.7
Kimble	141	1 091	147	218	196	D	31	19	17 722	485	12.2	52.6	51.8
King	1	D	0	0	0	0	0	D	D	43	2.3	62.8	51.2
Kinney	31	210	D	0	D	0	D	3	14 152	128	6.2	76.6	53.9
Kleberg	541	5 673	1 027	389	1 410	276	104	97	17 077	272	41.5	16.9	32.7
Knox	131	747	226	0	107	D	3	13	17 505	296	8.1	52.0	58.8
Lamar	1 197	16 515	3 043	4 141	2 790	479	344	402	24 370	1 539	24.9	14.4	39.3
Lamb	314	2 680	374	608	488	155	21	57	21 354	865	7.4	42.1	63.6
Lampasas	368	3 242	456	398	653	105	92	60	18 572	746	21.0	26.7	45.2
La Salle	90	694	74	0	159	25	D	13	19 146	280	5.7	53.2	43.6
Lavaca	508	6 280	913	2 444	788	267	77	116	18 449	2 558	26.5	7.7	37.7
Lee	412	3 404	301	457	661	171	82	77	22 587	1 685	26.2	8.5	38.6
Leon	329	3 319	191	518	469	92	55	96	28 793	1 633	24.9	15.5	42.1
Liberty	1 035	11 212	1 721	1 201	2 487	337	295	244	21 754	1 138	44.6	11.5	36.2
Limestone	415	4 316	865	825	761	164	76	83	19 173	1 212	19.7	16.8	41.6
Lipscomb	105	480	D	D	96	D	18	9	18 567	302	7.0	61.3	57.3
Live Oak	197	1 715	161	D	422	88	33	36	20 760	732	15.7	33.2	37.4
Llano	434	3 215	626	78	390	139	96	68	21 095	565	17.0	40.9	43.9
Loving	1	D	0	0	0	0	0	D	D	14	7.1	92.9	50.0
Lubbock	6 459	90 780	17 118	6 533	14 815	3 854	3 006	2 045	22 522	1 068	29.1	32.1	55.3
Lynn	106	781	133	35	108	73	13	18	23 291	490	7.3	60.6	75.9
McCulloch	231	2 039	391	166	457	94	91	37	18 312	545	7.9	43.7	46.2
McLennan	4 831	87 895	13 385	16 688	10 452	4 230	2 377	2 117	24 082	2 006	38.8	11.1	36.8
McMullen	16	82	D	0	D	D	D	3	31 305	210	2.4	74.8	52.4
Madison	217	1 840	458	35	444	92	56	35	18 906	816	24.4	12.5	39.5
Marion	185	1 249	190	293	226	D	11	22	17 900	207	19.3	16.4	42.0
Martin	91	588	161	0	131	35	12	14	23 230	353	8.5	57.2	63.5

Items 104—116

STATE County	Acreage (1,000)	Percent change, 1992-1997	Average size of farm	Total irrigated (1,000)	Total cropland (1,000)	Average per farm ($1,000)	Average per acre (dollars)	Value of machinery and equipment average per farm ($1,000)	Total (mil dol)	Average per farm (dollars)	Crops	Live-stock and poultry products	$10,000 or more	$100,000 or more	Percent of land owned by fed. gov. 1997	Water consumption 1995 (mil gal/day)
	117	118	119	120	121	122	123	124	125	126	127	128	129	130	131	132
TEXAS—Cont'd																
Guadalupe	348	0.2	189	1	165	268	1 680	25	31	17 035	44.4	55.6	20.5	2.7	0.2	9.5
Hale	587	4.7	698	310	512	414	568	115	240	285 213	48.7	51.3	69.6	44.4	0.0	354.0
Hall	448	1.1	1 440	9	172	323	235	65	24	75 873	76.2	23.8	55.3	24.1	0.0	11.6
Hamilton	466	1.1	482	1	134	337	779	31	52	54 254	5.6	94.4	37.6	6.8	0.0	3.3
Hansford	582	1.1	2 086	125	314	856	424	140	346	1 241 020	11.4	88.6	77.1	53.8	0.0	166.8
Hardeman	323	2.8	944	5	167	243	285	38	16	46 454	44.1	55.9	48.2	10.2	0.0	10.7
Hardin	65	104.5	185	1	18	209	1 239	23	3	8 116	33.3	66.7	15.5	0.6	8.1	184.3
Harris	311	1.0	180	10	119	343	2 225	29	43	25 073	69.9	30.1	21.2	4.5	2.6	498.9
Harrison	214	6.2	194	0	96	195	1 139	23	12	10 916	14.5	85.5	23.8	1.6	1.5	81.1
Hartley	823	19.8	3 359	126	D	1 240	367	158	350	1 428 449	15.0	85.0	75.1	53.9	0.0	211.4
Haskell	469	-5.1	767	28	292	282	404	58	40	65 033	71.7	28.3	57.4	18.3	0.0	97.5
Hays	298	-35.5	366	1	74	668	1 928	25	11	13 185	41.2	58.8	18.0	2.2	0.0	17.3
Hemphill	624	14.2	2 711	5	D	717	258	42	103	448 302	1.5	98.5	63.0	23.9	0.0	3.8
Henderson	367	3.1	225	1	155	219	1 016	29	29	18 096	34.3	65.7	25.3	2.3	0.0	125.1
Hidalgo	636	-3.7	463	185	439	609	1 360	63	197	143 652	91.8	8.2	41.1	17.3	1.8	932.3
Hill	464	-1.3	297	1	292	247	854	44	58	36 923	59.7	40.3	34.2	6.5	0.6	5.7
Hockley	572	16.4	847	143	430	349	417	107	89	132 319	75.7	24.3	56.7	35.1	0.0	155.9
Hood	225	-0.2	282	5	78	341	1 253	30	18	22 843	47.7	52.3	25.3	2.5	0.0	3 333.4
Hopkins	386	-0.1	220	4	222	211	1 031	38	127	72 298	3.0	97.0	40.4	16.4	1.7	12.4
Houston	440	5.6	322	2	168	279	888	30	27	20 006	14.5	85.5	31.2	2.8	11.9	5.7
Howard	544	11.2	1 247	3	202	480	350	65	31	72 217	69.4	30.6	48.2	19.7	0.0	6.7
Hudspeth	2 503	12.0	17 026	31	40	2 450	144	94	25	170 021	66.2	33.8	72.1	34.7	0.6	157.5
Hunt	353	2.4	172	0	215	200	1 183	24	24	11 754	44.3	55.7	20.8	2.0	0.0	97.2
Hutchinson	400	-0.7	2 106	48	126	671	343	88	43	226 152	31.9	68.1	56.3	28.4	1.0	145.6
Irion	652	-0.8	4 464	1	D	833	193	30	6	40 960	8.8	91.2	51.4	10.3	0.0	3.5
Jack	532	2.5	728	0	71	450	592	23	17	23 177	6.0	94.0	33.4	4.8	0.0	2.4
Jackson	463	0.2	586	22	240	492	809	72	47	59 819	79.6	20.4	40.9	16.3	1.5	87.0
Jasper	87	24.4	136	0	26	190	1 480	29	3	5 446	28.5	71.5	12.4	0.3	5.2	56.7
Jeff Davis	1 482	-2.8	17 851	0	D	2 821	158	53	9	112 582	0.7	99.3	65.1	26.5	0.0	1.2
Jefferson	434	34.7	772	32	181	616	825	42	26	46 187	70.8	29.2	37.2	13.9	7.8	168.5
Jim Hogg	768	4.4	4 086	D	25	1 092	276	26	6	34 577	0.1	99.9	38.8	8.5	0.0	1.6
Jim Wells	496	-4.2	673	3	199	353	612	35	36	48 263	50.1	49.9	28.7	8.3	0.3	4.8
Johnson	333	0.9	161	1	175	301	1 976	25	48	23 336	13.5	86.5	20.7	3.7	0.3	13.3
Jones	459	-10.5	530	4	300	238	426	44	39	45 136	56.2	43.8	42.6	10.5	0.0	285.9
Karnes	417	8.6	397	3	162	251	660	18	16	15 119	23.7	76.3	29.4	2.2	0.0	4.6
Kaufman	389	0.5	206	1	181	262	1 389	24	29	15 412	18.1	81.9	19.4	2.1	0.0	6.7
Kendall	325	-8.3	446	0	49	618	1 426	23	6	8 888	14.2	85.8	19.7	1.2	0.0	4.4
Kenedy	563	1.8	18 159	D	D	5 444	300	49	7	220 380	D	D	74.2	22.6	6.7	0.7
Kent	561	-5.7	3 280	1	51	557	178	42	7	42 565	16.0	84.0	44.4	11.7	0.0	2.1
Kerr	548	3.2	704	2	51	634	886	25	7	9 244	14.6	85.4	21.0	0.9	0.0	7.7
Kimble	773	-0.3	1 594	2	33	800	515	21	7	14 893	11.6	88.4	32.0	2.3	0.0	3.0
King	D	D	D	D	22	1 885	150	54	7	153 438	9.0	91.0	55.8	20.9	0.0	0.7
Kinney	629	-10.0	4 913	3	20	1 576	323	34	6	47 600	D	D	53.1	12.5	0.0	8.5
Kleberg	D	D	D	D	116	2 158	D	94	44	162 712	D	D	25.4	7.0	3.6	7.4
Knox	658	14.1	2 224	31	220	501	233	73	49	165 667	31.5	68.5	65.2	29.1	0.4	26.4
Lamar	431	1.4	280	1	248	217	750	28	35	22 992	31.8	68.2	34.6	5.3	1.6	22.3
Lamb	539	4.1	624	218	439	340	564	96	253	293 022	39.8	60.2	61.8	39.7	0.0	293.3
Lampasas	435	0.6	583	0	71	477	805	27	13	17 361	13.8	86.2	31.8	2.4	0.0	1.7
La Salle	527	-31.2	1 882	4	72	767	424	31	19	66 747	22.1	77.9	38.6	7.1	0.0	6.8
Lavaca	526	-0.4	206	5	220	220	1 017	24	43	16 676	9.8	90.2	22.8	1.6	0.0	16.4
Lee	344	8.0	204	1	130	210	1 116	24	23	13 373	23.9	76.1	28.4	1.0	2.5	4.8
Leon	515	6.8	315	2	183	259	866	27	27	16 572	12.3	87.7	27.7	2.4	0.0	7.1
Liberty	307	-10.3	270	14	160	278	1 152	38	24	20 847	69.6	30.4	19.3	4.2	0.2	611.9
Limestone	443	3.5	365	0	174	274	766	33	26	21 295	11.8	88.2	31.8	3.1	0.0	23.7
Lipscomb	529	-10.2	1 751	22	146	443	256	63	45	150 069	25.0	75.0	58.9	19.9	0.0	17.2
Live Oak	520	-6.9	711	3	128	431	651	34	12	16 077	36.7	63.3	31.0	2.7	0.4	9.3
Llano	532	5.0	942	1	44	752	796	22	10	17 362	5.2	94.8	37.3	2.8	0.4	4.7
Loving	352	1.5	25 148			1 735	69	25	1	62 872	0.0	100.0	71.4	14.3	0.0	0.6
Lubbock	541	12.2	506	212	456	441	808	104	134	125 239	70.6	29.4	53.0	27.7	0.4	217.8
Lynn	563	14.7	1 149	74	421	628	532	120	71	145 749	97.2	2.8	74.7	47.3	0.0	50.9
McCulloch	641	-5.2	1 175	2	135	562	468	47	18	33 089	29.0	71.0	47.5	9.2	0.0	6.4
McLennan	493	4.4	246	2	299	237	968	34	93	46 337	36.7	63.3	24.8	5.4	1.6	57.4
McMullen	521	1.0	2 481	D	26	979	403	30	6	26 439	6.6	93.4	42.4	5.7	1.8	1.3
Madison	224	-8.3	274	0	79	325	1 171	37	43	52 340	D	D	29.7	2.7	0.0	2.8
Marion	62	24.0	299	0	27	300	1 024	26	2	9 896	24.0	76.0	22.7	1.4	1.7	5.1
Martin	539	5.3	1 527	11	272	502	329	95	40	113 116	91.4	8.6	59.5	38.5	0.0	9.2

STATE County	Value of Residential Construction Authorized by Building Permits, 2000		Wholesale Trade, 1997				Retail Trade[1], 1997				Real Estate and Rental and Leasing, 1997			
	New Construction ($1,000)	Number of Housing Units	Number of Establishments	Number of Employees	Sales (mil dol)	Annual Payroll (mil dol)	Number of Establishments	Number of Employees	Sales (mil dol)	Annual Payroll (mil dol)	Number of Establishments	Number of Employees	Receipts (mil dol)	Annual Payroll (mil dol)
	133	134	135	136	137	138	139	140	141	142	143	144	145	146
TEXAS—Cont'd														
Guadalupe	56 907	473	82	681	366.1	20.6	215	2 665	498.1	41.7	58	205	21.4	3.5
Hale	6 075	124	74	540	294.5	13.3	164	1 566	264.7	23.6	31	111	6.2	1.4
Hall	0	0	6	25	10.1	0.5	22	137	43.1	2.1	NA	NA	NA	NA
Hamilton	460	8	10	118	42.1	2.2	57	301	45.4	4.0	4	D	D	D
Hansford	193	2	23	139	116.1	4.3	38	233	39.0	3.6	3	8	0.5	0.0
Hardeman	0	0	9	41	12.2	0.6	21	115	16.3	1.5	1	D	D	D
Hardin	1 384	21	28	150	33.4	3.3	152	1 630	350.6	24.5	24	90	6.8	0.8
Harris	2 745 796	24 565	7 564	101 357	110 399.7	4 129.7	11 596	168 038	31 045.1	2 921.9	4 039	33 808	4 154.7	829.5
Harrison	2 295	28	65	747	321.2	20.8	220	2 270	378.6	33.2	36	181	13.3	4.0
Hartley	NA	NA	5	D	D	D	10	84	14.4	1.2	7	D	D	D
Haskell	100	1	8	40	23.3	0.6	41	238	58.9	3.3	5	13	1.0	0.3
Hays	126 118	1 724	75	559	174.1	15.9	382	4 056	698.0	61.0	91	312	40.8	7.5
Hemphill	0	0	7	33	10.5	0.8	22	132	19.7	2.0	2	D	D	D
Henderson	11 956	115	42	215	98.3	4.6	221	2 586	381.1	34.3	52	191	18.3	2.8
Hidalgo	310 947	5 659	600	6 395	1 981.7	124.6	1 582	20 862	3 337.6	313.1	346	1 347	116.3	18.5
Hill	1 160	16	26	119	46.8	2.5	229	1 800	331.1	26.4	20	44	4.1	0.4
Hockley	1 173	16	40	255	81.5	6.3	86	725	150.6	11.3	21	42	3.6	0.6
Hood	3 891	33	29	83	32.5	2.0	159	1 702	346.6	30.3	44	274	14.5	3.6
Hopkins	3 204	33	48	1 088	607.1	27.0	174	1 753	357.2	27.8	23	123	9.2	1.6
Houston	433	5	16	136	49.4	2.4	91	772	122.4	10.6	10	17	1.2	0.2
Howard	964	15	50	559	215.5	22.0	149	1 509	248.6	21.1	37	121	9.5	2.0
Hudspeth	NA	NA	4	7	1.9	0.1	9	52	6.1	0.5	1	D	D	D
Hunt	6 021	67	54	447	263.6	10.1	258	3 013	479.9	41.7	56	214	14.3	3.8
Hutchinson	380	1	31	192	163.9	5.5	104	1 028	151.0	13.8	16	47	4.7	0.8
Irion	NA	NA	3	19	5.1	0.4	4	19	1.5	0.1	1	D	D	D
Jack	0	0	7	64	13.0	1.8	35	181	21.3	2.3	6	11	0.5	0.1
Jackson	2 361	25	22	177	58.4	3.3	63	479	90.6	7.6	11	25	1.6	0.2
Jasper	613	9	49	247	103.4	6.5	190	1 658	301.0	23.7	23	71	11.7	1.4
Jeff Davis	NA	NA	NA	NA	NA	NA	8	37	3.7	0.5	1	D	D	D
Jefferson	73 176	615	368	4 827	2 081.2	163.7	1 084	14 964	2 570.9	230.1	260	1 597	194.2	34.2
Jim Hogg	NA	NA	5	40	25.3	0.8	34	207	31.4	2.5	1	D	D	D
Jim Wells	2 199	24	56	522	139.8	14.1	160	1 531	258.1	23.4	41	258	35.3	7.5
Johnson	65 138	665	87	762	261.3	18.2	358	3 995	706.8	62.2	69	239	22.7	3.1
Jones	0	0	24	140	145.1	3.4	58	498	163.1	8.0	9	19	0.9	0.2
Karnes	17	2	14	168	45.8	2.4	54	434	59.8	5.1	5	19	1.1	0.1
Kaufman	21 812	330	77	665	189.3	16.8	286	2 693	573.3	43.0	34	103	8.2	1.3
Kendall	57 801	278	31	378	141.1	8.5	93	1 012	305.8	20.1	30	66	7.7	0.8
Kenedy	NA	NA	NA	NA	NA	NA	NA	NA	NA	NA	NA	NA	NA	NA
Kent	NA	NA	1	D	D	D	4	D	D	D	NA	NA	NA	NA
Kerr	14 996	167	48	271	65.6	6.4	210	2 467	436.1	38.4	63	180	18.2	3.2
Kimble	0	0	5	D	D	D	33	201	31.4	2.8	4	7	0.2	0.0
King	NA	NA	NA	NA	NA	NA	NA	NA	NA	NA	NA	NA	NA	NA
Kinney	327	3	2	D	D	D	9	41	4.2	0.4	3	4	0.4	0.0
Kleberg	848	11	10	42	8.2	0.9	113	1 414	214.3	20.0	24	65	7.0	0.8
Knox	NA	NA	13	79	29.8	1.7	31	163	24.7	2.0	1	D	D	D
Lamar	8 521	117	68	519	152.4	12.7	242	2 591	482.5	40.0	46	134	15.3	1.8
Lamb	215	4	25	146	72.6	3.1	63	450	75.4	5.9	5	11	0.5	0.1
Lampasas	392	12	16	79	36.3	0.7	65	562	94.4	7.8	12	32	2.1	0.3
La Salle	62	1	3	D	D	D	27	142	20.0	1.8	3	4	0.2	0.0
Lavaca	974	10	30	818	202.6	14.6	108	797	118.1	10.7	11	19	1.3	0.1
Lee	1 127	10	35	324	322.4	7.1	59	665	79.9	9.0	7	16	2.9	0.4
Leon	NA	NA	15	149	56.2	3.2	72	494	77.4	6.0	8	43	2.3	0.5
Liberty	14 407	213	53	D	D	D	204	2 472	441.7	36.5	45	179	17.7	4.2
Limestone	1 105	11	15	D	D	D	91	831	137.6	11.3	10	16	0.8	0.2
Lipscomb	0	0	11	32	12.5	0.6	17	82	10.6	0.8	1	D	D	D
Live Oak	147	4	9	77	25.4	0.9	45	397	75.0	5.1	7	14	1.3	0.2
Llano	2 268	24	15	222	85.5	5.4	77	380	69.1	5.3	17	56	6.0	1.0
Loving	NA	NA	1	D	D	D	NA	NA	NA	NA	NA	NA	NA	NA
Lubbock	94 120	924	505	6 628	3 867.8	181.3	1 084	14 538	2 673.0	238.0	296	1 905	133.8	30.7
Lynn	313	3	7	D	D	D	24	122	30.6	2.1	1	D	D	D
McCulloch	275	6	14	91	14.9	1.4	55	473	75.5	5.9	8	40	3.1	0.7
McLennan	75 871	701	315	3 755	1 716.3	102.1	862	10 227	1 797.8	162.7	212	1 086	131.4	21.4
McMullen	NA	NA	NA	NA	NA	NA	5	13	1.9	0.2	NA	NA	NA	NA
Madison	535	6	5	23	12.1	0.8	46	462	137.0	7.5	11	16	1.4	0.2
Marion	0	0	9	31	19.1	1.0	41	246	37.4	2.8	3	2	0.2	0.0
Martin	20	1	10	53	22.2	1.4	17	116	27.9	2.1	NA	NA	NA	NA

1. Establishments with payroll.

STATE County	Professional, Scientific, and Technical Services[1], 1997				Manufacturing, 1997				Accommodation and Foodservices, 1997			
	Number of Establishments	Number of Employees	Receipts (mil dol)	Annual Payroll (mil dol)	Number of Establishments	Number of Employees	Receipts (mil dol)	Annual Payroll (mil dol)	Number of Establishments	Number of Employees	Sales (mil dol)	Annual Payroll (mil dol)
	147	148	149	150	151	152	153	154	155	156	157	158
TEXAS—Cont'd												
Guadalupe	64	204	13.8	4.8	90	5 592	1 320.3	150.4	127	D	D	D
Hale	38	151	9.7	2.7	32	D	D	D	67	923	25.9	6.9
Hall	3	3	0.2	0.0	NA	NA	NA	NA	10	D	D	D
Hamilton	17	37	2.3	0.5	NA	NA	NA	NA	13	103	2.6	0.7
Hansford	6	19	1.3	0.5	NA	NA	NA	NA	11	D	D	D
Hardeman	7	10	0.4	0.1	NA	NA	NA	NA	10	D	D	D
Hardin	38	245	15.3	4.8	37	1 016	173.1	30.0	50	538	16.4	4.5
Harris	9 944	106 124	15 512.9	5 478.2	4 374	158 572	73 227.7	5 991.2	5 470	111 869	4 379.0	1 160.7
Harrison	86	506	83.6	27.3	90	3 128	600.4	83.2	75	1 017	35.1	9.3
Hartley	4	D	D	D	NA	NA	NA	NA	4	15	0.3	0.1
Haskell	7	13	0.6	0.1	NA	NA	NA	NA	8	97	2.3	0.7
Hays	140	459	42.9	14.1	108	3 389	477.0	96.2	177	2 890	88.4	25.4
Hemphill	7	14	1.4	0.2	NA	NA	NA	NA	12	69	1.4	0.3
Henderson	70	220	17.9	6.0	49	1 880	214.3	38.3	95	1 389	40.7	10.3
Hidalgo	482	2 682	193.4	62.7	261	10 284	1 428.2	178.3	626	10 871	352.1	90.1
Hill	29	89	6.2	1.5	37	1 237	174.4	30.7	67	785	25.3	6.4
Hockley	23	148	9.9	3.2	NA	NA	NA	NA	38	544	13.3	3.5
Hood	48	136	11.6	3.0	NA	NA	NA	NA	74	966	28.1	7.6
Hopkins	36	148	11.2	4.2	43	1 463	526.1	41.4	56	747	25.5	7.4
Houston	27	112	4.8	1.5	24	618	131.8	13.3	27	231	7.2	2.0
Howard	41	125	9.3	3.1	27	1 124	726.2	34.6	73	981	24.2	6.7
Hudspeth	NA	NA	NA	NA	NA	NA	NA	NA	5	35	1.4	0.2
Hunt	67	422	24.2	8.4	58	7 223	1 478.9	256.0	117	1 729	50.9	15.1
Hutchinson	24	115	7.4	2.7	30	1 718	1 949.1	89.1	48	578	15.1	4.0
Irion	1	D	D	D	NA	NA	NA	NA	5	D	D	D
Jack	12	27	1.2	0.5	NA	NA	NA	NA	11	D	D	D
Jackson	13	50	2.7	1.2	11	D	D	D	18	205	7.0	1.5
Jasper	32	126	10.3	1.9	29	1 911	543.2	76.6	49	714	21.6	5.6
Jeff Davis	1	D	D	D	NA	NA	NA	NA	12	138	4.5	1.3
Jefferson	469	4 143	490.9	204.3	230	14 471	15 920.2	727.0	426	8 206	261.9	69.9
Jim Hogg	3	14	0.7	0.3	NA	NA	NA	NA	14	106	3.0	0.9
Jim Wells	44	321	23.1	9.9	NA	NA	NA	NA	68	823	25.6	6.6
Johnson	113	499	39.3	12.2	170	5 942	981.4	161.3	134	1 885	60.2	16.6
Jones	13	46	2.2	0.8	NA	NA	NA	NA	24	119	3.7	1.0
Karnes	13	48	2.5	0.6	NA	NA	NA	NA	23	192	5.1	1.3
Kaufman	68	206	14.1	4.8	109	4 274	521.3	120.4	91	1 342	39.9	10.7
Kendall	57	158	11.6	3.9	NA	NA	NA	NA	50	858	27.7	8.5
Kenedy	1	D	D	D	NA	NA	NA	NA	1	D	D	D
Kent	NA	NA	NA	NA	NA	NA	NA	NA	1	D	D	D
Kerr	104	390	35.4	11.6	49	960	92.9	24.9	100	1 417	54.3	15.3
Kimble	7	43	1.7	0.5	NA	NA	NA	NA	27	212	6.7	1.9
King	NA	NA	NA	NA	NA	NA	NA	NA	1	D	D	D
Kinney	1	D	D	D	NA	NA	NA	NA	3	18	0.4	0.1
Kleberg	23	80	4.9	1.4	NA	NA	NA	NA	74	1 048	31.6	8.5
Knox	3	15	0.6	0.2	NA	NA	NA	NA	13	D	D	D
Lamar	52	243	13.6	4.3	60	4 809	2 056.3	161.0	96	1 466	45.9	13.0
Lamb	13	18	1.1	0.2	14	678	123.6	16.7	27	D	D	D
Lampasas	17	65	2.8	1.0	NA	NA	NA	NA	28	D	D	D
La Salle	3	8	0.7	0.1	NA	NA	NA	NA	8	93	3.4	0.9
Lavaca	28	100	19.9	2.2	46	2 127	192.5	37.2	32	375	9.2	2.6
Lee	24	87	6.4	2.5	NA	NA	NA	NA	24	252	8.2	2.1
Leon	15	42	2.4	0.7	NA	NA	NA	NA	24	385	9.3	2.6
Liberty	70	274	24.0	6.9	41	1 220	209.8	36.1	65	984	32.9	8.5
Limestone	22	48	3.4	0.9	17	790	80.1	15.4	33	290	9.7	2.4
Lipscomb	9	18	1.3	0.3	NA	NA	NA	NA	4	D	D	D
Live Oak	13	37	1.9	0.6	NA	NA	NA	NA	29	278	9.5	2.2
Llano	21	72	4.2	1.8	NA	NA	NA	NA	47	298	10.5	2.8
Loving	NA	NA	NA	NA	NA	NA	NA	NA	NA	NA	NA	NA
Lubbock	483	2 516	198.6	67.7	258	7 286	1 566.4	203.8	522	11 154	332.1	87.6
Lynn	4	13	0.4	0.2	NA	NA	NA	NA	7	48	1.0	0.3
McCulloch	17	95	6.7	2.4	NA	NA	NA	NA	23	181	7.1	1.6
McLennan	292	2 039	133.0	57.4	261	16 474	3 855.6	481.7	400	6 900	220.7	59.8
McMullen	1	D	D	D	NA	NA	NA	NA	2	D	D	D
Madison	15	60	4.5	1.3	NA	NA	NA	NA	19	213	7.9	2.1
Marion	4	8	0.8	0.1	NA	NA	NA	NA	35	185	5.0	1.3
Martin	4	11	0.7	0.3	NA	NA	NA	NA	4	28	0.6	0.2

1. Firms subject to federal tax.

STATE County	Health Care and Social Assistance[1], 1997				Other Services[1], 1997				Federal funds and grants, fiscal 2001[2] Expenditures (mil dol)			
										Direct payments for individuals[3]		
	Number of Establishments	Number of Employees	Receipts (mil dol)	Annual Payroll (mil dol)	Number of Establishments	Number of Employees	Receipts (mil dol)	Annual Payroll (mil dol)	Total	Social Security and government retirement	Medicare	Food stamps and Supplemental Security Income
	159	160	161	162	163	164	165	166	167	168	169	170
TEXAS—Cont'd												
Guadalupe	109	1 150	55.9	23.4	76	453	25.7	7.5	362.6	227.8	47.6	9.2
Hale	51	496	26.1	9.1	67	234	13.6	3.5	235.3	62.3	37.7	6.7
Hall	5	89	2.4	0.8	1	D	D	D	55.3	9.6	6.2	0.8
Hamilton	18	306	12.7	6.3	13	27	3.1	0.6	48.9	21.4	13.9	0.9
Hansford	4	D	D	D	14	53	3.6	1.2	51.0	10.8	4.4	0.5
Hardeman	11	83	3.3	1.0	8	22	2.2	0.4	45.4	12.5	7.0	0.7
Hardin	66	1 589	49.3	22.7	46	248	12.9	2.9	186.3	97.7	48.3	5.9
Harris	6 996	92 982	6 784.1	2 802.4	5 209	45 636	3 189.5	978.4	15 616.5	3 977.3	2 001.8	554.5
Harrison	89	946	46.6	19.0	74	369	28.9	7.1	290.4	113.6	50.3	10.9
Hartley	9	42	2.6	0.9	7	42	4.3	0.7	32.2	2.2	0.8	0.1
Haskell	12	163	6.0	2.3	14	65	3.2	0.7	72.4	17.9	9.6	1.0
Hays	135	1 412	77.9	32.7	93	434	22.2	5.9	355.5	142.5	38.3	6.6
Hemphill	3	17	1.1	0.5	6	12	1.5	0.3	13.1	6.1	3.5	0.2
Henderson	86	1 201	63.7	31.8	68	255	13.9	3.7	273.1	142.8	61.8	9.4
Hidalgo	833	15 858	1 167.0	431.0	479	2 465	114.3	30.6	2 151.8	536.9	322.6	204.4
Hill	29	533	30.0	10.4	44	172	9.5	2.5	186.0	84.0	35.3	5.1
Hockley	28	331	14.3	5.9	29	87	5.9	1.3	155.0	40.2	22.2	2.3
Hood	70	595	31.8	14.1	56	319	13.3	4.3	200.5	130.6	34.3	3.2
Hopkins	63	692	35.5	12.0	56	244	13.8	3.5	146.1	66.5	33.5	4.4
Houston	29	880	23.7	11.2	27	126	8.9	2.1	146.7	56.0	29.1	5.4
Howard	60	1 000	63.6	24.7	55	265	11.9	3.4	279.9	77.4	41.9	6.5
Hudspeth	NA	NA	NA	NA	3	5	0.3	0.1	45.9	4.3	2.1	0.4
Hunt	111	1 607	79.5	34.2	90	320	20.4	4.7	824.6	158.0	70.3	12.3
Hutchinson	39	769	31.5	12.5	33	219	17.3	3.8	106.0	54.7	23.2	2.8
Irion	NA	NA	NA	NA	NA	NA	NA	NA	7.2	3.5	1.4	0.2
Jack	7	74	2.8	1.1	9	12	1.1	0.2	31.3	16.0	8.0	0.7
Jackson	13	237	8.5	3.2	20	70	4.4	1.4	100.0	27.2	17.3	1.5
Jasper	65	1 412	42.3	21.7	47	238	12.1	3.6	186.9	77.9	45.4	7.5
Jeff Davis	5	15	0.8	0.2	NA	NA	NA	NA	16.6	5.0	1.6	0.3
Jefferson	707	11 019	681.3	287.9	471	3 318	188.7	56.0	1 690.7	510.4	322.8	54.4
Jim Hogg	3	73	1.4	0.9	3	6	0.5	0.1	47.2	8.3	7.6	1.8
Jim Wells	72	2 680	95.2	42.9	60	320	16.0	4.4	212.2	74.5	46.6	6.5
Johnson	135	1 711	82.7	38.2	145	633	43.2	10.7	419.1	242.3	87.7	11.3
Jones	17	362	13.4	4.9	15	35	2.6	0.5	128.2	40.1	20.3	2.6
Karnes	17	214	7.2	3.0	17	61	3.4	0.7	84.2	27.7	16.8	3.6
Kaufman	120	1 868	91.8	37.5	96	671	56.1	14.7	341.4	177.7	81.3	10.5
Kendall	40	527	19.8	9.2	37	153	8.2	2.7	121.7	84.3	17.5	1.1
Kenedy	NA	NA	NA	NA	NA	NA	NA	NA	1.4	0.5	0.3	0.0
Kent	NA	NA	NA	NA	NA	NA	NA	NA	9.1	2.6	1.1	0.1
Kerr	106	1 446	79.0	31.7	90	458	28.8	8.5	273.4	174.0	49.5	5.0
Kimble	3	D	D	D	7	29	1.6	0.4	21.8	11.0	4.7	1.0
King	NA	NA	NA	NA	NA	NA	NA	NA	3.5	0.3	0.2	0.0
Kinney	1	D	D	D	NA	NA	NA	NA	24.9	11.4	3.7	0.9
Kleberg	52	503	26.4	11.1	48	212	9.8	2.6	294.4	53.8	24.4	8.1
Knox	8	161	5.7	3.0	10	41	3.5	0.8	43.3	10.6	7.2	0.8
Lamar	148	2 772	101.2	46.8	84	394	18.9	5.2	264.9	111.3	48.4	10.1
Lamb	13	178	5.3	2.3	27	62	4.0	0.9	128.4	30.1	19.2	2.8
Lampasas	20	407	15.2	8.5	16	81	4.4	1.3	100.2	62.0	19.0	1.9
La Salle	5	D	D	D	7	24	1.4	0.2	53.5	9.1	5.5	2.0
Lavaca	34	354	15.4	6.2	32	107	6.9	1.7	125.0	56.8	29.6	2.0
Lee	21	178	8.1	2.8	24	75	6.0	1.2	60.4	27.1	11.0	2.0
Leon	16	192	7.8	3.5	20	59	3.2	0.7	103.9	49.5	20.9	2.1
Liberty	87	1 635	90.7	33.2	61	317	15.9	4.5	302.8	128.2	79.1	8.5
Limestone	31	456	17.0	6.6	25	65	4.9	1.2	118.6	51.8	22.8	4.2
Lipscomb	2	D	D	D	5	30	0.7	0.4	19.1	6.6	3.2	0.2
Live Oak	9	170	6.9	2.3	18	49	3.2	0.6	91.3	18.7	10.2	1.3
Llano	21	322	13.5	6.6	13	35	1.6	0.6	97.9	66.4	21.6	1.0
Loving	NA	NA	NA	NA	1	D	D	D	0.6	0.2	0.0	0.0
Lubbock	622	8 383	566.2	239.1	405	3 053	178.4	53.2	1 495.8	420.4	237.1	41.5
Lynn	4	9	0.5	0.2	7	20	1.3	0.3	100.8	12.4	8.0	1.3
McCulloch	12	261	8.9	4.8	17	63	2.8	0.6	55.0	21.3	12.2	1.5
McLennan	353	4 861	265.9	126.4	329	2 065	114.1	34.4	1 096.2	470.4	130.0	34.8
McMullen	NA	NA	NA	NA	NA	NA	NA	NA	4.0	1.6	0.5	0.0
Madison	13	235	6.8	3.5	10	78	12.4	1.7	46.4	21.8	9.0	1.9
Marion	10	177	4.9	2.4	16	43	2.1	0.5	68.4	25.7	9.9	3.0
Martin	7	92	4.5	1.6	5	D	D	D	70.1	7.8	4.5	1.2

1. Firms subject to federal tax.   2. October 1, 2000 to September 30, 2001.   3. State totals may include programs not allocated by county.

	Federal funds and grants, fiscal 2001[1] (cont'd)							Local government finances, 1997				
	Expenditures (mil dol) (cont'd)							General revenue				
	Procurement contract awards			Grants[2]						Taxes		
											Per capita[3] (dollars)	
STATE County	Salaries and wages	Defense	Other	Medicaid and other health-related	Nutrition and family welfare	Education	Other	Total (mil dol)	Intergovern-mental (mil dol)	Total (mil dol)	Total	Property
	171	172	173	174	175	176	177	178	179	180	181	182
TEXAS—Cont'd												
Guadalupe	12.2	0.9	2.2	33.4	5.2	2.5	9.5	116.9	53.9	47.7	612	504
Hale	6.2	0.0	1.9	26.0	4.7	1.9	25.7	82.0	40.8	27.4	750	527
Hall	1.1	0.0	0.2	4.6	0.5	0.3	12.1	10.3	4.5	3.8	1 037	869
Hamilton	1.8	0.0	0.4	5.1	0.2	0.3	2.6	13.6	7.5	4.4	580	465
Hansford	0.9	0.0	0.2	1.0	0.2	0.2	4.4	24.4	4.3	13.2	2 442	2 299
Hardeman	0.9	0.0	0.2	4.5	0.5	0.2	9.6	14.8	4.2	6.5	1 374	1 155
Hardin	3.3	0.0	1.0	20.8	3.0	1.7	1.9	78.2	41.3	26.3	544	486
Harris	1 489.2	869.9	3 654.8	1 390.4	289.8	174.5	479.5	8 382.8	2 056.8	4 158.1	1 317	1 038
Harrison	7.8	3.4	6.2	58.3	6.8	4.8	13.7	102.5	29.4	50.4	844	806
Hartley	0.3	0.0	0.1	0.2	0.1	0.1	2.5	4.1	1.2	2.6	511	444
Haskell	1.5	0.0	0.4	5.1	0.5	0.3	9.1	14.8	6.3	5.6	914	783
Hays	10.8	3.1	62.5	32.2	8.5	7.6	25.5	167.7	58.2	70.2	814	633
Hemphill	0.6	0.0	0.1	0.4	0.2	0.1	0.1	15.9	0.7	10.6	2 938	2 750
Henderson	6.3	0.0	1.6	35.5	3.0	1.9	3.9	112.7	47.7	47.6	707	578
Hidalgo	122.1	72.3	33.3	421.2	101.5	66.3	134.3	1 210.8	769.1	282.0	552	421
Hill	5.3	1.8	2.5	24.3	1.9	1.4	5.3	68.4	32.7	20.9	696	490
Hockley	2.5	0.0	0.7	11.1	7.1	1.6	12.7	88.8	28.1	36.8	1 540	1 450
Hood	5.7	2.7	1.5	5.8	1.1	0.8	14.1	69.0	20.0	27.5	760	637
Hopkins	4.9	0.0	1.2	21.7	2.2	1.0	6.4	69.2	20.0	21.1	691	541
Houston	3.9	5.8	2.5	31.3	2.2	1.3	2.9	32.6	16.5	12.6	575	468
Howard	37.7	24.8	7.2	22.9	3.2	1.8	14.4	90.2	28.5	32.3	992	772
Hudspeth	4.2	5.4	0.1	0.4	0.4	0.3	26.2	12.5	4.7	3.3	993	905
Hunt	18.7	461.1	30.8	44.4	4.7	2.9	6.0	165.1	63.7	51.2	739	585
Hutchinson	3.7	0.0	1.7	6.8	0.7	0.9	2.0	60.3	15.4	27.4	1 144	942
Irion	0.3	0.0	0.1	0.6	0.0	0.1	0.1	5.9	0.4	4.5	2 657	2 548
Jack	1.1	0.0	0.3	2.7	0.3	0.3	1.3	19.5	6.5	7.1	974	817
Jackson	1.7	0.0	0.4	9.1	1.5	0.5	8.1	44.4	10.7	13.8	1 014	861
Jasper	4.3	1.5	0.9	29.9	3.8	1.4	7.7	74.4	33.6	29.4	886	751
Jeff Davis	1.1	0.0	0.3	1.2	0.1	0.2	6.2	3.9	1.9	1.8	825	735
Jefferson	151.6	254.8	71.0	148.5	28.9	11.8	31.1	553.3	112.3	332.6	1 375	1 041
Jim Hogg	3.2	0.0	0.1	11.4	0.9	0.4	12.1	12.5	5.3	6.3	1 270	1 218
Jim Wells	6.1	0.0	0.9	50.5	9.8	2.3	1.3	76.4	41.5	24.0	602	425
Johnson	13.9	0.1	3.5	30.0	3.8	3.1	13.0	184.3	83.8	70.6	619	530
Jones	2.9	0.1	0.6	11.5	1.5	0.7	16.5	43.1	21.7	10.0	529	415
Karnes	1.9	0.0	0.5	23.7	4.0	1.0	1.3	33.7	16.1	9.9	792	656
Kaufman	10.8	0.0	2.8	26.6	4.6	3.2	7.9	122.6	64.1	43.7	684	560
Kendall	3.4	9.0	1.5	2.7	0.5	0.6	0.2	38.4	9.5	23.4	1 145	994
Kenedy	0.2	0.0	0.2	0.2	0.0	0.0	0.0	2.7	0.0	2.6	6 077	6 000
Kent	0.3	0.0	0.0	0.8	0.1	0.0	0.5	11.9	0.2	10.7	12 446	12 311
Kerr	24.7	1.8	1.3	9.5	1.6	1.8	0.4	66.9	19.9	35.8	839	654
Kimble	0.8	0.0	0.2	1.9	0.4	0.2	0.0	13.4	3.4	3.0	703	557
King	0.2	0.0	0.0	0.0	0.0	0.0	0.3	3.7	0.0	3.1	8 945	8 546
Kinney	4.8	0.0	0.0	2.7	0.4	0.2	0.0	6.8	3.7	2.3	655	557
Kleberg	44.8	101.3	1.1	24.3	4.9	4.1	1.2	67.6	30.1	26.0	860	710
Knox	1.4	0.2	0.5	4.9	0.6	0.3	3.0	20.2	7.3	3.7	848	715
Lamar	9.0	0.7	2.1	54.4	4.1	2.7	4.0	84.8	37.7	34.6	756	636
Lamb	2.1	0.0	0.8	11.7	1.4	1.0	8.6	41.3	14.7	17.3	1 164	1 055
Lampasas	2.4	0.1	0.6	7.0	1.3	0.9	2.7	27.3	14.7	8.4	482	382
La Salle	2.5	0.0	0.1	12.5	1.3	0.4	17.8	15.9	7.9	4.1	697	586
Lavaca	3.3	0.0	0.8	25.5	1.2	0.3	0.9	24.6	6.6	12.1	649	553
Lee	1.8	0.0	0.5	8.0	0.7	0.5	7.1	25.2	10.1	11.6	786	665
Leon	2.9	0.0	0.8	20.8	0.9	0.5	2.9	25.7	9.1	14.3	988	864
Liberty	6.8	0.0	1.8	33.6	7.9	2.1	9.0	99.2	41.9	44.2	691	586
Limestone	3.6	0.1	1.2	24.7	1.8	0.9	3.2	51.9	15.0	28.3	1 343	1 229
Lipscomb	1.1	0.0	0.2	0.8	0.1	0.1	0.4	10.9	2.0	7.2	2 390	2 240
Live Oak	14.6	32.2	1.4	6.0	0.5	0.4	1.3	20.2	4.3	13.3	1 310	1 216
Llano	2.1	0.0	0.6	4.5	0.1	0.3	0.1	33.5	1.6	14.7	1 125	1 033
Loving	0.2	0.0	0.0	0.0	0.0	0.0	0.0	1.3	0.0	1.1	10 094	9 962
Lubbock	74.1	8.7	16.3	100.0	22.5	11.6	57.7	644.4	274.3	179.0	776	586
Lynn	1.1	0.0	0.3	5.4	0.9	0.5	12.5	17.9	9.1	5.6	849	759
McCulloch	1.7	0.0	0.3	8.9	0.8	0.5	2.6	23.5	10.9	5.6	640	491
McLennan	108.1	48.8	13.4	128.5	18.3	9.9	33.7	607.1	185.8	162.8	802	575
McMullen	0.2	0.5	0.1	0.2	0.1	0.0	0.2	5.3	0.0	4.4	5 589	5 381
Madison	1.3	0.0	0.4	8.7	0.9	0.5	1.3	18.7	7.8	7.2	602	465
Marion	2.5	4.0	0.4	15.4	1.7	0.6	0.8	14.2	6.0	7.0	654	420
Martin	0.8	0.0	0.2	3.9	1.0	0.3	9.7	15.7	6.5	6.8	1 349	1 246

1. October 1, 2000 to September 30, 2001. 2. State totals may include programs not allocated by county. 3. Based on the resident population estimated as of July 1 of the year shown.

STATE County	Local government finances, 1997 (cont'd)									Government employment, 1999			Presidential election, 2000[2]		
	Direct general expenditure							Debt outstanding					Percent of vote cast —		
			Percent of total for —												
	Total (mil dol)	Per capita[1] (dollars)	Educa-tion	Health and hospitals	Police protec-tion	Public welfare	High-ways	Total (mil dol)	Per capita[1] (dollars)	Federal civilian	Federal military	State and local	Demo-cratic	Republi-can	All other
	183	184	185	186	187	188	189	190	191	192	193	194	195	196	197
TEXAS—Cont'd															
Guadalupe	119.6	1 534	68.7	0.8	4.2	0.1	3.9	75.0	962	183	217	4 280	27.2	70.3	2.5
Hale	76.1	2 079	58.1	10.1	7.9	0.6	3.0	8.7	238	128	96	2 518	23.7	75.4	0.9
Hall	9.4	2 539	62.7	7.2	3.3	0.1	4.3	3.7	1 006	28	0	340	32.6	66.8	0.5
Hamilton	13.2	1 736	79.6	0.0	4.2	0.0	5.3	6.0	789	32	20	530	26.0	72.5	1.5
Hansford	16.3	3 013	53.9	22.5	2.4	0.0	6.3	21.7	4 026	22	14	534	9.5	89.8	0.8
Hardeman	15.0	3 197	46.7	28.4	2.7	0.1	6.4	1.6	350	23	12	427	36.4	62.7	0.9
Hardin	79.8	1 649	77.3	0.7	3.1	0.6	3.9	34.0	703	80	130	2 274	31.4	67.1	1.5
Harris	8 165.3	2 586	44.5	9.4	7.0	0.3	3.5	15 724.2	4 979	24 466	9 669	196 729	42.9	54.3	2.9
Harrison	94.7	1 587	68.3	0.2	4.3	0.6	2.4	83.2	1 395	125	157	3 007	38.7	60.2	1.1
Hartley	4.4	852	66.6	0.1	4.1	0.0	8.9	0.8	151	11	14	465	17.7	81.0	1.3
Haskell	14.7	2 409	60.8	14.5	1.7	0.3	8.0	0.4	60	36	16	481	47.9	50.8	1.3
Hays	185.0	2 144	53.1	0.5	3.6	1.3	5.6	285.0	3 303	146	250	9 032	33.2	58.8	8.0
Hemphill	17.1	4 735	47.9	25.4	3.4	0.0	9.5	2.4	672	15	0	341	17.0	81.6	1.4
Henderson	110.7	1 644	74.0	0.1	5.7	0.3	4.8	63.4	941	103	186	2 837	34.0	64.8	1.2
Hidalgo	1 109.5	2 172	72.7	2.8	3.5	0.7	1.7	572.4	1 120	2 653	1 414	36 641	60.8	37.9	1.4
Hill	75.8	2 523	73.5	5.3	3.0	0.0	3.7	38.4	1 279	95	82	1 986	32.8	65.7	1.4
Hockley	86.2	3 604	73.4	0.6	2.0	0.3	2.4	137.2	5 734	58	61	1 685	21.0	77.8	1.1
Hood	67.9	1 876	52.2	24.8	2.9	0.0	3.2	50.8	1 404	95	102	1 549	26.9	71.0	2.2
Hopkins	65.2	2 136	46.9	28.1	4.3	0.0	4.9	24.1	788	99	80	1 930	33.8	64.9	1.4
Houston	30.2	1 381	73.8	0.1	4.4	0.0	5.2	16.8	769	85	58	2 088	34.4	64.4	1.1
Howard	88.3	2 712	60.6	1.5	3.9	2.4	3.1	224.8	6 904	783	83	2 916	28.7	69.8	1.4
Hudspeth	10.6	3 186	58.5	0.1	4.2	0.1	5.8	2.6	782	74	0	291	41.2	55.7	3.0
Hunt	167.8	2 421	46.8	25.4	3.8	0.0	4.0	109.8	1 585	306	246	6 091	32.1	66.1	1.8
Hutchinson	62.3	2 599	56.1	14.9	3.9	0.4	3.7	9.3	390	74	62	1 721	19.2	79.6	1.2
Irion	3.9	2 301	79.5	0.2	1.5	0.2	4.7	0.0	23	0	0	125	20.4	78.7	0.9
Jack	18.2	2 482	61.7	10.2	3.6	0.0	7.4	11.3	1 543	20	20	519	27.6	70.8	1.5
Jackson	41.3	3 027	50.7	13.7	3.1	0.0	5.3	69.8	5 110	36	36	1 056	29.8	69.3	0.9
Jasper	69.1	2 081	68.4	6.5	3.7	0.2	4.8	26.9	809	84	88	2 057	38.6	60.2	1.1
Jeff Davis	4.1	1 839	76.5	0.1	2.9	1.2	2.8	0.2	76	27	0	228	26.7	66.8	6.5
Jefferson	565.5	2 337	46.5	3.4	6.6	0.5	5.4	777.7	3 214	2 656	762	16 650	52.2	46.4	1.3
Jim Hogg	12.1	2 465	63.2	0.0	6.7	1.9	5.4	7.5	1 516	55	13	451	70.1	28.9	1.0
Jim Wells	70.4	1 767	71.1	0.1	4.1	0.8	3.8	19.6	492	90	144	2 159	61.7	37.4	0.9
Johnson	204.2	1 790	67.1	0.1	3.9	1.3	4.2	154.7	1 357	229	322	5 089	30.4	67.7	1.9
Jones	39.1	2 081	60.1	15.5	4.3	0.0	5.1	6.1	324	98	51	2 586	31.4	67.5	1.1
Karnes	28.5	2 283	65.7	11.3	2.8	0.2	2.2	8.8	707	37	40	1 665	37.5	61.2	1.3
Kaufman	120.4	1 885	76.2	0.0	3.9	0.7	2.6	64.1	1 003	175	179	4 386	32.3	66.3	1.4
Kendall	40.8	2 003	72.0	0.6	4.6	0.1	4.0	30.6	1 501	53	57	1 191	17.2	79.4	3.5
Kenedy	2.1	4 806	93.5	0.1	0.7	0.1	2.1	0.0	0	0	0	79	52.2	46.5	1.3
Kent	11.2	13 006	72.6	1.1	2.4	2.7	9.1	0.0	0	0	0	200	34.5	64.5	0.9
Kerr	60.3	1 415	60.8	0.6	6.3	0.9	4.2	40.5	950	568	114	2 702	20.8	76.1	3.1
Kimble	13.4	3 196	34.9	21.6	2.4	0.1	3.9	1.8	428	17	11	327	19.7	78.8	1.5
King	3.3	9 474	68.7	0.0	2.2	0.0	11.0	0.0	0	0	0	54	10.2	67.6	2.2
Kinney	6.4	1 840	67.7	0.0	1.7	2.2	1.6	2.9	829	72	0	247	33.7	64.5	1.8
Kleberg	67.1	2 219	57.7	1.2	7.4	2.6	3.8	20.9	692	641	669	3 658	48.7	49.2	2.0
Knox	17.7	4 108	48.0	25.2	2.5	0.0	3.0	2.3	542	39	11	416	39.1	60.1	0.8
Lamar	85.1	1 860	74.6	0.6	3.5	0.4	4.0	33.8	739	162	121	2 902	36.0	63.4	0.5
Lamb	39.8	2 678	63.5	16.2	3.8	0.1	3.4	4.0	267	47	39	1 003	24.2	75.1	0.7
Lampasas	31.2	1 781	71.1	0.4	5.6	0.5	4.7	8.4	481	46	46	911	25.2	72.8	2.0
La Salle	15.4	2 603	56.9	2.3	4.2	0.0	6.9	2.5	424	36	16	502	62.9	36.3	0.8
Lavaca	25.0	1 337	51.3	5.3	6.1	0.4	7.7	6.3	337	59	50	839	28.8	70.1	1.2
Lee	30.7	2 072	70.6	0.5	4.3	0.1	5.4	17.4	1 179	33	39	1 180	31.3	66.8	1.9
Leon	24.3	1 682	73.4	0.0	2.4	0.6	7.0	11.9	823	51	39	692	29.9	69.0	1.1
Liberty	98.3	1 537	64.7	0.2	4.5	0.4	5.8	47.6	745	123	176	3 882	36.4	62.1	1.5
Limestone	48.8	2 320	66.5	9.7	5.0	0.3	4.6	12.0	568	62	54	2 871	39.1	59.5	1.3
Lipscomb	10.5	3 458	59.7	11.7	3.7	0.1	7.6	0.3	87	22	0	330	15.9	82.8	1.2
Live Oak	21.2	2 092	65.5	1.7	7.1	0.4	11.0	5.0	493	322	27	624	27.8	70.6	1.6
Llano	35.0	2 669	33.3	39.0	3.1	0.0	3.6	4.8	366	38	36	920	24.8	73.0	2.1
Loving	1.9	17 943	0.0	0.0	8.2	0.0	3.6	0.0	0	0	0	16	18.6	79.5	1.9
Lubbock	567.6	2 461	42.2	28.0	4.5	0.1	2.5	429.7	1 863	1 256	643	21 271	24.3	73.7	2.0
Lynn	17.3	2 622	67.1	13.7	3.7	0.1	3.3	2.4	359	27	17	515	27.0	72.3	0.7
McCulloch	22.3	2 540	52.7	17.6	3.3	0.8	2.3	13.8	1 569	32	23	656	27.2	71.4	1.4
McLennan	591.5	2 914	40.6	3.6	4.2	0.2	3.0	2 887.4	14 225	3 084	573	12 032	34.1	63.9	2.0
McMullen	3.6	4 564	63.4	0.0	3.2	0.5	17.4	0.0	5	0	0	116	17.5	81.5	0.9
Madison	16.7	1 399	71.7	0.0	4.7	0.4	7.5	15.4	1 293	24	31	1 187	34.3	64.4	1.3
Marion	12.9	1 208	68.8	0.5	6.8	0.0	5.9	4.6	429	34	29	432	47.1	51.9	1.0
Martin	15.2	2 999	51.2	24.7	2.4	0.1	7.7	1.6	321	23	13	380	21.3	78.0	0.7

1. Based on the resident population estimated as of July 1 of the year shown.   2. Data subject to copyright.

Table B. States and Counties — **Land Area and Population**

STATE/ County code	MSA/ PMSA/ NECMA code[1]	County Type[2]	STATE County	Land area[3] (sq km) 2000	Population and population characteristics, 2000			Race alone or in combination (percent)					Age (percent)					
					Total persons	Rank	Per square kilometer	White	Black	Am. Indian, Alaska Native	Asian and Pacific Islander	Percent Hispanic[4]	Under 5 years	5 to 17 years	18 to 24 years	25 to 34 years	35 to 44 years	45 to 54 years
				1	2	3	4	5	6	7	8	9	10	11	12	13	14	15
			TEXAS—Cont'd															
48 319	...	9	Mason	2 414	3 738	2 939	1.5	93.3	0.2	1.3	0.1	20.9	5.1	17.3	4.7	8.9	11.8	15.3
48 321	...	4	Matagorda	2 886	37 957	1 166	13.2	69.9	13.2	1.2	2.7	31.3	7.4	22.6	8.9	11.4	15.5	13.0
48 323	...	5	Maverick	3 315	47 297	961	14.3	73.6	0.4	1.5	0.6	95.0	10.0	27.0	9.2	13.6	13.0	10.8
48 325	...	6	Medina	3 439	39 304	1 130	11.4	82.0	2.4	1.2	0.6	45.5	7.2	21.8	8.4	13.6	15.1	12.8
48 327	...	6	Menard	2 336	2 360	3 035	1.0	88.4	0.7	0.8	0.6	31.7	4.7	19.6	5.3	8.3	13.6	14.3
48 329	5800	3	Midland	2 332	116 009	465	49.7	79.0	7.3	1.0	1.2	29.0	7.5	22.7	8.8	12.1	16.3	13.3
48 331	...	6	Milam	2 633	24 238	1 587	9.2	80.3	11.3	1.1	0.3	18.6	6.8	20.6	7.7	10.8	13.9	12.7
48 333	...	9	Mills	1 938	5 151	2 840	2.7	90.5	1.4	0.8	0.2	13.0	5.4	20.2	4.7	8.5	12.0	14.0
48 335	...	7	Mitchell	2 357	9 698	2 470	4.1	76.1	13.0	0.7	0.4	31.0	4.7	15.1	11.5	14.4	16.3	14.1
48 337	...	6	Montague	2 410	19 117	1 841	7.9	97.1	0.3	1.5	0.5	5.4	6.0	18.0	6.8	10.5	13.8	13.0
48 339	3360	1	Montgomery	2 704	293 768	193	108.6	89.9	3.7	1.0	1.5	12.6	7.7	21.8	8.0	13.3	17.3	14.4
48 341	...	6	Moore	2 330	20 121	1 785	8.6	66.3	0.8	1.4	1.2	47.5	9.3	24.3	9.2	14.1	14.3	11.0
48 343	...	6	Morris	659	13 048	2 228	19.8	72.7	24.4	1.1	0.4	3.7	5.9	19.3	7.8	10.1	14.2	13.8
48 345	...	9	Motley	2 562	1 426	3 096	0.6	88.7	4.2	1.3	0.3	12.1	5.9	18.1	6.0	8.0	13.1	12.8
48 347	...	5	Nacogdoches	2 452	59 203	812	24.1	76.3	17.0	0.8	1.0	11.2	6.5	17.5	20.0	12.2	12.5	11.6
48 349	...	4	Navarro	2 610	45 124	995	17.3	72.2	17.2	0.9	1.1	15.8	7.2	20.1	9.9	12.4	14.3	12.2
48 351	...	8	Newton	2 416	15 072	2 085	6.2	76.7	20.9	1.2	0.4	3.8	6.5	19.7	9.0	12.2	14.4	13.7
48 353	...	6	Nolan	2 362	15 802	2 032	6.7	80.3	5.1	0.8	0.5	28.0	6.7	20.4	8.5	11.4	14.0	12.9
48 355	1880	2	Nueces	2 165	313 645	182	144.9	74.8	4.6	1.1	1.7	55.8	7.7	20.7	10.5	13.4	15.5	13.1
48 357	...	7	Ochiltree	2 376	9 006	2 528	3.8	88.2	0.2	1.6	0.5	31.8	8.1	22.5	8.4	12.7	15.9	12.5
48 359	...	8	Oldham	3 887	2 185	3 052	0.6	91.7	2.2	1.5	0.7	11.0	6.5	28.5	7.2	9.6	13.7	14.2
48 361	0840	2	Orange	923	84 966	613	92.1	89.0	8.6	1.1	1.0	3.6	6.7	20.6	8.7	12.4	15.7	13.7
48 363	...	6	Palo Pinto	2 468	27 026	1 481	11.0	89.8	2.6	1.3	0.8	13.6	6.7	19.3	8.2	11.3	14.6	13.1
48 365	...	6	Panola	2 074	22 756	1 660	11.0	79.7	17.9	0.8	0.5	3.5	6.2	19.0	9.2	10.6	14.5	14.4
48 367	2800	1	Parker	2 340	88 495	590	37.8	93.9	1.9	1.3	0.5	7.0	6.3	21.2	7.9	12.1	17.6	14.7
48 369	...	7	Parmer	2 283	10 016	2 444	4.4	68.1	1.2	1.1	0.5	49.2	8.6	24.3	8.5	12.2	14.0	11.1
48 371	...	7	Pecos	12 338	16 809	1 967	1.4	78.3	4.5	0.9	0.8	61.1	6.6	21.1	13.8	13.0	14.2	12.0
48 373	...	6	Polk	2 738	41 133	1 077	15.0	80.8	13.4	2.3	0.5	9.4	5.9	17.0	8.1	12.8	14.0	12.4
48 375	0320	3	Potter	2 355	113 546	474	48.2	70.8	10.6	1.6	2.9	28.1	8.3	19.7	11.1	14.8	15.3	11.6
48 377	...	7	Presidio	9 986	7 304	2 655	0.7	85.8	0.4	0.5	0.2	84.4	7.8	24.9	8.3	11.9	13.0	11.2
48 379	...	8	Rains	601	9 139	2 518	15.2	93.2	3.1	1.4	0.4	5.5	5.6	18.2	7.4	10.6	14.5	14.3
48 381	0320	3	Randall	2 368	104 312	507	44.1	92.0	1.7	1.2	1.3	10.3	6.8	19.2	11.2	12.8	15.7	13.7
48 383	...	6	Reagan	3 044	3 326	2 970	1.1	66.4	3.4	0.7	0.5	49.5	8.2	26.0	7.6	12.0	16.1	12.8
48 385	...	9	Real	1 813	3 047	2 990	1.7	92.9	0.3	1.4	0.4	22.6	4.9	18.6	5.4	8.8	12.7	13.3
48 387	...	6	Red River	2 720	14 314	2 139	5.3	79.1	18.1	1.2	0.2	4.7	5.8	18.0	7.8	11.0	13.4	13.2
48 389	...	7	Reeves	6 827	13 137	2 219	1.9	81.8	2.2	0.7	0.5	73.4	7.0	22.9	11.3	11.9	13.2	11.8
48 391	...	6	Refugio	1 995	7 828	2 621	3.9	81.7	7.0	0.9	0.5	44.6	6.0	20.2	7.4	11.2	14.8	13.1
48 393	...	9	Roberts	2 393	887	3 116	0.4	97.5	0.3	0.9	0.7	3.2	5.0	20.1	4.8	8.2	16.6	18.5
48 395	...	6	Robertson	2 213	16 000	2 022	7.2	67.9	24.5	1.1	0.3	14.7	7.2	21.0	7.5	11.0	13.2	12.8
48 397	1920	1	Rockwall	334	43 080	1 035	129.0	90.4	3.4	0.8	1.7	11.1	7.5	22.6	7.0	12.4	18.7	14.7
48 399	...	6	Runnels	2 721	11 495	2 336	4.2	83.1	1.7	0.9	0.6	29.3	6.3	20.6	6.4	10.8	13.4	12.7
48 401	...	6	Rusk	2 392	47 372	960	19.8	75.9	19.5	0.7	0.4	8.4	6.1	18.8	8.3	12.0	15.8	13.6
48 403	...	9	Sabine	1 270	10 469	2 400	8.2	88.7	10.1	1.0	0.1	1.8	5.2	15.9	5.6	8.9	12.2	11.9
48 405	...	9	San Augustine	1 367	8 946	2 530	6.5	69.9	28.1	0.6	0.2	3.6	5.7	18.0	6.8	10.3	12.6	12.8
48 407	...	8	San Jacinto	1 478	22 246	1 683	15.1	84.8	12.9	1.2	0.5	4.9	6.0	19.1	7.4	10.4	14.6	13.8
48 409	1880	3	San Patricio	1 791	67 138	732	37.5	79.5	3.2	1.2	1.1	49.4	8.1	23.0	10.0	13.1	15.1	12.1
48 411	...	7	San Saba	2 938	6 186	2 763	2.1	85.5	2.8	1.3	0.2	21.5	5.3	22.6	8.2	9.0	14.4	12.6
48 413	...	8	Schleicher	3 394	2 935	2 996	0.9	78.8	1.8	0.3	0.3	43.5	6.2	21.8	7.3	9.5	14.4	14.7
48 415	...	7	Scurry	2 337	16 361	2 000	7.0	82.6	6.3	0.8	0.3	27.8	6.3	18.9	10.7	11.4	14.8	13.5
48 417	...	8	Shackelford	2 367	3 302	2 973	1.4	94.8	0.6	0.8	0.0	7.6	5.4	21.3	6.0	9.5	15.3	14.2
48 419	...	7	Shelby	2 057	25 224	1 557	12.3	73.5	19.7	0.7	0.9	9.9	7.0	19.6	8.8	12.1	13.7	12.3
48 421	...	9	Sherman	2 391	3 186	2 980	1.3	84.0	0.6	1.0	0.2	27.4	6.9	24.5	7.0	12.5	14.0	12.6
48 423	8640	3	Smith	2 405	174 706	312	72.6	73.9	19.4	0.9	1.0	11.2	7.1	19.5	9.8	12.9	14.5	12.9
48 425	...	8	Somervell	485	6 809	2 711	14.0	93.5	0.4	1.3	0.4	13.4	6.4	22.0	7.7	11.1	15.7	14.9
48 427	...	6	Starr	3 168	53 597	871	16.9	89.3	0.2	0.3	0.4	97.5	10.4	27.0	11.0	14.4	12.7	9.5
48 429	...	7	Stephens	2 317	9 674	2 471	4.2	88.2	3.1	0.8	0.3	14.7	5.6	18.8	9.1	11.2	14.4	12.8
48 431	...	8	Sterling	2 391	1 393	3 098	0.6	87.7	0.1	0.5	0.1	31.0	5.1	23.6	6.1	10.3	19.5	13.1
48 433	...	9	Stonewall	2 379	1 693	3 085	0.7	89.7	3.5	1.0	0.6	11.8	5.1	17.7	6.2	9.5	13.1	13.1
48 435	...	7	Sutton	3 765	4 077	2 911	1.1	90.4	0.5	0.4	0.4	51.7	7.2	21.6	6.7	12.6	15.1	15.3
48 437	...	6	Swisher	2 332	8 378	2 575	3.6	73.9	6.1	1.3	0.2	35.2	7.4	20.5	10.3	12.5	13.0	11.0
48 439	2800	0	Tarrant	2 236	1 446 219	20	646.8	73.4	13.3	1.1	4.3	19.7	8.0	20.1	10.0	16.3	17.2	12.9
48 441	0040	3	Taylor	2 371	126 555	428	53.4	82.7	7.4	1.2	1.9	17.6	7.2	19.4	13.8	13.1	14.7	11.5
48 443	...	9	Terrell	6 106	1 081	3 106	0.2	89.4	0.0	1.9	0.6	48.6	5.6	21.0	5.0	8.7	14.7	14.6
48 445	...	6	Terry	2 305	12 761	2 247	5.5	79.7	5.3	0.9	0.3	44.1	7.3	21.0	9.5	12.2	14.8	11.7
48 447	...	9	Throckmorton	2 363	1 850	3 076	0.8	93.9	0.1	1.0	0.1	9.4	5.5	19.7	5.7	8.4	14.4	11.7
48 449	...	7	Titus	1 063	28 118	1 447	26.5	71.6	11.0	0.9	0.7	28.3	8.6	21.7	9.8	14.2	13.7	11.3

1. MSA = Metropolitan Statistical Area. PMSA = Primary MSA. NECMA = New England County Metropolitan Area. See Appendix A for explanation of these concepts. See Appendix B for list of metropolitan areas identified by type, with component counties. 2. County typology code from the Economic Research Service of USDA. See Appendix A for definition. 3. Dry land or land partially or temporarily covered by water. 4. Hispanic persons may be of any race.

Table B. States and Counties — Population and Households

STATE County	Age (percent) (cont'd)				Population — change and components of change, 1990–2001							Households, 2000				
					Total persons		Percent change		Components of change, 2000–2001						Percent	
	55 to 64 years	65 to 74 years	75 years and over	Percent female	2001	1990	1990–2000	2000–2001	Births	Deaths	Net migration	Number	Percent change, 1990–2000	Persons per household	Female family householder[1]	One person
	16	17	18	19	20	21	22	23	24	25	26	27	28	29	30	31
TEXAS—Cont'd																
Mason	13.5	12.0	11.5	52.0	3 805	3 423	9.2	1.8	39	76	103	1 607	12.0	2.31	7.7	29.2
Matagorda	8.8	6.9	5.5	50.4	38 157	36 928	2.8	0.5	732	452	-68	13 901	5.6	2.70	12.7	25.1
Maverick	6.9	5.7	3.8	52.1	48 259	36 378	30.0	2.0	1 363	341	-63	13 089	34.2	3.60	16.0	12.9
Medina	8.7	6.8	5.6	48.6	40 246	27 312	43.9	2.4	689	363	617	12 880	41.4	2.91	11.1	18.2
Menard	12.2	10.8	11.2	50.1	2 324	2 252	4.8	-1.5	28	42	-24	990	5.7	2.34	8.8	30.4
Midland	7.6	6.5	5.1	51.7	116 318	106 611	8.8	0.3	2 465	1 047	-1 100	42 745	9.8	2.68	11.4	24.2
Milam	10.2	8.3	8.9	51.0	24 644	22 946	5.6	1.7	417	420	412	9 199	5.9	2.59	11.3	25.9
Mills	12.2	10.6	12.5	49.4	5 128	4 531	13.7	-0.4	78	91	-9	2 001	12.3	2.43	7.0	27.8
Mitchell	8.8	7.6	7.6	38.6	9 524	8 016	21.0	-1.8	139	138	-176	2 837	-7.1	2.48	11.4	27.5
Montague	12.0	10.4	9.4	52.0	19 156	17 274	10.7	0.2	293	402	156	7 770	13.3	2.41	8.8	27.1
Montgomery	8.7	5.2	3.4	50.4	315 418	182 201	61.2	7.4	5 459	2 347	18 073	103 296	62.5	2.83	9.5	18.3
Moore	7.2	6.0	4.5	49.8	20 140	17 865	12.6	0.1	462	167	-286	6 774	11.0	2.94	9.0	18.2
Morris	10.7	10.0	8.3	51.9	13 260	13 200	-1.2	1.6	210	240	242	5 215	4.6	2.47	14.1	25.8
Motley	12.4	12.6	11.1	49.6	1 338	1 532	-6.9	-6.2	16	26	-80	606	-6.3	2.35	8.7	25.7
Nacogdoches	7.6	6.3	5.8	51.8	58 874	54 753	8.1	-0.6	1 109	681	-755	22 006	9.4	2.49	11.8	27.6
Navarro	9.3	7.1	7.3	50.8	45 971	39 926	13.0	1.9	860	634	633	16 491	10.9	2.65	12.2	24.1
Newton	10.4	8.4	5.7	49.0	15 139	13 569	11.1	0.4	224	167	12	5 583	13.7	2.59	11.5	24.1
Nolan	9.7	8.5	7.9	51.4	15 266	16 594	-4.8	-3.4	287	251	-581	6 170	-0.2	2.48	12.6	27.1
Nueces	7.9	6.2	5.0	51.1	312 470	291 145	7.7	-0.4	6 733	3 033	-4 883	110 365	10.7	2.79	15.3	22.6
Ochiltree	8.2	6.7	5.0	50.1	9 053	9 128	-1.3	0.5	223	115	-61	3 261	-2.0	2.74	7.9	21.0
Oldham	8.9	6.8	4.4	48.1	2 149	2 278	-4.1	-1.6	36	29	-44	735	7.9	2.61	8.8	21.0
Orange	9.5	7.3	5.3	50.9	84 582	80 509	5.5	-0.5	1 484	1 061	-793	31 642	9.0	2.65	12.1	21.7
Palo Pinto	10.5	8.7	7.7	50.8	27 211	25 055	7.9	0.7	499	403	94	10 594	11.2	2.52	10.4	26.2
Panola	10.3	8.3	7.5	52.0	22 719	22 035	3.3	-0.2	357	328	-55	8 821	7.0	2.53	11.3	25.1
Parker	9.6	6.1	4.4	49.0	92 700	64 785	36.6	4.8	1 278	904	3 747	31 131	35.1	2.75	8.7	18.3
Parmer	8.6	6.1	6.6	50.5	9 674	9 863	1.6	-3.4	209	113	-451	3 322	2.5	2.97	8.3	19.3
Pecos	8.5	6.3	4.5	44.8	16 362	14 675	14.5	-2.7	281	158	-584	5 153	9.4	2.86	11.6	19.6
Polk	11.8	10.5	7.4	47.9	43 479	30 687	34.0	5.7	590	645	2 342	15 119	27.5	2.50	10.8	24.6
Potter	7.5	5.9	5.8	49.8	113 705	97 841	16.1	0.1	2 728	1 527	-1 065	40 760	9.1	2.61	15.0	27.6
Presidio	9.0	7.8	6.2	51.5	7 466	6 637	10.0	2.2	173	67	52	2 530	12.2	2.85	13.6	24.2
Rains	13.4	9.5	6.6	50.1	10 006	6 715	36.1	9.5	93	147	895	3 617	38.6	2.51	9.1	22.3
Randall	8.6	6.9	5.0	51.4	105 671	89 673	16.3	1.3	1 611	832	613	41 240	19.4	2.49	9.2	25.4
Reagan	7.1	5.8	4.5	49.9	3 214	4 514	-26.3	-3.4	64	27	-154	1 107	-18.5	2.96	7.2	19.8
Real	15.5	12.2	8.6	50.5	3 083	2 412	26.3	1.2	43	61	54	1 245	34.7	2.38	7.6	28.2
Red River	11.1	9.6	10.1	51.8	14 185	14 317	0.0	-0.9	221	274	-73	5 827	2.4	2.41	11.8	27.7
Reeves	9.2	7.2	5.4	47.2	12 772	15 852	-17.1	-2.8	263	154	-488	4 091	-15.4	2.93	12.4	21.6
Refugio	10.8	8.8	7.8	51.1	7 729	7 976	-1.9	-1.3	122	113	-108	2 985	1.6	2.59	12.8	24.6
Roberts	12.4	8.5	6.0	49.9	854	1 025	-13.5	-3.7	14	16	-32	362	-7.4	2.45	3.9	23.8
Robertson	10.3	8.4	8.5	52.4	15 929	15 511	3.2	-0.4	292	300	-56	6 179	6.7	2.55	15.5	26.9
Rockwall	8.5	4.8	3.7	49.8	47 983	25 604	68.3	11.4	776	335	4 333	14 530	64.4	2.92	8.0	14.4
Runnels	10.2	9.3	10.3	51.8	11 089	11 294	1.8	-3.5	187	178	-423	4 428	1.9	2.53	9.6	26.7
Rusk	9.7	8.0	7.6	49.0	47 384	43 735	8.3	0.0	743	663	-51	17 364	6.4	2.57	11.2	24.2
Sabine	15.3	14.3	10.7	51.7	10 524	9 586	9.2	0.5	156	228	122	4 485	12.5	2.31	8.7	27.0
San Augustine	12.3	11.3	10.0	52.1	8 772	7 999	11.8	-1.9	146	171	-151	3 575	16.3	2.43	13.5	27.0
San Jacinto	12.7	10.2	5.8	49.9	22 897	16 372	35.9	2.9	280	270	625	8 651	38.5	2.55	9.7	22.6
San Patricio	8.1	6.2	4.3	49.9	67 120	58 749	14.3	0.0	1 499	698	-817	22 093	17.7	2.97	12.7	18.7
San Saba	10.2	9.6	10.7	48.2	6 219	5 401	14.5	0.5	79	87	44	2 289	7.9	2.45	8.4	27.5
Schleicher	9.8	8.1	8.3	50.3	2 963	2 990	-1.8	1.0	43	37	20	1 115	6.1	2.59	7.5	25.4
Scurry	8.9	8.2	7.2	48.1	15 899	18 634	-12.2	-2.8	280	245	-506	5 756	-9.6	2.55	10.4	25.1
Shackelford	10.1	9.5	8.7	52.6	3 310	3 316	-0.4	0.2	58	65	17	1 300	-2.7	2.49	8.7	26.2
Shelby	10.0	8.5	8.0	52.0	25 347	22 034	14.5	0.5	461	416	91	9 595	13.2	2.59	12.9	25.4
Sherman	8.8	7.2	6.4	49.4	3 185	2 858	11.5	0.0	45	20	-24	1 124	6.7	2.76	6.0	21.5
Smith	9.2	7.5	6.6	52.1	178 855	151 309	15.5	2.4	3 335	2 230	3 044	65 692	15.7	2.59	12.3	24.7
Somervell	8.8	6.6	6.7	50.1	7 080	5 360	27.0	4.0	114	75	228	2 438	28.2	2.73	9.6	21.3
Starr	6.8	4.9	3.3	51.5	54 671	40 518	32.3	2.0	1 729	268	-398	14 410	39.5	3.69	17.4	11.3
Stephens	10.5	9.3	8.4	49.2	9 470	9 010	7.4	-2.1	148	151	-203	3 661	3.0	2.47	9.9	26.4
Sterling	7.7	7.4	7.3	50.9	1 336	1 438	-3.1	-4.1	14	19	-53	513	3.8	2.67	7.0	23.2
Stonewall	11.4	12.0	11.9	52.6	1 576	2 013	-15.9	-6.9	28	39	-108	713	-11.5	2.32	8.8	29.0
Sutton	9.1	7.6	4.8	50.1	4 046	4 135	-1.4	-0.8	80	44	-69	1 515	3.3	2.67	7.7	22.6
Swisher	9.4	8.7	7.2	47.8	8 106	8 133	3.0	-3.2	157	116	-322	2 925	-2.3	2.65	9.5	24.1
Tarrant	7.3	4.6	3.7	50.5	1 486 392	1 170 103	23.6	2.8	30 961	11 643	21 176	533 864	21.7	2.67	12.2	24.9
Taylor	7.8	6.5	5.9	51.5	124 024	119 655	5.8	-2.0	2 625	1 474	-3 717	47 274	9.2	2.54	11.5	25.7
Terrell	12.9	10.5	7.0	49.2	1 005	1 410	-23.3	-7.0	10	18	-71	443	-15.5	2.44	7.4	31.8
Terry	8.9	7.9	6.7	48.1	12 576	13 218	-3.5	-1.4	297	163	-326	4 278	-4.5	2.76	11.9	22.1
Throckmorton	14.0	9.9	10.6	50.7	1 757	1 880	-1.6	-5.0	21	38	-79	765	-3.2	2.39	8.2	28.0
Titus	8.2	6.2	6.4	50.6	27 995	24 009	17.1	-0.4	604	342	-395	9 552	12.3	2.88	11.4	22.1

1. No spouse present.

Table B. States and Counties — **Vital Statistics, Health Resources, and Crime**

STATE County	Births, average 1997–1999 Total	Births, average 1997–1999 Rate[1]	Deaths, average 1997–1999 Number Total	Deaths, average 1997–1999 Number Infant[2]	Deaths, average 1997–1999 Rate Total[1]	Deaths, average 1997–1999 Rate Infant[3]	Physicians,[4] 2000 Number	Physicians,[4] 2000 Rate[5]	Hospitals,[4] 1998 Number	Hospitals,[4] 1998 Beds Number	Hospitals,[4] 1998 Beds Rate[5]	Medicare enrollees 2000	Serious crimes known to police, 2000[6] Total Number	Serious crimes known to police, 2000[6] Total Rate[7]
	32	33	34	35	36	37	38	39	40	41	42	43	44	45
TEXAS—Cont'd														
Mason	36	9.7	59	NA	16.0	NA	2	54	0	0	0	900	13	348
Matagorda	608	16.1	357	NA	9.4	NA	31	82	2	68	179	5 132	2 204	5 807
Maverick	1 050	21.9	259	NA	5.4	NA	33	70	1	60	125	5 747	1 584	3 349
Medina	535	14.3	305	NA	8.2	NA	18	46	1	27	72	4 753	864	2 198
Menard	29	12.4	35	NA	15.3	NA	0	0	0	0	0	539	33	1 398
Midland	1 972	16.6	822	16	6.9	8.1	179	154	2	318	266	13 924	3 913	3 373
Milam	319	13.2	295	NA	12.2	NA	12	50	2	81	334	4 433	525	2 166
Mills	58	12.3	74	NA	15.6	NA	2	39	0	0	0	1 168	18	349
Mitchell	107	11.4	110	NA	11.7	NA	7	72	1	37	381	1 595	217	2 238
Montague	229	12.3	318	NA	17.2	NA	14	73	2	80	432	4 192	661	3 644
Montgomery	4 072	14.9	1 791	26	6.6	6.4	346	118	2	211	78	27 610	10 031	3 415
Moore	415	21.2	138	NA	7.1	NA	13	65	1	111	564	2 162	427	2 122
Morris	169	12.7	171	NA	12.9	NA	4	31	0	0	0	2 852	424	3 643
Motley	17	13.0	22	NA	17.0	NA	1	70	0	0	0	347	5	351
Nacogdoches	792	14.0	546	NA	9.7	NA	105	177	2	293	521	8 121	2 198	3 713
Navarro	638	15.3	514	NA	12.3	NA	54	120	1	134	321	7 389	1 994	4 419
Newton	173	12.1	142	NA	9.9	NA	3	20	0	0	0	2 113	136	902
Nolan	242	14.8	200	NA	12.2	NA	10	63	1	54	327	3 055	NA	NA
Nueces	5 355	16.9	2 365	33	7.5	6.1	747	238	8	1 549	490	39 090	22 527	7 182
Ochiltree	146	16.6	78	NA	8.9	NA	3	33	1	44	498	1 095	269	2 987
Oldham	26	11.7	22	NA	10.2	NA	0	0	0	0	0	358	26	1 190
Orange	1 144	13.5	819	11	9.6	9.3	48	56	1	136	160	12 461	3 562	4 192
Palo Pinto	386	14.9	323	NA	12.5	NA	20	74	1	44	171	4 545	1 028	3 804
Panola	282	12.2	244	NA	10.6	NA	7	31	1	30	130	3 674	628	2 760
Parker	1 003	12.2	667	NA	8.1	NA	45	51	1	80	98	9 638	1 991	2 250
Parmer	176	17.0	91	NA	8.8	NA	4	40	1	26	252	1 266	108	1 248
Pecos	233	14.5	111	NA	6.9	NA	8	48	2	37	231	1 862	412	2 451
Polk	505	10.1	499	NA	10.0	NA	21	51	1	28	56	12 272	954	2 319
Potter	2 023	18.6	1 186	23	10.9	11.2	387	341	3	927	851	22 555	8 255	7 270
Presidio	146	17.0	46	NA	5.3	NA	1	14	0	0	0	1 304	47	643
Rains	86	10.0	101	NA	11.7	NA	2	22	0	0	0	1 334	251	2 746
Randall	1 353	13.6	640	8	6.5	5.7	100	96	2	99	99	4 930	6 451	6 184
Reagan	75	18.4	27	NA	6.6	NA	3	90	1	61	1 451	367	32	962
Real	33	12.2	48	NA	18.0	NA	2	66	0	0	0	763	28	919
Red River	162	11.8	205	NA	14.9	NA	6	42	1	36	262	3 061	293	2 047
Reeves	225	15.7	115	NA	8.1	NA	7	53	1	46	318	1 846	408	3 106
Refugio	98	12.5	88	NA	11.3	NA	3	38	1	20	253	1 479	148	1 891
Roberts	8	8.1	10	NA	10.6	NA	1	113	0	0	0	124	17	1 917
Robertson	240	15.4	209	NA	13.4	NA	3	19	0	0	0	2 856	165	1 031
Rockwall	546	14.6	242	NA	6.5	NA	54	125	0	0	0	3 675	1 017	2 361
Runnels	155	13.6	145	NA	12.7	NA	9	78	2	38	330	2 440	254	2 210
Rusk	565	12.3	538	NA	11.8	NA	31	65	1	96	209	6 747	1 746	3 686
Sabine	101	9.6	169	NA	16.0	NA	4	38	1	36	341	3 201	124	1 184
San Augustine	97	11.9	136	NA	16.7	NA	4	45	1	16	198	1 916	184	2 057
San Jacinto	231	10.6	200	NA	9.2	NA	1	4	0	0	0	2 879	498	2 239
San Patricio	1 147	16.2	533	NA	7.5	NA	41	61	1	68	95	8 644	2 147	3 198
San Saba	58	10.2	70	NA	12.3	NA	1	16	0	0	0	1 234	83	1 342
Schleicher	40	13.4	34	NA	11.5	NA	2	68	1	17	570	483	38	1 295
Scurry	217	12.1	180	NA	10.0	NA	13	79	1	72	398	2 775	416	2 543
Shackelford	39	11.8	45	NA	13.7	NA	2	61	1	24	727	631	17	515
Shelby	329	14.5	340	NA	15.0	NA	8	32	1	48	211	4 602	522	2 069
Sherman	43	14.8	23	NA	8.1	NA	1	31	0	0	0	465	19	596
Smith	2 419	14.4	1 670	15	9.9	6.1	492	282	3	558	331	27 453	8 491	4 914
Somervell	91	14.2	62	NA	9.6	NA	5	73	1	58	903	855	221	3 246
Starr	1 349	24.2	220	NA	3.9	NA	8	15	1	44	79	5 231	1 174	2 190
Stephens	130	13.2	121	NA	12.3	NA	5	52	1	35	357	1 764	180	1 861
Sterling	19	13.9	13	NA	9.4	NA	0	0	0	0	0	178	9	646
Stonewall	23	12.9	29	NA	16.5	NA	1	59	1	16	897	413	17	1 004
Sutton	68	15.4	36	NA	8.1	NA	4	98	1	52	1 165	554	96	2 355
Swisher	129	15.6	84	NA	10.1	NA	4	48	1	30	361	1 531	162	1 934
Tarrant	23 328	17.2	9 035	174	6.7	7.4	2 312	160	16	3 465	256	132 307	80 888	5 593
Taylor	2 013	16.5	1 118	16	9.2	7.8	253	200	2	494	405	18 393	4 923	3 890
Terrell	11	9.3	14	NA	12.1	NA	0	0	0	0	0	212	0	0
Terry	215	16.7	122	NA	9.5	NA	10	78	1	42	326	2 045	282	2 210
Throckmorton	17	9.7	27	NA	15.6	NA	3	162	1	20	1 158	374	6	324
Titus	489	19.3	275	NA	10.8	NA	35	124	1	145	570	3 756	1 029	3 660

1. Per 1,000 estimated resident population, average 1997–1999.   2. Deaths of infants under 1 year old.   3. Deaths of infants under 1 year old per 1,000 live births.   4. Data subject to copyright.   5. Per 100,000 resident population as of July 1 of the year shown.   6. Data for serious crimes have not been adjusted for underreporting; this may affect comparability between geographic areas and over time.   7. Per 100,000 population estimated by the FBI.

Table B. States and Counties — Crime, Education, Money Income, and Poverty

STATE County	Serious crimes known to police, 2000¹ (cont'd) Rate² Violent	Property	Education School enrollment and attainment, 1990 Enrollment³ Total	Percent private	Attainment⁴ (percent) High school graduate or more	Bachelor's degree or more	Local government expenditures, fiscal 1999⁵ Total current expenditures (mil dol)	Current expenditures per student (dollars)	Money income 1989 Per capita⁶ (dollars)	Households Median Dollars	Percent change, 1979–1989 (constant 1989 dollars)	Percent with $100,000 or more	Income and poverty, 1998 Median household income	Percent below poverty level All persons	Persons under 18	Persons 5–17 in families
	46	47	48	49	50	51	52	53	54	55	56	57	58	59	60	61
TEXAS—Cont'd																
Mason	54	294	646	7.6	65.1	12.9	5.0	8 398	8 575	15 366	-20.6	0.4	22 701	19.8	27.3	29.0
Matagorda	543	5 264	10 030	5.6	67.4	12.6	51.3	6 219	11 374	25 368	-20.7	2.6	32 788	17.6	25.3	23.6
Maverick	140	3 210	12 465	4.3	35.7	7.3	64.7	5 303	5 184	12 262	-24.6	1.2	17 857	38.9	47.1	44.2
Medina	267	1 931	7 048	6.5	61.7	11.0	44.1	5 408	9 820	22 455	4.6	2.3	31 149	17.9	23.9	24.5
Menard	85	1 314	415	1.0	58.0	11.3	4.4	8 836	9 318	14 271	-12.2	1.6	19 696	25.8	37.3	40.5
Midland	387	2 986	29 324	9.7	76.8	26.4	134.5	5 472	15 417	31 164	-11.7	5.2	39 427	14.1	19.9	19.0
Milam	297	1 869	5 491	3.5	61.0	10.0	27.6	5 866	10 341	18 355	-6.7	1.2	28 011	18.4	24.7	25.6
Mills	19	330	899	4.4	61.6	12.8	7.6	7 557	10 374	17 558	-1.7	1.8	24 486	17.7	24.7	27.6
Mitchell	124	2 114	1 942	3.4	59.3	10.6	11.0	7 157	9 581	17 600	-10.7	1.6	25 716	23.6	27.7	29.5
Montague	237	3 407	3 577	6.0	63.6	10.2	21.7	6 554	10 420	19 054	-5.4	2.0	27 653	15.9	21.5	22.0
Montgomery	381	3 034	49 023	9.7	75.5	19.4	287.2	5 262	14 283	32 254	-14.0	5.0	47 857	9.2	13.4	12.1
Moore	189	1 933	4 438	2.1	61.9	10.8	24.6	5 250	11 195	27 466	-11.3	2.0	35 932	12.9	18.5	18.3
Morris	369	3 274	3 148	1.7	68.6	10.5	17.1	6 373	10 344	19 895	-27.1	1.3	28 408	18.6	28.3	26.2
Motley	70	281	271	0.0	62.2	10.8	2.3	9 687	9 004	16 780	3.7	0.5	22 474	17.7	26.0	28.3
Nacogdoches	490	3 223	21 117	4.8	69.7	20.0	57.5	5 695	9 829	19 340	-3.8	2.0	29 412	19.6	27.5	26.4
Navarro	224	4 195	10 400	5.9	64.6	12.7	47.3	5 560	10 468	21 479	9.1	2.4	29 584	17.9	25.0	24.7
Newton	80	823	3 373	2.9	59.1	5.5	17.0	6 231	7 760	16 656	-23.4	0.6	27 239	20.3	25.1	29.5
Nolan	NA	NA	4 305	6.0	62.3	12.0	22.5	6 387	9 738	20 350	-8.4	1.1	26 950	21.1	30.0	30.2
Nueces	709	6 474	87 425	8.0	68.9	17.0	364.2	5 804	11 396	25 337	-8.7	2.6	30 387	20.1	27.3	25.7
Ochiltree	422	2 565	2 245	2.6	71.2	13.8	11.4	5 550	13 325	26 352	-22.7	3.2	38 394	12.5	18.4	18.4
Oldham	92	1 098	919	5.3	73.7	18.6	8.7	10 996	10 577	28 167	23.1	3.7	36 973	16.2	23.8	29.5
Orange	484	3 709	21 996	7.5	72.6	10.4	98.2	5 684	11 493	26 563	-23.2	1.5	36 985	14.5	22.2	19.7
Palo Pinto	311	3 493	5 797	6.0	65.0	11.1	29.8	6 076	9 979	20 389	-9.7	1.6	28 018	16.7	24.0	24.5
Panola	259	2 500	5 679	4.5	67.6	12.0	25.6	6 393	10 695	21 027	-15.1	2.1	32 016	15.9	21.8	21.8
Parker	148	2 102	16 566	8.4	74.5	13.9	80.4	5 243	12 966	30 592	5.8	2.7	42 528	8.8	13.7	11.5
Parmer	208	1 040	2 656	1.9	55.7	8.9	16.0	6 243	9 087	19 742	-16.0	2.0	31 194	17.2	23.1	23.4
Pecos	250	2 201	4 444	2.3	58.0	12.1	27.0	7 820	9 133	21 170	-22.6	1.7	27 209	24.0	29.3	30.4
Polk	204	2 115	6 562	4.1	59.7	8.6	37.9	5 787	9 974	18 968	1.8	1.9	29 789	15.5	22.7	25.2
Potter	753	6 517	24 643	6.5	67.8	11.5	179.5	5 619	10 230	20 472	-14.6	1.7	29 171	19.3	28.7	26.6
Presidio	164	479	1 848	1.8	43.9	11.8	11.1	5 922	6 347	13 016	-9.6	0.5	18 390	32.9	43.7	42.1
Rains	197	2 550	1 493	5.2	62.4	7.5	7.8	5 374	10 711	21 741	6.9	1.3	29 271	14.4	21.5	21.0
Randall	632	5 553	26 739	9.2	85.7	26.4	31.2	4 264	15 369	31 472	-11.6	3.6	46 950	7.8	10.8	10.5
Reagan	90	872	1 397	1.6	64.1	10.4	7.6	7 669	10 243	28 586	0.1	2.1	34 710	13.8	16.0	18.6
Real	33	886	521	1.7	60.2	10.0	2.0	7 612	8 184	17 428	13.3	0.7	22 855	28.2	47.4	49.2
Red River	356	1 691	3 235	4.7	57.0	7.3	17.7	6 160	8 482	16 217	1.0	0.5	22 670	23.1	34.1	32.8
Reeves	137	2 969	4 346	1.5	45.3	6.9	18.4	5 624	7 765	17 952	-15.3	0.6	23 676	26.7	32.0	35.1
Refugio	307	1 584	2 044	2.4	61.9	11.3	11.6	6 812	10 496	20 733	-14.2	3.0	30 265	18.7	27.3	27.1
Roberts	113	1 804	260	3.8	81.4	17.4	1.7	9 489	15 679	30 203	3.7	2.3	38 570	8.2	10.3	12.8
Robertson	138	894	3 661	8.9	57.2	9.5	21.0	6 371	9 705	17 206	-0.9	1.5	24 541	22.7	31.8	32.5
Rockwall	146	2 214	6 884	11.2	84.1	28.5	44.9	4 947	17 982	42 417	9.8	8.1	59 923	6.1	8.6	8.9
Runnels	278	1 931	2 725	2.4	56.8	10.0	17.3	6 661	9 602	19 348	-4.5	1.6	25 507	18.6	25.8	25.4
Rusk	488	3 198	11 008	4.7	66.6	10.7	48.3	6 279	10 127	22 211	-9.1	1.2	30 633	15.8	21.4	21.8
Sabine	134	1 051	1 762	4.9	60.8	9.5	10.4	6 492	10 539	17 512	7.9	1.3	26 700	17.3	29.8	30.0
San Augustine	235	1 822	1 677	1.9	57.2	8.3	10.6	6 968	8 151	15 134	-12.7	1.0	23 302	23.9	35.8	34.8
San Jacinto	198	2 041	3 706	3.4	58.9	7.7	19.7	5 499	9 657	19 867	0.0	2.2	29 689	17.5	23.1	26.1
San Patricio	213	2 985	17 368	4.1	60.6	11.0	88.5	5 623	9 425	22 864	-20.0	1.9	30 019	20.9	27.0	27.1
San Saba	162	1 180	1 153	5.3	61.7	11.9	7.9	6 823	10 785	14 462	-14.3	1.8	23 452	22.8	33.0	39.4
Schleicher	34	1 261	822	3.0	62.4	13.4	5.0	6 915	10 615	21 696	-10.4	2.7	28 556	19.0	25.3	27.0
Scurry	202	2 341	5 171	5.5	64.3	10.0	21.8	6 309	10 333	24 046	-12.1	1.6	32 509	18.3	24.8	25.5
Shackelford	0	515	790	6.8	66.1	15.0	4.6	6 654	11 487	18 773	-17.1	1.8	28 734	17.1	23.3	24.5
Shelby	289	1 780	5 064	3.7	57.3	8.8	28.3	5 825	9 510	17 446	-5.3	2.2	26 414	21.2	30.7	29.8
Sherman	31	565	678	4.3	70.5	13.2	5.2	6 534	10 396	23 005	-17.3	1.3	37 557	11.3	16.9	17.9
Smith	481	4 432	42 179	9.5	75.7	19.8	154.9	5 144	12 742	25 769	-5.9	3.2	35 630	14.3	21.7	19.2
Somervell	587	2 658	1 482	9.5	66.9	13.8	14.2	9 106	11 892	29 539	7.8	1.5	38 712	13.3	19.1	20.0
Starr	265	1 925	15 074	2.2	31.6	6.7	81.9	5 678	4 152	10 182	-20.3	0.5	16 363	43.8	47.3	49.7
Stephens	114	1 747	2 172	7.6	67.5	11.8	9.8	5 194	10 343	19 203	-9.6	2.1	27 833	18.7	25.5	25.3
Sterling	144	503	379	0.5	68.3	13.5	2.8	7 983	12 698	25 208	9.6	3.3	33 958	12.4	16.3	18.0
Stonewall	177	827	417	2.6	65.1	9.8	2.9	8 408	10 240	21 210	4.3	1.3	26 845	18.8	27.2	29.5
Sutton	221	2 134	1 168	3.9	62.0	20.4	7.1	7 146	10 926	20 933	-30.5	5.0	32 745	16.4	23.3	23.2
Swisher	310	1 623	2 069	2.0	61.8	11.5	12.0	6 713	9 692	19 569	-6.3	2.3	29 701	21.0	28.7	30.2
Tarrant	519	5 074	305 649	14.6	79.9	24.0	1 355.6	5 299	15 178	32 335	3.5	4.2	44 669	10.6	16.3	13.9
Taylor	332	3 558	34 059	26.4	75.4	20.7	141.3	5 785	11 791	24 661	-2.4	2.2	32 434	16.3	23.0	21.7
Terrell	0	0	364	1.4	66.3	12.0	2.4	10 617	10 146	21 213	-16.8	0.4	24 061	20.7	26.5	31.4
Terry	243	1 967	3 838	3.4	59.7	9.7	18.2	6 332	10 859	22 392	-6.8	3.0	28 322	24.3	31.9	33.8
Throckmorton	0	324	368	2.7	69.8	15.3	3.1	8 059	10 505	18 844	5.0	1.0	27 846	18.7	28.5	26.4
Titus	434	3 226	6 088	5.8	65.4	12.3	38.6	6 741	11 163	22 173	-13.4	2.0	29 907	16.6	24.2	23.5

1. Data for serious crimes have not been adjusted for underreporting; this may affect comparability between geographic areas and over time. 2. Per 100,000 population estimated by the FBI. 3. All persons 3 years old and over enrolled in nursery school through college. 4. Persons 25 years old and over. 5. Elementary and secondary education expenditures, local government fiscal years ending between July 1, 1998 and June 30, 1999. 6. Based on population enumerated as of April 1, 1990.

Table B. States and Counties — **Personal Income**

STATE County	Total (mil dol)	Percent change, 1998–1999	Per capita[1] Dollars	Per capita[1] Rank	Wages and salaries[2] (mil dol)	Proprietor's income (mil dol)	Dividends, interest, and rent (mil dol)	Transfer payments Total (mil dol)	Government payments to individuals Total (mil dol)	Social Security (mil dol)	Medical payments (mil dol)	Income mainte- nance (mil dol)	Unemploy- ment insurance (mil dol)
	62	63	64	65	66	67	68	69	70	71	72	73	74
TEXAS—Cont'd													
Mason	64	4.1	17 443	2 660	18	6	19	17	16	8	6	1	0
Matagorda	767	3.4	20 286	1 897	435	90	128	144	138	61	54	14	5
Maverick	527	6.2	10 826	3 102	277	34	51	174	165	34	83	40	4
Medina	722	6.9	19 139	2 247	210	51	114	127	121	42	57	13	1
Menard	36	4.7	15 948	2 901	13	0	11	12	11	5	5	2	0
Midland	3 635	-1.3	30 681	188	1 766	913	770	359	338	149	139	26	13
Milam	494	9.4	20 312	1 887	232	52	89	104	100	40	40	13	1
Mills	101	7.6	21 457	1 532	34	14	22	27	26	10	12	2	0
Mitchell	154	8.1	17 489	2 648	66	16	31	40	38	15	17	4	1
Montague	368	4.1	19 610	2 111	108	53	73	94	91	40	39	7	1
Montgomery	7 993	8.1	27 788	349	2 464	537	1 119	745	695	303	304	43	14
Moore	444	8.8	22 475	1 221	247	116	61	53	49	23	21	4	1
Morris	267	1.8	20 346	1 875	155	33	49	69	66	26	28	7	2
Motley	24	20.2	18 299	2 470	9	2	5	7	7	3	3	1	0
Nacogdoches	1 156	4.9	20 585	1 817	565	160	220	216	206	75	93	24	2
Navarro	909	5.7	21 720	1 443	452	75	173	185	178	68	77	20	2
Newton	232	4.1	16 163	2 879	60	18	28	59	57	19	24	9	2
Nolan	315	3.3	19 382	2 186	159	40	58	77	74	28	33	8	1
Nueces	7 213	2.3	22 864	1 121	4 656	816	1 227	1 139	1 084	354	507	145	26
Ochiltree	254	9.9	29 301	243	110	87	43	25	23	12	9	2	1
Oldham	58	11.1	26 023	511	25	18	7	6	6	3	2	0	0
Orange	1 866	1.5	21 886	1 394	906	106	292	367	352	136	160	31	13
Palo Pinto	543	4.9	20 758	1 754	214	44	105	110	105	45	45	8	1
Panola	452	5.9	19 685	2 089	176	69	96	95	91	36	38	9	2
Parker	2 110	8.1	24 699	714	477	211	315	234	219	107	80	13	3
Parmer	261	16.8	25 185	641	132	104	43	32	30	13	11	5	0
Pecos	223	3.7	13 910	3 051	130	23	36	49	46	16	21	6	1
Polk	933	4.1	17 759	2 584	274	84	253	278	269	132	105	17	3
Potter	2 607	3.5	23 897	880	2 335	499	490	513	494	189	215	41	10
Presidio	96	5.6	10 739	3 103	45	6	17	28	26	8	9	7	2
Rains	151	7.0	16 867	2 762	34	18	26	35	34	16	13	3	0
Randall	2 537	4.1	25 480	584	564	229	443	170	152	80	42	10	3
Reagan	54	1.6	14 058	3 046	32	2	11	11	10	4	4	1	0
Real	50	6.1	18 466	2 422	13	4	15	17	16	7	6	2	0
Red River	261	7.7	19 044	2 272	82	33	42	76	73	25	35	10	1
Reeves	205	4.1	14 643	3 015	106	21	29	52	49	16	21	9	2
Refugio	196	5.6	25 276	618	56	29	62	36	35	14	16	4	0
Roberts	17	-0.7	18 537	2 406	5	3	4	3	3	1	1	0	0
Robertson	272	7.4	17 260	2 693	102	19	58	74	71	26	29	10	1
Rockwall	1 293	10.6	32 744	135	376	113	169	91	84	41	35	4	1
Runnels	221	5.9	19 457	2 154	94	32	44	53	51	22	22	5	1
Rusk	937	4.5	20 449	1 853	409	106	181	178	170	74	70	15	3
Sabine	219	3.3	20 741	1 762	71	23	47	71	69	30	30	6	1
San Augustine	159	4.2	19 728	2 082	46	22	29	53	51	19	24	6	1
San Jacinto	400	6.6	17 733	2 594	54	25	53	87	83	37	33	9	1
San Patricio	1 279	5.3	17 847	2 568	656	93	169	239	228	77	104	32	5
San Saba	107	2.8	18 477	2 418	43	13	25	29	28	10	13	3	0
Schleicher	45	1.4	15 197	2 971	20	2	12	11	11	4	4	1	0
Scurry	338	-0.3	19 159	2 243	175	32	70	69	66	27	28	6	2
Shackelford	73	2.0	22 720	1 160	21	15	20	15	14	7	6	1	0
Shelby	520	5.2	22 916	1 106	189	128	75	121	117	41	55	15	2
Sherman	133	18.6	46 027	17	26	88	11	9	8	4	3	1	0
Smith	4 533	4.3	26 711	439	2 680	566	947	653	624	265	260	50	11
Somervell	189	10.4	28 582	278	155	17	30	22	21	8	10	1	0
Starr	486	5.6	8 588	3 108	206	57	46	185	175	30	86	53	4
Stephens	201	2.6	20 621	1 800	82	31	44	44	43	18	20	4	1
Sterling	21	-0.7	15 845	2 916	13	0	7	4	4	2	2	0	0
Stonewall	37	-2.3	21 468	1 528	15	5	10	9	9	4	4	1	0
Sutton	76	-2.0	17 676	2 604	47	2	21	14	14	5	6	2	0
Swisher	222	6.8	26 912	423	62	93	33	34	32	14	12	5	0
Tarrant	39 863	5.9	28 835	269	26 861	3 439	5 631	3 492	3 253	1 342	1 356	259	80
Taylor	3 010	4.2	24 579	735	1 718	478	565	463	442	174	189	38	6
Terrell	26	23.8	21 887	1 391	14	0	8	5	5	2	2	1	0
Terry	278	10.0	21 712	1 447	106	61	48	60	58	19	29	8	1
Throckmorton	51	15.6	29 829	217	11	16	13	9	9	4	3	1	0
Titus	559	5.4	22 065	1 344	431	56	88	98	94	35	45	8	2

1. Based on the resident population estimated as of July 1 of the year shown.   2. Includes other labor income.

Table B. States and Counties — Earnings, Social Security, and Housing

STATE County	Earnings, 1999									Social Security beneficiaries, December 2000		Supplemental Security Income recipients, December 2000	Housing units, 1990	
			Percent by selected industries											
			Goods-related[1]		Service-related and other[2]									
	Total (mil dol)	Farm	Total	Manu-facturing	Total	Retail trade	Finance, insur-ance, and real estate	Services	Govern-ment	Number	Rate[3]		Total	Percent change, 1980–1990
	75	76	77	78	79	80	81	82	83	84	85	86	87	88
TEXAS—Cont'd														
Mason	25	1.1	D	3.4	D	14.7	7.3	16.3	28.5	977	261	97	2 356	17.2
Matagorda	525	7.5	16.6	6.5	60.5	9.8	2.4	17.2	15.3	7 165	189	811	18 540	14.4
Maverick	311	0.8	9.7	6.6	49.5	12.9	3.9	17.2	40.0	6 633	140	3 438	11 143	28.5
Medina	261	3.7	14.1	5.1	51.6	14.2	4.9	17.3	30.7	5 954	151	583	10 860	23.9
Menard	13	-23.5	D	D	D	21.7	6.0	13.1	45.4	601	255	85	1 562	10.9
Midland	2 680	0.0	41.5	2.6	47.6	8.6	5.5	18.4	10.9	16 766	145	1 840	45 181	44.1
Milam	285	4.9	46.9	35.8	35.3	8.0	4.1	12.8	12.8	5 060	209	642	10 511	12.0
Mills	48	9.7	10.1	5.8	D	16.4	5.6	21.4	21.0	1 344	261	148	2 582	13.4
Mitchell	82	1.4	11.8	1.9	38.7	10.2	3.0	12.0	48.1	1 753	181	228	4 559	4.7
Montague	161	2.1	D	11.0	D	13.7	4.8	17.0	23.7	4 775	250	403	9 262	8.5
Montgomery	3 001	0.3	25.6	10.5	61.0	13.2	6.1	29.2	13.1	35 118	120	3 266	73 871	48.0
Moore	362	20.9	35.2	28.0	31.9	6.8	2.0	9.4	12.0	2 554	127	195	6 837	12.4
Morris	188	5.5	48.6	43.6	34.0	5.4	2.8	13.6	11.9	3 138	240	418	5 800	2.0
Motley	11	15.7	D	D	D	14.2	4.4	11.8	27.1	364	255	41	1 026	7.1
Nacogdoches	726	7.3	25.1	18.7	45.3	13.0	3.7	21.1	22.3	9 143	154	1 539	22 768	24.3
Navarro	526	1.8	23.3	15.9	58.1	16.9	4.0	22.9	16.8	8 393	186	1 311	17 219	15.2
Newton	78	-0.4	D	31.4	D	8.9	D	16.4	25.7	2 479	164	473	6 378	4.4
Nolan	199	2.6	24.2	15.7	47.6	9.7	4.0	16.6	25.6	3 345	212	407	7 462	-0.1
Nueces	5 472	0.8	22.0	9.8	55.8	12.3	4.9	28.1	21.4	45 244	144	8 928	114 326	21.1
Ochiltree	196	32.2	28.3	1.5	D	5.8	D	8.8	10.4	1 294	144	92	3 996	3.4
Oldham	43	42.2	D	D	D	4.4	D	D	20.9	366	168	25	861	8.0
Orange	1 012	0.0	48.7	39.2	37.4	9.2	2.5	17.8	14.0	15 263	180	1 557	32 032	4.5
Palo Pinto	258	0.4	D	19.6	D	14.8	4.6	20.8	21.7	5 513	204	409	13 349	9.1
Panola	245	10.0	33.7	14.4	38.7	8.1	3.6	14.2	17.6	4 468	196	553	9 700	10.6
Parker	688	1.3	25.4	13.7	54.5	14.9	6.8	20.3	18.7	13 130	148	521	26 044	47.0
Parmer	236	45.0	D	D	D	1.7	1.3	4.8	10.0	1 528	153	163	3 685	-7.4
Pecos	153	3.7	18.3	1.9	40.5	10.1	4.1	14.2	37.5	2 153	128	452	5 841	9.7
Polk	358	0.3	27.8	19.6	50.0	15.2	4.2	18.3	22.0	15 791	384	1 153	18 662	31.6
Potter	2 835	0.0	23.3	8.3	60.8	11.4	6.3	28.2	16.0	16 486	145	2 658	42 927	4.6
Presidio	50	3.5	D	1.2	D	9.0	3.7	13.2	57.0	1 356	186	623	2 890	36.6
Rains	51	15.7	D	4.6	D	13.6	5.0	16.0	20.2	1 987	217	140	3 533	43.0
Randall	793	4.4	22.0	8.9	56.6	11.7	5.5	22.8	17.0	14 546	139	476	37 807	32.5
Reagan	34	-5.2	D	D	D	6.2	3.9	11.5	30.8	469	141	38	1 685	12.4
Real	17	-8.0	D	D	D	14.2	4.2	27.6	32.1	942	309	113	2 049	33.3
Red River	115	10.6	D	25.2	D	10.8	5.3	16.4	20.2	3 393	237	572	6 650	-2.2
Reeves	128	7.8	22.4	13.8	40.8	11.0	2.7	10.6	29.0	2 145	163	541	6 044	7.5
Refugio	85	12.7	29.8	1.4	35.0	11.9	4.3	10.3	22.6	1 683	215	233	3 739	3.5
Roberts	8	25.3	D	D	D	5.1	D	D	31.1	215	242	5	492	0.0
Robertson	122	3.9	D	16.8	D	10.1	4.3	12.2	23.4	3 269	204	600	7 338	5.8
Rockwall	489	0.3	19.5	9.1	69.1	13.2	7.5	29.0	11.2	4 691	109	204	9 816	77.6
Runnels	126	9.2	32.1	26.4	39.0	9.8	6.4	12.3	19.7	2 761	240	303	5 345	-3.2
Rusk	514	4.6	37.9	12.5	43.9	8.3	3.2	18.4	13.6	8 849	187	973	19 092	12.3
Sabine	94	4.8	D	28.2	D	9.7	3.0	14.5	17.8	3 472	332	355	6 996	10.7
San Augustine	68	15.3	13.7	8.3	50.7	9.7	3.1	20.5	20.4	2 333	261	450	4 168	-2.3
San Jacinto	79	2.3	D	9.3	D	10.1	3.7	19.4	30.0	4 389	197	491	9 823	51.0
San Patricio	749	4.6	31.2	21.7	26.1	6.9	2.0	12.4	38.2	10 060	150	1 896	22 126	13.6
San Saba	56	4.1	D	1.5	D	17.0	D	18.6	35.0	1 384	224	178	3 078	2.1
Schleicher	23	-9.3	D	0.2	D	5.0	3.8	17.1	34.2	563	192	74	1 288	6.4
Scurry	207	1.7	33.8	5.0	39.7	8.8	4.3	12.1	24.7	3 102	190	326	7 702	6.4
Shackelford	36	-2.7	54.6	1.2	30.8	5.0	4.9	15.2	17.3	761	230	51	1 755	-0.9
Shelby	317	23.5	D	18.4	D	8.8	3.5	14.1	11.9	5 273	209	913	10 616	1.3
Sherman	114	76.9	D	1.0	D	2.4	D	3.3	6.8	394	124	16	1 293	0.5
Smith	3 246	1.1	26.9	15.5	59.1	13.3	6.5	27.7	12.9	31 042	178	3 629	64 369	25.8
Somervell	172	0.1	D	2.7	D	3.5	2.3	19.6	11.2	1 042	153	90	2 429	29.4
Starr	263	9.4	D	0.6	D	13.2	1.9	19.6	44.5	6 410	120	3 320	12 209	55.9
Stephens	113	-1.7	D	17.2	D	10.0	3.4	14.5	20.4	2 087	216	215	4 982	1.7
Sterling	13	-16.9	D	D	D	12.6	6.0	18.6	31.0	207	149	27	623	12.7
Stonewall	20	1.0	D	D	D	7.5	D	13.1	26.4	479	283	33	1 085	-4.7
Sutton	49	-11.3	D	D	D	10.3	4.9	16.0	24.9	646	158	99	1 924	-4.3
Swisher	154	56.4	D	2.2	25.6	4.7	2.3	6.2	14.3	1 724	206	152	3 497	-10.5
Tarrant	30 300	0.0	25.2	16.9	63.0	10.9	6.5	24.9	11.7	154 169	107	17 277	491 152	45.4
Taylor	2 196	0.8	20.1	12.4	53.9	10.6	4.7	26.4	25.1	20 777	164	2 561	49 988	20.1
Terrell	14	-8.7	D	D	D	4.6	2.3	16.0	52.4	225	208	35	810	-14.6
Terry	167	31.7	12.9	1.1	D	8.8	3.4	D	20.7	2 371	186	329	5 296	-2.7
Throckmorton	27	37.9	D	D	D	3.7	1.6	5.5	18.1	427	231	38	1 106	-0.5
Titus	487	2.2	D	34.4	D	10.0	2.6	12.9	16.7	4 208	150	595	9 357	10.8

1. Covers mining, construction, and manufacturing. 2. Covers private sector earnings in agricultural services, forestry, and fisheries; transportation and public utilities; wholesale trade; retail trade; finance, insurance, and real estate; and services. 3. Per 1,000 resident population estimated as of July 1 of the year shown.

STATE County	Housing units, 1990 (cont'd)								Civilian labor force, 2001				Civilian employment, 1990[5]		
	Occupied units										Unemployment		Percent		
		Owner-occupied				Renter-occupied									
				Owner cost as a percent of income											
	Total	Percent	Median value[1]	With a mortgage	Without a mortgage	Median rent[2]	Rent as percent of income	Substandard units[3] (percent)	Total	Percent change, 2000–2001	Total	Rate[4]	Total	Professional, managerial, and technical	Precision production, craft, and repair
	89	90	91	92	93	94	95	96	97	98	99	100	101	102	103
TEXAS—Cont'd															
Mason	1 435	77.4	35 200	19.9	15.1	207	22.8	7.0	1 487	-2.3	24	1.6	1 424	18.4	14.3
Matagorda	13 164	65.0	53 000	17.3	13.2	352	22.9	10.0	15 572	3.1	1 682	10.8	14 780	25.3	17.3
Maverick	9 756	67.0	36 200	24.6	13.5	241	27.2	32.0	18 676	0.5	4 346	23.3	10 287	19.7	8.8
Medina	9 109	78.3	45 300	20.7	13.4	288	26.3	11.3	15 578	-1.2	676	4.3	10 570	22.3	15.2
Menard	937	73.6	25 700	25.0	14.9	272	28.3	5.5	948	-5.7	38	4.0	869	13.3	11.4
Midland	38 920	65.9	62 300	20.2	12.8	367	22.6	6.4	60 427	1.2	2 047	3.4	48 715	34.3	11.9
Milam	8 686	72.2	40 000	18.6	12.9	278	28.2	8.0	9 592	0.7	420	4.4	8 494	18.2	13.7
Mills	1 782	79.3	34 100	23.6	14.2	219	22.6	4.6	2 347	0.7	34	1.4	1 775	14.3	12.1
Mitchell	3 054	76.1	25 700	17.6	13.7	238	28.4	5.0	3 287	2.5	124	3.8	2 908	18.9	12.4
Montague	6 858	78.1	35 000	20.4	13.6	284	28.5	3.5	6 847	-5.1	305	4.5	6 826	17.6	16.5
Montgomery	63 563	71.9	69 400	20.8	13.4	424	23.5	5.7	147 521	1.7	4 907	3.3	83 442	29.7	15.0
Moore	6 101	69.4	46 400	16.2	12.2	334	18.7	9.1	9 298	3.3	261	2.8	7 952	17.4	23.0
Morris	4 988	75.9	35 300	20.1	13.7	292	27.0	6.2	6 192	1.9	421	6.8	5 044	20.3	14.6
Motley	647	76.7	23 700	20.0	13.1	200	18.6	4.5	573	0.4	10	1.7	620	14.8	10.6
Nacogdoches	20 124	58.1	54 100	21.3	13.2	343	34.0	4.7	26 311	4.0	928	3.5	23 595	25.8	10.0
Navarro	14 874	69.5	40 900	20.1	14.5	331	25.8	5.9	21 468	-0.6	1 065	5.0	16 218	22.1	11.4
Newton	4 910	83.2	30 500	21.5	14.0	269	24.3	9.9	5 582	0.1	701	12.6	4 269	18.0	16.2
Nolan	6 183	70.4	29 300	18.9	13.3	281	27.6	5.0	6 835	-1.3	335	4.9	6 721	20.3	13.8
Nueces	99 740	58.2	54 700	21.3	12.8	369	25.7	10.1	144 506	-0.2	8 273	5.7	121 837	27.6	14.5
Ochiltree	3 328	71.4	45 400	20.8	12.0	349	23.3	4.1	4 911	1.2	115	2.3	4 079	19.0	17.1
Oldham	681	64.9	42 100	17.4	12.4	332	21.1	6.0	1 232	-1.3	17	1.4	942	24.8	8.0
Orange	29 025	75.6	44 400	16.1	12.6	347	25.1	4.9	40 678	-0.8	3 975	9.8	32 858	24.3	21.4
Palo Pinto	9 531	72.5	37 400	20.5	13.5	320	26.3	4.8	11 934	-1.5	523	4.4	9 947	22.1	17.2
Panola	8 241	80.4	43 100	20.3	13.4	336	28.6	6.1	7 784	1.8	529	6.8	8 457	19.4	18.9
Parker	23 048	79.0	67 600	20.6	12.8	393	24.5	4.3	44 032	0.8	1 426	3.2	29 647	26.9	16.5
Parmer	3 241	69.9	39 100	19.0	13.2	316	22.8	9.2	4 391	-1.3	136	3.1	3 959	12.8	13.7
Pecos	4 712	69.8	38 100	16.8	12.9	280	22.3	13.1	6 111	-3.0	305	5.0	5 608	22.3	16.8
Polk	11 855	80.3	39 900	22.4	14.8	331	27.9	6.5	14 434	-2.0	729	5.1	10 445	20.3	16.3
Potter	37 344	60.2	39 100	19.0	13.1	332	25.7	7.3	54 446	-1.4	2 789	5.1	41 895	21.4	15.7
Presidio	2 255	69.1	28 200	17.1	15.0	208	24.4	15.9	3 400	-5.8	799	23.5	2 028	19.4	13.9
Rains	2 609	81.6	42 500	23.0	14.3	340	27.1	3.9	3 756	0.8	164	4.4	2 670	19.0	15.6
Randall	34 553	68.4	64 800	20.3	12.0	381	24.0	2.7	57 071	-1.0	711	1.2	45 900	32.4	10.1
Reagan	1 358	73.0	44 000	19.6	11.1	322	20.4	13.2	1 678	-0.3	50	3.0	1 788	14.8	22.6
Real	924	77.7	38 300	25.2	14.5	268	21.1	6.2	1 350	1.3	51	3.8	832	17.8	12.0
Red River	5 688	75.6	25 700	18.2	14.2	224	25.4	7.6	5 648	-2.1	591	10.5	5 153	17.3	14.2
Reeves	4 838	74.5	25 800	17.8	13.9	261	25.1	11.0	6 693	-6.3	452	6.8	5 406	18.2	15.4
Refugio	2 937	71.4	39 300	17.3	13.3	283	23.1	8.5	2 649	-4.4	123	4.6	3 100	19.6	19.0
Roberts	391	71.9	42 200	19.5	12.1	330	16.0	3.0	410	-0.5	6	1.5	507	18.3	13.2
Robertson	5 793	71.1	37 400	21.8	15.4	258	24.1	8.8	6 457	1.5	321	5.0	5 716	19.4	14.6
Rockwall	8 838	77.4	97 900	23.1	12.6	535	23.7	3.8	23 715	2.1	872	3.7	13 241	37.0	11.1
Runnels	4 346	75.7	30 300	20.1	14.6	281	21.4	4.9	4 868	-0.1	183	3.8	4 722	17.1	12.1
Rusk	16 327	79.0	41 800	19.0	13.8	316	24.9	7.1	21 497	1.1	949	4.4	17 073	20.8	16.9
Sabine	3 985	84.5	36 200	24.6	12.9	258	33.8	5.0	4 060	-0.4	402	9.9	3 023	19.0	13.0
San Augustine	3 073	79.2	35 200	21.6	14.2	210	33.9	8.7	3 122	1.4	172	5.5	2 705	15.5	10.2
San Jacinto	6 247	84.6	40 300	21.1	15.2	309	27.3	10.5	9 285	3.1	372	4.0	5 505	21.3	17.8
San Patricio	18 776	68.3	47 000	19.2	13.4	336	23.7	12.8	29 836	-0.2	1 727	5.8	22 339	22.1	17.3
San Saba	2 122	73.0	33 100	17.8	16.5	220	25.1	6.2	2 581	3.4	75	2.9	1 991	17.5	8.7
Schleicher	1 051	71.6	33 300	19.1	11.8	285	23.2	5.4	1 559	1.3	36	2.3	1 144	17.9	21.3
Scurry	6 368	73.4	38 100	19.4	13.3	329	22.4	7.1	6 988	1.6	346	5.0	7 171	22.6	17.1
Shackelford	1 336	75.4	32 800	19.8	14.2	302	21.9	4.2	1 341	4.9	30	2.2	1 406	23.0	14.3
Shelby	8 476	77.7	35 200	22.2	14.1	258	29.5	6.1	8 954	0.4	541	6.0	7 846	16.8	13.9
Sherman	1 053	70.1	36 900	16.6	12.5	322	20.1	3.4	1 822	5.1	28	1.5	1 301	16.0	12.9
Smith	56 800	66.5	59 900	20.2	13.2	372	25.9	5.4	91 992	0.9	3 803	4.1	67 128	28.2	10.6
Somervell	1 902	70.9	55 300	15.9	13.0	338	26.7	8.3	2 154	3.2	141	6.5	2 009	27.1	17.9
Starr	10 331	78.8	21 900	26.7	13.3	224	34.9	35.5	20 831	-1.6	4 160	20.0	11 273	17.3	12.4
Stephens	3 556	74.8	35 900	22.7	14.7	308	26.5	3.1	3 774	-3.8	119	3.2	3 465	16.9	17.3
Sterling	494	69.2	48 100	21.6	11.7	313	22.8	5.9	630	-3.1	24	3.8	608	18.3	20.1
Stonewall	806	76.9	29 600	20.2	13.7	238	19.2	4.5	618	-2.4	29	4.7	809	17.7	13.3
Sutton	1 466	67.5	39 500	21.2	14.6	299	22.5	8.5	2 031	6.2	56	2.8	1 847	20.5	11.6
Swisher	2 993	68.4	34 200	19.7	13.0	284	23.6	8.7	3 541	-1.9	136	3.8	3 396	16.9	10.0
Tarrant	438 634	58.1	72 900	21.5	12.6	430	23.9	5.4	804 827	1.6	33 601	4.2	598 945	32.2	11.2
Taylor	43 301	62.2	45 500	20.5	12.9	379	25.8	4.4	57 335	-3.3	2 210	3.9	50 278	30.6	10.6
Terrell	524	65.5	27 200	18.8	13.7	235	18.0	6.9	661	-9.5	20	3.0	605	22.5	12.7
Terry	4 478	72.6	38 600	21.6	12.3	304	27.8	10.6	5 457	1.5	326	6.0	5 047	20.0	13.0
Throckmorton	790	76.2	28 700	17.7	13.9	240	24.8	2.7	702	-2.5	15	2.1	803	20.7	10.2
Titus	8 508	72.3	44 400	19.4	14.5	349	24.4	7.9	12 739	1.7	527	4.1	10 066	19.8	19.0

1. Specified owner-occupied units.　2. Specified renter-occupied units.　3. Overcrowded or lacking complete plumbing facilities.　4. Percent of civilian labor force.　5. Persons 16 years and older.

Table B. States and Counties — Nonfarm Employment and Agriculture

STATE County	Private nonfarm establishments, employment and payroll, 1999									Agriculture, 1997			
	Number of establishments	Employment						Annual payroll		Farms			Farm operators
		Total	Health Care and Social Assistance	Manufacturing	Retail trade	Finance and Insurance	Professional Scientific and Technical Services	Total (mil dol)	Average per employee (dollars)	Number	Percent with—		Whose principal occupation is farming (percent)
											Less than 50 acres	500 acres and over	
	104	105	106	107	108	109	110	111	112	113	114	115	116

TEXAS—Cont'd

STATE County	104	105	106	107	108	109	110	111	112	113	114	115	116
Mason	107	511	72	30	78	D	11	8	15 824	565	11.5	48.5	50.6
Matagorda	770	9 588	1 195	760	1 494	216	204	343	35 821	768	24.1	31.2	48.4
Maverick	801	7 630	1 049	1 256	1 785	368	168	135	17 647	169	28.4	33.1	46.2
Medina	566	4 874	980	482	1 103	196	284	91	18 676	1 570	26.2	22.7	42.2
Menard	49	276	D	D	75	D	D	4	14 616	291	12.4	53.3	54.3
Midland	4 060	44 868	5 287	2 194	6 369	1 646	2 071	1 265	28 188	411	44.5	24.1	40.1
Milam	416	5 234	704	1 712	653	221	123	147	28 060	1 655	24.4	14.4	44.7
Mills	131	962	356	70	186	56	14	18	18 236	731	12.7	32.7	48.6
Mitchell	147	1 142	394	0	258	57	31	24	21 444	378	12.4	42.9	46.8
Montague	450	3 432	797	454	618	165	95	59	17 311	1 234	18.4	18.4	39.1
Montgomery	5 572	73 781	5 923	7 280	13 631	2 303	4 101	2 042	27 682	1 163	56.1	6.0	31.2
Moore	445	6 439	573	2 756	743	131	77	155	24 099	263	8.0	69.6	67.3
Morris	276	3 433	302	1 582	293	120	82	106	30 735	372	29.6	9.1	38.2
Motley	49	170	D	D	D	D	D	3	19 741	214	4.7	62.1	59.3
Nacogdoches	1 319	18 032	3 502	3 774	3 352	510	822	365	20 222	1 200	27.2	7.3	44.8
Navarro	930	12 919	1 598	2 385	2 251	426	366	275	21 272	1 513	22.5	15.5	40.9
Newton	151	1 483	110	555	193	D	D	30	19 995	294	49.7	3.1	33.3
Nolan	387	4 479	892	907	703	161	142	96	21 350	445	10.3	42.7	47.6
Nueces	7 960	117 216	21 363	8 295	17 079	4 035	4 938	2 892	24 670	569	30.4	32.9	49.6
Ochiltree	301	2 341	261	130	392	112	108	49	21 095	361	5.3	68.7	64.3
Oldham	44	481	D	D	54	D	D	10	21 087	140	1.4	76.4	62.9
Orange	1 456	20 450	2 112	5 837	3 267	573	508	580	28 360	334	65.3	8.7	30.8
Palo Pinto	635	6 561	1 028	1 400	1 158	205	102	141	21 442	830	25.8	24.0	38.6
Panola	482	5 087	672	1 165	787	164	145	108	21 154	866	23.7	12.1	40.2
Parker	1 540	15 513	1 813	2 517	3 494	441	505	336	21 688	2 301	50.8	8.2	32.9
Parmer	207	3 237	96	D	298	95	37	71	22 041	599	7.2	74.1	74.1
Pecos	314	2 993	349	77	604	122	72	63	21 203	284	14.1	70.8	54.9
Polk	711	7 295	683	1 541	1 803	238	285	164	22 468	551	35.4	9.3	34.3
Potter	3 631	59 571	11 132	9 559	7 892	2 765	2 574	1 568	26 325	214	28.0	33.6	34.6
Presidio	117	612	D	D	151	40	20	10	16 059	138	11.6	73.2	54.3
Rains	131	904	84	D	255	D	24	16	17 543	493	36.5	8.5	45.8
Randall	1 945	21 546	1 875	1 610	4 822	929	477	468	21 707	583	22.3	39.5	44.4
Reagan	97	802	123	D	101	D	8	20	25 162	123	3.3	79.7	69.1
Real	72	404	165	52	52	D	6	6	15 200	207	8.7	60.4	44.9
Red River	216	2 604	584	981	449	73	27	44	16 779	1 088	19.4	17.9	43.8
Reeves	232	2 794	263	D	470	148	117	52	18 633	176	12.5	59.7	44.9
Refugio	166	1 188	158	D	237	67	38	25	20 736	230	17.0	33.5	53.5
Roberts	11	66	0	0	20	D	0	1	21 303	96	1.0	85.4	71.9
Robertson	232	2 168	302	375	312	151	23	48	22 255	1 289	23.0	15.4	40.3
Rockwall	948	9 271	1 068	1 134	2 105	265	651	223	24 041	265	47.9	5.3	27.2
Runnels	287	2 945	329	1 427	378	116	31	58	19 591	896	12.4	34.8	50.0
Rusk	769	9 092	1 078	1 303	1 226	350	240	235	25 835	1 296	24.2	9.0	38.0
Sabine	168	1 631	197	D	375	67	18	34	21 121	194	36.1	4.6	36.6
San Augustine	141	1 310	407	130	248	56	17	22	16 624	291	26.8	10.3	48.1
San Jacinto	152	1 163	113	D	230	26	30	23	19 741	398	43.5	7.0	36.2
San Patricio	1 002	12 247	1 311	3 239	1 992	379	429	296	24 155	496	30.2	36.9	57.3
San Saba	165	1 166	235	54	277	D	23	23	19 819	653	11.2	42.4	50.4
Schleicher	61	519	174	D	60	D	6	11	20 738	284	7.4	69.0	52.1
Scurry	419	4 104	474	406	719	159	51	83	20 342	606	15.0	35.6	48.2
Shackelford	100	500	71	D	70	D	14	11	21 048	250	7.6	48.8	45.6
Shelby	541	5 934	647	1 980	1 063	233	138	122	20 632	1 047	24.6	7.0	50.0
Sherman	62	394	D	D	64	D	0	8	21 411	293	5.8	70.3	70.0
Smith	4 863	71 725	14 141	9 908	11 147	2 822	2 977	1 940	27 045	1 844	43.0	4.6	31.3
Somervell	152	3 291	417	123	178	32	18	113	34 393	245	32.7	17.1	29.0
Starr	398	4 836	1 921	37	1 449	177	73	63	13 119	609	8.5	33.2	37.1
Stephens	270	2 386	290	667	429	91	48	48	20 247	454	7.5	42.3	39.2
Sterling	33	145	D	0	D	D	4	2	13 317	67	9.0	73.1	68.7
Stonewall	56	393	84	0	D	D	D	8	19 903	305	4.9	49.8	58.0
Sutton	138	1 079	109	D	228	D	15	24	21 918	211	5.2	80.6	58.3
Swisher	173	1 153	212	138	251	67	21	21	18 031	529	7.2	53.9	59.9
Tarrant	33 045	613 868	64 067	92 999	79 666	25 076	27 548	18 634	30 355	1 048	60.6	6.5	33.0
Taylor	3 543	48 514	10 145	3 702	7 339	1 893	1 323	1 040	21 437	1 048	27.5	23.8	35.4
Terrell	23	55	0	0	D	D	D	1	13 582	85	4.7	88.2	54.1
Terry	243	2 137	413	D	400	122	D	49	22 964	562	13.0	52.5	67.1
Throckmorton	58	337	104	D	36	D	D	5	16 083	249	4.0	57.0	61.0
Titus	672	11 984	1 854	4 366	1 551	265	141	292	24 393	722	30.3	8.4	38.4

Table B. States and Counties — **Agriculture, Land, and Water**

	Agriculture, 1997 (cont'd)															
STATE County	Land in farms					Value of land and buildings		Value of machinery and equipment average per farm ($1,000)	Value of products sold				Percent of farms with sales of —		Percent of land owned by fed. gov. 1997	Water consumption 1995 (mil gal/day)
			Acres								Percent from —					
	Acreage (1,000)	Percent change, 1992–1997	Average size of farm	Total irrigated (1,000)	Total cropland (1,000)	Average per farm ($1,000)	Average per acre (dollars)		Total (mil dol)	Average per farm (dollars)	Crops	Live-stock and poultry products	$10,000 or more	$100,000 or more		
	117	118	119	120	121	122	123	124	125	126	127	128	129	130	131	132
TEXAS—Cont'd																
Mason	595	8.8	1 054	6	65	674	709	25	20	34 647	21.0	79.0	45.5	6.9	0.0	12.7
Matagorda	551	-2.2	717	37	240	494	770	67	58	75 547	73.1	26.9	44.3	18.9	0.3	123.7
Maverick	470	-30.7	2 783	25	29	909	322	82	20	115 837	29.7	70.3	49.1	13.6	0.0	133.9
Medina	750	13.9	477	44	226	453	940	31	60	38 177	43.7	56.3	29.0	5.8	0.0	50.1
Menard	496	1.6	1 704	2	25	684	439	28	13	44 177	6.0	94.0	49.1	6.5	0.0	6.3
Midland	863	19.0	2 100	12	69	508	236	47	19	45 602	44.8	55.2	29.2	10.9	0.0	51.0
Milam	545	-1.1	329	1	248	267	780	29	63	37 815	29.7	70.3	32.1	5.1	0.0	50.1
Mills	425	-0.6	582	4	91	369	585	27	23	31 330	20.0	80.0	39.5	3.3	0.0	3.9
Mitchell	541	-7.8	1 432	1	162	336	269	58	20	53 758	63.4	36.6	42.1	13.5	0.0	4.7
Montague	494	-0.3	400	1	163	292	756	29	30	23 953	11.8	88.2	35.2	4.9	0.1	4.6
Montgomery	193	-0.3	166	0	48	322	2 157	28	16	13 479	59.3	40.7	17.5	1.2	8.0	37.6
Moore	555	-5.4	2 112	120	258	804	385	132	294	1 118 443	15.2	84.8	70.7	50.2	0.9	311.8
Morris	66	-10.2	179	D	36	206	1 136	32	15	39 323	3.0	97.0	32.5	5.6	0.0	85.9
Motley	590	22.9	2 757	6	D	540	199	54	19	87 109	49.5	50.5	55.1	20.1	0.0	5.9
Nacogdoches	372	69.3	310	0	102	299	1 004	35	167	139 076	0.7	99.3	38.7	15.8	2.1	13.9
Navarro	516	-1.8	341	0	237	236	795	39	34	22 190	37.3	62.7	29.9	3.8	0.8	8.6
Newton	62	107.0	211	0	10	209	1 027	23	1	4 917	25.9	74.2	13.3	0.0	0.3	3.9
Nolan	520	-3.0	1 169	7	153	412	358	43	32	72 858	37.8	62.2	40.0	12.1	0.0	4.2
Nueces	438	-1.1	770	1	351	673	910	93	66	116 440	95.3	4.7	48.9	24.1	0.4	155.7
Ochiltree	564	-5.0	1 563	73	348	717	435	116	104	288 089	25.2	74.8	67.6	29.1	0.0	84.9
Oldham	842	-0.7	6 014	8	D	1 305	220	70	88	632 073	4.7	95.3	65.7	33.6	0.0	6.4
Orange	88	54.2	263	2	26	317	1 095	24	3	9 933	42.8	57.2	12.0	2.4	0.8	80.0
Palo Pinto	524	1.4	632	0	83	418	642	28	15	18 038	10.9	89.1	29.5	3.1	0.0	461.8
Panola	202	3.7	234	2	84	196	899	31	46	53 000	1.8	98.2	32.2	7.5	0.0	11.4
Parker	480	15.3	209	1	170	386	1 760	21	44	19 051	24.6	75.4	20.3	2.5	0.7	18.9
Parmer	547	4.0	913	216	434	564	621	141	551	919 750	18.2	81.8	82.1	57.9	0.0	342.3
Pecos	2 943	1.8	10 363	25	D	1 662	160	48	40	141 659	41.8	58.2	56.7	18.7	0.0	70.2
Polk	136	-3.6	247	0	42	222	869	32	4	8 097	10.0	90.0	20.3	0.7	2.3	8.9
Potter	450	11.9	494	8	D	494	231	39	19	87 011	14.4	85.6	32.7	14.0	4.6	28.3
Presidio	1 690	-0.3	12 247	5	D	1 588	131	41	14	98 406	36.4	63.6	55.8	21.7	0.0	22.1
Rains	94	-3.6	192	0	46	240	1 323	24	16	32 138	25.7	74.3	31.6	6.3	0.0	1.4
Randall	460	-7.4	789	38	277	493	587	51	203	348 112	9.4	90.6	48.2	16.0	1.4	54.5
Reagan	624	0.9	5 072	24	57	1 028	197	87	12	101 615	65.9	34.1	73.2	32.5	0.0	30.4
Real	378	4.1	1 826	0	10	914	525	20	2	11 994	5.9	94.1	28.0	1.0	0.0	1.0
Red River	445	4.6	409	3	173	300	714	34	39	36 205	16.6	83.4	34.7	4.9	0.0	4.8
Reeves	1 014	-34.8	5 760	18	D	771	131	56	42	239 071	31.1	68.9	51.7	21.0	0.0	97.4
Refugio	550	-17.5	2 392	D	111	961	416	71	24	103 622	68.5	31.5	46.5	18.7	0.1	1.5
Roberts	566	11.0	5 896	8	51	1 256	217	74	14	146 505	13.1	86.9	72.9	34.4	0.0	5.6
Robertson	425	8.3	329	15	177	281	1 016	40	31	24 421	35.6	64.4	32.0	4.2	0.0	23.0
Rockwall	46	-2.1	174	0	32	410	1 979	29	4	14 093	53.8	46.2	17.4	1.9	0.0	0.2
Runnels	581	1.4	649	2	293	289	506	41	27	30 581	56.7	43.3	45.1	8.4	0.0	6.2
Rusk	267	-0.2	206	0	131	207	955	24	29	22 416	29.0	71.0	27.9	2.2	0.0	24.6
Sabine	25	-26.2	129	D	13	173	1 232	30	11	56 395	2.1	97.9	21.6	2.6	26.0	1.9
San Augustine	65	18.6	224	0	26	283	1 337	37	25	86 347	4.0	96.0	36.4	10.3	18.9	1.5
San Jacinto	85	2.0	213	0	28	276	1 148	23	5	11 590	22.8	77.2	21.4	2.3	14.9	2.3
San Patricio	406	13.3	818	3	265	686	797	92	74	149 866	77.0	23.0	51.8	30.4	0.0	11.7
San Saba	733	-1.5	1 122	3	139	714	634	32	25	38 488	18.6	81.4	47.5	7.0	0.0	5.3
Schleicher	739	-3.4	2 601	1	45	744	290	29	12	41 138	15.1	84.9	60.6	9.9	0.0	2.9
Scurry	479	-7.6	790	1	210	309	373	53	24	40 190	57.7	42.3	41.1	11.1	0.0	18.9
Shackelford	516	-8.5	2 063	1	54	604	292	34	11	45 085	17.3	82.7	44.4	12.4	0.0	1.3
Shelby	201	7.1	192	0	86	273	1 520	40	181	173 107	1.2	98.8	41.1	20.9	15.0	6.4
Sherman	607	19.8	2 072	162	355	1 166	584	183	295	1 006 870	17.4	82.6	73.4	56.0	0.0	244.0
Smith	251	1.2	136	1	127	223	1 794	25	38	20 798	52.0	48.0	23.1	2.6	0.0	37.9
Somervell	72	13.8	293	0	20	301	1 235	19	2	8 955	17.1	82.9	23.3	0.4	0.0	6.0
Starr	636	0.5	1 044	10	127	534	506	31	51	83 019	41.8	58.2	28.6	5.1	1.0	49.6
Stephens	465	-13.5	1 024	0	60	402	455	19	8	17 586	7.3	92.7	36.6	2.9	0.0	6.3
Sterling	706	-15.5	10 532	0	14	3 110	295	48	9	127 336	2.0	98.0	58.2	25.4	0.0	1.7
Stonewall	484	-5.6	1 585	0	109	339	215	37	11	34 890	30.4	69.6	43.3	9.5	0.0	1.5
Sutton	925	-0.1	4 383	0	9	1 067	247	35	9	43 525	2.1	97.9	60.7	11.4	0.0	3.2
Swisher	516	2.2	975	115	355	445	437	98	364	688 268	12.8	87.2	64.7	37.4	0.0	181.3
Tarrant	184	9.6	176	1	70	387	2 298	22	21	19 914	50.5	49.5	21.8	3.4	1.3	175.7
Taylor	492	-3.4	469	2	207	280	582	31	53	50 446	17.9	82.1	27.8	4.1	0.9	25.1
Terrell	1 291	-7.5	15 186	D	D	2 238	147	46	5	54 119	D	D	52.9	15.3	0.0	1.1
Terry	468	2.0	833	137	378	424	489	132	92	164 214	95.0	5.0	61.7	42.5	0.1	150.7
Throckmorton	562	-3.4	2 257		115	717	312	55	20	82 204	28.9	71.1	65.9	15.7	0.0	1.1
Titus	174	-3.1	242	0	73	242	1 170	28	41	57 331	2.0	98.0	27.1	6.1	0.0	1 420.4

Table B. States and Counties — Residential Construction, Wholesale and Retail Trade, and Real Estate

STATE County	Value of Residential Construction Authorized by Building Permits, 2000		Wholesale Trade, 1997				Retail Trade[1], 1997				Real Estate and Rental and Leasing, 1997			
	New Construction ($1,000)	Number of Housing Units	Number of Establishments	Number of Employees	Sales (mil dol)	Annual Payroll (mil dol)	Number of Establishments	Number of Employees	Sales (mil dol)	Annual Payroll (mil dol)	Number of Establishments	Number of Employees	Receipts (mil dol)	Annual Payroll (mil dol)
	133	134	135	136	137	138	139	140	141	142	143	144	145	146
TEXAS—Cont'd														
Mason	321	3	9	56	38.3	1.1	20	107	10.9	1.0	2	D	D	D
Matagorda	9 842	118	33	D	D	D	152	1 443	224.7	21.7	30	109	6.6	1.6
Maverick	9 012	179	35	165	85.3	3.7	184	1 716	233.3	21.1	29	184	10.3	2.0
Medina	2 617	35	28	241	75.7	4.4	117	955	215.2	18.0	16	37	2.9	0.4
Menard	NA	NA	4	34	13.9	1.0	11	60	10.2	0.7	1	D	D	D
Midland	17 182	158	297	2 708	1 938.6	93.9	549	6 649	1 226.3	108.5	185	899	90.0	17.8
Milam	770	10	22	177	119.8	3.2	82	701	106.8	9.8	16	31	1.7	0.3
Mills	NA	NA	7	75	28.2	0.4	36	159	32.3	2.4	3	3	0.1	0.0
Mitchell	0	0	9	93	5.2	0.8	38	226	35.8	3.5	4	11	1.2	0.2
Montague	360	8	30	118	53.7	1.9	86	640	97.9	8.0	11	16	0.9	0.2
Montgomery	636 115	4 197	337	3 271	2 129.7	118.8	835	11 926	2 224.8	187.4	184	861	140.5	24.9
Moore	1 930	14	26	187	137.7	6.0	83	724	127.5	11.0	19	43	3.3	0.5
Morris	115	2	15	230	100.2	6.9	53	342	38.9	4.2	6	7	2.3	0.3
Motley	0	0	3	24	2.4	0.4	11	37	6.1	0.5	1	D	D	D
Nacogdoches	5 100	100	57	593	161.6	14.1	279	3 036	501.2	45.0	59	174	18.5	3.0
Navarro	4 247	39	45	409	227.5	10.7	196	2 007	347.9	29.4	34	99	9.9	1.6
Newton	0	0	3	22	9.4	0.5	36	185	26.8	2.1	4	13	0.3	0.1
Nolan	154	2	24	171	48.7	4.5	83	786	121.1	10.2	11	32	2.3	0.3
Nueces	93 483	939	493	5 029	1 803.1	154.0	1 286	17 018	2 783.5	265.9	388	2 526	334.1	63.2
Ochiltree	470	3	33	175	78.3	4.3	44	377	63.3	5.5	6	15	1.2	0.1
Oldham	0	0	5	27	5.2	0.5	11	60	8.0	0.8	NA	NA	NA	NA
Orange	23 944	174	49	316	61.6	7.4	290	3 310	546.1	44.8	61	337	20.2	4.9
Palo Pinto	289	4	30	223	62.4	4.7	132	1 072	171.9	14.5	23	87	8.8	1.4
Panola	428	6	25	161	135.3	3.9	90	696	97.1	8.1	13	37	2.6	0.4
Parker	29 702	282	75	579	231.6	15.6	236	2 657	602.3	49.3	58	144	17.9	2.4
Parmer	620	5	28	186	122.0	4.1	42	279	48.3	3.8	6	5	0.4	0.1
Pecos	262	4	15	101	28.2	2.8	75	576	84.1	8.3	7	28	2.2	0.3
Polk	3 143	117	26	214	114.6	3.7	132	1 701	272.1	24.8	21	79	3.9	1.2
Potter	66 601	520	247	3 204	1 209.8	105.5	641	7 939	1 531.3	137.3	159	803	96.0	14.4
Presidio	5 911	67	6	14	4.1	0.2	27	152	21.4	1.6	2	D	D	D
Rains	368	9	5	D	D	D	33	186	22.3	2.4	1	D	D	D
Randall	5 191	37	110	1 620	1 180.9	47.5	346	4 299	838.3	72.4	97	370	34.8	6.9
Reagan	38	3	4	D	D	D	16	84	19.5	1.3	NA	NA	NA	NA
Real	3 028	31	3	D	D	D	19	57	6.3	0.6	2	D	D	D
Red River	419	5	4	D	D	D	59	482	61.2	4.8	4	7	1.8	0.1
Reeves	180	1	13	138	12.0	1.7	43	383	64.2	5.7	6	7	0.3	0.1
Refugio	135	1	12	60	19.3	1.3	38	258	49.6	4.0	6	18	1.2	0.3
Roberts	NA	NA	2	D	D	D	4	20	1.7	0.2	NA	NA	NA	NA
Robertson	660	9	11	49	84.2	0.7	55	364	52.0	4.5	9	47	3.2	0.3
Rockwall	185 615	955	58	343	133.2	7.8	112	1 488	266.9	24.1	39	256	17.8	3.9
Runnels	36	1	17	614	64.8	12.6	57	413	69.5	5.5	6	10	0.3	0.1
Rusk	1 400	13	41	516	137.0	11.9	144	1 305	188.0	17.0	21	64	5.0	0.7
Sabine	0	0	5	18	4.0	0.4	47	284	40.6	4.0	6	7	0.7	0.1
San Augustine	0	0	11	67	13.3	1.1	42	312	45.0	3.6	2	D	D	D
San Jacinto	935	11	6	31	4.8	0.5	33	235	29.7	2.9	3	3	0.2	0.0
San Patricio	29 400	495	42	262	105.9	6.8	200	1 988	348.7	29.6	46	150	10.9	1.6
San Saba	1 528	23	15	105	48.2	1.2	38	254	51.1	3.6	NA	NA	NA	NA
Schleicher	0	0	2	D	D	D	11	45	7.7	0.7	2	D	D	D
Scurry	268	8	27	215	50.0	5.9	80	762	135.3	10.9	15	51	3.2	0.7
Shackelford	NA	NA	6	13	2.7	0.3	22	86	14.8	1.0	NA	NA	NA	NA
Shelby	60	1	27	168	99.7	4.3	103	984	155.0	12.4	14	27	4.2	0.3
Sherman	1 623	16	9	40	35.1	0.9	12	47	8.1	0.8	1	D	D	D
Smith	71 030	543	297	3 103	1 237.7	93.9	805	9 773	1 868.6	170.2	189	895	93.2	20.7
Somervell	1 980	40	4	D	D	D	29	220	29.1	2.5	5	10	0.5	0.1
Starr	0	0	21	105	37.2	2.3	131	1 379	201.2	16.3	10	51	2.7	0.5
Stephens	120	1	16	45	10.9	1.2	47	421	56.1	5.8	7	22	0.9	0.2
Sterling	NA	NA	3	8	1.5	0.2	5	38	5.8	0.4	NA	NA	NA	NA
Stonewall	NA	NA	2	D	D	D	10	39	5.7	0.5	1	D	D	D
Sutton	0	0	14	63	18.9	1.7	31	206	56.3	4.0	5	9	0.5	0.1
Swisher	0	0	15	94	42.2	2.1	39	255	41.2	3.2	5	10	0.9	0.1
Tarrant	1 321 010	11 685	2 399	33 372	22 102.4	1 219.5	5 015	71 758	14 097.9	1 326.3	1 384	8 249	1 132.8	196.3
Taylor	33 646	374	219	1 996	933.9	54.1	635	7 211	1 297.7	116.7	168	876	88.4	16.7
Terrell	NA	NA	1	D	D	D	7	26	2.7	0.3	3	3	0.1	0.0
Terry	435	3	22	216	108.6	5.2	46	458	81.3	7.3	6	26	2.3	0.6
Throckmorton	NA	NA	5	8	2.1	0.2	11	37	4.9	0.4	NA	NA	NA	NA
Titus	1 768	28	48	539	203.3	14.2	147	1 483	271.1	23.7	24	85	6.9	1.2

1. Establishments with payroll.

STATE County	Professional, Scientific, and Technical Services[1], 1997				Manufacturing, 1997				Accommodation and Foodservices, 1997			
	Number of Establishments	Number of Employees	Receipts (mil dol)	Annual Payroll (mil dol)	Number of Establishments	Number of Employees	Receipts (mil dol)	Annual Payroll (mil dol)	Number of Establishments	Number of Employees	Sales (mil dol)	Annual Payroll (mil dol)
	147	148	149	150	151	152	153	154	155	156	157	158
TEXAS—Cont'd												
Mason	6	10	0.7	0.1	NA	NA	NA	NA	8	46	1.3	0.3
Matagorda	47	144	8.2	3.4	29	D	D	D	77	804	26.6	7.0
Maverick	28	158	11.7	3.6	19	1 091	78.0	13.2	46	670	23.7	6.1
Medina	34	281	12.1	4.8	23	556	50.5	13.8	46	413	12.9	3.2
Menard	1	D	D	D	NA	NA	NA	NA	9	42	1.9	0.4
Midland	350	2 088	245.0	75.6	135	2 435	326.1	76.5	231	3 814	123.9	34.2
Milam	27	114	8.8	3.7	9	1 559	456.0	65.3	43	342	10.7	2.9
Mills	6	13	1.0	0.1	NA	NA	NA	NA	6	55	1.4	0.4
Mitchell	9	31	1.6	0.4	NA	NA	NA	NA	17	146	3.9	0.9
Montague	30	85	4.9	1.5	21	505	44.1	8.9	38	360	10.4	2.2
Montgomery	498	2 279	251.0	96.4	285	6 706	1 540.8	219.1	284	6 044	230.2	62.6
Moore	20	84	6.0	1.9	19	2 865	2 663.2	72.5	46	630	20.3	5.2
Morris	16	155	18.5	3.4	16	2 224	688.0	95.7	21	D	D	D
Motley	1	D	D	D	NA	NA	NA	NA	3	15	0.3	0.1
Nacogdoches	69	240	18.7	4.6	60	3 475	771.3	99.3	87	1 897	57.1	15.6
Navarro	45	270	13.3	6.2	49	2 191	336.0	58.5	54	878	25.5	6.7
Newton	5	9	0.4	0.1	10	620	133.2	15.8	15	87	3.0	0.8
Nolan	32	104	8.5	3.3	17	1 043	176.7	27.7	35	426	11.7	2.9
Nueces	690	4 415	415.4	150.1	223	8 925	9 988.5	373.8	730	12 846	418.6	111.6
Ochiltree	20	89	5.3	2.4	NA	NA	NA	NA	20	254	7.0	1.8
Oldham	2	D	D	D	NA	NA	NA	NA	3	60	1.2	0.4
Orange	93	442	37.2	14.6	82	6 137	2 893.4	302.4	115	2 096	58.6	16.2
Palo Pinto	29	78	5.4	1.5	37	1 183	134.2	32.6	66	657	21.3	5.6
Panola	35	110	10.2	2.1	12	1 092	125.0	19.7	26	342	10.9	3.2
Parker	104	407	52.2	19.8	101	2 538	310.8	63.5	93	1 316	41.5	10.8
Parmer	10	33	1.7	0.5	6	D	D	D	15	D	D	D
Pecos	15	61	3.1	0.9	NA	NA	NA	NA	32	392	12.7	3.1
Polk	45	248	11.9	4.1	25	1 693	295.8	54.6	55	732	21.5	6.2
Potter	271	2 556	180.1	78.2	145	D	D	D	337	5 864	191.0	51.3
Presidio	5	7	1.3	0.1	NA	NA	NA	NA	15	130	3.3	1.0
Rains	8	19	1.2	0.3	NA	NA	NA	NA	14	87	2.9	0.7
Randall	92	323	19.6	7.1	58	D	D	D	143	2 428	71.6	19.6
Reagan	4	38	1.0	0.8	NA	NA	NA	NA	9	D	D	D
Real	5	10	0.3	0.1	NA	NA	NA	NA	6	42	2.1	0.5
Red River	6	11	1.1	0.3	18	1 171	127.0	24.4	15	D	D	D
Reeves	12	147	6.2	2.2	4	D	D	D	28	285	8.4	2.3
Refugio	7	32	3.1	0.9	NA	NA	NA	NA	23	215	6.1	1.7
Roberts	NA	NA	NA	NA	NA	NA	NA	NA	1	D	D	D
Robertson	9	25	1.5	0.3	NA	NA	NA	NA	18	211	5.9	2.1
Rockwall	72	254	24.1	8.5	56	927	114.8	24.0	44	831	26.7	8.1
Runnels	13	31	1.1	0.3	15	1 453	151.1	28.1	21	119	3.2	0.7
Rusk	40	204	38.7	4.5	51	1 302	170.3	29.4	45	518	15.3	4.3
Sabine	6	14	0.8	0.2	NA	NA	NA	NA	19	166	4.3	1.2
San Augustine	7	15	0.6	0.2	NA	NA	NA	NA	8	57	1.9	0.4
San Jacinto	11	17	1.3	0.5	NA	NA	NA	NA	9	126	4.6	1.1
San Patricio	46	260	20.1	8.6	45	2 510	1 235.3	103.2	109	1 037	31.8	8.3
San Saba	10	19	0.9	0.3	NA	NA	NA	NA	12	D	D	D
Schleicher	2	D	D	D	NA	NA	NA	NA	6	D	D	D
Scurry	18	44	2.5	0.6	NA	NA	NA	NA	36	418	9.5	3.0
Shackelford	9	17	1.4	0.2	NA	NA	NA	NA	8	65	1.8	0.5
Shelby	24	132	10.3	2.0	29	1 989	303.2	39.3	23	243	8.5	2.0
Sherman	2	D	D	D	NA	NA	NA	NA	9	46	0.8	0.2
Smith	392	2 464	284.0	93.0	213	10 969	2 299.1	381.1	294	5 834	175.1	47.8
Somervell	6	15	1.3	0.3	NA	NA	NA	NA	21	197	6.1	1.9
Starr	19	80	5.0	1.4	NA	NA	NA	NA	35	326	10.9	2.4
Stephens	18	36	7.5	0.7	18	562	94.3	13.0	20	158	5.6	1.3
Sterling	4	6	0.3	0.1	NA	NA	NA	NA	4	19	0.7	0.2
Stonewall	1	D	D	D	NA	NA	NA	NA	6	23	0.6	0.1
Sutton	5	11	0.9	0.2	NA	NA	NA	NA	11	151	4.7	1.4
Swisher	4	24	1.2	0.6	NA	NA	NA	NA	12	D	D	D
Tarrant	2 965	19 656	1 912.7	734.6	2 009	95 970	18 621.6	3 583.2	2 330	49 749	1 821.5	499.8
Taylor	229	1 123	93.2	30.4	118	3 062	1 010.7	79.9	269	5 497	151.6	41.8
Terrell	3	3	0.2	0.0	NA	NA	NA	NA	2	D	D	D
Terry	15	43	2.5	0.9	NA	NA	NA	NA	24	272	7.9	2.1
Throckmorton	3	7	0.2	0.1	NA	NA	NA	NA	2	D	D	D
Titus	33	132	7.1	2.6	42	4 792	845.3	102.4	41	689	21.1	5.5

1. Firms subject to federal tax.

Table B. States and Counties — Health and Other Services and Federal Funds

STATE County	Health Care and Social Assistance[1], 1997				Other Services[1], 1997				Federal funds and grants, fiscal 2001[2] Expenditures (mil dol)			
										Direct payments for individuals[3]		
	Number of Establishments	Number of Employees	Receipts (mil dol)	Annual Payroll (mil dol)	Number of Establishments	Number of Employees	Receipts (mil dol)	Annual Payroll (mil dol)	Total	Social Security and government retirement	Medicare	Food stamps and Supplemental Security Income
	159	160	161	162	163	164	165	166	167	168	169	170
TEXAS—Cont'd												
Mason	2	D	D	D	3	D	D	D	21.0	10.5	4.7	0.5
Matagorda	50	434	21.7	8.1	63	288	20.9	7.5	195.1	69.0	29.4	6.8
Maverick	45	358	28.1	8.7	29	83	3.8	0.8	211.1	48.8	34.0	24.0
Medina	41	455	16.8	7.1	34	68	5.1	1.3	155.2	80.5	26.1	5.5
Menard	1	D	D	D	1	D	D	D	15.0	6.3	3.6	0.5
Midland	245	2 971	251.9	102.6	228	1 509	112.2	29.3	391.7	191.8	81.2	16.3
Milam	26	360	12.5	6.2	22	68	4.8	1.1	136.6	56.9	20.3	3.7
Mills	8	153	4.8	2.2	9	15	1.8	0.2	28.5	13.4	7.5	0.5
Mitchell	6	116	3.6	1.6	9	17	2.1	0.3	59.3	18.6	10.4	0.9
Montague	21	438	16.5	8.2	30	88	5.9	1.2	109.6	57.3	24.6	2.4
Montgomery	365	4 857	354.2	139.3	293	2 439	129.1	42.5	815.6	438.9	178.7	29.7
Moore	22	229	11.4	4.8	36	130	12.0	2.5	78.5	28.8	10.2	1.5
Morris	23	392	12.1	5.9	23	91	6.8	2.1	77.8	39.1	17.5	2.8
Motley	NA	NA	NA	NA	4	4	0.1	0.0	17.5	4.0	2.4	0.2
Nacogdoches	159	2 348	133.0	50.1	86	499	23.7	7.2	270.6	108.2	54.1	11.0
Navarro	59	1 510	99.8	34.8	57	278	15.0	3.9	222.9	95.7	41.4	8.6
Newton	3	D	D	D	5	14	1.3	0.2	66.8	28.2	14.2	3.5
Nolan	32	320	15.1	5.7	24	144	7.6	2.4	103.3	37.9	19.4	3.2
Nueces	853	14 979	795.0	357.7	545	3 669	216.3	66.8	1 811.9	602.3	262.4	71.3
Ochiltree	13	59	3.3	1.2	19	103	7.3	2.4	53.0	13.9	5.6	0.8
Oldham	1	D	D	D	4	9	0.3	0.1	17.1	4.5	1.9	0.2
Orange	148	1 622	82.6	35.8	97	509	34.9	10.6	377.3	182.7	97.3	14.0
Palo Pinto	48	406	18.7	7.0	49	190	17.4	3.7	125.9	65.0	28.5	3.8
Panola	33	525	16.9	7.3	28	107	6.1	1.5	122.9	49.0	23.8	3.4
Parker	101	969	46.0	18.4	100	498	30.5	8.9	277.4	169.8	48.5	4.5
Parmer	6	29	1.7	1.0	20	45	4.1	0.8	84.9	15.2	6.9	1.1
Pecos	14	191	6.9	3.2	29	214	9.5	3.4	59.3	20.2	9.1	3.0
Polk	41	590	22.3	8.5	37	128	12.4	2.5	306.0	194.6	57.9	9.6
Potter	357	5 450	440.6	191.7	232	1 524	95.5	27.7	933.2	347.9	118.6	25.2
Presidio	1	D	D	D	5	9	0.7	0.1	51.3	11.1	4.6	4.3
Rains	4	70	0.7	0.3	11	50	3.6	0.4	36.6	20.7	7.4	0.7
Randall	146	1 056	72.4	25.7	147	964	51.1	14.9	150.5	57.0	30.8	2.3
Reagan	5	29	1.2	0.7	11	29	2.9	0.7	21.1	4.9	2.1	0.3
Real	2	D	D	D	1	D	D	D	18.6	10.2	3.4	0.9
Red River	12	372	15.1	6.7	12	63	3.2	1.1	114.2	38.7	20.6	2.9
Reeves	17	163	5.7	1.8	16	36	2.4	0.7	62.4	19.8	11.2	3.7
Refugio	8	124	2.5	1.1	5	17	0.9	0.2	54.6	18.8	10.1	1.5
Roberts	1	D	D	D	NA	NA	NA	NA	5.2	1.7	0.9	0.0
Robertson	14	274	9.9	4.2	16	37	2.7	0.5	103.6	35.8	16.0	4.5
Rockwall	82	736	45.2	19.4	48	211	12.2	3.6	138.2	62.7	17.9	1.5
Runnels	26	242	11.5	5.7	16	38	2.7	0.7	91.0	28.3	14.0	1.9
Rusk	62	756	29.0	11.9	44	201	11.2	3.3	192.0	86.5	41.3	6.7
Sabine	9	338	5.6	2.7	10	19	1.7	0.4	81.7	44.1	19.9	2.0
San Augustine	13	280	11.5	5.3	9	41	1.9	0.4	58.2	23.1	12.4	2.4
San Jacinto	10	50	3.8	1.7	6	25	1.1	0.3	87.5	39.5	19.0	7.2
San Patricio	75	1 085	57.0	23.8	66	229	12.7	3.3	414.5	124.5	57.2	14.9
San Saba	7	165	5.0	2.6	8	21	1.1	0.3	44.8	13.9	8.9	1.0
Schleicher	3	D	D	D	5	10	0.8	0.1	16.3	5.6	2.9	0.4
Scurry	21	236	8.9	3.8	37	174	9.7	2.7	90.5	33.1	17.5	2.4
Shackelford	4	43	1.8	0.8	7	15	1.0	0.2	25.4	9.2	3.5	0.4
Shelby	34	697	32.7	12.8	35	115	7.7	1.8	156.5	58.3	32.6	6.0
Sherman	NA	NA	NA	NA	5	8	0.9	0.1	50.7	5.4	2.6	0.1
Smith	430	5 047	396.8	186.2	288	2 032	116.3	35.4	776.2	383.0	156.3	24.9
Somervell	11	115	5.1	2.6	6	19	0.9	0.3	32.9	12.1	5.2	1.0
Starr	41	1 150	28.2	13.6	32	98	4.2	0.9	205.5	41.4	28.5	21.2
Stephens	15	154	6.1	2.8	12	35	2.1	0.5	45.3	20.9	12.5	1.3
Sterling	2	D	D	D	2	D	D	D	14.1	2.0	1.1	0.1
Stonewall	3	D	D	D	3	13	1.0	0.4	16.7	4.7	2.5	0.2
Sutton	6	30	2.0	0.6	5	38	1.7	0.5	13.3	6.0	2.8	0.5
Swisher	5	61	2.5	1.0	13	34	2.4	0.4	70.8	17.4	8.8	1.4
Tarrant	2 847	35 845	2 381.1	1 039.4	2 145	14 698	948.3	296.2	6 805.8	2 162.8	820.2	144.4
Taylor	314	5 225	310.4	123.2	225	1 892	109.5	34.6	867.0	291.0	100.7	18.3
Terrell	NA	NA	NA	NA	1	D	D	D	7.1	3.1	1.1	0.2
Terry	11	152	7.0	2.7	20	58	4.4	1.2	117.1	24.4	16.5	2.1
Throckmorton	4	46	1.8	0.7	NA	NA	NA	NA	15.8	5.0	2.5	0.2
Titus	76	1 048	48.4	24.4	34	172	9.7	2.2	117.9	49.5	27.4	3.9

1. Firms subject to federal tax.   2. October 1, 2000 to September 30, 2001.   3. State totals may include programs not allocated by county.

	Federal funds and grants, fiscal 2001[1] (cont'd)							Local government finances, 1997				
	Expenditures (mil dol) (cont'd)							General revenue				
	Procurement contract awards			Grants[2]							Taxes	
STATE County	Salaries and wages	Defense	Other	Medicaid and other health-related	Nutrition and family welfare	Education	Other	Total (mil dol)	Intergovern-mental (mil dol)	Total (mil dol)	Per capita[3] (dollars) Total	Property
	171	172	173	174	175	176	177	178	179	180	181	182
TEXAS—Cont'd												
Mason	0.7	0.0	0.2	3.0	0.2	0.1	0.2	7.3	3.6	2.6	718	640
Matagorda	4.6	3.3	1.1	19.8	10.9	1.7	7.7	141.0	27.6	79.7	2 101	2 008
Maverick	23.8	0.0	1.5	55.2	6.9	4.7	6.7	113.6	55.3	14.8	310	231
Medina	4.6	0.2	0.9	21.0	3.1	1.5	4.1	59.8	33.4	18.3	498	390
Menard	0.4	0.0	0.1	2.5	0.1	0.1	0.2	8.1	2.9	3.1	1 311	926
Midland	28.7	5.6	6.7	21.7	4.0	6.5	12.5	370.5	88.6	123.7	1 043	806
Milam	3.3	0.0	0.9	25.3	2.0	1.1	8.6	43.2	15.1	18.4	757	627
Mills	0.9	0.0	0.3	3.7	0.2	0.4	0.6	9.5	6.0	2.5	530	447
Mitchell	1.2	0.0	0.3	7.0	0.3	0.4	4.5	22.5	5.9	10.7	1 218	1 083
Montague	3.2	0.0	0.8	11.3	0.9	0.6	4.3	46.9	27.9	10.7	587	479
Montgomery	31.8	2.5	9.9	47.2	4.9	5.7	21.2	472.9	155.0	245.3	950	848
Moore	3.7	0.0	0.3	2.7	0.3	0.6	2.6	34.3	5.0	23.5	1 205	1 116
Morris	1.7	0.0	0.5	13.0	1.6	0.7	0.3	24.2	6.6	14.2	1 071	896
Motley	0.3	0.0	0.1	1.4	0.0	0.1	2.0	2.6	1.2	1.3	1 022	908
Nacogdoches	10.8	0.4	1.9	45.5	7.6	4.4	1.9	149.5	57.6	36.2	638	457
Newton	1.5	0.0	0.5	13.4	1.9	0.7	2.6	22.6	12.3	8.1	560	498
Nolan	2.3	0.0	0.6	10.8	2.2	0.8	10.1	48.5	13.8	17.2	1 041	866
Nueces	316.7	150.4	20.1	198.8	40.9	20.1	36.9	875.9	270.9	343.0	1 080	868
Ochiltree	1.1	0.0	0.3	1.0	0.1	0.2	8.4	23.3	4.9	10.6	1 190	1 037
Oldham	0.4	0.0	0.1	0.4	0.1	0.4	3.6	6.5	2.9	2.7	1 228	1 042
Orange	8.6	0.6	2.2	34.8	5.9	2.8	16.7	192.5	57.0	85.3	1 008	835
Palo Pinto	3.1	1.0	0.8	13.8	5.5	1.0	1.7	67.7	18.2	22.9	897	690
Panola	3.8	0.0	1.1	18.3	1.3	0.8	17.8	60.3	8.8	33.6	1 461	1 432
Parker	9.6	0.9	15.1	13.6	1.9	2.5	4.4	181.7	53.7	46.5	591	491
Parmer	2.7	0.0	0.3	3.3	0.6	0.5	6.1	20.6	11.5	7.5	717	596
Pecos	2.1	0.0	0.4	7.0	2.2	1.0	7.3	70.4	7.5	44.5	2 749	2 587
Polk	4.5	0.0	1.2	24.8	3.5	1.7	5.5	68.1	23.0	31.3	659	549
Potter	98.6	126.1	124.5	43.0	11.9	5.8	23.5	357.8	123.2	146.5	1 341	982
Presidio	8.6	3.2	2.9	10.9	0.8	0.7	3.4	13.4	7.7	3.5	412	312
Rains	1.0	0.0	0.3	4.1	0.3	0.2	0.9	11.2	5.0	5.2	630	531
Randall	2.7	0.0	0.5	6.0	1.4	2.5	18.1	48.2	16.6	24.5	247	219
Reagan	0.5	0.0	0.1	0.4	0.4	0.2	2.1	14.4	2.6	7.8	1 835	1 710
Real	0.4	0.1	0.2	2.9	0.2	0.1	0.0	6.1	1.4	2.0	755	644
Red River	2.3	0.0	0.9	31.1	2.3	0.7	7.2	35.4	13.7	7.2	521	428
Reeves	2.5	0.4	1.0	13.8	2.1	1.0	1.9	50.9	22.7	12.3	831	686
Refugio	1.7	0.0	0.4	6.0	0.9	0.4	5.3	23.0	5.1	11.8	1 492	1 333
Roberts	0.3	0.0	0.1	0.2	0.0	0.0	0.1	4.3	0.1	3.8	3 869	3 761
Robertson	2.5	0.1	0.6	27.4	2.0	0.9	2.7	33.2	13.1	16.0	1 028	958
Rockwall	4.7	13.4	5.3	3.3	0.4	0.5	1.4	61.3	16.1	35.9	998	881
Runnels	2.3	0.0	0.6	10.3	0.9	0.5	10.8	31.2	16.3	7.6	665	579
Rusk	5.7	0.0	1.3	32.5	5.8	1.6	7.3	66.2	26.1	32.3	708	638
Sabine	2.4	0.0	0.6	10.9	0.8	0.4	0.5	19.6	7.1	5.8	550	431
San Augustine	1.1	0.0	0.4	15.0	0.8	0.4	1.3	13.8	7.9	3.8	468	361
San Jacinto	1.4	0.0	0.4	13.0	1.4	0.8	1.1	27.4	10.8	13.2	634	575
San Patricio	83.1	36.4	1.5	48.0	10.1	4.8	2.0	131.1	55.3	54.4	781	702
San Saba	1.2	0.2	0.3	7.8	6.6	0.4	2.9	11.2	6.4	3.4	523	425
Schleicher	0.4	0.0	0.1	1.6	0.3	0.1	0.8	10.4	2.7	5.0	1 629	1 526
Scurry	2.2	0.0	0.5	8.9	1.7	0.7	5.4	40.7	14.9	17.2	947	788
Shackelford	0.7	0.1	0.1	1.0	0.2	0.1	7.6	6.9	3.1	3.1	943	830
Shelby	4.3	0.1	1.3	37.1	5.3	1.1	7.9	41.7	24.7	11.0	487	403
Sherman	0.3	0.0	0.2	0.2	0.1	0.1	11.2	9.3	1.3	5.9	2 036	1 900
Smith	51.3	0.6	14.0	89.9	11.3	6.4	13.9	303.6	114.7	133.3	800	601
Somervell	0.9	0.0	0.2	2.7	0.1	0.2	9.9	79.1	1.3	72.0	11 545	11 462
Starr	13.3	3.5	1.7	58.0	15.4	8.1	3.8	118.3	75.3	25.4	457	396
Stephens	1.3	0.2	0.3	5.1	0.5	0.4	0.4	26.2	8.6	9.3	939	776
Sterling	0.3	0.0	0.0	0.4	0.1	0.0	9.2	5.4	0.2	4.8	3 472	3 364
Stonewall	0.5	0.0	0.1	0.8	0.1	0.1	1.9	5.7	1.1	3.4	1 883	1 726
Sutton	0.4	0.0	0.1	1.6	0.1	0.2	0.1	13.9	2.2	8.7	1 951	1 769
Swisher	1.4	0.0	0.3	4.2	1.3	0.5	4.8	20.9	10.0	6.2	737	619
Tarrant	825.1	1 768.6	316.8	330.1	64.6	37.3	181.0	3 083.7	789.8	1 568.7	1 182	927
Taylor	195.0	79.6	7.6	51.7	11.3	5.7	78.5	242.0	104.8	97.6	804	596
Terrell	0.5	0.2	0.0	1.0	0.1	0.1	0.0	5.1	0.3	3.9	3 305	3 155
Terry	1.7	0.0	0.4	10.5	1.9	0.9	14.0	36.3	11.1	14.2	1 092	989
Throckmorton	0.5	0.0	0.1	1.2	0.0	0.1	1.3	4.2	1.9	1.8	1 076	988
Titus	5.8	0.7	0.8	17.5	2.5	1.7	5.0	113.3	23.2	25.8	1 023	796

1. October 1, 2000 to September 30, 2001. 2. State totals may include programs not allocated by county. 3. Based on the resident population estimated as of July 1 of the year shown.

STATE County	Total (mil dol)	Per capita[1] (dollars)	Education	Health and hospitals	Police protection	Public welfare	Highways	Total (mil dol)	Per capita[1] (dollars)	Federal civilian	Federal military	State and local	Democratic	Republican	All other
	183	184	185	186	187	188	189	190	191	192	193	194	195	196	197
TEXAS—Cont'd															
Mason	7.5	2 044	69.9	1.0	2.7	0.3	5.7	0.4	116	16	10	259	23.2	75.1	1.8
Matagorda	137.5	3 626	54.6	17.0	3.2	0.1	4.2	41.1	1 085	94	99	2 788	37.7	60.9	1.4
Maverick	115.7	2 418	57.8	21.6	2.2	0.3	1.3	28.5	595	419	128	3 249	65.0	34.1	1.0
Medina	54.9	1 491	75.9	0.8	3.2	1.3	2.7	27.8	755	64	100	2 678	31.3	66.7	2.0
Menard	7.4	3 168	59.6	1.0	2.1	16.3	6.0	0.8	322	0	0	202	33.7	64.8	1.4
Midland	357.6	3 014	38.6	32.3	4.9	0.0	1.8	210.5	1 774	562	311	7 818	19.0	79.3	1.7
Milam	43.1	1 774	60.8	13.0	4.4	0.1	7.6	11.4	470	67	64	1 245	41.5	56.9	1.6
Mills	9.6	2 006	77.1	1.2	1.2	0.2	4.9	1.2	249	23	12	330	23.7	75.1	1.2
Mitchell	22.3	2 542	57.6	19.8	1.4	0.0	6.7	7.9	895	26	23	1 317	32.5	66.4	1.1
Montague	40.3	2 203	56.7	24.3	3.8	0.3	3.7	23.8	1 299	62	49	1 237	30.8	67.5	1.7
Montgomery	466.6	1 807	59.9	6.9	5.2	0.2	3.0	786.4	3 047	512	756	11 020	21.9	75.9	2.2
Moore	41.2	2 109	71.8	0.1	4.8	0.0	1.3	13.3	683	72	52	1 406	19.7	79.4	1.0
Morris	23.4	1 758	74.3	0.2	5.3	0.5	1.7	2.9	221	30	36	677	50.2	48.7	1.1
Motley	2.4	1 904	77.9	0.0	0.0	0.0	9.1	0.1	90	12	0	107	18.4	80.1	1.6
Nacogdoches	150.2	2 648	38.0	37.6	3.1	0.1	1.8	80.4	1 418	192	153	4 534	31.3	66.4	2.3
Navarro	99.0	2 392	66.4	1.3	4.5	0.0	5.3	46.3	1 120	112	110	2 864	38.6	60.2	1.2
Newton	20.0	1 388	79.9	0.7	4.0	0.5	1.7	2.2	154	27	38	695	50.2	48.6	1.3
Nolan	46.1	2 799	50.4	22.9	4.0	0.8	2.9	14.6	884	51	43	1 823	35.3	62.8	1.9
Nueces	790.2	2 489	49.7	15.7	6.6	0.3	2.1	730.8	2 302	5 298	3 721	21 013	46.6	51.3	2.1
Ochiltree	23.6	2 655	44.3	27.5	4.1	0.0	7.1	1.1	121	31	23	663	8.5	90.7	0.8
Oldham	6.2	2 816	66.7	0.0	6.6	0.0	5.0	0.3	119	0	0	270	14.0	85.1	0.9
Orange	195.3	2 308	50.9	0.3	4.6	0.3	3.6	636.8	7 523	139	235	4 283	40.1	58.4	1.5
Palo Pinto	71.7	2 812	38.9	37.4	3.4	0.2	2.7	31.9	1 250	60	69	1 743	35.8	62.4	1.8
Panola	56.2	2 445	61.4	16.5	2.7	0.2	4.8	12.3	536	77	60	1 334	33.2	65.8	1.0
Parker	149.0	1 891	62.2	13.7	4.0	0.1	4.1	85.1	1 079	168	224	3 889	26.7	71.2	2.1
Parmer	20.1	1 919	77.9	2.5	3.6	0.1	5.7	2.1	197	68	27	798	16.3	82.9	0.8
Pecos	79.7	4 919	50.2	19.1	1.2	0.2	2.5	9.8	602	47	42	1 880	35.8	62.7	1.5
Polk	66.5	1 401	63.3	0.0	1.9	0.0	5.9	263.0	5 542	81	138	2 608	36.2	61.8	2.0
Potter	356.0	3 259	56.4	2.6	6.8	0.0	5.9	440.4	4 032	1 861	322	10 341	28.5	69.5	2.0
Presidio	17.4	2 025	63.4	0.5	3.1	0.1	7.0	11.1	1 297	189	24	538	60.6	35.2	4.3
Rains	9.7	1 185	72.7	0.0	3.1	0.2	6.9	3.0	367	17	24	352	36.8	61.5	1.8
Randall	45.0	455	62.2	0.0	13.9	0.2	3.9	20.3	205	46	262	4 388	17.3	81.2	1.6
Reagan	12.9	3 055	54.2	16.8	3.5	0.0	4.6	1.3	298	14	10	391	22.5	76.4	1.1
Real	5.7	2 137	33.4	0.0	0.8	38.3	1.8	3.6	1 333	0	0	213	21.2	76.9	1.9
Red River	30.2	2 192	59.1	25.6	1.6	0.4	3.9	4.8	348	45	36	790	42.7	56.5	0.8
Reeves	45.0	3 028	44.6	14.3	3.3	0.1	1.8	10.3	692	72	37	1 257	58.9	40.1	1.0
Refugio	21.0	2 667	51.2	22.4	2.3	0.1	4.1	2.1	267	44	20	636	40.1	58.9	1.0
Roberts	3.9	3 947	62.5	0.3	5.3	0.1	11.0	0.3	304	10	0	87	13.1	86.0	0.9
Robertson	35.7	2 299	70.9	0.6	4.8	0.3	3.8	13.3	853	46	41	931	51.5	47.2	1.2
Rockwall	67.4	1 875	62.5	0.3	6.3	0.0	4.9	86.8	2 417	75	104	1 629	20.6	77.4	1.9
Runnels	27.8	2 426	60.5	20.9	2.4	0.0	4.7	9.5	826	42	30	861	23.9	74.6	1.4
Rusk	72.4	1 587	76.2	0.0	3.9	0.5	5.2	29.3	641	108	120	2 054	29.1	69.8	1.1
Sabine	15.0	1 422	64.1	8.8	5.0	0.0	7.1	4.8	458	56	28	501	38.2	60.2	1.6
San Augustine	13.4	1 634	76.0	0.0	4.0	0.1	4.7	0.9	110	25	21	470	43.0	55.6	1.4
San Jacinto	27.4	1 314	71.5	0.1	4.2	1.2	7.6	19.0	909	35	59	736	38.2	59.9	1.8
San Patricio	129.5	1 860	69.4	2.9	4.3	0.4	4.6	45.8	657	352	3 433	3 653	41.9	56.7	1.4
San Saba	11.4	1 776	70.8	0.8	2.3	0.3	6.7	4.6	712	27	15	688	26.5	72.5	1.0
Schleicher	9.6	3 155	52.1	24.4	2.2	0.4	6.2	1.6	527	10	0	276	28.8	70.4	0.7
Scurry	40.1	2 205	68.5	0.7	3.8	0.5	4.9	9.8	540	44	46	1 702	22.4	76.2	1.3
Shackelford	8.2	2 445	75.8	0.0	3.2	0.0	3.7	3.1	942	14	0	213	19.6	79.1	1.3
Shelby	39.8	1 759	78.5	0.0	3.2	0.4	4.3	20.8	919	91	60	1 186	35.8	63.2	0.9
Sherman	8.8	3 019	61.2	13.4	4.8	0.1	8.1	0.8	270	12	0	278	12.4	85.8	1.8
Smith	294.7	1 768	59.4	7.8	5.1	1.8	3.3	248.4	1 490	991	449	11 027	27.2	71.5	1.4
Somervell	76.7	12 298	85.0	3.6	1.1	0.0	3.1	1.3	203	16	17	567	25.8	72.7	1.6
Starr	120.9	2 176	76.9	8.6	2.6	0.2	2.5	23.4	422	243	149	3 915	76.9	22.6	0.5
Stephens	25.9	2 615	38.9	21.2	3.5	0.1	3.4	9.4	948	26	26	767	24.6	73.7	1.7
Sterling	5.4	3 864	68.6	0.2	2.8	7.7	3.4	0.5	383	0	0	155	20.0	78.9	1.1
Stonewall	5.7	3 164	47.8	29.0	3.7	0.0	3.4	0.3	180	11	0	182	36.8	62.1	1.2
Sutton	12.6	2 833	52.6	13.7	7.0	0.6	6.2	0.1	14	0	11	459	30.4	69.0	0.6
Swisher	22.2	2 660	63.8	13.2	2.4	0.1	4.0	0.6	71	35	22	726	34.2	64.5	1.3
Tarrant	3 119.2	2 350	46.9	9.1	6.3	0.3	4.2	6 035.0	4 547	13 496	4 776	71 776	36.8	60.7	2.5
Taylor	240.2	1 978	55.5	5.6	6.1	0.7	4.0	124.8	1 027	1 461	4 956	8 488	24.4	73.7	1.9
Terrell	4.8	4 019	68.6	4.1	1.8	0.0	6.1	0.2	177	10	0	234	45.9	50.9	3.2
Terry	36.6	2 817	51.0	21.9	4.7	2.6	4.6	7.4	570	36	34	1 135	27.3	71.8	0.8
Throckmorton	4.6	2 673	78.7	0.0	0.5	1.6	1.5	0.7	408	12	0	192	27.1	72.2	0.7
Titus	109.6	4 342	36.9	40.8	1.9	0.1	2.5	115.6	4 577	123	67	2 568	37.1	61.6	1.2

1. Based on the resident population estimated as of July 1 of the year shown.   2. Data subject to copyright.

Table B. States and Counties — Land Area and Population

					Population and population characteristics, 2000													
								Race alone or in combination (percent)					Age (percent)					
STATE/ County code	MSA/ PMSA/ NECMA code[1]	County Type[2]	STATE County	Land area,[3] (sq km) 2000	Total persons	Rank	Per square kilometer	White	Black	Am. Indian, Alaska Native	Asian and Pacific Islander	Percent Hispanic[4]	Under 5 years	5 to 17 years	18 to 24 years	25 to 34 years	35 to 44 years	45 to 54 years
				1	2	3	4	5	6	7	8	9	10	11	12	13	14	15
			TEXAS—Cont'd															
48 451	7200	3	Tom Green	3 942	104 010	509	26.4	81.1	4.6	1.2	1.3	30.7	6.9	19.2	12.8	12.6	14.5	12.3
48 453	0640	2	Travis	2 562	812 280	56	317.0	70.6	9.8	1.1	5.3	28.2	7.2	16.5	14.7	19.9	16.7	12.3
48 455	...	7	Trinity	1 794	13 779	2 174	7.7	84.6	12.1	0.8	0.4	4.8	5.9	17.0	7.0	9.9	12.5	12.5
48 457	...	6	Tyler	2 390	20 871	1 741	8.7	84.9	12.2	1.0	0.4	3.6	5.8	17.4	8.0	13.0	14.2	12.3
48 459	4420	3	Upshur	1 522	35 291	1 239	23.2	86.8	10.4	1.2	0.4	4.0	6.6	20.4	8.0	11.1	15.5	13.4
48 461	...	8	Upton	3 216	3 404	2 962	1.1	78.9	1.8	1.6	0.4	42.6	5.5	23.8	7.9	9.1	15.8	13.4
48 463	...	7	Uvalde	4 031	25 926	1 520	6.4	78.6	0.5	1.0	0.7	65.9	8.4	23.0	9.8	12.3	13.0	11.6
48 465	...	5	Val Verde	8 211	44 856	1 002	5.5	78.8	1.7	1.1	0.9	75.5	8.9	23.1	9.4	14.7	13.2	11.0
48 467	...	6	Van Zandt	2 198	48 140	946	21.9	93.4	3.1	1.2	0.3	6.6	6.3	19.2	7.3	10.9	14.3	13.5
48 469	8750	3	Victoria	2 286	84 088	618	36.8	76.2	6.7	0.9	1.0	39.2	7.6	21.5	9.2	12.8	15.4	13.2
48 471	...	4	Walker	2 039	61 758	786	30.3	70.3	24.3	0.7	1.1	14.1	4.9	13.1	23.0	15.3	11.9	11.9
48 473	3360	1	Waller	1 330	32 663	1 326	24.6	59.3	29.7	0.9	0.7	19.4	6.9	18.8	18.1	12.3	14.1	12.5
48 475	...	6	Ward	2 164	10 909	2 374	5.0	81.7	4.9	1.2	0.3	42.0	6.6	24.0	7.8	10.3	14.8	13.0
48 477	...	6	Washington	1 578	30 373	1 388	19.2	75.7	19.0	0.5	1.3	8.7	6.0	18.7	11.1	11.1	14.2	13.1
48 479	4080	3	Webb	8 694	193 117	284	22.2	84.5	0.5	0.6	0.6	94.3	10.6	25.6	11.4	15.9	13.4	9.6
48 481	...	6	Wharton	2 823	41 188	1 075	14.6	70.4	15.3	0.6	0.6	31.3	7.0	21.7	9.3	11.6	14.4	12.7
48 483	...	9	Wheeler	2 368	5 284	2 831	2.2	89.1	2.9	1.3	0.9	12.6	6.0	18.9	6.5	9.1	13.4	13.5
48 485	9080	3	Wichita	1 626	131 664	405	81.0	81.0	10.9	1.7	2.6	12.2	7.0	18.2	13.7	13.6	15.4	11.6
48 487	...	6	Wilbarger	2 515	14 676	2 109	5.8	79.9	9.2	1.1	1.0	20.5	6.6	21.3	9.5	11.1	13.7	12.2
48 489	...	6	Willacy	1 545	20 082	1 790	13.0	72.6	2.3	0.6	0.2	85.7	8.2	23.4	11.9	12.9	13.7	10.8
48 491	0640	2	Williamson	2 908	249 967	232	86.0	84.3	5.5	0.9	3.3	17.2	8.5	21.4	8.1	16.8	18.8	12.6
48 493	7240	1	Wilson	2 090	32 408	1 336	15.5	83.5	1.4	1.1	0.6	36.5	6.9	22.3	7.6	11.9	16.7	14.2
48 495	...	6	Winkler	2 178	7 173	2 669	3.3	76.9	2.0	0.8	0.3	44.0	7.0	22.8	8.7	11.2	14.9	12.3
48 497	...	6	Wise	2 343	48 793	935	20.8	92.6	1.4	1.5	0.5	10.8	6.8	21.5	7.8	13.1	17.2	13.4
48 499	...	6	Wood	1 684	36 752	1 196	21.8	90.1	6.3	1.0	0.3	5.7	5.2	16.6	7.9	9.8	13.2	13.2
48 501	...	7	Yoakum	2 071	7 322	2 653	3.5	72.2	1.4	1.1	0.1	45.9	7.5	24.6	8.3	10.7	16.1	12.7
48 503	...	7	Young	2 389	17 943	1 903	7.5	92.5	1.4	1.3	0.4	10.6	6.0	19.0	7.0	10.0	14.7	13.4
48 505	...	6	Zapata	2 582	12 182	2 285	4.7	86.3	0.5	0.5	0.4	84.8	9.2	23.9	10.0	12.2	11.9	10.5
48 507	...	7	Zavala	3 363	11 600	2 324	3.4	67.6	0.6	0.7	0.3	91.2	8.9	25.2	10.2	13.6	12.1	11.4
49 000	...	X	UTAH	212 751	2 233 169	X	10.5	91.1	1.1	1.8	3.2	9.0	9.4	22.8	14.2	14.6	13.4	10.6
49 001	...	9	Beaver	6 708	6 005	2 778	0.9	94.7	0.4	1.9	1.3	5.5	9.3	24.2	9.4	11.5	12.5	11.7
49 003	...	6	Box Elder	14 823	42 745	1 042	2.9	94.3	0.3	1.4	1.6	6.5	9.3	26.8	10.5	11.4	13.9	10.4
49 005	...	4	Cache	3 016	91 391	562	30.3	93.4	0.6	0.9	2.6	6.3	9.9	21.4	22.2	14.8	11.0	8.6
49 007	...	7	Carbon	3 829	20 422	1 764	5.3	93.4	0.5	1.5	0.6	10.3	7.2	21.5	12.3	10.4	14.0	13.4
49 009	...	9	Daggett	1 809	921	3 114	0.5	95.7	1.2	1.2	0.9	5.1	6.6	16.6	8.9	12.7	14.7	15.4
49 011	7160	0	Davis	789	238 994	241	302.9	94.0	1.4	1.0	2.8	5.4	9.8	25.4	12.2	13.9	14.3	10.8
49 013	...	7	Duchesne	8 387	14 371	2 135	1.7	92.4	0.3	7.2	0.5	3.5	9.1	27.7	9.4	11.1	13.6	11.3
49 015	...	9	Emery	11 530	10 860	2 376	0.9	96.8	0.3	1.3	0.7	5.2	8.1	27.2	9.6	9.9	14.2	12.5
49 017	...	9	Garfield	13 401	4 735	2 865	0.4	96.3	0.2	2.5	0.8	2.9	8.6	24.1	7.8	10.7	12.5	12.8
49 019	...	7	Grand	9 545	8 485	2 566	0.9	93.8	0.4	4.7	0.5	5.6	7.0	19.9	8.2	12.3	15.6	15.5
49 021	...	7	Iron	8 542	33 779	1 288	4.0	94.5	0.5	2.8	1.4	4.1	9.4	21.9	20.6	12.5	11.1	9.7
49 023	...	6	Juab	8 785	8 238	2 588	0.9	97.4	0.2	1.5	0.6	2.6	11.2	27.4	9.4	13.1	12.2	10.1
49 025	2620	7	Kane	10 339	6 046	2 776	0.6	97.3	0.1	2.4	0.6	2.3	6.6	22.8	6.8	9.0	12.2	14.8
49 027	...	7	Millard	17 066	12 405	2 271	0.7	95.0	0.2	1.9	0.9	7.2	8.1	29.2	8.0	9.3	13.6	11.5
49 029	...	8	Morgan	1 578	7 129	2 676	4.5	99.2	0.2	0.6	0.5	1.4	8.1	28.9	8.0	9.3	13.6	11.5
49 031	...	9	Piute	1 963	1 435	3 095	0.7	96.4	0.1	1.9	0.4	4.5	8.2	22.5	6.6	8.6	11.0	12.8
49 033	...	9	Rich	2 664	1 961	3 067	0.7	98.6	0.1	0.3	0.6	1.8	7.2	27.4	7.2	8.9	13.3	12.5
49 035	7160	0	Salt Lake	1 910	898 387	43	470.4	88.6	1.4	1.3	4.8	11.9	8.9	21.6	12.9	16.1	14.5	11.5
49 037	...	7	San Juan	20 254	14 413	2 129	0.7	42.1	0.4	56.6	0.5	3.7	9.7	29.6	10.0	12.1	13.1	10.1
49 039	...	6	Sanpete	4 113	22 763	1 658	5.5	93.8	0.4	1.5	1.2	6.6	8.3	24.9	16.4	10.4	11.4	10.1
49 041	...	7	Sevier	4 948	18 842	1 850	3.8	96.5	0.3	2.6	0.6	2.6	8.8	25.7	10.1	9.9	12.9	11.2
49 043	...	6	Summit	4 846	29 736	1 406	6.1	92.9	0.4	0.6	1.4	8.1	7.1	22.7	8.4	14.4	19.6	15.6
49 045	...	6	Tooele	17 950	40 735	1 092	2.3	91.5	1.6	2.5	1.4	10.3	11.0	24.0	11.5	15.6	13.9	10.3
49 047	...	7	Uintah	11 596	25 224	1 557	2.2	89.1	0.2	10.3	0.5	3.5	8.4	26.3	10.7	11.0	14.4	11.7
49 049	6520	2	Utah	5 176	368 536	159	71.2	94.0	0.5	1.0	2.6	7.0	11.0	23.1	21.0	15.2	10.6	7.9
49 051	...	6	Wasatch	3 049	15 215	2 074	5.0	96.9	0.3	1.2	0.9	5.1	9.2	25.0	9.9	13.8	15.2	11.6
49 053	...	4	Washington	6 285	90 354	572	14.4	95.1	0.4	2.1	1.5	5.2	9.1	22.1	11.6	11.3	11.1	9.6
49 055	...	9	Wayne	6 372	2 509	3 026	0.4	98.0	0.3	0.8	0.4	2.0	8.8	23.6	8.1	10.4	12.1	13.4
49 057	7160	0	Weber	1 491	196 533	282	131.8	89.6	1.8	1.3	2.1	12.6	9.0	22.0	12.6	13.9	14.0	11.3
50 000	...	X	VERMONT	23 956	608 827	X	25.4	97.9	0.7	1.1	1.2	0.9	5.6	18.6	9.3	12.2	16.7	15.4
50 001	...	6	Addison	1 995	35 974	1 219	18.0	98.0	0.8	0.9	1.2	1.1	5.7	19.2	12.5	11.0	15.9	15.5
50 003	...	6	Bennington	1 752	36 994	1 190	21.1	98.5	0.6	0.6	0.8	0.9	5.2	18.5	7.7	10.6	15.7	15.1
50 005	...	7	Caledonia	1 685	29 702	1 409	17.6	98.5	0.5	1.3	0.5	0.7	5.5	19.8	8.8	11.0	15.3	16.1

1. MSA = Metropolitan Statistical Area. PMSA = Primary MSA. NECMA = New England County Metropolitan Area. See Appendix A for explanation of these concepts. See Appendix B for list of metropolitan areas identified by type, with component counties. 2. County typology code from the Economic Research Service of USDA. See Appendix A for definition. 3. Dry land or land partially or temporarily covered by water. 4. Hispanic persons may be of any race.

Table B. States and Counties — Population and Households

STATE County	55 to 64 years	65 to 74 years	75 years and over	Percent female	2001	1990	1990–2000	2000–2001	Births	Deaths	Net migration	Number	Percent change, 1990–2000	Persons per household	Female family householder[1]	One person
	Age (percent) (cont'd)				**Total persons**		**Percent change**		**Components of change, 2000–2001**						**Percent**	
	16	17	18	19	20	21	22	23	24	25	26	27	28	29	30	31
TEXAS—Cont'd																
Tom Green	8.3	6.9	6.5	51.6	103 079	98 458	5.6	-0.9	2 006	1 299	-1 624	39 503	11.6	2.52	11.9	27.2
Travis	5.9	3.7	3.1	48.8	833 797	576 407	40.9	2.6	16 520	4 787	10 049	320 766	37.7	2.47	10.4	30.1
Trinity	13.3	12.7	9.3	51.7	13 903	11 445	20.4	0.9	199	268	198	5 723	23.2	2.38	11.2	26.8
Tyler	11.5	10.1	7.7	48.3	20 603	16 646	25.4	-1.3	294	296	-266	7 775	20.4	2.48	10.0	24.3
Upshur	10.6	8.0	6.3	51.1	35 888	31 370	12.5	1.7	577	481	503	13 290	17.0	2.62	11.0	21.8
Upton	10.4	8.0	6.2	51.1	3 283	4 447	-23.5	-3.6	70	46	-149	1 256	-14.7	2.68	9.1	23.5
Uvalde	8.3	7.1	6.5	51.3	26 192	23 340	11.1	1.0	614	284	-60	8 559	13.3	2.96	13.7	19.9
Val Verde	8.6	6.3	4.6	50.8	45 776	38 721	15.8	2.1	1 191	420	146	14 151	19.5	3.11	13.9	17.5
Van Zandt	11.4	9.3	7.8	50.8	49 625	37 944	26.9	3.1	751	723	1 439	18 195	26.8	2.59	8.7	22.0
Victoria	8.3	6.6	5.4	51.3	84 710	74 361	13.1	0.7	1 781	846	-293	30 071	14.7	2.75	12.7	22.4
Walker	7.1	5.1	3.8	39.8	61 350	50 917	21.3	-0.7	801	520	-688	18 303	22.7	2.44	11.7	27.0
Waller	8.0	5.1	4.2	50.3	33 591	23 374	39.7	2.8	626	298	599	10 557	42.6	2.79	13.0	21.0
Ward	9.2	8.2	6.1	50.1	10 454	13 115	-16.8	-4.2	200	134	-533	3 964	-10.8	2.66	11.6	23.6
Washington	9.0	8.3	8.5	51.4	30 621	26 154	16.1	0.8	482	439	217	11 322	17.7	2.53	11.4	25.7
Webb	6.0	4.3	3.3	51.8	201 292	133 239	44.9	4.2	6 860	1 083	2 475	50 740	47.3	3.75	18.3	12.4
Wharton	8.8	7.1	6.8	50.8	41 202	39 955	3.1	0.0	807	529	-257	14 799	4.1	2.73	12.5	24.4
Wheeler	11.7	10.3	10.5	52.1	5 101	5 879	-10.1	-3.5	80	126	-139	2 152	-8.4	2.39	7.7	29.1
Wichita	7.9	6.9	5.8	49.1	128 461	122 378	7.6	-2.4	2 427	1 697	-3 970	48 441	7.0	2.49	11.9	27.2
Wilbarger	9.4	7.4	8.8	50.5	14 114	15 121	-2.9	-3.8	240	214	-602	5 537	-3.6	2.48	10.8	29.0
Willacy	7.5	6.7	4.9	48.7	19 905	17 705	13.4	-0.9	485	155	-518	5 584	10.6	3.40	16.1	16.5
Williamson	6.5	4.0	3.3	50.2	278 067	139 551	79.1	11.2	4 821	1 410	23 985	86 766	77.8	2.82	9.6	17.6
Wilson	9.0	6.3	5.2	50.1	33 721	22 650	43.1	4.1	524	297	1 067	11 038	41.1	2.89	9.2	17.1
Winkler	8.7	7.7	6.7	50.9	7 039	8 626	-16.8	-1.9	131	109	-159	2 584	-12.1	2.72	10.1	21.7
Wise	9.6	6.1	4.5	49.6	51 475	34 679	40.7	5.5	778	534	2 384	17 178	41.1	2.77	8.2	18.3
Wood	13.2	11.6	9.2	50.7	37 646	29 380	25.1	2.4	541	651	994	14 583	27.6	2.42	8.2	24.1
Yoakum	8.5	6.5	5.0	51.4	7 285	8 786	-16.7	-0.5	133	81	-93	2 469	-13.0	2.95	8.5	17.3
Young	10.2	9.9	9.7	52.2	17 723	18 126	-1.0	-1.2	267	337	-145	7 167	0.9	2.45	9.4	26.3
Zapata	8.0	8.0	6.3	50.8	12 461	9 279	31.3	2.3	315	119	86	3 921	37.0	3.10	13.0	17.5
Zavala	7.3	6.2	5.1	50.6	11 584	12 162	-4.6	-0.1	284	125	-177	3 428	2.1	3.28	21.8	16.6
UTAH	6.4	4.5	4.0	49.9	2 269 789	1 722 850	29.6	1.6	57 516	15 429	-5 549	701 281	30.5	3.13	9.4	17.8
Beaver	7.5	7.2	6.7	48.5	6 059	4 765	26.0	0.9	164	74	-35	1 982	24.3	2.93	7.0	20.5
Box Elder	7.3	5.7	4.7	49.6	43 397	36 485	17.2	1.5	990	350	30	13 144	20.0	3.22	7.9	16.0
Cache	5.1	3.5	3.7	50.8	91 208	70 183	30.2	-0.2	2 628	503	-2 356	27 543	31.0	3.24	7.2	14.5
Carbon	7.9	6.6	6.6	51.1	19 703	20 228	1.0	-3.5	412	230	-921	7 413	7.3	2.68	10.0	23.8
Daggett	11.6	10.0	3.5	44.4	905	690	33.5	-1.7	16	6	-29	340	34.4	2.48	4.4	25.9
Davis	6.3	4.2	3.2	49.8	244 840	187 941	27.2	2.4	6 087	1 318	1 178	71 201	32.8	3.31	9.2	13.6
Duchesne	8.5	5.7	3.6	49.3	14 709	12 645	13.6	2.4	383	110	67	4 559	23.0	3.11	8.9	16.8
Emery	8.4	5.5	4.5	49.8	10 609	10 332	5.1	-2.3	198	85	-373	3 468	15.7	3.10	7.2	17.6
Garfield	8.6	8.0	6.1	48.9	4 724	3 980	19.0	-0.2	103	53	-61	1 576	19.3	2.92	6.8	20.5
Grand	9.0	7.2	5.3	50.9	8 633	6 620	28.2	1.7	137	69	82	3 434	38.0	2.44	10.7	29.5
Iron	6.4	4.8	3.7	50.4	34 448	20 789	62.5	2.0	958	227	-54	10 627	69.5	3.11	8.5	15.9
Juab	6.8	4.8	5.0	49.9	8 489	5 817	41.6	3.0	239	80	92	2 456	36.4	3.31	7.9	17.5
Kane	11.1	9.3	7.4	50.4	6 058	5 169	17.0	0.2	102	71	-20	2 237	29.8	2.67	6.0	23.3
Millard	7.9	6.6	5.7	48.8	12 424	11 333	9.5	0.2	231	144	-71	3 840	14.7	3.19	7.1	18.3
Morgan	8.5	5.3	3.4	49.3	7 337	5 528	29.0	2.9	118	42	130	2 046	31.6	3.48	5.6	11.7
Piute	13.2	9.1	8.0	48.9	1 387	1 277	12.4	-3.3	26	18	-58	509	13.4	2.79	5.7	22.4
Rich	9.4	7.5	6.6	49.1	1 979	1 725	13.7	0.9	34	16	0	645	13.8	3.01	3.7	17.1
Salt Lake	6.5	4.2	3.9	49.6	904 331	725 956	23.8	0.7	21 990	6 360	-9 734	295 141	22.6	3.00	10.4	20.8
San Juan	7.0	4.8	3.6	50.1	13 836	12 621	14.2	-4.0	374	67	-908	4 089	21.2	3.46	14.1	18.7
Sanpete	7.3	5.8	5.0	49.4	23 376	16 259	40.0	2.7	491	179	304	6 547	34.7	3.27	7.2	17.8
Sevier	8.6	6.7	6.2	50.2	18 961	15 431	22.1	0.6	418	234	-57	6 081	24.7	3.03	7.8	17.6
Summit	7.2	3.1	1.7	48.0	31 103	15 518	91.6	4.6	520	128	960	10 332	96.0	2.87	6.2	18.4
Tooele	6.3	4.2	3.1	50.8	44 157	26 601	53.1	8.4	1 027	274	2 603	12 677	47.5	3.11	9.5	16.8
Uintah	7.6	5.7	4.2	50.2	25 926	22 211	13.6	2.8	545	199	355	8 187	22.7	3.05	10.6	17.2
Utah	4.8	3.4	3.0	50.4	377 411	263 590	39.8	2.4	11 939	1 896	-1 110	99 937	42.4	3.59	8.0	11.2
Wasatch	6.9	4.9	3.6	49.2	16 200	10 089	50.8	6.5	329	96	734	4 743	54.3	3.18	7.5	14.3
Washington	8.3	9.1	7.8	50.7	95 590	48 560	86.1	5.8	2 211	873	3 806	29 939	96.2	2.97	8.0	17.5
Wayne	9.2	7.5	7.0	49.1	2 554	2 177	15.3	1.8	53	34	26	890	27.3	2.81	5.3	21.5
Weber	6.9	5.4	5.0	49.8	199 435	158 330	24.1	1.5	4 793	1 693	-129	65 698	23.4	2.95	10.7	20.0
VERMONT	9.3	6.7	6.0	51.0	613 090	562 758	8.2	0.7	7 872	6 428	2 981	240 634	14.2	2.44	9.3	26.2
Addison	8.8	6.0	5.3	50.6	36 263	32 953	9.2	0.8	423	348	225	13 068	14.5	2.55	8.3	23.4
Bennington	10.6	8.8	7.9	52.0	37 148	35 845	3.2	0.4	444	504	224	14 846	9.2	2.41	10.1	26.8
Caledonia	9.2	7.4	7.0	50.6	29 770	27 846	6.7	0.2	372	350	59	11 663	12.5	2.46	10.4	25.6

1. No spouse present.

Table B. States and Counties — **Vital Statistics, Health Resources, and Crime**

STATE County	Births, average 1997–1999 Total	Rate[1]	Deaths, average 1997–1999 Number Total	Number Infant[2]	Rate Total[1]	Rate Infant[3]	Physicians,[4] 2000 Number	Rate[5]	Hospitals,[4] 1998 Number	Beds Number	Beds Rate[5]	Medicare enrollees 2000	Serious crimes known to police, 2000[6] Total Number	Rate[7]
	32	33	34	35	36	37	38	39	40	41	42	43	44	45
TEXAS—Cont'd														
Tom Green	1 587	15.5	977	12	9.5	7.4	213	205	3	478	465	15 721	5 203	5 002
Travis	12 242	17.2	3 753	69	5.3	5.6	1 771	218	7	1 517	213	61 380	44 316	5 456
Trinity	154	12.2	197	NA	15.6	NA	4	29	1	22	174	3 162	408	2 961
Tyler	213	10.5	242	NA	11.9	NA	11	53	1	36	176	3 840	270	1 294
Upshur	452	12.6	382	NA	10.6	NA	8	23	0	0	0	6 001	871	2 468
Upton	59	16.0	30	NA	8.1	NA	3	88	2	66	1 760	520	39	1 146
Uvalde	471	18.3	223	NA	8.7	NA	28	108	1	64	250	3 835	1 400	5 400
Val Verde	931	21.3	300	7	6.9	7.2	42	94	1	78	178	4 005	1 655	3 690
Van Zandt	555	12.6	570	NA	12.9	NA	15	31	1	26	59	8 255	1 232	2 559
Victoria	1 372	16.7	663	NA	8.1	NA	183	218	3	588	711	11 326	4 081	4 853
Walker	575	10.5	440	NA	8.0	NA	44	71	1	119	216	5 838	2 108	3 413
Waller	438	16.0	226	NA	8.2	NA	12	37	0	0	0	3 026	968	2 964
Ward	174	14.9	107	NA	9.2	NA	9	83	1	41	347	1 744	209	1 916
Washington	363	12.5	330	NA	11.4	NA	40	132	1	60	206	5 591	1 223	4 027
Webb	4 991	26.5	886	27	4.7	5.4	167	86	2	377	200	16 780	13 778	7 135
Wharton	611	15.2	396	NA	9.9	NA	69	168	2	221	551	6 298	2 096	5 089
Wheeler	58	11.0	90	NA	16.9	NA	6	114	2	63	1 190	1 226	41	776
Wichita	1 869	14.5	1 262	17	9.8	8.9	279	212	3	423	328	19 279	6 950	5 279
Wilbarger	196	14.0	172	NA	12.3	NA	28	191	1	52	379	2 668	699	4 763
Willacy	380	19.4	122	NA	6.2	NA	8	40	0	0	0	2 584	481	2 395
Williamson	3 720	16.5	1 063	17	4.7	4.7	211	84	3	213	95	18 414	5 788	2 316
Wilson	422	13.5	240	NA	7.7	NA	9	28	1	30	95	3 652	347	1 071
Winkler	129	16.4	77	NA	9.8	NA	6	84	1	16	201	1 105	102	1 422
Wise	618	13.9	398	NA	9.0	NA	18	37	1	50	113	5 367	801	1 642
Wood	400	11.6	487	NA	14.2	NA	25	68	2	78	227	8 021	976	2 656
Yoakum	125	15.8	63	NA	7.9	NA	3	41	1	24	300	967	132	1 803
Young	229	13.0	262	NA	14.9	NA	14	78	2	83	469	3 810	481	2 681
Zapata	234	20.6	89	NA	7.9	NA	3	25	0	0	0	1 362	74	607
Zavala	226	19.0	92	NA	7.8	NA	4	34	0	0	0	1 594	283	2 440
UTAH	44 065	21.0	11 820	243	5.6	5.5	3 665	164	39	4 269	203	206 056	99 958	4 476
Beaver	114	19.2	58	NA	9.8	NA	5	83	2	70	1 187	919	98	1 889
Box Elder	785	18.7	266	NA	6.3	NA	34	80	2	57	136	4 867	1 248	3 119
Cache	2 087	24.1	397	12	4.6	5.9	114	125	1	139	160	6 985	2 271	2 485
Carbon	334	16.0	195	NA	9.3	NA	21	103	1	88	420	3 255	685	3 354
Daggett	8	10.4	NA	NA	NA	NA	0	0	0	0	0	126	15	1 629
Davis	4 738	20.3	997	23	4.3	4.8	214	90	2	248	106	18 447	6 761	2 829
Duchesne	256	17.6	90	NA	6.2	NA	18	125	1	42	290	1 820	480	3 340
Emery	199	18.1	72	NA	6.6	NA	0	0	0	0	0	1 276	301	2 772
Garfield	80	18.7	42	NA	9.9	NA	3	63	1	20	468	778	NA	NA
Grand	126	15.5	63	NA	7.8	NA	9	106	1	34	421	1 172	481	5 669
Iron	668	23.2	174	NA	6.1	NA	17	50	1	47	164	3 440	1 124	3 339
Juab	164	21.6	62	NA	8.1	NA	4	49	1	20	264	881	NA	NA
Kane	99	16.1	52	NA	8.5	NA	6	99	1	33	532	1 118	NA	NA
Millard	217	17.7	103	NA	8.4	NA	5	40	2	40	327	1 606	379	3 055
Morgan	115	16.4	29	NA	4.1	NA	4	56	0	0	0	680	88	1 234
Piute	19	13.3	17	NA	11.9	NA	0	0	0	0	0	281	38	2 648
Rich	36	19.6	14	NA	7.6	NA	0	0	0	0	0	275	38	1 938
Salt Lake	17 086	20.2	4 877	101	5.8	5.9	2 264	252	9	1 924	226	79 611	49 171	5 476
San Juan	280	20.5	65	NA	4.8	NA	5	35	1	25	182	1 215	99	687
Sanpete	369	17.1	146	NA	6.8	NA	15	66	2	41	191	2 686	557	2 741
Sevier	315	17.2	158	NA	8.6	NA	12	64	1	27	146	2 776	793	4 209
Summit	437	16.4	83	NA	3.1	NA	47	158	0	0	0	1 555	1 237	4 160
Tooele	680	20.2	205	NA	6.1	NA	19	47	1	38	114	3 123	933	2 290
Uintah	448	17.4	156	NA	6.1	NA	18	71	1	39	152	2 711	694	2 751
Utah	8 794	26.0	1 473	42	4.4	4.8	398	108	4	610	182	26 276	12 549	3 405
Wasatch	264	19.9	77	NA	5.8	NA	9	59	1	40	301	1 365	247	1 623
Washington	1 658	20.1	629	9	7.6	5.6	115	127	1	103	125	14 032	2 158	2 388
Wayne	41	17.2	23	NA	9.5	NA	0	0	0	0	0	388	63	2 511
Weber	3 648	19.8	1 291	23	7.0	6.2	309	157	2	584	317	22 258	9 592	4 881
VERMONT	6 530	11.0	4 998	41	8.5	6.3	1 535	252	15	1 566	265	89 028	18 185	2 987
Addison	369	10.5	259	NA	7.4	NA	59	164	1	45	128	4 452	669	1 860
Bennington	374	10.4	396	NA	11.0	NA	105	284	1	140	389	6 690	824	2 227
Caledonia	303	10.6	268	NA	9.3	NA	40	135	1	37	130	4 874	699	2 001

1. Per 1,000 estimated resident population, average 1997–1999.   2. Deaths of infants under 1 year old.   3. Deaths of infants under 1 year old per 1,000 live births.   4. Data subject to copyright.   5. Per 100,000 resident population as of July 1 of the year shown.   6. Data for serious crimes have not been adjusted for underreporting; this may affect comparability between geographic areas and over time.   7. Per 100,000 population estimated by the FBI.

Table B. States and Counties — Crime, Education, Money Income, and Poverty

	Serious crimes known to police, 2000[1] (cont'd)		Education						Money income				Income and poverty, 1998			
	Rate[2]		School enrollment and attainment, 1990				Local government expenditures, fiscal 1999[5]		1989					Percent below poverty level		
			Enrollment[3]		Attainment[4] (percent)					Households						
										Median						
STATE County	Violent	Property	Total	Percent private	High school graduate or more	Bachelor's degree or more	Total current expenditures (mil dol)	Current expenditures per student (dollars)	Per capita[6] (dollars)	Dollars	Percent change, 1979–1989 (constant 1989 dollars)	Percent with $100,000 or more	Median household income	All persons	Persons under 18	Persons 5–17 in families
	46	47	48	49	50	51	52	53	54	55	56	57	58	59	60	61

TEXAS—Cont'd																
Tom Green	393	4 609	28 123	5.9	71.0	17.0	114.6	5 830	11 482	24 349	0.1	2.3	32 423	16.7	23.8	22.5
Travis	430	5 026	182 331	10.3	83.4	34.7	627.3	5 612	15 123	27 488	4.2	4.4	43 489	10.9	16.7	15.0
Trinity	414	2 547	2 345	2.1	60.7	9.0	15.5	6 560	9 605	16 963	-3.5	1.3	25 508	20.2	32.2	33.6
Tyler	225	1 068	3 694	3.2	62.2	8.5	23.1	6 031	9 733	20 647	1.5	0.5	28 173	18.3	26.0	25.5
Upshur	207	2 261	8 175	11.7	67.1	8.8	38.4	5 676	10 254	21 889	-13.1	1.7	30 276	15.6	20.9	21.7
Upton	235	911	1 325	4.0	62.5	10.3	9.0	9 265	9 500	24 342	-0.9	0.7	32 640	16.3	21.7	22.9
Uvalde	482	4 918	6 905	5.0	56.1	13.5	38.4	6 107	8 625	18 001	-7.2	2.1	23 603	27.7	36.6	38.3
Val Verde	337	3 353	11 484	7.5	56.1	13.0	54.6	5 364	7 904	18 042	-6.6	1.5	25 002	28.1	35.8	36.3
Van Zandt	239	2 320	8 188	4.2	62.1	8.7	46.6	5 073	10 130	21 072	-2.0	1.0	30 777	14.3	20.1	19.6
Victoria	558	4 295	21 249	10.1	70.2	14.1	98.0	6 050	12 196	26 945	-12.4	3.0	36 678	15.1	22.1	21.4
Walker	421	2 992	17 934	7.7	73.3	19.0	47.8	6 333	10 090	21 631	0.0	2.4	32 566	17.3	21.8	21.1
Waller	272	2 691	8 414	7.2	69.6	16.2	39.1	5 867	10 294	22 334	-23.3	2.2	31 098	17.0	22.0	23.2
Ward	183	1 733	3 744	2.6	63.2	10.4	16.7	6 396	9 971	22 270	-17.9	1.8	30 511	19.3	25.8	27.7
Washington	533	3 493	7 103	8.4	62.9	15.1	29.0	5 586	11 036	23 052	-1.0	2.5	34 808	14.4	21.2	20.7
Webb	528	6 606	48 323	7.0	47.8	11.1	263.5	5 577	6 771	18 074	-3.3	2.1	24 194	30.4	37.0	36.3
Wharton	568	4 521	10 781	7.7	61.2	11.8	48.9	5 628	10 911	23 896	-7.2	2.7	31 428	16.5	23.3	22.0
Wheeler	57	719	1 439	3.3	65.2	12.7	9.7	9 204	10 370	20 108	-12.4	1.2	29 044	17.2	23.7	24.0
Wichita	491	4 788	30 985	8.7	75.1	16.5	129.2	5 691	11 635	23 899	-7.2	2.2	33 755	15.2	21.7	20.3
Wilbarger	368	4 395	3 525	5.1	62.9	12.7	15.6	5 445	9 823	20 886	3.9	0.9	28 872	17.7	25.3	25.8
Willacy	368	2 027	6 016	1.9	42.9	8.8	32.7	6 554	6 074	14 590	-13.7	1.3	19 423	37.8	44.8	49.1
Williamson	184	2 132	40 989	12.0	81.4	24.6	296.2	5 344	13 490	33 695	2.7	2.7	53 894	5.7	7.9	7.7
Wilson	133	938	5 889	8.0	61.2	8.8	35.9	5 385	9 728	23 184	2.8	1.9	35 530	13.9	18.1	19.4
Winkler	223	1 199	2 463	1.7	57.5	10.1	14.3	7 535	9 843	22 366	-20.3	1.3	31 812	16.8	21.4	22.8
Wise	164	1 478	8 369	7.7	67.1	10.0	45.1	5 732	11 307	25 885	-5.7	2.4	38 685	9.9	13.3	12.8
Wood	430	2 226	6 456	8.4	65.7	9.6	34.1	5 653	10 937	20 927	-2.4	2.1	28 493	15.6	21.3	23.5
Yoakum	300	1 502	2 443	1.2	64.0	10.4	16.7	7 693	10 592	26 442	-10.9	4.0	34 095	16.9	22.6	22.6
Young	262	2 419	4 071	6.0	60.7	11.2	20.1	5 582	11 368	21 710	-9.4	2.7	29 414	17.3	23.5	24.3
Zapata	41	566	2 943	2.8	50.1	6.9	18.3	6 246	6 541	14 926	-13.4	1.1	21 924	30.2	35.7	42.0
Zavala	517	1 922	3 795	1.7	38.6	6.9	17.4	6 870	4 818	11 822	-20.8	0.8	16 096	43.1	47.5	53.9
UTAH	256	4 220	610 696	11.1	85.1	22.3	2 025.7	4 210	11 029	29 470	-0.5	2.5	41 380	10.0	12.7	10.7
Beaver	116	1 773	1 514	4.4	83.4	9.0	6.7	4 593	8 558	21 092	-1.3	0.6	32 273	12.4	15.5	14.1
Box Elder	150	2 969	12 531	4.2	83.6	17.6	46.1	4 117	11 045	33 468	14.6	1.6	45 460	8.4	10.9	9.5
Cache	83	2 402	29 988	2.7	89.3	30.0	76.2	3 996	9 544	26 949	7.9	1.6	38 849	10.6	12.3	11.2
Carbon	211	3 144	6 750	6.2	74.3	12.5	23.0	4 968	10 225	25 555	-24.3	1.1	35 723	15.9	19.8	18.1
Daggett	109	1 520	213	0.0	75.4	11.7	2.0	10 847	9 575	22 941	-17.0	0.0	37 557	10.7	13.2	14.3
Davis	145	2 684	67 833	6.1	89.9	23.5	242.0	4 082	11 611	35 108	0.4	3.0	50 168	6.6	8.5	6.7
Duchesne	237	3 103	4 591	2.4	74.8	11.8	20.8	4 820	8 197	23 653	-18.6	1.1	32 265	18.7	21.0	20.2
Emery	46	2 726	3 874	2.8	82.4	10.4	15.3	4 924	9 257	30 525	-10.3	0.3	40 022	13.1	15.3	14.0
Garfield	NA	NA	1 141	2.4	79.9	15.0	6.9	6 219	8 248	21 160	2.1	1.1	29 469	15.3	20.8	19.2
Grand	389	5 280	1 835	6.2	79.9	15.4	7.9	4 859	9 899	21 695	-24.6	0.9	29 886	17.7	22.0	23.0
Iron	101	3 238	8 405	2.4	85.8	21.9	32.0	4 606	8 539	23 185	-4.4	1.0	33 386	15.8	19.9	17.8
Juab	NA	NA	1 958	3.4	77.3	8.8	10.3	4 774	8 332	23 569	-6.8	0.0	36 129	11.7	14.5	13.1
Kane	NA	NA	1 602	2.6	82.5	11.8	7.7	5 303	8 721	21 134	3.0	0.6	31 442	15.7	19.1	19.4
Millard	121	2 934	4 160	5.0	84.9	15.9	19.4	5 375	8 574	26 376	21.0	0.3	35 969	14.7	17.2	16.2
Morgan	0	1 234	2 061	4.5	90.1	19.0	9.0	4 419	10 448	33 274	-4.9	2.6	51 844	5.2	7.0	6.0
Piute	488	2 160	407	1.0	79.8	12.5	2.9	6 921	8 160	19 125	-0.1	0.9	26 774	19.0	23.3	22.5
Rich	0	1 938	569	3.5	81.8	15.1	3.6	7 154	8 610	24 940	-7.8	1.0	36 297	11.5	13.3	14.2
Salt Lake	359	5 116	239 033	8.7	85.3	23.8	736.5	4 113	12 222	30 149	-2.3	3.2	45 484	9.1	12.2	9.7
San Juan	83	604	4 755	2.0	59.7	13.1	25.2	7 357	5 907	17 289	-21.9	1.0	28 674	25.6	24.8	28.8
Sanpete	128	2 613	6 532	1.5	82.0	15.6	24.6	4 489	7 585	20 197	-1.4	1.0	30 896	16.2	19.1	16.5
Sevier	255	3 954	5 264	5.1	81.9	12.6	20.9	4 374	8 615	23 300	-11.6	0.5	33 245	14.6	17.3	16.2
Summit	98	4 062	4 785	7.6	91.6	32.9	31.5	5 179	16 739	36 756	12.0	7.4	57 019	5.2	6.7	6.1
Tooele	133	2 158	8 396	4.6	77.3	11.3	33.6	4 112	10 568	30 178	-8.5	0.5	45 633	8.5	12.3	10.2
Uintah	159	2 593	7 622	3.4	73.7	11.2	28.2	4 361	8 379	23 968	-22.9	1.0	33 711	17.0	19.3	18.9
Utah	94	3 311	114 352	30.5	87.9	26.2	308.8	3 932	9 051	27 432	1.1	2.2	42 419	10.1	11.7	9.6
Wasatch	46	1 577	3 158	5.2	83.2	18.5	13.9	3 889	10 722	27 981	7.6	3.5	44 558	7.7	9.6	8.9
Washington	266	2 123	16 064	3.4	84.5	17.7	71.6	3 868	9 450	24 602	8.7	1.9	35 522	12.4	15.9	14.6
Wayne	199	2 312	736	1.4	82.0	20.0	3.6	6 569	7 692	20 000	8.0	0.7	29 319	16.2	19.8	19.7
Weber	324	4 556	50 567	5.6	82.5	18.0	175.5	4 302	11 637	30 125	4.0	1.6	43 744	11.1	15.3	13.0
VERMONT	114	2 873	145 988	17.3	80.8	24.3	792.7	7 541	13 527	29 792	20.2	2.8	37 947	9.6	12.6	10.3
Addison	53	1 807	9 338	29.2	82.0	25.1	51.1	8 621	12 717	30 112	21.8	2.6	39 828	9.3	11.3	9.3
Bennington	92	2 135	8 718	21.9	77.8	23.5	47.5	8 390	13 543	28 485	15.5	3.3	37 144	10.3	14.2	11.8
Caledonia	89	1 912	7 117	18.5	77.4	19.0	36.7	9 082	11 425	25 356	15.2	1.6	32 847	12.9	16.8	13.9

1. Data for serious crimes have not been adjusted for underreporting; this may affect comparability between geographic areas and over time. 2. Per 100,000 population estimated by the FBI. 3. All persons 3 years old and over enrolled in nursery school through college. 4. Persons 25 years old and over. 5. Elementary and secondary education expenditures, local government fiscal years ending between July 1, 1998 and June 30, 1999. 6. Based on population enumerated as of April 1, 1990.

Table B. States and Counties — **Personal Income**

STATE County	Personal income, 1999												
			Per capita[1]						Transfer payments				
										Government payments to individuals			
	Total (mil dol)	Percent change, 1998–1999	Dollars	Rank	Wages and salaries[2] (mil dol)	Proprietor's income (mil dol)	Dividends, interest, and rent (mil dol)	Total (mil dol)	Total (mil dol)	Social Security (mil dol)	Medical payments (mil dol)	Income mainte-nance (mil dol)	Unemploy-ment insurance (mil dol)
	62	63	64	65	66	67	68	69	70	71	72	73	74
TEXAS—Cont'd													
Tom Green	2 399	3.3	23 453	974	1 390	222	505	378	360	146	150	31	5
Travis	25 905	11.1	35 632	76	22 626	2 322	4 041	1 642	1 516	612	598	152	30
Trinity	241	6.1	18 918	2 309	59	26	47	72	70	31	28	7	1
Tyler	346	2.1	16 889	2 757	93	32	57	97	93	40	39	9	2
Upshur	692	5.0	18 932	2 305	156	90	104	150	143	62	60	11	3
Upton	66	-0.5	18 460	2 424	40	1	15	14	13	6	5	2	0
Uvalde	465	4.6	17 872	2 563	221	46	103	107	103	31	45	17	2
Val Verde	704	5.5	15 926	2 904	451	35	105	144	137	37	58	30	3
Van Zandt	933	6.4	20 771	1 748	216	87	136	200	192	83	87	12	2
Victoria	2 075	3.6	25 273	620	1 091	186	443	293	279	109	126	27	5
Walker	977	4.3	17 769	2 583	631	57	183	156	147	55	59	15	1
Waller	604	5.5	21 534	1 514	274	33	66	100	95	32	38	8	1
Ward	203	-4.0	17 621	2 618	97	16	43	44	42	18	16	5	1
Washington	810	4.3	27 827	346	360	80	271	124	119	51	52	10	1
Webb	2 726	5.5	14 112	3 044	1 785	260	303	547	513	112	248	117	9
Wharton	925	6.1	22 956	1 100	379	143	170	161	154	59	68	17	3
Wheeler	149	5.8	28 090	325	41	51	24	30	29	11	14	2	0
Wichita	3 142	3.9	24 499	757	1 905	398	635	466	445	175	182	43	8
Wilbarger	325	9.6	23 145	1 059	179	38	61	68	65	25	29	7	0
Willacy	250	6.3	12 746	3 088	88	25	31	86	83	19	40	20	2
Williamson	6 878	16.9	28 552	279	4 179	429	704	436	395	187	152	24	7
Wilson	686	10.5	21 113	1 634	117	54	79	95	89	33	40	10	1
Winkler	135	-0.3	17 456	2 657	64	13	25	32	31	12	14	3	1
Wise	1 057	10.2	22 635	1 183	355	106	132	127	119	57	45	8	2
Wood	687	4.8	19 942	2 010	216	105	123	176	170	74	71	10	2
Yoakum	161	13.2	20 587	1 816	97	31	28	26	25	10	10	3	1
Young	428	1.2	24 364	789	171	74	105	89	86	38	38	7	2
Zapata	143	-0.8	12 494	3 090	64	8	31	42	40	10	20	7	1
Zavala	135	10.2	11 351	3 097	53	20	13	50	48	11	21	14	1
UTAH	49 573	5.9	23 276	X	34 015	3 998	8 696	5 040	4 665	2 025	1 692	393	103
Beaver	113	10.6	18 740	2 357	54	27	19	20	19	7	8	1	0
Box Elder	922	6.2	21 551	1 505	659	86	139	102	94	48	32	6	2
Cache	1 675	5.5	19 177	2 235	1 043	141	302	180	164	71	56	12	3
Carbon	432	2.8	20 684	1 782	274	25	65	88	84	33	32	7	2
Daggett	13	3.4	18 710	2 365	13	1	3	2	2	1	1	0	0
Davis	5 417	7.1	22 631	1 184	2 852	312	865	428	387	172	133	28	8
Duchesne	242	1.8	16 369	2 851	126	20	38	49	46	17	19	6	2
Emery	184	3.1	16 635	2 803	141	14	25	32	30	14	11	3	1
Garfield	81	7.1	18 865	2 330	49	7	15	15	14	7	5	1	1
Grand	173	8.0	21 106	1 637	100	20	39	27	25	12	8	3	1
Iron	534	5.0	18 124	2 517	326	52	89	79	74	33	26	6	1
Juab	122	3.7	15 653	2 934	60	11	19	24	23	9	10	2	1
Kane	134	4.3	21 840	1 402	55	17	27	23	21	11	7	2	0
Millard	208	3.8	16 757	2 788	114	36	37	35	33	15	12	3	1
Morgan	147	6.5	20 469	1 845	46	17	27	12	11	6	3	1	0
Piute	23	6.8	15 481	2 945	6	5	4	5	5	3	2	1	0
Rich	33	10.0	16 958	2 741	12	6	9	5	5	3	1	0	0
Salt Lake	23 254	5.2	27 350	390	18 573	1 902	4 203	2 031	1 880	826	665	156	41
San Juan	186	4.9	13 639	3 065	116	17	27	42	39	10	15	12	1
Sanpete	318	5.8	14 419	3 027	146	37	55	61	57	27	21	5	1
Sevier	315	4.7	16 873	2 760	180	28	56	63	60	27	24	5	1
Summit	1 153	8.1	41 642	35	416	156	223	40	35	18	10	1	2
Tooele	692	11.5	19 327	2 202	406	35	90	69	63	25	24	6	2
Uintah	401	4.3	15 453	2 946	245	41	63	76	71	29	28	8	3
Utah	6 521	6.9	18 793	2 350	4 324	545	939	705	644	270	262	55	14
Wasatch	312	9.6	22 643	1 180	115	26	54	30	28	15	8	2	1
Washington	1 629	6.7	19 072	2 266	816	189	406	275	260	140	88	14	3
Wayne	45	4.3	18 754	2 355	23	8	8	7	7	3	2	1	0
Weber	4 295	5.3	23 160	1 057	2 724	218	852	513	480	174	180	45	13
VERMONT	15 345	4.7	25 845	X	9 249	1 333	3 138	2 195	2 060	873	809	230	46
Addison	829	5.2	23 382	991	410	86	175	102	93	44	31	11	4
Bennington	989	3.9	27 512	371	532	88	277	148	139	68	48	15	3
Caledonia	609	3.9	21 119	1 628	295	79	119	111	105	46	35	14	4

1. Based on the resident population estimated as of July 1 of the year shown.   2. Includes other labor income.

Table B. States and Counties — Earnings, Social Security, and Housing

STATE County	Earnings, 1999 Total (mil dol)	Farm	Goods-related[1] Total	Goods-related[1] Manu-facturing	Service-related and other[2] Total	Retail trade	Finance, insurance, and real estate	Services	Govern-ment	Social Security beneficiaries, December 2000 Number	Rate[3]	Supplemental Security Income recipients, December 2000	Housing units, 1990 Total	Percent change, 1980–1990
	75	76	77	78	79	80	81	82	83	84	85	86	87	88
TEXAS—Cont'd														
Tom Green	1 612	0.5	19.9	11.8	54.3	10.6	5.8	24.6	25.4	17 975	173	2 204	40 135	22.1
Travis	24 947	0.0	25.5	19.8	57.8	7.4	7.1	30.9	16.6	70 652	87	9 351	264 173	50.9
Trinity	85	7.2	20.6	13.8	49.9	11.2	4.5	19.1	22.3	3 720	270	453	7 200	22.8
Tyler	125	0.1	D	12.6	D	12.1	5.4	14.1	34.6	4 687	225	506	9 047	8.1
Upshur	246	4.0	22.5	9.8	54.6	15.4	5.6	20.0	19.0	7 438	211	770	12 887	12.1
Upton	41	-8.7	D	D	D	5.3	D	7.6	32.2	647	190	64	1 868	-0.4
Uvalde	267	2.5	15.2	7.1	53.0	12.3	3.6	20.3	29.3	4 435	171	1 024	9 692	16.1
Val Verde	486	-1.5	D	2.9	D	10.8	3.3	14.8	53.9	6 340	141	2 107	13 905	13.4
Van Zandt	303	6.8	20.1	2.8	53.7	15.0	4.0	19.2	19.4	9 948	207	859	17 013	24.8
Victoria	1 277	0.6	25.7	11.4	57.7	13.3	5.8	27.0	16.0	13 283	158	1 882	29 162	18.3
Walker	688	0.2	10.0	6.4	31.6	10.6	2.8	13.3	58.2	6 509	105	807	18 349	26.9
Waller	307	-0.4	31.0	21.9	39.4	14.2	3.7	11.4	29.9	3 778	116	474	8 824	31.3
Ward	113	-3.4	32.4	1.5	D	10.5	3.7	13.5	29.6	2 095	192	277	5 365	2.0
Washington	439	1.6	30.1	21.0	49.6	11.7	7.3	16.6	18.7	6 247	206	813	11 717	21.5
Webb	2 045	0.0	D	2.5	D	13.6	5.7	19.1	26.6	19 242	100	7 983	37 197	34.0
Wharton	522	16.3	20.3	10.7	45.8	11.1	4.0	18.1	17.6	7 346	178	1 074	16 277	6.4
Wheeler	92	41.3	8.1	2.0	34.5	7.6	2.3	13.7	16.2	1 359	257	114	3 071	-4.1
Wichita	2 303	0.5	26.5	14.7	41.9	9.4	4.2	20.0	31.1	20 989	159	2 501	51 413	6.3
Wilbarger	217	6.7	23.1	16.2	34.2	8.8	4.2	11.7	36.0	2 973	203	417	6 812	4.2
Willacy	113	12.9	D	D	47.9	10.6	2.8	19.0	34.1	3 007	150	1 123	6 072	13.6
Williamson	4 608	0.3	15.4	8.1	76.0	5.9	3.5	13.2	8.3	22 845	91	1 729	54 466	92.9
Wilson	171	5.2	19.6	5.8	45.8	13.0	3.9	19.0	29.5	4 603	142	584	8 516	37.2
Winkler	77	-0.4	37.5	0.5	D	7.4	2.6	13.9	23.8	1 357	189	181	3 708	-3.8
Wise	461	1.0	32.1	15.6	51.8	14.0	4.0	14.9	15.2	6 827	140	419	14 219	29.1
Wood	321	12.9	18.2	7.3	53.0	12.3	4.6	23.4	15.8	8 839	241	730	14 541	27.1
Yoakum	128	12.6	31.2	3.2	39.1	4.8	1.5	15.9	17.0	1 157	158	105	3 372	11.5
Young	245	0.4	D	18.4	D	8.7	4.9	14.6	16.3	4 299	240	349	8 523	3.4
Zapata	72	-0.8	33.0	0.8	D	8.7	3.8	12.5	35.0	1 618	133	454	4 225	38.3
Zavala	74	23.2	D	D	D	5.9	2.0	18.0	30.9	1 953	168	873	4 180	18.4
UTAH	38 013	0.7	22.1	13.1	59.2	10.5	7.7	27.7	18.0	241 086	108	20 174	598 388	22.1
Beaver	81	29.4	9.5	4.1	D	10.3	1.5	10.8	21.7	951	158	55	2 200	21.1
Box Elder	745	3.7	D	53.8	D	11.0	1.8	9.0	10.3	5 827	136	280	11 890	15.5
Cache	1 184	3.1	D	26.0	D	8.7	3.6	21.8	23.5	8 425	92	446	22 053	16.9
Carbon	299	-0.6	30.2	4.7	D	9.7	D	22.1	21.4	3 781	185	354	8 713	6.4
Daggett	14	-0.8	D	D	D	3.7	1.4	23.7	55.0	148	161	3	825	11.9
Davis	3 165	0.3	20.5	11.9	43.3	11.4	4.4	20.0	35.9	21 923	92	1 206	55 777	34.2
Duchesne	145	1.0	24.1	4.0	44.0	9.1	2.4	14.5	30.9	2 285	159	222	5 860	30.9
Emery	155	0.5	39.8	1.0	D	4.3	1.0	10.3	17.6	1 598	147	132	3 928	6.1
Garfield	56	-0.8	D	6.2	D	7.3	2.9	33.4	31.8	894	189	30	2 488	40.6
Grand	120	0.2	D	D	D	20.1	D	28.8	22.1	1 442	170	100	2 992	-1.8
Iron	378	4.2	D	13.3	D	11.9	6.4	20.9	27.9	4 016	119	324	8 499	36.0
Juab	71	6.7	24.6	17.4	47.8	12.1	1.4	28.6	20.9	1 124	136	77	2 311	17.4
Kane	73	1.1	D	D	D	14.1	3.1	24.9	26.3	1 308	216	57	3 237	48.1
Millard	150	16.9	34.4	3.8	D	8.5	D	14.5	21.3	1 869	151	119	4 125	25.4
Morgan	62	12.4	34.4	15.3	D	6.1	2.8	10.5	16.8	774	109	21	1 681	20.1
Piute	11	37.3	D	D	D	4.4	D	11.4	31.5	340	237	18	704	13.7
Rich	18	25.8	D	D	D	6.5	D	21.5	29.6	311	159	8	1 859	24.2
Salt Lake	20 474	0.0	19.9	11.3	65.5	10.2	10.3	27.8	14.5	92 918	103	8 800	257 339	19.9
San Juan	133	2.3	23.3	5.2	D	8.8	D	19.5	35.8	1 482	103	685	4 650	24.1
Sanpete	183	11.0	D	12.2	D	9.0	3.0	15.2	33.2	3 345	147	224	6 570	16.5
Sevier	208	3.7	D	8.2	D	12.2	2.8	19.5	23.3	3 443	183	201	6 059	11.7
Summit	572	2.6	15.8	4.8	70.5	15.0	15.8	34.4	11.2	2 064	69	50	11 256	91.5
Tooele	441	0.5	19.9	13.1	43.9	6.2	2.3	18.0	35.8	3 641	89	245	9 510	11.0
Uintah	286	1.5	26.7	1.9	D	10.0	D	23.1	22.1	3 519	140	351	8 142	23.0
Utah	4 869	0.6	21.1	12.9	65.1	10.0	4.8	42.2	13.2	31 655	86	2 879	72 820	16.8
Wasatch	141	1.5	D	6.6	D	13.6	4.4	25.6	20.8	1 693	111	68	4 465	-0.2
Washington	1 005	0.0	22.1	6.9	61.8	17.0	7.2	27.5	16.1	16 897	187	691	19 523	100.8
Wayne	31	16.4	11.5	2.2	D	9.2	D	27.7	28.4	461	184	18	1 061	25.1
Weber	2 942	0.2	D	21.2	D	10.6	4.9	25.8	23.1	22 951	117	2 451	57 851	14.6
VERMONT	10 583	1.3	27.0	19.7	55.7	10.1	5.6	29.3	16.0	104 476	172	12 492	271 214	21.5
Addison	496	5.2	26.5	18.5	56.3	11.4	3.1	34.2	12.0	5 344	149	583	14 022	16.8
Bennington	620	0.5	D	25.2	D	14.1	4.5	30.3	11.8	7 876	213	827	18 501	18.6
Caledonia	374	3.0	31.3	22.1	50.3	10.6	3.6	25.9	15.4	5 673	191	746	13 449	15.8

1. Covers mining, construction, and manufacturing. 2. Covers private sector earnings in agricultural services, forestry, and fisheries; transportation and public utilities; wholesale trade; retail trade; finance, insurance, and real estate; and services. 3. Per 1,000 resident population estimated as of July 1 of the year shown.

Table B. States and Counties — Housing, Labor Force, and Employment

STATE County	Housing units, 1990 (cont'd) Occupied units — Owner-occupied Total	Percent	Median value[1]	Owner cost as a percent of income — With a mortgage	Without a mortgage	Renter-occupied — Median rent[2]	Rent as percent of income	Substandard units[3] (percent)	Civilian labor force, 2001 Total	Percent change, 2000–2001	Unemployment Total	Rate[4]	Civilian employment, 1990[5] Total	Percent — Professional, managerial, and technical	Precision production, craft, and repair
	89	90	91	92	93	94	95	96	97	98	99	100	101	102	103
TEXAS—Cont'd															
Tom Green	35 408	62.3	49 600	19.8	12.8	365	25.1	6.2	49 988	0.6	1 423	2.8	41 808	26.9	11.2
Travis	232 861	45.7	78 300	23.1	12.5	416	26.8	6.3	493 605	2.2	20 047	4.1	302 536	40.2	7.9
Trinity	4 647	78.9	38 700	23.0	16.5	314	29.7	6.2	4 982	-4.2	250	5.0	4 011	18.8	11.0
Tyler	6 459	83.0	37 900	21.0	12.7	313	28.9	7.6	6 495	1.2	536	8.3	5 845	20.3	16.0
Upshur	11 360	80.4	42 100	20.2	13.6	305	27.1	5.8	16 909	0.1	830	4.9	12 668	19.4	15.7
Upton	1 472	75.2	27 600	17.2	12.1	273	13.8	11.6	1 488	2.1	61	4.1	1 747	20.9	19.9
Uvalde	7 553	69.1	38 600	20.2	12.8	263	24.3	14.2	10 919	-1.3	831	7.6	8 519	23.9	13.2
Val Verde	11 840	61.1	43 400	21.0	12.8	333	25.9	16.6	18 237	1.4	1 138	6.2	12 494	23.0	14.3
Van Zandt	14 349	80.5	45 600	21.2	14.6	341	26.5	5.3	20 728	1.5	757	3.7	14 795	18.8	15.9
Victoria	26 228	64.6	54 700	19.5	12.9	351	24.5	7.3	43 989	1.7	1 766	4.0	32 462	25.6	15.4
Walker	14 918	57.4	60 300	20.5	16.4	390	31.4	7.3	22 696	-1.5	618	2.7	18 228	30.3	7.4
Waller	7 402	68.7	54 300	20.0	15.1	335	27.3	8.6	13 129	1.2	609	4.6	9 636	23.7	11.8
Ward	4 444	76.9	33 300	18.0	12.1	280	22.0	9.8	3 865	-1.4	240	6.2	4 904	23.2	19.7
Washington	9 619	72.4	58 600	20.3	12.5	342	23.8	7.3	14 828	-1.2	291	2.0	11 919	23.6	12.1
Webb	34 438	60.6	49 800	22.5	12.7	314	27.6	28.1	75 221	1.6	5 319	7.1	45 819	23.3	10.0
Wharton	14 210	66.4	49 300	19.5	13.4	313	24.3	9.0	18 943	0.0	908	4.8	16 933	20.2	14.7
Wheeler	2 350	78.5	31 200	18.4	13.5	252	23.8	4.3	2 624	-1.5	79	3.0	2 511	24.0	11.0
Wichita	45 271	63.4	46 400	19.8	13.1	362	25.5	3.6	59 212	0.4	2 105	3.6	51 055	27.6	11.4
Wilbarger	5 741	67.3	36 300	18.9	14.3	312	24.6	4.8	7 401	2.4	179	2.4	6 504	22.1	12.5
Willacy	5 049	75.5	25 800	19.8	13.7	202	22.0	24.7	6 198	-4.7	1 018	16.4	5 521	19.1	12.2
Williamson	48 792	64.0	72 300	23.5	13.3	442	23.8	4.4	157 866	2.1	5 247	3.3	71 243	34.8	11.0
Wilson	7 481	80.6	49 900	23.1	13.0	278	24.5	9.5	16 034	1.7	505	3.1	9 447	19.7	16.7
Winkler	2 941	80.3	29 200	15.7	13.1	290	23.3	8.1	2 767	-0.8	162	5.9	3 102	22.5	23.5
Wise	12 175	79.2	49 700	20.3	13.7	338	24.5	6.7	25 005	4.0	858	3.4	14 453	19.5	16.9
Wood	11 426	79.6	47 400	20.1	13.4	335	28.3	4.7	14 077	0.9	692	4.9	11 309	21.0	14.1
Yoakum	2 839	74.1	45 100	16.4	12.2	371	21.4	10.6	3 076	-9.3	143	4.6	3 546	22.0	18.3
Young	7 101	73.1	41 200	20.9	13.5	300	26.3	3.3	7 914	-2.5	389	4.9	7 839	19.6	16.7
Zapata	2 862	82.0	35 500	24.1	12.6	239	31.8	19.9	4 619	2.0	316	6.8	2 550	20.0	19.9
Zavala	3 356	69.4	20 300	18.0	13.3	210	31.9	32.1	4 149	-3.0	654	15.8	3 631	18.5	8.3
UTAH	537 273	68.1	68 900	20.9	12.1	369	23.8	5.4	1 115 380	1.0	48 719	4.4	736 059	30.8	11.4
Beaver	1 594	85.1	51 200	21.8	13.8	294	26.5	4.5	2 351	-2.4	98	4.2	1 681	18.3	10.6
Box Elder	10 954	79.0	65 000	16.7	12.0	343	18.3	4.4	16 988	-1.7	948	5.6	14 601	28.1	14.1
Cache	21 021	62.6	67 100	19.7	11.9	335	24.0	6.7	44 765	1.5	1 435	3.2	30 374	31.5	10.7
Carbon	6 907	75.7	51 500	17.8	12.5	313	25.2	3.3	8 869	-2.6	563	6.3	7 587	26.5	19.1
Daggett	253	60.1	50 400	25.0	13.2	270	14.2	4.3	413	-9.8	19	4.6	295	18.3	15.3
Davis	53 598	74.1	75 700	20.4	11.3	394	22.1	4.6	123 005	0.3	4 695	3.8	77 921	34.1	11.1
Duchesne	3 707	81.5	43 400	21.4	13.2	335	24.4	8.5	6 048	6.5	377	6.2	4 506	22.8	14.5
Emery	2 998	82.3	48 500	15.8	11.9	311	18.8	6.1	3 696	-2.6	355	9.6	3 702	23.0	22.6
Garfield	1 321	81.9	49 800	21.5	12.8	292	17.8	6.3	2 731	-0.1	251	9.2	1 605	16.9	11.7
Grand	2 489	73.6	49 700	21.0	12.8	315	24.5	5.0	5 197	0.4	350	6.7	2 804	23.0	13.3
Iron	6 269	69.8	63 400	21.0	12.2	343	27.9	6.4	14 865	-0.5	681	4.6	8 402	25.1	10.5
Juab	1 801	80.1	43 300	17.7	12.2	285	16.3	4.4	3 694	6.4	184	5.0	2 378	16.9	17.3
Kane	1 724	77.4	63 100	24.4	12.3	308	18.8	7.3	2 859	0.2	101	3.5	1 961	21.7	14.4
Millard	3 349	79.3	50 400	19.7	13.8	290	19.4	7.2	4 291	-1.1	209	4.9	4 209	23.2	12.8
Morgan	1 555	82.7	78 000	18.1	12.2	355	14.9	7.6	3 580	2.3	130	3.6	2 282	25.2	13.5
Piute	449	85.7	45 500	22.3	14.1	242	26.0	6.0	613	18.8	47	7.7	424	21.0	7.3
Rich	521	78.7	45 900	19.0	12.9	304	19.6	4.0	952	-1.4	37	3.9	646	18.4	11.8
Salt Lake	240 680	65.1	71 000	21.3	12.1	379	24.0	4.4	486 166	0.8	20 946	4.3	333 193	31.6	10.7
San Juan	3 375	77.3	37 800	15.6	13.2	254	23.1	38.5	4 303	-6.3	390	9.1	3 668	30.1	11.7
Sanpete	4 859	79.7	49 000	20.9	14.1	310	26.4	6.9	8 811	-0.3	505	5.7	5 417	23.2	14.9
Sevier	4 877	82.4	51 600	20.2	13.0	324	22.1	4.9	8 160	-0.8	375	4.6	5 622	22.5	13.7
Summit	5 271	71.2	107 800	22.9	12.6	517	23.2	4.5	15 092	3.7	876	5.8	7 593	37.5	9.1
Tooele	8 581	70.2	60 400	18.0	11.8	351	18.4	5.3	12 834	5.7	946	7.4	11 037	23.2	17.3
Uintah	6 670	75.7	44 400	19.6	13.6	296	24.2	7.5	11 707	5.4	542	4.6	7 563	24.8	17.3
Utah	70 168	62.7	70 000	21.3	11.8	349	25.1	8.0	172 455	1.4	6 522	3.8	105 102	32.1	10.2
Wasatch	3 074	76.0	69 900	21.7	12.9	393	22.6	4.0	6 577	3.0	364	5.5	4 340	23.3	16.7
Washington	15 256	70.8	78 400	25.1	11.9	414	24.9	6.9	41 139	5.2	1 559	3.8	17 224	24.5	11.8
Wayne	699	81.7	54 000	22.8	12.8	257	15.5	5.1	1 553	0.8	82	5.3	795	22.3	10.4
Weber	53 253	70.7	66 000	20.1	12.0	356	23.3	4.3	101 669	0.3	5 134	5.0	69 127	31.2	12.2
VERMONT	210 650	69.0	95 500	21.9	14.7	446	27.1	2.5	334 695	0.9	12 021	3.6	283 146	31.3	12.3
Addison	11 410	74.2	93 400	22.6	15.3	455	27.5	3.5	20 127	-0.5	662	3.3	16 914	29.6	13.0
Bennington	13 595	70.0	97 100	23.0	14.2	434	29.1	2.3	20 111	0.5	928	4.6	16 995	28.0	14.3
Caledonia	10 368	71.3	72 700	19.8	13.6	349	27.1	2.8	15 251	0.4	789	5.2	13 040	26.6	12.7

1. Specified owner-occupied units.   2. Specified renter-occupied units.   3. Overcrowded or lacking complete plumbing facilities.   4. Percent of civilian labor force.   5. Persons 16 years and older.

Table B. States and Counties — Nonfarm Employment and Agriculture

| | Private nonfarm establishments, employment and payroll, 1999 | | | | | | | | | Agriculture, 1997 | | | |
| | | Employment | | | | | | Annual payroll | | Farms | | | Farm operators |
STATE County	Number of establishments	Total	Health Care and Social Assistance	Manufacturing	Retail trade	Finance and Insurance	Professional Scientific and Technical Services	Total (mil dol)	Average per employee (dollars)	Number	Percent with— Less than 50 acres	500 acres and over	Whose principal occupation is farming (percent)
	104	105	106	107	108	109	110	111	112	113	114	115	116
TEXAS—Cont'd													
Tom Green	2 584	34 394	5 985	3 917	5 375	1 355	1 130	764	22 213	880	34.9	33.2	46.8
Travis	22 855	411 597	40 442	53 728	50 813	20 336	37 406	16 508	40 106	1 038	39.4	12.8	36.8
Trinity	229	1 746	238	206	327	66	64	31	17 584	518	26.8	6.8	40.7
Tyler	288	4 059	479	426	594	67	94	66	16 190	463	50.3	3.9	36.5
Upshur	434	3 833	372	488	825	189	163	75	19 595	1 110	35.9	5.0	35.0
Upton	72	619	162	0	90	D	D	16	25 234	96	10.4	69.8	58.3
Uvalde	576	6 011	1 097	843	1 171	203	99	108	17 967	593	17.5	44.7	50.9
Val Verde	817	8 519	2 133	296	1 872	395	168	146	17 090	238	24.8	63.4	54.2
Van Zandt	740	6 502	1 102	685	1 392	289	164	122	18 727	2 423	39.7	5.3	40.0
Victoria	2 201	29 093	5 525	2 752	5 191	1 083	836	696	23 928	1 084	32.4	16.6	39.4
Walker	857	10 016	1 862	696	2 274	341	264	179	17 854	826	38.3	8.7	32.9
Waller	512	7 099	401	1 528	2 257	141	286	177	24 874	1 066	43.6	9.3	39.6
Ward	235	2 194	269	36	336	86	42	48	21 899	85	23.5	51.8	41.2
Washington	763	10 402	1 418	2 774	1 722	571	273	237	22 795	1 986	32.2	5.8	38.7
Webb	4 014	48 694	6 603	1 385	9 676	1 952	1 266	995	20 428	453	6.0	61.1	38.4
Wharton	965	10 684	1 935	1 946	1 848	416	193	234	21 870	1 347	24.3	28.1	53.6
Wheeler	183	1 244	389	41	210	50	21	18	14 700	505	9.7	45.0	48.7
Wichita	3 321	47 236	9 540	7 873	7 261	1 765	1 133	1 090	23 077	560	38.4	20.4	34.8
Wilbarger	350	3 712	558	831	679	271	86	85	22 787	476	13.9	38.2	54.6
Willacy	209	1 988	429	D	389	80	31	38	18 931	243	21.0	49.4	67.1
Williamson	4 549	59 954	5 887	9 685	11 207	4 994	2 038	1 723	28 743	2 034	36.8	12.7	41.1
Wilson	383	2 821	699	271	689	118	58	48	17 078	1 794	27.5	9.9	37.6
Winkler	161	1 047	176	0	203	57	18	24	22 669	39	28.2	59.0	46.2
Wise	865	10 530	1 058	1 330	1 728	304	279	301	28 579	2 075	41.1	8.4	35.3
Wood	742	5 784	863	737	1 261	323	153	115	19 859	1 331	35.8	5.9	43.6
Yoakum	191	1 659	90	99	227	33	35	45	27 109	278	9.4	58.6	61.9
Young	591	4 806	766	708	741	210	136	115	23 889	709	12.0	32.4	43.4
Zapata	140	1 414	133	D	250	61	10	25	17 562	323	2.8	57.6	45.2
Zavala	101	1 863	1 064	D	148	D	19	23	12 393	232	4.3	62.5	53.9
UTAH	53 809	889 355	83 961	121 939	119 433	45 679	47 160	23 364	26 271	14 181	46.3	16.4	42.2
Beaver	136	1 312	244	D	253	39	10	19	14 311	219	31.1	21.5	56.6
Box Elder	775	15 697	1 015	8 286	1 527	435	148	525	33 469	1 077	36.9	26.7	46.8
Cache	2 258	30 272	2 866	9 607	4 660	722	1 233	632	20 887	1 232	42.1	9.5	43.1
Carbon	515	6 455	844	324	1 352	121	286	169	26 241	199	48.2	18.1	38.2
Daggett	23	137	0	0	17	0	3	3	22 737	36	8.3	36.1	58.3
Davis	4 467	60 482	6 595	8 144	10 747	3 857	2 564	1 372	22 680	559	74.4	3.0	35.2
Duchesne	362	2 785	481	80	621	83	128	59	21 255	811	29.6	17.8	44.9
Emery	178	2 731	80	D	384	D	D	99	36 090	450	33.8	19.1	38.4
Garfield	132	1 024	D	150	112	D	D	21	20 701	285	30.2	18.9	40.7
Grand	364	2 772	246	34	585	50	82	44	16 039	85	52.9	15.3	48.2
Iron	823	9 285	663	1 688	1 847	320	422	164	17 668	375	32.0	34.4	41.6
Juab	147	1 771	283	337	266	24	D	36	20 075	228	22.8	32.5	39.9
Kane	177	1 351	145	169	336	D	14	23	17 025	143	21.0	43.4	46.2
Millard	232	2 490	256	283	552	65	97	64	25 589	650	23.1	30.3	53.8
Morgan	135	1 092	D	255	162	D	10	27	25 057	243	55.1	18.5	39.9
Piute	21	87	0	D	22	D	0	2	18 126	106	12.3	24.5	74.5
Rich	59	318	D	D	51	D	0	6	18 975	162	20.4	53.1	60.5
Salt Lake	25 333	475 802	41 139	53 976	54 290	32 542	26 569	13 782	28 966	593	78.9	3.9	34.1
San Juan	248	2 023	376	176	266	32	D	38	18 968	231	12.6	55.0	49.8
Sanpete	350	3 247	529	645	677	124	31	57	17 450	776	34.9	18.6	49.4
Sevier	470	4 889	607	469	1 008	95	111	101	20 679	478	44.4	9.2	41.4
Summit	1 423	14 753	323	662	2 496	337	564	285	19 321	476	46.6	20.0	38.4
Tooele	459	6 288	479	1 392	1 179	201	296	184	29 296	332	40.7	23.2	43.4
Uintah	713	5 374	490	199	1 188	146	254	126	23 380	795	41.5	15.6	39.5
Utah	6 835	137 583	14 491	15 808	17 881	3 183	9 641	3 219	23 396	1 790	68.2	6.5	37.0
Wasatch	443	3 151	333	269	608	78	170	58	18 496	294	60.9	5.8	33.7
Washington	2 393	25 270	3 174	2 195	5 410	759	771	503	19 896	429	46.9	20.0	38.0
Wayne	73	449	64	D	129	D	D	7	14 599	191	28.8	9.9	52.4
Weber	4 227	69 290	8 116	16 662	10 807	2 326	3 400	1 689	24 373	936	73.8	2.1	36.2
VERMONT	21 598	246 320	34 983	44 675	38 160	9 791	10 027	6 336	25 724	5 828	25.0	10.0	56.6
Addison	1 075	10 800	1 666	1 963	1 714	274	333	263	24 317	683	20.8	18.7	65.9
Bennington	1 566	16 336	2 552	3 127	3 198	402	293	387	23 717	171	38.0	6.4	50.3
Caledonia	975	9 128	1 396	1 878	1 834	367	274	210	22 969	452	21.5	9.5	54.9

STATE County	Acreage (1,000)	Percent change, 1992–1997	Average size of farm	Total irrigated (1,000)	Total cropland (1,000)	Average per farm ($1,000)	Average per acre (dollars)	Value of machinery and equipment average per farm ($1,000)	Total (mil dol)	Average per farm (dollars)	Crops	Livestock and poultry products	$10,000 or more	$100,000 or more	Percent of land owned by fed. gov. 1997	Water consumption 1995 (mil gal/day)
	117	118	119	120	121	122	123	124	125	126	127	128	129	130	131	132
TEXAS—Cont'd																
Tom Green	959	-6.1	1 089	44	217	554	564	52	86	97 587	31.4	68.6	43.6	14.4	1.2	256.8
Travis	396	19.0	382	3	113	495	1 285	23	16	15 831	58.7	41.3	24.0	3.5	0.5	590.5
Trinity	99	-10.2	191	0	49	245	1 084	33	6	11 744	6.8	93.2	25.7	2.1	14.9	1.9
Tyler	53	-9.8	115	0	25	204	1 954	20	3	6 729	20.8	79.2	17.7	0.4	2.4	2.7
Upshur	175	-9.6	158	1	72	189	1 253	25	31	27 850	3.6	96.4	26.1	5.0	0.0	6.8
Upton	746	7.4	7 774	12	D	1 263	163	79	8	79 714	53.5	46.5	61.5	25.0	0.0	20.1
Uvalde	943	2.8	1 590	53	159	765	488	50	68	115 490	40.9	59.1	40.0	17.7	0.0	60.8
Val Verde	1 748	-3.3	7 345	1	11	1 311	183	24	19	81 723	1.2	98.8	46.2	15.5	0.5	12.4
Van Zandt	361	-4.5	149	2	201	222	1 411	26	56	23 087	36.7	63.3	25.7	3.2	0.0	8.1
Victoria	458	6.3	423	4	155	318	716	33	29	26 419	59.8	40.2	28.0	6.0	0.0	47.4
Walker	184	-14.0	223	0	60	279	1 402	24	11	13 186	25.3	74.7	19.6	1.3	10.5	5.2
Waller	238	-2.0	223	8	116	430	1 958	38	29	27 323	51.5	48.5	27.4	4.2	0.0	24.4
Ward	363	-20.4	4 271	2	D	628	147	32	2	21 181	48.1	51.9	35.3	2.4	0.0	34.7
Washington	336	2.5	169	1	162	274	1 769	23	26	13 135	20.3	79.7	21.6	2.0	1.0	5.7
Webb	2 176	27.1	4 804	6	52	1 594	330	50	28	62 246	9.9	90.1	37.1	6.8	0.0	42.9
Wharton	679	5.3	504	91	443	484	966	73	134	99 146	79.7	20.3	49.4	21.5	0.0	272.0
Wheeler	514	2.4	1 018	6	155	301	275	44	81	159 706	4.7	95.3	46.9	7.3	0.0	5.7
Wichita	339	9.9	605	6	143	443	782	39	22	39 037	33.7	66.3	32.5	6.1	0.9	28.3
Wilbarger	884	2.4	1 857	14	260	545	294	74	33	69 825	57.0	43.0	55.3	13.7	0.0	27.9
Willacy	286	9.7	1 178	18	234	1 171	1 034	166	49	203 689	91.2	8.8	65.0	45.3	2.5	0.1
Williamson	538	-1.4	265	1	296	384	1 569	31	48	23 634	65.8	34.2	27.6	5.3	1.8	25.9
Wilson	446	-6.3	248	19	217	292	1 131	33	46	25 667	30.2	69.8	23.0	3.5	0.0	16.4
Winkler	488	12.6	12 506	D	D	1 311	105	29	2	47 206	D	D	46.2	10.3	0.0	4.0
Wise	412	-10.7	198	1	177	323	1 620	24	34	16 518	12.7	87.3	23.8	3.1	3.4	21.0
Wood	215	5.2	161	3	107	216	1 294	33	75	56 027	17.9	82.1	29.2	8.3	0.0	9.1
Yoakum	343	-0.6	1 234	82	247	616	568	133	52	187 751	93.7	6.3	63.3	39.2	0.0	104.6
Young	553	-1.7	781	0	155	349	452	25	23	32 712	22.6	77.4	41.9	4.7	0.0	7.8
Zapata	403	-16.9	1 249	2	33	434	373	20	7	22 545	D	D	36.5	2.8	0.0	5.8
Zavala	591	-18.3	2 546	20	78	1 021	434	64	45	195 625	40.0	60.0	56.0	22.8	0.0	70.0
UTAH	12 025	24.9	848	1 212	2 070	486	575	51	877	61 864	28.2	71.8	43.6	11.5	63.1	4 301.4
Beaver	131	-31.8	598	35	39	649	1 102	64	59	267 239	11.2	88.8	64.8	26.5	78.0	129.3
Box Elder	1 358	-6.4	1 261	137	344	547	437	80	102	94 868	35.6	64.4	54.0	18.4	31.9	370.9
Cache	266	-0.6	216	93	177	330	1 742	60	105	85 072	13.4	86.6	49.9	18.7	35.1	292.9
Carbon	202	-30.9	1 013	11	17	612	586	35	4	18 200	11.2	88.8	31.7	4.5	49.5	72.0
Daggett	26	20.4	736	8	13	472	641	52	1	40 000	29.7	70.3	63.9	11.1	77.5	15.4
Davis	68	35.8	121	22	27	376	3 296	35	33	59 722	82.2	17.8	31.5	9.5	10.8	159.2
Duchesne	1 328	232.9	1 638	115	125	521	310	44	28	33 992	16.9	83.1	50.8	9.0	44.7	171.5
Emery	159	-34.1	353	41	53	220	683	38	11	24 378	18.3	81.7	38.4	3.1	80.9	152.6
Garfield	121	-12.0	426	25	36	359	762	47	8	26 608	17.7	82.3	48.8	4.2	87.2	70.9
Grand	76	20.3	892	4	6	439	492	42	2	26 935	37.1	62.9	42.4	5.9	71.2	10.3
Iron	405	-6.8	1 079	60	71	609	667	79	42	112 336	66.9	33.1	51.2	17.9	57.3	154.1
Juab	276	-17.2	1 209	22	66	547	467	70	8	36 635	34.5	65.5	44.7	10.1	72.6	110.6
Kane	175	-16.5	1 226	7	15	626	508	33	3	22 590	7.6	92.4	37.8	5.6	80.1	10.0
Millard	458	-5.4	704	99	163	504	668	86	71	109 302	39.7	60.3	66.3	20.0	74.1	284.5
Morgan	179	-23.7	738	9	22	691	941	33	13	54 375	9.1	90.9	46.1	16.5	4.4	107.0
Piute	45	-24.5	420	14	21	377	985	66	7	68 071	9.1	90.8	72.6	14.2	72.3	71.6
Rich	524	6.2	3 233	75	87	854	269	90	16	95 913	7.1	92.9	68.5	20.4	31.7	152.8
Salt Lake	114	5.5	192	15	40	431	2 092	39	23	38 757	55.0	45.0	28.7	7.6	20.4	386.0
San Juan	1 673	414.8	7 243	9	150	1 787	241	60	9	39 381	38.5	61.5	46.8	10.4	59.1	42.1
Sanpete	360	-19.5	464	72	113	339	800	62	83	106 682	9.3	90.7	51.3	18.0	50.5	149.2
Sevier	147	-6.9	308	44	50	235	931	40	40	82 988	16.3	83.7	50.4	12.1	73.7	209.4
Summit	590	57.6	1 239	28	40	740	603	37	17	35 834	5.7	94.3	39.9	9.0	42.9	90.9
Tooele	292	-33.2	879	19	42	586	584	42	17	52 353	13.5	86.5	37.0	6.6	77.7	103.1
Uintah	2 268	75.1	2 853	84	91	695	244	45	21	27 001	26.2	73.8	39.6	5.0	60.2	195.5
Utah	375	-16.7	209	81	150	433	2 244	40	97	54 195	40.4	59.6	32.8	9.4	43.3	298.8
Wasatch	106	-23.6	361	15	17	564	1 544	27	8	26 351	14.4	85.6	29.6	7.8	48.1	96.5
Washington	163	-2.3	380	16	35	418	1 156	37	9	21 777	34.3	65.7	32.9	4.0	73.8	84.2
Wayne	60	-43.8	312	18	18	320	1 080	44	11	58 637	8.9	91.1	59.7	11.0	84.2	58.3
Weber	81	-68.3	87	33	40	328	2 210	44	28	30 420	25.0	75.0	28.8	6.8	15.6	252.1
VERMONT	1 262	-1.3	217	3	617	323	1 520	49	476	81 734	12.5	87.5	50.9	22.9	6.4	565.3
Addison	205	-2.4	300	0	135	389	1 281	75	113	165 034	8.6	91.4	65.6	40.6	17.8	6.7
Bennington	32	-4.8	189	0	12	325	1 833	44	8	47 277	29.0	71.0	40.4	12.3	33.2	8.2
Caledonia	94	-2.8	209	0	43	271	1 475	40	29	64 949	10.6	89.4	49.3	18.4	0.0	6.6

Table B. States and Counties — **Residential Construction, Wholesale and Retail Trade, and Real Estate**

STATE County	Value of Residential Construction Authorized by Building Permits, 2000		Wholesale Trade, 1997				Retail Trade[1], 1997				Real Estate and Rental and Leasing, 1997			
	New Construction ($1,000)	Number of Housing Units	Number of Establishments	Number of Employees	Sales (mil dol)	Annual Payroll (mil dol)	Number of Establishments	Number of Employees	Sales (mil dol)	Annual Payroll (mil dol)	Number of Establishments	Number of Employees	Receipts (mil dol)	Annual Payroll (mil dol)
	133	134	135	136	137	138	139	140	141	142	143	144	145	146
TEXAS—Cont'd														
Tom Green	25 994	247	159	D	D	D	471	5 404	890.7	84.3	134	550	51.7	8.3
Travis	1 364 341	14 269	1 268	18 345	8 991.9	717.9	2 925	45 335	16 072.8	916.0	1 212	6 484	820.3	159.0
Trinity	0	0	5	D	D	D	60	365	56.1	4.5	4	7	0.9	0.1
Tyler	30	1	5	D	D	D	72	612	85.2	7.5	5	10	1.2	0.1
Upshur	1 478	13	17	49	104.5	2.3	101	895	145.1	11.7	9	29	1.5	0.2
Upton	0	0	8	41	24.7	0.9	16	94	14.7	1.1	NA	NA	NA	NA
Uvalde	1 705	31	40	318	165.3	6.2	124	1 054	178.0	15.5	26	85	6.2	0.9
Val Verde	6 951	127	30	291	54.5	5.1	173	1 798	278.1	25.3	31	105	8.5	1.4
Van Zandt	3 866	32	31	179	70.8	4.1	145	1 339	245.2	20.2	23	46	4.6	0.5
Victoria	18 335	167	141	1 665	422.1	46.0	398	5 052	868.7	80.1	91	455	60.5	10.5
Walker	6 681	56	36	247	89.5	4.4	174	2 245	386.7	32.0	47	218	39.1	4.1
Waller	6 785	287	38	D	D	D	80	1 280	480.4	25.6	9	91	3.9	1.3
Ward	288	2	15	103	74.4	2.9	49	381	54.0	5.5	12	83	7.1	2.1
Washington	3 133	26	36	543	289.2	14.6	143	1 565	270.3	22.8	32	155	13.4	2.7
Webb	111 755	1 863	339	2 453	1 105.4	51.1	730	9 051	1 524.6	138.8	155	574	64.3	10.0
Wharton	6 984	132	69	1 005	326.6	23.7	217	1 799	301.0	27.4	34	174	12.8	3.0
Wheeler	204	1	11	80	30.8	1.6	45	226	33.1	2.7	2	D	D	D
Wichita	25 118	221	211	1 906	434.6	44.8	598	7 268	1 198.7	107.3	151	D	D	D
Wilbarger	173	3	21	81	30.6	1.9	76	737	111.5	8.9	13	38	3.6	0.6
Willacy	1 929	42	10	68	16.9	1.6	43	386	61.8	4.6	4	28	1.8	0.3
Williamson	534 011	5 691	217	1 723	750.3	57.6	623	8 402	1 582.1	152.9	183	639	73.6	12.8
Wilson	845	11	16	82	36.7	1.6	68	625	109.5	8.9	8	46	3.7	0.6
Winkler	0	0	6	26	7.6	0.9	32	225	43.6	3.3	8	32	3.8	0.9
Wise	9 458	90	38	343	197.2	6.8	122	1 692	689.2	31.3	29	80	13.0	1.7
Wood	1 168	13	47	364	189.5	10.0	146	1 173	211.1	17.3	26	60	3.8	0.9
Yoakum	72	1	22	119	73.4	2.9	42	246	34.0	3.2	7	19	0.7	0.2
Young	761	7	39	194	83.9	3.3	100	737	113.5	10.1	21	53	12.4	1.2
Zapata	NA	NA	3	D	D	D	37	221	26.8	2.3	2	D	D	D
Zavala	250	4	3	42	6.8	0.7	20	178	22.5	2.3	1	D	D	D
UTAH	2 137 953	17 638	3 278	44 319	21 115.5	1 420.5	7 656	114 474	19 964.6	1 856.9	2 169	12 318	1 342.6	236.0
Beaver	4 116	37	3	19	4.0	0.3	30	205	29.4	2.1	1	D	D	D
Box Elder	31 023	287	28	245	73.4	6.1	126	1 452	250.1	19.5	21	67	7.9	1.1
Cache	70 514	644	85	696	146.4	12.4	349	5 242	682.7	70.7	67	439	24.5	6.7
Carbon	7 074	116	46	348	175.3	9.4	94	1 310	174.9	17.6	16	65	5.1	0.9
Daggett	709	8	NA	NA	NA	NA	6	16	1.6	0.3	1	D	D	D
Davis	230 954	1 788	241	2 868	1 184.9	70.7	582	9 488	1 809.7	157.6	165	784	96.1	13.0
Duchesne	8 512	141	20	103	31.1	1.9	62	541	96.3	8.4	9	40	3.8	0.6
Emery	2 683	40	7	15	5.8	0.3	37	359	48.4	3.7	4	8	0.2	0.0
Garfield	5 631	68	3	D	D	D	23	122	16.9	1.4	NA	NA	NA	NA
Grand	7 331	91	11	46	8.8	1.2	74	528	77.0	8.4	20	85	5.8	1.4
Iron	37 601	452	32	266	113.6	6.1	135	1 663	286.9	24.2	43	151	17.0	1.7
Juab	9 305	85	8	52	10.7	0.7	29	267	40.3	3.0	2	D	D	D
Kane	7 132	85	5	D	D	D	42	308	35.0	4.0	9	18	2.0	0.5
Millard	3 312	53	16	82	28.8	1.4	58	495	82.2	6.4	NA	NA	NA	NA
Morgan	9 005	58	7	D	D	D	20	151	24.7	1.9	1	D	D	D
Piute	435	6	1	D	D	D	7	25	2.0	0.2	NA	NA	NA	NA
Rich	8 032	95	1	D	D	D	13	43	6.0	0.6	2	D	D	D
Salt Lake	543 646	4 435	2 013	29 521	15 365.4	1 018.0	3 230	53 236	10 139.4	937.0	1 114	7 528	878.2	158.8
San Juan	4 130	52	11	105	12.6	1.2	41	304	33.7	3.4	3	3	0.3	0.0
Sanpete	9 235	162	8	36	15.1	0.6	73	688	90.1	7.3	10	29	1.9	0.3
Sevier	9 808	92	19	238	78.1	3.9	102	1 067	167.5	14.1	9	47	3.8	1.0
Summit	98 018	539	47	147	116.9	6.0	242	2 520	307.9	32.0	94	634	56.6	11.0
Tooele	88 790	849	9	120	10.3	1.4	74	1 170	182.8	16.7	12	51	4.7	0.8
Uintah	16 658	121	49	291	77.6	4.7	104	1 190	180.4	16.9	23	115	15.4	3.3
Utah	509 146	3 731	320	6 272	2 763.6	190.4	978	15 868	2 486.4	245.1	239	1 085	108.0	16.9
Wasatch	62 324	318	14	65	14.3	2.5	56	454	69.1	6.3	17	29	3.4	0.2
Washington	173 834	1 551	85	641	238.5	18.0	406	4 829	879.4	77.3	102	332	31.8	4.6
Wayne	0	0	1	D	D	D	16	86	9.9	0.8	NA	NA	NA	NA
Weber	184 572	1 784	187	2 025	640.6	57.3	647	10 847	1 753.5	170.3	185	781	74.7	12.7
VERMONT	319 486	2 506	941	10 987	4 731.4	330.6	4 093	36 306	5 898.6	603.3	701	2 362	240.6	42.2
Addison	21 869	185	41	296	90.2	7.7	186	1 523	316.1	30.3	34	87	8.0	1.0
Bennington	25 084	213	49	250	87.0	6.2	359	3 160	553.4	53.0	48	135	13.6	2.3
Caledonia	11 653	111	34	431	179.4	10.2	199	1 644	232.8	24.3	32	81	6.2	1.0

1. Establishments with payroll.

STATE County	Professional, Scientific, and Technical Services[1], 1997				Manufacturing, 1997				Accommodation and Foodservices, 1997			
	Number of Establishments	Number of Employees	Receipts (mil dol)	Annual Payroll (mil dol)	Number of Establishments	Number of Employees	Receipts (mil dol)	Annual Payroll (mil dol)	Number of Establishments	Number of Employees	Sales (mil dol)	Annual Payroll (mil dol)
	147	148	149	150	151	152	153	154	155	156	157	158
TEXAS—Cont'd												
Tom Green	154	767	60.2	17.2	100	4 452	827.6	105.1	192	3 763	110.8	32.7
Travis	3 128	27 621	3 169.1	1 299.3	774	52 353	14 692.9	1 986.2	1 643	36 951	1 322.6	375.5
Trinity	9	49	3.4	0.9	NA	NA	NA	NA	15	213	7.5	2.5
Tyler	17	41	3.8	0.9	13	565	42.1	8.9	17	D	D	D
Upshur	20	118	9.4	3.1	31	603	81.1	13.2	28	371	11.4	2.9
Upton	2	D	D	D	NA	NA	NA	NA	8	D	D	D
Uvalde	31	70	6.1	1.7	17	710	50.7	9.4	54	636	20.6	5.7
Val Verde	39	122	8.3	2.3	24	522	125.4	10.2	88	1 046	33.3	8.5
Van Zandt	37	120	10.5	3.0	38	622	68.2	16.2	54	586	19.4	5.3
Victoria	141	712	59.5	21.1	71	3 064	1 245.3	119.5	155	2 711	79.6	21.7
Walker	54	208	33.4	4.9	38	677	90.8	14.7	77	1 545	45.4	12.9
Waller	22	45	3.1	0.9	43	1 283	245.6	43.3	40	722	18.0	4.5
Ward	16	69	3.5	1.2	NA	NA	NA	NA	23	198	5.8	1.7
Washington	41	176	12.5	5.0	41	2 982	529.2	81.9	60	767	23.4	6.1
Webb	210	1 029	69.6	23.1	87	1 402	258.6	28.1	253	4 350	144.7	37.4
Wharton	47	169	12.4	4.0	46	2 152	372.3	51.9	59	780	24.8	6.0
Wheeler	10	18	1.5	0.4	NA	NA	NA	NA	17	D	D	D
Wichita	212	1 071	87.6	32.8	153	7 927	1 435.9	254.9	277	5 225	159.6	47.1
Wilbarger	15	46	3.0	0.8	9	681	236.7	19.8	37	444	10.8	3.4
Willacy	10	25	1.3	0.4	NA	NA	NA	NA	20	194	5.7	1.4
Williamson	355	1 874	233.4	73.6	240	11 727	9 637.4	418.8	287	4 499	155.0	41.9
Wilson	20	43	2.1	0.4	NA	NA	NA	NA	26	D	D	D
Winkler	8	19	4.1	0.4	NA	NA	NA	NA	13	100	2.4	0.7
Wise	36	130	8.8	2.7	54	1 340	180.3	37.8	53	861	23.4	6.7
Wood	40	113	7.1	2.0	45	649	143.4	13.5	59	599	16.8	4.3
Yoakum	8	18	1.0	0.3	NA	NA	NA	NA	19	D	D	D
Young	30	87	6.2	2.3	28	1 043	248.4	28.3	38	353	10.0	2.7
Zapata	5	9	0.5	0.1	NA	NA	NA	NA	21	188	7.2	1.6
Zavala	7	19	1.4	0.2	NA	NA	NA	NA	12	66	2.7	0.5
UTAH	4 282	36 468	3 306.1	1 303.1	2 860	119 140	24 014.4	3 726.1	3 780	74 390	2 309.0	648.8
Beaver	4	5	0.1	0.0	NA	NA	NA	NA	34	462	10.3	3.2
Box Elder	33	128	7.4	2.1	51	5 725	1 271.6	270.7	61	1 063	26.0	8.5
Cache	152	905	51.1	20.3	149	8 355	1 785.6	195.0	112	1 991	50.5	13.2
Carbon	27	217	6.8	2.1	NA	NA	NA	NA	54	641	16.9	4.3
Daggett	2	D	D	D	NA	NA	NA	NA	5	72	4.0	1.6
Davis	321	2 158	127.8	56.1	227	7 170	1 592.1	202.8	267	5 752	151.6	42.9
Duchesne	14	97	3.1	1.1	NA	NA	NA	NA	30	274	8.5	1.9
Emery	5	37	1.9	0.9	NA	NA	NA	NA	19	108	4.7	1.3
Garfield	3	5	0.1	0.0	NA	NA	NA	NA	46	425	22.4	7.6
Grand	22	72	4.2	1.3	NA	NA	NA	NA	82	1 141	38.3	9.9
Iron	40	332	10.5	4.2	50	1 520	206.4	37.9	82	1 349	42.0	12.6
Juab	10	D	D	D	NA	NA	NA	NA	22	292	6.8	2.0
Kane	6	18	1.0	0.2	NA	NA	NA	NA	34	328	14.0	3.7
Millard	5	D	D	D	NA	NA	NA	NA	24	328	6.0	1.8
Morgan	7	13	0.7	0.3	NA	NA	NA	NA	9	89	1.9	0.5
Piute	NA	NA	NA	NA	NA	NA	NA	NA	3	38	0.5	0.2
Rich	NA	NA	NA	NA	NA	NA	NA	NA	14	42	2.2	0.6
Salt Lake	2 367	21 993	2 312.1	887.6	1 441	53 424	10 012.2	1 706.4	1 570	35 480	1 200.5	333.7
San Juan	9	67	2.7	2.3	NA	NA	NA	NA	38	382	20.0	3.9
Sanpete	11	24	1.9	0.4	18	908	116.7	16.9	40	439	7.1	1.8
Sevier	25	91	4.9	2.5	NA	NA	NA	NA	43	628	15.7	4.4
Summit	131	479	55.9	22.7	40	861	86.2	21.4	131	3 481	105.1	33.8
Tooele	22	300	25.6	12.8	27	1 737	342.8	56.8	43	475	16.0	3.8
Uintah	43	171	11.7	3.9	NA	NA	NA	NA	52	657	18.1	4.8
Utah	582	6 094	463.3	195.3	390	15 949	2 667.3	461.0	392	8 270	228.0	64.3
Wasatch	31	95	6.4	2.4	NA	NA	NA	NA	36	682	19.7	6.7
Washington	131	605	38.8	15.4	92	1 949	243.4	48.4	195	3 580	113.2	31.6
Wayne	1	D	D	D	NA	NA	NA	NA	22	113	4.0	0.8
Weber	278	2 307	150.3	61.6	210	18 446	5 242.4	635.0	320	5 808	155.1	43.4
VERMONT	1 622	7 792	719.1	279.0	1 226	42 533	7 803.0	1 459.6	1 932	27 088	910.2	277.2
Addison	77	244	17.9	7.4	61	1 871	321.9	59.4	88	948	32.4	11.0
Bennington	86	237	17.2	6.4	88	3 090	504.8	94.1	163	2 044	76.6	21.3
Caledonia	58	229	14.4	7.6	55	1 950	198.0	54.0	72	767	24.4	6.9

1. Firms subject to federal tax.

STATE County	Health Care and Social Assistance[1], 1997				Other Services[1], 1997				Federal funds and grants, fiscal 2001[2]			
									Expenditures (mil dol)			
										Direct payments for individuals[3]		
	Number of Establishments	Number of Employees	Receipts (mil dol)	Annual Payroll (mil dol)	Number of Establishments	Number of Employees	Receipts (mil dol)	Annual Payroll (mil dol)	Total	Social Security and government retirement	Medicare	Food stamps and Supplemental Security Income
	159	160	161	162	163	164	165	166	167	168	169	170
TEXAS—Cont'd												
Tom Green	186	3 404	208.9	91.7	180	961	58.3	16.1	633.2	237.1	76.1	14.9
Travis	1 705	29 036	1 985.2	805.8	1 336	9 356	590.9	192.2	6 913.1	1 212.8	316.3	79.4
Trinity	5	125	5.1	1.7	18	48	3.1	0.6	86.1	42.0	21.9	2.0
Tyler	22	389	15.5	6.9	10	24	1.8	0.4	137.3	51.7	26.0	3.5
Upshur	22	430	14.6	6.8	24	86	7.5	1.4	158.8	86.1	35.8	5.5
Upton	3	72	2.4	1.5	NA	NA	NA	NA	18.4	6.6	3.8	0.6
Uvalde	43	452	20.4	8.7	39	204	10.4	3.4	131.2	43.3	18.9	8.1
Val Verde	55	2 055	36.6	17.7	49	220	11.4	3.2	321.7	77.3	21.8	14.5
Van Zandt	53	1 004	31.0	15.0	41	238	16.1	4.7	206.6	110.2	53.4	4.4
Victoria	230	3 383	230.0	93.5	151	973	61.8	17.8	339.5	152.5	69.1	13.6
Walker	72	763	31.6	14.0	47	279	13.3	4.2	202.1	83.7	33.0	6.3
Waller	24	442	12.2	6.9	35	125	9.9	2.6	132.4	40.7	19.3	4.9
Ward	11	110	4.3	2.0	16	101	6.1	1.9	50.5	22.5	10.2	2.2
Washington	42	898	30.3	14.8	48	179	11.7	2.7	148.2	67.1	24.9	4.1
Webb	227	4 330	207.1	94.8	190	951	48.0	13.3	746.0	173.2	101.8	59.0
Wharton	55	1 645	84.7	30.6	71	273	17.6	4.4	256.9	78.8	42.5	8.4
Wheeler	13	174	6.1	3.4	7	23	1.3	0.2	71.6	14.3	10.5	0.6
Wichita	273	D	D	D	223	1 518	85.1	28.5	1 073.1	348.9	108.0	10.1
Wilbarger	29	402	19.8	7.8	18	60	4.0	1.1	90.2	32.9	19.9	1.9
Willacy	17	203	8.8	4.1	13	40	1.8	0.5	132.8	24.5	16.2	5.9
Williamson	293	3 179	180.9	72.2	269	1 508	95.9	29.7	868.9	327.6	74.3	11.3
Wilson	25	327	10.7	4.8	24	91	6.1	1.8	117.9	63.2	17.4	3.6
Winkler	10	108	4.1	1.7	10	37	2.5	0.5	30.5	14.8	9.3	1.4
Wise	51	615	24.2	10.8	51	243	16.5	4.3	137.4	79.3	26.6	3.2
Wood	54	660	25.0	11.2	38	141	7.5	2.1	194.5	109.5	43.3	4.3
Yoakum	5	24	1.2	0.4	12	44	3.5	0.9	60.6	12.4	6.1	0.9
Young	30	364	16.8	6.4	40	107	7.4	1.8	98.2	47.6	23.5	2.0
Zapata	6	75	2.1	1.0	6	15	1.1	0.2	48.6	14.5	12.8	4.1
Zavala	4	689	9.1	6.2	5	10	0.4	0.1	63.1	14.4	9.9	7.5
UTAH	3 851	46 989	2 988.8	1 226.7	2 728	17 612	1 090.5	312.6	11 377.4	3 490.8	903.2	180.7
Beaver	6	20	2.2	0.8	7	13	0.8	0.2	27.6	12.3	4.6	0.3
Box Elder	57	678	39.6	15.4	39	147	7.9	1.5	554.7	86.1	18.7	2.7
Cache	166	1 293	82.5	29.1	125	628	35.4	9.5	304.3	107.1	29.1	4.9
Carbon	53	829	55.8	18.8	34	220	19.3	4.9	91.6	49.6	17.6	4.1
Daggett	NA	NA	NA	NA	NA	NA	NA	NA	8.8	2.3	0.6	0.0
Davis	329	4 717	292.4	127.9	243	1 501	90.6	27.8	2 182.4	430.9	68.5	12.8
Duchesne	21	154	6.6	2.5	19	76	4.9	1.1	65.6	26.6	8.2	2.7
Emery	7	67	3.1	1.3	13	92	11.0	2.9	40.2	19.3	5.4	1.4
Garfield	1	D	D	D	2	D	D	D	38.2	10.6	3.0	0.5
Grand	10	36	2.2	0.7	13	21	1.9	0.3	48.2	17.2	3.6	1.1
Iron	47	343	15.9	5.7	42	136	9.1	2.0	115.4	52.3	12.5	3.1
Juab	8	145	4.6	1.5	7	27	2.6	0.6	28.0	13.9	5.1	0.6
Kane	7	35	1.5	0.7	12	52	2.8	0.7	31.5	15.9	4.6	0.5
Millard	16	70	3.4	1.2	9	28	3.0	0.6	50.8	20.8	7.4	1.3
Morgan	1	D	D	D	1	D	D	D	20.3	15.2	2.4	0.1
Piute	NA	NA	NA	NA	NA	NA	NA	NA	9.1	3.8	1.4	0.1
Rich	1	D	D	D	3	D	D	D	19.8	3.8	0.8	0.1
Salt Lake	1 766	23 094	1 579.6	652.7	1 285	9 616	622.4	185.2	3 975.0	1 245.4	377.3	74.3
San Juan	12	198	8.3	3.1	9	24	1.8	0.4	94.3	14.5	4.9	5.6
Sanpete	23	138	6.5	2.6	23	67	5.9	1.0	83.3	37.3	11.4	2.1
Sevier	33	299	12.2	5.1	28	141	13.1	2.1	79.9	39.2	13.9	2.0
Summit	41	285	14.9	5.4	34	157	8.7	2.2	86.2	27.4	5.0	0.5
Tooele	28	138	6.6	2.4	18	84	4.8	1.5	302.7	86.8	14.5	2.2
Uintah	47	412	26.6	9.3	42	134	16.0	2.6	98.0	40.0	11.4	2.8
Utah	596	7 371	421.0	178.8	340	2 256	103.9	29.1	910.1	393.5	120.2	21.6
Wasatch	17	183	6.6	2.8	15	43	3.7	0.9	37.5	20.1	4.8	0.6
Washington	193	1 722	114.0	41.2	98	433	32.9	8.4	356.2	213.2	48.4	9.6
Wayne	3	D	D	D	3	12	0.7	0.1	13.5	5.1	1.5	0.1
Weber	362	4 431	277.0	113.2	264	1 687	86.2	27.0	1 125.6	478.8	96.4	23.3
VERMONT	1 262	11 481	631.6	273.9	1 171	4 490	304.7	76.4	3 733.8	1 221.5	400.1	83.9
Addison	65	380	19.6	6.7	61	160	11.5	2.2	154.1	57.4	19.6	3.9
Bennington	107	1 132	56.3	26.5	78	282	18.2	4.9	183.9	87.2	30.0	6.5
Caledonia	48	459	21.9	9.8	53	160	11.6	2.7	146.4	64.8	21.3	5.1

1. Firms subject to federal tax.   2. October 1, 2000 to September 30, 2001.   3. State totals may include programs not allocated by county.

Table B. States and Counties — Federal Funds and Local Government Finances

	Federal funds and grants, fiscal 2001[1] (cont'd)							Local government finances, 1997				
	Expenditures (mil dol) (cont'd)							General revenue				
	Procurement contract awards		Grants[2]								Taxes	
											Per capita[3] (dollars)	
STATE County	Salaries and wages	Defense	Other	Medicaid and other health-related	Nutrition and family welfare	Education	Other	Total (mil dol)	Intergovern-mental (mil dol)	Total (mil dol)	Total	Property
	171	172	173	174	175	176	177	178	179	180	181	182
TEXAS—Cont'd												
Tom Green	147.3	24.2	3.2	45.5	10.7	4.1	24.2	174.2	69.8	74.3	724	553
Travis	480.4	320.4	167.6	637.9	873.6	790.6	1 898.8	1 773.9	302.8	986.2	1 422	1 086
Trinity	2.4	0.0	0.6	14.1	1.0	0.6	0.3	25.9	11.6	8.4	676	594
Tyler	2.4	37.3	0.6	12.6	1.4	0.8	0.2	34.3	15.3	11.1	551	484
Upshur	3.6	0.0	1.0	21.6	1.8	1.2	0.8	50.3	26.9	18.8	530	459
Upton	0.4	0.0	0.1	1.4	0.3	0.2	0.8	22.8	1.3	16.6	4 350	4 244
Uvalde	5.8	0.0	3.1	22.1	5.1	2.7	5.4	94.5	38.9	14.4	562	401
Val Verde	109.8	43.6	3.3	34.4	7.8	3.4	0.7	87.4	52.8	20.0	463	336
Van Zandt	5.8	0.0	1.5	19.4	1.9	1.5	6.0	65.6	32.2	23.3	542	456
Victoria	12.4	1.8	2.7	40.3	8.4	5.6	12.1	255.3	61.4	85.8	1 046	818
Walker	10.0	1.6	1.5	24.5	3.2	4.4	21.6	167.2	31.9	28.0	514	376
Waller	3.8	7.1	0.9	11.9	2.4	4.6	15.4	51.3	21.5	23.9	893	772
Ward	1.3	0.0	0.3	7.6	0.5	0.5	4.0	31.4	5.0	16.5	1 388	1 273
Washington	4.2	0.2	0.9	30.3	1.3	0.8	6.3	80.2	30.1	27.0	932	852
Webb	85.4	2.7	25.8	172.2	51.5	20.4	28.7	516.1	305.2	128.1	699	543
Wharton	5.4	0.0	1.3	35.0	3.6	1.9	4.0	97.2	40.3	37.6	936	768
Wheeler	1.3	0.0	0.4	3.3	0.3	0.2	32.5	20.1	3.4	10.3	1 949	1 814
Wichita	366.0	96.3	11.2	54.8	9.6	7.5	27.1	224.2	76.2	100.2	778	617
Wilbarger	2.8	0.0	0.5	9.3	1.1	0.5	3.3	52.3	18.3	16.6	1 173	1 069
Willacy	1.8	0.2	0.5	28.0	3.3	2.1	16.8	41.7	26.8	11.4	581	489
Williamson	24.1	196.6	107.6	35.9	8.0	6.7	33.3	421.8	120.5	227.0	1 078	962
Wilson	3.0	0.0	0.8	16.9	0.9	1.1	6.4	47.6	25.0	13.8	458	402
Winkler	0.6	0.0	0.2	3.3	0.2	0.4	0.0	27.0	6.3	13.5	1 680	1 562
Wise	6.2	0.7	1.6	9.3	1.0	0.8	4.4	65.1	27.2	28.3	667	595
Wood	5.8	0.1	1.3	19.8	1.7	2.7	1.8	62.2	18.5	26.3	769	666
Yoakum	0.7	0.0	0.2	2.3	0.8	0.4	8.6	39.1	3.3	29.7	3 630	3 519
Young	2.7	0.1	0.7	10.5	1.0	0.6	1.9	36.7	13.9	12.4	705	550
Zapata	1.5	0.0	0.2	12.4	0.9	1.0	0.2	25.9	7.0	17.3	1 536	1 516
Zavala	0.7	0.0	0.2	20.0	1.9	1.6	0.9	22.6	14.3	6.1	507	333
UTAH	1 765.3	1 275.1	808.9	915.3	344.1	225.6	759.2	X	X	X	X	X
Beaver	1.7	0.0	0.6	6.3	0.6	0.1	0.5	23.8	11.5	4.9	838	679
Box Elder	11.1	23.0	379.7	10.4	3.6	0.8	4.3	85.1	41.0	27.5	668	537
Cache	18.1	30.2	14.7	26.4	11.0	10.8	30.2	137.6	68.2	39.0	459	308
Carbon	8.3	0.0	-16.0	10.5	6.7	1.2	2.2	52.1	26.6	13.7	656	502
Daggett	2.6	0.0	1.8	0.5	0.1	0.1	0.8	3.9	2.1	1.2	1 626	1 405
Davis	679.8	821.8	84.3	33.4	17.2	7.3	8.4	430.4	206.6	125.7	556	408
Duchesne	3.3	0.7	0.6	6.4	2.2	0.9	12.0	55.2	23.5	9.5	655	530
Emery	2.6	0.0	1.1	4.0	1.5	0.3	3.6	67.2	16.8	22.0	2 024	1 876
Garfield	5.4	0.0	14.2	2.4	0.6	0.1	1.0	14.1	8.5	3.5	830	543
Grand	9.1	0.0	1.8	3.1	1.5	0.3	10.1	27.0	13.3	9.3	1 150	670
Iron	14.6	0.3	7.3	5.7	5.5	2.4	1.9	63.6	26.0	22.7	820	602
Juab	1.1	0.0	0.5	2.5	0.6	0.2	1.9	21.5	10.9	5.4	745	620
Kane	4.2	0.0	3.9	0.5	0.6	0.2	0.9	24.9	9.0	5.9	1 019	636
Millard	4.4	0.2	0.7	4.0	1.6	0.4	6.2	48.8	12.8	28.3	2 298	2 177
Morgan	0.7	0.0	0.2	1.0	0.3	0.1	0.1	13.2	7.3	3.9	571	445
Piute	0.3	0.0	0.2	2.4	0.3	0.1	0.3	4.2	3.3	0.7	523	438
Rich	0.6	0.0	0.1	0.5	0.2	0.1	13.3	6.6	3.5	2.3	1 280	1 132
Salt Lake	536.8	248.7	153.5	497.5	200.2	93.8	437.6	1 905.0	707.6	719.5	857	588
San Juan	6.7	0.9	5.2	34.0	4.4	8.5	5.7	46.7	28.9	9.2	675	551
Sanpete	4.1	0.1	6.0	10.8	2.7	2.1	2.5	47.7	24.5	9.5	452	327
Sevier	9.1	0.0	1.3	7.9	2.7	0.5	1.8	41.0	23.3	10.1	561	405
Summit	7.1	4.6	1.1	1.3	0.8	0.2	38.0	99.0	13.9	54.1	2 102	1 607
Tooele	53.7	68.0	57.8	8.6	4.0	0.9	2.7	95.4	36.5	18.3	584	441
Uintah	17.0	0.0	4.1	7.9	5.0	1.9	5.4	76.6	35.4	18.2	714	564
Utah	67.7	46.1	32.8	101.9	30.1	10.3	37.4	615.9	305.1	185.8	566	405
Wasatch	2.9	0.1	1.2	3.5	1.0	0.2	2.9	31.9	13.5	11.3	882	697
Washington	38.7	0.0	4.7	12.0	4.8	2.6	12.6	158.7	61.8	52.7	670	471
Wayne	3.7	0.0	0.6	1.4	0.3	0.1	0.2	6.4	4.4	1.2	514	364
Weber	250.1	30.2	45.0	108.9	27.8	5.1	21.2	350.5	160.6	116.8	643	463
VERMONT	319.4	307.2	83.9	517.7	143.8	98.5	309.4	X	X	X	X	X
Addison	7.6	18.3	11.6	19.8	4.5	1.5	3.7	70.8	19.1	44.8	1 283	1 276
Bennington	8.0	0.1	1.9	22.7	6.2	2.0	14.0	76.9	23.5	47.9	1 332	1 319
Caledonia	6.6	0.4	1.5	26.0	5.3	2.5	7.1	56.4	20.9	30.8	1 074	1 070

1. October 1, 2000 to September 30, 2001. 2. State totals may include programs not allocated by county. 3. Based on the resident population estimated as of July 1 of the year shown.

STATE County	Local government finances, 1997 (cont'd) Direct general expenditure Total (mil dol)	Per capita[1] (dollars)	Percent of total for — Educa- tion	Health and hospitals	Police protec- tion	Public welfare	High- ways	Debt outstanding Total (mil dol)	Per capita[1] (dollars)	Government employment, 1999 Federal civilian	Federal military	State and local	Presidential election, 2000[2] Percent of vote cast — Demo- cratic	Republi- can	All other
	183	184	185	186	187	188	189	190	191	192	193	194	195	196	197
TEXAS—Cont'd															
Tom Green	183.4	1 786	59.3	2.9	8.2	0.1	3.4	161.2	1 571	1 329	3 092	7 581	26.8	71.4	1.7
Travis	1 654.7	2 386	40.2	6.4	6.0	1.4	3.7	6 322.5	9 115	9 084	2 130	98 243	41.7	46.9	11.5
Trinity	24.4	1 969	63.3	20.2	2.5	0.1	3.7	7.0	566	47	33	656	40.4	58.4	1.2
Tyler	34.3	1 708	64.9	14.6	2.6	0.1	4.9	6.2	310	49	54	1 475	39.0	59.5	1.5
Upshur	47.5	1 340	78.0	0.3	3.0	0.1	4.3	20.6	581	65	96	1 523	32.6	66.0	1.4
Upton	22.1	5 783	48.1	28.1	2.5	0.0	5.0	1.2	316	0	0	459	20.9	77.1	2.0
Uvalde	93.1	3 635	56.7	33.0	1.9	0.6	1.1	10.5	410	111	68	2 431	40.8	57.7	1.5
Val Verde	86.8	2 012	59.9	3.7	5.3	1.2	3.2	48.4	1 123	1 764	1 462	3 017	44.1	54.2	1.7
Van Zandt	67.2	1 564	72.4	0.1	3.1	0.2	7.5	40.8	948	90	118	1 993	29.3	69.2	1.5
Victoria	239.4	2 918	38.5	31.9	5.6	0.0	3.0	142.9	1 742	233	217	6 171	29.8	68.5	1.6
Walker	153.8	2 821	26.6	3.3	3.6	0.2	2.7	700.2	12 841	198	151	12 491	34.4	63.1	2.5
Waller	57.2	2 133	72.6	0.1	4.0	0.4	6.9	39.3	1 467	56	86	3 102	46.5	52.4	1.2
Ward	32.4	2 728	46.1	21.1	5.3	0.8	4.7	2.8	235	25	30	1 128	32.4	65.4	2.2
Washington	85.0	2 928	79.3	1.0	3.4	0.1	3.4	63.9	2 200	72	76	2 757	25.4	73.2	1.4
Webb	515.0	2 811	52.4	1.2	4.6	0.5	5.3	352.8	1 926	1 902	508	13 049	57.4	41.4	1.2
Wharton	106.4	2 651	67.0	5.4	3.8	0.9	6.0	41.9	1 044	103	106	3 099	36.0	63.0	1.0
Wheeler	18.9	3 555	52.2	26.8	2.3	0.0	6.3	0.4	84	29	14	526	24.2	74.8	0.9
Wichita	228.2	1 771	50.4	4.4	6.2	0.6	4.0	141.7	1 100	2 566	8 571	9 144	33.0	65.1	1.9
Wilbarger	50.5	3 575	47.8	22.3	2.1	0.2	2.6	19.1	1 353	64	37	2 687	29.6	68.6	1.8
Willacy	40.3	2 050	79.2	0.5	3.9	0.1	4.8	7.2	365	36	57	1 379	63.6	35.3	1.1
Williamson	449.3	2 135	69.5	1.2	3.2	0.5	3.4	613.5	2 915	376	633	11 221	27.7	67.8	4.5
Wilson	48.5	1 607	66.8	10.8	2.8	0.0	3.3	23.9	790	55	85	1 646	34.2	64.2	1.6
Winkler	25.6	3 184	58.5	13.6	2.7	0.3	1.5	1.2	144	12	20	637	27.2	71.9	0.9
Wise	65.4	1 542	66.6	1.4	6.4	0.2	5.0	29.4	695	70	123	2 257	29.5	68.6	1.8
Wood	55.1	1 613	59.2	13.3	3.6	0.2	6.1	14.1	413	82	90	1 692	28.0	70.7	1.3
Yoakum	31.4	3 840	56.8	12.3	4.3	0.1	5.9	0.7	85	16	21	700	21.5	77.5	0.9
Young	33.8	1 921	58.9	9.0	4.8	0.3	4.9	12.5	710	51	46	1 391	26.5	72.2	1.3
Zapata	26.5	2 352	61.4	1.0	4.4	1.0	4.1	3.8	336	30	30	932	62.6	36.4	0.9
Zavala	23.4	1 955	68.4	0.6	3.9	0.4	1.9	4.9	410	13	31	895	77.1	22.1	0.7
UTAH	X	X	X	X	X	X	X	X	X	30 634	15 952	149 438	26.3	66.8	6.9
Beaver	17.3	2 945	39.4	13.1	6.6	0.0	10.4	19.0	3 248	35	32	563	24.0	73.4	2.6
Box Elder	87.5	2 130	52.8	0.8	4.1	0.5	5.3	67.9	1 651	209	229	2 017	16.5	79.4	4.1
Cache	134.1	1 581	57.2	3.3	4.8	0.0	4.5	88.1	1 038	308	476	8 285	15.6	78.2	6.2
Carbon	53.3	2 548	42.6	11.5	5.3	0.0	11.0	71.0	3 394	163	111	2 048	44.7	50.9	4.5
Daggett	3.5	4 671	64.3	0.5	5.6	0.0	4.5	2.4	3 180	69	0	136	23.9	72.9	3.2
Davis	412.8	1 826	58.2	1.7	6.4	0.5	3.7	284.0	1 256	10 156	5 349	10 080	21.5	73.3	5.3
Duchesne	55.8	3 863	43.8	28.0	4.4	0.0	5.5	35.8	2 478	86	78	1 518	17.1	79.7	3.2
Emery	66.0	6 066	30.6	1.3	3.2	0.6	9.0	352.5	32 418	50	59	812	21.8	73.7	4.4
Garfield	13.3	3 169	53.1	0.5	2.6	0.0	10.0	15.6	3 715	152	23	370	9.0	87.3	3.6
Grand	30.6	3 766	45.2	3.0	5.3	1.2	7.3	22.3	2 743	195	44	565	32.0	50.4	17.5
Iron	62.1	2 240	54.3	0.2	4.3	0.0	6.6	64.8	2 337	297	157	3 206	14.2	80.2	5.5
Juab	21.0	2 897	51.4	0.5	7.3	0.0	9.5	28.3	3 904	18	41	555	22.2	72.6	5.2
Kane	23.4	4 013	33.9	20.7	5.5	0.0	6.1	26.7	4 582	85	33	542	13.8	80.4	5.7
Millard	39.6	3 215	49.5	2.3	4.5	0.0	7.4	21.8	1 767	91	66	922	14.6	80.6	4.8
Morgan	13.1	1 891	68.4	0.0	5.3	0.0	4.7	7.3	1 053	11	38	334	17.4	77.7	4.8
Piute	3.8	2 708	81.9	0.2	1.6	0.0	4.5	1.9	1 341	0	0	108	17.0	80.2	2.8
Rich	6.6	3 624	64.2	1.1	2.7	0.0	5.4	4.5	2 472	14	10	169	16.8	81.5	1.7
Salt Lake	1 800.5	2 144	43.6	4.5	6.9	0.0	4.7	6 599.9	7 858	8 368	4 879	71 408	35.0	55.8	9.1
San Juan	38.8	2 837	62.7	1.8	2.7	0.0	8.7	24.9	1 820	182	72	1 378	38.7	57.4	3.9
Sanpete	48.8	2 338	52.5	13.5	3.3	0.0	10.1	36.3	1 738	73	117	2 142	16.3	77.8	5.9
Sevier	39.8	2 201	52.6	8.9	5.6	0.0	6.2	35.7	1 974	173	99	1 403	14.8	81.4	3.8
Summit	125.7	4 882	42.5	1.0	4.1	0.0	4.9	123.2	4 783	89	216	1 787	38.0	50.9	11.1
Tooele	88.5	2 818	38.1	15.3	4.9	0.1	5.9	90.5	2 881	1 709	262	1 515	32.1	62.6	5.4
Uintah	76.1	2 982	39.6	5.9	4.9	3.5	13.0	149.1	5 844	400	138	1 414	16.5	80.2	3.3
Utah	592.2	1 805	54.6	1.6	5.2	0.1	3.6	878.7	2 678	1 037	1 863	18 642	13.7	81.7	4.6
Wasatch	28.1	2 193	47.2	3.2	6.5	0.4	5.0	28.2	2 207	58	73	829	26.0	67.3	6.7
Washington	160.9	2 047	51.8	2.0	4.2	0.0	4.1	229.8	2 924	449	454	4 024	16.8	78.5	4.7
Wayne	6.7	2 812	56.5	1.1	3.9	0.0	18.0	1.5	651	102	13	165	16.5	77.8	5.7
Weber	351.9	1 938	51.1	2.0	4.5	3.4	3.2	228.1	1 256	6 049	1 008	12 501	31.7	62.6	5.8
VERMONT	X	X	X	X	X	X	X	X	X	5 529	4 596	40 344	50.6	40.7	8.6
Addison	76.2	2 181	78.1	0.1	1.6	0.2	8.0	27.1	774	135	270	1 711	51.3	39.9	8.8
Bennington	70.2	1 952	65.0	0.1	3.6	0.0	10.6	10.7	298	128	274	1 997	51.0	41.2	7.8
Caledonia	51.6	1 800	64.0	0.4	1.7	0.0	13.9	17.2	599	111	220	1 812	43.0	49.5	7.6

1. Based on the resident population estimated as of July 1 of the year shown.   2. Data subject to copyright.

Table B. States and Counties — **Land Area and Population**

STATE/ County code	MSA/ PMSA/ NECMA code[1]	County Type[2]	STATE County	Land area,[3] (sq km) 2000	Total persons	Rank	Per square kilometer	White	Black	Am. Indian, Alaska Native	Asian and Pacific Islander	Percent Hispanic[4]	Under 5 years	5 to 17 years	18 to 24 years	25 to 34 years	35 to 44 years	45 to 54 years
					1	2	3	4	5	6	7	8	9	10	11	12	13	14	15
			VERMONT—Cont'd															
50 007	1303	3	Chittenden	1 396	146 571	371	105.0	96.3	1.3	0.8	2.5	1.1	5.8	17.8	13.1	14.5	17.6	14.2
50 009	...	9	Essex	1 723	6 459	2 741	3.7	98.7	0.2	2.2	0.4	0.5	5.4	20.2	6.5	11.3	15.9	14.5
50 011	1303	3	Franklin	1 650	45 417	992	27.5	97.7	0.5	2.8	0.4	0.6	7.1	21.0	7.0	13.6	17.8	14.0
50 013	1303	3	Grand Isle	214	6 901	2 695	32.2	98.7	0.2	1.9	0.4	0.4	5.5	19.3	5.6	10.8	17.9	17.0
50 015	...	8	Lamoille	1 194	23 233	1 631	19.5	98.6	0.6	1.3	0.7	0.8	5.5	18.8	10.0	13.2	16.7	15.0
50 017	...	9	Orange	1 783	28 226	1 443	15.8	98.9	0.4	0.8	0.6	0.6	5.6	20.0	7.8	10.9	17.3	15.8
50 019	...	7	Orleans	1 807	26 277	1 507	14.5	98.5	0.5	1.7	0.4	0.7	5.7	19.5	7.1	11.5	15.3	15.3
50 021	...	7	Rutland	2 415	63 400	764	26.3	98.8	0.5	0.6	0.5	0.7	5.2	18.1	8.3	11.4	16.3	15.7
50 023	...	6	Washington	1 785	58 039	824	32.5	98.3	0.7	1.1	0.8	1.3	5.4	18.1	8.9	12.1	16.7	16.6
50 025	...	7	Windham	2 043	44 216	1 012	21.6	98.1	0.8	0.9	1.2	1.1	5.3	18.3	7.1	11.3	16.9	17.0
50 027	...	7	Windsor	2 515	57 418	831	22.8	98.6	0.5	0.7	0.9	0.8	5.0	18.4	5.9	10.8	16.5	16.7
51 000	...	X	**VIRGINIA**	102 548	7 078 515	X	69.0	73.9	20.4	0.7	4.4	4.7	6.5	18.0	9.6	14.6	17.0	14.1
51 001	...	7	Accomack	1 179	38 305	1 156	32.5	64.1	31.9	0.7	0.4	5.4	6.1	18.2	8.2	11.3	14.9	13.5
51 003	1540	3	Albemarle	1 872	79 236	646	42.3	86.3	10.2	0.5	3.2	2.6	6.3	18.6	7.3	14.0	16.9	15.2
51 005	...	6	Alleghany	1 152	12 926	2 239	11.2	96.9	2.6	0.5	0.3	0.4	5.6	17.3	6.2	11.7	15.1	15.8
51 007	...	8	Amelia	924	11 400	2 341	12.3	71.2	28.3	0.7	0.2	0.8	6.3	19.1	6.7	12.0	17.3	14.1
51 009	4640	3	Amherst	1 231	31 894	1 348	25.9	78.3	20.3	1.2	0.5	1.0	5.7	17.8	9.7	12.2	15.5	14.5
51 011	...	8	Appomattox	864	13 705	2 183	15.9	76.4	23.3	0.3	0.2	0.5	6.1	18.5	7.1	12.1	15.7	13.8
51 013	8840	0	Arlington	67	189 453	291	2 827.7	72.3	10.3	0.8	10.1	18.6	5.5	11.0	10.4	25.2	17.2	13.6
51 015	...	4	Augusta	2 513	65 615	744	26.1	95.6	3.7	0.4	0.5	0.9	5.7	18.1	6.9	12.4	17.4	15.7
51 017	...	9	Bath	1 378	5 048	2 849	3.7	92.9	6.5	0.5	0.6	0.4	4.4	16.6	5.5	12.0	16.3	14.9
51 019	4640	3	Bedford	1 954	60 371	801	30.9	92.8	6.5	0.5	0.6	0.7	5.8	18.2	5.8	12.1	17.8	16.1
51 021	...	9	Bland	929	6 871	2 700	7.4	95.5	4.2	0.4	0.2	0.5	4.5	14.9	7.6	14.6	16.1	16.3
51 023	6800	3	Botetourt	1 405	30 496	1 385	21.7	95.5	3.7	0.5	0.6	0.6	5.7	17.7	5.8	11.0	17.8	17.2
51 025	...	8	Brunswick	1 466	18 419	1 872	12.6	42.4	57.1	0.3	0.3	1.3	5.0	15.5	9.9	14.6	16.1	14.1
51 027	...	9	Buchanan	1 305	26 978	1 484	20.7	97.1	2.7	0.2	0.2	0.5	4.8	16.6	8.5	13.6	17.6	16.0
51 029	...	8	Buckingham	1 504	15 623	2 048	10.4	60.0	39.6	0.8	0.2	0.8	5.0	17.4	7.5	14.4	17.6	14.6
51 031	4640	3	Campbell	1 307	51 078	907	39.1	84.0	15.2	0.5	0.8	0.8	5.8	18.1	7.7	13.3	16.0	14.7
51 033	...	8	Caroline	1 379	22 121	1 686	16.0	63.6	35.2	1.4	0.6	1.3	6.2	18.5	7.4	13.2	16.7	14.4
51 035	...	7	Carroll	1 234	29 245	1 421	23.7	98.5	0.5	0.4	0.2	1.6	5.6	15.5	7.2	13.1	14.8	14.9
51 036	6760	2	Charles City County	473	6 926	2 694	14.6	36.6	55.7	8.9	0.2	0.6	5.6	16.5	7.5	11.3	17.5	17.4
51 037	...	8	Charlotte	1 230	12 472	2 267	10.1	65.9	33.2	0.5	0.2	1.7	5.5	18.8	7.2	11.3	14.9	13.3
51 041	6760	2	Chesterfield	1 103	259 903	214	235.6	77.8	18.4	0.7	2.8	2.9	6.7	21.5	7.7	13.0	18.2	16.4
51 043	8840	1	Clarke	457	12 652	2 252	27.7	91.9	7.1	0.6	0.9	1.5	5.2	18.2	5.8	10.7	18.3	15.7
51 045	...	8	Craig	856	5 091	2 844	5.9	98.2	0.2	0.4	0.3	0.3	5.7	17.9	6.4	12.4	17.2	15.3
51 047	8840	1	Culpeper	987	34 262	1 273	34.7	79.5	18.9	0.8	1.0	2.5	6.4	19.3	8.1	13.5	17.6	13.9
51 049	...	8	Cumberland	773	9 017	2 527	11.7	61.4	37.8	0.7	0.5	1.7	6.3	18.5	7.3	12.5	15.5	14.2
51 051	...	9	Dickenson	859	16 395	1 998	19.1	99.4	0.4	0.3	0.2	0.4	5.3	16.7	8.9	12.0	15.7	15.8
51 053	6760	1	Dinwiddie	1 305	24 533	1 574	18.8	65.2	34.0	0.6	0.6	1.0	5.6	18.4	6.7	12.8	18.1	15.1
51 057	...	8	Essex	668	9 989	2 447	15.0	59.0	39.8	1.2	0.9	0.7	5.2	17.7	7.0	11.8	15.2	14.9
51 059	8840	0	Fairfax	1 023	969 749	36	947.9	72.9	9.3	0.7	14.7	11.0	7.0	18.4	7.5	15.5	18.4	16.2
51 061	8840	1	Fauquier	1 683	55 139	855	32.8	89.6	9.4	0.7	0.9	2.0	6.4	20.4	6.4	11.5	18.8	15.8
51 063	...	8	Floyd	987	13 874	2 169	14.1	97.4	2.2	0.5	0.2	1.3	5.6	16.6	6.9	12.8	14.8	15.4
51 065	1540	3	Fluvanna	744	20 047	1 791	26.9	80.6	19.1	0.6	0.7	1.2	6.5	17.1	6.4	14.0	17.7	13.8
51 067	...	6	Franklin	1 792	47 286	962	26.4	89.6	9.7	0.4	0.6	1.2	5.4	16.8	8.1	12.1	16.1	15.3
51 069	...	4	Frederick	1 074	59 209	811	55.1	95.9	3.0	0.5	1.0	1.7	6.5	19.9	7.0	13.4	18.4	14.4
51 071	...	9	Giles	925	16 657	1 980	18.0	97.9	1.7	0.3	0.3	0.6	5.7	16.4	6.8	13.2	15.2	14.6
51 073	5720	1	Gloucester	561	34 780	1 259	62.0	88.0	10.8	1.0	1.2	1.6	5.8	20.4	6.8	11.8	18.6	14.6
51 075	6760	2	Goochland	737	16 863	1 963	22.9	73.4	26.0	0.5	0.6	0.9	5.2	16.1	5.3	12.8	19.3	17.1
51 077	...	9	Grayson	1 146	17 917	1 906	15.6	92.3	6.9	0.5	0.2	1.5	4.8	14.7	7.6	14.1	15.7	14.6
51 079	1540	3	Greene	406	15 244	2 073	37.5	92.1	7.0	0.6	0.7	1.3	7.5	19.8	6.7	14.9	18.3	13.9
51 081	...	6	Greensville	765	11 560	2 328	15.1	39.2	59.9	0.2	0.5	0.9	3.8	14.4	7.4	18.1	20.6	15.2
51 083	...	6	Halifax	2 122	37 355	1 181	17.6	60.9	38.5	0.5	0.3	1.2	5.9	17.5	6.9	11.6	14.8	14.8
51 085	6760	2	Hanover	1 224	86 320	602	70.5	89.0	9.7	0.7	1.0	1.0	6.5	20.6	6.9	11.8	18.9	15.5
51 087	6760	2	Henrico	617	262 300	210	425.1	70.0	25.3	0.7	4.1	2.3	6.8	17.8	7.8	15.7	17.2	14.2
51 089	...	4	Henry	990	57 930	825	58.5	75.2	23.1	0.4	0.6	3.5	5.5	16.8	7.5	13.2	15.8	14.2
51 091	...	9	Highland	1 077	2 536	3 023	2.4	99.5	0.1	0.3	0.3	0.5	3.7	16.2	4.1	8.6	15.9	16.6
51 093	5720	3	Isle of Wight	818	29 728	1 407	36.3	71.8	27.6	0.7	0.5	0.9	6.0	19.4	6.6	11.1	18.6	15.3
51 095	5720	0	James City County	370	48 102	948	130.0	83.2	14.9	0.7	2.1	1.7	5.6	17.7	6.4	11.0	16.4	14.6
51 097	...	8	King and Queen	819	6 630	2 724	8.1	62.1	36.5	2.2	0.5	0.9	5.4	17.4	7.0	10.7	16.2	15.2
51 099	8840	1	King George	466	16 803	1 968	36.1	79.1	19.4	1.1	1.4	1.8	7.6	20.2	8.2	13.8	17.9	13.7
51 101	...	6	King William	713	13 146	2 216	18.4	74.8	23.4	2.2	0.5	0.9	6.9	19.2	5.9	14.2	17.3	14.9
51 103	...	9	Lancaster	345	11 567	2 326	33.5	70.4	29.1	0.4	0.5	0.6	4.2	14.8	5.0	7.2	12.5	13.6
51 105	...	9	Lee	1 132	23 589	1 607	20.8	99.1	0.5	0.7	0.3	0.5	5.8	16.9	8.0	12.6	14.9	14.9
51 107	8840	1	Loudoun	1 346	169 599	320	126.0	84.9	7.6	0.6	6.4	5.9	9.7	20.1	5.7	17.6	21.3	13.1

1. MSA = Metropolitan Statistical Area. PMSA = Primary MSA. NECMA = New England County Metropolitan Area. See Appendix A for explanation of these concepts. See Appendix B for list of metropolitan areas identified by type, with component counties.   2. County typology code from the Economic Research Service of USDA. See Appendix A for definition.   3. Dry land or land partially or temporarily covered by water.   4. Hispanic persons may be of any race.

Table B. States and Counties — Population and Households

STATE County	Age (percent) (cont'd)				Population — change and components of change, 1990–2001							Households, 2000				
					Total persons		Percent change		Components of change, 2000–2001						Percent	
	55 to 64 years	65 to 74 years	75 years and over	Percent female	2001	1990	1990–2000	2000–2001	Births	Deaths	Net migration	Number	Percent change, 1990–2000	Persons per house-hold	Female family house-holder[1]	One person
	16	17	18	19	20	21	22	23	24	25	26	27	28	29	30	31
VERMONT—Cont'd																
Chittenden	7.7	5.0	4.4	51.3	147 591	131 761	11.2	0.7	2 041	1 138	160	56 452	16.5	2.47	8.7	26.1
Essex	11.0	8.9	6.3	50.0	6 507	6 405	0.8	0.7	99	78	28	2 602	11.0	2.47	8.3	24.1
Franklin	8.4	6.1	4.9	50.4	46 184	39 980	13.6	1.7	735	438	477	16 765	17.0	2.67	9.9	20.6
Grand Isle	11.5	7.5	4.8	50.0	7 220	5 318	29.8	4.6	88	63	285	2 761	36.8	2.50	7.1	22.2
Lamoille	9.5	6.0	5.4	50.0	23 602	19 735	17.7	1.6	283	220	308	9 221	24.7	2.45	8.9	25.0
Orange	9.7	7.1	5.7	50.2	28 786	26 149	7.9	2.0	364	294	488	10 936	15.7	2.52	8.9	23.4
Orleans	10.6	7.7	7.4	50.4	26 536	24 053	9.2	1.0	331	332	264	10 446	17.7	2.45	9.6	25.2
Rutland	10.1	7.6	7.3	51.4	63 250	62 142	2.0	-0.2	742	812	-49	25 678	8.4	2.39	10.1	27.9
Washington	9.4	6.5	6.3	51.0	58 503	54 928	5.7	0.8	718	638	397	23 659	12.9	2.36	9.2	28.5
Windham	10.2	7.2	6.8	51.3	44 055	41 588	6.3	-0.4	556	506	-197	18 375	13.0	2.35	9.6	29.7
Windsor	10.9	8.1	7.7	51.3	57 675	54 055	6.2	0.4	676	707	312	24 162	12.3	2.35	9.0	28.1
VIRGINIA	8.9	6.1	5.1	51.0	7 187 734	6 189 197	14.4	1.5	124 540	70 495	54 758	2 699 173	17.8	2.54	11.9	25.1
Accomack	11.2	9.2	7.5	51.5	38 414	31 703	20.8	0.3	543	576	158	15 299	20.9	2.45	14.4	27.7
Albemarle	9.2	6.7	5.8	52.0	80 413	68 177	16.2	1.5	1 274	634	566	31 876	30.5	2.44	9.1	27.0
Alleghany	12.7	8.5	7.1	50.1	12 840	12 815	0.9	-0.7	169	139	-114	5 149	4.2	2.46	8.1	22.2
Amelia	11.3	7.2	6.1	50.7	11 652	8 787	29.7	2.2	167	147	229	4 240	35.4	2.66	11.4	20.7
Amherst	10.9	7.9	5.9	52.3	32 139	28 578	11.6	0.8	476	369	143	11 941	21.5	2.51	12.4	24.0
Appomattox	11.8	8.2	6.5	51.3	13 885	12 300	11.4	1.3	210	184	157	5 322	17.5	2.55	11.5	21.3
Arlington	7.7	4.4	5.0	49.6	187 469	170 895	10.9	-1.0	3 457	1 369	-4 218	86 352	10.0	2.15	7.0	40.8
Augusta	11.1	7.4	5.4	49.7	66 621	54 557	20.3	1.5	848	663	822	24 818	25.5	2.56	8.6	20.1
Bath	13.6	10.2	6.5	49.8	5 073	4 799	5.2	0.5	60	82	47	2 053	8.3	2.34	7.8	26.3
Bedford	11.4	7.8	5.0	50.1	61 194	45 553	32.5	1.4	728	571	664	23 838	37.9	2.52	7.5	20.2
Bland	11.6	8.2	6.3	45.5	6 844	6 514	5.5	-0.4	57	83	1	2 568	14.4	2.43	8.7	23.3
Botetourt	11.6	8.1	5.0	50.1	30 812	24 992	22.0	1.0	397	279	198	11 700	27.9	2.56	7.0	19.2
Brunswick	10.2	8.3	6.2	46.9	18 292	15 987	15.2	-0.7	227	216	-138	6 277	14.1	2.47	16.6	27.6
Buchanan	11.6	6.9	4.6	49.3	26 331	31 333	-13.9	-2.4	351	339	-671	10 464	-5.4	2.46	10.6	22.5
Buckingham	10.1	7.4	6.1	45.1	15 786	12 873	21.4	1.0	176	187	169	5 324	22.6	2.52	14.2	25.1
Campbell	10.9	7.9	5.6	51.2	51 295	47 499	7.5	0.4	908	585	-87	20 639	15.0	2.45	11.4	24.6
Caroline	10.6	7.1	5.8	50.2	22 463	19 217	15.1	1.5	388	269	228	8 021	21.0	2.69	13.2	20.5
Carroll	11.8	9.5	7.5	50.7	29 381	26 519	10.3	0.5	346	388	183	12 186	16.5	2.36	8.6	25.4
Charles City County	11.4	8.0	4.6	50.9	6 969	6 282	10.3	0.6	115	102	30	2 670	23.6	2.59	15.2	22.5
Charlotte	11.4	9.3	8.2	52.1	12 451	11 688	6.7	-0.2	217	227	-5	4 951	14.8	2.47	13.0	27.4
Chesterfield	8.5	4.8	3.3	51.3	266 549	209 599	24.0	2.6	4 227	1 719	4 098	93 772	27.7	2.73	11.2	18.5
Clarke	11.4	8.1	6.5	50.5	13 111	12 101	4.6	3.6	150	160	460	4 942	16.7	2.50	8.9	24.1
Craig	11.5	7.7	5.9	49.2	5 090	4 372	16.4	0.0	62	48	-12	2 060	22.9	2.45	7.0	23.9
Culpeper	9.4	6.7	5.2	49.2	35 715	27 791	23.3	4.2	547	369	1 249	12 141	24.4	2.68	11.3	20.6
Cumberland	10.9	8.6	6.2	52.4	9 017	7 825	15.2	0.0	122	160	41	3 528	25.4	2.55	14.3	24.8
Dickenson	11.1	8.2	6.2	51.1	16 329	17 620	-7.0	-0.4	212	238	-35	6 732	4.3	2.42	10.6	25.3
Dinwiddie	11.1	7.0	5.2	50.3	24 630	22 279	10.1	0.4	313	275	60	9 107	21.6	2.58	13.9	22.2
Essex	10.8	9.0	8.3	52.6	10 020	8 689	15.0	0.3	159	163	35	3 995	22.6	2.46	14.0	26.1
Fairfax	9.1	4.6	3.3	50.4	985 161	818 310	18.5	1.6	18 298	5 204	2 580	350 714	20.0	2.74	8.6	21.4
Fauquier	10.2	5.9	4.6	50.6	57 820	48 700	13.2	4.9	849	512	2 300	19 842	20.2	2.75	8.6	18.7
Floyd	11.9	8.0	7.9	50.6	14 195	11 965	16.0	2.3	192	200	325	5 791	21.6	2.39	8.1	24.7
Fluvanna	10.6	9.2	4.8	53.6	21 257	12 429	61.3	6.0	251	177	1 108	7 387	63.5	2.59	9.9	18.8
Franklin	11.9	8.4	5.9	50.7	47 927	39 549	19.6	1.4	638	538	547	18 963	29.4	2.44	9.4	22.6
Frederick	9.7	6.2	4.5	50.0	61 315	45 723	29.5	3.6	925	511	1 665	22 097	34.2	2.64	8.8	19.2
Giles	11.5	8.7	8.0	51.1	16 816	16 366	1.8	1.0	261	237	138	6 994	8.2	2.37	9.7	26.6
Gloucester	10.2	6.6	5.2	50.9	35 410	30 131	15.4	1.8	472	410	567	13 127	19.7	2.62	9.9	20.3
Goochland	11.8	7.7	4.8	49.6	17 323	14 163	19.1	2.7	219	183	417	6 158	26.2	2.51	8.4	19.9
Grayson	11.6	9.5	7.4	48.2	17 727	16 278	10.1	-1.1	206	263	-125	7 259	12.2	2.31	8.5	26.8
Greene	9.1	5.4	4.3	50.4	15 945	10 297	48.0	4.6	290	115	516	5 574	48.7	2.71	10.4	18.0
Greensville	9.0	6.7	4.8	38.3	11 536	8 553	35.2	-0.2	125	112	-32	3 375	7.1	2.51	16.0	25.4
Halifax	11.5	8.7	8.3	52.4	37 074	36 030	3.7	-0.8	602	681	-190	15 018	40.0	2.43	14.8	27.4
Hanover	9.3	6.1	4.6	50.8	89 714	63 306	36.4	3.9	1 362	760	2 733	31 121	37.5	2.71	9.3	17.7
Henrico	8.0	6.2	6.2	53.1	264 973	217 878	20.4	1.0	4 748	2 860	886	108 121	21.3	2.39	13.1	28.9
Henry	11.9	8.7	6.3	51.3	57 332	56 942	1.7	-1.0	758	750	-600	23 910	9.8	2.40	12.2	25.8
Highland	14.6	10.4	9.9	50.6	2 518	2 635	-3.8	-0.7	23	40	0	1 131	4.6	2.24	7.1	29.1
Isle of Wight	10.9	7.2	5.0	51.1	30 659	25 053	18.7	3.1	469	336	788	11 319	25.3	2.61	12.2	20.0
James City County	11.5	9.5	7.3	51.6	50 249	34 779	38.3	4.5	601	431	1 934	19 003	46.5	2.47	8.9	21.4
King and Queen	11.8	8.8	7.6	51.2	6 572	6 289	5.4	-0.9	75	115	-16	2 673	14.3	2.48	13.5	24.6
King George	9.0	5.3	4.3	49.8	17 319	13 527	24.2	3.1	308	162	368	6 091	28.6	2.70	10.5	20.4
King William	9.9	6.6	5.1	50.8	13 577	10 913	20.5	3.3	218	139	347	4 846	26.4	2.69	10.2	18.3
Lancaster	14.4	14.1	14.4	53.5	11 553	10 896	6.2	-0.1	154	280	116	5 004	9.6	2.23	11.1	28.7
Lee	11.4	8.2	7.3	51.5	23 431	24 496	-3.7	-0.7	299	422	-27	9 706	5.1	2.41	11.7	27.0
Loudoun	6.8	3.2	2.4	50.6	190 903	86 185	96.8	12.6	3 772	809	17 816	59 900	96.5	2.82	7.8	18.4

1. No spouse present.

Table B. States and Counties — Vital Statistics, Health Resources, and Crime

STATE County	Births, average 1997–1999		Deaths, average 1997–1999				Physicians[4] 2000		Hospitals[4] 1998			Medicare enrollees 2000	Serious crimes known to police, 2000[6]	
			Number		Rate					Beds			Total	
	Total	Rate[1]	Total	Infant[2]	Total[1]	Infant[3]	Number	Rate[5]	Number	Number	Rate[5]		Number	Rate[7]
	32	33	34	35	36	37	38	39	40	41	42	43	44	45

VERMONT—Cont'd														
Chittenden	1 663	11.6	874	11	6.1	6.6	656	448	2	582	408	16 093	5 776	3 941
Essex	50	7.6	60	NA	9.2	NA	3	46	0	0	0	1 268	NA	NA
Franklin	597	13.6	342	NA	7.8	NA	61	134	1	70	159	5 634	1 147	2 525
Grand Isle	272	42.2	46	NA	7.1	NA	6	87	0	0	0	997	NA	NA
Lamoille	267	12.3	169	NA	7.8	NA	52	224	1	49	227	3 065	621	2 673
Orange	253	9.1	230	NA	8.3	NA	40	142	1	42	150	4 010	354	1 254
Orleans	283	11.2	258	NA	10.2	NA	34	129	1	46	182	4 640	577	2 196
Rutland	642	10.3	632	NA	10.1	NA	131	207	1	188	301	11 275	2 063	3 254
Washington	585	10.4	517	NA	9.2	NA	123	212	1	122	217	8 999	1 805	3 110
Windham	434	10.2	400	NA	9.3	NA	98	222	2	81	190	6 926	1 308	2 958
Windsor	438	7.9	548	NA	9.9	NA	127	221	2	164	296	10 058	876	1 526
VIRGINIA	92 559	13.6	54 539	710	8.0	7.7	14 280	202	92	18 211	268	893 048	214 348	3 028
Accomack	399	12.4	451	NA	14.0	NA	24	63	0	0	0	6 720	909	2 426
Albemarle	948	12.1	502	NA	6.4	NA	426	538	0	0	0	8 252	2 554	3 223
Alleghany	139	11.4	123	NA	10.1	NA	31	240	1	174	1 433	423	183	1 416
Amelia	126	12.1	107	NA	10.3	NA	2	18	0	0	0	1 634	106	930
Amherst	340	11.3	270	NA	9.0	NA	14	44	0	0	0	2 129	373	1 169
Appomattox	160	12.2	134	NA	10.2	NA	6	44	0	0	0	2 129	131	956
Arlington	2 579	14.6	1 100	16	6.2	6.1	569	300	3	690	389	17 672	2 725	1 438
Augusta	703	11.4	504	NA	8.2	NA	86	131	1	131	212	6 541	864	1 317
Bath	48	9.9	59	NA	12.1	NA	6	119	1	25	511	1 061	32	634
Bedford	639	11.4	445	NA	7.9	NA	31	51	0	0	0	8 916	550	911
Bland	55	8.0	68	NA	10.0	NA	5	73	0	0	0	1 238	68	990
Botetourt	294	10.3	228	NA	7.9	NA	12	39	0	0	0	4 482	384	1 259
Brunswick	180	10.4	196	NA	11.4	NA	2	11	0	0	0	3 075	142	771
Buchanan	275	9.5	283	NA	9.8	NA	17	63	1	99	342	6 589	360	1 334
Buckingham	147	10.1	142	NA	9.7	NA	6	38	0	0	0	2 011	205	1 312
Campbell	629	12.5	427	NA	8.5	NA	19	37	0	0	0	6 332	894	1 750
Caroline	300	13.7	199	NA	9.1	NA	9	41	0	0	0	3 072	343	1 619
Carroll	285	10.2	315	NA	11.3	NA	14	48	0	0	0	4 502	459	1 723
Charles City County	83	11.6	70	NA	9.9	NA	3	43	0	0	0	812	NA	NA
Charlotte	138	11.2	172	NA	14.0	NA	5	40	0	0	0	3 077	137	1 098
Chesterfield	3 314	13.4	1 365	20	5.5	5.9	337	130	1	284	115	21 410	7 683	2 956
Clarke	118	9.2	124	NA	9.7	NA	9	71	0	0	0	1 785	256	2 023
Craig	51	10.5	42	NA	8.5	NA	4	79	0	0	0	766	22	432
Culpeper	458	13.9	293	NA	8.9	NA	47	137	1	70	212	4 781	NA	NA
Cumberland	107	13.6	102	NA	13.0	NA	5	55	0	0	0	967	97	1 076
Dickenson	182	10.7	187	NA	11.0	NA	13	79	1	50	296	3 755	171	1 043
Dinwiddie	260	10.4	225	NA	9.0	NA	26	106	0	0	0	2 883	615	2 553
Essex	106	11.5	119	NA	13.0	NA	21	210	1	100	1 096	1 749	213	2 132
Fairfax	13 089	14.1	3 918	62	4.2	4.7	2 292	236	3	507	55	59 356	11 916	1 229
Fauquier	691	12.8	392	NA	7.3	NA	75	136	1	106	196	6 021	937	1 699
Floyd	138	10.5	152	NA	11.6	NA	5	36	0	0	0	2 272	148	1 067
Fluvanna	240	12.9	140	NA	7.5	NA	13	65	0	0	0	3 124	206	1 028
Franklin	474	10.6	419	NA	9.4	NA	35	74	1	37	83	6 997	820	1 734
Frederick	738	13.3	396	NA	7.2	NA	12	20	0	0	0	6 114	1 275	2 153
Giles	180	11.1	201	NA	12.3	NA	13	78	1	53	326	3 612	182	1 149
Gloucester	382	10.9	297	NA	8.5	NA	35	101	1	71	202	4 450	629	1 809
Goochland	181	10.2	127	NA	7.2	NA	16	95	0	0	0	1 994	170	1 008
Grayson	162	10.0	207	NA	12.8	NA	8	45	0	0	0	2 985	124	692
Greene	219	15.6	96	NA	6.9	NA	4	26	0	0	0	1 636	209	1 371
Greensville	105	9.2	89	NA	7.9	NA	1	9	0	0	0	801	129	1 116
Halifax	420	11.4	495	NA	13.4	NA	9	24	1	192	521	7 383	661	1 838
Hanover	977	11.9	581	NA	7.1	NA	87	101	0	0	0	12 129	1 603	1 857
Henrico	3 296	13.4	2 218	29	9.0	8.9	831	317	4	1 231	500	28 638	11 035	4 207
Henry	622	11.2	585	NA	10.5	NA	13	22	0	0	0	8 402	1 588	2 741
Highland	18	7.2	34	NA	13.7	NA	3	118	0	0	0	543	24	946
Isle of Wight	344	11.8	251	NA	8.6	NA	10	34	0	0	0	4 109	691	2 324
James City County	456	10.3	321	NA	7.2	NA	96	200	0	0	0	2 030	928	1 929
King and Queen	77	11.8	80	NA	12.2	NA	0	0	0	0	0	1 076	NA	NA
King George	247	14.3	123	NA	7.1	NA	7	42	0	0	0	1 772	420	2 500
King William	170	13.3	100	NA	7.8	NA	6	46	0	0	0	1 847	217	1 651
Lancaster	103	9.1	203	NA	17.9	NA	42	363	1	76	668	3 615	149	1 437
Lee	269	11.2	308	NA	12.9	NA	24	102	1	80	336	5 115	484	2 052
Loudoun	2 680	18.5	596	10	4.1	3.6	194	114	1	119	83	9 955	3 726	2 197

1. Per 1,000 estimated resident population, average 1997–1999.   2. Deaths of infants under 1 year old.   3. Deaths of infants under 1 year old per 1,000 live births.   4. Data subject to copyright.   5. Per 100,000 resident population as of July 1 of the year shown.   6. Data for serious crimes have not been adjusted for underreporting; this may affect comparability between geographic areas and over time.   7. Per 100,000 population estimated by the FBI.

STATE County	Serious crimes known to police, 2000[1] (cont'd) Rate[2] Violent	Property	Education — School enrollment and attainment, 1990 — Enrollment[3] Total	Percent private	Attainment[4] (percent) High school graduate or more	Bachelor's degree or more	Local government expenditures, fiscal 1999[5] Total current expenditures (mil dol)	Current expenditures per student (dollars)	Money income — 1989 Per capita[6] (dollars)	Households Median Dollars	Percent change, 1979–1989 (constant 1989 dollars)	Percent with $100,000 or more	Income and poverty, 1998 Median household income	Percent below poverty level All persons	Persons under 18	Persons 5–17 in families
	46	47	48	49	50	51	52	53	54	55	56	57	58	59	60	61
VERMONT—Cont'd																
Chittenden	166	3 775	39 777	21.0	86.7	34.0	176.5	7 549	16 096	36 877	25.2	4.5	48 007	7.1	9.6	7.2
Essex	NA	NA	1 511	10.3	68.0	8.5	7.9	8 169	9 854	22 358	7.9	0.3	30 029	13.8	18.7	16.8
Franklin	112	2 413	10 336	7.3	74.8	14.3	55.2	6 756	11 678	28 401	20.8	1.7	37 169	10.3	12.3	11.2
Grand Isle	NA	NA	1 192	11.3	79.0	20.3	6.7	8 426	13 940	30 536	23.4	3.3	42 269	8.9	12.4	11.3
Lamoille	108	2 565	5 265	6.1	80.2	23.9	29.2	7 405	12 519	27 315	23.1	2.4	35 381	10.7	13.8	12.0
Orange	78	1 176	6 614	9.9	80.4	21.9	40.1	7 754	11 898	28 004	29.9	1.9	37 065	9.7	12.4	10.5
Orleans	88	2 108	6 126	8.9	70.7	14.2	36.3	7 751	10 458	22 809	9.3	1.8	30 282	14.7	18.4	15.6
Rutland	82	3 172	14 714	15.7	79.4	20.6	82.0	7 597	12 780	28 229	14.1	1.9	34 624	10.5	13.9	11.2
Washington	109	3 001	13 391	21.9	81.3	24.4	77.7	7 669	13 547	29 623	22.9	2.6	38 880	9.2	11.8	9.7
Windham	127	2 832	9 743	18.5	81.7	25.2	66.6	9 396	13 134	27 767	21.0	2.2	38 666	9.8	12.9	10.7
Windsor	40	1 486	12 146	11.0	81.3	23.6	79.0	8 251	14 262	29 258	13.7	3.2	38 696	9.3	12.4	9.7
VIRGINIA	282	2 746	1 546 257	13.9	75.2	24.5	7 137.4	6 350	15 713	33 328	13.8	5.2	42 622	10.2	14.2	13.3
Accomack	248	2 178	6 327	9.5	59.5	9.2	31.7	5 826	10 506	20 431	12.1	1.2	26 338	20.4	29.2	26.6
Albemarle	178	3 045	21 567	11.5	81.5	39.4	80.2	6 466	17 448	36 886	23.6	7.3	49 171	8.0	12.3	9.8
Alleghany	441	975	3 046	5.4	67.4	9.3	[7]18.4	[7]6 233	11 606	26 486	-0.8	0.9	39 135	10.7	16.2	14.4
Amelia	70	860	1 909	9.3	56.3	7.2	10.4	5 738	11 605	26 612	11.4	1.4	35 628	11.6	17.5	15.6
Amherst	103	1 066	6 675	12.5	58.9	10.7	23.8	5 112	11 185	27 771	-0.1	0.8	36 112	10.7	15.1	13.8
Appomattox	51	905	2 794	7.2	61.1	8.7	12.5	5 266	10 795	25 612	-6.4	1.1	33 893	13.1	18.4	17.2
Arlington	105	1 334	34 765	31.9	87.5	52.3	187.0	10 321	25 633	44 600	22.6	10.7	60 591	6.3	11.6	11.0
Augusta	117	1 199	12 064	8.2	69.0	11.7	61.8	5 669	12 751	29 474	9.7	1.9	41 116	8.7	12.9	9.9
Bath	20	614	973	4.2	67.3	12.8	7.5	8 379	11 369	24 203	8.6	1.7	33 910	10.0	14.9	14.2
Bedford	99	812	10 173	13.7	68.8	15.6	[8]51.7	[8]5 014	14 305	30 712	13.5	2.8	45 474	7.3	11.2	9.1
Bland	58	931	1 524	5.1	62.6	4.6	5.7	5 919	9 765	23 587	1.5	0.9	33 140	10.4	11.7	11.2
Botetourt	108	1 151	5 706	10.0	72.9	13.6	26.9	5 828	13 810	33 079	15.1	2.3	47 667	6.2	9.8	7.6
Brunswick	71	700	4 305	15.9	50.5	7.0	17.0	6 567	8 872	19 424	5.8	1.2	26 692	20.2	25.4	24.1
Buchanan	222	1 112	8 251	5.8	42.5	6.4	29.8	6 652	9 621	19 851	-23.3	1.7	25 395	22.8	24.9	26.5
Buckingham	173	1 139	2 838	10.7	53.6	7.9	13.6	6 034	9 165	22 661	18.0	0.9	29 243	18.0	21.4	23.8
Campbell	151	1 600	11 250	17.0	66.1	12.9	44.8	5 267	12 061	27 212	-2.9	1.7	37 291	10.6	16.8	14.7
Caroline	387	1 232	4 244	7.6	58.8	8.3	21.3	5 594	11 837	28 934	19.2	2.7	37 020	13.0	18.2	16.8
Carroll	169	1 554	5 126	4.0	49.7	6.5	22.2	5 546	9 693	21 564	6.4	0.7	29 523	13.9	20.8	18.5
Charles City County	NA	NA	1 396	10.9	56.4	8.4	7.9	7 725	11 384	29 544	3.0	1.7	40 058	10.5	16.3	15.4
Charlotte	233	866	2 572	3.7	52.1	6.5	13.3	5 899	9 008	20 481	10.4	1.2	27 549	16.9	22.9	22.1
Chesterfield	216	2 740	59 331	9.8	84.2	29.2	276.4	5 461	17 423	43 604	8.7	5.7	58 423	5.8	8.4	6.8
Clarke	348	1 676	2 433	15.3	75.0	18.6	11.5	6 089	15 657	34 636	24.1	6.0	47 323	8.1	11.4	11.4
Craig	137	295	860	5.9	68.4	7.7	4.5	6 190	11 186	25 106	10.5	1.4	36 874	8.9	12.3	13.2
Culpeper	NA	NA	6 324	12.1	66.7	14.9	32.9	5 952	14 122	33 523	28.7	4.3	44 174	10.5	14.2	13.9
Cumberland	177	898	1 812	16.2	57.6	11.2	8.2	6 371	10 295	22 115	15.8	2.3	29 814	17.1	24.0	23.2
Dickenson	49	994	4 504	4.0	47.1	6.0	18.1	6 077	8 067	16 292	-28.2	1.2	23 653	22.0	24.6	26.7
Dinwiddie	212	2 341	4 535	9.1	59.2	8.4	22.7	5 319	12 212	29 388	15.0	1.6	37 244	10.8	15.4	15.5
Essex	140	1 992	1 816	8.4	64.7	16.4	10.3	6 159	11 529	26 074	10.7	1.6	32 047	14.6	21.2	20.3
Fairfax	26	1 202	217 447	19.0	91.4	49.0	[9]1 153.1	[9]7 737	24 833	59 284	17.9	16.4	73 337	4.7	7.0	5.5
Fauquier	165	1 534	11 380	14.3	78.9	21.5	59.3	6 371	19 195	45 222	39.6	8.9	59 654	6.2	8.7	8.4
Floyd	65	1 002	2 391	5.4	60.2	10.4	10.5	5 508	10 532	22 968	12.1	0.8	33 604	12.0	16.2	15.1
Fluvanna	95	933	2 808	6.6	68.5	16.3	16.3	5 638	12 977	31 378	41.0	2.9	43 198	7.2	9.7	10.5
Franklin	203	1 531	8 923	19.7	59.9	10.1	38.3	5 494	11 936	26 357	5.6	2.0	35 750	11.3	16.5	14.8
Frederick	76	2 077	10 552	10.2	70.1	14.7	62.4	6 016	13 671	32 806	14.4	2.4	45 394	7.4	10.8	9.1
Giles	126	1 023	3 402	2.7	64.5	8.9	14.7	5 732	11 462	24 125	5.9	1.1	33 825	11.6	17.3	16.9
Gloucester	118	1 691	7 335	11.2	74.0	14.7	35.8	5 379	13 122	31 591	16.9	2.3	42 350	9.8	13.3	12.9
Goochland	154	854	2 831	21.3	66.7	19.3	13.0	6 551	18 312	36 239	19.2	9.3	54 007	7.3	11.9	9.9
Grayson	84	608	3 087	8.1	51.1	4.2	13.8	5 972	8 966	19 324	-1.7	0.2	28 521	15.1	19.6	19.3
Greene	92	1 279	2 364	8.4	63.5	12.7	15.6	6 122	12 268	29 799	9.1	1.7	40 095	10.0	13.9	14.7
Greensville	372	744	2 124	5.6	50.0	5.3	[10]16.1	[10]5 862	9 504	22 116	13.2	0.9	29 208	19.1	25.4	21.2
Halifax	286	1 551	6 418	4.3	51.6	6.4	37.7	6 065	9 568	22 296	9.2	0.7	29 399	16.0	20.6	18.7
Hanover	107	1 750	15 822	15.2	77.5	18.9	80.6	5 094	16 463	40 683	13.7	4.3	57 367	4.4	6.1	5.2
Henrico	228	3 979	51 199	14.2	81.3	28.0	227.6	5 692	18 019	35 604	5.7	4.7	47 155	7.4	12.1	9.6
Henry	392	2 349	11 443	7.3	53.9	6.7	51.4	5 566	11 491	25 834	-3.0	1.2	32 129	12.2	19.2	16.6
Highland	118	828	477	4.0	61.8	13.0	2.6	7 503	10 828	20 903	-8.1	1.3	29 767	13.5	17.1	18.1
Isle of Wight	141	2 183	5 973	13.4	65.4	10.4	28.5	5 687	12 274	29 168	3.2	1.3	42 002	10.4	15.2	14.2
James City County	148	1 782	8 942	16.8	82.5	32.9	[11]NA	[11]NA	18 139	39 785	26.9	7.4	53 977	7.0	11.2	9.4
King and Queen	NA	NA	1 247	7.9	57.6	7.5	7.2	7 763	11 278	25 755	27.0	1.3	33 836	14.6	20.1	23.3
King George	161	2 339	3 400	6.8	73.1	20.4	17.9	6 021	15 365	35 556	17.5	3.7	49 017	8.1	11.4	11.5
King William	137	1 514	2 687	6.8	68.5	13.0	16.0	6 257	13 294	33 676	15.0	2.5	45 000	8.1	11.6	11.2
Lancaster	145	1 292	2 000	16.0	64.8	18.9	9.2	5 720	17 698	27 275	23.1	7.4	34 031	15.3	24.6	23.1
Lee	161	1 891	5 684	3.2	48.0	6.5	25.3	6 351	7 837	14 618	-16.4	0.9	22 604	25.4	28.9	31.0
Loudoun	177	2 019	21 224	13.4	86.6	32.7	181.8	6 972	20 757	52 064	27.1	9.3	75 886	3.2	4.7	4.2

1. Data for serious crimes have not been adjusted for underreporting; this may affect comparability between geographic areas and over time.   2. Per 100,000 population estimated by the FBI.   3. All persons 3 years old and over enrolled in nursery school through college.   4. Persons 25 years old and over.   5. Elementary and secondary education expenditures, local government fiscal years ending between July 1, 1998 and June 30, 1999.   6. Based on population enumerated as of April 1, 1990.   7. Clifton Forge City included with Allegheny County.   8. Bedford City included with Bedford County.   9. Fairfax City included with Fairfax County.   10. Emporia included with Greensville County.   11. Williamsburg included with James City County.

Table B. States and Counties — Personal Income

STATE County	Total (mil dol)	Percent change, 1998–1999	Per capita[1] Dollars	Per capita[1] Rank	Wages and salaries[2] (mil dol)	Proprietor's income (mil dol)	Dividends, interest, and rent (mil dol)	Transfer payments Total (mil dol)	Government payments to individuals Total (mil dol)	Social Security (mil dol)	Medical payments (mil dol)	Income maintenance (mil dol)	Unemployment insurance (mil dol)
	62	63	64	65	66	67	68	69	70	71	72	73	74
VERMONT—Cont'd													
Chittenden	4 375	5.7	30 391	198	3 487	292	829	431	398	167	162	42	6
Essex	109	3.1	16 340	2 852	53	18	16	25	23	11	5	3	2
Franklin	919	5.5	20 679	1 785	435	86	130	141	131	49	47	21	4
Grand Isle	167	9.7	26 243	490	23	14	32	20	19	10	4	2	2
Lamoille	538	5.0	24 529	750	257	69	114	77	72	29	28	8	3
Orange	590	4.0	21 165	1 611	204	56	122	90	83	38	28	11	1
Orleans	514	5.0	20 146	1 954	236	73	97	117	111	41	45	15	3
Rutland	1 515	2.4	24 272	811	851	108	296	324	310	110	155	29	5
Washington	1 504	6.4	26 726	437	987	138	278	235	222	88	97	23	4
Windham	1 130	3.2	26 480	467	759	98	251	167	157	71	60	16	4
Windsor	1 559	3.8	28 109	320	721	130	403	209	196	101	64	19	2
VIRGINIA	204 769	6.3	29 794	X	136 868	11 410	37 880	19 671	18 386	8 481	6 521	1 717	180
Accomack	649	4.1	20 194	1 935	333	53	160	136	130	61	46	15	2
Albemarle	(3)3 920	(3)3.9	(3)33 513	(3)121	(3)2 701	(3)390	(3)1 081	(3)342	(3)319	(3)158	(3)118	(3)24	(3)2
Alleghany	(4)514	(4)-0.8	(4)22 136	(4)1 313	(4)347	(4)26	(4)91	(4)109	(4)105	(4)44	(4)33	(4)9	(4)1
Amelia	220	5.3	20 768	1 750	65	25	34	34	32	16	12	3	0
Amherst	561	3.4	18 482	2 416	278	34	90	95	89	48	27	7	0
Appomattox	261	3.5	19 587	2 113	102	20	44	45	43	22	14	4	0
Arlington	8 763	6.6	50 111	8	10 526	498	1 880	362	334	148	133	25	2
Augusta	(5)2 478	(5)4.4	(5)23 612	(5)940	(5)1 467	(5)183	(5)495	(5)357	(5)337	(5)186	(5)110	(5)22	(5)3
Bath	119	6.3	24 067	847	70	8	31	21	20	9	8	1	0
Bedford	(6)1 656	(6)7.1	(6)25 782	(6)544	(6)471	(6)78	(6)374	(6)200	(6)188	(6)101	(6)53	(6)11	(6)1
Bland	113	1.8	16 650	2 800	50	9	17	25	24	11	9	2	0
Botetourt	734	5.9	25 166	647	217	44	148	89	83	45	22	4	1
Brunswick	291	4.3	15 860	2 914	130	19	49	71	68	28	26	8	0
Buchanan	513	1.1	17 999	2 540	256	48	100	170	164	75	51	21	3
Buckingham	246	3.2	16 659	2 798	83	25	36	53	50	22	19	6	1
Campbell	(7)2 722	(7)4.5	(7)23 823	(7)891	(7)2 394	(7)157	(7)491	(7)480	(7)458	(7)202	(7)185	(7)36	(7)2
Caroline	483	8.7	21 887	1 391	135	37	77	70	66	31	24	7	1
Carroll	(8)666	(8)5.0	(8)19 419	(8)2 171	(8)378	(8)49	(8)108	(8)161	(8)154	(8)64	(8)68	(8)14	(8)3
Charles City County	141	4.1	19 419	2 171	39	6	25	21	20	10	7	2	0
Charlotte	224	3.0	18 045	2 531	89	23	42	55	52	23	19	7	0
Chesterfield	8 013	7.4	31 627	164	3 868	306	1 228	507	458	269	129	28	3
Clarke	385	6.2	29 958	213	121	19	83	33	30	17	11	2	0
Craig	101	5.5	20 454	1 850	15	6	14	15	14	8	4	1	0
Culpeper	896	7.8	26 699	441	409	52	157	97	90	44	34	8	1
Cumberland	155	4.9	19 690	2 088	31	14	26	31	29	13	9	4	0
Dickenson	270	3.0	16 172	2 878	93	23	45	99	96	40	32	12	1
Dinwiddie	(9)1 970	(9)5.0	(9)25 824	(9)539	(9)1 005	(9)85	(9)271	(9)390	(9)375	(9)128	(9)177	(9)36	(9)2
Essex	199	6.5	21 783	1 418	97	14	44	40	38	18	15	3	0
Fairfax	(10)46 124	(10)7.7	(10)47 241	(10)13	(10)30 664	(10)2 580	(10)8 532	(10)1 653	(10)1 467	(10)716	(10)505	(10)92	(10)10
Fauquier	2 008	7.2	36 373	71	505	104	498	121	110	59	39	8	0
Floyd	232	4.9	17 466	2 653	61	19	48	45	42	21	14	4	1
Fluvanna	415	8.2	21 157	1 615	97	25	79	60	56	30	19	3	0
Franklin	939	4.4	20 765	1 751	370	47	189	143	135	75	38	10	2
Frederick	(11)2 091	(11)6.9	(11)26 451	(11)473	(11)1 435	(11)166	(11)385	(11)215	(11)200	(11)109	(11)64	(11)14	(11)2
Giles	326	3.2	19 963	2 000	183	22	54	70	67	34	23	5	1
Gloucester	798	4.5	22 516	1 214	213	39	159	94	87	42	31	7	1
Goochland	606	4.5	34 306	98	241	39	166	46	42	24	12	3	0
Grayson	289	3.0	17 570	2 636	69	25	51	65	61	32	20	6	1
Greene	281	7.5	19 166	2 241	85	19	36	35	32	16	12	3	0
Greensville	(12)308	(12)2.6	(12)18 100	(12)2 520	(12)229	(12)15	(12)49	(12)66	(12)62	(12)27	(12)25	(12)7	(12)0
Halifax	(13)698	(13)4.8	(13)18 897	(13)2 318	(13)395	(13)38	(13)113	(13)151	(13)144	(13)65	(13)51	(13)18	(13)3
Hanover	2 429	7.4	28 437	286	1 245	152	394	216	200	111	67	8	1
Henrico	8 367	6.6	34 198	104	6 444	342	1 838	675	628	375	189	33	4
Henry	(14)1 541	(14)2.0	(14)21 813	(14)1 409	(14)985	(14)100	(14)343	(14)289	(14)275	(14)148	(14)84	(14)21	(14)11
Highland	55	1.4	22 348	1 262	12	8	18	10	10	5	4	1	0
Isle of Wight	765	6.1	25 810	541	449	34	114	95	89	42	34	8	1
James City County	(15)2 039	(15)6.9	(15)34 888	(15)87	(15)1 103	(15)134	(15)538	(15)187	(15)176	(15)95	(15)62	(15)7	(15)1
King and Queen	141	4.8	21 610	1 482	33	10	22	23	21	10	8	2	0
King George	473	7.8	26 769	433	542	24	90	34	31	14	12	3	0
King William	313	5.5	24 008	856	124	13	56	38	35	19	12	3	0
Lancaster	334	4.4	29 430	236	120	16	148	64	62	33	22	4	1
Lee	392	1.2	16 449	2 834	137	22	57	134	130	46	48	22	2
Loudoun	5 861	14.6	37 500	64	4 758	192	822	211	182	100	62	10	1

1. Based on the resident population estimated as of July 1 of the year shown.   2. Includes other labor income.   3. Charlottesville included with Albemarle County.   4. Clifton Forge and Covington included with Alleghany County.   5. Staunton and Waynesboro included with Augusta County.   6. Bedford City included with Bedford County.   7. Lynchburg included with Campbell County.   8. Galax included with Carroll County.   9. Petersburg and Colonial Heights included with Dinwiddie County.   10. Fairfax City and Falls Church included with Fairfax County.   11. Winchester included with Frederick County.   12. Emporia included with Greensville County.   13. South Boston included with Halifax County.   14. Martinsville included with Henry County.   15. Williamsburg included with James City County.

Table B. States and Counties — Earnings, Social Security, and Housing

STATE County	Earnings, 1999									Social Security beneficiaries, December 2000		Housing units, 1990	
			Goods-related[1]		Service-related and other[2]								
	Total (mil dol)	Farm	Total	Manufacturing	Total	Retail trade	Finance, insurance, and real estate	Services	Government	Number	Rate[3]	Supplemental Security Income recipients, December 2000	Total	Percent change, 1980–1990
	75	76	77	78	79	80	81	82	83	84	85	86	87	88
VERMONT—Cont'd														
Chittenden	3 780	0.2	29.7	23.0	56.0	8.6	6.4	30.2	14.2	19 227	131	2 053	52 095	26.0
Essex	71	2.3	D	D	D	3.7	0.9	7.5	15.1	1 469	227	168	4 403	18.9
Franklin	521	5.6	26.2	20.7	46.9	12.1	3.3	21.4	21.3	6 246	138	1 109	17 250	19.3
Grand Isle	37	8.5	D	D	D	9.3	2.9	25.2	23.2	1 156	168	103	4 135	16.3
Lamoille	325	1.9	23.2	13.2	60.1	14.1	3.6	36.3	14.9	3 629	156	438	9 872	31.0
Orange	259	3.2	23.9	12.2	51.7	9.7	3.3	27.5	21.1	4 773	169	536	12 336	17.7
Orleans	308	6.2	27.7	19.6	47.8	10.7	3.8	23.1	18.3	5 476	208	847	12 997	16.3
Rutland	959	0.6	27.4	19.5	57.3	11.9	3.8	29.8	14.7	13 118	207	1 834	31 181	21.0
Washington	1 124	0.4	18.4	12.4	57.3	9.6	11.1	27.7	23.9	10 516	181	1 370	25 328	14.5
Windham	857	1.1	D	15.5	D	9.6	5.2	31.2	9.7	8 250	187	845	25 796	31.9
Windsor	851	0.5	25.9	16.6	52.2	10.0	4.1	29.5	21.5	11 722	204	1 023	29 849	23.0
VIRGINIA	148 278	0.2	17.2	10.8	58.9	8.3	7.3	30.6	23.7	1 036 281	146	132 064	2 496 334	23.5
Accomack	386	3.8	D	20.4	D	8.2	D	20.4	29.0	8 024	209	1 299	15 840	14.7
Albemarle	(4)3 091	(4)0.2	(4)19.5	(4)9.9	(4)48.2	(4)9.8	(4)8.1	(4)23.8	(4)32.1	11 855	150	738	25 958	27.5
Alleghany	(5)373	(5)0.1	(5)D	(5)D	(5)D	(5)8.5	(5)D	(5)16.9	(5)13.6	2 376	184	207	5 481	0.9
Amelia	90	10.3	D	11.3	D	6.9	D	15.1	19.2	2 096	184	291	3 439	14.0
Amherst	312	0.3	35.1	25.7	D	9.5	D	15.2	28.1	5 934	186	688	10 598	9.6
Appomattox	122	-0.2	D	30.9	D	10.3	4.1	11.1	20.6	2 885	211	356	4 913	9.0
Arlington	11 024	0.0	D	2.3	D	4.1	5.2	34.2	40.6	17 025	90	1 928	84 847	12.9
Augusta	(6)1 650	(6)1.1	(6)D	(6)26.8	(6)D	(6)11.1	(6)3.5	(6)18.3	(6)17.0	11 840	180	626	21 202	8.1
Bath	78	0.2	13.1	6.8	D	3.4	1.7	51.1	15.3	1 118	221	108	2 596	2.3
Bedford	(7)549	(7)0.1	(7)D	(7)25.5	(7)D	(7)7.5	(7)D	(7)24.7	(7)14.3	10 297	171	732	19 641	41.4
Bland	59	0.0	D	32.9	D	4.9	1.2	10.6	31.8	1 481	216	158	2 706	19.5
Botetourt	262	0.7	38.2	19.8	46.4	8.8	3.3	15.6	14.7	5 419	178	279	9 785	12.3
Brunswick	149	1.4	D	18.0	D	6.0	2.0	20.5	27.6	3 758	204	697	6 456	4.2
Buchanan	303	0.0	43.1	4.8	39.4	7.9	2.2	16.4	17.4	9 406	349	1 770	12 222	-4.3
Buckingham	109	2.7	27.0	12.1	D	6.6	D	18.3	30.9	2 895	185	489	5 013	10.4
Campbell	(8)2 551	(8)0.0	(8)D	(8)34.3	(8)D	(8)9.1	(8)7.6	(8)24.9	(8)9.8	9 989	196	945	19 008	16.3
Caroline	172	1.0	D	12.6	D	10.4	5.0	14.9	27.7	3 879	175	348	7 292	11.7
Carroll	(9)427	(9)0.7	(9)D	(9)35.8	(9)D	(9)11.6	(9)2.1	(9)20.2	(9)15.3	6 633	227	795	12 209	4.5
Charles City County	46	1.1	D	18.0	D	4.2	1.9	14.1	23.5	1 290	186	143	2 314	6.5
Charlotte	112	1.2	45.6	40.6	32.8	6.2	2.9	12.0	20.4	3 134	251	630	4 947	8.5
Chesterfield	4 174	0.1	25.7	17.4	57.7	11.2	7.5	22.0	16.5	30 782	118	2 409	77 329	58.2
Clarke	140	0.6	D	30.7	D	6.3	4.5	25.0	14.3	2 096	166	143	4 531	14.4
Craig	21	2.5	D	5.6	D	7.4	5.7	12.7	33.6	1 026	202	115	1 993	6.4
Culpeper	461	0.8	20.9	12.5	58.0	8.9	5.7	29.7	20.2	5 606	164	657	10 471	26.6
Cumberland	45	8.7	22.7	8.0	D	12.5	D	16.6	24.1	1 681	186	247	3 170	3.6
Dickenson	116	0.2	38.7	0.8	D	8.5	1.6	18.2	22.8	5 152	314	1 037	7 112	3.0
Dinwiddie	(10)1 091	(10)0.1	(10)D	(10)12.9	(10)D	(10)17.5	(10)4.0	(10)17.7	(10)29.8	4 416	180	773	8 023	17.3
Essex	111	1.0	30.7	24.7	54.1	17.7	5.0	24.6	14.2	2 289	229	245	4 073	-0.2
Fairfax	(11)33 244	(11)0.0	(11)D	(11)D	(11)D	(11)6.3	(11)8.8	(11)45.7	(11)14.6	81 506	84	7 013	307 966	42.7
Fauquier	609	0.9	D	6.3	D	10.6	6.8	30.0	16.1	2 873	207	251	5 505	12.0
Floyd	80	3.1	27.9	17.6	49.0	10.0	5.9	18.3	20.0	3 608	180	253	5 035	31.5
Fluvanna	122	0.9	D	D	D	5.6	D	23.9	27.5	3 466	180	253	5 035	31.5
Franklin	417	1.3	44.1	35.4	41.1	9.3	2.9	18.3	10.5	9 466	200	865	17 526	29.7
Frederick	(12)1 601	(12)0.4	(12)D	(12)29.3	(12)D	(12)11.4	(12)D	(12)26.9	(12)10.5	8 663	146	568	17 864	40.0
Giles	205	-0.4	52.4	45.3	D	8.8	2.2	14.7	11.3	4 089	245	524	7 098	5.4
Gloucester	253	0.0	D	4.0	D	15.6	4.3	23.2	28.7	5 388	155	495	12 451	49.8
Goochland	280	0.2	D	3.3	D	24.7	7.3	21.4	14.1	2 840	168	199	5 203	29.1
Grayson	93	3.3	38.5	32.8	37.1	6.3	3.4	17.6	21.2	4 487	250	556	7 529	10.9
Greene	105	3.3	D	D	D	9.2	D	18.9	22.1	2 078	136	211	4 154	35.8
Greensville	(13)244	(13)1.5	(13)D	(13)33.7	(13)D	(13)8.1	(13)1.4	(13)17.8	(13)24.3	2 035	176	365	3 393	-10.5
Halifax	(14)432	(14)1.1	(14)D	(14)33.3	(14)D	(14)12.1	(14)1.9	(14)19.1	(14)14.9	8 897	238	1 780	11 790	3.9
Hanover	1 397	0.3	D	12.2	D	9.1	4.8	24.4	10.3	12 117	140	557	23 727	37.3
Henrico	6 786	0.1	17.5	11.8	75.0	13.3	20.6	26.7	7.4	40 133	153	1 826	94 539	34.2
Henry	(15)1 085	(15)0.3	(15)D	(15)44.5	(15)D	(15)9.4	(15)3.1	(15)18.4	(15)11.5	13 019	225	1 057	23 169	10.5
Highland	20	9.9	D	20.1	D	4.6	4.4	18.2	19.1	661	261	43	1 759	20.2
Isle of Wight	483	0.5	D	58.1	D	4.1	10.1	8.0	8.5	5 242	176	558	9 753	26.6
James City County	(16)1 237	(16)0.0	(16)16.1	(16)9.7	(16)D	(16)13.7	(16)10.5	(16)32.9	(16)23.0	9 129	190	214	14 330	65.2
King and Queen	44	-0.4	D	18.5	D	3.9	D	13.2	35.9	1 201	181	162	2 698	7.5
King George	566	0.1	4.7	1.7	29.5	1.8	0.9	23.8	65.7	2 006	119	187	5 280	32.1
King William	137	0.9	51.2	41.5	33.3	8.3	5.5	12.7	14.6	2 240	170	191	4 193	21.9
Lancaster	136	0.1	13.4	4.1	74.9	12.3	10.8	41.8	11.6	3 784	327	222	5 918	15.9
Lee	139	0.9	27.4	9.8	46.9	9.4	3.5	23.6	24.7	6 696	284	1 961	10 263	6.3
Loudoun	4 950	0.1	11.4	4.2	75.6	6.3	2.5	51.7	12.9	12 073	71	622	32 932	66.8

1. Covers mining, construction, and manufacturing.   2. Covers private sector earnings in agricultural services, forestry, and fisheries; transportation and public utilities; wholesale trade; retail trade; finance, insurance, and real estate; and services.   3. Per 1,000 resident population estimated as of July 1 of the year shown.   4. Charlottesville included with Albemarle County.   5. Clifton Forge and Covington included with Alleghany County.   6. Staunton and Waynesboro included with Augusta County.   7. Bedford City included with Bedford County.   8. Lynchburg included with Campbell County.   9. Galax included with Carroll County.   10. Petersburg and Colonial Heights included with Dinwiddie County.   11. Fairfax City and Falls Church included with Fairfax County.   12. Winchester included with Frederick County.   13. Emporia included with Greensville County.   14. South Boston included with Halifax County.   15. Martinsville included with Henry County.   16. Williamsburg included with James City County.

Table B. States and Counties — Housing, Labor Force, and Employment

STATE County	Housing units, 1990 (cont'd) Occupied units Owner-occupied Total	Percent	Median value[1]	With a mortgage	Without a mortgage	Renter-occupied Median rent[2]	Rent as percent of income	Sub-standard units[3] (percent)	Civilian labor force, 2001 Total	Percent change, 2000–2001	Unemployment Total	Rate[4]	Civilian employment, 1990[5] Total	Percent Professional, managerial, and technical	Precision production, craft, and repair
	89	90	91	92	93	94	95	96	97	98	99	100	101	102	103
VERMONT—Cont'd															
Chittenden	48 439	64.4	117 500	21.8	13.7	526	27.0	1.7	90 582	1.2	2 187	2.4	72 417	39.7	9.4
Essex	2 344	78.3	56 500	18.5	13.9	319	25.0	4.0	2 950	0.9	194	6.6	2 489	18.4	16.5
Franklin	14 326	72.5	81 700	21.4	14.5	412	27.1	3.0	24 270	0.9	1 014	4.2	19 065	23.5	14.1
Grand Isle	2 018	77.7	105 100	21.6	15.1	462	24.8	1.9	3 529	0.3	180	5.1	2 538	28.6	15.5
Lamoille	7 397	69.8	89 900	23.2	15.8	414	28.2	3.1	11 793	0.0	577	4.9	9 709	29.0	13.0
Orange	9 455	77.6	86 400	22.7	15.2	417	25.6	4.0	15 845	1.2	425	2.7	12 992	28.5	13.9
Orleans	8 873	73.7	66 500	20.5	14.0	326	27.0	2.9	12 946	2.1	923	7.1	10 627	22.6	13.6
Rutland	23 690	68.5	94 000	22.5	14.9	440	27.6	2.2	31 419	1.4	1 290	4.1	30 798	27.1	13.4
Washington	20 948	68.7	89 900	21.1	14.8	411	25.6	2.1	32 012	1.7	1 223	3.8	27 345	34.1	11.3
Windham	16 264	64.2	97 200	22.1	15.9	458	27.0	3.2	22 417	-0.7	743	3.3	20 972	29.0	13.3
Windsor	21 523	69.4	97 300	21.8	15.8	457	27.0	2.4	31 443	1.5	886	2.8	27 245	30.4	14.1
VIRGINIA	2 291 830	66.3	91 000	21.9	12.5	495	25.8	4.1	3 675 345	1.8	127 298	3.5	3 028 362	33.8	11.5
Accomack	12 653	74.8	52 700	22.4	14.2	335	25.1	9.8	15 253	2.2	654	4.3	13 690	19.6	12.6
Albemarle	24 433	64.1	111 200	22.0	11.7	530	24.1	3.7	41 262	0.3	730	1.8	34 422	42.3	9.6
Alleghany	4 942	82.1	50 100	14.7	12.2	293	22.6	6.0	8 141	0.7	307	3.8	6 060	18.7	15.8
Amelia	3 131	80.5	54 900	18.7	11.6	327	18.6	8.9	5 558	5.7	153	2.8	4 213	15.6	15.9
Amherst	9 827	78.6	56 900	16.2	11.7	327	19.9	4.9	14 813	-1.0	567	3.8	13 342	19.7	13.9
Appomattox	4 531	81.1	51 000	15.9	11.8	295	23.9	5.2	5 365	1.8	362	6.7	5 810	19.0	16.2
Arlington	78 520	44.6	231 000	21.5	11.7	703	25.9	5.4	114 350	2.3	2 578	2.3	105 584	55.0	5.1
Augusta	19 781	80.5	70 500	17.9	11.8	357	21.8	4.5	32 396	1.6	916	2.8	27 611	20.8	15.3
Bath	1 895	76.6	46 700	18.6	11.3	312	18.4	7.0	2 476	2.0	115	4.6	2 177	22.9	12.8
Bedford	17 292	85.8	75 800	18.0	11.3	346	20.3	3.6	30 711	-1.2	1 070	3.5	23 433	24.7	14.8
Bland	2 244	84.8	43 800	19.7	11.2	235	14.7	6.5	3 472	-0.8	206	5.9	2 751	15.9	14.8
Botetourt	9 148	85.7	73 400	18.0	12.1	329	18.2	4.1	16 977	0.7	407	2.4	12 895	25.0	13.3
Brunswick	5 499	74.8	42 900	17.2	13.6	232	22.1	11.6	7 964	3.4	420	5.3	6 421	15.8	13.6
Buchanan	11 061	80.8	41 700	21.7	11.8	270	22.1	6.6	7 884	1.0	608	7.7	9 887	17.8	28.0
Buckingham	4 341	78.2	44 900	18.0	13.5	266	24.9	11.7	6 340	4.1	168	2.6	5 178	17.3	14.4
Campbell	17 952	77.5	61 800	16.5	11.6	330	21.0	4.2	26 939	-0.3	1 340	5.0	24 048	23.0	15.5
Caroline	6 631	80.0	64 700	21.8	13.4	400	21.4	11.8	11 690	8.5	357	3.1	9 055	18.1	16.0
Carroll	10 463	82.7	44 000	16.1	11.8	268	22.3	6.4	13 758	0.8	1 505	10.9	12 641	15.9	15.5
Charles City County	2 161	86.2	52 100	20.9	12.2	358	16.9	9.6	3 984	4.0	242	6.1	3 152	14.4	14.1
Charlotte	4 312	77.9	43 100	21.6	12.3	224	19.4	11.4	6 303	2.6	266	4.2	5 182	13.3	12.9
Chesterfield	73 441	79.5	87 200	20.5	12.1	541	24.3	1.3	145 467	1.3	3 707	2.5	113 694	36.1	11.9
Clarke	4 236	74.2	104 300	22.3	12.4	441	21.3	5.7	6 928	1.9	126	1.8	6 190	22.8	16.6
Craig	1 676	83.1	49 500	17.1	12.6	278	17.2	5.8	2 131	-2.1	71	3.3	2 111	17.0	17.7
Culpeper	9 757	67.3	95 200	22.3	13.0	514	24.0	5.4	17 301	1.9	361	2.1	13 524	25.0	15.5
Cumberland	2 813	79.3	50 600	18.5	11.4	338	25.7	13.1	3 967	2.7	93	2.3	3 637	20.1	12.2
Dickenson	6 457	81.4	39 300	24.1	12.5	262	29.5	8.0	5 834	10.4	986	16.9	5 076	19.5	22.2
Dinwiddie	7 492	80.1	56 900	17.0	12.5	352	23.0	5.5	12 483	1.4	365	2.9	10 218	19.6	16.8
Essex	3 258	78.9	68 200	21.5	12.7	376	22.2	8.2	4 404	3.5	201	4.6	4 022	21.6	15.8
Fairfax	292 345	70.7	213 800	23.4	11.7	834	26.4	3.4	575 691	2.3	13 221	2.3	468 776	51.9	6.3
Fauquier	16 509	73.3	146 500	23.5	12.3	634	24.1	3.5	30 428	1.9	508	1.7	25 531	31.9	14.0
Floyd	4 763	84.1	51 000	20.1	12.7	270	25.4	7.5	6 778	0.3	305	4.5	5 637	17.3	16.9
Fluvanna	4 518	79.8	75 100	20.7	12.7	429	24.6	6.8	9 982	0.5	205	2.1	6 178	24.5	16.3
Franklin	14 655	81.2	63 400	19.4	11.6	281	18.1	5.0	24 906	-0.7	1 172	4.7	20 091	18.0	15.5
Frederick	16 470	79.1	90 100	21.4	12.0	456	21.3	5.6	34 550	2.9	893	2.6	23 845	25.2	16.5
Giles	6 461	80.5	46 300	16.9	11.4	282	22.9	4.8	8 488	2.5	589	6.9	7 652	18.5	16.1
Gloucester	10 966	80.5	84 000	23.5	13.5	444	27.6	4.0	18 344	0.9	433	2.4	14 091	27.6	18.5
Goochland	4 880	84.2	90 100	20.1	13.2	461	21.5	5.8	9 364	1.3	208	2.2	7 028	29.6	13.0
Grayson	6 468	82.5	39 700	17.1	11.7	241	22.0	7.1	8 214	-1.0	870	10.6	7 843	13.6	14.2
Greene	3 749	76.8	73 700	21.6	13.3	419	24.0	7.4	7 961	0.4	159	2.0	5 473	23.1	19.3
Greensville	3 150	78.6	45 200	20.0	12.8	258	16.8	11.4	5 575	3.0	199	3.6	3 939	15.8	13.9
Halifax	10 728	76.9	45 200	16.6	13.1	227	19.2	12.9	19 450	6.9	1 816	9.3	13 568	14.5	14.6
Hanover	22 628	83.5	91 300	18.6	12.1	526	23.9	2.6	49 073	1.5	1 158	2.4	34 407	30.2	14.5
Henrico	89 138	63.8	83 900	20.4	12.6	509	24.4	1.5	144 058	2.0	4 727	3.3	120 294	35.5	9.8
Henry	21 771	77.9	51 800	16.0	11.7	314	19.7	4.4	26 711	0.1	2 292	8.6	29 513	15.0	14.1
Highland	1 081	81.2	51 400	20.4	11.5	269	17.1	9.0	1 313	4.9	30	2.3	1 293	15.4	13.8
Isle of Wight	9 032	79.5	83 200	21.4	13.0	363	24.3	5.4	15 401	0.8	425	2.8	11 740	23.6	18.5
James City County	12 968	73.3	119 500	22.2	11.5	528	25.8	2.2	25 562	0.9	547	2.1	17 537	38.1	10.9
King and Queen	2 339	81.9	55 600	17.5	13.6	375	18.4	8.7	3 006	2.8	116	3.9	2 919	15.8	18.1
King George	4 736	69.6	90 000	22.2	12.0	491	23.1	5.3	9 192	1.5	170	1.8	6 603	36.7	15.4
King William	3 834	81.2	70 200	21.2	13.4	364	18.5	7.7	6 509	3.6	239	3.7	5 504	26.0	14.3
Lancaster	4 564	81.7	90 000	22.4	13.0	431	23.7	6.7	5 151	2.8	402	7.8	4 236	23.1	13.5
Lee	9 231	75.7	34 400	20.4	12.7	267	29.7	10.4	9 445	3.4	516	5.5	7 927	17.2	15.7
Loudoun	30 490	73.3	170 200	25.4	13.5	813	25.6	2.0	97 935	3.2	2 795	2.9	50 525	42.4	10.1

1. Specified owner-occupied units.   2. Specified renter-occupied units.   3. Overcrowded or lacking complete plumbing facilities.   4. Percent of civilian labor force.   5. Persons 16 years and older.

	Private nonfarm establishments, employment and payroll, 1999								Agriculture, 1997			
	Employment						Annual payroll		Farms			Farm operators
										Percent with—		
STATE County	Number of establishments	Total	Health Care and Social Assistance	Manufacturing	Retail trade	Finance and Insurance	Professional Scientific and Technical Services	Total (mil dol)	Average per employee (dollars)	Number	Less than 50 acres	500 acres and over	Whose principal occupation is farming (percent)
	104	105	106	107	108	109	110	111	112	113	114	115	116

VERMONT—Cont'd													
Chittenden	5 383	80 438	11 127	15 462	11 728	3 668	5 191	2 411	29 975	456	35.7	7.2	49.6
Essex	132	1 369	D	D	61	D	12	35	25 874	79	15.2	17.7	70.9
Franklin	1 053	11 084	1 873	2 901	1 960	259	271	275	24 798	740	18.5	12.8	64.6
Grand Isle	171	579	D	D	143	D	26	12	20 062	107	29.0	13.1	64.5
Lamoille	961	9 267	1 276	775	1 443	200	213	174	18 797	297	31.0	6.1	46.8
Orange	773	6 438	1 382	1 299	988	D	219	138	21 508	537	20.9	6.9	55.3
Orleans	825	7 072	1 297	1 524	1 256	235	126	150	21 147	569	18.5	11.8	66.3
Rutland	2 269	26 297	3 514	4 753	4 288	681	787	612	23 276	530	23.4	12.8	55.3
Washington	2 248	24 892	3 377	3 474	4 007	2 203	798	620	24 919	344	28.8	3.5	51.7
Windham	1 838	22 450	2 433	3 327	2 785	812	500	557	24 795	305	34.8	4.6	47.9
Windsor	2 329	20 170	2 977	3 255	2 755	485	984	492	24 404	558	30.8	5.4	46.1
VIRGINIA	173 550	2 791 977	296 012	366 360	396 336	136 580	271 952	93 168	33 370	41 095	32.0	9.0	44.8
Accomack	823	9 050	753	3 291	1 263	257	534	163	18 066	268	38.1	21.3	64.2
Albemarle	1 778	21 367	1 961	2 291	4 330	768	1 423	521	24 378	747	30.4	10.4	44.2
Alleghany	155	2 529	742	615	391	D	15	60	23 878	160	22.5	5.6	27.5
Amelia	258	1 681	150	291	242	31	43	36	21 239	336	24.1	11.6	44.9
Amherst	580	6 775	392	1 629	1 243	200	113	166	24 463	406	21.4	9.9	36.5
Appomattox	269	2 893	163	1 173	520	83	D	61	21 034	353	16.1	8.8	40.2
Arlington	5 189	114 292	7 275	391	9 422	2 126	27 534	5 288	46 264	1	100.0	0.0	100.0
Augusta	1 151	17 351	3 009	5 213	1 799	205	366	462	26 655	1 499	36.6	9.1	48.3
Bath	140	699	111	38	106	22	21	21	29 911	129	14.7	28.7	51.9
Bedford	869	7 611	304	1 781	738	79	444	188	24 732	1 198	27.4	6.1	39.6
Bland	102	1 506	157	638	110	17	D	39	25 587	346	21.7	11.6	46.2
Botetourt	589	6 375	340	1 076	834	152	143	169	26 502	505	26.9	7.9	43.4
Brunswick	321	3 692	166	698	441	69	35	67	18 045	294	20.1	13.9	50.3
Buchanan	611	6 480	879	392	961	219	269	170	26 304	70	42.9	1.4	21.4
Buckingham	218	1 792	420	226	293	35	80	38	21 407	370	20.8	8.4	45.4
Campbell	978	14 007	523	4 733	2 022	204	339	328	23 448	621	18.4	10.8	44.9
Caroline	368	3 007	161	459	665	182	42	62	20 628	179	31.3	18.4	44.1
Carroll	468	5 095	456	1 867	957	57	77	98	19 249	913	33.8	3.0	34.9
Charles City County	121	1 462	D	166	31	D	11	38	26 122	59	30.5	37.3	47.5
Charlotte	242	2 640	113	1 267	266	55	33	50	19 100	493	20.5	12.4	47.5
Chesterfield	5 470	77 429	5 430	10 357	14 665	3 804	3 117	2 220	28 675	159	47.8	7.5	32.7
Clarke	298	3 074	214	1 146	278	91	77	84	27 187	325	31.1	10.5	47.4
Craig	58	280	D	D	32	D	3	6	20 607	176	17.6	11.9	44.3
Culpeper	809	9 684	1 244	1 408	1 864	535	696	267	27 584	521	32.4	10.6	46.4
Cumberland	134	821	98	81	231	D	28	15	18 302	248	20.6	12.5	44.0
Dickenson	282	2 200	360	D	444	63	56	53	23 914	102	39.2	2.0	29.4
Dinwiddie	261	4 678	D	496	369	66	D	115	24 482	351	25.9	11.7	43.9
Essex	323	3 923	542	1 334	799	168	79	73	18 666	114	21.1	36.0	63.2
Fairfax	25 142	469 801	29 793	13 050	49 614	23 364	112 678	27 491	58 515	121	60.3	4.1	43.0
Fauquier	1 483	12 540	1 775	972	2 056	564	828	331	26 397	957	35.2	10.3	47.6
Floyd	246	1 605	146	414	309	D	44	30	18 722	731	25.4	5.6	43.4
Fluvanna	317	1 998	209	85	245	30	92	43	21 703	256	19.5	9.0	42.2
Franklin	914	11 219	550	5 042	1 634	203	212	257	22 899	890	23.5	7.8	47.2
Frederick	1 179	18 238	1 356	4 490	2 875	307	624	466	25 550	568	31.0	7.9	42.8
Giles	330	4 864	461	2 420	754	89	80	125	25 785	341	20.8	8.2	41.6
Gloucester	777	6 301	984	243	1 575	166	226	111	17 558	108	45.4	12.0	50.9
Goochland	422	3 611	296	D	394	493	138	96	26 583	229	35.8	10.5	40.6
Grayson	176	1 685	64	981	179	74	21	38	22 321	854	35.6	7.1	37.6
Greene	245	1 600	104	28	362	28	118	35	21 997	198	22.2	6.6	49.0
Greensville	124	1 864	222	779	95	0	3	39	20 692	134	20.1	23.9	61.2
Halifax	773	11 563	1 373	4 570	1 525	165	133	268	23 143	940	21.7	11.1	53.7
Hanover	2 629	33 178	2 370	3 746	4 331	825	1 024	872	26 283	501	39.1	8.6	45.5
Henrico	7 197	143 249	15 700	10 768	18 953	20 478	8 028	4 805	33 546	154	49.4	6.5	35.1
Henry	895	14 945	557	7 614	2 008	356	137	333	22 249	288	27.4	6.2	38.5
Highland	99	390	17	D	30	21	D	6	16 538	283	11.0	17.0	53.7
Isle of Wight	527	9 275	395	4 474	1 096	136	183	274	29 517	190	24.7	32.6	65.8
James City County	1 015	11 642	815	1 238	2 103	180	791	275	23 646	58	48.3	10.3	46.6
King and Queen	99	569	25	126	39	D	23	11	18 953	127	15.7	18.1	52.8
King George	376	4 081	237	285	405	100	1 779	135	32 992	139	29.5	11.5	40.3
King William	305	3 329	230	1 148	497	130	100	108	32 314	123	17.9	26.0	48.0
Lancaster	492	3 799	964	135	666	231	130	85	22 391	70	25.7	14.3	60.0
Lee	360	3 572	857	510	611	193	43	75	20 860	1 106	37.9	2.9	43.9
Loudoun	4 122	56 995	4 143	3 609	8 346	1 875	4 474	2 081	36 513	1 032	53.3	7.4	38.3

STATE County	Land in farms — Acreage (1,000)	Percent change, 1992–1997	Acres — Average size of farm	Total irrigated (1,000)	Total cropland (1,000)	Value of land and buildings — Average per farm ($1,000)	Average per acre (dollars)	Value of machinery and equipment average per farm ($1,000)	Value of products sold — Total (mil dol)	Average per farm (dollars)	Percent from — Crops	Livestock and poultry products	Percent of farms with sales of — $10,000 or more	$100,000 or more	Percent of land owned by fed. gov. 1997	Water consumption 1995 (mil gal/day)
	117	118	119	120	121	122	123	124	125	126	127	128	129	130	131	132
VERMONT—Cont'd																
Chittenden	83	0.4	183	0	42	443	2 214	42	26	56 017	28.9	71.1	41.4	16.2	3.1	20.1
Essex	25	41.7	323	D	9	303	939	54	7	85 687	19.2	80.8	54.4	19.0	0.0	2.5
Franklin	190	-6.8	257	0	99	328	1 247	63	100	134 608	4.3	95.7	66.6	40.4	1.5	7.7
Grand Isle	21	-15.9	197	0	16	474	2 463	89	10	89 766	11.2	88.8	48.6	28.0	0.0	7.0
Lamoille	49	19.4	165	0	20	252	1 626	28	15	52 087	14.1	85.9	43.4	17.2	0.0	4.2
Orange	98	5.8	183	D	42	256	1 509	40	26	48 565	16.9	83.1	46.0	17.9	0.2	3.2
Orleans	144	-3.9	253	0	74	285	1 193	60	60	104 607	6.4	93.6	61.7	29.0	0.0	4.6
Rutland	126	-5.4	237	0	53	295	1 278	41	28	53 504	11.3	88.7	50.0	18.5	11.6	15.8
Washington	56	-4.6	164	0	23	306	1 853	37	15	43 724	21.4	78.6	40.4	11.0	1.4	7.9
Windham	47	6.4	154	0	19	337	2 177	53	20	66 775	44.8	55.2	42.6	16.1	6.8	460.3
Windsor	90	0.0	161	0	30	324	2 098	27	20	35 520	22.6	77.4	33.5	6.6	4.0	10.6
VIRGINIA	8 228	-0.8	200	85	4 322	385	1 920	42	2 344	57 027	33.3	66.7	39.3	10.0	9.8	5 466.9
Accomack	92	0.5	345	9	75	560	1 722	93	85	316 601	41.4	58.6	70.9	41.4	2.2	8.9
Albemarle	172	-8.9	231	1	75	841	3 605	41	21	28 715	21.6	78.4	34.5	3.7	(1)2.9	16.5
Alleghany	31	19.5	194	D	13	239	1 185	38	2	13 323	10.6	89.4	22.5	1.2	(2)59.0	57.1
Amelia	78	12.1	234	1	37	312	1 367	37	58	171 259	7.1	92.9	39.3	18.5	0.0	2.3
Amherst	93	3.0	228	D	34	318	1 240	33	5	12 575	29.4	70.6	25.4	1.0	21.6	18.2
Appomattox	77	-3.0	217	0	39	224	1 014	30	7	19 161	27.9	72.1	34.8	4.2	0.6	1.9
Arlington	D	D	D	D	D	D	D	D	D	D	D	D	100.0	100.0	(3)NA	0.1
Augusta	282	-1.7	188	3	147	479	2 509	41	139	92 510	9.9	90.1	47.8	15.1	(4)34.9	17.5
Bath	58	24.0	452	D	21	577	1 333	32	2	15 586	13.7	86.2	35.7	3.1	56.9	2.1
Bedford	195	-3.0	163	1	102	283	1 877	33	20	16 490	12.6	87.4	25.0	3.3	(5)5.3	17.0
Bland	83	1.7	241		28	218	862	26	7	20 486	6.8	93.2	35.5	3.8	39.9	1.2
Botetourt	91	-6.7	179	0	41	333	1 870	37	11	21 253	16.5	83.5	27.9	4.2	39.6	18.4
Brunswick	79	-6.9	269	2	33	331	1 136	51	18	61 439	67.9	32.1	45.2	13.9	1.7	4.0
Buchanan	6	-30.0	90	D	2	D	D	26	0	4 874	58.7	41.3	11.4	0.0	0.0	3.6
Buckingham	76	14.9	205	D	38	329	1 576	27	18	48 876	4.8	95.2	30.8	7.8	0.0	2.3
Campbell	141	5.0	227	1	63	300	1 272	36	15	23 531	40.9	59.1	32.7	5.3	0.0	11.3
Caroline	55	6.5	310	1	39	524	1 706	62	12	64 799	86.4	13.6	40.8	15.6	21.7	3.1
Carroll	110	-2.5	121	0	63	170	1 466	28	18	20 108	24.7	75.3	32.6	3.6	(6)4.4	3.5
Charles City County	D	D	D	0	D	737	1 471	106	7	112 597	89.9	10.1	49.2	32.2	0.4	1.7
Charlotte	132	16.4	267	2	54	317	1 170	42	17	33 504	57.4	42.6	39.1	9.5	0.3	1.9
Chesterfield	20	18.5	127	0	10	374	2 952	44	9	53 730	60.1	39.9	27.0	8.2	(7)0.7	1 007.8
Clarke	71	5.0	220	0	48	877	4 171	38	13	40 174	33.6	66.4	40.9	8.9	0.0	2.0
Craig	46	1.5	260	0	20	365	1 251	34	3	14 970	10.1	89.9	38.6	2.3	62.1	0.6
Culpeper	115	0.0	221	1	72	539	2 598	50	22	41 424	35.3	64.7	38.2	7.5	0.0	3.8
Cumberland	61	-1.5	246	0	29	341	1 510	44	25	100 689	7.7	92.3	36.7	16.1	0.0	0.9
Dickenson	9	0.0	89	D	5	88	1 013	15	0	4 790	33.5	66.5	11.8	0.0	7.2	3.3
Dinwiddie	89	4.0	254	2	44	356	1 395	54	18	51 691	76.3	23.7	36.8	11.7	4.5	4.2
Essex	62	9.9	540	D	43	686	1 282	110	10	90 239	95.1	4.9	61.4	28.9	0.1	1.1
Fairfax	12	-23.0	102	0	4	375	3 403	35	5	43 245	68.5	31.5	18.2	5.8	(3)6.3	76.7
Fauquier	239	1.3	250	3	122	969	3 787	53	47	49 607	28.4	71.6	36.3	7.6	1.1	6.6
Floyd	123	4.8	168	0	61	227	1 523	41	30	41 126	38.7	61.3	37.6	4.9	2.0	1.6
Fluvanna	59	1.6	230	0	26	433	1 937	39	6	24 536	12.5	87.5	27.0	2.7	0.0	117.6
Franklin	159	-4.4	178	2	82	282	1 534	46	41	45 982	18.4	81.6	37.6	11.8	0.7	5.7
Frederick	100	2.0	176	0	60	466	2 640	40	21	36 144	69.6	30.4	30.5	7.2	(8)1.8	5.5
Giles	67	-7.9	197	0	28	300	1 183	38	4	12 089	13.0	87.0	30.5	1.2	32.9	309.3
Gloucester	23	-3.3	215	0	17	524	2 598	59	5	46 928	95.5	4.5	43.5	13.9	0.0	2.8
Goochland	47	-8.3	204	0	26	591	3 136	58	7	29 942	29.3	70.6	29.3	4.4	0.0	2.9
Grayson	136	0.2	160	0	65	233	1 462	22	19	22 616	21.1	78.9	38.4	4.7	19.0	2.1
Greene	34	-9.0	170	0	18	471	2 599	37	4	22 475	9.2	90.8	39.9	3.0	14.8	1.6
Greensville	58	14.4	435	0	40	423	963	69	14	107 949	88.9	11.1	65.7	31.3	(9)0.0	3.4
Halifax	228	-2.2	242	4	92	253	1 015	41	40	42 743	81.7	18.3	54.6	11.8	1.5	7.1
Hanover	98	2.3	196	3	61	570	2 678	49	29	57 338	75.6	24.4	39.9	10.8	0.1	26.4
Henrico	26	10.0	171	0	14	478	2 724	42	10	63 866	64.3	35.7	37.0	8.4	0.4	8.0
Henry	48	-1.2	168	1	24	242	1 384	36	8	27 834	39.2	60.8	23.3	3.5	(10)0.0	41.6
Highland	91	-5.8	323	D	35	374	1 247	36	12	43 308	2.2	97.8	54.1	7.8	21.9	5.9
Isle of Wight	88	2.4	463	2	61	740	1 558	106	41	215 922	51.9	48.1	77.9	38.4	0.0	56.3
James City County	9	-11.4	153	0	6	527	3 448	48	2	32 615	79.5	20.5	34.5	8.6	(11)3.4	33.0
King and Queen	51	-4.1	400	0	34	442	1 077	66	10	80 083	80.9	19.1	55.1	16.5	0.0	0.7
King George	34	-10.1	246	1	20	572	2 334	50	5	33 719	89.4	10.6	33.8	5.0	3.5	3.7
King William	56	-4.8	457	1	38	705	1 500	84	12	94 780	78.4	21.6	48.0	22.0	0.0	22.4
Lancaster	17	-14.0	246	D	14	539	2 193	57	3	47 016	97.5	2.5	68.6	15.7	0.0	2.3
Lee	127	-1.2	115	0	63	137	1 184	29	13	11 844	50.8	49.2	32.5	1.1	6.9	3.8
Loudoun	185	-5.1	179	1	117	918	4 746	49	26	25 173	42.5	57.5	31.9	5.0	0.1	18.2

1. Charlottesville included with Albemarle County. 2. Clifton Forge and Covington included with Alleghany County. 3. Arlington County, Alexandria City, Fairfax, and falls Church City included with Fairfax County. 4. Staunton and Waynesboro included with Augusta County. 5. Bedford City included with Bedford County. 6. Galax included with Carroll County. 7. Colonial Heights included with Chesterfield County. 8. Winchester included with Frederick County. 9. Emporia included with Greensville County. 10. Martinsville included with Henry County. 11. Williamsburg included with James City County.

STATE County	Value of Residential Construction Authorized by Building Permits, 2000 New Construction ($1,000)	Number of Housing Units	Wholesale Trade, 1997 Number of Establishments	Number of Employees	Sales (mil dol)	Annual Payroll (mil dol)	Retail Trade[1], 1997 Number of Establishments	Number of Employees	Sales (mil dol)	Annual Payroll (mil dol)	Real Estate and Rental and Leasing, 1997 Number of Establishments	Number of Employees	Receipts (mil dol)	Annual Payroll (mil dol)
	133	134	135	136	137	138	139	140	141	142	143	144	145	146
VERMONT—Cont'd														
Chittenden	91 408	661	303	4 167	1 834.9	140.4	958	11 254	1 863.7	189.6	208	913	118.7	19.4
Essex	1 057	16	3	D	D	D	18	D	D	D	3	10	0.3	0.1
Franklin	22 310	225	49	582	381.6	15.8	237	1 734	324.4	28.6	37	102	7.8	1.3
Grand Isle	4 504	38	7	D	D	D	33	D	D	D	3	3	0.5	0.1
Lamoille	19 561	121	30	270	57.7	8.3	183	1 380	169.6	19.8	25	61	5.8	1.0
Orange	5 758	52	33	D	D	D	109	798	145.8	15.6	19	58	2.6	0.7
Orleans	6 829	77	36	D	D	D	174	1 161	220.4	19.9	18	27	2.7	0.3
Rutland	16 515	135	97	934	218.3	22.0	502	4 344	646.3	66.6	71	243	21.8	4.5
Washington	23 914	211	99	D	D	D	421	3 614	542.4	58.9	66	213	14.0	3.3
Windham	35 474	208	73	1 920	1 244.0	62.5	342	2 950	444.8	50.0	61	210	21.1	3.5
Windsor	33 550	253	87	704	242.9	19.1	372	2 559	415.5	44.7	76	219	17.5	3.7
VIRGINIA	5 051 601	48 402	7 868	106 365	61 046.7	3 784.4	29 032	379 039	62 569.9	6 202.6	6 717	43 976	5 749.2	1 028.4
Accomack	14 137	132	36	250	47.1	5.5	208	1 335	180.5	18.6	31	76	7.8	1.2
Albemarle	108 958	587	64	547	181.6	20.5	314	4 270	718.0	67.4	86	389	38.0	8.2
Alleghany	2 368	27	8	31	2.8	0.7	38	430	65.3	6.1	4	10	1.4	0.2
Amelia	8 485	69	9	167	41.1	4.8	36	226	41.0	4.0	3	6	0.9	0.1
Amherst	9 831	106	18	D	D	D	104	1 082	190.2	18.0	15	49	2.7	0.6
Appomattox	5 797	65	9	50	5.7	0.9	60	536	75.5	8.3	9	17	1.0	0.2
Arlington	46 246	811	110	1 208	819.8	57.2	665	10 098	1 819.4	188.7	257	3 137	690.6	84.2
Augusta	52 100	467	54	622	153.8	16.8	214	1 925	310.8	29.4	48	200	16.0	4.0
Bath	8 130	51	2	D	D	D	25	105	10.8	1.2	5	9	2.0	0.3
Bedford	76 474	468	34	170	281.9	4.8	92	604	83.9	10.0	28	55	6.9	0.9
Bland	2 508	54	6	D	D	D	18	145	19.8	1.4	NA	NA	NA	NA
Botetourt	27 483	203	34	464	213.9	12.5	81	796	130.2	11.0	17	47	2.6	0.5
Brunswick	5 504	47	7	54	27.6	1.3	60	455	49.6	5.3	4	D	D	D
Buchanan	1 638	21	34	296	140.3	8.7	130	1 018	135.2	13.7	14	32	2.4	0.9
Buckingham	5 322	55	5	16	6.6	0.3	42	254	34.4	3.7	7	D	D	D
Campbell	23 658	187	53	D	D	D	209	2 169	338.0	31.3	33	88	9.1	1.2
Caroline	10 418	97	16	74	27.8	2.0	69	608	118.4	8.5	10	26	2.0	0.3
Carroll	14 980	166	25	164	42.9	3.2	114	957	162.6	13.8	14	42	2.3	0.5
Charles City County	4 279	44	1	D	D	D	6	24	3.3	0.3	5	16	2.7	0.3
Charlotte	5 290	94	10	108	18.4	2.4	46	286	42.2	3.7	3	6	0.2	0.1
Chesterfield	227 037	1 958	372	3 154	1 447.5	116.3	938	15 275	2 412.6	230.7	201	1 151	183.9	27.9
Clarke	15 674	101	13	D	D	D	44	297	44.8	3.7	8	D	D	D
Craig	3 459	42	3	5	0.5	0.1	8	25	3.7	0.3	6	8	0.4	0.1
Culpeper	35 653	334	24	287	122.5	7.6	153	1 812	307.0	28.4	28	84	10.2	2.0
Cumberland	3 202	34	6	22	2.1	0.3	29	230	31.4	3.6	1	D	D	D
Dickenson	1 187	24	6	30	4.7	1.2	71	447	64.2	6.1	2	D	D	D
Dinwiddie	14 973	144	9	D	D	D	44	514	64.5	6.0	4	4	0.9	0.1
Essex	5 754	41	7	46	21.4	1.2	68	787	126.0	12.1	13	44	2.6	0.6
Fairfax	554 483	5 816	1 142	18 462	15 659.4	944.7	3 025	48 037	9 261.0	980.6	1 050	9 310	1 481.0	273.7
Fauquier	97 039	533	45	434	171.6	13.8	223	2 052	353.1	36.6	46	150	14.8	3.0
Floyd	7 859	97	6	18	10.7	0.4	45	364	55.3	4.3	7	8	0.8	0.1
Fluvanna	40 337	336	10	D	D	D	33	196	24.5	2.6	9	D	D	D
Franklin	58 069	392	33	186	85.4	5.2	180	1 707	257.7	23.4	20	99	9.8	1.8
Frederick	59 906	500	82	1 246	302.0	33.2	211	2 574	464.7	46.1	35	160	14.6	3.2
Giles	4 795	53	6	D	D	D	71	563	91.2	8.2	10	18	1.7	0.2
Gloucester	19 822	182	30	360	42.5	5.6	134	1 505	228.1	20.7	33	102	8.1	1.5
Goochland	36 043	223	25	168	72.8	4.9	50	391	72.5	6.7	11	15	2.7	0.4
Grayson	8 152	122	3	5	0.9	0.1	38	176	33.4	2.3	3	9	0.3	0.1
Greene	16 969	201	5	D	D	D	37	254	33.8	4.1	7	D	D	D
Greensville	4 516	72	10	45	18.4	0.9	26	179	23.0	1.9	4	21	1.1	0.2
Halifax	6 523	72	24	262	76.9	5.3	164	1 570	215.9	20.6	26	74	7.1	1.0
Hanover	94 618	966	240	4 199	3 044.5	150.2	309	4 693	830.0	80.6	72	249	33.0	5.2
Henrico	179 316	1 566	474	7 602	5 902.5	310.0	1 148	19 119	2 974.4	302.4	323	2 167	285.9	54.1
Henry	12 735	112	45	408	136.4	9.8	240	2 263	346.3	30.7	21	67	6.0	1.1
Highland	1 219	20	5	D	D	D	18	36	4.1	0.3	NA	NA	NA	NA
Isle of Wight	32 057	257	28	D	D	D	97	1 049	141.9	12.4	27	141	12.6	2.5
James City County	203 376	1 071	27	71	27.0	2.2	190	2 064	303.8	31.0	50	517	29.6	8.8
King and Queen	3 220	24	1	D	D	D	9	40	5.2	0.5	1	D	D	D
King George	14 628	129	7	46	7.3	0.9	48	306	53.2	4.8	15	D	D	D
King William	9 559	117	7	D	D	D	58	485	88.8	8.9	5	7	0.7	0.1
Lancaster	14 373	91	26	171	38.4	3.4	89	687	98.5	10.9	14	24	3.1	0.4
Lee	4 426	65	18	171	47.0	1.5	90	578	86.4	7.7	9	16	0.8	0.1
Loudoun	525 130	6 300	177	1 773	1 301.3	70.8	478	6 933	1 282.0	129.0	143	770	241.5	20.9

1. Establishments with payroll.

Table B. States and Counties — Professional, Manufacturing, and Accommodation and Foodservices

STATE County	Professional, Scientific, and Technical Services[1], 1997				Manufacturing, 1997				Accommodation and Foodservices, 1997			
	Number of Establishments	Number of Employees	Receipts (mil dol)	Annual Payroll (mil dol)	Number of Establishments	Number of Employees	Receipts (mil dol)	Annual Payroll (mil dol)	Number of Establishments	Number of Employees	Sales (mil dol)	Annual Payroll (mil dol)
	147	148	149	150	151	152	153	154	155	156	157	158
VERMONT—Cont'd												
Chittenden	514	3 854	429.4	157.5	234	14 302	3 942.1	624.0	392	6 211	207.7	61.1
Essex	4	3	0.7	0.3	11	883	86.0	25.7	21	D	D	D
Franklin	50	174	11.7	5.1	68	2 603	546.6	78.8	93	854	25.1	7.1
Grand Isle	9	16	0.9	0.3	NA	NA	NA	NA	21	D	D	D
Lamoille	78	166	11.3	4.3	51	697	85.2	18.0	112	3 415	122.2	36.5
Orange	56	164	12.0	5.0	58	1 220	128.5	29.3	58	626	20.8	6.4
Orleans	39	105	5.9	2.5	45	1 565	138.1	37.2	68	867	23.8	7.4
Rutland	155	580	42.7	19.8	123	4 635	542.2	150.5	234	3 358	108.6	31.7
Washington	191	729	54.3	21.9	152	2 901	446.2	84.7	176	2 200	63.0	20.2
Windham	124	442	29.1	10.8	120	3 473	442.8	99.5	218	3 194	106.1	36.6
Windsor	181	849	71.7	30.1	155	3 300	417.1	103.2	216	2 458	92.6	28.9
VIRGINIA	17 539	212 632	24 151.7	9 729.8	5 986	370 595	83 814.0	11 557.8	12 343	233 639	8 281.2	2 320.7
Accomack	42	476	49.7	16.0	32	3 209	244.5	52.6	100	892	32.9	9.0
Albemarle	178	1 030	80.9	32.2	54	D	D	D	140	3 054	114.8	35.1
Alleghany	3	7	0.5	0.2	NA	NA	NA	NA	15	199	6.9	2.3
Amelia	7	24	0.8	0.3	NA	NA	NA	NA	7	78	2.2	0.6
Amherst	27	80	4.7	2.0	44	1 678	395.1	53.8	44	615	19.3	4.9
Appomattox	10	34	2.3	0.5	18	1 216	112.7	28.5	19	185	5.6	1.5
Arlington	1 197	25 914	3 024.7	1 298.8	57	509	59.5	16.3	473	11 365	617.7	164.6
Augusta	56	280	15.6	6.0	66	5 372	1 312.4	175.1	66	1 112	33.0	10.0
Bath	7	13	1.3	0.2	3	D	D	D	16	81	2.6	0.9
Bedford	53	270	24.5	9.2	45	1 489	262.0	49.7	27	D	D	D
Bland	3	8	0.3	0.1	7	656	85.5	15.8	3	D	D	D
Botetourt	28	101	5.9	2.7	23	1 422	210.4	39.3	34	723	27.6	7.6
Brunswick	13	34	1.5	0.7	19	937	84.3	18.7	12	D	D	D
Buchanan	32	310	9.4	3.4	NA	NA	NA	NA	25	304	9.8	2.6
Buckingham	10	116	4.2	2.0	NA	NA	NA	NA	4	D	D	D
Campbell	51	243	29.5	9.4	62	5 098	1 383.7	123.5	55	D	D	D
Caroline	12	24	1.7	0.5	NA	NA	NA	NA	28	292	11.9	3.2
Carroll	20	64	3.3	1.0	35	2 430	286.3	45.3	41	498	15.6	4.0
Charles City County	2	D	D	D	10	680	62.2	16.0	6	D	D	D
Charlotte	8	33	1.2	0.3	15	1 178	143.6	25.4	13	117	3.1	1.0
Chesterfield	499	2 644	218.8	93.0	164	10 166	2 671.2	412.6	326	6 966	222.5	61.7
Clarke	18	47	4.4	1.5	13	1 167	190.3	33.7	20	D	D	D
Craig	2	D	D	D	NA	NA	NA	NA	4	D	D	D
Culpeper	50	620	46.6	17.0	28	1 484	278.9	45.3	52	629	22.0	5.9
Cumberland	7	14	0.6	0.2	NA	NA	NA	NA	4	19	0.4	0.1
Dickenson	11	65	2.8	1.6	NA	NA	NA	NA	13	99	3.0	0.8
Dinwiddie	7	D	D	D	NA	NA	NA	NA	16	154	5.9	1.3
Essex	17	66	2.9	1.2	18	1 140	119.4	24.8	23	356	12.4	3.8
Fairfax	4 748	88 929	11 813.4	4 743.6	478	13 181	2 594.5	551.9	1 523	31 596	1 368.8	382.6
Fauquier	131	561	53.4	23.7	36	867	107.8	25.7	70	1 415	47.6	13.9
Floyd	13	23	1.8	0.6	22	547	48.0	11.2	14	D	D	D
Fluvanna	22	47	2.3	0.9	NA	NA	NA	NA	9	107	5.0	1.5
Franklin	43	128	7.4	2.2	66	4 677	519.6	113.0	52	560	16.4	4.8
Frederick	50	441	13.1	5.9	69	3 416	741.1	97.0	72	1 317	45.6	12.8
Giles	11	65	2.8	1.6	15	2 731	538.6	90.5	17	187	6.1	1.7
Gloucester	46	172	9.7	3.8	NA	NA	NA	NA	43	686	19.3	5.1
Goochland	30	49	3.4	1.3	NA	NA	NA	NA	15	173	3.9	1.1
Grayson	7	34	0.8	0.4	18	1 085	123.4	25.8	14	65	1.8	0.6
Greene	9	37	4.7	1.7	NA	NA	NA	NA	10	134	4.5	1.3
Greensville	3	D	D	D	5	733	120.3	15.0	14	221	6.6	1.8
Halifax	32	102	5.6	1.9	42	4 707	652.9	113.8	61	773	23.7	5.9
Hanover	194	769	69.7	24.6	150	3 803	579.7	111.8	110	2 053	69.0	19.2
Henrico	726	5 767	519.4	238.5	216	10 857	2 432.3	379.0	458	9 892	350.6	96.8
Henry	29	97	4.5	1.2	70	7 970	858.4	189.1	73	1 105	31.6	8.4
Highland	3	3	0.1	0.0	NA	NA	NA	NA	6	50	1.0	0.3
Isle of Wight	22	145	8.6	4.0	17	4 698	1 546.8	106.6	34	D	D	D
James City County	106	541	40.2	16.7	26	D	D	D	77	1 715	74.6	21.0
King and Queen	1	D	D	D	NA	NA	NA	NA	2	D	D	D
King George	66	1 401	159.2	56.9	NA	NA	NA	NA	18	D	D	D
King William	17	55	2.5	0.9	13	1 114	357.2	56.5	10	136	3.9	1.1
Lancaster	36	117	9.5	4.0	NA	NA	NA	NA	25	452	17.4	6.2
Lee	20	49	2.6	0.8	17	784	70.8	10.8	18	200	5.7	1.5
Loudoun	530	3 624	618.6	187.5	128	3 459	480.8	132.8	212	3 877	154.8	45.8

1. Firms subject to federal tax.

STATE County	Health Care and Social Assistance[1], 1997				Other Services[1], 1997				Federal funds and grants, fiscal 2001[2] Expenditures (mil dol)			
										Direct payments for individuals[3]		
	Number of Establishments	Number of Employees	Receipts (mil dol)	Annual Payroll (mil dol)	Number of Establishments	Number of Employees	Receipts (mil dol)	Annual Payroll (mil dol)	Total	Social Security and government retirement	Medicare	Food stamps and Supplemental Security Income
	159	160	161	162	163	164	165	166	167	168	169	170
VERMONT—Cont'd												
Chittenden	372	3 978	242.3	105.6	284	1 439	96.3	28.3	986.3	234.6	71.7	14.5
Essex	3	D	D	D	4	D	D	D	46.3	17.1	5.4	1.2
Franklin	72	746	32.1	14.4	73	219	13.6	3.7	222.1	78.3	27.1	7.0
Grand Isle	6	D	D	D	5	D	D	D	30.9	14.1	4.2	0.7
Lamoille	49	468	23.5	8.9	53	143	10.1	2.4	93.7	41.9	13.9	2.9
Orange	34	D	D	D	46	134	11.4	2.5	120.1	56.1	17.4	3.7
Orleans	30	390	14.2	7.0	60	131	10.7	2.1	137.6	58.7	19.4	6.0
Rutland	147	1 376	77.7	34.7	132	737	30.3	9.0	339.4	146.9	53.2	11.3
Washington	134	1 062	60.6	27.0	124	354	26.3	5.8	532.6	127.6	38.6	8.1
Windham	103	591	34.1	14.1	84	345	33.9	6.3	198.9	93.9	32.8	6.7
Windsor	92	621	36.5	13.9	114	365	26.9	6.4	361.3	141.8	45.4	6.4
VIRGINIA	12 014	150 797	9 859.6	4 417.9	11 301	68 807	4 397.2	1 360.3	71 257.3	17 399.2	4 385.3	934.8
Accomack	29	160	7.7	2.7	49	133	7.9	1.8	290.6	93.3	33.6	8.1
Albemarle	130	1 393	79.6	35.6	90	572	35.7	12.4	227.4	130.6	47.8	4.2
Alleghany	28	752	51.8	20.3	9	46	2.3	0.7	28.2	13.7	2.7	1.9
Amelia	8	110	3.5	1.8	23	44	2.6	0.6	43.0	24.0	6.0	2.0
Amherst	27	462	16.0	5.5	54	169	9.7	2.6	120.3	70.9	18.0	3.9
Appomattox	15	129	3.9	1.5	19	47	2.8	0.7	52.4	29.4	7.8	1.8
Arlington	321	5 064	393.6	160.4	355	1 996	141.4	40.0	6 759.3	465.2	111.0	13.8
Augusta	70	756	61.4	24.9	62	235	15.3	4.5	171.5	99.5	31.7	3.3
Bath	5	16	1.2	0.6	2	D	D	D	27.4	14.9	6.9	0.4
Bedford	28	224	11.3	5.4	25	111	5.4	1.9	219.7	154.6	28.9	4.9
Bland	7	89	4.4	1.7	5	26	3.6	0.7	41.4	17.6	6.8	0.8
Botetourt	28	280	10.0	4.1	49	175	10.5	2.5	112.8	71.1	17.2	1.8
Brunswick	9	120	4.1	1.9	23	94	3.7	1.2	95.8	47.1	15.8	5.0
Buchanan	35	470	22.1	8.7	40	140	8.8	2.3	191.6	111.2	32.3	11.8
Buckingham	10	332	12.8	5.3	14	34	2.4	0.5	60.2	26.8	11.2	3.0
Campbell	46	330	15.1	5.2	72	321	16.8	5.6	147.2	88.7	22.7	5.4
Caroline	11	118	4.3	1.9	27	130	10.2	2.5	104.9	54.5	15.7	2.3
Carroll	29	435	17.5	8.3	26	100	8.5	1.9	115.4	57.4	21.1	4.8
Charles City County	1	D	D	D	5	22	0.9	0.2	27.8	13.8	4.7	1.0
Charlotte	4	99	3.1	1.2	13	40	1.8	0.4	84.7	38.6	12.7	3.4
Chesterfield	383	4 392	241.1	118.4	342	2 383	175.8	50.1	509.1	315.8	74.1	16.7
Clarke	14	192	6.9	3.6	17	58	3.6	1.2	49.7	30.0	7.9	0.7
Craig	4	D	D	D	2	D	D	D	30.9	11.0	3.0	0.6
Culpeper	43	456	29.6	12.7	40	436	24.5	8.7	139.5	79.7	24.3	4.5
Cumberland	4	58	1.2	0.7	9	25	1.1	0.3	33.7	14.6	4.8	1.3
Dickenson	14	389	24.1	8.2	24	65	4.5	1.1	108.1	61.3	19.3	6.2
Dinwiddie	10	73	4.2	1.9	18	54	3.6	0.6	91.7	49.8	15.3	3.0
Essex	25	274	13.4	4.5	24	63	3.0	0.9	52.7	25.9	12.7	1.5
Fairfax	1 867	19 772	1 643.6	709.8	1 329	9 204	772.7	225.8	11 279.4	1 965.5	232.2	56.6
Fauquier	93	890	46.8	20.4	89	450	30.2	9.3	245.8	130.5	28.5	3.4
Floyd	15	155	5.0	2.2	13	34	2.3	0.4	53.6	30.3	10.2	1.3
Fluvanna	8	72	2.4	1.2	13	48	3.0	0.7	76.4	51.2	13.0	1.2
Franklin	35	503	21.9	9.8	75	224	13.0	3.3	166.0	98.8	28.1	5.5
Frederick	47	766	42.7	23.8	74	367	25.5	7.4	156.0	109.5	19.0	4.0
Giles	24	226	9.2	4.0	28	96	5.7	1.4	89.2	49.0	17.8	3.0
Gloucester	44	552	21.8	10.2	52	247	11.8	3.7	149.6	98.0	22.2	3.3
Goochland	18	100	4.5	2.4	18	43	3.4	0.8	58.8	30.0	8.4	1.2
Grayson	10	71	3.2	1.6	16	87	3.1	1.2	73.3	35.5	14.0	4.0
Greene	7	171	4.5	2.5	22	71	3.3	1.2	42.7	25.1	8.0	1.2
Greensville	4	D	D	D	5	11	1.3	0.3	28.0	12.6	3.2	2.5
Halifax	59	558	33.1	18.0	62	230	11.6	3.1	211.2	93.5	34.1	8.7
Hanover	124	1 273	70.8	35.3	180	1 032	64.0	20.6	277.7	184.9	49.0	4.1
Henrico	565	8 260	559.3	280.5	411	3 156	199.2	64.6	564.6	270.7	142.0	12.2
Henry	48	591	24.8	12.9	62	229	11.2	3.6	196.4	118.5	37.6	5.8
Highland	3	D	D	D	5	16	0.8	0.1	16.4	7.3	3.4	0.2
Isle of Wight	20	218	12.1	6.2	49	194	10.6	3.1	140.6	76.6	20.9	3.9
James City County	66	556	28.4	13.3	43	288	14.1	6.5	101.0	72.3	11.5	2.0
King and Queen	2	D	D	D	8	14	0.9	0.3	30.8	15.8	5.4	1.2
King George	16	188	10.2	3.4	24	91	6.2	1.5	551.5	46.1	8.5	1.3
King William	16	118	4.0	1.8	26	64	5.6	1.2	53.1	27.6	9.9	1.3
Lancaster	37	358	19.5	10.1	26	125	7.3	2.6	89.7	59.4	17.4	1.3
Lee	31	560	37.3	14.1	22	82	3.7	1.0	378.2	69.7	30.7	12.3
Loudoun	245	2 035	140.4	54.9	200	1 341	105.5	32.6	1 164.2	262.9	38.7	3.9

1. Firms subject to federal tax.   2. October 1, 2000 to September 30, 2001.   3. State totals may include programs not allocated by county.

	Federal funds and grants, fiscal 2001[1] (cont'd)							Local government finances, 1997				
	Expenditures (mil dol) (cont'd)							General revenue				
	Procurement contract awards			Grants[2]							Taxes	
STATE County	Salaries and wages	Defense	Other	Medicaid and other health-related	Nutrition and family welfare	Education	Other	Total (mil dol)	Intergovernmental (mil dol)	Total (mil dol)	Per capita[3] (dollars) Total	Property
	171	172	173	174	175	176	177	178	179	180	181	182

VERMONT—Cont'd

Chittenden	111.6	276.8	17.3	132.7	17.1	10.6	53.1	279.6	48.0	177.9	1 258	1 224
Essex	3.3	0.0	0.4	5.6	1.3	0.3	10.9	12.2	5.0	6.2	939	920
Franklin	35.2	0.1	7.9	39.8	7.9	1.9	11.2	77.6	34.2	36.4	837	830
Grand Isle	1.3	0.0	3.0	3.5	0.7	0.2	2.3	11.1	1.7	8.5	1 375	1 363
Lamoille	4.2	0.0	1.0	17.5	2.9	1.4	3.0	43.2	11.4	27.5	1 285	1 279
Orange	5.8	1.6	1.4	20.6	3.8	1.4	3.9	54.2	19.3	31.4	1 131	1 125
Orleans	9.9	1.0	1.5	27.1	7.1	1.7	1.5	48.8	20.7	24.1	954	939
Rutland	19.5	3.5	4.6	64.7	10.9	3.4	9.3	122.3	34.2	73.8	1 177	1 166
Washington	22.6	1.3	13.1	72.4	59.2	47.7	117.6	113.9	35.3	65.5	1 161	1 156
Windham	9.9	0.9	2.9	24.3	7.7	2.7	7.7	100.5	19.7	70.8	1 653	1 643
Windsor	73.8	3.3	15.8	36.6	7.0	1.7	21.5	114.5	27.0	74.9	1 358	1 347
VIRGINIA	12 344.5	18 596.8	8 338.4	2 343.4	814.6	665.9	2 084.6	X	X	X	X	X
Accomack	40.0	19.7	48.2	25.6	5.6	1.9	7.3	63.8	30.3	25.0	778	599
Albemarle	4.2	1.3	10.3	14.6	1.8	2.9	6.7	134.9	41.9	78.4	1 011	737
Alleghany	0.3	0.0	0.1	5.9	1.4	1.0	0.9	33.0	14.3	12.5	1 012	830
Amelia	1.5	0.0	0.4	5.7	0.8	0.6	0.5	15.9	8.3	5.1	494	377
Amherst	2.9	0.0	2.6	11.0	1.5	1.4	7.3	39.6	21.1	14.5	485	333
Appomattox	2.6	0.0	0.5	7.1	1.0	0.7	0.1	18.5	11.0	6.3	486	339
Arlington	2 672.0	1 419.0	1 744.3	30.1	41.7	33.9	187.6	939.6	248.3	347.4	2 013	1 408
Augusta	6.2	0.1	1.6	14.4	2.3	2.3	3.8	93.9	43.2	36.7	594	392
Bath	1.8	0.0	0.3	2.4	0.3	0.3	0.1	13.9	3.3	9.4	1 900	1 768
Bedford	6.2	0.9	1.7	10.6	2.5	2.6	1.3	72.8	38.3	27.3	490	405
Bland	1.6	0.1	7.0	3.3	0.3	0.3	3.3	10.7	7.6	2.5	371	298
Botetourt	3.5	0.0	1.2	5.3	0.8	0.9	10.3	42.6	19.0	19.7	698	501
Brunswick	2.5	0.0	0.7	13.2	2.2	2.6	0.7	24.4	15.0	7.9	473	366
Buchanan	3.1	1.2	1.3	20.5	5.1	2.4	2.3	49.6	27.6	18.7	636	363
Buckingham	1.6	0.2	0.5	12.6	1.7	0.9	0.7	19.2	13.1	4.8	330	263
Campbell	6.5	0.5	1.6	16.0	3.0	2.7	-1.4	74.0	37.6	27.0	537	402
Caroline	11.7	5.6	1.5	6.9	1.8	1.7	0.4	32.5	17.4	13.5	623	477
Carroll	2.8	0.0	1.1	16.6	1.9	1.8	3.5	35.4	22.0	10.2	366	259
Charles City County	1.1	0.0	0.4	3.4	0.8	0.4	0.3	16.3	6.0	7.8	1 117	475
Charlotte	2.7	0.0	14.4	9.5	1.5	0.7	0.2	18.9	12.3	5.8	477	391
Chesterfield	23.9	10.3	6.2	11.4	6.4	8.6	23.4	509.3	174.1	257.0	1 058	826
Clarke	2.0	0.1	2.4	3.6	0.3	0.4	1.2	20.0	6.5	11.7	905	774
Craig	1.0	11.1	2.1	1.3	0.3	0.2	0.1	6.5	3.9	2.0	404	317
Culpeper	6.6	0.3	2.0	12.2	2.4	1.5	1.9	56.0	23.1	26.1	801	604
Cumberland	0.8	1.7	0.2	6.1	3.0	0.5	0.4	14.4	10.0	3.9	495	391
Dickenson	2.1	0.7	0.6	12.7	2.0	1.4	1.4	33.3	19.8	8.6	499	335
Dinwiddie	2.4	3.3	1.0	11.8	2.0	1.2	0.1	38.9	20.8	14.3	586	461
Essex	1.4	0.8	0.2	4.6	0.6	0.6	0.3	14.8	6.9	7.2	779	557
Fairfax	1 000.1	4 659.1	2 515.6	82.4	24.1	33.0	198.4	2 373.5	425.7	1 537.6	1 682	1 330
Fauquier	10.3	18.7	35.8	8.2	2.0	1.8	4.7	104.8	27.8	66.4	1 248	1 019
Floyd	2.5	0.0	0.7	5.2	0.6	0.7	1.7	16.3	8.7	6.6	504	384
Fluvanna	2.2	0.1	0.6	6.1	0.8	0.7	0.0	23.2	11.3	10.0	561	476
Franklin	6.6	0.0	1.4	15.2	2.8	2.3	1.1	59.4	29.8	24.1	543	394
Frederick	3.3	0.1	1.3	7.9	1.7	2.4	4.2	97.4	33.9	46.7	855	652
Giles	2.8	0.0	0.8	8.7	1.0	0.9	4.4	26.0	12.6	10.2	634	502
Gloucester	5.4	1.2	1.6	5.4	1.6	1.5	7.7	52.9	26.5	23.2	672	516
Goochland	1.5	0.0	0.4	4.0	0.7	0.9	6.0	24.3	7.9	14.2	807	654
Grayson	2.1	0.5	0.6	12.4	1.1	1.3	1.0	19.8	12.9	5.5	338	254
Greene	2.0	0.0	0.3	4.4	0.6	0.8	0.0	24.3	12.4	8.2	612	482
Greensville	0.1	0.2	0.0	4.4	1.8	0.8	0.3	22.1	14.0	5.5	483	362
Halifax	5.4	0.1	18.1	36.1	4.9	2.1	3.6	57.6	35.2	18.8	506	320
Hanover	9.3	4.1	5.0	8.2	1.7	2.1	4.4	130.3	44.9	74.5	944	726
Henrico	38.8	16.0	9.0	20.0	7.2	7.1	16.7	522.3	154.0	267.3	1 096	759
Henry	4.0	0.8	3.0	15.3	3.3	3.0	3.8	77.7	40.4	28.3	506	321
Highland	0.6	0.0	1.7	1.3	0.1	0.2	1.3	4.6	2.2	1.8	710	600
Isle of Wight	5.4	0.4	9.9	10.2	2.2	1.2	3.9	50.0	19.2	27.8	973	775
James City County	1.4	0.0	1.2	4.6	2.6	0.0	4.3	78.2	12.7	56.4	1 316	998
King and Queen	1.1	0.0	0.3	2.2	0.8	0.4	0.8	11.6	6.3	4.5	681	612
King George	248.0	237.4	4.2	3.0	0.8	0.6	0.2	24.5	11.2	11.3	669	521
King William	1.8	0.4	4.3	2.9	1.1	0.5	0.3	24.3	10.1	12.5	1 000	838
Lancaster	2.4	0.0	1.3	4.2	1.1	0.5	0.4	18.8	6.6	8.8	783	656
Lee	3.7	0.2	208.4	33.4	4.8	2.2	10.3	36.9	26.5	8.3	347	241
Loudoun	274.3	433.2	118.2	9.3	2.3	3.2	5.2	294.1	55.3	194.5	1 457	1 190

1. October 1, 2000 to September 30, 2001. 2. State totals may include programs not allocated by county. 3. Based on the resident population estimated as of July 1 of the year shown.

Table B. States and Counties — Local Government Finances, Government Employment, and Elections

STATE County	Local government finances, 1997 (cont'd)									Government employment, 1999			Presidential election, 2000[2]		
	Direct general expenditure							Debt outstanding					Percent of vote cast —		
	Total (mil dol)	Per capita[1] (dollars)	Percent of total for —					Total (mil dol)	Per capita[1] (dollars)	Federal civilian	Federal military	State and local	Democratic	Republican	All other
			Education	Health and hospitals	Police protection	Public welfare	Highways								
	183	184	185	186	187	188	189	190	191	192	193	194	195	196	197
VERMONT—Cont'd															
Chittenden	284.3	2 011	60.3	0.2	5.0	0.0	4.9	295.9	2 093	1 735	1 126	10 744	54.4	36.2	9.4
Essex	10.1	1 549	69.6	0.4	0.4	0.0	12.8	0.6	94	66	51	297	39.0	54.1	6.9
Franklin	68.5	1 574	77.2	0.2	1.6	0.0	8.1	49.0	1 126	720	338	2 169	49.6	43.7	6.7
Grand Isle	8.3	1 343	75.5	0.0	0.4	0.0	8.7	6.9	1 119	22	48	248	50.4	42.6	7.0
Lamoille	45.6	2 128	67.4	0.5	3.3	0.0	11.2	19.6	915	72	167	1 491	50.5	39.6	9.9
Orange	50.1	1 801	75.7	0.6	1.3	0.0	11.7	10.6	382	99	212	1 705	45.6	46.7	7.7
Orleans	45.3	1 787	75.4	0.1	1.6	0.0	10.4	22.1	874	202	194	1 561	45.1	47.8	7.0
Rutland	123.4	1 968	65.7	0.2	2.5	0.1	9.2	50.9	811	376	475	3 773	47.6	46.1	6.2
Washington	121.4	2 150	70.4	0.5	2.7	0.0	7.9	56.6	1 001	311	468	7 116	51.4	38.5	10.2
Windham	101.1	2 359	62.6	0.6	2.5	0.1	10.8	26.1	609	188	325	2 379	52.7	34.2	13.1
Windsor	114.8	2 082	67.3	0.3	3.3	0.2	9.2	27.4	496	1 364	428	3 341	51.9	40.2	7.8
VIRGINIA	X	X	X	X	X	X	X	X	X	161 159	165 461	465 057	44.5	52.5	3.0
Accomack	66.0	2 057	55.8	0.8	2.5	10.9	0.7	29.9	933	647	363	1 711	42.7	53.3	4.0
Albemarle	148.0	1 909	64.3	2.7	5.5	3.4	1.1	95.5	1 232	(3)1 247	(3)685	(3)24 047	44.2	49.7	6.2
Alleghany	31.6	2 567	57.9	0.7	2.7	4.5	0.0	25.5	2 075	(4)97	(4)89	(4)1 622	43.2	54.8	2.0
Amelia	15.0	1 458	64.6	0.9	7.1	5.4	0.0	7.1	692	30	41	500	36.6	61.6	1.8
Amherst	42.8	1 428	63.5	0.1	4.2	5.5	0.0	19.1	638	52	116	2 850	41.1	56.9	2.1
Appomattox	17.8	1 372	71.5	0.7	6.5	4.7	0.9	7.0	543	55	51	781	36.0	61.7	2.3
Arlington	1 165.3	6 752	15.7	2.5	3.2	3.8	2.0	1 847.7	10 707	31 857	15 768	9 471	60.3	34.2	5.5
Augusta	104.1	1 684	66.0	0.5	2.5	2.0	0.2	72.6	1 175	(5)310	(5)403	(5)8 487	26.3	70.2	3.5
Bath	13.0	2 640	57.3	1.1	4.7	3.5	0.0	11.0	2 232	45	19	365	37.2	59.3	3.5
Bedford	80.3	1 443	65.8	1.2	3.2	6.6	0.6	65.7	1 180	(6)172	(6)246	(6)2 300	31.2	65.9	2.9
Bland	8.4	1 227	70.0	1.0	6.9	4.6	0.8	3.0	430	18	26	569	31.7	65.4	2.9
Botetourt	41.0	1 450	65.9	0.1	6.6	2.7	0.1	30.1	1 066	59	112	1 122	33.4	64.1	2.5
Brunswick	24.2	1 438	63.2	0.2	4.1	6.6	0.0	3.3	199	50	70	1 400	56.5	42.7	0.9
Buchanan	52.1	1 776	59.0	0.7	3.3	6.4	7.8	27.0	921	62	109	1 906	58.3	39.2	2.5
Buckingham	20.1	1 382	65.4	0.4	3.4	3.9	0.0	4.6	317	31	56	1 059	47.0	50.2	2.9
Campbell	71.5	1 425	63.1	2.1	3.7	4.2	1.2	44.3	883	(7)887	(7)452	(7)7 011	32.8	64.8	2.5
Caroline	30.6	1 408	64.0	1.1	0.6	6.0	0.0	25.8	1 188	300	107	1 059	51.7	46.4	1.9
Carroll	33.8	1 207	67.0	0.9	5.3	6.6	0.5	22.2	794	(8)93	(8)131	(8)2 272	33.1	64.9	2.0
Charles City County	15.8	2 264	54.9	1.3	3.5	8.1	0.0	27.1	3 883	20	28	349	64.6	33.4	2.0
Charlotte	17.1	1 407	70.9	0.7	2.1	8.7	0.3	7.8	639	73	48	776	40.4	57.2	2.5
Chesterfield	532.4	2 191	54.5	3.3	5.6	5.1	0.9	546.7	2 250	3 380	970	14 061	34.9	63.2	2.0
Clarke	18.2	1 406	63.8	1.5	5.1	3.4	1.5	6.9	537	31	49	663	41.0	54.6	4.4
Craig	6.0	1 224	64.0	1.1	6.8	4.3	0.2	2.0	404	28	19	205	34.1	63.4	2.5
Culpeper	62.9	1 931	62.4	0.5	5.1	5.3	3.4	30.0	920	110	128	2 680	35.6	60.8	3.6
Cumberland	15.2	1 941	47.9	1.1	3.3	5.0	0.0	12.7	1 628	12	30	373	40.1	56.3	3.7
Dickenson	32.6	1 893	55.7	4.8	5.2	6.2	4.4	12.8	747	45	64	912	54.7	43.2	2.1
Dinwiddie	46.5	1 912	64.5	0.3	4.2	3.4	0.1	14.1	579	(9)321	(9)298	(9)9 840	43.8	54.3	1.9
Essex	15.9	1 722	56.8	0.5	8.7	3.6	0.6	10.2	1 106	28	35	416	45.7	52.1	2.2
Fairfax	2 500.1	2 735	46.4	4.6	4.8	5.8	2.2	2 582.1	2 824	(10)34 545	(10)6 867	(10)50 146	47.5	48.9	3.6
Fauquier	99.1	1 863	60.0	0.5	7.4	4.1	1.5	77.4	1 456	157	211	2 691	35.4	61.7	2.9
Floyd	14.2	1 086	72.4	2.0	3.0	0.2	0.4	4.6	349	35	75	989	39.4	57.0	3.6
Fluvanna	20.5	1 155	71.6	1.1	3.4	5.6	0.0	7.2	405	114	173	1 587	37.9	59.6	2.4
Franklin	63.4	1 428	71.4	3.2	4.0	2.7	1.0	35.1	791	156	327	4 007	32.0	65.1	3.0
Frederick	98.1	1 794	66.8	0.7	3.8	3.2	0.0	77.0	1 408	(11)441	(11)309	(11)4 302	44.0	52.4	3.5
Giles	25.3	1 567	57.9	0.9	7.2	5.2	1.0	11.2	695	47	62	786	33.2	63.6	3.1
Gloucester	55.6	1 613	70.1	0.7	4.1	3.4	0.0	56.6	1 642	88	136	2 466	33.2	63.6	3.1
Goochland	22.5	1 280	53.0	12.8	2.8	4.3	2.7	9.0	513	30	68	1 200	36.4	61.3	2.3
Grayson	19.5	1 209	66.9	1.1	5.9	7.7	0.5	3.2	198	36	63	609	36.0	61.8	2.2
Greene	21.8	1 627	66.2	0.6	5.0	3.3	0.0	25.3	1 888	49	56	711	32.8	62.4	4.8
Greensville	26.0	2 274	66.3	0.4	2.8	0.2	0.1	21.1	1 845	(12)65	(12)31	(12)1 897	59.2	40.1	0.7
Halifax	64.6	1 741	55.1	0.9	6.5	4.6	2.3	17.2	463	(13)112	(13)141	(13)2 058	42.4	54.9	2.7
Hanover	154.2	1 953	53.0	2.9	6.8	1.6	0.8	169.0	2 141	156	327	4 007	29.0	68.8	2.2
Henrico	551.9	2 263	43.1	2.9	6.4	2.1	6.3	538.0	2 206	810	942	11 890	42.7	55.2	2.2
Henry	83.9	1 498	62.0	0.9	3.8	5.4	0.3	104.0	1 857	(14)150	(14)270	(14)3 766	41.5	55.3	3.2
Highland	6.8	2 707	74.6	0.8	5.6	2.8	0.1	2.5	991	10	0	149	31.5	65.6	2.9
Isle of Wight	46.5	1 627	63.9	0.7	4.6	4.9	2.2	34.8	1 220	99	113	1 166	39.9	58.6	1.5
James City County	67.9	1 584	43.5	1.6	5.6	3.8	0.0	143.7	3 353	(15)271	(15)549	(15)7 827	37.1	59.8	3.1
King and Queen	12.6	1 932	61.6	0.0	2.1	4.8	0.0	10.0	1 529	17	184	265	48.5	49.8	1.8
King George	24.3	1 434	66.2	1.0	5.6	4.7	2.3	43.3	2 555	3 746	927	679	35.4	61.4	3.2
King William	22.5	1 807	69.3	0.2	4.9	3.0	0.5	9.2	738	26	50	636	36.8	61.5	1.7
Lancaster	17.0	1 506	48.5	1.9	5.7	5.0	0.0	40.4	3 578	41	43	471	46.1	52.0	1.9
Lee	36.3	1 509	70.4	0.9	4.1	7.4	1.6	13.9	577	56	91	1 240	46.1	52.0	1.9
Loudoun	314.5	2 356	52.7	3.4	5.7	4.3	1.9	331.3	2 482	4 114	615	8 043	41.0	56.2	2.8

1. Based on the resident population estimated as of July 1 of the year shown. 2. Data subject to copyright. 3. Charlottesville included with Albemarle County. 4. Clifton Forge and Covington included with Alleghany County. 5. Staunton and Waynesboro included with Augusta County. 6. Bedford City included with Bedford County. 7. Lynchburg included with Campbell County. 8. Galax included with Carroll County. 9. Petersburg and Colonial Heights included with Dinwiddie County. 10. Fairfax City and Falls Church included with Fairfax County. 11. Winchester included with Frederick County. 12. Emporia included with Greensville County. 13. South Boston included with Halifax County. 14. Martinsville included with Henry County. 15. Williamsburg included with James City County.

Table B. States and Counties — Land Area and Population

STATE/ County code	MSA/ PMSA/ NECMA code[1]	County Type[2]	STATE County	Land area,[3] (sq km) 2000	Total persons	Rank	Per square kilometer	White	Black	Am. Indian, Alaska Native	Asian and Pacific Islander	Percent Hispanic[4]	Under 5 years	5 to 17 years	18 to 24 years	25 to 34 years	35 to 44 years	45 to 54 years
					1	2	3	4	5	6	7	8	9	10	11	12	13	14	15
			VIRGINIA—Cont'd															
51 109	...	8	Louisa	1 288	25 627	1 529	19.9	77.4	22.2	0.9	0.3	0.7	5.9	18.5	6.6	12.1	17.8	15.2
51 111	...	9	Lunenburg	1 118	13 146	2 216	11.8	60.0	39.2	0.6	0.5	1.8	4.9	16.4	8.0	12.0	16.1	15.1
51 113	...	8	Madison	832	12 520	2 263	15.0	87.6	11.9	0.4	0.8	0.8	5.8	18.3	6.9	11.1	16.5	15.3
51 115	5720	1	Mathews	222	9 207	2 512	41.5	87.8	11.5	0.6	0.4	0.8	4.6	15.3	5.2	9.2	13.9	15.2
51 117	...	7	Mecklenburg	1 616	32 380	1 337	20.0	59.7	39.4	0.5	0.4	1.2	5.4	16.2	7.2	12.1	15.3	14.2
51 119	...	8	Middlesex	337	9 932	2 453	29.5	79.0	20.4	0.5	0.2	0.6	3.8	15.4	5.1	9.0	13.9	15.3
51 121	...	4	Montgomery	1 005	83 629	621	83.2	91.3	4.0	0.5	4.6	1.6	4.8	12.4	31.3	14.0	11.6	10.4
51 125	...	8	Nelson	1 223	14 445	2 126	11.8	83.7	15.6	1.0	0.5	2.1	5.3	16.4	6.4	10.2	15.3	17.1
51 127	6760	2	New Kent	543	13 462	2 196	24.8	81.2	16.6	1.9	0.7	1.3	5.6	19.3	5.9	12.4	19.7	15.3
51 131	...	9	Northampton	537	13 093	2 222	24.4	54.2	43.5	0.4	0.4	3.5	5.5	17.7	7.1	9.3	14.4	13.8
51 133	...	9	Northumberland	498	12 259	2 281	24.6	72.6	27.0	0.4	0.2	0.9	4.3	14.3	4.8	7.7	12.5	13.1
51 135	...	6	Nottoway	815	15 725	2 037	19.3	57.7	40.9	0.4	0.6	1.6	5.6	17.3	8.1	13.3	15.9	12.9
51 137	...	6	Orange	885	25 881	1 522	29.2	85.2	14.2	0.5	0.6	1.3	6.0	17.0	6.5	11.6	16.1	13.8
51 139	...	6	Page	806	23 177	1 635	28.8	96.9	2.3	0.5	0.4	1.1	5.5	16.0	7.7	12.9	15.4	14.0
51 141	...	9	Patrick	1 251	19 407	1 823	15.5	92.4	6.5	0.5	0.4	1.9	5.7	16.0	7.1	12.9	15.1	14.3
51 143	1950	3	Pittsylvania	2 514	61 745	787	24.6	75.5	23.9	0.4	0.3	1.2	5.7	17.4	7.2	12.1	16.7	15.4
51 145	6760	2	Powhatan	677	22 377	1 675	33.1	82.2	17.2	0.6	0.3	0.8	5.8	18.1	7.3	15.2	19.5	15.8
51 147	...	7	Prince Edward	914	19 720	1 808	21.6	62.9	36.3	0.5	1.0	0.9	5.0	15.3	23.5	10.1	12.4	11.5
51 149	6760	2	Prince George	688	33 047	1 318	48.0	62.4	33.5	0.8	2.6	4.9	6.0	19.1	13.6	16.2	17.1	13.0
51 153	8840	0	Prince William	875	280 813	200	320.9	71.8	20.1	1.0	5.2	9.7	8.5	21.9	8.8	16.1	19.1	13.7
51 155	...	7	Pulaski	830	35 127	1 245	42.3	93.5	5.9	0.6	0.4	1.0	5.5	15.1	7.3	14.1	15.1	15.9
51 157	...	8	Rappahannock	690	6 983	2 687	10.1	93.7	5.9	0.7	0.4	1.3	5.1	17.2	5.6	10.0	16.4	18.4
51 159	...	9	Richmond	496	8 809	2 545	17.8	65.4	33.4	0.4	0.6	2.1	4.1	14.3	8.0	14.1	17.8	14.0
51 161	6800	3	Roanoke	650	85 778	610	132.0	94.4	3.6	0.4	1.8	1.0	5.3	17.4	6.6	11.4	16.1	16.6
51 163	...	6	Rockbridge	1 553	20 808	1 748	13.4	96.2	3.2	0.6	0.6	0.6	5.4	16.8	7.9	11.6	15.5	15.1
51 165	...	5	Rockingham	2 204	67 725	724	30.7	97.3	1.6	0.3	0.4	3.3	6.3	18.4	8.7	12.6	16.3	14.2
51 167	...	6	Russell	1 229	30 308	1 390	24.7	96.5	3.2	0.3	0.1	0.8	5.4	15.8	8.6	14.6	16.3	15.1
51 169	3660	2	Scott	1 390	23 403	1 623	16.8	99.0	0.7	0.5	0.2	0.4	5.1	15.5	7.5	12.6	14.7	14.6
51 171	...	6	Shenandoah	1 327	35 075	1 248	26.4	96.4	1.4	0.6	0.6	3.4	5.6	16.7	6.6	12.1	15.5	14.3
51 173	...	6	Smyth	1 171	33 081	1 316	28.3	97.4	2.1	0.5	0.4	0.9	5.3	16.3	8.0	13.0	15.1	14.5
51 175	...	6	Southampton	1 553	17 482	1 925	11.3	56.3	43.2	0.4	0.3	0.7	5.1	17.6	8.8	12.2	17.0	14.1
51 177	8840	0	Spotsylvania	1 038	90 395	570	87.1	84.4	13.3	0.9	2.0	2.8	7.6	22.4	7.3	13.9	18.3	14.2
51 179	8840	1	Stafford	700	92 446	552	132.1	84.1	13.1	1.2	2.6	3.6	7.8	23.8	7.8	13.9	19.8	14.0
51 181	...	8	Surry	723	6 829	2 708	9.4	47.5	52.2	0.8	0.2	0.7	5.6	19.6	7.2	10.3	17.5	14.3
51 183	...	8	Sussex	1 271	12 504	2 264	9.8	36.9	62.4	0.5	0.4	0.8	4.6	15.0	9.0	16.4	17.9	14.4
51 185	...	7	Tazewell	1 346	44 598	1 006	33.1	96.7	2.4	0.5	0.8	0.5	5.3	16.2	8.4	11.8	15.4	16.2
51 187	8840	1	Warren	553	31 584	1 358	57.1	93.9	5.3	0.7	0.8	1.6	6.6	18.9	7.6	12.9	17.7	14.1
51 191	3660	2	Washington	1 458	51 103	906	35.1	98.1	1.5	0.4	0.5	0.6	5.1	15.7	8.7	12.4	15.9	15.2
51 193	...	6	Westmoreland	594	16 718	1 974	28.1	66.4	31.5	0.8	0.5	3.5	5.2	17.6	6.3	9.8	14.2	14.4
51 195	...	7	Wise	1 046	40 123	1 111	38.4	97.5	2.0	0.4	0.4	0.7	5.8	17.2	10.2	13.0	15.0	14.9
51 197	...	7	Wythe	1 200	27 599	1 463	23.0	96.3	3.1	0.4	0.5	0.6	5.5	16.4	7.6	13.8	15.0	14.8
51 199	5720	0	York	274	56 297	840	205.5	81.6	14.1	0.9	4.2	2.7	6.3	22.8	6.6	11.4	19.2	15.1
	...		**Independent Cities**															
51 510	8840	NA	Alexandria City	39	128 283	421	3 289.3	62.7	24.0	0.7	6.9	14.7	6.2	10.6	9.2	25.4	18.1	13.8
51 515	4640	NA	Bedford City	18	6 299	2 757	349.9	76.3	23.0	0.8	0.8	0.9	5.6	16.0	7.2	12.3	15.5	12.0
51 520	3660	NA	Bristol City	33	17 367	1 932	526.3	93.6	6.0	0.7	0.5	1.0	5.3	15.0	8.6	12.5	13.7	13.4
51 530	...	NA	Buena Vista City	18	6 349	2 751	352.7	94.3	5.2	0.4	0.7	1.0	6.2	16.3	10.6	13.0	13.0	13.7
51 540	1540	NA	Charlottesville City	27	45 049	997	1 668.5	71.2	23.2	0.5	5.9	2.4	4.4	10.8	33.8	14.6	11.2	9.3
51 550	5720	0	Chesapeake City	882	199 184	278	225.8	68.1	29.2	0.9	2.5	2.0	7.2	21.6	8.2	13.5	18.9	13.8
51 560	...	NA	Clifton Forge City	8	4 289	2 897	536.1	84.4	15.9	0.8	0.3	0.9	5.3	15.8	6.7	11.1	14.3	12.2
51 570	6760	NA	Colonial Heights City	19	16 897	1 960	889.3	90.0	6.6	0.4	3.2	1.6	5.3	17.3	8.3	12.0	14.8	13.3
51 580	...	NA	Covington City	15	6 303	2 756	420.2	85.5	13.9	0.8	1.1	0.6	6.3	15.2	8.2	13.0	13.3	13.0
51 590	1950	NA	Danville City	112	48 411	942	432.2	54.5	44.5	0.4	0.8	1.3	6.0	17.3	8.0	11.5	14.0	13.8
51 595	...	NA	Emporia City	18	5 665	2 810	314.7	42.7	56.4	0.3	0.7	1.5	6.2	19.0	8.1	11.4	14.2	11.4
51 600	8840	NA	Fairfax City	16	21 498	1 715	1 343.6	75.6	5.8	0.8	13.5	13.6	6.0	14.5	9.2	16.7	17.0	14.2
51 610	8840	NA	Falls Church City	5	10 377	2 406	2 075.4	87.2	3.8	0.8	7.8	8.4	5.5	17.9	5.1	13.3	17.8	14.2
51 620	...	NA	Franklin City	22	8 346	2 577	379.4	46.4	52.7	0.4	0.9	0.6	5.1	20.1	7.7	10.4	14.5	13.7
51 630	8840	NA	Fredericksburg City	27	19 279	1 829	714.0	74.8	21.3	0.8	2.0	4.9	5.8	11.9	23.8	14.8	12.4	11.1
51 640	...	NA	Galax City	21	6 837	2 706	325.6	87.0	6.6	0.8	0.7	11.1	6.4	16.6	7.9	12.8	13.6	13.2
51 650	5720	NA	Hampton City	134	146 437	374	1 092.8	51.1	46.1	1.1	2.7	2.8	6.3	17.9	12.6	14.8	17.7	12.4
51 660	...	NA	Harrisonburg City	45	40 468	1 104	899.3	87.1	6.7	0.5	4.2	8.8	4.7	10.7	40.9	11.3	9.9	8.0
51 670	6760	NA	Hopewell City	27	22 354	1 676	827.9	63.7	34.3	0.9	1.5	2.9	7.5	17.8	9.1	14.1	14.5	11.9
51 678	...	NA	Lexington City	6	6 867	2 701	1 144.5	86.8	10.7	0.5	2.4	1.6	3.0	8.0	41.4	7.7	6.8	9.0
51 680	4640	NA	Lynchburg City	128	65 269	747	509.9	67.8	30.6	0.7	1.6	1.3	5.8	16.3	15.5	12.2	13.1	12.4

1. MSA = Metropolitan Statistical Area. PMSA = Primary MSA. NECMA = New England County Metropolitan Area. See Appendix A for explanation of these concepts. See Appendix B for list of metropolitan areas identified by type, with component counties. 2. County typology code from the Economic Research Service of USDA. See Appendix A for definition. 3. Dry land or land partially or temporarily covered by water. 4. Hispanic persons may be of any race.

Table B. States and Counties — **Population and Households**

STATE County	Population, 2000 (cont'd) Age (percent) (cont'd)				Population — change and components of change, 1990–2001							Households, 2000				
					Total persons		Percent change		Components of change, 2000–2001						Percent	
	55 to 64 years	65 to 74 years	75 years and over	Percent female	2001	1990	1990–2000	2000–2001	Births	Deaths	Net migration	Number	Percent change, 1990–2000	Persons per household	Female family householder[1]	One person
	16	17	18	19	20	21	22	23	24	25	26	27	28	29	30	31
VIRGINIA—Cont'd																
Louisa	10.9	7.5	5.4	50.8	26 539	20 325	26.1	3.6	391	303	809	9 945	33.9	2.56	10.8	22.1
Lunenburg	10.7	9.2	7.6	46.8	13 080	11 419	15.1	-0.5	150	166	-56	4 998	13.0	2.39	13.3	28.7
Madison	11.1	8.2	6.8	51.3	12 761	11 949	4.8	1.9	159	181	261	4 739	14.4	2.60	8.8	21.8
Mathews	15.0	11.4	10.2	51.8	9 300	8 348	10.3	1.0	80	169	182	3 932	11.4	2.32	7.9	24.9
Mecklenburg	11.8	10.2	7.6	50.7	32 325	29 241	10.7	-0.2	485	506	-20	12 951	15.2	2.38	14.1	27.2
Middlesex	15.0	12.5	9.9	51.9	10 013	8 653	14.8	0.8	98	180	162	4 253	20.5	2.27	9.5	27.1
Montgomery	6.9	4.7	3.9	47.6	83 142	73 913	13.1	-0.6	1 033	597	-913	30 997	18.1	2.40	7.6	25.5
Nelson	12.5	9.8	7.0	51.3	14 678	12 778	13.0	1.6	230	209	215	5 887	22.5	2.42	10.7	25.0
New Kent	10.4	5.8	3.6	49.3	13 986	10 466	28.6	3.9	177	125	464	4 925	32.5	2.65	9.0	16.6
Northampton	11.0	11.5	9.7	53.2	13 125	13 061	0.2	0.2	227	256	67	5 321	3.7	2.39	17.5	29.4
Northumberland	17.0	15.0	11.1	52.3	12 417	10 524	16.5	1.3	147	265	274	5 470	21.8	2.24	8.7	27.7
Nottoway	9.8	8.8	8.3	48.4	15 650	14 993	4.9	-0.5	245	308	-4	5 664	8.0	2.48	15.4	27.6
Orange	11.8	9.9	7.3	51.6	26 705	21 421	20.8	3.2	420	363	753	10 150	28.0	2.50	10.7	22.1
Page	11.2	8.7	7.0	51.0	23 195	21 690	6.9	0.1	309	320	40	9 305	15.5	2.46	10.5	24.4
Patrick	12.4	8.9	7.6	50.8	19 470	17 473	11.1	0.3	234	299	133	8 141	17.8	2.36	8.6	25.8
Pittsylvania	11.3	8.1	6.2	51.2	61 878	55 672	10.9	0.2	920	720	-49	24 684	19.7	2.49	11.7	23.4
Powhatan	9.8	5.2	3.3	45.0	23 425	15 328	46.0	4.7	325	182	884	7 258	55.4	2.74	8.1	14.6
Prince Edward	8.1	6.9	7.3	51.1	19 659	17 320	13.9	-0.3	293	283	-64	6 561	22.1	2.43	14.9	28.9
Prince George	7.7	4.5	2.7	46.1	33 723	27 390	20.7	2.0	492	245	444	10 159	23.1	2.76	12.2	17.2
Prince William	7.1	3.0	1.8	50.1	298 707	214 954	30.6	6.4	6 118	1 173	12 757	94 570	35.7	2.94	11.2	17.1
Pulaski	11.8	8.2	7.0	50.7	35 024	34 496	1.8	-0.3	513	548	-54	14 643	9.7	2.32	10.5	27.0
Rappahannock	13.4	8.1	5.7	50.3	7 218	6 622	5.5	3.4	120	80	194	2 788	11.7	2.50	7.1	23.4
Richmond	10.1	8.6	9.1	43.9	8 874	7 273	21.1	0.7	105	149	110	2 937	11.0	2.40	11.8	28.3
Roanoke	10.6	8.4	7.5	52.7	86 220	79 278	8.2	0.5	1 068	976	373	34 686	14.3	2.41	8.5	25.1
Rockbridge	11.9	9.3	6.3	49.9	20 861	18 350	13.4	0.3	279	282	63	8 486	17.8	2.43	9.5	23.9
Rockingham	9.7	7.5	6.5	50.8	68 505	57 482	17.8	1.2	1 095	658	359	25 355	22.2	2.61	7.9	21.2
Russell	10.9	7.6	5.7	49.3	30 098	28 667	5.7	-0.7	376	430	-145	11 789	10.8	2.44	10.1	23.1
Scott	12.2	9.6	8.2	51.7	23 402	23 204	0.9	0.0	340	372	43	9 795	9.2	2.35	9.0	26.1
Shenandoah	11.9	9.4	7.9	51.3	35 851	31 636	10.9	2.2	482	490	780	14 296	14.8	2.42	9.3	25.1
Smyth	11.5	8.9	7.4	51.6	32 888	32 370	2.2	-0.6	440	494	-124	13 493	10.3	2.37	11.2	26.0
Southampton	10.9	7.4	6.8	47.2	17 412	17 022	2.7	-0.4	272	238	-101	6 279	4.5	2.53	13.5	24.9
Spotsylvania	8.0	4.8	3.5	50.7	97 760	57 397	57.5	8.1	1 469	644	6 370	31 308	65.3	2.87	9.9	16.4
Stafford	7.1	3.5	2.4	49.7	99 692	62 255	48.5	7.8	1 684	491	5 914	30 187	55.5	3.01	9.3	13.8
Surry	11.4	7.7	6.3	51.6	6 848	6 145	11.1	0.3	81	98	39	2 619	14.7	2.61	14.1	23.7
Sussex	9.2	7.1	6.3	42.5	12 373	10 248	22.0	-1.0	177	190	-117	4 126	8.7	2.41	18.9	28.2
Tazewell	11.3	8.6	7.0	52.1	44 175	45 960	-3.0	-0.9	580	650	-341	18 277	5.6	2.40	10.8	25.2
Warren	9.8	6.8	5.6	50.8	32 349	26 142	20.8	2.4	517	351	593	12 087	22.4	2.57	10.0	24.0
Washington	11.7	8.7	6.6	51.5	51 253	45 887	11.4	0.3	637	662	191	21 056	20.4	2.36	8.7	25.8
Westmoreland	13.4	10.6	8.3	52.0	16 788	15 480	8.0	0.4	282	288	82	6 846	13.0	2.43	13.5	26.9
Wise	9.9	7.6	6.4	51.3	39 925	39 573	1.4	-0.5	637	595	-227	16 013	10.3	2.44	12.0	25.5
Wythe	11.1	8.7	7.2	52.3	27 776	25 471	8.4	0.6	390	420	215	11 511	16.8	2.36	10.5	26.3
York	9.4	5.6	3.5	50.9	58 293	42 434	32.7	3.5	774	365	1 577	20 000	38.2	2.78	9.4	16.7
Independent Cities																
Alexandria City	7.8	4.4	4.6	51.7	128 773	111 183	15.4	0.4	2 833	1 065	-1 328	61 889	16.2	2.04	9.2	43.4
Bedford City	8.8	9.7	12.9	52.5	6 282	6 176	2.0	-0.3	115	156	24	2 519	1.8	2.26	17.2	33.0
Bristol City	10.9	10.2	10.3	54.9	17 342	18 426	-5.7	-0.1	263	348	62	7 678	1.1	2.18	13.6	34.3
Buena Vista City	10.9	8.5	7.7	53.6	6 334	6 406	-0.9	-0.2	111	110	-14	2 547	5.9	2.38	14.3	27.6
Charlottesville City	5.9	5.1	5.0	53.3	44 372	40 470	11.3	-1.5	640	545	-795	16 851	5.3	2.27	13.1	34.9
Chesapeake City	7.9	5.1	3.8	51.4	203 796	151 982	31.1	2.3	3 696	1 761	2 704	69 900	34.5	2.79	14.0	18.0
Clifton Forge City	10.9	10.6	13.1	55.9	4 181	4 679	-8.3	-2.5	74	102	-81	1 841	-4.6	2.22	14.9	34.4
Colonial Heights City	10.4	9.6	9.0	53.2	17 006	16 064	5.2	0.6	278	271	109	7 027	10.4	2.37	13.0	27.6
Covington City	10.9	9.9	10.3	52.2	6 286	7 352	-14.3	-0.3	106	124	6	2 835	-5.4	2.22	12.5	34.0
Danville City	9.8	9.7	9.9	54.5	47 780	53 056	-8.8	-1.3	858	953	-535	20 607	-5.1	2.27	19.6	33.9
Emporia City	9.2	8.9	11.7	54.5	5 621	5 556	2.0	-0.8	119	134	-28	2 226	9.6	2.43	21.0	32.2
Fairfax City	9.6	6.8	6.0	51.2	21 674	19 945	7.8	0.8	349	180	13	8 035	9.1	2.61	9.3	23.4
Falls Church City	9.2	5.1	7.1	51.3	10 612	9 464	9.6	2.3	120	88	206	4 471	6.6	2.31	8.6	33.8
Franklin City	10.2	8.6	9.8	55.8	8 196	8 392	-0.5	-1.8	135	190	-98	3 384	12.6	2.39	21.9	28.9
Fredericksburg City	7.3	6.3	6.5	55.0	19 952	19 033	1.3	3.5	460	272	473	8 102	8.8	2.09	13.1	39.2
Galax City	10.4	9.8	9.4	52.5	6 650	6 745	1.4	-2.7	157	145	-206	2 950	7.3	2.27	12.7	34.2
Hampton City	8.0	5.8	4.5	50.4	145 665	133 773	9.5	-0.5	2 832	1 399	-2 153	53 887	8.5	2.49	16.4	26.6
Harrisonburg City	5.2	4.3	5.0	52.6	39 932	30 707	31.8	-1.3	529	318	-758	13 133	27.4	2.53	9.3	28.3
Hopewell City	9.1	7.8	6.8	53.3	22 241	23 101	-3.2	-0.5	461	315	-254	9 055	0.5	2.43	21.2	24.5
Lexington City	7.6	7.7	8.7	44.8	6 864	6 959	-1.3	0.0	58	110	47	2 232	2.8	2.06	8.8	41.0
Lynchburg City	8.4	7.5	8.8	54.3	64 108	66 120	-1.3	-1.8	963	1 102	-1 050	25 477	1.3	2.30	16.0	32.7

1. No spouse present.

Table B. States and Counties — **Vital Statistics, Health Resources, and Crime**

STATE County	Births, average 1997–1999		Deaths, average 1997–1999				Physicians,[4] 2000		Hospitals,[4] 1998			Medicare enrollees 2000	Serious crimes known to police, 2000[6]	
			Number		Rate					Beds			Total	
	Total	Rate[1]	Total	Infant[2]	Total[1]	Infant[3]	Number	Rate[5]	Number	Number	Rate[5]		Number	Rate[7]
	32	33	34	35	36	37	38	39	40	41	42	43	44	45

STATE County	32	33	34	35	36	37	38	39	40	41	42	43	44	45
VIRGINIA—Cont'd														
Louisa	300	12.2	239	NA	9.8	NA	9	35	0	0	0	3 738	329	1 358
Lunenburg	117	9.8	143	NA	11.9	NA	5	38	0	0	0	2 043	131	997
Madison	132	10.5	123	NA	9.7	NA	9	72	0	0	0	1 806	114	911
Mathews	78	8.5	136	NA	14.9	NA	7	76	0	0	0	2 108	94	1 021
Mecklenburg	364	11.7	421	NA	13.6	NA	32	99	1	138	444	6 681	816	2 569
Middlesex	76	7.9	131	NA	13.6	NA	14	141	0	0	0	2 404	138	1 389
Montgomery	814	10.7	477	NA	6.3	NA	89	106	1	90	119	8 437	1 840	2 200
Nelson	173	12.3	159	NA	11.3	NA	13	90	0	0	0	3 048	243	1 682
New Kent	149	11.5	92	NA	7.0	NA	4	30	0	0	0	1 807	235	1 746
Northampton	152	11.9	181	NA	14.2	NA	41	313	1	158	1 243	2 954	338	2 582
Northumberland	94	8.1	184	NA	16.0	NA	9	73	0	0	0	2 891	92	753
Nottoway	167	11.0	221	NA	14.6	NA	22	140	0	0	0	3 107	356	2 337
Orange	294	11.6	287	NA	11.3	NA	25	97	0	0	0	5 491	212	819
Page	250	10.9	248	NA	10.8	NA	32	138	1	54	235	4 038	222	958
Patrick	183	9.9	226	NA	12.3	NA	15	77	1	61	331	3 605	397	2 046
Pittsylvania	657	11.5	572	NA	10.0	NA	11	18	0	0	0	8 073	534	865
Powhatan	241	11.0	133	NA	6.1	NA	8	36	0	0	0	2 301	258	1 153
Prince Edward	203	10.6	209	NA	11.0	NA	36	183	1	108	568	3 621	72	365
Prince George	356	12.0	168	NA	5.7	NA	19	57	0	0	0	2 049	463	1 401
Prince William	4 574	17.5	956	30	3.6	6.5	203	72	1	153	59	11 789	7 873	2 804
Pulaski	374	10.9	411	NA	11.9	NA	52	148	1	77	223	6 177	960	2 733
Rappahannock	77	10.4	62	NA	8.4	NA	2	29	0	0	0	1 300	88	1 260
Richmond	73	8.4	117	NA	13.5	NA	2	23	0	0	0	1 545	62	834
Roanoke	722	8.9	782	NA	9.6	NA	159	185	0	0	0	5 781	1 422	1 658
Rockbridge	202	10.4	194	NA	10.0	NA	8	38	0	0	0	2 249	331	1 591
Rockingham	770	12.2	539	NA	8.5	NA	25	37	0	0	0	8 758	709	1 047
Russell	298	10.3	319	NA	11.0	NA	21	69	1	78	269	5 261	234	778
Scott	230	10.2	296	NA	13.1	NA	11	47	0	0	0	5 112	241	1 030
Shenandoah	374	10.8	386	NA	11.1	NA	30	86	1	129	372	6 571	478	1 539
Smyth	350	10.7	407	NA	12.4	NA	53	160	1	176	537	6 777	520	1 572
Southampton	181	10.3	177	NA	10.1	NA	11	63	0	0	0	2 296	302	1 937
Spotsylvania	1 245	14.8	487	NA	5.8	NA	53	59	0	0	0	4 282	2 372	2 624
Stafford	1 317	14.8	373	NA	4.2	NA	36	39	0	0	0	4 260	1 894	2 049
Surry	69	10.6	69	NA	10.6	NA	0	0	0	0	0	991	125	1 830
Sussex	113	10.5	137	NA	12.7	NA	4	32	0	0	0	2 247	206	2 021
Tazewell	474	10.1	537	NA	11.5	NA	93	209	2	243	520	10 425	1 460	3 274
Warren	407	13.5	297	NA	9.8	NA	30	95	1	87	289	4 091	851	2 694
Washington	508	10.3	538	NA	10.9	NA	65	127	1	138	281	7 779	778	1 552
Westmoreland	195	12.0	215	NA	13.2	NA	8	48	0	0	0	3 334	245	1 465
Wise	499	12.7	454	NA	11.6	NA	38	95	2	127	329	8 487	567	1 441
Wythe	278	10.5	338	NA	12.8	NA	31	112	1	106	404	5 732	774	2 949
York	568	9.8	293	NA	5.0	NA	59	105	0	0	0	7 086	1 231	2 187
Independent Cities														
Alexandria City	2 017	17.1	825	13	7.0	6.4	409	319	1	347	293	19 869	5 299	4 131
Bedford City	76	11.9	117	NA	18.2	NA	17	270	1	166	2 628	3 310	189	3 000
Bristol City	164	9.5	254	NA	14.8	NA	6	35	0	0	0	5 693	501	2 885
Buena Vista City	72	11.4	89	NA	14.1	NA	3	47	0	0	0	1 428	35	551
Charlottesville City	460	12.2	399	NA	10.6	NA	515	1 143	2	734	1 920	7 327	2 335	5 183
Chesapeake City	2 817	14.1	1 315	28	6.6	9.9	377	189	1	260	130	19 984	6 894	3 461
Clifton Forge City	52	12.1	92	NA	21.3	NA	4	93	0	0	0	1 545	87	2 028
Colonial Heights City	187	11.2	215	NA	12.8	NA	46	272	0	0	0	3 723	1 226	7 256
Covington City	71	10.3	108	NA	15.6	NA	6	95	0	0	0	2 996	181	2 872
Danville City	617	12.1	776	NA	15.2	NA	155	320	1	336	661	13 288	2 195	4 534
Emporia City	70	12.6	118	NA	21.3	NA	16	282	1	182	3 325	2 034	451	7 961
Fairfax City	283	13.7	209	NA	10.1	NA	67	312	0	0	0	9 365	743	3 456
Falls Church City	129	12.9	81	NA	8.1	NA	79	761	1	656	6 533	3 617	258	3 091
Franklin City	96	11.3	128	NA	15.1	NA	25	300	1	208	2 395	2 359	258	3 091
Fredericksburg City	303	14.8	214	NA	10.4	NA	147	762	1	288	1 328	8 419	1 169	6 064
Galax City	97	14.4	110	NA	16.3	NA	40	585	1	149	2 171	3 293	294	4 300
Hampton City	1 983	14.4	1 090	15	7.9	7.7	240	164	1	289	211	17 643	5 608	3 830
Harrisonburg City	374	11.1	270	NA	8.0	NA	116	287	1	264	790	4 541	1 536	3 796
Hopewell City	334	14.8	263	NA	11.7	NA	49	219	1	140	621	4 043	1 282	5 735
Lexington City	43	5.9	81	NA	11.1	NA	24	349	1	98	1 332	2 599	96	1 398
Lynchburg City	760	11.7	818	NA	12.6	NA	214	328	2	529	808	14 671	2 779	4 258

1. Per 1,000 estimated resident population, average 1997–1999. 2. Deaths of infants under 1 year old. 3. Deaths of infants under 1 year old per 1,000 live births. 4. Data subject to copyright. 5. Per 100,000 resident population as of July 1 of the year shown. 6. Data for serious crimes have not been adjusted for underreporting; this may affect comparability between geographic areas and over time. 7. Per 100,000 population estimated by the FBI.

Table B. States and Counties — Crime, Education, Money Income, and Poverty

STATE County	Serious crimes known to police, 2000 (cont'd) Rate[2] Violent	Property	Education School enrollment and attainment, 1990 Enrollment[3] Total	Percent private	Attainment[4] (percent) High school graduate or more	Bach-elor's degree or more	Local government expenditures, fiscal 1999[5] Total current expenditures (mil dol)	Current expenditures per student (dollars)	Money income 1989 Per capita[6] (dollars)	Households Median Dollars	Percent change, 1979–1989 (constant 1989 dollars)	Percent with $100,000 or more	Income and poverty, 1998 Median house-hold income	Percent below poverty level All persons	Persons under 18	Persons 5–17 in families
	46	47	48	49	50	51	52	53	54	55	56	57	58	59	60	61
VIRGINIA—Cont'd																
Louisa	120	1 238	4 582	7.5	59.8	8.7	23.6	5 739	12 390	26 169	12.6	2.6	37 247	10.3	13.8	13.7
Lunenburg	167	829	2 516	3.5	52.2	6.6	11.6	6 052	9 158	19 459	-0.2	0.8	26 872	18.4	23.4	23.6
Madison	112	799	2 652	15.5	62.7	15.4	11.7	6 261	11 145	26 662	19.9	2.3	36 986	11.3	14.9	15.3
Mathews	98	923	1 623	8.9	70.0	15.5	7.5	5 668	13 671	27 428	8.7	1.5	38 908	10.2	15.2	15.2
Mecklenburg	280	2 289	6 072	6.8	58.1	10.0	27.0	5 347	10 508	20 901	-0.7	1.1	29 005	14.7	20.5	19.4
Middlesex	111	1 279	1 515	15.9	66.6	14.7	7.9	5 759	14 834	25 167	23.4	3.8	34 942	12.1	18.2	18.6
Montgomery	153	2 047	32 874	5.0	73.6	31.6	55.0	5 959	10 979	22 949	4.7	1.9	37 095	12.8	14.7	14.5
Nelson	145	1 537	2 699	8.2	57.0	13.4	12.8	6 148	11 419	23 705	15.8	2.8	33 943	11.8	15.6	15.9
New Kent	156	1 590	2 446	7.2	72.8	13.4	12.3	5 361	14 993	38 403	23.0	3.3	52 470	5.6	8.2	7.7
Northampton	252	2 329	2 913	7.3	57.3	12.4	15.0	6 270	10 176	18 117	8.9	2.5	23 718	23.4	30.2	30.6
Northumberland	41	712	1 923	12.6	63.9	13.5	9.8	6 340	13 712	23 065	1.3	3.4	33 197	12.8	20.5	20.8
Nottoway	190	2 146	3 031	7.8	53.2	8.8	14.6	5 886	10 036	21 774	-3.2	1.5	28 559	18.5	24.7	23.7
Orange	81	738	4 624	8.9	65.9	16.1	23.6	6 185	13 545	31 782	38.2	3.0	41 458	8.8	12.4	12.1
Page	108	850	4 181	8.7	55.4	7.9	18.9	5 215	11 304	24 971	17.8	1.7	32 595	11.7	16.5	15.9
Patrick	113	1 932	3 597	3.7	54.1	7.0	14.9	5 443	10 411	22 287	2.2	1.1	30 731	13.5	17.8	18.7
Pittsylvania	152	713	12 364	8.1	56.1	7.4	48.6	5 215	11 196	25 585	7.7	1.3	33 729	12.8	19.8	15.2
Powhatan	121	1 032	3 184	18.7	66.3	12.2	19.7	5 886	15 683	37 394	14.4	4.6	52 656	5.6	7.2	7.3
Prince Edward	101	264	6 254	21.7	60.5	14.2	14.3	5 335	9 031	21 395	3.8	1.1	29 087	19.2	21.5	23.6
Prince George	127	1 274	7 028	9.5	77.9	16.2	30.5	5 377	12 714	34 825	19.1	1.8	46 774	7.9	10.7	9.5
Prince William	206	2 598	59 451	12.6	87.8	27.6	318.3	6 227	17 833	49 370	15.8	6.5	62 037	5.7	8.2	6.9
Pulaski	216	2 517	7 490	3.9	59.6	11.5	29.0	5 750	11 074	23 319	-3.9	1.1	33 995	12.6	18.4	17.9
Rappahannock	14	1 246	1 266	10.3	67.2	18.9	6.4	6 127	17 260	32 377	32.5	5.8	42 638	9.3	12.8	13.1
Richmond	135	699	1 491	5.5	56.8	11.8	7.5	5 739	11 036	24 583	5.2	2.2	30 559	16.7	21.0	21.0
Roanoke	225	1 433	19 159	15.5	79.4	22.6	86.7	6 237	16 627	36 886	7.6	4.4	48 926	5.7	8.9	6.5
Rockbridge	144	1 447	3 624	11.5	62.1	12.9	18.8	5 887	11 287	24 955	10.1	1.4	35 572	11.2	17.6	14.9
Rockingham	50	997	12 657	16.9	64.7	14.6	59.9	5 653	12 647	29 637	14.0	2.1	39 752	8.9	13.5	10.7
Russell	70	708	6 568	2.5	50.6	6.7	23.9	5 423	8 753	17 853	-22.7	1.0	27 128	19.4	23.4	23.2
Scott	145	885	4 676	3.0	51.2	5.9	21.6	5 782	9 100	18 346	0.9	0.4	28 241	16.5	22.0	21.1
Shenandoah	180	1 359	5 774	6.8	65.2	11.2	31.3	5 789	12 686	26 527	17.4	1.7	36 486	9.8	14.1	13.2
Smyth	145	1 427	6 809	3.3	53.3	7.8	28.4	5 333	9 613	20 912	-0.8	0.8	30 109	15.6	21.5	20.1
Southampton	148	1 789	3 940	10.7	58.4	11.4	17.7	6 138	10 948	26 376	13.3	1.4	35 748	15.1	21.4	19.8
Spotsylvania	131	2 494	15 146	9.1	76.6	19.0	99.2	5 744	15 192	41 342	28.3	4.0	54 650	5.9	7.8	7.1
Stafford	143	1 906	16 060	8.2	80.9	21.6	106.3	5 594	15 917	44 661	23.0	5.2	62 837	5.1	6.8	6.1
Surry	278	1 552	1 461	10.7	58.0	11.0	11.3	9 268	11 495	25 027	11.7	1.4	32 678	14.3	19.3	19.1
Sussex	363	1 658	2 139	14.6	54.2	8.6	11.2	7 455	9 856	20 833	-3.2	1.7	28 227	20.1	25.3	25.3
Tazewell	792	2 482	11 338	7.5	57.3	9.1	41.5	5 360	9 995	19 670	-20.0	1.4	28 504	17.4	20.7	21.6
Warren	123	2 571	5 332	14.0	64.6	11.8	25.6	5 386	13 580	31 062	24.2	1.8	42 096	9.8	13.9	13.5
Washington	116	1 436	10 342	12.2	60.4	12.2	42.2	5 664	11 057	22 179	0.7	2.3	33 448	13.5	18.6	16.6
Westmoreland	185	1 280	3 148	9.4	59.0	10.9	14.8	5 117	12 268	24 654	10.1	1.7	31 866	14.9	21.6	21.6
Wise	239	1 202	10 202	3.5	52.1	8.6	41.3	5 623	9 392	19 594	-21.1	1.2	27 200	21.0	24.4	24.1
Wythe	229	2 720	5 751	4.6	61.8	10.0	24.0	5 478	10 404	20 964	-4.8	0.7	30 879	14.5	20.1	19.7
York	281	1 906	12 899	11.7	88.3	28.9	61.5	5 370	15 742	40 363	15.1	4.2	56 275	5.3	7.1	6.4
Independent Cities																
Alexandria City	245	3 886	21 083	28.1	86.9	48.5	107.8	9 977	25 509	41 472	17.7	8.9	54 631	8.7	17.1	17.0
Bedford City	286	2 715	1 149	12.7	60.1	15.0	(7)NA	(7)NA	11 070	22 787	8.8	2.0	29 040	16.9	23.5	23.9
Bristol City	351	2 534	4 103	16.4	60.8	13.8	15.6	6 542	10 290	19 226	-13.6	0.7	28 974	18.3	24.3	27.9
Buena Vista City	63	488	1 483	16.6	55.5	8.7	6.8	6 133	10 241	23 929	-0.3	0.9	32 328	12.6	16.7	19.6
Charlottesville City	890	4 293	14 747	7.4	75.5	34.1	38.8	8 824	12 928	24 190	3.5	2.6	34 270	16.7	19.2	25.4
Chesapeake City	536	2 925	40 639	12.1	77.1	16.9	216.4	5 891	13 817	35 737	13.2	2.4	47 919	9.0	12.5	11.2
Clifton Forge City	350	1 679	1 050	7.2	69.0	8.9	(8)NA	(8)NA	11 562	20 659	-7.8	3.2	29 820	16.8	25.9	26.2
Colonial Heights City	219	7 037	3 384	6.7	77.8	16.7	18.7	6 811	15 639	34 472	-2.4	2.5	42 682	6.5	9.7	9.6
Covington City	111	2 761	1 365	4.5	64.5	7.0	7.9	8 359	10 814	20 913	-8.7	0.8	28 991	14.2	20.0	23.1
Danville City	496	4 038	10 964	11.4	57.4	12.4	44.9	5 702	11 344	20 413	-11.2	1.3	27 590	17.9	22.3	27.1
Emporia City	1 183	6 778	1 189	9.3	58.1	13.4	(9)NA	(9)NA	10 478	21 009	3.9	1.6	25 489	19.9	22.2	30.0
Fairfax City	158	3 298	5 040	18.2	87.5	41.3	(10)NA	(10)NA	21 929	50 913	17.7	9.0	61 226	4.4	6.1	6.4
Falls Church City	NA	NA	2 281	18.5	91.4	52.8	15.5	10 042	26 709	51 011	24.1	12.4	65 623	3.2	4.6	4.3
Franklin City	240	2 852	1 902	11.5	61.9	14.4	10.4	6 141	11 212	20 357	-9.8	2.7	28 632	21.0	27.8	29.1
Fredericksburg City	545	5 519	5 149	6.4	73.8	26.1	16.7	7 643	13 825	26 614	11.3	2.9	37 357	14.1	19.3	25.3
Galax City	570	3 730	1 204	6.4	56.2	11.3	6.8	5 319	10 490	20 263	7.7	1.6	26 450	20.1	29.1	32.1
Hampton City	332	3 498	36 567	20.8	79.7	19.1	140.3	5 961	13 099	30 144	6.0	1.6	37 586	13.0	19.3	17.4
Harrisonburg City	351	3 445	13 711	11.3	76.8	28.7	25.2	7 055	11 607	25 312	8.8	3.0	36 667	17.2	18.6	19.3
Hopewell City	828	4 907	5 223	8.8	67.4	10.0	25.2	6 292	11 897	26 934	-1.5	1.3	33 213	16.4	24.3	25.7
Lexington City	146	1 252	3 415	48.1	72.8	32.1	3.8	8 384	10 077	21 361	4.1	1.9	29 785	15.9	15.4	20.4
Lynchburg City	458	3 800	19 204	37.7	69.5	21.7	59.9	6 383	12 657	23 726	-7.5	2.8	30 574	17.5	22.7	24.0

1. Data for serious crimes have not been adjusted for underreporting; this may affect comparability between geographic areas and over time. 2. Per 100,000 population estimated by the FBI. 3. All persons 3 years old and over enrolled in nursery school through college. 4. Persons 25 years old and over. 5. Elementary and secondary education expenditures, local government fiscal years ending between July 1, 1998 and June 30, 1999. 6. Based on population enumerated as of April 1, 1990. 7. Bedford City included with Bedford County. 8. Clifton Forge City included with Allegheny County. 9. Emporia included with Greensville County. 10. Fairfax City included with Fairfax County.

Table B. States and Counties — Personal Income

STATE County	Total (mil dol) [62]	Percent change, 1998–1999 [63]	Per capita[1] Dollars [64]	Per capita[1] Rank [65]	Wages and salaries[2] (mil dol) [66]	Proprietor's income (mil dol) [67]	Dividends, interest, and rent (mil dol) [68]	Transfer payments Total (mil dol) [69]	Gov't payments to individuals Total (mil dol) [70]	Social Security (mil dol) [71]	Medical payments (mil dol) [72]	Income maintenance (mil dol) [73]	Unemployment insurance (mil dol) [74]
VIRGINIA—Cont'd													
Louisa	576	6.8	23 026	1 082	204	69	82	80	75	35	29	6	1
Lunenburg	206	4.2	17 488	2 649	75	12	40	47	45	20	15	5	0
Madison	263	6.6	20 853	1 713	83	24	58	39	37	17	14	3	0
Mathews	251	5.0	27 081	411	36	14	73	39	38	20	14	2	0
Mecklenburg	634	3.4	20 450	1 852	355	38	123	134	128	60	48	13	2
Middlesex	242	5.0	24 774	709	70	13	78	45	43	24	14	3	0
Montgomery	(3)1 836	(3)6.7	(3)19 817	(3)2 052	(3)1 316	(3)110	(3)314	(3)225	(3)207	(3)100	(3)65	(3)18	(3)1
Nelson	295	5.6	20 806	1 734	81	29	66	57	54	25	20	4	0
New Kent	339	7.4	25 612	570	66	18	49	33	31	16	11	2	0
Northampton	259	4.2	20 233	1 913	121	22	64	61	58	25	21	9	1
Northumberland	273	4.1	23 425	981	63	27	101	58	56	30	20	2	1
Nottoway	305	7.2	19 950	2 006	176	20	57	71	68	24	29	6	1
Orange	579	5.2	22 470	1 223	208	36	149	97	92	47	34	6	1
Page	448	3.9	19 337	2 199	168	42	81	81	76	37	27	6	1
Patrick	345	3.0	18 605	2 393	137	29	54	69	66	32	23	6	2
Pittsylvania	(4)2 241	(4)3.6	(4)20 833	(4)1 722	(4)1 303	(4)123	(4)399	(4)423	(4)402	(4)202	(4)130	(4)45	(4)9
Powhatan	494	8.8	22 039	1 351	148	28	66	46	41	23	13	2	0
Prince Edward	314	5.2	16 331	2 856	218	24	62	67	63	28	23	8	0
Prince George	(5)1 194	(5)5.3	(5)23 192	(5)1 047	(5)996	(5)50	(5)183	(5)152	(5)144	(5)67	(5)48	(5)16	(5)1
Prince William	(6)8 976	(6)8.7	(6)28 747	(6)272	(6)3 803	(6)366	(6)1 109	(6)459	(6)400	(6)174	(6)143	(6)39	(6)4
Pulaski	721	6.8	20 952	1 681	538	43	107	140	133	64	49	11	1
Rappahannock	199	8.6	26 001	515	48	16	50	22	21	10	8	1	0
Richmond	156	4.6	17 795	2 576	85	10	36	31	30	14	12	2	0
Roanoke	(7)3 364	(7)3.6	(7)31 978	(7)155	(7)1 943	(7)214	(7)773	(7)322	(7)301	(7)185	(7)72	(7)12	(7)2
Rockbridge	(8)702	(8)5.2	(8)21 046	(8)1 655	(8)386	(8)42	(8)163	(8)117	(8)111	(8)60	(8)35	(8)9	(8)1
Rockingham	(9)2 261	(9)4.9	(9)23 262	(9)1 025	(9)1 611	(9)198	(9)419	(9)260	(9)242	(9)136	(9)73	(9)17	(9)1
Russell	521	4.2	18 137	2 512	240	33	78	151	145	62	51	17	2
Scott	380	2.5	16 882	2 758	101	19	61	109	104	45	38	15	1
Shenandoah	766	5.6	21 796	1 413	376	58	157	114	107	60	34	7	1
Smyth	644	5.1	19 702	2 084	410	50	98	133	127	61	44	12	2
Southampton	(10)601	(10)2.9	(10)23 072	(10)1 022	(10)259	(10)27	(10)99	(10)109	(10)104	(10)43	(10)42	(10)13	(10)1
Spotsylvania	(11)2 967	(11)9.8	(11)27 945	(11)336	(11)1 321	(11)175	(11)426	(11)249	(11)228	(11)108	(11)85	(11)15	(11)2
Stafford	2 289	10.2	24 567	740	813	95	318	128	111	57	35	8	2
Surry	121	2.6	18 700	2 367	98	5	26	22	20	9	8	2	0
Sussex	232	7.8	18 832	2 338	110	9	35	48	45	18	20	6	0
Tazewell	859	2.3	18 534	2 407	421	55	155	231	222	87	75	24	2
Warren	782	7.8	25 541	577	267	49	129	85	79	43	25	6	1
Washington	(12)1 489	(12)5.6	(12)22 385	(12)1 249	(12)943	(12)103	(12)290	(12)269	(12)256	(12)129	(12)80	(12)25	(12)2
Westmoreland	358	5.5	22 019	1 362	77	23	78	68	64	30	25	5	1
Wise	(13)826	(13)3.6	(13)18 677	(13)2 375	(13)537		(13)125	(13)248	(13)239	(13)92	(13)84	(13)30	(13)3
Wythe	548	5.2	20 673	1 787	292	36	87	109	104	50	37	9	1
York	(14)1 815	(14)5.3	(14)25 922	(14)527	(14)544	(14)74	(14)321	(14)148	(14)135	(14)72	(14)40	(14)6	(14)1
Independent Cities													
Alexandria City	5 824	8.1	49 609	10	4 402	275	1 152	326	304	100	141	32	3
Bedford City	(15)	(15)	(15)	(15)	(15)	(15)	(15)	(15)	(15)	(15)	(15)	(15)	(15)
Bristol City	(12)	(12)	(12)	(12)	(12)	(12)	(12)	(12)	(12)	(12)	(12)	(12)	(12)
Buena Vista City	(8)	(8)	(8)	(8)	(8)	(8)	(8)	(8)	(8)	(8)	(8)	(8)	(8)
Charlottesville City	(16)	(16)	(16)	(16)	(16)	(16)	(16)	(16)	(16)	(16)	(16)	(16)	(16)
Chesapeake City	4 997	6.8	24 646	723	2 455	174	639	467	429	190	149	42	6
Clifton Forge City	(17)	(17)	(17)	(17)	(17)	(17)	(17)	(17)	(17)	(17)	(17)	(17)	(17)
Colonial Heights City	(18)	(18)	(18)	(18)	(18)	(18)	(18)	(18)	(18)	(18)	(18)	(18)	(18)
Covington City	(17)	(17)	(17)	(17)	(17)	(17)	(17)	(17)	(17)	(17)	(17)	(17)	(17)
Danville City	(4)	(4)	(4)	(4)	(4)	(4)	(4)	(4)	(4)	(4)	(4)	(4)	(4)
Emporia City	(19)	(19)	(19)	(19)	(19)	(19)	(19)	(19)	(19)	(19)	(19)	(19)	(19)
Fairfax City	(20)	(20)	(20)	(20)	(20)	(20)	(20)	(20)	(20)	(20)	(20)	(20)	(20)
Falls Church City	(20)	(20)	(20)	(20)	(20)	(20)	(20)	(20)	(20)	(20)	(20)	(20)	(20)
Franklin City	(10)	(10)	(10)	(10)	(10)	(10)	(10)	(10)	(10)	(10)	(10)	(10)	(10)
Fredericksburg City	(11)	(11)	(11)	(11)	(11)	(11)	(11)	(11)	(11)	(11)	(11)	(11)	(11)
Galax City	(21)	(21)	(21)	(21)	(21)	(21)	(21)	(21)	(21)	(21)	(21)	(21)	(21)
Hampton City	3 053	5.3	22 250	1 285	2 778	113	511	421	397	162	136	45	4
Harrisonburg City	(9)	(9)	(9)	(9)	(9)	(9)	(9)	(9)	(9)	(9)	(9)	(9)	(9)
Hopewell City	(5)	(5)	(5)	(5)	(5)	(5)	(5)	(5)	(5)	(5)	(5)	(5)	(5)
Lexington City	(8)	(8)	(8)	(8)	(8)	(8)	(8)	(8)	(8)	(8)	(8)	(8)	(8)
Lynchburg City	(22)	(22)	(22)	(22)	(22)	(22)	(22)	(22)	(22)	(22)	(22)	(22)	(22)

1. Based on the resident population estimated as of July 1 of the year shown.   2. Includes other labor income.   3. Radford included with Montgomery County.   4. Danville included with Pittsylvania County.   5. Hopewell included with Prince George County.   6. Manassas and Manassas Park included with Prince William County.   7. Salem included with Roanoke County.   8. Buena Vista and Lexington included with Rockbridge County.   9. Harrisonburg included with Rockingham County.   10. Franklin included with Southhampton County.   11. Fredericksburg included with Spotsylvania County.   12. Bristol included with Washington County.   13. Norton included with Wise County.   14. Poquoson included with York County.   15. Bedford City included with Bedford County.   16. Charlottesville included with Albemarle County.   17. Clifton Forge and Covington included with Alleghany County.   18. Petersburg and Colonial Heights included with Dinwiddie County.   19. Emporia included with Greensville County.   20. Fairfax City and Falls Church included with Fairfax County.   21. Galax included with Carroll County.   22. Lynchburg included with Campbell County.

Table B. States and Counties — Earnings, Social Security, and Housing

STATE County	Earnings, 1999									Social Security beneficiaries, December 2000		Housing units, 1990		
			Goods-related[1]		Service-related and other[2]							Supplemental Security Income recipients, December 2000		
	Total (mil dol)	Farm	Total	Manufacturing	Total	Retail trade	Finance, insurance, and real estate	Services	Government	Number	Rate[3]		Total	Percent change, 1980–1990
	75	76	77	78	79	80	81	82	83	84	85	86	87	88
VIRGINIA—Cont'd														
Louisa	273	-0.2	D	20.7	D	4.8	4.1	17.6	13.1	4 582	179	563	9 080	28.6
Lunenburg	87	1.2	32.4	18.6	35.9	9.0	3.3	12.9	30.5	2 698	205	485	5 065	5.3
Madison	107	0.4	31.7	22.4	52.2	19.3	1.3	23.9	15.7	2 262	181	254	4 547	13.8
Mathews	50	1.6	24.4	10.0	50.6	14.1	4.0	19.2	23.3	2 378	258	116	4 725	11.8
Mecklenburg	393	1.8	D	25.8	D	13.4	D	18.6	17.9	7 863	243	1 311	14 589	11.9
Middlesex	84	0.6	20.4	10.6	49.7	12.4	6.4	21.6	29.3	2 780	280	203	5 486	11.1
Montgomery	(4)1 426	(4)0.1	(4)D	(4)20.8	(4)D	(4)10.4	(4)5.1	(4)19.3	(4)35.4	9 582	115	1 007	27 770	24.1
Nelson	110	2.5	D	7.8	D	6.5	3.2	35.2	16.9	3 185	220	401	7 063	28.4
New Kent	84	0.0	28.9	7.2	49.1	10.9	3.1	28.5	22.0	1 932	144	135	3 968	21.9
Northampton	143	7.0	12.7	8.8	56.6	10.1	2.6	33.9	23.8	3 339	255	699	6 183	0.8
Northumberland	89	1.5	26.1	D	D	7.6	5.1	20.9	16.0	3 580	292	201	6 841	22.5
Nottoway	196	1.9	D	17.6	D	9.6	2.4	11.5	37.2	3 327	212	574	5 732	2.0
Orange	245	2.0	D	22.0	D	11.3	D	14.6	21.3	5 842	226	531	9 038	22.8
Page	210	7.2	38.9	29.6	36.2	8.3	2.5	17.9	17.8	4 934	213	545	8 948	7.4
Patrick	166	1.0	47.3	42.6	38.7	7.2	2.2	17.0	13.0	4 222	218	518	8 125	15.2
Pittsylvania	(5)1 426	(5)0.4	(5)D	(5)37.0	(5)D	(5)10.7	(5)3.6	(5)21.1	(5)13.8	14 228	230	1 772	22 861	-5.7
Powhatan	176	0.8	D	2.8	D	8.0	4.2	13.6	41.2	2 799	125	209	4 910	27.9
Prince Edward	242	1.1	D	7.9	D	19.4	3.1	30.1	24.6	3 569	181	842	6 075	9.5
Prince George	(6)1 046	(6)0.0	(6)D	(6)17.1	(6)D	(6)6.2	(6)1.2	(6)12.4	(6)50.8	3 480	105	272	8 640	24.4
Prince William	(7)4 168	(7)0.0	(7)D	(7)4.6	(7)D	(7)14.0	(7)D	(7)26.4	(7)26.8	18 719	67	2 033	74 759	60.8
Pulaski	581	0.1	D	47.2	D	6.9	1.6	13.7	11.6	7 693	219	1 016	14 740	7.3
Rappahannock	64	0.1	15.3	1.4	D	16.7	D	37.8	15.8	1 308	187	110	2 964	9.6
Richmond	96	1.7	D	12.7	D	7.7	3.0	17.2	30.6	1 790	203	200	3 179	5.7
Roanoke	(8)2 157	(8)0.0	(8)D	(8)21.9	(8)D	(8)8.8	(8)8.9	(8)26.5	(8)15.7	16 040	187	502	31 689	18.2
Rockbridge	(9)427	(9)0.3	(9)D	(9)24.9	(9)D	(9)11.9	(9)2.9	(9)25.6	(9)20.9	4 018	193	312	7 975	11.9
Rockingham	(10)1 808	(10)2.9	(10)D	(10)28.5	(10)D	(10)9.9	(10)4.0	(10)20.5	(10)15.1	12 044	178	832	22 614	8.4
Russell	273	0.5	36.6	19.1	43.3	8.6	2.5	15.7	19.6	8 327	275	1 670	11 558	0.3
Scott	120	1.2	D	11.8	D	15.8	4.4	19.8	27.5	6 119	261	1 537	10 003	2.3
Shenandoah	434	3.0	D	36.5	D	10.2	3.1	15.8	12.5	7 520	214	497	15 160	26.3
Smyth	460	0.3	D	43.0	D	7.2	1.8	16.1	17.6	8 045	243	1 297	13 132	6.7
Southampton	(11)286	(11)2.0	(11)D	(11)14.5	(11)D	(11)9.3	(11)D	(11)21.2	(11)27.5	3 474	199	531	6 560	4.9
Spotsylvania	(12)1 497	(12)0.0	(12)D	(12)8.5	(12)D	(12)16.8	(12)7.1	(12)30.2	(12)16.2	10 391	115	626	20 483	72.9
Stafford	908	0.0	14.2	3.2	57.9	6.5	18.4	16.1	27.9	7 436	80	489	20 529	54.7
Surry	103	0.9	8.5	3.4	D	1.9	D	6.0	13.6	1 176	172	153	2 982	9.5
Sussex	119	1.8	D	13.1	D	10.7	2.4	13.7	39.4	2 344	187	513	4 252	7.4
Tazewell	476	0.5	D	10.1	D	16.0	3.3	26.8	19.4	10 790	242	2 159	18 901	3.4
Warren	316	0.1	30.3	18.7	53.6	13.4	3.3	26.1	16.0	5 077	161	429	11 223	17.9
Washington	(13)1 047	(13)0.5	(13)D	(13)27.2	(13)D	(13)12.5	(13)6.5	(13)19.9	(13)15.2	11 694	229	1 728	19 183	7.3
Westmoreland	100	3.5	D	18.7	D	12.4	5.0	18.8	22.3	3 842	230	357	8 378	12.1
Wise	(14)582	(14)0.1	(14)26.0	(14)3.2	(14)52.5	(14)2.4		(14)23.0	(14)21.5	10 193	254	2 527	15 927	1.7
Wythe	328	0.3	28.6	23.3	51.5	13.9	2.8	22.2	19.6	6 401	232	919	10 659	8.4
York	(15)618	(15)0.1	(15)19.1	(15)5.7	(15)D	(15)10.0	(15)3.3	(15)19.9	(15)39.0	7 245	129	259	15 284	33.8
Independent Cities														
Alexandria City	4 677	0.0	6.0	2.5	68.7	7.6	7.1	45.4	25.3	11 385	89	2 570	58 252	11.9
Bedford City	(16)	(16)	(16)	(16)	(16)	(16)	(16)	(16)	(16)	1 939	308	263	2 625	0.7
Bristol City	(13)	(13)	(13)	(13)	(13)	(13)	(13)	(13)	(13)	4 593	264	835	8 174	5.6
Buena Vista City	(9)	(9)	(9)	(9)	(9)	(9)	(9)	(9)	(9)	1 409	222	203	2 494	3.7
Charlottesville City	(17)	(17)	(17)	(17)	(17)	(17)	(17)	(17)	(17)	5 925	132	1 065	16 785	4.9
Chesapeake City	2 629	0.2	21.6	8.3	56.7	13.6	4.8	24.0	21.4	24 408	123	2 603	55 742	46.5
Clifton Forge City	(18)	(18)	(18)	(18)	(18)	(18)	(18)	(18)	(18)	999	233	215	2 131	3.2
Colonial Heights City	(19)	(19)	(19)	(19)	(19)	(19)	(19)	(19)	(19)	3 782	224	239	6 592	8.5
Covington City	(18)	(18)	(18)	(18)	(18)	(18)	(18)	(18)	(18)	1 808	287	283	3 269	-12.5
Danville City	(5)	(5)	(5)	(5)	(5)	(5)	(5)	(5)	(5)	11 278	233	2 344	23 297	26.6
Emporia City	(20)	(20)	(20)	(20)	(20)	(20)	(20)	(20)	(20)	1 488	263	377	2 178	11.6
Fairfax City	(21)	(21)	(21)	(21)	(21)	(21)	(21)	(21)	(21)	2 480	115	905	7 677	8.9
Falls Church City	(21)	(21)	(21)	(21)	(21)	(21)	(21)	(21)	(21)	1 348	130	338	4 668	3.7
Franklin City	(11)	(11)	(11)	(11)	(11)	(11)	(11)	(11)	(11)	1 949	234	542	3 166	17.8
Fredericksburg City	(12)	(12)	(12)	(12)	(12)	(12)	(12)	(12)	(12)	3 278	170	525	8 063	27.0
Galax City	(22)	(22)	(22)	(22)	(22)	(22)	(22)	(22)	(22)	1 961	287	444	2 943	4.7
Hampton City	2 891	0.0	13.0	9.4	39.3	8.6	2.7	20.5	47.7	20 192	138	2 400	53 623	22.8
Harrisonburg City	(10)	(10)	(10)	(10)	(10)	(10)	(10)	(10)	(10)	4 330	107	499	10 900	76.7
Hopewell City	(6)	(6)	(6)	(6)	(6)	(6)	(6)	(6)	(6)	4 417	198	758	9 625	3.6
Lexington City	(9)	(9)	(9)	(9)	(9)	(9)	(9)	(9)	(9)	1 846	269	206	2 311	-3.3
Lynchburg City	(23)	(23)	(23)	(23)	(23)	(23)	(23)	(23)	(23)	13 869	212	1 969	27 233	7.1

1. Covers mining, construction, and manufacturing.   2. Covers private sector earnings in agricultural services, forestry, and fisheries; transportation and public utilities; wholesale trade; retail trade; finance, insurance, and real estate; and services.   3. Per 1,000 resident population estimated as of July 1 of the year shown.   4. Radford included with Montgomery County.   5. Danville included with Pittsylvania County.   6. Hopewell included with Prince George County.   7. Manassas and Manassas Park included with Prince William County.   8. Salem included with Roanoke County.   9. Buena Vista and Lexington included with Rockbridge County.   10. Harrisonburg included with Rockingham County.   11. Franklin included with Southhampton County.   12. Fredericksburg included with Spotsylvania County.   13. Bristol included with Washington County.   14. Norton included with Wise County.   15. Poquoson included with York County.   16. Bedford City included with Bedford County.   17. Charlottesville included with Albemarle County.   18. Clifton Forge and Covington included with Alleghany County.   19. Petersburg and Colonial Heights included with Dinwiddie County.   20. Emporia included with Greensville County.   21. Fairfax City and Falls Church included with Fairfax County.   22. Galax included with Carroll County.   23. Lynchburg included with Campbell County.

Table B. States and Counties — Housing, Labor Force, and Employment

STATE County	Housing units, 1990 (cont'd)								Civilian labor force, 2001				Civilian employment, 1990[5]		
	Occupied units										Unemployment			Percent	
	Owner-occupied					Renter-occupied									
				Owner cost as a percent of income											
	Total	Percent	Median value[1]	With a mortgage	Without a mortgage	Median rent[2]	Rent as percent of income	Substandard units[3] (percent)	Total	Percent change, 2000–2001	Total	Rate[4]	Total	Professional, managerial, and technical	Precision production, craft, and repair
	89	90	91	92	93	94	95	96	97	98	99	100	101	102	103
VIRGINIA—Cont'd															
Louisa	7 427	79.9	64 400	20.7	12.3	399	24.7	8.8	10 150	2.9	454	4.5	9 646	18.8	19.3
Lunenburg	4 423	77.6	37 600	17.8	13.5	246	20.5	9.0	4 801	3.4	293	6.1	5 121	13.2	14.1
Madison	4 144	77.1	72 200	21.0	12.7	361	17.0	11.3	9 270	2.8	165	1.8	5 511	21.3	12.8
Mathews	3 530	83.3	79 900	23.0	12.3	391	26.8	7.5	4 742	1.2	127	2.7	3 865	20.9	16.2
Mecklenburg	11 244	71.7	50 700	17.0	13.0	244	18.8	10.3	15 120	1.4	1 093	7.2	13 355	17.9	13.3
Middlesex	3 530	82.8	77 500	21.1	13.2	338	24.0	6.2	5 560	3.5	97	1.7	3 884	23.0	15.3
Montgomery	26 241	55.4	71 700	19.2	11.6	397	30.0	3.1	38 151	1.9	1 187	3.1	34 250	37.1	10.3
Nelson	4 807	79.1	53 100	19.2	12.6	308	19.8	11.8	7 179	2.5	254	3.5	5 849	20.3	14.4
New Kent	3 718	87.8	86 500	20.1	12.1	459	18.6	3.8	7 211	2.2	246	3.4	5 326	28.6	16.6
Northampton	5 129	65.7	47 700	19.1	14.7	260	24.8	15.2	5 547	3.4	223	4.0	5 160	24.3	10.9
Northumberland	4 492	87.1	80 300	22.3	12.7	327	22.4	8.1	5 366	3.2	367	6.8	4 192	18.3	13.2
Nottoway	5 244	73.1	43 000	19.3	13.4	294	21.8	6.8	6 634	0.8	243	3.7	6 137	18.9	11.0
Orange	7 930	76.3	83 200	20.8	12.1	419	22.6	4.4	11 281	2.2	342	3.0	10 519	24.3	16.4
Page	8 055	76.9	61 500	20.9	12.8	359	23.8	6.5	12 315	4.1	406	3.3	9 590	14.4	21.5
Patrick	6 908	81.5	51 700	17.6	11.3	230	16.5	4.7	8 769	2.6	741	8.5	8 933	16.3	16.1
Pittsylvania	20 613	79.6	48 800	15.3	12.5	276	18.0	7.7	32 203	2.2	2 718	8.4	27 399	15.6	14.5
Powhatan	4 672	85.1	74 700	20.2	12.0	448	20.5	3.7	11 465	1.2	242	2.1	7 115	26.0	18.2
Prince Edward	5 373	70.9	54 200	18.9	12.7	310	22.3	7.8	8 542	3.3	334	3.9	6 969	23.9	10.0
Prince George	8 250	68.8	75 800	18.3	11.6	434	19.2	5.4	12 452	1.6	421	3.4	10 994	24.1	14.4
Prince William	69 709	71.0	138 500	25.6	12.5	736	26.6	2.4	152 086	2.1	3 688	2.4	112 964	37.3	12.1
Pulaski	13 349	73.0	51 400	16.8	11.9	297	21.7	3.9	18 006	5.1	1 821	10.1	15 673	21.9	13.6
Rappahannock	2 496	72.2	89 300	22.9	14.9	413	23.2	10.0	4 151	3.8	68	1.6	3 375	22.6	19.3
Richmond	2 645	81.5	63 100	18.1	12.6	336	17.2	10.8	4 022	2.0	141	3.5	3 215	17.4	14.3
Roanoke	30 355	77.3	80 500	17.5	11.8	420	21.8	1.1	48 754	0.3	949	1.9	42 577	33.8	9.8
Rockbridge	7 202	74.9	54 700	18.6	12.1	310	21.6	6.8	10 880	4.1	297	2.7	8 679	20.4	14.4
Rockingham	20 750	78.2	71 800	18.8	12.0	362	20.4	5.3	39 075	4.3	750	1.9	30 026	19.7	15.8
Russell	10 641	80.2	45 000	19.3	12.1	269	26.8	6.3	13 686	-0.2	1 000	7.3	10 414	16.8	21.0
Scott	8 966	77.8	41 400	15.6	11.9	250	25.5	9.9	9 066	0.7	448	4.9	8 550	15.8	16.5
Shenandoah	12 452	71.5	73 600	20.8	12.4	359	23.2	5.8	17 948	2.3	374	2.1	15 622	18.7	17.8
Smyth	12 234	74.3	42 600	16.3	11.9	266	20.9	4.8	15 954	-0.7	1 397	8.8	14 326	18.4	13.8
Southampton	6 009	71.5	57 000	19.1	13.4	265	20.9	12.3	8 319	0.0	219	2.6	7 316	18.7	14.9
Spotsylvania	18 945	81.9	104 000	22.2	12.5	684	24.1	3.4	47 389	1.6	795	1.7	29 479	29.5	15.3
Stafford	19 415	81.9	125 400	24.3	12.5	669	26.8	2.6	49 765	1.8	863	1.7	30 440	32.8	15.3
Surry	2 283	76.5	59 400	19.5	13.5	296	24.7	8.8	2 339	2.6	127	5.4	2 693	17.6	19.9
Sussex	3 795	69.3	48 200	18.2	13.0	293	24.7	10.2	6 099	-1.0	244	4.0	4 571	17.3	11.3
Tazewell	17 309	77.0	48 600	19.2	12.1	298	27.6	4.5	19 675	1.7	864	4.4	16 749	24.6	17.7
Warren	9 879	72.3	85 100	21.1	11.9	407	22.5	3.0	16 043	2.2	451	2.8	12 856	23.5	20.7
Washington	17 483	77.1	52 500	18.8	12.2	299	22.2	4.7	25 132	1.9	1 492	5.9	20 932	22.3	12.9
Westmoreland	6 057	79.3	68 800	19.6	12.7	397	26.3	9.4	7 515	1.6	380	5.1	6 745	24.4	13.0
Wise	14 513	76.4	43 500	18.8	12.5	302	29.7	5.8	14 651	0.0	825	5.6	13 514	23.9	20.1
Wythe	9 852	77.1	48 900	17.6	11.8	272	23.5	5.1	14 982	2.1	1 449	9.7	11 757	20.6	12.8
York	14 474	71.6	121 600	21.9	11.6	513	24.7	2.3	29 289	0.9	644	2.2	18 949	40.7	12.0
Independent Cities															
Alexandria City	53 280	40.5	228 600	22.2	12.0	701	25.4	4.8	79 614	2.5	2 226	2.8	70 756	53.1	4.9
Bedford City	2 475	62.3	55 700	15.6	12.4	251	24.5	1.5	2 878	-1.4	100	3.5	2 504	24.2	10.2
Bristol City	7 591	63.1	48 400	19.3	13.6	317	27.9	1.8	7 667	1.0	309	4.0	7 825	23.0	10.8
Buena Vista City	2 404	72.2	43 300	20.2	13.6	294	20.9	3.6	3 593	4.7	120	3.3	3 006	19.4	12.0
Charlottesville City	16 009	42.4	85 600	20.5	12.4	469	29.7	3.0	18 803	0.4	482	2.6	20 198	38.2	8.4
Chesapeake City	51 965	73.0	88 200	23.9	13.1	494	26.7	2.9	108 360	1.0	3 193	2.9	72 486	30.4	16.1
Clifton Forge City	1 930	62.0	35 200	16.5	12.6	290	29.0	1.5	NA	NA	NA	NA	1 685	22.5	13.5
Colonial Heights City	6 363	72.2	71 000	17.7	12.8	458	23.3	1.1	8 694	1.5	300	3.5	8 063	31.0	13.6
Covington City	2 998	69.2	38 700	17.3	12.9	313	24.2	1.2	3 283	1.4	177	5.4	2 869	19.2	11.0
Danville City	21 712	59.4	47 000	16.4	12.7	278	23.6	3.0	25 689	1.4	2 207	8.6	23 259	21.9	11.5
Emporia City	2 031	56.7	52 000	19.5	14.6	345	24.1	5.6	2 552	3.2	113	4.4	2 270	23.7	10.8
Fairfax City	7 362	65.9	184 300	20.5	11.9	823	27.3	2.5	13 062	1.2	87	0.7	11 890	45.0	8.3
Falls Church City	4 195	58.8	226 000	20.7	12.3	809	27.6	4.1	6 277	2.7	164	2.6	5 660	58.5	4.8
Franklin City	3 006	53.8	67 900	18.9	16.5	324	26.0	5.3	3 896	1.1	175	4.5	3 272	24.3	12.2
Fredericksburg City	7 450	37.3	104 900	20.6	12.4	530	27.2	2.7	10 262	3.0	415	4.0	9 629	32.4	12.6
Galax City	2 750	68.3	45 200	17.3	13.2	264	26.9	4.1	3 173	-0.8	262	8.3	3 236	21.8	11.3
Hampton City	49 673	59.2	78 200	22.4	13.2	470	26.1	2.6	67 271	1.2	2 550	3.8	58 561	30.0	15.1
Harrisonburg City	10 310	42.1	89 300	21.3	11.6	410	25.9	1.3	19 449	4.2	380	2.0	14 735	32.0	8.2
Hopewell City	9 014	56.9	54 300	17.3	12.4	389	24.5	3.1	11 065	2.8	592	5.4	10 372	21.8	15.1
Lexington City	2 172	54.9	74 500	19.7	12.5	355	28.8	1.1	3 185	3.6	52	1.6	2 586	34.2	4.9
Lynchburg City	25 143	58.2	56 900	16.9	12.6	346	24.7	2.2	30 021	-0.7	1 357	4.5	29 569	30.7	8.6

1. Specified owner-occupied units.   2. Specified renter-occupied units.   3. Overcrowded or lacking complete plumbing facilities.   4. Percent of civilian labor force.   5. Persons 16 years and older.

	Private nonfarm establishments, employment and payroll, 1999								Agriculture, 1997			Farm operators
	Employment						Annual payroll		Farms			
										Percent with—		Whose principal occupation is farming (percent)
STATE County	Number of establishments	Total	Health Care and Social Assistance	Manufacturing	Retail trade	Finance and Insurance	Professional Scientific and Technical Services	Total (mil dol)	Average per employee (dollars)	Number	Less than 50 acres	500 acres and over	
	104	105	106	107	108	109	110	111	112	113	114	115	116
VIRGINIA—Cont'd													
Louisa	487	4 072	217	653	572	131	177	130	32 018	385	26.0	10.9	43.4
Lunenburg	203	1 862	102	709	355	77	D	37	19 886	339	20.1	10.0	44.8
Madison	258	2 280	225	522	617	28	59	43	19 075	422	30.6	12.1	46.7
Mathews	205	1 184	98	142	274	D	24	21	17 981	58	50.0	8.6	36.2
Mecklenburg	839	12 000	1 235	4 270	1 961	248	326	231	19 245	604	20.7	14.4	51.7
Middlesex	357	2 181	352	233	415	115	74	40	18 434	67	29.9	19.4	56.7
Montgomery	1 748	22 730	2 019	4 923	4 929	741	1 510	521	22 904	517	32.9	7.4	37.7
Nelson	373	3 193	161	307	274	33	167	51	15 868	357	23.5	8.1	41.2
New Kent	263	1 937	331	157	427	D	59	42	21 709	64	29.7	14.1	42.2
Northampton	324	3 161	812	529	567	53	60	68	21 398	152	30.3	24.3	68.4
Northumberland	333	2 056	57	409	361	70	59	41	20 062	122	26.2	15.6	60.7
Nottoway	352	3 615	324	776	803	111	108	64	17 666	317	15.1	10.1	46.1
Orange	595	6 674	166	2 557	974	91	189	162	24 344	437	28.4	11.2	43.9
Page	463	5 953	516	2 611	704	125	80	111	18 591	541	43.8	4.3	54.0
Patrick	310	4 506	595	2 198	407	95	64	94	20 931	536	32.6	3.4	41.6
Pittsylvania	962	11 478	1 073	4 039	1 835	169	120	260	22 612	1 235	20.4	10.3	50.0
Powhatan	457	4 110	191	133	458	98	175	94	22 879	208	33.7	8.7	43.8
Prince Edward	531	7 351	1 844	656	1 563	220	117	141	19 127	312	17.6	10.9	45.2
Prince George	363	4 517	233	362	632	66	142	105	23 220	133	28.6	16.5	43.6
Prince William	4 451	60 121	5 138	3 278	14 079	1 106	2 878	1 470	24 451	261	47.9	4.6	43.7
Pulaski	672	14 086	1 142	7 214	1 708	175	104	363	25 749	370	31.6	8.9	38.4
Rappahannock	213	1 325	42	D	251	21	82	34	25 824	335	34.6	11.9	43.9
Richmond	227	2 054	359	462	372	75	37	51	24 753	139	27.3	18.7	49.6
Roanoke	1 458	21 459	2 132	2 565	2 361	2 765	539	550	25 645	273	48.7	1.8	42.9
Rockbridge	304	4 406	125	2 211	724	11	40	96	21 823	631	24.1	8.9	41.7
Rockingham	1 159	22 580	1 282	9 927	1 972	239	233	595	26 332	1 834	38.5	3.8	55.8
Russell	575	6 477	799	1 685	882	165	317	153	23 550	1 026	37.0	5.1	43.1
Scott	333	2 996	794	218	792	80	255	56	18 802	1 400	39.5	1.7	35.2
Shenandoah	889	12 320	1 054	5 307	1 949	291	190	277	22 485	841	35.3	5.5	44.2
Smyth	683	12 554	2 030	6 440	1 499	227	205	277	22 040	774	41.7	7.0	38.9
Southampton	281	4 413	219	2 706	348	37	47	155	35 039	277	13.4	41.2	69.3
Spotsylvania	1 375	16 293	1 023	1 853	3 518	358	657	392	24 084	253	34.4	8.7	42.3
Stafford	1 392	17 288	983	1 001	2 306	3 921	664	466	26 954	158	44.3	4.4	45.6
Surry	80	1 476	D	148	59	D	D	70	47 123	115	27.0	28.7	63.5
Sussex	216	3 822	382	1 376	426	56	7	88	22 951	134	19.4	35.8	70.1
Tazewell	1 220	13 354	2 017	1 190	3 118	366	579	269	20 112	488	30.7	13.3	38.7
Warren	758	8 138	757	1 195	1 201	241	155	173	21 248	259	35.5	9.3	37.1
Washington	1 160	14 097	2 273	2 355	2 335	408	493	316	22 449	1 744	51.3	3.6	36.6
Westmoreland	373	2 369	170	621	490	69	88	40	16 977	160	24.4	23.8	56.9
Wise	917	9 303	1 096	494	1 910	259	342	222	23 866	137	53.3	5.8	36.5
Wythe	714	8 831	1 205	2 267	1 948	170	118	181	20 530	734	27.9	9.3	42.8
York	1 181	13 521	683	455	2 554	151	448	249	18 383	39	64.1	2.6	35.9
Independent Cities													
Alexandria City	4 614	77 168	6 176	1 659	8 442	4 585	14 904	2 965	38 425	NA	NA	NA	NA
Bedford City	495	6 003	828	2 123	927	134	114	132	21 980	NA	NA	NA	NA
Bristol City	688	14 967	449	6 450	2 297	347	276	346	23 148	NA	NA	NA	NA
Buena Vista City	119	2 139	182	1 053	222	16	17	46	21 551	NA	NA	NA	NA
Charlottesville City	2 261	41 114	9 289	5 079	4 713	4 253	2 243	1 223	29 749	NA	NA	NA	NA
Chesapeake City	4 450	70 784	5 952	4 394	13 648	1 803	3 786	1 687	23 828	201	53.7	15.4	51.7
Clifton Forge City	134	1 334	275	D	343	66	24	21	15 504	NA	NA	NA	NA
Colonial Heights City	645	10 450	742	919	3 946	248	331	186	17 832	NA	NA	NA	NA
Covington City	265	4 624	96	2 507	722	104	55	157	33 962	NA	NA	NA	NA
Danville City	1 492	26 866	3 983	9 555	4 173	1 044	652	656	24 404	NA	NA	NA	NA
Emporia City	268	4 413	652	1 373	812	77	87	93	21 175	NA	NA	NA	NA
Fairfax City	2 132	35 756	2 219	255	5 883	1 856	13 181	1 499	41 931	NA	NA	NA	NA
Falls Church City	865	14 246	5 133	299	1 941	629	1 515	526	36 946	NA	NA	NA	NA
Franklin City	237	3 124	845	65	911	128	105	59	18 864	NA	NA	NA	NA
Fredericksburg City	1 585	21 426	4 382	1 060	5 106	856	820	522	24 373	NA	NA	NA	NA
Galax City	324	7 872	1 190	4 363	865	120	100	162	20 596	NA	NA	NA	NA
Hampton City	2 467	48 646	6 079	5 497	10 439	1 549	4 019	1 082	22 251	NA	NA	NA	NA
Harrisonburg City	1 483	23 859	3 830	3 727	4 668	693	1 022	540	22 639	NA	NA	NA	NA
Hopewell City	477	8 104	1 465	2 757	776	151	174	268	33 090	NA	NA	NA	NA
Lexington City	446	5 674	685	27	1 019	80	157	95	16 717	NA	NA	NA	NA
Lynchburg City	2 510	54 272	7 935	12 634	7 674	3 640	2 807	1 588	29 253	NA	NA	NA	NA

Table B. States and Counties — **Agriculture, Land, and Water**

STATE County	Land in farms Acreage (1,000) [117]	Land in farms Percent change, 1992–1997 [118]	Acres Average size of farm [119]	Acres Total irrigated (1,000) [120]	Acres Total cropland (1,000) [121]	Value of land and buildings Average per farm ($1,000) [122]	Value of land and buildings Average per acre (dollars) [123]	Value of machinery and equipment average per farm ($1,000) [124]	Value of products sold Total (mil dol) [125]	Value of products sold Average per farm (dollars) [126]	Percent from — Crops [127]	Percent from — Livestock and poultry products [128]	Percent of farms with sales of — $10,000 or more [129]	Percent of farms with sales of — $100,000 or more [130]	Percent of land owned by fed. gov. 1997 [131]	Water consumption 1995 (mil gal/day) [132]
VIRGINIA—Cont'd																
Louisa	79	-2.4	205	0	41	371	2 056	44	10	24 785	25.8	74.2	36.6	6.0	0.0	2 077.5
Lunenburg	78	-9.6	229	1	31	243	1 086	36	16	48 592	57.4	42.6	36.3	7.7	0.1	1.8
Madison	100	-1.0	237	0	55	478	2 348	45	17	39 773	17.6	82.4	43.8	9.0	15.6	1.8
Mathews	8	40.3	145	D	6	301	2 075	43	4	61 471	95.0	5.0	41.4	8.6	0.0	0.8
Mecklenburg	167	-0.7	276	5	83	300	1 197	54	42	69 450	78.1	21.9	49.2	17.1	2.4	10.7
Middlesex	18	-17.0	273	D	15	458	1 680	81	5	77 441	96.7	3.3	50.7	16.4	0.0	1.1
Montgomery	93	-6.0	180	0	44	325	1 764	38	15	28 610	14.9	85.1	36.6	6.6	(1)12.0	24.6
Nelson	73	0.3	205	1	35	330	1 624	27	7	19 172	58.4	41.6	29.7	2.8	5.4	2.8
New Kent	16	-8.9	256	0	12	496	1 935	51	3	45 955	94.8	5.2	46.9	10.9	0.4	40.1
Northampton	56	8.5	371	9	50	731	1 995	98	39	253 929	70.3	29.7	72.4	35.5	0.4	6.4
Northumberland	38	-6.9	313	D	31	475	1 616	104	10	79 056	98.4	1.6	59.8	20.5	0.0	1.2
Nottoway	69	8.1	218	0	36	286	1 456	38	22	69 579	15.4	84.6	37.5	11.7	12.5	3.2
Orange	101	-6.1	232	0	56	557	2 364	45	26	59 205	39.2	60.8	38.2	8.0	0.3	3.4
Page	68	4.4	125	0	39	335	2 660	44	115	212 955	2.0	98.0	56.9	29.6	32.1	4.6
Patrick	74	-6.1	138	0	36	201	1 710	38	13	24 837	51.8	48.2	28.9	3.9	2.4	2.4
Pittsylvania	267	-10.1	216	7	124	280	1 273	47	59	47 663	75.0	25.0	43.2	13.0	(2)0.0	10.6
Powhatan	43	0.2	207	0	19	445	2 280	35	7	33 014	21.2	78.8	33.2	7.7	0.0	1.7
Prince Edward	73	5.7	234	0	35	283	1 232	31	14	43 336	13.7	86.3	34.3	8.0	0.0	2.8
Prince George	45	-8.2	338	D	21	504	1 373	53	6	43 828	88.0	12.0	42.1	9.8	(3)6.4	22.1
Prince William	36	8.9	138	1	26	568	4 372	43	10	37 290	50.2	49.8	24.9	6.1	(4)17.9	330.1
Pulaski	80	11.7	217	D	40	341	1 414	41	13	35 062	7.5	92.5	38.1	7.0	14.1	8.7
Rappahannock	72	-8.7	215	0	36	728	3 183	38	6	16 535	35.4	64.6	31.9	3.6	18.2	0.9
Richmond	36	-6.8	262	0	26	368	1 395	72	9	63 921	94.5	5.5	56.1	16.5	0.7	2.1
Roanoke	27	6.8	98	0	12	243	2 491	26	5	18 470	51.2	48.8	24.9	4.0	(5)3.6	8.1
Rockbridge	140	-1.3	222	0	64	394	1 911	30	15	24 478	10.8	89.2	37.1	4.9	(6)20.1	7.2
Rockingham	230	-2.4	126	3	145	383	3 069	47	438	238 879	2.7	97.3	61.0	38.2	(7)35.9	29.1
Russell	153	-4.9	149	0	62	189	1 184	26	19	18 128	31.0	69.0	40.9	2.8	0.2	15.7
Scott	138	2.6	98	0	54	119	1 071	28	14	10 147	58.3	41.7	26.2	1.0	12.6	2.7
Shenandoah	127	1.5	151	1	73	371	2 365	32	73	86 853	10.2	89.8	40.5	13.1	23.7	6.9
Smyth	125	4.3	162	0	57	196	1 232	29	20	25 295	18.1	81.9	39.5	5.3	30.8	5.7
Southampton	185	4.2	670	2	103	1 030	1 594	123	55	198 881	76.3	23.7	75.5	44.8	(8)0.0	25.4
Spotsylvania	48	-9.5	190	D	24	526	2 473	39	6	23 988	36.7	63.3	37.2	4.0	(9)2.0	8.0
Stafford	20	-0.5	126	0	11	435	4 413	44	2	12 928	60.1	39.9	21.5	2.5	18.1	10.8
Surry	45	-15.3	390	2	32	606	1 583	94	20	169 878	44.5	55.5	56.5	27.8	0.1	1.3
Sussex	82	-1.8	608	2	45	787	1 284	84	D	D	D	D	61.9	34.3	0.0	1.6
Tazewell	134	-3.9	274	0	50	304	1 015	30	13	26 715	6.1	93.9	38.7	6.4	2.9	6.8
Warren	45	14.8	173	0	23	428	2 808	40	6	21 386	10.8	89.2	27.0	3.5	17.3	8.3
Washington	178	-6.1	102	0	91	213	2 110	30	51	29 134	25.5	74.5	34.8	3.6	(10)8.8	12.5
Westmoreland	63	11.9	392	2	42	640	1 677	99	20	123 397	93.9	6.1	57.5	21.2	0.3	2.6
Wise	16	24.3	118	D	7	223	1 790	25	1	9 228	30.5	69.5	22.6	0.7	(11)18.2	8.3
Wythe	140	6.5	190	0	78	263	1 469	36	24	33 263	7.1	92.9	40.2	7.4	21.5	5.0
York	2	-1.2	51	0	1	577	D	D	2	58 822	D	D	30.8	10.3	(12)11.3	25.2
Independent Cities																
Alexandria City	NA	NA	NA	NA	NA	NA	NA	NA	NA	NA	NA	NA	NA	NA	(13)NA	282.1
Bedford City	NA	NA	NA	NA	NA	NA	NA	NA	NA	NA	NA	NA	NA	NA	(14)NA	0.0
Bristol City	NA	NA	NA	NA	NA	NA	NA	NA	NA	NA	NA	NA	NA	NA	(10)NA	0.0
Buena Vista City	NA	NA	NA	NA	NA	NA	NA	NA	NA	NA	NA	NA	NA	NA	(6)NA	0.4
Charlottesville City	NA	NA	NA	NA	NA	NA	NA	NA	NA	NA	NA	NA	NA	NA	(15)NA	0.0
Chesapeake City	61	12.3	302	1	51	676	2 205	66	36	180 665	90.3	9.7	49.8	20.9	22.9	12.0
Clifton Forge City	NA	NA	NA	NA	NA	NA	NA	NA	NA	NA	NA	NA	NA	NA	(16)NA	0.0
Colonial Heights City	NA	NA	NA	NA	NA	NA	NA	NA	NA	NA	NA	NA	NA	NA	(17)NA	0.0
Covington City	NA	NA	NA	NA	NA	NA	NA	NA	NA	NA	NA	NA	NA	NA	(16)NA	3.4
Danville City	NA	NA	NA	NA	NA	NA	NA	NA	NA	NA	NA	NA	NA	NA	(2)NA	18.9
Emporia City	NA	NA	NA	NA	NA	NA	NA	NA	NA	NA	NA	NA	NA	NA	(18)NA	1.4
Fairfax City	NA	NA	NA	NA	NA	NA	NA	NA	NA	NA	NA	NA	NA	NA	(13)NA	0.1
Falls Church City	NA	NA	NA	NA	NA	NA	NA	NA	NA	NA	NA	NA	NA	NA	(13)NA	0.0
Franklin City	NA	NA	NA	NA	NA	NA	NA	NA	NA	NA	NA	NA	NA	NA	(8)NA	1.2
Fredericksburg City	NA	NA	NA	NA	NA	NA	NA	NA	NA	NA	NA	NA	NA	NA	(9)NA	4.2
Galax City	NA	NA	NA	NA	NA	NA	NA	NA	NA	NA	NA	NA	NA	NA	(19)NA	2.6
Hampton City	NA	NA	NA	NA	NA	NA	NA	NA	NA	NA	NA	NA	NA	NA	(12)NA	1.6
Harrisonburg City	NA	NA	NA	NA	NA	NA	NA	NA	NA	NA	NA	NA	NA	NA	(7)NA	
Hopewell City	NA	NA	NA	NA	NA	NA	NA	NA	NA	NA	NA	NA	NA	NA	(3)NA	156.0
Lexington City	NA	NA	NA	NA	NA	NA	NA	NA	NA	NA	NA	NA	NA	NA	(6)NA	0.0
Lynchburg City	NA	NA	NA	NA	NA	NA	NA	NA	NA	NA	NA	NA	NA	NA	0.0	1.4

1. Radford included with Montgomery County.   2. Danville included with Pittsylvania County.   3. Hopewell and Petersburg included with Prince George County.   4. Manassas and Manassas Park included with Prince William County.   5. Roanoke City and Salem included with Roanoke County.   6. Buena Vista and Lexington included with Rockbridge County.   7. Harrisonburg included with Rockingham County.   8. Franklin included with Southhampton County.   9. Fredericksburg included with Spotsylvania County.   10. Bristol included with Washington County.   11. Norton included with Wise County.   12. Hampton, Newport News, and Poquoson included with York County.   13. Arlington County, Alexandria City, Fairfax, and falls Church City included with Fairfax County.   14. Bedford City included with Bedford County.   15. Charlottesville included with Albemarle County.   16. Clifton Forge and Covington included with Alleghany County.   17. Colonial Heights included with Chesterfield County.   18. Emporia included with Greensville County.   19. Galax included with Carroll County.

Table B. States and Counties — Residential Construction, Wholesale and Retail Trade, and Real Estate

STATE County	Value of Residential Construction Authorized by Building Permits, 2000		Wholesale Trade, 1997				Retail Trade[1], 1997				Real Estate and Rental and Leasing, 1997			
	New Construction ($1,000)	Number of Housing Units	Number of Establishments	Number of Employees	Sales (mil dol)	Annual Payroll (mil dol)	Number of Establishments	Number of Employees	Sales (mil dol)	Annual Payroll (mil dol)	Number of Establishments	Number of Employees	Receipts (mil dol)	Annual Payroll (mil dol)
	133	134	135	136	137	138	139	140	141	142	143	144	145	146
VIRGINIA—Cont'd														
Louisa	27 136	262	14	105	29.1	2.9	73	530	77.7	7.4	12	24	2.7	0.3
Lunenburg	1 764	18	11	55	25.9	1.3	56	368	39.7	4.9	2	D	D	D
Madison	11 728	106	9	30	7.6	0.6	48	418	86.9	7.4	4	6	0.3	0.1
Mathews	6 808	45	9	D	D	D	42	287	33.5	3.6	6	13	1.2	0.2
Mecklenburg	16 862	186	38	230	71.1	4.9	200	2 109	272.5	26.3	25	78	6.6	1.3
Middlesex	11 038	74	17	121	26.2	2.7	53	358	48.4	5.4	21	95	3.7	0.8
Montgomery	36 079	330	39	581	169.8	16.6	355	4 976	749.7	74.4	70	497	53.1	10.5
Nelson	17 629	112	7	13	6.1	0.3	51	225	27.6	2.6	11	76	5.9	2.2
New Kent	18 427	157	9	D	D	D	39	412	53.7	4.9	5	11	0.7	0.1
Northampton	10 720	109	22	D	D	D	79	594	73.0	7.5	6	D	D	D
Northumberland	19 907	124	13	D	D	D	54	338	42.4	5.0	10	51	3.2	0.8
Nottoway	4 843	51	14	D	D	D	80	676	86.3	8.8	4	9	0.4	0.2
Orange	31 264	247	23	163	68.4	4.1	104	946	160.1	15.8	20	44	3.1	0.5
Page	6 436	80	13	49	4.5	0.7	83	645	97.2	8.9	8	27	1.9	0.5
Patrick	9 186	87	11	194	24.5	3.7	59	432	66.1	6.1	10	16	1.4	0.2
Pittsylvania	25 544	269	46	D	D	D	213	2 170	300.5	27.9	23	91	11.1	1.8
Powhatan	30 481	260	21	D	D	D	55	391	78.8	7.3	11	45	2.1	0.4
Prince Edward	6 855	67	20	143	30.9	3.4	125	1 703	267.4	24.4	19	80	5.3	1.3
Prince George	20 467	181	16	189	62.4	5.8	66	632	91.8	8.4	14	30	2.8	0.5
Prince William	445 644	4 758	150	1 736	1 191.2	61.7	915	13 936	2 563.1	240.5	160	767	84.0	15.5
Pulaski	13 980	145	21	299	152.0	7.9	133	1 541	250.9	21.6	22	63	4.5	1.0
Rappahannock	4 691	44	6	D	D	D	33	244	49.0	4.3	5	11	1.3	0.2
Richmond	4 441	38	17	89	18.7	2.2	49	460	62.6	5.8	7	25	1.1	0.3
Roanoke	29 167	580	95	796	399.4	24.5	202	2 559	461.8	41.7	52	231	25.2	3.7
Rockbridge	18 245	219	10	D	D	D	79	961	165.3	13.9	11	19	1.8	0.2
Rockingham	54 384	438	57	1 140	539.7	30.6	242	2 075	356.2	35.4	34	452	65.5	12.3
Russell	4 437	58	15	98	93.9	2.6	102	910	154.2	14.5	11	29	3.1	0.7
Scott	4 564	67	11	D	D	D	91	788	143.0	11.0	11	44	11.0	1.1
Shenandoah	23 302	270	24	241	85.9	4.9	158	1 574	279.3	23.6	24	98	16.0	1.3
Smyth	7 265	71	25	237	65.7	6.8	170	1 560	232.1	20.8	16	78	4.3	1.1
Southampton	6 311	68	17	D	D	D	56	378	41.3	4.6	10	19	1.0	0.2
Spotsylvania	208 574	1 460	67	821	686.0	19.5	261	4 038	737.6	66.6	52	455	33.4	7.9
Stafford	188 937	1 694	47	D	D	D	202	2 336	413.5	39.7	42	193	19.8	3.2
Surry	3 048	53	3	52	8.6	0.8	17	84	8.9	1.0	NA	NA	NA	NA
Sussex	1 100	13	14	106	30.7	2.1	47	358	71.5	5.6	5	16	1.9	0.5
Tazewell	8 841	94	81	781	215.1	15.8	267	3 193	565.5	47.2	72	199	29.9	3.4
Warren	22 512	201	18	D	D	D	142	1 354	199.7	19.6	20	44	4.6	0.8
Washington	19 677	294	51	1 125	847.5	29.3	253	2 609	408.9	40.8	41	159	11.9	2.7
Westmoreland	6 389	58	17	64	35.9	1.6	71	546	83.4	8.0	9	18	1.9	0.3
Wise	3 818	49	46	354	177.5	9.7	183	1 961	310.9	28.3	25	89	5.4	1.3
Wythe	10 054	108	21	184	73.0	4.9	204	1 933	346.1	27.2	16	30	3.5	0.5
York	77 143	783	45	415	137.9	10.5	255	2 681	326.9	32.6	41	158	20.8	2.7
Independent Cities														
Alexandria City	109 267	1 100	137	1 830	899.6	75.1	593	7 746	1 507.6	160.0	202	2 023	354.1	57.9
Bedford City	1 417	15	19	D	D	D	81	975	136.3	13.5	15	34	2.2	0.5
Bristol City	2 821	37	40	D	D	D	155	2 266	331.7	29.2	23	104	11.4	2.2
Buena Vista City	1 295	20	2	D	D	D	32	257	33.2	3.5	6	12	0.8	0.1
Charlottesville City	5 331	64	81	954	265.9	29.7	360	4 345	730.3	73.2	97	458	50.1	9.8
Chesapeake City	125 057	1 081	246	3 833	1 768.2	115.7	779	12 554	1 993.3	184.5	144	704	98.0	15.9
Clifton Forge City	65	1	2	D	D	D	34	321	47.4	4.6	4	7	0.6	0.1
Colonial Heights City	4 844	41	12	D	D	D	205	3 776	496.4	46.5	35	146	15.4	2.8
Covington City	150	3	9	44	15.3	1.1	61	539	90.4	7.9	13	27	1.7	0.3
Danville City	6 473	89	55	964	211.8	22.6	334	3 787	585.5	56.9	59	242	18.1	3.5
Emporia City	2 140	58	8	D	D	D	81	714	97.3	9.7	9	28	2.5	0.4
Fairfax City	17 915	166	48	519	515.2	22.3	305	5 870	1 288.0	115.5	68	345	48.3	9.4
Falls Church City	187	1	22	D	D	D	120	1 536	355.6	34.7	38	137	20.4	3.7
Franklin City	808	6	7	121	48.9	2.3	57	635	95.0	9.3	10	39	3.4	0.6
Fredericksburg City	4 520	41	53	723	427.3	23.3	317	3 701	567.3	60.7	57	297	43.2	6.5
Galax City	1 322	15	6	42	6.0	1.0	71	906	134.6	12.6	10	22	2.0	0.4
Hampton City	21 041	324	94	1 073	370.7	31.3	514	9 930	1 638.9	150.5	113	1 241	89.2	20.6
Harrisonburg City	13 343	193	62	971	749.2	25.5	308	4 161	690.8	64.0	48	263	30.8	5.5
Hopewell City	4 931	66	18	268	92.7	9.5	83	754	100.9	10.6	28	121	10.7	1.8
Lexington City	1 562	17	5	27	16.9	1.4	68	686	108.9	9.6	20	62	7.4	1.1
Lynchburg City	35 314	364	100	1 292	504.6	43.8	446	7 209	1 228.5	115.8	95	390	37.4	8.2

1. Establishments with payroll.

Table B. States and Counties — **Professional, Manufacturing, and Accommodation and Foodservices**

STATE County	Professional, Scientific, and Technical Services[1], 1997				Manufacturing, 1997				Accommodation and Foodservices, 1997			
	Number of Establishments	Number of Employees	Receipts (mil dol)	Annual Payroll (mil dol)	Number of Establishments	Number of Employees	Receipts (mil dol)	Annual Payroll (mil dol)	Number of Establishments	Number of Employees	Sales (mil dol)	Annual Payroll (mil dol)
	147	148	149	150	151	152	153	154	155	156	157	158
VIRGINIA—Cont'd												
Louisa	33	89	5.7	2.4	29	633	89.3	16.4	20	320	8.9	2.6
Lunenburg	7	27	1.1	0.6	16	900	76.3	16.2	5	41	1.0	0.3
Madison	18	32	1.5	0.5	NA	NA	NA	NA	12	126	5.7	1.7
Mathews	9	21	0.9	0.4	NA	NA	NA	NA	8	D	D	D
Mecklenburg	30	218	7.4	3.0	41	4 589	859.1	102.7	66	1 086	29.1	8.3
Middlesex	21	59	3.7	1.4	NA	NA	NA	NA	22	265	8.8	2.3
Montgomery	150	1 231	115.3	41.9	68	4 836	699.1	153.9	150	3 446	96.1	26.1
Nelson	25	81	5.0	2.2	14	621	41.2	8.7	21	708	23.6	8.3
New Kent	20	34	2.3	0.9	NA	NA	NA	NA	14	121	4.8	1.5
Northampton	14	39	1.6	0.4	NA	NA	NA	NA	29	408	15.6	4.0
Northumberland	11	30	1.7	0.7	19	575	59.6	12.9	16	115	3.1	1.1
Nottoway	15	69	2.2	0.8	18	681	139.9	11.3	29	391	9.7	2.5
Orange	42	145	9.7	3.8	35	2 529	445.6	68.8	34	478	14.6	3.9
Page	20	65	3.1	1.0	16	2 883	461.8	47.5	49	543	21.9	5.8
Patrick	10	37	1.4	0.5	38	2 610	249.7	55.7	22	D	D	D
Pittsylvania	26	182	4.1	1.2	59	D	D	D	56	608	19.7	5.6
Powhatan	30	55	3.8	1.6	NA	NA	NA	NA	9	124	3.9	0.9
Prince Edward	23	83	3.8	1.7	18	D	D	D	44	1 056	27.9	7.6
Prince George	36	277	31.7	13.1	NA	NA	NA	NA	27	674	20.9	5.2
Prince William	403	2 322	189.6	81.8	109	2 974	378.1	115.9	364	7 882	266.0	72.6
Pulaski	30	91	5.7	1.8	41	6 509	1 655.8	169.6	54	749	21.5	5.4
Rappahannock	18	58	6.4	2.3	NA	NA	NA	NA	13	206	8.7	2.9
Richmond	13	30	1.6	0.7	NA	NA	NA	NA	11	D	D	D
Roanoke	117	461	34.2	14.9	64	3 450	598.7	107.6	89	1 302	43.6	12.4
Rockbridge	14	31	2.0	0.7	24	2 090	335.4	50.0	44	525	19.9	5.7
Rockingham	46	214	13.5	5.4	74	9 272	4 112.5	269.7	79	1 706	54.2	14.4
Russell	28	339	9.1	4.6	26	1 614	129.2	28.8	29	339	9.7	2.7
Scott	20	D	D	D	NA	NA	NA	NA	18	D	D	D
Shenandoah	47	176	6.2	2.4	47	5 436	840.5	139.4	72	1 160	30.7	9.3
Smyth	34	165	11.2	4.6	53	4 913	692.6	109.2	47	526	16.5	4.4
Southampton	14	39	3.3	0.9	16	2 874	710.0	131.1	13	147	4.1	1.2
Spotsylvania	80	569	55.7	15.7	40	1 698	304.9	60.4	89	1 741	61.9	16.8
Stafford	96	351	37.9	12.8	47	711	99.2	17.2	95	1 809	57.3	14.9
Surry	5	14	1.0	0.3	NA	NA	NA	NA	5	D	D	D
Sussex	5	7	0.4	0.1	9	1 138	283.5	26.5	14	236	6.8	2.0
Tazewell	64	517	44.7	14.8	58	1 517	161.2	30.6	66	1 091	32.5	8.7
Warren	52	232	28.2	12.1	27	1 540	511.0	37.7	61	763	25.6	7.0
Washington	81	395	26.7	11.1	65	2 031	315.8	53.2	84	1 680	48.5	14.3
Westmoreland	28	73	5.3	1.6	16	694	124.6	13.5	37	253	9.7	2.6
Wise	53	299	18.5	8.6	24	556	64.2	10.1	49	688	20.5	5.6
Wythe	31	159	8.4	3.1	45	2 129	276.9	51.6	65	1 275	38.4	10.1
York	76	241	15.0	5.9	28	D	D	D	93	2 303	77.9	20.7
Independent Cities												
Alexandria City	894	12 710	1 456.2	634.2	114	1 907	328.1	59.4	310	6 616	308.3	92.3
Bedford City	38	114	6.9	2.4	30	2 278	254.3	62.2	24	D	D	D
Bristol City	54	D	D	D	41	6 954	1 222.9	184.4	52	D	D	D
Buena Vista City	8	19	0.6	0.2	10	D	D	D	11	162	4.4	1.4
Charlottesville City	206	1 448	118.7	49.7	67	D	D	D	179	3 521	121.5	34.7
Chesapeake City	263	2 653	198.1	84.5	132	4 558	1 085.0	147.0	305	6 321	187.4	51.6
Clifton Forge City	6	23	0.5	0.1	NA	NA	NA	NA	12	D	D	D
Colonial Heights City	35	219	8.3	3.5	14	838	215.4	20.4	63	1 431	40.8	10.9
Covington City	13	39	2.8	0.9	11	2 615	1 004.9	113.4	16	209	6.7	1.8
Danville City	76	577	27.3	11.6	47	D	D	D	114	2 159	65.7	18.8
Emporia City	13	49	3.1	1.2	13	1 055	158.7	29.0	24	490	16.2	4.4
Fairfax City	504	4 979	887.1	240.3	NA	NA	NA	NA	150	3 029	108.0	29.4
Falls Church City	127	1 600	157.7	68.0	NA	NA	NA	NA	68	D	D	D
Franklin City	12	79	2.6	1.1	NA	NA	NA	NA	18	321	10.1	2.5
Fredericksburg City	134	658	44.7	17.4	41	1 059	240.7	28.6	141	2 748	92.0	24.4
Galax City	13	62	3.3	1.2	24	4 460	380.2	86.8	28	D	D	D
Hampton City	211	3 190	270.9	120.4	80	4 636	971.0	123.4	229	5 002	149.9	41.1
Harrisonburg City	95	618	50.9	19.6	38	3 687	725.8	102.6	109	2 318	70.2	19.0
Hopewell City	25	153	11.5	5.4	19	2 907	1 328.1	147.4	46	D	D	D
Lexington City	34	102	5.1	2.1	NA	NA	NA	NA	57	787	27.4	6.9
Lynchburg City	182	2 715	260.3	107.1	117	12 535	3 096.4	481.1	173	3 808	110.8	30.9

1. Firms subject to federal tax.

Table B. States and Counties — Health and Other Services and Federal Funds

	Health Care and Social Assistance[1], 1997				Other Services[1], 1997				Federal funds and grants, fiscal 2001[2]			
									Expenditures (mil dol)			
										Direct payments for individuals[3]		
STATE County	Number of Establishments	Number of Employees	Receipts (mil dol)	Annual Payroll (mil dol)	Number of Establishments	Number of Employees	Receipts (mil dol)	Annual Payroll (mil dol)	Total	Social Security and government retirement	Medicare	Food stamps and Supplemental Security Income
	159	160	161	162	163	164	165	166	167	168	169	170
VIRGINIA—Cont'd												
Louisa	20	277	14.8	5.1	31	97	5.9	1.6	103.9	61.6	19.2	3.4
Lunenburg	5	13	1.1	0.4	18	57	2.3	0.6	54.1	28.2	10.4	3.2
Madison	10	155	4.9	2.3	9	23	2.3	0.5	50.9	26.0	9.9	1.2
Mathews	9	48	1.6	0.4	11	60	3.9	1.2	28.9	38.4	11.7	0.9
Mecklenburg	50	330	20.1	10.4	74	238	12.7	2.7	201.2	88.4	32.9	6.3
Middlesex	12	140	5.4	2.8	14	41	2.2	0.5	60.1	37.0	10.8	1.4
Montgomery	122	1 973	115.9	47.3	116	655	32.5	10.7	391.1	125.5	37.9	7.7
Nelson	13	131	7.1	2.5	13	30	2.3	0.6	86.3	45.6	13.9	2.0
New Kent	10	315	17.4	9.0	13	22	1.4	0.3	60.3	33.5	9.2	0.5
Northampton	26	286	17.0	7.8	16	49	2.5	0.6	209.6	36.3	13.3	4.0
Northumberland	8	68	3.1	1.3	29	108	6.8	1.8	78.5	49.2	14.7	1.4
Nottoway	17	316	10.8	4.2	36	87	5.8	1.5	123.7	45.7	15.6	3.3
Orange	31	240	17.3	5.6	38	147	10.0	2.4	143.6	95.1	24.6	3.1
Page	26	285	13.2	5.1	36	78	4.6	1.3	145.5	58.8	19.8	2.7
Patrick	21	300	10.6	5.4	16	56	3.8	0.9	83.7	44.9	14.6	3.0
Pittsylvania	46	472	30.8	13.8	81	293	14.2	4.0	243.0	104.5	36.7	9.2
Powhatan	13	99	4.2	2.0	15	42	2.9	0.9	56.9	38.4	8.9	1.3
Prince Edward	62	886	33.7	16.1	42	142	6.8	1.9	94.0	47.8	15.6	4.8
Prince George	11	D	D	D	24	103	6.0	2.2	440.8	59.2	9.1	1.7
Prince William	321	3 036	176.6	85.9	341	2 085	127.7	44.7	1 446.5	508.5	45.6	17.6
Pulaski	55	888	50.5	21.2	45	221	11.2	3.3	169.9	86.7	36.3	6.3
Rappahannock	4	15	1.0	0.2	9	25	2.4	0.5	39.1	24.4	6.6	0.6
Richmond	6	282	9.0	4.1	9	27	2.4	0.8	84.7	22.4	10.0	1.3
Roanoke	102	868	59.2	30.1	90	573	28.9	10.8	157.6	103.9	25.5	7.0
Rockbridge	14	156	5.5	2.9	16	54	3.9	1.0	73.8	34.9	10.1	1.8
Rockingham	51	375	20.7	10.6	95	483	33.1	9.6	197.1	117.8	37.0	5.1
Russell	39	650	28.8	12.8	32	136	6.7	2.3	164.3	79.7	33.9	11.6
Scott	24	506	29.7	10.5	20	88	3.4	1.2	147.4	63.4	27.0	8.8
Shenandoah	62	486	18.3	8.6	62	209	11.5	3.4	155.9	101.1	26.8	3.1
Smyth	48	448	25.6	13.1	45	185	12.6	2.8	207.5	86.8	30.4	7.4
Southampton	18	182	9.3	4.7	22	83	7.9	2.2	80.2	32.0	14.7	2.9
Spotsylvania	67	886	37.2	16.8	108	526	32.5	10.1	171.9	132.3	16.2	4.6
Stafford	89	982	47.1	21.2	120	581	35.1	10.3	232.3	172.2	19.0	3.1
Surry	4	20	1.5	0.7	2	D	D	D	30.5	15.2	5.5	0.8
Sussex	7	247	6.2	3.2	16	57	4.7	0.9	69.3	29.3	14.1	3.3
Tazewell	113	1 454	107.8	40.6	93	709	44.1	13.2	287.3	161.6	55.1	15.2
Warren	46	414	19.8	8.2	52	404	23.8	7.3	120.6	72.5	18.6	3.4
Washington	90	971	49.9	26.7	75	304	15.2	4.7	229.6	113.6	33.6	8.9
Westmoreland	11	63	2.1	1.3	19	62	3.6	0.8	104.3	61.8	20.6	2.6
Wise	58	601	33.1	13.1	72	212	15.2	3.6	326.9	131.7	47.4	16.5
Wythe	42	455	24.0	11.7	46	147	8.0	1.9	144.4	74.9	27.4	6.2
York	53	533	20.9	8.9	98	519	31.9	9.6	377.1	194.5	21.2	3.4
Independent Cities												
Alexandria City	323	2 788	216.5	105.2	267	1 919	122.4	42.9	2 648.1	556.6	119.2	18.5
Bedford City	30	206	10.4	5.0	44	219	14.8	4.4	61.7	42.9	8.9	1.8
Bristol City	26	344	13.6	6.2	44	195	12.0	3.2	147.2	70.0	26.6	6.3
Buena Vista City	5	28	1.5	0.7	9	16	0.9	0.2	35.5	18.6	6.5	1.4
Charlottesville City	162	2 092	138.9	54.6	133	827	41.6	14.5	484.9	101.8	38.3	8.2
Chesapeake City	338	3 228	195.7	87.9	305	2 846	241.4	53.0	902.3	485.0	101.6	19.0
Clifton Forge City	11	216	9.6	4.8	14	49	2.3	0.7	35.6	18.7	9.4	1.5
Colonial Heights City	64	629	39.1	17.1	50	390	19.3	6.7	248.4	72.9	17.5	0.8
Covington City	12	63	3.4	1.7	15	59	5.6	1.1	67.4	39.8	16.1	1.4
Danville City	126	1 459	89.6	42.0	123	735	36.0	10.2	307.8	158.4	56.1	10.6
Emporia City	18	191	13.2	6.1	21	59	2.6	0.7	47.8	22.3	12.9	1.3
Fairfax City	149	1 180	86.4	39.6	126	686	49.5	16.6	2 605.3	285.5	36.2	2.9
Falls Church City	73	915	84.2	35.9	64	323	25.0	8.3	977.8	85.7	34.5	2.8
Franklin City	24	160	13.9	6.8	16	75	4.3	1.2	89.7	37.1	12.9	3.7
Fredericksburg City	140	1 805	132.1	67.2	93	633	37.2	12.3	253.0	151.0	39.0	4.7
Galax City	33	469	24.2	12.0	16	73	4.5	1.3	63.4	36.9	13.8	1.2
Hampton City	192	1 976	106.4	51.9	178	1 129	64.8	20.9	1 913.1	440.8	89.7	23.7
Harrisonburg City	116	1 538	90.7	41.6	84	434	28.1	7.5	118.9	58.9	21.2	3.3
Hopewell City	50	1 444	92.7	40.0	36	409	12.7	4.8	192.0	74.3	22.7	7.4
Lexington City	35	213	11.6	5.0	22	100	3.4	1.1	58.9	36.4	8.0	0.7
Lynchburg City	177	2 893	171.0	86.8	152	933	51.6	15.6	903.0	192.6	63.8	18.5

1. Firms subject to federal tax.   2. October 1, 2000 to September 30, 2001.   3. State totals may include programs not allocated by county.

Table B. States and Counties — Federal Funds and Local Government Finances

STATE County	Federal funds and grants, fiscal 2001[1] (cont'd) — Expenditures (mil dol) (cont'd)							Local government finances, 1997 — General revenue				
	Procurement contract awards			Grants[2]						Taxes		
	Salaries and wages	Defense	Other	Medicaid and other health-related	Nutrition and family welfare	Education	Other	Total (mil dol)	Intergovern-mental (mil dol)	Total (mil dol)	Per capita[3] (dollars) Total	Property
	171	172	173	174	175	176	177	178	179	180	181	182
VIRGINIA—Cont'd												
Louisa	2.7	0.1	0.7	11.1	1.8	1.2	0.5	41.1	12.4	23.8	999	932
Lunenburg	1.4	0.0	0.4	7.4	1.3	0.6	0.1	17.0	10.4	5.4	441	347
Madison	3.6	0.0	0.5	6.1	1.2	0.6	0.4	16.1	8.5	7.0	557	443
Mathews	2.7	-29.3	0.7	2.2	0.5	0.4	0.0	12.3	5.0	6.5	718	617
Mecklenburg	6.5	23.8	1.2	25.5	2.4	1.5	10.0	45.6	26.7	15.2	490	313
Middlesex	1.4	2.7	0.4	2.4	0.6	0.7	1.2	13.2	5.0	7.2	751	611
Montgomery	16.0	28.5	9.7	21.1	3.7	7.2	117.0	110.8	46.1	43.2	569	391
Nelson	3.2	4.4	6.0	9.0	1.0	0.6	0.1	21.0	9.2	10.7	778	631
New Kent	2.1	0.1	1.1	2.5	1.6	0.5	8.0	21.7	10.3	9.7	788	675
Northampton	3.2	67.6	57.2	12.6	2.4	1.7	5.3	70.6	16.1	8.8	689	522
Northumberland	1.7	0.4	0.5	3.4	0.9	0.6	1.9	17.9	7.3	8.7	758	655
Nottoway	19.0	11.8	0.6	8.6	1.7	1.1	15.9	25.7	15.5	7.6	505	347
Orange	3.3	0.0	1.4	10.6	1.6	1.1	0.3	40.3	19.8	18.1	723	589
Page	7.9	14.8	27.7	8.7	1.2	1.1	1.4	34.3	19.9	10.3	451	332
Patrick	2.5	5.4	1.2	8.5	1.0	1.0	1.1	21.5	12.8	7.2	397	276
Pittsylvania	5.6	6.8	7.7	40.3	4.9	2.9	20.3	71.3	44.8	23.2	402	293
Powhatan	3.4	0.0	0.7	2.5	0.4	0.6	0.3	26.3	11.0	14.5	685	470
Prince Edward	4.0	0.2	0.8	10.8	2.0	1.6	0.8	27.3	14.2	10.4	549	305
Prince George	291.7	65.5	3.3	3.3	1.2	3.4	0.1	46.8	25.5	16.1	543	439
Prince William	411.2	284.9	63.6	12.7	7.7	7.9	69.6	589.9	196.7	309.1	1 215	945
Pulaski	4.4	4.4	1.0	13.8	2.6	2.1	6.7	64.6	29.4	19.6	571	396
Rappahannock	2.1	0.2	1.2	3.0	0.2	0.3	0.1	9.6	3.6	5.5	785	656
Richmond	1.4	1.2	5.3	3.7	33.3	0.7	2.1	13.4	7.7	4.7	553	410
Roanoke	2.7	0.6	0.7	7.7	2.1	2.5	2.8	156.7	51.4	86.2	1 060	788
Rockbridge	2.6	2.7	3.9	6.9	1.2	0.9	7.0	30.9	12.5	13.1	676	450
Rockingham	9.8	0.1	0.4	15.1	1.7	2.4	3.3	103.4	45.4	39.5	620	507
Russell	3.7	0.2	0.8	21.0	2.8	2.0	5.2	45.7	25.5	12.2	419	282
Scott	4.6	0.0	0.9	25.0	3.4	1.5	10.2	31.5	20.9	8.2	361	254
Shenandoah	8.0	0.0	2.0	8.7	1.3	1.6	0.3	49.5	19.1	25.5	744	546
Smyth	5.3	9.1	36.4	22.4	3.5	1.7	0.8	49.6	28.3	15.1	458	288
Southampton	2.4	0.9	2.3	12.6	1.9	1.0	1.0	26.7	15.5	9.4	530	474
Spotsylvania	3.0	0.0	1.1	5.8	1.9	2.3	2.4	136.6	52.3	72.3	892	658
Stafford	9.7	9.7	3.4	4.9	2.2	3.3	1.6	150.6	60.4	75.3	858	692
Surry	1.3	0.0	0.3	2.8	0.7	0.4	0.4	17.0	3.8	12.5	1 939	1 884
Sussex	3.4	1.7	0.5	9.1	2.6	0.7	0.9	21.8	9.2	6.4	636	519
Tazewell	7.0	0.1	1.6	21.7	4.9	4.7	4.1	68.3	40.0	22.2	474	324
Warren	9.3	2.3	2.0	6.2	1.4	1.4	2.6	44.6	19.3	20.7	690	534
Washington	6.0	3.4	1.5	30.1	5.6	4.2	15.8	67.9	34.7	26.5	542	351
Westmoreland	3.5	0.0	1.1	5.3	2.2	0.9	1.9	27.1	14.2	10.8	660	571
Wise	7.8	3.9	63.7	27.8	5.1	4.8	8.5	73.8	40.6	25.9	658	328
Wythe	5.7	0.2	1.2	15.3	2.2	2.7	5.0	46.5	24.2	15.7	595	333
York	102.5	18.7	17.2	4.6	2.5	8.9	2.2	107.3	36.9	52.5	919	683
Independent Cities												
Alexandria City	534.0	835.4	363.7	47.3	8.7	27.8	102.2	355.7	75.8	216.4	1 859	1 338
Bedford City	2.0	0.0	1.1	1.7	0.0	0.5	0.1	7.8	1.2	4.4	700	426
Bristol City	15.3	0.0	3.6	14.9	1.6	1.1	1.1	43.7	18.8	17.8	1 028	594
Buena Vista City	1.3	0.0	0.3	4.1	0.5	0.4	1.6	12.0	6.5	4.1	676	477
Charlottesville City	71.3	23.3	17.6	142.3	5.7	6.5	58.4	83.6	26.0	44.3	1 169	732
Chesapeake City	77.9	120.8	13.9	32.9	11.0	9.0	5.4	547.0	163.4	221.5	1 132	780
Clifton Forge City	1.0	0.0	0.2	1.6	0.4	0.5	0.0	2.9	0.4	1.9	440	167
Colonial Heights City	2.4	149.6	0.7	2.4	0.5	0.7	0.4	35.2	9.9	23.4	1 401	771
Covington City	3.4	0.3	0.6	4.0	0.5	0.5	0.0	14.6	4.8	7.5	1 073	736
Danville City	9.7	0.5	2.4	32.5	5.8	5.5	10.7	106.7	50.0	32.2	631	352
Emporia City	1.4	0.0	0.4	7.8	0.3	0.0	0.4	11.2	2.2	6.4	1 159	578
Fairfax City	45.5	973.2	1 181.8	7.7	4.2	10.4	38.3	60.2	6.7	45.3	2 227	1 269
Falls Church City	213.5	305.5	233.4	11.3	0.8	0.5	86.0	34.9	4.4	24.1	2 443	1 643
Franklin City	1.2	0.0	0.3	10.0	2.8	0.9	4.2	19.3	9.5	7.6	866	530
Fredericksburg City	14.5	9.8	11.6	6.8	2.6	0.9	3.8	63.8	16.7	30.3	1 436	799
Galax City	2.6	0.1	0.8	4.9	1.3	0.4	0.1	17.6	9.1	6.8	993	461
Hampton City	725.8	231.5	250.5	28.7	11.6	13.3	58.2	299.8	122.3	125.3	904	608
Harrisonburg City	8.9	0.4	2.2	5.7	1.7	1.6	4.5	58.8	14.9	31.7	945	449
Hopewell City	2.1	33.3	33.9	8.7	3.5	2.0	0.5	69.4	23.9	24.3	1 095	824
Lexington City	5.2	0.3	0.6	4.4	0.4	1.6	0.1	10.7	3.7	4.2	590	374
Lynchburg City	27.0	12.5	506.7	29.2	8.2	3.9	14.2	159.2	55.2	68.6	1 049	1 043

1. October 1, 2000 to September 30, 2001. 2. State totals may include programs not allocated by county. 3. Based on the resident population estimated as of July 1 of the year shown.

Table B. States and Counties — Local Government Finances, Government Employment, and Elections

STATE County	Local govt finances 1997 — Direct general expenditure: Total (mil dol)	Per capita[1] (dollars)	Education	Health and hospitals	Police protection	Public welfare	Highways	Debt outstanding: Total (mil dol)	Per capita[1] (dollars)	Govt employment 1999: Federal civilian	Federal military	State and local	Presidential election 2000[2] Percent of vote cast — Democratic	Republican	All other
	183	184	185	186	187	188	189	190	191	192	193	194	195	196	197
VIRGINIA—Cont'd															
Louisa	39.6	1 660	60.9	2.2	4.3	4.9	0.2	60.5	2 539	46	96	1 163	42.7	54.1	3.2
Lunenburg	15.8	1 297	70.5	1.7	6.0	4.2	1.0	6.7	550	29	45	845	44.1	54.7	1.2
Madison	15.7	1 259	69.4	1.6	4.0	6.5	0.0	4.0	323	86	48	458	36.7	58.5	4.8
Mathews	11.4	1 250	60.0	10.3	5.7	0.2	0.8	1.4	148	31	64	328	32.5	64.0	3.4
Mecklenburg	44.0	1 421	58.7	0.9	7.3	4.5	3.3	12.4	399	142	119	2 274	41.2	56.6	2.2
Middlesex	12.3	1 292	62.1	1.4	4.7	6.0	0.0	0.3	32	23	37	842	35.7	60.7	3.7
Montgomery	111.7	1 469	49.5	2.2	6.2	3.6	2.3	67.5	888	(3)385	(3)402	(3)15 435	43.2	51.5	5.3
Nelson	19.7	1 435	66.4	1.1	4.1	4.7	0.0	6.1	441	57	54	541	47.4	47.5	5.1
New Kent	18.6	1 521	61.5	0.9	6.5	6.3	3.7	9.3	755	33	51	535	33.7	64.5	1.8
Northampton	137.2	10 728	10.2	0.3	0.7	1.5	72.6	267.8	20 940	46	70	1 238	47.8	47.0	5.2
Northumberland	18.3	1 600	50.0	1.0	3.1	5.2	0.1	6.8	591	29	45	439	37.8	60.0	2.1
Nottoway	23.7	1 579	58.4	0.6	7.0	4.3	1.9	8.6	571	349	60	1 928	44.8	52.3	2.9
Orange	40.2	1 610	57.2	0.7	4.9	4.9	2.2	17.3	694	61	99	1 858	39.4	57.2	3.5
Page	32.2	1 410	55.3	1.1	6.2	6.6	2.6	11.4	500	175	89	973	34.1	63.7	2.2
Patrick	22.7	1 253	61.3	1.6	4.1	4.6	0.2	1.7	95	47	71	704	30.5	66.4	3.1
Pittsylvania	79.7	1 384	71.7	1.1	5.4	6.6	0.0	35.9	624	(4)270	(4)412	(4)5 702	32.3	65.0	2.8
Powhatan	27.8	1 310	74.1	0.6	4.9	4.0	0.0	13.1	619	46	86	2 120	27.9	70.3	1.9
Prince Edward	30.3	1 606	51.6	0.6	6.8	4.2	4.4	27.6	1 463	81	74	1 880	45.9	50.5	3.6
Prince George	70.9	2 383	42.5	0.4	3.1	2.1	0.0	112.5	3 781	(5)3 618	(5)5 148	(5)2 509	38.4	60.4	1.2
Prince William	589.9	2 318	51.9	3.0	5.8	3.4	1.9	846.5	3 327	(6)4 377	(6)6 905	(6)14 881	44.5	52.5	2.9
Pulaski	64.7	1 882	43.6	0.7	7.0	3.5	2.2	57.5	1 672	64	132	2 091	41.4	55.8	2.7
Rappahannock	9.9	1 402	61.1	1.3	3.6	6.5	0.3	2.1	298	43	29	293	41.7	52.8	5.5
Richmond	12.2	1 425	58.7	1.7	6.1	5.6	0.0	1.3	156	29	33	842	36.5	60.5	3.0
Roanoke	157.0	1 930	62.0	0.3	5.3	3.1	0.5	256.8	3 158	(7)1 939	(7)403	(7)6 340	37.7	60.1	2.2
Rockbridge	36.1	1 858	48.5	10.7	2.9	4.0	0.7	26.1	1 342	(8)144	(8)164	(8)2 498	37.7	57.8	4.5
Rockingham	109.7	1 721	67.1	0.6	2.8	5.4	1.4	49.8	781	(9)363	(9)381	(9)8 644	24.3	72.9	2.7
Russell	47.0	1 621	54.2	0.8	2.9	5.4	2.1	84.5	2 913	63	110	1 627	50.4	46.9	2.6
Scott	31.0	1 366	67.2	0.7	5.4	6.1	2.6	7.1	315	65	86	1 014	38.1	59.3	2.6
Shenandoah	44.5	1 298	66.7	0.8	6.4	3.6	1.5	39.6	1 155	155	135	1 552	30.6	66.7	2.7
Smyth	55.4	1 683	63.7	1.5	5.7	6.8	3.0	30.9	940	103	125	2 726	41.2	56.0	2.7
Southampton	29.7	1 678	56.5	1.3	3.6	5.7	1.2	18.2	1 032	(10)70	(10)99	(10)2 419	50.0	49.1	0.9
Spotsylvania	136.3	1 681	69.3	0.7	3.0	2.8	0.0	136.5	1 684	(11)305	(11)408	(11)6 527	38.5	59.3	2.3
Stafford	153.3	1 745	68.1	0.5	3.5	3.2	0.2	161.2	1 835	153	2 000	3 858	36.8	60.6	2.5
Surry	15.9	2 469	64.8	2.5	3.8	7.6	0.4	7.2	1 121	16	25	452	57.1	40.7	2.2
Sussex	28.4	2 821	37.9	0.6	6.2	5.2	0.2	21.7	2 149	58	47	1 374	51.4	44.7	3.9
Tazewell	66.8	1 425	62.9	1.2	4.7	5.1	3.1	28.1	600	117	177	3 099	44.2	53.0	2.8
Warren	44.5	1 484	49.4	0.4	7.8	4.5	9.6	34.5	1 150	165	118	1 301	38.6	56.7	4.6
Washington	60.9	1 248	61.4	1.7	5.7	6.0	0.9	29.3	601	(12)407	(12)258	(12)4 119	37.3	59.7	3.0
Westmoreland	26.5	1 626	59.5	1.1	5.7	5.7	0.8	15.0	921	74	62	689	48.5	48.7	2.9
Wise	74.3	1 892	58.3	1.0	4.3	5.8	3.5	26.1	665	(13)273	(13)169	(13)3 654	48.2	48.9	3.0
Wythe	45.3	1 724	50.9	1.3	7.0	7.5	2.6	25.2	959	115	102	2 001	34.0	64.2	1.8
York	121.8	2 133	52.9	0.8	2.4	2.4	0.2	112.4	1 968	(14)1 010	(14)1 878	(14)3 237	35.1	62.3	2.6
Independent Cities															
Alexandria City	344.1	2 956	29.6	6.9	7.9	8.7	6.0	182.9	1 572	7 221	3 676	8 464	61.0	34.6	4.4
Bedford City	8.2	1 295	0.0	1.4	15.7	1.5	12.8	30.2	4 798	(15)	(15)	(15)	44.2	52.0	3.9
Bristol City	44.1	2 552	40.5	0.9	7.2	3.8	5.6	19.2	1 111	(12)	(12)	(12)	42.2	55.7	2.1
Buena Vista City	10.9	1 769	56.4	1.2	6.6	1.6	12.1	5.7	933	(8)	(8)	(8)	47.6	49.6	2.8
Charlottesville City	96.5	2 547	37.9	5.0	7.1	5.6	4.7	52.1	1 374	(16)	(16)	(16)	59.1	30.7	10.1
Chesapeake City	586.2	2 997	42.8	20.7	3.7	1.9	7.1	704.6	3 602	1 272	1 944	12 978	45.1	53.3	1.6
Clifton Forge City	3.5	786	0.0	0.0	21.7	0.0	6.9	0.0	0	(17)	(17)	(17)	56.7	40.0	3.2
Colonial Heights City	33.3	1 997	54.3	0.3	7.1	1.0	3.8	16.7	1 000	(18)	(18)	(18)	27.0	71.0	2.0
Covington City	15.3	2 204	50.4	0.5	7.0	3.7	6.7	11.2	1 605	(17)	(17)	(17)	52.8	43.6	3.6
Danville City	119.6	2 344	38.9	0.5	5.0	4.8	5.4	272.1	5 333	(4)	(4)	(4)	44.9	51.5	3.6
Emporia City	10.1	1 825	25.2	0.0	12.9	2.3	10.9	0.5	87	(19)	(19)	(19)	53.7	45.1	1.2
Fairfax City	54.8	2 692	34.3	0.7	11.5	1.8	12.4	34.0	1 671	(20)	(20)	(20)	45.7	49.9	4.5
Falls Church City	32.7	3 314	49.1	0.4	8.0	3.5	4.7	25.4	2 571	(20)	(20)	(20)	55.7	38.2	6.1
Franklin City	20.8	2 357	51.0	0.8	8.3	4.5	7.9	11.5	1 310	(10)	(10)	(10)	55.2	43.7	1.1
Fredericksburg City	68.9	3 269	23.2	2.7	5.7	4.8	4.8	168.9	8 009	(11)	(11)	(11)	50.4	44.0	5.7
Galax City	13.4	1 948	47.9	1.0	6.9	5.1	11.5	0.0	0	(21)	(21)	(21)	45.0	52.4	2.6
Hampton City	296.8	2 142	45.5	0.0	6.0	4.7	2.4	215.8	1 558	8 055	9 448	8 770	57.4	40.9	1.7
Harrisonburg City	60.0	1 790	38.4	1.7	5.1	0.0	7.9	45.8	1 367	(9)	(9)	(9)	35.0	57.7	7.2
Hopewell City	62.5	2 818	41.7	0.2	5.0	4.8	5.3	66.0	2 976	(5)	(5)	(5)	43.3	53.7	2.9
Lexington City	14.6	2 027	24.8	1.5	6.9	2.9	6.3	20.5	2 843	(8)	(8)	(8)	49.0	44.7	6.2
Lynchburg City	152.7	2 338	37.6	6.2	5.4	1.7	7.9	231.8	3 547	(22)	(22)	(22)	44.2	53.3	2.6

1. Based on the resident population estimated as of July 1 of the year shown. 2. Data subject to copyright. 3. Radford included with Montgomery County. 4. Danville included with Pittsylvania County. 5. Hopewell included with Prince George County. 6. Manassas and Manassas Park included with Prince William County. 7. Salem included with Roanoke County. 8. Buena Vista and Lexington included with Rockbridge County. 9. Harrisonburg included with Rockingham County. 10. Franklin included with Southhampton County. 11. Fredericksburg included with Spotsylvania County. 12. Bristol included with Washington County. 13. Norton included with Wise County. 14. Poquoson included with York County. 15. Bedford City included with Bedford County. 16. Charlottesville included with Albemarle County. 17. Clifton Forge and Covington included with Alleghany County. 18. Petersburg and Colonial Heights included with Dinwiddie County. 19. Emporia included with Greensville County. 20. Fairfax City and Falls Church included with Fairfax County. 21. Galax included with Carroll County. 22. Lynchburg included with Campbell County.

Table B. States and Counties — **Land Area and Population**

					Population and population characteristics, 2000													
								Race alone or in combination (percent)						Age (percent)					
STATE/ County code	MSA/ PMSA/ NECMA code[1]	County Type[2]	STATE County	Land area,[3] (sq km) 2000	Total persons	Rank	Per square kilometer	White	Black	Am. Indian, Alaska Native	Asian and Pacific Islander	Percent Hispanic[4]	Under 5 years	5 to 17 years	18 to 24 years	25 to 34 years	35 to 44 years	45 to 54 years
				1	2	3	4	5	6	7	8	9	10	11	12	13	14	15
			VIRGINIA—Cont'd															
51 683	8840	NA	Manassas City	26	35 135	1 244	1 351.3	74.8	13.9	0.8	4.2	15.1	8.6	21.0	9.8	17.4	18.4	13.1
51 685	8840	NA	Manassas Park City	6	10 290	2 417	1 715.0	75.7	12.0	0.9	5.1	15.0	10.0	21.1	8.7	20.7	19.4	10.2
51 690	...	NA	Martinsville City	28	15 416	2 058	550.6	56.0	43.0	0.4	0.6	2.3	5.6	16.9	7.0	11.5	15.1	13.1
51 700	5720	NA	Newport News City	177	180 150	306	1 017.8	55.4	40.6	1.1	3.4	4.2	7.9	19.6	11.5	15.8	16.4	11.5
51 710	5720	NA	Norfolk City	139	234 403	247	1 686.4	50.1	45.3	1.1	3.9	3.8	7.1	17.0	18.2	15.6	14.3	10.7
51 720	...	NA	Norton City	20	3 904	2 922	195.2	92.4	6.6	0.4	1.3	0.9	5.1	16.6	10.2	13.0	14.3	14.9
51 730	6760	NA	Petersburg City	59	33 740	1 289	571.9	19.1	79.6	0.5	1.0	1.4	6.4	18.7	8.9	13.0	14.5	13.2
51 735	5720	NA	Poquoson City	40	11 566	2 327	289.2	97.2	0.8	0.6	2.0	1.1	5.1	21.7	6.4	9.0	17.7	16.9
51 740	5720	NA	Portsmouth City	86	100 565	522	1 169.4	47.0	51.5	1.1	1.3	1.7	7.1	18.6	11.1	14.0	15.1	12.3
51 750	...	NA	Radford City	25	15 859	2 028	634.4	89.4	8.7	0.6	2.0	1.2	3.5	9.4	44.0	10.8	8.8	8.2
51 760	6760	NA	Richmond City	156	197 790	280	1 267.9	39.2	58.1	0.7	1.7	2.6	6.3	15.5	13.1	16.6	15.1	12.6
51 770	6800	NA	Roanoke City	111	94 911	542	855.1	70.8	27.7	0.7	1.5	1.5	6.5	16.1	8.2	15.2	15.3	13.8
51 775	6800	NA	Salem City	38	24 747	1 566	651.2	92.6	6.2	0.4	1.2	0.8	4.9	16.0	11.7	11.8	15.0	14.0
51 790	...	NA	Staunton City	51	23 853	1 597	467.7	84.6	14.8	0.6	0.9	1.1	5.2	14.6	10.2	13.0	14.8	14.0
51 800	5720	0	Suffolk City	1 036	63 677	763	61.5	54.7	44.1	0.8	1.2	1.3	7.3	20.6	7.1	13.4	17.8	13.4
51 810	5720	0	Virginia Beach City	643	425 257	141	661.4	73.6	20.0	1.0	6.3	4.2	7.2	20.3	10.0	16.4	17.8	12.7
51 820	...	NA	Waynesboro City	40	19 520	1 819	488.0	87.9	10.8	0.8	0.9	3.3	6.6	17.3	7.9	12.9	14.5	12.9
51 830	5720	NA	Williamsburg City	22	11 998	2 294	545.4	80.8	13.8	0.6	5.3	2.5	2.7	6.9	46.0	9.7	8.1	8.0
51 840	...	NA	Winchester City	24	23 585	1 609	982.7	83.9	11.5	0.9	1.9	6.5	6.1	15.6	13.1	14.9	14.9	12.8
53 000	...	X	WASHINGTON	172 348	5 894 121	X	34.2	84.9	4.0	2.7	7.4	7.5	6.7	19.0	9.5	14.3	16.5	14.4
53 001	...	6	Adams	4 986	16 428	1 995	3.3	67.4	0.4	1.3	1.1	47.1	9.4	24.7	9.8	13.2	13.1	11.6
53 003	...	7	Asotin	1 646	20 551	1 758	12.5	97.3	0.4	2.4	0.8	2.0	6.8	18.7	8.1	11.3	14.8	13.5
53 005	6740	3	Benton	4 411	142 475	383	32.3	88.7	1.3	1.6	3.0	12.5	7.6	22.2	8.6	12.5	16.1	14.4
53 007	...	5	Chelan	7 566	66 616	734	8.8	85.6	0.4	1.8	1.3	19.3	7.1	20.8	8.3	12.0	15.2	14.0
53 009	...	5	Clallam	4 505	64 525	753	14.3	91.4	1.1	6.5	2.0	3.4	5.1	16.8	7.1	9.1	13.6	15.1
53 011	6440	1	Clark	1 627	345 238	169	212.2	91.6	2.3	1.8	4.8	4.7	7.8	20.9	8.4	14.1	16.7	14.4
53 013	...	9	Columbia	2 250	4 064	2 915	1.8	95.5	0.3	2.0	0.8	6.3	5.4	18.6	7.0	8.9	13.9	15.7
53 015	...	4	Cowlitz	2 949	92 948	550	31.5	94.3	0.8	3.0	2.1	4.6	6.7	20.1	8.3	12.3	15.2	14.5
53 017	...	7	Douglas	4 715	32 603	1 328	6.9	87.0	0.6	1.9	1.0	19.7	7.6	21.9	8.2	11.5	15.8	13.6
53 019	...	9	Ferry	5 708	7 260	2 658	1.3	78.7	0.4	20.9	0.8	2.8	5.4	21.4	7.6	9.3	14.1	17.3
53 021	6740	3	Franklin	3 218	49 347	926	15.3	65.6	2.9	1.3	2.2	46.7	10.0	24.6	10.9	14.5	13.7	11.4
53 023	...	9	Garfield	1 840	2 397	3 030	1.3	97.5	0.0	1.0	1.0	2.0	4.6	21.4	5.4	7.8	14.1	16.0
53 025	...	5	Grant	6 944	74 698	669	10.8	79.2	1.3	2.0	1.5	30.1	8.7	23.3	9.8	13.1	13.9	11.8
53 027	...	4	Grays Harbor	4 965	67 194	729	13.5	91.2	0.7	6.4	2.1	4.8	6.2	19.4	7.9	11.3	14.7	14.7
53 029	7600	1	Island	540	71 558	690	132.5	90.1	3.0	2.1	6.5	4.0	6.7	18.8	8.5	12.8	15.2	13.5
53 031	...	6	Jefferson	4 699	25 953	1 518	5.5	95.1	0.7	3.8	2.1	2.1	4.1	15.7	5.0	7.6	14.0	18.4
53 033	7600	0	King	5 506	1 737 034	12	315.5	78.9	6.5	1.9	13.4	5.5	6.1	16.4	9.3	17.0	17.8	14.9
53 035	1150	3	Kitsap	1 026	231 969	249	226.1	88.3	3.8	3.2	7.6	4.1	6.7	20.1	9.2	12.9	16.8	15.2
53 037	...	6	Kittitas	5 950	33 362	1 302	5.6	93.5	1.0	1.8	3.1	5.0	5.1	15.5	21.6	11.6	13.0	12.5
53 039	...	7	Klickitat	4 849	19 161	1 838	4.0	90.1	0.5	5.0	1.5	7.8	6.4	20.7	6.5	10.3	15.4	16.1
53 041	...	6	Lewis	6 236	68 600	720	11.0	94.8	0.6	2.2	1.3	5.4	6.4	20.1	8.2	10.8	14.5	14.3
53 043	...	8	Lincoln	5 986	10 184	2 430	1.7	97.1	0.6	2.7	0.5	1.9	5.7	19.5	5.2	8.7	14.5	15.1
53 045	...	6	Mason	2 489	49 405	925	19.8	91.2	1.5	5.4	2.3	4.8	5.4	18.1	7.7	11.1	15.4	14.6
53 047	...	7	Okanogan	13 644	39 564	1 125	2.9	77.9	0.5	13.2	1.0	14.4	6.3	21.4	7.3	10.9	14.6	15.0
53 049	...	7	Pacific	2 416	20 984	1 736	8.7	93.2	0.4	4.2	2.7	5.0	4.6	16.9	6.0	8.4	12.8	15.1
53 051	...	8	Pend Oreille	3 627	11 732	2 314	3.2	95.4	0.4	4.0	1.4	2.1	5.4	20.0	5.5	8.2	15.6	17.1
53 053	8200	2	Pierce	4 348	700 820	71	161.2	82.7	8.6	2.8	8.4	5.5	7.1	20.1	9.8	14.4	16.9	13.5
53 055	...	8	San Juan	453	14 077	2 156	31.1	96.9	0.4	1.7	1.6	2.4	3.7	15.4	4.5	7.3	14.4	20.5
53 057	...	4	Skagit	4 494	102 979	516	22.9	88.7	0.7	2.7	2.3	11.2	6.5	19.8	8.6	12.0	14.9	14.4
53 059	...	8	Skamania	4 290	9 872	2 458	2.3	94.3	0.5	3.5	1.3	4.0	6.4	20.2	6.7	10.7	17.9	16.9
53 061	7600	0	Snohomish	5 411	606 024	90	112.0	88.6	2.3	2.4	7.6	4.7	7.2	20.2	8.5	14.6	18.3	14.3
53 063	7840	2	Spokane	4 568	417 939	144	91.5	93.9	2.2	2.4	2.9	2.8	6.6	19.1	10.6	13.1	15.8	14.2
53 065	...	6	Stevens	6 419	40 066	1 112	6.2	92.6	0.5	7.4	1.3	1.8	6.1	22.6	6.4	9.3	15.6	16.1
53 067	5910	3	Thurston	1 883	207 355	268	110.1	89.0	3.1	2.8	6.7	4.5	6.2	19.1	9.3	13.0	16.3	15.7
53 069	...	9	Wahkiakum	684	3 824	2 927	5.6	95.9	0.3	3.5	1.0	2.6	5.3	18.1	5.3	8.4	13.8	16.5
53 071	...	4	Walla Walla	3 291	55 180	854	16.8	87.7	2.0	1.7	2.1	15.7	6.3	18.3	13.4	12.2	14.2	12.8
53 073	0860	3	Whatcom	5 490	166 814	324	30.4	90.8	1.1	3.8	4.0	5.2	6.1	18.0	14.2	12.8	14.6	14.4
53 075	...	5	Whitman	5 593	40 740	1 091	7.3	90.3	2.0	1.5	7.1	3.0	4.8	13.2	32.6	13.1	10.9	9.6
53 077	9260	3	Yakima	11 127	222 581	255	20.0	68.6	1.4	5.6	1.7	35.9	8.7	23.1	9.8	13.3	14.2	12.0
54 000	...	X	WEST VIRGINIA	62 361	1 808 344	X	29.0	95.9	3.5	0.6	0.7	0.7	5.6	16.6	9.5	12.7	15.1	15.0
54 001	...	7	Barbour	883	15 557	2 050	17.6	98.3	0.8	1.4	0.4	0.5	5.3	17.7	9.4	12.3	14.5	14.4
54 003	8840	3	Berkeley	832	75 905	660	91.2	93.9	5.3	0.6	0.8	1.5	6.6	19.1	8.3	14.6	16.7	14.4
54 005	...	6	Boone	1 303	25 535	1 538	19.6	99.1	1.0	0.4	0.1	0.5	6.3	16.9	9.0	12.8	15.2	16.5

1. MSA = Metropolitan Statistical Area. PMSA = Primary MSA. NECMA = New England County Metropolitan Area. See Appendix A for explanation of these concepts. See Appendix B for list of metropolitan areas identified by type, with component counties. 2. County typology code from the Economic Research Service of USDA. See Appendix A for definition. 3. Dry land or land partially or temporarily covered by water. 4. Hispanic persons may be of any race.

Table B. States and Counties — Population and Households

STATE County	55 to 64 years (16)	65 to 74 years (17)	75 years and over (18)	Percent female (19)	2001 (20)	1990 (21)	1990–2000 (22)	2000–2001 (23)	Births (24)	Deaths (25)	Net migration (26)	Number (27)	Percent change, 1990–2000 (28)	Persons per household (29)	Female family householder[1] (30)	One person (31)
VIRGINIA—Cont'd																
Manassas City	6.3	3.1	2.3	49.1	35 814	27 757	26.6	1.9	841	234	69	11 757	24.0	2.92	11.3	21.1
Manassas Park City	5.7	3.0	1.3	49.1	10 589	6 798	51.4	2.9	252	41	89	3 254	49.1	3.16	12.1	14.4
Martinsville City	10.0	9.7	10.9	54.8	15 311	16 162	-4.6	-0.7	315	327	-94	6 498	-5.0	2.27	19.1	34.2
Newport News City	7.3	5.4	4.7	51.6	180 305	171 477	5.1	0.1	4 359	1 808	-2 323	69 686	9.0	2.50	17.9	27.0
Norfolk City	6.2	5.5	5.4	48.9	233 147	261 250	-10.3	-0.5	5 354	2 693	-3 679	86 210	-3.7	2.45	18.8	30.2
Norton City	10.6	8.1	7.2	55.0	3 886	4 247	-8.1	-0.5	71	71	-17	1 730	1.9	2.23	15.7	34.9
Petersburg City	9.7	8.0	7.6	54.3	33 457	37 071	-9.0	-0.8	813	653	-446	13 799	-6.3	2.38	26.1	32.2
Poquoson City....................	11.8	6.6	4.7	49.9	11 694	11 005	5.1	1.1	124	119	125	4 166	10.5	2.75	8.4	15.9
Portsmouth City	8.0	6.8	6.9	51.7	99 494	103 910	-3.2	-1.1	2 267	1 522	-1 805	38 170	-1.5	2.51	20.9	27.5
Radford City	6.1	4.9	4.4	54.5	15 352	15 940	-0.5	-3.2	182	111	-589	5 809	11.6	2.25	8.9	32.0
Richmond City	7.5	6.5	6.7	53.5	195 966	202 713	-2.4	-0.9	4 141	2 958	-3 059	84 549	-0.9	2.21	20.4	37.6
Roanoke City	8.5	7.8	8.6	53.1	93 889	96 487	-1.6	-1.1	1 773	1 677	-1 133	42 003	2.4	2.20	16.5	35.9
Salem City	10.0	8.8	7.9	52.8	24 635	23 835	3.8	-0.5	324	381	-48	9 954	8.7	2.32	11.5	29.0
Staunton City	10.1	8.9	9.2	52.9	23 875	24 581	-3.0	0.1	318	368	76	9 676	2.6	2.19	11.7	34.7
Suffolk City	9.2	6.3	5.2	52.2	67 107	52 143	22.1	5.4	1 256	875	2 982	23 283	25.7	2.69	16.8	20.2
Virginia Beach City	7.1	4.9	3.6	50.5	426 931	393 089	8.2	0.4	8 182	3 063	-3 201	154 455	13.9	2.70	12.4	20.4
Waynesboro City	10.3	8.9	8.7	53.2	19 918	18 549	5.2	2.0	371	265	294	8 332	10.1	2.31	14.5	30.1
Williamsburg City	7.0	5.9	5.8	55.1	12 102	11 600	3.4	0.9	147	192	146	3 619	4.4	2.07	9.6	35.9
Winchester City	8.1	7.7	6.8	51.5	24 141	21 947	7.5	2.4	421	340	475	10 001	10.1	2.28	11.7	34.4
WASHINGTON	8.4	5.7	5.5	50.2	5 987 973	4 866 669	21.1	1.6	99 727	55 046	49 721	2 271 398	21.3	2.53	9.9	26.2
Adams	7.8	5.7	4.7	48.9	16 286	13 603	20.8	-0.9	395	156	-396	5 229	14.0	3.09	10.1	18.7
Asotin	10.5	8.0	8.3	52.3	20 560	17 605	16.7	0.0	343	297	-28	8 364	19.4	2.42	11.9	27.0
Benton	8.5	5.5	4.8	50.3	146 634	112 560	26.6	2.9	2 590	1 127	2 696	52 866	25.2	2.68	10.2	23.2
Chelan	8.7	6.9	6.9	50.2	67 133	52 250	27.5	0.8	1 243	715	2	25 021	21.2	2.62	8.7	25.1
Clallam	11.8	10.8	10.5	50.3	65 759	56 210	14.8	1.9	807	1 035	1 450	27 164	18.9	2.31	9.0	28.1
Clark	8.2	5.0	4.5	50.4	360 760	238 053	45.0	4.5	6 323	2 765	11 780	127 208	43.8	2.69	10.3	21.8
Columbia	12.0	9.2	9.3	51.2	4 113	4 024	1.0	1.2	51	75	72	1 687	6.6	2.36	8.5	29.0
Cowlitz	9.6	6.8	6.5	50.5	93 716	82 119	13.2	0.8	1 530	1 116	390	35 850	13.3	2.55	10.7	24.3
Douglas	8.8	6.8	5.9	50.4	32 967	26 205	24.4	1.1	531	290	128	11 726	21.0	2.76	9.7	20.0
Ferry	12.2	7.7	4.9	48.2	7 296	6 295	15.3	0.5	100	79	16	2 823	25.6	2.49	10.2	24.8
Franklin	6.5	4.7	3.8	47.8	51 015	37 473	31.7	3.4	1 291	380	772	14 840	21.7	3.26	11.4	17.8
Garfield	9.8	10.2	10.7	50.5	2 342	2 248	6.6	-2.3	28	36	-47	987	7.0	2.39	6.7	28.3
Grant	7.8	6.3	5.3	48.9	76 221	54 798	36.3	2.0	1 631	670	591	25 204	27.6	2.92	9.8	21.2
Grays Harbor	10.3	8.0	7.4	50.3	68 331	64 175	4.7	1.7	1 077	905	964	26 808	5.1	2.48	11.1	26.7
Island	10.2	7.7	6.5	49.9	74 114	60 195	18.9	3.6	1 112	686	2 151	27 784	27.5	2.52	7.8	21.5
Jefferson	14.1	11.7	9.4	51.1	26 584	20 406	27.2	2.4	240	367	749	11 645	35.0	2.21	8.2	28.5
King	8.1	5.1	5.3	50.2	1 741 785	1 507 305	15.2	0.3	28 254	14 897	-8 394	710 916	15.4	2.39	9.0	30.5
Kitsap	8.6	5.4	5.2	49.3	233 372	189 731	22.3	0.6	3 670	2 173	55	86 416	24.8	2.60	9.5	22.6
Kittitas	9.0	5.9	5.7	50.3	33 875	26 725	24.8	1.5	431	312	400	13 382	27.9	2.33	7.2	28.4
Klickitat	10.9	7.5	6.3	50.1	19 339	16 616	15.3	0.9	293	190	84	7 473	20.3	2.54	9.1	23.8
Lewis	10.2	7.9	7.7	50.4	69 273	59 358	15.6	1.0	1 117	920	503	26 306	17.0	2.57	9.9	24.0
Lincoln	12.3	9.7	9.3	50.4	10 257	8 864	14.9	0.7	140	144	81	4 151	15.1	2.42	6.4	26.0
Mason	11.2	9.5	7.0	48.3	50 425	38 341	28.9	2.1	666	671	1 011	18 912	29.8	2.49	9.2	23.3
Okanogan	10.5	7.8	6.3	50.2	39 543	33 350	18.6	-0.1	700	477	-238	15 027	18.8	2.58	11.0	24.5
Pacific	13.8	12.4	10.1	50.4	20 844	18 882	11.1	-0.7	211	332	-20	9 096	15.2	2.27	7.9	29.5
Pend Oreille	12.4	8.9	6.0	49.9	11 965	8 915	31.6	2.0	157	145	219	4 639	36.6	2.51	8.4	25.0
Pierce	8.0	5.4	4.8	50.3	719 407	586 203	19.6	2.7	12 685	6 405	12 464	260 800	21.5	2.60	11.8	24.3
San Juan	15.2	10.1	8.9	51.3	14 515	10 035	40.3	3.1	129	132	432	6 466	47.2	2.16	6.9	30.6
Skagit	9.1	7.3	7.3	50.5	105 247	79 545	29.5	2.2	1 663	1 179	1 794	38 852	27.1	2.60	9.7	23.3
Skamania	10.3	6.4	4.6	49.7	10 027	8 289	19.1	1.6	149	84	90	3 755	22.5	2.61	8.2	21.1
Snohomish	7.7	4.7	4.4	50.0	622 900	465 628	30.2	2.8	10 505	4 695	11 060	224 852	30.9	2.65	9.8	22.6
Spokane	8.2	6.0	6.4	50.9	423 261	361 333	15.7	1.3	6 761	4 471	3 197	163 611	15.5	2.46	11.0	28.1
Stevens	11.0	7.1	5.8	50.2	40 641	30 948	29.5	1.4	518	400	462	15 017	33.6	2.64	8.7	22.0
Thurston	8.9	5.8	5.6	51.0	213 546	161 238	28.6	3.0	3 166	2 009	4 988	81 625	31.3	2.50	10.3	25.1
Wahkiakum	14.2	9.9	8.6	50.0	3 787	3 327	14.9	-1.0	46	60	-23	1 553	17.6	2.42	6.3	24.4
Walla Walla	8.0	6.6	8.2	49.1	55 519	48 439	13.9	0.6	835	699	212	19 647	11.5	2.54	9.5	27.1
Whatcom	8.2	5.9	5.7	50.7	170 849	127 780	30.5	2.4	2 527	1 480	2 989	64 446	32.8	2.51	8.8	25.6
Whitman	6.4	4.4	4.8	49.4	39 879	38 775	5.1	-2.1	508	287	-1 102	15 257	12.6	2.31	6.2	29.4
Yakima	7.7	5.6	5.6	50.1	223 886	188 823	17.9	0.6	5 304	2 185	-1 833	73 993	12.1	2.96	12.5	21.5
WEST VIRGINIA...............	10.2	8.2	7.1	51.4	1 801 916	1 793 477	0.8	-0.4	25 477	26 372	-5 233	736 481	7.0	2.40	10.7	27.1
Barbour	10.8	8.2	7.4	50.7	15 514	15 699	-0.9	-0.3	204	260	22	6 123	4.9	2.47	10.3	25.1
Berkeley	9.1	6.6	4.6	50.2	79 202	59 253	28.1	4.3	1 206	756	2 791	29 569	32.3	2.53	10.7	24.2
Boone	9.8	7.5	6.1	51.2	25 427	25 870	-1.3	-0.4	361	356	-108	10 291	6.6	2.47	10.5	24.6

1. No spouse present.

STATE County	Births, average 1997–1999		Deaths, average 1997–1999				Physicians,⁴ 2000		Hospitals,⁴ 1998			Medicare enrollees 2000	Serious crimes known to police, 2000⁶	
			Number		Rate					Beds			Total	
	Total	Rate¹	Total	Infant²	Total¹	Infant³	Number	Rate⁵	Number	Number	Rate⁵		Number	Rate⁷
	32	33	34	35	36	37	38	39	40	41	42	43	44	45
VIRGINIA—Cont'd														
Manassas City	667	19.4	184	NA	5.3	NA	19	54	1	152	430	5 744	1 431	4 073
Manassas Park City	164	19.6	36	NA	4.3	NA	13	126	0	0	0	12	309	3 003
Martinsville City	186	12.0	263	NA	17.0	NA	75	487	1	182	1 162	6 709	772	5 008
Newport News City	3 123	17.6	1 411	40	7.9	12.7	373	207	3	794	445	20 830	9 995	5 548
Norfolk City	3 925	17.5	2 114	56	9.4	14.2	852	363	5	1 321	614	28 781	15 985	6 819
Norton City	35	8.6	47	NA	11.4	NA	50	1 281	2	121	2 912	1 361	236	6 045
Petersburg City	524	15.1	499	NA	14.4	NA	94	279	1	296	852	8 250	2 631	7 798
Poquoson City	103	9.0	89	NA	7.8	NA	10	86	0	0	0	964	99	856
Portsmouth City	1 610	16.3	1 136	19	11.5	11.6	251	250	2	505	510	15 944	6 537	6 500
Radford City	120	7.7	96	NA	6.2	NA	62	391	1	159	1 011	2 222	NA	NA
Richmond City	2 853	14.8	2 396	35	12.4	12.2	1 160	586	7	1 853	954	37 506	17 322	8 758
Roanoke City	1 411	15.0	1 281	11	13.6	7.6	341	359	2	744	794	24 281	4 742	4 996
Salem City	246	10.0	289	NA	11.8	NA	179	723	1	335	1 357	6 242	585	2 364
Staunton City	253	10.7	295	NA	12.4	NA	71	298	0	0	0	6 401	719	3 014
Suffolk City	876	13.9	599	10	9.5	11.0	130	204	1	185	295	6 899	2 905	4 562
Virginia Beach City	6 716	15.6	2 306	58	5.3	8.6	751	177	2	430	99	39 164	17 893	4 208
Waynesboro City	271	14.4	219	NA	11.7	NA	33	169	0	0	0	5 143	365	1 870
Williamsburg City	116	9.5	137	NA	11.3	NA	94	783	1	105	877	6 442	240	2 000
Winchester City	312	13.9	258	NA	11.5	NA	193	818	1	365	1 611	4 938	1 296	5 495
WASHINGTON	78 598	13.8	42 678	432	7.5	5.5	16 660	283	92	12 093	213	735 648	300 932	5 106
Adams	302	19.8	109	NA	7.1	NA	13	79	2	61	398	1 514	664	4 042
Asotin	276	13.0	227	NA	10.7	NA	23	112	1	41	193	3 816	895	4 355
Benton	2 030	14.9	856	12	6.3	5.7	246	173	3	290	213	16 374	5 370	3 769
Chelan	985	16.4	557	NA	9.3	NA	199	299	3	246	410	7 553	3 028	4 545
Clallam	663	10.3	771	NA	12.0	NA	136	211	2	198	309	15 515	1 987	3 079
Clark	4 910	15.0	2 186	24	6.7	5.0	430	125	1	310	95	36 852	13 336	3 863
Columbia	41	9.9	54	NA	12.9	NA	4	98	1	18	433	827	186	4 577
Cowlitz	1 193	13.1	881	8	9.6	7.0	159	171	1	209	228	14 578	5 205	5 846
Douglas	443	13.2	229	NA	6.8	NA	15	46	0	0	0	6 845	1 112	3 411
Ferry	83	11.6	67	NA	9.3	NA	2	28	1	25	349	999	93	1 281
Franklin	958	20.6	288	NA	6.2	NA	54	109	1	140	301	4 657	1 864	3 777
Garfield	16	6.7	30	NA	12.8	NA	0	0	1	54	2 318	525	98	4 088
Grant	1 274	18.0	522	NA	7.4	NA	66	88	4	201	285	10 117	3 450	4 786
Grays Harbor	851	12.6	752	NA	11.1	NA	83	124	2	188	278	12 533	3 232	4 859
Island	1 009	14.2	520	NA	7.3	NA	109	152	1	51	73	8 671	1 491	2 084
Jefferson	216	8.2	274	NA	10.4	NA	47	181	1	43	164	5 891	914	3 522
King	21 752	13.2	11 593	113	7.0	5.2	6 018	346	19	4 155	251	198 517	98 839	5 690
Kitsap	3 244	13.9	1 630	15	7.0	4.7	435	188	1	252	108	27 131	10 031	4 324
Kittitas	341	10.7	247	NA	7.8	NA	39	117	1	39	123	4 295	1 909	5 918
Klickitat	239	12.4	148	NA	7.7	NA	11	57	2	58	301	3 074	529	2 761
Lewis	874	12.8	730	NA	10.7	NA	68	99	2	204	299	12 506	3 260	4 752
Lincoln	110	11.3	111	NA	11.4	NA	8	79	2	139	1 428	2 098	173	1 875
Mason	540	10.8	484	NA	9.7	NA	42	85	1	58	116	9 293	2 755	5 660
Okanogan	530	13.8	376	NA	9.8	NA	47	119	3	171	447	6 422	1 014	3 189
Pacific	219	10.5	266	NA	12.8	NA	22	105	2	43	207	5 151	704	3 355
Pend Oreille	136	11.9	111	NA	9.7	NA	7	60	2	96	833	2 076	402	3 572
Pierce	9 918	14.7	4 953	59	7.3	6.0	1 392	199	7	1 058	156	81 646	46 423	6 683
San Juan	109	8.7	102	NA	8.2	NA	42	298	0	0	0	2 525	226	1 605
Skagit	1 314	13.2	900	9	9.1	6.6	211	205	3	307	309	16 664	6 071	5 895
Skamania	103	10.6	73	NA	7.5	NA	4	41	0	0	0	966	266	2 694
Snohomish	8 380	14.3	3 621	46	6.2	5.5	777	128	5	621	106	61 239	20 486	3 471
Spokane	5 420	13.3	3 527	30	8.6	5.5	993	238	4	1 274	312	58 983	25 061	6 051
Stevens	455	11.5	319	NA	8.0	NA	34	85	2	100	253	5 778	1 058	2 682
Thurston	2 459	12.1	1 508	12	7.4	4.7	446	215	2	437	216	26 991	8 507	4 103
Wahkiakum	39	10.2	49	NA	12.6	NA	2	52	0	0	0	748	70	1 831
Walla Walla	673	12.5	521	NA	9.7	NA	169	306	2	207	385	8 675	2 454	4 447
Whatcom	1 976	12.6	1 152	6	7.3	3.2	298	179	1	228	145	21 523	7 687	4 608
Whitman	383	9.8	220	NA	5.6	NA	46	113	2	90	228	4 086	951	2 501
Yakima	4 132	18.9	1 716	28	7.9	6.9	370	166	4	481	221	27 824	13 495	6 063
WEST VIRGINIA	20 430	11.3	20 899	173	11.5	8.5	3 593	199	56	8 397	464	337 811	47 067	2 603
Barbour	167	10.4	204	NA	12.7	NA	8	51	1	72	446	2 885	174	1 118
Berkeley	971	13.7	625	9	8.8	8.9	108	142	1	209	294	10 244	2 607	3 435
Boone	300	11.4	300	NA	11.4	NA	12	47	1	38	145	4 702	436	1 707

1. Per 1,000 estimated resident population, average 1997–1999. 2. Deaths of infants under 1 year old. 3. Deaths of infants under 1 year old per 1,000 live births. 4. Data subject to copyright. 5. Per 100,000 resident population as of July 1 of the year shown. 6. Data for serious crimes have not been adjusted for underreporting; this may affect comparability between geographic areas and over time. 7. Per 100,000 population estimated by the FBI.

STATE County	Serious crimes known to police, 2000[1] (cont'd) Rate[2] Violent	Property	Education School enrollment and attainment, 1990 Enrollment[3] Total	Percent private	Attainment[4] (percent) High school graduate or more	Bachelor's degree or more	Local government expenditures, fiscal 1999[5] Total current expenditures (mil dol)	Current expenditures per student (dollars)	Money income 1989 Per capita[6] (dollars)	Households Median Dollars	Percent change, 1979–1989 (constant 1989 dollars)	Percent with $100,000 or more	Income and poverty, 1998 Median household income	Percent below poverty level All persons	Persons under 18	Persons 5–17 in families
	46	47	48	49	50	51	52	53	54	55	56	57	58	59	60	61
VIRGINIA—Cont'd																
Manassas City	387	3 686	6 788	13.8	84.2	25.8	40.0	6 466	18 554	46 674	12.7	6.6	61 030	6.2	8.5	8.0
Manassas Park City	165	2 838	1 781	8.3	70.4	7.9	11.4	6 354	13 428	39 076	12.8	0.6	46 032	7.9	10.5	12.0
Martinsville City	545	4 463	3 279	10.7	62.9	15.8	18.1	6 662	13 742	22 446	-7.8	3.0	29 230	15.2	21.8	24.4
Newport News City	748	4 800	44 002	12.0	79.3	18.4	187.8	5 635	12 711	27 469	2.6	2.0	35 623	14.3	20.8	19.9
Norfolk City	712	6 108	60 528	12.8	72.7	16.8	240.8	6 362	11 643	23 563	12.4	2.2	29 679	22.3	29.5	28.8
Norton City	717	5 328	1 087	5.3	54.3	11.6	4.5	5 821	9 214	15 460	-29.7	1.5	23 929	21.7	26.8	29.4
Petersburg City	1 091	6 707	8 931	10.1	62.2	13.5	35.2	5 558	10 547	21 309	-5.4	1.2	26 324	22.5	33.1	32.0
Poquoson City	69	787	3 274	9.0	84.4	29.4	12.6	5 166	16 930	43 236	7.7	4.9	59 943	4.2	5.7	5.1
Portsmouth City	980	5 520	25 677	10.6	66.6	11.6	102.9	5 879	11 158	24 601	3.4	1.3	30 801	18.4	26.0	25.7
Radford City	NA	NA	9 233	3.0	75.4	29.1	9.0	5 756	9 704	19 487	-19.4	2.3	31 832	15.7	15.6	17.2
Richmond City	1 276	7 482	49 343	17.9	68.1	24.2	207.7	7 518	13 993	23 551	3.3	3.4	31 081	21.4	31.3	31.6
Roanoke City	567	4 429	19 198	11.1	68.0	15.6	91.1	6 743	12 513	22 591	1.6	2.3	29 008	17.6	24.4	26.7
Salem City	57	2 307	5 665	25.6	76.1	17.8	28.0	7 095	14 467	29 047	7.8	2.7	39 228	7.7	9.8	11.1
Staunton City	164	2 851	5 350	23.6	71.4	17.8	18.3	6 286	12 912	25 366	-5.4	1.8	33 926	12.5	15.5	19.3
Suffolk City	554	4 008	13 002	14.3	63.9	12.3	61.8	5 495	11 831	26 125	2.5	2.5	37 010	14.3	19.8	18.7
Virginia Beach City	222	3 986	105 358	14.5	88.0	25.5	421.3	5 440	15 242	36 271	7.1	4.2	46 465	7.8	10.8	9.7
Waynesboro City	236	1 634	3 679	9.3	71.2	18.2	18.2	6 089	13 469	26 668	-1.1	2.1	34 587	13.3	19.2	21.8
Williamsburg City	417	1 584	6 225	4.8	83.7	42.9	[7]53.6	[7]6 680	11 822	25 393	1.0	4.7	36 605	14.5	16.6	23.7
Winchester City	458	5 037	4 528	17.7	68.8	18.8	26.8	8 060	14 214	26 086	11.5	2.9	35 322	12.7	16.4	19.7
WASHINGTON	370	4 736	1 252 312	12.8	83.8	22.9	6 098.0	6 110	14 923	31 183	1.3	3.7	44 307	9.9	13.7	12.7
Adams	243	3 798	3 707	3.1	66.4	12.3	24.1	6 392	10 083	24 604	-12.8	2.1	32 579	16.0	19.7	19.3
Asotin	209	4 146	4 518	7.2	77.2	12.4	22.5	6 175	11 379	22 897	-10.7	1.5	33 330	15.1	20.1	21.1
Benton	246	3 523	31 738	9.0	83.9	23.3	168.6	5 933	14 027	32 593	-15.1	2.5	47 496	9.7	13.3	12.0
Chelan	216	4 329	12 315	7.3	74.3	16.7	83.8	6 385	12 533	24 312	-6.0	2.2	35 109	13.6	18.8	17.5
Clallam	177	2 903	12 755	9.4	79.7	16.1	63.6	5 980	12 798	25 434	-10.2	1.8	35 816	12.3	17.2	16.9
Clark	276	3 587	62 323	9.9	83.9	16.8	387.9	6 128	13 993	31 800	0.1	2.8	47 916	8.8	12.2	10.8
Columbia	123	4 454	984	2.5	71.8	15.1	4.8	6 722	11 108	22 418	-4.9	0.9	33 471	13.3	19.2	17.1
Cowlitz	349	5 497	20 066	8.3	77.3	11.3	106.3	5 929	12 638	27 866	-10.6	1.7	38 819	12.8	17.5	16.7
Douglas	147	3 264	6 464	5.9	75.9	13.8	38.2	5 865	12 071	27 054	-1.5	2.0	36 812	10.0	13.8	13.4
Ferry	96	1 185	1 745	3.5	72.6	12.0	9.4	7 479	9 860	25 170	2.4	0.3	30 389	18.9	21.3	25.0
Franklin	272	3 506	11 393	6.3	68.1	13.4	66.2	6 346	10 407	24 604	-18.8	2.4	32 801	17.3	20.4	21.3
Garfield	334	3 755	467	3.9	81.8	13.7	3.4	7 156	12 209	25 156	-7.7	1.3	33 201	10.5	12.3	15.0
Grant	327	4 458	14 517	4.6	71.6	11.9	97.7	5 896	10 376	22 372	-12.1	1.6	33 885	14.9	18.7	18.6
Grays Harbor	185	4 674	15 380	6.2	74.0	11.0	81.8	6 140	11 787	23 042	-19.5	1.8	34 831	16.1	21.1	21.0
Island	82	2 001	13 667	10.6	88.3	20.0	54.4	5 400	13 940	29 161	11.1	2.7	43 768	7.6	11.2	10.5
Jefferson	220	3 302	3 782	7.9	82.7	21.8	22.9	6 116	13 551	25 197	-2.1	2.7	37 745	11.5	16.5	17.8
King	428	5 262	369 847	17.1	88.2	32.8	1 572.6	6 259	18 587	36 179	4.2	5.9	52 435	7.6	11.1	9.5
Kitsap	432	3 892	47 813	10.7	86.6	19.8	253.9	5 983	14 311	32 043	0.9	2.7	45 759	8.7	11.8	11.1
Kittitas	189	5 729	10 412	2.9	81.2	22.2	29.6	6 035	10 781	20 489	-3.8	1.5	34 365	13.1	15.9	16.0
Klickitat	245	2 516	4 084	5.3	70.4	10.9	25.1	6 524	10 776	23 012	-13.9	1.4	34 315	14.9	19.1	20.3
Lewis	315	4 437	14 855	7.8	75.4	11.8	79.4	6 066	11 205	24 410	-3.6	1.7	33 205	14.1	17.8	17.4
Lincoln	238	1 637	2 085	8.0	81.9	16.0	19.0	8 157	11 977	24 617	-11.3	1.5	35 574	12.4	16.6	16.7
Mason	294	5 366	8 914	7.8	79.2	13.6	51.0	5 978	12 050	26 304	-2.7	1.6	37 575	11.8	16.2	16.3
Okanogan	252	2 938	8 050	9.6	71.3	12.0	48.1	6 124	10 346	20 303	-12.5	1.3	28 010	19.6	25.2	24.6
Pacific	234	3 121	3 934	10.5	74.2	11.3	25.2	7 024	10 952	20 029	-15.3	1.6	28 946	15.6	22.2	23.7
Pend Oreille	142	3 430	2 199	5.3	74.8	12.0	14.4	6 636	9 556	20 808	1.3	0.7	30 960	18.0	25.2	23.0
Pierce	654	6 030	150 262	14.8	83.2	17.5	741.5	5 924	13 439	30 412	5.4	2.7	44 389	10.3	14.0	12.4
San Juan	43	1 563	1 887	10.5	91.2	33.5	13.0	6 725	21 013	31 278	16.5	8.7	42 916	7.8	11.2	11.6
Skagit	137	5 758	18 837	9.6	81.0	16.3	119.9	6 492	13 804	28 389	2.8	3.1	39 992	10.9	15.6	14.3
Skamania	91	2 603	2 302	12.3	77.4	11.7	9.5	6 995	11 621	28 778	-12.0	1.4	40 735	9.7	11.2	13.1
Snohomish	240	3 232	116 244	12.5	85.7	19.3	589.4	5 751	15 769	36 847	5.9	3.6	51 560	6.6	9.1	8.3
Spokane	422	5 628	100 683	14.3	84.4	20.6	461.1	6 290	12 804	25 769	-3.5	2.4	37 188	12.3	16.2	14.5
Stevens	81	2 601	8 539	6.7	80.9	12.1	41.8	6 292	10 584	24 440	-1.4	1.3	33 545	15.2	18.1	18.9
Thurston	269	3 834	43 319	9.9	86.5	24.7	244.2	6 421	13 901	30 976	3.0	2.2	44 474	8.8	12.3	11.1
Wahkiakum	26	1 804	719	9.3	77.8	10.4	3.2	5 784	12 332	26 969	-17.3	3.1	37 465	10.7	12.6	13.9
Walla Walla	397	4 050	14 390	27.8	79.1	18.8	60.2	6 556	11 500	24 414	-7.0	2.0	35 974	13.7	17.6	17.2
Whatcom	223	4 385	37 132	10.4	83.2	22.0	147.0	5 712	13 753	28 367	5.3	3.4	39 261	11.1	14.0	13.5
Whitman	153	2 349	20 404	3.0	91.0	42.6	37.2	7 391	10 653	21 674	-8.3	1.7	35 068	14.2	15.2	14.7
Yakima	291	5 772	49 580	7.8	66.1	13.7	281.9	5 901	10 735	23 612	-4.7	2.1	31 624	18.0	22.3	21.6
WEST VIRGINIA	317	2 286	436 513	7.5	66.0	12.3	1 986.6	6 677	10 520	20 795	-14.8	1.5	28 460	16.8	24.2	21.7
Barbour	225	893	3 945	15.5	59.8	10.1	16.8	5 938	8 036	15 607	-22.4	0.5	24 013	21.4	27.7	27.4
Berkeley	406	3 029	13 045	9.3	68.4	11.9	80.1	6 352	11 832	27 412	6.3	1.9	37 690	11.3	17.6	14.9
Boone	427	1 281	6 319	2.4	54.1	6.4	35.4	7 561	9 189	17 073	-37.7	1.0	28 530	20.4	28.6	24.8

1. Data for serious crimes have not been adjusted for underreporting; this may affect comparability between geographic areas and over time.   2. Per 100,000 population estimated by the FBI.   3. All persons 3 years old and over enrolled in nursery school through college.   4. Persons 25 years old and over.   5. Elementary and secondary education expenditures, local government fiscal years ending between July 1, 1998 and June 30, 1999.   6. Based on population enumerated as of April 1, 1990.   7. Williamsburg included with James City County.

Table B. States and Counties — **Personal Income**

STATE County	Personal income, 1999												
			Per capita[1]					Transfer payments					
									Government payments to individuals				
	Total (mil dol)	Percent change, 1998–1999	Dollars	Rank	Wages and salaries[2] (mil dol)	Proprietor's income (mil dol)	Dividends, interest, and rent (mil dol)	Total (mil dol)	Total (mil dol)	Social Security (mil dol)	Medical payments (mil dol)	Income mainte-nance (mil dol)	Unemploy-ment insurance (mil dol)
	62	63	64	65	66	67	68	69	70	71	72	73	74
VIRGINIA—Cont'd													
Manassas City	(3)	(3)	(3)	(3)	(3)	(3)	(3)	(3)	(3)	(3)	(3)	(3)	(3)
Manassas Park City	(3)	(3)	(3)	(3)	(3)	(3)	(3)	(3)	(3)	(3)	(3)	(3)	(3)
Martinsville City	(4)	(4)	(4)	(4)	(4)	(4)	(4)	(4)	(4)	(4)	(4)	(4)	(4)
Newport News City	3 959	2.9	22 099	1 334	3 534	176	674	530	497	199	178	65	6
Norfolk City	5 057	2.8	22 390	1 246	8 267	256	1 095	796	767	253	302	127	9
Norton City	(5)	(5)	(5)	(5)	(5)	(5)	(5)	(5)	(5)	(5)	(5)	(5)	(5)
Petersburg City	(6)	(6)	(6)	(6)	(6)	(6)	(6)	(6)	(6)	(6)	(6)	(6)	(6)
Poquoson City	(7)	(7)	(7)	(7)	(7)	(7)	(7)	(7)	(7)	(7)	(7)	(7)	(7)
Portsmouth City	2 077	4.1	21 130	1 621	1 856	55	344	395	377	131	150	64	5
Radford City	(8)	(8)	(8)	(8)	(8)	(8)	(8)	(8)	(8)	(8)	(8)	(8)	(8)
Richmond City	5 862	2.5	30 900	181	7 304	574	1 355	922	886	293	391	128	6
Roanoke City	2 390	3.4	25 600	572	2 602	140	396	453	435	157	159	46	3
Salem City	(9)	(9)	(9)	(9)	(9)	(9)	(9)	(9)	(9)	(9)	(9)	(9)	(9)
Staunton City	(10)	(10)	(10)	(10)	(10)	(10)	(10)	(10)	(10)	(10)	(10)	(10)	(10)
Suffolk City	1 505	7.7	23 224	1 037	609	54	228	212	200	81	79	26	2
Virginia Beach City	12 291	4.7	28 356	291	5 745	685	2 206	910	828	387	269	67	9
Waynesboro City	(10)	(10)	(10)	(10)	(10)	(10)	(10)	(10)	(10)	(10)	(10)	(10)	(10)
Williamsburg City	(11)	(11)	(11)	(11)	(11)	(11)	(11)	(11)	(11)	(11)	(11)	(11)	(11)
Winchester City	(12)	(12)	(12)	(12)	(12)	(12)	(12)	(12)	(12)	(12)	(12)	(12)	(12)
WASHINGTON	174 877	7.6	30 380	X	114 587	13 388	32 265	20 437	19 244	7 460	6 838	1 708	983
Adams	319	0.3	20 941	1 684	174	10	74	70	67	19	33	6	6
Asotin	458	3.1	21 615	1 481	133	31	100	95	91	38	34	11	2
Benton	3 447	4.8	25 004	671	2 349	162	576	452	423	179	140	38	25
Chelan	1 550	3.8	25 483	583	1 000	177	339	254	242	101	84	20	18
Clallam	1 517	4.2	23 454	972	596	142	489	329	316	152	104	23	14
Clark	9 454	8.8	28 116	318	4 136	775	1 768	1 026	955	374	320	95	51
Columbia	84	0.1	20 257	1 903	44	4	23	18	17	8	5	2	1
Cowlitz	2 095	5.6	22 783	1 147	1 327	133	373	397	378	155	131	43	21
Douglas	657	3.4	19 204	2 232	223	10	138	114	107	43	39	9	8
Ferry	117	3.6	16 305	2 859	51	13	22	32	31	10	12	5	2
Franklin	840	0.1	17 961	2 546	617	68	140	179	169	45	75	20	14
Garfield	43	-8.8	18 237	2 485	23	-4	16	10	10	5	3	1	0
Grant	1 399	-1.3	19 424	2 167	801	119	271	276	261	94	95	28	26
Grays Harbor	1 409	4.2	21 004	1 666	729	109	272	340	326	130	127	34	14
Island	1 899	9.2	25 834	537	798	116	513	197	183	85	54	12	8
Jefferson	675	6.4	25 223	632	211	52	231	127	122	62	38	8	5
King	74 450	11.1	44 719	24	60 816	6 519	13 061	5 632	5 284	2 061	1 859	404	226
Kitsap	5 654	5.2	23 902	878	3 264	329	1 273	697	650	240	229	57	36
Kittitas	665	4.5	20 771	1 748	317	72	157	111	104	45	31	8	5
Klickitat	387	2.8	19 815	2 054	192	28	102	80	76	30	25	8	6
Lewis	1 431	5.6	20 851	1 715	776	126	279	320	306	124	116	29	17
Lincoln	203	-1.1	20 839	1 720	79	6	68	44	42	20	14	3	2
Mason	1 014	4.9	20 146	1 954	374	83	249	225	215	96	76	18	8
Okanogan	771	1.3	20 068	1 974	411	71	143	184	176	61	73	18	14
Pacific	426	2.3	20 523	1 829	154	47	107	116	111	53	38	9	5
Pend Oreille	219	6.9	18 911	2 312	82	27	49	57	55	18	22	8	2
Pierce	17 420	5.4	25 289	615	9 089	1 058	2 917	2 435	2 295	811	828	240	102
San Juan	488	6.4	37 843	59	129	59	243	50	47	26	14	2	2
Skagit	2 548	6.4	25 184	643	1 289	260	615	414	393	169	143	27	22
Skamania	213	5.0	21 702	1 452	64	9	38	30	28	12	9	3	2
Snohomish	16 767	5.6	28 105	322	8 791	881	2 421	1 737	1 613	671	541	115	86
Spokane	9 985	4.7	24 368	787	6 438	703	1 973	1 679	1 593	571	600	158	75
Stevens	695	3.8	17 316	2 678	295	60	129	163	155	60	55	17	10
Thurston	5 293	5.2	25 760	546	2 949	334	971	725	682	276	219	54	34
Wahkiakum	81	4.9	21 061	1 649	26	7	21	16	15	8	4	1	1
Walla Walla	1 151	2.5	21 366	1 557	723	68	251	211	200	83	69	16	11
Whatcom	3 724	5.0	23 228	1 036	2 078	373	827	558	525	216	178	45	28
Whitman	732	2.0	19 082	2 262	474	25	172	115	107	42	31	7	4
Yakima	4 595	1.6	20 811	1 731	2 568	327	856	920	873	267	374	105	70
WEST VIRGINIA	37 802	3.2	20 921	X	21 103	2 335	6 881	8 583	8 265	3 342	2 869	790	138
Barbour	244	3.7	15 263	2 963	80	14	45	75	73	27	24	9	3
Berkeley	1 678	8.2	23 040	1 079	853	87	243	238	225	97	64	17	3
Boone	522	4.9	19 843	2 039	298	55	67	130	126	51	36	16	5

1. Based on the resident population estimated as of July 1 of the year shown.　2. Includes other labor income.　3. Manassas and Manassas Park included with Prince William County.　4. Martinsville included with Henry County.　5. Norton included with Wise County.　6. Petersburg and Colonial Heights included with Dinwiddie County.　7. Poquoson included with York County.　8. Radford included with Montgomery County.　9. Salem included with Roanoke County.　10. Staunton and Waynesboro included with Augusta County.　11. Williamsburg included with James City County.　12. Winchester included with Frederick County.

Table B. States and Counties — Earnings, Social Security, and Housing

STATE County	Earnings, 1999									Social Security beneficiaries, December 2000		Housing units, 1990	
			Goods-related[1]		Service-related and other[2]							Supplemental Security Income recipients, December 2000		
	Total (mil dol)	Farm	Total	Manu-facturing	Total	Retail trade	Finance, insur-ance, and real estate	Services	Govern-ment	Number	Rate[3]		Total	Percent change, 1980–1990
	75	76	77	78	79	80	81	82	83	84	85	86	87	88
VIRGINIA—Cont'd														
Manassas City	(4)	(4)	(4)	(4)	(4)	(4)	(4)	(4)	(4)	2 720	77	470	10 232	85.7
Manassas Park City	(4)	(4)	(4)	(4)	(4)	(4)	(4)	(4)	(4)	696	68	NA	2 252	16.6
Martinsville City	(5)	(5)	(5)	(5)	(5)	(5)	(5)	(5)	(5)	5 015	325	547	7 310	3.3
Newport News City	3 710	0.0	32.3	28.1	40.5	6.8	3.8	22.9	27.3	24 142	134	4 154	69 728	26.8
Norfolk City	8 523	0.0	D	6.7	D	4.6	5.5	18.1	51.2	32 225	137	7 541	98 762	4.1
Norton City	(6)	(6)	(6)	(6)	(6)	(6)	(6)	(6)	(6)	1 494	383	298	1 845	0.3
Petersburg City	(7)	(7)	(7)	(7)	(7)	(7)	(7)	(7)	(7)	7 782	231	2 220	16 196	0.4
Poquoson City	(8)	(8)	(8)	(8)	(8)	(8)	(8)	(8)	(8)	1 602	139	NA	3 890	31.7
Portsmouth City	1 911	0.0	D	4.9	D	4.2	2.1	18.2	57.9	17 756	177	4 062	42 283	9.5
Radford City	(9)	(9)	(9)	(9)	(9)	(9)	(9)	(9)	(9)	2 053	129	188	5 496	32.1
Richmond City	7 878	0.0	18.0	13.5	55.6	4.4	13.1	25.1	26.4	33 806	171	8 393	94 141	2.9
Roanoke City	2 742	0.0	D	10.1	D	12.7	9.5	28.7	12.2	18 652	197	3 818	44 384	4.0
Salem City	(10)	(10)	(10)	(10)	(10)	(10)	(10)	(10)	(10)	5 107	206	349	9 609	6.6
Staunton City	(11)	(11)	(11)	(11)	(11)	(11)	(11)	(11)	(11)	5 492	230	649	10 003	15.9
Suffolk City	662	0.7	20.1	13.2	56.0	9.9	3.2	24.6	23.1	10 840	170	2 144	20 011	19.7
Virginia Beach City	6 431	0.0	D	3.1	D	11.0	9.4	29.3	30.5	47 007	111	4 593	147 037	59.8
Waynesboro City	(11)	(11)	(11)	(11)	(11)	(11)	(11)	(11)	(11)	4 701	241	479	7 902	27.4
Williamsburg City	(12)	(12)	(12)	(12)	(12)	(12)	(12)	(12)	(12)	1 976	165	194	3 960	30.2
Winchester City	(13)	(13)	(13)	(13)	(13)	(13)	(13)	(13)	(13)	4 488	190	587	9 808	17.0
WASHINGTON	127 975	0.9	21.4	14.8	60.5	9.2	6.4	31.9	17.2	844 367	143	100 572	2 032 378	20.3
Adams	184	10.3	D	17.0	D	9.2	1.9	11.3	22.9	2 243	137	254	5 263	4.2
Asotin	165	-1.6	D	7.7	D	15.4	4.2	30.0	20.6	4 541	221	556	7 519	6.8
Benton	2 510	3.5	D	8.1	D	8.4	3.0	31.1	18.3	19 795	139	1 786	44 877	5.2
Chelan	1 176	6.1	D	9.0	D	12.0	D	24.7	20.5	11 667	175	985	25 048	13.1
Clallam	737	0.3	20.4	11.0	50.7	12.7	5.1	23.0	28.6	17 653	274	1 342	25 225	15.4
Clark	4 911	0.2	30.0	18.6	53.6	10.2	6.1	24.1	16.1	43 268	125	5 280	92 849	27.5
Columbia	48	3.7	D	D	D	5.0	2.7	D	34.9	978	241	116	2 046	12.5
Cowlitz	1 460	0.6	41.9	33.0	43.4	10.3	3.5	19.3	14.1	17 115	184	2 172	33 304	4.9
Douglas	234	-5.8	11.5	3.2	52.5	15.8	2.8	17.0	30.2	5 007	154	383	10 640	16.4
Ferry	63	3.6	D	12.1	D	7.8	2.8	D	35.7	1 336	184	176	3 239	35.3
Franklin	684	12.3	16.2	8.4	49.8	9.0	1.8	20.4	21.6	5 362	109	806	13 664	2.6
Garfield	19	-33.2	D	D	D	6.7	4.1	11.2	75.6	613	256	25	1 209	5.9
Grant	919	14.7	D	16.7	D	10.2	D	13.0	24.3	11 416	153	1 468	22 809	12.5
Grays Harbor	839	1.2	D	23.4	D	12.5	4.2	19.8	20.6	14 584	217	2 060	29 932	4.7
Island	914	0.5	D	3.2	D	7.6	4.9	12.4	60.8	12 603	176	609	25 860	23.9
Jefferson	262	1.1	D	14.6	D	12.3	4.4	22.8	26.5	6 970	269	371	11 014	24.8
King	67 334	0.0	19.0	13.5	70.8	8.1	7.3	40.5	10.1	215 095	124	27 789	647 343	23.2
Kitsap	3 593	0.1	7.9	2.1	36.6	8.5	3.5	19.9	55.5	30 856	133	3 588	74 038	29.2
Kittitas	389	1.7	D	8.2	D	14.1	D	15.0	35.8	5 090	153	388	13 215	12.9
Klickitat	219	4.4	33.1	27.4	38.0	5.7	3.5	10.4	24.5	3 712	194	401	7 213	11.0
Lewis	902	2.5	D	17.2	D	16.0	D	17.8	19.0	14 505	211	1 585	25 487	10.2
Lincoln	85	-1.8	6.2	2.0	53.2	9.6	5.5	15.7	42.5	2 299	226	151	4 607	6.2
Mason	457	0.4	30.4	18.7	41.0	10.2	3.9	17.4	28.2	11 266	228	944	22 292	27.2
Okanogan	482	7.8	14.2	9.6	48.9	10.4	2.3	23.8	29.2	7 773	196	967	16 629	22.4
Pacific	201	6.5	21.6	16.6	43.2	11.0	3.9	19.8	28.7	5 968	284	533	12 404	13.3
Pend Oreille	109	0.7	D	36.9	D	7.6	2.0	11.8	29.2	2 303	196	436	5 404	15.3
Pierce	10 147	0.3	18.6	11.1	51.6	10.3	7.2	23.6	29.5	95 057	136	14 263	228 842	22.1
San Juan	188	0.1	D	4.8	D	13.8	7.9	27.8	17.6	2 949	209	72	6 075	14.4
Skagit	1 549	5.1	24.3	14.0	51.8	13.1	4.5	21.7	18.9	19 278	187	1 646	33 580	20.9
Skamania	72	-0.9	D	16.8	D	5.3	1.9	17.3	42.8	1 401	142	137	3 922	14.2
Snohomish	9 671	0.2	44.2	35.4	39.4	9.4	5.5	17.0	16.2	72 316	119	7 132	183 942	40.2
Spokane	7 141	0.1	20.0	12.6	60.3	10.6	7.6	28.0	19.6	66 647	159	8 863	150 105	9.0
Stevens	355	1.4	32.1	26.3	43.3	9.0	2.6	22.3	23.1	7 546	188	849	14 601	16.3
Thurston	3 283	0.8	11.7	5.5	45.6	11.1	4.6	22.9	41.9	32 459	157	3 329	66 464	31.1
Wahkiakum	33	1.1	40.0	36.0	34.8	6.2	3.2	10.8	24.0	923	241	42	1 496	-0.5
Walla Walla	791	4.3	22.3	17.8	D	9.1	4.0	24.1	24.1	9 686	176	927	19 029	4.9
Whatcom	2 452	2.7	29.1	16.3	53.2	11.4	6.3	23.5	15.0	25 329	152	2 666	55 742	17.4
Whitman	499	-1.4	D	4.7	34.0	6.9	3.1	12.6	59.9	4 497	110	272	14 598	1.2
Yakima	2 896	10.4	D	13.1	D	10.1	D	24.5	18.1	32 260	145	5 185	70 852	6.0
WEST VIRGINIA	23 438	0.1	26.2	14.4	52.0	9.6	4.3	25.5	21.9	393 593	218	71 414	781 295	4.5
Barbour	95	-0.4	27.7	8.9	D	9.0	3.8	25.9	27.1	3 467	223	841	6 956	12.4
Berkeley	940	0.4	D	13.5	D	9.0	4.1	D	33.4	12 030	158	1 482	25 385	36.7
Boone	353	0.0	D	D	D	6.1	D	8.9	13.9	5 898	231	1 293	10 705	-0.5

1. Covers mining, construction, and manufacturing.   2. Covers private sector earnings in agricultural services, forestry, and fisheries; transportation and public utilities; wholesale trade; retail trade; finance, insurance, and real estate; and services.   3. Per 1,000 resident population estimated as of July 1 of the year shown.   4. Manassas and Manassas Park included with Prince William County.   5. Martinsville included with Henry County.   6. Norton included with Wise County.   7. Petersburg and Colonial Heights included with Dinwiddie County.   8. Poquoson included with York County.   9. Radford included with Montgomery County.   10. Salem included with Roanoke County.   11. Staunton and Waynesboro included with Augusta County.   12. Williamsburg included with James City County.   13. Winchester included with Frederick County.

STATE County	Total	Percent	Median value[1]	With a mortgage	Without a mortgage	Median rent[2]	Rent as percent of income	Sub-standard units[3] (percent)	Total	Percent change, 2000–2001	Total	Rate[4]	Total	Professional, managerial, and technical	Precision production, craft, and repair
	89	90	91	92	93	94	95	96	97	98	99	100	101	102	103
VIRGINIA—Cont'd															
Manassas City	9 481	66.1	150 700	25.3	13.7	695	25.5	3.5	20 355	3.4	677	3.3	15 808	37.0	10.5
Manassas Park City	2 182	71.8	101 800	24.4	13.1	739	26.9	3.4	4 544	1.7	69	1.5	3 692	23.6	21.3
Martinsville City	6 839	60.7	52 700	18.9	13.2	320	23.7	2.6	6 539	-2.3	725	11.1	7 401	25.4	10.4
Newport News City	63 952	50.0	85 200	22.7	13.0	439	26.2	3.8	85 777	1.5	3 490	4.1	72 950	30.6	14.6
Norfolk City	89 478	44.0	74 500	23.4	13.5	438	28.5	5.7	85 344	1.8	4 851	5.7	89 580	27.2	12.4
Norton City	1 697	60.9	48 000	18.9	11.7	279	32.0	2.3	1 448	0.1	74	5.1	1 445	28.2	9.3
Petersburg City	14 730	50.9	52 000	21.4	12.7	360	27.7	4.4	16 184	3.1	1 030	6.4	15 920	21.7	8.2
Poquoson City	3 769	82.7	113 700	22.2	12.2	574	25.6	0.1	6 220	0.8	144	2.3	5 359	39.2	12.8
Portsmouth City	38 741	55.9	67 400	22.9	13.6	416	28.3	4.6	45 118	1.5	2 434	5.4	42 053	25.1	16.6
Radford City	5 207	47.8	64 500	15.8	12.6	410	35.1	1.2	6 743	2.3	311	4.6	6 319	35.1	8.1
Richmond City	85 337	46.3	66 600	21.4	14.5	413	27.5	3.2	97 422	2.5	4 891	5.0	96 229	31.0	7.3
Roanoke City	41 030	56.6	54 000	18.8	12.7	336	24.3	2.2	49 940	0.9	1 811	3.6	45 400	24.6	10.4
Salem City	9 161	67.4	69 100	16.8	11.8	404	25.2	0.4	13 697	0.7	332	2.4	12 061	28.0	9.6
Staunton City	9 432	61.2	62 700	17.0	12.6	359	24.1	1.6	11 649	1.2	295	2.5	11 161	27.0	10.7
Suffolk City	18 516	67.7	70 700	22.4	14.3	376	28.7	6.9	31 226	1.1	1 079	3.5	22 463	26.1	15.8
Virginia Beach City	135 566	62.5	96 500	24.9	12.2	577	27.0	2.3	216 083	1.1	6 546	3.0	174 616	35.0	11.2
Waynesboro City	7 568	62.3	68 100	18.3	12.7	374	22.4	2.5	9 477	2.0	385	4.1	8 607	28.2	12.4
Williamsburg City	3 468	36.4	121 000	20.3	12.1	492	28.3	1.7	6 250	1.9	378	6.0	4 974	41.6	4.9
Winchester City	9 084	45.4	89 100	19.1	12.7	425	24.2	2.8	13 730	3.2	409	3.0	11 405	27.6	12.5
WASHINGTON	1 872 431	62.6	93 400	20.4	11.8	445	25.7	4.0	2 995 696	-1.6	191 610	6.4	2 293 961	31.7	11.6
Adams	4 586	65.5	45 900	16.2	11.5	284	22.7	10.0	8 048	-0.5	869	10.8	5 847	16.8	10.0
Asotin	7 003	65.6	53 900	18.3	11.5	327	28.0	2.7	11 623	-3.3	558	4.8	7 111	23.9	13.7
Benton	42 227	63.1	66 200	16.0	11.4	363	21.5	3.7	71 834	1.0	4 694	6.5	52 440	36.5	10.6
Chelan	20 645	61.9	71 500	19.0	11.2	343	25.4	5.0	33 862	-0.9	3 218	9.5	23 004	24.3	10.9
Clallam	22 837	70.2	79 200	19.1	12.0	377	24.8	3.9	24 016	-3.3	1 868	7.8	20 874	25.9	10.6
Clark	88 440	64.3	74 200	19.3	11.4	447	24.7	3.2	179 194	-0.3	12 698	7.1	110 967	27.5	13.0
Columbia	1 582	67.6	37 400	15.2	12.1	278	18.5	4.6	1 338	-11.0	153	11.4	1 570	23.0	6.1
Cowlitz	31 640	65.4	61 300	15.2	11.1	348	24.6	3.8	40 138	-2.2	4 408	11.0	34 306	21.9	14.7
Douglas	9 687	68.7	68 700	17.3	11.0	375	23.0	7.1	18 834	-1.5	1 427	7.6	11 664	23.4	10.7
Ferry	2 247	69.8	50 100	14.2	12.1	257	15.9	12.7	2 433	-5.0	352	14.5	2 296	24.7	16.6
Franklin	12 196	59.7	56 000	17.6	11.9	295	25.5	12.6	22 602	0.7	2 128	9.4	15 686	21.0	10.6
Garfield	922	68.8	36 900	15.1	11.9	279	16.6	2.4	1 126	-1.4	42	3.7	969	20.5	9.8
Grant	19 745	64.6	51 600	16.9	11.2	281	22.3	7.0	36 337	-1.5	3 726	10.3	22 289	20.6	11.8
Grays Harbor	25 514	67.0	49 100	17.2	12.0	322	25.9	3.2	25 799	-2.8	2 729	10.6	24 390	21.7	11.0
Island	21 787	65.6	103 400	22.7	11.3	463	25.8	3.8	28 540	-3.0	1 335	4.7	21 236	29.9	16.0
Jefferson	8 627	73.9	88 700	19.6	11.5	384	25.1	6.4	11 003	0.3	643	5.8	7 664	29.7	14.1
King	615 792	58.8	140 100	21.1	11.6	510	25.8	3.4	999 609	-2.0	51 154	5.1	818 326	38.1	9.7
Kitsap	69 267	64.3	89 100	21.4	11.9	450	24.7	3.9	92 402	-1.2	5 541	6.0	78 930	32.9	16.0
Kittitas	10 460	57.2	60 500	18.5	12.7	318	29.9	4.0	14 915	1.4	971	6.5	11 882	24.5	9.4
Klickitat	6 210	66.0	52 700	16.5	12.3	331	23.0	5.1	8 423	-3.0	1 268	15.1	6 437	20.2	10.0
Lewis	22 478	70.0	57 600	18.0	12.4	348	24.6	4.0	27 886	-3.2	2 626	9.4	23 427	22.0	12.5
Lincoln	3 605	72.6	41 100	17.5	12.2	288	22.6	2.8	4 551	1.2	240	5.3	3 614	21.4	9.3
Mason	14 565	76.7	70 100	19.5	11.7	382	25.7	5.5	18 268	-3.3	1 448	7.9	14 224	24.6	15.3
Okanogan	12 654	66.7	50 300	17.0	12.2	277	23.0	8.1	20 207	-1.5	2 180	10.8	13 632	20.8	9.2
Pacific	7 896	71.9	49 300	17.3	12.9	315	25.0	4.3	7 570	-2.2	679	9.0	6 867	20.4	10.8
Pend Oreille	3 395	73.6	49 800	18.1	11.5	292	26.2	6.3	4 210	2.2	426	10.1	2 841	22.9	14.5
Pierce	214 652	60.3	82 500	21.1	12.4	436	26.2	4.3	328 401	-1.4	20 928	6.4	251 833	28.4	13.2
San Juan	4 392	71.9	166 400	25.1	10.6	475	23.0	6.4	6 526	-0.2	260	4.0	4 418	26.1	16.5
Skagit	30 573	69.9	81 500	19.6	11.7	422	25.3	4.3	51 043	-0.9	3 779	7.4	34 121	25.3	14.5
Skamania	3 066	73.5	67 100	17.2	11.8	328	17.4	5.3	3 777	-6.1	418	11.1	3 328	21.2	13.7
Snohomish	171 713	66.3	127 200	21.6	11.9	536	25.6	3.7	334 886	-2.3	17 918	5.4	235 752	28.6	15.9
Spokane	141 619	63.7	59 000	19.4	12.2	356	26.9	2.7	207 081	-1.0	13 629	6.6	157 142	30.9	9.9
Stevens	11 241	76.2	55 900	17.8	11.8	306	23.4	6.2	16 228	-2.5	1 765	10.9	11 583	23.4	12.5
Thurston	62 150	64.7	79 700	21.0	11.7	460	26.0	3.6	98 857	-1.2	5 610	5.7	74 539	36.4	9.6
Wahkiakum	1 321	75.5	62 300	16.5	12.6	300	19.3	2.2	1 697	-5.8	124	7.3	1 486	15.6	8.3
Walla Walla	17 623	62.3	56 500	17.4	11.7	319	25.5	4.3	25 794	-1.2	1 683	6.5	21 076	27.2	9.1
Whatcom	48 543	64.3	90 800	19.9	11.9	425	27.1	3.6	80 298	-1.2	5 460	6.8	61 657	26.3	13.0
Whitman	13 546	48.2	61 900	16.3	11.5	347	32.0	2.0	18 394	-4.1	455	2.5	17 167	41.7	4.9
Yakima	65 985	63.2	55 200	17.9	12.1	339	25.5	10.1	107 961	-1.6	12 203	11.3	77 366	22.9	9.5
WEST VIRGINIA	688 557	74.1	47 900	17.5	12.0	303	26.8	4.0	833 315	1.1	40 948	4.9	671 085	25.4	14.5
Barbour	5 835	77.5	35 200	23.7	13.1	271	30.4	6.0	6 077	-4.1	477	7.8	5 170	23.9	14.9
Berkeley	22 350	73.0	70 600	18.0	11.8	368	24.0	3.9	38 055	3.6	1 422	3.7	27 449	22.4	15.4
Boone	9 656	76.3	41 800	16.3	12.0	286	33.3	4.0	8 186	2.1	452	5.5	7 327	19.2	20.8

1. Specified owner-occupied units.   2. Specified renter-occupied units.   3. Overcrowded or lacking complete plumbing facilities.   4. Percent of civilian labor force.   5. Persons 16 years and older.

STATE County	Number of establishments	Total	Health Care and Social Assistance	Manufacturing	Retail trade	Finance and Insurance	Professional Scientific and Technical Services	Total (mil dol)	Average per employee (dollars)	Number	Less than 50 acres	500 acres and over	Whose principal occupation is farming (percent)
	104	105	106	107	108	109	110	111	112	113	114	115	116
VIRGINIA—Cont'd													
Manassas City	1 759	21 652	2 685	2 581	3 847	600	1 454	765	35 332	NA	NA	NA	NA
Manassas Park City	146	2 059	0	60	151	D	59	71	34 353	NA	NA	NA	NA
Martinsville City	761	17 740	1 726	8 139	1 971	448	243	407	22 959	NA	NA	NA	NA
Newport News City	3 717	84 667	10 122	24 845	10 183	2 040	4 495	2 243	26 489	NA	NA	NA	NA
Norfolk City	5 378	116 011	17 149	9 700	14 748	8 622	8 199	3 296	28 415	NA	NA	NA	NA
Norton City	296	4 755	1 161	425	935	112	190	125	26 375	NA	NA	NA	NA
Petersburg City	900	13 213	2 988	2 478	1 752	321	632	355	26 837	NA	NA	NA	NA
Poquoson City	170	1 385	235	50	333	32	78	24	17 298	NA	NA	NA	NA
Portsmouth City	1 703	25 119	6 184	1 742	3 876	678	1 559	595	23 707	NA	NA	NA	NA
Radford City	363	6 726	1 158	2 822	603	184	161	193	28 678	NA	NA	NA	NA
Richmond City	7 281	157 169	23 296	20 727	12 825	13 785	10 403	5 397	34 339	NA	NA	NA	NA
Roanoke City	4 136	74 556	9 977	8 887	12 631	3 770	2 986	1 918	25 720	NA	NA	NA	NA
Salem City	954	23 102	4 912	6 311	3 307	353	343	645	27 927	NA	NA	NA	NA
Staunton City	888	11 729	1 670	468	2 429	482	271	241	20 552	NA	NA	NA	NA
Suffolk City	1 136	16 229	2 670	2 613	2 751	339	482	382	23 523	218	34.4	20.2	64.2
Virginia Beach City	10 185	139 147	12 887	6 312	25 234	7 785	13 219	3 224	23 170	147	61.9	8.8	48.3
Waynesboro City	625	10 313	515	3 215	1 479	298	146	295	28 600	NA	NA	NA	NA
Williamsburg City	775	16 551	3 166	D	2 667	293	439	413	24 944	NA	NA	NA	NA
Winchester City	1 220	23 205	4 173	7 025	4 139	621	562	632	27 250	NA	NA	NA	NA
WASHINGTON	162 932	2 209 129	272 604	331 206	302 828	98 832	127 011	78 711	35 630	29 011	51.4	16.2	53.3
Adams	407	3 877	492	1 103	562	104	59	82	21 248	628	10.5	56.7	74.4
Asotin	436	3 941	787	379	748	101	147	88	22 344	140	22.1	62.1	53.6
Benton	3 293	48 406	5 645	3 724	7 250	1 251	7 385	1 585	32 734	1 078	67.3	10.4	43.5
Chelan	2 271	24 210	4 004	2 517	3 976	786	663	615	25 389	1 113	71.1	3.3	58.8
Clallam	2 072	15 567	3 093	1 062	2 902	566	544	348	22 360	292	66.8	2.1	43.8
Clark	7 876	93 265	11 556	17 641	13 612	3 432	3 808	2 708	29 038	1 175	71.5	1.6	38.4
Columbia	134	735	36	146	151	29	14	19	25 925	198	20.7	51.5	65.2
Cowlitz	2 377	32 561	3 981	7 924	4 920	835	816	969	29 775	349	59.3	2.6	37.0
Douglas	551	3 860	421	173	1 016	161	104	90	23 376	853	51.3	27.8	64.6
Ferry	158	1 028	99	157	223	18	21	27	26 294	179	18.4	31.3	56.4
Franklin	1 093	13 469	1 648	3 237	2 196	242	201	335	24 909	848	30.8	26.5	68.6
Garfield	53	362	82	0	65	20	D	7	20 470	182	11.0	65.9	73.1
Grant	1 686	16 514	2 075	3 848	3 140	400	451	406	24 563	1 699	28.5	28.0	69.7
Grays Harbor	1 945	17 433	2 338	3 368	3 021	593	468	459	26 338	389	50.9	5.4	46.0
Island	1 573	11 000	1 704	658	2 339	767	353	231	20 987	261	67.8	0.8	42.9
Jefferson	1 029	6 358	994	915	1 023	185	155	136	21 365	144	54.9	2.1	34.0
King	59 335	1 004 382	99 258	139 330	111 652	50 532	77 217	45 143	44 946	1 091	83.9	1.0	43.3
Kitsap	5 202	47 427	9 064	1 393	10 345	2 175	2 942	1 105	23 308	359	84.7	0.6	34.8
Kittitas	1 002	7 138	1 030	463	1 385	144	144	149	20 877	757	50.3	12.2	47.2
Klickitat	511	3 473	468	1 118	404	114	139	98	28 340	530	30.6	30.0	53.0
Lewis	1 969	19 126	2 510	3 549	3 661	473	362	480	25 091	1 117	51.7	1.8	44.6
Lincoln	301	1 846	512	D	321	95	103	42	23 014	707	7.1	73.8	79.8
Mason	1 026	8 532	1 015	1 619	1 338	307	242	198	23 250	211	75.4	1.9	47.9
Okanogan	1 037	8 617	1 415	584	1 595	204	208	174	20 191	1 270	47.5	18.0	57.2
Pacific	665	4 253	566	769	640	189	76	79	18 639	253	48.6	7.1	59.3
Pend Oreille	233	1 524	292	321	197	38	54	42	27 488	225	30.7	14.7	42.7
Pierce	15 416	199 454	33 881	21 450	30 167	7 936	6 767	5 566	27 908	989	75.4	0.9	42.8
San Juan	836	3 561	186	D	646	114	161	95	26 542	174	56.3	2.9	40.2
Skagit	3 256	33 953	4 978	4 909	6 673	905	1 092	906	26 678	714	53.8	5.5	52.7
Skamania	176	1 192	63	259	129	26	D	26	21 811	63	52.4	0.0	38.1
Snohomish	15 020	206 830	20 137	62 102	29 079	8 281	7 322	6 874	33 236	1 139	75.9	1.8	45.4
Spokane	11 717	162 962	26 344	20 166	23 868	10 560	6 397	4 537	27 841	1 643	44.1	17.3	43.4
Stevens	843	7 155	1 158	1 571	1 191	175	125	172	24 068	989	27.8	16.8	44.5
Thurston	5 012	51 695	8 893	3 180	9 198	2 596	3 140	1 323	25 587	832	72.7	2.4	39.1
Wahkiakum	104	584	108	D	81	15	D	14	23 402	108	33.3	5.6	43.5
Walla Walla	1 234	16 759	3 711	2 022	2 371	607	364	400	23 843	716	39.0	36.3	60.5
Whatcom	5 386	58 488	6 691	9 495	9 322	1 962	2 937	1 509	25 805	1 228	57.1	2.4	54.3
Whitman	876	7 004	1 236	D	1 394	317	232	147	21 009	1 003	12.4	68.3	80.2
Yakima	4 800	59 762	10 133	9 364	10 027	1 563	1 456	1 493	24 984	3 365	63.0	6.6	55.3
WEST VIRGINIA	41 451	545 495	100 330	73 103	89 629	21 920	19 091	13 514	24 774	17 772	21.1	7.5	40.2
Barbour	274	2 642	556	103	431	109	57	40	15 064	437	14.4	7.8	46.0
Berkeley	1 469	19 530	3 785	3 217	3 791	605	801	486	24 905	509	36.5	3.9	36.7
Boone	387	5 559	644	52	972	169	145	190	34 171	23	39.1	0.0	30.4

Table B. States and Counties — Agriculture, Land, and Water

	Agriculture, 1997 (cont'd)															
	Land in farms					Value of land and buildings		Value of machinery and equipment average per farm ($1,000)	Value of products sold				Percent of farms with sales of —		Percent of land owned by fed. gov. 1997	Water consumption 1995 (mil gal/day)
			Acres								Percent from —					
STATE County	Acreage (1,000)	Percent change, 1992–1997	Average size of farm	Total irrigated (1,000)	Total cropland (1,000)	Average per farm ($1,000)	Average per acre (dollars)		Total (mil dol)	Average per farm (dollars)	Crops	Live-stock and poultry products	$10,000 or more	$100,000 or more		
	117	118	119	120	121	122	123	124	125	126	127	128	129	130	131	132

STATE County	117	118	119	120	121	122	123	124	125	126	127	128	129	130	131	132
VIRGINIA—Cont'd																
Manassas City	NA	NA	NA	NA	NA	NA	NA	NA	NA	NA	NA	NA	NA	NA	(1)NA	0.1
Manassas Park City	NA	NA	NA	NA	NA	NA	NA	NA	NA	NA	NA	NA	NA	NA	(1)NA	0.4
Martinsville City	NA	NA	NA	NA	NA	NA	NA	NA	NA	NA	NA	NA	NA	NA	(2)NA	0.1
Newport News City	NA	NA	NA	NA	NA	NA	NA	NA	NA	NA	NA	NA	NA	NA	(3)NA	32.6
Norfolk City	NA	NA	NA	NA	NA	NA	NA	NA	NA	NA	NA	NA	NA	NA	6.0	13.6
Norton City	NA	NA	NA	NA	NA	NA	NA	NA	NA	NA	NA	NA	NA	NA	(4)NA	0.9
Petersburg City	NA	NA	NA	NA	NA	NA	NA	NA	NA	NA	NA	NA	NA	NA	(5)NA	0.1
Poquoson City	NA	NA	NA	NA	NA	NA	NA	NA	NA	NA	NA	NA	NA	NA	(3)NA	0.0
Portsmouth City	NA	NA	NA	NA	NA	NA	NA	NA	NA	NA	NA	NA	NA	NA	4.0	2.5
Radford City	NA	NA	NA	NA	NA	NA	NA	NA	NA	NA	NA	NA	NA	NA	(6)NA	3.1
Richmond City	NA	NA	NA	NA	NA	NA	NA	NA	NA	NA	NA	NA	NA	NA	0.0	70.4
Roanoke City	NA	NA	NA	NA	NA	NA	NA	NA	NA	NA	NA	NA	NA	NA	(7)NA	9.2
Salem City	NA	NA	NA	NA	NA	NA	NA	NA	NA	NA	NA	NA	NA	NA	(7)NA	3.4
Staunton City	NA	NA	NA	NA	NA	NA	NA	NA	NA	NA	NA	NA	NA	NA	(8)NA	0.0
Suffolk City	76	-8.2	350	1	57	688	1 869	125	39	177 392	84.1	15.9	67.9	31.7	13.0	88.9
Virginia Beach City	30	-30.3	204	0	25	455	2 529	51	14	92 778	76.8	23.2	46.9	14.3	6.6	8.2
Waynesboro City	NA	NA	NA	NA	NA	NA	NA	NA	NA	NA	NA	NA	NA	NA	(8)NA	11.5
Williamsburg City	NA	NA	NA	NA	NA	NA	NA	NA	NA	NA	NA	NA	NA	NA	(9)NA	1.6
Winchester City	NA	NA	NA	NA	NA	NA	NA	NA	NA	NA	NA	NA	NA	NA	(10)NA	0.2
WASHINGTON	15 180	-3.5	523	1 705	7 914	635	1 192	70	4 768	164 342	68.2	31.8	48.5	23.3	27.1	8 822.5
Adams	1 096	10.0	1 746	148	809	1 307	714	165	202	321 454	92.0	8.0	75.2	47.6	1.0	346.3
Asotin	304	10.7	2 175	0	87	1 003	439	81	10	69 593	65.5	34.5	58.6	25.0	16.1	5.7
Benton	612	-4.4	568	153	440	1 122	2 169	95	301	278 785	97.1	2.9	41.5	22.3	26.6	1 078.1
Chelan	124	10.5	111	31	41	415	3 148	52	146	131 539	99.5	0.5	70.8	35.3	77.2	127.6
Clallam	21	-12.4	72	4	12	400	3 753	26	6	20 584	45.4	54.6	18.8	5.5	45.2	101.6
Clark	73	-12.2	62	4	43	325	5 801	24	43	36 667	39.6	60.4	23.7	5.6	1.7	195.1
Columbia	310	1.7	1 567	4	178	775	514	134	24	123 619	92.0	8.0	61.6	33.3	28.6	17.1
Cowlitz	31	-13.6	89	3	15	365	4 150	34	16	45 612	45.6	54.4	16.9	6.0	3.8	208.4
Douglas	906	-1.3	1 063	21	533	778	668	87	118	137 894	95.5	4.5	69.6	33.2	3.1	63.0
Ferry	810	8.3	4 524	5	22	1 835	400	38	5	28 007	26.5	73.5	44.1	6.7	34.1	13.3
Franklin	564	-15.9	665	221	D	969	1 469	130	333	392 612	86.5	13.5	74.8	51.5	7.3	844.4
Garfield	325	0.0	1 787	1	192	974	543	157	25	135 633	88.9	11.1	75.3	46.7	20.8	2.0
Grant	1 095	0.8	645	446	786	1 001	1 596	149	804	473 368	68.9	31.1	73.4	48.4	14.1	1 795.1
Grays Harbor	42	-5.9	109	3	24	262	2 769	32	15	38 635	32.6	67.4	31.1	8.0	11.4	93.2
Island	16	-20.5	61	1	11	394	6 836	25	11	40 376	14.8	85.2	25.3	5.4	2.9	14.3
Jefferson	13	30.9	91	1	8	270	3 673	19	4	30 007	12.9	87.1	26.4	5.6	56.8	25.6
King	42	-0.8	38	3	24	379	8 839	36	94	85 968	41.1	58.9	28.7	11.0	23.1	291.6
Kitsap	19	91.3	53	0	6	267	5 591	26	12	34 074	32.6	67.4	19.5	2.5	2.5	40.4
Kittitas	178	-49.9	235	76	87	540	2 433	61	80	105 196	60.4	39.6	47.4	15.1	30.1	452.6
Klickitat	589	-14.7	1 111	20	186	627	579	47	33	62 701	71.4	28.6	43.6	12.6	2.9	98.9
Lewis	118	5.1	105	6	62	387	3 635	33	83	74 108	28.3	71.7	28.6	8.7	30.8	54.3
Lincoln	1 376	-6.1	1 946	48	876	1 079	537	139	108	152 486	91.9	8.1	77.2	49.6	0.9	71.6
Mason	20	81.7	95	0	7	302	4 100	17	13	63 340	D	D	26.1	3.3	24.5	18.7
Okanogan	1 179	-8.7	928	48	142	855	808	52	134	105 194	87.1	12.9	54.7	19.9	46.0	139.7
Pacific	40	21.9	159	3	15	368	2 369	35	17	67 052	48.5	51.5	50.2	19.4	1.2	9.8
Pend Oreille	63	14.8	281	2	27	348	1 494	35	3	12 794	40.0	60.0	29.3	1.3	56.5	5.1
Pierce	51	-13.8	51	5	24	336	7 273	30	70	70 612	39.7	60.3	25.5	7.7	28.8	198.3
San Juan	17	-19.6	97	1	12	487	5 419	15	3	15 246	14.1	85.9	21.8	1.1	2.1	3.0
Skagit	93	1.6	131	10	73	610	4 645	71	172	240 463	52.6	47.4	46.4	23.8	43.1	45.9
Skamania	4	5.5	67	0	2	334	4 988	28	2	24 316	86.7	13.3	20.6	4.8	76.7	13.3
Snohomish	61	-18.1	53	4	40	387	6 627	33	113	99 105	30.8	69.2	29.1	11.2	45.4	173.2
Spokane	590	-5.8	359	11	398	469	1 351	52	79	47 903	74.2	25.8	35.2	13.1	1.8	188.7
Stevens	525	-3.8	531	10	123	510	910	37	23	23 069	39.5	60.5	35.0	4.3	18.3	29.4
Thurston	56	-6.2	68	6	27	381	6 278	44	121	145 086	29.9	70.1	23.6	7.1	3.9	49.6
Wahkiakum	13	2.9	124	0	9	348	2 348	31	3	25 135	3.3	96.7	30.6	6.5	1.3	3.3
Walla Walla	715	0.5	998	97	598	891	856	108	257	358 841	D	D	58.7	37.3	0.7	353.6
Whatcom	104	-12.2	84	26	81	449	5 321	56	242	196 778	16.5	83.5	53.3	29.2	61.5	160.8
Whitman	1 301	-7.3	1 297	5	1 067	1 120	874	161	173	172 964	93.5	6.5	80.0	55.1	0.9	15.5
Yakima	1 683	2.6	500	278	605	1 220	1 220	73	873	259 582	66.5	33.5	61.4	28.9	17.6	1 475.0
WEST VIRGINIA	3 456	5.8	194	3	1 337	213	1 090	24	447	25 176	14.5	85.5	20.7	3.6	7.8	4 618.3
Barbour	87	13.9	198	0	39	168	903	23	4	8 985	11.7	88.3	21.7	0.9	0.4	2.2
Berkeley	73	-0.5	143	0	47	384	2 863	22	18	35 699	64.3	35.7	28.3	7.7	0.1	20.8
Boone	2	-22.2	102		0	116	1 141	19	0	1 944	71.1	28.9	4.3	0.0	0.0	4.0

1. Manassas and Manassas Park included with Prince William County. 2. Martinsville included with Henry County. 3. Hampton, Newport News, and Poquoson included with York County. 4. Norton included with Wise County. 5. Hopewell and Petersburg included with Prince George County. 6. Radford included with Montgomery County. 7. Roanoke City and Salem included with Roanoke County. 8. Staunton and Waynesboro included with Augusta County. 9. Williamsburg included with James City County. 10. Winchester included with Frederick County.

Table B. States and Counties — Residential Construction, Wholesale and Retail Trade, and Real Estate

STATE County	Value of Residential Construction Authorized by Building Permits, 2000		Wholesale Trade, 1997				Retail Trade[1], 1997				Real Estate and Rental and Leasing, 1997			
	New Construction ($1,000)	Number of Housing Units	Number of Establishments	Number of Employees	Sales (mil dol)	Annual Payroll (mil dol)	Number of Establishments	Number of Employees	Sales (mil dol)	Annual Payroll (mil dol)	Number of Establishments	Number of Employees	Receipts (mil dol)	Annual Payroll (mil dol)
	133	134	135	136	137	138	139	140	141	142	143	144	145	146
VIRGINIA—Cont'd														
Manassas City	3 529	54	59	1 008	626.3	41.0	230	3 355	647.5	64.9	51	302	41.1	5.5
Manassas Park City	22 770	207	13	180	36.7	6.4	16	142	28.7	2.9	2	D	D	D
Martinsville City	1 863	56	23	202	143.7	6.9	142	1 927	248.8	25.3	36	151	18.1	2.5
Newport News City	25 035	407	132	1 634	604.2	50.3	681	9 284	1 488.6	143.6	226	1 720	169.9	35.8
Norfolk City	26 356	287	324	5 845	2 914.6	183.9	918	12 628	1 900.4	207.3	273	2 128	203.8	44.2
Norton City	193	3	15	292	174.9	9.9	66	921	127.8	11.9	9	12	2.3	0.2
Petersburg City	510	11	35	538	139.2	16.8	189	1 764	290.0	29.5	28	131	11.1	2.2
Poquoson City	3 054	20	11	D	D	D	28	247	29.8	3.0	6	30	2.8	0.6
Portsmouth City	15 660	213	63	712	167.3	23.6	295	3 291	468.4	51.2	84	457	37.8	7.4
Radford City	2 494	15	8	296	51.7	3.3	58	561	79.2	8.6	21	108	11.3	1.4
Richmond City	21 230	270	464	7 572	5 979.5	283.5	1 013	11 579	1 738.1	193.5	265	2 166	213.5	54.8
Roanoke City	21 002	310	299	3 768	1 292.7	121.0	792	12 425	1 843.7	191.3	158	1 861	114.5	31.8
Salem City	8 859	73	86	1 809	635.8	58.6	174	3 089	452.5	51.8	26	179	13.9	4.0
Staunton City	3 817	65	33	327	132.0	7.4	168	2 213	330.5	32.0	43	214	15.9	3.3
Suffolk City	83 013	773	61	1 305	822.5	43.7	212	2 697	380.0	38.0	43	210	24.1	3.4
Virginia Beach City	181 594	1 464	479	5 642	1 922.8	159.4	1 621	21 987	3 342.7	337.2	472	3 101	333.0	66.8
Waynesboro City	7 964	100	21	D	D	D	115	1 512	216.6	22.2	29	131	9.4	1.9
Williamsburg City	21 533	182	16	D	D	D	163	2 262	330.2	33.7	32	201	40.9	8.3
Winchester City	11 914	116	39	569	301.1	16.4	283	3 667	571.3	58.7	55	208	24.5	5.3
WASHINGTON	4 426 088	39 021	10 039	118 810	75 397.8	4 376.0	22 841	283 653	52 472.9	5 385.9	7 544	41 899	5 352.8	935.3
Adams	3 098	27	36	408	158.5	11.2	71	526	100.2	9.7	11	25	1.8	0.2
Asotin	5 369	50	15	D	D	D	66	714	160.1	13.7	20	80	7.2	1.4
Benton	121 500	737	106	1 050	305.3	22.7	574	7 091	1 208.8	115.6	153	907	102.3	18.9
Chelan	36 185	266	115	1 760	782.5	53.1	415	4 030	697.7	73.3	121	526	38.9	9.2
Clallam	38 565	379	51	358	299.8	11.0	292	2 990	453.6	50.3	70	251	21.9	3.2
Clark	383 296	3 205	458	3 751	2 138.8	137.3	868	12 284	2 214.7	230.9	344	1 910	209.8	39.8
Columbia	2 170	38	14	D	D	D	29	147	23.2	2.5	2	D	D	D
Cowlitz	55 807	514	81	D	D	D	414	4 744	811.5	82.1	98	396	49.8	7.2
Douglas	16 347	127	31	188	81.8	5.6	91	1 109	184.9	17.4	18	99	9.9	1.5
Ferry	4 093	46	2	D	D	D	32	212	33.9	2.9	1	D	D	D
Franklin	34 272	281	93	1 111	550.7	33.0	196	2 205	487.4	45.9	40	219	23.1	4.6
Garfield	100	1	5	D	D	D	12	75	10.9	1.2	1	D	D	D
Grant	27 035	222	109	1 089	365.5	28.5	326	3 291	576.4	58.0	63	178	18.4	2.5
Grays Harbor	26 084	220	68	566	139.0	15.9	324	3 005	473.4	52.0	69	233	16.0	2.9
Island	77 410	569	33	126	40.9	3.2	231	2 000	311.9	33.5	80	226	23.6	3.5
Jefferson	32 864	274	23	D	D	D	149	974	146.0	14.3	34	100	7.9	1.1
King	1 378 380	11 726	4 937	63 696	50 226.1	2 641.6	7 031	99 542	19 399.8	2 025.3	3 119	20 887	3 219.0	560.3
Kitsap	134 078	1 111	135	925	330.9	29.9	773	10 338	1 722.1	179.5	240	1 053	103.4	16.3
Kittitas	34 268	315	36	350	129.9	9.2	178	1 427	230.8	23.0	40	135	12.1	1.7
Klickitat	9 859	86	22	120	33.9	2.2	69	346	47.4	5.4	24	58	5.4	0.6
Lewis	19 181	184	90	D	D	D	388	3 699	597.7	63.5	64	261	19.9	3.9
Lincoln	2 788	33	37	272	131.4	7.3	54	305	57.2	4.9	3	9	0.4	0.1
Mason	29 642	404	35	271	105.1	8.8	148	1 530	233.5	21.9	54	249	15.8	3.4
Okanogan	19 867	219	44	1 472	368.7	20.5	204	1 657	263.2	25.9	39	120	5.1	0.9
Pacific	6 532	63	14	D	D	D	115	680	87.1	11.0	21	37	3.6	0.3
Pend Oreille	6 163	91	5	D	D	D	44	247	35.8	3.3	7	16	0.9	0.2
Pierce	514 133	4 688	781	9 324	4 618.9	327.0	2 289	28 956	5 468.2	550.1	707	4 407	395.8	81.2
San Juan	41 041	392	17	D	D	D	115	561	81.7	10.1	48	92	13.0	1.8
Skagit	88 192	677	122	1 018	344.4	30.2	614	6 096	1 070.7	107.0	114	406	48.3	7.3
Skamania	3 961	36	2	D	D	D	15	137	14.2	1.7	5	10	0.9	0.1
Snohomish	639 866	6 111	755	6 808	3 561.6	232.3	2 027	26 302	5 303.0	524.2	670	3 061	366.2	65.2
Spokane	209 244	2 094	788	11 268	4 878.5	360.9	1 730	22 246	4 122.6	433.9	503	2 674	289.1	47.4
Stevens	12 727	131	28	133	39.8	3.2	141	1 239	184.0	18.6	26	96	10.2	1.3
Thurston	165 903	1 299	201	1 805	580.3	57.5	730	9 008	1 616.8	166.3	218	884	89.7	13.5
Wahkiakum	1 080	12	NA	NA	NA	NA	14	62	7.3	0.9	1	D	D	D
Walla Walla	25 928	199	78	726	318.1	16.4	222	2 426	376.4	41.9	45	187	17.0	2.6
Whatcom	170 603	1 625	308	2 451	1 042.7	76.0	840	9 758	1 673.3	165.7	220	877	91.8	12.3
Whitman	15 407	247	73	D	D	D	156	1 520	243.9	24.0	39	196	13.9	1.9
Yakima	52 078	484	291	4 871	1 853.8	141.9	854	10 174	1 741.6	174.9	212	1 018	99.9	17.0
WEST VIRGINIA	359 559	3 763	1 956	23 805	10 290.4	681.1	8 082	90 087	14 057.9	1 309.3	1 449	5 812	665.0	100.8
Barbour	664	9	9	75	12.7	1.2	57	509	69.3	6.7	4	6	1.9	0.0
Berkeley	85 128	777	52	D	D	D	335	4 000	546.7	52.2	67	241	18.9	3.4
Boone	1 609	17	19	121	52.9	3.5	110	984	146.3	14.4	15	26	4.4	0.3

1. Establishments with payroll.

Table B. States and Counties — **Professional, Manufacturing, and Accommodation and Foodservices**

STATE County	Professional, Scientific, and Technical Services[1], 1997				Manufacturing, 1997				Accommodation and Foodservices, 1997			
	Number of Establishments	Number of Employees	Receipts (mil dol)	Annual Payroll (mil dol)	Number of Establishments	Number of Employees	Receipts (mil dol)	Annual Payroll (mil dol)	Number of Establishments	Number of Employees	Sales (mil dol)	Annual Payroll (mil dol)
	147	148	149	150	151	152	153	154	155	156	157	158
VIRGINIA—Cont'd												
Manassas City	153	1 058	126.9	44.8	34	2 822	791.6	188.5	74	D	D	D
Manassas Park City	7	74	4.9	2.0	NA	NA	NA	NA	5	136	3.2	1.2
Martinsville City	54	223	16.6	7.7	39	8 726	724.1	203.0	46	768	25.1	6.6
Newport News City	286	3 023	218.8	88.6	131	24 707	3 300.5	898.4	312	5 464	170.1	47.7
Norfolk City	439	6 582	468.7	207.0	199	10 996	5 737.3	402.2	539	9 980	299.4	85.1
Norton City	19	188	8.9	4.0	NA	NA	NA	NA	23	D	D	D
Petersburg City	45	1 122	79.8	42.1	43	2 553	409.6	72.4	83	1 194	34.2	10.1
Poquoson City	13	79	5.6	2.8	NA	NA	NA	NA	20	193	4.3	1.2
Portsmouth City	105	1 023	82.1	31.5	71	1 812	368.7	52.0	137	2 040	58.7	15.8
Radford City	31	151	13.9	4.9	21	2 838	393.4	84.6	34	567	14.3	3.6
Richmond City	732	8 113	853.7	356.0	325	21 879	11 748.3	941.2	551	9 087	304.2	91.4
Roanoke City	331	2 632	211.6	88.7	152	8 489	2 156.3	242.9	325	6 380	203.4	58.7
Salem City	65	325	28.8	8.7	73	6 478	1 035.6	202.3	86	1 751	45.2	13.2
Staunton City	45	199	12.5	6.1	NA	NA	NA	NA	72	1 029	34.4	9.4
Suffolk City	59	273	21.4	9.2	52	2 257	1 103.5	63.8	62	1 027	32.8	8.9
Virginia Beach City	895	8 910	726.1	302.6	236	5 806	967.2	139.2	888	18 145	576.3	163.3
Waynesboro City	26	100	5.2	2.4	31	4 558	802.5	160.2	51	838	26.1	7.7
Williamsburg City	34	281	28.5	10.0	14	D	D	D	140	4 581	204.8	55.5
Winchester City	97	479	34.0	15.6	43	6 047	1 431.3	196.1	99	1 713	58.0	18.4
WASHINGTON	13 411	101 848	10 564.8	4 247.3	7 801	328 511	78 852.5	13 004.1	13 105	194 955	6 995.1	1 962.9
Adams	16	54	5.7	1.0	13	1 088	274.7	25.9	37	387	12.2	3.0
Asotin	30	106	7.4	2.7	NA	NA	NA	NA	40	516	16.1	4.9
Benton	274	7 403	926.0	364.4	121	3 672	885.5	139.5	256	4 223	136.1	36.8
Chelan	118	593	45.2	18.6	88	2 535	552.2	76.2	240	2 946	98.8	27.1
Clallam	105	434	33.5	12.0	75	1 481	359.2	49.0	214	2 104	75.9	19.6
Clark	564	2 929	234.2	98.3	421	19 537	3 854.3	715.2	506	8 570	271.7	76.8
Columbia	1	D	D	D	NA	NA	NA	NA	12	D	D	D
Cowlitz	116	677	43.7	18.9	125	8 309	2 496.5	364.4	214	3 208	97.1	28.7
Douglas	23	83	5.1	2.3	NA	NA	NA	NA	46	733	21.6	6.3
Ferry	7	27	1.9	0.8	NA	NA	NA	NA	21	126	5.1	1.1
Franklin	44	134	12.9	4.6	47	3 092	1 160.5	69.1	87	1 105	34.6	9.3
Garfield	1	D	D	D	NA	NA	NA	NA	3	D	D	D
Grant	93	407	25.6	9.5	56	4 090	806.9	111.3	170	1 930	58.8	15.3
Grays Harbor	84	320	22.3	11.1	97	3 792	822.9	125.7	238	2 150	74.2	20.3
Island	98	261	20.0	6.5	49	625	62.5	17.0	122	1 410	44.3	11.9
Jefferson	62	118	7.2	2.3	56	D	D	D	98	1 105	35.1	10.3
King	6 767	61 617	6 900.4	2 784.9	2 993	134 028	26 480.3	5 682.6	4 456	76 070	3 161.2	896.4
Kitsap	443	2 226	169.0	65.5	143	1 441	142.7	36.8	399	5 998	180.2	50.6
Kittitas	37	116	9.5	3.1	32	662	102.4	15.6	125	1 431	45.6	13.0
Klickitat	32	77	5.3	1.9	25	D	D	D	48	297	9.5	2.9
Lewis	81	301	19.9	7.0	115	3 630	648.0	97.1	196	1 919	62.9	17.5
Lincoln	10	78	4.6	2.4	NA	NA	NA	NA	33	154	4.2	1.1
Mason	58	284	17.1	5.9	52	1 664	343.9	51.7	98	953	29.9	7.8
Okanogan	46	150	9.7	3.4	28	794	123.6	20.9	122	1 192	42.4	12.4
Pacific	33	56	4.2	1.6	36	848	112.8	19.0	110	818	26.9	7.6
Pend Oreille	11	56	3.5	1.4	NA	NA	NA	NA	27	167	4.8	1.4
Pierce	974	4 965	444.3	174.0	680	22 283	4 275.9	705.2	1 218	18 808	603.6	169.3
San Juan	53	135	11.8	5.2	NA	NA	NA	NA	99	778	40.1	13.1
Skagit	209	732	55.7	20.6	185	5 026	2 917.7	148.9	277	3 614	118.1	31.5
Skamania	9	13	1.1	0.3	NA	NA	NA	NA	17	221	4.4	1.2
Snohomish	958	4 690	472.5	177.7	837	58 170	19 903.2	2 918.1	1 108	16 699	558.4	153.9
Spokane	886	5 738	444.5	186.9	572	20 892	3 994.6	681.4	904	14 456	453.2	128.5
Stevens	31	93	5.4	2.1	40	1 546	363.6	53.6	82	689	23.5	5.4
Thurston	401	2 571	198.1	86.2	156	3 218	761.0	100.7	406	6 076	193.0	56.6
Wahkiakum	4	D	D	D	NA	NA	NA	NA	13	50	1.5	0.4
Walla Walla	76	314	20.5	8.0	66	2 400	544.7	89.4	113	1 482	42.8	12.0
Whatcom	390	2 615	246.5	109.0	314	9 184	3 947.0	281.4	429	5 926	195.5	52.8
Whitman	43	156	10.3	3.5	NA	NA	NA	NA	110	1 196	30.9	7.6
Yakima	223	1 298	119.4	43.2	239	10 163	2 090.5	264.6	411	5 371	178.6	47.8
WEST VIRGINIA	2 517	15 714	1 166.9	395.2	1 505	72 813	18 293.3	2 460.7	3 290	51 529	1 633.2	462.3
Barbour	15	53	1.8	0.7	NA	NA	NA	NA	22	D	D	D
Berkeley	81	610	55.2	18.1	38	3 093	470.4	85.1	129	1 947	67.6	17.0
Boone	17	104	7.5	2.9	NA	NA	NA	NA	22	259	8.3	2.4

1. Firms subject to federal tax.

	Health Care and Social Assistance[1], 1997				Other Services[1], 1997				Federal funds and grants, fiscal 2001[2]			
									Expenditures (mil dol)			
										Direct payments for individuals[3]		
STATE County	Number of Establishments	Number of Employees	Receipts (mil dol)	Annual Payroll (mil dol)	Number of Establishments	Number of Employees	Receipts (mil dol)	Annual Payroll (mil dol)	Total	Social Security and government retirement	Medicare	Food stamps and Supplemental Security Income
	159	160	161	162	163	164	165	166	167	168	169	170
VIRGINIA—Cont'd												
Manassas City	106	1 161	67.1	34.9	108	832	60.2	22.2	644.1	118.0	23.6	3.1
Manassas Park City	NA	NA	NA	NA	6	72	4.6	1.5	14.2	2.4	0.0	0.3
Martinsville City	78	712	46.8	21.4	40	196	8.8	2.5	138.5	78.2	25.0	5.3
Newport News City	324	3 878	217.6	122.3	306	2 234	116.3	41.1	7 225.8	445.9	112.2	33.6
Norfolk City	400	6 583	451.7	219.1	388	2 569	147.8	49.7	4 896.8	560.2	182.4	62.1
Norton City	35	248	23.3	13.0	19	73	3.6	1.3	45.0	20.4	7.3	2.2
Petersburg City	89	1 438	64.1	32.6	76	620	32.6	12.0	324.0	136.4	54.7	13.4
Poquoson City	10	150	6.0	3.0	16	74	3.1	1.2	27.7	21.3	4.1	0.4
Portsmouth City	170	2 393	134.8	71.8	163	1 364	74.6	27.2	1 477.8	304.3	104.5	30.6
Radford City	47	360	22.1	12.7	19	102	3.5	1.2	97.0	29.3	12.0	1.6
Richmond City	540	14 788	1 111.6	414.8	504	3 887	256.6	82.0	3 407.6	910.0	283.7	78.6
Roanoke City	274	3 623	274.3	127.4	337	2 403	123.8	43.2	816.6	349.2	124.0	26.8
Salem City	64	2 817	224.2	72.7	81	349	19.0	6.2	233.9	90.0	26.6	0.9
Staunton City	63	646	38.4	17.3	53	404	19.7	6.9	153.9	83.0	31.4	4.2
Suffolk City	89	1 334	69.9	34.9	85	453	22.2	6.7	378.3	161.3	47.7	16.4
Virginia Beach City	809	8 315	473.4	223.9	716	4 870	254.7	89.2	2 823.8	1 122.1	170.5	40.5
Waynesboro City	47	446	26.6	10.6	51	311	19.3	5.2	107.5	69.8	21.3	3.3
Williamsburg City	61	697	45.1	23.5	35	184	7.1	2.6	225.8	138.8	31.5	1.7
Winchester City	126	1 018	98.2	53.5	77	400	21.2	7.3	150.9	71.4	27.0	3.6
WASHINGTON	12 310	122 813	7 797.7	3 390.2	8 771	49 756	3 492.0	1 033.0	36 903.4	12 116.2	3 603.5	840.7
Adams	15	205	8.3	4.2	22	45	4.2	0.8	123.7	20.7	7.8	2.8
Asotin	41	459	18.6	6.7	21	68	3.7	1.1	109.6	55.1	17.6	4.6
Benton	335	2 841	183.0	74.1	178	1 008	55.3	17.2	2 519.7	263.8	71.1	14.6
Chelan	134	1 984	162.8	65.7	118	396	29.1	7.7	305.9	144.6	41.0	7.9
Clallam	173	1 335	72.2	28.6	99	394	27.2	6.8	434.8	241.5	65.6	12.0
Clark	475	6 155	369.2	170.5	414	2 117	141.8	43.3	1 273.3	608.5	164.4	45.3
Columbia	6	21	0.8	0.4	13	33	2.3	0.6	40.0	11.6	3.9	0.8
Cowlitz	168	1 933	110.4	48.6	138	706	43.7	13.4	479.6	212.5	70.0	19.1
Douglas	33	367	23.6	7.8	36	122	9.5	2.5	137.6	58.1	25.5	3.2
Ferry	9	30	0.9	0.2	3	D	D	D	39.0	17.2	4.0	1.5
Franklin	81	669	40.5	15.7	67	343	28.5	7.7	212.6	67.8	24.9	8.2
Garfield	4	9	0.6	0.2	5	8	0.7	0.1	43.3	7.7	2.5	0.2
Grant	84	781	53.0	19.4	88	371	28.8	7.2	357.3	140.5	39.8	12.0
Grays Harbor	147	1 201	69.5	33.2	98	347	22.1	6.0	397.3	180.1	69.1	17.8
Island	115	796	38.3	14.6	62	266	14.8	4.7	627.4	202.1	36.3	5.0
Jefferson	61	715	28.3	13.0	58	220	12.2	3.2	155.5	95.9	25.0	3.2
King	4 360	41 887	2 913.7	1 247.1	3 244	20 986	1 642.9	474.2	10 228.5	2 970.9	1 092.4	229.4
Kitsap	473	4 466	245.3	104.1	264	1 300	77.7	23.9	2 340.0	662.8	119.7	28.5
Kittitas	51	468	25.4	9.5	55	261	12.6	3.2	130.9	64.6	19.9	2.6
Klickitat	22	165	8.1	3.5	18	64	5.7	1.0	108.8	46.0	12.6	3.4
Lewis	138	1 451	84.3	35.4	84	443	40.2	10.2	353.1	183.8	64.8	12.9
Lincoln	14	60	4.0	1.9	17	24	2.0	0.4	105.4	31.5	9.9	0.8
Mason	60	458	27.2	9.5	51	194	10.5	3.1	266.5	161.2	42.8	8.4
Okanogan	69	594	33.3	14.1	51	138	10.7	2.2	229.0	94.9	26.2	8.6
Pacific	33	209	10.1	3.9	26	72	4.3	1.2	141.6	73.3	24.5	4.3
Pend Oreille	11	70	3.8	1.6	9	28	1.4	0.4	62.8	33.8	7.6	3.3
Pierce	1 439	14 037	865.7	384.0	908	5 430	354.7	114.5	4 171.2	1 636.4	378.2	118.7
San Juan	20	62	3.8	0.9	20	41	3.2	0.8	58.5	39.1	9.6	0.7
Skagit	219	2 291	142.9	67.5	151	880	60.6	18.6	492.7	251.7	82.6	12.5
Skamania	6	23	1.2	0.3	5	9	0.6	0.2	42.9	16.1	3.5	1.2
Snohomish	1 067	10 785	623.5	293.5	827	4 502	292.6	93.7	2 045.8	963.3	291.0	56.4
Spokane	991	11 137	681.4	306.8	699	4 355	258.4	78.5	2 263.1	954.5	317.4	73.2
Stevens	41	475	20.5	9.7	44	189	12.2	3.8	189.4	92.0	24.1	6.5
Thurston	459	4 551	322.8	137.0	264	1 356	79.0	24.2	1 842.3	575.3	121.0	30.1
Wahkiakum	4	72	2.7	1.2	2	D	D	D	21.6	11.0	4.0	0.3
Walla Walla	96	1 183	67.7	29.4	54	256	17.3	4.8	311.8	127.5	40.0	7.5
Whatcom	406	3 627	201.2	82.1	225	1 161	81.3	22.1	904.4	319.7	85.4	24.0
Whitman	59	647	30.7	14.4	56	207	11.4	3.0	275.4	57.7	20.5	2.4
Yakima	391	4 594	298.6	129.8	277	1 408	87.6	26.8	1 002.9	371.6	137.5	46.7
WEST VIRGINIA	3 266	40 085	2 575.0	1 056.9	2 512	14 805	867.4	255.9	12 540.8	4 965.2	1 802.1	572.1
Barbour	15	124	5.4	1.8	12	29	1.5	0.3	89.1	37.5	16.1	6.4
Berkeley	114	863	55.4	19.8	94	410	22.6	6.8	516.9	182.8	45.7	8.7
Boone	22	209	9.9	4.0	23	101	6.3	1.8	144.2	73.9	23.6	11.6

1. Firms subject to federal tax.   2. October 1, 2000 to September 30, 2001.   3. State totals may include programs not allocated by county.

	Federal funds and grants, fiscal 2001[1] (cont'd)							Local government finances, 1997				
	Expenditures (mil dol) (cont'd)							General revenue				
	Procurement contract awards			Grants[2]						Taxes		
											Per capita[3] (dollars)	
STATE County	Salaries and wages	Defense	Other	Medicaid and other health-related	Nutrition and family welfare	Education	Other	Total (mil dol)	Intergovern-mental (mil dol)	Total (mil dol)	Total	Property
	171	172	173	174	175	176	177	178	179	180	181	182
VIRGINIA—Cont'd												
Manassas City	28.1	379.1	65.8	3.8	2.4	1.9	8.7	76.6	21.7	40.7	1 186	913
Manassas Park City	0.7	1.7	0.1	6.3	0.4	0.5	0.5	22.4	7.6	9.0	1 063	848
Martinsville City	4.2	1.5	1.7	10.2	1.3	1.2	3.4	36.6	15.8	12.7	806	458
Newport News City	378.0	5 919.4	136.3	50.1	19.8	15.3	65.3	396.2	168.1	171.0	972	663
Norfolk City	2 447.5	1 285.7	20.9	132.6	44.0	32.4	55.7	812.6	302.1	245.3	1 070	627
Norton City	5.8	2.7	0.2	3.3	2.1	0.4	0.3	9.0	4.5	3.6	846	352
Petersburg City	11.0	16.6	14.9	32.8	7.8	5.8	10.7	174.8	43.5	30.5	894	581
Poquoson City	0.8	0.0	0.0	0.4	0.1	0.6	0.0	20.5	7.9	10.6	923	773
Portsmouth City	563.5	276.8	28.2	63.9	17.3	8.4	49.3	245.9	121.8	85.2	856	572
Radford City	6.2	28.7	1.0	4.1	1.5	0.5	9.7	34.3	7.9	19.8	1 291	994
Richmond City	506.1	135.2	159.7	327.3	281.6	183.6	371.8	746.1	299.9	276.1	1 435	951
Roanoke City	97.5	53.5	25.7	58.8	15.8	6.9	24.5	272.3	112.4	114.3	1 214	691
Salem City	86.8	0.1	12.7	7.4	0.8	1.4	0.4	57.7	14.8	33.0	1 332	805
Staunton City	7.3	0.4	1.2	11.5	3.2	1.9	7.0	43.1	17.5	19.4	833	495
Suffolk City	22.5	57.1	6.0	36.6	7.2	3.5	7.0	120.7	59.0	48.9	802	579
Virginia Beach City	925.2	336.2	88.6	31.9	14.8	24.9	22.1	952.8	316.9	437.8	1 012	690
Waynesboro City	2.9	0.2	0.8	4.8	1.5	0.8	0.1	42.7	15.2	20.1	1 083	726
Williamsburg City	17.1	7.8	5.3	2.2	1.1	4.0	14.2	41.9	20.2	18.4	1 558	519
Winchester City	18.3	1.3	11.5	9.4	1.4	2.8	2.0	68.6	18.3	29.4	1 312	623
WASHINGTON	4 945.2	2 403.6	3 076.9	3 407.0	1 023.5	580.7	1 782.5	X	X	X	X	X
Adams	2.1	0.0	8.9	23.0	3.4	0.7	16.2	59.9	35.2	11.6	747	574
Asotin	2.9	2.8	0.9	10.8	4.1	1.6	3.2	53.7	33.7	9.9	469	352
Benton	57.3	14.6	2 007.0	35.5	14.0	5.4	10.5	499.3	238.9	94.8	698	442
Chelan	32.0	1.0	7.8	35.4	9.9	5.3	8.7	178.7	79.6	52.1	872	595
Clallam	31.3	0.6	13.6	27.6	11.6	6.4	7.0	209.5	67.4	40.4	632	457
Clark	158.5	12.6	39.2	109.6	39.8	14.7	47.4	746.4	373.6	225.4	712	524
Columbia	2.5	0.7	0.3	4.0	0.8	0.1	1.6	20.6	10.9	2.6	610	471
Cowlitz	14.5	0.3	71.5	47.4	16.6	13.6	4.9	237.8	104.7	69.8	769	509
Douglas	6.3	3.9	0.5	9.4	3.1	1.0	2.1	81.0	49.3	18.0	536	434
Ferry	5.1	0.0	1.2	2.4	1.6	1.7	3.6	19.3	14.1	2.9	396	297
Franklin	24.9	6.3	7.2	20.1	11.6	5.1	10.8	142.0	75.3	32.8	697	445
Garfield	3.7	14.3	0.5	0.6	0.3	0.1	0.0	11.9	7.3	1.7	733	595
Grant	34.2	2.4	21.8	30.9	12.4	5.1	17.5	250.4	115.9	44.2	634	456
Grays Harbor	12.6	10.8	6.6	44.6	15.3	5.8	13.9	190.1	98.2	50.1	737	405
Island	288.6	66.7	2.6	9.9	3.5	5.1	3.2	111.5	61.1	31.9	452	308
Jefferson	7.5	1.0	2.8	9.6	3.1	1.5	4.5	78.8	30.3	21.1	812	591
King	1 226.7	1 378.9	532.7	1 465.3	181.7	76.6	747.5	5 864.6	1 760.6	2 283.7	1 399	804
Kitsap	999.8	306.1	39.8	70.5	23.4	27.0	23.4	493.4	253.0	153.2	653	490
Kittitas	7.6	0.1	1.8	11.1	4.3	3.7	5.5	85.7	34.9	20.5	653	391
Klickitat	4.8	7.0	1.2	9.0	3.5	1.3	10.3	64.0	33.3	9.6	506	387
Lewis	13.1	1.0	5.3	43.7	11.6	7.1	2.7	175.7	89.7	48.0	710	443
Lincoln	3.3	0.0	0.6	2.2	1.1	1.0	3.5	54.4	24.4	9.2	943	785
Mason	4.7	3.5	4.6	16.1	7.7	3.3	6.7	130.2	55.6	32.0	646	464
Okanogan	19.2	0.4	8.7	21.9	11.1	5.7	15.1	123.3	58.3	21.7	561	393
Pacific	6.1	1.2	9.7	11.8	3.5	1.2	3.7	65.9	31.8	15.6	740	446
Pend Oreille	4.0	0.0	0.9	7.2	2.1	0.5	1.8	49.3	19.8	10.5	928	731
Pierce	1 114.3	194.0	66.1	371.7	104.0	39.2	58.4	1 692.8	818.3	516.1	776	551
San Juan	3.5	0.0	1.5	0.9	0.6	0.2	2.0	36.8	14.0	16.2	1 324	904
Skagit	19.7	6.8	10.6	36.5	13.4	10.5	33.3	361.1	116.9	77.8	796	560
Skamania	7.2	1.4	6.0	2.4	1.3	0.2	3.0	26.8	16.9	3.7	387	290
Snohomish	261.9	37.7	55.5	183.2	48.7	19.4	61.2	1 440.6	597.1	460.5	816	535
Spokane	319.5	41.0	51.6	252.6	65.2	30.8	64.6	944.3	463.4	295.3	730	456
Stevens	16.3	0.0	11.5	17.8	7.1	3.8	4.8	75.0	50.2	15.4	392	274
Thurston	66.0	2.2	16.9	173.8	255.6	193.3	358.9	505.5	248.5	163.6	817	574
Wahkiakum	0.9	0.0	0.3	1.4	0.3	0.1	3.1	12.6	5.8	2.7	702	492
Walla Walla	36.5	5.8	5.1	24.9	8.0	4.3	8.5	127.7	70.7	33.4	625	450
Whatcom	45.1	261.9	18.0	64.3	19.6	10.6	20.1	363.0	155.4	129.3	838	559
Whitman	13.7	0.7	3.9	26.5	3.4	5.1	51.3	107.3	49.1	23.9	608	421
Yakima	67.5	15.7	32.0	171.4	73.5	29.2	20.7	528.1	328.0	116.2	532	342
WEST VIRGINIA	1 005.2	104.6	422.8	1 403.7	353.9	242.9	970.3	X	X	X	X	X
Barbour	2.4	0.0	0.8	17.8	2.4	1.3	1.8	26.8	16.6	3.3	205	170
Berkeley	156.4	2.4	76.2	22.6	4.4	2.9	4.3	106.5	55.8	33.1	479	413
Boone	5.3	0.6	1.3	17.6	4.1	2.4	0.1	59.4	27.2	18.0	680	656

1. October 1, 2000 to September 30, 2001. 2. State totals may include programs not allocated by county. 3. Based on the resident population estimated as of July 1 of the year shown.

Table B. States and Counties — **Local Government Finances, Government Employment, and Elections**

STATE County	Local government finances, 1997 (cont'd)									Government employment, 1999			Presidential election, 2000[2]		
	Direct general expenditure							Debt outstanding					Percent of vote cast —		
			Percent of total for —												
	Total (mil dol)	Per capita[1] (dollars)	Education	Health and hospitals	Police protection	Public welfare	Highways	Total (mil dol)	Per capita[1] (dollars)	Federal civilian	Federal military	State and local	Democratic	Republican	All other
	183	184	185	186	187	188	189	190	191	192	193	194	195	196	197
VIRGINIA—Cont'd															
Manassas City	79.5	2 317	56.4	1.7	7.1	3.6	4.0	80.3	2 341	(3)	(3)	(3)	42.4	54.4	3.2
Manassas Park City	22.7	2 679	44.9	1.0	5.9	6.1	2.4	26.9	3 181	(3)	(3)	(3)	40.6	56.6	2.8
Martinsville City	40.6	2 569	41.8	0.5	8.4	4.2	5.9	13.9	880	(4)	(4)	(4)	53.6	45.0	1.3
Newport News City	428.8	2 439	42.5	0.5	7.1	5.5	5.3	545.9	3 104	4 919	9 242	10 792	51.5	46.7	1.7
Norfolk City	850.5	3 708	37.4	5.3	5.2	4.7	2.6	1 485.6	6 476	15 332	57 471	19 996	61.9	35.5	2.7
Norton City	9.0	2 118	49.8	0.0	9.9	7.3	8.4	2.0	474	(5)	(5)	(5)	56.7	41.8	1.4
Petersburg City	152.8	4 476	23.5	49.7	3.8	5.5	2.2	76.9	2 252	(6)	(6)	(6)	79.1	19.1	1.8
Poquoson City	19.0	1 660	61.9	2.1	12.7	0.0	4.4	19.9	1 736	(7)	(7)	(7)	24.7	72.9	2.4
Portsmouth City	298.4	2 998	39.6	3.3	4.1	4.0	2.7	270.8	2 721	9 653	5 137	6 165	62.9	35.6	1.5
Radford City	25.8	1 684	41.8	2.5	10.7	5.4	6.1	0.0	0	(8)	(8)	(8)	46.4	49.2	4.4
Richmond City	808.6	4 203	28.3	4.6	5.5	8.4	3.5	1 010.5	5 252	6 823	1 312	42 038	64.8	30.8	4.4
Roanoke City	259.9	2 761	37.7	0.6	5.0	8.3	3.5	356.2	3 783	1 739	398	6 315	53.6	43.8	2.6
Salem City	77.6	3 129	41.6	0.1	5.5	0.7	4.3	33.3	1 343	(9)	(9)	(9)	40.4	57.5	2.1
Staunton City	39.9	1 709	45.8	0.7	6.4	7.5	7.5	16.1	688	(10)	(10)	(10)	39.0	57.3	3.7
Suffolk City	136.1	2 229	51.3	0.1	4.1	4.8	3.3	162.4	2 660	214	293	4 034	50.6	48.0	1.4
Virginia Beach City	908.1	2 099	46.6	2.4	5.1	1.9	2.4	1 025.9	2 372	4 973	22 714	19 640	41.7	56.0	2.3
Waynesboro City	40.0	2 158	42.5	0.5	6.3	9.6	4.9	22.3	1 202	(10)	(10)	(10)	38.6	57.5	3.9
Williamsburg City	106.2	9 003	65.6	0.3	2.5	0.8	1.3	40.1	3 401	(11)	(11)	(11)	46.3	47.7	5.9
Winchester City	73.8	3 289	41.1	0.3	4.2	2.5	2.3	149.0	6 642	(12)	(12)	(12)	42.1	54.7	3.3
WASHINGTON	X	X	X	X	X	X	X	X	X	66 271	72 636	396 968	50.2	44.6	5.2
Adams	59.9	3 854	52.4	5.4	4.5	0.0	7.4	18.9	1 218	52	57	1 373	28.3	69.2	2.6
Asotin	51.0	2 409	42.0	6.6	4.5	0.1	13.3	21.0	992	70	79	946	34.3	61.5	4.3
Benton	391.1	2 881	44.2	14.6	3.6	0.0	8.3	7 433.4	54 749	827	524	9 075	32.6	64.2	3.2
Chelan	165.9	2 777	50.5	6.0	4.7	0.0	5.3	836.0	14 000	697	227	5 469	31.7	64.0	4.2
Clallam	181.9	2 849	37.0	26.7	4.1	0.0	4.7	92.9	1 455	438	497	4 852	42.8	50.4	6.8
Clark	753.2	2 380	57.1	2.5	3.8	0.2	3.9	981.9	3 102	2 456	1 256	16 358	45.6	49.6	4.8
Columbia	22.2	5 192	23.7	29.0	4.0	0.3	24.4	3.8	885	59	15	460	24.4	72.3	3.2
Cowlitz	261.8	2 882	45.4	2.9	5.1	0.0	8.3	113.5	1 250	268	342	5 422	49.3	45.6	5.1
Douglas	67.1	2 005	54.3	6.8	3.9	0.0	12.5	235.8	7 042	147	134	1 719	29.7	66.4	4.0
Ferry	19.3	2 653	52.7	4.3	3.6	0.0	12.3	11.6	1 604	141	27	577	30.7	62.4	7.0
Franklin	136.2	2 896	48.0	2.1	5.1	0.0	4.3	121.4	2 582	470	174	3 577	34.2	63.1	2.7
Garfield	12.0	5 258	28.6	21.2	3.3	0.0	25.3	1.6	706	121	0	279	22.6	73.9	3.5
Grant	236.1	3 387	47.4	18.6	3.0	1.3	7.3	677.4	9 716	286	268	5 890	29.7	66.5	3.7
Grays Harbor	195.6	2 879	44.8	5.3	5.2	0.1	9.0	76.8	1 130	213	290	4 594	51.2	43.2	5.6
Island	112.8	1 597	53.8	2.8	4.8	0.0	8.1	85.7	1 213	1 419	7 879	2 972	44.8	49.7	5.5
Jefferson	77.6	2 989	30.4	23.9	2.7	0.0	10.6	54.9	2 114	161	110	1 842	52.3	38.5	9.2
King	5 896.8	3 611	29.1	9.5	5.2	0.1	5.5	6 853.8	4 197	20 879	7 581	128 156	60.0	34.4	5.6
Kitsap	491.9	2 097	54.8	4.4	3.4	0.0	3.6	405.8	1 730	14 248	13 265	11 347	49.0	45.3	5.7
Kittitas	86.4	2 752	35.8	20.2	4.2	0.0	12.1	36.0	1 146	161	130	3 872	39.2	54.9	6.0
Klickitat	63.5	3 329	47.0	12.2	2.9	0.0	9.4	63.9	3 351	107	73	1 489	37.5	55.9	6.7
Lewis	172.6	2 553	46.1	5.2	4.5	0.0	13.1	239.7	3 546	298	255	4 676	33.0	61.9	5.1
Lincoln	54.3	5 539	35.0	20.6	2.6	0.0	13.8	12.0	1 227	71	36	1 232	27.3	68.2	4.5
Mason	114.4	2 313	43.4	18.2	3.4	0.0	6.5	77.0	1 556	109	187	3 372	48.4	45.6	6.0
Okanogan	116.8	3 022	43.2	24.6	4.2	0.1	4.3	56.9	1 472	796	143	3 005	29.3	63.4	7.3
Pacific	64.3	3 047	41.7	21.5	4.0	0.0	8.5	19.2	907	62	160	1 533	51.4	42.5	6.1
Pend Oreille	44.8	3 976	32.4	32.5	2.6	0.0	7.9	38.6	3 429	113	43	800	36.3	56.6	7.2
Pierce	1 668.3	2 510	45.9	4.9	5.5	0.3	5.1	1 486.4	2 236	9 398	23 054	38 699	51.5	44.1	4.4
San Juan	35.1	2 861	35.4	3.3	4.7	0.2	8.6	34.8	2 835	63	48	886	52.6	35.7	11.6
Skagit	368.1	3 767	39.5	28.6	3.0	0.0	4.3	237.1	2 427	395	379	7 696	45.2	49.0	5.8
Skamania	23.1	2 398	41.8	3.7	5.0	0.1	15.6	2.7	276	192	37	596	41.3	50.6	8.1
Snohomish	1 424.3	2 523	44.8	9.8	4.0	0.7	6.7	2 008.0	3 557	2 432	7 575	29 273	51.6	43.7	4.7
Spokane	925.5	2 287	51.7	3.3	4.3	0.0	5.1	631.4	1 560	4 323	4 974	26 271	43.3	51.9	4.7
Stevens	70.5	1 798	59.1	3.3	4.5	0.0	10.3	38.7	985	383	149	2 061	30.9	62.8	6.3
Thurston	486.5	2 428	50.4	4.1	3.9	0.1	5.1	353.4	1 764	988	792	32 085	51.8	41.0	7.2
Wahkiakum	10.8	2 784	29.0	9.6	4.4	0.1	19.3	1.9	499	16	14	239	40.7	52.4	6.9
Walla Walla	133.4	2 493	46.6	4.5	4.6	0.0	10.9	79.1	1 479	852	203	3 854	33.6	62.3	4.1
Whatcom	323.7	2 098	48.4	2.7	4.8	0.0	7.8	301.5	1 955	845	617	10 043	46.1	46.5	7.4
Whitman	105.1	2 672	44.2	21.2	3.5	0.0	9.2	29.8	757	276	157	8 068	40.1	55.4	4.5
Yakima	560.2	2 566	57.3	1.2	5.2	0.0	5.8	307.9	1 410	1 439	876	12 310	38.0	58.7	3.4
WEST VIRGINIA	X	X	X	X	X	X	X	X	X	21 361	9 905	118 536	45.6	51.9	2.4
Barbour	25.8	1 590	62.3	4.9	1.8	0.0	1.0	38.5	2 373	45	83	737	41.4	56.4	2.3
Berkeley	108.2	1 567	72.8	1.5	3.1	0.0	0.8	110.2	1 595	3 028	404	3 105	38.2	59.2	2.6
Boone	58.4	2 209	60.3	19.8	1.6	0.0	0.6	5.2	198	93	135	1 406	61.9	36.7	1.4

1. Based on the resident population estimated as of July 1 of the year shown. 2. Data subject to copyright. 3. Manassas and Manassas Park included with Prince William County. 4. Martinsville included with Henry County. 5. Norton included with Wise County. 6. Petersburg and Colonial Heights included with Dinwiddie County. 7. Poquoson included with York County. 8. Radford included with Montgomery County. 9. Salem included with Roanoke County. 10. Staunton and Waynesboro included with Augusta County. 11. Williamsburg included with James City County. 12. Winchester included with Frederick County.

Table B. States and Counties — Land Area and Population

STATE/ County code	MSA/ PMSA/ NECMA code[1]	County Type[2]	STATE County	Land area,[3] (sq km) 2000	Total persons	Rank	Per square kilometer	White	Black	Am. Indian, Alaska Native	Asian and Pacific Islander	Percent Hispanic[4]	Under 5 years	5 to 17 years	18 to 24 years	25 to 34 years	35 to 44 years	45 to 54 years
					1	2	3	4	5	6	7	8	9	10	11	12	13	14	15
			WEST VIRGINIA—Cont'd															
54 007	...	9	Braxton	1 330	14 702	2 107	11.1	98.7	0.8	0.9	0.2	0.4	5.3	17.5	7.5	13.0	15.1	15.0
54 009	8080	3	Brooke	230	25 447	1 543	110.6	98.5	1.1	0.4	0.5	0.4	5.0	15.4	9.4	11.4	14.4	15.5
54 011	3400	2	Cabell	729	96 784	534	132.8	94.4	4.7	0.6	1.1	0.7	5.4	14.6	13.5	13.1	13.6	13.8
54 013	...	9	Calhoun	727	7 582	2 637	10.4	99.3	0.1	0.6	0.1	0.6	5.1	17.3	8.0	10.3	15.5	15.9
54 015	...	8	Clay	887	10 330	2 412	11.6	99.1	0.2	1.5	0.1	0.4	6.1	19.5	9.0	12.7	14.8	14.3
54 017	...	9	Doddridge	830	7 403	2 648	8.9	99.1	0.4	0.9	0.3	0.6	5.9	19.1	8.4	10.9	15.7	14.6
54 019	...	6	Fayette	1 720	47 579	958	27.7	93.6	5.9	0.8	0.5	0.7	5.6	16.1	9.6	12.4	14.7	15.3
54 021	...	9	Gilmer	881	7 160	2 671	8.1	98.2	1.1	0.7	0.7	0.7	4.9	15.4	16.4	10.9	13.5	13.2
54 023	...	8	Grant	1 236	11 299	2 350	9.1	98.8	0.9	0.4	0.1	0.5	6.3	16.4	7.8	13.3	14.2	15.1
54 025	...	7	Greenbrier	2 645	34 453	1 265	13.0	96.2	3.4	1.0	0.3	0.7	5.5	16.1	7.7	11.2	14.9	15.4
54 027	...	8	Hampshire	1 662	20 203	1 780	12.2	98.6	0.9	0.6	0.3	0.6	6.1	19.0	7.1	12.4	15.2	14.6
54 029	8080	3	Hancock	215	32 667	1 325	151.9	97.0	2.5	0.4	0.5	0.7	5.3	15.5	7.2	11.8	15.3	15.8
54 031	...	9	Hardy	1 511	12 669	2 250	8.4	97.5	2.1	0.5	0.2	0.7	6.0	17.4	7.6	13.0	15.9	14.4
54 033	...	5	Harrison	1 078	68 652	719	63.7	97.4	1.9	0.5	0.8	1.0	5.7	17.4	8.3	12.4	15.1	14.4
54 035	...	6	Jackson	1 206	28 000	1 451	23.2	99.4	0.2	0.5	0.3	0.3	6.1	18.1	7.9	12.4	15.4	13.8
54 037	8840	1	Jefferson	543	42 190	1 054	77.7	92.2	6.7	0.8	1.0	1.7	6.3	17.6	10.0	13.1	16.8	15.5
54 039	1480	2	Kanawha	2 339	200 073	276	85.5	91.6	7.6	0.7	1.0	0.6	5.7	15.6	8.4	12.7	15.4	15.6
54 041	...	7	Lewis	990	16 919	1 957	17.1	99.3	0.2	0.7	0.4	0.5	5.3	16.8	7.7	12.7	15.2	15.0
54 043	...	8	Lincoln	1 133	22 108	1 687	19.5	99.6	0.2	0.6	0.2	0.5	6.0	17.6	9.3	13.7	15.4	14.7
54 045	...	7	Logan	1 176	37 710	1 169	32.1	96.9	2.8	0.4	0.4	0.5	5.7	16.4	9.3	12.9	15.1	16.3
54 047	...	7	McDowell	1 385	27 329	1 473	19.7	87.7	12.2	0.6	0.1	0.5	5.1	18.0	7.9	11.4	15.4	15.8
54 049	...	5	Marion	802	56 598	837	70.6	96.0	3.6	0.6	0.5	0.7	5.1	15.5	10.5	12.6	13.8	14.4
54 051	9000	3	Marshall	795	35 519	1 231	44.7	99.0	0.6	0.4	0.4	0.6	5.3	17.5	7.3	12.0	15.1	16.0
54 053	...	6	Mason	1 118	25 957	1 517	23.2	98.9	0.7	0.5	0.3	0.5	5.9	16.9	8.3	12.1	15.6	14.9
54 055	...	7	Mercer	1 089	62 980	770	57.8	93.4	6.0	0.6	0.6	0.5	5.8	15.3	9.8	12.5	13.7	15.0
54 057	1900	3	Mineral	849	27 078	1 479	31.9	96.9	2.9	0.4	0.3	0.6	5.5	17.8	8.6	12.6	14.5	14.7
54 059	...	7	Mingo	1 095	28 253	1 440	25.8	97.1	2.5	0.7	0.3	0.5	5.8	18.4	9.2	13.3	15.9	15.6
54 061	...	5	Monongalia	935	81 866	639	87.6	93.5	3.8	0.6	3.0	1.0	4.9	13.3	23.4	14.3	13.4	12.5
54 063	...	9	Monroe	1 226	14 583	2 113	11.9	93.6	6.3	0.7	0.2	0.5	5.0	15.2	8.1	14.4	16.0	15.0
54 065	...	8	Morgan	593	14 943	2 096	25.2	98.9	0.8	0.4	0.2	0.8	6.1	16.3	6.8	11.9	15.4	15.4
54 067	...	7	Nicholas	1 680	26 562	1 497	15.8	99.4	0.1	0.6	0.3	0.5	5.4	17.9	8.1	12.2	15.4	15.4
54 069	9000	3	Ohio	275	47 427	959	172.5	95.3	4.0	0.3	1.1	0.5	5.2	16.1	10.5	10.8	14.3	14.8
54 071	...	9	Pendleton	1 807	8 196	2 593	4.5	97.0	2.6	0.4	0.4	0.9	5.4	16.5	7.3	12.1	14.4	14.8
54 073	...	8	Pleasants	339	7 514	2 641	22.2	98.8	0.6	0.8	0.2	0.4	5.9	17.9	7.8	12.7	16.1	14.7
54 075	...	9	Pocahontas	2 435	9 131	2 520	3.7	99.0	0.8	0.5	0.2	0.4	5.0	15.9	7.0	11.9	15.6	15.3
54 077	...	7	Preston	1 679	29 334	1 418	17.5	99.4	0.4	0.4	0.3	0.6	5.6	18.1	8.0	12.3	15.4	15.1
54 079	1480	2	Putnam	897	51 589	899	57.5	98.5	0.7	0.4	0.7	0.5	6.5	18.4	7.6	13.2	17.2	15.5
54 081	...	5	Raleigh	1 572	79 220	647	50.4	90.3	8.9	0.5	0.9	0.9	5.5	16.0	8.7	13.6	15.0	15.8
54 083	...	7	Randolph	2 693	28 262	1 439	10.5	98.2	1.2	0.4	0.5	0.7	5.2	17.1	8.7	13.1	15.4	14.6
54 085	...	8	Ritchie	1 175	10 343	2 410	8.8	99.4	0.2	0.8	0.2	0.5	5.5	17.5	7.7	12.0	15.9	14.9
54 087	...	8	Roane	1 252	15 446	2 056	12.3	99.1	0.4	0.6	0.3	0.7	5.7	17.7	8.7	11.7	14.9	15.2
54 089	...	7	Summers	935	12 999	2 234	13.9	97.4	2.4	0.6	0.3	0.5	4.6	15.9	7.5	10.6	14.1	15.7
54 091	...	7	Taylor	448	16 089	2 017	35.9	98.7	1.0	0.5	0.3	0.6	5.4	17.5	7.9	12.9	15.6	14.9
54 093	...	9	Tucker	1 085	7 321	2 654	6.7	99.5	0.3	0.5	0.3	0.2	4.8	16.4	6.7	11.5	14.8	15.1
54 095	...	9	Tyler	667	9 592	2 479	14.4	99.8	0.1	0.4	0.2	0.4	5.2	18.0	6.5	11.9	15.0	15.3
54 097	...	7	Upshur	919	23 404	1 622	25.5	98.7	0.8	0.5	0.4	0.6	5.3	17.2	12.6	11.6	14.1	14.3
54 099	3400	2	Wayne	1 310	42 903	1 039	32.8	99.3	0.2	0.6	0.3	0.5	5.8	17.6	8.7	13.2	14.5	14.4
54 101	...	9	Webster	1 440	9 719	2 469	6.7	99.8	0.1	0.5	0.2	0.4	5.1	17.8	8.0	11.8	14.9	16.1
54 103	...	6	Wetzel	930	17 693	1 917	19.0	99.4	0.2	0.4	0.4	0.4	5.7	18.1	6.8	11.6	14.9	14.9
54 105	...	8	Wirt	603	5 873	2 796	9.7	99.3	0.3	0.6	0.2	0.3	5.6	19.8	7.6	12.1	17.5	13.2
54 107	6020	3	Wood	951	87 986	592	92.5	98.1	1.3	0.6	0.7	0.6	5.8	17.2	8.0	12.5	15.4	14.7
54 109	...	9	Wyoming	1 297	25 708	1 527	19.8	99.1	0.8	0.4	0.1	0.5	5.7	16.7	8.7	11.9	15.6	17.2
55 000	...	X	**WISCONSIN**	140 663	5 363 675	X	38.1	90.0	6.1	1.3	2.0	3.6	6.4	19.1	9.7	13.2	16.3	13.7
55 001	...	9	Adams	1 678	18 643	1 864	11.1	98.5	0.4	1.1	0.5	1.4	4.8	16.0	5.6	9.3	15.0	15.8
55 003	...	7	Ashland	2 703	16 866	1 962	6.2	86.6	0.4	11.7	0.6	1.1	6.3	19.1	11.2	10.9	14.9	12.9
55 005	...	7	Barron	2 235	44 963	999	20.1	98.3	0.3	1.2	0.5	1.0	5.7	19.7	8.1	10.9	15.8	13.7
55 007	...	8	Bayfield	3 823	15 013	2 089	3.9	89.9	0.2	10.6	0.4	0.6	5.3	19.4	5.3	9.3	15.8	16.3
55 009	3080	3	Brown	1 369	226 778	251	165.7	92.2	1.5	2.9	2.5	3.8	6.9	19.2	10.5	14.8	17.1	13.4
55 011	...	8	Buffalo	1 773	13 804	2 172	7.8	99.1	0.2	0.5	0.5	0.6	5.8	19.3	6.9	11.7	16.0	14.0
55 013	...	8	Burnett	2 128	15 674	2 040	7.4	94.6	0.5	5.6	0.5	0.8	4.9	17.2	6.0	9.1	14.1	14.6
55 015	0460	2	Calumet	828	40 631	1 097	49.1	97.3	0.5	0.6	1.9	1.1	7.0	21.6	7.2	13.7	18.3	13.5
55 017	2290	3	Chippewa	2 617	55 195	853	21.1	98.4	0.3	0.6	1.1	0.5	6.3	20.2	7.7	11.7	16.5	14.1
55 019	...	6	Clark	3 148	33 557	1 299	10.7	98.5	0.2	0.8	0.4	1.2	7.6	22.3	7.7	11.3	15.0	12.0
55 021	...	6	Columbia	2 004	52 468	890	26.2	97.9	1.0	0.7	0.6	1.6	6.1	19.1	7.1	12.7	17.2	14.2
55 023	...	7	Crawford	1 483	17 243	1 937	11.6	97.9	1.5	0.5	0.5	0.7	5.9	20.2	8.1	10.4	14.6	14.5

1. MSA = Metropolitan Statistical Area. PMSA = Primary MSA. NECMA = New England County Metropolitan Area. See Appendix A for explanation of these concepts. See Appendix B for list of metropolitan areas identified by type, with component counties.   2. County typology code from the Economic Research Service of USDA. See Appendix A for definition.   3. Dry land or land partially or temporarily covered by water.   4. Hispanic persons may be of any race.

STATE County	Population, 2000 (cont'd) Age (percent) (cont'd)				Population — change and components of change, 1990–2001							Households, 2000				
	55 to 64 years	65 to 74 years	75 years and over	Percent female	Total persons 2001	Total persons 1990	Percent change 1990–2000	Percent change 2000–2001	Births	Deaths	Net migration	Number	Percent change, 1990–2000	Persons per house-hold	Female family house-holder[1]	One person
	16	17	18	19	20	21	22	23	24	25	26	27	28	29	30	31
WEST VIRGINIA—Cont'd																
Braxton	10.8	8.2	7.7	49.4	14 747	12 998	13.1	0.3	198	190	38	5 771	16.6	2.46	9.2	25.2
Brooke	10.5	9.6	8.7	52.1	25 117	26 992	-5.7	-1.3	309	439	-193	10 396	2.6	2.36	9.9	27.9
Cabell	9.8	8.4	7.7	52.2	95 682	96 827	0.0	-1.1	1 447	1 574	-964	41 180	5.2	2.27	11.6	31.3
Calhoun	11.2	9.0	7.7	50.1	7 392	7 885	-3.8	-2.5	93	136	-149	3 071	3.1	2.46	10.3	24.9
Clay	9.9	8.0	5.6	50.5	10 324	9 983	3.5	-0.1	165	162	-3	4 020	10.8	2.55	10.4	24.3
Doddridge	10.5	8.4	6.4	49.5	7 745	6 994	5.8	4.6	94	106	346	2 845	8.5	2.56	10.3	22.5
Fayette	9.8	8.6	7.8	50.5	47 089	47 952	-0.8	-1.0	697	759	-415	18 945	3.6	2.41	13.2	26.9
Gilmer	10.4	8.2	7.2	49.7	7 120	7 669	-6.6	-0.6	86	127	3	2 768	1.9	2.43	8.6	25.5
Grant	11.7	8.2	7.1	50.6	11 340	10 428	8.4	0.4	169	129	0	4 591	17.0	2.43	8.2	24.5
Greenbrier	11.5	9.5	8.2	51.9	34 479	34 693	-0.7	0.1	489	544	98	14 571	5.8	2.32	10.7	28.6
Hampshire	11.0	8.4	6.2	50.1	20 798	16 498	22.5	2.9	274	244	556	7 955	28.7	2.49	9.5	24.6
Hancock	10.6	9.9	8.5	52.0	32 258	35 233	-7.3	-1.3	396	500	-294	13 678	-0.7	2.36	10.7	26.6
Hardy	10.9	8.5	6.4	50.6	12 740	10 977	15.4	0.6	174	181	80	5 204	21.4	2.42	8.6	27.0
Harrison	10.1	8.3	8.3	52.1	67 989	69 371	-1.0	-1.0	1 003	1 160	-483	27 867	3.2	2.42	11.4	27.7
Jackson	11.2	8.9	6.4	51.3	28 099	25 938	7.9	0.4	401	395	105	11 061	14.7	2.50	9.4	22.7
Jefferson	9.7	6.3	4.9	50.5	43 545	35 926	17.4	3.2	626	456	1 167	16 165	25.2	2.54	10.0	23.2
Kanawha	10.1	8.7	7.9	52.4	197 338	207 619	-3.6	-1.4	3 045	3 235	-2 512	86 226	1.8	2.28	12.3	30.8
Lewis	10.9	8.6	7.8	51.5	16 897	17 223	-1.8	-0.1	222	296	58	6 946	5.0	2.40	10.5	26.9
Lincoln	10.2	7.7	5.4	50.7	22 316	21 382	3.4	0.9	328	282	165	8 664	13.3	2.54	10.8	22.2
Logan	9.7	8.4	6.1	51.5	36 897	43 032	-12.4	-2.2	559	647	-729	14 880	-3.5	2.50	12.6	24.0
McDowell	10.3	8.5	7.6	52.5	26 568	35 233	-22.4	-2.8	426	489	-711	11 169	-13.3	2.42	14.9	27.3
Marion	10.3	8.7	9.1	52.5	56 373	57 249	-1.1	-0.4	752	883	-63	23 652	4.3	2.34	10.7	28.9
Marshall	10.4	8.8	7.5	51.3	35 171	37 356	-4.9	-1.0	428	518	-247	14 207	1.1	2.44	10.8	25.6
Mason	11.3	8.7	6.5	51.0	26 175	25 178	3.1	0.8	369	379	236	10 587	10.2	2.42	10.1	25.5
Mercer	10.5	9.0	8.4	52.3	62 355	64 980	-3.1	-1.0	968	1 009	-567	26 509	4.4	2.33	11.2	28.7
Mineral	11.3	8.1	7.0	51.1	27 059	26 697	1.4	-0.1	375	369	-11	10 784	8.0	2.46	9.7	25.0
Mingo	9.3	7.2	5.2	51.6	27 714	33 739	-16.3	-1.9	528	412	-662	11 303	-4.5	2.49	12.7	25.2
Monongalia	7.5	5.6	5.1	49.6	81 820	75 509	8.4	-0.1	1 054	772	-300	33 446	15.0	2.28	8.3	31.3
Monroe	11.1	8.4	7.0	50.9	14 610	12 406	17.5	0.2	162	186	53	5 447	14.7	2.41	7.9	24.8
Morgan	11.5	9.8	6.8	50.9	15 275	12 128	23.2	2.2	175	218	367	6 145	29.9	2.40	8.2	24.5
Nicholas	10.6	8.3	6.7	51.1	26 420	26 775	-0.8	-0.5	335	397	-70	10 722	7.5	2.46	10.0	24.8
Ohio	9.6	9.3	9.5	53.2	46 750	50 871	-6.8	-1.4	634	807	-494	19 733	-4.4	2.27	11.2	33.7
Pendleton	11.2	9.5	8.4	49.7	8 070	8 054	1.8	-1.5	109	129	-104	3 350	9.4	2.40	8.1	25.8
Pleasants	10.1	7.9	7.0	50.0	7 589	7 546	-0.4	1.0	122	107	62	2 887	4.3	2.51	10.4	22.9
Pocahontas	12.1	9.3	7.9	48.5	8 996	9 008	1.4	-1.5	134	141	-128	3 835	5.7	2.30	7.9	29.6
Preston	10.5	8.1	6.8	50.4	29 443	29 037	1.0	0.4	363	416	170	11 544	8.7	2.50	9.1	23.7
Putnam	10.0	6.7	4.9	50.8	51 680	42 835	20.4	0.2	735	560	-73	20 028	27.6	2.56	8.9	20.6
Raleigh	9.8	8.3	7.1	50.8	78 548	76 819	3.1	-0.8	1 085	1 116	-619	31 793	7.8	2.38	11.9	27.1
Randolph	10.8	7.6	7.5	49.7	28 231	27 803	1.7	-0.1	363	406	23	11 072	6.8	2.41	9.8	26.3
Ritchie	11.3	8.0	7.2	51.0	10 291	10 233	1.1	-0.5	121	175	3	4 184	6.5	2.45	9.7	25.0
Roane	11.3	8.1	6.7	50.5	15 364	15 120	2.2	-0.5	194	218	-56	6 161	7.3	2.49	9.3	23.5
Summers	11.6	10.7	9.2	51.1	12 796	14 204	-8.5	-1.6	127	248	-77	5 530	5.5	2.32	10.0	29.1
Taylor	10.0	8.3	7.5	51.1	16 017	15 144	6.2	-0.4	195	221	-40	6 320	10.1	2.47	10.9	25.5
Tucker	12.6	9.5	8.4	51.2	7 214	7 728	-5.3	-1.5	91	123	-74	3 052	1.2	2.35	7.8	27.2
Tyler	11.6	9.2	7.2	51.1	9 460	9 796	-2.1	-1.4	116	145	-101	3 836	3.4	2.47	8.6	23.1
Upshur	10.2	7.6	7.1	51.5	23 374	22 867	2.3	-0.1	309	337	10	8 972	8.8	2.45	9.1	25.2
Wayne	10.9	8.6	6.4	51.1	42 665	41 636	3.0	-0.6	630	568	-289	17 239	10.3	2.48	10.8	24.1
Webster	11.0	8.2	7.1	50.8	9 642	10 729	-9.4	-0.8	104	140	-40	4 010	0.4	2.41	10.6	25.7
Wetzel	12.0	9.0	7.2	51.5	17 395	19 258	-8.1	-1.7	255	288	-263	7 164	-1.9	2.45	9.3	25.7
Wirt	11.2	7.3	5.7	50.0	5 935	5 192	13.1	1.1	86	63	39	2 284	17.6	2.56	8.9	22.2
Wood	10.9	8.1	7.4	52.0	87 541	86 915	1.2	-0.5	1 236	1 246	-401	36 275	6.2	2.39	10.8	27.1
Wyoming	10.3	8.4	5.5	50.8	25 320	28 990	-11.3	-1.5	350	352	-385	10 454	-0.2	2.45	10.5	24.4
WISCONSIN	8.5	6.6	6.5	50.6	5 401 906	4 891 954	9.6	0.7	85 327	58 334	12 137	2 084 544	14.4	2.50	9.6	26.8
Adams	14.5	12.9	8.1	49.3	19 164	15 682	18.9	2.8	208	252	551	7 900	32.3	2.33	6.7	25.5
Ashland	8.9	7.3	8.6	50.7	16 881	16 307	3.4	0.1	260	239	-1	6 718	7.4	2.39	10.9	30.8
Barron	9.7	8.1	8.3	50.5	45 365	40 750	10.3	0.9	632	637	417	17 851	15.7	2.48	8.2	25.4
Bayfield	12.1	8.9	7.5	49.4	15 114	14 008	7.2	0.7	183	192	103	6 207	12.5	2.40	7.8	26.4
Brown	7.6	5.4	5.3	50.3	229 212	194 594	16.5	1.1	3 939	2 020	623	87 295	20.8	2.51	8.9	26.5
Buffalo	9.6	8.9	7.9	49.8	13 814	13 584	1.6	0.1	185	179	7	5 511	7.6	2.47	6.2	27.1
Burnett	13.9	11.8	8.5	49.6	15 966	13 084	19.8	1.9	190	227	320	6 613	26.2	2.33	7.5	26.9
Calumet	7.9	5.7	5.1	50.0	41 506	34 291	18.5	2.2	595	333	614	14 910	26.7	2.70	6.5	20.4
Chippewa	8.9	7.4	7.1	50.2	55 960	52 360	5.4	1.4	819	691	646	21 356	11.9	2.53	8.0	24.7
Clark	8.2	7.6	8.4	49.9	33 849	31 647	6.0	0.9	617	397	88	12 047	7.5	2.73	6.5	23.8
Columbia	9.2	7.2	7.2	49.6	53 365	45 088	16.4	1.7	762	652	792	20 439	21.2	2.49	7.4	25.5
Crawford	10.2	8.1	7.9	49.4	17 062	15 940	8.2	-1.0	242	236	-184	6 677	12.9	2.48	8.4	26.7

1. No spouse present.

Table B. States and Counties — **Vital Statistics, Health Resources, and Crime**

STATE County	Births, average 1997–1999 Total	Births, average 1997–1999 Rate[1]	Deaths, average 1997–1999 Number Total	Deaths, average 1997–1999 Number Infant[2]	Deaths, average 1997–1999 Rate Total[1]	Deaths, average 1997–1999 Rate Infant[3]	Physicians,[4] 2000 Number	Physicians,[4] 2000 Rate[5]	Hospitals,[4] 1998 Number	Hospitals,[4] 1998 Beds Number	Hospitals,[4] 1998 Beds Rate[5]	Medicare enrollees 2000	Serious crimes known to police, 2000[6] Total Number	Serious crimes known to police, 2000[6] Total Rate[7]
	32	33	34	35	36	37	38	39	40	41	42	43	44	45
WEST VIRGINIA—Cont'd														
Braxton	158	12.0	165	NA	12.5	NA	11	75	1	30	228	2 632	217	1 476
Brooke	250	9.6	335	NA	12.9	NA	38	149	0	0	0	4 301	194	860
Cabell	1 087	11.5	1 242	12	13.1	11.3	384	397	2	738	783	19 965	5 311	5 487
Calhoun	79	9.9	91	NA	11.5	NA	5	66	0	0	0	1 600	63	831
Clay	129	12.3	126	NA	11.9	NA	6	58	0	0	0	1 929	111	1 140
Doddridge	80	10.7	81	NA	10.8	NA	1	14	0	0	0	952	36	486
Fayette	532	11.1	620	NA	13.0	NA	66	139	2	181	378	10 250	977	2 180
Gilmer	74	10.3	92	NA	12.9	NA	1	14	0	0	0	1 336	82	1 145
Grant	139	12.5	117	NA	10.5	NA	10	89	1	65	586	1 941	141	1 282
Greenbrier	377	10.7	448	NA	12.7	NA	86	250	1	132	373	7 462	397	1 152
Hampshire	234	12.3	189	NA	9.9	NA	12	59	1	47	247	3 303	312	1 544
Hancock	316	9.3	383	NA	11.3	NA	25	77	1	269	792	7 567	NA	NA
Hardy	152	12.9	134	NA	11.3	NA	6	47	0	0	0	2 114	164	1 294
Harrison	783	11.1	904	NA	12.8	NA	147	214	1	309	436	13 997	881	1 332
Jackson	328	11.7	290	NA	10.4	NA	17	61	1	72	257	5 059	502	1 793
Jefferson	507	12.3	354	NA	8.6	NA	38	90	1	56	135	5 463	582	1 569
Kanawha	2 359	11.7	2 511	11	12.4	4.8	641	320	5	1 278	633	39 852	9 087	4 542
Lewis	193	11.0	221	NA	12.7	NA	21	124	1	77	442	3 626	153	904
Lincoln	280	12.6	249	NA	11.2	NA	8	36	0	0	0	3 926	567	2 565
Logan	450	11.0	489	9	12.0	19.2	80	212	3	209	509	8 239	NA	NA
McDowell	334	11.2	408	NA	13.6	NA	24	88	1	124	414	7 213	441	1 741
Marion	597	10.6	710	NA	12.6	NA	105	186	1	217	385	11 879	965	1 753
Marshall	377	10.6	413	NA	11.7	NA	41	115	1	143	403	5 852	NA	NA
Mason	281	10.8	305	NA	11.7	NA	29	112	1	201	777	4 658	520	2 100
Mercer	760	11.8	823	NA	12.8	NA	163	259	3	555	870	13 966	2 604	4 135
Mineral	299	11.1	295	NA	10.9	NA	22	81	1	63	236	4 768	NA	NA
Mingo	412	12.9	342	NA	10.7	NA	36	127	1	76	238	6 006	361	1 309
Monongalia	801	10.4	614	NA	7.9	NA	472	577	2	562	725	9 549	2 413	2 947
Monroe	136	10.3	146	NA	11.1	NA	6	41	0	0	0	2 957	99	679
Morgan	155	11.3	154	NA	11.3	NA	13	87	1	44	323	2 657	314	2 101
Nicholas	282	10.2	295	NA	10.7	NA	36	136	2	170	616	5 283	682	2 832
Ohio	519	10.7	664	NA	13.7	NA	238	502	2	664	1 375	10 472	1 234	2 719
Pendleton	88	10.9	99	NA	12.3	NA	5	61	0	0	0	1 617	64	781
Pleasants	76	10.2	85	NA	11.4	NA	2	27	0	0	0	1 329	NA	NA
Pocahontas	96	10.5	105	NA	11.5	NA	12	131	1	40	432	1 893	145	1 588
Preston	315	10.6	323	NA	10.8	NA	29	99	1	58	195	5 187	244	832
Putnam	597	11.7	428	NA	8.4	NA	50	97	1	68	133	6 536	1 242	2 456
Raleigh	853	10.8	890	7	11.3	8.6	193	244	3	486	615	15 554	2 580	3 257
Randolph	307	10.7	334	NA	11.7	NA	55	195	1	131	457	5 449	626	2 215
Ritchie	108	10.5	135	NA	13.1	NA	7	68	0	0	0	1 895	NA	NA
Roane	165	10.7	177	NA	11.5	NA	19	123	1	73	476	2 759	339	2 195
Summers	124	9.1	192	NA	14.2	NA	9	69	1	95	723	2 798	163	1 254
Taylor	166	10.8	183	NA	11.9	NA	10	62	1	131	855	2 646	158	982
Tucker	73	9.6	98	NA	12.9	NA	3	41	0	0	0	1 473	103	1 758
Tyler	93	9.5	117	NA	11.9	NA	5	52	1	18	183	1 559	114	1 188
Upshur	261	11.0	268	NA	11.4	NA	28	120	1	95	404	3 997	323	1 380
Wayne	475	11.3	447	NA	10.6	NA	40	93	0	0	0	6 312	1 133	2 883
Webster	104	10.2	118	NA	11.6	NA	8	82	1	35	342	2 067	196	2 334
Wetzel	218	11.9	221	NA	12.0	NA	18	102	1	58	318	3 852	149	859
Wirt	68	11.9	53	NA	9.4	NA	1	17	0	0	0	990	95	1 618
Wood	1 037	11.9	1 000	8	11.5	7.4	176	200	2	508	585	15 722	2 467	2 804
Wyoming	309	11.3	288	NA	10.5	NA	7	27	0	0	0	5 503	461	1 793
WISCONSIN	66 622	12.7	45 837	460	8.8	6.9	10 763	201	126	17 111	328	783 003	172 124	3 209
Adams	162	8.8	199	NA	10.7	NA	9	48	1	58	314	2 879	130	697
Ashland	207	12.6	189	NA	11.5	NA	47	279	1	101	613	3 315	547	3 243
Barron	487	11.1	477	NA	10.9	NA	59	131	3	252	574	8 214	778	1 818
Bayfield	152	10.0	162	NA	10.6	NA	16	107	0	0	0	2 597	358	2 385
Brown	3 024	14.0	1 562	23	7.2	7.5	392	173	3	632	293	26 915	6 234	2 749
Buffalo	150	10.5	153	NA	10.8	NA	3	22	0	0	0	2 604	182	1 318
Burnett	150	10.2	184	NA	12.5	NA	6	38	1	84	574	3 185	103	657
Calumet	490	12.8	252	NA	6.6	NA	22	54	1	47	122	3 677	695	1 711
Chippewa	649	11.9	534	NA	9.8	NA	60	109	3	358	656	9 101	1 256	2 276
Clark	471	14.2	315	NA	9.5	NA	22	66	1	199	600	5 986	412	1 228
Columbia	612	12.0	516	NA	10.1	NA	65	124	2	213	416	9 355	1 618	3 084
Crawford	198	12.0	178	NA	10.8	NA	16	93	1	62	374	2 977	215	1 247

1. Per 1,000 estimated resident population, average 1997–1999.   2. Deaths of infants under 1 year old.   3. Deaths of infants under 1 year old per 1,000 live births.   4. Data subject to copyright.   5. Per 100,000 resident population as of July 1 of the year shown.   6. Data for serious crimes have not been adjusted for underreporting; this may affect comparability between geographic areas and over time.   7. Per 100,000 population estimated by the FBI.

Table B. States and Counties — Crime, Education, Money Income, and Poverty

STATE County	Serious crimes known to police, 2000[1] (cont'd) Rate[2] Violent	Property	Education — School enrollment and attainment, 1990 Enrollment[3] Total	Percent private	Attainment[4] (percent) High school graduate or more	Bachelor's degree or more	Local government expenditures, fiscal 1999[5] Total current expenditures (mil dol)	Current expenditures per student (dollars)	Money income 1989 Per capita[6] (dollars)	Households Median Dollars	Percent change, 1979–1989 (constant 1989 dollars)	Percent with $100,000 or more	Income and poverty, 1998 Median household income	Percent below poverty level All persons	Persons under 18	Persons 5–17 in families
	46	47	48	49	50	51	52	53	54	55	56	57	58	59	60	61
WEST VIRGINIA—Cont'd																
Braxton	320	1 156	2 723	1.1	56.8	8.1	17.1	6 179	8 249	16 359	-5.1	0.5	25 044	21.6	29.6	28.7
Brooke	124	736	6 967	20.0	71.6	12.2	26.8	6 829	11 656	26 500	-19.3	0.9	33 362	12.2	20.9	15.8
Cabell	376	5 111	25 571	7.3	71.9	18.9	91.1	6 880	12 068	21 255	-11.3	2.5	30 565	16.6	26.6	21.3
Calhoun	106	725	1 851	1.0	56.3	6.8	10.1	6 864	7 223	14 496	-13.5	0.4	23 450	22.3	26.7	29.9
Clay	380	760	2 490	2.5	49.4	6.2	13.7	6 361	6 722	12 855	-22.0	0.2	23 296	25.5	30.8	33.0
Doddridge	203	284	1 546	5.0	64.6	10.3	9.0	6 821	8 297	17 159	-4.4	0.6	28 131	20.5	28.6	26.5
Fayette	241	1 939	12 179	4.8	57.1	8.8	52.3	6 726	8 653	16 774	-20.3	0.8	24 565	21.8	30.4	26.0
Gilmer	251	894	2 250	1.0	56.6	14.2	8.3	6 973	7 872	14 539	-13.8	1.0	23 808	24.3	31.1	33.4
Grant	236	1 045	2 329	4.0	60.2	8.6	12.1	6 161	10 394	20 923	6.9	1.6	28 627	14.4	20.6	18.8
Greenbrier	139	1 013	7 274	6.8	63.0	11.5	36.2	6 191	10 057	19 411	-5.0	1.4	28 302	16.5	23.8	21.5
Hampshire	267	1 277	3 708	2.7	61.8	9.0	20.5	5 909	9 996	20 753	3.8	1.3	29 776	16.3	24.2	22.5
Hancock	NA	NA	8 220	11.7	72.5	8.9	31.0	6 617	12 464	26 031	-25.0	0.9	33 440	11.5	18.6	16.1
Hardy	253	1 042	2 156	3.5	55.3	7.3	13.1	6 131	10 096	20 745	6.9	0.5	30 975	12.8	19.2	17.8
Harrison	204	1 128	15 973	9.4	70.6	13.5	79.0	6 602	10 281	20 367	-11.9	1.7	30 468	17.2	25.8	21.6
Jackson	246	1 546	6 172	4.4	65.4	8.7	33.8	6 643	9 832	21 655	-25.0	0.7	31 897	16.0	23.2	20.5
Jefferson	167	1 402	8 786	7.9	68.2	16.2	43.0	6 170	13 249	30 941	16.8	3.0	42 289	9.6	14.7	12.8
Kanawha	481	4 061	46 753	9.4	72.4	17.6	210.5	6 837	12 887	23 999	-17.2	2.5	34 242	14.8	24.1	18.9
Lewis	189	715	3 605	4.9	62.1	8.2	17.6	6 170	8 561	17 972	-13.4	0.8	26 216	19.9	27.3	26.4
Lincoln	715	1 850	5 108	1.4	49.1	4.7	29.2	7 101	7 224	14 659	-25.8	0.3	24 260	24.1	29.9	29.8
Logan	NA	NA	11 142	3.8	53.4	6.3	46.3	6 834	8 786	17 942	-26.3	1.2	25 061	22.4	27.5	26.6
McDowell	359	1 382	9 329	3.4	42.3	4.6	38.5	7 137	6 961	13 141	-35.2	0.7	19 104	29.8	31.9	37.5
Marion	156	1 597	13 633	7.0	71.4	12.5	60.1	6 730	10 328	20 386	-15.6	1.0	28 988	16.3	25.5	20.9
Marshall	NA	NA	8 777	14.3	70.9	9.7	41.3	7 126	10 946	22 687	-21.9	1.5	30 432	15.5	22.9	20.2
Mason	307	1 793	5 657	3.1	61.1	6.8	30.7	6 978	9 543	20 135	-20.3	1.0	29 965	17.6	24.8	22.3
Mercer	537	3 598	15 786	4.9	63.1	11.6	64.9	6 593	10 405	19 365	-16.5	1.6	27 095	18.9	28.0	24.2
Mineral	NA	NA	6 555	6.8	72.8	10.4	31.0	6 476	10 398	22 036	-10.3	0.9	30 669	15.2	23.3	20.6
Mingo	352	958	9 089	3.0	50.4	6.6	40.1	7 089	8 328	16 066	-23.6	1.5	25 576	24.4	28.1	28.3
Monongalia	436	2 511	27 645	5.4	75.4	28.1	67.9	6 545	11 772	22 183	-1.0	2.3	34 124	14.2	18.7	16.5
Monroe	171	507	2 682	6.0	62.1	8.0	12.7	6 200	8 959	18 217	-4.6	0.9	27 763	15.4	20.4	20.1
Morgan	301	1 800	2 264	3.1	64.8	11.8	13.8	6 041	11 420	24 372	6.7	1.3	32 159	12.1	18.8	16.4
Nicholas	353	2 479	6 379	3.5	61.2	8.0	32.7	6 865	8 652	18 116	-20.3	0.9	25 737	20.3	26.5	24.6
Ohio	282	2 437	12 437	24.3	75.1	18.4	42.8	6 921	12 348	22 489	-11.0	2.8	32 973	13.8	22.5	18.5
Pendleton	98	683	1 563	2.7	60.6	8.2	8.8	6 538	9 391	19 565	6.6	0.7	28 679	13.8	18.8	17.3
Pleasants	NA	NA	1 718	5.6	68.7	8.5	12.3	8 572	9 958	20 910	-22.9	1.9	30 943	14.5	20.7	18.7
Pocahontas	405	1 183	1 732	7.2	60.6	9.7	10.1	6 822	8 860	17 237	-16.8	0.9	25 474	17.6	24.2	23.6
Preston	112	719	6 800	2.8	62.7	8.3	30.6	6 013	9 158	19 940	-8.3	0.9	27 380	17.7	23.5	21.7
Putnam	312	2 143	10 238	7.6	73.8	13.3	54.2	6 170	11 840	27 405	-10.1	1.6	43 000	8.7	12.5	11.7
Raleigh	355	2 902	19 322	10.3	63.2	10.7	86.4	6 897	10 316	19 656	-23.0	1.6	28 968	17.6	24.2	21.0
Randolph	290	1 925	6 365	13.7	65.9	11.9	30.5	6 215	9 009	18 278	-14.8	1.2	26 185	18.8	27.5	24.6
Ritchie	NA	NA	2 209	1.0	61.5	6.0	12.6	6 842	9 117	17 333	-9.1	0.9	26 807	18.9	28.3	25.2
Roane	291	1 903	3 484	2.4	57.2	6.6	18.0	6 216	7 801	15 375	-21.1	0.5	25 717	20.8	28.2	27.3
Summers	277	977	2 974	6.2	58.0	8.5	11.4	6 539	8 203	16 457	-8.6	0.5	22 179	22.7	29.0	30.0
Taylor	44	939	3 369	6.4	66.0	8.1	17.3	6 392	8 746	17 963	-15.5	0.4	25 695	19.7	25.7	26.3
Tucker	119	1 639	1 648	5.7	64.0	8.6	8.1	6 353	8 978	17 949	-7.1	0.9	25 532	15.8	23.3	22.0
Tyler	156	1 032	2 282	3.8	68.7	9.0	11.8	7 349	9 692	20 360	-19.6	0.4	30 585	15.1	21.8	20.2
Upshur	150	1 231	6 121	22.6	64.3	12.0	25.1	6 130	8 748	18 739	-14.5	1.0	28 454	20.4	26.7	25.8
Wayne	290	2 593	10 322	3.0	63.1	9.0	51.0	6 486	9 430	19 688	-15.8	1.0	30 104	17.8	24.4	23.4
Webster	607	1 727	2 502	1.7	46.5	5.6	12.6	6 860	6 793	13 371	-18.6	0.5	20 536	28.3	34.2	37.3
Wetzel	63	795	4 404	1.7	70.1	10.4	24.0	6 487	10 454	21 545	-20.4	1.2	31 009	17.7	25.8	23.7
Wirt	204	1 413	1 184	1.9	66.2	8.0	7.5	6 345	8 163	16 951	-17.2	0.0	27 796	19.8	29.3	25.8
Wood	298	2 506	20 092	8.3	73.2	13.5	93.8	6 499	12 011	25 161	-9.5	1.6	34 334	14.2	22.1	18.3
Wyoming	268	1 525	7 839	2.1	53.0	6.2	35.5	7 584	8 268	17 248	-35.2	0.8	24 886	22.2	26.8	26.8
WISCONSIN	237	2 972	1 302 230	16.4	78.6	17.7	6 620.7	7 527	13 276	29 442	-0.6	2.6	42 169	8.9	13.6	11.8
Adams	54	644	3 057	6.4	67.0	7.4	15.5	7 651	10 926	21 548	-1.0	1.3	31 658	12.8	20.9	18.5
Ashland	130	3 113	4 231	19.2	75.3	12.8	26.2	7 917	9 661	19 012	-2.8	1.3	31 091	13.9	20.3	17.9
Barron	145	1 674	9 716	7.2	73.0	11.7	58.9	6 804	10 377	22 570	0.3	1.3	33 883	10.7	15.7	13.8
Bayfield	180	2 205	3 269	8.9	78.5	18.3	17.4	7 788	9 933	20 666	4.8	0.6	31 419	11.9	16.5	17.2
Brown	163	2 586	51 864	21.1	82.6	17.7	264.5	7 115	13 906	31 303	0.4	2.8	46 433	7.4	11.6	9.3
Buffalo	43	1 275	3 215	7.6	72.6	10.8	18.1	6 956	10 947	23 573	4.8	1.5	35 382	10.7	16.1	14.5
Burnett	70	587	2 876	5.0	72.3	8.9	16.4	7 216	9 623	20 153	8.0	0.4	31 317	11.9	19.1	16.8
Calumet	89	1 622	9 075	16.2	79.7	12.9	27.8	6 391	12 904	34 050	-0.7	2.0	51 334	4.5	6.5	5.3
Chippewa	85	2 190	12 967	13.1	74.9	10.8	64.0	6 958	11 170	25 858	1.5	1.7	38 560	9.4	14.2	12.2
Clark	69	1 159	7 738	13.4	67.5	8.6	42.8	7 084	9 810	22 177	3.3	1.5	33 135	11.2	16.3	14.0
Columbia	90	2 994	10 466	13.2	78.3	12.9	77.1	6 748	12 356	28 360	3.3	1.7	42 153	6.5	9.9	8.3
Crawford	12	1 235	3 884	13.9	72.4	10.8	19.9	7 027	9 661	21 436	4.0	0.8	31 033	11.9	16.7	15.1

1. Data for serious crimes have not been adjusted for underreporting; this may affect comparability between geographic areas and over time. 2. Per 100,000 population estimated by the FBI. 3. All persons 3 years old and over enrolled in nursery school through college. 4. Persons 25 years old and over. 5. Elementary and secondary education expenditures, local government fiscal years ending between July 1, 1998 and June 30, 1999. 6. Based on population enumerated as of April 1, 1990.

Table B. States and Counties — Personal Income

STATE County	Total (mil dol)	Percent change, 1998–1999	Per capita[1] Dollars	Rank	Wages and salaries[2] (mil dol)	Proprietor's income (mil dol)	Dividends, interest, and rent (mil dol)	Transfer payments Total (mil dol)	Government payments to individuals Total (mil dol)	Social Security (mil dol)	Medical payments (mil dol)	Income maintenance (mil dol)	Unemployment insurance (mil dol)
	62	63	64	65	66	67	68	69	70	71	72	73	74
WEST VIRGINIA—Cont'd													
Braxton	218	3.2	16 522	2 824	97	19	34	64	62	23	20	9	2
Brooke	524	2.3	20 248	1 908	271	29	111	113	108	55	36	5	1
Cabell	2 226	2.2	23 794	898	1 625	112	477	490	474	176	169	41	5
Calhoun	110	3.5	13 841	3 055	34	13	17	38	36	14	12	6	1
Clay	149	3.9	14 048	3 047	64	9	18	45	44	17	11	9	1
Doddridge	126	5.4	16 902	2 755	24	6	23	24	23	12	4	3	1
Fayette	832	1.5	17 787	2 578	340	40	127	278	269	101	98	27	5
Gilmer	122	1.5	17 088	2 720	44	10	27	35	34	12	12	4	1
Grant	211	4.0	18 913	2 311	121	25	40	48	46	18	19	4	1
Greenbrier	693	1.9	19 630	2 102	335	52	147	178	172	65	69	14	3
Hampshire	315	4.9	16 246	2 868	93	26	58	71	67	31	21	7	0
Hancock	769	2.4	22 786	1 145	499	37	123	170	164	78	63	7	2
Hardy	233	6.4	19 469	2 149	139	16	37	40	38	19	9	4	1
Harrison	1 677	5.1	23 851	886	1 052	129	331	342	329	137	113	31	8
Jackson	519	2.1	18 361	2 454	281	31	89	118	113	52	37	11	3
Jefferson	1 121	7.6	26 529	461	350	42	184	129	121	53	34	8	1
Kanawha	5 481	2.6	27 508	372	3 938	379	1 073	1 044	1 008	411	394	71	14
Lewis	298	4.0	17 058	2 724	147	23	63	77	73	32	24	9	1
Lincoln	319	3.8	14 261	3 037	71	20	40	95	91	37	21	18	2
Logan	695	-1.7	17 291	2 684	375	29	101	245	238	84	89	26	4
McDowell	410	-0.3	14 002	3 049	151	13	67	191	186	70	49	38	3
Marion	1 123	3.4	20 077	1 971	591	68	224	277	267	119	83	22	4
Marshall	681	4.1	19 485	2 145	421	25	118	151	145	63	49	12	3
Mason	449	2.3	17 263	2 690	228	10	75	120	115	47	43	12	3
Mercer	1 363	2.8	21 256	1 583	679	72	273	380	368	128	142	34	4
Mineral	507	3.7	18 722	2 361	172	29	81	123	118	43	43	9	1
Mingo	544	-0.4	17 268	2 688	309	61	86	175	169	62	50	29	4
Monongalia	1 868	4.1	24 258	814	1 285	118	369	306	293	99	127	18	2
Monroe	203	2.9	15 281	2 960	54	18	33	56	54	24	16	6	0
Morgan	284	5.9	20 455	1 849	76	22	52	63	61	26	23	4	1
Nicholas	463	5.6	16 814	2 776	228	52	81	130	125	54	42	13	3
Ohio	1 294	2.0	27 118	407	823	100	377	253	244	108	95	16	2
Pendleton	157	5.0	19 581	2 116	61	17	31	33	32	13	12	3	0
Pleasants	149	-0.9	19 843	2 039	99	6	25	40	39	14	19	3	0
Pocahontas	180	2.0	19 811	2 057	90	16	32	52	51	17	25	3	1
Preston	473	3.4	15 855	2 915	172	36	83	124	119	50	39	13	2
Putnam	1 228	5.6	23 642	927	584	54	158	168	159	74	44	10	4
Raleigh	1 633	2.8	20 687	1 781	931	85	263	423	409	160	140	36	9
Randolph	543	5.0	18 934	2 304	281	47	96	146	141	47	62	13	3
Ritchie	169	3.6	16 124	2 882	75	12	28	45	44	19	14	5	1
Roane	245	2.3	15 878	2 910	93	23	39	69	66	28	23	8	1
Summers	203	1.5	14 647	3 014	62	7	35	79	76	21	31	9	1
Taylor	234	2.6	15 259	2 965	85	10	37	69	66	23	21	7	2
Tucker	127	3.2	16 931	2 747	63	11	22	37	36	15	14	3	1
Tyler	159	2.7	16 336	2 855	87	7	34	38	36	18	10	3	1
Upshur	388	3.5	16 499	2 828	205	29	74	94	90	37	27	12	2
Wayne	669	2.5	15 988	2 899	312	27	96	158	151	70	28	24	3
Webster	132	1.5	13 183	3 079	64	5	18	51	49	19	14	9	1
Wetzel	351	1.9	19 271	2 216	121	16	66	90	87	37	32	8	2
Wirt	89	5.0	15 382	2 954	16	5	12	21	20	9	5	3	1
Wood	2 004	2.2	23 212	1 040	1 381	118	367	394	379	165	136	30	5
Wyoming	394	-1.3	14 606	3 017	174	12	56	142	137	60	33	21	2
WISCONSIN	143 705	4.9	27 370	X	92 350	8 287	29 254	17 648	16 622	7 964	6 107	1 289	468
Adams	349	5.9	18 606	2 391	118	34	68	79	76	42	22	5	2
Ashland	346	4.1	21 120	1 627	235	29	76	72	69	28	28	5	2
Barron	960	4.0	21 761	1 430	556	97	196	163	154	76	56	10	4
Bayfield	298	4.0	19 390	2 185	83	32	67	60	57	28	19	4	2
Brown	6 301	4.4	29 102	255	4 983	387	1 288	584	542	276	178	34	17
Buffalo	320	3.1	22 381	1 251	158	29	69	49	46	23	17	4	1
Burnett	289	6.1	19 355	2 195	109	29	69	68	65	34	21	4	1
Calumet	1 001	8.2	25 643	565	392	55	195	91	83	49	24	3	4
Chippewa	1 313	5.1	23 986	862	684	103	262	198	187	87	74	11	6
Clark	650	4.2	19 464	2 152	267	73	141	117	111	51	45	8	3
Columbia	1 242	5.3	23 975	865	565	107	263	176	166	85	61	7	5
Crawford	332	5.0	20 111	1 961	187	21	71	60	57	27	21	4	2

1. Based on the resident population estimated as of July 1 of the year shown. 2. Includes other labor income.

STATE County	Total (mil dol)	Farm	Goods-related[1] Total	Manu-facturing	Service-related and other[2] Total	Retail trade	Finance, insurance, and real estate	Services	Govern-ment	Number	Rate[3]	Supplemental Security Income recipients, December 2000	Total	Percent change, 1980–1990
	75	76	77	78	79	80	81	82	83	84	85	86	87	88
WEST VIRGINIA—Cont'd														
Braxton	116	-0.8	D	D	D	16.5	2.2	21.5	22.4	3 147	214	825	5 708	2.2
Brooke	300	0.0	D	40.3	D	8.3	2.9	17.8	11.4	5 792	228	421	10 838	-3.2
Cabell	1 737	0.0	20.2	13.8	62.9	10.3	5.6	33.7	17.0	20 186	209	3 957	43 596	0.0
Calhoun	47	-0.7	40.3	4.2	D	7.0	D	18.9	25.9	1 889	249	610	3 446	8.1
Clay	73	0.0	45.5	4.1	D	5.9	D	13.2	25.5	2 303	223	712	4 359	5.2
Doddridge	30	-4.3	25.3	7.6	D	8.5	6.8	14.8	34.7	1 591	215	246	3 251	2.0
Fayette	381	0.0	21.6	11.7	49.9	11.4	3.0	25.7	28.5	12 044	253	2 387	20 841	-2.9
Gilmer	54	-2.3	35.6	11.9	D	7.1	2.0	12.4	40.1	1 646	230	382	3 243	2.8
Grant	146	1.4	33.9	19.7	43.2	5.4	3.0	12.2	21.5	2 338	207	437	4 746	15.9
Greenbrier	387	0.3	16.6	10.2	63.8	12.2	3.2	38.8	19.3	8 135	236	1 436	16 757	10.2
Hampshire	119	2.2	D	9.2	D	9.2	4.5	22.4	30.6	4 108	203	713	8 817	26.0
Hancock	535	0.0	D	53.7	D	5.8	2.2	21.1	9.4	8 061	247	612	14 697	-1.8
Hardy	155	2.3	D	51.9	D	9.1	2.9	9.6	13.3	2 516	199	434	5 573	24.6
Harrison	1 181	-0.2	19.8	8.0	50.8	9.2	2.9	22.0	29.6	15 694	229	2 717	29 988	-0.7
Jackson	312	-1.3	D	37.5	D	12.5	2.6	15.9	14.8	6 087	217	1 022	10 571	13.1
Jefferson	393	0.5	D	19.6	D	12.7	3.8	23.6	27.3	6 500	154	622	14 606	26.5
Kanawha	4 316	0.0	20.0	11.3	61.6	8.7	7.3	30.4	18.5	45 103	225	6 558	92 747	2.1
Lewis	170	-0.5	24.2	11.1	48.8	11.9	2.1	22.6	27.5	4 081	241	952	7 454	3.7
Lincoln	91	0.4	29.1	3.9	D	8.2	D	17.2	34.2	4 897	222	1 847	8 429	3.7
Logan	404	0.0	27.2	5.7	D	12.3	D	29.5	17.9	9 679	257	2 250	16 848	-1.9
McDowell	164	0.0	24.6	1.1	39.0	9.9	4.0	14.3	36.4	8 858	324	3 573	15 330	-11.1
Marion	659	-0.2	27.9	9.0	51.1	9.7	3.9	24.6	21.1	13 253	234	1 762	25 491	-2.8
Marshall	447	-0.3	D	33.6	D	7.2	1.6	D	15.1	6 989	197	752	15 630	0.8
Mason	238	-1.1	D	20.5	D	6.4	2.1	19.2	20.5	5 575	215	1 101	10 932	6.8
Mercer	751	-0.2	14.0	7.8	62.8	12.4	4.0	31.0	23.4	15 512	246	3 263	28 426	-0.1
Mineral	201	0.3	30.6	23.0	44.4	11.6	2.6	20.3	24.7	5 116	189	603	10 930	6.7
Mingo	369	0.0	45.8	3.7	39.7	4.9	2.4	14.4	14.5	7 576	268	2 499	13 087	4.3
Monongalia	1 403	-0.2	D	8.1	D	8.3	3.2	27.2	39.8	11 175	137	1 445	31 563	8.5
Monroe	71	-2.2	27.4	17.6	D	5.8	D	13.3	41.1	3 127	214	672	5 994	15.9
Morgan	99	-0.2	D	13.3	D	10.5	3.7	20.8	23.1	3 155	211	293	6 757	38.3
Nicholas	280	-0.2	38.5	12.5	40.4	12.1	1.9	14.7	21.3	6 427	242	1 153	11 235	7.8
Ohio	922	0.0	D	7.9	D	9.0	6.5	44.7	14.7	11 828	249	1 306	23 229	-4.8
Pendleton	78	8.8	D	12.6	D	5.5	2.6	16.3	36.7	1 841	225	292	4 516	22.2
Pleasants	105	0.1	43.2	35.0	39.7	5.3	2.0	8.5	17.2	1 547	206	217	3 134	3.4
Pocahontas	107	-0.7	D	16.6	D	7.9	2.2	32.8	21.4	2 214	242	341	5 579	1.9
Preston	208	-0.3	29.3	13.8	46.1	10.0	3.2	15.9	25.0	6 126	209	1 110	12 137	5.6
Putnam	638	0.1	28.0	15.4	59.5	11.0	3.4	20.6	12.6	8 387	163	892	16 884	22.8
Raleigh	1 016	0.1	20.2	3.3	58.5	13.0	3.7	30.3	21.4	18 668	236	3 284	33 278	3.7
Randolph	329	0.0	D	13.3	D	11.4	3.2	31.1	22.1	6 035	214	1 375	12 548	13.4
Ritchie	87	-2.2	D	43.4	D	7.9	2.7	9.8	18.9	2 453	237	481	4 936	1.9
Roane	116	-1.6	43.5	22.6	D	9.6	4.6	19.0	20.3	3 654	237	867	6 611	9.4
Summers	69	-3.0	D	4.1	D	12.1	4.2	22.0	30.7	2 896	223	812	6 769	3.1
Taylor	95	1.5	D	25.9	D	8.4	1.7	12.5	35.4	3 022	188	611	6 528	0.2
Tucker	74	-0.4	D	15.9	D	7.2	5.1	21.1	23.6	1 841	251	215	3 900	2.0
Tyler	94	0.6	D	53.1	D	4.7	1.8	8.8	17.7	2 140	223	249	4 441	-3.4
Upshur	234	-1.2	36.9	19.1	46.4	11.1	2.3	25.0	17.8	4 744	203	989	9 506	5.4
Wayne	339	0.0	27.6	12.1	D	7.3	D	13.1	36.5	8 829	206	2 208	16 991	1.0
Webster	70	0.0	39.6	9.4	D	5.4	D	12.9	28.7	2 464	254	771	5 072	6.1
Wetzel	137	-0.3	D	4.2	D	18.9	3.5	16.0	27.5	4 168	236	730	8 129	-1.3
Wirt	21	-2.4	22.5	10.7	D	8.8	2.7	21.2	43.7	1 210	206	259	2 795	38.2
Wood	1 499	0.1	33.4	25.6	49.9	11.2	4.7	24.5	16.8	18 480	210	2 663	37 620	4.0
Wyoming	186	0.0	39.3	3.9	D	9.2	2.1	13.0	23.5	7 088	276	1 813	11 756	-3.2
WISCONSIN	100 638	0.8	32.9	26.3	52.5	9.1	6.8	24.1	13.8	901 712	168	84 892	2 055 774	10.3
Adams	152	7.9	19.9	14.4	42.4	8.5	2.6	18.2	29.8	5 031	270	329	12 418	23.1
Ashland	264	-0.3	28.2	22.0	D	D	2.5	28.6	18.6	3 535	210	390	8 371	7.6
Barron	653	4.1	D	31.0	D	10.8	2.9	19.7	15.8	9 539	212	900	19 363	12.9
Bayfield	115	0.3	16.7	6.1	56.7	12.0	4.4	28.1	26.4	3 406	227	219	10 918	13.2
Brown	5 370	0.6	31.3	24.3	58.5	9.9	7.6	24.0	9.6	31 263	138	2 842	74 740	20.0
Buffalo	187	3.8	13.9	9.6	D	6.1	2.8	12.6	16.6	2 935	213	225	5 586	2.0
Burnett	138	0.9	D	28.5	D	11.1	2.7	23.5	15.7	4 175	266	266	11 743	13.4
Calumet	447	3.1	D	49.8	D	6.8	3.0	10.2	10.0	5 624	138	187	12 465	19.5
Chippewa	786	1.6	44.4	35.3	38.3	10.2	2.2	16.3	15.7	10 598	192	883	21 024	9.5
Clark	340	8.0	D	28.7	D	7.7	D	14.6	17.8	6 613	197	547	12 904	4.2
Columbia	672	0.5	D	27.4	D	10.8	2.7	21.4	17.0	9 801	187	551	19 258	8.2
Crawford	208	0.0	D	32.9	D	16.8	3.0	22.3	13.4	3 453	200	350	7 315	8.1

1. Covers mining, construction, and manufacturing.   2. Covers private sector earnings in agricultural services, forestry, and fisheries; transportation and public utilities; wholesale trade; retail trade; finance, insurance, and real estate; and services.   3. Per 1,000 resident population estimated as of July 1 of the year shown.

Table B. States and Counties — Housing, Labor Force, and Employment

	Housing units, 1990 (cont'd)								Civilian labor force, 2001				Civilian employment, 1990[5]		
	Occupied units										Unemployment			Percent	
	Owner-occupied					Renter-occupied									
				Owner cost as a percent of income											
STATE County	Total	Percent	Median value[1]	With a mort-gage	Without a mort-gage	Median rent[2]	Rent as per-cent of income	Sub-stand-ard units[3] (percent)	Total	Percent change, 2000–2001	Total	Rate[4]	Total	Professional, managerial, and technical	Precision production, craft, and repair
	89	90	91	92	93	94	95	96	97	98	99	100	101	102	103

WEST VIRGINIA—Cont'd															
Braxton	4 950	77.9	39 300	21.3	13.3	264	25.3	8.1	5 261	-0.3	420	8.0	4 105	20.1	17.2
Brooke	10 131	79.1	44 100	15.5	11.7	306	20.7	2.0	11 388	1.1	508	4.5	10 858	23.7	14.3
Cabell	39 146	64.7	52 800	16.4	11.8	319	28.5	2.1	44 067	1.1	2 062	4.7	38 829	32.4	10.4
Calhoun	2 978	76.7	33 200	19.7	12.3	195	28.1	12.1	2 728	-0.3	421	15.4	2 423	21.5	15.1
Clay	3 627	76.0	33 000	21.5	12.0	246	35.1	10.0	4 250	0.8	303	7.1	2 346	21.1	17.4
Doddridge	2 623	82.4	33 800	18.9	11.4	238	27.6	6.4	3 395	1.1	151	4.4	2 387	20.1	18.0
Fayette	18 292	76.4	34 500	19.6	12.4	266	27.2	5.1	17 285	-0.9	1 159	6.7	14 337	25.2	16.0
Gilmer	2 717	71.4	42 100	17.0	11.7	282	31.6	9.5	2 620	-2.6	134	5.1	2 370	26.2	17.7
Grant	3 925	81.5	49 900	19.1	11.7	253	22.0	4.7	4 747	9.8	244	5.1	4 486	18.3	18.7
Greenbrier	13 775	75.6	44 000	18.8	12.2	275	25.7	3.7	15 812	1.3	987	6.2	13 500	23.0	13.5
Hampshire	6 182	81.1	50 500	18.5	12.6	267	24.4	8.9	9 549	4.1	432	4.5	6 536	19.8	19.6
Hancock	13 781	76.7	45 600	14.0	11.7	320	21.8	1.7	14 988	0.1	558	3.7	14 424	19.6	14.0
Hardy	4 286	82.2	49 300	17.7	13.0	260	23.9	8.6	7 921	5.4	217	2.7	4 861	14.4	17.0
Harrison	27 009	74.0	45 000	19.7	12.5	299	28.1	2.4	35 432	0.4	1 781	5.0	26 011	26.1	13.2
Jackson	9 645	78.4	51 400	16.5	12.0	314	27.8	4.3	13 044	0.6	778	6.0	9 637	21.4	15.2
Jefferson	0	71.9	84 100	18.1	12.0	376	23.9	3.4	23 106	2.9	586	2.5	17 631	25.0	15.2
Kanawha	84 713	68.5	56 400	16.0	11.5	339	24.1	1.8	109 845	0.4	4 381	4.0	87 615	31.0	11.2
Lewis	6 615	69.8	42 200	18.2	12.4	250	27.5	4.8	7 201	-0.3	425	5.9	6 071	21.1	14.9
Lincoln	7 647	77.1	38 200	18.0	11.5	253	35.1	9.9	6 829	-1.8	581	8.5	5 891	17.1	19.6
Logan	15 425	73.2	42 100	20.5	12.5	278	27.4	5.0	12 695	-1.7	694	5.5	12 253	21.2	20.3
McDowell	12 880	78.7	15 800	22.0	12.9	221	31.6	8.5	7 186	-2.3	499	6.9	7 398	19.7	21.2
Marion	22 667	75.5	42 300	17.0	12.7	300	29.0	2.0	24 756	0.1	1 328	5.4	20 932	23.5	17.9
Marshall	14 051	77.9	42 700	15.2	11.6	269	26.5	2.3	16 791	1.1	1 034	6.2	14 267	23.0	15.5
Mason	9 603	78.5	44 800	16.8	12.2	262	26.7	5.8	9 266	-0.3	1 003	10.8	8 867	17.8	16.4
Mercer	25 390	76.3	44 600	19.1	11.7	280	28.6	3.4	28 809	0.9	1 283	4.5	23 646	25.9	14.7
Mineral	9 981	77.5	49 300	18.3	12.1	270	23.4	2.6	13 017	0.7	813	6.2	10 987	22.6	15.2
Mingo	11 830	72.8	39 400	20.7	12.6	272	34.8	6.6	8 359	1.1	574	6.9	8 396	19.9	22.3
Monongalia	29 087	62.1	64 600	17.4	11.9	359	32.1	2.3	42 216	3.9	916	2.2	33 025	36.7	11.3
Monroe	4 749	84.3	42 500	21.1	12.3	261	21.3	6.9	5 524	2.0	221	4.0	4 586	19.0	15.1
Morgan	4 731	83.0	61 900	17.5	11.9	310	24.3	4.6	6 625	2.4	233	3.5	5 142	18.9	18.7
Nicholas	9 970	81.2	42 300	20.0	11.8	288	31.7	5.2	11 176	-0.9	667	6.0	8 575	21.2	18.2
Ohio	20 646	66.7	48 800	16.9	11.7	280	26.2	1.7	25 292	0.9	880	3.5	22 058	30.2	10.9
Pendleton	3 061	79.3	51 600	20.1	11.0	274	24.6	8.4	4 225	-2.6	131	3.1	3 391	16.0	16.9
Pleasants	2 769	79.6	51 100	16.0	12.0	259	24.5	5.4	2 975	4.0	202	6.8	2 792	22.4	18.7
Pocahontas	3 628	79.4	42 000	21.8	12.3	249	26.9	7.4	4 431	1.7	325	7.3	3 465	19.2	10.6
Preston	10 619	81.3	44 200	19.0	12.2	250	25.1	7.1	13 891	3.6	639	4.6	10 525	18.5	20.3
Putnam	15 695	83.3	62 700	16.6	11.6	345	25.4	3.9	28 338	0.0	1 035	3.7	17 954	27.0	13.7
Raleigh	29 483	75.5	44 100	19.8	11.8	296	28.5	3.3	36 101	2.1	1 524	4.2	25 344	26.9	14.7
Randolph	10 366	74.5	46 000	21.1	12.2	274	27.6	5.0	14 140	2.0	837	5.9	9 861	24.7	12.9
Ritchie	3 928	80.0	32 400	21.5	12.0	226	27.9	6.3	4 509	1.6	365	8.1	3 740	16.0	16.3
Roane	5 740	78.0	36 600	22.8	11.6	241	27.1	8.5	6 240	-3.5	837	13.4	4 823	18.5	16.5
Summers	5 240	76.7	34 800	19.5	11.5	228	29.9	7.8	4 441	0.4	285	6.4	3 946	21.4	13.8
Taylor	5 741	76.2	34 200	18.6	12.5	254	28.6	4.0	7 209	1.2	399	5.5	5 260	17.3	15.6
Tucker	3 017	80.4	38 200	20.4	11.9	256	23.1	5.4	3 621	-0.4	202	5.6	2 927	20.3	17.4
Tyler	3 709	82.0	43 200	16.2	11.6	283	28.8	4.8	4 357	-0.7	230	5.3	3 540	21.2	15.8
Upshur	8 245	75.5	47 900	20.0	12.2	281	27.7	5.5	11 255	2.7	599	5.3	8 364	23.8	14.9
Wayne	15 626	76.6	46 700	17.3	11.9	288	28.3	5.6	17 411	1.5	980	5.6	14 598	24.1	14.5
Webster	3 996	78.4	29 700	23.2	12.6	229	33.1	10.2	3 180	0.3	231	7.3	2 645	15.3	20.3
Wetzel	7 303	77.3	50 200	15.0	12.3	269	24.3	5.5	7 966	-1.0	674	8.5	6 556	20.2	18.8
Wirt	1 942	81.3	36 300	18.9	11.6	211	26.9	13.6	2 123	5.2	213	10.0	1 861	18.2	13.9
Wood	34 168	73.8	49 500	15.9	12.4	333	25.5	2.0	45 262	0.5	2 148	4.7	37 725	27.1	12.1
Wyoming	10 474	80.5	34 300	18.1	11.8	257	30.8	5.8	8 147	0.3	471	5.8	7 372	20.3	24.2
WISCONSIN	1 822 118	66.7	62 500	20.1	13.4	399	24.9	2.6	2 990 578	1.9	136 105	4.6	2 386 439	26.4	11.5
Adams	5 972	81.4	46 500	21.2	14.1	320	26.0	3.4	8 085	1.7	377	4.7	5 640	17.2	13.0
Ashland	6 255	70.6	37 300	19.2	15.6	278	27.3	3.9	8 005	2.3	605	7.6	6 628	24.1	8.6
Barron	15 435	73.5	47 000	20.6	14.3	313	27.5	2.6	23 850	0.7	1 308	5.5	18 462	19.0	11.6
Bayfield	5 515	78.8	44 700	20.8	14.9	272	27.0	5.8	7 560	1.9	480	6.3	5 814	26.4	11.5
Brown	72 280	65.6	62 600	20.3	13.0	373	23.9	2.1	138 623	2.4	5 290	3.8	99 142	26.6	11.2
Buffalo	5 123	75.2	43 000	19.0	13.0	286	22.4	2.7	8 072	1.1	341	4.2	6 499	17.6	11.3
Burnett	5 242	80.7	44 600	22.0	15.0	276	25.4	4.1	7 374	2.9	408	5.5	5 243	17.9	16.9
Calumet	11 772	78.6	62 100	20.5	12.1	346	21.0	2.4	25 899	2.2	1 000	3.9	17 478	21.3	12.9
Chippewa	19 077	74.2	46 500	18.3	13.5	325	24.9	2.4	31 050	1.9	1 794	5.8	23 870	20.6	12.0
Clark	11 209	78.7	36 900	20.0	13.9	269	23.5	4.3	15 971	1.8	1 208	7.6	13 956	17.0	10.4
Columbia	16 868	72.9	55 700	19.8	13.2	356	23.1	1.6	27 722	3.5	1 397	5.0	21 857	21.5	13.2
Crawford	5 914	74.2	42 900	20.5	14.3	298	25.3	3.1	10 322	2.9	529	5.1	7 142	16.0	10.4

1. Specified owner-occupied units.　　2. Specified renter-occupied units.　　3. Overcrowded or lacking complete plumbing facilities.　　4. Percent of civilian labor force.　　5. Persons 16 years and older.

	Private nonfarm establishments, employment and payroll, 1999									Agriculture, 1997			
	Employment						Annual payroll		Farms			Farm operators
											Percent with—		Whose principal occupation is farming (percent)
STATE County	Number of establishments	Total	Health Care and Social Assistance	Manufacturing	Retail trade	Finance and Insurance	Professional Scientific and Technical Services	Total (mil dol)	Average per employee (dollars)	Number	Less than 50 acres	500 acres and over	
	104	105	106	107	108	109	110	111	112	113	114	115	116
WEST VIRGINIA—Cont'd													
Braxton	321	3 074	513	471	779	72	72	58	18 875	280	11.8	7.9	41.4
Brooke	442	7 421	1 666	1 560	572	136	80	159	21 446	95	25.3	4.2	37.9
Cabell	2 785	45 228	10 012	5 871	7 154	2 672	1 947	1 098	24 277	305	28.9	1.0	37.0
Calhoun	137	989	210	220	121	52	D	19	18 754	171	8.2	7.6	38.0
Clay	136	1 304	252	76	96	D	0	36	27 953	100	7.0	3.0	43.0
Doddridge	74	539	143	D	229	D	3	8	15 184	302	10.3	10.3	34.4
Fayette	951	9 818	1 745	879	2 301	315	173	221	22 531	205	25.9	2.0	36.6
Gilmer	141	942	170	185	116	34	44	17	18 318	214	5.1	17.3	37.4
Grant	278	2 895	551	526	344	116	62	68	23 479	375	17.9	22.1	55.2
Greenbrier	1 009	9 786	2 285	944	2 062	235	167	207	21 140	727	23.0	12.1	41.7
Hampshire	331	2 697	733	190	437	137	54	47	17 280	547	21.8	12.4	44.4
Hancock	689	14 166	1 122	7 757	1 515	337	215	397	28 057	64	37.5	1.6	43.8
Hardy	257	5 036	259	3 365	597	126	D	101	20 015	467	22.9	15.8	57.8
Harrison	1 921	24 694	4 781	1 743	5 039	766	862	637	25 784	601	23.5	6.0	35.3
Jackson	527	7 245	928	2 407	1 429	250	113	189	26 062	730	18.9	4.0	36.0
Jefferson	833	10 084	796	2 358	1 666	343	452	214	21 191	357	40.9	10.4	53.2
Kanawha	6 011	92 869	15 124	6 447	14 248	5 928	5 052	2 642	28 448	154	35.1	1.9	29.9
Lewis	404	4 240	1 049	609	886	109	80	90	21 269	364	16.5	10.2	45.6
Lincoln	235	1 690	405	23	361	83	76	33	19 765	214	30.4	3.3	39.7
Logan	825	9 666	2 016	678	2 211	259	329	250	25 854	10	40.0	0.0	20.0
McDowell	421	3 972	1 052	13	871	161	94	94	23 686	7	42.9	0.0	57.1
Marion	1 292	15 568	2 658	1 449	2 428	650	816	370	23 763	317	19.6	1.6	34.4
Marshall	582	6 729	1 472	529	1 333	195	141	156	23 189	536	16.2	1.5	32.6
Mason	361	4 889	982	1 039	535	170	85	145	29 625	742	22.6	5.1	38.7
Mercer	1 445	19 727	4 586	1 855	3 805	655	592	457	23 155	409	29.3	3.4	39.4
Mineral	480	4 682	929	963	933	139	78	100	21 444	343	22.2	11.1	38.5
Mingo	623	6 847	810	278	860	240	210	189	27 674	5	80.0	0.0	0.0
Monongalia	2 018	29 335	7 660	2 182	4 905	723	990	703	23 968	430	24.9	2.8	33.0
Monroe	201	1 139	219	D	173	55	D	23	19 874	617	18.0	9.9	41.3
Morgan	243	2 286	466	286	394	110	54	48	21 107	161	21.7	5.0	41.0
Nicholas	660	6 915	1 236	816	1 539	171	241	142	20 528	304	28.9	3.0	38.5
Ohio	1 595	26 130	6 451	1 435	2 498	1 292	1 176	627	23 987	136	14.7	3.7	46.3
Pendleton	169	1 884	321	D	208	50	D	51	27 313	590	19.5	17.3	50.8
Pleasants	131	1 624	171	D	239	73	51	55	33 778	132	15.9	6.1	28.8
Pocahontas	248	3 217	316	460	289	54	D	53	16 343	357	14.0	18.5	44.0
Preston	604	4 872	996	791	798	172	142	103	21 043	866	20.3	4.5	40.2
Putnam	1 095	12 943	1 323	1 043	1 931	454	600	346	26 759	454	24.7	0.9	37.7
Raleigh	2 019	24 640	4 642	1 008	4 917	707	915	578	23 473	260	33.8	4.2	36.9
Randolph	777	8 618	1 894	1 531	1 468	237	222	166	23 268	352	8.8	11.1	40.5
Ritchie	229	2 442	219	1 286	246	68	39	57	23 268	454	12.1	6.6	39.5
Roane	299	2 670	511	724	478	138	63	50	18 594	454	12.1	6.6	39.0
Summers	198	1 471	439	70	284	60	51	26	17 610	316	19.0	5.7	40.5
Taylor	206	1 935	625	422	264	59	12	36	18 654	278	29.5	6.5	35.6
Tucker	210	2 296	268	317	244	59	11	38	16 571	191	19.9	5.8	39.3
Tyler	153	1 849	294	849	197	85	10	61	32 738	234	13.7	6.8	43.2
Upshur	527	6 554	1 098	1 014	812	149	132	127	19 433	399	23.8	4.5	41.1
Wayne	649	7 628	1 565	1 606	1 010	177	145	214	28 096	151	17.9	7.9	35.1
Webster	194	1 708	453	234	195	47	35	41	23 834	74	28.4	0.0	31.1
Wetzel	444	5 313	413	D	1 273	194	95	173	32 550	260	9.2	3.8	31.9
Wirt	82	377	28	65	D	20	9	5	12 424	199	15.1	6.0	38.7
Wood	2 395	37 069	5 835	7 502	6 274	1 482	1 000	934	25 185	520	21.5	1.3	36.9
Wyoming	438	4 244	653	127	783	113	80	89	21 086	31	38.7	6.5	32.3
WISCONSIN	139 646	2 368 404	296 494	573 353	316 102	128 200	87 696	69 271	29 248	65 602	19.5	9.2	59.5
Adams	283	2 359	396	479	341	56	60	50	21 288	360	15.3	14.7	53.9
Ashland	590	7 162	1 652	1 450	1 030	179	133	160	22 368	186	10.8	9.7	34.9
Barron	1 279	16 640	2 130	5 723	2 860	416	285	379	22 767	1 384	13.5	7.9	65.8
Bayfield	414	2 195	199	187	351	85	D	40	18 222	325	13.8	12.0	51.4
Brown	6 193	128 706	14 041	27 817	16 114	9 964	4 260	3 901	30 312	1 059	31.4	6.2	62.5
Buffalo	354	3 352	338	351	309	134	63	100	29 764	1 000	11.2	17.7	66.5
Burnett	435	3 365	629	1 008	537	90	68	70	20 821	351	12.5	10.3	51.3
Calumet	771	12 046	776	5 697	1 517	314	155	329	27 329	703	23.0	6.5	67.4
Chippewa	1 241	18 188	2 703	6 041	2 846	406	333	427	23 492	1 471	10.7	10.5	70.5
Clark	783	8 387	1 419	3 236	1 060	260	138	176	21 007	1 883	11.3	6.5	74.0
Columbia	1 460	17 318	1 977	5 357	2 524	458	430	423	24 435	1 359	21.5	12.2	58.0
Crawford	382	6 080	1 172	2 083	1 355	139	62	129	21 167	958	12.8	9.3	59.5

Table B. States and Counties — **Agriculture, Land, and Water**

STATE County	\multicolumn{6}{c}{Agriculture, 1997 (cont'd)}											
	\multicolumn{4}{c}{Land in farms}	Value of land and buildings		Value of machinery and equipment average per farm ($1,000)	\multicolumn{4}{c}{Value of products sold}		Percent of farms with sales of —		Percent of land owned by fed. gov. 1997	Water consumption 1995 (mil gal/day)
	Acreage (1,000)	Percent change, 1992–1997	\multicolumn{3}{c}{Acres}						Percent from —					
			Average size of farm	Total irrigated (1,000)	Total cropland (1,000)	Average per farm ($1,000)	Average per acre (dollars)		Total (mil dol)	Average per farm (dollars)	Crops	Livestock and poultry products	$10,000 or more	$100,000 or more		
	117	118	119	120	121	122	123	124	125	126	127	128	129	130	131	132
WEST VIRGINIA—Cont'd																
Braxton	67	-8.1	240		24	178	770	24	2	6 182	9.9	90.1	10.0	0.0	9.0	5.7
Brooke	14	13.2	143		7	170	1 187	27	1	11 583	30.9	69.2	15.8	3.2	0.0	50.3
Cabell	32	-11.1	105	0	10	136	1 342	19	2	7 421	81.0	19.0	9.8	1.3	0.8	82.5
Calhoun	38	9.8	225		12	160	654	16	1	4 013	8.9	91.3	9.4	0.0	0.0	1.6
Clay	17	15.3	173	D	5	186	1 078	23	1	5 397	24.6	75.2	12.0	0.0	0.0	1.4
Doddridge	71	19.6	234	D	27	142	647	16	1	3 465	18.1	81.9	6.6	0.0	0.0	0.9
Fayette	23	15.3	113	0	10	122	1 093	16	2	7 673	27.9	72.1	12.2	1.5	5.1	33.5
Gilmer	63	19.5	296	0	25	166	572	23	2	9 110	8.7	91.3	18.7	0.5	0.0	1.2
Grant	122	15.1	325	0	34	422	1 141	28	34	91 766	1.2	98.8	38.9	13.9	6.6	1 005.8
Greenbrier	184	2.4	254	0	62	275	1 070	34	40	55 403	2.7	97.3	38.5	7.2	15.4	11.2
Hampshire	140	3.2	257	1	50	353	1 321	34	16	28 719	18.5	81.5	30.7	4.6	0.8	2.7
Hancock	7	-10.8	112	D	3	137	1 228	28	1	9 038	74.2	25.8	17.2	0.0	0.0	175.8
Hardy	143	0.7	306	0	43	423	1 195	43	109	234 392	1.5	98.5	50.1	26.1	13.0	13.5
Harrison	103	15.9	172	0	48	158	1 062	22	5	7 914	14.3	85.7	12.6	1.3	0.0	59.5
Jackson	117	15.5	160	0	48	152	855	20	4	5 975	30.0	70.0	12.7	0.4	0.1	50.5
Jefferson	73	-1.4	204	0	56	716	3 722	45	19	54 375	42.7	57.3	42.3	13.2	2.1	13.7
Kanawha	19	-3.2	126	D	6	214	1 527	16	1	9 213	74.0	25.9	9.1	1.9	0.0	637.6
Lewis	79	-1.9	218	D	33	208	890	28	3	8 230	15.6	84.4	20.9	0.8	6.9	5.6
Lincoln	27	-8.6	128	0	9	102	825	15	1	5 545	85.5	14.5	14.0	0.0	0.0	2.1
Logan	D	D	D	D	D	243	1 789	11	D	D	D	D	20.0	0.0	0.0	6.2
McDowell	0	-51.2	70		0	97	1 393	21	D	D	D	D	28.6	0.0	0.0	7.3
Marion	39	-4.0	124	0	19	148	1 297	16	2	5 139	43.8	56.3	6.9	0.9	0.0	55.6
Marshall	78	22.0	146	0	32	115	777	19	3	5 453	19.0	81.0	8.8	0.9	0.0	750.5
Mason	121	3.0	162	0	49	179	1 120	29	15	20 340	49.3	50.7	19.5	3.1	0.2	661.7
Mercer	53	-6.2	131	0	18	136	883	22	3	6 207	28.0	72.0	12.5	0.7	0.3	21.9
Mineral	80	6.2	232	0	27	193	926	22	8	24 408	8.5	91.5	21.3	4.7	0.8	5.2
Mingo	D	D	D		D	22	925	11	0	1 211	0.0	100.0	0.0	0.0	1.4	6.5
Monongalia	58	5.6	135	0	28	176	1 141	26	3	6 721	18.5	81.5	14.7	0.9	0.2	132.1
Monroe	139	-6.9	225	0	48	208	1 049	26	19	31 315	9.9	90.1	36.0	5.8	6.3	3.4
Morgan	28	28.1	175	0	11	285	1 433	21	1	8 126	63.1	36.9	13.0	1.9	0.0	2.7
Nicholas	40	20.2	130	0	17	174	1 586	29	3	8 363	12.7	87.3	17.4	1.0	7.2	5.2
Ohio	21	0.5	155	D	13	139	882	23	2	13 159	12.7	87.3	16.9	5.1	0.0	43.8
Pendleton	175	-1.5	297	0	45	356	1 134	31	68	114 667	1.1	98.9	43.1	16.1	29.3	4.9
Pleasants	21	33.4	162	D	6	115	740	19	1	5 800	22.2	77.8	11.4	0.8	0.3	123.4
Pocahontas	129	12.1	361	0	38	289	844	30	5	14 401	11.5	88.5	33.1	2.2	51.8	5.1
Preston	152	9.1	175	D	74	169	987	22	11	12 237	22.1	77.9	20.2	2.3	1.0	147.2
Putnam	57	2.0	126	D	21	167	1 426	19	4	9 629	77.9	22.1	13.4	0.7	0.2	70.1
Raleigh	35	7.4	136	D	14	156	1 091	23	2	7 743	38.6	61.4	18.1	0.8	3.1	14.6
Randolph	104	0.1	263	D	36	214	846	31	6	14 258	13.7	86.3	24.2	2.0	30.1	15.1
Ritchie	87	22.5	247	0	35	153	607	21	2	6 376	17.4	82.7	13.1	0.3	0.0	4.0
Roane	93	13.1	204	0	41	141	646	18	3	5 785	11.5	88.5	16.1	0.0	0.0	3.5
Summers	57	-1.4	181	0	20	192	1 013	25	4	11 526	20.5	79.6	15.2	0.0	10.8	1.6
Taylor	44	4.0	157	D	17	199	1 305	25	4	13 218	42.2	57.7	15.8	2.9	2.2	7.3
Tucker	35	9.7	184	D	11	192	1 067	17	1	5 956	19.0	80.9	14.1	0.0	37.4	16.8
Tyler	48	2.2	205	D	20	107	621	16	1	4 764	16.4	83.6	9.4	0.0	0.1	25.0
Upshur	64	9.0	161	D	28	179	984	19	3	6 345	16.5	83.5	17.5	0.0	0.0	3.9
Wayne	29	-1.3	190	0	8	185	1 115	29	1	9 581	45.7	54.3	19.2	0.0	10.9	20.8
Webster	8	-10.6	109	D	3	94	862	22	0	2 620	23.7	76.3	5.4	0.0	18.6	1.7
Wetzel	48	29.1	184	D	13	117	674	15	1	2 826	25.9	74.1	3.5	0.0	0.0	91.8
Wirt	37	3.0	186	0	15	155	895	19	3	13 231	54.2	45.8	15.1	1.0	0.0	2.5
Wood	67	10.9	128	0	29	142	1 105	18	3	5 454	35.3	64.7	8.8	0.6	0.0	168.6
Wyoming	4	-33.7	128	D	1	91	709	13	0	5 797	58.3	41.7	6.5	0.0	5.1	6.5
WISCONSIN	14 900	-3.6	227	342	10 353	282	1 244	67	5 580	85 056	29.4	70.6	61.4	24.0	5.1	7 251.7
Adams	122	2.2	338	42	84	404	1 263	113	58	161 962	90.4	9.6	52.5	19.2	0.2	38.2
Ashland	47	-8.8	250		24	166	621	37	5	26 458	11.0	89.0	31.2	5.9	31.9	34.5
Barron	325	-7.4	235	9	218	197	866	62	165	118 900	14.1	85.9	66.8	26.3	0.0	16.4
Bayfield	84	-14.1	259	0	48	216	925	45	10	30 275	19.6	80.4	41.5	7.7	31.8	5.4
Brown	196	-4.4	185	0	168	333	1 770	74	128	121 309	13.9	86.1	66.8	31.6	0.0	496.5
Buffalo	309	-4.5	309	5	171	224	746	68	102	102 160	15.1	84.9	67.9	27.1	1.9	178.2
Burnett	83	-1.5	236	0	45	200	692	73	14	40 418	39.0	61.0	41.3	12.3	0.9	2.2
Calumet	144	-11.4	204	0	122	272	1 359	84	76	108 086	17.1	82.9	74.0	34.9	0.0	5.9
Chippewa	373	-3.7	253	2	238	199	765	65	119	80 686	15.8	84.2	68.3	26.1	0.0	11.2
Clark	414	-3.1	220	1	289	175	794	58	159	84 511	9.7	90.3	71.9	30.0	0.0	5.1
Columbia	326	-0.4	240	1	253	362	1 514	71	107	78 639	43.2	56.8	66.1	23.8	0.2	17.1
Crawford	233	-6.2	244	0	114	202	820	42	40	41 736	21.5	78.5	58.5	12.5	2.7	2.8

STATE County	Value of Residential Construction Authorized by Building Permits, 2000		Wholesale Trade, 1997				Retail Trade[1], 1997				Real Estate and Rental and Leasing, 1997			
	New Construction ($1,000)	Number of Housing Units	Number of Establishments	Number of Employees	Sales (mil dol)	Annual Payroll (mil dol)	Number of Establishments	Number of Employees	Sales (mil dol)	Annual Payroll (mil dol)	Number of Establishments	Number of Employees	Receipts (mil dol)	Annual Payroll (mil dol)
	133	134	135	136	137	138	139	140	141	142	143	144	145	146
WEST VIRGINIA—Cont'd														
Braxton	0	0	17	119	38.8	3.5	87	678	111.1	10.2	6	20	1.7	0.4
Brooke	1 652	13	10	D	D	D	86	684	91.3	8.7	9	27	2.5	0.4
Cabell	6 162	50	169	D	D	D	553	7 592	1 120.1	113.1	113	D	D	D
Calhoun	NA	NA	1	D	D	D	29	168	20.7	1.9	4	5	0.2	0.0
Clay	1 314	25	1	D	D	D	33	208	37.9	2.6	2	D	D	D
Doddridge	NA	NA	2	D	D	D	15	47	7.0	0.6	1	D	D	D
Fayette	5 477	89	29	402	84.6	11.4	206	2 103	328.6	31.3	25	53	6.3	0.6
Gilmer	0	0	5	16	5.7	0.3	25	164	23.4	2.3	2	D	D	D
Grant	2 463	53	8	D	D	D	54	349	53.0	4.9	7	31	2.0	0.5
Greenbrier	8 262	105	32	211	47.0	5.0	217	2 176	329.0	31.1	33	175	10.2	2.7
Hampshire	12 527	111	14	67	11.5	1.2	59	440	67.8	5.9	5	17	0.7	0.1
Hancock	2 810	21	21	133	42.6	3.5	135	1 682	206.0	20.2	27	85	6.5	1.4
Hardy	6 076	102	5	D	D	D	50	426	53.2	6.0	11	19	1.3	0.3
Harrison	14 338	166	91	1 434	452.2	43.2	391	4 956	766.7	70.2	53	154	15.0	2.3
Jackson	3 791	47	28	394	145.5	8.9	115	1 442	293.5	23.2	13	31	3.3	0.3
Jefferson	52 419	483	19	D	D	D	142	1 291	197.7	21.0	32	73	13.2	1.4
Kanawha	15 008	96	388	4 807	2 162.1	146.8	976	14 450	2 428.6	217.7	285	1 575	204.1	32.0
Lewis	0	0	15	125	26.8	2.9	89	946	143.6	12.7	12	29	3.6	1.0
Lincoln	1 521	29	5	D	D	D	51	358	52.3	4.7	5	12	0.6	0.3
Logan	99	7	46	398	158.7	11.4	204	1 996	335.7	31.0	23	87	7.4	1.7
McDowell	386	10	14	102	157.6	3.0	97	860	108.3	11.9	18	55	5.6	1.0
Marion	1 410	21	67	695	154.8	18.3	236	2 567	421.5	35.7	43	144	9.1	1.6
Marshall	420	6	21	D	D	D	114	1 523	204.3	18.3	14	D	D	D
Mason	673	10	6	75	47.9	1.9	80	557	79.5	7.2	15	45	4.8	0.7
Mercer	2 499	33	72	1 265	354.4	31.1	321	3 683	588.2	53.0	42	134	76.7	3.2
Mineral	39 005	328	18	D	D	D	103	982	142.7	12.6	12	34	2.6	0.3
Mingo	418	8	30	234	54.0	5.7	122	1 006	176.1	15.9	16	38	3.1	0.4
Monongalia	3 361	79	81	688	439.0	19.7	373	4 750	677.2	70.5	108	442	41.8	6.2
Monroe	27	1	10	56	14.1	0.9	37	192	27.7	2.1	3	3	0.2	0.0
Morgan	12 465	155	7	D	D	D	53	355	59.7	6.2	5	11	0.7	0.2
Nicholas	650	7	31	255	64.1	5.9	139	1 333	213.7	18.6	20	35	4.0	0.6
Ohio	2 757	18	110	D	D	D	247	2 706	387.0	43.2	59	D	D	D
Pendleton	2 992	49	5	24	2.9	0.3	33	210	29.4	2.8	2	D	D	D
Pleasants	180	4	3	D	D	D	28	248	41.8	3.5	5	18	1.3	0.2
Pocahontas	0	0	4	25	8.7	0.4	55	373	46.4	4.5	8	41	3.1	0.7
Preston	324	5	26	199	97.3	4.7	87	828	147.0	11.6	20	61	3.5	0.8
Putnam	27 103	271	60	1 255	423.2	43.4	201	2 119	365.0	30.1	27	83	9.2	1.0
Raleigh	10 393	89	131	1 146	378.1	32.8	390	4 889	826.8	75.9	92	335	37.0	6.4
Randolph	1 566	29	37	355	152.5	8.6	149	1 343	201.1	18.4	20	80	4.2	0.8
Ritchie	203	4	8	52	11.2	1.2	48	282	42.0	3.7	4	D	D	D
Roane	0	0	10	D	D	D	58	475	75.1	7.1	4	D	D	D
Summers	2 053	24	10	121	29.5	2.4	45	247	36.0	3.9	2	D	D	D
Taylor	91	2	5	D	D	D	47	318	55.7	4.5	4	14	0.4	0.1
Tucker	583	9	3	D	D	D	38	266	40.9	3.8	8	77	3.1	0.8
Tyler	40	1	2	D	D	D	32	191	25.6	2.1	1	D	D	D
Upshur	6 246	101	20	310	75.7	3.6	101	837	155.2	14.0	14	33	2.5	0.4
Wayne	2 660	50	31	D	D	D	111	1 127	168.5	15.4	21	D	D	D
Webster	0	0	7	D	D	D	32	212	31.2	2.8	2	D	D	D
Wetzel	668	10	14	69	32.7	1.4	112	1 070	145.5	14.1	17	36	5.2	0.8
Wirt	0	0	2	D	D	D	14	72	10.6	0.7	3	4	0.4	0.1
Wood	18 872	237	116	1 357	489.8	34.0	462	6 058	990.2	91.0	76	400	42.1	7.9
Wyoming	195	2	9	53	47.9	1.7	98	759	108.4	11.3	10	62	3.8	1.0
WISCONSIN	3 916 822	34 154	8 025	110 309	57 192.9	3 764.9	21 717	305 255	50 520.5	4 826.2	4 598	23 924	2 637.5	464.1
Adams	26 162	244	11	146	28.0	2.8	37	327	64.7	5.5	9	D	D	D
Ashland	4 015	49	18	130	40.5	3.3	113	1 041	149.7	13.4	11	36	2.1	0.4
Barron	30 193	337	66	763	153.8	17.6	254	2 812	451.6	41.9	30	84	8.6	1.3
Bayfield	12 259	146	7	36	5.6	0.8	66	328	51.0	4.2	8	25	1.7	0.3
Brown	197 641	1 559	461	6 480	2 848.1	212.1	950	14 976	2 569.1	239.7	197	1 048	116.3	18.7
Buffalo	7 739	81	17	180	47.6	4.2	46	305	45.7	3.8	6	17	0.7	0.1
Burnett	22 565	225	9	20	10.2	0.5	71	530	77.1	7.6	10	D	D	D
Calumet	50 582	388	45	474	98.6	12.1	106	1 615	232.7	20.1	18	56	3.2	0.3
Chippewa	48 469	442	49	654	237.4	21.7	205	2 475	481.3	39.9	26	87	5.2	0.8
Clark	12 910	134	51	278	71.3	6.6	137	1 071	198.0	16.1	13	27	1.9	0.4
Columbia	44 684	381	64	735	352.5	18.5	228	2 434	407.4	37.7	32	55	7.1	1.0
Crawford	5 014	57	19	118	220.9	3.9	88	915	133.6	12.3	16	D	D	D

1. Establishments with payroll.

Table B. States and Counties — **Professional, Manufacturing, and Accommodation and Foodservices**

STATE County	Professional, Scientific, and Technical Services[1], 1997				Manufacturing, 1997				Accommodation and Foodservices, 1997			
	Number of Establishments	Number of Employees	Receipts (mil dol)	Annual Payroll (mil dol)	Number of Establishments	Number of Employees	Receipts (mil dol)	Annual Payroll (mil dol)	Number of Establishments	Number of Employees	Sales (mil dol)	Annual Payroll (mil dol)
	147	148	149	150	151	152	153	154	155	156	157	158
WEST VIRGINIA—Cont'd												
Braxton	17	49	2.4	0.6	NA	NA	NA	NA	32	444	14.3	4.0
Brooke	18	85	4.5	1.5	22	1 275	637.6	49.6	58	D	D	D
Cabell	179	1 206	76.3	27.7	112	5 766	1 199.5	199.9	253	4 933	140.9	39.3
Calhoun	5	16	0.6	0.2	NA	NA	NA	NA	5	88	3.9	0.7
Clay	3	D	D	D	NA	NA	NA	NA	7	12	0.5	0.1
Doddridge	3	3	0.1	0.0	NA	NA	NA	NA	4	D	D	D
Fayette	46	200	11.9	4.2	34	807	169.4	27.5	65	918	27.9	8.5
Gilmer	6	37	2.1	0.5	NA	NA	NA	NA	11	92	2.5	0.6
Grant	14	34	2.1	0.7	18	929	106.2	15.6	21	166	4.4	1.0
Greenbrier	48	123	8.1	2.4	38	923	99.7	26.2	78	2 098	118.4	41.8
Hampshire	15	48	2.0	0.7	NA	NA	NA	NA	32	311	11.2	3.3
Hancock	47	190	20.1	4.6	37	8 011	2 105.3	330.3	84	D	D	D
Hardy	10	24	1.8	0.3	20	2 940	435.6	57.7	21	341	7.5	2.0
Harrison	115	836	61.4	21.7	68	2 022	394.0	72.7	151	2 340	73.0	20.6
Jackson	25	90	5.8	2.3	16	D	D	D	36	637	20.1	5.2
Jefferson	53	283	16.1	8.4	26	2 172	444.1	60.1	82	1 114	37.6	10.2
Kanawha	525	4 387	384.5	125.5	141	6 590	3 071.3	273.3	420	8 287	280.7	75.9
Lewis	14	77	5.0	1.2	18	538	52.6	13.5	30	341	12.4	3.3
Lincoln	15	78	4.4	2.0	NA	NA	NA	NA	11	D	D	D
Logan	45	341	16.2	7.0	39	853	82.6	20.2	63	751	24.0	6.1
McDowell	22	128	6.4	2.0	NA	NA	NA	NA	17	176	5.6	1.4
Marion	80	581	48.0	17.8	62	1 501	347.0	42.0	96	1 295	36.9	10.5
Marshall	24	100	9.6	3.4	NA	NA	NA	NA	61	661	19.6	5.5
Mason	22	68	3.8	1.1	16	1 173	466.3	47.1	30	307	7.6	2.1
Mercer	81	543	37.7	11.0	56	1 908	298.5	61.8	100	2 010	64.3	17.1
Mineral	20	66	3.1	0.7	16	1 138	136.3	40.4	48	486	13.2	3.4
Mingo	56	248	12.0	4.0	NA	NA	NA	NA	42	346	10.8	3.1
Monongalia	143	902	70.8	23.0	58	2 055	598.0	77.8	207	3 795	95.5	28.4
Monroe	9	10	0.8	0.1	NA	NA	NA	NA	13	D	D	D
Morgan	10	20	1.5	0.4	NA	NA	NA	NA	20	375	11.8	4.2
Nicholas	45	197	9.9	3.4	27	768	123.1	18.2	45	590	18.6	5.3
Ohio	115	923	81.0	23.4	58	D	D	D	148	2 136	60.3	17.5
Pendleton	6	7	0.5	0.1	7	595	47.3	10.4	11	105	2.7	0.7
Pleasants	7	20	0.5	0.1	6	D	D	D	11	127	3.6	1.1
Pocahontas	4	7	0.5	0.1	NA	NA	NA	NA	29	1 011	40.3	11.0
Preston	33	112	5.5	1.9	28	664	69.0	14.1	30	244	6.7	1.7
Putnam	66	414	26.1	9.9	35	1 091	234.0	38.5	67	1 050	32.2	8.5
Raleigh	116	765	53.4	23.2	56	999	164.9	32.6	140	2 489	84.4	23.3
Randolph	47	185	9.2	3.7	29	1 397	169.4	27.3	62	876	23.6	6.6
Ritchie	10	32	1.7	0.3	21	1 035	116.6	27.2	10	97	2.2	0.5
Roane	16	76	3.7	1.3	18	790	170.4	12.9	14	133	4.5	1.3
Summers	8	53	3.2	0.5	NA	NA	NA	NA	18	202	7.4	2.2
Taylor	7	10	0.5	0.1	NA	NA	NA	NA	15	119	3.6	0.9
Tucker	7	17	0.9	0.3	NA	NA	NA	NA	28	326	11.8	3.5
Tyler	7	13	0.6	0.2	12	D	D	D	15	D	D	D
Upshur	32	119	6.9	2.5	26	947	152.5	22.5	42	552	13.7	4.2
Wayne	23	132	8.1	3.3	33	1 770	325.0	47.3	49	443	12.4	3.4
Webster	7	25	1.3	0.3	NA	NA	NA	NA	12	D	D	D
Wetzel	17	87	4.8	1.5	18	D	D	D	42	420	12.3	3.6
Wirt	4	D	D	D	NA	NA	NA	NA	4	13	0.6	0.1
Wood	134	885	59.0	20.6	78	7 010	2 301.9	293.3	198	3 767	110.7	32.1
Wyoming	23	83	4.6	1.6	NA	NA	NA	NA	29	267	8.2	1.8
WISCONSIN	9 281	70 689	6 398.9	2 542.3	9 936	562 479	117 383.0	18 766.4	13 252	190 411	5 641.0	1 548.5
Adams	16	38	1.7	0.7	NA	NA	NA	NA	42	416	14.6	4.0
Ashland	30	102	5.9	2.3	28	1 661	150.7	44.8	73	753	20.8	5.7
Barron	46	230	13.8	5.8	96	5 430	891.5	133.9	146	1 395	39.5	10.4
Bayfield	13	22	1.9	0.5	NA	NA	NA	NA	92	620	22.2	5.5
Brown	373	3 348	270.8	118.7	396	25 825	6 457.4	1 015.7	533	10 183	283.4	81.9
Buffalo	19	39	1.6	0.6	NA	NA	NA	NA	45	D	D	D
Burnett	15	48	2.4	0.9	32	1 106	176.7	30.3	66	D	D	D
Calumet	33	258	18.3	10.2	64	6 078	1 018.9	190.9	75	932	24.9	6.4
Chippewa	54	230	17.0	7.1	112	6 442	989.8	203.7	132	1 322	34.3	8.5
Clark	30	78	4.1	1.5	87	2 863	799.6	70.7	66	D	D	D
Columbia	70	247	20.2	6.0	108	5 311	1 262.4	159.1	190	1 717	62.3	15.1
Crawford	11	38	1.9	1.2	20	2 252	509.1	50.8	54	614	15.7	4.3

1. Firms subject to federal tax.

STATE County	Health Care and Social Assistance[1], 1997				Other Services[1], 1997				Federal funds and grants, fiscal 2001[2] Expenditures (mil dol)			
										Direct payments for individuals[3]		
	Number of Establishments	Number of Employees	Receipts (mil dol)	Annual Payroll (mil dol)	Number of Establishments	Number of Employees	Receipts (mil dol)	Annual Payroll (mil dol)	Total	Social Security and government retirement	Medicare	Food stamps and Supplemental Security Income
	159	160	161	162	163	164	165	166	167	168	169	170
WEST VIRGINIA—Cont'd												
Braxton	12	140	4.4	1.8	14	43	3.1	1.0	83.9	34.5	11.8	5.0
Brooke	50	713	30.7	13.6	30	128	4.8	1.5	143.6	60.0	28.6	5.9
Cabell	238	3 609	273.0	129.9	166	1 249	58.1	20.3	669.2	291.6	97.9	32.5
Calhoun	4	18	1.0	0.3	8	32	1.0	0.3	51.7	19.2	8.5	4.2
Clay	4	75	3.5	1.0	7	45	3.5	1.4	63.2	25.3	9.7	6.0
Doddridge	2	D	D	D	3	D	D	D	29.5	13.3	4.7	2.0
Fayette	64	1 298	62.5	22.6	53	244	17.5	4.6	328.8	150.0	65.0	19.4
Gilmer	6	95	3.9	1.1	6	14	0.8	0.1	45.3	16.8	6.8	2.7
Grant	15	77	4.1	1.3	18	59	3.1	0.9	58.6	26.0	8.6	2.4
Greenbrier	82	1 659	106.4	44.2	65	178	8.5	2.1	222.9	105.7	37.8	9.6
Hampshire	19	327	13.6	5.1	20	49	3.0	0.7	91.2	48.1	14.8	4.7
Hancock	71	814	36.7	16.6	46	218	10.9	2.9	186.1	103.5	52.3	4.0
Hardy	12	104	4.4	1.7	16	40	2.4	0.5	95.9	28.3	8.2	2.3
Harrison	169	1 976	101.3	39.1	115	527	28.0	8.4	460.5	196.9	76.0	22.6
Jackson	35	411	17.7	5.8	34	83	4.5	1.3	135.8	69.3	23.1	8.5
Jefferson	46	297	13.5	5.8	42	187	8.3	2.5	235.0	104.9	24.9	5.3
Kanawha	555	6 286	513.0	210.2	340	2 361	129.6	39.8	1 923.2	607.0	226.8	53.8
Lewis	27	412	29.3	9.4	34	88	5.3	1.3	102.2	47.2	18.9	6.6
Lincoln	8	122	5.5	2.4	20	71	3.7	1.4	134.3	54.4	18.7	14.3
Logan	51	551	31.1	13.4	68	493	43.3	11.9	270.5	130.3	50.1	18.4
McDowell	24	213	10.4	3.9	21	70	5.2	1.4	268.5	107.0	41.3	28.8
Marion	101	1 028	73.3	30.7	105	564	32.2	9.3	384.9	170.8	61.5	16.1
Marshall	57	790	34.0	14.3	31	178	8.8	3.0	153.7	82.0	33.0	7.3
Mason	31	220	13.8	5.1	27	98	5.5	1.6	137.7	64.8	23.7	7.6
Mercer	174	1 620	126.4	55.8	105	997	57.2	19.9	435.6	201.4	81.3	27.8
Mineral	37	548	28.4	10.1	38	128	7.1	2.0	161.0	71.4	31.4	5.6
Mingo	48	574	44.6	14.9	30	149	8.5	2.7	216.3	98.2	31.4	23.1
Monongalia	146	2 716	186.2	92.2	138	1 163	71.2	21.8	532.9	143.5	55.2	14.2
Monroe	5	103	3.6	1.5	8	12	1.4	0.3	91.8	40.1	15.1	4.7
Morgan	11	253	8.8	3.7	12	27	2.1	0.5	68.6	42.8	10.9	2.3
Nicholas	41	365	20.7	6.7	36	167	9.2	2.8	151.0	78.7	25.3	9.2
Ohio	179	1 592	107.0	45.0	104	855	44.7	15.1	326.6	140.1	60.3	10.9
Pendleton	9	56	1.6	0.5	7	19	1.0	0.2	54.8	20.1	7.6	1.4
Pleasants	11	207	5.0	2.2	6	52	4.7	1.1	33.7	18.0	6.9	1.8
Pocahontas	16	174	6.0	2.0	10	19	1.2	0.2	115.5	24.7	10.9	1.9
Preston	25	320	13.6	5.3	40	130	9.0	1.8	155.3	74.6	25.8	8.9
Putnam	63	918	63.5	20.7	49	243	12.9	4.2	184.0	99.0	28.8	6.5
Raleigh	209	3 068	227.3	79.9	120	697	42.8	13.3	559.6	247.5	84.8	29.2
Randolph	71	685	33.7	11.9	35	127	6.2	1.5	172.7	75.8	29.1	10.3
Ritchie	8	156	5.6	2.3	9	24	1.6	0.3	52.1	25.5	9.3	3.2
Roane	13	167	7.1	3.0	7	17	1.5	0.4	82.2	36.5	14.3	6.6
Summers	15	171	7.3	2.5	13	38	2.1	0.7	97.6	39.8	14.1	5.9
Taylor	15	183	7.2	3.8	16	64	3.3	0.8	84.1	38.4	12.9	4.8
Tucker	5	16	0.9	0.2	10	24	1.7	0.3	58.8	21.2	6.2	1.2
Tyler	7	96	2.5	0.8	10	28	1.7	0.4	41.5	21.7	7.6	2.2
Upshur	35	404	18.4	7.2	19	98	4.7	1.6	113.8	55.4	16.8	8.7
Wayne	27	229	10.1	4.3	51	296	20.5	5.3	240.3	86.6	28.5	15.3
Webster	9	108	3.3	1.3	6	18	1.3	0.2	69.4	28.9	10.8	5.5
Wetzel	32	306	13.8	5.0	28	97	4.0	1.0	101.7	52.1	17.3	6.2
Wirt	2	D	D	D	3	D	D	D	33.2	13.9	4.7	1.5
Wood	194	2 376	152.9	64.5	165	1 656	119.1	28.9	606.1	224.9	89.2	21.9
Wyoming	25	220	10.9	4.5	19	86	4.4	1.3	196.0	89.9	27.6	14.2
WISCONSIN	9 315	114 562	6 917.4	3 447.3	8 648	49 101	2 991.3	886.4	26 645.3	10 432.0	3 667.8	604.7
Adams	13	71	3.4	1.4	12	38	2.2	0.6	97.6	40.4	13.6	1.9
Ashland	41	778	33.6	19.7	31	91	5.7	1.4	117.9	42.5	16.4	2.5
Barron	73	879	37.9	17.7	89	303	17.2	4.5	209.9	100.2	30.8	5.4
Bayfield	13	D	D	D	12	28	1.5	0.4	81.0	36.0	11.6	1.5
Brown	380	5 467	359.7	190.1	391	2 650	143.4	46.4	843.9	370.0	107.1	19.9
Buffalo	15	169	10.6	5.1	21	38	3.0	0.5	72.6	30.8	9.5	1.0
Burnett	13	83	3.8	2.1	23	57	4.4	0.9	85.3	42.9	11.5	2.1
Calumet	50	450	21.5	10.2	48	130	8.1	2.1	97.6	48.4	16.3	1.1
Chippewa	77	1 130	46.0	21.5	74	283	20.1	5.0	236.8	112.4	39.4	5.7
Clark	39	364	12.2	5.5	51	127	9.3	1.4	151.0	65.7	29.4	2.4
Columbia	89	846	42.7	17.8	86	320	20.6	5.6	285.0	121.7	43.1	2.6
Crawford	28	590	19.2	9.9	22	87	4.9	1.1	80.5	35.8	11.9	1.5

1. Firms subject to federal tax.   2. October 1, 2000 to September 30, 2001.   3. State totals may include programs not allocated by county.

Table B. States and Counties — **Federal Funds and Local Government Finances**

	Federal funds and grants, fiscal 2001[1] (cont'd)							Local government finances, 1997				
	Expenditures (mil dol) (cont'd)							General revenue				
	Procurement contract awards			Grants[2]						Taxes		
STATE County											Per capita[3] (dollars)	
	Salaries and wages	Defense	Other	Medicaid and other health-related	Nutrition and family welfare	Education	Other	Total (mil dol)	Intergovern-mental (mil dol)	Total (mil dol)	Total	Property
	171	172	173	174	175	176	177	178	179	180	181	182
WEST VIRGINIA—Cont'd												
Braxton	2.8	0.5	0.5	19.5	2.3	1.3	5.1	23.0	14.1	3.5	266	243
Brooke	2.9	0.0	0.7	8.2	2.0	1.4	31.0	37.7	17.7	13.7	523	458
Cabell	51.4	2.8	16.2	98.6	12.1	6.2	27.6	180.6	76.8	66.4	698	514
Calhoun	1.4	0.0	0.3	14.0	1.1	1.6	0.7	10.5	7.5	1.7	213	208
Clay	1.5	0.0	0.4	15.0	2.6	1.2	1.3	17.1	11.6	2.5	236	231
Doddridge	0.8	0.0	0.2	6.3	0.8	0.5	0.2	10.3	6.4	3.0	412	407
Fayette	16.3	1.0	3.7	45.4	8.0	4.3	9.6	71.5	38.3	20.1	414	362
Gilmer	1.8	0.0	1.5	9.7	1.0	0.7	1.0	10.5	6.6	3.2	452	434
Grant	2.8	0.0	0.8	10.8	1.9	0.6	3.6	44.0	9.1	5.8	521	510
Greenbrier	7.0	10.3	2.7	29.8	3.2	2.0	10.2	56.7	28.0	11.6	326	299
Hampshire	2.6	0.0	1.6	13.5	1.5	1.1	1.7	22.7	15.1	5.5	293	283
Hancock	4.0	2.5	1.3	9.1	2.9	1.6	0.9	61.7	23.1	22.9	665	542
Hardy	3.1	0.0	2.3	13.7	0.8	0.7	35.4	18.0	10.9	4.8	405	383
Harrison	60.7	1.2	20.4	39.9	8.4	5.3	17.6	139.5	61.8	48.5	686	552
Jackson	5.5	0.0	2.8	16.1	2.6	1.7	1.8	49.5	27.0	14.3	517	470
Jefferson	39.9	1.3	24.1	11.6	2.0	1.4	12.6	54.6	24.7	21.8	545	506
Kanawha	150.9	11.1	55.3	168.0	112.8	89.3	386.7	421.7	148.8	169.3	831	606
Lewis	3.6	0.0	0.7	19.3	1.9	1.3	1.4	24.1	14.2	6.5	370	340
Lincoln	2.6	0.1	0.7	33.4	4.8	3.4	0.4	32.1	24.6	5.5	247	244
Logan	7.4	0.5	1.6	36.3	8.2	4.5	5.0	63.5	42.8	16.3	395	368
McDowell	5.0	5.5	2.2	54.8	12.3	4.4	3.4	47.0	33.8	10.1	329	290
Marion	12.0	3.1	21.9	29.4	7.8	9.9	35.7	174.8	45.2	27.7	487	410
Marshall	5.6	0.0	1.0	14.4	3.7	2.7	2.5	78.2	27.9	21.5	604	518
Mason	8.4	4.4	1.0	18.2	3.2	1.8	1.2	46.1	20.4	13.0	500	467
Mercer	16.9	1.1	4.1	53.5	10.0	9.7	16.4	151.9	53.0	24.8	385	301
Mineral	3.5	12.4	11.4	12.7	2.7	2.4	3.9	45.9	32.2	10.0	371	344
Mingo	5.0	0.7	3.3	39.3	8.9	3.1	-3.7	58.8	33.9	17.2	529	473
Monongalia	84.1	4.1	77.2	63.6	5.2	7.2	57.7	126.2	47.7	44.2	571	464
Monroe	10.9	0.0	0.5	15.4	1.2	1.4	1.7	13.5	10.2	2.3	174	162
Morgan	1.6	1.5	0.5	4.5	0.7	0.9	2.7	27.3	11.3	5.8	431	407
Nicholas	5.7	2.1	1.6	18.1	3.8	2.7	1.8	64.9	26.8	12.5	454	339
Ohio	26.0	4.6	7.7	26.3	6.0	5.4	23.1	89.5	35.0	29.2	597	390
Pendleton	9.0	1.7	2.5	9.4	0.6	0.6	1.0	12.3	9.5	2.0	255	243
Pleasants	0.9	0.0	0.3	3.9	0.7	0.4	0.2	31.4	6.0	7.9	1 052	1 013
Pocahontas	3.0	1.0	1.8	8.5	0.9	1.0	61.6	18.4	9.1	3.3	360	287
Preston	8.9	0.4	4.8	20.7	3.4	2.2	3.7	38.4	26.1	7.5	251	237
Putnam	8.6	0.9	2.0	16.1	3.0	2.1	15.9	77.2	36.1	23.0	457	430
Raleigh	76.4	0.9	12.3	49.8	10.7	4.8	25.1	146.2	83.1	36.0	455	355
Randolph	12.7	0.0	3.1	27.9	3.1	3.2	1.6	43.2	29.9	6.9	241	193
Ritchie	1.9	0.0	0.7	8.8	0.9	0.9	0.3	13.9	9.0	3.6	350	343
Roane	2.4	0.2	0.5	15.3	2.0	1.6	2.2	21.8	15.8	3.9	254	224
Summers	2.3	8.7	2.0	20.3	2.2	1.1	0.1	16.6	13.1	2.6	190	144
Taylor	2.8	0.0	0.7	11.8	2.0	1.4	8.5	28.0	18.6	5.7	368	322
Tucker	3.1	0.0	0.4	7.1	0.6	0.6	18.0	15.0	8.2	3.4	444	382
Tyler	1.3	0.0	0.5	5.1	1.1	0.7	1.2	20.5	9.6	5.3	524	509
Upshur	5.0	0.0	2.6	15.0	2.9	1.9	1.4	32.9	21.5	5.9	249	227
Wayne	44.1	0.8	7.6	43.4	4.7	2.8	2.4	71.9	44.3	17.2	408	382
Webster	1.2	0.0	0.3	17.6	2.1	1.3	0.9	15.2	10.7	3.5	338	318
Wetzel	2.8	0.0	0.7	15.5	2.3	1.3	1.1	48.6	18.4	10.9	588	504
Wirt	0.8	4.1	0.2	5.3	0.7	0.4	1.4	8.5	6.2	1.6	287	276
Wood	95.4	1.4	28.7	43.0	8.3	5.0	72.0	210.6	64.6	45.3	521	410
Wyoming	5.1	10.6	3.1	24.4	7.3	2.8	3.5	43.2	28.6	11.0	398	372
WISCONSIN	1 626.4	905.8	911.4	2 932.5	893.2	533.3	1 483.5	X	X	X	X	X
Adams	16.6	0.0	0.6	13.3	2.3	1.2	3.0	39.2	18.7	15.8	868	819
Ashland	8.0	4.4	1.4	15.3	3.5	3.5	11.1	55.1	36.3	11.4	694	631
Barron	8.4	0.0	1.8	33.5	9.9	3.0	4.7	123.6	71.0	31.5	720	656
Bayfield	5.7	0.0	1.5	11.0	3.1	1.8	7.7	46.8	25.1	15.4	1 012	954
Brown	62.0	8.1	102.6	76.3	18.1	12.9	26.1	633.5	278.0	208.0	971	946
Buffalo	5.3	2.2	2.8	8.6	1.6	0.6	1.1	34.9	23.1	8.8	622	585
Burnett	1.9	5.7	0.6	11.4	2.5	0.8	2.4	36.8	19.8	12.5	859	806
Calumet	9.5	0.2	0.9	6.2	1.6	0.8	3.5	66.7	33.8	20.6	540	529
Chippewa	11.0	4.8	2.0	29.6	7.1	3.3	8.4	128.7	82.0	32.3	596	541
Clark	6.2	0.3	3.1	21.0	3.5	2.4	5.6	100.2	56.8	20.1	611	600
Columbia	11.8	0.9	47.9	20.6	6.9	2.2	4.9	152.0	73.7	51.8	1 028	949
Crawford	3.9	0.4	0.7	14.2	2.1	1.0	3.0	45.2	27.2	11.5	696	633

1. October 1, 2000 to September 30, 2001.   2. State totals may include programs not allocated by county.   3. Based on the resident population estimated as of July 1 of the year shown.

STATE County	Total (mil dol)	Per capita[1] (dollars)	Educa-tion	Health and hospitals	Police protec-tion	Public welfare	High-ways	Total (mil dol)	Per capita[1] (dollars)	Federal civilian	Federal military	State and local	Demo-cratic	Republi-can	All other
	183	184	185	186	187	188	189	190	191	192	193	194	195	196	197
WEST VIRGINIA—Cont'd															
Braxton	22.3	1 674	71.1	1.2	1.0	0.0	0.4	92.7	6 973	66	68	750	51.0	47.5	1.5
Brooke	37.4	1 424	68.7	4.1	3.9	0.0	2.9	24.7	941	42	133	985	49.7	44.6	5.6
Cabell	175.8	1 849	54.8	2.6	4.7	0.0	1.5	127.2	1 338	1 089	514	6 460	46.2	51.0	2.8
Calhoun	13.8	1 751	87.9	0.1	1.0	0.0	0.4	3.9	496	23	41	349	42.5	54.5	3.0
Clay	17.0	1 621	72.5	14.2	0.8	0.0	0.2	1.2	119	27	55	571	45.1	52.7	2.2
Doddridge	10.1	1 363	85.9	3.9	0.6	0.0	0.4	0.0	0	15	38	298	27.5	69.4	3.1
Fayette	70.2	1 449	68.7	0.5	3.5	0.0	1.5	103.2	2 131	289	241	3 174	57.3	40.3	2.4
Gilmer	10.7	1 492	75.6	2.3	2.0	0.0	0.6	0.4	53	30	37	725	39.9	56.9	3.2
Grant	46.0	4 152	23.2	46.5	0.8	0.0	0.2	166.9	15 052	57	57	916	19.7	78.8	1.6
Greenbrier	52.9	1 491	62.3	3.5	3.3	0.0	1.3	69.3	1 953	127	182	2 133	43.9	53.6	2.4
Hampshire	23.2	1 226	82.6	1.2	1.6	0.0	0.7	7.0	373	46	100	1 083	33.9	63.6	2.5
Hancock	58.7	1 703	48.8	0.7	5.3	0.0	4.2	96.2	2 789	74	174	1 359	46.4	47.9	5.6
Hardy	19.6	1 660	78.4	1.4	3.0	0.0	1.7	3.4	291	70	62	549	35.9	62.4	1.7
Harrison	134.7	1 904	58.1	2.1	3.9	0.0	2.2	181.1	2 561	4 086	364	3 539	48.9	48.7	2.3
Jackson	47.1	1 710	68.3	5.8	2.6	0.0	0.4	27.3	991	81	146	1 326	42.9	55.1	2.0
Jefferson	49.3	1 230	73.9	1.5	3.7	0.1	0.6	43.3	1 081	641	218	2 362	47.7	49.0	3.3
Kanawha	398.8	1 958	48.2	3.2	4.7	0.0	2.1	479.0	2 352	2 393	1 129	19 208	50.2	48.0	1.7
Lewis	23.3	1 330	72.7	7.6	2.5	0.0	1.1	1.1	65	66	90	1 466	38.4	58.8	2.9
Lincoln	30.2	1 359	87.4	0.7	0.5	0.0	0.0	7.2	322	50	115	866	52.8	45.4	1.8
Logan	62.2	1 505	83.1	2.5	2.2	0.0	0.7	6.4	154	127	207	2 001	61.8	36.9	1.2
McDowell	45.6	1 490	84.1	0.5	2.1	0.0	0.9	0.4	12	94	151	1 932	66.3	32.2	1.5
Marion	171.4	3 013	33.5	0.9	1.7	0.0	0.9	502.8	8 840	180	288	3 970	53.8	43.6	2.5
Marshall	77.5	2 172	49.8	0.8	2.9	0.0	1.1	318.8	8 929	78	193	1 957	44.5	50.8	4.7
Mason	45.4	1 747	63.4	0.8	2.1	0.0	1.0	73.9	2 845	181	134	1 240	44.2	53.2	2.5
Mercer	159.4	2 478	39.4	34.6	2.0	0.0	0.9	105.9	1 646	302	330	4 533	44.2	54.1	1.7
Mineral	46.2	1 723	79.9	0.9	1.6	0.0	1.0	9.2	342	72	139	1 411	34.2	63.2	2.7
Mingo	55.1	1 693	75.9	1.3	2.3	0.0	0.5	16.5	506	95	162	1 420	60.2	38.5	1.2
Monongalia	123.0	1 587	55.9	4.5	3.7	0.1	1.6	212.0	2 736	1 414	422	14 718	46.1	49.7	4.2
Monroe	13.4	1 019	86.7	1.0	1.9	0.0	0.3	2.9	218	224	68	494	40.7	57.2	2.0
Morgan	27.7	2 056	54.6	29.6	1.2	0.0	0.1	7.9	583	26	72	742	33.6	63.0	3.4
Nicholas	64.3	2 332	48.3	32.9	3.4	0.9	1.5	13.6	492	122	142	1 676	47.3	50.8	1.9
Ohio	79.0	1 616	51.3	1.5	5.7	0.0	3.0	119.2	2 439	482	247	3 597	42.6	53.5	3.9
Pendleton	11.8	1 474	79.6	2.6	1.2	0.0	0.1	1.6	198	176	230	343	36.4	62.0	1.6
Pleasants	31.3	4 186	36.1	0.3	1.0	0.0	0.4	220.0	29 382	16	39	566	39.5	58.7	1.8
Pocahontas	19.7	2 176	49.5	23.2	1.4	0.0	0.5	8.3	917	72	47	740	40.2	56.8	3.0
Preston	38.3	1 287	76.9	1.1	2.6	0.0	0.8	7.4	249	94	154	1 526	33.7	63.3	3.0
Putnam	75.2	1 498	68.8	2.4	2.3	0.0	0.4	144.2	2 873	159	268	2 109	38.6	59.6	1.7
Raleigh	122.5	1 551	69.3	0.7	4.0	0.0	2.1	58.3	738	1 403	608	3 628	45.9	52.3	1.7
Randolph	42.6	1 479	66.2	3.5	1.9	0.0	1.6	10.3	358	285	148	1 825	42.2	55.0	2.8
Ritchie	14.0	1 362	82.9	0.1	1.7	0.0	0.8	0.1	14	31	54	505	26.9	71.3	1.8
Roane	21.8	1 422	79.0	0.1	1.7	0.0	1.0	15.1	987	38	79	635	41.5	56.4	2.2
Summers	16.6	1 208	68.9	1.2	1.7	0.4	0.9	0.5	33	41	71	745	48.8	48.9	2.3
Taylor	26.8	1 747	74.2	3.5	1.4	0.0	1.4	11.9	774	44	79	1 090	43.3	54.7	2.0
Tucker	14.7	1 903	56.7	0.8	1.8	0.0	1.2	3.6	472	65	39	642	39.4	57.8	2.8
Tyler	17.7	1 761	72.4	12.0	1.5	0.0	0.8	10.5	1 044	29	50	490	30.9	65.7	3.3
Upshur	35.1	1 474	67.7	0.7	1.6	0.0	0.9	13.3	558	109	121	1 184	34.1	63.6	2.3
Wayne	70.8	1 682	77.0	1.4	1.5	0.0	0.4	26.4	627	905	216	2 237	48.9	49.2	1.9
Webster	15.0	1 454	76.0	1.4	1.3	0.0	0.8	0.5	45	21	52	633	53.3	44.9	1.9
Wetzel	44.6	2 411	49.6	34.7	2.4	0.0	1.3	33.4	1 807	54	94	1 081	45.3	51.5	3.2
Wirt	8.2	1 454	86.0	0.0	0.6	0.0	0.5	1.3	223	16	30	261	34.3	63.7	1.9
Wood	202.4	2 325	43.4	36.6	3.1	0.0	2.0	118.6	1 362	1 868	446	4 074	37.4	60.3	2.2
Wyoming	42.7	1 543	83.2	0.5	3.0	0.1	0.7	1.3	47	100	139	1 164	54.4	44.1	1.4
WISCONSIN	X	X	X	X	X	X	X	X	X	29 537	19 388	347 826	47.8	47.6	4.5
Adams	47.1	2 595	45.8	3.7	4.8	4.8	14.4	37.0	2 039	353	66	750	52.9	43.0	4.1
Ashland	58.0	3 516	43.9	2.2	3.9	8.1	14.8	44.5	2 696	175	58	1 345	55.2	38.5	6.3
Barron	130.1	2 979	50.6	5.3	3.3	6.8	15.4	77.5	1 776	159	157	3 281	44.9	49.5	5.7
Bayfield	45.7	2 999	39.5	8.2	3.5	3.9	19.6	24.0	1 579	133	67	901	53.6	39.5	6.9
Brown	651.6	3 041	47.2	4.7	5.2	5.1	7.9	515.0	2 404	978	817	12 476	45.6	50.3	4.1
Buffalo	37.0	2 608	50.2	3.6	2.5	5.7	21.3	10.6	748	169	50	769	48.7	45.7	5.6
Burnett	40.0	2 752	44.6	4.8	2.7	6.2	18.0	18.1	1 247	41	53	744	44.5	48.7	6.8
Calumet	75.0	1 971	39.6	4.1	4.4	8.5	14.3	33.5	880	118	138	1 244	41.1	54.3	4.6
Chippewa	131.7	2 428	50.2	6.7	4.8	3.6	15.4	72.1	1 329	214	194	3 529	46.2	49.0	4.7
Clark	107.4	3 256	47.8	6.5	3.2	14.9	10.8	52.3	1 584	113	118	1 981	41.9	52.7	5.4
Columbia	175.5	3 485	53.0	2.1	3.4	7.3	13.6	116.5	2 313	196	183	3 266	49.4	46.8	3.8
Crawford	49.5	2 989	44.5	1.9	6.3	10.2	15.1	44.1	2 662	75	58	827	54.2	40.9	5.0

1. Based on the resident population estimated as of July 1 of the year shown.   2. Data subject to copyright.

Table B. States and Counties — **Land Area and Population**

STATE/ County code	MSA/ PMSA/ NECMA code[1]	County Type[2]	STATE County	Land area,[3] (sq km) 2000	Population and population characteristics, 2000			Race alone or in combination (percent)					Age (percent)					
					Total persons	Rank	Per square kilometer	White	Black	Am. Indian, Alaska Native	Asian and Pacific Islander	Percent Hispanic[4]	Under 5 years	5 to 17 years	18 to 24 years	25 to 34 years	35 to 44 years	45 to 54 years
				1	2	3	4	5	6	7	8	9	10	11	12	13	14	15
			WISCONSIN—Cont'd															
55 025	4720	2	Dane	3 113	426 526	140	137.0	90.5	4.7	0.8	4.0	3.4	6.1	16.5	14.3	16.0	16.4	14.1
55 027	...	4	Dodge	2 285	85 897	609	37.6	95.8	2.6	0.6	0.6	2.5	5.9	18.8	8.3	13.7	17.5	13.2
55 029	...	7	Door	1 250	27 961	1 452	22.4	98.5	0.3	1.1	0.4	1.0	4.6	17.5	6.1	9.6	15.8	15.6
55 031	2240	3	Douglas	3 391	43 287	1 032	12.8	96.7	0.8	2.7	1.0	0.7	5.9	17.7	10.3	12.1	15.9	14.7
55 033	...	6	Dunn	2 207	39 858	1 115	18.1	96.8	0.5	0.6	2.5	0.8	5.7	17.6	19.8	12.1	13.7	12.5
55 035	2290	3	Eau Claire	1 651	93 142	549	56.4	95.9	0.8	0.9	3.1	0.9	6.0	17.5	17.1	12.6	14.1	13.1
55 037	...	9	Florence	1 264	5 088	2 845	4.0	99.0	0.4	0.9	0.4	0.5	4.5	18.4	5.3	10.2	16.8	14.8
55 039	...	4	Fond du Lac	1 872	97 296	533	52.0	96.9	1.1	0.7	1.1	2.0	6.0	19.2	9.4	12.6	16.2	13.9
55 041	...	9	Forest	2 626	10 024	2 442	3.8	87.0	1.3	12.2	0.3	1.1	5.7	19.6	7.8	10.1	13.8	12.3
55 043	...	6	Grant	2 973	49 597	924	16.7	98.7	0.6	0.3	0.6	0.6	5.2	18.5	14.6	10.5	14.3	12.6
55 045	...	6	Green	1 513	33 647	1 292	22.2	98.8	0.5	0.5	0.4	1.0	6.4	20.1	6.7	12.1	17.1	14.2
55 047	...	6	Green Lake	918	19 105	1 843	20.8	98.3	0.3	0.4	0.6	2.1	5.6	18.5	6.6	10.4	15.9	14.1
55 049	...	6	Iowa	1 975	22 780	1 656	11.5	99.2	0.3	0.4	0.5	0.3	6.4	20.6	6.6	12.7	17.8	14.4
55 051	...	9	Iron	1 961	6 861	2 702	3.5	99.1	0.2	1.1	0.3	0.7	4.0	15.4	5.9	9.0	15.7	14.2
55 053	...	6	Jackson	2 557	19 100	1 844	7.5	90.3	2.3	6.7	0.4	1.9	5.6	18.5	8.8	13.2	16.2	13.1
55 055	...	4	Jefferson	1 443	74 021	674	51.3	97.2	0.4	0.7	0.7	4.1	6.3	18.9	8.5	13.6	16.8	14.1
55 057	...	7	Juneau	1 988	24 316	1 583	12.2	97.3	0.5	1.7	0.5	1.4	5.9	19.5	6.9	10.8	15.8	13.5
55 059	3800	1	Kenosha	707	149 577	360	211.6	90.1	5.8	0.9	1.3	7.2	6.9	20.1	9.4	13.9	17.4	12.9
55 061	...	6	Kewaunee	887	20 187	1 781	22.8	99.1	0.2	0.6	0.2	0.8	5.9	19.9	8.0	12.1	16.1	13.7
55 063	3870	3	La Crosse	1 173	107 120	500	91.3	95.0	1.3	0.7	3.6	0.9	5.9	17.6	15.6	12.8	14.7	13.1
55 065	...	9	Lafayette	1 641	16 137	2 014	9.8	99.4	0.2	0.2	0.4	0.6	5.9	21.3	7.6	10.5	16.8	13.0
55 067	...	6	Langlade	2 260	20 740	1 751	9.2	98.8	0.3	1.1	0.4	0.8	5.4	19.0	6.5	10.6	15.4	13.5
55 069	...	6	Lincoln	2 288	29 641	1 411	13.0	98.4	0.6	0.8	0.6	0.8	5.7	19.7	6.9	11.6	16.3	13.0
55 071	...	4	Manitowoc	1 532	82 887	625	54.1	96.6	0.5	0.8	2.3	1.6	5.8	19.6	7.6	11.7	16.4	13.9
55 073	8940	3	Marathon	4 001	125 834	431	31.5	94.4	0.4	0.6	4.9	0.8	6.4	20.4	8.2	13.0	16.5	13.9
55 075	...	7	Marinette	3 631	43 384	1 031	11.9	98.7	0.3	0.9	0.5	0.7	5.1	18.4	8.1	9.9	15.9	14.0
55 077	...	9	Marquette	1 180	15 832	2 030	13.4	94.6	3.7	1.5	0.6	2.7	4.8	16.2	6.7	12.3	16.6	13.7
55 078	...	NA	Menominee	927	4 562	2 874	4.9	12.1	0.3	87.9		2.7	9.5	29.4	8.4	11.0	13.7	10.2
55 079	5080	0	Milwaukee	626	940 164	39	1 501.9	67.4	25.5	1.3	3.1	8.8	7.1	19.2	10.5	15.0	15.3	12.6
55 081	...	6	Monroe	2 333	40 899	1 085	17.5	97.2	0.6	1.3	0.8	1.8	6.7	21.4	7.7	11.5	15.9	14.0
55 083	...	6	Oconto	2 585	35 634	1 226	13.8	98.6	0.2	1.4	0.3	0.7	5.7	20.0	6.4	11.4	17.3	13.7
55 085	...	7	Oneida	2 912	36 776	1 195	12.6	98.4	0.4	1.1	0.5	0.7	4.7	17.6	5.7	10.2	16.2	14.7
55 087	0460	2	Outagamie	1 658	160 971	331	97.1	94.7	0.7	2.0	2.6	2.0	6.9	20.8	8.9	14.4	17.5	13.0
55 089	5080	0	Ozaukee	601	82 317	629	137.0	97.4	1.1	0.4	1.3	1.3	6.2	20.5	6.8	10.2	17.8	16.0
55 091	...	8	Pepin	602	7 213	2 665	12.0	99.4	0.1	0.6	0.3	0.3	5.9	20.6	7.9	10.8	15.2	13.6
55 093	5120	1	Pierce	1 493	36 804	1 194	24.7	98.7	0.4	0.6	0.6	0.8	5.7	18.7	17.0	12.1	16.0	13.3
55 095	...	6	Polk	2 376	41 319	1 071	17.4	98.3	0.3	1.4	0.4	0.8	5.9	20.3	6.7	11.2	16.4	14.4
55 097	...	4	Portage	2 088	67 182	730	32.2	96.4	0.5	0.6	2.7	1.4	5.9	18.2	16.2	12.4	15.3	13.3
55 099	...	7	Price	3 244	15 822	2 031	4.9	98.8	0.2	1.0	0.5	0.7	4.9	19.0	5.8	10.2	15.6	14.9
55 101	6600	3	Racine	863	188 831	293	218.8	84.5	11.2	0.8	1.0	7.9	7.0	20.0	8.3	13.0	16.9	13.9
55 103	...	7	Richland	1 518	17 924	1 905	11.8	99.0	0.4	0.5	0.4	0.9	5.6	19.6	8.4	10.5	15.0	14.1
55 105	3620	3	Rock	1 866	152 307	351	81.6	92.4	5.2	0.7	1.1	3.9	6.7	19.8	8.6	13.5	16.3	13.6
55 107	...	7	Rusk	2 365	15 347	2 065	6.5	98.3	0.7	0.8	0.4	0.8	5.4	19.4	7.9	10.2	14.6	13.8
55 109	5120	1	St. Croix	1 870	63 155	768	33.8	98.6	0.5	0.5	0.9	0.8	7.0	20.9	8.2	14.0	18.2	14.1
55 111	...	6	Sauk	2 169	55 225	852	25.5	98.0	0.4	1.1	0.5	1.7	6.5	19.6	7.4	12.9	16.4	13.8
55 113	...	9	Sawyer	3 254	16 196	2 007	5.0	82.9	0.4	17.1	0.4	0.9	5.5	18.6	6.0	9.4	15.2	14.7
55 115	...	6	Shawano	2 312	40 664	1 095	17.6	92.4	0.4	7.2	0.5	1.0	6.1	19.5	6.9	11.9	15.7	12.8
55 117	7620	3	Sheboygan	1 330	112 646	477	84.7	93.5	1.3	0.7	3.7	3.4	6.4	19.1	8.4	13.0	16.8	13.7
55 119	...	6	Taylor	2 525	19 680	1 813	7.8	99.3	0.2	0.5	0.4	0.6	5.8	21.3	7.6	11.6	16.8	13.0
55 121	...	8	Trempealeau	1 901	27 010	1 482	14.2	99.3	0.2	0.4	0.2	0.9	6.2	19.2	6.9	12.3	15.9	13.7
55 123	...	6	Vernon	2 059	28 056	1 450	13.6	99.3	0.2	0.4	0.3	0.7	6.5	20.9	6.8	10.0	15.2	13.7
55 125	...	9	Vilas	2 263	21 033	1 734	9.3	90.3	0.3	9.6	0.3	0.9	4.3	16.4	5.0	8.8	14.3	14.2
55 127	...	4	Walworth	1 438	93 759	548	65.2	95.5	1.0	0.5	1.0	6.5	5.9	18.3	13.8	11.9	15.6	13.1
55 129	...	9	Washburn	2 097	16 036	2 020	7.6	98.5	0.3	1.9	0.3	0.9	5.1	18.7	5.8	9.4	15.3	14.8
55 131	5080	1	Washington	1 116	117 493	461	105.3	98.3	0.5	0.5	0.8	1.3	6.8	19.9	7.2	13.1	18.4	14.5
55 133	5080	0	Waukesha	1 439	360 767	164	250.7	96.6	1.0	0.5	1.8	2.6	6.4	19.9	6.8	11.7	18.1	15.7
55 135	...	6	Waupaca	1 945	51 731	897	26.6	98.6	0.3	0.7	0.4	1.4	6.0	19.6	7.1	11.6	16.2	13.5
55 137	...	8	Waushara	1 621	23 154	1 636	14.3	97.7	0.3	0.8	0.5	3.7	5.0	18.5	6.0	9.5	15.4	14.2
55 139	0460	2	Winnebago	1 136	156 763	340	138.0	95.7	1.3	0.8	2.2	2.0	6.0	17.8	11.8	13.7	16.7	13.3
55 141	...	4	Wood	2 053	75 555	664	36.8	97.1	0.4	1.0	1.7	0.9	6.1	19.5	7.7	11.9	16.4	13.8
56 000	...	X	WYOMING	251 489	493 782	X	2.0	93.7	1.0	3.0	0.9	6.4	6.3	19.8	10.1	12.1	16.0	15.0
56 001	...	5	Albany	11 066	32 014	1 345	2.9	93.4	1.4	1.9	2.2	7.5	5.1	13.3	28.2	14.3	11.7	12.3
56 003	...	9	Big Horn	8 125	11 461	2 337	1.4	95.5	0.2	1.4	0.4	6.2	6.8	21.9	7.3	9.6	15.4	14.0
56 005	...	7	Campbell	12 424	33 698	1 290	2.7	97.3	0.3	1.7	0.6	3.5	7.4	23.7	9.5	12.9	19.4	15.6
56 007	...	7	Carbon	20 451	15 639	2 045	0.8	92.0	0.8	1.9	1.0	13.8	5.7	18.4	8.6	11.4	16.9	16.5

1. MSA = Metropolitan Statistical Area. PMSA = Primary MSA. NECMA = New England County Metropolitan Area. See Appendix A for explanation of these concepts. See Appendix B for list of metropolitan areas identified by type, with component counties. 2. County typology code from the Economic Research Service of USDA. See Appendix A for definition. 3. Dry land or land partially or temporarily covered by water. 4. Hispanic persons may be of any race.

STATE County	55 to 64 years	65 to 74 years	75 years and over	Percent female	2001	1990	1990–2000	2000–2001	Births	Deaths	Net migration	Number	Percent change, 1990–2000	Persons per house-hold	Female family house-holder[1]	One person
	16	17	18	19	20	21	22	23	24	25	26	27	28	29	30	31
WISCONSIN—Cont'd																
Dane	7.2	4.7	4.6	50.5	432 654	367 085	16.2	1.4	6 428	3 195	3 033	173 484	21.5	2.37	7.9	29.4
Dodge	8.7	6.8	7.2	47.7	86 447	76 559	12.2	0.6	1 210	1 017	393	31 417	17.0	2.56	7.5	24.1
Door	12.1	9.9	8.9	50.7	28 339	25 690	8.8	1.4	302	394	470	11 828	17.5	2.33	6.5	28.1
Douglas	9.0	7.0	7.5	50.7	43 468	41 758	3.7	0.4	604	587	178	17 808	8.8	2.36	10.1	29.8
Dunn	7.3	5.6	5.6	49.6	40 352	35 909	11.0	1.2	554	362	309	14 337	17.0	2.57	6.9	24.4
Eau Claire	7.4	5.9	6.4	51.6	93 278	85 183	9.3	0.1	1 375	819	-386	35 822	14.5	2.46	8.6	27.1
Florence	12.5	9.4	8.0	49.0	5 088	4 590	10.8	0.0	51	66	14	2 133	21.5	2.35	6.0	27.9
Fond du Lac	8.5	7.0	7.4	51.2	97 781	90 083	8.0	0.5	1 449	1 127	208	36 931	13.1	2.52	7.8	25.4
Forest	11.5	10.7	8.5	50.0	10 020	8 776	14.2	0.0	132	153	21	4 043	22.9	2.39	9.8	28.2
Grant	8.9	7.6	7.7	49.3	49 270	49 266	0.7	-0.7	588	599	-306	18 465	7.5	2.51	7.5	26.0
Green	8.7	7.0	7.7	50.8	34 022	30 339	10.9	1.1	502	390	271	13 212	14.5	2.51	7.5	25.0
Green Lake	10.1	9.3	9.6	50.8	19 260	18 651	2.4	0.8	283	287	163	7 703	7.1	2.43	6.9	27.0
Iowa	8.1	6.9	6.5	50.2	23 073	20 150	13.1	1.3	365	254	187	8 764	18.3	2.56	7.6	24.3
Iron	12.5	11.7	11.5	51.0	6 806	6 153	11.5	-0.8	37	122	31	3 083	18.5	2.19	7.0	32.0
Jackson	9.7	7.5	7.4	46.6	19 224	16 588	15.1	0.6	240	232	118	7 070	13.1	2.49	8.6	26.2
Jefferson	9.1	6.4	6.2	50.4	74 588	67 783	9.2	0.8	1 150	740	181	28 205	17.4	2.55	8.2	23.6
Juneau	10.8	8.8	8.0	50.0	24 577	21 650	12.3	1.1	345	355	274	9 696	17.3	2.47	8.8	26.0
Kenosha	7.9	5.9	5.6	50.4	152 524	128 181	16.7	2.0	2 693	1 513	1 794	56 057	19.2	2.60	11.5	25.5
Kewaunee	9.0	7.1	8.2	49.8	20 310	18 878	6.9	0.6	295	232	67	7 623	12.8	2.61	6.6	23.5
La Crosse	7.7	6.2	6.4	51.5	107 705	97 904	9.4	0.5	1 541	1 117	208	41 599	13.5	2.45	8.4	28.4
Lafayette	9.1	8.3	7.5	50.1	16 155	16 074	0.4	0.1	211	193	1	6 211	5.7	2.57	7.6	25.4
Langlade	10.7	9.4	9.4	50.4	20 744	19 505	6.3	0.0	272	285	20	8 452	11.8	2.42	8.2	26.7
Lincoln	10.3	8.2	8.2	50.0	29 873	26 993	9.8	0.8	388	386	237	11 721	15.4	2.46	8.1	25.5
Manitowoc	9.1	7.7	8.0	50.5	82 618	80 421	3.1	-0.3	1 124	1 074	-286	32 721	8.7	2.49	7.5	26.8
Marathon	8.6	6.4	6.6	50.1	126 031	115 400	9.0	0.2	1 873	1 133	-497	47 702	14.8	2.60	7.4	23.6
Marinette	10.9	8.7	8.9	50.6	43 417	40 548	7.0	0.1	521	662	192	17 585	13.1	2.38	7.4	28.3
Marquette	11.3	10.8	7.5	45.7	15 900	12 321	28.5	0.4	199	214	83	5 986	23.9	2.41	6.7	25.4
Menominee	9.4	6.0	2.4	50.7	4 621	4 075	12.0	1.3	135	58	-7	1 345	24.7	3.35	26.6	16.5
Milwaukee	7.4	6.4	6.6	52.1	932 012	959 212	-2.0	-0.9	19 363	11 503	-16 159	377 729	1.3	2.43	16.3	33.0
Monroe	8.9	6.9	7.0	49.6	41 258	36 633	11.6	0.9	676	498	200	15 399	17.2	2.60	8.8	25.0
Oconto	10.3	8.0	7.2	49.7	36 320	30 226	17.9	1.9	460	424	640	13 979	23.9	2.52	6.9	23.5
Oneida	12.1	10.7	8.0	50.2	37 045	31 679	16.1	0.7	391	505	380	15 333	21.1	2.34	7.1	26.4
Outagamie	7.7	5.5	5.4	50.1	164 115	140 510	14.6	2.0	2 766	1 437	1 835	60 530	19.8	2.61	7.6	24.2
Ozaukee	9.9	6.9	5.7	50.7	83 555	72 894	12.9	1.5	1 133	743	865	30 857	20.0	2.61	6.5	21.4
Pepin	9.3	7.8	9.1	49.7	7 330	7 107	1.5	1.6	116	94	95	2 759	5.6	2.57	6.8	26.1
Pierce	7.5	4.8	4.8	50.7	37 290	32 765	12.3	1.3	500	319	311	13 015	18.2	2.65	7.5	21.3
Polk	9.9	7.5	7.6	50.0	42 285	34 773	18.8	2.3	527	474	906	16 254	24.5	2.51	7.4	25.2
Portage	7.8	5.6	5.3	50.2	66 921	61 405	9.4	-0.4	939	562	-624	25 040	17.5	2.54	7.3	24.5
Price	10.8	9.2	9.7	49.8	15 602	15 600	1.4	-1.4	177	258	-136	6 564	8.4	2.37	6.6	28.5
Racine	8.6	6.4	5.9	50.5	189 613	175 034	7.9	0.4	3 204	1 963	-383	70 819	11.1	2.59	12.3	24.5
Richland	9.6	8.4	8.8	50.4	18 133	17 521	2.3	1.2	231	194	170	7 118	8.0	2.48	7.4	27.2
Rock	8.8	6.7	6.0	50.8	153 324	139 510	9.2	0.7	2 543	1 656	207	58 617	12.2	2.54	10.9	25.1
Rusk	10.3	9.1	9.3	50.4	15 331	15 079	1.8	-0.1	209	211	-5	6 095	7.1	2.45	7.9	27.0
St. Croix	7.7	5.0	4.8	50.0	66 319	50 251	25.7	5.0	1 073	571	2 601	23 410	32.7	2.66	7.0	21.2
Sauk	9.0	7.0	7.4	50.6	55 904	46 975	17.6	1.2	845	626	474	21 644	22.3	2.51	8.1	25.2
Sawyer	12.7	10.2	7.7	49.6	16 433	14 181	14.2	1.5	207	238	269	6 640	19.2	2.39	10.0	26.2
Shawano	10.3	8.4	8.4	50.1	40 925	37 157	9.4	0.6	581	556	246	15 815	14.8	2.51	8.0	24.9
Sheboygan	8.5	6.7	7.2	49.8	113 109	103 877	8.4	0.4	1 670	1 328	181	43 545	12.8	2.50	7.3	26.1
Taylor	8.8	7.3	7.9	49.4	19 637	18 901	4.1	-0.2	273	246	-64	7 529	12.5	2.58	7.1	24.7
Trempealeau	9.4	7.5	8.9	49.9	27 062	25 263	6.9	0.2	404	374	34	10 747	13.2	2.45	7.4	27.6
Vernon	9.8	8.2	8.8	50.6	28 260	25 617	9.5	0.7	447	396	164	10 825	11.3	2.55	6.8	26.7
Vilas	14.3	13.1	9.7	50.2	21 535	17 707	18.8	2.4	207	346	630	9 066	24.3	2.29	7.5	26.0
Walworth	8.6	6.4	6.3	50.3	95 605	75 000	25.0	2.0	1 347	1 040	1 539	34 522	25.0	2.57	8.2	24.7
Washburn	12.3	9.7	8.8	49.7	16 373	13 772	16.4	2.1	186	263	410	6 604	21.0	2.39	7.0	26.7
Washington	8.9	5.9	5.4	50.1	119 829	95 328	23.3	2.0	1 875	1 002	1 472	43 842	32.9	2.65	7.2	20.3
Waukesha	9.4	6.5	5.5	50.8	367 065	304 715	18.4	1.7	5 203	3 228	4 358	135 229	27.6	2.63	6.8	20.9
Waupaca	9.2	7.8	8.9	49.9	52 198	46 104	12.2	0.9	754	868	588	19 863	16.6	2.51	7.4	25.2
Waushara	12.1	10.7	8.5	49.6	23 497	19 385	19.4	1.5	280	315	366	9 336	22.6	2.43	6.7	24.4
Winnebago	8.2	6.3	6.3	50.1	157 312	140 320	11.7	0.4	2 166	1 582	44	61 157	14.9	2.43	8.3	27.6
Wood	9.1	7.3	8.0	51.0	75 306	73 605	2.6	-0.3	1 075	893	-413	30 135	9.7	2.47	8.0	27.2
WYOMING	9.0	6.3	5.3	49.7	494 423	453 589	8.9	0.1	7 610	4 956	-1 950	193 608	14.7	2.48	8.7	26.3
Albany	6.8	4.4	3.9	48.4	31 313	30 797	4.0	-2.2	424	214	-929	13 269	11.0	2.23	7.5	31.4
Big Horn	10.7	8.4	8.4	50.0	11 255	10 525	8.9	-1.8	175	171	-213	4 312	10.4	2.60	6.8	25.0
Campbell	6.3	3.2	2.0	48.6	34 853	29 370	14.7	3.4	578	178	745	12 207	22.5	2.73	8.8	20.2
Carbon	10.2	6.8	5.5	46.4	15 505	16 659	-6.1	-0.9	198	185	-147	6 129	2.1	2.39	8.3	27.5

1. No spouse present.

STATE County	Births, average 1997–1999		Deaths, average 1997–1999				Physicians,[4] 2000		Hospitals,[4] 1998			Medicare enrollees 2000	Serious crimes known to police, 2000[6]	
			Number		Rate					Beds			Total	
	Total	Rate[1]	Total	Infant[2]	Total[1]	Infant[3]	Number	Rate[5]	Number	Number	Rate[5]		Number	Rate[7]
	32	33	34	35	36	37	38	39	40	41	42	43	44	45
WISCONSIN—Cont'd														
Dane	5 171	12.2	2 522	35	5.9	6.8	1 625	381	4	1 246	293	45 098	12 787	3 581
Dodge	954	11.5	817	NA	9.8	NA	97	113	3	353	424	9 793	1 465	1 706
Door	245	9.1	322	NA	11.9	NA	42	150	1	77	285	5 625	547	1 956
Douglas	508	11.8	493	NA	11.5	NA	24	55	1	42	98	7 380	1 828	4 223
Dunn	457	11.7	275	NA	7.1	NA	21	53	1	55	141	5 010	NA	NA
Eau Claire	1 100	12.3	672	NA	7.5	NA	255	274	2	519	581	12 921	3 262	3 558
Florence	45	8.7	50	NA	9.6	NA	4	79	0	0	0	833	69	1 356
Fond du Lac	1 110	11.7	863	8	9.1	7.5	145	149	2	220	232	15 833	2 310	2 374
Forest	112	11.7	113	NA	11.8	NA	2	20	0	0	0	2 070	386	3 851
Grant	527	10.7	481	NA	9.8	NA	43	87	3	260	527	9 122	897	1 852
Green	384	11.5	312	NA	9.3	NA	85	253	1	143	428	5 335	629	1 869
Green Lake	217	11.1	239	NA	12.3	NA	29	152	1	163	839	3 992	370	1 937
Iowa	279	12.4	191	NA	8.5	NA	15	66	1	82	366	3 072	304	1 508
Iron	49	7.6	91	NA	14.2	NA	6	87	0	0	0	1 593	196	2 857
Jackson	205	11.5	185	NA	10.4	NA	10	52	1	38	214	3 047	366	1 916
Jefferson	896	12.2	602	NA	8.2	NA	61	82	1	92	125	12 062	1 808	2 443
Juneau	268	11.2	275	NA	11.5	NA	14	58	1	95	399	4 794	447	1 838
Kenosha	2 119	14.7	1 178	15	8.1	7.2	204	136	2	307	213	18 647	4 742	3 170
Kewaunee	224	11.3	182	NA	9.2	NA	11	54	1	17	86	3 319	242	1 199
La Crosse	1 283	12.5	906	11	8.8	8.3	357	333	2	552	538	14 958	3 135	3 150
Lafayette	180	11.1	167	NA	10.3	NA	5	31	1	28	172	2 684	187	1 234
Langlade	218	10.6	224	NA	10.9	NA	24	116	1	49	239	4 180	629	3 033
Lincoln	318	10.7	314	NA	10.5	NA	26	88	2	125	420	5 747	632	2 132
Manitowoc	918	11.1	834	NA	10.1	NA	116	140	2	354	430	14 458	1 880	2 268
Marathon	1 541	12.5	916	6	7.4	3.9	219	174	1	270	219	16 937	2 669	2 154
Marinette	444	10.3	515	NA	12.0	NA	56	129	1	115	267	8 954	805	1 856
Marquette	154	10.2	162	NA	10.7	NA	6	38	0	0	0	3 808	311	1 964
Menominee	93	19.2	41	NA	8.5	NA	4	88	0	0	0	494	400	8 768
Milwaukee	13 950	15.3	8 905	139	9.8	10.0	3 113	331	14	3 537	388	138 926	56 924	6 055
Monroe	535	13.5	384	NA	9.7	NA	42	103	2	105	266	6 099	1 047	2 560
Oconto	378	11.1	337	NA	10.0	NA	20	56	2	49	144	5 462	669	1 877
Oneida	343	9.6	395	NA	11.0	NA	92	250	2	132	370	8 199	850	2 311
Outagamie	2 124	13.6	1 160	13	7.4	6.3	261	162	3	426	273	20 119	3 466	2 153
Ozaukee	931	11.5	577	NA	7.1	NA	162	197	1	82	101	11 288	1 048	1 273
Pepin	85	11.9	81	NA	11.3	NA	7	97	1	88	1 236	1 379	58	804
Pierce	410	11.5	239	NA	6.7	NA	6	16	1	36	101	4 654	752	2 043
Polk	437	11.3	397	NA	10.2	NA	43	104	3	141	364	6 560	595	1 478
Portage	744	11.5	459	NA	7.1	NA	82	122	1	122	188	8 293	1 663	2 475
Price	166	10.6	207	NA	13.2	NA	12	76	1	42	266	3 244	247	1 561
Racine	2 574	13.9	1 561	20	8.4	7.6	251	133	3	561	301	27 713	8 057	4 267
Richland	204	11.5	176	NA	9.9	NA	24	134	1	38	212	2 963	256	1 428
Rock	1 993	13.2	1 328	14	8.8	7.2	281	184	3	474	314	21 843	5 579	3 663
Rusk	168	11.1	173	NA	11.4	NA	16	104	1	142	931	3 051	381	2 483
St. Croix	807	13.7	452	NA	7.7	NA	45	71	3	106	180	6 110	1 198	1 980
Sauk	696	13.0	493	NA	9.2	NA	74	134	3	186	349	8 862	1 694	3 067
Sawyer	169	10.5	182	NA	11.3	NA	13	80	1	117	726	3 149	388	2 758
Shawano	456	11.7	433	NA	11.1	NA	19	47	1	53	137	7 112	918	2 258
Sheboygan	1 335	12.1	1 042	9	9.5	6.5	150	133	3	421	382	17 377	3 309	2 938
Taylor	227	11.8	198	NA	10.3	NA	20	102	1	155	803	3 059	329	1 672
Trempealeau	326	12.3	289	NA	10.9	NA	17	63	3	298	1 126	5 170	368	1 362
Vernon	343	12.5	311	NA	11.3	NA	22	78	2	102	373	5 201	318	1 150
Vilas	186	8.7	266	NA	12.5	NA	35	166	2	114	536	5 073	543	2 772
Walworth	1 023	12.0	798	NA	9.3	NA	89	95	1	88	103	12 485	2 544	2 713
Washburn	151	9.7	191	NA	12.3	NA	18	112	2	185	1 200	4 086	328	2 045
Washington	1 445	12.7	775	NA	6.8	NA	105	89	2	191	168	14 566	2 583	2 198
Waukesha	4 119	11.7	2 534	21	7.2	5.1	799	221	4	682	193	47 567	5 890	1 736
Waupaca	578	11.4	656	NA	13.0	NA	39	75	1	40	79	10 408	1 115	2 155
Waushara	237	10.9	246	NA	11.4	NA	11	48	1	26	120	4 396	429	1 853
Winnebago	1 786	11.9	1 245	8	8.3	4.3	320	204	2	456	304	21 994	3 860	2 462
Wood	924	12.2	686	NA	9.0	NA	352	466	2	708	931	13 878	2 142	2 835
WYOMING	6 237	13.0	3 880	41	8.1	6.6	762	154	26	2 309	480	65 437	16 285	3 298
Albany	345	11.7	171	NA	5.8	NA	56	175	1	110	377	3 051	1 045	3 264
Big Horn	142	12.6	134	NA	11.9	NA	7	61	1	118	1 037	2 031	197	1 719
Campbell	473	14.6	149	NA	4.6	NA	44	131	1	119	367	2 163	1 383	4 104
Carbon	166	10.6	134	NA	8.6	NA	20	128	1	50	321	2 175	508	3 248

1. Per 1,000 estimated resident population, average 1997–1999.   2. Deaths of infants under 1 year old.   3. Deaths of infants under 1 year old per 1,000 live births.   4. Data subject to copyright.   5. Per 100,000 resident population as of July 1 of the year shown.   6. Data for serious crimes have not been adjusted for underreporting; this may affect comparability between geographic areas and over time.   7. Per 100,000 population estimated by the FBI.

Table B. States and Counties — Crime, Education, Money Income, and Poverty

	Serious crimes known to police, 2000[1] (cont'd)		Education						Money income				Income and poverty, 1998			
	Rate[2]		School enrollment and attainment, 1990				Local government expenditures, fiscal 1999[5]		1989				Percent below poverty level			
			Enrollment[3]		Attainment[4] (percent)					Households						
											Median					
STATE County	Violent	Property	Total	Percent private	High school graduate or more	Bachelor's degree or more	Total current expenditures (mil dol)	Current expenditures per student (dollars)	Per capita[6] (dollars)	Dollars	Percent change, 1979–1989 (constant 1989 dollars)	Percent with $100,000 or more	Median household income	All persons	Persons under 18	Persons 5–17 in families
	46	47	48	49	50	51	52	53	54	55	56	57	58	59	60	61

STATE County	46	47	48	49	50	51	52	53	54	55	56	57	58	59	60	61
WISCONSIN—Cont'd																
Dane	253	3 328	115 595	9.2	88.9	34.2	497.8	7 939	15 542	32 703	6.6	3.9	49 619	6.9	9.9	8.6
Dodge	68	1 638	18 094	19.3	72.3	10.2	63.3	7 229	12 050	29 166	-4.0	1.8	44 435	5.6	7.8	6.6
Door	75	1 881	5 832	13.0	79.6	16.4	34.1	7 927	12 458	26 259	-0.9	1.9	38 461	7.8	11.4	10.5
Douglas	162	4 061	10 910	6.7	77.2	14.8	50.3	7 064	10 744	22 122	-12.4	0.8	33 658	12.6	18.8	18.0
Dunn	NA	NA	13 694	4.3	77.7	19.4	43.2	7 012	10 364	24 452	5.2	1.6	38 307	11.3	15.1	13.7
Eau Claire	169	3 389	27 624	8.2	82.8	20.9	104.0	7 226	11 801	25 886	0.9	2.0	39 552	9.9	14.7	13.4
Florence	216	1 140	1 110	3.3	75.2	8.9	6.3	6 892	10 352	22 416	12.4	0.7	33 577	9.7	13.3	13.5
Fond du Lac	67	2 307	23 436	21.6	77.5	13.3	106.3	6 651	12 574	29 441	-3.3	2.0	44 369	6.5	9.4	7.9
Forest	419	3 432	2 064	2.7	64.1	7.6	14.4	6 759	8 339	16 907	-10.0	1.0	29 908	12.4	17.8	18.5
Grant	112	1 741	15 331	9.2	77.9	14.7	66.1	7 431	10 704	24 505	-3.3	1.8	35 316	9.6	13.5	11.3
Green	71	1 798	7 284	6.9	76.8	12.0	42.7	7 123	13 006	28 435	1.2	2.0	41 649	7.1	10.6	9.3
Green Lake	126	1 811	4 287	13.9	74.6	11.4	24.9	6 413	11 840	25 708	1.9	1.7	38 336	8.2	12.3	11.0
Iowa	99	1 409	4 836	5.3	80.6	13.3	30.0	7 535	11 339	25 914	7.7	2.1	39 785	8.2	11.2	10.6
Iron	117	2 740	1 162	7.1	74.7	10.5	8.0	7 607	9 280	17 537	5.2	0.7	28 068	11.0	16.6	15.6
Jackson	105	1 812	3 836	2.8	68.8	8.8	22.6	6 694	10 173	21 409	1.6	1.2	33 091	11.4	16.9	15.6
Jefferson	109	2 333	18 627	20.7	77.0	15.1	92.4	7 592	12 770	30 749	0.8	2.4	44 363	5.4	7.8	6.4
Juneau	123	1 715	4 923	10.8	70.6	8.6	32.0	7 173	10 304	22 073	5.1	1.4	32 209	10.7	15.7	14.3
Kenosha	415	2 755	34 027	17.6	75.1	12.7	183.0	6 985	13 265	30 638	-9.0	1.9	45 054	8.9	13.8	12.4
Kewaunee	154	1 045	4 649	17.2	73.5	8.2	24.5	6 677	11 299	26 927	-2.7	1.7	40 742	6.3	8.2	7.6
La Crosse	126	3 025	30 119	13.9	82.6	21.1	119.0	7 611	12 141	26 857	0.8	2.0	40 485	9.4	13.8	12.3
Lafayette	92	1 142	4 035	4.9	77.0	10.1	26.9	7 224	10 641	24 479	-4.1	2.0	34 764	9.2	12.7	11.6
Langlade	116	2 917	4 441	11.7	71.5	8.8	29.4	7 620	10 172	20 703	-3.0	1.8	32 285	11.5	16.8	16.1
Lincoln	152	1 980	6 478	11.7	71.1	10.8	36.8	7 000	11 282	25 175	5.3	1.3	38 291	7.7	11.5	10.2
Manitowoc	75	2 193	19 541	23.4	75.4	12.1	79.4	6 335	12 235	27 467	-7.0	1.9	43 057	5.9	9.5	8.0
Marathon	123	2 031	29 586	13.2	75.9	13.5	145.1	7 314	12 718	30 143	3.7	2.5	43 599	7.2	11.7	9.8
Marinette	157	1 699	10 035	13.6	73.6	10.1	55.5	7 319	10 420	22 396	-4.2	0.8	34 538	9.7	14.1	12.6
Marquette	139	1 825	2 542	10.4	69.7	8.8	15.0	6 455	10 652	22 234	5.4	1.0	31 818	9.6	14.2	14.2
Menominee	1 600	7 168	1 334	4.0	62.7	3.7	11.7	10 755	5 674	14 122	-36.9	0.4	23 969	25.1	29.3	33.3
Milwaukee	671	5 384	255 180	24.3	76.3	19.3	1 259.9	8 323	13 383	27 867	-8.2	2.4	37 952	15.9	26.0	22.7
Monroe	134	2 425	9 161	15.4	75.7	10.8	46.1	6 532	10 744	24 799	-2.0	1.3	36 050	11.0	16.4	15.0
Oconto	73	1 804	7 069	7.4	69.4	8.5	34.2	6 475	10 375	22 927	1.6	1.4	36 414	8.2	11.5	10.4
Oneida	136	2 175	6 979	8.8	77.6	14.9	48.9	7 532	11 681	23 901	-1.8	1.9	36 477	8.7	13.7	12.2
Outagamie	79	2 074	37 415	20.8	81.5	16.7	199.1	6 748	13 893	33 770	3.8	2.7	49 110	4.9	7.4	6.1
Ozaukee	35	1 238	19 679	26.2	86.9	29.7	99.9	7 840	19 249	42 695	-0.3	9.5	64 056	2.7	3.8	3.1
Pepin	28	776	1 745	15.4	71.0	9.6	13.3	7 967	10 751	22 992	-1.3	1.6	34 086	8.6	10.8	11.4
Pierce	92	1 951	10 471	6.8	81.1	17.8	54.6	7 302	12 203	30 520	8.4	2.4	46 325	6.2	8.2	7.3
Polk	75	1 403	8 607	4.5	78.0	11.4	56.2	6 831	11 291	24 267	2.6	1.6	39 142	8.4	11.9	10.9
Portage	86	2 389	20 204	9.2	79.7	19.1	73.4	6 963	11 730	28 686	2.7	1.9	43 438	8.8	12.7	11.0
Price	120	1 441	3 520	8.6	73.3	10.6	19.1	6 804	10 564	22 662	13.2	1.3	35 827	10.4	14.8	13.9
Racine	327	3 940	46 118	18.3	76.4	16.5	218.1	7 245	14 023	32 751	-6.7	2.9	45 915	8.7	13.6	11.3
Richland	201	1 227	4 222	9.2	73.7	10.8	16.5	7 784	10 287	21 946	-1.0	1.4	33 969	11.3	16.5	15.6
Rock	228	3 435	34 529	11.7	78.2	13.3	197.9	7 231	13 428	30 632	-4.6	2.0	43 150	8.6	13.6	11.9
Rusk	306	2 176	3 822	13.6	70.3	10.9	23.5	8 343	9 127	19 617	1.2	0.8	30 279	13.6	18.9	18.3
St. Croix	127	1 853	13 626	9.3	84.4	20.3	72.7	6 890	14 912	36 716	12.0	4.1	54 541	4.4	6.0	5.4
Sauk	130	2 937	10 973	14.0	74.7	12.9	70.4	6 964	11 697	26 217	0.9	1.5	39 783	8.0	11.7	10.5
Sawyer	57	2 701	3 217	6.7	73.7	12.9	18.3	7 409	9 232	18 094	-2.9	1.1	29 011	14.7	20.6	21.2
Shawano	32	2 226	8 349	12.2	69.5	9.4	43.3	6 765	10 586	23 841	2.1	1.4	35 384	9.2	12.7	12.1
Sheboygan	118	2 819	25 856	19.4	77.4	13.8	141.6	7 196	13 425	31 603	0.7	2.3	46 428	5.5	8.1	6.8
Taylor	61	1 611	4 731	10.6	68.8	9.2	24.6	6 547	10 452	24 304	2.0	2.0	36 788	9.8	12.8	12.7
Trempealeau	78	1 285	5 766	9.7	71.7	10.1	42.3	7 292	10 674	23 864	5.0	1.3	34 987	9.5	13.4	13.3
Vernon	51	1 099	5 916	10.3	69.2	11.2	34.7	7 373	10 132	21 548	2.5	1.4	31 999	12.5	17.7	17.5
Vilas	117	2 654	3 637	8.2	76.1	13.7	24.4	9 420	10 866	20 352	-1.9	1.3	31 292	9.2	14.4	14.3
Walworth	106	2 608	21 454	10.2	79.0	17.5	103.3	7 222	13 526	30 345	3.7	2.5	43 924	6.6	9.6	8.2
Washburn	125	1 921	3 153	7.4	74.9	12.8	22.4	7 281	9 847	19 962	-1.1	1.0	30 056	11.9	17.1	17.2
Washington	55	2 143	24 539	20.0	81.3	15.9	137.1	7 077	14 736	38 431	4.3	3.1	56 936	3.4	5.0	4.2
Waukesha	70	1 666	82 751	23.0	88.0	27.1	458.9	7 844	18 148	44 565	3.0	6.8	63 749	3.1	4.6	3.5
Waupaca	73	2 082	10 891	10.3	72.1	11.0	69.7	6 557	11 455	26 083	1.8	1.4	39 128	7.0	9.7	8.7
Waushara	86	1 766	3 979	6.4	70.0	10.0	20.6	6 253	10 408	21 888	2.6	1.1	32 628	12.1	18.6	18.0
Winnebago	131	2 332	37 970	12.3	80.6	18.2	161.7	6 762	13 696	30 007	-0.9	2.5	46 254	6.4	10.2	8.8
Wood	49	2 786	18 911	15.9	78.3	13.5	99.7	7 053	13 130	29 735	1.5	2.5	42 889	8.1	12.1	10.8
WYOMING	267	3 032	134 739	5.6	83.0	18.8	651.6	6 842	12 311	27 096	-19.1	2.0	35 868	11.4	15.4	12.6
Albany	294	2 971	14 368	5.8	89.3	38.5	28.1	7 276	11 825	20 715	-15.6	2.0	34 192	13.6	17.6	15.0
Big Horn	192	1 527	2 944	2.4	77.1	15.0	19.0	7 487	9 717	21 454	-12.8	0.9	32 995	12.4	17.0	14.1
Campbell	326	3 778	9 398	4.4	85.6	15.7	53.4	6 932	13 596	37 055	-15.2	2.5	50 891	7.6	9.6	7.6
Carbon	416	2 833	4 622	3.4	81.7	14.2	23.4	8 103	11 592	27 109	-26.4	1.0	37 227	11.8	14.4	12.1

1. Data for serious crimes have not been adjusted for underreporting; this may affect comparability between geographic areas and over time. 2. Per 100,000 population estimated by the FBI. 3. All persons 3 years old and over enrolled in nursery school through college. 4. Persons 25 years old and over. 5. Elementary and secondary education expenditures, local government fiscal years ending between July 1, 1998 and June 30, 1999. 6. Based on population enumerated as of April 1, 1990.

Table B. States and Counties — **Personal Income**

	Personal income, 1999												
			Per capita[1]						Transfer payments				
										Government payments to individuals			
STATE County	Total (mil dol)	Percent change, 1998–1999	Dollars	Rank	Wages and salaries[2] (mil dol)	Proprietor's income (mil dol)	Dividends, interest, and rent (mil dol)	Total (mil dol)	Total (mil dol)	Social Security (mil dol)	Medical payments (mil dol)	Income maintenance (mil dol)	Unemployment insurance (mil dol)
	62	63	64	65	66	67	68	69	70	71	72	73	74
WISCONSIN—Cont'd													
Dane	13 714	5.5	31 999	154	9 816	857	2 988	1 057	974	476	358	65	23
Dodge	1 886	4.1	22 585	1 199	1 127	138	384	246	229	127	79	9	6
Door	737	5.9	27 201	402	315	85	247	108	103	59	33	4	5
Douglas	926	3.5	21 542	1 510	508	54	166	181	173	65	64	14	4
Dunn	825	5.8	21 052	1 654	464	56	149	110	103	47	35	8	3
Eau Claire	2 259	5.4	25 174	646	1 609	141	447	291	273	129	97	20	6
Florence	107	4.7	20 764	1 752	25	5	21	19	18	9	6	1	0
Fond du Lac	2 572	3.2	27 129	406	1 558	157	496	309	290	148	103	13	7
Forest	183	5.1	18 948	2 295	75	24	40	42	40	19	13	3	1
Grant	1 023	2.4	20 747	1 758	458	89	241	175	166	80	62	10	4
Green	798	4.1	23 572	946	397	73	200	104	98	52	36	5	3
Green Lake	481	2.6	24 603	729	201	49	122	75	71	39	24	3	2
Iowa	504	6.9	22 204	1 298	314	37	101	62	57	29	20	4	2
Iron	134	3.9	21 305	1 569	53	17	29	32	31	16	11	2	1
Jackson	391	9.1	21 920	1 382	197	33	86	64	60	28	22	5	2
Jefferson	1 850	5.0	24 988	673	1 092	98	367	246	232	114	96	9	6
Juneau	474	4.7	19 672	2 094	248	42	100	97	92	45	32	6	3
Kenosha	3 820	5.9	26 111	501	1 831	138	601	455	426	208	158	30	10
Kewaunee	430	3.0	21 544	1 508	186	38	94	61	58	32	19	3	2
La Crosse	2 667	3.7	26 034	508	2 015	171	546	328	308	146	107	20	8
Lafayette	303	3.0	18 923	2 306	102	27	76	50	47	25	16	3	1
Langlade	417	4.3	20 295	1 892	208	42	84	85	81	40	28	5	2
Lincoln	610	0.1	20 379	1 867	335	35	123	112	106	54	39	5	4
Manitowoc	2 057	3.2	24 865	692	1 189	129	397	292	276	148	94	11	10
Marathon	3 214	5.1	26 009	514	2 151	180	621	365	341	175	114	24	13
Marinette	914	3.9	21 236	1 588	565	67	178	176	167	84	62	8	5
Marquette	279	4.4	18 158	2 508	96	24	57	63	60	34	18	3	2
Menominee	(3)69	(3)6.7	(3)13 797	(3)3 059	(3)53	(3)4	(3)18	(3)18	(3)17	(3)5	(3)7	(3)3	(3)1
Milwaukee	25 992	3.9	28 681	274	20 986	1 270	5 170	4 083	3 906	1 430	1 669	576	92
Monroe	816	4.2	20 529	1 827	495	68	169	127	119	53	41	8	5
Oconto	666	5.7	19 381	2 187	235	76	135	115	108	58	35	6	3
Oneida	904	4.3	25 076	657	503	63	232	161	154	82	53	7	5
Outagamie	4 451	8.2	28 084	326	3 165	231	802	402	371	203	119	20	14
Ozaukee	3 463	5.7	42 223	32	1 433	153	865	221	205	126	63	5	4
Pepin	148	5.8	20 227	1 918	62	16	30	27	26	12	11	1	1
Pierce	909	6.6	25 207	636	261	51	153	90	83	41	29	4	2
Polk	882	6.0	22 411	1 237	384	80	151	134	126	63	47	7	3
Portage	1 495	3.3	22 999	1 090	985	91	294	185	172	82	54	11	7
Price	347	1.6	22 292	1 277	182	29	81	69	66	31	25	4	3
Racine	5 335	4.8	28 720	273	3 042	199	1 020	614	578	291	206	42	23
Richland	348	3.9	19 599	2 112	155	26	77	59	56	29	20	4	2
Rock	3 794	3.7	25 103	652	2 428	171	672	491	461	232	161	32	18
Rusk	286	4.7	18 943	2 299	160	23	56	62	59	28	20	5	1
St. Croix	1 802	7.4	29 893	216	720	102	278	143	131	66	48	6	2
Sauk	1 322	5.7	24 355	793	911	84	276	179	168	86	62	9	5
Sawyer	326	5.4	20 058	1 977	160	31	78	68	65	31	23	5	2
Shawano	(3)808	(3)3.9	(3)20 611	(3)1 804	(3)329	(3)76	(3)142	(3)139	(3)132	(3)69	(3)44	(3)8	(3)3
Sheboygan	3 051	6.3	27 705	356	2 061	178	646	346	324	182	107	14	10
Taylor	392	4.1	20 334	1 880	242	35	75	63	59	28	22	4	2
Trempealeau	580	6.6	21 730	1 439	328	55	99	101	96	44	40	6	2
Vernon	497	4.2	17 923	2 554	184	49	98	99	93	45	34	7	2
Vilas	489	6.3	22 544	1 206	187	55	146	101	97	55	30	5	2
Walworth	2 160	5.7	25 064	659	1 183	131	464	265	248	133	84	10	6
Washburn	313	6.1	19 875	2 028	146	23	72	76	73	34	24	4	2
Washington	3 496	6.2	30 210	204	1 584	163	685	298	276	158	90	9	8
Waukesha	13 561	6.1	37 834	60	8 593	563	2 889	957	887	528	276	24	22
Waupaca	1 269	4.5	24 956	678	584	81	229	212	202	93	83	8	5
Waushara	421	3.5	19 309	2 204	135	35	93	87	82	46	26	5	2
Winnebago	4 180	3.9	27 759	352	3 330	153	924	459	430	232	145	22	11
Wood	2 150	5.4	28 205	306	1 668	123	410	275	260	131	97	14	9
WYOMING	12 644	5.7	26 363	X	7 096	1 266	3 301	1 517	1 422	652	435	106	31
Albany	704	4.8	24 239	818	391	58	182	85	80	29	25	6	1
Big Horn	221	6.0	19 738	2 078	124	23	53	40	38	20	10	3	1
Campbell	855	6.5	26 112	500	680	61	141	64	58	24	19	3	2
Carbon	349	2.2	22 613	1 191	189	26	92	50	47	21	13	3	1

1. Based on the resident population estimated as of July 1 of the year shown.   2. Includes other labor income.   3. Menominee County included with Shawano County.

Table B. States and Counties — Earnings, Social Security, and Housing

STATE County	Earnings, 1999 Total (mil dol)	Farm	Goods-related[1] Total	Manu-facturing	Service-related and other[2] Total	Retail trade	Finance, insurance, and real estate	Services	Govern-ment	Social Security beneficiaries, December 2000 Number	Rate[3]	Supplemental Security Income recipients, December 2000	Housing units, 1990 Total	Percent change, 1980–1990
	75	76	77	78	79	80	81	82	83	84	85	86	87	88
WISCONSIN—Cont'd														
Dane	10 673	0.3	19.1	12.0	55.2	8.9	9.6	25.3	25.4	51 999	122	5 245	147 851	17.1
Dodge	1 265	2.4	D	40.6	D	6.7	2.3	15.8	12.1	14 496	169	561	28 720	6.4
Door	401	2.3	D	17.2	D	16.0	5.5	27.4	13.3	6 585	236	222	18 037	17.7
Douglas	562	0.0	18.0	10.5	62.4	10.4	2.6	18.2	19.5	7 695	178	1 073	20 610	2.3
Dunn	521	2.6	23.6	16.7	48.5	19.2	2.4	15.6	25.3	5 924	149	586	13 252	11.5
Eau Claire	1 751	0.5	18.1	11.8	65.4	20.5	4.4	27.9	16.0	14 716	158	1 643	32 741	13.0
Florence	29	-0.8	29.4	20.4	40.0	10.8	2.1	16.4	31.4	1 151	226	87	3 775	13.0
Fond du Lac	1 716	1.4	44.9	36.1	42.4	9.1	3.4	18.3	11.3	16 728	172	1 028	34 548	8.9
Forest	99	0.1	D	19.7	D	8.1	2.8	26.5	22.5	2 336	233	192	7 203	6.7
Grant	547	2.8	24.5	18.0	47.1	11.6	4.6	19.8	25.7	10 150	205	811	18 450	1.4
Green	469	2.4	29.4	22.6	55.6	17.2	3.3	24.2	12.7	6 025	179	299	12 087	6.8
Green Lake	250	4.6	36.0	22.6	46.7	9.7	3.4	24.0	12.7	4 449	233	212	9 202	10.6
Iowa	351	2.2	D	6.8	D	D	D	14.2	12.2	3 722	163	210	8 220	8.6
Iron	70	-0.3	D	20.0	D	13.0	2.2	26.7	16.8	1 957	285	122	5 243	2.8
Jackson	230	8.4	D	12.4	D	9.4	3.2	13.0	17.1	3 617	189	384	7 627	9.3
Jefferson	1 190	1.2	D	40.0	D	10.4	2.8	16.7	11.6	12 763	172	695	25 719	7.0
Juneau	291	3.9	40.1	34.6	37.2	9.5	2.8	17.2	18.8	5 533	228	485	11 422	14.9
Kenosha	1 970	0.0	D	32.5	D	9.1	3.4	20.5	15.4	22 854	153	2 178	51 262	7.9
Kewaunee	225	6.2	D	32.0	D	7.1	3.7	13.3	14.7	3 692	183	162	7 544	7.4
La Crosse	2 186	0.2	D	18.8	D	9.9	5.9	29.3	13.7	16 987	159	1 699	38 239	14.9
Lafayette	129	10.0	18.2	12.3	44.3	6.9	6.2	12.2	27.5	3 163	196	182	6 313	0.3
Langlade	250	3.2	D	22.1	D	13.5	D	19.9	15.7	4 923	237	394	10 825	10.2
Lincoln	370	0.3	D	39.4	D	9.6	2.5	12.9	17.1	6 374	215	366	13 256	3.7
Manitowoc	1 318	2.7	46.2	39.4	39.6	7.1	2.5	17.8	11.6	16 534	199	970	31 843	5.7
Marathon	2 331	1.7	37.6	30.8	49.6	8.7	9.8	17.3	11.1	20 259	161	1 818	43 774	10.1
Marinette	632	1.8	D	42.6	D	9.2	2.4	17.9	12.4	9 953	229	714	25 650	13.7
Marquette	121	1.3	41.0	30.9	40.1	9.0	4.0	14.3	17.6	4 031	255	205	8 035	12.7
Menominee	[4]57	[4]0.0	[4]D	[4]D	[4]D	[4]2.2	[4]D	[4]52.2	[4]19.3	723	158	143	1 742	31.3
Milwaukee	22 256	0.0	24.5	21.0	62.9	7.4	10.7	32.4	12.6	155 488	165	30 855	390 715	3.4
Monroe	563	3.5	D	18.2	D	8.2	3.2	13.8	32.2	7 060	173	676	14 135	10.9
Oconto	311	3.9	D	28.3	D	9.5	2.7	16.2	18.0	7 122	200	426	18 832	11.2
Oneida	566	0.6	D	16.8	D	14.8	4.2	28.2	17.0	9 444	257	546	25 173	8.7
Outagamie	3 396	1.0	D	25.0	D	10.1	8.5	21.1	9.2	22 981	143	1 449	51 923	18.2
Ozaukee	1 586	0.2	D	35.8	D	8.2	9.9	22.1	8.8	13 080	159	278	26 482	17.6
Pepin	78	6.5	D	D	D	11.0	2.8	18.1	20.3	1 496	207	104	2 919	1.3
Pierce	312	1.3	D	14.8	D	9.3	4.3	18.2	32.8	4 805	131	244	11 536	11.4
Polk	464	1.8	D	31.1	D	9.7	4.0	19.2	15.7	7 814	189	478	18 562	14.4
Portage	1 076	2.0	D	19.9	D	9.0	13.9	17.6	16.4	9 715	145	735	22 910	15.1
Price	211	1.1	D	45.9	D	7.4	2.5	14.3	15.4	3 763	238	301	9 052	3.7
Racine	3 241	0.3	48.7	42.8	39.8	7.6	2.7	20.6	11.1	31 504	167	3 359	66 945	7.0
Richland	181	2.6	D	31.9	D	11.5	3.1	18.2	16.8	3 664	204	345	7 325	4.9
Rock	2 599	0.4	44.0	37.2	43.3	10.0	3.1	19.5	12.3	25 742	169	2 675	54 840	5.3
Rusk	182	2.8	D	37.5	D	9.4	2.0	12.9	20.4	3 550	231	359	7 904	9.9
St. Croix	822	1.0	D	30.5	D	11.6	3.8	21.9	12.5	7 685	122	347	18 519	24.1
Sauk	995	0.8	D	24.6	D	12.5	4.1	25.1	10.2	10 248	186	615	20 439	17.1
Sawyer	192	0.9	24.4	15.1	57.7	14.7	4.8	30.5	17.0	3 864	239	338	13 025	17.8
Shawano	[4]405	[4]6.9	[4]D	[4]21.0	[4]D	[4]11.7	[4]4.3	[4]23.4	[4]15.6	8 444	208	553	16 737	9.8
Sheboygan	2 240	0.8	53.3	47.2	36.2	7.6	4.7	16.8	9.7	19 574	174	1 213	40 695	9.0
Taylor	278	0.7	D	40.9	D	8.2	3.3	13.4	11.2	3 590	182	234	7 710	7.6
Trempealeau	383	4.0	D	41.0	D	6.2	2.7	14.4	15.5	5 671	210	496	10 097	3.6
Vernon	233	2.3	D	11.4	D	11.2	7.3	23.4	21.5	5 890	210	535	10 830	6.8
Vilas	242	1.3	D	8.8	D	16.4	5.0	31.3	15.1	6 430	306	224	20 225	10.0
Walworth	1 314	0.5	D	29.9	D	9.5	4.0	20.2	16.4	14 739	157	701	36 937	10.6
Washburn	170	2.1	23.6	17.6	49.6	12.6	5.5	20.7	24.7	4 219	263	369	9 829	12.8
Washington	1 747	0.3	43.7	35.8	43.4	8.8	5.3	16.7	12.6	17 299	147	564	34 382	21.2
Waukesha	9 156	0.0	37.1	27.7	55.8	7.7	6.9	24.0	7.1	54 934	152	1 581	110 452	19.3
Waupaca	665	2.2	D	36.6	D	10.3	3.7	14.9	16.0	10 683	207	659	20 141	11.0
Waushara	170	7.9	D	11.8	D	12.3	3.8	18.0	19.5	5 539	239	354	12 246	8.9
Winnebago	3 483	0.1	D	45.9	D	6.3	4.7	17.9	11.0	25 538	163	1 744	56 123	12.9
Wood	1 791	1.3	31.7	26.6	D	8.6	D	35.7	9.2	14 823	196	1 071	28 839	10.1
WYOMING	8 361	1.7	27.4	5.2	47.1	9.7	5.2	19.3	23.8	76 116	154	5 827	203 411	8.1
Albany	449	1.0	D	7.9	D	10.6	4.0	23.2	42.1	3 307	103	258	13 844	15.8
Big Horn	147	6.9	31.8	6.3	36.4	6.9	2.9	9.1	24.9	2 335	204	180	5 048	4.4
Campbell	741	0.3	51.7	2.9	34.6	7.0	2.3	12.0	13.4	2 814	84	201	11 538	21.4
Carbon	215	2.4	23.9	9.6	46.8	10.7	3.4	16.5	27.0	2 411	154	148	8 190	-5.4

1. Covers mining, construction, and manufacturing.   2. Covers private sector earnings in agricultural services, forestry, and fisheries; transportation and public utilities; wholesale trade; retail trade; finance, insurance, and real estate; and services.   3. Per 1,000 resident population estimated as of July 1 of the year shown.   4. Menominee County included with Shawano County.

Table B. States and Counties — **Housing, Labor Force, and Employment**

STATE County	Housing units, 1990 (cont'd) Occupied units Owner-occupied Total	Percent	Median value[1]	Owner cost as a percent of income With a mortgage	Without a mortgage	Renter-occupied Median rent[2]	Rent as percent of income	Sub-stand-ard units[3] (percent)	Civilian labor force, 2001 Total	Percent change, 2000–2001	Unemployment Total	Rate[4]	Civilian employment, 1990[5] Total	Percent Professional, managerial, and technical	Precision production, craft, and repair
	89	90	91	92	93	94	95	96	97	98	99	100	101	102	103
WISCONSIN—Cont'd															
Dane	142 786	55.2	78 400	20.9	13.1	465	26.0	2.6	272 673	3.5	5 557	2.0	208 069	38.0	7.7
Dodge	26 853	73.1	54 800	20.2	14.1	370	22.6	1.9	48 384	1.5	2 547	5.3	36 376	18.1	13.1
Door	10 066	77.5	66 500	22.5	14.3	348	23.8	1.6	16 132	4.2	833	5.2	11 889	22.3	16.7
Douglas	16 374	69.6	38 700	17.9	13.2	300	27.2	2.6	22 870	0.3	1 156	5.1	17 697	24.4	10.2
Dunn	12 250	67.2	49 000	18.1	13.2	343	28.7	3.2	21 945	1.1	896	4.1	16 950	24.0	9.7
Eau Claire	31 282	64.5	53 500	18.9	13.2	356	27.2	2.5	52 338	1.2	2 124	4.1	40 643	28.6	8.6
Florence	1 755	82.8	45 400	20.0	15.3	302	24.1	4.1	1 712	6.4	115	6.7	1 955	19.8	14.4
Fond du Lac	32 644	71.8	56 000	19.1	12.8	367	23.7	1.5	55 616	3.1	2 377	4.3	44 902	21.6	13.2
Forest	3 290	76.9	38 400	21.3	15.5	272	25.8	4.1	4 935	8.0	322	6.5	3 227	18.7	10.9
Grant	17 169	69.5	43 600	17.5	13.2	305	24.0	2.3	24 644	2.5	1 314	5.3	23 266	20.9	11.8
Green	11 541	69.3	53 600	20.9	13.4	340	22.5	1.7	18 226	-0.4	875	4.8	15 527	19.4	12.2
Green Lake	7 189	75.1	48 400	20.5	13.6	306	22.5	1.8	10 781	3.5	601	5.6	8 615	18.2	15.0
Iowa	7 406	72.5	45 900	18.6	14.3	323	23.0	2.8	14 146	3.6	525	3.7	10 311	18.3	12.1
Iron	2 602	79.2	30 800	19.9	15.1	242	25.7	2.2	3 440	5.3	237	6.9	2 451	21.0	14.5
Jackson	6 253	72.7	39 600	19.9	14.7	290	24.3	3.7	11 586	-1.2	599	5.2	7 264	17.2	10.2
Jefferson	24 019	70.6	59 800	19.9	13.5	376	22.1	1.8	43 216	1.0	1 670	3.9	35 187	21.9	12.7
Juneau	8 265	75.9	40 700	20.4	14.5	310	23.8	3.0	10 504	0.8	951	9.1	9 478	18.1	13.9
Kenosha	47 029	68.8	65 100	19.4	12.9	411	24.6	2.8	81 825	0.4	4 006	4.9	59 827	23.9	14.3
Kewaunee	6 756	80.8	50 000	19.2	14.5	277	20.2	2.2	10 881	3.3	456	4.2	9 323	15.7	15.3
La Crosse	36 662	62.9	58 400	20.0	13.7	353	25.3	2.4	61 272	1.9	2 266	3.7	49 988	28.0	9.2
Lafayette	5 876	72.5	39 400	19.8	13.6	308	22.1	2.4	7 382	1.4	387	5.2	7 808	15.1	12.2
Langlade	7 563	77.5	37 600	19.6	13.8	284	24.5	3.1	9 431	1.5	731	7.8	8 226	16.9	13.0
Lincoln	10 159	76.3	43 200	18.3	14.5	297	21.0	2.6	14 721	0.5	859	5.8	12 363	20.5	11.9
Manitowoc	30 112	73.9	49 500	16.6	12.3	295	22.5	2.0	45 674	3.0	2 616	5.7	38 381	20.2	13.9
Marathon	41 547	74.7	54 800	18.1	13.1	365	23.0	2.6	74 627	1.6	3 095	4.1	57 719	23.0	11.0
Marinette	15 542	77.4	41 400	18.5	15.0	298	25.0	2.8	21 826	3.3	1 467	6.7	17 221	19.4	13.1
Marquette	4 831	80.6	45 600	20.0	14.4	304	22.6	2.4	7 323	4.1	537	7.3	5 196	16.2	14.3
Menominee	1 079	64.4	48 600	16.8	13.3	226	27.8	16.1	2 329	0.5	271	11.6	971	21.1	9.1
Milwaukee	373 048	52.1	65 300	20.7	14.0	434	26.7	3.5	480 641	1.2	27 037	5.6	446 630	29.0	10.2
Monroe	13 144	72.8	48 600	20.8	13.8	323	23.1	3.4	20 456	3.4	1 106	5.4	16 616	20.3	10.9
Oconto	11 283	81.6	43 200	20.8	16.2	294	23.5	2.7	16 896	6.0	1 144	6.8	13 113	18.1	14.5
Oneida	12 666	77.4	52 900	20.3	13.8	332	24.6	2.5	20 721	2.4	1 118	5.4	13 958	27.2	12.3
Outagamie	50 527	72.3	64 400	18.8	13.0	385	22.1	1.9	104 326	2.0	3 910	3.7	71 130	25.5	12.4
Ozaukee	25 707	74.4	100 500	20.8	13.3	495	23.6	1.4	48 817	1.1	1 482	3.0	39 100	34.2	12.5
Pepin	2 612	76.4	40 700	20.5	15.4	280	26.1	1.8	3 118	-0.7	185	5.9	3 126	16.9	11.0
Pierce	11 011	70.7	65 500	20.6	13.4	387	24.5	2.2	21 253	1.9	840	4.0	17 195	22.4	10.3
Polk	13 056	77.9	53 600	20.5	14.3	318	28.0	2.9	23 163	4.4	1 390	6.0	15 455	20.0	13.7
Portage	21 306	70.3	58 800	18.4	13.3	372	25.9	3.1	37 115	0.6	1 653	4.5	30 150	25.4	10.3
Price	6 054	79.6	40 900	20.1	14.4	286	22.4	5.0	6 949	0.9	489	7.0	6 725	20.8	11.8
Racine	63 736	68.3	64 200	19.3	12.6	402	24.9	2.6	92 439	1.7	6 175	6.7	84 059	26.3	14.0
Richland	6 593	71.9	40 500	20.4	13.7	299	24.2	3.7	8 369	0.8	403	4.8	8 003	16.8	13.0
Rock	52 252	68.2	52 300	17.0	12.9	387	24.7	2.0	78 771	1.1	5 048	6.4	67 826	22.7	12.8
Rusk	5 693	75.0	36 700	19.8	14.3	278	24.4	4.8	7 113	0.7	520	7.3	6 194	19.7	10.8
St. Croix	17 638	74.9	74 400	20.6	14.0	429	24.2	1.8	34 831	3.0	1 566	4.5	25 705	27.0	11.9
Sauk	17 703	72.3	55 600	20.4	13.5	353	24.3	2.1	36 512	4.2	1 313	3.6	22 987	20.6	13.3
Sawyer	5 569	74.9	49 500	23.6	16.1	261	26.4	4.0	9 824	3.5	563	5.7	5 231	24.3	12.8
Shawano	13 775	77.1	45 500	19.8	13.6	305	23.3	3.5	20 291	1.2	1 093	5.4	16 708	17.6	12.2
Sheboygan	38 592	70.3	59 400	18.5	13.0	361	21.5	1.7	63 298	1.5	2 411	3.8	52 159	22.5	12.9
Taylor	6 692	78.9	43 500	17.8	13.8	292	21.3	5.0	10 582	1.0	618	5.8	8 716	15.7	10.4
Trempealeau	9 495	73.0	40 900	19.8	14.3	276	22.8	3.0	14 660	1.3	853	5.8	12 039	18.9	11.2
Vernon	9 725	76.2	43 600	20.7	14.4	257	25.8	4.3	13 853	0.8	699	5.0	11 547	18.0	10.9
Vilas	7 294	79.2	58 900	23.4	14.5	302	26.3	2.9	11 373	2.2	590	5.2	7 129	24.7	14.1
Walworth	27 620	66.9	69 100	20.7	13.6	413	25.0	2.1	53 534	2.9	1 980	3.7	38 093	23.9	13.1
Washburn	5 456	76.3	46 900	21.1	15.0	288	27.3	3.8	8 161	2.4	518	6.3	5 653	22.6	13.4
Washington	32 977	73.9	83 900	21.2	12.9	455	21.9	1.7	68 492	1.3	2 593	3.8	50 498	24.9	16.0
Waukesha	105 990	77.3	96 300	21.1	12.8	541	23.5	1.4	215 161	1.1	7 124	3.3	164 509	34.5	12.0
Waupaca	17 037	76.1	50 000	20.2	14.1	328	23.3	2.6	26 695	1.8	1 322	5.0	20 961	20.2	12.4
Waushara	7 616	80.3	45 300	20.3	13.9	307	24.9	3.0	11 553	7.1	668	5.8	8 089	18.9	13.3
Winnebago	53 216	66.6	60 200	20.0	12.8	382	24.0	1.5	98 004	1.9	3 437	3.5	70 401	26.5	11.1
Wood	27 473	73.3	50 500	16.7	12.6	343	23.6	2.0	40 644	1.9	2 138	5.3	34 173	24.2	11.9
WYOMING	168 839	67.8	61 600	18.8	11.9	333	23.7	3.1	271 262	1.6	10 666	3.9	207 868	27.2	13.2
Albany	11 957	49.2	67 300	19.0	11.1	343	32.3	3.0	19 187	2.8	379	2.0	14 927	39.0	7.0
Big Horn	3 905	73.9	44 300	18.4	12.8	289	23.0	4.5	5 948	-0.8	296	5.0	4 277	24.1	11.5
Campbell	9 968	70.5	68 500	16.8	13.6	362	20.5	2.8	22 360	8.5	654	2.9	14 531	23.6	17.1
Carbon	6 001	69.1	52 700	16.1	12.0	301	20.0	3.1	8 222	-1.2	364	4.4	7 602	20.4	15.3

1. Specified owner-occupied units.   2. Specified renter-occupied units.   3. Overcrowded or lacking complete plumbing facilities.   4. Percent of civilian labor force.   5. Persons 16 years and older.

Table B. States and Counties — Nonfarm Employment and Agriculture

STATE County	Private nonfarm establishments, employment and payroll, 1999									Agriculture, 1997			
	Number of establishments	Employment						Annual payroll		Farms			Farm operators
		Total	Health Care and Social Assistance	Manufacturing	Retail trade	Finance and Insurance	Professional Scientific and Technical Services	Total (mil dol)	Average per employee (dollars)	Number	Percent with—		Whose principal occupation is farming (percent)
											Less than 50 acres	500 acres and over	
	104	105	106	107	108	109	110	111	112	113	114	115	116
WISCONSIN—Cont'd													
Dane	12 191	219 244	28 568	26 681	31 208	19 183	13 092	6 481	29 561	2 595	30.1	8.1	54.3
Dodge	1 825	29 802	3 357	13 432	3 307	598	560	854	28 664	1 807	20.0	8.7	65.8
Door	1 307	10 307	720	2 464	1 735	312	275	227	22 001	702	23.4	4.1	56.0
Douglas	1 107	13 495	1 912	1 589	2 027	375	433	293	21 700	267	15.0	11.6	39.0
Dunn	961	13 095	1 845	2 639	1 947	387	382	300	22 913	1 397	14.3	11.3	58.8
Eau Claire	2 639	43 904	7 404	6 307	7 475	1 881	1 557	1 064	24 242	927	17.0	5.7	58.8
Florence	110	567	D	164	93	D	D	11	18 767	86	10.5	9.3	51.2
Fond du Lac	2 524	43 570	4 562	11 995	6 204	1 546	2 039	1 175	26 971	1 488	17.6	8.2	62.8
Forest	305	2 350	291	425	320	72	81	48	20 259	111	17.1	8.1	47.7
Grant	1 278	13 619	1 956	3 079	2 378	526	398	264	19 399	2 238	13.7	12.0	65.9
Green	943	12 931	1 866	3 416	3 172	381	247	311	24 032	1 295	17.4	9.8	68.2
Green Lake	630	6 633	994	1 824	1 232	182	120	157	23 694	584	17.5	8.7	57.9
Iowa	572	10 049	846	1 236	5 152	172	176	244	24 297	1 394	14.1	11.6	59.8
Iron	230	2 017	385	352	349	31	36	36	17 750	38	7.9	10.5	42.1
Jackson	410	4 986	490	951	854	196	119	133	26 626	774	13.2	13.4	58.0
Jefferson	1 889	32 943	3 384	12 728	3 761	710	535	822	24 965	1 240	25.8	7.0	52.2
Juneau	642	8 360	897	3 002	1 035	166	118	186	22 292	654	16.5	10.1	53.7
Kenosha	3 074	50 214	6 442	12 159	6 995	990	1 115	1 427	28 421	388	40.5	12.4	49.5
Kewaunee	490	5 538	480	2 316	716	207	138	132	23 767	795	16.4	6.4	66.2
La Crosse	2 939	56 107	9 924	10 188	9 142	1 995	1 854	1 454	25 912	759	14.9	9.2	53.1
Lafayette	343	2 870	D	618	599	143	D	61	21 152	1 127	16.0	14.2	71.6
Langlade	611	6 684	838	1 577	1 401	202	89	145	21 665	453	19.4	13.0	63.8
Lincoln	777	9 536	955	3 298	1 558	222	140	223	23 433	425	15.1	6.4	56.7
Manitowoc	1 905	33 758	3 947	14 147	4 086	752	556	951	28 176	1 227	23.3	8.1	60.1
Marathon	3 429	62 164	6 387	18 368	9 587	4 462	1 685	1 730	27 822	2 703	23.3	6.2	60.6
Marinette	1 076	16 527	2 254	6 547	2 062	423	198	419	25 355	551	15.6	11.1	54.6
Marquette	338	3 150	237	1 227	448	80	34	75	23 893	443	17.8	14.4	50.3
Menominee	97	1 831	D	D	143	D	D	35	19 117	5	60.0	0.0	60.0
Milwaukee	21 394	472 647	73 711	84 905	51 646	37 278	23 986	15 675	33 165	83	67.5	2.4	43.4
Monroe	881	13 012	2 193	3 867	1 657	340	202	308	23 692	1 567	14.3	7.0	61.2
Oconto	846	8 954	909	2 733	993	211	184	209	23 346	940	15.1	8.1	55.7
Oneida	1 584	16 245	3 414	2 291	3 376	414	424	400	24 624	117	25.6	14.5	55.6
Outagamie	4 621	92 464	8 061	21 422	11 982	6 512	3 142	2 744	29 673	1 286	26.4	7.6	59.2
Ozaukee	2 831	37 075	3 149	13 053	4 573	1 510	1 822	1 159	31 263	427	34.7	6.1	49.4
Pepin	193	1 781	288	D	342	80	33	39	22 001	425	15.8	10.4	64.0
Pierce	786	6 325	627	954	1 080	303	200	134	21 256	1 265	20.5	7.9	52.4
Polk	1 073	11 795	1 746	3 910	1 684	392	269	270	22 925	1 301	17.6	8.2	51.5
Portage	1 635	26 549	2 455	5 313	4 114	3 443	890	672	25 329	913	14.8	12.2	56.7
Price	460	5 551	913	2 462	750	153	73	138	24 844	370	10.0	10.5	53.0
Racine	4 164	73 607	8 546	20 032	10 041	3 951	2 194	2 279	30 955	554	41.0	9.4	55.1
Richland	350	4 408	555	1 731	879	125	60	101	22 872	1 032	13.2	8.5	57.6
Rock	3 331	61 440	7 108	18 049	8 805	1 578	1 008	1 864	30 339	1 324	32.6	12.9	52.3
Rusk	352	4 411	605	1 966	512	103	29	100	22 695	578	9.3	10.7	68.9
St. Croix	1 635	20 870	2 276	5 965	3 182	507	975	545	26 123	1 520	23.9	7.4	48.2
Sauk	1 683	24 988	2 771	6 666	4 241	884	734	649	25 977	1 452	16.9	10.6	57.2
Sawyer	622	4 699	546	812	844	154	105	101	21 598	184	16.8	13.6	54.9
Shawano	915	10 117	1 312	2 193	1 711	323	184	206	20 336	1 337	15.3	6.4	65.9
Sheboygan	2 594	55 101	5 458	21 386	6 176	1 851	1 820	1 632	29 614	968	32.2	8.5	61.7
Taylor	477	7 273	829	3 166	904	245	85	183	25 164	887	13.0	10.5	69.3
Trempealeau	688	10 325	1 269	5 093	1 000	313	145	250	24 259	1 408	11.4	9.4	57.7
Vernon	643	6 025	1 526	946	1 145	296	126	116	19 191	1 893	17.9	5.7	59.1
Vilas	800	4 278	383	369	641	155	65	87	20 442	44	31.8	4.5	54.5
Walworth	2 596	35 401	3 138	10 970	4 131	806	875	858	24 239	853	32.6	15.1	56.6
Washburn	575	4 579	762	1 014	1 007	147	138	91	19 913	354	12.4	13.0	46.3
Washington	3 092	45 940	4 314	15 333	5 726	2 077	1 165	1 290	28 080	787	30.9	5.6	58.7
Waukesha	12 461	219 599	19 016	50 562	25 101	11 032	11 305	7 474	34 036	630	46.8	7.8	47.5
Waupaca	1 356	16 636	2 290	5 917	2 527	577	248	402	24 175	1 129	19.8	7.2	57.5
Waushara	519	4 297	503	786	830	136	313	81	18 859	634	22.7	12.0	53.0
Winnebago	3 726	80 940	9 254	27 018	9 377	2 447	2 147	2 564	31 678	860	24.0	9.0	57.9
Wood	1 916	38 402	7 951	9 462	5 295	1 052	637	1 179	30 697	968	16.9	8.6	63.1
WYOMING	17 909	169 188	24 481	9 518	28 136	6 826	6 214	4 288	25 346	9 232	16.9	50.5	60.5
Albany	999	9 734	1 635	608	1 802	376	629	191	19 603	315	10.5	65.1	54.3
Big Horn	293	2 463	302	285	325	83	D	64	26 118	495	17.6	32.7	59.4
Campbell	1 148	13 253	1 301	201	1 736	271	405	451	34 003	531	11.9	72.3	59.7
Carbon	550	4 608	489	339	838	142	92	110	23 950	310	12.9	66.8	69.0

Items 104—116

STATE County	Agriculture, 1997 (cont'd)														
	Land in farms					Value of land and buildings		Value of machinery and equipment average per farm ($1,000)	Value of products sold				Percent of farms with sales of —		Percent of land owned by fed. gov. 1997	Water consumption 1995 (mil gal/day)
			Acres								Percent from —				
	Acreage (1,000)	Percent change, 1992– 1997	Average size of farm	Total irrigated (1,000)	Total cropland (1,000)	Average per farm ($1,000)	Average per acre (dollars)		Total (mil dol)	Average per farm (dollars)	Crops	Live-stock and poultry products	$10,000 or more	$100,000 or more		
	117	118	119	120	121	122	123	124	125	126	127	128	129	130	131	132
WISCONSIN—Cont'd																
Dane	513	-4.8	198	7	414	367	1 853	73	285	109 687	31.1	68.9	59.5	25.6	0.2	112.7
Dodge	392	-5.3	217	1	331	329	1 537	86	194	107 131	26.4	73.6	74.4	32.4	3.4	13.7
Door	122	-6.2	174	1	93	262	1 383	59	38	54 552	31.2	68.8	53.7	17.1	0.2	4.9
Douglas	71	-0.3	265	D	34	177	608	24	6	21 307	21.2	78.8	28.1	4.9	0.2	6.7
Dunn	369	0.4	264	13	235	242	934	71	114	81 872	25.6	74.4	57.1	23.2	0.0	15.1
Eau Claire	191	0.7	206	3	133	196	943	52	58	62 328	30.0	70.0	55.4	19.8	0.0	18.1
Florence	19	-7.8	225	D	11	152	673	44	2	21 513	26.2	73.8	38.4	5.8	26.8	0.6
Fond du Lac	325	-7.7	218	1	273	306	1 388	76	151	101 573	25.5	74.5	71.4	33.3	0.2	17.2
Forest	26	0.6	236	D	12	167	716	36	4	33 313	11.4	88.6	36.9	6.3	51.0	1.0
Grant	600	-3.4	268	D	376	288	1 112	68	204	91 287	17.9	82.1	71.9	33.0	0.5	251.5
Green	305	4.1	235	5	249	313	1 385	74	125	96 813	23.3	76.7	72.0	37.0	0.0	6.5
Green Lake	134	-17.6	230	3	106	306	1 453	62	45	77 493	36.8	63.2	64.6	25.2	0.0	5.3
Iowa	367	1.3	263	8	232	335	1 235	62	111	79 559	20.6	79.4	61.7	25.3	0.0	3.3
Iron	10	-3.7	254	D	5	183	720	41	1	21 553	38.0	62.0	34.2	2.6	0.0	0.8
Jackson	244	11.9	315	4	133	336	1 068	62	78	100 666	53.2	46.8	58.3	22.2	0.3	9.3
Jefferson	242	4.0	195	9	200	375	1 917	67	131	105 860	45.2	54.8	59.3	20.2	0.1	22.7
Juneau	169	-13.2	259	10	110	321	1 288	66	53	80 338	54.3	45.7	56.1	16.5	14.6	8.4
Kenosha	85	-8.9	218	0	74	613	2 961	98	33	85 699	63.9	36.1	59.0	25.5	0.0	35.1
Kewaunee	161	-5.1	203	0	132	288	1 351	88	81	101 548	18.6	81.4	65.2	32.3	0.0	725.9
La Crosse	170	-6.8	223	1	89	233	1 075	51	46	60 287	19.7	80.3	54.8	19.8	3.1	69.0
Lafayette	338	-5.2	300	0	263	345	1 146	84	136	120 859	28.6	71.4	77.4	40.1	0.0	3.2
Langlade	124	3.2	273	13	82	300	1 060	100	51	112 395	57.3	42.7	60.7	23.2	6.2	13.3
Lincoln	84	-2.4	197	0	44	180	928	56	20	47 741	33.4	66.6	49.4	12.5	0.0	10.9
Manitowoc	245	-1.7	200	1	206	256	1 325	72	138	112 841	13.6	86.4	63.0	32.4	0.0	1 260.8
Marathon	516	-2.7	191	6	337	202	1 039	68	204	75 578	24.7	75.3	68.2	24.0	0.0	183.4
Marinette	132	-9.8	239	2	83	217	1 038	48	40	71 845	18.4	81.6	53.5	18.5	0.0	22.3
Marquette	125	-8.2	282	4	86	334	1 137	55	32	72 870	53.5	46.5	51.5	16.9	0.3	1.6
Menominee	0	0.0	77		D	189	2 446	13	0	2 506	D	D	0.0	0.0	0.0	0.3
Milwaukee	6	-30.0	76	0	D	319	4 180	44	7	82 173	D	D	51.8	26.5	0.0	1 974.0
Monroe	330	-4.8	210	3	178	255	1 165	66	102	64 958	33.5	66.5	57.9	17.4	13.2	6.4
Oconto	204	-2.5	217	0	144	225	1 062	63	67	70 870	19.4	80.6	59.4	21.8	21.6	6.2
Oneida	39	22.0	334	2	16	421	1 262	65	13	113 594	85.5	14.5	38.5	17.9	1.3	32.8
Outagamie	252	-4.4	196	0	212	305	1 557	83	142	110 563	23.7	76.3	68.8	33.3	0.0	67.7
Ozaukee	70	-11.5	164	0	59	424	2 509	58	32	75 052	34.5	65.5	52.9	22.7	0.1	223.5
Pepin	104	-8.7	245	1	66	198	879	62	29	69 226	27.0	73.0	70.6	24.0	0.0	1.4
Pierce	268	-2.0	212	0	184	244	1 130	49	76	60 375	30.2	69.8	55.1	21.3	0.0	4.3
Polk	268	-5.1	206	1	171	216	969	68	68	52 225	23.5	76.5	50.8	16.7	0.7	4.8
Portage	263	-1.2	288	76	189	355	1 194	101	115	126 060	67.6	32.4	56.2	22.2	0.0	85.2
Price	93	-2.5	250	D	40	215	739	48	15	40 960	27.6	72.4	43.5	8.9	18.6	9.3
Racine	123	-7.5	222	5	110	520	2 396	77	78	141 584	53.7	46.3	52.5	20.6	0.0	37.7
Richland	238	-12.1	231	2	128	211	922	49	61	59 247	14.9	85.1	51.6	18.5	0.0	2.7
Rock	351	2.3	265	10	308	453	1 727	79	130	97 906	56.9	43.1	58.5	24.7	0.1	152.0
Rusk	159	-5.3	275	0	83	172	615	55	32	56 192	6.9	93.1	59.2	18.0	0.0	4.2
St. Croix	312	1.3	205	4	237	282	1 368	53	92	60 267	28.2	71.8	49.7	17.1	1.0	7.7
Sauk	333	-0.9	229	10	213	286	1 212	77	121	83 487	18.2	81.8	60.9	24.6	1.3	13.2
Sawyer	48	3.1	263	0	27	207	769	55	10	55 544	33.6	66.4	50.0	17.4	14.7	1.5
Shawano	270	-9.2	202	0	184	213	1 082	71	127	94 640	10.0	90.0	67.2	27.0	0.0	6.0
Sheboygan	182	-11.9	188	0	153	313	1 668	78	92	95 254	19.1	80.9	63.8	29.1	0.0	464.7
Taylor	224	-3.2	252	0	122	177	679	51	62	69 621	9.0	91.0	66.3	23.3	18.8	2.2
Trempealeau	341	-2.4	242	4	211	204	829	57	124	88 315	16.2	83.8	57.0	21.2	0.4	5.6
Vernon	344	-6.0	182	0	203	198	1 135	46	86	45 690	16.1	83.9	58.7	13.3	2.1	200.6
Vilas	8	0.0	172	1	D	369	2 143	98	6	140 675	97.9	2.1	43.2	15.9	8.3	1.5
Walworth	220	-3.0	258	1	187	537	2 107	80	93	109 484	48.3	51.7	61.5	28.1	0.0	14.6
Washburn	98	13.8	276	2	46	233	891	51	16	45 010	37.8	62.2	43.8	10.7	0.7	2.5
Washington	127	-13.5	162	0	105	359	2 165	69	61	78 075	33.1	66.9	63.5	21.7	0.0	12.8
Waukesha	106	-7.4	168	1	88	461	2 982	53	42	66 823	64.2	35.8	47.0	16.0	0.0	43.5
Waupaca	227	-6.3	201	9	162	227	1 210	56	86	76 334	26.2	73.8	58.5	22.8	0.0	10.2
Waushara	175	4.5	275	49	127	383	1 308	85	75	118 298	75.3	24.7	49.2	18.6	0.0	25.7
Winnebago	167	-1.5	195	0	136	331	1 722	76	62	71 731	31.7	68.3	57.7	21.7	0.2	68.7
Wood	219	-0.8	227	6	138	320	1 482	77	91	93 834	47.5	52.5	65.8	26.0	0.5	121.9
WYOMING	34 089	3.7	3 692	1 719	2 968	808	222	61	899	97 327	19.3	80.7	62.6	20.6	45.9	7 040.2
Albany	1 922	2.9	6 103	155	133	1 433	243	59	34	108 598	4.9	95.1	61.9	24.8	24.3	179.7
Big Horn	443	0.6	896	116	131	642	666	72	43	87 710	57.9	42.1	63.0	22.4	73.3	740.9
Campbell	2 944	8.9	5 544	5	157	634	119	54	35	65 770	5.8	94.2	65.7	17.1	12.6	52.0
Carbon	2 282	-16.1	7 360	182	158	1 383	191	73	43	140 141	5.8	94.2	65.2	32.9	56.7	786.1

STATE County	New Construction ($1,000)	Number of Housing Units	Number of Establishments	Number of Employees	Sales (mil dol)	Annual Payroll (mil dol)	Number of Establishments	Number of Employees	Sales (mil dol)	Annual Payroll (mil dol)	Number of Establishments	Number of Employees	Receipts (mil dol)	Annual Payroll (mil dol)
	Value of Residential Construction Authorized by Building Permits, 2000		Wholesale Trade, 1997				Retail Trade[1], 1997				Real Estate and Rental and Leasing, 1997			
	133	134	135	136	137	138	139	140	141	142	143	144	145	146
WISCONSIN—Cont'd														
Dane	465 509	3 986	675	10 048	4 350.1	342.7	1 845	30 150	4 860.9	507.2	520	3 519	371.4	71.1
Dodge	48 628	384	86	1 087	528.9	33.7	277	3 220	544.2	49.6	39	161	9.8	1.7
Door	45 236	458	34	159	38.9	3.3	281	1 581	258.9	24.8	55	107	14.5	1.8
Douglas	21 337	251	59	D	D	D	161	2 075	334.1	31.1	40	146	10.0	1.8
Dunn	27 771	305	43	433	98.2	9.5	156	2 060	324.0	30.0	28	50	5.1	0.5
Eau Claire	80 940	731	135	1 463	613.5	42.2	459	7 405	1 036.0	100.7	100	456	45.5	7.1
Florence	0	0	5	D	D	D	12	78	15.1	0.8	5	6	0.5	0.1
Fond du Lac	56 665	415	116	1 204	528.2	36.0	413	5 744	891.2	86.6	73	297	27.9	4.5
Forest	7 341	96	11	76	13.5	1.9	42	345	50.9	4.9	9	30	2.3	0.2
Grant	16 571	159	66	613	174.5	11.2	243	2 310	357.6	32.3	50	126	9.7	1.1
Green	26 579	211	66	588	208.8	14.1	181	3 025	572.9	66.3	18	41	7.0	0.4
Green Lake	13 433	82	19	149	32.6	3.8	113	1 297	161.4	15.7	15	42	3.0	0.4
Iowa	18 211	198	39	331	109.9	10.7	105	4 409	1 211.4	107.7	9	30	2.9	0.2
Iron	7 908	73	8	48	11.9	1.1	38	337	49.4	4.5	11	50	3.2	0.6
Jackson	8 177	89	10	74	8.7	1.1	83	919	124.7	11.6	12	24	3.9	0.6
Jefferson	61 845	577	92	1 483	466.5	42.2	253	3 519	568.2	53.1	54	177	16.5	3.0
Juneau	16 360	187	22	200	77.5	4.5	102	1 056	170.5	15.1	15	31	1.9	0.2
Kenosha	105 536	1 014	135	2 515	1 385.3	91.5	546	6 442	1 072.4	95.7	112	412	43.8	6.6
Kewaunee	17 004	131	20	139	35.5	3.4	72	655	113.6	10.3	8	11	1.0	0.1
La Crosse	65 042	571	154	3 217	1 921.6	102.5	509	9 005	1 452.6	135.6	120	774	59.2	13.3
Lafayette	5 836	61	23	170	62.2	4.0	62	526	94.8	8.8	4	4	0.3	0.0
Langlade	12 590	153	39	348	217.8	11.0	114	1 270	255.7	20.5	10	38	2.0	0.4
Lincoln	22 853	219	25	D	D	D	142	1 504	220.1	20.6	26	82	3.9	0.6
Manitowoc	52 354	468	67	611	257.1	22.0	295	3 856	561.0	55.1	50	183	14.1	2.2
Marathon	88 641	803	221	3 395	1 002.0	102.5	565	9 236	1 421.6	142.6	86	439	39.9	7.1
Marinette	21 991	271	33	485	93.2	14.8	187	2 008	285.9	27.4	26	45	5.3	0.6
Marquette	12 640	128	10	D	D	D	47	444	56.6	5.6	10	32	1.5	0.3
Menominee	3 241	28	2	D	D	D	13	113	15.2	1.2	1	D	D	D
Milwaukee	160 776	1 750	1 393	22 559	13 007.5	845.3	3 224	52 471	8 065.2	839.2	875	6 745	827.5	145.6
Monroe	21 502	235	46	465	241.6	12.2	139	1 618	261.8	22.8	25	85	5.6	1.1
Oconto	44 092	461	28	121	45.1	3.8	118	1 017	178.6	14.2	22	37	2.3	0.4
Oneida	44 390	411	45	441	119.9	12.8	294	3 030	471.5	45.3	63	212	24.9	4.0
Outagamie	168 997	1 488	291	4 066	1 694.0	147.5	712	11 218	1 936.3	182.2	124	702	75.6	15.0
Ozaukee	95 126	502	204	1 314	627.1	49.6	352	4 453	940.1	75.3	78	322	36.7	7.9
Pepin	5 014	46	11	90	27.4	2.1	38	434	88.7	8.6	3	6	0.6	0.1
Pierce	38 229	309	29	D	D	D	112	1 047	151.6	13.6	19	185	27.7	6.0
Polk	44 491	431	38	432	112.5	11.0	183	1 552	221.6	19.7	26	73	7.5	0.6
Portage	48 227	468	93	1 307	380.9	39.8	262	3 916	603.2	56.8	53	191	18.8	2.9
Price	16 045	173	19	211	41.5	3.3	97	726	106.9	9.9	4	12	1.5	0.2
Racine	104 598	867	234	4 560	3 816.9	142.4	664	9 693	1 564.1	142.0	132	746	57.7	12.1
Richland	11 129	132	16	122	32.2	1.6	76	821	128.5	11.4	11	25	1.6	0.2
Rock	78 065	848	152	2 823	1 706.4	95.8	584	8 484	1 599.7	148.4	105	364	52.9	5.6
Rusk	11 685	116	9	35	4.8	0.6	62	486	78.7	6.7	8	23	1.6	0.3
St. Croix	124 277	1 099	80	484	210.3	14.9	224	3 053	590.3	52.2	59	333	21.1	5.1
Sauk	58 829	575	68	1 090	426.4	33.6	295	4 083	582.6	62.2	45	184	22.6	3.4
Sawyer	24 537	274	8	79	23.8	3.4	100	778	133.6	12.0	24	53	5.3	0.6
Shawano	21 581	216	40	450	191.8	12.3	153	1 747	267.5	26.2	20	67	4.4	0.8
Sheboygan	78 950	675	119	2 041	1 185.0	65.4	398	5 831	911.0	88.0	85	400	38.2	6.2
Taylor	6 655	73	19	467	80.8	9.1	88	896	141.8	11.4	11	54	4.3	1.0
Trempealeau	15 429	153	39	215	125.6	5.2	126	1 017	169.4	13.5	18	49	7.3	0.8
Vernon	9 911	110	37	217	75.6	4.5	108	1 139	161.1	16.9	17	32	1.7	0.2
Vilas	31 868	360	20	69	17.0	1.5	150	764	122.8	12.8	24	D	D	D
Walworth	123 565	971	128	1 554	883.1	46.8	371	3 880	627.2	59.2	94	299	33.0	5.2
Washburn	18 566	241	16	90	21.9	2.1	96	975	173.6	15.4	23	70	7.0	0.9
Washington	122 470	931	181	2 658	1 107.9	97.0	390	5 184	1 201.5	86.0	76	276	35.0	4.1
Waukesha	419 525	2 448	1 272	16 570	11 523.8	672.1	1 385	24 345	4 094.2	392.4	413	2 432	352.9	65.0
Waupaca	29 286	272	58	406	116.3	9.5	242	2 473	416.3	36.8	34	98	7.2	1.3
Waushara	23 627	262	21	156	54.5	3.6	91	817	148.3	12.9	17	31	3.8	0.5
Winnebago	85 861	811	194	3 387	1 088.8	111.9	611	8 712	1 489.6	141.4	148	711	65.2	11.5
Wood	41 072	392	85	1 421	636.9	44.1	355	5 177	950.5	83.0	60	248	19.8	3.3
WYOMING	313 653	1 582	800	5 761	2 547.1	161.9	2 939	26 934	4 530.5	426.7	717	2 463	220.8	39.5
Albany	12 192	107	24	132	84.9	2.7	168	1 663	339.7	27.5	47	129	9.5	1.5
Big Horn	999	12	15	64	14.9	1.2	59	340	50.7	5.0	10	D	D	D
Campbell	7 769	61	78	658	235.4	22.9	179	1 733	280.3	28.0	37	142	11.4	1.8
Carbon	4 080	33	18	70	25.5	1.3	103	847	141.2	11.7	22	46	3.5	0.5

1. Establishments with payroll.

STATE County	Professional, Scientific, and Technical Services[1], 1997				Manufacturing, 1997				Accommodation and Foodservices, 1997			
	Number of Establish-ments	Number of Employees	Receipts (mil dol)	Annual Payroll (mil dol)	Number of Establish-ments	Number of Employees	Receipts (mil dol)	Annual Payroll (mil dol)	Number of Establish-ments	Number of Employees	Sales (mil dol)	Annual Payroll (mil dol)
	147	148	149	150	151	152	153	154	155	156	157	158
WISCONSIN—Cont'd												
Dane	1 132	10 748	943.4	412.4	564	26 568	4 840.5	864.4	993	18 607	554.1	156.9
Dodge	64	417	33.6	10.9	164	12 667	3 159.9	413.8	165	1 637	41.6	10.7
Door	64	251	14.7	5.0	63	2 222	267.5	59.7	243	1 796	96.4	25.1
Douglas	52	317	21.5	8.2	56	1 543	500.2	45.4	178	1 818	50.9	13.1
Dunn	43	289	17.5	7.9	60	2 910	875.4	92.0	107	1 383	33.4	9.4
Eau Claire	165	1 485	112.2	48.5	107	4 182	651.3	110.9	247	4 932	115.9	34.6
Florence	4	9	0.3	0.1	NA	NA	NA	NA	16	D	D	D
Fond du Lac	137	630	45.9	18.0	158	11 150	2 115.7	393.2	227	3 584	92.9	25.6
Forest	9	66	3.8	2.0	NA	NA	NA	NA	35	D	D	D
Grant	50	298	18.9	7.8	57	2 996	718.1	68.5	139	1 431	34.7	8.5
Green	43	180	14.2	4.4	77	3 667	840.2	93.5	92	1 182	29.1	8.3
Green Lake	24	89	5.4	1.4	61	2 383	262.0	55.8	62	707	20.0	5.7
Iowa	31	106	5.5	2.2	34	815	156.7	18.4	52	D	D	D
Iron	13	25	1.8	0.6	12	534	64.2	10.5	53	440	11.3	2.7
Jackson	25	103	4.3	2.2	20	810	134.2	17.8	52	685	17.1	4.5
Jefferson	90	598	33.0	13.6	165	12 201	2 431.5	371.8	187	2 098	52.8	13.9
Juneau	26	118	5.7	2.8	47	3 503	522.7	103.0	86	979	34.2	10.1
Kenosha	176	687	47.7	20.4	204	9 526	2 031.0	396.2	340	4 546	133.3	37.1
Kewaunee	23	73	4.3	1.4	45	2 359	314.0	67.1	53	512	11.6	2.8
La Crosse	191	1 531	117.1	52.5	161	10 171	1 382.6	313.7	300	5 533	141.9	41.4
Lafayette	15	23	1.6	0.4	21	661	134.4	14.5	36	256	5.5	1.5
Langlade	15	79	3.8	2.1	39	1 493	184.0	35.9	75	677	18.8	5.2
Lincoln	31	81	5.1	1.6	63	3 637	532.4	101.2	98	894	21.3	6.3
Manitowoc	86	538	41.8	11.9	180	13 474	2 134.1	407.2	179	2 512	59.4	16.4
Marathon	181	1 264	127.4	46.6	232	16 839	3 181.9	502.6	276	3 779	105.2	29.7
Marinette	42	132	9.1	4.0	82	6 766	1 139.1	217.9	140	1 386	36.2	9.9
Marquette	12	27	1.9	0.4	24	996	135.8	27.3	59	D	D	D
Menominee	NA	NA	NA	NA	6	705	51.0	16.6	9	D	D	D
Milwaukee	2 027	20 568	2 101.0	837.7	1 463	86 933	16 535.5	3 213.2	1 838	31 293	1 005.6	280.5
Monroe	36	143	8.7	3.4	58	3 397	745.0	79.9	110	1 186	35.8	9.3
Oconto	33	129	7.0	2.9	61	2 445	297.7	56.6	107	953	26.2	6.3
Oneida	89	363	25.7	10.3	68	2 526	395.3	78.3	209	1 903	61.6	16.9
Outagamie	275	2 371	199.9	86.7	303	21 410	5 315.4	750.7	361	6 755	192.1	53.5
Ozaukee	321	1 443	156.2	55.8	242	13 420	2 763.1	485.8	182	2 900	75.0	22.0
Pepin	6	29	1.4	0.4	NA	NA	NA	NA	26	D	D	D
Pierce	47	158	10.0	4.3	40	942	216.7	24.7	102	994	24.3	6.1
Polk	55	198	11.2	3.8	95	3 912	628.1	90.7	118	904	26.4	7.0
Portage	80	521	33.3	14.6	83	5 534	1 265.8	178.3	202	3 337	86.2	24.6
Price	23	80	4.6	1.8	46	2 957	449.6	91.7	42	D	D	D
Racine	296	1 821	134.3	55.6	379	18 869	5 229.5	664.1	360	5 324	154.7	42.2
Richland	19	67	2.9	1.1	26	1 851	373.3	52.7	32	D	D	D
Rock	182	1 002	65.1	23.5	234	19 547	10 105.6	785.3	343	5 295	151.2	41.3
Rusk	12	30	1.2	0.4	30	1 722	203.1	41.0	42	D	D	D
St. Croix	124	754	93.7	36.0	150	5 867	827.0	174.3	142	1 962	52.9	15.3
Sauk	76	549	37.0	16.8	114	6 570	1 121.2	180.8	241	3 276	123.6	32.9
Sawyer	24	76	4.2	1.6	39	859	137.3	22.4	109	613	24.3	6.1
Shawano	27	144	5.5	3.1	67	1 985	330.3	51.0	109	1 147	32.9	8.6
Sheboygan	150	1 235	92.2	40.5	239	20 047	4 252.7	628.3	237	3 714	105.9	29.1
Taylor	17	59	2.9	1.4	43	2 987	592.7	83.8	39	D	D	D
Trempealeau	29	177	7.7	3.9	62	4 678	799.9	121.8	85	713	17.1	4.9
Vernon	24	103	3.6	1.3	37	970	168.1	20.7	66	D	D	D
Vilas	20	54	3.2	1.1	NA	NA	NA	NA	188	1 451	69.9	17.3
Walworth	158	649	57.3	20.0	218	10 377	1 496.2	311.7	276	5 518	168.1	53.1
Washburn	25	126	7.7	3.2	35	793	94.7	17.1	80	521	17.6	4.3
Washington	162	1 254	102.0	26.3	321	15 660	2 360.2	499.2	217	3 737	93.7	25.7
Waukesha	1 142	9 380	1 031.1	377.8	1 148	49 130	9 434.6	1 760.3	635	11 945	372.6	104.4
Waupaca	51	165	8.7	3.1	105	5 995	1 235.3	176.0	139	1 583	41.8	11.1
Waushara	18	51	2.5	0.9	32	746	79.2	14.9	70	D	D	D
Winnebago	202	1 630	142.9	46.0	316	27 191	6 026.6	976.5	341	5 832	153.7	43.4
Wood	77	518	33.0	12.2	117	9 421	2 535.6	363.3	191	2 468	65.3	17.3
WYOMING	1 264	5 274	388.8	146.9	503	8 448	2 955.1	256.4	1 751	24 950	808.9	219.0
Albany	108	549	40.6	17.1	33	531	89.1	13.5	104	1 922	45.1	12.8
Big Horn	10	33	2.4	1.0	NA	NA	NA	NA	32	215	4.8	1.5
Campbell	80	336	22.3	8.2	NA	NA	NA	NA	77	1 346	41.9	11.1
Carbon	26	73	6.6	1.4	NA	NA	NA	NA	85	781	25.8	6.8

1. Firms subject to federal tax.

Table B. States and Counties — **Health and Other Services and Federal Funds**

STATE County	Health Care and Social Assistance[1], 1997 — Number of Establishments	Number of Employees	Receipts (mil dol)	Annual Payroll (mil dol)	Other Services[1], 1997 — Number of Establishments	Number of Employees	Receipts (mil dol)	Annual Payroll (mil dol)	Federal funds and grants, fiscal 2001[2] — Total	Direct payments for individuals[3] — Social Security and government retirement	Medicare	Food stamps and Supplemental Security Income
	159	160	161	162	163	164	165	166	167	168	169	170
WISCONSIN—Cont'd												
Dane	785	9 899	735.9	320.2	664	4 412	258.5	88.8	2 977.3	711.8	199.7	33.8
Dodge	137	1 252	70.0	34.5	113	402	22.2	6.0	244.5	126.3	44.3	3.1
Door	56	512	23.8	11.2	55	207	12.7	2.8	146.2	74.2	26.7	1.4
Douglas	53	718	33.5	16.0	68	397	22.5	6.0	228.5	109.1	35.5	7.4
Dunn	39	1 003	31.5	16.3	59	268	13.2	3.5	149.5	62.0	17.8	2.3
Eau Claire	180	3 052	196.1	111.8	205	1 242	64.2	19.3	380.0	168.6	57.4	11.3
Florence	4	92	3.3	1.8	3	D	D	D	22.3	12.0	3.9	0.6
Fond du Lac	157	1 748	181.2	54.2	162	945	44.4	13.7	380.5	201.2	66.6	5.6
Forest	10	326	7.5	3.3	10	21	1.4	0.4	61.5	27.0	7.6	1.2
Grant	78	969	35.0	14.4	103	331	18.7	4.2	231.3	104.6	38.4	4.3
Green	52	767	55.7	25.8	73	271	19.0	5.3	138.6	64.6	24.1	1.6
Green Lake	46	334	15.5	7.3	32	104	6.9	1.6	93.5	47.9	17.2	1.1
Iowa	39	303	18.7	7.8	27	81	5.7	1.2	97.0	35.4	11.7	1.3
Iron	10	251	8.2	3.9	10	36	1.2	0.3	38.9	20.3	7.1	0.6
Jackson	18	221	12.3	5.1	25	66	3.4	0.7	92.0	39.4	11.8	2.3
Jefferson	135	1 397	70.7	32.8	129	553	28.3	8.3	310.7	152.7	55.3	2.5
Juneau	31	300	13.9	5.8	40	155	9.4	2.5	140.8	66.6	20.1	2.2
Kenosha	263	2 517	136.9	65.9	222	1 262	68.1	19.3	557.7	267.1	103.1	16.9
Kewaunee	34	251	7.4	3.3	28	76	4.8	1.0	135.3	40.2	14.4	1.1
La Crosse	139	1 013	57.5	26.8	193	1 271	65.1	20.7	441.0	197.8	59.9	12.3
Lafayette	17	79	5.4	1.4	25	68	5.2	0.9	88.6	29.5	11.7	1.1
Langlade	26	374	17.9	8.2	41	150	7.5	1.9	104.2	52.5	18.7	2.5
Lincoln	40	453	22.2	11.8	43	190	10.3	3.1	135.6	73.7	25.1	2.6
Manitowoc	129	1 362	78.1	41.3	129	496	27.9	7.9	344.3	180.0	63.3	5.9
Marathon	200	2 672	188.8	104.9	222	1 201	79.2	20.9	480.8	214.5	73.7	12.5
Marinette	68	1 006	50.0	26.1	53	202	11.8	3.3	311.4	116.1	35.8	4.1
Marquette	18	216	8.8	4.5	21	64	3.9	1.0	92.4	48.4	14.9	0.9
Menominee	1	D	D	D	3	D	D	D	35.7	7.0	2.2	0.9
Milwaukee	2 074	27 274	1 753.0	942.9	1 412	9 778	580.6	187.3	5 373.3	1 819.3	895.1	264.2
Monroe	38	360	15.7	7.6	65	310	14.4	4.6	289.3	104.8	22.8	4.0
Oconto	40	559	19.8	9.7	50	86	6.4	1.1	141.5	70.2	22.4	2.4
Oneida	80	1 272	67.5	30.2	89	336	24.0	6.0	193.5	109.4	34.0	3.2
Outagamie	287	3 049	217.2	111.8	303	2 270	130.9	38.9	513.1	278.0	72.4	9.2
Ozaukee	209	1 958	112.6	53.2	161	877	41.9	13.8	293.4	161.8	48.5	1.6
Pepin	9	117	4.8	2.6	8	29	1.7	0.4	39.2	16.1	6.5	0.6
Pierce	48	646	22.1	11.5	46	168	9.8	2.7	126.2	60.0	18.5	1.4
Polk	58	652	33.8	15.9	63	226	12.3	3.2	173.0	84.0	28.5	2.8
Portage	93	1 220	68.3	39.5	101	554	44.5	10.8	242.0	108.6	33.0	4.8
Price	21	328	10.8	5.2	22	59	3.6	0.8	81.7	41.6	14.0	1.7
Racine	265	3 771	263.8	132.8	291	2 195	125.4	40.3	766.4	376.1	126.9	24.1
Richland	20	156	10.4	5.6	19	58	4.5	0.9	79.5	35.8	12.5	2.0
Rock	223	3 402	196.2	97.5	241	1 052	63.8	16.8	650.4	292.3	101.6	19.8
Rusk	21	248	7.3	3.3	21	44	3.3	0.7	80.1	36.3	11.3	2.1
St. Croix	80	787	44.6	21.7	90	324	21.3	5.6	170.6	86.5	26.2	2.0
Sauk	98	1 358	67.3	33.9	97	345	23.1	5.8	231.9	110.8	39.6	3.3
Sawyer	26	199	8.7	4.3	33	112	6.4	1.7	98.1	42.8	13.7	2.3
Shawano	44	902	28.5	12.7	56	203	13.3	2.9	172.7	86.9	28.0	3.0
Sheboygan	176	2 412	134.3	74.8	172	967	56.5	14.6	428.7	221.2	69.7	7.9
Taylor	23	276	11.4	6.3	31	97	7.1	1.5	72.2	35.6	13.4	1.4
Trempealeau	32	207	7.6	3.6	50	168	10.6	2.4	136.6	59.2	20.5	2.5
Vernon	38	259	12.0	5.8	46	72	4.5	0.9	137.1	59.7	18.2	2.7
Vilas	20	99	4.9	2.0	34	99	6.0	1.4	124.8	66.9	21.5	1.6
Walworth	168	1 504	71.9	33.9	137	496	26.8	7.9	309.5	165.9	56.8	4.7
Washburn	22	264	12.0	6.1	31	95	5.9	1.3	110.1	54.5	13.6	1.8
Washington	168	1 700	82.6	37.6	195	1 374	85.8	24.1	332.5	201.7	60.2	3.5
Waukesha	800	9 241	551.7	274.0	648	5 262	423.2	126.2	1 176.1	687.2	203.2	9.5
Waupaca	80	1 086	53.0	22.2	94	277	18.1	4.6	254.0	135.5	41.9	3.7
Waushara	19	339	10.3	4.7	35	92	6.6	1.5	104.9	57.1	17.7	2.2
Winnebago	318	3 623	264.4	132.3	260	1 778	97.3	28.9	1 106.3	282.6	106.5	11.2
Wood	121	1 308	69.7	33.1	129	651	54.0	11.4	343.5	179.5	60.4	6.8
WYOMING	1 006	7 875	493.6	210.3	980	4 866	422.8	94.8	3 583.6	1 037.7	299.4	48.0
Albany	72	601	34.9	16.1	61	358	16.7	5.3	156.6	48.9	17.1	2.5
Big Horn	7	31	2.2	0.9	18	48	2.7	0.5	65.8	28.4	10.1	1.3
Campbell	54	272	21.2	8.8	84	545	48.0	15.1	85.3	33.7	9.5	1.8
Carbon	32	255	11.3	4.9	27	71	4.8	1.2	218.1	32.6	11.3	1.2

1. Firms subject to federal tax. 2. October 1, 2000 to September 30, 2001. 3. State totals may include programs not allocated by county.

STATE County	Salaries and wages	Defense	Other	Medicaid and other health-related	Nutrition and family welfare	Education	Other	Total (mil dol)	Intergovernmental (mil dol)	Total (mil dol)	Total	Property
											Per capita[3] (dollars)	
	171	172	173	174	175	176	177	178	179	180	181	182
WISCONSIN—Cont'd												
Dane	239.5	18.5	92.8	424.3	244.1	196.5	660.7	1 241.6	461.4	558.9	1 406	1 306
Dodge	10.8	1.3	4.8	19.9	4.4	1.7	6.1	188.9	85.1	58.6	711	657
Door	15.8	1.2	2.0	11.4	1.9	1.1	4.3	79.8	28.4	38.8	1 444	1 348
Douglas	9.2	0.3	1.3	33.5	10.7	3.6	6.4	161.7	85.5	47.5	1 099	1 015
Dunn	5.5	0.3	3.4	20.7	5.0	3.8	7.5	106.5	58.5	26.7	690	641
Eau Claire	23.9	5.2	4.9	52.2	10.5	5.6	17.3	268.4	138.2	77.8	872	840
Florence	0.9	0.0	0.2	2.6	0.7	0.2	0.1	14.3	8.5	4.1	780	771
Fond du Lac	14.1	2.0	7.9	35.0	8.6	4.0	5.1	263.9	126.1	87.6	928	908
Forest	4.4	0.0	1.7	12.0	2.6	1.5	1.7	28.2	17.3	8.0	834	789
Grant	9.9	0.1	2.2	29.2	4.3	3.7	2.7	151.0	83.4	36.2	732	723
Green	5.2	0.0	1.2	11.4	2.5	1.6	6.9	86.2	43.2	26.2	789	771
Green Lake	3.4	0.2	1.2	9.6	1.6	0.8	1.6	55.4	26.8	20.7	1 066	1 039
Iowa	5.3	0.2	1.5	9.5	3.2	0.9	12.4	57.1	28.9	19.9	899	839
Iron	1.2	0.1	0.3	6.4	1.0	0.8	0.7	21.0	11.7	6.3	970	900
Jackson	3.4	0.0	0.7	17.0	3.8	1.5	4.4	55.6	31.0	12.6	715	665
Jefferson	11.6	1.1	4.1	30.6	4.6	2.9	23.2	196.3	90.2	65.5	892	830
Juneau	15.1	2.1	1.2	16.9	3.2	1.5	5.2	68.8	39.1	17.4	727	669
Kenosha	25.2	8.8	14.2	55.1	18.3	7.0	9.8	444.2	210.3	169.0	1 183	1 108
Kewaunee	3.6	0.0	52.6	6.8	1.3	0.8	6.9	51.0	27.9	14.7	746	734
La Crosse	28.5	22.1	8.8	48.3	12.2	7.7	19.6	315.8	142.9	97.9	958	867
Lafayette	3.0	3.8	0.8	9.7	1.5	0.8	4.1	60.5	31.3	15.3	936	928
Langlade	3.0	0.5	0.7	17.8	3.6	1.4	0.9	58.7	32.6	17.5	849	790
Lincoln	4.8	0.0	1.1	17.4	3.4	1.3	3.8	84.1	44.8	22.7	767	716
Manitowoc	12.2	0.6	3.6	35.3	6.6	2.6	15.6	190.5	96.6	52.5	639	619
Marathon	32.8	0.2	29.1	55.0	10.7	7.4	23.9	372.6	180.2	114.2	933	859
Marinette	10.0	0.4	96.7	28.8	5.0	2.2	4.4	113.6	65.3	30.6	710	696
Marquette	3.0	3.6	5.0	6.4	1.5	0.6	3.4	32.0	15.6	12.3	831	786
Menominee	0.5	0.0	0.1	5.4	4.2	7.6	2.5	19.6	16.3	2.6	551	547
Milwaukee	552.5	80.7	178.1	817.1	256.2	91.1	181.5	3 478.1	1 758.8	1 206.8	1 328	1 241
Monroe	69.9	16.4	14.1	26.0	4.4	2.2	15.2	103.6	57.7	26.3	668	606
Oconto	5.6	0.1	1.3	17.5	3.6	1.4	8.8	82.9	50.5	20.0	600	557
Oneida	12.7	0.0	1.7	18.5	5.0	1.7	3.2	114.6	41.0	58.1	1 629	1 530
Outagamie	21.7	6.4	13.7	46.2	10.1	7.6	22.0	483.9	212.7	166.8	1 082	1 054
Ozaukee	9.9	33.4	3.1	9.3	1.9	1.9	10.5	202.6	58.8	101.6	1 258	1 186
Pepin	1.4	0.0	3.8	5.1	0.8	0.4	0.1	25.1	16.1	6.5	908	863
Pierce	6.7	0.6	2.2	15.6	2.6	2.5	1.1	100.3	59.8	27.0	767	724
Polk	7.6	1.5	1.8	20.2	4.9	1.8	10.2	116.6	63.6	30.8	805	755
Portage	12.3	0.2	19.7	24.6	6.8	3.1	8.6	163.0	84.2	52.8	816	742
Price	5.3	0.0	1.0	12.7	2.0	0.7	1.2	44.5	26.5	11.9	758	712
Racine	25.0	9.2	6.9	87.9	25.7	9.5	43.2	476.4	254.7	154.5	833	814
Richland	2.9	0.1	0.7	14.2	2.3	0.7	1.4	47.3	25.3	11.5	643	598
Rock	20.0	42.4	8.4	79.3	22.3	10.0	9.8	445.3	253.4	124.8	830	810
Rusk	3.1	0.0	0.8	14.6	4.8	1.2	2.8	62.0	35.2	9.7	636	540
St. Croix	9.1	0.6	4.1	13.5	2.9	1.4	8.8	146.1	72.3	47.2	824	756
Sauk	8.9	6.8	2.4	24.8	4.5	2.5	11.4	154.7	74.8	54.1	1 021	910
Sawyer	4.4	0.0	0.9	13.4	4.3	3.3	5.4	42.3	21.9	15.7	983	901
Shawano	6.4	0.0	1.6	27.1	4.2	2.4	3.0	93.9	50.8	24.8	643	596
Sheboygan	13.7	5.5	34.8	35.2	8.7	3.8	12.1	334.0	157.6	107.5	978	957
Taylor	4.5	0.1	0.8	9.2	1.7	1.1	0.5	52.4	34.4	11.0	569	559
Trempealeau	6.3	0.1	1.2	23.0	4.5	1.5	3.7	91.2	50.0	20.7	785	746
Vernon	5.8	4.4	2.2	24.7	3.1	1.6	5.6	73.1	42.8	17.3	637	626
Vilas	3.8	0.0	0.9	11.2	3.6	4.9	8.1	52.7	17.8	28.7	1 357	1 277
Walworth	12.2	0.6	3.1	25.2	5.1	3.4	6.0	268.5	80.4	110.9	1 313	1 210
Washburn	7.0	4.6	1.9	14.1	2.4	1.9	3.3	44.3	22.6	16.7	1 090	1 033
Washington	18.8	0.2	3.6	22.6	5.1	2.9	4.2	268.6	107.9	112.9	1 002	970
Waukesha	53.9	38.6	56.3	53.1	10.5	8.8	27.2	948.0	288.9	495.8	1 421	1 377
Waupaca	8.9	4.4	14.4	24.2	4.4	2.2	4.1	133.5	73.5	40.9	818	765
Waushara	3.3	0.0	1.0	14.6	2.5	1.2	0.7	48.5	24.1	18.3	851	806
Winnebago	34.9	548.9	11.7	49.5	11.9	6.2	19.3	400.6	171.7	133.8	892	866
Wood	12.0	0.0	3.7	44.1	7.2	3.6	13.2	226.5	118.0	71.5	943	922
WYOMING	434.5	95.6	245.5	218.4	82.1	102.6	810.0	X	X	X	X	X
Albany	12.1	1.3	6.8	19.3	3.5	5.9	28.3	97.3	36.2	14.5	489	238
Big Horn	4.5	0.0	4.3	7.1	1.2	0.7	5.6	44.9	20.7	11.1	1 003	668
Campbell	4.9	0.0	14.7	2.8	2.4	1.1	9.0	128.1	28.5	76.6	2 389	2 080
Carbon	8.1	1.0	129.3	8.2	2.8	1.1	19.7	58.1	19.1	21.1	1 333	1 069

1. October 1, 2000 to September 30, 2001.   2. State totals may include programs not allocated by county.   3. Based on the resident population estimated as of July 1 of the year shown.

STATE County	Total (mil dol)	Per capita[1] (dollars)	Education	Health and hospitals	Police protection	Public welfare	Highways	Total (mil dol)	Per capita[1] (dollars)	Federal civilian	Federal military	State and local	Democratic	Republican	All other
	183	184	185	186	187	188	189	190	191	192	193	194	195	196	197
WISCONSIN—Cont'd															
Dane	1 305.1	3 283	48.5	2.1	5.5	9.8	5.4	1 280.3	3 221	4 209	1 583	68 140	61.1	32.6	6.3
Dodge	205.7	2 495	36.1	3.6	5.1	14.1	11.9	125.6	1 524	198	295	4 248	38.7	57.5	3.8
Door	88.1	3 275	43.0	5.0	4.0	3.1	12.6	61.1	2 271	83	148	1 555	43.1	51.3	5.6
Douglas	157.1	3 638	51.5	5.2	4.8	3.6	7.8	129.7	3 002	116	153	3 184	62.6	31.9	5.5
Dunn	118.7	3 063	44.0	1.5	3.5	14.9	15.9	87.7	2 263	98	138	4 386	47.4	46.1	6.4
Eau Claire	274.0	3 070	51.2	5.3	5.0	7.2	7.8	149.5	1 675	380	317	7 648	50.3	43.7	6.0
Florence	13.6	2 614	44.9	8.5	5.2	0.4	16.7	11.1	2 124	22	18	297	33.9	63.5	2.5
Fond du Lac	269.4	2 856	52.1	7.3	4.2	6.7	7.9	138.9	1 472	252	336	5 199	39.0	57.0	4.0
Forest	33.8	3 528	52.7	2.2	10.4	4.4	13.0	21.4	2 232	118	34	654	45.8	51.0	3.3
Grant	154.7	3 126	53.7	7.0	3.3	8.1	11.2	87.3	1 763	171	174	4 699	48.7	46.6	4.7
Green	95.1	2 869	46.2	3.0	5.1	11.3	14.1	52.5	1 583	95	119	1 794	51.5	44.4	4.1
Green Lake	57.2	2 942	50.8	4.7	5.5	3.8	10.7	44.3	2 276	63	69	1 026	36.2	59.9	3.9
Iowa	63.1	2 847	54.6	0.8	3.2	8.3	14.7	43.7	1 973	94	80	1 296	55.4	40.0	4.6
Iron	19.4	2 995	43.0	6.9	4.6	0.5	19.3	10.6	1 632	24	22	340	46.2	49.4	4.3
Jackson	59.0	3 350	44.2	7.3	3.3	14.2	12.5	28.8	1 633	56	63	1 388	52.0	43.6	4.3
Jefferson	200.0	2 725	47.0	4.4	5.2	9.7	11.0	120.7	1 645	192	261	3 830	42.1	53.2	4.7
Juneau	71.9	2 998	46.2	1.4	3.7	9.5	14.2	43.0	1 792	262	86	1 471	47.1	48.1	4.8
Kenosha	454.2	3 179	51.0	3.9	5.9	7.3	4.9	429.8	3 008	289	539	8 016	50.9	45.3	3.7
Kewaunee	53.9	2 738	46.4	10.1	3.7	1.5	19.9	29.9	1 521	79	70	940	46.3	48.4	5.2
La Crosse	330.5	3 232	49.0	5.0	4.9	7.9	6.8	234.8	2 296	500	377	8 497	51.2	43.8	5.0
Lafayette	65.3	3 988	44.8	7.8	2.6	10.6	16.2	36.3	2 216	65	57	1 158	51.1	45.9	2.9
Langlade	62.9	3 059	45.2	4.0	4.0	5.3	15.9	32.5	1 582	50	73	1 183	43.2	52.7	4.1
Lincoln	88.5	2 987	43.7	4.6	4.9	11.0	13.8	76.3	2 574	78	106	1 805	46.8	47.2	6.0
Manitowoc	210.8	2 564	42.2	3.2	5.2	9.9	12.1	132.7	1 613	193	308	4 156	45.5	49.9	4.7
Marathon	399.6	3 264	46.8	13.0	3.7	3.1	9.5	225.0	1 838	529	438	6 734	45.5	49.5	5.1
Marinette	117.0	2 720	50.0	4.6	4.9	5.1	10.7	73.4	1 707	124	205	2 092	43.6	52.9	3.5
Marquette	44.6	3 009	52.4	5.7	6.9	3.4	13.5	25.6	1 732	54	54	689	47.8	49.0	3.3
Menominee	19.5	4 094	58.6	2.3	3.2	17.2	8.3	1.6	332	[3]0	[3]18	[3]358	77.0	18.2	4.8
Milwaukee	3 337.2	3 672	41.2	5.1	7.1	6.4	4.1	2 732.8	3 007	9 226	3 606	53 594	58.2	37.7	4.1
Monroe	106.1	2 697	43.1	3.0	4.1	13.8	15.4	74.6	1 895	2 348	259	2 121	45.7	50.3	4.0
Oconto	89.8	2 691	42.6	6.4	3.4	4.3	15.6	64.6	1 936	116	121	1 624	43.7	52.5	3.8
Oneida	115.9	3 247	57.0	1.8	4.6	4.1	11.5	80.3	2 248	264	128	2 369	44.1	50.4	5.5
Outagamie	494.5	3 207	50.7	4.4	4.4	5.6	10.4	406.1	2 634	372	559	7 963	43.2	52.1	4.7
Ozaukee	246.2	3 049	41.6	3.4	5.5	5.1	7.5	160.0	1 982	162	289	3 430	31.5	65.2	3.3
Pepin	29.1	4 049	53.9	5.5	3.1	5.5	17.4	14.3	1 992	32	26	518	50.6	44.5	4.8
Pierce	109.5	3 111	51.6	5.4	3.7	2.8	13.7	61.3	1 743	107	127	3 280	47.7	45.5	6.9
Polk	126.9	3 314	54.1	4.5	2.4	7.5	11.9	90.1	2 354	147	139	2 252	45.3	48.4	6.3
Portage	164.5	2 540	45.4	5.7	4.6	6.2	11.2	124.0	1 916	210	233	5 408	53.1	39.1	7.7
Price	43.6	2 771	46.2	2.5	4.2	9.6	17.3	28.9	1 839	119	55	959	43.0	52.2	4.8
Racine	479.1	2 584	43.2	4.4	8.3	10.3	6.1	284.0	1 532	422	657	8 486	46.8	49.5	3.7
Richland	49.0	2 734	37.8	5.6	3.4	14.8	15.7	41.6	2 319	60	63	1 029	46.3	48.2	5.6
Rock	465.5	3 097	46.7	5.1	5.4	12.2	6.5	271.6	1 807	347	533	8 288	57.5	39.0	3.5
Rusk	67.6	4 415	38.2	13.8	2.3	9.7	9.7	33.4	2 181	56	53	1 235	42.9	51.0	6.1
St. Croix	156.3	2 728	49.3	7.1	3.7	5.0	14.8	143.9	2 511	160	213	3 163	43.7	50.9	5.5
Sauk	175.9	3 320	51.0	6.3	4.1	5.5	8.8	130.8	2 469	151	192	3 102	50.8	45.2	4.0
Sawyer	48.8	3 052	45.1	6.2	3.3	5.7	19.3	12.2	763	73	57	1 030	42.9	51.1	5.9
Shawano	116.3	3 020	49.5	3.2	4.0	6.2	14.5	78.2	2 032	[3]122	[3]138	[3]2 041	41.7	54.2	4.1
Sheboygan	354.9	3 229	47.9	4.6	4.4	12.0	7.5	238.9	2 174	229	400	5 834	42.7	53.7	3.6
Taylor	55.5	2 883	47.8	2.3	3.6	7.2	16.3	29.0	1 506	93	68	905	36.2	58.7	5.1
Trempealeau	97.8	3 710	49.4	3.8	2.2	12.9	11.7	61.8	2 345	127	94	1 837	54.9	41.1	4.0
Vernon	77.9	2 865	49.9	0.9	2.7	13.8	14.1	51.3	1 888	116	98	1 721	50.4	43.6	6.0
Vilas	60.3	2 854	51.8	1.9	4.2	3.7	14.4	50.5	2 391	75	77	1 044	38.2	56.5	5.3
Walworth	283.4	3 357	36.4	15.4	6.8	8.1	7.5	221.9	2 628	203	305	6 330	38.3	56.8	4.9
Washburn	45.6	2 980	50.8	4.7	3.0	4.7	14.1	23.2	1 517	129	56	1 167	45.9	48.6	5.4
Washington	279.4	2 480	49.1	4.8	5.4	6.4	8.2	238.2	2 114	1 055	409	4 798	29.5	67.0	3.4
Waukesha	1 010.6	2 897	51.8	2.5	5.5	3.0	6.0	854.9	2 451	887	1 266	15 408	31.6	65.3	3.1
Waupaca	144.0	2 877	51.7	2.2	5.4	8.6	12.5	118.1	2 360	147	179	3 234	38.5	56.9	4.5
Waushara	56.6	2 631	48.2	6.3	3.2	5.5	14.3	40.2	1 868	69	77	995	41.4	54.4	4.2
Winnebago	434.1	2 895	40.4	4.6	5.1	7.1	9.2	345.0	2 301	580	542	10 423	44.7	50.4	5.0
Wood	223.1	2 944	51.7	7.2	4.7	6.0	9.4	112.9	1 490	210	269	4 342	44.6	49.8	5.7
WYOMING	X	X	X	X	X	X	X	X	X	7 066	6 237	48 821	28.3	69.2	2.5
Albany	89.3	3 005	29.9	34.3	3.9	1.5	2.5	33.0	1 112	245	184	6 110	38.5	59.4	2.1
Big Horn	43.8	3 972	49.2	26.5	3.2	0.2	3.6	27.4	2 486	106	66	1 231	20.6	76.3	3.2
Campbell	143.4	4 469	47.8	3.0	3.5	0.1	5.5	90.7	2 828	85	193	3 080	15.8	81.9	2.3
Carbon	55.6	3 507	43.0	20.0	6.2	0.5	4.5	17.4	1 101	142	91	1 745	32.1	65.5	2.3

1. Based on the resident population estimated as of July 1 of the year shown.   2. Data subject to copyright.   3. Menominee County included with Shawano County.

STATE/ County code	MSA/ PMSA/ NECMA code[1]	County Type[2]	STATE County	Land area,[3] (sq km) 2000	Population and population characteristics, 2000													
								Race alone or in combination (percent)					Age (percent)					
					Total persons	Rank	Per square kilometer	White	Black	Am. Indian, Alaska Native	Asian and Pacific Islander	Percent Hispanic[4]	Under 5 years	5 to 17 years	18 to 24 years	25 to 34 years	35 to 44 years	45 to 54 years
				1	2	3	4	5	6	7	8	9	10	11	12	13	14	15
			WYOMING—Cont'd															
56 009	...	6	Converse	11 020	12 052	2 292	1.1	96.2	0.3	1.8	0.4	5.5	6.4	22.1	7.0	11.0	17.1	16.1
56 011	...	9	Crook	7 404	5 887	2 795	0.8	98.6	0.2	1.5	0.3	0.9	5.2	21.7	6.6	8.4	16.2	15.6
56 013	...	7	Fremont	23 782	35 804	1 225	1.5	78.6	0.2	20.9	0.6	4.4	6.5	20.9	8.3	10.7	15.2	14.8
56 015	...	7	Goshen	5 764	12 538	2 262	2.2	94.9	0.3	1.4	0.4	8.8	5.8	18.4	9.4	9.9	14.4	14.0
56 017	...	7	Hot Springs	5 190	4 882	2 855	0.9	97.2	0.3	2.6	0.3	2.4	4.8	17.2	5.9	8.4	14.9	15.1
56 019	...	7	Johnson	10 791	7 075	2 677	0.7	98.5	0.2	1.5	0.3	2.1	5.2	19.0	5.6	9.7	13.8	16.3
56 021	1580	3	Laramie	6 957	81 607	637	11.7	91.2	3.2	1.7	1.7	10.9	6.6	19.2	9.6	14.2	16.3	14.1
56 023	...	7	Lincoln	10 539	14 573	2 114	1.4	98.3	0.2	1.3	0.5	2.2	6.8	24.1	7.2	9.8	15.6	14.6
56 025	1350	3	Natrona	13 830	66 533	735	4.8	95.7	1.1	1.8	0.7	4.9	6.5	19.5	10.1	12.1	15.8	14.7
56 027	...	9	Niobrara	6 801	2 407	3 028	0.4	98.8	0.2	0.9	0.1	1.5	4.8	17.8	6.1	9.4	16.6	14.4
56 029	...	7	Park	17 981	25 786	1 524	1.4	97.5	0.2	1.0	0.7	3.7	5.5	18.9	9.1	9.8	15.5	16.0
56 031	...	7	Platte	5 400	8 807	2 546	1.6	97.4	0.2	1.2	0.4	5.3	5.2	20.2	6.6	9.5	14.7	15.8
56 033	...	7	Sheridan	6 535	26 560	1 498	4.1	97.2	0.3	1.9	0.8	2.4	5.3	18.8	8.0	10.1	15.2	16.7
56 035	...	9	Sublette	12 646	5 920	2 791	0.5	98.4	0.4	1.0	0.5	1.9	5.9	19.9	6.0	10.2	17.2	17.7
56 037	...	5	Sweetwater	27 001	37 613	1 173	1.4	93.9	1.0	1.8	1.0	9.4	6.9	22.0	10.1	12.0	17.3	15.8
56 039	...	7	Teton	10 380	18 251	1 883	1.8	94.7	0.2	1.0	1.0	6.5	5.2	14.7	9.8	20.2	18.1	16.7
56 041	...	7	Uinta	5 391	19 742	1 807	3.7	95.7	0.2	1.6	0.6	5.3	8.2	25.2	9.0	11.9	17.3	14.5
56 043	...	7	Washakie	5 802	8 289	2 580	1.4	92.2	0.3	1.6	1.1	11.5	5.9	21.4	6.4	10.0	14.3	14.8
56 045	...	7	Weston	6 210	6 644	2 721	1.1	97.4	0.2	2.3	0.3	2.1	5.2	18.8	7.4	9.9	16.4	15.9

1. MSA = Metropolitan Statistical Area. PMSA = Primary MSA. NECMA = New England County Metropolitan Area. See Appendix A for explanation of these concepts. See Appendix B for list of metropolitan areas identified by type, with component counties.   2. County typology code from the Economic Research Service of USDA. See Appendix A for definition.   3. Dry land or land partially or temporarily covered by water.   4. Hispanic persons may be of any race.

STATE County	Population, 2000 (cont'd)				Population — change and components of change, 1990–2001							Households, 2000				
	Age (percent) (cont'd)				Total persons		Percent change		Components of change, 2000–2001						Percent	
	55 to 64 years	65 to 74 years	75 years and over	Percent female	2001	1990	1990–2000	2000–2001	Births	Deaths	Net migration	Number	Percent change, 1990–2000	Persons per house-hold	Female family house-holder[1]	One person
	16	17	18	19	20	21	22	23	24	25	26	27	28	29	30	31
WYOMING—Cont'd																
Converse	9.2	6.5	4.5	50.2	12 186	11 128	8.3	1.1	195	123	65	4 694	16.0	2.55	8.4	23.4
Crook	11.6	8.4	6.4	49.4	5 836	5 294	11.2	-0.9	69	63	-56	2 308	22.0	2.51	5.4	24.9
Fremont	10.2	7.6	5.7	50.5	35 967	33 662	6.4	0.5	630	440	-9	13 545	12.9	2.58	10.9	25.5
Goshen	10.8	8.4	8.9	50.3	12 389	12 373	1.3	-1.2	182	161	-169	5 061	5.7	2.38	7.7	27.6
Hot Springs	13.6	10.1	9.9	51.9	4 805	4 809	1.5	-1.6	73	84	-65	2 108	8.5	2.25	7.4	31.7
Johnson	12.4	9.7	8.4	50.9	7 245	6 145	15.1	2.4	74	89	183	2 959	23.4	2.36	7.1	28.5
Laramie	8.6	6.1	5.3	49.8	81 958	73 142	11.6	0.4	1 340	789	-143	31 927	13.7	2.45	9.9	27.2
Lincoln	9.6	6.9	5.5	49.5	14 793	12 625	15.4	1.5	227	122	113	5 266	27.3	2.75	5.1	21.0
Natrona	8.6	7.1	5.6	50.6	66 798	61 226	8.7	0.4	1 042	678	-70	26 819	12.5	2.42	10.6	27.5
Niobrara	12.3	10.3	8.5	51.2	2 396	2 499	-3.7	-0.5	34	38	-7	1 011	-2.0	2.28	6.0	29.5
Park	10.8	7.6	7.0	51.3	25 974	23 178	11.3	0.7	337	313	173	10 312	17.8	2.42	7.1	26.2
Platte	11.5	8.5	8.0	50.7	8 782	8 145	8.1	-0.3	112	131	-4	3 625	14.0	2.40	6.8	27.3
Sheridan	10.4	7.8	7.7	51.1	26 833	23 562	12.7	1.0	343	358	292	11 167	18.5	2.31	8.2	30.9
Sublette	11.0	7.2	4.8	48.9	6 018	4 843	22.2	1.7	74	69	94	2 371	29.3	2.47	5.3	23.6
Sweetwater	7.9	4.3	3.7	49.4	36 873	38 823	-3.1	-2.0	695	303	-1 151	14 105	3.6	2.62	9.2	23.6
Teton	8.4	4.4	2.5	46.7	18 437	11 173	63.3	1.0	214	89	63	7 688	68.3	2.36	5.7	27.3
Uinta	6.9	4.0	2.9	49.1	19 572	18 705	5.5	-0.9	376	145	-409	6 823	15.9	2.84	9.9	20.9
Washakie	10.5	8.3	7.6	50.2	8 102	8 388	-1.2	-2.3	136	128	-200	3 278	3.9	2.47	7.3	26.5
Weston	10.7	7.9	7.6	49.2	6 533	6 518	1.9	-1.7	82	85	-106	2 624	8.5	2.42	7.3	25.0

1. No spouse present.

Table B. States and Counties — **Vital Statistics, Health Resources, and Crime**

| STATE County | Births, average 1997–1999 | | Deaths, average 1997–1999 | | | | Physicians,[4] 2000 | | Hospitals,[4] 1998 | | | Medicare enrollees 2000 | Serious crimes known to police, 2000[6] | |
| | | | Number | | Rate | | | | | Beds | | | Total | |
	Total	Rate[1]	Total	Infant[2]	Total[1]	Infant[3]	Number	Rate[5]	Number	Number	Rate[5]		Number	Rate[7]
	32	33	34	35	36	37	38	39	40	41	42	43	44	45
WYOMING—Cont'd														
Converse	152	12.3	85	NA	6.9	NA	5	41	1	34	276	1 499	250	2 074
Crook	67	11.6	43	NA	7.5	NA	2	34	1	48	823	895	113	2 062
Fremont	486	13.5	359	NA	10.0	NA	64	179	2	177	491	5 506	1 072	2 994
Goshen	152	11.8	128	NA	10.0	NA	10	80	1	36	279	2 342	241	1 922
Hot Springs	45	9.7	65	NA	13.9	NA	6	123	1	49	1 037	1 071	162	3 318
Johnson	65	9.6	74	NA	10.9	NA	8	113	1	83	1 216	1 402	165	2 332
Laramie	1 141	14.5	621	8	7.9	7.0	178	218	2	266	337	10 710	2 869	3 516
Lincoln	182	13.1	94	NA	6.8	NA	6	41	2	33	238	1 907	231	1 642
Natrona	833	13.1	545	NA	8.6	NA	115	173	1	282	445	9 629	2 745	4 126
Niobrara	27	10.2	31	NA	11.6	NA	3	125	1	52	1 922	502	28	1 163
Park	305	11.9	243	NA	9.5	NA	52	202	2	356	1 381	4 082	668	2 591
Platte	96	11.2	104	NA	12.1	NA	6	68	1	86	997	1 681	203	2 305
Sheridan	258	10.3	282	NA	11.2	NA	50	188	1	64	254	4 564	745	2 805
Sublette	64	11.2	54	NA	9.5	NA	6	101	0	0	0	796	164	2 770
Sweetwater	547	13.8	241	NA	6.1	NA	41	109	1	99	249	3 617	1 802	4 791
Teton	185	13.0	64	NA	4.5	NA	47	258	1	104	734	1 364	603	3 304
Uinta	336	16.5	106	NA	5.2	NA	22	111	1	42	205	1 667	717	3 632
Washakie	103	12.0	88	NA	10.2	NA	11	133	1	30	346	1 468	141	1 701
Weston	66	10.3	65	NA	10.1	NA	3	45	1	71	1 097	1 185	155	2 685

1. Per 1,000 estimated resident population, average 1997–1999.   2. Deaths of infants under 1 year old.   3. Deaths of infants under 1 year old per 1,000 live births.   4. Data subject to copyright.   5. Per 100,000 resident population as of July 1 of the year shown.   6. Data for serious crimes have not been adjusted for underreporting; this may affect comparability between geographic areas and over time.   7. Per 100,000 population estimated by the FBI.

STATE County	Serious crimes known to police, 2000[1] (cont'd) Rate[2]		Education						Money income				Income and poverty, 1998			
			School enrollment and attainment, 1990				Local government expenditures, fiscal 1999[5]		1989				Percent below poverty level			
			Enrollment[3]		Attainment[4] (percent)					Households						
										Median						
	Violent	Property	Total	Percent private	High school graduate or more	Bachelor's degree or more	Total current expenditures (mil dol)	Current expenditures per student (dollars)	Per capita[6] (dollars)	Dollars	Percent change, 1979–1989 (constant 1989 dollars)	Percent with $100,000 or more	Median household income	All persons	Persons under 18	Persons 5–17 in families
	46	47	48	49	50	51	52	53	54	55	56	57	58	59	60	61
WYOMING—Cont'd																
Converse	108	1 966	3 240	3.5	83.4	12.7	18.6	7 095	12 023	27 713	-27.1	2.6	39 893	12.4	16.4	14.7
Crook	529	1 533	1 472	7.8	79.7	15.6	9.6	7 533	10 322	23 440	-15.5	1.0	35 684	9.7	12.4	11.2
Fremont	198	2 796	9 450	5.7	77.5	16.5	57.8	8 031	9 806	22 260	-35.1	1.4	30 417	17.0	22.4	18.7
Goshen	152	1 771	3 524	6.9	76.5	14.5	16.5	7 683	10 598	21 750	-7.5	1.6	30 650	16.0	22.2	19.4
Hot Springs	389	2 929	1 227	0.9	76.1	14.3	6.1	7 036	11 940	24 500	-9.5	2.1	30 080	13.3	18.6	14.5
Johnson	184	2 148	1 533	7.2	79.8	17.9	9.0	6 708	11 563	22 157	-19.9	2.5	32 674	12.4	17.7	15.0
Laramie	217	3 299	20 076	7.9	84.2	20.7	91.2	6 250	12 932	27 571	-6.7	1.7	39 728	10.7	16.1	12.7
Lincoln	235	1 408	4 069	2.5	83.2	15.2	24.3	7 087	10 558	28 488	-5.6	1.0	41 609	9.3	12.0	9.5
Natrona	355	3 771	17 410	5.6	85.3	20.4	79.8	6 505	12 992	27 586	-28.0	2.6	36 026	12.4	18.1	14.3
Niobrara	166	997	555	1.6	75.7	13.0	3.7	7 650	11 816	20 947	-2.6	2.5	27 637	17.3	22.4	20.2
Park	175	2 416	6 461	6.9	82.6	18.8	28.0	6 039	12 147	25 942	-12.7	2.2	36 920	12.2	16.9	13.8
Platte	114	2 191	2 155	5.7	79.7	11.4	12.1	6 962	10 757	21 822	-33.4	0.9	32 573	13.3	18.8	15.8
Sheridan	256	2 549	6 329	6.0	81.6	17.6	30.0	6 790	12 457	24 772	-18.4	2.1	35 418	11.5	16.8	13.3
Sublette	253	2 517	1 152	2.7	84.2	21.4	10.1	7 850	12 567	26 825	-10.4	3.2	40 599	8.4	11.7	9.8
Sweetwater	354	4 437	12 366	5.7	81.5	13.3	59.2	7 015	13 698	36 210	-10.4	1.9	51 090	8.1	10.5	7.9
Teton	411	2 893	2 182	9.3	91.9	30.0	14.7	6 364	17 234	31 586	2.2	4.3	47 058	4.9	6.7	6.1
Uinta	86	3 546	6 282	2.4	84.1	14.3	35.5	6 788	12 245	33 259	-12.1	2.6	43 952	10.4	12.6	10.8
Washakie	314	1 387	2 130	4.6	78.8	18.4	11.9	6 514	11 017	25 172	-17.7	1.5	38 286	10.7	15.4	12.3
Weston	295	2 391	1 794	5.6	83.2	12.7	8.9	6 876	11 263	26 213	-21.9	1.7	36 608	11.1	14.6	12.4

1. Data for serious crimes have not been adjusted for underreporting; this may affect comparability between geographic areas and over time. 2. Per 100,000 population estimated by the FBI. 3. All persons 3 years old and over enrolled in nursery school through college. 4. Persons 25 years old and over. 5. Elementary and secondary education expenditures, local government fiscal years ending between July 1, 1998 and June 30, 1999. 6. Based on population enumerated as of April 1, 1990.

STATE County	Total (mil dol)	Percent change, 1998–1999	Per capita[1] Dollars	Per capita[1] Rank	Wages and salaries[2] (mil dol)	Proprietor's income (mil dol)	Dividends, interest, and rent (mil dol)	Transfer payments Total (mil dol)	Government payments to individuals Total (mil dol)	Social Security (mil dol)	Medical payments (mil dol)	Income mainte-nance (mil dol)	Unemploy-ment insurance (mil dol)
	62	63	64	65	66	67	68	69	70	71	72	73	74
WYOMING—Cont'd													
Converse	266	5.5	21 453	1 533	150	22	69	34	31	16	8	2	1
Crook	131	6.8	22 714	1 165	51	15	35	16	15	8	4	1	0
Fremont	753	5.7	20 808	1 732	377	59	189	147	140	55	56	15	3
Goshen	273	5.6	21 565	1 497	101	51	66	48	45	22	14	4	1
Hot Springs	105	4.8	23 392	988	46	10	27	23	22	11	8	1	0
Johnson	162	8.0	23 652	925	66	14	57	24	23	14	5	1	0
Laramie	2 158	5.8	27 361	387	1 326	125	526	250	235	98	67	19	3
Lincoln	292	7.8	20 870	1 709	156	25	87	38	35	19	9	3	1
Natrona	1 922	5.2	30 427	194	958	312	472	223	211	103	66	16	4
Niobrara	58	12.6	21 662	1 465	21	7	18	11	10	5	3	1	0
Park	662	6.0	25 965	522	328	70	209	87	82	42	25	5	2
Platte	195	9.0	22 654	1 179	108	24	49	32	30	16	8	2	0
Sheridan	711	4.1	28 344	292	301	58	266	93	88	43	25	5	2
Sublette	145	7.5	24 992	672	60	17	52	16	15	8	4	1	0
Sweetwater	1 036	2.4	26 347	481	754	100	193	99	91	39	24	6	3
Teton	867	12.3	59 632	3	498	105	362	32	29	14	8	1	1
Uinta	416	2.7	20 486	1 841	239	34	60	52	48	17	19	3	1
Washakie	203	3.6	23 795	897	108	18	60	30	28	15	9	1	1
Weston	159	8.1	24 872	691	63	32	36	23	22	12	6	1	0

1. Based on the resident population estimated as of July 1 of the year shown.   2. Includes other labor income.

STATE County	Earnings, 1999									Social Security beneficiaries, December 2000			Housing units, 1990	
					Percent by selected industries									
			Goods-related[1]		Service-related and other[2]							Supplemental Security Income recipients, December 2000		
	Total (mil dol)	Farm	Total	Manufacturing	Total	Retail trade	Finance, insurance, and real estate	Services	Government	Number	Rate[3]		Total	Percent change, 1980–1990
	75	76	77	78	79	80	81	82	83	84	85	86	87	88
WYOMING—Cont'd														
Converse	172	2.6	30.7	1.6	D	7.6	2.2	D	20.0	1 865	155	112	5 234	-2.2
Crook	66	7.1	33.0	10.1	D	8.0	2.4	8.6	27.3	1 057	180	36	2 605	7.0
Fremont	437	2.4	20.6	3.9	50.8	12.7	3.3	24.7	26.3	6 748	188	751	14 437	-0.9
Goshen	152	18.4	D	6.2	D	7.2	4.2	17.9	22.6	2 676	213	201	5 551	10.6
Hot Springs	56	1.8	D	D	D	9.1	4.9	26.7	25.8	1 247	255	79	2 429	-4.3
Johnson	80	-1.1	D	D	D	12.8	6.2	21.0	28.2	1 664	235	47	3 112	2.7
Laramie	1 451	1.3	11.2	4.6	47.6	10.3	6.2	17.5	39.9	11 874	146	1 065	30 507	11.4
Lincoln	181	1.7	37.8	8.0	38.6	9.1	2.8	9.4	21.9	2 295	157	84	5 409	15.8
Natrona	1 269	0.3	34.3	4.1	50.9	9.1	5.2	22.6	14.6	11 333	170	1 199	29 082	2.1
Niobrara	28	9.9	D	7.8	D	9.5	2.8	8.8	35.7	570	237	25	1 456	1.5
Park	398	3.8	21.8	4.3	47.9	10.5	5.1	23.0	26.5	4 944	192	243	10 306	17.5
Platte	132	7.3	D	1.1	D	9.3	2.5	14.5	18.6	1 946	221	98	4 026	-20.3
Sheridan	359	1.3	12.3	3.5	57.4	11.1	7.0	24.6	29.0	5 113	193	336	11 154	2.1
Sublette	77	5.8	29.0	1.3	D	10.2	4.3	20.0	24.5	957	162	21	2 911	21.6
Sweetwater	855	0.1	49.8	10.2	35.0	7.7	3.0	11.3	15.1	4 286	114	322	15 444	2.2
Teton	603	0.0	20.0	2.2	68.3	13.4	15.7	34.0	11.7	1 554	85	64	7 060	44.3
Uinta	273	0.3	D	3.7	D	9.8	3.1	D	21.8	2 015	102	215	7 246	61.1
Washakie	126	4.4	29.7	16.2	45.2	8.0	3.4	20.0	20.7	1 700	205	84	3 732	-1.4
Weston	95	4.4	33.5	8.3	D	8.0	4.0	16.9	19.3	1 404	211	56	3 090	6.6

1. Covers mining, construction, and manufacturing. finance, insurance, and real estate; and services. 2. Covers private sector earnings in agricultural services, forestry, and fisheries; transportation and public utilities; wholesale trade; retail trade; 3. Per 1,000 resident population estimated as of July 1 of the year shown.

Table B. States and Counties — Housing, Labor Force, and Employment

STATE County	Housing units, 1990 (cont'd)								Civilian labor force, 2001				Civilian employment, 1990[5]		
	Occupied units										Unemployment			Percent	
	Owner-occupied					Renter-occupied									
				Owner cost as a percent of income											
	Total	Percent	Median value[1]	With a mortgage	Without a mortgage	Median rent[2]	Rent as percent of income	Sub-standard units[3] (percent)	Total	Percent change, 2000–2001	Total	Rate[4]	Total	Professional, managerial, and technical	Precision production, craft, and repair
	89	90	91	92	93	94	95	96	97	98	99	100	101	102	103
WYOMING—Cont'd															
Converse	4 046	71.0	51 000	15.6	11.6	285	20.4	2.2	6 575	-2.9	277	4.2	5 071	20.7	17.1
Crook	1 892	78.3	54 400	19.7	12.4	312	17.9	5.3	2 995	-5.0	114	3.8	2 411	20.2	11.5
Fremont	12 002	69.6	50 600	17.1	12.3	299	23.9	6.3	18 547	2.0	1 187	6.4	13 745	27.9	12.2
Goshen	4 790	70.1	52 100	21.7	11.6	287	23.7	2.7	6 407	-3.3	232	3.6	5 405	21.1	11.0
Hot Springs	1 943	67.1	53 400	20.5	11.6	285	23.8	3.5	2 466	0.7	105	4.3	2 216	26.8	12.5
Johnson	2 397	69.7	56 600	21.1	12.2	298	23.1	3.5	3 853	-2.6	118	3.1	2 972	21.2	9.8
Laramie	28 092	65.5	69 800	20.5	11.6	362	24.6	2.1	42 186	2.1	1 494	3.5	32 914	31.3	9.5
Lincoln	4 137	80.0	60 200	20.1	12.5	339	19.1	4.4	6 797	3.5	364	5.4	5 037	23.6	17.0
Natrona	23 837	68.9	53 100	18.6	11.7	298	23.5	1.9	35 239	2.6	1 429	4.1	28 391	31.0	11.8
Niobrara	1 032	71.4	33 700	19.6	11.9	245	21.1	1.8	1 244	-4.1	41	3.3	1 112	24.6	6.7
Park	8 757	67.7	65 600	18.7	12.2	340	21.6	2.4	15 436	0.0	680	4.4	10 781	28.1	12.4
Platte	3 179	75.6	52 100	17.0	12.3	292	23.2	1.7	4 465	-4.3	173	3.9	3 572	22.4	13.0
Sheridan	9 426	68.4	58 200	19.7	12.8	326	24.9	2.9	14 048	-0.6	563	4.0	10 789	25.8	12.6
Sublette	1 834	69.8	64 400	21.2	13.2	359	19.4	4.2	3 347	3.5	69	2.1	2 330	20.3	16.7
Sweetwater	13 616	70.2	70 900	17.0	11.5	350	18.6	3.4	20 388	0.9	941	4.6	18 115	22.5	20.8
Teton	4 568	58.9	133 400	22.0	12.5	457	23.2	3.9	12 633	2.8	284	2.2	6 633	27.8	16.4
Uinta	5 885	72.2	59 300	20.2	11.9	356	21.5	5.3	11 005	4.0	552	5.0	8 308	23.6	19.1
Washakie	3 156	71.8	54 600	20.7	11.4	297	21.2	2.8	4 599	-3.0	208	4.5	3 752	27.6	12.3
Weston	2 419	78.1	44 700	14.9	11.6	297	21.6	1.8	3 316	-2.2	143	4.3	2 977	17.8	15.7

1. Specified owner-occupied units.　　2. Specified renter-occupied units.　　3. Overcrowded or lacking complete plumbing facilities.　　4. Percent of civilian labor force.　　5. Persons 16 years and older.

Table B. States and Counties — Nonfarm Employment and Agriculture

STATE County	Private nonfarm establishments, employment and payroll, 1999									Agriculture, 1997			
	Number of establishments	Employment						Annual payroll		Farms			Farm operators
		Total	Health Care and Social Assistance	Manufacturing	Retail trade	Finance and Insurance	Professional Scientific and Technical Services	Total (mil dol)	Average per employee (dollars)	Number	Percent with—		Whose principal occupation is farming (percent)
											Less than 50 acres	500 acres and over	
	104	105	106	107	108	109	110	111	112	113	114	115	116
WYOMING—Cont'd													
Converse	370	2 704	393	60	416	84	99	67	24 822	348	8.6	69.0	65.5
Crook	185	1 479	166	221	176	D	D	37	24 951	498	6.2	73.3	68.1
Fremont	1 288	9 759	1 833	496	1 841	381	310	199	20 343	983	25.8	29.1	58.7
Goshen	374	2 926	738	233	526	137	67	52	17 868	688	12.9	51.0	67.9
Hot Springs	198	1 466	444	33	211	D	D	25	16 970	147	21.1	35.4	57.8
Johnson	305	1 664	256	D	320	95	70	33	19 888	315	10.5	71.7	68.3
Laramie	2 287	26 708	4 643	1 587	5 387	1 964	1 034	622	23 302	615	10.4	55.9	56.7
Lincoln	481	3 791	360	591	569	111	86	97	25 698	504	27.8	25.4	48.4
Natrona	2 580	26 574	3 800	1 702	4 058	1 085	1 101	667	25 094	311	20.6	48.9	58.5
Niobrara	94	467	84	D	79	D	D	7	15 572	278	3.6	84.9	80.9
Park	1 159	8 765	1 185	545	1 669	436	286	215	24 499	588	24.3	29.3	55.8
Platte	285	2 132	328	84	335	77	58	50	23 283	461	15.2	56.0	68.1
Sheridan	1 078	8 740	2 080	300	1 565	375	408	180	20 550	568	23.2	45.6	53.3
Sublette	315	1 296	152	58	201	51	52	30	22 785	275	18.9	54.2	61.8
Sweetwater	1 099	14 748	1 110	977	2 399	361	283	501	33 963	160	13.8	39.4	48.8
Teton	1 612	13 528	1 063	244	1 900	375	730	351	25 976	104	27.9	25.0	53.8
Uinta	570	5 763	1 216	293	1 127	121	143	149	25 776	300	23.0	40.3	55.3
Washakie	375	2 986	656	426	419	112	79	65	21 918	205	28.3	45.9	61.5
Weston	220	1 513	247	D	237	63	23	32	20 915	233	7.7	77.7	57.9

Items 104—116

Table B. States and Counties — **Agriculture, Land, and Water**

STATE County	Land in farms Acreage (1,000)	Percent change, 1992–1997	Acres Average size of farm	Total irrigated (1,000)	Total cropland (1,000)	Value of land and buildings Average per farm ($1,000)	Average per acre (dollars)	Value of machinery and equipment average per farm ($1,000)	Value of products sold Total (mil dol)	Average per farm (dollars)	Percent from — Crops	Live-stock and poultry products	Percent of farms with sales of — $10,000 or more	$100,000 or more	Percent of land owned by fed. gov. 1997	Water con-sump-tion 1995 (mil gal/ day)
	117	118	119	120	121	122	123	124	125	126	127	128	129	130	131	132
WYOMING—Cont'd																
Converse	2 515	6.4	7 228	46	79	836	122	71	27	76 968	6.1	93.9	67.8	25.6	14.3	224.5
Crook	1 690	9.6	3 393	4	181	746	203	70	32	63 345	7.1	92.9	71.3	16.3	13.2	44.6
Fremont	2 619	8.4	2 664	154	D	552	210	47	61	62 560	27.8	72.2	57.9	15.9	51.7	594.0
Goshen	1 266	2.5	1 840	134	289	629	337	65	131	190 197	20.2	79.8	74.1	29.9	1.8	165.5
Hot Springs	944	4.0	6 423	38	36	910	142	52	10	65 035	10.3	89.7	59.2	17.7	41.9	204.4
Johnson	2 132	3.7	6 767	45	61	1 250	192	70	28	88 314	4.9	95.1	73.7	28.3	31.1	299.9
Laramie	1 728	1.7	2 810	61	D	659	241	70	96	156 031	20.8	79.2	59.5	18.5	0.9	112.8
Lincoln	408	-26.9	810	89	115	455	571	54	23	45 574	13.2	86.8	51.4	12.3	71.6	498.7
Natrona	2 807	11.9	9 025	49	52	1 806	190	54	27	86 135	11.7	88.3	54.3	20.3	41.7	190.3
Niobrara	1 608	19.6	5 785	11	91	681	129	59	28	99 876	4.3	95.7	83.1	27.0	7.5	28.4
Park	1 011	26.9	1 720	114	121	632	395	63	66	111 485	47.8	52.2	53.2	21.6	63.6	868.0
Platte	1 285	-5.9	2 787	67	170	645	231	82	68	148 031	16.5	83.5	63.6	20.8	8.1	129.7
Sheridan	1 608	33.0	2 831	60	129	1 019	365	48	38	67 582	9.8	90.2	54.8	13.7	27.2	856.9
Sublette	592	-0.2	2 152	174	169	1 374	673	69	27	98 937	4.7	95.3	58.9	28.4	75.1	448.9
Sweetwater	1 421	-17.4	8 881	34	42	773	87	39	7	43 517	18.7	81.3	61.2	9.4	65.9	73.1
Teton	52	-15.5	504	17	21	444	939	43	5	44 749	29.8	70.2	49.0	13.5	88.9	89.0
Uinta	940	6.8	3 133	110	108	752	254	50	22	74 417	2.5	97.5	62.0	16.3	38.6	180.0
Washakie	450	13.1	2 195	50	58	887	448	85	29	140 201	45.5	54.5	62.9	30.7	66.8	259.0
Weston	1 421	-4.3	6 097	3	96	741	122	44	19	81 191	4.3	95.7	70.8	15.9	20.6	14.0

STATE County	Value of Residential Construction Authorized by Building Permits, 2000		Wholesale Trade, 1997				Retail Trade[1], 1997				Real Estate and Rental and Leasing, 1997			
	New Construction ($1,000)	Number of Housing Units	Number of Establish-ments	Number of Employees	Sales (mil dol)	Annual Payroll (mil dol)	Number of Establish-ments	Number of Employees	Sales (mil dol)	Annual Payroll (mil dol)	Number of Establish-ments	Number of Employees	Receipts (mil dol)	Annual Payroll (mil dol)
	133	134	135	136	137	138	139	140	141	142	143	144	145	146
WYOMING—Cont'd														
Converse	877	11	15	128	42.0	2.2	59	430	64.2	5.6	11	19	1.7	0.1
Crook	664	7	2	D	D	D	27	180	25.7	2.4	1	D	D	D
Fremont	2 574	43	43	260	85.2	3.9	204	1 735	296.8	27.8	55	217	15.8	3.4
Goshen	89	1	21	240	210.9	4.1	65	509	69.3	7.7	14	33	2.1	0.3
Hot Springs	352	4	3	D	D	D	32	229	20.4	2.2	5	D	D	D
Johnson	1 548	12	12	53	6.9	0.9	56	287	38.5	3.9	11	27	2.4	0.5
Laramie	33 835	245	81	665	267.5	18.6	358	4 851	855.5	77.8	88	321	27.7	5.2
Lincoln	19 480	145	10	23	9.8	0.5	80	623	86.4	7.3	12	29	1.2	0.2
Natrona	16 904	145	206	1 853	984.1	59.2	399	3 985	645.6	65.2	106	414	39.2	8.4
Niobrara	0	0	3	D	D	D	14	84	11.9	1.0	NA	NA	NA	NA
Park	18 204	137	44	178	51.8	4.1	219	1 528	271.3	24.5	35	123	10.8	2.0
Platte	622	8	8	D	D	D	46	374	68.5	4.8	13	24	1.3	0.2
Sheridan	9 792	99	40	246	146.1	6.4	179	1 561	240.8	23.9	76	177	12.5	1.9
Sublette	7 052	54	7	26	10.8	0.6	33	189	26.4	2.7	10	21	2.3	0.4
Sweetwater	4 951	41	82	469	188.5	15.0	212	2 399	402.8	38.6	51	181	15.2	3.0
Teton	164 019	326	35	201	49.3	5.7	242	1 619	300.9	33.7	67	322	46.4	6.0
Uinta	6 590	72	32	226	73.2	7.3	96	1 027	174.5	15.0	29	163	12.7	3.3
Washakie	595	8	15	156	31.8	2.4	70	474	80.7	7.2	12	37	3.2	0.5
Weston	468	11	6	26	4.2	0.9	39	267	38.4	3.3	5	9	0.9	0.1

1. Establishments with payroll.

STATE County	Professional, Scientific, and Technical Services[1], 1997				Manufacturing, 1997				Accommodation and Foodservices, 1997			
	Number of Establish-ments	Number of Employees	Receipts (mil dol)	Annual Payroll (mil dol)	Number of Establish-ments	Number of Employees	Receipts (mil dol)	Annual Payroll (mil dol)	Number of Establish-ments	Number of Employees	Sales (mil dol)	Annual Payroll (mil dol)
	147	148	149	150	151	152	153	154	155	156	157	158
WYOMING—Cont'd												
Converse	21	68	4.1	1.4	NA	NA	NA	NA	45	474	12.7	3.3
Crook	7	14	0.9	0.3	NA	NA	NA	NA	27	120	4.6	1.1
Fremont	78	283	16.7	6.7	41	D	D	D	152	1 397	39.9	11.4
Goshen	18	39	2.9	0.7	NA	NA	NA	NA	35	369	9.0	2.3
Hot Springs	9	28	1.3	0.5	NA	NA	NA	NA	31	234	7.2	1.8
Johnson	21	48	3.1	1.2	NA	NA	NA	NA	35	305	9.7	3.1
Laramie	199	843	64.5	24.7	48	1 349	606.3	45.2	183	3 930	106.3	31.1
Lincoln	24	84	4.2	1.7	20	579	200.8	17.4	53	369	11.5	2.7
Natrona	205	1 213	81.0	30.7	91	1 440	328.3	40.7	172	2 924	79.0	21.8
Niobrara	7	8	0.5	0.1	NA	NA	NA	NA	18	107	3.6	0.8
Park	64	218	12.2	4.3	41	524	66.1	13.9	130	1 283	90.0	21.7
Platte	19	37	3.5	1.0	NA	NA	NA	NA	40	352	9.1	2.4
Sheridan	73	304	24.1	7.4	NA	NA	NA	NA	88	1 199	36.8	10.5
Sublette	17	52	4.5	1.4	NA	NA	NA	NA	46	178	7.6	1.8
Sweetwater	58	236	17.0	7.6	29	696	458.2	36.1	109	1 838	61.3	17.5
Teton	165	577	61.8	23.6	NA	NA	NA	NA	180	4 303	166.3	43.8
Uinta	27	142	10.7	4.3	NA	NA	NA	NA	50	829	24.2	6.5
Washakie	21	70	3.0	1.2	NA	NA	NA	NA	35	320	8.4	2.1
Weston	7	19	0.9	0.3	NA	NA	NA	NA	24	155	4.1	1.1

1. Firms subject to federal tax.

STATE County	Health Care and Social Assistance[1], 1997				Other Services[1], 1997				Federal funds and grants, fiscal 2001[2]			
									Expenditures (mil dol)			
									Total	Direct payments for individuals[3]		
	Number of Establishments	Number of Employees	Receipts (mil dol)	Annual Payroll (mil dol)	Number of Establishments	Number of Employees	Receipts (mil dol)	Annual Payroll (mil dol)	Total	Social Security and government retirement	Medicare	Food stamps and Supplemental Security Income
	159	160	161	162	163	164	165	166	167	168	169	170
WYOMING—Cont'd												
Converse	16	96	4.4	1.4	18	47	3.6	0.7	60.6	21.8	5.9	1.0
Crook	6	D	D	D	7	D	D	D	37.4	12.4	3.7	0.2
Fremont	87	1 144	73.7	28.2	64	219	17.7	4.4	213.5	78.3	29.2	6.9
Goshen	17	60	3.9	1.2	30	71	4.1	0.8	76.7	31.3	9.9	1.1
Hot Springs	11	114	5.2	2.1	14	55	1.9	0.5	29.6	15.4	5.5	0.2
Johnson	12	27	2.5	1.0	12	50	2.5	0.8	43.3	19.3	4.5	0.4
Laramie	153	1 576	105.7	51.0	127	1 122	165.2	24.3	900.6	223.2	49.7	8.8
Lincoln	16	53	2.8	0.6	21	43	3.4	0.7	50.2	28.9	7.5	0.6
Natrona	168	1 524	93.3	40.8	154	808	57.2	15.2	303.9	139.0	44.2	9.8
Niobrara	2	D	D	D	3	D	D	D	18.3	5.9	2.2	0.9
Park	63	293	20.3	9.3	60	248	23.9	5.7	177.3	61.1	17.3	1.6
Platte	15	84	4.3	1.9	19	50	3.3	0.6	52.4	25.1	7.7	0.8
Sheridan	69	537	28.9	11.8	45	214	10.5	2.9	162.6	74.7	17.5	2.6
Sublette	15	52	2.6	1.2	12	18	1.2	0.2	23.2	11.8	2.6	0.2
Sweetwater	61	457	27.5	11.5	76	359	24.0	6.6	135.8	59.9	18.7	2.1
Teton	76	288	28.1	9.1	53	242	14.4	4.6	62.8	21.7	5.6	0.3
Uinta	30	147	9.8	4.3	39	142	8.6	2.1	55.3	27.1	6.1	2.5
Washakie	15	170	6.3	2.0	28	105	6.3	1.8	47.5	20.0	8.2	0.6
Weston	9	70	3.6	1.7	8	30	1.3	0.4	30.7	16.7	5.3	0.5

1. Firms subject to federal tax.   2. October 1, 2000 to September 30, 2001.   3. State totals may include programs not allocated by county.

Table B. States and Counties — Federal Funds and Local Government Finances

	Federal funds and grants, fiscal 2001[1] (cont'd)							Local government finances, 1997				
	Expenditures (mil dol) (cont'd)							General revenue				
	Procurement contract awards			Grants[2]							Taxes	
STATE County											Per capita[3] (dollars)	
	Salaries and wages	Defense	Other	Medicaid and other health-related	Nutrition and family welfare	Education	Other	Total (mil dol)	Intergovern-mental (mil dol)	Total (mil dol)	Total	Property
	171	172	173	174	175	176	177	178	179	180	181	182
WYOMING—Cont'd												
Converse	2.8	0.0	0.4	3.3	1.2	0.7	19.6	39.2	13.4	14.7	1 192	1 003
Crook	2.5	0.0	1.9	2.2	0.3	0.3	11.5	16.5	9.1	5.7	978	837
Fremont	19.1	0.3	6.3	22.2	7.3	23.4	10.3	100.9	62.7	24.3	678	568
Goshen	5.0	0.0	0.7	10.9	1.8	1.0	2.1	34.8	20.2	8.2	639	413
Hot Springs	1.0	0.0	0.2	4.2	0.5	0.3	1.6	13.0	4.9	6.0	1 282	1 096
Johnson	3.7	0.0	0.8	2.2	0.4	1.0	9.5	30.1	14.9	5.7	846	665
Laramie	222.1	89.7	18.1	63.8	33.0	40.0	126.7	251.1	109.5	42.9	547	361
Lincoln	5.1	0.0	1.4	2.7	1.0	0.7	0.9	59.3	23.0	18.4	1 324	1 187
Natrona	39.1	1.6	8.3	20.6	8.1	4.4	17.1	170.5	100.0	31.4	494	285
Niobrara	1.2	0.0	0.2	1.1	0.2	0.3	4.4	11.5	4.9	2.8	1 057	842
Park	28.5	0.0	28.8	9.4	1.9	1.3	22.4	73.2	32.3	21.3	830	767
Platte	5.2	0.0	1.1	3.8	2.0	0.6	1.1	27.3	10.7	6.9	813	650
Sheridan	25.7	0.0	4.8	15.3	2.6	1.2	11.7	84.6	38.3	15.3	608	315
Sublette	4.5	0.0	1.0	0.6	0.3	0.4	1.6	20.8	4.0	12.5	2 198	2 118
Sweetwater	13.6	0.1	3.1	7.8	3.8	1.5	19.2	170.4	41.1	73.8	1 858	1 604
Teton	13.9	1.4	10.6	1.8	0.4	0.5	6.2	84.5	11.8	31.0	2 228	1 304
Uinta	3.4	0.0	1.0	1.7	2.3	1.3	7.3	67.2	23.3	29.6	1 458	1 272
Washakie	6.6	0.0	1.3	4.4	2.9	0.4	1.0	20.4	11.4	6.2	723	676
Weston	2.0	0.0	0.4	2.8	0.5	0.4	1.2	16.1	9.7	4.9	755	588

1. October 1, 2000 to September 30, 2001.   2. State totals may include programs not allocated by county.   3. Based on the resident population estimated as of July 1 of the year shown.

STATE County	Local government finances, 1997 (cont'd)							Debt outstanding		Government employment, 1999			Presidential election, 2000[2]		
	Direct general expenditure												Percent of vote cast —		
			Percent of total for —												
	Total (mil dol)	Per capita[1] (dollars)	Educa- tion	Health and hospitals	Police protec- tion	Public welfare	High- ways	Total (mil dol)	Per capita[1] (dollars)	Federal civilian	Federal military	State and local	Demo- cratic	Republi- can	All other
	183	184	185	186	187	188	189	190	191	192	193	194	195	196	197
WYOMING—Cont'd															
Converse	43.2	3 512	46.4	15.5	4.7	0.4	4.4	33.6	2 732	68	73	1 135	20.9	76.2	2.9
Crook	15.6	2 690	65.7	1.7	5.3	0.1	6.9	3.9	674	72	34	558	13.3	84.6	2.1
Fremont	100.5	2 801	67.1	0.7	4.1	0.8	2.4	32.1	894	440	213	3 185	27.6	69.7	2.7
Goshen	34.2	2 664	63.4	4.2	3.4	0.2	2.7	12.3	956	92	74	1 166	26.2	71.4	2.4
Hot Springs	19.4	4 152	71.6	0.5	3.6	0.3	3.5	6.8	1 455	14	26	526	23.3	74.1	2.7
Johnson	23.0	3 393	40.5	35.2	3.6	0.1	4.2	9.4	1 383	68	40	686	15.8	82.1	2.2
Laramie	251.6	3 206	45.0	26.7	3.3	0.2	4.3	114.4	1 458	2 393	3 855	8 803	35.0	62.8	2.2
Lincoln	63.7	4 592	50.6	8.4	3.3	0.2	3.6	147.9	10 666	109	82	1 263	17.5	80.1	2.4
Natrona	176.6	2 775	53.0	1.2	5.0	0.4	3.5	62.0	974	657	374	4 596	31.1	66.3	2.6
Niobrara	10.9	4 154	37.2	24.4	2.7	0.1	2.9	19.6	7 499	23	16	348	17.1	79.9	3.0
Park	73.9	2 880	56.9	9.3	3.8	0.0	3.5	61.9	2 412	810	150	2 407	19.2	78.4	2.4
Platte	27.4	3 206	48.3	1.1	3.3	0.1	3.9	94.3	11 037	98	51	777	29.0	68.0	3.0
Sheridan	84.5	3 353	48.6	26.9	3.8	0.0	4.8	8.2	325	601	148	2 226	27.7	70.0	2.3
Sublette	23.0	4 035	52.1	4.1	6.4	0.7	6.8	34.8	6 117	95	41	485	14.5	82.8	2.7
Sweetwater	195.4	4 917	48.8	17.1	3.9	0.2	3.5	199.8	5 029	259	231	3 790	35.7	60.9	3.4
Teton	79.6	5 715	22.6	43.1	5.2	0.6	2.8	40.5	2 907	412	86	1 489	41.6	56.4	2.0
Uinta	72.5	3 575	57.6	0.5	5.3	0.4	5.5	159.7	7 872	77	119	1 946	22.5	74.5	3.0
Washakie	20.0	2 316	56.8	0.6	5.8	0.4	4.2	13.5	1 563	141	50	643	20.0	78.0	1.9
Weston	16.2	2 486	62.1	2.4	4.6	0.6	6.5	5.4	834	59	40	626	14.8	83.1	2.1

1. Based on the resident population estimated as of July 1 of the year shown.   2. Data subject to copyright.

Metropolitan Areas

(For explanation of symbols, see page xii)

Table C. Metropolitan Areas — **Land Area and Population**

CMSA/ MSA/ PMSA/ NECMA code[1]	Area Name	Land area,[2] (sq km) 2000	Population and population characteristics, 2000													
			Total persons	Rank	Per square kilometer	Race alone or in combination (percent)				Percent Hispanic[3]	Age (percent)					
						White	Black	Am. Indian, Alaska Native	Asian and Pacific Islander		Under 5 years	5 to 17 years	18 to 24 years	25 to 34 years	35 to 44 years	45 to 54 years
		1	2	3	4	5	6	7	8	9	10	11	12	13	14	15
0040	Abilene, TX	2 371	126 555	269	53.4	82.7	7.4	1.2	1.9	17.6	7.2	19.4	13.8	13.1	14.7	11.5
0120	Albany, GA	1 775	120 822	277	68.1	47.4	51.4	0.5	0.9	1.3	7.6	20.7	11.4	14.0	14.8	13.1
0160	Albany-Schenectady-Troy, NY	8 345	875 583	69	104.9	90.6	6.8	0.6	2.2	2.7	6.0	17.9	9.5	13.0	16.1	14.4
0200	Albuquerque, NM	15 392	712 738	75	46.3	73.2	3.1	6.6	2.4	41.6	7.0	19.3	9.8	14.0	16.3	14.0
0220	Alexandria, LA	3 425	126 337	270	36.9	67.3	30.8	1.2	1.1	1.4	7.1	20.2	9.5	12.6	15.3	13.2
0240	Allentown-Bethlehem-Easton, PA	2 853	637 958	81	223.6	91.1	3.5	0.4	2.0	7.9	5.7	17.8	8.4	12.4	16.4	14.1
0280	Altoona, PA	1 362	129 144	265	94.8	98.2	1.4	0.3	0.5	0.5	5.6	17.1	8.9	12.0	15.0	14.3
0320	Amarillo, TX	4 723	217 858	192	46.1	80.9	6.3	1.4	2.2	19.6	7.6	19.5	11.1	13.8	15.5	12.6
0380	Anchorage, AK	4 396	260 283	168	59.2	77.2	7.2	10.4	8.5	5.7	7.7	21.5	9.6	15.4	18.5	14.9
0450	Anniston, AL	1 576	112 249	288	71.2	79.7	18.8	0.8	0.9	1.6	6.2	17.4	10.4	12.9	15.0	14.2
0460	Appleton-Oshkosh-Neenah, WI	3 623	358 365	139	98.9	95.4	1.0	1.3	2.3	1.9	6.5	19.6	10.0	14.0	17.2	13.2
0480	Asheville, NC	2 863	225 965	188	78.9	90.9	7.3	0.9	0.9	2.7	5.7	16.2	8.8	13.5	15.6	14.8
0500	Athens, GA	1 529	153 444	233	100.4	74.2	20.9	0.5	2.8	5.1	5.8	15.6	23.3	15.3	13.1	11.3
0520	Atlanta, GA	15 861	4 112 198	9	259.3	64.2	29.6	0.7	3.8	6.5	7.5	19.1	9.5	17.6	17.8	13.5
0580	Auburn-Opalika, AL	1 577	115 092	283	73.0	74.9	22.9	0.6	2.0	1.4	6.3	17.0	22.7	14.5	13.6	11.0
0600	Augusta-Aiken, GA-SC	6 341	477 441	107	75.3	62.6	35.0	0.8	2.1	2.4	6.9	20.2	9.9	13.7	16.1	13.7
0640	Austin-San Marcos, TX	10 940	1 249 763	48	114.2	74.7	8.5	1.1	4.3	26.2	7.4	17.9	13.4	18.3	17.0	12.5
0680	Bakersfield, CA	21 085	661 645	80	31.4	65.1	6.6	2.6	4.5	38.4	8.4	23.5	10.2	14.1	15.7	11.6
0733	Bangor, ME	8 795	144 919	248	16.5	97.5	0.7	1.4	1.0	0.6	5.4	17.5	11.3	12.5	16.5	14.6
0743	Barnstable-Yarmouth, MA	1 024	222 230	190	216.9	95.6	2.4	1.0	0.9	1.3	4.8	15.7	5.2	9.7	15.3	14.8
0760	Baton Rouge, LA	4 108	602 894	88	146.8	65.6	32.2	0.5	1.8	1.8	7.3	20.0	12.8	14.2	15.4	13.1
0840	Beaumont-Port Arthur, TX	5 580	385 090	130	69.0	69.3	25.1	0.8	2.4	8.0	6.7	19.7	9.6	13.1	15.8	13.2
0860	Bellingham, WA	5 490	166 814	224	30.4	90.8	1.1	3.8	4.0	5.2	6.1	18.0	14.2	12.8	14.6	14.4
0870	Benton Harbor, MI	1 479	162 453	227	109.8	81.0	16.7	1.0	1.5	3.0	6.5	19.5	8.3	12.1	15.4	14.1
0880	Billings, MT	6 825	129 352	264	19.0	94.5	0.8	4.1	0.9	3.7	6.6	18.9	9.3	12.6	16.2	14.4
0920	Biloxi-Gulfport-Pascagoula, MS	4 623	363 988	137	78.7	77.1	19.8	0.9	2.5	2.3	7.0	19.5	10.0	13.8	16.1	13.2
0960	Binghamton, NY	3 174	252 320	172	79.5	93.9	3.3	0.6	2.7	1.8	5.8	18.1	10.2	11.3	16.0	13.6
1000	Birmingham, AL	8 253	921 106	67	111.6	68.0	30.3	0.6	1.1	1.8	6.7	18.4	9.2	14.3	16.0	14.0
1010	Bismarck, ND	9 219	94 719	305	10.3	96.1	0.4	3.6	0.5	0.7	6.3	19.0	10.2	12.6	16.4	14.3
1020	Bloomington, IN	1 021	120 563	278	118.0	92.3	3.5	0.7	4.0	1.9	5.1	12.9	27.7	14.7	12.6	11.1
1040	Bloomington-Normal, IL	3 065	150 433	238	49.1	90.4	6.8	0.5	2.4	2.5	6.5	17.0	18.6	14.2	15.0	12.2
1080	Boise City, ID	4 260	432 345	119	101.5	92.1	0.8	1.5	2.4	8.8	8.1	20.3	10.4	15.5	15.8	13.0
1123	Boston-Worcester-Lawrence-Lowell-Brockton, MA-NH	16 711	6 057 826	4	362.5	87.0	5.8	0.6	4.4	6.0	6.4	17.6	8.9	15.0	17.2	13.8
1240	Brownsville-Harlingen-San Benito, TX	2 346	335 227	147	142.9	82.4	0.6	0.6	0.7	84.3	9.5	24.3	10.5	13.8	12.9	10.7
1260	Bryan-College Station, TX	1 517	152 415	235	100.5	76.2	11.0	0.8	4.5	17.9	6.2	15.3	32.0	14.5	11.4	8.6
1280	Buffalo-Niagara Falls, NY	4 059	1 170 111	51	288.3	84.8	12.3	1.0	1.6	2.9	6.1	18.3	8.7	12.4	16.0	13.7
1303	Burlington, VT	3 260	198 889	202	61.0	96.7	1.0	1.3	1.9	0.9	6.1	18.6	11.5	14.2	17.6	14.2
1320	Canton-Massillon, OH	2 514	406 934	123	161.8	92.1	7.4	0.7	0.7	0.9	6.4	18.5	8.2	12.1	15.6	14.5
1350	Casper, WY	13 830	66 533	317	4.8	95.7	1.1	1.8	0.7	4.9	6.5	19.5	10.1	12.1	15.8	14.7
1360	Cedar Rapids, IA	1 858	191 701	207	103.2	95.2	3.3	0.6	1.8	1.4	7.0	18.3	10.1	14.3	15.9	13.6
1400	Champaign-Urbana, IL	2 582	179 669	214	69.6	80.4	12.0	0.7	7.2	2.9	5.8	15.3	23.1	14.7	13.5	11.4
1480	Charleston, WV	3 236	251 662	173	77.8	93.0	6.2	0.6	1.0	0.6	5.9	16.2	8.2	12.8	15.8	15.6
1440	Charleston-North Charleston, SC	6 711	549 033	96	81.8	66.1	31.3	0.8	1.8	2.4	6.7	19.1	11.2	14.7	16.1	13.4
1520	Charlotte-Gastonia-Rock Hill, NC-SC	8 746	1 499 293	43	171.4	74.6	21.0	0.7	2.3	5.1	7.1	18.3	9.1	16.7	17.1	13.4
1540	Charlottesville, VA	3 048	159 576	229	52.4	81.9	14.7	0.5	3.5	2.2	5.9	16.3	14.6	14.3	15.5	13.3
1560	Chattanooga, TN-GA	4 723	465 161	110	98.5	83.7	14.6	0.7	1.3	1.5	6.2	17.6	9.3	13.6	15.5	14.5
1580	Cheyenne, WY	6 957	81 607	313	11.7	91.2	3.2	1.7	1.7	10.9	6.6	19.2	9.6	14.2	16.3	14.1
14	Chicago-Gary-Kenosha, IL-IN-WI	17 941	9 157 540		510.4	68.7	19.2	0.6	4.8	16.4	7.4	19.5	9.5	15.3	16.3	13.0
1600	Chicago, IL	13 111	8 272 768	3	631.0	67.7	19.4	0.6	5.2	17.1	7.5	19.5	9.5	15.6	16.3	13.0
2960	Gary, IN	2 370	631 362	82	266.4	74.8	20.1	0.7	1.2	10.5	7.0	19.6	9.4	12.6	15.8	14.1
3740	Kankakee, IL	1 753	103 833	296	59.2	81.1	16.0	0.6	1.0	4.8	7.0	20.1	9.7	12.9	15.3	13.2
3800	Kenosha, WI	707	149 577	240	211.7	90.1	5.8	0.9	1.3	7.2	6.9	20.1	9.4	13.9	17.4	12.9
1620	Chico-Paradise, CA	4 246	203 171	200	47.8	88.0	1.9	3.6	4.4	10.5	5.7	18.3	13.6	11.4	13.4	13.2
21	Cincinnati-Hamilton, OH-KY-IN	9 865	1 979 202		200.6	86.3	12.1	0.6	1.6	1.1	7.0	19.4	9.5	14.1	16.6	13.5
1640	Cincinnati, OH-KY-IN	8 655	1 646 395	33	190.2	85.0	13.5	0.6	1.5	1.1	7.1	19.5	9.0	14.2	16.6	13.4
3200	Hamilton-Middletown, OH	1 210	332 807	149	275.0	92.2	5.7	0.6	1.9	1.4	6.9	19.0	11.9	13.4	16.4	13.6
1660	Clarksville-Hopkinsville, TN-KY	3 265	207 033	199	63.4	74.2	21.9	1.2	2.6	5.0	9.0	19.4	13.5	17.9	15.0	10.2
28	Cleveland-Akron, OH	9 355	2 945 831		314.9	80.3	17.4	0.6	1.7	2.7	6.6	18.7	8.2	13.2	16.1	14.0
0080	Akron, OH	2 344	694 960	77	296.5	87.0	11.6	0.7	1.6	0.8	6.5	18.2	9.5	13.2	16.2	14.2
1680	Cleveland-Lorain-Elyria, OH	7 011	2 250 871	24	321.1	78.2	19.2	0.6	1.7	3.3	6.6	18.8	7.8	13.1	16.1	13.9
1720	Colorado Springs, CO	5 507	516 929	101	93.9	84.5	7.7	2.0	4.1	11.3	7.6	20.0	10.5	14.9	17.6	13.4
1740	Columbia, MO	1 775	135 454	258	76.3	87.1	9.4	1.0	3.5	1.8	6.2	16.6	19.9	15.2	14.7	12.1

1. MSA = Metropolitan Statistical Area. CMSA = Consolidated MSA. PMSA = Primary MSA. NECMA = New England County Metropolitan Area. See Appendix A for explanation of these concepts. See Appendix B for list of metropolitan areas identified by type, with component counties.   2. Dry land or land partially or temporarily covered by water.   3. Hispanic persons may be of any race.

Table C. Metropolitan Areas — **Population and Households**

Area Name	Population, 2000 (cont'd)				Population — change and components of change, 1990–2001							Households, 2000				
	Age (percent) (cont'd)				Total persons		Percent change		Components of change, 2000–2001						Percent	
	55 to 64 years	65 to 74 years	75 years and over	Percent female	2001	1990	1990–2000	2000–2001	Births	Deaths	Net migration	Number	Percent change, 1990–2000	Persons per house-hold	Female family house-holder[1]	One person
	16	17	18	19	20	21	22	23	24	25	26	27	28	29	30	31
Abilene, TX	7.8	6.5	5.9	51.5	124 024	119 655	5.8	-2.0	2 625	1 474	-3 717	47 274	9.2	2.54	11.5	25.7
Albany, GA	7.9	5.9	4.7	52.6	121 262	112 571	7.3	0.4	2 803	1 314	-1 055	43 781	11.2	2.64	21.3	24.4
Albany-Schenectady-Troy, NY	8.8	7.1	7.2	51.5	877 895	861 623	1.6	0.3	12 338	10 264	524	350 284	6.0	2.41	11.3	29.4
Albuquerque, NM	8.4	6.0	5.3	51.0	723 296	589 131	21.0	1.5	13 265	6 557	4 080	275 028	24.1	2.55	12.8	26.7
Alexandria, LA	9.2	7.1	6.0	52.2	126 566	131 556	-4.0	0.2	2 493	1 667	-539	47 120	2.6	2.56	16.8	26.0
Allentown-Bethlehem-Easton, PA	9.1	8.0	8.1	51.5	643 489	595 043	7.2	0.9	8 720	7 785	4 847	247 148	9.4	2.49	10.2	26.0
Altoona, PA	9.7	8.6	8.8	52.1	128 391	130 542	-1.1	-0.6	1 797	2 051	-456	51 518	2.4	2.43	11.2	27.8
Amarillo, TX	8.0	6.4	5.4	50.5	219 376	187 514	16.2	0.7	4 339	2 359	-452	82 000	14.1	2.55	12.1	26.5
Anchorage, AK	7.0	3.4	2.1	49.4	264 937	226 338	15.0	1.8	5 283	1 370	852	94 822	14.7	2.67	11.5	23.4
Anniston, AL	9.8	8.0	6.2	52.2	111 338	116 032	-3.3	-0.8	2 091	1 550	-1 433	45 307	5.4	2.42	13.4	26.9
Appleton-Oshkosh-Neenah, WI	7.9	5.9	5.7	50.1	362 933	315 121	13.7	1.3	5 527	3 352	2 493	136 597	18.3	2.54	7.8	25.3
Asheville, NC	10.1	8.0	7.5	51.9	228 820	191 310	18.1	1.3	3 569	3 170	2 498	93 776	21.3	2.33	10.6	28.7
Athens, GA	6.9	4.6	4.1	51.1	155 073	126 262	21.5	1.1	2 505	1 313	437	58 557	24.4	2.47	12.3	26.1
Atlanta, GA	7.4	4.2	3.3	50.6	4 262 584	2 959 500	38.9	3.7	87 030	31 149	91 727	1 504 871	36.5	2.68	13.6	23.3
Auburn-Opalika, AL	6.8	4.6	3.5	50.8	116 572	87 146	32.1	1.3	1 800	910	629	45 702	38.1	2.42	11.8	27.8
Augusta-Aiken, GA-SC	8.5	6.2	4.8	51.5	480 454	415 220	15.0	0.6	9 149	5 354	-691	176 867	18.6	2.61	16.5	24.3
Austin-San Marcos, TX	6.3	4.0	3.3	49.2	1 313 231	846 227	47.7	5.1	24 724	7 688	45 701	471 855	44.7	2.57	10.2	26.6
Bakersfield, CA	7.1	5.2	4.2	48.7	676 367	544 981	21.4	2.2	14 327	5 938	6 571	208 652	15.0	3.03	14.5	20.3
Bangor, ME	9.2	7.2	5.8	51.2	145 385	146 601	-1.1	0.3	1 837	1 671	360	58 096	7.5	2.38	10.0	27.0
Barnstable-Yarmouth, MA	11.5	11.9	11.2	52.7	226 809	186 605	19.1	2.1	2 621	3 458	5 374	94 822	22.2	2.28	9.0	30.0
Baton Rouge, LA	7.8	5.2	4.2	51.6	607 523	528 261	14.1	0.8	11 904	5 569	-1 860	223 349	18.6	2.63	15.6	24.4
Beaumont-Port Arthur, TX	8.6	7.1	6.1	50.1	382 952	361 218	6.6	-0.6	7 027	4 973	-4 185	142 327	6.0	2.59	14.5	25.2
Bellingham, WA	8.2	5.9	5.7	50.7	170 849	127 780	30.5	2.4	2 527	1 480	2 989	64 446	32.8	2.51	8.8	25.6
Benton Harbor, MI	9.6	7.5	6.9	51.5	161 820	161 378	0.7	-0.4	2 802	2 099	-1 293	63 569	4.2	2.49	13.2	27.1
Billings, MT	8.8	6.8	6.5	51.2	130 398	113 419	14.0	0.8	2 048	1 357	409	52 084	16.5	2.43	10.1	27.9
Biloxi-Gulfport-Pascagoula, MS	9.1	6.6	4.6	50.3	366 263	312 368	16.5	0.6	6 875	4 253	-206	136 111	21.7	2.60	14.4	23.9
Binghamton, NY	9.5	7.9	7.8	51.5	250 887	264 497	-4.6	-0.6	3 456	3 127	-1 691	100 474	-0.2	2.42	10.6	29.3
Birmingham, AL	8.7	6.8	5.9	52.2	928 108	839 942	9.7	0.8	17 042	11 817	1 837	361 304	13.0	2.49	14.8	26.7
Bismarck, ND	8.2	6.8	6.2	50.9	95 218	83 831	13.0	0.5	1 346	846	31	37 559	19.8	2.44	8.7	27.5
Bloomington, IN	6.7	4.9	4.3	50.9	119 880	108 978	10.6	-0.6	1 611	910	-1 385	46 898	19.2	2.27	8.1	32.4
Bloomington-Normal, IL	6.9	5.0	4.7	51.7	151 878	129 180	16.5	1.0	2 429	1 252	331	56 746	21.3	2.45	8.8	27.6
Boise City, ID	7.3	4.9	4.8	50.0	452 158	295 851	46.1	4.6	8 607	3 437	14 394	158 426	45.7	2.67	9.6	22.6
Boston-Worcester-Lawrence-Lowell-Brockton, MA-NH	8.5	6.4	6.3	51.6	6 099 037	5 685 769	6.5	0.7	98 483	63 416	7 279	2 313 452	9.6	2.54	11.0	27.0
Brownsville-Harlingen-San Benito, TX	7.1	6.3	4.8	52.1	344 782	260 120	28.9	2.9	10 262	2 275	1 695	97 267	32.7	3.40	17.4	15.4
Bryan-College Station, TX	5.2	3.5	3.2	49.5	151 660	121 862	25.1	-0.5	2 751	826	-2 730	55 202	26.2	2.52	10.0	25.5
Buffalo-Niagara Falls, NY	9.1	8.0	7.8	52.1	1 162 917	1 189 340	-1.6	-0.6	17 378	15 601	-8 643	468 719	1.5	2.42	13.5	30.2
Burlington, VT	8.1	5.4	4.5	51.0	200 995	177 059	12.3	1.1	2 864	1 639	922	75 978	17.3	2.51	9.0	25.0
Canton-Massillon, OH	9.6	7.7	7.3	51.9	406 524	394 106	3.3	0.1	6 513	5 192	-1 576	159 442	6.8	2.49	11.2	25.9
Casper, WY	8.6	7.1	5.6	50.6	66 798	61 226	8.7	0.4	1 042	678	-70	26 819	12.5	2.42	10.6	27.5
Cedar Rapids, IA	8.5	6.2	6.1	51.0	193 165	168 767	13.6	0.8	3 373	1 823	5	76 753	17.2	2.43	9.0	27.5
Champaign-Urbana, IL	6.6	5.1	4.7	49.7	179 643	173 025	3.8	0.0	2 781	1 301	-1 473	70 597	10.5	2.33	9.2	31.4
Charleston, WV	10.1	8.2	7.2	52.1	249 018	250 454	0.5	-1.1	3 780	3 795	-2 585	106 254	5.8	2.34	11.6	28.9
Charleston-North Charleston, SC	8.6	5.8	4.5	50.9	554 831	506 877	8.3	1.1	10 181	5 339	1 203	207 957	17.0	2.55	15.3	24.8
Charlotte-Gastonia-Rock Hill, NC-SC	8.2	5.6	4.6	50.9	1 544 944	1 161 546	29.1	3.0	28 991	14 667	31 172	575 293	30.5	2.55	12.1	24.5
Charlottesville, VA	8.4	6.5	5.3	52.4	161 987	131 373	21.5	1.5	2 455	1 471	1 395	61 688	26.6	2.43	10.4	27.4
Chattanooga, TN-GA	9.8	7.4	6.1	51.9	467 716	424 176	9.7	0.5	7 354	6 027	1 333	185 144	13.5	2.46	12.8	26.1
Cheyenne, WY	8.6	6.1	5.3	49.8	81 958	73 142	11.6	0.4	1 340	789	-143	31 927	13.7	2.45	9.9	27.2
Chicago-Gary-Kenosha, IL-IN-WI	8.1	5.7	5.2	51.1	9 233 053	8 239 820	11.1	0.8	181 834	91 005	-17 482	3 302 211	11.2	2.72	13.4	26.2
Chicago, IL	8.0	5.6	5.1	51.1	8 342 190	7 410 858	11.6	0.8	165 854	80 903	-17 936	2 971 690	11.2	2.73	13.3	26.4
Gary, IN	9.0	6.8	5.8	51.6	634 217	604 526	4.4	0.5	11 390	7 256	-1 102	236 282	9.4	2.63	14.9	24.9
Kankakee, IL	8.8	6.7	6.3	51.1	104 122	96 255	7.9	0.3	1 897	1 333	-238	38 182	10.3	2.61	13.1	24.9
Kenosha, WI	7.9	5.9	5.6	50.4	152 524	128 181	16.7	2.0	2 693	1 513	1 794	56 057	19.2	2.60	11.5	25.5
Chico-Paradise, CA	8.6	7.5	8.3	51.0	205 973	182 120	11.6	1.4	2 809	2 679	2 710	79 566	11.0	2.48	11.2	27.2
Cincinnati-Hamilton, OH-KY-IN	8.2	6.3	5.4	51.4	1 994 521	1 817 542	8.9	0.8	36 172	21 569	518	768 130	13.1	2.52	12.2	27.3
Cincinnati, OH-KY-IN	8.3	6.3	5.6	51.5	1 657 508	1 526 063	7.9	0.7	30 271	18 349	-1 130	645 048	12.3	2.50	12.4	28.2
Hamilton-Middletown, OH	8.1	6.1	4.6	51.2	337 013	291 479	14.2	1.3	5 901	3 220	1 648	123 082	17.7	2.61	10.7	22.7
Clarksville-Hopkinsville, TN-KY	6.6	4.8	3.7	49.3	206 672	169 439	22.2	-0.2	5 108	1 795	-3 584	73 187	30.7	2.69	12.7	20.9
Cleveland-Akron, OH	9.0	7.3	7.0	52.0	2 942 641	2 859 662	3.0	0.1	49 600	36 406	-15 800	1 166 799	6.6	2.47	13.4	28.7
Akron, OH	8.7	7.1	6.4	51.7	696 960	657 575	5.7	0.3	11 417	8 043	-1 078	274 237	10.0	2.47	12.1	27.0
Cleveland-Lorain-Elyria, OH	9.0	7.4	7.2	52.1	2 245 681	2 202 087	2.2	-0.2	38 183	28 363	-14 722	892 562	5.6	2.47	13.8	29.2
Colorado Springs, CO	7.3	4.9	3.8	49.8	533 428	397 014	30.2	3.2	10 615	3 602	9 610	192 409	30.9	2.61	10.2	23.9
Columbia, MO	6.6	4.4	4.2	51.7	136 774	112 379	20.5	1.0	2 133	1 024	261	53 094	26.6	2.38	10.4	28.7

1. No spouse present.

Area Name	Births, average 1997–1999 Total	Rate[1]	Deaths, average 1997–1999 Number Total	Infant[2]	Rate Total[1]	Infant[3]	Physicians,[4] 1998 Number	Rate[5]	Hospitals,[4] 1998 Number	Beds Number	Rate[5]	Medicare enrollees 1999	Serious crimes known to police, 2000[6] Total Number	Rate[7]
	32	33	34	35	36	37	38	39	40	41	42	43	44	45
Abilene, TX	2 013	16.5	1 118	16	9.2	7.9	268	220	2	494	405	18 142	4 923	3 890
Albany, GA	1 940	16.5	976	NA	8.3	NA	226	191	2	601	509	15 118	6 762	5 597
Albany-Schenectady-Troy, NY	10 427	12.0	8 220	NA	9.4	NA	2 372	272	12	3 235	371	140 499	28 528	3 258
Albuquerque, NM	10 659	15.3	5 044	70	7.3	6.6	2 065	304	8	1 619	239	87 249	48 794	6 873
Alexandria, LA	1 863	14.7	1 309	18	10.3	9.7	306	241	3	746	588	19 949	8 742	7 108
Allentown-Bethlehem-Easton, PA	7 161	11.6	6 180	NA	10.0	NA	1 498	243	9	2 227	361	110 456	17 672	3 033
Altoona, PA	1 386	10.6	1 573	10	12.1	7.2	283	217	4	593	454	24 773	3 539	2 740
Amarillo, TX	3 376	16.2	1 826	31	8.8	9.2	490	235	5	1 026	492	27 042	14 706	6 750
Anchorage, AK	NA	NA	NA	NA	NA	NA	655	257	2	603	236	16 091	NA	NA
Anniston, AL	1 556	13.3	1 248	18	10.7	11.6	176	150	3	366	313	20 378	5 420	5 982
Appleton-Oshkosh-Neenah, WI	4 400	12.8	2 657	NA	7.7	NA	632	183	6	929	270	45 035	8 021	2 238
Asheville, NC	2 617	12.3	2 337	22	10.9	8.4	697	326	2	714	334	39 384	8 555	3 852
Athens, GA	1 873	13.5	996	NA	7.2	NA	283	204	2	486	350	15 983	8 566	5 600
Atlanta, GA	60 954	16.3	23 927	NA	6.4	NA	8 138	217	44	9 404	251	345 389	198 438	4 857
Auburn-Opalika, AL	1 372	13.7	699	13	7.0	9.5	137	136	1	289	288	10 319	6 506	5 653
Augusta-Aiken, GA-SC	6 726	14.7	3 986	NA	8.7	NA	1 482	323	7	1 891	413	59 409	21 936	4 594
Austin-San Marcos, TX	18 482	16.7	5 934	NA	5.4	NA	2 214	200	13	1 892	171	95 875	56 196	4 497
Bakersfield, CA	11 312	17.9	4 590	78	7.3	6.9	868	137	11	1 649	261	72 391	25 533	3 859
Bangor, ME	1 536	10.7	1 328	12	9.3	7.8	350	246	4	633	445	23 525	4 230	2 930
Barnstable-Yarmouth, MA	2 108	10.1	2 633	10	12.6	4.7	581	279	2	385	185	55 123	6 654	2 994
Baton Rouge, LA	8 817	15.3	4 396	NA	7.6	NA	1 101	191	8	1 746	304	62 918	43 325	7 473
Beaumont-Port Arthur, TX	5 121	13.6	3 853	NA	10.3	NA	610	162	9	1 782	474	57 174	18 473	4 797
Bellingham, WA	1 976	12.6	1 152	6	7.3	3.0	325	207	1	228	145	20 976	7 687	4 608
Benton Harbor, MI	2 123	13.2	1 596	22	10.0	10.4	242	151	4	733	457	28 086	6 207	3 835
Billings, MT	1 618	12.8	1 065	13	8.4	8.0	357	283	2	520	412	19 040	7 349	5 681
Biloxi-Gulfport-Pascagoula, MS	5 236	15.0	3 236	NA	9.3	NA	762	218	7	1 234	353	46 960	20 794	6 190
Binghamton, NY	2 867	11.5	2 579	NA	10.4	NA	541	217	3	802	322	45 477	6 492	2 581
Birmingham, AL	12 768	14.1	9 190	NA	10.1	NA	2 756	303	16	4 942	544	134 321	40 453	5 087
Bismarck, ND	1 118	12.2	681	NA	7.4	NA	267	292	3	549	600	13 636	2 628	2 775
Bloomington, IN	1 277	11.0	703	9	6.1	7.0	239	208	1	265	230	12 352	4 316	3 580
Bloomington-Normal, IL	1 905	13.3	971	15	6.8	7.9	264	185	2	322	226	16 265	NA	NA
Boise City, ID	6 396	16.1	2 622	38	6.6	5.9	801	202	5	870	220	45 740	17 222	3 983
Boston-Worcester-Lawrence-Lowell-Brockton, MA-NH....	78 239	13.3	49 609	396	8.5	5.1	19 998	341	82	18 725	319	853 150	164 057	2 896
Brownsville-Harlingen-San Benito, TX	7 453	22.9	1 841	33	5.7	4.4	383	117	5	951	291	35 311	20 720	6 181
Bryan-College Station, TX	1 998	15.0	643	12	4.8	6.0	271	203	2	256	192	10 788	8 277	5 431
Buffalo-Niagara Falls, NY	14 211	12.3	12 400	111	10.8	7.8	3 257	283	17	5 074	440	208 202	39 869	3 908
Burlington, VT	2 532	13.1	1 262	NA	6.5	NA	722	374	3	652	338	21 230	6 923	3 606
Canton-Massillon, OH	5 075	12.6	4 056	32	10.1	6.3	792	197	5	1 710	425	69 684	NA	NA
Casper, WY	833	13.1	545	NA	8.6	NA	124	196	1	282	445	9 592	2 745	4 126
Cedar Rapids, IA	2 556	14.0	1 400	14	7.6	5.5	354	194	2	877	480	26 037	7 240	3 909
Champaign-Urbana, IL	2 219	13.1	1 058	17	6.3	7.7	437	260	2	555	331	18 628	NA	NA
Charleston, WV	2 956	11.7	2 939	NA	11.6	NA	735	290	6	1 346	532	46 087	10 329	4 121
Charleston-North Charleston, SC	7 922	14.6	4 027	83	7.4	10.5	1 579	292	8	1 871	346	64 144	32 582	5 934
Charlotte-Gastonia-Rock Hill, NC-SC	20 960	15.1	11 065	157	8.0	7.5	2 645	191	12	3 445	249	172 920	82 367	5 867
Charlottesville, VA	1 867	12.5	1 137	NA	7.6	NA	1 044	700	2	734	492	19 850	5 304	3 324
Chattanooga, TN-GA	5 860	13.0	4 612	NA	10.2	NA	1 053	234	12	1 966	437	71 163	27 953	6 009
Cheyenne, WY	1 141	14.5	621	8	7.9	7.0	197	250	2	266	337	10 500	2 869	3 516
Chicago-Gary-Kenosha, IL-IN-WI	140 615	15.9	71 117	1 247	8.1	8.9	21 849	248	104	28 440	323	1 071 989	NA	NA
Chicago, IL	128 274	16.1	63 126	1 138	7.9	8.9	20 506	258	91	24 995	315	948 937	NA	NA
Gary, IN	8 716	13.9	5 757	83	9.2	9.5	1 000	160	9	2 656	426	88 485	22 457	4 185
Kankakee, IL	1 506	14.7	1 056	11	10.3	7.3	158	155	2	482	472	16 174	NA	NA
Kenosha, WI	2 119	14.7	1 178	15	8.1	7.1	185	128	2	307	213	18 393	4 742	3 170
Chico-Paradise, CA	2 265	11.7	2 161	13	11.1	5.7	383	197	5	661	340	35 957	7 213	3 550
Cincinnati-Hamilton, OH-KY-IN	28 143	14.4	16 954	NA	8.7	NA	4 409	226	25	6 164	316	264 319	61 342	3 928
Cincinnati, OH-KY-IN	23 633	14.6	14 404	NA	8.9	NA	4 034	249	20	5 372	332	223 760	46 785	3 760
Hamilton-Middletown, OH .	4 510	13.7	2 550	41	7.7	9.1	375	113	5	792	240	40 559	14 557	4 589
Clarksville-Hopkinsville, TN-KY	3 907	19.6	1 364	29	6.8	7.4	303	152	2	390	195	19 494	NA	NA
Cleveland-Akron, OH	38 766	13.3	28 544	313	9.8	8.1	8 263	284	44	11 528	396	458 068	NA	NA
Akron, OH	8 958	13.0	6 290	63	9.1	7.0	1 535	223	7	2 221	322	101 745	17 541	2 631
Cleveland-Lorain-Elyria, OH	29 808	13.4	22 254	250	10.0	8.4	6 728	303	37	9 307	419	356 323	NA	NA
Colorado Springs, CO	7 818	15.9	2 785	68	5.7	8.7	1 016	207	4	1 008	206	50 821	21 439	4 155
Columbia, MO	1 773	13.7	785	10	6.1	5.6	813	630	3	931	721	13 703	4 809	3 550

1. Per 1,000 estimated resident population, average 1997–1999.   2. Deaths of infants under 1 year old.   3. Deaths of infants under 1 year old per 1,000 live births.   4. Data subject to copyright.   5. Per 100,000 resident population as of July 1 of the year shown.   6. Data for serious crimes have not been adjusted for underreporting; this may affect comparability between geographic areas and over time.   7. Per 100,000 population estimated by the FBI.

Area Name	Rate[2] Violent	Property	Enrollment[3] Total	Percent private	Attainment[4] (percent) High school graduate or more	Bach-elor's degree or more	Local government expenditures, fiscal 1999[5] Total current expenditures (mil dol)	Current expenditures per student (dollars)	Money income 1989 Per capita[6] (dollars)	Households Median Dollars	Percent change, 1979–1989 (constant 1989 dollars)	Percent with $100,000 or more	Income and poverty, 1998 Median house-hold income	Percent below poverty level All persons	Persons under 18	Persons 5–17 in families
	46	47	48	49	50	51	52	53	54	55	56	57	58	59	60	61
Abilene, TX	332	3 558	34 059	26.4	75.4	20.7	141.3	5 785	11 791	24 660	-2.4	2.2	NA	16.3	23.0	21.7
Albany, GA	509	5 088	33 336	11.2	67.9	16.5	138.7	6 148	10 919	24 699	-5.2	2.3	NA	21.3	30.4	29.3
Albany-Schenectady-Troy, NY	317	2 941	221 422	22.8	79.8	23.6	1 185.9	8 745	15 152	32 427	15.8	3.7	NA	10.6	16.8	16.4
Albuquerque, NM	924	5 949	162 926	10.6	81.1	24.8	596.9	5 237	13 042	27 317	NA	3.1	NA	14.3	21.5	18.4
Alexandria, LA	708	6 400	34 655	13.5	69.0	14.6	129.9	5 427	10 014	20 810	-7.3	2.1	NA	20.1	28.9	26.4
Allentown-Bethlehem-Easton, PA	286	2 747	137 602	24.4	73.5	17.4	699.0	7 434	14 730	31 875	4.3	3.3	NA	8.0	13.5	12.4
Altoona, PA	245	2 495	29 518	13.6	75.0	10.5	130.9	6 299	11 233	23 270	-6.0	1.3	NA	13.1	18.6	18.2
Amarillo, TX	695	6 055	51 382	7.9	76.4	18.7	210.7	5 367	12 687	25 424	-10.7	2.6	NA	13.7	20.1	18.6
Anchorage, AK	NA	NA	63 357	11.5	90.4	26.9	333.0	6 715	19 620	43 946	-4.2	9.4	NA	8.7	12.9	10.8
Anniston, AL	753	5 229	30 580	7.5	67.4	14.2	97.4	5 057	10 704	23 802	3.9	1.2	NA	16.1	24.6	20.6
Appleton-Oshkosh-Neenah, WI	103	2 135	84 460	16.5	80.9	17.0	388.6	6 727	13 698	31 954	1.0	2.5	NA	5.5	8.4	7.0
Asheville, NC	367	3 485	42 476	14.2	73.0	18.5	189.7	5 979	12 852	25 295	11.5	2.2	NA	13.3	20.3	18.6
Athens, GA	313	5 287	47 163	7.2	73.7	30.7	138.0	6 636	11 999	22 957	6.1	3.2	NA	15.5	22.0	21.7
Atlanta, GA	569	4 288	743 923	15.6	78.7	26.1	4 256.2	6 299	16 670	35 606	18.7	5.8	NA	10.5	16.9	15.3
Auburn-Opalika, AL	791	4 862	35 831	5.3	73.2	25.3	92.6	5 408	11 409	21 227	8.7	2.7	NA	14.6	20.9	18.1
Augusta-Aiken, GA-SC	383	4 211	109 908	12.0	71.4	17.7	469.6	5 335	12 629	28 244	14.7	2.9	NA	16.1	24.6	22.7
Austin-San Marcos, TX	369	4 128	266 120	9.8	81.2	30.7	1 116.2	5 537	14 166	27 956	6.3	3.8	NA	10.1	14.8	13.7
Bakersfield, CA	489	3 370	153 512	7.7	67.6	13.3	880.8	6 131	12 154	28 633	4.4	3.2	NA	20.5	28.5	28.3
Bangor, ME	107	2 823	41 743	9.7	79.1	17.7	157.7	6 873	12 231	26 630	12.0	2.3	NA	11.8	16.1	13.4
Barnstable-Yarmouth, MA	526	2 468	37 509	13.9	88.4	28.1	248.9	7 721	16 402	31 766	21.9	4.1	NA	7.1	12.1	12.4
Baton Rouge, LA	697	6 776	161 296	17.6	76.8	22.4	520.1	5 512	12 305	26 920	-10.8	3.1	NA	14.5	21.1	18.6
Beaumont-Port Arthur, TX	544	4 253	97 680	9.7	73.6	13.7	429.7	5 858	12 024	25 466	-20.0	2.2	NA	16.2	24.4	21.1
Bellingham, WA	223	4 385	37 132	10.4	83.2	22.0	147.0	5 712	13 753	28 367	5.4	3.4	NA	11.1	14.0	13.5
Benton Harbor, MI	431	3 404	42 700	17.9	74.7	16.7	216.4	7 374	12 636	27 244	-0.1	2.4	NA	14.4	21.7	20.2
Billings, MT	302	5 379	30 202	11.0	83.7	21.5	120.7	5 462	12 416	25 942	-11.3	2.3	NA	12.4	18.4	15.1
Biloxi-Gulfport-Pascagoula, MS	353	5 837	83 588	11.5	73.9	15.4	292.7	4 704	10 708	23 551	-5.4	1.7	NA	14.1	20.1	17.3
Binghamton, NY	178	2 403	69 340	10.9	79.2	20.2	350.5	8 086	13 515	29 245	6.1	2.5	NA	13.2	20.5	19.7
Birmingham, AL	585	4 502	210 978	14.2	73.0	19.7	805.5	5 373	13 322	26 613	1.6	3.5	NA	12.8	19.8	16.4
Bismarck, ND	77	2 698	22 710	14.2	79.4	21.9	78.4	4 891	12 316	27 001	-11.4	2.1	NA	10.0	14.1	11.1
Bloomington, IN	173	3 407	47 386	4.6	82.1	32.9	86.3	6 486	12 017	24 780	7.8	2.9	NA	11.7	13.5	13.0
Bloomington-Normal, IL	NA	NA	45 875	11.4	84.7	29.0	136.6	5 961	14 138	31 366	0.9	3.2	NA	8.2	10.9	10.1
Boise City, ID	298	3 685	82 080	10.3	82.4	21.1	372.9	4 983	12 943	27 790	1.8	2.7	NA	10.7	15.3	12.7
Boston-Worcester-Lawrence-Lowell-Brockton, MA-NH	462	2 434	1 439 096	28.7	80.5	27.8	7 216.4	7 893	17 644	38 529	27.7	7.0	NA	8.4	13.1	13.0
Brownsville-Harlingen-San Benito, TX	470	5 711	89 414	5.4	50.0	12.0	485.4	5 909	7 125	17 335	-11.8	1.6	NA	33.2	39.5	38.3
Bryan-College Station, TX	400	5 031	58 837	5.3	79.8	35.8	120.3	5 769	10 987	20 410	-1.0	2.6	NA	16.3	21.4	20.5
Buffalo-Niagara Falls, NY	497	3 411	301 716	18.2	76.3	18.8	1 631.1	9 014	13 403	28 083	-2.9	2.6	NA	13.7	21.9	20.2
Burlington, VT	153	3 453	51 305	18.0	83.7	29.0	238.4	7 371	15 034	34 663	24.4	3.8	NA	7.9	10.4	8.4
Canton-Massillon, OH	NA	NA	94 863	15.5	75.7	13.9	412.6	5 972	12 848	27 684	-10.6	2.2	NA	10.3	16.5	13.9
Casper, WY	355	3 771	17 410	5.6	85.3	20.4	79.8	6 505	12 992	27 586	-28.0	2.6	NA	12.4	18.1	14.3
Cedar Rapids, IA	221	3 688	44 286	18.3	84.9	21.5	187.2	5 791	14 902	32 137	-4.5	2.8	NA	7.3	11.2	9.4
Champaign-Urbana, IL	NA	NA	67 446	5.9	87.5	34.1	147.3	6 177	13 130	26 540	-3.6	3.0	NA	11.3	14.9	14.7
Charleston, WV	447	3 674	56 991	9.1	72.7	16.9	264.7	6 689	12 708	24 578	-15.8	2.4	NA	13.5	21.4	17.2
Charleston-North Charleston, SC	762	5 172	134 889	14.2	75.7	18.9	480.8	5 385	12 334	28 065	8.3	2.3	NA	14.3	20.9	20.8
Charlotte-Gastonia-Rock Hill, NC-SC	798	5 069	283 880	13.4	72.5	19.6	1 311.1	5 702	14 611	31 124	10.9	3.6	NA	10.3	15.9	14.5
Charlottesville, VA	360	2 964	41 486	9.5	76.9	33.3	150.9	6 917	15 227	31 396	18.1	4.9	NA	10.2	13.5	13.5
Chattanooga, TN-GA	784	5 225	101 482	15.7	68.0	15.9	374.1	5 458	12 558	25 593	0.1	2.7	NA	12.7	18.8	16.0
Cheyenne, WY	217	3 299	20 076	7.9	84.2	20.7	91.2	6 250	12 932	27 571	-6.7	1.8	NA	10.7	16.1	12.7
Chicago-Gary-Kenosha, IL-IN-WI	NA	NA	2 189 520	22.8	76.6	23.4	10 552.9	7 241	16 319	35 771	2.8	6.0	NA	10.3	15.2	13.2
Chicago, IL	NA	NA	1 962 005	23.5	76.7	24.5	9 480.4	7 278	16 683	36 301	4.5	6.5	NA	10.2	15.1	13.1
Gary, IN	469	3 716	167 424	16.0	75.4	14.0	776.5	7 061	13 174	31 628	-13.4	2.4	NA	11.4	16.5	14.2
Kankakee, IL	NA	NA	26 064	17.1	73.1	11.9	112.9	6 074	12 142	28 284	-2.9	1.8	NA	12.3	17.2	16.6
Kenosha, WI	415	2 755	34 027	17.6	75.1	12.7	183.0	6 985	13 265	30 638	-9.0	1.9	NA	8.9	13.8	12.4
Chico-Paradise, CA	344	3 206	56 394	5.7	77.6	19.5	216.6	6 139	12 083	22 775	4.4	2.4	NA	19.4	27.2	29.6
Cincinnati-Hamilton, OH-KY-IN	334	3 594	473 524	19.7	74.6	19.7	1 956.9	6 297	14 329	30 695	1.4	3.8	NA	9.3	14.0	11.8
Cincinnati, OH-KY-IN	336	3 424	392 024	21.2	74.4	19.9	1 635.5	6 370	14 401	30 370	1.7	3.9	NA	9.6	14.6	12.4
Hamilton-Middletown, OH	329	4 260	81 500	12.7	76.0	18.7	321.3	5 949	13 947	32 439	-1.2	3.3	NA	7.7	11.3	9.2
Clarksville-Hopkinsville, TN-KY	NA	NA	42 530	7.1	75.6	14.0	158.8	4 885	10 508	23 730	6.8	1.2	NA	13.3	18.5	16.1
Cleveland-Akron, OH	NA	NA	727 277	20.1	76.2	18.7	3 250.1	7 227	14 462	30 128	-5.4	3.7	NA	11.1	17.8	15.0
Akron, OH	173	2 458	177 922	12.6	78.5	19.3	723.1	6 605	13 997	29 279	-5.4	3.4	NA	10.2	16.2	13.7
Cleveland-Lorain-Elyria, OH	NA	NA	549 355	22.5	75.5	18.5	2 527.0	7 427	14 601	30 350	-5.5	3.7	NA	11.4	18.3	15.5
Colorado Springs, CO	386	3 769	109 787	14.5	88.3	25.8	508.2	5 703	13 664	29 603	8.8	2.9	NA	9.7	14.3	11.9
Columbia, MO	332	3 218	42 951	9.7	84.8	36.5	113.8	5 510	12 707	25 646	-1.4	2.6	NA	10.8	14.3	12.9

1. Data for serious crimes have not been adjusted for underreporting; this may affect comparability between geographic areas and over time. 2. Per 100,000 population estimated by the FBI. 3. All persons 3 years old and over enrolled in nursery school through college. 4. Persons 25 years old and over. 5. Elementary and secondary education expenditures, local government fiscal years ending between July 1, 1998 and June 30, 1999. 6. Based on population enumerated as of April 1, 1990.

Table C. Metropolitan Areas — **Personal Income**

Area Name	Personal income, 1999												
			Per capita[1]						Transfer payments				
										Government payments to individuals			
	Total (mil dol)	Percent change, 1998–1999	Dollars	Rank	Wages and salaries[2] (mil dol)	Proprietor's income (mil dol)	Dividends, interest, and rent (mil dol)	Total (mil dol)	Total (mil dol)	Social Security (mil dol)	Medical payments (mil dol)	Income mainte-nance (mil dol)	Unemploy-ment insurance (mil dol)
	62	63	64	65	66	67	68	69	70	71	72	73	74
Abilene, TX	3 010	4.2	24 579	189	1 718	478	565	463	442	174	189	38	6
Albany, GA	2 630	2.6	22 394	266	1 906	188	460	437	412	139	158	77	8
Albany-Schenectady-Troy, NY	25 136	4.2	28 909	78	16 178	1 626	4 890	3 875	3 692	1 437	1 473	326	56
Albuquerque, NM	17 391	3.8	25 619	154	11 787	985	3 321	2 190	2 065	841	743	242	33
Alexandria, LA	2 918	3.3	23 020	246	1 640	256	552	660	637	167	359	69	4
Allentown-Bethlehem-Easton, PA	17 613	5.1	28 483	86	10 141	1 255	3 353	2 621	2 496	1 154	1 007	153	76
Altoona, PA	3 034	4.8	23 352	235	1 827	322	495	633	606	203	250	55	16
Amarillo, TX	5 145	3.8	24 652	187	2 899	728	932	683	647	269	257	51	13
Anchorage, AK	8 717	3.4	33 813	25	5 897	841	1 536	1 082	1 042	168	237	97	39
Anniston, AL	2 388	0.9	20 492	302	1 559	116	455	462	441	183	163	49	6
Appleton-Oshkosh-Neenah, WI	9 632	6.3	27 670	101	6 888	438	1 922	951	883	484	288	44	28
Asheville, NC	5 747	4.1	26 706	128	3 415	394	1 384	887	848	376	337	74	10
Athens, GA	3 445	5.0	24 539	191	2 336	276	694	390	359	153	134	44	2
Atlanta, GA	125 302	7.9	32 486	33	93 163	11 338	19 864	9 230	8 399	3 677	3 177	917	112
Auburn-Opalika, AL	2 012	5.5	19 696	308	1 202	126	382	266	248	112	81	29	3
Augusta-Aiken, GA-SC	10 852	3.7	23 549	229	7 264	507	2 021	1 635	1 543	598	587	198	27
Austin-San Marcos, TX	36 437	11.8	31 794	39	28 126	3 024	5 312	2 548	2 350	968	931	219	43
Bakersfield, CA	12 777	2.6	19 886	307	7 850	1 377	1 989	2 249	2 126	698	755	434	106
Bangor, ME	3 267	4.3	22 617	261	2 141	251	493	602	577	214	238	64	10
Barnstable-Yarmouth, MA	7 326	7.7	34 470	24	3 020	647	2 108	1 163	1 124	552	441	48	38
Baton Rouge, LA	14 657	3.8	25 316	162	10 007	929	2 504	1 870	1 767	636	796	200	20
Beaumont-Port Arthur, TX	8 803	1.0	23 395	232	5 518	616	1 547	1 687	1 622	603	752	158	44
Bellingham, WA	3 724	5.0	23 228	241	2 078	373	827	558	525	216	178	45	28
Benton Harbor, MI	4 065	5.5	25 454	159	2 459	275	791	671	640	282	249	74	13
Billings, MT	3 214	4.1	25 253	169	2 024	250	701	417	393	187	120	29	8
Biloxi-Gulfport-Pascagoula, MS	8 020	4.4	22 707	258	5 718	406	1 401	1 240	1 172	476	486	107	11
Binghamton, NY	6 073	4.3	24 542	190	3 810	402	1 151	1 106	1 054	471	408	108	17
Birmingham, AL	25 527	5.0	27 896	98	17 584	1 799	4 857	3 338	3 171	1 398	1 223	309	33
Bismarck, ND	2 267	4.3	24 660	186	1 452	138	436	325	309	129	119	17	5
Bloomington, IN	2 801	4.6	23 957	212	1 905	200	584	304	281	133	102	21	5
Bloomington-Normal, IL	4 211	7.7	28 947	77	3 261	231	749	357	328	168	98	23	9
Boise City, ID	11 178	7.8	27 408	110	7 388	1 376	2 051	1 101	1 032	452	357	79	31
Boston-Worcester-Lawrence-Lowell-Brockton, MA-NH	214 141	7.3	36 285	15	147 378	17 090	37 332	24 192	23 113	8 318	11 284	1 844	701
Brownsville-Harlingen-San Benito, TX	4 700	4.0	14 280	316	2 609	405	702	1 171	1 114	271	536	237	21
Bryan-College Station, TX	2 846	3.9	21 206	292	1 998	230	499	292	268	110	102	31	2
Buffalo-Niagara Falls, NY	30 506	3.5	26 710	126	19 065	1 791	5 411	5 648	5 407	2 162	2 171	661	108
Burlington, VT	5 461	5.8	28 039	94	3 946	392	990	592	548	226	214	65	11
Canton-Massillon, OH	10 043	2.4	24 955	178	5 817	529	2 005	1 595	1 509	693	557	115	25
Casper, WY	1 922	5.2	30 427	56	958	312	472	223	211	103	66	16	4
Cedar Rapids, IA	5 719	6.0	30 932	46	4 428	318	1 101	571	532	280	175	37	12
Champaign-Urbana, IL	4 296	4.6	25 233	170	3 084	197	1 042	416	381	170	126	41	12
Charleston, WV	6 709	3.1	26 709	127	4 522	433	1 231	1 212	1 167	485	438	82	17
Charleston-North Charleston, SC	12 684	7.5	22 944	247	8 297	885	2 433	1 690	1 592	611	653	189	21
Charlotte-Gastonia-Rock Hill, NC-SC	42 998	7.3	30 340	59	32 052	3 035	7 423	4 235	3 978	1 819	1 546	354	71
Charlottesville, VA	4 616	4.5	30 517	53	2 883	435	1 195	436	407	204	149	30	2
Chattanooga, TN-GA	11 856	5.5	26 228	138	7 698	1 023	2 042	1 829	1 746	738	737	150	23
Cheyenne, WY	2 158	5.8	27 361	112	1 326	125	526	250	235	98	67	19	3
Chicago-Gary-Kenosha, IL-IN-WI	300 846	4.8	33 857	X	201 597	25 930	58 160	30 024	28 211	11 321	11 672	3 316	832
Chicago, IL	278 241	4.8	34 743	22	189 002	24 952	54 423	26 822	25 182	9 958	10 500	3 008	775
Gary, IN	16 396	4.6	26 093	142	9 400	741	2 695	2 330	2 208	991	854	235	36
Kankakee, IL	2 389	3.6	23 256	238	1 364	99	442	416	395	164	160	42	11
Kenosha, WI	3 820	5.9	26 111	141	1 831	138	601	455	426	208	158	30	10
Chico-Paradise, CA	4 297	5.7	22 012	275	2 023	465	945	918	880	344	309	147	17
Cincinnati-Hamilton, OH-KY-IN	57 819	5.0	29 485	X	38 308	3 516	11 779	6 714	6 303	2 714	2 400	525	97
Cincinnati, OH-KY-IN	48 996	5.0	30 105	62	33 858	3 141	10 160	5 672	5 333	2 277	2 045	453	83
Hamilton-Middletown, OH	8 823	5.1	26 456	133	4 450	375	1 619	1 042	970	438	354	72	14
Clarksville-Hopkinsville, TN-KY	4 329	5.8	21 500	289	3 031	270	690	552	523	190	205	54	8
Cleveland-Akron, OH	87 042	3.7	29 905	X	56 193	5 764	17 827	12 035	11 408	4 726	4 561	1 038	184
Akron, OH	19 359	3.9	28 079	93	11 537	902	3 763	2 649	2 500	1 075	962	215	42
Cleveland-Lorain-Elyria, OH	67 683	3.7	30 472	55	44 657	4 863	14 064	9 386	8 908	3 651	3 599	822	142
Colorado Springs, CO	13 627	6.7	27 255	116	9 531	829	2 561	1 301	1 217	481	457	116	18
Columbia, MO	3 459	4.1	26 568	129	2 397	230	689	364	340	138	148	29	2

1. Based on the resident population estimated as of July 1 of the year shown. 2. Includes other labor income.

Table C. Metropolitan Areas — **Earnings, Social Security, and Housing**

Area Name	Earnings, 1999									Social Security beneficiaries, December 2000		Supplemental Security Income recipients, December 2000	Housing units, 1990	
			Goods-related[1]		Service-related and other[2]									
	Total (mil dol)	Farm	Total	Manufacturing	Total	Retail trade	Finance, insurance, and real estate	Services	Government	Number	Rate[3]		Total	Percent change, 1980–1990
	75	76	77	78	79	80	81	82	83	84	85	86	87	88
Abilene, TX	2 196	0.8	20.1	12.4	53.9	10.6	4.7	26.4	25.1	20 777	164	2 561	49 988	20.1
Albany, GA	2 095	1.8	D	18.2	D	9.4	D	24.0	23.2	18 106	150	5 199	42 910	11.1
Albany-Schenectady-Troy, NY	17 804	0.2	D	11.1	D	8.9	7.5	30.0	26.2	160 076	183	17 923	361 002	10.4
Albuquerque, NM	12 773	0.2	D	D	D	10.6	6.6	32.4	22.0	103 964	146	14 467	241 683	22.8
Alexandria, LA	1 897	0.5	18.6	10.9	56.1	10.0	4.6	28.9	24.7	22 863	181	6 121	51 239	6.2
Allentown-Bethlehem-Easton, PA	11 396	0.0	D	24.9	D	9.0	6.4	28.2	10.6	126 178	198	10 640	241 060	12.9
Altoona, PA	2 148	0.5	D	17.5	D	14.6	3.4	26.3	14.7	24 572	190	4 125	54 349	4.4
Amarillo, TX	3 628	0.9	23.0	8.4	59.9	11.5	6.1	27.1	16.2	31 032	142	3 134	80 734	16.0
Anchorage, AK	6 738	0.0	14.9	1.5	55.8	9.7	5.4	24.9	29.2	20 935	80	4 022	94 153	33.8
Anniston, AL	1 676	0.4	24.1	19.6	42.3	10.1	2.8	17.8	33.3	24 228	216	4 411	46 753	9.8
Appleton-Oshkosh-Neenah, WI	7 325	0.7	D	36.5	D	8.1	6.3	18.9	10.1	54 143	151	3 380	120 511	15.8
Asheville, NC	3 809	1.3	24.9	17.1	D	11.0	4.7	31.1	15.9	46 251	205	5 309	85 618	16.8
Athens, GA	2 613	2.2	D	16.0	D	9.9	4.4	23.4	30.7	18 695	122	3 420	50 960	32.1
Atlanta, GA	104 501	0.2	D	11.0	D	8.6	9.2	30.2	10.9	428 238	104	52 760	1 224 367	45.1
Auburn-Opalika, AL	1 328	0.8	25.5	19.1	39.0	10.8	4.0	16.8	34.6	14 160	123	2 638	36 636	23.5
Augusta-Aiken, GA-SC	7 771	0.4	D	15.9	D	9.1	3.6	21.1	26.5	74 449	156	12 861	165 632	25.6
Austin-San Marcos, TX	31 150	0.1	D	17.6	D	7.6	6.5	27.8	15.9	115 123	92	13 862	370 310	56.5
Bakersfield, CA	9 227	4.2	17.8	5.1	50.4	9.2	3.9	20.4	27.6	88 399	134	25 914	198 636	27.6
Bangor, ME	2 392	0.4	21.0	15.2	58.5	11.8	4.0	28.5	20.1	27 597	190	4 137	61 359	14.9
Barnstable-Yarmouth, MA	3 666	0.1	D	9.4	D	16.9	7.2	31.1	16.7	61 851	278	3 625	135 192	35.3
Baton Rouge, LA	10 937	0.1	D	13.5	D	9.0	6.6	25.5	18.6	77 100	128	14 184	212 078	19.2
Beaumont-Port Arthur, TX	6 134	0.1	34.2	23.4	50.6	10.1	3.5	26.4	15.1	67 554	175	8 809	149 807	4.2
Bellingham, WA	2 452	2.7	29.1	16.3	53.2	11.4	6.3	23.5	15.0	25 329	152	2 666	55 742	17.4
Benton Harbor, MI	2 733	0.8	40.6	35.5	47.1	8.4	3.2	23.4	11.6	31 371	193	4 662	69 532	1.1
Billings, MT	2 274	0.6	14.9	6.3	69.9	12.4	6.3	32.1	14.5	21 565	167	1 864	48 781	14.1
Biloxi-Gulfport-Pascagoula, MS	6 124	0.0	D	18.8	D	8.7	3.0	25.7	29.2	60 558	166	9 476	129 916	14.8
Binghamton, NY	4 212	0.3	D	27.9	D	8.6	4.1	24.6	18.6	52 839	209	6 175	108 223	8.3
Birmingham, AL	19 382	0.3	19.2	10.8	66.1	8.8	9.8	28.7	14.3	162 326	176	25 813	348 470	11.0
Bismarck, ND	1 591	0.1	D	7.1	D	10.7	6.0	30.5	21.0	15 727	166	1 236	33 270	10.1
Bloomington, IN	2 105	0.0	23.9	17.2	46.3	10.1	5.3	23.2	29.9	14 746	122	1 300	41 948	15.8
Bloomington-Normal, IL	3 492	0.1	19.3	13.1	67.9	8.0	31.3	19.8	12.9	18 508	123	1 269	49 164	8.3
Boise City, ID	8 764	1.4	33.6	23.9	51.1	9.6	6.0	21.9	13.9	54 830	127	5 903	113 986	15.8
Boston-Worcester-Lawrence-Lowell-Brockton, MA-NH	164 467	0.1	D	16.1	D	8.2	11.4	35.4	11.2	953 854	157	141 642	2 270 865	13.3
Brownsville-Harlingen-San Benito, TX	3 014	2.4	14.5	11.1	56.0	12.7	5.3	26.3	27.1	41 810	125	15 977	88 759	34.5
Bryan-College Station, TX	2 228	0.4	15.4	7.0	46.8	11.3	5.8	23.9	37.4	12 969	85	1 686	48 799	36.7
Buffalo-Niagara Falls, NY	20 855	0.2	D	21.6	D	9.2	7.2	27.3	17.8	236 307	202	30 073	492 516	3.9
Burlington, VT	4 338	0.9	D	D	D	9.0	6.0	29.1	15.1	26 629	134	3 265	73 480	23.8
Canton-Massillon, OH	6 346	0.8	38.3	30.8	49.0	10.3	4.4	23.1	11.9	76 372	188	6 868	158 446	3.2
Casper, WY	1 269	0.3	34.3	4.1	50.9	9.1	5.2	22.6	14.6	11 333	170	1 199	29 082	2.1
Cedar Rapids, IA	4 746	0.2	31.9	25.1	58.7	8.4	7.1	25.7	9.2	30 447	159	2 099	68 357	5.5
Champaign-Urbana, IL	3 281	0.1	18.5	12.8	46.1	9.4	4.5	23.7	35.2	21 055	117	2 205	68 416	9.4
Charleston, WV	4 954	0.0	21.0	11.8	61.3	9.0	6.8	29.2	17.7	53 490	213	7 450	109 631	4.8
Charleston-North Charleston, SC	9 182	0.2	D	10.9	D	10.8	6.1	26.3	27.3	79 352	145	13 258	199 879	31.6
Charlotte-Gastonia-Rock Hill, NC-SC	35 087	0.7	D	16.6	D	9.0	D	24.3	10.3	210 532	140	21 887	472 913	29.9
Charlottesville, VA	3 317	0.3	D	D	D	9.6	D	23.7	31.6	23 466	147	2 267	51 932	20.1
Chattanooga, TN-GA	8 721	0.3	D	19.4	D	11.0	8.3	24.4	15.4	84 986	183	11 362	177 706	12.5
Cheyenne, WY	1 451	1.3	11.2	4.6	47.6	10.3	6.2	17.5	39.9	11 874	146	1 065	30 507	11.4
Chicago-Gary-Kenosha, IL-IN-WI	227 527	0.0	D	17.2	D	7.4	11.1	31.8	11.7	1 214 819	133	186 067	3 170 271	5.6
Chicago, IL	213 954	0.0	D	16.5	D	7.3	11.5	32.3	11.5	1 067 203	129	169 677	2 851 754	6.0
Gary, IN	10 140	0.1	D	27.5	D	9.4	3.8	25.3	13.2	106 154	168	11 641	230 254	1.0
Kankakee, IL	1 463	0.7	D	21.9	D	11.5	4.5	24.6	16.0	18 608	179	2 571	37 001	-1.6
Kenosha, WI	1 970	0.0	D	32.5	D	9.1	3.4	20.5	15.4	22 854	153	2 178	51 262	7.9
Chico-Paradise, CA	2 488	2.0	D	8.4	D	12.6	6.2	31.8	21.2	41 551	205	9 092	76 115	24.0
Cincinnati-Hamilton, OH-KY-IN	41 825	0.0	D	D	D	9.0	8.0	D	12.0	305 102	154	38 105	722 225	11.2
Cincinnati, OH-KY-IN	36 999	0.0	D	D	D	8.9	8.1	D	11.6	256 067	156	32 897	611 872	9.9
Hamilton-Middletown, OH	4 825	0.1	33.8	24.9	51.9	9.6	7.8	19.9	14.4	49 035	147	5 208	110 353	19.3
Clarksville-Hopkinsville, TN-KY	3 301	0.1	D	15.0	D	8.7	2.6	14.6	48.7	24 834	120	4 335	60 662	19.1
Cleveland-Akron, OH	61 957	0.2	D	23.9	D	8.2	7.7	28.3	13.2	512 090	174	62 293	1 163 911	4.1
Akron, OH	12 438	0.1	31.8	25.8	53.3	9.8	5.3	23.9	14.8	117 102	169	12 647	263 776	6.4
Cleveland-Lorain-Elyria, OH	49 519	0.2	D	23.4	D	7.8	8.3	29.4	12.8	394 988	175	49 646	900 135	3.4
Colorado Springs, CO	10 360	0.0	18.4	12.1	54.3	9.0	6.5	28.2	27.3	60 746	118	40	165 056	40.4
Columbia, MO	2 628	-0.2	14.4	8.5	48.2	9.8	8.7	21.6	37.6	16 448	121	1 800	44 695	19.4

1. Covers mining, construction, and manufacturing.   2. Covers private sector earnings in agricultural services, forestry, and fisheries; transportation and public utilities; wholesale trade; retail trade; finance, insurance, and real estate; and services.   3. Per 1,000 resident population estimated as of July 1 of the year shown.

Table C. Metropolitan Areas — **Housing, Labor Force, and Employment**

Area Name	Housing units, 1990 (cont'd) Occupied units Owner-occupied Total	Percent	Median value[1]	Owner cost as a percent of income With a mortgage	Without a mortgage	Renter-occupied Median rent[2]	Rent as percent of income	Sub-standard units[3] (percent)	Civilian labor force, 2001 Total	Percent change, 2000–2001	Unemployment Total	Rate[4]	Civilian employment, 1990[5] Total	Percent Professional, managerial, and technical	Precision production, craft, and repair
	89	90	91	92	93	94	95	96	97	98	99	100	101	102	103
Abilene, TX	43 301	62.2	45 500	20.5	12.9	378	25.8	4.4	57 335	-3.3	2 210	3.9	50 278	30.6	10.6
Albany, GA	39 362	55.7	58 800	18.7	13.2	336	26.1	6.6	53 992	-4.4	2 993	5.5	46 281	27.7	11.9
Albany-Schenectady-Troy, NY	330 484	64.0	99 000	NA	NA	456	NA	1.8	442 141	-1.1	14 137	3.2	424 003	34.0	9.5
Albuquerque, NM	221 619	64.3	82 400	NA	NA	401	NA	6.0	370 845	0.9	13 468	3.6	271 567	35.1	10.6
Alexandria, LA	45 941	66.5	52 600	19.6	13.4	337	27.6	5.2	59 746	-1.5	3 608	6.0	48 788	29.2	10.5
Allentown-Bethlehem-Easton, PA	225 831	71.9	97 500	21.9	13.0	448	26.1	1.8	325 732	2.9	14 070	4.3	286 502	27.9	12.2
Altoona, PA	50 332	72.6	41 100	17.0	13.2	298	26.8	1.6	63 742	1.7	3 737	5.9	55 022	23.0	13.2
Amarillo, TX	71 897	64.2	52 700	19.9	12.7	347	24.8	5.1	111 517	-1.2	3 500	3.1	87 795	27.2	12.8
Anchorage, AK	82 702	52.8	109 700	22.6	11.4	563	24.8	4.3	144 851	0.4	6 165	4.3	111 242	37.5	9.5
Anniston, AL	42 983	70.3	51 600	19.3	12.7	310	23.8	2.3	52 206	-2.7	2 916	5.6	46 899	23.6	14.0
Appleton-Oshkosh-Neenah, WI	115 515	70.3	62 400	19.5	12.8	380	23.0	1.8	228 229	2.0	8 347	3.7	159 009	25.5	11.9
Asheville, NC	77 290	71.0	63 500	NA	NA	366	NA	2.7	111 064	-0.3	4 170	3.8	93 226	27.4	13.3
Athens, GA	47 066	54.8	70 800	NA	NA	387	NA	3.8	73 376	-0.9	2 295	3.1	60 422	33.3	10.4
Atlanta, GA	1 102 578	62.7	88 800	NA	NA	524	NA	3.6	2 280 400	0.2	79 640	3.5	1 563 539	32.7	10.4
Auburn-Opalika, AL	33 097	58.1	64 900	16.9	12.4	339	35.1	3.7	50 511	0.9	1 918	3.8	40 043	30.8	10.5
Augusta-Aiken, GA-SC	149 093	66.7	63 300	NA	NA	383	NA	4.7	204 903	-2.3	10 167	5.0	184 471	29.5	13.9
Austin-San Marcos, TX	325 995	51.2	74 800	NA	NA	414	NA	6.3	754 270	2.0	29 021	3.8	432 006	37.7	9.0
Bakersfield, CA	181 480	59.3	82 800	22.5	12.4	439	27.4	10.9	291 683	0.1	30 718	10.5	214 668	26.2	13.3
Bangor, ME	54 063	69.7	69 100	19.3	13.1	396	25.9	3.2	79 882	0.1	3 305	4.1	67 389	28.1	12.8
Barnstable-Yarmouth, MA.....	77 586	72.4	162 800	NA	NA	645	NA	1.4	107 916	1.8	4 250	3.9	82 526	31.0	12.4
Baton Rouge, LA	188 377	65.3	66 600	18.2	12.5	369	26.5	5.0	309 448	1.2	16 673	5.4	233 090	32.1	12.7
Beaumont-Port Arthur, TX	134 238	69.7	42 900	17.0	13.0	359	25.6	5.1	177 717	-1.3	14 564	8.2	148 500	26.6	15.3
Bellingham, WA	48 543	64.3	90 800	19.9	11.9	424	27.1	3.6	80 298	-1.2	5 460	6.8	61 657	26.3	13.0
Benton Harbor, MI	61 025	69.6	52 800	16.9	13.2	367	26.9	2.9	84 313	-0.5	4 780	5.7	73 154	27.7	13.5
Billings, MT	44 689	65.7	62 800	21.4	12.0	342	25.5	1.6	71 160	-1.4	2 353	3.3	54 760	28.6	9.9
Biloxi-Gulfport-Pascagoula, MS	111 828	67.6	53 200	NA	NA	344	NA	4.8	174 573	-3.2	7 236	4.1	123 014	28.8	14.6
Binghamton, NY	100 681	67.9	78 000	19.8	12.9	386	26.7	1.6	121 020	-0.7	5 059	4.2	123 419	34.5	10.9
Birmingham, AL	319 774	68.1	60 600	NA	NA	361	NA	3.2	476 209	0.3	16 429	3.4	379 295	30.4	11.2
Bismarck, ND	31 361	67.1	63 600	20.6	12.4	339	23.7	2.0	54 045	1.1	1 363	2.5	42 237	31.5	9.2
Bloomington, IN	39 351	54.8	66 600	18.5	12.0	400	32.2	2.5	61 386	1.1	1 915	3.1	52 564	36.6	9.2
Bloomington-Normal, IL	46 796	63.5	65 900	17.3	11.8	386	24.8	1.5	91 903	-0.6	2 250	2.4	68 058	29.5	8.4
Boise City, ID	108 759	69.0	66 300	NA	NA	372	NA	3.6	249 243	4.7	9 962	4.0	143 604	30.9	10.7
Boston-Worcester-Lawrence-Lowell-Brockton, MA-NH....	2 111 440	59.3	165 200	NA	NA	595	NA	2.7	3 211 688	1.4	118 657	3.7	2 912 225	36.9	10.0
Brownsville-Harlingen-San Benito, TX	73 278	64.4	38 400	20.7	12.6	294	27.6	25.2	133 165	2.1	12 269	9.2	86 302	25.4	10.5
Bryan-College Station, TX	43 725	41.9	66 600	20.1	13.0	410	34.0	6.6	77 554	1.1	1 269	1.6	56 368	38.9	8.2
Buffalo-Niagara Falls, NY	461 803	64.5	71 900	NA	NA	380	NA	1.7	547 000	-2.0	29 475	5.4	542 686	29.4	11.0
Burlington, VT	64 783	66.6	109 000	NA	NA	498	NA	2.0	118 381	1.1	3 381	2.9	94 020	36.1	10.5
Canton-Massillon, OH..........	149 240	70.7	57 100	16.9	12.0	352	24.4	1.5	206 036	1.3	8 386	4.1	175 340	26.4	11.4
Casper, WY	23 837	68.9	53 100	18.6	11.7	297	23.5	1.9	35 239	2.6	1 429	4.1	28 391	31.0	11.8
Cedar Rapids, IA	65 501	70.4	58 500	16.5	12.1	368	23.2	1.4	114 357	-0.7	3 204	2.8	87 606	30.8	10.8
Champaign-Urbana, IL..........	63 900	54.5	67 700	20.1	12.2	410	29.6	2.6	99 009	-0.2	2 755	2.8	87 114	39.0	7.4
Charleston, WV	100 408	70.8	57 400	16.1	11.5	339	24.2	2.1	138 183	0.3	5 416	3.9	105 569	30.3	11.6
Charleston-North Charleston, SC	177 668	62.6	72 200	21.8	13.4	432	25.4	4.5	272 251	-1.8	10 187	3.7	220 922	28.6	15.1
Charlotte-Gastonia-Rock Hill, NC-SC	440 670	66.8	72 300	19.7	12.6	424	23.6	3.3	811 046	0.6	41 651	5.1	613 891	27.0	12.7
Charlottesville, VA..............	48 709	59.4	93 800	20.6	12.2	496	26.5	4.1	78 008	0.4	1 576	2.0	66 271	37.8	10.7
Chattanooga, TN-GA	163 117	68.3	57 300	NA	NA	362	NA	3.0	231 572	0.2	7 463	3.2	197 611	26.2	12.0
Cheyenne, WY	28 092	65.5	69 800	20.5	11.6	361	24.6	2.2	42 186	2.1	1 494	3.5	32 914	31.3	9.5
Chicago-Gary-Kenosha, IL-IN-WI	2 969 099	61.8	101 900	NA	NA	483	NA	5.1	4 668 140	-0.8	249 731	5.3	3 979 255	31.5	10.5
Chicago, IL	2 671 540	61.0	109 900	NA	NA	491	NA	5.3	4 240 788	-0.9	227 691	5.4	3 611 434	32.2	10.1
Gary, IN	215 907	69.3	58 100	16.4	13.1	400	24.7	3.6	293 592	0.1	15 008	5.1	265 789	25.3	14.5
Kankakee, IL	34 623	66.8	54 700	16.9	12.8	375	24.2	3.3	51 935	-1.0	3 026	5.8	42 205	25.2	12.1
Kenosha, WI	47 029	68.8	65 100	19.4	12.9	410	24.6	2.8	81 825	0.4	4 006	4.9	59 827	23.9	14.3
Chico-Paradise, CA	71 665	60.9	94 000	22.4	11.9	438	32.6	5.1	87 996	0.6	6 191	7.0	70 880	29.6	11.0
Cincinnati-Hamilton, OH-KY-IN	679 137	64.5	70 800	NA	NA	371	NA	2.8	1 062 355	1.4	40 104	3.8	860 318	30.9	10.9
Cincinnati, OH-KY-IN	574 602	63.7	70 400	NA	NA	364	NA	2.9	866 171	1.1	33 763	3.9	723 002	31.1	10.8
Hamilton-Middletown, OH .	104 535	69.2	73 000	18.9	12.3	414	25.8	2.0	196 184	3.1	6 341	3.2	137 316	30.0	11.4
Clarksville-Hopkinsville, TN-KY	55 981	58.1	54 000	20.6	12.4	352	24.1	4.2	89 760	1.5	4 370	4.9	59 591	24.7	12.2
Cleveland-Akron, OH	1 094 413	67.0	70 300	NA	NA	398	NA	1.9	1 492 825	0.5	67 917	4.5	1 307 775	30.3	11.4
Akron, OH.......................	249 227	69.0	63 600	18.9	12.6	396	26.7	1.6	366 573	0.4	15 583	4.3	305 611	29.7	11.7
Cleveland-Lorain-Elyria, OH...	845 186	66.5	72 100	NA	NA	399	NA	2.0	1 126 252	0.5	52 334	4.6	1 002 164	30.4	11.3
Colorado Springs, CO..........	146 965	57.4	81 700	22.8	12.2	418	26.0	2.8	263 863	1.7	11 727	4.4	172 530	34.8	10.0
Columbia, MO	41 937	55.0	65 700	17.5	12.0	380	27.3	2.1	87 354	3.4	1 557	1.8	58 017	38.3	7.8

1. Specified owner-occupied units. 2. Specified renter-occupied units. 3. Overcrowded or lacking complete plumbing facilities. 4. Percent of civilian labor force. 5. Persons 16 years and older.

Table C. Metropolitan Areas — Nonfarm Employment and Agriculture

Area Name	Private nonfarm establishments, employment and payroll, 1999									Agriculture, 1997			
	Number of establish-ments	Employment						Annual payroll		Farms			Farm operators
		Total	Health Care and Social Assistance	Manufac-turing	Retail trade	Finance and Insurance	Professional Scientific and Technical Services	Total (mil dol)	Average per employee (dollars)	Number	Percent with—		Whose principal occu-pation is farming (percent)
											Less than 50 acres	500 acres and over	
	104	105	106	107	108	109	110	111	112	113	114	115	116
Abilene, TX	3 543	48 514	10 145	3 702	7 339	1 893	1 323	1 040	21 437	1 048	27.5	23.8	35.4
Albany, GA	2 810	46 939	7 400	8 217	7 499	1 423	1 475	1 245	26 524	296	36.5	32.8	48.0
Albany-Schenectady-Troy, NY	20 370	331 972	55 296	32 325	49 672	25 570	21 119	9 723	29 289	2 538	27.4	8.1	54.5
Albuquerque, NM	17 778	277 059	34 853	24 756	40 555	13 882	25 187	7 705	27 810	1 460	71.7	9.6	37.9
Alexandria, LA	3 122	45 955	12 171	2 890	7 677	1 756	1 846	1 062	23 110	817	39.4	11.9	46.5
Allentown-Bethlehem-Eas-ton, PA	14 883	253 061	34 773	42 893	31 449	13 353	7 921	7 955	31 435	988	42.9	9.6	56.9
Altoona, PA	3 264	50 331	8 647	9 177	8 078	1 897	2 176	1 223	24 299	422	20.6	10.2	68.5
Amarillo, TX	5 576	81 117	13 007	11 169	12 714	3 694	3 051	2 036	25 100	797	23.8	37.9	41.8
Anchorage, AK	7 929	108 021	15 451	1 741	14 965	4 945	6 888	4 317	39 964	NA	NA	NA	NA
Anniston, AL	2 568	40 241	5 080	11 024	6 392	1 026	889	864	21 471	629	39.1	3.8	35.3
Appleton-Oshkosh-Neenah, WI	9 118	185 450	18 091	54 137	22 876	9 273	5 444	5 637	30 396	2 849	24.9	7.8	60.8
Asheville, NC	6 629	97 841	16 826	18 535	14 709	2 682	2 978	2 408	24 611	1 916	54.6	1.9	42.4
Athens, GA	3 639	52 816	7 270	11 361	9 205	1 680	1 780	1 262	23 894	1 007	37.7	4.7	42.8
Atlanta, GA	111 021	2 021 497	163 876	187 738	237 215	113 446	151 047	71 523	35 381	5 572	48.0	3.5	38.2
Auburn-Opalika, AL	2 021	30 768	4 470	7 081	5 407	827	668	660	21 451	347	32.9	10.7	31.7
Augusta-Aiken, GA-SC	9 751	169 591	26 092	42 299	24 685	4 511	7 039	4 754	28 032	1 492	36.9	8.7	35.7
Austin-San Marcos, TX	30 735	505 265	52 018	67 970	68 790	26 279	40 418	18 937	37 479	6 721	34.1	12.1	39.8
Bakersfield, CA	10 756	146 999	19 597	13 140	24 826	6 641	7 517	3 903	26 551	1 997	35.1	30.3	63.8
Bangor, ME	4 088	57 241	11 200	8 931	9 853	1 962	1 843	1 459	25 489	525	31.0	11.4	47.2
Barnstable-Yarmouth, MA	8 253	69 028	12 139	3 008	13 909	3 117	3 618	2 002	29 003	221	89.6	0.0	49.8
Baton Rouge, LA	14 631	255 077	30 916	21 128	36 470	12 833	15 936	7 109	27 870	1 160	51.2	7.4	35.4
Beaumont-Port Arthur, TX	8 146	131 126	19 847	21 330	20 122	3 842	5 039	3 802	28 995	1 250	52.3	15.4	36.2
Bellingham, WA	5 386	58 488	6 691	9 495	9 322	1 962	2 937	1 509	25 800	1 228	57.1	2.4	54.3
Benton Harbor, MI	4 021	61 186	7 534	16 121	8 274	1 438	1 570	1 795	29 337	1 182	49.1	5.8	54.2
Billings, MT	4 857	56 986	8 557	2 955	9 483	2 935	3 618	1 418	24 883	1 097	32.5	32.0	53.5
Biloxi-Gulfport-Pascagoula, MS	7 481	135 096	17 933	21 697	18 459	3 821	5 136	3 340	24 723	835	49.9	3.2	30.7
Binghamton, NY	5 116	91 859	12 823	23 849	12 903	3 438	3 914	2 638	28 718	1 008	22.7	7.2	53.9
Birmingham, AL	23 074	432 567	56 507	48 069	51 610	32 906	21 997	13 061	30 194	2 646	40.7	3.6	36.4
Bismarck, ND	2 955	40 785	8 844	2 138	6 410	2 099	2 440	958	23 489	1 774	10.9	56.4	62.6
Bloomington, IN	2 929	45 718	6 416	8 143	7 482	1 526	1 747	1 129	24 695	473	33.4	5.5	35.1
Bloomington-Normal, IL	3 533	80 254	7 266	8 271	9 700	20 824	2 023	2 566	31 973	1 475	18.0	35.5	66.0
Boise City, ID	12 724	183 263	20 920	29 959	23 113	8 790	7 477	5 220	28 484	3 119	62.0	6.8	46.0
Boston-Worcester-Lawrence-Lowell-Brockton, MA-NH	164 960	2 923 913	414 945	411 536	345 364	205 370	215 534	115 361	39 454	4 421	57.5	1.9	51.8
Brownsville-Harlingen-San Benito, TX	5 751	83 540	18 924	12 106	13 406	2 635	2 058	1 554	18 602	902	55.0	16.9	48.1
Bryan-College Station, TX	3 177	45 391	5 647	4 801	8 251	1 867	3 259	1 015	22 361	1 084	35.4	11.5	35.1
Buffalo-Niagara Falls, NY	26 960	460 436	64 116	79 524	63 546	25 060	23 887	13 035	28 310	1 660	38.3	6.4	51.7
Burlington, VT	6 607	92 101	13 000	18 363	13 831	3 927	5 488	2 698	29 294	1 303	25.4	10.9	59.3
Canton-Massillon, OH	9 902	163 072	23 539	41 624	23 059	5 599	4 544	4 331	26 559	1 769	36.2	4.5	43.5
Casper, WY	2 580	26 574	3 800	1 702	4 058	1 085	1 101	667	25 100	311	20.6	48.9	58.5
Cedar Rapids, IA	5 317	109 920	11 278	20 752	13 359	6 171	4 447	3 529	32 105	1 480	28.9	11.6	51.8
Champaign-Urbana, IL	4 101	68 571	9 709	9 745	10 860	2 990	3 041	1 673	24 398	1 371	17.4	31.1	63.8
Charleston, WV	7 106	105 812	16 447	7 490	16 179	6 382	5 652	2 988	28 239	608	27.3	1.2	35.7
Charleston-North Charles-ton, SC	13 850	214 598	29 685	21 544	30 308	6 488	11 230	5 425	25 280	872	47.4	8.5	39.9
Charlotte-Gastonia-Rock Hill, NC-SC	41 367	757 708	68 218	127 171	87 464	46 958	40 433	24 393	32 193	4 253	40.0	4.7	41.3
Charlottesville, VA	4 601	66 079	11 563	7 483	9 650	5 079	3 876	1 822	27 573	1 201	26.7	9.5	44.5
Chattanooga, TN-GA	11 294	205 532	22 958	44 815	26 269	15 876	8 352	5 522	26 867	1 766	41.2	4.5	32.4
Cheyenne, WY	2 287	26 708	4 643	1 587	5 387	1 964	1 034	622	23 289	615	10.4	55.9	56.7
Chicago-Gary-Kenosha, IL-IN-WI	227 107	4 177 809	446 337	640 380	468 712	273 322	301 849	157 732	37 755	7 015	32.8	21.7	56.1
Chicago, IL	208 299	3 847 229	403 303	574 233	422 846	263 751	292 688	148 044	38 481	4 878	34.3	21.2	57.0
Gary, IN	13 429	225 276	30 950	47 229	33 019	7 098	7 369	6 770	30 052	918	32.0	19.9	49.5
Kankakee, IL	2 305	55 090	5 642	6 759	5 852	1 483	677	1 491	27 065	831	21.8	31.0	61.1
Kenosha, WI	3 074	50 214	6 442	12 159	6 995	990	1 115	1 427	28 418	388	40.5	12.4	49.5
Chico-Paradise, CA	4 534	52 142	10 142	4 512	9 352	1 825	2 556	1 143	21 921	1 942	58.7	9.4	54.8
Cincinnati-Hamilton, OH-KY-IN	46 760	917 611	114 262	137 985	111 681	48 356	50 632	29 409	32 050	8 586	38.3	4.0	37.2
Cincinnati, OH-KY-IN	40 532	809 222	100 006	117 077	98 438	41 360	46 253	26 130	32 290	7 737	38.0	3.8	36.4
Hamilton-Middletown, OH	6 228	108 389	14 256	20 908	13 243	6 996	4 379	3 279	30 252	849	40.8	6.6	43.7
Clarksville-Hopkinsville, TN-KY	3 649	54 928	8 465	12 227	10 138	1 653	1 453	1 218	22 174	2 146	29.7	10.5	44.9
Cleveland-Akron, OH	76 991	1 348 990	181 076	256 788	162 097	73 840	68 482	43 466	32 221	4 645	45.3	4.0	44.7
Akron, OH	17 603	290 061	36 909	55 559	38 311	10 527	12 001	9 179	31 645	970	50.7	3.3	42.2
Cleveland-Lorain-Elyria, OH	59 388	1 058 929	144 167	201 229	123 786	63 313	56 481	34 287	32 379	3 675	43.9	4.2	45.4
Colorado Springs, CO	13 387	202 377	23 093	22 992	28 749	10 148	14 564	6 037	29 830	851	32.2	32.0	42.0
Columbia, MO	3 775	60 320	13 509	5 757	9 268	5 220	2 101	1 428	23 674	1 227	28.8	10.8	35.6

Table C. Metropolitan Areas — Agriculture, Land, and Water

	Agriculture, 1997 (cont'd)														
	Land in farms				Value of land and buildings			Value of products sold				Percent of farms with sales of —			
		Acres					Value of machinery and equipment			Percent from —					
Area Name	Acreage (1,000)	Percent change, 1992–1997	Average size of farm	Total irrigated (1,000)	Total cropland (1,000)	Average per farm ($1,000)	Average per acre (dollars)	Average per farm ($1,000)	Total (mil dol)	Average per farm (dollars)	Crops	Live-stock and poultry products	$10,000 or more	$100,000 or more	Percent of land owned by Fed. Gov. 1997	Water con-sump-tion 1995 (mil gal/day)
	117	118	119	120	121	122	123	124	125	126	127	128	129	130	131	132
Abilene, TX	492	-3.4	469	2	207	280	582	31	53	50 446	18.0	82.0	27.8	4.1	0.9	25.1
Albany, GA	221	25.7	747	29	120	1 089	1 422	118	64	217 821	85.0	15.0	49.7	27.7	0.8	160.3
Albany-Schenectady-Troy, NY	493	-0.9	194	3	327	288	1 501	49	156	61 517	28.0	72.0	48.0	16.2	0.4	801.2
Albuquerque, NM	1 628	6.1	1 115	38	67	349	326	24	68	46 311	21.0	79.0	20.3	3.8	29.7	437.3
Alexandria, LA	194	-7.8	238	7	122	333	1 464	56	55	67 534	88.0	12.0	39.8	16.4	11.6	497.7
Allentown-Bethlehem-Easton, PA	190	3.7	192	1	164	645	3 480	64	93	94 080	70.0	30.0	55.4	17.8	0.6	558.1
Altoona, PA	84	10.3	199	0	60	379	2 008	57	51	120 855	14.0	86.0	65.2	38.2	0.1	35.7
Amarillo, TX	910	1.2	1 142	47	D	493	411	48	222	278 004	10.0	90.0	44.0	15.4	3.0	82.8
Anchorage, AK	NA	NA	NA	NA	NA	NA	NA	NA	NA	NA	NA	NA	NA	NA	NA	45.2
Anniston, AL	77	4.6	123	1	39	260	1 896	32	54	85 668	12.0	87.0	22.9	7.6	21.3	26.3
Appleton-Oshkosh-Neenah, WI	564	-5.5	198	1	470	305	1 556	81	280	98 230	24.0	76.0	66.7	30.2	0.1	142.2
Asheville, NC	167	-10.5	87	1	63	263	3 021	20	45	23 243	74.0	26.0	23.7	2.1	15.4	42.0
Athens, GA	134	6.9	133	1	60	320	2 367	29	163	161 742	7.0	93.0	37.1	19.0	0.3	24.3
Atlanta, GA	640	1.4	115	D	283	385	3 514	25	455	81 724	12.0	88.0	27.3	11.2	1.1	1 364.1
Auburn-Opalika, AL	76	11.5	218	1	22	409	1 847	47	20	57 226	86.4	13.6	30.5	3.5	0.0	18.9
Augusta-Aiken, GA-SC	291	3.0	195	D	127	287	1 435	35	98	65 515	D	D	27.4	8.9	9.6	449.4
Austin-San Marcos, TX	1 890	-5.5	281	8	729	401	1 498	26	136	20 175	43.0	57.0	23.7	3.5	1.1	651.0
Bakersfield, CA	2 851	0.4	1 428	913	1 054	2 162	1 605	189	1 969	985 735	91.0	9.0	66.8	45.6	27.9	2 462.7
Bangor, ME	117	-1.2	222	2	49	226	1 058	43	30	57 101	37.0	63.0	40.6	13.5	0.4	21.5
Barnstable-Yarmouth, MA	5	-5.1	21	2	2	329	15 774	32	18	82 466	94.0	6.0	57.9	14.5	15.5	39.5
Baton Rouge, LA	191	-12.2	164	D	106	361	2 047	41	62	53 061	D	D	23.1	6.2	0.0	404.2
Beaumont-Port Arthur, TX	587	42.5	470	34	224	421	912	32	32	25 718	65.0	35.0	24.3	7.0	6.8	432.9
Bellingham, WA	104	-12.2	84	26	81	449	5 321	56	242	196 778	17.0	83.0	53.3	29.2	61.5	160.8
Benton Harbor, MI	174	4.2	147	11	146	283	1 913	63	81	68 846	89.0	11.0	52.9	16.2	0.0	2 195.8
Billings, MT	1 526	4.9	1 391	80	381	524	372	57	96	87 552	31.0	69.0	51.3	16.7	5.2	440.4
Biloxi-Gulfport-Pascagoula, MS	87	20.4	104	0	39	246	2 344	27	10	11 381	49.0	51.0	17.4	1.9	10.6	228.0
Binghamton, NY	195	-8.4	194	1	110	168	929	41	52	51 143	15.0	85.0	39.3	14.3	0.1	141.5
Birmingham, AL	325	0.7	123	4	169	293	2 384	30	217	82 001	10.0	90.0	26.6	10.6	0.0	870.5
Bismarck, ND	2 124	0.6	1 197	7	1 045	388	311	65	96	54 313	39.0	61.0	64.1	15.4	1.0	49.7
Bloomington, IN	62	5.3	131	0	36	296	2 344	27	8	17 772	58.0	42.0	25.8	4.4	8.7	14.6
Bloomington-Normal, IL	697	-1.8	472	1	666	1 278	2 657	130	238	161 521	89.0	11.0	81.9	46.8	0.0	17.0
Boise City, ID	586	-6.1	188	299	325	384	2 093	56	405	129 887	48.0	52.0	44.6	17.3	28.4	1 737.3
Boston-Worcester-Lawrence-Lowell-Brockton, MA-NH....	379	-2.0	86	20	D	472	5 771	42	348	78 736	81.0	19.0	45.7	14.6	1.1	916.0
Brownsville-Harlingen-San Benito, TX	369	12.0	409	109	230	446	1 143	62	79	88 042	88.0	12.0	40.7	18.1	4.4	456.5
Bryan-College Station, TX	265	-10.4	245	6	104	402	1 517	34	41	37 993	19.0	81.0	26.8	3.5	0.0	33.5
Buffalo-Niagara Falls, NY	271	-3.7	163	4	214	239	1 474	63	136	81 660	51.0	49.0	47.9	17.0	0.1	1 529.1
Burlington, VT	295	-5.3	226	1	158	380	1 607	58	135	103 422	9.0	91.0	56.3	30.9	1.9	34.8
Canton-Massillon, OH	250	-3.4	141	1	175	304	2 374	43	94	53 293	40.0	60.0	42.6	11.1	1.0	48.2
Casper, WY	2 807	11.9	9 025	49	52	1 806	190	54	27	86 135	12.0	88.0	54.3	20.3	41.7	190.3
Cedar Rapids, IA	339	-2.8	229	0	292	526	2 347	60	113	76 662	66.0	34.0	60.6	20.8	0.0	259.9
Champaign-Urbana, IL	568	-0.8	414	6	549	1 201	2 940	117	190	138 614	96.0	4.0	85.7	42.0	0.3	36.1
Charleston, WV	76	0.6	126	D	27	179	1 452	19	6	9 525	77.0	23.0	12.3	1.0	0.0	707.7
Charleston-North Charleston, SC	161	10.2	184	D	73	301	1 828	40	70	80 835	76.0	24.0	34.4	9.6	16.8	645.1
Charlotte-Gastonia-Rock Hill, NC-SC	591	2.5	139	3	374	383	2 803	37	450	105 711	23.0	77.0	32.1	12.9	0.1	3 504.9
Charlottesville, VA	265	-6.7	221	1	119	693	3 106	40	32	26 795	18.0	82.0	33.8	3.4	3.8	135.7
Chattanooga, TN-GA	241	-6.2	137	1	123	296	1 967	26	81	45 834	8.0	92.0	23.9	6.4	3.0	1 559.7
Cheyenne, WY	1 728	1.7	2 810	61	D	659	241	70	96	156 031	21.0	79.0	59.5	18.5	0.9	112.8
Chicago-Gary-Kenosha, IL-IN-WI	2 310	-4.9	329	43	2 155	1 080	3 374	100	968	137 969	81.0	19.0	69.4	33.0	1.2	13 655.0
Chicago, IL	1 590	-6.0	326	16	1 481	1 169	3 681	101	712	145 893	79.0	21.0	69.4	33.4	1.2	10 738.3
Gary, IN	283	-1.3	309	13	262	789	2 539	68	90	98 098	88.0	12.0	61.8	27.5	2.3	2 852.6
Kankakee, IL	352	-2.1	423	14	338	1 102	2 759	132	133	159 906	89.0	11.0	82.6	40.2	0.0	29.0
Kenosha, WI	85	-8.9	218	0	74	613	2 961	98	33	85 698	64.0	36.0	59.0	25.5	0.0	35.1
Chico-Paradise, CA	404	-10.6	208	224	247	754	3 589	73	286	147 388	97.0	3.0	57.3	26.7	14.1	957.7
Cincinnati-Hamilton, OH-KY-IN	1 109	-6.1	129	5	748	318	2 502	36	217	25 246	75.0	25.0	37.0	5.4	0.5	1 632.8
Cincinnati, OH-KY-IN	974	-6.6	126	4	641	296	2 430	34	182	23 489	78.0	22.0	36.3	4.7	0.6	1 559.0
Hamilton-Middletown, OH .	135	-2.5	158	0	108	517	3 024	50	35	41 263	61.0	39.0	43.0	11.7	0.3	73.9
Clarksville-Hopkinsville, TN-KY	474	0.0	221	2	339	346	1 615	47	113	52 827	76.0	24.0	46.0	12.0	7.0	35.4
Cleveland-Akron, OH	571	-5.4	123	7	421	370	3 182	51	294	63 223	75.0	25.0	41.3	9.9	1.7	2 112.9
Akron, OH......................	105	-9.0	108	1	73	364	3 536	38	33	33 722	64.0	36.0	37.5	8.0	6.3	99.9
Cleveland-Lorain-Elyria, OH.................................	467	-4.6	127	6	348	372	3 103	54	261	71 010	77.0	23.0	42.3	10.4	0.2	2 013.0
Colorado Springs, CO	867	1.2	1 019	15	78	410	443	27	30	35 640	41.0	59.0	36.1	6.2	14.9	134.7
Columbia, MO	250	-8.1	204	4	172	331	1 599	37	40	32 684	42.0	58.0	34.8	5.9	0.8	18.2

Area Name	Value of Residential Construction Authorized by Building Permits, 2000		Wholesale Trade, 1997				Retail Trade[1], 1997				Real Estate and Rental and Leasing, 1997			
	New Construction ($1,000)	Number of Housing Units	Number of Establishments	Number of Employees	Sales (mil dol)	Annual Payroll (mil dol)	Number of Establishments	Number of Employees	Sales (mil dol)	Annual Payroll (mil dol)	Number of Establishments	Number of Employees	Receipts (mil dol)	Annual Payroll (mil dol)
	133	134	135	136	137	138	139	140	141	142	143	144	145	146
Abilene, TX	33 646	374	219	1 996	933.9	54.1	635	7 211	1 297.7	116.7	168	876	88.4	16.7
Albany, GA	59 565	681	191	2 398	1 029.5	70.7	613	8 069	1 208.7	118.3	133	636	83.4	12.5
Albany-Schenectady-Troy, NY	336 963	2 650	1 094	14 639	7 447.2	507.2	3 582	47 672	7 673.7	744.7	669	4 116	580.3	91.5
Albuquerque, NM	473 991	4 773	1 110	13 384	4 880.7	401.0	2 593	38 256	7 107.8	685.0	823	4 808	530.8	89.2
Alexandria, LA	44 876	440	173	1 789	581.1	45.6	586	7 397	1 188.3	108.5	92	660	57.8	12.4
Allentown-Bethlehem-Easton, PA	336 169	2 863	906	12 174	6 826.3	430.3	2 427	31 129	5 657.8	532.3	406	2 388	291.9	51.1
Altoona, PA	20 947	226	160	2 836	1 641.3	82.3	639	8 310	1 331.2	117.7	90	419	34.8	6.9
Amarillo, TX	71 792	557	357	4 824	2 390.8	153.0	987	12 238	2 369.5	209.7	256	1 173	130.8	21.4
Anchorage, AK	202 855	1 190	434	4 748	1 989.1	181.4	1 001	15 115	3 114.9	319.3	356	2 145	322.2	56.8
Anniston, AL	43 645	336	130	1 688	890.9	47.0	578	6 747	982.0	92.5	73	298	24.5	4.4
Appleton-Oshkosh-Neenah, WI	305 440	2 687	530	7 927	2 881.4	271.5	1 429	21 545	3 658.6	343.7	290	1 469	143.9	26.8
Asheville, NC	174 663	1 470	349	4 358	1 369.7	128.4	1 187	13 506	2 242.4	214.4	229	1 053	132.5	21.9
Athens, GA	136 009	1 358	150	D	D	D	669	9 012	1 361.8	130.9	168	661	71.3	11.5
Atlanta, GA	6 071 988	64 216	9 263	140 471	138 768.4	6 098.7	14 631	221 587	40 479.3	3 984.0	4 742	34 506	5 451.9	1 061.2
Auburn-Opalika, AL	59 568	574	86	727	308.0	18.6	425	5 437	774.4	73.7	84	464	35.0	6.9
Augusta-Aiken, GA-SC	264 080	2 277	455	3 774	1 536.8	112.8	1 883	24 355	3 850.6	367.9	415	1 699	179.0	32.3
Austin-San Marcos, TX	2 038 645	21 889	1 613	20 998	10 048.4	797.7	4 157	60 049	18 878.3	1 160.8	1 532	7 554	945.7	180.9
Bakersfield, CA	371 103	3 070	612	7 930	4 313.9	256.4	1 918	22 792	4 224.4	412.1	419	2 479	220.5	43.8
Bangor, ME	38 476	482	196	2 786	938.0	85.6	796	9 433	1 654.6	148.0	146	620	66.9	9.5
Barnstable-Yarmouth, MA	363 416	1 882	259	1 361	462.8	45.5	1 592	13 675	2 518.8	256.5	286	917	138.1	21.4
Baton Rouge, LA	293 552	3 222	951	11 993	4 904.9	404.6	2 402	34 451	5 540.0	516.9	606	4 330	404.0	84.2
Beaumont-Port Arthur, TX	98 504	810	445	5 293	2 176.2	174.5	1 526	19 904	3 467.6	299.4	345	2 024	221.3	39.9
Bellingham, WA	170 603	1 625	308	2 451	1 042.7	76.0	840	9 758	1 673.3	165.7	220	877	91.8	12.3
Benton Harbor, MI	84 030	507	193	1 887	938.3	60.0	674	8 078	1 302.5	125.6	164	627	186.3	10.5
Billings, MT	54 381	464	389	4 915	2 648.9	143.4	717	8 736	1 575.6	144.9	195	770	85.9	12.3
Biloxi-Gulfport-Pascagoula, MS	290 651	3 819	295	2 909	992.3	76.2	1 523	18 255	2 776.7	255.4	342	1 332	113.8	20.1
Binghamton, NY	31 063	253	292	D	D	D	974	13 086	1 981.4	184.3	141	668	86.3	10.7
Birmingham, AL	611 752	5 133	1 971	29 990	18 884.2	1 038.0	3 844	52 390	9 000.7	830.0	815	6 919	945.4	168.8
Bismarck, ND	63 687	502	192	1 983	813.2	52.6	467	6 058	1 010.6	100.9	113	616	52.8	7.4
Bloomington, IN	73 296	620	102	D	D	D	514	6 846	1 073.7	97.5	162	869	83.1	15.3
Bloomington-Normal, IL	78 742	909	212	2 268	1 348.4	87.1	632	9 242	1 474.6	142.3	134	704	99.8	14.6
Boise City, ID	777 249	6 042	735	9 122	5 917.9	312.0	1 693	21 387	4 177.3	389.9	467	2 128	220.0	37.1
Boston-Worcester-Lawrence-Lowell-Brockton, MA-NH	2 649 511	18 184	10 229	150 552	114 849.2	6 714.1	24 369	331 207	59 245.8	5 820.2	5 656	41 467	5 844.8	1 228.5
Brownsville-Harlingen-San Benito, TX	194 470	3 111	387	3 772	1 218.9	81.6	1 117	13 089	1 904.0	179.3	283	1 208	98.5	18.1
Bryan-College Station, TX	101 964	1 372	130	1 655	426.5	41.9	569	7 994	1 336.2	122.2	181	1 090	78.5	17.2
Buffalo-Niagara Falls, NY	311 999	2 672	1 917	28 285	15 619.1	949.1	4 514	66 786	9 643.8	957.2	849	5 834	769.9	134.2
Burlington, VT	118 222	924	359	4 749	2 216.5	156.2	1 228	12 998	2 188.1	218.2	248	1 018	127.0	20.8
Canton-Massillon, OH	191 180	1 279	542	8 422	4 235.3	281.0	1 697	23 989	3 800.8	368.5	281	1 296	127.6	23.1
Casper, WY	16 904	145	206	1 853	984.1	59.2	399	3 985	645.6	65.2	106	414	39.2	8.4
Cedar Rapids, IA	131 869	1 679	375	5 653	2 324.1	166.0	874	13 337	2 040.9	213.9	199	1 135	128.8	25.6
Champaign-Urbana, IL	105 873	1 049	199	3 737	2 419.0	111.5	675	10 645	1 556.7	151.9	203	1 356	179.7	27.3
Charleston, WV	42 111	367	448	6 062	2 585.3	190.2	1 177	16 569	2 793.6	247.8	312	1 658	213.3	33.0
Charleston-North Charleston, SC	744 172	5 387	606	6 644	4 402.0	209.1	2 424	29 095	4 538.1	441.1	590	3 352	366.3	62.6
Charlotte-Gastonia-Rock Hill, NC-SC	2 417 584	23 928	3 762	50 099	41 925.7	1 956.1	5 866	79 252	14 439.8	1 358.7	1 507	11 445	1 656.4	332.2
Charlottesville, VA	171 594	1 188	160	1 676	525.9	56.6	744	9 065	1 506.7	147.3	199	887	91.9	18.4
Chattanooga, TN-GA	273 856	2 510	814	10 120	4 889.3	302.3	2 048	25 869	4 194.6	404.7	419	2 315	255.9	62.3
Cheyenne, WY	33 835	245	81	665	267.5	18.6	358	4 851	855.5	77.8	88	321	27.7	5.2
Chicago-Gary-Kenosha, IL-IN-WI	5 643 625	42 511	17 360	271 372	237 956.8	11 660.0	30 327	442 052	81 073.8	8 015.9	9 032	63 269	11 824.8	1 933.6
Chicago, IL	5 097 208	38 073	16 373	258 217	230 934.2	11 214.5	27 221	398 282	73 673.5	7 334.5	8 299	59 915	11 431.1	1 866.8
Gary, IN	390 415	3 035	721	8 917	4 818.0	305.8	2 172	31 734	5 420.9	497.2	536	2 594	315.0	54.3
Kankakee, IL	50 466	389	126	1 628	809.3	47.2	388	5 594	907.0	88.5	85	348	34.9	5.9
Kenosha, WI	105 536	1 014	135	2 515	1 385.3	91.5	546	6 442	1 072.4	95.7	112	412	43.8	6.6
Chico-Paradise, CA	130 380	1 134	179	1 792	637.9	56.9	777	9 004	1 502.6	154.0	212	1 012	80.5	13.4
Cincinnati-Hamilton, OH-KY-IN	1 341 718	12 109	3 352	D	D	D	7 287	111 122	18 144.7	1 735.0	1 888	12 308	1 725.1	298.7
Cincinnati, OH-KY-IN	1 088 338	9 724	2 898	48 487	43 669.5	1 817.7	6 365	97 593	15 956.2	1 526.5	1 653	10 984	1 575.4	273.0
Hamilton-Middletown, OH	253 380	2 385	454	D	D	D	922	13 529	2 188.6	208.5	235	1 324	149.7	25.7
Clarksville-Hopkinsville, TN-KY	97 331	1 672	172	1 997	964.3	59.0	824	9 731	1 640.7	151.8	179	644	76.4	9.9
Cleveland-Akron, OH	1 618 456	10 745	5 790	80 340	45 381.4	3 113.1	11 511	162 090	27 129.8	2 668.4	2 725	22 109	2 614.9	468.0
Akron, OH	459 187	3 342	1 253	16 023	9 624.2	598.1	2 637	38 291	6 633.6	639.5	580	3 403	413.2	74.7
Cleveland-Lorain-Elyria, OH	1 159 269	7 403	4 537	64 317	35 757.1	2 515.0	8 874	123 799	20 496.2	2 028.9	2 145	18 706	2 201.7	393.2
Colorado Springs, CO	710 778	6 264	498	6 513	1 417.9	213.3	1 901	27 806	5 015.1	503.6	735	3 064	362.3	62.8
Columbia, MO	118 678	1 263	138	1 651	684.7	49.9	602	8 880	1 469.7	135.3	173	642	75.2	11.0

1. Establishments with payroll.

Table C. Metropolitan Areas — Professional, Manufacturing, Accommodation and Foodservices, Finance and Insurance

Area Name	Professional, Scientific, and Technical Services[1], 1997				Manufacturing, 1997				Accommodation and Foodservices, 1997			
	Number of Establishments	Number of Employees	Sales (mil dol)	Annual Payroll (mil dol)	Number of Establishments	Number of Employees	Sales (mil dol)	Annual Payroll (mil dol)	Number of Establishments	Number of Employees	Sales (mil dol)	Annual Payroll (mil dol)
	147	148	149	150	151	152	153	154	155	156	157	158
Abilene, TX	229	1 123	93.2	30.4	118	3 062	1 011	80	269	5 497	151.6	41.8
Albany, GA	179	1 334	98.7	37.9	98	9 046	4 331	320	201	3 830	120.5	32.4
Albany-Schenectady-Troy, NY	1 768	16 154	1 617.7	636.1	752	31 436	6 970	1 128	1 969	25 692	896.4	251.5
Albuquerque, NM	2 032	23 668	2 619.1	1 054.9	800	25 743	14 171	788	1 374	29 191	952.4	267.3
Alexandria, LA	247	1 956	124.2	42.2	73	3 179	1 166	103	224	3 985	119.8	31.7
Allentown-Bethlehem-Easton, PA	1 136	7 230	677.1	248.9	920	45 167	10 640	1 500	1 258	18 589	649.5	176.0
Altoona, PA	181	1 838	151.6	53.5	157	8 966	1 592	252	254	4 003	108.8	29.6
Amarillo, TX	363	2 879	199.7	85.3	203	11 110	3 625	359	480	8 292	262.6	70.9
Anchorage, AK	907	5 939	767.2	301.3	187	2 022	322	63	640	11 364	574.0	165.8
Anniston, AL	149	702	45.2	13.2	149	10 841	1 505	258	185	4 262	114.4	31.3
Appleton-Oshkosh-Neenah, WI	510	4 259	361.2	142.9	683	54 679	12 361	1 918	777	13 519	370.7	103.3
Asheville, NC	477	2 409	174.9	77.5	347	18 516	3 111	518	530	9 360	340.4	100.8
Athens, GA	258	1 433	116.2	59.3	151	10 960	1 646	275	303	5 537	162.5	44.4
Atlanta, GA	12 807	113 482	13 392.6	5 216.8	4 394	190 720	49 692	6 386	7 296	158 518	6 002.3	1 681.2
Auburn-Opalika, AL	129	589	50.6	16.3	88	7 016	1 233	195	199	4 165	110.3	29.6
Augusta-Aiken, GA-SC	688	6 578	651.3	247.7	364	41 124	10 336	1 561	769	14 593	442.2	119.5
Austin-San Marcos, TX	3 699	30 168	3 460.5	1 392.2	1 192	68 826	24 925	2 529	2 211	45 599	1 605.8	453.9
Bakersfield, CA	753	6 296	525.7	224.6	390	14 306	2 825	379	1 013	14 724	493.2	129.1
Bangor, ME	271	1 388	102.7	45.9	155	8 897	1 659	286	344	4 778	151.3	45.8
Barnstable-Yarmouth, MA	571	1 919	173.7	63.9	226	2 561	349	82	1 144	11 852	624.3	177.3
Baton Rouge, LA	1 548	13 337	1 263.3	475.8	533	21 530	18 449	994	972	20 054	618.6	168.2
Beaumont-Port Arthur, TX	600	4 830	543.3	223.8	349	21 624	18 987	1 059	591	10 840	336.8	90.6
Bellingham, WA	390	2 615	246.5	109.0	314	9 184	3 947	281	429	5 926	195.5	52.8
Benton Harbor, MI	255	1 338	124.6	48.9	397	16 996	2 394	539	383	5 328	163.5	44.0
Billings, MT	404	2 664	199.7	74.9	182	3 223	1 798	110	365	6 691	205.3	58.7
Biloxi-Gulfport-Pascagoula, MS	551	4 266	340.5	140.6	260	21 327	5 786	686	640	13 826	445.5	119.5
Binghamton, NY	369	2 751	244.6	82.7	290	25 484	4 717	1 028	560	7 689	228.5	64.9
Birmingham, AL	2 073	17 463	1 813.0	716.2	1 120	47 970	9 236	1 478	1 505	30 643	961.3	269.4
Bismarck, ND	206	1 890	96.1	40.9	81	2 193	673	74	205	4 065	112.5	31.9
Bloomington, IN	196	1 360	97.0	34.0	122	8 817	2 444	303	302	6 312	176.6	48.8
Bloomington-Normal, IL	234	1 382	111.6	57.9	112	8 388	3 870	358	336	7 104	200.5	58.3
Boise City, ID	933	6 972	938.6	276.9	571	30 667	9 900	1 131	836	14 724	441.5	123.0
Boston-Worcester-Lawrence-Lowell-Brockton, MA-NH	18 317	178 861	23 091.4	9 440.2	9 384	422 764	83 290	16 622	13 151	211 551	8 494.5	2 352.5
Brownsville-Harlingen-San Benito, TX	339	2 278	126.5	42.7	235	12 694	1 733	242	513	8 349	278.2	71.7
Bryan-College Station, TX	279	2 086	200.9	74.8	101	3 126	382	80	275	5 668	170.7	48.2
Buffalo-Niagara Falls, NY	2 043	16 820	1 542.6	563.3	1 561	81 398	18 458	3 259	2 735	38 792	1 143.1	329.9
Burlington, VT	573	4 044	442.0	162.9	302	16 905	4 489	703	506	7 065	232.8	68.2
Canton-Massillon, OH	660	3 662	316.1	110.0	669	41 134	8 525	1 381	806	14 761	400.3	110.3
Casper, WY	205	1 213	81.0	30.7	91	1 440	328	41	172	2 924	79.0	21.8
Cedar Rapids, IA	369	2 936	268.6	106.7	239	22 877	6 376	935	439	7 853	240.1	68.2
Champaign-Urbana, IL	336	2 660	263.2	91.6	152	10 857	2 690	292	449	8 944	248.6	70.6
Charleston, WV	591	4 801	410.6	135.5	176	7 681	3 305	312	487	9 337	312.9	84.3
Charleston-North Charleston, SC	1 110	8 539	784.1	314.6	415	20 595	6 589	688	1 097	24 251	836.2	232.8
Charlotte-Gastonia-Rock Hill, NC-SC	3 302	32 123	3 264.0	1 258.3	2 422	133 983	32 134	4 062	2 651	53 527	1 811.8	491.3
Charlottesville, VA	415	2 562	206.6	84.6	142	6 980	1 163	236	338	6 816	245.8	72.6
Chattanooga, TN-GA	776	4 980	425.2	170.7	707	44 038	7 471	1 266	882	15 946	538.4	149.5
Cheyenne, WY	199	843	64.5	24.7	48	1 349	606	45	183	3 930	106.3	31.1
Chicago-Gary-Kenosha, IL-IN-WI	25 710	244 468	31 494.4	12 091.9	14 080	660 689	145 632	24 785	16 640	292 805	11 833.2	3 195.2
Chicago, IL	24 437	236 655	30 848.6	11 862.4	13 191	594 764	122 696	21 753	14 881	264 904	11 009.9	2 968.9
Gary, IN	965	6 619	565.4	196.4	569	49 462	18 651	2 373	1 190	19 792	589.6	161.9
Kankakee, IL	132	507	32.7	12.7	116	6 937	2 253	264	229	3 563	100.4	27.4
Kenosha, WI	176	687	47.7	20.4	204	9 526	2 031	396	340	4 546	133.3	37.1
Chico-Paradise, CA	308	1 513	130.7	45.0	232	4 944	772	128	380	5 920	156.2	43.3
Cincinnati-Hamilton, OH-KY-IN	4 039	40 006	4 145.8	1 571.7	2 686	139 924	35 239	5 358	3 793	77 902	2 668.8	735.5
Cincinnati, OH-KY-IN	3 595	36 858	3 853.9	1 482.5	2 290	119 533	28 671	4 539	3 274	67 983	2 382.5	655.8
Hamilton-Middletown, OH	444	3 148	291.9	89.2	396	20 391	6 568	819	519	9 919	286.3	79.6
Clarksville-Hopkinsville, TN-KY	199	1 076	66.3	20.0	139	10 988	2 052	298	338	6 907	187.8	55.5
Cleveland-Akron, OH	6 880	57 578	5 971.1	2 393.8	6 021	255 158	53 189	9 468	6 035	106 193	3 316.3	898.4
Akron, OH	1 499	10 377	1 052.4	401.7	1 389	55 296	9 001	1 924	1 423	24 958	736.8	208.1
Cleveland-Lorain-Elyria, OH	5 381	47 201	4 918.7	1 992.1	4 632	199 862	44 188	7 544	4 612	81 235	2 579.5	690.3
Colorado Springs, CO	1 384	10 515	1 199.2	467.1	499	21 593	5 699	701	998	21 480	771.9	216.9
Columbia, MO	272	1 588	112.4	39.1	87	5 703	1 595	165	312	5 983	180.1	48.4

1. Firms subject to federal tax.

Table C. Metropolitan Areas — Health and Other Services and Federal Funds

Area Name	Health Care and Social Assistance[1], 1997				Other Services[1], 1997				Federal funds and grants, fiscal 2001[2] Expenditures (mil dol)			
									Total	Direct payments for individuals		
	Number of Establishments	Number of Employees	Receipts (mil dol)	Annual Payroll (mil dol)	Number of Establishments	Number of Employees	Receipts (mil dol)	Annual Payroll (mil dol)		Social Security and government retirement	Medicare	Food stamps and Supplemental Security Income
	159	160	161	162	163	164	165	166	167	168	169	170
Abilene, TX	314	5 225	310.4	123.2	225	1 892	109.5	34.6	867.0	291.0	100.7	18.3
Albany, GA	257	3 419	243.2	111.9	185	1 214	74.5	23.6	772.3	253.4	88.7	42.0
Albany-Schenectady-Troy, NY	1 578	17 556	1 145.9	515.4	1 228	7 046	494.4	139.2	9 274.4	2 223.2	700.5	121.1
Albuquerque, NM	1 261	17 318	1 181.3	491.2	991	7 049	397.5	128.3	6 270.6	1 608.3	418.2	119.6
Alexandria, LA	335	5 666	306.0	129.1	170	984	55.3	16.7	813.0	292.4	142.6	41.1
Allentown-Bethlehem-Easton, PA	1 461	13 639	946.9	437.7	1 051	6 719	447.8	137.6	3 025.5	1 391.0	720.9	75.9
Altoona, PA	284	2 816	200.5	83.6	251	1 319	72.7	18.9	745.2	343.0	149.6	28.5
Amarillo, TX	503	6 506	513.0	217.3	379	2 488	146.5	42.7	1 083.7	404.9	149.4	27.4
Anchorage, AK	599	5 053	508.6	203.9	393	2 576	185.8	54.8	2 532.2	399.9	72.0	33.1
Anniston, AL	212	2 824	185.1	81.1	206	855	45.3	15.1	938.3	392.1	116.3	32.3
Appleton-Oshkosh-Neenah, WI	655	7 122	503.0	254.4	611	4 178	236.3	69.9	1 717.0	609.0	195.2	21.5
Asheville, NC	478	6 310	440.9	220.4	361	1 873	108.3	34.0	1 275.4	569.1	186.8	40.0
Athens, GA	327	2 530	212.4	103.7	203	1 333	72.2	21.6	706.8	239.2	84.4	22.7
Atlanta, GA	7 456	88 125	6 422.8	2 756.6	6 401	42 758	2 981.9	937.5	21 328.1	5 878.8	2 116.6	533.2
Auburn-Opalika, AL	133	1 478	104.9	51.3	125	661	35.6	10.2	399.8	177.5	53.7	18.8
Augusta-Aiken, GA-SC	892	11 392	824.1	349.9	638	3 889	204.8	63.4	4 394.7	1 130.3	319.4	104.4
Austin-San Marcos, TX	2 199	34 516	2 278.3	924.9	1 772	11 569	726.2	232.5	8 478.3	1 845.3	489.5	109.0
Bakersfield, CA	938	9 631	755.0	278.5	694	4 192	348.6	92.2	3 740.9	1 062.7	517.7	157.8
Bangor, ME	310	3 432	209.8	98.2	208	980	82.3	20.4	863.7	336.4	109.1	31.6
Barnstable-Yarmouth, MA	482	5 989	336.5	163.8	439	1 819	124.6	36.0	1 559.8	757.8	339.6	19.4
Baton Rouge, LA	1 166	18 146	1 096.0	481.6	899	6 714	424.2	132.3	3 499.5	969.0	498.2	131.8
Beaumont-Port Arthur, TX	921	14 230	813.2	346.5	614	4 075	236.6	69.4	2 254.3	790.9	468.4	74.3
Bellingham, WA	406	3 627	201.2	82.1	225	1 161	81.3	22.1	904.4	319.7	85.4	24.0
Benton Harbor, MI	281	2 395	154.1	71.3	262	1 452	77.6	25.1	821.1	369.6	149.2	40.7
Billings, MT	334	2 942	228.1	114.5	291	1 788	114.1	34.1	687.9	275.7	85.7	15.3
Biloxi-Gulfport-Pascagoula, MS	657	7 588	551.0	218.8	491	2 594	139.4	43.2	3 331.8	941.5	303.0	81.4
Binghamton, NY	389	4 234	300.8	137.4	346	1 573	103.9	27.5	1 591.1	585.5	214.0	44.4
Birmingham, AL	1 644	27 544	2 153.8	940.2	1 488	11 194	767.4	226.9	5 034.7	2 020.3	952.2	207.4
Bismarck, ND	161	1 589	128.6	59.3	184	1 030	59.7	17.9	778.9	194.1	62.8	9.2
Bloomington, IN	243	2 384	162.1	76.2	160	1 124	64.3	20.0	541.5	181.6	57.5	11.3
Bloomington-Normal, IL	228	2 901	190.8	91.6	226	1 433	85.6	26.8	551.2	218.2	73.6	11.9
Boise City, ID	893	9 685	646.0	303.7	620	3 882	210.0	62.2	2 095.2	755.4	193.1	44.8
Boston-Worcester-Lawrence-Lowell-Brockton, MA-NH	11 498	175 268	10 936.6	5 118.4	10 348	60 832	4 316.8	1 336.9	39 436.8	11 491.5	6 314.2	840.3
Brownsville-Harlingen-San Benito, TX	509	11 065	498.3	216.2	338	2 279	96.3	30.0	1 467.0	389.7	216.4	123.7
Bryan-College Station, TX	263	2 838	212.1	84.9	196	1 244	64.8	18.4	639.2	171.6	52.7	11.1
Buffalo-Niagara Falls, NY	2 275	29 298	1 579.8	703.1	1 908	10 373	664.7	189.8	6 683.2	2 802.0	1 100.2	225.9
Burlington, VT	450	4 724	274.4	120.0	362	1 658	109.9	32.0	1 239.3	326.9	103.0	22.1
Canton-Massillon, OH	756	9 782	617.2	296.8	710	4 693	273.9	85.0	1 785.6	900.8	357.1	60.1
Casper, WY	168	1 524	93.3	40.8	154	808	57.2	15.2	303.9	139.0	44.2	9.8
Cedar Rapids, IA	340	3 925	267.5	138.3	350	2 296	143.5	43.3	1 115.3	363.9	108.7	17.1
Champaign-Urbana, IL	204	4 973	367.9	182.4	244	1 241	65.0	21.0	930.7	262.1	80.4	21.2
Charleston, WV	618	7 204	576.5	230.8	389	2 604	142.4	44.1	2 107.2	706.1	255.7	60.4
Charleston-North Charleston, SC	1 050	12 478	812.1	329.6	863	5 636	320.9	102.9	3 939.7	1 358.8	344.7	104.2
Charlotte-Gastonia-Rock Hill, NC-SC	2 246	31 937	2 226.8	1 004.3	2 417	15 794	1 010.9	315.6	5 653.7	2 539.0	860.8	179.6
Charlottesville, VA	307	3 728	225.4	93.8	258	1 518	83.6	28.8	831.3	308.6	107.1	14.9
Chattanooga, TN-GA	908	12 904	949.7	422.6	690	4 483	267.1	81.0	3 090.5	1 085.9	464.7	92.1
Cheyenne, WY	153	1 576	105.7	51.0	127	1 122	165.2	24.3	900.6	223.2	49.7	8.8
Chicago-Gary-Kenosha, IL-IN-WI	16 389	181 324	13 092.7	5 736.1	13 631	93 958	6 738.5	2 069.3	41 568.8	14 618.6	7 617.0	1 813.0
Chicago, IL	14 682	164 115	11 992.3	5 225.2	12 268	84 406	6 159.4	1 883.7	37 549.6	12 862.9	6 808.2	1 648.2
Gary, IN	1 276	12 962	856.0	392.0	979	7 336	451.2	148.0	2 962.5	1 275.0	599.3	126.0
Kankakee, IL	168	1 730	107.6	53.0	162	954	59.8	18.3	498.9	213.6	106.4	21.9
Kenosha, WI	263	2 517	136.9	65.9	222	1 262	68.1	19.3	557.7	267.1	103.1	16.9
Chico-Paradise, CA	553	5 261	299.4	114.3	261	1 454	147.1	25.3	1 094.0	481.4	222.0	54.8
Cincinnati-Hamilton, OH-KY-IN	3 378	46 309	2 770.4	1 377.9	3 009	20 569	1 303.9	410.8	10 215.1	3 669.3	1 502.3	313.1
Cincinnati, OH-KY-IN	2 914	40 680	2 441.3	1 213.4	2 587	17 645	1 111.3	351.2	9 063.8	3 104.1	1 293.9	272.2
Hamilton-Middletown, OH	464	5 629	329.1	164.6	422	2 924	192.6	59.6	1 151.4	565.3	208.4	40.9
Clarksville-Hopkinsville, TN-KY	249	3 422	188.5	80.6	256	1 141	61.7	16.7	1 845.9	435.5	100.1	36.1
Cleveland-Akron, OH	5 791	69 515	4 290.2	2 062.6	5 032	34 570	2 329.6	666.1	15 062.4	5 972.4	3 059.1	549.6
Akron, OH	1 304	15 741	964.6	484.4	NA	NA	NA	NA	3 184.5	1 318.0	650.2	110.8
Cleveland-Lorain-Elyria, OH	4 487	53 774	3 325.6	1 578.2	3 873	26 825	1 911.5	532.6	11 878.0	4 654.4	2 408.9	438.8
Colorado Springs, CO	1 134	10 522	710.1	311.1	754	4 558	264.9	89.7	4 337.1	1 277.0	240.2	48.2
Columbia, MO	328	4 024	321.4	129.7	230	1 269	67.1	20.6	655.6	214.6	83.1	17.8

1. Firms subject to federal tax.   2. October 1, 1998 to September 30, 1999.

	Federal funds and grants, fiscal 2001[1] (cont'd)							Local government finances, 1997				
	Expenditures (mil dol) (cont'd)							General revenue				
	Procurement contract awards		Grants[2]							Taxes		
											Per capita[3] (dollars)	
Area Name	Salaries and wages	Defense	Other	Medicaid and other health-related	Nutrition and family welfare	Education	Other	Total (mil dol)	Intergovernmental (mil dol)	Total (mil dol)	Total	Property
	171	172	173	174	175	176	177	178	179	180	181	182
Abilene, TX	195.0	79.6	7.6	51.7	11.3	5.7	78.5	242.0	104.8	97.6	804	596
Albany, GA	141.1	42.9	30.0	80.6	32.9	12.9	12.9	300.2	132.2	109.6	931	552
Albany-Schenectady-Troy, NY	509.7	222.1	363.7	990.2	1 528.4	663.4	1 612.5	2 819.6	930.7	1 368.9	1 562	1 148
Albuquerque, NM	842.5	379.8	1 860.6	471.2	97.0	60.7	295.6	1 492.3	794.3	389.9	578	346
Alexandria, LA	101.6	21.5	13.6	101.4	17.1	11.1	43.2	251.4	107.2	113.8	900	376
Allentown-Bethlehem-Easton, PA	144.6	165.2	45.1	217.2	44.0	15.3	116.6	1 590.8	542.5	657.5	1 071	839
Altoona, PA	49.5	0.3	8.4	87.9	20.4	5.8	30.2	243.5	120.0	78.2	598	430
Amarillo, TX	101.3	126.1	125.0	49.0	13.3	8.3	41.6	406.1	139.8	171.0	822	620
Anchorage, AK	785.0	399.5	118.2	246.6	62.1	34.4	328.5	747.0	306.7	234.7	935	835
Anniston, AL	107.5	156.5	11.6	55.3	9.2	8.7	27.4	301.6	98.5	51.1	436	125
Appleton-Oshkosh-Neenah, WI	66.1	555.5	26.3	101.9	23.6	14.6	44.7	951.2	418.1	321.1	938	914
Asheville, NC	134.6	14.7	44.1	134.1	19.9	14.2	78.9	455.2	204.1	151.4	717	531
Athens, GA	98.9	5.5	22.4	87.4	21.7	12.2	81.4	434.7	108.3	113.0	816	549
Atlanta, GA	2 735.4	5 056.3	970.4	1 299.7	642.7	436.0	1 045.6	9 887.1	3 083.8	4 233.6	1 167	829
Auburn-Opalika, AL	23.2	3.4	3.4	35.5	8.7	6.6	49.7	272.4	66.3	53.8	546	170
Augusta-Aiken, GA-SC	608.0	117.6	1 623.6	277.3	64.3	28.2	49.4	881.1	388.4	309.8	678	437
Austin-San Marcos, TX	536.6	520.5	340.6	761.8	895.7	808.8	1 966.3	2 514.5	548.5	1 325.3	1 237	976
Bakersfield, CA	641.9	278.9	112.8	326.0	141.5	55.2	80.9	2 258.4	1 111.7	475.7	757	618
Bangor, ME	93.5	23.4	15.2	122.5	18.4	13.8	58.4	315.8	121.4	137.6	960	908
Barnstable-Yarmouth, MA	130.7	78.8	29.7	83.1	17.0	10.5	69.0	522.1	107.6	331.0	1 614	1 548
Baton Rouge, LA	153.5	250.7	33.6	288.3	301.6	214.2	533.9	1 129.7	383.7	523.9	919	308
Beaumont-Port Arthur, TX	163.5	255.4	74.2	204.1	37.8	16.2	49.8	824.0	210.5	444.2	1 185	923
Bellingham, WA	45.1	261.9	18.0	64.3	19.6	10.6	20.1	363.0	155.4	129.3	838	559
Benton Harbor, MI	24.7	2.6	12.9	115.4	26.8	13.5	35.6	404.7	221.7	101.0	629	610
Billings, MT	102.5	1.6	27.1	65.6	15.2	8.8	42.5	248.1	82.9	83.5	664	613
Biloxi-Gulfport-Pascagoula, MS	758.4	829.4	181.5	94.8	29.8	19.0	43.3	948.5	265.3	246.1	717	605
Binghamton, NY	58.2	412.6	18.6	134.6	33.1	18.0	43.7	830.0	324.9	368.8	1 465	1 101
Birmingham, AL	495.2	103.9	176.3	572.2	82.0	54.9	220.3	2 007.8	741.1	841.0	934	359
Bismarck, ND	62.5	26.4	13.6	52.4	49.9	46.7	185.1	177.5	61.2	67.3	739	641
Bloomington, IN	25.2	1.0	13.3	146.1	7.5	8.8	54.8	209.9	67.1	83.6	716	589
Bloomington-Normal, IL	48.0	1.6	12.1	25.5	7.8	6.0	49.2	287.4	91.3	149.2	1 060	903
Boise City, ID	277.8	39.3	117.6	205.7	72.4	58.2	267.0	716.5	297.1	258.9	675	625
Boston-Worcester-Lawrence-Lowell-Brockton, MA-NH	2 966.6	5 461.7	1 440.0	5 466.9	1 020.5	579.8	1 902.2	14 197.1	5 667.3	6 747.6	1 158	1 126
Brownsville-Harlingen-San Benito, TX	108.3	3.7	16.3	314.8	68.6	39.3	99.9	726.9	441.5	157.7	492	367
Bryan-College Station, TX	54.5	12.0	22.6	80.7	9.9	9.1	160.3	246.1	60.9	125.8	946	712
Buffalo-Niagara Falls, NY	557.5	212.1	137.1	908.6	240.0	84.6	163.9	4 038.1	1 458.7	1 737.1	1 491	1 061
Burlington, VT	148.1	276.9	28.1	176.0	25.8	12.6	66.7	368.3	83.9	222.9	1 166	1 139
Canton-Massillon, OH	81.6	15.6	30.9	162.9	45.1	25.6	40.7	837.3	356.8	339.6	843	591
Casper, WY	39.1	1.6	8.3	20.6	8.1	4.4	17.1	170.5	100.0	31.4	494	285
Cedar Rapids, IA	60.4	355.6	32.5	68.3	20.0	6.4	25.6	464.3	173.9	175.0	963	924
Champaign-Urbana, IL	76.5	36.7	16.1	90.3	15.3	12.4	223.0	372.4	147.4	150.3	892	780
Charleston, WV	159.5	12.0	57.2	184.1	115.8	91.4	402.6	498.9	184.9	192.2	757	571
Charleston-North Charleston, SC	701.9	582.5	134.9	348.9	55.7	37.0	179.8	1 079.6	410.7	391.8	768	585
Charlotte-Gastonia-Rock Hill, NC-SC	468.1	57.4	568.4	446.8	123.8	78.4	150.7	4 024.7	1 320.7	1 129.3	836	654
Charlottesville, VA	79.7	24.7	28.8	167.3	8.9	10.9	65.1	266.0	91.6	140.9	961	681
Chattanooga, TN-GA	456.6	12.7	508.7	250.7	47.9	37.9	68.9	1 268.1	347.9	336.3	751	517
Cheyenne, WY	222.1	89.7	18.1	63.8	33.0	40.0	126.7	251.1	109.5	42.9	547	361
Chicago-Gary-Kenosha, IL-IN-WI	4 636.2	1 202.6	1 926.5	4 389.6	1 108.8	390.7	1 680.8	26 946.9	8 321.0	13 719.7	1 588	1 271
Chicago, IL	4 465.1	1 115.4	1 871.7	3 909.6	973.4	357.1	1 556.5	24 443.5	7 352.2	12 684.0	1 632	1 284
Gary, IN	121.1	78.0	36.4	379.7	102.2	21.5	103.4	1 832.0	651.5	785.8	1 260	1 235
Kankakee, IL	24.8	0.4	4.3	45.2	14.9	5.1	11.0	227.2	107.0	80.9	793	721
Kenosha, WI	25.2	8.8	14.2	55.1	18.3	7.0	9.8	444.2	210.3	169.0	1 183	1 108
Chico-Paradise, CA	27.9	2.4	22.8	120.5	38.8	16.0	11.1	568.4	340.3	112.7	580	416
Cincinnati-Hamilton, OH-KY-IN	910.4	1 124.8	526.1	1 030.9	217.8	100.4	307.8	4 930.2	1 666.8	2 150.3	1 112	754
Cincinnati, OH-KY-IN	876.0	1 084.0	515.1	915.4	189.4	87.5	254.4	4 256.6	1 415.0	1 867.4	1 162	776
Hamilton-Middletown, OH	34.4	40.8	11.0	115.5	28.4	12.9	53.4	673.7	251.8	283.0	866	645
Clarksville-Hopkinsville, TN-KY	915.2	169.2	8.5	76.4	19.3	12.2	15.9	350.8	127.8	99.2	502	255
Cleveland-Akron, OH	1 287.7	404.9	465.6	1 631.4	415.1	188.8	435.9	8 834.8	2 975.7	4 065.5	1 398	889
Akron, OH	185.6	191.0	57.9	282.3	87.7	43.9	109.0	1 903.2	611.4	866.3	1 269	806
Cleveland-Lorain-Elyria, OH	1 102.1	213.9	407.7	1 349.1	327.4	144.9	326.9	6 931.6	2 364.3	3 199.2	1 437	914
Colorado Springs, CO	1 331.2	1 029.2	126.6	105.4	43.2	30.7	51.7	1 187.2	404.2	379.5	791	492
Columbia, MO	99.1	5.5	18.9	77.8	8.7	18.7	73.1	223.9	79.2	93.9	731	424

1. October 1, 1998 to September 30, 1999. 2. State totals may include programs not allocated by county. 3. Based on the resident population estimated as of July 1 of the year shown.

Area Name	Local government finances, 1997 (cont'd)									Government employment, 1999			Presidential election, 2000²		
	Direct general expenditure							Debt outstanding					Percent of vote cast —		
	Total (mil dol)	Per capita¹ (dollars)	Percent of total for —					Total (mil dol)	Per capita¹ (dollars)	Federal civilian	Federal military	State and local	Democratic	Republican	All other
			Education	Health and hospitals	Police protection	Public welfare	Highways								
	183	184	185	186	187	188	189	190	191	192	193	194	195	196	197
Abilene, TX	240.2	1 978	55.5	5.6	6.1	0.7	4.0	124.8	1 027	1 461	4 956	8 488	24.4	73.7	1.9
Albany, GA	301.7	2 564	44.4	11.9	5.0	0.2	2.1	101.4	862	2 721	1 155	9 429	50.4	49.1	0.4
Albany-Schenectady-Troy, NY	2 885.1	3 292	47.4	2.4	3.4	13.7	4.6	2 001.3	2 284	7 962	3 451	100 290	52.8	41.5	5.6
Albuquerque, NM	1 552.0	2 300	44.1	2.2	7.4	0.6	5.4	1 508.3	2 235	13 600	6 646	51 437	48.2	47.2	4.6
Alexandria, LA	250.5	1 981	51.6	0.1	7.9	0.0	4.4	201.5	1 593	2 143	706	11 473	38.5	58.8	2.6
Allentown-Bethlehem-Easton, PA	1 668.2	2 718	48.4	2.4	2.8	8.4	2.9	3 154.0	5 138	2 847	2 106	28 074	49.7	46.5	3.8
Altoona, PA	242.1	1 849	59.3	0.3	2.9	5.5	3.7	328.0	2 505	962	437	7 463	34.9	62.9	2.2
Amarillo, TX	401.0	1 926	57.1	2.3	7.6	0.1	5.6	460.7	2 213	1 907	584	14 729	21.5	76.8	1.7
Anchorage, AK	796.1	3 171	47.4	3.8	5.0	1.1	7.7	1 314.8	5 237	9 696	10 542	17 704	NA	NA	NA
Anniston, AL	295.2	2 521	33.0	36.3	3.6	0.0	3.0	131.3	1 121	4 403	2 374	7 511	40.6	57.3	2.1
Appleton-Oshkosh-Neenah, WI	1 003.6	2 933	45.4	4.5	4.7	6.5	10.2	784.5	2 293	1 070	1 239	19 630	43.6	51.6	4.8
Asheville, NC	461.9	2 186	45.0	9.4	5.3	6.0	2.4	328.8	1 556	2 552	732	13 469	44.8	54.1	1.0
Athens, GA	401.3	2 897	31.4	32.5	5.1	0.8	2.8	253.2	1 828	1 673	881	18 016	44.3	53.6	2.1
Atlanta, GA	9 365.1	2 582	44.2	13.0	4.9	0.8	4.4	13 625.6	3 757	45 042	18 189	214 862	44.9	52.6	2.5
Auburn-Opalika, AL	269.9	2 741	40.6	31.9	3.5	0.0	3.9	317.7	3 225	345	704	12 885	38.1	58.6	3.3
Augusta-Aiken, GA-SC	874.6	1 913	52.7	6.4	4.9	0.3	3.9	663.5	1 451	7 302	11 114	34 163	39.7	59.0	1.3
Austin-San Marcos, TX	2 431.0	2 270	47.7	5.2	5.2	1.1	3.8	7 326.8	6 841	10 028	3 237	123 114	38.0	52.7	9.3
Bakersfield, CA	2 097.2	3 336	42.5	10.0	3.9	11.5	2.4	1 046.2	1 664	10 663	5 581	40 054	36.2	60.7	3.1
Bangor, ME	299.3	2 089	51.8	3.9	3.8	1.9	5.9	139.2	971	1 413	724	12 266	44.9	48.7	6.5
Barnstable-Yarmouth, MA	579.2	2 823	47.9	0.9	5.6	0.5	6.2	414.6	2 021	1 832	1 302	11 272	51.5	41.0	7.5
Baton Rouge, LA	1 136.6	1 993	42.8	3.8	7.2	0.2	5.9	1 190.2	2 088	2 628	3 287	58 767	42.9	55.0	2.1
Beaumont-Port Arthur, TX	840.7	2 242	50.5	2.4	5.8	0.4	4.9	1 448.5	3 863	2 875	1 127	23 207	46.8	51.8	1.4
Bellingham, WA	323.7	2 098	48.4	2.7	4.8	0.0	7.8	301.5	1 955	845	617	10 043	46.1	46.5	7.4
Benton Harbor, MI	397.8	2 475	57.8	7.5	4.1	0.9	4.9	189.4	1 178	439	332	8 571	43.2	54.7	2.2
Billings, MT	245.0	1 948	51.1	3.9	7.0	1.0	3.1	122.8	976	1 724	735	6 793	35.4	59.0	5.5
Biloxi-Gulfport-Pascagoula, MS	1 009.9	2 941	31.4	30.2	4.1	0.6	4.6	1 098.3	3 198	8 723	15 336	22 068	34.0	63.8	2.2
Binghamton, NY	822.1	3 266	47.5	2.6	2.7	13.2	4.9	330.4	1 313	1 011	512	20 018	49.8	44.9	5.3
Birmingham, AL	1 977.5	2 197	40.5	8.3	6.5	1.1	4.7	2 523.5	2 804	9 577	5 955	58 644	40.9	57.1	2.0
Bismarck, ND	169.1	1 857	45.5	1.1	5.1	3.8	8.7	128.0	1 406	1 032	737	8 898	29.1	64.5	6.5
Bloomington, IN	196.8	1 687	48.0	1.2	3.0	4.3	4.4	139.5	1 196	413	425	19 097	43.6	47.6	8.8
Bloomington-Normal, IL	271.8	1 931	47.3	1.5	6.8	1.7	7.9	221.9	1 576	973	332	12 968	40.9	55.8	3.2
Boise City, ID	772.0	2 011	51.5	1.7	5.9	0.9	6.0	331.0	862	4 832	1 837	27 206	30.8	63.4	5.8
Boston-Worcester-Lawrence-Lowell-Brockton, MA-NH	13 277.3	2 278	50.4	2.4	6.4	1.7	4.1	10 295.2	1 767	51 320	22 447	336 451	58.7	34.4	7.0
Brownsville-Harlingen-San Benito, TX	693.3	2 161	66.3	1.4	3.8	0.7	2.6	787.6	2 455	2 121	958	21 836	53.5	44.8	1.7
Bryan-College Station, TX	273.9	2 060	49.1	3.1	4.8	0.3	3.9	325.7	2 448	967	462	26 801	26.3	70.0	3.7
Buffalo-Niagara Falls, NY	4 160.4	3 572	42.5	6.0	4.0	14.0	4.0	2 336.8	2 006	10 096	2 701	75 314	55.6	38.8	5.6
Burlington, VT	361.1	1 890	63.9	0.2	4.2	0.0	5.6	351.8	1 841	2 477	1 512	13 161	53.2	38.0	8.7
Canton-Massillon, OH	817.0	2 029	50.9	6.6	5.7	5.6	5.1	301.7	749	1 313	1 026	18 898	46.6	49.3	4.0
Casper, WY	176.6	2 775	53.0	1.2	5.0	0.4	3.5	62.0	974	657	374	4 596	31.1	66.3	2.6
Cedar Rapids, IA	450.7	2 480	51.4	4.5	6.3	1.2	6.9	272.4	1 499	1 148	867	10 503	53.1	43.9	3.0
Champaign-Urbana, IL	353.7	2 099	49.8	0.6	5.7	2.7	6.9	124.5	739	1 371	444	31 076	47.8	46.6	5.6
Charleston, WV	474.0	1 867	51.4	3.1	4.4	0.0	1.8	623.3	2 455	2 552	1 397	21 317	47.8	50.4	1.7
Charleston-North Charleston, SC	1 041.3	2 042	46.6	2.2	6.3	0.3	2.3	1 510.9	2 963	8 427	13 806	43 560	42.1	55.1	2.8
Charlotte-Gastonia-Rock Hill, NC-SC	3 856.1	2 856	35.1	24.5	4.8	5.2	2.2	4 149.4	3 073	7 966	4 720	87 741	40.6	58.4	1.0
Charlottesville, VA	286.9	1 957	56.1	3.2	5.9	4.3	2.1	180.1	1 228	1 331	816	25 747	45.6	47.9	6.5
Chattanooga, TN-GA	1 296.2	2 897	28.2	31.3	4.6	3.4	3.6	1 091.5	2 439	6 585	1 776	25 722	41.0	57.5	1.6
Cheyenne, WY	251.6	3 206	45.0	26.7	3.3	0.2	4.3	114.4	1 458	2 393	3 855	8 803	35.0	62.8	2.2
Chicago-Gary-Kenosha, IL-IN-WI	25 408.2	2 940	42.4	4.2	7.1	1.7	4.8	25 504.2	2 951	67 159	46 048	487 251	58.9	38.3	2.8
Chicago, IL	22 972.8	2 955	41.8	4.0	7.4	1.1	4.9	24 031.0	3 091	64 078	43 087	438 080	59.3	37.9	2.8
Gary, IN	1 766.0	2 833	45.2	7.7	3.9	8.2	2.9	915.2	1 468	2 449	2 195	34 974	57.7	40.2	2.2
Kankakee, IL	215.3	2 111	58.1	1.3	6.2	0.4	8.2	128.2	1 257	343	227	6 181	47.7	49.9	2.4
Kenosha, WI	454.2	3 179	51.0	3.9	5.9	7.3	4.9	429.8	3 008	289	539	8 016	50.9	45.3	3.7
Chico-Paradise, CA	588.4	3 031	43.5	4.7	3.8	14.3	2.4	196.0	1 010	558	386	13 779	37.4	54.4	8.1
Cincinnati-Hamilton, OH-KY-IN	4 945.0	2 557	40.3	7.0	5.8	4.4	4.8	4 102.2	2 121	16 362	5 480	105 163	37.1	60.0	2.9
Cincinnati, OH-KY-IN	4 260.1	2 650	38.3	7.3	5.8	4.3	4.6	3 343.7	2 080	15 794	4 606	86 772	37.7	59.4	2.9
Hamilton-Middletown, OH	685.0	2 096	52.2	5.4	5.7	5.0	5.6	758.6	2 322	568	874	18 391	33.9	63.3	2.8
Clarksville-Hopkinsville, TN-KY	342.9	1 736	48.5	21.4	4.3	0.9	3.8	337.5	1 709	4 530	24 954	10 683	45.0	53.6	1.4
Cleveland-Akron, OH	8 369.3	2 878	41.7	11.2	6.0	4.7	4.5	6 558.2	2 255	23 093	8 087	165 866	55.3	40.6	4.0
Akron, OH	1 827.7	2 678	39.8	13.2	5.5	4.7	5.7	1 107.3	1 623	2 997	1 798	43 125	52.5	43.4	4.0
Cleveland-Lorain-Elyria, OH	6 541.7	2 939	42.2	10.6	6.1	4.7	4.2	5 450.9	2 449	20 096	6 289	122 741	56.2	39.7	4.1
Colorado Springs, CO	1 144.8	2 385	46.6	14.3	5.3	5.0	5.4	1 299.3	2 707	10 130	29 063	27 281	30.8	63.9	5.3
Columbia, MO	227.7	1 775	52.0	1.3	5.0	2.0	8.3	248.9	1 940	2 028	657	26 435	48.3	47.7	4.0

1. Based on the resident population estimated as of July 1 of the year shown.   2. Data subject to copyright.

Table C. Metropolitan Areas — Land Area and Population

CMSA/ MSA/ PMSA/ NECMA code[1]	Area Name	Land area[2] (sq km) 2000	Total persons	Rank	Per square kilometer	White	Black	Am. Indian, Alaska Native	Asian and Pacific Islander	Percent Hispanic[3]	Under 5 years	5 to 17 years	18 to 24 years	25 to 34 years	35 to 44 years	45 to 54 years
		1	2	3	4	5	6	7	8	9	10	11	12	13	14	15
1760	Columbia, SC	3 770	536 691	99	142.4	64.8	32.6	0.6	1.9	2.4	6.5	18.4	11.6	15.1	16.5	13.8
1800	Columbus, GA-AL	4 066	274 624	165	67.5	55.7	41.2	0.8	2.0	4.0	7.2	19.5	11.8	14.7	15.2	12.2
1840	Columbus, OH	8 136	1 540 157	41	189.3	82.7	14.4	0.8	2.8	1.8	7.2	18.3	10.7	16.0	16.6	13.3
1880	Corpus Christi, TX	3 956	380 783	132	96.3	75.6	4.4	1.1	1.6	54.7	7.8	21.1	10.4	13.3	15.4	13.0
1890	Corvallis, OR	1 752	78 153	315	44.6	91.5	1.2	1.7	5.9	4.7	5.1	16.2	20.2	12.9	13.8	14.2
1900	Cumberland, MD-WV	1 951	102 008	300	52.3	94.5	5.0	0.4	0.7	0.7	5.2	16.2	10.5	12.5	14.4	13.6
31	Dallas-Fort Worth, TX	23 579	5 221 801		221.5	71.5	14.3	1.1	4.4	21.5	8.0	20.0	10.0	16.8	17.2	12.6
1920	Dallas, TX	16 021	3 519 176	10	219.7	69.2	15.5	1.1	4.6	23.0	8.1	19.9	10.1	17.4	17.2	12.5
2800	Fort Worth-Arlington, TX	7 557	1 702 625	31	225.3	76.3	11.6	1.2	3.8	18.2	7.8	20.2	9.7	15.7	17.1	13.0
1950	Danville, VA	2 626	110 156	292	42.0	66.3	33.0	0.4	0.5	1.2	5.8	17.3	7.6	11.8	15.5	14.7
1960	Davenport-Moline-Rock Island, IA-IL	4 423	359 062	138	81.2	89.9	6.7	0.7	1.5	5.8	6.6	18.6	9.3	12.8	15.4	14.2
2000	Dayton-Springfield, OH	4 360	950 558	65	218.0	83.6	15.0	0.7	1.7	1.2	6.5	18.3	10.0	13.0	15.4	14.0
2020	Daytona Beach, FL	4 114	493 175	103	119.9	87.4	9.7	0.8	1.4	6.4	4.8	15.2	7.8	10.6	14.2	13.3
2030	Decatur, AL	3 304	145 867	247	44.2	84.9	12.0	3.0	0.6	2.8	6.5	18.9	8.4	13.8	16.3	14.0
2040	Decatur, IL	1 504	114 706	285	76.3	84.7	14.9	0.5	0.8	1.0	6.4	18.2	9.8	11.6	14.8	14.4
34	Denver-Boulder-Greeley, CO	22 003	2 581 506		117.3	83.0	5.3	1.6	3.7	18.5	7.1	18.6	9.8	16.4	17.4	14.2
1125	Boulder-Longmont, CO	1 923	291 288	161	151.5	90.5	1.2	1.2	3.9	10.5	6.0	16.9	13.4	16.0	17.6	15.0
2080	Denver, CO	9 740	2 109 282	25	216.6	81.9	6.2	1.7	3.8	18.8	7.2	18.6	9.0	16.7	17.5	14.3
3060	Greeley, CO	10 340	180 936	213	17.5	84.1	0.8	1.6	1.4	27.0	7.8	20.4	13.2	14.3	15.4	12.6
2120	Des Moines, IA	4 474	456 022	112	101.9	91.1	4.6	0.6	2.7	4.2	7.5	18.6	9.2	15.3	16.5	13.6
35	Detroit-Ann Arbor-Flint, MI	17 004	5 456 428		320.9	74.8	21.7	1.0	2.8	2.9	7.0	19.4	8.7	14.5	16.5	13.9
0440	Ann Arbor, MI	5 255	578 736	93	110.1	87.1	8.0	1.0	4.3	3.1	6.5	18.0	12.9	14.8	16.6	14.3
2160	Detroit, MI	10 093	4 441 551	7	440.1	73.0	23.5	0.9	2.8	2.9	7.0	19.5	8.1	14.6	16.5	13.8
2640	Flint, MI	1 657	436 141	118	263.3	77.1	21.3	1.6	1.2	2.3	7.3	20.2	8.9	13.6	16.0	13.7
2180	Dothan, AL	2 956	137 916	256	46.7	74.7	23.5	1.0	1.2	2.0	7.0	19.1	8.7	13.8	15.5	13.4
2190	Dover, DE	1 527	126 697	268	83.0	75.1	21.8	1.3	2.3	3.2	7.2	20.0	10.1	13.5	16.2	12.5
2200	Dubuque, IA	1 575	89 143	308	56.6	97.8	1.1	0.4	0.8	1.2	6.6	18.9	10.2	12.0	15.3	13.4
2240	Duluth-Superior, MN-WI	19 514	243 815	179	12.5	96.2	1.1	2.8	1.0	0.8	5.3	17.2	11.2	11.0	15.3	15.0
2290	Eau Claire, WI	4 268	148 337	242	34.8	96.8	0.6	0.8	2.3	0.8	6.1	18.5	13.6	12.3	15.0	13.5
2320	El Paso, TX	2 624	679 622	79	259.0	76.8	3.5	1.1	1.5	78.2	8.7	23.3	10.6	14.5	14.8	11.3
2330	Elkhart-Goshen, IN	1 201	182 791	211	152.2	88.0	5.8	0.7	1.3	8.9	8.1	20.8	9.5	14.5	15.3	12.8
2335	Elmira, NY	1 057	91 070	307	86.1	92.3	6.7	0.6	1.0	1.8	6.0	18.4	8.8	12.3	16.0	13.9
2340	Enid, OK	2 741	57 813	318	21.1	91.0	3.8	3.6	1.8	4.1	6.7	18.3	9.1	12.1	15.3	13.0
2360	Erie, PA	2 077	280 843	163	135.2	92.0	6.7	0.5	1.0	2.2	6.2	18.8	10.8	12.5	15.1	13.6
2400	Eugene-Springfield, OR	11 795	322 959	151	27.4	93.7	1.3	2.6	3.2	4.6	5.8	17.1	12.0	13.0	14.5	15.3
2440	Evansville-Henderson, IN-KY	3 800	296 195	159	77.9	92.7	6.5	0.5	0.9	0.9	6.3	18.1	9.9	12.6	16.1	14.0
2520	Fargo-Moorhead, ND-MN	7 279	174 367	218	24.0	96.0	1.0	1.7	1.6	1.9	6.5	17.4	16.3	14.5	15.2	12.7
2560	Fayetteville, NC	1 691	302 963	157	179.2	57.4	36.3	2.4	3.2	6.9	8.2	19.7	13.7	17.3	15.6	10.9
2580	Fayetteville-Springdale-Rogers, AR	4 651	311 121	156	66.9	91.2	1.6	2.5	2.0	8.5	7.5	18.3	12.0	15.0	14.9	12.0
2620	Flagstaff, AZ-UT	58 558	122 366	276	2.1	66.7	1.3	28.4	1.3	10.5	7.2	21.5	14.1	13.7	15.0	13.5
2650	Florence, AL	3 274	142 950	250	43.7	86.5	12.7	0.7	0.4	1.1	6.0	17.3	9.3	12.9	15.0	13.8
2655	Florence, SC	2 072	125 761	272	60.7	59.2	39.6	0.5	1.0	1.1	6.5	19.4	9.7	13.6	15.3	14.4
2670	Fort Collins-Loveland, CO	6 737	251 494	174	37.3	93.5	1.0	1.4	2.3	8.3	6.1	17.7	14.2	14.4	16.3	14.2
2700	Fort Myers-Cape Coral, FL	2 081	440 888	116	211.8	88.9	7.1	0.6	1.1	9.5	5.2	14.4	6.2	10.5	13.4	12.4
2710	Fort Pierce-Port St. Lucie, FL	2 922	319 426	153	109.3	84.5	12.0	0.6	1.2	7.9	5.1	15.9	6.1	9.9	14.3	12.6
2720	Fort Smith, AR-OK	4 676	207 290	198	44.3	85.8	4.4	8.0	2.7	4.9	7.3	19.5	8.8	13.5	15.5	13.2
2750	Fort Walton Beach, FL	2 423	170 498	220	70.4	85.9	9.9	1.4	4.0	4.3	6.4	18.4	9.6	13.9	17.2	13.1
2760	Fort Wayne, IN	6 339	502 141	102	79.2	89.4	8.1	0.7	1.3	3.3	7.5	20.3	9.2	13.6	15.8	13.5
2840	Fresno, CA	20 975	922 516	66	44.0	59.2	5.7	2.8	8.5	44.0	8.4	23.4	10.9	13.9	14.6	11.7
2880	Gadsden, AL	1 385	103 459	298	74.7	83.7	14.9	0.8	0.6	1.7	6.4	17.4	8.7	13.0	14.3	14.1
2900	Gainesville, FL	2 264	217 955	191	96.3	75.1	20.0	0.8	4.2	5.7	5.1	15.0	23.2	14.4	13.3	12.2
2975	Glens Falls, NY	4 415	124 345	273	28.2	97.0	2.0	0.6	0.7	1.5	5.5	18.8	7.9	12.5	16.3	14.4
2980	Goldsboro, NC	1 431	113 329	286	79.2	62.2	33.6	0.7	1.4	4.9	7.0	19.2	9.9	14.2	16.3	13.0
2985	Grand Forks, ND-MN	8 827	97 478	303	11.0	94.7	1.4	2.7	1.2	2.9	6.3	17.9	17.7	12.9	14.6	12.2
2995	Grand Junction, CO	8 619	116 255	282	13.5	94.2	0.7	1.8	1.0	10.0	6.3	18.8	9.4	11.4	15.4	14.4
3000	Grand Rapids-Muskegon-Holland, MI	7 144	1 088 514	59	152.4	87.3	8.0	1.1	1.9	6.3	7.5	20.8	10.3	14.1	16.2	12.8
3040	Great Falls, MT	6 988	80 357	314	11.5	92.9	1.5	5.7	1.5	2.4	6.6	19.4	9.1	12.3	15.8	13.3
3080	Green Bay, WI	1 369	226 778	187	165.6	92.2	1.5	2.9	2.5	3.8	6.9	19.2	10.5	14.8	17.1	13.4
3120	Greensboro—Winston-Salem—High Point, NC	10 052	1 251 509	47	124.5	75.4	20.7	0.7	1.7	5.0	6.6	17.4	9.5	14.9	16.1	13.8
3150	Greenville, NC	1 688	133 798	260	79.3	62.9	34.1	0.5	1.4	3.2	6.5	17.1	17.5	15.4	14.5	12.3
3160	Greenville-Spartanburg-Anderson, SC	8 310	962 441	64	115.8	79.9	17.8	0.5	1.5	2.7	6.6	17.8	10.2	14.3	15.7	13.7
3240	Harrisburg-Lebanon-Carlisle, PA	5 156	629 401	83	122.1	88.9	8.5	0.4	1.9	3.1	5.9	17.6	8.7	13.0	16.1	14.7

1. MSA = Metropolitan Statistical Area. CMSA = Consolidated MSA. PMSA = Primary MSA. NECMA = New England County Metropolitan Area. See Appendix A for explanation of these concepts. See Appendix B for list of metropolitan areas identified by type, with component counties.   2. Dry land or land partially or temporarily covered by water.   3. Hispanic persons may be of any race.

Table C. Metropolitan Areas — **Population and Households**

Area Name	Population, 2000 (cont'd) Age (percent) (cont'd) 55 to 64 years	65 to 74 years	75 years and over	Percent female	Population — change and components of change, 1990–2001 Total persons 2001	1990	Percent change 1990–2000	2000–2001	Components of change, 2000–2001 Births	Deaths	Net migration	Households, 2000 Number	Percent change, 1990–2000	Persons per household	Percent Female family householder[1]	One person
	16	17	18	19	20	21	22	23	24	25	26	27	28	29	30	31
Columbia, SC	8.1	5.4	4.5	51.6	543 543	453 847	18.3	1.3	9 709	5 286	2 636	203 341	24.6	2.49	14.4	26.4
Columbus, GA-AL	7.8	6.5	5.0	50.7	273 481	260 862	5.3	-0.4	5 966	3 232	-3 777	101 314	9.3	2.56	18.4	25.7
Columbus, OH	7.9	5.5	4.5	50.9	1 559 597	1 345 460	14.5	1.3	29 313	14 831	4 942	610 757	18.9	2.45	11.9	28.1
Corpus Christi, TX	8.0	6.2	4.9	50.9	379 590	349 894	8.8	-0.3	8 232	3 731	-5 700	132 458	11.8	2.82	14.9	22.0
Corvallis, OR	7.2	5.1	5.2	50.2	77 926	70 811	10.4	-0.3	1 037	591	-674	30 145	15.4	2.43	7.2	26.1
Cumberland, MD-WV	10.6	8.8	8.4	50.4	101 164	101 643	0.4	-0.8	1 292	1 598	-495	40 106	1.2	2.38	10.1	28.7
Dallas-Fort Worth, TX	7.3	4.5	3.6	50.2	5 400 737	4 037 282	29.3	3.4	113 128	39 936	103 708	1 906 764	26.4	2.70	12.0	24.7
Dallas, TX	7.1	4.3	3.4	50.1	3 646 217	2 676 248	31.5	3.6	78 150	25 579	72 326	1 281 957	28.0	2.70	12.1	25.1
Fort Worth-Arlington, TX	7.6	4.9	3.9	50.4	1 754 520	1 361 034	25.1	3.0	34 978	14 357	31 382	624 807	23.4	2.68	11.7	24.0
Danville, VA	10.6	8.8	7.9	52.6	109 658	108 728	1.3	-0.5	1 778	1 673	-584	45 291	7.0	2.39	15.3	28.2
Davenport-Moline-Rock Island, IA-IL	9.3	7.0	6.8	51.2	357 641	350 855	2.3	-0.4	6 228	4 298	-3 287	143 102	5.0	2.45	11.0	28.0
Dayton-Springfield, OH	9.4	7.2	6.3	51.8	946 085	951 262	0.1	-0.5	16 460	11 942	-8 790	379 626	4.2	2.43	12.7	27.9
Daytona Beach, FL	11.3	11.9	10.9	51.5	509 545	399 438	23.5	3.3	6 130	7 939	17 892	206 017	24.6	2.32	10.6	27.3
Decatur, AL	9.8	6.9	5.3	51.0	146 357	131 556	10.9	0.3	2 406	1 714	-140	57 140	16.1	2.52	11.2	24.3
Decatur, IL	9.6	7.9	7.3	52.3	112 964	117 206	-2.1	-1.5	1 911	1 486	-2 179	46 561	1.2	2.39	12.2	28.8
Denver-Boulder-Greeley, CO	7.6	4.8	4.1	49.9	2 653 476	1 980 140	30.4	2.8	49 845	19 481	40 856	1 003 218	27.8	2.53	9.9	27.4
Boulder-Longmont, CO	7.2	4.2	3.6	49.4	297 686	225 339	29.3	2.2	4 658	1 773	3 573	114 680	29.7	2.47	7.7	26.3
Denver, CO	7.7	4.9	4.1	50.0	2 160 841	1 622 980	30.0	2.4	41 549	16 321	25 789	825 291	27.1	2.52	10.2	28.0
Greeley, CO	7.4	4.8	4.1	49.9	194 949	131 821	37.3	7.7	3 638	1 387	11 494	63 247	33.2	2.78	9.4	21.0
Des Moines, IA	8.1	5.7	5.5	51.4	463 092	392 928	16.1	1.6	8 692	4 205	2 729	179 404	17.2	2.48	10.0	27.0
Detroit-Ann Arbor-Flint, MI	8.4	6.2	5.5	51.3	5 478 262	5 187 171	5.2	0.4	96 655	59 847	-14 535	2 081 797	8.6	2.58	14.2	27.0
Ann Arbor, MI	8.0	4.8	4.1	50.0	590 910	490 058	18.1	2.1	8 857	4 499	7 783	216 641	23.8	2.54	8.8	25.3
Detroit, MI	8.4	6.3	5.8	51.4	4 448 235	4 266 654	4.1	0.2	79 685	50 552	-22 178	1 695 331	7.3	2.58	14.6	27.2
Flint, MI	8.7	6.6	5.0	51.9	439 117	430 459	1.3	0.7	8 113	4 796	-140	169 825	5.3	2.54	16.3	26.6
Dothan, AL	9.5	7.2	5.9	51.8	138 217	130 964	5.3	0.2	2 563	1 590	-604	54 712	13.0	2.47	13.9	25.7
Dover, DE	8.7	6.6	5.0	51.8	129 066	110 993	14.1	1.9	2 445	1 401	1 364	47 224	19.1	2.61	13.8	23.0
Dubuque, IA	8.9	7.3	7.4	51.4	88 856	86 403	3.2	-0.3	1 386	1 114	-533	33 690	9.4	2.51	8.7	26.7
Duluth-Superior, MN-WI	9.2	7.5	8.4	50.8	242 928	239 990	1.6	-0.4	3 101	3 321	-571	100 427	5.4	2.33	9.5	31.0
Eau Claire, WI	8.0	6.5	6.6	51.1	149 238	137 543	7.8	0.6	2 194	1 510	260	57 178	13.5	2.49	8.4	26.2
El Paso, TX	7.1	5.7	4.0	51.8	688 039	591 610	14.9	1.2	18 056	4 976	-4 616	210 022	17.7	3.18	18.0	17.8
Elkhart-Goshen, IN	8.1	5.6	5.2	50.3	184 186	156 198	17.0	0.8	3 801	1 719	-640	66 154	16.6	2.72	10.5	22.6
Elmira, NY	9.0	7.8	7.8	50.6	90 675	95 195	-4.3	-0.4	1 273	1 225	-406	35 049	-0.6	2.44	12.4	27.9
Enid, OK	9.4	7.9	8.1	51.6	57 114	56 735	1.9	-1.2	997	828	-863	23 175	3.2	2.42	10.5	27.7
Erie, PA	8.6	7.1	7.2	51.2	279 636	275 575	1.9	-0.4	4 277	3 443	-1 966	106 507	4.9	2.51	12.1	27.6
Eugene-Springfield, OR	9.0	6.6	6.7	50.8	324 316	282 912	14.2	0.4	4 655	3 511	376	130 453	17.7	2.42	10.0	26.6
Evansville-Henderson, IN-KY	9.0	7.2	6.8	51.9	296 250	278 990	6.2	0.0	4 622	3 926	-542	118 361	8.9	2.43	10.9	27.5
Fargo-Moorhead, ND-MN	6.9	5.3	5.3	50.4	175 630	153 296	13.7	0.7	2 766	1 410	-16	69 985	21.1	2.38	8.0	29.9
Fayetteville, NC	6.8	4.8	2.9	49.4	299 203	274 713	10.3	-1.2	7 561	2 392	-8 835	107 358	17.3	2.65	15.5	22.4
Fayetteville-Springdale-Rogers, AR	8.3	6.6	5.5	50.3	321 861	210 939	47.5	3.5	5 807	2 859	7 701	118 363	46.3	2.56	8.8	23.5
Flagstaff, AZ-UT	7.4	4.6	2.9	50.1	123 974	101 760	20.2	1.3	2 526	719	-155	42 685	34.9	2.79	11.9	22.1
Florence, AL	10.5	8.2	7.0	52.2	142 528	131 327	8.9	-0.3	2 235	1 875	-729	58 549	14.8	2.40	11.3	26.3
Florence, SC	9.2	6.3	5.5	53.0	126 607	114 344	10.0	0.7	2 503	1 638	35	47 147	17.2	2.59	18.1	24.5
Fort Collins-Loveland, CO	7.6	5.1	4.5	50.0	259 472	186 136	35.1	3.2	3 917	1 832	5 831	97 164	37.9	2.52	7.9	23.4
Fort Myers-Cape Coral, FL	12.4	13.7	11.7	51.1	462 455	335 113	31.6	4.9	6 003	6 024	21 207	188 599	34.6	2.31	8.7	25.8
Fort Pierce-Port St. Lucie, FL	11.2	10.4	11.9	51.1	330 331	251 071	27.2	3.4	4 346	4 692	11 118	132 221	30.7	2.37	9.5	25.8
Fort Smith, AR-OK	9.5	6.8	5.8	50.9	209 182	175 911	17.8	0.9	3 711	2 413	650	79 763	19.3	2.56	11.3	24.7
Fort Walton Beach, FL	9.3	7.4	4.7	49.5	173 065	143 777	18.6	1.5	2 927	1 585	1 336	66 269	24.3	2.49	10.2	23.5
Fort Wayne, IN	8.1	6.1	5.9	50.9	504 279	456 281	10.1	0.4	9 364	5 355	-1 710	192 052	13.8	2.57	10.7	26.1
Fresno, CA	7.1	5.3	4.8	50.2	942 149	755 569	22.1	2.1	20 102	7 994	7 870	289 095	16.0	3.10	14.9	20.1
Gadsden, AL	10.0	8.5	7.5	52.1	103 014	99 840	3.6	-0.4	1 670	1 642	-432	41 615	7.6	2.44	13.1	26.3
Gainesville, FL	7.1	5.0	4.6	51.2	218 795	181 596	20.0	0.4	3 184	2 014	-277	87 509	22.8	2.34	12.3	29.1
Glens Falls, NY	10.0	7.8	6.8	50.1	124 996	118 539	4.9	0.5	1 549	1 441	586	48 184	12.5	2.48	10.4	25.8
Goldsboro, NC	8.9	6.8	4.8	50.7	112 736	104 666	8.3	-0.5	2 357	1 416	-1 489	42 612	15.5	2.55	15.4	24.5
Grand Forks, ND-MN	7.2	5.7	6.5	49.5	95 550	103 272	-5.6	-2.0	1 500	941	-2 502	37 505	0.5	2.44	8.7	28.5
Grand Junction, CO	9.3	7.9	7.3	51.0	119 281	93 145	24.8	2.6	1 868	1 314	2 449	45 823	26.4	2.47	9.8	25.1
GrandRapids-Muskegon-Holland, MI	7.5	5.5	5.3	50.7	1 103 488	937 891	16.1	1.4	20 849	10 026	4 455	396 047	18.6	2.67	10.9	23.8
Great Falls, MT	9.4	7.2	6.7	50.5	79 298	77 691	3.4	-1.3	1 353	936	-1 461	32 547	8.0	2.41	9.9	28.8
Green Bay, WI	7.6	5.4	5.3	50.3	229 212	194 594	16.5	1.1	3 939	2 020	623	87 295	20.8	2.51	8.9	26.5
Greensboro-Winston-Salem—High Point, NC	9.2	6.8	5.7	51.7	1 268 603	1 050 304	19.2	1.4	22 479	13 938	8 999	498 751	20.2	2.44	12.3	26.4
Greenville, NC	7.1	5.2	4.3	52.6	134 977	108 480	23.3	0.9	2 613	1 269	-110	52 539	29.8	2.43	14.4	28.3
Greenville-Spartanburg-Anderson, SC	9.4	6.6	5.7	51.3	978 213	830 499	15.9	1.6	16 468	11 315	10 813	374 741	19.8	2.49	12.6	25.4
Harrisburg-Lebanon-Carlisle, PA	9.3	7.6	7.1	51.5	631 761	587 986	7.0	0.4	8 988	7 751	1 335	248 931	10.0	2.43	10.3	27.5

1. No spouse present.

Area Name	Births, average 1997-1999		Deaths, average 1997-1999				Physicians,[4] 1998		Hospitals,[4] 1998			Medicare enrollees 1999	Serious crimes known to police, 2000[6]	
			Number		Rate					Beds			Total	
	Total	Rate[1]	Total	Infant[2]	Total[1]	Infant[3]	Number	Rate[5]	Number	Number	Rate[5]		Number	Rate[7]
	32	33	34	35	36	37	38	39	40	41	42	43	44	45
Columbia, SC	7 028	13.7	3 999	69	7.8	9.8	1 339	261	5	1 554	303	60 941	28 175	5 250
Columbus, GA-AL	4 215	15.5	2 509	NA	9.2	NA	507	186	4	991	364	36 585	13 760	5 020
Columbus, OH	21 781	14.8	11 517	178	7.8	8.2	3 497	238	17	4 624	315	174 730	85 367	6 367
Corpus Christi, TX	6 502	16.8	2 898	NA	7.5	NA	786	203	9	1 617	417	47 088	24 674	6 480
Corvallis, OR	829	10.7	452	NA	5.8	NA	188	242	1	124	159	7 996	3 601	4 608
Cumberland, MD-WV	1 030	10.5	1 287	NA	13.1	NA	194	198	3	525	535	20 019	2 797	3 453
Dallas-Fort Worth, TX	83 043	17.3	30 905	515	6.4	6.2	8 847	184	61	11 335	236	455 851	280 817	5 381
Dallas, TX	56 600	17.6	19 809	330	6.2	5.8	6 366	198	42	7 633	238	294 166	192 505	5 476
Fort Worth-Arlington, TX	26 443	16.6	11 096	185	7.0	7.0	2 481	156	19	3 702	232	161 685	88 312	5 187
Danville, VA	1 274	11.8	1 348	NA	12.4	NA	166	153	1	336	310	21 288	2 729	2 477
Davenport-Moline-Rock Island, IA-IL	4 799	13.4	3 370	NA	9.4	NA	624	174	8	1 476	413	55 174	NA	NA
Dayton-Springfield, OH	12 531	13.1	9 162	NA	9.6	NA	2 152	227	13	3 918	413	146 313	43 043	5 263
Daytona Beach, FL	4 877	10.4	6 161	NA	13.1	NA	830	176	9	1 574	334	113 756	22 928	4 649
Decatur, AL	1 955	13.7	1 323	NA	9.3	NA	182	127	4	497	348	20 987	NA	NA
Decatur, IL	1 485	13.1	1 212	15	10.7	10.1	198	174	2	581	511	20 007	NA	NA
Denver-Boulder-Greeley, CO	35 903	15.2	15 053	240	6.4	6.7	6 458	273	20	4 997	211	252 173	97 798	3 882
Boulder-Longmont, CO	3 419	12.8	1 363	17	5.1	5.0	754	282	3	360	135	27 015	9 146	3 140
Denver, CO	29 878	15.4	12 635	204	6.5	6.8	5 457	281	16	4 311	222	207 649	81 990	3 987
Greeley, CO	2 606	16.3	1 055	19	6.6	7.3	247	155	1	326	204	17 509	6 662	3 877
Des Moines, IA	6 672	15.2	3 400	NA	7.8	NA	1 086	249	7	1 932	442	56 098	21 462	4 706
Detroit-Ann Arbor-Flint, MI	74 750	13.7	46 621	647	8.5	8.7	14 008	257	67	17 810	326	729 017	247 180	4 569
Ann Arbor, MI	7 128	13.0	3 450	NA	6.3	NA	2 502	457	10	2 047	374	56 266	16 752	2 895
Detroit, MI	61 421	13.7	39 359	535	8.8	8.7	10 678	239	52	13 984	313	611 731	206 365	4 688
Flint, MI	6 201	14.2	3 812	79	8.7	12.7	828	190	5	1 779	408	61 020	24 063	5 603
Dothan, AL	1 974	14.7	1 240	21	9.2	10.6	290	215	3	718	533	20 507	4 774	3 607
Dover, DE	1 827	14.7	1 032	14	8.3	7.7	181	146	1	190	153	15 837	5 223	4 122
Dubuque, IA	1 128	12.8	851	NA	9.7	NA	187	213	3	670	763	14 454	2 298	2 578
Duluth-Superior, MN-WI	2 516	10.6	2 694	NA	11.4	NA	488	206	9	1 410	596	43 598	8 487	3 481
Eau Claire, WI	1 749	12.2	1 206	NA	8.4	NA	337	234	5	877	610	21 909	4 518	3 076
El Paso, TX	14 379	20.6	3 853	75	5.5	5.2	1 059	151	6	1 829	260	72 503	37 913	5 579
Elkhart-Goshen, IN	2 943	17.0	1 369	23	7.9	7.8	228	132	2	476	276	21 856	9 718	5 316
Elmira, NY	1 072	11.7	972	NA	10.6	NA	232	252	2	495	538	16 581	2 724	2 991
Enid, OK	796	14.0	669	7	11.8	8.8	121	213	2	298	524	10 223	2 925	5 059
Erie, PA	3 507	12.7	2 730	28	9.9	8.0	631	228	6	1 167	422	44 902	7 534	2 683
Eugene-Springfield, OR	3 709	11.8	2 806	22	9.0	5.9	650	207	4	620	197	47 785	18 224	5 643
Evansville-Henderson, IN-KY	3 777	13.0	2 959	NA	10.2	NA	680	234	5	1 394	479	46 815	8 549	3 688
Fargo-Moorhead, ND-MN	2 201	13.1	1 154	NA	6.8	NA	447	265	3	667	396	20 493	4 773	2 737
Fayetteville, NC	5 600	19.7	1 843	64	6.5	11.4	534	188	2	515	181	28 345	18 375	6 065
Fayetteville-Springdale-Rogers, AR	4 376	15.9	2 317	32	8.4	7.3	483	177	6	735	270	42 086	9 087	2 921
Flagstaff, AZ-UT	1 910	15.9	555	NA	4.6	NA	280	233	3	174	145	13 449	6 718	5 740
Florence, AL	1 736	12.7	1 431	NA	10.4	NA	232	169	4	907	661	25 146	3 757	2 690
Florence, SC	1 748	14.0	1 286	20	10.3	11.4	278	223	4	765	612	18 410	8 887	7 120
Fort Collins-Loveland, CO	2 945	12.7	1 371	15	5.9	5.1	442	191	3	375	162	25 902	9 020	3 587
Fort Myers-Cape Coral, FL	4 568	11.6	4 810	35	12.2	7.7	1 026	261	6	1 707	434	99 107	21 332	4 838
Fort Pierce-Port St. Lucie, FL	3 359	11.4	3 662	26	12.4	7.7	671	227	4	792	268	73 479	13 231	4 142
Fort Smith, AR-OK	3 037	15.6	1 982	NA	10.2	NA	375	193	4	829	427	31 308	10 560	5 094
Fort Walton Beach, FL	2 361	14.0	1 213	19	7.2	8.0	356	210	3	433	256	23 429	4 774	3 006
Fort Wayne, IN	7 490	15.6	4 096	NA	8.5	NA	851	177	9	1 493	310	66 299	16 018	3 875
Fresno, CA	15 927	18.3	6 170	109	7.1	6.8	1 492	171	16	2 242	258	106 105	52 847	5 729
Gadsden, AL	1 312	12.6	1 297	12	12.5	9.1	164	158	2	538	517	19 168	NA	NA
Gainesville, FL	2 485	12.5	1 494	24	7.5	9.7	1 325	667	3	1 057	532	25 051	14 741	6 763
Glens Falls, NY	1 351	11.1	1 151	NA	9.5	NA	237	195	2	553	454	20 537	2 826	2 402
Goldsboro, NC	1 689	15.1	1 028	20	9.2	11.8	165	147	1	267	238	16 621	5 842	5 155
Grand Forks, ND-MN	1 368	13.9	785	NA	8.0	NA	204	209	4	665	680	12 817	3 355	3 496
Grand Junction, CO	1 428	12.6	1 064	15	9.4	10.5	312	276	3	422	374	19 622	4 541	3 919
GrandRapids-Muskegon-Holland, MI	16 213	15.6	7 802	121	7.5	7.5	1 979	191	12	2 465	237	133 028	40 359	3 710
Great Falls, MT	1 086	13.8	730	9	9.3	8.3	201	254	2	402	509	12 698	4 939	6 146
Green Bay, WI	3 024	14.0	1 562	23	7.2	7.6	401	186	3	632	293	26 605	6 234	2 749
Greensboro—Winston-Salem—High Point, NC	16 159	13.8	10 548	148	9.0	9.2	2 449	210	13	3 512	301	175 256	64 014	5 146
Greenville, NC	1 866	14.8	1 010	22	8.0	11.8	559	441	1	571	451	15 761	9 302	6 952
Greenville-Spartanburg-Anderson, SC	12 258	13.3	8 470	105	9.2	8.6	1 628	177	11	2 697	294	139 622	46 485	4 834
Harrisburg-Lebanon-Carlisle, PA	7 308	11.9	5 961	42	9.7	5.7	1 783	289	9	2 203	358	99 371	15 443	2 498

1. Per 1,000 estimated resident population, average 1997-1999.   2. Deaths of infants under 1 year old.   3. Deaths of infants under 1 year old per 1,000 live births.   4. Data subject to copyright.   5. Per 100,000 resident population as of July 1 of the year shown.   6. Data for serious crimes have not been adjusted for underreporting; this may affect comparability between geographic areas and over time.   7. Per 100,000 population estimated by the FBI.

Table C. Metropolitan Areas — Crime, Education, Money Income, and Poverty

Area Name	Serious crimes known to police, 2000¹ (cont'd) Rate² Violent	Property	Education — School enrollment and attainment, 1990 — Enrollment³ Total	Percent private	Attainment⁴ (percent) High school graduate or more	Bachelor's degree or more	Local government expenditures, fiscal 1999⁵ Total current expenditures (mil dol)	Current expenditures per student (dollars)	Money income 1989 Per capita⁶ (dollars)	Households Median Dollars	Percent change, 1979–1989 (constant 1989 dollars)	Percent with $100,000 or more	Median household income	Income and poverty, 1998 Percent below poverty level All persons	Persons under 18	Persons 5–17 in families
	46	47	48	49	50	51	52	53	54	55	56	57	58	59	60	61
Columbia, SC	736	4 514	127 116	11.9	78.6	25.3	547.1	6 235	13 618	30 473	9.7	3.1	NA	11.8	18.1	16.1
Columbus, GA-AL	473	4 547	64 390	10.8	69.0	15.0	282.8	6 035	11 409	23 622	8.3	2.4	NA	18.0	27.7	25.4
Columbus, OH	530	5 837	358 609	15.1	79.8	23.3	1 603.9	6 584	14 537	30 609	5.3	3.5	NA	9.9	15.3	13.4
Corpus Christi, TX	621	5 859	104 793	7.4	67.6	16.0	452.8	5 767	11 065	24 952	-10.5	2.5	NA	20.2	27.2	26.0
Corvallis, OR	243	4 365	29 624	5.8	89.3	41.3	76.6	7 498	12 994	27 295	0.6	3.3	NA	10.1	12.5	10.7
Cumberland, MD-WV	428	3 025	24 873	8.7	71.4	11.5	108.9	6 908	11 131	21 691	-8.0	1.5	NA	15.1	21.7	21.2
Dallas-Fort Worth, TX	592	4 789	1 066 267	13.8	78.6	25.4	4 893.5	5 393	15 755	32 446	3.7	5.1	NA	10.5	16.1	13.6
Dallas, TX	652	4 824	711 757	13.8	78.4	26.9	3 297.5	5 447	16 218	32 667	4.1	5.7	NA	10.5	16.1	13.5
Fort Worth-Arlington, TX	469	4 718	354 510	13.9	78.9	22.4	1 596.0	5 284	14 845	32 112	3.3	4.0	NA	10.5	16.1	13.8
Danville, VA	303	2 174	23 328	9.7	56.8	9.9	93.4	5 438	11 268	23 086	-1.4	1.3	NA	15.2	20.9	20.5
Davenport-Moline-Rock Island, IA-IL	NA	NA	93 483	16.8	79.1	17.4	387.7	6 355	13 251	27 940	-17.3	2.3	NA	10.5	15.7	14.2
Dayton-Springfield, OH	470	4 793	253 276	18.2	77.6	19.1	1 035.1	6 848	14 087	30 471	1.9	2.8	NA	10.1	16.1	13.7
Daytona Beach, FL	709	3 940	83 636	20.2	75.7	15.0	366.2	5 554	13 420	25 130	20.2	2.5	NA	12.6	20.2	18.7
Decatur, AL	NA	NA	31 660	7.2	66.2	13.3	145.1	5 673	12 104	26 643	5.6	1.9	NA	12.2	18.5	16.3
Decatur, IL	NA	NA	29 951	15.7	76.2	14.8	107.4	5 723	13 762	28 598	-8.7	2.5	NA	13.5	20.3	19.3
Denver-Boulder-Greeley, CO	329	3 553	533 845	13.7	85.5	29.7	2 439.7	5 941	16 287	32 541	-1.3	4.6	NA	8.7	12.7	11.4
Boulder-Longmont, CO	268	2 872	72 009	9.7	91.3	42.1	251.4	5 552	17 359	35 322	6.6	5.5	NA	7.7	10.3	8.7
Denver, CO	340	3 647	420 586	15.1	85.5	28.9	2 032.4	6 027	16 539	32 851	-2.1	4.7	NA	8.6	12.8	11.5
Greeley, CO	305	3 572	41 250	6.0	74.9	18.4	156.0	5 532	11 350	25 642	-3.2	2.0	NA	11.4	15.2	13.5
Des Moines, IA	245	4 461	99 862	18.5	85.4	22.6	507.5	6 640	14 972	31 181	-1.8	3.3	NA	7.8	11.9	9.8
Detroit-Ann Arbor-Flint, MI	699	3 870	1 423 735	14.0	76.4	18.5	6 924.9	7 609	15 542	34 289	-3.2	4.9	NA	11.3	17.4	15.6
Ann Arbor, MI	247	2 648	162 946	10.5	84.7	30.9	648.5	7 258	16 333	37 097	5.4	5.7	NA	7.1	9.6	9.0
Detroit, MI	761	3 927	1 138 104	14.8	75.4	17.7	5 692.3	7 717	15 649	34 300	-3.3	5.1	NA	11.5	17.7	15.9
Flint, MI	666	4 937	122 685	10.5	76.8	12.8	584.1	7 025	13 583	31 029	-11.8	2.5	NA	14.6	22.8	20.4
Dothan, AL	411	3 196	34 718	8.6	70.4	14.5	121.4	5 284	11 535	24 485	8.0	1.8	NA	16.5	24.0	22.8
Dover, DE	638	3 484	29 454	13.8	73.1	15.0	147.4	7 076	12 726	29 497	14.7	2.4	NA	11.9	17.2	16.6
Dubuque, IA	165	2 413	23 997	41.1	77.7	16.8	76.2	6 167	12 331	28 276	-13.0	2.4	NA	8.9	12.9	10.4
Duluth-Superior, MN-WI	221	3 260	64 901	8.2	79.7	16.8	263.6	6 900	11 644	23 690	-16.1	1.3	NA	11.9	16.9	14.4
Eau Claire, WI	138	2 938	40 591	9.8	79.6	16.9	168.0	7 122	11 560	25 875	1.2	1.9	NA	9.7	14.5	12.9
El Paso, TX	705	4 874	199 118	7.1	63.7	15.2	863.0	5 626	9 150	22 643	-3.5	2.2	NA	26.8	35.6	31.8
Elkhart-Goshen, IN	408	4 908	36 915	15.3	72.8	14.2	215.8	6 747	13 825	30 973	5.1	3.2	NA	8.9	13.4	11.7
Elmira, NY	284	2 707	23 886	17.8	77.2	15.4	114.4	8 165	12 069	26 134	2.5	2.0	NA	13.9	20.6	20.5
Enid, OK	391	4 668	13 899	14.1	76.5	17.3	56.3	5 371	11 564	23 243	-16.3	2.2	NA	14.9	22.2	20.1
Erie, PA	261	2 422	74 816	25.9	77.5	16.2	304.5	7 137	12 317	26 581	-5.4	2.3	NA	12.4	18.2	17.3
Eugene-Springfield, OR	314	5 329	80 983	8.3	83.0	22.2	350.9	7 147	12 570	25 267	-7.3	2.4	NA	13.7	18.3	16.2
Evansville-Henderson, IN-KY	404	3 284	68 019	18.6	75.1	14.8	284.3	6 375	13 265	27 228	-4.2	2.6	NA	10.9	15.9	14.3
Fargo-Moorhead, ND-MN	122	2 615	50 047	10.6	85.1	25.0	158.8	5 560	12 449	26 551	-8.2	2.4	NA	9.8	13.2	10.9
Fayetteville, NC	544	5 521	73 885	9.7	80.3	16.6	264.8	5 163	11 100	25 461	13.1	1.6	NA	16.3	22.8	20.9
Fayetteville-Springdale-Rogers, AR	226	2 695	54 023	8.2	74.0	17.3	242.0	4 978	11 925	24 462	9.3	2.1	NA	11.3	16.6	13.4
Flagstaff, AZ-UT	421	5 319	38 724	5.8	79.2	23.9	109.3	5 231	10 486	NA	NA	2.3	NA	19.6	25.0	25.2
Florence, AL	175	2 515	31 874	8.5	66.8	14.5	126.1	5 754	11 582	23 106	-9.6	1.9	NA	13.7	21.4	19.3
Florence, SC	989	6 131	32 153	8.9	64.3	14.8	121.6	5 415	11 007	24 264	4.0	2.4	NA	18.7	26.6	24.7
Fort Collins-Loveland, CO	233	3 354	62 261	7.4	88.6	32.3	219.5	5 675	13 968	29 685	3.2	3.0	NA	8.3	10.5	9.4
Fort Myers-Cape Coral, FL	590	4 248	59 636	13.1	76.9	16.4	329.5	6 015	15 623	28 447	16.2	4.0	NA	10.9	19.9	18.4
Fort Pierce-Port St. Lucie, FL	604	3 538	49 320	15.8	75.1	16.1	256.6	5 726	16 177	29 416	19.6	4.7	NA	12.9	23.0	21.9
Fort Smith, AR-OK	524	4 570	42 398	8.0	67.5	11.8	188.6	5 071	11 083	22 400	2.4	2.0	NA	15.9	22.9	19.7
Fort Walton Beach, FL	360	2 646	37 715	7.7	83.8	21.0	158.8	5 221	13 147	27 941	10.0	2.0	NA	10.7	16.5	15.4
Fort Wayne, IN	251	3 624	118 712	17.8	80.0	16.2	534.9	6 580	13 883	31 298	0.0	2.7	NA	8.4	12.1	10.4
Fresno, CA	742	4 987	229 019	6.5	65.9	16.3	1 166.5	5 784	11 711	26 481	0.7	3.5	NA	24.1	34.0	33.8
Gadsden, AL	NA	NA	23 854	8.5	64.1	10.2	84.4	5 148	10 997	22 314	0.0	1.5	NA	16.2	24.1	21.4
Gainesville, FL	961	5 802	71 842	7.3	82.7	34.6	165.9	5 592	12 252	22 084	6.7	3.0	NA	17.1	23.3	23.1
Glens Falls, NY	266	2 136	28 933	11.6	76.2	15.5	187.4	8 465	13 298	29 641	20.4	2.4	NA	12.4	18.1	18.4
Goldsboro, NC	592	4 563	27 469	11.4	71.2	12.7	101.4	5 271	10 843	23 559	8.7	1.2	NA	16.9	23.0	22.5
Grand Forks, ND-MN	175	3 321	33 581	5.9	81.2	21.4	96.8	5 662	11 031	24 353	-3.5	1.6	NA	12.7	16.5	14.6
Grand Junction, CO	203	3 716	24 299	7.4	79.5	17.4	104.6	5 261	11 850	23 698	-14.8	1.8	NA	13.0	18.0	16.0
Grand Rapids-Muskegon-Holland, MI	402	3 308	260 702	19.9	78.6	17.8	1 349.5	7 040	13 676	31 796	3.5	3.1	NA	8.8	12.8	11.6
Great Falls, MT	815	5 331	18 971	12.3	82.9	18.4	72.8	5 060	12 011	23 700	-11.9	2.3	NA	14.7	21.6	18.0
Green Bay, WI	163	2 586	51 864	21.1	82.6	17.7	264.5	7 115	13 906	31 302	0.4	2.8	NA	7.4	11.6	9.3
Greensboro—Winston-Salem—High Point, NC	551	4 595	248 233	14.1	71.6	18.7	1 067.6	5 714	14 454	29 043	8.2	3.4	NA	10.8	17.3	15.0
Greenville, NC	655	6 297	35 790	6.7	71.0	21.9	108.7	5 428	11 642	23 324	7.8	2.3	NA	17.8	23.2	23.1
Greenville-Spartanburg-Anderson, SC	737	4 097	208 948	15.1	66.5	16.7	834.1	5 583	12 653	27 236	4.6	2.3	NA	11.0	17.2	14.9
Harrisburg-Lebanon-Carlisle, PA	230	2 268	134 963	17.1	76.9	18.0	702.1	7 049	14 659	31 637	5.8	2.9	NA	7.8	12.9	11.7

1. Data for serious crimes have not been adjusted for underreporting; this may affect comparability between geographic areas and over time. 2. Per 100,000 population estimated by the FBI. 3. All persons 3 years old and over enrolled in nursery school through college. 4. Persons 25 years old and over. 5. Elementary and secondary education expenditures, local government fiscal years ending between July 1, 1998 and June 30, 1999. 6. Based on population enumerated as of April 1, 1990.

Table C. Metropolitan Areas — **Personal Income**

Area Name	Personal income, 1999							Transfer payments					
			Per capita[1]						Government payments to individuals				
	Total (mil dol)	Percent change, 1998–1999	Dollars	Rank	Wages and salaries[2] (mil dol)	Proprietor's income (mil dol)	Dividends, interest, and rent (mil dol)	Total (mil dol)	Total (mil dol)	Social Security (mil dol)	Medical payments (mil dol)	Income maintenance (mil dol)	Unemployment insurance (mil dol)
	62	63	64	65	66	67	68	69	70	71	72	73	74
Columbia, SC........................	14 168	5.9	27 444	109	10 246	810	2 434	1 668	1 575	614	640	139	16
Columbus, GA-AL	6 500	4.5	23 950	213	4 480	354	1 168	960	904	343	304	139	14
Columbus, OH	44 353	5.5	29 777	63	32 063	2 694	7 633	4 694	4 374	1 717	1 701	422	62
Corpus Christi, TX	8 491	2.8	21 936	276	5 312	909	1 396	1 378	1 312	431	610	177	31
Corvallis, OR	2 184	1.8	28 291	88	1 344	121	594	203	190	90	47	15	3
Cumberland, MD-WV	2 033	3.2	20 700	298	1 071	108	372	535	516	181	221	37	12
Dallas-Fort Worth, TX	159 469	7.0	32 482	X	113 729	20 246	22 742	12 368	11 518	4 737	4 856	961	313
Dallas, TX	113 794	7.4	34 690	23	85 258	16 297	16 243	8 100	7 533	3 068	3 205	664	221
Fort Worth-Arlington, TX ...	45 675	6.2	28 035	95	28 471	3 948	6 499	4 268	3 986	1 669	1 650	296	92
Danville, VA	2 241	3.6	20 833	295	1 303	123	399	423	402	202	130	45	9
Davenport-Moline-Rock Island, IA-IL	9 397	1.4	26 186	139	6 291	562	2 078	1 209	1 135	563	372	108	34
Dayton-Springfield, OH	26 238	3.2	27 369	111	18 089	1 094	5 368	3 560	3 355	1 425	1 275	292	45
Daytona Beach, FL	10 691	4.3	22 520	262	4 326	490	3 169	2 267	2 180	1 141	796	126	16
Decatur, AL	3 395	3.8	23 668	223	1 941	221	518	528	502	209	219	43	7
Decatur, IL	3 078	5.2	27 188	119	2 199	163	618	464	440	203	146	48	11
Denver-Boulder-Greeley, CO	85 396	8.6	35 318	X	59 900	9 098	15 145	6 242	5 813	2 507	2 346	503	85
Boulder-Longmont, CO	10 248	8.1	37 523	14	7 699	752	2 237	542	494	245	166	37	10
Denver, CO	71 359	8.7	36 058	16	50 039	7 820	12 304	5 249	4 898	2 090	1 998	428	69
Greeley, CO	3 789	8.2	22 852	252	2 162	526	603	451	422	172	182	38	6
Des Moines, IA	13 801	6.1	31 118	45	10 432	847	2 551	1 312	1 219	596	431	97	27
Detroit-Ann Arbor-Flint, MI....	170 312	5.4	31 140	X	118 274	9 329	30 415	21 003	19 953	8 095	8 655	2 143	460
Ann Arbor, MI	18 811	8.0	33 750	27	11 537	961	3 290	1 476	1 369	660	521	95	29
Detroit, MI	140 825	5.2	31 472	42	99 602	7 955	25 243	17 668	16 807	6 740	7 390	1 823	370
Flint, MI	10 677	3.3	24 412	200	7 136	414	1 882	1 860	1 776	695	744	225	61
Dothan, AL	3 064	4.6	22 653	260	2 314	193	545	483	459	191	163	58	7
Dover, DE	2 876	3.7	22 819	254	1 873	166	471	401	375	166	139	28	12
Dubuque, IA	2 237	2.2	25 385	161	1 544	175	559	300	282	144	98	19	7
Duluth-Superior, MN-WI........	6 044	4.5	25 566	157	3 591	395	1 262	1 058	1 010	408	392	89	23
Eau Claire, WI	3 572	5.3	24 724	183	2 293	244	709	489	460	216	172	31	13
El Paso, TX	12 084	3.7	17 216	314	7 649	1 245	1 928	2 134	2 014	566	851	365	14
Elkhart-Goshen, IN	4 605	5.9	26 360	136	4 203	245	863	500	466	235	170	34	7
Elmira, NY	2 162	4.0	23 563	226	1 309	113	375	440	420	170	175	42	7
Enid, OK..............................	1 342	1.1	23 559	227	732	129	287	253	243	102	108	16	2
Erie, PA...............................	6 768	4.0	24 433	198	4 258	544	1 254	1 144	1 089	461	418	115	35
Eugene-Springfield, OR	7 972	4.7	25 315	163	4 425	698	1 899	1 226	1 170	493	409	110	40
Evansville-Henderson, IN-KY	7 918	4.1	27 191	118	5 259	546	1 650	1 109	1 053	487	415	83	15
Fargo-Moorhead, ND-MN	4 450	5.9	26 155	140	2 997	352	878	504	472	198	164	33	7
Fayetteville, NC....................	7 172	4.3	25 285	167	5 401	324	1 072	888	845	267	306	128	14
Fayetteville-Springdale-Rogers, AR	6 901	8.1	24 213	206	4 681	610	1 444	823	770	412	225	52	13
Flagstaff, AZ-UT...................	2 573	5.3	21 325	290	1 492	252	584	354	333	105	127	48	8
Florence, AL	2 959	3.0	21 617	284	1 630	194	570	555	530	259	185	46	10
Florence, SC	2 925	4.9	23 360	234	2 033	177	446	555	532	160	257	72	9
Fort Collins-Loveland, CO	6 723	6.8	28 386	87	4 021	579	1 327	564	522	253	188	34	9
Fort Myers-Cape Coral, FL ..	11 160	4.9	27 861	99	5 028	704	4 077	1 959	1 886	1 018	697	76	11
Fort Pierce-Port St. Lucie, FL.	8 891	4.0	29 641	64	3 090	516	3 547	1 581	1 526	790	568	81	23
Fort Smith, AR-OK...............	4 366	5.9	22 326	268	2 861	462	769	708	671	300	241	68	13
Fort Walton Beach, FL..........	4 204	3.7	24 720	184	2 911	203	1 051	560	532	218	194	36	6
Fort Wayne, IN.....................	13 248	4.1	27 355	113	9 444	738	2 594	1 478	1 384	706	504	92	17
Fresno, CA...........................	18 279	5.7	20 776	297	10 428	2 188	2 952	3 452	3 282	938	1 261	696	185
Gadsden, AL.........................	2 123	2.2	20 518	301	1 112	137	338	455	436	194	169	43	7
Gainesville, FL	5 091	3.3	25 648	152	3 596	236	1 026	710	674	231	288	77	5
Glens Falls, NY	2 789	3.2	22 939	248	1 524	258	585	507	481	208	191	45	10
Goldsboro, NC	2 240	1.2	20 050	306	1 463	127	378	419	399	148	167	53	6
Grand Forks, ND-MN............	2 279	1.1	23 870	217	1 473	148	444	319	301	118	111	23	5
Grand Junction, CO.............	2 712	5.9	23 557	228	1 483	260	593	423	402	183	152	29	5
GrandRapids-Muskegon-Holland, MI	29 055	5.2	27 616	106	20 942	1 707	5 302	3 217	3 015	1 424	1 101	277	89
Great Falls, MT	1 915	2.5	24 463	195	1 101	155	440	294	280	123	91	23	5
Green Bay, WI	6 301	4.4	29 102	75	4 983	387	1 288	584	542	276	178	34	17
Greensboro—Winston-Salem—High Point, NC	34 080	5.0	28 896	79	22 484	2 334	7 136	4 080	3 865	1 819	1 497	315	69
Greenville, NC......................	2 974	1.4	23 239	239	2 003	113	480	439	416	145	180	62	9
Greenville-Spartanburg-Anderson, SC	23 117	5.3	24 869	180	16 093	1 476	4 121	3 016	2 846	1 432	970	235	40
Harrisburg-Lebanon-Carlisle, PA	17 780	3.9	28 753	81	13 041	1 110	3 277	2 251	2 127	964	804	142	57

1. Based on the resident population estimated as of July 1 of the year shown.   2. Includes other labor income.

Table C. Metropolitan Areas — **Earnings, Social Security, and Housing**

Area Name	Earnings, 1999									Social Security beneficiaries, December 2000		Supplemental Security Income recipients, December 2000	Housing units, 1990	
			Goods-related[1]		Service-related and other[2]									
	Total (mil dol)	Farm	Total	Manu-facturing	Total	Retail trade	Finance, insurance, and real estate	Services	Govern-ment	Number	Rate[3]		Total	Percent change, 1980–1990
	75	76	77	78	79	80	81	82	83	84	85	86	87	88
Columbia, SC	11 056	0.2	16.4	10.3	56.0	9.5	10.0	24.0	27.5	74 336	139	10 269	177 120	22.5
Columbus, GA-AL	4 834	0.3	D	D	D	NA	D	23.2	30.7	43 188	157	8 407	101 457	11.6
Columbus, OH	34 757	0.0	D	13.7	D	12.2	11.2	27.1	17.4	199 891	130	28 550	547 847	16.2
Corpus Christi, TX	6 221	1.2	23.1	11.2	52.2	11.6	4.6	26.2	23.4	55 304	145	10 824	136 452	19.8
Corvallis, OR	1 465	1.6	D	31.2	D	6.9	3.3	22.7	24.5	9 926	127	610	27 024	7.3
Cumberland, MD-WV	1 179	0.0	24.6	18.3	D	11.9	3.9	25.8	23.1	21 308	209	2 418	43 443	3.1
Dallas-Fort Worth, TX	133 975	0.1	D	14.7	D	9.0	9.8	29.0	9.2	544 126	104	82 676	1 702 751	40.8
Dallas, TX	101 555	0.1	D	14.0	D	8.3	10.9	30.4	8.3	350 658	100	62 929	1 133 568	38.3
Fort Worth-Arlington, TX	32 420	0.1	25.4	16.9	62.5	11.2	6.4	24.7	12.0	193 468	114	19 747	569 183	46.3
Danville, VA	1 426	0.4	D	37.0	D	10.7	3.6	21.1	13.8	25 506	232	4 116	46 158	8.2
Davenport-Moline-Rock Island, IA-IL	6 853	0.2	D	21.4	D	9.9	5.0	24.9	16.4	63 146	176	5 816	145 587	0.5
Dayton-Springfield, OH	19 184	0.0	D	26.2	D	8.5	4.5	25.7	19.3	164 227	173	19 862	385 420	6.3
Daytona Beach, FL	4 816	1.7	D	8.8	D	14.6	6.3	35.2	17.6	132 797	269	9 294	196 187	50.5
Decatur, AL	2 162	3.0	D	D	D	9.0	3.7	15.7	13.4	25 986	178	4 190	52 631	17.5
Decatur, IL	2 362	0.1	39.5	31.5	51.1	9.1	3.6	21.2	9.3	22 322	195	2 899	50 049	-3.0
Denver-Boulder-Greeley, CO	68 998	0.4	18.9	10.3	68.4	8.2	10.3	30.1	12.3	290 972	113	29 495	861 909	23.4
Boulder-Longmont, CO	8 451	0.1	27.9	22.7	59.6	7.9	5.6	36.5	12.4	27 961	96	2 347	94 621	26.8
Denver, CO	57 859	0.0	17.0	8.0	70.7	8.3	11.2	29.7	12.2	240 779	114	24 876	716 150	24.0
Greeley, CO	2 687	9.4	30.9	19.7	46.0	8.5	7.3	17.2	13.7	22 232	123	2 272	51 138	10.0
Des Moines, IA	11 279	0.3	D	9.1	D	8.7	D	26.2	13.2	65 576	144	5 747	160 948	10.3
Detroit-Ann Arbor-Flint, MI	127 603	0.1	D	30.5	D	7.7	6.0	26.7	11.5	856 070	157	122 166	2 031 519	5.0
Ann Arbor, MI	12 497	0.2	D	28.4	D	8.5	4.1	23.6	22.1	70 260	121	5 665	188 223	12.8
Detroit, MI	107 556	0.0	35.8	30.5	54.0	7.5	6.3	27.1	10.2	710 515	160	103 891	1 672 488	4.2
Flint, MI	7 550	0.0	38.3	32.8	47.9	8.8	4.2	25.3	13.7	75 295	173	12 610	170 808	4.8
Dothan, AL	2 507	1.7	D	18.4	D	9.7	2.9	20.3	29.0	25 527	185	5 136	52 628	16.6
Dover, DE	2 039	1.3	D	12.6	D	10.7	4.1	19.2	38.8	20 124	159	2 487	42 106	19.1
Dubuque, IA	1 719	1.3	34.8	28.5	56.0	9.6	4.7	29.8	7.9	16 579	186	1 310	32 053	1.7
Duluth-Superior, MN-WI	3 986	0.0	21.2	8.8	58.7	10.5	3.8	28.0	20.1	47 916	197	5 381	116 013	0.5
Eau Claire, WI	2 537	0.9	26.2	19.1	57.0	17.3	3.7	24.3	15.9	25 314	171	2 526	53 765	11.6
El Paso, TX	8 893	0.4	17.9	13.0	54.2	10.5	8.4	21.1	27.5	83 893	123	1 549	187 473	26.7
Elkhart-Goshen, IN	4 448	0.0	D	55.9	D	7.0	2.8	12.9	6.1	25 650	140	1 991	60 182	16.0
Elmira, NY	1 422	0.3	31.1	25.0	49.8	10.6	3.9	24.5	18.8	19 272	212	2 787	37 290	1.6
Enid, OK	861	1.9	19.6	8.7	54.1	10.4	4.1	23.3	24.5	11 528	199	1 160	26 502	3.6
Erie, PA	4 802	0.4	37.4	31.6	48.9	10.0	5.8	23.9	13.2	51 507	183	7 486	108 585	4.7
Eugene-Springfield, OR	5 123	0.2	D	18.5	D	12.1	5.6	26.5	17.6	55 706	172	5 095	116 676	5.0
Evansville-Henderson, IN-KY	5 805	0.1	D	26.0	D	9.4	5.7	25.6	9.7	54 598	184	5 831	117 896	9.5
Fargo-Moorhead, ND-MN	3 349	2.0	D	8.7	D	10.1	8.3	28.6	15.2	23 055	132	1 950	60 953	14.9
Fayetteville, NC	5 726	0.1	D	8.8	D	8.5	2.7	13.3	57.1	36 219	120	7 460	98 360	20.9
Fayetteville-Springdale-Rogers, AR	5 291	3.9	D	20.8	D	22.1	4.1	17.4	12.4	51 025	164	4 399	88 793	25.6
Flagstaff, AZ-UT	1 744	0.6	D	D	D	13.9	3.2	28.8	32.5	13 714	112	3 045	46 151	42.2
Florence, AL	1 823	1.1	29.5	21.8	44.3	11.2	4.1	18.8	25.2	30 764	215	4 408	55 334	7.8
Florence, SC	2 210	0.5	D	19.3	D	10.6	8.4	25.2	18.9	20 989	167	5 880	43 209	10.3
Fort Collins-Loveland, CO	4 599	0.5	32.3	23.3	48.0	11.8	5.3	24.1	19.3	30 553	121	1 845	77 811	25.1
Fort Myers-Cape Coral, FL	5 732	1.0	15.3	4.3	65.3	15.6	9.8	29.0	18.4	115 298	262	6 086	189 051	70.3
Fort Pierce-Port St. Lucie, FL	3 605	4.3	D	6.1	D	12.6	7.9	30.7	16.1	88 377	277	5 955	128 042	70.9
Fort Smith, AR-OK	3 322	1.0	D	28.0	D	9.6	3.5	28.3	10.7	38 957	188	6 078	74 646	15.2
Fort Walton Beach, FL	3 114	0.1	8.3	3.8	46.2	10.4	5.0	25.2	45.4	27 883	164	2 402	62 569	45.2
Fort Wayne, IN	10 182	0.1	D	33.9	D	8.5	7.6	21.2	9.4	77 771	155	5 538	181 864	9.4
Fresno, CA	12 616	6.0	D	9.4	D	10.1	D	23.5	21.0	119 306	129	40 401	266 394	22.1
Gadsden, AL	1 249	1.9	D	25.1	D	11.3	4.0	27.7	14.5	23 675	229	4 254	41 787	4.8
Gainesville, FL	3 833	0.6	D	5.2	D	9.5	6.7	30.5	37.3	28 357	130	4 855	79 022	34.1
Glens Falls, NY	1 782	1.0	D	19.1	D	11.7	5.6	28.3	19.9	24 163	194	2 990	55 953	14.8
Goldsboro, NC	1 590	2.1	D	14.5	D	9.4	4.7	18.7	33.1	19 960	176	4 460	39 483	12.7
Grand Forks, ND-MN	1 621	2.6	D	7.1	D	10.5	3.6	23.3	31.5	14 178	145	1 095	41 360	5.2
Grand Junction, CO	1 742	0.3	19.8	8.1	62.3	14.1	7.0	28.4	17.6	22 690	195	2 103	39 208	20.4
GrandRapids-Muskegon-Holland, MI	22 649	0.7	D	34.2	D	9.3	5.1	21.4	9.8	157 287	144	18 249	357 679	15.6
Great Falls, MT	1 256	0.7	D	3.4	D	11.8	7.4	28.6	29.2	14 652	182	1 434	33 063	2.7
Green Bay, WI	5 370	0.6	31.3	24.3	58.5	9.9	7.6	24.0	9.6	31 263	138	2 842	74 740	20.0
Greensboro—Winston-Salem—High Point, NC	24 818	0.7	D	25.7	D	9.7	7.6	25.7	10.0	210 547	168	20 845	444 316	21.0
Greenville, NC	2 116	-0.8	D	18.7	D	10.0	4.4	21.3	32.0	19 446	145	4 702	43 070	30.6
Greenville-Spartanburg-Anderson, SC	17 569	0.3	D	28.8	D	11.5	4.8	21.4	12.9	170 326	177	19 181	335 792	20.6
Harrisburg-Lebanon-Carlisle, PA	14 151	0.3	D	14.5	D	8.5	8.7	24.6	21.7	109 865	175	8 727	241 489	11.6

1. Covers mining, construction, and manufacturing. 2. Covers private sector earnings in agricultural services, forestry, and fisheries; transportation and public utilities; wholesale trade; retail trade; finance, insurance, and real estate; and services. 3. Per 1,000 resident population estimated as of July 1 of the year shown.

Table C. Metropolitan Areas — Housing, Labor Force, and Employment

Area Name	Housing units, 1990 (cont'd)								Civilian labor force, 2001				Civilian employment, 1990[5]		
	Occupied units										Unemployment			Percent	
	Owner-occupied					Renter-occupied									
				Owner cost as a percent of income											
	Total	Percent	Median value[1]	With a mortgage	Without a mortgage	Median rent[2]	Rent as percent of income	Sub-standard units[3] (percent)	Total	Percent change, 2000–2001	Total	Rate[4]	Total	Professional, managerial, and technical	Precision production, craft, and repair
	89	90	91	92	93	94	95	96	97	98	99	100	101	102	103
Columbia, SC	163 223	65.6	72 600	20.3	12.5	427	24.7	3.7	272 400	-2.8	8 628	3.2	226 655	33.9	10.4
Columbus, GA-AL	92 695	56.9	56 600	NA	NA	349	NA	5.0	124 455	-2.1	6 020	4.8	101 920	26.1	12.3
Columbus, OH	513 498	59.8	72 300	NA	NA	420	NA	2.1	875 515	2.5	24 624	2.8	675 076	32.7	9.1
Corpus Christi, TX	118 516	59.8	53 600	21.0	12.9	364	25.4	10.5	174 342	-0.2	10 000	5.7	144 176	26.8	14.9
Corvallis, OR	26 126	55.1	72 900	20.1	12.2	387	29.4	3.7	40 034	0.1	1 185	3.0	32 984	41.2	6.8
Cumberland, MD-WV	39 615	71.8	47 400	17.2	12.7	280	25.5	1.7	45 257	-0.2	3 260	7.2	40 718	25.4	12.5
Dallas-Fort Worth, TX	1 508 031	57.6	77 800	NA	NA	444	NA	6.5	2 937 800	2.0	133 805	4.6	2 073 309	32.5	10.6
Dallas, TX	1 001 750	56.0	81 500	NA	NA	453	NA	7.1	2 006 801	2.2	95 378	4.8	1 388 158	33.1	9.9
Fort Worth-Arlington, TX	506 281	60.7	72 000	NA	NA	428	NA	5.3	930 999	1.6	38 427	4.1	685 151	31.4	11.8
Danville, VA	42 325	69.3	47 900	15.8	12.6	277	22.4	5.3	57 892	1.8	4 925	8.5	50 658	18.5	13.1
Davenport-Moline-Rock Island, IA-IL	136 269	67.8	49 800	16.9	12.6	343	24.8	1.7	185 325	-1.4	8 536	4.6	161 975	26.5	11.3
Dayton-Springfield, OH	364 300	65.7	65 000	17.5	12.4	398	25.2	2.0	480 678	1.8	20 660	4.3	438 828	31.9	10.8
Daytona Beach, FL	165 296	72.3	71 000	NA	NA	468	NA	2.4	195 094	1.4	8 425	4.3	166 071	27.4	12.7
Decatur, AL	49 209	73.9	57 700	17.3	12.4	330	22.4	3.3	73 589	-0.4	4 285	5.8	60 004	23.9	16.9
Decatur, IL	45 996	70.2	45 400	15.5	12.5	339	25.0	1.6	57 687	-4.5	3 647	6.3	52 639	26.3	11.7
Denver-Boulder-Greeley, CO	785 276	61.5	88 400	NA	NA	434	NA	2.9	1 430 761	0.8	50 749	3.5	1 038 930	36.3	9.1
Boulder-Longmont, CO	88 402	61.1	102 800	22.3	12.3	501	28.7	2.4	189 963	3.3	6 679	3.5	124 542	45.0	8.1
Denver, CO	649 404	61.6	87 800	22.6	12.5	431	25.5	2.8	1 152 616	0.3	40 493	3.5	851 275	35.9	9.0
Greeley, CO	47 470	61.2	67 500	22.2	13.0	356	26.6	4.2	88 182	2.7	3 577	4.1	63 113	24.3	12.5
Des Moines, IA	153 100	66.9	59 100	19.5	13.2	426	24.7	2.3	260 980	1.6	6 727	2.6	210 506	30.4	8.6
Detroit-Ann Arbor-Flint, MI	1 916 409	69.2	67 200	NA	NA	454	NA	3.1	2 821 469	-1.0	141 951	5.0	2 344 516	30.3	11.8
Ann Arbor, MI	175 050	65.5	87 300	NA	NA	514	NA	2.8	312 776	0.4	9 612	3.1	250 928	36.7	10.3
Detroit, MI	1 580 063	69.5	67 600	18.2	13.6	453	27.3	3.1	2 317 541	-1.2	117 785	5.1	1 914 501	30.0	11.8
Flint, MI	161 296	70.4	50 500	16.0	13.3	400	31.3	3.0	191 152	-0.5	14 554	7.6	179 087	24.6	13.6
Dothan, AL	48 418	65.2	51 400	17.3	12.8	313	22.9	3.9	66 978	-0.4	3 054	4.6	57 113	24.8	14.1
Dover, DE	39 655	69.2	80 800	NA	NA	421	NA	3.4	72 364	1.9	2 649	3.7	51 615	25.9	14.0
Dubuque, IA	30 799	71.2	53 600	16.2	12.1	314	23.8	1.7	48 237	-0.2	2 061	4.3	42 025	25.3	10.5
Duluth-Superior, MN-WI	95 275	73.4	41 600	15.6	12.6	292	28.3	2.3	128 356	1.9	6 930	5.4	101 011	27.8	12.2
Eau Claire, WI	50 359	68.2	50 600	18.7	13.3	345	26.5	2.5	83 388	1.5	3 918	4.7	64 513	25.6	9.9
El Paso, TX	178 366	58.7	57 300	20.6	12.0	346	26.0	15.4	284 190	-0.4	23 266	8.2	216 790	27.7	11.0
Elkhart-Goshen, IN	56 713	71.8	62 300	17.0	11.6	404	23.3	2.3	94 834	-2.5	5 142	5.4	80 588	22.6	13.8
Elmira, NY	35 275	68.3	53 600	17.5	14.6	360	27.3	1.6	42 027	-1.7	2 217	5.3	41 063	28.5	11.8
Enid, OK	22 460	69.1	38 100	19.9	12.3	338	24.0	2.0	26 014	-1.9	744	2.9	24 402	24.7	12.5
Erie, PA	101 564	68.6	54 000	17.5	12.7	328	25.5	1.9	140 711	0.3	8 228	5.8	122 635	26.8	12.4
Eugene-Springfield, OR	110 799	60.8	65 800	20.2	13.3	417	28.5	3.7	165 257	-0.9	11 182	6.8	129 698	28.3	10.4
Evansville-Henderson, IN-KY	108 663	68.9	54 500	17.4	12.4	337	24.9	2.3	158 739	1.0	6 032	3.8	132 407	26.2	12.6
Fargo-Moorhead, ND-MN	57 771	58.9	64 500	20.2	12.4	346	26.3	2.1	104 927	1.7	1 969	1.9	79 205	29.6	8.5
Fayetteville, NC	91 500	57.7	63 500	23.1	13.9	405	26.1	4.3	120 051	-0.2	6 514	5.4	96 204	26.5	11.8
Fayetteville-Springdale-Rogers, AR	80 927	66.9	57 600	NA	NA	356	NA	3.6	152 570	2.6	3 484	2.3	99 938	24.6	12.5
Flagstaff, AZ-UT	31 642	61.4	NA	NA	NA	NA	NA	18.6	64 486	1.8	3 424	5.3	43 951	28.2	11.8
Florence, AL	51 001	74.1	49 700	18.1	12.4	295	25.4	2.5	66 380	-0.7	5 457	8.2	56 819	23.1	16.2
Florence, SC	40 217	70.5	54 900	18.6	13.7	341	25.0	6.6	62 274	-2.6	3 640	5.8	51 984	24.7	13.4
Fort Collins-Loveland, CO	70 472	62.9	83 900	22.0	12.5	419	28.4	2.4	146 144	2.6	5 154	3.5	94 102	36.6	10.4
Fort Myers-Cape Coral, FL	140 124	72.1	84 300	22.6	11.8	503	26.2	3.0	192 223	4.9	6 163	3.2	144 465	25.7	13.3
Fort Pierce-Port St. Lucie, FL	101 196	74.0	84 100	21.8	11.7	516	26.4	3.7	130 700	2.1	9 496	7.3	102 436	25.4	14.5
Fort Smith, AR-OK	66 884	69.4	45 200	19.0	12.8	308	24.4	4.3	96 959	-1.0	4 125	4.3	77 931	21.9	14.2
Fort Walton Beach, FL	53 313	62.2	70 600	21.6	11.5	412	25.6	2.8	83 690	1.7	2 796	3.3	58 554	31.7	11.4
Fort Wayne, IN	168 806	73.2	57 000	NA	NA	377	NA	2.3	262 920	0.1	12 696	4.8	228 442	26.3	12.6
Fresno, CA	249 303	55.5	83 900	NA	NA	432	NA	13.5	441 744	-1.8	59 646	13.5	303 089	26.6	10.0
Gadsden, AL	38 675	74.0	42 700	17.8	12.9	280	24.0	2.5	48 309	-3.1	3 560	7.4	40 902	20.8	14.4
Gainesville, FL	71 258	54.1	66 000	NA	NA	395	NA	4.7	107 664	1.0	2 810	2.6	85 785	41.8	7.6
Glens Falls, NY	42 815	71.4	81 000	20.5	13.7	432	27.2	2.1	57 960	-1.9	2 535	4.4	52 870	26.0	12.5
Goldsboro, NC	36 889	62.7	58 000	NA	NA	321	NA	4.1	49 593	0.8	2 663	5.4	44 564	23.2	13.1
Grand Forks, ND-MN	37 324	57.1	57 100	NA	NA	352	NA	2.2	52 638	0.7	1 672	3.2	45 333	29.1	8.8
Grand Junction, CO	36 250	64.9	62 700	21.3	12.2	333	25.4	2.7	57 814	0.1	2 285	4.0	41 219	28.1	11.5
GrandRapids-Muskegon-Holland, MI	333 911	73.6	65 700	NA	NA	420	NA	2.5	625 951	0.2	31 739	5.1	451 193	25.9	12.4
Great Falls, MT	30 133	63.7	60 200	20.5	11.9	317	25.7	2.5	36 833	-1.7	1 663	4.5	31 669	27.9	10.2
Green Bay, WI	72 280	65.6	62 600	20.3	13.0	372	23.9	2.1	138 623	2.4	5 290	3.8	99 142	26.6	11.2
Greensboro—Winston-Salem—High Point, NC	414 793	67.8	70 700	NA	NA	390	NA	2.6	644 206	-0.8	32 432	5.0	559 047	26.0	13.1
Greenville, NC	40 491	58.1	65 300	NA	NA	349	NA	5.4	69 128	0.1	4 184	6.1	53 492	30.0	10.5
Greenville-Spartanburg-Anderson, SC	312 740	70.0	58 700	NA	NA	358	NA	3.2	496 109	-0.9	22 826	4.6	410 204	25.8	13.8
Harrisburg-Lebanon-Carlisle, PA	226 353	68.8	75 400	19.2	12.0	418	23.3	1.9	352 521	1.9	12 036	3.4	298 729	28.8	10.8

1. Specified owner-occupied units.　2. Specified renter-occupied units.　3. Overcrowded or lacking complete plumbing facilities.　4. Percent of civilian labor force.　5. Persons 16 years and older.

Table C. Metropolitan Areas — **Nonfarm Employment and Agriculture**

Area Name	Private nonfarm establishments, employment and payroll, 1999									Agriculture, 1997			
		Employment						Annual payroll		Farms			Farm operators
											Percent with—		
	Number of establishments	Total	Health Care and Social Assistance	Manufacturing	Retail trade	Finance and Insurance	Professional Scientific and Technical Services	Total (mil dol)	Average per employee (dollars)	Number	Less than 50 acres	500 acres and over	Whose principal occupation is farming (percent)
	104	105	106	107	108	109	110	111	112	113	114	115	116
Columbia, SC	14 005	237 158	29 234	23 967	33 191	20 013	11 964	6 372	26 868	1 149	43.6	4.6	41.3
Columbus, GA-AL	5 668	103 917	10 951	21 880	14 518	6 974	2 935	2 643	25 434	505	31.1	16.0	36.8
Columbus, OH	37 056	754 033	81 715	80 715	100 170	77 203	40 556	23 655	31 371	4 646	36.0	13.9	48.9
Corpus Christi, TX	8 962	129 463	22 674	11 534	19 071	4 414	5 367	3 188	24 625	1 065	30.3	34.7	53.1
Corvallis, OR	1 931	28 396	3 819	8 712	3 203	565	1 585	840	29 582	726	65.4	7.4	41.5
Cumberland, MD-WV	2 334	29 047	5 794	5 192	5 483	1 047	751	661	22 756	582	22.0	10.0	40.4
Dallas-Fort Worth, TX	126 046	2 465 145	213 719	317 716	270 612	145 241	158 147	88 679	35 973	17 707	46.1	8.1	33.5
Dallas, TX	88 431	1 802 462	144 261	215 385	181 454	118 391	129 254	68 965	38 262	11 497	43.7	8.3	33.7
Fort Worth-Arlington, TX	37 615	662 683	69 458	102 331	89 158	26 850	28 893	19 714	29 749	6 210	50.5	7.7	33.3
Danville, VA	2 454	38 344	5 056	13 594	6 008	1 213	772	916	23 889	1 235	20.4	10.3	50.0
Davenport-Moline-Rock Island, IA-IL	9 380	161 182	19 071	27 308	23 563	6 563	5 352	4 586	28 452	2 761	25.0	21.1	60.2
Dayton-Springfield, OH	21 234	414 677	56 990	85 834	54 837	13 939	21 111	12 696	30 617	3 178	44.0	11.5	43.3
Daytona Beach, FL	11 693	138 000	21 049	11 653	25 923	4 416	5 381	2 948	21 362	1 001	69.9	6.2	50.0
Decatur, AL	3 214	51 236	4 924	16 581	7 324	1 662	1 189	1 403	27 383	2 501	40.9	4.4	31.6
Decatur, IL	2 745	54 983	6 836	10 930	6 906	1 606	1 032	1 641	29 846	665	24.7	36.7	62.1
Denver-Boulder-Greeley, CO	79 050	1 201 670	115 977	109 215	144 052	78 005	101 543	43 919	36 548	5 537	37.9	21.5	50.6
Boulder-Longmont, CO	10 772	145 191	12 798	25 510	18 073	4 111	22 006	5 897	40 615	657	60.4	6.7	42.0
Denver, CO	64 416	1 002 277	97 295	72 838	119 019	69 921	78 095	36 456	36 373	1 921	44.5	21.7	43.2
Greeley, CO	3 862	54 202	5 884	10 867	6 960	3 973	1 442	1 566	28 892	2 959	28.6	24.6	57.4
Des Moines, IA	13 131	256 660	30 389	21 875	32 194	42 541	10 843	7 867	30 651	2 932	30.2	18.0	48.0
Detroit-Ann Arbor-Flint, MI	127 554	2 347 194	282 598	416 727	296 936	108 000	147 847	90 257	38 453	8 168	43.2	8.6	45.1
Ann Arbor, MI	14 031	228 775	35 119	50 105	30 958	6 847	13 280	8 197	35 830	2 984	38.1	11.0	45.2
Detroit, MI	104 370	1 965 764	225 291	338 130	240 382	95 851	129 467	77 181	39 263	4 388	45.6	7.3	45.2
Flint, MI	9 153	152 655	22 188	28 492	25 596	5 302	5 100	4 879	31 961	796	49.5	6.4	44.5
Dothan, AL	3 690	57 076	8 713	10 183	8 937	1 472	1 329	1 382	24 213	1 112	28.3	15.9	45.7
Dover, DE	2 979	43 783	5 810	7 339	8 333	2 722	1 541	1 064	24 302	767	40.3	12.0	59.8
Dubuque, IA	2 627	48 230	6 382	11 562	6 672	2 020	1 056	1 202	24 922	1 579	17.9	7.3	64.1
Duluth-Superior, MN-WI	6 623	92 095	18 705	6 718	14 576	3 446	3 135	2 292	24 887	980	18.3	9.3	33.7
Eau Claire, WI	3 880	62 092	10 107	12 348	10 321	2 287	1 890	1 491	24 013	2 398	13.1	8.7	66.0
El Paso, TX	12 379	195 303	25 446	34 141	28 747	5 887	6 782	4 285	21 940	415	67.7	11.6	40.7
Elkhart-Goshen, IN	5 016	114 299	7 625	58 940	11 353	1 749	1 658	3 303	28 898	1 335	45.9	6.2	46.7
Elmira, NY	1 899	35 641	6 100	9 014	5 807	849	969	908	25 476	313	23.3	4.8	39.0
Enid, OK	1 655	18 913	3 812	1 429	3 448	653	507	403	21 308	1 069	13.5	35.3	55.1
Erie, PA	6 824	120 107	17 574	34 253	15 694	4 790	3 473	3 233	26 918	1 123	31.7	4.2	55.8
Eugene-Springfield, OR	9 698	119 071	15 634	21 187	18 915	4 125	6 281	3 072	25 800	2 104	65.3	4.2	37.2
Evansville-Henderson, IN-KY	7 958	146 238	20 671	31 117	19 282	5 644	5 160	4 041	27 633	1 590	32.1	19.6	50.4
Fargo-Moorhead, ND-MN	5 306	87 671	12 312	7 766	13 443	6 097	3 094	2 198	25 071	1 806	12.3	51.0	75.8
Fayetteville, NC	5 340	89 199	13 328	13 252	15 699	3 040	2 833	2 020	22 646	433	37.9	12.9	43.0
Fayetteville-Springdale-Rogers, AR	7 664	130 092	12 686	28 233	16 358	3 889	3 866	3 516	27 027	4 799	41.1	4.4	45.2
Flagstaff, AZ-UT	3 585	38 853	4 379	2 491	7 399	716	1 051	820	21 105	342	30.4	37.4	44.4
Florence, AL	3 404	49 755	6 912	11 869	7 780	1 452	1 068	1 074	21 586	1 912	39.6	6.7	31.2
Florence, SC	3 329	55 933	10 617	10 808	9 556	4 307	1 510	1 405	25 119	615	33.3	15.4	52.7
Fort Collins-Loveland, CO	7 842	90 677	9 874	12 718	15 181	2 806	5 199	2 435	26 854	1 298	50.5	13.0	39.3
Fort Myers-Cape Coral, FL	12 099	140 147	16 624	5 293	26 933	4 938	8 634	3 379	24 110	509	70.9	10.0	40.3
Fort Pierce-Port St. Lucie, FL	7 973	86 261	13 744	5 255	16 551	3 204	4 325	2 069	23 985	805	53.9	15.8	48.6
Fort Smith, AR-OK	4 869	90 219	11 882	27 470	10 827	2 416	3 709	2 199	24 374	2 655	32.8	7.5	38.5
Fort Walton Beach, FL	4 813	57 204	7 023	3 442	10 965	2 200	4 263	1 281	22 394	342	37.1	6.4	36.5
Fort Wayne, IN	12 822	253 663	28 571	72 438	30 455	12 276	9 650	7 374	29 070	5 416	33.9	12.1	42.5
Fresno, CA	16 990	230 629	32 639	30 370	34 678	10 177	9 254	6 026	26 129	8 265	55.8	11.7	61.5
Gadsden, AL	2 198	33 152	5 181	8 066	4 783	955	643	766	23 106	904	47.3	3.1	31.9
Gainesville, FL	5 076	78 917	16 699	5 109	13 401	2 544	4 854	1 889	23 937	1 086	57.9	6.2	40.8
Glens Falls, NY	3 375	41 800	6 103	7 516	7 208	1 711	1 157	1 106	26 459	796	19.5	14.1	63.1
Goldsboro, NC	2 364	37 017	6 884	8 837	6 046	1 215	728	824	22 260	827	39.5	13.1	62.8
Grand Forks, ND-MN	2 646	36 514	7 935	3 234	7 042	1 207	1 082	807	22 101	2 134	8.4	48.6	68.6
Grand Junction, CO	3 622	40 427	6 753	3 837	7 088	1 211	1 604	996	24 637	1 489	64.1	8.3	44.3
Grand Rapids-Muskegon-Holland, MI	26 792	526 698	53 916	155 573	64 425	17 771	19 056	16 570	31 460	4 175	43.9	6.9	47.3
Great Falls, MT	2 534	27 093	5 515	926	5 352	1 940	1 197	573	21 149	903	20.3	44.3	57.5
Green Bay, WI	6 193	128 706	14 041	27 817	16 114	9 964	4 260	3 901	30 309	1 059	31.4	6.2	62.5
Greensboro—Winston-Salem—High Point, NC	32 590	609 681	62 016	148 727	72 866	33 242	21 370	17 486	28 681	6 934	41.0	3.5	45.6
Greenville, NC	3 148	51 832	9 760	9 262	8 061	1 764	1 518	1 224	23 615	474	26.8	23.0	67.1
Greenville-Spartanburg-Anderson, SC	24 809	477 308	42 495	115 686	56 803	13 411	17 640	13 447	28 173	4 043	44.6	3.3	32.5
Harrisburg-Lebanon-Carlisle, PA	15 296	290 794	41 603	37 228	37 596	22 291	12 882	8 440	29 024	3 098	31.6	4.3	57.7

Table C. Metropolitan Areas — Agriculture, Land, and Water

Area Name	Land in farms — Acreage (1,000)	Percent change, 1992–1997	Average size of farm	Total irrigated (1,000)	Total cropland (1,000)	Value of land and buildings — Average per farm ($1,000)	Average per acre (dollars)	Value of machinery and equipment Average per farm ($1,000)	Value of products sold — Total (mil dol)	Average per farm (dollars)	Percent from — Crops	Percent from — Livestock and poultry products	Percent of farms with sales of — $10,000 or more	$100,000 or more	Percent of land owned by Fed. Gov. 1997	Water consumption 1995 (mil gal/day)
	117	118	119	120	121	122	123	124	125	126	127	128	129	130	131	132
Columbia, SC	150	0.7	131	7	77	269	2 381	35	119	103 794	23.0	77.0	31.7	12.7	7.2	683.8
Columbus, GA-AL	156	1.0	308	2	48	399	1 335	31	11	21 513	D	D	23.8	4.6	17.7	97.7
Columbus, OH	1 204	-0.7	259	1	1 038	612	2 392	65	435	93 580	68.0	32.0	53.6	18.7	0.6	251.8
Corpus Christi, TX	844	5.3	792	4	616	679	856	93	141	132 008	86.0	14.0	50.2	27.0	0.2	167.3
Corvallis, OR	131	9.9	180	20	92	413	2 527	55	70	96 697	87.3	12.7	31.5	11.3	17.6	80.9
Cumberland, MD-WV	122	7.6	209	0	47	222	1 167	25	12	20 093	16.0	84.0	22.5	3.8	1.9	50.3
Dallas-Fort Worth, TX	3 585	3.4	202	14	1 795	338	1 668	28	368	20 764	38.0	62.0	21.8	3.1	0.9	5 019.9
Dallas, TX	2 363	1.6	206	6	1 301	330	1 597	30	237	20 578	44.0	56.0	22.1	3.2	1.0	1 478.6
Fort Worth-Arlington, TX	1 222	7.3	197	8	493	352	1 806	24	131	21 108	28.0	72.0	21.3	3.1	0.7	3 541.2
Danville, VA	267	-10.1	216	7	124	280	1 273	47	59	47 663	75.0	25.0	43.2	13.0	0.0	29.5
Davenport-Moline-Rock Island, IA-IL	852	-1.3	309	10	754	705	2 324	89	324	117 332	62.0	38.0	72.6	33.2	0.9	1 034.8
Dayton-Springfield, OH	649	-3.3	204	4	577	529	2 602	62	232	73 093	83.0	17.0	53.9	17.4	0.9	264.6
Daytona Beach, FL	199	4.9	199	18	43	519	2 837	35	148	148 047	95.0	5.0	47.0	19.3	2.3	170.8
Decatur, AL	364	10.5	145	2	234	264	1 811	28	158	63 213	13.0	87.0	25.8	9.1	13.1	202.3
Decatur, IL	323	3.8	486	D	303	1 354	2 803	125	106	158 998	96.0	4.0	74.3	44.1	0.0	46.6
Denver-Boulder-Greeley, CO	3 350	NA	605	470	D	D	D	74	1 480	267 370	24.0	76.0	49.3	17.2	11.9	1 802.2
Boulder-Longmont, CO	128	-18.4	195	39	59	534	2 054	55	44	66 470	64.0	36.0	34.7	7.8	35.0	173.6
Denver, CO	1 309	D	681	38	D	D	D	48	150	78 146	75.0	25.0	38.2	10.5	11.4	466.7
Greeley, CO	1 914	-8.3	647	393	882	567	807	95	1 287	434 821	16.0	84.0	59.8	23.7	8.1	1 161.9
Des Moines, IA	849	0.6	290	1	708	573	2 005	67	248	84 740	71.0	29.0	56.6	21.1	2.0	70.2
Detroit-Ann Arbor-Flint, MI	1 437	-5.1	176	21	1 234	432	2 467	63	505	61 782	78.0	22.0	46.8	13.2	0.1	5 854.0
Ann Arbor, MI	615	-4.5	206	9	531	456	2 166	66	188	62 944	70.0	30.0	49.7	15.4	0.0	103.8
Detroit, MI	704	-4.1	160	11	604	440	2 790	64	289	65 819	84.0	16.0	46.8	12.7	0.1	5 695.8
Flint, MI	118	-13.9	148	1	99	301	2 106	52	28	35 170	73.0	27.0	36.2	7.8	0.0	54.5
Dothan, AL	329	1.0	296	11	200	349	1 143	60	91	81 501	55.0	45.0	45.3	15.2	6.1	133.8
Dover, DE	195	-1.2	254	21	168	647	2 556	74	154	200 379	41.0	59.0	64.4	29.9	3.7	33.9
Dubuque, IA	336	-2.2	213	0	258	336	1 623	69	172	108 709	18.0	82.0	76.0	34.6	0.4	81.5
Duluth-Superior, MN-WI	226	1.0	231	D	121	147	625	25	15	15 682	40.0	60.0	23.2	3.2	16.9	210.3
Eau Claire, WI	564	-2.2	235	4	371	197	825	60	176	73 589	20.0	80.0	63.3	23.7	0.0	29.3
El Paso, TX	244	D	587	41	47	404	720	72	77	184 754	48.0	52.0	37.6	19.5	13.7	392.6
Elkhart-Goshen, IN	183	-4.8	137	24	160	376	2 738	48	124	92 912	28.0	72.0	64.6	24.7	0.0	43.4
Elmira, NY	59	0.5	189	0	36	186	983	41	13	41 208	31.0	69.0	33.9	12.1	0.0	18.2
Enid, OK	615	-7.1	575	0	459	384	693	59	83	77 621	47.0	53.0	66.5	19.0	0.3	6.1
Erie, PA	168	-0.2	149	1	114	290	1 892	63	69	61 366	63.0	37.0	51.0	14.4	0.0	97.2
Eugene-Springfield, OR	224	-7.6	106	23	120	336	3 428	34	87	41 431	62.0	38.0	24.3	6.7	53.5	350.1
Evansville-Henderson, IN-KY	562	-5.7	354	D	491	613	1 761	93	154	97 143	82.0	18.0	58.4	24.7	0.4	875.7
Fargo-Moorhead, ND-MN	1 649	0.7	913	12	1 542	807	900	146	307	169 826	87.0	13.0	76.0	45.8	0.6	26.7
Fayetteville, NC	103	4.2	238	2	57	461	2 205	66	68	156 314	33.0	67.0	45.7	18.9	10.4	35.7
Fayetteville-Springdale-Rogers, AR	631	-2.3	132	2	343	302	2 380	33	697	145 227	1.0	99.0	39.9	19.5	3.8	363.7
Flagstaff, AZ-UT	6 385	3.0	18 669	10	D	2 831	152	33	14	40 693	5.0	95.0	34.8	8.5	46.3	57.4
Florence, AL	327	-3.8	171	3	203	249	1 443	29	62	32 254	42.0	58.0	22.3	6.6	3.3	107.2
Florence, SC	169	-13.5	274	2	114	337	1 230	67	69	112 367	89.0	11.0	53.2	21.5	0.0	50.0
Fort Collins-Loveland, CO	542	0.4	418	78	127	657	1 602	49	100	77 414	38.0	62.0	37.1	10.2	46.9	270.2
Fort Myers-Cape Coral, FL	129	20.6	253	26	34	724	2 664	38	116	228 678	98.0	2.0	39.9	10.6	0.6	134.0
Fort Pierce-Port St. Lucie, FL	411	-16.3	511	201	211	1 348	2 748	77	318	395 230	88.0	12.0	58.9	23.6	0.1	479.9
Fort Smith, AR-OK	547	14.9	206	6	237	228	1 142	29	136	51 215	13.0	87.0	28.7	7.7	14.8	62.3
Fort Walton Beach, FL	51	-10.8	149	0	21	249	1 608	25	9	25 471	61.0	39.0	21.3	3.8	38.8	29.9
Fort Wayne, IN	1 193	0.6	220	3	1 063	458	2 188	58	420	77 504	62.0	38.0	58.8	20.0	0.9	83.0
Fresno, CA	2 523	0.0	305	1 462	1 584	1 009	3 386	77	3 400	411 373	77.0	23.0	72.2	36.7	37.8	4 528.7
Gadsden, AL	95	10.4	105	0	47	207	2 253	28	55	60 779	6.0	94.0	25.3	9.4	0.0	264.5
Gainesville, FL	198	3.8	182	8	75	361	2 209	22	50	46 276	62.0	38.0	32.5	7.7	0.0	48.3
Glens Falls, NY	204	-3.7	256	1	125	318	1 263	61	80	100 156	14.0	86.0	58.7	26.6	0.0	24.3
Goldsboro, NC	229	27.5	277	2	147	542	2 025	83	337	407 605	21.0	79.0	71.0	41.8	0.8	32.0
Grand Forks, ND-MN	1 827	0.8	856	22	1 656	662	780	151	323	151 481	92.0	8.0	67.4	37.7	1.1	33.9
Grand Junction, CO	417	-0.8	280	88	92	487	2 045	30	50	33 882	40.0	60.0	33.2	5.9	72.1	972.9
GrandRapids-Muskegon-Holland, MI	667	-2.9	160	42	543	387	2 416	75	652	156 220	54.0	46.0	52.3	22.1	1.0	1 196.3
Great Falls, MT	1 441	1.2	1 596	33	508	620	373	61	67	73 899	48.0	52.0	55.6	16.1	12.5	153.2
Green Bay, WI	196	-4.4	185	0	168	333	1 770	74	128	121 309	14.0	86.0	66.8	31.6	0.0	496.5
Greensboro—Winston-Salem—High Point, NC	800	3.0	115	11	443	307	2 731	35	370	53 405	37.0	63.0	37.7	12.4	0.4	1 140.2
Greenville, NC	193	-0.3	408	2	144	767	1 865	112	196	413 795	50.0	50.0	76.8	49.6	0.8	26.0
Greenville-Spartanburg-Anderson, SC	455	2.2	113	D	248	277	2 730	27	94	23 316	50.0	50.0	17.3	2.6	0.4	351.0
Harrisburg-Lebanon-Carlisle, PA	455	3.2	147	3	367	446	3 070	59	368	118 752	16.0	84.0	61.9	28.6	0.6	205.5

Table C. Metropolitan Areas — Residential Construction, Wholesale and Retail Trade, and Real Estate

Area Name	Value of Residential Construction Authorized by Building Permits, 2000		Wholesale Trade, 1997				Retail Trade[1], 1997				Real Estate and Rental and Leasing, 1997			
	New Construction ($1,000)	Number of Housing Units	Number of Establishments	Number of Employees	Sales (mil dol)	Annual Payroll (mil dol)	Number of Establishments	Number of Employees	Sales (mil dol)	Annual Payroll (mil dol)	Number of Establishments	Number of Employees	Receipts (mil dol)	Annual Payroll (mil dol)
	133	134	135	136	137	138	139	140	141	142	143	144	145	146
Columbia, SC	373 737	4 319	841	12 095	5 272.0	403.7	2 361	32 643	5 279.2	507.3	533	3 298	396.8	74.9
Columbus, GA-AL	148 147	1 638	241	3 382	1 422.4	104.0	1 078	13 800	2 216.0	213.3	271	1 343	158.2	29.1
Columbus, OH	1 729 840	14 853	2 340	41 517	24 477.8	1 572.9	5 710	95 130	16 922.7	1 657.9	1 588	11 553	1 207.6	259.5
Corpus Christi, TX	122 883	1 434	535	5 291	1 909.0	160.7	1 486	19 006	3 132.2	295.5	434	2 676	345.0	64.8
Corvallis, OR	43 104	264	63	681	112.6	15.9	294	3 175	473.9	53.2	111	379	38.9	5.5
Cumberland, MD-WV	47 099	407	89	1 014	291.6	26.8	488	5 701	806.2	76.1	68	232	26.3	3.7
Dallas-Fort Worth, TX	6 160 574	44 753	10 129	156 656	134 407.6	6 404.3	17 277	248 035	49 966.2	4 751.2	5 928	43 562	6 076.9	1 242.8
Dallas, TX	4 740 833	32 088	7 539	121 860	111 779.3	5 149.0	11 509	167 923	34 212.6	3 283.0	4 373	34 656	4 889.0	1 037.6
Fort Worth-Arlington, TX	1 419 741	12 665	2 590	34 796	22 628.3	1 255.3	5 768	80 112	15 753.6	1 468.2	1 555	8 906	1 187.8	205.3
Danville, VA	32 018	358	101	D	D	D	547	5 957	886.0	84.8	82	333	29.2	5.3
Davenport-Moline-Rock Island, IA-IL	120 118	1 028	709	9 840	5 930.7	319.9	1 587	22 573	3 630.9	366.5	329	2 157	230.8	48.2
Dayton-Springfield, OH	346 601	2 793	1 232	17 765	13 286.9	660.9	3 606	57 315	8 873.7	855.1	801	4 371	511.6	92.8
Daytona Beach, FL	521 750	5 032	527	4 586	1 724.3	113.3	1 984	24 859	4 131.8	382.7	599	3 040	305.9	53.3
Decatur, AL	40 843	399	199	2 179	1 337.0	61.2	683	7 147	1 253.1	105.2	104	465	41.4	8.3
Decatur, IL	38 745	361	158	1 815	3 249.3	57.4	506	6 967	1 129.6	110.4	98	515	39.9	8.5
Denver-Boulder-Greeley, CO	3 803 015	33 828	5 324	69 748	54 606.9	2 762.2	9 631	135 043	25 211.0	2 592.2	3 906	25 501	3 610.1	648.6
Boulder-Longmont, CO	372 872	2 780	539	5 558	3 906.0	234.9	1 275	17 269	2 915.0	309.9	486	2 189	287.9	49.2
Denver, CO	2 850 969	26 679	4 538	61 361	49 366.4	2 442.4	7 851	111 579	21 140.5	2 173.1	3 266	22 736	3 256.7	590.0
Greeley, CO	579 174	4 369	247	2 829	1 334.6	84.9	505	6 195	1 155.5	109.2	154	576	65.4	9.5
Des Moines, IA	393 981	3 017	1 008	14 715	9 828.3	507.0	1 927	30 808	4 919.6	503.3	488	3 500	591.5	85.4
Detroit-Ann Arbor-Flint, MI	3 413 274	25 317	8 413	114 303	121 286.3	5 073.5	20 340	288 550	54 531.5	5 178.0	4 743	32 001	4 486.0	783.5
Ann Arbor, MI	645 242	4 645	773	7 322	4 832.0	278.2	2 055	29 758	5 506.6	527.0	512	2 856	271.5	59.7
Detroit, MI	2 499 355	18 348	7 218	101 097	114 554.9	4 578.2	16 476	233 423	44 503.7	4 241.7	3 881	27 532	4 020.9	695.1
Flint, MI	268 677	2 324	422	5 884	1 899.4	217.2	1 809	25 369	4 521.3	409.3	350	1 613	193.6	28.7
Dothan, AL	35 118	706	243	2 686	823.6	62.9	838	9 203	1 490.0	142.7	127	496	43.4	8.6
Dover, DE	75 131	858	110	D	D	D	594	7 864	1 325.4	128.3	128	506	49.4	8.0
Dubuque, IA	44 983	341	157	1 845	926.5	50.8	525	6 583	935.5	100.2	89	341	32.8	4.9
Duluth-Superior, MN-WI	76 042	832	339	3 486	2 263.0	110.8	1 248	14 460	2 226.1	217.3	215	1 064	95.3	16.6
Eau Claire, WI	129 409	1 173	184	2 117	851.0	63.9	664	9 880	1 517.4	140.6	126	543	50.8	7.8
El Paso, TX	166 593	3 203	1 000	11 129	6 089.3	309.6	2 134	28 986	4 698.9	430.5	550	2 458	285.3	48.1
Elkhart-Goshen, IN	125 684	1 296	382	5 031	2 246.1	160.0	751	10 866	1 973.6	179.6	171	884	78.1	13.9
Elmira, NY	22 604	178	107	1 667	447.2	49.2	412	5 963	875.9	82.9	66	345	47.9	7.4
Enid, OK	9 770	59	122	1 967	570.1	48.9	302	3 423	501.7	47.8	70	287	24.6	4.8
Erie, PA	72 802	704	334	4 069	1 277.8	131.9	1 225	16 323	2 562.1	239.0	180	834	75.5	13.8
Eugene-Springfield, OR	183 158	1 330	535	6 144	2 498.6	179.6	1 462	18 145	3 322.6	328.3	463	2 042	226.5	35.0
Evansville-Henderson, IN-KY	154 763	1 747	501	6 301	5 940.7	188.2	1 405	19 403	3 075.6	300.5	306	1 842	202.7	32.8
Fargo-Moorhead, ND-MN	100 022	1 304	433	6 710	3 166.1	200.4	765	12 525	2 127.2	199.1	201	1 194	121.7	18.6
Fayetteville, NC	104 664	1 544	205	2 454	845.3	66.5	1 061	14 929	2 563.3	239.3	272	1 182	137.5	23.4
Fayetteville-Springdale-Rogers, AR	253 018	2 842	445	5 089	9 295.6	154.0	1 310	15 772	2 460.5	234.8	322	1 210	141.8	19.6
Flagstaff, AZ-UT	106 143	768	117	1 090	557.8	25.4	695	7 525	1 116.2	116.1	184	680	77.3	13.5
Florence, AL	25 734	324	209	3 132	773.2	75.7	735	8 461	1 308.3	119.9	121	434	41.9	7.5
Florence, SC	50 243	645	206	2 847	1 017.6	81.6	759	8 935	1 467.3	138.4	114	387	40.7	7.3
Fort Collins-Loveland, CO	427 366	3 524	311	2 630	805.6	75.9	1 201	13 810	2 440.5	234.2	360	1 497	190.0	27.8
Fort Myers-Cape Coral, FL	1 283 813	9 210	586	4 593	1 450.3	135.3	1 924	25 417	4 367.0	430.5	642	3 328	461.1	72.2
Fort Pierce-Port St. Lucie, FL	442 382	3 477	372	2 957	1 005.3	77.5	1 322	16 069	2 841.3	272.5	389	1 638	204.5	39.8
Fort Smith, AR-OK	59 039	664	318	2 584	926.2	67.4	989	11 707	1 848.1	167.9	189	828	93.6	14.6
Fort Walton Beach, FL	177 457	1 489	139	959	248.3	23.9	931	11 322	1 754.9	165.7	280	1 582	140.3	29.0
Fort Wayne, IN	367 066	2 592	899	14 048	7 880.4	437.8	2 037	30 121	4 868.8	471.0	455	2 403	302.9	50.4
Fresno, CA	490 770	3 804	1 058	13 627	6 111.0	434.3	2 805	33 404	6 102.0	601.9	653	3 713	398.9	71.1
Gadsden, AL	22 940	263	135	D	D	D	452	4 935	737.8	65.9	68	273	23.9	4.4
Gainesville, FL	164 574	1 973	224	1 824	738.0	54.5	923	12 726	1 934.5	186.2	279	1 630	155.2	28.2
Glens Falls, NY	70 517	550	137	D	D	D	675	6 929	1 115.8	109.9	87	341	45.3	6.1
Goldsboro, NC	40 778	428	151	2 217	891.1	59.4	523	6 169	1 033.0	88.1	81	263	21.0	4.5
Grand Forks, ND-MN	17 001	155	187	1 926	758.7	51.4	503	6 973	1 146.4	101.1	85	590	37.2	7.9
Grand Junction, CO	128 285	1 316	198	1 461	531.1	42.8	600	6 409	1 152.7	115.0	133	658	62.6	11.6
GrandRapids-Muskegon-Holland, MI	800 666	6 614	1 902	34 712	19 356.4	1 241.3	3 978	63 004	10 419.9	1 042.9	911	5 531	666.6	115.3
Great Falls, MT	11 989	99	141	1 231	1 114.8	32.6	427	5 049	803.0	81.8	100	395	30.4	4.6
Green Bay, WI	197 641	1 559	461	6 480	2 848.1	212.1	950	14 976	2 569.1	239.7	197	1 048	116.3	18.7
Greensboro—Winston-Salem—High Point, NC	1 000 663	9 806	2 447	34 363	19 221.1	1 285.8	5 511	70 814	12 362.1	1 198.9	1 171	6 626	848.5	140.6
Greenville, NC	123 846	1 766	181	2 153	1 246.8	66.4	643	7 956	1 384.8	124.8	121	495	51.4	7.9
Greenville-Spartanburg-Anderson, SC	631 905	6 850	1 728	21 306	15 790.1	742.7	4 316	53 794	9 178.9	806.8	814	3 818	464.2	78.2
Harrisburg-Lebanon-Carlisle, PA	265 586	2 467	736	15 165	11 751.0	489.4	2 711	38 661	6 706.7	638.6	439	3 066	425.7	69.5

1. Establishments with payroll.

Table C. Metropolitan Areas — Professional, Manufacturing, Accommodation and Foodservices, Finance and Insurance

Area Name	Professional, Scientific, and Technical Services[1], 1997				Manufacturing, 1997				Accommodation and Foodservices, 1997			
	Number of Establishments	Number of Employees	Sales (mil dol)	Annual Payroll (mil dol)	Number of Establishments	Number of Employees	Sales (mil dol)	Annual Payroll (mil dol)	Number of Establishments	Number of Employees	Sales (mil dol)	Annual Payroll (mil dol)
	147	148	149	150	151	152	153	154	155	156	157	158
Columbia, SC..................	1 243	9 455	1 059.8	370.9	460	23 522	5 302	785	1 033	21 176	621.9	172.4
Columbus, GA-AL............	325	1 841	163.4	49.3	230	19 930	4 358	597	473	8 942	292.4	84.6
Columbus, OH.................	3 552	34 157	3 619.4	1 336.2	1 577	77 263	18 153	2 743	3 074	62 081	2 051.6	593.6
Corpus Christi, TX...........	736	4 675	435.5	158.7	268	11 435	11 224	477	839	13 883	450.3	119.9
Corvallis, OR..................	210	1 367	116.7	50.1	106	8 547	1 392	495	205	2 807	85.9	24.0
Cumberland, MD-WV.........	114	581	28.6	14.6	83	5 307	922	180	213	2 920	88.6	23.2
Dallas-Fort Worth, TX.......	13 418	123 856	14 630.4	6 005.7	6 764	315 240	63 617	11 471	8 336	181 083	6 963.9	1 906.4
Dallas, TX......................	10 188	103 158	12 614.6	5 236.1	4 452	210 507	43 668	7 655	5 705	127 167	5 012.6	1 371.6
Fort Worth-Arlington, TX ...	3 230	20 698	2 015.8	769.7	2 312	104 733	19 950	3 816	2 631	53 916	1 951.3	534.7
Danville, VA....................	102	759	31.4	12.7	106	15 092	2 846	420	170	2 767	85.5	24.4
Davenport-Moline-Rock Island, IA-IL............	605	4 308	353.3	134.4	460	26 539	9 412	1 096	864	15 139	428.5	123.1
Dayton-Springfield, OH........	1 815	19 167	1 940.4	707.3	1 563	88 330	23 156	3 478	1 803	36 044	1 099.1	309.8
Daytona Beach, FL............	914	4 290	366.5	128.2	434	11 776	1 473	309	1 139	21 223	677.9	179.9
Decatur, AL.....................	193	984	74.4	28.9	243	16 307	5 627	610	218	4 276	114.6	32.6
Decatur, IL.....................	156	1 101	90.0	36.1	134	11 616	6 114	479	233	4 105	123.6	35.7
Denver-Boulder-Greeley, CO	9 909	79 903	10 676.2	3 768.9	3 533	115 133	26 466	4 302	5 114	102 537	3 562.3	1 019.0
Boulder-Longmont, CO	1 612	15 458	3 081.9	760.2	686	26 225	5 196	1 052	708	13 824	453.1	131.0
Denver, CO	8 076	63 481	7 522.0	2 980.8	2 639	78 135	16 931	2 905	4 135	84 666	3 002.5	858.5
Greeley, CO	221	964	72.2	27.9	208	10 773	4 339	345	271	4 047	106.8	29.4
Des Moines, IA	1 027	10 837	860.5	350.9	476	22 735	5 543	760	1 010	18 473	565.8	165.1
Detroit-Ann Arbor-Flint, MI...	11 780	118 407	12 601.9	5 347.1	8 637	430 461	134 710	19 470	9 532	173 690	5 800.1	1 596.4
Ann Arbor, MI	1 387	9 818	1 081.6	439.9	839	48 754	11 869	2 129	1 002	19 245	619.7	169.0
Detroit, MI......................	9 733	104 440	11 246.1	4 782.0	7 443	347 293	111 601	15 596	7 736	140 827	4 776.5	1 316.2
Flint, MI.........................	660	4 149	274.3	125.2	355	34 414	11 240	1 745	794	13 618	403.9	111.2
Dothan, AL......................	224	1 380	84.0	30.9	151	10 487	1 528	255	280	5 149	148.5	38.3
Dover, DE.......................	155	1 091	69.4	30.3	82	7 985	1 966	210	234	3 796	118.4	31.9
Dubuque, IA....................	117	802	56.4	23.5	133	10 687	3 075	387	233	3 838	94.7	27.4
Duluth-Superior, MN-WI.......	370	2 503	169.3	74.8	284	6 989	1 380	201	769	10 428	340.6	86.4
Eau Claire, WI.................	219	1 715	129.2	55.6	219	10 624	1 641	315	379	6 254	150.3	43.1
El Paso, TX.....................	927	5 777	398.1	161.7	652	36 723	7 967	774	1 094	19 292	703.3	194.0
Elkhart-Goshen, IN	246	1 465	111.6	36.0	894	56 087	9 000	1 611	354	6 202	189.4	51.7
Elmira, NY......................	104	827	56.5	18.3	94	9 098	1 357	278	213	2 965	86.2	24.4
Enid, OK........................	92	432	33.6	12.1	66	2 389	506	63	123	1 896	51.9	14.7
Erie, PA.........................	379	2 330	177.7	62.4	570	32 813	5 779	1 142	614	9 599	265.2	73.3
Eugene-Springfield, OR........	797	4 682	374.3	138.8	624	19 262	3 882	590	809	12 022	387.8	110.5
Evansville-Henderson, IN-KY	579	4 379	307.7	118.6	433	30 411	8 946	1 102	610	11 510	345.7	101.2
Fargo-Moorhead, ND-MN	328	2 625	189.1	75.6	221	7 982	1 742	209	401	8 799	235.7	66.6
Fayetteville, NC...............	329	2 084	142.1	47.7	121	12 282	2 767	385	495	10 654	318.4	91.2
Fayetteville-Springdale-Rogers, AR	586	2 868	276.9	90.3	387	29 015	4 881	704	602	9 766	282.3	77.8
Flagstaff, AZ-UT................	187	795	59.9	21.8	101	2 487	604	82	511	9 737	421.7	109.5
Florence, AL....................	225	963	67.7	22.5	233	13 126	2 377	376	249	4 324	113.5	31.7
Florence, SC....................	179	1 194	83.8	33.0	139	11 011	2 114	328	245	4 857	147.1	40.5
Fort Collins-Loveland, CO	711	3 815	336.3	134.2	384	15 840	3 891	645	647	10 779	343.6	95.0
Fort Myers-Cape Coral, FL...	997	6 053	458.2	197.4	357	5 363	742	141	824	17 424	699.1	175.2
Fort Pierce-Port St. Lucie, FL	666	3 040	233.4	94.1	296	5 504	1 098	162	503	8 635	315.4	83.0
Fort Smith, AR-OK..............	309	2 182	134.7	49.1	314	27 144	5 010	675	396	6 530	195.4	52.3
Fort Walton Beach, FL.........	417	3 181	264.0	113.5	133	3 448	297	82	401	8 450	261.7	73.0
Fort Wayne, IN.................	838	6 336	512.0	180.1	955	69 514	15 296	2 347	947	18 311	546.4	159.0
Fresno, CA......................	1 265	11 520	626.4	245.0	790	31 465	6 620	825	1 418	22 022	704.9	188.3
Gadsden, AL....................	122	621	36.6	13.7	136	8 775	1 577	277	169	3 223	85.0	23.6
Gainesville, FL.................	570	3 788	292.8	126.4	151	5 251	1 010	157	431	8 981	263.0	67.8
Glens Falls, NY................	210	1 239	136.3	42.7	183	7 866	1 463	267	507	4 662	199.4	56.5
Goldsboro, NC..................	129	596	43.4	16.0	101	9 495	1 418	231	158	2 953	84.4	23.1
Grand Forks, ND-MN..........	138	925	61.0	28.6	92	3 087	552	75	260	5 253	118.8	33.7
Grand Junction, CO............	275	1 283	91.3	39.2	167	3 605	484	99	247	4 555	124.7	36.3
Grand Rapids-Muskegon-Holland, MI	1 958	15 704	1 413.7	596.9	2 334	150 646	28 466	5 649	1 777	34 206	1 010.1	292.2
Great Falls, MT.................	176	994	69.3	28.6	80	925	229	24	267	3 592	109.7	29.4
Green Bay, WI..................	373	3 348	270.8	118.7	396	25 825	6 457	1 016	533	10 183	283.4	81.9
Greensboro—Winston-Salem—High Point, NC	2 449	15 760	1 455.7	537.6	2 401	149 443	30 771	4 217	2 279	45 265	1 411.1	404.6
Greenville, NC..................	219	1 303	88.0	35.3	119	9 305	2 742	281	237	5 342	153.5	41.8
Greenville-Spartanburg-Anderson, SC..................	1 719	15 003	3 678.6	672.5	1 603	121 048	24 906	3 689	1 844	37 201	1 033.9	285.7
Harrisburg-Lebanon-Carlisle, PA	1 106	9 966	934.3	372.7	674	38 896	8 691	1 241	1 296	21 233	720.4	198.5

1. Firms subject to federal tax.

Area Name	Health Care and Social Assistance[1], 1997				Other Services[1], 1997				Federal funds and grants, fiscal 2001[2] Expenditures (mil dol)			
										Direct payments for individuals		
	Number of Establishments	Number of Employees	Receipts (mil dol)	Annual Payroll (mil dol)	Number of Establishments	Number of Employees	Receipts (mil dol)	Annual Payroll (mil dol)	Total	Social Security and government retirement	Medicare	Food stamps and Supplemental Security Income
	159	160	161	162	163	164	165	166	167	168	169	170
Columbia, SC	967	12 786	917.2	420.7	855	5 898	344.9	104.3	3 856.2	1 188.9	290.3	81.3
Columbus, GA-AL	393	6 141	481.5	186.5	399	2 488	130.3	43.8	2 185.9	719.6	191.6	71.2
Columbus, OH	2 820	37 189	2 339.0	1 159.5	2 091	15 594	940.6	301.6	8 608.2	2 597.1	950.4	239.6
Corpus Christi, TX	928	16 064	852.1	381.5	611	3 898	228.9	70.1	2 226.4	726.9	319.6	86.2
Corvallis, OR	148	1 994	140.5	52.6	88	461	26.3	7.9	352.9	125.4	33.4	6.3
Cumberland, MD-WV	207	1 896	126.8	58.0	173	918	46.3	13.7	668.9	281.8	149.4	19.5
Dallas-Fort Worth, TX	10 290	132 820	9 968.3	4 094.9	7 440	53 833	3 569.9	1 118.6	20 869.3	7 168.3	2 917.3	532.2
Dallas, TX	7 137	93 700	7 426.7	2 984.9	4 994	37 685	2 534.6	798.5	13 166.4	4 462.7	1 926.4	368.8
Fort Worth-Arlington, TX	3 153	39 120	2 541.6	1 110.1	2 446	16 148	1 035.3	320.1	7 702.9	2 705.6	990.8	163.4
Danville, VA	172	1 931	120.4	55.8	204	1 028	50.3	14.1	550.8	262.9	92.7	19.8
Davenport-Moline-Rock Island, IA-IL	664	6 598	445.5	205.5	635	4 097	249.3	73.9	1 917.1	835.8	266.9	57.0
Dayton-Springfield, OH	1 770	22 628	1 413.9	682.0	1 487	13 421	685.8	243.5	7 082.0	2 278.5	800.5	159.4
Daytona Beach, FL	968	10 384	618.1	263.1	754	3 261	173.6	49.9	2 876.3	1 628.0	634.7	68.6
Decatur, AL	262	3 263	197.5	92.1	197	1 417	74.4	23.5	694.8	312.0	117.1	26.3
Decatur, IL	204	2 546	155.6	70.3	189	1 456	86.0	28.7	600.1	268.0	98.2	25.7
Denver-Boulder-Greeley, CO	5 256	55 361	3 951.9	1 728.3	4 199	26 714	1 800.1	540.2	13 686.2	4 020.8	1 422.2	229.1
Boulder-Longmont, CO	715	6 087	405.5	170.7	482	2 945	192.2	60.9	1 569.4	410.7	133.5	17.2
Denver, CO	4 332	46 995	3 408.1	1 501.2	3 502	22 639	1 540.2	461.4	11 548.1	3 370.1	1 197.8	196.7
Greeley, CO	209	2 279	138.2	56.5	215	1 130	67.8	17.9	568.7	240.0	90.9	15.2
Des Moines, IA	876	10 385	694.5	341.4	772	4 934	313.9	94.6	2 598.7	854.8	282.9	51.6
Detroit-Ann Arbor-Flint, MI	11 047	109 879	7 204.7	3 466.6	7 935	56 425	3 827.5	1 208.4	27 245.9	10 322.7	5 427.3	1 062.8
Ann Arbor, MI	1 132	9 886	694.6	310.5	735	4 342	279.8	91.1	2 394.5	845.3	332.4	42.9
Detroit, MI	8 878	90 527	5 899.6	2 845.4	6 573	47 918	3 292.4	1 042.8	22 773.8	8 584.3	4 654.1	905.3
Flint, MI	1 037	9 466	610.5	310.7	627	4 165	255.2	74.4	2 077.5	893.1	440.8	114.5
Dothan, AL	283	5 213	402.9	184.3	246	1 273	65.8	19.6	968.9	364.8	114.9	37.4
Dover, DE	192	2 157	137.6	59.6	215	1 016	56.0	16.8	935.8	317.9	74.5	18.0
Dubuque, IA	124	2 376	185.8	89.3	172	889	51.2	14.9	402.0	186.9	70.5	8.5
Duluth-Superior, MN-WI	429	6 052	274.1	141.7	395	2 204	146.8	42.0	1 386.7	599.1	206.4	41.6
Eau Claire, WI	257	4 182	242.2	133.2	279	1 525	84.3	24.3	616.8	281.0	96.8	17.0
El Paso, TX	984	16 524	1 165.3	455.8	824	5 779	265.7	87.6	3 580.5	1 127.6	409.9	184.8
Elkhart-Goshen, IN	233	3 281	187.7	78.0	345	2 427	164.1	47.3	536.7	298.7	94.9	16.5
Elmira, NY	162	1 675	123.1	60.7	108	553	36.1	9.8	519.7	219.9	79.3	18.6
Enid, OK	145	1 487	90.8	40.6	104	476	26.0	7.0	418.3	147.7	56.7	10.1
Erie, PA	560	5 498	423.4	190.6	476	2 174	135.0	39.6	1 324.6	596.3	258.9	61.5
Eugene-Springfield, OR	751	7 176	492.8	217.7	473	3 210	194.0	57.1	1 550.8	703.3	211.8	58.4
Evansville-Henderson, IN-KY	586	9 740	603.1	279.5	494	3 863	233.3	73.0	1 423.7	637.5	260.0	49.4
Fargo-Moorhead, ND-MN	300	6 435	499.1	203.1	337	2 358	133.4	41.0	852.2	292.1	83.8	16.8
Fayetteville, NC	407	6 135	366.5	159.9	402	2 631	145.7	45.1	3 426.3	786.5	124.1	65.2
Fayetteville-Springdale-Rogers, AR	497	5 223	314.4	152.2	425	2 583	144.2	44.5	1 120.7	616.2	167.3	30.8
Flagstaff, AZ-UT	247	1 662	109.0	46.5	195	951	57.5	14.9	724.1	220.3	58.5	25.3
Florence, AL	295	3 607	256.2	110.4	234	1 367	71.5	21.0	844.1	399.1	136.5	25.5
Florence, SC	276	5 558	399.9	193.5	191	1 268	73.1	21.7	665.2	261.1	105.3	44.5
Fort Collins-Loveland, CO	530	4 957	296.2	133.5	384	2 151	127.6	39.0	906.4	387.6	122.4	13.9
Fort Myers-Cape Coral, FL	825	12 968	954.5	408.4	695	3 599	224.9	68.5	2 334.1	1 400.1	579.0	44.4
Fort Pierce-Port St. Lucie, FL	677	10 392	756.4	294.9	517	2 226	138.1	38.8	1 845.1	1 111.7	467.3	46.9
Fort Smith, AR-OK	391	6 467	419.5	186.5	290	1 749	110.9	28.5	965.5	462.4	163.9	42.0
Fort Walton Beach, FL	356	5 134	412.2	142.7	313	1 531	86.3	25.5	2 219.3	717.8	116.5	17.4
Fort Wayne, IN	774	11 627	744.9	338.4	850	5 707	343.4	107.4	2 290.2	913.8	314.4	54.7
Fresno, CA	1 769	16 742	1 173.5	489.9	1 042	6 412	486.7	127.1	4 121.6	1 333.7	543.8	252.8
Gadsden, AL	199	4 291	312.8	127.9	132	570	34.8	9.5	565.6	277.3	126.9	26.5
Gainesville, FL	502	6 499	435.3	201.2	318	1 631	94.1	28.0	1 307.6	395.9	151.3	39.8
Glens Falls, NY	191	1 985	130.0	64.3	169	668	51.3	14.7	546.3	279.7	92.5	17.0
Goldsboro, NC	181	2 357	114.4	56.0	151	998	58.5	18.5	805.6	273.3	83.5	27.0
Grand Forks, ND-MN	133	1 967	81.4	51.1	168	968	49.3	14.5	728.9	161.7	61.5	9.9
Grand Junction, CO	264	2 504	150.7	69.9	188	1 018	73.9	19.1	613.3	283.7	83.9	14.1
Grand Rapids-Muskegon-Holland, MI	1 777	20 530	1 267.5	640.6	1 680	11 037	745.7	221.2	4 125.2	1 814.4	620.5	138.4
Great Falls, MT	205	1 729	104.2	40.5	153	690	43.3	11.4	689.5	220.1	62.8	11.5
Green Bay, WI	380	5 467	359.7	190.1	391	2 650	143.4	46.4	843.9	370.0	107.1	19.9
Greensboro—Winston-Salem—High Point, NC	1 942	27 699	1 973.0	864.1	1 921	12 122	750.9	224.1	5 367.1	2 440.8	838.4	152.5
Greenville, NC	205	3 334	216.7	115.5	158	875	49.1	13.7	549.6	218.7	82.4	35.9
Greenville-Spartanburg-Anderson, SC	1 486	18 322	1 290.9	629.0	1 449	8 464	554.0	163.3	3 969.5	2 011.4	631.1	135.3
Harrisburg-Lebanon-Carlisle, PA	1 209	12 926	855.9	403.4	1 040	5 746	365.7	111.4	5 904.6	1 734.5	528.9	62.9

1. Firms subject to federal tax.   2. October 1, 1998 to September 30, 1999.

Table C. Metropolitan Areas — Federal Funds and Local Government Finances

	Federal funds and grants, fiscal 2001[1] (cont'd)							Local government finances, 1997				
	Expenditures (mil dol) (cont'd)							General revenue				
	Procurement contract awards			Grants[2]							Taxes	
											Per capita[3] (dollars)	
Area Name	Salaries and wages	Defense	Other	Medicaid and other health-related	Nutrition and family welfare	Education	Other	Total (mil dol)	Intergovern-mental (mil dol)	Total (mil dol)	Total	Property
	171	172	173	174	175	176	177	178	179	180	181	182
Columbia, SC....................	824.7	167.6	97.2	328.2	192.7	155.7	392.1	1 342.7	430.4	295.8	587	520
Columbus, GA-AL..............	775.3	138.1	12.4	139.3	42.4	19.7	30.6	575.5	246.7	224.9	827	471
Columbus, OH	748.3	379.5	243.6	957.8	824.1	428.1	822.7	3 978.5	1 333.2	1 933.5	1 324	851
Corpus Christi, TX	399.8	186.8	21.6	246.8	51.0	24.9	38.9	1 006.9	326.2	397.3	1 026	838
Corvallis, OR	37.7	2.7	8.8	35.5	5.3	4.4	76.1	158.2	62.1	64.3	841	723
Cumberland, MD-WV	35.3	15.1	20.1	84.1	10.9	7.6	27.4	213.2	112.1	61.2	618	425
Dallas-Fort Worth, TX	2 499.4	3 978.8	896.4	1 376.1	249.8	143.3	556.8	11 531.0	2 614.6	5 900.1	1 260	964
Dallas, TX	1 645.1	2 206.6	559.5	996.6	178.4	99.6	344.2	8 012.2	1 667.2	4 186.8	1 339	1 011
Fort Worth-Arlington, TX ...	854.3	1 772.2	336.9	379.5	71.4	43.8	212.5	3 518.8	947.3	1 713.3	1 101	869
Danville, VA......................	15.3	7.3	10.1	72.8	10.7	8.5	31.0	178.0	94.8	55.4	510	321
Davenport-Moline-Rock Island, IA-IL........................	266.8	95.4	19.2	116.3	42.7	14.2	42.3	857.9	355.1	303.6	850	749
Dayton-Springfield, OH	1 231.0	1 263.5	277.2	485.1	129.9	67.4	139.8	2 594.3	940.4	1 083.1	1 146	728
Daytona Beach, FL	88.2	150.1	27.5	104.1	33.1	27.1	61.6	1 212.8	342.8	406.7	873	709
Decatur, AL.......................	94.5	6.3	5.9	67.0	10.3	7.9	22.0	342.1	119.2	61.9	437	195
Decatur, IL........................	23.2	0.0	44.4	51.4	12.3	5.5	18.3	270.8	134.0	79.6	697	658
Denver-Boulder-Greeley, CO	2 065.7	1 188.8	1 821.9	1 030.6	362.9	241.8	835.4	6 873.8	1 940.5	3 063.3	1 321	792
Boulder-Longmont, CO	193.0	119.3	262.3	82.9	12.6	16.2	287.1	657.8	156.2	368.1	1 407	893
Denver, CO	1 837.1	1 068.9	1 548.5	880.8	331.3	212.8	531.5	5 831.1	1 634.8	2 541.1	1 337	782
Greeley, CO	35.6	0.5	11.2	66.9	19.0	12.8	16.8	385.0	149.5	154.2	991	735
Des Moines, IA	329.6	34.7	72.0	247.9	183.4	90.8	303.6	1 211.5	421.8	458.7	1 067	1 019
Detroit-Ann Arbor-Flint, MI...	1 964.1	1 852.1	681.8	2 980.0	864.4	357.0	952.4	16 419.3	8 524.2	4 569.9	840	740
Ann Arbor, MI	198.5	55.5	63.3	464.1	40.2	28.8	201.2	1 372.9	640.4	427.0	792	759
Detroit, MI........................	1 678.6	1 795.6	583.8	2 276.8	731.9	290.1	702.8	13 579.6	7 093.4	3 886.6	871	754
Flint, MI...........................	87.1	1.0	34.7	239.1	92.4	38.1	48.4	1 466.8	790.4	256.3	589	571
Dothan, AL........................	231.8	34.4	32.6	67.1	12.5	10.4	16.4	388.3	118.0	72.9	543	182
Dover, DE	199.9	50.7	4.6	71.9	21.2	49.4	86.4	220.2	144.7	37.8	308	280
Dubuque, IA	18.4	0.6	4.4	40.5	9.2	2.4	22.0	195.7	82.2	72.6	824	688
Duluth-Superior, MN-WI........	132.0	4.3	26.5	193.8	51.7	18.5	54.8	872.4	421.1	207.7	872	797
Eau Claire, WI	34.9	10.1	6.9	81.8	17.5	8.9	25.7	397.2	220.3	110.1	767	727
El Paso, TX	645.5	369.9	74.1	370.0	82.6	54.5	120.1	1 582.9	756.8	507.8	724	557
Elkhart-Goshen, IN	17.4	3.0	6.1	51.0	9.5	4.0	6.3	350.5	135.9	161.4	946	814
Elmira, NY........................	27.7	1.3	33.5	72.2	16.6	7.0	25.0	284.8	128.5	107.2	1 151	822
Enid, OK...........................	66.8	71.2	2.9	18.4	4.6	3.7	3.3	99.4	42.6	35.9	633	324
Erie, PA............................	84.6	37.5	16.1	137.7	39.7	11.3	30.1	628.4	305.3	212.1	759	598
Eugene-Springfield, OR	101.6	9.7	32.3	234.2	44.0	41.8	56.2	846.7	365.1	256.5	824	689
Evansville-Henderson, IN-KY	70.8	57.4	17.3	158.3	29.0	8.5	39.4	615.1	229.1	256.2	887	761
Fargo-Moorhead, ND-MN	118.8	15.3	21.1	66.2	16.6	6.9	72.1	381.8	149.2	125.7	755	657
Fayetteville, NC..................	1 722.7	398.4	35.5	136.7	47.0	25.7	29.4	709.7	294.8	158.4	558	407
Fayetteville-Springdale-Rogers, AR	84.2	18.6	23.4	54.9	14.4	17.3	61.6	447.9	175.8	167.6	628	370
Flagstaff, AZ-UT.................	127.3	4.6	36.2	87.5	22.0	45.3	66.3	302.4	131.9	100.1	838	572
Florence, AL......................	101.1	1.5	34.3	65.2	9.7	8.7	20.0	407.0	118.2	82.9	604	322
Florence, SC.....................	41.0	2.0	8.3	134.4	18.5	9.9	10.5	208.8	107.8	62.9	505	339
Fort Collins-Loveland, CO	120.2	6.6	50.8	73.3	15.3	12.8	73.7	708.1	144.5	250.2	1 107	741
Fort Myers-Cape Coral, FL...	108.7	6.9	24.6	62.6	28.6	19.3	24.6	1 548.2	259.2	458.5	1 184	1 041
Fort Pierce-Port St. Lucie, FL..................................	47.0	2.6	13.1	51.0	27.4	18.1	35.2	767.7	217.5	343.2	1 161	1 037
Fort Smith, AR-OK..............	75.3	26.5	11.1	91.9	15.0	13.7	37.1	316.5	151.6	106.8	555	309
Fort Walton Beach, FL.........	772.8	471.5	21.1	36.8	14.1	13.6	20.7	354.9	167.7	108.4	647	548
Fort Wayne, IN..................	159.9	351.5	81.0	168.0	38.8	11.3	61.3	1 053.1	369.4	459.2	962	878
Fresno, CA.......................	458.9	10.8	126.4	525.9	247.1	94.7	88.7	2 971.1	1 680.2	547.7	630	452
Gadsden, AL.....................	16.6	0.5	17.3	63.4	7.1	8.4	6.5	184.1	91.8	58.4	560	152
Gainesville, FL...................	160.8	5.9	35.2	193.3	29.2	20.6	200.8	469.0	198.4	135.7	684	581
Glens Falls, NY..................	25.4	1.8	6.0	74.0	15.2	8.2	8.8	417.1	154.6	192.5	1 570	1 219
Goldsboro, NC...................	192.4	34.4	13.2	93.4	22.2	9.7	20.7	200.0	123.1	47.0	420	291
Grand Forks, ND-MN..........	138.2	47.1	12.7	57.3	16.7	17.9	45.1	249.1	114.1	78.7	774	652
Grand Junction, CO............	57.5	29.6	48.9	44.2	10.5	6.0	11.9	248.0	103.1	97.9	884	501
Grand Rapids-Muskegon-Holland, MI.....................	246.8	178.4	165.1	352.7	100.1	171.4	196.0	2 725.9	1 425.2	700.6	683	606
Great Falls, MT..................	169.2	60.9	8.0	66.8	11.6	5.1	31.8	135.2	61.8	42.8	541	514
Green Bay, WI...................	62.0	8.1	102.6	76.3	18.1	12.9	26.1	633.5	278.0	208.0	971	946
Greensboro—Winston-Salem—High Point, NC	371.1	297.3	149.5	567.9	101.6	76.3	193.7	2 638.1	1 151.6	968.7	840	655
Greenville, NC...................	22.5	14.4	7.4	102.8	17.8	9.2	10.9	615.5	129.6	64.9	536	396
Greenville-Spartanburg-Anderson, SC...................	182.3	111.4	79.8	405.8	63.6	56.6	152.3	1 916.2	630.2	571.1	631	556
Harrisburg-Lebanon-Carlisle, PA	613.5	191.6	86.4	438.9	730.0	368.1	979.7	1 450.0	514.7	601.4	978	690

1. October 1, 1998 to September 30, 1999.   2. State totals may include programs not allocated by county.   3. Based on the resident population estimated as of July 1 of the year shown.

Area Name	Total (mil dol)	Per capita[1] (dollars)	Education	Health and hospitals	Police protection	Public welfare	Highways	Total (mil dol)	Per capita[1] (dollars)	Federal civilian	Federal military	State and local	Democratic	Republican	All other
	183	184	185	186	187	188	189	190	191	192	193	194	195	196	197
Columbia, SC	1 391.5	2 761	37.5	34.7	3.6	0.2	1.0	1 013.1	2 010	8 201	12 985	65 135	43.1	54.3	2.6
Columbus, GA-AL	544.3	2 001	47.3	9.4	5.8	0.2	3.1	496.9	1 827	5 772	18 082	15 776	52.5	46.9	0.7
Columbus, OH	3 909.7	2 677	41.7	8.2	6.4	4.9	5.1	3 243.4	2 221	14 104	4 471	126 792	44.2	52.5	3.2
Corpus Christi, TX	919.7	2 376	52.5	13.9	6.3	0.2	2.5	776.5	2 006	5 650	7 154	24 666	45.8	52.1	2.0
Corvallis, OR	139.9	1 828	45.9	8.3	9.3	1.7	5.9	27.2	355	659	331	9 857	50.9	41.4	7.7
Cumberland, MD-WV	224.5	2 265	58.5	0.9	2.8	2.7	5.1	108.4	1 093	656	402	6 925	39.4	57.6	3.0
Dallas-Fort Worth, TX	11 243.6	2 401	47.6	9.4	5.9	0.3	3.8	16 824.4	3 593	44 931	15 787	260 145	36.7	60.9	2.4
Dallas, TX	7 703.3	2 464	47.0	9.6	5.8	0.2	3.7	10 498.7	3 358	30 943	10 363	177 842	37.3	60.2	2.4
Fort Worth-Arlington, TX	3 540.3	2 275	48.8	9.0	6.0	0.4	4.2	6 325.6	4 064	13 988	5 424	82 303	35.4	62.2	2.4
Danville, VA	199.3	1 835	52.0	0.7	5.2	5.5	3.2	308.0	2 836	270	412	5 702	37.7	59.2	3.1
Davenport-Moline-Rock Island, IA-IL	832.0	2 329	53.1	4.0	4.4	2.0	7.4	531.8	1 489	7 212	1 341	19 444	53.9	43.3	2.8
Dayton-Springfield, OH	2 485.6	2 630	43.7	4.6	6.5	6.4	4.7	1 406.1	1 488	18 820	8 335	51 321	46.2	50.8	3.0
Daytona Beach, FL	1 156.9	2 483	36.3	21.4	6.4	0.4	4.6	1 058.8	2 272	1 389	1 059	21 630	52.8	45.1	2.2
Decatur, AL	354.2	2 500	40.1	29.3	4.0	0.2	3.4	429.3	3 030	393	867	8 061	40.7	57.3	1.9
Decatur, IL	264.6	2 316	45.5	2.0	5.7	0.6	6.7	167.2	1 463	371	260	6 144	49.0	48.1	2.9
Denver-Boulder-Greeley, CO	6 839.0	2 950	35.4	4.0	5.6	5.4	7.1	11 407.3	4 920	33 241	9 636	157 773	47.1	46.1	6.9
Boulder-Longmont, CO	681.5	2 605	38.9	1.0	6.3	3.5	7.7	620.6	2 372	2 649	853	23 567	50.1	36.4	13.4
Denver, CO	5 769.9	3 035	33.9	4.5	5.5	5.7	7.1	10 581.2	5 566	30 011	8 322	123 266	47.4	46.8	5.8
Greeley, CO	387.6	2 491	51.6	2.0	5.2	5.1	6.7	205.5	1 321	581	461	10 940	36.3	58.0	5.7
Des Moines, IA	1 188.8	2 766	48.3	10.3	4.6	1.3	5.5	1 010.6	2 352	5 859	2 385	29 882	50.6	46.8	2.6
Detroit-Ann Arbor-Flint, MI	16 347.6	3 006	46.8	7.5	5.8	1.2	5.1	11 954.5	2 198	34 498	11 823	303 948	57.2	40.3	2.4
Ann Arbor, MI	1 411.6	2 617	53.7	5.6	4.3	1.3	4.5	1 285.8	2 384	3 164	1 170	73 035	51.4	45.2	3.4
Detroit, MI	13 492.8	3 023	46.0	6.0	6.2	1.2	5.3	10 016.2	2 244	29 856	9 790	207 360	57.5	40.2	2.3
Flint, MI	1 443.2	3 315	47.5	22.9	4.3	1.2	3.6	652.5	1 499	1 478	863	23 553	62.8	34.9	2.3
Dothan, AL	395.1	2 942	30.5	37.3	3.8	0.2	3.9	358.1	2 667	3 282	4 954	9 550	29.9	68.4	1.7
Dover, DE	218.1	1 778	71.3	0.0	5.3	0.2	1.7	105.5	860	1 682	4 610	13 646	47.2	49.9	2.8
Dubuque, IA	191.6	2 175	38.1	5.8	4.4	5.3	10.5	52.5	596	297	433	3 564	55.4	40.8	3.7
Duluth-Superior, MN-WI	867.3	3 641	36.0	7.0	4.9	8.4	11.1	670.5	2 815	2 104	1 037	20 093	60.3	32.8	6.9
Eau Claire, WI	405.7	2 827	50.9	5.7	5.0	6.0	10.3	221.6	1 544	594	511	11 177	48.9	45.6	5.5
El Paso, TX	1 543.2	2 200	60.6	10.3	5.7	0.6	1.6	1 258.7	1 794	8 493	11 588	45 063	57.8	39.7	2.5
Elkhart-Goshen, IN	364.3	2 134	60.9	1.3	4.8	4.8	3.5	157.6	923	308	609	6 889	30.1	67.5	2.4
Elmira, NY	297.6	3 197	43.8	2.8	2.8	17.0	5.2	123.1	1 322	447	195	6 992	46.2	49.8	4.0
Enid, OK	99.7	1 758	54.5	0.6	4.7	0.0	6.7	128.6	2 268	393	1 485	3 633	30.2	68.7	1.1
Erie, PA	657.1	2 352	51.9	5.6	3.9	5.4	3.4	883.8	3 163	1 639	982	14 240	52.9	43.6	3.5
Eugene-Springfield, OR	874.9	2 810	47.8	3.5	4.9	1.1	7.3	757.5	2 433	2 004	1 079	23 532	51.6	40.5	7.9
Evansville-Henderson, IN-KY	592.5	2 051	48.7	1.4	5.4	2.9	4.1	871.8	3 017	1 288	1 022	13 879	43.6	54.7	1.8
Fargo-Moorhead, ND-MN	385.3	2 316	42.4	1.4	4.1	5.2	6.5	483.8	2 908	2 166	1 192	12 842	38.3	54.9	6.7
Fayetteville, NC	746.1	2 627	37.7	26.6	5.8	5.7	1.4	475.3	1 673	10 028	44 938	20 376	50.1	49.4	0.5
Fayetteville-Springdale-Rogers, AR	450.0	1 685	51.9	2.8	5.4	0.0	5.0	355.2	1 331	1 566	1 599	17 676	36.8	60.0	3.2
Flagstaff, AZ-UT	285.8	2 390	43.5	3.2	6.3	5.7	5.4	400.0	3 346	3 263	323	11 994	47.3	45.4	7.3
Florence, AL	396.6	2 889	35.7	37.2	3.2	0.1	4.1	175.3	1 277	1 679	833	10 662	45.5	52.2	2.3
Florence, SC	195.4	1 571	63.5	1.1	5.0	0.6	1.8	270.0	2 171	702	673	11 384	41.4	57.1	1.5
Fort Collins-Loveland, CO	577.9	2 557	34.1	17.4	4.7	4.2	8.5	1 031.1	4 562	2 092	690	21 556	38.9	52.7	8.5
Fort Myers-Cape Coral, FL	1 485.2	3 837	25.8	15.4	3.9	0.4	7.9	2 032.5	5 251	1 910	930	24 096	39.9	57.6	2.5
Fort Pierce-Port St. Lucie, FL	790.7	2 674	43.2	1.4	7.8	0.8	3.8	1 356.0	4 587	815	720	14 017	48.7	49.1	2.3
Fort Smith, AR-OK	298.2	1 550	62.3	0.2	4.9	0.0	8.7	189.7	986	1 270	1 085	8 875	38.9	58.4	2.6
Fort Walton Beach, FL	346.9	2 070	61.9	2.2	5.0	0.4	4.2	155.5	928	6 427	15 289	7 425	24.0	73.7	2.3
Fort Wayne, IN	996.8	2 087	52.5	6.6	4.3	3.6	4.4	402.1	842	2 542	1 700	23 959	34.5	63.5	2.0
Fresno, CA	2 910.7	3 351	40.7	10.4	4.6	13.2	2.9	1 831.8	2 109	9 933	1 760	55 332	42.0	54.1	3.9
Gadsden, AL	177.1	1 698	49.6	1.9	7.7	0.3	6.0	79.1	758	347	627	5 013	44.3	53.6	2.1
Gainesville, FL	479.9	2 420	47.0	1.5	8.0	0.1	2.6	1 023.6	5 161	2 855	511	36 967	55.2	39.8	5.0
Glens Falls, NY	417.8	3 409	50.3	3.6	2.4	11.2	7.6	242.1	1 975	413	251	9 113	41.8	52.9	5.3
Goldsboro, NC	192.4	1 718	58.5	4.8	4.1	6.9	3.0	104.1	929	1 443	4 604	8 277	38.4	61.3	0.4
Grand Forks, ND-MN	260.6	2 562	40.8	1.7	4.0	6.5	8.6	189.7	1 865	1 384	3 456	10 857	38.5	55.2	6.3
Grand Junction, CO	237.6	2 147	45.0	1.3	6.4	8.4	7.7	240.6	2 174	1 161	319	6 689	30.3	63.5	6.3
Grand Rapids-Muskegon-Holland, MI	2 931.3	2 856	55.5	7.5	3.6	1.7	5.3	2 899.8	2 825	4 169	2 167	49 555	37.6	60.1	2.4
Great Falls, MT	145.9	1 843	53.3	1.9	4.1	0.8	3.0	71.9	908	1 458	3 954	3 889	39.4	54.5	6.0
Green Bay, WI	651.6	3 041	47.2	4.7	5.2	5.1	7.9	515.0	2 404	978	817	12 476	45.6	50.3	4.1
Greensboro—Winston-Salem—High Point, NC	2 497.9	2 167	45.2	7.5	5.7	5.6	2.4	1 524.6	1 323	6 405	3 611	65 173	40.1	59.2	0.7
Greenville, NC	538.9	4 452	21.3	56.9	2.9	3.2	1.0	243.6	2 012	390	400	17 176	45.7	53.8	0.5
Greenville-Spartanburg-Anderson, SC	1 850.8	2 046	45.7	23.2	3.9	0.1	1.8	3 378.9	3 735	2 975	5 034	58 887	32.6	64.9	2.5
Harrisburg-Lebanon-Carlisle, PA	1 516.1	2 465	54.6	3.9	2.8	5.9	3.4	2 052.3	3 337	11 663	2 951	56 423	38.3	59.1	2.6

1. Based on the resident population estimated as of July 1 of the year shown.   2. Data subject to copyright.

Table C. Metropolitan Areas — **Land Area and Population**

CMSA/MSA/PMSA/NECMA code[1]	Area Name	Land area[2] (sq km) 2000	Total persons	Rank	Per square kilometer	White	Black	Am. Indian, Alaska Native	Asian and Pacific Islander	Percent Hispanic[3]	Under 5 years	5 to 17 years	18 to 24 years	25 to 34 years	35 to 44 years	45 to 54 years
			1	2	3	4	5	6	7	8	9	10	11	12	13	14	15
3283	Hartford, CT	3 923	1 148 618	53	292.8	82.2	10.5	0.6	2.8	9.4	6.3	17.9	8.3	13.1	16.9	14.3
3285	Hattiesburg, MS	2 496	111 674	289	44.7	72.3	26.6	0.5	0.8	1.2	7.1	18.7	15.6	14.4	14.2	11.7
3290	Hickory-Morganton-Lenoir, NC	4 244	341 851	145	80.6	88.3	7.2	0.5	2.7	4.0	6.5	17.6	8.5	14.7	15.8	14.1
3320	Honolulu, HI	1 553	876 156	68	564.0	35.2	3.4	1.8	83.2	6.7	6.5	17.3	10.1	14.9	15.7	13.4
3350	Houma, LA	6 060	194 477	204	32.1	79.2	15.7	4.7	1.0	1.5	7.2	21.1	10.3	13.7	16.1	12.7
42	Houston-Galveston-Brazoria, TX	19 956	4 669 571		234.0	64.8	17.4	0.8	5.5	28.9	8.1	21.0	9.8	15.9	16.9	13.3
1145	Brazoria, TX	3 591	241 767	181	67.3	79.1	8.8	1.0	2.4	22.8	7.7	20.8	8.6	14.4	18.0	13.6
2920	Galveston-Texas City, TX	1 032	250 158	177	242.4	74.5	15.8	0.9	2.6	18.0	7.0	19.7	8.7	13.2	17.0	14.4
3360	Houston, TX	15 333	4 177 646	8	272.5	63.4	17.9	0.8	5.9	29.9	8.1	21.1	10.0	16.2	16.8	13.2
3400	Huntington-Ashland, WV-KY-OH	5 592	315 538	154	56.4	97.0	2.5	0.6	0.5	0.7	5.8	16.7	10.2	13.1	14.6	14.1
3440	Huntsville, AL	3 556	342 376	144	96.3	75.7	21.5	1.5	2.0	2.0	6.8	18.7	9.3	14.0	17.6	13.5
3480	Indianapolis, IN	9 125	1 607 486	37	176.2	83.1	14.5	0.6	1.6	2.7	7.4	19.2	8.8	15.3	17.0	13.3
3500	Iowa City, IA	1 591	111 006	290	69.7	91.5	3.4	0.6	4.7	2.5	5.8	14.3	23.4	16.6	14.1	12.2
3520	Jackson, MI	1 830	158 422	230	86.6	90.1	8.7	1.1	0.8	2.2	6.6	19.1	8.1	13.6	16.8	14.2
3560	Jackson, MS	6 114	440 801	117	72.1	53.1	45.9	0.3	1.0	1.0	7.4	20.1	10.8	14.5	15.9	13.1
3580	Jackson, TN	2 190	107 377	293	49.0	69.2	29.6	0.5	0.8	1.6	6.9	18.7	11.5	13.4	15.4	13.3
3600	Jacksonville, FL	6 825	1 100 491	57	161.2	74.1	22.2	0.8	3.1	3.8	6.9	19.2	9.0	14.5	16.9	13.8
3605	Jacksonville, NC	1 986	150 355	239	75.7	74.6	19.7	1.6	3.0	7.2	8.8	17.3	23.8	15.8	13.4	8.6
3610	Jamestown, NY	2 751	139 750	254	50.8	95.2	2.6	0.8	0.6	4.2	5.8	18.7	10.3	11.3	15.0	13.6
3620	Janesville-Beloit, WI	1 866	152 307	236	81.6	92.4	5.2	0.7	1.1	3.9	6.7	19.8	8.6	13.5	16.3	13.6
3660	Johnson City-Kingsport-Bristol, TN-VA	7 422	480 091	105	64.7	96.9	2.3	0.6	0.5	0.9	5.6	15.9	8.6	13.6	15.2	14.5
3680	Johnstown, PA	4 565	232 621	185	51.0	96.9	2.7	0.2	0.4	0.8	5.1	16.4	8.5	11.8	15.0	14.4
3700	Jonesboro, AR	1 841	82 148	312	44.6	90.2	8.0	0.8	0.9	2.1	6.9	17.2	14.0	14.4	14.3	12.8
3710	Joplin, MO	3 279	157 322	231	48.0	94.9	1.6	3.1	0.9	3.0	7.2	18.7	10.3	12.9	14.8	12.9
3720	Kalamazoo-Battle Creek, MI	4 873	452 851	113	92.9	86.8	10.3	1.4	1.7	3.6	6.5	18.8	12.1	13.1	15.2	13.6
3760	Kansas City, MO-KS	14 002	1 776 062	28	126.8	82.5	13.4	1.2	2.2	5.2	7.2	19.4	8.6	14.6	16.9	13.7
3810	Killeen-Temple, TX	5 469	312 952	155	57.2	66.7	22.2	1.5	4.2	15.7	8.6	19.6	14.5	17.7	15.3	10.1
3840	Knoxville, TN	6 344	687 249	78	108.3	92.3	6.1	0.8	1.3	1.3	6.0	16.6	10.0	13.8	15.9	14.4
3850	Kokomo, IN	1 433	101 541	301	70.8	92.4	6.1	0.7	1.2	1.9	6.9	18.6	8.1	13.0	15.2	14.4
3870	La Crosse, WI-MN	2 619	126 838	267	48.4	95.6	1.1	0.7	3.2	0.9	5.9	18.2	14.2	12.4	15.0	13.3
3920	Lafayette, IN	2 344	182 821	210	78.0	91.0	2.4	0.6	4.1	5.6	6.1	16.0	22.4	14.3	13.1	11.2
3880	Lafayette, LA	6 717	385 647	129	57.4	70.3	28.5	0.5	1.0	1.3	7.5	21.0	10.6	13.5	15.9	12.6
3960	Lake Charles, LA	2 774	183 577	209	66.2	74.5	24.4	0.7	0.9	1.3	7.2	20.2	10.3	13.0	15.7	13.2
3980	Lakeland-Winter Haven, FL	4 855	483 924	104	99.7	80.9	14.1	0.8	1.3	9.5	6.4	18.0	8.3	12.3	14.2	12.3
4000	Lancaster, PA	2 458	470 658	109	191.5	92.5	3.3	0.4	1.7	5.7	6.9	19.7	9.2	12.6	15.7	13.2
4040	Lansing-East Lansing, MI	4 421	447 728	114	101.3	86.5	9.1	1.2	3.1	4.7	6.4	18.3	14.7	13.6	15.1	13.8
4080	Laredo, TX	8 694	193 117	205	22.2	84.5	0.5	0.6	0.6	94.3	10.6	25.6	11.4	15.9	13.4	9.6
4100	Las Cruces, NM	9 861	174 682	217	17.7	71.0	2.0	2.2	1.3	63.4	7.8	21.9	13.3	12.9	14.1	11.5
4120	Las Vegas, NV-AZ	101 964	1 563 282	40	15.3	77.1	8.9	1.7	6.8	20.6	7.3	18.0	8.8	15.5	15.7	13.9
4150	Lawrence, KS	1 183	99 962	302	84.5	88.5	5.2	3.6	3.9	3.3	5.6	14.8	26.4	15.2	13.1	11.2
4200	Lawton, OK	2 770	114 996	284	41.5	69.0	20.6	7.0	3.9	8.4	7.9	19.8	13.9	15.5	15.2	10.7
4243	Lewiston-Auburn, ME	1 218	103 793	297	85.2	98.1	1.0	0.8	0.9	1.0	5.9	18.0	9.1	13.2	16.5	13.9
4280	Lexington, KY	4 971	479 198	106	96.4	87.6	10.0	0.6	1.9	2.5	6.4	16.3	13.8	16.0	15.9	13.3
4320	Lima, OH	2 087	155 084	232	74.3	90.1	9.3	0.6	0.7	1.2	6.7	19.7	9.3	12.3	15.5	13.7
4360	Lincoln, NE	2 173	250 291	176	115.2	91.7	3.5	1.1	3.4	3.4	6.7	16.8	15.4	15.3	15.1	13.1
4400	Little Rock-North Little Rock, AR	7 531	583 845	92	77.5	75.6	22.3	1.0	1.4	2.1	7.0	18.6	10.0	14.8	16.0	13.7
4420	Longview-Marshall, TX	4 559	208 780	196	45.8	75.8	19.8	1.0	0.7	7.1	6.8	20.0	9.8	12.2	15.4	13.2
49	Los Angeles-Riverside-Orange County, CA	87 944	16 373 645		186.2	59.1	8.3	1.6	12.0	40.3	7.8	20.7	10.0	15.9	16.1	12.2
4480	Los Angeles-Long Beach, CA	10 518	9 519 338	1	905.1	52.8	10.5	1.5	13.6	44.6	7.7	20.3	10.3	16.6	15.9	12.1
5945	Orange County, CA	2 045	2 846 289	14	1 392.1	68.3	2.1	1.3	15.5	30.8	7.6	19.4	9.4	16.4	16.8	12.7
6780	Riverside-San Bernardino, CA	70 603	3 254 821	11	46.1	66.0	8.6	2.1	5.7	37.8	8.1	23.2	9.8	13.7	15.8	11.7
8735	Ventura, CA	4 779	753 197	72	157.6	73.3	2.4	1.8	7.0	33.4	7.5	21.0	9.0	13.8	16.9	13.6
4520	Louisville, KY-IN	5 366	1 025 598	61	191.1	83.9	14.5	0.6	1.4	1.6	6.7	18.0	8.8	14.0	16.7	14.3
4600	Lubbock, TX	2 330	242 628	180	104.1	76.0	8.0	1.0	1.7	27.5	7.2	18.5	16.3	13.8	14.0	11.7
4640	Lynchburg, VA	4 637	214 911	193	46.3	80.5	18.4	0.7	1.0	1.0	5.8	17.5	9.8	12.4	15.5	14.3
4680	Macon, GA	3 967	322 549	152	81.3	60.0	38.0	0.6	1.6	2.1	7.1	20.0	10.0	13.8	16.2	13.3
4720	Madison, WI	3 113	426 526	120	137.0	90.5	4.7	0.8	4.0	3.4	6.1	16.5	14.3	16.0	16.4	14.1
4800	Mansfield, OH	2 328	175 818	215	75.5	91.8	7.6	0.7	0.7	0.9	6.4	18.4	8.3	12.8	15.5	14.1
4880	McAllen-Edinburg-Mission, TX	4 066	569 463	94	140.1	79.7	0.6	0.6	0.7	88.3	10.2	25.1	11.3	14.9	12.8	9.8
4890	Medford-Ashland, OR	7 214	181 269	212	25.1	94.4	0.7	2.4	1.8	6.7	6.0	18.4	8.7	11.2	14.3	15.4
4900	Melbourne-Titusville-Palm Bay, FL	2 637	476 230	108	180.6	88.3	9.0	0.9	2.2	4.6	5.2	16.8	6.8	10.6	16.5	13.3
4920	Memphis, TN-AR-MS	7 787	1 135 614	54	145.8	53.6	43.8	0.5	1.7	2.4	7.6	20.7	9.5	14.9	16.1	13.4

1. MSA = Metropolitan Statistical Area. CMSA = Consolidated MSA. PMSA = Primary MSA. NECMA = New England County Metropolitan Area. See Appendix A for explanation of these concepts. See Appendix B for list of metropolitan areas identified by type, with component counties.   2. Dry land or land partially or temporarily covered by water.   3. Hispanic persons may be of any race.

Table C. Metropolitan Areas — **Population and Households**

Area Name	55 to 64 years	65 to 74 years	75 years and over	Percent female	Total persons 2001	Total persons 1990	Percent change 1990–2000	Percent change 2000–2001	Births	Deaths	Net migration	Households Number	Percent change, 1990–2000	Persons per house-hold	Female family house-holder[1]	One person
	16	17	18	19	20	21	22	23	24	25	26	27	28	29	30	31
Hartford, CT	9.1	6.9	7.1	51.6	1 157 645	1 123 678	2.2	0.8	17 211	13 039	5 280	445 870	5.2	2.48	12.0	27.0
Hattiesburg, MS	7.6	5.8	5.0	52.4	113 372	98 738	13.1	1.5	2 198	1 310	816	41 579	15.4	2.54	15.3	25.7
Hickory-Morganton-Lenoir, NC	10.0	7.2	5.6	50.4	346 573	292 405	16.9	1.4	5 904	3 967	2 862	133 966	19.2	2.50	10.8	24.2
Honolulu, HI	8.7	7.1	6.3	49.7	881 295	836 231	4.8	0.6	17 436	7 346	-4 517	286 450	8.0	2.95	12.3	21.6
Houma, LA	8.5	6.0	4.4	51.0	195 396	182 842	6.4	0.5	3 775	1 872	-920	68 054	12.2	2.81	13.3	19.4
Houston-Galveston-Brazoria, TX	7.3	4.5	3.2	50.2	4 795 974	3 731 014	25.2	2.7	102 990	34 275	57 456	1 639 401	22.5	2.80	13.0	23.4
Brazoria, TX	7.9	5.3	3.6	48.4	249 832	191 707	26.1	3.3	4 762	1 925	5 197	81 954	28.0	2.82	10.4	19.1
Galveston-Texas City, TX	8.9	6.3	4.8	50.4	255 865	217 396	15.1	2.3	4 768	2 649	3 625	94 782	16.4	2.60	13.1	25.1
Houston, TX	7.1	4.3	3.1	50.2	4 290 277	3 321 911	25.8	2.7	93 460	29 701	48 634	1 462 665	22.6	2.82	13.2	23.6
Huntington-Ashland, WV-KY-OH	10.5	8.3	6.7	51.7	313 930	312 529	1.0	-0.5	4 630	4 651	-1 509	128 039	7.0	2.41	11.3	26.5
Huntsville, AL	9.3	6.4	4.5	50.8	348 911	293 047	16.8	1.9	5 938	3 363	4 017	134 643	21.4	2.47	11.6	26.5
Indianapolis, IN	8.1	5.8	5.1	51.2	1 632 452	1 380 491	16.4	1.6	30 940	16 753	10 237	629 655	18.8	2.50	12.1	27.0
Iowa City, IA	6.1	3.9	3.5	50.2	111 230	96 119	15.5	0.2	1 641	608	-797	44 080	22.2	2.34	6.8	30.2
Jackson, MI	8.8	6.6	6.2	49.0	159 665	149 756	5.8	0.8	2 530	1 772	546	58 168	8.4	2.55	12.0	24.6
Jackson, MS	7.8	5.6	4.8	52.4	445 344	395 396	11.5	1.0	8 978	4 776	293	160 338	14.4	2.64	18.7	25.1
Jackson, TN	8.4	6.5	6.0	52.0	108 100	90 801	18.3	0.7	1 952	1 373	187	41 212	20.6	2.50	15.3	25.7
Jacksonville, FL	8.6	6.1	5.0	51.4	1 131 490	906 727	21.4	2.8	21 014	11 645	21 567	425 584	23.9	2.54	14.0	24.8
Jacksonville, NC	5.8	4.0	2.3	44.8	145 988	149 838	0.3	-2.9	4 168	979	-7 451	48 122	18.4	2.72	11.6	18.6
Jamestown, NY	9.3	8.0	8.0	51.2	138 662	141 895	-1.5	-0.8	1 865	1 815	-1 099	54 515	1.5	2.45	10.8	28.1
Janesville-Beloit, WI	8.8	6.7	6.0	50.8	153 324	139 510	9.2	0.7	2 543	1 656	207	58 617	12.2	2.54	10.9	25.1
Johnson City-Kingsport-Bristol, TN-VA	11.2	8.3	7.0	51.6	482 174	436 068	10.1	0.4	6 884	6 542	1 905	199 218	16.8	2.35	10.2	26.8
Johnstown, PA	9.7	9.4	9.8	51.0	230 279	241 280	-3.6	-1.0	2 796	3 608	-1 444	91 753	0.2	2.41	9.8	28.5
Jonesboro, AR	8.6	6.2	5.5	51.6	83 008	68 956	19.1	1.0	1 439	882	335	32 301	22.9	2.46	11.4	25.2
Joplin, MO	9.2	7.2	6.7	51.4	158 516	134 910	16.6	0.8	2 849	2 036	451	61 552	16.1	2.50	10.4	25.7
Kalamazoo-Battle Creek, MI	8.5	6.4	5.8	51.3	453 455	429 453	5.4	0.1	7 637	4 966	-1 924	175 561	9.1	2.48	11.6	27.1
Kansas City, MO-KS	8.3	6.0	5.4	51.2	1 803 445	1 582 874	12.2	1.5	33 292	18 096	12 240	694 468	14.1	2.51	11.8	27.1
Killeen-Temple, TX	6.1	4.4	3.7	49.5	313 997	255 299	22.6	0.3	7 946	2 293	-4 428	105 457	25.7	2.72	12.1	21.3
Knoxville, TN	9.9	7.3	6.2	51.6	697 656	585 960	17.3	1.5	10 498	8 184	8 183	281 472	21.7	2.38	10.6	27.2
Kokomo, IN	10.3	7.3	6.3	51.6	101 464	96 946	4.7	0.1	1 726	1 231	-546	41 269	9.9	2.43	10.9	27.4
La Crosse, WI-MN	7.8	6.4	6.7	51.4	127 645	116 401	9.0	0.6	1 777	1 358	438	49 232	13.2	2.46	8.2	27.9
Lafayette, IN	6.9	5.0	5.1	49.1	182 785	161 572	13.2	0.0	2 917	1 784	-1 145	67 771	18.8	2.46	8.4	27.2
Lafayette, LA	8.1	6.1	4.8	51.6	387 171	345 053	11.8	0.4	7 843	4 079	-2 138	143 006	17.4	2.64	15.3	24.4
Lake Charles, LA	8.6	6.8	5.1	51.3	182 842	168 134	9.2	-0.4	3 635	2 150	-2 195	68 613	13.7	2.61	14.7	24.0
Lakeland-Winter Haven, FL	10.3	9.9	8.4	50.9	492 751	405 382	19.4	1.8	8 446	6 641	7 075	187 233	20.0	2.52	12.0	24.1
Lancaster, PA	8.6	6.9	7.1	51.2	474 601	422 822	11.3	0.8	8 045	5 250	1 322	172 560	14.3	2.64	8.6	23.1
Lansing-East Lansing, MI	8.0	5.3	4.8	51.4	449 118	432 684	3.5	0.3	7 165	3 996	-1 750	172 413	9.9	2.48	11.1	27.4
Laredo, TX	6.0	4.3	3.3	51.8	201 292	133 239	44.9	4.2	6 860	1 083	2 475	50 740	47.3	3.75	18.3	12.4
Las Cruces, NM	7.7	6.2	4.4	50.7	176 790	135 510	28.9	1.2	3 576	1 285	-142	59 556	32.2	2.85	14.7	21.3
Las Vegas, NV-AZ	9.9	7.2	4.6	49.2	1 660 516	852 646	83.3	6.2	29 459	15 199	81 340	588 371	78.0	2.62	11.4	24.5
Lawrence, KS	5.8	4.1	3.9	50.3	100 005	81 798	22.2	0.0	1 503	661	-796	38 486	27.7	2.37	8.5	28.5
Lawton, OK	7.2	5.6	4.1	48.2	112 466	111 486	3.1	-2.2	2 535	1 062	-3 987	39 808	6.0	2.63	14.1	23.4
Lewiston-Auburn, ME	9.0	7.1	7.3	51.5	104 131	105 259	-1.4	0.3	1 445	1 357	292	42 028	5.0	2.38	11.0	28.0
Lexington, KY	8.0	5.5	4.7	51.1	483 575	405 936	18.0	0.9	8 181	4 736	955	191 006	24.0	2.39	11.4	27.7
Lima, OH	8.6	7.2	7.0	50.3	155 073	154 340	0.5	0.0	2 786	2 012	-734	58 022	4.8	2.55	11.0	26.3
Lincoln, NE	7.2	5.3	5.1	50.0	252 090	213 641	17.2	0.7	4 448	1 988	-573	99 187	19.9	2.40	9.1	29.1
Little Rock-North Little Rock, AR	8.7	6.0	5.2	51.6	590 024	513 026	13.8	1.1	11 101	6 295	1 435	230 864	18.1	2.47	13.3	26.6
Longview-Marshall, TX	9.2	7.2	6.2	51.5	210 428	193 801	7.7	0.8	3 961	2 740	489	79 064	9.7	2.57	13.1	24.7
Los Angeles-Riverside-Orange County, CA	7.4	5.3	4.6	50.4	16 700 693	14 531 529	12.7	2.0	338 272	128 830	117 584	5 347 107	9.1	3.00	13.5	22.8
Los Angeles-Long Beach, CA	7.3	5.2	4.6	50.6	9 637 494	8 863 052	7.4	1.2	199 594	74 407	-6 422	3 133 774	4.8	2.98	14.7	24.6
Orange County, CA	7.9	5.2	4.6	50.2	2 890 444	2 410 668	18.1	1.6	58 810	20 628	6 311	935 287	13.1	3.00	10.7	21.1
Riverside-San Bernardino, CA	7.1	5.7	4.9	50.2	3 402 125	2 588 793	25.7	4.5	65 433	28 070	108 656	1 034 812	19.4	3.07	13.4	19.5
Ventura, CA	8.1	5.3	4.9	50.1	770 630	669 016	12.6	2.3	14 435	5 725	9 039	243 234	11.9	3.04	10.9	18.9
Louisville, KY-IN	8.9	6.8	5.8	51.4	1 030 841	949 012	8.1	0.5	18 031	12 495	-81	412 050	12.5	2.44	13.6	27.8
Lubbock, TX	7.5	6.0	5.1	51.1	243 999	222 636	9.0	0.6	4 729	2 427	-850	92 516	13.5	2.52	12.6	26.9
Lynchburg, VA	10.2	7.8	6.7	52.0	215 018	193 926	10.8	0.0	3 190	2 783	-306	84 414	16.1	2.43	12.0	26.0
Macon, GA	8.5	6.2	4.9	52.5	325 928	291 079	10.8	1.0	6 616	3 962	773	121 505	14.1	2.58	17.7	25.0
Madison, WI	7.2	4.7	4.6	50.5	432 654	367 085	16.2	1.4	6 428	3 195	3 033	173 484	21.5	2.37	7.9	29.4
Mansfield, OH	10.0	7.7	6.7	50.2	174 645	174 007	1.0	-0.7	2 899	2 348	-1 684	68 491	3.8	2.46	11.1	26.5
McAllen-Edinburg-Mission, TX	6.2	5.5	4.2	51.4	590 285	383 545	48.5	3.7	17 678	3 364	6 772	156 824	51.6	3.60	15.7	13.1
Medford-Ashland, OR	10.0	7.9	8.1	51.4	184 963	146 387	23.8	2.0	2 592	2 273	3 372	71 532	25.0	2.48	10.5	25.1
Melbourne-Titusville-Palm Bay, FL	11.0	10.9	9.0	51.0	489 522	398 978	19.4	2.8	6 126	6 084	13 117	198 195	22.8	2.35	10.2	26.9
Memphis, TN-AR-MS	7.8	5.4	4.5	52.0	1 144 971	1 007 306	12.7	0.8	24 788	12 384	-3 199	424 202	16.1	2.63	18.9	25.5

1. No spouse present.

Table C. Metropolitan Areas — **Vital Statistics, Health Resources, and Crime**

Area Name	Births, average 1997–1999		Deaths, average 1997–1999				Physicians,[4] 1998		Hospitals,[4] 1998			Medicare enrollees 1999	Serious crimes known to police, 2000[6]	
			Number		Rate					Beds			Total	
	Total	Rate[1]	Total	Infant[2]	Total[1]	Infant[3]	Number	Rate[5]	Number	Number	Rate[5]		Number	Rate[7]
	32	33	34	35	36	37	38	39	40	41	42	43	44	45
Hartford, CT	14 593	13.1	10 354	117	9.3	8.0	3 322	299	12	2 690	242	175 658	36 747	3 759
Hattiesburg, MS	1 737	15.6	1 010	NA	9.1	NA	262	236	3	695	625	15 044	3 718	4 172
Hickory-Morganton-Lenoir, NC	4 334	13.4	3 015	NA	9.3	NA	497	154	6	812	252	49 217	12 673	3 716
Honolulu, HI	12 494	14.3	5 708	88	6.6	7.0	2 526	290	10	2 316	265	117 980	46 659	5 325
Houma, LA	2 970	15.4	1 458	30	7.5	10.1	249	128	5	647	334	24 961	9 106	4 746
Houston-Galveston-Brazoria, TX	76 893	17.4	26 710	474	6.1	6.2	9 853	224	57	12 767	290	384 009	229 992	4 926
Brazoria, TX	3 580	15.6	1 520	21	6.6	5.9	255	111	4	310	135	22 988	6 832	2 835
Galveston-Texas City, TX	3 640	14.8	2 020	23	8.2	6.3	889	362	2	927	378	30 422	12 907	5 160
Houston, TX	69 673	17.7	23 170	430	5.9	6.2	8 709	222	51	11 530	293	330 599	210 253	5 033
Huntington-Ashland, WV-KY-OH	3 673	11.7	3 648	NA	11.6	NA	667	212	5	1 460	465	57 861	NA	NA
Huntsville, AL	4 819	14.2	2 564	NA	7.6	NA	538	158	4	960	282	40 554	16 092	4 723
Indianapolis, IN	23 357	15.4	13 142	NA	8.6	NA	4 113	271	24	5 571	367	196 760	NA	NA
Iowa City, IA	1 295	12.6	496	9	4.8	6.9	1 063	1 035	2	1 002	975	9 007	3 460	3 117
Jackson, MI	2 039	13.0	1 405	22	9.0	10.8	195	125	2	507	325	23 609	6 426	4 243
Jackson, MS	6 698	15.6	3 717	72	8.7	10.7	1 321	307	9	2 398	558	53 041	24 500	6 797
Jackson, TN	1 413	14.0	1 023	NA	10.2	NA	286	284	2	710	705	15 158	6 103	5 684
Jacksonville, FL	15 590	14.9	8 958	143	8.6	9.2	2 481	237	12	3 177	304	135 572	65 258	6 026
Jacksonville, NC	3 196	22.4	736	23	5.2	7.2	182	128	1	133	93	11 422	5 840	3 884
Jamestown, NY	1 608	11.6	1 476	11	10.7	6.8	193	140	4	687	497	25 821	3 800	2 719
Janesville-Beloit, WI	1 993	13.2	1 328	14	8.8	7.0	251	167	3	474	314	21 678	5 579	3 663
Johnson City-Kingsport-Bristol, TN-VA	5 263	11.4	5 107	NA	11.1	NA	1 156	250	10	1 729	374	85 751	15 033	3 138
Johnstown, PA	2 322	9.8	2 826	NA	12.0	NA	439	186	7	1 102	466	49 427	3 514	1 646
Jonesboro, AR	1 143	14.8	725	8	9.4	7.0	214	276	2	425	548	11 220	3 646	4 438
Joplin, MO	2 179	14.6	1 617	NA	10.9	NA	287	193	5	759	510	25 309	NA	NA
Kalamazoo-Battle Creek, MI	5 974	13.4	3 931	51	8.8	8.5	1 015	227	8	1 568	351	64 230	23 089	5 153
Kansas City, MO-KS	25 570	14.7	14 337	NA	8.3	NA	4 205	242	33	6 333	365	224 771	81 732	5 233
Killeen-Temple, TX	5 973	20.0	1 784	44	6.0	7.4	753	250	5	803	266	26 461	11 912	3 820
Knoxville, TN	8 309	12.6	6 465	NA	9.8	NA	1 662	252	10	2 481	376	105 107	28 283	4 131
Kokomo, IN	1 357	13.5	958	NA	9.6	NA	141	141	3	416	415	15 683	3 581	3 527
La Crosse, WI-MN	1 498	12.3	1 087	NA	8.9	NA	372	305	3	641	526	18 139	3 377	2 832
Lafayette, IN	2 312	13.4	1 350	NA	7.8	NA	319	185	3	530	308	20 107	6 113	3 344
Lafayette, LA	5 995	16.0	3 149	NA	8.4	NA	620	165	11	1 527	406	49 341	17 056	4 560
Lake Charles, LA	2 734	15.2	1 643	26	9.1	9.5	300	166	6	862	478	25 334	10 451	5 800
Lakeland-Winter Haven, FL	6 363	14.1	5 086	55	11.2	8.6	725	160	5	1 430	316	88 530	28 140	5 850
Lancaster, PA	6 577	14.1	4 103	46	9.0	7.0	787	172	5	1 118	245	68 534	11 989	2 554
Lansing-East Lansing, MI	5 846	13.0	3 010	NA	6.7	NA	1 061	236	7	1 632	363	51 768	16 233	3 714
Laredo, TX	4 991	26.5	886	27	4.7	5.4	170	90	2	377	200	16 260	13 778	7 135
Las Cruces, NM	3 037	18.0	1 021	19	6.1	6.3	239	141	1	221	131	19 601	NA	NA
Las Vegas, NV-AZ	21 335	16.1	11 643	146	8.8	6.8	2 204	167	13	2 577	195	189 175	70 012	4 479
Lawrence, KS	1 143	12.1	483	NA	5.1	NA	152	163	1	167	179	8 802	743	743
Lawton, OK	2 049	18.4	855	20	7.7	9.8	200	176	2	339	299	12 333	5 563	4 438
Lewiston-Auburn, ME	1 170	11.6	1 037	7	10.2	6.0	238	235	2	440	434	17 884	3 662	3 528
Lexington, KY	6 247	13.9	3 648	NA	8.1	NA	1 591	354	11	2 455	546	56 053	NA	NA
Lima, OH	2 094	13.6	1 528	NA	9.9	NA	243	158	4	703	456	25 085	5 281	3 962
Lincoln, NE	3 259	13.8	1 609	22	6.8	6.8	508	216	3	702	298	29 038	15 254	6 095
Little Rock-North Little Rock, AR	8 298	14.9	4 958	NA	8.9	NA	1 792	322	10	2 805	504	73 445	36 277	6 213
Longview-Marshall, TX	2 940	14.1	2 157	NA	10.3	NA	272	130	4	568	272	32 960	9 958	4 770
Los Angeles-Riverside-Orange County, CA	267 223	16.9	103 388	1 569	6.5	5.9	35 766	227	194	45 417	288	1 701 644	597 089	3 647
Los Angeles-Long Beach, CA	157 474	17.1	59 833	911	6.5	5.8	22 895	248	114	30 364	330	975 304	379 451	3 986
Orange County, CA	45 422	16.7	16 404	208	6.0	4.6	6 940	255	37	6 889	253	282 452	74 298	2 610
Riverside-San Bernardino, CA	52 988	17.0	22 575	381	7.2	7.2	4 710	151	35	6 713	216	361 067	125 828	3 866
Ventura, CA	11 339	15.5	4 576	69	6.2	6.1	1 221	167	8	1 451	198	82 821	17 512	2 325
Louisville, KY-IN	13 638	13.6	9 666	NA	9.7	NA	2 596	260	16	4 525	453	151 257	31 438	3 790
Lubbock, TX	3 688	16.1	1 881	32	8.2	8.7	705	307	6	1 551	676	29 062	16 057	6 618
Lynchburg, VA	2 444	11.7	2 077	NA	10.0	NA	343	165	3	695	334	37 553	4 785	2 227
Macon, GA	4 764	14.9	2 875	NA	9.0	NA	676	212	7	1 236	387	43 792	20 025	6 208
Madison, WI	5 171	12.2	2 522	35	5.9	6.8	1 703	401	4	1 246	293	44 320	12 787	3 581
Mansfield, OH	2 234	12.7	1 798	NA	10.2	NA	225	129	6	653	374	29 284	6 080	3 763
McAllen-Edinburg-Mission, TX	12 762	24.4	2 667	61	5.1	4.8	520	100	5	1 036	198	52 177	32 306	5 673
Medford-Ashland, OR	2 120	12.2	1 755	11	10.1	5.2	429	248	3	471	272	31 590	8 137	4 489
Melbourne-Titusville-Palm Bay, FL	5 050	10.9	4 771	22	10.3	4.4	872	187	5	1 190	255	93 639	17 204	4 249
Memphis, TN-AR-MS	18 079	16.5	9 778	221	8.9	12.2	2 560	234	17	5 330	487	131 219	77 805	6 851

1. Per 1,000 estimated resident population, average 1997–1999. 2. Deaths of infants under 1 year old. 3. Deaths of infants under 1 year old per 1,000 live births. 4. Data subject to copyright. 5. Per 100,000 resident population as of July 1 of the year shown. 6. Data for serious crimes have not been adjusted for underreporting; this may affect comparability between geographic areas and over time. 7. Per 100,000 population estimated by the FBI.

Table C. Metropolitan Areas — Crime, Education, Money Income, and Poverty

Area Name	Serious crimes known to police, 2000[1] (cont'd) Rate[2] Violent	Property	Education — School enrollment and attainment, 1990 — Enrollment[3] Total	Percent private	Attainment[4] (percent) High school graduate or more	Bachelor's degree or more	Local government expenditures, fiscal 1999[5] Total current expenditures (mil dol)	Current expenditures per student (dollars)	Money income 1989 Per capita[6] (dollars)	Households Median Dollars	Percent change, 1979–1989 (constant 1989 dollars)	Percent with $100,000 or more	Income and poverty, 1998 Median household income	Percent below poverty level All persons	Persons under 18	Persons 5–17 in families
	46	47	48	49	50	51	52	53	54	55	56	57	58	59	60	61
Hartford, CT	327	3 432	282 344	18.4	79.1	26.5	1 604.5	8 887	18 939	41 428	21.8	7.1	NA	8.8	13.8	13.5
Hattiesburg, MS	183	3 989	32 126	7.7	72.5	20.1	87.7	4 533	10 028	NA	NA	0.7	NA	17.2	23.1	20.2
Hickory-Morganton-Lenoir, NC	259	3 457	64 496	8.1	61.9	11.4	290.2	5 341	12 461	27 177	6.8	1.9	NA	11.0	17.7	15.6
Honolulu, HI	263	5 062	221 821	21.6	81.2	24.6	1 143.9	6 082	16 256	40 580	14.9	7.9	NA	9.7	14.3	12.5
Houma, LA	546	4 200	51 354	12.3	58.0	9.7	196.5	5 406	9 385	21 599	-30.6	1.6	NA	15.6	21.3	20.2
Houston-Galveston-Brazoria, TX	680	4 246	1 059 519	11.0	75.1	24.1	4 935.0	5 520	14 928	31 487	-10.6	5.3	NA	12.8	18.5	15.5
Brazoria, TX	257	2 578	55 183	8.0	75.5	15.1	253.1	5 339	13 468	34 418	-12.0	2.9	NA	10.3	14.8	13.0
Galveston-Texas City, TX .	494	4 666	61 025	8.5	75.8	19.3	352.2	5 416	13 993	29 465	-9.7	3.6	NA	12.2	19.0	16.7
Houston, TX	716	4 317	943 311	11.3	75.1	25.0	4 329.7	5 540	15 073	31 473	-10.4	5.5	NA	13.0	18.7	15.6
Huntington-Ashland, WV-KY-OH	NA	NA	78 189	5.7	66.7	12.6	316.5	6 107	10 744	21 057	-14.8	1.7	NA	17.8	26.1	23.3
Huntsville, AL	477	4 246	77 827	12.2	77.1	27.1	305.5	5 542	14 750	31 964	16.2	3.6	NA	11.1	18.0	15.4
Indianapolis, IN	NA	NA	335 267	16.1	78.1	20.2	1 713.8	6 804	14 936	31 314	0.5	3.6	NA	9.2	13.6	11.6
Iowa City, IA	403	2 714	40 420	6.1	90.6	44.0	76.0	5 814	14 113	27 862	2.3	4.6	NA	8.5	10.2	9.2
Jackson, MI	468	3 775	38 772	14.2	77.7	12.9	197.4	7 639	12 556	29 155	-6.1	2.3	NA	11.7	16.9	15.8
Jackson, MS	621	6 176	116 736	19.0	74.4	25.1	335.6	4 528	12 311	26 364	2.9	3.2	NA	15.0	21.5	17.8
Jackson, TN	1 040	4 644	23 496	21.5	66.4	15.5	90.3	5 592	11 179	NA	NA	2.1	NA	14.0	18.7	16.5
Jacksonville, FL	954	5 072	222 340	16.0	77.4	18.6	953.1	5 197	14 141	29 513	15.5	3.2	NA	11.5	17.7	15.8
Jacksonville, NC	297	3 587	33 122	8.6	83.0	13.4	107.2	5 025	10 713	23 385	13.1	1.0	NA	16.1	20.2	20.3
Jamestown, NY	205	2 514	37 059	7.9	74.4	14.2	214.8	8 510	11 287	24 183	-3.2	1.4	NA	16.5	23.8	24.1
Janesville-Beloit, WI	228	3 435	34 529	11.7	78.2	13.3	197.9	7 231	13 428	30 632	-4.6	2.0	NA	8.6	13.6	11.9
Johnson City-Kingsport-Bristol, TN-VA	363	2 775	96 813	8.5	63.1	13.8	393.0	5 641	11 427	22 385	-2.3	1.9	NA	13.7	19.7	17.4
Johnstown, PA	197	1 449	54 908	15.9	70.5	10.2	250.4	7 537	10 448	21 529	-16.8	1.3	NA	13.1	19.0	18.2
Jonesboro, AR	297	4 141	19 048	5.2	67.5	16.4	64.3	5 019	11 301	22 150	1.3	2.2	NA	15.2	21.2	17.7
Joplin, MO	NA	NA	32 378	8.5	71.8	13.0	124.6	4 693	10 790	21 393	2.1	1.6	NA	13.4	18.8	16.7
Kalamazoo-Battle Creek, MI.	624	4 529	125 496	11.1	79.4	20.3	544.0	7 236	13 431	28 974	-2.4	3.0	NA	12.3	17.8	17.6
Kansas City, MO-KS	627	4 606	402 457	15.9	82.3	23.2	1 790.6	5 992	15 030	31 559	0.1	3.8	NA	8.6	12.8	11.0
Killeen-Temple, TX	370	3 450	66 886	8.5	79.4	15.7	323.7	5 467	10 409	23 698	9.3	1.7	NA	14.4	20.7	19.1
Knoxville, TN	533	3 598	141 152	8.6	71.1	19.5	547.8	5 330	13 201	25 464	3.2	2.8	NA	11.6	16.8	14.5
Kokomo, IN	301	3 226	24 685	9.3	78.2	13.6	119.7	7 066	14 234	31 452	-2.0	2.1	NA	9.7	14.9	13.0
La Crosse, WI-MN	117	2 715	34 739	14.0	81.5	20.0	140.3	7 277	12 053	26 685	1.1	1.9	NA	9.2	13.2	11.8
Lafayette, IN	167	3 177	61 148	7.1	83.2	26.3	162.9	6 455	12 432	27 253	-0.6	2.7	NA	9.5	11.8	10.8
Lafayette, LA	598	3 962	99 048	14.5	63.6	15.2	335.0	5 092	9 817	19 948	-23.0	2.4	NA	18.3	24.8	23.6
Lake Charles, LA	649	5 151	47 034	12.1	70.3	14.7	176.3	5 323	11 233	24 374	-22.3	2.3	NA	14.5	21.1	18.1
Lakeland-Winter Haven, FL ..	606	5 244	89 009	13.4	68.0	12.9	422.2	5 462	12 392	25 215	5.6	2.4	NA	15.5	24.9	22.6
Lancaster, PA	238	2 316	97 202	22.1	70.5	16.7	487.6	7 160	14 235	33 254	10.6	3.4	NA	7.6	12.1	10.9
Lansing-East Lansing, MI ...	428	3 286	148 916	9.1	84.2	24.7	556.8	7 450	14 044	32 155	-1.3	3.2	NA	10.7	14.8	14.2
Laredo, TX	528	6 607	48 323	7.0	47.8	11.1	263.5	5 577	6 771	18 074	-3.3	2.1	NA	30.4	37.0	36.3
Las Cruces, NM	NA	NA	46 488	4.4	70.4	21.9	196.2	5 370	9 374	21 858	5.5	1.4	NA	25.6	34.6	31.2
Las Vegas, NV-AZ	559	3 920	190 291	9.1	76.8	13.3	1 225.9	5 310	14 768	30 022	2.1	3.5	NA	11.5	17.0	15.7
Lawrence, KS	35	708	36 059	6.7	88.8	38.4	77.6	6 027	12 003	25 244	6.4	2.7	NA	11.4	13.7	13.1
Lawton, OK	573	4 265	30 373	6.9	81.1	18.4	121.7	5 275	10 602	24 378	5.5	1.5	NA	18.3	26.0	24.5
Lewiston-Auburn, ME..........	172	3 356	25 878	18.0	71.8	12.6	109.9	6 875	12 397	26 979	19.0	2.0	NA	10.6	14.6	13.0
Lexington, KY	NA	NA	116 334	13.3	74.5	24.5	408.6	5 987	13 390	26 854	5.0	3.3	NA	11.9	17.1	14.7
Lima, OH	368	3 594	39 899	15.2	76.2	10.9	162.7	5 815	11 994	28 141	-3.6	1.8	NA	9.8	14.3	12.5
Lincoln, NE	490	5 605	67 322	12.9	88.1	27.6	218.7	6 161	13 803	28 908	-1.0	2.5	NA	9.0	11.9	9.7
Little Rock-North Little Rock, AR	572	5 641	133 355	15.2	76.6	20.4	506.4	5 643	12 809	26 500	2.0	2.8	NA	12.4	18.6	14.8
Longview-Marshall, TX	387	4 383	52 132	11.5	72.8	14.8	238.0	5 431	11 423	23 969	-10.3	2.3	NA	16.0	23.5	21.4
Los Angeles-Riverside-Orange County, CA	730	2 917	4 089 214	14.7	73.2	22.0	16 515.7	5 730	16 444	36 710	18.4	7.9	NA	16.3	24.3	22.6
Los Angeles-Long Beach, CA	945	3 041	2 521 219	15.9	70.0	22.3	9 648.6	5 968	16 149	34 964	18.9	7.9	NA	18.9	28.1	26.0
Orange County, CA	302	2 308	666 355	13.5	81.2	27.8	2 545.3	5 399	19 890	45 921	21.5	11.3	NA	10.1	16.4	14.3
Riverside-San Bernardino, CA	576	3 290	713 348	11.4	74.8	14.8	3 592.0	5 442	13 879	33 278	18.0	4.2	NA	15.6	22.0	21.6
Ventura, CA	280	2 045	188 292	14.7	79.4	23.0	729.8	5 435	17 861	45 612	28.2	9.3	NA	10.0	16.3	15.1
Louisville, KY-IN..............	486	3 304	237 510	19.0	73.3	17.2	967.9	6 165	13 529	27 435	-2.8	2.9	NA	11.1	17.2	13.5
Lubbock, TX	1 067	5 551	74 111	7.6	74.2	23.4	247.9	5 876	12 008	24 328	-7.6	2.9	NA	17.8	25.2	23.7
Lynchburg, VA	227	2 000	48 451	23.8	66.6	16.2	180.2	5 485	12 632	26 776	0.0	2.2	NA	11.9	16.8	15.8
Macon, GA	517	5 691	77 090	17.5	71.1	15.8	333.0	5 875	12 731	27 887	7.5	2.7	NA	16.8	26.6	25.1
Madison, WI	253	3 328	115 595	9.2	88.9	34.2	497.8	7 939	15 542	32 703	6.6	3.9	NA	6.9	9.9	8.6
Mansfield, OH	153	3 610	41 131	12.4	73.6	11.0	198.6	6 545	12 208	26 579	-6.0	1.6	NA	10.8	16.1	14.9
McAllen-Edinburg-Mission, TX	483	5 190	134 820	4.4	46.6	11.5	805.3	5 937	6 630	16 702	-11.3	1.7	NA	35.3	40.9	39.1
Medford-Ashland, OR	245	4 244	34 122	9.6	80.1	17.6	187.8	6 517	12 492	25 068	-3.3	2.2	NA	14.7	20.5	17.8
Melbourne-Titusville-Palm Bay,FL	696	3 553	90 909	17.5	82.3	20.4	345.0	5 024	15 093	30 534	8.1	2.8	NA	10.5	17.5	15.8
Memphis, TN-AR-MS..........	1 015	5 836	267 233	15.5	73.1	18.7	1 043.5	5 133	12 851	26 899	6.2	3.6	NA	15.0	21.5	17.2

1. Data for serious crimes have not been adjusted for underreporting; this may affect comparability between geographic areas and over time.   2. Per 100,000 population estimated by the FBI.   3. All persons 3 years old and over enrolled in nursery school through college.   4. Persons 25 years old and over.   5. Elementary and secondary education expenditures, local government fiscal years ending between July 1, 1998 and June 30, 1999.   6. Based on population enumerated as of April 1, 1990.

Table C. Metropolitan Areas — **Personal Income**

	Personal income, 1999												
			Per capita[1]					Transfer payments					
									Government payments to individuals				
Area Name	Total (mil dol)	Percent change, 1998–1999	Dollars	Rank	Wages and salaries[2] (mil dol)	Proprietor's income (mil dol)	Dividends, interest, and rent (mil dol)	Total (mil dol)	Total (mil dol)	Social Security (mil dol)	Medical payments (mil dol)	Income mainte-nance (mil dol)	Unemploy-ment insurance (mil dol)
	62	63	64	65	66	67	68	69	70	71	72	73	74
Hartford, CT	39 104	4.9	35 109	21	28 119	2 737	6 719	4 886	4 683	1 858	2 120	409	123
Hattiesburg, MS	2 290	4.5	20 256	303	1 405	202	424	397	375	143	153	42	3
Hickory-Morganton-Lenoir, NC	8 145	5.2	24 997	176	5 408	577	1 509	1 129	1 070	507	428	78	17
Honolulu, HI	25 475	2.0	29 465	69	16 821	1 998	4 915	2 733	2 604	1 076	865	428	89
Houma, LA	3 998	-1.3	20 547	299	2 360	215	683	689	654	260	290	75	7
Houston-Galveston-Brazoria, TX	141 745	4.9	31 543	X	93 426	24 466	19 499	11 687	10 909	4 040	4 996	1 070	327
Brazoria, TX	5 559	4.1	23 724	221	2 822	353	786	624	584	242	254	44	21
Galveston-Texas City, TX	6 285	2.3	25 296	165	2 943	370	1 072	837	794	314	354	68	22
Houston, TX	129 901	5.1	32 386	34	87 661	23 743	17 641	10 226	9 531	3 484	4 388	959	284
Huntington-Ashland, WV-KY-OH	6 415	2.7	20 533	300	3 661	314	1 158	1 482	1 423	538	498	165	24
Huntsville, AL	8 926	4.0	25 993	145	7 283	477	1 681	900	837	379	289	85	13
Indianapolis, IN	46 904	5.4	30 523	52	33 677	3 034	8 562	4 887	4 588	2 113	1 802	365	63
Iowa City, IA	3 055	6.5	29 425	71	2 221	206	606	218	196	99	61	15	4
Jackson, MI	3 730	6.5	23 719	222	2 170	229	692	584	554	253	214	51	12
Jackson, MS	11 123	4.7	25 709	151	7 614	840	2 014	1 425	1 337	542	527	164	13
Jackson, TN	2 524	5.2	24 840	181	1 892	214	370	402	385	147	172	38	5
Jacksonville, FL	29 182	2.3	27 625	104	19 931	1 644	5 515	3 470	3 282	1 339	1 283	315	38
Jacksonville, NC	3 299	4.1	23 157	245	2 502	135	449	334	315	104	125	41	5
Jamestown, NY	2 869	1.8	20 877	294	1 627	194	515	652	623	258	249	74	12
Janesville-Beloit, WI	3 794	3.7	25 103	172	2 428	171	672	491	461	232	161	32	18
Johnson City-Kingsport-Bristol, TN-VA	10 236	3.6	22 119	272	6 068	677	1 796	1 998	1 917	841	761	169	24
Johnstown, PA	5 042	4.6	21 564	285	2 450	503	858	1 315	1 268	465	587	87	34
Jonesboro, AR	1 697	5.9	21 853	279	1 136	137	295	267	253	105	100	25	4
Joplin, MO	3 366	4.4	22 441	265	2 185	262	621	598	570	240	246	49	7
Kalamazoo-Battle Creek, MI	11 440	3.1	25 583	156	7 656	706	2 142	1 662	1 576	689	622	158	34
Kansas City, MO-KS	53 072	6.3	30 225	60	36 759	3 999	9 768	5 638	5 318	2 330	2 152	416	96
Killeen-Temple, TX	6 713	5.9	22 654	259	4 801	369	977	768	726	238	270	85	16
Knoxville, TN	17 207	4.6	25 603	155	10 969	1 594	3 087	2 543	2 429	1 072	992	201	36
Kokomo, IN	2 734	5.5	27 233	117	2 377	121	451	368	348	175	134	24	4
La Crosse, WI-MN	3 156	3.8	25 886	148	2 143	217	647	397	373	176	133	24	10
Lafayette, IN	4 187	3.6	23 867	218	3 094	199	830	461	427	209	142	28	5
Lafayette, LA	8 121	-0.3	21 528	287	4 884	654	1 437	1 401	1 334	446	620	181	17
Lake Charles, LA	4 116	2.0	22 792	255	2 761	289	722	692	659	257	299	57	8
Lakeland-Winter Haven, FL	10 653	5.9	23 294	236	5 756	782	2 274	1 890	1 806	889	630	162	21
Lancaster, PA	12 563	4.6	27 309	114	7 413	1 390	2 439	1 464	1 372	725	470	94	27
Lansing-East Lansing, MI	11 458	5.8	25 419	160	8 327	658	2 015	1 373	1 287	572	501	130	29
Laredo, TX	2 726	5.5	14 112	317	1 785	260	303	547	513	112	248	117	9
Las Cruces, NM	2 897	3.8	17 003	315	1 574	252	549	519	488	170	183	84	8
Las Vegas, NV-AZ	40 723	8.8	29 486	68	26 194	3 498	8 393	4 561	4 334	2 001	1 492	313	136
Lawrence, KS	2 130	5.6	21 658	283	1 307	112	434	218	201	92	69	17	5
Lawton, OK	2 360	2.6	22 134	270	1 650	135	352	341	324	114	98	47	2
Lewiston-Auburn, ME	2 388	3.0	23 570	225	1 403	144	346	459	441	166	199	47	9
Lexington, KY	12 831	5.4	28 161	91	9 148	1 278	2 425	1 351	1 265	550	457	122	15
Lima, OH	3 709	4.6	24 072	209	2 555	180	812	562	529	246	191	40	8
Lincoln, NE	6 772	5.2	28 493	84	4 726	451	1 367	694	651	292	240	47	5
Little Rock-North Little Rock, AR	15 414	5.2	27 571	107	10 709	1 028	2 800	2 010	1 906	751	789	156	34
Longview-Marshall, TX	4 792	2.8	22 872	251	2 746	524	887	849	813	323	346	77	20
Los Angeles-Riverside-Orange County, CA	449 834	5.6	28 050	X	282 256	52 622	80 245	54 250	51 168	15 922	21 327	9 744	1 139
Los Angeles-Long Beach, CA	263 815	4.8	28 276	89	179 143	32 718	48 089	34 251	32 454	8 687	14 344	7 022	688
Orange County, CA	93 333	6.5	33 805	26	59 062	11 280	17 287	7 411	6 880	2 830	2 541	862	129
Riverside-San Bernardino, CA	70 604	6.8	22 060	274	32 740	6 324	10 815	10 496	9 884	3 586	3 749	1 636	251
Ventura, CA	22 083	7.2	29 639	65	11 311	2 301	4 054	2 092	1 950	818	692	224	71
Louisville, KY-IN	29 514	5.4	29 342	73	19 999	1 630	6 194	3 747	3 556	1 550	1 395	298	64
Lubbock, TX	5 574	2.9	24 459	196	3 280	719	961	858	818	286	397	79	7
Lynchburg, VA	4 939	5.2	23 649	224	3 143	269	955	775	735	352	264	54	4
Macon, GA	7 857	5.0	24 433	198	5 388	539	1 432	1 132	1 064	382	442	153	15
Madison, WI	13 714	5.5	31 999	37	9 816	857	2 988	1 057	974	476	358	65	23
Mansfield, OH	3 975	3.0	22 509	263	2 503	213	755	684	646	296	230	51	14
McAllen-Edinburg-Mission, TX	7 135	5.8	13 339	318	3 831	813	988	1 768	1 675	380	811	384	39
Medford-Ashland, OR	4 220	6.0	24 004	211	2 146	388	1 128	708	677	323	216	56	26
Melbourne-Titusville-Palm Bay, FL	11 421	3.4	24 282	205	6 537	501	2 778	2 003	1 917	969	695	99	22
Memphis, TN-AR-MS	31 857	4.9	28 828	80	22 189	2 998	4 820	3 855	3 664	1 287	1 601	527	51

1. Based on the resident population estimated as of July 1 of the year shown.   2. Includes other labor income.

Table C. Metropolitan Areas — **Earnings, Social Security, and Housing**

Area Name	Total (mil dol)	Farm	Goods-related[1] Total	Manu- facturing	Service-related and other[2] Total	Retail trade	Finance, insur- ance, and real estate	Services	Govern- ment	Social Security beneficiaries, December 2000 Number	Rate[3]	Supple- mental Security Income recipients, December 2000	Housing units, 1990 Total	Percent change, 1980- 1990
	75	76	77	78	79	80	81	82	83	84	85	86	87	88
Hartford, CT	30 856	0.3	D	17.3	D	7.7	16.8	27.2	14.4	199 743	174	17 757	450 082	15.4
Hattiesburg, MS	1 607	1.1	18.1	10.9	54.2	12.9	5.0	25.6	26.5	18 107	162	3 723	39 589	NA
Hickory-Morganton-Lenoir, NC	5 984	1.8	D	43.0	D	8.8	2.4	16.7	12.0	61 030	179	5 703	121 418	17.6
Honolulu, HI	18 819	0.3	8.3	2.8	58.2	10.3	8.5	27.2	33.2	130 535	149	15 646	281 683	11.8
Houma, LA	2 575	0.4	30.0	12.6	53.4	9.8	3.1	21.1	16.2	32 573	167	6 435	66 748	15.4
Houston-Galveston- Brazoria, TX	117 892	0.1	28.6	12.4	61.2	7.7	7.3	29.0	10.0	462 204	99	74 221	1 537 837	22.6
Brazoria, TX	3 175	0.4	48.4	32.0	36.6	8.7	2.9	16.1	14.6	27 007	112	2 785	74 504	23.2
Galveston-Texas City, TX	3 313	0.0	22.4	14.6	46.3	10.9	7.0	19.6	31.4	35 301	141	3 974	99 451	19.9
Houston, TX	111 404	0.1	28.3	11.8	62.4	7.6	7.5	29.6	9.2	399 896	96	67 462	1 363 882	22.7
Huntington-Ashland, WV-KY-OH	3 975	0.0	D	16.9	D	10.5	D	28.2	18.7	64 538	205	15 535	130 687	2.0
Huntsville, AL	7 760	0.4	D	23.1	D	7.2	2.9	29.0	27.4	49 198	144	7 245	119 310	36.2
Indianapolis, IN	36 711	0.1	D	21.2	D	9.4	9.5	26.0	12.3	233 013	145	22 212	571 246	13.2
Iowa City, IA	2 427	0.3	D	8.5	D	8.7	3.9	20.2	45.3	10 887	98	907	37 210	17.8
Jackson, MI	2 400	0.2	33.5	26.9	49.6	9.8	3.3	21.7	16.7	27 742	175	3 339	57 979	4.0
Jackson, MS	8 454	0.5	15.6	9.0	62.7	10.3	9.2	26.3	21.2	67 097	152	14 675	152 493	17.7
Jackson, TN	2 106	-0.2	D	25.7	D	10.0	D	23.7	17.9	18 277	170	3 264	36 753	10.4
Jacksonville, FL	21 575	0.3	D	7.7	D	9.9	13.3	28.5	18.6	164 089	149	22 220	384 360	33.7
Jacksonville, NC	2 637	0.3	D	2.8	D	6.6	1.6	8.2	73.2	14 565	97	2 313	47 526	34.1
Jamestown, NY	1 821	1.5	33.4	28.9	45.3	10.6	2.7	21.8	19.9	29 535	211	3 970	62 682	2.9
Janesville-Beloit, WI	2 599	0.4	44.0	37.2	43.3	10.0	3.1	19.5	12.3	25 742	169	2 675	54 840	5.3
Johnson City-Kingsport-Bristol, TN-VA	6 746	0.0	D	28.5	D	11.1	4.8	24.1	14.4	104 729	218	15 903	183 995	10.3
Johnstown, PA	2 952	0.6	25.7	15.2	55.7	11.0	5.5	26.6	18.1	54 461	234	6 437	103 087	2.5
Jonesboro, AR	1 272	2.3	D	22.4	D	10.8	4.4	26.7	15.4	13 252	161	2 496	28 434	17.8
Joplin, MO	2 448	0.7	D	24.5	D	11.4	3.3	23.1	10.5	30 074	191	3 522	57 938	10.8
Kalamazoo-Battle Creek, MI	8 362	0.6	D	32.9	D	8.8	D	21.7	16.4	76 455	169	10 034	176 104	8.1
Kansas City, MO-KS	40 758	0.1	D	12.2	D	8.8	9.4	27.9	14.3	261 853	147	23 036	663 910	15.2
Killeen-Temple, TX	5 170	0.3	D	7.1	D	7.8	2.9	15.6	55.1	31 987	102	4 119	94 927	25.4
Knoxville, TN	12 563	0.1	D	16.6	D	12.8	5.7	30.2	15.2	127 073	185	17 359	252 294	17.0
Kokomo, IN	2 498	0.4	D	61.5	D	7.1	2.4	11.5	9.2	18 831	185	1 626	40 247	2.2
La Crosse, WI-MN	2 360	0.6	D	18.4	D	9.8	5.8	28.9	14.0	20 739	164	1 906	45 496	13.9
Lafayette, IN	3 293	0.1	D	32.1	D	8.6	4.9	19.7	23.1	23 058	126	1 581	60 234	9.0
Lafayette, LA	5 538	0.8	29.4	9.8	55.8	10.8	4.1	27.5	14.1	60 433	157	15 849	137 601	19.0
Lake Charles, LA	3 050	0.0	38.6	22.9	47.6	8.3	3.1	25.0	13.7	30 421	166	4 780	66 426	9.2
Lakeland-Winter Haven, FL	6 538	2.7	22.2	13.3	60.9	15.2	6.1	25.8	14.2	105 981	219	12 260	186 225	38.1
Lancaster, PA	8 802	1.0	39.6	29.2	50.9	10.4	5.9	21.5	8.5	79 045	168	6 357	156 462	20.9
Lansing-East Lansing, MI	8 985	0.4	23.5	17.6	49.7	8.4	8.1	25.1	26.3	62 579	140	7 672	165 018	10.4
Laredo, TX	2 045	0.0	D	2.5	D	13.6	5.7	19.1	26.6	19 242	100	7 983	37 197	34.0
Las Cruces, NM	1 826	7.1	10.9	5.1	45.7	9.7	3.8	23.2	36.3	23 611	135	4 969	49 148	NA
Las Vegas, NV-AZ	29 693	0.1	15.4	3.2	71.4	10.1	9.4	41.8	13.1	240 347	154	21 483	376 083	68.1
Lawrence, KS	1 418	0.1	21.1	13.6	47.7	12.4	6.2	21.5	31.1	10 307	103	909	31 782	24.7
Lawton, OK	1 784	0.5	D	9.9	D	7.7	2.8	14.4	55.9	15 021	131	2 197	43 589	9.1
Lewiston-Auburn, ME	1 548	0.9	D	17.8	63.6	11.4	5.7	34.0	11.8	20 771	200	3 123	43 815	14.2
Lexington, KY	10 426	3.9	D	22.1	D	9.2	D	23.8	17.0	67 134	140	9 955	166 685	18.6
Lima, OH	2 735	0.1	40.5	34.1	45.1	9.1	3.0	21.8	14.3	27 465	177	2 812	59 665	4.0
Lincoln, NE	5 178	0.4	20.2	13.9	58.0	8.3	8.8	27.5	21.4	32 984	132	3 124	86 734	13.6
Little Rock-North Little Rock, AR	11 737	0.5	D	10.4	D	9.1	7.6	27.3	21.7	92 886	159	13 398	214 546	18.6
Longview-Marshall, TX	3 270	0.5	34.7	21.1	53.6	12.2	4.4	23.6	11.2	37 973	182	5 385	81 057	13.7
Los Angeles-Riverside-Orange County, CA	334 878	0.5	19.9	14.6	66.5	9.0	9.6	34.1	13.1	1 836 675	112	524 541	5 293 072	19.6
Los Angeles-Long Beach, CA	211 861	0.1	18.1	14.0	69.0	8.3	9.6	37.2	12.8	999 598	105	359 866	3 163 343	10.8
Orange County, CA	70 341	0.3	23.1	16.9	67.4	9.5	12.5	31.0	9.2	309 994	109	56 271	875 072	21.3
Riverside-San Bernardino, CA	39 064	1.5	21.8	12.2	55.5	12.0	5.3	25.1	21.1	431 332	133	94 339	1 026 179	54.3
Ventura, CA	13 612	4.1	25.5	18.8	53.7	9.8	6.9	26.3	16.8	95 751	127	14 065	228 478	24.6
Louisville, KY-IN	21 629	0.0	D	19.3	D	10.2	7.1	26.8	12.4	175 488	171	24 250	390 494	8.1
Lubbock, TX	3 998	1.0	12.8	6.9	65.4	14.6	6.3	29.1	20.8	34 088	140	4 712	91 770	14.0
Lynchburg, VA	3 412	0.1	D	32.1	D	8.9	D	24.0	12.2	42 028	196	4 597	79 105	16.4
Macon, GA	5 927	0.8	D	15.0	D	9.1	6.5	23.9	29.2	51 274	159	10 804	115 154	16.8
Madison, WI	10 673	0.3	19.1	12.0	55.2	8.9	9.6	25.3	25.4	51 999	122	5 245	147 851	17.1
Mansfield, OH	2 715	0.3	D	35.9	D	10.0	3.9	18.7	15.4	33 072	188	3 513	69 864	1.7
McAllen-Edinburg-Mission, TX	4 644	2.3	15.2	7.4	55.3	15.4	4.1	22.9	27.2	63 055	111	26 057	128 241	44.0
Medford-Ashland, OR	2 534	0.2	22.5	14.4	61.0	16.5	5.9	26.3	16.3	37 469	207	2 746	60 376	15.5
Melbourne-Titusville-Palm Bay, FL	7 038	0.3	D	19.0	D	9.9	4.4	35.6	17.5	112 990	237	7 736	185 150	62.6
Memphis, TN-AR-MS	25 187	0.1	D	11.8	D	9.7	7.9	27.7	13.5	158 054	139	37 837	394 329	15.9

1. Covers mining, construction, and manufacturing.   2. Covers private sector earnings in agricultural services, forestry, and fisheries; transportation and public utilities; wholesale trade; retail trade; finance, insurance, and real estate; and services.   3. Per 1,000 resident population estimated as of July 1 of the year shown.

Table C. Metropolitan Areas — Housing, Labor Force, and Employment

Area Name	Housing units, 1990 (cont'd)								Civilian labor force, 2001				Civilian employment, 1990 [5]		
	Occupied units														
	Owner-occupied					Renter-occupied					Unemployment			Percent	
				Owner cost as a percent of income											
	Total	Percent	Median value[1]	With a mortgage	Without a mortgage	Median rent[2]	Rent as percent of income	Sub-standard units[3] (percent)	Total	Percent change, 2000–2001	Total	Rate[4]	Total	Professional, managerial, and technical	Precision production, craft, and repair
	89	90	91	92	93	94	95	96	97	98	99	100	101	102	103
Hartford, CT	423 651	64.7	169 300	22.0	13.2	576	25.0	2.4	572 269	-1.6	18 698	3.3	590 735	35.4	10.9
Hattiesburg, MS	36 033	65.3	NA	NA	NA	NA	NA	NA	53 192	0.1	1 672	3.1	41 252	25.6	12.3
Hickory-Morganton-Lenoir, NC	112 387	74.7	57 000	NA	NA	341	NA	3.2	182 592	3.2	12 096	6.6	158 993	19.0	15.6
Honolulu, HI	265 304	52.0	283 600	21.5	10.7	662	27.6	15.9	429 252	1.3	17 517	4.1	395 811	31.5	9.9
Houma, LA	60 672	74.4	52 600	20.0	12.6	319	26.2	8.3	94 011	2.5	3 538	3.8	67 524	22.2	17.6
Houston-Galveston-Brazoria, TX	1 338 775	56.2	63 700	NA	NA	405	NA	9.0	2 425 894	1.6	107 740	4.4	1 800 508	32.9	12.0
Brazoria, TX	64 019	69.2	61 800	18.2	12.3	400	21.6	6.9	106 660	0.3	6 324	5.9	86 663	28.9	18.1
Galveston-Texas City, TX	81 451	62.0	59 700	19.6	13.4	400	25.4	5.7	117 791	-0.5	7 039	6.0	99 670	33.1	13.5
Houston, TX	1 193 305	55.1	64 200	NA	NA	406	NA	9.4	2 201 443	1.8	94 377	4.3	1 614 175	33.1	11.6
Huntington-Ashland, WV-KY-OH	119 640	72.0	46 600	16.6	12.1	305	27.8	3.6	138 575	0.4	8 632	6.2	118 603	26.1	13.4
Huntsville, AL	110 893	67.1	73 900	NA	NA	397	NA	3.1	178 082	1.5	6 311	3.5	144 186	39.3	11.1
Indianapolis, IN	529 814	64.7	64 100	NA	NA	407	NA	2.2	865 305	1.6	29 009	3.4	692 323	29.6	11.4
Iowa City, IA	36 067	52.7	76 900	19.0	12.2	411	28.3	2.9	70 883	3.7	1 723	2.4	54 591	40.8	6.3
Jackson, MI	53 660	73.7	47 900	16.1	12.7	375	25.0	2.1	80 869	1.2	4 309	5.3	64 317	24.7	12.5
Jackson, MS	140 157	65.7	59 900	21.0	13.8	399	27.6	6.3	234 676	0.5	8 443	3.6	180 802	32.0	9.8
Jackson, TN	34 167	67.0	NA	NA	NA	NA	NA	NA	59 078	-0.6	2 718	4.6	41 115	NA	11.0
Jacksonville, FL	343 526	64.8	67 800	20.8	12.3	438	25.6	4.1	567 164	2.0	23 983	4.2	422 421	28.9	11.5
Jacksonville, NC	40 658	53.7	62 200	23.4	13.2	397	25.3	4.7	48 654	-0.9	2 199	4.5	38 674	24.0	13.8
Jamestown, NY	53 696	68.6	47 800	18.0	13.5	325	28.6	1.6	64 029	-2.3	3 466	5.4	62 263	24.1	12.0
Janesville-Beloit, WI	52 252	68.2	52 300	17.0	12.9	386	24.7	2.0	78 771	1.1	5 048	6.4	67 826	22.7	12.8
Johnson City-Kingsport-Bristol, TN-VA	170 569	73.7	52 000	17.9	12.3	301	24.4	3.3	223 855	1.0	10 440	4.7	194 639	24.2	13.7
Johnstown, PA	91 578	74.6	40 900	19.1	13.1	277	24.9	2.0	102 480	0.1	6 797	6.6	91 968	23.4	13.3
Jonesboro, AR	26 285	65.4	50 200	19.3	13.1	335	26.8	2.2	42 456	-1.5	1 886	4.4	32 772	23.6	11.2
Joplin, MO	53 020	71.7	39 400	17.2	12.0	297	24.5	2.6	84 439	1.7	3 745	4.4	61 567	22.5	13.0
Kalamazoo-Battle Creek, MI.	160 916	68.5	53 800	NA	NA	394	NA	2.5	238 301	0.5	11 442	4.8	199 521	29.4	10.4
Kansas City, MO-KS	608 459	65.6	66 300	NA	NA	424	NA	2.4	1 009 014	0.7	44 161	4.4	784 951	31.1	10.0
Killeen-Temple, TX	83 927	52.1	57 300	21.5	12.9	378	25.2	5.5	116 509	0.7	5 046	4.3	83 561	27.9	11.5
Knoxville, TN	231 254	68.3	61 100	NA	NA	341	NA	2.6	359 947	2.2	11 957	3.3	278 110	30.3	11.9
Kokomo, IN	37 549	72.8	51 600	14.6	12.1	357	24.5	1.8	50 145	0.0	3 074	6.1	44 821	23.7	15.9
La Crosse, WI-MN	43 506	65.5	57 500	NA	NA	348	NA	2.4	72 766	2.0	2 706	3.7	59 030	27.4	9.5
Lafayette, IN	57 068	60.1	59 400	NA	NA	388	NA	3.2	90 426	1.2	2 960	3.3	77 998	32.5	10.3
Lafayette, LA	121 807	67.5	50 500	NA	NA	297	NA	7.4	179 671	3.4	9 646	5.4	132 264	27.3	13.3
Lake Charles, LA	60 328	70.4	54 700	17.6	12.8	337	26.3	4.5	90 247	0.5	5 465	6.1	67 327	26.2	17.1
Lakeland-Winter Haven, FL.	155 969	70.5	61 000	19.7	11.9	385	25.4	4.4	205 627	0.8	12 787	6.2	171 677	23.2	13.3
Lancaster, PA	150 956	69.4	89 400	20.7	11.9	440	23.8	2.9	249 866	1.6	7 984	3.2	215 292	24.0	13.6
Lansing-East Lansing, MI ...	156 887	64.7	64 500	18.4	13.1	421	26.0	2.6	248 660	0.4	8 531	3.4	216 826	31.6	9.6
Laredo, TX	34 438	60.6	49 800	22.5	12.7	313	27.6	28.1	75 221	1.6	5 319	7.1	45 819	23.3	10.0
Las Cruces, NM	45 029	NA	67 300	20.7	12.3	346	28.2	9.7	71 301	0.5	4 785	6.7	53 059	32.1	10.5
Las Vegas, NV-AZ	330 490	54.5	91 500	NA	NA	511	NA	6.7	803 157	4.7	43 840	5.5	416 030	23.4	11.5
Lawrence, KS	30 138	52.5	68 000	19.7	12.3	412	33.8	3.0	56 150	1.4	2 474	4.4	41 086	35.1	8.1
Lawton, OK	37 569	60.2	54 000	21.3	12.3	376	25.7	4.8	40 669	-0.6	1 352	3.3	37 640	31.0	8.9
Lewiston-Auburn, ME	40 017	62.2	86 800	21.1	13.9	373	24.9	2.4	60 144	-2.2	2 444	4.1	50 588	23.4	14.5
Lexington, KY	154 089	58.4	69 000	NA	NA	370	NA	3.0	260 960	-1.3	8 860	3.4	204 827	32.2	9.4
Lima, OH	55 384	73.2	54 200	15.9	11.9	345	23.9	2.1	76 449	-0.2	3 741	4.9	67 465	22.8	13.1
Lincoln, NE	82 759	60.5	62 200	18.9	11.9	377	25.6	1.4	145 823	1.1	4 151	2.8	117 484	32.7	9.5
Little Rock-North Little Rock, AR	195 437	64.8	59 700	19.8	13.0	391	26.3	3.7	298 327	-1.1	12 069	4.0	241 622	30.1	10.6
Longview-Marshall, TX	72 092	69.4	51 100	NA	NA	340	NA	5.5	102 541	-0.2	5 523	5.4	82 363	24.0	14.6
Los Angeles-Riverside-Orange County, CA	4 900 720	54.0	211 700	NA	NA	645	NA	15.5	8 397 370	2.3	420 133	5.0	6 912 664	31.1	11.4
Los Angeles-Long Beach, CA	2 989 552	48.2	226 400	25.2	11.6	625	29.5	18.9	4 875 237	2.4	277 010	5.7	4 203 792	30.9	11.0
Orange County, CA	827 066	60.1	252 700	NA	NA	789	NA	10.7	1 537 105	1.7	46 277	3.0	1 292 472	35.0	10.3
Riverside-San Bernardino, CA	866 804	65.2	133 900	25.8	12.2	561	29.7	9.8	1 565 165	3.0	77 926	5.0	1 079 628	26.6	14.4
Ventura, CA	217 298	65.5	245 300	NA	NA	753	NA	10.3	419 863	1.6	18 920	4.5	336 772	33.1	11.7
Louisville, KY-IN	366 364	67.6	56 100	NA	NA	345	NA	2.6	562 071	-1.4	24 672	4.4	450 019	27.6	11.6
Lubbock, TX	81 534	58.2	54 500	20.0	12.6	376	29.5	6.6	126 786	2.4	3 239	2.6	102 790	30.9	9.9
Lynchburg, VA	72 689	72.4	61 692	16.6	12.1	335	23.6	3.4	105 362	-0.8	4 434	4.2	92 896	25.5	12.8
Macon, GA	106 478	63.1	59 100	NA	NA	361	NA	4.5	144 038	-1.6	5 537	3.8	129 317	28.2	13.4
Madison, WI	142 786	55.2	78 400	20.9	13.1	464	26.0	2.6	272 673	3.5	5 557	2.0	208 069	38.0	7.7
Mansfield, OH	65 956	70.9	49 300	NA	NA	330	NA	2.0	83 865	1.2	4 750	5.7	76 988	22.1	14.7
McAllen-Edinburg-Mission, TX	103 479	70.3	35 900	21.5	12.7	281	26.5	28.4	208 182	2.1	27 277	13.1	122 112	23.3	10.5
Medford-Ashland, OR	57 238	66.2	74 900	22.0	13.3	412	27.6	4.4	91 923	0.0	5 757	6.3	62 704	25.1	10.7
Melbourne-Titusville-Palm Bay, FL	161 365	69.2	75 200	21.0	11.5	482	26.2	2.2	211 968	1.8	9 018	4.3	183 692	34.7	12.8
Memphis, TN-AR-MS	365 450	61.7	64 600	NA	NA	388	NA	5.3	564 488	0.7	23 628	4.2	456 421	29.0	9.8

1. Specified owner-occupied units.   2. Specified renter-occupied units.   3. Overcrowded or lacking complete plumbing facilities.   4. Percent of civilian labor force.   5. Persons 16 years and older.

Table C. Metropolitan Areas — Nonfarm Employment and Agriculture

Area Name	Private nonfarm establishments, employment and payroll, 1999									Agriculture, 1997			
		Employment						Annual payroll		Farms			Farm operators
											Percent with—		
	Number of establishments	Total	Health Care and Social Assistance	Manufacturing	Retail trade	Finance and Insurance	Professional Scientific and Technical Services	Total (mil dol)	Average per employee (dollars)	Number	Less than 50 acres	500 acres and over	Whose principal occupation is farming (percent)
	104	105	106	107	108	109	110	111	112	113	114	115	116
Hartford, CT	29 995	559 334	77 533	86 642	66 940	73 130	29 933	21 338	38 149	1 270	57.9	2.3	50.2
Hattiesburg, MS	2 869	40 923	7 861	5 461	7 826	1 542	1 280	909	22 212	692	33.7	5.9	38.7
Hickory-Morganton-Lenoir, NC	8 087	164 141	13 953	78 999	17 959	2 605	2 390	4 180	25 466	1 846	44.3	3.0	40.7
Honolulu, HI	20 583	307 514	37 259	10 806	41 145	17 329	15 605	8 924	29 020	880	93.2	1.7	100.0
Houma, LA	4 499	63 744	7 765	7 465	10 501	1 807	2 907	1 644	25 791	535	34.8	18.5	41.9
Houston-Galveston-Brazoria, TX	105 933	1 924 869	186 668	198 537	224 668	85 364	136 083	68 865	35 776	9 112	47.9	11.2	36.3
Brazoria, TX	3 796	58 119	4 868	14 415	9 079	1 436	1 526	1 934	33 277	1 783	45.4	13.8	33.6
Galveston-Texas City, TX	4 791	69 272	13 462	6 952	11 301	3 904	1 910	1 791	25 855	519	59.3	8.3	30.8
Houston, TX	97 346	1 797 478	168 338	177 170	204 288	80 024	132 647	65 140	36 240	6 810	47.7	10.8	37.4
Huntington-Ashland, WV-KY-OH	6 827	98 487	19 639	14 823	17 368	4 399	3 474	2 551	25 902	2 758	30.7	2.9	32.9
Huntsville, AL	8 206	139 910	14 223	30 246	19 097	3 952	18 785	4 365	31 199	2 100	40.1	9.9	35.5
Indianapolis, IN	41 821	778 597	98 896	107 257	98 569	52 939	36 771	25 973	33 359	5 113	40.2	17.3	47.9
Iowa City, IA	2 677	48 632	12 411	4 961	8 207	1 427	1 487	1 188	24 428	1 261	24.0	13.3	55.7
Jackson, MI	3 439	53 997	7 555	11 974	8 388	1 446	1 477	1 558	28 853	987	34.7	8.0	38.0
Jackson, MS	11 108	199 127	31 251	17 419	26 952	13 243	8 240	5 298	26 606	1 746	24.2	14.5	34.0
Jackson, TN	2 888	53 057	8 102	13 540	7 694	1 300	1 106	1 397	26 330	981	28.2	9.6	36.6
Jacksonville, FL	28 084	476 106	53 791	34 069	62 235	49 298	25 089	13 060	27 431	918	62.5	8.6	46.4
Jacksonville, NC	2 610	28 213	4 464	1 835	6 479	941	846	505	17 900	369	40.7	8.4	56.9
Jamestown, NY	3 129	47 379	7 224	13 795	6 791	956	1 141	1 091	23 027	1 557	33.2	5.3	56.0
Janesville-Beloit, WI	3 331	61 440	7 108	18 049	8 805	1 578	1 008	1 864	30 339	1 324	32.6	12.9	52.3
Johnson City-Kingsport-Bristol, TN-VA	10 238	176 119	23 717	46 495	25 816	9 429	3 947	4 446	25 244	8 856	53.9	1.7	35.1
Johnstown, PA	5 473	72 276	12 474	13 219	11 430	4 151	2 866	1 622	22 442	1 483	19.5	8.0	57.0
Jonesboro, AR	2 252	33 463	5 888	7 758	5 480	893	752	789	23 578	754	21.6	33.8	63.8
Joplin, MO	4 060	69 463	10 363	15 960	9 681	1 637	1 294	1 599	23 019	2 977	30.7	7.2	39.3
Kalamazoo-Battle Creek, MI.	10 555	188 527	25 132	41 485	25 814	8 591	6 461	5 675	30 102	2 840	34.1	9.6	47.9
Kansas City, MO-KS	48 215	865 967	97 982	92 806	104 326	58 780	56 315	27 663	31 945	9 774	32.1	11.2	40.5
Killeen-Temple, TX	4 773	82 225	19 264	8 525	12 308	3 552	3 290	1 873	22 779	2 816	29.0	16.7	39.1
Knoxville, TN	18 475	299 601	38 065	43 823	46 658	11 116	22 389	8 365	27 920	4 816	51.5	1.8	33.6
Kokomo, IN	2 349	47 325	5 023	20 060	6 451	1 237	632	1 959	41 395	901	28.4	22.1	57.0
La Crosse, WI-MN	3 351	60 368	10 977	10 856	9 623	2 161	1 939	1 538	25 477	1 713	13.0	14.0	57.8
Lafayette, IN	3 845	73 936	8 676	22 256	11 104	3 616	2 015	2 059	27 848	1 250	31.0	25.3	52.5
Lafayette, LA	9 835	135 959	20 458	12 848	21 810	4 729	7 861	3 333	24 515	2 424	45.9	17.7	48.1
Lake Charles, LA	4 272	70 100	10 422	11 083	10 653	2 005	2 901	1 832	26 134	749	35.6	17.5	34.6
Lakeland-Winter Haven, FL	9 619	157 276	17 356	19 464	22 787	10 998	5 479	3 937	25 032	2 464	62.3	8.6	39.3
Lancaster, PA	11 289	204 872	24 445	52 670	30 475	6 683	6 909	5 582	27 246	4 556	39.6	1.3	74.2
Lansing-East Lansing, MI	10 304	168 975	22 201	26 156	26 734	10 947	7 435	5 131	30 365	3 012	34.5	9.9	44.1
Laredo, TX	4 014	48 694	6 603	1 385	9 676	1 952	1 266	995	20 434	453	6.0	61.1	38.4
Las Cruces, NM	3 260	35 749	5 863	2 303	6 608	1 324	2 634	724	20 252	1 290	75.7	7.8	40.4
Las Vegas, NV-AZ	32 384	636 444	44 349	22 627	76 648	22 872	26 519	17 862	28 065	565	49.7	23.0	48.1
Lawrence, KS	2 594	36 795	4 629	4 315	6 211	1 325	1 791	780	21 199	839	30.3	13.8	42.9
Lawton, OK	2 199	27 491	4 994	3 662	5 119	1 068	1 168	598	21 753	1 030	18.2	25.2	44.3
Lewiston-Auburn, ME	2 732	43 092	7 404	8 387	6 387	2 197	2 034	1 054	24 459	288	27.4	9.7	52.1
Lexington, KY	12 387	222 480	30 975	46 361	32 519	7 333	10 687	6 259	28 133	6 229	39.7	7.6	47.6
Lima, OH	3 883	68 633	10 900	18 041	9 726	1 790	1 240	1 910	27 829	1 919	27.5	11.4	47.9
Lincoln, NE	6 894	122 307	16 504	16 224	16 742	9 808	8 006	3 188	26 066	1 457	32.3	19.1	46.0
Little Rock-North Little Rock, AR	15 919	272 601	41 790	31 411	34 500	13 663	13 522	7 298	26 772	2 730	30.0	15.2	40.9
Longview-Marshall, TX	5 569	77 224	9 848	17 129	11 982	2 878	2 576	1 885	24 410	2 580	37.0	7.1	33.2
Los Angeles-Riverside-Orange County, CA	368 275	6 110 848	585 313	996 683	646 041	307 904	520 090	206 750	33 833	8 292	78.2	4.7	44.6
Los Angeles-Long Beach, CA	222 513	3 747 755	359 599	622 885	355 417	179 710	394 384	130 919	34 933	1 226	84.7	4.7	39.9
Orange County, CA	76 532	1 330 960	104 096	224 520	137 246	90 695	91 517	47 541	35 719	349	74.8	3.2	49.3
Riverside-San Bernardino, CA	52 440	807 316	98 840	118 418	121 319	23 601	21 216	21 246	26 317	4 503	79.2	4.3	44.5
Ventura, CA	16 790	224 817	22 778	30 860	32 059	13 898	12 973	7 044	31 332	2 214	73.3	5.6	46.5
Louisville, KY-IN	26 907	507 600	62 653	80 340	63 564	29 581	21 123	15 167	29 880	3 844	41.6	5.1	38.5
Lubbock, TX	6 459	90 780	17 118	6 533	14 815	3 854	3 006	2 045	22 527	1 068	29.1	32.1	55.3
Lynchburg, VA	5 432	88 668	9 982	22 900	12 604	4 257	3 817	2 402	27 090	2 225	23.8	8.1	40.5
Macon, GA	7 349	116 473	17 739	16 895	18 711	8 570	5 175	3 047	26 161	810	34.1	12.2	36.7
Madison, WI	12 191	219 244	28 568	26 681	31 208	19 183	13 092	6 481	29 561	2 595	30.1	8.1	54.3
Mansfield, OH	4 056	69 520	8 535	22 299	9 843	1 726	1 512	1 810	26 036	1 620	27.2	11.7	49.9
McAllen-Edinburg-Mission, TX	8 187	108 951	19 533	11 865	22 671	4 252	3 218	2 061	18 917	1 373	49.5	18.9	45.4
Medford-Ashland, OR	5 248	60 898	8 433	7 349	10 268	2 214	1 892	1 517	24 911	1 623	66.7	4.7	41.0
Melbourne-Titusville-Palm Bay, FL	11 358	158 062	20 746	20 127	25 659	4 057	13 050	4 400	27 837	470	74.9	8.7	36.2
Memphis, TN-AR-MS	25 257	521 597	60 262	53 294	64 317	22 964	22 619	15 796	30 284	2 717	38.6	17.4	40.9

Table C. Metropolitan Areas — **Agriculture, Land, and Water**

Area Name	Land in farms					Value of land and buildings		Value of machinery and equipment Average per farm ($1,000)	Value of products sold				Percent of farms with sales of —		Percent of land owned by Fed. Gov. 1997	Water consumption 1995 (mil gal/day)
	Acreage (1,000)	Percent change, 1992-1997	Acres			Average per farm ($1,000)	Average per acre (dollars)		Total (mil dol)	Average per farm (dollars)	Percent from —		$10,000 or more	$100,000 or more		
			Average size of farm	Total irrigated (1,000)	Total cropland (1,000)						Crops	Livestock and poultry products				
	117	118	119	120	121	122	123	124	125	126	127	128	129	130	131	132
Hartford, CT	108	-6.2	85	5	58	548	6 662	43	173	136 536	83.0	17.0	40.6	13.1	0.2	737.0
Hattiesburg, MS	120	32.1	174	1	41	321	1 739	29	46	65 978	11.0	89.0	27.6	8.5	9.9	50.4
Hickory-Morganton-Lenoir, NC	199	10.9	108	2	115	266	2 630	30	123	66 707	28.0	72.0	32.6	12.7	9.2	853.4
Honolulu, HI	80	-13.1	91	16	29	565	6 225	33	143	162 460	72.0	28.0	57.5	14.5	12.5	278.9
Houma, LA	188	6.2	351	1	100	531	1 419	70	46	86 705	84.0	16.0	43.4	14.0	0.0	62.7
Houston-Galveston-Brazoria, TX	2 395	-1.3	263	106	988	371	1 492	36	253	27 804	69.0	31.0	24.4	5.1	2.6	1 858.4
Brazoria, TX	567	0.5	318	30	203	403	1 293	38	43	23 904	59.0	41.0	22.5	5.0	2.7	286.0
Galveston-Texas City, TX	105	2.9	202	1	30	251	1 053	28	7	13 112	31.0	69.0	18.3	1.9	0.1	61.1
Houston, TX	1 723	-2.2	253	75	754	372	1 584	36	204	29 945	72.0	28.0	25.3	5.4	2.9	1 511.4
Huntington-Ashland, WV-KY-OH	353	-3.9	128	0	131	128	1 084	22	28	10 011	61.0	39.0	22.1	1.1	8.3	211.6
Huntsville, AL	464	7.5	221	8	339	467	2 101	42	82	39 136	49.0	51.0	28.0	7.1	5.8	846.3
Indianapolis, IN	1 423	-4.8	278	D	1 295	758	2 714	73	504	98 523	80.0	20.0	57.5	22.6	0.3	609.7
Iowa City, IA	288	1.1	229	1	249	416	1 816	56	100	79 612	51.0	49.0	64.0	24.0	4.0	62.9
Jackson, MI	181	-14.1	184	3	138	272	1 600	51	44	44 895	54.0	46.0	41.7	9.1	0.0	37.3
Jackson, MS	496	-9.5	284	D	229	370	1 247	42	127	72 737	27.0	73.0	29.1	9.3	0.4	73.2
Jackson, TN	219	2.7	223	D	146	228	1 073	44	35	35 433	78.0	22.0	27.1	7.4	0.0	20.2
Jacksonville, FL	191	-13.1	208	22	50	472	2 319	45	130	141 830	44.0	56.0	31.7	13.7	5.1	257.6
Jacksonville, NC	63	-0.9	172	0	42	291	1 729	48	102	275 201	22.0	78.0	55.6	31.4	15.4	14.8
Jamestown, NY	245	-5.8	157	1	145	172	1 145	46	89	56 951	33.0	67.0	52.0	15.5	0.0	1 204.1
Janesville-Beloit, WI	351	2.3	265	10	308	453	1 727	79	130	97 906	57.0	43.0	58.5	24.7	0.1	152.0
Johnson City-Kingsport-Bristol, TN-VA	715	-3.1	81	2	389	201	2 390	27	152	17 196	43.0	57.0	25.8	2.1	14.6	1 155.4
Johnstown, PA	294	-1.0	198	1	187	259	1 255	55	82	55 241	24.0	76.0	50.5	15.6	0.1	62.7
Jonesboro, AR	363	3.8	482	222	335	612	1 365	119	123	162 763	98.0	2.0	68.4	41.4	0.6	349.6
Joplin, MO	527	-1.9	177	6	348	231	1 272	26	200	67 115	17.0	83.0	35.3	8.9	0.0	33.2
Kalamazoo-Battle Creek, MI	567	-6.4	200	47	444	343	1 658	63	267	94 056	71.0	29.0	51.9	16.2	0.7	274.5
Kansas City, MO-KS	2 256	-1.0	231	13	1 626	359	1 601	41	451	46 160	58.0	42.0	40.6	9.2	1.1	1 459.1
Killeen-Temple, TX	1 053	3.1	374	2	370	329	775	30	80	28 237	29.0	71.0	27.6	4.0	16.7	49.9
Knoxville, TN	419	-2.6	87	1	253	307	3 465	30	98	20 326	D	D	18.0	2.1	14.2	613.8
Kokomo, IN	306	-1.2	340	D	286	921	2 780	97	128	142 536	75.0	25.0	74.1	35.7	0.0	25.1
La Crosse, WI-MN	468	3.0	273	1	276	273	1 086	57	123	72 047	31.0	69.0	61.6	22.4	2.8	72.0
Lafayette, IN	478	-3.1	382	4	443	919	2 389	93	186	148 405	68.0	32.0	71.4	34.6	0.0	51.3
Lafayette, LA	704	-0.8	290	147	604	372	1 399	62	185	76 361	91.0	9.0	38.3	17.0	0.8	235.7
Lake Charles, LA	312	-5.0	416	30	140	500	1 301	33	20	27 307	69.0	31.0	28.8	8.3	0.0	312.0
Lakeland-Winter Haven, FL	621	1.7	252	118	187	532	2 110	31	253	102 865	81.0	19.0	48.0	12.5	2.5	391.9
Lancaster, PA	392	1.0	86	5	331	472	5 578	52	767	168 293	13.0	87.0	82.1	43.5	0.0	165.7
Lansing-East Lansing, MI	666	-2.6	221	6	559	358	1 590	65	200	66 354	57.0	43.0	49.4	14.4	0.0	192.8
Laredo, TX	2 176	27.1	4 804	6	52	1 594	330	50	28	62 247	10.0	90.0	37.1	6.8	0.0	42.9
Las Cruces, NM	581	10.5	451	82	91	541	1 305	65	235	182 546	55.0	45.0	32.7	13.3	76.1	441.4
Las Vegas, NV-AZ	1 153	-47.7	2 041	36	56	908	392	54	62	109 205	35.0	65.0	35.4	9.6	85.8	625.6
Lawrence, KS	219	-1.6	260	2	147	297	1 135	53	39	46 347	56.0	44.0	39.8	10.1	3.1	21.6
Lawton, OK	435	7.0	422	1	194	309	720	39	32	31 380	35.0	65.0	42.1	7.2	23.4	21.1
Lewiston-Auburn, ME	56	-9.8	194	1	23	304	1 715	71	62	216 587	13.0	87.0	47.9	19.4	0.0	14.0
Lexington, KY	1 058	-5.7	170	9	715	416	2 469	37	556	89 301	27.0	73.0	57.4	12.7	1.2	190.4
Lima, OH	403	1.0	210	D	368	456	2 110	74	145	75 525	64.0	36.0	70.0	22.1	0.1	54.4
Lincoln, NE	421	1.5	289	13	344	400	1 410	51	82	56 545	72.0	28.0	51.6	17.4	1.4	21.0
Little Rock-North Little Rock, AR	763	1.6	280	234	551	387	1 364	52	176	64 420	68.0	32.0	34.5	13.6	3.7	480.8
Longview-Marshall, TX	441	-0.4	171	1	193	203	1 212	25	46	17 736	7.0	93.0	24.0	2.9	0.8	112.3
Los Angeles-Riverside-Orange County, CA	1 968	-13.6	237	412	536	705	3 201	56	2 978	359 083	65.0	35.0	48.4	21.9	62.3	4 583.4
Los Angeles-Long Beach, CA	131	-28.9	107	27	49	507	4 475	39	238	193 854	94.0	6.0	37.1	14.1	29.6	1 683.0
Orange County, CA	58	-4.7	167	13	17	871	6 010	90	229	655 819	99.0	1.0	53.0	29.2	13.1	517.3
Riverside-San Bernardino, CA	1 433	-16.2	318	261	338	659	2 087	63	1 665	369 833	39.0	61.0	46.7	20.7	69.5	2 010.4
Ventura, CA	346	7.9	156	111	132	883	6 860	46	846	381 939	98.0	2.0	57.3	27.5	50.0	372.7
Louisville, KY-IN	517	-6.1	135	D	343	325	2 531	35	117	30 382	52.0	48.0	32.1	6.0	3.6	1 246.3
Lubbock, TX	541	12.2	506	212	456	441	808	104	134	125 239	71.0	29.0	53.0	27.7	0.4	217.8
Lynchburg, VA	428	0.8	193	D	199	294	1 540	34	39	17 741	25.0	75.0	27.2	3.4	8.0	47.8
Macon, GA	217	9.7	268	13	115	397	1 474	55	75	92 489	61.0	39.0	34.2	11.6	5.4	168.6
Madison, WI	513	-4.8	198	7	414	367	1 853	73	285	109 687	31.0	69.0	59.5	25.6	0.2	112.7
Mansfield, OH	382	-0.5	236	0	327	438	1 895	67	122	75 524	63.0	37.0	60.2	19.9	0.0	22.0
McAllen-Edinburg-Mission, TX	636	-3.7	463	185	439	609	1 360	63	197	143 653	92.0	8.0	41.1	17.3	1.8	932.3
Medford-Ashland, OR	246	-6.1	152	53	70	353	1 784	32	51	31 397	75.0	25.0	22.1	3.4	47.7	363.6
Melbourne-Titusville-Palm Bay, FL	277	38.3	588	31	27	909	1 474	33	38	80 757	86.0	14.0	36.0	9.8	12.7	135.5
Memphis, TN-AR-MS	1 038	-1.5	382	110	835	594	1 630	69	228	84 060	90.0	10.0	34.3	15.2	1.3	778.7

Table C. Metropolitan Areas — Residential Construction, Wholesale and Retail Trade, and Real Estate

Area Name	Value of Residential Construction Authorized by Building Permits, 2000		Wholesale Trade, 1997				Retail Trade[1], 1997				Real Estate and Rental and Leasing, 1997			
	New Construction ($1,000)	Number of Housing Units	Number of Establishments	Number of Employees	Sales (mil dol)	Annual Payroll (mil dol)	Number of Establishments	Number of Employees	Sales (mil dol)	Annual Payroll (mil dol)	Number of Establishments	Number of Employees	Receipts (mil dol)	Annual Payroll (mil dol)
	133	134	135	136	137	138	139	140	141	142	143	144	145	146
Hartford, CT	409 800	3 265	1 676	28 388	17 900.5	1 205.6	4 853	64 199	10 937.9	1 168.5	1 102	7 492	1 142.5	205.4
Hattiesburg, MS	24 910	326	142	D	D	D	597	7 759	1 135.9	106.0	119	477	41.5	6.8
Hickory-Morganton-Lenoir, NC	267 854	2 190	487	7 360	3 606.1	227.1	1 524	17 319	2 935.2	264.7	236	883	103.3	16.8
Honolulu, HI	288 748	1 969	1 463	15 423	6 079.9	487.0	3 269	44 960	8 264.7	823.6	1 221	7 746	1 219.9	208.4
Houma, LA	68 316	696	300	3 189	1 119.0	88.3	805	10 106	1 634.1	143.7	218	2 077	303.7	63.4
Houston-Galveston-Brazoria, TX	4 207 090	35 900	8 837	113 506	117 381.3	4 566.5	15 173	215 892	39 877.0	3 679.1	4 932	38 177	4 691.3	934.5
Brazoria, TX	292 168	2 085	220	2 524	840.2	102.1	629	8 945	1 534.4	136.0	196	1 231	142.8	29.3
Galveston-Texas City, TX	338 069	2 931	198	1 522	561.3	46.6	921	10 591	1 786.9	165.8	224	1 160	128.5	25.4
Houston, TX	3 576 853	30 884	8 419	109 460	115 979.8	4 417.8	13 623	196 356	36 555.7	3 377.3	4 512	35 786	4 420.0	879.8
Huntington-Ashland, WV-KY-OH	23 590	288	361	4 570	1 656.2	125.3	1 456	17 394	2 589.8	247.0	250	942	94.0	16.3
Huntsville, AL	67 761	1 210	520	5 494	3 485.9	189.0	1 479	19 814	3 015.3	291.4	366	1 735	178.2	31.7
Indianapolis, IN	2 007 906	15 356	3 040	42 968	28 933.9	1 613.7	6 203	95 437	16 941.0	1 603.9	1 715	12 032	1 467.6	267.7
Iowa City, IA	122 604	1 151	89	D	D	D	467	6 924	990.9	104.7	120	566	66.7	10.2
Jackson, MI	85 630	919	196	2 339	1 047.2	83.7	564	8 108	1 289.4	126.9	96	465	41.9	7.3
Jackson, MS	234 518	2 270	772	11 386	5 390.5	363.6	1 819	27 344	4 249.5	422.9	459	2 224	255.5	38.7
Jackson, TN	66 340	656	171	2 248	790.8	61.8	647	8 650	1 296.3	122.7	95	443	44.0	7.6
Jacksonville, FL	1 312 360	10 571	1 717	23 651	17 396.9	813.0	4 414	59 044	10 329.4	977.0	1 196	7 570	1 092.1	182.3
Jacksonville, NC	67 461	915	69	D	D	D	564	6 542	1 090.1	96.7	129	497	53.0	7.5
Jamestown, NY	28 983	236	159	2 171	748.6	57.6	591	7 096	1 011.1	96.6	86	395	41.9	7.0
Janesville-Beloit, WI	78 065	848	152	2 823	1 706.4	95.8	584	8 484	1 599.7	148.4	105	364	52.9	5.6
Johnson City-Kingsport-Bristol, TN-VA	126 891	1 501	548	7 332	3 732.2	194.4	2 137	24 655	4 041.4	369.4	369	1 534	157.0	25.6
Johnstown, PA	41 345	460	231	2 955	855.2	79.3	1 060	11 916	1 787.9	157.7	115	483	48.4	7.3
Jonesboro, AR	30 695	320	140	1 548	509.7	35.6	480	5 589	854.3	80.8	86	349	41.5	5.9
Joplin, MO	39 859	481	250	2 575	1 092.1	64.3	790	9 302	1 444.4	133.7	151	585	50.4	9.3
Kalamazoo-Battle Creek, MI	267 307	2 417	543	8 329	3 423.0	305.7	1 812	25 894	4 130.9	389.1	373	2 626	236.8	49.6
Kansas City, MO-KS	1 476 335	12 877	3 647	53 535	46 070.8	2 011.0	6 750	98 293	18 112.0	1 723.5	1 930	13 008	1 881.8	311.2
Killeen-Temple, TX	176 072	1 885	167	2 658	1 457.7	81.6	973	12 190	2 002.2	185.4	284	1 228	100.6	17.4
Knoxville, TN	379 689	4 007	1 198	14 821	8 438.0	509.7	3 518	45 022	8 077.2	748.7	788	4 390	492.1	95.0
Kokomo, IN	62 396	461	130	999	958.7	34.8	461	6 556	1 077.7	96.4	95	329	39.7	5.6
La Crosse, WI-MN	75 478	644	185	3 753	1 991.6	112.6	579	9 505	1 528.9	141.6	125	785	61.0	13.4
Lafayette, IN	148 757	1 787	164	1 618	551.3	41.5	690	10 888	1 673.3	156.6	171	818	86.9	13.0
Lafayette, LA	158 219	1 458	666	8 138	3 432.8	266.2	1 637	21 337	3 451.6	320.6	456	3 419	438.9	94.0
Lake Charles, LA	70 748	959	244	3 136	1 732.7	90.8	775	10 400	1 606.2	147.1	210	1 164	106.0	20.6
Lakeland-Winter Haven, FL	330 680	4 746	639	8 329	4 176.2	212.7	1 816	22 751	3 844.3	360.9	431	2 001	217.3	39.8
Lancaster, PA	250 470	2 016	663	11 020	10 936.6	341.6	2 012	29 237	4 671.7	480.8	281	1 906	247.2	41.9
Lansing-East Lansing, MI	260 673	2 316	507	7 289	4 509.5	261.8	1 756	26 727	4 317.5	424.4	410	3 493	281.6	63.8
Laredo, TX	111 755	1 863	339	2 453	1 105.4	51.1	730	9 051	1 524.6	138.8	155	574	64.3	10.0
Las Cruces, NM	95 920	982	122	978	283.6	25.0	511	6 266	1 059.1	98.1	175	530	44.8	7.4
Las Vegas, NV-AZ	2 841 015	28 162	1 423	16 654	6 661.7	547.8	4 488	66 198	13 698.9	1 325.7	1 689	12 985	1 726.8	299.7
Lawrence, KS	83 869	803	88	777	248.8	21.0	453	5 664	758.5	80.3	122	434	46.4	6.6
Lawton, OK	15 161	138	84	766	200.6	16.4	436	5 216	691.8	67.8	133	523	48.7	8.1
Lewiston-Auburn, ME	34 697	321	126	1 244	277.8	35.7	533	6 362	1 247.1	96.4	109	418	46.9	7.2
Lexington, KY	416 893	4 241	684	10 214	5 750.8	316.3	2 083	31 088	4 923.7	460.5	517	2 520	358.8	46.9
Lima, OH	53 867	395	236	3 782	3 967.5	107.6	734	10 022	1 632.9	146.1	139	551	47.7	8.1
Lincoln, NE	187 802	1 697	304	D	D	D	996	15 734	2 270.4	232.0	267	1 480	150.3	25.4
Little Rock-North Little Rock, AR	333 880	2 738	1 073	16 315	10 350.4	494.1	2 584	34 803	6 218.0	541.8	618	3 750	430.5	68.9
Longview-Marshall, TX	24 571	201	424	4 360	2 289.3	137.0	1 055	11 990	2 073.4	190.0	179	859	89.7	21.1
Los Angeles-Riverside-Orange County, CA	8 787 912	54 944	32 538	413 546	303 020.6	15 195.0	47 411	616 435	124 135.4	12 079.1	17 465	121 581	20 184.4	3 521.9
Los Angeles-Long Beach, CA	2 364 387	16 968	21 474	259 217	177 244.9	9 450.4	27 577	343 656	69 534.2	6 769.0	10 932	76 904	13 608.6	2 256.3
Orange County, CA	1 981 282	12 520	7 029	103 113	94 403.4	3 999.6	9 084	126 575	26 172.8	2 572.0	3 537	29 156	4 714.8	939.1
Riverside-San Bernardino, CA	3 626 948	21 496	2 947	37 405	20 969.7	1 222.4	8 402	115 373	21 951.8	2 129.4	2 324	12 267	1 452.1	253.0
Ventura, CA	815 295	3 960	1 088	13 811	10 402.7	522.6	2 348	30 831	6 476.6	608.7	672	3 254	409.0	73.4
Louisville, KY-IN	740 222	6 751	1 865	28 299	17 367.6	950.2	4 154	63 200	9 631.4	991.4	1 054	6 823	881.4	143.3
Lubbock, TX	94 120	924	505	6 628	3 867.8	181.3	1 084	14 538	2 673.0	238.0	296	1 905	133.8	30.7
Lynchburg, VA	146 695	1 140	224	2 674	1 531.8	79.3	932	12 039	1 977.0	188.5	186	616	58.4	11.3
Macon, GA	209 898	2 692	362	4 127	1 786.2	128.1	1 475	19 930	3 120.1	297.4	298	1 472	201.8	32.6
Madison, WI	465 509	3 986	675	10 048	4 350.1	342.7	1 845	30 150	4 860.9	507.2	520	3 519	371.4	71.1
Mansfield, OH	63 294	631	209	2 422	808.6	67.1	763	10 574	1 549.5	151.3	125	490	49.9	7.4
McAllen-Edinburg-Mission, TX	310 947	5 659	600	6 395	1 981.7	124.6	1 582	20 862	3 337.6	313.1	346	1 347	116.3	18.5
Medford-Ashland, OR	160 010	1 351	284	2 678	1 022.7	69.8	835	9 564	2 075.3	172.2	248	1 003	95.9	15.2
Melbourne-Titusville-Palm Bay, FL	509 727	4 284	577	4 389	1 362.4	136.2	1 856	23 867	3 900.5	370.3	525	2 443	220.0	45.3
Memphis, TN-AR-MS	1 087 390	10 259	2 050	36 575	37 008.2	1 277.5	4 296	65 612	10 476.4	1 012.9	951	7 504	907.3	176.5

1. Establishments with payroll.

Table C. Metropolitan Areas —

Professional, Manufacturing, Accommodation and Foodservices, Finance and Insurance

Area Name	Professional, Scientific, and Technical Services[1], 1997				Manufacturing, 1997				Accommodation and Foodservices, 1997			
	Number of Establishments	Number of Employees	Sales (mil dol)	Annual Payroll (mil dol)	Number of Establishments	Number of Employees	Sales (mil dol)	Annual Payroll (mil dol)	Number of Establishments	Number of Employees	Sales (mil dol)	Annual Payroll (mil dol)
	147	148	149	150	151	152	153	154	155	156	157	158
Hartford, CT	2 720	23 268	2 760.9	1 086.4	2 053	89 601	15 058	3 772	2 341	35 958	1 268.8	371.0
Hattiesburg, MS	202	994	75.2	26.2	106	5 940	1 154	133	211	4 755	125.7	33.2
Hickory-Morganton-Lenoir, NC	415	1 921	135.5	50.3	1 012	78 514	9 908	1 925	573	10 632	299.2	84.0
Honolulu, HI	1 917	13 729	1 400.6	546.8	685	11 161	2 692	301	2 125	53 916	3 036.8	852.8
Houma, LA	329	2 597	216.8	78.3	185	6 454	964	202	302	4 687	154.6	42.0
Houston-Galveston-Brazoria, TX	11 650	116 232	17 046.6	5 979.1	5 387	202 631	99 862	7 902	6 989	140 028	5 330.4	1 420.6
Brazoria, TX	246	1 212	93.4	38.8	199	14 149	10 761	683	295	4 787	148.4	41.8
Galveston-Texas City, TX .	333	1 375	131.6	52.5	160	7 279	9 183	393	485	9 156	301.5	82.4
Houston, TX	11 071	113 645	16 821.6	5 887.8	5 028	181 203	79 919	6 826	6 209	126 085	4 880.5	1 296.4
Huntington-Ashland, WV-KY-OH	392	2 314	155.9	63.9	262	15 112	5 602	548	550	9 860	288.5	78.8
Huntsville, AL	835	13 490	1 629.7	619.6	404	35 060	8 313	1 388	584	12 811	391.8	107.5
Indianapolis, IN	3 582	30 739	3 085.3	1 159.3	2 014	106 283	26 773	4 306	3 031	65 908	2 178.1	620.4
Iowa City, IA	164	1 085	81.9	29.3	89	3 639	2 510	121	271	5 496	144.3	40.8
Jackson, MI	200	1 354	90.8	45.5	351	12 248	2 272	422	267	4 467	137.0	37.7
Jackson, MS	912	7 182	721.5	273.1	392	19 717	3 969	522	689	15 039	479.4	134.1
Jackson, TN	148	1 009	79.1	37.1	162	13 282	3 549	401	202	4 416	144.3	39.2
Jacksonville, FL	2 506	19 393	1 727.5	756.1	950	33 883	8 408	1 119	2 047	42 445	1 438.6	385.5
Jacksonville, NC	137	725	34.9	11.9	37	1 829	346	38	249	4 420	127.9	34.5
Jamestown, NY	168	815	48.5	19.2	222	13 084	2 974	409	368	4 323	124.9	35.4
Janesville-Beloit, WI	182	1 002	65.1	23.5	234	19 547	10 106	785	343	5 295	151.2	41.3
Johnson City-Kingsport-Bristol, TN-VA	663	3 861	305.6	117.3	571	48 454	8 653	1 628	721	15 467	445.0	127.7
Johnstown, PA	269	2 090	125.6	51.2	271	12 231	1 994	303	482	6 045	165.7	46.0
Jonesboro, AR	148	675	53.4	19.3	122	6 886	1 258	185	133	2 720	80.2	21.6
Joplin, MO	182	1 092	60.7	25.4	261	16 219	2 847	400	309	5 764	159.5	46.0
Kalamazoo-Battle Creek, MI .	726	4 641	412.0	177.2	748	43 859	9 631	1 587	905	16 004	459.7	135.9
Kansas City, MO-KS	4 407	44 494	4 769.8	1 907.9	2 201	95 231	31 015	3 328	3 270	70 663	2 553.0	731.2
Killeen-Temple, TX	228	2 166	182.5	56.3	160	7 921	1 404	237	436	7 874	233.3	63.3
Knoxville, TN	1 397	17 148	1 750.3	699.9	894	43 228	8 609	1 311	1 584	31 961	1 133.2	317.5
Kokomo, IN	122	503	35.4	11.7	102	20 972	4 931	1 108	207	4 232	124.3	34.3
La Crosse, WI-MN	211	1 584	121.7	53.2	184	10 668	1 433	324	333	5 793	148.7	42.8
Lafayette, IN	242	1 336	110.4	38.2	162	21 654	9 084	840	375	7 475	213.7	61.2
Lafayette, LA	995	6 607	601.0	229.5	363	13 086	3 317	309	568	11 632	344.5	97.8
Lake Charles, LA	348	2 432	183.4	69.2	134	11 274	10 154	542	294	8 019	306.4	75.4
Lakeland-Winter Haven, FL ..	712	4 006	347.6	135.4	480	20 627	6 000	634	711	13 383	419.3	113.2
Lancaster, PA	639	5 130	439.8	165.6	918	52 908	10 585	1 752	877	15 724	506.4	145.6
Lansing-East Lansing, MI	897	6 161	598.0	253.6	428	29 104	8 893	1 471	836	17 358	489.7	139.3
Laredo, TX	210	1 029	69.6	23.1	87	1 402	259	28	253	4 350	144.7	37.4
Las Cruces, NM	222	1 334	107.3	45.7	111	2 290	396	47	253	4 278	121.7	32.6
Las Vegas, NV-AZ	2 560	20 871	2 152.4	845.2	990	21 588	3 924	637	2 542	190 873	12 597.4	3 823.1
Lawrence, KS	192	1 280	84.5	33.1	76	4 240	729	120	240	4 627	120.7	34.2
Lawton, OK	127	1 062	63.0	30.5	51	3 325	901	120	203	3 660	96.9	28.9
Lewiston-Auburn, ME	151	1 672	191.6	54.3	183	8 233	1 219	227	180	2 438	77.4	23.3
Lexington, KY	1 040	9 563	1 150.2	316.9	550	44 382	15 908	1 675	957	21 830	706.4	202.0
Lima, OH	217	1 158	77.9	26.6	225	17 765	8 369	697	333	5 793	165.4	43.6
Lincoln, NE	483	7 161	688.0	211.6	267	15 322	3 855	502	545	11 230	318.5	91.8
Little Rock-North Little Rock, AR	1 433	10 922	991.0	428.9	635	31 679	6 195	864	1 049	21 213	644.8	181.1
Longview-Marshall, TX	383	2 140	206.5	74.4	326	16 739	4 090	544	377	5 963	192.8	53.7
Los Angeles-Riverside-Orange County, CA	35 753	449 814	44 285.7	17 310.0	28 102	981 382	171 359	32 251	26 797	473 565	18 990.5	5 116.8
Los Angeles-Long Beach, CA	22 194	346 290	31 678.8	12 767.4	17 915	622 302	106 706	20 311	15 718	267 157	11 074.3	2 991.3
Orange County, CA	8 838	75 635	9 728.8	3 540.6	5 767	215 936	39 134	7 644	5 397	105 298	4 241.7	1 133.2
Riverside-San Bernardino, CA	3 124	17 060	1 648.8	537.2	3 412	109 582	19 355	3 160	4 482	79 231	2 899.1	782.9
Ventura, CA	1 597	10 829	1 229.3	464.9	1 008	33 562	6 163	1 136	1 200	21 879	775.3	209.4
Louisville, KY-IN	2 262	17 402	1 639.8	559.3	1 333	80 938	34 197	2 882	1 882	43 541	1 364.7	395.7
Lubbock, TX	483	2 516	198.6	67.7	258	7 286	1 566	204	522	11 154	332.1	87.6
Lynchburg, VA	351	3 422	325.9	130.0	298	23 078	5 392	770	323	6 030	174.8	48.6
Macon, GA	530	3 737	307.7	109.4	292	18 617	7 022	688	579	11 830	357.8	96.7
Madison, WI	1 132	10 748	943.4	412.4	564	26 568	4 841	864	993	18 607	554.1	156.9
Mansfield, OH	209	1 092	82.5	26.6	310	21 787	3 639	779	366	5 773	170.7	46.4
McAllen-Edinburg-Mission, TX	482	2 682	193.4	62.7	261	10 284	1 428	178	626	10 871	352.1	90.1
Medford-Ashland, OR	341	1 917	99.5	35.4	301	7 428	1 424	202	474	6 253	205.3	60.3
Melbourne-Titusville-Palm Bay,FL	1 073	11 192	1 195.6	455.0	494	20 832	3 451	754	860	16 207	495.3	136.3
Memphis, TN-AR-MS	1 864	16 144	1 555.7	583.1	1 156	58 220	14 625	1 868	1 689	40 218	1 509.6	409.5

1. Firms subject to federal tax.

Table C. Metropolitan Areas — Health and Other Services and Federal Funds

Area Name	Health Care and Social Assistance[1], 1997				Other Services[1], 1997				Federal funds and grants, fiscal 2001[2]			
									Expenditures (mil dol)			
									Total	Direct payments for individuals		
	Number of Establishments	Number of Employees	Receipts (mil dol)	Annual Payroll (mil dol)	Number of Establishments	Number of Employees	Receipts (mil dol)	Annual Payroll (mil dol)	Total	Social Security and government retirement	Medicare	Food stamps and Supplemental Security Income
	159	160	161	162	163	164	165	166	167	168	169	170
Hartford, CT	2 490	34 766	2 323.9	1 117.7	2 136	12 552	871.9	269.8	7 493.2	2 366.7	1 119.9	150.9
Hattiesburg, MS	183	3 307	226.7	121.0	128	860	53.6	15.0	559.6	229.9	88.6	28.0
Hickory-Morganton-Lenoir, NC	498	7 610	491.1	220.8	459	2 462	147.7	45.0	1 234.2	666.3	223.9	37.6
Honolulu, HI	1 730	13 474	1 231.7	563.1	1 097	8 402	560.8	170.7	7 775.6	2 046.2	555.7	183.5
Houma, LA	319	3 564	230.7	110.6	267	2 468	212.0	59.0	815.6	344.8	173.5	53.8
Houston-Galveston-Brazoria, TX	8 592	112 349	7 912.8	3 268.2	6 611	54 362	3 715.9	1 138.4	19 941.1	5 732.4	2 738.8	682.9
Brazoria, TX	306	2 905	155.5	65.8	298	1 312	88.5	24.1	703.4	353.6	136.0	22.0
Galveston-Texas City, TX	360	4 424	215.2	97.2	358	2 159	134.4	39.7	1 295.4	460.5	220.2	36.8
Houston, TX	7 926	105 020	7 542.1	3 105.2	5 955	50 891	3 493.0	1 074.7	17 942.2	4 918.2	2 382.6	624.1
Huntington-Ashland, WV-KY-OH	554	7 006	474.1	231.8	437	2 595	135.0	41.9	1 931.7	841.5	305.0	108.2
Huntsville, AL	658	7 547	539.0	225.7	530	2 873	152.8	50.8	5 057.5	860.1	196.1	56.6
Indianapolis, IN	2 997	40 791	2 652.3	1 221.8	2 489	18 324	1 094.5	343.4	9 082.2	3 064.0	1 185.3	215.3
Iowa City, IA	181	1 907	97.5	41.4	152	767	43.3	12.5	595.6	136.8	38.3	6.1
Jackson, MI	299	2 649	180.0	85.7	238	1 294	77.2	22.2	663.6	322.5	128.0	27.9
Jackson, MS	769	11 744	878.5	376.6	608	4 229	277.1	80.6	3 104.5	853.2	300.3	111.1
Jackson, TN	214	3 917	299.9	152.7	182	1 106	60.3	18.9	515.6	206.1	92.0	24.3
Jacksonville, FL	2 134	29 760	2 180.5	991.4	1 859	11 003	714.9	217.1	6 878.1	2 611.7	879.4	172.5
Jacksonville, NC	188	2 489	127.1	57.5	195	914	45.5	13.4	1 624.5	328.2	48.3	18.8
Jamestown, NY	243	2 304	109.8	49.9	178	721	45.2	11.3	750.1	323.1	121.2	27.2
Janesville-Beloit, WI	223	3 402	196.2	97.5	241	1 052	63.8	16.8	650.4	292.3	101.6	19.8
Johnson City-Kingsport-Bristol, TN-VA	859	12 513	847.1	388.8	663	3 823	199.5	63.8	2 598.0	1 235.4	433.2	103.7
Johnstown, PA	484	3 732	233.7	114.7	345	1 492	96.1	24.7	1 502.8	630.4	328.9	49.1
Jonesboro, AR	214	3 357	245.4	115.8	118	623	39.5	10.0	407.4	153.9	53.8	17.5
Joplin, MO	298	3 468	204.8	86.7	299	1 411	79.4	21.4	1 038.9	336.1	132.9	27.7
Kalamazoo-Battle Creek, MI.	861	9 534	618.1	300.4	714	4 577	286.5	88.1	2 144.9	909.4	344.5	74.1
Kansas City, MO-KS	3 389	45 900	3 101.9	1 410.5	3 045	19 363	1 217.6	372.6	9 684.8	3 505.4	1 449.3	220.6
Killeen-Temple, TX	325	6 424	432.2	148.1	378	1 965	94.1	29.6	3 027.6	710.8	136.5	31.2
Knoxville, TN	1 348	15 182	1 241.9	583.3	1 071	6 437	346.9	109.6	6 018.9	1 620.5	563.6	136.5
Kokomo, IN	189	2 163	127.5	57.5	152	1 090	51.2	16.4	469.4	228.9	90.4	15.2
La Crosse, WI-MN	156	1 187	65.1	30.1	226	1 348	71.7	22.0	529.3	238.0	72.6	13.6
Lafayette, IN	212	3 067	229.9	107.7	273	1 795	113.7	33.6	740.1	284.4	95.9	14.9
Lafayette, LA	887	11 407	779.2	306.4	552	3 271	215.0	64.4	1 826.8	617.1	321.3	113.6
Lake Charles, LA	405	4 756	319.7	131.7	262	1 914	122.2	35.7	803.7	355.8	175.5	38.8
Lakeland-Winter Haven, FL..	643	9 886	657.7	279.4	611	3 224	199.6	60.6	2 234.6	1 240.9	463.8	95.1
Lancaster, PA	710	8 212	523.8	252.0	808	4 429	276.4	81.6	1 796.5	921.2	317.8	43.8
Lansing-East Lansing, MI	882	7 532	497.6	237.9	612	3 933	212.9	68.2	3 961.3	937.4	297.4	63.5
Laredo, TX	227	4 330	207.1	94.8	190	951	48.0	13.3	746.0	173.2	101.8	59.0
Las Cruces, NM	272	3 149	177.9	75.3	169	1 025	43.9	13.2	1 088.9	321.3	82.3	49.9
Las Vegas, NV-AZ	2 330	31 173	2 708.3	1 047.0	1 540	12 172	784.8	241.2	6 888.2	3 351.3	983.8	178.9
Lawrence, KS	175	1 648	88.7	41.8	132	782	42.5	13.5	349.5	136.2	39.4	7.1
Lawton, OK	208	2 349	141.5	52.8	146	778	36.3	10.9	1 224.2	323.2	59.6	21.6
Lewiston-Auburn, ME	221	2 542	149.6	68.4	191	714	46.2	12.9	536.8	234.0	90.2	24.4
Lexington, KY	925	13 727	946.7	413.5	721	4 533	239.1	75.4	2 258.4	845.5	267.8	87.0
Lima, OH	268	3 440	203.1	103.9	256	1 502	86.6	25.6	819.6	447.2	129.5	26.8
Lincoln, NE	548	6 380	376.7	184.1	418	2 512	134.2	42.0	1 436.7	461.4	116.4	25.1
Little Rock-North Little Rock, AR	1 277	15 592	1 114.6	521.4	913	5 497	333.5	96.2	3 952.0	1 334.1	420.2	100.9
Longview-Marshall, TX	441	6 511	366.4	155.4	330	2 092	141.7	38.4	971.9	466.0	200.4	37.4
Los Angeles-Riverside-Orange County, CA	33 476	327 415	26 324.3	10 252.6	21 477	141 666	10 056.3	2 867.1	76 494.4	21 820.3	13 732.5	3 328.7
Los Angeles-Long Beach, CA	20 278	196 543	15 709.6	6 162.8	13 134	86 614	6 086.4	1 734.3	48 957.5	11 382.0	8 544.5	2 330.6
Orange County, CA	6 986	66 269	5 571.4	2 170.8	4 249	28 174	2 101.9	600.0	10 905.9	3 884.7	2 097.1	342.3
Riverside-San Bernardino, CA	4 621	51 493	3 956.7	1 505.8	3 219	21 301	1 425.5	406.0	12 968.0	5 296.2	2 544.8	584.8
Ventura, CA	1 591	13 110	1 086.6	413.1	875	5 577	442.5	126.7	3 663.0	1 257.4	546.1	71.0
Louisville, KY-IN	2 103	33 050	2 164.8	960.4	1 752	11 917	729.2	232.6	5 517.5	2 208.3	899.6	100.0
Lubbock, TX	622	8 383	566.2	239.1	405	3 053	178.4	53.2	1 495.8	420.4	237.1	41.5
Lynchburg, VA	308	4 115	223.8	107.9	347	1 753	98.4	30.1	1 451.8	549.6	142.2	34.5
Macon, GA	695	10 878	806.2	323.2	516	2 660	155.5	47.1	2 741.8	877.5	280.6	84.5
Madison, WI	785	9 899	735.9	320.2	664	4 412	258.5	88.8	2 977.3	711.8	199.7	33.8
Mansfield, OH	333	3 607	192.8	88.8	252	1 838	100.9	37.0	805.1	379.3	150.8	27.5
McAllen-Edinburg-Mission, TX	833	15 858	1 167.0	431.0	479	2 465	114.3	30.6	2 151.8	536.9	322.6	204.4
Medford-Ashland, OR	384	3 810	244.3	110.5	222	1 192	80.6	21.6	927.4	467.4	122.0	29.7
Melbourne-Titusville-Palm Bay, FL	1 017	10 631	783.2	358.0	728	3 778	206.4	63.8	4 566.9	1 724.7	524.2	62.8
Memphis, TN-AR-MS	1 960	25 156	2 127.2	896.9	1 599	12 008	763.7	240.1	6 558.2	2 021.2	824.3	341.6

1. Firms subject to federal tax.   2. October 1, 1998 to September 30, 1999.

	Federal funds and grants, fiscal 2001[1] (cont'd)							Local government finances, 1997				
	Expenditures (mil dol) (cont'd)							General revenue				
	Procurement contract awards			Grants[2]						Taxes		
Area Name											Per capita[3] (dollars)	
	Salaries and wages	Defense	Other	Medicaid and other health-related	Nutrition and family welfare	Education	Other	Total (mil dol)	Intergovernmental (mil dol)	Total (mil dol)	Total	Property
	171	172	173	174	175	176	177	178	179	180	181	182
Hartford, CT	421.6	979.1	221.5	805.3	370.5	145.8	607.1	2 831.2	916.6	1 617.2	1 463	1 448
Hattiesburg, MS	48.5	12.4	5.8	50.1	10.5	8.5	43.0	332.0	85.8	55.2	503	463
Hickory-Morganton-Lenoir, NC	50.7	13.7	14.7	117.8	22.5	20.8	36.7	674.7	319.6	161.2	506	383
Honolulu, HI	2 424.9	1 182.8	127.3	403.4	173.4	145.5	385.5	996.0	150.0	526.9	606	476
Houma, LA	32.8	21.0	20.0	89.0	20.2	16.7	16.7	507.9	165.1	128.6	673	245
Houston-Galveston-Brazoria, TX	1 652.6	1 068.9	3 735.3	1 728.7	339.8	209.4	620.4	10 824.0	2 713.5	5 502.7	1 274	1 036
Brazoria, TX	28.0	11.8	8.5	45.7	6.0	5.8	26.3	460.1	111.3	246.4	1 093	978
Galveston-Texas City, TX .	58.6	173.6	49.6	160.2	18.5	9.7	29.0	701.8	155.0	395.5	1 628	1 437
Houston, TX	1 566.0	883.5	3 677.2	1 522.7	315.2	193.9	565.0	9 662.2	2 447.2	4 860.9	1 262	1 014
Huntington-Ashland, WV-KY-OH	140.2	11.8	49.6	290.4	48.6	23.1	52.4	539.6	284.9	153.1	486	363
Huntsville, AL	745.5	2 286.0	591.5	102.7	16.0	24.0	102.6	607.8	225.3	197.4	593	226
Indianapolis, IN	876.2	897.5	251.2	826.7	385.9	202.0	625.2	3 923.4	1 351.6	1 632.2	1 086	945
Iowa City, IA	73.4	1.7	73.1	174.4	4.1	5.9	32.4	199.1	69.1	84.8	829	768
Jackson, MI	27.5	11.2	7.2	64.4	21.5	9.0	15.1	370.0	218.4	75.9	489	432
Jackson, MS	290.6	228.2	106.6	319.3	228.6	147.5	376.3	825.6	367.6	268.9	632	592
Jackson, TN	32.4	0.6	6.9	88.8	7.8	7.6	10.8	383.8	72.8	77.6	781	444
Jacksonville, FL	1 534.4	441.3	215.7	384.4	129.9	69.6	205.2	2 368.7	882.9	823.9	796	614
Jacksonville, NC	928.6	209.9	5.1	40.9	11.2	7.5	6.4	222.6	130.6	48.8	341	218
Jamestown, NY	26.3	22.4	46.1	96.2	27.1	13.3	24.0	483.0	200.9	189.6	1 354	1 078
Janesville-Beloit, WI	20.0	42.4	8.4	79.3	22.3	10.0	9.8	445.3	253.4	124.8	830	810
Johnson City-Kingsport-Bristol, TN-VA	170.9	8.1	107.4	335.6	45.8	30.8	52.2	734.5	287.5	298.4	648	412
Johnstown, PA	91.8	110.1	26.2	146.0	26.4	10.3	44.0	514.4	239.8	144.0	606	472
Jonesboro, AR	24.1	0.0	5.4	36.0	11.3	8.1	24.1	110.0	53.7	36.3	471	305
Joplin, MO	31.6	17.4	336.7	90.3	15.4	10.2	14.0	247.9	92.5	89.0	605	335
Kalamazoo-Battle Creek, MI.	229.8	26.6	66.9	251.1	71.2	35.1	45.1	1 231.2	646.4	309.6	693	646
Kansas City, MO-KS	1 593.4	300.2	925.0	731.1	150.8	85.9	289.1	4 568.5	1 373.2	1 960.3	1 147	719
Killeen-Temple, TX	1 583.3	260.5	38.8	76.0	18.1	54.6	24.6	641.6	328.3	174.9	584	426
Knoxville, TN	350.9	36.3	2 528.4	375.8	58.1	49.7	130.8	1 267.7	381.3	570.4	872	456
Kokomo, IN	21.0	0.1	5.7	45.5	10.2	2.2	8.9	333.0	91.1	118.9	1 190	1 089
La Crosse, WI-MN	31.9	26.3	9.5	57.4	13.7	8.5	20.8	360.6	170.3	107.4	884	806
Lafayette, IN	37.4	7.7	10.8	78.2	10.7	7.7	103.1	326.4	121.4	139.7	815	716
Lafayette, LA	79.9	20.3	42.8	355.1	45.5	30.3	57.1	571.6	259.4	199.7	537	163
Lake Charles, LA	36.4	8.5	15.8	84.5	16.1	11.6	15.9	480.0	111.0	238.5	1 334	449
Lakeland-Winter Haven, FL ..	81.2	7.4	23.5	134.0	56.6	29.6	55.8	896.4	388.5	274.6	612	505
Lancaster, PA	100.0	86.2	54.0	124.0	28.3	12.4	60.6	904.6	306.8	395.6	871	677
Lansing-East Lansing, MI	168.6	64.5	33.5	360.7	606.7	283.8	975.2	1 198.7	633.6	312.9	700	629
Laredo, TX	85.4	2.7	25.8	172.2	51.5	20.4	28.7	516.1	305.2	128.1	699	543
Las Cruces, NM	143.6	160.4	63.2	110.9	26.9	18.8	71.6	371.2	203.5	61.6	365	198
Las Vegas, NV-AZ	743.7	157.9	655.6	317.1	110.0	61.7	195.9	3 791.3	1 416.0	1 173.1	929	545
Lawrence, KS	30.9	2.1	7.1	41.5	6.6	23.4	31.1	214.2	55.5	76.4	839	656
Lawton, OK	577.9	119.9	10.7	41.0	15.7	13.6	15.7	265.5	104.9	49.1	431	208
Lewiston-Auburn, ME	22.1	1.9	4.5	88.1	14.7	7.3	14.5	207.6	72.2	111.1	1 099	1 053
Lexington, KY	239.2	135.3	93.9	245.5	38.8	33.8	116.1	855.7	244.3	337.9	761	339
Lima, OH	33.3	13.2	10.0	58.6	19.2	8.7	16.8	319.8	134.1	123.8	799	527
Lincoln, NE	148.9	27.9	26.4	162.5	116.7	75.7	191.1	605.8	149.9	273.2	1 171	924
Little Rock-North Little Rock, AR	604.3	139.0	81.5	302.0	171.6	139.1	495.0	1 098.3	416.5	360.2	652	394
Longview-Marshall, TX	31.5	5.1	7.0	140.1	16.6	9.9	26.4	409.4	140.9	199.7	959	786
Los Angeles-Riverside-Orange County, CA	5 660.8	10 441.2	3 843.6	8 198.5	3 152.6	1 078.8	2 303.7	52 345.9	27 358.9	13 323.6	854	578
Los Angeles-Long Beach, CA	3 074.6	7 583.4	2 949.5	6 248.8	2 348.4	694.4	1 695.2	33 598.5	18 386.9	8 143.3	890	573
Orange County, CA	704.5	1 758.7	462.8	734.5	246.6	129.8	167.2	7 098.7	2 844.4	2 392.0	895	637
Riverside-San Bernardino, CA	1 238.4	557.8	370.6	1 011.2	475.9	215.3	326.7	9 537.1	5 269.0	2 160.1	705	519
Ventura, CA	643.3	541.4	60.7	204.0	81.7	39.2	114.6	2 111.5	858.6	628.3	865	668
Louisville, KY-IN	500.7	685.4	121.0	469.8	113.3	61.5	158.5	2 118.6	657.4	802.6	808	471
Lubbock, TX	74.1	8.7	16.3	100.0	22.5	11.6	57.7	644.4	274.3	179.0	776	586
Lynchburg, VA	44.6	4.9	513.6	68.4	15.1	11.2	21.6	353.5	153.4	141.7	683	595
Macon, GA	880.0	183.1	66.9	174.6	52.8	27.7	44.4	730.1	270.8	257.5	815	528
Madison, WI	239.5	18.5	92.8	424.3	244.1	196.5	660.7	1 241.6	461.4	558.9	1 406	1 306
Mansfield, OH	54.3	11.0	8.2	72.7	20.2	11.4	26.6	397.5	180.7	156.7	896	621
McAllen-Edinburg-Mission, TX	122.1	72.3	33.3	421.2	101.5	66.3	134.3	1 210.8	769.1	282.0	552	421
Medford-Ashland, OR	83.7	0.9	45.2	90.5	20.8	9.8	31.9	386.3	176.3	123.7	724	630
Melbourne-Titusville-Palm Bay, FL	387.0	1 005.5	633.6	67.9	31.9	23.3	66.5	992.6	322.6	330.2	716	569
Memphis, TN-AR-MS	826.9	382.5	519.4	920.1	180.7	69.2	177.9	2 428.3	833.1	903.2	834	507

1. October 1, 1998 to September 30, 1999.   2. State totals may include programs not allocated by county.   3. Based on the resident population estimated as of July 1 of the year shown.

Area Name	Local government finances, 1997 (cont'd)									Government employment, 1999			Presidential election, 2000[2]		
	Direct general expenditure							Debt outstanding					Percent of vote cast —		
			Percent of total for —												
	Total (mil dol)	Per capita[1] (dollars)	Education	Health and hospitals	Police protection	Public welfare	Highways	Total (mil dol)	Per capita[1] (dollars)	Federal civilian	Federal military	State and local	Democratic	Republican	All other
	183	184	185	186	187	188	189	190	191	192	193	194	195	196	197
Hartford, CT	2 852.3	2 581	54.2	0.9	5.7	1.6	4.2	1 457.8	1 319	7 761	2 862	83 925	58.7	35.7	5.5
Hattiesburg, MS	349.3	3 188	24.1	51.9	2.8	0.2	3.3	161.2	1 471	756	980	12 440	30.8	67.1	2.1
Hickory-Morganton-Lenoir, NC	663.2	2 083	47.1	16.1	4.3	7.3	2.7	262.0	823	888	978	21 501	33.8	65.5	0.7
Honolulu, HI	972.6	1 118	0.0	1.3	13.4	0.0	2.6	1 698.5	1 953	27 908	50 274	61 100	54.5	39.6	5.9
Houma, LA	465.6	2 435	38.2	36.9	4.1	0.5	3.8	211.1	1 104	436	1 124	13 440	40.8	56.1	3.1
Houston-Galveston-Brazoria, TX	10 632.2	2 461	48.0	8.3	6.5	0.3	3.6	18 544.6	4 293	27 123	13 349	275 159	40.1	57.3	2.7
Brazoria, TX	453.6	2 012	61.7	6.0	4.8	0.5	5.1	409.3	1 816	462	657	14 007	31.1	66.8	2.1
Galveston-Texas City, TX	704.7	2 900	54.3	7.1	5.3	0.3	3.4	794.6	3 270	923	1 013	28 066	43.0	54.2	2.7
Houston, TX	9 473.9	2 460	46.9	8.5	6.7	0.3	3.5	17 340.7	4 502	25 738	11 679	233 086	40.5	56.9	2.6
Huntington-Ashland, WV-KY-OH	549.5	1 743	59.1	2.9	3.4	1.6	2.6	518.5	1 645	2 856	1 276	17 747	47.6	50.2	2.3
Huntsville, AL	692.9	2 081	42.8	6.5	5.1	0.2	4.9	885.3	2 659	15 246	3 469	24 319	41.8	55.8	2.5
Indianapolis, IN	4 009.2	2 667	45.0	12.7	4.0	2.9	3.5	4 552.1	3 028	14 847	6 302	94 391	38.9	58.7	2.4
Iowa City, IA	217.3	2 124	38.7	3.8	4.5	3.4	13.1	200.7	1 961	1 572	504	26 180	59.1	33.9	7.0
Jackson, MI	396.5	2 552	58.8	7.3	3.4	3.4	5.1	218.2	1 404	453	311	9 327	45.5	51.8	2.7
Jackson, MS	852.7	2 004	48.2	7.8	6.5	0.8	6.2	642.9	1 511	5 323	3 093	45 565	41.0	56.5	2.4
Jackson, TN	414.9	4 178	20.2	48.1	2.8	0.1	2.9	242.3	2 439	578	394	10 723	45.3	53.8	0.8
Jacksonville, FL	2 394.3	2 314	44.3	2.8	6.1	0.5	3.0	5 726.5	5 535	17 657	25 127	46 847	36.6	61.4	1.9
Jacksonville, NC	245.6	1 717	54.8	7.5	4.2	4.9	1.4	93.6	655	5 284	37 114	7 289	34.0	65.1	1.0
Jamestown, NY	511.1	3 650	49.3	1.7	2.8	13.4	7.8	276.8	1 977	414	278	9 491	46.0	49.5	4.5
Janesville-Beloit, WI	465.5	3 097	46.7	5.1	5.4	12.2	6.5	271.6	1 807	347	533	8 288	57.5	39.0	3.5
Johnson City-Kingsport-Bristol, TN-VA	731.5	1 590	53.1	4.9	5.4	1.3	6.3	582.6	1 266	3 318	1 800	26 219	38.3	59.9	1.8
Johnstown, PA	531.5	2 236	51.5	3.4	1.7	6.6	3.8	972.4	4 091	1 469	924	12 735	45.4	51.7	2.9
Jonesboro, AR	111.5	1 449	60.6	0.5	4.6	0.0	6.7	139.4	1 812	427	436	5 726	49.2	48.3	2.5
Joplin, MO	251.2	1 708	53.5	8.0	4.8	0.4	7.8	60.1	408	502	721	7 876	31.0	66.7	2.2
Kalamazoo-Battle Creek, MI.	1 306.7	2 925	51.1	8.0	5.1	1.5	5.9	1 083.0	2 424	5 078	928	30 087	48.5	48.2	3.2
Kansas City, MO-KS	4 597.7	2 690	44.8	7.6	6.6	0.6	5.2	5 859.7	3 428	28 031	12 535	107 389	49.1	47.8	3.1
Killeen-Temple, TX	596.8	1 991	65.2	4.8	3.8	0.4	2.5	705.1	2 352	8 079	42 839	20 395	32.5	65.7	1.7
Knoxville, TN	1 343.9	2 054	43.5	7.2	5.0	0.8	5.8	1 272.6	1 945	5 776	2 704	46 125	39.6	58.7	1.8
Kokomo, IN	291.7	2 918	40.0	24.6	3.9	2.0	4.0	126.2	1 263	369	350	6 533	36.9	60.6	2.4
La Crosse, WI-MN	376.5	3 098	49.2	4.4	4.7	7.7	8.0	249.6	2 054	574	455	9 465	50.1	44.7	5.1
Lafayette, IN	322.8	1 882	53.0	5.0	4.4	5.7	4.6	120.6	703	609	650	21 178	38.1	57.9	4.0
Lafayette, LA	561.9	1 510	55.8	8.0	5.5	0.1	4.0	664.8	1 787	1 406	2 099	22 318	40.9	56.1	3.0
Lake Charles, LA	455.7	2 548	39.3	7.7	8.3	0.4	7.4	617.0	3 450	644	1 007	12 597	46.1	51.7	2.2
Lakeland-Winter Haven, FL..	895.2	1 995	48.6	2.8	7.8	1.0	4.2	1 182.9	2 637	1 411	1 011	25 247	44.6	53.6	1.8
Lancaster, PA	1 006.5	2 217	55.1	2.5	3.2	4.2	3.5	1 478.9	3 257	1 606	1 545	16 971	31.4	66.1	2.5
Lansing-East Lansing, MI	1 302.0	2 911	57.8	1.7	4.2	2.7	4.2	1 126.7	2 519	2 874	1 308	52 781	52.4	44.6	3.0
Laredo, TX	515.0	2 811	52.4	1.2	4.6	0.5	5.3	352.8	1 926	1 902	508	13 049	57.4	41.4	1.2
Las Cruces, NM	387.8	2 302	48.7	22.3	3.4	1.1	3.6	251.1	1 490	3 440	672	14 713	51.3	45.6	3.2
Las Vegas, NV-AZ	4 067.4	3 223	32.4	8.1	7.3	1.3	7.3	6 394.0	5 066	9 280	9 458	65 208	49.7	46.1	4.2
Lawrence, KS	204.5	2 245	35.9	26.7	5.0	0.3	4.5	182.6	2 004	561	509	14 751	45.8	42.8	11.4
Lawton, OK	259.6	2 044	44.8	33.8	3.9	0.0	2.7	87.0	763	3 672	13 949	7 930	40.8	58.3	0.9
Lewiston-Auburn, ME	206.5	2 044	54.0	0.1	3.8	0.4	5.8	144.9	1 434	376	499	4 768	53.3	40.5	6.1
Lexington, KY	791.7	1 783	50.3	2.5	5.9	0.8	4.0	1 426.0	3 211	5 209	1 595	40 680	41.9	55.0	3.1
Lima, OH	309.6	1 998	52.5	2.7	4.6	5.7	4.7	138.4	893	576	398	9 788	30.7	66.6	2.7
Lincoln, NE	589.1	2 525	45.1	13.3	3.6	2.8	5.0	639.3	2 740	2 506	1 039	27 306	41.7	51.8	6.5
Little Rock-North Little Rock, AR	1 075.8	1 948	45.7	7.6	6.3	0.0	5.3	1 116.7	2 022	9 387	7 639	49 297	48.3	48.9	2.8
Longview-Marshall, TX	408.1	1 960	60.6	6.3	5.4	0.7	4.4	309.9	1 488	525	551	11 378	32.7	66.1	1.2
Los Angeles-Riverside-Orange County, CA	50 639.7	3 244	32.9	7.7	8.2	11.6	2.9	58 476.8	3 746	94 066	56 600	831 992	54.6	41.3	4.1
Los Angeles-Long Beach, CA	31 842.4	3 482	30.2	8.3	8.9	12.9	2.3	36 250.4	3 964	55 832	21 020	506 753	63.5	32.4	4.2
Orange County, CA	6 992.4	2 615	37.4	3.2	8.2	7.5	4.5	9 731.1	3 639	12 572	7 039	132 267	40.4	55.8	3.9
Riverside-San Bernardino, CA	9 723.8	3 174	37.6	8.8	6.1	11.6	3.5	11 158.6	3 642	17 248	21 467	160 250	46.1	50.1	3.9
Ventura, CA	2 081.2	2 867	37.2	8.8	7.1	6.5	3.7	1 336.7	1 841	8 414	7 074	32 722	47.1	48.2	4.7
Louisville, KY-IN	2 204.9	2 220	39.3	9.4	5.0	1.6	2.4	3 522.4	3 546	10 483	3 632	58 094	47.0	50.8	2.2
Lubbock, TX	567.6	2 461	42.2	28.0	4.5	0.1	2.5	429.7	1 863	1 256	643	21 271	24.3	73.7	2.0
Lynchburg, VA	355.5	1 714	51.3	3.4	4.6	3.8	4.0	391.1	1 885	1 111	814	12 161	37.0	60.4	2.7
Macon, GA	722.3	2 285	44.2	16.9	5.7	0.3	4.1	440.1	1 392	13 343	5 829	19 426	44.6	54.4	1.1
Madison, WI	1 305.1	3 283	48.5	2.1	5.5	9.8	5.4	1 280.3	3 221	4 209	1 583	68 140	61.1	32.6	6.3
Mansfield, OH	395.8	2 264	48.5	6.9	5.1	5.2	6.4	89.6	513	786	450	10 310	37.9	58.1	4.0
McAllen-Edinburg-Mission, TX	1 109.5	2 172	72.7	2.8	3.5	0.7	1.7	572.4	1 120	2 653	1 414	36 641	60.8	37.9	1.4
Medford-Ashland, OR	398.8	2 333	49.9	8.6	6.6	0.0	5.7	125.9	736	1 722	593	8 984	39.1	54.3	6.6
Melbourne-Titusville-Palm Bay, FL	964.9	2 093	45.0	7.6	6.9	0.5	4.7	1 111.7	2 412	5 415	3 425	19 851	44.6	52.7	2.7
Memphis, TN-AR-MS	2 572.9	2 375	39.0	11.6	7.9	0.3	3.7	3 054.7	2 820	15 693	6 283	66 660	52.9	45.8	1.3

1. Based on the resident population estimated as of July 1 of the year shown.   2. Data subject to copyright.

Table C. Metropolitan Areas — **Land Area and Population**

CMSA/ MSA/ PMSA/ NECMA code[1]	Area Name	Land area,[2] (sq km) 2000	Population and population characteristics, 2000													
			Total persons	Rank	Per square kilometer	Race alone or in combination (percent)				Percent Hispanic[3]	Age (percent)					
						White	Black	Am. Indian, Alaska Native	Asian and Pacific Islander		Under 5 years	5 to 17 years	18 to 24 years	25 to 34 years	35 to 44 years	45 to 54 years
		1	2	3	4	5	6	7	8	9	10	11	12	13	14	15
4940	Merced, CA....................	4 995	210 554	195	42.2	60.9	4.5	2.3	8.5	45.3	8.9	25.6	10.3	13.4	14.4	10.9
56	Miami-Fort Lauderdale, FL ..	8 162	3 876 380		474.9	72.4	21.9	0.5	2.4	40.3	6.4	17.9	8.3	14.7	16.5	12.8
2680	Fort Lauderdale, FL	3 122	1 623 018	36	519.9	72.4	22.2	0.5	3.0	16.7	6.3	17.2	7.2	14.2	17.2	13.3
5000	Miami, FL	5 040	2 253 362	23	447.1	72.3	21.6	0.4	2.0	57.3	6.5	18.3	9.1	15.0	16.1	12.5
63	Milwaukee-Racine, WI	4 644	1 689 572		363.8	79.1	15.8	0.9	2.3	6.5	6.9	19.6	9.0	13.7	16.4	13.7
5080	Milwaukee-Waukesha, WI	3 781	1 500 741	42	396.9	78.5	16.3	1.0	2.5	6.3	6.9	19.5	9.1	13.8	16.3	13.7
6600	Racine, WI....................	863	188 831	208	218.9	84.5	11.2	0.8	1.0	7.9	7.0	20.0	8.3	13.0	16.9	13.9
	Minneapolis-St. Paul, MN-															
5120	WI	15 703	2 968 806	13	189.1	87.7	6.2	1.3	4.8	3.3	7.2	19.6	9.2	15.4	17.8	13.7
5140	Missoula, MT	6 729	95 802	304	14.2	95.8	0.5	3.4	1.6	1.6	5.7	17.2	15.4	14.0	15.1	14.6
5160	Mobile, AL	7 328	540 258	98	73.7	70.2	27.7	1.1	1.4	1.4	7.0	19.7	9.3	13.0	15.4	13.3
5170	Modesto, CA..................	3 869	446 997	115	115.5	73.9	3.2	2.5	6.3	31.7	8.0	23.2	9.8	13.6	15.4	12.1
5200	Monroe, LA	1 581	147 250	245	93.1	65.0	33.8	0.5	0.9	1.2	7.2	20.7	12.0	13.5	14.4	12.2
5240	Montgomery, AL	5 198	333 055	148	64.1	59.3	39.3	0.7	1.2	1.2	6.9	19.3	10.7	14.4	15.9	13.1
5280	Muncie, IN...................	1 019	118 769	281	116.6	91.8	7.2	0.6	1.0	1.1	5.9	16.2	16.9	12.4	13.2	12.5
5330	Myrtle Beach, SC..............	2 936	196 629	203	67.0	82.0	15.9	0.8	1.1	2.6	5.7	15.6	9.4	14.2	15.1	13.7
5345	Naples, FL	5 246	251 377	175	47.9	87.4	5.5	0.5	0.9	19.6	5.3	14.5	6.6	11.2	13.3	11.7
5360	Nashville, TN	10 548	1 231 311	49	116.7	80.6	16.0	0.7	2.1	3.3	6.9	17.9	10.2	15.8	17.1	13.8
5523	New London-Norwich, CT ...	1 725	259 088	169	150.2	89.1	6.5	1.9	2.7	5.1	6.3	18.1	8.6	13.6	17.6	13.9
5560	New Orleans, LA	8 805	1 337 726	45	151.9	58.4	38.0	0.8	2.5	4.4	6.9	19.9	9.7	13.8	16.0	13.9
	New York-Northern New Jer- sey-Long Island, NY-															
70	NJ-CT-PA	27 065	21 199 865		783.3	66.3	18.4	0.8	7.7	18.2	6.8	18.0	8.7	15.0	16.6	13.5
0875	Bergen-Passaic, NJ	1 086	1 373 167	44	1 264.0	74.9	8.8	0.5	8.9	17.3	6.7	17.4	7.6	13.9	16.9	14.0
2281	Dutchess County, NY......	2 076	280 150	164	134.9	85.1	10.2	0.7	3.0	6.4	6.2	18.8	9.4	12.5	17.7	14.2
3640	Jersey City, NJ	121	608 975	86	5 036.2	59.9	14.7	0.8	10.5	39.8	6.4	16.2	10.4	19.6	16.0	11.9
	Middlesex-Somerset-															
5015	Hunterdon, NJ	2 705	1 169 641	52	432.4	75.5	8.6	0.5	12.0	11.2	6.8	17.6	8.2	14.8	18.1	14.1
5190	Monmouth-Ocean, NJ	2 870	1 126 217	56	392.4	89.5	6.3	0.4	3.2	5.7	6.6	18.2	6.8	11.8	16.7	13.8
5380	Nassau-Suffolk, NY.........	3 105	2 753 913	16	886.9	83.5	9.2	0.5	4.1	10.3	6.8	18.6	7.5	12.9	17.2	14.3
	New Haven-Bridgeport- Stamford-Danbury-															
5483	Waterbury, CT	3 189	1 706 575	30	535.1	81.1	11.5	0.6	3.3	11.0	6.9	18.2	7.8	13.5	16.9	13.9
5600	New York, NY	2 957	9 314 235	2	3 150.1	54.1	26.3	1.0	10.3	25.1	6.8	17.6	9.6	16.5	15.9	12.9
5640	Newark, NJ	4 086	2 032 989	26	497.5	67.7	23.3	0.5	4.6	13.3	7.1	18.5	7.9	14.2	17.2	13.9
5660	Newburgh, NY-PA	2 114	387 669	128	183.4	86.5	8.4	0.8	1.8	10.8	7.4	21.4	8.3	12.4	17.4	13.9
8480	Trenton, NJ	585	350 761	141	599.4	70.0	20.7	0.5	5.7	9.7	6.3	17.7	10.2	14.0	16.5	14.0
	Norfolk-Virginia Beach-New- port News, VA-NC															
5720		6 083	1 569 541	39	258.0	64.1	31.9	1.0	3.7	3.1	7.0	19.4	11.2	14.7	17.0	12.6
5790	Ocala, FL	4 089	258 916	170	63.3	85.3	12.0	1.0	1.0	6.0	5.2	16.2	6.4	10.2	13.6	12.1
5800	Odessa-Midland, TX..........	4 665	237 132	182	50.8	77.6	6.1	1.2	1.1	35.8	7.8	22.5	9.7	12.5	15.7	12.9
5880	Oklahoma City, OK...........	10 999	1 083 346	60	98.5	79.0	11.4	6.6	3.2	6.7	7.0	18.6	11.4	14.2	15.7	13.3
5920	Omaha, NE-IA	6 411	716 998	74	111.8	86.7	8.9	1.0	2.0	5.5	7.4	19.8	9.8	14.8	16.3	13.3
5960	Orlando, FL	9 041	1 644 561	34	181.9	77.0	14.9	0.8	3.5	16.5	6.5	18.3	9.5	15.1	16.7	13.0
5990	Owensboro, KY...............	1 198	91 545	306	76.4	94.6	4.8	0.4	0.7	0.9	6.7	19.1	9.0	12.6	15.8	13.7
6015	Panama City, FL..............	1 978	148 217	243	74.9	85.8	11.2	1.5	2.5	2.4	6.1	18.0	8.7	13.3	16.9	13.7
	Parkersburg-Marietta, WV-															
6020	OH	2 596	151 237	237	58.3	98.1	1.3	0.6	0.7	0.6	5.8	17.4	8.3	12.2	15.6	14.7
6080	Pensacola, FL.................	4 349	412 153	122	94.8	79.4	17.0	1.8	2.8	2.6	6.2	18.2	10.8	13.5	16.1	13.2
6120	Peoria-Pekin, IL	4 652	347 387	142	74.7	89.1	9.4	0.6	1.4	1.6	6.6	18.4	9.4	12.8	15.0	14.1
	Philadelphia-Wilmington- Atlantic City, PA-NJ-															
77	DE-MD	15 372	6 188 463		402.6	73.7	20.3	0.6	3.7	5.6	6.5	18.9	8.8	13.7	16.5	13.6
0560	Atlantic-Cape May, NJ	2 114	354 878	140	167.9	76.6	14.9	0.7	4.3	9.6	6.1	18.3	7.6	12.4	16.7	13.6
6160	Philadelphia, PA-NJ	9 985	5 100 931	5	510.9	73.3	20.9	0.5	3.9	5.1	6.5	18.9	8.8	13.6	16.4	13.6
	Vineland-Millville-Bridge-															
8760	ton, NJ	1 267	146 438	246	115.6	67.9	21.5	1.7	1.4	19.0	6.3	19.1	8.5	15.1	16.1	13.2
	Wilmington-Newark, DE-															
9160	MD	2 006	586 216	91	292.3	77.3	18.5	0.6	2.7	4.7	6.7	18.6	9.9	14.6	16.8	13.5
6200	Phoenix-Mesa, AZ	37 743	3 251 876	12	86.2	79.4	4.2	2.8	2.9	25.1	7.8	19.0	10.1	15.7	15.4	11.9
6240	Pine Bluff, AR	2 292	84 278	310	36.8	49.0	49.9	0.5	0.9	1.0	6.9	19.4	10.8	12.8	15.1	13.4
6280	Pittsburgh, PA................	11 980	2 358 695	22	196.9	90.3	8.6	0.4	1.4	0.7	5.6	16.7	8.1	12.2	15.9	14.4
6323	Pittsfield, MA.................	2 412	134 953	259	55.9	96.1	2.5	0.5	1.4	1.7	5.2	17.2	8.4	10.9	15.4	14.9
6340	Pocatello, ID	2 883	75 565	316	26.2	93.1	0.9	3.6	1.8	4.7	8.1	20.0	14.6	13.7	13.5	12.7
6403	Portland, ME	2 164	265 612	166	122.7	96.7	1.4	0.7	1.8	1.0	5.8	17.5	8.4	13.9	17.5	14.9
79	Portland-Salem, OR-WA......	18 007	2 265 223		125.8	87.2	3.0	2.0	5.7	8.7	7.1	18.6	9.5	15.2	16.2	14.6
	Portland-Vancouver, OR-															
6440	WA	13 022	1 918 009	27	147.3	87.4	3.4	1.9	6.2	7.4	7.0	18.5	9.3	15.5	16.5	14.8
7080	Salem, OR....................	4 986	347 214	143	69.6	85.9	1.2	2.7	2.7	15.6	7.4	19.6	10.5	13.6	14.4	13.4
	Providence-Warwick-Paw-															
6483	tucket, RI	2 437	962 886	63	395.1	86.3	5.6	1.0	3.0	9.2	6.1	17.6	10.3	13.4	16.2	13.4
6520	Provo-Orem, UT	5 176	368 536	135	71.2	94.0	0.5	1.0	2.6	7.0	11.0	23.1	21.0	15.2	10.6	7.9
6560	Pueblo, CO	6 187	141 472	252	22.9	82.4	2.3	2.6	1.2	38.0	6.7	19.1	9.4	12.4	14.8	13.5
6580	Punta Gorda, FL..............	1 796	141 627	251	78.8	93.5	4.8	0.5	1.2	3.3	3.7	12.0	4.5	7.6	11.2	11.8
	Raleigh-Durham-Chapel															
6640	Hill, NC	9 036	1 187 941	50	131.5	70.6	23.3	0.8	3.4	6.1	6.9	17.3	11.6	17.6	17.3	13.3
6660	Rapid City, SD	7 190	88 565	309	12.3	89.2	1.4	9.9	1.4	2.6	7.1	19.5	10.5	12.9	16.3	13.7

1. MSA = Metropolitan Statistical Area. CMSA = Consolidated MSA. PMSA = Primary MSA. NECMA = New England County Metropolitan Area. See Appendix A for explanation of these concepts. See Appendix B for list of metropolitan areas identified by type, with component counties.   2. Dry land or land partially or temporarily covered by water.   3. Hispanic persons may be of any race.

Table C. Metropolitan Areas — **Population and Households**

Area Name	55 to 64 years	65 to 74 years	75 years and over	Percent female	2001	1990	1990–2000	2000–2001	Births	Deaths	Net migration	Number	Percent change, 1990–2000	Persons per household	Female family householder[1]	One person
	16	17	18	19	20	21	22	23	24	25	26	27	28	29	30	31
Merced, CA........................	7.0	5.3	4.2	50.2	219 096	178 403	18.0	4.1	4 517	1 730	5 742	63 815	15.3	3.25	14.1	17.7
Miami-Fort Lauderdale, FL ...	8.9	7.2	7.3	51.7	3 958 243	3 192 725	21.4	2.1	69 063	44 239	56 981	1 431 219	17.2	2.66	15.1	26.2
Fort Lauderdale, FL..........	8.4	7.2	8.9	51.7	1 668 560	1 255 531	29.3	2.8	27 574	20 344	38 431	654 445	23.8	2.45	12.5	29.6
Miami, FL......................	9.2	7.2	6.1	51.7	2 289 683	1 937 194	16.3	1.6	41 489	23 895	18 550	776 774	12.2	2.84	17.2	23.3
Milwaukee-Racine, WI	8.2	6.4	6.2	51.4	1 692 074	1 607 183	5.1	0.1	30 778	18 439	-9 847	658 476	9.5	2.51	12.8	28.2
Milwaukee-Waukesha, WI.	8.1	6.4	6.2	51.5	1 502 461	1 432 149	4.8	0.1	27 574	16 476	-9 464	587 657	9.3	2.50	12.9	28.7
Racine, WI....................	8.6	6.4	5.9	50.5	189 613	175 034	7.9	0.4	3 204	1 963	-383	70 819	11.1	2.59	12.3	24.5
Minneapolis-St. Paul, MN-WI	7.6	4.9	4.7	50.6	3 015 573	2 538 776	16.9	1.6	54 473	23 535	15 294	1 136 615	18.4	2.56	9.7	26.7
Missoula, MT.....................	7.9	5.0	5.0	50.0	96 303	78 687	21.8	0.5	1 328	844	51	38 439	24.9	2.40	9.2	28.0
Mobile, AL........................	9.3	7.1	5.8	51.9	545 572	476 923	13.3	1.0	10 424	6 511	1 406	205 515	18.2	2.58	15.7	24.4
Modesto, CA	7.4	5.5	5.0	50.8	468 566	370 522	20.6	4.8	8 802	4 204	16 758	145 146	15.8	3.03	13.7	19.4
Monroe, LA	8.1	6.5	5.4	52.8	146 678	142 191	3.6	-0.4	2 926	1 683	-1 795	55 216	9.3	2.58	17.9	25.8
Montgomery, AL.................	8.4	6.1	5.2	51.7	334 310	292 517	13.9	0.4	6 634	3 822	-1 568	124 808	18.3	2.53	16.7	26.5
Muncie, IN........................	9.4	7.1	6.4	52.0	118 531	119 659	-0.7	-0.2	1 799	1 491	-503	47 131	4.3	2.37	10.9	28.2
Myrtle Beach, SC..............	11.3	9.4	5.6	50.9	202 425	144 053	36.5	2.9	3 041	2 274	4 994	81 800	46.7	2.37	11.5	25.8
Naples, FL........................	12.7	14.0	10.5	49.9	265 769	152 099	65.3	5.7	3 570	2 694	13 275	102 973	66.9	2.39	7.2	24.5
Nashville, TN.....................	8.3	5.5	4.5	51.1	1 251 830	985 026	25.0	1.7	22 547	12 215	9 783	479 569	27.6	2.49	12.3	26.3
New London-Norwich, CT.....	8.9	6.7	6.3	50.5	259 065	254 957	1.6	0.0	3 830	2 673	-1 051	99 835	7.1	2.48	11.0	26.0
New Orleans, LA.................	8.5	6.2	5.2	52.2	1 332 694	1 285 262	4.1	-0.4	26 061	15 627	-15 687	505 579	7.6	2.59	18.2	27.1
New York-Northern New Jersey-Long Island, NY-NJ-CT-PA	8.9	6.6	6.1	51.9	21 217 880	19 480 002	8.8	0.5	374 072	212 670	-48 374	7 735 264	8.5	2.68	14.7	26.7
Bergen-Passaic, NJ.......	9.4	7.2	6.9	51.8	1 377 757	1 296 252	5.9	0.3	22 285	15 152	-2 365	494 673	6.6	2.73	11.8	23.8
Dutchess County, NY.......	9.0	6.5	5.5	50.0	284 447	259 462	8.0	1.5	4 058	2 625	2 943	99 536	11.1	2.63	10.3	24.6
Jersey City, NJ	8.2	6.0	5.3	50.9	607 554	553 099	10.1	-0.2	10 958	5 798	-6 871	230 546	10.4	2.60	16.6	29.5
Middlesex-Somerset-Hunterdon, NJ	8.6	6.3	5.5	50.9	1 184 281	1 019 786	14.7	1.3	19 299	10 235	5 865	418 477	14.6	2.72	9.7	22.3
Monmouth-Ocean, NJ	9.3	8.4	8.5	51.9	1 150 184	986 395	14.2	2.1	17 121	14 628	21 440	424 638	16.1	2.61	9.6	25.3
Nassau-Suffolk, NY........	9.4	7.2	6.2	51.4	2 773 621	2 609 212	5.5	0.7	45 809	27 522	2 267	916 686	7.1	2.95	10.9	18.6
New Haven-Bridgeport-Stamford-Danbury-Waterbury, CT	9.0	6.8	7.1	51.8	1 713 742	1 631 864	4.6	0.4	28 336	18 793	-1 809	643 272	5.5	2.58	13.0	26.0
New York, NY..................	8.7	6.3	5.6	52.5	9 333 651	8 546 846	9.0	0.2	178 288	90 211	-70 960	3 484 108	7.1	2.61	18.1	30.8
Newark, NJ.....................	9.0	6.3	5.9	51.8	2 041 824	1 915 724	6.1	0.4	36 082	20 755	-6 549	729 062	6.3	2.73	14.4	24.0
Newburgh, NY-PA	8.4	5.9	5.0	49.9	397 290	335 603	15.5	2.5	6 261	3 438	6 811	132 221	18.0	2.83	10.9	21.4
Trenton, NJ.....................	8.6	6.4	6.1	51.3	353 529	325 759	7.7	0.8	5 575	3 513	854	125 807	7.6	2.62	13.8	25.6
Norfolk-Virginia Beach-Newport News, VA-NC	7.8	5.7	4.6	50.7	1 583 170	1 444 710	8.6	0.9	30 870	15 381	-1 367	577 659	13.0	2.60	14.9	23.4
Ocala, FL..........................	11.8	13.6	10.9	51.7	267 889	194 835	32.9	3.5	3 565	3 941	9 199	106 755	36.6	2.36	10.7	25.0
Odessa-Midland, TX	7.7	6.5	4.8	51.5	237 616	225 545	5.1	0.2	5 409	2 280	-2 641	86 591	6.6	2.70	12.6	24.1
Oklahoma City, OK	8.5	6.2	5.2	51.0	1 092 342	958 839	13.0	0.8	19 455	12 083	1 822	424 764	15.5	2.47	12.3	27.5
Omaha, NE-IA....................	7.8	5.7	4.9	50.9	723 210	639 580	12.1	0.9	13 924	6 525	-983	275 565	14.7	2.55	11.4	26.9
Orlando, FL.......................	8.5	6.8	5.6	50.8	1 707 175	1 224 844	34.3	3.8	28 627	15 582	48 976	625 248	34.4	2.58	12.4	23.5
Owensboro, KY..................	9.2	7.3	6.5	51.9	91 793	87 189	5.0	0.3	1 709	1 092	-330	36 033	9.1	2.47	11.8	27.1
Panama City, FL.................	10.0	7.9	5.4	50.5	150 316	126 994	16.7	1.4	2 536	1 739	1 354	59 597	21.8	2.43	12.0	26.0
Parkersburg-Marietta, WV-OH	10.7	8.1	7.2	51.7	150 532	149 169	1.4	-0.5	2 191	2 123	-721	61 412	6.2	2.41	10.1	26.4
Pensacola, FL....................	9.4	7.2	5.5	50.2	416 306	344 406	19.7	1.0	7 188	4 768	1 742	154 842	20.5	2.50	13.8	24.7
Peoria-Pekin, IL	9.2	7.4	7.1	51.4	345 824	339 172	2.4	-0.4	5 868	4 207	-3 170	135 857	5.0	2.47	10.7	27.0
Philadelphia-Wilmington-Atlantic City, PA-NJ-DE-MD	8.7	6.9	6.5	51.9	6 215 629	5 893 019	5.0	0.4	103 206	74 011	-1 314	2 320 719	7.4	2.58	14.2	26.9
Atlantic-Cape May, NJ	9.7	8.1	7.4	51.7	357 831	319 416	11.1	0.8	5 497	4 459	2 080	137 172	11.5	2.52	13.6	28.0
Philadelphia, PA-NJ	8.7	6.9	6.6	52.1	5 116 830	4 922 257	3.6	0.3	84 845	61 828	-6 818	1 914 246	6.3	2.58	14.3	27.1
Vineland-Millville-Bridgeton, NJ	8.7	6.6	6.4	49.0	146 289	138 053	6.1	0.1	2 441	1 749	-808	49 143	4.3	2.73	17.3	23.6
Wilmington-Newark, DE-MD	8.4	6.1	5.3	51.3	594 679	513 293	14.2	1.4	10 423	5 975	4 232	220 158	16.6	2.58	13.1	24.9
Phoenix-Mesa, AZ	8.0	6.4	5.6	49.8	3 383 644	2 238 498	45.3	4.1	69 368	30 398	91 971	1 194 250	41.0	2.67	10.8	24.4
Pine Bluff, AR	8.7	6.6	6.3	51.1	83 565	85 487	-1.4	-0.8	1 794	1 142	-1 368	30 555	1.8	2.59	18.8	26.2
Pittsburgh, PA	9.5	8.8	8.9	52.3	2 347 163	2 394 811	-1.5	-0.5	31 830	35 231	-7 319	966 500	2.0	2.37	11.4	30.0
Pittsfield, MA	10.1	8.6	9.3	52.2	134 137	139 352	-3.2	-0.6	1 702	2 068	-391	56 006	3.1	2.30	11.0	32.0
Pocatello, ID	7.4	5.2	4.9	50.6	75 323	66 026	14.4	-0.3	1 713	750	-1 207	27 192	16.1	2.69	10.0	22.8
Portland, ME	8.7	6.6	6.7	51.6	266 988	243 135	9.2	0.5	3 609	2 937	-330	107 989	14.3	2.38	10.0	28.0
Portland-Salem, OR-WA.......	8.0	5.2	5.5	50.3	2 317 384	1 793 476	26.3	2.3	40 209	21 373	33 470	866 475	25.4	2.56	10.0	25.9
Portland-Vancouver, OR-WA	8.0	5.1	5.3	50.4	1 965 436	1 515 452	26.6	2.5	33 841	17 658	31 270	741 776	25.8	2.54	9.9	26.3
Salem, OR	8.2	6.2	6.6	50.0	351 948	278 024	24.9	1.4	6 368	3 715	2 200	124 699	22.7	2.68	10.7	23.7
Providence-Warwick-Pawtucket, RI	8.4	7.0	7.5	52.0	973 702	916 270	5.1	1.1	14 239	11 660	8 582	373 196	8.1	2.48	13.0	26.0
Provo-Orem, UT..................	4.8	3.4	3.0	50.4	377 411	263 590	39.8	2.4	11 939	1 896	-1 110	99 937	42.4	3.59	8.0	11.2
Pueblo, CO	8.9	8.0	7.2	51.1	144 955	123 051	15.0	2.5	2 514	1 767	2 728	54 579	16.0	2.52	13.3	26.6
Punta Gorda, FL	14.5	18.4	16.3	52.2	147 009	110 975	27.6	3.8	1 248	2 614	6 631	63 864	31.9	2.18	7.2	26.0
Raleigh-Durham-Chapel Hill, NC	7.3	4.7	3.9	50.9	1 231 528	858 516	38.4	3.7	22 733	9 794	30 350	461 097	37.8	2.48	11.0	26.4
Rapid City, SD	8.2	6.4	5.4	50.4	89 829	81 343	8.9	1.4	1 656	876	526	34 641	13.4	2.49	11.7	26.1

1. No spouse present.

Table C. Metropolitan Areas — **Vital Statistics, Health Resources, and Crime**

Area Name	Births, average 1997–1999		Deaths, average 1997–1999				Physicians[4] 1998		Hospitals[4] 1998	Beds		Medicare enrollees 1999	Serious crimes known to police, 2000[6] Total	
			Number		Rate									
	Total	Rate[1]	Total	Infant[2]	Total[1]	Infant[3]	Number	Rate[5]	Number	Number	Rate[5]		Number	Rate[7]
	32	33	34	35	36	37	38	39	40	41	42	43	44	45
Merced, CA	3 662	18.6	1 366	24	6.9	6.6	208	105	4	402	203	19 515	8 993	4 271
Miami-Fort Lauderdale, FL	51 393	14.1	34 646	317	9.5	6.2	10 605	290	45	14 195	388	555 395	262 781	6 779
Fort Lauderdale, FL	20 321	13.5	15 925	143	10.6	7.0	3 758	250	20	5 538	368	251 056	77 241	4 759
Miami, FL	31 072	14.4	18 721	174	8.7	5.6	6 847	318	25	8 657	402	304 339	185 540	8 234
Milwaukee-Racine, WI	23 019	14.0	14 352	NA	8.7	NA	4 478	272	24	5 053	307	239 390	74 502	4 466
Milwaukee-Waukesha, WI	20 445	14.0	12 791	NA	8.8	NA	4 227	290	21	4 492	308	211 807	66 445	4 492
Racine, WI	2 574	13.9	1 561	20	8.4	7.8	251	135	3	561	301	27 583	8 057	4 267
Minneapolis-St. Paul, MN-WI	41 937	14.8	18 641	NA	6.6	NA	6 448	228	32	6 454	228	311 942	119 781	4 038
Missoula, MT	1 044	11.7	650	NA	7.3	NA	273	307	2	336	378	10 947	NA	NA
Mobile, AL	7 951	15.0	5 159	96	9.7	12.1	1 083	203	9	1 997	375	79 155	29 676	6 675
Modesto, CA	6 993	16.4	3 342	48	7.8	6.9	642	151	7	1 478	347	53 593	23 840	5 333
Monroe, LA	2 237	15.2	1 330	21	9.1	9.4	332	226	5	1 012	689	19 459	9 568	7 209
Montgomery, AL	4 914	15.3	2 953	NA	9.2	NA	579	180	7	1 346	418	44 686	20 670	6 315
Muncie, IN	1 412	12.1	1 134	10	9.7	7.1	255	218	1	428	366	18 131	1 293	1 089
Myrtle Beach, SC	2 206	12.7	1 685	19	9.7	8.6	290	166	3	480	275	28 923	16 129	8 203
Naples, FL	2 599	13.0	2 158	20	10.8	7.7	772	387	2	500	251	47 572	9 954	3 960
Nashville, TN	17 156	14.9	9 416	NA	8.2	NA	3 288	284	20	4 620	400	138 150	73 778	5 992
New London-Norwich, CT	2 794	11.3	1 893	17	7.7	6.1	568	231	2	428	174	37 856	NA	NA
New Orleans, LA	19 414	14.8	12 215	141	9.3	0.0	4 280	327	30	6 084	465	176 100	74 355	5 852
New York-Northern New Jersey-Long Island, NY-NJ-CT-PA	289 737	14.5	170 273	1 843	8.5	6.4	68 326	341	209	78 109	390	2 871 592	596 056	3 213
Bergen-Passaic, NJ	18 074	13.5	11 710	95	8.7	5.3	4 808	358	12	5 100	379	205 188	32 683	2 380
Dutchess County, NY	3 383	12.7	2 172	18	8.2	5.3	610	230	3	686	259	39 721	5 905	2 169
Jersey City, NJ	8 518	15.3	4 789	68	8.6	8.0	903	162	9	2 435	437	72 790	23 990	3 939
Middlesex-Somerset-Hunterdon, NJ	15 613	13.9	8 311	78	7.4	5.0	3 278	292	8	2 478	221	141 127	26 414	2 258
Monmouth-Ocean, NJ	14 290	13.1	11 809	80	10.8	5.6	2 460	225	10	3 290	301	202 878	26 281	2 334
Nassau-Suffolk, NY	35 606	13.3	21 977	199	8.2	5.6	10 416	390	28	10 161	380	413 344	NA	NA
New Haven-Bridgeport-Stamford-Danbury-Waterbury, CT	22 485	13.8	14 679	141	9.0	6.3	6 015	369	16	4 233	259	254 330	57 265	3 506
New York, NY	133 915	15.4	71 942	895	8.3	6.7	32 328	372	84	37 201	428	1 174 061	315 783	3 418
Newark, NJ	27 973	14.3	17 087	202	8.8	7.2	5 814	298	28	9 797	502	270 024	74 600	3 669
Newburgh, NY-PA	5 465	14.8	2 819	NA	7.6	NA	601	163	6	1 054	285	47 027	9 471	2 556
Trenton, NJ	4 415	13.3	2 978	36	9.0	8.2	1 093	330	5	1 674	505	51 102	14 069	4 011
Norfolk-Virginia Beach-Newport News, VA-NC	23 306	15.0	11 659	NA	7.5	NA	3 377	219	17	3 960	257	175 380	70 188	4 472
Ocala, FL	2 754	11.4	3 096	23	12.8	8.4	385	159	2	534	221	66 595	11 853	4 578
Odessa-Midland, TX	4 250	17.5	1 785	31	7.4	7.3	369	150	4	719	293	28 744	10 376	4 361
Oklahoma City, OK	15 700	15.1	9 316	NA	9.0	NA	2 402	231	19	3 839	369	131 165	68 281	6 303
Omaha, NE-IA	10 635	15.3	5 316	78	7.7	7.3	1 884	272	12	3 380	487	84 892	38 183	5 325
Orlando, FL	21 201	14.1	12 225	143	8.1	6.7	2 925	194	19	4 593	305	221 252	97 547	5 940
Owensboro, KY	1 287	14.1	871	NA	9.6	NA	163	179	2	526	577	14 918	3 368	3 679
Panama City, FL	1 987	13.5	1 331	19	9.0	9.6	256	174	2	478	325	22 484	7 986	5 388
Parkersburg-Marietta, WV-OH	1 761	11.7	1 672	NA	11.1	NA	259	172	4	758	505	26 335	3 667	2 456
Pensacola, FL	5 495	13.8	3 556	47	8.9	8.6	845	211	6	1 792	448	57 141	13 817	3 882
Peoria-Pekin, IL	4 529	13.1	3 270	NA	9.5	NA	740	215	6	1 262	366	55 521	NA	NA
Philadelphia-Wilmington-Atlantic City, PA-NJ-DE-MD	80 874	13.5	58 889	651	9.8	8.0	19 431	324	89	22 024	368	908 766	246 143	3 992
Atlantic-Cape May, NJ	4 588	13.7	3 710	NA	11.0	NA	652	194	5	1 282	381	59 180	19 446	5 480
Philadelphia, PA-NJ	66 488	13.4	49 103	547	9.9	8.2	17 218	348	75	18 522	374	754 357	193 224	3 805
Vineland-Millville-Bridgeton, NJ	1 948	13.9	1 432	21	10.2	10.8	219	156	3	631	450	22 159	6 583	4 495
Wilmington-Newark, DE-MD	7 850	13.9	4 644	NA	8.2	NA	1 342	237	6	1 589	281	73 070	26 890	4 587
Phoenix-Mesa, AZ	50 193	17.1	22 803	377	7.8	7.5	6 392	218	29	6 561	224	379 791	200 403	6 169
Pine Bluff, AR	1 231	15.1	942	16	11.5	13.0	146	179	1	484	593	12 901	6 879	8 162
Pittsburgh, PA	25 719	11.0	27 502	178	11.7	6.9	7 028	300	37	10 636	453	451 678	55 558	2 536
Pittsfield, MA	1 330	10.0	1 570	5	11.8	3.8	374	281	4	595	447	26 555	2 951	2 439
Pocatello, ID	1 252	16.8	567	9	7.6	7.2	146	195	2	248	331	8 935	2 561	3 389
Portland, ME	2 921	11.5	2 296	13	9.0	4.5	1 007	397	6	1 049	414	40 254	7 850	2 955
Portland-Salem, OR-WA	31 467	14.6	16 863	161	7.8	5.1	5 271	245	22	4 140	193	267 786	113 632	5 023
Portland-Vancouver, OR-WA	26 380	14.5	13 949	134	7.7	5.1	4 710	259	18	3 623	199	218 812	95 353	4 979
Salem, OR	5 087	15.4	2 914	NA	8.8	NA	561	170	4	517	157	48 974	18 279	5 264
Providence-Warwick-Pawtucket, RI	11 489	12.7	8 974	76	9.9	6.6	2 722	301	9	2 614	289	156 769	33 506	3 480
Provo-Orem, UT	8 794	26.0	1 473	42	4.4	4.8	401	119	4	610	182	25 494	12 549	3 405
Pueblo, CO	1 838	13.6	1 372	15	10.2	8.2	324	240	2	563	417	24 749	6 338	4 480
Punta Gorda, FL	1 049	7.8	2 060	4	15.3	3.8	401	297	3	652	483	38 452	3 297	2 328
Raleigh-Durham-Chapel Hill, NC	16 265	15.1	7 355	133	6.8	8.2	4 405	408	13	3 374	312	117 113	61 358	5 240
Rapid City, SD	1 362	15.6	663	10	7.6	7.3	251	286	1	328	374	11 859	4 359	4 922

1. Per 1,000 estimated resident population, average 1997–1999. 2. Deaths of infants under 1 year old. 3. Deaths of infants under 1 year old per 1,000 live births. 4. Data subject to copyright. 5. Per 100,000 resident population as of July 1 of the year shown. 6. Data for serious crimes have not been adjusted for underreporting; this may affect comparability between geographic areas and over time. 7. Per 100,000 population estimated by the FBI.

Table C. Metropolitan Areas — Crime, Education, Money Income, and Poverty

Area Name	Serious crimes known to police, 2000[1] (cont'd) Rate[2] Violent	Property	Education — Enrollment[3] Total	Percent private	Attainment[4] (percent) High school graduate or more	Bachelor's degree or more	Local government expenditures, fiscal 1999[5] Total current expenditures (mil dol)	Current expenditures per student (dollars)	Money income 1989 Per capita[6] (dollars)	Households Median Dollars	Percent change, 1979–1989 (constant 1989 dollars)	Percent with $100,000 or more	Income and poverty, 1998 Median household income	Percent below poverty level All persons	Persons under 18	Persons 5–17 in families
	46	47	48	49	50	51	52	53	54	55	56	57	58	59	60	61
Merced, CA	621	3 650	56 282	6.6	63.1	12.0	295.6	5 943	10 606	25 547	3.9	2.8	NA	24.7	33.2	35.6
Miami-Fort Lauderdale, FL	969	5 810	778 956	20.6	69.9	18.8	3 471.2	5 947	14 943	28 502	6.2	4.8	NA	16.2	25.0	22.0
Fort Lauderdale, FL	603	4 156	263 345	20.1	76.8	18.8	1 306.1	5 650	16 883	30 570	10.0	4.7	NA	11.0	17.9	15.4
Miami, FL	1 233	7 001	515 611	20.8	65.0	18.8	2 165.1	6 141	13 686	26 908	3.1	4.9	NA	19.8	29.6	26.3
Milwaukee-Racine, WI	435	4 031	428 267	23.2	79.3	20.8	2 174.0	7 990	14 702	32 358	-4.4	3.6	NA	10.7	17.4	14.7
Milwaukee-Waukesha, WI	449	4 043	382 149	23.8	79.7	21.3	1 955.8	8 082	14 785	32 315	-4.1	3.6	NA	11.0	17.9	15.2
Racine, WI	327	3 940	46 118	18.3	76.4	16.5	218.1	7 245	14 023	32 750	-6.7	2.9	NA	8.7	13.6	11.3
Minneapolis-St. Paul, MN-WI	354	3 684	673 370	16.6	87.1	26.9	3 440.1	6 941	16 721	36 467	5.6	5.1	NA	7.6	11.2	9.4
Missoula, MT	NA	NA	25 497	6.4	85.4	27.7	79.9	5 692	11 944	23 388	-14.2	2.1	NA	14.7	20.0	17.3
Mobile, AL	606	6 069	128 674	17.4	70.8	15.8	444.6	5 081	11 388	23 644	-3.9	2.4	NA	17.0	24.8	22.0
Modesto, CA	691	4 642	102 957	7.8	68.4	13.0	533.1	5 707	12 731	29 793	10.6	3.5	NA	17.2	24.2	24.7
Monroe, LA	935	6 274	42 399	9.1	71.6	18.9	141.3	5 017	10 593	21 129	-9.2	2.3	NA	19.9	28.3	26.7
Montgomery, AL	602	5 713	82 106	15.5	73.2	21.1	261.4	4 817	12 258	26 685	5.5	2.6	NA	15.4	23.8	20.8
Muncie, IN	93	996	37 870	5.0	74.5	16.5	121.7	7 177	12 168	24 436	-11.4	2.0	NA	13.6	18.5	16.8
Myrtle Beach, SC	1 007	7 196	33 637	7.7	74.3	16.0	170.2	6 342	12 385	24 959	10.4	2.4	NA	13.7	21.4	21.0
Naples, FL	548	3 412	27 492	11.9	79.0	22.3	197.5	6 415	21 386	34 001	22.1	9.1	NA	10.3	19.2	18.4
Nashville, TN	969	5 023	242 440	20.1	74.0	21.4	994.3	5 515	14 567	30 222	7.6	3.7	NA	9.5	13.6	11.2
New London-Norwich, CT	NA	NA	61 393	19.8	80.9	21.8	349.0	8 938	16 702	37 487	23.4	4.7	NA	8.0	11.6	12.1
New Orleans, LA	773	5 079	360 095	29.6	71.9	19.3	1 161.4	5 699	12 005	24 415	-9.7	3.2	NA	17.8	26.2	23.5
New York-Northern New Jersey-Long Island, NY-NJ-CT-PA	609	2 604	4 878 393	25.9	75.1	25.7	30 371.0	10 020	18 864	38 513	26.8	9.4	NA	13.4	20.3	19.8
Bergen-Passaic, NJ	261	2 119	296 616	25.8	77.3	27.3	2 062.8	10 913	21 234	45 039	23.2	12.0	NA	7.8	11.9	11.8
Dutchess County, NY	198	1 971	67 685	24.7	79.8	24.8	399.4	8 940	17 420	42 249	24.4	6.1	NA	8.2	12.6	11.8
Jersey City, NJ	654	3 285	128 644	29.0	64.1	19.7	807.8	10 387	14 480	30 916	28.3	4.2	NA	16.2	24.1	25.0
Middlesex-Somerset-Hunterdon, NJ	188	2 070	250 426	19.0	81.8	30.2	1 679.2	10 159	20 699	48 701	22.7	10.9	NA	5.4	8.1	7.8
Monmouth-Ocean, NJ	189	2 145	229 583	21.9	79.3	22.5	1 612.3	9 462	18 383	39 830	26.8	7.7	NA	6.7	9.9	9.7
Nassau-Suffolk, NY	NA	NA	665 563	23.0	83.2	26.5	5 134.3	11 764	20 884	51 670	27.3	13.9	NA	6.9	11.3	9.3
New Haven-Bridgeport-Stamford-Danbury-Waterbury, CT	370	3 136	395 168	26.5	79.3	29.3	2 362.0	9 172	21 975	43 268	25.7	11.8	NA	9.0	14.0	13.6
New York, NY	854	2 564	2 195 241	28.6	70.3	24.6	11 771.9	9 320	17 397	31 658	26.6	7.8	NA	20.0	30.1	30.1
Newark, NJ	560	3 109	472 978	22.6	76.5	26.9	3 375.6	10 943	19 810	42 174	24.4	10.9	NA	9.8	14.6	14.8
Newburgh, NY-PA	283	2 273	90 364	19.0	77.4	19.1	584.4	8 881	15 080	38 161	28.5	5.0	NA	11.2	16.2	15.5
Trenton, NJ	517	3 494	86 125	29.5	77.1	29.5	581.4	11 078	18 936	41 227	25.1	9.0	NA	9.2	13.9	14.3
Norfolk-Virginia Beach-Newport News, VA-NC	464	4 008	375 122	13.6	78.6	19.8	1 591.1	5 772	13 467	30 766	12.0	2.8	NA	12.1	16.7	15.6
Ocala, FL	781	3 797	37 941	11.7	69.6	11.5	201.2	5 306	11 782	22 451	13.6	2.0	NA	15.2	25.3	23.9
Odessa-Midland, TX	451	3 925	64 011	7.6	71.6	18.5	276.5	5 220	13 034	26 744	-19.0	3.6	NA	16.2	22.5	21.6
Oklahoma City, OK	518	5 785	268 693	12.2	79.2	21.6	941.8	5 112	13 269	26 882	-3.7	2.7	NA	14.1	20.8	18.3
Omaha, NE-IA	547	4 778	180 577	19.1	84.4	22.5	707.5	5 863	13 916	30 258	0.6	3.2	NA	9.0	12.9	10.5
Orlando, FL	882	5 058	287 286	14.6	78.6	20.4	1 365.8	5 357	14 591	30 211	18.1	3.6	NA	11.8	19.0	16.8
Owensboro, KY	188	3 491	21 955	22.3	72.3	14.1	82.7	5 688	11 456	24 399	-8.5	1.9	NA	12.7	18.7	15.6
Panama City, FL	617	4 771	32 011	9.5	74.7	15.7	137.1	5 285	12 225	24 684	11.0	2.0	NA	14.6	22.5	22.1
Parkersburg-Marietta, WV-OH	225	2 231	35 570	11.3	75.0	13.4	156.9	6 214	11 772	24 882	-9.5	1.6	NA	13.6	20.3	17.9
Pensacola, FL	622	3 260	89 901	12.3	76.7	18.3	362.0	5 348	12 278	25 735	5.5	2.3	NA	15.2	22.8	21.5
Peoria-Pekin, IL	NA	NA	91 361	18.1	78.4	16.9	340.7	6 095	13 796	29 836	-12.2	2.8	NA	10.5	15.5	14.2
Philadelphia-Wilmington-Atlantic City, PA-NJ-DE-MD	641	3 351	1 463 758	28.9	75.8	22.1	7 833.6	8 684	16 296	35 385	18.2	5.7	NA	10.7	16.2	15.5
Atlantic-Cape May, NJ	424	5 056	69 177	16.5	73.2	16.7	543.7	9 650	15 873	32 407	27.4	4.5	NA	10.6	16.4	16.8
Philadelphia, PA-NJ	654	3 151	1 226 846	30.6	75.9	22.6	6 407.8	8 675	16 354	35 406	17.5	5.9	NA	10.9	16.4	15.6
Vineland-Millville-Bridgeton, NJ	717	3 778	33 115	13.3	63.4	10.8	265.3	10 531	12 560	29 985	16.3	2.6	NA	14.8	20.8	22.7
Wilmington-Newark, DE-MD	635	3 952	134 620	23.6	79.5	23.4	616.8	7 533	17 008	38 216	17.2	5.3	NA	8.4	12.8	11.7
Phoenix-Mesa, AZ	556	5 613	588 764	10.6	80.7	21.4	2 426.3	4 773	14 671	30 350	3.2	4.1	NA	12.3	19.0	17.2
Pine Bluff, AR	1 450	6 712	23 015	6.0	65.9	14.6	80.2	5 189	9 852	21 322	-0.3	1.6	NA	22.5	31.0	26.0
Pittsburgh, PA	329	2 207	554 565	20.1	77.3	18.7	2 693.2	7 928	13 785	26 656	-10.9	3.1	NA	11.0	17.7	15.9
Pittsfield, MA	387	2 052	34 224	21.7	77.9	20.9	174.4	8 155	14 857	30 469	14.5	3.5	NA	9.7	15.6	15.1
Pocatello, ID	282	3 107	23 087	4.3	82.9	19.8	71.7	4 940	10 976	26 275	-10.2	1.6	NA	13.4	17.4	14.7
Portland, ME	135	2 820	58 915	16.5	85.0	27.6	293.1	7 385	15 816	32 285	25.4	4.5	NA	7.8	11.7	9.3
Portland-Salem, OR-WA	421	4 602	456 026	14.4	83.5	22.5	2 403.6	6 658	14 593	30 451	1.0	3.4	NA	10.0	14.2	12.1
Portland-Vancouver, OR-WA	448	4 531	383 949	14.6	84.3	23.3	2 032.5	6 684	15 021	31 037	0.9	3.6	NA	9.4	13.3	11.2
Salem, OR	272	4 992	72 077	13.2	78.9	18.2	371.1	6 521	12 260	26 770	-1.5	2.2	NA	13.5	19.1	16.6
Providence-Warwick-Pawtucket, RI	298	3 182	232 837	24.6	71.0	20.4	1 120.4	7 895	14 806	31 908	18.8	4.0	NA	10.9	16.8	16.0
Provo-Orem, UT	94	3 311	114 352	30.5	87.9	26.2	308.8	3 921	9 051	27 431	1.1	2.2	NA	10.1	11.7	9.6
Pueblo, CO	720	3 760	32 691	6.1	73.9	14.0	127.8	5 271	10 347	21 552	-16.9	1.3	NA	17.3	24.0	22.3
Punta Gorda, FL	220	2 108	16 107	11.9	75.7	13.4	92.5	5 585	14 431	25 745	16.5	2.7	NA	9.5	18.3	17.7
Raleigh-Durham-Chapel Hill, NC	474	4 766	236 433	16.3	80.0	31.7	992.7	5 860	15 629	32 046	18.0	4.2	NA	9.5	14.6	13.3
Rapid City, SD	351	4 571	21 946	9.7	84.8	21.2	90.4	5 140	12 031	25 340	1.5	2.4	NA	13.1	18.2	15.5

1. Data for serious crimes have not been adjusted for underreporting; this may affect comparability between geographic areas and over time. 2. Per 100,000 population estimated by the FBI. 3. All persons 3 years old and over enrolled in nursery school through college. 4. Persons 25 years old and over. 5. Elementary and secondary education expenditures, local government fiscal years ending between July 1, 1998 and June 30, 1999. 6. Based on population enumerated as of April 1, 1990.

Table C. Metropolitan Areas — **Personal Income**

| | Personal income, 1999 | | | | | | | | | | | | |
Area Name	Total (mil dol)	Percent change, 1998–1999	Per capita[1] Dollars	Per capita[1] Rank	Wages and salaries[2] (mil dol)	Proprietor's income (mil dol)	Dividends, interest, and rent (mil dol)	Transfer payments Total (mil dol)	Government payments to individuals Total (mil dol)	Social Security (mil dol)	Medical payments (mil dol)	Income mainte- nance (mil dol)	Unemploy- ment insurance (mil dol)
	62	63	64	65	66	67	68	69	70	71	72	73	74
Merced, CA	3 687	4.8	18 367	312	1 780	526	535	791	752	199	316	157	37
Miami-Fort Lauderdale, FL	99 018	4.5	26 682	X	60 992	5 958	22 355	15 091	14 413	4 983	7 179	1 535	237
Fort Lauderdale, FL	45 208	4.6	29 442	70	23 588	1 844	12 026	5 945	5 664	2 558	2 468	323	96
Miami, FL	53 811	4.4	24 733	182	37 404	4 114	10 328	9 146	8 748	2 425	4 711	1 212	141
Milwaukee-Racine, WI	51 847	4.8	31 457	X	35 638	2 348	10 629	6 174	5 852	2 533	2 304	656	150
Milwaukee-Waukesha, WI.	46 512	4.8	31 805	38	32 596	2 149	9 609	5 560	5 274	2 242	2 098	614	127
Racine, WI	5 335	4.8	28 720	82	3 042	199	1 020	614	578	291	206	42	23
Minneapolis-St. Paul, MN-WI	101 242	6.0	35 250	20	72 170	5 706	20 481	8 628	8 044	3 234	3 366	772	193
Missoula, MT	2 187	4.9	24 476	194	1 402	232	466	267	250	108	77	23	5
Mobile, AL	11 681	3.6	21 814	280	7 064	700	2 213	1 986	1 888	804	727	214	27
Modesto, CA	9 517	4.6	21 790	282	4 981	1 060	1 524	1 621	1 537	511	589	276	71
Monroe, LA	3 246	4.7	22 128	271	2 081	277	599	559	533	182	235	72	7
Montgomery, AL	8 266	5.2	25 637	153	5 566	526	1 569	1 165	1 107	423	429	142	13
Muncie, IN	2 813	3.6	24 362	203	1 744	162	522	453	430	196	162	40	6
Myrtle Beach, SC	4 373	7.7	24 492	193	2 589	463	937	657	624	327	200	55	12
Naples, FL	9 288	5.1	44 862	4	3 249	845	4 317	916	878	530	287	33	7
Nashville, TN	35 750	5.6	30 510	54	24 632	4 027	5 657	3 774	3 575	1 441	1 608	279	69
New London-Norwich, CT	7 817	2.2	31 771	40	5 428	575	1 412	1 005	962	390	422	78	29
New Orleans, LA	33 890	2.2	25 960	146	21 346	3 370	6 077	5 290	5 058	1 736	2 341	688	48
New York-Northern New Jer- sey-Long Island, NY-NJ- CT-PA	774 748	5.6	38 539	X	496 351	76 652	140 924	101 807	97 715	29 570	50 166	11 664	2 128
Bergen-Passaic, NJ	54 521	5.7	40 623	6	30 531	6 537	10 977	5 070	4 807	2 233	1 885	312	173
Dutchess County, NY	8 268	7.0	30 822	47	4 374	446	1 520	1 062	1 006	430	420	79	15
Jersey City, NJ	15 292	3.8	27 662	102	11 978	1 138	1 820	2 452	2 344	674	1 114	323	129
Middlesex-Somerset- Hunterdon, NJ	45 189	5.3	39 969	7	32 611	3 480	7 258	3 557	3 335	1 607	1 263	153	120
Monmouth-Ocean, NJ	36 620	4.9	33 021	30	15 005	2 325	7 581	4 679	4 463	2 181	1 761	182	133
Nassau-Suffolk, NY	104 197	4.4	38 751	11	49 828	7 175	23 162	11 652	11 086	4 632	4 951	724	164
New Haven-Bridgeport- Stamford-Danbury-Water- bury, CT	73 991	5.0	45 267	3	43 382	6 162	13 767	7 473	7 174	2 692	3 387	633	177
New York, NY	338 168	6.3	38 814	10	246 040	42 595	56 628	55 166	53 330	11 202	30 954	8 225	906
Newark, NJ	75 676	4.8	38 715	12	48 719	5 416	14 043	7 885	7 502	2 871	3 261	780	253
Newburgh, NY-PA	9 596	5.3	25 553	158	4 327	503	1 659	1 407	1 330	515	583	139	21
Trenton, NJ	13 230	6.3	39 626	9	9 556	875	2 507	1 404	1 339	535	586	113	36
Norfolk-Virginia Beach-New- port News, VA-NC	39 034	4.8	24 979	177	27 687	1 833	6 973	4 351	4 072	1 697	1 465	470	45
Ocala, FL	5 440	4.5	22 115	273	2 384	359	1 387	1 231	1 186	657	407	80	8
Odessa-Midland, TX	6 056	-2.3	24 999	175	3 217	1 111	1 179	788	746	305	314	70	34
Oklahoma City, OK	25 568	4.6	24 437	197	17 187	2 121	4 522	3 276	3 088	1 293	1 147	311	39
Omaha, NE-IA	21 450	6.2	30 692	48	15 045	1 744	3 952	2 191	2 066	855	816	182	19
Orlando, FL	40 782	6.2	26 568	129	29 037	2 828	7 146	5 138	4 857	2 171	1 928	378	52
Owensboro, KY	2 132	4.5	23 383	233	1 271	130	443	354	337	151	130	29	8
Panama City, FL	3 361	2.9	22 719	257	2 023	252	686	567	541	214	214	51	9
Parkersburg-Marietta, WV- OH	3 409	2.2	22 826	253	2 140	229	624	644	615	270	225	49	11
Pensacola, FL	9 067	3.1	22 476	264	5 401	437	1 746	1 436	1 364	545	518	155	12
Peoria-Pekin, IL	9 458	2.9	27 297	115	6 348	516	2 040	1 239	1 168	580	399	105	35
Philadelphia-Wilmington- Atlantic City, PA-NJ-DE- MD	194 352	4.5	32 397	X	123 206	15 547	35 751	26 616	25 413	9 504	11 259	2 771	740
Atlantic-Cape May, NJ	10 576	3.5	31 322	44	6 304	1 801	1 799	1 565	1 499	608	635	94	92
Philadelphia, PA-NJ	161 501	4.3	32 627	31	101 078	12 504	29 719	22 525	21 535	7 862	9 701	2 446	573
Vineland-Millville-Bridge- ton, NJ	3 208	3.1	22 894	249	2 021	248	494	651	624	225	271	64	39
Wilmington-Newark, DE- MD	19 067	7.2	33 368	29	13 803	995	3 739	1 876	1 755	808	651	166	35
Phoenix-Mesa, AZ	83 228	7.2	27 617	105	56 465	6 139	15 411	9 278	8 733	3 978	3 265	697	87
Pine Bluff, AR	1 627	2.9	20 141	305	1 117	77	291	320	304	109	100	50	7
Pittsburgh, PA	68 977	5.0	29 587	66	41 448	6 689	12 539	11 774	11 303	4 617	4 904	873	317
Pittsfield, MA	3 848	3.8	29 103	74	2 129	319	883	710	686	266	331	48	19
Pocatello, ID	1 516	4.1	20 252	304	893	96	238	223	210	80	64	19	6
Portland, ME	8 074	6.1	31 484	41	5 999	547	1 690	976	931	385	393	88	9
Portland-Salem, OR-WA	64 589	5.5	29 615	X	42 228	4 883	13 371	7 042	6 640	2 759	2 347	576	275
Portland-Vancouver, OR- WA	56 616	5.6	30 672	49	37 770	4 305	11 583	5 795	5 453	2 268	1 902	470	234
Salem, OR	7 973	5.4	23 789	219	4 458	577	1 788	1 247	1 187	492	445	106	42
Providence-Warwick-Paw- tucket, RI	26 326	4.9	29 000	76	15 126	1 711	5 083	4 483	4 311	1 533	1 966	413	145
Provo-Orem, UT	6 521	6.9	18 793	310	4 324	545	939	705	644	270	262	55	14
Pueblo, CO	3 003	4.4	21 924	277	1 620	176	531	750	725	212	387	73	6
Punta Gorda, FL	3 337	4.5	24 356	204	1 019	182	1 316	810	785	450	273	20	3
Raleigh-Durham-Chapel Hill, NC	35 436	7.6	32 054	36	26 389	2 186	6 523	2 992	2 792	1 196	1 136	260	38
Rapid City, SD	2 211	6.6	25 088	173	1 476	177	548	283	269	119	95	21	2

1. Based on the resident population estimated as of July 1 of the year shown.   2. Includes other labor income.

Table C. Metropolitan Areas — **Earnings, Social Security, and Housing**

Area Name	Earnings, 1999									Social Security beneficiaries, December 2000			Housing units, 1990	
	Total (mil dol)	Farm	Percent by selected industries							Number	Rate³	Supplemental Security Income recipients, December 2000	Total	Percent change, 1980–1990
			Goods-related¹		Service-related and other²									
			Total	Manufacturing	Total	Retail trade	Finance, insurance, and real estate	Services	Government					
	75	76	77	78	79	80	81	82	83	84	85	86	87	88
Merced, CA	2 306	13.8	22.3	17.2	44.7	10.5	3.6	16.3	19.2	26 857	128	8 987	58 410	16.7
Miami-Fort Lauderdale, FL	66 950	0.4	10.9	6.3	72.9	10.8	11.0	33.1	15.8	598 856	154	143 847	1 399 948	21.6
Fort Lauderdale, FL	25 432	0.1	12.8	6.6	72.1	12.6	10.8	33.8	15.0	278 996	172	27 597	628 660	29.3
Miami, FL	41 518	0.6	9.7	6.1	73.4	9.6	11.0	32.7	16.3	319 860	142	116 250	771 288	15.9
Milwaukee-Racine, WI	37 986	0.1	D	25.8	D	7.6	8.8	28.2	11.0	272 305	161	36 637	628 976	7.7
Milwaukee-Waukesha, WI	34 745	0.0	D	24.2	D	7.6	9.4	28.9	11.0	240 801	160	33 278	562 031	7.8
Racine, WI	3 241	0.3	48.7	42.8	39.8	7.6	2.7	20.6	11.1	31 504	167	3 359	66 945	7.0
Minneapolis-St. Paul, MN-WI	77 876	0.1	D	19.4	D	9.1	10.6	27.9	11.6	359 430	121	36 504	1 015 235	23.0
Missoula, MT	1 634	-0.2	16.2	8.5	64.9	12.6	6.4	30.7	19.2	12 787	133	1 562	33 466	9.6
Mobile, AL	7 764	0.8	24.0	14.6	58.0	11.4	5.7	27.3	17.1	98 095	182	16 244	202 153	22.4
Modesto, CA	6 042	3.9	26.0	18.8	53.8	11.4	4.1	23.6	16.4	63 879	143	18 696	132 027	28.8
Monroe, LA	2 358	0.3	22.0	16.2	62.0	10.5	10.4	26.4	15.6	22 543	153	4 876	56 300	9.4
Montgomery, AL	6 092	0.6	D	11.2	D	9.0	8.5	24.5	29.6	53 798	162	12 248	116 754	14.6
Muncie, IN	1 906	0.6	D	24.0	D	10.4	4.5	26.8	18.2	21 646	182	2 613	48 793	2.5
Myrtle Beach, SC	3 051	0.6	D	8.3	D	20.1	9.9	32.3	12.3	40 118	204	4 260	89 960	63.6
Naples, FL	4 095	4.2	14.5	2.8	71.6	12.7	14.6	35.3	9.7	56 935	226	1 931	94 165	85.6
Nashville, TN	28 658	0.1	D	14.8	D	10.8	8.8	34.3	10.8	168 227	137	20 436	410 968	28.5
New London-Norwich, CT	6 003	0.8	27.4	21.8	52.8	8.0	2.7	33.3	19.0	43 359	167	3 166	104 461	15.7
New Orleans, LA	24 717	0.1	20.0	10.0	62.8	9.2	6.4	32.6	17.1	209 379	157	48 965	540 422	9.3
New York-Northern New Jersey-Long Island, NY-NJ-CT-PA	573 003	0.0	D	11.0	D	6.4	20.5	32.1	12.5	3 160 957	150	601 131	7 658 812	6.5
Bergen-Passaic, NJ	37 068	0.0	D	16.3	D	8.2	8.3	33.3	9.1	225 294	164	22 106	487 329	4.5
Dutchess County, NY	4 820	0.2	32.7	27.4	48.9	8.2	4.8	28.8	18.2	46 909	167	4 927	97 632	12.4
Jersey City, NJ	13 116	0.0	D	8.8	D	6.8	21.5	22.9	16.8	77 741	128	21 467	229 682	3.8
Middlesex-Somerset-Hunterdon, NJ	36 091	0.1	D	18.1	D	6.7	10.1	29.7	10.1	164 491	141	11 836	382 814	26.2
Monmouth-Ocean, NJ	17 330	0.2	D	5.1	D	11.2	8.2	34.8	18.7	230 567	205	11 398	438 271	22.0
Nassau-Suffolk, NY	57 003	0.1	D	9.8	D	9.8	11.2	32.9	16.2	474 662	172	38 210	927 609	7.1
New Haven-Bridgeport-Stamford-Danbury-Waterbury, CT	49 544	0.1	D	19.6	D	7.7	15.3	31.2	8.9	283 795	166	24 729	651 434	11.9
New York, NY	288 635	0.0	D	7.3	D	4.8	29.6	32.7	11.4	1 242 348	133	411 843	3 449 058	2.3
Newark, NJ	54 136	0.0	D	16.6	D	6.6	10.8	30.7	13.4	299 493	147	39 951	729 651	2.3
Newburgh, NY-PA	4 831	0.5	14.7	9.4	56.7	11.9	5.4	24.9	28.1	58 756	152	6 664	141 666	27.6
Trenton, NJ	10 431	0.0	D	11.9	D	5.8	8.6	35.9	25.7	56 901	162	8 000	123 666	10.8
Norfolk-Virginia Beach-Newport News, VA-NC	29 520	0.1	D	10.0	D	8.2	5.7	22.6	38.0	212 510	135	29 588	558 946	29.8
Ocala, FL	2 743	2.5	22.5	13.5	56.3	13.9	6.5	24.0	18.7	78 163	302	6 074	94 567	70.9
Odessa-Midland, TX	4 327	0.1	36.8	6.2	49.5	10.1	4.8	19.7	13.8	34 875	147	4 685	93 970	27.0
Oklahoma City, OK	19 308	0.1	20.5	11.7	55.0	9.8	6.0	27.4	24.4	156 200	144	18 259	425 043	20.6
Omaha, NE-IA	16 789	0.2	D	10.4	D	8.6	9.6	30.7	14.5	98 236	137	9 507	256 489	11.6
Orlando, FL	31 865	0.8	14.8	7.9	72.9	11.4	8.6	38.5	11.4	263 027	160	31 350	524 197	60.2
Owensboro, KY	1 400	-0.2	29.7	19.3	52.6	11.6	4.5	24.1	17.8	17 631	193	2 793	35 041	10.7
Panama City, FL	2 275	0.1	D	6.5	D	13.3	5.6	27.7	27.9	27 694	187	3 557	65 999	53.8
Parkersburg-Marietta, WV-OH	2 369	0.1	35.2	26.5	49.1	10.8	4.3	23.8	15.6	30 843	204	4 289	63 372	5.4
Pensacola, FL	5 838	0.3	14.9	7.5	52.3	10.0	4.7	27.4	32.5	71 157	173	10 092	145 061	33.1
Peoria-Pekin, IL	6 864	0.5	D	29.0	D	8.6	5.4	27.0	10.8	62 794	181	6 293	136 458	-2.6
Philadelphia-Wilmington-Atlantic City, PA-NJ-DE-MD	138 753	0.2	D	16.3	D	8.2	10.3	34.3	12.9	1 034 598	167	146 064	2 376 423	9.8
Atlantic-Cape May, NJ	8 106	0.3	D	2.7	D	9.3	3.8	53.4	16.9	68 085	192	6 564	192 414	19.2
Philadelphia, PA-NJ	113 581	0.2	D	16.4	D	8.2	10.1	34.4	12.7	853 025	167	126 902	1 932 499	8.4
Vineland-Millville-Bridgeton, NJ	2 269	1.5	26.9	20.8	47.6	9.1	4.6	20.2	24.0	25 658	175	4 400	50 294	6.2
Wilmington-Newark, DE-MD	14 797	0.3	D	22.6	D	7.7	16.8	25.6	11.1	87 830	150	8 198	201 216	17.3
Phoenix-Mesa, AZ	62 604	0.7	21.9	13.7	65.2	10.3	11.4	29.5	12.2	459 851	141	41 944	1 004 773	55.8
Pine Bluff, AR	1 193	1.7	27.3	24.2	46.1	9.1	3.5	20.6	24.9	14 573	173	3 636	33 311	0.8
Pittsburgh, PA	48 137	0.0	25.4	18.1	63.2	8.7	7.9	32.3	11.4	503 736	214	57 357	1 015 208	2.6
Pittsfield, MA	2 448	0.1	25.4	19.0	62.1	12.0	7.1	33.6	12.4	30 012	222	3 609	64 324	8.6
Pocatello, ID	989	0.5	D	11.4	D	12.3	5.5	19.8	27.2	9 697	128	1 311	25 694	3.5
Portland, ME	6 547	0.1	16.9	11.0	68.6	12.1	13.0	30.6	14.3	45 790	172	4 816	109 890	19.7
Portland-Salem, OR-WA	47 111	1.1	D	17.8	D	9.8	7.5	26.2	14.2	307 522	136	32 903	725 936	13.9
Portland-Vancouver, OR-WA	42 075	0.7	D	18.4	D	9.7	7.8	26.7	12.5	250 999	131	27 447	620 089	14.8
Salem, OR	5 035	4.2	D	12.3	D	10.5	5.5	22.3	28.0	56 523	163	5 456	105 847	8.9
Providence-Warwick-Pawtucket, RI	16 837	0.1	D	17.2	D	9.5	8.5	31.9	15.7	177 457	184	26 330	377 097	11.0
Provo-Orem, UT	4 869	0.6	21.1	12.9	65.1	10.0	4.8	42.2	13.2	31 655	86	2 879	72 820	16.8
Pueblo, CO	1 796	-0.2	19.3	10.7	58.1	15.0	6.7	26.1	22.8	27 702	196	4 869	50 872	3.6
Punta Gorda, FL	1 200	2.0	D	3.1	D	16.3	6.7	37.8	16.1	50 192	354	1 498	64 641	85.8
Raleigh-Durham-Chapel Hill, NC	28 575	0.6	D	19.0	D	8.4	D	29.9	17.3	142 590	120	18 856	359 310	42.3
Rapid City, SD	1 653	0.4	16.2	8.1	60.0	13.1	6.9	28.4	23.4	14 822	167	1 621	33 741	19.6

1. Covers mining, construction, and manufacturing.   2. Covers private sector earnings in agricultural services, forestry, and fisheries; transportation and public utilities; wholesale trade; retail trade; finance, insurance, and real estate; and services.   3. Per 1,000 resident population estimated as of July 1 of the year shown.

Table C. Metropolitan Areas — **Housing, Labor Force, and Employment**

Area Name	Occupied units — Total (89)	Owner-occupied Percent (90)	Median value[1] (91)	Owner cost as a percent of income — With a mortgage (92)	Without a mortgage (93)	Renter-occupied Median rent[2] (94)	Rent as percent of income (95)	Sub-standard units[3] (percent) (96)	Civilian labor force 2001 — Total (97)	Percent change, 2000–2001 (98)	Unemployment Total (99)	Rate[4] (100)	Civilian employment 1990[5] — Total (101)	Percent Professional, managerial, and technical (102)	Precision production, craft, and repair (103)
Merced, CA	55 331	54.4	90 800	22.7	12.1	429	28.2	15.7	84 218	-1.5	11 791	14.0	66 116	21.7	11.5
Miami-Fort Lauderdale, FL	1 220 797	60.2	88 700	NA	NA	523	NA	12.2	1 892 296	3.3	114 436	6.0	1 500 947	28.6	11.1
Fort Lauderdale, FL	528 442	68.0	91 800	23.6	13.1	574	29.0	5.2	811 864	3.7	39 814	4.9	599 119	29.9	11.7
Miami, FL	692 355	54.3	86 500	23.1	13.0	492	31.3	17.6	1 080 432	3.0	74 622	6.9	901 828	27.8	10.7
Milwaukee-Racine, WI	601 458	60.4	74 800	NA	NA	441	NA	2.9	905 550	1.2	44 411	4.9	784 796	29.8	11.5
Milwaukee-Waukesha, WI	537 722	59.4	76 900	20.9	13.6	446	26.0	2.9	813 111	1.2	38 236	4.7	700 737	30.3	11.2
Racine, WI	63 736	68.3	64 200	19.3	12.6	401	24.9	2.6	92 439	1.7	6 175	6.7	84 059	26.3	14.0
Minneapolis-St. Paul, MN-WI	960 170	68.9	88 300	NA	NA	477	NA	2.3	1 771 222	2.9	57 803	3.3	1 366 976	33.8	9.5
Missoula, MT	30 782	60.1	66 200	20.3	12.2	334	28.0	3.3	54 198	-1.9	1 960	3.6	37 122	30.8	9.1
Mobile, AL	173 943	69.3	55 300	19.1	12.8	328	26.2	4.7	273 215	0.2	14 926	5.5	198 070	27.2	13.0
Modesto, CA	125 375	60.7	124 300	23.3	11.7	481	28.9	10.5	210 264	2.1	21 472	10.2	151 010	23.8	14.0
Monroe, LA	50 518	64.8	52 800	21.0	13.2	333	28.0	6.3	73 626	2.5	4 082	5.5	58 100	29.7	11.0
Montgomery, AL	105 531	67.1	61 500	19.2	12.6	372	24.5	5.4	164 289	0.3	6 575	4.0	128 656	29.7	10.0
Muncie, IN	45 177	66.8	42 300	15.5	12.7	333	27.5	2.0	59 735	1.8	2 734	4.6	55 097	25.1	12.0
Myrtle Beach, SC	55 764	68.5	75 600	NA	NA	424	NA	4.2	103 361	-2.7	4 903	4.7	66 730	24.8	13.6
Naples, FL	61 703	70.2	121 400	22.7	11.7	571	26.5	5.5	108 014	7.6	4 221	3.9	68 449	25.9	12.9
Nashville, TN	375 831	63.2	76 000	21.2	12.6	425	25.3	2.8	670 434	1.4	22 258	3.3	501 819	30.5	10.8
New London-Norwich, CT	93 245	64.7	149 200	22.7	13.0	571	24.8	1.9	132 250	-0.8	3 709	2.8	120 161	33.0	13.6
New Orleans, LA	469 823	58.7	69 800	NA	NA	396	NA	6.4	612 452	0.8	31 761	5.2	533 656	31.2	10.5
New York-Northern New Jersey-Long Island, NY-NJ-CT-PA	7 126 646	51.9	187 300	NA	NA	546	NA	7.2	10 012 608	-0.8	455 688	4.6	9 405 581	35.1	9.1
Bergen-Passaic, NJ	464 149	63.9	214 400	23.6	15.2	645	26.2	4.1	655 184	-1.3	28 425	4.3	661 994	35.2	9.8
Dutchess County, NY	89 567	69.1	149 200	NA	NA	599	NA	2.0	120 387	0.6	3 904	3.2	127 925	39.1	10.6
Jersey City, NJ	208 739	32.5	157 000	24.0	15.6	524	25.0	9.9	280 386	-0.4	17 482	6.2	268 816	27.2	8.8
Middlesex-Somerset-Hunterdon, NJ	365 085	70.7	173 500	23.7	14.8	679	25.3	2.8	659 397	0.9	21 372	3.2	555 733	38.3	9.5
Monmouth-Ocean, NJ	365 717	77.4	150 600	25.1	16.3	647	29.0	1.9	529 990	1.1	20 134	3.8	456 555	34.4	11.4
Nassau-Suffolk, NY	856 234	80.3	187 000	23.6	16.3	777	29.0	2.7	1 391 713	-0.8	45 797	3.3	1 326 668	35.1	10.4
New Haven-Bridgeport-Stamford-Danbury-Waterbury, CT	609 741	65.5	198 400	NA	NA	630	NA	2.7	856 659	-1.9	28 864	3.4	837 868	36.6	10.6
New York, NY	3 252 399	33.3	209 000	22.4	14.5	502	25.7	11.5	4 150 103	-1.3	233 601	5.6	3 884 751	34.9	7.7
Newark, NJ	686 032	59.6	188 400	NA	NA	581	NA	5.1	1 014 239	-0.7	43 433	4.3	964 896	34.4	9.4
Newburgh, NY-PA	112 042	68.9	139 100	NA	NA	592	NA	3.3	176 377	0.3	6 641	3.8	153 943	30.5	12.5
Trenton, NJ	116 941	66.5	137 900	22.2	14.4	569	25.7	3.1	178 173	2.2	6 035	3.4	166 432	38.8	8.0
Norfolk-Virginia Beach-Newport News, VA-NC	511 136	59.6	86 800	NA	NA	479	NA	3.6	754 090	1.2	27 092	3.6	615 581	31.0	13.7
Ocala, FL	78 177	75.6	61 800	22.0	11.7	385	25.4	4.2	98 572	0.0	4 786	4.9	74 958	23.8	12.9
Odessa-Midland, TX	81 242	65.9	51 700	NA	NA	337	NA	7.8	119 539	1.3	5 119	4.3	98 666	28.9	14.5
Oklahoma City, OK	367 775	64.3	54 500	20.1	12.5	368	25.6	3.7	554 929	0.8	21 511	3.9	450 696	30.8	10.8
Omaha, NE-IA	240 149	64.6	59 000	NA	NA	399	NA	2.1	395 631	0.8	12 673	3.2	316 628	30.4	9.5
Orlando, FL	465 275	64.2	82 500	NA	NA	515	NA	4.1	907 287	1.2	36 591	4.0	612 750	29.3	10.8
Owensboro, KY	33 036	68.8	48 000	16.3	11.8	285	24.9	2.7	49 525	-1.3	2 694	5.4	39 290	23.9	13.5
Panama City, FL	48 938	65.5	61 600	20.0	12.3	369	25.2	2.9	65 013	0.4	3 873	6.0	53 222	28.3	11.4
Parkersburg-Marietta, WV-OH	57 804	74.1	50 400	16.2	12.2	318	25.0	2.2	77 544	0.1	3 381	4.4	64 976	27.1	12.3
Pensacola, FL	128 508	67.2	59 600	20.2	12.3	383	25.8	3.7	170 672	-1.0	8 217	4.8	143 322	29.0	13.5
Peoria-Pekin, IL	129 363	68.0	49 700	15.5	12.3	348	23.1	1.8	183 443	-1.4	8 487	4.6	154 817	28.7	10.9
Philadelphia-Wilmington-Atlantic City, PA-NJ-DE-MD	2 160 142	69.4	100 800	NA	NA	517	NA	3.0	3 077 214	1.1	136 095	4.4	2 818 996	32.8	10.5
Atlantic-Cape May, NJ	122 979	66.8	107 700	22.8	15.6	570	27.6	3.5	167 926	-0.6	10 256	6.1	154 687	26.5	10.4
Philadelphia, PA-NJ	1 801 159	69.6	100 400	NA	NA	514	NA	3.0	2 534 787	1.1	109 697	4.3	2 337 323	33.5	10.3
Vineland-Millville-Bridgeton, NJ	47 118	68.5	73 900	20.8	14.4	479	27.9	4.7	62 138	-1.7	4 660	7.5	60 937	22.8	12.6
Wilmington-Newark, DE-MD	188 886	69.1	109 000	20.0	12.2	519	24.7	2.1	312 363	2.1	11 482	3.7	266 049	32.8	11.3
Phoenix-Mesa, AZ	846 714	63.7	84 200	NA	NA	461	NA	6.3	1 620 060	3.7	63 610	3.9	1 046 251	31.6	11.2
Pine Bluff, AR	30 001	67.1	43 300	17.0	15.0	336	28.1	5.7	35 674	-1.2	2 926	8.2	33 236	25.2	11.6
Pittsburgh, PA	947 248	70.0	55 600	NA	NA	362	NA	1.5	1 175 869	1.8	51 109	4.3	1 041 067	31.3	10.8
Pittsfield, MA	54 315	65.2	114 900	20.8	13.3	436	25.2	1.0	63 369	1.3	2 324	3.7	65 136	32.0	12.7
Pocatello, ID	23 412	68.7	53 300	18.5	11.6	294	24.3	3.8	40 750	3.6	1 932	4.7	29 061	30.2	11.0
Portland, ME	94 512	64.3	118 300	22.2	13.2	521	26.2	1.7	145 578	-0.7	3 379	2.3	123 322	33.9	10.2
Portland-Salem, OR-WA	691 102	61.9	70 700	NA	NA	430	NA	3.5	1 244 266	-0.2	74 084	6.0	877 443	30.9	10.9
Portland-Vancouver, OR-WA	589 441	61.6	72 400	NA	NA	436	NA	3.3	1 071 843	0.1	63 209	5.9	754 650	31.2	11.0
Salem, OR	101 661	63.5	60 600	20.7	13.1	394	25.9	4.4	172 423	-1.7	10 875	6.3	122 793	28.8	10.2
Providence-Warwick-Pawtucket, RI	345 290	59.5	131 300	22.2	13.9	480	26.4	2.7	462 312	-0.3	22 178	4.8	447 642	29.4	12.1
Provo-Orem, UT	70 168	62.7	70 000	21.3	11.8	348	25.1	8.0	172 455	1.4	6 522	3.8	105 102	32.1	10.2
Pueblo, CO	47 057	67.9	51 300	21.1	12.7	307	27.7	3.7	58 198	-0.4	2 997	5.1	47 431	26.7	10.7
Punta Gorda, FL	48 433	79.6	77 200	NA	NA	499	NA	2.1	52 044	4.9	1 744	3.4	38 468	26.2	13.8
Raleigh-Durham-Chapel Hill, NC	334 506	60.8	89 100	NA	NA	456	NA	3.0	652 309	1.7	21 746	3.3	468 008	37.9	10.1
Rapid City, SD	30 553	61.4	56 600	22.3	13.1	385	26.1	2.9	48 315	1.7	1 483	3.1	36 145	27.9	13.0

1. Specified owner-occupied units. 2. Specified renter-occupied units. 3. Overcrowded or lacking complete plumbing facilities. 4. Percent of civilian labor force. 5. Persons 16 years and older.

Table C. Metropolitan Areas — **Nonfarm Employment and Agriculture**

	Private nonfarm establishments, employment and payroll, 1999								Agriculture, 1997			
	Employment						Annual payroll		Farms			Farm operators
										Percent with—		Whose principal occupation is farming (percent)
Area Name	Number of establishments	Total	Health Care and Social Assistance	Manufacturing	Retail trade	Finance and Insurance	Professional Scientific and Technical Services	Total (mil dol)	Average per employee (dollars)	Number	Less than 50 acres	500 acres and over	
	104	105	106	107	108	109	110	111	112	113	114	115	116
Merced, CA	2 931	38 209	5 216	8 322	6 609	975	852	871	22 796	2 831	52.5	10.8	61.9
Miami-Fort Lauderdale, FL ...	116 048	1 459 472	176 949	94 931	208 780	78 877	84 232	43 114	29 541	1 923	87.0	2.8	53.3
Fort Lauderdale, FL	49 501	596 218	75 225	36 232	95 113	34 693	35 920	17 250	28 932	347	86.2	2.3	55.6
Miami, FL	66 547	863 254	101 724	58 699	113 667	44 184	48 312	25 864	29 961	1 576	87.2	2.9	52.7
Milwaukee-Racine, WI	43 942	848 868	108 736	183 885	97 087	55 848	40 472	27 877	32 840	2 481	39.1	7.0	52.9
Milwaukee-Waukesha, WI .	39 778	775 261	100 190	163 853	87 046	51 897	38 278	25 598	33 019	1 927	38.5	6.3	52.3
Racine, WI	4 164	73 607	8 546	20 032	10 041	3 951	2 194	2 279	30 962	554	41.0	9.4	55.1
Minneapolis-St. Paul, MN-WI	83 094	1 594 560	176 766	227 431	181 421	114 288	96 605	56 999	35 746	10 460	34.3	7.5	46.2
Missoula, MT	3 576	39 548	5 939	2 969	7 517	1 610	1 982	905	22 884	482	53.1	13.9	35.5
Mobile, AL	13 271	204 389	26 332	27 446	30 318	7 007	8 956	4 971	24 321	1 732	49.9	8.1	41.1
Modesto, CA	8 176	117 156	16 354	23 307	18 629	3 454	3 550	3 098	26 443	4 009	65.5	6.5	55.8
Monroe, LA	4 093	62 353	9 902	7 692	9 348	5 525	3 482	1 548	24 826	377	37.9	11.9	42.4
Montgomery, AL	7 933	128 438	17 752	15 434	19 331	8 335	6 100	3 184	24 790	1 562	26.5	15.2	39.1
Muncie, IN	2 764	47 613	7 194	9 391	7 420	1 696	1 729	1 240	26 043	635	38.0	13.7	47.7
Myrtle Beach, SC	7 152	82 166	6 435	6 084	15 198	3 239	2 278	1 732	21 079	896	31.1	9.8	54.9
Naples, FL	8 198	87 955	10 422	2 762	16 470	3 422	3 884	2 319	26 366	235	53.6	23.0	46.8
Nashville, TN	33 247	616 275	73 367	81 815	77 057	38 434	27 611	19 228	31 200	10 049	39.7	3.9	35.6
New London-Norwich, CT.....	5 705	103 728	14 350	18 805	13 782	2 052	4 347	3 414	32 913	610	45.4	3.1	51.0
New Orleans, LA	31 794	537 865	74 509	43 287	72 213	24 835	28 362	14 988	27 866	840	58.7	8.5	43.6
New York-Northern New Jersey-Long Island, NY-NJ-CT-PA	584 423	8 464 645	1 244 734	758 971	915 325	702 513	680 142	378 958	44 770	8 296	64.1	3.7	46.3
Bergen-Passaic, NJ	44 975	617 736	67 801	86 186	76 936	31 302	36 589	24 550	39 742	176	88.6	0.6	47.2
Dutchess County, NY	6 634	85 854	15 780	13 491	13 485	3 336	4 623	2 541	29 597	539	33.0	9.8	54.7
Jersey City, NJ	13 294	214 721	20 191	20 840	20 189	23 245	9 639	8 349	38 883	0	X	X	X
Middlesex-Somerset-Hunterdon, NJ	33 914	589 647	52 201	71 017	61 884	39 080	61 391	26 196	44 427	2 025	66.4	3.7	38.2
Monmouth-Ocean, NJ	29 252	310 907	53 861	17 928	59 615	12 348	22 269	10 088	32 447	1 109	80.7	3.2	44.7
Nassau-Suffolk, NY	89 163	1 043 276	162 997	104 024	152 696	67 953	73 115	36 559	35 043	661	72.6	2.1	65.5
New Haven-Bridgeport-Stamford-Danbury-Waterbury, CT	49 393	779 470	107 510	108 780	100 302	50 850	50 628	34 704	44 523	678	69.9	0.7	52.1
New York, NY	241 648	3 653 788	613 933	206 291	302 072	397 470	331 426	188 625	51 625	179	65.4	1.7	41.9
Newark, NJ	58 097	907 723	114 054	110 932	90 832	62 691	70 638	38 417	42 322	1 980	62.1	3.5	38.3
Newburgh, NY-PA	8 618	96 494	14 985	9 677	19 226	4 317	4 003	2 580	26 737	664	38.9	5.1	68.2
Trenton, NJ	9 435	165 029	21 421	9 805	18 088	9 921	15 821	6 349	38 472	285	64.9	4.6	42.5
Norfolk-Virginia Beach-Newport News, VA-NC	34 133	563 193	67 599	61 834	92 311	23 823	38 005	13 930	24 734	1 105	44.1	18.1	55.3
Ocala, FL	5 408	71 483	10 583	9 420	13 599	2 291	2 439	1 600	22 383	1 669	62.1	5.0	47.0
Odessa-Midland, TX	7 138	83 682	11 838	5 276	12 959	2 649	3 310	2 164	25 860	619	51.1	22.6	38.9
Oklahoma City, OK	29 412	425 956	57 876	50 863	58 107	21 590	20 719	10 955	25 719	6 655	30.5	14.2	40.0
Omaha, NE-IA	18 853	364 226	44 068	35 925	46 075	31 094	18 217	11 063	30 374	3 446	25.1	25.8	61.9
Orlando, FL	44 048	786 453	68 735	47 400	105 319	31 950	43 765	21 487	27 321	3 080	70.6	7.4	46.1
Owensboro, KY	2 386	40 236	5 668	8 751	6 140	1 290	1 136	998	24 804	1 042	43.2	11.8	43.2
Panama City, FL	4 195	53 939	7 622	3 363	10 032	2 783	2 731	1 132	20 987	70	60.0	4.3	40.0
Parkersburg-Marietta, WV-OH	3 947	59 094	8 884	12 868	9 255	2 186	1 561	1 508	25 519	1 420	20.3	3.0	38.1
Pensacola, FL	8 640	127 836	20 099	8 558	20 198	3 839	5 524	2 952	23 092	904	51.5	8.0	45.7
Peoria-Pekin, IL	8 446	159 346	22 471	22 735	19 783	6 568	6 382	4 979	31 246	2 756	25.8	22.8	54.6
Philadelphia-Wilmington-Atlantic City, PA-NJ-DE-MD	154 687	2 653 267	376 236	286 398	328 171	187 415	199 374	93 160	35 111	7 014	56.9	4.9	51.5
Atlantic-Cape May, NJ	10 210	146 636	15 916	5 366	20 294	3 411	5 640	4 047	27 599	573	70.0	1.9	44.5
Philadelphia, PA-NJ	123 944	2 175 053	322 096	242 485	265 295	148 179	175 425	76 913	35 361	5 077	56.7	4.3	52.2
Vineland-Millville-Bridgeton, NJ	3 030	44 706	6 620	11 955	7 065	1 508	1 479	1 291	28 878	573	61.8	4.7	53.1
Wilmington-Newark, DE-MD	17 503	286 872	31 604	26 592	35 517	34 317	16 830	10 909	38 027	791	44.9	10.7	51.5
Phoenix-Mesa, AZ	72 460	1 333 037	123 046	145 246	163 366	89 240	83 581	40 760	30 577	2 184	57.2	20.5	52.4
Pine Bluff, AR	1 616	27 421	4 330	7 832	4 461	843	639	643	23 449	362	25.7	37.0	60.2
Pittsburgh, PA	59 469	1 022 647	152 921	121 654	131 652	56 573	65 032	32 329	31 613	4 894	29.6	3.3	44.6
Pittsfield, MA	4 356	56 586	10 060	8 447	8 797	2 067	2 077	1 587	28 046	387	39.5	7.0	50.1
Pocatello, ID	1 882	23 616	3 245	3 695	4 420	1 444	1 055	551	23 332	664	44.0	20.6	40.5
Portland, ME	10 057	145 538	22 969	15 486	20 799	12 375	8 081	4 311	29 621	455	47.3	3.5	47.3
Portland-Salem, OR-WA	64 622	950 019	99 771	143 558	143 558	55 264	50 845	30 708	32 324	13 370	70.9	3.4	39.4
Portland-Vancouver, OR-WA	56 031	845 582	85 319	129 795	103 487	47 798	47 370	28 089	33 219	9 677	73.8	2.3	36.8
Salem, OR	8 591	104 437	14 452	13 763	16 254	7 466	3 475	2 619	25 077	3 693	63.5	6.1	46.3
Providence-Warwick-Pawtucket, RI	25 534	377 369	59 880	69 132	43 820	22 724	14 574	11 098	29 409	596	60.4	2.0	47.5
Provo-Orem, UT	6 835	137 583	14 491	15 808	17 881	3 183	9 641	3 219	23 397	1 790	68.2	6.5	37.0
Pueblo, CO	3 206	46 711	9 569	4 103	7 320	1 454	1 316	1 040	22 265	664	31.3	34.2	48.3
Punta Gorda, FL	2 997	32 143	6 513	677	7 283	1 156	1 380	670	20 844	209	47.8	22.0	47.4
Raleigh-Durham-Chapel Hill, NC	32 767	561 063	65 588	71 915	69 564	23 591	42 950	18 523	33 014	4 112	37.4	6.8	50.9
Rapid City, SD	3 216	38 420	6 765	4 239	6 670	1 728	1 325	897	23 347	637	16.2	46.8	64.1

Table C. Metropolitan Areas — **Agriculture, Land, and Water**

Area Name	Land in farms					Value of land and buildings		Value of machinery and equipment Average per farm ($1,000)	Value of products sold		Percent from —		Percent of farms with sales of —		Percent of land owned by Fed. Gov. 1997	Water consumption 1995 (mil gal/day)
	Acreage (1,000)	Percent change, 1992–1997	Average size of farm	Total irrigated (1,000)	Total cropland (1,000)	Average per farm ($1,000)	Average per acre (dollars)		Total (mil dol)	Average per farm (dollars)	Crops	Live-stock and poultry products	$10,000 or more	$100,000 or more		
				Acres												
	117	118	119	120	121	122	123	124	125	126	127	128	129	130	131	132
Merced, CA	882	-9.9	311	493	532	951	3 149	96	1 273	449 832	45.0	55.0	72.3	38.6	1.9	1 688.4
Miami-Fort Lauderdale, FL ...	116	7.4	60	60	74	409	7 180	46	466	242 083	97.0	3.0	52.4	22.8	0.2	856.6
Fort Lauderdale, FL..........	31	28.7	89	2	7	414	4 791	33	49	141 280	86.0	14.0	57.6	21.3	0.2	287.3
Miami, FL.......................	85	1.3	54	58	68	408	8 047	49	417	264 278	98.0	2.0	51.2	23.2	NA	569.3
Milwaukee-Racine, WI.........	432	-10.4	174	7	D	431	2 516	64	221	89 016	D	D	54.7	20.4	0.0	2 291.5
Milwaukee-Waukesha, WI..	309	-11.5	160	2	D	405	2 563	60	142	73 903	D	D	55.3	20.3	0.0	2 253.8
Racine, WI.....................	123	-7.5	222	5	110	520	2 396	77	78	141 585	54.0	46.0	52.5	20.6	0.0	37.7
Minneapolis-St. Paul, MN-WI	1 906	-4.9	182	85	1 470	358	1 977	62	701	67 014	53.0	47.0	49.0	17.1	1.3	1 554.5
Missoula, MT.....................	262	5.6	544	22	47	494	993	34	8	16 643	27.0	73.0	28.2	3.1	42.1	113.6
Mobile, AL........................	287	5.5	166	11	178	369	2 354	41	125	72 143	81.0	19.0	31.9	9.7	1.3	1 146.4
Modesto, CA.....................	733	-3.6	183	359	382	779	4 508	61	1 209	301 453	46.0	54.0	63.5	29.4	0.3	1 437.9
Monroe, LA.......................	89	18.8	236	11	60	277	1 239	68	26	68 247	65.0	35.0	35.0	13.3	2.1	111.9
Montgomery, AL.................	470	6.1	301	2	210	463	1 581	39	64	40 786	47.0	53.0	31.0	7.4	0.3	106.5
Muncie, IN........................	173	2.6	273	0	160	585	2 219	65	53	82 874	84.0	16.0	57.2	19.8	0.0	18.8
Myrtle Beach, SC...............	184	-6.3	205	1	117	384	1 943	72	83	92 397	87.0	13.0	55.6	24.0	0.5	94.1
Naples, FL........................	277	-8.2	1 180	53	69	2 152	1 796	166	277	1 178 400	97.0	3.0	66.8	34.0	35.5	208.2
Nashville, TN.....................	1 291	0.8	128	3	788	324	2 562	31	204	20 266	53.0	47.0	27.5	3.4	0.6	991.4
New London-Norwich, CT.....	68	2.9	111	0	30	445	4 220	41	126	206 238	44.0	56.0	34.9	12.5	0.3	41.2
New Orleans, LA.................	163	-9.4	194	D	80	384	2 047	60	55	65 664	D	D	33.5	11.2	3.8	5 152.3
New York-Northern New Jersey-Long Island, NY-NJ-CT-PA	754	-2.7	91	D	D	D	D	D	D	D	D	D	42.1	13.7	2.2	4 462.1
Bergen-Passaic, NJ..........	5	21.6	28	0	2	561	18 134	29	13	73 131	95.0	5.0	51.7	14.2	0.0	422.1
Dutchess County, NY.......	107	-3.0	198	1	63	791	4 619	53	34	63 013	49.0	51.0	53.6	15.2	0.4	39.2
Jersey City, NJ	0	X	X	0	0	X	X	X	0	X	X	X	X	X	1.5	0.2
Middlesex-Somerset-Hunterdon, NJ..................	180	2.6	89	3	131	652	7 769	40	84	41 698	84.0	16.0	32.4	7.3	0.3	249.4
Monmouth-Ocean, NJ........	71	2.6	64	7	52	606	9 241	46	76	68 659	90.0	10.0	39.4	11.5	5.7	139.1
Nassau-Suffolk, NY	37	0.7	56	16	30	671	11 719	70	171	258 664	93.0	7.0	71.0	33.7	0.9	390.1
New Haven-Bridgeport-Stamford-Danbury-Waterbury, CT	36	1.4	54	1	20	640	11 080	36	60	88 674	79.0	21.0	41.7	11.8	0.2	389.0
New York, NY..................	D	D	D	D	D	D	D	D	D	D	D	D	55.9	20.1	0.9	705.1
Newark, NJ.....................	D	D	D	3	113	624	6 973	34	106	53 716	67.0	33.0	30.4	9.9	4.5	249.0
Newburgh, NY-PA	100	-7.9	151	5	D	573	3 816	74	71	107 277	64.0	36.0	68.2	28.2	4.1	1 372.9
Trenton, NJ.....................	28	-21.1	100	1	23	1 359	13 871	44	13	46 509	92.0	8.0	38.2	10.5	0.0	506.1
Norfolk-Virginia Beach-Newport News, VA-NC	337	-4.0	305	D	258	626	D	D	D	D	D	D	55.9	24.0	7.4	281.3
Ocala, FL..........................	266	-10.3	159	6	100	491	3 094	27	102	60 833	23.0	77.0	31.3	9.3	28.3	52.1
Odessa-Midland, TX	1 325	6.6	2 141	14	D	438	201	38	22	35 771	39.0	61.0	25.5	8.4	0.0	68.9
Oklahoma City, OK	1 775	3.7	267	10	900	271	1 030	33	198	29 688	27.0	73.0	32.5	5.5	0.8	135.4
Omaha, NE-IA....................	1 271	0.2	369	D	1 115	681	1 943	84	451	130 893	60.0	40.0	70.7	32.4	0.8	1 358.7
Orlando, FL.......................	1 008	-9.5	327	113	181	649	2 037	38	525	170 340	89.0	11.0	45.8	16.9	3.7	493.9
Owensboro, KY	251	0.4	241	3	207	388	1 650	57	71	68 406	82.0	18.0	48.8	15.1	0.0	220.2
Panama City, FL	7	-25.2	96	0	3	179	1 858	23	3	38 171	92.0	8.0	24.3	4.3	5.1	58.9
Parkersburg-Marietta, WV-OH.................................	213	6.5	150	0	102	188	1 312	31	23	16 383	37.0	63.0	21.9	3.2	5.0	859.1
Pensacola, FL....................	143	4.8	158	7	94	272	1 761	43	46	51 055	81.0	19.0	33.8	13.4	7.2	292.8
Peoria-Pekin, IL	895	0.1	325	34	805	855	2 621	86	308	111 613	79.0	21.0	70.6	31.0	0.0	919.7
Philadelphia-Wilmington-Atlantic City, PA-NJ-DE-MD.................................	839	-0.7	120	85	D	580	4 819	62	950	135 459	D	D	50.7	20.6	1.5	3 118.7
Atlantic-Cape May, NJ	41	-0.7	71	13	25	345	5 113	61	70	122 646	99.0	1.0	43.3	16.8	3.9	71.8
Philadelphia, PA-NJ	569	0.1	112	48	D	594	5 254	60	690	135 846	D	D	51.8	20.6	1.3	2 325.8
Vineland-Millville-Bridgeton, NJ	66	-3.9	116	19	51	421	3 738	77	94	164 314	96.0	4.0	53.8	27.9	0.0	87.4
Wilmington-Newark, DE-MD.................................	163	-2.4	206	4	130	776	3 666	68	96	121 359	51.0	49.0	47.0	17.4	0.8	633.8
Phoenix-Mesa, AZ	2 012	-23.6	921	525	D	1 509	1 529	96	1 028	470 484	56.0	44.0	51.2	32.4	41.2	3 649.2
Pine Bluff, AR	289	2.4	797	147	258	761	976	155	95	263 116	85.0	15.0	60.5	40.3	2.5	454.5
Pittsburgh, PA...................	642	-6.0	131	2	421	290	2 219	43	132	27 012	45.0	55.0	35.4	6.5	0.2	2 245.7
Pittsfield, MA....................	63	3.0	162	0	31	547	3 150	35	21	53 553	40.0	60.0	35.9	11.9	0.0	24.0
Pocatello, ID.....................	309	-4.8	466	42	167	257	658	43	25	37 699	62.0	38.0	35.7	8.1	27.4	313.5
Portland, ME	50	-7.7	110	1	26	322	2 600	35	17	38 062	64.0	36.0	38.9	10.5	0.6	36.9
Portland-Salem, OR-WA......	1 147	2.0	86	190	799	422	5 002	48	1 264	94 529	81.0	19.0	33.5	11.2	22.0	1 317.3
Portland-Vancouver, OR-WA	670	2.3	69	84	420	393	5 804	38	734	75 891	81.0	19.0	30.5	8.9	22.2	983.4
Salem, OR	478	1.6	129	106	379	499	3 877	75	529	143 369	83.0	17.0	41.2	17.3	21.7	334.0
Providence-Warwick-Pawtucket, RI	45	12.1	75	3	19	410	5 453	37	34	56 525	82.0	18.0	44.1	11.2	0.2	126.1
Provo-Orem, UT.................	375	-16.7	209	81	150	433	2 244	40	97	54 195	40.0	60.0	32.8	9.4	43.3	298.8
Pueblo, CO........................	823	-8.3	1 239	36	90	533	471	38	34	50 666	42.0	58.0	45.6	10.5	7.9	246.1
Punta Gorda, FL	290	27.9	1 389	26	45	1 878	1 359	45	50	240 010	89.0	11.0	51.2	22.0	0.0	49.9
Raleigh-Durham-Chapel Hill, NC	669	0.7	163	17	375	423	2 712	44	465	113 039	47.0	53.0	47.6	19.9	1.0	545.3
Rapid City, SD	1 044	-2.1	1 639	9	288	512	325	49	40	62 289	29.0	71.0	61.2	14.1	43.1	30.2

Table C. Metropolitan Areas — **Residential Construction, Wholesale and Retail Trade, and Real Estate**

Area Name	Value of Residential Construction Authorized by Building Permits, 2000		Wholesale Trade, 1997				Retail Trade[1], 1997				Real Estate and Rental and Leasing, 1997			
	New Construction ($1,000)	Number of Housing Units	Number of Establishments	Number of Employees	Sales (mil dol)	Annual Payroll (mil dol)	Number of Establishments	Number of Employees	Sales (mil dol)	Annual Payroll (mil dol)	Number of Establishments	Number of Employees	Receipts (mil dol)	Annual Payroll (mil dol)
	133	134	135	136	137	138	139	140	141	142	143	144	145	146
Merced, CA	184 032	1 380	117	1 333	699.9	36.4	551	6 122	1 102.1	108.0	121	461	46.0	5.7
Miami-Fort Lauderdale, FL	2 708 381	24 445	13 294	108 664	69 726.6	3 650.6	16 618	199 582	38 700.4	3 635.7	5 641	34 187	5 050.5	817.4
Fort Lauderdale, FL	1 486 624	11 970	4 359	38 614	26 122.2	1 414.7	6 804	89 290	17 979.8	1 639.9	2 263	14 394	2 196.6	351.6
Miami, FL	1 221 757	12 475	8 935	70 050	43 604.4	2 235.9	9 814	110 292	20 720.6	1 995.8	3 378	19 793	2 853.9	465.8
Milwaukee-Racine, WI	902 495	6 498	3 284	47 661	30 083.3	1 806.4	6 015	96 146	15 865.1	1 535.0	1 574	10 521	1 309.8	234.6
Milwaukee-Waukesha, WI	797 897	5 631	3 050	43 101	26 266.4	1 664.1	5 351	86 453	14 301.0	1 392.9	1 442	9 775	1 252.1	222.6
Racine, WI	104 598	867	234	4 560	3 816.9	142.4	664	9 693	1 564.1	142.0	132	746	57.7	12.1
Minneapolis-St. Paul, MN-WI	3 119 222	22 306	6 464	98 760	81 849.0	4 106.1	10 519	173 134	31 195.8	2 969.6	3 518	24 708	3 360.5	614.7
Missoula, MT	40 177	571	183	1 991	775.9	50.0	540	6 800	1 069.0	105.2	138	593	46.2	8.2
Mobile, AL	474 850	4 630	850	9 895	3 826.4	295.0	2 482	30 710	4 619.9	452.9	575	3 309	310.5	62.9
Modesto, CA	400 922	3 023	417	5 118	2 264.4	159.1	1 368	17 706	3 282.2	319.2	340	2 033	244.5	42.4
Monroe, LA	48 742	395	248	2 912	1 257.2	82.4	753	9 649	1 483.5	134.0	176	805	79.7	12.7
Montgomery, AL	120 470	1 270	468	5 850	3 095.1	166.2	1 504	19 978	3 146.9	293.6	350	2 365	193.5	42.0
Muncie, IN	51 957	402	119	1 501	653.4	45.8	548	7 340	1 118.7	105.4	119	433	46.9	8.4
Myrtle Beach, SC	406 482	4 492	230	1 824	481.5	49.5	1 522	14 457	2 505.2	230.7	360	3 026	259.6	59.7
Naples, FL	1 188 311	7 970	350	2 076	813.8	63.0	1 343	15 366	2 627.1	274.1	509	2 874	305.2	66.0
Nashville, TN	1 297 925	10 640	2 213	35 488	23 385.2	1 288.8	5 282	73 125	12 780.5	1 257.9	1 408	9 822	1 557.2	245.4
New London-Norwich, CT	108 777	814	201	2 279	801.6	81.9	1 182	13 923	2 405.0	240.3	188	723	82.4	13.8
New Orleans, LA	517 318	4 183	2 182	27 247	24 973.6	909.6	5 241	69 416	11 032.9	1 073.5	1 320	10 690	1 241.7	231.9
New York-Northern New Jersey-Long Island, NY-NJ-CT-PA	6 629 631	58 588	47 914	D	D	D	85 012	904 682	172 895.5	17 814.0	31 494	168 324	34 036.6	5 390.8
Bergen-Passaic, NJ	419 775	3 304	4 882	68 811	71 520.4	3 315.4	6 127	77 533	15 426.0	1 521.8	1 775	10 482	2 073.1	324.7
Dutchess County, NY	172 169	1 003	274	D	D	D	1 097	13 506	2 259.5	225.7	256	1 502	165.9	28.5
Jersey City, NJ	83 481	1 338	1 065	21 629	11 271.5	864.6	2 327	22 670	3 842.9	384.9	542	3 070	628.1	96.1
Middlesex-Somerset-Hunterdon, NJ	561 626	5 358	2 746	49 781	43 743.1	2 272.7	4 563	61 187	12 124.3	1 171.2	985	5 923	1 050.5	181.7
Monmouth-Ocean, NJ	816 140	8 545	1 626	12 480	7 235.3	505.6	4 793	58 270	11 128.8	1 059.1	985	4 140	634.7	105.0
Nassau-Suffolk, NY	1 113 237	6 438	7 524	78 508	45 747.2	3 214.0	13 144	149 961	29 993.3	2 968.7	3 438	15 766	2 904.1	453.7
New Haven-Bridgeport-Stamford-Danbury-Waterbury, CT	751 007	4 196	3 084	44 031	56 353.7	2 192.4	7 343	95 954	19 289.1	1 993.9	1 859	11 669	2 225.6	377.2
New York, NY	1 637 321	18 082	21 217	223 228	212 129.3	10 175.2	34 081	293 786	53 828.7	5 967.7	18 735	99 627	21 329.5	3 374.2
Newark, NJ	648 631	6 566	4 407	69 478	58 304.7	3 279.2	8 128	90 246	17 642.9	1 796.1	2 255	12 882	2 533.4	374.2
Newburgh, NY-PA	291 211	2 475	471	D	D	D	1 545	18 334	3 230.3	307.3	305	1 349	196.9	25.6
Trenton, NJ	135 034	1 283	472	8 480	4 403.0	291.5	1 442	18 217	3 183.1	326.1	289	1 685	256.7	43.1
Norfolk-Virginia Beach-Newport News, VA-NC	909 011	7 429	1 585	21 645	8 973.1	649.3	6 010	83 007	12 705.1	1 259.5	1 570	10 833	1 082.8	222.3
Ocala, FL	363 776	2 354	309	3 219	999.6	80.0	1 014	13 159	2 221.4	202.1	244	786	88.4	13.8
Odessa-Midland, TX	37 803	396	652	6 226	2 986.2	211.8	1 087	12 709	2 366.2	212.9	321	1 752	177.8	35.8
Oklahoma City, OK	576 147	5 401	1 844	23 760	16 611.1	703.7	4 394	56 273	10 141.6	905.3	1 276	6 716	734.8	128.5
Omaha, NE-IA	482 677	5 727	1 274	19 950	13 721.6	655.7	2 753	46 740	7 655.9	765.6	738	5 107	622.2	116.8
Orlando, FL	2 402 069	24 924	3 149	36 667	29 509.2	1 201.0	6 795	93 025	16 865.1	1 538.6	2 200	19 964	2 647.1	473.6
Owensboro, KY	53 720	835	141	1 678	872.9	43.7	470	6 011	853.8	84.5	75	476	33.9	7.7
Panama City, FL	167 156	1 452	173	1 406	422.1	34.2	832	9 558	1 496.8	148.1	229	1 018	76.8	15.6
Parkersburg-Marietta, WV-OH	21 740	256	190	2 183	656.4	53.3	741	9 121	1 491.2	136.9	124	546	59.8	10.6
Pensacola, FL	251 154	2 511	470	5 065	1 719.0	135.4	1 620	20 217	3 435.8	305.6	389	1 625	159.4	27.8
Peoria-Pekin, IL	166 429	1 564	494	8 924	9 499.5	372.0	1 375	19 639	3 352.0	311.5	289	1 648	164.0	31.2
Philadelphia-Wilmington-Atlantic City, PA-NJ-DE-MD	2 303 379	22 642	9 964	D	D	D	24 437	320 158	58 373.5	5 869.5	5 373	38 918	10 040.8	1 036.1
Atlantic-Cape May, NJ	254 627	2 867	308	3 219	1 032.5	102.6	2 042	19 298	3 474.2	356.5	444	2 013	329.8	45.9
Philadelphia, PA-NJ	1 787 156	16 421	8 777	119 671	97 035.0	5 011.9	19 454	259 802	47 692.4	4 801.6	3 987	32 530	4 814.3	887.7
Vineland-Millville-Bridgeton, NJ	22 446	255	189	2 230	989.4	69.4	578	7 157	1 226.5	130.1	115	486	52.0	9.4
Wilmington-Newark, DE-MD	239 150	3 099	690	D	D	D	2 363	33 901	5 980.4	581.3	827	3 889	4 844.6	93.1
Phoenix-Mesa, AZ	5 297 816	45 310	4 840	62 284	39 724.9	2 284.0	9 618	149 267	30 011.9	2 856.2	3 502	22 551	3 079.9	558.2
Pine Bluff, AR	8 539	139	77	780	309.9	18.9	393	4 785	726.6	71.8	58	368	23.8	5.8
Pittsburgh, PA	788 093	6 430	3 811	51 132	39 222.1	1 839.2	9 664	132 247	21 462.3	1 998.1	1 909	12 344	1 971.8	292.3
Pittsfield, MA	50 246	314	136	D	D	D	832	8 513	1 280.7	137.7	122	410	43.9	7.5
Pocatello, ID	23 347	235	104	935	282.6	25.2	343	4 177	705.7	65.1	64	255	23.5	3.5
Portland, ME	221 126	1 680	574	8 884	3 673.3	296.8	1 570	20 735	3 825.9	346.5	407	2 731	293.4	63.5
Portland-Salem, OR-WA	1 812 694	14 646	4 494	58 798	48 456.3	2 192.6	8 114	114 249	22 182.9	2 217.8	3 007	17 856	2 175.2	402.1
Portland-Vancouver, OR-WA	1 623 152	12 962	4 127	55 126	47 185.0	2 092.1	6 890	98 020	19 278.0	1 927.3	2 573	15 963	1 966.1	363.9
Salem, OR	189 542	1 684	367	3 672	1 271.3	100.5	1 224	16 229	2 904.9	290.5	434	1 893	209.0	38.2
Providence-Warwick-Pawtucket, RI	254 426	2 289	1 488	18 201	7 360.3	616.4	3 684	41 903	6 879.5	686.1	825	4 298	526.1	95.6
Provo-Orem, UT	509 146	3 731	320	6 272	2 763.6	190.4	978	15 868	2 486.4	245.1	239	1 085	108.0	16.9
Pueblo, CO	106 645	1 098	113	1 101	390.3	27.5	600	7 040	1 180.7	121.7	131	486	58.8	8.2
Punta Gorda, FL	182 298	1 670	103	446	117.2	11.2	515	6 840	1 063.3	100.4	167	601	60.7	10.1
Raleigh-Durham-Chapel Hill, NC	2 102 832	18 553	1 785	25 877	17 143.5	1 049.3	4 906	64 714	11 521.9	1 080.4	1 268	6 834	1 112.6	174.9
Rapid City, SD	44 883	427	173	2 027	675.7	57.8	581	6 870	1 132.0	112.2	126	530	52.7	9.0

1. Establishments with payroll.

Table C. Metropolitan Areas — **Professional, Manufacturing, Accommodation and Foodservices, Finance and Insurance**

Area Name	Professional, Scientific, and Technical Services[1], 1997				Manufacturing, 1997				Accommodation and Foodservices, 1997			
	Number of Establishments	Number of Employees	Sales (mil dol)	Annual Payroll (mil dol)	Number of Establishments	Number of Employees	Sales (mil dol)	Annual Payroll (mil dol)	Number of Establishments	Number of Employees	Sales (mil dol)	Annual Payroll (mil dol)
	147	148	149	150	151	152	153	154	155	156	157	158
Merced, CA	138	668	41.0	15.8	123	8 381	2 432	198	269	3 265	108.4	27.2
Miami-Fort Lauderdale, FL	13 446	70 277	7 580.8	2 959.6	4 998	103 525	14 312	2 779	7 041	136 840	5 673.9	1 493.9
Fort Lauderdale, FL	5 625	27 496	2 940.7	1 103.7	1 967	37 134	5 788	1 115	3 206	61 243	2 474.5	615.5
Miami, FL	7 821	42 781	4 640.0	1 856.0	3 031	66 391	8 524	1 664	3 835	75 597	3 199.5	878.5
Milwaukee-Racine, WI	3 948	34 466	3 524.7	1 353.2	3 553	184 012	36 323	6 623	3 232	55 199	1 701.6	474.9
Milwaukee-Waukesha, WI.	3 652	32 645	3 390.4	1 297.6	3 174	165 143	31 094	5 958	2 872	49 875	1 546.9	432.7
Racine, WI	296	1 821	134.3	55.6	379	18 869	5 230	664	360	5 324	154.7	42.2
Minneapolis-St. Paul, MN-WI	9 814	81 621	9 422.4	3 672.8	5 348	234 192	44 600	8 761	5 131	111 217	3 757.3	1 111.4
Missoula, MT	276	1 617	109.7	45.2	136	2 690	562	89	329	4 782	145.6	40.4
Mobile, AL	994	6 930	588.2	235.1	583	27 280	6 304	962	952	19 104	594.5	163.3
Modesto, CA	478	2 974	232.5	81.3	435	25 056	6 887	823	676	9 877	312.7	80.4
Monroe, LA	358	2 042	145.3	50.7	152	8 235	1 983	288	265	5 360	170.1	42.6
Montgomery, AL	646	4 780	445.5	201.4	303	15 813	2 671	426	534	12 217	340.5	94.8
Muncie, IN	153	1 691	87.8	37.3	176	9 972	1 765	403	228	4 981	126.7	35.6
Myrtle Beach, SC	400	1 766	135.5	53.8	160	6 687	928	173	1 044	20 246	881.7	228.5
Naples, FL	743	3 074	414.1	196.5	205	2 305	259	62	518	11 599	536.7	140.9
Nashville, TN	2 682	21 278	2 219.5	832.0	1 544	84 573	21 496	2 792	2 248	55 500	2 076.5	586.4
New London-Norwich, CT	463	3 944	338.9	162.2	237	19 888	2 963	1 035	590	8 652	333.0	95.7
New Orleans, LA	3 406	24 941	2 478.9	967.9	1 022	43 738	26 356	1 673	2 653	60 890	2 369.6	652.8
New York-Northern New Jersey-Long Island, NY-NJ-CT-PA	63 083	569 807	78 862.1	30 606.6	29 610	837 259	164 000	29 316	39 803	494 546	24 535.3	6 816.5
Bergen-Passaic, NJ	5 217	31 665	3 904.1	1 405.8	2 865	94 466	16 884	3 461	2 674	32 527	1 455.9	395.0
Dutchess County, NY	591	3 149	284.3	113.6	210	11 848	3 033	521	558	6 243	252.1	64.4
Jersey City, NJ	977	7 208	931.7	342.8	979	26 470	4 221	788	1 127	10 056	466.5	119.6
Middlesex-Somerset-Hunterdon, NJ	4 676	60 045	6 881.8	2 872.0	1 528	71 336	19 941	3 002	2 173	28 472	1 220.8	332.0
Monmouth-Ocean, NJ	3 026	17 617	1 808.0	768.7	896	19 994	3 258	604	2 323	28 700	1 110.0	303.2
Nassau-Suffolk, NY	9 464	55 636	5 982.3	2 198.9	4 188	113 034	19 126	3 984	5 676	64 915	2 811.1	767.6
New Haven-Bridgeport-Stamford-Danbury-Waterbury, CT	5 719	42 336	5 849.6	2 398.8	2 908	116 940	24 189	4 781	3 416	46 224	1 918.0	532.7
New York, NY	24 511	275 541	43 493.7	16 577.9	11 821	239 106	34 657	6 604	16 261	208 970	12 310.8	3 481.2
Newark, NJ	6 804	62 207	7 958.3	3 214.4	3 261	110 238	32 134	4 341	3 942	48 837	2 219.6	608.6
Newburgh, NY-PA	658	2 780	280.9	100.4	346	D	D	D	778	7 984	305.5	82.2
Trenton, NJ	1 223	10 930	1 407.3	586.2	352	13 537	2 414	580	703	9 870	394.0	109.9
Norfolk-Virginia Beach-Newport News, VA-NC	2 583	27 170	2 097.1	888.0	1 043	62 701	16 721	2 067	2 932	58 484	1 888.0	526.6
Ocala, FL	361	1 882	132.9	52.8	215	9 620	1 288	238	363	6 558	200.9	54.1
Odessa-Midland, TX	542	3 093	314.1	102.1	338	5 961	1 612	192	465	7 620	243.8	67.1
Oklahoma City, OK	2 932	16 522	1 462.5	567.3	1 181	51 318	12 605	1 620	2 161	41 765	1 263.8	349.6
Omaha, NE-IA	1 529	14 710	1 364.3	544.9	709	34 735	8 809	1 100	1 475	26 895	899.4	258.9
Orlando, FL	4 465	34 147	3 378.8	1 344.4	1 564	47 086	8 327	1 628	3 013	103 403	5 399.3	1 274.7
Owensboro, KY	145	857	56.4	23.3	114	8 011	2 938	277	150	3 331	100.6	26.6
Panama City, FL	268	1 730	138.9	56.1	136	3 492	719	109	483	9 268	336.3	84.8
Parkersburg-Marietta, WV-OH	211	1 270	88.8	31.5	182	12 252	4 203	481	320	5 790	176.1	50.7
Pensacola, FL	669	4 446	340.1	143.7	295	9 421	2 642	336	612	13 071	404.6	106.9
Peoria-Pekin, IL	549	5 510	446.9	200.6	350	23 638	7 551	996	822	13 322	381.0	109.1
Philadelphia-Wilmington-Atlantic City, PA-NJ-DE-MD	15 494	164 081	19 882.8	8 074.3	7 571	296 009	78 628	11 145	12 299	216 197	11 327.8	3 047.0
Atlantic-Cape May, NJ	724	4 680	449.9	184.1	242	5 740	711	162	1 727	60 280	5 383.3	1 423.3
Philadelphia, PA-NJ	13 093	147 380	18 002.6	7 343.3	6 606	251 908	66 608	9 483	9 294	133 515	5 134.5	1 395.2
Vineland-Millville-Bridgeton, NJ	200	1 061	88.9	34.1	210	12 985	1 896	398	218	2 554	78.8	21.1
Wilmington-Newark, DE-MD	1 477	10 960	1 341.4	512.8	513	25 376	9 413	1 101	1 060	19 848	731.3	207.4
Phoenix-Mesa, AZ	7 228	58 051	5 136.8	2 141.5	3 438	148 277	35 313	5 200	5 134	116 068	4 335.8	1 207.2
Pine Bluff, AR	85	619	38.1	14.5	84	7 774	1 742	219	131	2 049	57.9	15.0
Pittsburgh, PA	4 925	54 512	6 040.7	2 297.1	3 000	120 793	24 173	4 355	4 875	83 749	2 587.6	728.3
Pittsfield, MA	247	1 420	129.3	50.6	207	9 176	1 423	345	485	7 060	247.3	75.6
Pocatello, ID	108	934	47.4	22.5	62	3 482	775	119	188	2 792	75.3	20.5
Portland, ME	973	6 408	614.6	253.8	382	14 304	2 233	477	792	11 749	429.9	121.3
Portland-Salem, OR-WA	5 923	41 488	3 986.4	1 654.2	3 828	149 132	35 464	5 102	4 639	79 468	2 808.5	795.7
Portland-Vancouver, OR-WA	5 341	38 580	3 762.0	1 565.9	3 363	134 123	32 874	4 684	4 033	69 599	2 496.2	709.8
Salem, OR	582	2 908	224.5	88.3	465	15 009	2 590	418	606	9 869	312.3	85.9
Providence-Warwick-Pawtucket, RI	2 114	12 465	1 162.0	449.1	2 437	73 295	10 186	2 189	2 289	29 519	1 013.8	280.7
Provo-Orem, UT	582	6 094	463.3	195.3	390	15 949	2 667	461	392	8 270	228.0	64.3
Pueblo, CO	192	981	49.7	19.3	107	4 688	1 021	147	321	4 969	142.4	38.1
Punta Gorda, FL	194	1 083	73.3	37.3	74	587	78	14	218	3 935	123.5	31.9
Raleigh-Durham-Chapel Hill, NC	3 560	28 633	3 324.0	1 253.3	1 143	72 443	24 867	2 264	2 219	42 253	1 551.2	432.9
Rapid City, SD	207	1 119	91.0	30.6	134	4 263	867	101	326	5 125	163.7	44.3

1. Firms subject to federal tax.

Area Name	Health Care and Social Assistance[1], 1997				Other Services[1], 1997				Federal funds and grants, fiscal 2001[2] Expenditures (mil dol)				
										Direct payments for individuals			
	Number of Establishments	Number of Employees	Receipts (mil dol)	Annual Payroll (mil dol)	Number of Establishments	Number of Employees	Receipts (mil dol)	Annual Payroll (mil dol)	Total	Social Security and government retirement	Medicare	Food stamps and Supplemental Security Income
	159	160	161	162	163	164	165	166	167	168	169	170
Merced, CA	323	2 668	167.8	64.2	171	813	49.2	14.3	843.7	320.6	127.3	59.9
Miami-Fort Lauderdale, FL	10 383	112 426	8 661.5	3 480.5	7 147	41 623	2 788.3	759.1	19 841.1	6 423.0	5 504.1	1 047.4
Fort Lauderdale, FL	4 226	51 708	3 879.0	1 603.0	3 246	19 188	1 397.3	373.4	7 322.5	3 284.0	2 369.1	216.9
Miami, FL	6 157	60 718	4 782.5	1 877.5	3 901	22 435	1 391.0	385.8	12 518.6	3 139.0	3 135.0	830.5
Milwaukee-Racine, WI	3 516	43 944	2 763.7	1 440.5	2 707	19 486	1 256.9	391.9	7 941.8	3 246.1	1 333.9	303.0
Milwaukee-Waukesha, WI	3 251	40 173	2 499.9	1 307.6	2 416	17 291	1 131.6	351.5	7 175.4	2 869.9	1 207.0	278.9
Racine, WI	265	3 771	263.8	132.8	291	2 195	125.4	40.3	766.4	376.1	126.9	24.1
Minneapolis-St. Paul, MN-WI	5 073	70 207	4 109.1	2 082.1	4 471	41 363	2 493.7	875.8	13 234.2	4 482.8	1 639.6	324.9
Missoula, MT	285	2 305	151.7	70.7	184	956	61.9	17.0	465.6	177.4	49.1	13.4
Mobile, AL	783	12 466	847.7	398.9	838	5 584	354.8	105.8	3 221.9	1 277.5	513.6	143.6
Modesto, CA	805	9 346	656.1	253.2	538	3 154	210.7	58.7	1 775.3	720.4	337.7	111.0
Monroe, LA	355	5 465	339.6	153.9	224	1 332	74.1	22.2	680.3	250.9	150.6	42.6
Montgomery, AL	654	10 312	708.4	290.7	499	3 228	168.3	51.8	3 271.8	901.7	255.7	93.5
Muncie, IN	223	3 304	200.9	94.2	186	1 530	98.7	24.4	539.7	249.0	93.4	23.0
Myrtle Beach, SC	326	4 036	295.9	117.8	336	1 477	91.5	25.5	877.5	475.0	127.6	31.7
Naples, FL	492	5 124	404.9	175.0	431	2 035	109.6	34.8	1 080.5	691.4	234.3	16.1
Nashville, TN	2 468	44 414	3 172.4	1 370.4	1 858	13 207	882.6	267.5	6 793.0	2 206.2	893.7	175.4
New London-Norwich, CT	490	7 493	521.3	227.8	391	2 113	137.6	37.8	3 185.5	597.5	228.2	25.1
New Orleans, LA	2 910	47 063	3 015.5	1 248.4	1 930	14 036	897.7	271.8	8 865.6	2 490.3	1 515.4	439.4
New York-Northern New Jersey-Long Island, NY-NJ-CT-PA	45 338	432 570	34 143.2	14 472.5	36 922	182 440	12 687.4	3 768.1	116 416.4	37 790.7	22 009.8	4 615.9
Bergen-Passaic, NJ	3 773	33 327	2 974.0	1 226.5	2 911	14 935	1 095.2	345.6	6 104.5	2 752.8	1 310.1	150.4
Dutchess County, NY	583	4 966	347.0	145.8	448	1 802	125.0	33.3	1 160.3	566.3	201.7	28.3
Jersey City, NJ	1 002	6 936	522.6	213.3	915	4 477	264.3	77.8	3 194.0	809.6	543.3	153.9
Middlesex-Somerset-Hunterdon, NJ	2 365	23 883	2 090.2	825.3	1 959	9 915	752.7	220.5	4 484.6	1 993.7	878.4	72.1
Monmouth-Ocean, NJ	2 682	26 349	1 916.5	825.3	1 944	9 035	567.7	170.4	6 496.3	2 950.9	1 300.5	73.0
Nassau-Suffolk, NY	7 532	77 693	6 073.7	2 540.5	6 187	29 595	2 050.3	608.4	14 249.9	6 018.3	2 857.3	230.7
New Haven-Bridgeport-Stamford-Danbury-Waterbury, CT	3 979	51 826	3 665.7	1 700.5	3 131	17 526	1 230.0	383.8	9 974.9	3 377.5	1 791.0	215.5
New York, NY	16 803	154 220	12 321.5	5 102.1	14 201	67 473	4 595.2	1 320.0	55 334.0	14 081.0	10 546.8	3 277.7
Newark, NJ	4 940	43 453	3 385.6	1 461.0	3 942	21 313	1 546.9	479.1	10 045.8	3 704.2	1 915.1	315.1
Newburgh, NY-PA	697	5 727	383.1	164.4	577	2 679	196.4	52.1	1 931.1	721.0	276.8	47.0
Trenton, NJ	796	7 200	583.3	262.6	538	2 985	210.3	62.1	3 441.0	815.5	388.8	52.0
Norfolk-Virginia Beach-Newport News, VA-NC	2 601	30 528	1 788.9	878.1	2 465	17 087	1 008.4	316.7	20 749.5	4 209.5	943.4	243.9
Ocala, FL	466	6 512	466.6	185.9	369	1 680	93.9	29.4	1 495.6	919.2	312.6	45.5
Odessa-Midland, TX	472	6 645	415.6	171.5	461	3 286	306.6	70.1	820.8	394.1	182.1	40.3
Oklahoma City, OK	2 547	33 079	2 058.9	907.2	1 609	11 495	650.5	196.8	8 002.8	2 432.3	765.3	173.8
Omaha, NE-IA	1 226	15 265	996.6	480.8	1 234	8 294	497.8	156.4	3 783.7	1 428.2	451.0	85.0
Orlando, FL	3 136	38 208	2 746.2	1 240.1	2 626	16 893	1 040.0	314.7	8 410.3	3 550.9	1 369.3	241.0
Owensboro, KY	202	2 568	184.0	76.4	144	829	50.4	14.5	423.4	199.2	77.1	22.3
Panama City, FL	317	4 398	315.8	131.2	246	1 569	85.5	27.6	1 460.5	484.3	136.3	26.3
Parkersburg-Marietta, WV-OH	295	3 795	234.7	100.5	278	2 165	150.8	37.2	904.3	367.1	144.7	34.7
Pensacola, FL	662	11 163	748.8	344.1	557	3 672	210.4	73.6	2 999.5	1 314.0	325.2	83.9
Peoria-Pekin, IL	544	6 673	467.7	239.2	559	3 672	255.1	81.2	1 701.1	728.6	286.6	57.4
Philadelphia-Wilmington-Atlantic City, PA-NJ-DE-MD	12 730	139 603	9 857.3	4 559.7	9 969	58 475	3 898.1	1 202.4	37 523.0	13 129.1	7 050.2	1 229.7
Atlantic-Cape May, NJ	748	6 313	470.8	218.6	597	3 288	173.3	56.8	2 029.5	836.8	422.6	44.3
Philadelphia, PA-NJ	10 631	118 672	8 318.9	3 840.5	8 254	48 485	3 316.7	1 007.5	32 063.6	10 878.1	6 026.7	1 086.3
Vineland-Millville-Bridgeton, NJ	238	2 191	161.8	74.8	243	1 156	65.2	20.6	776.1	292.3	162.3	30.8
Wilmington-Newark, DE-MD	1 113	12 427	905.7	425.9	875	5 546	342.9	117.5	2 653.8	1 121.9	438.7	68.2
Phoenix-Mesa, AZ	5 980	65 092	4 618.5	2 016.1	4 168	30 680	2 040.5	606.3	16 016.6	5 991.6	2 231.0	399.6
Pine Bluff, AR	191	1 709	110.3	48.3	110	750	40.7	12.6	648.8	192.6	70.8	33.4
Pittsburgh, PA	5 433	59 633	4 112.6	1 814.6	4 303	25 001	1 652.9	465.3	16 289.8	6 086.0	3 542.6	446.2
Pittsfield, MA	268	4 334	254.6	113.7	231	1 074	62.7	18.7	952.7	331.3	186.0	19.7
Pocatello, ID	157	1 421	79.8	39.1	108	564	33.5	9.5	327.1	144.7	36.8	12.4
Portland, ME	764	9 092	602.3	303.5	503	3 458	226.7	71.3	1 488.8	566.2	191.2	36.9
Portland-Salem, OR-WA	4 608	46 839	3 043.0	1 329.2	3 248	20 378	1 413.9	429.2	10 520.8	4 010.2	1 355.0	312.4
Portland-Vancouver, OR-WA	3 887	40 364	2 663.4	1 162.7	2 817	18 146	1 282.8	388.3	8 311.7	3 279.2	1 143.2	257.8
Salem, OR	721	6 475	379.6	166.5	431	2 232	131.2	40.9	2 209.1	731.0	211.9	54.6
Providence-Warwick-Pawtucket, RI	1 923	23 642	1 380.0	613.6	1 793	7 820	500.2	150.2	5 621.1	2 077.9	956.6	183.9
Provo-Orem, UT	596	7 371	421.0	178.8	340	2 256	103.9	29.1	910.1	393.5	120.2	21.6
Pueblo, CO	299	3 459	203.9	98.4	194	912	47.5	13.9	822.5	369.3	128.7	37.9
Punta Gorda, FL	305	4 286	306.9	134.7	189	674	37.4	10.2	884.7	569.3	249.5	10.3
Raleigh-Durham-Chapel Hill, NC	2 019	28 385	1 734.6	796.4	1 713	10 843	775.0	224.0	6 949.1	1 877.8	630.3	131.2
Rapid City, SD	226	2 315	163.6	65.6	191	1 049	55.5	17.4	612.1	224.5	48.0	14.0

1. Firms subject to federal tax.　　2. October 1, 1998 to September 30, 1999.

Table C. Metropolitan Areas — **Federal Funds and Local Government Finances**

Area Name	Federal funds and grants, fiscal 2001[1] (cont'd) — Expenditures (mil dol) (cont'd) — Procurement contract awards: Salaries and wages	Defense	Other	Grants[2]: Medicaid and other health-related	Nutrition and family welfare	Education	Other	Local government finances, 1997 — General revenue: Total (mil dol)	Intergovernmental (mil dol)	Taxes: Total (mil dol)	Per capita[3] (dollars): Total	Property
	171	172	173	174	175	176	177	178	179	180	181	182
Merced, CA	29.3	2.2	24.1	116.8	60.1	20.8	30.7	764.1	458.6	102.0	520	413
Miami-Fort Lauderdale, FL ...	1 538.3	205.8	393.4	2 789.8	437.2	208.4	414.6	12 361.3	3 571.4	4 168.9	1 157	890
Fort Lauderdale, FL..........	428.3	92.4	137.2	270.1	103.1	68.8	166.7	4 746.9	1 168.5	1 714.5	1 166	921
Miami, FL.......................	1 110.0	113.4	256.1	2 519.7	334.1	139.6	247.8	7 614.5	2 402.8	2 454.4	1 151	869
Milwaukee-Racine, WI	660.2	162.0	248.0	990.0	299.5	114.3	266.5	5 373.7	2 469.1	2 071.6	1 266	1 200
Milwaukee-Waukesha, WI.	635.2	152.8	241.1	902.1	273.8	104.8	223.4	4 897.3	2 214.4	1 917.0	1 321	1 249
Racine, WI...................	25.0	9.2	6.9	87.9	25.7	9.5	43.2	476.4	254.7	154.5	833	814
Minneapolis-St. Paul, MN-WI	1 279.9	1 322.7	481.5	1 410.0	485.6	286.7	892.4	9 216.7	3 517.2	3 108.2	1 113	1 044
Missoula, MT	69.9	5.6	22.2	55.6	12.7	10.6	27.7	158.2	57.6	74.9	843	814
Mobile, AL	170.5	107.8	485.3	213.6	59.1	36.8	102.6	1 040.8	421.0	350.6	665	209
Modesto, CA	70.6	6.4	66.9	246.7	94.6	30.8	25.4	1 342.0	740.0	254.6	604	412
Monroe, LA	29.0	3.0	7.8	102.8	16.6	11.0	17.5	289.6	116.9	136.3	927	353
Montgomery, AL	517.9	290.4	47.7	247.9	203.3	165.7	395.9	524.7	261.1	179.3	562	142
Muncie, IN	23.4	0.0	8.2	77.5	14.4	4.5	11.5	214.2	97.2	86.0	731	670
Myrtle Beach, SC	27.6	4.7	7.7	83.0	15.5	9.6	67.0	409.2	115.7	165.7	980	789
Naples, FL........................	36.4	5.7	14.3	29.1	17.4	7.4	12.2	502.7	92.3	285.7	1 459	1 257
Nashville, TN	619.8	44.6	702.4	774.3	312.2	245.0	555.7	2 544.2	712.5	1 124.0	991	553
New London-Norwich, CT.....	333.0	1 718.0	43.2	114.3	24.1	21.2	36.2	663.2	233.3	332.3	1 314	1 285
New Orleans, LA...............	915.1	858.2	914.6	903.0	172.7	113.3	251.9	3 397.8	935.0	1 426.9	1 091	403
New York-Northern New Jersey-Long Island, NY-NJ-CT-PA	8 814.6	4 823.2	3 243.4	19 912.2	4 135.2	983.5	4 406.3	89 095.4	28 154.8	44 590.0	2 243	1 519
Bergen-Passaic, NJ..........	296.9	357.8	174.9	541.9	94.0	26.3	167.6	3 853.6	956.4	2 316.4	1 735	1 715
Dutchess County, NY........	66.1	6.7	12.6	184.0	21.4	12.4	16.4	866.8	254.0	462.0	1 745	1 391
Jersey City, NJ	463.4	19.7	162.2	624.1	108.0	18.1	60.7	1 636.7	711.2	666.5	1 209	1 191
Middlesex-Somerset-Hunterdon, NJ	353.5	106.3	267.1	370.8	47.3	26.1	225.3	3 115.4	733.5	1 894.2	1 713	1 687
Monmouth-Ocean, NJ	646.6	766.2	100.2	360.4	69.1	32.8	66.6	3 114.9	869.7	1 752.8	1 628	1 598
Nassau-Suffolk, NY	1 186.2	964.8	744.8	1 364.1	214.1	125.8	193.0	11 467.3	2 675.3	7 405.1	2 777	2 255
New Haven-Bridgeport-Stamford-Danbury-Waterbury, CT	575.4	1 471.1	250.3	1 239.5	220.5	106.5	321.6	4 423.6	1 263.1	2 670.0	1 643	1 621
New York, NY	3 769.1	593.7	1 148.9	13 388.0	2 675.8	331.8	2 098.4	51 582.0	17 839.5	22 881.7	2 657	1 195
Newark, NJ	865.8	244.3	225.0	1 244.2	285.0	63.5	642.6	6 260.0	2 008.5	3 389.4	1 744	1 707
Newburgh, NY-PA	411.9	145.8	31.1	175.4	38.1	20.8	21.5	1 562.6	408.8	591.1	1 614	1 309
Trenton, NJ	179.5	146.6	126.2	419.9	362.0	219.4	592.5	1 212.4	434.8	560.9	1 701	1 678
Norfolk-Virginia Beach-Newport News, VA-NC	5 278.3	8 226.1	582.2	412.2	137.5	124.3	297.3	3 778.8	1 398.1	1 550.2	1 003	676
Ocala, FL.........................	37.1	2.9	25.6	70.9	27.7	13.5	13.0	411.8	199.1	119.9	505	446
Odessa-Midland, TX	40.2	6.9	9.7	60.4	15.8	17.3	19.4	785.7	198.1	239.6	984	751
Oklahoma City, OK...........	1 622.2	931.1	357.7	455.3	291.9	177.0	580.3	2 115.4	693.5	757.3	735	351
Omaha, NE-IA...................	662.4	128.6	128.4	416.0	88.3	54.9	134.6	1 631.9	529.9	779.2	1 134	864
Orlando, FL......................	558.7	1 662.2	177.6	307.2	118.8	81.7	188.6	4 004.9	1 175.4	1 502.4	1 024	759
Owensboro, KY	17.8	5.6	4.9	35.3	16.2	5.0	9.3	189.8	66.1	43.6	479	299
Panama City, FL...............	288.7	146.2	11.3	47.0	19.0	13.6	8.3	460.6	158.6	108.1	739	475
Parkersburg-Marietta, WV-OH....................................	107.0	2.7	34.2	77.1	16.6	11.3	80.9	333.6	115.6	99.8	663	487
Pensacola, FL	693.5	168.0	37.6	159.1	60.7	29.8	51.6	860.9	411.0	238.1	600	400
Peoria-Pekin, IL	168.2	81.8	32.0	92.7	31.8	12.3	41.7	753.4	328.0	282.6	817	692
Philadelphia-Wilmington-Atlantic City, PA-NJ-DE-MD...................................	3 694.0	3 128.9	1 394.7	4 495.4	883.5	279.8	1 102.8	18 746.8	7 421.8	7 916.9	1 326	986
Atlantic-Cape May, NJ	240.5	34.4	67.5	182.5	34.4	13.7	65.5	1 309.3	396.5	729.7	2 180	2 145
Philadelphia, PA-NJ	3 148.4	3 024.5	1 251.1	3 911.6	739.7	229.0	860.8	15 877.0	6 282.1	6 687.3	1 354	962
Vineland-Millville-Bridgeton, NJ.........................	40.1	22.7	8.7	126.1	29.7	10.4	10.9	463.2	280.5	121.7	864	853
Wilmington-Newark, DE-MD.............................	265.0	47.3	67.4	275.2	79.7	26.7	165.5	1 097.3	462.7	378.2	681	533
Phoenix-Mesa, AZ	1 315.9	2 562.9	373.2	1 195.4	498.6	312.9	668.0	7 142.3	3 011.5	2 452.5	864	594
Pine Bluff, AR	65.1	96.6	7.6	76.5	14.8	9.5	18.6	148.9	72.7	47.6	579	343
Pittsburgh, PA..................	1 119.5	770.3	953.3	1 805.9	300.9	86.4	557.3	6 449.1	2 682.2	2 479.8	1 050	796
Pittsfield, MA...................	40.3	105.8	102.3	87.5	20.5	9.8	18.2	303.3	146.3	129.8	967	934
Pocatello, ID	24.6	0.0	9.0	43.6	4.3	3.2	16.7	177.4	69.3	39.1	530	505
Portland, ME	241.5	110.2	34.8	162.0	25.1	10.5	29.7	611.2	131.2	364.6	1 450	1 414
Portland-Salem, OR-WA.....	1 092.5	194.2	354.8	1 422.3	405.4	228.3	810.1	6 258.0	2 473.3	2 198.5	1 041	810
Portland-Vancouver, OR-WA................................	1 001.1	191.3	334.1	1 165.2	205.9	102.4	384.1	5 514.4	2 115.1	1 978.5	1 107	846
Salem, OR	91.5	2.9	20.6	257.1	199.5	125.9	426.0	743.6	358.3	220.0	676	609
Providence-Warwick-Pawtucket, RI......................	383.6	35.2	101.2	804.6	208.1	110.1	374.1	1 940.7	639.2	1 117.4	1 235	1 220
Provo-Orem, UT	67.7	46.1	32.8	101.9	30.1	10.3	37.4	615.9	305.1	185.8	566	405
Pueblo, CO	38.2	18.8	11.3	115.5	38.6	12.6	17.4	303.9	144.2	112.1	844	517
Punta Gorda, FL	15.9	0.1	4.6	7.1	7.7	3.9	8.7	268.9	54.4	131.5	984	744
Raleigh-Durham-Chapel Hill, NC....................................	584.7	109.1	444.0	1 175.7	461.6	279.0	953.7	2 553.7	922.4	879.7	838	642
Rapid City, SD	170.2	5.1	26.6	35.3	12.6	10.2	29.1	192.8	68.0	91.5	1 050	748

1. October 1, 1998 to September 30, 1999.   2. State totals may include programs not allocated by county.   3. Based on the resident population estimated as of July 1 of the year shown.

Table C. Metropolitan Areas — Local Government Finances, Government Employment, and Elections

Area Name	Local government finances, 1997 (cont'd)									Government employment, 1999			Presidential election, 2000[2]		
	Direct general expenditure							Debt outstanding					Percent of vote cast —		
			Percent of total for —												
	Total (mil dol)	Per capita[1] (dollars)	Education	Health and hospitals	Police protection	Public welfare	Highways	Total (mil dol)	Per capita[1] (dollars)	Federal civilian	Federal military	State and local	Democratic	Republican	All other
	183	184	185	186	187	188	189	190	191	192	193	194	195	196	197
Merced, CA	735.8	3 752	44.4	12.9	3.2	14.4	1.7	149.4	762	466	387	12 306	45.1	51.8	3.1
Miami-Fort Lauderdale, FL	12 492.7	3 467	33.3	14.2	7.8	0.7	1.9	14 094.2	3 912	25 375	10 875	195 156	59.7	38.9	1.3
Fort Lauderdale, FL	4 649.6	3 161	31.9	22.2	8.4	0.6	1.9	4 913.8	3 341	7 202	3 735	75 255	67.4	30.9	1.6
Miami, FL	7 843.1	3 679	34.1	9.4	7.5	0.8	1.9	9 180.4	4 306	18 173	7 140	119 901	52.6	46.3	1.2
Milwaukee-Racine, WI	5 352.5	3 271	43.8	4.4	6.8	6.0	5.0	4 269.9	2 609	11 752	6 227	85 716	46.9	49.4	3.7
Milwaukee-Waukesha, WI	4 873.4	3 358	43.9	4.4	6.6	5.6	4.9	3 985.9	2 747	11 330	5 570	77 230	46.9	49.4	3.7
Racine, WI	479.1	2 584	43.2	4.4	8.3	10.3	6.1	284.0	1 532	422	657	8 486	46.8	49.5	3.7
Minneapolis-St. Paul, MN-WI	9 608.2	3 441	40.3	6.5	4.3	5.7	6.0	12 459.2	4 462	21 628	12 191	194 384	50.0	43.5	6.5
Missoula, MT	163.4	1 839	56.4	4.7	5.4	0.4	3.6	111.4	1 254	1 302	515	7 731	37.0	46.1	16.9
Mobile, AL	1 035.5	1 964	42.0	10.2	5.4	0.3	7.2	1 223.6	2 321	2 760	4 015	33 105	37.0	60.7	2.3
Modesto, CA	1 293.6	3 067	42.7	12.1	4.9	11.6	2.2	1 786.6	4 235	1 216	842	22 857	44.0	52.4	3.6
Monroe, LA	299.4	2 036	48.8	0.7	7.9	0.3	7.7	168.6	1 147	494	815	12 005	36.9	60.3	2.8
Montgomery, AL	531.9	1 667	52.9	4.2	7.4	0.3	7.8	454.4	1 424	7 046	6 886	29 457	42.8	55.7	1.5
Muncie, IN	213.6	1 816	55.4	1.0	4.1	6.3	4.1	77.7	660	426	413	9 695	47.4	50.2	2.5
Myrtle Beach, SC	446.4	2 639	45.2	9.2	4.8	0.3	4.0	435.0	2 571	446	957	9 788	40.9	56.5	2.6
Naples, FL	530.4	2 710	46.9	2.9	7.6	0.6	6.7	559.5	2 859	622	454	8 977	32.5	65.6	1.9
Nashville, TN	2 604.2	2 295	36.6	7.0	6.4	0.8	3.9	4 200.4	3 702	11 371	5 120	68 738	49.6	48.7	1.7
New London-Norwich, CT	673.9	2 664	55.5	0.8	5.8	1.1	5.7	441.4	1 745	2 615	8 614	14 293	55.4	37.7	6.9
New Orleans, LA	3 128.0	2 392	35.4	17.2	6.8	0.6	3.3	4 021.4	3 075	16 108	11 578	90 169	51.0	46.7	2.3
New York-Northern New Jersey-Long Island, NY-NJ-CT-PA	86 303.8	4 342	34.3	6.8	6.5	11.8	2.9	79 281.6	3 989	160 412	55 274	1 241 904	62.0	34.0	4.0
Bergen-Passaic, NJ	3 804.9	2 849	47.3	3.9	6.9	5.3	3.2	1 741.2	1 304	5 238	3 261	62 491	56.0	40.9	3.2
Dutchess County, NY	889.0	3 359	48.6	5.3	4.1	9.0	4.7	485.9	1 836	1 364	536	20 490	46.9	47.1	6.0
Jersey City, NJ	1 555.6	2 821	28.9	5.2	7.7	7.3	2.3	1 414.7	2 565	7 842	1 458	33 814	70.6	26.2	3.2
Middlesex-Somerset-Hunterdon, NJ	3 159.1	2 858	54.6	3.3	5.7	3.0	3.4	2 110.6	1 909	6 875	2 886	67 906	53.4	42.6	4.1
Monmouth-Ocean, NJ	3 126.5	2 903	53.2	1.7	5.9	3.4	3.3	2 414.9	2 242	11 614	6 336	50 927	48.8	47.0	4.1
Nassau-Suffolk, NY	11 892.4	4 460	46.2	4.6	7.8	6.9	3.1	8 447.7	3 168	20 037	6 002	158 968	55.7	40.2	4.1
New Haven-Bridgeport-Stamford-Danbury-Waterbury, CT	4 467.2	2 748	50.1	1.3	5.9	2.1	3.7	2 395.7	1 474	10 998	4 163	81 510	55.1	39.7	5.2
New York, NY	48 318.8	5 611	24.4	9.5	6.5	16.6	2.5	55 276.9	6 419	70 597	18 449	569 969	73.8	22.3	3.9
Newark, NJ	6 294.6	3 239	45.3	3.5	6.5	6.5	3.5	3 244.5	1 669	17 333	4 838	125 539	56.4	40.2	3.4
Newburgh, NY-PA	1 595.0	4 355	39.0	1.9	2.8	9.9	3.2	720.9	1 968	5 536	6 491	21 854	45.5	50.2	4.3
Trenton, NJ	1 200.7	3 641	49.0	2.4	5.9	5.8	3.0	1 028.7	3 119	2 978	854	48 436	61.4	34.4	4.2
Norfolk-Virginia Beach-Newport News, VA-NC	3 974.1	2 572	44.6	5.2	4.9	3.4	3.3	4 845.4	3 136	45 964	109 044	98 355	47.6	50.3	2.1
Ocala, FL	416.0	1 753	51.9	0.8	8.5	0.4	9.1	334.0	1 408	690	540	13 917	43.4	53.6	3.1
Odessa-Midland, TX	765.3	3 145	39.2	34.9	4.4	0.1	2.0	456.6	1 876	776	638	16 976	23.3	74.9	1.8
Oklahoma City, OK	2 044.6	1 984	45.7	11.0	7.3	0.2	4.5	2 025.4	1 965	25 605	13 088	77 814	35.8	63.1	1.2
Omaha, NE-IA	1 572.9	2 288	51.2	2.5	5.1	0.5	6.3	1 835.9	2 671	8 332	10 956	40 605	38.6	57.0	4.3
Orlando, FL	4 030.3	2 747	39.7	2.0	6.5	0.7	6.9	8 852.8	6 034	9 530	4 170	80 024	47.0	51.0	2.0
Owensboro, KY	186.5	2 050	40.6	6.7	3.6	0.0	2.8	883.5	9 707	293	340	7 302	39.0	58.9	2.1
Panama City, FL	472.5	3 232	38.8	23.9	6.6	0.0	3.4	247.6	1 693	3 011	4 532	6 955	32.1	65.7	2.2
Parkersburg-Marietta, WV-OH	323.1	2 145	46.5	26.0	3.9	2.1	5.2	142.1	943	2 126	606	7 215	38.2	59.2	2.6
Pensacola, FL	835.6	2 104	51.0	1.4	6.8	0.6	5.1	1 246.6	3 139	7 486	15 449	21 425	32.2	65.5	2.4
Peoria-Pekin, IL	714.0	2 064	51.2	1.4	4.8	1.3	6.5	386.1	1 116	2 410	811	17 469	45.7	51.9	2.3
Philadelphia-Wilmington-Atlantic City, PA-NJ-DE-MD	18 181.9	3 045	45.3	4.6	5.6	4.3	3.7	22 143.6	3 708	63 909	29 148	309 204	60.1	37.0	2.8
Atlantic-Cape May, NJ	1 448.6	4 328	40.1	1.3	7.4	4.3	4.1	1 158.3	3 461	2 890	2 298	25 570	54.1	42.8	3.0
Philadelphia, PA-NJ	15 192.6	3 075	44.6	5.3	5.4	4.5	3.4	19 767.0	4 001	55 446	22 813	238 442	60.8	36.3	2.8
Vineland-Millville-Bridgeton, NJ	441.6	3 134	55.9	3.2	4.0	7.7	4.3	153.1	1 086	755	341	11 644	57.9	38.8	3.4
Wilmington-Newark, DE-MD	1 099.0	1 978	57.8	0.7	6.1	0.1	6.8	1 065.2	1 917	4 818	3 696	33 548	57.8	38.9	3.3
Phoenix-Mesa, AZ	7 125.2	2 509	37.5	3.4	7.1	7.6	4.3	14 214.6	5 006	19 899	13 240	163 107	43.2	53.1	3.7
Pine Bluff, AR	150.9	1 835	53.0	0.3	7.5	0.0	4.3	109.7	1 334	1 588	504	6 459	65.1	32.2	2.6
Pittsburgh, PA	6 382.0	2 703	48.0	5.7	3.7	3.8	3.6	10 199.6	4 320	19 090	8 535	105 330	53.0	44.2	2.8
Pittsfield, MA	324.7	2 418	55.8	0.6	3.7	0.1	6.8	145.7	1 085	461	421	7 361	63.9	26.6	9.5
Pocatello, ID	171.1	2 317	40.7	26.7	5.0	0.7	4.2	43.1	584	523	329	7 565	35.3	59.1	5.6
Portland, ME	569.7	2 266	44.4	0.4	4.8	3.3	5.1	420.3	1 671	3 112	4 162	17 185	52.0	41.0	6.9
Portland-Salem, OR-WA	6 164.3	2 918	43.6	4.6	5.0	0.3	5.3	5 957.7	2 820	19 165	8 077	135 850	51.4	42.4	6.2
Portland-Vancouver, OR-WA	5 392.9	3 017	42.2	4.4	5.0	0.3	5.3	5 508.9	3 082	17 620	6 951	101 943	52.8	41.0	6.2
Salem, OR	771.4	2 372	53.6	6.1	4.9	0.0	5.7	448.9	1 380	1 545	1 126	33 907	43.3	51.1	5.6
Providence-Warwick-Pawtucket, RI	1 856.7	2 052	56.2	0.2	7.0	0.4	3.0	1 035.1	1 144	6 184	5 297	52 223	61.6	31.3	7.1
Provo-Orem, UT	592.2	1 805	54.6	1.6	5.2	0.1	3.6	878.7	2 678	1 037	1 863	18 642	13.7	81.7	4.6
Pueblo, CO	298.9	2 249	43.8	1.9	4.8	12.0	5.9	413.0	3 107	707	379	10 569	53.5	42.3	4.1
Punta Gorda, FL	239.6	1 792	40.7	3.4	7.5	1.5	8.7	365.3	2 732	284	301	5 020	44.3	53.0	2.7
Raleigh-Durham-Chapel Hill, NC	2 454.2	2 337	43.7	12.0	4.9	4.8	2.2	8 587.2	8 178	9 687	4 142	113 058	49.8	49.1	1.2
Rapid City, SD	193.4	2 218	44.5	0.9	5.1	0.5	4.9	108.9	1 249	1 296	3 660	5 309	30.4	67.6	2.0

1. Based on the resident population estimated as of July 1 of the year shown. 2. Data subject to copyright.

Table C. Metropolitan Areas — Land Area and Population

CMSA/MSA/PMSA/NECMA code[1]	Area Name	Land area,[2] (sq km) 2000	Total persons	Rank	Per square kilometer	White	Black	Am. Indian, Alaska Native	Asian and Pacific Islander	Percent Hispanic[3]	Under 5 years	5 to 17 years	18 to 24 years	25 to 34 years	35 to 44 years	45 to 54 years
			1	2	3	4	5	6	7	8	9	10	11	12	13	14	15
6680	Reading, PA	2 224	373 638	133	168.0	89.4	4.3	0.4	1.3	9.7	6.2	18.4	8.8	12.7	16.2	13.7
6690	Redding, CA	9 804	163 256	226	16.7	92.5	1.1	4.8	2.7	5.5	5.9	20.2	8.2	10.3	15.0	14.7
6720	Reno, NV	16 426	339 486	146	20.7	83.2	2.6	2.7	5.9	16.6	7.0	17.9	9.8	14.5	16.5	14.7
	Richland-Kennewick-Pasco, WA															
6740		7 629	191 822	206	25.1	82.8	1.7	1.5	2.8	21.3	8.2	22.8	9.2	13.0	15.4	13.6
6760	Richmond-Petersburg, VA	7 626	996 512	62	130.7	65.9	30.8	0.8	2.5	2.3	6.5	18.7	8.9	14.5	17.1	14.6
6800	Roanoke, VA	2 204	235 932	183	107.0	84.9	13.6	0.5	1.5	1.1	5.8	16.8	7.7	12.9	15.9	15.3
6820	Rochester, MN	1 691	124 277	274	73.5	91.4	3.2	0.6	4.9	2.4	7.2	19.8	8.5	14.5	17.7	13.3
6840	Rochester, NY	8 872	1 098 201	58	123.8	85.3	11.0	0.7	2.2	4.3	6.3	19.4	9.3	12.9	16.4	14.1
6880	Rockford, IL	4 024	371 236	134	92.2	86.6	8.6	0.7	1.8	7.4	7.0	19.9	8.1	13.5	16.2	13.7
6895	Rocky Mount, NC	2 707	143 026	249	52.8	54.0	43.5	0.6	0.7	3.1	6.7	19.4	8.5	13.3	16.1	14.5
82	Sacramento-Yolo, CA	13 194	1 796 857		136.2	74.1	8.2	2.4	11.7	15.5	6.9	20.1	9.7	13.8	16.3	13.7
6920	Sacramento, CA	10 569	1 628 197	35	154.0	74.3	8.8	2.4	11.6	14.4	7.0	20.3	8.8	13.8	16.6	13.8
9270	Yolo, CA	2 624	168 660	222	64.3	72.0	2.6	2.2	12.3	25.9	6.5	18.7	18.3	14.0	14.2	12.0
	Saginaw-Bay City-Midland, MI															
6960		4 596	403 070	124	87.7	86.3	10.9	1.0	1.1	4.9	6.5	19.6	8.8	12.4	15.7	14.2
7120	Salinas, CA	8 604	401 762	125	46.7	60.0	4.5	1.9	8.5	46.8	7.8	20.6	10.9	15.9	15.4	12.3
7160	Salt Lake City-Ogden, UT		1 333 914	46	318.4	89.7	1.5	1.3	4.0	10.8	9.1	22.3	12.7	15.4	14.4	11.4
7200	San Angelo, TX	3 942	104 010	295	26.4	81.1	4.6	1.2	1.3	30.7	6.9	19.2	12.8	12.6	14.5	12.3
7240	San Antonio, TX	8 615	1 592 383	38	184.8	73.6	7.2	1.3	2.2	51.2	7.8	20.6	10.3	14.7	15.6	12.6
7320	San Diego, CA	10 878	2 813 833	15	258.7	70.3	6.6	1.6	11.4	26.7	7.1	18.7	11.3	15.8	16.3	12.5
	San Francisco-Oakland-San Jose, CA															
84		19 083	7 039 362		368.9	62.7	8.1	1.5	21.3	19.7	6.4	17.2	8.9	16.4	17.3	14.3
5775	Oakland, CA	3 775	2 392 557	21	633.8	59.7	13.8	1.6	19.8	18.5	6.9	18.5	8.8	15.4	17.2	14.3
7360	San Francisco, CA	2 630	1 731 183	29	658.2	62.1	6.0	1.1	25.7	16.8	5.2	13.6	8.1	18.7	17.4	14.8
7400	San Jose, CA	3 343	1 682 585	32	503.3	57.6	3.4	1.3	28.2	24.0	7.1	17.7	9.3	17.8	17.6	13.0
7485	Santa Cruz-Watsonville, CA	1 153	255 602	171	221.7	78.9	1.5	2.1	5.1	26.8	6.1	17.7	11.9	14.4	16.5	15.9
7500	Santa Rosa, CA	4 082	458 614	111	112.4	85.2	2.0	2.4	4.6	17.3	6.0	18.4	8.8	12.7	16.5	16.1
8720	Vallejo-Fairfield-Napa, CA	4 100	518 821	100	126.5	66.5	13.0	2.0	13.9	19.1	7.0	20.3	9.0	13.8	16.7	14.2
	San Luis Obispo-Atascadero-Paso Robles, CA															
7460		8 558	246 681	178	28.8	87.7	2.4	2.1	3.9	16.3	5.0	16.6	13.6	11.4	15.6	14.7
	Santa Barbara-Santa Maria-Lompoc, CA															
7480		7 089	399 347	126	56.3	76.4	2.8	2.2	5.6	34.2	6.5	18.4	13.3	13.9	15.1	12.3
7490	Santa Fe, NM	5 228	147 635	244	28.2	79.0	0.9	3.8	1.8	44.4	6.1	18.2	7.7	12.8	16.7	17.3
7510	Sarasota-Bradenton, FL	3 400	589 959	90	173.5	90.8	6.3	0.6	1.2	6.6	4.7	13.5	5.7	9.9	13.1	12.6
7520	Savannah, GA	3 520	293 000	160	83.2	62.2	35.4	0.6	2.0	2.2	6.9	19.2	10.6	14.4	15.7	13.0
7560	Scranton—Wilkes-Barre—Hazleton, PA	5 781	624 776	84	108.1	97.4	1.7	0.3	0.7	1.2	5.1	16.4	9.0	12.0	14.9	13.9
	Seattle-Tacoma-Bremerton, WA															
91		18 714	3 554 760		190.0	82.7	5.7	2.3	10.5	5.2	6.5	18.2	9.2	15.5	17.5	14.6
1150	Bremerton, WA	1 026	231 969	186	226.2	88.3	3.8	3.2	7.6	4.1	6.7	20.1	9.2	12.9	16.8	15.2
5910	Olympia, WA	1 883	207 355	197	110.1	89.0	3.1	2.8	6.7	4.5	6.2	19.1	9.3	13.0	16.3	15.7
	Seattle-Bellevue-Everett, WA															
7600		11 457	2 414 616	19	210.8	81.7	5.3	2.0	11.7	5.2	6.4	17.5	9.0	16.2	17.8	14.7
8200	Tacoma, WA	4 348	700 820	76	161.2	82.7	8.6	2.8	8.4	5.5	7.1	20.1	9.8	14.4	16.9	13.5
7610	Sharon, PA	1 740	120 293	279	69.1	94.0	5.7	0.4	0.5	0.7	5.7	17.7	8.9	11.2	14.8	13.7
7620	Sheboygan, WI	1 330	112 646	287	84.7	93.5	1.3	0.7	3.7	3.4	6.4	19.1	8.4	13.0	16.8	13.7
7640	Sherman-Denison, TX	2 418	110 595	291	45.7	89.1	6.3	2.4	0.9	6.8	6.5	18.8	9.3	12.1	15.4	13.2
7680	Shreveport-Bossier City, LA	6 000	392 302	127	65.4	60.6	37.8	0.9	1.1	1.8	7.0	19.9	9.9	13.0	15.0	13.1
7720	Sioux City, IA-NE	2 943	124 130	275	42.2	87.9	2.4	2.4	3.0	11.3	7.8	20.0	10.2	13.7	14.7	12.8
7760	Sioux Falls, SD	3 594	172 412	219	48.0	94.9	1.8	2.1	1.3	1.9	7.4	19.3	10.4	15.2	16.8	12.9
7800	South Bend, IN	1 185	265 559	167	224.2	84.1	12.3	0.9	1.8	4.7	7.0	18.7	11.8	13.2	14.8	13.1
7840	Spokane, WA	4 568	417 939	121	91.5	93.9	2.2	2.4	2.9	2.8	6.6	19.1	10.6	13.1	15.8	14.2
7880	Springfield, IL	3 062	201 437	201	65.8	89.1	9.7	0.6	1.4	1.0	6.4	18.7	8.0	13.1	16.5	14.8
8003	Springfield, MA	2 972	608 479	87	204.7	83.8	7.4	0.7	2.4	12.2	6.0	18.4	11.7	12.4	15.5	13.7
7920	Springfield, MO	4 743	325 721	150	68.7	95.9	2.2	1.5	1.3	1.7	6.5	17.3	12.3	13.9	15.3	13.1
6980	St. Cloud, MN	4 540	167 392	223	36.9	96.8	1.1	0.6	1.8	1.3	6.6	19.4	15.3	13.4	15.3	12.0
7000	St. Joseph, MO	2 188	102 490	299	46.8	94.8	4.2	0.9	0.7	2.2	6.3	18.4	10.5	12.8	15.6	12.9
7040	St. Louis, MO-IL	16 555	2 603 607	17	157.3	79.3	18.8	0.6	1.8	1.5	6.7	19.6	8.8	13.3	16.6	13.5
8050	State College, PA	2 868	135 758	257	47.3	92.3	2.9	0.4	4.6	1.7	4.6	13.4	26.8	13.4	13.1	11.1
	Steubenville-Weirton, OH-WV															
8080		1 506	132 008	261	87.7	95.3	4.3	0.5	0.5	0.6	5.2	15.9	8.4	11.3	14.8	15.4
8120	Stockton-Lodi, CA	3 624	563 598	95	155.5	62.7	7.5	2.3	14.4	30.5	8.0	23.0	10.0	13.4	15.4	12.2
8140	Sumter, SC	1 723	104 646	294	60.7	51.0	47.2	0.6	1.3	1.8	7.5	20.6	10.5	13.7	15.7	12.4
8160	Syracuse, NY	7 984	732 117	73	91.7	90.3	7.2	1.2	1.8	2.1	6.3	19.4	9.8	12.6	16.2	13.7
8240	Tallahassee, FL	3 064	284 539	162	92.9	63.1	34.1	0.7	2.1	3.9	5.9	16.2	19.5	14.5	14.4	13.2
	Tampa-St. Petersburg-Clearwater, FL															
8280		6 615	2 395 997	20	362.2	84.5	10.8	0.8	2.4	10.4	5.8	16.2	7.5	12.8	15.5	13.3
8320	Terre Haute, IN	2 636	149 192	241	56.6	94.0	4.8	0.7	1.2	1.0	6.2	17.3	12.6	12.8	14.6	13.2
	Texarkana, TX-Texarkana, AR															
8360		3 916	129 749	263	33.1	74.6	23.7	1.2	0.7	3.6	6.7	18.6	9.5	13.9	14.4	13.3
8400	Toledo, OH	3 534	618 203	85	174.9	83.8	13.5	0.7	1.5	4.4	6.7	19.2	11.1	13.4	15.3	13.5
8440	Topeka, KS	1 424	169 871	221	119.3	85.2	10.2	2.2	1.4	7.3	6.8	18.5	8.8	12.8	15.6	14.6

1. MSA = Metropolitan Statistical Area. CMSA = Consolidated MSA. PMSA = Primary MSA. NECMA = New England County Metropolitan Area. See Appendix A for explanation of these concepts. See Appendix B for list of metropolitan areas identified by type, with component counties.   2. Dry land or land partially or temporarily covered by water.   3. Hispanic persons may be of any race.

Table C. Metropolitan Areas — **Population and Households**

Area Name	Age (percent) (cont'd)				Total persons		Percent change		Components of change, 2000–2001			Households, 2000				
	55 to 64 years	65 to 74 years	75 years and over	Percent female	2001	1990	1990–2000	2000–2001	Births	Deaths	Net migration	Number	Percent change, 1990–2000	Persons per household	Female family householder[1]	One person
	16	17	18	19	20	21	22	23	24	25	26	27	28	29	30	31
Reading, PA	8.9	7.7	7.3	51.0	377 679	336 523	11.0	1.1	5 526	4 608	3 250	141 570	10.9	2.55	9.9	24.6
Redding, CA	10.5	7.9	7.3	51.3	168 478	147 036	11.0	3.2	2 393	2 159	4 911	63 426	13.3	2.52	11.9	24.7
Reno, NV	9.1	6.0	4.6	49.3	353 336	254 667	33.3	4.1	6 041	3 278	10 990	132 084	29.1	2.53	10.3	27.0
Richland-Kennewick-Pasco, WA	8.0	5.3	4.5	49.7	197 649	150 033	27.9	3.0	3 881	1 507	3 468	67 706	24.4	2.81	10.4	22.0
Richmond-Petersburg, VA	8.5	6.0	5.2	51.9	1 009 962	865 640	15.1	1.3	17 671	10 648	6 366	387 721	16.8	2.48	14.4	26.4
Roanoke, VA	9.8	8.1	7.7	52.6	235 556	224 592	5.0	-0.2	3 562	3 313	-610	98 343	9.6	2.33	12.0	29.4
Rochester, MN	8.3	5.4	5.4	50.9	126 275	106 470	16.7	1.6	2 305	1 004	746	47 807	19.3	2.53	8.0	25.8
Rochester, NY	8.7	6.4	6.5	51.4	1 096 741	1 062 470	3.4	0.1	16 964	11 681	-6 494	420 073	6.1	2.51	12.4	27.1
Rockford, IL	9.0	6.5	6.1	50.9	375 144	329 676	12.6	1.1	6 518	3 961	1 460	141 855	13.7	2.57	11.0	25.0
Rocky Mount, NC	9.0	6.9	5.6	52.5	143 197	133 369	7.2	0.1	2 773	1 843	-762	54 036	9.5	2.59	17.1	24.6
Sacramento-Yolo, CA	8.1	6.0	5.4	51.0	1 874 683	1 506 792	19.3	4.3	31 040	16 167	62 092	665 298	19.6	2.65	12.7	25.0
Sacramento, CA	8.2	6.1	5.4	50.9	1 699 868	1 365 580	19.2	4.4	28 323	14 839	57 352	605 923	19.9	2.64	12.8	25.2
Yolo, CA	6.9	4.8	4.6	51.1	174 815	141 212	19.4	3.6	2 717	1 328	4 740	59 375	16.5	2.71	11.1	23.3
Saginaw-Bay City-Midland, MI	9.3	6.9	6.6	51.6	402 999	399 320	0.9	0.0	6 470	4 474	-1 949	156 129	5.3	2.53	12.7	25.8
Salinas, CA	7.1	5.3	4.7	48.2	407 629	355 660	13.0	1.5	8 435	2 970	507	121 236	7.3	3.14	11.6	21.2
Salt Lake City-Ogden, UT	6.5	4.4	3.9	49.7	1 348 606	1 072 227	24.4	1.1	32 870	9 371	-8 685	432 040	24.3	3.04	10.2	19.5
San Angelo, TX	8.3	6.9	6.5	51.6	103 079	98 458	5.6	-0.9	2 006	1 299	-1 624	39 503	11.6	2.52	11.9	27.2
San Antonio, TX	7.8	5.8	4.9	51.3	1 626 538	1 324 749	20.2	2.1	33 365	14 512	15 999	559 946	22.1	2.78	14.8	23.4
San Diego, CA	7.3	5.7	5.5	49.7	2 862 819	2 498 016	12.6	1.7	54 974	23 530	19 381	994 677	12.1	2.73	11.6	24.2
San Francisco-Oakland-San Jose, CA	8.4	5.7	5.4	50.2	7 073 364	6 277 523	12.1	0.5	125 094	61 044	-31 082	2 557 158	9.8	2.69	10.8	25.8
Oakland, CA	8.2	5.5	5.2	51.0	2 433 952	2 108 078	13.5	1.7	43 526	20 903	19 165	867 495	11.2	2.71	12.4	24.8
San Francisco, CA	9.0	6.7	6.5	49.9	1 720 450	1 603 678	8.0	-0.6	27 221	17 469	-20 992	684 453	6.5	2.47	9.3	32.1
San Jose, CA	8.0	5.2	4.4	49.3	1 668 309	1 497 577	12.4	-0.8	34 201	11 487	-38 127	565 863	8.8	2.92	10.0	21.4
Santa Cruz-Watsonville, CA	7.6	4.8	5.1	50.1	254 538	229 734	11.3	-0.4	4 217	2 073	-3 278	91 139	9.1	2.71	10.2	25.1
Santa Rosa, CA	8.8	6.0	6.7	50.8	464 024	388 222	18.1	1.2	6 838	4 592	3 327	172 403	15.7	2.60	10.4	25.7
Vallejo-Fairfield-Napa, CA	8.1	5.6	5.3	49.7	532 091	450 234	15.2	2.6	9 091	4 520	8 823	175 805	13.6	2.83	12.8	21.2
San Luis Obispo-Atascadero-Paso Robles, CA	8.6	7.3	7.1	48.6	250 727	217 162	13.6	1.6	2 915	2 528	3 693	92 739	15.5	2.49	9.1	26.0
Santa Barbara-Santa Maria-Lompoc, CA	7.8	6.3	6.4	50.0	399 543	369 608	8.0	0.0	6 927	3 697	-3 025	136 622	5.3	2.80	10.0	24.3
Santa Fe, NM	10.3	6.2	4.7	50.9	148 713	117 043	26.1	0.7	2 174	1 121	60	59 979	33.1	2.42	11.0	28.8
Sarasota-Bradenton, FL	12.0	14.0	14.5	52.2	609 846	489 483	20.5	3.4	7 224	10 601	22 941	262 397	21.2	2.20	8.4	29.6
Savannah, GA	8.5	6.3	5.5	51.5	296 232	257 899	13.6	1.1	6 196	3 350	408	111 105	17.0	2.56	15.9	25.2
Scranton—Wilkes-Barre—Hazleton, PA	9.8	9.1	9.8	52.2	619 790	638 524	-2.2	-0.8	7 488	10 265	-1 938	252 582	2.5	2.37	11.2	30.5
Seattle-Tacoma-Bremerton, WA	8.1	5.2	5.1	50.2	3 605 124	2 970 300	19.7	1.4	59 392	30 865	22 324	1 392 393	20.5	2.50	9.8	27.1
Bremerton, WA	8.6	5.4	5.2	49.3	233 372	189 731	22.3	0.6	3 670	2 173	95	86 416	24.8	2.60	9.5	22.6
Olympia, WA	8.9	5.8	5.6	51.0	213 546	161 238	28.6	3.0	3 166	2 009	4 988	81 625	31.3	2.50	10.3	25.1
Seattle-Bellevue-Everett, WA	8.1	5.1	5.1	50.2	2 438 799	2 033 128	18.8	1.0	39 871	20 278	4 817	963 552	19.1	2.46	9.2	28.4
Tacoma, WA	8.0	5.4	4.8	50.3	719 407	586 203	19.6	2.7	12 685	6 405	12 464	260 800	21.5	2.60	11.8	24.3
Sharon, PA	9.7	9.1	9.0	51.3	119 682	121 003	-0.6	-0.5	1 624	1 856	-319	46 712	2.5	2.44	10.9	27.0
Sheboygan, WI	8.5	6.7	7.2	49.8	113 109	103 877	8.4	0.4	1 670	1 328	181	43 545	12.8	2.50	7.3	26.1
Sherman-Denison, TX	9.5	7.7	7.4	51.6	113 184	95 019	16.4	2.3	1 858	1 606	2 322	42 849	16.3	2.51	11.4	25.5
Shreveport-Bossier City, LA	8.9	7.0	6.2	52.2	391 501	376 330	4.2	-0.2	7 341	4 920	-3 106	151 103	8.1	2.53	18.0	27.2
Sioux City, IA-NE	7.8	6.4	6.4	50.8	123 380	115 018	7.9	-0.6	2 623	1 397	-2 004	46 246	7.7	2.62	11.4	26.1
Sioux Falls, SD	7.2	5.5	5.4	50.4	176 649	139 236	23.8	2.5	3 086	1 599	2 740	66 778	25.7	2.50	9.1	26.7
South Bend, IN	7.8	6.7	6.9	51.7	264 779	247 052	7.5	-0.3	4 929	3 101	-2 565	100 743	9.1	2.50	12.4	27.9
Spokane, WA	8.2	6.0	6.4	50.9	423 261	361 333	15.7	1.3	6 761	4 471	3 197	163 611	15.5	2.46	11.0	28.1
Springfield, IL	9.0	6.8	6.7	52.2	201 935	189 550	6.3	0.2	3 261	2 377	-296	83 595	9.5	2.37	11.5	30.5
Springfield, MA	8.2	6.7	7.2	52.4	608 738	602 878	0.9	0.0	8 721	7 449	-776	231 279	5.1	2.49	14.0	28.0
Springfield, MO	8.6	6.6	6.3	51.3	331 379	264 346	23.2	1.7	5 418	3 505	3 781	129 357	27.1	2.41	9.6	26.8
St. Cloud, MN	7.0	5.7	5.3	49.8	169 930	149 509	12.0	1.5	2 694	1 292	1 181	60 669	19.6	2.63	7.8	24.1
St. Joseph, MO	8.7	7.2	7.7	50.9	102 061	97 715	4.9	-0.4	1 615	1 425	-594	39 830	5.1	2.45	11.2	27.9
St. Louis, MO-IL	8.6	6.7	6.1	52.0	2 617 637	2 492 348	4.5	0.5	45 162	31 014	7	1 012 419	7.5	2.52	13.5	27.4
State College, PA	7.2	5.6	4.8	48.9	135 940	124 812	8.8	0.1	1 509	1 002	-273	49 323	15.6	2.45	6.1	26.6
Steubenville-Weirton, OH-WV	10.7	9.7	8.8	52.2	130 230	142 523	-7.4	-1.3	1 614	2 190	-1 167	54 491	-1.3	2.36	11.1	27.9
Stockton-Lodi, CA	7.4	5.4	5.2	50.0	595 324	480 628	17.3	5.6	11 289	5 453	25 469	181 629	14.8	3.00	14.0	20.7
Sumter, SC	8.3	6.1	5.1	51.6	104 237	101 276	3.3	-0.4	2 287	1 205	-1 449	37 728	15.3	2.68	18.3	23.2
Syracuse, NY	8.6	6.8	6.5	51.5	731 252	742 237	-1.4	0.1	11 296	7 898	-4 039	282 601	3.5	2.50	12.1	27.8
Tallahassee, FL	7.3	4.7	4.2	52.4	284 697	233 609	21.8	0.1	5 009	2 342	-2 473	112 388	27.4	2.39	14.3	28.8
Tampa-St. Petersburg-Clearwater, FL	9.8	9.4	9.8	51.8	2 450 337	2 067 959	15.9	2.3	36 647	36 122	53 505	1 009 316	16.1	2.33	11.2	29.7
Terre Haute, IN	8.8	7.1	7.4	51.0	147 961	147 585	1.1	-0.8	2 407	2 085	-1 531	57 976	3.9	2.42	11.0	28.5
Texarkana, TX-Texarkana, AR	9.0	7.0	6.6	50.1	130 679	120 132	8.0	0.7	2 358	1 759	380	48 695	8.5	2.50	15.3	25.9
Toledo, OH	8.2	6.5	6.2	51.8	617 554	614 128	0.7	0.1	10 801	7 205	-4 098	243 499	5.6	2.47	13.1	28.7
Topeka, KS	9.1	7.1	6.6	51.6	170 080	160 976	5.5	0.1	3 027	2 177	-581	68 920	8.1	2.39	11.6	29.8

1. No spouse present.

Table C. Metropolitan Areas — **Vital Statistics, Health Resources, and Crime**

Area Name	Births, average 1997–1999		Deaths, average 1997–1999				Physicians[4] 1998		Hospitals[4] 1998	Beds		Medicare enrollees 1999	Serious crimes known to police, 2000[6] Total	
			Number		Rate									
	Total	Rate[1]	Total	Infant[2]	Total[1]	Infant[3]	Number	Rate[5]	Number	Number	Rate[5]		Number	Rate[7]
	32	33	34	35	36	37	38	39	40	41	42	43	44	45
Reading, PA	4 423	12.4	3 675	33	10.3	7.5	676	190	3	874	246	60 126	11 263	3 381
Redding, CA	1 993	12.2	1 694	12	10.3	6.0	399	243	5	656	399	30 619	5 341	3 272
Reno, NV	4 864	15.5	2 522	36	8.1	7.4	801	255	4	1 009	322	38 743	15 335	4 517
Richland-Kennewick-Pasco, WA	2 988	16.3	1 144	NA	6.3	NA	287	157	4	430	235	20 435	7 234	3 771
Richmond-Petersburg, VA	12 755	13.3	8 352	NA	8.7	NA	2 692	281	14	3 804	397	125 756	44 527	4 502
Roanoke, VA	2 673	11.7	2 580	NA	11.3	NA	727	319	3	1 079	474	40 570	7 133	3 023
Rochester, MN	1 767	15.1	762	10	6.5	5.7	1 438	1 232	3	1 343	1 151	13 725	3 065	2 466
Rochester, NY	14 282	13.2	9 291	NA	8.6	NA	3 055	282	16	3 823	353	162 392	39 573	3 645
Rockford, IL	5 066	14.2	3 156	NA	8.8	NA	710	199	6	1 068	299	51 449	NA	NA
Rocky Mount, NC	1 998	13.7	1 442	NA	9.9	NA	194	133	3	412	282	22 338	8 156	5 768
Sacramento-Yolo, CA	23 839	14.1	12 682	141	7.5	5.9	3 954	235	17	3 841	228	220 087	77 288	4 301
Sacramento, CA	21 702	14.1	11 650	132	7.6	6.1	3 449	225	15	3 672	240	203 071	71 307	4 380
Yolo, CA	2 137	13.9	1 032	9	6.7	4.2	505	328	2	169	110	17 016	5 981	3 546
Saginaw-Bay City-Midland, MI	5 242	13.1	3 556	41	8.9	7.8	774	193	5	1 496	372	61 617	15 471	3 838
Salinas, CA	6 530	17.9	2 290	38	6.3	5.8	743	203	4	675	185	42 526	12 960	3 226
Salt Lake City-Ogden, UT	25 472	20.1	7 165	147	5.7	5.8	2 799	221	13	2 756	217	118 101	65 524	4 914
San Angelo, TX	1 587	15.5	977	12	9.5	7.6	203	198	3	478	465	15 679	5 203	5 002
San Antonio, TX	25 997	16.9	11 211	NA	7.3	NA	4 173	271	19	4 312	280	184 261	103 480	6 560
San Diego, CA	43 019	15.5	18 984	230	6.8	5.3	7 405	266	25	6 828	246	336 516	94 408	3 355
San Francisco-Oakland-San Jose, CA	94 092	13.8	47 900	482	7.0	5.1	20 681	303	81	20 160	296	829 269	256 406	3 642
Oakland, CA	32 540	14.1	16 350	182	7.1	5.6	5 517	238	27	5 829	251	270 633	103 450	4 324
San Francisco, CA	20 091	12.0	13 530	89	8.1	4.4	8 054	478	22	6 608	393	243 093	67 636	3 907
San Jose, CA	25 410	15.5	8 984	126	5.5	5.0	4 356	265	15	4 488	273	164 906	44 507	2 645
Santa Cruz-Watsonville, CA	3 529	14.6	1 656	18	6.8	5.1	564	232	2	395	163	28 364	8 690	3 400
Santa Rosa, CA	5 481	12.7	3 748	28	8.7	5.1	1 142	264	8	889	205	62 630	13 512	2 946
Vallejo-Fairfield-Napa, CA	7 041	14.2	3 632	39	7.3	5.5	1 048	211	7	1 951	393	59 643	18 611	3 587
San Luis Obispo-Atascadero-Paso Robles, CA	2 522	10.8	1 988	12	8.5	4.8	619	264	6	636	271	38 602	7 156	2 901
Santa Barbara-Santa Maria-Lompoc, CA	5 707	14.7	2 878	28	7.4	4.9	1 083	278	8	1 314	337	54 627	10 195	2 553
Santa Fe, NM	1 789	12.7	867	NA	6.1	NA	453	320	2	261	184	16 756	6 496	4 526
Sarasota-Bradenton, FL	5 473	10.1	8 029	32	14.8	5.8	1 723	317	6	2 175	400	156 931	27 443	4 652
Savannah, GA	4 417	15.4	2 516	NA	8.8	NA	673	236	4	1 256	440	38 955	18 011	6 147
Scranton—Wilkes-Barre—Hazleton, PA	6 211	10.1	8 212	NA	13.3	NA	1 375	223	14	2 934	477	130 608	7 780	1 553
Seattle-Tacoma-Bremerton, WA	46 762	13.7	23 825	245	7.0	5.2	9 350	273	35	6 574	192	398 831	185 777	5 259
Bremerton, WA	3 244	13.8	1 630	15	7.0	4.6	454	195	1	252	108	26 495	10 031	4 324
Olympia, WA	2 459	12.1	1 508	12	7.4	4.9	461	228	2	437	216	26 187	8 507	4 103
Seattle-Bellevue-Everett, WA	31 141	13.5	15 734	159	6.8	5.1	7 059	305	25	4 827	209	266 193	120 816	5 037
Tacoma, WA	9 918	14.7	4 953	59	7.3	5.9	1 376	203	7	1 058	156	79 956	46 423	6 683
Sharon, PA	1 339	11.0	1 439	8	11.8	6.0	237	194	4	638	523	24 230	2 311	1 949
Sheboygan, WI	1 335	12.1	1 042	9	9.5	6.7	149	135	3	421	382	17 373	3 309	2 938
Sherman-Denison, TX	1 408	13.7	1 227	10	11.9	7.1	177	172	3	540	525	18 340	4 663	4 216
Shreveport-Bossier City, LA	5 598	14.8	3 859	NA	10.2	NA	1 070	283	12	2 091	552	57 257	24 661	6 286
Sioux City, IA-NE	1 965	16.3	1 123	NA	9.3	NA	227	188	2	681	565	18 414	6 541	5 269
Sioux Falls, SD	2 356	14.4	1 194	NA	7.3	NA	503	308	4	849	520	20 967	4 705	2 959
South Bend, IN	3 821	14.8	2 445	36	9.5	9.4	564	219	4	836	324	40 741	15 492	5 834
Spokane, WA	5 420	13.3	3 527	30	8.6	5.5	1 025	251	4	1 274	312	58 435	25 061	6 051
Springfield, IL	2 656	13.0	1 888	22	9.3	8.3	674	331	3	1 336	655	30 575	NA	NA
Springfield, MA	7 319	12.4	5 793	42	9.8	5.7	1 435	244	9	1 973	335	95 715	26 278	4 390
Springfield, MO	4 097	13.4	2 878	NA	9.4	NA	704	231	5	1 657	544	47 670	16 167	4 963
St. Cloud, MN	2 138	13.1	1 038	NA	6.4	NA	312	192	5	655	404	21 029	2 838	1 695
St. Joseph, MO	1 304	13.4	1 137	NA	11.7	NA	174	179	2	482	495	17 152	4 055	4 731
St. Louis, MO-IL	35 474	13.8	24 749	288	9.7	8.1	6 673	260	44	10 556	412	376 668	NA	NA
State College, PA	1 290	9.7	802	6	6.1	4.7	235	177	2	232	175	15 106	3 476	2 560
Steubenville-Weirton, OH-WV	1 342	10.0	1 718	NA	12.7	NA	156	116	3	643	478	28 129	NA	NA
Stockton-Lodi, CA	8 797	16.0	4 208	52	7.6	5.9	750	136	8	1 140	207	66 446	29 644	5 260
Sumter, SC	1 682	15.5	875	18	8.0	10.7	110	103	1	230	215	13 265	5 793	5 589
Syracuse, NY	9 372	12.8	6 464	NA	8.8	NA	1 951	266	9	2 545	346	111 972	21 176	2 947
Tallahassee, FL	3 476	13.3	1 842	45	7.1	12.9	573	220	2	812	311	28 200	18 665	6 636
Tampa-St. Petersburg-Clearwater, FL	27 689	12.3	27 930	219	12.4	7.9	5 762	255	33	8 131	360	464 530	140 257	5 854
Terre Haute, IN	1 891	12.7	1 643	NA	11.1	NA	257	173	4	661	445	25 105	NA	NA
Texarkana, TX-Texarkana, AR	1 710	13.9	1 350	NA	10.9	NA	215	174	4	711	576	19 654	5 851	4 509
Toledo, OH	8 513	14.0	5 753	55	9.4	6.5	1 647	270	10	2 860	469	88 429	31 755	5 857
Topeka, KS	2 338	14.0	1 645	23	9.8	9.8	482	292	2	642	388	27 122	14 477	8 643

1. Per 1,000 estimated resident population, average 1997–1999.   2. Deaths of infants under 1 year old.   3. Deaths of infants under 1 year old per 1,000 live births.   4. Data subject to copyright.   5. Per 100,000 resident population as of July 1 of the year shown.   6. Data for serious crimes have not been adjusted for underreporting; this may affect comparability between geographic areas and over time.   7. Per 100,000 population estimated by the FBI.

Table C. Metropolitan Areas — Crime, Education, Money Income, and Poverty

Area Name	Serious crimes known to police, 2000[1] (cont'd) Rate[2] Violent	Property	Education: School enrollment and attainment, 1990 — Enrollment[3] Total	Percent private	Attainment[4] (percent) High school graduate or more	Bachelor's degree or more	Local government expenditures, fiscal 1999[5] Total current expenditures (mil dol)	Current expenditures per student (dollars)	Money income 1989 Per capita[6] (dollars)	Households Median Dollars	Percent change, 1979–1989 (constant 1989 dollars)	Percent with $100,000 or more	Income and poverty, 1998 Median household income	Percent below poverty level All persons	Persons under 18	Persons 5–17 in families
	46	47	48	49	50	51	52	53	54	55	56	57	58	59	60	61
Reading, PA	413	2 968	75 295	18.3	70.0	15.1	450.7	7 130	14 604	32 047	9.1	3.1	NA	8.9	14.8	13.0
Redding, CA	505	2 767	39 216	9.9	78.4	13.7	192.5	6 314	12 381	25 581	3.8	2.4	NA	17.2	24.8	27.0
Reno, NV	413	4 104	61 679	8.9	82.5	20.7	283.8	5 374	16 365	31 890	-2.7	4.5	NA	9.9	14.1	13.2
Richland-Kennewick-Pasco, WA	253	3 518	43 131	8.3	80.2	21.0	234.8	6 044	13 123	30 729	-16.0	2.5	NA	11.6	15.4	14.6
Richmond-Petersburg, VA	458	4 044	214 653	13.3	75.8	23.8	977.6	5 898	15 848	33 488	10.4	4.2	NA	10.2	14.5	13.0
Roanoke, VA	330	2 693	49 728	14.3	73.4	18.1	232.7	6 469	14 318	28 943	6.8	3.0	NA	10.9	15.4	14.9
Rochester, MN	232	2 234	28 118	15.4	88.0	29.5	150.1	7 118	16 214	35 788	6.4	5.2	NA	6.9	9.7	8.4
Rochester, NY	231	3 414	279 066	21.6	79.0	22.9	1 679.1	8 790	15 205	34 001	5.0	4.0	NA	12.0	18.9	17.9
Rockford, IL	NA	NA	82 011	16.4	76.4	15.6	399.3	6 486	14 273	31 567	-6.4	2.9	NA	9.2	13.5	12.5
Rocky Mount, NC	554	5 214	33 014	9.3	62.3	11.4	145.1	5 568	11 345	24 020	7.1	1.9	NA	17.3	25.7	23.3
Sacramento-Yolo, CA	523	3 778	418 766	10.8	82.6	23.4	1 812.6	5 713	15 407	32 733	12.7	4.3	NA	13.9	21.4	21.3
Sacramento, CA	518	3 862	367 436	11.2	83.0	22.7	1 661.5	5 723	15 570	33 195	13.0	4.3	NA	13.8	21.4	21.2
Yolo, CA	565	2 981	51 330	7.6	79.1	30.3	151.0	5 605	13 861	28 866	11.9	4.2	NA	14.4	21.6	22.2
Saginaw-Bay City-Midland, MI	515	3 323	113 353	13.2	76.2	15.1	499.4	7 151	13 040	29 156	-12.5	2.7	NA	13.1	19.8	18.8
Salinas, CA	575	2 651	97 096	10.0	72.9	21.5	421.4	6 060	14 578	33 519	13.3	5.3	NA	15.4	24.2	22.9
Salt Lake City-Ogden, UT	316	4 598	357 433	7.7	85.6	22.9	1 154.0	4 134	12 029	30 881	-1.0	2.9	NA	8.9	11.9	9.5
San Angelo, TX	393	4 609	28 123	5.9	71.0	17.0	114.6	5 830	11 482	24 348	0.1	2.3	NA	16.7	23.8	22.5
San Antonio, TX	587	5 973	380 795	12.8	72.5	19.3	1 723.0	5 907	11 828	26 048	2.7	2.9	NA	17.1	24.7	21.9
San Diego, CA	489	2 866	678 445	12.5	81.9	25.3	2 716.6	5 774	16 220	35 021	22.2	6.0	NA	13.1	20.2	18.6
San Francisco-Oakland-San Jose, CA	509	3 133	1 683 435	16.4	82.7	30.9	6 021.5	5 971	19 629	41 458	20.8	9.1	NA	9.1	14.7	14.0
Oakland, CA	587	3 737	565 117	14.8	83.4	29.9	2 108.1	5 723	18 782	40 620	19.6	8.1	NA	9.7	15.9	14.8
San Francisco, CA	531	3 376	395 462	21.3	82.4	34.9	1 203.4	6 547	22 049	40 493	22.6	10.5	NA	8.6	13.7	13.5
San Jose, CA	429	2 216	429 640	17.4	82.0	32.6	1 548.2	6 111	20 423	48 115	22.9	11.4	NA	8.2	13.5	12.4
Santa Cruz-Watsonville, CA	464	2 936	67 978	10.7	81.9	29.7	237.4	5 870	17 347	37 112	31.2	7.5	NA	12.0	18.8	18.4
Santa Rosa, CA	296	2 650	101 892	11.3	84.4	24.5	437.3	6 103	17 239	36 298	22.1	5.2	NA	8.4	12.5	12.9
Vallejo-Fairfield-Napa, CA	545	3 042	123 346	12.5	82.2	19.7	487.2	5 359	15 522	38 453	19.8	4.4	NA	10.1	15.9	15.4
San Luis Obispo-Atascadero-Paso Robles, CA	283	2 618	65 365	9.3	83.3	22.9	211.9	5 789	15 237	31 164	25.6	4.4	NA	12.2	17.7	17.8
Santa Barbara-Santa Maria-Lompoc, CA	329	2 224	109 709	11.8	80.0	26.6	386.8	5 997	17 155	35 676	18.5	7.4	NA	14.1	21.7	21.5
Santa Fe, NM	478	4 048	30 763	16.4	84.5	35.7	108.2	5 584	16 499	32 294	7.9	5.6	NA	10.5	15.4	13.6
Sarasota-Bradenton, FL	654	3 998	81 667	13.6	78.9	19.2	414.9	6 098	16 712	28 124	16.1	4.3	NA	9.5	17.6	17.0
Savannah, GA	725	5 422	66 320	18.4	72.7	17.2	285.1	5 712	12 659	27 038	12.6	2.8	NA	16.6	25.3	23.9
Scranton—Wilkes-Barre—Hazleton, PA	165	1 388	145 217	24.1	72.8	13.6	631.2	7 525	12 004	24 231	2.2	2.0	NA	10.8	16.6	15.2
Seattle-Tacoma-Bremerton, WA	425	4 834	741 152	15.0	86.7	26.4	3 456.0	6 069	16 507	34 421	4.1	4.5	NA	8.1	11.5	10.2
Bremerton, WA	432	3 892	47 813	10.7	86.6	19.8	253.9	5 983	14 311	32 042	0.9	2.7	NA	8.7	11.8	11.1
Olympia, WA	269	3 834	43 319	9.9	86.5	24.7	244.2	6 421	13 901	30 976	3.0	2.2	NA	8.8	12.3	11.1
Seattle-Bellevue-Everett, WA	371	4 666	499 758	15.9	87.7	29.5	2 216.4	6 092	17 804	36 126	4.7	5.3	NA	7.3	10.5	9.2
Tacoma, WA	654	6 029	150 262	14.8	83.2	17.5	741.5	5 924	13 439	30 411	5.4	2.7	NA	10.3	14.0	12.4
Sharon, PA	156	1 793	28 594	20.5	75.1	13.6	159.9	8 284	11 336	24 598	-14.5	1.6	NA	13.0	19.9	19.4
Sheboygan, WI	118	2 820	25 856	19.4	77.4	13.8	141.6	7 196	13 425	31 603	0.7	2.4	NA	5.5	8.1	6.8
Sherman-Denison, TX	307	3 909	23 758	10.3	72.1	14.0	112.8	5 665	12 201	25 240	-1.3	2.3	NA	13.2	19.8	17.8
Shreveport-Bossier City, LA	742	5 544	102 591	9.8	73.5	16.7	407.1	5 523	11 269	22 808	-11.2	2.4	NA	18.2	26.7	24.5
Sioux City, IA-NE	514	4 755	30 460	21.8	77.9	16.0	141.0	6 364	11 988	25 216	-7.2	2.3	NA	10.7	15.7	13.4
Sioux Falls, SD	270	2 689	35 231	20.8	82.7	20.7	138.6	4 990	13 223	27 843	-0.4	2.7	NA	7.4	10.7	7.8
South Bend, IN	442	5 392	67 863	31.6	76.1	19.2	276.6	7 056	13 277	28 235	-4.1	2.6	NA	11.0	16.2	14.2
Spokane, WA	422	5 629	100 683	14.3	84.4	16.6	461.1	6 290	12 804	25 768	-3.5	2.4	NA	12.3	16.2	14.5
Springfield, IL	NA	NA	47 550	17.0	81.5	21.9	195.4	6 154	14 829	30 299	-0.3	2.8	NA	9.7	14.6	13.8
Springfield, MA	916	3 474	170 224	22.5	75.7	20.8	790.3	8 140	14 122	31 750	16.3	3.5	NA	12.7	19.6	20.6
Springfield, MO	330	4 633	71 088	14.4	77.5	18.6	246.1	4 907	11 968	24 204	2.0	2.4	NA	11.8	17.2	14.7
St. Cloud, MN	123	1 572	48 493	16.6	78.1	16.9	188.0	6 368	11 498	27 328	2.5	2.3	NA	8.4	10.9	9.5
St. Joseph, MO	265	4 466	23 695	8.9	73.1	13.5	90.0	5 216	11 162	23 494	-2.9	1.7	NA	12.8	18.1	16.3
St. Louis, MO-IL	NA	NA	649 189	24.9	75.9	20.5	2 663.2	6 420	14 847	31 718	2.6	3.9	NA	10.3	15.5	13.5
State College, PA	134	2 426	50 857	5.9	83.6	32.3	118.0	8 181	11 854	26 060	4.6	2.9	NA	9.6	12.0	11.7
Steubenville-Weirton, OH-WV	NA	NA	34 367	17.5	72.0	9.5	132.8	6 524	11 487	24 110	-24.6	1.1	NA	13.5	21.4	18.9
Stockton-Lodi, CA	815	4 445	137 025	11.3	68.6	13.2	622.5	5 540	12 705	30 634	13.7	3.6	NA	17.6	24.8	26.1
Sumter, SC	964	4 625	28 487	12.2	69.8	15.0	100.1	5 284	9 997	22 386	9.6	1.4	NA	18.3	24.6	24.4
Syracuse, NY	326	2 621	203 913	21.3	78.8	20.8	1 088.7	8 312	13 668	30 705	7.7	3.0	NA	12.8	19.1	18.4
Tallahassee, FL	1 016	5 620	82 977	9.8	80.3	32.4	228.3	5 711	13 122	26 208	14.2	3.2	NA	14.6	20.7	19.8
Tampa-St. Petersburg-Clearwater, FL	892	4 962	424 681	16.2	75.1	17.3	1 881.0	5 708	14 374	26 035	14.8	3.0	NA	12.9	21.6	19.3
Terre Haute, IN	NA	NA	40 238	9.3	75.5	15.4	149.1	6 081	11 647	23 368	-7.3	1.8	NA	13.7	18.7	17.0
Texarkana, TX-Texarkana, AR	585	3 924	30 716	5.2	69.6	12.8	122.9	5 241	11 147	22 947	0.4	2.0	NA	17.8	26.3	23.6
Toledo, OH	489	5 368	175 227	16.7	77.6	17.4	691.2	7 064	13 710	29 120	-3.4	3.4	NA	11.7	17.5	15.2
Topeka, KS	845	7 798	40 682	12.8	84.4	22.3	162.4	6 023	14 091	29 878	0.7	2.5	NA	10.4	15.8	14.6

1. Data for serious crimes have not been adjusted for underreporting; this may affect comparability between geographic areas and over time.   2. Per 100,000 population estimated by the FBI.   3. All persons 3 years old and over enrolled in nursery school through college.   4. Persons 25 years old and over.   5. Elementary and secondary education expenditures, local government fiscal years ending between July 1, 1998 and June 30, 1999.   6. Based on population enumerated as of April 1, 1990.

Table C. Metropolitan Areas — **Personal Income**

Area Name	Personal income, 1999 Total (mil dol)	Percent change, 1998–1999	Per capita[1] Dollars	Per capita[1] Rank	Wages and salaries[2] (mil dol)	Proprietor's income (mil dol)	Dividends, interest, and rent (mil dol)	Transfer payments Total (mil dol)	Government payments to individuals Total (mil dol)	Social Security (mil dol)	Medical payments (mil dol)	Income mainte-nance (mil dol)	Unemploy-ment insurance (mil dol)
	62	63	64	65	66	67	68	69	70	71	72	73	74
Reading, PA	10 002	3.8	27 921	97	6 000	724	1 898	1 472	1 400	631	583	95	38
Redding, CA	3 764	5.1	22 880	250	1 826	548	712	814	782	293	295	117	19
Reno, NV	11 303	6.7	35 343	19	6 812	1 041	3 109	939	886	389	300	60	32
Richland-Kennewick-Pasco, WA	4 287	3.8	23 219	243	2 965	229	717	631	592	224	215	58	38
Richmond-Petersburg, VA	29 413	5.9	30 593	51	21 358	1 600	5 575	3 008	2 825	1 316	1 044	259	18
Roanoke, VA	6 488	3.7	28 491	85	4 762	399	1 316	863	820	386	253	63	5
Rochester, MN	3 853	7.4	32 359	35	3 213	197	755	350	325	147	131	26	6
Rochester, NY	30 389	3.2	28 162	90	19 816	1 783	5 768	4 738	4 511	1 752	1 862	586	88
Rockford, IL	9 498	3.5	26 484	132	6 417	514	1 826	1 164	1 090	564	364	92	40
Rocky Mount, NC	3 163	-3.7	21 510	288	2 070	237	362	579	552	198	233	80	12
Sacramento-Yolo, CA	49 736	7.1	28 568	X	31 882	4 816	8 350	6 608	6 274	2 029	2 479	1 148	135
Sacramento, CA	45 530	7.4	28 718	83	28 663	4 294	7 539	6 106	5 802	1 869	2 301	1 067	122
Yolo, CA	4 206	4.3	27 037	122	3 219	523	811	502	472	160	178	81	13
Saginaw-Bay City-Midland, MI	10 424	4.2	26 012	143	6 934	550	2 048	1 618	1 541	678	593	174	39
Salinas, CA	10 927	5.5	29 393	72	5 674	1 894	2 423	1 178	1 107	401	395	157	63
Salt Lake City-Ogden, UT	32 967	5.5	25 855	149	24 149	2 432	5 920	2 972	2 747	1 172	978	228	62
San Angelo, TX	2 399	3.3	23 453	231	1 390	222	505	378	360	146	150	31	5
San Antonio, TX	38 680	5.2	24 716	185	24 658	4 683	6 541	5 048	4 783	1 600	2 074	617	62
San Diego, CA	83 183	8.3	29 489	67	52 156	8 140	16 838	9 026	8 502	3 122	3 305	1 222	139
San Francisco-Oakland-San Jose, CA	280 844	10.3	40 858	X	195 859	26 469	52 842	22 319	20 996	7 790	7 934	3 193	447
Oakland, CA	83 769	8.4	35 666	18	48 187	7 015	15 006	8 034	7 582	2 601	3 045	1 234	149
San Francisco, CA	83 768	8.0	49 695	1	62 193	10 093	18 798	5 939	5 614	2 179	2 019	921	92
San Jose, CA	76 850	15.8	46 649	2	68 466	5 850	11 830	4 539	4 221	1 567	1 592	604	99
Santa Cruz-Watsonville, CA	8 224	8.4	33 539	28	3 622	853	1 652	741	694	269	246	88	31
Santa Rosa, CA	14 296	8.1	32 492	32	7 003	1 600	3 180	1 477	1 392	625	493	140	28
Vallejo-Fairfield-Napa, CA	13 937	9.7	27 506	108	6 388	1 059	2 375	1 589	1 493	549	539	207	47
San Luis Obispo-Atascadero-Paso Robles, CA	6 134	5.3	25 888	147	2 926	892	1 575	815	769	377	230	84	14
Santa Barbara-Santa Maria-Lompoc, CA	11 817	5.0	30 218	61	6 301	1 378	3 458	1 231	1 156	529	366	141	26
Santa Fe, NM	4 366	4.0	30 634	50	2 749	384	1 190	379	353	167	118	32	5
Sarasota-Bradenton, FL	19 626	4.1	35 679	17	7 957	1 205	7 507	2 910	2 810	1 557	1 017	102	15
Savannah, GA	7 653	4.4	26 534	131	4 746	486	1 592	1 027	966	393	368	121	11
Scranton—Wilkes-Barre—Hazleton, PA	15 031	3.3	24 581	188	8 585	1 206	2 932	3 257	3 134	1 239	1 357	200	99
Seattle-Tacoma-Bremerton, WA	121 483	8.9	35 052	X	85 706	9 237	21 155	11 423	10 708	4 143	3 730	884	493
Bremerton, WA	5 654	5.2	23 902	215	3 264	329	1 273	697	650	240	229	57	36
Olympia, WA	5 293	5.2	25 760	150	2 949	334	971	725	682	276	219	54	34
Seattle-Bellevue-Everett, WA	93 116	10.0	39 880	8	70 404	7 516	15 995	7 566	7 081	2 816	2 454	532	320
Tacoma, WA	17 420	5.4	25 289	166	9 089	1 058	2 917	2 435	2 295	811	828	240	102
Sharon, PA	2 656	3.5	21 864	278	1 449	217	483	578	553	248	221	46	13
Sheboygan, WI	3 051	6.3	27 705	100	2 061	178	646	346	324	182	107	14	10
Sherman-Denison, TX	2 440	5.4	23 521	230	1 424	173	407	440	422	173	179	28	7
Shreveport-Bossier City, LA	9 084	3.6	24 053	210	5 595	671	1 795	1 545	1 479	534	663	174	14
Sioux City, IA-NE	3 032	3.2	25 144	171	1 931	233	574	407	382	177	141	34	6
Sioux Falls, SD	4 991	7.0	30 341	58	3 428	468	961	448	421	211	157	21	2
South Bend, IN	6 919	3.9	26 761	124	4 402	434	1 422	906	855	419	327	72	10
Spokane, WA	9 985	4.7	24 368	202	6 438	703	1 973	1 679	1 593	571	600	158	75
Springfield, IL	5 713	3.6	28 000	96	3 951	358	1 218	691	649	311	228	62	16
Springfield, MA	15 995	4.6	27 149	120	9 158	985	2 749	3 072	2 964	910	1 551	297	80
Springfield, MO	7 562	4.7	24 525	192	4 822	779	1 534	1 081	1 024	446	402	84	11
St. Cloud, MN	3 831	3.3	23 231	240	2 729	311	783	464	430	181	158	34	13
St. Joseph, MO	2 310	5.1	23 764	220	1 386	163	440	408	390	164	165	31	5
St. Louis, MO-IL	78 051	3.9	30 382	57	51 339	4 378	17 192	9 552	9 067	3 927	3 666	860	155
State College, PA	3 187	4.4	24 107	208	2 187	326	591	367	341	154	106	24	9
Steubenville-Weirton, OH-WV	2 819	2.0	21 151	293	1 561	143	566	671	645	293	243	47	8
Stockton-Lodi, CA	12 133	6.2	21 544	286	6 455	1 229	1 946	2 262	2 153	622	924	419	69
Sumter, SC	2 050	4.3	18 238	313	1 372	101	343	377	358	125	137	59	5
Syracuse, NY	18 335	3.5	25 017	174	11 817	1 192	3 162	3 039	2 884	1 178	1 161	318	52
Tallahassee, FL	6 825	4.6	26 252	137	5 226	340	1 141	767	719	271	260	102	8
Tampa-St. Petersburg-Clearwater, FL	64 120	5.3	28 145	92	39 304	3 268	14 738	10 282	9 866	4 576	3 923	661	89
Terre Haute, IN	3 286	4.1	22 170	269	2 052	184	685	598	569	249	225	46	8
Texarkana, TX-Texarkana, AR	2 680	4.2	21 811	281	1 535	289	503	490	468	169	206	58	7
Toledo, OH	16 496	3.8	27 087	121	11 529	938	3 204	2 434	2 302	890	931	236	40
Topeka, KS	4 507	3.9	26 394	134	3 397	245	922	617	587	257	189	50	10

1. Based on the resident population estimated as of July 1 of the year shown.   2. Includes other labor income.

Table C. Metropolitan Areas — **Earnings, Social Security, and Housing**

	Earnings, 1999									Social Security bene-ficiaries, December 2000		Housing units, 1990	
			Goods-related[1]		Service-related and other[2]							Supple-mental Security Income recipients, December 2000	
Area Name	Total (mil dol)	Farm	Total	Manu-facturing	Total	Retail trade	Finance, insur-ance, and real estate	Services	Govern-ment	Number	Rate[3]		Total	Percent change, 1980–1990
	75	76	77	78	79	80	81	82	83	84	85	86	87	88
Reading, PA	6 723	0.9	34.6	28.4	53.5	9.7	6.6	24.5	11.1	68 831	184	5 615	134 482	12.1
Redding, CA	2 374	0.4	D	8.7	D	12.6	4.0	30.1	19.0	36 125	221	8 117	60 552	27.6
Reno, NV	7 852	0.0	17.7	7.7	68.2	9.8	7.6	35.9	14.1	46 770	138	3 963	112 193	30.4
Richland-Kennewick-Pasco, WA	3 195	5.4	D	8.2	D	8.5	2.8	28.8	19.0	25 157	131	2 592	58 541	4.6
Richmond-Petersburg, VA	22 958	0.1	D	13.6	D	9.5	12.6	23.9	19.2	149 576	150	18 133	355 207	23.9
Roanoke, VA	5 161	0.0	D	15.5	D	10.9	9.0	27.1	13.8	45 218	192	4 948	95 467	9.5
Rochester, MN	3 409	0.6	D	21.7	D	7.2	3.6	46.4	8.8	17 035	137	1 355	41 603	21.1
Rochester, NY	21 598	0.6	34.2	29.5	51.1	8.6	5.2	26.6	14.1	191 817	175	24 043	421 684	8.9
Rockford, IL	6 931	0.4	D	37.0	D	7.8	5.2	21.4	9.9	61 414	165	5 485	131 195	8.8
Rocky Mount, NC	2 306	3.8	D	24.9	D	9.3	D	18.2	15.8	26 768	187	6 200	52 851	14.9
Sacramento-Yolo, CA	36 698	0.7	16.4	8.9	54.2	9.4	8.6	25.5	28.7	250 854	140	62 076	609 904	30.8
Sacramento, CA	32 957	0.3	16.6	8.9	54.6	9.2	9.1	26.5	28.5	230 906	142	57 363	556 904	31.7
Yolo, CA	3 741	4.3	15.1	8.6	50.4	10.9	4.4	16.4	30.3	19 948	118	4 713	53 000	21.5
Saginaw-Bay City-Midland, MI	7 484	0.5	D	38.3	D	8.8	3.8	22.1	11.6	74 581	185	10 062	155 508	4.2
Salinas, CA	7 568	15.0	10.3	5.2	54.0	9.1	6.4	22.8	20.7	49 035	122	8 720	121 224	17.1
Salt Lake City-Ogden, UT	26 580	0.1	D	12.5	D	10.4	9.0	26.6	18.0	137 792	103	12 457	370 967	21.0
San Angelo, TX	1 612	0.5	19.9	11.8	54.3	10.6	5.8	24.6	25.4	17 975	173	2 204	40 135	22.1
San Antonio, TX	29 341	0.3	15.4	7.2	60.3	10.5	8.9	25.4	24.1	216 953	136	38 475	512 927	33.2
San Diego, CA	60 296	0.6	17.3	11.4	59.3	8.9	7.9	30.2	22.8	370 870	132	76 889	946 240	31.4
San Francisco-Oakland-San Jose, CA	222 328	0.3	D	19.9	D	7.8	9.3	34.1	10.9	867 881	123	199 427	2 457 201	14.7
Oakland, CA	55 202	0.1	21.7	14.0	63.1	9.3	7.2	30.9	15.1	292 088	122	69 353	820 279	17.8
San Francisco, CA	72 286	0.1	D	7.5	D	8.2	17.4	39.0	10.3	236 071	136	62 507	680 010	5.8
San Jose, CA	74 315	0.2	41.6	37.3	51.7	5.4	3.8	33.4	6.4	169 766	101	40 971	540 240	14.0
Santa Cruz-Watsonville, CA	4 475	4.3	21.4	13.7	58.9	11.6	5.4	31.6	15.5	31 133	122	5 353	91 878	13.6
Santa Rosa, CA	8 603	1.5	28.5	18.2	56.9	10.9	7.9	27.8	13.1	70 643	154	9 208	161 062	29.7
Vallejo-Fairfield-Napa, CA	7 447	1.6	D	14.3	D	11.8	4.5	24.7	23.8	68 180	131	12 035	163 732	31.7
San Luis Obispo-Atascad-ero-Paso Robles, CA	3 818	3.0	17.6	8.0	58.7	13.4	6.0	26.3	20.7	44 075	179	5 186	90 200	35.1
Santa Barbara-Santa Maria-Lompoc, CA	7 679	4.8	17.7	10.6	58.2	10.6	6.6	30.7	19.3	61 083	153	9 050	138 149	20.2
Santa Fe, NM	3 132	0.1	8.3	2.1	D	10.2	7.2	30.4	39.4	20 290	137	1 838	49 029	40.5
Sarasota-Bradenton, FL	9 162	2.0	D	9.8	D	12.3	8.7	42.0	10.2	170 972	290	6 712	272 300	38.3
Savannah, GA	5 232	0.1	D	19.1	D	10.5	5.0	26.8	18.6	45 821	156	7 554	106 219	21.6
Scranton—Wilkes-Barre—Hazleton, PA	9 791	0.1	D	D	D	10.0	6.3	26.1	14.7	145 131	232	14 542	267 886	2.9
Seattle-Tacoma-Bremerton, WA	94 943	0.1	D	14.7	D	8.6	6.9	34.7	16.1	458 386	129	56 710	1 226 489	26.0
Bremerton, WA	3 593	0.1	7.9	2.1	36.6	8.5	3.5	19.9	55.5	30 856	133	3 588	74 038	29.2
Olympia, WA	3 283	0.8	11.7	5.5	45.6	11.1	4.6	22.9	41.9	32 459	157	3 329	66 464	31.1
Seattle-Bellevue-Everett, WA	77 919	0.1	D	16.1	D	8.3	7.1	37.3	11.5	300 014	124	35 530	857 145	26.5
Tacoma, WA	10 147	0.3	18.6	11.1	51.6	10.3	7.2	23.6	29.5	95 057	136	14 263	228 842	22.1
Sharon, PA	1 666	0.4	35.3	28.9	52.0	11.5	4.0	25.9	12.3	27 438	228	3 233	48 689	2.2
Sheboygan, WI	2 240	0.8	53.3	47.2	36.2	7.6	4.7	16.8	9.7	19 574	174	1 213	40 695	9.0
Sherman-Denison, TX	1 597	0.6	37.5	29.1	50.2	11.7	6.5	23.8	11.6	20 736	187	1 944	44 223	12.0
Shreveport-Bossier City, LA	6 265	0.1	23.0	14.0	53.3	9.2	4.0	27.8	23.6	65 762	168	13 337	160 974	11.5
Sioux City, IA-NE	2 163	0.9	D	D	D	9.9	5.6	28.0	12.4	20 496	165	2 153	45 557	0.9
Sioux Falls, SD	3 895	1.5	D	13.3	D	10.2	12.8	29.2	9.3	24 814	144	1 983	55 603	15.8
South Bend, IN	4 837	0.1	D	21.0	D	9.8	6.3	32.3	10.3	44 888	169	3 933	97 956	7.4
Spokane, WA	7 141	0.1	20.0	12.6	60.3	10.6	7.6	28.0	19.6	66 647	159	8 863	150 105	9.0
Springfield, IL	4 309	0.4	D	D	D	7.5	9.3	30.3	32.0	35 778	178	4 786	81 523	5.2
Springfield, MA	10 143	0.2	22.7	16.7	56.6	9.9	7.6	29.1	20.5	108 558	178	22 650	233 093	9.0
Springfield, MO	5 601	0.0	D	15.7	D	13.0	6.9	28.4	12.8	56 225	173	6 318	109 789	20.3
St. Cloud, MN	3 040	2.2	27.3	19.7	55.4	14.0	4.7	23.9	15.1	23 597	141	1 704	55 327	23.6
St. Joseph, MO	1 548	0.0	D	D	D	10.4	D	25.4	15.9	19 386	189	2 173	41 493	-0.5
St. Louis, MO-IL	55 717	0.1	D	18.3	D	8.7	8.6	29.2	12.6	439 032	169	48 682	1 027 136	11.2
State College, PA	2 513	0.4	18.1	13.0	41.6	7.7	4.1	22.1	40.0	17 568	129	1 534	46 195	16.8
Steubenville-Weirton, OH-WV	1 703	0.1	D	36.1	D	8.8	2.7	23.0	12.8	31 437	238	3 496	59 446	-3.8
Stockton-Lodi, CA	7 684	3.9	20.6	13.1	56.6	10.4	6.3	21.6	18.9	77 655	138	24 799	166 274	22.3
Sumter, SC	1 472	0.5	D	24.1	D	8.6	3.4	17.4	32.0	16 819	161	4 267	35 016	18.4
Syracuse, NY	13 009	0.4	D	19.2	D	9.0	7.2	26.2	17.1	131 322	179	17 161	299 347	8.9
Tallahassee, FL	5 566	1.0	D	2.9	D	8.3	5.3	28.5	42.0	33 849	119	6 615	96 184	31.9
Tampa-St. Petersburg-Clear-water, FL	42 572	0.7	D	8.3	D	10.7	10.5	37.1	13.4	529 543	221	50 035	1 025 064	34.2
Terre Haute, IN	2 236	0.1	D	D	D	13.9	3.9	22.6	17.3	28 754	193	3 276	62 097	2.1
Texarkana, TX-Texarkana, AR	1 824	2.4	D	14.0	D	12.7	4.2	25.1	22.7	22 402	173	4 024	50 406	13.3
Toledo, OH	12 467	0.5	D	26.4	D	9.0	4.4	25.5	14.8	98 755	160	15 428	247 243	4.7
Topeka, KS	3 642	0.0	18.2	11.8	59.0	11.2	8.3	26.1	22.8	29 837	176	3 532	68 991	7.1

1. Covers mining, construction, and manufacturing.   2. Covers private sector earnings in agricultural services, forestry, and fisheries; transportation and public utilities; wholesale trade; retail trade; finance, insurance, and real estate; and services.   3. Per 1,000 resident population estimated as of July 1 of the year shown.

Table C. Metropolitan Areas — **Housing, Labor Force, and Employment**

Area Name	Housing units, 1990 (cont'd)								Civilian labor force, 2001				Civilian employment, 1990[5]		
	Occupied units										Unemployment			Percent	
			Owner-occupied			Renter-occupied										
				Owner cost as a percent of income												
	Total	Percent	Median value[1]	With a mortgage	Without a mortgage	Median rent[2]	Rent as percent of income	Sub-standard units[3] (percent)	Total	Percent change, 2000–2001	Total	Rate[4]	Total	Professional, managerial, and technical	Precision production, craft, and repair
	89	90	91	92	93	94	95	96	97	98	99	100	101	102	103
Reading, PA	127 649	73.9	81 800	19.7	12.5	412	24.7	2.2	186 241	1.3	9 166	4.9	166 292	25.2	13.1
Redding, CA	55 966	64.5	91 300	21.7	11.9	431	29.2	5.1	76 487	2.3	5 155	6.7	58 578	26.8	12.6
Reno, NV	102 294	54.1	111 200	23.4	12.2	508	26.6	5.7	183 058	2.7	7 561	4.1	140 734	27.7	9.5
Richland-Kennewick-Pasco, WA	54 423	62.4	64 400	16.3	11.5	348	22.1	5.7	94 436	0.9	6 822	7.2	68 126	32.9	10.6
Richmond-Petersburg, VA	331 824	65.0	79 300	20.3	12.9	458	25.5	2.5	528 922	1.9	18 129	3.4	442 812	32.3	10.9
Roanoke, VA	89 694	67.7	67 700	17.9	12.2	363	23.6	1.8	129 368	0.6	3 499	2.7	112 933	28.5	10.4
Rochester, MN	40 058	72.4	72 300	18.6	11.8	409	23.4	2.1	78 135	4.3	1 955	2.5	57 318	40.1	7.6
Rochester, NY	396 089	67.9	85 500	NA	NA	462	NA	1.7	555 041	-1.5	25 138	4.5	520 469	33.0	11.4
Rockford, IL	124 809	68.8	60 900	NA	NA	373	NA	2.4	197 597	-2.2	12 934	6.5	162 794	25.8	13.6
Rocky Mount, NC	49 360	63.3	55 600	NA	NA	327	NA	7.1	67 461	0.0	5 197	7.7	64 829	21.5	12.9
Sacramento-Yolo, CA	556 448	59.0	136 700	NA	NA	530	NA	5.9	923 031	2.0	37 539	4.1	693 136	33.3	10.5
Sacramento, CA	505 476	59.7	136 700	23.4	11.7	532	29.3	5.7	829 833	2.4	33 584	4.0	626 876	32.9	10.7
Yolo, CA	50 972	51.9	137 800	NA	NA	509	NA	7.9	93 198	-0.9	3 955	4.2	66 260	37.1	8.8
Saginaw-Bay City-Midland, MI	148 235	73.6	49 100	16.7	13.2	380	29.1	2.5	202 771	-0.2	10 980	5.4	169 787	26.9	12.8
Salinas, CA	112 965	50.6	198 200	24.8	11.4	624	28.5	14.6	195 850	-0.2	18 133	9.3	146 885	26.8	8.7
Salt Lake City-Ogden, UT	347 531	67.4	71 000	21.0	12.0	377	23.7	4.4	710 840	0.6	30 775	4.3	480 241	31.9	11.0
San Angelo, TX	35 408	62.3	49 600	19.8	12.8	364	25.1	6.2	49 988	0.6	1 423	2.8	41 808	26.9	11.2
San Antonio, TX	458 502	59.6	57 200	NA	NA	379	NA	9.4	788 521	1.7	31 223	4.0	559 142	30.2	11.0
San Diego, CA	887 403	53.8	186 700	25.9	11.5	610	29.8	9.1	1 424 852	1.6	45 698	3.2	1 145 266	34.5	11.1
San Francisco-Oakland-San Jose, CA	2 329 808	56.5	257 700	NA	NA	689	NA	8.3	3 934 668	0.9	160 059	4.1	3 229 687	37.8	10.0
Oakland, CA	779 806	58.8	224 400	25.3	11.8	641	28.6	7.0	1 264 666	1.7	50 578	4.0	1 042 347	37.7	10.2
San Francisco, CA	642 504	48.3	332 400	25.6	11.7	708	28.0	9.2	982 909	0.1	37 403	3.8	865 380	38.4	7.9
San Jose, CA	520 180	59.1	289 400	24.9	11.5	772	27.4	10.6	1 012 671	0.4	45 190	4.5	806 917	41.1	10.6
Santa Cruz-Watsonville, CA	83 566	59.9	256 100	27.2	11.7	712	31.4	9.4	143 814	1.2	8 761	6.1	117 904	36.3	10.7
Santa Rosa, CA	149 011	62.9	201 400	26.2	11.7	644	29.5	4.6	262 617	1.3	7 678	2.9	193 296	31.7	12.3
Vallejo-Fairfield-Napa, CA	154 741	63.3	155 300	25.2	11.8	600	27.9	6.2	267 991	2.1	10 449	3.9	203 843	29.2	13.4
San Luis Obispo-Atascadero-Paso Robles, CA	80 281	59.8	215 300	NA	NA	572	NA	5.7	118 603	2.2	3 306	2.8	97 417	29.3	12.3
Santa Barbara-Santa Maria-Lompoc, CA	129 802	54.7	250 000	25.0	11.3	653	31.3	9.7	202 668	-0.7	7 003	3.5	180 217	32.7	10.7
Santa Fe, NM	45 053	68.8	109 900	21.6	11.8	485	26.5	5.8	74 902	-0.3	1 805	2.4	59 394	42.6	9.2
Sarasota-Bradenton, FL	216 553	74.0	84 300	NA	NA	515	NA	2.2	288 099	3.6	8 668	3.0	201 798	28.0	12.5
Savannah, GA	94 940	61.8	63 400	NA	NA	401	NA	4.6	135 132	-1.4	4 315	3.2	112 046	27.8	12.8
Scranton—Wilkes-Barre—Hazleton, PA	246 491	69.2	60 400	NA	NA	322	NA	1.6	309 546	1.1	16 810	5.4	282 064	24.7	12.3
Seattle-Tacoma-Bremerton, WA	1 155 361	61.0	118 100	NA	NA	492	NA	3.7	1 882 695	-1.9	102 486	5.4	1 480 616	34.4	11.7
Bremerton, WA	69 267	64.3	89 100	21.4	11.9	449	24.7	3.9	92 402	-1.2	5 541	6.0	78 930	32.9	16.0
Olympia, WA	62 150	64.7	79 700	21.0	11.7	459	26.0	3.6	98 857	-1.2	5 610	5.7	74 539	36.4	9.6
Seattle-Bellevue-Everett, WA	809 292	60.6	135 900	NA	NA	514	NA	3.5	1 363 035	-2.1	70 407	5.2	1 075 314	35.8	11.2
Tacoma, WA	214 652	60.3	82 500	21.1	12.4	435	26.2	4.3	328 401	-1.4	20 928	6.4	251 833	28.4	13.2
Sharon, PA	45 591	75.0	41 900	17.1	13.0	320	26.4	2.3	58 621	0.9	2 998	5.1	50 027	23.3	11.8
Sheboygan, WI	38 592	70.3	59 400	18.5	13.0	360	21.5	1.7	63 298	1.5	2 411	3.8	52 159	22.5	12.9
Sherman-Denison, TX	36 847	69.3	46 600	18.3	13.5	367	23.8	3.4	50 095	-0.6	2 709	5.4	42 133	26.1	13.8
Shreveport-Bossier City, LA	139 815	66.0	55 100	NA	NA	346	NA	5.5	186 521	2.3	11 885	6.4	149 039	28.3	11.4
Sioux City, IA-NE	42 934	68.5	41 300	17.5	13.1	328	24.8	2.8	63 830	1.5	2 042	3.2	54 471	24.6	13.0
Sioux Falls, SD	53 142	64.0	57 600	NA	NA	372	NA	1.8	105 835	1.8	2 417	2.3	74 222	27.2	10.2
South Bend, IN	92 365	72.0	50 800	17.1	12.4	401	25.3	2.2	135 359	0.4	6 245	4.6	117 132	28.9	10.8
Spokane, WA	141 619	63.7	58 900	19.4	12.2	355	26.9	2.7	207 081	-1.0	13 629	6.6	157 142	30.9	9.9
Springfield, IL	76 345	67.1	60 200	16.7	12.0	379	23.4	1.8	106 571	-1.2	4 213	4.0	97 332	34.4	8.7
Springfield, MA	219 958	60.7	125 600	20.8	13.4	493	26.3	2.9	289 894	1.6	11 051	3.8	287 529	30.5	10.8
Springfield, MO	101 791	66.4	57 200	NA	NA	340	NA	2.5	173 371	-1.2	6 017	3.5	127 700	25.6	11.1
St. Cloud, MN	50 711	70.5	61 300	19.8	12.5	389	26.9	2.5	101 777	2.4	4 126	4.1	73 824	24.1	10.7
St. Joseph, MO	37 915	69.5	41 500	NA	NA	303	NA	1.8	52 415	4.1	2 723	5.2	42 597	23.1	11.7
St. Louis, MO-IL	942 119	68.8	69 800	NA	NA	413	NA	3.0	1 359 506	0.0	66 060	4.9	1 176 958	31.3	10.6
State College, PA	42 683	59.8	74 700	20.3	11.8	447	31.3	4.5	67 355	3.2	1 958	2.9	57 809	35.9	8.1
Steubenville-Weirton, OH-WV	55 223	75.4	43 900	15.3	12.2	300	24.4	2.0	55 615	0.8	2 625	4.7	54 810	21.0	15.4
Stockton-Lodi, CA	158 156	57.6	121 700	23.3	11.8	488	28.2	12.4	264 782	1.9	23 134	8.7	195 575	24.2	12.5
Sumter, SC	32 723	65.2	56 900	NA	NA	355	NA	7.1	46 785	-2.6	3 372	7.2	37 746	21.8	14.9
Syracuse, NY	272 974	66.7	75 300	NA	NA	426	NA	2.0	354 587	-1.1	16 614	4.7	348 527	31.2	11.0
Tallahassee, FL	88 233	59.7	70 500	19.8	12.5	429	29.7	5.1	151 407	0.8	4 710	3.1	119 309	38.7	7.2
Tampa-St. Petersburg-Clearwater, FL	869 481	69.3	71 300	22.6	12.1	447	27.2	3.1	1 269 704	2.5	47 531	3.7	923 652	29.3	11.0
Terre Haute, IN	55 824	72.2	38 100	NA	NA	305	NA	2.8	69 899	0.0	3 895	5.6	63 645	25.8	11.9
Texarkana, TX-Texarkana, AR	44 868	70.0	46 400	17.8	13.2	344	25.6	4.4	55 394	-0.5	2 513	4.5	49 659	25.1	13.7
Toledo, OH	230 681	66.6	59 700	17.4	13.3	390	25.9	1.9	324 171	0.7	14 968	4.6	279 224	28.8	11.0
Topeka, KS	63 768	66.6	55 700	18.4	12.1	385	24.5	2.2	88 744	-1.9	3 595	4.1	80 143	32.4	8.6

1. Specified owner-occupied units.   2. Specified renter-occupied units.   3. Overcrowded or lacking complete plumbing facilities.   4. Percent of civilian labor force.   5. Persons 16 years and older.

Table C. Metropolitan Areas — Nonfarm Employment and Agriculture

Area Name	Private nonfarm establishments, employment and payroll, 1999									Agriculture, 1997			
	Number of establishments	Employment						Annual payroll		Farms			Farm operators
		Total	Health Care and Social Assistance	Manufacturing	Retail trade	Finance and Insurance	Professional Scientific and Technical Services	Total (mil dol)	Average per employee (dollars)	Number	Percent with—		Whose principal occupation is farming (percent)
											Less than 50 acres	500 acres and over	
	104	105	106	107	108	109	110	111	112	113	114	115	116
Reading, PA	8 079	145 991	16 011	39 884	20 146	5 585	6 452	4 331	29 666	1 586	39.0	5.0	63.0
Redding, CA	4 380	43 952	8 858	3 555	8 200	1 343	1 891	1 109	25 232	850	61.3	14.0	41.6
Reno, NV	10 958	167 777	15 541	11 773	20 976	5 584	7 956	4 916	29 301	285	56.1	17.5	36.8
Richland-Kennewick-Pasco, WA	4 386	61 875	7 293	6 961	9 446	1 493	7 586	1 920	31 030	1 926	51.2	17.5	54.6
Richmond-Petersburg, VA	26 486	463 107	53 042	53 066	59 559	40 335	24 234	14 593	31 511	1 858	35.8	10.8	42.2
Roanoke, VA	7 137	125 492	17 361	18 839	19 133	7 040	4 011	3 282	26 153	778	34.6	5.8	43.2
Rochester, MN	2 926	70 786	26 415	10 786	9 486	1 564	2 492	2 490	35 176	1 317	28.3	10.9	51.3
Rochester, NY	24 133	464 369	64 866	95 859	60 012	16 159	20 340	15 095	32 506	3 609	30.6	14.0	56.8
Rockford, IL	8 798	160 213	19 110	49 732	19 601	6 397	5 252	4 820	30 085	2 276	29.8	20.8	55.3
Rocky Mount, NC	3 275	56 832	6 632	15 703	7 447	2 176	1 455	1 477	25 989	787	31.4	22.9	63.7
Sacramento-Yolo, CA	39 496	588 809	70 084	48 072	79 557	40 404	34 758	18 280	31 046	3 971	63.3	10.9	48.9
Sacramento, CA	36 075	533 585	65 621	42 038	73 223	37 673	32 247	16 629	31 165	3 048	68.7	7.7	46.6
Yolo, CA	3 421	55 224	4 463	6 034	6 334	2 731	2 511	1 651	29 896	923	45.6	21.1	56.4
Saginaw-Bay City-Midland, MI	9 602	161 026	25 340	32 678	27 456	4 879	5 477	5 358	33 274	2 311	30.1	13.2	52.7
Salinas, CA	8 519	104 520	12 099	6 755	16 970	4 794	3 714	2 993	28 636	1 209	40.7	29.9	66.3
Salt Lake City-Ogden, UT	34 027	605 574	55 850	78 782	75 844	38 725	32 533	16 843	27 813	2 088	75.4	2.9	35.3
San Angelo, TX	2 584	34 394	5 985	3 917	5 375	1 355	1 130	764	22 213	880	34.9	33.2	46.8
San Antonio, TX	33 375	591 205	83 225	50 097	77 180	37 569	34 351	15 664	26 495	6 256	36.8	9.2	38.5
San Diego, CA	65 905	1 015 773	107 615	116 648	129 028	47 963	83 377	33 860	33 334	5 925	90.2	2.0	37.2
San Francisco-Oakland-San Jose, CA	193 942	3 210 688	318 775	451 561	331 512	175 525	281 471	150 569	46 896	8 135	65.3	9.5	49.4
Oakland, CA	57 492	913 250	101 536	108 171	100 370	48 935	64 132	36 262	39 707	1 045	58.0	13.9	45.6
San Francisco, CA	61 600	982 019	90 373	57 755	91 332	88 737	110 059	46 809	47 656	525	47.4	21.7	58.3
San Jose, CA	44 909	941 476	71 520	231 338	81 280	21 178	91 218	56 160	59 651	985	74.5	7.8	47.6
Santa Cruz-Watsonville, CA	6 813	75 617	9 548	8 685	12 305	2 035	4 468	2 364	31 263	722	75.8	3.5	59.8
Santa Rosa, CA	13 147	159 421	22 328	26 391	24 643	10 612	7 117	4 953	31 069	2 745	66.3	7.3	49.0
Vallejo-Fairfield-Napa, CA	9 981	138 705	23 470	19 221	21 582	4 028	4 477	4 021	28 990	2 113	64.3	9.9	47.0
San Luis Obispo-Atascadero-Paso Robles, CA	6 736	72 677	12 426	6 894	12 020	2 385	3 145	1 832	25 207	1 916	49.3	19.7	48.4
Santa Barbara-Santa Maria-Lompoc, CA	10 675	135 515	16 737	16 464	20 154	6 191	7 929	4 069	30 026	1 451	59.0	16.1	52.0
Santa Fe, NM	5 033	49 541	6 774	1 352	8 938	2 101	3 379	1 271	25 656	340	54.4	22.9	37.4
Sarasota-Bradenton, FL	16 513	259 622	30 959	19 354	34 056	7 568	12 109	6 085	23 438	1 012	59.2	12.2	47.2
Savannah, GA	7 464	113 846	15 549	15 827	17 633	3 415	3 775	3 074	27 001	306	35.0	13.4	41.5
Scranton—Wilkes-Barre—Hazleton, PA	15 152	244 341	40 899	48 797	35 658	10 899	7 383	6 006	24 580	1 698	26.7	4.7	52.5
Seattle-Tacoma-Bremerton, WA	101 558	1 520 788	172 937	228 113	192 780	72 287	97 741	60 242	39 612	4 671	77.3	1.4	42.3
Bremerton, WA	5 202	47 427	9 064	1 393	10 345	2 175	2 942	1 105	23 299	359	84.7	0.6	34.8
Olympia, WA	5 012	51 695	8 893	3 180	9 198	2 596	3 140	1 323	25 592	832	72.7	2.4	39.1
Seattle-Bellevue-Everett, WA	75 928	1 222 212	121 099	202 090	143 070	59 580	84 892	52 248	42 749	2 491	78.6	1.3	44.2
Tacoma, WA	15 416	199 454	33 881	21 450	30 167	7 936	6 767	5 566	27 906	989	75.4	0.9	42.8
Sharon, PA	2 951	44 414	8 413	10 883	7 341	1 228	788	1 060	23 866	1 030	20.4	4.7	51.7
Sheboygan, WI	2 594	55 101	5 458	21 386	6 176	1 851	1 820	1 632	29 618	968	32.2	8.5	61.7
Sherman-Denison, TX	2 540	38 147	6 762	9 952	6 115	2 264	872	1 013	26 555	2 080	39.6	8.7	36.6
Shreveport-Bossier City, LA	9 136	149 249	26 398	17 550	20 879	5 042	4 713	3 695	24 757	1 186	34.7	14.2	38.5
Sioux City, IA-NE	3 370	59 919	8 107	12 469	8 383	2 131	1 089	1 481	24 717	1 595	19.6	24.8	59.6
Sioux Falls, SD	5 637	101 801	16 571	13 522	13 673	12 593	2 981	2 605	25 589	1 931	22.6	26.3	60.4
South Bend, IN	6 585	123 952	14 574	21 236	18 431	5 382	5 378	3 423	27 616	666	41.3	13.7	45.6
Spokane, WA	11 717	162 962	26 344	20 166	23 868	10 560	6 397	4 537	27 841	1 643	44.1	17.3	43.4
Springfield, IL	5 609	83 916	18 127	4 042	12 332	7 190	4 205	2 238	26 670	1 345	28.8	31.9	60.4
Springfield, MA	14 700	225 070	40 398	36 929	34 209	12 067	7 961	6 218	27 627	957	52.7	2.6	50.9
Springfield, MO	9 361	146 852	23 173	22 312	22 080	6 424	5 285	3 560	24 242	4 897	36.0	5.6	39.1
St. Cloud, MN	4 636	78 232	10 426	16 144	13 756	2 561	1 910	2 011	25 706	3 816	17.9	6.8	63.8
St. Joseph, MO	2 619	38 065	6 287	6 945	5 511	1 997	1 021	964	25 325	1 596	23.3	14.0	48.0
St. Louis, MO-IL	66 609	1 195 533	150 762	170 777	144 709	67 380	67 928	38 841	32 488	8 702	28.6	13.7	45.0
State College, PA	3 090	44 897	5 425	8 227	7 741	1 761	2 844	1 063	23 676	788	26.8	6.1	57.0
Steubenville-Weirton, OH-WV	2 738	43 971	6 844	13 290	5 802	1 160	654	1 096	24 926	569	20.6	5.6	39.2
Stockton-Lodi, CA	9 980	147 642	20 034	22 673	21 167	6 170	4 302	4 047	27 411	3 862	62.6	8.3	59.3
Sumter, SC	1 900	34 751	3 639	12 483	4 944	908	570	800	23 021	396	35.9	16.7	46.2
Syracuse, NY	16 577	290 632	40 596	45 298	39 843	14 773	13 869	8 508	29 274	2 745	22.3	12.2	59.7
Tallahassee, FL	7 007	97 118	16 246	3 976	16 932	4 501	8 095	2 426	24 980	533	44.3	8.4	34.7
Tampa-St. Petersburg-Clearwater, FL	60 933	998 626	119 268	77 614	135 510	66 550	68 294	27 779	27 817	4 151	72.4	4.3	35.8
Terre Haute, IN	3 514	57 324	8 391	11 663	12 085	1 743	1 214	1 412	24 632	1 224	30.2	20.3	50.4
Texarkana, TX-Texarkana, AR	2 873	41 779	8 232	6 243	7 268	1 228	863	997	23 864	1 640	29.9	11.6	38.8
Toledo, OH	14 964	282 296	45 550	55 508	37 261	8 812	12 858	8 639	30 603	2 194	32.8	16.7	49.0
Topeka, KS	4 605	84 717	16 202	7 643	10 908	5 420	4 400	2 263	26 712	823	30.6	14.2	40.8

Table C. Metropolitan Areas — **Agriculture, Land, and Water**

Area Name	Acreage (1,000)	Percent change, 1992–1997	Average size of farm	Total irrigated (1,000)	Total cropland (1,000)	Average per farm ($1,000)	Average per acre (dollars)	Value of machinery and equipment Average per farm ($1,000)	Total (mil dol)	Average per farm (dollars)	Crops	Live-stock and poultry products	$10,000 or more	$100,000 or more	Percent of land owned by Fed. Gov. 1997	Water consumption 1995 (mil gal/day)
	117	118	119	120	121	122	123	124	125	126	127	128	129	130	131	132
Reading, PA	222	-0.2	140	1	188	547	3 673	71	248	156 235	48.0	52.0	65.0	29.4	1.0	85.1
Redding, CA	317	-18.4	373	39	59	420	1 021	22	31	36 881	59.0	41.0	29.1	5.1	38.0	310.8
Reno, NV	772	8.6	2 709	35	42	1 326	498	32	23	79 011	67.0	33.0	34.4	7.0	68.9	153.2
Richland-Kennewick-Pasco, WA	1 176	-10.3	610	374	D	1 055	1 833	110	633	328 902	92.0	8.0	56.1	35.2	18.5	1 922.5
Richmond-Petersburg, VA	385	-7.2	207	D	207	492	2 225	51	94	50 799	68.0	32.0	36.6	10.0	1.6	1 341.3
Roanoke, VA	117	-3.9	151	0	53	301	2 011	33	16	20 276	28.0	72.0	26.9	4.1	26.6	39.1
Rochester, MN	304	-0.8	231	0	245	328	1 425	75	106	80 729	48.0	52.0	57.3	22.6	0.0	41.3
Rochester, NY	968	-0.9	268	14	787	348	1 339	84	478	132 497	58.0	42.0	55.5	24.1	0.5	873.6
Rockford, IL	716	-2.0	315	4	651	720	2 524	79	272	119 290	70.0	30.0	67.8	33.0	0.0	83.7
Rocky Mount, NC	347	-3.4	441	19	226	766	1 746	119	317	402 210	47.0	53.0	69.0	43.5	0.0	36.4
Sacramento-Yolo, CA	1 087	-4.5	274	456	615	775	3 038	57	613	154 465	82.0	18.0	40.2	16.1	27.0	2 240.1
Sacramento, CA	550	-11.1	181	162	234	580	3 336	36	268	88 086	64.0	36.0	33.6	11.7	32.5	1 150.1
Yolo, CA	537	3.4	581	294	381	1 420	2 732	126	345	373 666	97.0	3.0	62.1	30.6	4.1	1 090.1
Saginaw-Bay City-Midland, MI	553	-5.9	239	9	493	416	1 668	80	163	70 407	89.0	11.0	59.8	18.5	0.7	746.7
Salinas, CA	1 544	12.5	1 277	260	389	2 685	2 358	226	1 750	1 447 268	98.0	2.0	69.9	44.4	27.5	632.6
Salt Lake City-Ogden, UT	263	-36.6	126	69	107	370	2 439	40	85	40 633	56.0	44.0	29.5	7.8	16.0	797.3
San Angelo, TX	959	-6.1	1 089	44	217	554	564	52	86	97 586	31.0	69.0	43.6	14.4	1.2	256.8
San Antonio, TX	1 425	-1.1	228	33	601	310	1 403	28	151	24 114	50.0	50.0	19.9	2.8	2.5	891.5
San Diego, CA	475	-8.3	80	70	113	407	5 504	23	633	106 790	87.0	13.0	34.7	10.9	22.9	776.5
San Francisco-Oakland-San Jose, CA	2 135	-1.3	262	351	D	1 025	4 217	52	1 602	196 980	82.0	18.0	53.1	22.8	4.2	2 154.8
Oakland, CA	406	-9.6	388	41	85	920	2 172	31	109	104 280	75.0	25.0	43.3	13.0	2.7	758.1
San Francisco, CA	194	-14.0	370	5	D	1 063	2 766	55	193	368 434	73.0	27.0	61.7	25.7	10.8	254.3
San Jose, CA	319	-7.1	324	19	32	606	2 425	50	188	191 355	90.0	10.0	41.5	13.6	1.4	350.3
Santa Cruz-Watsonville, CA	71	34.2	98	21	28	573	6 234	67	248	343 234	95.0	5.0	57.9	29.8	0.1	72.2
Santa Rosa, CA	571	10.4	208	57	145	1 025	5 211	47	464	168 895	69.0	31.0	53.3	23.8	2.5	126.1
Vallejo-Fairfield-Napa, CA	575	-0.3	272	208	284	1 419	5 909	63	400	189 358	92.0	8.0	59.2	27.4	5.5	593.8
San Luis Obispo-Atascadero-Paso Robles, CA	1 302	-1.7	679	61	281	1 046	1 591	49	313	163 335	90.0	10.0	47.2	17.6	16.7	188.4
Santa Barbara-Santa Maria-Lompoc, CA	817	-2.4	563	104	157	1 378	2 716	82	660	454 680	94.0	6.0	52.9	27.0	49.5	322.2
Santa Fe, NM	D	D	D	D	D	D	D	29	D	D	53.0	D	20.0	4.7	28.5	51.0
Sarasota-Bradenton, FL	397	-12.1	392	63	125	915	2 465	57	264	260 643	90.0	10.0	45.4	16.1	0.0	170.6
Savannah, GA	87	27.4	283	D	32	360	1 342	45	13	42 278	79.0	21.0	32.0	8.8	14.2	753.1
Scranton—Wilkes-Barre—Hazleton, PA	258	2.9	152	2	176	303	2 060	51	98	57 551	45.0	55.0	45.7	12.1	0.1	183.3
Seattle-Tacoma-Bremerton, WA	244	-7.8	52	20	132	364	6 991	34	420	89 914	34.0	66.0	26.3	8.7	26.1	767.3
Bremerton, WA	19	91.3	53	0	6	267	5 011	26	12	34 075	33.0	67.0	19.5	2.5	2.5	40.4
Olympia, WA	56	-6.2	68	6	27	381	6 278	44	121	145 087	30.0	70.0	23.6	7.1	3.9	49.6
Seattle-Bellevue-Everett, WA	118	-13.1	47	9	75	384	7 435	33	217	87 198	34.0	66.0	28.5	10.5	31.3	479.0
Tacoma, WA	51	-13.8	51	5	24	336	7 273	30	70	70 612	40.0	60.0	25.5	7.7	28.8	198.3
Sharon, PA	167	3.5	162	0	113	248	1 595	45	46	44 753	39.0	61.0	48.8	11.5	0.3	85.4
Sheboygan, WI	182	-11.9	188	0	153	313	1 668	78	92	95 254	19.0	81.0	63.8	29.1	0.0	464.7
Sherman-Denison, TX	417	1.8	201	2	245	293	1 508	29	35	17 056	44.0	56.0	23.4	3.0	2.9	27.3
Shreveport-Bossier City, LA	335	-1.6	282	3	173	330	1 209	40	42	35 406	56.0	44.0	30.3	7.3	5.2	106.3
Sioux City, IA-NE	639	10.2	401	20	547	506	1 262	78	180	113 027	63.0	37.0	68.0	30.0	0.5	692.8
Sioux Falls, SD	725	-3.1	375	2	643	435	1 183	87	204	105 692	60.0	40.0	74.1	31.2	0.6	27.7
South Bend, IN	154	-10.4	231	13	140	537	2 258	68	55	82 850	73.0	27.0	56.5	18.8	0.0	94.3
Spokane, WA	590	-5.8	359	11	398	469	1 351	52	79	47 903	74.0	26.0	35.2	13.1	1.8	188.7
Springfield, IL	637	4.3	474	1	589	1 112	2 448	112	215	159 810	87.0	13.0	68.3	38.8	0.0	338.9
Springfield, MA	90	-1.6	94	2	43	326	4 176	33	65	67 525	78.0	22.0	41.5	13.0	1.5	258.1
Springfield, MO	777	-1.2	159	1	464	274	1 702	24	106	21 544	9.0	91.0	31.9	4.4	4.5	184.8
St. Cloud, MN	822	-0.7	216	42	623	223	1 075	72	392	102 687	19.0	81.0	67.1	29.0	0.4	46.0
St. Joseph, MO	408	0.1	256	0	323	312	1 193	51	73	45 510	74.0	26.0	51.2	13.0	0.0	60.7
St. Louis, MO-IL	2 159	-2.5	248	11	1 671	474	1 951	58	555	63 769	63.0	37.0	48.7	15.5	0.4	2 951.6
State College, PA	136	-2.9	173	0	93	522	2 761	51	51	64 109	26.0	74.0	58.8	23.2	0.0	33.6
Steubenville-Weirton, OH-WV	92	4.6	162	D	50	156	1 086	27	8	14 729	32.0	68.0	21.4	2.8	0.0	2 372.9
Stockton-Lodi, CA	809	3.2	209	519	559	1 017	4 667	82	1 180	305 465	73.0	27.0	65.3	33.6	0.3	1 816.8
Sumter, SC	139	0.3	352	5	95	362	994	66	60	151 952	52.0	48.0	38.4	20.2	0.9	32.1
Syracuse, NY	687	-2.8	250	3	484	264	1 099	67	284	103 291	30.0	70.0	57.9	24.6	0.1	1 369.5
Tallahassee, FL	125	-21.1	235	8	40	505	2 012	46	96	180 291	90.0	10.0	31.1	7.3	13.3	55.7
Tampa-St. Petersburg-Clearwater, FL	464	-15.9	112	61	183	415	3 788	29	452	108 869	69.0	31.0	38.5	12.1	0.9	474.5
Terre Haute, IN	392	-7.9	321	D	335	554	1 706	75	99	80 928	76.0	24.0	57.8	20.8	1.4	799.8
Texarkana, TX-Texarkana, AR	435	-0.5	265	11	240	295	1 285	34	87	52 898	22.0	78.0	32.7	9.9	3.7	157.9
Toledo, OH	581	-0.2	265	2	548	604	2 275	82	245	111 748	77.0	23.0	72.5	27.3	0.4	771.3
Topeka, KS	224	-1.3	272	12	148	280	1 084	39	29	35 362	74.0	26.0	42.0	9.7	0.6	42.9

Table C. Metropolitan Areas — Residential Construction, Wholesale and Retail Trade, and Real Estate

Area Name	Value of Residential Construction Authorized by Building Permits, 2000		Wholesale Trade, 1997				Retail Trade[1], 1997				Real Estate and Rental and Leasing, 1997			
	New Construction ($1,000)	Number of Housing Units	Number of Establishments	Number of Employees	Sales (mil dol)	Annual Payroll (mil dol)	Number of Establishments	Number of Employees	Sales (mil dol)	Annual Payroll (mil dol)	Number of Establishments	Number of Employees	Receipts (mil dol)	Annual Payroll (mil dol)
	133	134	135	136	137	138	139	140	141	142	143	144	145	146
Reading, PA	192 359	1 809	439	7 051	3 121.7	253.0	1 468	19 302	3 330.7	326.2	215	1 324	191.3	28.1
Redding, CA	125 542	970	217	1 786	566.6	51.9	713	8 113	1 354.5	140.3	199	878	80.3	14.6
Reno, NV	463 001	4 544	639	9 339	5 663.6	324.9	1 328	19 418	3 751.1	389.5	614	3 058	444.5	66.1
Richland-Kennewick-Pasco, WA	155 772	1 018	199	2 161	856.0	55.7	770	9 296	1 696.2	161.5	193	1 126	125.4	23.5
Richmond-Petersburg, VA	657 155	5 887	1 696	24 147	16 973.7	910.7	4 145	59 324	9 207.1	927.5	1 002	6 252	765.4	150.7
Roanoke, VA	86 511	1 166	514	6 837	2 541.8	216.7	1 249	18 869	2 888.3	295.7	253	2 318	156.1	40.0
Rochester, MN	167 555	1 552	125	1 176	605.4	37.5	583	9 254	1 431.6	136.5	124	654	72.9	9.7
Rochester, NY	418 739	3 391	1 536	19 113	10 744.4	751.2	3 977	61 350	9 177.5	886.7	815	6 678	754.3	139.4
Rockford, IL	165 987	1 835	607	8 000	3 183.7	256.8	1 331	19 691	3 221.4	313.8	286	1 335	179.6	26.5
Rocky Mount, NC	60 326	790	172	2 806	1 493.1	87.8	720	7 516	1 249.8	114.5	123	758	95.8	15.0
Sacramento-Yolo, CA	2 677 146	16 793	1 960	30 491	15 598.2	1 051.5	5 466	74 401	14 122.4	1 446.5	1 851	12 578	1 359.6	266.0
Sacramento, CA	2 493 082	15 591	1 678	22 662	10 598.1	793.7	5 008	68 625	13 095.7	1 335.9	1 662	11 273	1 181.7	236.0
Yolo, CA	184 065	1 202	282	7 829	5 000.2	257.8	458	5 776	1 026.7	110.6	189	1 305	177.9	30.0
Saginaw-Bay City-Midland, MI	155 960	1 545	465	5 794	2 525.4	190.8	1 995	26 027	4 300.9	405.2	304	1 407	142.7	24.3
Salinas, CA	375 397	1 714	473	7 530	4 747.4	267.9	1 558	16 413	3 035.9	327.9	386	1 837	236.4	38.9
Salt Lake City-Ogden, UT	959 172	8 007	2 441	34 414	17 191.0	1 146.0	4 459	73 571	13 702.6	1 264.8	1 464	9 093	1 049.0	184.6
San Angelo, TX	25 994	247	159	D	D	D	471	5 404	890.7	84.3	134	550	51.7	8.3
San Antonio, TX	868 207	10 594	2 026	26 607	13 362.1	852.9	5 105	71 460	12 898.4	1 217.3	1 492	9 360	1 168.9	212.6
San Diego, CA	2 732 529	15 592	4 159	53 589	26 543.9	2 273.7	9 109	119 022	22 215.3	2 241.1	3 742	23 069	3 250.0	573.9
San Francisco-Oakland-San Jose, CA	4 824 809	27 577	13 392	189 537	167 465.4	9 195.8	24 198	319 325	63 219.8	6 608.4	9 220	61 943	10 593.5	1 761.6
Oakland, CA	1 898 408	9 533	4 391	62 404	62 758.8	2 673.7	7 068	96 839	19 781.8	1 980.7	2 721	16 493	2 618.2	438.3
San Francisco, CA	941 067	5 580	4 157	43 484	29 296.5	2 038.6	7 417	88 243	16 906.1	1 888.0	3 167	26 410	4 773.9	834.7
San Jose, CA	936 630	6 639	3 468	66 542	68 095.4	3 891.8	5 278	79 921	16 673.6	1 696.7	1 968	12 585	2 456.4	372.8
Santa Cruz-Watsonville, CA	115 222	545	342	4 472	1 541.8	140.3	986	11 794	1 970.2	215.5	314	1 649	166.5	27.1
Santa Rosa, CA	369 134	2 505	619	7 430	3 069.7	259.4	1 808	22 190	4 146.2	443.7	576	2 394	329.3	48.5
Vallejo-Fairfield-Napa, CA	564 348	2 775	415	5 205	2 703.1	192.0	1 641	20 338	3 742.0	383.8	474	2 412	249.1	40.2
San Luis Obispo-Atascadero-Paso Robles, CA	269 987	1 673	244	1 904	561.5	46.8	1 132	10 917	1 780.7	182.4	319	1 243	149.7	20.9
Santa Barbara-Santa Maria-Lompoc, CA	174 684	867	469	4 282	1 636.0	137.5	1 653	19 187	3 183.5	354.0	557	2 613	357.8	64.3
Santa Fe, NM	77 461	591	176	1 335	381.6	43.4	905	8 423	1 497.0	157.4	216	921	122.6	20.5
Sarasota-Bradenton, FL	892 147	7 110	797	5 470	2 123.5	162.7	2 607	32 476	5 747.5	538.2	836	3 322	449.0	68.3
Savannah, GA	275 825	2 708	374	4 464	2 489.2	146.6	1 413	17 355	2 718.0	267.1	312	1 540	202.1	36.9
Scranton—Wilkes-Barre—Hazleton, PA	151 050	1 480	747	9 994	3 447.2	264.6	2 888	36 815	5 570.9	521.4	410	2 197	206.1	43.1
Seattle-Tacoma-Bremerton, WA	2 909 770	25 504	6 842	82 684	59 358.6	3 291.6	13 081	176 146	33 821.7	3 479.0	5 034	30 518	4 197.7	740.0
Bremerton, WA	134 078	1 111	135	925	330.9	29.9	773	10 338	1 722.1	179.5	240	1 053	103.4	16.3
Olympia, WA	165 903	1 299	201	1 805	580.3	57.5	730	9 008	1 616.8	166.3	218	884	89.7	13.5
Seattle-Bellevue-Everett, WA	2 095 656	18 406	5 725	70 630	53 828.5	2 877.1	9 289	127 844	25 014.6	2 583.0	3 869	24 174	3 608.8	629.0
Tacoma, WA	514 133	4 688	781	9 324	4 618.9	327.0	2 289	28 956	5 468.2	550.1	707	4 407	395.8	81.2
Sharon, PA	38 372	432	124	1 692	656.3	41.9	618	7 852	1 285.0	112.8	84	281	29.6	5.0
Sheboygan, WI	78 950	675	119	2 041	1 185.0	65.4	398	5 831	911.0	88.0	85	400	38.2	6.2
Sherman-Denison, TX	20 604	200	132	958	406.1	25.1	474	6 213	1 092.0	98.5	104	351	32.0	5.8
Shreveport-Bossier City, LA	133 709	1 020	608	7 673	4 066.8	224.1	1 613	20 627	3 465.8	318.9	345	1 628	158.4	29.7
Sioux City, IA-NE	31 524	280	239	D	D	D	603	8 649	1 248.5	127.5	127	747	68.7	12.3
Sioux Falls, SD	187 132	2 305	395	5 717	2 345.5	171.3	842	12 863	2 149.9	202.8	192	1 012	100.3	19.0
South Bend, IN	162 876	1 665	472	7 080	3 389.0	230.7	1 069	16 822	2 782.9	249.0	215	1 274	127.8	25.5
Spokane, WA	209 244	2 094	788	11 268	4 878.5	360.9	1 730	22 246	4 122.6	433.9	503	2 674	289.1	47.4
Springfield, IL	95 656	929	274	3 621	1 588.1	122.4	877	12 374	2 050.2	191.6	215	885	87.4	14.7
Springfield, MA	160 530	1 120	682	D	D	D	2 466	31 651	4 884.5	492.2	501	2 352	299.1	48.9
Springfield, MO	255 974	2 558	657	9 379	5 261.8	274.7	1 592	19 993	3 665.7	326.6	397	1 891	162.1	34.1
St. Cloud, MN	141 037	1 354	238	4 771	1 604.2	145.5	763	11 222	1 851.1	170.0	150	733	64.2	11.5
St. Joseph, MO	28 316	286	162	1 673	1 186.0	45.8	446	5 354	884.7	80.5	95	454	33.8	6.0
St. Louis, MO-IL	1 404 043	12 129	4 805	66 406	57 134.3	2 875.6	9 870	141 603	24 122.5	2 499.1	2 612	17 872	2 404.1	427.6
State College, PA	67 780	653	100	D	D	D	617	7 861	1 153.9	108.7	111	704	83.1	14.0
Steubenville-Weirton, OH-WV	10 457	146	100	1 021	335.9	26.1	556	6 335	828.7	81.7	86	310	24.9	5.0
Stockton-Lodi, CA	828 298	5 392	560	9 751	7 651.7	319.3	1 594	19 957	3 679.6	364.7	436	2 602	257.7	52.3
Sumter, SC	28 197	294	84	671	208.6	18.1	425	4 841	782.0	72.8	74	277	26.6	4.3
Syracuse, NY	196 959	1 739	1 206	15 611	11 660.9	571.3	2 895	40 997	6 099.5	606.6	553	4 605	428.2	100.4
Tallahassee, FL	210 409	2 280	281	2 990	1 102.7	88.7	1 195	16 706	2 424.2	245.9	316	1 894	206.4	33.9
Tampa-St. Petersburg-Clearwater, FL	1 881 485	19 244	4 304	53 358	35 721.0	1 808.6	9 142	128 351	24 184.1	2 199.6	2 759	15 239	1 804.9	323.2
Terre Haute, IN	43 118	415	176	1 838	774.7	47.0	675	11 487	2 635.1	184.0	106	545	45.0	9.3
Texarkana, TX-Texarkana, AR	23 009	419	183	2 601	1 212.1	75.5	612	6 734	1 194.8	104.0	112	585	65.1	9.3
Toledo, OH	252 874	2 144	988	13 914	8 164.5	476.7	2 475	37 164	6 083.6	583.4	532	3 298	382.7	72.3
Topeka, KS	83 668	591	204	2 298	947.1	65.9	768	10 625	1 619.6	166.7	199	1 216	88.8	22.4

1. Establishments with payroll.

Area Name	Professional, Scientific, and Technical Services[1], 1997				Manufacturing, 1997				Accommodation and Foodservices, 1997			
	Number of Establishments	Number of Employees	Sales (mil dol)	Annual Payroll (mil dol)	Number of Establishments	Number of Employees	Sales (mil dol)	Annual Payroll (mil dol)	Number of Establishments	Number of Employees	Sales (mil dol)	Annual Payroll (mil dol)
	147	148	149	150	151	152	153	154	155	156	157	158
Reading, PA	546	5 520	476.6	215.2	587	41 614	7 729	1 511	706	10 091	330.4	90.9
Redding, CA	304	1 636	127.0	51.6	177	3 526	635	119	402	5 070	161.7	41.7
Reno, NV	1 193	6 422	659.7	259.7	418	11 522	1 931	362	778	34 517	1 815.8	583.1
Richland-Kennewick-Pasco, WA	318	7 537	939.0	369.0	168	6 764	2 046	209	343	5 328	170.7	46.1
Richmond-Petersburg, VA	2 381	19 222	1 803.5	780.5	1 004	54 752	19 725	2 123	1 724	32 448	1 082.5	306.1
Roanoke, VA	541	3 519	280.5	115.0	312	19 839	4 001	592	534	10 156	319.8	91.9
Rochester, MN	206	2 145	164.4	84.1	77	10 477	3 085	482	274	5 924	204.3	58.5
Rochester, NY	2 063	17 773	1 826.2	684.7	1 516	106 140	25 984	4 228	2 176	31 670	1 023.5	292.2
Rockford, IL	653	5 722	417.0	202.4	912	51 445	9 929	1 934	702	11 248	352.4	96.0
Rocky Mount, NC	155	989	77.8	27.1	154	17 599	3 328	502	220	4 228	133.8	36.4
Sacramento-Yolo, CA	3 750	27 466	2 973.5	1 121.9	1 489	47 690	14 551	1 689	3 443	56 414	1 878.5	505.7
Sacramento, CA	3 519	25 925	2 769.4	1 062.5	1 314	41 512	13 036	1 477	3 141	52 035	1 738.4	469.5
Yolo, CA	231	1 541	204.1	59.4	175	6 178	1 515	212	302	4 379	140.1	36.2
Saginaw-Bay City-Midland, MI	600	4 439	329.4	138.5	462	33 753	8 792	1 781	781	15 846	455.1	131.5
Salinas, CA	694	2 998	293.1	109.2	302	7 070	1 329	224	905	16 869	835.3	226.0
Salt Lake City-Ogden, UT	2 966	26 458	2 590.2	1 005.3	1 878	79 040	16 847	2 544	2 157	47 040	1 507.2	420.0
San Angelo, TX	154	767	60.2	17.2	100	4 452	828	105	192	3 763	110.8	32.7
San Antonio, TX	3 046	22 370	2 098.8	822.2	1 296	45 807	7 481	1 245	2 883	60 511	2 164.8	600.9
San Diego, CA	7 144	59 761	7 072.3	2 725.7	3 407	118 868	22 234	4 224	5 426	105 069	4 237.9	1 157.4
San Francisco-Oakland-San Jose, CA	24 040	221 672	31 368.0	12 686.9	11 035	479 063	130 727	22 174	15 727	257 563	11 514.6	3 162.4
Oakland, CA	6 345	49 557	6 362.8	2 518.4	3 230	113 175	33 983	4 692	4 288	61 734	2 475.3	656.3
San Francisco, CA	8 849	87 847	13 133.6	5 174.9	2 607	64 080	11 325	2 452	5 433	98 286	5 074.8	1 461.3
San Jose, CA	6 338	71 612	10 440.6	4 424.1	3 464	249 947	72 528	13 094	3 495	60 330	2 590.7	677.7
Santa Cruz-Watsonville, CA	678	3 073	384.1	132.1	387	10 011	2 135	315	591	8 223	305.5	80.8
Santa Rosa, CA	1 171	5 682	565.8	239.1	793	24 209	5 120	969	1 005	13 993	490.2	132.2
Vallejo-Fairfield-Napa, CA	659	3 901	481.0	198.4	554	17 641	5 636	652	915	14 997	578.2	154.1
San Luis Obispo-Atascadero-Paso Robles, CA	529	2 292	212.2	76.7	323	6 322	1 156	182	674	10 534	382.5	101.7
Santa Barbara-Santa Maria-Lompoc, CA	981	6 344	711.2	270.6	502	14 985	2 770	584	952	17 195	633.1	177.1
Santa Fe, NM	531	2 692	282.1	117.1	177	1 501	132	34	403	8 194	325.2	95.4
Sarasota-Bradenton, FL	1 515	7 664	663.0	263.1	663	18 965	2 988	571	1 077	20 531	723.3	196.6
Savannah, GA	528	2 908	224.6	88.4	227	14 606	5 326	609	641	13 513	452.0	123.3
Scranton—Wilkes-Barre—Hazleton, PA	923	6 985	519.3	204.4	849	51 202	9 883	1 421	1 424	20 141	590.3	160.0
Seattle-Tacoma-Bremerton, WA	9 641	76 330	8 204.3	3 294.8	4 858	219 765	51 626	9 460	7 709	125 061	4 740.7	1 338.8
Bremerton, WA	443	2 226	169.0	65.5	143	1 441	143	37	399	5 998	180.2	50.6
Olympia, WA	401	2 571	198.1	86.2	156	3 218	761	101	406	6 076	193.0	56.6
Seattle-Bellevue-Everett, WA	7 823	66 568	7 392.9	2 969.1	3 879	192 823	46 446	8 618	5 686	94 179	3 763.9	1 062.3
Tacoma, WA	974	4 965	444.3	174.0	680	22 283	4 276	705	1 218	18 808	603.6	169.3
Sharon, PA	130	679	49.4	22.0	198	10 457	2 441	327	270	3 953	113.3	32.6
Sheboygan, WI	150	1 235	92.2	40.5	239	20 047	4 253	628	237	3 714	105.9	29.1
Sherman-Denison, TX	162	715	52.6	19.6	140	10 223	3 557	365	200	3 312	104.8	30.7
Shreveport-Bossier City, LA	695	3 908	315.1	116.5	337	16 911	5 397	578	637	13 990	555.8	140.0
Sioux City, IA-NE	204	1 043	79.1	25.7	136	11 977	4 503	301	287	4 468	130.4	36.0
Sioux Falls, SD	381	2 437	186.6	74.4	198	12 978	3 203	340	419	8 418	231.2	66.0
South Bend, IN	520	4 003	369.9	154.8	457	20 435	4 150	699	537	10 620	305.2	86.9
Spokane, WA	886	5 738	444.5	186.9	572	20 892	3 995	681	904	14 456	453.2	128.5
Springfield, IL	489	3 323	280.3	118.8	142	3 986	743	117	521	8 379	255.3	74.6
Springfield, MA	1 003	6 519	492.1	207.9	982	39 110	7 002	1 396	1 263	18 308	578.1	162.5
Springfield, MO	642	4 259	375.1	125.4	516	23 359	4 170	594	695	13 073	382.3	109.1
St. Cloud, MN	249	1 504	113.7	47.4	272	15 406	2 517	441	362	6 520	177.3	47.5
St. Joseph, MO	143	797	65.2	22.0	103	7 382	2 295	235	210	3 357	99.7	27.7
St. Louis, MO-IL	5 911	59 511	6 679.3	2 414.2	3 320	170 766	51 488	6 590	5 065	100 455	3 281.6	943.2
State College, PA	211	2 332	167.5	85.9	159	8 546	1 409	255	287	5 241	154.8	41.2
Steubenville-Weirton, OH-WV	153	627	42.2	13.0	104	11 530	3 206	459	308	3 266	89.9	25.5
Stockton-Lodi, CA	575	3 531	277.7	111.2	553	24 646	5 879	750	826	11 413	376.9	96.5
Sumter, SC	116	471	29.1	8.9	84	12 655	2 050	303	133	2 311	70.0	19.1
Syracuse, NY	1 344	11 797	1 044.2	410.3	787	44 756	9 950	1 681	1 667	22 773	709.3	208.6
Tallahassee, FL	877	6 998	710.4	295.4	159	4 075	745	100	495	10 205	307.5	79.6
Tampa-St. Petersburg-Clearwater, FL	6 398	62 828	6 186.3	2 318.5	2 580	77 098	12 701	2 246	4 138	81 729	2 952.0	780.6
Terre Haute, IN	193	1 072	75.3	23.1	181	10 684	2 922	377	353	6 006	176.3	49.9
Texarkana, TX-Texarkana, AR	162	733	65.9	20.2	100	6 330	1 471	228	221	3 819	128.7	31.6
Toledo, OH	1 152	11 064	1 100.2	385.1	954	55 581	16 347	2 194	1 382	24 590	764.2	205.9
Topeka, KS	405	3 227	233.6	94.7	140	7 722	1 806	265	374	6 745	199.2	54.3

1. Firms subject to federal tax.

Table C. Metropolitan Areas — **Health and Other Services and Federal Funds**

Area Name	Health Care and Social Assistance[1], 1997				Other Services[1], 1997				Federal funds and grants, fiscal 2001[2] Expenditures (mil dol)			
										Direct payments for individuals		
	Number of Establishments	Number of Employees	Receipts (mil dol)	Annual Payroll (mil dol)	Number of Establishments	Number of Employees	Receipts (mil dol)	Annual Payroll (mil dol)	Total	Social Security and government retirement	Medicare	Food stamps and Supplemental Security Income
	159	160	161	162	163	164	165	166	167	168	169	170
Reading, PA..................	601	6 387	412.6	200.5	559	3 102	183.2	56.4	1 528.4	782.9	322.6	42.9
Redding, CA..................	487	5 441	387.9	156.8	241	1 289	86.4	22.8	958.8	443.6	174.8	47.8
Reno, NV......................	779	7 430	649.9	288.0	518	3 269	217.6	68.7	1 519.9	648.5	194.6	29.4
Richland-Kennewick-Pasco, WA	416	3 510	223.5	89.8	245	1 351	83.7	24.9	2 732.4	331.6	95.9	22.8
Richmond-Petersburg, VA	1 878	32 981	2 214.3	956.5	1 692	12 163	778.4	245.8	6 259.8	2 189.6	699.4	141.8
Roanoke, VA..................	468	7 588	567.8	234.3	557	3 500	182.3	62.7	1 321.0	614.3	193.3	36.5
Rochester, MN................	168	2 241	102.8	50.7	180	1 363	69.8	20.4	544.4	185.1	67.1	10.6
Rochester, NY................	1 771	18 344	1 175.8	491.7	1 502	7 780	513.3	147.9	5 473.3	2 217.8	902.0	176.6
Rockford, IL..................	525	6 787	503.0	241.5	607	4 163	260.1	82.7	1 442.5	690.7	232.8	49.5
Rocky Mount, NC.............	205	4 459	279.9	115.3	211	1 247	74.6	20.9	731.0	297.5	114.4	40.9
Sacramento-Yolo, CA	3 549	33 932	2 659.3	1 118.5	2 237	15 481	1 116.3	336.3	16 444.4	3 981.4	1 295.5	406.6
Sacramento, CA..............	3 282	31 500	2 522.6	1 060.0	2 028	14 340	1 024.1	310.9	15 446.3	3 741.1	1 195.1	378.9
Yolo, CA	267	2 432	136.7	58.6	209	1 141	92.3	25.4	998.1	240.3	100.5	27.7
Saginaw-Bay City-Midland, MI	822	7 512	493.6	243.1	658	3 829	229.0	67.3	1 841.3	855.8	343.5	82.9
Salinas, CA	708	5 613	430.5	177.7	445	2 416	172.1	48.0	1 894.6	706.7	274.8	46.2
Salt Lake City-Ogden, UT.....	2 457	32 242	2 148.9	893.8	1 792	12 804	799.2	240.0	7 283.0	2 155.1	542.2	110.4
San Angelo, TX...............	186	3 404	208.9	91.7	180	961	58.3	16.1	633.2	237.1	76.1	14.9
San Antonio, TX..............	3 185	54 720	3 188.8	1 308.8	2 393	16 535	911.1	293.5	11 419.4	3 881.4	1 165.4	299.3
San Diego, CA................	5 508	53 541	4 232.7	1 656.5	3 811	24 273	1 648.1	466.0	19 825.2	5 542.6	2 300.8	448.1
San Francisco-Oakland-San Jose, CA	16 455	150 688	11 833.0	4 863.3	10 604	66 407	5 126.3	1 511.3	38 665.8	11 335.2	5 524.6	1 186.4
Oakland, CA.................	5 158	51 394	4 144.8	1 697.8	3 365	21 627	1 712.7	503.8	13 040.5	3 796.6	1 951.1	429.9
San Francisco, CA	4 698	35 597	2 870.0	1 193.5	3 151	18 692	1 426.1	414.5	10 543.2	2 991.7	1 625.1	344.7
San Jose, CA	3 742	38 283	3 032.2	1 240.9	2 471	16 850	1 352.9	400.5	9 495.7	2 133.0	1 005.2	265.2
Santa Cruz-Watsonville, CA	631	4 739	309.8	121.7	330	1 614	112.1	31.3	928.7	359.9	190.0	29.5
Santa Rosa, CA	1 241	11 357	766.6	319.5	676	3 604	252.0	74.0	1 881.0	884.5	398.4	47.1
Vallejo-Fairfield-Napa, CA.	985	9 318	709.6	289.8	611	4 020	270.5	87.2	2 776.8	1 169.6	354.7	70.0
San Luis Obispo-Atascadero-Paso Robles, CA	599	5 083	375.3	161.3	294	1 446	96.2	25.9	994.3	519.9	206.4	25.4
Santa Barbara-Santa Maria-Lompoc, CA	934	6 609	516.9	199.8	536	3 054	192.1	57.4	2 385.3	771.7	305.2	49.2
Santa Fe, NM.................	346	3 183	184.2	84.0	186	922	58.8	17.3	3 120.6	289.2	68.7	12.1
Sarasota-Bradenton, FL.......	1 504	21 183	1 513.0	613.1	939	4 701	259.8	81.9	3 613.1	2 166.8	958.3	51.7
Savannah, GA................	493	6 733	487.2	243.2	439	2 921	184.2	61.1	2 340.5	638.1	253.2	62.6
Scranton—Wilkes-Barre—Hazleton, PA................	1 431	14 933	925.9	408.4	980	4 828	273.8	74.2	3 817.7	1 712.2	885.2	98.8
Seattle-Tacoma-Bremerton, WA	7 913	76 522	5 009.3	2 180.4	5 569	33 840	2 461.7	735.2	21 255.3	7 010.8	2 038.5	468.2
Bremerton, WA................	473	4 466	245.3	104.1	264	1 300	77.7	23.9	2 340.0	662.8	119.7	28.5
Olympia, WA.................	459	4 551	322.8	137.0	264	1 356	79.0	24.2	1 842.3	575.3	121.0	30.1
Seattle-Bellevue-Everett, WA	5 542	53 468	3 575.5	1 555.2	4 133	25 754	1 950.3	572.6	12 901.7	4 136.3	1 419.7	290.8
Tacoma, WA.................	1 439	14 037	865.7	384.0	908	5 430	354.7	114.5	4 171.2	1 636.4	378.2	118.7
Sharon, PA...................	303	2 686	162.7	72.5	203	876	44.3	12.9	660.6	330.0	160.1	25.7
Sheboygan, WI................	176	2 412	134.3	74.8	172	967	56.5	14.6	428.7	221.2	69.7	7.9
Sherman-Denison, TX	278	4 362	225.0	104.6	123	649	32.9	9.6	532.3	282.7	109.7	14.6
Shreveport-Bossier City, LA .	720	12 092	798.1	351.1	574	3 592	226.4	66.1	2 326.9	865.1	380.0	108.6
Sioux City, IA-NE.............	243	2 346	198.6	95.1	213	1 594	96.1	29.7	616.9	240.1	93.0	15.5
Sioux Falls, SD...............	303	4 644	364.8	200.4	316	1 993	112.2	34.0	882.7	307.4	87.5	15.3
South Bend, IN...............	496	5 999	458.0	212.7	452	3 851	256.3	81.0	1 723.3	530.0	211.4	38.1
Spokane, WA.................	991	11 137	681.4	306.8	699	4 355	258.4	78.5	2 263.1	954.5	317.4	73.2
Springfield, IL................	370	7 740	482.4	206.5	362	2 352	146.2	47.4	2 798.7	560.0	174.6	40.4
Springfield, MA...............	1 031	15 668	937.6	433.3	937	4 910	334.8	101.3	3 484.1	1 227.8	591.1	145.0
Springfield, MO...............	528	8 067	559.1	264.0	617	3 887	209.5	62.5	1 416.2	687.8	224.5	49.8
St. Cloud, MN	267	3 669	258.3	130.5	281	1 667	102.7	27.6	632.9	277.5	79.3	12.9
St. Joseph, MO	188	2 366	143.7	65.3	179	855	50.9	14.4	508.8	226.6	99.6	20.7
St. Louis, MO-IL..............	5 241	62 262	3 946.7	1 806.2	4 472	27 486	1 743.6	554.6	19 046.1	5 633.1	2 429.9	473.5
State College, PA	212	2 520	169.1	72.4	159	958	52.2	14.5	799.9	211.1	77.6	10.3
Steubenville-Weirton, OH-WV	256	3 315	154.3	69.3	197	1 166	54.4	16.8	792.4	383.4	186.8	30.0
Stockton-Lodi, CA	949	9 252	664.0	273.5	690	3 838	265.3	74.2	2 439.4	933.2	398.7	158.0
Sumter, SC	128	1 347	81.0	40.6	123	827	47.5	14.1	752.4	254.5	62.6	33.6
Syracuse, NY.................	1 236	12 308	887.0	412.5	1 061	6 796	494.7	138.3	3 740.0	1 547.9	545.3	123.9
Tallahassee, FL	467	6 635	470.5	214.0	427	2 712	151.5	49.0	3 826.4	555.6	151.6	49.5
Tampa-St. Petersburg-Clearwater, FL	5 794	80 476	5 822.3	2 384.3	3 972	23 499	1 466.0	441.2	14 481.0	6 661.6	3 356.2	388.2
Terre Haute, IN...............	302	3 901	264.9	85.3	222	1 560	74.2	22.4	883.6	341.9	152.9	25.4
Texarkana, TX-Texarkana, AR	267	4 304	255.0	119.1	179	1 170	69.3	20.0	939.9	334.2	140.8	31.3
Toledo, OH...................	1 149	16 531	1 021.8	515.0	1 030	6 734	419.2	125.8	2 871.8	1 133.5	596.4	132.5
Topeka, KS	322	5 720	309.5	159.9	296	1 914	127.2	41.7	1 477.7	469.6	125.3	26.1

1. Firms subject to federal tax.   2. October 1, 1998 to September 30, 1999.

	Federal funds and grants, fiscal 2001[1] (cont'd)							Local government finances, 1997				
	Expenditures (mil dol) (cont'd)							General revenue				
	Procurement contract awards			Grants[2]						Taxes		
Area Name											Per capita[3] (dollars)	
	Salaries and wages	Defense	Other	Medicaid and other health-related	Nutrition and family welfare	Education	Other	Total (mil dol)	Intergovern-mental (mil dol)	Total (mil dol)	Total	Property
	171	172	173	174	175	176	177	178	179	180	181	182
Reading, PA	72.5	25.5	21.5	118.0	26.5	10.9	60.6	888.2	318.7	394.0	1 113	880
Redding, CA	64.2	3.0	24.5	91.2	41.4	14.7	27.3	535.3	281.8	115.6	709	548
Reno, NV	175.3	35.6	43.6	113.1	25.3	17.7	179.5	874.3	369.6	293.3	959	668
Richland-Kennewick-Pasco, WA	82.2	20.9	2 014.1	55.5	25.7	10.5	21.3	641.4	314.2	127.6	698	442
Richmond-Petersburg, VA	895.5	434.0	236.3	438.2	315.6	217.0	442.7	2 361.6	831.7	1 029.6	1 092	779
Roanoke, VA	190.4	54.2	40.3	79.2	19.5	11.7	37.9	529.4	197.5	253.3	1 108	714
Rochester, MN	50.2	6.2	8.6	154.2	8.8	6.0	11.3	326.5	131.8	102.9	898	812
Rochester, NY	318.7	146.9	120.7	715.5	170.6	109.9	206.4	3 867.0	1 427.1	1 695.6	1 561	1 154
Rockford, IL	77.3	78.1	33.7	94.2	24.7	14.6	28.1	808.4	301.9	367.7	1 036	993
Rocky Mount, NC	40.2	2.6	13.8	125.0	28.9	11.2	13.6	384.5	175.6	74.0	508	391
Sacramento-Yolo, CA	761.5	1 185.4	261.7	1 445.6	2 663.1	1 093.9	2 796.5	5 461.0	2 528.5	1 370.8	828	560
Sacramento, CA	611.1	1 151.1	217.3	1 291.5	2 636.8	1 081.3	2 673.6	5 015.9	2 309.6	1 249.0	831	567
Yolo, CA	150.5	34.3	44.4	154.1	26.4	12.6	122.8	445.1	218.9	121.8	797	490
Saginaw-Bay City-Midland, MI	105.9	6.6	26.5	193.2	71.6	29.8	46.6	1 109.7	576.4	269.3	668	615
Salinas, CA	357.2	115.5	27.8	132.4	64.7	32.0	85.0	1 447.7	558.4	319.6	883	585
Salt Lake City-Ogden, UT	1 466.7	1 100.7	282.8	639.7	245.2	106.2	467.2	2 685.9	1 074.8	962.0	771	537
San Angelo, TX	147.3	24.2	3.2	45.5	10.7	4.1	24.2	174.2	69.8	74.3	724	553
San Antonio, TX	2 224.7	1 510.1	534.5	948.1	179.6	108.0	312.3	3 393.4	1 327.2	1 285.0	850	703
San Diego, CA	4 715.6	2 863.2	665.8	1 552.4	425.1	198.3	603.9	8 204.5	3 812.5	2 084.2	766	544
San Francisco-Oakland-San Jose, CA	3 804.1	4 000.1	3 593.4	4 536.9	904.1	403.7	1 678.5	24 707.9	9 596.8	8 138.6	1 215	782
Oakland, CA	1 096.3	345.4	2 191.2	1 505.0	387.6	150.9	641.4	8 708.3	3 468.0	2 600.5	1 145	740
San Francisco, CA	1 414.9	578.5	512.5	1 760.6	182.4	90.3	491.5	6 983.1	2 434.1	2 456.4	1 478	903
San Jose, CA	680.2	2 741.0	813.8	822.0	190.3	90.9	374.4	5 453.7	2 104.5	2 060.5	1 281	826
Santa Cruz-Watsonville, CA	33.0	13.2	14.4	115.6	30.8	18.2	57.4	804.9	339.1	228.5	950	629
Santa Rosa, CA	132.5	23.1	34.7	166.2	52.4	22.6	58.3	1 276.7	511.5	384.6	897	665
Vallejo-Fairfield-Napa, CA	447.1	298.9	27.0	167.6	60.7	30.8	55.4	1 481.1	739.7	408.2	833	591
San Luis Obispo-Atascad-ero-Paso Robles, CA	40.6	12.3	10.4	80.3	31.9	11.7	15.5	676.0	233.4	248.9	1 067	849
Santa Barbara-Santa Maria-Lompoc, CA	271.0	507.6	57.0	147.3	48.7	27.1	126.1	1 210.2	497.5	347.8	891	672
Santa Fe, NM	81.5	13.2	2 155.8	138.1	118.0	79.3	132.2	294.9	154.2	86.6	618	246
Sarasota-Bradenton, FL	116.8	57.1	33.4	78.9	35.2	24.6	53.5	1 556.9	284.1	551.6	1 024	830
Savannah, GA	796.4	218.6	67.6	144.4	50.2	22.1	33.0	769.9	265.0	339.0	1 193	780
Scranton—Wilkes-Barre—Hazleton, PA	243.6	155.6	61.5	344.3	67.7	19.8	94.7	1 249.4	492.3	506.3	814	590
Seattle-Tacoma-Bremerton, WA	3 957.2	1 985.6	713.5	2 274.4	617.0	360.6	1 252.5	10 108.2	3 738.5	3 609.1	1 072	663
Bremerton, WA	999.8	306.1	39.8	70.5	23.4	27.0	23.4	493.4	253.0	153.2	653	490
Olympia, WA	66.0	2.2	16.9	173.8	255.6	193.3	358.9	505.5	248.5	163.6	817	574
Seattle-Bellevue-Everett, WA	1 777.2	1 483.3	590.7	1 658.4	233.9	101.1	811.9	7 416.6	2 418.7	2 776.2	1 224	722
Tacoma, WA	1 114.3	194.0	66.1	371.7	104.0	39.2	58.4	1 692.8	818.3	516.1	776	551
Sharon, PA	18.7	0.5	4.1	58.8	15.9	4.2	19.6	237.6	127.1	74.1	607	449
Sheboygan, WI	13.7	5.5	34.8	35.2	8.7	3.8	12.1	334.0	157.6	107.5	978	957
Sherman-Denison, TX	17.1	1.6	6.0	50.7	7.0	2.7	20.7	217.3	82.9	85.6	843	680
Shreveport-Bossier City, LA	393.5	65.3	38.1	265.1	47.9	28.7	54.9	861.9	332.6	360.4	952	419
Sioux City, IA-NE	55.1	3.2	7.5	68.4	16.7	8.6	32.5	291.0	134.2	102.1	845	776
Sioux Falls, SD	119.4	6.8	48.1	62.0	8.1	3.1	47.8	305.2	67.2	180.7	1 125	777
South Bend, IN	68.0	175.6	414.5	129.6	24.2	9.9	40.5	544.7	219.9	204.9	794	776
Spokane, WA	319.5	41.0	51.6	252.6	65.2	30.8	64.6	944.3	463.4	295.3	730	456
Springfield, IL	133.2	19.6	22.1	269.0	702.5	325.2	439.8	422.5	171.8	174.8	857	755
Springfield, MA	450.2	64.0	126.1	384.5	125.0	59.2	115.8	1 456.0	777.2	488.7	827	814
Springfield, MO	142.0	3.2	38.6	145.2	26.6	15.8	33.4	475.0	179.1	189.8	630	368
St. Cloud, MN	77.8	0.3	19.2	62.2	14.8	9.2	16.9	446.0	221.4	117.6	729	691
St. Joseph, MO	31.7	0.4	4.4	62.7	11.1	4.9	10.2	169.3	68.1	71.6	737	399
St. Louis, MO-IL	1 685.3	4 769.5	662.4	1 681.3	288.9	136.7	730.5	5 706.3	2 031.3	2 564.6	1 003	634
State College, PA	37.7	72.0	14.5	74.7	8.0	13.9	222.4	229.7	80.9	92.8	698	468
Steubenville-Weirton, OH-WV	22.1	3.7	6.2	70.6	19.0	9.0	38.8	239.8	107.2	89.0	651	553
Stockton-Lodi, CA	163.3	40.2	54.6	342.5	139.3	41.0	70.2	1 709.9	922.8	354.1	653	458
Sumter, SC	203.8	29.7	4.9	100.1	19.3	11.9	6.4	163.3	93.2	51.4	482	399
Syracuse, NY	287.9	287.1	73.4	439.0	103.0	53.8	145.0	2 467.2	988.3	1 098.7	1 483	1 172
Tallahassee, FL	100.9	29.3	19.5	476.0	575.7	486.7	1 207.5	663.8	260.3	207.0	794	539
Tampa-St. Petersburg-Clear-water, FL	1 196.2	1 003.2	250.2	642.4	223.3	136.7	343.3	5 719.7	1 912.6	2 046.8	919	723
Terre Haute, IN	85.7	45.8	15.8	107.7	16.1	6.1	36.6	273.3	116.2	112.5	758	737
Texarkana, TX-Texarkana, AR	98.9	48.8	8.2	90.0	16.0	6.2	124.4	239.4	115.6	77.9	631	427
Toledo, OH	157.3	55.7	37.0	332.0	86.3	43.6	114.6	1 700.5	608.2	770.7	1 260	758
Topeka, KS	171.4	5.7	36.0	134.9	158.2	92.1	216.0	423.2	144.6	175.0	1 061	836

1. October 1, 1998 to September 30, 1999.   2. State totals may include programs not allocated by county.   3. Based on the resident population estimated as of July 1 of the year shown.

Table C. Metropolitan Areas — **Local Government Finances, Government Employment, and Elections**

Area Name	Direct general expenditure							Debt outstanding		Government employment, 1999			Presidential election, 2000[2]		
													Percent of vote cast —		
	Total (mil dol)	Per capita[1] (dollars)	Education	Health and hospitals	Police protection	Public welfare	Highways	Total (mil dol)	Per capita[1] (dollars)	Federal civilian	Federal military	State and local	Democratic	Republican	All other
	183	184	185	186	187	188	189	190	191	192	193	194	195	196	197
Reading, PA..............	906.5	2 560	55.6	3.1	2.9	6.8	2.9	1 461.7	4 129	1 168	1 220	18 012	43.8	52.7	3.5
Redding, CA..............	520.3	3 189	42.7	6.9	4.7	11.6	4.8	456.1	2 795	1 221	318	10 526	30.2	65.0	4.7
Reno, NV.................	877.3	2 869	32.5	2.5	7.8	2.5	5.9	985.2	3 222	3 156	676	18 547	42.6	52.0	5.3
Richland-Kennewick-Pasco, WA	527.3	2 884	45.2	11.4	4.0	0.0	7.2	7 554.8	41 329	1 297	698	12 652	32.9	64.0	3.1
Richmond-Petersburg, VA.....	2 497.7	2 648	41.3	6.2	5.6	5.1	3.1	2 608.7	2 766	15 237	9 230	88 549	42.9	54.7	2.5
Roanoke, VA..............	535.5	2 343	47.6	0.4	5.3	5.2	2.5	676.4	2 960	3 737	913	13 777	42.7	55.0	2.4
Rochester, MN............	335.5	2 927	51.7	1.4	4.4	7.7	6.8	254.0	2 216	908	478	6 530	43.5	51.6	4.9
Rochester, NY............	3 971.1	3 656	46.2	4.1	3.4	14.6	4.1	2 546.4	2 345	5 362	2 252	73 349	47.4	47.9	4.7
Rockford, IL.............	801.1	2 258	51.9	1.1	6.4	2.5	6.0	527.4	1 487	1 396	797	16 905	45.5	51.4	3.2
Rocky Mount, NC..........	386.1	2 652	42.5	28.7	4.0	6.5	1.7	50.7	348	582	442	10 023	48.6	51.0	0.4
Sacramento-Yolo, CA......	5 417.5	3 272	36.8	3.7	4.7	12.0	4.7	9 522.3	5 751	16 960	5 652	199 892	46.2	48.4	5.5
Sacramento, CA.........	4 955.2	3 297	37.2	3.6	4.7	12.0	4.4	9 269.2	6 167	14 502	5 345	177 242	45.3	49.5	5.2
Yolo, CA...............	462.2	3 025	31.9	4.5	5.4	11.7	7.6	253.1	1 657	2 458	307	22 650	54.9	37.5	7.6
Saginaw-Bay City-Midland, MI	1 102.0	2 735	50.4	9.1	4.1	2.0	5.3	856.0	2 124	1 802	830	19 872	51.6	46.2	2.2
Salinas, CA..............	1 453.5	4 016	30.8	26.3	4.2	6.0	3.2	538.4	1 488	4 897	5 745	23 857	57.5	37.2	5.2
Salt Lake City-Ogden, UT.....	2 565.2	2 056	47.0	3.7	6.5	0.6	4.3	7 112.0	5 701	24 573	11 236	93 989	32.0	60.1	7.9
San Angelo, TX...........	183.4	1 786	59.3	2.9	8.2	0.1	3.4	161.2	1 571	1 329	3 092	7 581	26.8	71.4	1.7
San Antonio, TX..........	3 428.7	2 269	50.3	10.8	5.7	2.3	3.2	6 839.3	4 525	33 517	36 276	98 199	41.9	55.2	2.8
San Diego, CA............	8 408.2	3 088	34.2	7.9	5.3	9.5	3.2	7 951.5	2 920	41 608	105 281	155 228	45.7	49.6	4.7
San Francisco-Oakland-San Jose, CA	24 551.2	3 664	28.1	12.0	5.8	8.1	3.5	24 816.0	3 703	62 263	24 003	408 902	64.0	29.9	6.1
Oakland, CA............	8 524.0	3 755	27.9	13.3	5.5	8.1	3.8	10 365.9	4 566	18 591	6 291	145 371	64.8	29.8	5.4
San Francisco, CA......	7 019.7	4 224	20.3	15.1	6.5	7.6	2.7	7 209.2	4 338	24 276	3 853	112 374	69.4	23.7	6.9
San Jose, CA...........	5 376.2	3 341	32.6	8.6	5.5	9.2	3.5	4 548.0	2 827	12 180	3 771	80 289	60.7	34.4	4.9
Santa Cruz-Watsonville, CA	812.3	3 378	33.2	9.6	5.4	6.7	3.1	432.9	1 800	552	473	16 886	61.5	27.3	11.2
Santa Rosa, CA.........	1 357.0	3 166	40.4	10.0	5.3	5.9	4.8	947.4	2 210	1 885	1 433	25 132	59.5	32.2	8.2
Vallejo-Fairfield-Napa, CA.	1 462.0	2 982	36.5	4.8	6.9	10.0	4.2	1 312.6	2 677	4 779	8 182	28 850	56.3	39.4	4.4
San Luis Obispo-Atascadero-Paso Robles, CA........	664.8	2 850	39.4	8.4	4.8	8.4	4.4	258.3	1 107	682	478	18 934	40.9	52.2	6.9
Santa Barbara-Santa Maria-Lompoc, CA	1 179.2	3 022	36.8	8.6	6.4	7.4	3.8	516.1	1 323	3 823	4 096	27 150	47.4	46.1	6.5
Santa Fe, NM...........	317.5	2 266	40.5	1.2	6.3	3.3	8.6	459.8	3 283	1 430	518	23 971	60.6	32.8	6.5
Sarasota-Bradenton, FL........	1 508.9	2 801	35.0	18.9	6.1	0.4	4.9	1 511.1	2 805	2 036	1 242	21 433	45.0	52.0	3.0
Savannah, GA............	751.7	2 646	41.1	5.8	6.3	0.4	7.0	622.6	2 192	2 689	5 411	17 680	45.9	53.4	0.6
Scranton—Wilkes-Barre—Hazleton, PA	1 320.3	2 124	56.2	0.2	3.0	4.3	3.8	1 676.6	2 697	4 841	2 104	29 951	53.3	42.7	4.0
Seattle-Tacoma-Bremerton, WA	10 080.6	2 993	36.6	8.2	4.9	0.2	5.5	11 193.1	3 323	49 364	60 146	242 532	55.6	39.1	5.3
Bremerton, WA.........	491.9	2 097	54.8	4.4	3.4	0.0	3.6	405.8	1 730	14 248	13 265	11 347	49.0	45.3	5.7
Olympia, WA...........	486.5	2 428	50.4	4.1	3.9	0.1	5.1	353.4	1 764	988	792	32 085	51.8	41.0	7.2
Seattle-Bellevue-Everett, WA	7 433.9	3 278	32.4	9.4	5.0	0.2	5.8	8 947.5	3 945	24 730	23 035	160 401	57.6	37.0	5.3
Tacoma, WA............	1 668.3	2 510	45.9	4.9	5.5	0.3	5.1	1 486.4	2 236	9 398	23 054	38 699	51.5	44.1	4.4
Sharon, PA..............	253.9	2 080	63.9	4.1	2.4	1.8	4.2	227.7	1 866	299	408	5 396	48.9	47.5	3.6
Sheboygan, WI...........	354.9	3 229	47.9	4.6	4.4	12.0	7.5	238.9	2 174	229	400	5 834	42.7	53.7	3.6
Sherman-Denison, TX.........	230.0	2 265	63.1	3.3	4.9	1.3	3.6	313.4	3 086	347	273	5 369	34.2	64.1	1.7
Shreveport-Bossier City, LA.	818.0	2 160	46.7	7.3	6.9	0.7	3.8	535.2	1 413	4 674	7 462	27 087	44.8	53.5	1.7
Sioux City, IA-NE........	301.7	2 497	51.1	2.2	4.8	0.8	6.7	178.4	1 477	907	558	6 277	46.4	50.0	3.6
Sioux Falls, SD..........	287.6	1 790	47.4	1.2	5.0	1.1	10.4	294.9	1 836	2 138	1 229	7 198	42.9	55.6	1.5
South Bend, IN...........	554.5	2 149	48.9	1.0	4.1	4.8	4.3	394.6	1 529	1 186	952	12 554	48.9	48.8	2.2
Spokane, WA.............	925.5	2 287	51.7	3.3	4.3	0.0	5.1	631.4	1 560	4 323	4 974	26 271	43.3	51.9	4.7
Springfield, IL...........	406.8	1 995	51.1	1.3	7.8	0.9	6.3	458.8	2 250	2 205	467	28 543	41.5	55.5	3.0
Springfield, MA...........	1 454.4	2 460	52.8	1.4	5.3	1.4	3.6	1 887.7	3 193	6 695	1 964	42 598	57.6	32.7	9.6
Springfield, MO..........	463.9	1 541	54.5	1.4	4.7	1.7	8.5	441.7	1 468	2 406	1 517	17 160	38.5	58.9	2.6
St. Cloud, MN............	444.5	2 757	44.9	3.7	3.5	7.2	10.4	659.0	4 088	1 544	663	10 745	39.8	51.8	8.5
St. Joseph, MO...........	175.4	1 806	48.3	1.4	5.5	0.2	6.7	32.4	334	571	472	6 733	47.3	49.2	3.5
St. Louis, MO-IL..........	5 553.1	2 171	50.9	2.8	6.6	0.4	4.8	3 698.2	1 446	30 053	17 370	132 482	52.8	44.7	2.5
State College, PA.........	225.8	1 698	54.9	3.5	2.9	3.9	3.7	243.4	1 830	495	532	32 822	43.2	52.8	4.0
Steubenville-Weirton, OH-WV	233.2	1 706	53.7	1.5	4.8	7.4	5.1	155.3	1 136	380	495	6 070	49.4	44.7	5.9
Stockton-Lodi, CA..........	1 703.2	3 139	38.6	10.0	5.4	13.2	3.4	1 050.8	1 937	3 872	1 122	29 952	47.7	48.9	3.4
Sumter, SC...............	160.6	1 507	63.3	2.3	6.3	0.5	1.9	82.5	774	1 165	5 507	5 668	46.8	51.9	1.3
Syracuse, NY.............	2 605.4	3 517	46.5	2.5	3.2	12.7	5.6	1 594.1	2 152	4 977	1 799	53 531	51.5	43.5	5.0
Tallahassee, FL...........	667.4	2 561	43.7	0.5	8.1	0.3	5.1	1 232.8	4 730	1 800	724	58 288	60.4	37.2	2.5
Tampa-St. Petersburg-Clearwater, FL	5 569.8	2 501	38.8	7.6	7.1	1.9	4.0	6 952.0	3 122	18 099	11 437	111 167	48.9	48.1	3.0
Terre Haute, IN..........	307.8	2 073	63.2	3.7	2.4	2.0	3.7	136.0	916	1 360	546	9 839	46.3	52.0	1.8
Texarkana, TX-Texarkana, AR	233.3	1 891	60.2	2.7	5.5	0.4	3.7	192.2	1 558	3 340	453	7 728	40.7	58.1	1.2
Toledo, OH...............	1 735.7	2 837	38.3	7.5	5.6	5.0	4.3	1 050.7	1 717	2 487	1 642	43 526	53.3	43.5	3.2
Topeka, KS...............	418.9	2 540	48.6	4.4	6.2	0.0	5.6	498.3	3 021	2 872	1 069	18 964	46.8	48.3	4.9

1. Based on the resident population estimated as of July 1 of the year shown.   2. Data subject to copyright.

Table C. Metropolitan Areas — **Land Area and Population**

CMSA/ MSA/ PMSA/ NECMA code[1]	Area Name	Land area,[2] (sq km) 2000	Population and population characteristics, 2000												
						Race alone or in combination (percent)					Age (percent)					
			Total persons	Rank	Per square kilometer	White	Black	Am. Indian, Alaska Native	Asian and Pacific Islander	Percent Hispanic[3]	Under 5 years	5 to 17 years	18 to 24 years	25 to 34 years	35 to 44 years	45 to 54 years
		1	2	3	4	5	6	7	8	9	10	11	12	13	14	15
8520	Tucson, AZ	23 792	843 746	70	35.5	77.8	3.7	4.0	2.9	29.3	6.6	18.0	10.9	13.5	14.9	13.1
8560	Tulsa, OK	12 987	803 235	71	61.8	80.4	9.5	10.7	1.7	4.8	7.2	19.5	9.3	13.8	15.8	13.7
8600	Tuscaloosa, AL	3 430	164 875	225	48.1	68.8	29.6	0.6	1.2	1.3	6.4	17.0	16.5	13.9	14.1	13.0
8640	Tyler, TX	2 405	174 706	216	72.7	73.9	19.4	0.9	1.0	11.2	7.1	19.5	9.8	12.9	14.5	12.9
8680	Utica-Rome, NY	6 796	299 896	158	44.1	93.1	5.1	0.6	1.3	2.7	5.6	18.3	8.5	12.3	15.5	13.7
8750	Victoria, TX	2 286	84 088	311	36.8	76.2	6.7	0.9	1.0	39.2	7.6	21.5	9.2	12.8	15.4	13.2
8780	Visalia-Tulare-Porterville, CA	12 494	368 021	136	29.5	62.0	2.0	2.5	4.3	50.8	8.9	24.8	10.6	13.6	14.0	11.2
8800	Waco, TX	2 698	213 517	194	79.1	73.7	15.6	0.9	1.4	17.9	7.1	19.5	14.6	12.4	14.0	11.8
97	Washington-Baltimore, DC-MD-VA-WV	24 803	7 608 070		306.7	64.8	27.1	0.8	6.1	6.4	6.8	18.5	8.7	15.3	17.6	14.4
0720	Baltimore, MD	6 757	2 552 994	18	377.8	68.5	28.1	0.7	3.2	2.0	6.5	18.8	8.6	13.9	17.2	14.2
3180	Hagerstown, MD	1 187	131 923	262	111.2	90.7	8.2	0.5	1.1	1.2	6.1	17.3	8.1	14.4	16.9	13.8
8840	Washington, DC-MD-VA-WV	16 859	4 923 153	6	292.0	62.2	27.1	0.8	7.8	8.8	7.0	18.3	8.7	16.1	17.8	14.5
8920	Waterloo-Cedar Falls, IA	1 469	128 012	266	87.2	89.8	8.6	0.5	1.3	1.8	6.1	17.0	15.7	11.9	13.3	13.6
8940	Wausau, WI	4 001	125 834	271	31.4	94.4	0.4	0.6	4.9	0.8	6.4	20.4	8.2	13.0	16.5	13.9
8960	West Palm Beach-Boca Raton, FL	5 113	1 131 184	55	221.2	80.4	14.9	0.5	2.1	12.4	5.6	15.7	6.6	11.8	15.2	12.5
9000	Wheeling, WV-OH	2 462	153 172	234	62.2	96.4	3.2	0.4	0.6	0.5	5.1	16.7	8.5	11.6	15.0	15.2
9080	Wichita Falls, TX	3 982	140 518	253	35.3	82.0	10.2	1.7	2.4	11.8	6.9	18.4	13.2	13.4	15.5	11.8
9040	Wichita, KS	7 683	545 220	97	71.0	84.1	8.6	2.1	3.4	7.4	7.7	20.4	9.4	13.8	16.2	13.2
9140	Williamsport, PA	3 198	120 044	280	37.5	94.7	4.8	0.5	0.5	0.7	5.5	17.8	9.7	12.0	15.6	14.1
9200	Wilmington, NC	2 729	233 450	184	85.5	81.5	16.5	0.9	0.9	2.2	5.6	15.4	10.4	14.0	14.9	14.3
9260	Yakima, WA	11 127	222 581	189	20.0	68.6	1.4	5.6	1.7	35.9	8.7	23.1	9.8	13.3	14.2	12.0
9280	York, PA	2 343	381 751	131	163.0	93.7	4.2	0.4	1.1	3.0	6.1	18.5	7.5	13.1	17.2	14.6
9320	Youngstown-Warren, OH	4 051	594 746	89	146.8	88.4	10.8	0.6	0.6	1.8	6.0	18.1	8.0	12.0	15.2	14.6
9340	Yuba City, CA	3 194	139 149	255	43.6	73.0	3.1	3.9	11.7	20.1	7.7	22.2	9.8	13.2	14.9	12.2
9360	Yuma, AZ	14 281	160 026	228	11.2	71.1	2.6	2.2	1.7	50.5	7.9	21.0	10.0	12.5	13.1	9.9

1. MSA = Metropolitan Statistical Area. CMSA = Consolidated MSA. PMSA = Primary MSA. NECMA = New England County Metropolitan Area. See Appendix A for explanation of these concepts. See Appendix B for list of metropolitan areas identified by type, with component counties.   2. Dry land or land partially or temporarily covered by water.   3. Hispanic persons may be of any race.

Table C. Metropolitan Areas — **Population and Households**

Area Name	Population, 2000 (cont'd)				Population — change and components of change, 1990–2001								Households, 2000				
	Age (percent) (cont'd)				Total persons		Percent change		Components of change, 2000–2001							Percent		
	55 to 64 years	65 to 74 years	75 years and over	Percent female	2001	1990	1990–2000	2000–2001	Births	Deaths	Net migration		Number	Percent change, 1990–2000	Persons per house-hold	Female family house-holder[1]	One person
	16	17	18	19	20	21	22	23	24	25	26		27	28	29	30	31
Tucson, AZ	8.8	7.5	6.7	51.1	863 049	666 957	26.5	2.3	15 242	9 053	13 238		332 350	27.0	2.47	11.8	28.5
Tulsa, OK	8.8	6.4	5.4	51.2	810 726	708 954	13.3	0.9	14 775	8 734	1 463		315 532	13.8	2.50	11.5	27.0
Tuscaloosa, AL	7.8	6.3	5.0	51.9	165 062	150 500	9.6	0.1	2 904	1 791	-877		64 517	16.6	2.42	14.0	28.4
Tyler, TX	9.2	7.5	6.6	52.1	178 855	151 309	15.5	2.4	3 335	2 230	3 044		65 692	15.7	2.59	12.3	24.7
Utica-Rome, NY	9.4	7.8	8.7	50.6	297 725	316 645	-5.3	-0.7	4 001	4 030	-2 053		116 230	-1.1	2.44	11.6	29.1
Victoria, TX	8.3	6.6	5.4	51.3	84 710	74 361	13.1	0.7	1 781	846	-293		30 071	14.7	2.75	12.7	22.4
Visalia-Tulare-Porterville, CA	7.0	5.2	4.6	50.0	374 249	311 932	18.0	1.7	8 528	3 184	980		110 385	12.8	3.28	14.5	17.1
Waco, TX	7.8	6.5	6.3	51.5	215 104	189 123	12.9	0.7	4 182	2 567	58		78 859	12.3	2.59	13.6	26.0
Washington-Baltimore, DC-MD-VA-WV	8.6	5.5	4.7	51.5	7 759 736	6 726 395	13.1	2.0	140 238	69 706	80 634		2 871 861	15.3	2.59	13.2	26.4
Baltimore, MD	8.9	6.4	5.7	51.9	2 572 945	2 382 172	7.2	0.8	44 887	30 080	5 213		974 071	10.7	2.55	14.9	26.4
Hagerstown, MD	9.2	7.4	6.7	48.9	133 197	121 393	8.7	1.0	2 074	1 613	863		49 726	11.1	2.46	10.7	26.0
Washington, DC-MD-VA-WV	8.5	5.0	4.1	51.3	5 053 594	4 222 830	16.6	2.6	93 277	38 013	74 558		1 848 064	18.0	2.61	12.4	26.4
Waterloo-Cedar Falls, IA	8.4	6.8	7.2	52.0	126 483	123 798	3.4	-1.2	1 961	1 388	-2 115		49 683	5.9	2.45	10.8	27.1
Wausau, WI	8.6	6.4	6.6	50.1	126 031	115 400	9.0	0.2	1 873	1 133	-497		47 702	14.8	2.60	7.4	23.6
West Palm Beach-Boca Raton, FL	9.6	10.8	12.3	51.7	1 165 049	863 503	31.0	3.0	17 057	16 200	32 835		474 175	29.7	2.34	9.7	29.2
Wheeling, WV-OH	9.9	9.0	8.9	51.7	151 372	159 301	-3.8	-1.2	1 969	2 514	-1 208		62 249	-1.0	2.35	11.1	29.6
Wichita Falls, TX	8.0	7.0	5.8	49.1	137 387	130 351	7.8	-2.2	2 580	1 792	-3 961		51 786	7.4	2.50	11.6	26.8
Wichita, KS	7.6	6.1	5.7	50.5	548 741	485 270	12.4	0.6	11 055	5 679	-1 708		210 552	12.8	2.54	10.5	27.4
Williamsport, PA	9.4	8.2	7.8	51.1	118 977	118 710	1.1	-0.9	1 658	1 515	-1 184		47 003	4.6	2.44	10.3	26.9
Wilmington, NC	11.2	8.4	5.7	51.5	240 513	171 269	36.3	3.0	3 636	2 587	5 947		98 621	44.6	2.32	11.1	27.0
Yakima, WA	7.7	5.6	5.6	50.1	223 886	188 823	17.9	0.6	5 304	2 185	-1 833		73 993	12.1	2.96	12.5	21.5
York, PA	9.4	7.1	6.4	50.8	386 299	339 574	12.4	1.2	5 399	4 032	3 292		148 219	15.2	2.52	9.0	23.3
Youngstown-Warren, OH	9.7	8.4	8.1	51.6	590 618	600 877	-1.0	-0.7	9 013	8 593	-4 364		234 580	2.9	2.47	12.8	27.5
Yuba City, CA	8.4	6.4	5.2	50.1	141 432	122 643	13.5	1.6	2 687	1 505	1 176		47 568	10.9	2.87	12.4	21.4
Yuma, AZ	9.0	10.0	6.6	49.5	164 942	106 895	49.7	3.1	3 709	1 217	2 488		53 848	50.5	2.86	11.2	18.5

1. No spouse present.

Table C. Metropolitan Areas — **Vital Statistics, Health Resources, and Crime**

Area Name	Births, average 1997–1999		Deaths, average 1997–1999				Physicians,[4] 1998		Hospitals,[4] 1998			Medicare enrollees 1999	Serious crimes known to police, 2000[6]	
			Number		Rate					Beds			Total	
	Total	Rate[1]	Total	Infant[2]	Total[1]	Infant[3]	Number	Rate[5]	Number	Number	Rate[5]		Number	Rate[7]
	32	33	34	35	36	37	38	39	40	41	42	43	44	45
Tucson, AZ...........................	11 691	14.8	7 104	70	9.0	6.0	2 446	309	9	2 078	263	123 255	59 039	6 997
Tulsa, OK.............................	11 757	15.1	6 839	NA	8.8	NA	1 695	218	14	2 715	349	106 091	37 631	4 685
Tuscaloosa, AL	2 125	13.2	1 371	22	8.5	10.4	333	207	2	680	423	22 174	14 649	8 912
Tyler, TX..............................	2 419	14.4	1 670	15	9.9	6.2	519	307	3	558	331	26 726	8 491	4 914
Utica-Rome, NY	3 406	11.5	3 243	NA	11.0	NA	582	198	6	1 279	434	56 976	7 742	2 605
Victoria, TX	1 372	16.7	663	NA	8.1	NA	189	229	3	588	711	11 171	4 081	4 853
Visalia-Tulare-Porterville, CA	6 747	19.0	2 587	41	7.3	6.1	421	119	7	854	240	40 519	16 089	4 372
Waco, TX	3 124	15.3	1 953	21	9.6	6.7	368	181	3	638	314	30 158	12 883	6 034
Washington-Baltimore, DC-MD-VA-WV	103 759	14.2	54 192	797	7.4	7.7	24 813	341	64	19 722	271	807 100	323 389	4 279
Baltimore, MD.....................	33 636	13.5	23 228	299	9.3	8.9	8 748	352	23	8 330	335	333 809	143 492	5 621
Hagerstown, MD..............	1 528	12.0	1 239	8	9.7	5.2	236	185	1	320	251	19 944	3 600	2 729
Washington, DC-MD-VA-WV	68 595	14.7	29 725	NA	6.4	NA	15 829	339	40	11 072	237	453 347	176 297	3 618
Waterloo-Cedar Falls, IA	1 545	12.8	1 161	11	9.6	7.1	272	225	3	609	503	19 923	5 501	4 297
Wausau, WI	1 541	12.5	916	6	7.4	3.9	219	178	1	270	219	16 844	2 669	2 154
West Palm Beach-Boca Raton, FL	12 850	12.5	12 805	82	12.4	6.4	3 403	330	14	3 294	319	239 091	71 962	6 554
Wheeling, WV-OH................	1 620	10.5	2 006	NA	13.0	NA	359	235	6	1 198	784	30 624	1 843	1 493
Wichita Falls, TX	1 979	14.4	1 328	17	9.7	8.6	291	212	3	423	308	20 037	7 066	5 029
Wichita, KS	8 547	15.8	4 367	NA	8.1	NA	1 075	197	9	2 225	409	70 904	25 965	5 295
Williamsport, PA..................	1 332	11.4	1 197	10	10.2	7.5	250	213	4	612	522	21 386	1 726	1 576
Wilmington, NC	2 691	12.4	1 967	NA	9.0	NA	517	237	4	711	326	36 945	14 215	6 187
Yakima, WA	4 132	18.9	1 716	28	7.9	6.8	361	166	4	481	221	27 567	13 495	6 063
York, PA	4 505	12.1	3 174	19	8.5	4.2	638	171	3	768	206	54 564	7 790	2 393
Youngstown-Warren, OH......	7 127	12.0	6 713	75	11.3	10.5	1 079	182	8	2 305	390	109 935	NA	NA
Yuba City, CA	2 211	16.1	1 158	NA	8.4	NA	220	161	2	260	190	18 741	5 772	4 148
Yuma, AZ.............................	2 934	20.6	1 089	19	7.6	6.5	154	116	1	275	208	17 758	5 455	3 770

1. Per 1,000 estimated resident population, average 1997–1999.   2. Deaths of infants under 1 year old.   3. Deaths of infants under 1 year old per 1,000 live births.   4. Data subject to copyright.   5. Per 100,000 resident population as of July 1 of the year shown.   6. Data for serious crimes have not been adjusted for underreporting; this may affect comparability between geographic areas and over time.   7. Per 100,000 population estimated by the FBI.

Table C. Metropolitan Areas — Crime, Education, Money Income, and Poverty

Area Name	Serious crimes known to police, 2000 (cont'd) Rate[2] Violent	Property	Education School enrollment and attainment, 1990 Enrollment[3] Total	Percent private	Attainment[4] (percent) High school graduate or more	Bachelor's degree or more	Local government expenditures, fiscal 1999[5] Total current expenditures (mil dol)	Current expenditures per student (dollars)	Money income 1989 Per capita[6] (dollars)	Households Median Dollars	Percent change, 1979–1989 (constant 1989 dollars)	Percent with $100,000 or more	Income and poverty, 1998 Median household income	Percent below poverty level All persons	Persons under 18	Persons 5–17 in families
	46	47	48	49	50	51	52	53	54	55	56	57	58	59	60	61
Tucson, AZ	658	6 339	188 198	9.8	80.5	23.3	622.1	4 962	13 177	25 400	-4.0	3.1	NA	15.9	24.4	23.2
Tulsa, OK	666	4 019	187 682	17.1	79.4	20.3	710.2	5 020	13 783	26 990	-6.4	3.3	NA	12.7	19.5	17.2
Tuscaloosa, AL	802	8 110	49 658	7.9	69.6	20.0	139.5	5 412	11 406	23 056	4.9	2.5	NA	16.2	24.0	20.8
Tyler, TX	481	4 433	42 179	9.5	75.7	19.8	154.9	5 144	12 742	25 769	-5.9	3.2	NA	14.3	21.7	19.2
Utica-Rome, NY	246	2 359	79 376	13.8	74.6	15.9	425.9	8 392	11 877	25 958	3.3	1.9	NA	15.0	22.7	22.3
Victoria, TX	558	4 295	21 249	10.1	70.2	14.1	98.0	6 050	12 196	26 945	-12.4	3.0	NA	15.1	22.1	21.4
Visalia-Tulare-Porterville, CA	646	3 726	92 825	5.7	60.2	11.8	504.8	5 958	10 302	24 449	3.1	2.6	NA	26.6	35.3	36.2
Waco, TX	565	5 469	57 779	25.3	71.6	16.6	225.1	5 775	11 185	22 664	-0.5	2.0	NA	17.0	25.0	22.7
Washington-Baltimore, DC-MD-VA-WV	667	3 612	1 703 511	20.5	80.6	31.6	8 632.8	7 368	19 255	41 921	18.3	8.5	NA	8.4	12.1	11.4
Baltimore, MD	1 072	4 549	593 146	19.8	74.7	23.1	2 803.2	6 983	16 596	36 549	15.2	5.6	NA	10.0	14.1	13.7
Hagerstown, MD	333	2 396	25 860	10.8	69.3	11.4	126.8	6 290	12 970	29 632	6.4	2.0	NA	9.7	14.0	13.7
Washington, DC-MD-VA-WV	464	3 154	1 084 505	21.2	84.3	37.0	5 702.8	7 603	20 935	45 900	20.3	10.3	NA	11.0	11.0	10.1
Waterloo-Cedar Falls, IA	374	3 923	37 637	12.4	80.4	17.3	132.6	7 932	12 321	25 682	-21.4	2.0	NA	11.8	17.6	15.4
Wausau, WI	123	2 031	29 586	13.2	75.9	13.5	145.1	7 314	12 718	30 143	3.7	2.5	NA	7.2	11.7	9.8
West Palm Beach-Boca Raton, FL	742	5 812	171 097	20.2	78.8	22.1	860.5	5 871	19 937	32 523	16.4	7.2	NA	11.0	19.2	17.3
Wheeling, WV-OH	145	1 348	37 660	15.6	72.9	12.2	144.6	6 585	11 119	21 830	-19.9	1.7	NA	15.2	23.4	20.2
Wichita Falls, TX	470	4 559	33 012	8.4	75.0	16.3	141.5	5 717	11 640	23 982	-7.1	2.2	NA	14.9	21.3	19.9
Wichita, KS	479	4 816	127 866	14.4	82.2	21.5	529.1	5 559	14 303	30 151	-0.8	2.9	NA	10.1	14.4	12.5
Williamsport, PA	106	1 470	27 909	12.3	74.5	12.3	139.5	7 055	11 714	25 552	1.5	1.8	NA	11.6	17.7	16.9
Wilmington, NC	498	5 689	42 226	8.6	75.4	18.0	189.7	6 017	13 215	26 086	5.4	2.6	NA	13.6	20.5	19.8
Yakima, WA	291	5 772	49 580	7.8	66.1	13.7	281.9	5 901	10 735	23 612	-4.7	2.1	NA	18.0	22.3	21.6
York, PA	174	2 219	72 386	15.9	72.8	13.9	342.0	6 129	14 544	32 604	5.8	2.7	NA	6.8	10.8	9.6
Youngstown-Warren, OH	NA	NA	146 914	12.5	74.3	12.0	603.5	6 386	11 936	25 471	-16.0	1.8	NA	12.7	19.7	17.3
Yuba City, CA	435	3 713	34 454	6.2	70.5	12.7	175.9	6 089	11 391	24 312	6.1	2.4	NA	19.6	27.6	32.1
Yuma, AZ	466	3 304	28 755	5.9	64.9	12.7	132.7	4 587	10 428	23 634	NA	1.8	NA	27.3	42.4	37.0

1. Data for serious crimes have not been adjusted for underreporting; this may affect comparability between geographic areas and over time.   2. Per 100,000 population estimated by the FBI.   3. All persons 3 years old and over enrolled in nursery school through college.   4. Persons 25 years old and over.   5. Elementary and secondary education expenditures, local government fiscal years ending between July 1, 1998 and June 30, 1999.   6. Based on population enumerated as of April 1, 1990.

Table C. Metropolitan Areas — **Personal Income**

Area Name	Personal income, 1999												
			Per capita[1]						Transfer payments				
										Government payments to individuals			
	Total (mil dol)	Percent change, 1998–1999	Dollars	Rank	Wages and salaries[2] (mil dol)	Proprietor's income (mil dol)	Dividends, interest, and rent (mil dol)	Total (mil dol)	Total (mil dol)	Social Security (mil dol)	Medical payments (mil dol)	Income mainte-nance (mil dol)	Unemploy-ment insurance (mil dol)
	62	63	64	65	66	67	68	69	70	71	72	73	74
Tucson, AZ	19 215	6.5	23 911	214	10 903	1 281	4 661	2 951	2 806	1 219	1 089	250	21
Tulsa, OK	21 740	2.8	27 654	103	13 381	3 352	3 773	2 624	2 482	1 114	953	190	37
Tuscaloosa, AL	3 746	4.4	23 207	244	2 588	183	668	647	617	225	281	61	6
Tyler, TX	4 533	4.3	26 711	125	2 680	566	947	653	624	265	260	50	11
Utica-Rome, NY	6 806	3.8	23 225	242	3 891	404	1 282	1 435	1 373	546	576	151	22
Victoria, TX	2 075	3.6	25 273	168	1 091	186	443	293	279	109	126	27	5
Visalia-Tulare-Porterville, CA	6 929	5.0	19 329	309	3 429	1 130	1 009	1 412	1 343	370	526	284	96
Waco, TX	4 755	5.7	23 281	237	2 969	513	819	723	687	278	248	77	8
Washington-Baltimore, DC-MD-VA-WV	263 429	6.8	35 797	X	191 932	15 721	48 625	21 606	20 222	7 683	8 730	2 019	346
Baltimore, MD	78 309	5.8	31 434	43	49 734	4 365	14 500	9 516	9 036	3 399	4 003	955	182
Hagerstown, MD	3 088	5.3	24 162	207	2 015	127	582	467	442	199	170	32	10
Washington, DC-MD-VA-WV	182 032	7.3	38 403	13	140 182	11 228	33 544	11 623	10 743	4 085	4 557	1 032	154
Waterloo-Cedar Falls, IA	2 988	0.6	24 905	179	2 140	170	618	473	448	208	157	44	13
Wausau, WI	3 214	5.1	26 009	144	2 151	180	621	365	341	175	114	24	13
West Palm Beach-Boca Raton, FL	43 978	4.3	41 907	5	18 150	3 207	17 918	5 153	4 961	2 567	1 963	199	72
Wheeling, WV-OH	3 440	3.4	22 349	267	1 852	210	814	749	719	315	271	55	10
Wichita Falls, TX	3 331	3.8	24 406	201	1 947	430	670	492	469	188	190	44	8
Wichita, KS	14 769	2.4	26 916	123	10 215	1 128	2 849	1 714	1 616	749	595	143	35
Williamsport, PA	2 659	4.0	22 784	256	1 612	228	520	484	461	209	166	41	20
Wilmington, NC	5 621	6.0	25 309	164	3 434	403	1 322	891	851	387	328	77	15
Yakima, WA	4 595	1.6	20 811	296	2 568	327	856	920	873	267	374	105	70
York, PA	9 931	3.9	26 370	135	5 758	881	1 810	1 166	1 091	587	346	76	33
Youngstown-Warren, OH	14 080	3.0	23 895	216	7 988	790	2 760	2 686	2 559	1 126	998	220	43
Yuba City, CA	2 942	8.8	21 313	291	1 381	425	457	611	585	171	231	109	23
Yuma, AZ	2 502	1.8	18 452	311	1 457	367	387	449	425	163	145	48	36

1. Based on the resident population estimated as of July 1 of the year shown.   2. Includes other labor income.

Table C. Metropolitan Areas — Earnings, Social Security, and Housing

Area Name	Earnings, 1999									Social Security beneficiaries, December 2000		Supplemental Security Income recipients, December 2000	Housing units, 1990	
	Total (mil dol)	Farm	Goods-related[1]		Service-related and other[2]					Number	Rate[3]		Total	Percent change, 1980–1990
			Total	Manu-facturing	Total	Retail trade	Finance, insurance, and real estate	Services	Govern-ment					
	75	76	77	78	79	80	81	82	83	84	85	86	87	88
Tucson, AZ	12 184	0.1	21.1	13.0	56.9	10.2	5.6	32.8	21.9	143 679	170	14 396	298 207	36.4
Tulsa, OK	16 733	0.0	32.8	21.5	58.4	8.6	5.9	26.1	8.8	125 050	156	12 092	311 890	16.8
Tuscaloosa, AL	2 772	0.3	35.4	22.1	38.5	9.9	3.6	17.4	25.8	27 726	168	5 674	58 740	16.7
Tyler, TX	3 246	1.1	26.9	15.5	59.1	13.3	6.5	27.7	12.9	31 142	178	3 629	64 369	25.8
Utica-Rome, NY	4 296	0.6	D	15.9	D	10.7	7.4	27.8	24.6	64 683	216	9 129	132 050	6.2
Victoria, TX	1 277	0.6	25.7	11.4	57.7	13.3	5.8	27.0	16.0	13 283	158	1 882	29 162	18.3
Visalia-Tulare-Porterville, CA	4 559	15.3	D	9.8	D	10.8	D	16.3	21.4	48 818	133	15 792	105 013	18.3
Waco, TX	3 482	0.7	25.1	18.6	58.2	10.2	11.7	25.0	16.0	34 507	162	4 568	78 857	19.6
Washington-Baltimore, DC-MD-VA-WV	207 653	0.1	D	D	D	6.8	D	D	26.7	909 150	119	119 629	2 660 934	21.8
Baltimore, MD	54 100	0.2	D	9.2	D	8.3	9.4	31.7	21.9	384 542	151	52 384	938 979	16.0
Hagerstown, MD	2 142	0.4	D	19.3	D	11.2	7.7	27.0	13.8	22 705	172	2 030	47 448	11.9
Washington, DC-MD-VA-WV	151 411	0.1	D	D	D	6.1	D	D	28.6	501 903	102	65 215	1 674 507	25.6
Waterloo-Cedar Falls, IA	2 311	0.6	D	26.9	D	9.8	5.2	25.2	16.7	23 010	180	2 749	49 688	-1.2
Wausau, WI	2 331	1.7	37.6	30.8	49.6	8.7	9.8	17.3	11.1	20 259	161	1 818	43 774	10.1
West Palm Beach-Boca Raton, FL	21 357	2.2	15.0	9.1	71.3	10.2	13.6	35.6	11.5	265 788	235	14 066	461 665	56.1
Wheeling, WV-OH	2 062	-0.2	D	14.3	D	11.6	4.8	D	16.7	35 071	229	4 020	69 434	-3.3
Wichita Falls, TX	2 377	1.2	26.2	14.2	41.8	9.4	4.2	19.7	30.7	22 518	160	2 591	55 093	6.6
Wichita, KS	11 343	0.3	39.4	32.7	48.3	8.6	4.6	23.9	12.0	82 223	151	8 007	202 521	16.1
Williamsport, PA	1 840	0.4	30.8	25.2	54.8	9.9	6.1	24.9	14.1	23 950	200	3 010	49 580	4.3
Wilmington, NC	3 836	0.2	D	16.4	D	13.2	6.8	24.5	17.8	45 598	195	5 489	94 190	45.2
Yakima, WA	2 896	10.4	D	13.1	D	10.1	D	24.5	18.1	32 260	145	5 185	70 852	6.0
York, PA	6 639	0.1	41.9	34.0	47.5	10.6	4.5	20.9	10.5	65 031	170	5 274	134 761	14.6
Youngstown-Warren, OH	8 778	0.3	36.8	30.7	49.2	11.1	4.5	22.6	13.6	124 047	209	14 514	242 483	1.1
Yuba City, CA	1 807	9.2	15.1	7.6	46.2	10.0	3.2	20.3	29.5	22 150	159	6 527	45 408	14.5
Yuma, AZ	1 824	12.8	D	3.8	D	9.8	D	18.1	28.0	22 008	138	2 603	46 541	24.1

1. Covers mining, construction, and manufacturing. 2. Covers private sector earnings in agricultural services, forestry, and fisheries; transportation and public utilities; wholesale trade; retail trade; finance, insurance, and real estate; and services. 3. Per 1,000 resident population estimated as of July 1 of the year shown.

Table C. Metropolitan Areas — Housing, Labor Force, and Employment

Area Name	Housing units, 1990 (cont'd)								Civilian labor force, 2001				Civilian employment, 1990[5]		
	Occupied units							Sub-stand-ard units[3] (percent)			Unemployment			Percent	
	Owner-occupied					Renter-occupied									
				Owner cost as a percent of income											
	Total	Percent	Median value[1]	With a mort-gage	Without a mort-gage	Median rent[2]	Rent as per-cent of income		Total	Percent change, 2000–2001	Total	Rate[4]	Total	Professional, managerial, and technical	Precision production, craft, and repair
	89	90	91	92	93	94	95	96	97	98	99	100	101	102	103
Tucson, AZ	261 792	60.9	76 500	22.2	12.0	389	28.7	6.5	392 593	2.1	13 561	3.5	290 058	33.1	10.8
Tulsa, OK	277 202	65.5	58 900	20.2	12.7	360	24.6	3.1	421 169	0.3	14 227	3.4	336 445	30.2	12.6
Tuscaloosa, AL	55 354	61.5	62 100	18.5	12.7	343	29.5	3.8	84 318	0.1	2 746	3.3	65 917	29.2	12.5
Tyler, TX	56 800	66.5	59 900	20.2	13.2	371	25.9	5.4	91 992	0.9	3 803	4.1	67 128	28.2	10.6
Utica-Rome, NY	117 498	66.5	69 000	18.4	13.9	360	27.0	2.0	138 770	-2.3	6 386	4.6	133 749	28.1	11.5
Victoria, TX	26 228	64.6	54 700	19.5	12.9	350	24.5	7.3	43 989	1.7	1 766	4.0	32 462	25.6	15.4
Visalia-Tulare-Porterville, CA	97 861	60.1	73 900	22.6	12.1	402	29.2	14.5	170 908	-0.3	26 396	15.4	118 964	21.8	9.6
Waco, TX	70 208	58.9	50 300	18.6	12.8	359	27.9	5.2	100 901	-0.4	3 938	3.9	82 485	27.5	11.6
Washington-Baltimore, DC-MD-VA-WV	2 491 041	62.2	136 098	NA	NA	590	NA	3.9	4 139 686	1.4	148 407	3.6	3 581 926	40.8	9.1
Baltimore, MD	880 145	63.7	101 200	20.7	12.6	489	25.3	2.8	1 330 732	1.3	60 724	4.6	1 192 182	35.1	10.7
Hagerstown, MD	44 762	63.8	83 000	18.7	12.4	357	21.7	2.2	69 280	1.4	2 842	4.1	56 191	23.0	14.4
Washington, DC-MD-VA-WV	1 566 134	61.3	160 939	NA	NA	658	NA	4.6	2 739 674	1.5	84 841	3.1	2 333 553	44.2	8.2
Waterloo-Cedar Falls, IA	46 932	67.3	44 100	NA	NA	325	NA	2.2	67 628	0.7	2 548	3.8	56 595	26.2	11.0
Wausau, WI	41 547	74.7	54 800	18.1	13.1	364	23.0	2.6	74 627	1.6	3 095	4.1	57 719	23.0	11.0
West Palm Beach-Boca Raton, FL	365 558	71.9	98 400	23.4	12.4	586	28.1	4.3	540 276	4.0	29 779	5.5	387 274	31.4	11.2
Wheeling, WV-OH	62 858	72.4	44 100	16.8	12.0	279	26.6	2.1	74 628	0.9	3 240	4.3	63 304	25.8	13.4
Wichita Falls, TX	48 228	64.5	46 300	NA	NA	360	NA	3.5	63 235	0.5	2 201	3.5	54 608	27.3	11.7
Wichita, KS	186 640	65.2	57 300	19.5	12.5	391	24.8	3.4	278 362	-2.1	11 452	4.1	237 187	30.8	13.9
Williamsport, PA	44 949	69.7	54 900	18.9	12.9	333	25.3	2.2	57 977	2.3	3 381	5.8	52 566	22.6	12.3
Wilmington, NC	68 208	68.2	71 600	NA	NA	410	NA	2.6	116 990	0.9	5 733	4.9	82 489	27.4	13.5
Yakima, WA	65 985	63.2	55 200	17.9	12.1	338	25.5	10.1	107 961	-1.6	12 203	11.3	77 366	22.9	9.5
York, PA	128 666	74.4	79 700	NA	NA	408	NA	1.7	198 245	1.4	8 920	4.5	176 908	24.0	14.2
Youngstown-Warren, OH	227 967	72.8	49 000	NA	NA	336	NA	1.7	277 972	-0.4	16 614	6.0	249 622	23.6	13.1
Yuba City, CA	42 887	55.9	80 900	21.6	12.0	384	27.7	9.3	58 446	-0.3	7 088	12.1	44 688	24.5	13.1
Yuma, AZ	35 791	66.0	64 000	21.3	13.5	435	27.7	14.6	64 487	-2.2	15 716	24.4	37 189	24.2	10.2

1. Specified owner-occupied units.   2. Specified renter-occupied units.   3. Overcrowded or lacking complete plumbing facilities.   4. Percent of civilian labor force.   5. Persons 16 years and older.

Table C. Metropolitan Areas — Nonfarm Employment and Agriculture

Area Name	Private nonfarm establishments, employment and payroll, 1999									Agriculture, 1997			
	Number of establishments	Employment						Annual payroll		Farms			Farm operators
		Total	Health Care and Social Assistance	Manufacturing	Retail trade	Finance and Insurance	Professional Scientific and Technical Services	Total (mil dol)	Average per employee (dollars)	Number	Percent with—		Whose principal occupation is farming (percent)
											Less than 50 acres	500 acres and over	
	104	105	106	107	108	109	110	111	112	113	114	115	116
Tucson, AZ..................	18 507	278 669	40 371	29 214	40 823	8 241	14 351	7 368	26 440	419	60.1	22.0	45.6
Tulsa, OK...................	22 014	361 718	40 608	53 122	43 726	19 227	17 256	10 711	29 611	6 006	34.3	13.3	34.9
Tuscaloosa, AL	3 956	67 473	10 679	12 460	9 763	1 775	2 252	1 782	26 411	510	30.8	10.0	37.3
Tyler, TX	4 863	71 725	14 141	9 908	11 147	2 822	2 977	1 940	27 048	1 844	43.0	4.6	31.3
Utica-Rome, NY	6 166	99 116	17 882	19 276	15 073	7 993	3 031	2 393	24 143	1 511	17.5	11.4	65.3
Victoria, TX	2 201	29 093	5 525	2 752	5 191	1 083	836	696	23 923	1 084	32.4	16.6	39.4
Visalia-Tulare-Porterville, CA	5 862	72 991	10 678	12 048	12 674	3 000	2 089	1 753	24 017	5 446	59.7	8.2	55.5
Waco, TX	4 831	87 895	13 385	16 688	10 452	4 230	2 377	2 117	24 086	2 006	38.8	11.1	36.8
Washington-Baltimore, DC-MD-VA-WV........................	191 171	3 195 495	371 523	176 178	392 498	163 049	431 832	123 411	38 620	12 345	44.5	7.0	46.5
Baltimore, MD..................	61 903	1 017 774	150 524	87 202	135 111	58 354	81 795	32 697	32 126	3 622	50.9	7.4	48.4
Hagerstown, MD..............	3 246	53 662	7 947	9 821	8 385	4 563	1 182	1 397	26 033	768	34.1	4.7	54.9
Washington, DC-MD-VA-WV	126 022	2 124 059	213 052	79 155	249 002	100 132	348 855	89 317	42 050	7 955	42.6	7.1	44.8
Waterloo-Cedar Falls, IA	3 178	59 199	9 062	13 132	9 238	2 804	1 737	1 514	25 575	1 002	25.1	18.2	52.5
Wausau, WI	3 429	62 164	6 387	18 368	9 587	4 462	1 685	1 730	27 830	2 703	23.3	6.2	60.6
West Palm Beach-Boca Raton, FL	35 926	427 874	57 929	25 084	65 360	22 886	27 707	13 058	30 518	855	76.0	10.4	57.0
Wheeling, WV-OH...............	3 805	52 324	11 660	3 767	9 108	2 360	1 697	1 187	22 686	1 294	16.3	5.6	39.6
Wichita Falls, TX................	3 470	47 880	9 616	7 889	7 378	1 765	1 145	1 103	23 037	1 056	25.8	29.6	42.5
Wichita, KS	13 900	260 669	33 544	65 396	31 060	9 011	9 998	7 874	30 207	3 430	25.5	24.9	48.4
Williamsport, PA..............	2 849	47 149	7 667	12 792	7 264	1 965	1 094	1 109	23 521	841	19.9	4.8	52.3
Wilmington, NC	7 712	92 259	12 090	10 362	15 797	2 946	5 299	2 343	25 396	275	49.8	6.5	47.3
Yakima, WA	4 800	59 762	10 133	9 364	10 027	1 563	1 456	1 493	24 982	3 365	63.0	6.6	55.3
York, PA	8 206	149 398	16 226	44 221	20 897	4 031	4 017	4 287	28 695	1 698	43.9	6.8	50.7
Youngstown-Warren, OH......	13 659	208 592	31 810	50 850	31 430	7 184	6 024	5 879	28 184	2 310	35.9	4.2	43.8
Yuba City, CA	2 454	26 054	5 036	2 873	5 124	940	693	628	24 104	2 020	47.0	12.2	58.9
Yuma, AZ....................	2 489	31 256	4 461	2 164	6 476	964	745	610	19 516	465	44.7	25.6	59.4

Items 104—116

Table C. Metropolitan Areas — **Agriculture, Land, and Water**

Area Name	Agriculture, 1997 (cont'd)															
	Land in farms					Value of land and buildings		Value of machinery and equipment Average per farm ($1,000)	Value of products sold				Percent of farms with sales of —		Percent of land owned by Fed. Gov. 1997	Water consumption 1995 (mil gal/day)
			Acres								Percent from —					
	Acreage (1,000)	Percent change, 1992–1997	Average size of farm	Total irrigated (1,000)	Total cropland (1,000)	Average per farm ($1,000)	Average per acre (dollars)		Total (mil dol)	Average per farm (dollars)	Crops	Live-stock and poultry products	$10,000 or more	$100,000 or more		
	117	118	119	120	121	122	123	124	125	126	127	128	129	130	131	132
Tucson, AZ	2 914	-16.1	6 954	29	D	2 346	340	38	47	111 840	81.0	19.0	41.1	13.6	29.0	263.8
Tulsa, OK	2 255	6.7	376	6	617	267	716	24	193	32 165	23.0	77.0	27.2	4.3	2.5	143.0
Tuscaloosa, AL	100	4.0	196	1	43	294	1 569	29	21	40 253	30.0	70.0	25.1	6.7	1.5	35.3
Tyler, TX	251	1.2	136	1	127	223	1 794	25	38	20 798	52.0	48.0	23.1	2.6	0.0	37.9
Utica-Rome, NY	358	-11.8	237	1	229	227	970	56	120	79 338	16.0	84.0	61.1	27.5	0.3	55.3
Victoria, TX	458	6.3	423	4	155	318	716	33	29	26 419	60.0	40.0	28.0	6.0	0.0	47.4
Visalia-Tulare-Porterville, CA	1 310	-3.3	240	625	703	835	3 444	68	1 921	352 806	58.0	42.0	67.4	35.7	48.5	2 208.7
Waco, TX	493	4.4	246	2	299	237	968	34	93	46 337	37.0	63.0	24.8	5.4	1.6	57.4
Washington-Baltimore, DC-MD-VA-WV	2 080	-2.4	168	23	1 424	634	3 713	51	669	54 213	45.0	55.0	39.1	11.9	3.8	2 090.0
Baltimore, MD.................	573	-3.1	158	13	450	633	3 900	60	262	72 398	54.0	46.0	42.7	15.0	3.1	388.8
Hagerstown, MD.............	126	1.8	164	1	95	454	2 819	68	61	78 911	21.0	79.0	50.5	27.9	4.8	60.0
Washington, DC-MD-VA-WV	1 381	-2.5	174	10	879	651	3 718	46	346	43 548	41.0	59.0	36.3	9.0	4.1	1 641.2
Waterloo-Cedar Falls, IA	286	-4.7	285	1	263	622	2 321	82	128	127 637	60.0	40.0	76.6	35.9	0.0	57.3
Wausau, WI	516	-2.7	191	6	337	202	1 039	68	204	75 578	25.0	75.0	68.2	24.0	0.0	183.4
West Palm Beach-Boca Raton, FL	605	-5.2	707	417	529	2 398	3 404	84	873	1 020 909	100.0	0.0	64.1	33.9	10.1	959.8
Wheeling, WV-OH............	247	16.7	191	D	110	165	881	30	17	13 154	18.0	82.0	20.8	3.5	0.0	1 034.0
Wichita Falls, TX	950	3.1	899	6	266	509	604	44	85	80 734	14.0	86.0	45.9	14.4	0.4	50.4
Wichita, KS	1 620	1.5	472	57	1 009	456	976	58	287	83 572	45.0	55.0	54.8	18.0	0.4	144.0
Williamsport, PA	136	1.9	161	2	87	283	1 873	50	43	51 357	37.0	63.0	50.7	15.2	0.3	16.3
Wilmington, NC	42	-1.8	153	1	28	419	2 574	39	35	125 931	D	D	46.2	16.7	1.3	78.5
Yakima, WA	1 683	2.6	500	278	D	605	1 220	73	873	259 582	67.0	33.0	61.4	28.9	17.6	1 475.0
York, PA	261	3.6	154	1	217	472	3 187	57	129	75 748	40.0	60.0	50.0	17.3	0.2	2 350.0
Youngstown-Warren, OH	324	-4.1	140	2	237	285	2 131	50	104	45 189	47.0	53.0	42.0	11.1	1.2	253.4
Yuba City, CA	557	0.7	276	327	394	1 050	3 882	97	386	191 208	95.0	5.0	62.1	32.8	9.1	1 408.6
Yuma, AZ	238	3.8	511	196	215	2 266	4 496	145	522	1 122 716	D	D	68.4	43.0	81.5	1 398.6

Table C. Metropolitan Areas — Residential Construction, Wholesale and Retail Trade, and Real Estate

Area Name	Value of Residential Construction Authorized by Building Permits, 2000		Wholesale Trade, 1997				Retail Trade[1], 1997				Real Estate and Rental and Leasing, 1997			
	New Construction ($1,000)	Number of Housing Units	Number of Establishments	Number of Employees	Sales (mil dol)	Annual Payroll (mil dol)	Number of Establishments	Number of Employees	Sales (mil dol)	Annual Payroll (mil dol)	Number of Establishments	Number of Employees	Receipts (mil dol)	Annual Payroll (mil dol)
	133	134	135	136	137	138	139	140	141	142	143	144	145	146
Tucson, AZ	995 002	7 779	929	9 257	2 759.8	266.0	2 785	39 285	6 853.8	693.4	978	6 631	676.6	130.5
Tulsa, OK	456 809	3 740	1 637	20 463	10 168.5	707.8	3 039	41 087	7 293.0	663.9	914	4 836	540.2	99.2
Tuscaloosa, AL	71 427	709	185	1 981	858.1	61.1	790	10 852	1 543.2	151.0	161	1 079	82.6	13.7
Tyler, TX	71 030	543	297	3 103	1 237.7	93.9	805	9 773	1 868.6	170.2	189	895	93.2	20.7
Utica-Rome, NY	41 627	405	278	3 248	1 056.3	86.3	1 225	14 847	2 159.5	210.2	208	748	88.9	12.6
Victoria, TX	18 335	167	141	1 665	422.1	46.0	398	5 052	868.7	80.1	91	455	60.5	10.5
Visalia-Tulare-Porterville, CA	162 800	1 627	343	5 120	2 527.7	135.1	1 107	12 742	2 135.7	211.8	206	809	97.7	12.6
Waco, TX	75 871	701	315	3 755	1 716.3	102.1	862	10 227	1 797.8	162.7	212	1 086	131.4	21.4
Washington-Baltimore, DC-MD-VA-WV	5 253 769	51 614	8 247	123 675	80 810.2	5 174.0	27 318	383 694	66 662.6	7 050.4	7 759	62 797	9 018.8	1 701.0
Baltimore, MD	1 278 630	11 804	3 494	51 526	32 627.0	1 974.6	9 585	132 311	21 687.7	2 340.4	2 331	18 521	2 397.0	476.2
Hagerstown, MD	67 537	721	156	2 184	922.7	62.9	598	7 450	1 220.5	117.3	105	479	43.4	7.3
Washington, DC-MD-VA-WV	3 907 601	39 089	4 597	69 965	47 260.4	3 136.5	17 135	243 933	43 754.3	4 592.6	5 323	43 797	6 578.4	1 217.5
Waterloo-Cedar Falls, IA	39 574	379	169	2 690	952.7	77.0	598	9 386	1 344.8	139.3	126	549	60.9	10.3
Wausau, WI	88 641	803	221	3 395	1 002.0	102.5	565	9 236	1 421.6	142.6	86	439	39.9	7.1
West Palm Beach-Boca Raton, FL	1 331 563	10 504	2 187	17 864	11 544.5	707.0	4 967	61 563	11 731.2	1 126.1	1 716	9 409	1 323.8	248.3
Wheeling, WV-OH	5 772	49	189	2 472	1 734.8	66.7	744	9 588	1 328.9	129.8	121	554	45.0	8.7
Wichita Falls, TX	26 363	231	229	2 048	476.0	47.1	625	7 379	1 222.2	109.3	152	521	51.5	8.0
Wichita, KS	256 007	2 595	900	10 551	6 192.5	352.9	2 154	28 706	4 801.5	471.5	606	2 815	352.3	56.3
Williamsport, PA	31 726	313	137	2 195	481.9	51.4	605	7 600	1 149.3	108.4	78	299	32.2	4.7
Wilmington, NC	369 346	3 309	381	3 895	1 293.9	104.0	1 302	14 842	2 903.0	249.0	338	2 089	182.3	37.3
Yakima, WA	52 078	484	291	4 871	1 853.8	141.9	854	10 174	1 741.6	174.9	212	1 018	99.9	17.0
York, PA	216 475	2 009	450	9 498	3 428.1	275.9	1 447	20 356	3 250.6	315.4	236	1 138	128.3	21.5
Youngstown-Warren, OH	152 997	1 324	749	9 292	3 622.4	282.3	2 568	33 971	5 314.5	497.2	413	2 470	248.8	45.9
Yuba City, CA	47 860	322	130	1 018	453.3	31.9	446	5 129	851.3	86.7	118	592	51.9	7.4
Yuma, AZ	96 296	1 288	132	2 376	512.9	41.3	455	5 984	1 035.7	94.5	113	485	48.4	7.0

1. Establishments with payroll.

Area Name	Professional, Scientific, and Technical Services[1], 1997				Manufacturing, 1997			.	Accommodation and Foodservices, 1997			
	Number of Establish-ments	Number of Employees	Sales (mil dol)	Annual Payroll (mil dol)	Number of Establish-ments	Number of Employees	Sales (mil dol)	Annual Payroll (mil dol)	Number of Establish-ments	Number of Employees	Sales (mil dol)	Annual Payroll (mil dol)
	147	148	149	150	151	152	153	154	155	156	157	158
Tucson, AZ	1 811	12 214	1 124.2	430.9	764	26 746	4 455	1 065	1 524	32 305	1 041.9	292.2
Tulsa, OK	2 177	14 688	1 489.2	549.6	1 441	50 859	9 954	1 656	1 593	27 153	873.1	233.0
Tuscaloosa, AL	257	1 733	134.0	51.6	160	10 738	2 558	379	317	7 396	202.5	55.6
Tyler, TX	392	2 464	284.0	93.0	213	10 969	2 299	381	294	5 834	175.1	47.8
Utica-Rome, NY	402	2 504	185.8	65.6	351	20 050	3 148	583	681	7 156	220.7	61.4
Victoria, TX	141	712	59.5	21.1	71	3 064	1 245	120	155	2 711	79.6	21.7
Visalia-Tulare-Porterville, CA	335	1 788	265.6	45.0	282	11 439	3 167	315	510	7 020	232.3	56.8
Waco, TX	292	2 039	133.0	57.4	261	16 474	3 856	482	400	6 900	220.7	59.8
Washington-Baltimore, DC-MD-VA-WV	26 290	346 773	44 475.0	17 623.8	4 979	180 692	39 149	6 730	13 376	263 545	10 802.8	3 067.6
Baltimore, MD	6 666	60 715	6 654.6	2 613.7	2 177	93 594	22 685	3 449	4 492	80 323	2 923.1	808.3
Hagerstown, MD	163	854	63.5	22.7	147	9 173	1 924	294	230	4 135	127.6	36.4
Washington, DC-MD-VA-WV	19 461	285 204	37 757.0	14 987.4	2 655	77 925	14 540	2 987	8 654	179 087	7 752.1	2 222.9
Waterloo-Cedar Falls, IA	193	1 530	100.9	44.9	165	13 542	5 133	556	293	5 544	135.8	39.2
Wausau, WI	181	1 264	127.4	46.6	232	16 839	3 182	503	276	3 779	105.2	29.7
West Palm Beach-Boca Raton, FL	4 211	21 787	2 352.0	985.5	1 051	26 262	6 345	1 138	2 087	41 031	1 659.8	440.9
Wheeling, WV-OH	220	1 350	114.3	34.0	137	3 511	649	90	361	5 078	147.4	41.0
Wichita Falls, TX	217	1 087	88.2	33.0	156	7 939	1 437	255	282	5 256	160.6	47.3
Wichita, KS	1 060	6 705	558.6	225.4	702	66 234	12 218	2 716	1 130	20 170	648.7	184.8
Williamsport, PA	137	1 014	68.8	27.1	208	12 982	2 460	370	283	3 571	106.1	28.5
Wilmington, NC	586	3 404	272.4	110.3	260	10 718	3 711	426	610	10 677	348.7	93.5
Yakima, WA	223	1 298	119.4	43.2	239	10 163	2 091	265	411	5 371	178.6	47.8
York, PA	502	3 457	268.4	105.2	661	45 754	8 157	1 558	635	10 721	318.7	91.1
Youngstown-Warren, OH	831	5 393	370.4	157.0	896	55 718	14 455	2 267	1 195	18 502	529.3	144.2
Yuba City, CA	143	572	37.3	14.3	114	2 792	602	76	187	2 383	75.9	21.9
Yuma, AZ	148	666	48.1	17.3	66	3 041	390	55	245	4 158	130.0	31.3

1. Firms subject to federal tax.

Table C. Metropolitan Areas — **Health and Other Services and Federal Funds**

Area Name	Health Care and Social Assistance[1], 1997				Other Services[1], 1997				Federal funds and grants, fiscal 2001[2]			
									Expenditures (mil dol)			
										Direct payments for individuals		
	Number of Establish-ments	Number of Employees	Receipts (mil dol)	Annual Payroll (mil dol)	Number of Establish-ments	Number of Employees	Receipts (mil dol)	Annual Payroll (mil dol)	Total	Social Security and government retirement	Medicare	Food stamps and Supplemental Security Income
	159	160	161	162	163	164	165	166	167	168	169	170
Tucson, AZ..........................	1 614	19 280	1 283.3	563.9	1 171	7 575	437.9	138.1	6 360.2	2 062.9	676.0	128.3
Tulsa, OK............................	1 747	24 266	1 537.5	681.2	1 202	7 626	526.4	154.2	3 434.3	1 543.6	605.2	110.5
Tuscaloosa, AL	274	3 580	223.9	116.2	248	1 481	79.3	25.1	839.2	328.7	136.2	41.5
Tyler, TX	430	5 047	396.8	186.2	288	2 032	116.3	35.4	776.2	383.0	156.3	24.9
Utica-Rome, NY	484	4 753	312.2	143.5	414	2 245	174.7	44.2	1 830.3	771.0	280.0	60.9
Victoria, TX	230	3 383	230.0	93.5	151	973	61.8	17.8	339.5	152.5	69.1	13.6
Visalia-Tulare-Porterville, CA	588	5 102	334.0	127.8	308	1 544	115.2	28.7	1 459.6	488.7	239.5	90.6
Waco, TX	353	4 861	265.9	126.4	329	2 065	114.1	34.4	1 096.2	470.4	130.0	34.8
Washington-Baltimore, DC-MD-VA-WV......................	15 462	162 986	11 741.6	5 140.1	11 491	79 223	5 341.6	1 668.9	101 678.6	17 587.0	5 392.5	960.6
Baltimore, MD..................	5 234	64 227	4 262.9	1 879.9	3 885	27 412	1 724.4	541.1	19 575.0	5 598.2	2 536.0	426.7
Hagerstown, MD...............	225	3 006	208.0	95.5	207	1 524	81.7	25.4	575.5	294.7	108.0	16.9
Washington, DC-MD-VA-WV	10 003	95 753	7 270.7	3 164.6	7 399	50 287	3 535.4	1 102.3	81 528.1	11 694.2	2 748.4	517.0
Waterloo-Cedar Falls, IA	228	2 173	167.9	83.0	213	1 513	80.2	25.9	605.4	265.8	102.9	22.2
Wausau, WI	200	2 672	188.8	104.9	222	1 201	79.2	20.9	480.8	214.5	73.7	12.5
West Palm Beach-Boca Raton, FL	3 280	39 623	2 981.7	1 257.5	2 113	11 678	726.5	209.6	7 332.5	3 190.7	1 792.9	114.4
Wheeling, WV-OH................	357	4 025	207.0	88.9	228	1 451	75.0	24.4	867.7	413.8	176.6	34.0
Wichita Falls, TX..................	278	3 935	211.8	85.8	233	1 552	87.5	28.9	1 127.4	366.2	113.8	20.9
Wichita, KS	909	17 460	1 261.2	521.8	913	5 640	352.2	107.9	3 095.3	1 062.9	400.1	70.6
Williamsport, PA..................	218	2 050	134.4	58.6	176	887	57.5	15.2	593.9	274.6	113.1	22.7
Wilmington, NC	496	6 823	440.1	183.2	399	2 128	133.0	39.1	1 251.3	602.3	170.7	41.9
Yakima, WA	391	4 594	298.6	129.8	277	1 408	87.6	26.8	1 002.9	371.6	137.5	46.7
York, PA.............................	586	6 842	469.4	214.2	585	3 058	202.4	58.0	1 948.2	780.7	256.4	35.3
Youngstown-Warren, OH......	1 287	15 298	838.1	388.8	889	5 394	299.5	89.6	3 011.3	1 427.5	675.5	129.7
Yuba City, CA	252	2 702	248.1	79.0	148	821	53.9	14.3	903.0	298.1	116.2	38.2
Yuma, AZ............................	224	2 428	154.1	60.1	158	855	46.5	13.6	815.4	292.9	109.9	26.0

1. Firms subject to federal tax.   2. October 1, 1998 to September 30, 1999.

	Federal funds and grants, fiscal 2001[1] (cont'd)							Local government finances, 1997				
	Expenditures (mil dol) (cont'd)							General revenue				
	Procurement contract awards			Grants[2]							Taxes		
											Per capita[3] (dollars)	
Area Name	Salaries and wages	Defense	Other	Medicaid and other health-related	Nutrition and family welfare	Education	Other	Total (mil dol)	Intergovern-mental (mil dol)	Total (mil dol)	Total	Property
	171	172	173	174	175	176	177	178	179	180	181	182
Tucson, AZ	635.8	1 765.9	100.5	496.4	94.8	78.7	207.3	1 850.7	837.9	671.3	860	654
Tulsa, OK	277.3	171.9	91.3	250.0	75.6	55.8	123.3	1 518.7	503.4	570.3	746	391
Tuscaloosa, AL	70.1	14.3	53.6	78.8	18.0	15.9	40.6	476.7	141.7	64.7	402	206
Tyler, TX	51.3	0.6	14.0	89.9	11.3	6.4	13.9	303.6	114.7	133.3	800	601
Utica-Rome, NY	138.2	104.8	35.4	248.2	39.6	22.4	52.8	1 032.8	431.1	405.8	1 358	1 004
Victoria, TX	12.4	1.8	2.7	40.3	8.4	5.6	12.1	255.3	61.4	85.8	1 046	818
Visalia-Tulare-Porterville, CA	56.2	4.5	30.4	260.2	107.3	38.6	51.5	1 468.0	786.8	190.2	539	364
Waco, TX	108.1	48.8	13.4	128.5	18.3	9.9	33.7	607.1	185.8	162.8	802	575
Washington-Baltimore, DC-MD-VA-WV	26 566.3	15 097.0	20 827.5	5 183.8	1 133.6	812.3	5 004.3	22 316.2	7 112.1	11 447.2	1 588	885
Baltimore, MD	2 905.8	1 963.6	1 180.4	2 631.2	619.6	261.0	821.9	5 969.2	2 174.5	2 874.9	1 161	685
Hagerstown, MD	29.0	4.2	11.7	66.7	10.0	3.8	11.8	237.6	87.8	104.0	811	520
Washington, DC-MD-VA-WV	23 631.5	13 129.2	19 635.4	2 485.9	504.0	547.6	4 170.6	16 109.4	4 849.8	8 468.4	1 840	1 003
Waterloo-Cedar Falls, IA	34.2	1.9	0.9	73.8	19.9	10.4	15.4	351.5	147.2	104.2	857	735
Wausau, WI	32.8	0.2	29.1	55.0	10.7	7.4	23.9	372.6	180.2	114.2	933	859
West Palm Beach-Boca Raton, FL	317.8	1 146.4	132.2	182.1	77.7	39.1	244.7	3 140.0	632.2	1 523.2	1 495	1 256
Wheeling, WV-OH	42.9	4.8	12.5	79.1	22.2	12.5	38.2	299.2	128.4	93.6	607	437
Wichita Falls, TX	376.3	96.3	11.4	58.0	9.8	7.7	28.1	240.7	83.8	107.2	782	620
Wichita, KS	396.3	606.3	94.4	218.9	60.6	21.5	61.1	1 171.4	484.5	410.3	773	561
Williamsport, PA	36.1	19.7	14.9	55.8	13.7	4.1	14.9	254.6	105.3	97.0	819	555
Wilmington, NC	66.4	139.1	27.9	114.5	21.7	10.2	17.5	693.0	222.8	180.6	846	621
Yakima, WA	67.5	15.7	32.0	171.4	73.5	29.2	20.7	528.1	328.0	116.2	532	342
York, PA	111.1	545.6	26.4	109.5	19.2	6.6	28.5	735.0	264.7	307.6	830	614
Youngstown-Warren, OH	147.2	16.3	39.1	309.5	95.0	41.6	44.7	1 252.6	581.2	476.7	801	570
Yuba City, CA	155.9	5.0	19.3	92.1	37.4	18.8	16.6	406.0	247.5	87.4	627	506
Yuma, AZ	206.5	27.3	10.8	54.2	25.3	14.0	18.1	336.4	182.6	93.8	721	481

1. October 1, 1998 to September 30, 1999.   2. State totals may include programs not allocated by county.   3. Based on the resident population estimated as of July 1 of the year shown.

Area Name	Local government finances, 1997 (cont'd)									Government employment, 1999			Presidential election, 2000[2]		
	Direct general expenditure							Debt outstanding					Percent of vote cast —		
			Percent of total for —												
	Total (mil dol)	Per capita[1] (dollars)	Education	Health and hospitals	Police protection	Public welfare	High-ways	Total (mil dol)	Per capita[1] (dollars)	Federal civilian	Federal military	State and local	Demo-cratic	Republi-can	All other
	183	184	185	186	187	188	189	190	191	192	193	194	195	196	197
Tucson, AZ........................	2 026.7	2 598	36.8	5.1	5.5	7.0	3.9	2 077.0	2 662	8 835	7 512	56 154	51.3	43.3	5.3
Tulsa, OK........................	1 522.5	1 992	45.5	2.5	6.0	0.0	3.5	2 364.7	3 094	5 033	3 968	37 116	38.2	60.4	1.4
Tuscaloosa, AL	431.2	2 682	35.6	32.7	3.9	0.0	4.1	333.6	2 075	1 454	1 001	18 678	40.9	56.6	2.5
Tyler, TX	294.7	1 768	59.4	7.8	5.1	1.8	3.3	248.4	1 490	991	449	11 027	27.2	71.5	1.4
Utica-Rome, NY	1 056.5	3 535	46.1	2.4	2.6	11.2	5.6	513.7	1 719	2 321	706	25 044	45.4	49.9	4.7
Victoria, TX	239.4	2 918	38.5	31.9	5.6	0.0	3.0	142.9	1 742	233	217	6 171	29.8	68.5	1.6
Visalia-Tulare-Porterville, CA	1 436.4	4 067	38.3	20.1	3.0	12.0	1.5	565.2	1 600	1 244	689	25 325	36.7	60.2	3.0
Waco, TX	591.5	2 914	40.6	3.6	4.2	0.2	3.0	2 887.4	14 225	3 084	573	12 032	34.1	63.9	2.0
Washington-Baltimore, DC-MD-VA-WV........................	21 614.3	2 999	40.2	4.4	5.7	7.1	3.5	23 084.2	3 203	416 563	107 129	434 898	56.4	40.0	3.5
Baltimore, MD..................	5 977.3	2 415	48.0	2.4	6.7	0.5	4.8	5 738.6	2 318	69 830	26 323	165 796	53.9	42.6	3.4
Hagerstown, MD..............	234.3	1 828	58.6	0.8	3.9	0.3	4.8	230.5	1 799	662	514	7 130	38.4	58.9	2.8
Washington, DC-MD-VA-WV	15 402.7	3 346	36.9	5.2	5.3	9.8	3.0	17 115.1	3 718	346 071	80 292	261 972	58.1	38.3	3.6
Waterloo-Cedar Falls, IA	380.5	3 131	44.8	7.7	4.1	4.2	7.8	232.1	1 910	563	578	11 065	54.7	42.6	2.8
Wausau, WI	399.6	3 264	46.8	13.0	3.7	3.1	9.5	225.0	1 838	529	438	6 734	45.5	49.5	5.1
West Palm Beach-Boca Raton, FL	3 052.6	2 997	32.4	4.1	8.0	0.7	3.8	3 439.3	3 377	5 519	2 379	52 139	62.3	35.3	2.4
Wheeling, WV-OH................	284.2	1 843	49.8	4.9	4.4	3.2	4.0	481.4	3 123	732	621	9 580	48.1	47.2	4.7
Wichita Falls, TX	243.4	1 775	51.9	4.1	5.9	0.6	4.2	142.8	1 042	2 589	8 594	9 627	32.3	65.8	1.8
Wichita, KS	1 190.9	2 245	44.2	2.6	5.1	1.2	8.5	1 691.6	3 189	4 751	5 277	29 817	37.3	58.2	4.5
Williamsport, PA................	245.0	2 070	56.5	0.1	2.3	3.2	4.7	326.2	2 755	646	394	5 572	34.0	62.8	3.2
Wilmington, NC	702.2	3 288	29.8	36.3	3.6	4.8	1.2	362.3	1 696	1 199	897	17 394	44.6	54.6	0.9
Yakima, WA	560.2	2 566	57.3	1.2	5.2	0.0	5.8	307.9	1 410	1 439	876	12 310	38.0	58.7	3.4
York, PA	690.5	1 864	50.9	3.9	3.7	4.5	3.5	964.9	2 604	3 679	1 707	12 651	36.0	60.8	3.2
Youngstown-Warren, OH......	1 219.3	2 049	49.5	5.5	6.1	6.1	4.7	504.0	847	2 658	1 525	31 105	57.9	38.0	4.1
Yuba City, CA	410.8	2 949	46.3	4.4	3.9	12.4	3.8	149.4	1 072	1 462	3 411	8 438	32.7	63.7	3.6
Yuma, AZ	334.0	2 569	46.4	1.4	6.7	2.1	7.3	266.5	2 049	2 342	4 181	6 743	42.1	54.8	3.1

1. Based on the resident population estimated as of July 1 of the year shown.   2. Data subject to copyright.

TABLE D:

Cities of 25,000 or More

(For explanation of symbols, see page xii)

Page

Table D. Cities — Land Area and Population

STATE Place code	City	Land area, 2000[1] (sq km)	Total persons	Rank	Per square kilometer	Total persons 1990	Percent change 1990–2000	Total persons 1980	Percent change 1980–1990	White	Black	Am. Indian, Alaska Native	Asian and Pacific Islander	Other race	His-panic[2]	Non-His-panic White
		1	2	3	4	5	6	7	8	9	10	11	12	13	14	15
01 00000	ALABAMA	131 426.4	4 447 100	X	33.8	4 040 389	10.1	3 894 025	3.8	72.0	26.3	1.0	1.0	0.9	1.7	70.3
01 03076	Auburn	101.3	42 987	712	424.4	33 830	27.1	28 471	18.8	79.0	17.1	0.6	3.8	0.8	1.5	77.2
01 05980	Bessemer	105.4	29 672	1 050	281.5	33 581	-11.6	31 729	5.8	29.4	70.0	0.6	0.4	0.5	1.1	28.5
01 07000	Birmingham	388.3	242 820	71	625.3	265 347	-8.5	284 413	-6.7	24.6	74.0	0.5	1.1	0.9	1.6	23.5
01 20104	Decatur	138.3	53 929	551	389.9	49 917	8.0	42 002	18.8	76.6	20.0	1.1	1.1	2.6	5.6	72.6
01 21184	Dothan	224.3	57 737	493	257.4	54 131	6.6	48 750	11.1	68.1	30.5	0.6	1.1	0.7	1.3	66.7
01 26896	Florence	64.6	36 264	858	561.4	36 426	-0.4	37 029	-1.6	79.3	19.5	0.6	0.9	0.8	1.3	77.7
01 28696	Gadsden	93.2	38 978	797	418.2	42 523	-8.3	47 565	-10.6	63.6	34.5	0.7	0.9	1.5	2.7	61.6
01 35800	Homewood	21.5	25 043	1 236	1 164.8	23 644	5.9	21 412	10.4	80.7	15.6	0.5	3.0	1.4	2.8	78.1
01 35896	Hoover	111.7	62 742	439	561.7	39 988	56.9	19 792	102.1	88.5	7.0	0.4	3.4	1.9	3.8	85.5
01 37000	Huntsville	450.8	158 216	127	351.0	159 880	-1.0	142 513	12.2	65.9	30.9	1.3	2.8	1.0	2.0	63.4
01 45784	Madison	60.0	29 329	1 063	488.8	14 792	98.3	NA	NA	81.8	13.4	1.4	4.3	1.1	2.3	78.6
01 50000	Mobile	305.4	198 915	92	651.3	199 973	1.4	200 396	-2.1	51.1	46.7	0.6	1.8	0.8	1.4	49.8
01 51000	Montgomery	402.4	201 568	87	500.9	190 350	5.9	177 857	7.0	48.4	50.1	0.5	1.5	0.6	1.2	47.1
01 59472	Phenix City	63.7	28 265	1 094	443.7	25 311	11.7	26 941	-6.1	53.5	45.3	0.5	0.9	0.8	1.5	52.3
01 62496	Prichard	65.8	28 633	1 080	435.2	34 320	-16.6	39 518	-13.2	14.6	85.1	0.7	0.4	0.2	0.6	14.1
01 77256	Tuscaloosa	145.7	77 906	338	534.7	77 866	0.2	75 211	3.4	54.8	43.1	0.4	1.9	0.9	1.4	53.5
02 00000	ALASKA	1 481 346.9	626 932	X	0.4	550 043	14.0	401 851	36.9	74.0	4.3	19.0	6.1	2.4	4.1	67.6
02 03000	Anchorage	4 395.8	260 283	65	59.2	226 338	15.0	174 431	29.8	77.2	7.2	10.4	8.5	3.3	5.7	69.9
02 24230	Fairbanks	82.5	30 224	1 027	366.4	30 843	-2.0	22 645	36.2	72.3	12.9	13.3	5.0	3.6	6.1	64.2
02 36400	Juneau	7 036.1	30 711	1 016	4.4	26 751	14.8	19 528	37.0	80.5	1.4	16.6	7.4	1.8	3.4	73.3
04 00000	ARIZONA	294 312.2	5 130 632	X	17.4	3 665 339	40.0	2 716 546	34.9	77.9	3.6	5.7	2.6	13.2	25.3	63.8
04 02830	Apache Junction	88.7	31 814	977	358.7	18 092	75.8	NA	NA	94.5	0.8	1.8	1.1	3.9	8.8	87.9
04 04720	Avondale	106.9	35 883	868	335.7	17 595	103.9	NA	NA	66.6	5.9	2.0	2.9	26.7	46.2	44.5
04 08220	Bullhead City	117.1	33 769	932	288.4	21 951	53.8	10 364	111.8	88.1	1.2	2.1	1.6	9.8	20.2	75.4
04 10530	Casa Grande	124.8	25 224	1 228	202.1	19 076	32.2	NA	NA	67.8	4.9	6.0	1.6	23.4	39.1	50.4
04 12000	Chandler	149.9	176 581	114	1 178.0	89 862	96.5	29 720	202.4	79.7	4.1	1.8	5.4	12.3	21.0	68.6
04 23620	Flagstaff	164.7	52 894	563	321.2	45 857	15.3	34 743	32.0	80.4	2.2	11.3	1.9	7.3	16.1	69.5
04 27400	Gilbert	111.3	109 697	204	985.6	29 149	276.3	NA	NA	88.2	3.0	1.1	4.7	6.0	11.9	79.9
04 27820	Glendale	144.2	218 812	80	1 517.4	147 070	48.0	97 172	52.2	78.5	5.5	2.1	3.8	13.8	24.8	64.7
04 39370	Lake Havasu City	111.5	41 938	730	376.1	24 363	72.1	NA	NA	95.7	0.4	1.3	1.1	3.0	7.9	89.5
04 46000	Mesa	323.7	396 375	42	1 224.5	289 199	37.1	152 453	89.7	84.1	3.1	2.3	2.4	11.1	19.7	73.2
04 51600	Oro Valley town	82.4	29 700	1 047	360.4	8 627	244.3	NA	NA	94.5	1.4	0.7	2.6	2.4	7.5	88.2
04 54050	Peoria	358.0	108 364	210	302.7	51 080	113.8	12 251	313.6	87.1	3.3	1.2	2.9	8.2	15.4	77.9
04 55000	Phoenix	1 229.9	1 321 045	6	1 074.1	988 015	34.2	789 704	24.6	73.8	5.8	2.7	2.8	18.4	34.1	55.8
04 57380	Prescott	96.0	33 938	923	353.5	26 592	27.6	20 055	32.6	94.4	0.7	2.0	1.4	3.3	8.2	88.2
04 65000	Scottsdale	477.1	202 705	86	424.9	130 099	55.8	88 412	47.1	93.6	1.5	1.0	2.7	2.9	7.0	88.0
04 66820	Sierra Vista	397.5	37 775	824	95.0	32 983	14.5	24 937	32.3	77.3	12.5	1.9	6.3	7.5	15.8	65.4
04 71510	Surprise city	180.0	30 848	1 013	171.4	7 122	333.1	NA	NA	87.8	3.0	0.8	1.5	8.9	23.3	71.8
04 73000	Tempe	103.8	158 625	126	1 528.2	141 993	11.7	106 743	33.0	80.2	4.4	2.7	6.1	10.2	17.9	69.7
04 77000	Tucson	504.2	486 699	30	965.3	415 444	18.3	330 537	24.5	73.3	5.1	3.2	3.5	19.0	35.7	54.2
04 85540	Yuma	276.2	77 515	340	280.6	56 966	36.1	42 433	34.2	71.7	3.8	2.2	2.4	23.9	45.7	47.5
05 00000	ARKANSAS	134 855.9	2 673 400	X	19.8	2 350 624	13.7	2 286 357	2.8	81.2	16.0	1.4	1.1	1.8	3.2	78.6
05 15190	Conway	90.8	43 167	708	475.4	26 481	63.0	20 375	30.0	85.1	12.5	0.7	1.6	1.3	2.3	83.0
05 23290	Fayetteville	112.5	58 047	489	516.0	42 247	37.4	36 608	15.4	88.6	5.8	2.3	3.5	2.5	4.9	84.0
05 24550	Fort Smith	130.4	80 268	321	615.6	72 798	10.3	71 626	1.6	79.6	9.4	3.2	5.2	5.8	8.8	74.0
05 33400	Hot Springs	85.2	35 750	872	419.6	33 095	10.1	35 781	-9.3	80.5	17.5	1.5	1.1	1.3	3.8	76.5
05 34750	Jacksonville	68.3	29 916	1 038	438.0	29 101	2.8	NA	NA	71.0	25.9	1.1	3.0	1.7	3.4	67.2
05 35710	Jonesboro	206.3	55 515	530	269.1	46 535	19.3	31 530	47.6	86.4	11.6	0.8	1.2	1.3	2.3	84.2
05 41000	Little Rock	301.0	183 133	110	608.4	175 727	4.2	158 461	10.9	56.1	41.0	0.7	2.0	1.6	2.7	54.0
05 50450	North Little Rock	116.1	60 433	459	520.5	61 829	-2.3	64 288	-3.8	63.5	34.6	1.0	0.9	1.4	2.4	61.5
05 55310	Pine Bluff	118.1	55 085	535	466.4	57 140	-3.6	56 636	0.9	32.8	66.3	0.5	1.0	0.3	0.8	32.0
05 60410	Rogers	86.8	38 829	801	447.3	24 692	57.3	17 429	41.7	87.4	0.7	1.7	1.8	10.3	19.3	76.9
05 66080	Springdale	81.1	45 798	665	564.7	29 945	52.9	23 440	27.8	83.4	1.1	1.8	4.0	12.2	19.7	74.1
05 68810	Texarkana	82.5	26 448	1 168	320.6	22 631	16.9	21 459	5.5	67.2	31.5	1.2	0.6	1.0	1.8	65.0
05 74540	West Memphis	68.6	27 666	1 118	403.3	28 259	-2.1	28 138	0.4	42.6	56.3	0.5	0.7	0.6	1.0	41.8
06 00000	CALIFORNIA	403 932.8	33 871 648	X	83.9	29 785 857	13.8	23 667 765	25.7	63.4	7.4	1.9	13.0	19.4	32.4	46.7
06 00562	Alameda	28.0	72 259	368	2 580.7	73 979	-2.3	63 852	15.9	61.9	7.5	1.6	30.1	5.5	9.3	52.5
06 00884	Alhambra	19.7	85 804	293	4 355.5	82 087	4.5	64 615	27.0	33.0	2.1	1.2	49.1	18.8	35.5	13.8
06 02000	Anaheim	126.8	328 014	55	2 586.9	266 406	23.1	219 311	21.5	59.0	3.2	1.5	13.9	27.6	46.8	35.9
06 02252	Antioch	69.8	90 532	271	1 297.0	62 195	45.6	42 683	45.7	71.2	11.1	2.3	10.5	12.5	22.1	55.9
06 02364	Apple Valley	189.9	54 239	547	285.6	46 079	17.7	14 305	222.1	80.3	8.8	2.3	3.4	9.9	18.6	67.7
06 02462	Arcadia	28.4	53 054	558	1 868.1	48 284	9.9	45 994	5.0	47.9	1.5	0.7	47.7	5.9	10.6	40.1
06 03064	Atascadero	69.2	26 411	1 170	381.7	23 138	14.1	16 232	42.5	91.9	2.8	2.2	2.3	4.4	10.5	82.7
06 03386	Azusa	23.1	44 712	687	1 935.6	41 203	8.5	29 380	40.2	57.2	4.4	2.1	7.7	34.7	63.8	24.2
06 03526	Bakersfield	292.9	247 057	69	843.5	176 264	40.2	105 611	66.9	65.5	10.0	2.5	5.6	21.1	32.5	51.1

1. Dry land or land partially or temporarily covered by water.   2. Hispanic persons may be of any race.

Table D. Cities — **Population and Households**

City	Population characteristics, 2000 (cont'd)										Households, 2000				
	Age of population (percent)													Percent	
	Under 5 years	5 to 17 years	18 to 24 years	25 to 34 years	35 to 44 years	45 to 54 years	55 to 64 years	65 to 74 years	75 years and over	Percent female	Number	Percent change, 1990–2000	Persons per household	Female family householder[1]	One-person
	16	17	18	19	20	21	22	23	24	25	26	27	28	29	30
ALABAMA	6.7	18.6	9.9	13.6	15.4	13.5	9.3	7.1	5.9	51.7	1 737 080	15.3	2.49	14.2	26.1
Auburn	4.1	11.2	44.6	12.7	9.2	7.4	4.3	3.2	3.2	50.1	18 421	37.0	2.12	7.7	36.8
Bessemer	7.7	19.1	9.6	12.3	13.7	12.6	8.5	8.2	8.2	54.7	11 537	-8.3	2.52	29.2	29.0
Birmingham	6.8	18.2	11.1	14.9	15.1	12.9	7.5	6.7	6.7	53.9	98 782	-6.3	2.37	24.6	34.4
Decatur	6.8	18.6	8.8	13.7	15.9	13.8	9.3	7.0	6.1	52.0	21 824	14.1	2.43	13.4	28.9
Dothan	6.9	18.6	8.4	12.9	15.3	14.0	9.4	7.6	6.9	53.1	23 685	14.5	2.39	15.4	28.4
Florence	5.8	15.7	13.7	12.4	13.2	12.5	9.2	8.7	8.8	54.3	15 820	6.1	2.20	14.0	33.8
Gadsden	6.6	16.5	9.5	12.7	12.6	12.8	9.2	9.7	10.4	54.0	16 456	-6.0	2.28	18.1	33.9
Homewood	6.3	14.0	17.8	19.6	14.3	11.5	5.8	4.5	6.1	53.8	10 688	4.9	2.16	11.4	36.2
Hoover	6.6	18.2	7.9	15.3	17.4	15.3	8.4	5.8	5.1	51.3	25 191	56.8	2.47	7.2	25.9
Huntsville	6.2	17.0	10.7	13.5	15.9	13.3	10.1	7.7	5.7	51.9	66 742	5.8	2.29	13.7	32.3
Madison	7.8	22.5	6.8	13.9	21.9	14.5	7.1	3.4	2.1	50.6	11 143	86.7	2.61	9.6	23.9
Mobile	7.3	19.2	10.8	13.6	14.4	12.7	8.3	6.9	6.8	53.2	78 480	4.0	2.46	19.9	30.2
Montgomery	7.1	18.9	12.1	14.7	15.0	12.6	7.7	6.1	5.7	53.1	78 384	12.0	2.44	19.1	30.1
Phenix City	7.1	19.2	9.6	14.0	14.7	12.4	8.8	8.0	6.3	53.7	11 517	18.2	2.40	22.1	30.4
Prichard	7.8	23.6	11.4	10.3	14.3	12.7	8.3	6.0	5.5	54.3	9 841	-11.5	2.84	36.0	23.4
Tuscaloosa	5.7	14.1	24.5	13.5	11.9	11.5	6.9	6.3	5.5	52.4	31 381	6.5	2.22	15.7	35.2
ALASKA	7.6	22.8	9.1	14.3	18.2	15.1	7.1	3.6	2.1	48.3	221 600	17.3	2.74	10.8	23.5
Anchorage	7.7	21.5	9.6	15.4	18.5	14.9	7.0	3.4	2.1	49.4	94 822	14.7	2.67	11.5	23.4
Fairbanks	9.6	19.8	14.7	18.5	14.4	10.8	5.6	3.6	3.0	48.7	11 075	1.7	2.56	12.6	27.4
Juneau	6.5	20.9	8.1	14.0	18.8	18.0	7.7	3.5	2.6	49.6	11 543	16.6	2.60	10.5	24.4
ARIZONA	7.5	19.2	10.0	14.5	15.0	12.2	8.6	7.1	5.9	50.1	1 901 327	38.9	2.64	11.1	24.8
Apache Junction	6.3	14.2	6.9	11.6	12.1	11.0	12.6	14.4	10.9	51.1	13 775	78.8	2.29	8.5	27.2
Avondale	9.8	24.5	9.7	16.8	16.2	11.5	6.2	3.2	2.1	49.4	10 640	116.4	3.36	12.7	12.9
Bullhead City	6.4	16.1	7.3	11.3	13.2	13.0	13.6	11.5	7.7	50.3	13 909	57.6	2.42	11.1	25.3
Casa Grande	8.7	22.2	9.3	13.1	13.3	11.0	8.6	8.2	5.6	50.7	8 920	37.3	2.80	15.1	21.7
Chandler	9.1	20.7	8.6	19.0	19.0	11.8	6.0	3.4	2.4	50.1	62 377	98.1	2.82	10.5	19.3
Flagstaff	6.7	17.6	21.7	16.4	14.1	12.2	6.1	3.1	2.2	50.4	19 306	33.9	2.59	11.6	23.2
Gilbert	10.3	23.9	7.4	18.4	19.4	11.7	5.2	2.4	1.4	50.3	35 405	277.4	3.10	8.3	12.7
Glendale	8.5	21.6	10.8	15.5	16.4	12.7	7.1	4.0	3.4	50.1	75 700	41.0	2.85	12.8	21.3
Lake Havasu City	4.7	14.8	5.7	8.8	12.8	12.7	15.0	15.2	10.3	50.8	17 911	80.6	2.32	7.7	22.8
Mesa	8.2	19.1	11.2	15.5	14.2	11.1	7.3	6.7	6.6	50.5	146 643	36.0	2.68	10.6	24.2
Oro Valley town	5.0	16.5	4.5	8.3	15.3	14.8	12.9	14.3	8.4	51.5	12 249	330.4	2.41	4.9	19.4
Peoria	7.4	21.0	6.7	13.9	16.8	11.9	8.0	6.9	7.5	52.0	39 184	114.7	2.73	9.1	20.5
Phoenix	8.7	20.3	10.9	17.2	16.0	11.9	6.9	4.4	3.7	49.1	465 834	25.9	2.79	12.9	25.4
Prescott	3.7	12.1	11.2	8.1	10.8	13.9	13.4	13.8	13.0	50.8	15 098	31.5	2.11	7.9	32.1
Scottsdale	5.2	14.2	6.6	14.3	16.1	15.1	11.9	9.2	7.5	51.8	90 669	57.5	2.22	7.5	30.8
Sierra Vista	7.7	18.1	13.0	15.4	13.8	11.0	8.9	7.1	5.0	49.8	14 196	21.6	2.48	10.4	25.1
Surprise city	7.3	12.6	7.0	13.6	8.8	8.9	16.4	17.1	8.4	50.9	12 484	453.9	2.46	5.4	17.9
Tempe	5.7	14.1	21.3	19.4	13.8	11.8	6.7	3.9	3.3	48.3	63 602	14.5	2.41	9.7	28.5
Tucson	7.2	17.3	13.8	15.7	14.9	11.8	7.3	6.0	5.9	51.0	192 891	18.6	2.42	13.8	32.3
Yuma	8.7	20.9	11.9	13.5	13.6	10.1	7.4	7.4	6.5	50.2	26 649	38.2	2.79	13.1	21.7
ARKANSAS	6.8	18.7	9.8	13.2	14.9	13.1	9.6	7.4	6.6	51.2	1 042 696	17.0	2.49	12.1	25.6
Conway	6.9	16.4	22.4	15.7	13.5	10.3	5.8	4.3	4.7	52.5	16 039	70.0	2.44	11.2	26.1
Fayetteville	6.5	13.4	25.7	17.3	12.6	10.5	5.3	4.1	4.6	49.3	23 798	40.9	2.21	9.6	34.0
Fort Smith	7.6	17.8	9.8	14.3	15.0	13.1	8.7	6.7	7.0	51.5	32 398	9.3	2.42	12.3	30.7
Hot Springs	5.9	14.3	8.2	11.4	13.9	12.9	10.1	10.7	12.6	53.1	16 096	11.1	2.12	12.4	38.4
Jacksonville	9.5	19.5	12.8	17.7	15.6	10.6	7.1	4.7	2.7	49.9	10 890	10.5	2.64	14.6	22.0
Jonesboro	6.7	16.2	16.6	14.5	13.6	12.5	8.1	6.2	5.6	52.1	22 219	23.6	2.38	12.2	27.5
Little Rock	7.1	17.6	10.0	16.1	15.6	14.1	7.9	5.7	5.9	52.9	77 352	6.6	2.30	16.1	33.8
North Little Rock	7.1	18.3	9.0	13.4	14.9	13.8	8.7	7.3	7.3	53.3	25 542	2.2	2.35	17.6	32.0
Pine Bluff	7.4	20.1	12.2	12.7	14.2	12.0	7.7	6.6	7.1	52.7	19 956	-4.4	2.57	23.8	29.2
Rogers	8.9	20.6	9.0	15.9	15.6	11.1	7.2	5.7	6.1	51.2	14 005	44.3	2.74	10.1	22.2
Springdale	9.3	19.7	10.7	16.3	15.1	11.1	7.6	5.2	5.0	50.4	16 149	41.3	2.80	10.5	22.0
Texarkana	7.6	18.3	10.1	14.2	14.3	12.8	8.7	6.9	7.1	52.1	10 384	19.4	2.45	18.7	28.3
West Memphis	8.5	23.0	9.8	13.7	14.5	11.9	8.1	5.4	5.0	53.6	10 051	1.7	2.70	25.1	24.8
CALIFORNIA	7.3	20.0	9.9	15.4	16.2	12.8	7.7	5.6	5.0	50.2	11 502 870	10.8	2.87	12.6	23.5
Alameda	5.6	15.9	7.0	15.3	18.2	15.8	8.8	6.5	6.8	52.0	30 226	3.9	2.35	11.4	32.2
Alhambra	6.2	16.1	9.7	18.0	16.0	12.9	7.9	6.4	6.8	52.9	29 111	3.1	2.88	16.4	22.5
Anaheim	9.2	21.0	10.5	17.8	15.7	11.0	6.7	4.4	3.8	50.0	96 969	10.7	3.34	13.1	18.1
Antioch	8.6	23.6	8.2	14.0	18.4	13.0	6.7	4.1	3.3	51.0	29 338	37.1	3.07	13.5	15.9
Apple Valley	7.1	24.4	7.8	10.0	15.1	12.7	9.0	7.9	5.9	51.6	18 557	19.0	2.90	14.2	18.0
Arcadia	4.6	18.7	7.5	10.8	16.4	16.3	10.3	7.5	8.0	53.0	19 149	4.3	2.74	11.9	22.3
Atascadero	5.4	20.3	8.3	10.9	17.8	17.1	8.7	6.1	5.4	48.5	9 531	12.3	2.62	11.4	22.0
Azusa	9.3	21.6	15.5	17.2	14.2	9.5	5.8	3.9	3.0	50.6	12 549	-0.8	3.41	17.1	18.7
Bakersfield	8.8	23.9	10.1	14.4	15.5	12.0	6.6	4.5	4.2	51.4	83 441	33.6	2.92	15.5	21.5

1. No spouse present.

City	Persons in group quarters, 2000 Total	Institutional Total	Persons in nursing homes	Non-Institutional[1]	Serious crimes known to police, 2000[2] Total Number	Rate[3]	Rate[3] Violent	Property	Education, 1990 School enrollment Public	Private	Attainment[4] (percent) High school graduate or more	Bachelor's degree or more	Money income, 1989 Households Per capita (dollars)[5]	Median Dollars	Percent change, 1979–1989 (constant 1989 dollars)
	31	32	33	34	35	36	37	38	39	40	41	42	43	44	45
ALABAMA	114 720	65 363	26 697	49 357	202 159	4 546	486	4 060	940 143	116 259	66.9	15.7	11 486	23 597	3.0
Auburn	3 855	177	104	3 678	2 049	4 767	291	4 476	19 968	934	88.1	50.1	10 278	12 931	-11.4
Bessemer	629	594	305	35	3 930	13 245	1 506	11 738	7 261	808	57.8	7.2	8 433	16 331	-15.6
Birmingham	8 852	3 902	1 895	4 950	20 749	8 545	1 214	7 331	58 988	9 258	69.3	16.2	10 127	19 193	-4.2
Decatur	923	621	299	302	NA	NA	NA	NA	10 803	1 268	74.0	20.5	14 374	30 005	4.5
Dothan	1 127	1 030	556	97	3 144	5 445	537	4 908	12 498	1 624	70.5	19.3	13 047	25 790	2.4
Florence	1 477	736	474	741	1 811	4 994	378	4 616	8 578	1 148	70.2	22.6	11 854	21 459	-13.6
Gadsden	1 430	878	454	552	NA	NA	NA	NA	8 305	1 072	61.5	10.7	10 772	19 187	-2.0
Homewood	1 937	134	0	1 803	1 807	7 216	415	6 800	5 358	1 337	90.6	42.0	17 582	30 516	0.0
Hoover	491	454	440	37	2 017	3 215	177	3 038	8 417	2 259	94.2	45.8	21 961	44 747	2.8
Huntsville	5 575	1 666	736	3 909	12 239	7 736	786	6 949	38 355	6 335	82.0	33.3	16 204	32 295	8.0
Madison	254	208	179	46	871	2 970	201	2 769	3 125	488	92.4	49.0	19 743	42 911	NA
Mobile	6 180	2 727	1 512	3 453	17 614	6 913	587	6 326	42 297	11 800	74.8	21.4	12 509	22 446	-8.2
Montgomery	10 187	2 870	1 134	7 317	16 261	8 067	775	7 292	45 032	9 062	75.7	24.6	12 755	26 311	5.4
Phenix City	674	609	314	65	1 153	4 079	495	3 584	5 340	658	59.1	10.6	9 954	20 478	10.7
Prichard	733	423	180	310	3 437	12 004	1 757	10 247	10 087	1 096	53.7	5.1	5 820	11 576	-18.3
Tuscaloosa	8 102	1 934	704	6 168	11 210	14 389	1 159	13 230	27 482	2 546	72.1	27.3	11 469	19 568	1.2
ALASKA	19 349	4 824	803	14 525	26 641	4 249	567	3 683	141 933	14 424	86.6	23.0	17 610	41 408	-2.8
Anchorage	7 014	1 915	291	5 099	12 866	4 943	586	4 358	56 060	7 297	90.4	26.9	19 620	43 946	-4.2
Fairbanks	1 899	327	81	1 572	1 680	5 558	682	4 877	6 876	880	86.2	18.3	14 665	32 033	-9.8
Juneau	678	229	39	449	NA	NA	NA	NA	6 825	813	89.9	30.7	19 920	47 924	-7.3
ARIZONA	109 850	63 768	13 607	46 082	299 092	5 830	532	5 298	896 427	94 695	78.7	20.3	13 461	27 540	-0.1
Apache Junction	223	0	0	223	1 428	4 489	255	4 234	3 238	257	70.1	7.2	9 946	19 686	NA
Avondale	146	146	121	0	2 056	5 730	429	5 301	4 263	215	57.1	9.4	8 990	24 292	NA
Bullhead City	117	79	77	38	1 734	5 135	589	4 546	3 226	232	72.4	10.1	12 486	24 814	22.2
Casa Grande	274	123	123	151	2 657	10 534	753	9 780	5 324	289	72.0	14.2	11 388	25 926	NA
Chandler	782	478	392	304	8 301	4 701	252	4 449	23 900	2 395	85.8	26.2	14 720	38 124	27.7
Flagstaff	2 853	177	73	2 676	4 844	9 158	605	8 553	20 097	1 083	86.9	32.7	11 517	28 382	0.4
Gilbert	66	54	54	12	3 766	3 433	112	3 321	9 173	762	90.8	29.0	14 665	41 081	NA
Glendale	2 857	1 014	987	1 843	14 521	6 636	598	6 039	38 015	5 142	82.6	17.7	13 524	31 665	-0.2
Lake Havasu City	321	236	233	85	1 375	3 279	160	3 119	4 278	272	79.0	13.3	14 418	28 826	NA
Mesa	3 949	2 189	1 705	1 760	25 525	6 440	604	5 836	74 891	7 088	84.8	21.0	13 506	30 273	1.2
Oro Valley town	159	27	27	132	473	1 593	51	1 542	NA	NA	NA	NA	NA	NA	NA
Peoria	1 514	873	855	641	4 950	4 568	245	4 323	11 443	1 009	83.5	16.9	14 059	34 205	33.2
Phoenix	22 468	12 948	1 674	9 520	97 498	7 380	738	6 642	221 676	30 872	78.7	19.9	14 096	29 291	0.3
Prescott	2 044	862	733	1 182	1 857	5 472	377	5 095	5 012	1 278	83.3	23.5	13 851	22 517	-4.6
Scottsdale	1 677	479	409	1 198	9 303	4 589	282	4 308	24 551	4 531	90.8	34.5	23 482	39 037	4.8
Sierra Vista	2 575	259	259	2 316	1 652	4 373	254	4 119	8 273	684	90.1	23.8	13 449	29 590	5.5
Surprise city	124	66	54	58	893	2 895	292	2 603	NA	NA	NA	NA	NA	NA	NA
Tempe	5 242	406	394	4 836	15 208	9 587	617	8 971	47 375	4 546	89.9	36.8	15 530	31 885	-4.1
Tucson	19 182	7 942	1 202	11 240	44 525	9 148	933	8 215	108 663	11 562	78.6	20.7	11 184	21 748	-7.9
Yuma	3 144	1 065	581	2 079	5 226	3 854	487	3 367	13 405	989	73.6	15.6	11 529	26 753	1.2
ARKANSAS	73 908	45 152	21 379	28 756	110 019	4 115	445	3 670	530 045	52 360	66.3	13.3	10 520	21 147	3.3
Conway	4 037	533	382	3 504	2 222	5 147	185	4 962	8 083	1 696	76.3	27.4	10 457	22 291	-1.9
Fayetteville	5 350	1 420	823	3 930	2 893	4 984	346	4 638	15 401	795	84.3	36.0	12 184	21 202	10.4
Fort Smith	1 990	1 632	618	358	7 174	8 938	749	8 189	14 584	2 112	73.3	16.7	12 994	23 835	2.4
Hot Springs	1 586	1 086	704	500	4 068	11 939	1 010	10 369	5 569	639	64.4	13.2	11 461	15 708	-6.5
Jacksonville	1 204	41	40	1 163	1 557	5 205	582	4 623	6 929	884	82.9	12.2	10 337	25 009	2.9
Jonesboro	2 575	712	480	1 863	3 122	5 624	346	5 278	13 083	783	73.3	21.2	12 360	23 318	1.9
Little Rock	4 915	2 774	1 026	2 141	17 551	9 584	1 030	8 553	35 746	10 211	82.0	30.3	15 307	26 889	1.6
North Little Rock	520	403	403	117	5 655	9 357	731	8 626	12 403	1 968	73.0	17.5	12 390	23 958	-5.9
Pine Bluff	3 821	2 644	745	1 177	6 301	11 439	2 109	9 329	15 274	1 012	65.5	16.6	9 530	19 143	-5.3
Rogers	476	420	409	56	1 450	3 734	203	3 531	4 946	457	77.6	15.1	12 779	26 198	6.2
Springdale	574	509	286	65	1 624	3 546	231	3 315	6 261	555	70.1	13.7	11 837	25 376	0.7
Texarkana	1 057	902	287	155	1 963	7 422	817	6 605	5 224	378	67.4	12.4	9 990	19 016	-6.3
West Memphis	514	462	211	52	1 585	5 729	1 164	4 565	6 755	658	62.5	10.8	10 009	22 052	-2.3
CALIFORNIA	819 754	413 656	120 724	406 098	1 266 714	3 740	622	3 118	7 177 045	1 123 001	76.2	23.4	16 409	35 798	17.1
Alameda	1 077	469	331	608	2 835	3 923	418	3 505	14 112	2 970	88.1	31.3	19 833	38 122	25.7
Alhambra	1 923	971	931	952	2 120	2 471	295	2 176	20 630	3 970	72.1	22.9	13 436	31 368	15.0
Anaheim	3 796	1 290	1 215	2 506	9 909	3 021	431	2 590	62 255	8 608	75.4	18.8	15 746	39 620	18.0
Antioch	416	262	252	154	2 806	3 099	581	2 518	16 086	1 775	82.6	14.9	15 153	40 936	16.9
Apple Valley	363	176	136	187	1 911	3 523	343	3 180	11 167	1 479	80.1	14.9	14 643	34 050	-1.9
Arcadia	581	419	419	162	1 500	2 827	262	2 565	10 797	2 325	88.9	36.4	25 441	47 347	13.5
Atascadero	1 466	1 282	65	184	771	2 919	507	2 412	5 767	718	86.3	20.6	14 639	35 140	13.2
Azusa	1 949	69	45	1 880	1 213	2 713	324	2 389	10 093	2 518	62.7	12.1	11 038	31 889	15.7
Bakersfield	3 813	2 018	1 125	1 795	10 279	4 161	290	3 871	46 179	4 892	77.8	19.6	14 183	32 154	5.0

1. Persons in emergency shelters and persons visible in street locations. 2. Data for serious crimes have not been adjusted for underreporting. This may affect comparability between geographic areas and over time. 3. Per 100,000 population estimated by the FBI. 4. Persons 25 years old and older. 5. Based on population enumerated as of April 1, 1990.

Table D. Cities — Income, Poverty, and Housing

City	Money income, 1989 (cont'd) Households (cont'd) Percent with $100,000 or more	Percent below poverty, 1989 Persons Total	Persons Percent change in rate, 1979–1989	Families Total	Housing units, 2000 Total	Percent change, 1990–2000	Vacant units Vacant units for sale or rent[1]	For seasonal use (percent)	Home owner vacancy rate	Renter vacancy rate	Occupied units Total	Percent owner occupied	Percent renter occupied	Average size owner occupied	Average size renter occupied
	46	47	48	49	50	51	52	53	54	55	56	57	58	59	60
ALABAMA	2.3	18.3	-3.0	14.3	1 963 711	17.6	226 631	2.4	2.0	11.8	1 737 080	72.5	27.5	2.57	2.30
Auburn	2.9	39.9	18.4	14.8	20 043	36.6	1 622	0.5	3.0	8.8	18 421	40.9	59.1	2.45	1.90
Bessemer	0.7	29.7	15.1	24.3	12 790	-7.2	1 253	0.1	1.9	7.0	11 537	59.2	40.8	2.53	2.49
Birmingham	1.4	24.8	12.7	20.8	111 927	-4.9	13 145	0.3	2.7	11.6	98 782	53.7	46.3	2.49	2.23
Decatur	3.0	12.7	-4.5	10.0	23 950	16.0	2 126	0.3	2.3	12.9	21 824	63.8	36.2	2.52	2.26
Dothan	2.8	17.0	5.6	13.2	25 920	16.8	2 235	0.5	2.3	10.5	23 685	62.9	37.1	2.47	2.26
Florence	1.9	18.5	18.6	14.3	17 707	11.3	1 887	0.6	3.0	12.6	15 820	58.5	41.5	2.33	2.02
Gadsden	1.6	20.4	10.9	16.5	18 797	-1.8	2 341	0.3	3.5	10.8	16 456	63.6	36.4	2.29	2.27
Homewood	3.7	6.7	4.7	3.2	11 494	7.1	806	0.3	1.6	9.5	10 688	54.6	45.4	2.34	1.95
Hoover	9.0	3.0	-25.0	2.2	27 150	59.3	1 959	0.7	1.9	12.1	25 191	66.0	34.0	2.68	2.07
Huntsville	4.6	11.6	-9.4	8.9	73 670	8.6	6 928	0.7	2.7	12.8	66 742	61.6	38.4	2.42	2.07
Madison	5.4	4.2	NA	3.1	12 121	83.2	978	0.7	3.2	13.4	11 143	70.3	29.7	2.81	2.13
Mobile	3.1	22.4	20.4	18.4	86 187	4.1	7 707	0.5	1.7	9.1	78 480	59.3	40.7	2.55	2.32
Montgomery	2.8	18.1	-6.7	14.4	86 787	13.2	8 403	0.3	2.5	9.9	78 384	61.9	38.1	2.51	2.33
Phenix City	1.1	22.2	-10.1	18.3	13 250	22.5	1 733	0.2	3.6	15.9	11 517	52.7	47.3	2.47	2.31
Prichard	0.4	44.1	13.7	40.4	11 336	-13.0	1 495	0.2	1.7	12.6	9 841	58.4	41.6	2.81	2.87
Tuscaloosa	3.1	26.7	3.1	17.1	34 857	11.7	3 476	0.4	2.1	11.3	31 381	47.7	52.3	2.43	2.04
ALASKA	7.7	9.0	-15.9	6.8	260 978	12.2	39 378	8.2	1.9	7.8	221 600	62.5	37.5	2.89	2.49
Anchorage	9.3	7.1	-4.1	5.4	100 368	6.6	5 546	1.1	1.4	5.3	94 822	60.1	39.9	2.81	2.46
Fairbanks	3.6	10.4	-1.9	8.1	12 357	-1.4	1 282	1.0	2.4	10.0	11 075	34.9	65.1	2.62	2.53
Juneau	8.6	5.6	36.6	3.7	12 282	15.5	739	1.5	0.9	5.7	11 543	63.7	36.3	2.78	2.29
ARIZONA	3.4	15.7	19.3	11.4	2 189 189	31.9	287 862	6.5	2.1	9.2	1 901 327	68.0	32.0	2.69	2.53
Apache Junction	0.6	16.7	NA	11.8	22 771	78.5	8 996	29.8	5.3	26.7	13 775	82.1	17.9	2.27	2.38
Avondale	1.3	28.2	NA	23.9	11 419	104.7	779	0.5	2.7	12.2	10 640	77.6	22.4	3.35	3.39
Bullhead City	1.9	12.8	19.6	6.8	18 430	37.0	4 521	13.3	4.4	9.2	13 909	60.3	39.7	2.31	2.58
Casa Grande	2.6	17.4	NA	16.1	11 041	49.1	2 121	7.8	2.7	18.4	8 920	64.0	36.0	2.80	2.79
Chandler	3.2	9.7	-25.4	7.1	66 592	90.4	4 215	1.6	1.5	10.2	62 377	73.6	26.4	2.86	2.70
Flagstaff	2.6	17.2	17.0	10.4	21 396	31.2	2 090	4.6	2.1	5.3	19 306	48.2	51.8	2.74	2.46
Gilbert	4.3	6.2	NA	5.4	37 007	247.3	1 602	0.7	2.1	5.2	35 405	84.9	15.1	3.16	2.72
Glendale	2.4	11.5	27.8	9.0	79 667	30.1	3 967	0.4	1.4	6.7	75 700	64.8	35.2	2.97	2.63
Lake Havasu City	2.7	8.1	NA	5.1	23 018	79.2	5 107	17.3	2.3	7.8	17 911	77.6	22.4	2.29	2.45
Mesa	2.5	9.5	11.8	6.9	175 701	25.1	29 058	10.3	2.4	10.7	146 643	66.4	33.6	2.74	2.54
Oro Valley town	NA	NA	NA	NA	13 946	290.0	1 697	6.3	2.2	14.5	12 249	84.2	15.8	2.47	2.12
Peoria	2.1	7.9	-29.5	5.7	42 573	94.0	3 389	3.0	2.3	10.0	39 184	84.3	15.7	2.78	2.45
Phoenix	3.9	14.2	27.9	10.5	495 832	17.5	29 998	0.9	1.4	7.9	465 834	60.7	39.3	2.89	2.63
Prescott	2.9	13.3	5.6	8.1	17 144	28.0	2 046	6.0	2.7	6.1	15 098	65.2	34.8	2.14	2.07
Scottsdale	10.9	5.9	5.4	3.5	104 974	52.1	14 305	7.6	2.3	10.6	90 669	69.6	30.4	2.32	1.97
Sierra Vista	2.6	10.7	33.8	8.7	15 685	21.3	1 489	1.1	2.0	10.7	14 196	52.2	47.8	2.43	2.53
Surprise city	NA	NA	NA	NA	16 260	209.4	3 776	13.3	3.2	31.6	12 484	88.3	11.7	2.37	3.14
Tempe	3.9	13.6	24.8	7.0	67 068	9.1	3 466	0.8	1.0	6.1	63 602	51.0	49.0	2.59	2.22
Tucson	1.5	20.2	37.4	14.4	209 609	14.3	16 718	1.7	1.6	8.1	192 891	53.4	46.6	2.58	2.24
Yuma	1.8	16.0	35.6	12.8	34 475	51.9	7 826	11.7	1.6	12.3	26 649	63.5	36.5	2.80	2.78
ARKANSAS	1.8	19.1	0.4	14.8	1 173 043	17.2	130 347	2.5	2.5	9.6	1 042 696	69.4	30.6	2.54	2.40
Conway	1.9	16.9	18.2	10.2	17 289	70.5	1 250	0.3	3.2	8.3	16 039	55.1	44.9	2.66	2.17
Fayetteville	2.8	19.8	4.8	10.9	25 467	35.2	1 669	0.5	2.7	6.1	23 798	42.2	57.8	2.45	2.04
Fort Smith	3.1	13.8	2.2	10.5	35 341	6.9	2 943	0.4	2.5	8.1	32 398	56.3	43.7	2.52	2.29
Hot Springs	1.3	24.9	23.9	18.5	18 813	7.2	2 717	2.9	3.2	11.9	16 096	57.3	42.7	2.18	2.05
Jacksonville	0.8	11.6	33.3	10.6	11 890	9.2	1 000	0.5	2.3	8.9	10 890	47.3	52.7	2.58	2.69
Jonesboro	2.9	16.5	18.7	12.5	24 263	24.2	2 044	0.4	2.5	10.4	22 219	57.7	42.3	2.49	2.24
Little Rock	4.4	14.6	3.5	10.8	84 793	4.7	7 441	0.5	1.7	9.7	77 352	57.4	42.6	2.46	2.10
North Little Rock	2.2	17.2	35.4	12.8	27 567	1.1	2 025	0.3	2.2	8.4	25 542	57.5	42.5	2.39	2.29
Pine Bluff	1.6	27.7	14.0	22.9	22 484	-3.0	2 528	0.3	2.0	9.2	19 956	58.8	41.2	2.56	2.58
Rogers	2.4	8.7	3.6	6.2	14 836	44.2	831	0.4	2.6	5.9	14 005	63.2	36.8	2.77	2.69
Springdale	2.0	9.4	-16.8	7.1	16 962	41.3	813	0.3	2.3	4.4	16 149	60.4	39.6	2.77	2.85
Texarkana	1.8	25.2	34.8	21.0	11 721	18.9	1 337	0.4	2.8	15.1	10 384	60.9	39.1	2.46	2.42
West Memphis	1.3	22.9	-12.6	18.4	11 022	4.9	971	0.3	1.7	10.2	10 051	56.0	44.0	2.73	2.66
CALIFORNIA	7.1	12.5	9.7	9.3	12 214 549	9.2	711 679	1.9	1.4	3.7	11 502 870	56.9	43.1	2.93	2.79
Alameda	7.7	6.8	-16.0	5.7	31 644	3.7	1 418	0.5	0.5	2.4	30 226	47.9	52.1	2.50	2.22
Alhambra	3.1	14.8	25.4	11.5	30 069	1.6	958	0.3	1.3	2.1	29 111	39.2	60.8	3.04	2.78
Anaheim	6.2	10.6	37.7	7.4	99 719	7.0	2 750	0.2	0.9	3.2	96 969	50.0	50.0	3.24	3.45
Antioch	3.6	9.1	24.7	8.1	30 116	31.1	778	0.1	0.9	3.4	29 338	71.0	29.0	3.14	2.90
Apple Valley	4.2	10.7	28.9	9.2	20 163	20.9	1 606	0.7	3.4	7.8	18 557	70.0	30.0	2.83	3.08
Arcadia	16.6	5.2	30.0	3.5	19 970	2.5	821	0.6	1.8	2.4	19 149	62.3	37.7	2.91	2.47
Atascadero	3.1	7.8	13.0	6.4	9 848	11.0	317	0.7	0.9	2.7	9 531	65.6	34.4	2.71	2.44
Azusa	2.0	14.3	25.4	10.9	13 013	-1.7	464	0.2	1.1	4.0	12 549	50.5	49.5	3.34	3.48
Bakersfield	4.5	15.0	32.7	12.4	88 262	33.4	4 821	0.3	2.0	6.2	83 441	60.5	39.5	3.01	2.77

1. Includes units rented or sold but not occupied. 2. Specified owner-occupied units. 3. Specified renter-occupied units. 4. Overcrowded or lacking complete plumbing facilities.

City	Civilian labor force, 2001		Unemployment		Civilian employment, 1990[2]		Percent		Disability 1990 Work disabled persons[3] (percent)	Value of residential construction authorized by building permits, 2000		
	Total	Percent change, 2000–2001	Total	Rate[1]	Total	Professional, managerial, and technical	Precision production, craft, and repair			New construction ($1,000)	Number of housing units	Percent single family
	61	62	63	64	65	66	67	68		69	70	71
ALABAMA	2 147 552	-0.3	114 360	5.3	1 741 794	26.1	13.0	9.7		1 718 032	17 406	78.5
Auburn	18 093	1.0	703	3.9	14 330	43.9	4.8	4.1		51 085	504	52.0
Bessemer	14 191	0.6	898	6.3	11 903	19.1	11.7	12.7		3 419	37	100.0
Birmingham	130 421	0.5	7 149	5.5	110 156	27.5	8.6	10.3		29 260	446	26.5
Decatur	28 165	-0.3	1 683	6.0	22 815	32.3	13.2	8.3		27 577	227	100.0
Dothan	29 910	-0.6	1 305	4.4	25 011	29.5	11.3	8.2		28 156	625	48.8
Florence	19 303	0.1	2 081	10.8	15 625	29.7	12.3	9.4		15 065	173	67.6
Gadsden	18 303	-3.0	1 710	9.3	15 914	21.6	12.3	12.3		903	12	100.0
Homewood	13 653	0.1	250	1.8	12 002	49.0	4.5	3.6		9 201	62	100.0
Hoover	26 938	0.1	376	1.4	22 053	49.6	4.8	3.8		110 223	525	96.6
Huntsville	100 620	1.4	3 526	3.5	81 396	44.9	8.2	7.1		18 027	531	100.0
Madison	10 449	1.1	193	1.8	8 598	59.2	7.5	4.6		31 404	530	71.3
Mobile	103 266	0.0	6 772	6.6	81 976	33.0	9.1	8.9		38 318	540	53.3
Montgomery	100 700	0.3	4 228	4.2	83 026	32.4	8.1	8.3		81 882	787	97.0
Phenix City	13 673	-0.3	795	5.8	10 576	21.4	14.5	10.7		21 807	358	30.2
Prichard	12 011	-1.2	739	6.2	10 515	15.1	13.3	12.1		12 018	104	100.0
Tuscaloosa	43 118	0.0	1 724	4.0	32 724	35.0	8.6	7.2		64 791	557	77.2
ALASKA	321 983	0.0	20 191	6.3	245 379	34.3	11.2	6.6		332 575	2 147	74.8
Anchorage	144 851	0.4	6 165	4.3	111 242	37.5	9.5	6.7		202 855	1 190	69.0
Fairbanks	16 091	0.1	1 047	6.5	11 425	28.9	10.5	6.5		1 010	11	100.0
Juneau	16 868	-1.6	817	4.8	14 482	42.0	8.3	5.4		19 313	98	87.8
ARIZONA	2 419 619	3.1	113 025	4.7	1 603 896	30.8	11.4	8.3		7 157 588	61 485	79.4
Apache Junction	9 893	3.1	376	3.8	6 584	17.7	20.2	17.7		22 590	297	98.7
Avondale	9 351	4.9	696	7.4	5 811	21.3	13.1	10.8		112 769	1 486	86.5
Bullhead City	17 653	5.5	884	5.0	9 779	18.7	12.8	12.1		29 891	295	100.0
Casa Grande	12 345	3.2	542	4.4	8 167	25.9	12.6	8.2		34 881	326	100.0
Chandler	72 537	3.4	2 119	2.9	47 282	36.3	10.8	5.4		507 048	4 550	54.2
Flagstaff	33 218	2.0	1 406	4.2	22 911	30.9	8.5	4.9		41 580	345	70.4
Gilbert	22 402	3.3	613	2.7	14 631	33.9	11.9	4.1		513 196	3 434	96.3
Glendale	114 075	3.7	4 445	3.9	73 610	29.8	11.5	7.9		259 952	2 900	43.1
Lake Havasu City	18 555	5.3	443	2.4	10 562	22.5	17.4	10.5		93 289	993	95.5
Mesa	208 743	3.5	6 892	3.3	135 531	31.7	12.3	6.9		687 712	6 510	70.4
Oro Valley town	3 973	1.8	92	2.3	NA	NA	NA	NA		152 098	994	100.0
Peoria	33 484	3.4	1 004	3.0	21 809	29.3	13.2	7.3		339 480	3 148	89.1
Phoenix	748 360	3.8	32 068	4.3	480 945	30.4	11.4	8.0		899 266	7 998	59.2
Prescott	17 824	4.2	582	3.3	10 120	32.1	10.6	10.1		76 956	498	94.4
Scottsdale	107 695	3.3	3 022	2.8	70 281	41.3	6.2	5.9		437 385	3 553	71.5
Sierra Vista	14 518	4.4	507	3.5	12 086	38.1	7.8	8.4		19 894	297	100.0
Surprise city	3 656	4.5	232	6.3	NA	NA	NA	NA		322 838	3 252	100.0
Tempe	123 249	3.5	4 100	3.3	80 002	39.7	8.4	5.6		9 895	48	100.0
Tucson	244 151	2.1	9 326	3.8	179 702	31.0	10.8	9.2		374 133	3 549	77.9
Yuma	34 255	-1.0	5 818	17.0	21 684	28.1	9.8	7.7		47 702	541	85.2
ARKANSAS	1 226 661	-0.9	62 796	5.1	994 289	23.3	12.5	11.2		858 615	9 203	75.3
Conway	19 234	-0.3	969	5.0	12 569	30.3	8.8	6.8		52 521	428	86.0
Fayetteville	30 950	2.5	743	2.4	21 133	37.4	7.2	6.3		50 988	529	59.0
Fort Smith	40 668	-1.0	1 635	4.0	33 999	27.1	12.4	9.1		34 030	362	57.5
Hot Springs	15 141	-0.4	806	5.3	12 411	26.4	8.4	14.7		11 500	105	100.0
Jacksonville	12 370	-0.9	780	6.3	10 648	26.2	9.0	9.5		13 183	239	29.7
Jonesboro	29 741	-1.5	1 308	4.4	22 968	27.0	9.9	10.0		28 727	280	87.9
Little Rock	99 159	-1.2	4 018	4.1	87 408	37.8	6.5	7.9		112 099	723	71.2
North Little Rock	31 516	-1.2	1 321	4.2	27 741	28.7	10.1	10.2		10 416	63	100.0
Pine Bluff	23 527	-1.1	2 162	9.2	21 683	26.4	9.5	11.1		2 720	78	64.1
Rogers	19 182	2.7	409	2.1	11 958	24.2	11.8	8.7		35 061	331	95.5
Springdale	21 814	2.5	446	2.0	14 898	24.4	12.8	10.1		64 438	971	47.1
Texarkana	9 956	-1.2	405	4.1	9 107	23.2	11.9	11.0		10 736	161	100.0
West Memphis	13 578	0.1	704	5.2	12 071	22.9	10.4	10.3		15 751	300	37.3
CALIFORNIA	17 362 231	1.6	927 058	5.3	13 996 309	32.3	11.1	7.4		23 343 965	145 575	72.1
Alameda	41 626	1.7	1 346	3.2	35 523	41.0	8.4	6.6		763	5	60.0
Alhambra	44 397	2.3	2 064	4.6	38 702	31.9	9.5	5.4		4 398	28	71.4
Anaheim	169 682	1.8	5 936	3.5	141 959	27.4	12.4	6.2		40 718	314	36.3
Antioch	37 587	1.3	1 644	4.4	29 631	27.1	16.0	8.4		217 233	1 157	100.0
Apple Valley	25 131	3.1	1 276	5.1	18 185	26.8	16.5	10.4		41 562	277	100.0
Arcadia	26 508	2.2	736	2.8	23 561	45.1	6.2	5.3		49 023	135	100.0
Atascadero	13 974	2.3	298	2.1	11 555	29.3	14.2	8.9		24 611	137	92.0
Azusa	22 827	2.4	1 462	6.4	19 532	20.9	13.3	7.1		11 128	63	96.8
Bakersfield	102 265	0.3	7 915	7.7	77 612	31.3	11.4	8.5		259 986	2 111	93.9

1. Percent of civilian labor force.   2. Persons 16 years and older.   3. Persons 16 to 64 years old.

Table D. Cities — Wholesale Trade, Retail Trade, and Real Estate

City	Wholesale Trade, 1997				Retail Trade[1], 1997				Real Estate and Rental and Leasing, 1997			
	Number of Establishments	Number of Employees	Sales (mil dol)	Annual Payroll (mil dol)	Number of Establishments	Number of Employees	Sales (mil dol)	Annual Payroll (mil dol)	Number of Establishments	Number of Employees	Receipts (mil dol)	Annual Payroll (mil dol)
	72	73	74	75	76	77	78	79	80	81	82	83
ALABAMA	6 315	79 229	40 986.3	2 394.7	20 163	231 665	36 623.3	3 381.7	3 664	20 629	2 130.3	396.7
Auburn	26	D	D	D	198	2 851	385.1	37.2	53	357	27.0	5.4
Bessemer	70	1 423	922.7	47.8	209	2 773	519.0	45.1	26	96	9.2	1.7
Birmingham	736	14 656	6 744.4	494.1	1 150	16 618	3 085.5	294.7	275	3 000	442.9	81.9
Decatur	138	1 785	868.5	51.9	410	4 920	921.9	74.2	81	404	35.2	7.3
Dothan	180	1 918	643.2	49.1	547	7 148	1 199.2	116.0	84	313	32.8	5.8
Florence	72	1 842	349.0	43.6	353	5 049	710.0	68.7	63	261	25.4	5.3
Gadsden	70	1 031	283.2	28.3	290	3 148	503.5	45.2	43	162	18.7	3.3
Homewood	154	1 998	1 083.3	68.3	254	4 276	565.0	61.6	57	502	73.3	12.1
Hoover	126	1 240	1 767.6	57.1	203	4 812	874.2	82.0	44	282	28.3	5.2
Huntsville	361	3 968	2 828.5	143.7	945	14 647	2 268.6	219.3	278	1 339	138.7	24.6
Madison	56	563	332.0	20.9	77	1 211	146.3	15.8	28	206	22.9	4.2
Mobile	491	6 314	2 669.0	195.4	1 140	17 003	2 573.2	261.2	291	1 685	175.6	31.9
Montgomery	365	4 733	2 701.0	141.0	1 091	15 619	2 425.3	232.3	287	2 140	175.4	39.3
Phenix City	17	453	91.2	11.6	127	1 470	181.1	18.6	33	109	11.5	1.4
Prichard	27	476	147.7	15.5	77	566	71.1	8.8	8	26	2.7	0.4
Tuscaloosa	117	1 153	516.6	37.2	577	8 496	1 250.9	122.3	129	985	66.6	12.5
ALASKA	784	6 860	2 989.8	256.8	2 866	32 502	6 251.4	670.5	716	4 014	543.2	98.3
Anchorage	434	4 748	1 989.1	181.4	1 001	15 115	3 114.9	319.3	356	2 145	322.2	56.8
Fairbanks	51	590	178.3	21.8	248	3 356	727.0	77.2	64	408	38.9	9.2
Juneau	33	196	96.3	8.2	173	1 807	312.7	37.2	49	249	38.3	4.0
ARIZONA	6 689	80 155	45 763.9	2 748.9	16 283	232 050	43 960.9	4 223.9	5 450	32 529	4 110.1	747.4
Apache Junction	12	D	D	D	80	980	143.5	14.7	36	94	10.5	1.0
Avondale	7	D	D	D	38	582	141.8	10.1	14	33	4.4	0.8
Bullhead City	NA	NA	NA	NA	NA	NA	NA	NA	NA	NA	NA	NA
Casa Grande	35	326	93.5	8.5	182	2 103	336.6	31.6	34	120	12.3	2.1
Chandler	162	1 952	1 254.0	59.2	283	5 528	1 190.7	127.1	101	449	66.2	9.1
Flagstaff	80	739	505.0	18.2	367	5 011	784.6	79.0	116	439	53.3	9.4
Gilbert	74	301	119.1	9.4	110	1 870	362.7	39.2	54	205	23.0	3.8
Glendale	160	2 130	848.8	57.3	598	11 308	2 311.9	203.3	150	897	101.4	15.5
Lake Havasu City	42	189	44.0	4.4	228	2 290	377.6	37.9	54	126	15.9	2.2
Mesa	347	2 797	1 280.8	109.0	1 405	23 747	4 348.7	420.2	367	1 576	194.3	28.1
Oro Valley town	NA	NA	NA	NA	NA	NA	NA	NA	NA	NA	NA	NA
Peoria	25	113	37.6	3.3	149	2 558	454.5	46.6	48	349	31.1	5.5
Phoenix	2 447	37 073	21 861.7	1 383.9	3 807	58 531	11 407.6	1 123.2	1 485	13 109	1 768.6	331.3
Prescott	47	302	113.6	7.8	251	2 822	513.7	52.5	101	272	35.4	5.2
Scottsdale	634	3 997	2 749.3	164.0	1 232	16 189	3 614.6	342.4	570	2 480	430.0	81.2
Sierra Vista	15	D	D	D	145	2 321	371.4	37.1	48	236	18.6	3.4
Surprise city	NA	NA	NA	NA	NA	NA	NA	NA	NA	NA	NA	NA
Tempe	659	10 322	9 609.2	370.2	728	13 575	3 491.9	295.3	293	2 069	274.4	50.3
Tucson	615	6 532	1 801.0	190.1	2 079	30 607	5 370.2	547.7	647	4 879	485.7	98.2
Yuma	65	635	207.9	19.8	300	4 376	697.9	66.2	78	323	24.7	4.2
ARKANSAS	3 619	41 385	27 515.4	1 136.6	12 600	132 335	21 643.7	1 904.4	2 269	9 761	1 001.6	163.2
Conway	54	D	D	D	248	3 111	526.2	47.8	57	133	17.8	2.0
Fayetteville	88	1 202	6 024.6	43.7	401	5 711	790.0	79.9	116	507	61.8	7.9
Fort Smith	219	1 942	660.3	52.1	599	8 197	1 282.6	121.4	120	557	63.9	10.2
Hot Springs	NA	NA	NA	NA	NA	NA	NA	NA	NA	NA	NA	NA
Jacksonville	17	D	D	D	109	1 394	239.8	22.5	35	D	D	D
Jonesboro	111	1 342	458.1	30.6	410	5 146	770.3	73.8	79	D	D	D
Little Rock	555	10 270	4 550.3	332.1	1 101	15 944	2 590.5	236.9	323	2 685	290.6	50.2
North Little Rock	219	3 255	4 712.8	91.6	466	7 671	1 328.5	121.9	68	356	28.8	6.1
Pine Bluff	69	D	D	D	349	4 359	653.5	66.0	52	334	22.8	5.6
Rogers	44	495	712.8	14.8	204	2 669	418.5	39.1	56	245	27.2	3.8
Springdale	163	1 775	673.2	51.4	278	3 463	615.0	58.8	57	175	27.9	3.4
Texarkana	46	739	200.8	18.1	147	1 413	243.3	20.2	24	75	4.9	0.8
West Memphis	41	477	281.9	14.5	151	2 170	402.2	27.0	24	111	12.3	2.2
CALIFORNIA	57 842	755 513	551 230.6	29 900.2	106 357	1 354 797	263 118.3	26 362.7	37 244	243 288	38 288.4	6 570.5
Alameda	68	538	353.4	24.5	204	2 329	408.5	48.5	81	313	49.5	6.5
Alhambra	427	1 972	747.1	46.3	249	3 672	983.2	76.0	95	343	43.4	7.7
Anaheim	962	12 779	15 533.1	457.4	963	13 119	2 773.7	278.2	335	3 019	358.3	88.3
Antioch	32	273	85.6	9.1	197	2 898	500.1	51.4	42	270	35.8	4.2
Apple Valley	21	109	14.8	2.0	68	960	146.6	14.6	35	140	14.9	3.3
Arcadia	309	1 131	569.8	30.2	283	4 000	509.7	59.8	112	492	63.9	10.4
Atascadero	14	95	36.0	2.8	129	1 374	226.0	21.3	26	82	9.3	0.9
Azusa	56	939	412.9	26.6	89	1 226	307.0	26.7	28	107	14.7	2.4
Bakersfield	291	3 891	2 747.6	144.2	918	12 207	2 382.2	230.0	229	1 333	117.2	23.2

1. Establishments with payroll.

City	Professional, Scientific, and Technical Services, 1997[1]				Manufacturing, 1997				Accommodation and Foodservices, 1997			
	Number of Establishments	Number of Employees	Receipts (mil dol)	Annual Payroll (mil dol)	Number of Establishments	Number of Employees	Receipts (mil dol)	Annual Payroll (mil dol)	Number of Establishments	Number of Employees	Sales (mil dol)	Annual Payroll (mil dol)
	84	85	86	87	88	89	90	91	92	93	94	95
ALABAMA	7 076	54 413	5 295.6	2 051.4	5 444	352 618	67 970.1	10 187.8	6 955	134 719	3 881.8	1 059.6
Auburn	63	340	32.1	11.7	28	1 708	270.3	34.8	125	3 013	76.3	20.2
Bessemer	53	180	10.9	3.9	45	2 164	367.9	70.0	52	1 459	33.3	9.3
Birmingham	815	9 020	991.8	390.3	382	19 057	3 179.5	621.0	524	10 504	346.8	99.6
Decatur	139	822	63.8	25.5	124	8 495	3 219.0	291.1	137	3 117	86.5	25.3
Dothan	160	1 147	69.1	26.4	102	8 269	1 311.0	212.8	176	3 527	111.0	28.3
Florence	136	718	49.3	16.9	83	6 049	743.8	140.9	109	2 242	59.6	17.4
Gadsden	103	468	32.1	12.6	67	6 067	1 241.0	217.5	102	1 953	56.7	15.7
Homewood	179	1 568	113.9	44.9	40	1 472	403.1	43.6	107	2 467	99.1	25.9
Hoover	168	858	96.1	32.8	NA	NA	NA	NA	90	1 916	60.3	17.2
Huntsville	666	12 461	1 532.3	571.7	240	25 793	6 694.3	1 014.6	400	8 853	282.1	76.6
Madison	53	191	24.3	8.9	28	NA	D	D	56	1 432	39.1	11.3
Mobile	674	5 495	496.7	196.6	213	11 631	1 907.4	445.0	482	10 102	301.6	84.8
Montgomery	540	4 295	407.0	189.2	190	10 312	1 798.7	269.0	411	9 983	277.3	76.5
Phenix City	38	D	D	D	34	2 566	864.2	91.6	60	882	30.4	7.9
Prichard	2	D	D	D	22	1 038	340.1	40.2	26	D	D	D
Tuscaloosa	210	1 556	107.6	44.2	89	6 020	1 058.9	179.1	252	6 355	171.6	47.4
ALASKA	1 437	7 892	945.9	370.8	488	10 770	3 305.0	331.2	1 763	20 587	1 065.5	301.5
Anchorage	907	5 939	767.2	301.3	187	2 022	322.3	62.9	640	11 364	574.0	165.8
Fairbanks	118	592	52.5	21.9	NA	NA	NA	NA	121	1 989	86.7	23.4
Juneau	96	415	44.9	18.5	NA	NA	NA	NA	94	1 117	57.7	16.1
ARIZONA	10 163	75 789	6 669.4	2 724.7	4 917	193 616	43 030.3	6 753.6	9 089	184 323	6 633.0	1 823.2
Apache Junction	12	28	1.7	0.8	NA	NA	NA	NA	48	809	20.6	5.5
Avondale	14	46	4.1	1.5	NA	NA	NA	NA	18	179	6.4	1.6
Bullhead City	NA	NA	NA	NA	NA	NA	NA	NA	NA	NA	NA	NA
Casa Grande	22	342	9.5	4.7	27	1 626	307.1	52.1	68	1 240	40.8	9.4
Chandler	208	746	69.3	25.0	135	9 668	4 744.3	352.0	207	3 846	130.2	35.9
Flagstaff	143	702	53.7	19.9	62	1 798	505.2	67.7	268	5 144	179.7	47.0
Gilbert	111	494	64.8	23.1	78	2 228	311.5	57.4	44	783	24.3	6.3
Glendale	167	768	36.9	14.5	156	6 398	1 075.9	244.0	293	6 042	187.0	51.1
Lake Havasu City	55	171	12.8	3.6	82	1 845	274.7	37.4	117	1 911	54.7	15.8
Mesa	628	4 950	282.8	128.5	258	13 921	3 367.1	530.7	577	12 355	411.4	108.9
Oro Valley town	NA	NA	NA	NA	NA	NA	NA	NA	NA	NA	NA	NA
Peoria	46	430	9.1	3.5	34	558	54.3	13.8	74	1 128	35.4	10.0
Phoenix	3 664	36 761	3 328.5	1 470.5	1 706	69 401	14 649.6	2 532.4	2 223	50 275	2 008.7	555.1
Prescott	144	547	41.0	13.9	65	1 509	178.0	36.7	140	2 037	64.1	17.3
Scottsdale	1 222	6 295	713.2	252.4	257	8 254	1 128.2	192.1	563	18 396	723.5	211.8
Sierra Vista	72	1 196	103.1	43.1	NA	NA	NA	NA	77	1 455	38.4	10.1
Surprise city	NA	NA	NA	NA	NA	NA	NA	NA	NA	NA	NA	NA
Tempe	671	5 531	454.7	160.2	498	24 105	5 414.8	865.2	514	10 694	345.4	95.9
Tucson	1 331	9 883	886.9	349.6	520	20 152	3 483.6	841.2	1 151	23 782	704.4	199.1
Yuma	125	597	44.2	16.1	36	2 481	348.1	44.5	174	3 274	97.4	24.5
ARKANSAS	4 125	23 094	1 825.8	719.6	3 316	230 153	45 186.0	5 778.4	4 663	73 397	2 179.7	589.9
Conway	70	482	40.7	11.6	67	7 242	1 205.9	183.1	91	2 125	61.0	16.8
Fayetteville	217	1 023	80.5	26.7	68	5 962	948.9	144.2	222	3 881	110.7	31.4
Fort Smith	209	1 197	91.6	27.3	206	20 817	3 949.8	521.5	239	4 463	133.1	36.6
Hot Springs	NA	NA	NA	NA	66	2 756	610.0	68.2	NA	NA	NA	NA
Jacksonville	29	99	5.5	2.2	32	1 995	309.5	53.7	52	893	27.3	6.9
Jonesboro	137	652	51.9	18.9	97	6 234	1 126.9	170.7	118	D	D	D
Little Rock	979	8 734	827.9	372.9	251	12 570	2 457.9	365.9	490	10 389	329.0	95.8
North Little Rock	125	898	64.0	24.7	91	4 073	1 095.8	110.4	186	4 378	126.0	34.4
Pine Bluff	79	387	27.2	7.6	75	D	D	D	118	D	D	D
Rogers	104	485	38.9	14.6	71	7 083	1 047.8	181.4	78	1 369	37.8	10.2
Springdale	97	560	37.4	16.3	106	D	D	D	124	2 099	66.2	17.9
Texarkana	36	D	D	D	20	2 230	491.5	98.7	71	1 290	44.2	11.3
West Memphis	43	292	13.2	4.4	33	D	D	D	65	1 307	45.6	11.7
CALIFORNIA	78 635	805 856	89 555.7	35 258.6	49 418	1 809 667	379 612.4	65 762.8	62 532	1 052 715	42 261.1	11 437.2
Alameda	209	1 576	221.4	89.0	56	2 298	1 009.1	127.3	165	1 908	66.9	17.9
Alhambra	170	1 000	55.7	18.6	125	3 248	308.5	81.8	172	2 627	91.0	24.2
Anaheim	556	4 422	451.5	165.3	896	38 330	6 019.8	1 358.7	689	18 054	818.6	222.9
Antioch	68	254	15.2	5.4	38	577	117.7	20.2	109	1 501	54.1	13.5
Apple Valley	26	69	5.4	2.4	NA	NA	NA	NA	41	612	17.2	4.2
Arcadia	141	804	83.6	29.5	72	971	201.2	29.0	134	2 232	84.4	21.0
Atascadero	38	119	9.1	2.7	NA	NA	NA	NA	46	616	18.5	4.9
Azusa	14	36	2.9	1.4	126	5 017	905.9	197.7	63	894	31.4	7.8
Bakersfield	519	2 793	249.5	89.5	160	4 560	416.0	107.9	472	7 956	272.6	72.8

1. Firms subject to federal tax.

Table D. Cities — **Entertainment, Health Care, and Other Services**

City	Arts, Entertainment, and Recreation[1], 1997				Health Care and Social Assistance[1], 1997				Other Services[1], 1997			
	Number of Establish-ments	Number of Employees	Receipts (mil dol)	Annual Payroll (mil dol)	Number of Establish-ments	Number of Employees	Receipts (mil dol)	Annual Payroll (mil dol)	Number of Establish-ments	Number of Employees	Receipts (mil dol)	Annual Payroll (mil dol)
	96	97	98	99	100	101	102	103	104	105	106	107
ALABAMA	791	9 381	435.7	105.0	7 121	104 492	7 116.7	3 104.8	6 329	37 061	2 241.7	659.3
Auburn	12	0	0.0	0.0	48	316	20.2	8.7	53	326	16.0	4.9
Bessemer	5	55	1.6	0.5	71	851	46.3	25.1	65	406	28.7	8.4
Birmingham	41	1 092	58.2	13.1	675	10 682	985.1	442.3	456	4 311	265.4	85.5
Decatur	20	134	4.8	1.1	196	2 088	146.4	67.7	115	1 054	51.5	18.1
Dothan	21	233	8.2	2.6	209	4 502	370.9	170.3	160	921	50.2	14.9
Florence	15	0	0.0	0.0	176	2 120	153.1	64.4	101	673	29.7	10.1
Gadsden	10	103	4.0	1.4	156	3 611	285.8	114.8	79	379	22.4	6.0
Homewood	12	51	1.8	0.5	158	5 628	498.8	184.9	90	766	55.4	17.3
Hoover	12	112	3.4	0.9	99	1 628	82.5	36.2	71	512	23.7	8.5
Huntsville	50	884	22.4	6.6	502	5 883	457.4	193.9	358	2 234	120.9	41.1
Madison	6	58	0.9	0.3	39	548	28.3	11.3	31	170	7.9	2.7
Mobile	51	849	37.8	7.2	490	9 662	697.9	328.5	429	3 308	215.2	63.1
Montgomery	35	526	19.4	4.8	534	8 898	637.4	262.1	371	2 688	138.6	43.7
Phenix City	3	0	0.0	0.0	36	691	33.7	11.0	63	328	18.2	5.6
Prichard	NA	NA	NA	NA	13	320	13.6	6.1	35	183	7.9	2.4
Tuscaloosa	20	204	4.9	1.7	203	1 920	157.6	84.6	182	1 234	64.9	20.7
ALASKA	320	3 055	168.3	34.9	1 143	8 156	758.1	309.4	852	4 364	331.0	93.4
Anchorage	101	1 455	81.2	16.2	599	5 053	508.6	203.8	393	2 576	185.8	54.8
Fairbanks	26	312	17.4	2.3	99	768	79.0	39.9	83	459	33.5	9.9
Juneau	21	232	14.4	3.0	81	437	40.1	16.6	56	240	15.8	4.5
ARIZONA	1 071	24 416	2 033.3	475.1	9 155	97 091	6 687.9	2 893.3	6 494	43 669	2 794.0	829.6
Apache Junction	4	53	2.1	0.8	24	600	30.0	14.3	33	120	5.2	1.5
Avondale	4	0	0.0	0.0	14	223	10.4	4.6	19	83	6.0	1.3
Bullhead City	NA	NA	NA	NA	NA	NA	NA	NA	NA	NA	NA	NA
Casa Grande	5	36	2.6	0.3	73	584	42.9	18.1	35	284	12.1	4.4
Chandler	25	0	0.0	0.0	235	2 420	148.7	69.4	157	1 010	54.0	18.5
Flagstaff	24	687	19.7	6.2	205	1 485	98.8	42.9	132	726	44.1	11.7
Gilbert	14	286	14.6	3.5	78	1 255	71.6	31.4	68	321	20.4	8.4
Glendale	21	492	24.4	5.5	373	4 208	288.3	124.4	271	1 442	93.0	25.3
Lake Havasu City	14	130	8.2	2.1	96	797	51.9	22.3	72	473	32.5	9.4
Mesa	59	975	45.4	11.4	799	9 068	585.8	248.8	548	3 686	220.9	71.2
Oro Valley town	NA	NA	NA	NA	NA	NA	NA	NA	NA	NA	NA	NA
Peoria	8	102	6.0	1.5	106	1 791	112.5	50.6	77	454	24.8	7.6
Phoenix	255	6 004	462.3	158.4	2 677	30 034	2 243.6	994.8	1 836	15 938	1 141.9	321.2
Prescott	12	117	9.0	2.0	175	1 480	86.6	32.9	104	548	27.5	8.2
Scottsdale	113	3 408	276.0	58.8	773	7 095	525.0	226.4	410	2 733	159.9	52.2
Sierra Vista	6	78	1.8	0.5	77	946	59.6	22.7	40	207	8.6	2.7
Surprise city	NA	NA	NA	NA	NA	NA	NA	NA	NA	NA	NA	NA
Tempe	60	1 069	126.1	57.1	369	3 613	262.3	104.7	324	2 511	184.1	57.9
Tucson	116	2 174	109.3	25.6	1 196	14 955	1 045.8	457.0	852	5 858	340.0	107.1
Yuma	20	0	0.0	0.0	195	2 274	140.2	55.0	114	649	32.8	9.8
ARKANSAS	594	5 343	228.7	56.8	4 571	59 960	3 655.1	1 609.7	3 553	18 809	1 113.9	310.5
Conway	13	0	0.0	0.0	122	1 231	72.1	33.2	69	484	25.5	7.5
Fayetteville	23	227	8.0	2.1	167	1 690	121.0	60.1	107	774	33.5	11.1
Fort Smith	19	0	0.0	0.0	263	4 345	326.9	147.4	171	1 225	68.8	19.8
Hot Springs	NA	NA	NA	NA	NA	NA	NA	NA	NA	NA	NA	NA
Jacksonville	6	68	1.5	0.7	44	614	28.3	14.5	42	162	8.1	2.4
Jonesboro	29	181	8.2	2.2	198	3 087	237.9	112.4	103	561	34.7	9.1
Little Rock	55	640	28.6	8.3	704	9 469	777.5	361.7	428	2 983	183.5	52.5
North Little Rock	19	192	10.1	3.6	188	1 610	117.4	52.3	149	960	60.0	18.1
Pine Bluff	12	0	0.0	0.0	181	1 671	108.4	47.5	101	728	39.1	12.3
Rogers	8	168	7.0	2.6	95	1 159	63.6	33.6	65	370	18.6	5.7
Springdale	14	90	3.2	0.7	105	1 120	67.0	29.6	97	573	32.1	10.1
Texarkana	5	0	0.0	0.0	32	0	0.0	0.0	37	290	13.6	4.4
West Memphis	9	0	0.0	0.0	55	660	38.1	15.0	52	391	23.0	6.6
CALIFORNIA	12 015	182 004	15 913.8	6 296.6	69 857	664 539	51 968.0	20 619.3	44 642	282 762	20 521.5	5 852.2
Alameda	24	583	95.8	53.9	159	1 631	84.6	36.0	93	479	33.1	9.4
Alhambra	15	103	4.8	1.4	197	2 031	133.4	49.7	100	497	37.5	11.1
Anaheim	50	0	0.0	0.0	730	8 305	726.8	264.4	473	3 487	305.4	77.4
Antioch	19	191	6.7	1.7	136	1 297	102.8	40.3	79	452	32.4	9.7
Apple Valley	1	0	0.0	0.0	142	750	123.3	49.6	21	123	6.9	1.5
Arcadia	45	2 114	105.6	35.4	244	1 806	140.2	62.3	92	303	18.7	4.8
Atascadero	5	81	1.9	0.5	71	315	20.1	6.5	41	180	12.7	2.9
Azusa	4	106	4.3	1.2	34	445	12.5	5.2	53	279	19.1	5.0
Bakersfield	50	1 027	35.6	10.6	639	7 112	600.4	217.4	346	2 300	168.0	45.7

1. Firms subject to federal tax.

City	Procurement contracts Defense	Other	Grants Total[2]	Health and family welfare	Energy and environment	Education	Housing and community development	Direct payments for individuals Educational assistance	Housing assistance	Intergovernmental Total (mil dol)	Total (mil dol)	Percent from state government	Taxes Total (mil dol)	Per capita[3] (dollars) Total	Property	Sales and gross receipts
	108	109	110	111	112	113	114	115	116	117	118	119	120	121	122	123
ALABAMA	3 427.0	1 777.2	5 297.5	3 005.9	86.5	499.9	73.5	211.9	279.9	X	X	X	X	X	X	X
Auburn	2.9	0.6	42.1	7.0	1.3	2.3	0.5	8.5	2.3	37.2	1.2	89.7	25.9	640	144	301
Bessemer	0.1	0.2	1.7	0.1	0.0	0.2	0.9	1.3	4.9	26.6	3.0	94.8	19.8	643	360	47
Birmingham	98.5	117.7	349.2	259.1	24.8	9.6	3.7	29.5	50.0	355.7	44.0	40.0	237.6	939	139	401
Decatur	2.3	0.3	6.2	2.3	0.0	0.6	1.2	0.0	7.4	152.4	4.1	28.8	22.5	412	36	321
Dothan	14.5	0.3	10.0	3.1	0.0	1.4	0.4	4.0	4.7	48.3	2.0	71.0	37.5	656	39	588
Florence	0.2	0.6	1.7	1.0	0.0	0.0	0.3	4.1	8.6	61.6	2.7	45.9	44.6	1 141	776	305
Gadsden	0.0	14.5	10.6	4.3	0.0	2.6	2.0	3.9	4.3	50.0	3.9	16.3	35.4	840	56	391
Homewood	0.0	1.2	0.0	0.0	0.0	0.0	0.0	0.0	0.0	30.9	2.2	28.9	24.8	1 105	265	640
Hoover	0.0	0.3	-0.3	0.0	0.0	0.0	0.0	0.0	0.0	59.6	2.1	53.9	51.7	867	79	685
Huntsville	2 198.1	196.0	71.7	5.1	3.0	5.0	2.3	6.5	11.4	178.3	18.3	54.0	102.8	584	88	424
Madison	6.0	0.4	0.1	0.0	0.0	0.1	0.0	0.0	0.9	15.5	1.1	79.1	9.9	392	85	245
Mobile	102.4	460.6	71.7	35.8	0.5	7.3	4.6	27.2	34.4	248.8	13.8	85.5	159.6	789	69	599
Montgomery	190.1	27.3	762.8	235.7	42.7	148.9	49.0	21.0	17.2	150.5	21.1	27.2	104.6	531	75	334
Phenix City	0.1	0.0	0.6	0.4	0.0	0.1	0.0	2.1	3.8	38.6	4.9	86.0	11.3	414	20	318
Prichard	0.5	0.0	0.0	0.0	0.0	0.0	0.0	0.0	6.9	15.1	2.3	56.6	7.4	228	73	142
Tuscaloosa	12.6	48.3	43.4	14.0	4.4	7.8	2.2	19.9	10.9	75.7	14.6	8.2	42.5	510	70	316
ALASKA	833.9	296.5	2 313.7	937.8	96.3	264.7	12.1	9.2	56.6	X	X	X	X	X	X	X
Anchorage	251.3	89.0	396.3	132.4	11.5	19.2	7.1	5.2	24.4	852.1	361.9	93.9	271.4	1 064	957	76
Fairbanks	13.4	21.0	113.7	34.9	1.5	11.6	0.5	3.1	11.6	21.2	5.6	98.1	10.0	299	187	94
Juneau	0.4	3.6	372.8	81.9	60.3	74.5	0.0	0.5	5.2	147.8	39.3	94.2	53.2	1 761	837	871
ARIZONA	4 583.6	676.3	5 190.3	2 911.8	74.9	653.3	78.6	219.8	207.5	X	X	X	X	X	X	X
Apache Junction	0.0	0.2	0.2	0.0	0.0	0.0	0.0	0.0	0.1	NA	NA	NA	NA	NA	NA	NA
Avondale	0.0	0.0	1.2	0.0	0.0	0.6	0.0	1.6	0.7	27.9	7.0	92.6	9.8	357	69	205
Bullhead City	0.0	0.0	1.4	0.0	0.0	0.0	0.0	0.0	0.5	31.4	13.7	70.6	8.6	307	32	252
Casa Grande	0.0	0.6	5.2	1.2	0.0	1.8	0.0	0.0	1.4	27.2	7.2	85.5	12.3	535	80	408
Chandler	68.9	39.7	3.4	0.0	0.1	0.8	2.0	1.2	6.3	175.3	53.0	70.5	64.8	404	97	272
Flagstaff	2.2	6.7	49.9	9.6	4.6	11.6	0.0	12.5	2.5	70.0	27.0	92.7	21.9	387	133	231
Gilbert	117.5	18.2	1.4	0.0	0.0	0.2	0.3	16.8	0.0	73.6	18.2	86.4	27.1	305	89	169
Glendale	1.8	2.4	3.0	0.0	-0.2	1.0	1.6	7.3	12.7	188.7	60.4	81.0	67.8	351	96	217
Lake Havasu City	0.1	0.5	3.0	0.0	0.0	0.1	0.0	0.1	0.7	44.4	13.8	84.5	22.6	558	245	277
Mesa	772.2	7.7	19.1	0.2	0.0	1.7	2.1	7.2	16.6	350.7	116.8	81.1	127.2	353	31	264
Oro Valley town	0.0	0.0	0.0	0.0	0.0	0.0	0.0	0.0	0.0	NA	NA	NA	NA	NA	NA	NA
Peoria	0.1	0.6	0.7	0.0	0.0	0.2	0.5	0.0	1.8	98.8	24.2	81.0	41.3	475	105	297
Phoenix	836.4	83.4	856.6	314.1	39.7	137.9	34.5	74.4	67.4	1 636.4	496.9	70.8	553.0	462	124	305
Prescott	1.5	8.5	8.2	0.6	0.1	2.1	0.0	2.9	0.6	49.7	11.9	85.1	20.5	600	83	459
Scottsdale	280.2	26.6	24.0	4.7	1.3	2.0	1.0	8.9	6.8	318.4	46.4	94.5	162.6	832	186	567
Sierra Vista	3.5	0.2	0.8	0.0	0.0	0.8	0.0	0.1	2.3	30.8	14.4	91.7	9.5	249	29	200
Surprise city	0.0	0.0	2.3	1.9	0.0	0.0	0.0	0.0	0.3	NA	NA	NA	NA	NA	NA	NA
Tempe	427.2	6.4	81.3	16.8	3.4	12.0	1.8	29.2	6.1	222.5	56.2	72.1	110.8	661	129	513
Tucson	1 733.4	55.6	295.6	123.7	10.3	22.7	13.5	38.1	37.8	534.7	203.2	66.8	203.0	441	73	343
Yuma	24.5	4.9	12.5	5.4	0.1	2.6	1.0	5.3	7.6	62.1	20.7	92.7	28.9	463	105	333
ARKANSAS	384.8	306.8	3 448.5	1 932.1	38.7	310.8	32.8	118.9	198.3	X	X	X	X	X	X	X
Conway	0.2	0.1	12.5	3.5	0.0	0.4	0.7	8.5	1.7	34.4	3.6	76.4	11.3	289	26	257
Fayetteville	1.0	3.5	59.8	6.4	0.1	7.1	0.6	9.8	5.3	51.2	14.1	33.5	15.7	294	9	273
Fort Smith	10.3	2.0	8.1	0.0	0.0	0.1	1.1	3.1	10.9	76.7	21.2	36.6	27.6	365	93	259
Hot Springs	0.0	0.5	0.9	0.0	0.0	0.0	0.0	0.0	7.7	37.6	4.5	68.8	16.1	425	18	389
Jacksonville	0.3	0.0	0.3	0.0	0.0	0.0	0.3	0.3	6.0	105.2	6.9	25.1	10.5	366	7	355
Jonesboro	0.0	1.9	11.7	6.2	0.0	3.6	1.1	11.5	8.6	30.4	12.4	34.5	4.7	89	44	27
Little Rock	77.3	39.5	592.8	214.8	38.2	109.2	23.5	18.3	22.9	200.2	68.7	19.9	35.4	202	58	111
North Little Rock	9.5	0.8	4.0	1.5	0.0	0.0	1.5	4.7	11.9	45.5	15.4	29.7	6.0	102	45	38
Pine Bluff	2.1	0.1	24.4	6.3	0.0	3.7	2.0	10.1	11.5	41.2	13.9	45.1	14.2	268	55	198
Rogers	0.1	2.5	3.7	2.3	0.0	0.0	0.4	0.0	1.2	35.7	5.0	44.5	16.8	454	49	389
Springdale	14.7	3.4	1.2	0.0	0.0	0.7	0.3	0.3	2.4	32.2	9.0	36.5	12.2	302	59	230
Texarkana	0.6	0.6	5.7	1.5	0.0	0.3	0.3	0.0	8.1	22.9	4.8	65.3	8.8	370	78	284
West Memphis	0.6	0.1	4.4	1.7	0.0	0.6	0.6	1.7	4.2	23.7	7.8	54.7	7.6	285	28	248
CALIFORNIA	19 864.2	9 084.4	39 797.1	25 233.8	502.8	3 492.7	761.4	1 409.7	4 291.0	X	X	X	X	X	X	X
Alameda	5.3	23.9	3.6	1.5	0.0	0.1	1.5	2.4	19.1	76.5	12.4	63.4	40.4	513	215	239
Alhambra	0.0	21.9	6.9	3.8	0.0	0.0	3.0	0.6	1.3	63.5	10.0	60.9	30.8	367	119	217
Anaheim	616.9	45.1	9.6	0.0	0.0	0.9	8.0	3.3	45.5	354.2	62.5	41.0	147.3	499	129	334
Antioch	0.7	0.2	4.7	0.0	0.0	0.6	0.5	1.4	3.3	42.6	7.6	78.3	18.0	221	102	97
Apple Valley	0.3	0.8	0.5	0.0	0.0	0.3	0.0	0.0	0.0	22.1	6.1	88.0	6.2	110	19	59
Arcadia	1.6	0.6	26.6	24.6	1.9	0.0	0.0	0.0	2.5	NA	NA	NA	NA	NA	NA	NA
Atascadero	0.2	0.1	0.0	0.0	0.0	0.0	0.0	0.0	0.1	NA	NA	NA	NA	NA	NA	NA
Azusa	75.0	23.4	1.0	0.1	0.0	0.8	0.0	2.8	6.0	34.7	6.3	85.6	17.7	415	119	226
Bakersfield	2.2	5.1	47.7	13.4	0.1	2.8	15.3	20.6	9.0	163.0	30.7	77.5	67.6	321	97	198

1. October 1, 2000 to September 30, 2001. 2. Includes program categories not shown separately. State totals include additional categories not allocated by city. 3. Based on population estimated as of July 1 of the year shown.

Table D. Cities — City Government Finances

City	City government finances, 1999 (cont'd)												
	General expenditure												
	Per capita[1] (dollars)			Percent of total for —									
	Total (mil dol)	Total	Capital outlays	Public welfare	Highways	Parking facilities	Education	Health and hospitals	Police protection	Sewerage and sanitation	Parks and recreation	Housing and community development	Interest on debt
	124	125	126	127	128	129	130	131	132	133	134	135	136
ALABAMA	X	X	X	X	X	X	X	X	X	X	X	X	X
Auburn	33.4	826	118	0.3	18.1	0.1	9.0	2.4	11.1	18.5	7.5	1.1	11.0
Bessemer	28.7	931	0	0.0	1.4	0.1	0.0	0.0	23.5	9.4	2.6	23.0	2.8
Birmingham	318.2	1 258	73	0.1	4.2	6.6	3.9	1.5	19.2	4.7	1.5	3.9	14.7
Decatur	141.1	2 580	260	0.0	3.0	0.0	0.0	60.4	5.0	8.1	4.1	0.8	7.3
Dothan	50.1	877	119	0.0	6.7	0.0	0.6	0.5	19.0	22.0	9.9	0.0	2.5
Florence	82.8	2 118	875	0.0	5.1	0.0	4.7	0.1	6.6	39.7	4.5	0.9	2.0
Gadsden	48.5	1 152	61	1.0	10.1	0.0	3.0	0.8	16.7	15.0	9.7	4.0	4.2
Homewood	36.6	1 628	674	0.0	5.7	0.0	6.7	0.5	16.1	6.1	4.6	0.0	0.6
Hoover	50.0	840	126	0.0	5.3	0.5	0.0	0.7	19.9	13.2	6.6	0.0	7.7
Huntsville	222.3	1 263	420	0.2	4.6	0.5	0.0	2.4	10.1	11.3	6.4	1.9	12.8
Madison	23.4	922	318	0.0	9.0	0.0	0.1	0.0	8.8	41.9	9.1	0.0	7.0
Mobile	246.9	1 221	252	0.0	4.2	0.1	0.0	0.4	13.2	14.6	6.9	0.0	13.5
Montgomery	141.9	720	70	0.1	12.5	0.2	1.3	1.4	19.6	10.0	13.7	2.8	3.1
Phenix City	40.6	1 484	128	0.0	3.5	0.0	0.0	40.6	7.9	5.3	5.2	2.8	3.8
Prichard	13.0	398	40	0.5	4.4	0.0	0.0	3.8	20.7	30.6	1.4	0.1	0.7
Tuscaloosa	76.8	921	293	0.0	5.3	1.3	0.0	0.2	13.4	26.7	5.6	2.4	1.0
ALASKA	X	X	X	X	X	X	X	X	X	X	X	X	X
Anchorage	959.4	3 762	998	0.0	14.0	0.3	44.6	3.6	6.5	2.9	4.0	0.0	5.3
Fairbanks	23.8	715	21	0.0	19.5	0.0	0.0	0.3	21.5	0.0	0.0	0.0	0.3
Juneau	132.3	4 383	420	0.0	6.4	0.1	35.5	24.3	6.4	3.4	3.9	2.2	1.8
ARIZONA	X	X	X	X	X	X	X	X	X	X	X	X	X
Apache Junction	NA	NA	NA	NA	NA	NA	NA	NA	NA	NA	NA	NA	NA
Avondale	29.0	1 052	414	1.1	9.4	0.0	0.0	0.0	11.9	13.2	2.4	0.1	5.9
Bullhead City	25.5	906	147	0.0	8.7	0.0	0.0	0.0	29.2	5.3	4.8	6.5	9.6
Casa Grande	27.0	1 173	214	0.0	11.3	0.0	0.0	0.0	19.6	14.0	9.8	3.5	1.5
Chandler	123.8	772	109	0.0	11.7	0.0	0.0	0.0	19.2	12.4	3.6	8.2	5.8
Flagstaff	57.4	1 012	162	0.0	9.3	0.0	0.0	0.0	13.4	17.3	8.0	5.2	8.2
Gilbert	75.3	847	210	0.0	11.3	0.0	0.0	0.0	15.7	27.8	15.9	0.3	8.8
Glendale	192.3	994	284	0.1	7.6	0.0	0.0	0.0	15.8	26.9	5.8	5.2	4.7
Lake Havasu City	42.6	1 051	131	0.0	12.6	0.0	0.6	0.0	12.6	14.7	6.9	0.7	3.1
Mesa	370.8	1 030	301	0.6	12.4	0.0	0.0	0.0	23.9	18.9	11.6	2.3	4.7
Oro Valley town	NA	NA	NA	NA	NA	NA	NA	NA	NA	NA	NA	NA	NA
Peoria	84.8	975	235	0.0	14.4	0.0	0.3	0.0	9.8	8.9	13.4	2.2	8.1
Phoenix	1 667.4	1 392	514	0.0	6.0	0.2	0.9	0.0	14.3	12.4	9.9	4.6	8.6
Prescott	37.5	1 098	269	0.0	14.0	0.0	0.0	0.4	12.6	26.3	10.0	0.0	5.3
Scottsdale	471.6	2 414	912	0.0	4.5	0.0	0.0	0.0	8.0	6.2	5.6	0.9	7.4
Sierra Vista	32.1	842	297	0.0	7.7	0.0	0.1	3.7	14.5	9.3	10.0	0.0	8.8
Surprise city	NA	NA	NA	NA	NA	NA	NA	NA	NA	NA	NA	NA	NA
Tempe	207.6	1 238	442	0.0	11.1	0.0	0.0	0.0	16.1	5.8	9.8	19.6	3.4
Tucson	453.8	986	168	3.0	11.0	0.3	0.0	0.0	16.8	5.4	11.5	11.3	6.5
Yuma	65.1	1 043	334	0.0	15.6	0.0	0.0	0.0	26.5	10.6	15.8	2.2	2.9
ARKANSAS	X	X	X	X	X	X	X	X	X	X	X	X	X
Conway	47.1	1 204	496	0.7	20.0	0.0	0.0	0.2	10.6	10.4	2.0	1.3	12.9
Fayetteville	47.1	884	189	0.0	6.9	0.3	0.0	0.0	12.0	24.1	5.1	2.5	4.6
Fort Smith	63.2	835	153	0.0	21.3	0.3	0.0	0.1	14.4	16.3	3.0	1.3	4.8
Hot Springs	49.7	1 310	607	0.0	16.3	0.1	0.0	0.6	9.0	15.1	2.5	1.0	8.3
Jacksonville	87.0	3 015	158	0.0	2.1	0.0	0.0	81.8	3.0	3.0	1.7	0.6	1.2
Jonesboro	25.1	480	65	0.0	15.9	0.2	0.0	2.0	19.0	23.8	2.9	0.0	7.4
Little Rock	225.1	1 284	182	0.0	7.3	0.2	0.0	3.3	15.1	10.2	16.6	1.7	11.0
North Little Rock	53.2	899	0	0.0	9.3	0.9	0.0	1.4	23.6	16.7	6.9	2.6	7.0
Pine Bluff	40.5	764	87	0.0	11.4	0.0	0.0	0.7	21.4	20.9	11.7	4.6	4.4
Rogers	36.5	986	323	0.0	24.6	0.0	0.0	0.0	13.3	11.1	4.7	0.5	11.2
Springdale	29.0	720	140	0.0	9.4	0.0	0.0	0.6	18.0	15.5	3.2	1.8	1.7
Texarkana	23.9	1 008	284	0.3	5.0	0.0	0.0	0.3	19.3	14.4	0.8	1.6	14.5
West Memphis	23.0	866	166	0.0	10.6	0.0	0.0	1.1	17.8	17.4	2.4	3.8	4.4
CALIFORNIA	X	X	X	X	X	X	X	X	X	X	X	X	X
Alameda	85.6	1 088	191	0.0	20.2	0.1	0.0	0.3	20.2	4.0	8.9	9.4	2.6
Alhambra	54.2	645	75	0.0	7.9	1.5	0.0	3.2	24.4	10.7	8.5	12.7	9.9
Anaheim	525.2	1 780	711	0.0	5.9	0.0	0.0	0.1	11.7	6.6	7.6	7.6	13.4
Antioch	52.2	641	150	0.0	17.9	0.0	0.0	0.7	23.1	4.1	5.1	8.3	22.9
Apple Valley	18.9	335	48	0.0	22.1	0.0	0.0	1.1	22.6	28.1	0.0	2.5	5.3
Arcadia	NA	NA	NA	NA	NA	NA	NA	NA	NA	NA	NA	NA	NA
Atascadero	NA	NA	NA	NA	NA	NA	NA	NA	NA	NA	NA	NA	NA
Azusa	31.1	730	35	0.0	6.1	0.0	0.0	0.7	32.6	7.5	2.7	9.6	14.2
Bakersfield	189.5	901	248	0.0	10.6	0.4	0.0	0.3	18.9	26.6	4.6	2.4	5.4

1. Based on population estimated as of July 1 of the year shown.

City Government Finances, City Government Employment, and Climate

City	Debt outstanding Total (mil dol) 137	Per capita[1] (dollars) 138	Percent utility 139	City government employment, 2001 140	Climate[2] Mean January 141	July 142	Limits January[3] 143	July[4] 144	Annual precipitation (inches) 145	Heating degree days 146	Cooling degree days 147
ALABAMA	X	X	X	X	X	X	X	X	X	X	X
Auburn	70.8	1 752	11.0	462	43.1	79.2	32.7	89.3	56.47	2 612	1 865
Bessemer	31.0	1 005	51.4	445	41.7	79.7	30.5	91.4	59.11	2 893	1 777
Birmingham	810.6	3 204	0.0	4 036	41.5	79.8	31.3	89.9	54.58	2 918	1 797
Decatur	231.3	4 229	14.4	1 766	38.8	79.0	29.2	89.0	57.18	3 323	1 651
Dothan	41.6	730	22.2	1 048	48.2	80.0	37.2	91.0	55.61	1 903	2 204
Florence	83.8	2 143	63.2	829	38.7	79.7	29.0	90.3	53.85	3 325	1 736
Gadsden	40.7	966	21.2	625	39.1	78.9	28.7	89.5	55.31	3 317	1 610
Homewood	21.6	962	0.0	326	NA	NA	NA	NA	NA	NA	NA
Hoover	58.4	980	0.0	564	41.5	79.8	31.3	89.9	54.58	2 918	1 797
Huntsville	542.1	3 080	11.1	2 578	38.8	79.0	29.2	89.0	57.18	3 323	1 651
Madison	61.3	2 413	36.4	NA	NA	NA	NA	NA	NA	NA	NA
Mobile	673.2	3 330	6.3	3 006	49.9	82.3	40.0	91.3	63.96	1 702	2 627
Montgomery	149.4	758	56.4	3 106	46.1	81.3	35.8	91.1	53.43	2 224	2 212
Phenix City	46.0	1 680	54.0	385	45.7	81.9	35.2	91.8	51.00	2 261	2 284
Prichard	17.4	532	88.7	NA	49.9	82.3	40.0	91.3	63.96	1 702	2 627
Tuscaloosa	100.6	1 207	85.3	1 033	42.8	81.1	32.4	91.1	54.90	2 661	2 070
ALASKA	X	X	X	X	X	X	X	X	X	X	X
Anchorage	1 286.6	5 046	31.8	8 793	14.9	58.4	8.4	65.2	15.91	10 570	0
Fairbanks	0.7	22	0.0	178	10.1	62.5	18.5	72.3	10.87	13 940	84
Juneau	36.5	1 210	0.0	1 508	24.2	56.0	19.0	63.9	54.31	8 897	0
ARIZONA	X	X	X	X	X	X	X	X	X	X	X
Apache Junction	NA	NA	NA	NA	NA	NA	NA	NA	NA	NA	NA
Avondale	60.7	2 199	23.7	NA	NA	NA	NA	NA	NA	NA	NA
Bullhead City	46.1	1 638	0.0	NA	NA	NA	NA	NA	NA	NA	NA
Casa Grande	11.0	477	0.0	NA	NA	NA	NA	NA	NA	NA	NA
Chandler	239.8	1 495	51.4	1 334	51.9	90.2	38.1	104.8	9.04	1 490	3 476
Flagstaff	114.7	2 024	28.7	NA	28.7	66.3	15.2	81.9	22.80	7 131	145
Gilbert	98.4	1 108	0.0	NA	51.9	90.2	38.1	104.8	9.04	1 490	3 476
Glendale	187.4	968	12.4	1 556	53.6	93.5	41.2	105.9	7.66	1 350	4 162
Lake Havasu City	34.6	853	19.6	NA	NA	NA	NA	NA	NA	NA	NA
Mesa	553.6	1 537	38.6	3 637	52.9	91.2	39.5	105.5	8.50	1 366	3 635
Oro Valley town	NA	NA	NA	NA	NA	NA	NA	NA	NA	NA	NA
Peoria	191.5	2 200	30.2	838	53.6	93.5	41.2	105.9	7.66	1 350	4 162
Phoenix	3 475.3	2 901	6.8	13 035	53.6	93.5	41.2	105.9	7.66	1 350	4 162
Prescott	50.3	1 473	13.9	NA	36.2	73.1	21.9	88.1	19.63	4 995	631
Scottsdale	697.4	3 569	15.9	1 982	53.6	93.5	41.2	105.9	7.66	1 350	4 162
Sierra Vista	55.9	1 468	0.0	NA	45.1	78.5	26.8	93.5	18.63	2 928	1 441
Surprise city	NA	NA	NA	NA	NA	NA	NA	NA	NA	NA	NA
Tempe	153.0	913	44.4	1 814	52.6	90.6	37.8	106.7	8.88	1 464	3 530
Tucson	707.9	1 537	34.5	6 018	51.3	86.6	38.6	99.4	12.00	1 678	2 954
Yuma	49.6	795	27.6	NA	56.5	93.7	44.2	106.6	3.17	927	4 305
ARKANSAS	X	X	X	X	X	X	X	X	X	X	X
Conway	131.7	3 364	27.1	362	39.0	81.4	27.9	93.1	49.36	3 147	1 917
Fayetteville	52.3	982	23.8	600	34.0	78.7	22.9	89.3	44.04	4 141	1 401
Fort Smith	81.7	1 080	28.4	724	36.9	81.5	25.5	93.0	40.90	3 478	1 894
Hot Springs	72.3	1 905	21.4	532	39.3	81.7	28.5	93.3	56.52	3 181	1 958
Jacksonville	23.2	804	6.0	731	38.5	81.4	29.4	91.5	49.25	3 228	1 916
Jonesboro	93.5	1 790	72.7	572	36.6	81.7	27.9	92.3	47.19	3 504	1 940
Little Rock	378.7	2 160	0.0	2 846	39.1	81.9	29.1	92.4	50.86	3 155	2 005
North Little Rock	198.8	3 360	76.1	1 059	38.5	81.4	29.4	91.5	49.25	3 228	1 916
Pine Bluff	31.4	592	0.0	413	40.0	81.8	29.6	92.4	52.36	3 016	2 050
Rogers	98.3	2 652	3.7	357	NA	NA	NA	NA	NA	NA	NA
Springdale	6.6	163	0.0	462	34.0	78.7	22.9	89.3	44.04	4 141	1 401
Texarkana	65.9	2 782	29.9	212	NA	NA	NA	NA	NA	NA	NA
West Memphis	30.0	1 127	52.5	368	37.0	81.1	27.4	90.9	50.77	3 438	1 871
CALIFORNIA	X	X	X	X	X	X	X	X	X	X	X
Alameda	35.2	447	15.8	649	49.9	62.1	43.3	70.0	24.30	2 902	115
Alhambra	53.7	639	1.7	462	55.7	75.2	41.7	89.2	17.90	1 433	1 427
Anaheim	1 178.9	3 994	31.0	2 706	57.4	72.6	45.6	82.6	12.27	1 238	1 175
Antioch	165.7	2 034	10.2	340	44.5	73.8	35.9	90.8	12.80	2 837	1 066
Apple Valley	13.1	232	0.0	NA	44.2	79.3	30.0	97.4	5.51	3 127	1 525
Arcadia	NA	NA	NA	NA	55.7	75.2	41.7	89.2	17.90	1 433	1 427
Atascadero	NA	NA	NA	NA	NA	NA	NA	NA	NA	NA	NA
Azusa	57.6	1 351	0.0	NA	55.8	75.0	43.6	89.0	19.37	1 453	1 394
Bakersfield	259.9	1 236	2.7	1 249	47.8	84.1	38.6	98.5	5.72	2 182	2 365

1. Based on the population estimated as of July 1 of the year shown.   2. Represents normal values based on the 30-year period, 1961–1990.   3. Average daily minimum.   4. Average daily maximum.

Table D. Cities — Land Area and Population

STATE Place code	City	Land area, 2000[1] (sq km)	Population, 2000			Population				Population characteristics, 2000 — Percent						
													Race (alone or in combination)			
			Total persons	Rank	Per square kilometer	Total persons 1990	Percent change 1990–2000	Total persons 1980	Percent change 1980–1990	White	Black	Am. Indian, Alaska Native	Asian and Pacific Islander	Other race	His-panic[2]	Non-His-panic White
		1	2	3	4	5	6	7	8	9	10	11	12	13	14	15
	CALIFORNIA—Cont'd															
06 03666	Baldwin Park	17.3	75 837	351	4 383.6	69 330	9.4	50 554	37.1	43.9	1.9	2.0	12.6	44.2	78.7	7.3
06 04870	Bell	6.4	36 664	846	5 728.8	34 365	6.7	25 450	35.0	52.9	1.5	1.6	1.5	47.4	90.9	5.8
06 04982	Bellflower	15.7	72 878	364	4 641.9	61 815	17.9	53 441	15.7	50.1	14.1	1.7	11.9	27.6	43.2	30.7
06 04996	Bell Gardens	6.4	44 054	696	6 883.4	42 315	4.1	34 117	24.0	52.3	1.1	2.0	1.0	48.2	93.4	4.7
06 05108	Belmont	11.7	25 123	1 234	2 147.3	24 165	4.0	24 505	-1.4	78.8	2.0	0.8	18.7	4.3	8.3	70.4
06 05290	Benicia	33.4	26 865	1 151	804.3	24 437	9.9	15 376	58.9	83.5	5.8	2.0	10.4	4.2	9.0	73.9
06 06000	Berkeley	27.1	102 743	227	3 791.3	102 724	0.0	103 328	-0.6	63.7	15.3	1.6	19.1	6.5	9.7	55.2
06 06308	Beverly Hills	14.7	33 784	931	2 298.2	31 971	5.7	32 367	-1.2	89.3	2.1	0.4	8.8	4.1	4.6	82.0
06 08100	Brea	27.3	35 410	881	1 297.1	32 873	7.7	27 913	17.8	80.7	1.6	1.2	10.7	9.9	20.3	66.5
06 08786	Buena Park	27.4	78 282	335	2 857.0	68 784	13.8	64 165	7.2	57.4	4.5	1.8	23.6	18.5	33.5	38.2
06 08954	Burbank	44.9	100 316	239	2 234.2	93 649	7.1	84 625	10.7	77.7	2.6	1.2	10.8	14.0	24.9	59.4
06 09066	Burlingame	11.2	28 158	1 096	2 514.1	26 666	5.6	26 173	1.9	80.3	1.4	0.7	16.2	5.5	10.6	71.3
06 09710	Calexico	16.1	27 109	1 141	1 683.8	18 633	45.5	14 412	29.3	49.5	0.6	0.9	2.4	50.2	95.3	2.4
06 10046	Camarillo	49.0	57 077	501	1 164.8	52 297	9.1	37 797	38.4	83.8	1.9	1.2	9.2	7.7	15.5	72.8
06 10345	Campbell	14.5	38 138	816	2 630.2	36 088	5.7	27 067	33.3	77.0	3.0	1.4	16.6	6.9	13.3	66.0
06 11194	Carlsbad	97.0	78 247	336	806.7	63 292	23.6	35 490	78.3	89.2	1.3	1.1	5.9	5.7	11.7	80.5
06 11530	Carson	48.8	89 730	276	1 838.7	83 995	6.8	81 221	3.4	29.0	26.6	1.3	28.0	20.6	34.9	12.0
06 12048	Cathedral City	49.7	42 647	719	858.1	30 085	41.8	NA	NA	68.9	3.3	1.6	4.7	25.9	50.0	42.0
06 12524	Ceres	18.0	34 609	908	1 922.7	26 413	31.0	13 281	98.9	69.0	3.3	2.8	7.0	23.7	37.9	50.2
06 12552	Cerritos	22.3	51 488	580	2 308.9	53 244	-3.3	53 020	0.4	29.5	7.2	0.8	61.4	5.1	10.4	21.4
06 13014	Chico	71.9	59 954	468	833.9	39 970	50.0	26 603	50.2	86.1	2.8	2.6	5.6	7.5	12.3	77.2
06 13210	Chino	54.5	67 168	406	1 232.4	59 682	12.5	40 165	48.6	59.8	8.3	1.7	6.4	28.9	47.4	37.6
06 13392	Chula Vista	126.6	173 556	120	1 370.9	135 160	28.4	83 927	61.0	59.5	5.4	1.4	14.1	25.4	49.6	31.7
06 13756	Claremont	34.0	33 998	922	999.9	32 610	4.3	30 950	5.4	77.1	5.8	1.3	13.6	6.7	15.4	65.0
06 14218	Clovis	44.3	68 468	394	1 545.6	50 323	36.1	33 021	52.4	79.8	2.4	2.8	8.0	11.8	20.3	67.5
06 14890	Colton	39.1	47 662	635	1 219.0	40 213	18.3	21 310	89.0	46.7	12.0	2.0	6.8	37.9	60.7	20.8
06 15044	Compton	26.2	93 493	258	3 568.4	90 454	3.4	81 286	11.3	19.4	41.2	1.2	1.7	40.3	56.8	1.0
06 16000	Concord	78.1	121 780	177	1 559.3	111 308	9.4	103 255	7.8	75.8	3.8	1.8	12.6	12.5	21.8	60.9
06 16350	Corona	91.0	124 966	170	1 373.3	75 943	64.6	37 791	101.0	66.5	7.2	1.6	9.6	20.7	35.7	47.0
06 16532	Costa Mesa	40.5	108 724	209	2 684.5	96 357	12.8	82 562	16.7	73.2	1.8	1.4	8.9	19.1	31.8	56.8
06 16742	Covina	18.0	46 837	647	2 602.1	43 332	8.1	33 751	28.4	62.2	5.6	1.7	11.7	20.0	40.3	42.3
06 17568	Culver City	13.2	38 816	803	2 940.6	38 793	0.1	38 139	1.7	63.8	13.6	1.8	14.5	12.8	23.7	48.1
06 17610	Cupertino	28.3	50 546	592	1 786.1	39 967	26.5	34 015	17.5	52.8	1.0	0.6	46.6	2.2	4.0	47.8
06 17750	Cypress	17.1	46 229	659	2 703.5	42 655	8.4	40 391	5.6	69.3	3.4	1.4	23.5	7.1	15.7	57.1
06 17918	Daly City	19.6	103 621	223	5 286.8	92 088	12.5	78 594	17.2	30.2	5.4	1.0	55.2	14.8	22.3	17.7
06 17946	Dana Point	17.2	35 110	890	2 041.3	31 896	10.1	10 602	200.8	89.8	1.2	1.2	3.8	7.0	15.5	78.8
06 17988	Danville	46.9	41 715	733	889.4	31 306	33.2	26 446	18.4	88.6	1.1	0.6	10.7	1.8	4.7	83.0
06 18100	Davis	27.1	60 308	462	2 225.4	46 322	30.2	36 640	26.4	74.2	3.1	1.5	20.4	6.0	9.6	65.9
06 18394	Delano	26.2	38 824	802	1 481.8	22 762	70.6	16 491	38.0	29.2	5.8	1.4	17.8	50.4	68.5	9.2
06 19192	Diamond Bar	38.2	56 287	514	1 473.5	53 672	4.9	28 045	91.4	44.1	5.3	0.9	45.3	8.9	18.5	31.0
06 19766	Downey	32.2	107 323	212	3 333.0	91 444	17.4	82 602	10.7	57.6	4.2	1.4	9.0	32.8	57.9	28.7
06 20018	Dublin	32.6	29 973	1 037	919.4	23 229	29.0	13 496	72.1	72.7	10.5	1.4	12.8	6.7	13.5	62.3
06 20956	East Palo Alto	6.6	29 506	1 055	4 470.6	23 451	25.8	18 191	28.9	30.0	24.2	1.6	11.8	37.5	58.8	6.5
06 21712	El Cajon	37.7	94 869	252	2 516.4	88 918	6.7	73 892	20.3	79.3	6.5	2.0	4.9	13.7	22.5	64.5
06 21782	El Centro	24.8	37 835	822	1 525.6	31 405	20.5	23 996	30.9	50.0	3.5	1.5	4.2	44.6	74.6	18.1
06 22230	El Monte	24.7	115 965	192	4 694.9	106 162	9.2	79 494	33.5	39.2	1.0	1.9	19.4	42.8	72.4	7.4
06 22678	Encinitas	49.5	58 014	490	1 172.0	55 406	4.7	10 796	413.2	89.3	0.9	1.0	4.5	7.4	14.8	79.0
06 22804	Escondido	94.0	133 559	160	1 420.8	108 648	22.9	64 355	68.8	72.0	2.9	2.3	5.9	22.0	38.7	51.9
06 23042	Eureka	24.5	26 128	1 190	1 066.4	27 025	-3.3	24 074	12.3	86.9	2.5	7.3	5.0	3.8	7.8	78.6
06 23182	Fairfield	97.5	96 178	246	986.4	78 650	22.3	58 099	35.4	61.9	17.1	2.1	15.8	11.4	18.8	49.0
06 24638	Folsom	56.3	51 884	574	921.6	29 802	74.1	11 003	170.9	80.4	6.4	1.3	9.1	6.1	9.5	74.2
06 24680	Fontana	93.5	128 929	163	1 378.9	87 535	47.3	37 111	135.9	49.3	12.9	2.0	5.8	35.6	57.7	23.9
06 25338	Foster City	9.7	28 803	1 075	2 969.4	28 176	2.2	23 287	21.0	62.8	2.5	0.6	36.0	2.6	5.3	55.9
06 25380	Fountain Valley	23.1	54 978	536	2 380.0	53 691	2.4	55 080	-2.5	67.8	1.5	1.2	28.5	5.6	10.7	58.5
06 26000	Fremont	198.6	203 413	85	1 024.2	173 339	17.3	131 945	31.4	52.4	3.8	1.3	40.8	8.0	13.5	41.4
06 27000	Fresno	270.3	427 652	37	1 582.1	354 091	20.8	218 202	62.3	54.0	9.2	2.6	13.0	26.6	39.9	37.3
06 28000	Fullerton	57.5	126 003	169	2 191.4	114 144	10.4	102 034	11.9	65.2	2.7	1.4	17.9	17.2	30.2	48.7
06 28168	Gardena	15.1	57 746	492	3 824.2	51 481	12.2	45 165	14.0	27.5	27.2	1.3	30.1	19.5	31.8	12.2
06 29000	Garden Grove	46.7	165 196	124	3 537.4	142 965	15.5	123 307	15.9	50.3	1.8	1.4	33.2	17.7	32.5	32.5
06 29504	Gilroy	41.1	41 464	738	1 008.9	31 487	31.7	21 641	45.5	63.6	2.3	2.4	6.3	31.2	53.8	38.0
06 30000	Glendale	79.4	194 973	98	2 455.6	180 038	8.3	139 060	29.5	73.1	1.6	0.7	17.9	17.0	19.7	54.2
06 30014	Glendora	49.6	49 415	606	996.3	47 832	3.3	38 654	23.7	83.9	1.8	1.2	7.9	9.5	21.7	60.3
06 31960	Hanford	33.9	41 686	734	1 229.7	30 463	36.8	20 995	45.1	69.2	5.6	2.3	4.3	24.6	38.7	49.9
06 32548	Hawthorne	15.7	84 112	302	5 357.5	71 349	17.9	56 447	26.4	33.0	34.4	1.4	8.9	27.8	44.3	13.0
06 33000	Hayward	114.8	140 030	150	1 219.8	114 705	22.1	94 167	21.8	48.2	12.3	1.9	25.2	20.6	34.2	29.2
06 33182	Hemet	66.4	58 812	480	885.7	43 366	35.6	22 454	93.1	83.6	3.2	2.1	2.4	12.4	23.1	70.3
06 33434	Hesperia	174.4	62 582	441	358.8	50 418	24.1	13 540	272.4	78.5	4.7	2.5	2.2	17.1	29.4	62.4
06 33588	Highland	35.3	44 605	688	1 263.6	34 439	29.5	NA	NA	60.5	13.3	2.4	7.9	21.5	36.6	41.7
06 34120	Hollister	17.0	34 413	914	2 024.3	19 318	78.1	11 488	68.2	63.8	1.8	2.2	4.7	33.4	55.1	38.5
06 36000	Huntington Beach	68.4	189 594	101	2 771.8	181 519	4.4	170 505	6.5	82.7	1.1	1.5	11.5	7.4	14.7	71.9
06 36056	Huntington Park	7.8	61 348	451	7 865.1	56 129	9.3	46 223	21.4	45.9	1.0	1.3	1.1	55.6	95.6	2.7

1. Dry land or land partially or temporarily covered by water. 2. Hispanic persons may be of any race.

Table D. Cities — **Population and Households**

	Population characteristics, 2000 (cont'd)										Households, 2000				
	Age of population (percent)													Percent	
City	Under 5 years	5 to 17 years	18 to 24 years	25 to 34 years	35 to 44 years	45 to 54 years	55 to 64 years	65 to 74 years	75 years and over	Percent female	Number	Percent change, 1990–2000	Persons per house-hold	Female family house-holder[1]	One-person
	16	17	18	19	20	21	22	23	24	25	26	27	28	29	30
CALIFORNIA—Cont'd															
Baldwin Park	9.7	25.3	11.9	16.4	14.2	10.6	5.9	3.6	2.5	50.0	16 961	2.1	4.44	17.5	8.1
Bell	10.8	24.5	12.9	19.0	13.3	9.3	4.8	3.0	2.4	49.5	8 918	-1.1	4.05	18.3	11.0
Bellflower	9.5	22.3	10.3	16.8	15.2	11.0	6.4	4.3	4.1	51.3	23 367	2.0	3.09	19.0	21.1
Bell Gardens	11.4	28.0	12.9	18.2	13.3	8.1	4.1	2.4	1.6	49.4	9 466	2.4	4.61	19.6	7.2
Belmont	6.0	13.3	6.5	16.8	19.1	15.0	10.1	7.0	6.2	50.8	10 418	3.1	2.35	7.1	27.2
Benicia	5.6	21.5	6.5	10.2	18.1	19.2	9.6	5.2	4.1	51.4	10 328	12.2	2.60	11.9	23.6
Berkeley	4.0	10.1	21.6	17.9	13.9	13.9	8.4	4.9	5.3	50.9	44 955	3.5	2.16	9.5	38.1
Beverly Hills	3.7	16.2	6.3	14.1	15.2	15.8	10.9	8.1	9.5	54.5	15 035	3.2	2.24	8.1	38.2
Brea	6.1	19.6	8.5	13.7	16.7	14.9	9.3	6.4	4.9	51.2	13 067	6.9	2.70	10.5	23.0
Buena Park	8.1	21.4	9.7	15.8	16.6	11.9	7.3	5.5	3.8	50.4	23 332	5.1	3.32	14.8	14.4
Burbank	5.7	16.5	7.7	17.3	18.1	13.3	8.5	6.0	6.8	51.5	41 608	5.9	2.39	11.5	33.6
Burlingame	5.6	13.6	5.5	18.1	18.7	14.4	8.7	6.5	8.8	52.2	12 511	1.5	2.21	7.7	35.6
Calexico	7.8	27.1	9.9	12.5	14.7	11.0	6.6	6.4	4.0	53.4	6 814	44.1	3.96	22.0	10.4
Camarillo	6.6	18.7	6.5	11.9	16.6	13.7	9.0	7.2	9.8	51.6	21 438	18.4	2.62	8.2	24.1
Campbell	6.5	15.0	7.6	20.4	19.9	13.5	7.4	5.0	4.7	50.4	15 920	4.0	2.38	10.1	30.4
Carlsbad	6.4	16.9	6.2	13.4	18.5	16.0	8.6	7.1	6.9	51.1	31 521	26.1	2.46	8.6	24.8
Carson	6.9	21.5	9.9	13.5	15.0	12.7	9.8	6.6	4.1	51.7	24 648	3.5	3.59	17.2	14.2
Cathedral City	8.8	22.3	8.8	15.0	15.6	10.1	7.1	6.7	5.5	49.3	14 027	28.5	3.03	11.9	23.2
Ceres	8.6	25.7	10.1	13.7	16.3	11.2	6.3	4.7	3.4	50.8	10 435	21.6	3.31	15.5	14.1
Cerritos	4.7	19.8	8.8	10.9	14.9	17.9	13.4	6.1	3.6	51.3	15 390	2.4	3.34	10.9	8.9
Chico	6.0	15.1	27.0	15.1	11.7	10.2	5.0	3.9	6.0	50.9	23 476	51.4	2.42	11.3	29.3
Chino	7.2	21.3	12.3	16.3	17.9	13.1	6.1	3.3	2.5	44.6	17 304	10.7	3.43	12.9	14.1
Chula Vista	7.8	20.9	9.4	15.2	16.4	11.8	7.4	6.0	5.0	51.5	57 705	20.7	2.99	14.9	19.5
Claremont	4.3	16.3	18.6	9.8	14.2	14.7	9.1	7.1	7.5	53.0	11 281	7.7	2.56	10.4	24.9
Clovis	7.6	23.1	9.2	13.2	17.2	13.5	6.9	4.7	4.6	52.0	24 347	33.3	2.79	13.2	22.3
Colton	10.0	24.9	11.9	16.7	14.9	10.0	5.2	3.7	2.7	50.7	14 520	7.8	3.26	19.5	19.4
Compton	10.4	28.1	11.5	15.0	13.7	8.8	5.6	4.2	2.7	51.0	22 327	0.0	4.16	27.7	13.2
Concord	7.1	18.2	9.0	15.5	17.3	13.9	8.3	5.7	5.0	50.6	44 020	5.0	2.74	12.3	23.2
Corona	9.8	23.6	8.9	17.3	17.8	11.1	5.7	3.2	2.6	50.5	37 839	58.2	3.29	11.2	14.4
Costa Mesa	7.1	16.1	11.2	21.5	17.5	11.5	6.5	4.6	3.9	48.8	39 206	4.6	2.69	10.3	28.1
Covina	7.4	20.7	9.5	14.7	16.4	12.6	7.8	6.0	4.9	52.1	15 971	2.8	2.89	16.3	20.8
Culver City	5.5	15.4	6.6	15.1	18.2	15.8	9.5	7.0	6.9	53.3	16 611	2.8	2.31	12.8	34.5
Cupertino	6.1	20.6	5.2	12.1	21.0	15.4	8.7	5.8	5.2	50.1	18 204	18.5	2.75	7.8	19.6
Cypress	6.0	21.0	7.9	12.4	17.8	14.3	10.1	6.6	4.0	51.3	15 654	9.6	2.93	13.3	17.6
Daly City	6.0	16.4	10.5	16.4	15.8	13.7	9.0	6.9	5.2	50.8	30 775	6.1	3.34	14.2	18.1
Dana Point	5.6	15.0	7.1	14.2	17.1	17.2	10.8	7.4	5.7	50.0	14 456	13.8	2.41	8.8	26.0
Danville	7.1	21.5	4.2	8.2	19.4	18.6	10.7	5.3	5.0	51.5	14 816	33.9	2.78	7.1	15.5
Davis	4.6	14.0	30.9	14.9	12.2	11.3	5.4	3.3	3.4	52.3	22 948	28.0	2.50	8.2	25.0
Delano	9.1	23.4	12.4	17.2	15.5	9.3	5.6	4.1	3.4	43.5	8 409	34.8	4.02	18.4	10.8
Diamond Bar	5.7	21.3	8.8	11.9	17.7	17.6	9.5	4.7	2.8	51.0	17 651	4.4	3.18	11.1	12.5
Downey	8.0	21.2	9.8	16.5	14.7	11.5	7.3	5.3	5.7	51.4	33 989	3.0	3.11	15.8	19.1
Dublin	5.9	15.1	9.3	21.4	22.8	14.2	6.7	3.1	1.5	47.3	9 325	37.1	2.65	9.1	21.3
East Palo Alto	10.0	25.0	13.4	18.6	13.9	8.8	5.1	3.2	1.9	48.5	6 976	0.3	4.20	19.8	18.2
El Cajon	8.2	19.7	11.2	15.5	15.8	11.3	7.0	5.6	5.8	51.2	34 199	4.0	2.70	16.0	24.1
El Centro	8.4	25.3	9.7	13.8	15.1	11.7	6.7	5.5	3.9	50.9	11 439	18.7	3.23	18.7	18.8
El Monte	10.0	24.1	12.1	17.4	14.1	9.7	5.7	4.0	3.0	49.5	27 034	3.5	4.24	18.5	10.9
Encinitas	5.9	17.2	7.2	14.7	18.6	18.1	7.8	4.9	5.5	50.2	22 830	9.9	2.52	8.8	25.7
Escondido	8.8	20.9	10.4	15.9	15.5	11.0	6.5	4.9	6.1	50.4	43 817	11.6	3.01	11.7	22.4
Eureka	5.7	16.6	11.6	13.8	15.0	15.2	8.3	6.5	7.2	50.5	10 957	-1.6	2.26	14.0	35.3
Fairfield	8.5	21.3	11.1	14.9	16.4	12.0	6.8	5.0	3.9	50.2	30 870	21.4	2.98	14.2	17.0
Folsom	6.9	17.3	6.6	17.2	21.8	14.6	6.8	4.4	4.4	44.8	17 196	96.4	2.61	8.0	21.8
Fontana	10.3	27.5	10.3	16.3	16.0	10.1	4.6	2.7	2.0	50.4	34 014	28.9	3.78	15.5	10.9
Foster City	5.9	15.3	5.9	16.8	18.5	16.2	11.4	6.1	4.0	50.8	11 613	3.6	2.47	7.7	23.6
Fountain Valley	6.0	17.5	7.9	13.4	16.7	14.8	12.4	6.6	4.7	51.1	18 162	4.3	3.00	10.5	16.0
Fremont	7.4	18.3	7.7	17.3	19.5	13.7	7.7	4.9	3.5	49.7	68 237	13.4	2.96	9.2	16.5
Fresno	9.1	23.8	11.8	14.8	14.1	11.0	6.2	4.7	4.6	50.9	140 079	15.0	2.99	17.6	23.3
Fullerton	7.0	18.2	11.5	16.6	15.7	12.0	7.7	5.9	5.5	50.6	43 609	6.7	2.83	11.0	23.5
Gardena	7.5	18.3	8.7	16.5	15.8	12.0	8.8	7.0	5.4	51.3	20 324	12.1	2.80	18.1	25.5
Garden Grove	7.9	20.5	9.2	16.9	16.6	11.6	7.7	5.5	4.0	49.9	45 791	2.8	3.56	13.0	15.2
Gilroy	9.4	23.1	10.0	16.4	16.3	11.9	6.1	3.7	3.1	50.2	11 869	24.8	3.46	14.2	14.3
Glendale	5.7	16.7	8.4	14.9	17.3	14.1	9.0	7.2	6.7	52.3	71 805	4.7	2.68	11.8	25.7
Glendora	6.3	21.3	7.6	12.0	17.1	14.1	9.1	6.7	5.9	51.7	16 819	3.0	2.88	12.1	19.1
Hanford	8.7	22.9	9.8	14.7	14.9	11.6	7.1	5.2	5.1	51.0	13 931	28.3	2.93	15.4	20.6
Hawthorne	10.1	21.6	11.3	19.5	15.3	10.3	5.8	3.5	2.7	51.9	28 536	5.2	2.93	23.5	24.5
Hayward	7.9	18.9	10.9	17.5	15.8	11.9	6.9	5.2	4.9	50.4	44 804	11.7	3.08	14.5	20.9
Hemet	6.5	16.0	7.2	10.2	10.4	8.6	8.0	12.8	20.2	54.2	25 252	45.2	2.26	11.2	34.4
Hesperia	7.9	24.9	9.3	11.6	15.7	12.2	7.4	6.1	4.9	50.7	19 966	20.6	3.12	13.8	16.5
Highland	9.5	26.1	9.0	14.1	15.9	12.2	6.7	4.0	2.5	51.2	13 478	19.1	3.29	19.0	15.4
Hollister	10.0	24.6	9.5	16.4	17.4	10.7	5.1	3.6	2.7	49.5	9 716	64.8	3.52	12.2	12.7
Huntington Beach	6.2	16.1	8.4	17.4	17.5	14.2	9.8	5.9	4.5	49.9	73 657	6.9	2.56	9.6	24.3
Huntington Park	10.4	25.4	13.0	18.7	13.6	9.0	4.8	3.1	2.0	49.9	14 860	6.9	4.12	20.3	10.9

1. No spouse present.

Table D. Cities — **Group Quarters, Crime, Education, and Income**

City	Persons in group quarters, 2000 Total	Institutional Total	Persons in nursing homes	Non-Institutional[1]	Serious crimes known to police, 2000[2] Total Number	Rate[3]	Violent	Property	Education, 1990 School enrollment Public	Private	Attainment[4] (percent) High school graduate or more	Bachelor's degree or more	Money income, 1989 Per capita (dollars)[5]	Households Median Dollars	Percent change 1979–1989 (constant 1989 dollars)
	31	32	33	34	35	36	37	38	39	40	41	42	43	44	45
CALIFORNIA—Cont'd															
Baldwin Park	606	278	260	328	1 725	2 275	398	1 876	21 055	1 942	50.5	9.7	8 858	32 684	18.6
Bell	538	97	97	441	891	2 430	706	1 724	9 473	762	33.6	3.7	7 104	22 515	6.3
Bellflower	623	253	253	370	2 482	3 406	598	2 807	13 342	2 690	72.3	12.0	14 304	32 711	16.5
Bell Gardens	456	301	123	155	1 215	2 758	856	1 902	15 062	466	26.3	1.7	6 125	23 819	17.1
Belmont	627	103	103	524	480	1 911	322	1 588	4 523	1 444	91.5	36.8	25 827	50 859	15.5
Benicia	54	27	27	27	538	2 003	190	1 813	5 842	1 038	90.4	32.6	20 663	49 660	27.2
Berkeley	5 822	246	185	5 576	7 688	7 483	734	6 749	33 379	5 963	90.3	58.7	18 720	29 737	31.4
Beverly Hills	39	1	0	38	1 530	4 529	364	4 165	5 389	2 080	89.4	47.0	55 463	54 348	29.5
Brea	128	22	0	106	1 454	4 106	441	3 666	7 779	1 196	87.4	31.0	21 407	51 253	18.6
Buena Park	934	325	306	609	2 028	2 591	365	2 225	16 570	2 440	76.7	15.9	15 176	41 435	11.3
Burbank	826	476	462	350	3 172	3 162	296	2 866	17 715	3 769	79.7	22.9	18 897	35 959	17.8
Burlingame	486	428	428	58	914	3 246	227	3 019	4 669	1 087	88.3	33.5	25 031	42 487	25.1
Calexico	103	0	0	103	1 174	4 331	240	4 091	7 075	346	35.9	5.6	6 595	18 635	-8.3
Camarillo	939	393	211	546	1 165	2 041	147	1 894	11 591	2 232	87.9	27.2	19 930	48 219	19.6
Campbell	290	106	106	184	1 024	2 685	252	2 433	7 317	1 296	88.6	31.0	20 759	42 489	28.4
Carlsbad	787	535	535	252	2 055	2 626	229	2 398	13 006	2 204	89.6	35.8	21 764	45 739	22.1
Carson	1 210	242	236	968	3 398	3 787	929	2 857	21 574	3 685	71.4	17.1	13 749	43 882	10.0
Cathedral City	145	0	0	145	1 790	4 197	624	3 574	6 530	527	69.6	13.0	13 331	30 908	NA
Ceres	99	57	52	42	2 265	6 545	517	6 027	6 727	596	67.1	8.8	11 603	30 876	17.9
Cerritos	93	30	30	63	2 354	4 572	394	4 178	16 067	2 696	89.2	37.0	18 966	59 076	12.6
Chico	3 063	497	486	2 566	2 070	3 453	320	3 132	19 251	595	86.3	31.8	10 584	19 005	1.7
Chino	7 816	7 634	0	182	2 043	3 042	386	2 656	18 730	2 528	74.2	11.8	12 916	41 958	5.3
Chula Vista	1 079	647	165	432	7 048	4 061	487	3 573	33 584	3 926	75.7	17.7	14 102	32 012	6.1
Claremont	5 104	465	384	4 639	1 027	3 021	188	2 833	6 803	5 675	92.8	51.2	22 161	53 479	18.8
Clovis	480	253	224	227	2 987	4 363	140	4 222	14 762	1 215	81.8	20.1	13 160	31 699	15.1
Colton	264	123	123	141	1 867	3 917	434	3 483	10 697	1 228	70.3	13.4	10 924	28 838	20.4
Compton	650	93	73	557	4 938	5 282	1 631	3 651	26 873	2 917	51.2	6.2	7 842	24 971	10.7
Concord	1 354	706	706	648	4 949	4 064	388	3 676	24 578	4 845	88.1	26.1	17 566	41 675	12.4
Corona	632	431	337	201	3 612	2 890	261	2 630	18 607	2 212	76.1	18.0	15 292	43 555	25.6
Costa Mesa	3 270	1 268	260	2 002	3 462	3 184	253	2 931	20 013	4 313	83.5	27.3	18 750	40 313	24.6
Covina	602	279	247	323	2 188	4 672	576	4 095	9 773	1 966	82.5	16.4	16 259	38 907	11.2
Culver City	524	241	170	283	1 584	4 081	423	3 658	8 065	1 651	84.1	35.0	21 471	42 971	15.9
Cupertino	448	377	377	71	1 164	2 303	206	2 097	9 609	1 652	94.5	52.1	29 118	64 587	27.1
Cypress	321	5	5	316	1 012	2 189	234	1 955	11 215	1 702	87.5	26.6	19 147	50 981	11.2
Daly City	790	532	524	258	2 128	2 054	317	1 737	21 430	4 887	78.8	24.2	14 744	41 533	14.9
Dana Point	242	95	95	147	707	2 014	197	1 817	6 208	1 128	90.3	35.8	27 986	54 516	44.3
Danville	464	94	94	370	575	1 378	110	1 268	7 660	1 342	95.7	48.3	31 265	74 472	18.9
Davis	2 970	254	254	2 716	1 808	2 998	421	2 577	22 712	1 171	95.0	63.8	15 269	29 044	18.0
Delano	5 057	4 982	177	75	1 615	4 160	245	3 915	6 269	404	41.9	7.6	7 491	21 054	-6.5
Diamond Bar	118	51	48	67	893	1 587	210	1 377	15 049	2 611	90.6	37.0	21 497	60 651	17.5
Downey	1 765	1 423	412	342	3 079	2 869	317	2 552	20 400	3 645	76.3	16.3	16 696	36 991	9.3
Dublin	5 292	5 262	0	30	641	2 139	310	1 828	4 630	1 087	85.9	24.1	17 056	53 710	23.4
East Palo Alto	189	41	41	148	1 289	4 369	973	3 396	6 355	1 222	60.6	15.6	9 968	29 206	23.2
El Cajon	2 483	1 429	1 388	1 054	3 817	4 023	660	3 364	20 107	2 486	78.5	14.4	13 518	28 108	10.1
El Centro	887	749	112	138	2 095	5 537	946	4 591	10 192	699	59.5	13.5	9 898	25 147	-8.3
El Monte	1 270	623	572	647	3 668	3 163	923	2 240	29 844	2 293	44.3	6.0	8 056	28 034	21.0
Encinitas	559	415	393	144	1 366	2 355	300	2 055	11 940	2 248	88.6	39.7	22 451	46 069	56.9
Escondido	1 765	696	696	1 069	5 099	3 818	501	3 317	23 628	3 293	77.9	18.3	14 647	32 895	28.6
Eureka	1 355	487	110	868	2 162	8 275	559	7 716	6 973	425	79.3	18.0	12 915	21 812	-4.9
Fairfield	4 229	1 886	986	2 343	4 287	4 457	562	3 895	20 745	1 753	84.2	15.4	13 713	36 886	22.4
Folsom	6 944	3 228	87	3 716	1 211	2 334	123	2 211	6 263	786	84.2	24.2	17 617	46 726	69.5
Fontana	499	218	189	281	4 067	3 154	697	2 457	23 338	2 486	72.0	9.4	11 585	35 558	16.1
Foster City	87	67	67	20	490	1 701	90	1 611	6 224	1 348	95.0	46.7	28 399	60 462	19.7
Fountain Valley	512	169	167	343	1 646	2 994	266	2 728	14 346	2 544	88.7	31.3	20 699	56 255	13.4
Fremont	1 759	755	484	1 004	5 309	2 610	190	2 420	41 577	6 417	86.6	29.9	20 101	51 231	20.6
Fresno	8 187	4 527	1 691	3 660	32 868	7 686	899	6 787	104 708	8 198	69.0	19.1	11 528	24 923	3.1
Fullerton	2 770	884	846	1 886	4 098	3 252	248	3 005	28 702	4 867	82.7	29.8	19 098	41 921	15.5
Gardena	804	556	509	248	2 675	4 632	1 145	3 488	11 326	1 695	73.4	16.5	14 601	33 683	6.8
Garden Grove	2 234	788	701	1 446	5 140	3 111	439	2 672	34 198	4 363	74.4	16.1	13 976	39 882	11.3
Gilroy	430	219	143	211	1 676	4 042	733	3 309	9 124	844	68.5	16.2	14 241	40 955	27.7
Glendale	2 864	1 715	1 689	1 149	4 909	2 518	372	2 145	39 208	9 304	77.2	28.6	17 966	34 372	19.2
Glendora	1 007	786	671	221	993	2 010	174	1 835	11 726	2 052	83.7	22.2	18 573	46 116	13.6
Hanford	848	718	358	130	1 791	4 296	365	3 932	7 531	765	71.0	11.9	11 283	26 629	8.2
Hawthorne	500	308	308	192	3 739	4 445	1 512	2 933	16 468	3 078	73.9	15.7	13 880	30 967	6.7
Hayward	2 138	755	751	1 383	5 667	4 047	553	3 494	26 035	3 443	76.3	17.0	15 048	36 058	7.6
Hemet	1 679	919	871	760	2 768	4 707	551	4 156	4 873	514	67.3	9.2	12 270	20 382	11.6
Hesperia	331	196	104	135	1 853	2 961	260	2 700	12 993	1 363	71.3	6.7	11 472	30 795	27.3
Highland	240	8	8	232	1 511	3 388	448	2 939	8 762	1 163	74.4	13.7	12 567	31 561	NA
Hollister	171	159	62	12	1 008	2 929	860	2 069	5 072	670	63.3	11.6	11 415	32 857	26.4
Huntington Beach	792	496	434	296	4 526	2 387	199	2 188	42 235	6 873	89.2	32.1	23 500	50 633	25.8
Huntington Park	181	16	0	165	3 009	4 905	1 001	3 904	16 507	1 399	30.6	5.3	7 238	23 595	24.1

1. Persons in emergency shelters and persons visible in street locations.   2. Data for serious crimes have not been adjusted for underreporting. This may affect comparability between geographic areas and over time.   3. Per 100,000 population estimated by the FBI.   4. Persons 25 years old and older.   5. Based on population enumerated as of April 1, 1990.

City	Percent with $100,000 or more	Persons Total	Percent change in rate, 1979–1989	Families Total	Housing units 2000 Total	Percent change, 1990–2000	Vacant units for sale or rent[1]	For seasonal use (percent)	Home owner vacancy rate	Renter vacancy rate	Occupied units Total	Percent owner occupied	Percent renter occupied	Average size owner occupied	Average size renter occupied
	46	47	48	49	50	51	52	53	54	55	56	57	58	59	60
CALIFORNIA—Cont'd															
Baldwin Park	2.3	15.7	3.3	12.8	17 430	1.5	469	0.1	1.2	1.9	16 961	61.0	39.0	4.43	4.45
Bell	0.9	26.1	33.8	22.9	9 215	-2.0	297	0.5	1.7	1.9	8 918	30.9	69.1	4.36	3.91
Bellflower	3.1	9.6	-3.0	7.4	24 247	0.5	880	0.2	1.8	3.0	23 367	40.3	59.7	3.20	3.02
Bell Gardens	1.1	26.1	3.2	23.8	9 788	2.5	322	0.1	2.7	1.7	9 466	23.8	76.2	4.67	4.59
Belmont	13.8	4.7	20.5	2.8	10 577	2.5	159	0.2	0.3	1.0	10 418	60.2	39.8	2.59	1.99
Benicia	9.3	5.4	12.5	3.7	10 547	10.0	219	0.4	0.5	2.4	10 328	70.7	29.3	2.73	2.27
Berkeley	8.5	17.5	-16.7	9.4	46 875	2.5	1 920	0.6	0.7	2.8	44 955	42.7	57.3	2.40	1.98
Beverly Hills	30.0	6.6	-25.8	4.2	15 856	0.8	821	0.9	1.6	3.3	15 035	43.4	56.6	2.73	1.87
Brea	11.4	3.5	2.9	1.7	13 327	5.4	260	0.3	0.5	2.1	13 067	64.2	35.8	2.88	2.37
Buena Park	5.4	8.0	6.7	5.9	23 826	2.7	494	0.1	0.8	2.2	23 332	57.1	42.9	3.28	3.36
Burbank	6.1	8.3	7.8	5.9	42 847	4.0	1 239	0.4	0.9	2.1	41 608	43.5	56.5	2.61	2.22
Burlingame	11.3	4.7	-19.0	2.9	12 869	-0.3	358	0.6	0.4	2.2	12 511	47.9	52.1	2.58	1.87
Calexico	1.5	32.3	35.7	29.9	6 983	44.5	169	0.3	1.0	1.1	6 814	55.2	44.8	4.19	3.68
Camarillo	9.6	4.4	4.8	2.5	21 946	17.2	508	0.3	0.9	1.9	21 438	73.5	26.5	2.63	2.59
Campbell	7.5	5.8	-23.7	3.8	16 286	2.7	366	0.6	0.4	1.5	15 920	48.2	51.8	2.55	2.22
Carlsbad	9.4	6.8	-9.3	3.6	33 798	24.1	2 277	2.6	2.2	4.1	31 521	67.4	32.6	2.52	2.33
Carson	5.7	6.9	-12.7	5.0	25 337	3.7	689	0.1	1.1	2.6	24 648	77.9	22.1	3.57	3.68
Cathedral City	3.4	13.6	NA	9.6	17 893	17.5	3 866	10.5	4.1	5.2	14 027	65.2	34.8	2.95	3.18
Ceres	1.8	15.5	31.4	12.6	10 773	18.7	338	0.1	1.0	3.8	10 435	66.2	33.8	3.29	3.34
Cerritos	15.1	4.0	25.0	3.0	15 607	1.6	217	0.2	0.4	1.7	15 390	83.5	16.5	3.30	3.56
Chico	2.0	32.0	22.6	15.9	24 386	49.7	910	0.3	1.8	2.6	23 476	40.4	59.6	2.52	2.35
Chino	4.6	7.4	-6.3	6.0	17 898	10.9	594	0.1	0.9	5.2	17 304	68.7	31.3	3.51	3.26
Chula Vista	3.5	9.8	16.7	8.6	59 495	19.4	1 790	0.4	1.0	3.1	57 705	57.4	42.6	3.09	2.85
Claremont	16.2	5.3	-8.6	2.2	11 559	6.7	278	0.4	0.7	2.2	11 281	66.7	33.3	2.74	2.20
Clovis	1.9	10.3	12.0	8.6	25 250	33.7	903	0.2	1.5	4.0	24 347	60.4	39.6	2.95	2.56
Colton	1.5	15.6	11.4	13.4	15 680	6.2	1 160	0.3	3.4	7.0	14 520	52.0	48.0	3.53	2.97
Compton	1.6	27.5	4.2	24.2	23 795	2.4	1 468	0.1	3.7	5.1	22 327	56.3	43.7	4.16	4.15
Concord	4.7	6.7	11.7	4.9	45 083	3.1	1 063	0.3	0.5	2.3	44 020	62.6	37.4	2.69	2.81
Corona	5.1	8.3	-16.2	5.7	39 271	48.0	1 432	0.2	1.9	3.8	37 839	67.5	32.5	3.39	3.06
Costa Mesa	7.2	9.2	8.2	6.0	40 406	2.0	1 200	0.3	0.8	2.8	39 206	40.5	59.5	2.66	2.71
Covina	5.0	7.6	20.6	5.3	16 364	1.6	393	0.1	0.8	2.5	15 971	58.4	41.6	3.02	2.72
Culver City	8.7	6.7	-1.5	4.6	17 130	1.1	519	0.2	1.2	2.1	16 611	54.4	45.6	2.34	2.26
Cupertino	22.4	3.2	-13.5	2.1	18 682	16.4	478	0.4	0.6	1.8	18 204	63.6	36.4	2.83	2.62
Cypress	10.3	4.5	-8.2	3.4	16 028	8.9	374	0.6	0.6	2.9	15 654	69.4	30.6	2.96	2.87
Daly City	5.3	7.2	2.9	5.9	31 311	3.8	536	0.3	0.3	1.7	30 775	59.8	40.2	3.48	3.13
Dana Point	18.8	7.2	-10.0	4.4	15 682	6.9	1 226	4.6	1.2	4.2	14 456	62.0	38.0	2.38	2.46
Danville	28.3	2.1	-4.5	1.2	15 130	32.0	314	0.3	0.6	5.5	14 816	89.1	10.9	2.83	2.38
Davis	5.5	25.5	1.6	7.1	23 617	29.2	669	0.4	0.8	2.7	22 948	44.6	55.4	2.64	2.39
Delano	1.6	23.7	27.4	21.0	8 830	36.2	421	0.3	1.1	5.6	8 409	59.4	40.6	4.16	3.80
Diamond Bar	13.8	3.5	-5.4	2.4	17 959	1.7	308	0.2	0.7	1.9	17 651	82.6	17.4	3.21	3.05
Downey	6.5	8.1	15.7	5.7	34 759	1.3	770	0.2	1.0	1.5	33 989	51.8	48.2	3.26	2.94
Dublin	7.5	4.2	23.5	3.0	9 872	41.2	547	0.4	0.7	8.1	9 325	64.9	35.1	2.80	2.37
East Palo Alto	1.7	17.5	2.9	14.7	7 091	-3.5	115	0.2	0.3	1.0	6 976	43.5	56.5	4.69	3.83
El Cajon	3.2	12.9	9.3	10.7	35 190	2.1	991	0.3	0.6	2.7	34 199	40.5	59.5	2.67	2.72
El Centro	2.1	23.3	102.6	20.6	12 263	20.5	824	2.4	1.2	4.9	11 439	50.2	49.8	3.34	3.12
El Monte	1.6	22.5	13.1	18.5	27 758	2.2	724	0.2	1.2	1.4	27 034	41.0	59.0	4.03	4.39
Encinitas	12.6	8.3	-17.0	3.5	23 843	7.8	1 013	1.9	0.9	2.6	22 830	64.2	35.8	2.61	2.35
Escondido	4.1	11.2	0.9	7.8	45 050	7.2	1 233	0.2	1.0	2.7	43 817	53.2	46.8	2.93	3.10
Eureka	1.8	18.7	34.5	14.6	11 637	-1.2	680	0.5	2.0	4.7	10 957	46.5	53.5	2.29	2.23
Fairfield	2.4	7.4	-21.3	6.3	31 792	20.6	922	0.2	0.7	3.9	30 870	59.7	40.3	2.99	2.97
Folsom	9.8	5.2	-45.8	4.3	17 968	90.8	772	0.4	1.6	7.1	17 196	76.3	23.7	2.75	2.18
Fontana	1.7	11.4	-1.7	10.2	35 908	22.2	1 894	0.1	3.1	4.2	34 014	68.1	31.9	3.87	3.58
Foster City	17.3	2.9	-17.1	1.6	12 009	2.2	396	1.1	0.3	2.6	11 613	61.5	38.5	2.64	2.21
Fountain Valley	14.5	3.5	-7.9	2.2	18 473	2.5	311	0.3	0.5	2.3	18 162	74.7	25.3	3.07	2.79
Fremont	9.4	4.3	-10.4	3.0	69 452	11.3	1 215	0.3	0.6	1.7	68 237	64.5	35.5	3.08	2.73
Fresno	3.0	24.0	52.9	19.3	149 025	15.2	8 946	0.2	1.9	6.4	140 079	50.6	49.4	2.94	3.05
Fullerton	9.6	9.8	30.7	5.6	44 771	4.2	1 162	0.2	0.8	2.8	43 609	53.9	46.1	2.87	2.77
Gardena	3.4	9.8	6.5	8.2	21 041	10.5	717	0.2	1.2	3.3	20 324	47.3	52.7	2.85	2.76
Garden Grove	3.9	10.4	25.3	7.8	46 703	1.6	912	0.2	0.7	2.0	45 791	59.6	40.4	3.49	3.67
Gilroy	6.1	12.9	-0.8	10.7	12 152	24.4	283	0.1	0.6	1.6	11 869	61.2	38.8	3.27	3.75
Glendale	8.6	14.4	42.6	12.3	73 713	2.2	1 908	0.3	0.9	1.9	71 805	38.4	61.6	2.72	2.65
Glendora	9.5	5.0	-3.8	3.7	17 145	1.6	326	0.2	0.6	2.1	16 819	73.6	26.4	2.97	2.62
Hanford	1.8	15.7	-1.9	13.1	14 721	26.8	790	0.4	2.1	6.0	13 931	59.0	41.0	2.96	2.89
Hawthorne	2.4	13.9	51.1	11.8	29 629	1.4	1 093	0.2	1.4	3.3	28 536	25.9	74.1	3.36	2.78
Hayward	3.5	9.7	5.4	7.6	45 922	8.8	1 118	0.2	0.6	2.6	44 804	53.2	46.8	3.13	3.02
Hemet	0.7	14.0	34.6	10.1	29 401	49.3	4 149	2.6	3.1	19.2	25 252	64.6	35.4	2.15	2.46
Hesperia	1.9	12.5	35.9	10.9	21 348	23.0	1 382	0.4	2.7	7.3	19 966	72.3	27.7	3.08	3.23
Highland	3.4	15.8	NA	12.2	14 858	18.3	1 380	0.2	3.7	12.6	13 478	66.6	33.4	3.22	3.44
Hollister	1.9	11.7	-16.4	9.3	9 924	59.5	208	0.2	0.6	2.3	9 716	67.0	33.0	3.51	3.55
Huntington Beach	12.3	5.2	-20.0	3.2	75 662	4.0	2 005	0.7	0.9	2.0	73 657	60.6	39.4	2.58	2.54
Huntington Park	1.1	24.3	3.8	21.7	15 335	5.6	475	0.1	2.3	1.9	14 860	27.4	72.6	4.65	3.92

1. Includes units rented or sold but not occupied. 2. Specified owner-occupied units. 3. Specified renter-occupied units. 4. Overcrowded or lacking complete plumbing facilities.

Table D. Cities — **Labor Force, Employment, Disability, and Construction**

City	Civilian labor force, 2001				Civilian employment, 1990[2]			Disability 1990	Value of residential construction authorized by building permits, 2000		
	Total	Percent change, 2000–2001	Unemployment		Total	Percent		Work disabled persons[3] (percent)	New construction ($1,000)	Number of housing units	Percent single family
			Total	Rate[1]		Professional, managerial, and technical	Precision production, craft, and repair				
	61	62	63	64	65	66	67	68	69	70	71

CALIFORNIA—Cont'd											
Baldwin Park	33 438	2.4	2 184	6.5	28 573	16.3	14.7	6.2	3 256	30	90.0
Bell	15 640	2.6	1 510	9.7	12 918	10.4	15.6	7.5	68	1	100.0
Bellflower	34 781	2.3	1 576	4.5	30 357	24.0	14.1	8.2	2 855	23	100.0
Bell Gardens	18 488	2.7	1 935	10.5	15 133	8.1	14.8	6.5	814	9	55.6
Belmont	17 099	-0.9	388	2.3	14 877	41.2	11.0	4.3	1 384	4	100.0
Benicia	17 021	2.1	463	2.7	12 974	40.0	10.6	7.3	7 780	47	76.6
Berkeley	66 240	2.0	2 753	4.2	55 990	56.4	4.2	7.8	7 142	47	21.3
Beverly Hills	18 937	2.2	550	2.9	16 810	53.8	2.8	3.3	2 146	4	100.0
Brea	22 350	1.6	461	2.1	18 977	40.3	9.7	5.5	16 392	99	83.8
Buena Park	42 229	1.8	1 513	3.6	35 299	27.3	14.4	6.9	3 533	17	52.9
Burbank	57 091	2.3	2 242	3.9	50 144	35.8	10.3	6.4	25 308	73	87.7
Burlingame	17 250	-1.0	320	1.9	15 072	38.0	7.9	4.9	9 322	42	52.4
Calexico	8 895	-7.0	2 545	28.6	5 294	16.2	7.0	8.9	37 419	347	99.4
Camarillo	30 820	1.6	1 096	3.6	24 967	39.5	10.1	6.3	56 542	361	55.7
Campbell	27 031	-0.3	874	3.2	21 816	40.5	11.0	6.3	11 893	64	100.0
Carlsbad	40 786	1.6	1 047	2.6	33 000	42.2	7.8	6.1	379 481	1 826	95.1
Carson	47 557	2.4	2 637	5.5	41 067	25.4	13.6	7.6	19 380	163	96.9
Cathedral City	21 309	2.8	990	4.6	13 944	21.1	14.9	8.4	30 240	246	89.0
Ceres	14 705	2.1	1 510	10.3	10 554	20.8	16.3	10.8	11 085	99	100.0
Cerritos	31 552	2.2	889	2.8	28 033	42.0	9.8	4.3	5 814	15	100.0
Chico	22 734	0.6	1 545	6.8	18 359	29.9	9.0	7.0	59 118	508	66.7
Chino	34 202	3.1	1 169	3.4	25 181	25.7	13.0	6.4	17 586	97	100.0
Chula Vista	74 622	1.7	2 531	3.4	59 865	30.7	12.1	8.0	393 542	2 639	67.3
Claremont	18 817	2.2	607	3.2	16 648	50.0	5.7	5.5	16 664	76	80.3
Clovis	33 410	-1.7	2 838	8.5	24 675	30.2	11.0	7.3	94 800	507	100.0
Colton	24 129	3.1	1 484	6.2	17 262	24.5	14.3	7.8	10 030	65	95.4
Compton	37 520	2.7	4 216	11.2	30 447	15.4	13.4	10.2	578	6	100.0
Concord	75 468	1.1	2 282	3.0	60 333	34.2	12.0	7.1	50 940	321	44.5
Corona	56 959	2.9	2 447	4.3	37 410	30.3	13.1	5.9	300 888	1 323	100.0
Costa Mesa	69 727	1.7	1 816	2.6	58 875	34.3	10.0	5.3	8 413	58	100.0
Covina	25 292	2.3	1 039	4.1	22 173	30.0	11.7	7.6	8 440	42	100.0
Culver City	24 835	2.2	785	3.2	21 987	44.1	7.9	5.2	5 910	35	100.0
Cupertino	28 891	-0.6	752	2.6	23 469	59.1	5.8	4.5	34 216	126	88.9
Cypress	28 030	1.7	789	2.8	23 616	37.0	11.2	6.2	7 500	34	100.0
Daly City	56 765	-0.2	2 069	3.6	48 693	25.1	9.0	6.3	19 217	84	96.4
Dana Point	21 554	1.6	514	2.4	18 241	40.2	9.3	4.4	34 426	116	70.7
Danville	21 237	0.8	333	1.6	17 233	48.8	6.3	3.6	9 322	55	100.0
Davis	34 460	-0.8	1 105	3.2	24 765	56.0	4.1	4.4	100 628	554	71.3
Delano	12 482	-0.9	3 194	25.6	7 640	16.8	6.3	9.1	14 883	163	97.5
Diamond Bar	33 114	2.2	899	2.7	29 452	43.7	7.3	4.0	19 175	27	100.0
Downey	51 159	2.3	2 135	4.2	44 819	27.1	12.8	6.5	7 715	51	31.4
Dublin	12 730	1.5	331	2.6	10 935	35.3	11.7	6.9	222 983	867	86.9
East Palo Alto	12 163	1.4	882	7.3	10 043	25.0	10.3	10.4	49 058	480	23.3
El Cajon	49 791	1.7	1 945	3.9	39 732	27.0	15.2	10.5	10 939	74	100.0
El Centro	16 869	-4.8	3 478	20.6	11 165	28.9	9.0	8.5	4 260	46	100.0
El Monte	50 681	2.5	3 694	7.3	42 956	13.4	16.1	6.2	11 099	97	94.8
Encinitas	38 935	1.6	842	2.2	31 633	43.7	8.1	4.4	67 602	269	96.3
Escondido	64 636	1.6	2 143	3.3	51 895	28.9	13.6	8.2	63 552	306	92.2
Eureka	13 056	-1.6	800	6.1	11 220	25.9	10.8	15.7	1 666	15	100.0
Fairfield	44 113	2.1	1 987	4.5	33 008	26.1	14.5	8.4	96 335	587	100.0
Folsom	14 738	2.3	408	2.8	11 741	43.1	7.9	5.9	276 401	1 243	100.0
Fontana	50 759	3.1	2 336	4.6	36 913	21.1	15.9	6.8	260 402	1 435	100.0
Foster City	20 247	-0.9	458	2.3	17 617	47.3	6.4	3.5	500	1	100.0
Fountain Valley	35 826	1.6	886	2.5	30 291	41.0	10.0	5.6	796	3	100.0
Fremont	112 642	1.7	3 490	3.1	96 262	39.0	11.8	5.5	109 351	489	48.3
Fresno	197 243	-1.9	24 270	12.3	139 607	31.0	9.2	9.6	197 258	1 446	96.7
Fullerton	73 973	1.7	2 153	2.9	62 264	35.0	9.7	5.9	50 314	259	95.8
Gardena	29 340	2.3	1 328	4.5	25 609	26.0	12.6	7.6	27 798	181	97.8
Garden Grove	86 037	1.9	3 370	3.9	71 668	26.7	14.1	7.3	16 655	136	97.8
Gilroy	19 044	2.2	1 413	7.4	14 705	26.2	12.6	6.1	63 044	307	94.8
Glendale	100 678	2.4	5 392	5.4	87 112	37.5	9.5	6.5	17 082	71	59.2
Glendora	27 355	2.2	900	3.3	24 186	34.8	12.7	6.9	8 409	39	87.2
Hanford	16 975	-0.5	2 049	12.1	12 400	23.5	10.1	9.5	21 298	235	100.0
Hawthorne	42 721	2.4	2 278	5.3	36 974	26.1	11.9	6.9	1 539	9	100.0
Hayward	65 911	2.2	3 001	4.6	55 481	26.3	13.4	7.8	68 421	294	100.0
Hemet	15 423	2.7	1 137	7.4	9 804	22.5	17.1	14.6	100 307	627	88.7
Hesperia	25 797	3.1	1 499	5.8	18 522	19.7	22.7	11.3	27 362	210	100.0
Highland	20 088	3.1	1 128	5.6	14 453	24.0	14.2	8.3	12 942	53	100.0
Hollister	14 453	2.7	1 512	10.5	8 457	21.7	14.2	5.7	51 734	358	100.0
Huntington Beach	127 966	1.6	2 896	2.3	108 429	39.5	10.2	5.4	107 277	433	98.6
Huntington Park	27 524	2.7	2 750	10.0	22 649	10.8	15.0	4.7	0	0	0.0

1. Percent of civilian labor force. 2. Persons 16 years and older. 3. Persons 16 to 64 years old.

City	Wholesale Trade, 1997				Retail Trade[1], 1997				Real Estate and Rental and Leasing, 1997			
	Number of Establish- ments	Number of Employees	Sales (mil dol)	Annual Payroll (mil dol)	Number of Establish- ments	Number of Employees	Sales (mil dol)	Annual Payroll (mil dol)	Number of Establish- ments	Number of Employees	Receipts (mil dol)	Annual Payroll (mil dol)
	72	73	74	75	76	77	78	79	80	81	82	83
CALIFORNIA—Cont'd												
Baldwin Park	152	1 323	744.9	40.7	125	1 041	204.5	21.2	26	94	12.5	1.9
Bell	71	1 287	591.7	39.2	62	483	102.1	10.3	12	90	15.8	2.9
Bellflower	44	316	62.6	6.9	169	2 116	439.4	41.0	84	340	40.8	5.9
Bell Gardens	35	319	147.1	7.9	80	584	104.0	9.5	10	26	2.0	0.2
Belmont	46	779	428.9	58.0	64	810	228.1	23.4	35	320	28.0	4.9
Benicia	78	1 542	747.9	68.0	76	825	137.1	16.0	40	172	28.5	4.6
Berkeley	136	1 389	438.2	61.0	536	6 313	1 238.7	131.9	162	681	108.8	15.4
Beverly Hills	186	1 256	928.6	60.1	414	5 910	1 377.4	170.8	424	2 214	423.9	77.5
Brea	235	2 926	2 548.1	121.4	296	5 094	765.5	75.6	53	351	43.8	9.1
Buena Park	157	2 150	1 322.6	74.7	235	3 793	966.6	88.5	49	398	55.6	12.5
Burbank	261	3 956	5 069.4	162.2	381	5 981	1 306.1	110.6	173	1 853	709.6	81.5
Burlingame	244	1 597	2 062.5	70.2	192	2 282	546.3	59.3	147	966	183.2	24.0
Calexico	62	352	167.8	6.5	182	2 091	291.3	28.2	19	84	5.1	1.2
Camarillo	128	1 892	632.8	82.1	249	3 110	607.9	58.9	58	316	41.1	9.3
Campbell	NA	NA	NA	NA	NA	NA	NA	NA	NA	NA	NA	NA
Carlsbad	266	4 290	2 140.3	174.8	355	4 855	1 120.5	106.7	139	1 054	134.8	29.7
Carson	338	7 029	5 176.5	273.5	216	4 505	949.5	100.0	70	2 884	544.1	103.7
Cathedral City	35	250	52.5	7.9	169	2 421	574.0	52.6	36	223	25.6	3.9
Ceres	20	D	D	D	81	1 350	222.7	20.9	24	99	8.3	1.4
Cerritos	276	5 313	3 940.4	201.6	279	7 822	1 934.3	159.8	55	282	41.6	6.7
Chico	109	1 300	469.1	44.3	420	5 812	987.8	97.7	101	531	48.9	8.0
Chino	217	2 830	1 296.1	107.0	184	2 963	554.2	55.6	40	209	38.3	4.4
Chula Vista	265	1 717	681.3	46.0	546	7 502	1 276.6	125.7	161	750	93.6	11.9
Claremont	29	210	91.1	7.9	97	1 251	321.6	26.7	28	149	14.2	3.4
Clovis	44	219	89.1	5.6	262	4 319	853.0	78.4	46	256	29.4	3.9
Colton	60	846	279.4	27.3	103	1 682	327.6	33.1	28	144	14.8	3.3
Compton	135	3 114	1 325.1	108.7	148	1 811	375.2	33.5	23	166	25.7	3.6
Concord	203	1 677	1 264.6	68.7	481	7 295	1 654.9	164.3	119	620	123.2	18.4
Corona	220	2 958	2 396.6	102.7	270	4 513	1 066.4	96.0	86	861	69.3	18.4
Costa Mesa	373	5 888	7 388.3	289.9	693	12 297	2 343.3	251.8	216	1 751	312.8	58.2
Covina	97	652	333.2	20.4	177	2 632	537.9	52.3	74	358	41.5	7.6
Culver City	201	3 449	1 638.7	160.4	341	4 970	884.9	97.6	100	1 040	91.6	26.0
Cupertino	92	1 464	1 935.2	117.9	248	3 355	509.2	55.0	78	373	67.1	11.7
Cypress	99	3 799	7 999.8	230.9	100	1 254	310.6	25.7	45	152	27.5	3.8
Daly City	47	550	209.7	21.4	240	3 214	524.9	52.3	49	208	43.1	3.9
Dana Point	46	143	136.8	5.1	114	1 295	306.3	27.6	36	158	25.3	3.3
Danville	75	286	328.4	13.2	139	1 599	352.8	31.1	83	597	70.6	12.9
Davis	27	93	29.5	4.1	139	1 885	324.6	37.4	71	487	42.3	8.5
Delano	16	160	67.1	5.3	99	1 016	161.9	16.1	13	38	3.7	0.5
Diamond Bar	174	1 100	1 241.9	31.3	102	1 031	204.3	17.4	54	395	41.2	14.2
Downey	98	1 112	635.1	43.5	295	4 694	1 061.1	103.6	111	533	62.7	10.9
Dublin	81	546	270.6	20.4	154	2 499	614.1	57.2	31	204	31.6	2.9
East Palo Alto	7	D	D	D	20	79	16.2	1.2	16	40	6.1	0.6
El Cajon	116	1 262	369.2	34.0	497	6 539	1 211.8	123.6	145	656	62.8	12.5
El Centro	47	334	137.5	8.6	172	2 393	417.7	43.0	31	128	10.6	1.4
El Monte	314	3 461	2 389.6	129.8	245	3 320	1 335.3	96.6	46	267	39.5	5.5
Encinitas	81	461	234.6	17.0	224	2 525	493.4	50.6	90	296	51.3	6.8
Escondido	171	1 172	377.2	38.9	600	9 390	1 765.6	186.0	163	964	157.4	20.8
Eureka	56	587	166.3	17.3	271	3 173	539.7	53.9	48	231	14.7	3.8
Fairfield	60	1 016	913.8	37.1	336	5 090	940.9	93.0	84	395	41.4	6.6
Folsom	23	D	D	D	162	2 134	444.9	41.6	34	105	14.2	2.4
Fontana	69	2 432	1 925.2	64.6	209	4 001	773.6	75.1	47	271	42.4	6.2
Foster City	97	1 595	862.6	98.2	60	1 171	246.9	23.9	46	719	115.4	36.6
Fountain Valley	157	1 429	1 951.1	63.4	218	3 242	632.2	57.4	55	327	45.8	9.6
Fremont	656	10 975	15 406.2	477.3	440	6 544	1 705.1	152.1	195	1 168	186.4	26.5
Fresno	655	8 209	3 934.0	269.4	1 546	19 850	3 589.5	362.8	398	2 598	273.1	51.1
Fullerton	225	3 596	2 331.2	134.9	292	4 361	938.6	88.0	122	700	82.1	15.5
Gardena	198	1 708	606.8	51.2	175	2 196	439.3	44.1	49	211	41.2	5.3
Garden Grove	240	3 031	1 469.9	101.4	413	5 618	1 247.9	116.3	103	555	85.0	13.1
Gilroy	43	D	D	D	273	3 118	664.8	60.1	42	136	21.6	2.8
Glendale	315	2 813	1 057.6	101.1	725	9 426	1 844.2	188.1	226	1 421	299.0	43.4
Glendora	50	546	322.9	22.8	133	1 758	341.5	34.7	58	207	22.9	3.5
Hanford	27	218	114.5	4.7	184	2 512	414.6	41.2	38	161	12.4	2.2
Hawthorne	55	821	218.9	28.2	187	2 581	528.4	49.1	56	151	16.9	1.9
Hayward	598	9 655	5 283.1	364.3	438	6 541	1 460.6	147.6	163	1 217	217.4	32.9
Hemet	19	87	49.1	3.3	221	3 349	561.7	60.0	61	328	31.4	5.0
Hesperia	38	187	98.2	4.9	129	1 161	200.2	21.4	30	88	8.4	1.2
Highland	6	148	25.1	3.0	50	578	109.1	9.2	18	61	5.7	0.8
Hollister	27	687	161.6	19.4	93	1 400	233.1	25.5	22	67	12.0	1.1
Huntington Beach	477	4 819	2 484.3	171.6	601	8 063	1 700.6	160.6	228	1 188	262.2	38.0
Huntington Park	58	1 167	374.8	35.9	173	1 658	296.2	30.9	12	77	6.4	0.7

1. Establishments with payroll.

City	Professional, Scientific, and Technical Services, 1997[1]				Manufacturing, 1997				Accommodation and Foodservices, 1997			
	Number of Establishments	Number of Employees	Receipts (mil dol)	Annual Payroll (mil dol)	Number of Establishments	Number of Employees	Receipts (mil dol)	Annual Payroll (mil dol)	Number of Establishments	Number of Employees	Sales (mil dol)	Annual Payroll (mil dol)
	84	85	86	87	88	89	90	91	92	93	94	95
CALIFORNIA—Cont'd												
Baldwin Park	14	122	9.6	3.0	141	2 854	232.1	68.5	60	839	32.6	7.6
Bell	10	192	7.6	3.9	29	940	177.3	28.8	50	684	25.5	5.5
Bellflower	47	227	15.4	5.8	NA	NA	NA	NA	88	1 057	38.9	8.8
Bell Gardens	4	D	D	D	70	1 672	163.3	42.2	37	382	15.7	3.3
Belmont	81	408	49.8	19.6	NA	NA	NA	NA	60	619	28.3	7.2
Benicia	79	758	74.4	26.2	85	2 063	1 650.0	88.1	54	D	D	D
Berkeley	464	2 554	332.6	130.2	199	5 247	996.6	212.8	367	4 711	198.6	56.9
Beverly Hills	908	4 940	909.9	319.0	64	501	45.1	10.9	188	6 230	297.9	92.7
Brea	151	1 724	162.6	47.0	187	8 461	1 145.1	316.5	103	2 393	85.0	21.9
Buena Park	67	887	97.0	43.3	126	7 108	1 358.5	227.8	119	2 750	102.0	27.9
Burbank	368	126 307	4 972.4	2 707.5	298	9 355	1 131.2	306.9	236	4 756	201.0	53.0
Burlingame	255	1 802	247.6	108.0	83	2 286	408.5	90.9	123	4 988	287.4	83.8
Calexico	20	79	5.2	2.3	NA	NA	NA	NA	54	625	21.7	5.7
Camarillo	176	1 468	176.2	68.1	173	8 487	1 513.5	296.9	112	1 846	69.7	17.6
Campbell	NA	NA	NA	NA	156	3 307	613.5	133.6	NA	NA	NA	NA
Carlsbad	351	3 377	423.7	136.3	205	12 384	2 418.9	458.0	165	4 176	186.3	50.3
Carson	77	775	94.1	32.4	321	13 958	5 207.9	477.5	118	1 606	63.6	15.7
Cathedral City	30	100	10.5	2.6	NA	NA	NA	NA	86	957	32.4	8.3
Ceres	11	51	2.9	1.2	32	835	131.1	24.0	43	566	20.4	4.8
Cerritos	111	1 627	342.0	111.6	117	5 463	801.1	169.4	99	1 972	72.9	21.6
Chico	171	1 026	99.3	34.4	107	2 455	403.7	63.1	210	3 754	94.1	26.0
Chino	80	585	60.6	17.2	259	9 897	1 294.7	245.8	89	1 816	56.9	14.9
Chula Vista	156	706	57.8	19.4	158	5 626	1 029.2	210.9	280	4 370	157.2	39.9
Claremont	114	726	75.5	22.7	29	1 309	177.6	58.0	70	1 235	40.0	11.5
Clovis	72	355	23.4	8.6	55	2 320	259.4	56.0	133	D	D	D
Colton	31	438	43.6	13.9	54	1 668	278.2	45.4	75	1 021	33.5	8.6
Compton	23	D	D	D	179	8 188	1 108.1	215.3	63	687	23.4	5.5
Concord	256	2 044	246.9	102.2	145	2 554	353.3	97.6	217	3 607	141.2	38.0
Corona	133	733	81.3	25.2	291	10 424	1 817.4	313.2	136	2 311	77.8	19.7
Costa Mesa	552	6 031	908.1	338.7	310	11 091	1 757.6	429.6	315	6 638	282.7	75.4
Covina	142	783	50.4	18.5	119	3 226	359.5	114.5	106	1 603	63.3	16.0
Culver City	249	2 290	243.0	82.3	119	2 789	253.7	76.1	153	2 491	118.9	33.5
Cupertino	296	2 091	343.7	141.2	49	2 626	295.1	112.9	138	2 657	109.4	30.5
Cypress	75	924	104.5	42.4	40	1 341	200.4	41.8	89	1 400	48.5	12.4
Daly City	69	215	19.9	7.2	NA	NA	NA	NA	115	2 049	82.4	21.4
Dana Point	85	276	31.1	10.2	NA	NA	NA	NA	72	2 515	140.5	34.8
Danville	182	862	104.9	48.0	NA	NA	NA	NA	99	D	D	D
Davis	110	588	95.0	24.7	NA	NA	NA	NA	118	1 930	57.1	14.3
Delano	10	172	7.3	5.2	NA	NA	NA	NA	43	D	D	D
Diamond Bar	135	1 020	133.8	47.2	NA	NA	NA	NA	69	1 021	35.2	9.1
Downey	123	458	38.1	14.0	102	7 464	1 419.0	372.8	183	2 964	116.6	30.0
Dublin	100	666	98.3	27.4	26	606	75.1	23.4	55	1 285	46.1	11.3
East Palo Alto	4	D	D	D	13	767	196.5	42.5	13	182	9.0	2.0
El Cajon	150	1 481	62.4	27.7	187	6 102	654.3	194.1	211	2 819	103.4	25.4
El Centro	56	334	34.3	11.2	NA	NA	NA	NA	96	1 294	43.0	10.9
El Monte	81	293	38.3	10.4	238	8 068	882.2	211.8	128	1 317	53.2	11.7
Encinitas	213	711	85.6	34.7	NA	NA	NA	NA	148	2 207	73.4	20.7
Escondido	260	1 173	109.1	39.0	190	4 330	563.8	114.5	233	3 505	123.8	32.9
Eureka	107	565	39.8	14.7	44	686	128.5	20.6	146	1 951	64.7	17.1
Fairfield	111	520	41.9	15.6	53	2 955	1 036.1	121.7	133	2 346	79.5	20.2
Folsom	78	329	39.7	16.2	23	648	79.2	26.2	103	D	D	D
Fontana	20	66	3.8	1.2	111	4 811	1 128.7	153.9	119	1 530	55.8	13.5
Foster City	148	1 858	349.2	142.4	26	1 866	563.4	115.8	62	1 206	51.2	13.4
Fountain Valley	164	1 350	191.5	55.5	111	2 645	1 302.2	84.6	128	1 974	74.1	18.0
Fremont	497	4 632	512.0	226.0	464	34 623	10 765.3	1 593.4	290	4 612	176.8	44.2
Fresno	913	10 110	505.0	205.4	412	15 225	3 099.8	395.1	799	13 915	433.4	119.8
Fullerton	260	2 543	427.3	120.0	228	10 916	2 217.1	375.8	199	3 792	137.0	37.0
Gardena	54	227	20.1	6.9	339	7 739	849.2	208.3	162	1 734	68.0	16.8
Garden Grove	184	1 228	95.2	29.2	354	9 710	2 255.3	269.5	278	3 868	138.1	36.5
Gilroy	46	221	18.1	8.4	61	2 538	426.9	76.7	83	1 147	48.3	10.4
Glendale	585	4 637	469.8	186.6	329	7 280	784.7	217.7	304	4 915	191.2	51.4
Glendora	77	329	44.8	12.8	53	1 321	194.4	49.3	78	1 149	39.2	10.4
Hanford	55	274	21.3	7.0	27	1 672	376.3	62.6	91	1 256	40.7	10.3
Hawthorne	33	241	19.1	10.3	114	5 719	1 006.6	234.6	98	1 272	57.8	12.4
Hayward	215	1 525	164.7	64.6	385	11 817	2 287.2	430.1	236	2 959	112.9	27.9
Hemet	72	270	19.8	7.0	25	972	106.5	19.9	106	1 332	44.5	11.2
Hesperia	35	115	10.2	2.1	66	1 212	157.6	26.3	68	873	26.7	7.1
Highland	11	33	1.7	0.5	NA	NA	NA	NA	35	D	D	D
Hollister	41	133	12.1	4.7	49	1 346	231.1	39.7	50	653	22.3	5.8
Huntington Beach	460	2 632	258.9	100.8	417	14 927	2 377.3	594.8	378	6 467	237.9	64.3
Huntington Park	18	92	8.0	2.6	163	5 042	575.4	133.5	74	D	D	D

1. Firms subject to federal tax.

City	Arts, Entertainment, and Recreation[1], 1997				Health Care and Social Assistance[1], 1997				Other Services[1], 1997			
	Number of Establishments	Number of Employees	Receipts (mil dol)	Annual Payroll (mil dol)	Number of Establishments	Number of Employees	Receipts (mil dol)	Annual Payroll (mil dol)	Number of Establishments	Number of Employees	Receipts (mil dol)	Annual Payroll (mil dol)
	96	97	98	99	100	101	102	103	104	105	106	107
CALIFORNIA—Cont'd												
Baldwin Park	3	0	0.0	0.0	56	1 505	85.0	42.7	59	234	15.7	4.7
Bell	NA	NA	NA	NA	23	210	12.9	4.9	34	138	13.2	3.8
Bellflower	9	79	6.0	1.4	115	2 474	255.0	86.3	117	599	42.6	11.9
Bell Gardens	5	0	0.0	0.0	20	371	15.4	7.0	33	240	14.8	4.7
Belmont	5	49	1.7	0.5	48	361	24.1	9.4	47	239	16.2	4.3
Benicia	9	22	1.8	0.2	49	286	17.3	5.8	52	705	55.0	21.4
Berkeley	38	447	25.4	6.6	420	2 272	203.9	78.6	203	1 353	84.4	27.3
Beverly Hills	573	2 856	975.1	551.7	769	3 162	443.4	165.8	221	1 546	86.6	28.0
Brea	6	0	0.0	0.0	100	1 059	88.8	30.6	91	941	71.6	26.7
Buena Park	14	3 603	157.3	61.4	80	818	53.1	19.5	66	384	19.5	5.7
Burbank	167	1 831	296.0	190.2	326	2 921	258.4	103.2	218	1 805	146.6	42.0
Burlingame	18	246	17.0	3.0	151	1 441	92.2	40.3	106	587	47.5	14.4
Calexico	1	0	0.0	0.0	19	108	5.7	1.6	14	37	3.3	0.9
Camarillo	16	194	12.6	3.1	144	826	65.1	24.9	82	719	59.1	18.7
Campbell	NA	NA	NA	NA	NA	NA	NA	NA	NA	NA	NA	NA
Carlsbad	14	204	15.9	4.0	119	767	51.9	20.3	86	650	38.7	11.0
Carson	7	60	4.0	0.7	116	1 009	63.5	21.6	97	1 177	90.1	29.8
Cathedral City	7	570	46.8	12.3	38	355	26.9	8.2	84	506	35.8	10.4
Ceres	3	0	0.0	0.0	36	311	13.7	4.7	33	139	9.8	1.9
Cerritos	8	202	9.3	2.0	114	1 128	64.9	25.7	63	585	35.2	12.8
Chico	23	479	13.3	4.2	300	3 478	208.1	80.1	136	1 016	112.6	17.6
Chino	9	275	11.2	3.4	102	1 441	110.9	39.4	97	1 159	70.5	23.4
Chula Vista	26	408	27.1	6.6	319	2 169	190.0	68.2	184	1 118	67.0	20.5
Claremont	10	278	12.4	4.4	92	701	40.7	15.8	31	164	6.3	2.2
Clovis	11	0	0.0	0.0	124	1 026	55.5	22.0	102	568	36.6	9.9
Colton	7	10	11.2	1.1	56	838	52.5	21.8	42	514	23.4	7.8
Compton	6	0	0.0	0.0	50	370	24.8	8.3	60	425	23.1	6.6
Concord	15	426	12.5	4.3	327	3 277	213.1	87.4	209	1 382	113.9	35.3
Corona	18	230	14.5	3.3	168	1 720	103.8	40.6	135	1 080	108.0	31.0
Costa Mesa	37	686	35.1	11.7	210	1 730	132.4	46.2	292	1 610	117.7	34.6
Covina	8	131	5.5	1.8	181	2 400	163.1	72.9	116	571	40.2	11.4
Culver City	80	174	67.2	37.7	176	3 249	265.2	89.8	132	1 053	77.3	25.7
Cupertino	6	114	5.5	1.4	138	1 158	80.8	27.7	53	277	21.9	4.6
Cypress	16	882	66.3	25.6	72	912	59.7	26.1	82	608	49.0	13.6
Daly City	14	394	12.5	3.9	195	1 623	133.2	53.8	89	428	30.9	8.9
Dana Point	14	120	17.3	2.8	62	338	25.9	10.5	33	130	7.8	2.3
Danville	11	801	20.2	6.9	97	636	45.0	17.9	44	192	11.9	3.7
Davis	12	171	5.8	1.8	132	989	72.5	34.8	48	252	16.9	5.0
Delano	1	0	0.0	0.0	46	366	21.7	8.4	20	48	3.9	0.9
Diamond Bar	7	148	7.3	1.6	122	893	74.7	20.5	48	204	16.5	4.9
Downey	10	169	6.6	2.0	239	3 288	228.7	93.4	140	1 475	80.0	25.3
Dublin	6	74	3.3	1.0	42	713	90.7	30.3	64	451	44.3	15.4
East Palo Alto	NA	NA	NA	NA	4	3	0.3	0.0	6	11	1.4	0.2
El Cajon	15	270	11.0	2.8	210	2 970	199.4	80.7	170	1 160	84.5	21.6
El Centro	3	58	1.1	0.4	96	1 065	74.4	28.7	43	265	13.8	4.6
El Monte	5	33	1.4	0.5	112	1 448	77.5	30.6	132	738	46.4	12.8
Encinitas	23	163	9.9	2.9	228	1 666	152.1	54.3	92	790	42.4	13.3
Escondido	20	413	17.9	4.7	272	3 026	185.9	79.8	242	1 222	84.7	24.6
Eureka	11	121	3.0	0.8	124	1 164	89.8	32.4	88	504	33.2	9.6
Fairfield	14	284	11.0	3.5	179	1 563	122.5	48.8	118	659	40.1	13.6
Folsom	8	136	4.6	1.5	81	1 137	71.0	30.0	46	244	14.3	3.2
Fontana	3	0	0.0	0.0	71	2 494	233.5	85.1	103	578	37.2	12.6
Foster City	10	165	8.7	2.8	53	356	21.4	9.1	24	141	8.7	4.3
Fountain Valley	11	611	19.1	5.7	259	3 313	312.7	124.0	102	851	52.5	19.0
Fremont	27	782	25.4	7.8	431	4 438	368.1	140.0	293	1 742	129.7	38.1
Fresno	63	1 118	50.3	13.3	1 189	12 047	919.3	385.7	626	4 602	358.9	94.9
Fullerton	17	434	23.8	7.5	268	2 615	229.5	100.3	172	798	68.5	19.0
Gardena	5	0	0.0	0.0	152	2 163	131.7	53.2	136	820	56.0	17.8
Garden Grove	15	0	0.0	0.0	353	3 847	274.8	94.8	228	1 373	94.7	23.8
Gilroy	4	75	1.6	0.5	99	1 235	77.9	34.4	63	733	42.7	12.8
Glendale	70	583	54.6	18.9	618	5 699	422.9	160.7	304	2 164	135.2	49.8
Glendora	5	58	2.1	0.6	147	1 710	101.6	43.4	81	660	34.7	10.2
Hanford	6	83	2.4	0.5	94	1 310	84.7	34.7	50	207	13.8	3.3
Hawthorne	4	16	0.8	0.1	123	1 295	89.7	35.8	112	442	36.6	8.7
Hayward	16	204	9.0	2.5	197	3 352	285.4	128.4	243	2 490	211.8	56.0
Hemet	8	141	5.0	1.5	177	1 973	143.3	55.1	70	399	22.2	6.1
Hesperia	4	39	1.5	0.6	63	308	25.7	6.8	93	466	28.7	7.1
Highland	1	0	0.0	0.0	30	577	37.5	16.8	23	88	4.7	1.7
Hollister	2	0	0.0	0.0	54	339	18.2	6.9	40	171	16.1	2.7
Huntington Beach	35	843	54.4	14.6	460	3 937	274.7	106.3	344	1 807	138.1	37.3
Huntington Park	4	124	4.2	1.2	116	1 260	96.2	36.3	63	299	20.8	5.8

1. Firms subject to federal tax.

Table D. Cities — Federal Funds and City Government Finances

City	Selected federal funds, fiscal 2001[1] (mil dol)									City government finances, 1999						
	Procurement contracts		Grants					Direct payments for individuals		General revenue						
										Intergovernmental			Taxes			
														Per capita[3] (dollars)		
	Defense	Other	Total[2]	Health and family welfare	Energy and environment	Education	Housing and community development	Educational assistance	Housing assistance	Total (mil dol)	Total (mil dol)	Percent from state government	Total (mil dol)	Total	Property	Sales and gross receipts
	108	109	110	111	112	113	114	115	116	117	118	119	120	121	122	123
CALIFORNIA—Cont'd																
Baldwin Park	0.3	0.2	4.8	0.0	0.0	2.2	1.7	0.2	13.5	28.4	8.6	62.9	13.9	194	110	72
Bell	0.3	3.1	0.1	0.0	0.0	0.0	0.0	1.5	0.3	NA	NA	NA	NA	NA	NA	NA
Bellflower	0.3	0.2	2.6	0.0	0.0	0.8	1.6	0.1	0.7	22.1	6.7	69.9	12.8	201	31	157
Bell Gardens	0.2	0.8	0.3	0.0	0.0	0.0	0.0	0.0	1.1	NA	NA	NA	NA	NA	NA	NA
Belmont	0.3	16.7	1.1	0.8	0.0	0.3	0.0	1.0	0.7	NA	NA	NA	NA	NA	NA	NA
Benicia	164.5	1.1	0.2	0.1	0.0	0.1	0.0	0.0	2.5	NA	NA	NA	NA	NA	NA	NA
Berkeley	12.3	1 783.6	348.9	148.8	12.0	23.0	5.1	22.3	37.3	210.5	48.4	66.1	83.5	773	242	307
Beverly Hills	0.7	24.4	0.4	0.0	0.0	0.0	0.0	0.7	2.7	125.5	3.9	84.5	78.9	2 435	510	1 000
Brea	15.9	3.1	0.1	0.0	0.0	0.1	0.0	34.5	0.0	66.3	3.9	73.8	38.1	1 070	581	426
Buena Park	3.9	0.2	1.5	0.0	0.0	0.3	1.0	0.0	2.0	46.8	7.3	80.7	28.4	388	125	242
Burbank	15.8	1.5	17.4	0.0	0.0	0.7	3.1	1.7	13.9	152.3	16.7	58.5	77.6	797	344	379
Burlingame	16.4	3.8	1.9	1.0	0.0	0.0	0.0	0.0	0.0	NA	NA	NA	NA	NA	NA	NA
Calexico	0.2	0.0	0.4	0.0	0.0	0.3	0.0	0.0	3.0	18.3	2.8	70.7	9.3	350	138	165
Camarillo	58.7	3.5	1.0	0.0	0.0	0.6	0.4	8.2	4.0	NA	NA	NA	NA	NA	NA	NA
Campbell	0.0	0.0	0.4	0.0	0.0	0.2	0.0	0.0	8.3	NA	NA	NA	NA	NA	NA	NA
Carlsbad	32.6	12.1	4.0	2.5	0.4	0.6	0.4	0.2	4.1	126.0	18.3	81.6	50.8	680	202	349
Carson	314.5	2.7	7.3	2.2	0.0	2.3	1.6	10.4	3.6	73.1	11.3	80.3	45.7	522	222	248
Cathedral City	0.0	0.0	0.2	0.0	0.0	0.2	0.0	0.0	0.2	35.3	4.7	70.8	22.0	586	337	218
Ceres	0.1	0.5	0.2	0.0	0.0	0.1	0.0	0.0	2.4	NA	NA	NA	NA	NA	NA	NA
Cerritos	3.4	0.8	2.9	0.0	0.0	0.0	0.0	0.5	0.0	85.1	4.0	100.0	45.9	852	352	465
Chico	2.4	5.1	7.2	0.4	0.1	2.8	1.1	12.9	4.5	73.7	30.2	87.2	26.9	572	220	343
Chino	0.5	0.2	2.9	0.0	0.0	0.0	0.8	0.0	0.7	NA	NA	NA	NA	NA	NA	NA
Chula Vista	23.8	2.5	8.1	0.0	0.0	1.1	2.7	6.0	6.5	155.5	19.6	69.3	63.7	397	96	172
Claremont	1.4	0.2	7.6	1.7	0.1	2.0	0.0	4.6	5.5	NA	NA	NA	NA	NA	NA	NA
Clovis	0.0	9.9	1.5	0.7	0.0	0.7	0.0	1.9	0.0	NA	NA	NA	NA	NA	NA	NA
Colton	0.5	0.1	0.4	0.1	0.0	0.2	0.0	1.4	3.6	33.5	4.3	74.2	15.6	350	150	175
Compton	13.9	0.4	7.6	0.4	0.0	1.9	3.2	3.7	34.7	94.1	25.2	35.6	44.2	479	259	179
Concord	19.1	1.1	16.8	0.5	0.1	0.8	1.3	0.4	9.6	105.6	10.0	89.4	50.0	425	143	223
Corona	8.0	2.9	2.3	0.0	0.0	0.0	1.2	0.0	1.4	107.6	12.7	85.2	50.6	448	158	180
Costa Mesa	32.5	3.0	7.3	0.0	0.8	1.7	4.2	8.4	1.6	76.6	13.1	62.9	48.5	474	105	344
Covina	1.7	1.2	0.1	0.0	0.0	0.0	0.0	0.1	2.8	33.6	4.6	81.2	19.7	444	167	259
Culver City	7.2	3.7	6.7	4.0	0.0	0.5	0.0	2.7	5.2	107.9	20.8	25.4	57.1	1 438	477	730
Cupertino	1.7	0.9	0.7	0.0	0.0	0.0	0.0	3.8	1.9	NA	NA	NA	NA	NA	NA	NA
Cypress	1.6	5.5	5.0	0.0	0.0	0.0	0.0	5.2	0.5	30.6	5.4	69.8	18.1	379	145	187
Daly City	0.5	0.3	1.2	0.0	0.0	0.0	1.3	0.3	10.3	61.6	13.9	49.3	24.9	251	83	140
Dana Point	0.0	0.0	1.7	0.0	0.0	1.7	0.0	0.0	0.0	20.9	4.1	97.7	13.7	398	77	290
Danville	0.0	0.0	0.1	0.0	0.0	0.0	0.0	0.0	0.1	23.9	3.7	72.1	12.1	300	93	108
Davis	2.5	8.0	196.4	91.5	28.9	3.5	1.8	17.8	9.7	NA	NA	NA	NA	NA	NA	NA
Delano	0.0	1.0	1.2	0.0	0.0	0.0	0.0	0.0	2.4	21.2	9.3	89.0	6.0	174	77	66
Diamond Bar	0.0	0.5	0.1	0.0	0.0	0.0	0.0	0.0	0.0	23.5	5.8	90.5	7.9	145	37	89
Downey	206.2	-3.9	134.0	117.9	0.0	11.1	1.1	0.0	0.0	56.9	10.8	83.7	29.6	316	82	214
Dublin	3.3	2.2	0.0	0.0	0.0	0.0	0.0	0.0	0.2	NA	NA	NA	NA	NA	NA	NA
East Palo Alto	0.0	0.0	1.4	0.0	0.0	0.3	0.0	0.0	4.6	NA	NA	NA	NA	NA	NA	NA
El Cajon	7.8	2.6	4.5	0.0	0.0	1.6	1.7	8.0	10.9	60.6	13.0	89.7	29.1	309	100	193
El Centro	12.0	1.7	18.9	1.6	0.0	5.7	0.0	0.0	3.4	74.9	5.4	56.7	11.3	301	93	195
El Monte	14.5	1.2	5.2	0.0	0.0	0.2	5.2	3.8	4.4	50.9	13.9	72.4	31.2	279	72	185
Encinitas	3.1	0.8	4.4	0.0	2.6	0.3	1.1	0.0	0.4	NA	NA	NA	NA	NA	NA	NA
Escondido	7.7	0.5	5.1	1.0	0.0	1.1	2.8	0.0	4.2	98.2	15.5	58.8	42.5	352	110	224
Eureka	1.0	3.3	6.8	2.0	0.9	1.3	0.1	5.4	5.4	NA	NA	NA	NA	NA	NA	NA
Fairfield	28.5	0.2	10.8	0.1	0.9	5.4	0.9	0.0	12.8	85.9	16.3	46.1	44.3	493	232	188
Folsom	3.0	1.3	0.2	0.0	0.0	0.0	0.0	0.0	1.4	NA	NA	NA	NA	NA	NA	NA
Fontana	0.6	0.2	7.4	0.0	0.0	0.6	1.5	0.0	5.6	97.6	11.2	66.7	51.8	472	190	148
Foster City	2.0	8.0	2.0	2.0	0.0	0.0	0.0	0.0	0.0	40.0	2.3	99.5	26.0	853	604	218
Fountain Valley	1.4	2.3	1.0	0.2	0.0	0.4	0.4	0.7	1.0	33.9	4.1	86.8	19.4	343	75	246
Fremont	6.2	2.8	5.1	1.4	0.0	0.6	1.7	4.8	3.8	160.4	20.3	81.2	96.4	472	190	170
Fresno	1.0	38.8	85.5	26.2	1.7	13.6	22.1	42.2	58.2	374.5	80.6	55.6	117.1	294	94	160
Fullerton	113.1	4.6	11.6	2.6	0.1	2.5	3.2	25.7	2.7	77.8	14.5	67.5	41.3	339	152	163
Gardena	28.5	2.5	11.7	0.0	0.0	0.0	0.9	2.6	2.4	NA	NA	NA	NA	NA	NA	NA
Garden Grove	8.9	0.3	4.8	0.9	0.0	0.0	2.5	2.2	22.0	85.6	29.5	45.5	40.9	270	116	124
Gilroy	0.0	0.5	1.2	0.0	0.0	0.8	0.3	1.1	5.0	NA	NA	NA	NA	NA	NA	NA
Glendale	2.8	5.0	8.0	0.0	0.0	3.1	4.4	12.6	18.8	199.9	40.7	57.7	84.6	457	148	255
Glendora	0.3	0.1	0.7	0.0	0.0	0.0	0.6	3.5	0.7	NA	NA	NA	NA	NA	NA	NA
Hanford	0.0	12.5	4.7	3.2	0.0	0.5	0.0	0.0	3.2	NA	NA	NA	NA	NA	NA	NA
Hawthorne	2.2	12.7	4.8	0.3	0.0	0.0	2.4	0.1	6.7	70.5	26.0	35.5	26.9	366	88	222
Hayward	5.6	1.0	20.3	9.0	0.2	7.0	1.6	13.2	7.8	109.7	24.9	78.2	53.4	414	125	266
Hemet	0.2	0.2	0.5	0.0	0.0	0.1	0.1	0.3	3.8	NA	NA	NA	NA	NA	NA	NA
Hesperia	1.4	0.3	0.6	0.0	0.0	0.2	0.4	0.0	0.3	15.6	5.6	74.4	8.2	132	5	108
Highland	1.1	0.0	0.3	0.3	0.0	0.0	0.0	0.0	0.0	11.9	3.5	85.4	5.9	141	43	45
Hollister	14.9	0.9	0.5	0.5	0.0	0.0	0.0	0.0	2.7	NA	NA	NA	NA	NA	NA	NA
Huntington Beach	454.9	135.3	3.5	0.0	0.0	1.1	1.9	4.9	3.1	150.1	21.9	73.6	80.2	411	142	220
Huntington Park	0.0	1.6	2.5	0.0	0.0	0.0	2.3	0.0	1.4	40.7	12.5	49.6	21.4	367	160	158

1. October 1, 2000 to September 30, 2001.   2. Includes program categories not shown separately. State totals include additional categories not allocated by city.   3. Based on population estimated as of July 1 of the year shown.

City	City government finances, 1999 (cont'd)												
	General expenditure												
	Per capita[1] (dollars)			Percent of total for —									
	Total (mil dol)	Total	Capital outlays	Public welfare	Highways	Parking facilities	Education	Health and hospitals	Police protection	Sewerage and sanitation	Parks and recreation	Housing and community develop-ment	Interest on debt
	124	125	126	127	128	129	130	131	132	133	134	135	136
CALIFORNIA—Cont'd													
Baldwin Park	35.5	493	106	0.0	10.5	0.0	0.0	0.0	24.5	0.2	3.9	40.8	6.1
Bell	NA	NA	NA	NA	NA	NA	NA	NA	NA	NA	NA	NA	NA
Bellflower	19.6	308	40	0.0	17.3	0.1	0.0	0.4	36.5	0.0	13.9	8.7	3.3
Bell Gardens	NA	NA	NA	NA	NA	NA	NA	NA	NA	NA	NA	NA	NA
Belmont	NA	NA	NA	NA	NA	NA	NA	NA	NA	NA	NA	NA	NA
Benicia	NA	NA	NA	NA	NA	NA	NA	NA	NA	NA	NA	NA	NA
Berkeley	218.3	2 019	186	0.0	5.6	1.4	0.0	9.6	15.0	16.2	6.4	5.4	5.3
Beverly Hills	120.6	3 722	413	0.0	9.3	3.4	0.0	2.5	21.3	6.7	10.4	1.4	10.7
Brea	69.8	1 963	495	0.0	9.3	0.0	0.0	1.5	18.2	2.9	4.8	18.5	19.7
Buena Park	48.3	658	171	0.0	13.1	0.0	0.0	0.0	26.5	4.4	5.5	17.2	8.0
Burbank	167.7	1 721	321	0.0	9.1	0.2	0.0	4.3	15.4	8.5	5.1	21.9	7.5
Burlingame	NA	NA	NA	NA	NA	NA	NA	NA	NA	NA	NA	NA	NA
Calexico	25.6	963	114	0.0	23.0	1.1	0.0	0.2	14.2	13.5	2.1	12.7	8.0
Camarillo	NA	NA	NA	NA	NA	NA	NA	NA	NA	NA	NA	NA	NA
Campbell	NA	NA	NA	NA	NA	NA	NA	NA	NA	NA	NA	NA	NA
Carlsbad	90.3	1 208	311	0.0	9.0	6.4	0.0	1.9	13.3	3.6	11.1	4.3	6.5
Carson	65.6	749	154	0.0	17.7	0.0	0.0	0.2	30.6	0.0	10.4	15.4	6.0
Cathedral City	39.9	1 060	138	0.0	15.2	0.0	0.0	1.1	15.5	0.0	0.6	24.1	6.0
Ceres	NA	NA	NA	NA	NA	NA	NA	NA	NA	NA	NA	NA	NA
Cerritos	66.1	1 226	196	0.0	16.3	0.0	0.0	0.1	8.5	3.2	5.7	14.2	18.9
Chico	66.2	1 410	745	0.0	2.0	1.0	0.0	0.0	13.1	4.1	2.8	15.3	4.6
Chino	NA	NA	NA	NA	NA	NA	NA	NA	NA	NA	NA	NA	NA
Chula Vista	124.5	776	62	0.0	10.1	0.2	0.0	0.7	18.2	10.9	6.1	2.7	24.1
Claremont	NA	NA	NA	NA	NA	NA	NA	NA	NA	NA	NA	NA	NA
Clovis	NA	NA	NA	NA	NA	NA	NA	NA	NA	NA	NA	NA	NA
Colton	42.9	959	199	0.0	2.6	0.0	0.0	0.7	15.6	16.1	1.0	10.8	25.4
Compton	79.1	857	113	0.0	11.7	0.0	0.0	2.0	22.9	1.1	2.2	18.4	10.3
Concord	108.3	920	187	0.0	12.7	0.0	0.0	0.0	27.3	9.4	19.3	7.6	5.8
Corona	114.8	1 018	176	0.0	11.5	0.1	0.0	0.7	15.7	16.9	5.3	9.5	15.7
Costa Mesa	73.4	717	38	0.0	8.4	0.0	0.0	6.2	32.4	1.2	9.4	4.2	2.3
Covina	33.1	744	126	0.0	11.7	0.0	0.0	3.4	27.7	5.1	5.8	14.2	9.5
Culver City	93.5	2 354	580	0.0	5.3	0.2	0.0	2.2	18.6	14.6	3.8	17.7	10.0
Cupertino	NA	NA	NA	NA	NA	NA	NA	NA	NA	NA	NA	NA	NA
Cypress	31.3	653	173	0.0	32.5	0.0	0.0	0.0	27.1	0.4	13.8	8.5	1.5
Daly City	61.1	616	116	0.0	10.3	0.0	0.0	0.0	20.1	15.2	11.6	3.5	0.0
Dana Point	14.9	433	74	0.0	20.1	0.0	0.0	1.3	32.4	0.2	8.3	0.0	0.0
Danville	17.3	429	21	0.0	17.5	0.0	0.0	0.4	16.5	1.9	14.4	2.0	6.5
Davis	NA	NA	NA	NA	NA	NA	NA	NA	NA	NA	NA	NA	NA
Delano	24.8	722	230	0.0	4.2	0.0	0.0	1.3	13.5	6.9	2.8	26.1	2.7
Diamond Bar	21.6	396	210	0.0	10.1	0.0	0.0	0.3	17.8	0.0	8.7	47.2	0.0
Downey	52.8	564	61	0.0	11.7	0.0	0.0	2.8	33.4	1.1	8.6	5.7	2.9
Dublin	NA	NA	NA	NA	NA	NA	NA	NA	NA	NA	NA	NA	NA
East Palo Alto	NA	NA	NA	NA	NA	NA	NA	NA	NA	NA	NA	NA	NA
El Cajon	58.9	625	51	0.0	10.4	0.0	0.0	4.5	28.6	14.2	5.6	6.2	4.6
El Centro	77.2	2 066	296	0.0	6.2	0.0	0.0	63.9	5.8	6.7	1.5	2.9	1.9
El Monte	55.4	496	34	0.0	11.8	1.0	0.0	0.2	29.2	0.0	6.0	12.1	4.3
Encinitas	NA	NA	NA	NA	NA	NA	NA	NA	NA	NA	NA	NA	NA
Escondido	104.9	870	192	0.0	12.6	0.0	0.0	2.2	17.8	9.6	4.2	17.4	12.5
Eureka	NA	NA	NA	NA	NA	NA	NA	NA	NA	NA	NA	NA	NA
Fairfield	86.7	965	124	0.0	14.3	0.0	0.0	0.2	15.9	0.2	7.9	14.3	24.9
Folsom	NA	NA	NA	NA	NA	NA	NA	NA	NA	NA	NA	NA	NA
Fontana	101.3	923	91	0.0	10.0	0.0	0.0	0.3	16.6	5.1	2.0	16.8	16.9
Foster City	42.2	1 386	144	0.0	3.5	0.0	0.0	0.0	13.3	6.5	9.5	19.4	8.4
Fountain Valley	35.2	622	15	0.0	20.9	0.0	0.0	3.6	26.2	7.1	4.9	7.8	6.3
Fremont	166.1	813	309	0.0	8.5	0.0	0.0	4.5	21.4	3.5	19.0	10.2	6.2
Fresno	400.1	1 005	260	0.0	7.6	0.7	0.0	0.6	18.8	27.5	9.6	3.2	10.0
Fullerton	78.0	640	146	0.0	14.3	0.0	0.0	1.5	27.4	9.3	6.8	10.9	1.7
Gardena	NA	NA	NA	NA	NA	NA	NA	NA	NA	NA	NA	NA	NA
Garden Grove	88.2	583	100	0.0	12.3	0.0	0.0	3.9	27.7	0.0	2.5	26.1	7.2
Gilroy	NA	NA	NA	NA	NA	NA	NA	NA	NA	NA	NA	NA	NA
Glendale	184.1	995	187	0.0	7.1	4.0	0.0	0.5	19.7	14.9	6.9	11.4	2.3
Glendora	NA	NA	NA	NA	NA	NA	NA	NA	NA	NA	NA	NA	NA
Hanford	NA	NA	NA	NA	NA	NA	NA	NA	NA	NA	NA	NA	NA
Hawthorne	85.8	1 169	324	0.0	3.1	0.0	0.0	0.0	45.0	10.3	4.7	13.8	4.9
Hayward	125.9	977	331	0.0	7.0	0.0	0.0	0.9	24.2	15.1	1.2	14.9	3.5
Hemet	NA	NA	NA	NA	NA	NA	NA	NA	NA	NA	NA	NA	NA
Hesperia	16.0	258	23	0.0	16.8	0.0	0.0	5.0	32.6	0.0	0.0	7.0	13.3
Highland	14.0	334	90	0.0	32.5	0.0	0.0	1.1	23.6	0.0	0.1	14.5	9.0
Hollister	NA	NA	NA	NA	NA	NA	NA	NA	NA	NA	NA	NA	NA
Huntington Beach	132.8	680	72	0.0	17.4	0.7	0.0	3.7	28.9	5.9	8.5	3.2	1.9
Huntington Park	40.0	688	7	0.0	5.5	0.9	0.0	0.2	28.0	0.5	3.1	8.8	26.0

1. Based on population estimated as of July 1 of the year shown.

City	City government finances, 1999 (cont'd)			City government employment, 2001	Climate[2]						
	Debt outstanding				Average daily temperature (degrees Fahrenheit)						
					Mean		Limits				
	Total (mil dol)	Per capita[1] (dollars)	Percent utility		January	July	January[3]	July[4]	Annual precipitation (inches)	Heating degree days	Cooling degree days
	137	138	139	140	141	142	143	144	145	146	147
CALIFORNIA—Cont'd											
Baldwin Park	54.3	755	0.0	NA	55.7	75.2	41.7	89.2	17.90	1 433	1 427
Bell	NA	NA	NA	NA	58.3	74.3	48.9	84.0	14.77	1 154	1 537
Bellflower	3.5	56	0.0	NA	55.9	73.1	44.9	82.7	11.80	1 430	1 201
Bell Gardens	NA	NA	NA	NA	58.3	74.3	48.9	84.0	14.77	1 154	1 537
Belmont	NA	NA	NA	NA	NA	NA	NA	NA	NA	NA	NA
Benicia	NA	NA	NA	NA	NA	NA	NA	NA	NA	NA	NA
Berkeley	212.4	1 965	0.0	1 438	49.9	62.1	43.3	70.0	24.30	2 902	115
Beverly Hills	255.4	7 883	8.3	846	57.2	70.4	46.5	79.2	13.06	1 391	986
Brea	229.0	6 439	9.3	NA	57.4	72.6	45.6	82.6	12.27	1 238	1 175
Buena Park	38.9	531	0.0	NA	57.4	72.6	45.6	82.6	12.27	1 238	1 175
Burbank	257.1	2 638	27.8	1 321	54.5	75.6	41.3	90.2	15.87	1 609	1 424
Burlingame	NA	NA	NA	NA	48.7	62.7	41.8	71.6	19.70	3 016	145
Calexico	27.3	1 029	16.9	NA	NA	NA	NA	NA	NA	NA	NA
Camarillo	NA	NA	NA	NA	55.3	66.1	44.2	74.4	14.38	1 992	416
Campbell	NA	NA	NA	NA	49.4	69.5	40.6	82.4	14.42	2 387	594
Carlsbad	103.8	1 388	5.2	NA	54.5	67.6	44.1	73.5	10.93	2 010	555
Carson	78.6	897	0.0	530	56.1	69.7	45.3	78.8	13.57	1 568	794
Cathedral City	101.3	2 690	0.0	NA	56.4	92.0	42.5	108.7	5.31	985	4 014
Ceres	NA	NA	NA	NA	45.6	77.1	37.4	94.2	12.10	2 605	1 401
Cerritos	133.4	2 475	0.0	396	55.9	73.1	44.9	82.7	11.80	1 430	1 201
Chico	64.9	1 383	0.0	406	44.0	77.4	34.5	94.2	26.32	2 953	1 360
Chino	NA	NA	NA	NA	54.3	74.6	40.7	90.4	16.62	1 713	1 273
Chula Vista	502.9	3 132	0.0	1 427	55.3	68.2	45.3	73.1	9.34	1 798	638
Claremont	NA	NA	NA	NA	54.3	74.6	40.7	90.4	16.62	1 713	1 273
Clovis	NA	NA	NA	NA	45.7	81.9	37.4	98.6	10.60	2 556	1 967
Colton	131.4	2 940	13.6	NA	53.6	79.4	40.3	97.0	15.42	1 719	1 804
Compton	130.0	1 409	0.0	755	56.1	69.7	45.3	78.8	13.57	1 568	794
Concord	138.3	1 175	0.0	579	44.5	73.8	35.9	90.8	12.80	2 837	1 066
Corona	326.8	2 897	11.6	783	53.9	75.4	40.5	92.1	11.83	1 747	1 339
Costa Mesa	24.8	242	0.0	641	55.2	67.1	46.8	71.8	10.85	1 866	500
Covina	51.8	1 165	5.4	NA	54.3	74.6	40.7	90.4	16.62	1 713	1 273
Culver City	168.3	4 238	0.0	773	57.2	70.4	46.5	79.2	13.06	1 391	986
Cupertino	NA	NA	NA	NA	49.4	69.5	40.6	82.4	14.42	2 387	594
Cypress	7.6	158	0.0	NA	57.4	72.6	45.6	82.6	12.27	1 238	1 175
Daly City	0.3	3	0.0	595	48.7	62.7	41.8	71.6	19.70	3 016	145
Dana Point	0.0	0	0.0	30	53.7	67.2	41.5	75.8	12.19	2 157	493
Danville	17.5	434	0.0	NA	46.1	71.6	35.5	89.8	14.21	2 909	780
Davis	NA	NA	NA	NA	44.5	74.1	36.3	92.7	18.13	2 911	1 041
Delano	11.0	320	0.0	NA	NA	NA	NA	NA	NA	NA	NA
Diamond Bar	0.0	0	0.0	NA	54.3	74.6	40.7	90.4	16.62	1 713	1 273
Downey	14.4	154	0.0	491	58.3	74.3	48.9	84.0	14.77	1 154	1 537
Dublin	NA	NA	NA	NA	NA	NA	NA	NA	NA	NA	NA
East Palo Alto	NA	NA	NA	NA	NA	NA	NA	NA	NA	NA	NA
El Cajon	48.8	518	0.0	548	56.6	72.5	44.6	83.4	12.80	1 400	1 110
El Centro	25.6	685	4.2	NA	54.6	91.3	39.3	107.5	2.71	1 156	3 741
El Monte	61.3	549	0.0	384	55.7	75.2	41.7	89.2	17.90	1 433	1 427
Encinitas	NA	NA	NA	NA	54.5	67.6	44.1	73.5	10.93	2 010	555
Escondido	176.8	1 467	4.2	937	55.2	70.5	43.1	81.3	13.04	1 802	868
Eureka	NA	NA	NA	NA	48.0	57.0	41.5	61.8	37.53	4 496	0
Fairfield	235.7	2 623	26.2	547	45.5	72.0	36.2	88.5	21.38	2 767	898
Folsom	NA	NA	NA	NA	45.6	77.2	37.7	94.2	23.91	2 683	1 422
Fontana	499.0	4 546	0.0	442	56.0	78.6	44.5	94.8	15.63	1 478	1 922
Foster City	54.2	1 779	0.0	NA	48.7	68.7	38.9	83.4	19.74	2 563	486
Fountain Valley	36.6	646	0.0	NA	57.4	72.6	45.6	82.6	12.27	1 238	1 175
Fremont	247.1	1 210	0.0	1 189	49.0	66.7	41.1	76.1	13.73	2 578	410
Fresno	718.2	1 804	7.4	3 316	45.7	81.9	37.4	98.6	10.60	2 556	1 967
Fullerton	23.3	191	0.0	705	57.4	72.6	45.6	82.6	12.27	1 238	1 175
Gardena	NA	NA	NA	NA	56.1	69.7	45.3	78.8	13.57	1 568	794
Garden Grove	101.0	667	18.5	731	57.4	72.6	45.6	82.6	12.27	1 238	1 175
Gilroy	NA	NA	NA	NA	47.4	70.9	35.6	88.3	19.77	2 668	719
Glendale	96.9	523	0.0	1 858	54.5	75.6	41.3	90.2	15.87	1 609	1 424
Glendora	NA	NA	NA	NA	54.3	74.6	40.7	90.4	16.62	1 713	1 273
Hanford	NA	NA	NA	NA	43.9	78.8	34.3	95.9	7.95	2 816	1 551
Hawthorne	35.6	485	0.0	382	56.8	69.1	47.8	75.3	12.01	1 458	727
Hayward	71.9	558	0.0	860	49.0	66.7	41.1	76.1	13.73	2 578	410
Hemet	NA	NA	NA	NA	50.2	77.6	39.3	96.2	17.33	2 432	1 451
Hesperia	59.9	961	0.0	NA	44.2	79.3	30.0	97.4	5.51	3 127	1 525
Highland	20.8	495	0.0	NA	53.6	79.4	40.3	97.0	15.42	1 719	1 804
Hollister	NA	NA	NA	NA	NA	NA	NA	NA	NA	NA	NA
Huntington Beach	93.4	478	41.4	1 188	55.2	67.1	46.8	71.8	10.85	1 866	500
Huntington Park	151.3	2 599	0.0	NA	58.3	74.3	48.9	84.0	14.77	1 154	1 537

1. Based on the population estimated as of July 1 of the year shown.   2. Represents normal values based on the 30-year period, 1961–1990.   3. Average daily minimum.   4. Average daily maximum.

Table D. Cities — Land Area and Population

STATE Place code	City	Land area, 2000[1] (sq km)	Population, 2000 Total persons	Rank	Per square kilometer	Population Total persons 1990	Percent change 1990–2000	Total persons 1980	Percent change 1980–1990	Population characteristics, 2000 Percent — Race (alone or in combination) White	Black	Am. Indian, Alaska Native	Asian and Pacific Islander	Other race	Hispanic[2]	Non-Hispanic White
		1	2	3	4	5	6	7	8	9	10	11	12	13	14	15
	CALIFORNIA—Cont'd															
06 36294	Imperial Beach	11.1	26 992	1 146	2 431.7	26 512	1.8	22 689	16.8	67.5	6.4	2.1	10.5	20.5	40.1	43.5
06 36448	Indio	69.1	49 116	616	710.8	36 850	33.3	21 611	70.5	52.1	3.1	1.5	2.2	45.2	75.4	19.5
06 36546	Inglewood	23.7	112 580	200	4 750.2	109 602	2.7	94 245	16.3	21.9	48.7	1.4	2.1	30.4	46.0	4.1
06 36770	Irvine	119.6	143 072	146	1 196.3	110 330	29.7	62 134	77.6	65.2	1.8	0.6	32.7	4.7	7.4	57.0
06 39248	Laguna Niguel	38.0	61 891	445	1 628.7	44 723	38.4	12 237	265.5	86.8	1.6	0.8	9.5	5.2	10.4	77.4
06 39290	La Habra	19.0	58 974	477	3 103.9	51 266	15.0	45 232	13.3	67.1	2.0	1.6	7.4	26.9	49.0	41.4
06 39486	Lake Elsinore	87.6	28 928	1 073	330.2	19 733	46.6	NA	NA	69.8	6.2	2.5	3.7	23.3	38.0	51.4
06 39496	Lake Forest	32.4	58 707	483	1 811.9	56 065	4.7	NA	NA	79.8	2.3	1.2	11.8	9.4	18.6	66.7
06 39892	Lakewood	24.4	79 345	329	3 251.8	73 553	7.9	74 654	-1.5	66.8	8.1	1.6	16.7	12.4	22.8	52.4
06 40004	La Mesa	24.0	54 749	539	2 281.2	52 911	3.5	50 308	5.2	84.4	5.8	1.5	6.1	6.8	13.5	73.7
06 40032	La Mirada	20.3	46 783	650	2 304.6	40 452	15.7	40 986	-1.3	67.9	2.3	1.4	16.5	16.0	33.5	47.1
06 40130	Lancaster	243.5	118 718	184	487.5	97 300	22.0	48 027	102.6	67.0	17.5	2.3	5.4	13.4	24.1	52.4
06 40340	La Puente	9.0	41 063	749	4 562.6	36 955	11.1	30 882	19.7	43.4	2.4	.9	8.3	49.4	83.1	6.7
06 40830	La Verne	21.5	31 638	986	1 471.5	30 843	2.6	23 508	31.2	80.9	3.7	1.3	8.8	9.8	23.1	63.6
06 40886	Lawndale	5.1	31 711	982	6 217.8	27 331	16.0	23 460	16.5	47.5	13.6	1.8	12.3	31.7	52.1	21.9
06 41992	Livermore	62.0	73 345	361	1 183.0	56 741	29.3	48 349	17.4	85.9	2.1	1.6	8.2	7.1	14.4	74.4
06 42202	Lodi	31.7	56 999	503	1 798.1	51 874	9.9	35 221	47.3	78.4	0.9	1.8	7.1	17.0	27.1	63.5
06 42524	Lompoc	30.1	41 103	748	1 365.5	37 649	9.2	26 267	43.3	70.3	8.4	3.0	6.0	18.1	37.3	47.9
06 43000	Long Beach	130.6	461 522	34	3 533.9	429 321	7.5	361 334	18.8	48.9	16.0	1.7	15.4	23.6	35.8	33.1
06 43280	Los Altos	16.4	27 693	1 117	1 688.6	26 599	4.1	25 769	3.2	82.9	0.6	0.5	17.5	1.5	3.0	78.2
06 44000	Los Angeles	1 214.9	3 694 820	2	3 041.3	3 485 557	6.0	2 966 850	17.5	51.2	12.0	1.4	11.4	29.4	46.5	29.7
06 44028	Los Banos	20.8	25 869	1 204	1 243.7	14 519	78.2	10 341	40.4	63.7	5.1	2.5	4.4	30.8	50.4	39.8
06 44112	Los Gatos	27.7	28 592	1 083	1 032.2	27 357	4.5	26 906	1.7	89.7	1.1	0.8	9.5	2.5	5.2	83.3
06 44574	Lynwood	12.6	69 845	384	5 543.3	61 945	12.8	48 548	27.6	37.3	14.0	1.7	1.5	50.0	82.3	2.9
06 45022	Madera	31.8	43 207	707	1 358.7	29 283	47.5	21 732	34.7	52.9	4.4	3.9	2.3	42.3	67.8	25.1
06 45400	Manhattan Beach	10.2	33 852	928	3 318.8	32 063	5.6	31 542	1.7	91.6	0.9	0.6	7.9	1.9	5.2	85.4
06 45484	Manteca	41.2	49 258	613	1 195.6	40 773	20.8	24 925	63.6	79.6	3.5	2.8	6.0	14.8	25.1	64.1
06 45778	Marina	22.7	25 101	1 235	1 105.8	26 512	-5.3	20 647	28.4	49.4	16.3	2.2	23.8	17.1	23.2	37.8
06 46114	Martinez	31.7	35 866	869	1 131.4	31 800	12.8	22 582	40.9	85.2	4.0	2.0	9.0	4.9	10.2	75.5
06 46492	Maywood	3.0	28 083	1 099	9 361.0	27 893	0.7	21 810	27.9	47.2	0.5	1.4	0.7	54.8	96.3	2.6
06 46870	Menlo Park	26.2	30 785	1 014	1 175.0	28 403	8.4	26 369	7.7	74.9	7.6	1.0	10.1	9.9	15.6	66.4
06 46898	Merced	51.4	63 893	427	1 243.1	56 155	13.8	36 499	53.9	56.3	7.3	2.5	13.2	26.2	41.4	37.8
06 47766	Milpitas	35.1	62 698	440	1 786.3	50 690	23.7	37 820	34.0	34.4	4.4	1.3	55.5	9.7	16.6	23.8
06 48256	Mission Viejo	48.3	93 102	259	1 927.6	79 464	27.9	50 666	43.7	86.4	1.6	0.9	9.6	5.3	12.1	76.0
06 48354	Modesto	92.7	188 856	102	2 037.3	164 746	14.6	106 602	54.5	74.2	4.8	2.6	8.9	15.8	25.6	59.6
06 48648	Monrovia	35.6	36 929	838	1 037.3	35 733	3.3	30 531	17.0	66.9	9.5	1.8	8.6	18.2	35.2	46.6
06 48788	Montclair	13.2	33 049	948	2 503.7	28 434	16.2	22 628	25.7	48.7	6.9	1.7	9.6	38.1	60.0	23.6
06 48816	Montebello	21.4	62 150	444	2 904.2	59 564	4.3	52 929	12.5	51.5	1.1	1.8	12.7	38.5	74.6	11.1
06 48872	Monterey	21.9	29 674	1 049	1 355.0	31 954	-7.1	27 558	16.0	84.8	3.2	1.5	9.9	5.4	10.9	75.0
06 48914	Monterey Park	19.8	60 051	466	3 032.9	60 738	-1.1	54 338	11.8	23.7	0.7	1.0	63.9	14.3	28.9	7.3
06 49138	Moorpark	49.3	31 415	994	637.2	25 494	23.2	NA	NA	77.8	1.9	1.2	7.2	15.9	27.8	62.4
06 49270	Moreno Valley	132.7	142 381	148	1 073.0	118 779	19.9	NA	NA	51.4	21.6	1.9	8.3	23.1	38.4	32.2
06 49278	Morgan Hill	30.2	33 556	938	1 111.1	23 928	40.2	17 060	40.3	76.7	2.2	2.1	8.6	16.1	27.5	61.3
06 49670	Mountain View	31.2	70 708	378	2 266.3	67 365	5.0	58 655	14.8	67.2	3.1	0.9	23.1	10.1	18.3	55.2
06 50076	Murrieta	73.5	44 282	692	602.5	18 557	138.6	NA	NA	85.4	4.1	1.6	6.1	7.5	17.5	71.8
06 50258	Napa	45.8	72 585	367	1 584.8	61 865	17.3	50 879	21.6	83.8	0.8	2.0	2.9	14.6	26.8	68.2
06 50398	National City	19.1	54 260	546	2 840.8	54 249	0.0	48 772	11.2	39.1	6.6	1.6	21.7	36.9	59.1	14.1
06 50916	Newark	36.2	42 471	721	1 173.2	37 861	12.2	32 126	17.9	57.8	4.7	1.6	26.4	17.2	28.6	40.3
06 51182	Newport Beach	38.3	70 032	383	1 828.5	66 643	5.1	62 556	6.5	93.8	0.7	0.6	5.1	1.7	4.7	89.0
06 52526	Norwalk	25.1	103 298	225	4 115.5	94 279	9.6	85 286	10.5	48.6	5.1	1.8	13.1	36.2	62.9	18.9
06 52582	Novato	71.8	47 630	636	663.4	47 585	0.1	43 916	8.4	86.2	2.7	1.3	7.1	6.9	13.1	76.3
06 53000	Oakland	145.2	399 484	41	2 751.3	372 242	7.3	339 337	9.7	34.7	37.6	1.7	17.4	14.1	21.9	23.5
06 53322	Oceanside	105.1	161 029	125	1 532.2	128 090	25.7	76 698	67.0	70.6	7.4	1.7	9.3	16.7	30.2	53.6
06 53896	Ontario	128.9	158 007	128	1 225.8	133 179	18.6	88 820	49.9	52.2	8.3	1.8	5.4	37.9	59.9	26.6
06 53980	Orange	60.6	128 821	164	2 125.8	110 658	16.4	91 788	20.6	73.7	2.0	1.4	10.9	15.9	32.2	54.6
06 54652	Oxnard	65.6	170 358	122	2 596.9	142 560	19.5	108 195	31.8	45.9	4.4	2.0	9.3	43.4	66.2	20.6
06 54806	Pacifica	32.7	38 390	809	1 174.0	37 670	1.9	36 866	2.2	75.0	4.2	1.6	20.1	6.3	14.6	61.3
06 55156	Palmdale	271.8	116 670	190	429.2	73 314	66.0	12 277	472.3	59.1	15.8	1.9	5.3	23.5	37.7	41.0
06 55184	Palm Desert	63.1	41 155	745	652.2	23 252	77.0	11 801	97.0	88.9	1.6	0.9	3.3	7.8	17.1	77.6
06 55254	Palm Springs	244.1	42 807	715	175.4	40 144	6.6	32 271	24.4	81.0	4.4	1.6	4.7	11.5	23.7	66.5
06 55282	Palo Alto	61.3	58 598	484	955.9	55 900	4.8	55 225	1.2	78.6	2.5	0.7	19.4	2.3	4.6	72.8
06 55520	Paradise	47.3	26 408	1 171	558.3	25 401	4.0	22 571	12.5	96.2	0.4	2.3	1.9	2.0	4.3	91.2
06 55618	Paramount	12.3	55 266	533	4 493.2	47 669	15.9	36 407	30.9	38.5	14.3	1.7	5.0	45.5	72.3	9.0
06 56000	Pasadena	59.8	133 936	159	2 239.7	131 586	1.8	118 550	11.0	57.7	15.6	1.5	11.6	19.3	33.4	39.1
06 56700	Perris	81.3	36 189	860	445.1	21 500	68.3	NA	NA	45.8	17.3	2.5	4.3	36.2	56.2	22.8
06 56784	Petaluma	35.7	54 548	543	1 528.0	43 166	26.4	33 834	27.6	87.8	1.7	1.5	5.7	7.7	14.6	77.0
06 56924	Pico Rivera	21.5	63 428	432	2 950.1	59 177	7.2	53 459	10.7	54.3	0.9	1.9	3.3	45.1	88.3	7.7
06 57456	Pittsburg	40.4	56 769	505	1 405.2	47 607	19.2	33 034	44.1	48.9	20.7	1.9	16.5	19.8	33.2	31.2
06 57526	Placentia	17.1	46 488	654	2 718.6	41 259	12.7	35 041	17.7	70.8	2.1	1.5	12.6	16.8	31.1	53.7
06 57764	Pleasant Hill	18.4	32 837	954	1 784.6	31 583	4.0	25 124	25.7	85.4	2.1	1.3	11.9	3.8	8.4	76.6
06 57792	Pleasanton	56.1	63 654	429	1 134.7	50 570	25.9	35 160	43.8	83.6	1.7	0.9	14.0	3.7	7.9	75.8

1. Dry land or land partially or temporarily covered by water.   2. Hispanic persons may be of any race.

City	Population characteristics, 2000 (cont'd)										Households, 2000				
	Age of population (percent)													Percent	
	Under 5 years	5 to 17 years	18 to 24 years	25 to 34 years	35 to 44 years	45 to 54 years	55 to 64 years	65 to 74 years	75 years and over	Percent female	Number	Percent change, 1990–2000	Persons per household	Female family householder[1]	One-person
	16	17	18	19	20	21	22	23	24	25	26	27	28	29	30
CALIFORNIA—Cont'd															
Imperial Beach	8.4	21.1	13.9	17.0	15.3	11.0	5.8	4.4	3.1	50.1	9 272	2.1	2.84	18.1	21.4
Indio	10.4	24.9	11.1	15.7	13.7	8.9	6.3	5.2	3.9	49.7	13 871	29.1	3.48	16.7	16.0
Inglewood	9.1	23.3	10.2	16.4	15.5	11.5	6.9	4.1	3.0	52.5	36 805	1.9	3.02	24.9	25.3
Irvine	5.6	17.9	14.4	15.0	17.3	14.9	7.7	3.9	3.3	51.6	51 199	27.2	2.66	9.8	22.8
Laguna Niguel	7.0	19.6	6.0	12.7	20.2	16.8	8.8	5.1	3.8	51.3	23 217	35.2	2.65	8.8	20.6
La Habra	8.4	20.7	10.3	16.4	15.3	11.2	7.0	5.4	5.4	50.7	18 947	4.6	3.08	13.5	21.0
Lake Elsinore	9.8	26.2	9.3	14.7	17.4	10.5	5.4	3.9	2.8	50.1	8 817	45.4	3.27	13.8	16.2
Lake Forest	7.1	19.9	8.0	15.0	18.3	15.1	8.1	4.0	4.6	50.8	20 008	-7.9	2.89	10.3	19.4
Lakewood	7.1	20.5	8.1	13.9	17.2	13.6	7.8	6.1	5.8	51.6	26 853	2.9	2.95	13.4	18.4
La Mesa	5.7	14.1	9.9	16.5	16.4	12.8	7.5	7.1	10.0	52.8	24 186	4.2	2.22	11.6	34.2
La Mirada	6.3	19.9	10.7	12.4	16.1	12.1	8.7	7.7	6.1	51.7	14 580	14.5	3.10	10.4	17.3
Lancaster	8.0	24.3	9.5	13.8	17.5	11.6	6.6	4.6	4.0	49.2	38 224	16.2	2.92	17.0	22.1
La Puente	9.0	24.8	11.6	16.7	14.3	9.7	6.2	4.7	2.9	50.0	9 461	4.9	4.34	17.9	10.1
La Verne	5.8	19.4	9.7	11.2	16.2	15.1	9.4	6.6	6.6	51.9	11 070	3.1	2.79	11.5	19.6
Lawndale	9.3	22.6	10.2	19.5	16.4	10.6	5.9	3.5	2.1	49.4	9 555	3.6	3.31	19.0	18.8
Livermore	7.7	20.4	7.1	14.8	20.3	14.0	8.1	4.3	3.2	50.0	26 123	26.5	2.80	9.3	18.8
Lodi	7.9	20.3	9.6	13.3	14.8	12.1	7.7	6.5	7.8	51.2	20 692	8.9	2.71	12.2	25.4
Lompoc	8.0	22.0	8.9	15.6	17.7	11.4	7.1	5.3	4.0	46.9	13 059	4.4	2.88	14.8	23.5
Long Beach	8.4	20.8	10.9	17.2	15.7	11.6	6.4	4.4	4.7	50.9	163 088	2.6	2.77	16.1	29.6
Los Altos	5.9	17.8	3.5	7.2	17.3	16.9	12.2	9.0	10.3	51.8	10 462	6.4	2.61	5.4	18.7
Los Angeles	7.7	18.8	11.1	18.2	15.8	11.6	7.0	5.1	4.6	50.2	1 275 412	4.8	2.83	14.5	28.5
Los Banos	9.4	25.8	8.9	13.7	16.1	10.6	6.2	5.0	4.3	50.2	7 721	61.8	3.33	12.4	15.8
Los Gatos	5.0	16.2	4.3	12.9	18.5	16.1	11.7	7.4	7.9	52.5	11 988	6.3	2.33	7.2	29.7
Lynwood	10.6	27.4	13.1	17.3	13.9	9.0	4.5	2.4	1.8	48.9	14 395	1.7	4.70	20.6	7.7
Madera	10.7	24.7	12.5	15.7	12.6	9.4	5.5	4.7	4.2	49.3	11 978	30.8	3.57	17.5	16.8
Manhattan Beach	6.5	15.8	4.1	17.7	19.8	16.1	9.6	5.9	4.5	49.6	14 474	3.4	2.34	5.8	29.3
Manteca	7.5	24.1	8.8	13.1	17.4	12.8	7.0	4.9	4.4	51.0	16 368	21.8	2.98	13.0	18.6
Marina	5.7	15.6	14.0	19.7	18.7	11.6	6.8	5.2	2.7	42.8	6 745	-14.7	2.79	15.1	21.4
Martinez	5.6	17.1	7.3	13.4	19.2	17.5	9.8	5.4	4.4	50.4	14 300	14.3	2.41	11.0	27.4
Maywood	11.4	25.6	13.2	19.4	13.2	8.5	4.5	2.5	1.7	49.0	6 469	-0.4	4.33	16.9	8.4
Menlo Park	6.6	15.3	6.2	17.4	17.4	13.3	8.0	6.7	9.2	51.5	12 387	4.8	2.41	8.5	32.1
Merced	9.2	25.5	11.4	13.8	13.6	10.8	6.3	4.9	4.6	51.1	20 435	11.8	3.06	18.2	22.6
Milpitas	7.2	17.5	9.5	19.0	19.0	13.3	7.5	4.6	2.4	47.4	17 132	21.5	3.47	10.9	11.5
Mission Viejo	6.9	20.2	6.6	11.7	18.8	15.5	9.4	5.5	5.4	51.1	32 449	28.9	2.84	8.1	17.3
Modesto	7.6	22.5	9.6	13.5	15.5	12.8	7.6	5.6	5.5	51.5	64 959	12.1	2.86	14.7	22.5
Monrovia	8.0	19.3	8.0	16.9	17.1	12.7	7.5	5.0	5.4	52.0	13 502	2.0	2.71	15.4	26.0
Montclair	8.9	24.3	10.7	15.7	14.7	11.0	6.5	4.4	3.9	50.1	8 800	3.1	3.69	16.3	15.0
Montebello	8.1	20.5	10.4	16.6	13.8	10.6	7.6	6.7	5.7	52.0	18 844	1.2	3.28	20.1	17.1
Monterey	5.0	11.6	13.1	18.1	15.6	13.6	8.1	6.7	8.2	50.8	12 600	-0.7	2.13	8.4	37.0
Monterey Park	5.6	15.7	8.4	15.0	15.2	13.0	9.3	9.3	9.6	52.0	19 564	0.3	3.06	15.8	17.3
Moorpark	8.1	26.1	8.6	12.4	19.9	14.8	5.6	2.7	1.8	50.1	8 994	18.0	3.49	9.7	9.9
Moreno Valley	8.8	28.0	10.5	12.9	16.6	12.1	5.6	3.4	2.0	51.1	39 225	12.2	3.61	17.1	11.0
Morgan Hill	8.1	22.4	7.6	13.5	18.2	14.8	7.9	3.9	3.6	50.4	10 846	38.9	3.05	11.1	15.1
Mountain View	6.0	11.9	8.3	24.6	18.8	12.6	7.2	5.3	5.2	48.3	31 242	4.2	2.25	7.3	35.6
Murrieta	7.5	26.2	6.4	10.9	19.9	11.0	6.6	7.1	4.3	51.0	14 320	2 421.1	3.08	8.1	14.5
Napa	6.8	19.0	8.5	14.1	15.5	13.9	8.5	6.2	7.6	50.9	26 978	12.8	2.64	11.1	26.8
National City	8.1	22.0	14.0	15.0	14.0	10.0	5.9	6.0	5.1	49.4	15 018	1.7	3.39	21.1	16.7
Newark	7.2	20.0	9.5	16.5	17.8	12.8	8.3	4.9	3.0	49.6	12 992	8.1	3.26	11.6	14.1
Newport Beach	4.0	11.7	6.5	17.0	16.0	15.2	12.0	8.8	8.8	50.5	33 071	7.2	2.09	6.1	35.3
Norwalk	8.6	23.5	10.7	15.7	14.8	10.9	6.7	5.1	3.9	50.5	26 887	2.1	3.79	16.6	12.7
Novato	5.9	17.2	6.4	12.6	17.4	16.9	10.7	6.6	6.4	51.6	18 524	1.6	2.52	10.3	25.2
Oakland	7.1	17.9	9.7	18.1	15.8	13.5	7.4	5.2	5.3	51.7	150 790	4.3	2.60	17.7	32.5
Oceanside	7.6	20.0	10.2	14.8	16.2	11.1	6.5	6.7	6.9	50.5	56 488	20.9	2.83	11.0	22.7
Ontario	9.7	24.7	11.2	16.9	15.4	10.6	5.5	3.3	2.6	49.9	43 525	8.1	3.60	15.5	15.1
Orange	7.4	19.3	9.9	16.5	16.8	12.6	7.9	5.4	4.3	49.8	40 930	11.3	3.02	11.6	19.5
Oxnard	8.9	22.8	11.8	16.2	14.7	10.8	6.5	4.7	3.4	48.9	43 576	10.9	3.85	14.1	14.6
Pacifica	5.7	17.5	7.7	14.4	18.4	17.3	9.3	5.8	4.0	50.7	13 994	4.9	2.73	11.0	21.2
Palmdale	9.3	28.7	8.5	12.7	18.4	11.3	5.4	3.4	2.2	50.9	34 285	56.2	3.40	16.2	13.9
Palm Desert	4.5	12.8	6.2	10.1	12.5	12.8	13.4	14.6	12.9	51.9	19 184	81.1	2.13	7.7	32.4
Palm Springs	4.7	12.3	6.1	10.4	13.8	13.8	12.6	12.9	13.4	48.1	20 516	10.2	2.05	8.5	41.6
Palo Alto	5.1	16.1	4.9	14.5	17.9	16.0	9.9	7.1	8.5	51.1	25 216	4.2	2.30	7.0	32.6
Paradise	4.3	16.1	5.9	7.8	13.3	14.6	10.8	11.3	15.9	53.4	11 591	4.9	2.22	10.3	32.0
Paramount	11.0	25.9	12.0	18.1	13.8	8.9	5.1	2.9	2.2	50.9	13 972	7.5	3.93	21.7	14.6
Pasadena	6.9	16.2	9.3	18.5	16.4	12.5	8.0	5.8	6.3	51.1	51 844	3.3	2.52	12.1	33.7
Perris	10.8	28.8	9.9	15.7	15.1	8.7	4.8	3.4	2.8	51.0	9 652	43.5	3.73	18.8	12.2
Petaluma	6.6	19.6	7.2	12.9	18.6	15.7	8.4	5.2	5.9	51.1	19 932	24.1	2.70	10.6	22.6
Pico Rivera	8.2	22.7	10.5	15.5	14.2	10.6	7.2	6.3	4.7	50.9	16 468	2.9	3.83	17.8	12.8
Pittsburg	8.3	22.5	10.4	14.9	16.3	12.5	6.8	4.5	3.7	50.9	17 741	13.4	3.17	17.2	18.0
Placentia	7.4	19.6	9.5	16.2	15.8	13.2	9.2	5.4	3.7	50.4	15 037	12.5	3.07	11.2	16.0
Pleasant Hill	6.1	15.3	7.2	14.4	18.0	16.8	9.0	6.2	7.0	51.5	13 753	5.8	2.35	9.1	29.1
Pleasanton	6.8	21.4	5.5	12.5	20.8	16.5	8.9	4.3	3.3	50.9	23 311	26.1	2.72	7.8	19.3

1. No spouse present.

	Persons in group quarters, 2000				Serious crimes known to police, 2000[2]				Education, 1990				Money income, 1989		
		Institutional			Total		Rate[3]		School enrollment		Attainment[4] (percent)			Households	
														Median	
City	Total	Total	Persons in nursing homes	Non-Institutional[1]	Number	Rate[3]	Violent	Property	Public	Private	High school graduate or more	Bachelor's degree or more	Per capita (dollars)[5]	Dollars	Percent change, 1979–1989 (constant 1989 dollars)
	31	32	33	34	35	36	37	38	39	40	41	42	43	44	45
CALIFORNIA—Cont'd															
Imperial Beach	666	0	0	666	876	3 245	578	2 667	6 435	449	77.9	12.1	10 731	26 464	21.6
Indio	856	551	197	305	2 234	4 548	711	3 838	10 010	582	52.0	9.2	9 244	25 976	1.7
Inglewood	1 370	745	409	625	4 668	4 146	1 222	2 924	27 957	5 702	66.0	14.9	11 899	29 881	18.7
Irvine	7 112	103	103	7 009	3 208	2 242	154	2 088	35 018	3 982	95.1	52.8	25 332	56 307	7.3
Laguna Niguel	303	41	41	262	886	1 432	121	1 310	9 335	2 018	95.9	44.6	28 614	61 501	22.2
La Habra	595	252	252	343	1 475	2 501	232	2 269	11 764	1 965	76.3	18.4	16 196	39 967	13.2
Lake Elsinore	73	0	0	73	1 360	4 701	947	3 754	4 479	389	72.8	8.1	11 765	30 801	NA
Lake Forest	838	558	558	280	1 196	2 037	221	1 816	NA	NA	NA	NA	NA	NA	NA
Lakewood	194	112	112	82	2 801	3 530	461	3 069	16 418	2 991	81.4	17.7	17 446	44 700	15.7
La Mesa	1 046	820	781	226	2 086	3 810	398	3 412	11 959	1 403	86.7	24.3	16 700	31 171	10.7
La Mirada	1 639	222	222	1 417	1 027	2 195	338	1 858	8 578	2 929	81.1	17.8	16 415	47 143	7.9
Lancaster	7 015	6 402	749	613	4 323	3 641	991	2 651	22 304	4 222	80.3	16.2	14 842	38 388	13.6
La Puente	32	0	0	32	1 127	2 709	740	1 969	10 440	1 085	50.6	7.5	9 060	33 273	8.4
La Verne	708	159	156	549	741	2 342	297	2 045	7 866	1 986	84.6	27.1	18 622	46 587	30.5
Lawndale	86	0	0	86	998	3 147	993	2 154	6 254	801	69.4	13.1	13 550	34 552	18.7
Livermore	201	128	128	73	1 738	2 370	180	2 190	13 920	1 932	88.2	27.3	19 330	49 149	17.5
Lodi	1 024	683	628	341	2 836	4 976	788	4 188	10 743	1 669	72.3	13.9	14 638	30 739	14.4
Lompoc	3 439	3 245	106	194	1 374	3 343	348	2 995	9 380	1 080	78.4	14.2	13 384	31 702	15.7
Long Beach	10 181	3 378	2 371	6 803	17 667	3 828	697	3 131	104 593	13 481	75.5	23.2	15 639	31 938	23.8
Los Altos	419	297	297	122	329	1 188	83	1 105	4 914	1 468	95.7	59.6	37 776	79 579	30.0
Los Angeles	82 597	30 446	12 853	52 151	180 538	4 886	1 360	3 526	806 534	172 104	67.0	23.0	16 188	30 925	17.3
Los Banos	175	149	149	26	636	2 459	329	2 130	3 818	291	63.0	12.1	11 345	24 649	0.9
Los Gatos	702	553	553	149	685	2 396	192	2 203	5 803	1 171	93.5	47.9	33 714	57 815	31.0
Lynwood	2 200	1 622	391	578	2 682	3 840	1 321	2 518	18 255	1 722	40.9	3.9	7 260	25 961	2.6
Madera	438	201	201	237	2 444	5 656	1 405	4 252	8 203	447	52.5	8.9	8 883	21 401	-5.5
Manhattan Beach	14	0	0	14	1 205	3 560	207	3 353	5 141	1 659	96.0	56.4	38 932	67 723	37.4
Manteca	477	288	288	189	1 949	3 957	414	3 543	11 117	979	74.9	10.1	12 813	35 083	15.2
Marina	6 307	4 087	0	2 220	471	1 876	307	1 570	6 745	700	84.2	17.0	11 338	29 043	11.6
Martinez	1 350	1 217	219	133	1 031	2 875	137	2 738	6 891	1 380	88.3	29.3	20 060	45 964	13.8
Maywood	94	90	90	4	626	2 229	442	1 788	8 699	589	27.9	1.6	6 927	25 567	21.5
Menlo Park	952	625	312	327	789	2 563	205	2 358	4 338	1 936	89.7	54.8	30 130	50 468	37.4
Merced	1 370	810	222	560	4 090	6 401	654	5 747	17 527	1 197	69.1	15.8	10 237	24 727	4.4
Milpitas	3 174	3 116	24	58	2 047	3 265	396	2 869	12 516	2 015	81.0	24.9	17 520	55 730	33.3
Mission Viejo	1 065	32	32	1 033	1 433	1 539	144	1 395	19 074	3 242	93.7	39.1	24 160	61 058	19.9
Modesto	3 208	1 853	1 261	1 355	10 663	5 646	512	5 134	42 844	4 022	74.8	15.8	13 572	31 701	7.2
Monrovia	293	93	85	200	1 174	3 179	395	2 784	7 520	1 697	77.3	19.7	15 495	35 684	32.6
Montclair	612	181	181	431	1 879	5 685	638	5 047	6 925	919	68.1	10.1	11 530	33 084	8.1
Montebello	309	277	256	32	2 204	3 546	536	3 010	15 222	2 718	60.8	14.6	12 276	31 441	5.8
Monterey	2 842	300	290	2 542	1 319	4 445	657	3 788	6 250	2 000	88.5	39.8	18 174	34 727	18.0
Monterey Park	277	85	85	192	1 338	2 228	301	1 927	15 474	2 612	70.0	22.4	13 290	32 605	-3.3
Moorpark	12	5	0	7	329	1 047	169	879	6 776	1 144	85.3	28.4	19 183	60 368	NA
Moreno Valley	697	6	0	691	6 302	4 426	795	3 631	34 759	3 850	81.8	14.3	13 474	42 186	NA
Morgan Hill	505	306	155	199	1 059	3 156	170	2 986	6 729	718	83.4	28.1	19 560	53 480	29.1
Mountain View	504	307	278	197	2 315	3 274	511	2 763	12 117	3 071	86.6	40.7	22 436	42 431	27.9
Murrieta	186	63	63	123	817	1 845	156	1 689	NA	NA	NA	NA	NA	NA	NA
Napa	1 459	689	467	770	1 742	2 400	285	2 115	14 117	1 878	80.8	19.2	16 219	35 479	11.3
National City	3 343	215	215	3 128	2 668	4 917	796	4 121	13 643	1 048	58.9	9.1	8 658	22 129	12.0
Newark	89	0	0	89	1 750	4 120	306	3 814	9 626	1 395	78.6	21.1	16 721	50 471	14.2
Newport Beach	940	427	418	513	2 349	3 354	149	3 206	11 679	2 991	95.3	50.3	45 434	60 374	30.9
Norwalk	1 349	961	588	388	3 090	2 991	630	2 361	24 483	3 547	64.7	9.9	11 713	38 124	16.8
Novato	982	618	521	364	1 341	2 815	325	2 490	10 308	2 009	91.7	31.8	21 518	45 890	11.6
Oakland	7 175	2 894	1 475	4 281	25 060	6 273	1 261	5 012	84 860	16 611	74.4	27.2	14 676	27 095	17.3
Oceanside	1 280	181	156	1 099	5 853	3 635	528	3 106	27 133	3 569	81.2	18.8	14 522	33 453	33.3
Ontario	1 141	428	412	713	7 653	4 843	713	4 131	33 744	3 830	68.5	11.0	12 120	35 788	12.3
Orange	5 332	3 297	268	2 035	3 349	2 600	259	2 340	24 557	6 304	81.7	25.6	19 064	46 539	25.6
Oxnard	2 597	503	475	2 094	5 661	3 323	507	2 816	36 567	4 356	61.3	13.0	12 096	37 174	25.8
Pacifica	181	142	133	39	700	1 823	284	1 539	8 540	1 376	86.5	22.8	18 553	47 533	17.3
Palmdale	94	3	3	91	4 392	3 764	841	2 924	16 749	2 325	79.8	13.3	14 606	41 974	32.8
Palm Desert	227	152	152	75	1 837	4 464	403	4 060	3 865	613	86.2	23.6	25 926	37 315	13.3
Palm Springs	696	279	279	417	3 237	7 562	1 068	6 494	5 625	744	77.1	20.4	19 725	27 538	1.7
Palo Alto	668	433	343	235	1 905	3 251	159	3 092	10 227	3 739	94.7	65.2	32 489	55 333	33.4
Paradise	620	317	287	303	981	3 715	413	3 302	4 823	415	77.5	15.1	12 887	22 954	9.1
Paramount	320	300	143	20	2 592	4 690	890	3 800	13 942	1 353	50.1	6.9	9 429	29 015	15.7
Pasadena	3 518	1 333	1 236	2 185	5 637	4 209	547	3 662	25 951	10 994	77.5	36.3	19 588	35 103	28.6
Perris	232	111	105	121	1 952	5 394	1 080	4 313	4 938	534	64.1	7.3	9 773	28 611	NA
Petaluma	740	321	321	419	1 426	2 614	152	2 462	10 199	1 427	86.4	24.4	17 170	40 926	15.7
Pico Rivera	350	335	335	15	1 563	2 464	639	1 826	16 096	1 897	52.3	6.1	10 454	34 383	11.5
Pittsburg	506	179	163	327	2 279	4 015	451	3 564	12 128	1 705	70.5	14.4	13 686	38 532	17.1
Placentia	303	89	89	214	925	1 990	282	1 708	11 405	1 215	81.7	30.2	18 924	50 945	13.1
Pleasant Hill	460	305	305	155	1 446	4 404	426	3 977	6 555	1 117	92.4	35.4	21 950	46 885	20.6
Pleasanton	235	161	161	74	1 509	2 371	130	2 240	12 552	1 522	93.0	37.2	24 812	59 458	23.5

1. Persons in emergency shelters and persons visible in street locations. 2. Data for serious crimes have not been adjusted for underreporting. This may affect comparability between geographic areas and over time. 3. Per 100,000 population estimated by the FBI. 4. Persons 25 years old and older. 5. Based on population enumerated as of April 1, 1990.

Table D. Cities — Income, Poverty, and Housing

City	Money income, 1989 (cont'd)				Housing units, 2000										
	Households (cont'd)	Percent below poverty, 1989					Vacant units				Occupied units				
		Persons		Families											
	Percent with $100,000 or more	Total	Percent change in rate, 1979–1989	Total	Total	Percent change, 1990–2000	Vacant units for sale or rent[1]	For seasonal use (percent)	Home owner vacancy rate	Renter vacancy rate	Total	Percent owner occupied	Percent renter occupied	Average size owner occupied	Average size renter occupied
	46	47	48	49	50	51	52	53	54	55	56	57	58	59	60
CALIFORNIA—Cont'd															
Imperial Beach	1.4	17.7	4.7	14.9	9 739	2.2	467	1.8	0.8	3.0	9 272	30.0	70.0	2.79	2.86
Indio	1.6	21.2	34.2	17.0	16 909	29.8	3 038	12.8	2.4	4.9	13 871	56.2	43.8	3.45	3.51
Inglewood	2.5	16.5	7.1	14.1	38 648	-0.2	1 843	0.1	1.5	3.5	36 805	36.3	63.7	3.24	2.90
Irvine	18.5	6.4	77.8	2.6	53 711	27.2	2 512	0.7	1.1	3.5	51 199	60.0	40.0	2.78	2.46
Laguna Niguel	22.1	3.1	-3.1	2.2	23 885	26.4	668	0.8	0.8	3.3	23 217	75.0	25.0	2.68	2.56
La Habra	6.4	8.0	31.1	5.9	19 441	4.1	494	0.2	1.3	2.1	18 947	56.6	43.4	3.04	3.13
Lake Elsinore	2.1	11.9	NA	8.4	9 505	36.2	688	0.9	3.3	7.0	8 817	64.6	35.4	3.29	3.25
Lake Forest	NA	NA	NA	NA	20 486	NA	478	0.1	0.8	4.1	20 008	72.0	28.0	2.93	2.79
Lakewood	5.2	4.9	-5.8	3.2	27 310	1.9	457	0.1	0.6	1.9	26 853	72.0	28.0	2.94	2.97
La Mesa	3.0	9.2	-7.1	6.0	24 943	3.3	757	0.3	0.7	2.8	24 186	47.2	52.8	2.35	2.10
La Mirada	6.3	3.9	-20.4	2.4	14 811	10.9	231	0.2	0.7	1.7	14 580	82.0	18.0	3.15	2.85
Lancaster	4.1	9.9	13.8	7.7	41 745	15.3	3 521	0.3	3.4	8.8	38 224	61.4	38.6	3.01	2.78
La Puente	1.5	14.0	18.6	12.4	9 660	4.0	199	0.1	1.2	1.3	9 461	60.9	39.1	4.50	4.09
La Verne	7.8	4.4	-25.4	3.1	11 286	1.6	216	0.2	0.6	2.6	11 070	77.5	22.5	2.84	2.63
Lawndale	2.2	13.1	2.3	10.4	9 869	0.9	314	0.3	1.3	2.5	9 555	33.2	66.8	3.41	3.26
Livermore	6.9	5.2	18.2	4.4	26 610	23.8	487	0.2	0.4	2.0	26 123	72.2	27.8	2.86	2.65
Lodi	3.0	12.6	34.0	10.0	21 378	8.7	686	0.2	1.2	2.9	20 692	54.6	45.4	2.65	2.77
Lompoc	1.8	15.1	15.3	12.9	13 621	2.7	562	0.2	0.8	4.0	13 059	51.6	48.4	2.83	2.94
Long Beach	5.5	16.8	18.3	13.5	171 632	0.7	8 544	0.4	2.2	4.2	163 088	41.0	59.0	2.81	2.74
Los Altos	37.0	1.2	-53.8	0.5	10 727	6.1	265	0.3	0.3	6.2	10 462	85.6	14.4	2.67	2.21
Los Angeles	7.9	18.9	15.2	14.9	1 337 706	2.9	62 294	0.4	1.8	3.5	1 275 412	38.6	61.4	2.99	2.73
Los Banos	2.5	19.4	55.2	15.8	8 049	58.8	328	0.6	1.3	3.1	7 721	67.9	32.1	3.29	3.40
Los Gatos	21.6	4.6	-14.8	2.1	12 367	4.6	379	0.9	0.5	2.3	11 988	65.3	34.7	2.54	1.92
Lynwood	1.4	21.8	5.8	20.1	14 987	3.2	592	0.2	2.4	2.7	14 395	47.1	52.9	5.09	4.35
Madera	1.9	26.9	38.7	21.4	12 521	31.4	543	0.2	1.5	3.8	11 978	52.7	47.3	3.38	3.78
Manhattan Beach	30.0	3.8	-13.6	1.5	15 034	2.3	560	1.1	1.0	3.0	14 474	65.1	34.9	2.60	1.85
Manteca	2.7	9.9	5.3	8.6	16 937	21.1	569	0.2	1.1	3.1	16 368	63.0	37.0	3.06	2.85
Marina	1.3	9.7	-28.7	8.5	8 537	3.3	1 792	0.3	6.4	2.9	6 745	45.8	54.2	2.77	2.80
Martinez	6.0	5.9	3.5	4.2	14 597	12.5	297	0.1	0.5	2.0	14 300	68.8	31.2	2.53	2.16
Maywood	1.1	21.3	0.0	19.1	6 701	0.3	232	0.1	1.8	1.6	6 469	29.4	70.6	4.74	4.15
Menlo Park	18.6	6.5	-18.8	3.9	12 714	3.8	327	0.8	0.3	1.5	12 387	57.0	43.0	2.67	2.07
Merced	2.4	25.1	51.2	20.2	21 532	13.5	1 097	0.2	1.6	5.1	20 435	46.5	53.5	2.93	3.18
Milpitas	11.6	4.9	-23.4	3.1	17 364	20.0	232	0.1	0.4	2.1	17 132	69.8	30.2	3.49	3.44
Mission Viejo	17.2	2.0	-39.4	1.0	32 985	25.0	536	0.3	0.6	2.3	32 449	81.4	18.6	2.87	2.71
Modesto	3.5	13.0	26.2	10.5	67 179	10.4	2 220	0.2	1.2	3.3	64 959	58.7	41.3	2.89	2.81
Monrovia	5.0	12.4	11.7	8.2	13 957	0.1	455	0.2	1.0	2.5	13 502	47.9	52.1	2.75	2.68
Montclair	2.6	16.7	38.0	13.0	9 066	1.7	266	0.1	1.2	3.6	8 800	60.6	39.4	3.59	3.84
Montebello	5.5	14.0	17.6	11.6	19 416	1.2	572	0.2	1.0	2.7	18 844	47.5	52.5	3.28	3.28
Monterey	5.2	6.6	-7.0	3.6	13 382	-0.9	782	2.7	1.0	2.3	12 600	38.5	61.5	2.29	2.03
Monterey Park	5.9	16.4	62.4	13.4	20 209	-0.4	645	0.3	1.9	1.9	19 564	54.0	46.0	2.97	3.16
Moorpark	10.7	4.3	NA	2.6	9 094	14.9	100	0.1	0.5	1.2	8 994	82.1	17.9	3.43	3.78
Moreno Valley	2.9	8.4	NA	6.9	41 431	9.2	2 206	0.2	2.8	5.9	39 225	71.1	28.9	3.63	3.56
Morgan Hill	12.5	4.5	-47.1	3.5	11 091	36.0	245	0.3	0.6	2.6	10 846	72.5	27.5	2.98	3.21
Mountain View	8.0	6.2	-10.1	3.8	32 432	3.0	1 190	0.9	0.6	1.6	31 242	41.5	58.5	2.30	2.21
Murrieta	NA	NA	NA	NA	14 921	NA	601	0.7	1.7	5.1	14 320	79.7	20.3	3.18	2.70
Napa	4.2	7.7	-11.5	5.2	27 776	11.5	798	0.6	0.8	1.9	26 978	60.6	39.4	2.59	2.71
National City	0.9	21.3	12.1	20.2	15 422	1.2	404	0.1	0.5	2.3	15 018	35.0	65.0	3.63	3.26
Newark	6.1	5.0	-5.7	4.1	13 150	7.0	158	0.2	0.4	1.2	12 992	70.6	29.4	3.22	3.37
Newport Beach	28.7	5.7	-17.4	2.3	37 288	7.0	4 217	5.3	1.8	8.0	33 071	55.7	44.3	2.30	1.83
Norwalk	2.2	9.3	-11.4	7.2	27 554	1.1	667	0.1	1.4	2.0	26 887	65.8	34.2	3.85	3.67
Novato	11.1	4.2	-23.6	2.5	18 994	1.1	470	0.3	0.9	2.5	18 524	67.6	32.4	2.50	2.56
Oakland	4.9	18.8	1.6	16.7	157 508	1.8	6 718	0.3	1.0	2.7	150 790	41.4	58.6	2.76	2.49
Oceanside	3.2	10.1	-17.9	6.7	59 581	16.6	3 093	2.4	1.0	3.2	56 488	62.1	37.9	2.82	2.85
Ontario	2.3	13.6	28.3	10.6	45 182	6.2	1 657	0.2	1.6	3.3	43 525	57.6	42.4	3.64	3.55
Orange	11.2	8.0	19.4	4.7	41 904	10.2	974	0.2	1.1	2.0	40 930	62.6	37.4	2.91	3.20
Oxnard	3.9	12.5	1.6	9.6	45 166	9.5	1 590	1.6	1.0	1.8	43 576	57.3	42.7	3.79	3.94
Pacifica	6.7	4.5	-22.4	3.2	14 245	3.7	251	0.3	0.2	1.9	13 994	68.6	31.4	2.88	2.41
Palmdale	3.9	8.9	-15.2	7.7	37 096	52.0	2 811	0.3	3.1	9.6	34 285	71.0	29.0	3.43	3.33
Palm Desert	11.1	7.1	-2.7	4.2	28 021	53.6	8 837	23.0	2.3	8.3	19 184	66.9	33.1	2.12	2.16
Palm Springs	7.2	12.6	21.2	8.8	30 823	1.0	10 307	23.5	3.2	11.0	20 516	60.8	39.2	2.03	2.09
Palo Alto	20.5	4.6	-23.3	1.9	26 048	3.4	832	0.8	0.6	2.0	25 216	57.2	42.8	2.55	1.96
Paradise	1.5	11.1	11.0	8.2	12 374	6.4	783	0.8	2.5	6.2	11 591	70.9	29.1	2.23	2.21
Paramount	1.9	17.6	-6.9	15.0	14 591	6.3	619	0.2	3.4	3.1	13 972	42.9	57.1	3.91	3.95
Pasadena	10.1	14.9	5.7	11.1	54 132	2.1	2 288	0.6	1.4	2.9	51 844	45.8	54.2	2.64	2.41
Perris	0.5	15.7	NA	12.2	10 553	36.0	901	1.0	4.0	7.2	9 652	68.1	31.9	3.79	3.58
Petaluma	4.5	4.2	-33.3	2.7	20 304	22.7	372	0.3	0.5	1.7	19 932	70.1	29.9	2.75	2.59
Pico Rivera	2.0	11.6	8.4	9.3	16 807	3.0	339	0.0	0.9	2.3	16 468	70.4	29.6	3.90	3.67
Pittsburg	2.2	10.8	-16.3	8.5	18 300	9.5	559	0.2	0.9	3.8	17 741	62.8	37.2	3.24	3.05
Placentia	9.9	7.7	51.0	5.2	15 326	11.6	289	0.2	0.6	2.3	15 037	69.0	31.0	2.92	3.40
Pleasant Hill	8.3	3.6	-20.0	2.1	14 034	2.8	281	0.2	0.5	1.4	13 753	63.5	36.5	2.53	2.05
Pleasanton	14.6	2.4	-31.4	1.5	23 968	23.8	657	0.7	0.5	3.2	23 311	73.4	26.6	2.87	2.30

1. Includes units rented or sold but not occupied.   2. Specified owner-occupied units.   3. Specified renter-occupied units.   4. Overcrowded or lacking complete plumbing facilities.

Table D. Cities — Labor Force, Employment, Disability, and Construction

City	Civilian labor force, 2001				Civilian employment, 1990[2]			Disability 1990	Value of residential construction authorized by building permits, 2000		
			Unemployment			Percent					
	Total	Percent change, 2000–2001	Total	Rate[1]	Total	Professional, managerial, and technical	Precision production, craft, and repair	Work disabled persons[3] (percent)	New construction ($1,000)	Number of housing units	Percent single family
	61	62	63	64	65	66	67	68	69	70	71
CALIFORNIA—Cont'd											
Imperial Beach	12 814	1.8	706	5.5	10 055	22.3	17.8	9.0	6 531	35	54.3
Indio	23 738	2.7	1 755	7.4	15 086	17.0	11.4	8.4	59 002	464	100.0
Inglewood	59 376	2.5	4 620	7.8	50 059	24.3	10.7	6.7	2 456	22	59.1
Irvine	72 718	1.6	1 519	2.1	61 726	52.8	3.6	3.4	423 046	4 050	28.1
Laguna Niguel	30 155	1.5	535	1.8	25 679	46.5	6.0	3.6	28 048	110	100.0
La Habra	32 053	1.8	1 109	3.5	26 827	28.4	11.6	6.9	29 017	100	100.0
Lake Elsinore	11 459	2.8	666	5.8	7 407	20.0	23.3	9.9	51 216	275	100.0
Lake Forest	41 262	1.6	917	2.2	NA	NA	NA	NA	NA	NA	NA
Lakewood	42 234	2.2	1 405	3.3	37 327	31.6	13.4	6.7	2 105	20	15.0
La Mesa	33 437	1.6	878	2.6	27 037	35.5	10.6	7.5	1 284	7	100.0
La Mirada	23 316	2.3	817	3.5	20 569	29.7	12.6	6.6	5 300	132	3.0
Lancaster	49 478	2.4	2 673	5.4	42 790	33.3	15.7	7.9	40 605	411	67.9
La Puente	18 555	2.5	1 327	7.2	15 750	15.8	15.9	7.3	649	12	0.0
La Verne	17 530	2.2	529	3.0	15 543	37.5	9.1	5.7	9 798	73	58.9
Lawndale	16 165	2.4	940	5.8	13 919	24.5	17.2	6.1	611	5	100.0
Livermore	36 589	1.7	1 132	3.1	31 270	38.1	12.8	6.4	105 776	511	89.2
Lodi	31 151	1.9	2 006	6.4	23 588	24.2	13.2	8.0	46 808	302	99.3
Lompoc	18 141	-0.8	869	4.8	15 908	26.0	14.9	9.6	237	1	100.0
Long Beach	227 635	2.4	12 022	5.3	197 118	32.5	10.8	8.3	26 847	181	63.0
Los Altos	16 886	-0.6	459	2.7	13 701	64.4	4.4	3.5	23 472	49	100.0
Los Angeles	1 953 375	2.4	126 148	6.5	1 670 488	30.4	10.3	6.7	558 740	6 567	25.7
Los Banos	7 172	-1.4	965	13.5	5 666	22.9	11.8	11.3	74 581	537	100.0
Los Gatos	19 761	-0.5	546	2.8	16 026	53.6	6.0	4.4	22 778	89	95.5
Lynwood	26 718	2.6	2 600	9.7	22 049	13.0	16.4	7.6	3 109	30	100.0
Madera	17 642	-0.8	3 065	17.4	10 147	17.2	11.7	10.3	19 719	176	98.9
Manhattan Beach	22 727	2.2	410	1.8	20 403	57.9	4.5	4.0	58 784	184	96.7
Manteca	23 758	1.9	1 657	7.0	17 887	22.5	17.4	9.6	168 183	1 147	100.0
Marina	11 783	-0.1	712	6.0	9 150	23.3	7.7	6.3	1 380	7	100.0
Martinez	21 720	1.0	576	2.7	17 431	40.5	10.2	6.5	28 462	133	100.0
Maywood	13 652	2.6	1 302	9.5	11 291	8.0	15.5	5.8	231	4	50.0
Menlo Park	16 609	-0.9	357	2.1	14 468	57.1	4.7	5.9	14 738	38	100.0
Merced	25 582	-1.5	3 549	13.9	20 113	28.0	11.2	8.8	38 008	331	100.0
Milpitas	32 792	0.5	1 514	4.6	26 087	37.1	12.3	5.4	39 164	238	7.1
Mission Viejo	46 257	1.5	837	1.8	39 377	43.9	7.5	4.4	64 614	656	23.8
Modesto	95 819	2.1	8 726	9.1	69 663	27.5	13.1	9.4	188 329	1 320	98.9
Monrovia	20 717	2.3	990	4.8	18 035	32.0	10.9	7.3	10 812	56	100.0
Montclair	18 045	3.1	852	4.7	13 106	20.3	14.7	8.5	186	1	100.0
Montebello	30 375	2.4	1 576	5.2	26 329	24.7	11.5	6.5	0	0	0.0
Monterey	17 627	0.0	588	3.3	14 083	39.7	6.4	5.1	5 202	29	72.4
Monterey Park	31 001	2.3	1 466	4.7	27 001	32.3	8.9	6.2	16 787	65	100.0
Moorpark	16 542	1.6	561	3.4	13 423	39.4	11.8	4.4	78 375	491	36.5
Moreno Valley	79 767	2.8	4 467	5.6	51 676	26.5	15.5	6.8	53 499	323	100.0
Morgan Hill	15 296	-0.1	535	3.5	12 311	38.1	10.6	6.3	42 149	201	83.1
Mountain View	51 652	-0.4	1 588	3.1	41 755	49.0	7.6	5.5	23 280	121	100.0
Murrieta	12 767	2.9	495	3.9	NA	NA	NA	NA	168 714	886	100.0
Napa	37 742	2.3	1 434	3.8	29 601	30.2	13.2	9.4	49 827	232	98.3
National City	22 832	1.8	1 355	5.9	17 835	17.1	16.0	8.4	378	3	100.0
Newark	24 245	2.0	952	3.9	20 542	29.0	14.9	6.0	33 777	107	100.0
Newport Beach	46 699	1.5	874	1.9	39 728	51.4	4.7	3.9	87 901	533	30.2
Norwalk	48 831	2.4	2 499	5.1	42 358	21.0	15.5	6.7	8 534	140	8.6
Novato	27 538	-1.1	625	2.3	25 165	37.2	9.4	5.1	83 478	268	100.0
Oakland	198 309	3.1	14 063	7.1	162 488	36.2	7.9	10.4	42 013	449	33.0
Oceanside	68 388	1.7	2 666	3.9	54 576	27.2	13.1	8.0	116 165	654	77.1
Ontario	83 444	3.1	3 806	4.6	60 708	20.9	15.9	6.8	46 691	238	99.2
Orange	71 859	1.7	2 058	2.9	60 514	35.0	9.8	5.2	67 609	373	82.0
Oxnard	85 201	1.6	5 527	6.5	66 922	21.7	13.1	7.5	168 095	1 032	58.9
Pacifica	24 615	-0.9	550	2.2	21 424	31.7	13.3	7.5	9 741	38	94.7
Palmdale	35 732	2.4	1 906	5.3	30 924	28.9	18.7	7.0	104 941	661	100.0
Palm Desert	17 472	2.9	535	3.1	11 623	31.4	9.0	6.2	150 738	533	78.2
Palm Springs	28 292	2.9	1 136	4.0	18 636	30.1	8.8	8.5	39 686	181	98.9
Palo Alto	39 567	-0.8	898	2.3	32 251	66.6	3.8	4.5	32 991	94	100.0
Paradise	10 356	0.6	569	5.5	8 480	28.3	14.7	13.6	9 655	74	100.0
Paramount	23 244	2.5	1 783	7.7	19 620	15.3	15.0	7.7	111	1	100.0
Pasadena	75 487	2.3	3 661	4.8	65 665	42.8	7.2	6.9	52 810	644	5.1
Perris	12 293	2.7	930	7.6	7 798	20.1	17.3	11.6	5 201	79	11.4
Petaluma	30 640	1.3	726	2.4	22 681	33.1	12.7	6.8	42 653	300	75.0
Pico Rivera	29 316	2.4	1 913	6.5	25 052	16.7	13.8	7.5	470	4	100.0
Pittsburg	27 803	1.4	1 292	4.6	21 853	24.6	13.2	9.2	54 289	467	56.3
Placentia	27 254	1.7	733	2.7	22 992	36.9	9.5	5.2	23 065	136	67.6
Pleasant Hill	22 449	0.9	469	2.1	18 120	43.8	9.1	6.4	10 758	49	100.0
Pleasanton	34 757	1.4	784	2.3	29 961	42.7	8.3	4.8	166 627	368	100.0

1. Percent of civilian labor force.   2. Persons 16 years and older.   3. Persons 16 to 64 years old.

City	Wholesale Trade, 1997				Retail Trade[1], 1997				Real Estate and Rental and Leasing, 1997			
	Number of Establishments	Number of Employees	Sales (mil dol)	Annual Payroll (mil dol)	Number of Establishments	Number of Employees	Sales (mil dol)	Annual Payroll (mil dol)	Number of Establishments	Number of Employees	Receipts (mil dol)	Annual Payroll (mil dol)
	72	73	74	75	76	77	78	79	80	81	82	83
CALIFORNIA—Cont'd												
Imperial Beach	6	34	6.6	0.5	43	254	34.1	3.5	25	D	D	D
Indio	33	D	D	D	136	1 752	327.0	32.3	32	177	22.9	3.7
Inglewood	102	1 455	509.8	48.9	231	2 567	527.9	47.2	71	636	124.8	15.1
Irvine	894	17 641	29 723.1	881.0	400	6 137	1 368.5	137.1	320	4 308	678.7	157.1
Laguna Niguel	102	337	462.7	14.3	146	2 911	526.8	50.2	61	315	51.6	9.4
La Habra	67	479	175.2	14.8	158	2 378	392.2	43.6	40	163	19.3	2.7
Lake Elsinore	12	53	14.6	1.6	162	1 826	269.4	26.5	21	76	8.7	1.2
Lake Forest	NA	NA	NA	NA	NA	NA	NA	NA	NA	NA	NA	NA
Lakewood	43	315	58.6	7.4	250	4 211	637.0	66.1	40	224	40.7	4.1
La Mesa	36	222	70.3	7.5	281	4 491	872.1	84.6	116	648	65.6	12.2
La Mirada	114	2 755	2 521.4	118.2	95	1 394	287.7	29.0	24	177	25.9	6.4
Lancaster	61	652	198.1	17.2	326	3 906	715.8	75.5	76	420	54.6	8.6
La Puente	18	D	D	D	100	1 125	228.2	19.9	18	122	9.0	1.6
La Verne	45	340	220.7	11.3	84	1 229	212.8	21.1	17	171	15.6	3.5
Lawndale	22	D	D	D	96	1 108	303.9	21.8	27	237	23.4	3.6
Livermore	129	1 708	1 133.7	74.4	188	2 931	593.7	55.4	57	306	46.9	8.9
Lodi	58	1 050	415.4	30.3	218	2 970	529.7	53.8	68	763	51.9	15.2
Lompoc	17	D	D	D	111	1 439	245.7	23.9	33	144	13.2	2.4
Long Beach	402	5 257	8 218.0	200.8	998	11 047	1 939.9	197.4	404	2 934	372.0	62.8
Los Altos	51	D	D	D	115	920	163.6	20.0	78	199	57.1	6.8
Los Angeles	8 327	87 405	49 609.3	3 065.1	10 639	118 117	22 932.8	2 342.9	4 998	39 094	7 382.2	1 219.5
Los Banos	15	D	D	D	75	939	143.9	17.3	16	46	7.7	0.5
Los Gatos	65	440	272.6	24.2	199	2 216	484.9	53.6	102	402	61.2	12.1
Lynwood	44	747	259.6	23.3	83	925	179.9	17.1	13	78	8.2	1.2
Madera	33	D	D	D	141	1 918	302.5	31.5	19	89	8.9	1.4
Manhattan Beach	54	442	403.3	27.1	159	2 794	612.3	51.1	89	356	46.5	11.3
Manteca	23	D	D	D	147	1 996	359.3	36.2	45	213	19.8	3.8
Marina	9	59	18.7	1.9	41	475	59.9	6.7	22	D	D	D
Martinez	41	446	654.3	20.1	78	1 224	281.7	27.9	33	187	27.6	4.7
Maywood	16	164	54.3	4.7	47	572	86.7	8.9	5	D	D	D
Menlo Park	68	1 674	779.9	107.2	139	1 930	558.1	49.8	91	796	120.8	32.6
Merced	37	576	416.7	18.7	265	3 722	674.7	65.8	67	320	30.5	4.5
Milpitas	224	4 470	3 747.0	206.3	318	4 934	804.5	89.2	45	236	71.9	9.4
Mission Viejo	142	783	465.7	38.5	256	3 702	775.0	67.7	85	862	131.0	29.2
Modesto	164	2 111	870.5	66.9	704	10 008	1 765.7	177.1	171	1 003	136.2	22.0
Monrovia	109	1 020	282.7	32.9	141	2 617	553.2	48.3	26	98	9.6	2.0
Montclair	57	499	129.2	14.1	290	5 363	709.9	84.8	20	144	11.4	2.9
Montebello	123	1 929	1 474.6	77.0	242	3 468	630.0	62.2	60	294	49.3	7.5
Monterey	56	1 324	1 460.5	49.7	264	2 785	381.0	44.5	100	581	60.4	10.6
Monterey Park	268	1 656	864.8	44.3	169	1 683	275.2	26.2	81	350	82.8	7.5
Moorpark	56	773	242.3	31.4	33	452	77.9	9.5	13	43	7.4	1.3
Moreno Valley	25	80	47.0	2.5	277	3 997	691.2	74.9	49	207	18.3	3.1
Morgan Hill	48	1 593	625.5	66.5	94	1 453	278.8	28.4	41	115	27.0	2.9
Mountain View	180	5 479	2 612.0	283.5	296	4 458	977.6	98.8	121	771	102.8	16.4
Murrieta	NA	NA	NA	NA	NA	NA	NA	NA	NA	NA	NA	NA
Napa	84	568	202.5	17.0	319	3 712	648.8	69.6	85	712	53.4	10.5
National City	119	1 302	814.1	39.9	324	5 030	1 052.3	105.7	46	197	30.1	3.7
Newark	83	1 410	683.9	56.6	218	3 470	626.8	60.2	34	224	64.4	5.1
Newport Beach	289	7 136	2 642.8	140.7	440	5 947	1 140.2	125.1	521	5 612	1 233.7	229.0
Norwalk	84	815	610.1	28.7	172	2 810	630.1	57.4	44	206	25.7	4.1
Novato	111	981	423.1	34.9	192	2 619	543.8	59.5	79	434	64.0	10.1
Oakland	526	7 662	3 553.2	285.6	1 030	10 190	2 146.5	213.1	476	2 712	406.9	66.7
Oceanside	125	1 694	925.6	42.1	388	4 916	781.2	82.4	94	445	59.7	7.8
Ontario	371	7 262	5 425.5	251.6	461	7 653	1 769.1	152.1	115	1 008	201.5	25.1
Orange	403	5 751	4 685.5	228.2	484	5 519	1 227.3	123.8	164	947	140.4	24.4
Oxnard	175	2 818	922.9	110.6	487	6 821	1 398.7	135.8	100	464	57.2	9.5
Pacifica	7	14	7.3	0.6	70	721	127.3	12.1	21	58	12.0	1.1
Palmdale	36	268	71.7	8.4	208	2 852	543.0	53.3	58	193	24.7	3.4
Palm Desert	68	403	125.6	11.0	364	4 024	669.7	71.7	89	425	51.1	10.7
Palm Springs	40	D	D	D	225	2 759	438.1	49.1	113	518	91.4	12.3
Palo Alto	104	1 382	1 019.1	126.5	307	6 097	1 337.7	139.9	155	1 336	258.1	44.1
Paradise	8	D	D	D	84	859	120.9	13.3	37	D	D	D
Paramount	200	2 752	888.6	83.4	115	1 515	230.2	24.5	42	232	28.6	4.6
Pasadena	200	2 492	2 219.5	108.6	567	8 330	1 553.1	160.9	239	2 059	244.6	40.8
Perris	13	106	29.6	2.7	66	2 544	471.0	39.6	17	58	4.8	0.8
Petaluma	113	1 948	579.8	60.5	276	3 307	618.6	65.7	71	399	41.9	6.9
Pico Rivera	86	1 532	620.1	51.9	108	1 554	303.9	33.8	24	240	45.9	6.7
Pittsburg	31	378	147.4	14.6	111	2 158	369.0	38.6	22	170	35.4	3.6
Placentia	129	1 264	477.6	45.6	110	1 525	334.6	38.1	36	411	23.4	6.6
Pleasant Hill	35	338	153.9	15.3	159	2 383	382.2	36.2	49	204	26.6	4.8
Pleasanton	253	5 868	13 804.0	331.2	349	5 665	1 068.2	107.5	101	442	92.0	17.7

1. Establishments with payroll.

City	Professional, Scientific, and Technical Services, 1997[1]				Manufacturing, 1997				Accommodation and Foodservices, 1997			
	Number of Establishments	Number of Employees	Receipts (mil dol)	Annual Payroll (mil dol)	Number of Establishments	Number of Employees	Receipts (mil dol)	Annual Payroll (mil dol)	Number of Establishments	Number of Employees	Sales (mil dol)	Annual Payroll (mil dol)
	84	85	86	87	88	89	90	91	92	93	94	95
CALIFORNIA—Cont'd												
Imperial Beach	7	17	1.1	0.3	NA	NA	NA	NA	47	430	13.9	3.7
Indio	34	85	10.6	2.5	NA	NA	NA	NA	74	1 050	42.0	9.5
Inglewood	51	576	161.8	40.1	74	2 554	384.3	79.7	127	1 694	74.1	15.9
Irvine	1 419	18 430	2 874.4	1 057.0	479	34 067	8 500.6	1 319.0	300	8 073	338.2	91.4
Laguna Niguel	170	575	68.6	29.0	NA	NA	NA	NA	109	D	D	D
La Habra	58	233	22.9	8.8	87	1 371	155.0	39.4	98	1 526	49.8	12.9
Lake Elsinore	17	40	3.0	1.1	53	778	61.0	17.7	53	759	23.1	6.3
Lake Forest	NA	NA	NA	NA	NA	NA	NA	NA	NA	NA	NA	NA
Lakewood	57	702	44.4	15.0	NA	NA	NA	NA	147	2 837	91.7	23.5
La Mesa	163	536	46.3	14.9	NA	NA	NA	NA	152	3 516	120.9	35.2
La Mirada	52	256	56.6	10.2	74	4 323	757.0	132.1	72	1 084	44.3	11.0
Lancaster	87	438	42.2	16.5	50	845	79.0	15.3	148	2 716	92.4	23.0
La Puente	10	66	8.0	2.8	NA	NA	NA	NA	57	521	20.7	4.6
La Verne	42	339	36.2	10.2	43	1 062	188.6	35.0	43	744	25.2	6.3
Lawndale	25	184	11.4	4.8	NA	NA	NA	NA	46	594	22.9	5.8
Livermore	120	1 591	200.7	84.7	112	2 897	499.5	89.7	119	1 755	64.8	15.6
Lodi	86	440	24.1	11.1	99	3 149	475.3	88.6	124	1 561	51.1	12.8
Lompoc	26	108	8.1	3.3	NA	NA	NA	NA	77	1 109	37.7	8.9
Long Beach	740	8 083	788.2	308.4	332	27 548	8 786.9	1 400.3	678	11 571	445.8	120.7
Los Altos	213	903	137.2	53.6	NA	NA	NA	NA	60	1 250	47.5	13.3
Los Angeles	10 755	122 686	14 539.9	5 668.2	7 222	186 758	27 378.2	5 302.8	6 215	103 676	4 523.1	1 249.1
Los Banos	20	98	6.1	2.7	14	D	D	D	41	452	16.9	4.1
Los Gatos	261	1 307	217.4	94.0	61	1 055	136.4	50.2	120	2 282	79.4	23.4
Lynwood	11	48	7.8	1.9	62	2 516	289.0	56.6	56	478	21.0	4.4
Madera	34	204	16.7	6.3	38	1 260	190.9	33.9	64	D	D	D
Manhattan Beach	178	681	97.7	34.4	NA	NA	NA	NA	126	2 782	121.9	33.6
Manteca	28	96	8.5	2.8	28	1 779	208.2	38.4	80	D	D	D
Marina	12	28	1.6	0.6	NA	NA	NA	NA	29	341	13.9	3.1
Martinez	90	311	25.5	10.1	33	D	D	D	77	802	27.9	7.4
Maywood	3	D	D	D	31	514	32.7	9.1	27	278	12.3	2.6
Menlo Park	254	3 754	642.2	268.7	78	6 371	1 478.0	369.8	83	1 352	67.5	17.7
Merced	83	471	29.9	11.4	42	2 326	457.3	64.3	129	1 755	55.2	13.7
Milpitas	140	1 123	188.7	60.4	202	27 550	7 129.6	1 364.6	192	3 839	147.6	37.2
Mission Viejo	178	883	98.7	40.3	46	1 466	272.3	70.3	130	2 184	73.5	18.4
Modesto	328	2 342	181.0	64.2	137	7 462	2 124.8	265.5	334	5 931	182.2	48.3
Monrovia	92	736	79.1	31.7	130	5 150	725.6	199.4	73	1 502	56.7	15.8
Montclair	27	152	8.3	2.7	72	854	95.0	19.9	73	D	D	D
Montebello	57	205	15.5	3.9	112	4 850	642.2	133.7	118	1 579	55.9	13.4
Monterey	222	1 044	114.8	44.9	61	1 317	159.6	44.1	205	4 733	236.7	62.8
Monterey Park	113	334	28.8	8.7	79	1 841	170.4	43.9	128	2 039	84.0	22.8
Moorpark	41	554	82.7	20.5	52	2 578	370.1	79.4	26	D	D	D
Moreno Valley	43	196	10.3	2.5	19	1 095	143.7	20.8	129	2 149	66.6	18.0
Morgan Hill	77	482	41.2	17.4	68	2 304	365.3	91.8	80	1 038	39.3	8.8
Mountain View	446	7 957	1 238.2	497.9	235	20 837	9 372.0	1 298.7	221	3 463	173.7	41.4
Murrieta	NA	NA	NA	NA	NA	NA	NA	NA	NA	NA	NA	NA
Napa	160	1 248	244.0	109.3	104	2 694	591.2	84.7	189	2 720	111.3	30.5
National City	50	554	16.8	8.9	100	1 744	342.7	45.1	148	1 844	63.7	16.5
Newark	67	872	78.2	28.5	84	2 989	597.5	124.1	103	1 684	74.6	17.6
Newport Beach	1 031	7 343	1 120.3	413.7	109	5 136	1 481.8	255.6	339	8 404	371.7	106.7
Norwalk	51	435	13.5	5.6	75	1 234	159.9	28.9	118	1 651	64.4	14.8
Novato	177	1 446	151.4	62.1	82	1 669	263.1	65.2	109	1 341	50.4	13.2
Oakland	1 110	8 673	1 130.3	466.2	574	13 913	2 048.1	426.2	738	9 390	436.3	121.3
Oceanside	169	865	62.3	22.8	157	3 749	416.5	97.5	239	3 893	126.1	33.9
Ontario	119	1 048	121.9	47.2	420	16 296	3 257.5	483.4	210	4 760	217.0	58.8
Orange	497	6 459	611.3	217.4	338	10 463	1 452.6	309.4	246	4 307	171.0	45.5
Oxnard	175	1 069	102.5	35.4	172	6 935	1 440.7	220.8	220	4 487	166.6	47.0
Pacifica	45	97	11.3	4.4	NA	NA	NA	NA	62	575	24.9	6.0
Palmdale	47	227	18.5	6.3	44	D	D	D	111	2 286	74.6	19.2
Palm Desert	200	746	79.7	23.1	57	702	82.2	18.9	149	5 164	214.5	63.9
Palm Springs	130	596	54.3	20.6	37	734	107.6	22.5	220	4 974	197.4	57.4
Palo Alto	731	9 034	1 724.7	720.1	114	7 983	2 232.0	362.6	248	5 211	240.7	72.5
Paradise	28	74	4.5	1.1	NA	NA	NA	NA	52	658	16.3	4.3
Paramount	28	417	26.8	10.3	268	6 401	1 081.7	199.4	55	559	21.7	4.9
Pasadena	872	10 199	1 292.9	484.8	151	2 877	389.0	87.4	364	8 048	313.4	92.9
Perris	10	43	2.1	0.8	40	2 616	421.7	59.7	41	583	17.9	4.8
Petaluma	145	1 158	119.2	51.6	119	4 998	1 403.7	249.8	138	2 010	64.1	17.3
Pico Rivera	16	179	15.3	4.9	81	3 122	518.5	89.0	71	1 004	37.3	9.0
Pittsburg	26	150	12.4	3.5	46	2 362	1 503.1	118.3	66	864	30.3	8.2
Placentia	60	372	41.2	15.5	134	3 438	447.2	85.9	77	1 250	47.3	11.1
Pleasant Hill	116	1 058	104.8	65.0	NA	NA	NA	NA	72	1 268	49.1	12.2
Pleasanton	328	3 797	614.7	185.4	100	1 759	328.4	77.1	187	3 699	152.5	40.7

1. Firms subject to federal tax.

Table D. Cities — Entertainment, Health Care, and Other Services

City	Arts, Entertainment, and Recreation[1], 1997				Health Care and Social Assistance[1], 1997				Other Services[1], 1997			
	Number of Establishments	Number of Employees	Receipts (mil dol)	Annual Payroll (mil dol)	Number of Establishments	Number of Employees	Receipts (mil dol)	Annual Payroll (mil dol)	Number of Establishments	Number of Employees	Receipts (mil dol)	Annual Payroll (mil dol)
	96	97	98	99	100	101	102	103	104	105	106	107
CALIFORNIA—Cont'd												
Imperial Beach	2	0	0.0	0.0	14	339	16.2	6.2	21	116	3.9	1.0
Indio	10	0	0.0	0.0	80	1 011	82.3	30.9	54	288	17.3	5.6
Inglewood	33	2 581	393.7	118.8	274	4 043	314.1	131.0	139	1 037	62.0	17.6
Irvine	45	954	68.6	16.3	364	3 296	292.5	119.6	232	2 270	143.4	49.5
Laguna Niguel	11	177	8.6	3.3	129	563	42.6	17.2	58	411	26.0	7.9
La Habra	2	0	0.0	0.0	75	1 900	160.9	66.0	107	597	37.1	9.8
Lake Elsinore	6	176	3.3	2.1	35	206	13.0	4.5	31	129	7.9	1.9
Lake Forest	NA	NA	NA	NA	NA	NA	NA	NA	NA	NA	NA	NA
Lakewood	13	282	9.3	2.7	130	1 546	123.2	52.8	73	740	40.5	16.1
La Mesa	10	170	4.7	1.6	296	3 397	229.7	90.4	99	661	29.0	9.6
La Mirada	7	103	7.3	1.3	76	951	61.3	24.9	36	256	13.3	4.3
Lancaster	13	182	8.4	2.4	266	3 606	307.0	106.5	117	676	51.1	11.9
La Puente	1	0	0.0	0.0	38	206	16.8	4.6	34	100	7.0	1.3
La Verne	1	0	0.0	0.0	35	239	17.1	6.8	28	130	5.8	1.5
Lawndale	3	0	0.0	0.0	59	365	28.2	8.3	85	398	26.0	6.5
Livermore	11	205	8.6	2.0	119	1 159	60.9	31.7	93	734	82.4	26.9
Lodi	9	169	9.2	2.6	145	1 433	100.6	36.7	107	458	32.0	8.0
Lompoc	4	39	0.9	0.2	59	337	26.1	10.5	46	239	13.8	3.7
Long Beach	53	867	56.4	12.3	898	9 999	899.4	383.9	482	3 892	286.5	96.3
Los Altos	7	120	3.5	1.3	112	766	68.9	26.1	54	219	13.4	4.3
Los Angeles	4 229	23 403	4 530.8	2 178.7	7 491	74 565	6 051.2	2 351.7	5 358	33 761	2 397.4	631.4
Los Banos	3	0	0.0	0.0	41	225	12.8	3.9	23	102	6.2	2.2
Los Gatos	17	309	11.8	4.7	269	3 611	227.4	110.8	82	341	21.9	6.0
Lynwood	1	0	0.0	0.0	100	818	71.9	27.6	34	185	9.9	2.3
Madera	6	59	1.4	0.4	93	936	52.3	19.0	48	229	15.9	4.2
Manhattan Beach	23	303	18.6	7.2	129	587	55.4	24.7	67	388	21.7	5.8
Manteca	11	188	8.3	2.0	84	1 024	69.9	28.3	58	657	54.4	14.9
Marina	4	63	1.2	0.5	15	149	7.2	2.7	17	57	4.0	0.8
Martinez	4	12	0.7	0.1	39	1 214	98.8	45.2	42	152	13.3	3.6
Maywood	3	5	0.5	0.0	21	219	13.1	5.0	24	94	6.2	1.8
Menlo Park	15	89	8.3	2.3	114	1 284	109.5	47.2	53	359	27.2	9.0
Merced	13	159	3.4	0.9	204	1 929	127.8	48.7	71	460	25.7	8.2
Milpitas	16	329	14.9	3.1	123	1 065	99.2	35.9	96	721	74.8	18.4
Mission Viejo	19	316	12.8	3.6	268	2 229	207.1	82.7	122	655	70.7	16.5
Modesto	39	693	23.0	6.1	513	6 951	524.4	204.4	245	1 474	95.5	28.5
Monrovia	7	110	4.5	1.8	49	633	47.2	16.5	71	356	22.7	6.5
Montclair	5	124	5.3	1.0	70	1 526	98.6	40.4	67	599	43.1	14.1
Montebello	5	0	0.0	0.0	155	1 300	103.0	39.0	106	813	53.4	15.9
Monterey	25	261	24.0	10.3	230	2 053	168.4	71.8	80	540	30.9	9.2
Monterey Park	6	0	0.0	0.0	203	2 641	201.9	83.2	80	368	22.3	6.2
Moorpark	7	0	0.0	0.0	18	115	7.1	2.5	26	125	9.5	2.4
Moreno Valley	17	246	10.4	3.1	156	1 298	75.0	25.6	94	380	21.2	6.1
Morgan Hill	9	111	3.0	1.0	55	490	32.1	10.7	47	265	16.5	4.6
Mountain View	15	308	13.0	3.8	236	1 871	175.4	75.8	151	883	74.8	23.1
Murrieta	NA	NA	NA	NA	NA	NA	NA	NA	NA	NA	NA	NA
Napa	14	329	10.2	3.1	259	2 345	151.2	61.4	118	639	44.4	12.3
National City	6	119	7.2	1.3	112	1 088	66.4	27.2	123	838	54.9	17.0
Newark	4	60	1.4	0.3	38	208	14.9	4.6	60	360	29.6	8.1
Newport Beach	61	1 348	77.4	20.8	582	3 923	411.0	175.9	159	1 117	70.3	22.1
Norwalk	6	148	6.6	1.3	97	982	58.1	20.6	74	337	21.9	6.0
Novato	13	220	15.7	5.2	130	998	79.9	34.0	91	646	45.7	14.7
Oakland	62	1 218	183.1	103.0	886	8 669	854.1	338.6	597	3 524	268.3	78.3
Oceanside	14	482	18.2	6.6	215	1 448	131.3	44.8	149	1 022	66.0	18.4
Ontario	12	379	13.6	4.0	114	1 780	196.1	58.1	194	2 069	145.3	47.8
Orange	36	533	19.1	5.6	481	5 069	496.9	201.6	260	1 821	124.6	36.1
Oxnard	34	352	16.9	4.7	309	2 564	194.2	78.7	183	1 011	71.2	17.9
Pacifica	4	67	1.6	0.6	34	249	12.8	5.0	34	119	8.0	2.3
Palmdale	8	181	6.0	1.8	110	926	58.4	21.4	73	366	22.3	5.5
Palm Desert	29	720	35.7	11.7	121	855	53.8	20.4	95	704	36.5	11.3
Palm Springs	19	929	42.6	13.6	210	2 790	279.7	98.9	90	563	33.9	9.8
Palo Alto	16	230	16.2	9.2	285	1 900	188.4	70.1	107	964	101.1	29.4
Paradise	4	83	2.3	0.7	96	745	37.6	13.2	35	106	8.0	1.9
Paramount	2	0	0.0	0.0	76	1 199	86.2	30.9	68	677	53.7	16.0
Pasadena	68	853	56.2	19.7	562	6 453	547.7	216.5	300	1 843	133.9	33.9
Perris	1	0	0.0	0.0	30	285	13.2	4.7	18	61	7.0	2.1
Petaluma	15	264	11.3	3.7	151	1 375	77.0	33.4	97	543	44.6	12.3
Pico Rivera	3	0	0.0	0.0	80	887	49.0	22.6	59	708	32.7	10.1
Pittsburg	4	21	0.6	0.1	57	500	27.9	10.6	46	289	15.2	6.8
Placentia	5	0	0.0	0.0	67	584	47.0	18.7	60	298	24.5	7.3
Pleasant Hill	10	137	6.4	1.9	98	727	51.0	19.9	50	290	12.4	4.1
Pleasanton	31	531	39.4	15.3	198	1 903	234.6	64.3	107	722	63.5	18.8

1. Firms subject to federal tax.

City	Selected federal funds, fiscal 2001[1] (mil dol)									City government finances, 1999						
	Procurement contracts		Grants					Direct payments for individuals		General revenue						
										Intergovernmental			Taxes			
														Per capita[3] (dollars)		
	Defense	Other	Total[2]	Health and family welfare	Energy and environment	Education	Housing and community development	Educational assistance	Housing assistance	Total (mil dol)	Total (mil dol)	Percent from state government	Total (mil dol)	Total	Property	Sales and gross receipts
	108	109	110	111	112	113	114	115	116	117	118	119	120	121	122	123
CALIFORNIA—Cont'd																
Imperial Beach	2.6	0.3	0.6	0.0	0.0	0.5	0.0	0.0	0.9	NA	NA	NA	NA	NA	NA	NA
Indio	0.0	0.0	3.4	0.5	0.0	0.0	0.0	0.0	9.0	29.3	6.7	47.2	12.2	271	77	166
Inglewood	22.8	1.2	15.1	5.7	0.1	0.0	3.0	0.2	23.4	132.3	49.8	58.3	47.6	427	75	254
Irvine	196.3	39.1	131.9	83.7	9.6	3.2	0.8	18.1	5.2	141.7	19.2	70.7	80.7	591	83	373
Laguna Niguel	0.1	0.9	0.8	0.0	0.0	0.0	0.7	0.0	1.4	19.3	5.1	91.5	11.8	220	26	163
La Habra	0.0	0.0	1.1	0.0	0.0	0.3	0.8	0.0	2.6	36.0	10.2	74.7	15.3	282	83	175
Lake Elsinore	3.2	0.1	1.0	0.0	0.0	0.9	0.0	0.0	0.5	NA	NA	NA	NA	NA	NA	NA
Lake Forest	1.0	0.1	0.6	0.0	0.0	0.0	0.6	7.6	0.0	22.0	6.4	92.4	13.1	NA	NA	NA
Lakewood	95.7	0.0	1.5	0.0	0.0	0.0	1.3	0.0	2.2	39.1	9.1	84.2	18.5	243	72	159
La Mesa	0.3	2.5	1.6	0.7	0.0	0.1	0.7	3.2	3.4	33.8	6.6	84.8	16.7	299	81	205
La Mirada	21.3	2.6	0.1	0.0	0.0	0.0	0.0	2.0	0.6	NA	NA	NA	NA	NA	NA	NA
Lancaster	8.7	0.1	18.2	0.2	0.0	1.0	1.4	4.2	10.7	94.6	20.2	82.2	46.1	389	209	153
La Puente	0.6	0.0	0.1	0.0	0.0	0.0	0.0	0.6	9.2	NA	NA	NA	NA	NA	NA	NA
La Verne	10.7	0.1	0.4	0.0	0.0	0.0	0.0	3.4	0.8	NA	NA	NA	NA	NA	NA	NA
Lawndale	0.1	0.1	0.1	0.0	0.0	0.0	0.0	0.0	1.6	NA	NA	NA	NA	NA	NA	NA
Livermore	6.1	2.1	5.8	4.8	0.0	0.1	0.3	0.7	8.4	93.0	18.6	35.0	31.8	440	131	203
Lodi	0.7	10.6	0.2	0.0	0.0	0.0	0.0	0.0	0.5	NA	NA	NA	NA	NA	NA	NA
Lompoc	14.9	0.6	4.6	0.9	0.0	2.1	0.4	0.0	0.4	NA	NA	NA	NA	NA	NA	NA
Long Beach	3 030.1	111.3	61.5	7.9	0.0	11.6	13.1	62.0	93.7	844.9	146.9	49.2	186.7	433	141	251
Los Altos	1.3	1.9	1.3	0.8	0.0	0.0	0.0	1.3	0.0	NA	NA	NA	NA	NA	NA	NA
Los Angeles	420.6	297.8	1 540.8	532.8	32.2	52.7	203.1	136.4	886.4	5 064.4	940.1	48.3	2 128.9	592	190	263
Los Banos	0.0	0.5	2.0	0.0	0.0	0.0	0.0	0.0	0.7	NA	NA	NA	NA	NA	NA	NA
Los Gatos	0.6	0.9	2.1	0.0	0.3	0.0	0.0	0.0	0.9	NA	NA	NA	NA	NA	NA	NA
Lynwood	0.4	0.1	5.7	0.0	1.0	0.5	3.7	0.1	0.2	33.1	7.9	78.3	13.3	211	79	112
Madera	0.1	0.0	6.8	2.5	0.0	0.0	1.2	0.1	2.9	NA	NA	NA	NA	NA	NA	NA
Manhattan Beach	0.3	0.0	0.0	0.0	0.0	0.0	0.0	0.1	0.0	NA	NA	NA	NA	NA	NA	NA
Manteca	0.0	0.5	0.3	0.0	0.0	0.0	0.0	0.0	1.0	34.3	7.2	77.5	14.9	315	113	122
Marina	0.6	1.3	4.0	0.0	0.0	0.0	0.0	0.0	0.0	NA	NA	NA	NA	NA	NA	NA
Martinez	83.7	3.6	36.1	26.1	0.0	0.3	5.2	1.4	1.7	NA	NA	NA	NA	NA	NA	NA
Maywood	1.5	0.0	0.0	0.0	0.0	0.0	0.0	0.0	0.5	NA	NA	NA	NA	NA	NA	NA
Menlo Park	136.0	29.8	30.6	18.5	2.3	1.4	0.0	0.0	2.5	41.6	4.0	79.8	25.6	849	370	379
Merced	0.0	0.3	19.9	7.7	0.2	0.5	2.3	6.1	5.9	45.5	7.3	74.3	17.3	291	112	157
Milpitas	5.9	7.2	0.7	0.0	0.0	0.3	0.3	1.5	5.9	92.7	7.5	83.9	52.7	868	463	329
Mission Viejo	0.4	1.9	1.4	0.0	0.0	1.0	0.2	1.8	0.5	46.9	12.4	71.5	27.7	290	109	134
Modesto	5.6	36.5	26.9	13.8	0.0	2.1	4.2	7.4	13.5	125.4	25.9	52.5	59.2	325	37	220
Monrovia	6.8	2.3	1.0	0.1	0.4	0.0	0.0	1.4	3.5	NA	NA	NA	NA	NA	NA	NA
Montclair	0.0	0.1	0.1	0.0	0.0	0.0	0.0	0.0	1.1	NA	NA	NA	NA	NA	NA	NA
Montebello	9.3	0.8	8.1	0.0	0.0	1.2	1.6	0.3	1.7	65.7	14.0	46.6	35.0	579	242	303
Monterey	52.6	8.1	6.6	0.1	0.5	2.1	1.0	1.8	11.1	NA	NA	NA	NA	NA	NA	NA
Monterey Park	0.0	5.9	12.5	0.0	0.0	0.8	7.6	7.6	1.6	42.0	8.4	61.5	20.4	327	164	137
Moorpark	7.5	0.3	0.5	0.0	0.0	0.5	0.0	0.0	0.0	NA	NA	NA	NA	NA	NA	NA
Moreno Valley	7.3	0.3	5.4	0.0	0.0	3.9	1.6	0.4	0.6	58.4	11.7	79.9	30.1	208	58	140
Morgan Hill	2.3	0.1	0.4	0.0	0.0	0.0	0.0	0.0	0.6	NA	NA	NA	NA	NA	NA	NA
Mountain View	9.7	17.7	17.3	8.8	1.3	0.3	0.5	0.0	7.9	118.0	9.4	72.4	61.9	858	355	387
Murrieta	1.2	0.0	0.0	0.0	0.0	0.0	0.0	0.0	0.0	20.4	4.2	80.9	8.6	NA	NA	NA
Napa	0.8	0.1	10.7	1.2	0.0	2.0	0.5	1.5	12.6	54.9	17.9	48.8	26.9	404	112	212
National City	11.0	1.7	10.4	7.6	0.0	0.4	2.1	0.4	24.4	42.8	9.5	52.2	22.6	411	137	257
Newark	2.2	22.3	0.5	0.4	0.1	0.0	0.0	0.0	1.2	32.4	3.8	83.9	19.1	442	119	264
Newport Beach	21.9	8.4	6.1	0.1	0.0	0.0	0.2	0.4	0.6	100.0	15.1	87.0	61.5	849	313	384
Norwalk	3.0	1.0	14.1	0.1	0.0	1.4	2.1	10.9	7.6	51.9	13.7	75.6	25.4	261	72	175
Novato	2.9	7.3	7.8	7.2	0.3	0.1	0.2	0.0	0.9	NA	NA	NA	NA	NA	NA	NA
Oakland	59.4	36.1	345.0	66.7	2.8	12.4	31.5	12.4	157.2	731.2	106.9	44.0	255.1	697	234	245
Oceanside	6.2	1.1	27.8	0.0	0.1	3.8	2.2	1.5	7.5	142.6	21.3	93.5	34.5	226	87	101
Ontario	25.2	2.5	6.3	0.0	0.0	2.4	2.7	1.3	4.5	150.9	17.2	67.7	84.0	571	228	266
Orange	138.2	1.3	10.8	2.0	0.2	0.5	5.0	5.4	78.2	111.0	19.9	85.4	52.5	424	161	218
Oxnard	19.9	2.0	16.2	5.7	0.0	1.6	3.1	0.2	16.9	149.8	21.1	62.1	53.1	343	111	165
Pacifica	0.0	0.1	-0.5	0.0	0.0	0.0	0.0	0.0	6.4	NA	NA	NA	NA	NA	NA	NA
Palmdale	681.4	2.1	-20.9	0.0	0.0	0.4	2.4	0.0	7.0	72.7	19.6	62.6	41.1	411	206	150
Palm Desert	0.1	0.0	1.8	0.0	0.0	1.3	0.0	4.3	0.8	86.9	2.9	95.1	55.8	1 898	979	726
Palm Springs	0.2	1.5	7.5	1.0	0.1	0.2	0.0	0.3	3.7	81.0	12.8	38.1	37.9	863	283	539
Palo Alto	64.6	86.2	258.6	230.3	4.7	1.0	0.3	0.1	11.5	120.9	6.6	71.2	47.6	806	159	547
Paradise	0.0	0.0	0.3	0.0	0.0	0.1	0.2	0.0	0.6	NA	NA	NA	NA	NA	NA	NA
Paramount	9.1	0.2	2.8	0.0	1.2	0.0	1.5	0.2	1.4	29.4	8.4	60.5	15.3	299	132	143
Pasadena	125.7	1 438.7	135.4	38.0	16.3	4.4	3.5	13.5	50.3	212.0	39.2	65.8	96.4	716	227	378
Perris	0.0	0.0	0.5	0.0	0.0	0.4	0.0	0.0	0.6	NA	NA	NA	NA	NA	NA	NA
Petaluma	2.2	2.9	2.0	0.8	0.1	0.3	0.4	0.0	2.5	NA	NA	NA	NA	NA	NA	NA
Pico Rivera	185.3	1.0	9.5	0.0	0.0	0.2	1.3	0.0	6.4	38.7	10.1	46.0	20.4	336	123	189
Pittsburg	0.0	0.1	2.4	0.5	0.0	1.2	0.6	0.1	21.8	52.9	10.5	44.8	22.6	428	287	122
Placentia	2.5	2.3	0.8	0.0	0.0	0.7	0.0	0.0	1.2	NA	NA	NA	NA	NA	NA	NA
Pleasant Hill	0.0	0.2	1.1	0.2	0.0	0.7	0.0	6.2	2.0	18.8	2.3	89.2	12.0	359	79	223
Pleasanton	8.1	2.9	1.0	0.0	0.2	0.2	0.2	0.0	0.6	80.1	6.9	70.1	49.4	772	265	378

1. October 1, 2000 to September 30, 2001.   2. Includes program categories not shown separately. State totals include additional categories not allocated by city.   3. Based on population estimated as of July 1 of the year shown.

Table D. Cities — City Government Finances

City	Total (mil dol) 124	Total 125	Capital outlays 126	Public welfare 127	Highways 128	Parking facilities 129	Education 130	Health and hospitals 131	Police protection 132	Sewerage and sanitation 133	Parks and recreation 134	Housing and community development 135	Interest on debt 136
CALIFORNIA—Cont'd													
Imperial Beach	NA	NA	NA	NA	NA	NA	NA	NA	NA	NA	NA	NA	NA
Indio	28.5	632	105	0.0	9.1	0.0	0.0	0.5	22.7	0.8	2.5	17.3	16.8
Inglewood	139.4	1 249	83	0.0	5.6	0.2	0.0	1.6	19.6	7.9	4.0	15.7	3.4
Irvine	137.1	1 005	113	0.0	18.4	0.0	0.0	1.2	20.7	3.0	14.0	1.5	20.6
Laguna Niguel	19.2	358	135	0.0	31.2	0.0	0.0	0.8	25.1	0.0	12.2	5.0	0.0
La Habra	36.0	664	66	0.0	11.2	0.0	0.0	2.7	26.8	5.8	7.0	2.1	5.5
Lake Elsinore	NA	NA	NA	NA	NA	NA	NA	NA	NA	NA	NA	NA	NA
Lake Forest	17.3	NA	NA	0.0	30.8	0.0	0.0	0.7	32.7	0.0	8.9	1.0	0.0
Lakewood	28.8	378	36	0.0	13.3	0.0	0.0	0.2	18.1	9.9	23.5	9.7	4.7
La Mesa	29.1	520	40	0.0	9.9	0.3	0.0	0.2	23.8	19.5	8.5	2.3	2.2
La Mirada	NA	NA	NA	NA	NA	NA	NA	NA	NA	NA	NA	NA	NA
Lancaster	91.6	773	178	0.0	18.4	0.0	0.0	0.0	14.9	0.0	8.6	26.3	21.6
La Puente	NA	NA	NA	NA	NA	NA	NA	NA	NA	NA	NA	NA	NA
La Verne	NA	NA	NA	NA	NA	NA	NA	NA	NA	NA	NA	NA	NA
Lawndale	NA	NA	NA	NA	NA	NA	NA	NA	NA	NA	NA	NA	NA
Livermore	88.3	1 222	457	0.0	28.3	0.0	0.0	0.4	13.4	9.7	3.5	7.1	7.8
Lodi	NA	NA	NA	NA	NA	NA	NA	NA	NA	NA	NA	NA	NA
Lompoc	NA	NA	NA	NA	NA	NA	NA	NA	NA	NA	NA	NA	NA
Long Beach	766.7	1 779	82	0.0	9.1	0.0	0.0	3.5	16.5	7.8	3.1	11.8	7.8
Los Altos	NA	NA	NA	NA	NA	NA	NA	NA	NA	NA	NA	NA	NA
Los Angeles	4 913.3	1 366	288	0.0	3.9	0.1	0.3	0.7	18.9	8.0	4.7	3.9	8.1
Los Banos	NA	NA	NA	NA	NA	NA	NA	NA	NA	NA	NA	NA	NA
Los Gatos	NA	NA	NA	NA	NA	NA	NA	NA	NA	NA	NA	NA	NA
Lynwood	32.4	512	28	0.0	13.2	0.0	0.0	0.2	13.3	10.2	7.0	12.0	4.6
Madera	NA	NA	NA	NA	NA	NA	NA	NA	NA	NA	NA	NA	NA
Manhattan Beach	NA	NA	NA	NA	NA	NA	NA	NA	NA	NA	NA	NA	NA
Manteca	36.3	765	203	0.0	15.2	0.0	0.0	0.6	16.5	28.5	8.5	9.0	4.4
Marina	NA	NA	NA	NA	NA	NA	NA	NA	NA	NA	NA	NA	NA
Martinez	NA	NA	NA	NA	NA	NA	NA	NA	NA	NA	NA	NA	NA
Maywood	NA	NA	NA	NA	NA	NA	NA	NA	NA	NA	NA	NA	NA
Menlo Park	36.1	1 199	272	0.0	11.6	0.1	0.0	0.2	20.1	3.2	23.2	12.1	5.2
Merced	45.6	767	94	0.0	4.9	0.0	0.0	0.0	23.7	24.5	4.7	13.3	3.8
Milpitas	78.9	1 298	406	0.0	15.4	0.0	0.0	10.0	17.4	19.8	5.1	11.1	3.6
Mission Viejo	40.4	423	63	0.0	24.7	0.0	0.0	1.4	18.0	0.0	21.4	2.7	0.3
Modesto	146.5	805	264	0.0	11.4	0.1	0.0	2.5	23.5	20.3	7.5	10.2	4.2
Monrovia	NA	NA	NA	NA	NA	NA	NA	NA	NA	NA	NA	NA	NA
Montclair	NA	NA	NA	NA	NA	NA	NA	NA	NA	NA	NA	NA	NA
Montebello	58.3	964	290	0.0	4.1	0.0	0.0	0.0	20.2	3.9	17.0	24.3	10.4
Monterey	NA	NA	NA	NA	NA	NA	NA	NA	NA	NA	NA	NA	NA
Monterey Park	39.3	628	43	0.0	7.2	0.0	0.0	1.0	25.1	8.9	6.5	9.5	6.0
Moorpark	NA	NA	NA	NA	NA	NA	NA	NA	NA	NA	NA	NA	NA
Moreno Valley	73.7	510	63	0.0	9.9	0.0	0.0	2.4	39.5	0.0	4.7	3.2	0.4
Morgan Hill	NA	NA	NA	NA	NA	NA	NA	NA	NA	NA	NA	NA	NA
Mountain View	109.6	1 518	356	0.0	14.3	0.1	0.0	0.0	11.9	16.5	12.4	1.8	4.9
Murrieta	19.9	NA	NA	0.0	29.2	0.0	0.0	0.3	24.9	0.0	0.0	0.3	2.7
Napa	53.0	797	45	0.0	13.1	0.5	0.0	1.8	17.7	4.5	6.0	25.5	1.3
National City	43.8	797	225	0.0	13.1	0.0	0.0	0.2	24.1	8.6	4.1	22.9	3.5
Newark	34.1	789	149	0.0	10.7	0.0	0.0	10.3	22.9	0.8	23.1	1.9	11.3
Newport Beach	104.3	1 440	298	0.0	19.6	0.0	0.0	0.6	25.1	6.9	8.0	0.0	1.7
Norwalk	50.1	513	24	0.0	11.4	1.3	0.0	0.0	17.6	0.3	8.6	24.7	7.8
Novato	NA	NA	NA	NA	NA	NA	NA	NA	NA	NA	NA	NA	NA
Oakland	914.4	2 499	740	0.0	4.1	0.5	0.0	2.2	12.7	1.7	3.1	7.0	13.5
Oceanside	149.4	981	243	0.0	10.3	0.0	0.0	0.0	21.1	19.9	2.1	4.3	9.2
Ontario	152.4	1 035	199	0.0	8.4	0.0	0.0	3.5	22.4	11.7	3.9	16.4	6.5
Orange	102.6	828	219	0.0	7.0	0.0	0.0	0.1	22.0	8.2	6.3	8.8	7.0
Oxnard	135.0	873	142	0.0	16.1	0.0	0.0	0.0	18.6	30.2	5.0	5.9	5.5
Pacifica	NA	NA	NA	NA	NA	NA	NA	NA	NA	NA	NA	NA	NA
Palmdale	76.2	760	162	0.0	21.5	0.0	0.0	0.6	12.7	0.0	4.9	30.7	11.7
Palm Desert	80.2	2 727	777	0.0	10.5	0.1	0.0	0.1	8.9	0.0	10.9	37.7	16.3
Palm Springs	97.3	2 215	695	0.0	4.8	0.4	0.0	0.3	13.0	5.7	5.7	3.9	11.3
Palo Alto	134.0	2 268	369	0.0	10.6	0.5	0.0	1.7	11.2	30.2	13.5	3.8	1.4
Paradise	NA	NA	NA	NA	NA	NA	NA	NA	NA	NA	NA	NA	NA
Paramount	25.0	488	73	0.0	15.1	0.0	0.0	0.8	28.8	0.0	6.6	13.9	14.8
Pasadena	221.8	1 648	142	0.0	9.0	4.2	0.0	3.3	15.4	4.2	8.8	10.6	7.1
Perris	NA	NA	NA	NA	NA	NA	NA	NA	NA	NA	NA	NA	NA
Petaluma	NA	NA	NA	NA	NA	NA	NA	NA	NA	NA	NA	NA	NA
Pico Rivera	37.3	614	46	0.0	7.7	0.0	0.0	0.0	14.8	0.0	12.0	25.5	14.8
Pittsburg	49.0	929	120	0.0	9.2	0.0	0.0	2.3	20.0	1.3	5.4	24.9	22.0
Placentia	NA	NA	NA	NA	NA	NA	NA	NA	NA	NA	NA	NA	NA
Pleasant Hill	17.1	514	33	0.0	19.0	0.0	0.0	0.3	32.2	0.0	0.8	13.8	7.4
Pleasanton	81.1	1 266	197	0.0	13.0	0.0	0.0	0.7	16.0	9.6	13.1	1.3	15.8

1. Based on population estimated as of July 1 of the year shown.

Table D. Cities — **City Government Finances, City Government Employment, and Climate**

City	City government finances, 1999 (cont'd) Debt outstanding			City government employment, 2001	Climate[2] Average daily temperature (degrees Fahrenheit) Mean		Limits				
	Total (mil dol)	Per capita[1] (dollars)	Percent utility		January	July	January[3]	July[4]	Annual precipitation (inches)	Heating degree days	Cooling degree days
	137	138	139	140	141	142	143	144	145	146	147
CALIFORNIA—Cont'd											
Imperial Beach	NA	NA	NA	NA	55.3	68.2	45.3	73.1	9.34	1 798	638
Indio	79.0	1 755	0.0	NA	56.4	92.0	42.5	108.7	5.31	985	4 014
Inglewood	116.8	1 046	4.6	769	56.8	69.1	47.8	75.3	12.01	1 458	727
Irvine	611.8	4 484	0.0	778	54.5	71.6	41.4	83.7	11.81	1 784	973
Laguna Niguel	0.0	0	0.0	NA	53.7	67.2	41.5	75.8	12.19	2 157	493
La Habra	51.6	951	0.0	NA	57.4	72.6	45.6	82.6	12.27	1 238	1 175
Lake Elsinore	NA	NA	NA	NA	NA	NA	NA	NA	NA	NA	NA
Lake Forest	0.0	NA	NA	NA	NA	NA	NA	NA	NA	NA	NA
Lakewood	24.2	317	22.6	242	55.9	73.1	44.9	82.7	11.80	1 430	1 201
La Mesa	10.3	183	0.0	NA	56.6	72.5	44.6	83.4	12.80	1 400	1 110
La Mirada	NA	NA	NA	NA	57.4	72.6	45.6	82.6	12.27	1 238	1 175
Lancaster	270.6	2 283	0.0	281	45.1	80.7	31.9	97.1	6.92	2 948	1 720
La Puente	NA	NA	NA	NA	55.7	75.2	41.7	89.2	17.90	1 433	1 427
La Verne	NA	NA	NA	NA	54.3	74.6	40.7	90.4	16.62	1 713	1 273
Lawndale	NA	NA	NA	NA	56.1	69.7	45.3	78.8	13.57	1 568	794
Livermore	111.0	1 536	0.0	428	46.1	71.6	35.5	89.8	14.21	2 909	780
Lodi	NA	NA	NA	NA	45.1	73.9	36.4	91.4	17.11	2 809	1 020
Lompoc	NA	NA	NA	NA	52.9	62.9	40.1	72.9	13.95	2 651	265
Long Beach	1 489.6	3 457	3.9	5 785	55.9	73.1	44.9	82.7	11.80	1 430	1 201
Los Altos	NA	NA	NA	NA	47.5	66.4	37.7	78.4	14.96	2 911	297
Los Angeles	10 429.3	2 899	31.9	50 930	58.3	74.3	48.9	84.0	14.77	1 154	1 537
Los Banos	NA	NA	NA	NA	NA	NA	NA	NA	NA	NA	NA
Los Gatos	NA	NA	NA	NA	49.4	69.5	40.6	82.4	14.42	2 387	594
Lynwood	21.1	333	19.9	NA	58.3	74.3	48.9	84.0	14.77	1 154	1 537
Madera	NA	NA	NA	NA	44.7	79.7	35.5	97.8	11.15	2 741	1 632
Manhattan Beach	NA	NA	NA	NA	56.8	69.1	47.8	75.3	12.01	1 458	727
Manteca	26.4	556	0.0	NA	45.0	77.7	37.0	94.4	13.95	2 707	1 470
Marina	NA	NA	NA	NA	51.7	60.0	43.3	68.1	18.72	3 125	55
Martinez	NA	NA	NA	NA	49.9	63.2	42.0	71.0	22.20	2 574	199
Maywood	NA	NA	NA	NA	58.3	74.3	48.9	84.0	14.77	1 154	1 537
Menlo Park	35.1	1 165	0.0	NA	47.5	66.4	37.7	78.4	14.96	2 911	297
Merced	33.9	571	0.0	NA	45.1	78.6	35.7	96.9	12.01	2 692	1 500
Milpitas	94.3	1 552	0.0	NA	49.4	69.5	40.6	82.4	14.42	2 387	594
Mission Viejo	34.0	357	0.0	146	54.5	71.6	41.4	83.7	11.81	1 784	973
Modesto	206.0	1 132	13.2	1 227	45.6	77.1	37.4	94.2	12.10	2 605	1 401
Monrovia	NA	NA	NA	NA	55.8	75.0	43.6	89.0	19.37	1 453	1 394
Montclair	NA	NA	NA	NA	54.3	74.6	40.7	90.4	16.62	1 713	1 273
Montebello	86.5	1 428	0.0	NA	58.3	74.3	48.9	84.0	14.77	1 154	1 537
Monterey	NA	NA	NA	NA	51.7	60.0	43.3	68.1	18.72	3 125	55
Monterey Park	44.3	708	0.0	395	55.7	75.2	41.7	89.2	17.90	1 433	1 427
Moorpark	NA	NA	NA	NA	54.6	67.8	41.2	80.8	17.39	2 039	569
Moreno Valley	3.6	25	0.0	352	53.6	76.9	41.2	93.7	10.00	1 796	1 500
Morgan Hill	NA	NA	NA	NA	NA	NA	NA	NA	NA	NA	NA
Mountain View	121.1	1 677	0.0	NA	47.5	66.4	37.7	78.4	14.96	2 911	297
Murrieta	15.7	NA	0.0	NA	NA	NA	NA	NA	NA	NA	NA
Napa	22.4	337	52.2	NA	47.1	67.9	37.2	82.1	25.12	2 844	456
National City	30.8	560	0.0	NA	57.4	71.0	48.9	76.2	9.90	1 256	984
Newark	69.2	1 604	0.0	NA	49.0	66.7	41.1	76.1	13.73	2 578	410
Newport Beach	39.3	542	36.2	NA	55.2	67.1	46.8	71.8	10.85	1 866	500
Norwalk	66.2	679	0.0	306	55.9	73.1	44.9	82.7	11.80	1 430	1 201
Novato	NA	NA	NA	NA	46.4	67.0	36.8	82.5	24.60	3 050	335
Oakland	2 259.6	6 176	0.0	4 480	49.9	62.1	43.3	70.0	24.30	2 902	115
Oceanside	172.0	1 129	6.6	1 014	54.5	67.6	44.1	73.5	10.93	2 010	555
Ontario	212.9	1 446	0.0	1 139	54.3	74.6	40.7	90.4	16.62	1 713	1 273
Orange	120.0	969	2.3	702	57.4	72.6	45.6	82.6	12.27	1 238	1 175
Oxnard	181.9	1 176	3.5	1 257	55.3	66.1	44.2	74.4	14.38	1 992	416
Pacifica	NA	NA	NA	NA	48.7	62.7	41.8	71.6	19.70	3 016	145
Palmdale	195.6	1 952	0.0	339	45.1	80.7	31.9	97.1	6.92	2 948	1 720
Palm Desert	227.1	7 721	0.0	NA	NA	NA	NA	NA	NA	NA	NA
Palm Springs	179.5	4 085	0.0	NA	56.4	92.0	42.5	108.7	5.31	985	4 014
Palo Alto	28.7	486	0.0	NA	47.5	66.4	37.7	78.4	14.96	2 911	297
Paradise	NA	NA	NA	NA	45.4	77.2	36.9	90.8	52.71	3 214	1 342
Paramount	100.2	1 960	0.4	NA	55.9	73.1	44.9	82.7	11.80	1 430	1 201
Pasadena	309.7	2 301	30.9	1 764	55.8	75.0	43.6	89.0	19.37	1 453	1 394
Perris	NA	NA	NA	NA	NA	NA	NA	NA	NA	NA	NA
Petaluma	NA	NA	NA	NA	46.4	67.0	36.8	82.5	24.60	3 050	335
Pico Rivera	64.4	1 061	29.2	NA	58.3	74.3	48.9	84.0	14.77	1 154	1 537
Pittsburg	226.5	4 291	6.5	NA	44.5	73.8	35.9	90.8	12.80	2 837	1 066
Placentia	NA	NA	NA	NA	57.4	72.6	45.6	82.6	12.27	1 238	1 175
Pleasant Hill	27.1	813	0.0	NA	44.5	73.8	35.9	90.8	12.80	2 837	1 066
Pleasanton	203.6	3 180	0.0	NA	46.1	71.6	35.5	89.8	14.21	2 909	780

1. Based on the population estimated as of July 1 of the year shown.   2. Represents normal values based on the 30-year period, 1961–1990.   3. Average daily minimum.   4. Average daily maximum.

Table D. Cities — Land Area and Population

STATE Place code	City	Land area, 2000¹ (sq km)	Population, 2000 Total persons	Rank	Per square kilometer	Population Total persons 1990	Percent change 1990–2000	Total persons 1980	Percent change 1980–1990	White	Black	Am. Indian, Alaska Native	Asian and Pacific Islander	Other race	Hispanic²	Non-Hispanic White
			1	2	3	4	5	6	7	8	9	10	11	12	13
	CALIFORNIA—Cont'd															
06 58072	Pomona	59.2	149 473	137	2 524.9	131 700	13.5	92 742	42.0	45.6	10.4	2.0	8.6	38.6	64.5	17.0
06 58240	Porterville	36.3	39 615	783	1 091.3	29 521	34.2	19 692	49.9	58.6	1.7	2.9	5.9	35.9	49.4	42.0
06 58520	Poway	101.6	48 044	630	472.9	43 396	10.7	32 263	34.5	86.5	2.1	1.2	9.7	4.8	10.4	77.2
06 59451	Rancho Cucamonga	97.0	127 743	167	1 316.9	101 409	26.0	55 250	83.5	71.0	8.9	1.6	7.9	16.3	27.8	54.8
06 59514	Rancho Palos Verdes	35.4	41 145	746	1 162.3	41 667	-1.3	36 577	13.9	70.1	2.4	0.6	28.1	2.4	5.7	63.1
06 59920	Redding	151.4	80 865	318	534.1	66 176	21.7	41 995	58.3	91.7	1.5	3.8	4.0	2.5	5.4	85.7
06 59962	Redlands	91.9	63 591	430	692.0	62 667	1.5	43 619	43.7	77.4	5.1	1.8	6.8	13.5	24.1	63.3
06 60018	Redondo Beach	16.3	63 261	435	3 881.0	60 167	5.1	57 102	5.4	82.7	3.1	1.2	11.8	6.2	13.5	70.8
06 60102	Redwood City	50.4	75 402	353	1 496.1	66 072	14.1	54 951	20.2	72.6	3.0	1.2	11.6	16.1	31.2	53.9
06 60466	Rialto	56.6	91 873	265	1 623.2	72 395	26.9	37 474	93.2	43.3	23.7	2.1	4.0	32.4	51.2	21.5
06 60620	Richmond	77.6	99 216	240	1 278.6	86 019	15.3	74 676	15.2	35.0	37.8	1.6	14.6	16.7	26.5	21.2
06 62000	Riverside	202.3	255 166	67	1 261.3	226 546	12.6	170 876	32.6	63.6	8.4	2.1	7.4	23.9	38.1	45.6
06 62364	Rocklin	41.9	36 330	854	867.1	18 806	93.2	NA	NA	91.7	1.3	1.8	6.3	3.0	7.9	83.4
06 62546	Rohnert Park	16.7	42 236	724	2 529.1	36 326	16.3	22 965	58.2	84.9	2.9	2.1	8.3	7.6	13.6	74.0
06 62896	Rosemead	13.3	53 505	553	4 022.9	51 638	3.6	42 604	21.2	29.0	0.9	1.4	50.3	22.0	41.3	8.0
06 62938	Roseville	78.9	79 921	323	1 012.9	44 685	78.9	24 347	83.5	89.2	1.7	1.6	6.0	5.2	11.5	79.8
06 64000	Sacramento	251.6	407 018	40	1 617.7	369 365	10.2	275 741	34.0	52.6	17.3	2.8	20.6	13.7	21.6	40.5
06 64224	Salinas	49.2	151 060	134	3 070.3	108 777	38.9	80 479	35.2	49.4	3.9	2.0	8.3	41.9	64.1	24.2
06 65000	San Bernardino	152.3	185 401	108	1 217.3	170 036	9.0	117 490	44.7	49.4	17.8	2.5	5.7	30.4	47.5	28.9
06 65028	San Bruno	14.1	40 165	770	2 848.6	38 961	3.1	35 417	10.0	63.1	2.6	1.2	26.2	14.8	24.1	46.9
06 65042	San Buenaventura (Ventura)	54.6	100 916	236	1 848.3	92 557	9.0	74 393	24.4	82.7	2.0	2.5	4.5	13.0	24.3	68.1
06 65070	San Carlos	15.3	27 718	1 116	1 811.6	26 382	5.1	24 710	6.8	88.1	1.0	0.7	10.3	4.0	7.7	80.2
06 65084	San Clemente	45.6	49 936	599	1 095.1	41 100	21.5	27 325	50.4	90.4	1.1	1.3	4.0	6.2	15.9	78.4
06 66000	San Diego	840.0	1 223 400	7	1 456.4	1 110 623	10.2	875 538	26.9	63.9	8.9	1.3	16.4	14.7	25.4	49.4
06 66070	San Dimas	40.2	34 980	896	870.1	32 398	8.0	24 014	34.9	78.5	3.8	1.5	11.2	9.7	23.3	61.1
06 67000	San Francisco	120.9	776 733	13	6 424.6	723 959	7.3	678 974	6.6	53.0	8.6	1.2	33.4	8.5	14.1	43.6
06 67042	San Gabriel	10.7	39 804	778	3 720.0	37 120	7.2	30 072	23.4	35.9	1.3	1.3	50.8	14.2	30.7	17.4
06 68000	San Jose	452.9	894 943	11	1 976.0	782 224	14.4	629 442	24.3	51.5	4.1	1.5	29.6	18.7	30.2	36.0
06 68028	San Juan Capistrano	36.8	33 882	930	919.2	26 183	29.2	18 959	38.1	81.7	1.1	1.7	3.0	16.2	33.1	62.3
06 68084	San Leandro	34.0	79 452	327	2 336.8	68 223	16.5	63 952	6.7	55.9	11.0	1.7	26.5	11.3	20.1	42.3
06 68154	San Luis Obispo	27.6	44 114	694	1 600.5	41 958	5.3	34 252	22.5	87.2	1.9	1.5	6.9	6.3	11.7	78.7
06 68196	San Marcos	61.5	54 977	537	893.9	38 974	41.1	17 479	123.0	71.3	2.8	1.5	6.4	22.8	36.9	53.9
06 68252	San Mateo	31.6	92 482	262	2 926.6	85 619	8.0	77 561	10.4	70.2	3.1	1.1	19.6	11.4	20.5	56.5
06 68294	San Pablo	6.7	30 215	1 028	4 509.7	25 158	20.1	19 750	27.4	36.3	19.9	2.0	19.5	29.6	44.6	16.2
06 68364	San Rafael	43.0	56 063	518	1 303.8	48 410	15.8	44 800	8.1	79.6	3.0	1.3	7.3	13.7	23.3	65.9
06 68378	San Ramon	30.0	44 722	686	1 490.7	35 303	26.7	22 356	57.9	79.9	2.3	0.9	17.6	3.2	7.2	72.3
06 69000	Santa Ana	70.3	337 977	51	4 807.6	293 827	15.0	203 713	44.2	46.6	2.1	1.7	9.9	44.3	76.1	12.4
06 69070	Santa Barbara	49.1	92 325	263	1 880.3	85 571	7.9	74 414	15.0	77.5	2.2	1.9	3.9	18.6	35.0	58.3
06 69084	Santa Clara	47.6	102 361	228	2 150.4	93 613	9.3	87 746	6.7	59.6	2.8	1.1	32.3	9.4	16.0	48.3
06 69088	Santa Clarita	123.9	151 088	133	1 219.4	120 050	25.9	NA	NA	83.0	2.6	1.3	7.0	10.3	20.5	69.3
06 69112	Santa Cruz	32.5	54 593	542	1 679.8	49 711	9.8	41 483	19.8	82.7	2.5	2.1	7.0	10.8	17.4	72.0
06 69196	Santa Maria	50.1	77 423	342	1 545.4	61 552	25.8	39 685	55.1	62.5	2.3	3.1	6.2	31.4	59.7	32.0
06 70000	Santa Monica	21.4	84 084	303	3 929.2	86 905	-3.2	88 314	-1.6	81.9	4.5	1.1	9.0	7.9	13.4	71.9
06 70042	Santa Paula	11.9	28 598	1 082	2 403.2	25 062	14.1	20 552	21.9	59.4	0.7	2.1	1.5	41.0	71.2	26.4
06 70098	Santa Rosa	103.9	147 595	140	1 420.5	113 261	30.3	83 320	35.9	81.4	2.9	2.6	5.6	12.3	19.2	70.9
06 70224	Santee	41.6	52 975	561	1 273.4	52 902	0.1	47 080	12.4	90.3	2.0	1.7	4.9	5.4	11.4	80.8
06 70280	Saratoga	31.4	29 843	1 043	950.4	28 061	6.4	29 261	-4.1	69.4	0.5	0.4	31.0	1.2	3.1	65.1
06 70742	Seaside	22.9	31 696	984	1 384.1	38 826	-18.4	36 567	6.2	54.5	14.8	2.2	15.7	21.0	34.5	36.4
06 72016	Simi Valley	101.5	111 351	202	1 097.1	100 218	11.1	77 500	29.3	84.7	1.7	1.6	8.0	8.1	16.8	72.7
06 73080	South Gate	19.1	96 375	245	5 045.8	86 284	11.7	66 784	29.2	45.8	1.2	1.3	1.3	55.2	92.0	6.0
06 73262	South San Francisco	23.4	60 552	457	2 587.7	54 312	11.5	49 393	10.0	49.6	3.5	1.4	34.1	13.8	31.8	30.5
06 73962	Stanton	8.1	37 403	832	4 617.7	30 491	22.7	23 723	28.5	53.6	2.7	1.7	18.2	29.2	48.9	30.2
06 75000	Stockton	141.7	243 771	70	1 720.3	210 943	15.6	149 779	40.8	47.7	12.5	2.3	23.9	20.8	32.5	32.2
06 75630	Suisun City	10.4	26 118	1 191	2 511.3	22 704	15.0	11 087	104.8	50.6	21.7	2.1	23.7	11.3	17.8	38.6
06 77000	Sunnyvale	56.8	131 760	161	2 319.7	117 324	12.3	106 618	10.0	56.7	2.7	1.1	34.9	9.1	15.5	46.5
06 78120	Temecula	68.0	57 716	494	848.8	27 177	113.0	NA	NA	82.6	4.3	1.7	7.0	9.1	19.0	69.3
06 78148	Temple City	10.4	33 377	943	3 209.3	31 153	7.1	28 972	7.5	51.5	1.1	0.9	40.6	9.5	20.5	37.7
06 78582	Thousand Oaks	142.1	117 005	188	823.4	104 381	12.1	77 072	35.4	87.7	1.4	1.0	7.3	5.6	13.1	77.7
06 80000	Torrance	53.2	137 946	155	2 593.0	133 107	3.6	129 881	2.5	63.1	2.7	1.1	31.9	6.3	12.8	52.4
06 80238	Tracy	54.4	56 929	504	1 046.5	33 558	69.6	18 428	82.1	70.9	6.4	2.0	11.4	16.4	27.7	54.0
06 80644	Tulare	43.0	43 994	697	1 023.1	33 249	32.3	22 498	47.8	61.6	5.8	2.4	3.0	33.3	45.6	43.8
06 80812	Turlock	34.5	55 810	524	1 617.7	42 224	32.2	26 278	60.7	77.0	1.8	1.8	6.3	18.6	29.4	60.4
06 80854	Tustin	29.5	67 504	402	2 288.3	50 689	33.2	32 317	56.8	62.5	3.5	1.3	17.0	20.5	34.2	44.8
06 81204	Union City	49.9	66 869	408	1 340.1	53 762	24.4	39 406	36.4	34.9	7.6	1.3	48.8	14.7	24.0	20.4
06 81344	Upland	39.2	68 393	395	1 744.7	63 374	7.9	47 647	33.0	71.1	8.4	1.6	8.8	15.0	27.5	54.8
06 81554	Vacaville	70.1	88 625	279	1 264.3	71 476	24.0	43 367	64.8	76.8	11.2	2.1	7.3	8.7	17.9	63.2
06 81666	Vallejo	78.2	116 760	189	1 493.1	109 199	6.9	80 303	36.0	40.4	25.8	1.8	29.2	10.1	15.9	30.4
06 82590	Victorville	188.5	64 229	426	339.7	50 103	27.8	14 229	252.1	66.0	13.4	2.4	5.2	19.3	33.5	47.5
06 82954	Visalia	74.0	91 565	267	1 237.4	75 659	21.0	49 729	52.1	73.1	2.3	2.4	6.3	20.3	35.6	54.9
06 82996	Vista	48.4	89 857	274	1 856.5	71 861	25.0	35 834	100.5	68.3	5.1	1.9	6.1	23.8	38.9	49.9
06 83332	Walnut	23.3	30 004	1 035	1 287.7	29 105	3.1	12 478	133.3	30.8	4.6	0.6	58.2	9.7	19.3	18.2

1. Dry land or land partially or temporarily covered by water.   2. Hispanic persons may be of any race.

City	Population characteristics, 2000 (cont'd)										Households, 2000				
	Age of population (percent)													Percent	
	Under 5 years	5 to 17 years	18 to 24 years	25 to 34 years	35 to 44 years	45 to 54 years	55 to 64 years	65 to 74 years	75 years and over	Percent female	Number	Percent change, 1990–2000	Persons per house-hold	Female family house-holder[1]	One-person
	16	17	18	19	20	21	22	23	24	25	26	27	28	29	30
CALIFORNIA—Cont'd															
Pomona	9.4	25.2	13.0	15.9	14.6	10.2	5.3	3.5	2.9	49.4	37 855	3.9	3.82	16.3	15.4
Porterville	9.5	24.8	10.8	14.0	14.0	11.2	6.3	4.4	5.0	50.9	11 884	24.0	3.20	17.7	19.1
Poway	6.0	24.7	7.1	9.5	18.6	17.0	8.5	4.5	4.1	50.8	15 467	11.4	3.08	10.5	12.6
Rancho Cucamonga	7.0	22.9	9.9	14.6	18.6	14.4	6.6	3.5	2.6	50.0	40 863	21.5	3.04	12.8	16.8
Rancho Palos Verdes	4.9	18.1	4.7	7.0	16.0	16.5	14.2	11.1	7.6	51.6	15 256	2.1	2.66	6.8	16.8
Redding	6.6	19.5	9.7	11.8	14.6	13.4	8.9	7.5	8.0	52.1	32 103	23.0	2.44	13.0	27.6
Redlands	6.2	20.0	10.7	13.0	14.9	14.2	8.4	5.9	6.7	52.8	23 593	7.3	2.61	13.0	26.0
Redondo Beach	5.7	13.1	6.1	20.9	22.1	15.5	8.0	4.7	3.7	49.6	28 566	6.9	2.21	9.0	33.1
Redwood City	7.5	15.7	8.4	18.9	18.5	13.2	7.6	4.7	5.5	49.7	28 060	10.1	2.62	9.9	27.1
Rialto	9.5	28.2	10.4	13.8	15.3	10.8	5.6	3.9	2.6	51.1	24 659	12.6	3.69	18.6	13.4
Richmond	7.7	20.0	9.9	15.9	15.5	13.3	7.9	5.2	4.7	51.4	34 625	5.7	2.82	20.1	26.2
Riverside	8.0	22.1	12.9	14.6	15.3	11.6	6.4	4.6	4.4	50.7	82 005	8.7	3.02	14.8	21.5
Rocklin	7.9	22.1	7.0	13.9	19.8	13.8	7.0	4.9	3.7	51.1	13 258	87.7	2.74	9.4	18.7
Rohnert Park	6.3	19.0	14.8	15.1	16.9	13.4	6.4	3.9	4.2	51.5	15 503	15.6	2.65	11.9	24.0
Rosemead	7.5	20.0	10.5	16.3	15.3	12.0	7.7	6.1	4.6	50.9	13 913	1.5	3.80	17.4	12.6
Roseville	7.3	19.5	7.0	13.8	17.0	12.7	8.3	7.5	6.9	52.1	30 783	85.4	2.57	10.1	23.1
Sacramento	7.1	20.2	10.4	15.6	15.1	12.8	7.4	5.7	5.7	51.4	154 581	7.0	2.57	15.4	32.0
Salinas	9.3	22.8	11.8	17.9	15.7	10.2	5.3	3.8	3.3	46.8	38 298	14.8	3.66	14.8	17.1
San Bernardino	9.8	25.4	11.0	14.7	14.9	10.1	5.9	4.3	3.9	50.8	56 330	3.4	3.19	21.1	21.1
San Bruno	6.1	16.9	8.2	16.4	18.0	14.6	8.5	6.1	5.2	50.6	14 677	0.3	2.72	11.2	25.5
San Buenaventura (Ventura)	6.6	18.5	7.8	14.1	17.4	14.6	8.3	6.3	6.5	50.8	38 524	8.8	2.56	11.7	26.5
San Carlos	7.0	15.1	4.3	13.5	19.6	16.4	9.8	6.5	7.8	51.9	11 455	3.7	2.40	7.2	25.7
San Clemente	6.5	17.6	7.2	13.7	17.9	15.4	8.6	6.9	6.2	49.4	19 395	16.1	2.56	7.8	23.4
San Diego	6.7	17.3	12.4	17.7	16.2	12.1	7.0	5.4	5.1	49.6	450 691	11.0	2.61	11.4	28.0
San Dimas	5.9	19.7	8.9	12.0	16.1	15.8	9.8	5.8	6.1	52.0	12 163	11.1	2.78	11.6	21.0
San Francisco	4.1	10.5	9.1	23.2	17.2	13.9	8.4	6.9	6.7	49.2	329 700	7.9	2.30	8.9	38.6
San Gabriel	6.7	16.8	8.6	16.7	16.6	12.8	8.3	6.3	7.1	52.0	12 587	3.0	3.10	15.2	18.2
San Jose	7.6	18.8	9.9	18.0	17.4	12.4	7.6	4.7	3.6	49.2	276 598	10.5	3.20	11.7	18.4
San Juan Capistrano	7.2	20.9	7.8	12.0	15.4	14.6	9.1	6.2	6.9	50.8	10 930	21.2	3.06	12.3	19.7
San Leandro	6.3	15.9	7.8	15.2	16.8	13.7	8.3	7.4	8.6	51.8	30 642	5.2	2.57	12.7	28.5
San Luis Obispo	3.4	10.8	33.6	12.4	11.2	10.7	5.8	5.0	7.1	48.6	18 639	10.0	2.27	7.2	32.7
San Marcos	8.8	20.3	9.4	16.4	15.9	10.9	6.4	5.4	6.4	50.4	18 111	33.0	3.03	9.6	20.3
San Mateo	6.1	14.3	7.2	17.7	17.4	13.7	8.5	6.7	8.4	51.1	37 338	5.2	2.44	9.1	31.6
San Pablo	9.1	22.6	10.9	17.0	14.8	10.7	6.2	4.1	4.5	50.9	9 051	4.0	3.29	19.7	22.5
San Rafael	5.8	13.7	8.1	16.6	16.7	15.4	9.4	6.5	7.9	50.5	22 371	10.2	2.42	9.0	32.1
San Ramon	7.4	18.9	5.8	14.7	21.0	17.4	8.8	3.4	2.7	50.7	16 944	31.9	2.63	7.0	21.1
Santa Ana	10.3	23.9	12.8	19.5	14.5	8.7	4.8	3.1	2.4	48.2	73 002	1.9	4.55	13.5	12.7
Santa Barbara	5.6	14.1	13.8	17.1	15.2	13.1	7.3	5.8	7.9	50.8	35 605	3.7	2.47	9.5	32.9
Santa Clara	6.5	13.4	11.3	21.9	17.2	11.7	7.4	5.6	5.1	49.1	38 526	5.4	2.58	9.5	25.9
Santa Clarita	7.8	22.5	8.1	14.2	19.4	13.9	6.9	3.8	3.3	50.5	50 787	32.0	2.95	9.8	18.7
Santa Cruz	4.9	12.5	20.5	17.1	15.5	14.7	6.3	4.0	4.5	50.2	20 442	12.8	2.44	9.6	29.3
Santa Maria	9.0	22.6	11.6	15.7	13.9	9.7	6.2	5.6	5.7	49.2	22 146	11.2	3.40	13.3	20.0
Santa Monica	4.1	10.5	6.1	20.3	19.8	15.7	9.1	6.4	7.9	51.8	44 497	-0.8	1.83	7.5	51.2
Santa Paula	8.8	22.6	10.9	15.6	14.1	10.4	6.8	5.3	5.3	49.1	8 136	6.2	3.49	13.4	17.2
Santa Rosa	6.5	17.8	9.5	14.3	15.7	14.4	7.9	5.9	8.0	51.2	56 036	22.6	2.57	11.0	27.8
Santee	6.7	21.5	8.4	13.7	19.1	14.3	7.3	4.7	4.2	51.8	18 470	3.9	2.81	13.0	18.2
Saratoga	5.4	20.7	4.0	5.8	18.0	17.5	12.4	9.1	7.1	50.9	10 450	4.0	2.83	4.9	14.3
Seaside	9.7	20.6	11.1	19.4	15.1	10.1	5.7	5.2	3.3	49.1	9 833	-7.6	3.21	13.9	18.1
Simi Valley	7.3	21.1	7.9	14.1	18.7	14.7	8.4	4.5	3.1	50.5	36 421	13.8	3.04	10.7	14.7
South Gate	10.1	25.5	12.5	17.5	14.0	9.6	5.2	2.9	2.5	50.4	23 213	3.5	4.15	18.4	10.4
South San Francisco	6.5	17.8	9.2	15.4	16.6	13.3	8.6	7.0	5.6	50.4	19 677	6.3	3.05	13.2	19.9
Stanton	9.3	21.1	10.5	18.4	14.9	9.7	6.5	4.9	4.7	49.4	10 767	4.5	3.43	14.8	21.5
Stockton	8.6	23.8	11.0	13.6	13.8	11.8	7.1	5.2	5.0	51.3	78 556	14.2	3.04	17.3	22.9
Suisun City	7.7	24.9	8.9	13.3	19.1	13.9	6.4	3.4	2.3	50.5	7 987	19.3	3.26	13.1	14.3
Sunnyvale	7.0	13.4	7.7	23.2	18.1	11.9	8.0	5.7	4.9	48.6	52 539	8.8	2.49	8.2	27.1
Temecula	8.9	25.8	7.8	13.5	19.7	11.6	5.5	4.4	2.7	50.6	18 293	100.4	3.15	10.0	12.6
Temple City	5.7	18.3	8.1	12.5	16.4	15.5	9.6	6.6	7.3	52.4	11 338	2.6	2.90	14.3	19.7
Thousand Oaks	6.7	19.3	7.1	12.3	17.6	15.8	10.1	5.8	5.3	50.8	41 793	14.6	2.75	8.7	19.6
Torrance	5.7	17.3	6.8	13.4	18.9	14.6	9.2	7.5	6.5	51.4	54 542	3.7	2.51	10.3	27.5
Tracy	9.4	25.0	7.5	15.5	19.6	11.3	5.4	3.3	3.1	50.0	17 620	57.2	3.21	10.7	14.4
Tulare	9.6	25.0	10.5	14.2	14.5	10.4	6.4	4.9	4.4	51.4	13 543	24.7	3.22	17.1	16.7
Turlock	8.1	21.8	11.4	14.4	14.4	11.4	6.7	5.6	6.2	51.9	18 408	25.3	2.92	13.1	21.2
Tustin	8.6	18.2	9.3	20.4	17.7	11.5	7.1	4.1	3.1	51.0	23 831	30.0	2.82	12.3	24.1
Union City	7.3	20.5	9.8	16.0	16.8	13.8	7.8	4.6	3.5	50.3	18 642	18.7	3.57	12.2	11.3
Upland	7.0	20.3	9.6	13.8	15.4	14.3	8.8	5.9	4.9	51.9	24 551	6.4	2.76	14.3	21.1
Vacaville	6.6	20.3	9.0	16.3	19.2	13.4	6.9	4.5	3.7	45.8	28 105	24.2	2.83	12.4	19.2
Vallejo	7.2	20.4	9.0	13.6	16.0	14.6	8.0	5.6	5.6	51.6	39 601	5.9	2.90	16.5	22.7
Victorville	8.6	25.6	8.6	13.2	15.5	10.6	6.8	6.2	5.0	51.6	20 893	46.7	3.03	16.1	19.4
Visalia	8.1	23.2	9.6	13.7	14.8	12.4	7.3	5.3	5.5	51.8	30 883	18.3	2.91	14.1	20.7
Vista	8.6	21.1	11.4	16.5	16.2	10.7	5.5	4.8	5.2	50.0	28 877	13.8	3.03	12.7	20.5
Walnut	4.9	22.9	9.8	9.8	17.4	19.5	8.9	4.3	2.6	50.8	8 260	5.3	3.63	9.9	5.8

1. No spouse present.

City	Persons in group quarters, 2000				Serious crimes known to police, 2000[2]				Education, 1990				Money income, 1989		
		Institutional			Total		Rate[3]		School enrollment		Attainment[4] (percent)			Households	
														Median	
	Total	Total	Persons in nursing homes	Non-Institutional[1]	Number	Rate[3]	Violent	Property	Public	Private	High school graduate or more	Bachelor's degree or more	Per capita (dollars)[5]	Dollars	Percent change, 1979–1989 (constant 1989 dollars)
	31	32	33	34	35	36	37	38	39	40	41	42	43	44	45
CALIFORNIA—Cont'd															
Pomona	5 041	1 906	788	3 135	5 862	3 922	920	3 002	35 026	3 608	59.6	13.1	10 728	32 132	24.6
Porterville	1 632	1 123	276	509	1 761	4 445	439	4 006	7 677	420	60.8	12.5	9 666	22 168	-3.7
Poway	426	354	354	72	844	1 757	210	1 546	11 751	1 782	91.3	34.4	20 720	53 252	32.0
Rancho Cucamonga	3 626	1 858	0	1 768	3 509	2 747	201	2 546	28 107	4 059	86.0	21.1	17 239	46 193	10.9
Rancho Palos Verdes	509	166	166	343	488	1 186	182	1 004	8 813	2 342	95.2	53.6	36 509	79 797	13.4
Redding	2 377	1 216	478	1 161	3 040	3 759	470	3 289	15 928	1 795	81.0	16.6	13 040	25 828	4.3
Redlands	1 966	541	535	1 425	2 290	3 601	541	3 060	14 150	3 983	84.6	31.3	17 825	37 073	13.7
Redondo Beach	187	96	5	91	2 071	3 274	326	2 948	10 355	2 394	90.4	40.4	26 230	51 913	41.9
Redwood City	1 927	1 481	269	446	2 093	2 776	261	2 515	13 459	2 652	81.5	27.1	20 292	42 962	31.3
Rialto	804	265	248	539	3 466	3 773	712	3 061	20 166	2 087	73.2	10.2	11 862	36 233	6.1
Richmond	1 628	953	165	675	5 944	5 991	1 209	4 781	20 556	3 009	76.7	22.2	14 630	32 165	23.0
Riverside	7 798	2 881	1 180	4 917	12 228	4 792	786	4 006	60 348	9 147	77.8	19.3	14 235	34 801	16.3
Rocklin	20	6	6	14	712	1 960	91	1 869	4 738	706	89.3	26.1	17 729	40 417	NA
Rohnert Park	1 101	0	0	1 101	1 431	3 388	175	3 213	10 515	922	87.5	21.8	14 861	36 097	11.3
Rosemead	612	387	280	225	1 604	2 998	699	2 299	14 473	1 577	53.8	10.0	9 796	29 770	13.0
Roseville	928	713	646	215	3 082	3 856	293	3 564	10 563	1 430	86.9	24.0	17 430	39 975	35.1
Sacramento	9 002	4 831	1 917	4 171	27 338	6 717	766	5 951	92 299	12 126	76.9	23.5	14 087	28 183	15.1
Salinas	10 805	8 756	361	2 049	6 457	4 274	835	3 439	29 916	2 539	62.3	13.0	11 351	31 271	7.5
San Bernardino	5 849	3 765	664	2 084	11 870	6 402	1 135	5 268	41 817	4 451	68.1	12.7	10 865	25 533	8.1
San Bruno	221	122	122	99	984	2 450	202	2 248	7 977	1 880	84.0	21.3	18 289	42 019	10.6
San Buenaventura (Ventura)	2 370	1 376	426	994	3 349	3 319	340	2 979	20 228	3 396	84.1	24.6	19 091	40 307	28.0
San Carlos	183	145	145	38	533	1 923	155	1 768	4 088	1 374	91.6	35.8	28 161	54 658	28.9
San Clemente	292	62	62	230	825	1 652	204	1 448	7 359	1 691	90.4	32.4	23 841	46 374	44.4
San Diego	45 818	6 637	3 285	39 181	46 359	3 789	585	3 204	277 321	42 965	82.3	29.8	16 401	33 686	22.5
San Dimas	1 209	372	215	837	742	2 121	386	1 735	7 466	1 784	85.2	26.7	20 246	50 268	18.6
San Francisco	19 757	4 200	1 685	15 557	42 174	5 430	837	4 593	139 171	39 838	78.0	35.0	19 695	33 414	25.7
San Gabriel	755	681	510	74	937	2 354	452	1 902	8 487	1 648	70.9	21.8	13 733	32 559	14.3
San Jose	10 864	3 846	2 106	7 018	22 808	2 549	551	1 998	203 672	28 285	77.2	25.3	16 905	46 206	20.5
San Juan Capistrano	426	305	181	121	567	1 676	160	1 517	5 919	1 354	83.6	28.1	23 344	46 250	17.1
San Leandro	827	517	471	310	3 948	4 969	629	4 340	12 810	2 195	79.4	16.9	17 563	35 681	9.8
San Luis Obispo	1 862	362	362	1 500	2 082	4 713	303	4 410	18 936	918	89.0	34.9	14 760	25 982	18.2
San Marcos	148	15	15	133	1 446	2 630	375	2 255	9 390	818	76.1	14.8	13 590	31 961	4.7
San Mateo	1 316	609	477	707	2 494	2 697	371	2 326	16 194	3 466	85.3	30.2	22 746	42 894	15.3
San Pablo	465	367	367	98	2 241	7 417	1 542	5 875	6 327	620	65.8	11.6	10 505	25 479	17.7
San Rafael	2 020	1 083	765	937	1 835	3 273	449	2 824	8 173	2 350	89.0	38.4	24 230	41 922	16.8
San Ramon	85	47	5	38	998	2 232	195	2 037	8 817	1 176	95.4	42.9	25 196	63 607	19.3
Santa Ana	5 624	3 482	752	2 142	10 452	3 093	541	2 551	79 865	6 429	49.7	10.6	10 019	35 162	14.3
Santa Barbara	4 517	477	477	4 040	2 991	3 240	494	2 746	17 954	2 887	79.1	33.1	18 934	33 667	30.1
Santa Clara	2 787	459	427	2 328	3 121	3 049	285	2 764	19 358	6 735	83.5	30.8	19 676	44 707	22.8
Santa Clarita	1 393	370	370	1 023	2 681	1 774	222	1 553	26 974	5 117	87.9	25.9	21 073	52 970	NA
Santa Cruz	4 634	373	29	4 261	2 964	5 429	996	4 433	16 742	1 429	85.7	35.2	15 538	31 857	35.5
Santa Maria	2 162	1 438	380	724	2 496	3 224	400	2 823	14 912	1 529	65.7	10.7	12 118	29 492	9.9
Santa Monica	2 516	941	790	1 575	4 688	5 575	764	4 812	14 591	4 434	87.5	43.4	29 134	35 997	29.4
Santa Paula	243	129	129	114	744	2 602	367	2 234	6 147	705	60.0	9.9	11 650	31 605	19.8
Santa Rosa	3 806	1 558	649	2 248	5 289	3 583	370	3 214	25 935	3 540	85.7	26.9	17 259	35 237	21.0
Santee	1 043	899	211	144	1 314	2 480	317	2 163	13 652	1 353	84.5	13.1	14 179	39 073	14.0
Saratoga	251	215	208	36	340	1 139	141	999	5 984	1 486	95.0	57.9	40 660	86 674	25.7
Seaside	103	28	28	75	905	2 855	805	2 051	9 271	717	77.9	14.7	10 409	28 655	17.1
Simi Valley	800	163	133	637	1 683	1 511	120	1 391	25 343	4 393	86.7	21.1	18 630	53 967	21.3
South Gate	141	61	61	80	3 155	3 274	817	2 457	25 757	2 212	40.9	5.3	8 368	27 279	11.4
South San Francisco	443	148	148	295	1 715	2 832	251	2 581	11 736	2 353	77.5	19.7	15 857	42 920	15.1
Stanton	518	278	278	240	1 020	2 727	393	2 334	6 591	899	70.4	14.2	12 803	33 367	14.8
Stockton	5 316	1 739	1 643	3 577	16 849	6 912	1 219	5 693	58 278	7 947	66.6	15.0	11 331	26 876	8.4
Suisun City	94	61	61	33	585	2 240	257	1 983	7 060	470	82.1	12.8	12 539	40 865	14.2
Sunnyvale	875	499	484	376	2 638	2 002	145	1 857	23 928	4 766	87.1	37.1	22 309	46 403	20.1
Temecula	22	0	0	22	1 914	3 316	357	2 959	6 420	1 221	87.6	21.9	16 895	44 270	NA
Temple City	511	413	409	98	554	1 660	285	1 375	6 971	1 429	83.1	21.9	16 107	38 789	11.5
Thousand Oaks	1 951	270	253	1 681	1 940	1 658	156	1 502	24 336	6 223	89.8	35.0	23 682	56 856	26.0
Torrance	1 249	686	609	563	4 346	3 151	337	2 813	27 861	5 241	87.6	31.2	22 095	47 204	16.6
Tracy	345	153	153	192	1 954	3 432	214	3 218	8 862	659	77.1	12.1	14 298	40 256	44.4
Tulare	447	214	175	233	2 425	5 512	866	4 646	9 321	534	60.8	8.4	9 878	24 686	8.7
Turlock	2 080	504	504	1 576	3 145	5 635	532	5 103	10 953	972	69.6	17.1	11 936	27 293	10.7
Tustin	418	35	18	383	2 129	3 154	338	2 816	11 382	1 636	86.0	25.5	18 120	38 433	15.9
Union City	342	215	215	127	2 368	3 541	511	3 030	14 557	1 759	77.5	20.6	14 865	46 988	16.4
Upland	585	316	308	269	2 793	4 084	447	3 636	15 433	3 019	84.1	25.4	19 569	41 965	15.3
Vacaville	9 218	9 149	261	69	2 256	2 546	392	2 154	16 669	1 962	82.4	16.9	14 490	40 679	16.1
Vallejo	1 745	819	644	926	7 070	6 055	1 111	4 944	25 289	4 406	81.0	19.2	14 271	36 605	23.9
Victorville	670	406	266	264	3 410	5 326	517	4 809	9 958	978	75.0	10.5	11 474	28 698	12.8
Visalia	1 622	893	681	729	5 016	5 478	849	4 629	21 504	1 957	75.2	19.7	12 994	29 463	5.1
Vista	2 266	1 262	378	1 004	2 661	2 961	392	2 570	15 666	1 653	79.4	18.4	13 983	32 553	27.1
Walnut	40	24	24	16	525	1 750	230	1 520	9 115	1 704	87.5	35.1	18 749	64 333	27.0

1. Persons in emergency shelters and persons visible in street locations. 2. Data for serious crimes have not been adjusted for underreporting. This may affect comparability between geographic areas and over time. 3. Per 100,000 population estimated by the FBI. 4. Persons 25 years old and older. 5. Based on population enumerated as of April 1, 1990.

City	Percent with $100,000 or more	Persons Total	Percent change in rate, 1979–1989	Families Total	Total	Percent change, 1990–2000	Vacant units for sale or rent[1]	For seasonal use (percent)	Home owner vacancy rate	Renter vacancy rate	Total	Percent owner occupied	Percent renter occupied	Average size owner occupied	Average size renter occupied
	46	47	48	49	50	51	52	53	54	55	56	57	58	59	60
CALIFORNIA—Cont'd															
Pomona	3.5	18.4	7.0	14.0	39 598	2.9	1 743	0.2	2.2	3.2	37 855	57.3	42.7	3.86	3.76
Porterville	1.5	26.8	71.8	22.1	12 691	26.0	807	0.4	2.0	7.2	11 884	56.4	43.6	3.19	3.20
Poway	13.0	4.0	-23.1	2.9	15 714	9.2	247	0.2	0.3	2.1	15 467	77.7	22.3	3.12	2.95
Rancho Cucamonga	7.0	5.5	0.0	4.1	42 134	15.9	1 271	0.1	1.2	4.1	40 863	70.2	29.8	3.20	2.66
Rancho Palos Verdes	37.2	3.2	14.3	2.0	15 709	1.6	453	0.7	0.8	3.7	15 256	81.6	18.4	2.67	2.65
Redding	2.2	14.3	41.6	11.1	33 802	24.1	1 699	0.5	1.9	4.6	32 103	56.7	43.3	2.47	2.41
Redlands	6.9	9.0	-7.2	6.4	24 790	6.9	1 197	0.4	2.2	5.0	23 593	60.4	39.6	2.71	2.46
Redondo Beach	12.3	5.6	-28.2	3.6	29 543	4.7	977	0.6	1.2	2.6	28 566	49.5	50.5	2.37	2.05
Redwood City	9.1	8.3	15.3	6.1	28 921	7.7	861	0.8	0.4	2.3	28 060	53.0	47.0	2.61	2.63
Rialto	2.5	12.1	42.4	9.7	26 045	9.3	1 386	0.1	2.9	5.6	24 659	68.4	31.6	3.74	3.59
Richmond	3.5	16.1	-2.4	13.5	36 044	4.4	1 419	0.3	1.2	3.1	34 625	53.3	46.7	2.87	2.76
Riverside	4.7	11.9	5.3	8.4	85 974	7.1	3 969	0.3	1.9	4.8	82 005	56.6	43.4	3.18	2.81
Rocklin	5.7	5.6	NA	3.7	14 421	90.8	1 163	0.3	1.7	17.1	13 258	72.7	27.3	2.88	2.35
Rohnert Park	2.0	8.5	-25.4	4.5	15 808	13.6	305	0.4	0.5	2.2	15 503	58.4	41.6	2.83	2.40
Rosemead	2.7	20.0	34.2	16.2	14 345	1.5	432	0.2	1.0	2.2	13 913	48.8	51.2	3.67	3.92
Roseville	5.4	6.8	-35.2	5.2	31 925	79.5	1 142	0.4	1.3	4.5	30 783	69.5	30.5	2.67	2.34
Sacramento	3.0	17.2	14.7	13.8	163 957	6.9	9 376	0.4	2.0	5.4	154 581	50.1	49.9	2.65	2.50
Salinas	2.4	15.6	24.8	12.4	39 659	14.7	1 361	0.2	1.0	3.8	38 298	50.1	49.9	3.65	3.67
San Bernardino	2.1	22.8	39.9	19.5	63 535	8.0	7 205	0.2	6.1	9.7	56 330	52.4	47.6	3.25	3.12
San Bruno	6.4	4.8	-4.0	3.8	14 980	-1.3	303	0.5	0.4	1.7	14 677	63.0	37.0	2.76	2.66
San Buenaventura (Ventura)	6.7	6.6	-14.3	4.6	39 803	6.6	1 279	0.9	0.8	2.8	38 524	58.7	41.3	2.62	2.46
San Carlos	16.5	2.7	-6.9	1.7	11 691	3.1	236	0.3	0.3	2.0	11 455	72.7	27.3	2.55	2.02
San Clemente	12.1	7.0	-10.3	4.7	20 653	10.3	1 258	3.7	0.9	2.5	19 395	62.4	37.6	2.59	2.51
San Diego	5.9	13.4	8.1	9.7	469 689	8.8	18 998	1.1	0.8	3.2	450 691	49.5	50.5	2.71	2.52
San Dimas	10.9	5.4	8.0	3.7	12 503	8.9	340	0.4	1.0	2.6	12 163	73.7	26.3	2.87	2.51
San Francisco	7.4	12.7	-7.3	9.7	346 527	5.5	16 827	1.1	0.8	2.5	329 700	35.0	65.0	2.73	2.06
San Gabriel	4.9	15.2	36.9	12.6	12 909	1.4	322	0.3	0.9	1.8	12 587	47.6	52.4	3.15	3.06
San Jose	8.0	9.3	13.4	6.5	281 841	8.7	5 243	0.3	0.4	1.8	276 598	61.8	38.2	3.22	3.16
San Juan Capistrano	15.3	6.2	37.8	3.3	11 320	17.8	390	0.6	1.0	6.1	10 930	78.9	21.1	2.91	3.60
San Leandro	3.6	5.0	4.2	3.3	31 334	3.8	692	0.3	0.6	2.2	30 642	60.6	39.4	2.70	2.36
San Luis Obispo	3.8	27.4	17.6	6.7	19 306	8.0	667	0.6	1.1	2.3	18 639	41.9	58.1	2.35	2.22
San Marcos	3.1	10.9	26.7	7.9	18 862	30.3	751	0.3	1.4	3.3	18 111	66.0	34.0	2.83	3.40
San Mateo	9.5	6.2	6.9	3.9	38 249	3.6	911	0.6	0.5	1.6	37 338	53.9	46.1	2.53	2.34
San Pablo	1.0	19.0	3.3	17.1	9 340	-0.8	289	0.4	0.9	2.1	9 051	49.1	50.9	3.40	3.18
San Rafael	12.9	8.1	5.2	4.4	22 948	8.6	577	0.5	0.9	1.7	22 371	53.8	46.2	2.31	2.53
San Ramon	16.9	1.7	6.3	1.1	17 552	29.7	608	0.7	0.4	3.5	16 944	71.3	28.7	2.84	2.12
Santa Ana	3.0	18.1	29.3	12.5	74 588	-0.5	1 586	0.1	0.8	1.9	73 002	49.3	50.7	4.54	4.57
Santa Barbara	7.6	12.7	15.5	7.8	37 076	2.3	1 471	1.4	0.7	2.3	35 605	42.0	58.0	2.51	2.43
Santa Clara	6.6	6.2	6.9	3.7	39 630	4.6	1 104	0.6	0.4	1.8	38 526	46.1	53.9	2.69	2.49
Santa Clarita	10.8	3.7	NA	2.2	52 442	27.5	1 655	0.2	1.2	4.8	50 787	74.7	25.3	3.00	2.78
Santa Cruz	4.9	15.7	-4.8	7.2	21 504	11.1	1 062	2.4	0.7	1.4	20 442	46.6	53.4	2.51	2.39
Santa Maria	2.7	16.8	43.6	12.8	22 847	8.1	701	0.2	0.9	3.1	22 146	55.9	44.1	3.18	3.68
Santa Monica	12.2	9.4	-5.1	5.7	47 863	0.2	3 366	1.6	1.4	4.3	44 497	29.8	70.2	2.24	1.66
Santa Paula	2.9	12.2	-9.6	10.0	8 341	3.5	205	0.2	0.5	2.2	8 136	57.7	42.3	3.29	3.75
Santa Rosa	4.7	8.3	-10.8	5.5	57 578	20.6	1 542	0.5	0.7	2.1	56 036	58.5	41.5	2.56	2.57
Santee	2.1	5.4	-20.6	3.9	18 833	3.1	363	0.2	0.5	2.2	18 470	71.0	29.0	2.80	2.84
Saratoga	42.0	1.4	-36.4	0.5	10 649	3.2	199	0.3	0.3	3.4	10 450	90.0	10.0	2.88	2.37
Seaside	1.0	12.2	-17.0	9.9	11 005	-2.1	1 172	0.2	2.9	1.5	9 833	44.0	56.0	2.99	3.39
Simi Valley	8.9	3.6	-26.5	2.3	37 272	12.6	851	0.1	0.9	3.8	36 421	77.6	22.4	3.09	2.85
South Gate	1.5	17.4	22.5	15.2	24 269	5.8	1 056	1.5	2.1	1.7	23 213	46.9	53.1	4.42	3.90
South San Francisco	4.4	5.9	-4.8	4.7	20 138	5.5	461	0.3	0.7	1.3	19 677	62.5	37.5	3.02	3.11
Stanton	2.0	13.6	12.4	10.1	11 011	2.4	244	0.2	0.9	2.0	10 767	48.9	51.1	3.18	3.66
Stockton	3.1	21.4	28.9	16.9	82 042	13.1	3 486	0.2	1.4	4.3	78 556	51.6	48.4	2.99	3.08
Suisun City	1.4	9.4	-21.7	7.8	8 146	15.9	159	0.1	0.8	3.1	7 987	73.6	26.4	3.34	3.03
Sunnyvale	9.3	4.7	-2.1	3.3	53 753	5.8	1 214	0.6	0.5	1.3	52 539	47.6	52.4	2.60	2.39
Temecula	7.2	4.9	NA	3.6	19 099	79.2	806	0.4	1.4	7.2	18 293	73.4	26.6	3.27	2.84
Temple City	5.1	5.6	16.7	3.8	11 674	1.1	336	0.4	0.9	1.9	11 338	63.1	36.9	2.96	2.79
Thousand Oaks	16.5	4.2	-4.5	2.7	42 958	13.8	1 165	0.5	0.9	2.9	41 793	75.3	24.7	2.80	2.61
Torrance	10.6	5.1	8.5	3.6	55 967	1.9	1 425	0.3	1.0	2.4	54 542	56.0	44.0	2.68	2.29
Tracy	2.9	7.4	-49.7	5.8	18 087	48.6	467	0.2	1.1	2.8	17 620	72.2	27.8	3.28	3.02
Tulare	1.9	21.4	22.3	18.3	14 253	26.0	710	0.3	1.3	5.4	13 543	60.5	39.5	3.16	3.30
Turlock	2.4	13.2	2.3	10.2	19 095	24.0	687	0.3	1.7	2.8	18 408	55.8	44.2	2.98	2.85
Tustin	6.8	6.8	3.0	4.3	25 501	32.1	1 670	0.4	0.9	2.5	23 831	49.6	50.4	2.70	2.93
Union City	5.3	6.5	-8.5	5.1	18 877	16.1	235	0.1	0.5	1.3	18 642	71.3	28.7	3.59	3.52
Upland	9.9	7.8	14.7	5.8	25 467	4.0	916	0.2	1.6	3.9	24 551	58.9	41.1	2.83	2.66
Vacaville	3.2	6.1	-28.2	4.9	28 696	21.3	591	0.2	0.7	2.8	28 105	66.7	33.3	2.90	2.68
Vallejo	2.7	8.5	-20.6	6.9	41 219	3.3	1 618	0.3	1.2	4.5	39 601	63.2	36.8	2.99	2.76
Victorville	1.9	14.8	26.5	11.9	22 498	44.0	1 605	0.5	2.8	7.9	20 893	65.1	34.9	3.05	3.00
Visalia	3.6	17.6	63.0	14.1	32 654	20.3	1 771	0.3	2.2	6.4	30 883	62.7	37.3	2.88	2.97
Vista	3.7	11.7	6.4	8.0	29 814	8.7	937	0.2	1.0	3.3	28 877	54.2	45.8	2.89	3.20
Walnut	14.8	4.1	0.0	3.2	8 395	3.8	135	0.3	0.7	2.2	8 260	88.9	11.1	3.62	3.73

1. Includes units rented or sold but not occupied. 2. Specified owner-occupied units. 3. Specified renter-occupied units. 4. Overcrowded or lacking complete plumbing facilities.

Table D. Cities — Labor Force, Employment, Disability, and Construction

City	Civilian labor force, 2001		Unemployment		Civilian employment, 1990[2]	Percent		Disability 1990	Value of residential construction authorized by building permits, 2000		
	Total	Percent change, 2000–2001	Total	Rate[1]	Total	Professional, managerial, and technical	Precision production, craft, and repair	Work disabled persons[3] (percent)	New construction ($1,000)	Number of housing units	Percent single family
	61	62	63	64	65	66	67	68	69	70	71
CALIFORNIA—Cont'd											
Pomona	65 389	2.5	4 604	7.0	55 571	22.8	13.3	7.7	4 046	30	100.0
Porterville	15 624	-0.2	2 861	18.3	10 507	25.1	9.2	12.3	16 812	196	100.0
Poway	27 254	1.6	557	2.0	22 169	40.7	10.2	5.2	49 620	213	52.1
Rancho Cucamonga	68 922	3.1	2 069	3.0	50 962	33.2	12.7	5.7	242 764	1 411	64.1
Rancho Palos Verdes	23 803	2.2	425	1.8	21 373	57.1	3.9	4.4	25 889	40	100.0
Redding	36 324	2.3	2 447	6.7	27 820	30.9	10.3	12.2	74 964	603	70.3
Redlands	37 922	3.1	1 146	3.0	28 034	40.8	9.3	6.9	31 553	153	100.0
Redondo Beach	44 931	2.2	1 171	2.6	40 006	47.2	8.4	4.7	71 537	317	100.0
Redwood City	42 069	-0.7	1 073	2.6	36 496	34.1	11.0	6.7	36 000	220	6.4
Rialto	41 616	3.1	2 122	5.1	30 106	22.6	14.7	8.9	26 810	215	53.5
Richmond	50 255	1.7	3 162	6.3	38 823	32.6	8.8	11.1	71 855	581	46.0
Riverside	159 612	2.8	8 263	5.2	103 866	29.9	13.5	7.3	243 258	1 807	56.3
Rocklin	14 908	2.8	508	3.4	9 685	35.4	9.6	7.8	226 745	1 391	74.5
Rohnert Park	26 234	1.4	862	3.3	19 237	28.1	11.9	7.8	259	7	0.0
Rosemead	24 771	2.4	1 610	6.5	21 174	19.0	13.5	6.7	11 382	51	100.0
Roseville	33 646	2.8	1 287	3.8	21 763	35.3	11.3	6.5	396 915	2 509	55.5
Sacramento	208 167	2.3	10 668	5.1	161 812	34.7	8.5	10.8	334 801	2 789	70.1
Salinas	64 503	-0.3	7 821	12.1	46 848	20.8	9.3	8.9	116 117	651	88.9
San Bernardino	86 450	3.1	5 987	6.9	61 337	24.3	13.5	10.7	10 096	76	100.0
San Bruno	24 483	-0.6	675	2.8	21 195	29.6	12.9	6.2	0	0	0.0
San Buenaventura (Ventura)	58 977	1.6	2 080	3.5	47 791	36.1	12.2	8.4	42 225	219	79.5
San Carlos	17 214	-1.1	278	1.6	15 077	43.5	9.1	5.9	4 493	17	58.8
San Clemente	26 122	1.6	606	2.3	22 121	37.0	11.3	5.4	275 794	1 011	95.9
San Diego	653 365	1.6	21 340	3.3	524 841	37.5	9.4	7.1	970 189	6 459	31.2
San Dimas	19 552	2.2	511	2.6	17 408	38.4	10.0	5.2	5 568	26	100.0
San Francisco	436 902	0.6	22 508	5.2	386 530	38.5	6.3	8.0	413 414	2 766	2.9
San Gabriel	19 803	2.3	937	4.7	17 248	28.1	9.5	6.0	6 611	40	82.5
San Jose	516 083	0.9	27 063	5.2	407 862	34.4	12.5	6.0	452 478	4 426	30.2
San Juan Capistrano	15 709	1.6	359	2.3	13 308	35.5	10.0	4.6	15 360	47	100.0
San Leandro	40 008	2.0	1 576	3.9	33 893	29.0	12.2	7.8	34 759	175	100.0
San Luis Obispo	25 714	2.2	780	3.0	21 067	34.9	7.1	5.8	11 975	100	57.0
San Marcos	22 055	1.6	679	3.1	17 751	25.3	14.9	6.9	226 745	1 019	82.4
San Mateo	55 600	-0.6	1 580	2.8	48 091	35.3	9.6	4.9	49 575	498	11.4
San Pablo	13 146	1.7	891	6.8	10 103	18.3	14.3	12.7	8 549	90	8.9
San Rafael	29 465	-0.6	1 044	3.5	26 575	41.3	8.3	6.9	12 683	138	15.9
San Ramon	26 019	0.9	468	1.8	21 064	45.1	7.2	3.8	63 229	241	100.0
Santa Ana	171 744	2.1	9 303	5.4	140 823	16.8	13.9	5.2	31 984	329	16.7
Santa Barbara	52 301	-0.7	1 527	2.9	46 765	34.8	10.1	6.9	5 001	45	73.3
Santa Clara	68 300	0.3	2 868	4.2	54 573	41.2	10.7	5.5	24 299	217	76.5
Santa Clarita	68 697	2.2	1 843	2.7	61 119	37.5	11.9	5.1	126 154	826	55.8
Santa Cruz	32 042	1.1	1 705	5.3	26 485	38.8	9.0	8.3	11 194	61	72.1
Santa Maria	30 682	-0.8	1 537	5.0	26 844	19.8	11.8	8.9	51 542	333	100.0
Santa Monica	57 212	2.3	2 110	3.7	50 375	50.4	5.3	5.9	60 344	446	11.7
Santa Paula	14 359	1.6	1 044	7.3	11 184	20.8	13.0	7.5	391	2	100.0
Santa Rosa	75 166	1.3	2 134	2.8	55 373	32.3	11.0	8.1	150 055	1 098	78.8
Santee	32 347	1.6	875	2.7	26 135	27.9	15.7	7.2	0	0	0.0
Saratoga	17 790	-0.6	480	2.7	14 437	62.8	4.2	4.0	31 333	64	100.0
Seaside	17 034	-0.1	1 338	7.9	12 973	21.5	9.7	8.3	1 111	9	100.0
Simi Valley	69 662	1.6	2 715	3.9	56 232	34.6	13.2	6.4	185 501	776	100.0
South Gate	41 309	2.6	3 476	8.4	34 588	11.8	17.0	5.7	2 296	20	100.0
South San Francisco	32 695	-0.3	1 154	3.5	28 079	24.7	12.0	5.9	34 807	155	100.0
Stanton	18 506	2.1	992	5.4	15 184	24.6	14.7	6.6	166	1	100.0
Stockton	109 048	1.9	11 237	10.3	79 162	27.2	9.7	10.5	263 344	1 817	100.0
Suisun City	13 075	2.0	647	4.9	9 738	23.8	16.8	8.3	24 115	101	100.0
Sunnyvale	86 421	0.1	3 280	3.8	69 343	48.4	9.1	5.0	32 463	189	34.4
Temecula	19 794	2.9	644	3.3	13 142	32.3	14.2	5.4	153 681	1 386	82.4
Temple City	17 286	2.3	609	3.5	15 247	32.7	11.2	6.1	13 042	254	12.6
Thousand Oaks	70 954	1.6	2 655	3.7	57 368	42.4	7.9	5.2	175 798	666	95.9
Torrance	82 325	2.2	2 496	3.0	72 981	42.3	10.2	5.2	34 403	204	60.8
Tracy	21 122	1.9	1 537	7.3	15 851	23.5	16.1	8.6	232 649	1 433	100.0
Tulare	17 801	-0.3	2 369	13.3	12 704	20.0	12.0	10.8	18 751	224	100.0
Turlock	24 484	2.1	2 195	9.0	17 828	26.0	13.6	8.4	75 603	708	73.4
Tustin	32 455	1.7	995	3.1	27 274	33.9	10.4	5.7	22 702	61	100.0
Union City	32 544	1.7	1 081	3.3	27 747	26.6	13.2	6.6	91 276	497	68.4
Upland	43 951	3.1	1 409	3.2	32 430	35.5	9.9	6.1	13 503	94	100.0
Vacaville	40 901	2.1	1 357	3.3	30 985	27.0	16.1	7.2	119 727	704	75.1
Vallejo	63 414	2.1	2 889	4.6	47 425	28.3	12.9	9.2	102 737	487	100.0
Victorville	20 809	3.1	1 365	6.6	14 822	23.3	17.1	10.7	50 720	402	97.0
Visalia	42 881	-0.3	4 323	10.1	31 741	32.3	9.0	8.3	79 397	661	97.9
Vista	40 081	1.7	1 468	3.7	32 065	28.5	13.7	7.2	36 738	158	100.0
Walnut	16 842	2.2	552	3.3	14 893	43.2	8.1	4.1	13 229	33	100.0

1. Percent of civilian labor force.   2. Persons 16 years and older.   3. Persons 16 to 64 years old.

Table D. Cities — Wholesale Trade, Retail Trade, and Real Estate

City	Wholesale Trade, 1997				Retail Trade[1], 1997				Real Estate and Rental and Leasing, 1997			
	Number of Establishments	Number of Employees	Sales (mil dol)	Annual Payroll (mil dol)	Number of Establishments	Number of Employees	Sales (mil dol)	Annual Payroll (mil dol)	Number of Establishments	Number of Employees	Receipts (mil dol)	Annual Payroll (mil dol)
	72	73	74	75	76	77	78	79	80	81	82	83
CALIFORNIA—Cont'd												
Pomona	229	2 982	1 184.8	87.3	269	3 216	599.5	63.6	81	424	50.7	9.4
Porterville	23	398	150.5	6.3	165	2 097	340.6	35.1	32	105	16.7	1.3
Poway	60	530	263.4	20.3	139	2 036	442.8	38.9	54	225	25.3	4.1
Rancho Cucamonga	219	2 594	1 529.4	86.3	233	3 947	708.9	70.5	80	460	47.5	9.6
Rancho Palos Verdes	46	101	110.7	5.6	49	595	109.7	10.8	46	127	28.8	3.0
Redding	152	1 311	436.3	40.5	501	6 513	1 128.3	115.6	146	664	59.8	11.1
Redlands	37	496	161.2	16.3	208	3 313	560.8	60.4	67	247	32.5	3.9
Redondo Beach	77	552	366.7	23.2	287	3 968	538.5	62.8	91	295	51.7	5.8
Redwood City	128	1 376	1 099.4	72.6	256	4 199	1 097.2	104.5	88	1 279	114.1	31.6
Rialto	50	553	924.3	21.3	115	1 708	313.9	29.0	41	176	22.1	3.3
Richmond	105	1 396	690.9	47.6	224	2 510	453.7	45.6	54	242	46.7	6.7
Riverside	267	3 395	1 723.0	104.9	800	11 452	2 279.3	219.7	250	1 276	145.0	28.3
Rocklin	68	968	567.2	34.4	84	1 365	217.1	24.2	21	105	14.7	1.9
Rohnert Park	35	D	D	D	108	2 203	390.8	40.7	42	239	51.8	6.4
Rosemead	100	D	D	D	134	1 155	190.1	18.1	28	126	11.3	2.7
Roseville	77	1 520	668.4	66.1	279	5 514	1 545.9	134.7	79	922	82.3	21.6
Sacramento	594	10 553	5 538.2	369.9	1 296	18 093	3 039.6	329.7	415	3 058	367.3	80.1
Salinas	200	3 802	2 308.0	145.6	496	7 173	1 332.5	146.3	104	546	71.7	11.7
San Bernardino	150	2 728	1 050.2	88.0	640	9 571	1 903.9	181.0	152	556	68.7	11.7
San Bruno	35	244	452.9	10.8	138	2 833	656.6	57.9	29	138	49.6	4.4
San Buenaventura (Ventura)	201	2 816	639.9	98.2	483	6 334	1 249.8	128.2	175	790	94.5	19.4
San Carlos	129	1 504	671.4	57.1	142	1 503	315.9	36.4	52	246	32.1	6.9
San Clemente	144	1 293	748.4	48.7	173	1 587	286.7	27.5	65	236	35.6	4.7
San Diego	2 178	33 766	18 478.4	1 634.8	4 128	54 308	10 018.2	1 020.3	1 954	14 038	2 109.3	386.8
San Dimas	102	970	1 271.8	34.0	101	1 295	210.7	22.3	29	172	27.3	4.0
San Francisco	1 900	17 677	12 219.1	779.8	3 841	39 693	6 795.0	830.6	1 627	14 492	2 721.2	472.9
San Gabriel	156	599	195.5	12.8	173	1 475	306.7	26.7	65	223	29.0	4.5
San Jose	1 423	25 578	27 076.8	1 398.6	2 169	34 278	6 905.0	700.5	794	6 088	1 140.3	179.0
San Juan Capistrano	66	391	212.3	14.1	122	1 427	326.9	32.4	49	212	31.1	8.0
San Leandro	324	4 402	2 533.3	176.1	351	5 952	1 116.7	113.9	120	1 838	242.1	50.5
San Luis Obispo	69	554	161.6	14.4	319	3 845	606.1	62.8	106	501	53.5	7.8
San Marcos	155	1 843	495.5	63.8	229	2 275	525.1	48.7	40	232	25.6	4.4
San Mateo	156	2 138	1 840.2	179.4	400	6 247	1 082.8	120.7	161	1 892	252.5	54.5
San Pablo	13	41	11.5	0.8	139	1 552	315.2	31.7	26	132	22.8	2.7
San Rafael	221	1 775	754.6	66.1	411	4 637	1 075.2	115.7	152	1 458	203.0	41.9
San Ramon	162	2 759	7 459.8	175.5	143	1 962	380.0	38.7	68	548	146.3	24.8
Santa Ana	571	8 899	4 113.4	357.2	876	11 543	2 302.6	232.1	254	2 951	451.6	89.3
Santa Barbara	157	1 145	379.8	35.2	655	7 589	1 220.4	143.3	257	1 397	551.8	45.4
Santa Clara	593	13 779	20 791.0	892.0	414	6 703	1 758.7	187.6	146	973	307.9	30.1
Santa Clarita	75	576	392.6	37.4	297	3 720	736.6	66.9	111	506	74.4	10.9
Santa Cruz	92	888	170.1	23.7	282	3 626	578.9	62.3	80	327	41.9	5.5
Santa Maria	117	1 350	451.7	43.7	353	4 928	810.5	89.5	69	383	32.6	6.3
Santa Monica	234	2 608	3 792.3	124.3	726	8 018	2 200.3	190.0	334	1 932	338.8	70.0
Santa Paula	32	765	265.1	19.4	72	515	124.4	7.4	15	171	10.9	2.0
Santa Rosa	182	2 088	716.2	71.3	758	10 653	2 118.8	220.5	235	959	133.4	20.5
Santee	63	418	106.6	11.2	125	2 234	401.5	40.1	45	173	22.6	3.1
Saratoga	48	D	D	D	64	569	102.7	12.1	55	264	49.4	8.7
Seaside	15	123	23.6	2.9	83	1 204	353.3	32.5	12	58	7.4	1.0
Simi Valley	146	2 050	843.9	76.9	279	3 806	852.4	69.0	68	341	36.1	6.9
South Gate	86	1 417	1 327.5	41.1	154	1 738	361.1	32.0	27	129	83.2	4.4
South San Francisco	472	7 370	4 778.9	302.0	187	2 558	585.9	56.6	72	1 328	346.3	44.3
Stanton	39	732	127.9	18.7	96	1 136	238.9	21.6	25	101	18.2	2.0
Stockton	262	4 027	2 949.0	125.9	742	9 842	1 771.4	178.2	208	1 223	125.6	25.2
Suisun City	11	D	D	D	37	360	65.7	7.0	7	43	5.5	0.8
Sunnyvale	386	8 677	7 425.4	574.6	373	6 319	1 659.8	150.3	122	780	131.0	20.6
Temecula	77	973	579.6	37.4	211	2 817	687.7	63.0	51	287	29.9	4.8
Temple City	75	311	90.7	5.9	89	1 033	142.4	14.9	14	58	6.4	0.7
Thousand Oaks	202	1 997	6 480.3	96.3	504	7 185	1 706.4	153.1	145	731	114.8	16.5
Torrance	618	7 802	14 366.0	405.3	794	12 773	3 023.3	265.0	303	1 890	293.5	41.4
Tracy	30	299	219.5	9.7	196	2 464	401.0	38.4	34	115	15.8	1.9
Tulare	40	478	135.9	12.4	154	2 095	315.5	35.4	24	73	10.0	1.0
Turlock	53	409	166.4	12.5	166	1 898	352.6	34.6	33	128	21.5	2.3
Tustin	232	3 233	2 236.2	139.6	235	4 916	1 691.7	138.3	126	652	109.6	17.7
Union City	179	4 640	2 722.5	186.2	88	2 227	510.9	49.6	24	84	15.5	2.1
Upland	108	579	191.3	16.0	224	2 684	528.4	54.3	89	513	44.9	9.3
Vacaville	35	392	110.2	9.9	302	3 830	701.5	67.0	80	312	43.2	6.2
Vallejo	32	387	220.4	12.8	279	4 187	791.0	83.2	68	317	29.8	4.6
Victorville	29	227	63.6	8.3	304	4 766	839.9	80.6	44	221	24.2	5.1
Visalia	137	1 344	1 050.8	44.4	436	6 124	1 042.9	100.7	97	406	52.8	7.9
Vista	110	1 592	426.5	48.7	233	3 212	665.6	61.5	105	590	63.3	9.0
Walnut	247	1 212	1 278.7	33.7	60	553	91.4	9.9	18	106	15.1	3.2

1. Establishments with payroll.

City	Professional, Scientific, and Technical Services, 1997[1]				Manufacturing, 1997				Accommodation and Foodservices, 1997			
	Number of Establishments	Number of Employees	Receipts (mil dol)	Annual Payroll (mil dol)	Number of Establishments	Number of Employees	Receipts (mil dol)	Annual Payroll (mil dol)	Number of Establishments	Number of Employees	Sales (mil dol)	Annual Payroll (mil dol)
	84	85	86	87	88	89	90	91	92	93	94	95
CALIFORNIA—Cont'd												
Pomona	92	555	41.7	16.3	253	9 792	1 551.4	301.9	165	2 603	94.5	23.8
Porterville	38	113	9.0	2.2	35	1 045	161.4	28.1	79	1 143	35.4	8.0
Poway	97	366	51.4	15.6	52	1 397	227.6	41.2	80	1 086	39.5	10.2
Rancho Cucamonga	200	955	100.1	33.7	243	9 913	2 009.1	311.7	153	D	D	D
Rancho Palos Verdes	86	228	25.4	10.8	NA	NA	NA	NA	34	694	26.2	6.4
Redding	261	1 519	115.4	48.6	110	1 351	166.2	38.0	254	3 849	120.5	31.6
Redlands	122	656	56.6	22.4	54	1 803	196.1	41.3	119	1 865	59.1	16.1
Redondo Beach	197	4 408	740.9	278.7	40	D	D	D	161	3 122	126.1	34.8
Redwood City	301	3 687	552.7	232.1	98	4 606	930.1	238.6	173	3 138	130.4	35.2
Rialto	28	164	9.5	3.6	66	1 935	299.0	50.2	64	1 152	32.5	8.0
Richmond	115	923	89.0	43.9	137	4 640	2 979.0	207.8	83	947	29.8	7.4
Riverside	466	3 195	333.6	101.4	289	10 901	1 687.2	322.4	397	6 281	208.3	56.7
Rocklin	40	149	17.7	5.7	32	798	216.0	26.7	51	1 053	29.7	8.2
Rohnert Park	53	429	27.5	32.6	48	781	136.2	27.6	74	1 792	60.0	16.4
Rosemead	48	343	21.2	3.7	82	1 759	149.6	38.1	103	1 159	43.0	10.1
Roseville	188	1 357	132.6	55.8	57	D	D	D	167	3 185	102.0	27.2
Sacramento	1 456	11 899	1 355.5	544.8	423	15 763	3 582.7	579.1	877	14 847	528.8	142.9
Salinas	201	1 078	89.1	35.0	97	2 752	641.6	96.0	226	3 118	105.3	27.2
San Bernardino	264	1 877	176.7	66.1	150	4 140	589.5	106.1	322	5 345	177.5	47.7
San Bruno	69	394	41.9	20.0	NA	NA	NA	NA	59	971	38.1	10.2
San Buenaventura (Ventura)	389	2 574	234.3	91.6	157	3 126	374.7	90.9	251	4 544	166.4	47.0
San Carlos	132	805	66.7	27.8	148	3 712	561.6	144.4	83	755	32.0	9.1
San Clemente	157	767	107.0	31.3	91	1 452	189.3	49.3	117	1 269	56.8	14.3
San Diego	4 584	46 351	5 780.7	2 278.2	1 444	65 599	14 315.4	2 562.7	2 776	61 170	2 607.4	706.7
San Dimas	82	1 542	237.8	62.5	99	2 382	321.7	73.1	59	1 156	39.5	10.0
San Francisco	4 984	58 942	9 016.6	3 517.4	1 247	25 037	3 378.9	642.4	3 258	60 113	3 281.1	955.7
San Gabriel	69	211	15.6	4.0	54	628	36.5	11.0	134	1 535	57.2	15.2
San Jose	2 393	24 773	3 370.6	1 426.5	1 225	86 726	26 808.1	4 263.5	1 478	23 699	981.3	249.5
San Juan Capistrano	107	527	72.7	28.8	44	1 108	176.6	40.7	58	932	33.3	9.1
San Leandro	152	1 720	149.5	65.3	257	9 002	2 260.6	310.7	170	2 256	79.3	22.0
San Luis Obispo	236	1 214	120.9	46.8	78	1 521	195.0	43.9	173	3 535	114.4	30.9
San Marcos	69	320	25.1	9.5	227	5 981	872.1	172.1	92	1 555	48.5	14.0
San Mateo	462	2 997	396.6	179.4	77	531	67.5	18.4	235	3 428	148.7	44.0
San Pablo	15	101	11.6	4.6	NA	NA	NA	NA	60	788	29.4	7.0
San Rafael	433	1 893	231.2	94.6	149	1 809	223.2	58.3	198	2 429	93.4	23.8
San Ramon	282	3 271	558.6	203.7	NA	NA	NA	NA	99	D	D	D
Santa Ana	834	7 761	763.3	311.5	961	30 246	4 052.4	878.1	454	6 519	264.5	67.0
Santa Barbara	520	2 950	363.6	133.9	155	2 204	262.6	68.7	385	7 545	294.4	84.9
Santa Clara	583	10 210	1 378.6	588.8	711	46 029	12 884.0	2 398.9	309	6 513	316.3	82.6
Santa Clarita	140	777	79.4	23.1	66	1 136	164.3	39.5	151	2 432	80.8	22.6
Santa Cruz	239	985	109.7	39.1	122	2 969	866.8	101.2	216	3 339	124.5	33.9
Santa Maria	119	848	49.4	21.1	86	2 608	452.4	63.7	146	2 593	79.1	22.8
Santa Monica	995	7 478	1 124.9	444.8	147	4 065	560.6	141.0	375	9 894	461.9	127.1
Santa Paula	28	162	15.0	5.0	NA	NA	NA	NA	38	396	12.8	3.1
Santa Rosa	539	2 613	251.4	95.4	203	9 598	1 784.1	418.2	339	5 122	175.4	47.2
Santee	39	201	13.1	3.8	127	2 356	216.9	61.1	70	D	D	D
Saratoga	152	572	67.1	27.8	NA	NA	NA	NA	42	548	28.6	7.2
Seaside	14	40	2.9	1.1	NA	NA	NA	NA	54	953	35.8	9.6
Simi Valley	164	1 228	168.2	55.0	157	4 709	1 208.3	170.5	157	2 789	92.7	23.8
South Gate	21	394	78.9	14.1	200	7 603	1 330.9	214.9	98	966	36.6	8.1
South San Francisco	109	2 634	396.7	127.5	193	10 151	2 011.2	485.9	152	3 819	221.9	64.4
Stanton	13	98	6.5	2.9	64	1 251	117.2	31.4	75	785	29.9	7.2
Stockton	336	2 326	197.4	76.7	191	8 783	1 809.8	256.7	398	5 902	197.7	51.5
Suisun City	10	30	2.6	0.5	NA	NA	NA	NA	26	D	D	D
Sunnyvale	521	9 031	1 180.3	550.0	438	43 471	11 208.6	2 683.0	293	4 987	226.5	59.8
Temecula	116	1 009	93.7	26.4	107	4 321	1 113.4	145.6	107	2 274	75.3	20.9
Temple City	33	98	6.2	1.8	NA	NA	NA	NA	46	D	D	D
Thousand Oaks	464	2 279	274.0	105.6	137	4 172	602.0	158.9	234	5 150	179.9	47.7
Torrance	684	4 953	655.1	245.7	328	16 065	4 364.1	719.9	400	7 747	296.4	79.5
Tracy	58	299	19.9	7.4	48	2 527	651.2	77.5	88	1 368	43.8	10.8
Tulare	41	187	13.6	5.8	35	1 797	1 331.8	61.0	73	786	27.3	6.4
Turlock	45	229	19.5	6.3	69	3 636	857.2	93.0	87	1 146	35.9	9.2
Tustin	387	2 569	314.1	113.9	141	6 771	1 446.3	282.5	143	2 877	97.9	26.9
Union City	48	257	24.4	7.8	93	3 696	677.5	128.1	69	648	25.1	5.9
Upland	134	753	43.2	16.4	95	1 510	224.1	40.1	114	D	D	D
Vacaville	72	285	21.6	8.2	58	2 382	355.8	71.1	121	2 260	77.0	20.5
Vallejo	88	458	31.0	13.0	40	682	198.2	23.0	172	2 225	73.3	18.7
Victorville	66	355	26.1	9.4	29	773	216.3	27.8	143	2 588	83.8	22.8
Visalia	202	1 171	229.2	31.9	87	3 873	821.2	106.7	204	3 751	123.5	31.7
Vista	143	668	59.5	19.1	153	5 607	743.9	148.9	127	1 380	48.3	11.7
Walnut	54	347	20.8	6.7	48	665	146.7	23.0	30	D	D	D

1. Firms subject to federal tax.

Table D. Cities — **Entertainment, Health Care, and Other Services**

City	Arts, Entertainment, and Recreation[1], 1997				Health Care and Social Assistance[1], 1997				Other Services[1], 1997			
	Number of Establish-ments	Number of Employees	Receipts (mil dol)	Annual Payroll (mil dol)	Number of Establish-ments	Number of Employees	Receipts (mil dol)	Annual Payroll (mil dol)	Number of Establish-ments	Number of Employees	Receipts (mil dol)	Annual Payroll (mil dol)
	96	97	98	99	100	101	102	103	104	105	106	107
CALIFORNIA—Cont'd												
Pomona	11	365	47.5	12.0	214	2 315	150.9	60.3	141	813	62.7	16.3
Porterville	5	0	0.0	0.0	95	1 040	61.9	20.0	36	149	11.1	2.2
Poway	13	282	12.8	2.6	140	923	74.5	30.1	65	276	21.4	5.3
Rancho Cucamonga	14	298	15.0	4.3	148	1 524	88.7	31.3	131	1 016	63.7	19.7
Rancho Palos Verdes	4	74	5.3	1.1	71	275	24.1	11.4	24	181	15.4	4.8
Redding	22	261	8.5	2.6	413	4 908	355.9	143.8	171	1 064	69.7	18.6
Redlands	11	279	8.7	2.6	172	2 695	158.5	74.1	89	451	27.8	6.6
Redondo Beach	19	247	11.0	3.8	132	995	85.0	36.7	108	913	83.6	26.1
Redwood City	24	618	28.9	9.0	220	2 232	209.9	96.5	135	804	64.8	19.2
Rialto	4	0	0.0	0.0	78	792	33.1	12.3	58	456	53.0	11.2
Richmond	11	90	9.9	3.0	118	1 345	94.2	42.8	108	547	48.4	13.4
Riverside	34	573	23.8	6.5	540	7 486	622.4	244.5	327	2 316	154.0	41.8
Rocklin	7	180	4.3	1.7	45	202	15.0	4.7	36	177	9.7	2.1
Rohnert Park	10	169	6.3	2.3	54	336	18.7	7.4	43	243	15.5	4.8
Rosemead	4	0	0.0	0.0	76	742	44.1	17.6	72	265	15.7	3.6
Roseville	15	205	5.9	1.3	241	2 603	239.9	88.4	107	1 310	132.2	44.7
Sacramento	81	1 285	96.4	18.8	993	10 610	883.1	385.6	572	4 272	335.0	95.0
Salinas	17	247	17.8	2.8	281	2 272	192.3	78.2	155	943	74.0	21.3
San Bernardino	22	406	17.6	4.8	376	3 826	309.9	126.5	211	1 459	96.9	26.2
San Bruno	7	0	0.0	0.0	65	910	103.8	41.3	72	438	36.9	10.2
San Buenaventura (Ventura)	38	474	20.7	5.1	342	2 578	228.6	85.4	162	1 407	132.3	38.8
San Carlos	4	53	1.2	0.6	73	411	30.9	11.1	82	542	47.9	14.8
San Clemente	13	299	11.9	3.2	124	1 032	70.7	28.9	61	335	19.4	5.6
San Diego	267	6 439	479.5	188.9	2 642	28 497	2 464.6	977.0	1 827	12 658	867.9	239.3
San Dimas	15	331	26.4	6.9	78	899	52.2	23.2	62	566	46.6	16.3
San Francisco	332	6 402	632.3	240.8	2 260	14 360	1 209.7	478.5	1 477	8 794	634.9	179.0
San Gabriel	8	44	1.8	0.4	140	1 066	66.2	24.3	78	433	32.4	9.9
San Jose	106	2 907	209.4	82.8	1 701	18 436	1 371.8	567.1	1 146	7 214	546.3	156.7
San Juan Capistrano	14	294	12.9	5.2	71	464	55.4	19.1	43	215	16.3	4.6
San Leandro	11	134	5.2	1.5	198	3 891	242.4	106.2	155	1 057	99.8	29.6
San Luis Obispo	15	121	4.7	1.8	239	2 987	219.4	107.1	92	601	33.5	9.3
San Marcos	15	251	11.1	3.1	66	558	28.3	11.4	97	507	39.9	11.6
San Mateo	39	730	39.1	17.9	343	2 321	179.4	73.0	195	964	67.9	19.8
San Pablo	5	0	0.0	0.0	75	863	60.7	26.7	39	197	12.9	3.3
San Rafael	31	303	23.8	6.0	214	2 269	159.7	72.8	230	1 178	108.8	32.4
San Ramon	12	898	23.1	8.0	153	1 198	109.6	42.4	91	805	61.5	18.4
Santa Ana	28	542	53.0	16.1	677	5 708	426.3	168.0	432	3 105	267.0	79.4
Santa Barbara	43	395	28.3	10.3	416	3 277	286.2	109.5	205	1 130	70.6	20.7
Santa Clara	24	2 699	100.5	28.6	149	2 998	274.6	129.7	229	2 002	206.8	65.9
Santa Clarita	40	369	23.1	8.5	205	1 678	122.1	49.2	146	786	54.5	14.7
Santa Cruz	27	966	35.6	13.1	143	1 195	80.9	28.1	99	522	37.4	10.7
Santa Maria	10	114	4.7	1.0	219	1 706	118.7	45.8	121	750	45.5	12.5
Santa Monica	403	1 697	329.4	170.9	742	5 019	552.4	218.0	300	1 982	135.0	37.9
Santa Paula	1	0	0.0	0.0	33	353	12.0	4.4	28	94	7.5	1.4
Santa Rosa	39	688	36.5	11.7	609	6 325	479.8	208.0	274	1 594	106.0	32.8
Santee	12	207	9.0	2.9	62	401	21.9	9.3	101	517	36.3	10.3
Saratoga	6	95	3.8	1.7	61	410	26.9	10.3	30	215	10.8	4.0
Seaside	3	8	0.4	0.1	14	68	4.1	1.1	48	235	20.6	5.4
Simi Valley	21	555	18.5	5.7	196	1 283	120.4	46.6	130	659	49.5	13.6
South Gate	5	18	1.2	0.1	89	694	46.1	16.9	84	275	22.8	5.0
South San Francisco	13	153	11.0	2.7	105	1 635	163.0	71.8	137	1 472	106.9	33.6
Stanton	7	0	0.0	0.0	25	107	6.2	1.9	67	231	21.6	4.9
Stockton	42	660	22.4	7.2	558	5 597	432.7	184.4	318	1 733	111.6	34.0
Suisun City	4	38	0.5	0.2	27	160	6.3	2.5	18	114	6.7	2.0
Sunnyvale	20	227	12.7	3.3	235	2 474	249.6	80.0	192	1 459	111.7	34.0
Temecula	13	231	9.2	2.9	102	818	59.0	18.1	81	506	35.7	9.6
Temple City	4	10	0.7	0.2	45	712	27.2	11.1	39	202	9.7	3.7
Thousand Oaks	45	272	23.3	10.5	388	4 125	369.8	135.0	154	970	75.8	23.4
Torrance	37	923	53.4	20.3	795	6 134	520.6	221.2	270	1 467	111.8	31.7
Tracy	10	107	4.9	1.1	70	682	35.4	13.4	48	293	14.7	3.9
Tulare	6	0	0.0	0.0	82	638	45.3	14.4	53	232	17.4	4.3
Turlock	13	83	2.2	0.6	121	1 067	70.4	25.4	75	478	27.7	6.9
Tustin	17	721	34.1	9.0	237	2 551	172.9	68.3	95	771	61.9	17.0
Union City	1	0	0.0	0.0	64	550	50.2	15.0	47	496	63.2	13.2
Upland	14	229	11.4	2.5	244	1 644	132.0	57.0	80	410	28.0	7.5
Vacaville	8	188	4.5	1.6	119	1 115	90.6	31.2	84	423	29.2	7.6
Vallejo	15	484	42.4	6.9	215	2 725	232.6	107.0	134	906	54.7	17.6
Victorville	8	215	6.6	2.3	120	1 606	121.4	37.6	82	497	29.4	8.4
Visalia	15	0	0.0	0.0	283	2 532	183.7	77.2	140	877	67.1	17.3
Vista	9	306	18.8	5.5	167	2 233	174.0	61.7	101	594	38.4	11.8
Walnut	5	18	1.7	0.2	48	549	19.6	6.9	50	423	27.9	10.8

1. Firms subject to federal tax.

Table D. Cities — **Federal Funds and City Government Finances**

	Selected federal funds, fiscal 2001[1] (mil dol)									City government finances, 1999						
	Procurement contracts		Grants					Direct payments for individuals		General revenue						
										Intergovernmental			Taxes			
														Per capita[3] (dollars)		
City	Defense	Other	Total[2]	Health and family welfare	Energy and environment	Education	Housing and community development	Educational assistance	Housing assistance	Total (mil dol)	Total (mil dol)	Percent from state government	Total (mil dol)	Total	Property	Sales and gross receipts
	108	109	110	111	112	113	114	115	116	117	118	119	120	121	122	123
CALIFORNIA—Cont'd																
Pomona	32.6	1.6	13.7	2.8	2.3	1.9	4.0	29.7	10.6	112.3	29.3	48.1	57.8	426	174	217
Porterville	0.7	0.8	6.1	3.0	0.1	1.1	1.3	0.0	1.2	NA	NA	NA	NA	NA	NA	NA
Poway	3.3	1.3	3.3	0.3	0.0	2.1	0.0	0.2	0.9	63.8	4.3	92.7	29.1	593	384	134
Rancho Cucamonga	7.4	17.8	1.5	0.0	0.0	0.4	1.1	3.8	1.2	100.2	9.6	87.8	59.4	495	254	189
Rancho Palos Verdes	0.8	0.1	0.7	0.0	0.1	0.6	0.0	0.0	0.0	NA	NA	NA	NA	NA	NA	NA
Redding	2.4	4.8	15.4	6.9	0.0	3.4	1.5	6.4	8.0	87.9	16.2	38.4	30.4	390	141	209
Redlands	21.3	8.8	6.0	0.0	1.6	0.9	0.3	2.3	2.7	47.5	6.1	84.8	21.6	321	147	114
Redondo Beach	254.5	63.2	7.0	0.3	0.0	0.0	0.9	0.0	7.6	72.7	8.7	76.0	34.2	543	191	284
Redwood City	11.0	4.0	14.3	1.9	0.0	2.2	7.1	0.6	4.6	93.0	16.4	60.0	43.1	587	169	330
Rialto	0.2	0.1	1.7	0.0	0.0	0.0	1.5	0.0	4.0	55.4	7.8	75.1	20.9	249	121	93
Richmond	4.8	4.8	5.4	0.8	0.3	0.0	2.1	0.0	42.8	119.5	20.7	60.4	68.7	735	363	318
Riverside	8.6	4.1	79.4	13.6	3.9	6.0	21.1	27.6	72.2	211.8	31.8	64.3	84.7	323	90	203
Rocklin	0.3	0.0	0.0	0.0	0.0	0.0	0.0	4.7	3.1	28.8	2.9	70.2	18.9	611	105	127
Rohnert Park	7.1	0.4	4.8	0.1	0.0	3.6	0.0	4.2	0.4	31.6	3.2	96.9	10.9	265	46	180
Rosemead	5.0	0.0	1.3	0.0	0.1	0.0	1.3	0.6	0.0	NA	NA	NA	NA	NA	NA	NA
Roseville	3.4	2.8	1.5	0.0	0.0	0.8	0.5	0.0	3.4	139.4	10.0	59.6	55.4	773	114	405
Sacramento	873.1	104.5	6 410.5	2 568.4	239.2	968.8	95.3	164.8	160.4	495.5	95.0	81.0	198.3	491	160	274
Salinas	1.1	2.8	22.7	6.3	0.0	2.6	3.9	5.5	3.0	79.0	16.7	64.7	46.1	379	87	210
San Bernardino	57.2	7.0	75.1	11.9	0.0	8.0	18.7	28.2	36.8	177.0	30.6	61.7	74.5	400	123	231
San Bruno	33.1	1.1	20.7	0.0	0.0	0.8	0.0	1.7	0.0	NA	NA	NA	NA	NA	NA	NA
San Buenaventura (Ventura)	0.0	0.0	0.0	0.0	0.0	0.0	0.0	0.0	0.0	86.5	16.5	88.1	39.7	403	96	248
San Carlos	24.6	0.2	28.6	0.1	0.0	0.2	0.0	0.0	0.0	NA	NA	NA	NA	NA	NA	NA
San Clemente	11.0	1.2	0.6	0.0	0.5	0.0	0.0	0.0	0.5	NA	NA	NA	NA	NA	NA	NA
San Diego	2 332.3	480.0	1 016.3	615.4	17.3	35.0	29.1	66.7	197.9	1 483.0	413.1	27.3	508.9	417	127	242
San Dimas	2.0	0.5	0.0	0.0	0.0	0.0	0.0	0.4	0.8	NA	NA	NA	NA	NA	NA	NA
San Francisco	321.6	216.3	815.4	531.5	5.4	28.4	27.8	83.9	239.9	4 043.9	1 520.9	82.3	1 375.0	1 844	726	633
San Gabriel	7.9	0.0	0.5	0.2	0.0	0.0	0.0	0.0	0.2	NA	NA	NA	NA	NA	NA	NA
San Jose	125.5	57.6	88.0	15.6	2.3	21.7	18.3	27.2	88.2	1 094.9	136.6	49.6	522.3	606	199	260
San Juan Capistrano	5.1	2.5	0.3	0.0	0.0	0.0	0.0	0.0	0.0	NA	NA	NA	NA	NA	NA	NA
San Leandro	15.7	24.1	3.5	1.9	0.1	0.0	0.7	0.0	3.3	78.5	6.7	90.5	45.9	617	119	389
San Luis Obispo	6.7	0.6	24.0	15.1	0.0	2.2	0.0	13.5	13.3	NA	NA	NA	NA	NA	NA	NA
San Marcos	5.2	1.2	7.9	4.3	0.3	3.1	0.0	7.1	0.0	49.1	4.2	88.5	30.0	606	286	213
San Mateo	5.8	3.8	12.0	4.6	0.0	0.2	1.2	1.4	18.7	89.8	13.0	57.4	50.1	549	198	226
San Pablo	0.0	0.1	4.0	0.5	0.0	3.1	0.0	2.0	4.0	22.7	2.4	82.3	12.0	447	210	132
San Rafael	0.6	4.8	5.7	2.4	0.0	0.9	0.2	1.1	5.5	51.1	4.7	95.8	30.2	592	176	343
San Ramon	11.7	5.4	0.7	0.1	0.6	0.0	0.0	0.0	0.1	44.0	3.7	90.7	28.4	670	220	340
Santa Ana	42.6	79.5	61.0	13.9	2.4	5.2	9.8	7.1	35.0	257.2	66.7	62.0	108.5	355	111	221
Santa Barbara	103.7	16.6	116.1	19.7	6.1	2.7	4.2	18.4	37.0	133.4	14.8	63.9	53.4	617	192	400
Santa Clara	164.8	8.7	117.9	2.0	1.4	1.7	5.1	5.1	28.3	173.8	10.3	81.5	85.9	856	294	519
Santa Clarita	0.2	0.2	9.2	0.0	0.0	0.0	0.0	0.0	0.0	81.1	27.0	69.2	43.9	345	38	245
Santa Cruz	7.9	1.4	51.7	16.6	3.5	2.6	1.2	9.0	27.1	NA	NA	NA	NA	NA	NA	NA
Santa Maria	2.8	2.7	4.1	0.0	0.0	0.5	2.4	3.5	2.0	57.9	10.6	83.7	23.2	341	45	206
Santa Monica	86.6	5.6	56.5	41.7	0.6	2.4	3.7	7.8	17.2	267.0	43.1	38.0	125.0	1 397	278	818
Santa Paula	1.8	0.3	0.7	0.0	0.0	0.6	0.0	0.0	5.7	NA	NA	NA	NA	NA	NA	NA
Santa Rosa	3.9	3.3	31.4	9.3	1.1	2.1	1.3	5.4	18.2	160.6	29.4	40.6	56.8	448	91	300
Santee	20.4	0.3	0.7	0.0	0.0	0.3	0.3	0.0	3.8	27.7	5.1	76.0	16.0	276	133	99
Saratoga	0.0	0.3	1.7	0.0	1.7	0.0	0.0	1.5	2.2	NA	NA	NA	NA	NA	NA	NA
Seaside	0.6	1.1	3.9	0.0	0.0	3.0	0.4	2.9	2.7	NA	NA	NA	NA	NA	NA	NA
Simi Valley	19.8	1.5	0.4	0.0	0.0	0.0	0.4	0.2	0.3	83.4	20.1	59.5	35.9	325	114	134
South Gate	0.3	0.0	2.8	0.0	0.0	0.0	2.6	0.7	10.9	51.5	13.1	59.7	20.6	233	70	137
South San Francisco	2.4	1.9	11.1	7.0	0.0	0.0	0.9	0.0	3.1	86.2	13.5	34.8	34.2	582	211	318
Stanton	0.0	0.0	0.1	0.0	0.0	0.0	0.0	0.0	0.0	NA	NA	NA	NA	NA	NA	NA
Stockton	28.5	20.0	66.0	18.2	9.7	3.7	11.3	20.6	16.9	195.6	37.9	55.5	79.8	332	65	229
Suisun City	0.8	0.2	1.9	0.9	0.0	0.2	0.0	2.6	8.1	NA	NA	NA	NA	NA	NA	NA
Sunnyvale	2 291.6	12.2	13.8	6.0	0.2	0.1	4.4	0.2	7.2	167.9	22.6	90.9	64.0	502	137	322
Temecula	2.4	1.1	0.6	0.2	0.2	0.2	0.0	0.0	0.2	44.3	6.4	48.8	29.6	668	169	318
Temple City	0.0	0.0	0.2	0.0	0.0	0.2	0.0	0.0	0.0	NA	NA	NA	NA	NA	NA	NA
Thousand Oaks	51.5	2.4	8.8	0.2	0.9	1.4	1.3	1.2	2.5	106.2	13.9	63.1	54.5	465	135	232
Torrance	155.1	18.6	33.7	18.6	7.7	0.9	0.0	7.1	11.7	172.1	28.2	80.4	102.3	744	103	573
Tracy	5.8	0.1	3.3	0.0	0.0	0.2	0.0	0.0	3.7	80.5	23.5	16.2	14.3	301	93	174
Tulare	0.0	7.3	1.8	0.5	0.0	0.3	0.8	0.1	8.5	NA	NA	NA	NA	NA	NA	NA
Turlock	0.0	9.0	4.6	0.0	0.0	0.5	1.4	6.6	0.6	33.9	9.4	47.5	13.4	266	41	167
Tustin	8.3	4.1	1.3	0.2	0.0	0.0	0.6	0.0	1.8	48.1	13.3	38.0	27.7	430	127	270
Union City	0.9	12.7	13.7	12.5	0.0	0.4	0.7	0.0	1.1	43.7	8.4	58.7	23.3	364	153	143
Upland	0.1	12.8	1.4	0.0	0.0	0.9	0.4	0.0	6.6	48.5	7.0	71.4	18.3	270	129	102
Vacaville	0.4	7.6	1.8	0.0	0.0	0.2	0.6	0.0	5.9	86.2	11.8	55.4	44.3	531	242	135
Vallejo	1.6	0.7	2.7	0.0	0.0	0.2	1.6	0.5	20.0	120.0	11.8	100.0	34.8	312	73	207
Victorville	0.5	135.5	6.8	0.0	0.0	0.2	0.6	6.5	3.5	37.3	4.9	82.3	19.3	281	58	210
Visalia	2.7	0.0	33.6	9.9	0.0	2.2	1.8	11.8	4.1	89.1	12.9	80.0	28.0	314	96	187
Vista	19.6	1.1	3.0	0.8	0.0	0.3	1.7	1.9	0.2	64.9	9.0	78.4	31.7	391	132	168
Walnut	1.7	0.0	0.9	0.0	0.0	0.6	0.0	6.7	0.0	NA	NA	NA	NA	NA	NA	NA

1. October 1, 2000 to September 30, 2001.   2. Includes program categories not shown separately. State totals include additional categories not allocated by city.   3. Based on population estimated as of July 1 of the year shown.

Table D. Cities — **City Government Finances**

	City government finances, 1999 (cont'd)												
	General expenditure												
City	Per capita[1] (dollars)			Percent of total for —									
	Total (mil dol)	Total	Capital outlays	Public welfare	Highways	Parking facilities	Education	Health and hospitals	Police protection	Sewerage and sanitation	Parks and recreation	Housing and community development	Interest on debt
	124	125	126	127	128	129	130	131	132	133	134	135	136
CALIFORNIA—Cont'd													
Pomona	113.4	836	101	0.0	9.0	0.2	0.0	0.3	26.3	8.7	3.9	18.7	10.0
Porterville	NA	NA	NA	NA	NA	NA	NA	NA	NA	NA	NA	NA	NA
Poway	58.1	1 183	128	0.0	7.8	0.0	0.0	1.6	15.5	9.1	6.7	13.4	25.2
Rancho Cucamonga	82.0	683	58	0.0	15.8	0.0	0.0	0.0	15.0	0.0	5.6	16.2	16.7
Rancho Palos Verdes	NA	NA	NA	NA	NA	NA	NA	NA	NA	NA	NA	NA	NA
Redding	86.8	1 114	261	0.0	4.2	0.4	0.0	0.4	17.4	16.3	3.6	14.3	5.5
Redlands	45.6	678	43	0.0	8.8	0.0	0.0	3.5	21.4	19.6	4.0	1.5	13.6
Redondo Beach	67.1	1 064	26	0.0	4.4	0.0	0.0	5.0	22.5	1.6	8.3	9.8	3.9
Redwood City	89.9	1 224	344	0.0	22.3	0.4	0.0	0.3	18.3	10.2	5.1	4.5	3.6
Rialto	57.2	681	69	0.0	9.5	0.0	0.0	3.7	36.6	4.8	5.9	5.0	9.4
Richmond	129.3	1 383	295	0.0	5.4	0.0	0.0	0.0	24.3	4.3	4.1	9.2	4.9
Riverside	203.6	777	139	0.0	15.3	0.0	0.0	0.7	22.9	9.8	6.5	5.8	14.1
Rocklin	27.4	887	106	0.0	5.6	0.0	0.0	0.5	16.3	0.0	19.1	2.2	14.7
Rohnert Park	44.4	1 082	162	0.0	6.2	0.0	0.0	1.4	16.0	31.8	9.0	8.1	4.2
Rosemead	NA	NA	NA	NA	NA	NA	NA	NA	NA	NA	NA	NA	NA
Roseville	107.4	1 499	404	0.0	13.4	0.0	0.0	0.2	11.0	24.5	9.9	4.0	8.6
Sacramento	490.8	1 214	378	0.0	10.4	1.8	0.0	3.1	18.6	10.9	9.4	3.2	6.1
Salinas	76.1	627	115	0.0	14.6	0.0	0.0	2.9	26.7	3.6	13.5	3.5	6.3
San Bernardino	185.7	996	180	0.0	6.3	0.1	0.0	0.8	20.6	13.8	2.9	13.2	16.9
San Bruno	NA	NA	NA	NA	NA	NA	NA	NA	NA	NA	NA	NA	NA
San Buenaventura (Ventura)	98.8	1 005	302	0.0	19.7	0.2	0.0	0.1	17.2	15.9	9.7	3.0	4.8
San Carlos	NA	NA	NA	NA	NA	NA	NA	NA	NA	NA	NA	NA	NA
San Clemente	NA	NA	NA	NA	NA	NA	NA	NA	NA	NA	NA	NA	NA
San Diego	1 434.7	1 175	277	0.0	3.4	0.3	0.0	0.3	16.3	26.6	7.4	7.3	14.6
San Dimas	NA	NA	NA	NA	NA	NA	NA	NA	NA	NA	NA	NA	NA
San Francisco	4 578.2	6 139	1 918	8.5	3.6	0.1	2.3	17.3	6.7	2.8	5.7	2.7	6.6
San Gabriel	NA	NA	NA	NA	NA	NA	NA	NA	NA	NA	NA	NA	NA
San Jose	1 083.3	1 258	269	0.0	6.5	0.4	0.0	0.2	14.3	17.5	9.8	14.3	9.4
San Juan Capistrano	NA	NA	NA	NA	NA	NA	NA	NA	NA	NA	NA	NA	NA
San Leandro	78.0	1 048	76	0.0	11.0	0.4	0.0	0.2	18.7	16.1	8.2	4.8	3.6
San Luis Obispo	NA	NA	NA	NA	NA	NA	NA	NA	NA	NA	NA	NA	NA
San Marcos	56.4	1 137	388	0.0	10.8	0.0	0.0	0.0	10.8	0.0	4.3	19.9	16.2
San Mateo	86.5	948	248	0.0	11.6	4.2	0.0	0.0	18.2	12.7	10.1	7.6	3.8
San Pablo	19.3	715	203	0.0	16.3	0.0	0.0	0.0	31.1	0.0	3.2	21.2	13.1
San Rafael	51.0	998	139	0.0	15.3	0.0	0.0	5.3	22.3	0.0	11.6	6.9	2.9
San Ramon	40.9	963	200	0.0	19.3	0.0	0.0	0.2	11.2	0.3	13.5	11.9	13.8
Santa Ana	272.8	892	165	0.0	3.3	0.4	0.0	1.4	25.5	6.3	4.6	11.8	8.4
Santa Barbara	113.2	1 307	192	0.0	8.4	2.1	0.0	0.4	16.1	5.1	9.9	10.1	5.6
Santa Clara	163.6	1 630	439	0.0	7.7	0.6	0.0	0.2	13.3	16.0	5.1	9.6	7.9
Santa Clarita	73.2	576	150	0.0	7.5	0.0	0.0	0.0	15.6	2.2	17.3	11.1	2.0
Santa Cruz	NA	NA	NA	NA	NA	NA	NA	NA	NA	NA	NA	NA	NA
Santa Maria	60.1	882	264	0.0	14.4	0.0	0.0	0.0	17.0	37.3	4.3	1.3	7.0
Santa Monica	212.6	2 374	388	0.0	3.6	0.6	0.0	0.4	17.8	14.1	6.9	8.8	1.7
Santa Paula	NA	NA	NA	NA	NA	NA	NA	NA	NA	NA	NA	NA	NA
Santa Rosa	143.0	1 127	205	0.0	11.6	1.6	0.0	0.4	18.1	24.5	8.6	3.4	9.8
Santee	26.9	466	95	0.0	15.5	0.0	0.0	3.9	24.4	0.0	4.8	11.1	4.0
Saratoga	NA	NA	NA	NA	NA	NA	NA	NA	NA	NA	NA	NA	NA
Seaside	NA	NA	NA	NA	NA	NA	NA	NA	NA	NA	NA	NA	NA
Simi Valley	76.0	688	162	0.0	14.5	0.0	0.0	0.4	24.4	14.3	2.5	11.5	11.6
South Gate	46.7	528	39	0.0	19.3	0.0	0.0	0.0	30.7	6.6	6.9	15.1	7.2
South San Francisco	90.5	1 538	571	0.0	1.4	0.3	0.0	2.1	12.3	19.0	10.0	8.8	2.2
Stanton	NA	NA	NA	NA	NA	NA	NA	NA	NA	NA	NA	NA	NA
Stockton	239.1	996	275	0.0	7.3	0.1	0.0	0.0	21.0	32.7	3.7	5.9	5.8
Suisun City	NA	NA	NA	NA	NA	NA	NA	NA	NA	NA	NA	NA	NA
Sunnyvale	168.7	1 323	140	0.0	6.2	0.1	0.0	0.2	12.7	31.7	7.9	6.5	4.1
Temecula	55.0	1 242	694	0.0	35.9	0.0	0.0	0.1	9.6	0.0	9.4	25.1	1.9
Temple City	NA	NA	NA	NA	NA	NA	NA	NA	NA	NA	NA	NA	NA
Thousand Oaks	104.2	889	164	0.0	16.7	0.0	0.0	0.1	11.7	19.0	2.1	21.3	4.6
Torrance	147.7	1 074	12	0.0	5.8	0.0	0.0	3.6	25.0	4.7	6.3	5.6	6.0
Tracy	43.8	920	111	0.0	12.3	0.7	0.0	0.5	16.8	21.5	10.9	7.8	7.8
Tulare	NA	NA	NA	NA	NA	NA	NA	NA	NA	NA	NA	NA	NA
Turlock	35.0	697	207	0.0	11.6	0.0	0.0	0.4	32.5	20.3	4.0	5.8	1.9
Tustin	48.1	747	207	0.0	21.1	0.0	0.0	0.2	27.5	0.0	8.0	8.5	11.6
Union City	40.0	624	150	0.0	10.6	0.0	0.0	0.2	26.5	0.0	8.9	16.2	5.3
Upland	53.7	792	112	0.0	7.2	0.0	0.0	0.4	19.0	24.2	6.2	7.7	14.4
Vacaville	75.1	901	181	0.0	2.9	0.0	0.0	3.9	17.7	9.9	9.1	27.6	7.7
Vallejo	125.2	1 123	116	0.0	3.7	0.0	0.0	0.2	17.2	10.0	21.9	19.4	11.2
Victorville	33.9	492	10	0.0	7.4	0.0	0.0	1.3	20.5	26.8	6.0	2.0	7.8
Visalia	85.8	961	245	0.0	2.7	0.0	0.0	0.0	18.1	15.7	6.7	7.0	6.5
Vista	72.0	890	304	0.0	12.8	0.0	0.0	3.4	13.0	9.7	6.7	26.0	8.2
Walnut	NA	NA	NA	NA	NA	NA	NA	NA	NA	NA	NA	NA	NA

1. Based on population estimated as of July 1 of the year shown.

Table D. Cities — City Government Finances, City Government Employment, and Climate

City	City government finances, 1999 (cont'd) Debt outstanding			City government employment, 2001	Climate[2] Average daily temperature (degrees Fahrenheit) Mean		Limits		Annual precipitation (inches)	Heating degree days	Cooling degree days
	Total (mil dol)	Per capita[1] (dollars)	Percent utility		January	July	January[3]	July[4]			
	137	138	139	140	141	142	143	144	145	146	147
CALIFORNIA—Cont'd											
Pomona	213.7	1 575	3.2	730	54.3	74.6	40.7	90.4	16.62	1 713	1 273
Porterville	NA	NA	NA	NA	46.4	81.8	36.4	98.3	11.03	2 374	1 998
Poway	186.1	3 790	3.4	NA	56.6	72.5	44.6	83.4	12.80	1 400	1 110
Rancho Cucamonga	231.4	1 928	0.0	432	56.0	78.6	44.5	94.8	15.63	1 478	1 922
Rancho Palos Verdes	NA	NA	NA	NA	56.1	69.7	45.3	78.8	13.57	1 568	794
Redding	218.4	2 802	71.8	796	45.5	81.5	35.7	98.3	33.30	2 855	1 797
Redlands	99.9	1 484	23.4	499	52.8	78.4	39.6	95.8	12.80	1 875	1 673
Redondo Beach	47.2	749	0.0	NA	56.8	69.1	47.8	75.3	12.01	1 458	727
Redwood City	71.8	977	0.0	NA	48.7	68.7	38.9	83.4	19.74	2 563	486
Rialto	80.2	956	0.0	374	53.6	79.4	40.3	97.0	15.42	1 719	1 804
Richmond	93.6	1 002	0.0	951	49.9	63.2	42.0	71.0	22.20	2 574	199
Riverside	675.1	2 575	40.5	1 913	53.9	77.9	40.5	94.4	9.58	1 678	1 651
Rocklin	71.4	2 313	0.0	NA	NA	NA	NA	NA	NA	NA	NA
Rohnert Park	47.9	1 169	0.0	226	47.4	67.6	37.0	83.8	30.30	2 883	489
Rosemead	NA	NA	NA	NA	55.7	75.2	41.7	89.2	17.90	1 433	1 427
Roseville	195.4	2 729	21.5	NA	45.6	77.2	37.7	94.2	23.91	2 683	1 422
Sacramento	321.0	794	1.0	4 264	45.2	75.7	37.7	93.2	17.52	2 749	1 237
Salinas	96.9	798	0.0	760	50.5	62.5	40.0	71.1	12.44	2 964	181
San Bernardino	421.3	2 260	1.9	1 811	53.6	79.4	40.3	97.0	15.42	1 719	1 804
San Bruno	NA	NA	NA	NA	48.7	62.7	41.8	71.6	19.70	3 016	145
San Buenaventura (Ventura)	58.3	592	27.0	690	55.3	66.1	44.2	74.4	14.38	1 992	416
San Carlos	NA	NA	NA	NA	48.7	68.7	38.9	83.4	19.74	2 563	486
San Clemente	NA	NA	NA	NA	53.7	67.2	41.5	75.8	12.19	2 157	493
San Diego	2 392.1	1 960	0.0	11 775	57.4	71.0	48.9	76.2	9.90	1 256	984
San Dimas	NA	NA	NA	NA	54.3	74.6	40.7	90.4	16.62	1 713	1 273
San Francisco	6 660.2	8 931	3.5	29 286	51.1	59.1	45.8	64.6	19.71	3 005	65
San Gabriel	NA	NA	NA	NA	55.7	75.2	41.7	89.2	17.90	1 433	1 427
San Jose	2 096.3	2 434	0.0	7 185	49.4	69.5	40.6	82.4	14.42	2 387	594
San Juan Capistrano	NA	NA	NA	NA	53.7	67.2	41.5	75.8	12.19	2 157	493
San Leandro	35.0	470	0.0	454	49.9	62.1	43.3	70.0	24.30	2 902	115
San Luis Obispo	NA	NA	NA	NA	52.5	65.2	41.5	78.1	23.46	2 498	335
San Marcos	207.6	4 187	0.0	NA	55.2	70.5	43.1	81.3	13.04	1 802	868
San Mateo	87.2	955	0.0	684	48.7	68.7	38.9	83.4	19.74	2 563	486
San Pablo	53.7	1 992	0.0	NA	49.9	63.2	42.0	71.0	22.20	2 574	199
San Rafael	57.2	1 121	0.0	NA	48.8	67.7	40.6	81.6	35.74	2 581	449
San Ramon	70.2	1 653	0.0	NA	46.1	71.6	35.5	89.8	14.21	2 909	780
Santa Ana	414.0	1 353	4.8	2 288	57.4	72.6	45.6	82.6	12.27	1 238	1 175
Santa Barbara	118.1	1 363	46.6	1 233	52.0	65.4	40.3	73.9	16.25	2 438	289
Santa Clara	407.2	4 057	55.2	1 072	49.4	69.5	40.6	82.4	14.42	2 387	594
Santa Clarita	22.7	179	0.0	340	54.5	75.6	41.3	90.2	15.87	1 609	1 424
Santa Cruz	NA	NA	NA	NA	49.9	63.5	38.8	75.7	28.99	2 969	148
Santa Maria	69.2	1 016	0.0	NA	51.1	63.1	38.3	73.3	12.36	2 984	169
Santa Monica	74.3	829	0.0	1 792	57.2	65.5	49.6	69.3	13.21	1 819	446
Santa Paula	NA	NA	NA	NA	54.6	67.8	41.2	80.8	17.39	2 039	569
Santa Rosa	305.8	2 410	0.0	1 214	47.4	67.6	37.0	83.8	30.30	2 883	489
Santee	12.5	217	0.0	NA	56.6	72.5	44.6	83.4	12.80	1 400	1 110
Saratoga	NA	NA	NA	NA	49.4	69.5	40.6	82.4	14.42	2 387	594
Seaside	NA	NA	NA	NA	51.7	60.0	43.3	68.1	18.72	3 125	55
Simi Valley	152.6	1 382	0.0	630	54.6	67.8	41.2	80.8	17.39	2 039	569
South Gate	58.2	659	23.3	393	58.3	74.3	48.9	84.0	14.77	1 154	1 537
South San Francisco	48.9	831	2.2	NA	48.7	62.7	41.8	71.6	19.70	3 016	145
Stanton	NA	NA	NA	NA	57.4	72.6	45.6	82.6	12.27	1 238	1 175
Stockton	264.3	1 100	6.2	2 021	45.0	77.7	37.0	94.4	13.95	2 707	1 470
Suisun City	NA	NA	NA	NA	NA	NA	NA	NA	NA	NA	NA
Sunnyvale	70.1	550	0.0	893	49.4	69.5	40.6	82.4	14.42	2 387	594
Temecula	25.1	566	0.0	NA	53.9	75.4	40.5	92.1	11.83	1 747	1 339
Temple City	NA	NA	NA	NA	55.7	75.2	41.7	89.2	17.90	1 433	1 427
Thousand Oaks	134.4	1 147	0.0	524	55.3	66.1	44.2	74.4	14.38	1 992	416
Torrance	158.0	1 149	5.4	1 571	56.1	69.7	45.3	78.8	13.57	1 568	794
Tracy	91.7	1 925	2.7	NA	45.2	76.2	36.7	92.1	11.85	2 659	1 321
Tulare	NA	NA	NA	NA	45.4	80.4	37.0	96.0	10.15	2 511	1 762
Turlock	12.2	242	0.0	NA	45.6	77.1	37.4	94.2	12.10	2 605	1 401
Tustin	104.6	1 624	9.1	NA	54.5	71.6	41.4	83.7	11.81	1 784	973
Union City	50.2	783	0.0	NA	49.0	66.7	41.1	76.1	13.73	2 578	410
Upland	86.3	1 273	0.0	NA	54.3	74.6	40.7	90.4	16.62	1 713	1 273
Vacaville	170.9	2 050	0.0	699	45.2	75.2	36.1	94.1	23.84	2 764	1 154
Vallejo	278.3	2 496	18.7	591	49.9	63.2	42.0	71.0	22.20	2 574	199
Victorville	68.0	987	0.0	NA	44.2	79.3	30.0	97.4	5.51	3 127	1 525
Visalia	94.5	1 058	0.0	560	45.4	80.4	37.0	96.0	10.15	2 511	1 762
Vista	91.1	1 126	0.0	328	55.2	70.5	43.1	81.3	13.04	1 802	868
Walnut	NA	NA	NA	NA	54.3	74.6	40.7	90.4	16.62	1 713	1 273

1. Based on the population estimated as of July 1 of the year shown.   2. Represents normal values based on the 30-year period, 1961–1990.   3. Average daily minimum.   4. Average daily maximum.

Table D. Cities — Land Area and Population

STATE Place code	City	Land area, 2000[1] (sq km)	Total persons	Rank	Per square kilometer	Total persons 1990	Percent change 1990–2000	Total persons 1980	Percent change 1980–1990	White	Black	Am. Indian, Alaska Native	Asian and Pacific Islander	Other race	His-panic[2]	Non-His-panic White
		1	2	3	4	5	6	7	8	9	10	11	12	13	14	15
	CALIFORNIA—Cont'd															
06 83346	Walnut Creek	51.6	64 296	423	1 246.0	60 569	6.2	53 643	12.9	86.8	1.5	0.9	11.0	3.2	6.0	80.6
06 83668	Watsonville	16.4	44 265	693	2 699.1	31 099	42.3	23 543	32.1	47.3	1.1	2.6	4.6	49.9	75.1	19.4
06 84200	West Covina	41.7	105 080	220	2 519.9	96 226	9.2	80 291	19.8	47.5	7.1	1.4	24.8	24.4	45.7	23.0
06 84410	West Hollywood	4.9	35 716	873	7 289.0	36 118	-1.1	35 703	1.2	89.4	3.7	0.9	5.0	4.6	8.8	81.4
06 84550	Westminster	26.2	88 207	282	3 366.7	78 293	12.7	71 133	10.1	49.0	1.4	1.4	40.2	12.1	21.7	36.2
06 84816	West Sacramento	54.2	31 615	988	583.3	28 898	9.4	10 875	165.7	70.2	3.3	3.3	10.9	19.7	30.0	54.6
06 85292	Whittier	37.9	83 680	305	2 207.9	77 671	7.7	69 717	11.4	67.6	1.6	2.1	4.6	29.5	55.9	37.6
06 86328	Woodland	26.7	49 151	615	1 840.9	40 230	22.2	30 235	33.1	71.0	1.7	2.6	5.5	24.4	38.8	53.0
06 86832	Yorba Linda	50.2	58 918	479	1 173.7	52 422	12.4	28 254	85.5	84.2	1.5	1.0	12.8	3.9	10.3	74.8
06 86972	Yuba City	24.3	36 758	843	1 512.7	27 385	34.2	18 731	46.2	70.7	3.4	3.2	11.2	16.6	24.6	59.0
06 87042	Yucaipa	71.9	41 207	743	573.1	32 819	25.6	23 345	40.6	88.3	1.2	2.2	2.1	9.8	18.3	76.7
08 00000	**COLORADO**	268 627.2	4 301 261	X	16.0	3 294 473	30.6	2 889 735	14.0	85.2	4.4	1.9	3.0	8.5	17.1	74.5
08 03455	Arvada	84.6	102 153	231	1 207.5	89 261	14.4	84 619	5.5	93.1	1.0	1.4	3.0	4.1	9.8	85.5
08 04000	Aurora	369.1	276 393	61	748.8	222 103	24.4	158 588	40.1	72.3	15.0	1.8	5.7	9.9	19.8	59.2
08 07850	Boulder	63.1	94 673	253	1 500.4	85 127	11.2	76 685	11.0	90.5	1.6	1.0	5.1	4.4	8.2	84.2
08 09280	Broomfield	70.2	38 272	813	545.2	24 638	55.3	20 722	18.9	90.8	1.2	1.3	5.1	4.2	9.1	83.7
08 16000	Colorado Springs	481.1	360 890	48	750.1	280 430	28.7	215 150	30.3	83.9	7.8	1.9	4.3	6.3	12.0	75.3
08 20000	Denver	397.2	554 636	25	1 396.4	467 610	18.6	492 365	-5.0	68.3	12.1	2.2	3.6	17.7	31.7	51.9
08 24785	Englewood	17.0	31 727	980	1 866.3	29 396	7.9	30 021	-2.1	90.0	1.9	2.3	2.5	6.0	13.0	81.0
08 27425	Fort Collins	120.5	118 652	185	984.7	87 491	35.6	65 092	34.4	92.0	1.4	1.3	3.5	4.6	8.8	85.4
08 31660	Grand Junction	79.8	41 986	729	526.1	32 893	27.6	28 144	16.9	93.6	0.9	1.8	1.3	4.6	10.9	85.9
08 32155	Greeley	77.5	76 930	346	992.6	60 454	27.3	53 006	14.1	82.9	1.2	1.5	2.0	15.4	29.5	66.8
08 43000	Lakewood	107.7	144 126	144	1 338.2	126 475	14.0	112 860	12.1	89.5	1.9	2.0	3.5	5.9	14.5	78.9
08 45255	Littleton	35.0	40 340	767	1 152.6	33 711	19.7	28 655	17.6	93.6	1.5	1.4	2.3	3.3	8.4	86.8
08 45970	Longmont	56.4	71 093	377	1 260.5	51 976	36.8	42 942	21.0	86.7	0.8	1.6	2.3	10.9	19.1	76.8
08 46465	Loveland	63.6	50 608	591	795.7	37 357	35.5	30 244	23.5	94.7	0.6	1.4	1.3	4.1	8.6	88.6
08 54330	Northglenn	19.2	31 575	990	1 644.5	27 195	16.1	29 847	-8.9	85.7	2.0	2.0	4.0	9.6	20.3	72.9
08 62000	Pueblo	116.7	102 121	232	875.1	98 640	3.5	101 686	-3.0	79.4	2.9	2.7	1.2	17.6	44.1	51.1
08 77290	Thornton	69.6	82 384	310	1 183.7	55 031	49.7	40 343	36.4	85.5	1.9	2.0	3.4	10.5	21.3	72.4
08 83835	Westminster	81.6	100 940	235	1 237.0	74 619	35.3	50 176	48.7	86.6	1.6	1.5	6.5	6.7	15.2	75.9
08 84440	Wheat Ridge	23.5	32 913	950	1 400.6	29 419	11.9	30 280	-2.8	91.5	1.2	1.9	2.0	6.1	13.5	82.1
09 00000	**CONNECTICUT**	12 548.0	3 405 565	X	271.4	3 287 116	3.6	3 107 564	5.8	83.3	10.0	0.7	2.9	5.5	9.4	77.5
09 08000	Bridgeport	41.4	139 529	152	3 370.3	141 686	-1.5	142 546	-0.6	48.5	33.2	1.0	4.1	19.0	31.9	30.9
09 08420	Bristol	68.7	60 062	464	874.3	60 640	-1.0	57 370	5.7	93.0	3.4	0.7	1.8	2.8	5.3	89.3
09 18430	Danbury	109.1	74 848	356	686.0	65 585	14.1	60 470	8.5	79.2	7.6	0.7	6.2	10.3	15.8	68.1
09 37000	Hartford	44.8	121 578	179	2 713.8	139 739	-13.0	136 392	2.5	30.8	40.6	1.2	2.6	30.6	40.5	17.8
09 46450	Meriden	61.5	58 244	488	947.1	59 479	-2.1	57 118	4.1	82.7	7.7	0.8	1.7	10.2	21.1	69.9
09 47290	Middletown	105.9	43 167	708	407.6	42 762	0.9	39 040	9.5	82.2	13.7	0.8	3.3	3.0	5.3	77.5
09 47500	Milford	58.4	52 305	572	895.6	48 139	4.7	NA	NA	94.6	2.2	0.4	2.7	1.3	3.3	91.3
09 49880	Naugatuck Borough	42.4	30 989	1 006	730.9	30 625	1.2	26 456	15.8	93.4	3.5	0.7	1.9	2.4	4.5	88.9
09 50370	New Britain	34.5	71 538	373	2 073.6	75 491	-5.2	73 840	2.2	72.5	12.3	0.8	2.7	15.7	26.8	58.8
09 52000	New Haven	48.8	123 626	175	2 533.3	130 474	-5.2	126 109	3.5	45.9	39.3	1.2	4.7	13.0	21.4	35.6
09 52280	New London	14.3	25 671	1 211	1 795.2	28 540	-10.1	28 842	-1.0	67.6	21.8	2.3	3.2	11.5	19.7	56.1
09 55990	Norwalk	59.1	82 951	308	1 403.6	78 331	5.9	77 767	0.7	76.1	16.3	0.6	3.8	6.3	15.6	64.3
09 56200	Norwich	73.4	36 117	862	492.1	37 391	-3.4	38 074	-1.8	85.8	9.0	2.4	2.7	4.3	6.1	80.4
09 68100	Shelton	79.2	38 101	817	481.1	35 418	7.6	31 314	13.1	95.6	1.3	0.5	2.2	1.7	3.5	92.1
09 73000	Stamford	97.8	117 083	187	1 197.2	108 056	8.4	102 453	5.5	71.9	16.5	0.5	5.6	8.7	16.8	61.2
09 76500	Torrington	103.1	35 202	887	341.4	33 687	4.5	30 987	8.7	94.3	2.7	0.6	2.2	1.8	3.3	91.5
09 80000	Waterbury	74.0	107 271	213	1 449.6	108 961	-1.6	103 266	5.5	69.7	18.0	1.0	2.1	13.2	21.8	58.2
09 82800	West Haven	28.1	52 360	571	1 863.3	54 021	-3.1	53 184	1.6	76.2	17.4	0.7	3.4	5.2	9.1	69.7
10 00000	**DELAWARE**	5 059.7	783 600	X	154.9	666 168	17.6	594 338	12.1	75.9	20.1	0.8	2.5	2.6	4.8	72.5
10 21200	Dover	58.0	32 135	969	554.1	27 630	16.3	23 504	17.6	56.7	38.8	1.2	4.0	2.4	4.1	53.3
10 50670	Newark	23.1	28 547	1 086	1 235.8	26 463	7.9	25 247	4.8	88.7	6.5	0.5	4.8	1.3	2.5	85.7
10 77580	Wilmington	28.1	72 664	366	2 585.9	71 529	1.6	70 195	1.9	36.6	57.8	0.8	0.9	6.0	9.8	32.1
11 00000	**DISTRICT OF COLUMBIA**	159.0	572 059	X	3 597.9	606 900	-5.7	638 432	-4.9	32.2	61.3	0.8	3.2	5.0	7.9	27.8
11 50000	Washington	159.0	572 059	21	3 597.9	606 900	-5.7	638 432	-4.9	32.2	61.3	0.8	3.2	5.0	7.9	27.8
12 00000	**FLORIDA**	139 669.8	15 982 378	X	114.4	12 938 071	23.5	9 746 961	32.7	79.7	15.5	0.7	2.3	4.4	16.8	65.4
12 00950	Altamonte Springs	23.0	41 200	744	1 791.3	35 167	17.2	22 028	59.6	81.6	10.7	0.8	3.8	6.3	15.9	69.5
12 01700	Apopka	62.3	26 642	1 158	427.6	13 611	95.7	NA	NA	76.0	16.5	0.7	2.4	7.2	18.1	63.0
12 07300	Boca Raton	70.4	74 764	357	1 062.0	61 486	21.6	49 505	24.2	92.1	4.3	0.4	2.6	2.6	8.5	84.2
12 07875	Boynton Beach	41.1	60 389	460	1 469.3	46 284	30.5	35 624	29.9	71.4	24.6	0.4	2.1	4.2	9.2	64.4
12 07950	Bradenton	31.4	49 504	604	1 576.6	43 769	13.1	30 170	45.1	79.4	15.8	0.6	1.1	4.8	11.3	71.6
12 10275	Cape Coral	272.4	102 286	230	375.5	74 991	36.4	32 103	133.6	94.4	2.4	0.6	1.3	2.9	8.3	87.5
12 12875	Clearwater	65.5	108 787	208	1 660.9	98 669	10.3	85 528	15.4	85.4	10.4	0.7	2.0	3.3	9.0	78.1

1. Dry land or land partially or temporarily covered by water.   2. Hispanic persons may be of any race.

	Population characteristics, 2000 (cont'd)										Households, 2000				
	Age of population (percent)													Percent	
City	Under 5 years	5 to 17 years	18 to 24 years	25 to 34 years	35 to 44 years	45 to 54 years	55 to 64 years	65 to 74 years	75 years and over	Percent female	Number	Percent change, 1990–2000	Persons per house-hold	Female family house-holder[1]	One-person
	16	17	18	19	20	21	22	23	24	25	26	27	28	29	30
CALIFORNIA—Cont'd															
Walnut Creek	4.4	13.2	5.2	12.2	14.8	14.5	10.3	9.8	15.5	53.8	30 301	6.9	2.09	6.7	38.0
Watsonville	9.3	24.7	11.8	16.4	14.1	9.7	5.4	4.2	4.4	49.8	11 381	20.6	3.84	16.4	17.6
West Covina	7.6	20.9	10.0	14.9	15.6	12.7	7.9	5.8	4.5	51.4	31 411	4.4	3.32	15.8	14.8
West Hollywood	1.6	4.0	6.3	26.4	22.2	13.8	8.5	8.0	9.0	44.8	23 120	2.4	1.53	4.4	60.5
Westminster	7.3	18.7	8.8	16.8	15.8	12.4	9.2	6.6	4.5	50.0	26 406	5.3	3.32	12.4	16.9
West Sacramento	7.7	22.1	9.1	12.5	15.2	12.2	8.5	7.0	5.6	50.6	11 404	3.2	2.75	15.4	27.1
Whittier	7.8	20.5	10.0	15.1	15.5	11.7	6.9	5.8	6.7	51.4	28 271	2.3	2.88	14.3	22.4
Woodland	8.1	21.7	9.6	14.6	15.7	12.7	7.2	4.9	5.6	51.0	16 751	18.0	2.89	12.9	21.0
Yorba Linda	6.0	23.3	7.3	9.6	18.9	18.1	9.2	4.5	3.2	50.9	19 252	14.8	3.05	8.3	12.4
Yuba City	8.1	20.9	10.7	14.9	14.5	11.4	7.3	6.0	6.2	51.1	13 290	25.6	2.70	14.3	26.5
Yucaipa	6.5	22.0	7.6	11.0	16.2	13.0	8.2	7.0	8.4	51.7	15 193	14.1	2.67	11.6	25.3
COLORADO	6.9	18.7	10.0	15.4	17.1	14.3	7.9	5.3	4.4	49.6	1 658 238	29.3	2.53	9.6	26.3
Arvada	6.4	19.8	7.8	12.4	18.0	15.5	9.4	6.2	4.5	51.0	39 019	19.2	2.60	9.7	23.1
Aurora	8.1	19.5	10.1	17.7	17.0	13.3	6.9	4.1	3.3	50.5	105 625	18.5	2.60	13.1	27.4
Boulder	4.1	10.7	25.9	19.5	13.6	12.4	6.0	3.7	4.1	48.4	39 596	14.2	2.20	6.5	33.7
Broomfield	7.8	21.5	7.7	16.2	20.1	13.9	6.2	4.1	2.5	49.8	13 842	58.8	2.76	8.2	19.3
Colorado Springs	7.5	19.0	10.3	15.4	17.4	13.5	7.4	5.1	4.5	50.5	141 516	27.7	2.50	10.6	27.0
Denver	6.8	15.1	10.7	20.5	15.6	12.8	7.2	5.5	5.7	49.5	239 235	13.4	2.27	10.8	39.3
Englewood	5.8	14.5	9.6	18.2	17.7	12.9	7.1	5.6	8.6	50.5	14 392	8.6	2.15	10.8	37.9
Fort Collins	5.9	15.6	22.1	16.9	14.6	11.7	5.4	3.8	4.0	49.8	45 882	36.2	2.45	7.9	26.0
Grand Junction	5.6	15.6	11.9	11.9	14.4	13.9	8.8	8.3	9.6	51.3	17 865	39.5	2.23	9.4	33.2
Greeley	7.5	18.2	19.0	14.3	13.0	11.4	6.5	4.9	5.2	51.0	27 647	22.1	2.63	10.8	25.6
Lakewood	6.1	16.2	9.6	15.7	16.8	14.2	9.4	6.5	5.6	50.6	60 531	17.2	2.32	10.8	30.7
Littleton	5.7	17.6	8.2	13.0	17.1	15.1	9.1	7.2	7.0	51.4	17 313	24.5	2.29	9.2	33.3
Longmont	7.8	20.1	8.5	15.1	18.0	13.8	7.4	4.6	4.6	50.5	26 667	36.3	2.64	10.1	23.7
Loveland	7.0	19.9	7.8	13.6	17.0	14.0	8.1	6.3	6.2	51.0	19 741	40.5	2.55	9.8	23.4
Northglenn	7.3	19.4	9.9	16.1	16.8	11.4	8.8	6.7	3.5	50.0	11 610	18.1	2.71	11.8	23.0
Pueblo	6.7	18.4	10.3	12.5	14.1	13.0	8.4	8.2	8.4	51.6	40 307	5.2	2.44	15.1	30.0
Thornton	8.8	21.2	9.6	18.0	18.0	13.0	5.8	3.2	2.4	50.3	28 882	51.6	2.83	11.5	18.7
Westminster	7.3	19.6	9.6	17.6	18.4	14.3	6.8	3.8	2.7	50.0	38 343	37.8	2.62	9.6	23.7
Wheat Ridge	6.1	15.1	7.6	13.3	16.0	14.0	9.0	7.8	11.2	52.7	14 559	10.8	2.20	11.4	35.4
CONNECTICUT	6.6	18.2	8.0	13.3	17.1	14.1	9.1	6.8	7.0	51.6	1 301 670	5.8	2.53	12.1	26.4
Bridgeport	8.2	20.3	11.2	15.9	14.7	11.1	7.3	5.5	5.9	52.3	50 307	-3.9	2.70	24.0	29.0
Bristol	6.3	16.9	7.2	15.1	17.4	13.5	8.8	7.3	7.6	51.6	24 886	3.9	2.38	11.5	28.9
Danbury	6.5	15.1	10.2	17.8	17.6	13.4	8.3	5.6	5.4	51.0	27 183	12.8	2.64	10.5	26.2
Hartford	8.3	21.8	12.6	15.5	14.3	11.0	7.1	4.9	4.6	52.2	44 986	-12.6	2.58	29.6	33.2
Meriden	7.1	18.6	8.1	14.1	16.1	13.5	8.3	6.6	7.5	51.6	22 951	-1.2	2.49	15.2	28.9
Middletown	6.5	15.2	8.3	17.6	17.5	13.0	8.5	6.2	7.2	51.7	18 554	10.3	2.23	11.6	35.0
Milford	6.0	16.3	5.9	14.0	17.7	15.2	10.0	7.4	7.5	51.6	20 900	10.9	2.48	9.7	26.6
Naugatuck Borough	6.9	19.9	7.3	14.9	18.2	13.1	7.9	5.4	6.3	51.4	11 829	4.4	2.60	12.8	24.9
New Britain	6.6	17.5	12.5	14.9	14.0	11.5	7.1	6.9	8.8	52.1	28 558	-5.3	2.40	17.7	33.1
New Haven	7.1	18.4	16.4	17.8	13.4	10.2	6.6	4.8	5.4	52.1	47 094	-3.9	2.40	22.9	36.1
New London	6.7	16.2	17.6	15.0	14.6	11.2	6.7	5.6	6.5	51.1	10 181	-5.0	2.26	17.8	37.8
Norwalk	6.9	15.2	7.0	17.7	17.9	13.3	9.3	6.9	5.9	51.2	32 711	7.0	2.51	12.2	28.2
Norwich	6.4	17.7	8.9	14.0	16.2	13.4	8.1	7.3	8.1	52.5	15 091	0.5	2.34	15.0	32.0
Shelton	6.2	17.4	5.8	12.2	17.8	15.2	10.5	7.3	7.5	51.6	14 190	13.9	2.65	8.5	21.8
Stamford	6.9	15.2	7.4	17.8	17.3	12.9	8.7	7.1	6.8	51.6	45 399	8.2	2.54	11.5	28.7
Torrington	6.0	17.1	6.4	13.4	17.6	13.5	8.6	7.5	10.1	51.6	14 743	6.2	2.33	10.3	32.1
Waterbury	7.6	18.9	8.9	14.8	15.1	11.7	8.0	6.7	8.2	52.7	42 622	-1.3	2.46	19.1	31.4
West Haven	6.2	16.9	9.7	14.9	16.3	13.4	8.4	6.9	7.3	52.3	21 090	-0.9	2.42	15.6	31.0
DELAWARE	6.6	18.3	9.6	13.9	16.3	13.3	9.1	7.2	5.8	51.4	298 736	20.7	2.54	13.1	25.0
Dover	6.7	16.9	15.7	13.7	14.2	11.5	8.0	6.7	6.7	52.9	12 340	24.6	2.35	16.7	31.4
Newark	3.0	9.5	43.6	11.2	8.7	9.0	5.9	4.6	4.5	54.0	8 989	20.4	2.43	7.2	27.2
Wilmington	6.8	19.0	9.8	16.4	15.6	12.2	7.6	6.1	6.5	52.3	28 617	0.2	2.39	23.8	37.1
DISTRICT OF COLUMBIA	5.7	14.4	12.7	17.8	15.3	13.2	8.7	6.3	5.9	52.9	248 338	-0.5	2.16	18.9	43.8
Washington	5.7	14.4	12.7	17.8	15.3	13.2	8.7	6.3	5.9	52.9	248 338	-0.5	2.16	18.9	43.8
FLORIDA	5.9	16.9	8.3	13.0	15.5	12.9	9.8	9.1	8.5	51.2	6 337 929	23.4	2.46	12.0	26.6
Altamonte Springs	5.9	14.5	10.8	20.8	16.3	12.8	8.2	5.3	5.4	51.9	18 821	22.0	2.17	12.0	36.1
Apopka	8.5	19.7	8.6	16.2	17.4	11.9	7.6	5.7	4.4	51.6	9 562	87.1	2.76	14.4	18.6
Boca Raton	4.7	14.2	8.1	10.6	15.8	15.2	11.5	9.8	10.0	51.3	31 848	21.1	2.26	7.1	29.5
Boynton Beach	5.7	14.1	6.4	13.3	14.8	11.0	8.7	11.0	14.8	53.2	26 210	29.2	2.26	10.9	33.0
Bradenton	6.1	15.4	7.7	12.2	13.1	11.5	8.4	10.4	15.0	52.6	21 379	13.3	2.24	12.1	34.1
Cape Coral	5.5	17.1	5.8	11.2	15.6	13.9	11.4	10.5	9.1	51.5	40 768	37.0	2.49	9.3	19.7
Clearwater	5.2	14.0	8.0	12.8	14.8	13.7	10.1	9.7	11.8	52.1	48 449	9.8	2.17	11.3	35.5

1. No spouse present.

Table D. Cities — Group Quarters, Crime, Education, and Income

City	Persons in group quarters, 2000				Serious crimes known to police, 2000[2]				Education, 1990				Money income, 1989		
		Institutional			Total		Rate[3]		School enrollment		Attainment[4] (percent)			Households	
															Median
	Total	Total	Persons in nursing homes	Non-Institutional[1]	Number	Rate[3]	Violent	Property	Public	Private	High school graduate or more	Bachelor's degree or more	Per capita (dollars)[5]	Dollars	Percent change, 1979–1989 (constant 1989 dollars)
	31	32	33	34	35	36	37	38	39	40	41	42	43	44	45
CALIFORNIA—Cont'd															
Walnut Creek	964	513	513	451	2 246	3 493	201	3 293	10 716	2 438	94.4	46.9	26 354	45 529	9.5
Watsonville	553	223	212	330	1 891	4 272	685	3 587	7 716	673	53.6	10.7	10 422	27 980	15.6
West Covina	808	195	167	613	4 338	4 128	368	3 760	23 760	4 858	80.6	20.2	15 862	42 481	4.0
West Hollywood	230	0	0	230	1 972	5 521	1 019	4 502	3 814	1 232	84.9	37.4	24 386	29 314	27.3
Westminster	552	203	203	349	3 064	3 474	373	3 101	19 479	2 671	75.1	18.1	15 530	41 364	7.6
West Sacramento	206	112	112	94	1 672	5 289	1 268	4 020	6 138	780	66.3	8.9	11 510	23 287	9.1
Whittier	2 348	1 159	374	1 189	2 390	2 856	296	2 560	16 509	4 602	79.7	20.8	17 874	38 020	13.7
Woodland	790	451	413	339	1 308	2 661	527	2 134	9 247	1 360	76.2	17.0	13 854	31 671	3.3
Yorba Linda	135	6	0	129	950	1 612	231	1 382	13 803	2 913	92.9	37.0	25 791	67 892	32.9
Yuba City	916	701	449	215	2 044	5 561	495	5 066	6 953	585	74.3	16.4	11 815	23 491	8.3
Yucaipa	572	430	329	142	865	2 099	167	1 932	6 688	1 046	73.9	12.4	14 131	27 182	39.6
COLORADO	102 955	52 741	18 495	50 214	171 304	3 983	334	3 649	789 735	106 409	84.4	27.0	14 821	30 140	-0.4
Arvada	751	143	120	608	3 401	3 329	113	3 217	21 923	2 473	88.4	25.0	15 642	39 014	-5.9
Aurora	2 089	1 411	812	678	15 568	5 633	547	5 085	51 306	7 402	90.3	26.3	15 255	33 214	-8.7
Boulder	7 479	1 144	621	6 335	3 571	3 772	230	3 542	31 418	2 828	94.9	58.9	17 268	29 407	4.8
Broomfield	7	0	0	7	1 271	3 322	141	3 181	6 287	830	91.8	27.9	15 766	39 067	0.2
Colorado Springs	7 153	3 665	1 827	3 488	17 926	4 967	455	4 512	62 669	11 837	87.8	27.5	14 243	28 928	8.2
Denver	12 719	6 216	2 621	6 503	26 302	4 742	520	4 222	86 008	22 991	79.2	29.0	15 590	25 106	-3.4
Englewood	728	622	576	106	NA	NA	NA	NA	5 247	1 095	80.2	19.0	13 514	25 422	-2.9
Fort Collins	6 055	903	538	5 152	4 876	4 109	309	3 800	33 241	2 132	91.5	42.7	13 439	26 826	1.5
Grand Junction	2 180	823	224	1 357	3 028	7 212	360	6 852	6 862	593	77.1	17.9	11 723	19 042	-13.9
Greeley	4 221	1 177	658	3 044	4 162	5 410	351	5 059	19 582	1 372	76.6	25.1	11 461	23 462	-3.5
Lakewood	3 800	2 721	1 357	1 079	7 479	5 189	300	4 889	25 585	4 549	88.2	29.6	16 726	34 054	-12.6
Littleton	611	541	332	70	323	801	40	761	7 242	1 157	89.8	35.7	18 360	34 006	-4.7
Longmont	615	420	414	195	2 301	3 237	436	2 801	12 304	1 105	84.5	20.5	14 037	32 534	-1.2
Loveland	361	295	278	66	1 746	3 450	209	3 241	9 525	938	84.2	18.6	13 345	30 548	4.2
Northglenn	163	163	163	0	1 677	5 311	336	4 975	6 266	806	83.1	13.8	13 619	34 726	-11.3
Pueblo	3 894	2 942	1 115	952	5 194	5 086	962	4 125	24 669	1 584	73.2	13.8	10 168	20 501	-18.0
Thornton	550	490	430	60	4 472	5 428	506	4 922	13 765	1 478	82.6	14.1	12 799	34 146	-2.3
Westminster	487	380	290	107	1 576	1 561	72	1 489	18 763	2 462	88.4	23.8	15 456	36 716	-1.2
Wheat Ridge	844	505	477	339	1 922	5 840	428	5 411	4 830	889	82.7	20.6	15 451	28 338	-8.6
CONNECTICUT	107 939	55 256	32 223	52 683	110 091	3 233	325	2 908	626 637	178 849	79.2	27.2	20 189	41 721	24.0
Bridgeport	3 596	1 919	942	1 677	8 900	6 379	1 422	4 957	26 482	9 076	61.1	12.3	13 156	28 704	23.6
Bristol	771	588	588	183	1 731	2 882	395	2 487	11 180	2 287	75.0	15.4	16 909	38 261	17.9
Danbury	3 128	2 010	684	1 118	2 083	2 783	178	2 605	11 815	3 528	76.5	26.9	19 300	43 832	30.2
Hartford	5 355	2 290	920	3 065	11 220	9 229	1 226	8 003	33 231	8 323	59.4	14.4	11 081	22 140	14.7
Meriden	1 141	875	815	266	2 164	3 715	161	3 554	10 904	2 736	72.6	15.8	15 618	36 211	19.9
Middletown	1 874	1 427	557	447	1 485	3 440	111	3 329	6 840	4 492	77.3	26.4	17 814	37 644	29.8
Milford	537	420	420	117	1 914	3 659	96	3 564	8 725	2 663	81.9	23.4	19 099	44 142	NA
Naugatuck Borough	220	194	194	26	685	2 210	171	2 039	6 559	1 384	78.2	17.0	16 691	39 902	26.9
New Britain	3 071	897	897	2 174	3 973	5 554	509	5 045	15 222	3 097	64.7	16.7	14 715	30 121	14.0
New Haven	10 599	2 662	1 117	7 937	9 784	7 914	1 387	6 527	26 285	14 607	71.0	26.7	12 968	25 811	31.8
New London	2 706	247	247	2 459	1 258	4 900	830	4 071	4 907	3 257	75.4	17.9	12 971	26 336	14.5
Norwalk	865	527	527	338	3 297	3 975	448	3 526	13 496	3 764	79.5	29.5	23 075	48 171	29.8
Norwich	749	388	379	361	1 225	3 392	413	2 979	7 121	1 457	71.8	16.4	14 844	29 354	13.7
Shelton	561	541	351	20	627	1 646	89	1 556	6 140	2 553	83.1	23.9	20 256	49 965	27.5
Stamford	1 753	891	818	862	3 065	2 618	245	2 373	16 930	6 071	81.2	35.1	27 092	49 787	33.2
Torrington	834	653	653	181	1 036	2 943	347	2 596	5 782	1 109	72.5	15.7	16 407	35 230	28.4
Waterbury	2 214	1 562	1 362	652	6 984	6 511	509	6 002	18 018	6 124	66.8	14.1	14 209	30 533	22.6
West Haven	1 259	449	345	810	1 928	3 682	141	3 541	8 993	3 440	74.5	17.2	15 810	35 723	24.6
DELAWARE	24 583	11 510	4 852	13 073	35 090	4 478	684	3 794	135 362	35 857	77.5	21.4	15 854	34 875	16.6
Dover	3 118	842	699	2 276	2 296	7 145	650	6 494	6 691	1 537	82.2	26.5	14 105	31 308	9.6
Newark	6 727	141	141	6 586	1 408	4 932	603	4 330	11 556	2 201	89.6	47.6	14 076	38 584	27.5
Wilmington	4 228	2 785	553	1 443	6 758	9 300	1 773	7 528	13 799	3 298	67.7	18.9	14 256	26 389	34.6
DISTRICT OF COLUMBIA	35 562	7 964	3 759	27 598	41 626	7 277	1 508	5 769	97 160	54 088	73.1	33.3	18 881	30 727	13.1
Washington	35 562	7 964	3 759	27 598	41 604	7 273	1 507	5 765	97 160	54 088	73.1	33.3	18 881	30 727	13.1
FLORIDA	388 945	248 350	88 828	140 595	910 154	5 695	812	4 883	2 459 541	467 121	74.4	18.3	14 698	27 483	11.7
Altamonte Springs	428	419	405	9	1 941	4 711	342	4 369	6 807	1 402	89.8	30.0	16 284	31 538	1.2
Apopka	217	135	135	82	1 984	7 447	1 043	6 403	2 704	458	76.7	18.6	14 112	30 662	NA
Boca Raton	2 806	548	536	2 258	3 312	4 430	281	4 149	9 193	4 222	88.4	34.9	28 307	42 314	12.1
Boynton Beach	1 091	912	897	179	4 991	8 265	830	7 435	7 227	1 192	73.1	16.4	16 668	28 824	21.1
Bradenton	1 586	1 415	990	171	3 398	6 864	931	5 933	6 865	862	75.2	15.6	13 815	26 010	20.8
Cape Coral	591	550	550	41	3 630	3 549	208	3 341	12 658	1 591	81.4	15.2	14 934	31 177	8.1
Clearwater	3 863	1 457	1 437	2 406	5 794	5 326	795	4 531	16 257	2 950	80.2	20.4	16 726	26 473	8.2

1. Persons in emergency shelters and persons visible in street locations. 2. Data for serious crimes have not been adjusted for underreporting. This may affect comparability between geographic areas and over time. 3. Per 100,000 population estimated by the FBI. 4. Persons 25 years old and older. 5. Based on population enumerated as of April 1, 1990.

City	Money income, 1989 (cont'd) Households (cont'd) Percent with $100,000 or more	Percent below poverty, 1989 Persons Total	Percent change in rate, 1979–1989	Families Total	Housing units, 2000 Total	Percent change, 1990–2000	Vacant units Vacant units for sale or rent[1]	For seasonal use (percent)	Home owner vacancy rate	Renter vacancy rate	Occupied units Total	Percent owner occupied	Percent renter occupied	Average size owner occupied	Average size renter occupied
	46	47	48	49	50	51	52	53	54	55	56	57	58	59	60
CALIFORNIA—Cont'd															
Walnut Creek	11.7	3.8	-5.0	2.2	31 425	4.9	1 124	0.6	1.1	2.8	30 301	68.3	31.7	2.16	1.94
Watsonville	1.9	15.3	15.9	11.0	11 695	18.0	314	0.3	0.6	2.9	11 381	48.1	51.9	3.55	4.11
West Covina	6.7	7.7	45.3	5.7	32 058	3.0	647	0.1	0.7	2.2	31 411	66.5	33.5	3.38	3.19
West Hollywood	6.4	11.4	-14.9	11.0	24 110	1.2	990	0.8	1.7	2.4	23 120	21.6	78.4	1.55	1.53
Westminster	6.5	11.4	58.3	7.6	26 940	4.2	534	0.1	0.7	2.3	26 406	60.2	39.8	3.21	3.48
West Sacramento	1.5	18.5	103.3	15.7	12 133	4.1	729	0.3	1.3	6.6	11 404	54.5	45.5	2.60	2.94
Whittier	8.1	7.8	5.4	5.5	28 977	0.8	706	0.2	0.9	2.1	28 271	57.8	42.2	2.94	2.80
Woodland	3.0	9.6	15.7	8.1	17 120	15.5	369	0.2	0.7	2.1	16 751	58.5	41.5	2.93	2.82
Yorba Linda	22.9	4.9	-36.7	1.3	19 567	12.8	315	0.2	0.6	1.9	19 252	84.7	15.3	3.11	2.71
Yuba City	2.4	18.6	52.5	15.5	13 912	25.7	622	0.3	1.4	4.7	13 290	47.4	52.6	2.76	2.64
Yucaipa	2.9	7.6	-15.6	5.8	16 112	12.9	919	0.4	2.0	6.6	15 193	74.2	25.8	2.64	2.79
COLORADO	3.8	11.7	15.6	8.6	1 808 037	22.4	149 799	4.0	1.4	5.5	1 658 238	67.3	32.7	2.64	2.30
Arvada	2.9	6.3	61.5	4.9	39 733	15.0	714	0.1	0.6	2.5	39 019	75.7	24.3	2.70	2.30
Aurora	2.3	7.4	37.0	6.1	109 260	9.4	3 635	0.2	1.1	3.5	105 625	63.9	36.1	2.65	2.50
Boulder	5.6	19.0	16.6	7.5	40 726	12.3	1 130	0.6	0.6	2.2	39 596	49.5	50.5	2.30	2.11
Broomfield	3.7	5.1	30.8	4.2	14 322	57.4	480	0.4	1.0	6.3	13 842	76.8	23.2	2.90	2.32
Colorado Springs	3.0	10.9	5.8	8.6	148 690	19.5	7 174	0.5	1.2	6.2	141 516	60.8	39.2	2.65	2.27
Denver	3.9	17.1	24.8	13.1	251 435	4.9	12 200	0.6	1.7	4.5	239 235	52.5	47.5	2.41	2.10
Englewood	1.0	10.9	39.7	7.7	14 916	0.1	524	0.1	0.7	4.3	14 392	52.2	47.8	2.32	1.98
Fort Collins	2.9	17.0	11.1	8.0	47 755	35.1	1 873	0.4	1.4	4.1	45 882	57.0	43.0	2.61	2.24
Grand Junction	1.8	21.6	63.6	16.8	18 784	37.1	919	0.4	1.7	5.9	17 865	62.6	37.4	2.35	2.03
Greeley	2.3	19.5	10.8	12.2	28 972	20.8	1 325	0.2	1.9	4.8	27 647	58.4	41.6	2.76	2.45
Lakewood	3.5	7.6	52.0	5.2	62 422	12.1	1 891	0.3	0.7	3.6	60 531	60.9	39.1	2.41	2.17
Littleton	5.1	7.3	15.9	5.1	18 084	22.4	771	0.3	0.7	7.2	17 313	62.1	37.9	2.49	1.97
Longmont	2.3	7.8	27.9	6.0	27 394	33.8	727	0.3	1.1	2.6	26 667	65.6	34.4	2.72	2.50
Loveland	1.9	7.9	8.2	5.7	20 299	38.0	558	0.3	1.0	2.8	19 741	69.4	30.6	2.62	2.37
Northglenn	1.4	5.3	-5.4	3.7	12 051	15.4	441	0.2	0.7	6.8	11 610	67.4	32.6	2.88	2.34
Pueblo	1.2	21.6	51.0	18.0	43 121	5.5	2 814	0.2	1.7	8.5	40 307	65.6	34.4	2.49	2.34
Thornton	1.0	8.2	28.1	6.9	29 573	41.0	691	0.1	0.9	4.7	28 882	77.7	22.3	2.91	2.57
Westminster	2.9	6.6	17.9	5.6	39 318	31.6	975	0.3	0.5	4.3	38 343	69.7	30.3	2.75	2.31
Wheat Ridge	2.8	8.4	20.0	6.0	14 931	5.7	372	0.3	0.6	2.4	14 559	54.6	45.4	2.29	2.10
CONNECTICUT	9.2	6.8	-14.8	5.0	1 385 975	4.9	84 305	1.7	1.1	5.6	1 301 670	66.8	33.2	2.67	2.25
Bridgeport	2.7	17.1	-16.2	15.0	54 367	-5.0	4 060	0.2	1.9	5.6	50 307	43.2	56.8	2.74	2.67
Bristol	3.1	4.4	-25.4	2.9	26 125	4.5	1 239	0.3	1.1	5.2	24 886	61.9	38.1	2.60	2.03
Danbury	8.4	5.8	-13.4	4.7	28 519	9.9	1 336	1.3	1.1	3.4	27 183	58.3	41.7	2.67	2.59
Hartford	1.9	27.5	9.1	25.7	50 644	-9.7	5 658	0.3	2.0	9.2	44 986	24.6	75.4	2.76	2.52
Meriden	3.0	7.3	-1.4	6.3	24 631	-0.8	1 680	0.2	1.7	7.3	22 951	59.9	40.1	2.59	2.34
Middletown	4.2	7.0	-27.8	4.9	19 697	8.8	1 143	0.5	1.5	5.8	18 554	51.3	48.7	2.49	1.95
Milford	6.7	3.7	NA	2.5	21 962	9.0	1 062	1.6	0.7	6.1	20 900	77.3	22.7	2.61	2.02
Naugatuck Borough	4.2	4.2	-40.8	3.2	12 341	3.4	512	0.2	0.9	5.0	11 829	66.5	33.5	2.79	2.22
New Britain	2.2	12.8	8.5	10.7	31 164	-3.6	2 606	0.2	1.7	6.1	28 558	42.7	57.3	2.50	2.32
New Haven	3.7	21.3	-8.2	18.2	52 941	-2.1	5 847	0.3	3.7	7.1	47 094	29.6	70.4	2.60	2.32
New London	2.1	15.1	-10.7	12.0	11 560	-3.4	1 379	1.1	2.5	9.8	10 181	37.9	62.1	2.39	2.17
Norwalk	12.0	5.2	-25.7	3.8	33 753	4.7	1 042	0.6	0.6	2.9	32 711	62.0	38.0	2.61	2.35
Norwich	3.2	11.9	-5.6	9.7	16 600	0.8	1 509	1.3	2.3	7.0	15 091	52.5	47.5	2.51	2.16
Shelton	9.9	2.5	-28.6	1.6	14 707	13.3	517	0.7	0.9	5.8	14 190	81.8	18.2	2.76	2.15
Stamford	16.9	6.3	-18.2	3.9	47 317	6.9	1 918	1.0	0.6	3.0	45 399	56.7	43.3	2.65	2.39
Torrington	3.3	5.2	-24.6	3.1	16 147	6.5	1 404	2.7	1.9	7.0	14 743	64.6	35.4	2.50	2.02
Waterbury	2.4	12.1	-14.2	9.9	46 827	-0.8	4 205	0.3	2.2	7.6	42 622	47.6	52.4	2.58	2.36
West Haven	2.7	6.1	-35.1	4.2	22 336	-1.5	1 246	0.3	1.5	6.6	21 090	55.2	44.8	2.62	2.18
DELAWARE	4.5	8.7	-26.8	6.1	343 072	18.3	44 336	7.6	1.5	8.2	298 736	72.3	27.7	2.61	2.37
Dover	3.5	12.5	-8.8	10.1	13 195	25.8	855	0.4	2.0	6.7	12 340	52.3	47.7	2.50	2.19
Newark	5.4	17.4	-5.9	1.8	9 294	18.2	305	0.2	1.1	4.0	8 989	54.5	45.5	2.53	2.31
Wilmington	3.8	18.1	-26.4	15.1	32 138	2.9	3 521	0.2	2.6	8.4	28 617	50.1	49.9	2.45	2.33
DISTRICT OF COLUMBIA	7.8	16.9	-9.3	13.3	274 845	-1.3	26 507	0.8	2.9	5.9	248 338	40.8	59.2	2.31	2.06
Washington	7.8	16.9	-9.1	13.3	274 845	-1.3	26 507	0.8	2.9	5.9	248 338	40.8	59.2	2.31	2.06
FLORIDA	3.9	12.7	-6.0	9.0	7 302 947	19.7	965 018	6.6	2.2	9.3	6 337 929	70.1	29.9	2.49	2.39
Altamonte Springs	2.7	7.7	35.1	5.4	19 992	16.6	1 171	1.0	1.5	5.7	18 821	41.8	58.2	2.38	2.02
Apopka	3.7	11.5	NA	8.5	10 091	76.7	529	1.3	1.8	4.5	9 562	75.8	24.2	2.75	2.81
Boca Raton	16.2	5.5	7.8	3.6	37 547	13.6	5 699	11.2	1.4	7.0	31 848	75.6	24.4	2.33	2.04
Boynton Beach	3.1	9.6	-3.0	6.2	30 643	20.0	4 433	9.6	2.1	7.8	26 210	72.8	27.2	2.27	2.24
Bradenton	1.7	12.8	-11.1	8.8	24 887	12.5	3 508	7.5	2.1	9.4	21 379	61.7	38.3	2.25	2.22
Cape Coral	3.2	5.9	0.0	4.0	45 653	32.4	4 885	6.2	1.8	7.9	40 768	80.0	20.0	2.48	2.54
Clearwater	4.1	10.7	24.4	7.5	56 802	5.5	8 353	7.6	2.4	9.3	48 449	62.1	37.9	2.19	2.12

1. Includes units rented or sold but not occupied. 2. Specified owner-occupied units. 3. Specified renter-occupied units. 4. Overcrowded or lacking complete plumbing facilities.

Table D. Cities — Labor Force, Employment, Disability, and Construction

| City | Civilian labor force, 2001 | | Unemployment | | Civilian employment, 1990[2] | Percent | | Disability 1990 | Value of residential construction authorized by building permits, 2000 | | |
	Total	Percent change, 2000–2001	Total	Rate[1]	Total	Professional, managerial, and technical	Precision production, craft, and repair	Work disabled persons[3] (percent)	New construction ($1,000)	Number of housing units	Percent single family
	61	62	63	64	65	66	67	68	69	70	71
CALIFORNIA—Cont'd											
Walnut Creek	38 500	0.9	820	2.1	31 063	49.5	6.0	4.9	30 310	116	84.5
Watsonville	17 251	1.8	2 212	12.8	13 129	18.1	10.5	6.9	20 898	112	100.0
West Covina	54 271	2.3	2 066	3.8	47 727	29.1	11.5	5.8	25 229	71	100.0
West Hollywood	25 502	2.4	1 383	5.4	22 050	49.6	4.3	6.9	20 829	133	1.5
Westminster	47 663	1.8	1 718	3.6	39 832	30.2	13.1	7.1	410	2	100.0
West Sacramento	16 382	-0.9	912	5.6	11 486	21.3	13.1	13.2	66 325	546	99.6
Whittier	42 163	2.3	1 567	3.7	37 114	31.2	11.8	6.2	4 702	20	90.0
Woodland	26 567	-0.9	1 242	4.7	18 803	26.9	12.4	7.9	2 676	23	100.0
Yorba Linda	34 149	1.5	578	1.7	29 104	45.1	7.4	4.0	62 378	175	100.0
Yuba City	15 780	-0.7	2 250	14.3	11 004	27.0	13.3	12.1	21 803	138	98.6
Yucaipa	17 360	3.1	561	3.2	12 806	26.8	15.7	10.3	21 723	154	100.0
COLORADO	2 294 893	0.9	85 295	3.7	1 633 281	34.3	9.8	7.8	6 822 089	54 596	70.7
Arvada	62 483	0.2	2 184	3.5	48 488	34.3	10.6	7.0	55 958	388	99.0
Aurora	162 490	0.3	5 661	3.5	119 026	33.3	8.3	6.7	323 206	3 948	40.3
Boulder	72 975	3.4	2 766	3.8	47 707	51.0	4.2	4.4	21 807	123	88.6
Broomfield	19 550	2.0	513	2.6	13 393	36.7	11.7	5.1	75 362	459	91.3
Colorado Springs	196 035	1.7	8 749	4.5	128 155	36.1	9.3	8.9	NA	NA	NA
Denver	279 233	0.5	12 443	4.5	233 602	35.4	7.2	9.2	314 704	3 649	39.4
Englewood	21 064	0.4	776	3.7	15 419	27.9	12.8	9.6	30 669	480	3.5
Fort Collins	70 373	2.7	2 653	3.8	45 199	41.1	7.9	4.7	166 826	1 581	62.2
Grand Junction	17 294	-0.1	837	4.8	12 216	29.6	9.8	12.3	NA	NA	NA
Greeley	40 921	2.8	1 667	4.1	29 282	29.0	10.8	7.3	97 886	1 005	67.9
Lakewood	91 046	0.1	2 944	3.2	70 987	37.3	9.0	7.9	42 522	501	42.3
Littleton	24 198	0.3	827	3.4	17 718	40.5	8.0	7.6	41 785	187	84.0
Longmont	40 574	3.6	1 828	4.5	26 328	33.2	12.5	7.2	150 528	1 465	89.4
Loveland	27 748	2.6	933	3.4	17 897	29.9	13.7	7.3	116 594	1 099	85.2
Northglenn	20 237	0.1	633	3.1	14 688	24.4	13.3	7.3	38 253	560	35.2
Pueblo	45 882	-0.3	2 457	5.4	37 313	27.2	9.5	13.1	NA	NA	NA
Thornton	39 484	0.1	1 269	3.2	28 632	24.0	13.1	6.6	209 961	2 177	41.0
Westminster	55 713	-0.1	1 450	2.6	42 000	34.3	11.0	6.2	94 136	1 032	14.1
Wheat Ridge	19 162	0.2	650	3.4	14 916	32.0	12.2	10.2	3 561	22	50.0
CONNECTICUT	1 717 642	-1.7	56 352	3.3	1 692 874	35.5	11.2	6.4	1 425 046	9 376	87.0
Bridgeport	60 045	-0.6	3 644	6.1	62 443	22.0	11.9	8.8	4 095	106	52.8
Bristol	31 492	-1.0	1 219	3.9	33 112	27.9	15.5	7.0	9 158	77	100.0
Danbury	35 797	-2.2	1 086	3.0	35 764	34.5	11.2	5.7	43 940	381	82.7
Hartford	52 423	-0.7	3 453	6.6	56 870	24.3	9.0	9.7	3 494	61	18.0
Meriden	30 063	-1.8	1 245	4.1	30 347	26.9	14.3	7.6	4 901	68	100.0
Middletown	23 849	-1.6	775	3.2	23 923	36.2	11.7	5.5	7 415	179	54.2
Milford	25 827	-1.4	820	3.2	26 737	32.9	12.7	6.0	21 162	195	75.9
Naugatuck Borough	16 283	-2.2	676	4.2	16 137	29.5	14.5	6.6	6 555	68	100.0
New Britain	33 728	-0.9	1 841	5.5	36 681	26.1	13.2	7.1	628	13	100.0
New Haven	57 039	-1.8	2 440	4.3	58 178	34.7	8.2	8.8	1 826	25	100.0
New London	13 086	-0.6	526	4.0	12 371	26.2	11.0	10.4	93	1	100.0
Norwalk	48 387	-2.4	1 341	2.8	45 360	37.0	11.3	5.8	17 715	116	69.0
Norwich	18 754	-0.6	666	3.6	17 348	27.5	14.9	10.9	2 693	29	100.0
Shelton	19 939	-1.3	687	3.4	19 083	36.6	14.2	5.3	11 075	121	96.7
Stamford	65 817	-2.5	1 792	2.7	60 010	39.9	8.2	5.2	80 057	571	11.2
Torrington	18 143	-0.7	730	4.0	17 531	28.2	14.0	7.9	6 309	71	100.0
Waterbury	51 398	-1.1	3 095	6.0	51 384	26.6	12.7	9.8	5 332	114	88.6
West Haven	28 346	-1.7	1 029	3.6	28 527	27.6	12.0	7.2	2 506	43	100.0
DELAWARE	418 819	2.4	14 705	3.5	335 147	31.0	11.9	7.7	414 088	4 611	84.9
Dover	17 894	1.9	650	3.6	12 767	35.0	9.3	8.4	7 459	87	100.0
Newark	14 977	3.5	512	3.4	12 287	43.9	5.1	3.2	22 792	323	18.9
Wilmington	36 373	2.3	1 762	4.8	33 188	29.4	7.8	10.6	4 187	116	47.4
DISTRICT OF COLUMBIA	277 879	-0.4	18 135	6.5	303 994	44.0	4.5	8.4	53 992	806	23.2
Washington	277 879	-0.4	18 135	6.5	303 994	44.0	4.5	8.4	53 993	806	23.2
FLORIDA	7 673 565	2.4	364 665	4.8	5 810 467	28.8	11.5	8.7	17 462 412	155 269	68.6
Altamonte Springs	31 156	0.8	1 121	3.6	21 224	36.7	6.9	5.2	4 520	85	15.3
Apopka	9 921	1.2	399	4.0	6 934	29.1	11.0	7.2	41 012	582	95.9
Boca Raton	41 503	3.5	1 465	3.5	30 374	41.4	7.2	4.8	87 809	458	26.0
Boynton Beach	27 355	4.0	1 541	5.6	19 583	28.1	11.2	7.9	28 405	284	89.4
Bradenton	26 616	4.0	1 017	3.8	18 062	26.8	13.4	9.5	6 432	79	100.0
Cape Coral	43 866	4.9	1 376	3.1	32 991	26.3	13.1	8.4	196 868	2 198	79.8
Clearwater	58 469	2.6	2 307	3.9	45 175	29.4	9.9	8.9	6 602	107	15.0

1. Percent of civilian labor force. 2. Persons 16 years and older. 3. Persons 16 to 64 years old.

Table D. Cities — **Wholesale Trade, Retail Trade, and Real Estate**

City	Wholesale Trade, 1997				Retail Trade[1], 1997				Real Estate and Rental and Leasing, 1997			
	Number of Establishments	Number of Employees	Sales (mil dol)	Annual Payroll (mil dol)	Number of Establishments	Number of Employees	Sales (mil dol)	Annual Payroll (mil dol)	Number of Establishments	Number of Employees	Receipts (mil dol)	Annual Payroll (mil dol)
	72	73	74	75	76	77	78	79	80	81	82	83
CALIFORNIA—Cont'd												
Walnut Creek	121	1 177	2 402.7	64.5	339	5 859	1 240.9	132.8	230	1 342	233.6	42.0
Watsonville	57	1 641	750.6	57.2	142	1 551	302.1	31.5	48	234	19.2	3.4
West Covina	59	199	114.2	6.0	297	5 218	972.8	88.3	48	141	21.0	2.8
West Hollywood	135	862	457.9	34.3	324	2 794	571.2	69.2	97	752	139.3	21.0
Westminster	86	585	202.6	15.4	444	5 042	1 051.9	93.0	73	352	41.4	6.3
West Sacramento	154	4 361	3 109.2	145.5	101	1 098	215.7	23.0	51	435	90.5	14.8
Whittier	90	696	660.3	29.0	247	3 181	618.1	64.6	83	317	33.2	6.4
Woodland	74	2 953	1 561.0	92.8	165	2 372	406.5	43.6	50	291	30.2	4.5
Yorba Linda	157	4 351	1 700.6	65.0	116	1 726	371.3	34.1	54	208	63.8	5.1
Yuba City	48	390	181.5	14.1	231	3 273	528.8	54.7	69	449	36.1	5.7
Yucaipa	23	208	72.1	4.7	79	646	108.6	10.7	35	120	15.9	1.6
COLORADO	7 383	88 364	60 310.4	3 282.0	18 299	225 647	40 536.0	4 163.3	6 663	38 224	4 853.5	883.8
Arvada	122	1 075	282.1	30.2	294	4 106	660.1	70.2	110	558	47.0	9.5
Aurora	289	4 800	4 326.8	189.1	842	13 348	2 335.9	230.7	301	1 921	222.7	48.1
Boulder	251	2 548	1 598.3	100.1	699	9 587	1 544.9	169.8	281	1 425	201.4	35.5
Broomfield	64	527	202.6	22.4	90	1 384	290.4	27.9	44	123	12.9	1.9
Colorado Springs	417	5 911	1 205.2	200.8	1 644	25 565	4 669.3	466.5	661	2 826	333.1	58.4
Denver	1 681	26 604	16 177.1	972.8	2 410	30 080	5 600.9	628.0	1 201	11 339	1 771.9	287.0
Englewood	220	3 278	4 291.7	137.6	275	3 427	941.1	82.5	70	1 044	147.1	28.4
Fort Collins	110	D	D	D	603	8 644	1 437.0	141.5	194	928	111.6	17.3
Grand Junction	141	1 123	390.4	32.7	467	5 179	965.9	94.4	93	497	46.3	7.9
Greeley	107	1 098	442.2	33.9	297	4 511	764.8	75.3	107	447	50.6	7.5
Lakewood	221	1 326	957.5	53.3	654	9 359	1 801.6	179.4	257	1 330	129.3	28.8
Littleton	114	1 093	875.4	43.9	360	7 383	1 599.0	145.1	89	462	39.6	7.4
Longmont	79	1 519	1 751.6	81.3	300	4 269	776.4	76.8	78	348	41.1	5.9
Loveland	62	611	186.4	18.0	264	3 101	613.5	52.3	76	303	40.9	4.9
Northglenn	26	145	59.7	4.1	106	1 276	268.0	27.2	40	232	22.7	4.4
Pueblo	90	890	360.3	24.0	532	6 586	1 117.2	114.5	107	450	51.0	7.6
Thornton	47	438	557.6	18.8	158	4 013	729.2	80.0	34	325	20.8	6.2
Westminster	94	688	272.5	26.9	372	6 483	1 093.4	104.6	88	441	60.1	7.2
Wheat Ridge	66	648	268.3	18.1	198	2 747	589.2	57.6	49	226	40.5	4.1
CONNECTICUT	5 283	77 716	75 821.6	3 595.3	14 574	186 935	34 938.9	3 634.3	3 372	20 635	3 522.8	609.3
Bridgeport	131	1 665	601.2	63.7	342	3 755	665.8	81.6	94	342	57.0	8.3
Bristol	58	839	251.9	32.1	215	2 741	556.1	50.7	33	131	22.7	2.9
Danbury	125	2 150	904.0	69.9	497	8 262	1 715.5	166.6	76	1 739	535.3	66.1
Hartford	171	4 575	3 038.6	214.5	419	3 644	764.8	87.0	191	1 708	282.2	62.7
Meriden	67	745	220.4	25.1	256	3 678	570.1	59.6	66	307	36.0	6.4
Middletown	51	672	220.3	22.8	148	2 020	377.6	40.0	52	249	42.7	5.1
Milford	153	1 925	776.7	80.7	342	5 645	1 133.3	106.0	43	193	31.8	4.5
Naugatuck Borough	22	372	152.2	13.0	77	1 139	186.9	18.6	16	78	8.0	1.0
New Britain	41	575	279.0	24.0	203	2 068	435.7	42.8	37	223	26.0	5.6
New Haven	130	1 399	737.6	50.9	390	3 377	506.2	64.4	140	847	113.3	19.1
New London	22	223	63.8	8.3	146	1 799	428.6	43.8	23	147	14.7	3.6
Norwalk	210	4 143	3 682.2	338.1	411	7 133	1 792.5	180.7	94	443	144.3	18.2
Norwich	29	480	175.8	15.2	181	2 749	468.5	47.8	30	128	12.2	2.0
Shelton	47	1 111	921.7	54.0	94	1 626	381.2	30.7	22	473	80.5	18.1
Stamford	354	5 992	22 164.2	430.8	545	6 973	1 798.1	186.7	216	1 816	358.0	74.5
Torrington	52	603	209.8	23.9	201	2 531	454.5	43.5	26	127	10.3	2.1
Waterbury	113	1 462	494.9	51.7	481	5 527	982.0	96.4	100	436	58.5	10.6
West Haven	57	1 000	490.0	41.5	140	1 479	277.2	28.4	43	100	13.1	1.9
DELAWARE	906	13 509	12 585.5	619.5	3 736	47 116	8 237.0	798.7	1 101	5 243	5 006.5	118.3
Dover	40	D	D	D	310	5 026	802.9	77.2	71	294	30.6	4.7
Newark	52	D	D	D	204	3 796	760.8	70.1	60	335	73.9	6.5
Wilmington	106	1 736	1 158.1	70.1	354	3 674	708.5	71.7	269	1 015	2 425.1	24.8
DISTRICT OF COLUMBIA	348	5 008	3 918.6	223.0	2 075	19 608	2 788.8	351.5	934	7 725	1 354.2	275.4
Washington	348	5 008	3 918.6	223.0	2 075	19 608	2 788.8	351.5	934	7 725	1 354.2	275.4
FLORIDA	31 214	296 139	187 079.9	9 678.2	66 643	841 814	151 191.2	14 169.5	20 388	118 086	15 360.4	2 652.2
Altamonte Springs	152	1 137	897.2	51.0	407	6 342	896.6	94.8	102	533	85.6	15.2
Apopka	47	481	132.3	13.5	105	1 664	261.1	23.2	20	64	8.8	1.1
Boca Raton	525	6 440	4 325.7	322.1	744	9 092	1 438.2	163.8	344	2 096	378.2	69.8
Boynton Beach	92	498	171.1	14.4	219	2 757	405.0	42.2	76	276	41.3	6.6
Bradenton	37	219	98.3	6.5	241	3 294	519.6	50.1	76	261	39.0	4.9
Cape Coral	94	D	D	D	300	3 747	515.3	52.9	97	287	51.9	5.7
Clearwater	301	2 173	1 020.3	65.6	775	11 505	2 535.5	222.9	201	961	93.6	20.2

1. Establishments with payroll.

City	Professional, Scientific, and Technical Services, 1997[1]				Manufacturing, 1997				Accommodation and Foodservices, 1997			
	Number of Establish-ments	Number of Employees	Receipts (mil dol)	Annual Payroll (mil dol)	Number of Establish-ments	Number of Employees	Receipts (mil dol)	Annual Payroll (mil dol)	Number of Establish-ments	Number of Employees	Sales (mil dol)	Annual Payroll (mil dol)
	84	85	86	87	88	89	90	91	92	93	94	95
CALIFORNIA—Cont'd												
Walnut Creek	718	5 790	750.6	313.9	45	1 417	355.1	63.5	197	3 719	156.6	42.1
Watsonville	57	333	32.9	12.1	81	3 482	555.6	87.0	81	908	32.9	8.0
West Covina	109	660	42.7	16.2	NA	NA	NA	NA	146	2 285	82.1	23.7
West Hollywood	205	2 868	288.9	123.8	NA	NA	NA	NA	184	4 676	205.4	61.6
Westminster	95	257	16.5	4.6	128	1 984	168.5	43.7	206	2 288	81.2	20.2
West Sacramento	42	571	79.8	23.4	68	2 487	712.9	91.5	66	910	30.5	7.9
Whittier	144	649	55.2	21.6	76	2 733	298.3	69.4	140	2 443	77.7	20.0
Woodland	58	299	24.1	9.5	65	2 309	484.6	77.6	83	1 157	38.1	9.8
Yorba Linda	115	596	63.0	23.3	72	1 523	205.8	70.6	68	1 573	49.7	13.4
Yuba City	90	386	24.7	9.6	35	759	234.1	27.2	79	1 269	39.4	11.4
Yucaipa	28	64	4.0	1.2	NA	NA	NA	NA	40	627	19.1	5.0
COLORADO	14 315	103 008	12 887.7	4 625.1	5 480	173 069	40 012.8	6 176.8	10 064	195 126	6 705.5	1 937.4
Arvada	210	1 123	179.2	40.5	106	3 022	432.0	100.6	150	D	D	D
Aurora	451	3 226	379.3	128.9	139	2 360	342.4	75.3	424	8 844	278.3	76.8
Boulder	948	D	D	D	282	9 940	1 758.8	415.7	363	8 078	272.8	79.0
Broomfield	94	429	29.9	12.9	92	7 101	1 389.9	284.5	49	D	D	D
Colorado Springs	1 227	10 126	1 161.5	451.6	418	17 439	4 204.3	565.9	829	19 464	703.1	199.8
Denver	3 147	29 056	3 640.3	1 455.0	976	26 320	4 867.8	816.2	1 564	33 749	1 335.2	386.0
Englewood	195	898	103.7	38.7	200	4 684	617.2	145.2	96	D	D	D
Fort Collins	410	2 650	243.3	102.6	124	8 117	2 334.6	351.8	311	6 749	190.8	54.6
Grand Junction	210	1 174	80.7	36.3	113	3 212	446.0	91.0	180	3 697	102.8	30.0
Greeley	154	715	53.6	21.1	71	5 073	1 926.5	120.0	153	2 654	70.5	19.3
Lakewood	615	4 788	461.3	193.8	125	1 720	359.0	72.1	317	6 234	202.4	60.1
Littleton	269	1 054	91.8	37.3	67	1 860	279.0	60.0	139	D	D	D
Longmont	188	915	74.6	32.4	152	4 688	556.7	136.6	140	2 460	82.6	22.9
Loveland	123	543	38.5	13.0	66	5 214	1 260.8	225.2	103	1 728	53.9	13.6
Northglenn	42	232	21.3	7.4	42	616	102.8	17.4	49	1 128	39.2	10.9
Pueblo	176	939	46.5	17.9	70	2 818	578.4	96.2	280	4 547	131.6	35.3
Thornton	42	264	11.4	3.8	26	1 587	279.3	44.5	109	2 616	85.2	23.5
Westminster	187	968	67.6	28.5	70	2 450	659.3	95.7	170	3 812	118.0	33.9
Wheat Ridge	144	993	93.9	37.8	58	1 413	295.2	53.1	99	1 707	54.2	15.5
CONNECTICUT	9 393	71 058	9 115.8	3 700.1	5 844	252 330	46 938.2	10 452.1	6 903	96 556	3 746.6	1 062.8
Bridgeport	184	1 528	172.6	79.3	249	10 340	1 424.4	375.0	163	D	D	D
Bristol	73	292	20.7	8.2	158	4 542	580.5	159.0	98	D	D	D
Danbury	231	1 744	199.7	81.6	130	6 556	1 302.0	281.0	181	2 803	111.4	30.0
Hartford	405	6 197	891.3	322.3	112	2 183	254.5	60.6	313	4 733	172.8	50.4
Meriden	74	721	60.4	20.2	103	4 353	751.2	162.9	106	1 232	49.6	12.3
Middletown	88	686	76.4	32.5	58	5 256	1 662.2	222.0	103	1 094	44.5	12.0
Milford	158	1 081	126.0	49.3	206	6 100	1 104.5	258.8	168	2 647	99.0	25.6
Naugatuck Borough	32	83	8.5	2.6	63	2 957	737.5	109.8	42	D	D	D
New Britain	71	376	39.4	15.0	141	5 329	845.0	193.2	95	D	D	D
New Haven	418	2 855	339.9	137.1	106	4 177	750.6	147.2	262	3 327	137.8	37.8
New London	100	886	72.4	34.1	NA	NA	NA	NA	95	1 392	48.1	14.0
Norwalk	378	3 173	420.7	174.2	170	6 713	1 420.5	297.7	202	1 944	93.2	25.7
Norwich	75	407	34.1	16.8	48	1 403	254.5	44.8	78	1 379	47.9	13.4
Shelton	108	934	103.6	42.7	77	4 923	728.6	211.8	74	862	40.9	10.2
Stamford	720	10 898	1 713.6	787.5	183	6 126	2 515.3	229.6	281	3 980	198.4	55.0
Torrington	51	176	18.5	4.3	83	3 770	443.8	118.7	72	866	30.9	8.6
Waterbury	152	848	78.7	28.4	219	6 433	1 085.3	220.9	198	2 472	83.9	23.4
West Haven	53	463	25.3	8.8	62	5 258	1 623.1	276.5	97	1 238	42.6	12.1
DELAWARE	1 717	12 382	1 430.4	553.4	675	41 084	13 397.3	1 474.3	1 605	26 969	1 009.0	280.8
Dover	89	820	52.3	23.9	29	3 902	1 338.5	111.5	134	2 689	82.3	22.2
Newark	96	509	57.5	23.1	52	D	D	D	123	2 829	111.2	26.6
Wilmington	450	4 322	690.2	266.2	102	D	D	D	219	3 798	155.9	50.5
DISTRICT OF COLUMBIA	3 760	61 123	10 365.2	3 935.5	200	2 858	320.2	101.1	1 700	42 650	2 263.5	701.4
Washington	3 760	61 123	10 365.2	3 935.5	200	2 858	320.2	101.1	1 700	42 650	2 263.5	701.4
FLORIDA	42 403	276 263	27 231.1	10 803.5	15 992	433 149	77 477.5	13 185.1	28 999	608 834	24 165.3	6 239.5
Altamonte Springs	252	1 411	119.6	45.9	NA	NA	NA	NA	156	4 756	167.2	47.5
Apopka	43	213	12.1	3.8	28	808	123.7	35.5	52	1 097	28.2	7.1
Boca Raton	1 029	4 922	612.4	237.1	175	4 828	639.0	211.2	297	5 635	279.0	61.5
Boynton Beach	152	996	56.2	24.5	65	D	D	D	101	2 001	63.0	18.1
Bradenton	196	814	74.5	30.1	34	D	D	D	104	1 652	55.2	13.2
Cape Coral	164	1 469	68.7	36.9	77	549	46.5	12.9	122	1 787	60.0	16.5
Clearwater	634	4 100	397.1	169.3	182	3 191	342.9	84.8	401	7 830	339.3	84.1

1. Firms subject to federal tax.

City	Arts, Entertainment, and Recreation[1], 1997				Health Care and Social Assistance[1], 1997				Other Services[1], 1997			
	Number of Establishments	Number of Employees	Receipts (mil dol)	Annual Payroll (mil dol)	Number of Establishments	Number of Employees	Receipts (mil dol)	Annual Payroll (mil dol)	Number of Establishments	Number of Employees	Receipts (mil dol)	Annual Payroll (mil dol)
	96	97	98	99	100	101	102	103	104	105	106	107
CALIFORNIA—Cont'd												
Walnut Creek	25	469	16.2	5.1	353	4 391	369.2	178.9	177	1 051	71.7	21.3
Watsonville	4	167	4.7	1.5	101	774	45.7	16.6	53	188	12.4	3.1
West Covina	6	187	8.0	1.8	272	2 713	223.7	86.1	59	244	13.8	3.6
West Hollywood	254	1 001	264.0	140.7	191	934	139.4	53.3	146	883	47.8	14.7
Westminster	11	0	0.0	0.0	225	1 651	121.9	46.4	154	770	51.3	13.3
West Sacramento	1	0	0.0	0.0	40	408	17.5	8.2	62	372	36.2	9.5
Whittier	16	258	11.0	5.0	266	2 671	250.9	87.3	143	751	62.2	16.7
Woodland	10	0	0.0	0.0	76	913	41.4	13.5	79	379	26.9	7.5
Yorba Linda	6	199	18.6	4.4	108	705	52.1	19.4	76	516	29.4	8.9
Yuba City	10	149	4.6	1.4	169	1 778	198.3	56.5	78	527	31.9	9.2
Yucaipa	2	0	0.0	0.0	48	529	32.5	9.3	41	174	11.5	3.0
COLORADO	1 494	30 541	1 909.6	625.0	8 611	85 370	5 790.8	2 538.1	6 793	39 363	2 571.1	770.0
Arvada	18	234	7.0	2.4	168	1 255	74.0	27.7	158	768	53.8	15.1
Aurora	56	901	40.9	10.5	516	8 108	602.1	236.7	375	2 132	132.3	40.2
Boulder	53	692	34.7	13.5	391	2 990	225.1	93.2	235	1 652	114.9	36.3
Broomfield	10	104	4.0	1.2	45	303	17.6	7.7	54	446	23.7	8.0
Colorado Springs	122	1 522	66.1	18.6	1 048	10 148	690.0	302.8	659	4 163	241.0	82.0
Denver	150	1 772	291.8	146.8	1 478	15 938	1 197.2	562.3	1 101	8 212	604.5	172.8
Englewood	12	274	10.0	2.3	192	1 846	200.2	99.9	164	894	67.2	20.4
Fort Collins	26	529	14.3	4.1	344	3 354	206.7	95.1	184	1 160	70.3	21.7
Grand Junction	18	208	7.2	2.8	229	2 229	138.0	65.0	147	886	67.5	17.3
Greeley	25	260	6.1	2.0	157	1 785	118.2	47.6	123	734	40.2	11.6
Lakewood	44	957	50.7	12.2	350	3 861	227.8	96.5	299	1 550	85.8	27.9
Littleton	14	183	8.7	2.2	170	1 896	125.3	50.2	112	793	57.5	18.5
Longmont	22	278	12.6	2.5	151	1 845	103.3	44.4	120	583	33.1	10.5
Loveland	9	73	3.1	0.6	128	1 187	73.6	32.3	78	473	23.0	7.3
Northglenn	5	97	3.0	0.8	33	482	27.1	11.5	45	345	17.5	5.1
Pueblo	26	0	0.0	0.0	282	3 349	199.9	96.5	166	846	43.3	12.9
Thornton	12	194	7.6	1.9	105	1 324	87.0	37.6	67	743	49.5	14.5
Westminster	13	263	8.4	2.8	153	1 486	93.5	42.6	105	493	28.1	9.9
Wheat Ridge	15	96	4.2	1.1	186	1 818	147.9	72.5	105	600	45.3	13.6
CONNECTICUT	1 046	27 236	2 526.8	589.2	7 515	100 363	6 849.7	3 199.3	6 121	34 089	2 370.2	727.8
Bridgeport	20	166	19.6	3.4	252	4 422	332.3	144.2	161	932	71.9	22.1
Bristol	13	178	18.7	3.7	116	1 460	93.5	45.4	92	434	23.8	6.5
Danbury	27	224	11.4	3.2	192	3 359	232.0	129.4	152	853	59.2	17.8
Hartford	16	227	58.9	33.2	324	3 772	466.7	249.5	212	1 129	76.3	21.4
Meriden	6	0	0.0	0.0	113	1 567	107.8	47.3	96	447	29.9	10.2
Middletown	8	21	2.4	0.3	123	1 694	134.3	61.2	87	462	54.6	14.7
Milford	21	441	25.0	9.4	139	2 380	125.7	57.8	130	789	50.9	17.4
Naugatuck Borough	2	0	0.0	0.0	36	520	30.3	11.5	52	261	18.3	5.9
New Britain	7	68	5.2	1.2	118	2 004	154.0	84.7	100	530	40.7	11.5
New Haven	15	282	81.6	5.9	331	3 999	391.2	171.7	254	1 748	119.4	35.9
New London	8	0	0.0	0.0	103	1 953	195.7	71.5	66	409	23.3	8.1
Norwalk	41	314	40.4	7.7	234	2 389	203.9	99.9	179	880	73.9	23.5
Norwich	10	123	6.4	1.9	139	1 971	129.2	68.1	74	422	23.9	7.1
Shelton	4	21	1.1	0.3	61	1 036	70.8	35.5	47	237	14.5	4.7
Stamford	56	752	116.1	25.0	340	2 938	265.5	115.6	219	1 133	83.5	25.5
Torrington	8	68	7.9	0.7	94	1 601	86.9	37.0	76	303	17.5	4.8
Waterbury	22	190	19.0	2.5	248	4 374	316.6	153.6	188	1 001	62.9	19.4
West Haven	8	37	9.1	0.6	60	967	49.3	24.6	111	643	46.4	15.9
DELAWARE	216	4 074	240.1	62.0	1 465	15 980	1 131.6	526.4	1 198	7 006	420.5	140.7
Dover	10	0	0.0	0.0	128	1 428	94.3	42.6	103	678	36.1	11.4
Newark	9	138	5.5	1.4	126	1 456	167.5	73.8	69	473	27.4	11.6
Wilmington	21	754	24.2	7.8	249	2 106	190.5	90.0	166	1 236	72.4	27.0
DISTRICT OF COLUMBIA	171	1 564	161.9	56.1	1 464	13 692	1 054.8	476.7	978	6 218	404.8	111.1
Washington	171	1 564	161.9	56.1	1 464	13 692	1 054.8	476.7	978	6 218	404.8	111.1
FLORIDA	4 763	103 980	7 871.5	1 972.9	35 568	447 117	32 559.1	13 610.7	26 121	146 360	9 123.6	2 665.7
Altamonte Springs	17	164	9.1	2.1	192	2 032	166.3	70.2	110	778	48.9	15.3
Apopka	7	86	3.5	0.9	32	205	13.9	4.8	50	303	17.1	5.3
Boca Raton	76	1 502	73.6	23.1	547	5 483	470.9	194.5	310	1 823	129.2	37.3
Boynton Beach	15	26	6.6	0.9	190	2 277	165.9	70.6	114	469	27.1	7.1
Bradenton	13	37	4.4	1.4	226	6 301	470.7	176.5	99	531	29.3	8.6
Cape Coral	23	228	12.0	2.6	168	1 330	98.3	41.2	137	550	40.5	11.5
Clearwater	40	512	28.3	7.6	522	6 373	426.7	186.0	259	1 915	159.2	47.9

1. Firms subject to federal tax.

Table D. Cities — Federal Funds and City Government Finances

City	Selected federal funds, fiscal 2001[1] (mil dol)									City government finances, 1999						
	Procurement contracts		Grants					Direct payments for individuals		General revenue						
											Intergovernmental		Taxes			
														Per capita[3] (dollars)		
	Defense	Other	Total[2]	Health and family welfare	Energy and environment	Education	Housing and community development	Educational assistance	Housing assistance	Total (mil dol)	Total (mil dol)	Percent from state government	Total (mil dol)	Total	Property	Sales and gross receipts
	108	109	110	111	112	113	114	115	116	117	118	119	120	121	122	123
CALIFORNIA—Cont'd																
Walnut Creek	34.1	65.3	4.7	3.5	0.0	0.0	0.6	0.0	1.2	54.2	5.2	87.5	32.6	507	91	368
Watsonville	5.0	5.3	6.9	1.2	0.4	1.5	0.9	0.0	1.8	NA	NA	NA	NA	NA	NA	NA
West Covina	5.6	0.7	17.1	5.3	0.0	1.2	1.3	1.0	2.6	55.9	10.2	76.5	31.8	320	111	177
West Hollywood	0.4	0.0	1.1	0.0	0.0	0.0	0.0	0.0	2.4	47.5	3.3	88.6	27.3	750	139	523
Westminster	0.0	0.2	2.0	0.0	0.3	0.1	1.6	0.6	0.0	44.3	8.6	80.7	26.4	314	78	203
West Sacramento	30.0	0.1	2.0	1.0	0.9	0.0	0.0	0.0	0.8	NA	NA	NA	NA	NA	NA	NA
Whittier	2.6	0.1	2.3	0.0	0.0	0.9	1.0	8.5	2.8	55.5	9.1	70.5	22.7	287	71	197
Woodland	1.4	0.1	9.1	0.0	0.1	0.0	0.5	0.0	5.9	NA	NA	NA	NA	NA	NA	NA
Yorba Linda	9.2	1.2	0.0	0.0	0.0	0.0	0.0	0.0	0.0	46.8	5.6	80.8	28.5	473	305	126
Yuba City	0.5	12.0	1.4	0.0	0.0	0.7	0.2	0.0	4.0	NA	NA	NA	NA	NA	NA	NA
Yucaipa	0.0	0.0	0.5	0.0	0.5	0.0	0.0	0.0	0.0	13.1	3.7	95.4	5.1	139	60	50
COLORADO	2 277.1	2 190.5	3 915.6	2 062.7	102.5	370.2	63.9	161.3	322.4	X	X	X	X	X	X	X
Arvada	0.4	24.2	0.8	0.0	0.0	0.0	0.7	0.0	7.1	85.6	12.6	75.4	44.1	452	120	320
Aurora	5.3	7.6	10.1	0.2	0.0	3.3	2.6	1.7	13.2	222.8	21.7	53.5	143.6	573	65	492
Boulder	78.4	224.4	317.4	35.8	17.3	8.5	1.6	9.4	6.2	147.1	15.5	20.8	95.6	1 056	174	729
Broomfield	23.1	7.9	0.9	0.3	0.4	0.0	0.0	0.0	0.6	51.9	2.1	86.8	38.5	1 120	127	450
Colorado Springs	528.7	76.4	53.3	11.0	0.4	6.0	4.7	12.8	15.3	499.2	46.1	36.6	139.1	403	46	356
Denver	620.7	226.4	993.7	446.6	56.0	131.1	37.5	80.9	110.6	1 538.6	166.1	86.2	593.4	1 189	351	721
Englewood	111.1	61.8	8.4	0.8	0.4	1.2	0.0	0.0	2.9	44.4	3.5	59.5	25.7	815	77	717
Fort Collins	5.9	24.9	110.0	35.8	7.3	5.8	1.3	10.6	9.7	138.7	9.1	50.2	77.5	711	101	594
Grand Junction	29.6	42.2	4.4	0.3	0.1	0.4	0.4	4.9	13.3	52.6	8.0	20.0	28.4	688	86	598
Greeley	0.1	1.1	17.5	6.1	0.0	4.9	1.4	6.4	13.9	67.9	7.8	38.6	36.9	524	75	432
Lakewood	3.3	95.2	24.6	10.8	7.7	0.2	1.3	0.2	8.6	81.1	14.6	53.2	52.9	387	35	338
Littleton	171.3	57.7	5.1	0.2	2.0	0.0	1.4	1.5	3.5	40.9	10.2	18.3	21.3	518	58	442
Longmont	5.7	4.5	2.3	0.5	1.0	0.0	0.3	0.0	7.3	80.3	4.2	59.9	41.3	665	115	481
Loveland	0.6	10.9	3.3	0.7	0.0	0.6	0.4	0.0	2.7	55.9	4.6	42.5	29.1	617	72	413
Northglenn	0.9	0.3	0.0	0.0	0.0	0.0	0.0	0.0	0.5	20.4	1.8	81.5	11.1	372	55	302
Pueblo	3.5	6.7	14.9	5.1	0.0	4.5	1.5	9.4	18.5	73.0	10.6	41.9	47.4	441	61	378
Thornton	35.3	3.6	1.6	1.2	0.0	0.0	0.0	0.0	2.8	70.8	4.3	87.1	50.1	675	114	531
Westminster	2.5	3.6	1.2	0.0	0.2	0.9	0.0	4.2	2.9	125.5	8.3	39.5	58.0	606	29	559
Wheat Ridge	6.7	3.0	2.2	0.0	1.2	0.0	0.0	0.0	1.0	NA	NA	NA	NA	NA	NA	NA
CONNECTICUT	4 205.8	528.1	4 363.8	2 850.8	101.2	317.4	66.8	79.4	585.9	X	X	X	X	X	X	X
Bridgeport	42.1	4.8	27.0	12.3	0.4	3.7	5.1	4.6	49.2	465.9	246.2	100.0	155.6	1 132	1 115	11
Bristol	0.1	0.1	1.3	0.0	0.2	0.0	0.9	0.0	8.4	140.2	50.1	91.4	73.4	1 240	1 229	0
Danbury	31.0	15.4	36.1	1.5	28.2	0.7	0.6	1.8	16.8	149.7	41.3	98.1	90.7	1 377	1 343	0
Hartford	-2.6	7.1	578.5	278.6	46.0	93.1	32.5	3.6	122.5	591.8	356.1	87.1	183.9	1 398	1 375	0
Meriden	7.3	49.6	2.7	1.7	0.0	0.2	0.8	0.1	9.6	143.2	64.9	100.0	66.1	1 167	1 162	0
Middletown	1.8	0.2	10.3	6.4	0.0	0.5	0.5	3.0	11.5	98.2	30.3	100.0	56.6	1 297	1 263	7
Milford	5.0	0.6	1.7	0.0	0.0	0.8	0.5	0.0	3.4	NA	NA	NA	NA	NA	NA	NA
Naugatuck Borough	1.1	0.1	0.1	0.0	0.0	0.1	0.0	0.0	3.4	71.5	29.5	100.0	34.4	1 137	1 121	0
New Britain	2.1	0.2	8.9	3.1	1.4	1.6	2.4	4.1	14.9	157.6	71.9	100.0	73.9	1 048	1 041	0
New Haven	5.8	15.2	344.9	289.6	13.0	12.7	9.1	12.3	88.7	513.0	291.4	94.9	152.3	1 236	1 200	4
New London	5.1	21.5	5.7	0.2	0.0	2.4	1.0	1.5	18.1	74.7	37.9	96.6	25.5	1 067	1 057	0
Norwalk	26.0	4.0	29.5	24.4	0.1	0.7	1.0	2.3	16.1	214.2	46.3	99.6	158.1	2 026	1 986	0
Norwich	0.0	1.0	1.6	0.0	0.2	0.0	0.9	1.2	9.5	104.9	49.2	97.5	44.9	1 285	1 018	0
Shelton	10.6	19.2	1.0	0.0	0.0	0.0	0.0	0.0	1.9	69.4	10.0	97.9	49.5	1 308	1 286	0
Stamford	31.6	13.5	7.5	2.6	0.0	1.2	1.7	0.1	28.6	334.3	42.6	99.6	237.8	2 148	2 111	0
Torrington	2.2	0.0	0.1	0.0	0.0	0.0	0.0	0.0	6.6	72.9	24.4	98.4	43.5	1 262	1 245	0
Waterbury	3.2	1.5	13.9	4.0	0.0	3.1	4.1	3.1	37.1	284.2	145.3	94.0	119.5	1 134	1 123	0
West Haven	0.2	4.2	2.1	0.2	0.0	0.1	0.8	2.3	6.8	121.7	51.4	88.8	62.1	1 203	1 188	7
DELAWARE	83.8	64.2	891.5	488.1	34.4	94.2	13.1	17.1	88.3	X	X	X	X	X	X	X
Dover	0.8	0.6	116.5	3.3	24.6	36.4	5.9	7.8	15.8	20.4	3.2	73.0	8.6	284	187	6
Newark	5.3	8.1	78.8	17.7	4.9	4.4	0.0	4.0	9.6	15.1	1.7	79.6	4.8	171	131	0
Wilmington	17.2	11.1	52.9	24.9	2.6	1.1	7.2	0.9	28.1	123.4	16.8	78.1	71.6	999	347	19
DISTRICT OF COLUMBIA	1 633.8	8 628.9	4 020.3	1 490.5	157.4	324.2	50.6	45.1	301.8	X	X	X	X	X	X	X
Washington	1 633.8	8 628.9	4 020.3	1 490.5	157.4	324.2	50.6	45.1	301.8	5 240.0	1 551.2	0.0	2 973.6	5 684	1 299	1 875
FLORIDA	6 615.4	2 243.9	13 665.9	7 871.2	156.4	1 441.9	232.1	778.7	1 112.0	X	X	X	X	X	X	X
Altamonte Springs	0.9	1.1	0.3	0.0	0.0	0.0	0.0	0.1	0.0	44.3	5.1	72.0	18.8	477	201	243
Apopka	11.2	0.6	4.3	4.3	0.0	0.0	0.0	0.0	2.8	NA	NA	NA	NA	NA	NA	NA
Boca Raton	3.0	6.1	15.1	5.3	0.1	0.2	0.7	1.1	2.5	102.6	14.6	42.7	54.8	763	385	325
Boynton Beach	0.2	0.9	0.8	0.0	0.0	0.0	0.6	0.0	0.8	65.4	7.4	71.0	29.9	559	394	112
Bradenton	7.5	2.5	9.0	2.8	0.0	2.5	0.5	5.5	5.3	30.6	7.0	74.8	11.9	253	94	150
Cape Coral	0.2	0.1	0.6	0.0	0.0	0.0	0.6	0.1	0.1	114.1	17.0	57.9	33.3	366	249	92
Clearwater	98.7	21.2	33.7	0.5	0.0	3.1	1.2	6.8	8.5	122.5	10.0	28.0	53.6	528	203	300

1. October 1, 2000 to September 30, 2001. 2. Includes program categories not shown separately. State totals include additional categories not allocated by city. 3. Based on population estimated as of July 1 of the year shown.

Table D. Cities — **City Government Finances**

City	Total (mil dol)	Per capita[1] (dollars) Total	Capital outlays	Public welfare	Highways	Parking facilities	Education	Health and hospitals	Police protection	Sewerage and sanitation	Parks and recreation	Housing and community development	Interest on debt
	124	125	126	127	128	129	130	131	132	133	134	135	136
CALIFORNIA—Cont'd													
Walnut Creek	41.4	644	128	0.0	13.2	2.2	0.0	0.0	27.4	0.0	20.7	4.1	1.8
Watsonville	NA	NA	NA	NA	NA	NA	NA	NA	NA	NA	NA	NA	NA
West Covina	63.8	641	105	0.0	11.8	0.9	0.0	2.8	26.4	0.7	5.7	7.3	12.5
West Hollywood	45.3	1 248	127	0.0	17.0	6.0	0.0	0.0	23.5	4.4	3.9	8.3	3.3
Westminster	44.4	528	58	0.0	6.6	0.0	0.0	1.4	41.3	0.0	2.5	10.3	7.5
West Sacramento	NA	NA	NA	NA	NA	NA	NA	NA	NA	NA	NA	NA	NA
Whittier	50.2	634	74	0.0	12.3	0.2	0.0	0.0	35.2	14.4	9.8	7.1	3.9
Woodland	NA	NA	NA	NA	NA	NA	NA	NA	NA	NA	NA	NA	NA
Yorba Linda	43.2	718	115	0.0	25.8	0.0	0.0	8.7	14.1	0.0	6.6	17.7	8.2
Yuba City	NA	NA	NA	NA	NA	NA	NA	NA	NA	NA	NA	NA	NA
Yucaipa	7.1	194	31	0.0	6.7	0.0	0.0	0.8	40.3	0.0	15.9	15.6	5.6
COLORADO	X	X	X	X	X	X	X	X	X	X	X	X	X
Arvada	67.4	691	65	0.0	18.6	0.0	0.0	0.0	19.1	9.6	15.0	5.8	5.0
Aurora	214.9	857	145	0.0	11.6	0.0	0.0	0.0	23.9	9.8	9.5	3.4	4.3
Boulder	133.8	1 477	326	0.0	16.1	1.9	0.0	0.0	16.5	5.3	16.5	5.8	4.4
Broomfield	31.3	910	306	1.4	2.5	0.0	0.0	0.0	15.5	28.1	14.6	13.2	9.4
Colorado Springs	513.7	1 489	250	0.0	11.5	0.3	0.0	42.4	9.7	3.6	4.0	1.8	3.1
Denver	1 314.7	2 634	211	8.0	6.4	0.5	0.0	3.1	9.4	6.2	7.8	2.9	19.7
Englewood	53.7	1 700	597	0.0	9.3	0.0	0.0	0.0	11.9	8.6	10.0	6.1	2.4
Fort Collins	122.0	1 120	362	0.3	20.3	0.3	0.0	0.0	12.4	14.6	18.3	1.1	5.9
Grand Junction	49.2	1 192	224	0.0	23.0	0.3	0.0	0.3	16.7	14.5	14.6	4.7	1.0
Greeley	66.8	949	117	0.0	10.1	0.3	0.0	0.3	16.9	8.0	17.4	2.3	3.5
Lakewood	78.0	570	139	0.0	21.4	0.0	0.0	0.9	25.2	3.7	17.9	3.4	4.8
Littleton	42.4	1 032	18	0.3	11.8	0.0	0.0	0.0	16.3	14.3	5.6	1.9	2.6
Longmont	65.6	1 056	240	0.0	13.8	0.0	0.0	0.1	15.8	18.0	17.9	1.1	2.1
Loveland	44.6	947	190	1.7	13.7	0.0	0.0	0.0	17.5	16.3	15.2	1.5	0.8
Northglenn	16.7	557	68	0.0	14.9	0.0	0.0	0.0	25.5	13.1	18.5	3.5	1.1
Pueblo	58.3	544	40	0.0	11.5	0.4	0.0	1.1	19.1	7.6	10.6	5.0	9.3
Thornton	59.9	808	145	0.0	17.7	0.0	0.0	0.0	15.8	13.4	15.0	0.0	12.9
Westminster	108.4	1 133	320	0.0	10.3	0.0	0.0	0.0	10.4	0.0	20.2	0.3	16.8
Wheat Ridge	NA	NA	NA	NA	NA	NA	NA	NA	NA	NA	NA	NA	NA
CONNECTICUT	X	X	X	X	X	X	X	X	X	X	X	X	X
Bridgeport	439.4	3 197	209	0.7	1.5	0.0	41.2	2.0	7.6	5.7	1.2	8.5	2.8
Bristol	147.0	2 485	152	2.3	4.8	0.0	49.1	3.6	6.3	6.1	2.0	0.4	1.4
Danbury	157.0	2 385	117	0.4	3.3	0.3	53.0	1.4	7.1	4.2	1.7	0.5	2.5
Hartford	642.7	4 887	738	1.5	2.6	0.4	46.2	1.4	5.1	2.3	0.6	7.3	1.7
Meriden	152.1	2 683	528	0.1	2.9	0.1	48.6	1.2	5.2	4.3	1.3	1.0	3.4
Middletown	111.9	2 565	419	0.1	8.0	0.2	44.4	1.4	10.7	7.6	1.8	0.4	11.4
Milford	NA	NA	NA	NA	NA	NA	NA	NA	NA	NA	NA	NA	NA
Naugatuck Borough	65.5	2 165	127	0.0	2.3	0.0	57.0	1.7	5.3	1.4	1.3	0.0	2.1
New Britain	136.8	1 941	0	0.1	2.3	0.3	55.3	0.5	6.5	5.6	4.8	0.0	9.2
New Haven	484.4	3 932	453	4.7	2.9	1.6	45.9	0.6	5.0	3.6	2.5	1.8	3.3
New London	77.4	3 243	181	2.1	3.4	0.5	46.1	1.3	10.1	8.5	3.0	2.9	2.3
Norwalk	206.5	2 645	236	0.6	10.4	0.2	52.9	6.6	6.3	0.5	1.9	1.1	2.2
Norwich	99.3	2 843	113	0.0	1.7	0.4	55.0	0.9	5.9	6.1	5.7	1.3	2.7
Shelton	71.2	1 880	173	2.4	3.8	0.0	59.3	0.4	4.4	5.0	0.8	0.1	2.0
Stamford	341.2	3 083	345	0.1	2.5	0.2	40.6	3.2	8.7	5.3	3.6	0.9	3.5
Torrington	69.4	2 014	6	0.2	4.1	0.2	52.0	1.6	8.1	7.8	0.8	0.0	3.2
Waterbury	248.3	2 357	179	4.3	2.0	0.4	54.4	2.0	9.0	6.0	2.4	1.9	1.0
West Haven	119.9	2 322	236	1.1	3.6	0.0	53.6	0.9	9.5	5.1	1.3	0.6	3.3
DELAWARE	X	X	X	X	X	X	X	X	X	X	X	X	X
Dover	21.9	722	145	0.0	7.5	0.0	0.0	0.0	36.6	29.1	2.0	1.6	2.6
Newark	19.1	684	43	0.0	8.3	0.3	0.0	0.0	23.4	28.5	8.9	1.8	1.5
Wilmington	126.4	1 764	227	0.0	8.6	1.9	0.0	0.0	20.6	12.5	5.7	7.4	7.3
DISTRICT OF COLUMBIA	X	X	X	X	X	X	X	X	X	X	X	X	X
Washington	4 798.5	9 173	638	26.0	2.1	0.1	16.2	10.6	6.5	3.5	3.2	1.3	5.3
FLORIDA	X	X	X	X	X	X	X	X	X	X	X	X	X
Altamonte Springs	35.5	903	157	0.0	6.1	0.0	0.0	0.0	18.7	16.3	7.9	0.0	1.9
Apopka	NA	NA	NA	NA	NA	NA	NA	NA	NA	NA	NA	NA	NA
Boca Raton	94.9	1 322	214	0.0	11.0	0.0	0.0	0.0	15.6	7.1	12.5	2.2	9.5
Boynton Beach	60.8	1 134	249	0.0	1.3	0.0	0.0	0.0	16.6	13.9	14.6	0.7	4.1
Bradenton	27.3	579	105	0.0	3.3	0.2	0.0	0.0	14.2	36.8	8.6	4.9	3.2
Cape Coral	68.6	752	56	0.0	9.7	0.0	0.0	0.0	15.0	6.3	13.5	2.9	15.3
Clearwater	107.3	1 058	3	0.0	5.6	1.9	0.0	0.0	21.7	26.2	9.9	1.5	0.6

1. Based on population estimated as of July 1 of the year shown.

City	City government finances, 1999 (cont'd) Debt outstanding Total (mil dol)	Per capita[1] (dollars)	Percent utility	City government employment, 2001	Climate[2] Average daily temperature (degrees Fahrenheit) Mean January	July	Limits January[3]	July[4]	Annual precipitation (inches)	Heating degree days	Cooling degree days
	137	138	139	140	141	142	143	144	145	146	147
CALIFORNIA—Cont'd											
Walnut Creek	11.2	174	0.0	429	44.5	73.8	35.9	90.8	12.80	2 837	1 066
Watsonville	NA	NA	NA	NA	49.4	61.8	38.3	71.3	21.73	3 213	107
West Covina	84.8	852	13.5	456	55.7	75.2	41.7	89.2	17.90	1 433	1 427
West Hollywood	33.9	934	0.0	146	58.3	74.3	48.9	84.0	14.77	1 154	1 537
Westminster	57.9	689	8.0	340	57.4	72.6	45.6	82.6	12.27	1 238	1 175
West Sacramento	NA	NA	NA	NA	45.2	75.7	37.7	93.2	17.52	2 749	1 237
Whittier	35.9	453	20.6	464	55.7	75.2	41.7	89.2	17.90	1 433	1 427
Woodland	NA	NA	NA	NA	44.5	76.9	35.9	96.3	19.43	2 777	1 387
Yorba Linda	67.4	1 121	0.0	NA	57.4	72.6	45.6	82.6	12.27	1 238	1 175
Yuba City	NA	NA	NA	NA	45.6	78.8	37.2	96.0	21.04	2 524	1 607
Yucaipa	7.5	205	0.0	NA	52.8	78.4	39.6	95.8	12.80	1 875	1 673
COLORADO	X	X	X	X	X	X	X	X	X	X	X
Arvada	93.1	954	11.9	613	30.2	71.9	17.1	85.7	15.86	6 158	554
Aurora	269.6	1 076	42.7	2 436	29.7	73.5	16.1	88.2	15.40	6 020	679
Boulder	119.4	1 319	10.5	1 332	32.6	73.0	19.9	87.5	18.58	5 554	649
Broomfield	88.7	2 578	32.1	420	NA	NA	NA	NA	NA	NA	NA
Colorado Springs	844.4	2 448	64.0	7 018	28.8	70.8	16.1	84.4	16.24	6 415	419
Denver	5 105.8	10 231	5.4	12 765	29.7	73.5	16.1	88.2	15.40	6 020	679
Englewood	54.8	1 736	27.6	508	29.7	73.5	16.1	88.2	15.40	6 020	679
Fort Collins	189.6	1 741	38.2	1 596	27.7	71.5	14.1	85.5	15.07	6 368	479
Grand Junction	6.5	158	0.0	594	25.0	78.8	14.5	93.6	8.64	5 548	1 183
Greeley	69.2	983	41.4	711	26.1	73.5	12.3	89.1	13.97	6 306	645
Lakewood	60.3	440	0.3	763	30.2	71.9	17.1	85.7	15.86	6 158	554
Littleton	18.5	451	0.0	373	30.2	71.9	17.1	85.7	15.86	6 158	554
Longmont	34.9	563	29.3	799	26.6	72.4	11.7	88.7	13.60	6 443	562
Loveland	15.3	324	67.0	650	27.7	71.5	14.1	85.5	15.07	6 368	479
Northglenn	51.4	1 719	95.7	NA	29.7	73.5	16.1	88.2	15.40	6 020	679
Pueblo	95.9	894	14.1	815	29.8	77.1	14.2	93.0	11.19	5 413	973
Thornton	223.6	3 016	41.2	609	29.7	73.5	16.1	88.2	15.40	6 020	679
Westminster	337.5	3 527	11.8	803	30.2	71.9	17.1	85.7	15.86	6 158	554
Wheat Ridge	NA	NA	NA	NA	30.2	71.9	17.1	85.7	15.86	6 158	554
CONNECTICUT	X	X	X	X	X	X	X	X	X	X	X
Bridgeport	356.3	2 592	19.9	5 027	28.9	73.7	21.9	81.7	41.66	5 537	724
Bristol	33.9	573	31.6	NA	24.6	73.7	15.8	85.0	44.14	6 151	677
Danbury	88.6	1 345	24.9	1 875	23.8	71.3	13.2	83.6	44.50	6 492	486
Hartford	86.2	656	0.0	2 299	24.6	73.7	15.8	85.0	44.14	6 151	677
Meriden	70.7	1 248	1.1	1 776	27.1	72.8	19.2	83.3	49.72	5 945	633
Middletown	191.0	4 376	0.0	NA	27.1	72.8	19.2	83.3	49.72	5 945	633
Milford	NA	NA	NA	NA	NA	NA	NA	NA	NA	NA	NA
Naugatuck Borough	24.9	822	0.0	965	27.1	72.8	19.2	83.3	49.72	5 945	633
New Britain	110.8	1 572	0.5	2 087	24.6	73.7	15.8	85.0	44.14	6 151	677
New Haven	139.8	1 135	0.0	4 738	28.9	73.7	21.9	81.7	41.66	5 537	724
New London	27.6	1 154	17.4	949	27.7	71.4	18.5	80.7	48.16	5 951	472
Norwalk	76.2	976	0.0	2 131	27.5	72.9	17.9	83.5	46.80	5 865	613
Norwich	44.5	1 274	0.0	1 197	27.6	72.2	17.5	82.7	50.01	5 869	551
Shelton	17.8	471	0.0	NA	28.9	73.7	21.9	81.7	41.66	5 537	724
Stamford	247.1	2 232	0.0	3 706	27.4	72.6	17.6	84.4	49.43	5 778	613
Torrington	58.5	1 699	0.0	NA	23.6	70.7	13.5	82.0	49.28	6 636	418
Waterbury	56.0	532	14.0	3 525	27.1	72.8	19.2	83.3	49.72	5 945	633
West Haven	59.9	1 160	0.0	NA	28.9	73.7	21.9	81.7	41.66	5 537	724
DELAWARE	X	X	X	X	X	X	X	X	X	X	X
Dover	46.7	1 538	84.9	365	33.8	77.2	25.0	87.7	44.14	4 337	1 199
Newark	8.6	306	0.0	259	31.3	76.0	22.3	87.2	42.61	4 825	1 033
Wilmington	208.2	2 905	15.1	1 330	30.6	76.4	22.4	85.6	40.84	4 937	1 046
DISTRICT OF COLUMBIA	X	X	X	X	X	X	X	X	X	X	X
Washington	4 662.9	8 914	0.1	35 835	34.6	80.0	26.8	88.5	38.63	4 047	1 549
FLORIDA	X	X	X	X	X	X	X	X	X	X	X
Altamonte Springs	26.0	662	61.3	NA	59.7	82.3	48.6	91.5	48.11	686	3 381
Apopka	NA	NA	NA	NA	NA	NA	NA	NA	NA	NA	NA
Boca Raton	175.2	2 441	25.7	1 252	66.2	82.5	56.8	91.2	59.15	262	4 038
Boynton Beach	82.3	1 535	55.5	NA	65.1	82.2	55.7	89.9	60.75	323	3 891
Bradenton	41.0	871	64.8	NA	60.2	81.4	49.0	90.8	53.71	678	3 186
Cape Coral	245.8	2 695	36.6	1 179	63.8	82.8	53.2	91.1	53.37	418	3 855
Clearwater	116.0	1 143	90.5	1 717	59.9	82.1	50.0	90.2	43.92	726	3 396

1. Based on the population estimated as of July 1 of the year shown. 2. Represents normal values based on the 30-year period, 1961–1990. 3. Average daily minimum. 4. Average daily maximum.

STATE Place code	City	Land area, 2000[1] (sq km)	Population, 2000			Population				Population characteristics, 2000 — Percent						
												Race (alone or in combination)				
			Total persons	Rank	Per square kilometer	Total persons 1990	Percent change 1990–2000	Total persons 1980	Percent change 1980–1990	White	Black	Am. Indian, Alaska Native	Asian and Pacific Islander	Other race	Hispanic[2]	Non-Hispanic White
		1	2	3	4	5	6	7	8	9	10	11	12	13	14	15
	FLORIDA—Cont'd															
12 13275	Coconut Creek	29.9	43 566	703	1 457.1	27 269	59.8	NA	NA	87.9	6.8	0.3	3.1	4.2	11.7	77.8
12 14125	Cooper City	16.4	27 939	1 103	1 703.6	21 335	31.0	10 140	110.4	90.6	3.6	0.4	4.8	2.8	15.6	75.7
12 14250	Coral Gables	34.0	42 249	723	1 242.6	40 091	5.4	43 241	-7.3	93.2	3.6	0.3	2.1	2.4	46.6	47.7
12 14400	Coral Springs	61.9	117 549	186	1 899.0	78 864	49.1	37 349	111.2	83.3	10.2	0.4	4.2	4.6	15.5	69.9
12 16475	Davie	86.6	75 720	352	874.4	47 143	60.6	20 877	125.8	88.9	5.2	0.6	3.5	4.3	18.8	72.2
12 16525	Daytona Beach	152.0	64 112	425	421.8	61 991	3.4	54 176	14.4	63.6	33.5	0.8	2.3	1.7	3.5	60.3
12 16725	Deerfield Beach	34.8	64 583	422	1 855.8	46 997	37.4	39 193	19.9	78.9	17.2	0.4	1.8	4.6	8.7	71.2
12 17100	Delray Beach	39.8	60 020	467	1 508.0	47 184	27.2	34 325	37.5	67.5	29.7	0.4	1.9	4.6	7.0	61.8
12 18575	Dunedin	26.9	35 691	874	1 326.8	34 427	3.7	30 203	14.0	95.9	2.2	0.6	1.4	1.1	3.3	92.4
12 24000	Fort Lauderdale	82.2	152 397	130	1 854.0	149 238	2.1	153 279	-2.6	65.6	31.5	0.5	1.6	4.7	9.5	57.5
12 24125	Fort Myers	82.4	48 208	626	585.0	44 947	7.3	36 638	22.7	57.8	35.2	0.7	1.5	7.9	14.5	49.2
12 24300	Fort Pierce	38.2	37 516	830	982.1	36 830	1.9	33 802	9.0	50.9	42.8	0.7	1.2	7.6	15.0	41.4
12 25175	Gainesville	124.8	95 447	249	764.8	91 482	12.2	81 371	4.6	70.1	24.0	0.7	5.3	2.2	6.4	64.1
12 27322	Greenacres City	12.1	27 569	1 121	2 278.4	18 683	47.6	NA	NA	85.0	7.3	0.6	2.4	7.3	21.2	69.2
12 28450	Hallandale	10.9	34 282	915	3 145.1	30 997	10.6	36 511	-15.1	79.1	17.0	0.5	1.6	4.8	18.8	62.6
12 30000	Hialeah	49.8	226 419	75	4 546.6	188 008	20.4	145 254	29.4	91.2	2.9	0.3	0.7	8.6	90.3	8.1
12 32000	Hollywood	70.8	139 357	153	1 968.3	121 720	14.5	121 323	0.3	80.7	13.2	0.6	2.7	6.3	22.5	61.6
12 32275	Homestead	37.0	31 909	974	862.4	26 694	19.5	20 668	29.2	64.1	25.0	0.8	1.4	14.2	51.8	22.9
12 35000	Jacksonville	1 962.4	735 617	14	374.9	635 042	9.3	NA	NA	66.0	29.7	0.8	3.6	2.1	4.2	62.2
12 35875	Jupiter town	51.8	39 328	788	759.2	26 753	57.9	NA	NA	95.8	1.4	0.4	1.7	1.9	7.3	89.4
12 36550	Key West	15.4	25 478	1 219	1 654.4	24 832	2.6	24 382	1.8	86.7	10.0	0.8	1.8	3.0	16.5	71.4
12 36950	Kissimmee	43.2	47 814	634	1 106.8	30 337	57.6	15 487	95.9	70.8	11.3	1.0	4.3	17.5	41.7	43.7
12 38250	Lakeland	118.7	78 452	333	660.9	70 576	11.2	47 406	48.9	74.8	22.1	0.7	1.8	2.5	6.4	69.5
12 39075	Lake Worth	14.6	35 133	889	2 406.4	28 564	23.0	27 048	5.6	67.4	21.3	1.4	1.4	13.4	29.7	48.1
12 39425	Largo	40.6	69 371	386	1 708.6	65 910	5.3	58 977	11.8	94.0	3.1	0.7	2.1	1.6	4.2	89.9
12 39525	Lauderdale Lakes	9.3	31 705	983	3 409.1	27 341	16.0	25 426	7.5	25.1	72.0	0.4	1.8	6.0	5.5	21.2
12 39550	Lauderhill	18.9	57 585	496	3 046.8	49 015	17.5	37 271	31.5	35.0	61.9	0.4	2.4	4.5	6.9	29.5
12 43125	Margate	22.8	53 909	552	2 364.4	42 985	25.4	36 044	19.3	81.0	13.1	0.6	3.7	5.4	15.3	67.8
12 43975	Melbourne	78.2	71 382	374	912.8	60 034	18.9	46 497	29.1	86.4	10.1	0.9	3.2	1.9	5.5	80.7
12 45000	Miami	92.4	362 470	47	3 922.8	358 648	1.1	346 865	3.4	69.5	24.2	0.5	1.1	9.5	65.8	11.8
12 45025	Miami Beach	18.2	87 933	289	4 831.5	92 639	-5.1	96 298	-3.8	89.8	4.8	0.5	2.0	6.6	53.4	40.9
12 45975	Miramar	76.4	72 739	365	952.1	40 663	78.9	32 813	23.9	46.2	46.2	0.4	4.2	8.3	29.4	21.6
12 49425	North Lauderdale	10.0	32 264	965	3 226.4	26 473	21.9	NA	NA	52.7	38.3	0.6	4.2	9.9	21.1	36.7
12 49450	North Miami	21.9	59 880	469	2 734.2	50 001	19.8	42 566	17.5	36.7	58.1	0.7	3.0	6.6	23.2	18.1
12 49475	North Miami Beach	12.8	40 786	754	3 186.4	35 361	15.3	36 553	-3.3	49.3	41.8	0.6	5.2	8.6	30.0	24.8
12 50575	Oakland Park	16.3	30 966	1 008	1 899.8	26 326	17.6	23 035	14.3	68.4	25.1	0.6	2.8	7.9	17.9	53.9
12 50750	Ocala	100.1	45 943	663	459.0	42 045	9.3	37 161	13.1	74.2	22.7	0.9	1.5	2.5	5.7	69.6
12 53000	Orlando	242.2	185 951	105	767.8	164 674	12.9	128 291	28.4	63.4	28.3	0.7	3.6	7.7	17.5	50.8
12 53150	Ormond Beach	66.7	36 301	856	544.2	29 721	22.1	21 378	39.0	95.2	2.9	0.5	1.7	0.7	2.2	92.5
12 53575	Oviedo	39.2	26 316	1 175	671.3	11 114	136.8	NA	NA	85.3	9.5	0.7	3.3	3.6	12.2	75.0
12 54000	Palm Bay	164.8	79 413	328	481.9	62 543	27.0	18 560	237.0	83.6	12.2	0.8	2.5	3.7	8.6	76.2
12 54075	Palm Beach Gardens	144.2	35 058	894	243.1	24 139	45.2	14 407	67.6	94.6	2.6	0.3	2.5	1.1	5.6	89.1
12 54700	Panama City	53.1	36 417	850	685.8	34 396	5.9	33 346	3.1	75.2	22.0	1.4	2.3	1.1	2.9	72.3
12 55775	Pembroke Pines	85.6	137 427	157	1 605.5	65 566	109.6	35 776	83.3	78.0	14.6	0.4	4.9	5.9	28.2	52.7
12 55925	Pensacola	58.8	56 255	517	956.7	59 198	-5.0	57 619	2.7	66.1	31.2	1.1	2.3	0.9	2.1	63.7
12 56975	Pinellas Park	38.2	45 658	669	1 195.2	43 571	4.8	32 811	32.8	91.1	2.5	1.1	4.8	2.9	6.3	85.3
12 57425	Plantation	56.3	82 934	309	1 473.1	66 814	24.1	48 501	37.8	80.0	15.1	0.4	3.8	3.8	13.1	68.0
12 57550	Plant City	58.6	29 915	1 039	510.5	22 754	31.5	19 270	18.1	73.0	16.6	0.7	1.3	10.2	17.4	64.3
12 58050	Pompano Beach	53.2	78 191	337	1 469.8	72 411	8.0	52 618	37.6	69.3	27.7	0.5	1.4	4.9	9.9	60.8
12 58575	Port Orange	64.0	45 823	664	716.0	35 399	29.4	18 756	88.7	96.4	1.7	0.6	1.5	0.8	2.5	93.7
12 58715	Port St. Lucie	195.6	88 769	278	453.8	55 761	59.2	14 690	279.6	89.2	7.7	0.6	1.7	2.6	7.5	82.8
12 60975	Riviera Beach	21.6	29 884	1 041	1 383.5	27 646	8.1	26 473	4.4	28.5	69.4	0.5	1.4	2.5	4.5	25.4
12 63000	St. Petersburg	154.4	248 232	68	1 607.7	240 318	3.3	238 647	0.7	73.0	23.2	0.6	3.3	2.0	4.2	68.6
12 63650	Sanford	49.5	38 291	811	773.6	32 387	18.2	23 176	39.7	61.5	33.1	1.0	1.5	5.2	10.4	54.6
12 64175	Sarasota	38.6	52 715	567	1 365.7	50 897	3.6	48 876	4.1	78.4	16.8	0.9	1.4	4.5	11.9	69.8
12 69700	Sunrise	47.1	85 779	294	1 821.2	65 683	30.6	39 681	65.5	71.5	21.9	0.4	4.1	5.6	17.1	57.0
12 70600	Tallahassee	247.9	150 624	135	607.6	124 773	20.7	81 548	53.0	61.7	34.9	0.7	3.0	1.6	4.2	57.8
12 70675	Tamarac	29.5	55 588	528	1 884.3	44 822	24.0	29 376	52.6	84.0	11.6	0.4	2.1	4.9	14.9	71.4
12 71000	Tampa	290.2	303 447	57	1 045.6	280 015	8.4	271 523	3.1	66.3	27.2	0.9	2.9	5.8	19.3	51.0
12 71900	Titusville	55.1	40 670	757	738.1	39 394	3.2	31 910	23.5	85.0	13.2	0.9	1.4	1.1	3.5	81.3
12 76582	Weston city	61.5	49 286	612	801.4	9 829	401.4	NA	NA	89.7	4.2	0.2	3.8	4.5	30.2	61.8
12 76600	West Palm Beach	142.8	82 103	312	575.0	67 764	21.2	63 305	7.0	59.7	34.0	0.8	2.1	6.9	18.2	46.0
12 78275	Winter Haven	45.8	26 487	1 165	578.3	24 725	7.1	21 169	16.8	72.5	24.5	0.5	1.4	3.3	4.9	69.1
12 78325	Winter Springs	37.2	31 666	985	851.2	22 151	43.0	10 475	111.5	90.5	5.2	0.6	2.4	3.5	10.5	81.6
13 00000	**GEORGIA**	149 976.2	8 186 453	X	54.6	6 478 149	26.4	5 462 982	18.6	66.1	29.2	0.6	2.5	2.9	5.3	62.6
13 01052	Albany	143.8	76 939	345	535.0	78 804	-2.4	74 059	6.4	33.7	65.2	0.5	0.9	0.6	1.2	32.7
13 01696	Alpharetta	55.3	34 854	902	630.3	13 002	168.1	NA	NA	84.9	6.8	0.5	6.3	3.1	5.5	80.7
13 03436	Athens-Clarke County	312.8	101 489	233	324.5	86 522	15.9	42 549	103.3	66.1	27.8	0.5	3.7	3.5	6.3	62.0
13 04000	Atlanta	341.2	416 474	39	1 220.6	393 929	5.7	425 022	-7.3	34.0	62.1	0.5	2.3	2.5	4.5	31.3
13 04200	Augusta-Richmond County	839.3	199 775	89	238.0	NA	NA	NA	NA	46.8	50.7	0.7	2.2	1.5	2.8	44.4

1. Dry land or land partially or temporarily covered by water.   2. Hispanic persons may be of any race.

Table D. Cities — Population and Households

City	Population characteristics, 2000 (cont'd)										Households, 2000				
	Age of population (percent)													Percent	
	Under 5 years	5 to 17 years	18 to 24 years	25 to 34 years	35 to 44 years	45 to 54 years	55 to 64 years	65 to 74 years	75 years and over	Percent female	Number	Percent change, 1990–2000	Persons per household	Female family householder[1]	One-person
	16	17	18	19	20	21	22	23	24	25	26	27	28	29	30
FLORIDA—Cont'd															
Coconut Creek	6.2	11.8	5.6	16.0	15.3	10.5	8.1	9.5	17.0	53.5	20 093	48.0	2.16	7.7	32.5
Cooper City	6.1	25.3	6.3	9.4	20.8	18.1	7.5	4.1	2.6	51.5	9 123	30.8	3.06	11.9	10.8
Coral Gables	4.9	12.5	13.9	13.7	15.3	13.9	10.0	7.5	8.3	53.3	16 793	8.6	2.31	9.1	31.5
Coral Springs	6.9	23.8	7.9	13.2	19.1	16.4	6.7	3.1	2.9	51.3	39 522	46.3	2.96	13.3	15.2
Davie	6.7	19.7	8.2	14.5	18.9	14.5	8.2	5.4	4.0	51.3	28 682	60.2	2.64	12.6	22.3
Daytona Beach	5.0	12.6	16.6	13.1	12.5	11.5	9.0	9.4	10.4	50.1	28 605	3.8	2.06	14.5	39.4
Deerfield Beach	4.8	10.8	6.5	14.2	14.2	11.0	9.2	10.8	18.5	53.4	31 392	35.8	2.02	9.6	40.3
Delray Beach	5.0	13.2	6.3	12.4	14.7	12.6	9.8	10.8	15.1	52.3	26 787	25.2	2.22	10.2	35.3
Dunedin	3.8	11.8	5.4	10.3	14.2	13.6	11.0	12.9	17.0	54.2	17 258	8.6	2.01	8.8	37.9
Fort Lauderdale	5.3	14.1	7.7	15.1	17.7	14.9	9.9	7.8	7.5	47.6	68 468	3.1	2.14	11.5	40.3
Fort Myers	8.1	18.2	11.4	15.8	14.5	10.8	6.8	6.2	8.1	50.6	19 107	5.3	2.40	18.4	33.8
Fort Pierce	7.6	19.6	9.8	12.5	13.5	11.0	8.5	8.7	8.8	50.7	14 407	1.7	2.56	19.3	31.1
Gainesville	4.6	13.2	29.4	15.0	11.6	10.5	5.9	4.8	5.0	51.1	37 279	16.8	2.25	13.3	32.6
Greenacres City	6.1	14.8	7.6	14.7	13.8	10.7	8.7	11.9	11.7	53.2	12 059	46.4	2.29	12.5	29.7
Hallandale	4.0	9.2	5.3	11.0	11.9	11.1	11.7	14.7	21.1	53.9	18 051	5.3	1.88	9.1	45.2
Hialeah	5.8	17.2	8.2	14.2	15.1	12.0	10.9	9.5	7.1	51.9	70 704	19.1	3.15	17.4	14.7
Hollywood	5.9	15.4	7.0	14.4	16.9	13.7	9.4	8.0	9.4	51.5	59 673	12.8	2.31	11.9	34.4
Homestead	10.6	22.5	12.8	17.3	13.8	9.3	5.7	4.2	3.7	48.3	10 095	8.4	3.10	22.4	20.9
Jacksonville	7.3	19.4	9.7	15.5	16.8	13.1	7.8	5.5	4.8	51.6	284 499	10.6	2.53	16.0	26.2
Jupiter town	5.2	15.5	5.1	11.4	17.5	14.8	11.6	11.1	7.8	50.7	16 945	58.8	2.32	8.4	25.8
Key West	4.7	11.3	8.4	18.0	19.2	16.9	9.9	6.3	5.5	45.0	11 016	5.7	2.23	8.2	31.4
Kissimmee	7.8	19.2	12.0	18.7	16.2	11.5	6.9	4.5	3.1	50.5	17 121	51.3	2.77	15.8	20.9
Lakeland	6.2	15.2	10.3	12.5	12.2	11.2	9.4	10.6	12.4	53.5	33 509	13.0	2.23	13.7	32.9
Lake Worth	7.1	15.8	10.6	16.2	16.5	12.0	7.6	6.3	7.9	47.9	13 828	10.1	2.49	11.5	33.6
Largo	4.2	11.4	6.1	11.4	13.7	11.9	11.1	13.4	16.7	53.5	34 041	6.6	1.99	9.0	38.5
Lauderdale Lakes	7.6	20.1	8.7	12.7	14.2	10.8	8.1	7.1	10.7	55.2	12 099	1.1	2.59	22.2	30.1
Lauderhill	7.5	19.1	8.7	14.8	15.5	11.5	6.8	6.2	9.9	54.2	22 810	7.9	2.49	20.1	31.0
Margate	6.0	14.9	6.5	13.6	15.6	12.2	9.5	7.9	13.8	52.8	22 714	20.0	2.36	10.2	30.8
Melbourne	5.4	15.3	9.3	12.6	15.8	12.4	9.6	9.7	10.0	51.5	30 788	22.8	2.22	11.5	32.9
Miami	5.9	15.9	8.8	15.0	15.4	12.2	9.9	8.9	8.1	50.3	134 198	3.0	2.61	18.7	30.4
Miami Beach	3.9	9.5	7.8	20.9	17.3	12.4	8.9	8.8	10.5	48.8	46 194	-6.3	1.87	8.5	48.7
Miramar	8.7	22.3	8.6	16.4	19.0	12.1	6.6	3.8	2.5	52.4	23 058	60.2	3.15	19.1	14.3
North Lauderdale	8.0	21.8	10.7	17.5	17.7	11.7	5.6	3.2	3.7	51.6	10 799	19.0	2.99	19.3	19.6
North Miami	8.1	20.0	11.3	15.8	16.0	12.5	7.1	4.8	4.4	51.9	20 541	2.1	2.85	20.1	26.9
North Miami Beach	7.1	20.2	9.4	14.2	16.8	13.3	7.7	5.5	5.8	52.2	13 987	0.1	2.89	19.5	23.9
Oakland Park	6.7	14.1	9.0	18.6	20.2	13.7	7.6	5.4	4.7	47.8	13 502	11.6	2.26	13.3	35.1
Ocala	5.9	17.3	9.3	12.1	14.1	11.7	9.2	9.0	11.4	52.7	18 646	7.2	2.29	15.9	33.0
Orlando	6.6	15.4	10.7	21.1	16.2	11.6	7.0	5.7	5.7	51.6	80 883	23.1	2.25	15.4	35.0
Ormond Beach	4.2	15.0	4.5	8.5	13.9	14.8	11.7	13.3	14.2	53.3	15 629	23.0	2.27	8.8	27.1
Oviedo	8.4	23.6	7.1	15.1	21.5	12.8	5.8	3.6	2.2	50.5	8 556	125.5	3.07	9.9	10.5
Palm Bay	6.1	20.4	7.6	12.1	17.5	12.6	8.9	8.7	6.0	51.2	30 336	30.0	2.60	12.2	21.8
Palm Beach Gardens	4.5	14.2	5.1	10.6	15.6	15.4	13.4	11.4	9.7	52.6	15 599	63.2	2.23	8.9	27.7
Panama City	6.1	16.9	9.6	13.8	16.0	13.0	8.7	7.8	8.1	51.4	14 819	5.5	2.30	15.4	32.2
Pembroke Pines	7.1	18.5	6.4	14.9	18.6	12.2	7.1	7.0	8.2	53.4	51 989	94.6	2.62	11.1	24.1
Pensacola	5.7	17.2	8.9	12.1	14.8	14.5	9.6	8.9	8.3	53.0	24 524	2.3	2.27	16.7	32.9
Pinellas Park	5.5	15.8	6.7	13.3	15.9	12.3	9.8	9.5	11.0	52.3	19 444	6.9	2.31	11.6	30.2
Plantation	6.0	17.1	7.1	14.7	17.3	15.2	9.5	6.2	6.9	52.5	33 244	25.5	2.48	11.2	25.8
Plant City	8.3	21.1	8.9	14.2	14.9	12.0	8.2	6.6	5.7	51.8	10 849	29.2	2.73	14.8	22.9
Pompano Beach	5.3	12.5	7.4	13.5	15.6	12.5	10.0	9.9	13.5	50.7	35 197	9.5	2.13	10.9	38.6
Port Orange	4.5	15.3	5.9	10.3	14.6	14.2	11.5	12.4	11.2	52.4	19 574	30.8	2.32	9.6	25.7
Port St. Lucie	5.8	18.5	5.9	11.4	16.7	13.0	9.8	10.5	8.3	51.4	33 909	64.0	2.60	10.0	18.2
Riviera Beach	7.1	22.1	8.0	12.0	13.8	11.8	10.3	8.3	6.7	52.3	11 387	10.2	2.60	23.5	27.6
St. Petersburg	5.7	15.8	7.7	13.8	16.5	13.9	9.2	8.1	9.3	52.3	109 663	3.7	2.20	13.8	35.6
Sanford	7.5	19.3	10.7	16.6	15.9	12.2	7.2	5.5	5.0	50.3	14 237	17.5	2.57	19.2	27.0
Sarasota	5.3	13.1	9.2	13.4	14.6	12.8	9.6	9.6	12.4	51.4	23 427	2.7	2.12	12.3	38.3
Sunrise	6.4	18.5	7.3	14.7	16.9	11.9	6.5	6.5	11.2	53.2	33 308	26.6	2.54	13.8	27.2
Tallahassee	5.2	12.2	29.7	15.9	11.9	10.9	5.9	4.1	4.1	52.8	63 217	25.3	2.17	13.2	34.7
Tamarac	4.4	9.0	5.3	12.1	11.3	10.1	10.0	14.4	23.4	55.3	27 423	19.7	2.00	9.4	36.3
Tampa	6.8	17.9	10.0	15.8	16.5	12.7	7.9	6.4	6.1	51.2	124 758	8.7	2.36	16.1	33.7
Titusville	5.7	17.3	6.9	10.9	15.3	12.4	10.8	11.2	9.6	52.4	17 200	6.1	2.32	12.6	29.9
Weston city	9.0	23.4	5.0	14.5	21.7	13.3	6.4	4.2	2.5	51.5	16 576	NA	2.97	9.0	13.8
West Palm Beach	6.1	15.3	9.8	16.0	15.5	12.6	8.8	7.6	8.4	50.7	34 769	20.8	2.26	13.6	37.6
Winter Haven	5.7	15.2	6.8	11.0	12.5	11.5	9.8	11.8	15.6	54.0	11 833	8.2	2.17	12.8	36.0
Winter Springs	6.0	21.0	7.3	11.5	17.9	16.4	9.0	6.3	4.5	51.5	11 774	47.0	2.69	11.1	18.8
GEORGIA	7.3	19.2	10.2	15.9	16.5	13.2	8.1	5.3	4.3	50.8	3 006 369	27.0	2.65	14.5	23.6
Albany	7.8	20.0	13.0	14.2	13.5	12.0	7.6	6.3	5.6	54.0	28 620	2.5	2.54	25.2	28.8
Alpharetta	8.5	18.6	7.2	19.2	21.3	13.1	6.3	3.4	2.4	50.4	13 911	164.2	2.50	7.3	27.7
Athens-Clarke County	5.2	12.6	31.3	16.4	11.0	9.5	5.9	4.1	3.9	51.2	39 706	NA	2.35	13.3	29.7
Atlanta	6.4	15.9	13.3	19.7	15.5	12.0	7.4	5.0	4.7	50.4	168 147	8.0	2.30	20.7	38.5
Augusta-Richmond County	7.1	19.7	12.0	14.8	15.0	12.6	7.9	6.0	4.8	51.8	73 920	NA	2.55	20.8	27.7

1. No spouse present.

City	Persons in group quarters, 2000				Serious crimes known to police, 2000[2]				Education, 1990				Money income, 1989		
	Institutional			Non-Institutional[1]	Total		Rate[3]		School enrollment		Attainment[4] (percent)		Per capita (dollars)[5]	Households Median	
	Total	Total	Persons in nursing homes		Number	Rate[3]	Violent	Property	Public	Private	High school graduate or more	Bachelor's degree or more		Dollars	Percent change, 1979–1989 (constant 1989 dollars)
	31	32	33	34	35	36	37	38	39	40	41	42	43	44	45
FLORIDA—Cont'd															
Coconut Creek	197	113	113	84	1 103	2 532	209	2 323	2 739	987	84.3	21.7	19 347	33 191	NA
Cooper City	1	0	0	1	567	2 029	172	1 858	5 156	1 201	87.8	28.4	17 954	49 750	10.4
Coral Gables	3 510	97	51	3 413	2 944	6 968	551	6 417	4 099	7 975	89.6	49.1	30 852	47 506	29.6
Coral Springs	567	305	305	262	3 985	3 390	260	3 130	20 831	3 758	89.2	31.5	18 319	43 428	0.6
Davie	97	33	33	64	3 641	4 809	380	4 428	9 362	2 304	80.7	20.5	16 747	36 843	7.1
Daytona Beach	5 097	1 492	1 315	3 605	6 776	10 569	1 763	8 806	9 823	5 895	73.6	16.5	11 901	18 631	8.0
Deerfield Beach	1 168	659	305	509	2 161	3 346	461	2 885	5 142	1 810	74.3	16.1	17 093	26 950	16.1
Delray Beach	530	304	216	226	4 866	8 107	988	7 119	6 357	1 307	74.6	21.5	21 292	31 146	12.7
Dunedin	943	209	209	734	1 269	3 556	244	3 312	4 785	780	81.6	18.9	16 721	25 906	11.4
Fort Lauderdale	5 559	3 979	617	1 580	12 782	8 387	1 156	7 231	22 214	6 278	74.2	21.9	19 814	27 239	5.5
Fort Myers	2 307	2 205	784	102	6 050	12 550	2 338	10 212	8 871	1 230	68.4	16.1	12 329	22 102	10.4
Fort Pierce	705	8	0	697	4 129	11 006	2 124	8 882	7 822	662	56.9	11.3	9 961	18 913	4.3
Gainesville	11 507	1 989	386	9 518	6 771	7 094	1 030	6 064	35 803	2 617	84.8	40.5	11 549	21 077	-0.1
Greenacres City	0	0	0	0	NA	NA	NA	NA	2 787	561	76.4	13.0	14 640	29 241	NA
Hallandale	368	133	133	235	2 270	6 622	1 222	5 399	2 862	706	67.9	14.1	16 950	20 841	-9.4
Hialeah	3 652	2 304	1 603	1 348	13 946	6 159	737	5 422	38 812	7 282	46.3	7.3	8 914	23 443	-10.8
Hollywood	1 751	858	812	893	9 615	6 900	775	6 125	18 887	5 667	72.9	15.7	16 303	27 352	3.0
Homestead	575	432	400	143	3 895	12 207	2 222	9 985	5 935	693	55.6	8.5	9 792	20 594	7.9
Jacksonville	15 317	6 579	3 401	8 738	51 073	6 943	1 116	5 827	136 589	27 199	76.9	18.4	13 857	28 513	NA
Jupiter town	91	70	70	21	1 530	3 890	425	3 466	3 899	1 053	87.4	27.3	21 433	38 211	NA
Key West	893	518	95	375	2 472	9 702	997	8 706	4 065	490	79.9	20.8	15 547	28 121	30.1
Kissimmee	461	321	192	140	3 640	7 613	1 021	6 592	5 924	685	76.1	13.4	11 931	27 591	22.1
Lakeland	3 710	1 247	1 090	2 463	6 002	7 651	570	7 081	12 241	3 150	74.0	19.3	13 487	24 462	10.5
Lake Worth	761	645	645	116	3 023	8 604	1 130	7 474	4 543	848	67.1	12.5	12 130	21 665	7.6
Largo	1 786	922	696	864	2 806	4 045	473	3 572	8 011	1 877	77.1	13.8	14 539	24 296	4.8
Lauderdale Lakes	350	337	337	13	1 374	4 334	823	3 510	5 155	948	68.1	9.7	11 295	20 731	-12.4
Lauderhill	842	210	112	632	2 209	3 836	672	3 164	8 582	2 143	79.2	19.0	14 953	26 722	-3.1
Margate	345	247	247	98	1 758	3 261	362	2 899	6 294	1 114	74.6	12.3	14 897	28 465	6.3
Melbourne	3 064	1 451	694	1 613	NA	NA	NA	NA	10 843	3 871	79.2	18.8	13 224	25 893	5.8
Miami	11 611	8 333	1 517	3 278	39 756	10 968	2 173	8 795	74 008	13 310	47.6	12.8	9 799	16 925	-8.8
Miami Beach	1 336	796	671	540	12 393	14 094	1 505	12 589	12 727	4 088	65.5	21.2	16 504	15 312	7.4
Miramar	28	0	0	28	2 840	3 904	489	3 415	8 394	2 231	77.9	14.9	13 820	35 794	2.5
North Lauderdale	0	0	0	0	1 227	3 803	629	3 174	6 342	1 051	82.7	14.9	13 440	36 297	NA
North Miami	1 255	547	498	708	5 595	9 344	1 470	7 874	10 969	2 549	69.3	17.9	13 297	24 898	-2.1
North Miami Beach	426	386	382	40	2 551	6 255	792	5 463	7 195	1 596	68.7	14.9	13 531	24 963	3.0
Oakland Park	440	13	13	427	2 344	7 570	1 014	6 556	3 678	1 177	78.3	17.5	15 273	27 708	6.0
Ocala	3 260	2 537	1 070	723	5 244	11 414	1 576	9 838	7 851	836	71.6	16.7	12 783	21 766	7.7
Orlando	4 041	2 489	1 031	1 552	22 369	12 030	2 111	9 918	30 232	4 687	78.1	22.6	13 879	26 119	18.8
Ormond Beach	766	571	475	195	1 306	3 598	322	3 275	4 713	1 273	84.2	26.2	18 875	32 704	8.4
Oviedo	78	41	41	37	692	2 630	323	2 307	2 908	530	90.5	34.8	14 266	40 221	NA
Palm Bay	390	263	236	127	3 966	4 994	879	4 115	12 924	2 745	82.1	16.7	12 645	30 287	5.9
Palm Beach Gardens	325	142	142	183	2 025	5 776	265	5 511	3 894	1 327	90.9	38.2	26 185	44 688	5.8
Panama City	2 351	2 091	503	260	2 433	6 681	843	5 838	7 685	887	70.3	16.7	12 169	21 881	11.6
Pembroke Pines	1 288	1 261	105	27	3 853	2 804	293	2 511	11 439	3 041	81.8	20.9	16 747	36 431	-6.5
Pensacola	496	342	305	154	NA	NA	NA	NA	12 794	2 073	79.1	28.1	14 795	25 066	5.1
Pinellas Park	802	484	312	318	2 771	6 069	550	5 519	6 818	1 440	73.8	10.8	12 734	26 109	11.7
Plantation	475	417	417	58	4 321	5 210	295	4 915	11 895	3 782	87.7	31.7	21 702	41 832	-1.2
Plant City	337	269	269	68	2 844	9 507	1 277	8 230	4 818	590	68.0	13.4	12 292	25 268	16.3
Pompano Beach	3 239	2 647	453	592	5 176	6 620	1 123	5 497	10 047	2 605	73.7	18.4	17 382	29 683	5.2
Port Orange	504	414	399	90	1 031	2 250	72	2 178	6 514	1 018	79.8	15.3	13 391	26 472	21.5
Port St. Lucie	574	331	319	243	2 422	2 728	244	2 484	10 499	1 824	80.6	13.2	14 018	32 553	2.5
Riviera Beach	313	137	116	176	4 810	16 096	1 944	14 151	6 396	829	67.7	15.7	14 674	24 847	5.9
St. Petersburg	6 502	3 297	2 840	3 205	20 404	8 220	1 623	6 597	40 870	8 716	75.1	18.6	14 132	23 577	19.2
Sanford	1 696	1 302	50	394	4 088	10 676	1 520	9 156	7 106	732	70.8	11.9	11 115	25 029	27.8
Sarasota	3 122	1 870	1 083	1 252	4 278	8 115	1 151	6 964	7 874	1 266	76.4	21.0	16 151	24 884	13.5
Sunrise	1 066	771	685	295	4 770	5 561	426	5 135	11 575	2 564	79.2	16.7	14 593	31 540	13.5
Tallahassee	13 157	3 720	930	9 437	12 570	8 345	1 211	7 134	48 511	3 552	85.5	40.7	13 247	23 453	19.1
Tamarac	609	310	310	299	1 321	2 376	295	2 081	4 030	1 156	76.0	14.2	18 012	26 703	7.7
Tampa	8 918	3 000	763	5 918	33 666	11 095	2 103	8 992	54 676	11 045	70.6	18.7	13 277	22 772	10.3
Titusville	825	638	536	187	1 821	4 478	858	3 619	7 868	1 279	80.7	18.9	14 274	28 425	2.6
Weston city	0	0	0	0	NA	NA	NA	NA	NA	NA	NA	NA	NA	NA	NA
West Palm Beach	3 635	970	734	2 665	11 396	13 880	1 474	12 406	11 038	3 175	71.7	20.4	15 712	26 504	18.3
Winter Haven	762	442	436	320	2 014	7 604	755	6 849	3 946	834	71.3	17.8	14 154	23 695	11.0
Winter Springs	36	0	0	36	660	2 084	199	1 885	5 246	883	89.3	29.1	17 265	40 563	10.5
GEORGIA	233 822	126 023	34 812	107 799	388 949	4 751	505	4 246	1 433 862	209 997	70.9	19.3	13 631	29 021	15.2
Albany	4 237	1 614	490	2 623	5 654	7 349	704	6 644	20 885	2 449	66.4	17.8	10 496	21 885	-4.3
Alpharetta	80	2	0	78	2 461	7 061	298	6 762	2 371	566	92.5	36.1	20 540	44 335	NA
Athens-Clarke County	8 180	1 179	567	7 001	6 868	6 839	418	6 421	22 535	993	72.2	36.1	9 252	14 286	-14.9
Atlanta	28 947	8 938	1 225	20 009	55 468	13 318	2 781	10 537	83 204	19 991	69.9	26.6	15 279	22 275	17.7
Augusta-Richmond County	10 911	3 193	498	7 718	NA	NA	NA	NA	NA	NA	NA	NA	NA	NA	NA

1. Persons in emergency shelters and persons visible in street locations. 2. Data for serious crimes have not been adjusted for underreporting. This may affect comparability between geographic areas and over time. 3. Per 100,000 population estimated by the FBI. 4. Persons 25 years old and older. 5. Based on population enumerated as of April 1, 1990.

City	Money income, 1989 (cont'd)				Housing units, 2000										
	Households (cont'd)	Percent below poverty, 1989					Vacant units				Occupied units				
		Persons		Families											
	Percent with $100,000 or more	Total	Percent change in rate, 1979–1989	Total	Total	Percent change, 1990–2000	Vacant units for sale or rent[1]	For seasonal use (percent)	Home owner vacancy rate	Renter vacancy rate	Total	Percent owner occupied	Percent renter occupied	Average size owner occupied	Average size renter occupied
	46	47	48	49	50	51	52	53	54	55	56	57	58	59	60
FLORIDA—Cont'd															
Coconut Creek	2.9	4.1	NA	2.4	22 182	40.6	2 089	4.1	2.4	10.0	20 093	75.5	24.5	2.17	2.13
Cooper City	7.5	3.7	27.6	2.5	9 289	26.4	166	0.5	0.7	2.9	9 123	92.2	7.8	3.07	3.00
Coral Gables	22.5	6.5	-27.8	4.4	17 849	7.8	1 056	1.7	1.5	4.2	16 793	65.8	34.2	2.56	1.83
Coral Springs	10.2	5.2	26.8	4.3	41 337	38.8	1 815	0.7	1.6	5.1	39 522	65.0	35.0	3.08	2.73
Davie	4.9	7.8	-8.2	4.8	31 284	57.3	2 602	3.3	2.6	5.3	28 682	76.5	23.5	2.74	2.29
Daytona Beach	1.7	22.5	-0.9	16.0	33 345	3.7	4 740	6.4	2.6	8.4	28 605	47.3	52.7	2.15	1.98
Deerfield Beach	3.0	9.9	16.5	5.8	37 343	29.7	5 951	10.2	1.8	5.5	31 392	70.2	29.8	1.98	2.12
Delray Beach	8.2	11.3	-8.9	7.5	31 702	15.2	4 915	11.0	1.5	7.8	26 787	69.7	30.3	2.19	2.30
Dunedin	3.0	7.1	18.3	4.6	19 952	8.4	2 694	6.2	2.3	13.8	17 258	71.4	28.6	2.09	1.81
Fort Lauderdale	7.1	17.1	20.4	13.1	80 862	-0.5	12 394	8.5	2.5	7.7	68 468	55.4	44.6	2.18	2.10
Fort Myers	2.8	20.7	-4.6	17.2	21 836	2.1	2 729	3.7	3.7	10.0	19 107	39.7	60.3	2.50	2.34
Fort Pierce	1.8	29.2	5.8	20.1	17 170	-0.5	2 763	6.1	3.1	13.0	14 407	53.2	46.8	2.40	2.73
Gainesville	2.9	26.3	8.7	15.7	40 105	15.9	2 826	0.4	2.0	6.8	37 279	47.7	52.3	2.39	2.12
Greenacres City	1.7	7.1	NA	4.6	14 153	26.5	2 094	8.4	2.3	10.5	12 059	70.9	29.1	2.17	2.56
Hallandale	3.7	16.0	44.1	10.5	25 022	0.9	6 971	19.7	2.6	9.0	18 051	66.6	33.4	1.80	2.03
Hialeah	1.0	18.2	37.9	15.5	72 142	16.0	1 438	0.2	1.0	1.7	70 704	50.7	49.3	3.35	2.95
Hollywood	4.8	11.0	29.4	7.7	68 426	8.1	8 753	7.2	2.2	7.1	59 673	62.2	37.8	2.43	2.10
Homestead	1.3	29.9	9.9	24.6	11 162	3.6	1 067	1.3	3.7	8.0	10 095	36.0	64.0	2.74	3.31
Jacksonville	2.9	12.8	NA	9.8	308 826	8.5	24 327	0.3	1.8	9.0	284 499	63.2	36.8	2.64	2.34
Jupiter town	7.8	5.8	NA	3.9	20 943	43.4	3 998	14.4	1.4	11.1	16 945	81.3	18.7	2.31	2.33
Key West	3.8	10.4	-33.3	7.8	13 306	8.9	2 290	8.3	2.3	9.3	11 016	45.6	54.4	2.24	2.23
Kissimmee	0.8	11.8	-2.5	9.2	19 642	44.4	2 521	5.6	2.6	9.2	17 121	44.9	55.1	2.88	2.67
Lakeland	2.9	14.0	-8.5	10.2	38 980	11.6	5 471	5.5	3.5	9.4	33 509	60.3	39.7	2.24	2.22
Lake Worth	1.6	17.1	44.9	13.6	15 861	1.5	2 033	5.5	2.6	7.9	13 828	52.4	47.6	2.41	2.57
Largo	1.7	7.4	5.7	4.4	40 261	4.0	6 220	8.6	3.0	10.2	34 041	67.4	32.6	2.01	1.93
Lauderdale Lakes	0.7	14.2	69.0	10.4	14 325	2.9	2 226	9.7	2.9	6.8	12 099	62.2	37.8	2.41	2.89
Lauderhill	3.0	10.3	30.4	7.9	25 751	-2.0	2 941	5.3	3.1	5.8	22 810	59.4	40.6	2.40	2.62
Margate	2.1	7.7	75.0	5.3	24 740	14.3	2 026	3.9	2.3	6.2	22 714	80.1	19.9	2.37	2.33
Melbourne	1.6	12.8	7.6	8.7	33 678	20.0	2 890	2.5	2.3	8.5	30 788	62.1	37.9	2.34	2.02
Miami	2.6	31.2	27.3	25.7	148 388	2.7	14 190	2.0	2.9	6.6	134 198	34.9	65.1	2.79	2.52
Miami Beach	5.0	25.2	42.4	19.9	59 723	-4.3	13 529	12.8	7.6	8.8	46 194	36.6	63.4	2.00	1.80
Miramar	1.9	8.4	42.4	6.5	25 905	69.9	2 847	0.4	9.7	6.6	23 058	80.1	19.9	3.23	2.83
North Lauderdale	1.7	6.7	NA	4.7	11 444	16.8	645	0.9	3.1	5.8	10 799	63.7	36.3	3.03	2.92
North Miami	2.4	15.5	47.6	12.4	22 281	0.8	1 740	1.6	2.2	5.8	20 541	50.5	49.5	3.10	2.61
North Miami Beach	3.1	12.9	43.3	9.0	15 350	-3.0	1 363	3.9	2.6	4.7	13 987	61.8	38.2	2.98	2.74
Oakland Park	1.8	10.4	10.6	7.8	14 509	4.6	1 007	2.8	2.0	4.6	13 502	50.7	49.3	2.23	2.29
Ocala	2.9	19.9	-5.2	15.4	20 501	5.3	1 855	1.6	2.3	8.0	18 646	57.2	42.8	2.34	2.22
Orlando	2.7	15.8	-11.2	12.2	88 486	20.5	7 603	1.3	1.8	8.3	80 883	40.8	59.2	2.38	2.16
Ormond Beach	6.2	6.7	-6.9	4.5	17 258	21.6	1 629	4.7	1.7	10.4	15 629	81.7	18.3	2.32	2.06
Oviedo	1.8	7.8	NA	6.4	8 977	113.1	421	0.3	1.4	11.9	8 556	85.6	14.4	3.09	2.92
Palm Bay	1.5	8.7	26.1	6.1	32 902	25.2	2 566	2.0	2.6	9.0	30 336	75.3	24.7	2.63	2.54
Palm Beach Gardens	12.6	4.5	73.1	3.5	18 317	50.5	2 718	10.0	1.6	10.0	15 599	79.5	20.5	2.26	2.08
Panama City	2.0	19.6	-5.3	16.4	16 548	3.9	1 729	0.9	2.5	11.2	14 819	57.8	42.2	2.35	2.23
Pembroke Pines	3.4	5.1	45.7	3.5	55 296	87.2	3 307	2.1	2.1	5.8	51 989	80.2	19.8	2.65	2.48
Pensacola	3.8	18.9	-3.1	14.2	26 995	2.4	2 471	0.7	2.2	10.0	24 524	63.3	36.7	2.34	2.16
Pinellas Park	1.0	9.3	4.5	6.9	21 843	6.1	2 399	4.5	2.6	8.9	19 444	75.1	24.9	2.29	2.36
Plantation	9.3	3.5	-7.9	2.1	34 999	19.0	1 755	1.7	1.3	5.2	33 244	71.7	28.3	2.58	2.23
Plant City	2.8	17.8	-4.3	14.1	11 797	26.2	948	0.9	2.4	7.8	10 849	65.7	34.3	2.73	2.71
Pompano Beach	5.0	16.0	42.9	10.7	44 496	4.2	9 299	15.8	1.9	7.1	35 197	62.8	37.2	2.07	2.23
Port Orange	0.9	8.2	-16.3	5.1	21 102	24.0	1 528	3.5	1.7	5.6	19 574	82.1	17.9	2.33	2.24
Port St. Lucie	2.1	5.4	-16.9	4.2	36 785	51.7	2 876	3.6	2.0	8.1	33 909	83.3	16.7	2.55	2.83
Riviera Beach	4.5	22.6	39.5	17.9	14 220	1.0	2 833	13.8	1.9	8.6	11 387	59.2	40.8	2.47	2.78
St. Petersburg	2.8	13.6	-2.9	9.5	124 618	-0.7	14 955	3.9	2.4	9.1	109 663	63.5	36.5	2.32	2.00
Sanford	1.2	16.3	-25.9	12.1	15 623	12.9	1 386	0.9	2.7	6.6	14 237	55.4	44.6	2.63	2.49
Sarasota	4.4	13.3	-10.7	10.3	26 898	-0.3	3 471	6.6	2.2	7.8	23 427	58.4	41.6	2.08	2.17
Sunrise	1.6	6.5	30.0	4.5	35 661	21.7	2 353	1.9	2.4	5.8	33 308	73.8	26.2	2.58	2.43
Tallahassee	2.7	22.3	-7.1	11.9	68 417	23.9	5 200	0.6	2.1	7.7	63 217	43.8	56.2	2.35	2.04
Tamarac	3.2	5.8	28.9	3.4	29 750	13.8	2 327	3.3	2.7	4.8	27 423	79.9	20.1	1.94	2.27
Tampa	3.4	19.4	3.7	15.0	135 776	4.7	11 018	0.6	2.1	7.8	124 758	55.0	45.0	2.49	2.20
Titusville	1.5	10.6	-16.5	7.9	19 178	5.5	1 978	3.4	2.3	10.6	17 200	68.0	32.0	2.33	2.28
Weston city	NA	NA	NA	NA	18 943	NA	2 367	4.7	2.8	5.3	16 576	81.8	18.2	3.02	2.78
West Palm Beach	3.8	16.2	2.5	12.7	40 461	15.7	5 692	5.0	2.9	10.3	34 769	52.0	48.0	2.31	2.20
Winter Haven	2.4	13.5	-17.7	8.9	13 912	9.1	2 079	5.5	3.8	11.8	11 833	59.1	40.9	2.26	2.05
Winter Springs	6.0	3.3	-60.2	2.6	12 306	41.4	532	0.7	1.2	9.0	11 774	80.3	19.7	2.72	2.55
GEORGIA	3.8	14.7	-11.7	11.5	3 281 737	24.4	275 368	1.5	1.9	8.2	3 006 369	67.5	32.5	2.71	2.51
Albany	2.6	27.5	13.2	22.1	32 062	4.8	3 442	0.4	2.7	10.7	28 620	47.4	52.6	2.54	2.54
Alpharetta	9.3	3.7	NA	2.3	14 670	149.2	759	0.7	1.7	5.6	13 911	60.3	39.7	2.81	2.02
Athens-Clarke County	2.4	39.3	47.7	22.5	42 126	127.7	2 420	0.4	1.6	4.9	39 706	42.0	58.0	2.45	2.27
Atlanta	6.3	27.3	-0.7	24.6	186 925	2.3	18 778	0.6	4.1	7.2	168 147	43.7	56.3	2.37	2.25
Augusta-Richmond County	NA	NA	NA	NA	82 312	NA	8 392	0.3	2.6	10.7	73 920	58.0	42.0	2.62	2.46

1. Includes units rented or sold but not occupied.   2. Specified owner-occupied units.   3. Specified renter-occupied units.   4. Overcrowded or lacking complete plumbing facilities.

City	Civilian labor force, 2001				Civilian employment, 1990[2]			Disability 1990	Value of residential construction authorized by building permits, 2000		
			Unemployment			Percent					
	Total	Percent change, 2000–2001	Total	Rate[1]	Total	Professional, managerial, and technical	Precision production, craft, and repair	Work disabled persons[3] (percent)	New construction ($1,000)	Number of housing units	Percent single family
	61	62	63	64	65	66	67	68	69	70	71
FLORIDA—Cont'd											
Coconut Creek	15 772	3.9	902	5.7	11 539	35.4	9.5	7.6	83 832	1 176	47.3
Cooper City	14 951	3.1	397	2.7	11 294	39.9	9.9	4.0	8 635	57	100.0
Coral Gables	24 057	2.2	870	3.6	20 790	52.3	4.5	3.0	27 837	52	96.2
Coral Springs	55 588	3.3	1 962	3.5	41 614	36.8	8.7	4.5	93 707	978	63.5
Davie	34 873	3.5	1 491	4.3	25 905	32.0	13.2	6.9	93 805	719	82.3
Daytona Beach	30 892	1.9	1 760	5.7	26 724	26.5	10.0	10.9	26 927	152	55.3
Deerfield Beach	26 477	3.6	1 163	4.4	19 644	28.4	10.5	7.0	9 912	98	100.0
Delray Beach	27 949	4.5	2 148	7.7	19 573	29.3	9.5	6.9	39 622	307	76.5
Dunedin	18 719	2.4	598	3.2	14 576	29.6	10.6	7.9	45 241	511	7.2
Fort Lauderdale	99 726	4.0	6 115	6.1	72 643	28.7	10.1	8.0	71 356	594	31.6
Fort Myers	27 800	5.2	1 253	4.5	20 612	25.4	11.7	10.9	35 250	291	56.0
Fort Pierce	18 780	2.4	2 621	14.0	13 474	18.7	10.4	11.5	4 450	51	49.0
Gainesville	48 858	1.2	1 519	3.1	38 730	45.0	5.6	6.4	29 308	401	41.6
Greenacres City	13 015	3.9	667	5.1	9 367	23.5	15.2	7.6	44 248	683	39.5
Hallandale	13 807	4.2	926	6.7	9 996	27.7	9.5	9.8	8 514	230	5.2
Hialeah	107 891	3.1	7 784	7.2	89 758	15.6	16.1	6.6	10 892	160	20.6
Hollywood	76 922	3.9	4 279	5.6	56 372	28.3	13.6	8.8	36 088	302	96.7
Homestead	13 433	2.9	878	6.5	11 257	16.6	14.4	8.4	7 220	90	100.0
Jacksonville	398 854	2.1	17 869	4.5	314 432	28.9	11.1	9.1	511 146	5 587	62.6
Jupiter town	17 926	3.6	692	3.9	13 074	37.6	10.0	5.8	164 820	956	52.6
Key West	14 900	3.8	385	2.6	12 524	26.3	9.8	7.5	4 894	35	88.6
Kissimmee	27 810	1.8	1 467	5.3	16 552	21.8	10.2	7.0	40 469	386	100.0
Lakeland	35 883	0.7	2 043	5.7	30 126	29.7	10.6	8.9	59 727	1 025	16.3
Lake Worth	18 310	4.1	1 104	6.0	13 053	21.1	14.4	8.0	5 753	16	100.0
Largo	37 031	2.4	1 188	3.2	28 831	27.6	11.5	10.0	16 749	115	100.0
Lauderdale Lakes	15 105	4.2	1 039	6.9	10 915	20.5	11.3	6.5	0	0	0.0
Lauderhill	31 290	3.8	1 593	5.1	23 045	29.3	10.2	6.7	1 540	26	100.0
Margate	25 845	3.7	1 254	4.9	19 083	24.8	14.8	7.1	2 475	22	100.0
Melbourne	32 151	1.9	1 570	4.9	27 679	32.6	13.5	9.4	69 650	748	52.9
Miami	187 614	3.8	18 706	10.0	151 446	19.7	12.2	8.1	232 682	2 191	2.7
Miami Beach	45 930	3.3	3 697	8.0	37 867	32.2	6.6	8.6	172 784	843	1.9
Miramar	28 763	3.6	1 266	4.4	21 338	30.7	14.3	6.5	286 762	2 552	86.6
North Lauderdale	19 799	3.6	914	4.6	14 655	24.5	16.5	5.4	475	28	0.0
North Miami	29 697	3.2	2 206	7.4	24 649	26.8	10.4	6.6	193	7	0.0
North Miami Beach	19 376	2.7	1 099	5.7	16 388	27.7	11.1	7.9	2 300	5	100.0
Oakland Park	20 548	3.5	867	4.2	15 273	24.8	13.1	7.2	1 428	14	100.0
Ocala	22 772	0.1	1 173	5.2	17 263	28.9	9.9	12.4	22 559	149	100.0
Orlando	118 079	1.4	5 228	4.4	82 176	30.9	8.9	8.4	81 965	1 052	29.7
Ormond Beach	14 369	0.9	431	3.0	12 786	41.2	8.1	7.4	33 137	210	100.0
Oviedo	8 420	0.6	246	2.9	5 776	41.0	8.2	4.4	56 548	247	97.6
Palm Bay	34 549	1.8	1 525	4.4	29 890	31.1	15.8	8.4	56 978	530	100.0
Palm Beach Gardens	16 673	3.4	460	2.8	12 300	45.8	7.0	5.9	61 479	317	91.8
Panama City	17 469	0.5	1 247	7.1	14 121	29.6	10.2	11.7	14 685	149	91.3
Pembroke Pines	42 978	3.3	1 384	3.2	32 277	35.0	10.2	6.1	134 494	1 139	98.9
Pensacola	26 454	-0.9	1 444	5.5	24 099	38.7	7.5	9.3	12 158	109	63.3
Pinellas Park	25 885	2.4	889	3.4	20 106	24.3	16.2	11.4	6 997	76	100.0
Plantation	48 446	3.4	1 734	3.6	36 249	41.4	8.2	5.3	29 682	120	100.0
Plant City	14 282	2.4	510	3.6	10 134	24.9	12.3	9.1	16 334	222	91.9
Pompano Beach	43 585	3.9	2 534	5.8	31 856	27.7	11.6	8.8	6 491	78	100.0
Port Orange	18 090	1.0	587	3.2	16 056	28.6	11.5	10.1	67 491	630	67.0
Port St. Lucie	31 970	1.7	2 058	6.4	24 942	24.6	17.5	8.9	135 180	1 528	80.9
Riviera Beach	17 232	4.9	1 667	9.7	11 808	22.7	12.3	10.4	5 812	62	100.0
St. Petersburg	142 354	2.7	6 116	4.3	109 586	30.8	10.5	10.7	29 514	230	91.7
Sanford	22 036	1.2	1 034	4.7	14 841	24.2	14.9	9.8	52 590	857	38.2
Sarasota	33 163	3.6	1 136	3.4	23 554	28.4	11.0	9.0	12 499	187	36.9
Sunrise	40 248	3.6	1 797	4.5	29 838	31.2	10.8	6.1	27 403	347	100.0
Tallahassee	83 871	0.9	3 004	3.6	65 373	42.4	5.0	5.4	123 958	1 537	44.5
Tamarac	22 205	3.8	1 185	5.3	16 312	28.7	9.9	8.9	36 974	334	13.2
Tampa	184 736	2.6	8 294	4.5	129 830	29.2	9.8	10.9	246 614	2 703	53.2
Titusville	21 057	1.7	885	4.2	18 258	35.4	12.5	9.4	15 021	122	95.1
Weston city	NA	NA	NA	NA	NA	NA	NA	NA	NA	NA	NA
West Palm Beach	47 421	4.3	3 299	7.0	33 472	28.6	10.1	8.5	88 715	924	60.7
Winter Haven	11 949	0.7	680	5.7	10 032	29.0	9.9	9.1	5 316	68	52.9
Winter Springs	17 066	0.7	543	3.2	11 676	37.6	9.8	6.1	36 278	203	96.1
GEORGIA	4 131 569	-1.0	165 221	4.0	3 090 276	28.2	11.9	8.8	8 722 246	91 820	75.0
Albany	33 685	-4.6	2 222	6.6	30 689	27.9	10.6	9.8	14 031	230	50.9
Alpharetta	9 634	-0.1	154	1.6	7 657	42.0	8.2	4.3	35 349	175	100.0
Athens-Clarke County	46 275	-0.8	1 569	3.4	19 344	33.0	6.0	6.4	69 515	958	55.4
Atlanta	229 369	0.6	13 382	5.8	175 126	32.4	6.8	10.0	354 534	5 819	13.8
Augusta-Richmond County	79 030	-2.6	4 326	5.5	NA	NA	NA	NA	NA	NA	NA

1. Percent of civilian labor force. 2. Persons 16 years and older. 3. Persons 16 to 64 years old.

Table D. Cities — Wholesale Trade, Retail Trade, and Real Estate

City	Wholesale Trade, 1997				Retail Trade[1], 1997				Real Estate and Rental and Leasing, 1997			
	Number of Establishments	Number of Employees	Sales (mil dol)	Annual Payroll (mil dol)	Number of Establishments	Number of Employees	Sales (mil dol)	Annual Payroll (mil dol)	Number of Establishments	Number of Employees	Receipts (mil dol)	Annual Payroll (mil dol)
	72	73	74	75	76	77	78	79	80	81	82	83
FLORIDA—Cont'd												
Coconut Creek	41	85	61.1	3.9	55	1 016	420.4	27.5	25	85	15.7	2.1
Cooper City	49	158	116.5	5.3	72	1 079	136.9	13.6	28	78	13.7	1.7
Coral Gables	268	1 981	4 723.1	117.7	315	3 652	795.2	75.6	260	1 266	176.7	35.4
Coral Springs	259	2 588	915.1	88.7	417	6 395	950.0	92.3	136	452	86.7	12.5
Davie	267	2 285	1 406.1	56.1	303	3 690	684.8	71.6	113	401	57.9	10.2
Daytona Beach	90	1 028	393.2	27.6	546	7 481	1 466.9	126.7	151	975	106.9	18.2
Deerfield Beach	211	3 391	6 510.8	153.8	278	4 340	885.8	81.8	84	495	67.3	12.4
Delray Beach	120	569	231.5	19.2	344	4 265	1 467.3	102.4	85	356	41.4	8.0
Dunedin	41	217	81.8	8.4	129	1 346	175.4	20.0	28	107	17.9	2.5
Fort Lauderdale	761	8 279	6 347.6	336.0	1 203	13 080	3 192.2	287.9	495	4 013	799.5	117.2
Fort Myers	207	2 258	557.6	65.2	614	8 593	1 695.1	160.2	151	983	148.9	21.6
Fort Pierce	59	899	260.3	19.1	257	2 844	431.0	39.9	53	236	23.7	4.1
Gainesville	138	1 296	620.9	40.8	498	6 521	1 098.3	104.8	171	876	97.7	17.1
Greenacres City	NA	NA	NA	NA	NA	NA	NA	NA	NA	NA	NA	NA
Hallandale	90	524	121.7	12.1	134	1 932	263.0	29.1	50	109	21.0	2.1
Hialeah	576	4 040	1 114.6	99.0	945	10 430	1 530.9	151.2	252	884	199.3	21.1
Hollywood	361	2 408	1 191.1	80.0	556	6 758	1 234.9	121.6	219	1 351	160.8	29.7
Homestead	35	D	D	D	122	1 636	303.0	27.8	25	95	7.4	2.1
Jacksonville	1 394	21 860	16 590.0	760.3	3 134	44 276	8 034.1	761.4	886	6 374	918.5	158.4
Jupiter town	67	397	284.3	18.4	196	1 904	327.8	35.0	76	368	42.0	8.7
Key West	32	D	D	D	332	3 117	421.1	48.3	111	476	49.5	7.8
Kissimmee	43	D	D	D	309	3 517	531.7	52.3	130	2 347	207.3	47.6
Lakeland	164	2 468	2 191.2	66.1	621	9 559	1 559.9	148.6	139	689	81.7	13.0
Lake Worth	69	D	D	D	183	1 519	274.6	26.4	44	218	20.4	4.8
Largo	179	1 593	526.0	46.4	382	4 358	626.5	66.1	108	648	76.9	11.8
Lauderdale Lakes	19	D	D	D	78	713	142.1	13.2	22	928	123.5	23.3
Lauderhill	51	193	63.6	4.9	159	1 884	534.1	33.3	54	412	30.4	6.2
Margate	97	381	195.8	10.3	198	3 187	848.1	68.2	53	338	40.4	5.8
Melbourne	142	1 124	388.1	38.5	446	6 394	1 137.5	111.6	115	642	63.4	11.4
Miami	1 810	12 885	7 178.4	388.8	2 533	21 675	3 681.5	362.5	729	4 625	719.5	119.7
Miami Beach	136	470	255.9	12.5	466	3 680	504.2	62.1	313	1 909	189.7	33.1
Miramar	84	1 479	712.8	57.9	115	2 063	341.1	29.3	33	131	18.4	2.8
North Lauderdale	13	27	8.8	0.6	48	950	121.2	11.7	9	30	2.6	0.5
North Miami	108	574	183.1	16.2	235	3 402	705.8	83.2	95	535	57.7	10.7
North Miami Beach	96	379	180.7	11.3	217	2 775	541.4	47.8	69	242	33.5	4.8
Oakland Park	223	1 500	489.7	49.2	275	2 719	517.4	53.6	72	286	38.8	5.7
Ocala	198	2 243	680.8	54.6	602	8 560	1 470.4	136.7	145	487	57.5	8.5
Orlando	676	9 637	4 389.2	315.3	1 406	18 296	3 786.5	334.3	457	6 995	991.3	194.8
Ormond Beach	58	622	207.6	17.9	170	2 231	257.1	30.2	79	412	43.9	8.1
Oviedo	35	129	85.7	3.8	72	1 082	153.4	14.4	23	66	9.7	1.0
Palm Bay	46	264	117.5	11.0	150	2 174	307.1	28.1	47	335	25.2	6.3
Palm Beach Gardens	80	271	239.9	13.9	307	5 612	836.9	91.0	86	361	67.9	11.3
Panama City	88	686	246.5	18.1	415	5 461	916.9	88.6	86	363	32.4	6.0
Pembroke Pines	135	417	233.3	13.9	375	7 362	1 650.7	125.8	95	422	77.8	9.4
Pensacola	151	1 992	552.8	53.9	470	6 415	991.4	93.9	115	511	52.2	9.5
Pinellas Park	115	1 234	391.7	33.0	241	5 235	1 530.8	104.9	37	157	18.6	3.0
Plantation	229	878	629.3	35.0	441	6 511	1 137.4	109.9	145	788	94.2	15.4
Plant City	69	1 383	568.8	42.2	159	2 594	451.7	40.7	37	127	12.0	2.1
Pompano Beach	503	5 616	2 386.7	177.8	587	6 828	1 571.8	140.1	190	953	141.1	24.3
Port Orange	38	207	62.0	5.6	109	1 572	207.5	21.8	38	223	16.6	3.2
Port St. Lucie	NA	NA	NA	NA	NA	NA	NA	NA	NA	NA	NA	NA
Riviera Beach	101	1 627	1 088.9	55.3	114	847	157.3	17.9	42	136	24.3	3.1
St. Petersburg	293	3 147	2 221.3	112.5	933	12 942	2 128.7	208.2	287	1 531	177.4	31.2
Sanford	84	1 046	249.6	28.1	303	3 960	628.4	57.7	32	276	24.1	4.6
Sarasota	123	890	329.3	23.9	512	5 601	931.6	93.9	184	864	124.4	20.4
Sunrise	246	2 713	1 728.5	123.1	448	7 971	1 355.2	133.7	74	706	78.1	13.3
Tallahassee	204	2 181	602.2	62.6	864	13 270	1 721.2	188.5	241	1 659	179.5	30.0
Tamarac	95	706	433.5	24.9	208	2 516	350.8	38.4	62	452	43.7	10.1
Tampa	1 048	18 497	15 906.4	630.9	1 792	25 054	4 756.7	428.9	526	4 489	599.8	110.6
Titusville	29	186	42.3	4.0	182	2 602	386.5	37.1	36	127	10.3	1.4
Weston city	NA	NA	NA	NA	NA	NA	NA	NA	NA	NA	NA	NA
West Palm Beach	188	1 897	1 356.4	68.4	615	9 261	1 968.5	188.4	203	1 508	142.6	39.8
Winter Haven	69	1 098	359.7	24.1	269	3 253	552.5	54.5	67	431	42.6	9.3
Winter Springs	38	118	32.1	2.7	32	196	24.4	2.5	22	56	6.0	1.0
GEORGIA	13 978	191 078	163 647.5	7 519.7	33 073	420 676	72 212.5	6 943.6	7 794	47 669	6 912.9	1 308.8
Albany	171	2 151	971.2	63.8	548	7 595	1 134.8	112.6	122	618	79.3	12.1
Alpharetta	185	5 776	9 870.4	307.6	317	6 233	945.6	105.9	60	335	76.5	14.2
Athens-Clarke County	NA	NA	NA	NA	NA	NA	NA	NA	NA	NA	NA	NA
Atlanta	1 164	15 406	17 285.9	636.9	2 044	26 738	4 229.8	491.1	832	8 689	1 485.7	318.5
Augusta-Richmond County	NA	NA	NA	NA	NA	NA	NA	NA	NA	NA	NA	NA

1. Establishments with payroll.

City	Professional, Scientific, and Technical Services, 1997[1]				Manufacturing, 1997				Accommodation and Foodservices, 1997			
	Number of Establish- ments	Number of Employees	Receipts (mil dol)	Annual Payroll (mil dol)	Number of Establish- ments	Number of Employees	Receipts (mil dol)	Annual Payroll (mil dol)	Number of Establish- ments	Number of Employees	Sales (mil dol)	Annual Payroll (mil dol)
	84	85	86	87	88	89	90	91	92	93	94	95
FLORIDA—Cont'd												
Coconut Creek	57	128	15.3	4.6	NA	NA	NA	NA	19	116	5.3	1.3
Cooper City	69	213	12.5	5.0	NA	NA	NA	NA	31	611	16.1	4.7
Coral Gables	1 109	5 707	606.4	248.3	NA	NA	NA	NA	172	3 701	153.3	47.3
Coral Springs	421	1 587	127.9	45.8	82	1 186	139.8	34.5	179	3 218	109.9	27.5
Davie	214	669	68.7	22.8	111	1 447	156.1	39.0	138	D	D	D
Daytona Beach	280	1 761	152.3	53.4	63	1 931	200.4	44.4	321	7 016	247.2	62.6
Deerfield Beach	218	1 350	142.0	67.7	100	2 511	333.9	78.4	140	2 438	105.0	25.5
Delray Beach	180	1 773	197.9	89.0	67	613	84.3	18.2	138	2 233	84.2	21.8
Dunedin	122	2 328	257.0	75.7	NA	NA	NA	NA	77	916	32.0	7.9
Fort Lauderdale	1 656	8 971	1 086.8	448.4	352	7 546	1 001.7	247.2	698	19 971	941.5	221.9
Fort Myers	322	2 093	179.2	80.7	95	1 743	296.7	47.9	213	4 338	145.1	38.1
Fort Pierce	95	848	47.2	21.0	NA	NA	NA	NA	113	1 751	53.8	14.3
Gainesville	371	2 547	199.1	84.0	85	1 688	414.3	57.7	273	4 610	140.2	36.2
Greenacres City	NA	NA	NA	NA	NA	NA	NA	NA	NA	NA	NA	NA
Hallandale	66	243	20.8	8.4	55	733	78.3	18.7	67	1 610	46.0	13.3
Hialeah	237	1 710	81.2	31.9	690	18 397	1 822.3	425.4	268	3 248	129.7	31.2
Hollywood	607	3 377	307.9	136.6	169	3 498	769.6	92.6	320	4 871	163.4	44.6
Homestead	38	144	11.1	4.3	NA	NA	NA	NA	67	990	32.8	8.2
Jacksonville	1 959	17 491	1 552.9	690.0	754	28 237	7 231.0	944.1	1 420	28 354	917.2	244.2
Jupiter town	193	751	83.3	29.0	NA	NA	NA	NA	96	2 152	73.5	21.3
Key West	106	334	28.0	10.0	32	526	79.5	15.1	286	5 476	307.5	74.5
Kissimmee	93	382	28.6	9.6	32	526	79.5	15.1	205	6 281	480.2	80.2
Lakeland	256	1 911	172.6	66.6	81	4 007	652.3	127.5	222	5 146	160.4	42.8
Lake Worth	92	382	29.0	12.7	46	523	40.3	10.8	78	852	32.9	9.2
Largo	178	819	90.9	27.9	138	2 544	229.8	60.6	176	2 854	89.8	21.8
Lauderdale Lakes	17	60	5.9	1.9	NA	NA	NA	NA	27	326	11.6	3.0
Lauderhill	103	394	25.4	9.1	NA	NA	NA	NA	63	D	D	D
Margate	100	300	32.1	8.4	NA	NA	NA	NA	97	D	D	D
Melbourne	297	2 072	209.7	87.0	91	4 435	1 282.6	160.6	182	3 407	96.8	28.1
Miami	2 447	16 969	2 231.5	955.7	575	7 490	1 021.7	188.8	912	16 953	764.8	202.7
Miami Beach	298	1 048	107.2	36.4	NA	NA	NA	NA	466	12 714	551.0	160.3
Miramar	59	368	37.7	13.6	36	729	124.9	25.1	44	425	15.6	3.4
North Lauderdale	25	249	27.5	12.4	NA	NA	NA	NA	36	431	14.0	3.3
North Miami	123	716	36.8	14.5	63	529	44.6	10.3	107	1 952	66.6	16.7
North Miami Beach	185	722	72.7	34.4	48	647	100.9	16.0	74	911	32.8	8.4
Oakland Park	156	1 520	145.8	49.0	166	1 855	193.8	48.8	115	1 729	70.7	17.5
Ocala	252	1 557	112.0	47.1	138	7 680	1 023.1	185.3	203	4 763	141.2	39.0
Orlando	1 348	14 678	1 505.2	630.4	281	12 168	2 390.5	522.5	581	18 872	753.5	214.0
Ormond Beach	119	573	47.5	15.2	47	1 039	100.1	26.4	113	2 485	70.5	19.8
Oviedo	50	166	13.4	7.4	NA	NA	NA	NA	25	D	D	D
Palm Bay	76	306	27.3	11.5	61	8 325	1 171.6	358.6	80	1 152	35.5	9.4
Palm Beach Gardens	225	1 039	116.0	48.0	NA	NA	NA	NA	96	2 340	93.6	25.8
Panama City	155	840	63.1	25.0	63	2 255	514.8	74.8	175	3 471	129.5	33.3
Pembroke Pines	226	785	65.6	23.6	54	632	80.0	15.7	190	4 009	134.3	34.4
Pensacola	372	3 047	234.9	106.7	75	1 865	475.7	62.9	183	4 156	130.5	35.3
Pinellas Park	85	622	40.3	17.7	190	7 653	1 136.3	209.6	92	1 565	60.4	14.1
Plantation	489	2 583	280.2	77.4	53	D	D	D	164	3 601	136.1	35.5
Plant City	52	193	11.9	5.5	54	3 990	935.0	101.3	58	1 070	30.7	8.3
Pompano Beach	278	1 367	142.4	41.3	284	6 711	783.8	187.8	229	3 035	124.9	34.1
Port Orange	43	267	23.2	8.8	NA	NA	NA	NA	66	1 403	40.7	11.4
Port St. Lucie	NA	NA	NA	NA	NA	NA	NA	NA	NA	NA	NA	NA
Riviera Beach	58	240	31.1	13.2	73	1 439	213.2	42.1	41	741	33.1	8.2
St. Petersburg	842	10 581	792.7	373.1	203	7 389	1 237.3	227.1	432	7 827	268.8	76.2
Sanford	63	342	24.8	12.6	61	2 270	253.6	50.2	81	1 594	51.4	13.8
Sarasota	483	2 969	329.2	137.7	89	1 529	136.6	35.5	241	4 628	183.5	49.5
Sunrise	187	643	94.5	22.1	71	2 405	201.3	50.6	163	3 065	115.9	27.8
Tallahassee	704	6 304	654.0	277.3	102	D	D	D	401	8 819	268.9	69.8
Tamarac	175	724	74.5	28.6	NA	NA	NA	NA	102	D	D	D
Tampa	1 780	26 172	3 145.2	1 112.8	463	13 213	2 442.1	364.2	842	20 303	782.8	212.3
Titusville	79	286	25.2	11.4	46	614	49.9	12.3	80	2 005	52.8	15.8
Weston city	NA	NA	NA	NA	NA	NA	NA	NA	NA	NA	NA	NA
West Palm Beach	758	6 079	644.2	305.8	154	7 014	2 269.2	402.8	294	5 797	223.0	60.1
Winter Haven	115	510	41.1	17.6	42	818	188.3	24.1	116	2 223	63.0	15.8
Winter Springs	59	164	20.9	5.2	NA	NA	NA	NA	12	167	4.6	1.2
GEORGIA	17 810	138 198	15 266.4	5 908.8	9 083	533 830	124 526.8	15 534.1	13 829	274 322	9 689.9	2 695.1
Albany	164	1 286	94.6	36.6	76	D	D	D	188	3 688	116.6	31.2
Alpharetta	259	2 413	384.5	124.5	44	2 279	589.2	88.9	126	2 355	95.8	26.1
Athens-Clarke County	NA	NA	NA	NA	90	9 388	1 368.5	234.9	NA	NA	NA	NA
Atlanta	2 573	38 245	5 305.7	1 969.6	499	21 497	5 822.0	688.7	1 361	37 792	1 604.8	478.7
Augusta-Richmond County	NA	NA	NA	NA	NA	NA	NA	NA	NA	NA	NA	NA

1. Firms subject to federal tax.

City	Arts, Entertainment, and Recreation[1], 1997				Health Care and Social Assistance[1], 1997				Other Services[1], 1997			
	Number of Establishments	Number of Employees	Receipts (mil dol)	Annual Payroll (mil dol)	Number of Establishments	Number of Employees	Receipts (mil dol)	Annual Payroll (mil dol)	Number of Establishments	Number of Employees	Receipts (mil dol)	Annual Payroll (mil dol)
	96	97	98	99	100	101	102	103	104	105	106	107
FLORIDA—Cont'd												
Coconut Creek	7	21	1.1	0.2	39	351	15.8	7.0	29	131	7.0	2.3
Cooper City	8	42	4.0	0.6	65	498	28.2	13.0	28	104	5.5	1.3
Coral Gables	27	347	25.6	4.9	462	3 479	311.4	121.0	122	752	35.7	12.4
Coral Springs	46	731	33.5	10.0	362	2 500	189.9	76.6	192	747	34.8	9.7
Davie	33	439	99.7	49.5	110	880	48.7	20.9	205	962	84.9	24.5
Daytona Beach	29	1 007	101.0	17.9	221	3 362	202.2	92.9	138	788	36.6	12.6
Deerfield Beach	23	325	120.4	13.0	117	1 398	97.8	32.7	128	918	39.1	14.2
Delray Beach	23	247	9.6	4.3	200	1 880	125.5	55.7	157	860	57.9	16.8
Dunedin	9	121	4.7	1.3	130	1 232	81.0	41.1	62	297	14.7	4.3
Fort Lauderdale	117	1 481	116.7	52.2	699	8 023	570.5	267.4	524	3 508	392.4	73.3
Fort Myers	19	483	14.0	4.4	292	7 275	566.7	252.3	200	1 504	89.5	29.6
Fort Pierce	9	71	5.4	1.6	140	2 991	216.0	88.0	90	497	26.9	8.6
Gainesville	35	523	18.8	4.7	281	2 442	157.1	77.9	209	1 096	69.1	20.5
Greenacres City	NA	NA	NA	NA	NA	NA	NA	NA	NA	NA	NA	NA
Hallandale	17	0	0.0	0.0	107	767	59.2	23.1	90	470	28.6	9.3
Hialeah	31	282	30.1	5.8	680	9 124	698.4	233.9	465	1 893	113.4	29.5
Hollywood	72	1 419	103.5	18.3	450	6 097	514.4	211.2	288	2 096	143.6	42.5
Homestead	6	0	0.0	0.0	68	460	29.4	11.2	43	183	10.9	2.9
Jacksonville	173	2 808	187.6	94.3	1 579	23 107	1 729.8	810.5	1 448	9 054	604.7	184.3
Jupiter town	28	420	42.1	16.0	143	873	69.8	31.8	91	419	24.2	7.4
Key West	29	293	36.4	14.8	60	534	38.7	18.1	68	280	16.2	4.3
Kissimmee	34	1 065	52.9	16.0	182	2 772	195.0	80.6	97	552	29.4	9.7
Lakeland	24	321	12.2	3.5	265	4 898	329.3	133.3	161	941	44.6	14.7
Lake Worth	9	282	10.7	4.4	93	1 055	54.3	22.2	93	343	22.3	5.6
Largo	16	114	5.0	1.3	249	5 499	401.1	156.2	176	771	47.4	14.9
Lauderdale Lakes	2	0	0.0	0.0	81	2 560	219.5	83.6	29	77	3.8	0.9
Lauderhill	11	139	4.1	2.1	111	1 580	76.4	32.8	89	462	21.2	6.1
Margate	19	194	9.2	2.6	143	1 952	136.6	53.2	130	541	34.4	9.6
Melbourne	22	360	15.7	3.6	263	3 690	309.3	141.3	135	809	40.8	13.5
Miami	123	2 733	470.2	146.5	1 319	12 101	980.0	375.5	836	5 045	337.2	85.8
Miami Beach	56	409	51.0	10.8	330	3 313	292.4	123.4	163	1 023	41.7	13.6
Miramar	7	25	1.0	0.4	65	956	102.1	36.3	53	228	18.3	5.7
North Lauderdale	2	0	0.0	0.0	19	123	5.2	2.0	34	232	20.9	5.6
North Miami	23	117	8.1	1.8	115	2 044	132.1	63.0	116	418	20.3	5.6
North Miami Beach	16	344	28.1	6.9	194	3 116	237.7	113.8	105	514	27.0	8.4
Oakland Park	13	155	24.9	3.6	138	2 503	200.5	76.2	205	766	55.9	13.7
Ocala	16	204	7.7	1.8	346	5 464	416.1	167.4	223	1 171	65.7	21.0
Orlando	122	0	0.0	0.0	676	7 391	683.5	321.8	440	4 650	289.2	89.0
Ormond Beach	23	277	9.0	2.8	180	2 294	144.4	62.9	58	305	14.0	4.0
Oviedo	7	158	8.1	1.8	41	352	19.6	8.9	37	166	7.6	2.2
Palm Bay	13	119	5.2	1.2	121	1 032	70.3	31.2	81	286	17.5	5.1
Palm Beach Gardens	20	268	19.5	4.2	239	2 888	255.2	94.4	77	453	20.9	7.7
Panama City	24	271	10.4	2.6	200	3 295	257.7	104.1	112	798	38.6	11.9
Pembroke Pines	37	392	19.8	5.0	298	1 916	139.4	55.0	159	1 096	54.0	17.8
Pensacola	31	392	25.4	4.5	315	3 553	287.5	145.0	115	952	52.3	15.0
Pinellas Park	15	135	7.5	2.0	83	1 293	64.0	33.9	135	840	50.6	14.8
Plantation	33	320	17.9	4.6	505	7 694	649.6	267.0	154	1 178	71.7	21.8
Plant City	9	274	6.1	2.1	86	847	50.1	22.4	44	241	15.3	4.2
Pompano Beach	35	513	38.2	7.4	195	2 304	140.5	60.9	270	2 338	163.6	52.6
Port Orange	7	30	1.3	0.4	77	568	34.0	11.8	55	215	9.1	2.8
Port St. Lucie	NA	NA	NA	NA	NA	NA	NA	NA	NA	NA	NA	NA
Riviera Beach	11	58	5.3	1.5	29	145	6.7	2.4	51	220	19.5	4.9
St. Petersburg	50	825	20.2	11.6	783	9 333	656.0	289.4	412	2 116	125.0	40.0
Sanford	13	145	5.5	2.0	72	1 964	140.0	55.9	86	319	20.6	5.9
Sarasota	39	757	42.2	9.1	380	3 285	288.3	136.3	179	1 186	61.0	22.2
Sunrise	21	443	19.5	3.4	193	2 942	196.5	74.7	127	558	33.7	10.0
Tallahassee	42	385	13.5	3.7	393	5 607	405.0	189.0	322	2 179	121.6	40.2
Tamarac	12	141	8.2	2.0	207	3 294	225.5	86.0	99	469	24.7	6.9
Tampa	114	5 723	471.6	167.7	1 014	14 076	1 178.9	467.3	785	5 358	358.9	109.7
Titusville	14	151	7.5	1.9	119	1 302	85.5	39.5	81	388	23.4	7.3
Weston city	NA	NA	NA	NA	NA	NA	NA	NA	NA	NA	NA	NA
West Palm Beach	45	630	44.5	13.0	421	5 793	389.8	187.5	220	1 476	97.8	31.1
Winter Haven	7	17	0.6	0.1	149	2 460	182.0	85.8	83	408	24.6	7.5
Winter Springs	8	43	2.3	0.7	20	104	5.4	2.1	19	47	4.1	1.1
GEORGIA	1 653	23 437	1 533.7	408.9	13 960	173 768	12 065.1	5 158.0	11 482	69 422	4 580.7	4 407.5
Albany	11	156	7.4	1.6	245	3 266	238.2	109.6	159	1 110	66.0	21.3
Alpharetta	19	275	16.3	5.5	115	672	72.1	25.2	82	850	37.0	9.1
Athens-Clarke County	NA	NA	NA	NA	NA	NA	NA	NA	NA	NA	NA	NA
Atlanta	157	3 937	379.9	88.0	1 134	12 059	1 040.0	480.2	903	7 202	498.6	149.4
Augusta-Richmond County	NA	NA	NA	NA	NA	NA	NA	NA	NA	NA	NA	NA

1. Firms subject to federal tax.

Table D. Cities — Federal Funds and City Government Finances

	Selected federal funds, fiscal 2001[1] (mil dol)									City government finances, 1999						
	Procurement contracts		Grants					Direct payments for individuals		General revenue						
										Intergovernmental			Taxes			
														Per capita[3] (dollars)		
City	Defense	Other	Total[2]	Health and family welfare	Energy and environment	Education	Housing and community development	Educational assistance	Housing assistance	Total (mil dol)	Total (mil dol)	Percent from state government	Total (mil dol)	Total	Property	Sales and gross receipts
	108	109	110	111	112	113	114	115	116	117	118	119	120	121	122	123
FLORIDA—Cont'd																
Coconut Creek	0.1	0.2	0.0	0.0	0.0	0.0	0.0	0.0	0.0	23.9	2.8	96.0	13.8	369	159	163
Cooper City	0.3	0.1	0.1	0.0	0.0	0.0	0.0	0.0	0.0	NA	NA	NA	NA	NA	NA	NA
Coral Gables	0.7	3.1	105.5	98.9	0.4	0.4	0.0	0.0	0.0	79.0	5.5	64.2	46.5	1 138	666	319
Coral Springs	3.0	24.1	0.1	0.0	0.0	0.0	0.1	0.0	5.0	70.6	8.4	94.2	40.2	360	146	171
Davie	6.0	0.4	0.7	0.0	0.0	0.0	0.3	0.0	0.3	44.7	7.4	88.0	28.5	460	218	190
Daytona Beach	52.8	4.7	29.3	2.2	0.0	5.1	1.3	19.3	10.0	67.9	9.6	61.1	28.0	430	211	193
Deerfield Beach	2.6	2.0	0.2	0.0	0.0	0.0	0.1	0.0	2.3	NA	NA	NA	NA	NA	NA	NA
Delray Beach	0.9	1.1	1.0	0.1	0.0	0.0	0.5	0.0	5.8	61.7	7.4	71.6	34.8	649	401	208
Dunedin	0.3	0.1	0.0	0.0	0.0	0.0	0.0	0.2	0.4	32.8	3.2	96.9	13.2	378	133	225
Fort Lauderdale	28.5	20.7	61.8	23.2	0.8	8.4	3.3	56.8	23.6	202.4	27.5	46.6	101.2	658	368	248
Fort Myers	0.3	1.7	27.8	6.9	0.0	3.6	3.3	6.8	10.2	80.7	20.2	54.1	23.2	509	213	252
Fort Pierce	0.5	2.1	12.4	0.5	0.0	3.2	1.1	4.0	5.5	31.4	5.7	48.5	11.3	311	185	113
Gainesville	4.0	22.3	266.7	101.0	6.5	9.6	2.7	28.7	31.9	94.1	17.7	65.4	24.1	261	111	133
Greenacres City	0.0	0.0	0.0	0.0	0.0	0.0	0.0	0.0	0.0	NA	NA	NA	NA	NA	NA	NA
Hallandale	0.0	0.1	0.1	0.0	0.0	0.0	0.0	0.0	0.9	NA	NA	NA	NA	NA	NA	NA
Hialeah	2.3	3.4	7.1	0.0	0.0	0.2	6.4	8.7	31.2	159.5	26.7	51.3	81.2	384	165	194
Hollywood	0.8	0.8	4.8	0.1	2.2	0.2	1.9	0.8	6.1	144.3	22.3	64.7	59.2	456	224	197
Homestead	2.1	14.7	1.7	0.0	0.0	0.0	1.1	0.0	19.6	31.5	9.2	41.8	6.7	232	169	36
Jacksonville	283.0	119.8	83.0	25.7	0.6	7.4	14.3	26.4	150.8	1 030.7	139.2	77.7	469.6	677	380	279
Jupiter town	0.6	1.1	0.3	0.0	0.0	0.0	0.0	0.0	0.0	NA	NA	NA	NA	NA	NA	NA
Key West	8.4	4.9	5.8	0.8	0.0	0.2	0.0	0.5	5.1	NA	NA	NA	NA	NA	NA	NA
Kissimmee	1.3	0.1	4.9	0.8	0.0	1.4	0.0	0.6	4.2	49.5	12.6	37.8	15.4	400	129	248
Lakeland	4.2	1.2	3.5	0.7	0.0	0.0	1.5	4.5	6.8	101.4	13.5	49.3	25.2	339	112	192
Lake Worth	3.2	13.3	0.9	0.1	0.0	0.6	0.0	7.6	0.0	39.5	11.3	33.7	11.9	408	240	140
Largo	23.7	9.9	9.4	0.2	2.7	5.8	0.1	0.0	0.6	61.5	13.3	56.1	22.8	344	92	235
Lauderdale Lakes	0.0	0.0	0.1	0.0	0.0	0.0	0.0	0.3	9.7	13.9	2.5	91.1	9.1	321	152	158
Lauderhill	0.0	0.0	1.7	0.0	0.0	0.0	1.5	0.2	0.0	NA	NA	NA	NA	NA	NA	NA
Margate	0.0	0.0	0.6	0.0	0.0	0.0	0.5	0.1	0.0	NA	NA	NA	NA	NA	NA	NA
Melbourne	640.8	4.8	11.0	2.1	2.1	0.0	2.2	2.4	6.3	66.4	9.5	62.6	24.0	347	129	188
Miami	84.5	119.3	260.2	105.0	14.0	19.8	53.9	116.9	78.2	406.2	73.2	50.0	217.0	589	357	205
Miami Beach	2.4	0.6	8.6	3.9	0.0	0.1	4.2	0.1	36.3	208.0	26.3	24.4	102.5	1 057	589	226
Miramar	0.6	1.1	0.6	0.1	0.0	0.0	0.1	0.0	0.0	NA	NA	NA	NA	NA	NA	NA
North Lauderdale	0.0	0.0	0.0	0.0	0.0	0.0	0.0	0.0	0.0	16.9	2.7	84.3	7.3	246	76	155
North Miami	0.3	0.0	1.8	0.3	0.0	0.0	1.3	0.0	1.1	49.0	6.1	67.9	15.9	313	209	87
North Miami Beach	0.0	0.6	0.2	0.0	0.0	0.0	0.0	0.0	2.6	41.6	5.6	91.4	14.0	393	308	65
Oakland Park	34.4	0.5	0.7	0.6	0.0	0.0	0.0	0.0	0.0	NA	NA	NA	NA	NA	NA	NA
Ocala	2.2	12.2	6.8	2.0	0.0	1.5	0.8	3.6	19.6	56.2	10.6	47.8	15.0	318	180	78
Orlando	1 573.2	42.1	128.1	24.3	12.6	6.4	4.1	39.7	32.6	354.0	54.4	75.1	125.3	692	331	306
Ormond Beach	0.5	0.5	0.1	0.0	0.0	0.0	0.0	0.0	2.3	33.3	3.0	78.2	12.7	383	164	202
Oviedo	0.7	0.9	0.1	0.0	0.0	0.0	0.0	0.0	0.0	NA	NA	NA	NA	NA	NA	NA
Palm Bay	76.9	1.5	7.4	0.0	0.0	0.0	0.6	0.1	0.5	46.4	7.6	75.3	24.6	317	158	143
Palm Beach Gardens	0.4	1.3	0.9	0.0	0.0	0.0	0.0	0.0	0.0	NA	NA	NA	NA	NA	NA	NA
Panama City	41.5	3.6	7.2	3.1	0.5	3.6	0.3	4.3	15.5	NA	NA	NA	NA	NA	NA	NA
Pembroke Pines	0.1	0.0	0.9	0.2	0.0	0.0	0.6	0.0	0.6	NA	NA	NA	NA	NA	NA	NA
Pensacola	86.0	9.4	29.6	3.7	0.2	4.1	0.7	15.5	28.1	67.5	11.8	50.5	29.3	504	155	314
Pinellas Park	0.1	0.2	5.8	5.0	0.0	0.0	0.0	0.1	2.3	40.1	4.6	79.2	19.0	430	146	256
Plantation	0.0	5.1	0.3	0.1	0.0	0.0	0.1	0.0	0.0	48.7	5.2	92.4	27.4	336	177	117
Plant City	0.1	0.2	0.6	0.0	0.0	0.0	0.0	0.0	1.5	NA	NA	NA	NA	NA	NA	NA
Pompano Beach	10.1	0.5	60.6	0.9	0.0	0.0	1.3	0.7	10.0	86.6	11.3	76.1	42.9	564	325	186
Port Orange	0.1	0.0	0.0	0.0	0.0	0.0	0.0	0.0	0.5	29.2	1.5	85.7	10.4	242	107	123
Port St. Lucie	0.0	0.0	0.6	0.0	0.0	0.0	0.0	0.0	0.0	NA	NA	NA	NA	NA	NA	NA
Riviera Beach	0.6	0.7	1.2	0.0	0.0	0.0	0.0	0.0	9.3	NA	NA	NA	NA	NA	NA	NA
St. Petersburg	482.3	7.4	35.2	12.5	2.1	0.2	6.9	2.1	26.7	287.8	56.5	44.1	97.4	412	226	171
Sanford	2.3	0.6	8.8	1.2	0.4	1.6	1.3	4.3	4.0	NA	NA	NA	NA	NA	NA	NA
Sarasota	6.2	2.9	22.4	2.1	3.6	2.2	2.4	1.1	5.7	72.2	3.6	32.2	32.4	636	248	355
Sunrise	0.9	0.5	1.4	0.0	0.0	0.0	0.8	0.0	1.1	108.5	7.6	78.2	35.1	436	222	163
Tallahassee	26.3	7.5	2 080.1	798.9	98.6	468.2	41.2	37.9	28.3	168.4	16.5	69.5	49.7	364	104	229
Tamarac	0.0	0.1	0.2	0.0	0.0	0.0	0.1	0.0	0.0	38.1	5.4	75.9	14.4	271	160	78
Tampa	171.3	52.6	163.1	73.9	1.7	15.3	7.4	47.3	56.3	422.8	57.4	60.6	148.8	515	246	217
Titusville	3.8	2.9	14.2	0.0	0.1	0.5	4.0	0.0	1.3	NA	NA	NA	NA	NA	NA	NA
Weston city	NA	NA	NA	NA	NA	NA	NA	NA	NA	22.0	1.8	100.0	10.2	NA	NA	NA
West Palm Beach	1 122.3	46.0	104.4	23.5	2.0	3.2	1.5	4.2	18.9	111.5	16.1	48.6	56.1	735	449	224
Winter Haven	0.5	0.8	2.6	1.3	0.0	0.6	0.3	2.3	5.0	23.9	4.8	74.0	10.3	402	182	202
Winter Springs	0.0	0.0	0.0	0.0	0.0	0.0	0.0	0.0	0.0	15.4	2.4	97.4	6.8	237	104	111
GEORGIA	5 990.4	1 391.8	7 929.2	4 716.3	103.6	819.2	123.9	247.2	591.1	X	X	X	X	X	X	X
Albany	30.6	24.8	18.1	7.0	0.0	3.7	2.9	11.0	8.1	75.4	17.4	1.6	27.5	355	158	171
Alpharetta	19.5	8.3	0.5	0.2	0.2	0.0	0.0	0.0	0.7	NA	NA	NA	NA	NA	NA	NA
Athens-Clarke County	0.1	0.7	40.6	37.5	0.0	0.0	0.0	0.0	1.3	126.8	28.3	30.0	57.0	638	283	325
Atlanta	201.9	510.3	1 756.3	693.6	82.1	273.2	77.8	72.1	200.1	1 070.1	154.2	6.4	232.7	576	240	228
Augusta-Richmond County	NA	NA	NA	NA	NA	NA	NA	NA	NA	NA	NA	NA	NA	NA	NA	NA

1. October 1, 2000 to September 30, 2001.   2. Includes program categories not shown separately. State totals include additional categories not allocated by city.   3. Based on population estimated as of July 1 of the year shown.

Table D. Cities — **City Government Finances**

City	City government finances, 1999 (cont'd)												
	General expenditure												
	Per capita[1] (dollars)			Percent of total for —									
	Total (mil dol)	Total	Capital outlays	Public welfare	Highways	Parking facilities	Education	Health and hospitals	Police protection	Sewerage and sanitation	Parks and recreation	Housing and community development	Interest on debt
	124	125	126	127	128	129	130	131	132	133	134	135	136
FLORIDA—Cont'd													
Coconut Creek	22.5	601	77	0.0	4.3	0.0	0.0	0.0	27.8	10.6	16.4	0.0	5.0
Cooper City	NA	NA	NA	NA	NA	NA	NA	NA	NA	NA	NA	NA	NA
Coral Gables	77.5	1 896	179	0.0	7.2	3.3	0.0	0.0	24.6	13.9	7.8	0.0	0.5
Coral Springs	66.1	592	122	0.0	5.5	0.0	0.0	4.3	30.8	7.3	16.4	0.0	5.0
Davie	42.7	688	114	0.0	6.6	0.0	0.0	0.0	35.9	0.0	9.6	0.0	4.6
Daytona Beach	67.9	1 042	171	0.0	5.9	0.0	0.0	0.0	27.5	25.1	12.8	4.0	2.4
Deerfield Beach	NA	NA	NA	NA	NA	NA	NA	NA	NA	NA	NA	NA	NA
Delray Beach	65.6	1 223	78	0.3	4.3	0.1	0.0	0.0	23.5	6.1	15.3	6.2	4.2
Dunedin	28.2	805	38	0.0	6.3	0.0	0.0	0.0	9.9	27.3	14.6	0.0	13.7
Fort Lauderdale	193.3	1 258	125	0.0	2.2	3.4	0.0	0.0	28.9	10.6	13.6	5.2	3.2
Fort Myers	75.8	1 660	121	0.0	7.2	0.1	0.0	0.0	18.6	13.8	13.7	11.8	9.6
Fort Pierce	31.9	879	0	0.0	7.9	0.0	0.0	0.0	24.4	26.4	4.9	2.7	2.1
Gainesville	88.9	959	25	0.0	6.0	0.0	0.0	0.0	23.2	16.5	6.6	1.9	8.6
Greenacres City	NA	NA	NA	NA	NA	NA	NA	NA	NA	NA	NA	NA	NA
Hallandale	NA	NA	NA	NA	NA	NA	NA	NA	NA	NA	NA	NA	NA
Hialeah	152.8	723	101	0.0	5.5	0.0	0.0	0.0	18.7	25.5	5.1	5.2	2.7
Hollywood	130.9	1 006	78	0.0	6.1	1.2	0.0	0.0	28.6	19.5	6.4	2.2	0.4
Homestead	25.8	888	73	0.0	2.1	0.0	0.0	0.0	29.8	19.7	10.7	7.4	8.1
Jacksonville	1 103.1	1 590	366	2.6	5.2	0.2	0.0	4.0	12.1	15.7	3.2	1.2	15.1
Jupiter town	NA	NA	NA	NA	NA	NA	NA	NA	NA	NA	NA	NA	NA
Key West	NA	NA	NA	NA	NA	NA	NA	NA	NA	NA	NA	NA	NA
Kissimmee	37.1	963	90	0.0	17.0	0.0	0.0	0.0	22.5	4.8	10.7	4.5	1.9
Lakeland	112.4	1 514	297	0.0	11.5	0.3	0.0	0.0	16.7	16.7	13.3	1.5	9.9
Lake Worth	30.4	1 043	51	0.0	2.9	0.1	0.0	0.0	24.8	23.7	12.0	0.0	4.6
Largo	59.8	902	150	0.0	6.4	0.0	0.0	0.0	17.4	28.3	11.4	3.2	2.5
Lauderdale Lakes	12.4	441	0	0.7	6.5	0.0	0.0	0.0	29.3	12.6	9.0	2.9	8.7
Lauderhill	NA	NA	NA	NA	NA	NA	NA	NA	NA	NA	NA	NA	NA
Margate	NA	NA	NA	NA	NA	NA	NA	NA	NA	NA	NA	NA	NA
Melbourne	54.5	789	103	0.0	9.3	0.0	0.0	0.0	23.0	16.5	12.9	1.9	3.1
Miami	340.0	922	46	0.0	2.8	2.5	0.0	0.0	23.5	9.0	5.1	11.1	9.8
Miami Beach	236.3	2 434	551	0.0	1.1	7.7	0.0	3.1	15.4	11.1	14.6	17.5	8.8
Miramar	NA	NA	NA	NA	NA	NA	NA	NA	NA	NA	NA	NA	NA
North Lauderdale	18.0	612	31	0.0	4.2	0.0	0.0	0.0	28.8	14.2	11.6	4.2	0.3
North Miami	44.4	874	72	2.1	5.3	0.0	0.0	0.0	20.8	27.7	8.2	0.4	8.1
North Miami Beach	43.5	1 223	186	0.0	4.6	0.0	0.0	0.0	27.8	18.9	5.6	0.0	2.1
Oakland Park	NA	NA	NA	NA	NA	NA	NA	NA	NA	NA	NA	NA	NA
Ocala	57.6	1 225	128	0.0	12.6	0.1	0.0	0.0	19.9	21.4	8.4	1.0	3.4
Orlando	356.3	1 967	469	1.3	13.1	2.8	0.0	0.0	17.4	23.0	9.1	2.0	6.1
Ormond Beach	35.3	1 068	371	0.0	10.5	0.0	0.0	0.0	24.6	21.0	9.8	0.0	2.1
Oviedo	NA	NA	NA	NA	NA	NA	NA	NA	NA	NA	NA	NA	NA
Palm Bay	52.8	681	268	0.0	19.5	0.5	0.0	0.0	18.5	23.2	5.4	2.3	1.9
Palm Beach Gardens	NA	NA	NA	NA	NA	NA	NA	NA	NA	NA	NA	NA	NA
Panama City	NA	NA	NA	NA	NA	NA	NA	NA	NA	NA	NA	NA	NA
Pembroke Pines	NA	NA	NA	NA	NA	NA	NA	NA	NA	NA	NA	NA	NA
Pensacola	75.5	1 297	175	0.0	5.2	0.0	0.0	0.2	15.6	5.0	16.7	12.8	11.3
Pinellas Park	37.2	843	104	0.0	8.9	0.0	0.0	0.0	17.6	28.4	7.3	0.5	3.3
Plantation	47.1	578	18	0.0	3.2	0.0	0.0	0.0	37.6	11.0	12.6	0.0	3.9
Plant City	NA	NA	NA	NA	NA	NA	NA	NA	NA	NA	NA	NA	NA
Pompano Beach	81.1	1 067	34	0.0	2.3	0.3	0.0	5.8	30.5	17.4	9.5	1.1	2.7
Port Orange	32.3	751	184	0.0	6.3	0.0	0.0	0.0	12.8	25.8	8.6	0.0	6.3
Port St. Lucie	NA	NA	NA	NA	NA	NA	NA	NA	NA	NA	NA	NA	NA
Riviera Beach	NA	NA	NA	NA	NA	NA	NA	NA	NA	NA	NA	NA	NA
St. Petersburg	238.4	1 010	83	0.9	3.2	1.8	0.0	0.0	19.9	22.5	15.1	1.4	12.7
Sanford	NA	NA	NA	NA	NA	NA	NA	NA	NA	NA	NA	NA	NA
Sarasota	66.8	1 310	77	0.0	8.7	0.5	0.0	0.0	24.4	19.5	14.8	4.1	4.1
Sunrise	166.7	2 076	1 165	0.0	2.3	0.0	0.0	0.0	7.8	56.0	4.2	0.2	4.1
Tallahassee	212.2	1 553	449	0.6	18.4	0.7	0.0	0.1	13.2	22.8	5.9	1.4	4.5
Tamarac	27.7	523	46	0.0	7.7	0.0	0.0	0.0	24.6	18.5	4.5	0.3	1.2
Tampa	420.4	1 454	305	4.6	10.4	9.0	0.0	0.0	22.4	18.2	7.9	1.9	8.4
Titusville	NA	NA	NA	NA	NA	NA	NA	NA	NA	NA	NA	NA	NA
Weston city	15.1	NA	NA	0.0	0.0	0.0	0.0	0.0	18.6	15.4	6.6	0.0	0.0
West Palm Beach	104.1	1 364	166	0.0	6.1	1.4	0.0	1.9	24.7	4.8	8.1	6.0	5.6
Winter Haven	31.6	1 228	392	2.6	5.5	0.0	0.0	0.0	16.8	18.1	23.2	0.0	3.1
Winter Springs	14.2	498	92	0.0	20.0	0.0	0.0	0.3	19.9	8.1	9.6	0.0	5.3
GEORGIA	X	X	X	X	X	X	X	X	X	X	X	X	X
Albany	92.0	1 186	330	0.0	7.0	0.0	0.0	0.0	12.6	13.5	9.2	5.9	1.3
Alpharetta	NA	NA	NA	NA	NA	NA	NA	NA	NA	NA	NA	NA	NA
Athens-Clarke County	118.2	1 323	306	1.1	4.1	0.5	0.0	5.2	14.9	12.7	7.2	5.9	0.6
Atlanta	1 016.5	2 517	824	0.1	4.1	0.0	0.0	0.0	10.6	14.6	6.2	0.7	9.6
Augusta-Richmond County	NA	NA	NA	NA	NA	NA	NA	NA	NA	NA	NA	NA	NA

1. Based on population estimated as of July 1 of the year shown.

Table D. Cities — City Government Finances, City Government Employment, and Climate

	City government finances, 1999 (cont'd)				Climate[2]						
	Debt outstanding			City government employment, 2001	Average daily temperature (degrees Fahrenheit)				Annual precipitation (inches)	Heating degree days	Cooling degree days
					Mean		Limits				
City	Total (mil dol)	Per capita[1] (dollars)	Percent utility		January	July	January[3]	July[4]			
	137	138	139	140	141	142	143	144	145	146	147
FLORIDA—Cont'd											
Coconut Creek	20.8	556	0.0	NA	66.2	82.5	56.8	91.2	59.15	262	4 038
Cooper City	NA	NA	NA	NA	NA	NA	NA	NA	NA	NA	NA
Coral Gables	19.1	469	0.0	848	67.2	82.6	59.2	89.0	55.91	200	4 198
Coral Springs	107.7	964	27.5	777	66.2	82.5	56.8	91.2	59.15	262	4 038
Davie	75.4	1 215	72.0	NA	67.2	82.6	57.9	90.1	60.64	205	4 124
Daytona Beach	80.4	1 235	61.4	NA	57.5	81.2	46.9	89.8	47.89	909	2 919
Deerfield Beach	NA	NA	NA	NA	66.2	82.5	56.8	91.2	59.15	262	4 038
Delray Beach	89.6	1 671	50.8	NA	66.2	82.5	56.8	91.2	59.15	262	4 038
Dunedin	84.9	2 426	27.0	NA	59.9	82.1	50.0	90.2	43.92	726	3 396
Fort Lauderdale	123.6	804	17.5	2 708	67.2	82.6	57.9	90.1	60.64	205	4 124
Fort Myers	174.1	3 810	42.2	NA	63.8	82.8	53.2	91.1	53.37	418	3 855
Fort Pierce	104.9	2 886	84.1	NA	62.5	81.4	51.6	90.4	50.06	490	3 441
Gainesville	448.0	4 835	76.4	1 969	53.7	80.7	42.5	90.7	51.81	1 316	2 570
Greenacres City	NA	NA	NA	NA	NA	NA	NA	NA	NA	NA	NA
Hallandale	NA	NA	NA	NA	67.2	82.6	57.9	90.1	60.64	205	4 124
Hialeah	62.2	294	6.7	1 484	66.3	82.4	56.8	89.8	63.01	273	4 012
Hollywood	120.0	923	94.6	1 599	67.2	82.6	57.9	90.1	60.64	205	4 124
Homestead	30.9	1 062	0.0	383	65.3	81.1	54.5	90.1	58.74	277	3 603
Jacksonville	4 918.6	7 091	52.5	NA	NA	NA	NA	NA	NA	NA	NA
Jupiter town	NA	NA	NA	NA	NA	NA	NA	NA	NA	NA	NA
Key West	NA	NA	NA	NA	NA	NA	NA	NA	NA	NA	NA
Kissimmee	262.9	6 822	94.3	NA	61.0	81.7	48.7	91.4	46.11	603	3 324
Lakeland	625.9	8 435	73.8	2 116	61.1	82.5	50.4	92.2	47.54	588	3 546
Lake Worth	52.4	1 801	60.3	NA	65.1	82.2	55.7	89.9	60.75	323	3 891
Largo	38.8	585	0.0	NA	59.9	82.1	50.0	90.2	43.92	726	3 396
Lauderdale Lakes	14.6	519	0.0	NA	67.2	82.6	57.9	90.1	60.64	205	4 124
Lauderhill	NA	NA	NA	NA	67.2	82.6	57.9	90.1	60.64	205	4 124
Margate	NA	NA	NA	NA	66.2	82.5	56.8	91.2	59.15	262	4 038
Melbourne	85.0	1 231	73.6	NA	60.9	81.1	50.7	90.0	45.49	644	3 193
Miami	560.9	1 522	0.0	3 848	67.2	82.6	59.2	89.0	55.91	200	4 198
Miami Beach	337.1	3 473	0.0	1 722	68.1	82.6	62.3	86.9	45.35	139	4 157
Miramar	NA	NA	NA	NA	66.3	82.4	56.8	89.8	63.01	273	4 012
North Lauderdale	2.1	72	54.3	NA	66.2	82.5	56.8	91.2	59.15	262	4 038
North Miami	55.3	1 089	11.9	536	66.3	82.4	56.8	89.8	63.01	273	4 012
North Miami Beach	23.7	667	31.8	NA	68.1	82.6	62.3	86.9	45.35	139	4 157
Oakland Park	NA	NA	NA	NA	67.2	82.6	57.9	90.1	60.64	205	4 124
Ocala	109.6	2 331	68.5	NA	57.5	81.5	45.1	92.2	51.59	930	3 046
Orlando	375.9	2 075	0.0	3 472	59.7	82.3	48.6	91.5	48.11	686	3 381
Ormond Beach	41.7	1 262	73.6	NA	57.5	81.2	46.9	89.8	47.89	909	2 919
Oviedo	NA	NA	NA	NA	NA	NA	NA	NA	NA	NA	NA
Palm Bay	86.6	1 118	62.0	NA	60.9	81.1	50.7	90.0	45.49	644	3 193
Palm Beach Gardens	NA	NA	NA	NA	NA	NA	NA	NA	NA	NA	NA
Panama City	NA	NA	NA	NA	50.7	80.8	39.1	90.0	65.06	1 681	2 409
Pembroke Pines	NA	NA	NA	NA	66.3	82.4	56.8	89.8	63.01	273	4 012
Pensacola	149.5	2 569	6.9	NA	50.6	82.1	41.4	89.9	62.25	1 617	2 636
Pinellas Park	35.4	801	28.5	NA	60.7	83.1	52.9	89.8	48.62	603	3 626
Plantation	65.0	798	57.7	802	67.2	82.6	57.9	90.1	60.64	205	4 124
Plant City	NA	NA	NA	NA	NA	NA	NA	NA	NA	NA	NA
Pompano Beach	46.2	608	33.2	655	66.2	82.5	56.8	91.2	59.15	262	4 038
Port Orange	95.6	2 221	63.9	NA	57.5	81.2	46.9	89.8	47.89	909	2 919
Port St. Lucie	NA	NA	NA	NA	62.5	81.4	51.6	90.4	50.06	490	3 441
Riviera Beach	NA	NA	NA	NA	65.1	82.2	55.7	89.9	60.75	323	3 891
St. Petersburg	583.6	2 473	11.5	3 115	60.7	83.1	52.9	89.8	48.62	603	3 626
Sanford	NA	NA	NA	NA	58.2	81.5	46.8	91.6	48.81	831	3 004
Sarasota	104.7	2 052	62.0	NA	60.2	81.4	49.0	90.8	53.71	678	3 186
Sunrise	332.6	4 140	66.9	908	67.2	82.6	57.9	90.1	60.64	205	4 124
Tallahassee	268.3	1 964	45.3	3 197	50.5	81.3	38.1	91.3	65.71	1 705	2 518
Tamarac	24.1	456	77.8	NA	66.2	82.5	56.8	91.2	59.15	262	4 038
Tampa	846.5	2 927	5.5	4 261	59.9	82.1	50.0	90.2	43.92	726	3 396
Titusville	NA	NA	NA	NA	58.6	81.3	47.3	91.4	54.07	803	3 057
Weston city	0.0	NA	NA	NA	NA	NA	NA	NA	NA	NA	NA
West Palm Beach	140.7	1 843	30.6	1 356	65.1	82.2	55.7	89.9	60.75	323	3 891
Winter Haven	50.7	1 971	0.0	505	NA	NA	NA	NA	NA	NA	NA
Winter Springs	36.7	1 282	66.4	NA	NA	NA	NA	NA	NA	NA	NA
GEORGIA	X	X	X	X	X	X	X	X	X	X	X
Albany	60.9	785	68.3	1 070	46.5	80.8	33.8	91.9	51.48	2 205	2 206
Alpharetta	NA	NA	NA	NA	NA	NA	NA	NA	NA	NA	NA
Athens-Clarke County	61.1	684	87.5	NA	41.8	79.6	32.0	89.6	49.74	2 893	1 709
Atlanta	1 612.0	3 992	31.3	8 320	41.0	78.8	31.5	88.0	50.77	2 991	1 667
Augusta-Richmond County	NA	NA	NA	NA	NA	NA	NA	NA	NA	NA	NA

1. Based on the population estimated as of July 1 of the year shown.   2. Represents normal values based on the 30-year period, 1961–1990.   3. Average daily minimum.   4. Average daily maximum.

STATE Place code	City	Land area, 2000[1] (sq km)	Population, 2000 Total persons	Rank	Per square kilometer	Population Total persons 1990	Percent change 1990–2000	Total persons 1980	Percent change 1980–1990	White	Black	Am. Indian, Alaska Native	Asian and Pacific Islander	Other race	His-panic[2]	Non-His-panic White
										Population characteristics, 2000 — Percent — Race (alone or in combination)						
		1	2	3	4	5	6	7	8	9	10	11	12	13	14	15
	GEORGIA—Cont'd															
13 19000	Columbus	560.1	186 291	104	332.6	178 685	3.9	NA	NA	51.8	44.6	0.8	2.3	2.5	4.5	48.7
13 21380	Dalton city	51.3	27 912	1 104	544.1	22 218	25.6	20 939	6.1	68.6	8.2	0.7	2.2	23.2	40.2	49.7
13 25720	East Point	35.6	39 595	784	1 112.2	34 595	14.5	37 486	-7.7	16.9	79.0	0.6	1.1	4.0	7.6	13.0
13 31908	Gainesville	70.1	25 578	1 215	364.9	17 885	43.0	15 280	17.0	66.5	16.1	0.6	3.1	15.4	33.2	47.8
13 38964	Hinesville	42.0	30 392	1 022	723.6	21 596	40.7	11 309	91.0	44.2	48.2	1.1	4.2	6.7	9.1	38.8
13 44340	La Grange	75.0	25 998	1 195	346.6	25 574	1.7	24 163	5.8	50.0	47.9	0.5	1.2	1.5	2.4	48.4
13 49000	Macon	144.5	97 255	243	673.0	107 365	-9.4	116 903	-8.2	35.9	62.9	0.4	0.9	0.7	1.2	35.0
13 49756	Marietta	56.7	58 748	481	1 036.1	44 129	33.1	30 829	43.1	58.4	30.5	0.8	3.6	9.5	16.9	48.6
13 59724	Peachtree City	60.3	31 580	989	523.7	19 027	66.0	NA	NA	88.9	6.5	0.6	4.3	1.3	3.7	85.1
13 66668	Rome	76.1	34 980	896	459.7	30 425	15.3	29 609	2.4	64.5	28.2	0.7	1.9	6.4	10.3	59.2
13 67284	Roswell	98.5	79 334	330	805.4	47 986	65.3	23 337	105.6	82.9	9.1	0.6	4.4	5.0	10.6	75.5
13 69000	Savannah	193.6	131 510	162	679.3	137 812	-4.6	141 378	-2.5	39.8	57.8	0.6	2.1	1.3	2.2	37.9
13 71492	Smyrna	36.0	40 999	750	1 138.9	32 453	26.3	20 312	59.8	61.3	28.1	0.9	4.6	7.8	13.8	53.5
13 78800	Valdosta	77.5	43 724	702	564.2	40 038	9.2	37 533	6.7	48.6	49.0	0.6	1.8	1.3	2.2	46.7
13 80508	Warner Robins	59.0	48 804	618	827.2	43 861	11.3	39 879	10.0	64.1	32.8	0.8	2.7	1.7	3.8	60.5
15 00000	HAWAII	16 634.5	1 211 537	X	72.8	1 108 229	9.3	964 691	14.9	39.3	2.8	2.1	81.3	3.9	7.2	22.9
15 14650	Hilo CDP	140.6	40 759	755	289.9	37 808	7.8	35 269	7.2	38.7	1.2	2.6	96.0	4.3	8.8	15.9
15 17000	Honolulu CDP	222.0	371 657	46	1 674.1	377 059	-1.4	365 048	3.3	30.1	2.4	1.4	83.3	2.4	4.4	18.7
15 23150	Kailua CDP	17.2	36 513	848	2 122.8	36 818	-0.8	35 812	2.8	64.3	1.6	2.4	63.8	3.0	6.1	42.3
15 28250	Kaneohe CDP	17.0	34 970	898	2 057.1	35 448	-1.3	29 919	18.5	41.3	1.5	2.1	91.7	2.9	7.2	19.3
15 51050	Mililani CDP	10.1	28 608	1 081	2 832.5	29 359	-2.6	21 365	37.4	38.3	4.3	1.9	84.5	3.9	7.8	19.2
15 62600	Pearl City CDP	12.9	30 976	1 007	2 401.2	30 993	0.1	42 575	-27.2	30.1	3.6	1.6	86.8	3.9	7.3	16.0
15 77750	Waimalu CDP	15.3	29 371	1 061	1 919.7	29 967	-2.0	NA	NA	29.7	3.5	1.6	86.4	3.6	6.0	16.1
15 79700	Waipahu CDP	6.7	33 108	945	4 941.5	31 435	5.3	29 139	7.9	13.7	1.7	1.4	100.5	3.5	6.1	4.1
16 00000	IDAHO	214 314.3	1 293 953	X	6.0	1 006 734	28.5	944 127	6.6	92.8	0.6	2.1	1.5	5.0	7.9	88.0
16 08830	Boise City	165.2	185 787	106	1 124.6	126 685	46.7	102 451	23.7	94.4	1.1	1.4	3.0	2.6	4.5	89.9
16 12250	Caldwell	29.4	25 967	1 197	883.2	18 586	41.1	17 699	4.0	77.6	0.8	1.8	1.7	21.1	28.1	68.3
16 16750	Coeur d'Alene	34.0	34 514	910	1 015.1	24 561	40.5	20 054	22.5	97.6	0.4	1.8	1.2	1.0	2.7	94.1
16 39700	Idaho Falls	44.2	50 730	588	1 147.7	43 973	15.4	39 590	11.1	93.6	0.9	1.3	1.5	4.4	7.2	89.4
16 46540	Lewiston	42.7	30 904	1 012	723.7	28 082	10.0	27 986	0.3	96.7	0.4	2.6	1.3	0.8	1.9	94.1
16 52120	Meridian city	30.5	34 919	901	1 144.9	9 596	263.9	NA	NA	96.3	0.7	1.0	2.3	1.9	3.7	92.4
16 56260	Nampa	51.4	51 867	576	1 009.1	28 365	82.9	25 112	13.0	86.1	0.7	1.7	1.8	12.7	17.9	78.2
16 64090	Pocatello	73.1	51 466	582	704.0	46 117	11.6	46 340	-0.5	94.2	1.0	2.1	2.1	2.9	4.9	90.4
16 82810	Twin Falls	31.1	34 469	912	1 108.3	27 634	24.7	26 209	5.4	94.0	0.4	1.4	1.6	5.0	8.9	87.6
17 00000	ILLINOIS	143 960.8	12 419 293	X	86.3	11 430 602	8.6	11 427 409	0.0	75.1	15.6	0.6	3.9	6.8	12.3	67.8
17 00243	Addison	24.4	35 914	867	1 471.9	32 053	12.0	29 759	7.7	77.5	2.7	0.6	8.6	13.1	28.4	60.0
17 01114	Alton	40.5	30 496	1 021	753.0	33 060	-7.8	34 171	-3.2	73.8	25.7	0.7	0.7	1.0	1.5	71.6
17 02154	Arlington Heights	42.5	76 031	349	1 789.0	75 463	0.8	66 116	14.1	91.6	1.1	0.2	6.6	1.7	4.5	87.6
17 03012	Aurora	99.8	142 990	147	1 432.8	99 672	43.5	81 293	22.6	70.5	11.9	0.7	3.6	16.2	32.6	52.1
17 04013	Bartlett	38.4	36 706	844	955.9	19 395	89.3	13 254	46.3	88.4	2.3	0.4	8.5	2.0	5.5	83.6
17 04845	Belleville	48.8	41 410	739	848.4	42 806	-3.3	41 580	2.9	82.8	16.1	0.6	1.2	0.7	1.6	80.5
17 05573	Berwyn	10.1	54 016	550	5 348.1	45 426	18.9	46 849	-3.0	76.8	1.6	0.9	3.2	21.3	38.0	56.4
17 06613	Bloomington	58.3	64 808	421	1 111.6	51 889	24.9	44 189	17.4	86.5	9.5	0.5	3.5	1.9	3.3	83.3
17 07133	Bolingbrook	53.1	56 321	513	1 060.7	40 843	37.9	37 245	9.7	66.7	21.6	0.7	7.3	6.7	13.1	57.9
17 09447	Buffalo Grove	23.8	42 909	714	1 802.9	36 417	17.8	22 238	63.8	89.7	0.9	0.1	9.1	1.4	3.3	86.5
17 09642	Burbank	10.8	27 902	1 106	2 583.5	27 600	1.1	28 462	-3.0	93.8	0.4	0.5	2.2	6.4	11.1	84.3
17 10487	Calumet City	18.8	39 071	791	2 078.2	37 840	3.3	39 697	-4.7	40.3	53.9	0.7	0.8	6.7	10.9	34.4
17 11332	Carol Stream	23.0	40 438	763	1 758.2	31 759	27.3	15 514	104.7	80.2	4.7	0.5	12.0	4.8	10.0	73.0
17 11358	Carpentersville	19.3	30 586	1 018	1 584.8	23 049	32.7	23 275	-1.0	72.0	4.7	1.0	2.6	23.4	40.6	51.9
17 12385	Champaign	44.0	67 518	401	1 534.5	63 502	6.3	58 133	9.2	74.9	16.5	0.6	7.6	2.6	4.0	71.3
17 14000	Chicago	588.3	2 896 016	3	4 922.7	2 783 726	4.0	3 005 078	-7.4	44.3	37.4	0.7	5.1	15.6	26.0	31.3
17 14026	Chicago Heights	24.8	32 776	955	1 321.6	32 966	-0.6	37 026	-11.0	47.2	38.9	0.8	0.7	15.1	23.8	36.8
17 14351	Cicero	15.1	85 616	296	5 669.9	67 436	27.0	61 232	10.1	51.9	1.3	1.3	1.3	48.2	77.4	19.6
17 17887	Crystal Lake	42.1	38 000	819	902.6	24 692	53.9	18 590	32.8	95.0	0.7	0.4	2.5	2.6	7.0	89.6
17 18563	Danville	44.0	33 904	924	770.5	33 828	0.2	39 019	-13.3	71.8	25.5	0.6	1.5	2.7	4.6	68.3
17 18823	Decatur	107.6	81 860	314	760.8	83 900	-2.4	94 081	-10.8	79.1	20.6	0.5	0.9	0.7	1.2	77.0
17 19161	De Kalb	32.7	39 018	795	1 193.2	35 076	11.2	33 099	6.0	81.2	9.7	0.6	5.3	5.3	9.0	75.6
17 19642	Des Plaines	37.4	58 720	482	1 570.1	53 414	9.9	53 568	-0.3	86.1	1.2	0.6	8.3	5.8	14.0	76.0
17 20292	Dolton	11.8	25 614	1 213	2 170.7	23 956	6.9	24 766	-3.3	15.0	83.1	0.5	0.8	1.8	3.1	13.2
17 20591	Downers Grove	36.9	48 724	619	1 320.4	47 464	4.0	42 572	10.0	91.1	2.1	0.3	6.2	1.4	3.6	87.8
17 22255	East St. Louis	36.4	31 542	991	866.5	40 944	-23.0	55 200	-25.8	1.5	98.2	0.5	0.2	0.3	0.7	1.2
17 23074	Elgin	64.8	94 487	255	1 458.1	77 014	22.7	63 798	20.7	73.0	7.5	0.8	4.5	17.2	34.3	53.8
17 23256	Elk Grove Village	28.6	34 727	906	1 214.2	33 429	3.9	28 907	15.6	87.1	1.6	0.3	9.5	2.8	6.2	82.4
17 23620	Elmhurst	26.6	42 762	716	1 607.6	42 029	1.7	44 276	-5.1	94.2	1.0	0.3	4.2	1.3	4.0	90.5
17 23724	Elmwood Park	4.9	25 405	1 221	5 184.7	23 206	9.5	24 016	-3.4	93.8	0.7	0.4	2.5	5.1	11.0	84.6
17 24582	Evanston	20.1	74 239	359	3 693.5	73 233	1.4	73 706	-0.6	67.4	24.1	0.6	7.2	4.0	6.1	62.6

1. Dry land or land partially or temporarily covered by water.   2. Hispanic persons may be of any race.

City	Under 5 years	5 to 17 years	18 to 24 years	25 to 34 years	35 to 44 years	45 to 54 years	55 to 64 years	65 to 74 years	75 years and over	Percent female	Number	Percent change, 1990–2000	Persons per household	Female family householder[1]	One-person
					Age of population (percent)							Households, 2000			Percent
	16	17	18	19	20	21	22	23	24	25	26	27	28	29	30
GEORGIA—Cont'd															
Columbus	7.3	19.5	11.9	14.6	15.2	12.2	7.5	6.5	5.2	51.4	69 819	6.0	2.54	19.6	26.7
Dalton city	8.9	18.4	12.0	17.0	13.3	11.4	7.5	5.6	5.9	49.0	9 689	10.9	2.81	11.5	27.6
East Point	8.7	20.6	11.9	16.1	15.2	12.8	6.7	4.1	3.9	52.8	14 553	8.8	2.69	28.9	27.4
Gainesville	8.3	16.7	15.1	18.3	12.3	10.3	6.6	5.7	6.8	50.5	8 537	23.0	2.79	15.2	29.5
Hinesville	10.6	23.6	13.8	19.1	16.9	8.9	4.1	2.0	1.1	50.7	10 528	40.3	2.89	16.7	17.4
La Grange	7.7	20.7	11.0	13.8	13.1	11.7	7.5	6.8	7.7	53.9	10 022	2.6	2.50	23.5	30.1
Macon	7.8	19.2	11.3	13.6	13.8	12.3	7.8	7.1	7.2	55.6	38 444	-6.6	2.44	25.7	31.7
Marietta	7.9	14.5	14.1	24.1	15.4	10.2	5.5	3.7	4.6	49.7	23 895	20.3	2.39	13.8	32.8
Peachtree City	6.1	25.5	5.8	8.8	19.7	18.0	8.2	4.2	3.8	51.2	10 876	75.1	2.89	8.4	16.0
Rome	6.7	17.5	12.1	14.2	13.5	11.8	8.3	7.6	8.3	52.6	13 320	10.9	2.47	17.0	30.9
Roswell	6.9	17.5	8.2	17.0	18.1	16.3	8.4	4.0	3.5	50.0	30 207	66.1	2.61	8.6	23.1
Savannah	7.0	18.6	13.2	14.8	13.7	11.6	7.9	6.5	6.8	52.8	51 375	-1.1	2.45	21.7	31.4
Smyrna	6.9	12.6	10.8	26.7	17.1	11.3	6.2	4.4	3.9	51.2	18 372	23.8	2.21	11.4	37.5
Valdosta	7.7	18.4	18.4	14.6	12.6	11.0	6.8	5.4	5.0	53.7	16 692	18.0	2.50	19.5	28.4
Warner Robins	7.2	20.3	9.6	15.5	16.4	12.1	8.1	6.4	4.4	51.5	19 550	16.9	2.48	16.6	28.1
HAWAII	6.5	18.0	9.5	14.1	15.8	14.1	8.8	7.0	6.2	49.8	403 240	13.2	2.92	12.4	21.9
Hilo CDP	5.6	19.0	10.3	10.7	13.7	14.3	9.6	8.5	8.2	51.1	14 577	9.4	2.70	15.2	24.1
Honolulu CDP	5.1	14.1	8.9	14.5	15.4	14.4	9.7	8.7	9.1	50.9	140 337	4.3	2.57	12.1	29.7
Kailua CDP	5.7	18.4	7.2	12.0	16.6	16.5	9.7	7.6	6.1	50.5	12 229	3.3	2.98	12.2	16.6
Kaneohe CDP	5.8	18.8	8.2	12.6	16.5	14.1	9.3	8.3	6.5	51.0	10 976	3.4	3.14	13.7	15.4
Mililani CDP	5.8	21.4	9.2	11.9	16.5	18.6	9.5	4.6	2.5	50.1	9 010	2.7	3.17	10.2	10.6
Pearl City CDP	5.1	13.7	13.7	14.7	12.4	11.1	12.0	10.5	6.6	46.5	8 921	0.5	3.17	12.3	14.9
Waimalu CDP	5.4	16.0	9.5	14.8	16.6	17.2	10.2	6.3	3.8	49.4	10 524	1.5	2.78	11.1	21.0
Waipahu CDP	6.9	19.6	9.5	13.4	13.3	11.6	9.8	8.6	7.2	50.6	7 566	0.0	4.23	18.1	11.1
IDAHO	7.5	21.0	10.7	13.1	14.9	13.2	8.3	5.9	5.4	49.9	469 645	30.2	2.69	8.7	22.4
Boise City	7.1	18.3	11.7	16.3	16.1	13.6	7.0	4.8	5.3	50.5	74 438	46.4	2.44	10.0	28.0
Caldwell	9.6	21.3	13.1	14.6	12.7	10.6	7.0	5.1	5.9	51.1	8 963	33.7	2.79	13.9	23.3
Coeur d'Alene	6.9	18.1	11.7	13.7	14.3	13.0	7.6	6.6	8.2	51.6	13 985	35.7	2.39	11.5	28.2
Idaho Falls	8.2	22.1	10.1	12.9	14.6	13.0	7.9	5.8	5.4	50.5	18 793	17.3	2.65	10.2	25.3
Lewiston	5.9	17.3	10.7	12.3	14.5	13.4	8.9	8.0	9.1	51.2	12 795	11.1	2.36	9.3	27.9
Meridian city	11.4	22.3	6.9	19.8	17.3	10.4	5.4	3.6	2.9	50.9	11 829	227.5	2.93	8.8	14.5
Nampa	10.5	20.4	12.5	17.6	12.7	9.2	5.9	5.0	6.2	51.0	18 090	77.1	2.77	11.4	22.6
Pocatello	8.3	18.3	16.7	14.7	12.6	12.0	6.9	5.2	5.2	50.8	19 334	12.5	2.58	10.5	25.0
Twin Falls	7.8	18.6	12.1	12.8	13.4	12.1	8.1	6.7	8.3	52.0	13 274	26.8	2.51	11.0	26.8
ILLINOIS	7.1	19.1	9.8	14.6	16.0	13.1	8.4	6.2	5.9	51.0	4 591 779	9.3	2.63	12.3	26.8
Addison	7.6	18.6	11.3	16.6	15.4	12.8	9.3	5.3	3.1	49.2	11 649	8.6	3.07	10.2	16.9
Alton	7.2	18.5	9.1	14.5	14.5	12.0	8.0	7.3	8.7	53.1	12 518	-3.5	2.36	17.4	33.3
Arlington Heights	6.0	17.1	6.0	13.2	16.6	14.7	10.3	7.9	8.2	51.9	30 763	6.8	2.44	6.3	29.0
Aurora	10.6	21.2	10.2	19.4	16.5	10.6	5.4	3.1	3.1	49.6	46 489	37.9	3.04	12.0	20.6
Bartlett	10.7	21.1	5.4	16.4	21.4	13.4	6.1	3.3	2.3	50.6	12 179	91.3	3.00	7.0	14.2
Belleville	6.2	17.3	9.0	14.1	16.2	12.5	7.6	7.8	9.4	52.9	17 603	-0.8	2.27	13.5	35.1
Berwyn	7.9	18.3	9.6	16.1	15.6	11.7	7.3	6.0	7.4	51.3	19 702	2.1	2.73	12.8	29.4
Bloomington	7.4	17.6	12.5	16.8	16.5	12.8	6.5	5.0	5.0	51.5	26 642	24.0	2.34	9.7	32.8
Bolingbrook	9.5	22.7	8.4	16.8	18.4	13.5	6.4	2.4	1.9	50.1	17 416	40.6	3.22	10.9	14.2
Buffalo Grove	6.6	22.3	5.3	11.7	20.5	16.8	7.8	5.2	3.9	51.6	15 708	17.8	2.72	6.6	22.1
Burbank	5.9	19.3	9.9	12.2	15.9	13.2	9.6	7.7	6.3	51.2	9 317	1.6	2.98	12.1	18.9
Calumet City	7.7	21.0	8.6	14.7	16.0	11.6	7.6	6.3	6.4	53.5	15 139	-1.9	2.58	22.4	29.8
Carol Stream	8.2	22.7	9.1	16.5	20.2	12.6	5.0	2.6	3.1	50.7	13 872	22.4	2.91	9.6	21.1
Carpentersville	10.5	22.6	10.9	19.7	15.7	10.0	5.3	3.6	1.7	48.4	8 872	28.5	3.45	11.5	13.9
Champaign	5.0	12.8	31.7	15.1	11.6	10.0	5.4	4.5	3.9	49.3	27 071	12.0	2.23	9.0	36.6
Chicago	7.5	18.7	11.2	18.4	15.0	11.4	7.5	5.5	4.8	51.5	1 061 928	3.6	2.67	18.9	32.6
Chicago Heights	9.2	22.5	10.2	14.2	13.7	11.0	7.4	6.4	5.5	51.3	10 703	-2.1	3.00	22.3	22.9
Cicero	10.9	23.7	12.7	18.2	13.7	8.8	4.8	3.4	3.7	48.6	23 115	-0.3	3.70	13.7	17.5
Crystal Lake	8.1	23.5	6.7	13.4	19.7	13.0	6.6	4.5	4.5	50.6	13 070	51.1	2.89	8.4	20.2
Danville	7.1	17.8	9.5	13.6	14.1	12.7	8.6	7.9	8.7	50.2	13 327	-3.4	2.35	15.1	33.9
Decatur	6.7	17.3	11.1	12.1	13.9	13.5	9.0	8.2	8.2	53.2	34 086	0.2	2.30	14.1	32.7
De Kalb	5.4	11.6	39.2	14.0	9.7	7.6	4.4	3.8	4.3	50.5	13 081	23.9	2.42	9.4	29.6
Des Plaines	5.9	16.5	7.5	12.9	16.3	14.0	9.8	8.3	8.9	51.6	22 362	11.9	2.58	9.0	28.5
Dolton	7.5	24.5	8.3	12.3	17.5	13.5	7.1	4.8	4.4	53.6	8 512	2.1	2.98	26.1	20.8
Downers Grove	6.2	18.5	6.6	12.1	17.2	16.0	9.0	6.5	7.9	52.0	18 979	7.5	2.53	7.2	27.4
East St. Louis	8.6	24.2	9.7	11.9	12.7	11.8	8.5	7.1	5.4	55.1	11 178	-14.4	2.80	40.6	27.8
Elgin	9.2	19.8	10.7	17.5	16.1	11.8	6.4	4.2	4.4	50.0	31 543	17.4	2.94	11.3	23.3
Elk Grove Village	6.0	18.9	7.4	13.1	18.7	15.1	9.1	7.0	4.8	51.3	13 278	10.6	2.60	8.6	25.6
Elmhurst	7.0	18.6	7.0	11.3	17.2	14.0	9.0	7.1	8.9	51.9	15 627	3.3	2.63	7.4	24.6
Elmwood Park	5.7	16.2	8.2	13.9	16.6	13.4	9.4	8.1	8.5	52.4	9 858	4.1	2.55	12.4	29.2
Evanston	5.8	14.4	16.4	17.3	14.7	12.8	7.9	5.1	5.7	52.9	29 651	6.1	2.27	10.9	36.3

1. No spouse present.

Table D. Cities — Group Quarters, Crime, Education, and Income

City	Persons in group quarters, 2000				Serious crimes known to police, 2000[2]				Education, 1990				Money income, 1989		
		Institutional			Total		Rate[3]		School enrollment		Attainment[4] (percent)			Households	
														Median	
	Total	Total	Persons in nursing homes	Non-Institutional[1]	Number	Rate[3]	Violent	Property	Public	Private	High school graduate or more	Bachelor's degree or more	Per capita (dollars)[5]	Dollars	Percent change, 1979–1989 (constant 1989 dollars)
	31	32	33	34	35	36	37	38	39	40	41	42	43	44	45
GEORGIA—Cont'd															
Columbus	9 107	3 249	1 053	5 858	11 879	6 394	576	5 818	39 810	4 829	71.5	16.6	11 949	24 056	NA
Dalton city	685	508	365	177	2 127	7 620	709	6 911	4 016	337	61.9	20.0	15 284	24 517	-2.0
East Point	438	149	132	289	2 512	6 344	1 205	5 140	7 203	1 217	72.3	18.0	12 508	26 787	7.9
Gainesville	1 760	1 189	190	571	2 577	10 075	868	9 207	3 533	879	68.2	24.9	14 978	25 689	-0.3
Hinesville	12	0	0	12	2 240	7 370	721	6 650	5 526	443	87.8	19.2	9 905	24 584	8.6
La Grange	895	429	139	466	1 965	7 558	469	7 089	5 457	1 093	57.7	16.2	12 181	21 851	9.2
Macon	3 595	1 668	911	1 927	10 926	11 234	797	10 438	22 027	5 648	63.9	15.3	11 502	21 038	-3.4
Marietta	1 561	483	459	1 078	3 273	5 571	548	5 023	8 009	2 067	81.3	28.2	15 808	27 371	7.4
Peachtree City	152	152	152	0	281	890	35	855	5 279	747	94.3	37.9	19 047	53 514	NA
Rome	2 114	1 422	495	692	3 532	10 097	1 810	8 288	5 500	1 509	63.4	17.5	11 973	21 078	4.3
Roswell	628	53	0	575	447	563	47	517	10 090	2 521	92.3	45.6	24 080	52 205	11.9
Savannah	5 497	2 120	642	3 377	11 093	8 435	1 076	7 359	28 821	6 439	70.1	16.6	10 978	22 102	5.6
Smyrna	466	66	21	400	2 554	6 229	420	5 810	5 001	968	84.7	34.1	19 158	33 863	6.1
Valdosta	1 952	475	355	1 477	NA	NA	NA	NA	11 884	1 009	69.5	21.1	11 329	21 864	10.0
Warner Robins	409	292	292	117	3 367	6 899	551	6 348	10 021	1 190	80.7	14.8	12 531	29 722	-5.1
HAWAII	35 782	7 690	2 949	28 092	62 987	5 199	244	4 955	233 972	56 606	80.1	22.9	15 770	38 829	13.2
Hilo CDP	1 391	479	465	912	NA	NA	NA	NA	9 899	979	79.2	20.9	13 373	30 014	-1.4
Honolulu CDP	11 286	3 039	1 638	8 247	46 659	5 325	263	5 062	66 403	21 760	79.5	27.7	18 554	37 190	11.5
Kailua CDP	69	5	0	64	NA	NA	NA	NA	6 560	3 007	88.6	33.5	20 008	55 259	19.4
Kaneohe CDP	499	276	136	223	NA	NA	NA	NA	6 924	2 501	83.8	24.9	16 479	49 770	9.5
Mililani CDP	4	0	0	4	NA	NA	NA	NA	7 978	2 088	92.5	33.0	17 898	55 337	19.1
Pearl City CDP	2 727	117	110	2 610	NA	NA	NA	NA	6 803	1 604	83.9	15.9	15 580	50 752	3.2
Waimalu CDP	90	1	0	89	NA	NA	NA	NA	6 041	1 945	88.6	31.7	20 426	51 985	NA
Waipahu CDP	1 134	27	25	1 107	NA	NA	NA	NA	7 546	933	65.7	7.6	10 875	38 380	7.9
IDAHO	31 496	17 717	5 735	13 779	41 228	3 186	253	2 934	268 404	27 234	79.7	17.7	11 457	25 257	-1.4
Boise City	4 013	2 569	1 109	1 444	8 392	4 517	357	4 160	31 126	3 154	88.6	27.8	15 208	29 121	2.9
Caldwell	931	514	178	417	1 538	5 923	520	5 403	4 203	714	67.0	12.6	9 511	20 831	-2.4
Coeur d'Alene	1 062	867	526	195	2 400	6 954	620	6 334	5 436	675	80.5	17.1	12 107	22 268	3.5
Idaho Falls	946	672	93	274	2 320	4 573	262	4 311	11 614	1 114	84.2	25.7	13 107	29 887	-3.9
Lewiston	662	405	368	257	1 298	4 200	178	4 022	6 830	480	80.9	16.3	12 828	25 711	-4.6
Meridian city	263	153	153	110	NA	NA	NA	NA	NA	NA	NA	NA	NA	NA	NA
Nampa	1 844	688	496	1 156	2 779	5 358	389	4 968	6 158	1 285	70.4	10.7	8 810	19 696	-4.7
Pocatello	1 663	280	265	1 383	1 864	3 622	243	3 379	15 104	831	83.1	22.2	11 385	24 955	-12.2
Twin Falls	1 167	575	339	592	2 266	6 574	487	6 087	6 737	487	76.5	13.7	11 329	23 206	-6.6
ILLINOIS	321 781	174 727	91 887	147 054	532 315	4 286	657	3 629	2 440 505	591 168	76.2	21.0	15 201	32 252	-0.4
Addison	201	0	0	201	NA	NA	NA	NA	6 866	1 627	74.7	16.1	15 944	41 375	-1.1
Alton	942	633	429	309	NA	NA	NA	NA	6 926	1 079	72.4	11.6	10 904	22 948	-5.0
Arlington Heights	919	793	790	126	NA	NA	NA	NA	13 402	4 757	89.8	39.5	22 864	51 331	1.4
Aurora	1 889	1 015	824	874	5 942	4 156	550	3 606	21 198	6 097	71.2	18.6	13 335	35 039	3.5
Bartlett	113	49	0	64	NA	NA	NA	NA	4 795	996	90.2	28.4	18 324	51 524	13.2
Belleville	1 476	1 304	928	172	NA	NA	NA	NA	8 058	1 895	75.6	15.2	13 117	26 668	-4.5
Berwyn	181	140	140	41	NA	NA	NA	NA	7 075	2 268	73.1	15.0	15 097	31 326	3.9
Bloomington	2 447	555	330	1 892	NA	NA	NA	NA	10 713	3 423	83.9	31.7	15 667	29 354	9.1
Bolingbrook	279	270	270	9	NA	NA	NA	NA	11 265	1 982	85.6	23.1	14 766	46 166	3.7
Buffalo Grove	236	234	234	2	NA	NA	NA	NA	7 729	1 951	94.5	47.4	23 718	56 011	9.9
Burbank	117	71	56	46	NA	NA	NA	NA	5 572	1 456	70.1	7.5	13 294	37 449	-10.8
Calumet City	22	0	0	22	NA	NA	NA	NA	6 810	2 046	73.0	10.4	13 569	30 138	-17.0
Carol Stream	85	83	83	2	NA	NA	NA	NA	6 868	1 475	89.3	32.1	16 697	45 141	26.1
Carpentersville	4	0	0	4	NA	NA	NA	NA	6 162	491	69.5	6.4	11 803	36 410	-5.9
Champaign	7 239	307	253	6 932	NA	NA	NA	NA	27 633	1 534	88.2	40.0	13 025	22 967	-8.0
Chicago	59 547	27 323	13 839	32 224	210 702	7 276	1 606	5 669	544 092	200 101	66.0	19.5	12 899	26 301	2.6
Chicago Heights	644	236	236	408	NA	NA	NA	NA	7 689	1 533	65.1	11.6	11 047	27 551	-11.5
Cicero	198	190	190	8	NA	NA	NA	NA	13 991	3 295	56.3	7.1	10 687	27 170	-3.1
Crystal Lake	276	221	221	55	NA	NA	NA	NA	6 102	854	89.0	28.5	17 681	46 197	5.9
Danville	2 522	2 361	376	161	NA	NA	NA	NA	7 238	1 129	74.1	15.0	12 401	22 315	-13.6
Decatur	3 448	1 590	903	1 858	NA	NA	NA	NA	17 067	3 711	74.0	15.7	13 348	25 451	-12.5
De Kalb	7 374	380	380	6 994	NA	NA	NA	NA	18 692	866	87.0	39.5	10 826	25 387	-2.3
Des Plaines	1 000	858	858	142	NA	NA	NA	NA	9 395	2 294	83.1	21.6	18 231	42 176	-1.2
Dolton	231	231	231	0	NA	NA	NA	NA	5 303	1 181	78.6	12.6	14 063	36 724	-14.1
Downers Grove	768	381	381	387	NA	NA	NA	NA	9 015	3 159	89.7	40.0	20 891	48 226	3.0
East St. Louis	272	182	119	90	NA	NA	NA	NA	12 182	892	55.7	7.3	6 421	12 627	-2.3
Elgin	1 908	1 145	613	763	NA	NA	NA	NA	16 733	3 505	74.0	18.3	13 929	35 554	7.4
Elk Grove Village	221	149	149	72	NA	NA	NA	NA	6 956	1 437	87.8	26.5	19 262	48 863	3.3
Elmhurst	1 591	851	821	740	NA	NA	NA	NA	7 626	3 134	87.8	36.2	21 005	49 611	7.2
Elmwood Park	243	239	239	4	NA	NA	NA	NA	3 176	1 531	73.0	16.9	16 344	34 410	-3.8
Evanston	6 964	559	559	6 405	NA	NA	NA	NA	10 640	14 218	89.2	58.0	22 346	41 115	13.0

1. Persons in emergency shelters and persons visible in street locations. 2. Data for serious crimes have not been adjusted for underreporting. This may affect comparability between geographic areas and over time. 3. Per 100,000 population estimated by the FBI. 4. Persons 25 years old and older. 5. Based on population enumerated as of April 1, 1990.

Table D. Cities — Income, Poverty, and Housing

City	Money income, 1989 (cont'd)				Housing units, 2000										
	Households (cont'd)	Percent below poverty, 1989					Vacant units				Occupied units				
	Percent with $100,000 or more	Persons		Families										Average size owner occupied	Average size renter occupied
		Total	Percent change in rate, 1979–1989	Total	Total	Percent change, 1990–2000	Vacant units for sale or rent[1]	For seasonal use (percent)	Home owner vacancy rate	Renter vacancy rate	Total	Percent owner occupied	Percent renter occupied		
	46	47	48	49	50	51	52	53	54	55	56	57	58	59	60
GEORGIA—Cont'd															
Columbus	2.6	18.6	NA	14.9	76 182	7.4	6 363	0.3	1.7	10.5	69 819	56.4	43.6	2.57	2.49
Dalton city	4.5	14.8	10.4	10.1	10 229	7.1	540	0.2	1.5	5.3	9 689	47.9	52.1	2.71	2.90
East Point	1.7	16.9	28.0	14.5	15 637	-0.2	1 084	0.2	1.7	5.2	14 553	45.4	54.6	2.63	2.74
Gainesville	6.9	18.7	29.9	15.6	9 076	18.6	539	0.3	2.0	5.7	8 537	43.7	56.3	2.67	2.88
Hinesville	1.0	17.5	-1.1	16.3	11 742	46.1	1 214	0.3	4.9	10.0	10 528	49.6	50.4	3.02	2.75
La Grange	3.3	21.3	7.0	16.8	11 000	0.5	978	0.4	2.1	8.4	10 022	46.8	53.2	2.49	2.52
Macon	2.6	24.4	8.9	20.8	44 341	-2.5	5 897	0.2	2.9	14.2	38 444	50.1	49.9	2.46	2.41
Marietta	3.6	14.2	8.4	9.4	25 227	8.9	1 332	0.2	1.5	5.2	23 895	37.6	62.4	2.36	2.41
Peachtree City	9.7	2.2	NA	1.3	11 313	73.0	437	0.6	1.2	7.9	10 876	81.2	18.8	2.95	2.65
Rome	2.2	18.7	-3.1	15.4	14 508	10.8	1 188	0.3	2.2	9.1	13 320	53.0	47.0	2.50	2.43
Roswell	14.4	3.3	-10.8	2.2	31 300	54.1	1 093	0.3	1.0	5.3	30 207	67.0	33.0	2.68	2.46
Savannah	1.8	22.6	0.9	18.5	57 437	-2.3	6 062	0.3	1.7	9.1	51 375	50.3	49.7	2.52	2.38
Smyrna	3.5	6.6	11.9	4.1	19 633	16.7	1 261	0.4	3.3	4.5	18 372	50.1	49.9	2.18	2.23
Valdosta	2.8	23.8	3.5	19.1	18 907	21.1	2 215	0.3	3.1	13.2	16 692	47.7	52.3	2.56	2.45
Warner Robins	0.9	11.8	14.6	10.0	21 688	19.9	2 138	0.2	2.8	12.1	19 550	57.5	42.5	2.49	2.45
HAWAII	7.1	8.3	-16.6	6.0	460 542	18.1	57 302	5.6	1.6	8.2	403 240	56.5	43.5	3.07	2.71
Hilo CDP	3.7	14.5	4.3	11.3	16 026	13.4	1 449	1.3	1.2	10.0	14 577	60.9	39.1	2.78	2.58
Honolulu CDP	9.0	8.4	-16.0	5.5	158 663	8.8	18 326	3.3	1.7	10.2	140 337	46.9	53.1	2.75	2.40
Kailua CDP	12.8	3.4	-52.1	2.1	12 780	4.5	551	1.3	0.8	4.1	12 229	69.7	30.3	3.09	2.72
Kaneohe CDP	7.9	4.9	-5.8	2.9	11 472	5.7	496	0.4	0.8	5.5	10 976	68.1	31.9	3.19	3.03
Mililani CDP	7.0	1.7	-48.5	1.4	9 280	4.3	270	0.2	1.0	4.9	9 010	75.9	24.1	3.16	3.21
Pearl City CDP	8.1	3.5	-2.8	2.4	9 181	2.0	260	0.2	0.6	3.2	8 921	68.7	31.3	3.24	3.00
Waimalu CDP	10.4	3.1	NA	1.9	10 999	3.6	475	0.3	1.1	6.0	10 524	62.1	37.9	2.94	2.53
Waipahu CDP	5.9	13.4	-2.2	12.8	8 033	3.8	467	0.0	1.0	8.0	7 566	53.4	46.6	4.63	3.76
IDAHO	2.1	13.3	5.2	9.7	527 824	27.7	58 179	5.2	2.2	7.6	469 645	72.4	27.6	2.75	2.52
Boise City	3.3	9.4	6.8	6.3	77 850	46.1	3 412	0.5	1.5	5.2	74 438	64.0	36.0	2.58	2.19
Caldwell	1.3	16.0	3.2	11.6	9 603	34.7	640	0.2	2.5	7.9	8 963	65.3	34.7	2.83	2.72
Coeur d'Alene	1.4	14.1	17.5	9.8	14 929	36.3	944	0.6	2.4	7.6	13 985	61.8	38.2	2.48	2.25
Idaho Falls	2.1	10.5	32.9	8.8	19 771	17.4	978	0.4	1.5	5.9	18 793	68.3	31.7	2.80	2.32
Lewiston	1.8	11.3	-1.7	8.1	13 394	11.1	599	0.4	1.2	5.4	12 795	66.8	33.2	2.48	2.12
Meridian city	NA	NA	NA	NA	12 293	228.2	464	0.2	2.7	2.9	11 829	84.3	15.7	2.98	2.67
Nampa	0.7	18.5	6.9	13.6	19 379	80.1	1 289	0.3	3.4	7.5	18 090	69.5	30.5	2.80	2.69
Pocatello	1.8	15.3	59.4	11.1	20 627	9.9	1 293	0.4	2.3	7.8	19 334	66.2	33.8	2.72	2.30
Twin Falls	2.2	14.4	24.1	10.3	14 162	28.6	888	0.4	2.0	8.1	13 274	62.5	37.5	2.57	2.41
ILLINOIS	4.9	11.9	8.2	9.0	4 885 615	8.4	293 836	0.6	1.5	6.2	4 591 779	67.3	32.7	2.76	2.37
Addison	5.4	4.7	23.7	3.7	11 805	7.1	156	0.2	0.4	1.4	11 649	68.4	31.6	3.09	3.01
Alton	1.0	19.9	26.8	16.6	13 894	-2.2	1 376	0.2	2.3	10.1	12 518	65.4	34.6	2.42	2.24
Arlington Heights	12.1	2.4	-7.7	1.4	31 725	4.3	962	0.3	1.2	4.6	30 763	76.7	23.3	2.60	1.91
Aurora	2.9	10.5	20.7	8.1	48 797	37.0	2 308	0.2	1.6	6.1	46 489	70.1	29.9	3.17	2.71
Bartlett	7.1	2.6	-10.3	1.7	12 356	85.6	177	0.1	0.6	4.7	12 179	93.1	6.9	3.03	2.72
Belleville	1.6	9.0	15.4	5.9	19 142	0.3	1 539	0.1	2.1	8.9	17 603	60.2	39.8	2.44	2.00
Berwyn	1.9	5.7	5.6	3.8	20 691	3.2	989	0.2	1.3	4.4	19 702	61.5	38.5	3.05	2.23
Bloomington	3.6	10.0	1.0	7.1	28 431	25.6	1 789	0.2	2.1	8.1	26 642	63.1	36.9	2.59	1.92
Bolingbrook	2.8	3.2	-3.0	2.4	17 884	38.8	468	0.1	1.2	4.4	17 416	85.2	14.8	3.30	2.75
Buffalo Grove	12.8	1.5	-46.4	1.0	16 166	16.6	458	1.7	0.4	2.9	15 708	87.1	12.9	2.80	2.13
Burbank	2.1	4.3	7.5	2.6	9 518	2.4	201	0.1	0.8	2.2	9 317	83.0	17.0	3.09	2.46
Calumet City	1.1	9.8	63.3	7.8	15 947	-3.9	808	0.1	2.1	6.3	15 139	63.3	36.7	2.74	2.31
Carol Stream	2.2	3.5	-38.6	2.7	14 200	17.4	328	0.1	0.9	3.5	13 872	70.5	29.5	3.15	2.34
Carpentersville	2.0	10.6	47.2	8.9	9 113	27.1	241	0.1	0.9	3.1	8 872	79.9	20.1	3.46	3.40
Champaign	3.2	22.7	22.7	9.6	28 556	9.8	1 485	0.2	1.4	5.1	27 071	47.4	52.6	2.43	2.05
Chicago	3.5	21.6	6.4	18.3	1 152 868	1.8	90 940	0.4	1.7	5.7	1 061 928	43.8	56.2	2.90	2.49
Chicago Heights	2.4	20.1	36.7	17.1	11 444	-1.5	741	0.1	2.6	6.5	10 703	62.8	37.2	3.02	2.97
Cicero	1.0	13.9	56.2	11.2	24 640	-0.8	1 525	0.3	2.0	3.4	23 115	55.2	44.8	3.94	3.40
Crystal Lake	5.2	2.1	-51.2	1.6	13 459	50.0	389	0.3	1.1	4.3	13 070	79.3	20.7	3.04	2.30
Danville	2.4	19.3	44.0	15.3	14 886	-2.9	1 559	0.2	3.1	11.8	13 327	62.5	37.5	2.42	2.25
Decatur	2.5	15.9	34.7	12.3	37 239	-0.6	3 153	0.3	1.9	11.7	34 086	66.4	33.6	2.35	2.20
De Kalb	2.7	24.4	26.4	8.7	13 619	24.8	538	0.3	1.6	3.6	13 081	41.9	58.1	2.67	2.24
Des Plaines	5.8	2.2	-31.3	1.5	22 851	11.4	489	0.2	0.6	3.5	22 362	79.3	20.7	2.70	2.13
Dolton	2.1	4.9	53.1	4.1	8 944	4.1	432	0.1	2.7	4.9	8 512	81.6	18.4	3.10	2.47
Downers Grove	9.1	2.5	0.0	1.5	19 477	7.2	498	0.3	0.9	3.5	18 979	79.2	20.8	2.70	1.86
East St. Louis	0.4	43.9	1.4	39.5	12 899	-17.4	1 721	0.1	1.9	7.7	11 178	52.9	47.1	2.78	2.82
Elgin	3.0	7.8	2.6	5.9	32 665	16.9	1 122	0.2	1.1	4.9	31 543	70.2	29.8	3.01	2.77
Elk Grove Village	6.3	2.7	58.8	2.0	13 513	8.8	235	0.2	0.3	4.3	13 278	76.7	23.3	2.74	2.12
Elmhurst	10.3	1.4	-53.3	0.9	16 147	4.3	520	0.8	1.0	4.8	15 627	83.3	16.7	2.78	1.92
Elmwood Park	3.9	5.3	39.5	4.0	10 150	3.8	292	0.2	0.9	2.8	9 858	65.6	34.4	2.79	2.09
Evanston	12.1	9.8	38.0	5.3	30 817	5.7	1 166	0.4	1.2	3.2	29 651	52.7	47.3	2.50	2.01

1. Includes units rented or sold but not occupied.   2. Specified owner-occupied units.   3. Specified renter-occupied units.   4. Overcrowded or lacking complete plumbing facilities.

Table D. Cities — Labor Force, Employment, Disability, and Construction

City	Civilian labor force, 2001		Unemployment		Civilian employment, 1990[2]		Percent		Disability 1990	Value of residential construction authorized by building permits, 2000		
	Total	Percent change, 2000–2001	Total	Rate[1]	Total	Professional, managerial, and technical	Precision production, craft, and repair		Work disabled persons[3] (percent)	New construction ($1,000)	Number of housing units	Percent single family
	61	62	63	64	65	66	67		68	69	70	71
GEORGIA—Cont'd												
Columbus	84 676	-2.5	4 045	4.8	71 922	28.4	10.9		10.3	72 220	975	57.0
Dalton city	13 840	-3.3	784	5.7	11 132	26.1	8.8		9.0	23 849	482	20.1
East Point	21 615	0.5	1 162	5.4	16 519	24.7	8.4		9.2	1 275	12	100.0
Gainesville	13 467	-0.4	468	3.5	8 741	31.4	11.3		8.7	22 231	572	17.0
Hinesville	9 555	0.9	457	4.8	6 641	29.8	8.3		6.3	10 758	133	85.0
La Grange	14 184	1.4	920	6.5	10 975	24.4	11.9		11.2	22 451	353	24.6
Macon	46 668	-1.9	2 444	5.2	44 111	25.4	10.8		12.5	6 949	98	100.0
Marietta	35 436	0.4	1 384	3.9	24 226	33.0	10.3		6.4	70 863	643	44.3
Peachtree City	14 340	-0.2	374	2.6	8 749	48.5	7.4		3.8	30 288	131	100.0
Rome	15 225	0.1	857	5.6	12 928	27.8	8.3		11.4	NA	NA	NA
Roswell	35 074	-0.1	566	1.6	27 870	43.0	5.8		3.4	75 896	434	88.0
Savannah	63 190	-1.5	2 519	4.0	55 865	27.4	10.7		10.3	21 669	153	79.1
Smyrna	28 706	0.2	818	2.8	19 841	37.8	7.3		5.0	99 426	567	100.0
Valdosta	21 959	-4.7	996	4.5	16 688	29.2	7.6		10.2	16 068	512	24.8
Warner Robins	23 859	-1.5	780	3.3	19 757	30.5	16.4		9.5	43 264	842	69.5
HAWAII	605 524	1.7	28 081	4.6	529 059	29.9	10.5		6.6	823 363	4 905	86.7
Hilo CDP	NA	NA	NA	NA	17 062	29.5	10.1		9.3	NA	NA	NA
Honolulu CDP	429 252	1.3	17 517	4.1	191 891	33.6	8.0		5.9	NA	NA	NA
Kailua CDP	NA	NA	NA	NA	19 234	38.6	10.4		5.7	NA	NA	NA
Kaneohe CDP	NA	NA	NA	NA	18 426	33.3	11.5		5.5	NA	NA	NA
Mililani CDP	NA	NA	NA	NA	14 815	38.0	12.0		4.2	NA	NA	NA
Pearl City CDP	NA	NA	NA	NA	15 592	26.4	12.2		5.9	NA	NA	NA
Waimalu CDP	NA	NA	NA	NA	16 661	37.9	11.4		4.3	NA	NA	NA
Waipahu CDP	NA	NA	NA	NA	14 233	16.0	12.3		8.5	NA	NA	NA
IDAHO	682 228	3.7	33 836	5.0	443 703	27.1	11.3		9.0	1 358 934	10 915	88.7
Boise City	114 023	4.6	3 952	3.5	66 115	36.0	9.0		7.5	160 031	1 288	76.7
Caldwell	14 531	5.0	874	6.0	8 178	22.9	11.4		9.2	35 918	429	91.1
Coeur d'Alene	20 049	2.8	1 166	5.8	11 038	28.1	11.4		9.0	37 615	412	75.2
Idaho Falls	29 372	2.9	1 022	3.5	19 741	41.4	9.6		7.7	18 000	218	85.3
Lewiston	19 755	1.1	680	3.4	13 120	25.5	13.2		9.8	5 790	68	48.5
Meridian city	8 041	4.5	250	3.1	NA	NA	NA		NA	96 318	765	93.7
Nampa	21 114	5.0	1 199	5.7	11 925	22.5	14.1		14.3	122 148	1 278	91.7
Pocatello	29 178	3.6	1 362	4.7	20 824	31.9	10.1		9.2	10 564	101	94.1
Twin Falls	17 650	4.9	762	4.3	12 714	25.0	10.2		10.0	16 597	196	85.7
ILLINOIS	6 348 558	-1.1	342 580	5.4	5 417 967	30.0	10.7		6.9	6 527 956	51 944	72.8
Addison	20 649	-0.7	1 169	5.7	17 774	24.4	14.0		4.1	15 111	75	78.7
Alton	13 825	-1.0	1 116	8.1	13 004	24.3	12.9		12.1	5 494	74	16.2
Arlington Heights	44 982	-1.0	1 582	3.5	41 977	43.3	7.1		3.6	49 807	314	17.8
Aurora	69 947	-0.5	4 318	6.2	49 137	25.6	11.5		6.5	175 995	1 967	52.4
Bartlett	20 582	-0.6	832	4.0	10 642	36.6	9.8		3.7	20 063	121	100.0
Belleville	20 302	-1.5	1 819	9.0	18 942	29.0	10.3		8.6	10 483	149	67.1
Berwyn	22 720	-0.5	1 412	6.2	22 052	26.7	12.3		6.8	3 605	48	4.2
Bloomington	39 521	-0.6	1 056	2.7	28 115	31.8	8.1		6.2	43 466	470	77.2
Bolingbrook	32 286	-0.6	1 672	5.2	21 789	31.2	11.8		4.0	65 333	857	53.3
Buffalo Grove	25 967	-1.0	854	3.3	21 071	46.6	6.3		2.6	7 552	50	36.0
Burbank	14 698	-1.4	648	4.4	13 615	18.7	16.8		7.0	5 897	66	72.7
Calumet City	19 016	-1.0	1 345	7.1	17 664	22.8	12.1		6.9	1 366	14	100.0
Carol Stream	22 623	-0.7	934	4.1	17 773	35.1	10.9		3.3	3 624	19	100.0
Carpentersville	15 359	0.0	1 321	8.6	11 122	16.1	18.8		8.0	65 104	475	100.0
Champaign	38 693	-0.4	995	2.6	32 714	41.8	5.5		4.9	36 006	375	54.4
Chicago	1 334 026	-0.7	92 140	6.9	1 207 108	28.1	8.9		8.4	504 163	6 611	20.2
Chicago Heights	14 625	-0.9	1 263	8.6	13 612	22.3	10.6		9.1	838	8	100.0
Cicero	33 631	-0.4	2 855	8.5	28 832	15.0	14.0		7.0	58	1	100.0
Crystal Lake	19 724	-0.4	1 013	5.1	12 907	37.1	10.1		4.7	43 364	310	81.3
Danville	14 794	-1.3	1 474	10.0	13 627	28.3	9.2		11.1	3 750	30	100.0
Decatur	40 137	-4.1	3 094	7.7	36 125	27.3	10.3		9.7	12 279	188	36.2
De Kalb	21 801	-1.4	787	3.6	18 203	34.0	7.9		3.3	17 941	270	15.9
Des Plaines	34 264	0.2	2 163	6.3	29 257	30.9	12.2		5.4	5 868	29	100.0
Dolton	12 917	-0.7	1 086	8.4	11 580	26.0	11.5		7.0	662	11	27.3
Downers Grove	29 822	-0.9	1 087	3.6	25 318	44.7	8.2		3.9	17 740	90	55.6
East St. Louis	11 342	-2.6	1 276	11.3	10 888	19.7	6.0		15.6	2 399	27	100.0
Elgin	50 273	-0.3	3 618	7.2	39 227	26.5	11.9		5.9	21 847	194	100.0
Elk Grove Village	21 402	-0.7	863	4.0	19 167	35.0	10.0		3.7	14 693	116	51.7
Elmhurst	25 108	-0.9	881	3.5	22 446	40.3	8.6		4.8	41 597	176	86.4
Elmwood Park	12 171	-0.6	589	4.8	11 737	28.7	10.8		5.9	1 053	13	7.7
Evanston	42 265	-1.2	1 788	4.2	40 413	52.2	3.7		4.8	845	4	50.0

1. Percent of civilian labor force. 2. Persons 16 years and older. 3. Persons 16 to 64 years old.

City	Wholesale Trade, 1997				Retail Trade[1], 1997				Real Estate and Rental and Leasing, 1997			
	Number of Establishments	Number of Employees	Sales (mil dol)	Annual Payroll (mil dol)	Number of Establishments	Number of Employees	Sales (mil dol)	Annual Payroll (mil dol)	Number of Establishments	Number of Employees	Receipts (mil dol)	Annual Payroll (mil dol)
	72	73	74	75	76	77	78	79	80	81	82	83
GEORGIA—Cont'd												
Columbus	208	2 884	1 316.5	91.3	845	11 718	1 950.9	186.6	224	1 197	142.7	27.3
Dalton city	248	D	D	D	372	5 098	919.6	89.2	67	301	56.7	7.1
East Point	39	673	396.0	17.0	91	1 160	155.4	16.8	35	542	32.6	8.9
Gainesville	116	1 512	1 035.2	44.0	331	4 250	773.2	74.6	53	221	29.3	5.8
Hinesville	7	41	6.5	0.8	133	1 635	239.4	20.7	35	D	D	D
La Grange	42	397	189.3	12.9	202	2 809	445.6	43.5	34	135	14.1	2.5
Macon	210	2 776	984.0	81.8	765	10 586	1 630.2	159.5	157	986	137.1	24.3
Marietta	342	4 471	2 719.7	190.6	409	7 391	1 948.2	167.1	149	1 091	132.6	23.7
Peachtree City	70	680	378.1	24.3	80	1 354	174.9	19.1	31	84	13.0	1.9
Rome	76	795	309.9	25.5	343	4 389	707.0	65.8	40	266	20.6	4.5
Roswell	309	2 912	6 033.5	151.9	321	4 720	1 298.8	118.4	132	716	126.5	21.2
Savannah	220	2 737	1 487.2	90.9	962	12 394	1 894.3	188.8	194	974	115.7	23.0
Smyrna	117	1 906	3 411.0	82.4	226	4 820	927.2	81.0	92	527	158.0	18.5
Valdosta	109	1 027	408.0	27.5	379	4 892	758.2	72.7	73	438	31.4	6.9
Warner Robins	31	310	184.1	10.5	238	3 790	607.1	58.0	61	254	36.6	3.9
HAWAII	1 872	18 532	7 147.5	576.0	5 088	64 218	11 317.8	1 161.8	1 753	12 446	1 824.1	311.9
Hilo CDP	87	811	314.2	22.0	261	3 696	552.2	63.0	78	378	37.1	6.5
Honolulu CDP	1 114	11 332	4 537.5	354.2	2 258	27 812	5 483.5	534.7	973	6 707	968.4	179.3
Kailua CDP	26	81	58.4	3.9	104	1 758	227.9	27.5	30	114	15.6	2.7
Kaneohe CDP	22	84	23.1	1.9	137	2 171	371.8	37.7	30	114	10.2	2.4
Mililani CDP	14	115	37.5	6.3	50	1 181	176.8	19.5	12	36	3.4	0.6
Pearl City CDP	37	517	176.1	14.8	50	1 062	239.7	18.8	15	49	6.2	1.1
Waimalu CDP	18	86	10.0	1.5	84	1 259	251.7	27.0	22	151	10.2	3.3
Waipahu CDP	60	1 246	364.7	41.3	119	1 908	378.3	39.6	25	113	14.7	3.1
IDAHO	1 980	22 828	10 127.8	628.0	5 848	63 732	11 649.6	1 079.7	1 236	4 870	450.3	73.9
Boise City	367	5 235	4 637.4	200.1	939	12 880	2 505.9	230.0	294	1 536	167.7	28.2
Caldwell	35	263	76.0	5.8	120	1 270	287.0	26.7	18	100	6.2	1.2
Coeur d'Alene	53	398	247.0	13.3	292	3 576	692.1	66.3	83	252	32.6	4.3
Idaho Falls	125	1 529	572.0	38.9	398	4 758	790.0	76.9	65	365	18.9	3.5
Lewiston	55	557	183.1	14.7	220	2 749	453.6	47.2	39	178	11.5	2.5
Meridian city	NA	NA	NA	NA	NA	NA	NA	NA	NA	NA	NA	NA
Nampa	70	890	377.1	23.8	216	2 664	563.2	49.0	48	103	12.8	1.5
Pocatello	89	883	270.6	24.2	239	2 809	538.4	48.8	59	221	21.4	3.1
Twin Falls	109	1 190	330.7	26.9	299	4 013	726.7	65.6	58	218	24.6	3.5
ILLINOIS	21 956	325 847	275 978.4	13 325.5	44 568	610 790	108 002.2	10 596.0	11 411	73 819	12 830.0	2 101.4
Addison	257	4 566	2 649.9	182.1	123	2 754	801.0	63.9	34	239	39.6	8.4
Alton	27	327	79.2	11.6	207	2 404	392.6	36.8	33	121	14.3	2.1
Arlington Heights	326	3 664	4 427.1	192.3	326	4 970	1 302.5	92.7	104	913	139.9	27.2
Aurora	140	2 212	5 262.0	93.8	463	7 942	1 171.5	121.0	90	486	51.8	10.0
Bartlett	43	115	70.8	4.7	39	486	77.2	7.8	11	56	7.3	1.5
Belleville	42	D	D	D	231	3 073	543.4	55.4	58	247	22.8	4.1
Berwyn	29	141	98.1	4.7	147	1 578	272.8	27.8	25	106	9.1	1.5
Bloomington	109	1 137	566.5	50.5	364	5 300	905.1	85.6	78	323	43.1	5.5
Bolingbrook	54	1 076	1 102.0	34.9	102	2 786	456.9	43.9	29	158	15.2	2.2
Buffalo Grove	190	2 251	2 784.6	111.8	123	1 705	357.6	40.9	45	324	36.0	9.0
Burbank	10	84	9.1	1.4	91	1 794	290.2	26.0	12	68	5.5	1.0
Calumet City	20	D	D	D	194	4 775	715.1	72.1	22	108	9.8	1.3
Carol Stream	103	3 552	4 950.8	157.4	80	1 349	299.7	26.6	20	105	14.5	2.4
Carpentersville	12	D	D	D	38	401	57.4	6.1	13	96	13.5	2.3
Champaign	76	1 414	689.0	38.3	379	6 227	825.3	82.6	108	859	106.3	18.2
Chicago	3 312	50 029	31 971.1	1 970.1	7 885	86 703	13 882.1	1 553.2	2 971	25 827	5 226.4	899.1
Chicago Heights	51	890	371.9	25.6	93	1 165	308.7	26.4	21	132	11.5	2.4
Cicero	45	669	403.7	29.5	133	1 869	347.4	32.3	22	115	10.8	1.5
Crystal Lake	95	854	439.4	33.9	203	3 291	618.9	55.4	52	249	30.6	4.5
Danville	60	1 802	1 004.0	55.1	214	3 212	434.2	44.2	48	D	D	D
Decatur	129	1 609	3 119.0	50.6	372	5 334	882.6	87.8	88	498	38.7	8.3
De Kalb	20	D	D	D	130	2 153	297.9	32.1	36	200	26.4	3.1
Des Plaines	224	5 611	4 724.2	258.4	197	2 592	562.6	51.8	85	1 293	691.3	40.4
Dolton	8	91	21.3	3.3	60	851	116.8	12.6	12	75	10.8	1.7
Downers Grove	171	3 009	3 195.4	143.0	267	5 969	1 591.6	135.1	67	397	73.5	10.5
East St. Louis	23	D	D	D	73	617	71.2	8.6	20	69	6.2	1.3
Elgin	169	2 985	2 158.1	129.4	226	3 887	862.8	82.4	78	433	68.5	10.9
Elk Grove Village	621	10 899	8 110.0	479.7	152	3 039	550.1	68.2	55	467	86.9	14.7
Elmhurst	197	6 605	2 264.9	341.4	188	2 898	850.4	74.0	68	472	73.1	15.8
Elmwood Park	17	33	25.2	1.1	52	567	86.0	9.2	12	32	4.7	0.5
Evanston	95	992	403.3	30.0	292	4 370	746.0	87.1	128	603	101.5	15.1

1. Establishments with payroll.

City	Professional, Scientific, and Technical Services, 1997[1]				Manufacturing, 1997				Accommodation and Foodservices, 1997			
	Number of Establish-ments	Number of Employees	Receipts (mil dol)	Annual Payroll (mil dol)	Number of Establish-ments	Number of Employees	Receipts (mil dol)	Annual Payroll (mil dol)	Number of Establish-ments	Number of Employees	Sales (mil dol)	Annual Payroll (mil dol)
	84	85	86	87	88	89	90	91	92	93	94	95
GEORGIA—Cont'd												
Columbus	264	1 607	146.2	43.6	158	D	D	D	365	D	D	D
Dalton city	110	736	59.2	27.3	260	21 534	4 970.4	540.2	118	2 350	84.6	23.3
East Point	31	159	12.2	4.8	41	1 199	286.7	40.6	48	1 084	45.3	12.6
Gainesville	143	781	76.2	26.4	95	7 365	1 543.3	178.2	127	2 449	83.4	23.7
Hinesville	27	D	D	D	NA	NA	NA	NA	54	1 052	31.3	7.7
La Grange	50	221	15.8	6.9	70	8 540	1 634.0	257.6	59	1 026	31.3	7.9
Macon	308	1 792	163.4	51.7	154	10 650	5 388.6	419.5	273	5 786	175.0	47.3
Marietta	419	3 087	267.4	99.7	158	4 886	924.1	169.1	235	4 203	163.2	45.4
Peachtree City	82	274	30.4	11.4	37	5 277	1 304.1	161.8	50	1 442	61.3	16.6
Rome	108	579	53.9	17.4	88	5 342	1 070.6	154.1	118	2 246	78.9	20.2
Roswell	500	2 323	268.8	103.2	58	759	164.3	24.7	151	3 072	115.8	33.6
Savannah	367	2 239	188.1	75.7	131	4 579	1 279.7	139.3	413	9 619	334.6	90.1
Smyrna	173	1 327	153.2	75.6	50	1 032	136.8	36.6	142	3 028	109.5	30.7
Valdosta	117	674	41.6	16.9	70	4 816	1 272.4	118.9	138	2 787	83.0	23.6
Warner Robins	89	969	89.0	35.3	34	D	D	D	120	2 510	69.5	18.6
HAWAII	2 480	15 743	1 574.0	606.5	921	15 109	3 192.5	405.0	3 081	88 083	5 007.9	1 507.5
Hilo CDP	124	573	35.6	13.8	58	716	80.2	17.5	116	1 881	64.7	18.5
Honolulu CDP	1 650	12 014	1 282.5	503.2	491	7 639	904.9	187.7	1 503	42 549	2 604.0	733.4
Kailua CDP	67	202	20.4	7.8	NA	NA	NA	NA	83	D	D	D
Kaneohe CDP	25	97	7.6	2.6	NA	NA	NA	NA	60	1 009	36.9	9.5
Mililani CDP	14	87	11.1	5.7	NA	NA	NA	NA	27	D	D	D
Pearl City CDP	12	91	6.4	2.6	NA	NA	NA	NA	42	734	27.9	7.2
Waimalu CDP	22	380	12.3	6.1	NA	NA	NA	NA	43	884	39.8	10.2
Waipahu CDP	15	49	3.7	1.4	NA	NA	NA	NA	77	1 287	48.7	12.6
IDAHO	2 364	19 669	2 046.1	756.2	1 647	66 184	16 952.9	2 099.8	2 978	42 067	1 232.5	345.7
Boise City	675	5 927	868.9	252.1	210	16 823	5 780.6	753.4	511	10 138	316.3	89.0
Caldwell	40	124	10.0	3.4	64	1 956	239.1	41.1	59	749	21.2	5.6
Coeur d'Alene	155	790	59.2	24.6	61	1 169	193.6	32.5	173	2 943	101.0	27.7
Idaho Falls	187	7 210	740.5	334.8	79	2 107	217.8	44.9	170	3 335	88.6	25.4
Lewiston	65	D	D	D	44	D	D	D	97	1 415	42.0	12.3
Meridian city	NA	NA	NA	NA	NA	NA	NA	NA	NA	NA	NA	NA
Nampa	54	306	19.9	7.6	71	5 798	3 008.7	179.9	96	1 701	46.1	12.3
Pocatello	97	885	44.5	21.2	52	2 315	385.7	70.4	133	2 031	56.4	15.4
Twin Falls	119	493	35.2	12.4	64	2 400	512.1	51.8	125	2 160	58.3	17.1
ILLINOIS	30 378	274 714	33 855.1	13 105.4	17 953	887 350	200 020.0	31 837.9	23 984	397 300	14 826.8	4 018.7
Addison	99	1 146	77.9	21.4	388	10 598	1 461.1	346.9	53	990	39.2	8.7
Alton	63	350	25.8	11.0	31	1 716	358.4	66.1	99	1 821	57.1	15.0
Arlington Heights	430	4 523	446.5	146.0	120	10 976	3 052.9	645.6	147	2 953	124.2	32.5
Aurora	204	1 937	115.4	53.1	148	8 759	2 743.1	387.4	192	3 122	110.3	29.1
Bartlett	66	93	11.9	4.1	22	1 426	304.7	58.4	30	D	D	D
Belleville	177	1 119	101.2	43.2	60	2 239	307.7	65.7	132	2 260	61.8	17.0
Berwyn	59	128	10.3	3.3	22	585	79.5	23.6	101	D	D	D
Bloomington	173	1 005	89.4	38.2	59	D	D	D	192	4 221	124.7	37.1
Bolingbrook	78	291	24.9	10.2	21	2 453	807.9	153.8	57	988	34.4	8.7
Buffalo Grove	219	1 244	154.1	67.5	54	3 889	652.1	138.3	74	D	D	D
Burbank	17	85	4.3	1.1	NA	NA	NA	NA	69	D	D	D
Calumet City	34	119	7.1	2.0	19	757	155.3	23.4	106	1 674	51.4	12.8
Carol Stream	62	319	26.4	12.0	91	5 123	973.3	190.8	50	864	29.5	7.8
Carpentersville	17	46	3.6	1.5	40	2 066	294.4	73.7	27	679	23.0	6.7
Champaign	183	1 654	202.0	67.0	67	2 846	393.2	74.8	252	5 728	152.1	42.5
Chicago	8 115	118 842	17 205.3	6 757.5	3 195	130 372	26 745.9	4 178.4	5 148	92 348	4 481.9	1 194.1
Chicago Heights	42	327	27.5	12.4	71	4 061	982.5	149.0	54	762	23.5	6.2
Cicero	30	305	16.3	6.2	123	5 613	973.2	190.7	89	914	37.8	9.3
Crystal Lake	143	510	43.3	18.8	99	5 437	756.3	186.8	73	1 589	52.8	14.4
Danville	77	287	25.8	7.7	60	4 864	1 363.4	160.5	116	1 893	53.3	15.5
Decatur	144	1 026	81.1	33.4	98	D	D	D	196	D	D	D
De Kalb	49	149	12.5	3.5	47	2 648	535.3	71.2	94	1 719	45.4	11.1
Des Plaines	281	5 785	649.1	213.5	164	12 021	1 849.6	411.0	144	2 408	104.6	26.8
Dolton	9	38	3.0	1.5	23	1 196	263.3	38.2	36	530	14.8	3.9
Downers Grove	272	1 843	182.2	69.8	104	5 174	692.7	203.0	117	3 415	126.4	35.1
East St. Louis	8	D	D	D	22	564	134.9	20.9	37	476	18.6	4.1
Elgin	185	1 437	164.1	53.8	175	9 955	1 779.0	345.8	129	2 019	76.4	20.2
Elk Grove Village	146	2 803	339.3	115.5	550	23 239	3 916.5	864.4	85	1 442	63.6	16.6
Elmhurst	229	1 044	107.7	47.0	85	2 882	421.0	103.1	83	D	D	D
Elmwood Park	27	106	4.9	2.2	NA	NA	NA	NA	34	492	21.0	5.4
Evanston	357	2 085	227.6	80.7	67	2 310	321.7	74.4	177	2 491	110.1	30.1

1. Firms subject to federal tax.

City	Arts, Entertainment, and Recreation[1], 1997				Health Care and Social Assistance[1], 1997				Other Services[1], 1997			
	Number of Establishments	Number of Employees	Receipts (mil dol)	Annual Payroll (mil dol)	Number of Establishments	Number of Employees	Receipts (mil dol)	Annual Payroll (mil dol)	Number of Establishments	Number of Employees	Receipts (mil dol)	Annual Payroll (mil dol)
	96	97	98	99	100	101	102	103	104	105	106	107
GEORGIA—Cont'd												
Columbus	37	D	D	D	343	5 225	439.9	171.6	305	2 004	104.7	35.8
Dalton city	7	41	2.0	0.6	106	1 275	102.0	47.6	88	453	32.3	9.4
East Point	4	51	1.2	0.4	87	981	62.3	28.0	51	443	41.0	14.6
Gainesville	17	155	5.8	1.9	191	2 352	215.0	89.3	101	624	37.8	11.0
Hinesville	3	0	0.0	0.0	40	402	20.5	7.3	40	174	10.1	2.6
La Grange	3	60	1.0	0.4	62	970	65.0	32.3	61	320	19.7	6.3
Macon	25	275	8.2	2.2	430	7 536	627.8	247.8	247	1 385	82.9	26.7
Marietta	25	454	24.5	6.5	284	3 777	303.5	137.1	213	1 640	108.2	37.9
Peachtree City	10	42	1.5	0.6	49	398	25.6	11.2	35	297	12.5	4.4
Rome	10	56	4.7	0.8	147	3 735	330.8	125.1	73	642	35.9	12.4
Roswell	24	259	12.1	3.7	204	2 257	217.3	78.6	172	1 241	137.7	29.0
Savannah	42	475	21.0	5.8	370	5 400	405.8	216.0	270	1 877	110.5	37.2
Smyrna	13	241	13.1	2.4	121	1 458	104.3	38.3	75	491	34.4	10.4
Valdosta	15	120	5.1	1.1	165	2 399	148.0	65.9	107	572	30.1	8.6
Warner Robins	8	102	2.5	1.0	128	1 370	98.0	41.5	107	563	27.3	8.3
HAWAII	386	6 925	409.6	116.6	2 360	18 221	1 646.3	730.8	1 476	10 375	683.2	206.4
Hilo CDP	11	129	4.2	1.0	180	1 643	155.4	53.9	76	476	28.6	8.9
Honolulu CDP	159	2 592	143.5	43.2	1 194	9 866	925.5	427.4	748	5 786	395.5	117.0
Kailua CDP	9	248	11.8	3.4	108	526	44.1	20.8	36	229	13.3	4.7
Kaneohe CDP	6	72	4.1	1.4	63	587	37.6	16.3	55	729	37.0	12.2
Mililani CDP	3	149	6.8	2.2	25	169	15.6	7.2	18	91	3.6	1.2
Pearl City CDP	5	37	2.2	0.6	29	296	26.4	9.1	27	197	15.6	4.6
Waimalu CDP	9	208	11.2	3.0	66	463	49.1	25.3	28	220	13.5	4.3
Waipahu CDP	1	0	0.0	0.0	53	239	22.7	10.2	55	291	22.9	7.4
IDAHO	457	4 425	174.1	45.2	2 551	26 365	1 548.3	680.1	1 858	9 461	550.6	151.7
Boise City	56	825	28.2	8.2	587	5 728	433.0	204.9	319	2 584	132.7	39.8
Caldwell	6	73	1.4	0.5	58	982	69.7	26.9	41	214	13.4	3.8
Coeur d'Alene	22	266	13.2	4.1	183	1 886	111.0	44.0	89	529	28.2	7.7
Idaho Falls	19	203	3.8	1.2	225	3 094	226.9	90.4	112	591	38.1	10.4
Lewiston	11	0	0.0	0.0	109	0	0.0	0.0	82	527	27.7	8.0
Meridian city	NA	NA	NA	NA	NA	NA	NA	NA	NA	NA	NA	NA
Nampa	9	97	4.1	0.8	98	1 580	86.4	45.5	87	412	20.6	5.9
Pocatello	18	206	4.4	1.5	145	1 280	72.5	35.8	89	475	29.3	8.3
Twin Falls	19	96	4.0	0.9	127	2 028	108.7	49.4	83	542	26.3	7.9
ILLINOIS	3 097	46 972	3 640.3	1 040.6	21 122	248 667	16 870.2	7 441.8	18 806	118 317	8 296.8	2 503.0
Addison	9	57	2.8	0.8	40	233	16.1	7.0	110	855	74.8	22.4
Alton	11	0	0.0	0.0	111	1 344	93.1	47.7	70	393	25.8	7.5
Arlington Heights	23	398	35.7	9.1	269	3 153	246.5	121.9	149	1 055	56.5	19.9
Aurora	20	0	0.0	0.0	191	3 113	253.8	111.8	154	949	58.8	19.5
Bartlett	6	0	0.0	0.0	36	293	16.8	6.3	32	153	8.5	3.1
Belleville	13	220	7.1	2.0	198	2 228	147.3	75.6	119	652	38.1	13.2
Berwyn	6	65	5.1	1.7	107	763	67.2	30.6	66	333	25.0	6.2
Bloomington	19	226	8.3	1.8	145	1 814	129.6	64.1	136	965	60.2	19.1
Bolingbrook	7	54	1.9	0.5	54	673	30.0	12.1	56	351	25.7	6.8
Buffalo Grove	15	76	5.6	1.1	108	1 102	91.4	39.7	59	547	40.8	12.4
Burbank	3	0	0.0	0.0	25	469	27.8	11.6	31	124	9.5	2.7
Calumet City	5	98	6.0	1.1	57	917	42.6	14.9	45	224	14.1	4.0
Carol Stream	9	201	5.1	2.1	62	513	43.7	21.7	47	471	35.6	10.2
Carpentersville	3	34	1.0	0.3	11	48	3.8	1.3	16	53	3.4	1.1
Champaign	22	280	6.9	2.5	121	2 269	161.7	67.1	127	741	38.0	13.0
Chicago	563	7 547	864.0	361.1	4 019	43 898	3 217.3	1 284.8	3 333	23 886	1 820.5	502.9
Chicago Heights	2	0	0.0	0.0	46	1 130	95.3	40.8	52	349	17.4	5.4
Cicero	24	575	79.9	10.9	33	1 063	51.6	18.6	72	465	34.4	11.4
Crystal Lake	15	200	8.4	1.7	128	1 554	76.2	37.7	96	622	36.9	11.7
Danville	8	80	2.8	0.7	82	1 285	78.7	36.8	77	487	23.3	7.8
Decatur	16	213	5.6	2.0	185	2 354	147.7	67.0	144	1 278	73.6	25.6
De Kalb	5	0	0.0	0.0	34	385	26.5	13.2	58	282	13.0	3.8
Des Plaines	11	87	3.5	1.1	182	2 088	175.4	69.1	145	1 042	88.7	27.7
Dolton	6	40	1.2	0.3	24	597	23.5	11.2	26	190	13.4	4.4
Downers Grove	15	192	5.9	1.8	180	2 091	192.7	81.9	117	1 153	104.3	37.9
East St. Louis	2	0	0.0	0.0	41	419	26.1	7.5	28	177	10.0	2.8
Elgin	17	0	0.0	0.0	178	1 864	135.5	71.5	126	1 292	78.5	28.4
Elk Grove Village	8	65	5.8	1.2	105	1 228	120.3	57.9	97	918	77.7	28.0
Elmhurst	8	123	4.8	1.8	144	2 235	208.5	91.9	103	892	64.7	21.9
Elmwood Park	NA	NA	NA	NA	39	395	23.4	9.5	27	136	5.5	1.9
Evanston	29	157	8.4	3.0	237	2 145	220.7	114.5	98	529	32.2	11.1

1. Firms subject to federal tax.

Table D. Cities — Federal Funds and City Government Finances

City	Selected federal funds, fiscal 2001[1] (mil dol) Procurement contracts		Grants					Direct payments for individuals		City government finances, 1999 — General revenue	Intergovernmental		Taxes	Per capita[3] (dollars)		
	Defense	Other	Total[2]	Health and family welfare	Energy and environment	Education	Housing and community development	Educational assistance	Housing assistance	Total (mil dol)	Total (mil dol)	Percent from state government	Total (mil dol)	Total	Property	Sales and gross receipts
	108	109	110	111	112	113	114	115	116	117	118	119	120	121	122	123
GEORGIA—Cont'd																
Columbus	1.8	2.0	14.6	4.0	0.0	2.1	4.9	5.6	15.0	NA	NA	NA	NA	NA	NA	NA
Dalton city	1.3	1.1	1.7	0.7	0.0	0.7	0.0	1.8	3.9	45.9	3.0	15.0	18.1	784	600	138
East Point	0.1	0.3	1.7	0.0	0.0	0.0	0.0	0.0	2.4	29.9	9.4	2.3	10.7	318	220	79
Gainesville	6.9	4.8	15.2	14.2	0.0	0.0	0.0	2.4	3.9	39.2	7.3	34.9	11.5	576	263	241
Hinesville	19.8	0.0	7.0	0.0	0.0	6.9	0.0	0.0	3.1	13.1	2.2	12.0	5.7	215	118	84
La Grange	2.3	0.9	3.8	3.4	0.0	0.0	0.0	1.4	4.2	87.2	4.4	15.5	3.8	149	1	116
Macon	5.1	24.7	18.2	5.1	0.0	3.0	3.1	12.2	22.2	85.6	31.3	4.0	32.9	288	149	111
Marietta	4 640.0	58.6	24.3	1.1	0.0	1.7	7.4	3.3	7.8	58.2	8.0	2.5	23.5	458	151	199
Peachtree City	0.9	0.0	0.4	0.0	0.0	0.0	0.0	0.0	0.6	NA	NA	NA	NA	NA	NA	NA
Rome	0.5	0.4	2.8	0.1	0.1	0.2	0.0	4.2	4.5	37.3	9.7	39.9	13.7	442	221	153
Roswell	1.5	5.3	0.5	0.4	0.0	0.0	0.0	0.0	0.0	NA	NA	NA	NA	NA	NA	NA
Savannah	97.9	49.6	23.6	6.7	0.9	4.7	3.8	14.0	18.3	170.6	40.0	9.6	63.2	480	276	153
Smyrna	2.8	6.2	0.5	0.0	0.0	0.0	0.0	0.0	4.0	29.0	2.3	4.7	15.9	444	273	119
Valdosta	31.5	0.8	7.7	3.4	0.0	1.9	0.0	7.0	4.2	39.2	8.7	16.8	19.1	461	111	321
Warner Robins	52.9	2.4	5.1	4.3	0.0	0.0	0.3	1.0	0.6	27.1	1.7	68.5	13.7	294	160	107
HAWAII	1 294.4	172.5	1 513.7	688.2	30.8	209.4	25.7	29.2	144.0	X	X	X	X	X	X	X
Hilo CDP	NA	NA	NA	NA	NA	NA	NA	NA	NA	NA	NA	NA	NA	NA	NA	NA
Honolulu CDP	121.7	65.2	298.2	156.1	0.0	2.1	20.1	4.5	73.2	961.3	145.6	42.3	512.5	1 295	1 018	246
Kailua CDP	NA	NA	NA	NA	NA	NA	NA	NA	NA	NA	NA	NA	NA	NA	NA	NA
Kaneohe CDP	NA	NA	NA	NA	NA	NA	NA	NA	NA	NA	NA	NA	NA	NA	NA	NA
Mililani CDP	NA	NA	NA	NA	NA	NA	NA	NA	NA	NA	NA	NA	NA	NA	NA	NA
Pearl City CDP	NA	NA	NA	NA	NA	NA	NA	NA	NA	NA	NA	NA	NA	NA	NA	NA
Waimalu CDP	NA	NA	NA	NA	NA	NA	NA	NA	NA	NA	NA	NA	NA	NA	NA	NA
Waipahu CDP	NA	NA	NA	NA	NA	NA	NA	NA	NA	NA	NA	NA	NA	NA	NA	NA
IDAHO	145.9	1 051.2	1 505.4	734.0	39.7	141.1	14.5	56.9	70.3	X	X	X	X	X	X	X
Boise City	5.8	52.4	309.6	73.4	31.9	51.1	9.4	11.3	10.2	137.4	16.2	60.3	57.9	368	314	22
Caldwell	0.0	1.2	6.5	4.2	0.0	0.0	0.0	0.7	1.1	16.4	3.0	83.1	5.3	235	193	23
Coeur d'Alene	1.3	8.7	4.1	1.5	0.1	0.2	0.0	3.3	4.0	24.3	5.2	81.0	9.8	301	217	43
Idaho Falls	26.4	788.0	5.5	1.7	0.0	0.1	0.0	0.8	2.7	39.6	10.1	60.7	14.6	303	289	4
Lewiston	0.4	2.3	9.7	2.7	0.0	0.7	0.0	2.9	5.4	26.8	6.9	56.1	10.7	354	315	7
Meridian city	26.8	34.1	5.7	0.0	0.0	0.0	0.0	0.0	0.4	11.3	1.6	96.3	4.7	NA	NA	NA
Nampa	0.7	2.5	4.6	3.0	0.0	0.6	0.3	1.1	1.1	32.2	6.9	62.3	10.2	242	197	13
Pocatello	0.0	4.1	12.2	3.5	0.5	1.8	0.5	13.7	5.4	35.4	9.7	56.5	14.2	268	240	16
Twin Falls	0.1	2.6	8.2	5.5	0.0	0.4	0.0	4.8	1.6	20.4	5.4	73.9	8.5	255	231	7
ILLINOIS	1 716.4	2 418.8	11 883.4	7 228.0	236.4	1 221.7	264.2	405.6	1 308.9	X	X	X	X	X	X	X
Addison	7.3	0.5	0.0	0.0	0.0	0.0	0.0	0.0	3.6	30.4	8.9	99.5	8.6	251	110	104
Alton	2.2	0.1	6.1	5.1	0.0	0.0	0.0	0.0	4.4	33.7	17.1	100.0	7.4	236	133	96
Arlington Heights	16.0	0.1	29.0	0.0	0.2	0.2	0.5	0.0	4.7	70.6	18.3	93.1	39.0	509	371	98
Aurora	3.0	1.0	2.1	0.0	0.0	0.2	0.9	1.1	12.9	120.7	48.7	95.9	54.9	440	245	150
Bartlett	0.0	0.0	0.0	0.0	0.0	0.0	0.0	0.0	0.0	NA	NA	NA	NA	NA	NA	NA
Belleville	24.8	0.6	4.4	0.9	0.1	0.6	1.8	5.6	7.8	NA	NA	NA	NA	NA	NA	NA
Berwyn	0.0	0.1	1.0	0.0	0.0	0.3	0.4	0.0	0.0	40.7	12.8	98.4	17.5	406	279	94
Bloomington	1.6	2.7	12.0	4.0	0.0	0.0	0.8	1.3	4.5	55.2	20.6	94.3	24.2	411	217	174
Bolingbrook	1.7	0.2	0.2	0.0	0.0	0.0	0.1	0.0	3.4	39.7	12.8	94.6	17.1	316	141	139
Buffalo Grove	4.3	13.7	0.1	0.0	0.0	0.1	0.0	0.0	0.0	27.5	4.5	95.3	12.8	306	197	62
Burbank	0.0	0.0	0.0	0.0	0.0	0.0	0.0	0.0	0.0	17.6	5.3	100.0	10.4	374	208	136
Calumet City	1.5	0.1	0.1	0.0	0.0	0.0	0.0	0.0	3.1	30.9	15.4	100.0	12.0	325	185	121
Carol Stream	0.8	1.7	0.1	0.0	0.0	0.0	0.1	0.0	6.3	23.0	9.3	94.9	8.0	215	62	129
Carpentersville	1.8	0.0	0.0	0.0	0.0	0.0	0.0	0.0	14.7	NA	NA	NA	NA	NA	NA	NA
Champaign	14.6	3.2	231.2	51.8	17.3	0.7	0.0	3.9	5.9	50.4	16.1	90.1	25.0	389	160	201
Chicago	308.9	347.9	1 764.4	566.1	14.3	72.6	202.5	148.0	675.6	4 381.6	1 140.1	70.3	1 899.2	678	242	395
Chicago Heights	0.2	0.4	0.6	0.0	0.0	0.1	0.0	1.9	3.9	29.6	9.5	99.3	15.7	495	376	94
Cicero	0.3	0.1	3.5	0.0	0.0	0.0	3.3	0.0	1.4	62.4	16.3	100.0	33.5	470	306	87
Crystal Lake	0.1	0.3	1.0	0.9	0.0	0.1	0.0	0.9	1.7	27.1	11.9	100.0	6.6	200	168	13
Danville	6.9	6.3	3.9	2.4	0.0	1.0	0.0	1.9	8.4	27.7	12.8	88.2	7.2	226	108	104
Decatur	0.0	40.2	9.3	3.5	0.0	1.2	2.8	3.5	13.4	58.9	28.2	83.7	20.1	251	111	131
De Kalb	0.0	0.0	15.9	2.7	0.3	8.6	0.4	12.1	11.2	22.8	8.6	100.0	11.4	317	127	179
Des Plaines	0.8	6.1	18.5	0.6	15.6	0.5	0.7	1.4	0.2	52.6	18.3	94.8	23.3	421	291	92
Dolton	0.1	0.0	2.0	2.0	0.0	0.0	0.0	0.0	0.5	17.2	5.5	100.0	6.3	262	199	39
Downers Grove	19.8	2.6	2.1	1.2	0.1	0.0	0.0	0.6	4.2	39.4	17.8	99.4	12.9	250	133	98
East St. Louis	0.3	8.3	11.9	5.4	0.1	0.6	3.5	0.0	9.6	33.9	23.3	99.2	8.8	236	113	105
Elgin	5.4	0.4	2.2	0.0	0.0	1.1	0.9	2.5	11.3	89.3	38.0	95.4	29.3	335	264	55
Elk Grove Village	7.2	0.6	4.0	3.7	0.0	0.0	0.0	0.0	0.0	38.6	16.8	99.4	16.6	480	268	154
Elmhurst	5.8	0.2	0.2	0.1	0.1	0.0	0.0	1.7	0.7	50.3	20.1	98.5	15.4	354	173	159
Elmwood Park	0.0	0.1	0.0	0.0	0.0	0.0	0.0	0.0	0.0	15.1	3.7	100.0	9.7	430	260	101
Evanston	14.7	0.9	166.0	125.2	7.3	5.3	3.2	15.6	3.6	91.2	18.8	82.9	46.8	651	384	214

1. October 1, 2000 to September 30, 2001.   2. Includes program categories not shown separately. State totals include additional categories not allocated by city.   3. Based on population estimated as of July 1 of the year shown.

City	City government finances, 1999 (cont'd)												
	General expenditure												
	Per capita[1] (dollars)			Percent of total for —									
	Total (mil dol)	Total	Capital outlays	Public welfare	Highways	Parking facilities	Education	Health and hospitals	Police protection	Sewerage and sanitation	Parks and recreation	Housing and community development	Interest on debt
	124	125	126	127	128	129	130	131	132	133	134	135	136
GEORGIA—Cont'd													
Columbus	NA	NA	NA	NA	NA	NA	NA	NA	NA	NA	NA	NA	NA
Dalton city	63.6	2 751	1 025	0.4	7.5	0.0	0.8	0.0	6.9	58.7	11.0	0.1	1.0
East Point	32.4	961	23	0.0	3.4	0.0	0.0	0.0	24.6	15.8	3.7	3.1	4.1
Gainesville	36.7	1 844	560	3.6	2.9	0.0	0.0	0.0	12.6	37.6	6.3	0.8	1.5
Hinesville	13.0	493	28	0.0	11.6	0.0	0.0	0.1	26.8	31.0	3.0	1.6	0.0
La Grange	101.5	4 043	511	0.1	2.4	0.0	0.0	64.4	4.8	13.7	3.5	1.2	0.5
Macon	72.8	636	72	0.0	5.4	0.1	0.0	0.6	17.5	5.6	6.2	7.4	3.8
Marietta	76.4	1 488	349	4.2	7.5	0.0	0.0	0.0	12.5	11.4	5.1	3.6	7.4
Peachtree City	NA	NA	NA	NA	NA	NA	NA	NA	NA	NA	NA	NA	NA
Rome	36.1	1 168	367	2.5	14.0	0.0	0.0	0.2	14.5	21.7	3.5	3.3	3.4
Roswell	NA	NA	NA	NA	NA	NA	NA	NA	NA	NA	NA	NA	NA
Savannah	171.5	1 302	222	0.5	4.5	1.2	0.0	0.0	14.4	30.2	7.1	5.6	3.6
Smyrna	32.6	909	165	0.0	5.9	0.0	0.0	0.0	17.0	20.6	9.3	1.3	0.8
Valdosta	41.6	1 005	350	0.0	13.3	0.0	0.0	0.2	15.4	21.4	10.8	0.6	0.0
Warner Robins	29.6	633	69	0.0	9.7	0.0	0.0	0.0	23.7	21.0	3.8	7.8	0.3
HAWAII	X	X	X	X	X	X	X	X	X	X	X	X	X
Hilo CDP	NA	NA	NA	NA	NA	NA	NA	NA	NA	NA	NA	NA	NA
Honolulu CDP	904.7	2 286	365	0.0	7.7	0.0	0.0	1.7	16.9	18.2	8.9	4.2	9.6
Kailua CDP	NA	NA	NA	NA	NA	NA	NA	NA	NA	NA	NA	NA	NA
Kaneohe CDP	NA	NA	NA	NA	NA	NA	NA	NA	NA	NA	NA	NA	NA
Mililani CDP	NA	NA	NA	NA	NA	NA	NA	NA	NA	NA	NA	NA	NA
Pearl City CDP	NA	NA	NA	NA	NA	NA	NA	NA	NA	NA	NA	NA	NA
Waimalu CDP	NA	NA	NA	NA	NA	NA	NA	NA	NA	NA	NA	NA	NA
Waipahu CDP	NA	NA	NA	NA	NA	NA	NA	NA	NA	NA	NA	NA	NA
IDAHO	X	X	X	X	X	X	X	X	X	X	X	X	X
Boise City	142.3	904	245	0.0	0.8	0.7	0.0	0.4	14.8	22.3	12.3	2.4	1.2
Caldwell	16.2	726	166	0.0	12.0	0.0	0.0	0.0	14.7	29.2	10.0	2.9	0.8
Coeur d'Alene	21.9	674	113	0.0	17.3	0.4	0.0	0.0	16.8	24.9	5.4	0.0	4.1
Idaho Falls	38.0	789	112	0.0	6.5	0.0	0.0	3.9	18.3	16.3	14.1	0.0	0.4
Lewiston	26.5	871	144	0.0	18.4	0.0	0.0	0.0	14.2	24.1	9.9	0.0	0.0
Meridian city	10.5	NA	NA	0.0	0.7	0.0	0.0	0.0	23.7	40.7	9.5	0.0	0.0
Nampa	30.7	732	131	0.0	8.1	0.0	0.0	0.0	16.0	17.8	17.9	2.6	2.3
Pocatello	32.1	605	61	0.0	11.4	0.0	0.0	0.0	17.9	18.3	9.9	4.1	2.0
Twin Falls	19.0	572	77	0.0	13.1	0.0	0.0	0.0	18.6	20.9	11.9	0.1	2.6
ILLINOIS	X	X	X	X	X	X	X	X	X	X	X	X	X
Addison	37.5	1 100	245	0.0	9.0	0.0	0.0	0.0	18.6	12.2	0.0	4.7	14.2
Alton	29.1	926	162	0.0	12.4	0.0	0.0	0.4	15.6	14.0	13.1	0.6	7.8
Arlington Heights	73.0	954	279	0.0	23.2	0.6	0.0	1.9	16.1	2.5	0.0	0.4	6.7
Aurora	107.9	865	143	0.5	7.1	0.8	0.0	1.0	25.6	7.9	3.2	1.6	7.9
Bartlett	NA	NA	NA	NA	NA	NA	NA	NA	NA	NA	NA	NA	NA
Belleville	NA	NA	NA	NA	NA	NA	NA	NA	NA	NA	NA	NA	NA
Berwyn	42.4	986	37	0.6	9.6	0.0	0.0	0.6	25.9	8.8	2.1	7.4	4.6
Bloomington	49.5	842	116	0.0	7.1	1.7	0.0	0.0	14.6	10.1	10.2	7.0	3.9
Bolingbrook	52.2	962	337	0.0	10.2	0.0	0.0	0.0	16.6	12.8	1.2	0.0	4.7
Buffalo Grove	25.5	610	69	0.0	7.2	0.2	0.0	0.0	25.0	14.7	5.5	0.0	4.8
Burbank	15.9	573	227	0.0	6.6	0.0	0.0	0.0	26.1	0.0	0.0	0.2	0.3
Calumet City	30.3	820	77	0.0	20.7	0.0	0.0	1.1	19.3	3.6	0.6	2.0	8.0
Carol Stream	18.7	506	147	0.0	34.5	0.0	0.0	0.0	28.2	7.8	0.0	0.0	3.2
Carpentersville	NA	NA	NA	NA	NA	NA	NA	NA	NA	NA	NA	NA	NA
Champaign	74.0	1 151	414	0.3	21.8	2.1	0.0	0.3	18.4	6.8	6.0	2.6	1.0
Chicago	4 500.4	1 606	332	2.9	10.9	0.0	0.0	3.1	22.3	6.5	1.1	3.9	11.1
Chicago Heights	31.4	992	47	0.0	4.8	0.0	0.0	0.6	22.1	6.3	0.0	4.9	14.1
Cicero	50.3	705	109	0.3	16.4	0.0	0.0	1.6	19.5	4.7	0.0	3.8	8.4
Crystal Lake	22.9	693	105	0.0	19.7	0.0	0.0	0.7	21.2	8.1	0.0	0.0	13.7
Danville	27.2	858	63	0.0	14.5	0.7	0.0	0.0	21.8	8.7	1.2	8.3	5.3
Decatur	53.9	674	133	0.0	16.6	1.0	0.0	0.0	23.5	4.2	0.0	7.0	7.1
De Kalb	23.9	663	38	0.0	14.3	0.0	0.0	0.0	18.2	4.1	1.9	3.7	4.2
Des Plaines	47.2	854	179	1.0	11.2	1.0	0.0	0.0	18.0	5.4	0.6	0.6	8.8
Dolton	14.9	622	14	0.5	10.1	0.0	0.0	0.4	32.3	6.7	0.9	0.0	13.1
Downers Grove	46.2	893	235	0.0	12.2	1.0	0.0	0.0	15.4	1.5	0.0	1.6	7.4
East St. Louis	29.6	792	0	0.0	11.4	0.0	0.0	0.0	19.2	10.1	0.0	4.4	8.8
Elgin	73.4	838	110	0.0	16.5	0.0	0.0	0.0	22.3	5.4	12.1	6.7	7.1
Elk Grove Village	34.6	998	146	0.0	14.3	0.0	0.0	0.8	19.8	5.2	0.0	0.0	3.0
Elmhurst	45.7	1 050	318	0.2	28.6	0.6	0.0	0.4	16.7	10.3	0.7	14.0	5.1
Elmwood Park	13.9	620	276	0.0	3.6	0.0	0.0	2.1	19.2	8.9	15.9	0.0	2.1
Evanston	94.5	1 314	243	1.9	3.6	2.3	0.0	2.5	16.5	22.8	9.1	5.9	10.8

1. Based on population estimated as of July 1 of the year shown.

Table D. Cities — City Government Finances, City Government Employment, and Climate

City	City government finances, 1999 (cont'd) Debt outstanding Total (mil dol)	Per capita[1] (dollars)	Percent utility	City government employment, 2001	Climate[2] Average daily temperature (degrees Fahrenheit) Mean January	July	Limits January[3]	July[4]	Annual precipitation (inches)	Heating degree days	Cooling degree days
	137	138	139	140	141	142	143	144	145	146	147
GEORGIA—Cont'd											
Columbus	NA	NA	NA	NA	NA	NA	NA	NA	NA	NA	NA
Dalton city	182.6	7 897	85.1	250	NA	NA	NA	NA	NA	NA	NA
East Point	30.0	892	41.5	543	41.0	78.8	31.5	88.0	50.77	2 991	1 667
Gainesville	62.5	3 140	85.4	550	NA	NA	NA	NA	NA	NA	NA
Hinesville	11.0	416	100.0	NA	NA	NA	NA	NA	NA	NA	NA
La Grange	49.7	1 980	83.9	418	43.4	79.0	31.9	90.1	54.52	2 667	1 696
Macon	44.6	390	0.0	1 529	45.4	81.2	34.2	91.9	44.63	2 334	2 125
Marietta	85.2	1 659	0.0	731	41.0	78.8	31.5	88.0	50.77	2 991	1 667
Peachtree City	NA	NA	NA	NA	NA	NA	NA	NA	NA	NA	NA
Rome	41.7	1 349	57.9	644	38.4	76.9	27.0	87.3	55.33	3 467	1 337
Roswell	NA	NA	NA	NA	41.0	78.8	31.5	88.0	50.77	2 991	1 667
Savannah	229.5	1 743	39.0	2 248	48.9	81.8	38.1	91.1	49.22	1 847	2 365
Smyrna	30.1	838	25.8	346	41.0	78.8	31.5	88.0	50.77	2 991	1 667
Valdosta	8.9	214	100.0	513	49.0	80.7	36.7	92.1	52.24	1 844	2 350
Warner Robins	32.6	699	96.3	483	45.4	81.2	34.2	91.9	44.63	2 334	2 125
HAWAII	X	X	X	X	X	X	X	X	X	X	X
Hilo CDP	NA	NA	NA	NA	71.7	75.8	63.6	83.0	129.19	0	3 284
Honolulu CDP	1 780.6	4 499	2.2	NA	71.4	78.9	62.4	87.7	21.53	0	3 845
Kailua CDP	NA	NA	NA	NA	71.3	77.0	65.5	82.2	79.91	0	3 482
Kaneohe CDP	NA	NA	NA	NA	71.3	77.0	65.5	82.2	79.91	0	3 482
Mililani CDP	NA	NA	NA	NA	71.4	78.9	62.4	87.7	21.53	0	3 845
Pearl City CDP	NA	NA	NA	NA	71.4	78.9	62.4	87.7	21.53	0	3 845
Waimalu CDP	NA	NA	NA	NA	71.4	78.9	62.4	87.7	21.53	0	3 845
Waipahu CDP	NA	NA	NA	NA	71.4	78.9	62.4	87.7	21.53	0	3 845
IDAHO	X	X	X	X	X	X	X	X	X	X	X
Boise City	74.7	475	0.0	1 368	29.0	74.0	21.6	90.2	12.11	5 861	754
Caldwell	5.7	254	0.0	187	NA	NA	NA	NA	NA	NA	NA
Coeur d'Alene	20.5	631	12.8	555	NA	NA	NA	NA	NA	NA	NA
Idaho Falls	46.2	960	94.4	610	18.2	68.6	10.0	86.0	10.88	8 063	305
Lewiston	1.2	40	100.0	311	33.6	74.1	27.6	89.0	12.43	5 270	814
Meridian city	0.4	NA	100.0	146	NA	NA	NA	NA	NA	NA	NA
Nampa	13.8	330	0.0	527	29.0	74.0	21.6	90.2	12.11	5 861	754
Pocatello	8.5	161	0.0	550	23.3	70.6	14.4	88.1	12.14	7 180	421
Twin Falls	9.2	277	22.3	256	26.9	68.8	18.6	85.0	10.40	6 769	329
ILLINOIS	X	X	X	X	X	X	X	X	X	X	X
Addison	90.3	2 649	0.0	243	21.0	73.2	12.9	83.7	35.82	6 536	752
Alton	30.9	983	0.0	NA	27.0	78.5	17.9	88.4	38.43	5 214	1 346
Arlington Heights	88.1	1 152	9.6	625	21.0	73.2	12.9	83.7	35.82	6 536	752
Aurora	172.7	1 384	10.9	1 029	19.7	73.1	10.7	84.2	36.88	6 699	702
Bartlett	NA	NA	NA	NA	NA	NA	NA	NA	NA	NA	NA
Belleville	NA	NA	NA	NA	29.9	77.4	20.3	89.4	38.37	4 774	1 271
Berwyn	32.7	760	0.0	398	21.0	73.2	12.9	83.7	35.82	6 536	752
Bloomington	34.9	593	0.0	557	23.9	75.9	15.4	86.7	37.10	5 759	1 117
Bolingbrook	51.8	954	0.0	349	19.7	73.1	10.7	84.2	36.88	6 699	702
Buffalo Grove	30.7	733	0.0	255	21.0	73.2	12.9	83.7	35.82	6 536	752
Burbank	0.0	0	0.0	NA	22.4	75.1	14.9	84.4	37.38	6 176	940
Calumet City	39.9	1 080	0.0	402	23.7	74.1	15.2	85.5	36.82	6 043	857
Carol Stream	17.4	471	47.7	NA	21.0	73.2	12.9	83.7	35.82	6 536	752
Carpentersville	NA	NA	NA	NA	NA	NA	NA	NA	NA	NA	NA
Champaign	27.6	429	0.0	NA	23.8	75.0	16.0	85.3	39.71	5 854	985
Chicago	9 620.1	3 433	5.7	40 151	22.4	75.1	14.9	84.4	37.38	6 176	940
Chicago Heights	66.2	2 094	0.0	393	20.6	73.7	12.2	83.8	37.12	6 541	780
Cicero	70.2	985	0.0	630	22.4	75.1	14.9	84.4	37.38	6 176	940
Crystal Lake	51.3	1 551	6.3	286	NA	NA	NA	NA	NA	NA	NA
Danville	22.6	712	0.0	311	25.1	75.2	16.1	86.8	40.18	5 610	1 005
Decatur	93.9	1 174	37.1	593	25.2	76.2	16.0	87.9	40.16	5 522	1 120
De Kalb	23.5	651	14.1	237	17.7	73.0	8.9	83.8	36.35	7 034	682
Des Plaines	94.4	1 708	7.0	465	21.0	73.2	12.9	83.7	35.82	6 536	752
Dolton	15.0	628	0.0	NA	NA	NA	NA	NA	NA	NA	NA
Downers Grove	47.9	927	0.0	404	21.0	73.2	12.9	83.7	35.82	6 536	752
East St. Louis	44.4	1 186	0.0	249	28.4	78.4	18.9	89.6	37.86	5 001	1 329
Elgin	129.2	1 476	64.9	627	18.3	71.9	9.3	82.7	35.19	7 084	603
Elk Grove Village	21.3	614	0.0	390	21.0	73.2	12.9	83.7	35.82	6 536	752
Elmhurst	27.3	627	0.0	459	21.0	73.2	12.9	83.7	35.82	6 536	752
Elmwood Park	4.6	205	0.0	NA	NA	NA	NA	NA	NA	NA	NA
Evanston	236.0	3 282	6.4	897	21.0	73.2	12.9	83.7	35.82	6 536	752

1. Based on the population estimated as of July 1 of the year shown.   2. Represents normal values based on the 30-year period, 1961–1990.   3. Average daily minimum.   4. Average daily maximum.

Table D. Cities — **Land Area and Population**

STATE Place code	City	Land area, 2000[1] (sq km)	Population, 2000 Total persons	Rank	Per square kilometer	Population Total persons 1990	Percent change 1990–2000	Total persons 1980	Percent change 1980–1990	Population characteristics, 2000 — Percent — Race (alone or in combination) — White	Black	Am. Indian, Alaska Native	Asian and Pacific Islander	Other race	His-panic[2]	Non-His-panic White
		1	2	3	4	5	6	7	8	9	10	11	12	13	14	15
	ILLINOIS—Cont'd															
17 27884	Freeport	29.6	26 443	1 169	893.3	25 840	2.3	26 266	-1.6	83.8	15.2	0.5	1.4	1.5	2.1	80.9
17 28326	Galesburg	43.8	33 706	935	769.5	33 530	0.5	35 305	-5.0	85.9	11.3	0.6	1.3	2.9	5.0	82.1
17 29730	Glendale Heights	14.0	31 765	978	2 268.9	27 915	13.8	23 163	20.5	66.1	5.4	0.6	21.2	9.8	18.4	54.8
17 29756	Glen Ellyn	17.1	26 999	1 145	1 578.9	24 919	8.3	23 649	5.4	90.9	2.4	0.3	5.5	2.7	4.7	87.0
17 29938	Glenview	34.8	41 847	731	1 202.5	38 436	8.9	32 060	19.9	86.8	1.7	0.3	10.9	1.8	4.1	83.1
17 30926	Granite City	43.2	31 301	1 000	724.6	32 766	-4.5	36 815	-11.0	96.1	2.2	1.0	0.8	1.3	2.9	93.1
17 32018	Gurnee	34.7	28 834	1 074	831.0	13 715	110.2	NA	NA	83.9	5.6	0.6	9.1	3.0	6.0	78.7
17 32746	Hanover Park	17.6	38 278	812	2 174.9	32 918	16.3	28 850	14.1	70.7	6.6	0.7	13.0	12.2	26.7	53.5
17 33383	Harvey	16.0	30 000	1 036	1 875.0	29 771	0.8	35 779	-16.8	11.1	80.8	0.7	0.7	8.7	12.8	6.3
17 34722	Highland Park	32.0	31 365	996	980.2	30 575	2.6	30 611	0.1	92.2	2.1	0.3	2.8	3.9	8.9	86.4
17 35411	Hoffman Estates	51.0	49 495	605	970.5	46 363	6.8	37 272	24.4	76.1	4.8	0.5	16.2	4.7	10.5	68.3
17 38570	Joliet	98.6	106 221	217	1 077.3	77 217	37.6	77 956	-0.9	71.1	18.8	0.7	1.6	10.1	18.4	61.0
17 38934	Kankakee	31.8	27 491	1 124	864.5	27 541	-0.2	30 141	-8.6	52.5	42.1	0.8	0.6	6.1	9.3	47.8
17 42028	Lansing	17.5	28 332	1 092	1 619.0	28 131	0.7	29 039	-3.1	86.7	11.0	0.5	0.9	2.1	5.7	82.0
17 44407	Lombard	25.1	42 322	722	1 686.1	39 408	7.4	37 295	5.7	88.3	3.0	0.5	7.8	2.1	4.8	84.1
17 47774	Maywood	7.0	26 987	1 147	3 855.3	27 139	-0.6	27 998	-3.1	10.8	83.8	0.6	0.4	6.3	10.5	5.5
17 49867	Moline	40.4	43 768	701	1 083.4	43 080	1.6	45 709	-5.8	90.1	3.7	0.6	1.6	5.9	11.9	82.3
17 51089	Mount Prospect	26.4	56 265	516	2 131.3	53 168	5.8	52 634	1.0	82.2	2.1	0.5	11.9	5.3	11.8	73.8
17 51349	Mundelein	22.3	30 935	1 010	1 387.2	21 224	45.8	17 053	24.5	80.5	1.9	0.6	7.3	11.8	24.2	66.5
17 51622	Naperville	91.6	128 358	165	1 401.3	85 806	49.6	42 346	102.6	86.2	3.3	0.3	10.4	1.1	3.2	82.9
17 53000	Niles	15.2	30 068	1 033	1 978.2	28 375	6.0	30 363	-6.5	84.7	0.6	0.4	13.6	2.6	5.0	80.3
17 53234	Normal	35.3	45 386	674	1 285.7	40 023	13.4	35 672	12.2	88.8	8.4	0.4	2.6	1.3	2.6	86.2
17 53481	Northbrook	33.5	33 435	941	998.1	32 565	2.6	30 778	5.8	90.1	0.7	0.1	9.5	0.7	1.8	87.8
17 53559	North Chicago	20.3	35 918	866	1 769.4	34 978	2.7	38 774	-9.8	50.7	37.7	1.7	5.1	9.1	18.2	39.1
17 54638	Oak Forest	14.6	28 051	1 100	1 921.3	26 202	7.1	26 096	0.4	91.7	3.8	0.5	3.1	2.5	5.9	86.6
17 54820	Oak Lawn	22.3	55 245	534	2 477.4	56 182	-1.7	60 590	-7.3	95.1	1.3	0.4	2.1	2.9	5.3	89.9
17 54885	Oak Park	12.2	52 524	569	4 305.2	53 648	-2.1	54 887	-2.3	71.1	23.9	0.7	5.1	2.4	4.5	66.2
17 56640	Orland Park	49.6	51 077	585	1 029.8	35 720	43.0	23 045	55.0	94.6	0.8	0.2	3.9	1.7	3.7	91.0
17 57225	Palatine	33.6	65 479	417	1 948.8	41 554	57.6	32 166	29.2	84.7	2.5	0.4	8.3	6.0	14.1	74.9
17 57875	Park Ridge	18.2	37 775	824	2 075.5	37 075	1.9	38 704	-4.2	96.1	0.3	0.2	3.1	1.1	2.9	93.5
17 58447	Pekin	34.1	33 857	927	992.9	32 254	5.0	33 967	-5.0	96.5	2.7	0.7	0.5	0.3	1.3	94.8
17 59000	Peoria	115.0	112 936	199	982.1	113 508	-0.5	124 160	-8.6	71.1	26.2	0.6	2.7	1.7	2.5	68.3
17 62367	Quincy	37.9	40 366	766	1 065.1	39 682	1.7	42 554	-6.7	94.1	5.4	0.5	0.7	0.6	0.9	92.5
17 65000	Rockford	145.1	150 115	136	1 034.6	142 815	5.9	139 712	1.5	74.9	18.4	0.8	2.7	5.8	10.2	68.4
17 65078	Rock Island	41.2	39 684	779	963.2	40 630	-2.3	47 036	-13.6	79.1	18.5	0.7	1.1	3.0	5.9	74.3
17 66040	Round Lake Beach	12.9	25 859	1 205	2 004.6	16 406	57.6	12 921	27.0	77.0	3.6	1.2	2.7	18.5	31.3	62.1
17 66703	St. Charles	36.2	27 896	1 108	770.6	22 636	23.3	17 487	29.4	94.6	1.9	0.4	2.1	2.0	5.5	90.4
17 68003	Schaumburg	49.2	75 386	354	1 532.2	68 586	9.9	53 303	28.7	80.2	3.7	0.4	15.0	2.5	5.3	75.5
17 70122	Skokie	26.0	63 348	433	2 436.5	59 432	6.6	60 278	-1.4	71.6	5.0	0.4	22.7	3.6	5.7	65.6
17 72000	Springfield	139.9	111 454	201	796.7	105 412	5.7	99 637	5.8	82.3	16.2	0.6	1.8	0.7	1.2	80.3
17 73157	Streamwood	18.9	36 407	851	1 926.3	31 197	16.7	23 456	33.0	79.7	4.3	0.7	9.6	8.5	16.8	69.0
17 75484	Tinley Park	38.7	48 401	625	1 250.7	37 115	30.4	26 169	41.8	94.3	2.1	0.3	2.7	1.8	4.1	90.5
17 77005	Urbana	27.2	36 395	852	1 338.1	36 383	0.0	35 978	1.1	69.0	15.2	0.6	15.4	2.4	3.5	65.4
17 79293	Waukegan	59.6	87 901	285	1 474.8	69 481	26.5	67 653	2.7	53.0	20.3	1.0	4.2	25.2	44.8	30.9
17 81048	Wheaton	29.1	55 416	532	1 904.3	51 441	7.7	43 043	19.5	90.1	3.1	0.3	5.5	1.5	3.7	87.5
17 81087	Wheeling	21.8	34 496	911	1 582.4	29 911	15.3	23 270	28.5	78.5	2.7	0.5	9.9	10.6	20.7	66.4
17 82075	Wilmette	13.9	27 651	1 120	1 989.3	26 694	3.6	28 229	-5.4	90.7	0.7	0.2	9.0	0.6	2.1	88.0
17 83245	Woodridge	21.6	30 934	1 011	1 432.1	26 359	17.4	22 322	18.1	77.0	8.7	0.5	12.0	4.1	9.2	70.1
18 00000	INDIANA	92 894.8	6 080 485	X	65.5	5 544 156	9.7	5 490 214	1.0	88.6	8.8	0.6	1.3	2.0	3.5	85.8
18 01468	Anderson	103.7	59 734	470	576.0	59 518	0.4	64 714	-8.0	82.8	15.7	0.8	0.8	1.1	2.1	80.9
18 05860	Bloomington	51.1	69 291	388	1 356.0	62 735	11.7	52 044	19.2	88.8	4.9	0.8	6.2	1.6	2.5	85.7
18 10342	Carmel	46.1	37 733	826	818.5	25 380	48.7	18 272	38.9	93.4	1.7	0.4	4.8	0.6	1.7	91.3
18 14734	Columbus	67.2	39 059	793	581.2	33 948	15.1	30 614	10.9	92.4	3.2	0.4	3.6	1.7	2.8	90.0
18 19486	East Chicago	31.0	32 414	962	1 045.6	33 892	-4.4	39 786	-14.8	38.5	36.8	0.8	0.4	26.1	51.6	12.1
18 20728	Elkhart	55.3	51 874	575	938.0	44 661	16.2	41 305	8.1	74.1	16.0	1.1	1.6	10.3	14.8	66.8
18 22000	Evansville	105.4	121 582	178	1 153.5	126 272	-3.7	130 496	-3.2	87.5	11.7	0.6	1.0	0.7	1.1	85.6
18 23278	Fishers town	56.2	37 835	822	673.2	7 189	426.3	NA	NA	93.2	3.2	0.3	3.7	0.7	2.0	90.9
18 25000	Fort Wayne	204.5	205 727	84	1 006.0	195 680	7.2	172 196	11.4	77.4	18.5	0.9	2.0	3.6	5.8	73.1
18 27000	Gary	130.1	102 746	226	789.7	116 646	-11.9	151 953	-23.2	13.0	85.3	0.7	0.4	2.7	4.9	10.1
18 28386	Goshen	34.2	29 383	1 059	859.2	23 794	23.5	19 665	21.0	84.9	2.1	0.6	1.4	13.1	19.3	76.7
18 29898	Greenwood	37.0	36 037	864	974.0	26 507	36.0	19 327	37.2	97.2	0.6	0.4	1.7	0.8	1.9	95.4
18 31000	Hammond	59.3	83 048	307	1 400.5	84 236	-1.4	93 714	-10.1	74.8	15.3	1.0	0.8	11.0	21.0	62.4
18 34114	Hobart	67.9	25 363	1 223	373.5	24 440	3.8	22 987	6.3	95.1	1.6	0.6	0.8	3.4	8.1	89.0
18 36000	Indianapolis	949.2	791 926	12	834.3	731 726	6.7	NA	NA	70.7	26.1	0.7	1.8	2.4	3.9	67.7
18 38358	Jeffersonville	35.2	27 362	1 132	777.3	24 016	13.9	21 220	13.2	84.3	14.9	0.8	1.2	0.9	1.8	81.5
18 40392	Kokomo	41.9	46 113	661	1 100.5	44 996	2.5	47 808	-5.9	86.8	11.3	0.9	1.4	1.5	2.6	83.8
18 40788	Lafayette	52.0	56 397	510	1 084.6	45 393	24.6	43 011	3.7	90.4	3.6	0.9	1.5	5.2	9.1	84.9
18 42426	Lawrence	52.0	38 915	799	748.4	26 849	44.9	25 591	4.9	80.2	16.4	0.7	2.3	2.3	4.7	76.0
18 46908	Marion	34.4	31 320	999	910.5	32 607	-3.9	35 874	-9.1	81.6	16.8	1.1	1.0	2.0	3.6	77.8
18 48528	Merrillville	86.2	30 560	1 020	354.5	27 257	12.1	27 677	-1.5	71.6	23.6	0.8	1.9	4.6	9.7	64.5

1. Dry land or land partially or temporarily covered by water.   2. Hispanic persons may be of any race.

Items 1—15

Table D. Cities — **Population and Households**

City	Population characteristics, 2000 (cont'd)										Households, 2000				
	Age of population (percent)													Percent	
	Under 5 years	5 to 17 years	18 to 24 years	25 to 34 years	35 to 44 years	45 to 54 years	55 to 64 years	65 to 74 years	75 years and over	Percent female	Number	Percent change, 1990–2000	Persons per house-hold	Female family house-holder[1]	One-person
	16	17	18	19	20	21	22	23	24	25	26	27	28	29	30
ILLINOIS—Cont'd															
Freeport	6.6	17.8	8.5	12.8	15.0	12.4	8.8	8.1	10.0	53.4	11 222	3.5	2.29	12.6	33.7
Galesburg	5.7	15.4	11.8	12.9	14.1	13.2	8.7	8.4	9.7	49.9	13 237	-0.3	2.24	12.4	34.6
Glendale Heights	8.0	18.9	11.5	20.1	16.7	13.0	6.9	3.1	1.9	49.0	10 791	12.3	2.94	9.9	22.8
Glen Ellyn	7.8	20.5	6.2	12.1	17.9	15.3	8.7	6.2	5.1	51.2	10 207	8.4	2.63	6.8	25.2
Glenview	6.5	19.1	5.2	9.5	15.8	16.5	11.4	8.6	7.4	52.0	15 464	15.9	2.67	6.9	20.7
Granite City	6.0	18.7	8.3	12.9	16.2	12.7	8.8	8.5	7.8	52.0	12 773	-1.8	2.43	13.7	29.4
Gurnee	9.6	20.7	5.5	15.8	21.3	13.4	6.5	4.1	3.1	51.5	10 629	98.3	2.71	7.8	22.7
Hanover Park	8.8	22.7	10.9	17.3	17.8	12.3	6.2	2.6	1.5	48.5	11 105	10.5	3.44	11.8	13.5
Harvey	9.6	25.5	10.8	13.5	13.1	10.9	7.9	5.0	3.6	52.0	8 990	-0.7	3.30	31.8	20.7
Highland Park	7.4	19.6	4.6	9.6	15.9	16.4	11.4	8.5	6.5	51.0	11 521	4.5	2.71	5.8	19.5
Hoffman Estates	7.2	20.9	8.7	15.4	18.5	15.3	7.3	3.9	2.8	50.2	17 034	7.0	2.89	9.6	19.9
Joliet	9.3	20.2	10.1	17.6	15.5	10.1	6.2	5.1	6.0	50.5	36 182	35.1	2.81	13.3	24.7
Kankakee	8.3	21.1	9.7	14.3	14.4	11.6	7.1	5.9	7.4	52.1	10 020	-3.6	2.60	21.2	31.5
Lansing	6.4	17.9	7.8	12.8	16.3	13.7	9.4	8.0	7.7	52.6	11 416	4.9	2.48	11.4	27.9
Lombard	6.1	16.8	7.9	16.1	17.3	13.0	8.2	6.4	8.1	51.5	16 487	9.6	2.49	7.9	28.7
Maywood	8.0	23.7	10.4	13.6	14.1	11.8	8.7	6.0	3.6	53.2	7 937	-1.2	3.38	30.2	19.1
Moline	6.5	17.6	9.2	12.8	15.0	14.2	9.4	7.7	7.7	52.2	18 492	1.2	2.35	10.4	31.9
Mount Prospect	6.6	16.4	8.2	15.3	16.0	12.9	9.9	8.5	6.3	50.3	21 585	6.4	2.60	7.2	25.1
Mundelein	9.2	22.2	8.3	16.2	19.7	12.7	5.4	3.7	2.5	48.9	9 858	38.5	3.12	9.0	17.0
Naperville	8.4	23.4	6.4	13.1	20.6	15.4	6.5	3.1	3.1	51.1	43 751	50.3	2.89	5.9	18.8
Niles	3.8	12.9	6.9	10.5	13.5	13.4	11.3	12.4	15.4	53.3	12 002	11.4	2.39	8.5	30.6
Normal	4.9	12.6	38.1	12.3	10.8	8.7	5.0	3.9	3.7	53.0	15 157	27.8	2.43	9.3	26.6
Northbrook	5.7	19.8	4.4	6.7	15.1	17.0	12.6	9.9	8.7	51.7	12 203	7.1	2.68	5.3	18.9
North Chicago	8.0	16.1	34.7	17.0	10.5	5.7	3.5	2.5	2.0	39.0	7 661	7.3	3.09	18.9	21.8
Oak Forest	6.7	19.3	9.1	13.8	17.2	15.1	9.6	5.2	4.0	50.2	9 785	10.4	2.81	9.7	20.7
Oak Lawn	5.4	16.6	7.2	11.2	15.0	13.0	9.9	10.5	11.3	53.1	22 220	3.5	2.46	10.1	30.9
Oak Park	6.9	17.3	6.7	17.3	17.9	16.5	7.9	4.5	5.1	53.5	23 079	2.1	2.26	11.6	37.0
Orland Park	5.4	19.0	7.1	9.2	15.5	16.3	11.0	8.9	7.5	52.2	18 675	54.4	2.71	7.9	20.6
Palatine	7.3	17.5	8.5	18.0	17.8	13.7	8.3	5.0	3.8	50.2	25 518	68.3	2.56	8.3	27.5
Park Ridge	5.8	18.7	5.5	8.3	16.2	15.1	10.7	9.6	10.1	52.6	14 219	5.6	2.61	8.0	24.1
Pekin	6.5	16.7	9.3	14.4	15.9	12.9	8.5	8.1	7.6	50.9	13 380	2.3	2.37	11.4	29.5
Peoria	7.4	18.3	12.0	13.8	13.4	12.7	8.1	6.8	7.4	52.7	45 199	0.5	2.38	15.5	33.2
Quincy	5.9	17.4	10.0	12.1	13.8	12.3	8.7	8.5	11.4	53.1	16 546	2.9	2.30	11.6	33.7
Rockford	7.7	18.9	9.2	14.9	14.8	12.5	7.9	6.7	7.4	51.8	59 158	7.9	2.46	14.8	30.7
Rock Island	6.4	16.5	13.1	12.0	13.7	13.3	8.6	7.6	8.7	52.8	16 148	-0.6	2.31	14.2	34.5
Round Lake Beach	11.3	23.7	9.4	18.9	17.5	9.9	4.7	2.5	2.1	49.6	7 349	49.9	3.50	10.5	14.0
St. Charles	6.3	21.5	7.4	12.3	17.4	16.7	8.3	5.0	5.2	50.2	10 351	27.3	2.62	8.0	23.5
Schaumburg	6.0	15.9	8.3	19.2	17.1	14.9	9.1	4.7	4.8	51.3	31 799	15.3	2.36	8.1	32.3
Skokie	5.2	17.8	7.0	10.2	14.7	15.5	10.0	9.2	10.3	52.6	23 223	2.3	2.68	9.9	23.6
Springfield	6.6	17.4	8.8	14.3	15.5	14.4	8.6	7.0	7.4	53.0	48 621	8.0	2.24	12.9	36.1
Streamwood	8.7	19.4	8.2	18.7	18.6	12.8	7.5	3.8	2.3	49.9	12 095	21.8	2.99	9.2	17.3
Tinley Park	6.6	20.0	8.1	12.9	18.2	15.5	8.0	5.7	5.0	51.6	17 478	37.9	2.73	8.6	23.1
Urbana	4.4	10.5	36.2	16.3	10.1	8.4	4.8	4.2	5.2	47.3	14 327	8.5	2.14	8.7	36.6
Waukegan	9.6	20.6	12.1	18.4	15.0	10.6	5.8	4.2	3.7	49.2	27 787	13.2	3.09	14.6	24.2
Wheaton	6.3	19.8	10.5	12.2	16.5	15.4	8.0	5.4	5.8	51.3	19 377	9.0	2.64	7.3	24.5
Wheeling	6.6	16.8	9.4	18.0	17.1	13.9	7.8	5.3	4.9	50.8	13 280	6.5	2.57	9.0	30.1
Wilmette	7.1	22.6	3.6	5.5	16.2	17.2	10.6	8.6	8.6	52.1	10 039	3.3	2.73	6.4	21.1
Woodridge	7.6	19.7	9.2	17.2	18.8	14.7	7.5	3.3	2.0	50.3	11 382	18.3	2.71	10.5	23.5
INDIANA	7.0	18.9	10.1	13.7	15.8	13.4	8.7	6.5	5.9	51.0	2 336 306	13.1	2.53	11.1	25.9
Anderson	6.9	16.3	11.2	14.0	13.6	12.2	9.1	8.0	8.6	52.6	25 274	4.0	2.28	15.1	33.1
Bloomington	4.1	8.6	42.3	15.4	9.2	7.9	4.7	3.8	4.0	51.4	26 468	26.1	2.09	7.8	39.1
Carmel	7.9	22.4	4.8	11.0	18.9	16.4	8.9	5.1	4.6	51.4	13 597	49.2	2.74	6.6	18.9
Columbus	7.4	18.3	8.0	14.2	15.3	13.8	9.3	6.9	6.8	51.9	15 985	24.4	2.39	11.0	29.1
East Chicago	9.1	21.4	11.1	13.4	13.4	10.8	7.5	7.4	5.9	52.2	11 707	-3.4	2.75	26.7	28.6
Elkhart	9.4	19.0	11.1	17.1	14.6	11.0	6.9	5.2	5.5	50.8	20 072	14.6	2.55	15.3	30.3
Evansville	6.4	16.3	11.5	13.7	14.9	12.5	8.4	7.7	8.5	53.0	52 273	-1.3	2.24	13.7	35.1
Fishers town	11.9	20.3	5.4	23.4	21.4	10.2	4.0	2.2	1.2	51.1	14 044	423.6	2.69	6.6	20.7
Fort Wayne	7.8	19.2	10.7	15.2	14.9	12.4	7.3	6.0	6.4	51.6	83 333	19.7	2.41	14.6	32.6
Gary	8.4	21.5	10.1	11.5	13.5	13.1	9.0	7.5	5.3	54.2	38 244	-6.6	2.66	30.9	28.9
Goshen	7.9	18.0	12.9	16.3	13.7	10.5	7.0	5.6	8.0	49.8	10 675	18.2	2.61	10.1	27.5
Greenwood	7.7	17.6	9.6	16.5	15.6	12.6	8.1	5.8	6.5	52.1	14 931	40.9	2.37	9.9	29.9
Hammond	8.1	19.2	9.8	14.4	15.7	12.2	7.6	6.5	6.5	51.2	32 026	-0.4	2.58	16.9	29.7
Hobart	6.1	17.5	8.6	13.6	16.1	13.8	9.2	7.6	7.5	51.5	9 855	22.1	2.55	10.4	24.1
Indianapolis	7.3	18.3	10.1	16.5	16.3	12.7	7.6	5.8	5.2	51.6	324 342	9.5	2.39	15.0	32.0
Jeffersonville	6.7	16.9	8.7	15.1	16.2	14.6	9.2	6.9	5.7	52.0	11 643	33.1	2.30	14.8	32.1
Kokomo	7.8	17.1	9.4	14.7	14.3	13.1	9.2	7.2	7.2	52.7	20 273	8.6	2.24	14.1	35.2
Lafayette	7.0	16.2	14.2	17.4	13.9	11.8	7.4	5.9	6.1	50.6	24 060	33.1	2.31	10.2	33.2
Lawrence	9.1	20.9	7.7	17.3	18.9	11.8	6.2	4.5	3.7	51.2	14 853	40.0	2.60	13.0	24.8
Marion	6.5	16.7	12.5	12.5	13.5	12.1	9.2	8.3	8.7	53.0	12 462	-1.8	2.30	14.7	33.8
Merrillville	6.6	18.0	8.7	13.7	15.7	13.7	8.5	6.9	8.2	52.3	11 678	16.7	2.57	12.6	26.1

1. No spouse present.

Table D. Cities — Group Quarters, Crime, Education, and Income

City	Persons in group quarters, 2000				Serious crimes known to police, 2000[2]				Education, 1990				Money income, 1989		
		Institutional			Total		Rate[3]		School enrollment		Attainment[4] (percent)			Households	
														Median	
	Total	Total	Persons in nursing homes	Non-Institutional[1]	Number	Rate[3]	Violent	Property	Public	Private	High school graduate or more	Bachelor's degree or more	Per capita (dollars)[5]	Dollars	Percent change, 1979–1989 (constant 1989 dollars)
	31	32	33	34	35	36	37	38	39	40	41	42	43	44	45
ILLINOIS—Cont'd															
Freeport	730	548	460	182	NA	NA	NA	NA	5 090	587	74.3	14.4	12 631	24 758	-8.4
Galesburg	4 079	2 561	646	1 518	NA	NA	NA	NA	6 842	1 670	75.0	13.9	11 982	22 469	-17.2
Glendale Heights	16	6	0	10	NA	NA	NA	NA	6 900	1 203	84.2	23.9	15 715	42 822	-0.1
Glen Ellyn	109	22	22	87	NA	NA	NA	NA	5 240	1 584	94.0	51.3	24 151	51 916	5.3
Glenview	532	316	310	216	NA	NA	NA	NA	7 067	2 576	92.2	46.2	30 531	59 020	6.5
Granite City	294	209	209	85	NA	NA	NA	NA	7 132	857	69.9	8.6	12 326	25 598	-14.6
Gurnee	30	0	0	30	NA	NA	NA	NA	2 719	670	90.9	37.8	20 965	49 069	NA
Hanover Park	66	26	0	40	NA	NA	NA	NA	8 531	902	83.7	19.0	14 770	44 237	0.3
Harvey	362	154	88	208	NA	NA	NA	NA	8 670	957	66.7	8.0	8 690	23 201	-23.2
Highland Park	196	0	0	196	NA	NA	NA	NA	6 231	1 737	92.3	55.9	43 394	71 905	11.3
Hoffman Estates	263	263	259	0	NA	NA	NA	NA	10 808	2 156	90.3	33.5	19 072	49 475	6.6
Joliet	4 494	3 566	1 548	928	NA	NA	NA	NA	15 170	4 827	71.1	14.6	13 091	30 967	-2.6
Kankakee	1 447	1 252	302	195	NA	NA	NA	NA	6 196	1 199	65.9	11.6	10 349	20 328	-18.3
Lansing	0	0	0	0	NA	NA	NA	NA	4 875	1 783	81.9	15.5	16 112	36 641	-9.4
Lombard	1 341	688	688	653	NA	NA	NA	NA	6 865	2 967	88.3	30.4	18 281	44 210	1.8
Maywood	189	0	0	189	NA	NA	NA	NA	6 653	1 574	66.0	10.2	10 698	30 780	-4.3
Moline	350	290	222	60	NA	NA	NA	NA	9 196	1 631	81.2	19.3	14 939	27 512	-18.0
Mount Prospect	66	5	0	61	NA	NA	NA	NA	8 939	2 956	85.0	30.9	20 345	46 508	2.4
Mundelein	177	0	0	177	NA	NA	NA	NA	4 418	1 331	85.8	30.6	16 950	45 947	11.4
Naperville	1 986	943	812	1 043	2 295	1 788	74	1 714	20 702	5 738	95.5	54.4	23 934	60 979	6.6
Niles	1 350	1 163	1 163	187	NA	NA	NA	NA	3 718	1 541	75.0	20.2	17 422	38 718	-8.5
Normal	8 584	428	360	8 156	NA	NA	NA	NA	21 090	1 143	92.1	40.4	12 101	31 376	-7.6
Northbrook	751	515	515	236	NA	NA	NA	NA	6 536	2 188	93.9	55.1	38 100	73 362	9.6
North Chicago	12 282	1 691	0	10 591	NA	NA	NA	NA	6 501	1 152	79.2	10.2	9 165	25 500	-4.0
Oak Forest	534	485	0	49	NA	NA	NA	NA	5 619	1 677	87.2	17.8	15 745	43 387	-1.5
Oak Lawn	490	471	471	19	NA	NA	NA	NA	7 904	4 407	80.0	17.6	16 852	38 665	-4.7
Oak Park	379	225	225	154	NA	NA	NA	NA	10 100	3 876	90.9	51.2	21 269	40 453	17.2
Orland Park	437	411	411	26	NA	NA	NA	NA	7 862	2 367	88.5	28.8	20 521	51 748	4.5
Palatine	217	144	144	73	NA	NA	NA	NA	7 850	2 046	90.6	37.6	22 098	48 668	-4.5
Park Ridge	667	494	493	173	NA	NA	NA	NA	5 828	2 750	89.4	37.4	26 150	52 817	1.5
Pekin	2 209	2 001	299	208	NA	NA	NA	NA	7 055	678	75.7	10.5	12 246	25 198	-17.8
Peoria	5 428	1 795	1 261	3 633	10 254	9 079	815	8 265	23 270	9 717	77.9	23.6	14 039	26 074	-14.5
Quincy	2 364	1 618	1 428	746	NA	NA	NA	NA	7 166	2 613	73.6	14.5	11 708	21 325	-10.2
Rockford	4 326	2 945	1 875	1 381	12 417	8 272	807	7 465	27 221	6 684	74.8	18.7	14 109	28 282	-8.4
Rock Island	2 435	632	444	1 803	NA	NA	NA	NA	7 987	3 257	76.3	17.0	12 381	24 131	-19.0
Round Lake Beach	140	140	140	0	NA	NA	NA	NA	4 410	491	73.0	8.2	11 550	36 616	-4.7
St. Charles	810	677	171	133	NA	NA	NA	NA	5 541	791	88.4	36.1	20 794	46 655	13.6
Schaumburg	436	430	430	6	NA	NA	NA	NA	15 125	2 669	90.5	34.2	20 826	47 029	6.8
Skokie	1 139	722	655	417	NA	NA	NA	NA	10 550	3 511	85.5	36.7	20 595	42 276	-7.9
Springfield	2 556	1 515	1 035	1 041	8 394	7 531	1 007	6 525	20 012	5 644	81.7	24.9	14 813	27 995	0.2
Streamwood	225	211	189	14	NA	NA	NA	NA	6 857	1 110	83.4	19.9	16 416	48 758	10.1
Tinley Park	717	644	101	73	NA	NA	NA	NA	8 162	1 961	82.3	18.2	15 518	43 198	3.0
Urbana	5 735	618	400	5 117	NA	NA	NA	NA	17 462	653	89.2	53.8	11 439	21 705	-11.0
Waukegan	2 090	1 011	353	1 079	NA	NA	NA	NA	16 320	2 389	71.1	14.1	13 060	31 315	-2.1
Wheaton	4 200	1 710	932	2 490	NA	NA	NA	NA	10 537	5 328	92.2	49.4	22 433	52 208	11.3
Wheeling	370	366	366	4	NA	NA	NA	NA	5 085	1 114	85.9	30.0	18 480	39 848	1.2
Wilmette	223	126	126	97	NA	NA	NA	NA	4 965	1 931	95.1	63.7	38 465	71 274	15.0
Woodridge	86	0	0	86	NA	NA	NA	NA	5 940	1 252	91.6	32.4	17 730	44 570	1.3
INDIANA	178 154	90 885	48 745	87 269	228 135	3 752	349	3 403	1 233 973	202 215	75.6	15.6	13 149	28 797	-2.3
Anderson	2 179	856	599	1 323	NA	NA	NA	NA	11 127	2 876	71.3	12.0	12 161	23 221	-12.1
Bloomington	14 005	873	327	13 132	2 728	3 937	176	3 761	34 145	1 322	86.5	47.9	10 616	18 393	0.4
Carmel	521	454	454	67	754	1 998	29	1 969	5 906	1 320	95.0	51.3	24 956	54 505	5.0
Columbus	814	781	552	33	2 491	6 378	184	6 193	6 697	767	76.1	20.3	14 366	28 859	-4.4
East Chicago	192	106	106	86	NA	NA	NA	NA	9 030	1 359	57.7	6.6	9 090	19 391	-32.7
Elkhart	658	292	283	366	5 069	9 772	549	9 222	8 362	1 006	71.7	13.7	13 331	25 291	-1.0
Evansville	4 720	2 463	1 567	2 257	6 215	5 112	512	4 599	21 814	6 538	72.4	14.6	12 564	22 936	-6.0
Fishers town	1	0	0	1	664	1 755	100	1 655	NA	NA	NA	NA	NA	NA	NA
Fort Wayne	5 036	2 865	1 988	2 171	12 115	5 889	399	5 490	34 842	9 109	77.1	15.7	12 776	26 344	-2.0
Gary	849	535	481	314	6 301	6 133	1 035	5 098	32 701	2 915	64.8	8.8	8 994	19 390	-32.9
Goshen	1 524	856	369	668	1 713	5 830	963	4 867	4 144	1 463	72.2	17.7	13 047	28 932	11.9
Greenwood	577	439	376	138	1 875	5 203	497	4 706	5 045	876	82.7	18.7	16 367	32 994	-2.0
Hammond	394	116	116	278	6 211	7 479	1 084	6 395	17 236	3 488	69.3	9.2	11 576	26 883	-19.6
Hobart	248	211	211	37	NA	NA	NA	NA	4 839	778	78.7	11.7	14 596	34 602	-12.8
Indianapolis	17 915	11 375	5 425	6 540	37 389	4 710	862	3 848	142 850	33 552	76.5	21.9	14 605	29 083	NA
Jeffersonville	628	461	198	167	1 541	5 632	523	5 109	4 574	523	69.1	12.3	11 655	23 977	-4.7
Kokomo	694	556	422	138	2 736	5 933	514	5 419	9 749	1 074	74.0	13.0	12 619	26 272	-4.3
Lafayette	709	524	505	185	2 961	5 250	291	4 959	9 452	1 461	80.5	21.4	13 468	27 023	1.9
Lawrence	286	263	263	23	949	2 439	242	2 197	5 451	799	78.9	17.3	14 011	29 652	1.6
Marion	2 631	1 119	623	1 512	517	1 651	86	1 564	6 450	1 187	66.5	10.8	11 188	22 006	-12.1
Merrillville	555	432	396	123	1 106	3 619	232	3 387	5 645	1 060	80.2	15.1	15 131	36 221	-15.3

1. Persons in emergency shelters and persons visible in street locations. 2. Data for serious crimes have not been adjusted for underreporting. This may affect comparability between geographic areas and over time. 3. Per 100,000 population estimated by the FBI. 4. Persons 25 years old and older. 5. Based on population enumerated as of April 1, 1990.

City	Percent with $100,000 or more	Percent change in rate, 1979–1989 Total	Total	Families Total	Total	Percent change, 1990–2000	Vacant units for sale or rent[1]	For seasonal use (percent)	Home owner vacancy rate	Renter vacancy rate	Total	Percent owner occupied	Percent renter occupied	Average size owner occupied	Average size renter occupied
	46	47	48	49	50	51	52	53	54	55	56	57	58	59	60
ILLINOIS—Cont'd															
Freeport	1.2	12.5	58.2	9.6	12 471	6.4	1 249	0.3	2.0	14.6	11 222	68.2	31.8	2.42	2.02
Galesburg	1.9	17.9	90.4	12.9	14 133	-1.3	896	0.2	1.8	7.5	13 237	64.3	35.7	2.35	2.03
Glendale Heights	3.4	2.7	0.0	2.0	11 105	8.8	314	0.1	0.5	5.0	10 791	70.1	29.9	3.22	2.28
Glen Ellyn	14.6	2.2	-38.9	0.9	10 515	7.9	308	0.4	0.8	3.2	10 207	77.4	22.6	2.78	2.14
Glenview	24.7	1.7	-5.6	0.9	15 853	15.2	389	0.5	0.7	3.2	15 464	88.0	12.0	2.70	2.45
Granite City	1.3	13.2	23.4	10.5	14 022	1.0	1 249	0.1	1.7	13.6	12 773	70.5	29.5	2.51	2.23
Gurnee	7.0	2.9	NA	2.3	10 929	96.2	300	0.4	0.5	5.9	10 629	78.4	21.6	2.92	1.96
Hanover Park	3.9	2.8	-22.2	2.1	11 343	9.0	238	0.0	0.5	5.1	11 105	82.3	17.7	3.38	3.72
Harvey	1.0	25.6	40.7	23.1	10 158	-1.2	1 168	0.1	3.3	8.9	8 990	56.4	43.6	3.38	3.19
Highland Park	34.7	2.8	33.3	1.6	11 934	4.4	413	0.8	1.1	3.2	11 521	82.1	17.9	2.72	2.66
Hoffman Estates	8.3	2.0	-28.6	1.3	17 387	4.7	353	0.1	0.6	4.3	17 034	76.5	23.5	3.06	2.33
Joliet	2.5	13.0	8.3	9.6	38 176	31.4	1 994	0.1	1.6	6.7	36 182	70.4	29.6	2.93	2.52
Kankakee	1.1	23.5	30.6	20.3	10 965	-3.6	945	0.2	3.6	8.4	10 020	53.4	46.6	2.68	2.50
Lansing	2.6	2.7	-6.9	2.0	11 748	5.0	332	0.1	1.3	4.9	11 416	75.3	24.7	2.61	2.09
Lombard	4.3	2.6	4.0	1.6	17 019	7.4	532	0.4	0.7	6.0	16 487	74.9	25.1	2.64	2.02
Maywood	2.3	15.2	12.6	11.4	8 475	-0.8	538	0.1	2.3	6.9	7 937	62.8	37.2	3.65	2.91
Moline	3.4	10.3	51.5	8.1	19 487	1.3	995	0.4	1.1	6.4	18 492	67.3	32.7	2.47	2.09
Mount Prospect	7.7	3.3	26.9	2.1	21 952	4.8	367	0.1	0.5	2.5	21 585	71.5	28.5	2.67	2.43
Mundelein	6.2	4.9	-5.8	3.1	10 167	37.4	309	0.2	1.2	6.3	9 858	79.7	20.3	3.10	3.18
Naperville	16.8	1.5	-21.1	0.9	45 651	47.7	1 900	0.5	1.3	8.7	43 751	79.7	20.3	3.11	2.02
Niles	5.3	3.7	15.6	2.5	12 256	10.9	254	0.3	0.4	1.1	12 002	76.5	23.5	2.50	2.03
Normal	3.0	21.7	26.2	5.7	15 683	27.5	526	0.2	1.0	4.0	15 157	55.2	44.8	2.57	2.25
Northbrook	34.2	1.8	-10.0	1.1	12 492	7.0	289	0.5	0.7	2.5	12 203	91.7	8.3	2.74	1.97
North Chicago	1.1	14.9	58.5	12.4	8 377	5.7	716	0.3	2.0	5.2	7 661	36.3	63.7	3.14	3.06
Oak Forest	3.7	3.0	25.0	2.1	10 022	10.6	237	0.1	1.3	3.1	9 785	81.7	18.3	3.00	2.00
Oak Lawn	4.4	3.4	3.0	2.4	22 846	4.6	626	0.2	1.4	4.0	22 220	82.9	17.1	2.56	1.99
Oak Park	8.3	4.6	-9.8	3.1	23 723	0.6	644	0.2	0.8	2.7	23 079	56.3	43.7	2.67	1.73
Orland Park	10.6	2.4	-11.1	1.5	19 045	52.6	370	0.3	0.9	3.4	18 675	91.1	8.9	2.76	2.20
Palatine	10.4	2.5	25.0	1.8	26 223	65.4	705	0.3	0.6	4.5	25 518	69.3	30.7	2.65	2.34
Park Ridge	16.3	1.3	-31.6	0.9	14 646	6.0	427	0.3	1.2	4.3	14 219	87.6	12.4	2.71	1.88
Pekin	1.5	13.9	63.5	10.9	14 038	1.9	658	0.2	1.3	5.4	13 380	67.2	32.8	2.50	2.08
Peoria	3.9	18.9	53.7	15.1	49 125	1.8	3 926	0.2	1.9	10.3	45 199	59.7	40.3	2.49	2.21
Quincy	2.0	15.0	26.1	11.7	18 043	2.9	1 497	0.3	1.8	9.9	16 546	66.4	33.6	2.43	2.03
Rockford	3.1	13.4	30.1	10.5	63 570	9.3	4 412	0.2	1.7	8.4	59 158	61.1	38.9	2.59	2.26
Rock Island	2.2	19.3	56.9	13.9	17 542	-2.0	1 394	0.2	1.8	9.8	16 148	65.1	34.9	2.41	2.12
Round Lake Beach	1.9	6.8	33.3	6.2	7 608	50.9	259	0.3	1.6	3.2	7 349	84.6	15.4	3.54	3.27
St. Charles	10.2	2.5	-21.9	1.7	11 072	30.2	721	1.0	2.3	10.5	10 351	74.0	26.0	2.81	2.06
Schaumburg	6.5	2.7	3.8	2.2	33 093	12.2	1 294	0.4	0.5	6.8	31 799	69.4	30.6	2.52	1.99
Skokie	9.6	3.9	56.0	2.7	23 702	2.3	479	0.3	0.8	1.9	23 223	75.2	24.8	2.77	2.41
Springfield	2.5	12.6	20.0	9.7	53 733	10.7	5 112	0.3	2.4	11.0	48 621	62.8	37.2	2.38	2.01
Streamwood	3.1	2.6	13.0	1.7	12 371	19.8	276	0.1	1.3	3.2	12 095	89.6	10.4	3.00	2.96
Tinley Park	2.9	2.5	-35.9	1.4	18 037	36.4	559	0.1	1.6	3.4	17 478	84.9	15.1	2.86	1.99
Urbana	2.8	21.8	23.2	12.7	15 311	9.3	984	0.3	1.5	7.3	14 327	37.0	63.0	2.35	2.02
Waukegan	2.4	9.5	0.0	6.5	29 243	13.3	1 456	0.2	1.5	6.0	27 787	56.5	43.5	3.35	2.74
Wheaton	13.7	5.1	54.5	1.8	19 881	6.7	504	0.2	0.7	3.8	19 377	74.1	25.9	2.84	2.08
Wheeling	3.4	3.2	0.0	2.0	13 697	5.4	417	0.4	0.5	4.9	13 280	66.6	33.4	2.78	2.15
Wilmette	33.7	2.1	-25.0	1.2	10 319	2.7	280	0.7	0.7	2.7	10 039	86.8	13.2	2.83	2.11
Woodridge	4.2	2.9	-12.1	2.1	11 708	14.8	326	0.2	0.8	4.6	11 382	67.2	32.8	2.94	2.24
INDIANA	2.5	10.7	10.1	7.9	2 532 319	12.7	196 013	1.3	1.8	8.8	2 336 306	71.4	28.6	2.64	2.24
Anderson	1.4	18.0	41.7	15.2	27 643	4.9	2 369	0.4	2.3	9.2	25 274	63.8	36.2	2.31	2.21
Bloomington	3.0	31.5	35.2	15.3	28 400	28.9	1 932	0.6	2.7	6.3	26 468	35.3	64.7	2.30	1.97
Carmel	17.0	1.6	-44.8	1.0	14 107	46.3	510	0.3	1.5	7.0	13 597	79.1	20.9	2.92	2.03
Columbus	2.7	10.9	2.8	7.7	17 162	27.5	1 177	0.4	2.2	8.6	15 985	64.9	35.1	2.50	2.20
East Chicago	0.8	25.6	52.4	24.5	13 261	-1.7	1 554	0.2	2.2	8.8	11 707	44.6	55.4	2.95	2.59
Elkhart	2.9	12.5	4.2	10.3	21 688	13.3	1 616	0.4	2.4	8.2	20 072	53.5	46.5	2.64	2.45
Evansville	2.2	14.6	19.7	11.2	57 065	-1.9	4 792	0.4	2.2	8.1	52 273	60.0	40.0	2.38	2.02
Fishers town	NA	NA	NA	NA	15 241	NA	1 197	0.4	2.3	18.8	14 044	77.5	22.5	2.90	1.98
Fort Wayne	1.5	11.5	4.5	8.3	90 915	17.8	7 582	0.3	1.9	10.7	83 333	61.6	38.4	2.57	2.14
Gary	0.7	29.4	44.1	26.4	43 630	-7.3	5 386	0.2	2.5	8.3	38 244	55.8	44.2	2.66	2.68
Goshen	2.2	7.6	16.9	4.9	11 264	18.3	589	0.5	2.0	5.4	10 675	63.6	36.4	2.65	2.55
Greenwood	2.9	6.1	32.6	4.4	16 042	40.7	1 111	0.5	2.3	10.7	14 931	62.5	37.5	2.64	1.93
Hammond	0.9	13.5	45.2	11.8	34 139	0.6	2 113	0.2	1.6	6.4	32 026	63.2	36.8	2.70	2.37
Hobart	2.0	5.1	13.3	3.9	10 299	24.1	444	0.3	1.8	5.8	9 855	80.2	19.8	2.63	2.21
Indianapolis	3.3	12.5	NA	9.7	356 980	10.0	32 638	0.3	2.0	11.0	324 342	58.7	41.3	2.53	2.18
Jeffersonville	1.3	14.9	2.8	11.7	12 402	32.3	759	0.4	1.6	7.7	11 643	62.2	37.8	2.41	2.11
Kokomo	1.1	16.4	45.1	14.2	22 292	9.6	2 019	0.7	2.3	10.3	20 273	61.1	38.9	2.31	2.12
Lafayette	2.3	8.9	-1.1	5.7	25 602	32.9	1 542	0.3	1.6	6.8	24 060	52.9	47.1	2.45	2.16
Lawrence	1.2	7.4	0.0	5.9	16 292	40.2	1 439	0.4	3.4	15.3	14 853	75.8	24.2	2.68	2.37
Marion	1.3	18.9	39.0	15.4	13 820	-1.3	1 358	0.2	2.4	10.6	12 462	62.1	37.9	2.42	2.11
Merrillville	2.6	3.6	12.5	2.9	12 303	19.2	625	0.3	1.9	8.3	11 678	70.6	29.4	2.79	2.03

1. Includes units rented or sold but not occupied.   2. Specified owner-occupied units.   3. Specified renter-occupied units.   4. Overcrowded or lacking complete plumbing facilities.

Table D. Cities — **Labor Force, Employment, Disability, and Construction**

City	Civilian labor force, 2001		Unemployment		Civilian employment, 1990[2]	Percent		Disability 1990	Value of residential construction authorized by building permits, 2000		
	Total	Percent change, 2000–2001	Total	Rate[1]	Total	Professional, managerial, and technical	Precision production, craft, and repair	Work disabled persons[3] (percent)	New construction ($1,000)	Number of housing units	Percent single family
	61	62	63	64	65	66	67	68	69	70	71
ILLINOIS—Cont'd											
Freeport	12 749	-1.5	1 218	9.6	11 926	23.0	13.4	7.9	8 152	71	15.5
Galesburg	16 275	-1.6	940	5.8	14 086	25.9	11.1	10.0	3 170	30	100.0
Glendale Heights	19 058	-0.3	988	5.2	16 336	30.6	11.5	2.8	16 564	194	100.0
Glen Ellyn	15 460	-0.4	707	4.6	13 394	47.1	6.7	3.7	17 887	69	100.0
Glenview	22 202	-0.8	824	3.7	18 805	47.8	5.8	3.4	51 120	229	83.0
Granite City	14 952	-1.0	1 256	8.4	14 010	22.3	11.7	12.3	1 366	19	78.9
Gurnee	16 097	-1.0	597	3.7	7 955	46.7	8.0	3.4	27 754	159	94.3
Hanover Park	21 674	-0.5	1 206	5.6	18 209	25.7	12.4	4.9	120	1	100.0
Harvey	12 464	-1.4	1 249	10.0	11 187	20.1	10.7	11.6	460	6	100.0
Highland Park	17 150	-1.5	412	2.4	16 059	52.2	4.0	2.9	20 630	64	84.4
Hoffman Estates	29 814	-0.4	1 259	4.2	26 782	36.7	9.4	3.8	4 803	39	100.0
Joliet	46 004	-0.5	3 628	7.9	32 754	24.2	12.3	7.1	142 359	1 538	99.0
Kankakee	11 935	-0.4	1 133	9.5	10 322	27.8	8.7	11.9	935	11	100.0
Lansing	15 803	-1.3	680	4.3	14 507	28.0	15.7	5.3	1 255	6	100.0
Lombard	25 605	-1.0	1 047	4.1	21 895	37.5	11.0	3.6	8 178	120	31.7
Maywood	12 784	-0.6	1 178	9.2	11 957	21.2	6.8	9.8	2 198	23	4.3
Moline	21 999	-2.6	1 115	5.1	19 779	30.8	9.7	7.5	8 219	45	82.2
Mount Prospect	32 877	-0.7	1 282	3.9	30 621	36.2	9.5	4.4	2 980	16	50.0
Mundelein	17 406	-1.1	889	5.1	11 905	34.4	10.0	4.7	12 703	111	100.0
Naperville	69 977	-0.7	2 623	3.7	45 705	51.4	5.4	2.3	187 739	1 129	98.1
Niles	16 169	-1.1	629	3.9	14 316	29.8	11.3	4.0	1 624	9	100.0
Normal	28 903	-0.5	591	2.0	21 262	32.9	5.2	2.9	14 539	292	47.9
Northbrook	18 314	-1.2	551	3.0	16 669	51.4	3.9	3.4	31 119	94	100.0
North Chicago	8 967	-1.4	900	10.0	7 688	21.8	9.2	9.0	3 435	46	84.8
Oak Forest	16 785	-1.3	685	4.1	14 282	29.6	14.3	5.0	7 017	75	68.0
Oak Lawn	30 410	-1.4	1 158	3.8	27 689	29.1	13.2	5.9	8 832	96	70.8
Oak Park	33 038	-1.2	1 192	3.6	31 041	54.1	4.5	3.9	1 199	6	100.0
Orland Park	28 092	-1.1	1 025	3.6	18 330	38.2	10.0	4.0	85 764	465	76.8
Palatine	33 846	-0.5	1 724	5.1	22 917	40.7	7.4	3.6	35 069	245	85.3
Park Ridge	20 755	-1.1	638	3.1	18 781	45.6	7.1	3.8	21 674	68	100.0
Pekin	16 938	-1.1	1 057	6.2	13 941	25.1	11.9	8.0	7 012	56	100.0
Peoria	56 188	-1.3	3 101	5.5	49 082	35.1	7.2	9.0	59 787	689	58.2
Quincy	21 254	-1.2	1 156	5.4	17 362	27.1	10.0	9.2	12 333	99	65.7
Rockford	76 479	-1.5	6 505	8.5	65 168	28.3	11.6	8.5	20 679	301	70.4
Rock Island	18 220	-2.7	972	5.3	17 063	26.1	9.3	9.5	2 311	17	100.0
Round Lake Beach	12 740	-0.6	888	7.0	8 098	17.7	16.8	5.3	21 364	299	66.9
St. Charles	16 371	-0.3	846	5.2	12 200	40.4	9.9	4.2	60 394	441	97.7
Schaumburg	49 231	-0.6	1 935	3.9	42 148	37.7	8.1	3.7	720	3	100.0
Skokie	32 338	-0.7	1 258	3.9	30 818	41.6	7.2	4.7	10 130	41	26.8
Springfield	61 537	-1.1	2 891	4.7	53 528	37.6	7.1	7.7	52 629	486	69.1
Streamwood	22 234	-0.7	1 117	5.0	17 889	28.5	13.5	5.0	36 913	334	100.0
Tinley Park	26 014	-1.2	970	3.7	18 592	30.9	15.2	4.2	90 148	665	86.8
Urbana	21 381	-0.3	633	3.0	18 293	50.5	4.6	4.1	16 950	245	20.0
Waukegan	40 607	-1.3	3 031	7.5	33 556	24.4	12.0	7.6	27 979	373	43.4
Wheaton	31 962	-1.0	989	3.1	27 643	49.2	5.7	3.8	13 335	57	100.0
Wheeling	19 795	-0.4	953	4.8	18 200	33.9	9.4	4.0	20 753	182	44.5
Wilmette	13 723	-1.3	333	2.4	13 257	58.9	3.6	3.6	14 476	37	100.0
Woodridge	18 930	-1.0	726	3.8	15 715	39.6	9.6	3.9	25 919	164	100.0
INDIANA	3 106 388	0.7	135 891	4.4	2 628 695	25.6	12.9	7.9	4 414 439	37 903	80.2
Anderson	30 393	2.5	1 760	5.8	26 407	20.9	12.2	10.9	13 873	136	88.2
Bloomington	32 036	1.4	1 226	3.8	27 232	42.8	4.4	4.3	NA	NA	NA
Carmel	23 430	1.3	402	1.7	13 477	46.7	4.7	3.5	253 702	1 303	67.2
Columbus	18 658	-1.4	779	4.2	15 417	32.7	10.7	9.2	NA	NA	NA
East Chicago	12 878	0.7	1 199	9.3	11 490	16.9	11.7	10.7	1 336	16	100.0
Elkhart	26 265	-1.6	1 899	7.2	21 893	20.0	14.8	10.1	8 925	104	59.6
Evansville	68 486	1.5	2 813	4.1	58 474	25.8	10.3	8.8	10 952	159	84.9
Fishers town	17 269	1.0	135	0.8	NA	NA	NA	NA	170 860	1 254	100.0
Fort Wayne	97 941	0.4	5 616	5.7	85 039	26.8	10.9	8.9	20 304	227	58.6
Gary	45 241	1.0	4 974	11.0	39 616	21.3	9.6	12.8	634	6	100.0
Goshen	14 380	-2.7	718	5.0	12 275	23.8	11.2	7.2	17 408	185	68.6
Greenwood	20 464	1.1	356	1.7	14 531	30.8	13.0	5.4	68 171	598	97.7
Hammond	38 553	0.1	2 203	5.7	35 762	20.0	15.0	9.3	1 611	12	100.0
Hobart	10 945	-0.3	335	3.1	10 438	25.7	15.5	7.3	30 418	317	50.8
Indianapolis	426 632	1.7	16 646	3.9	372 602	31.1	9.8	8.2	557 812	4 787	73.8
Jeffersonville	13 123	0.7	561	4.3	10 291	24.9	10.2	12.0	23 390	229	86.0
Kokomo	22 375	0.8	1 724	7.7	19 652	24.0	14.6	10.8	26 958	220	90.0
Lafayette	26 456	1.1	813	3.1	22 767	28.5	11.1	7.9	36 700	583	44.9
Lawrence	15 616	1.6	545	3.5	13 697	27.9	12.9	6.1	54 111	402	100.0
Marion	13 391	2.0	1 270	9.5	13 607	21.1	13.8	12.8	NA	NA	NA
Merrillville	13 943	-0.4	364	2.6	13 359	25.7	14.8	6.6	9 696	120	43.3

1. Percent of civilian labor force.   2. Persons 16 years and older.   3. Persons 16 to 64 years old.

Table D. Cities — **Wholesale Trade, Retail Trade, and Real Estate**

City	Wholesale Trade, 1997				Retail Trade[1], 1997				Real Estate and Rental and Leasing, 1997			
	Number of Establishments	Number of Employees	Sales (mil dol)	Annual Payroll (mil dol)	Number of Establishments	Number of Employees	Sales (mil dol)	Annual Payroll (mil dol)	Number of Establishments	Number of Employees	Receipts (mil dol)	Annual Payroll (mil dol)
	72	73	74	75	76	77	78	79	80	81	82	83
ILLINOIS—Cont'd												
Freeport	25	230	80.1	5.6	135	2 155	346.3	34.9	23	97	9.0	1.5
Galesburg	42	527	210.5	14.5	198	3 304	409.3	45.9	35	148	11.0	1.8
Glendale Heights	79	2 417	1 337.5	96.7	63	1 390	332.8	29.7	8	82	16.1	1.4
Glen Ellyn	72	220	364.7	15.2	113	1 498	257.7	29.2	44	184	26.2	4.2
Glenview	146	1 753	866.8	77.3	166	1 909	515.6	45.4	54	178	29.7	4.4
Granite City	36	578	859.5	19.2	110	1 456	250.2	22.7	31	186	14.6	3.5
Gurnee	66	1 036	477.9	43.6	227	4 329	640.4	60.8	23	284	58.5	6.9
Hanover Park	26	558	333.7	26.0	76	1 094	157.6	18.5	15	71	13.3	1.1
Harvey	30	659	277.7	26.5	66	777	141.1	15.8	10	38	3.4	0.7
Highland Park	106	410	1 106.1	22.0	180	2 419	570.5	52.4	58	125	27.0	4.0
Hoffman Estates	107	1 094	1 790.1	67.9	104	1 657	332.8	36.7	35	158	24.1	3.1
Joliet	90	952	216.2	28.9	405	7 042	1 281.5	119.9	74	304	34.9	5.4
Kankakee	40	403	205.9	13.6	115	1 289	212.3	24.5	27	163	16.3	2.8
Lansing	43	589	310.3	23.1	158	3 073	472.9	48.1	42	163	17.5	3.0
Lombard	180	3 003	3 228.9	137.2	282	5 138	858.2	91.3	63	703	75.2	24.6
Maywood	10	68	21.3	1.7	45	332	90.3	7.0	9	41	5.5	1.1
Moline	73	1 072	766.8	43.6	325	5 164	805.5	81.6	61	370	52.8	9.1
Mount Prospect	136	2 164	3 162.7	109.9	232	4 285	573.1	66.2	46	224	31.0	5.2
Mundelein	82	755	269.5	31.3	135	1 762	292.0	32.3	16	435	19.9	4.8
Naperville	310	3 398	12 942.4	192.8	396	7 212	1 506.7	143.3	139	606	105.6	16.2
Niles	95	2 178	661.9	72.5	234	5 190	1 147.9	91.2	32	254	31.5	5.8
Normal	35	D	D	D	152	2 843	398.2	39.8	40	336	48.9	7.9
Northbrook	375	4 107	3 172.5	190.8	269	4 258	723.0	86.2	126	659	144.6	25.6
North Chicago	22	777	269.7	37.9	37	343	69.2	11.3	12	D	D	D
Oak Forest	31	323	173.7	12.4	58	549	155.3	14.3	21	86	6.9	2.2
Oak Lawn	39	139	71.2	3.9	239	4 298	1 039.9	92.0	60	271	29.5	4.5
Oak Park	57	242	146.1	9.4	181	1 624	240.0	26.7	59	383	40.5	7.3
Orland Park	73	476	150.1	16.4	374	7 389	1 244.9	117.8	64	253	57.9	6.5
Palatine	167	799	689.3	36.4	217	2 943	554.5	54.6	75	439	67.8	9.7
Park Ridge	108	457	605.4	18.1	117	1 432	305.0	29.0	54	318	59.0	9.3
Pekin	28	D	D	D	152	2 429	463.8	41.5	23	134	12.7	3.0
Peoria	231	3 831	5 321.3	138.6	566	9 434	1 501.0	149.3	154	753	92.9	16.8
Quincy	82	1 175	403.4	34.0	275	4 308	607.1	62.0	50	209	17.0	2.7
Rockford	320	4 838	1 812.5	167.6	679	11 718	1 875.3	185.9	150	806	104.7	18.1
Rock Island	80	1 728	543.6	53.9	128	1 365	201.1	20.0	41	185	17.1	3.1
Round Lake Beach	6	D	D	D	62	1 422	224.9	21.3	8	27	5.2	0.6
St. Charles	120	1 554	1 329.1	64.4	239	3 595	577.3	59.4	40	230	27.2	3.6
Schaumburg	431	9 640	12 007.5	536.1	523	12 331	2 262.6	227.5	132	1 130	299.0	39.4
Skokie	234	3 921	6 222.6	230.0	413	7 088	981.6	118.7	116	756	351.9	46.4
Springfield	162	2 370	963.3	80.0	618	9 812	1 634.3	154.7	145	624	69.8	11.3
Streamwood	32	184	93.9	7.3	64	891	163.7	12.4	13	107	3.5	1.0
Tinley Park	41	350	172.7	12.9	130	2 456	494.0	44.1	23	129	9.7	2.0
Urbana	32	D	D	D	109	1 836	287.3	30.4	36	138	48.3	4.1
Waukegan	73	2 423	1 016.1	94.6	288	4 373	735.2	78.2	61	335	47.8	8.0
Wheaton	115	369	408.2	15.1	217	2 919	513.3	51.7	59	253	40.1	6.7
Wheeling	203	3 111	1 473.3	134.3	101	1 707	366.7	31.7	36	307	41.6	13.2
Wilmette	47	134	214.6	6.8	133	1 571	241.0	27.0	56	242	31.7	6.4
Woodridge	33	1 109	536.7	41.0	64	1 308	203.3	19.3	30	160	20.6	3.1
INDIANA	8 896	112 705	66 350.1	3 737.8	24 954	337 867	57 241.6	5 273.8	5 427	28 948	3 269.1	572.6
Anderson	60	885	247.7	23.1	346	5 079	833.0	77.0	68	307	23.2	5.0
Bloomington	72	868	284.5	26.7	443	6 424	1 010.6	91.4	140	822	75.7	14.2
Carmel	175	1 670	2 788.6	90.4	184	3 663	720.9	69.9	74	519	82.6	13.8
Columbus	81	698	588.1	22.4	286	3 941	566.8	55.6	50	228	30.5	4.8
East Chicago	60	1 115	953.8	39.0	60	610	83.6	10.6	14	128	21.2	4.0
Elkhart	168	2 457	1 147.6	80.3	330	5 168	920.2	82.5	89	371	42.5	7.0
Evansville	296	4 051	1 480.3	123.3	870	13 655	2 092.6	211.3	198	1 327	148.7	23.5
Fishers town	NA	NA	NA	NA	NA	NA	NA	NA	NA	NA	NA	NA
Fort Wayne	531	8 532	4 041.7	281.3	1 058	17 653	2 859.6	283.0	238	1 582	193.2	35.5
Gary	65	1 480	534.5	52.1	218	2 361	359.8	30.8	62	272	32.2	4.5
Goshen	29	D	D	D	171	2 885	494.2	47.7	36	190	15.6	3.1
Greenwood	61	501	552.5	19.7	258	4 847	728.5	70.1	46	208	26.9	3.8
Hammond	95	1 366	961.1	44.5	251	3 388	556.3	52.0	62	553	77.2	17.6
Hobart	23	223	150.2	10.1	136	2 254	397.6	36.3	25	113	14.5	2.3
Indianapolis	1 863	D	D	D	3 405	56 872	10 305.6	990.4	1 048	D	D	D
Jeffersonville	59	831	430.2	23.0	108	1 608	264.4	24.7	46	206	34.0	2.7
Kokomo	73	601	553.3	22.3	346	5 564	878.7	81.5	73	281	35.3	5.2
Lafayette	83	1 027	218.2	26.3	410	6 608	1 060.4	100.8	87	411	45.4	7.0
Lawrence	34	346	110.7	11.0	116	1 418	241.4	25.6	33	149	12.6	2.7
Marion	43	431	118.8	13.4	233	3 131	524.9	46.2	39	154	11.4	2.2
Merrillville	63	681	284.0	24.3	308	5 485	965.6	87.5	60	302	26.7	4.6

1. Establishments with payroll.

City	Professional, Scientific, and Technical Services, 1997[1]				Manufacturing, 1997				Accommodation and Foodservices, 1997			
	Number of Establishments	Number of Employees	Receipts (mil dol)	Annual Payroll (mil dol)	Number of Establishments	Number of Employees	Receipts (mil dol)	Annual Payroll (mil dol)	Number of Establishments	Number of Employees	Sales (mil dol)	Annual Payroll (mil dol)
	84	85	86	87	88	89	90	91	92	93	94	95
ILLINOIS—Cont'd												
Freeport	49	223	16.3	6.5	40	7 645	1 058.2	280.7	78	1 108	31.4	7.5
Galesburg	47	257	19.3	7.0	48	D	D	D	104	D	D	D
Glendale Heights	41	176	23.8	6.6	48	2 304	327.2	87.7	43	D	D	D
Glen Ellyn	172	1 037	90.5	37.8	NA	NA	NA	NA	52	847	40.9	7.9
Glenview	214	523	82.3	23.8	68	1 481	222.9	54.2	104	1 842	76.3	21.7
Granite City	45	278	33.1	15.8	28	5 632	1 857.1	234.5	72	937	28.6	7.5
Gurnee	101	610	73.3	23.9	63	2 769	517.6	96.5	91	2 322	92.7	23.6
Hanover Park	30	79	6.3	2.9	NA	NA	NA	NA	47	626	23.3	6.0
Harvey	9	57	7.2	2.8	48	2 361	699.2	110.4	38	504	13.7	3.6
Highland Park	226	576	83.5	26.3	44	D	D	D	71	968	41.6	10.9
Hoffman Estates	160	1 676	268.0	89.1	23	971	191.2	45.6	83	1 653	72.1	18.4
Joliet	172	1 047	93.5	40.7	104	7 268	3 814.8	323.6	191	3 300	107.9	28.1
Kankakee	67	305	20.8	8.2	32	2 502	673.5	96.0	69	900	26.5	7.2
Lansing	56	220	35.3	8.8	34	870	171.4	29.7	75	1 331	46.3	12.5
Lombard	212	1 630	192.4	85.6	102	1 718	246.3	62.2	95	2 231	87.6	24.3
Maywood	8	52	4.2	1.6	28	603	74.0	19.1	33	363	19.3	4.7
Moline	91	576	43.1	18.6	61	2 150	500.4	89.7	163	3 304	90.5	25.7
Mount Prospect	181	849	95.0	29.3	46	3 457	553.4	134.8	101	D	D	D
Mundelein	79	438	64.7	23.0	92	3 691	553.3	124.5	61	D	D	D
Naperville	588	3 513	404.3	173.6	84	2 334	348.9	80.4	233	4 972	184.8	53.0
Niles	97	745	50.2	23.1	102	6 376	1 023.3	242.4	102	1 774	59.9	16.4
Normal	30	172	5.8	2.3	19	D	D	D	93	2 250	60.2	16.8
Northbrook	569	7 553	695.5	379.1	123	4 672	840.3	161.1	112	1 602	75.1	21.1
North Chicago	19	135	14.7	6.2	28	1 606	356.6	51.7	56	934	31.3	8.9
Oak Forest	46	188	13.6	5.1	22	519	85.7	16.1	36	532	16.1	4.5
Oak Lawn	110	271	23.9	8.2	31	527	57.1	17.5	96	2 205	74.4	20.2
Oak Park	226	915	88.4	34.4	43	679	82.8	22.3	81	1 458	49.3	14.6
Orland Park	167	632	58.3	19.9	55	2 195	477.7	92.4	127	2 676	98.7	26.2
Palatine	225	1 039	113.0	43.5	76	2 830	453.6	91.9	115	1 887	69.5	17.6
Park Ridge	229	1 517	150.3	64.9	NA	NA	NA	NA	61	755	25.9	6.3
Pekin	55	223	12.8	5.2	28	D	D	D	75	1 319	34.6	10.0
Peoria	299	4 031	337.5	154.2	113	5 666	1 381.6	197.3	344	6 592	203.4	59.1
Quincy	96	442	36.7	11.6	57	2 995	774.0	96.6	117	2 098	62.9	17.5
Rockford	440	4 666	258.8	107.6	477	26 100	4 467.4	998.8	347	6 984	223.7	61.1
Rock Island	101	1 022	69.1	30.6	58	1 927	238.5	47.7	92	1 178	33.6	8.3
Round Lake Beach	12	37	1.4	0.4	NA	NA	NA	NA	28	353	13.2	3.2
St. Charles	146	1 676	120.9	70.1	118	7 053	1 360.7	238.7	104	3 175	98.1	33.5
Schaumburg	457	4 468	592.6	238.8	190	8 709	1 448.1	404.8	210	5 836	239.2	62.7
Skokie	351	2 378	326.6	114.3	212	9 083	1 815.5	310.1	138	2 572	101.0	27.8
Springfield	398	3 008	255.1	108.9	84	2 850	462.9	82.2	373	6 820	209.9	62.0
Streamwood	38	62	5.0	2.0	45	918	148.4	36.8	38	612	24.2	6.3
Tinley Park	83	287	22.7	7.4	33	1 140	197.1	40.2	62	1 037	34.9	9.4
Urbana	61	534	27.1	11.4	33	D	D	D	104	2 038	62.9	18.4
Waukegan	143	1 293	116.9	59.9	95	6 037	986.8	213.6	152	2 101	79.5	19.7
Wheaton	381	1 859	191.9	82.1	34	508	63.1	19.0	84	2 007	62.2	16.6
Wheeling	144	1 022	124.4	45.4	186	10 194	2 306.9	415.8	57	D	D	D
Wilmette	146	258	36.6	15.6	NA	NA	NA	NA	45	D	D	D
Woodridge	49	208	22.9	11.6	16	741	192.6	30.5	25	466	15.3	4.5
INDIANA	9 795	69 393	5 974.2	2 207.5	9 303	625 692	142 270.7	22 121.4	11 705	215 710	6 646.3	1 865.3
Anderson	126	889	49.2	26.2	59	8 999	1 769.1	456.0	160	4 055	116.4	32.8
Bloomington	167	1 285	91.2	31.3	61	5 013	1 751.3	159.4	275	6 020	165.8	45.1
Carmel	235	2 517	251.2	105.1	53	1 304	177.8	44.2	79	1 636	57.7	16.3
Columbus	123	694	50.7	22.3	96	11 647	2 273.1	366.2	110	2 721	88.6	24.6
East Chicago	17	135	14.0	5.5	51	16 068	4 894.2	812.3	57	494	16.0	3.6
Elkhart	136	898	67.3	20.7	349	17 947	3 023.5	554.5	184	3 093	94.5	26.9
Evansville	359	3 237	231.8	89.9	213	15 029	3 446.0	528.1	396	D	D	D
Fishers town	NA	NA	NA	NA	NA	NA	NA	NA	NA	NA	NA	NA
Fort Wayne	505	4 954	412.1	144.6	390	22 830	4 258.9	846.3	506	11 413	350.9	103.0
Gary	46	403	54.8	12.6	62	10 066	3 377.4	511.3	120	1 465	43.7	11.4
Goshen	49	195	15.2	4.2	105	7 397	1 070.8	200.8	66	1 403	41.7	11.4
Greenwood	96	506	31.2	12.3	45	1 013	289.6	36.1	107	2 419	66.4	19.3
Hammond	101	1 364	79.7	30.2	76	4 195	1 468.0	171.4	164	2 024	71.3	17.3
Hobart	28	128	7.3	2.3	NA	NA	NA	NA	55	D	D	D
Indianapolis	2 174	22 189	2 356.5	875.1	1 094	D	D	D	1 751	D	D	D
Jeffersonville	86	316	26.5	7.9	75	3 671	584.0	105.3	66	D	D	D
Kokomo	87	393	30.1	10.1	66	D	D	D	160	3 637	109.6	29.9
Lafayette	134	972	79.1	27.8	71	D	D	D	152	3 092	94.7	27.6
Lawrence	39	146	14.8	4.3	30	626	61.9	19.6	52	802	23.2	6.6
Marion	53	320	14.5	4.9	56	8 037	1 537.0	356.6	92	1 901	54.9	15.3
Merrillville	177	1 609	167.0	56.3	35	641	82.1	17.7	134	3 640	118.2	33.5

1. Firms subject to federal tax.

City	Arts, Entertainment, and Recreation[1], 1997				Health Care and Social Assistance[1], 1997				Other Services[1], 1997			
	Number of Establish-ments	Number of Employees	Receipts (mil dol)	Annual Payroll (mil dol)	Number of Establish-ments	Number of Employees	Receipts (mil dol)	Annual Payroll (mil dol)	Number of Establish-ments	Number of Employees	Receipts (mil dol)	Annual Payroll (mil dol)
	96	97	98	99	100	101	102	103	104	105	106	107
ILLINOIS—Cont'd												
Freeport..............................	3	7	0.5	0.1	58	574	32.9	17.2	58	295	13.5	4.0
Galesburg............................	12	77	3.1	0.5	63	1 119	68.1	25.5	64	330	20.4	5.7
Glendale Heights	7	189	9.5	1.7	25	1 178	52.7	25.9	24	127	11.5	3.9
Glen Ellyn...........................	9	54	2.1	0.8	65	480	30.6	11.5	41	267	14.1	4.7
Glenview..............................	31	206	15.9	7.2	123	1 032	74.8	37.5	101	752	38.0	13.6
Granite City.........................	7	62	3.1	1.1	80	898	61.2	23.6	62	390	20.8	6.9
Gurnee................................	9	0	0.0	0.0	82	696	59.1	27.6	56	405	26.1	7.6
Hanover Park.......................	2	0	0.0	0.0	35	429	25.0	12.4	36	261	14.3	6.9
Harvey.................................	1	0	0.0	0.0	53	819	61.8	34.9	29	278	30.3	11.5
Highland Park......................	15	188	6.0	2.4	158	1 238	97.1	52.1	79	453	30.1	8.9
Hoffman Estates	15	194	10.0	2.8	169	3 590	305.3	121.8	45	277	14.8	4.4
Joliet...................................	16	0	0.0	0.0	232	2 607	225.9	108.3	128	888	59.2	16.9
Kankakee............................	8	102	5.9	1.2	86	777	58.3	28.7	60	361	23.8	7.1
Lansing...............................	9	68	3.9	1.0	39	259	14.2	6.1	78	678	38.4	13.6
Lombard.............................	16	380	49.8	5.0	104	1 475	91.6	38.9	117	1 049	104.5	35.9
Maywood............................	1	0	0.0	0.0	23	121	9.0	3.6	19	86	5.8	1.6
Moline.................................	16	103	6.6	1.2	137	1 515	113.0	54.2	105	681	51.2	13.4
Mount Prospect....................	6	92	5.7	1.4	82	1 053	62.3	24.8	84	365	24.9	6.1
Mundelein...........................	9	72	6.1	1.3	37	291	14.7	6.0	70	586	102.5	24.3
Naperville............................	33	650	22.0	6.9	309	3 625	247.7	100.3	173	1 311	72.4	24.0
Niles...................................	9	98	3.1	0.8	90	1 405	78.5	31.7	70	639	52.5	16.2
Normal................................	2	0	0.0	0.0	52	701	44.0	21.4	51	337	16.3	5.3
Northbrook..........................	25	551	20.2	9.7	168	1 935	133.6	71.2	69	686	47.3	17.4
North Chicago	1	0	0.0	0.0	10	71	5.1	2.8	11	94	4.7	1.8
Oak Forest...........................	4	18	1.2	0.3	49	397	34.8	16.5	43	315	31.8	7.5
Oak Lawn............................	6	77	5.4	1.3	214	2 249	207.2	109.4	111	656	39.3	12.5
Oak Park.............................	19	88	4.6	1.3	219	1 964	144.5	64.3	90	585	40.4	12.6
Orland Park.........................	16	515	18.1	5.6	170	1 408	91.9	39.3	104	833	44.0	14.0
Palatine..............................	26	209	11.5	2.9	103	842	58.5	28.5	127	915	68.7	20.2
Park Ridge..........................	9	88	5.3	2.4	179	1 523	189.6	84.4	73	402	21.0	7.0
Pekin..................................	7	59	1.5	0.5	67	803	45.2	21.4	66	352	18.5	5.4
Peoria.................................	33	690	28.7	9.6	311	4 072	349.3	186.0	202	1 996	146.6	48.0
Quincy................................	16	173	3.7	1.1	106	1 490	93.2	49.4	113	636	36.2	11.6
Rockford.............................	45	429	16.7	4.2	349	4 885	397.9	196.2	293	2 654	165.0	54.3
Rock Island.........................	12	530	24.6	8.1	77	816	46.1	19.7	79	618	33.8	10.0
Round Lake Beach	1	0	0.0	0.0	15	183	9.9	4.5	23	111	6.3	2.0
St. Charles..........................	12	60	5.6	0.8	64	428	31.7	14.7	73	455	26.8	8.4
Schaumburg........................	15	326	16.9	3.4	171	2 134	177.9	67.5	188	1 498	109.8	35.5
Skokie................................	34	266	11.3	2.6	252	3 679	218.6	91.4	172	1 403	81.8	26.3
Springfield...........................	45	553	39.7	7.8	307	7 266	466.0	199.5	248	1 813	112.8	37.3
Streamwood........................	5	93	2.9	0.9	35	399	24.7	8.3	47	241	16.4	4.7
Tinley Park..........................	14	208	29.9	4.2	75	529	31.8	13.0	52	311	17.5	5.7
Urbana................................	6	0	0.0	0.0	32	0	0.0	0.0	48	296	14.8	4.9
Waukegan...........................	18	312	9.5	3.1	124	1 448	93.4	46.1	111	493	33.7	9.7
Wheaton..............................	9	194	8.0	2.7	137	1 520	133.1	50.5	95	551	30.8	10.3
Wheeling.............................	7	29	1.9	0.5	38	342	23.7	8.5	65	545	72.3	14.7
Wilmette..............................	18	21	2.6	0.9	95	467	43.0	20.8	53	400	27.8	9.9
Woodridge...........................	8	249	9.8	3.0	56	404	26.3	11.3	27	148	8.5	2.3
INDIANA...........................	1 500	24 903	1 918.3	516.1	10 236	132 416	8 132.3	3 675.3	9 243	60 711	3 701.4	1 127.8
Anderson............................	21	0	0.0	0.0	158	1 520	91.5	41.3	127	784	43.3	14.2
Bloomington	17	56	7.9	0.7	200	2 054	148.2	69.9	119	725	35.1	11.3
Carmel................................	21	246	11.9	3.5	131	1 520	123.2	53.3	79	552	44.6	13.2
Columbus............................	10	59	2.7	0.5	133	1 519	102.0	54.9	81	574	34.0	12.1
East Chicago	3	0	0.0	0.0	28	253	11.6	5.2	40	492	41.3	15.8
Elkhart................................	14	140	4.3	1.5	114	1 500	106.4	41.7	145	1 163	69.1	20.6
Evansville............................	43	1 804	140.5	31.4	368	7 358	475.3	227.9	304	2 787	161.4	51.7
Fishers town........................	NA	NA	NA	NA	NA	NA	NA	NA	NA	NA	NA	NA
Fort Wayne..........................	58	674	28.1	8.8	434	7 242	424.5	191.2	447	3 741	237.4	74.6
Gary....................................	9	0	0.0	0.0	127	1 160	71.5	31.8	78	558	31.0	9.7
Goshen...............................	7	41	2.2	0.6	59	709	36.5	15.4	65	524	37.7	10.0
Greenwood..........................	18	229	9.5	2.4	83	1 232	76.2	31.9	85	681	39.9	14.4
Hammond............................	10	0	0.0	0.0	69	558	44.4	17.7	120	937	54.0	19.1
Hobart.................................	9	106	2.9	0.9	44	597	34.7	13.6	48	427	26.5	9.6
Indianapolis........................	230	4 451	428.7	175.8	1 752	26 194	1 802.7	829.6	1 320	11 727	702.1	221.8
Jeffersonville	8	35	2.1	0.6	98	1 475	88.9	38.9	53	485	28.4	10.0
Kokomo..............................	21	279	8.6	2.6	150	1 761	110.3	50.7	107	849	37.6	12.3
Lafayette.............................	13	220	5.8	1.7	129	2 390	188.5	94.0	146	1 118	78.2	22.4
Lawrence............................	10	0	0.0	0.0	30	0	0.0	0.0	48	256	15.0	4.6
Marion................................	8	73	3.0	0.6	96	1 531	67.5	33.1	67	335	15.5	4.8
Merrillville...........................	13	313	12.9	3.6	251	2 761	197.2	95.3	91	654	43.8	15.0

1. Firms subject to federal tax.

Table D. Cities — Federal Funds and City Government Finances

City	Selected federal funds, fiscal 2001[1] (mil dol)									City government finances, 1999						
	Procurement contracts		Grants					Direct payments for individuals		Intergovernmental			Taxes			
														Per capita[3] (dollars)		
	Defense	Other	Total[2]	Health and family welfare	Energy and environment	Education	Housing and community development	Educational assistance	Housing assistance	Total (mil dol)	Total (mil dol)	Percent from state government	Total (mil dol)	Total	Property	Sales and gross receipts
	108	109	110	111	112	113	114	115	116	117	118	119	120	121	122	123
ILLINOIS—Cont'd																
Freeport	0.5	0.0	2.8	1.0	0.3	1.1	0.0	1.3	1.9	NA	NA	NA	NA	NA	NA	NA
Galesburg	0.0	0.2	1.9	0.0	0.0	1.7	0.0	3.0	3.5	25.2	9.3	95.6	8.0	244	130	109
Glendale Heights	0.5	0.4	2.7	2.7	0.0	0.0	0.0	0.0	2.6	20.9	6.5	100.0	7.6	252	140	97
Glen Ellyn	0.0	0.3	0.0	0.0	0.0	0.0	0.0	2.9	1.7	NA	NA	NA	NA	NA	NA	NA
Glenview	0.4	1.2	0.1	0.0	0.0	0.1	0.0	0.0	0.6	37.1	12.6	74.5	13.8	346	195	118
Granite City	4.0	0.0	0.3	0.0	0.0	0.2	0.0	0.1	1.9	NA	NA	NA	NA	NA	NA	NA
Gurnee	0.3	0.2	0.0	0.0	0.0	0.0	0.0	0.0	2.0	23.6	14.2	89.2	4.8	190	65	69
Hanover Park	0.0	0.0	0.0	0.0	0.0	0.0	0.0	0.0	0.0	NA	NA	NA	NA	NA	NA	NA
Harvey	0.1	0.2	1.4	0.4	0.1	0.6	0.0	0.0	1.0	14.0	1.9	100.0	10.3	359	274	85
Highland Park	1.3	0.4	0.2	0.0	0.0	0.2	0.0	0.0	1.8	44.3	9.9	99.3	21.6	691	420	190
Hoffman Estates	0.3	0.4	0.4	0.4	0.0	0.0	0.0	1.4	0.3	64.0	10.0	100.0	43.8	904	834	56
Joliet	0.8	0.1	11.1	4.9	0.0	0.5	3.6	2.7	13.1	99.4	45.0	91.9	31.4	340	120	190
Kankakee	0.0	0.3	5.5	2.0	0.0	1.3	0.9	2.9	6.7	36.0	8.9	75.1	9.5	358	208	120
Lansing	0.0	0.0	0.0	0.0	0.0	0.0	0.0	0.0	0.5	26.8	17.6	100.0	4.7	166	84	66
Lombard	11.3	0.6	1.4	0.0	0.6	0.0	0.1	1.4	1.9	36.1	15.6	96.6	11.8	279	112	149
Maywood	0.5	0.0	15.3	13.2	0.3	1.4	0.0	0.0	6.6	NA	NA	NA	NA	NA	NA	NA
Moline	16.2	1.4	6.5	0.0	0.0	1.1	1.0	4.3	6.7	38.1	12.3	90.9	15.1	360	227	99
Mount Prospect	0.8	1.2	0.2	0.0	0.1	0.0	0.1	0.1	6.6	37.6	14.6	98.5	18.5	344	193	102
Mundelein	0.0	4.6	0.8	0.5	0.0	0.2	0.0	0.0	1.1	NA	NA	NA	NA	NA	NA	NA
Naperville	3.8	1.0	1.7	0.1	0.8	0.0	0.2	1.0	2.9	107.6	34.4	95.3	43.8	374	226	133
Niles	0.0	1.3	0.6	0.4	0.0	0.0	0.0	0.1	0.2	NA	NA	NA	NA	NA	NA	NA
Normal	0.0	0.0	7.7	0.8	0.0	3.2	0.5	11.4	1.9	32.4	11.3	93.2	12.5	283	100	160
Northbrook	1.6	1.2	1.2	0.1	0.0	0.1	0.0	0.0	1.1	33.3	12.7	90.3	13.4	405	302	32
North Chicago	2.3	14.7	15.6	5.7	0.0	9.5	0.3	0.1	14.7	NA	NA	NA	NA	NA	NA	NA
Oak Forest	0.0	0.0	0.0	0.0	0.0	0.0	0.0	0.3	0.0	11.9	5.3	98.8	4.1	148	119	19
Oak Lawn	0.0	0.1	0.3	0.0	0.0	0.0	0.3	1.9	0.0	40.6	15.3	98.0	12.7	220	159	36
Oak Park	0.0	0.0	4.4	1.4	0.0	0.0	2.9	0.0	7.8	45.9	11.8	80.6	23.1	456	320	105
Orland Park	0.3	0.1	0.3	0.0	0.0	0.2	0.0	0.1	0.0	35.5	17.7	100.0	6.2	129	76	18
Palatine	0.0	0.9	1.4	0.2	0.0	0.3	0.2	2.0	4.5	29.9	9.1	95.7	12.5	275	178	58
Park Ridge	0.0	0.2	0.1	0.0	0.0	0.0	0.0	0.0	0.0	26.9	7.6	93.1	16.8	449	268	121
Pekin	0.1	0.9	2.4	0.0	0.0	1.2	0.2	0.0	6.7	27.3	10.7	93.0	7.7	242	146	90
Peoria	17.8	2.5	30.7	3.7	6.8	0.9	3.2	6.6	51.0	108.9	47.4	92.8	40.3	363	111	240
Quincy	2.3	7.2	2.2	0.5	0.0	0.5	0.0	3.7	1.9	28.6	14.4	95.3	6.7	168	114	44
Rockford	56.5	9.4	26.5	5.5	0.0	5.7	4.5	3.9	23.6	123.3	61.1	82.1	45.2	315	248	44
Rock Island	12.5	0.6	6.8	2.6	0.0	0.3	1.4	1.4	11.6	45.0	13.4	85.5	11.7	301	229	59
Round Lake Beach	0.0	0.0	0.0	0.0	0.0	0.0	0.0	0.0	2.4	NA	NA	NA	NA	NA	NA	NA
St. Charles	0.7	0.0	0.5	0.0	0.3	0.0	0.0	0.0	1.0	31.5	11.3	90.8	8.6	324	149	153
Schaumburg	3.6	1.3	5.4	0.0	0.0	0.1	0.5	0.0	1.9	78.6	45.5	98.8	20.5	275	6	235
Skokie	5.4	11.2	0.7	0.0	0.0	0.0	0.0	0.7	1.5	58.4	21.1	96.3	32.4	553	375	149
Springfield	18.7	6.6	1 570.5	820.3	162.9	319.7	2.4	4.1	29.3	119.6	38.5	98.6	33.0	282	116	159
Streamwood	0.0	0.0	0.0	0.0	0.0	0.0	0.0	0.0	0.0	18.3	6.1	96.3	9.5	271	148	80
Tinley Park	0.0	0.1	0.0	0.0	0.0	0.0	0.0	0.0	0.7	27.2	12.5	90.8	9.7	212	159	16
Urbana	2.2	0.4	48.8	4.2	0.8	7.4	1.4	15.0	3.7	29.8	11.3	74.7	11.3	325	158	147
Waukegan	6.4	2.4	12.3	5.7	0.1	1.4	4.3	0.3	16.5	52.0	21.2	87.8	21.1	278	145	102
Wheaton	0.0	0.1	5.3	0.0	0.0	0.0	0.0	3.5	7.5	NA	NA	NA	NA	NA	NA	NA
Wheeling	4.0	0.1	0.3	0.1	0.0	0.0	0.0	0.0	0.7	22.9	8.1	95.0	9.6	313	193	111
Wilmette	1.0	0.4	0.3	0.0	0.0	0.0	0.2	0.0	0.8	22.3	5.9	100.0	11.7	447	302	111
Woodridge	0.0	0.2	0.0	0.0	0.0	0.0	0.0	0.0	0.5	15.3	6.5	92.5	4.7	161	66	64
INDIANA	1 749.7	984.6	5 849.6	3 674.6	111.0	525.2	102.7	325.7	599.9	X	X	X	X	X	X	X
Anderson	1.1	0.0	3.7	0.5	0.0	0.0	2.2	1.7	12.4	50.9	12.3	66.7	24.4	417	305	9
Bloomington	1.0	7.8	163.6	111.3	5.4	7.1	1.4	13.1	15.1	49.1	13.0	69.8	19.0	292	213	0
Carmel	0.6	0.5	1.2	1.0	0.0	0.0	0.0	0.0	0.0	30.7	5.4	62.4	17.2	409	154	0
Columbus	5.6	0.1	16.0	2.1	12.8	0.1	0.0	0.1	7.9	35.4	11.7	45.4	12.8	396	387	0
East Chicago	0.1	0.0	3.5	1.0	0.0	0.0	2.4	0.0	15.8	58.1	19.1	46.2	26.2	849	841	0
Elkhart	1.9	2.0	2.4	0.0	0.0	0.5	0.8	0.0	10.7	46.4	19.5	47.5	19.2	439	376	0
Evansville	53.0	4.0	14.8	3.3	1.9	0.7	3.5	6.9	19.6	134.1	37.7	74.0	39.8	324	234	0
Fishers town	0.0	0.2	0.0	0.0	0.0	0.0	0.0	0.4	0.0	NA	NA	NA	NA	NA	NA	NA
Fort Wayne	317.4	49.1	19.5	5.4	0.0	1.9	4.2	8.5	27.9	128.2	33.0	66.7	47.7	257	196	0
Gary	1.4	0.1	14.1	1.0	0.0	0.7	4.5	4.7	28.4	152.9	57.8	80.5	57.0	525	512	0
Goshen	1.1	0.0	1.6	0.0	0.0	0.0	0.9	0.8	4.1	17.3	4.7	58.6	6.1	240	205	0
Greenwood	0.0	0.0	0.6	0.0	0.0	0.0	0.0	0.1	4.6	NA	NA	NA	NA	NA	NA	NA
Hammond	2.3	0.6	6.4	0.2	0.0	1.7	2.9	4.5	8.3	110.4	46.7	85.1	29.9	382	366	0
Hobart	0.0	0.0	0.0	0.0	0.0	0.0	0.0	0.2	0.1	16.2	4.3	89.6	7.5	303	281	0
Indianapolis	854.6	122.4	941.8	333.1	74.4	171.7	63.4	209.0	136.8	1 396.9	300.0	83.6	613.9	828	660	48
Jeffersonville	0.7	2.8	1.8	1.1	0.0	0.3	0.0	0.1	9.0	NA	NA	NA	NA	NA	NA	NA
Kokomo	0.1	0.3	3.4	1.9	0.1	0.0	1.2	0.9	8.2	45.1	10.8	61.0	22.0	488	369	0
Lafayette	0.0	0.9	18.5	3.4	2.9	0.0	1.5	0.4	20.6	36.6	6.8	76.3	18.2	408	256	0
Lawrence	0.4	2.3	0.0	0.0	0.0	0.0	0.0	0.0	0.0	NA	NA	NA	NA	NA	NA	NA
Marion	0.0	5.2	2.1	1.3	0.0	0.5	0.0	2.9	11.1	25.2	4.8	79.7	12.8	445	271	0
Merrillville	0.0	0.9	0.4	0.0	0.0	0.3	0.0	0.4	0.5	10.9	3.1	89.9	5.5	180	161	0

1. October 1, 2000 to September 30, 2001. 2. Includes program categories not shown separately. State totals include additional categories not allocated by city. 3. Based on population estimated as of July 1 of the year shown.

Table D. Cities — **City Government Finances**

City	City government finances, 1999 (cont'd)												
	General expenditure												
	Per capita[1] (dollars)			Percent of total for —									
	Total (mil dol)	Total	Capital outlays	Public welfare	Highways	Parking facilities	Education	Health and hospitals	Police protection	Sewerage and sanitation	Parks and recreation	Housing and community development	Interest on debt
	124	125	126	127	128	129	130	131	132	133	134	135	136
ILLINOIS—Cont'd													
Freeport	NA	NA	NA	NA	NA	NA	NA	NA	NA	NA	NA	NA	NA
Galesburg	23.1	705	70	0.0	17.5	0.0	0.0	0.0	16.1	4.4	9.1	0.0	10.0
Glendale Heights	18.4	608	5	0.0	12.8	0.0	0.0	0.0	24.0	9.6	14.3	0.0	6.5
Glen Ellyn	NA	NA	NA	NA	NA	NA	NA	NA	NA	NA	NA	NA	NA
Glenview	50.1	1 256	486	0.0	3.7	0.3	0.0	0.4	12.6	3.3	0.0	0.0	6.3
Granite City	NA	NA	NA	NA	NA	NA	NA	NA	NA	NA	NA	NA	NA
Gurnee	21.8	872	217	0.0	17.1	0.0	0.0	0.0	25.4	4.5	0.2	0.0	1.1
Hanover Park	NA	NA	NA	NA	NA	NA	NA	NA	NA	NA	NA	NA	NA
Harvey	13.6	473	0	0.0	7.0	1.8	0.0	0.0	31.6	13.3	0.0	0.0	2.3
Highland Park	39.7	1 269	153	0.0	14.0	1.6	0.0	0.0	15.8	1.5	9.8	5.0	3.7
Hoffman Estates	45.5	938	162	0.0	6.6	0.0	0.0	1.0	19.3	3.4	0.5	0.4	26.3
Joliet	95.4	1 034	170	0.0	24.8	0.7	0.0	0.0	21.3	7.7	0.2	2.6	1.4
Kankakee	32.1	1 213	180	0.6	10.3	0.0	0.0	0.1	13.5	21.9	0.1	4.4	9.7
Lansing	22.2	779	124	0.0	11.5	0.0	0.0	0.0	21.9	12.4	0.0	2.2	15.4
Lombard	34.9	827	289	0.0	20.1	0.2	0.0	0.2	17.2	10.0	0.0	0.6	3.7
Maywood	NA	NA	NA	NA	NA	NA	NA	NA	NA	NA	NA	NA	NA
Moline	43.4	1 035	205	0.0	9.4	0.0	0.0	0.0	16.4	11.6	5.3	2.0	4.9
Mount Prospect	36.5	681	119	1.4	15.2	0.5	0.0	0.2	22.5	10.0	0.5	1.4	2.8
Mundelein	NA	NA	NA	NA	NA	NA	NA	NA	NA	NA	NA	NA	NA
Naperville	87.9	751	109	0.0	21.1	0.9	0.0	0.0	19.8	11.5	2.7	0.6	5.0
Niles	NA	NA	NA	NA	NA	NA	NA	NA	NA	NA	NA	NA	NA
Normal	27.8	628	121	0.0	14.0	0.0	0.0	0.0	14.8	5.4	13.3	1.8	6.4
Northbrook	31.2	942	79	0.0	16.4	0.6	0.0	0.0	21.2	5.1	0.0	2.1	2.5
North Chicago	NA	NA	NA	NA	NA	NA	NA	NA	NA	NA	NA	NA	NA
Oak Forest	13.0	468	102	0.0	24.9	2.1	0.0	0.0	27.7	4.3	0.0	0.0	7.5
Oak Lawn	40.2	696	108	0.3	12.6	4.9	0.0	0.0	21.2	7.4	2.6	0.8	2.9
Oak Park	44.6	881	82	0.0	8.2	5.1	0.0	1.8	23.5	7.3	0.0	12.0	3.2
Orland Park	42.5	888	293	0.0	12.9	0.2	0.0	0.0	19.6	11.8	13.0	1.2	1.5
Palatine	28.7	630	9	0.0	9.1	0.5	0.0	0.9	20.5	11.3	0.0	2.8	18.2
Park Ridge	27.3	730	128	0.0	12.6	0.9	0.0	0.5	18.3	13.3	0.6	0.7	1.7
Pekin	24.2	758	125	0.0	8.8	0.1	0.0	0.0	18.5	11.9	0.1	2.4	16.4
Peoria	115.1	1 035	240	0.0	12.1	9.0	0.0	0.0	14.4	4.8	3.7	13.5	5.9
Quincy	27.6	692	12	0.0	10.5	0.1	0.0	0.4	21.2	17.3	0.0	0.1	9.6
Rockford	120.9	842	108	5.6	15.3	0.7	0.0	0.2	22.3	8.5	0.5	6.0	2.5
Rock Island	40.2	1 038	112	0.0	9.9	0.8	0.0	0.0	16.7	8.9	15.2	6.7	5.4
Round Lake Beach	NA	NA	NA	NA	NA	NA	NA	NA	NA	NA	NA	NA	NA
St. Charles	33.0	1 244	253	0.0	21.5	2.7	0.0	7.3	17.6	7.7	0.1	1.7	2.0
Schaumburg	66.9	899	223	0.2	17.9	0.1	0.0	2.9	24.5	2.8	4.2	0.4	2.3
Skokie	51.1	872	137	0.0	9.7	0.2	0.0	1.5	17.1	13.6	3.0	0.9	7.1
Springfield	102.2	873	117	0.0	16.7	1.1	0.0	2.5	19.5	10.3	2.6	5.9	6.8
Streamwood	15.7	450	91	0.0	24.9	0.0	0.0	0.0	32.7	0.0	1.9	1.9	3.8
Tinley Park	20.7	451	77	0.0	17.2	1.9	0.0	0.0	34.2	4.0	0.0	0.0	2.5
Urbana	30.3	869	232	0.4	29.6	1.5	0.0	0.0	16.3	4.8	0.0	9.1	7.2
Waukegan	56.8	747	79	0.0	12.2	0.8	0.0	0.7	25.8	6.4	1.0	2.7	9.4
Wheaton	NA	NA	NA	NA	NA	NA	NA	NA	NA	NA	NA	NA	NA
Wheeling	20.0	653	115	0.8	17.3	0.2	0.0	0.0	29.1	7.8	0.0	4.3	3.2
Wilmette	24.0	916	119	0.0	14.4	0.7	0.0	0.6	19.9	21.5	0.4	4.6	5.4
Woodridge	16.6	565	112	0.0	5.6	0.0	0.0	0.0	29.7	2.1	0.2	0.0	6.4
INDIANA	X	X	X	X	X	X	X	X	X	X	X	X	X
Anderson	50.0	855	62	0.0	5.9	0.4	0.0	1.1	17.0	20.1	7.6	0.0	3.7
Bloomington	54.3	835	173	0.3	9.4	1.8	0.0	5.5	10.3	26.4	9.8	3.7	6.2
Carmel	33.2	788	93	0.0	8.8	0.0	0.0	0.0	19.5	21.0	0.1	0.0	3.3
Columbus	34.4	1 066	194	0.0	7.6	0.3	0.1	1.5	10.8	13.0	21.2	0.4	2.5
East Chicago	70.4	2 280	511	0.0	6.2	0.0	0.0	6.6	11.1	32.3	5.4	7.7	1.0
Elkhart	53.2	1 219	257	0.0	7.1	0.0	0.0	0.2	13.3	19.8	7.4	2.7	2.8
Evansville	121.1	986	230	0.1	3.8	8.1	0.0	2.0	15.5	17.6	8.6	3.7	4.6
Fishers town	NA	NA	NA	NA	NA	NA	NA	NA	NA	NA	NA	NA	NA
Fort Wayne	133.8	720	90	0.0	10.9	0.5	0.0	0.9	21.1	20.1	7.9	6.9	3.6
Gary	148.4	1 368	202	0.0	5.3	0.0	0.0	2.5	9.7	21.6	4.0	0.8	4.7
Goshen	18.8	745	41	0.0	12.2	0.0	0.0	2.7	13.3	15.1	3.7	1.2	1.7
Greenwood	NA	NA	NA	NA	NA	NA	NA	NA	NA	NA	NA	NA	NA
Hammond	119.4	1 527	113	0.0	3.9	0.0	0.0	0.7	10.6	12.8	3.0	5.1	4.4
Hobart	17.6	708	121	0.0	13.5	0.4	0.0	0.3	17.1	18.6	10.3	0.0	2.2
Indianapolis	1 607.3	2 168	539	3.9	4.5	0.2	0.0	18.6	8.1	7.6	8.4	7.6	10.3
Jeffersonville	NA	NA	NA	NA	NA	NA	NA	NA	NA	NA	NA	NA	NA
Kokomo	51.1	1 133	133	0.0	8.5	0.0	0.0	0.0	12.4	26.4	3.1	2.5	3.1
Lafayette	40.1	899	60	0.0	9.2	0.3	0.0	0.0	15.4	17.3	8.2	3.7	0.7
Lawrence	NA	NA	NA	NA	NA	NA	NA	NA	NA	NA	NA	NA	NA
Marion	22.1	768	60	0.0	8.0	0.1	0.0	0.0	20.2	17.0	3.3	4.3	1.3
Merrillville	10.6	347	22	0.0	21.0	0.0	0.0	7.8	24.3	0.0	2.0	0.0	1.2

1. Based on population estimated as of July 1 of the year shown.

City	City government finances, 1999 (cont'd)			City government employment, 2001	Climate[2]						
	Debt outstanding				Average daily temperature (degrees Fahrenheit)						
					Mean		Limits				
	Total (mil dol)	Per capita[1] (dollars)	Percent utility		January	July	January[3]	July[4]	Annual precipitation (inches)	Heating degree days	Cooling degree days
	137	138	139	140	141	142	143	144	145	146	147
ILLINOIS—Cont'd											
Freeport	NA	NA	NA	NA	17.1	72.9	7.8	84.2	33.08	7 169	645
Galesburg	33.8	1 031	0.0	NA	21.1	75.1	12.5	85.3	36.55	6 314	925
Glendale Heights	27.3	902	0.0	NA	21.0	73.2	12.9	83.7	35.82	6 536	752
Glen Ellyn	NA	NA	NA	NA	NA	NA	NA	NA	NA	NA	NA
Glenview	62.6	1 571	18.5	381	21.0	73.2	12.9	83.7	35.82	6 536	752
Granite City	NA	NA	NA	NA	28.4	78.4	18.9	89.6	37.86	5 001	1 329
Gurnee	6.6	265	35.7	NA	NA	NA	NA	NA	NA	NA	NA
Hanover Park	NA	NA	NA	NA	21.0	73.2	12.9	83.7	35.82	6 536	752
Harvey	18.9	657	0.0	NA	20.6	73.7	12.2	83.8	37.12	6 541	780
Highland Park	26.6	851	28.7	344	21.0	73.2	12.9	83.7	35.82	6 536	752
Hoffman Estates	307.5	6 338	0.0	369	18.3	71.9	9.3	82.7	35.19	7 084	603
Joliet	55.9	605	40.0	823	20.7	73.8	11.8	84.6	36.26	6 463	776
Kankakee	48.9	1 848	0.0	277	21.1	74.6	12.3	85.2	35.31	6 322	921
Lansing	54.4	1 907	1.9	NA	23.7	74.1	15.2	85.5	36.82	6 043	857
Lombard	15.1	357	0.0	326	21.0	73.2	12.9	83.7	35.82	6 536	752
Maywood	NA	NA	NA	NA	21.0	73.2	12.9	83.7	35.82	6 536	752
Moline	42.1	1 004	0.0	418	19.9	75.2	11.3	85.9	39.08	6 474	911
Mount Prospect	19.9	372	3.6	308	21.0	73.2	12.9	83.7	35.82	6 536	752
Mundelein	NA	NA	NA	NA	NA	NA	NA	NA	NA	NA	NA
Naperville	126.3	1 079	35.8	1 202	19.7	73.1	10.7	84.2	36.88	6 699	702
Niles	NA	NA	NA	NA	21.0	73.2	12.9	83.7	35.82	6 536	752
Normal	22.5	509	0.0	325	23.9	75.9	15.4	86.7	37.10	5 759	1 117
Northbrook	35.4	1 068	54.0	NA	21.0	73.2	12.9	83.7	35.82	6 536	752
North Chicago	NA	NA	NA	NA	19.3	71.2	10.8	81.1	34.20	7 136	542
Oak Forest	18.8	679	2.5	NA	20.6	73.7	12.2	83.8	37.12	6 541	780
Oak Lawn	35.3	611	31.1	427	22.4	75.1	14.9	84.4	37.38	6 176	940
Oak Park	32.0	632	8.4	512	22.4	75.1	14.9	84.4	37.38	6 176	940
Orland Park	21.1	440	0.0	369	20.6	73.7	12.2	83.8	37.12	6 541	780
Palatine	96.3	2 115	0.0	357	21.0	73.2	12.9	83.7	35.82	6 536	752
Park Ridge	6.1	162	0.0	278	21.0	73.2	12.9	83.7	35.82	6 536	752
Pekin	56.4	1 765	0.0	NA	21.6	75.5	13.2	85.7	36.25	6 148	982
Peoria	165.1	1 486	0.0	1 017	21.6	75.5	13.2	85.7	36.25	6 148	982
Quincy	38.3	960	0.0	446	23.9	76.7	15.6	86.8	39.66	5 763	1 106
Rockford	93.1	648	32.1	1 263	18.2	73.2	9.8	83.8	36.28	6 969	702
Rock Island	44.6	1 152	11.2	452	19.9	75.2	11.3	85.9	39.08	6 474	911
Round Lake Beach	NA	NA	NA	NA	NA	NA	NA	NA	NA	NA	NA
St. Charles	25.9	978	4.2	NA	NA	NA	NA	NA	NA	NA	NA
Schaumburg	17.1	230	0.0	751	21.0	73.2	12.9	83.7	35.82	6 536	752
Skokie	86.3	1 471	5.0	581	21.0	73.2	12.9	83.7	35.82	6 536	752
Springfield	229.9	1 963	51.2	1 741	24.2	76.5	15.9	86.9	35.25	5 688	1 141
Streamwood	13.1	376	32.8	NA	18.3	71.9	9.3	82.7	35.19	7 084	603
Tinley Park	19.7	430	18.3	244	20.6	73.7	12.2	83.8	37.12	6 541	780
Urbana	30.7	881	0.0	269	23.8	75.0	16.0	85.3	39.71	5 854	985
Waukegan	87.5	1 152	5.8	618	19.3	71.2	10.8	81.1	34.20	7 136	542
Wheaton	NA	NA	NA	NA	21.1	73.9	12.3	86.0	36.68	6 354	818
Wheeling	12.4	406	0.0	230	21.0	73.2	12.9	83.7	35.82	6 536	752
Wilmette	52.4	1 999	27.7	205	21.0	73.2	12.9	83.7	35.82	6 536	752
Woodridge	25.8	878	25.0	NA	19.7	73.1	10.7	84.2	36.88	6 699	702
INDIANA	X	X	X	X	X	X	X	X	X	X	X
Anderson	36.8	628	11.2	932	24.8	73.5	17.4	83.7	38.47	5 916	812
Bloomington	53.9	829	23.8	589	27.3	75.8	18.1	85.9	43.14	5 309	1 068
Carmel	33.1	787	15.8	391	25.5	75.4	17.2	85.5	39.94	5 615	1 014
Columbus	24.2	750	42.9	456	22.0	72.1	13.6	83.6	37.50	6 576	644
East Chicago	9.4	305	0.0	899	23.7	74.1	15.2	85.5	36.82	6 043	857
Elkhart	23.7	544	40.6	623	23.3	72.9	16.1	82.9	39.14	6 331	728
Evansville	121.8	992	11.2	1 382	30.1	78.4	21.2	89.1	43.14	4 708	1 376
Fishers town	NA	NA	NA	NA	NA	NA	NA	NA	NA	NA	NA
Fort Wayne	104.2	561	21.0	1 916	22.9	74.0	15.3	84.6	34.75	6 273	824
Gary	104.5	963	0.0	1 762	23.7	74.1	15.2	85.5	36.82	6 043	857
Goshen	9.2	364	19.3	NA	NA	NA	NA	NA	NA	NA	NA
Greenwood	NA	NA	NA	NA	25.5	75.4	17.2	85.5	39.94	5 615	1 014
Hammond	98.4	1 259	0.0	1 360	23.7	74.1	15.2	85.5	36.82	6 043	857
Hobart	7.6	305	0.0	225	NA	NA	NA	NA	NA	NA	NA
Indianapolis	2 891.6	3 901	10.4	NA	NA	NA	NA	NA	NA	NA	NA
Jeffersonville	NA	NA	NA	NA	NA	NA	NA	NA	NA	NA	NA
Kokomo	24.1	534	0.0	536	22.1	73.1	13.6	84.4	39.89	6 429	770
Lafayette	18.2	409	44.6	657	22.5	73.5	13.9	84.4	36.05	6 228	806
Lawrence	NA	NA	NA	NA	25.5	75.4	17.2	85.5	39.94	5 615	1 014
Marion	13.9	482	56.5	310	23.1	73.3	14.7	84.4	37.56	6 260	760
Merrillville	7.4	242	0.0	NA	23.7	74.1	15.2	85.5	36.82	6 043	857

1. Based on the population estimated as of July 1 of the year shown.   2. Represents normal values based on the 30-year period, 1961–1990.   3. Average daily minimum.   4. Average daily maximum.

Table D. Cities — Land Area and Population

STATE Place code	City	Land area, 2000[1] (sq km)	Population, 2000			Population				Population characteristics, 2000 — Percent						
			Total persons	Rank	Per square kilo-meter	Total persons 1990	Percent change 1990–2000	Total persons 1980	Percent change 1980–1990	White	Black	Am. Indian, Alaska Native	Asian and Pacific Islander	Other race	His-panic[2]	Non-His-panic White
		1	2	3	4	5	6	7	8	9	10	11	12	13	14	15
	INDIANA—Cont'd															
18 48798	Michigan City	50.8	32 900	951	647.6	33 822	-2.7	36 833	-8.2	71.4	27.7	0.9	0.8	1.7	3.1	67.8
18 49932	Mishawaka	40.7	46 557	652	1 143.9	42 635	9.2	40 201	6.1	93.3	4.3	1.0	1.8	1.6	2.8	90.2
18 51876	Muncie	62.6	67 430	403	1 077.2	71 170	-5.3	77 216	-7.8	87.1	11.7	0.7	1.3	0.9	1.4	85.0
18 52326	New Albany	37.9	37 603	829	992.2	36 322	3.5	37 103	-2.1	91.5	7.9	0.8	0.8	0.9	1.4	89.4
18 54180	Noblesville city, IN	46.4	28 590	1 084	616.2	17 655	61.9	12 056	46.4	97.2	1.4	0.5	1.2	0.8	1.4	95.7
18 61092	Portage	65.9	33 496	940	508.3	29 062	15.3	27 409	6.0	94.2	1.8	0.8	1.0	4.1	9.9	86.7
18 64260	Richmond	60.1	39 124	789	651.0	38 705	1.1	41 327	-6.3	88.8	10.2	0.8	1.1	1.4	2.0	85.9
18 71000	South Bend	100.2	107 789	211	1 075.7	105 511	2.2	109 727	-3.8	68.4	26.1	1.0	1.8	5.8	8.5	63.3
18 75428	Terre Haute	80.9	59 614	472	736.9	57 475	3.7	61 125	-6.0	88.0	10.7	0.9	1.6	0.9	1.6	85.3
18 78326	Valparaiso	28.2	27 428	1 127	972.6	24 414	12.3	22 247	9.7	95.7	1.9	0.7	2.0	1.4	3.3	92.1
18 82862	West Lafayette	14.3	28 778	1 076	2 012.4	26 144	10.1	21 247	23.0	84.6	2.7	0.4	12.4	1.7	3.2	81.5
19 00000	IOWA	144 701.0	2 926 324	X	20.2	2 776 831	5.4	2 913 808	-4.7	94.9	2.5	0.6	1.6	1.6	2.8	92.6
19 01855	Ames	55.9	50 731	587	907.5	47 198	7.5	45 775	3.1	88.4	3.0	0.4	8.4	1.1	2.0	86.3
19 02305	Ankeny	43.4	27 117	1 140	624.8	18 482	46.7	15 429	19.8	97.7	1.0	0.3	1.3	0.6	1.1	96.4
19 06355	Bettendorf	55.0	31 275	1 003	568.6	28 139	11.1	27 376	2.8	96.0	1.9	0.6	1.8	0.9	2.5	93.5
19 09550	Burlington	36.4	26 839	1 153	737.3	27 208	-1.4	29 529	-7.9	92.9	5.9	0.7	1.0	1.2	2.1	90.6
19 11755	Cedar Falls	73.3	36 145	861	493.1	34 298	5.4	36 310	-5.5	96.1	2.0	0.4	2.0	0.7	1.1	94.6
19 12000	Cedar Rapids	163.5	120 758	181	738.6	108 772	11.0	110 217	-1.3	93.5	4.6	0.7	2.2	0.9	1.7	90.9
19 14430	Clinton	92.1	27 772	1 113	301.5	29 201	-4.9	32 828	-11.0	95.1	3.8	0.8	0.9	0.8	1.7	92.9
19 16860	Council Bluffs	96.8	58 268	486	601.9	54 315	7.3	56 449	-3.8	95.9	1.4	0.9	0.9	2.2	4.5	92.5
19 19000	Davenport	162.6	98 359	241	604.9	95 333	3.2	103 264	-7.7	85.8	10.4	1.0	2.4	3.0	5.4	81.3
19 21000	Des Moines	196.3	198 682	93	1 012.1	193 189	2.8	191 003	1.1	84.1	8.9	0.8	4.1	4.4	6.6	79.6
19 22395	Dubuque	68.6	57 686	495	840.9	57 538	0.3	62 321	-7.7	97.0	1.5	0.5	1.1	0.9	1.6	95.4
19 28515	Fort Dodge	37.7	25 136	1 233	666.7	26 057	-2.9	29 423	-12.0	93.7	4.4	0.6	1.1	1.6	2.9	91.1
19 38595	Iowa City	62.6	62 220	442	993.9	59 735	4.2	50 508	18.3	88.8	4.4	0.6	6.3	1.7	2.9	85.8
19 49485	Marion	31.1	26 294	1 178	845.5	20 422	28.8	19 474	4.9	97.8	0.9	0.4	1.2	0.6	1.1	96.4
19 49755	Marshalltown	46.7	26 009	1 193	556.9	25 178	3.3	26 938	-6.5	88.4	1.8	0.7	1.4	9.6	12.6	83.6
19 50160	Mason City	66.8	29 172	1 067	436.7	29 040	0.5	30 144	-3.7	96.7	1.7	0.5	1.1	1.6	3.4	93.4
19 73335	Sioux City	141.9	85 013	299	599.1	80 505	5.6	82 003	-1.8	87.2	3.1	2.8	3.3	6.0	10.9	80.6
19 79950	Urbandale	53.6	29 072	1 069	542.4	23 775	22.3	17 869	33.1	96.0	1.9	0.3	2.1	0.8	1.6	94.3
19 82425	Waterloo	157.3	68 747	392	437.0	66 467	3.4	75 985	-12.5	83.4	14.7	0.6	1.2	2.2	2.6	80.6
19 83910	West Des Moines	69.4	46 403	656	668.6	31 702	46.4	21 894	44.8	93.8	2.2	0.4	3.2	1.7	3.0	91.1
20 00000	KANSAS	211 899.6	2 688 418	X	12.7	2 477 588	8.5	2 364 236	4.8	87.9	6.3	1.8	2.2	4.0	7.0	83.1
20 18250	Dodge City	32.7	25 176	1 230	769.9	21 129	19.2	18 001	17.4	73.7	2.4	1.2	2.8	22.6	42.9	51.5
20 21275	Emporia	25.6	26 760	1 155	1 045.3	25 512	4.9	25 287	0.9	80.9	3.6	1.2	3.0	13.9	21.5	71.1
20 25325	Garden City	22.1	28 451	1 090	1 287.4	24 097	18.1	18 256	32.0	71.1	1.9	1.6	4.1	24.1	43.9	49.8
20 33625	Hutchinson	54.7	40 787	753	745.6	39 308	3.8	40 284	-2.4	90.6	5.0	1.4	0.9	4.4	7.7	85.4
20 36000	Kansas City	321.8	146 866	142	456.4	151 521	-3.1	161 093	-5.9	58.1	31.3	1.7	2.2	9.9	16.8	48.9
20 38900	Lawrence	72.8	80 098	322	1 100.2	65 608	22.1	52 738	24.4	86.4	6.2	4.0	4.7	2.0	3.6	82.1
20 39000	Leavenworth	60.9	35 420	880	581.6	38 495	-8.0	33 656	14.4	79.1	17.6	1.6	2.5	2.4	5.1	74.1
20 39075	Leawood	39.1	27 656	1 119	707.3	19 693	40.4	13 360	47.4	95.9	1.6	0.3	2.5	0.4	1.3	94.2
20 39350	Lenexa	88.8	40 238	769	453.1	34 110	18.0	18 639	83.0	90.9	3.7	0.9	4.2	2.1	4.0	87.5
20 44250	Manhattan	38.9	44 831	684	1 152.5	43 081	4.1	32 645	32.0	89.0	5.6	1.0	4.8	1.8	3.5	85.4
20 52575	Olathe	140.3	92 962	260	662.6	63 402	46.6	37 258	70.2	90.2	4.3	0.9	3.3	3.2	5.4	86.2
20 53775	Overland Park	147.0	149 080	139	1 014.1	111 790	33.4	81 784	36.7	91.9	2.9	0.7	4.4	1.7	3.8	88.4
20 62700	Salina	58.9	45 679	668	775.5	42 299	8.0	41 843	1.1	89.8	4.5	1.3	2.4	4.4	6.7	85.4
20 64500	Shawnee	108.1	47 996	631	444.0	37 962	26.4	29 625	28.1	92.0	3.5	0.8	3.2	2.5	4.4	88.2
20 71000	Topeka	145.1	122 377	176	843.4	119 883	2.1	115 266	4.0	81.2	13.2	2.5	1.6	5.1	8.9	75.1
20 79000	Wichita	351.6	344 284	50	979.2	304 017	13.2	279 272	8.9	77.8	12.4	2.3	4.7	6.1	9.6	71.7
21 00000	KENTUCKY	102 895.5	4 041 769	X	39.3	3 686 892	9.6	3 660 324	0.7	91.0	7.7	0.6	1.0	0.8	1.5	89.3
21 08902	Bowling Green	91.7	49 296	611	537.6	41 688	18.2	40 450	3.1	82.6	13.3	0.6	2.6	3.0	4.1	79.1
21 17848	Covington	34.0	43 370	705	1 275.6	43 646	-0.6	49 569	-11.9	88.5	11.0	0.7	0.6	0.9	1.4	86.3
21 28900	Frankfort	38.2	27 741	1 115	726.2	26 535	4.5	25 973	2.2	83.2	15.7	0.5	1.4	1.0	1.5	81.1
21 35866	Henderson	38.8	27 373	1 130	705.5	25 945	5.5	24 834	4.5	88.2	11.0	0.5	0.5	0.8	1.3	86.7
21 37918	Hopkinsville	62.2	30 089	1 032	483.7	29 809	0.9	27 318	9.2	67.2	31.6	0.6	1.2	0.9	1.7	65.3
21 40222	Jeffersontown	25.8	26 633	1 159	1 032.3	23 223	14.7	15 736	47.6	88.0	9.2	0.6	2.1	1.7	2.5	85.5
21 46027	Lexington-Fayette	736.9	260 512	64	353.5	225 366	15.6	204 165	10.4	82.4	14.1	0.6	2.9	1.7	3.3	79.1
21 48000	Louisville	160.9	256 231	66	1 592.5	269 555	-4.9	298 455	-9.7	64.2	33.9	0.7	1.8	1.2	1.9	61.9
21 58620	Owensboro	45.1	54 067	549	1 198.8	53 577	0.9	54 450	-1.6	91.8	7.6	0.5	0.8	0.7	1.0	90.1
21 58836	Paducah	50.5	26 307	1 177	520.9	27 256	-3.5	29 315	-7.0	74.2	25.0	0.8	1.0	0.7	1.4	72.1
21 65226	Richmond	49.5	27 152	1 137	548.5	21 183	28.2	21 705	-2.4	89.7	9.1	0.8	1.4	0.7	1.2	87.5
22 00000	LOUISIANA	112 824.7	4 468 976	X	39.6	4 221 826	5.9	4 206 116	0.3	64.8	32.9	1.0	1.5	1.1	2.4	62.5
22 00975	Alexandria	68.4	46 342	657	677.5	49 049	-5.5	51 565	-4.9	43.2	55.3	0.6	1.5	0.5	1.0	42.0
22 05000	Baton Rouge	199.0	227 818	74	1 144.8	219 531	3.8	219 419	0.1	46.4	50.4	0.5	3.0	0.8	1.7	44.7
22 08920	Bossier City	105.8	56 461	509	533.7	52 721	7.1	50 861	3.7	73.1	23.4	1.1	2.6	1.9	4.0	69.4

1. Dry land or land partially or temporarily covered by water.   2. Hispanic persons may be of any race.

Table D. Cities — **Population and Households**

| | Population characteristics, 2000 (cont'd) | | | | | | | | | | Households, 2000 | | | | |
| | Age of population (percent) | | | | | | | | | | | | | Percent | |
City	Under 5 years	5 to 17 years	18 to 24 years	25 to 34 years	35 to 44 years	45 to 54 years	55 to 64 years	65 to 74 years	75 years and over	Percent female	Number	Percent change, 1990–2000	Persons per house-hold	Female family house-holder[1]	One-person
	16	17	18	19	20	21	22	23	24	25	26	27	28	29	30
INDIANA—Cont'd															
Michigan City	7.6	17.4	9.6	15.1	15.6	12.6	8.0	6.9	7.2	49.6	12 550	0.1	2.41	18.1	30.9
Mishawaka	7.1	16.9	11.8	16.3	14.4	12.0	7.4	6.5	7.5	52.7	20 248	12.5	2.23	13.0	35.8
Muncie	5.8	13.9	24.6	12.9	11.2	10.3	8.0	6.6	6.6	52.7	27 322	0.5	2.24	13.0	34.1
New Albany	6.9	17.2	9.6	14.0	15.2	13.2	8.6	7.6	7.8	53.1	15 959	8.6	2.31	16.1	30.8
Noblesville city, IN	9.3	20.2	7.3	17.0	17.5	13.0	7.2	4.4	4.1	50.9	10 576	59.0	2.64	9.2	21.3
Portage	7.2	18.9	9.4	13.8	16.1	14.2	8.6	6.0	5.8	51.5	12 746	21.2	2.60	12.2	23.9
Richmond	6.8	16.6	11.0	13.7	13.7	12.5	9.1	8.1	8.3	53.0	16 287	4.5	2.29	13.9	33.0
South Bend	8.3	19.0	10.4	15.5	13.8	11.5	6.7	6.8	8.0	52.3	42 908	1.5	2.45	17.0	32.5
Terre Haute	6.2	15.2	18.7	13.4	13.2	11.2	7.2	6.5	8.3	50.7	22 870	6.4	2.28	14.0	34.9
Valparaiso	5.9	15.3	17.4	14.5	13.6	13.0	7.2	5.8	7.3	52.1	10 867	21.0	2.27	9.7	33.4
West Lafayette	2.5	7.9	54.6	10.2	6.7	6.5	3.9	3.1	4.6	42.8	10 462	14.3	2.26	4.4	32.7
IOWA	6.4	18.6	10.2	12.4	15.2	13.4	8.8	7.2	7.7	50.9	1 149 276	8.0	2.46	8.6	27.2
Ames	4.4	10.2	40.0	14.2	9.6	8.7	5.2	3.9	3.8	47.8	18 085	15.8	2.30	5.3	28.5
Ankeny	8.4	18.8	11.4	16.9	16.5	13.0	7.1	4.2	3.7	51.5	10 339	53.0	2.57	7.3	21.8
Bettendorf	6.2	20.1	6.7	11.4	16.6	16.9	9.7	6.5	5.9	51.5	12 474	17.0	2.48	8.1	26.0
Burlington	6.6	17.9	8.9	12.4	14.3	13.7	9.0	7.9	9.3	52.4	11 102	1.1	2.36	12.0	31.0
Cedar Falls	4.4	13.6	30.6	9.5	11.0	12.0	7.0	5.4	6.5	53.1	12 833	9.8	2.45	7.5	25.5
Cedar Rapids	7.1	17.3	10.8	15.2	15.5	13.0	8.0	6.4	6.7	51.3	49 820	14.1	2.36	10.0	30.2
Clinton	6.6	18.0	9.1	11.6	15.1	13.1	9.4	8.0	9.1	52.3	11 427	-2.1	2.36	11.7	30.2
Council Bluffs	7.2	18.8	10.3	14.2	15.4	12.5	8.2	7.2	6.1	51.6	22 889	8.3	2.49	14.3	27.9
Davenport	7.4	18.8	10.7	15.1	14.9	13.0	7.9	6.0	6.2	51.4	39 124	5.2	2.44	13.4	29.5
Des Moines	7.5	17.3	10.6	16.3	15.5	12.6	7.8	6.0	6.4	51.6	80 504	2.6	2.39	12.6	31.9
Dubuque	6.2	17.4	11.8	11.9	14.6	13.1	8.5	7.7	8.9	52.6	22 560	5.2	2.37	10.0	31.0
Fort Dodge	6.8	17.5	10.7	11.3	13.9	12.8	8.5	8.2	10.4	52.5	10 470	-0.3	2.29	11.4	33.8
Iowa City	4.6	11.6	32.8	16.4	11.7	10.6	5.2	3.5	3.5	51.0	25 202	14.8	2.23	6.7	33.8
Marion	7.4	19.0	8.2	15.3	16.6	13.5	8.6	5.9	5.5	51.4	10 458	34.6	2.47	8.4	26.0
Marshalltown	6.7	17.8	8.9	12.3	13.7	13.7	9.2	8.1	9.5	50.5	10 175	2.0	2.44	10.8	29.7
Mason City	6.2	17.3	10.2	11.9	14.8	13.2	8.5	8.4	9.4	52.6	12 368	2.8	2.27	10.3	33.5
Sioux City	7.9	19.2	11.0	14.2	14.3	12.6	7.6	6.6	6.7	51.2	32 054	5.1	2.57	12.2	27.7
Urbandale	6.7	19.6	7.0	13.4	17.9	15.6	9.0	6.1	4.6	51.7	11 484	27.4	2.51	7.1	24.2
Waterloo	7.0	17.6	10.6	13.6	13.8	13.6	8.4	7.3	8.0	52.0	28 169	4.2	2.39	13.3	30.0
West Des Moines	7.7	16.9	9.7	19.2	16.3	13.0	7.3	5.3	4.5	52.1	19 826	52.8	2.33	7.7	30.5
KANSAS	7.0	19.5	10.3	13.0	15.6	13.2	8.2	6.5	6.7	50.6	1 037 891	9.9	2.51	9.3	27.0
Dodge City	9.9	21.3	12.3	16.3	13.7	10.3	6.2	4.6	5.3	48.4	8 395	10.3	2.94	10.3	23.5
Emporia	7.3	18.0	19.4	13.9	13.3	10.8	6.2	4.8	6.2	51.1	10 253	5.1	2.47	9.4	31.1
Garden City	10.2	22.5	11.6	16.2	14.9	10.5	6.1	4.1	4.1	49.4	9 338	15.7	2.99	10.8	22.1
Hutchinson	6.6	16.6	11.0	12.8	15.1	12.7	8.5	7.8	9.1	49.6	16 335	4.3	2.31	10.3	31.7
Kansas City	8.1	20.4	10.6	14.5	14.9	12.1	7.7	6.1	5.5	51.1	55 500	-2.9	2.62	18.2	29.2
Lawrence	5.4	13.1	30.7	16.2	12.2	10.2	4.9	3.6	3.6	50.3	31 388	28.0	2.30	8.7	30.6
Leavenworth	8.2	19.5	8.8	15.6	19.2	12.1	6.9	4.9	4.8	47.1	12 035	4.9	2.60	11.6	27.1
Leawood	6.3	23.8	4.2	5.9	17.4	19.6	10.1	7.0	5.6	51.0	9 841	42.9	2.81	5.1	15.2
Lenexa	6.4	19.3	9.5	14.7	17.3	16.5	7.7	3.5	5.1	51.1	15 574	22.5	2.54	7.6	24.3
Manhattan	4.6	11.2	39.2	14.0	10.0	8.6	4.6	3.6	4.2	48.5	16 949	15.4	2.30	6.6	30.5
Olathe	9.4	21.5	9.2	18.0	18.7	12.8	5.4	2.8	2.4	50.1	32 314	50.7	2.83	9.0	18.4
Overland Park	7.1	19.0	7.0	14.6	17.9	14.9	8.0	5.8	5.6	51.6	59 703	32.9	2.47	7.4	27.4
Salina	7.1	18.8	10.0	13.6	15.1	12.8	8.3	7.1	7.1	51.1	18 523	7.1	2.39	10.5	30.1
Shawnee	7.7	19.1	7.8	15.8	18.4	14.6	8.1	5.0	3.5	50.8	18 552	27.2	2.58	8.2	22.7
Topeka	7.0	17.2	9.9	14.0	14.8	13.5	8.4	7.4	7.7	52.0	52 190	4.5	2.27	13.1	35.0
Wichita	8.0	19.1	10.1	15.0	15.7	12.8	7.4	6.0	5.9	50.7	139 087	12.9	2.44	11.6	31.2
KENTUCKY	6.6	18.0	9.9	14.1	15.9	13.8	9.2	6.8	5.7	51.1	1 590 647	15.3	2.47	11.8	26.0
Bowling Green	6.0	14.2	23.5	14.5	12.4	10.4	7.1	5.9	6.0	51.6	19 277	20.7	2.27	13.1	33.5
Covington	7.8	18.0	10.0	17.3	16.0	11.9	7.1	5.9	6.0	51.1	18 257	5.4	2.31	16.5	36.5
Frankfort	6.2	15.4	11.7	15.3	15.0	13.6	8.8	7.0	6.9	52.3	12 314	11.6	2.14	14.1	37.6
Henderson	6.7	16.9	9.2	14.1	15.3	13.7	8.8	7.8	7.4	52.8	11 693	10.9	2.27	14.1	32.1
Hopkinsville	7.4	19.0	9.7	13.7	14.6	12.1	8.7	7.6	7.3	53.2	12 174	6.8	2.39	18.2	29.7
Jeffersontown	7.2	17.5	7.7	16.2	17.2	14.6	8.7	6.0	4.8	51.9	10 653	19.7	2.46	10.7	26.4
Lexington-Fayette	6.2	15.1	14.6	17.1	16.1	13.2	7.6	5.3	4.7	50.9	108 288	21.0	2.29	11.5	31.7
Louisville	6.6	17.0	10.4	14.7	15.7	13.2	7.8	7.3	7.4	52.7	111 414	-1.5	2.22	19.2	37.9
Owensboro	6.8	17.4	9.8	12.7	14.7	13.1	9.2	8.2	8.1	53.3	22 659	4.6	2.29	13.9	33.3
Paducah	6.5	16.0	8.5	12.3	13.9	13.2	9.2	8.8	11.4	54.5	11 825	-1.1	2.12	16.2	39.3
Richmond	6.0	11.6	31.7	16.6	10.9	8.3	5.5	4.6	4.9	52.5	10 795	49.7	2.14	12.8	34.7
LOUISIANA	7.1	20.2	10.6	13.5	15.5	13.1	8.5	6.3	5.2	51.6	1 656 053	10.5	2.62	16.6	25.3
Alexandria	7.3	20.8	9.2	11.8	14.4	12.7	8.7	7.5	7.6	54.5	17 816	-1.8	2.50	23.2	30.4
Baton Rouge	6.8	17.6	17.5	13.9	13.3	11.9	7.5	5.8	5.6	52.5	88 973	6.8	2.42	19.0	31.7
Bossier City	8.0	20.2	11.0	14.7	15.6	11.5	7.9	6.1	4.8	51.4	21 197	11.4	2.58	15.8	24.7

1. No spouse present.

Table D. Cities — Group Quarters, Crime, Education, and Income

City	Persons in group quarters, 2000				Serious crimes known to police, 2000[2]				Education, 1990				Money income, 1989		
		Institutional			Total		Rate[3]		School enrollment		Attainment[4] (percent)			Households	
														Median	
	Total	Total	Persons in nursing homes	Non-Institutional[1]	Number	Rate[3]	Violent	Property	Public	Private	High school graduate or more	Bach-elor's degree or more	Per capita (dollars)[5]	Dollars	Percent change, 1979–1989 (constant 1989 dollars)
	31	32	33	34	35	36	37	38	39	40	41	42	43	44	45
INDIANA—Cont'd															
Michigan City	2 661	2 585	385	76	2 690	8 176	471	7 705	7 025	1 111	69.1	9.4	10 868	23 127	-19.0
Mishawaka	1 305	354	215	951	4 282	9 197	573	8 624	8 434	1 893	74.2	14.8	12 823	24 302	-6.3
Muncie	6 201	1 036	574	5 165	356	528	110	418	24 616	1 155	70.1	16.0	10 686	19 353	-14.2
New Albany	680	615	509	65	2 922	7 771	630	7 140	7 474	846	68.3	12.9	11 781	23 933	-6.0
Noblesville city, IN	645	628	235	17	625	2 186	45	2 141	4 084	407	81.1	29.1	17 445	36 652	8.8
Portage	406	358	358	48	1 308	3 905	125	3 780	6 797	780	74.5	9.3	13 057	33 118	-19.6
Richmond	1 832	859	418	973	2 565	6 556	488	6 068	7 798	1 723	68.0	13.0	10 975	20 585	-12.0
South Bend	2 817	1 662	1 072	1 155	8 496	7 882	739	7 143	19 506	6 035	72.0	18.5	11 949	24 131	-8.2
Terre Haute	7 401	2 873	674	4 528	5 141	8 624	230	8 394	15 758	1 731	72.3	15.8	10 527	19 118	-11.3
Valparaiso	2 708	743	498	1 965	808	2 946	95	2 851	4 668	3 610	85.2	27.9	14 987	31 602	-8.7
West Lafayette	5 138	215	215	4 923	636	2 210	136	2 075	16 117	578	95.7	68.4	13 169	21 786	-10.0
IOWA	104 169	50 256	33 428	53 913	94 630	3 234	266	2 967	626 759	110 970	80.1	16.9	12 422	26 229	-6.8
Ames	9 122	186	137	8 936	1 592	3 138	138	3 000	25 919	790	95.1	54.1	11 347	24 636	-8.7
Ankeny	558	235	235	323	892	3 289	159	3 131	5 243	680	93.9	29.1	14 557	36 582	-4.2
Bettendorf	294	180	178	114	812	2 596	201	2 395	6 778	1 030	90.1	34.2	17 747	40 174	-8.6
Burlington	633	475	339	158	1 493	5 563	574	4 989	5 950	665	77.8	14.0	12 025	25 105	-7.6
Cedar Falls	4 694	524	524	4 170	1 002	2 772	335	2 437	14 217	858	88.5	31.4	12 114	28 003	-16.6
Cedar Rapids	3 369	1 407	985	1 962	6 297	5 215	292	4 922	22 774	5 248	84.5	23.3	15 246	31 458	-3.3
Clinton	787	326	107	461	NA	NA	NA	NA	6 273	924	76.2	14.4	11 830	23 562	-22.0
Council Bluffs	1 329	858	432	471	5 816	9 981	848	9 134	11 712	1 301	73.9	10.0	11 318	25 014	-6.5
Davenport	2 877	1 471	875	1 406	8 037	8 171	1 638	6 533	20 270	6 047	78.8	20.1	12 557	26 218	-16.9
Des Moines	6 537	2 670	1 586	3 867	13 688	6 889	361	6 529	36 096	10 629	81.0	18.9	13 710	26 703	-4.7
Dubuque	4 167	1 047	867	3 120	1 977	3 427	210	3 217	8 542	7 146	78.4	19.4	12 377	27 027	-13.6
Fort Dodge	1 165	815	599	350	1 995	7 937	648	7 288	4 884	1 248	78.3	16.1	11 639	22 783	-14.5
Iowa City	6 110	462	115	5 648	2 050	3 295	526	2 769	28 991	1 516	93.9	53.7	13 277	24 565	1.7
Marion	430	230	230	200	382	1 453	8	1 445	4 303	765	87.4	21.2	14 502	33 436	-7.3
Marshalltown	1 224	1 146	1 024	78	1 305	5 017	873	4 145	5 630	515	80.8	17.8	13 424	27 325	-7.1
Mason City	1 125	616	476	509	2 103	7 209	185	7 024	6 226	924	79.7	16.3	12 229	24 146	-7.1
Sioux City	2 674	1 172	777	1 502	5 697	6 701	654	6 047	15 735	5 393	77.9	17.5	12 339	25 045	-7.3
Urbandale	304	252	252	52	820	2 821	79	2 741	5 043	1 055	95.8	37.5	19 200	42 686	3.0
Waterloo	1 551	819	413	732	3 935	5 724	476	5 248	13 639	2 776	77.9	14.1	12 475	23 578	-24.2
West Des Moines	299	220	214	79	1 798	3 875	144	3 730	5 959	1 792	94.8	41.8	21 503	41 045	3.9
KANSAS	81 950	45 396	25 248	36 554	118 527	4 409	389	4 019	593 376	74 989	81.3	21.1	13 300	27 291	-0.5
Dodge City	493	274	202	219	1 970	7 825	632	7 193	4 883	1 087	74.9	18.8	11 064	24 789	-11.6
Emporia	1 465	318	196	1 147	1 899	7 096	340	6 756	8 755	405	83.1	24.7	11 159	22 621	-13.6
Garden City	572	237	151	335	2 237	7 863	671	7 191	6 660	647	71.8	15.7	11 853	27 981	-6.8
Hutchinson	2 974	2 711	571	263	2 863	7 019	468	6 551	8 499	1 021	77.2	14.3	11 849	23 557	-8.0
Kansas City	1 348	872	540	476	NA	NA	NA	NA	34 012	4 776	69.3	10.1	10 478	23 307	-8.6
Lawrence	7 957	437	343	7 520	39	49	2	46	30 002	1 450	90.9	44.0	11 760	22 900	3.7
Leavenworth	4 103	3 462	157	641	1 589	4 486	508	3 978	8 880	1 609	85.4	29.3	12 827	30 156	5.9
Leawood	45	42	38	3	626	2 264	98	2 166	3 965	1 325	97.9	60.1	34 275	74 980	14.1
Lenexa	670	668	668	2	NA	NA	NA	NA	7 892	1 907	95.8	45.5	20 202	46 935	0.4
Manhattan	5 794	369	294	5 425	NA	NA	NA	NA	17 017	607	92.6	42.2	11 273	21 531	-1.4
Olathe	1 595	742	625	853	3 526	3 793	314	3 479	16 435	3 078	90.9	31.2	14 696	39 742	5.6
Overland Park	1 588	1 433	1 139	155	91	61	1	60	23 677	5 233	94.1	44.8	21 214	44 246	1.4
Salina	1 367	685	429	682	3 103	6 793	342	6 452	8 348	1 609	81.9	17.6	13 044	25 084	-5.7
Shawnee	248	198	198	50	1 617	3 369	263	3 107	8 176	1 880	90.0	29.5	17 268	39 206	-3.3
Topeka	4 078	3 336	1 604	742	13 056	10 669	1 044	9 624	24 726	4 120	82.7	22.1	13 680	26 774	-0.4
Wichita	4 877	3 196	1 514	1 681	21 669	6 294	604	5 689	65 447	12 134	81.9	22.7	14 516	28 024	-2.9
KENTUCKY	114 804	62 057	29 266	52 747	119 626	2 960	295	2 665	807 842	110 473	64.6	13.6	11 153	22 534	-3.7
Bowling Green	5 489	1 101	573	4 388	2 961	6 007	566	5 441	12 816	489	71.5	23.4	11 760	20 043	-1.9
Covington	1 120	842	451	278	NA	NA	NA	NA	7 859	1 788	62.4	9.8	10 293	21 003	5.3
Frankfort	1 331	594	98	737	NA	NA	NA	NA	5 488	686	77.1	22.7	13 100	25 670	-2.7
Henderson	808	677	359	131	NA	NA	NA	NA	5 349	641	66.3	11.8	11 828	22 085	-13.7
Hopkinsville	999	894	451	105	NA	NA	NA	NA	6 528	487	69.4	13.4	10 440	21 352	-4.4
Jeffersontown	402	400	400	2	NA	NA	NA	NA	4 218	1 781	85.5	27.5	17 302	38 962	8.2
Lexington-Fayette	12 723	4 722	1 423	8 001	13 657	5 242	725	4 518	56 571	8 444	80.2	30.6	14 962	28 056	5.2
Louisville	8 527	3 664	2 065	4 863	15 061	5 878	796	5 082	51 805	13 390	67.2	17.2	11 527	20 141	-2.1
Owensboro	2 223	1 103	750	1 120	2 805	5 188	213	4 975	9 906	2 944	71.8	15.3	11 442	21 952	-10.4
Paducah	1 212	1 132	641	80	1 968	7 481	646	6 835	5 214	565	69.0	14.6	11 918	17 196	-13.4
Richmond	4 074	372	183	3 702	2 003	7 377	924	6 453	9 385	273	65.4	19.6	8 771	15 588	-11.4
LOUISIANA	135 965	90 002	31 521	45 963	242 344	5 423	681	4 742	979 200	206 559	68.3	16.1	10 635	21 949	-14.0
Alexandria	1 782	1 281	761	501	5 612	12 110	1 165	10 945	11 442	1 664	68.6	18.4	10 887	18 546	-7.9
Baton Rouge	12 453	3 406	1 397	9 047	21 858	9 595	1 129	8 466	58 990	11 453	76.8	28.3	12 398	21 898	-13.8
Bossier City	1 695	852	569	843	4 172	7 339	863	6 527	13 180	1 207	81.4	15.9	11 326	25 918	-5.6

1. Persons in emergency shelters and persons visible in street locations. areas and over time.   3. Per 100,000 population estimated by the FBI.   2. Data for serious crimes have not been adjusted for underreporting. This may affect comparability between geographic   4. Persons 25 years old and older.   5. Based on population enumerated as of April 1, 1990.

Table D. Cities — Income, Poverty, and Housing

City	Money income, 1989 (cont'd) House-holds (cont'd) Percent with $100,000 or more	Percent below poverty, 1989 Persons Total	Percent change in rate, 1979–1989	Families Total	Housing units, 2000 Total	Percent change, 1990–2000	Vacant units for sale or rent[1]	For seasonal use (percent)	Home owner vacancy rate	Renter vacancy rate	Occupied units Total	Percent owner occu-pied	Percent renter occu-pied	Average size owner occu-pied	Average size renter occu-pied
	46	47	48	49	50	51	52	53	54	55	56	57	58	59	60
INDIANA—Cont'd															
Michigan City	1.2	16.4	36.7	13.8	14 221	1.6	1 671	3.4	2.7	8.2	12 550	61.1	38.9	2.49	2.28
Mishawaka	1.5	9.1	-2.2	6.5	21 572	13.4	1 324	0.4	1.6	6.7	20 248	56.8	43.2	2.47	1.92
Muncie	1.6	23.8	34.5	14.3	30 205	1.3	2 883	0.3	2.2	9.3	27 322	55.8	44.2	2.27	2.20
New Albany	1.3	15.5	32.5	13.0	17 098	9.7	1 139	0.3	1.7	7.4	15 959	59.3	40.7	2.40	2.18
Noblesville city, IN	6.8	7.5	5.6	5.1	11 294	58.4	718	0.6	1.7	11.1	10 576	74.1	25.9	2.79	2.21
Portage	1.7	7.9	54.9	9.2	13 375	23.1	629	0.4	1.3	8.0	12 746	72.5	27.5	2.70	2.33
Richmond	1.8	20.5	44.4	16.3	17 647	4.2	1 360	0.4	2.0	9.4	16 287	58.7	41.3	2.33	2.23
South Bend	1.6	14.4	19.0	11.2	46 349	1.3	3 441	0.5	2.0	7.6	42 908	63.1	36.9	2.50	2.35
Terre Haute	1.3	20.4	48.9	15.5	25 636	6.5	2 766	0.3	3.2	11.9	22 870	59.5	40.5	2.38	2.14
Valparaiso	3.4	8.6	43.3	6.2	11 559	24.4	692	0.5	1.5	7.4	10 867	55.1	44.9	2.56	1.92
West Lafayette	5.0	34.2	62.9	7.3	10 819	14.3	357	0.2	1.4	2.5	10 462	32.2	67.8	2.57	2.11
IOWA	2.1	11.5	13.7	8.4	1 232 511	7.8	83 235	1.3	1.7	6.8	1 149 276	72.3	27.7	2.57	2.15
Ames	2.8	24.1	52.5	10.5	18 757	16.8	672	0.3	1.2	3.3	18 085	46.1	53.9	2.52	2.11
Ankeny	1.2	5.6	-21.1	3.4	10 882	55.8	543	0.2	3.4	5.5	10 339	71.8	28.2	2.79	2.00
Bettendorf	5.5	4.7	74.1	3.2	13 044	17.9	570	0.5	1.5	7.3	12 474	77.3	22.7	2.64	1.95
Burlington	1.2	13.7	45.7	11.3	11 985	1.8	883	0.4	2.0	9.1	11 102	70.2	29.8	2.49	2.06
Cedar Falls	2.5	16.8	102.4	9.1	13 271	10.0	438	0.2	0.8	3.4	12 833	64.3	35.7	2.55	2.27
Cedar Rapids	3.0	10.0	31.6	6.6	52 240	14.9	2 420	0.3	1.5	5.8	49 820	69.0	31.0	2.50	2.03
Clinton	1.1	12.7	67.1	10.2	12 412	-1.4	985	0.4	1.8	11.2	11 427	69.3	30.7	2.48	2.10
Council Bluffs	1.3	12.2	18.4	10.0	24 340	9.4	1 451	0.3	1.4	9.3	22 889	65.0	35.0	2.60	2.28
Davenport	1.8	15.6	57.6	12.4	41 350	2.5	2 226	0.3	1.6	7.3	39 124	65.2	34.8	2.58	2.18
Des Moines	2.3	12.9	21.7	9.5	85 067	2.1	4 563	0.2	1.4	6.8	80 504	64.7	35.3	2.53	2.12
Dubuque	2.2	10.9	32.9	7.6	23 819	6.4	1 259	0.3	0.8	8.0	22 560	67.5	32.5	2.58	1.95
Fort Dodge	1.2	12.8	24.3	9.5	11 168	-0.4	698	0.4	1.5	8.2	10 470	66.4	33.6	2.44	1.99
Iowa City	4.7	23.4	18.8	9.3	26 083	16.1	881	0.2	2.4	2.2	25 202	46.5	53.5	2.46	2.02
Marion	2.1	6.5	54.8	4.6	10 968	37.1	510	0.3	2.6	5.7	10 458	78.3	21.7	2.65	1.82
Marshalltown	1.7	9.5	15.9	6.8	10 857	2.1	682	0.6	1.7	7.8	10 175	70.1	29.9	2.53	2.20
Mason City	1.7	9.6	2.1	7.2	13 029	2.8	661	0.3	1.5	5.4	12 368	67.4	32.6	2.44	1.92
Sioux City	2.6	13.8	21.1	10.5	33 816	5.1	1 762	0.2	1.4	7.8	32 054	66.2	33.8	2.71	2.29
Urbandale	6.5	2.7	0.0	2.2	11 869	27.7	385	0.3	1.2	5.1	11 484	77.6	22.4	2.67	1.94
Waterloo	2.0	16.9	62.5	14.3	29 499	1.6	1 330	0.2	0.9	5.9	28 169	67.1	32.9	2.47	2.20
West Des Moines	9.2	3.3	-21.4	1.9	20 815	52.3	989	0.7	1.6	5.9	19 826	62.1	37.9	2.58	1.90
KANSAS	2.8	11.5	13.7	8.3	1 131 200	8.3	93 309	0.9	2.0	8.8	1 037 891	69.2	30.8	2.63	2.25
Dodge City	2.3	12.6	37.0	8.8	8 976	8.7	581	0.3	1.5	8.3	8 395	60.7	39.3	3.01	2.84
Emporia	1.9	16.7	46.5	11.1	11 019	2.7	766	0.3	1.5	7.5	10 253	53.6	46.4	2.71	2.18
Garden City	3.0	9.3	9.4	6.6	9 907	15.4	569	0.2	1.5	7.3	9 338	61.6	38.4	3.16	2.71
Hutchinson	1.6	12.0	23.7	9.1	17 693	3.1	1 358	0.3	1.7	10.1	16 335	64.7	35.3	2.43	2.11
Kansas City	0.7	17.9	24.3	14.6	61 446	-4.7	5 946	0.3	1.9	8.4	55 500	62.0	38.0	2.69	2.52
Lawrence	2.8	24.1	26.2	11.5	32 761	26.5	1 373	0.1	1.9	3.6	31 388	45.9	54.1	2.57	2.07
Leavenworth	1.3	9.5	-19.5	7.4	12 936	2.9	901	0.2	2.0	6.3	12 035	50.8	49.2	2.47	2.74
Leawood	32.4	1.3	8.3	1.0	10 129	40.5	288	0.7	0.7	7.4	9 841	92.8	7.2	2.87	2.01
Lenexa	7.9	4.3	19.4	2.9	16 378	21.4	804	0.4	0.7	8.4	15 574	62.7	37.3	2.85	2.01
Manhattan	1.7	24.6	43.0	10.1	17 690	13.7	741	0.3	1.3	3.4	16 949	42.9	57.1	2.54	2.12
Olathe	2.4	4.1	-22.6	3.3	33 343	48.2	1 029	0.1	1.6	3.3	32 314	71.5	28.5	3.02	2.36
Overland Park	8.6	2.8	0.0	1.9	62 586	30.3	2 883	0.6	1.0	8.1	59 703	68.3	31.7	2.72	1.94
Salina	2.5	12.2	45.2	8.6	19 599	6.5	1 076	0.3	1.6	7.3	18 523	66.1	33.9	2.51	2.16
Shawnee	4.6	4.1	5.1	3.3	19 086	25.4	564	0.2	1.0	4.9	18 522	74.4	25.6	2.78	1.98
Topeka	2.2	12.3	32.3	9.3	56 435	3.2	4 245	0.2	1.6	7.2	52 190	60.7	39.3	2.40	2.07
Wichita	2.8	12.5	22.5	9.5	152 119	12.6	13 032	0.3	2.0	12.0	139 087	61.6	38.4	2.61	2.17
KENTUCKY	2.0	19.0	8.1	16.0	1 750 927	16.2	160 280	1.7	1.8	8.7	1 590 647	70.8	29.2	2.55	2.27
Bowling Green	2.4	23.9	29.9	18.1	21 290	21.7	2 013	0.4	2.6	10.1	19 277	47.0	53.0	2.34	2.21
Covington	1.0	19.8	13.8	17.7	20 448	7.0	2 191	0.3	3.1	9.7	18 257	49.3	50.7	2.53	2.11
Frankfort	1.2	13.0	18.2	10.4	13 422	13.0	1 108	0.5	1.5	9.9	12 314	52.0	48.0	2.27	2.01
Henderson	1.5	17.0	34.9	14.9	12 652	11.4	959	0.5	1.9	7.2	11 693	57.3	42.7	2.39	2.11
Hopkinsville	1.5	21.8	15.3	17.1	13 260	8.4	1 086	0.2	2.7	7.9	12 174	57.9	42.1	2.39	2.39
Jeffersontown	4.0	3.4	-17.1	2.6	11 220	19.8	567	1.0	0.9	8.6	10 653	69.8	30.2	2.60	2.15
Lexington-Fayette	4.2	14.1	4.4	10.2	116 167	18.9	7 879	0.8	1.1	8.4	108 288	55.3	44.7	2.47	2.07
Louisville	1.9	22.6	17.1	18.6	121 275	-2.2	9 861	0.3	1.8	7.5	111 414	52.5	47.5	2.33	2.10
Owensboro	1.8	18.9	37.0	15.3	24 302	5.3	1 643	0.4	1.9	7.7	22 659	60.2	39.8	2.38	2.14
Paducah	2.5	23.8	27.3	19.1	13 221	0.5	1 396	0.5	3.3	10.4	11 825	52.9	47.1	2.22	2.01
Richmond	1.6	31.7	19.6	24.0	11 857	50.7	1 062	0.3	3.5	8.8	10 795	35.2	64.8	2.31	2.05
LOUISIANA	2.4	23.6	26.8	19.4	1 847 181	7.6	191 128	2.1	1.6	9.3	1 656 053	67.9	32.1	2.70	2.44
Alexandria	3.3	28.8	19.0	24.0	19 806	-2.7	1 990	0.3	2.0	10.7	17 816	57.4	42.6	2.53	2.47
Baton Rouge	4.0	26.2	40.1	20.3	97 388	0.3	8 415	0.3	1.6	8.8	88 973	52.2	47.8	2.58	2.25
Bossier City	1.4	16.0	37.9	12.8	23 026	5.6	1 829	0.5	2.1	9.8	21 197	60.0	40.0	2.60	2.56

1. Includes units rented or sold but not occupied. 2. Specified owner-occupied units. 3. Specified renter-occupied units. 4. Overcrowded or lacking complete plumbing facilities.

Table D. Cities — **Labor Force, Employment, Disability, and Construction**

City	Civilian labor force, 2001				Civilian employment, 1990[2]			Disability 1990	Value of residential construction authorized by building permits, 2000		
			Unemployment			Percent					
	Total	Percent change, 2000–2001	Total	Rate[1]	Total	Professional, managerial, and technical	Precision production, craft, and repair	Work disabled persons[3] (percent)	New construction ($1,000)	Number of housing units	Percent single family
	61	62	63	64	65	66	67	68	69	70	71
INDIANA—Cont'd											
Michigan City	16 699	2.8	1 140	6.8	14 582	20.4	11.4	9.5	4 981	72	69.4
Mishawaka	24 700	0.4	1 090	4.4	21 419	24.7	11.7	6.6	38 362	842	11.8
Muncie	34 245	2.1	1 999	5.8	31 169	24.7	9.7	9.7	9 511	173	23.7
New Albany	21 643	0.3	826	3.8	16 476	26.4	11.9	9.6	8 210	127	43.3
Noblesville city, IN	15 880	1.4	340	2.1	9 223	33.7	9.7	6.4	134 207	1 065	73.9
Portage	16 002	0.3	831	5.2	13 161	20.6	17.0	10.1	16 614	188	95.7
Richmond	18 962	-0.6	1 143	6.0	16 804	25.8	11.2	10.9	2 535	30	100.0
South Bend	55 913	0.9	3 551	6.4	47 503	29.0	9.4	8.2	NA	NA	NA
Terre Haute	25 264	0.1	1 670	6.6	23 222	27.2	9.4	10.2	10 206	134	76.9
Valparaiso	14 247	-0.1	449	3.2	11 970	37.6	11.7	6.0	19 750	256	27.3
West Lafayette	13 981	1.4	567	4.1	11 910	55.8	2.6	2.1	9 951	58	69.0
IOWA	1 587 790	1.6	52 954	3.3	1 340 242	25.3	10.5	7.6	1 333 184	12 500	67.8
Ames	29 602	0.1	810	2.7	25 307	46.7	4.0	3.2	25 997	541	26.1
Ankeny	13 472	1.3	186	1.4	11 130	35.6	9.0	5.2	43 627	456	85.5
Bettendorf	16 787	-0.3	416	2.5	14 582	38.9	8.9	5.2	24 986	155	92.3
Burlington	14 066	-1.1	803	5.7	12 348	26.2	13.9	9.0	4 238	34	73.5
Cedar Falls	20 277	0.5	640	3.2	17 077	31.7	7.8	5.5	20 431	167	64.1
Cedar Rapids	73 391	-0.6	2 204	3.0	56 107	32.0	10.2	6.8	65 382	965	36.2
Clinton	14 864	2.1	825	5.6	12 754	23.2	12.6	8.9	6 407	66	51.5
Council Bluffs	31 546	1.4	1 116	3.5	25 915	20.9	11.6	11.3	37 930	522	29.9
Davenport	51 591	0.1	2 149	4.2	44 039	27.9	10.4	7.8	30 353	327	59.9
Des Moines	123 271	1.8	4 119	3.3	99 816	26.9	9.2	9.1	38 742	327	95.4
Dubuque	31 884	-0.1	1 515	4.8	27 639	27.9	9.7	7.2	11 408	108	37.0
Fort Dodge	13 026	2.9	478	3.7	11 551	26.9	10.2	9.6	4 936	36	83.3
Iowa City	43 512	3.8	1 116	2.6	33 465	43.1	4.6	4.1	41 097	432	36.8
Marion	14 193	-1.0	268	1.9	10 975	31.6	10.5	6.3	23 764	343	52.5
Marshalltown	13 210	2.1	408	3.1	12 086	28.6	11.5	8.0	2 946	23	47.8
Mason City	15 572	-0.2	484	3.1	14 045	25.5	8.8	9.5	7 718	50	72.0
Sioux City	44 151	1.8	1 585	3.6	38 030	26.4	12.4	9.2	10 069	98	81.6
Urbandale	16 799	1.3	248	1.5	13 865	43.4	4.7	3.7	50 391	333	90.4
Waterloo	34 375	0.8	1 555	4.5	28 541	25.6	11.7	10.2	12 609	153	58.2
West Des Moines	22 301	1.4	424	1.9	18 327	46.1	3.9	4.1	75 348	475	63.4
KANSAS	1 381 325	-2.1	59 165	4.3	1 172 214	28.7	11.5	7.2	1 397 043	12 542	74.1
Dodge City	11 808	-3.1	368	3.1	10 352	24.5	14.9	8.0	4 736	51	88.2
Emporia	13 899	-2.0	715	5.1	12 074	25.4	15.4	5.6	2 373	31	67.7
Garden City	13 929	-4.1	1 475	10.6	12 115	22.7	19.9	6.0	4 355	62	58.1
Hutchinson	19 540	-2.9	951	4.9	17 962	23.8	12.2	8.7	7 624	69	79.7
Kansas City	70 071	-0.4	6 065	8.7	64 557	19.9	11.5	9.6	18 142	144	98.6
Lawrence	45 181	1.4	2 168	4.8	32 924	37.7	6.5	5.1	59 371	602	50.7
Leavenworth	14 632	-0.5	906	6.2	11 601	32.6	9.0	8.6	5 477	68	76.5
Leawood	12 411	-1.4	286	2.3	9 215	55.0	2.7	2.9	48 620	198	100.0
Lenexa	26 753	-1.1	855	3.2	19 682	44.4	5.7	3.3	61 492	270	100.0
Manhattan	20 736	-2.5	699	3.4	18 236	39.5	6.6	4.3	14 467	124	41.1
Olathe	46 971	-0.9	1 804	3.8	34 327	37.3	8.7	4.3	145 056	1 220	100.0
Overland Park	86 478	-1.1	2 614	3.0	63 736	45.0	4.8	3.8	240 157	2 192	38.1
Salina	25 416	-2.9	908	3.6	20 957	25.3	12.4	8.6	16 432	123	100.0
Shawnee	29 706	-0.9	1 166	3.9	21 690	34.5	10.1	4.4	91 296	1 075	50.3
Topeka	64 948	-1.9	3 042	4.7	58 267	32.2	7.7	9.2	34 586	266	86.8
Wichita	174 828	-2.1	7 998	4.6	149 768	31.7	13.1	8.5	97 833	1 114	92.5
KENTUCKY	1 967 572	-0.7	107 904	5.5	1 563 960	24.7	12.9	11.4	1 767 181	18 460	80.3
Bowling Green	24 794	-1.7	228	0.9	19 291	30.5	8.0	9.3	32 152	429	59.4
Covington	19 229	-0.4	989	5.1	18 636	22.6	12.4	12.2	10 523	236	63.6
Frankfort	14 522	-1.9	494	3.4	13 236	36.4	7.7	8.0	5 872	79	34.2
Henderson	14 307	-0.1	945	6.6	11 710	23.4	13.0	11.4	6 940	102	68.6
Hopkinsville	16 502	1.0	1 000	6.1	11 985	26.0	11.5	10.8	8 085	110	78.2
Jeffersontown	16 208	-2.3	481	3.0	13 224	35.8	8.4	4.9	5 290	44	88.6
Lexington-Fayette	144 218	-1.6	4 258	3.0	117 906	37.2	7.8	7.4	243 912	2 544	74.6
Louisville	127 583	-2.3	5 672	4.4	115 546	28.1	9.7	11.5	34 615	505	68.1
Owensboro	29 039	-1.1	1 766	6.1	23 746	25.9	11.5	10.1	40 103	594	78.5
Paducah	11 414	-2.1	264	2.3	10 489	26.5	9.7	14.0	6 360	39	94.9
Richmond	13 086	-0.2	849	6.5	9 474	27.1	8.4	8.0	11 968	189	56.1
LOUISIANA	2 050 323	1.0	122 390	6.0	1 641 614	28.1	12.5	10.3	1 552 991	14 720	89.1
Alexandria	22 182	-1.3	1 785	8.0	17 726	32.6	7.7	12.4	8 260	60	100.0
Baton Rouge	121 048	1.5	7 088	5.9	95 679	35.6	8.1	7.6	32 003	586	35.8
Bossier City	28 248	1.9	1 547	5.5	21 090	28.6	11.1	8.0	29 070	238	100.0

1. Percent of civilian labor force.   2. Persons 16 years and older.   3. Persons 16 to 64 years old.

City	Wholesale Trade, 1997				Retail Trade[1], 1997				Real Estate and Rental and Leasing, 1997			
	Number of Establishments	Number of Employees	Sales (mil dol)	Annual Payroll (mil dol)	Number of Establishments	Number of Employees	Sales (mil dol)	Annual Payroll (mil dol)	Number of Establishments	Number of Employees	Receipts (mil dol)	Annual Payroll (mil dol)
	72	73	74	75	76	77	78	79	80	81	82	83
INDIANA—Cont'd												
Michigan City	55	726	248.0	22.7	299	3 759	562.4	57.1	35	148	13.4	2.2
Mishawaka	87	1 278	667.0	41.4	393	8 081	1 479.9	116.8	56	248	29.7	4.6
Muncie	80	1 151	444.0	37.6	406	5 648	863.3	83.7	90	341	37.4	6.6
New Albany	69	D	D	D	174	1 886	265.7	30.0	43	214	17.2	3.4
Noblesville city, IN	103	1 178	771.7	42.0	115	1 766	320.0	28.4	28	115	26.3	2.3
Portage	27	612	364.5	18.3	80	1 185	197.2	17.5	26	148	22.3	3.0
Richmond	68	1 362	1 148.3	45.7	249	3 582	585.7	54.6	48	187	20.7	3.4
South Bend	250	4 759	2 191.4	155.5	440	6 597	939.1	98.6	104	853	80.4	18.0
Terre Haute	114	1 390	592.3	36.6	411	7 586	1 963.8	129.8	68	404	30.9	7.2
Valparaiso	44	403	254.6	13.0	177	3 403	534.3	53.0	48	257	31.2	4.2
West Lafayette	9	D	D	D	79	1 660	188.4	17.2	45	D	D	D
IOWA	5 399	63 596	35 453.7	1 820.1	14 695	175 694	26 723.8	2 633.4	2 518	12 619	1 457.5	249.0
Ames	50	380	129.6	10.8	246	3 922	510.8	54.6	48	304	20.7	5.0
Ankeny	58	1 094	411.4	34.3	93	1 677	284.0	25.2	24	94	10.6	1.5
Bettendorf	78	665	516.4	26.3	124	1 821	252.2	28.9	42	182	27.4	3.7
Burlington	33	330	152.2	7.9	132	2 108	259.3	31.0	37	394	46.6	9.7
Cedar Falls	38	723	420.6	22.3	180	2 611	429.5	41.4	35	96	13.1	1.7
Cedar Rapids	285	4 914	1 986.5	139.7	640	10 952	1 638.6	172.0	154	996	110.4	22.1
Clinton	36	277	77.4	6.0	153	1 883	321.5	34.3	35	141	9.4	1.3
Council Bluffs	68	1 155	836.3	36.0	287	4 400	717.2	67.5	52	273	24.8	4.5
Davenport	252	3 458	2 372.4	111.8	545	8 810	1 416.2	147.5	107	1 184	111.3	28.4
Des Moines	408	6 500	2 459.9	221.1	897	13 577	2 103.9	231.6	235	1 848	263.9	43.8
Dubuque	97	1 164	656.2	32.3	382	5 537	734.3	80.4	80	322	30.0	4.5
Fort Dodge	53	D	D	D	216	2 932	374.4	40.5	45	D	D	D
Iowa City	38	D	D	D	333	5 448	775.2	79.8	89	438	50.3	7.8
Marion	35	292	106.2	8.5	112	1 210	200.3	22.3	23	83	10.3	2.2
Marshalltown	39	D	D	D	155	2 296	295.0	31.8	27	239	20.2	6.1
Mason City	55	657	344.1	19.1	218	3 451	519.7	47.4	38	126	13.3	1.9
Sioux City	188	D	D	D	469	7 174	1 049.7	108.3	105	D	D	D
Urbandale	101	1 574	1 391.1	64.8	127	2 441	484.8	46.8	38	219	82.2	4.6
Waterloo	102	1 750	389.1	49.3	347	6 030	807.8	88.5	84	438	47.1	8.5
West Des Moines	118	1 665	3 625.2	68.3	274	5 081	608.2	68.4	87	853	163.2	23.4
KANSAS	5 085	59 954	42 209.9	1 946.8	12 271	140 412	22 571.9	2 191.1	2 602	13 005	1 525.8	259.6
Dodge City	43	506	286.0	14.5	146	1 832	323.6	28.6	33	106	10.7	1.6
Emporia	35	535	182.9	13.3	163	1 870	274.3	26.6	31	D	D	D
Garden City	33	D	D	D	155	2 284	335.9	33.7	34	111	9.4	1.8
Hutchinson	60	955	345.4	28.8	238	2 966	510.3	50.7	41	142	52.1	2.0
Kansas City	293	6 566	3 864.7	216.5	404	4 622	851.0	83.3	119	684	82.4	14.7
Lawrence	77	644	207.0	18.7	413	5 420	731.5	77.8	111	409	45.6	6.4
Leavenworth	13	D	D	D	128	1 638	272.0	24.3	25	113	13.0	1.8
Leawood	87	606	981.5	24.9	95	1 895	201.3	25.6	44	201	33.0	5.7
Lenexa	383	6 605	3 410.9	248.5	226	3 574	634.4	70.7	62	441	48.4	9.1
Manhattan	41	517	141.7	12.7	294	3 570	484.4	47.8	73	241	19.1	3.0
Olathe	181	3 333	1 536.1	130.5	319	4 695	1 106.9	97.8	75	381	46.9	8.1
Overland Park	513	5 130	12 533.4	244.3	745	13 018	2 208.7	222.6	281	2 692	430.0	72.1
Salina	81	989	421.4	28.4	302	4 285	663.4	62.7	64	268	32.3	4.1
Shawnee	75	593	376.5	18.7	165	2 439	459.1	44.2	49	226	29.1	4.2
Topeka	177	1 900	706.5	56.7	706	10 166	1 559.8	160.2	186	1 187	87.3	22.0
Wichita	682	8 221	4 005.0	274.3	1 580	22 657	3 834.5	381.9	480	2 483	317.6	50.4
KENTUCKY	5 051	69 309	37 242.9	2 071.2	17 369	212 189	33 332.7	3 128.1	3 227	16 284	1 961.6	314.3
Bowling Green	128	1 795	1 276.6	50.3	458	6 764	1 048.2	96.3	92	379	36.2	5.5
Covington	35	312	159.3	11.2	173	1 869	310.1	32.4	36	301	19.1	5.7
Frankfort	26	D	D	D	179	2 893	382.0	34.9	32	D	D	D
Henderson	59	D	D	D	192	2 203	415.4	36.1	39	172	15.2	3.3
Hopkinsville	66	D	D	D	241	2 498	406.0	39.6	57	212	23.3	3.4
Jeffersontown	221	3 629	1 512.5	128.7	172	4 097	767.6	73.1	45	751	100.4	18.7
Lexington-Fayette	NA	NA	NA	NA	NA	NA	NA	NA	NA	NA	NA	NA
Louisville	677	14 614	8 597.4	488.2	1 166	15 744	2 069.0	240.0	332	2 698	331.7	60.0
Owensboro	105	1 272	564.7	33.6	393	4 356	656.1	63.4	61	433	30.8	7.3
Paducah	112	D	D	D	432	5 688	914.3	81.8	63	373	56.9	10.5
Richmond	29	572	249.1	21.3	195	2 838	429.3	37.4	41	155	14.9	1.7
LOUISIANA	6 390	76 350	46 972.3	2 375.2	17 863	224 412	35 807.9	3 307.9	4 151	28 571	3 342.1	642.2
Alexandria	101	1 255	427.5	32.5	362	5 064	777.6	76.3	61	375	34.5	5.4
Baton Rouge	594	7 871	2 925.2	283.0	1 408	20 737	3 382.5	328.9	388	3 279	271.4	64.5
Bossier City	77	1 023	1 111.3	28.2	305	4 370	761.7	67.0	54	238	23.5	3.8

1. Establishments with payroll.

Table D. Cities — Professional Services, Manufacturing, Accommodation and Foodservices

City	Professional, Scientific, and Technical Services, 1997[1]				Manufacturing, 1997				Accommodation and Foodservices, 1997			
	Number of Establish-ments	Number of Employees	Receipts (mil dol)	Annual Payroll (mil dol)	Number of Establish-ments	Number of Employees	Receipts (mil dol)	Annual Payroll (mil dol)	Number of Establish-ments	Number of Employees	Sales (mil dol)	Annual Payroll (mil dol)
	84	85	86	87	88	89	90	91	92	93	94	95
INDIANA—Cont'd												
Michigan City	64	406	21.3	7.4	69	4 621	946.9	153.3	106	1 679	55.1	15.0
Mishawaka	113	1 067	99.9	40.6	128	5 253	636.5	162.9	164	3 655	104.8	29.8
Muncie	111	1 480	65.3	27.6	109	7 185	1 305.6	302.4	174	4 337	109.2	30.4
New Albany	114	877	69.8	25.3	100	6 779	1 168.7	188.2	87	1 408	44.5	12.8
Noblesville city, IN	78	428	52.3	17.3	38	1 419	292.7	45.5	51	1 050	29.3	8.7
Portage	43	228	22.7	10.1	22	2 172	1 124.5	112.6	56	951	28.1	8.0
Richmond	54	343	24.4	11.3	95	8 093	1 500.2	250.1	103	2 158	63.6	18.4
South Bend	292	2 564	235.7	99.2	200	10 066	1 850.1	361.8	257	4 868	142.8	40.8
Terre Haute	133	836	55.2	16.9	92	5 998	1 398.4	200.3	217	4 308	126.8	36.2
Valparaiso	90	527	42.5	15.6	54	2 134	552.2	82.4	90	1 672	49.5	14.0
West Lafayette	38	137	16.5	5.4	20	D	D	D	86	1 860	47.0	13.5
IOWA	4 670	31 115	2 435.6	887.9	3 749	235 880	62 413.7	7 573.3	6 830	99 148	2 762.8	769.5
Ames	104	808	88.3	31.2	44	2 344	824.1	75.3	168	3 173	79.0	21.7
Ankeny	49	251	17.6	7.6	14	2 225	879.6	111.2	50	1 022	29.5	8.1
Bettendorf	65	356	33.3	12.3	28	1 127	130.9	34.3	72	1 712	49.5	15.8
Burlington	49	219	15.8	5.0	37	4 089	891.2	142.0	89	D	D	D
Cedar Falls	61	627	35.3	16.8	50	1 911	261.7	61.5	99	2 182	47.9	15.3
Cedar Rapids	296	2 391	229.8	89.3	164	21 491	6 194.2	890.3	350	6 760	209.8	59.5
Clinton	41	156	9.8	3.2	28	3 649	1 780.1	126.9	91	1 184	32.1	9.0
Council Bluffs	78	458	39.1	12.5	41	D	D	D	146	3 338	174.2	45.1
Davenport	229	1 571	138.5	44.1	121	6 380	2 984.9	248.0	262	5 707	167.0	48.5
Des Moines	450	6 867	527.9	218.0	234	11 168	2 841.7	375.8	514	9 234	293.7	86.7
Dubuque	98	733	51.9	22.3	86	D	D	D	179	3 220	80.1	23.7
Fort Dodge	61	309	21.9	8.2	44	1 976	911.3	61.3	78	1 274	35.5	10.3
Iowa City	125	761	62.2	21.0	48	2 945	2 339.2	102.7	178	3 743	89.2	25.5
Marion	32	418	24.1	13.1	39	607	74.8	21.0	38	D	D	D
Marshalltown	45	193	12.6	4.7	38	D	D	D	70	981	27.3	7.9
Mason City	53	321	23.0	9.6	37	3 308	677.9	88.8	88	1 495	39.1	11.1
Sioux City	169	907	71.3	23.1	94	6 018	1 853.7	160.2	214	3 544	103.2	28.4
Urbandale	90	968	82.9	27.2	23	861	288.2	31.9	48	776	25.7	7.2
Waterloo	122	876	64.9	27.6	93	11 413	4 848.1	487.4	163	3 120	82.1	22.2
West Des Moines	214	1 911	167.4	74.8	43	1 390	194.6	43.6	118	2 641	78.4	24.8
KANSAS	5 345	39 534	3 559.3	1 396.0	3 309	193 742	46 296.4	6 532.5	5 677	91 173	2 685.7	757.1
Dodge City	49	439	27.6	12.5	19	D	D	D	64	D	D	D
Emporia	37	D	D	D	30	D	D	D	96	1 593	36.2	9.7
Garden City	53	320	20.2	8.0	NA	NA	NA	NA	61	1 261	37.6	10.6
Hutchinson	75	407	23.9	10.3	47	2 365	364.0	71.2	103	1 927	56.7	14.6
Kansas City	146	1 098	86.1	32.4	249	14 624	7 562.1	623.8	212	2 962	102.6	28.7
Lawrence	175	1 216	77.4	30.1	56	3 439	541.6	86.2	222	4 511	117.9	33.6
Leavenworth	51	637	73.1	19.4	NA	NA	NA	NA	63	1 104	27.6	8.3
Leawood	122	800	93.7	37.0	NA	NA	NA	NA	37	D	D	D
Lenexa	216	3 229	299.5	121.2	133	7 703	1 506.0	232.7	89	1 994	69.7	19.2
Manhattan	87	665	55.5	20.9	NA	NA	NA	NA	153	3 003	75.3	21.2
Olathe	182	636	62.0	22.4	117	4 902	842.3	181.4	128	2 785	79.2	23.7
Overland Park	795	11 091	1 306.2	527.1	106	1 632	226.4	50.7	340	8 788	316.7	93.8
Salina	80	697	51.6	20.2	68	5 496	985.3	160.7	127	2 357	66.1	20.0
Shawnee	95	201	19.2	7.7	42	D	D	D	77	D	D	D
Topeka	376	3 131	224.9	91.5	124	D	D	D	353	D	D	D
Wichita	865	6 100	518.0	210.6	496	52 170	8 579.6	2 158.6	852	15 891	528.1	151.1
KENTUCKY	6 189	41 991	3 820.3	1 260.1	4 218	288 405	86 636.1	9 198.1	6 546	129 442	4 056.1	1 140.6
Bowling Green	130	869	53.1	18.4	88	D	D	D	182	4 306	134.0	39.5
Covington	100	754	77.0	31.4	45	1 491	321.1	40.7	133	2 283	87.5	24.3
Frankfort	95	655	59.5	24.7	28	2 760	504.5	79.1	85	D	D	D
Henderson	62	265	17.1	5.4	62	6 189	1 557.8	192.9	75	1 392	40.8	11.8
Hopkinsville	71	272	21.4	6.6	48	4 406	775.0	114.5	72	1 713	42.4	14.9
Jeffersontown	117	1 615	182.6	47.6	107	4 447	632.0	139.8	79	2 869	98.7	27.4
Lexington-Fayette	NA	NA	NA	NA	283	17 403	4 313.9	654.0	NA	NA	NA	NA
Louisville	1 024	9 645	948.4	334.6	456	29 078	17 225.4	1 076.2	648	15 529	507.6	147.7
Owensboro	127	809	53.2	22.3	86	D	D	D	121	2 865	87.4	23.2
Paducah	120	886	62.7	20.4	40	1 634	300.9	51.9	167	3 808	117.5	33.3
Richmond	52	201	10.8	3.6	35	1 981	583.1	55.4	79	1 806	51.1	14.7
LOUISIANA	9 077	63 642	5 754.6	2 159.0	3 545	165 777	80 424.0	6 054.5	7 151	147 016	5 259.9	1 408.9
Alexandria	173	1 114	90.1	31.3	32	D	D	D	138	2 717	80.7	22.2
Baton Rouge	1 114	9 708	856.1	330.0	265	5 598	1 444.6	201.2	594	13 431	409.5	113.6
Bossier City	72	286	19.3	6.7	57	1 915	211.4	45.4	150	5 379	292.7	67.9

1. Firms subject to federal tax.

Table D. Cities — Entertainment, Health Care, and Other Services

City	Arts, Entertainment, and Recreation[1], 1997				Health Care and Social Assistance[1], 1997				Other Services[1], 1997			
	Number of Establishments	Number of Employees	Receipts (mil dol)	Annual Payroll (mil dol)	Number of Establishments	Number of Employees	Receipts (mil dol)	Annual Payroll (mil dol)	Number of Establishments	Number of Employees	Receipts (mil dol)	Annual Payroll (mil dol)
	96	97	98	99	100	101	102	103	104	105	106	107
INDIANA—Cont'd												
Michigan City	10	0	0.0	0.0	93	1 164	87.5	40.3	76	465	26.2	9.7
Mishawaka	17	270	7.5	2.3	102	1 129	73.3	32.3	102	693	43.4	13.3
Muncie	18	255	6.8	1.8	182	2 555	173.4	81.1	141	1 346	87.8	21.3
New Albany	11	69	2.1	0.8	135	1 730	103.1	43.7	82	543	28.8	10.0
Noblesville city, IN	12	177	6.7	2.0	60	649	40.5	18.6	45	287	18.8	5.1
Portage	8	43	1.8	0.4	46	494	24.6	10.6	52	357	21.4	7.0
Richmond	12	89	3.5	0.8	86	985	51.5	27.0	82	423	20.6	6.5
South Bend	16	178	7.1	1.7	303	4 036	344.7	165.3	220	2 470	172.6	55.3
Terre Haute	18	144	4.2	1.1	211	3 023	226.9	71.1	129	1 162	54.9	16.3
Valparaiso	8	83	3.4	0.8	139	1 369	101.5	47.7	90	552	30.7	8.9
West Lafayette	5	26	0.9	0.2	31	329	21.8	6.2	38	216	8.1	3.0
IOWA	875	14 169	919.8	220.3	4 876	56 374	3 183.2	1 540.6	5 234	24 383	1 486.5	411.3
Ames	15	289	9.0	2.7	62	1 142	76.9	41.1	78	472	27.8	7.7
Ankeny	11	47	2.5	0.5	41	641	21.1	9.7	40	220	21.3	4.6
Bettendorf	11	0	0.0	0.0	66	480	35.2	11.9	52	396	21.0	7.5
Burlington	8	96	3.4	0.7	79	643	45.2	19.6	44	222	12.1	3.3
Cedar Falls	6	0	0.0	0.0	62	616	33.4	16.9	50	308	18.4	6.0
Cedar Rapids	30	544	14.0	4.3	266	3 172	226.4	116.5	251	1 651	95.8	29.4
Clinton	11	0	0.0	0.0	69	646	39.8	15.0	59	248	14.4	3.9
Council Bluffs	19	0	0.0	0.0	93	1 220	71.4	40.2	100	536	31.8	9.6
Davenport	39	0	0.0	0.0	228	2 501	196.1	97.8	206	1 376	79.7	25.7
Des Moines	41	495	45.1	6.0	409	4 536	403.6	201.9	368	2 531	153.5	49.1
Dubuque	20	1 106	73.7	19.1	104	2 146	179.0	85.8	130	773	40.3	12.7
Fort Dodge	5	46	1.2	0.3	79	674	49.2	23.6	68	374	18.9	6.0
Iowa City	20	213	6.0	1.7	124	1 312	76.7	30.6	104	569	32.4	9.6
Marion	8	65	1.9	0.4	35	348	17.5	7.4	47	227	14.6	4.7
Marshalltown	8	0	0.0	0.0	48	532	29.0	14.2	50	236	13.9	3.7
Mason City	11	0	0.0	0.0	62	1 118	74.0	46.3	72	371	16.8	5.7
Sioux City	28	0	0.0	0.0	209	1 986	181.2	87.3	155	1 195	59.0	18.9
Urbandale	13	232	4.4	1.4	52	719	38.5	16.1	53	431	27.7	9.3
Waterloo	17	184	8.4	2.1	156	1 484	131.2	64.7	132	1 121	55.1	18.5
West Des Moines	16	275	10.3	3.6	158	2 146	121.3	63.7	75	586	26.7	8.5
KANSAS	652	7 618	374.5	91.0	4 793	66 613	4 116.1	1 771.8	4 604	24 081	1 548.4	452.9
Dodge City	6	81	1.6	0.6	57	765	64.8	24.3	45	213	12.5	3.4
Emporia	9	67	1.6	0.4	60	696	32.4	16.4	64	289	14.5	4.2
Garden City	6	0	0.0	0.0	48	576	40.4	19.0	63	319	16.1	4.9
Hutchinson	5	69	1.3	0.3	73	1 172	93.1	45.3	79	403	20.0	6.3
Kansas City	23	0	0.0	0.0	199	3 705	288.5	101.4	215	1 325	74.0	24.2
Lawrence	33	263	8.9	2.3	159	1 399	80.1	37.2	119	738	38.7	13.0
Leavenworth	7	39	1.0	0.3	56	429	21.7	10.5	50	241	11.9	4.0
Leawood	7	100	3.6	1.3	76	488	45.6	22.5	30	202	10.2	3.7
Lenexa	14	212	7.3	2.0	95	2 157	161.8	55.9	94	925	99.5	25.2
Manhattan	12	0	0.0	0.0	92	936	55.1	22.0	83	439	18.0	5.8
Olathe	15	96	4.7	1.5	154	1 897	106.9	53.2	141	814	49.1	15.5
Overland Park	56	1 105	45.0	13.5	447	7 629	570.2	243.5	261	1 823	109.3	38.1
Salina	11	0	0.0	0.0	123	0	0.0	0.0	99	526	31.9	9.9
Shawnee	13	110	3.7	1.1	58	661	31.9	13.5	71	384	26.1	8.7
Topeka	34	546	17.2	4.1	308	5 637	307.4	159.0	277	1 782	120.3	39.3
Wichita	78	0	0.0	0.0	701	14 506	1 103.3	450.4	675	4 622	283.2	89.0
KENTUCKY	906	10 580	550.2	126.3	6 805	94 720	5 936.2	2 620.3	5 383	31 164	1 870.3	551.4
Bowling Green	21	136	4.0	0.9	218	3 778	259.3	103.6	116	976	40.7	13.6
Covington	10	114	5.8	1.4	38	695	24.0	13.1	76	391	26.0	8.3
Frankfort	6	84	2.8	1.1	84	1 234	87.2	36.1	55	385	20.5	8.6
Henderson	7	0	0.0	0.0	89	680	48.3	19.2	57	475	30.2	10.0
Hopkinsville	10	38	1.6	0.4	91	0	0.0	0.0	67	247	16.0	4.0
Jeffersontown	13	176	12.8	2.4	65	1 467	128.5	37.5	74	730	57.8	16.8
Lexington-Fayette	NA	NA	NA	NA	NA	NA	NA	NA	NA	NA	NA	NA
Louisville	94	1 991	130.7	21.1	799	14 394	998.1	472.7	580	4 014	240.6	73.6
Owensboro	17	147	5.4	1.3	178	2 374	174.7	73.5	119	747	43.7	12.8
Paducah	15	142	4.9	1.7	157	1 927	167.2	85.5	93	645	43.7	10.8
Richmond	5	32	0.6	0.1	82	794	41.9	19.1	42	270	10.8	3.4
LOUISIANA	1 016	22 828	1 958.1	412.9	8 580	129 773	7 967.6	3 341.5	5 998	39 764	2 595.2	767.2
Alexandria	15	79	7.9	1.1	236	4 053	243.9	101.7	109	629	38.1	11.9
Baton Rouge	59	2 688	273.4	46.0	769	11 992	793.7	364.8	539	4 223	249.6	80.1
Bossier City	21	0	0.0	0.0	90	1 461	81.0	32.3	123	701	36.8	10.7

1. Firms subject to federal tax.

Table D. Cities — **Federal Funds and City Government Finances**

	Selected federal funds, fiscal 2001[1] (mil dol)									City government finances, 1999						
										General revenue						
	Procurement contracts		Grants					Direct payments for individuals		Intergovernmental			Taxes			
														Per capita[3] (dollars)		
City	Defense	Other	Total[2]	Health and family welfare	Energy and environment	Education	Housing and community development	Educational assistance	Housing assistance	Total (mil dol)	Total (mil dol)	Percent from state government	Total (mil dol)	Total	Property	Sales and gross receipts
	108	109	110	111	112	113	114	115	116	117	118	119	120	121	122	123
INDIANA—Cont'd																
Michigan City	2.0	0.2	2.8	0.4	0.3	0.8	0.1	0.2	5.6	46.5	18.5	88.2	15.6	479	367	0
Mishawaka	58.2	58.2	0.7	0.1	0.0	0.0	0.4	1.1	10.5	29.7	6.6	83.1	13.9	307	291	0
Muncie	0.0	3.0	10.2	1.7	0.0	1.7	3.0	8.4	6.6	41.7	11.6	76.5	20.0	297	236	0
New Albany	0.0	0.3	1.6	0.6	0.0	0.0	0.9	2.9	3.4	NA	NA	NA	NA	NA	NA	NA
Noblesville city, IN	0.0	0.5	0.1	0.0	0.0	0.0	0.0	0.1	4.9	25.0	3.4	78.6	12.8	493	222	0
Portage	0.2	0.0	2.7	0.0	0.0	0.0	0.0	0.0	1.2	19.0	4.9	94.4	6.9	210	199	0
Richmond	1.2	0.8	1.1	1.0	0.0	0.0	0.0	3.1	10.6	33.2	11.0	57.6	11.3	305	277	0
South Bend	115.8	342.0	27.5	4.8	4.6	0.3	4.5	4.6	38.0	100.5	20.1	72.3	41.0	412	358	4
Terre Haute	15.9	8.0	11.2	2.9	0.0	2.4	2.8	7.9	7.6	36.2	10.9	65.7	16.5	310	304	0
Valparaiso	0.9	3.9	1.5	0.0	0.2	0.0	0.0	2.2	6.8	20.0	4.0	78.0	8.0	308	290	0
West Lafayette	7.6	3.3	105.5	32.2	6.9	5.4	0.4	14.0	4.6	NA	NA	NA	NA	NA	NA	NA
IOWA	503.3	393.5	3 079.2	1 887.0	71.0	263.7	53.1	134.9	219.2	X	X	X	X	X	X	X
Ames	4.5	35.9	101.1	13.0	9.1	2.4	0.1	12.9	3.4	129.5	15.3	81.3	15.1	311	241	57
Ankeny	0.0	0.1	2.5	0.2	0.0	0.8	0.0	6.0	0.3	23.8	8.2	95.6	9.4	374	334	24
Bettendorf	0.7	0.2	0.3	0.0	0.0	0.0	0.0	0.0	1.5	32.6	6.6	82.4	17.9	565	358	190
Burlington	1.1	0.0	3.8	1.2	0.0	0.0	0.0	0.0	4.9	26.2	5.3	61.0	11.5	429	277	139
Cedar Falls	1.2	0.5	8.6	0.3	1.3	4.8	0.3	7.1	3.6	34.9	8.0	43.4	14.0	402	280	110
Cedar Rapids	354.7	21.2	23.1	5.7	0.2	3.0	2.0	12.1	11.0	156.6	31.9	58.8	56.1	489	447	27
Clinton	0.6	0.0	1.1	0.0	0.0	0.0	0.1	0.5	2.5	26.8	6.8	73.4	12.0	434	334	94
Council Bluffs	0.1	0.2	2.7	0.5	0.0	0.2	1.4	2.1	11.7	68.8	11.6	57.5	35.4	629	407	210
Davenport	47.4	1.1	16.1	9.7	0.4	2.4	2.5	9.7	11.0	104.4	25.5	73.6	46.8	483	378	91
Des Moines	14.3	18.3	512.0	182.3	49.3	76.7	37.4	20.6	32.5	248.9	57.4	49.7	90.5	473	429	36
Dubuque	0.4	0.9	9.7	1.3	0.0	0.6	3.0	3.7	10.1	66.8	13.9	47.7	25.3	448	303	126
Fort Dodge	6.3	0.2	4.5	0.7	0.0	0.4	0.0	3.0	5.1	19.7	4.0	67.6	8.5	345	327	10
Iowa City	1.6	69.5	186.0	153.3	4.4	4.4	1.7	9.0	11.8	72.2	16.4	48.6	23.2	381	356	14
Marion	0.4	0.0	0.0	0.0	0.0	0.0	0.0	0.0	0.9	15.7	2.6	96.3	8.0	337	303	12
Marshalltown	0.0	3.0	11.4	0.8	0.0	0.0	0.0	1.3	2.8	20.8	5.5	67.2	9.3	370	346	15
Mason City	0.4	3.1	4.1	2.0	1.0	0.2	0.0	1.8	4.8	28.2	6.3	62.8	12.9	448	294	136
Sioux City	0.9	1.3	19.3	4.0	1.4	4.3	2.3	5.9	11.5	96.9	20.8	47.1	43.7	529	387	134
Urbandale	0.0	0.8	0.0	0.0	0.0	0.0	0.0	0.0	0.0	15.6	3.1	92.9	10.5	378	330	28
Waterloo	0.6	-5.8	9.6	2.3	1.0	1.0	2.3	3.6	11.8	80.8	21.2	38.8	34.6	543	400	129
West Des Moines	10.7	5.9	6.3	6.0	0.0	0.0	0.0	0.0	1.3	48.0	6.5	60.3	27.2	643	573	45
KANSAS	960.0	422.9	2 721.1	1 500.1	49.6	318.0	42.3	100.5	141.8	X	X	X	X	X	X	X
Dodge City	0.0	0.0	5.0	0.4	0.0	1.4	0.0	1.2	1.2	19.5	2.9	86.2	10.6	472	226	236
Emporia	0.5	0.0	3.6	0.7	0.0	2.7	0.0	3.9	1.9	18.7	3.9	68.4	6.8	279	171	108
Garden City	0.0	0.0	4.4	0.8	0.0	3.5	0.0	1.2	0.9	21.8	4.1	41.0	7.5	287	108	173
Hutchinson	0.4	0.0	2.8	0.4	0.0	1.1	0.0	1.8	2.8	32.7	6.7	34.3	15.0	384	194	184
Kansas City	4.5	28.7	62.1	48.2	0.1	5.5	2.8	4.4	19.6	267.4	33.8	40.5	107.1	758	450	297
Lawrence	1.6	4.2	73.4	23.2	3.7	21.5	1.5	10.3	3.3	125.3	18.4	53.2	24.6	332	146	177
Leavenworth	3.7	7.8	1.1	0.0	0.0	0.5	0.6	0.4	8.2	23.1	6.0	44.1	11.9	304	173	124
Leawood	0.0	0.1	0.3	0.1	0.0	0.0	0.0	0.0	0.0	29.6	7.2	17.4	14.2	547	284	223
Lenexa	1.8	10.5	1.1	0.9	0.0	0.0	0.0	0.0	0.4	47.8	11.6	27.4	24.4	628	360	241
Manhattan	9.0	4.2	63.3	7.2	6.6	7.5	0.0	12.2	1.2	29.4	2.9	54.2	18.4	446	169	269
Olathe	28.6	1.5	6.7	0.2	0.0	0.0	2.2	1.1	4.3	83.8	16.0	24.6	30.9	363	174	171
Overland Park	11.3	14.9	1.5	0.3	0.0	0.0	0.5	0.1	5.2	107.8	22.0	49.3	63.5	455	111	302
Salina	1.0	0.9	2.1	1.6	0.0	0.2	0.1	2.5	2.6	41.9	13.6	22.6	10.5	239	178	54
Shawnee	0.7	17.3	1.5	0.7	0.0	0.0	0.0	0.0	1.4	31.6	8.4	22.5	15.0	331	175	135
Topeka	3.5	22.0	454.4	163.9	37.4	88.1	28.1	6.5	19.6	134.3	19.7	49.2	62.0	521	250	261
Wichita	568.0	49.1	42.8	12.4	0.4	7.4	5.6	12.0	16.4	302.6	78.9	50.1	94.4	287	177	96
KENTUCKY	1 133.8	1 625.4	5 100.1	3 217.8	52.2	474.6	90.7	185.2	309.9	X	X	X	X	X	X	X
Bowling Green	3.2	0.7	18.4	7.6	1.0	6.0	0.0	11.9	6.5	56.0	6.3	24.5	26.7	595	141	11
Covington	0.0	12.5	9.4	2.3	0.5	2.2	2.4	0.7	8.0	51.5	11.7	31.6	25.8	639	108	44
Frankfort	1.4	2.2	725.1	241.8	35.8	148.9	61.8	2.9	14.5	30.6	4.1	30.8	12.8	484	91	0
Henderson	0.0	0.0	3.2	0.7	0.3	0.4	0.3	0.1	4.4	26.2	6.5	20.4	7.9	300	120	30
Hopkinsville	0.9	0.8	1.4	0.0	0.0	0.4	0.4	0.0	4.6	22.5	1.7	90.0	11.9	371	81	12
Jeffersontown	0.0	0.0	0.0	0.0	0.0	0.0	0.0	0.0	0.3	17.4	0.9	57.6	11.3	440	121	12
Lexington-Fayette	114.6	22.4	159.6	84.8	4.5	10.3	3.0	73.8	18.0	312.5	35.7	29.5	171.7	710	128	33
Louisville	571.8	56.9	146.3	52.9	3.0	15.5	15.5	33.1	53.6	410.9	129.6	30.1	206.3	809	180	8
Owensboro	5.6	1.4	16.0	10.1	0.0	1.2	1.5	2.2	11.9	57.0	9.0	64.3	20.1	372	102	9
Paducah	0.5	56.1	3.4	0.9	0.0	1.0	0.0	0.0	7.6	39.7	7.5	33.6	20.4	788	188	12
Richmond	9.7	0.1	8.4	1.7	0.0	1.8	0.0	11.0	4.2	28.4	4.8	34.3	10.9	394	49	15
LOUISIANA	1 473.7	1 151.6	6 172.7	3 917.2	75.4	582.4	140.3	204.6	354.1	X	X	X	X	X	X	X
Alexandria	16.1	4.7	16.3	3.1	0.0	1.9	1.2	3.0	5.3	49.9	11.2	24.4	26.2	572	112	421
Baton Rouge	200.3	6.9	861.7	243.8	51.5	184.3	52.4	35.3	28.8	482.7	44.1	80.1	278.6	1 317	300	913
Bossier City	1.2	0.6	3.0	2.1	0.0	0.0	0.8	2.8	4.2	106.9	13.6	82.8	36.9	651	110	508

1. October 1, 2000 to September 30, 2001. 2. Includes program categories not shown separately. State totals include additional categories not allocated by city. 3. Based on population estimated as of July 1 of the year shown.

City	City government finances, 1999 (cont'd)												
	General expenditure												
	Per capita¹ (dollars)			Percent of total for —									
	Total (mil dol)	Total	Capital outlays	Public welfare	Highways	Parking facilities	Education	Health and hospitals	Police protection	Sewerage and sanitation	Parks and recreation	Housing and com-munity develop-ment	Interest on debt
	124	125	126	127	128	129	130	131	132	133	134	135	136
INDIANA—Cont'd													
Michigan City	51.5	1 578	328	0.0	3.0	0.0	0.0	0.2	8.0	30.2	17.8	2.3	4.0
Mishawaka	31.4	692	72	0.0	10.0	0.0	0.0	2.3	14.1	13.9	8.0	6.3	6.4
Muncie	40.9	606	29	0.0	7.9	0.0	0.0	0.6	14.2	34.3	2.7	4.5	0.2
New Albany	NA	NA	NA	NA	NA	NA	NA	NA	NA	NA	NA	NA	NA
Noblesville city, IN	25.0	963	239	0.0	8.8	0.2	0.0	0.6	10.5	13.2	5.9	0.0	8.8
Portage	17.3	524	109	0.0	10.4	0.0	0.0	0.3	14.0	28.0	6.3	0.0	4.1
Richmond	30.4	821	170	0.0	9.3	0.0	0.0	1.1	15.0	28.8	9.2	1.3	0.0
South Bend	113.8	1 145	219	0.0	6.3	15.0	0.0	1.7	15.9	10.2	17.5	0.0	3.4
Terre Haute	37.8	709	62	0.0	6.8	0.0	0.0	0.0	12.4	17.0	6.6	7.3	4.3
Valparaiso	18.8	727	83	0.0	9.4	0.6	0.0	0.0	12.1	25.8	18.9	0.0	3.4
West Lafayette	NA	NA	NA	NA	NA	NA	NA	NA	NA	NA	NA	NA	NA
IOWA	X	X	X	X	X	X	X	X	X	X	X	X	X
Ames	130.6	2 698	649	0.5	9.9	0.5	0.0	64.2	3.4	6.8	2.6	0.6	3.0
Ankeny	19.6	781	319	0.1	37.4	0.0	0.0	2.8	12.0	5.4	11.0	0.0	9.8
Bettendorf	35.3	1 111	356	0.0	27.6	0.0	0.0	0.0	11.6	7.2	9.9	1.0	8.3
Burlington	32.1	1 196	514	0.7	21.2	1.8	0.0	2.0	10.8	9.5	20.7	3.7	5.3
Cedar Falls	32.4	932	248	0.0	34.5	0.5	0.0	0.9	8.1	14.0	8.7	3.3	5.1
Cedar Rapids	164.7	1 438	476	0.0	18.2	2.4	0.0	0.6	10.6	26.2	8.7	4.2	6.4
Clinton	28.1	1 017	314	0.7	27.5	0.1	0.0	1.7	13.4	10.0	6.9	1.1	11.8
Council Bluffs	81.7	1 452	715	0.0	19.8	0.1	0.0	1.7	9.8	17.3	9.6	3.5	6.0
Davenport	96.7	998	161	0.0	21.1	0.6	0.0	0.7	6.6	11.3	11.7	6.9	15.4
Des Moines	228.0	1 192	163	0.0	9.5	1.3	0.0	1.2	13.7	21.4	5.5	1.2	8.5
Dubuque	61.8	1 094	323	0.2	20.8	0.9	0.0	1.8	10.9	9.6	8.2	6.5	3.8
Fort Dodge	19.6	791	164	0.6	10.6	0.4	0.0	5.2	12.5	24.7	8.8	5.4	5.6
Iowa City	81.7	1 342	492	0.0	12.8	4.6	0.0	0.5	7.7	21.4	6.2	7.7	9.8
Marion	14.4	607	130	0.3	24.1	0.0	0.0	0.1	19.2	18.6	4.5	1.4	3.7
Marshalltown	23.5	934	318	0.2	29.5	0.3	0.0	0.2	15.7	20.4	4.9	4.2	6.3
Mason City	24.2	844	199	0.3	16.1	0.4	0.0	0.5	14.0	13.4	8.7	6.6	8.4
Sioux City	94.8	1 146	266	0.0	9.5	0.7	0.0	0.3	11.0	13.3	10.0	11.3	6.4
Urbandale	15.1	542	63	0.0	19.0	0.0	0.0	2.3	20.0	7.6	14.8	1.8	5.8
Waterloo	76.1	1 194	326	0.3	19.8	1.0	0.0	3.5	11.7	14.8	7.3	7.5	10.9
West Des Moines	50.9	1 203	493	1.0	25.1	0.0	0.0	5.0	10.6	20.0	11.5	1.7	4.7
KANSAS	X	X	X	X	X	X	X	X	X	X	X	X	X
Dodge City	19.2	857	216	0.3	5.6	0.0	0.0	0.3	16.4	13.0	9.3	6.6	4.3
Emporia	20.5	839	127	0.0	10.7	0.4	0.0	0.3	15.8	19.7	9.0	1.8	6.4
Garden City	17.7	679	50	0.0	7.1	0.1	0.0	0.7	16.5	11.4	11.2	0.7	14.4
Hutchinson	35.6	912	210	0.0	5.2	0.0	0.0	0.6	10.7	16.8	5.9	0.0	3.2
Kansas City	274.6	1 943	199	0.0	7.0	0.0	0.0	1.2	11.5	4.8	2.8	1.6	34.6
Lawrence	133.1	1 793	367	0.2	1.6	0.4	0.0	46.2	5.6	10.7	5.8	4.1	4.0
Leavenworth	21.9	558	103	0.0	9.2	0.2	0.0	0.0	15.4	14.1	5.3	7.9	4.4
Leawood	26.1	1 009	243	0.0	17.2	0.0	0.0	0.2	16.8	11.3	7.9	0.0	4.4
Lenexa	43.6	1 122	293	0.0	23.6	0.0	0.0	0.4	14.5	0.7	10.9	0.0	23.5
Manhattan	44.5	1 076	382	0.0	2.4	0.0	0.0	0.5	11.0	8.2	4.5	7.2	5.9
Olathe	82.9	975	269	0.0	13.0	0.0	0.0	0.1	9.7	12.1	4.1	0.6	19.4
Overland Park	96.1	688	199	0.7	38.1	0.0	0.0	0.5	20.7	0.0	9.2	0.2	3.8
Salina	38.8	881	157	0.0	8.1	0.0	0.0	1.1	9.7	12.9	15.3	7.4	3.0
Shawnee	30.8	681	229	0.4	32.6	0.0	0.0	0.0	18.5	9.0	5.2	0.0	16.0
Topeka	138.8	1 167	125	0.8	10.7	2.1	0.0	6.0	14.3	11.6	6.7	6.3	12.8
Wichita	296.6	901	225	2.9	23.4	0.2	0.0	1.0	12.4	11.1	8.5	7.5	9.7
KENTUCKY	X	X	X	X	X	X	X	X	X	X	X	X	X
Bowling Green	44.3	987	70	1.0	8.6	0.0	0.0	0.0	12.0	9.2	11.2	7.1	23.2
Covington	48.6	1 204	70	0.0	11.0	1.1	0.0	0.0	20.0	4.0	1.1	19.9	11.5
Frankfort	31.0	1 175	199	0.0	4.9	1.0	0.0	8.8	9.1	15.2	5.5	1.6	3.3
Henderson	25.0	946	38	3.2	5.7	0.0	0.0	0.0	14.0	24.7	3.7	6.2	4.8
Hopkinsville	21.4	668	62	0.0	6.2	0.0	0.0	0.0	15.5	21.4	2.2	9.9	14.4
Jeffersontown	17.8	693	65	0.0	1.2	0.0	0.0	0.0	18.9	9.8	0.0	0.0	20.9
Lexington-Fayette	282.7	1 170	261	2.2	8.6	0.1	0.1	1.9	11.2	13.9	6.1	4.8	5.7
Louisville	304.4	1 194	203	1.7	5.8	1.6	0.0	0.6	16.6	4.9	8.9	6.7	7.2
Owensboro	53.1	982	128	0.0	4.4	0.1	0.0	0.0	12.2	8.5	3.4	7.2	17.8
Paducah	32.4	1 251	84	0.6	9.0	0.0	0.0	0.0	15.7	9.5	5.0	15.4	2.0
Richmond	22.6	819	85	10.4	1.6	0.0	0.0	0.0	9.9	15.6	7.0	7.0	30.8
LOUISIANA	X	X	X	X	X	X	X	X	X	X	X	X	X
Alexandria	64.5	1 408	603	0.0	19.1	0.7	0.0	0.3	22.3	28.1	3.5	5.4	1.8
Baton Rouge	489.7	2 315	358	0.5	13.1	0.1	0.0	9.8	11.3	16.2	3.7	4.2	9.0
Bossier City	113.2	1 998	564	0.0	11.6	0.0	0.0	42.6	7.0	11.3	3.6	4.1	3.9

1. Based on population estimated as of July 1 of the year shown.

Table D. Cities — City Government Finances, City Government Employment, and Climate

City	City government finances, 1999 (cont'd) Debt outstanding Total (mil dol)	Per capita[1] (dollars)	Percent utility	City government employment, 2001	Climate[2] Average daily temperature (degrees Fahrenheit) Mean January	July	Limits January[3]	July[4]	Annual precipitation (inches)	Heating degree days	Cooling degree days
	137	138	139	140	141	142	143	144	145	146	147
INDIANA—Cont'd											
Michigan City	65.8	2 016	18.1	459	23.7	74.1	15.2	85.5	36.82	6 043	857
Mishawaka	32.5	718	1.0	567	23.3	72.9	16.1	82.9	39.14	6 331	728
Muncie	1.2	18	0.0	551	23.6	74.4	15.7	84.4	37.88	6 027	878
New Albany	NA	NA	NA	NA	31.7	77.2	23.2	87.0	44.39	4 514	1 288
Noblesville city, IN	40.8	1 571	0.0	NA	NA	NA	NA	NA	NA	NA	NA
Portage	13.8	418	0.0	NA	23.7	74.1	15.2	85.5	36.82	6 043	857
Richmond	0.0	0	0.0	564	24.9	73.1	15.9	84.5	39.95	5 963	759
South Bend	136.8	1 376	18.5	1 527	23.3	72.9	16.1	82.9	39.14	6 331	728
Terre Haute	29.2	548	0.0	580	25.3	75.6	16.2	86.6	41.19	5 581	1 025
Valparaiso	17.2	663	3.5	366	NA	NA	NA	NA	NA	NA	NA
West Lafayette	NA	NA	NA	NA	23.8	74.9	15.8	86.0	35.80	5 940	935
IOWA	X	X	X	X	X	X	X	X	X	X	X
Ames	88.1	1 819	17.1	576	18.2	74.2	8.8	85.3	32.94	6 776	816
Ankeny	46.4	1 851	2.2	153	NA	NA	NA	NA	NA	NA	NA
Bettendorf	48.9	1 542	0.0	258	19.9	75.2	11.3	85.9	39.08	6 474	911
Burlington	30.1	1 120	1.1	259	21.8	75.7	13.1	85.8	36.06	6 158	992
Cedar Falls	37.8	1 089	18.4	413	14.6	73.1	5.4	83.9	33.70	7 406	702
Cedar Rapids	265.7	2 319	0.0	1 344	17.6	74.2	9.2	84.6	33.72	6 924	788
Clinton	52.8	1 911	0.0	228	20.3	75.1	11.3	86.1	35.21	6 324	941
Council Bluffs	74.9	1 330	5.4	513	21.1	76.9	10.9	87.9	29.86	6 300	1 072
Davenport	227.6	2 350	0.0	898	19.9	75.2	11.3	85.9	39.08	6 474	911
Des Moines	439.7	2 299	10.7	2 217	19.4	76.6	10.7	86.7	33.12	6 497	1 036
Dubuque	33.8	598	0.0	571	15.9	72.3	7.7	82.4	38.36	7 327	593
Fort Dodge	24.0	971	6.9	215	16.2	73.8	6.6	85.1	33.93	7 261	768
Iowa City	157.0	2 578	5.9	570	20.6	76.3	11.5	87.5	36.31	6 227	1 047
Marion	9.4	394	3.8	153	NA	NA	NA	NA	NA	NA	NA
Marshalltown	34.6	1 373	8.0	206	16.9	73.3	7.2	84.8	34.43	7 170	695
Mason City	26.1	909	8.6	314	13.2	72.5	4.2	83.6	32.74	7 837	623
Sioux City	104.0	1 258	8.9	853	17.7	75.7	7.7	86.5	25.86	6 893	907
Urbandale	15.3	547	0.0	166	NA	NA	NA	NA	NA	NA	NA
Waterloo	143.3	2 249	1.0	590	14.6	73.1	5.4	83.9	33.70	7 406	702
West Des Moines	65.2	1 541	38.3	340	19.4	76.6	10.7	86.7	33.12	6 497	1 036
KANSAS	X	X	X	X	X	X	X	X	X	X	X
Dodge City	24.7	1 102	12.3	223	NA	NA	NA	NA	NA	NA	NA
Emporia	22.0	899	33.8	285	28.7	79.3	17.9	91.3	36.84	4 856	1 414
Garden City	42.8	1 644	2.3	282	NA	NA	NA	NA	NA	NA	NA
Hutchinson	30.6	784	17.9	406	28.1	80.7	16.4	93.6	29.22	5 103	1 489
Kansas City	1 333.6	9 438	0.0	2 731	25.7	78.5	16.7	88.7	37.62	5 393	1 288
Lawrence	119.7	1 612	25.6	1 326	29.2	80.3	19.2	91.3	39.28	4 734	1 565
Leavenworth	18.5	473	4.0	311	27.0	78.5	16.7	90.1	40.54	5 192	1 313
Leawood	45.0	1 737	0.0	218	NA	NA	NA	NA	NA	NA	NA
Lenexa	163.4	4 209	0.0	379	28.0	78.2	18.3	88.7	39.56	5 029	1 308
Manhattan	58.5	1 415	0.0	308	27.8	80.0	17.3	91.4	33.82	5 043	1 478
Olathe	309.4	3 639	11.9	719	28.0	78.2	18.3	88.7	39.56	5 029	1 308
Overland Park	70.2	502	0.0	736	28.0	78.2	18.3	88.7	39.56	5 029	1 308
Salina	59.7	1 356	45.6	516	28.1	80.9	17.6	92.6	29.82	5 101	1 534
Shawnee	158.8	3 510	0.0	252	28.0	78.2	18.3	88.7	39.56	5 029	1 308
Topeka	328.5	2 761	13.0	1 751	26.7	78.5	16.3	89.3	35.23	5 265	1 304
Wichita	664.0	2 017	9.3	3 209	29.5	81.4	19.2	92.8	29.33	4 791	1 628
KENTUCKY	X	X	X	X	X	X	X	X	X	X	X
Bowling Green	177.5	3 961	6.3	617	32.9	77.9	23.6	88.7	50.93	4 328	1 370
Covington	87.8	2 175	0.0	418	28.1	75.1	19.5	85.5	41.33	5 248	996
Frankfort	13.2	498	0.0	524	29.8	75.5	19.4	87.3	42.52	5 002	1 038
Henderson	123.2	4 658	85.4	455	32.2	77.8	23.4	88.6	44.80	4 323	1 393
Hopkinsville	58.0	1 810	29.3	403	32.0	77.7	22.1	89.5	50.79	4 437	1 365
Jeffersontown	46.1	1 796	2.4	102	NA	NA	NA	NA	NA	NA	NA
Lexington-Fayette	499.9	2 068	0.0	NA	30.8	75.8	22.4	85.8	44.55	4 783	1 140
Louisville	308.4	1 209	21.3	4 429	31.7	77.2	23.2	87.0	44.39	4 514	1 288
Owensboro	319.6	5 914	62.6	830	32.2	77.9	23.1	89.3	46.65	4 334	1 415
Paducah	15.6	602	49.6	554	32.6	78.8	23.5	89.0	49.31	4 279	1 475
Richmond	123.5	4 468	23.4	233	NA	NA	NA	NA	NA	NA	NA
LOUISIANA	X	X	X	X	X	X	X	X	X	X	X
Alexandria	101.2	2 209	57.4	880	46.8	82.4	36.4	92.5	58.50	2 003	2 477
Baton Rouge	850.0	4 018	0.0	NA	49.8	82.3	39.6	91.4	60.89	1 669	2 690
Bossier City	121.7	2 150	11.3	717	45.1	82.7	34.8	93.0	46.11	2 264	2 368

1. Based on the population estimated as of July 1 of the year shown.   2. Represents normal values based on the 30-year period, 1961–1990.   3. Average daily minimum.   4. Average daily maximum.

Table D. Cities — **Land Area and Population**

STATE Place code	City	Land area, 2000[1] (sq km)	Population, 2000 — Total persons	Rank	Per square kilometer	Total persons 1990	Percent change 1990–2000	Total persons 1980	Percent change 1980–1990	White	Black	Am. Indian, Alaska Native	Asian and Pacific Islander	Other race	His-panic[2]	Non-His-panic White
		1	2	3	4	5	6	7	8	9	10	11	12	13	14	15
	LOUISIANA—Cont'd															
22 36255	Houma	36.3	32 393	963	892.4	30 495	6.2	32 608	-6.5	68.7	26.7	4.4	1.0	1.0	1.8	66.6
22 39475	Kenner	39.2	70 517	380	1 798.9	72 033	-2.1	66 382	8.5	70.1	22.9	0.8	3.3	5.3	13.6	59.8
22 40735	Lafayette	123.3	110 257	203	894.2	101 865	8.3	81 961	24.3	69.0	28.9	0.5	1.7	1.0	1.9	67.1
22 41155	Lake Charles	104.0	71 757	372	690.0	70 580	1.7	75 226	-6.2	51.1	47.5	0.7	1.3	0.8	1.4	49.5
22 51410	Monroe	74.3	53 107	556	714.8	54 909	-3.3	57 597	-4.7	37.2	61.4	0.3	1.3	0.4	1.0	36.4
22 54035	New Iberia	27.4	32 623	960	1 190.6	31 828	2.5	32 766	-2.9	57.8	38.9	0.6	3.1	0.9	1.5	56.3
22 55000	New Orleans	467.6	484 674	31	1 036.5	496 938	-2.5	557 515	-10.9	28.9	67.9	0.5	2.6	1.5	3.1	26.6
22 70000	Shreveport	267.1	200 145	88	749.3	198 518	0.8	205 776	-3.5	47.4	51.2	0.7	1.1	0.7	1.6	45.9
22 70805	Slidell	30.5	25 695	1 210	842.5	24 124	6.5	26 718	-9.7	84.4	14.0	1.0	1.1	1.0	2.7	81.2
23 00000	**MAINE**	79 931.1	1 274 923	X	16.0	1 227 928	3.8	1 125 043	9.1	97.9	0.7	1.0	1.0	0.4	0.7	96.5
23 02795	Bangor	89.2	31 473	992	352.8	33 181	-5.1	31 643	4.9	96.3	1.4	1.6	1.6	0.6	1.0	94.4
23 38740	Lewiston	88.3	35 690	875	404.2	39 757	-10.2	40 481	-1.8	97.3	1.6	1.0	1.2	0.7	1.3	95.0
23 60545	Portland	54.9	64 249	424	1 170.3	64 157	0.1	61 572	4.2	92.8	3.2	1.0	3.7	1.2	1.5	90.6
24 00000	**MARYLAND**	25 314.1	5 296 486	X	209.2	4 780 753	10.8	4 216 933	13.4	65.4	28.8	0.7	4.6	2.5	4.3	62.1
24 01600	Annapolis	17.4	35 838	870	2 059.7	33 195	8.0	31 740	4.6	63.8	32.1	0.6	2.4	2.8	6.4	59.0
24 04000	Baltimore	209.3	651 154	17	3 111.1	736 014	-11.5	786 775	-6.5	32.6	65.2	0.8	1.9	1.2	1.7	31.0
24 08775	Bowie	41.7	50 269	596	1 205.5	37 642	33.5	33 695	11.7	64.4	32.0	1.0	3.8	1.5	2.9	61.1
24 30325	Frederick	52.9	52 767	565	997.5	40 186	31.3	28 086	43.1	79.1	16.0	0.8	3.9	2.9	4.8	75.0
24 31175	Gaithersburg	26.1	52 613	568	2 015.8	39 676	32.6	26 424	50.2	61.6	15.7	0.8	15.2	11.2	19.8	49.1
24 36075	Hagerstown	27.6	36 687	845	1 329.2	35 306	3.9	34 132	3.4	87.6	11.2	0.7	1.3	1.1	1.8	85.2
24 67675	Rockville	34.8	47 388	639	1 361.7	44 830	5.7	43 811	2.3	70.2	9.9	0.9	16.3	6.2	11.7	61.9
25 00000	**MASSACHUSETTS**	20 305.6	6 349 097	X	312.7	6 016 425	5.5	5 737 093	4.9	86.2	6.3	0.6	4.3	5.1	6.8	81.9
25 00765	Agawam	60.2	28 144	1 098	467.5	27 323	3.0	NA	NA	97.4	1.1	0.4	1.2	0.7	1.8	95.5
25 02690	Attleboro	71.3	42 068	727	590.0	38 383	9.6	34 196	12.2	92.7	2.0	0.6	4.0	2.6	4.3	89.1
25 03600	Barnstable Town	155.5	47 821	633	307.5	40 949	16.8	NA	NA	93.8	3.5	1.1	1.2	3.0	1.7	90.8
25 05595	Beverly	43.0	39 862	776	927.0	38 195	4.4	37 655	1.4	96.9	1.4	0.4	1.6	0.7	1.8	94.8
25 07000	Boston	125.4	589 141	20	4 698.1	574 283	2.6	562 994	2.0	56.8	27.7	0.9	8.4	10.9	14.4	49.5
25 09000	Brockton	55.6	94 304	256	1 696.1	92 788	1.6	95 172	-2.5	64.4	23.3	0.9	2.9	16.5	8.0	58.2
25 11000	Cambridge	16.7	101 355	234	6 069.2	95 802	5.8	95 322	0.5	71.2	13.8	0.8	13.3	5.7	7.4	64.6
25 13205	Chelsea	5.7	35 080	892	6 154.4	28 710	22.2	25 431	12.9	63.3	8.7	0.9	5.4	28.5	48.4	38.3
25 13660	Chicopee	59.2	54 653	541	923.2	56 632	-3.5	55 112	2.8	91.4	2.8	0.5	1.3	5.9	8.8	86.9
25 21990	Everett	8.8	38 037	818	4 322.4	35 701	6.5	37 195	-4.0	84.1	7.5	0.7	3.9	9.4	9.5	75.2
25 23000	Fall River	80.3	91 938	264	1 144.9	92 703	-0.8	92 574	0.1	93.3	3.2	0.6	2.8	2.8	3.3	89.5
25 23875	Fitchburg	71.9	39 102	790	543.8	41 194	-5.1	39 580	4.1	84.2	4.7	0.9	5.0	8.4	15.0	75.2
25 25100	Franklin	69.3	29 560	1 054	426.6	22 095	33.8	NA	NA	96.7	1.3	0.3	2.1	0.5	1.1	95.3
25 26150	Gloucester	67.2	30 273	1 025	450.5	28 716	5.4	27 717	3.6	97.9	0.9	0.4	1.0	0.9	1.5	96.2
25 29405	Haverhill	86.3	58 969	478	683.3	51 418	14.7	46 865	9.7	91.4	3.0	0.6	1.8	5.3	8.8	86.3
25 30840	Holyoke	55.1	39 838	777	723.0	43 704	-8.8	44 678	-2.2	68.0	4.6	0.8	1.2	28.4	41.4	54.0
25 34550	Lawrence	18.0	72 043	370	4 002.4	70 207	2.6	63 175	11.1	53.5	7.6	1.3	3.3	41.0	59.7	34.1
25 35075	Leominster	74.8	41 303	740	552.2	38 145	8.3	34 508	10.5	88.9	4.4	0.5	3.0	5.6	11.0	81.5
25 37000	Lowell	35.7	105 167	218	2 945.9	103 439	1.7	92 418	11.9	71.4	5.0	0.6	18.2	9.0	14.0	62.5
25 37490	Lynn	28.0	89 050	277	3 180.4	81 245	9.6	78 471	3.5	71.0	12.6	0.9	7.7	12.8	18.4	62.5
25 37875	Malden	13.1	56 340	512	4 300.8	53 884	4.6	53 386	0.9	74.2	9.7	0.5	14.8	4.5	4.8	69.6
25 38715	MarlBorough	54.6	36 255	859	664.0	31 813	14.0	30 617	3.9	90.3	2.6	0.6	4.3	5.0	6.1	84.9
25 39835	Medford	21.1	55 765	525	2 642.9	57 407	-2.9	58 076	-1.2	88.2	7.1	0.4	4.4	2.4	2.6	85.0
25 40115	Melrose	12.2	27 134	1 139	2 224.1	28 150	-3.6	30 055	-6.3	96.4	1.3	0.4	2.5	1.0	1.0	94.5
25 40710	Methuen	58.0	43 789	699	755.0	39 990	9.5	NA	NA	90.9	1.8	0.4	2.8	6.0	9.6	85.8
25 45000	New Bedford	52.1	93 768	257	1 799.8	99 922	-6.2	98 478	1.5	82.9	6.8	1.4	1.2	14.0	10.2	75.2
25 45560	Newton	46.8	83 829	304	1 791.2	82 585	1.5	83 622	-1.2	89.3	2.4	0.3	8.4	1.2	2.5	86.4
25 46330	Northampton	89.2	28 978	1 071	324.9	29 289	-1.1	29 286	0.0	91.7	2.8	0.9	3.8	3.0	5.2	87.8
25 52490	Peabody	42.5	48 129	627	1 132.4	47 264	1.8	45 976	2.8	95.5	1.3	0.3	1.7	3.0	3.4	92.4
25 53960	Pittsfield	105.5	45 793	666	434.1	48 622	-5.8	51 974	-6.4	94.0	4.6	0.6	1.5	1.1	2.0	91.6
25 55745	Quincy	43.5	88 025	283	2 023.6	84 985	3.6	84 743	0.3	81.0	2.6	0.4	16.0	1.8	2.1	78.4
25 56585	Revere	15.3	47 283	643	3 090.4	42 786	10.5	42 423	0.9	86.9	3.6	0.6	6.0	6.9	9.4	79.4
25 59105	Salem	21.0	40 407	764	1 924.1	38 091	6.1	38 220	-0.3	87.4	3.9	0.6	2.6	8.2	11.2	82.4
25 62535	Somerville	10.6	77 478	341	7 309.2	76 210	1.7	77 372	-1.5	80.6	7.9	0.6	7.4	8.6	8.8	72.7
25 67000	Springfield	83.1	152 082	131	1 830.1	156 983	-3.1	152 319	3.1	58.7	22.9	1.0	2.8	18.9	27.2	48.8
25 69170	Taunton	120.7	55 976	521	463.8	49 832	12.3	45 001	10.7	93.4	3.5	0.5	1.1	3.8	3.9	89.8
25 72600	Waltham	32.9	59 226	475	1 800.2	57 878	2.3	58 200	-0.6	84.4	5.0	0.4	7.9	4.4	8.5	78.4
25 76030	Westfield	120.6	40 072	773	332.3	38 372	4.4	36 465	5.2	95.8	1.2	0.6	1.2	2.6	5.0	92.1
25 81035	Woburn	32.8	37 258	835	1 135.9	35 943	3.7	36 626	-1.9	91.5	2.2	0.3	5.3	1.9	3.1	89.0
25 82000	Worcester	97.3	172 648	121	1 774.4	169 759	1.7	161 799	4.9	79.8	8.0	1.0	5.5	9.3	15.1	70.8
26 00000	**MICHIGAN**	147 121.2	9 938 444	X	67.6	9 295 287	6.9	9 262 044	0.4	81.8	14.8	1.3	2.2	2.0	3.3	78.6
26 01380	Allen Park	18.2	29 376	1 060	1 614.1	31 092	-5.5	34 196	-9.1	96.8	0.8	0.9	1.1	1.7	4.7	92.5
26 03000	Ann Arbor	70.0	114 024	195	1 628.9	109 608	4.0	107 960	1.5	77.3	9.9	0.9	13.1	2.1	3.3	72.8

1. Dry land or land partially or temporarily covered by water.   2. Hispanic persons may be of any race.

Table D. Cities — **Population and Households**

	Population characteristics, 2000 (cont'd)										Households, 2000				
	Age of population (percent)													Percent	
City	Under 5 years	5 to 17 years	18 to 24 years	25 to 34 years	35 to 44 years	45 to 54 years	55 to 64 years	65 to 74 years	75 years and over	Percent female	Number	Percent change, 1990–2000	Persons per house-hold	Female family house-holder[1]	One-person
	16	17	18	19	20	21	22	23	24	25	26	27	28	29	30
LOUISIANA—Cont'd															
Houma	7.4	20.5	9.8	13.3	16.0	12.6	8.3	6.6	5.7	51.3	11 634	9.2	2.72	16.7	24.1
Kenner	7.0	20.3	9.4	14.1	16.4	15.1	8.7	5.2	3.7	52.0	25 652	2.4	2.72	16.3	23.2
Lafayette	6.4	18.6	13.3	14.0	15.5	13.3	7.7	6.3	4.9	51.8	43 506	19.8	2.43	14.6	29.4
Lake Charles	6.9	18.6	11.5	12.5	14.4	12.9	8.5	7.7	6.9	52.4	27 974	4.3	2.44	18.7	30.0
Monroe	7.6	22.0	15.0	12.4	12.7	11.0	6.5	6.2	6.6	54.3	19 421	1.5	2.54	25.3	31.3
New Iberia	8.2	21.6	9.7	12.4	14.4	12.2	8.1	6.8	6.6	53.2	11 756	5.5	2.70	20.5	25.2
New Orleans	6.9	19.8	11.4	14.5	14.8	13.1	7.8	6.0	5.7	53.1	188 251	0.0	2.48	24.5	33.2
Shreveport	7.1	19.8	10.7	13.2	14.1	13.0	8.2	6.9	7.0	53.4	78 662	4.0	2.48	21.5	30.8
Slidell	6.7	20.3	7.6	12.5	16.0	13.8	9.5	7.2	6.5	52.1	9 480	13.9	2.67	14.0	20.4
MAINE	5.5	18.1	8.1	12.4	16.7	15.1	9.7	7.5	6.8	51.3	518 200	11.4	2.39	9.5	27.0
Bangor	5.7	15.5	12.4	14.7	15.6	13.9	8.1	6.7	7.4	52.8	13 713	2.4	2.12	12.8	37.6
Lewiston	5.6	15.2	12.6	12.9	14.0	12.7	9.3	8.3	9.4	52.4	15 290	-3.4	2.17	11.8	35.9
Portland	5.1	13.6	10.7	19.3	16.8	13.3	7.3	6.3	7.6	52.1	29 714	5.2	2.08	10.5	40.1
MARYLAND	6.7	18.9	8.5	14.1	17.3	14.3	8.9	6.1	5.2	51.7	1 980 859	13.3	2.61	14.1	25.0
Annapolis	6.7	15.0	9.3	17.7	15.7	14.3	9.3	6.3	5.7	52.6	15 303	8.8	2.30	16.3	32.9
Baltimore	6.4	18.4	10.9	14.3	15.6	12.8	8.4	6.9	6.3	53.4	257 996	-6.7	2.42	25.0	34.9
Bowie	7.5	19.4	5.7	14.5	20.5	13.8	9.2	5.7	3.7	52.2	18 188	41.1	2.74	11.0	19.7
Frederick	7.5	17.7	9.3	17.7	17.6	12.4	6.7	5.3	6.0	52.4	20 891	33.3	2.42	12.8	30.0
Gaithersburg	8.2	16.8	9.0	18.9	18.8	13.4	6.6	3.5	4.8	51.3	19 621	29.1	2.65	11.2	27.8
Hagerstown	7.9	17.6	9.0	15.8	15.3	12.3	7.8	6.8	7.6	53.2	15 849	5.2	2.26	15.9	35.4
Rockville	6.3	17.1	7.0	14.2	17.9	14.8	9.7	6.8	6.3	51.2	17 247	10.1	2.65	9.5	23.8
MASSACHUSETTS	6.3	17.4	9.1	14.6	16.7	13.8	8.6	6.7	6.8	51.8	2 443 580	8.7	2.51	11.9	28.0
Agawam	5.5	16.5	6.5	12.6	17.0	15.4	9.7	7.4	9.3	52.5	11 260	7.9	2.43	9.8	28.0
Attleboro	7.0	18.4	6.8	15.7	18.2	12.7	8.3	6.4	6.5	51.4	16 019	13.0	2.57	10.6	25.7
Barnstable Town	5.2	16.7	5.6	10.4	16.4	14.9	10.6	10.5	9.6	52.2	19 626	18.2	2.38	10.7	27.7
Beverly	6.3	15.4	9.0	13.6	17.2	14.5	8.3	7.2	8.4	52.7	15 750	6.4	2.39	9.7	29.9
Boston	5.4	14.3	16.2	21.2	14.7	10.8	7.0	5.3	5.1	51.9	239 528	4.8	2.31	16.4	37.1
Brockton	7.3	20.6	9.1	14.6	15.9	12.4	8.4	5.8	5.9	52.1	33 675	2.5	2.74	19.9	26.6
Cambridge	4.1	9.2	21.2	24.9	13.8	11.0	6.8	4.6	4.5	51.0	42 615	8.1	2.03	9.7	41.4
Chelsea	8.1	19.2	10.6	19.0	15.6	9.8	6.5	5.4	5.8	49.8	11 888	12.7	2.87	20.1	28.8
Chicopee	5.5	17.2	8.5	13.2	15.6	13.3	9.2	8.5	9.1	52.4	23 117	2.2	2.32	14.2	32.7
Everett	5.9	15.7	8.9	18.4	16.4	11.8	8.1	7.5	7.2	52.4	15 435	6.2	2.45	15.2	31.3
Fall River	6.4	17.8	9.2	15.6	14.2	11.7	8.3	7.6	9.4	53.3	38 759	3.9	2.32	16.5	34.2
Fitchburg	6.7	19.1	11.6	13.9	14.9	11.7	7.5	6.7	7.9	52.3	14 943	-2.7	2.50	14.6	30.3
Franklin	9.4	20.9	6.5	13.6	21.5	13.3	6.6	4.6	3.6	51.0	10 152	194.4	2.85	8.5	18.3
Gloucester	5.8	16.2	6.5	12.5	17.4	16.1	9.9	8.3	7.3	52.1	12 592	8.7	2.38	10.6	30.7
Haverhill	7.4	18.3	7.7	15.7	17.8	12.8	7.6	5.9	6.9	52.5	22 976	17.4	2.51	13.4	28.6
Holyoke	7.9	21.5	9.0	13.0	13.8	11.5	7.7	6.7	8.9	53.2	14 967	-5.6	2.57	22.1	30.9
Lawrence	9.0	23.0	11.1	15.8	14.6	10.5	6.2	4.4	5.4	52.2	24 463	0.8	2.90	25.7	25.5
Leominster	7.1	18.4	7.2	14.9	17.5	13.1	8.2	6.8	6.9	51.9	16 491	11.2	2.48	12.5	27.9
Lowell	7.3	19.6	11.9	17.1	15.3	11.0	6.8	5.4	5.4	50.7	37 887	2.3	2.67	17.4	29.0
Lynn	7.3	19.7	9.1	15.1	15.9	12.4	7.7	6.3	6.5	51.6	33 511	6.2	2.62	17.6	31.0
Malden	5.8	14.1	8.5	20.2	16.7	12.5	8.3	7.0	6.8	51.9	23 009	5.0	2.42	12.3	32.2
MarlBorough	7.0	16.2	7.0	17.5	19.2	13.2	8.4	5.8	5.7	50.7	14 501	19.3	2.47	9.0	28.4
Medford	4.9	13.1	11.0	17.0	15.6	12.4	8.7	8.1	9.2	53.1	22 067	1.1	2.43	11.8	28.7
Melrose	6.7	15.3	5.4	14.5	17.5	15.2	9.1	7.6	8.7	53.0	10 982	0.4	2.44	8.7	29.7
Methuen	6.3	18.5	7.3	13.6	17.4	13.5	8.1	7.1	8.3	52.1	16 532	12.9	2.62	12.2	25.3
New Bedford	6.7	18.2	9.5	14.3	14.4	11.9	8.2	7.7	9.0	52.9	38 178	-1.6	2.40	18.9	31.6
Newton	5.2	16.0	10.3	12.9	15.3	16.0	9.2	7.1	8.0	53.5	31 201	5.9	2.51	8.0	25.5
Northampton	4.1	12.9	15.4	14.1	15.8	16.3	7.6	5.9	7.9	56.9	11 880	6.4	2.14	10.1	37.3
Peabody	5.8	16.4	6.2	12.4	17.1	14.5	10.2	9.1	8.4	52.1	18 581	5.8	2.55	10.4	25.4
Pittsfield	5.9	17.2	6.9	12.6	15.7	13.7	9.4	8.8	9.8	52.5	19 704	-1.1	2.26	13.1	34.0
Quincy	5.1	12.4	8.1	19.7	16.3	13.1	9.0	8.0	8.3	52.3	38 883	9.0	2.22	10.5	37.6
Revere	5.8	15.2	7.9	16.5	16.1	12.4	9.4	8.3	8.3	51.6	19 463	11.6	2.41	13.9	32.7
Salem	5.6	14.6	10.4	17.0	16.3	13.7	8.2	6.9	7.2	53.6	17 492	10.7	2.24	13.3	34.9
Somerville	4.5	10.3	15.9	27.6	15.0	10.1	6.2	5.2	5.2	51.3	31 555	4.1	2.38	10.3	31.0
Springfield	7.6	21.3	11.4	14.0	14.4	11.6	7.2	6.1	6.4	52.8	57 130	-1.1	2.57	23.8	30.2
Taunton	7.1	17.8	8.0	15.9	17.3	12.7	8.4	6.3	6.6	51.9	22 045	17.0	2.50	13.4	28.2
Waltham	4.7	10.8	16.8	19.1	15.3	12.0	8.2	6.6	6.5	50.7	23 207	12.0	2.29	8.9	34.2
Westfield	5.9	17.9	12.6	12.3	15.7	13.7	8.2	6.6	7.1	51.6	14 797	7.0	2.54	10.6	25.9
Woburn	5.8	15.3	6.9	17.3	17.6	12.9	8.8	8.6	6.8	51.1	14 997	11.2	2.47	10.9	28.7
Worcester	6.5	17.1	13.3	15.5	14.8	11.4	7.2	6.3	7.8	52.0	67 028	4.9	2.41	15.6	33.0
MICHIGAN	6.8	19.4	9.4	13.7	16.1	13.8	8.7	6.5	5.8	51.0	3 785 661	10.7	2.56	12.5	26.2
Allen Park	5.3	16.8	6.5	12.0	16.3	13.7	8.5	9.2	11.7	52.4	11 974	-0.5	2.43	9.9	28.2
Ann Arbor	5.0	11.7	26.8	18.3	13.0	11.3	6.0	4.1	3.8	50.6	45 693	9.7	2.22	7.5	35.5

1. No spouse present.

Table D. Cities — Group Quarters, Crime, Education, and Income

City	Persons in group quarters, 2000				Serious crimes known to police, 2000[2]				Education, 1990				Money income, 1989		
		Institutional			Total		Rate[3]		School enrollment		Attainment[4] (percent)			Households	
														Median	
	Total	Total	Persons in nursing homes	Non-Institutional[1]	Number	Rate[3]	Violent	Property	Public	Private	High school graduate or more	Bachelor's degree or more	Per capita (dollars)[5]	Dollars	Percent change, 1979–1989 (constant 1989 dollars)
	31	32	33	34	35	36	37	38	39	40	41	42	43	44	45
LOUISIANA—Cont'd															
Houma	800	681	119	119	2 316	7 150	1 343	5 807	7 138	1 211	62.6	12.6	9 790	19 397	-35.0
Kenner	698	437	414	261	3 883	5 506	569	4 938	13 205	7 665	77.5	21.3	12 884	30 389	-12.2
Lafayette	4 438	1 966	924	2 472	8 259	7 491	776	6 714	24 506	4 497	75.2	27.3	12 925	23 430	-17.3
Lake Charles	3 570	2 208	820	1 362	4 478	6 241	877	5 364	17 200	2 627	69.4	18.4	11 475	21 225	-24.8
Monroe	3 706	1 373	714	2 333	6 708	12 631	1 787	10 844	16 657	1 650	68.7	23.7	10 037	16 223	-7.5
New Iberia	932	467	362	465	960	2 943	239	2 704	7 560	966	57.1	9.9	8 740	18 506	-31.3
New Orleans	17 641	9 772	2 976	7 869	33 826	6 979	1 064	5 916	104 217	42 298	68.1	22.4	11 372	18 477	-6.7
Shreveport	5 391	3 476	1 979	1 915	17 059	8 523	937	7 586	49 670	5 988	74.1	19.6	11 663	22 079	-12.4
Slidell	347	324	305	23	2 272	8 842	662	8 181	5 415	1 336	80.6	23.7	13 396	34 492	-14.2
MAINE	34 912	13 091	9 339	21 821	33 400	2 620	110	2 510	267 445	37 423	78.8	18.8	12 957	27 854	20.3
Bangor	2 360	789	468	1 571	1 875	5 957	175	5 783	7 145	1 616	83.5	24.4	13 418	24 674	16.5
Lewiston	2 543	764	693	1 779	1 719	4 816	157	4 660	6 752	2 842	63.7	9.7	12 277	24 051	16.2
Portland	2 443	924	527	1 519	2 869	4 465	327	4 139	11 762	2 375	83.2	29.6	14 914	26 576	29.9
MARYLAND	134 056	69 318	26 716	64 738	255 085	4 816	787	4 030	982 507	229 826	78.4	26.5	17 730	39 386	15.9
Annapolis	706	212	212	494	2 418	6 747	1 479	5 268	6 147	1 899	80.2	32.8	18 358	35 516	19.8
Baltimore	25 753	12 634	4 204	13 119	65 886	10 118	2 458	7 661	142 587	38 971	60.7	15.5	11 994	24 045	12.0
Bowie	471	327	327	144	NA	NA	NA	NA	7 605	2 319	92.4	37.6	21 876	59 622	9.9
Frederick	2 110	969	969	1 141	2 544	4 821	1 179	3 642	7 673	1 684	77.9	24.0	15 410	34 891	18.7
Gaithersburg	623	268	268	355	NA	NA	NA	NA	8 554	1 316	86.7	39.6	18 845	43 644	23.3
Hagerstown	829	412	392	417	1 740	4 743	591	4 151	6 230	599	65.0	9.9	11 742	22 859	9.1
Rockville	1 642	1 269	643	373	NA	NA	NA	NA	9 056	2 437	86.4	45.4	21 484	52 073	11.4
MASSACHUSETTS	221 216	88 453	55 837	132 763	192 131	3 026	476	2 550	1 100 827	429 307	80.0	27.2	17 224	36 952	25.4
Agawam	726	726	726	0	719	2 555	725	1 830	NA	NA	NA	NA	NA	NA	NA
Attleboro	831	609	609	222	1 042	2 477	261	2 215	6 703	2 078	75.3	20.2	14 970	36 631	23.0
Barnstable Town	1 204	600	328	604	1 770	3 701	954	2 748	NA	NA	NA	NA	NA	NA	NA
Beverly	2 170	774	770	1 396	320	803	83	720	6 747	2 776	87.1	28.0	18 436	39 603	25.9
Boston	35 077	8 481	3 930	26 596	35 870	6 089	1 243	4 846	87 567	78 941	75.7	30.0	15 581	29 180	39.0
Brockton	1 876	1 367	927	509	4 873	5 167	1 056	4 111	19 297	3 424	74.4	12.9	13 455	31 712	23.6
Cambridge	14 663	505	272	14 158	4 390	4 331	513	3 818	10 994	23 172	84.4	54.2	19 879	33 140	39.1
Chelsea	953	878	878	75	1 585	4 518	1 425	3 093	4 867	1 899	63.2	12.0	11 559	25 144	33.9
Chicopee	1 006	310	310	696	2 291	4 192	1 310	2 882	9 156	3 376	66.3	10.4	13 525	28 905	11.6
Everett	231	214	214	17	1 222	3 213	854	2 358	5 369	2 151	72.9	11.3	14 220	30 786	17.9
Fall River	1 891	1 472	1 351	419	3 627	3 945	596	3 349	17 693	3 208	46.7	8.4	10 966	22 452	16.4
Fitchburg	1 745	567	517	1 178	2 123	5 429	1 102	4 327	8 714	1 671	68.8	13.1	12 140	27 101	14.4
Franklin	626	66	66	560	125	423	125	298	NA	NA	NA	NA	NA	NA	NA
Gloucester	360	265	265	95	498	1 645	112	1 533	4 850	1 075	75.6	20.4	16 044	32 690	24.7
Haverhill	1 397	851	794	546	2 022	3 429	415	3 013	9 533	2 324	78.0	21.0	15 464	36 945	46.5
Holyoke	1 381	1 188	1 180	193	2 785	6 991	1 157	5 834	8 634	2 083	68.0	15.2	11 088	22 858	10.4
Lawrence	1 044	801	551	243	4 080	5 663	901	4 762	15 852	3 437	57.0	9.7	9 686	22 183	10.5
Leominster	394	296	296	98	1 458	3 530	211	3 319	6 801	1 958	75.2	19.3	15 960	35 974	29.7
Lowell	3 841	1 120	1 120	2 721	4 070	3 870	768	3 102	23 926	5 033	65.8	15.5	12 701	29 351	21.5
Lynn	1 344	738	738	606	4 777	5 364	1 147	4 218	15 162	3 558	73.2	14.3	13 026	28 553	18.6
Malden	605	379	379	226	1 723	3 058	761	2 297	8 111	3 760	77.9	20.1	15 820	34 344	28.6
Marlborough	489	346	346	143	668	1 843	168	1 674	5 418	1 396	83.0	26.6	18 471	41 315	28.3
Medford	2 204	536	536	1 668	1 402	2 514	228	2 286	7 219	5 878	79.0	23.7	16 941	38 859	26.9
Melrose	329	291	291	38	375	1 382	41	1 341	4 722	1 494	87.7	31.4	20 202	44 109	24.5
Methuen	483	319	319	164	1 151	2 629	178	2 450	NA	NA	NA	NA	NA	NA	NA
New Bedford	1 986	1 507	1 291	479	3 333	3 555	894	2 661	19 739	2 854	49.7	9.7	10 923	22 647	16.1
Newton	5 578	621	612	4 957	1 090	1 300	74	1 226	11 272	11 642	91.7	57.2	28 840	59 719	33.6
Northampton	3 602	1 090	675	2 512	612	2 112	162	1 950	5 383	3 457	81.9	32.9	14 623	31 097	24.8
Peabody	720	535	524	185	1 272	2 643	330	2 313	7 650	2 813	79.2	20.9	17 002	39 800	14.8
Pittsfield	1 267	910	621	357	1 347	2 941	304	2 638	9 230	1 636	78.1	19.2	15 426	29 987	12.9
Quincy	1 586	780	655	806	2 300	2 613	267	2 346	11 658	6 183	82.7	23.2	17 436	35 858	23.1
Revere	318	255	255	63	1 682	3 557	829	2 728	6 255	2 076	73.9	12.3	14 723	30 659	20.7
Salem	1 160	162	149	998	1 287	3 185	240	2 945	6 835	1 756	78.2	24.5	16 155	32 645	28.6
Somerville	2 515	316	280	2 199	2 048	2 643	213	2 430	9 759	5 214	75.2	30.9	15 179	32 455	34.5
Springfield	5 533	1 648	829	3 885	12 589	8 278	1 835	6 443	31 044	11 959	69.6	15.0	11 584	25 656	15.0
Taunton	820	592	394	228	1 666	2 976	457	2 519	9 135	1 732	66.8	12.1	13 613	32 315	22.8
Waltham	5 991	749	459	5 242	1 019	1 721	52	1 668	7 457	8 422	79.0	26.5	16 777	38 514	23.4
Westfield	2 468	511	370	1 957	1 135	2 832	814	2 019	9 515	1 445	78.7	19.3	14 225	33 498	11.1
Woburn	244	100	100	144	905	2 429	183	2 246	6 176	1 901	86.4	23.7	18 155	42 679	23.4
Worcester	11 107	2 893	2 542	8 214	8 880	5 143	872	4 271	30 317	15 786	72.9	21.1	13 393	28 955	22.4
MICHIGAN	249 889	126 132	50 113	123 757	408 456	4 110	555	3 555	2 242 239	338 803	76.8	17.4	14 154	31 020	-3.7
Allen Park	306	295	292	11	744	2 533	204	2 328	5 507	1 776	78.7	16.5	17 013	39 925	-11.4
Ann Arbor	12 389	519	303	11 870	3 979	3 490	266	3 224	45 196	4 204	93.9	64.2	17 786	33 344	8.6

1. Persons in emergency shelters and persons visible in street locations. 2. Data for serious crimes have not been adjusted for underreporting. This may affect comparability between geographic areas and over time. 3. Per 100,000 population estimated by the FBI. 4. Persons 25 years old and older. 5. Based on population enumerated as of April 1, 1990.

Table D. Cities — Income, Poverty, and Housing

	Money income, 1989 (cont'd)				Housing units, 2000										
	Households (cont'd)	Percent below poverty, 1989					Vacant units				Occupied units				
		Persons		Families											
City	Percent with $100,000 or more	Total	Percent change in rate, 1979–1989	Total	Total	Percent change, 1990–2000	Vacant units for sale or rent[1]	For seasonal use (percent)	Home owner vacancy rate	Renter vacancy rate	Total	Percent owner occupied	Percent renter occupied	Average size owner occupied	Average size renter occupied
	46	47	48	49	50	51	52	53	54	55	56	57	58	59	60
LOUISIANA—Cont'd															
Houma	2.3	26.4	52.6	22.0	12 514	9.0	880	0.1	1.3	8.0	11 634	67.7	32.3	2.80	2.54
Kenner	3.5	14.2	44.9	12.2	27 378	0.4	1 726	0.3	0.9	10.1	25 652	60.8	39.2	2.87	2.49
Lafayette	4.1	21.9	42.2	17.0	46 865	16.1	3 359	0.5	1.4	9.1	43 506	58.3	41.7	2.63	2.15
Lake Charles	2.8	23.6	54.2	20.3	31 429	5.3	3 455	0.4	2.1	13.6	27 974	57.6	42.4	2.51	2.34
Monroe	3.3	37.8	27.7	31.6	21 278	-1.5	1 857	0.3	1.8	7.6	19 421	49.6	50.4	2.56	2.52
New Iberia	1.6	28.7	72.9	23.6	12 880	3.7	1 124	0.4	1.5	7.2	11 756	62.6	37.4	2.70	2.69
New Orleans	3.6	31.6	19.7	27.3	215 091	-4.6	26 840	1.1	2.2	7.9	188 251	46.5	53.5	2.60	2.37
Shreveport	3.0	25.3	42.9	20.2	86 802	-0.8	8 140	0.4	1.8	10.9	78 662	59.0	41.0	2.52	2.41
Slidell	3.1	10.1	16.1	9.1	10 133	11.5	653	0.4	1.5	11.2	9 480	76.1	23.9	2.71	2.57
MAINE	2.4	10.8	-16.9	8.0	651 901	11.0	133 701	15.6	1.7	7.0	518 200	71.6	28.4	2.54	2.03
Bangor	3.5	15.0	2.7	11.5	14 587	1.5	874	1.0	2.0	4.2	13 713	47.5	52.5	2.43	1.85
Lewiston	2.0	13.9	4.5	11.0	16 470	-3.8	1 180	0.4	1.3	8.8	15 290	47.2	52.8	2.44	1.92
Portland	2.9	14.0	-9.1	10.6	31 862	1.8	2 148	3.0	0.5	3.6	29 714	42.5	57.5	2.41	1.84
MARYLAND	6.9	8.3	-15.6	6.0	2 145 283	13.4	164 424	1.8	1.6	6.1	1 980 859	67.7	32.3	2.73	2.35
Annapolis	6.3	12.1	-21.4	9.9	16 165	6.0	862	1.2	1.4	3.8	15 303	51.7	48.3	2.36	2.23
Baltimore	2.4	21.9	-4.4	17.8	300 477	-1.1	42 481	0.5	3.6	7.6	257 996	50.3	49.7	2.57	2.27
Bowie	10.0	1.1	-35.3	0.5	18 718	43.3	530	0.2	1.2	4.5	18 188	85.0	15.0	2.79	2.45
Frederick	2.4	8.0	-22.3	6.1	22 106	33.1	1 215	0.3	2.7	5.3	20 891	55.6	44.4	2.59	2.22
Gaithersburg	5.7	6.0	-6.3	5.1	20 674	28.7	1 053	0.5	1.5	6.1	19 621	52.6	47.4	2.86	2.42
Hagerstown	1.1	15.8	-1.9	13.1	17 089	4.4	1 240	0.2	3.4	5.7	15 849	41.9	58.1	2.36	2.19
Rockville	14.3	5.8	18.4	3.7	17 786	9.5	539	0.2	0.8	4.5	17 247	67.7	32.3	2.71	2.54
MASSACHUSETTS	6.7	8.9	-6.9	6.7	2 621 989	6.0	178 409	3.6	0.7	3.5	2 443 580	61.7	38.3	2.72	2.17
Agawam	NA	NA	NA	NA	11 659	7.3	399	0.6	0.8	4.2	11 260	73.6	26.4	2.63	1.90
Attleboro	2.9	6.4	-8.6	4.3	16 554	10.0	535	0.2	0.7	3.8	16 019	63.8	36.2	2.81	2.16
Barnstable Town	NA	NA	NA	NA	25 018	7.1	5 392	19.0	1.1	3.7	19 626	76.2	23.8	2.43	2.19
Beverly	7.1	6.6	-9.6	5.3	16 275	4.0	525	0.8	0.4	3.1	15 750	60.0	40.0	2.70	1.93
Boston	4.8	18.7	-7.4	15.1	251 935	0.4	12 407	0.6	1.0	3.0	239 528	32.2	67.8	2.51	2.22
Brockton	3.1	13.6	7.9	11.7	34 837	-1.5	1 162	0.1	0.5	3.3	33 675	54.6	45.4	2.98	2.46
Cambridge	7.8	10.7	-29.1	7.2	44 725	6.5	2 110	1.3	0.9	2.6	42 615	32.3	67.7	2.16	1.97
Chelsea	2.3	24.1	12.6	22.9	12 337	6.6	449	0.2	1.1	1.6	11 888	28.9	71.1	2.87	2.87
Chicopee	1.6	9.8	11.4	8.1	24 424	3.1	1 307	0.4	0.9	4.8	23 117	59.3	40.7	2.46	2.11
Everett	2.0	9.6	-7.7	8.2	15 908	3.2	473	0.1	0.5	2.2	15 435	41.4	58.6	2.67	2.29
Fall River	0.9	14.3	-3.4	12.3	41 857	3.7	3 098	0.2	1.4	6.7	38 759	34.9	65.1	2.66	2.14
Fitchburg	1.8	14.0	8.5	11.7	16 002	-4.0	1 059	0.2	1.4	6.5	14 943	51.6	48.4	2.64	2.35
Franklin	NA	NA	NA	NA	10 327	34.3	175	0.3	0.3	2.9	10 152	81.2	18.8	3.06	1.92
Gloucester	5.3	7.5	-23.5	6.8	13 958	6.3	1 366	6.9	0.8	2.7	12 592	59.7	40.3	2.60	2.04
Haverhill	3.3	8.8	-16.2	7.4	23 737	11.3	761	0.3	0.5	3.1	22 976	60.2	39.8	2.69	2.23
Holyoke	2.2	25.7	33.2	22.9	16 210	-4.2	1 243	0.2	0.9	6.9	14 967	41.5	58.5	2.66	2.50
Lawrence	1.1	27.5	42.5	25.6	25 601	-4.9	1 138	0.2	1.0	3.0	24 463	32.2	67.8	3.02	2.85
Leominster	3.7	7.2	-22.6	5.8	16 976	9.3	485	0.2	0.5	2.6	16 491	57.9	42.1	2.71	2.16
Lowell	2.4	18.0	33.3	15.1	39 468	-2.1	1 581	0.2	1.2	3.1	37 887	43.0	57.0	2.87	2.53
Lynn	1.8	15.9	15.2	13.9	34 637	0.1	1 126	0.2	0.7	2.3	33 511	45.6	54.4	2.81	2.46
Malden	2.7	7.5	-20.2	5.5	23 634	1.8	625	0.3	0.4	2.1	23 009	43.3	56.7	2.86	2.08
MarlBorough	7.0	5.7	-21.9	4.3	14 903	14.4	402	0.4	0.5	2.4	14 501	61.0	39.0	2.68	2.13
Medford	5.3	6.9	-9.2	4.9	22 687	0.2	620	0.2	0.5	2.5	22 067	58.6	41.4	2.62	2.15
Melrose	8.0	4.2	-6.7	2.9	11 248	-0.4	266	0.4	0.4	1.6	10 982	67.0	33.0	2.78	1.75
Methuen	NA	NA	NA	NA	16 885	9.4	353	0.2	0.3	2.8	16 532	71.9	28.1	2.79	2.19
New Bedford	1.0	16.8	3.7	14.6	41 511	-0.6	3 333	0.3	1.9	6.9	38 178	43.8	56.2	2.60	2.25
Newton	23.8	4.3	-25.9	2.3	32 112	5.3	911	0.8	0.5	2.1	31 201	69.5	30.5	2.70	2.08
Northampton	3.0	11.5	-9.4	6.9	12 405	5.6	525	1.0	0.4	3.4	11 880	53.5	46.5	2.44	1.79
Peabody	5.6	4.6	-22.0	3.8	18 898	3.6	317	0.3	0.3	1.7	18 581	71.2	28.8	2.75	2.06
Pittsfield	3.3	9.7	-5.8	7.8	21 366	0.4	1 662	1.2	1.5	9.0	19 704	60.8	39.2	2.45	1.97
Quincy	4.5	6.8	-17.1	5.3	40 093	6.3	1 210	0.5	0.4	2.7	38 883	49.0	51.0	2.59	1.87
Revere	3.1	11.6	9.4	8.6	20 181	7.8	718	0.4	0.5	2.3	19 463	50.0	50.0	2.64	2.19
Salem	4.1	11.7	11.4	9.6	18 175	5.9	683	0.4	0.9	2.5	17 492	49.1	50.9	2.40	2.09
Somerville	3.2	11.5	-7.3	7.6	32 477	2.2	922	0.3	0.8	1.6	31 555	30.6	69.4	2.59	2.28
Springfield	1.5	20.1	12.9	17.7	61 172	-0.2	4 042	0.3	1.3	6.1	57 130	49.9	50.1	2.61	2.28
Taunton	1.8	8.3	-21.0	6.7	22 908	13.0	863	0.1	0.6	4.7	22 045	61.2	38.8	2.73	2.14
Waltham	5.5	6.5	-19.8	4.2	23 880	9.9	673	0.5	0.3	2.2	23 207	46.0	54.0	2.60	2.03
Westfield	2.9	8.0	2.6	7.2	15 441	6.7	644	0.5	1.0	2.8	14 797	67.8	32.2	2.68	2.25
Woburn	6.2	5.1	-12.1	4.5	15 391	9.1	394	0.5	0.4	2.2	14 997	61.2	38.8	2.74	2.04
Worcester	2.6	15.3	6.3	12.2	70 723	2.0	3 695	0.4	0.9	4.1	67 028	43.3	56.7	2.57	2.28
MICHIGAN	3.8	13.1	26.1	10.2	4 234 279	10.0	448 618	5.5	1.6	6.8	3 785 661	73.8	26.2	2.67	2.24
Allen Park	3.8	3.3	57.1	2.2	12 254	0.2	280	0.2	0.6	4.4	11 974	87.9	12.1	2.51	1.82
Ann Arbor	7.8	16.1	9.5	6.0	47 218	7.3	1 525	0.5	1.0	2.6	45 693	45.3	54.7	2.43	2.06

1. Includes units rented or sold but not occupied.   2. Specified owner-occupied units.   3. Specified renter-occupied units.   4. Overcrowded or lacking complete plumbing facilities.

Table D. Cities — Labor Force, Employment, Disability, and Construction

City	Civilian labor force, 2001		Unemployment		Civilian employment, 1990[2]	Percent		Disability 1990	Value of residential construction authorized by building permits, 2000		
	Total	Percent change, 2000–2001	Total	Rate[1]	Total	Professional, managerial, and technical	Precision production, craft, and repair	Work disabled persons[3] (percent)	New construction ($1,000)	Number of housing units	Percent single family
	61	62	63	64	65	66	67	68	69	70	71
LOUISIANA—Cont'd											
Houma	15 422	2.5	597	3.9	10 860	27.2	13.2	14.2	NA	NA	NA
Kenner	38 954	0.7	1 689	4.3	34 952	30.8	11.0	7.5	15 438	154	36.4
Lafayette	57 646	3.3	2 536	4.4	41 441	37.2	8.8	8.6	NA	NA	NA
Lake Charles	37 548	0.6	2 767	7.4	27 620	29.4	12.7	10.7	23 347	168	77.4
Monroe	24 985	3.0	1 947	7.8	19 247	34.2	5.9	8.9	5 122	32	93.8
New Iberia	14 953	1.7	1 039	6.9	11 288	21.0	15.8	11.9	5 903	39	100.0
New Orleans	195 752	0.9	11 570	5.9	186 036	34.1	7.0	10.7	93 433	679	51.3
Shreveport	95 983	2.4	6 358	6.6	78 900	30.4	9.3	9.1	58 181	345	100.0
Slidell	15 762	1.1	560	3.6	10 666	37.8	10.4	8.7	9 675	106	100.0
MAINE	683 907	-0.7	27 143	4.0	571 842	27.8	13.4	10.2	722 979	6 177	93.1
Bangor	18 477	-0.4	556	3.0	16 086	35.1	9.0	10.3	7 977	139	15.1
Lewiston	21 467	-2.2	845	3.9	18 827	21.5	13.2	12.4	3 107	26	100.0
Portland	37 647	-0.6	944	2.5	33 378	35.1	8.1	9.7	16 179	160	55.0
MARYLAND	2 837 433	1.2	115 709	4.1	2 481 342	37.0	10.3	7.0	3 232 127	30 358	82.8
Annapolis	21 776	1.7	1 206	5.5	18 188	40.2	7.3	7.9	10 000	132	98.5
Baltimore	295 303	0.9	23 273	7.9	314 688	27.6	9.3	11.7	21 224	257	85.2
Bowie	24 448	0.8	550	2.2	22 649	45.4	8.7	5.4	NA	NA	NA
Frederick	27 697	1.4	929	3.4	21 423	34.2	12.0	6.6	68 649	802	98.0
Gaithersburg	26 932	1.3	780	2.9	23 627	44.3	8.0	5.5	48 699	568	59.2
Hagerstown	20 567	1.5	888	4.3	16 644	20.6	12.5	10.3	4 308	105	60.0
Rockville	28 299	1.3	779	2.8	24 862	49.5	8.5	6.3	61 037	592	42.6
MASSACHUSETTS	3 283 709	1.5	120 605	3.7	3 027 950	36.2	10.0	7.2	2 741 243	18 000	78.9
Agawam	14 390	1.3	477	3.3	NA	NA	NA	NA	7 105	55	92.7
Attleboro	21 807	1.7	946	4.3	19 917	28.7	15.6	8.4	12 515	181	77.9
Barnstable Town	24 016	2.7	793	3.3	NA	NA	NA	NA	51 110	207	99.0
Beverly	21 781	1.4	616	2.8	20 256	36.2	10.1	6.8	12 139	56	100.0
Boston	296 883	1.5	12 067	4.1	288 704	37.1	6.4	8.0	73 648	567	16.9
Brockton	45 306	1.1	2 276	5.0	42 921	24.0	11.7	10.4	6 298	62	100.0
Cambridge	54 939	1.3	1 389	2.5	54 097	55.0	4.5	5.5	63 280	465	2.8
Chelsea	12 358	2.0	680	5.5	11 981	22.3	10.8	11.3	387	6	16.7
Chicopee	26 601	1.6	1 138	4.3	27 373	21.9	13.3	8.2	3 872	54	85.2
Everett	18 395	1.2	711	3.9	17 794	24.4	11.2	8.7	392	7	14.3
Fall River	42 019	1.1	2 429	5.8	40 226	18.5	12.9	11.2	8 631	161	73.9
Fitchburg	17 382	0.4	944	5.4	17 948	26.0	10.7	9.1	5 936	74	39.2
Franklin	16 084	1.4	454	2.8	NA	NA	NA	NA	15 512	88	97.7
Gloucester	16 115	1.7	822	5.1	14 470	30.1	13.0	8.5	9 991	77	75.3
Haverhill	29 161	1.6	1 412	4.8	25 492	33.7	12.5	6.9	12 920	144	77.8
Holyoke	15 853	1.9	851	5.4	16 446	28.0	11.1	12.6	8 139	58	10.3
Lawrence	28 561	3.8	2 864	10.0	25 644	22.2	13.4	9.8	1 336	13	53.8
Leominster	20 289	0.6	992	4.9	19 533	32.5	11.3	7.7	6 867	61	100.0
Lowell	53 035	3.9	3 034	5.7	45 912	28.2	13.1	9.3	8 071	106	92.5
Lynn	38 443	1.6	1 774	4.6	36 053	25.8	12.6	10.0	6 497	75	84.0
Malden	29 618	1.6	1 111	3.8	28 671	33.5	9.3	8.3	1 332	37	45.9
MarlBorough	20 067	1.6	705	3.5	18 070	40.3	10.4	5.8	33 343	575	16.2
Medford	31 017	1.4	947	3.1	30 450	34.5	9.6	6.4	660	9	77.8
Melrose	15 086	1.2	418	2.8	14 855	43.0	9.4	6.0	524	4	100.0
Methuen	21 623	1.5	1 112	5.1	NA	NA	NA	NA	14 123	121	100.0
New Bedford	39 528	0.7	3 070	7.8	40 185	19.7	11.9	12.0	5 242	82	100.0
Newton	47 086	1.3	1 103	2.3	46 439	57.0	4.4	4.0	17 705	107	48.6
Northampton	15 394	1.1	357	2.3	15 816	39.0	7.0	8.0	4 952	26	92.3
Peabody	27 367	1.4	861	3.1	24 949	31.2	11.9	7.5	21 208	226	11.1
Pittsfield	20 226	0.1	843	4.2	22 379	31.9	11.7	10.1	4 572	39	100.0
Quincy	49 632	1.2	1 719	3.5	46 523	33.3	9.9	7.4	33 703	395	13.2
Revere	21 191	1.2	888	4.2	20 393	25.6	10.8	9.9	4 863	77	16.9
Salem	21 321	1.7	823	3.9	19 958	34.5	10.6	7.0	22 771	220	40.0
Somerville	44 541	1.6	1 342	3.0	43 677	38.0	7.5	6.8	0	0	0.0
Springfield	63 423	1.7	3 428	5.4	65 274	26.8	9.9	10.6	4 937	66	93.9
Taunton	27 824	1.3	1 153	4.1	24 527	24.6	12.1	9.0	12 554	128	82.8
Waltham	34 540	1.5	1 097	3.2	32 353	35.6	10.9	5.8	4 309	46	91.3
Westfield	18 830	1.3	643	3.4	18 909	29.3	12.1	7.0	11 973	79	100.0
Woburn	22 450	1.5	690	3.1	20 485	35.8	11.3	6.1	26 135	116	100.0
Worcester	77 672	2.6	3 709	4.8	75 836	31.0	9.2	9.0	25 133	293	95.2
MICHIGAN	5 175 083	-0.5	274 360	5.3	4 166 196	28.3	12.0	9.0	6 255 867	52 489	81.8
Allen Park	15 469	-2.3	382	2.5	13 873	31.2	12.9	8.3	550	3	100.0
Ann Arbor	70 018	0.0	1 400	2.0	59 668	55.3	3.7	4.2	58 620	352	79.3

1. Percent of civilian labor force. 2. Persons 16 years and older. 3. Persons 16 to 64 years old.

Table D. Cities — Wholesale Trade, Retail Trade, and Real Estate

City	Wholesale Trade, 1997				Retail Trade¹, 1997				Real Estate and Rental and Leasing, 1997			
	Number of Establishments	Number of Employees	Sales (mil dol)	Annual Payroll (mil dol)	Number of Establishments	Number of Employees	Sales (mil dol)	Annual Payroll (mil dol)	Number of Establishments	Number of Employees	Receipts (mil dol)	Annual Payroll (mil dol)
	72	73	74	75	76	77	78	79	80	81	82	83
LOUISIANA—Cont'd					•							
Houma....................	102	1 276	429.7	38.6	246	3 088	437.5	42.4	70	1 269	199.9	43.9
Kenner....................	170	D	D	D	350	5 765	968.9	86.5	71	1 404	128.2	25.5
Lafayette................	321	4 159	1 864.0	137.4	818	12 689	2 104.3	198.9	252	1 850	238.5	51.0
Lake Charles..........	141	2 039	533.0	56.0	483	6 705	1 019.8	96.4	137	714	62.3	12.3
Monroe..................	139	1 867	680.8	56.9	470	6 314	1 058.1	94.4	113	628	58.0	9.7
New Iberia.............	82	1 139	279.8	36.2	214	2 748	505.3	43.3	62	998	175.9	36.4
New Orleans...........	484	6 086	2 450.5	210.2	1 871	20 405	2 771.3	315.6	481	3 538	407.4	72.3
Shreveport.............	422	5 186	1 723.0	154.9	930	12 010	2 056.5	198.3	213	1 069	110.4	20.4
Slidell...................	48	D	D	D	322	4 324	666.3	59.3	45	273	35.3	4.3
MAINE..................	1 726	19 932	7 305.6	616.2	7 074	72 897	12 737.1	1 164.2	1 343	5 929	601.7	114.2
Bangor..................	92	1 600	620.5	49.2	335	5 340	999.7	87.9	81	347	47.2	6.1
Lewiston................	60	D	D	D	202	2 548	593.1	40.1	50	172	16.4	2.7
Portland................	233	3 538	1 477.5	113.0	422	5 380	1 292.3	97.5	172	1 618	163.4	37.3
MARYLAND............	6 283	92 458	54 906.6	3 656.3	19 798	274 260	46 428.2	4 914.0	5 065	39 502	4 764.7	971.3
Annapolis..............	89	646	419.0	28.6	466	6 238	1 032.9	111.3	80	530	74.4	14.9
Baltimore..............	792	14 152	6 171.2	499.2	2 256	23 159	3 438.4	414.7	597	4 807	568.2	124.9
Bowie...................	26	D	D	D	104	2 284	339.1	35.5	39	175	34.0	3.4
Frederick...............	123	2 088	634.0	68.4	464	7 724	1 308.2	132.7	111	617	73.2	14.9
Gaithersburg..........	76	D	D	D	333	6 573	1 340.1	128.7	84	D	D	D
Hagerstown............	79	967	301.6	28.3	305	4 123	689.7	62.4	54	D	D	D
Rockville...............	131	2 656	2 937.3	150.0	305	4 250	983.6	97.4	74	1 172	183.4	32.7
MASSACHUSETTS..........	9 993	146 827	112 792.4	6 484.8	26 209	335 736	58 578.0	5 894.8	5 834	41 233	5 925.4	1 214.1
Agawam................	NA	NA	NA	NA	NA	NA	NA	NA	NA	NA	NA	NA
Attleboro...............	40	394	172.1	16.7	158	2 973	476.3	38.8	33	153	23.1	4.4
Barnstable Town.......	NA	NA	NA	NA	NA	NA	NA	NA	NA	NA	NA	NA
Beverly.................	46	331	210.8	18.0	146	1 820	350.5	34.2	36	140	20.4	3.2
Boston..................	770	9 857	7 574.9	437.2	2 262	26 624	4 255.7	472.0	826	12 736	1 550.8	426.5
Brockton...............	84	1 666	604.2	58.1	359	5 414	932.4	106.4	53	257	35.3	5.4
Cambridge..............	145	3 696	1 457.9	183.4	538	7 290	1 113.4	124.6	143	1 144	206.7	36.8
Chelsea.................	116	D	D	D	98	1 260	241.4	24.6	29	98	13.3	2.4
Chicopee...............	57	D	D	D	183	2 372	382.8	34.0	34	165	26.5	3.5
Everett.................	75	1 269	925.6	59.8	85	595	123.9	11.4	13	85	7.6	1.8
Fall River..............	87	1 079	401.8	27.4	349	3 408	592.4	61.1	76	302	33.2	5.3
Fitchburg..............	45	D	D	D	170	2 011	349.8	39.2	36	161	12.1	3.1
Franklin................	NA	NA	NA	NA	NA	NA	NA	NA	NA	NA	NA	NA
Gloucester.............	66	318	227.8	11.0	123	1 400	227.6	23.7	33	99	10.9	3.1
Haverhill...............	71	703	157.7	19.4	158	2 202	420.7	39.3	35	176	19.5	3.9
Holyoke................	47	765	245.6	24.3	218	3 305	451.3	46.8	37	271	18.3	3.9
Lawrence..............	72	1 119	344.5	37.1	158	1 255	328.4	29.9	38	206	20.7	3.7
Leominster.............	56	602	408.7	22.4	209	3 166	494.2	45.4	46	193	23.9	4.2
Lowell..................	88	1 159	353.9	41.5	256	2 514	472.4	44.1	63	466	41.9	7.3
Lynn....................	61	856	419.5	31.4	213	2 658	429.8	43.9	47	254	31.0	5.5
Malden.................	48	845	463.8	29.8	161	1 869	364.6	31.9	44	264	31.6	4.5
MarlBorough...........	104	3 725	2 244.5	201.3	219	3 074	494.3	59.0	31	174	35.6	4.6
Medford................	64	1 146	386.2	40.2	185	2 918	547.4	50.3	23	183	35.5	4.8
Melrose................	18	238	67.3	5.8	73	818	130.2	14.2	13	30	4.6	0.6
Methuen................	NA	NA	NA	NA	NA	NA	NA	NA	NA	NA	NA	NA
New Bedford...........	146	2 111	782.7	59.4	325	3 273	499.4	52.2	64	238	25.1	4.7
Newton.................	175	2 587	1 857.5	109.0	390	5 701	978.1	113.9	140	1 506	281.6	49.2
Northampton...........	22	D	D	D	206	2 525	380.0	41.5	52	152	22.2	2.3
Peabody................	109	2 817	2 689.7	132.4	282	4 899	886.4	86.4	42	263	20.8	4.9
Pittsfield...............	51	D	D	D	243	3 362	527.9	56.0	55	218	22.0	4.2
Quincy.................	89	859	384.8	28.0	271	5 146	822.5	84.0	72	691	158.6	18.2
Revere..................	30	D	D	D	140	1 882	302.8	31.3	26	152	18.3	3.3
Salem..................	49	456	175.3	20.7	172	1 880	292.7	32.1	36	157	20.7	4.3
Somerville..............	80	1 020	352.0	35.0	208	3 307	559.0	53.0	35	158	20.9	2.8
Springfield.............	166	2 524	1 989.4	116.4	565	7 313	1 123.3	120.1	119	688	101.4	18.0
Taunton................	73	1 364	644.5	56.2	252	3 261	417.2	44.5	35	180	35.3	3.8
Waltham................	158	4 158	4 387.3	279.2	258	3 185	587.5	64.8	96	779	227.7	30.8
Westfield...............	51	879	765.3	23.9	152	2 191	335.8	32.2	33	118	13.0	2.2
Woburn................	288	4 495	2 780.6	216.5	223	3 640	754.3	86.2	57	1 245	165.4	33.7
Worcester..............	216	2 085	803.4	70.0	722	8 854	1 530.5	157.3	139	1 313	201.7	33.8
MICHIGAN.............	13 936	189 057	158 757.3	7 629.6	39 564	529 441	93 706.1	8 922.3	8 302	50 941	6 492.7	1 126.2
Allen Park..............	30	399	272.4	27.0	104	852	115.4	13.5	26	109	14.0	1.7
Ann Arbor..............	174	1 767	1 399.0	80.6	647	9 645	1 369.5	154.4	147	1 414	107.4	33.2

1. Establishments with payroll.

Professional Services, Manufacturing, Accommodation and Foodservices

City	Professional, Scientific, and Technical Services, 1997[1]				Manufacturing, 1997				Accommodation and Foodservices, 1997			
	Number of Establishments	Number of Employees	Receipts (mil dol)	Annual Payroll (mil dol)	Number of Establishments	Number of Employees	Receipts (mil dol)	Annual Payroll (mil dol)	Number of Establishments	Number of Employees	Sales (mil dol)	Annual Payroll (mil dol)
	84	85	86	87	88	89	90	91	92	93	94	95
LOUISIANA—Cont'd												
Houma	118	737	65.4	24.7	57	2 086	269.5	74.5	86	1 262	41.8	13.2
Kenner	116	599	42.9	17.0	68	1 693	161.2	45.6	160	3 712	148.4	35.4
Lafayette	703	5 264	502.4	194.3	125	3 434	538.4	89.1	329	8 380	250.9	73.3
Lake Charles	273	1 738	127.6	45.4	66	D	D	D	183	6 092	239.5	59.7
Monroe	251	1 593	115.8	40.6	58	3 061	408.0	76.1	172	3 734	116.9	29.5
New Iberia	100	427	29.5	10.7	51	1 427	209.0	46.8	71	1 186	29.6	7.7
New Orleans	1 420	12 469	1 401.8	551.5	261	10 453	2 305.0	362.2	1 105	32 081	1 371.8	377.5
Shreveport	531	3 033	274.8	102.6	177	D	D	D	374	7 150	219.3	61.2
Slidell	102	546	45.5	15.0	31	611	73.0	11.1	147	2 637	83.5	20.9
MAINE	2 552	13 747	1 215.6	474.8	1 812	82 288	14 097.6	2 591.1	3 714	39 624	1 509.3	428.8
Bangor	147	869	70.4	33.0	46	D	D	D	144	2 709	88.4	27.2
Lewiston	73	1 215	153.4	38.2	79	D	D	D	77	1 032	32.2	9.7
Portland	436	3 645	363.9	152.7	119	3 905	624.9	107.0	275	4 084	147.4	42.4
MARYLAND	14 115	146 814	15 940.2	6 483.8	3 996	163 992	36 505.9	5 840.5	9 049	161 273	5 972.5	1 644.7
Annapolis	370	2 142	253.7	95.2	NA	NA	NA	NA	166	4 426	169.2	49.5
Baltimore	1 395	14 695	1 645.0	666.3	688	30 216	9 822.2	1 006.2	1 328	20 021	849.9	232.0
Bowie	113	1 662	66.9	39.8	NA	NA	NA	NA	44	1 031	33.4	9.1
Frederick	255	3 129	224.7	105.5	79	3 097	505.1	100.3	178	3 687	123.2	33.4
Gaithersburg	278	6 826	1 197.7	432.5	42	1 993	318.0	89.8	144	3 327	129.5	35.1
Hagerstown	107	607	36.3	15.4	64	3 361	593.1	96.9	124	2 604	78.5	22.3
Rockville	673	14 867	1 598.6	673.9	68	1 438	166.2	52.9	183	2 703	104.9	28.1
MASSACHUSETTS	18 086	177 345	22 744.1	9 261.4	9 554	417 135	77 876.6	16 379.0	14 800	227 476	9 269.9	2 575.6
Agawam	NA	NA	NA	NA	NA	NA	NA	NA	NA	NA	NA	NA
Attleboro	50	169	17.0	5.7	143	9 714	1 412.0	333.5	81	1 697	53.9	15.0
Barnstable Town	NA	NA	NA	NA	NA	NA	NA	NA	NA	NA	NA	NA
Beverly	91	325	43.0	15.9	83	3 861	726.1	168.1	79	909	33.3	8.8
Boston	3 053	49 765	7 871.3	2 949.9	536	18 944	3 941.5	671.5	1 907	39 831	2 049.1	576.1
Brockton	138	1 181	78.6	30.8	121	3 009	378.0	92.0	150	2 658	88.2	24.9
Cambridge	738	20 339	2 751.9	1 341.2	106	3 050	585.2	98.1	413	7 766	404.3	111.9
Chelsea	34	342	37.6	14.6	62	2 084	341.4	66.0	62	D	D	D
Chicopee	35	131	10.7	3.9	109	4 974	990.0	184.6	125	1 608	52.8	14.0
Everett	29	251	16.3	7.4	77	2 216	297.0	82.1	55	D	D	D
Fall River	145	586	48.2	16.7	199	12 366	1 364.5	337.3	181	2 276	78.3	20.9
Fitchburg	67	259	19.1	6.9	89	3 896	653.6	145.3	101	1 370	46.9	12.7
Franklin	NA	NA	NA	NA	NA	NA	NA	NA	NA	NA	NA	NA
Gloucester	69	215	26.2	9.5	64	3 948	846.8	137.2	101	1 031	42.4	13.0
Haverhill	99	631	45.4	19.0	119	3 885	545.9	130.8	123	D	D	D
Holyoke	51	459	25.4	9.1	88	4 223	886.8	139.0	81	1 153	39.7	10.0
Lawrence	63	424	23.9	9.0	120	6 252	1 052.4	207.9	84	D	D	D
Leominster	68	323	31.4	11.3	135	6 003	1 256.0	196.3	95	1 344	42.5	11.6
Lowell	144	1 389	138.2	48.3	101	5 709	888.1	193.3	174	D	D	D
Lynn	80	233	18.9	7.0	67	6 870	2 101.8	325.2	131	D	D	D
Malden	71	715	29.5	12.7	63	1 929	309.2	63.8	89	938	36.5	9.5
MarlBorough	138	2 020	338.4	125.5	90	4 959	1 592.9	258.0	115	2 024	80.0	23.4
Medford	85	429	52.3	20.2	52	924	98.3	24.9	87	1 201	42.6	11.4
Melrose	76	336	29.9	11.9	NA	NA	NA	NA	30	364	13.9	3.8
Methuen	NA	NA	NA	NA	NA	NA	NA	NA	NA	NA	NA	NA
New Bedford	165	653	49.0	19.1	151	9 839	1 259.9	273.8	209	2 019	70.7	17.4
Newton	540	4 235	451.7	209.0	87	2 999	542.6	110.2	163	3 699	172.1	49.1
Northampton	107	468	33.0	12.7	39	1 471	264.5	46.3	97	1 873	57.9	17.4
Peabody	114	836	85.6	35.3	98	4 028	690.1	164.5	135	2 408	97.9	27.4
Pittsfield	112	821	70.1	30.3	59	D	D	D	125	2 083	61.6	18.0
Quincy	222	1 972	209.5	84.6	72	753	127.3	25.9	201	2 943	115.2	30.9
Revere	35	102	10.1	3.7	NA	NA	NA	NA	84	D	D	D
Salem	154	511	46.3	15.4	70	1 733	190.2	54.9	116	1 556	51.5	14.9
Somerville	140	776	94.8	33.6	83	2 574	433.0	96.2	154	D	D	D
Springfield	321	2 198	188.1	82.4	174	7 199	1 161.1	258.9	278	4 770	146.3	43.3
Taunton	80	591	31.4	13.3	71	4 465	709.0	174.4	101	D	D	D
Waltham	308	5 834	737.4	329.4	161	7 431	1 217.2	351.5	172	2 852	123.3	30.9
Westfield	48	308	30.5	13.7	105	3 786	634.7	132.6	73	1 095	29.8	7.8
Woburn	195	2 113	243.4	99.7	195	5 778	876.7	226.8	77	1 528	74.5	18.0
Worcester	445	2 718	232.7	93.3	278	13 475	2 139.5	528.5	415	6 202	200.3	54.7
MICHIGAN	18 614	162 971	16 231.7	6 882.9	16 045	833 429	214 900.7	34 418.9	18 958	320 014	10 158.7	2 835.8
Allen Park	50	492	52.2	19.3	20	D	D	D	62	1 276	34.5	8.7
Ann Arbor	621	6 371	809.0	320.8	131	4 330	599.8	160.0	344	8 266	273.7	75.9

1. Firms subject to federal tax.

City	Arts, Entertainment, and Recreation[1], 1997				Health Care and Social Assistance[1], 1997				Other Services[1], 1997			
	Number of Establishments	Number of Employees	Receipts (mil dol)	Annual Payroll (mil dol)	Number of Establishments	Number of Employees	Receipts (mil dol)	Annual Payroll (mil dol)	Number of Establishments	Number of Employees	Receipts (mil dol)	Annual Payroll (mil dol)
	96	97	98	99	100	101	102	103	104	105	106	107
LOUISIANA—Cont'd												
Houma	14	130	6.9	1.6	112	1 181	102.1	53.3	94	857	87.0	22.1
Kenner	18	0	0.0	0.0	100	1 821	95.6	37.3	157	815	49.3	14.4
Lafayette	44	990	44.7	8.2	558	6 842	564.7	218.9	263	1 938	116.5	37.6
Lake Charles	25	0	0.0	0.0	299	3 622	268.0	111.3	165	1 213	68.5	20.8
Monroe	18	127	10.0	1.7	233	3 869	253.0	112.0	114	828	40.2	12.5
New Iberia	12	0	0.0	0.0	126	1 566	106.3	38.7	79	414	28.3	8.2
New Orleans	117	3 609	271.8	61.7	1 022	19 447	1 245.4	530.6	605	4 684	257.7	77.8
Shreveport	66	1 832	234.5	33.6	532	8 680	612.4	274.1	332	2 328	153.6	45.8
Slidell	16	175	8.7	1.5	159	2 196	132.6	56.4	93	439	29.5	7.7
MAINE	524	5 456	254.4	64.0	2 727	28 944	1 608.4	766.3	1 923	8 820	612.3	169.6
Bangor	20	212	39.9	1.9	181	2 230	154.4	74.5	87	553	47.2	11.8
Lewiston	10	148	4.4	1.4	133	1 460	97.3	45.2	75	0	0.0	0.0
Portland	38	353	19.1	5.0	284	3 230	245.0	125.1	179	1 171	84.8	24.3
MARYLAND	1 460	19 398	1 412.4	494.8	10 841	116 241	8 060.7	3 538.0	7 871	55 241	3 561.3	1 129.2
Annapolis	34	296	16.5	4.4	146	1 678	124.1	63.5	141	1 411	66.6	23.4
Baltimore	107	2 147	338.7	168.5	1 220	16 856	1 093.8	486.1	891	6 733	426.4	131.5
Bowie	18	209	17.9	6.6	111	652	43.3	18.3	47	244	10.9	3.7
Frederick	26	401	17.3	4.1	230	2 439	167.0	79.5	157	1 030	79.2	22.1
Gaithersburg	20	458	15.3	4.3	108	875	61.5	27.3	124	884	59.9	18.6
Hagerstown	13	135	7.2	1.2	143	1 748	146.0	67.0	108	717	30.5	10.0
Rockville	32	828	63.9	14.8	196	1 863	136.1	59.5	186	1 753	166.0	54.8
MASSACHUSETTS	1 781	22 598	1 578.5	518.6	11 887	182 902	11 361.4	5 310.5	10 806	61 557	4 359.8	1 338.6
Agawam	NA	NA	NA	NA	NA	NA	NA	NA	NA	NA	NA	NA
Attleboro	5	57	5.8	1.2	74	1 003	66.1	29.0	55	238	15.0	4.3
Barnstable Town	NA	NA	NA	NA	NA	NA	NA	NA	NA	NA	NA	NA
Beverly	13	123	7.6	2.2	108	2 108	125.3	74.5	55	294	19.0	5.9
Boston	165	3 463	433.2	186.3	963	19 284	1 437.5	701.5	1 021	7 625	519.3	150.1
Brockton	15	177	4.3	1.3	188	3 962	271.5	132.7	142	754	45.8	12.1
Cambridge	40	529	46.2	7.5	201	2 433	219.3	93.9	148	1 024	91.0	21.6
Chelsea	2	0	0.0	0.0	23	577	26.8	11.9	31	153	15.2	4.4
Chicopee	6	63	2.6	0.8	51	1 145	53.3	23.1	89	476	31.6	9.7
Everett	4	32	1.1	0.2	51	327	20.2	9.8	69	403	31.1	9.3
Fall River	11	34	1.9	0.3	202	2 493	154.3	80.8	154	730	39.8	12.1
Fitchburg	5	0	0.0	0.0	90	1 051	63.0	28.4	70	331	22.4	6.8
Franklin	NA	NA	NA	NA	NA	NA	NA	NA	NA	NA	NA	NA
Gloucester	11	74	5.1	1.6	45	432	26.1	12.3	55	201	12.6	4.1
Haverhill	15	464	15.9	4.7	76	1 858	100.4	54.5	85	466	26.3	8.5
Holyoke	11	58	6.4	1.7	95	1 287	86.0	40.7	59	294	16.0	5.2
Lawrence	4	0	0.0	0.0	57	0	0.0	0.0	94	842	56.3	19.1
Leominster	9	68	3.2	0.9	68	708	55.2	18.1	71	362	21.2	6.5
Lowell	10	154	6.1	2.2	145	2 311	146.5	69.6	149	738	46.4	13.6
Lynn	8	40	1.9	0.7	131	1 835	104.8	51.6	110	527	33.1	10.4
Malden	9	85	4.2	0.9	88	1 525	60.6	30.5	106	536	38.7	9.6
MarlBorough	11	158	4.6	1.3	59	881	54.8	22.5	77	696	91.1	23.3
Medford	3	61	2.7	0.6	93	1 051	70.9	31.3	96	698	55.3	18.8
Melrose	3	0	0.0	0.0	76	1 035	69.9	40.1	42	170	11.1	3.5
Methuen	NA	NA	NA	NA	NA	NA	NA	NA	NA	NA	NA	NA
New Bedford	14	87	4.3	1.0	153	3 383	163.6	80.5	142	890	66.6	17.8
Newton	37	347	22.4	6.8	338	4 519	247.4	118.9	159	1 057	73.4	21.7
Northampton	14	85	3.5	0.9	104	1 389	84.1	41.8	67	286	21.3	6.0
Peabody	7	77	3.6	1.6	90	1 792	84.5	41.2	110	543	34.8	10.7
Pittsfield	18	0	0.0	0.0	128	2 115	144.5	60.0	102	0	0.0	0.0
Quincy	20	217	11.8	3.0	203	3 576	180.9	80.6	161	934	62.8	19.6
Revere	3	0	0.0	0.0	50	710	34.3	15.1	78	285	19.5	5.2
Salem	16	67	5.3	1.5	122	1 187	79.8	41.1	76	330	26.3	6.7
Somerville	19	264	18.4	4.8	60	577	37.3	14.5	112	920	58.4	20.6
Springfield	16	191	8.5	2.9	333	5 394	358.0	168.0	223	1 636	108.0	35.0
Taunton	9	57	2.1	0.5	88	1 425	93.0	45.2	77	355	24.5	6.6
Waltham	18	225	12.7	2.7	131	1 759	177.9	60.2	137	710	70.2	19.0
Westfield	9	63	3.5	1.1	56	661	32.9	13.3	71	329	19.5	6.5
Woburn	13	109	6.8	2.9	79	2 458	140.1	55.1	101	765	62.5	26.3
Worcester	21	521	13.9	5.0	385	8 418	651.3	280.7	310	2 203	134.8	42.2
MICHIGAN	2 693	34 161	2 202.8	664.6	18 943	186 954	11 811.5	5 696.8	14 705	93 792	6 159.1	1 893.8
Allen Park	11	325	18.1	8.9	85	885	52.1	24.4	58	300	13.0	4.5
Ann Arbor	43	533	18.8	5.6	305	2 913	242.0	88.6	168	1 129	73.0	23.1

1. Firms subject to federal tax.

	Selected federal funds, fiscal 2001[1] (mil dol)									City government finances, 1999						
	Procurement contracts		Grants					Direct payments for individuals		Intergovernmental			Taxes			
														Per capita[3] (dollars)		
City	Defense	Other	Total[2]	Health and family welfare	Energy and environment	Education	Housing and community development	Educational assistance	Housing assistance	Total (mil dol)	Total (mil dol)	Percent from state government	Total (mil dol)	Total	Property	Sales and gross receipts
	108	109	110	111	112	113	114	115	116	117	118	119	120	121	122	123
LOUISIANA—Cont'd																
Houma	0.0	0.0	6.8	0.0	0.0	1.5	3.6	0.5	0.3	238.0	46.0	86.0	55.7	1 857	811	993
Kenner	1.1	0.5	1.2	0.0	0.0	0.0	1.1	0.9	4.7	65.1	42.8	6.4	11.7	164	71	47
Lafayette	6.9	14.7	25.8	12.3	0.0	2.6	2.2	13.7	10.2	167.2	18.9	53.6	79.9	703	185	473
Lake Charles	6.4	8.4	11.7	4.4	0.1	1.6	1.2	9.0	14.3	73.9	17.0	26.4	44.8	633	68	526
Monroe	2.7	2.8	21.1	5.5	1.2	0.9	1.5	10.7	16.6	88.5	18.8	33.4	51.9	968	135	791
New Iberia	4.5	2.1	3.1	1.0	1.0	0.0	0.2	0.4	6.5	NA	NA	NA	NA	NA	NA	NA
New Orleans	650.3	486.4	382.2	184.0	17.1	28.8	58.4	57.4	75.3	714.3	111.6	79.6	360.8	775	322	413
Shreveport	13.2	20.0	39.2	17.4	1.2	3.5	7.9	6.8	36.3	225.0	42.2	42.9	129.8	689	228	427
Slidell	11.8	0.9	0.2	0.0	0.0	0.0	0.0	0.3	2.1	25.6	2.2	72.7	19.3	740	157	523
MAINE	503.4	170.9	1 904.7	1 276.0	37.1	149.9	22.6	59.2	173.9	X	X	X	X	X	X	X
Bangor	3.9	1.9	21.8	2.0	0.0	3.3	1.5	3.2	8.0	125.2	45.4	43.5	35.5	1 164	1 053	99
Lewiston	0.1	0.0	5.8	2.1	0.0	0.0	0.8	1.8	14.8	73.9	25.5	100.0	38.6	1 068	1 061	0
Portland	59.7	5.9	26.8	10.5	1.0	2.2	2.8	19.2	26.0	192.3	37.8	98.2	93.1	1 483	1 454	0
MARYLAND	4 909.1	5 827.2	7 586.5	4 578.7	120.3	492.9	95.1	139.6	689.6	X	X	X	X	X	X	X
Annapolis	259.7	19.4	107.3	5.7	7.6	6.3	3.7	0.8	30.4	42.4	8.7	44.6	21.3	635	530	67
Baltimore	545.8	435.2	1 761.5	1 054.9	65.1	161.8	49.7	62.7	222.5	2 135.9	1 164.3	84.9	735.4	1 139	739	84
Bowie	3.1	17.5	8.0	0.4	0.0	3.1	0.0	3.3	0.3	NA	NA	NA	NA	NA	NA	NA
Frederick	98.6	43.4	18.7	8.8	0.3	0.2	0.2	2.1	5.8	41.9	9.1	41.0	20.3	428	396	11
Gaithersburg	80.3	199.6	16.2	10.3	1.5	0.0	0.0	0.1	5.4	NA	NA	NA	NA	NA	NA	NA
Hagerstown	2.9	3.5	7.6	2.8	0.1	0.4	0.9	2.2	8.2	32.7	9.3	36.5	12.0	351	328	7
Rockville	345.1	1 279.7	312.3	181.6	5.5	12.6	15.8	9.0	29.0	48.5	10.7	29.9	19.4	415	369	15
MASSACHUSETTS	5 280.5	1 570.3	9 718.3	6 731.1	262.3	666.6	186.4	356.5	1 516.9	X	X	X	X	X	X	X
Agawam	0.9	0.0	0.0	0.0	0.0	0.0	0.0	0.0	0.0	50.1	17.2	100.0	27.6	NA	NA	NA
Attleboro	2.7	2.6	6.1	0.2	0.0	0.0	0.4	0.0	2.9	77.7	38.0	99.1	32.9	831	817	0
Barnstable Town	0.0	0.0	3.1	0.0	0.0	0.0	0.0	0.0	0.0	108.6	22.0	91.5	67.6	NA	NA	NA
Beverly	7.8	2.2	6.1	5.6	0.0	0.0	0.0	1.1	10.9	79.8	20.2	90.5	46.6	1 195	1 181	3
Boston	134.8	157.4	2 305.0	1 399.5	126.2	62.3	101.1	61.0	617.1	2 294.0	1 116.1	93.2	883.1	1 590	1 477	69
Brockton	1.1	7.2	14.5	1.2	0.2	0.5	2.7	3.4	22.8	226.9	134.7	96.8	74.5	800	784	2
Cambridge	275.2	187.6	724.2	483.8	85.1	13.5	4.8	15.6	27.9	272.9	51.5	72.7	178.3	1 910	1 770	64
Chelsea	0.1	0.5	7.3	1.1	0.0	0.3	0.0	0.0	11.7	96.2	64.0	94.7	22.2	811	785	0
Chicopee	9.6	16.9	2.0	0.0	0.0	0.0	1.6	0.6	7.8	107.5	55.5	96.2	41.5	768	756	4
Everett	1.1	0.2	0.1	0.0	0.0	0.0	0.0	0.0	5.0	NA	NA	NA	NA	NA	NA	NA
Fall River	1.9	0.3	10.2	1.8	1.0	1.0	5.1	3.5	32.9	189.6	132.2	88.3	41.9	463	455	0
Fitchburg	0.3	0.7	8.2	0.0	0.7	0.8	2.1	1.4	6.0	84.0	48.6	95.7	25.0	624	614	1
Franklin	3.0	0.8	0.0	0.0	0.0	0.0	0.0	0.0	0.0	58.2	20.2	98.5	32.0	NA	NA	NA
Gloucester	4.4	3.0	1.9	0.2	0.0	0.0	0.9	0.0	4.7	66.1	18.1	89.0	38.6	1 301	1 275	8
Haverhill	0.0	0.3	7.1	1.2	0.0	0.3	1.2	3.1	15.0	159.7	58.4	95.5	49.4	893	876	5
Holyoke	0.0	0.3	24.0	13.7	0.0	1.7	3.2	3.1	13.8	139.6	87.7	95.9	30.5	744	731	4
Lawrence	1.0	0.1	12.0	5.2	0.4	1.5	3.3	0.0	27.1	188.4	143.9	96.0	31.7	457	445	3
Leominster	0.3	0.5	3.7	3.4	0.0	0.0	0.3	0.0	6.6	77.1	37.1	97.7	33.3	828	810	7
Lowell	15.0	4.4	30.9	8.8	5.2	3.6	3.7	7.1	25.9	246.6	161.6	95.7	66.9	661	647	5
Lynn	880.9	1.0	7.9	2.0	0.1	0.6	4.6	0.0	43.3	216.0	133.0	97.4	58.9	726	717	0
Malden	3.7	5.6	160.1	1.6	0.2	152.1	3.1	0.5	14.2	108.4	48.0	93.1	44.2	840	828	0
MarlBorough	129.5	10.3	2.5	1.1	0.6	0.0	0.0	0.1	5.9	73.8	15.2	92.0	52.2	1 570	1 512	25
Medford	1.7	0.1	7.6	0.7	0.9	0.8	1.6	3.3	12.5	107.4	39.4	90.6	56.4	1 008	995	0
Melrose	0.3	0.1	0.0	0.0	0.0	0.0	0.0	0.0	6.3	52.4	14.7	95.8	30.7	1 120	1 113	1
Methuen	0.4	1.3	0.0	0.0	0.0	0.0	0.0	0.0	0.0	85.3	39.5	93.3	37.5	NA	NA	NA
New Bedford	21.2	1.6	18.0	3.5	1.9	3.1	4.8	0.2	28.1	229.3	142.4	92.7	58.2	604	594	0
Newton	0.8	14.2	42.5	15.7	0.0	5.1	4.1	1.2	7.7	209.8	26.2	84.8	157.2	1 956	1 899	17
Northampton	19.3	0.6	6.4	1.4	0.0	2.8	1.3	0.1	4.3	NA	NA	NA	NA	NA	NA	NA
Peabody	4.3	10.2	2.6	0.0	0.1	0.8	1.8	0.0	9.5	97.8	32.0	85.7	48.3	981	948	12
Pittsfield	105.8	2.2	12.3	1.2	0.1	0.5	1.5	1.3	14.6	94.4	48.0	94.0	40.4	888	878	5
Quincy	222.7	20.5	7.8	1.6	0.0	0.0	3.8	2.9	23.5	304.5	97.9	80.2	95.2	1 111	1 089	0
Revere	0.0	0.0	0.2	0.0	0.0	0.0	0.1	0.0	11.1	87.4	42.7	94.7	41.8	1 004	970	12
Salem	2.4	0.7	4.9	0.6	0.0	1.6	1.3	3.7	7.3	91.9	29.8	93.5	47.7	1 244	1 230	5
Somerville	8.3	2.0	59.0	50.6	0.6	0.0	5.6	0.3	28.3	136.0	74.2	91.3	53.0	715	700	3
Springfield	1.7	16.9	35.2	4.3	0.4	9.9	7.3	10.8	74.4	443.1	292.1	89.6	108.0	729	711	7
Taunton	734.8	1.4	6.1	1.7	0.5	0.0	1.1	0.0	7.1	100.2	50.8	91.5	39.4	749	734	3
Waltham	33.0	25.9	60.2	41.2	5.4	2.7	0.9	6.7	14.2	130.3	27.8	95.0	87.4	1 493	1 414	33
Westfield	15.2	0.1	3.6	0.6	0.0	0.4	0.5	2.1	3.2	80.1	38.4	94.6	33.7	896	886	0
Woburn	18.2	12.5	8.0	5.1	0.0	0.0	0.1	0.2	4.0	78.3	15.9	97.0	51.2	1 382	1 323	33
Worcester	9.7	6.9	137.5	110.6	1.3	4.5	7.1	12.6	52.3	402.9	224.4	91.5	140.6	844	832	4
MICHIGAN	2 262.6	1 115.7	10 886.6	6 764.3	200.3	1 094.3	222.1	302.2	752.4	X	X	X	X	X	X	X
Allen Park	0.0	0.0	0.1	0.0	0.0	0.1	0.0	0.0	0.0	NA	NA	NA	NA	NA	NA	NA
Ann Arbor	46.6	39.2	468.9	319.4	18.8	8.4	2.1	19.1	11.2	137.3	30.5	68.1	58.0	528	490	0

1. October 1, 2000 to September 30, 2001.   2. Includes program categories not shown separately. State totals include additional categories not allocated by city.   3. Based on population estimated as of July 1 of the year shown.

Table D. Cities — City Government Finances

	City government finances, 1999 (cont'd)												
			General expenditure										
	Per capita[1] (dollars)			Percent of total for —									
City	Total (mil dol)	Total	Capital outlays	Public welfare	Highways	Parking facilities	Education	Health and hospitals	Police protection	Sewerage and sanitation	Parks and recreation	Housing and community development	Interest on debt
	124	125	126	127	128	129	130	131	132	133	134	135	136
LOUISIANA—Cont'd													
Houma	245.8	8 205	1 504	2.2	3.8	0.0	0.7	49.4	4.6	4.2	7.3	2.9	2.2
Kenner	58.5	817	151	1.2	9.6	0.0	0.0	0.1	24.1	12.0	9.0	5.2	4.2
Lafayette	184.3	1 622	501	0.1	19.8	0.2	0.8	0.0	17.0	7.8	8.3	6.3	5.7
Lake Charles	66.0	933	279	0.0	13.5	0.0	0.0	0.0	11.7	4.7	12.7	18.4	0.5
Monroe	85.2	1 589	265	0.2	23.0	0.0	0.0	1.1	11.0	9.7	5.0	13.1	2.6
New Iberia	NA	NA	NA	NA	NA	NA	NA	NA	NA	NA	NA	NA	NA
New Orleans	742.1	1 594	181	0.3	7.2	0.6	0.0	3.2	13.9	8.6	3.2	9.5	8.8
Shreveport	241.4	1 282	376	0.2	8.9	0.2	0.0	0.1	12.0	11.9	5.9	7.8	8.2
Slidell	19.9	762	50	0.0	19.7	0.0	0.0	1.1	24.8	15.8	6.1	1.4	10.4
MAINE	X	X	X	X	X	X	X	X	X	X	X	X	X
Bangor	90.0	2 949	131	5.4	6.2	0.4	31.7	0.0	5.2	3.1	3.2	3.3	3.0
Lewiston	68.6	1 897	139	0.5	8.5	0.5	42.8	0.3	5.1	6.7	2.3	4.4	3.0
Portland	208.3	3 318	246	6.9	4.6	0.0	33.5	0.9	5.5	5.8	2.5	0.6	3.2
MARYLAND	X	X	X	X	X	X	X	X	X	X	X	X	X
Annapolis	42.3	1 258	161	0.0	13.2	1.4	0.0	0.0	22.5	12.3	4.5	1.1	4.0
Baltimore	1 983.4	3 072	574	0.1	6.3	0.5	39.3	4.0	10.9	7.9	2.3	5.3	3.8
Bowie	NA	NA	NA	NA	NA	NA	NA	NA	NA	NA	NA	NA	NA
Frederick	41.2	869	119	0.0	16.6	1.5	0.0	0.0	23.3	13.1	10.6	3.1	8.6
Gaithersburg	NA	NA	NA	NA	NA	NA	NA	NA	NA	NA	NA	NA	NA
Hagerstown	35.4	1 038	219	0.0	8.6	2.2	0.0	0.0	20.3	24.8	12.0	2.6	2.2
Rockville	45.7	976	172	0.0	15.0	0.0	0.0	0.4	7.8	14.2	28.0	2.6	3.8
MASSACHUSETTS	X	X	X	X	X	X	X	X	X	X	X	X	X
Agawam	66.0	NA	NA	0.1	4.1	0.0	66.7	0.5	4.2	4.5	0.8	0.0	1.8
Attleboro	70.9	1 793	126	0.4	2.9	0.0	57.3	0.3	5.8	5.3	1.4	0.0	5.1
Barnstable Town	116.2	NA	NA	0.1	10.0	0.0	42.7	0.6	5.9	3.5	2.2	0.4	3.3
Beverly	79.7	2 043	230	0.1	5.1	0.1	45.5	0.3	5.5	8.1	0.8	0.9	1.4
Boston	2 103.0	3 786	469	5.3	3.1	0.2	33.5	3.2	10.9	7.2	3.6	4.8	2.4
Brockton	229.5	2 463	271	0.2	2.3	0.1	63.0	0.2	5.9	4.8	0.6	0.8	0.9
Cambridge	248.3	2 660	117	0.4	1.8	0.6	41.4	0.0	8.5	3.0	1.4	2.0	1.6
Chelsea	100.8	3 677	493	0.2	2.4	0.0	50.2	0.5	5.4	2.2	0.1	1.7	5.3
Chicopee	104.5	1 933	64	0.9	2.7	0.0	59.2	2.5	5.9	4.8	1.4	1.7	1.0
Everett	NA	NA	NA	NA	NA	NA	NA	NA	NA	NA	NA	NA	NA
Fall River	187.2	2 065	144	0.3	2.6	0.0	54.2	1.0	6.9	8.0	0.4	3.6	0.9
Fitchburg	99.0	2 473	509	0.1	3.2	0.1	56.5	0.3	5.4	5.8	0.4	1.5	1.3
Franklin	54.7	NA	NA	0.2	6.1	0.0	62.1	0.3	6.0	3.8	0.5	0.0	2.5
Gloucester	77.9	2 626	686	0.1	2.5	0.0	38.3	0.5	5.4	18.3	1.0	2.1	6.5
Haverhill	164.6	2 975	243	2.5	2.6	0.0	38.9	24.5	4.2	2.8	0.8	1.5	3.1
Holyoke	137.2	3 350	210	9.1	2.7	0.2	53.1	0.7	6.1	4.4	0.9	2.5	2.4
Lawrence	166.7	2 401	35	0.1	1.9	0.3	59.9	0.1	4.7	4.8	0.4	1.7	2.6
Leominster	67.2	1 672	109	0.2	4.5	0.0	62.4	0.4	6.3	5.1	0.6	0.8	2.6
Lowell	250.6	2 479	152	0.2	2.9	0.5	58.4	0.7	6.2	4.8	1.0	2.5	3.9
Lynn	234.2	2 889	367	2.4	3.4	0.3	63.0	0.3	5.4	3.5	0.3	1.4	1.5
Malden	158.5	3 010	1 053	1.2	2.4	1.5	60.2	0.2	4.3	2.0	0.2	3.1	2.1
MarlBorough	74.4	2 236	314	0.2	6.4	0.0	58.7	0.3	6.4	6.6	0.4	2.0	2.1
Medford	103.3	1 845	119	0.3	3.4	0.0	42.6	0.3	7.9	3.1	0.6	2.6	0.5
Melrose	51.1	1 867	81	0.0	5.5	0.1	52.2	0.1	5.5	3.0	2.0	0.7	0.6
Methuen	104.4	NA	NA	0.2	5.2	0.0	63.8	0.3	4.6	3.3	1.0	1.5	3.8
New Bedford	246.5	2 558	356	0.2	3.2	0.0	49.4	1.0	6.5	9.1	0.6	4.4	0.9
Newton	216.0	2 689	280	0.1	4.0	0.0	55.4	0.7	5.6	4.0	1.6	1.6	0.7
Northampton	NA	NA	NA	NA	NA	NA	NA	NA	NA	NA	NA	NA	NA
Peabody	97.9	1 989	141	0.0	3.6	0.0	47.3	0.5	5.8	3.6	1.1	5.1	0.8
Pittsfield	100.0	2 197	134	0.2	3.0	0.3	54.2	0.4	5.5	6.5	0.6	3.0	1.1
Quincy	314.4	3 666	489	0.1	3.9	0.0	26.6	27.5	5.6	3.2	0.7	3.6	1.8
Revere	90.8	2 178	105	0.3	3.0	0.0	50.7	0.5	6.2	2.5	0.7	0.9	0.8
Salem	89.6	2 337	59	0.2	1.9	0.5	47.1	0.4	7.1	2.8	2.9	1.6	2.4
Somerville	169.5	2 287	378	0.1	3.3	0.0	45.8	0.5	6.3	1.9	0.4	3.6	1.9
Springfield	471.9	3 186	300	0.1	3.2	0.1	57.0	0.3	6.7	5.4	1.0	2.3	2.1
Taunton	122.2	2 326	421	4.0	3.5	0.1	53.2	0.5	6.1	7.8	0.8	1.2	1.1
Waltham	120.3	2 055	233	0.2	6.1	0.2	46.3	0.4	8.4	9.8	0.8	1.1	0.6
Westfield	92.7	2 469	532	0.1	3.2	0.1	63.2	1.3	4.6	4.5	0.4	1.3	1.9
Woburn	77.9	2 100	137	0.2	8.2	0.0	48.4	0.3	8.1	2.5	0.8	0.0	0.9
Worcester	438.8	2 635	352	0.1	2.4	0.0	59.1	0.9	7.5	4.3	1.1	1.2	2.9
MICHIGAN	X	X	X	X	X	X	X	X	X	X	X	X	X
Allen Park	NA	NA	NA	NA	NA	NA	NA	NA	NA	NA	NA	NA	NA
Ann Arbor	134.3	1 222	241	1.0	5.8	9.8	0.0	0.0	12.8	17.2	3.1	0.0	3.4

1. Based on population estimated as of July 1 of the year shown.

City	City government finances, 1999 (cont'd) Debt outstanding			City government employment, 2001	Climate[2] Average daily temperature (degrees Fahrenheit)						
					Mean		Limits				
	Total (mil dol)	Per capita[1] (dollars)	Percent utility		January	July	January[3]	July[4]	Annual precipitation (inches)	Heating degree days	Cooling degree days
	137	138	139	140	141	142	143	144	145	146	147
LOUISIANA—Cont'd											
Houma	143.9	4 801	27.4	1 365	52.1	81.6	42.0	90.4	62.91	1 429	2 668
Kenner	48.9	683	0.0	648	51.3	81.9	41.8	90.6	61.88	1 513	2 655
Lafayette	389.3	3 427	39.0	2 601	50.6	82.1	41.2	90.6	58.36	1 587	2 673
Lake Charles	21.0	297	0.0	811	50.4	82.2	41.1	90.8	54.84	1 616	2 650
Monroe	56.6	1 055	0.0	1 144	44.2	82.3	34.6	92.4	51.48	2 407	2 323
New Iberia	NA	NA	NA	NA	50.4	81.7	40.5	90.7	59.56	1 609	2 596
New Orleans	1 130.8	2 429	1.9	9 403	51.3	81.9	41.8	90.6	61.88	1 513	2 655
Shreveport	407.9	2 166	28.6	2 833	45.1	82.7	34.8	93.0	46.11	2 264	2 368
Slidell	37.8	1 448	0.0	326	NA	NA	NA	NA	NA	NA	NA
MAINE	X	X	X	X	X	X	X	X	X	X	X
Bangor	13.8	451	0.0	1 227	17.5	68.2	8.2	78.1	41.23	7 930	251
Lewiston	42.2	1 165	15.2	1 070	20.2	70.7	11.1	80.7	45.30	7 244	398
Portland	117.2	1 867	0.0	2 754	20.8	68.6	11.4	78.8	44.34	7 378	268
MARYLAND	X	X	X	X	X	X	X	X	X	X	X
Annapolis	38.1	1 133	12.9	514	33.6	77.6	24.6	87.6	41.81	4 382	1 271
Baltimore	1 363.4	2 112	13.4	29 045	31.8	77.0	23.4	87.2	40.76	4 707	1 137
Bowie	NA	NA	NA	NA	33.6	77.6	24.6	87.6	41.81	4 382	1 271
Frederick	63.3	1 333	17.4	508	31.4	74.7	23.1	85.3	40.25	4 810	925
Gaithersburg	NA	NA	NA	NA	30.7	74.7	21.4	85.8	41.11	5 093	889
Hagerstown	18.3	536	20.8	446	28.7	74.9	20.3	85.8	38.60	5 293	909
Rockville	30.0	641	4.9	579	30.7	74.7	21.4	85.8	41.11	5 093	889
MASSACHUSETTS	X	X	X	X	X	X	X	X	X	X	X
Agawam	38.8	NA	0.0	769	NA	NA	NA	NA	NA	NA	NA
Attleboro	93.6	2 365	26.3	1 188	25.9	71.2	15.5	82.3	46.68	6 346	457
Barnstable Town	108.3	NA	0.0	1 548	NA	NA	NA	NA	NA	NA	NA
Beverly	30.9	791	10.5	1 043	28.6	73.5	21.6	81.8	41.51	5 641	678
Boston	1 111.9	2 002	0.0	22 950	28.6	73.5	21.6	81.8	41.51	5 641	678
Brockton	56.3	604	15.4	3 273	26.9	71.2	16.9	82.2	45.50	6 225	461
Cambridge	96.6	1 034	6.6	2 904	28.6	73.5	21.6	81.8	41.51	5 641	678
Chelsea	106.4	3 881	3.4	NA	28.6	73.5	21.6	81.8	41.51	5 641	678
Chicopee	19.8	367	5.7	2 059	26.8	74.1	17.6	85.4	43.88	5 754	751
Everett	NA	NA	NA	NA	28.6	73.5	21.6	81.8	41.51	5 641	678
Fall River	61.6	680	0.9	2 868	30.6	73.5	23.4	81.3	47.34	5 426	729
Fitchburg	77.1	1 926	2.1	NA	23.4	71.3	13.4	81.5	47.02	6 698	485
Franklin	33.5	NA	15.2	NA	NA	NA	NA	NA	NA	NA	NA
Gloucester	100.8	3 398	7.0	1 025	28.6	73.5	21.6	81.8	41.51	5 641	678
Haverhill	137.0	2 476	3.8	2 408	24.7	72.5	15.2	83.8	44.43	6 413	575
Holyoke	80.7	1 971	30.3	2 173	26.8	74.1	17.6	85.4	43.88	5 754	751
Lawrence	53.9	776	0.0	NA	24.7	72.5	15.4	82.6	42.80	6 322	555
Leominster	30.9	767	0.0	NA	23.4	71.3	13.4	81.5	47.02	6 698	485
Lowell	179.7	1 778	3.3	3 579	24.3	73.3	14.7	84.8	42.07	6 339	610
Lynn	175.7	2 167	48.8	2 982	28.6	73.5	21.6	81.8	41.51	5 641	678
Malden	120.0	2 279	0.0	1 437	28.6	73.5	21.6	81.8	41.51	5 641	678
MarlBorough	49.4	1 485	13.0	1 029	23.4	71.3	13.4	81.5	47.02	6 698	485
Medford	7.9	141	13.4	1 365	28.6	73.5	21.6	81.8	41.51	5 641	678
Melrose	4.6	169	3.1	891	28.6	73.5	21.6	81.8	41.51	5 641	678
Methuen	84.4	NA	2.7	1 307	NA	NA	NA	NA	NA	NA	NA
New Bedford	175.7	1 823	2.7	3 864	30.6	73.5	23.4	81.3	47.34	5 426	729
Newton	38.6	481	0.0	2 928	28.6	73.5	21.6	81.8	41.51	5 641	678
Northampton	NA	NA	NA	NA	23.6	71.8	12.2	84.6	42.50	6 404	522
Peabody	60.1	1 221	42.6	1 581	24.5	71.0	14.3	82.7	46.64	6 573	425
Pittsfield	41.8	919	15.4	NA	21.4	68.9	11.0	81.5	43.47	7 060	293
Quincy	118.9	1 387	2.9	2 174	27.4	71.5	18.5	81.5	47.69	6 072	450
Revere	13.6	325	2.5	NA	28.6	73.5	21.6	81.8	41.51	5 641	678
Salem	46.9	1 224	1.6	NA	28.6	73.5	21.6	81.8	41.51	5 641	678
Somerville	62.5	843	6.4	1 895	28.6	73.5	21.6	81.8	41.51	5 641	678
Springfield	282.6	1 908	0.0	7 110	26.8	74.1	17.6	85.4	43.88	5 754	751
Taunton	67.9	1 292	29.5	1 712	25.9	71.2	15.5	82.3	46.68	6 346	457
Waltham	12.7	217	17.1	1 511	28.6	73.5	21.6	81.8	41.51	5 641	678
Westfield	73.0	1 942	18.4	1 505	26.8	74.1	17.6	85.4	43.88	5 754	751
Woburn	15.0	405	0.0	NA	24.5	71.0	14.3	82.7	46.64	6 573	425
Worcester	554.7	3 331	12.8	5 908	22.8	69.7	15.0	79.3	47.75	6 979	333
MICHIGAN	X	X	X	X	X	X	X	X	X	X	X
Allen Park	NA	NA	NA	NA	22.9	72.9	15.5	83.8	32.71	6 500	677
Ann Arbor	133.8	1 217	30.1	1 565	23.2	73.0	16.2	83.7	32.81	6 379	713

1. Based on the population estimated as of July 1 of the year shown.   2. Represents normal values based on the 30-year period, 1961–1990.   3. Average daily minimum.   4. Average daily maximum.

Table D. Cities — **Land Area and Population**

STATE Place code	City	Land area, 2000[1] (sq km)	Population, 2000 Total persons	Rank	Per square kilometer	Population Total persons 1990	Percent change 1990–2000	Total persons 1980	Percent change 1980–1990	White	Black	Am. Indian, Alaska Native	Asian and Pacific Islander	Other race	Hispanic[2]	Non-Hispanic White
		1	2	3	4	5	6	7	8	9	10	11	12	13	14	15
	MICHIGAN—Cont'd															
26 05920	Battle Creek	110.9	53 364	555	481.2	53 516	-0.3	35 724	49.8	76.9	19.4	1.7	2.3	2.7	4.6	72.6
26 06020	Bay City	27.0	36 817	841	1 363.6	38 936	-5.4	41 593	-6.4	93.4	3.5	1.7	0.7	3.2	6.7	87.8
26 12060	Burton	60.8	30 308	1 024	498.5	27 437	10.5	29 976	-8.5	94.0	4.1	1.8	1.1	1.3	2.3	90.9
26 21000	Dearborn	63.1	97 775	242	1 549.5	89 286	9.5	90 660	-1.5	96.1	1.5	0.6	2.7	8.7	3.0	84.8
26 21020	Dearborn Heights	30.3	58 264	487	1 922.9	60 838	-4.2	67 706	-10.1	94.3	2.4	0.9	2.9	2.4	3.4	89.3
26 22000	Detroit	359.4	951 270	10	2 646.8	1 027 974	-7.5	1 203 339	-14.6	13.8	82.8	0.9	1.4	3.6	5.0	10.5
26 24120	East Lansing	29.1	46 525	653	1 598.8	50 677	-8.2	51 392	-1.4	82.7	8.1	0.7	9.1	1.6	2.7	79.4
26 24290	Eastpointe	13.2	34 077	919	2 581.6	35 283	-3.4	38 280	-7.8	93.7	5.1	1.2	1.2	0.5	1.3	91.2
26 27440	Farmington Hills	86.2	82 111	311	952.6	74 614	10.0	58 056	28.5	84.7	7.4	0.6	8.3	1.2	1.5	81.9
26 29000	Flint	87.1	124 943	171	1 434.5	140 925	-11.3	159 611	-11.7	43.7	55.3	2.2	0.8	1.8	3.0	40.0
26 31420	Garden City	15.2	30 047	1 034	1 976.8	31 846	-5.6	35 640	-10.6	97.4	1.3	0.9	1.0	0.7	2.0	94.6
26 34000	Grand Rapids	115.6	197 800	94	1 711.1	189 126	4.6	181 843	4.0	69.9	22.0	1.5	2.1	7.9	13.1	62.5
26 38640	Holland	42.9	35 048	895	817.0	30 745	14.0	26 281	17.0	80.4	3.2	1.1	4.1	14.0	22.2	70.0
26 40680	Inkster	16.2	30 115	1 031	1 859.0	30 772	-2.1	35 190	-12.6	27.1	69.5	1.4	3.8	1.3	1.6	24.5
26 41420	Jackson	28.7	36 316	855	1 266.4	37 425	-3.0	39 739	-5.8	77.0	22.0	1.7	0.9	2.4	4.0	72.2
26 42160	Kalamazoo	63.9	77 145	344	1 207.3	80 277	-3.9	79 722	0.7	73.5	22.4	1.6	3.1	3.2	4.3	69.5
26 42820	Kentwood	54.5	45 255	677	830.4	37 826	19.6	30 438	24.3	83.0	10.2	1.0	6.3	2.2	3.9	79.0
26 46000	Lansing	90.8	119 128	183	1 312.0	127 321	-6.4	130 414	-2.4	69.0	24.4	2.0	3.4	6.1	10.0	61.4
26 47800	Lincoln Park	15.2	40 008	774	2 632.1	41 832	-4.4	45 105	-7.3	94.9	2.4	1.3	0.7	2.5	6.4	89.2
26 49000	Livonia	92.5	100 545	238	1 087.0	100 850	-0.3	104 814	-3.8	96.5	1.1	0.6	2.3	0.7	1.7	94.1
26 50560	Madison Heights	18.6	31 101	1 005	1 672.1	32 196	-3.4	35 375	-9.0	92.1	2.1	1.1	5.7	1.8	1.6	88.5
26 53780	Midland	86.0	41 685	735	484.7	38 053	9.5	37 257	2.1	94.5	2.1	0.7	3.1	0.8	1.9	92.2
26 56020	Mount Pleasant	20.2	25 946	1 198	1 284.5	23 299	11.4	23 746	-1.9	90.7	4.3	2.2	3.3	1.4	2.5	88.0
26 56320	Muskegon	37.2	40 105	771	1 078.1	39 809	0.7	40 823	-2.5	63.5	33.4	2.3	0.9	3.6	6.4	57.9
26 59440	Novi	78.9	47 386	640	600.6	32 998	43.6	22 525	46.5	88.6	2.2	0.5	9.4	0.9	1.8	86.1
26 59920	Oak Park	13.0	29 793	1 044	2 291.8	30 468	-2.2	31 537	-3.4	50.5	47.3	0.8	2.8	3.0	1.3	46.4
26 65440	Pontiac	51.8	66 337	412	1 280.6	71 136	-6.7	76 715	-7.3	41.8	49.9	1.5	2.9	7.6	12.8	34.5
26 65560	Portage	83.4	44 897	683	538.3	41 042	9.4	38 157	7.6	92.4	4.5	0.9	3.1	1.1	1.9	89.6
26 65820	Port Huron	20.9	32 338	964	1 547.3	33 694	-4.0	33 981	-0.8	89.2	9.2	1.8	0.8	2.0	4.3	84.5
26 69035	Rochester Hills	85.1	68 825	390	808.8	61 766	11.4	NA	NA	90.0	2.7	0.6	7.3	0.8	2.3	87.1
26 69800	Roseville	25.4	48 129	627	1 894.8	51 412	-6.4	54 311	-5.3	94.9	3.0	1.1	2.0	0.7	1.5	92.4
26 70040	Royal Oak	30.6	60 062	464	1 962.8	65 410	-8.2	70 893	-7.7	96.1	1.8	0.7	2.1	0.8	1.3	93.9
26 70520	Saginaw	45.2	61 799	448	1 367.2	69 512	-11.1	77 508	-10.3	49.4	44.9	1.2	0.7	7.1	11.7	42.7
26 70760	St. Clair Shores	29.9	63 096	437	2 110.2	68 107	-7.4	76 210	-10.6	97.9	0.8	0.9	1.1	0.4	1.2	96.0
26 74900	Southfield	67.9	78 296	334	1 153.1	75 727	3.4	75 568	0.2	41.0	55.8	0.9	3.7	1.9	1.2	38.3
26 74960	Southgate	17.8	30 136	1 030	1 693.0	30 771	-2.1	32 058	-4.0	94.8	2.3	0.9	2.0	1.2	4.0	90.9
26 76460	Sterling Heights	94.9	124 471	173	1 311.6	117 810	5.7	108 999	8.1	93.0	1.5	0.6	5.5	1.9	1.3	89.8
26 79000	Taylor	61.2	65 868	415	1 076.3	70 811	-7.0	77 568	-8.7	87.9	9.5	1.5	2.0	1.3	3.2	84.0
26 80700	Troy	86.9	80 959	317	931.6	72 884	11.1	67 102	8.6	83.9	2.3	0.5	14.1	1.2	1.5	81.3
26 84000	Warren	88.8	138 247	154	1 556.8	144 864	-4.6	161 134	-10.1	93.3	3.1	1.1	3.7	1.1	1.4	90.4
26 86000	Westland	53.0	86 602	289	1 634.0	84 724	2.2	84 603	0.1	89.0	7.4	1.1	3.3	1.4	2.5	85.6
26 88900	Wyandotte	13.7	28 006	1 102	2 044.2	30 938	-9.5	34 006	-9.0	97.8	0.8	1.3	0.6	1.1	2.9	94.3
26 88940	Wyoming	63.3	69 368	387	1 095.9	63 891	8.6	59 616	7.2	86.6	5.8	1.3	3.4	5.7	9.7	80.4
27 00000	**MINNESOTA**	206 189.1	4 919 479	X	23.9	4 375 665	12.4	4 075 970	7.4	90.8	4.1	1.6	3.4	1.8	2.9	88.2
27 01486	Andover	88.3	26 588	1 161	301.1	15 216	74.7	NA	NA	97.6	0.9	0.8	1.4	0.5	1.0	95.8
27 01900	Apple Valley	44.9	45 527	670	1 014.0	34 598	31.6	21 818	58.6	93.3	2.5	0.6	4.1	1.3	2.0	90.9
27 06382	Blaine	87.7	44 942	680	512.5	38 975	15.3	28 558	36.5	95.1	1.4	1.3	3.1	1.0	1.7	92.6
27 06616	Bloomington	91.9	85 172	298	926.8	86 335	-1.3	81 831	5.5	89.5	4.1	0.7	5.8	1.7	2.7	86.9
27 07948	Brooklyn Center	20.6	29 172	1 067	1 416.1	28 887	1.0	31 230	-7.5	73.8	15.9	1.5	9.8	2.5	2.8	70.4
27 07966	Brooklyn Park	67.5	67 388	404	998.3	56 381	19.5	43 332	30.1	73.6	15.9	1.1	10.2	2.4	2.9	70.3
27 08794	Burnsville	64.4	60 220	463	935.1	51 288	17.4	35 674	43.8	89.5	5.2	0.9	5.0	2.0	2.9	86.3
27 13114	Coon Rapids	58.7	61 607	450	1 049.5	52 978	16.3	35 826	47.9	94.8	2.7	1.1	2.2	1.0	1.5	92.4
27 13456	Cottage Grove	88.0	30 582	1 019	347.5	22 935	33.3	18 994	20.7	94.7	2.8	0.8	1.9	1.2	2.5	92.2
27 17000	Duluth	176.1	86 918	286	493.6	85 493	1.7	92 811	-7.9	94.3	2.2	3.4	1.5	0.5	1.1	92.1
27 17288	Eagan	83.7	63 557	431	759.3	47 409	34.1	20 700	129.0	89.7	4.1	0.7	6.1	1.5	2.2	86.9
27 18116	Eden Prairie	83.9	54 901	538	654.4	39 311	39.7	16 263	141.7	91.9	2.8	0.4	5.5	0.9	1.6	89.7
27 18188	Edina	40.8	47 425	638	1 162.4	46 075	2.9	46 073	0.0	95.2	1.5	0.3	3.6	0.6	1.1	93.6
27 22814	Fridley	26.3	27 449	1 125	1 043.7	28 335	-3.1	30 228	-6.3	91.2	4.4	1.5	3.7	2.3	2.6	87.5
27 31076	Inver Grove Heights	74.2	29 751	1 046	401.0	22 477	32.4	17 147	31.1	93.5	2.8	0.9	2.6	2.3	4.2	89.8
27 35180	Lakeville	93.7	43 128	710	460.3	24 854	73.5	14 790	68.0	95.4	1.7	0.7	2.6	1.0	1.9	93.3
27 39878	Mankato	39.4	32 427	961	823.0	31 459	3.1	28 650	9.8	93.6	2.4	0.7	3.3	1.4	2.2	91.5
27 40166	Maple Grove	85.1	50 365	594	591.8	38 736	30.0	20 525	88.7	95.8	1.4	0.5	3.0	0.5	1.1	94.1
27 40382	Maplewood	44.9	34 947	900	778.3	30 954	12.9	26 990	14.7	90.3	4.4	1.0	5.1	1.2	2.2	87.6
27 43000	Minneapolis	142.2	382 618	45	2 690.7	368 383	3.9	370 951	-0.7	68.0	20.5	3.3	7.2	5.8	7.6	62.5
27 43252	Minnetonka	70.3	51 301	584	729.7	48 370	6.1	38 683	25.0	95.3	1.8	0.4	2.8	0.8	1.3	93.7
27 43864	Moorhead	34.8	32 177	967	924.6	32 295	-0.4	29 998	7.7	93.8	1.1	2.6	1.9	2.6	4.5	90.1
27 47680	Oakdale	28.7	26 653	1 157	928.7	18 377	45.0	12 126	51.6	93.9	3.0	0.8	3.0	1.3	2.7	90.7
27 51730	Plymouth	85.2	65 894	414	773.4	50 889	29.5	31 614	61.0	92.5	3.2	0.6	4.3	0.8	1.6	90.4
27 54214	Richfield	17.9	34 439	913	1 924.0	35 710	-3.6	37 851	-5.7	83.2	7.9	1.3	6.1	4.3	6.3	78.8

1. Dry land or land partially or temporarily covered by water.   2. Hispanic persons may be of any race.

Table D. Cities — **Population and Households**

City	Under 5 years	5 to 17 years	18 to 24 years	25 to 34 years	35 to 44 years	45 to 54 years	55 to 64 years	65 to 74 years	75 years and over	Percent female	Number	Percent change, 1990–2000	Persons per household	Female family householder[1]	One-person
	Population characteristics, 2000 (cont'd) — Age of population (percent)										Households, 2000			Percent	
	16	17	18	19	20	21	22	23	24	25	26	27	28	29	30
MICHIGAN—Cont'd															
Battle Creek	7.3	19.9	8.7	14.5	15.0	13.1	8.0	6.7	6.9	52.1	21 348	-0.5	2.43	16.1	31.6
Bay City	7.0	18.5	9.4	14.8	15.6	12.7	7.8	6.5	7.6	51.8	15 208	-2.3	2.38	14.7	32.9
Burton	7.3	20.1	8.4	14.9	17.1	12.8	8.2	6.5	4.6	51.1	11 699	12.0	2.58	12.8	25.3
Dearborn	8.3	19.6	8.3	14.5	14.6	11.9	7.2	6.5	9.0	50.3	36 770	3.7	2.65	9.4	30.9
Dearborn Heights	6.4	16.1	7.5	14.0	15.5	12.4	9.3	9.8	9.0	51.8	23 276	-0.7	2.47	10.8	28.0
Detroit	8.0	23.1	9.7	15.2	14.4	12.2	7.1	5.6	4.9	52.9	336 428	-10.1	2.77	31.6	29.7
East Lansing	2.5	6.5	58.6	10.6	5.8	6.2	3.7	2.5	3.6	51.9	14 390	6.6	2.22	5.7	36.2
Eastpointe	6.4	18.1	7.6	15.2	17.1	12.6	6.6	7.7	8.8	51.5	13 595	1.1	2.50	12.3	28.8
Farmington Hills	6.0	17.1	6.7	14.5	16.8	15.3	9.3	7.0	7.4	51.6	33 559	14.8	2.41	6.6	29.6
Flint	9.0	21.6	10.3	15.1	14.3	11.9	7.3	5.8	4.7	53.0	48 744	-9.6	2.51	27.5	31.9
Garden City	6.2	18.9	7.6	14.7	17.9	12.9	8.2	8.5	5.0	50.6	11 479	2.4	2.62	11.2	24.0
Grand Rapids	8.3	18.8	13.1	17.2	14.3	10.8	6.0	5.2	6.4	51.1	73 217	6.1	2.57	15.8	30.8
Holland	8.0	18.2	17.5	14.4	13.0	9.9	5.6	5.4	8.2	52.6	11 971	13.2	2.67	10.8	26.8
Inkster	8.0	21.8	9.2	15.8	14.5	11.9	7.9	6.1	4.7	52.3	11 169	-0.3	2.67	26.8	27.9
Jackson	9.1	20.6	9.8	15.8	14.6	11.4	6.8	5.6	6.4	52.3	14 210	-3.5	2.48	19.9	32.0
Kalamazoo	6.2	14.1	27.6	15.0	11.8	9.6	5.6	4.5	5.6	51.8	29 413	0.0	2.30	14.7	34.8
Kentwood	7.7	18.9	10.4	17.1	16.6	12.6	6.9	5.0	4.9	51.8	18 477	21.2	2.43	10.8	30.9
Lansing	8.2	18.6	11.4	17.6	15.2	12.4	6.9	5.2	4.5	52.0	49 505	-2.2	2.39	17.0	33.2
Lincoln Park	6.9	17.4	8.5	16.4	16.3	12.9	7.4	7.1	7.0	51.1	16 204	-0.3	2.46	13.3	29.3
Livonia	5.6	18.2	6.3	11.3	17.4	14.9	9.4	8.9	8.0	51.5	38 089	6.1	2.59	8.0	22.9
Madison Heights	6.2	15.9	8.1	17.9	17.5	12.3	7.9	8.0	6.2	51.1	13 299	3.5	2.33	10.5	33.8
Midland	6.5	19.4	10.2	12.2	15.7	14.0	8.2	6.8	7.1	52.1	16 743	13.0	2.42	8.7	28.6
Mount Pleasant	3.4	8.1	54.1	9.8	7.0	6.5	3.7	3.1	4.3	54.8	8 449	26.8	2.38	8.5	29.6
Muskegon	7.6	18.1	11.6	16.6	15.5	11.6	6.4	5.5	6.9	47.7	14 569	-1.4	2.42	20.2	34.4
Novi	7.4	20.2	6.7	15.2	20.4	14.7	7.2	4.3	3.8	50.8	18 726	47.5	2.52	7.1	28.1
Oak Park	6.8	21.4	8.0	14.4	15.4	14.0	7.8	5.9	6.3	53.2	11 104	2.0	2.68	19.5	26.6
Pontiac	8.9	21.7	10.3	17.4	14.9	11.5	6.8	4.7	3.8	51.3	24 234	-2.2	2.68	25.2	29.4
Portage	6.9	19.5	8.5	13.8	16.0	14.7	8.7	6.5	5.3	52.1	18 138	17.3	2.45	9.7	27.2
Port Huron	7.8	19.2	9.7	14.8	14.9	12.1	7.5	6.5	7.6	52.4	12 961	-1.5	2.43	17.5	31.9
Rochester Hills	6.5	19.4	6.7	12.1	18.0	17.1	9.5	5.5	5.2	51.3	26 315	17.7	2.59	6.8	24.0
Roseville	6.5	16.6	8.2	16.5	16.5	12.4	7.8	7.9	7.5	51.6	19 976	2.2	2.40	12.7	30.8
Royal Oak	5.2	12.6	7.5	21.2	17.6	13.6	7.4	6.7	8.3	51.2	28 880	1.9	2.06	7.5	40.8
Saginaw	8.6	23.0	9.9	14.1	14.2	12.1	6.6	5.8	5.6	53.4	23 182	-11.4	2.60	27.3	29.5
St. Clair Shores	5.1	15.1	6.2	12.6	16.2	13.7	9.4	11.1	10.7	52.4	27 434	0.8	2.28	10.0	32.7
Southfield	5.6	16.0	7.9	15.8	14.8	15.4	9.3	6.8	8.4	54.1	33 987	5.8	2.27	14.3	36.2
Southgate	5.4	16.1	8.3	14.8	15.9	14.2	9.1	8.4	7.8	51.8	12 836	5.8	2.33	9.7	32.3
Sterling Heights	6.2	17.9	8.5	14.3	16.1	15.0	10.3	5.8	5.9	51.0	46 319	13.4	2.66	8.5	24.1
Taylor	7.5	19.7	9.3	15.3	15.7	12.6	8.9	6.7	4.2	51.8	24 776	-0.3	2.63	17.4	23.1
Troy	6.2	20.0	6.7	12.1	17.6	17.0	10.1	5.8	4.5	50.5	30 018	14.7	2.69	6.0	22.8
Warren	6.4	16.6	7.6	14.9	15.9	11.8	9.7	9.1	8.2	51.1	55 551	1.7	2.47	11.7	28.8
Westland	6.9	16.3	9.0	17.3	16.5	12.4	8.2	7.0	6.3	51.9	36 533	10.3	2.34	12.1	32.6
Wyandotte	5.6	17.1	8.3	14.2	17.4	14.1	7.6	7.6	8.2	51.0	11 816	-4.1	2.36	11.9	31.9
Wyoming	8.0	20.0	10.9	17.3	16.4	11.8	6.2	5.1	4.3	50.6	26 536	9.8	2.60	12.0	26.6
MINNESOTA	6.7	19.5	9.6	13.7	16.8	13.5	8.2	6.0	6.1	50.5	1 895 127	15.0	2.52	8.9	26.9
Andover	9.2	26.3	6.0	14.5	21.9	13.1	6.1	1.7	1.1	49.2	8 107	83.0	3.28	5.5	8.4
Apple Valley	7.2	22.5	7.2	13.9	19.2	16.3	8.2	3.3	2.2	49.1	16 344	46.6	2.77	9.0	19.3
Blaine	7.8	21.3	8.7	15.8	19.1	14.2	7.8	3.7	1.6	49.9	15 898	24.0	2.82	11.1	17.0
Bloomington	5.3	15.3	8.0	13.6	15.8	15.1	11.3	8.7	7.0	51.7	36 400	5.5	2.30	8.2	29.6
Brooklyn Center	6.7	18.3	9.6	14.8	15.3	11.6	8.1	8.3	7.1	51.3	11 430	1.8	2.52	13.4	28.2
Brooklyn Park	8.1	20.7	9.7	16.8	18.2	14.0	6.9	3.7	1.9	50.3	24 432	19.8	2.75	12.1	22.0
Burnsville	7.1	19.1	10.1	16.9	17.1	13.7	8.7	4.4	2.8	50.7	23 687	23.8	2.53	10.0	24.8
Coon Rapids	7.5	21.2	8.9	15.2	18.1	13.6	8.2	4.6	2.7	51.3	22 578	29.4	2.71	12.2	20.1
Cottage Grove	8.5	24.2	7.4	15.6	18.8	13.6	7.2	3.6	1.3	50.2	9 932	44.9	3.07	8.8	11.0
Duluth	5.4	15.9	16.2	12.1	14.1	13.4	7.9	6.5	8.6	51.7	35 500	2.2	2.26	11.4	34.5
Eagan	8.1	21.9	7.4	16.7	21.6	14.2	6.0	2.7	1.5	50.8	23 773	36.4	2.67	8.4	23.0
Eden Prairie	7.8	22.6	6.2	14.6	21.0	16.1	6.8	3.0	1.9	50.9	20 457	41.6	2.68	7.7	22.0
Edina	5.4	17.5	4.4	8.8	14.8	15.9	10.6	10.1	12.6	54.2	20 996	5.7	2.24	5.8	34.0
Fridley	6.7	15.9	10.2	15.4	15.6	13.4	11.0	7.7	4.2	50.6	11 328	3.8	2.40	11.6	26.8
Inver Grove Heights	7.2	20.1	9.2	15.4	18.5	13.9	7.8	4.7	3.1	50.5	11 257	44.3	2.62	10.3	21.5
Lakeville	10.1	26.0	5.9	15.2	22.6	12.1	5.3	1.9	0.9	49.4	13 609	73.3	3.17	7.5	10.7
Mankato	4.9	12.0	32.5	13.1	10.8	9.8	5.6	4.9	6.4	50.8	12 367	10.2	2.31	8.8	32.2
Maple Grove	7.4	23.3	6.6	13.7	21.2	17.0	6.7	2.6	1.5	50.5	17 532	39.9	2.87	7.5	15.8
Maplewood	6.5	18.2	7.7	13.0	16.9	13.8	8.7	7.4	7.7	52.2	13 758	19.7	2.48	10.5	27.0
Minneapolis	6.6	15.4	14.4	20.6	15.9	12.0	5.9	4.0	5.1	49.8	162 352	1.0	2.25	12.3	40.3
Minnetonka	5.3	17.8	6.0	11.7	16.8	18.1	10.3	7.2	6.8	52.1	21 393	14.5	2.37	6.8	27.3
Moorhead	5.8	16.8	23.1	10.9	13.3	10.9	6.3	5.8	6.9	53.1	11 660	5.4	2.43	9.8	29.2
Oakdale	7.7	21.3	7.2	15.0	19.6	13.2	7.5	4.7	3.7	51.8	10 243	52.9	2.59	11.1	25.2
Plymouth	7.0	20.1	7.4	13.8	19.2	16.1	8.9	4.8	2.8	50.7	24 820	35.2	2.60	7.6	21.8
Richfield	6.0	14.2	9.3	16.9	16.5	12.7	8.0	7.1	9.3	51.0	15 073	-3.1	2.25	10.5	33.7

1. No spouse present.

Table D. Cities — **Group Quarters, Crime, Education, and Income**

City	Persons in group quarters, 2000				Serious crimes known to police, 2000[2]				Education, 1990				Money income, 1989		
		Institutional			Total		Rate[3]		School enrollment		Attainment[4] (percent)			Households	
															Median
	Total	Total	Persons in nursing homes	Non-Institutional[1]	Number	Rate[3]	Violent	Property	Public	Private	High school graduate or more	Bachelor's degree or more	Per capita (dollars)[5]	Dollars	Percent change, 1979–1989 (constant 1989 dollars)
	31	32	33	34	35	36	37	38	39	40	41	42	43	44	45
MICHIGAN—Cont'd															
Battle Creek	1 522	1 075	366	447	5 047	9 458	1 598	7 859	12 557	1 335	76.6	15.8	12 963	25 306	13.7
Bay City	585	197	4	388	1 726	4 688	516	4 172	8 932	1 529	70.0	9.4	10 782	21 380	-18.0
Burton	110	0	0	110	1 883	6 213	396	5 817	6 743	674	72.7	6.7	12 940	29 961	-14.6
Dearborn	401	224	154	177	5 834	5 967	786	5 180	19 659	3 603	75.9	21.7	16 852	34 909	-5.9
Dearborn Heights	687	527	367	160	1 887	3 239	245	2 993	10 888	3 045	74.1	13.7	16 493	36 771	-13.3
Detroit	19 701	10 509	4 597	9 192	95 761	10 067	2 324	7 742	244 105	46 262	62.1	9.6	9 443	18 742	-20.0
East Lansing	14 573	229	229	14 344	1 658	3 564	312	3 252	34 848	1 206	96.6	71.2	11 212	24 716	-1.7
Eastpointe	79	0	0	79	1 532	4 496	560	3 935	6 854	1 377	69.5	8.9	14 156	34 069	-5.8
Farmington Hills	1 313	547	417	766	1 951	2 376	196	2 180	15 282	3 967	89.2	42.0	25 499	51 986	0.7
Flint	2 559	1 013	186	1 546	11 007	8 810	1 463	7 347	37 455	4 565	69.3	10.3	10 415	20 176	-29.9
Garden City	18	2	0	16	673	2 240	113	2 127	7 066	812	75.0	7.1	14 257	38 717	-9.6
Grand Rapids	9 694	4 415	2 592	5 279	12 945	6 544	1 069	5 476	36 852	16 614	76.4	20.8	12 070	26 809	3.5
Holland	3 096	520	516	2 576	1 477	4 214	317	3 898	5 831	3 495	73.6	22.5	13 344	30 689	6.6
Inkster	252	77	73	175	1 615	5 363	1 332	4 031	7 486	1 106	66.7	7.3	10 723	25 198	-18.3
Jackson	1 104	599	327	505	3 168	8 723	1 002	7 721	8 316	1 675	71.5	10.8	10 410	20 830	-14.6
Kalamazoo	9 539	1 285	501	8 254	5 982	7 754	1 054	6 700	27 289	3 454	79.6	29.8	11 956	23 207	-5.3
Kentwood	362	180	125	182	1 632	3 606	276	3 330	8 264	1 861	83.9	26.0	15 453	34 324	4.7
Lansing	872	502	314	370	6 883	5 778	1 023	4 755	33 276	4 581	78.3	18.3	12 232	26 398	-7.2
Lincoln Park	128	116	110	12	2 076	5 189	510	4 679	7 879	1 962	67.6	6.8	13 338	30 638	-14.0
Livonia	1 891	1 181	1 019	710	3 042	3 026	189	2 837	21 482	4 718	84.7	23.8	19 145	48 645	-3.4
Madison Heights	160	139	139	21	1 435	4 614	254	4 360	6 754	838	72.4	11.0	14 192	31 757	-12.0
Midland	1 220	459	355	761	998	2 394	182	2 212	8 979	2 626	88.4	41.9	19 255	38 747	-1.8
Mount Pleasant	5 868	627	261	5 241	720	2 775	177	2 598	14 493	412	84.7	39.3	9 032	19 185	-15.7
Muskegon	4 827	4 459	333	368	3 521	8 779	950	7 829	9 468	1 290	68.7	8.2	8 890	18 748	-7.1
Novi	267	202	202	65	1 400	2 954	148	2 807	7 912	1 152	89.5	33.9	20 752	47 518	5.4
Oak Park	23	0	0	23	1 076	3 612	171	3 440	7 084	2 000	80.8	22.2	14 544	36 090	-3.1
Pontiac	1 441	647	283	794	4 634	6 986	1 899	5 086	17 191	1 642	62.4	7.9	9 847	21 962	-19.0
Portage	415	120	120	295	2 142	4 771	209	4 562	10 380	1 512	88.6	31.3	17 602	39 045	3.1
Port Huron	839	441	195	398	1 385	4 283	439	3 844	8 167	712	71.2	10.6	11 210	21 522	-13.1
Rochester Hills	783	280	280	503	NA	NA	NA	NA	14 788	2 863	89.4	39.5	23 209	54 996	NA
Roseville	184	153	153	31	2 390	4 966	349	4 617	10 659	1 959	69.4	6.9	13 437	32 337	-8.8
Royal Oak	506	223	194	283	1 858	3 093	230	2 864	12 168	3 049	86.0	28.4	18 065	36 835	-1.6
Saginaw	1 438	746	319	692	4 405	7 128	1 916	5 212	19 417	1 885	68.6	9.3	8 944	17 736	-27.2
St. Clair Shores	484	372	372	112	1 611	2 553	241	2 312	12 145	2 586	77.9	13.7	16 690	36 929	-9.4
Southfield	1 223	673	610	550	5 432	6 938	940	5 998	14 392	4 153	84.8	34.7	21 098	40 579	-8.5
Southgate	198	171	91	27	1 271	4 218	358	3 859	6 140	1 106	73.8	9.5	15 485	36 526	-13.6
Sterling Heights	1 198	672	650	526	3 613	2 903	206	2 697	31 317	4 132	80.7	18.5	17 084	46 470	0.4
Taylor	695	580	438	115	3 826	5 809	571	5 238	15 295	2 857	68.2	6.8	12 955	32 659	-12.9
Troy	235	0	0	235	2 424	2 994	130	2 864	18 495	3 217	88.9	39.9	23 249	55 407	7.0
Warren	1 302	1 002	996	300	4 092	2 960	457	2 503	29 107	4 142	71.7	10.3	15 224	35 980	-10.0
Westland	942	848	599	94	2 876	3 321	281	3 040	18 382	2 031	75.7	11.4	15 079	34 995	-8.6
Wyandotte	94	41	0	53	866	3 092	179	2 914	6 203	1 202	68.9	7.8	13 190	28 312	-13.1
Wyoming	358	87	87	271	2 647	3 816	381	3 435	13 538	2 949	78.6	13.2	13 271	31 103	-0.5
MINNESOTA	135 883	63 058	40 506	72 825	171 611	3 488	281	3 208	1 006 375	168 652	82.4	21.8	14 389	30 909	3.8
Andover	12	0	0	12	725	2 727	132	2 595	4 355	552	90.5	16.8	15 464	46 515	NA
Apple Valley	237	192	192	45	1 369	3 007	114	2 893	9 791	1 171	95.4	36.6	18 173	49 981	7.9
Blaine	103	0	0	103	1 831	4 074	100	3 974	10 419	894	87.3	14.6	13 841	40 404	0.5
Bloomington	1 326	727	665	599	4 724	5 546	283	5 263	16 656	3 691	91.2	31.7	20 032	41 736	-4.5
Brooklyn Center	387	183	171	204	2 283	7 826	466	7 360	6 128	438	83.8	14.1	14 645	34 168	-8.5
Brooklyn Park	218	15	15	203	3 437	5 100	462	4 639	14 211	1 464	90.7	20.9	15 541	40 018	7.7
Burnsville	343	131	29	212	1 958	3 251	103	3 148	11 925	1 810	94.5	34.3	18 523	43 620	-2.5
Coon Rapids	362	184	184	178	2 483	4 030	195	3 836	13 297	1 729	88.8	16.5	14 669	42 069	0.3
Cottage Grove	59	0	0	59	802	2 622	114	2 508	6 660	800	92.3	19.1	14 564	46 027	3.2
Duluth	6 561	2 154	1 119	4 407	3 801	4 373	361	4 012	22 227	2 868	81.4	22.5	12 484	23 370	-8.5
Eagan	165	0	0	165	1 895	2 982	120	2 862	10 643	1 872	96.0	39.2	18 662	46 612	15.4
Eden Prairie	174	77	77	97	1 579	2 876	111	2 765	8 759	1 825	97.0	46.8	23 898	52 956	5.5
Edina	290	262	262	28	1 397	2 946	65	2 880	8 318	2 306	94.7	52.6	32 301	48 936	-3.3
Fridley	218	53	53	165	1 481	5 395	215	5 181	5 977	875	87.1	20.5	16 347	36 855	-3.8
Inver Grove Heights	263	213	162	50	1 010	3 395	208	3 186	5 444	766	87.6	18.6	15 184	39 378	6.6
Lakeville	39	0	0	39	954	2 212	49	2 163	6 505	751	94.0	20.5	15 476	44 920	10.6
Mankato	3 839	328	254	3 511	1 878	5 791	234	5 557	13 745	985	84.9	29.2	10 376	22 480	-7.1
Maple Grove	68	0	0	68	1 251	2 484	127	2 357	10 837	1 266	95.4	28.5	17 481	50 611	8.8
Maplewood	817	337	337	480	1 350	3 863	189	3 674	5 677	1 541	85.4	20.3	16 459	37 856	-3.3
Minneapolis	18 064	5 701	4 199	12 363	27 489	7 184	1 151	6 033	78 444	17 368	82.6	30.3	14 830	25 324	5.3
Minnetonka	635	345	212	290	1 473	2 871	74	2 797	9 565	2 619	94.3	43.2	25 221	50 659	0.0
Moorhead	3 836	524	382	3 312	902	2 803	211	2 592	10 617	2 760	83.5	27.9	10 550	24 265	-11.8
Oakdale	109	0	0	109	1 029	3 861	191	3 669	4 674	695	89.5	20.3	16 207	41 049	8.4
Plymouth	1 450	935	97	515	1 561	2 369	138	2 231	11 725	2 332	94.4	41.4	21 908	51 314	10.0
Richfield	488	241	241	247	1 347	3 911	305	3 606	6 273	1 002	88.1	20.9	15 992	32 405	-5.3

1. Persons in emergency shelters and persons visible in street locations. 2. Data for serious crimes have not been adjusted for underreporting. This may affect comparability between geographic areas and over time. 3. Per 100,000 population estimated by the FBI. 4. Persons 25 years old and older. 5. Based on population enumerated as of April 1, 1990.

Table D. Cities — Income, Poverty, and Housing

| City | Money income, 1989 (cont'd) | | | | Housing units, 2000 | | | | | | | | | | |
	Households (cont'd) Percent with $100,000 or more	Percent below poverty, 1989 Persons Total	Percent change in rate, 1979–1989	Families Total	Total	Percent change, 1990–2000	Vacant units — Vacant units for sale or rent[1]	For seasonal use (percent)	Home owner vacancy rate	Renter vacancy rate	Occupied units Total	Percent owner occupied	Percent renter occupied	Average size owner occupied	Average size renter occupied
	46	47	48	49	50	51	52	53	54	55	56	57	58	59	60
MICHIGAN—Cont'd															
Battle Creek	2.3	18.3	2.2	14.1	23 525	1.2	2 177	0.4	2.5	12.1	21 348	65.8	34.2	2.52	2.25
Bay City	0.9	18.1	37.1	14.8	16 259	-0.7	1 051	0.4	1.7	7.4	15 208	69.5	30.5	2.51	2.09
Burton	1.6	14.3	60.7	11.0	12 348	13.9	649	0.2	2.7	5.3	11 699	80.8	19.2	2.67	2.23
Dearborn	5.2	10.8	80.0	8.2	38 981	5.6	2 211	1.2	1.5	6.1	36 770	73.4	26.6	2.75	2.38
Dearborn Heights	4.6	5.5	44.7	4.0	23 913	0.1	637	0.3	0.9	3.8	23 276	85.4	14.6	2.53	2.14
Detroit	1.2	32.4	47.9	29.0	375 096	-8.5	38 668	0.2	1.6	8.3	336 428	54.9	45.1	2.84	2.68
East Lansing	7.0	33.8	24.3	11.4	15 321	6.4	931	0.3	1.2	6.3	14 390	32.0	68.0	2.41	2.13
Eastpointe	1.8	4.9	8.9	3.7	13 965	2.1	370	0.2	0.9	4.5	13 595	88.0	12.0	2.56	2.09
Farmington Hills	15.6	3.0	-16.7	1.7	34 858	11.8	1 299	0.8	0.5	5.1	33 559	66.9	33.1	2.72	1.77
Flint	1.0	30.6	81.1	27.6	55 464	-5.6	6 720	0.3	2.7	13.1	48 744	58.8	41.2	2.45	2.59
Garden City	1.6	4.3	19.4	3.0	11 719	3.0	240	0.2	0.5	3.6	11 479	86.2	13.8	2.71	2.03
Grand Rapids	1.9	16.1	19.3	12.6	77 960	5.8	4 743	0.3	1.3	6.6	73 217	59.7	40.3	2.69	2.39
Holland	4.0	11.8	37.2	8.2	12 533	11.5	562	0.9	1.4	3.3	11 971	67.1	32.9	2.73	2.55
Inkster	1.4	23.2	50.6	19.6	12 013	-0.3	844	0.2	1.7	7.7	11 169	58.0	42.0	2.76	2.55
Jackson	1.0	24.7	55.3	21.2	15 241	-2.9	1 031	0.3	1.5	7.9	14 210	57.6	42.4	2.55	2.38
Kalamazoo	3.1	26.2	33.7	19.3	31 798	1.0	2 385	0.4	2.1	6.9	29 413	47.7	52.3	2.43	2.18
Kentwood	2.7	5.0	-26.5	3.7	19 507	19.4	1 030	0.5	1.3	7.0	18 477	61.0	39.0	2.71	1.99
Lansing	1.2	19.4	48.1	16.5	53 159	-1.4	3 654	0.4	2.0	7.2	49 505	57.5	42.5	2.49	2.26
Lincoln Park	1.7	8.5	70.0	6.2	16 821	0.3	617	0.3	1.0	5.8	16 204	79.1	20.9	2.57	2.06
Livonia	7.6	2.6	18.2	1.7	38 658	5.5	569	0.3	0.4	2.7	38 089	88.8	11.2	2.68	1.86
Madison Heights	1.5	8.4	35.5	6.9	13 623	3.0	324	0.3	0.8	3.0	13 299	70.1	29.9	2.50	1.93
Midland	8.3	9.5	66.7	6.1	17 773	15.1	1 030	0.8	1.7	6.7	16 743	69.7	30.3	2.63	1.92
Mount Pleasant	2.0	38.7	29.9	14.6	8 878	25.6	429	0.4	1.7	4.5	8 449	34.3	65.7	2.43	2.35
Muskegon	0.5	26.5	37.3	23.0	15 999	0.1	1 430	0.5	2.9	7.8	14 569	56.9	43.1	2.58	2.21
Novi	8.9	3.3	17.9	2.2	19 649	44.9	923	0.5	1.2	7.0	18 726	71.1	28.9	2.78	1.88
Oak Park	2.5	10.9	55.7	8.4	11 370	0.2	266	0.2	1.1	2.7	11 104	74.8	25.2	2.74	2.52
Pontiac	0.8	26.7	51.7	24.1	26 336	-1.0	2 102	0.2	2.0	8.6	24 234	52.8	47.2	2.76	2.59
Portage	5.8	4.2	16.7	2.8	18 880	17.0	742	0.4	1.4	5.2	18 138	68.9	31.1	2.71	1.88
Port Huron	2.0	22.1	38.1	20.0	14 003	-0.2	1 042	0.7	2.0	7.9	12 961	57.2	42.8	2.54	2.29
Rochester Hills	14.2	2.6	NA	1.7	27 263	15.8	948	0.5	1.0	6.1	26 315	79.1	20.9	2.76	1.92
Roseville	1.5	6.2	3.3	4.9	20 519	2.5	543	0.3	0.9	3.3	19 976	75.2	24.8	2.53	2.01
Royal Oak	3.4	4.6	9.5	2.9	29 942	2.7	1 062	0.7	0.8	4.5	28 880	70.1	29.9	2.24	1.65
Saginaw	0.7	31.7	52.4	28.5	25 639	-8.4	2 457	0.2	2.2	7.6	23 182	63.6	36.4	2.61	2.59
St. Clair Shores	3.4	3.6	2.9	2.6	28 208	1.0	774	0.5	0.8	4.0	27 434	85.8	14.2	2.36	1.81
Southfield	6.9	5.8	56.8	3.5	35 698	1.8	1 711	0.3	1.1	5.8	33 987	54.1	45.9	2.64	1.83
Southgate	2.1	4.6	48.4	3.3	13 361	6.9	525	0.5	1.2	4.8	12 836	70.6	29.4	2.58	1.73
Sterling Heights	4.5	3.6	12.5	2.8	47 547	12.4	1 228	0.3	0.9	3.7	46 319	79.0	21.0	2.87	1.88
Taylor	1.8	11.9	40.0	11.0	25 905	0.7	1 129	0.2	1.5	5.8	24 776	70.8	29.2	2.67	2.53
Troy	13.4	2.8	0.0	2.0	30 872	13.5	854	0.7	0.5	3.7	30 018	77.3	22.7	2.92	1.91
Warren	2.9	6.5	32.7	5.1	57 249	1.9	1 698	0.3	0.8	4.4	55 551	80.4	19.6	2.55	2.12
Westland	1.7	7.1	36.5	5.6	38 077	10.3	1 544	0.3	1.5	5.2	36 533	62.7	37.3	2.57	1.97
Wyandotte	1.4	9.7	26.0	8.0	12 303	-4.0	487	0.3	1.1	4.4	11 816	73.0	27.0	2.53	1.91
Wyoming	1.5	7.1	20.3	5.4	27 506	9.8	970	0.2	1.0	5.6	26 536	67.6	32.4	2.80	2.18
MINNESOTA	3.6	10.2	7.6	7.3	2 065 946	11.8	170 819	5.1	0.9	4.1	1 895 127	74.6	25.4	2.69	2.03
Andover	5.9	3.6	NA	2.2	8 205	81.6	98	0.1	0.6	1.1	8 107	95.7	4.3	3.32	2.34
Apple Valley	8.8	3.5	40.0	2.6	16 536	43.3	192	0.2	0.3	2.2	16 344	88.0	12.0	2.86	2.14
Blaine	1.3	5.2	13.0	4.1	16 169	22.7	271	0.1	0.8	0.9	15 898	90.5	9.5	2.87	2.32
Bloomington	7.4	3.7	23.3	2.3	37 104	3.6	704	0.4	0.3	3.0	36 400	70.6	29.4	2.48	1.88
Brooklyn Center	1.9	7.1	31.5	5.8	11 598	-1.0	168	0.2	0.4	2.3	11 430	68.7	31.3	2.70	2.13
Brooklyn Park	2.3	7.5	25.0	7.0	24 846	16.8	414	0.2	0.4	2.9	24 432	73.4	26.6	2.94	2.22
Burnsville	5.7	4.2	35.5	3.5	24 261	19.8	574	0.4	0.4	3.4	23 687	68.1	31.9	2.71	2.14
Coon Rapids	2.6	4.8	17.1	3.8	22 828	26.1	250	0.2	0.5	1.1	22 578	80.4	19.6	2.81	2.30
Cottage Grove	2.3	2.6	4.0	1.8	10 024	41.1	92	0.1	0.2	4.3	9 932	91.4	8.6	3.09	2.92
Duluth	2.1	16.6	38.3	10.5	36 996	2.7	1 494	0.5	1.0	3.4	35 500	64.1	35.9	2.46	1.91
Eagan	4.8	2.8	-22.2	2.2	24 390	32.2	617	0.3	0.2	5.6	23 773	75.0	25.0	2.85	2.11
Eden Prairie	12.7	3.1	14.8	2.4	21 026	36.5	569	0.7	0.4	3.9	20 457	78.3	21.7	2.83	2.11
Edina	19.7	3.2	28.0	1.8	21 669	3.3	673	1.4	0.5	2.5	20 996	76.5	23.5	2.42	1.66
Fridley	3.5	6.1	45.2	4.9	11 504	0.8	176	0.2	0.4	2.0	11 328	67.7	32.3	2.51	2.19
Inver Grove Heights	3.6	7.2	46.9	6.1	11 457	40.6	200	0.2	0.6	2.2	11 257	77.5	22.5	2.72	2.27
Lakeville	4.4	3.0	-25.0	2.1	13 799	70.3	190	0.2	0.5	2.3	13 609	91.8	8.2	3.22	2.55
Mankato	1.1	25.2	59.5	11.0	12 759	9.2	392	0.2	0.9	2.6	12 367	52.9	47.1	2.51	2.09
Maple Grove	5.4	2.3	-14.8	1.8	17 745	36.8	213	0.2	0.3	2.3	17 532	92.7	7.3	2.92	2.24
Maplewood	3.0	6.2	55.0	5.6	14 004	15.5	246	0.4	0.4	1.9	13 758	75.7	24.3	2.67	1.90
Minneapolis	3.2	18.5	37.0	14.1	168 606	-2.4	6 254	0.5	0.7	2.8	162 352	51.4	48.6	2.43	2.05
Minnetonka	14.6	2.1	-4.5	1.1	22 228	10.5	835	1.1	0.4	5.0	21 393	75.7	24.3	2.55	1.79
Moorhead	1.5	19.9	73.0	10.8	12 180	5.8	520	0.2	0.8	6.3	11 660	63.7	36.3	2.65	2.05
Oakdale	2.2	5.8	-1.7	4.8	10 394	49.9	151	0.2	0.5	1.8	10 243	80.5	19.5	2.75	1.94
Plymouth	12.5	3.4	21.4	2.4	25 258	28.8	438	0.5	0.3	2.1	24 820	76.5	23.5	2.76	2.08
Richfield	1.4	5.5	48.6	3.9	15 357	-4.6	284	0.2	0.4	2.4	15 073	67.6	32.4	2.42	1.91

1. Includes units rented or sold but not occupied.   2. Specified owner-occupied units.   3. Specified renter-occupied units.   4. Overcrowded or lacking complete plumbing facilities.

City	Civilian labor force, 2001				Civilian employment, 1990[2]			Disability 1990	Value of residential construction authorized by building permits, 2000		
			Unemployment			Percent					
	Total	Percent change, 2000–2001	Total	Rate[1]	Total	Professional, managerial, and technical	Precision production, craft, and repair	Work disabled persons[3] (percent)	New construction ($1,000)	Number of housing units	Percent single family
	61	62	63	64	65	66	67	68	69	70	71
MICHIGAN—Cont'd											
Battle Creek	26 507	0.4	1 656	6.2	21 874	27.0	10.2	12.7	16 044	214	46.3
Bay City	18 401	0.2	1 368	7.4	15 458	23.1	12.5	11.3	278	3	100.0
Burton	12 149	-0.3	1 032	8.5	11 273	18.7	15.4	10.6	13 447	122	100.0
Dearborn	43 624	-2.2	1 234	2.8	38 978	36.0	10.3	7.9	34 679	303	18.8
Dearborn Heights	31 713	-2.2	845	2.7	28 383	27.3	13.3	8.6	10 263	52	100.0
Detroit	403 916	0.2	39 088	9.7	335 462	22.1	8.8	13.8	38 118	366	19.7
East Lansing	29 518	0.6	1 208	4.1	26 344	41.5	2.1	2.0	2 045	17	100.0
Eastpointe	20 140	-1.5	873	4.3	16 006	23.0	15.0	9.5	386	5	100.0
Farmington Hills	49 628	-2.0	1 306	2.6	40 703	48.6	7.8	4.9	26 639	166	75.9
Flint	53 352	1.2	6 990	13.1	47 016	21.2	11.0	14.4	5 818	71	88.7
Garden City	17 676	-2.2	472	2.7	15 819	18.5	17.0	9.8	1 747	19	100.0
Grand Rapids	118 927	1.0	8 334	7.0	85 877	27.2	9.6	9.2	26 263	237	100.0
Holland	22 179	0.4	1 149	5.2	14 823	26.9	9.7	7.1	7 575	64	89.1
Inkster	13 970	-0.9	914	6.5	12 005	21.8	9.9	14.1	1 252	21	61.9
Jackson	19 148	2.3	1 486	7.8	14 838	22.5	9.6	15.2	1 440	12	100.0
Kalamazoo	43 423	1.2	2 711	6.2	36 210	33.0	6.8	8.1	6 555	46	47.8
Kentwood	28 044	-0.5	913	3.3	21 068	30.9	9.1	5.9	17 586	250	98.4
Lansing	67 914	0.7	3 115	4.6	60 089	27.8	9.2	10.7	11 022	206	17.5
Lincoln Park	21 195	-1.9	754	3.6	18 796	18.3	14.3	10.6	348	5	100.0
Livonia	57 003	-2.4	1 151	2.0	51 356	36.4	12.0	6.2	14 801	117	100.0
Madison Heights	20 559	-0.9	1 033	5.0	16 447	24.1	14.3	9.2	1 920	23	100.0
Midland	22 718	-1.0	672	3.0	18 103	49.4	8.1	5.8	15 239	137	52.6
Mount Pleasant	14 440	0.9	473	3.3	10 205	34.1	3.7	3.6	15 685	324	10.8
Muskegon	19 033	1.5	1 737	9.1	13 970	21.4	11.0	15.5	6 755	69	100.0
Novi	22 189	-1.9	634	2.9	18 156	41.2	9.4	5.0	59 325	544	48.7
Oak Park	17 733	-1.2	807	4.6	14 257	32.8	8.8	9.1	1 401	17	100.0
Pontiac	35 108	1.7	3 817	10.9	26 357	17.7	11.9	14.5	15 444	215	97.7
Portage	25 637	0.0	683	2.7	22 195	37.1	8.3	6.0	33 923	203	100.0
Port Huron	17 681	0.6	1 596	9.0	13 281	22.7	11.2	11.9	8 574	149	24.8
Rochester Hills	39 511	-1.8	1 180	3.0	32 287	48.2	7.8	4.5	34 950	167	100.0
Roseville	31 716	-0.8	1 947	6.1	24 731	20.2	15.9	9.8	9 673	172	86.0
Royal Oak	42 957	-1.8	1 373	3.2	35 027	38.9	9.6	7.0	1 931	16	100.0
Saginaw	28 127	1.5	2 912	10.4	22 721	20.6	9.2	12.6	296	5	100.0
St. Clair Shores	41 633	-1.4	1 909	4.6	33 001	28.8	12.9	8.1	4 460	39	100.0
Southfield	49 251	-1.3	2 090	4.2	39 725	44.1	6.6	7.2	11 383	125	100.0
Southgate	16 877	-2.2	465	2.8	15 091	23.0	14.3	9.2	15 890	123	67.5
Sterling Heights	78 448	-1.6	3 211	4.1	62 504	32.8	12.8	5.9	60 235	751	70.4
Taylor	36 190	-1.7	1 479	4.1	31 917	17.6	16.2	10.5	9 402	102	100.0
Troy	47 760	-2.1	1 113	2.3	39 292	48.6	8.1	3.9	37 842	291	73.9
Warren	88 426	-0.9	5 163	5.8	69 172	24.6	14.8	8.7	7 709	119	57.1
Westland	49 096	-2.2	1 391	2.8	43 865	23.0	14.6	8.7	9 758	93	100.0
Wyandotte	15 010	-1.9	555	3.7	13 291	21.5	14.5	11.8	2 554	16	100.0
Wyoming	45 470	0.2	2 224	4.9	33 581	20.9	12.6	7.7	21 792	239	86.6
MINNESOTA	2 814 357	2.8	104 059	3.7	2 192 417	30.3	10.1	7.4	4 203 928	32 814	77.9
Andover	15 392	3.0	440	2.9	8 163	27.6	15.9	4.9	46 222	342	100.0
Apple Valley	29 556	2.9	784	2.7	19 122	39.4	8.7	4.7	50 542	635	29.0
Blaine	29 879	3.1	950	3.2	21 899	23.8	14.9	7.1	76 766	564	100.0
Bloomington	59 037	3.0	1 737	2.9	51 813	36.2	7.8	5.9	4 008	54	24.1
Brooklyn Center	16 937	3.2	660	3.9	15 306	26.9	11.3	8.1	327	3	100.0
Brooklyn Park	42 438	3.1	1 471	3.5	32 716	30.1	11.0	5.8	35 324	321	91.3
Burnsville	41 358	3.1	1 169	2.8	30 795	36.6	7.6	5.0	20 979	159	74.2
Coon Rapids	40 612	3.0	1 278	3.1	29 489	28.2	12.2	6.7	18 585	148	91.2
Cottage Grove	18 807	2.7	487	2.6	11 969	28.2	9.8	6.4	21 942	143	90.9
Duluth	45 041	1.0	1 866	4.1	37 139	33.0	7.9	8.8	9 425	105	56.2
Eagan	41 400	2.8	970	2.3	28 797	42.8	7.8	4.1	49 819	332	78.0
Eden Prairie	33 018	3.1	953	2.9	23 463	45.9	5.8	4.0	97 528	591	44.7
Edina	26 499	3.0	689	2.6	23 495	52.5	2.8	3.7	15 437	28	100.0
Fridley	18 872	3.1	672	3.6	16 583	30.6	10.0	6.7	2 360	20	80.0
Inver Grove Heights	19 257	3.0	554	2.9	12 516	28.1	11.5	6.5	42 774	208	98.1
Lakeville	25 664	2.8	514	2.0	13 660	29.3	13.4	5.1	113 848	613	96.6
Mankato	21 225	2.7	659	3.1	16 806	25.7	8.4	6.9	19 759	194	45.9
Maple Grove	32 063	3.0	861	2.7	22 334	36.8	10.3	4.5	171 746	1 500	37.5
Maplewood	20 739	2.6	565	2.7	16 170	31.9	11.1	7.6	16 368	129	49.6
Minneapolis	212 736	3.0	8 245	3.9	192 508	36.4	6.3	9.8	32 793	347	27.4
Minnetonka	33 948	2.8	824	2.4	27 926	45.2	5.8	4.2	26 053	93	89.2
Moorhead	20 305	3.1	421	2.1	15 987	30.2	6.2	6.7	13 979	144	69.4
Oakdale	17 720	2.7	414	2.3	10 605	30.4	11.7	5.4	19 116	162	51.9
Plymouth	41 403	2.9	1 075	2.6	29 820	43.6	6.6	4.0	47 091	286	100.0
Richfield	21 885	2.9	645	2.9	20 327	29.9	8.5	6.3	24 837	273	12.5

1. Percent of civilian labor force. 2. Persons 16 years and older. 3. Persons 16 to 64 years old.

Table D. Cities — Wholesale Trade, Retail Trade, and Real Estate

City	Wholesale Trade, 1997				Retail Trade[1], 1997				Real Estate and Rental and Leasing, 1997			
	Number of Establish-ments	Number of Employees	Sales (mil dol)	Annual Payroll (mil dol)	Number of Establish-ments	Number of Employees	Sales (mil dol)	Annual Payroll (mil dol)	Number of Establish-ments	Number of Employees	Receipts (mil dol)	Annual Payroll (mil dol)
	72	73	74	75	76	77	78	79	80	81	82	83
MICHIGAN—Cont'd												
Battle Creek	59	976	1 139.7	37.5	266	3 825	632.7	58.2	53	270	32.0	5.2
Bay City	63	938	409.2	27.0	221	2 081	400.1	36.6	42	175	14.7	3.3
Burton	31	560	136.3	17.7	228	3 754	513.5	56.3	28	152	14.7	3.9
Dearborn	156	1 822	1 104.2	78.4	557	9 607	1 752.5	170.9	81	1 132	375.6	44.8
Dearborn Heights	30	237	101.6	8.4	187	2 455	391.6	38.8	35	192	19.2	2.6
Detroit	740	12 878	14 616.4	541.3	2 253	17 886	3 188.7	289.1	380	2 279	233.2	47.2
East Lansing	22	D	D	D	119	2 471	304.0	32.3	59	367	32.6	10.0
Eastpointe	NA	NA	NA	NA	NA	NA	NA	NA	NA	NA	NA	NA
Farmington Hills	416	5 457	7 318.4	266.7	328	4 696	1 100.4	104.2	206	3 754	429.5	89.1
Flint	139	1 970	728.3	62.0	531	5 157	864.6	86.3	101	476	59.8	8.7
Garden City	18	139	24.1	4.2	111	1 300	392.1	31.5	16	49	5.8	0.7
Grand Rapids	485	8 890	4 426.2	345.5	795	11 578	2 018.1	214.8	225	1 461	162.6	30.9
Holland	64	1 011	549.2	35.3	230	3 525	612.3	58.7	54	258	32.6	5.6
Inkster	8	79	27.0	3.0	55	470	86.7	7.9	8	47	4.7	0.7
Jackson	100	1 311	633.6	52.1	237	3 671	567.5	56.3	43	160	19.4	2.5
Kalamazoo	155	2 389	687.3	84.8	337	4 265	727.2	70.5	110	1 317	113.6	27.7
Kentwood	121	3 845	3 354.0	142.9	267	5 718	855.4	84.4	62	504	51.8	11.0
Lansing	190	3 186	933.4	103.9	523	8 178	1 486.6	150.2	105	1 730	103.8	27.5
Lincoln Park	22	187	40.0	5.2	159	2 644	352.5	35.9	26	100	11.8	1.4
Livonia	424	8 691	6 430.2	337.7	644	9 668	1 591.2	167.7	120	799	149.1	21.5
Madison Heights	141	2 960	2 722.8	152.0	193	3 744	717.8	66.4	48	510	57.3	9.6
Midland	54	478	240.4	19.6	256	3 673	584.7	59.4	45	168	22.1	2.8
Mount Pleasant	38	D	D	D	130	2 193	288.1	29.0	30	520	16.4	6.3
Muskegon	53	669	237.7	22.3	176	2 571	413.0	42.5	26	134	13.1	1.9
Novi	163	3 940	2 851.9	185.1	323	6 100	1 177.8	105.4	53	254	34.7	6.3
Oak Park	91	1 178	627.7	44.3	182	2 510	401.9	55.2	34	374	30.3	7.1
Pontiac	76	D	D	D	228	2 548	502.3	44.6	45	299	27.5	5.6
Portage	83	2 431	692.7	94.7	338	6 404	879.0	85.9	55	354	30.1	6.9
Port Huron	30	285	173.1	11.4	168	1 936	375.7	40.3	36	131	17.7	2.7
Rochester Hills	175	1 405	1 302.5	66.9	240	4 340	968.3	92.3	51	223	41.0	6.1
Roseville	78	973	383.6	39.0	293	5 807	966.3	91.2	47	179	20.6	2.8
Royal Oak	118	915	590.0	37.8	297	4 193	773.9	85.4	67	212	44.2	4.6
Saginaw	76	1 182	317.9	39.0	206	1 898	260.6	30.5	33	176	10.9	2.6
St. Clair Shores	86	548	605.4	23.5	234	3 306	547.8	58.4	47	244	40.0	4.1
Southfield	440	6 838	15 374.8	426.0	566	8 925	1 987.7	182.6	292	3 001	356.3	89.2
Southgate	17	D	D	D	171	3 836	888.7	70.3	19	87	8.8	2.1
Sterling Heights	155	2 409	952.0	106.0	495	9 680	1 598.9	160.0	87	410	64.3	9.7
Taylor	86	1 931	1 872.1	66.3	343	6 038	1 037.0	102.3	56	627	128.3	21.0
Troy	521	7 489	11 690.9	384.1	607	12 184	2 410.8	226.9	169	1 527	191.3	41.2
Warren	274	4 379	2 802.5	169.5	563	8 524	1 730.7	172.0	108	682	105.2	15.4
Westland	76	738	280.8	27.9	335	6 533	1 160.5	101.2	54	410	51.2	7.5
Wyandotte	31	286	59.5	9.4	107	753	122.2	13.3	13	99	4.3	2.3
Wyoming	223	7 193	3 330.3	272.5	308	5 510	934.6	101.4	63	851	150.2	23.3
MINNESOTA	9 348	131 787	99 444.5	5 024.0	20 883	282 282	48 077.7	4 525.7	5 051	30 172	3 886.4	687.2
Andover	14	47	10.3	1.2	35	430	72.0	6.3	4	D	D	D
Apple Valley	49	244	245.7	12.9	112	2 761	529.3	46.5	37	152	18.3	2.7
Blaine	59	964	316.5	33.0	199	3 100	504.4	45.5	36	282	33.9	4.6
Bloomington	485	8 222	10 687.5	402.2	587	12 036	2 079.0	201.3	191	2 224	211.3	67.1
Brooklyn Center	54	540	329.1	20.1	133	3 435	675.0	58.0	33	216	21.5	4.0
Brooklyn Park	97	1 270	580.1	52.7	154	4 656	1 220.1	93.6	41	283	28.3	5.5
Burnsville	225	2 563	1 605.0	88.5	372	7 850	1 272.9	123.4	90	507	69.6	10.0
Coon Rapids	39	456	172.3	19.7	151	3 412	573.7	49.3	58	293	25.8	4.7
Cottage Grove	5	15	7.1	0.5	44	1 066	151.6	13.3	19	77	7.2	1.1
Duluth	129	1 611	778.7	49.3	536	7 277	1 037.1	110.8	109	694	54.9	11.3
Eagan	163	3 496	2 059.3	144.7	140	3 251	555.1	57.4	69	367	56.3	8.3
Eden Prairie	319	6 208	5 447.1	303.0	188	3 597	676.4	61.9	96	1 562	399.5	68.4
Edina	300	2 906	5 783.3	145.7	377	8 123	1 182.9	132.6	199	1 253	166.9	33.6
Fridley	94	1 593	817.6	61.3	107	2 863	482.5	47.0	27	177	31.9	3.5
Inver Grove Heights	24	393	166.0	9.8	58	1 516	435.5	32.6	10	66	10.5	0.7
Lakeville	51	564	256.8	17.0	68	1 247	349.6	27.1	31	111	10.8	2.0
Mankato	74	1 179	415.5	32.9	266	4 823	702.4	66.1	57	333	28.5	6.1
Maple Grove	95	1 606	1 252.8	86.2	97	1 569	277.6	24.9	31	130	14.6	1.6
Maplewood	41	421	126.1	12.1	254	4 936	854.6	77.5	52	234	25.8	3.9
Minneapolis	841	14 152	13 527.1	644.3	1 333	15 860	2 344.0	287.7	518	4 246	587.8	121.4
Minnetonka	288	4 016	7 374.9	189.6	352	7 410	1 157.6	116.5	98	786	188.8	24.1
Moorhead	36	507	220.1	12.0	138	2 113	361.6	28.7	33	D	D	D
Oakdale	20	77	32.6	2.4	61	975	198.4	17.7	18	80	7.3	1.4
Plymouth	350	11 437	6 950.7	412.4	165	4 057	1 460.4	109.5	93	427	93.4	11.9
Richfield	37	322	110.1	11.6	148	2 746	438.7	46.2	36	367	34.4	5.2

1. Establishments with payroll.

City	Professional, Scientific, and Technical Services, 1997[1]				Manufacturing, 1997				Accommodation and Foodservices, 1997			
	Number of Establishments	Number of Employees	Receipts (mil dol)	Annual Payroll (mil dol)	Number of Establishments	Number of Employees	Receipts (mil dol)	Annual Payroll (mil dol)	Number of Establishments	Number of Employees	Sales (mil dol)	Annual Payroll (mil dol)
	84	85	86	87	88	89	90	91	92	93	94	95
MICHIGAN—Cont'd												
Battle Creek	96	568	51.6	22.3	81	10 194	3 337.7	409.4	162	3 033	91.4	26.9
Bay City	95	621	46.5	22.6	79	4 174	794.7	198.3	111	1 629	41.3	11.1
Burton	29	437	24.6	8.9	41	D	D	D	82	1 445	43.2	12.1
Dearborn	215	2 747	252.8	127.1	119	13 098	5 533.8	764.4	267	5 771	221.3	62.0
Dearborn Heights	67	348	20.3	10.9	NA	NA	NA	NA	104	1 814	57.0	14.3
Detroit	718	12 794	1 594.4	604.3	825	47 487	19 778.5	2 312.2	1 108	15 426	576.0	150.4
East Lansing	110	687	57.9	24.9	NA	NA	NA	NA	113	2 372	62.9	17.0
Eastpointe	NA	NA	NA	NA	NA	NA	NA	NA	NA	NA	NA	NA
Farmington Hills	656	7 600	829.1	359.6	155	5 109	993.8	225.3	181	3 779	131.4	38.2
Flint	253	1 497	101.8	46.6	94	D	D	D	266	3 824	112.9	29.8
Garden City	13	28	2.7	1.6	NA	NA	NA	NA	54	740	26.4	6.1
Grand Rapids	661	6 066	647.4	257.7	459	30 971	5 140.1	1 309.1	386	8 134	262.6	78.5
Holland	76	682	55.4	26.3	117	16 130	3 246.8	615.7	87	2 258	57.3	19.1
Inkster	9	30	1.8	0.7	NA	NA	NA	NA	28	164	8.9	2.0
Jackson	109	966	60.6	30.8	143	4 453	826.1	149.8	111	1 769	57.9	14.6
Kalamazoo	227	1 861	169.7	76.7	153	7 499	1 450.5	253.8	206	4 217	112.1	33.8
Kentwood	95	1 096	80.8	35.4	99	9 998	1 550.8	332.1	102	2 798	84.7	24.7
Lansing	279	2 201	240.7	108.0	131	D	D	D	260	5 620	159.8	47.7
Lincoln Park	24	530	62.4	27.5	NA	NA	NA	NA	79	D	D	D
Livonia	384	6 668	553.6	224.0	350	17 012	4 243.0	826.7	266	6 399	213.6	57.1
Madison Heights	118	2 302	235.2	95.6	227	6 683	1 060.2	282.2	102	2 250	77.9	19.6
Midland	108	603	61.6	19.9	49	5 289	1 671.1	278.9	93	2 330	68.0	20.5
Mount Pleasant	66	384	25.1	13.0	15	D	D	D	71	1 921	49.9	14.3
Muskegon	90	568	52.1	23.1	108	6 918	1 231.0	236.7	82	D	D	D
Novi	126	1 436	166.9	66.6	87	2 448	378.8	104.4	96	2 778	90.9	28.7
Oak Park	47	368	43.3	12.5	78	1 632	208.1	63.4	45	743	22.4	5.9
Pontiac	54	510	28.4	12.4	58	8 474	4 570.2	378.7	130	D	D	D
Portage	114	953	85.2	38.4	78	5 667	902.2	239.4	110	2 752	78.6	23.4
Port Huron	75	397	30.2	14.2	74	5 789	1 355.6	184.8	69	1 143	38.4	10.3
Rochester Hills	184	2 952	190.4	81.8	140	7 936	1 264.0	285.9	103	2 592	76.7	22.4
Roseville	58	846	28.6	14.0	202	6 582	930.5	257.1	111	2 563	83.2	22.3
Royal Oak	207	1 903	300.2	75.8	98	2 397	531.4	96.3	143	3 071	107.0	32.9
Saginaw	116	1 023	73.2	32.0	78	7 667	2 289.5	420.8	123	1 928	55.5	15.2
St. Clair Shores	160	862	59.9	31.4	68	2 756	335.0	76.7	128	D	D	D
Southfield	938	13 035	1 584.8	696.8	115	4 564	748.8	211.7	283	4 739	195.6	54.5
Southgate	26	335	15.8	9.3	NA	NA	NA	NA	74	D	D	D
Sterling Heights	234	2 657	302.7	136.2	314	21 628	6 777.9	1 241.7	202	4 083	126.3	36.7
Taylor	63	893	45.3	17.4	90	2 662	652.4	94.2	154	2 789	84.4	22.9
Troy	843	15 151	1 644.7	822.1	396	11 872	1 678.0	470.9	225	5 330	202.4	57.3
Warren	193	4 180	391.2	203.1	518	23 404	8 065.3	1 157.2	301	5 435	193.3	51.4
Westland	69	415	41.5	16.6	79	2 533	402.6	91.5	154	3 022	94.1	25.1
Wyandotte	43	161	9.9	4.0	49	2 227	511.1	96.0	68	901	26.8	7.2
Wyoming	80	967	63.4	25.6	185	11 933	2 055.0	539.2	131	2 557	78.1	21.9
MINNESOTA	12 391	96 677	10 447.9	4 091.3	8 091	382 530	76 244.9	13 126.1	9 982	179 487	5 934.2	1 688.8
Andover	41	95	8.0	3.7	NA	NA	NA	NA	8	193	5.0	1.2
Apple Valley	107	266	21.5	9.6	NA	NA	NA	NA	37	1 011	33.8	9.0
Blaine	81	334	27.6	11.3	134	3 147	368.3	106.2	52	1 568	43.9	12.7
Bloomington	578	7 762	967.6	376.6	209	10 538	1 655.5	420.8	246	9 049	383.3	106.7
Brooklyn Center	70	386	31.4	13.8	44	1 723	242.3	66.6	45	1 456	44.5	14.1
Brooklyn Park	116	865	86.2	41.8	109	5 406	860.9	226.8	68	D	D	D
Burnsville	212	956	96.4	33.9	113	4 055	723.6	148.1	108	3 101	92.2	27.0
Coon Rapids	95	452	35.0	13.4	61	2 613	379.1	102.8	77	1 705	53.7	15.5
Cottage Grove	27	54	7.1	2.0	10	D	D	D	23	357	10.1	2.7
Duluth	197	1 446	98.3	43.4	97	2 751	534.2	88.9	241	4 872	156.3	43.1
Eagan	214	879	105.8	42.2	85	4 169	3 294.1	169.5	102	2 541	82.7	26.6
Eden Prairie	330	3 902	441.0	170.8	146	9 873	1 528.6	412.6	106	2 189	85.9	24.6
Edina	522	4 975	699.1	238.0	93	3 007	479.4	109.4	89	D	D	D
Fridley	84	389	37.6	17.1	159	9 797	1 673.7	382.5	45	1 145	28.2	8.8
Inver Grove Heights	45	170	19.8	6.3	NA	NA	NA	NA	24	460	13.0	3.8
Lakeville	59	178	10.3	4.9	63	3 186	646.4	108.8	27	671	23.0	7.0
Mankato	81	569	46.1	15.7	62	3 721	1 476.4	116.6	111	2 295	62.4	17.1
Maple Grove	138	356	36.0	14.9	105	5 685	1 028.2	227.8	55	1 552	42.1	12.5
Maplewood	81	501	47.7	23.4	32	712	110.2	21.6	87	2 249	64.1	18.8
Minneapolis	1 977	27 509	3 565.9	1 384.7	699	25 906	3 953.5	951.1	921	20 653	828.9	246.8
Minnetonka	363	1 994	212.8	90.0	118	7 462	1 457.8	296.9	110	2 804	108.4	32.9
Moorhead	44	268	21.4	9.0	26	926	205.3	29.1	65	1 349	32.2	9.7
Oakdale	58	234	29.1	7.0	NA	NA	NA	NA	27	364	11.1	3.1
Plymouth	303	2 114	286.5	101.0	207	12 651	2 096.5	498.1	72	2 130	107.4	31.6
Richfield	60	423	19.8	7.7	NA	NA	NA	NA	52	1 414	45.4	12.6

1. Firms subject to federal tax.

City	Arts, Entertainment, and Recreation[1], 1997				Health Care and Social Assistance[1], 1997				Other Services[1], 1997			
	Number of Establish-ments	Number of Employees	Receipts (mil dol)	Annual Payroll (mil dol)	Number of Establish-ments	Number of Employees	Receipts (mil dol)	Annual Payroll (mil dol)	Number of Establish-ments	Number of Employees	Receipts (mil dol)	Annual Payroll (mil dol)
	96	97	98	99	100	101	102	103	104	105	106	107
MICHIGAN—Cont'd												
Battle Creek	15	187	7.6	2.0	181	1 988	113.0	53.0	94	892	52.8	16.2
Bay City	10	107	6.6	1.5	98	1 092	70.1	37.3	90	541	31.7	9.8
Burton	7	39	1.7	0.4	75	462	28.2	13.7	57	402	24.3	7.2
Dearborn	23	764	25.0	6.5	330	2 666	238.9	111.3	180	1 200	76.3	28.2
Dearborn Heights	9	107	3.9	1.2	95	791	46.9	20.9	98	619	37.1	12.2
Detroit	66	1 773	173.5	73.6	900	12 747	730.3	371.9	829	7 518	467.3	149.6
East Lansing	8	314	6.0	2.2	101	1 098	75.5	34.8	36	268	11.2	4.1
Eastpointe	NA	NA	NA	NA	NA	NA	NA	NA	NA	NA	NA	NA
Farmington Hills	34	374	24.2	6.6	313	2 982	224.2	97.7	155	1 205	69.4	24.3
Flint	10	107	3.6	1.1	292	2 900	206.0	100.9	199	1 384	84.1	23.4
Garden City	3	16	0.9	0.2	73	549	44.1	22.4	65	333	21.9	6.4
Grand Rapids	44	679	25.6	7.3	462	5 625	413.0	221.3	334	2 478	168.6	53.8
Holland	8	162	4.9	1.8	86	1 412	83.0	42.1	87	603	37.1	12.5
Inkster	2	0	0.0	0.0	20	104	3.9	1.7	19	93	6.2	1.7
Jackson	11	196	6.5	1.5	168	1 384	114.9	52.8	97	669	38.2	10.6
Kalamazoo	23	529	14.3	4.7	191	2 875	216.5	112.9	174	1 469	92.2	30.2
Kentwood	14	315	11.6	2.9	57	669	40.9	16.6	79	1 026	75.0	20.8
Lansing	25	462	41.7	6.3	254	2 316	184.3	95.5	204	1 413	77.6	24.2
Lincoln Park	11	119	3.4	0.8	68	965	58.8	27.1	87	523	30.1	9.5
Livonia	35	697	92.1	12.7	371	3 919	264.2	113.0	245	2 467	232.2	71.0
Madison Heights	15	245	14.6	3.9	82	703	56.9	24.3	85	956	62.6	20.9
Midland	13	181	8.6	3.2	176	1 599	105.1	52.8	83	556	37.3	9.9
Mount Pleasant	6	147	2.4	1.0	73	745	42.8	20.3	47	266	11.4	3.4
Muskegon	15	220	7.1	2.0	126	1 370	97.5	52.2	51	380	19.2	6.7
Novi	15	138	10.1	2.2	96	974	59.9	29.1	72	694	47.8	17.8
Oak Park	8	84	4.1	0.8	62	364	21.4	10.4	41	172	13.0	3.5
Pontiac	9	0	0.0	0.0	90	792	65.6	30.0	105	775	47.1	14.1
Portage	13	250	7.0	1.9	109	1 077	62.2	28.6	100	692	40.8	12.8
Port Huron	10	115	5.4	1.0	131	978	87.3	46.6	62	383	20.2	5.8
Rochester Hills	16	142	16.7	2.7	197	1 885	111.0	52.5	76	491	41.5	12.0
Roseville	12	254	10.2	2.4	96	789	59.5	27.6	110	559	38.9	13.1
Royal Oak	17	110	6.9	1.5	171	1 157	89.9	42.5	129	1 014	65.2	24.7
Saginaw	7	72	5.5	1.2	128	1 243	81.3	42.2	93	507	28.1	8.4
St. Clair Shores	25	218	12.6	3.2	202	1 473	119.8	58.6	136	778	36.6	11.5
Southfield	29	566	22.1	8.1	602	8 302	533.1	276.2	170	1 565	99.6	32.3
Southgate	9	31	1.2	0.3	69	795	58.0	27.3	56	546	54.1	13.6
Sterling Heights	21	173	14.1	4.0	210	2 114	140.7	61.6	169	1 217	82.0	29.2
Taylor	13	188	6.6	2.0	102	1 411	68.3	33.0	96	623	54.2	14.3
Troy	32	362	66.8	8.6	324	3 065	211.4	113.5	185	1 951	169.6	50.8
Warren	21	396	15.6	4.3	314	4 053	286.7	139.7	278	2 122	152.3	47.3
Westland	14	193	8.9	2.4	132	1 848	103.3	44.5	107	913	60.7	20.4
Wyandotte	8	79	2.9	0.7	46	317	28.4	12.7	62	422	21.0	7.1
Wyoming	12	191	6.7	2.1	75	1 097	57.9	23.4	165	1 161	75.3	24.5
MINNESOTA	1 593	27 958	1 469.7	477.9	8 033	106 839	5 864.5	2 946.0	7 614	55 723	3 394.6	1 103.6
Andover	3	0	0.0	0.0	17	86	2.6	0.9	21	93	4.1	1.5
Apple Valley	5	73	2.3	0.6	54	837	38.6	19.7	48	353	19.4	6.3
Blaine	9	133	4.4	1.1	56	576	27.0	11.5	63	429	26.3	9.3
Bloomington	37	1 896	87.3	26.0	153	2 105	112.1	66.5	177	5 563	200.1	136.3
Brooklyn Center	9	242	5.7	2.2	53	758	44.6	23.2	45	404	16.3	5.7
Brooklyn Park	12	261	7.6	2.2	70	1 017	41.0	18.4	84	679	39.6	12.3
Burnsville	20	461	7.2	3.0	121	2 359	106.4	50.8	120	1 019	55.4	19.1
Coon Rapids	17	423	12.3	2.7	110	2 280	121.4	64.0	70	431	26.2	7.5
Cottage Grove	4	72	2.6	0.9	30	338	16.7	8.3	22	242	7.1	2.6
Duluth	31	279	9.7	2.3	224	2 800	137.0	72.6	186	1 122	71.5	21.4
Eagan	16	426	14.2	3.8	98	855	47.9	18.4	95	1 634	102.7	41.9
Eden Prairie	23	1 837	125.7	68.0	86	1 349	113.6	36.7	83	1 777	155.9	61.0
Edina	26	114	10.4	2.7	327	4 058	301.4	154.4	104	1 356	63.3	25.6
Fridley	8	256	5.1	2.1	56	793	60.6	34.1	59	512	44.2	10.9
Inver Grove Heights	5	91	2.3	0.8	35	425	17.1	9.0	39	272	20.4	7.2
Lakeville	10	88	5.0	1.5	31	204	9.7	4.4	28	175	12.5	3.4
Mankato	15	86	3.2	0.7	102	1 840	91.5	46.8	82	579	30.5	9.2
Maple Grove	8	103	4.4	1.7	66	666	32.7	16.0	51	311	16.5	6.1
Maplewood	14	137	5.6	1.4	78	967	67.5	34.6	74	541	28.0	8.2
Minneapolis	139	2 506	233.4	77.4	672	9 019	622.7	318.0	672	7 965	499.0	155.1
Minnetonka	33	320	23.6	6.9	111	2 170	114.0	54.6	76	738	42.2	17.3
Moorhead	4	57	1.1	0.4	43	380	20.2	9.2	59	264	15.6	4.5
Oakdale	8	26	2.5	0.7	28	197	6.5	2.8	26	191	12.0	2.7
Plymouth	17	98	8.8	2.6	120	1 207	83.9	47.9	71	566	45.6	13.9
Richfield	7	69	2.9	0.6	63	686	33.7	14.2	59	396	27.1	9.0

1. Firms subject to federal tax.

Table D. Cities — Federal Funds and City Government Finances

City	Selected federal funds, fiscal 2001[1] (mil dol)									City government finances, 1999						
	Procurement contracts		Grants					Direct payments for individuals		General revenue						
											Intergovernmental		Taxes			
														Per capita[3] (dollars)		
	Defense	Other	Total[2]	Health and family welfare	Energy and environment	Education	Housing and community development	Educational assistance	Housing assistance	Total (mil dol)	Total (mil dol)	Percent from state government	Total (mil dol)	Total	Property	Sales and gross receipts
	108	109	110	111	112	113	114	115	116	117	118	119	120	121	122	123
MICHIGAN—Cont'd																
Battle Creek	20.4	23.0	13.2	6.4	0.0	2.1	2.5	2.8	3.2	89.5	19.7	71.5	40.7	761	509	0
Bay City	1.5	0.3	5.8	0.0	0.0	3.1	1.5	8.3	3.6	41.3	13.0	72.5	14.8	417	402	0
Burton	0.1	0.0	0.1	0.0	0.0	0.0	0.0	0.0	0.6	NA	NA	NA	NA	NA	NA	NA
Dearborn	0.2	175.7	23.4	0.4	8.2	1.6	2.9	14.7	3.8	147.0	23.6	76.8	63.4	691	651	0
Dearborn Heights	0.0	0.0	0.1	0.0	0.0	0.0	0.0	0.0	1.5	46.4	15.4	69.9	16.3	273	251	0
Detroit	13.5	68.2	502.3	151.4	16.1	11.9	82.1	27.0	128.6	3 485.4	2 172.2	85.3	817.4	842	387	53
East Lansing	1.4	0.5	126.8	31.8	8.6	6.4	0.6	19.1	4.5	NA	NA	NA	NA	NA	NA	NA
Eastpointe	0.1	0.0	0.1	0.0	0.0	0.0	0.0	0.0	0.0	NA	NA	NA	NA	NA	NA	NA
Farmington Hills	1.8	0.7	0.8	0.0	0.0	0.5	0.3	2.0	3.1	66.9	12.9	90.5	33.5	420	395	0
Flint	0.1	13.5	37.4	7.2	0.3	4.9	10.8	28.1	33.0	474.9	145.3	87.5	61.9	470	458	0
Garden City	0.1	0.0	0.0	0.0	0.0	0.0	0.0	0.0	0.7	25.9	5.8	93.2	9.2	280	261	0
Grand Rapids	33.1	27.6	53.2	13.1	0.0	2.6	8.2	21.2	26.5	213.2	57.1	70.8	81.6	440	148	0
Holland	13.7	20.5	4.1	1.3	0.0	1.8	0.6	1.2	4.2	40.5	9.0	73.3	13.1	394	386	0
Inkster	0.0	0.0	0.8	0.0	0.0	0.0	0.1	0.0	6.5	NA	NA	NA	NA	NA	NA	NA
Jackson	11.1	0.8	11.0	3.4	1.2	0.7	1.6	2.0	11.6	NA	NA	NA	NA	NA	NA	NA
Kalamazoo	4.7	2.2	26.2	8.4	0.5	8.2	0.0	14.7	27.9	104.7	26.3	80.6	27.3	358	348	0
Kentwood	0.0	0.0	0.0	0.0	0.0	0.0	0.0	0.0	7.6	20.5	6.0	94.8	9.5	224	196	0
Lansing	61.9	5.1	1 435.1	604.0	124.6	235.8	67.7	19.7	59.7	180.1	36.8	81.8	71.3	558	343	0
Lincoln Park	0.0	0.0	1.5	0.1	0.0	0.0	1.4	0.0	2.0	35.9	10.6	75.8	14.4	341	323	0
Livonia	13.3	2.9	0.9	0.0	0.0	0.5	0.2	4.2	6.1	93.3	17.3	95.7	40.1	395	372	0
Madison Heights	1.5	0.1	0.0	0.0	0.0	0.0	0.0	0.2	4.3	NA	NA	NA	NA	NA	NA	NA
Midland	0.1	0.2	3.0	0.0	0.8	0.1	0.4	3.5	3.3	54.4	9.3	85.1	26.5	664	653	0
Mount Pleasant	0.0	0.0	6.8	2.0	0.3	3.2	0.0	10.7	2.4	16.4	5.5	87.0	4.5	194	183	0
Muskegon	66.0	24.9	13.2	6.7	0.0	3.0	1.6	1.7	5.1	39.3	12.7	66.2	14.1	362	175	0
Novi	0.1	0.2	0.7	0.5	0.0	0.0	0.0	0.0	0.0	44.4	6.2	90.7	20.9	467	436	0
Oak Park	0.0	0.2	0.0	0.0	0.0	0.0	0.0	1.0	2.4	29.9	6.4	99.1	13.2	447	431	0
Pontiac	3.1	0.4	21.6	8.0	0.0	0.5	11.3	0.0	31.7	102.3	29.0	72.0	35.9	521	277	0
Portage	0.0	0.0	0.4	0.0	0.0	0.1	0.3	0.0	0.6	34.6	7.8	96.3	15.4	352	336	0
Port Huron	2.6	1.4	6.9	1.9	1.5	0.2	1.9	2.0	6.7	47.4	15.4	51.1	19.7	610	369	0
Rochester Hills	0.0	0.3	0.7	0.0	0.0	0.1	0.0	0.0	0.0	52.6	9.6	95.3	18.0	267	246	0
Roseville	10.5	1.1	1.5	0.0	0.0	0.0	1.5	0.0	7.5	42.2	11.8	77.8	17.0	331	317	0
Royal Oak	0.1	0.0	3.2	1.8	0.0	0.1	0.4	0.1	3.1	57.8	14.0	81.3	25.2	392	357	0
Saginaw	4.8	6.5	15.9	4.5	1.0	0.7	5.1	3.1	9.7	80.1	26.2	67.5	24.7	389	121	0
St. Clair Shores	0.0	0.0	1.3	0.0	0.0	0.2	1.0	0.1	0.4	52.9	13.2	80.8	19.5	295	276	0
Southfield	17.6	2.0	4.2	2.8	0.0	0.0	0.8	5.5	4.7	109.2	18.7	73.2	50.5	673	651	0
Southgate	0.0	0.0	0.8	0.4	0.0	0.0	0.0	1.2	2.5	NA	NA	NA	NA	NA	NA	NA
Sterling Heights	1 344.6	0.2	1.0	0.0	0.0	0.1	0.7	0.0	9.6	86.7	20.2	91.9	43.0	346	323	0
Taylor	0.9	0.7	1.1	0.0	0.0	0.0	0.7	0.0	26.9	122.7	38.4	35.9	34.6	477	455	0
Troy	19.3	26.3	29.7	20.1	8.9	0.0	0.0	0.8	6.0	77.0	12.4	95.6	44.1	556	519	0
Warren	277.2	2.3	5.3	0.0	0.0	0.6	1.3	3.3	1.4	143.3	32.1	90.1	63.6	447	431	0
Westland	0.3	0.2	11.4	9.6	0.0	0.0	1.7	0.1	5.7	67.6	17.9	75.3	23.3	271	260	0
Wyandotte	0.0	0.0	0.1	0.0	0.0	0.0	0.0	0.0	0.4	54.8	16.6	61.5	16.4	515	499	0
Wyoming	0.1	0.0	1.4	0.0	0.0	0.0	0.8	0.0	3.9	50.2	13.9	77.2	19.6	285	263	0
MINNESOTA	1 378.9	670.3	5 260.4	3 350.2	86.8	454.3	83.0	215.6	416.6	X	X	X	X	X	X	X
Andover	0.0	0.0	0.0	0.0	0.0	0.0	0.0	0.0	0.0	16.9	1.1	94.9	4.7	196	167	0
Apple Valley	0.0	0.3	0.6	0.4	0.0	0.0	0.0	0.0	2.4	31.5	4.6	87.8	13.0	286	248	11
Blaine	0.4	0.0	3.7	3.0	0.0	0.0	0.0	0.0	0.7	30.7	5.6	93.6	8.5	189	157	8
Bloomington	55.6	11.9	1.3	0.4	0.0	0.0	0.5	0.1	5.5	106.9	18.6	75.7	52.6	610	483	70
Brooklyn Center	0.0	1.1	0.0	0.0	0.0	0.0	0.0	0.0	1.0	32.0	5.8	96.4	10.7	385	342	24
Brooklyn Park	0.5	0.5	0.1	0.0	0.0	0.0	0.0	0.0	2.1	55.9	9.4	88.5	23.6	373	349	0
Burnsville	16.6	0.7	0.1	0.0	0.0	0.0	0.0	0.1	5.1	64.3	8.5	75.5	20.9	352	311	11
Coon Rapids	0.0	0.0	0.6	0.4	0.0	0.0	0.0	0.0	5.4	40.2	7.6	92.2	10.4	163	113	36
Cottage Grove	0.0	0.0	0.5	0.0	0.0	0.4	0.0	0.0	0.3	23.0	5.1	92.8	6.2	198	175	0
Duluth	1.2	3.9	29.3	5.1	0.4	2.7	7.8	9.1	12.5	149.6	50.2	80.4	31.8	392	209	177
Eagan	85.7	6.1	0.1	0.0	0.0	0.0	0.0	0.0	0.2	49.0	5.0	89.0	15.6	261	235	5
Eden Prairie	38.3	6.1	2.1	0.6	0.1	0.0	0.0	0.1	4.1	51.4	3.6	83.7	21.4	426	377	0
Edina	203.0	23.3	1.2	1.1	0.0	0.0	0.0	0.0	3.5	45.1	2.6	89.9	23.0	500	448	6
Fridley	0.1	0.8	0.0	0.0	0.0	0.0	0.0	0.0	1.1	23.9	5.6	89.9	7.9	284	253	4
Inver Grove Heights	0.4	0.0	0.0	0.0	0.0	0.0	0.0	0.0	0.2	23.1	3.9	56.1	7.7	264	224	0
Lakeville	0.3	3.6	0.1	0.0	0.0	0.0	0.0	2.4	0.1	31.9	6.4	94.1	7.6	195	163	4
Mankato	0.6	0.3	4.5	2.5	0.0	1.3	0.0	7.3	3.9	39.1	12.0	82.4	11.6	376	267	87
Maple Grove	0.4	7.5	0.2	0.0	0.1	0.0	0.0	0.0	0.3	64.0	5.6	91.3	15.9	339	283	0
Maplewood	0.0	0.0	0.0	0.0	0.0	0.0	0.0	0.0	3.9	34.1	4.6	100.0	9.5	272	242	0
Minneapolis	471.6	142.7	558.0	281.4	18.4	33.3	25.0	82.5	68.6	670.3	171.7	82.6	234.9	668	518	106
Minnetonka	2.9	1.2	1.5	0.4	0.5	0.0	0.0	0.0	2.8	35.9	4.2	92.3	17.3	340	294	6
Moorhead	0.1	0.4	5.5	3.1	0.1	0.1	0.9	6.9	1.5	35.1	13.9	80.6	3.9	119	104	8
Oakdale	0.1	0.4	0.1	0.1	0.0	0.0	0.0	0.0	2.6	19.9	3.3	78.2	6.1	228	204	0
Plymouth	22.3	0.8	0.5	0.0	0.0	0.0	0.0	0.0	1.6	47.7	8.9	80.6	15.1	245	208	0
Richfield	0.0	0.0	0.0	0.0	0.0	0.0	0.0	0.0	3.0	33.8	9.1	78.9	11.3	332	290	11

1. October 1, 2000 to September 30, 2001.   2. Includes program categories not shown separately. State totals include additional categories not allocated by city.   3. Based on population estimated as of July 1 of the year shown.

Table D. Cities — **City Government Finances**

City	City government finances, 1999 (cont'd)												
	General expenditure												
	Per capita[1] (dollars)			Percent of total for —									
	Total (mil dol)	Total	Capital outlays	Public welfare	Highways	Parking facilities	Education	Health and hospitals	Police protection	Sewerage and sanitation	Parks and recreation	Housing and community develop-ment	Interest on debt
	124	125	126	127	128	129	130	131	132	133	134	135	136
MICHIGAN—Cont'd													
Battle Creek	75.9	1 420	203	0.0	13.8	0.9	0.0	0.0	17.9	9.8	5.0	0.0	8.0
Bay City	35.2	992	110	0.0	15.5	0.0	0.0	0.0	18.3	18.9	3.0	0.0	4.3
Burton	NA	NA	NA	NA	NA	NA	NA	NA	NA	NA	NA	NA	NA
Dearborn	127.9	1 395	211	0.7	11.2	0.0	0.0	0.4	14.3	12.3	6.7	2.5	4.5
Dearborn Heights	49.6	829	120	0.0	9.8	0.0	0.0	0.0	18.1	28.2	2.1	0.0	1.4
Detroit	3 475.1	3 582	427	0.0	5.0	0.5	42.5	3.0	8.5	9.6	3.1	5.0	4.4
East Lansing	NA	NA	NA	NA	NA	NA	NA	NA	NA	NA	NA	NA	NA
Eastpointe	NA	NA	NA	NA	NA	NA	NA	NA	NA	NA	NA	NA	NA
Farmington Hills	55.1	690	109	0.0	17.0	0.0	0.0	0.0	21.2	5.1	8.7	0.0	3.1
Flint	426.6	3 240	259	0.0	2.6	0.0	0.0	63.8	7.5	5.4	2.2	1.8	2.0
Garden City	24.9	760	65	0.0	14.0	0.0	0.0	0.0	14.9	24.7	4.0	0.0	12.9
Grand Rapids	209.2	1 128	101	0.0	9.1	2.8	0.0	0.0	16.4	17.6	4.1	2.7	6.9
Holland	35.1	1 056	219	0.9	22.7	0.0	0.0	0.0	12.2	18.6	10.5	0.0	1.5
Inkster	NA	NA	NA	NA	NA	NA	NA	NA	NA	NA	NA	NA	NA
Jackson	NA	NA	NA	NA	NA	NA	NA	NA	NA	NA	NA	NA	NA
Kalamazoo	106.8	1 401	150	0.1	8.8	0.0	0.0	0.0	23.0	22.2	2.3	0.0	23.0
Kentwood	20.2	478	48	0.0	16.0	0.0	0.1	0.0	24.0	8.9	4.6	0.0	0.1
Lansing	201.7	1 578	376	0.8	4.8	1.8	0.0	0.0	9.0	12.7	7.1	0.2	9.7
Lincoln Park	31.4	742	32	1.0	13.1	0.1	0.0	0.0	21.5	19.9	4.1	4.7	0.6
Livonia	93.0	917	156	0.0	11.6	0.0	0.0	0.0	17.7	24.1	4.3	0.6	4.1
Madison Heights	NA	NA	NA	NA	NA	NA	NA	NA	NA	NA	NA	NA	NA
Midland	43.6	1 091	151	0.0	16.6	0.1	0.0	0.0	9.0	19.0	7.0	4.7	1.4
Mount Pleasant	16.7	715	72	0.0	11.4	0.6	0.0	0.0	16.4	13.1	5.1	0.0	5.3
Muskegon	40.0	1 026	182	0.0	19.5	0.0	0.0	0.0	16.7	16.2	4.4	0.5	3.1
Novi	48.8	1 090	280	0.0	10.0	0.0	0.0	0.0	14.8	31.1	3.9	0.0	9.6
Oak Park	27.2	919	12	0.3	9.1	0.0	0.0	0.0	27.4	21.7	4.2	0.0	7.5
Pontiac	108.0	1 567	123	0.0	4.7	1.3	0.0	0.1	17.1	7.1	9.0	3.1	6.3
Portage	35.1	803	117	1.8	17.6	0.0	0.0	0.0	18.4	14.9	4.4	0.0	7.1
Port Huron	44.8	1 389	393	0.1	10.2	0.3	0.0	0.0	12.9	26.6	5.9	8.3	0.2
Rochester Hills	57.4	851	83	0.0	10.1	0.0	0.0	0.0	16.8	34.9	3.2	0.0	3.6
Roseville	40.2	782	50	0.0	12.2	0.0	0.0	0.0	20.5	28.0	3.1	1.0	1.4
Royal Oak	60.8	945	213	0.0	7.2	1.3	0.0	0.7	13.1	18.6	5.8	1.6	3.1
Saginaw	82.8	1 305	171	0.3	11.4	0.7	0.0	0.0	17.7	17.4	5.0	16.7	7.8
St. Clair Shores	54.3	821	146	0.0	10.9	0.0	0.0	0.0	16.8	29.1	7.6	0.0	2.3
Southfield	105.6	1 406	248	0.4	16.9	3.5	0.0	0.0	14.3	20.7	6.5	1.4	1.2
Southgate	NA	NA	NA	NA	NA	NA	NA	NA	NA	NA	NA	NA	NA
Sterling Heights	82.2	661	98	0.0	10.4	0.0	0.0	0.0	21.2	10.1	2.1	0.9	2.4
Taylor	122.3	1 686	731	0.3	8.7	0.0	0.0	0.0	7.1	9.1	5.1	15.1	1.6
Troy	73.4	926	148	0.0	11.7	0.0	0.0	0.0	24.0	13.5	7.3	0.0	0.6
Warren	125.6	881	83	0.0	9.2	0.0	0.0	0.0	20.1	22.6	3.5	1.2	3.0
Westland	72.5	840	133	0.8	14.5	0.0	0.0	0.0	15.3	29.8	3.8	0.7	1.7
Wyandotte	38.5	1 207	0	0.8	6.6	3.9	0.0	0.0	9.7	15.3	2.6	0.0	14.5
Wyoming	58.9	857	278	0.0	15.5	0.0	0.0	0.0	24.8	21.8	4.3	3.7	2.0
MINNESOTA	X	X	X	X	X	X	X	X	X	X	X	X	X
Andover	9.2	385	11	0.0	10.0	0.0	0.0	0.1	7.8	11.9	4.6	0.0	34.4
Apple Valley	31.4	691	291	0.0	29.3	0.0	0.0	0.1	14.6	4.0	27.3	0.0	9.1
Blaine	28.3	629	214	0.0	3.3	0.0	0.0	0.0	12.4	20.3	6.8	12.4	12.1
Bloomington	77.3	897	186	0.0	19.4	0.0	0.0	7.5	14.4	16.9	11.4	1.2	4.9
Brooklyn Center	33.1	1 189	366	0.0	13.4	0.0	0.0	0.0	17.0	15.9	8.0	0.0	12.5
Brooklyn Park	48.8	773	261	0.0	27.1	0.0	0.0	0.0	16.2	10.5	21.1	1.8	7.3
Burnsville	59.2	998	146	0.0	15.3	0.0	0.0	0.1	11.2	6.4	6.2	0.0	34.5
Coon Rapids	44.6	700	182	0.0	6.8	0.0	0.0	0.5	10.7	10.6	13.4	3.4	22.4
Cottage Grove	23.0	737	160	0.0	36.7	0.0	0.0	2.5	13.2	6.4	11.5	0.0	5.0
Duluth	144.2	1 775	238	0.0	16.5	0.4	0.0	0.0	8.8	10.8	11.7	2.8	8.5
Eagan	41.7	694	193	0.0	9.2	0.0	0.0	0.0	14.4	10.4	9.5	2.9	15.9
Eden Prairie	39.1	778	121	0.0	11.2	0.0	0.0	0.0	11.5	13.1	11.3	1.8	28.3
Edina	44.3	966	184	1.1	12.8	0.0	0.0	0.4	8.5	11.0	17.9	7.9	12.6
Fridley	21.5	770	188	0.0	28.9	0.0	0.0	0.0	15.4	19.7	5.9	1.8	6.6
Inver Grove Heights	19.4	662	141	0.0	26.2	0.0	0.0	0.0	14.6	8.4	14.1	0.0	14.8
Lakeville	22.8	583	185	0.0	20.8	0.0	0.0	0.1	16.9	24.0	10.7	2.6	7.0
Mankato	55.8	1 813	780	0.0	15.3	0.5	0.0	0.0	6.5	25.7	9.8	10.5	6.6
Maple Grove	48.6	1 035	407	0.0	31.0	0.0	0.0	0.0	8.4	9.3	11.0	1.9	11.8
Maplewood	31.7	905	85	0.0	5.8	0.0	0.0	2.5	13.8	15.5	5.0	0.0	30.0
Minneapolis	631.4	1 795	304	0.0	5.8	4.5	0.0	1.7	14.0	11.3	10.8	6.7	18.0
Minnetonka	32.4	635	164	0.0	17.5	0.0	0.0	0.5	16.3	14.3	14.4	4.5	8.0
Moorhead	38.5	1 165	377	0.0	11.7	0.5	0.0	0.8	11.8	17.6	10.6	14.8	10.6
Oakdale	16.4	616	191	0.0	3.4	0.0	0.0	1.0	15.0	12.0	5.9	0.0	15.1
Plymouth	45.9	747	188	0.0	5.9	0.0	0.0	0.0	10.9	12.9	8.3	0.7	11.9
Richfield	34.5	1 012	162	0.0	11.9	0.0	0.0	0.4	15.1	10.8	14.7	17.9	8.4

1. Based on population estimated as of July 1 of the year shown.

City	City government finances, 1999 (cont'd) Debt outstanding			City government employment, 2001	Climate[2] Average daily temperature (degrees Fahrenheit)						
	Total (mil dol)	Per capita[1] (dollars)	Percent utility		Mean		Limits		Annual precipitation (inches)	Heating degree days	Cooling degree days
					January	July	January[3]	July[4]			
	137	138	139	140	141	142	143	144	145	146	147
MICHIGAN—Cont'd											
Battle Creek	118.7	2 219	15.0	674	22.5	71.7	14.9	83.2	35.70	6 677	575
Bay City	46.7	1 317	44.2	438	22.0	72.2	14.7	84.1	29.51	6 763	599
Burton	NA	NA	NA	NA	21.5	70.6	14.2	81.5	30.28	6 979	483
Dearborn	162.3	1 771	0.0	1 240	22.9	72.9	15.5	83.8	32.71	6 500	677
Dearborn Heights	13.5	226	0.0	NA	22.9	72.9	15.5	83.8	32.71	6 500	677
Detroit	3 258.6	3 359	20.8	35 851	24.7	74.2	18.7	83.3	32.09	6 167	805
East Lansing	NA	NA	NA	NA	20.1	70.5	12.4	81.9	29.68	7 228	458
Eastpointe	NA	NA	NA	NA	24.7	74.2	18.7	83.3	32.09	6 167	805
Farmington Hills	33.3	417	0.0	495	22.2	72.4	14.8	83.8	30.56	6 653	647
Flint	147.6	1 121	0.7	4 030	21.5	70.6	14.2	81.5	30.28	6 979	483
Garden City	75.8	2 314	0.0	NA	22.9	72.9	15.5	83.8	32.71	6 500	677
Grand Rapids	436.0	2 351	33.7	2 211	21.8	71.6	14.7	82.8	36.04	6 973	534
Holland	44.6	1 341	77.7	481	23.3	70.8	16.8	81.9	36.25	6 747	529
Inkster	NA	NA	NA	NA	22.9	72.3	15.6	83.3	32.62	6 569	626
Jackson	NA	NA	NA	NA	21.5	72.2	14.3	83.2	29.73	6 791	621
Kalamazoo	440.6	5 778	2.9	1 004	23.7	73.5	16.4	84.9	37.03	6 230	764
Kentwood	1.1	27	74.5	NA	21.8	71.6	14.7	82.8	36.04	6 973	534
Lansing	338.0	2 644	8.5	2 069	20.9	70.8	13.3	82.6	30.62	7 101	490
Lincoln Park	6.6	156	45.1	NA	22.9	72.9	15.5	83.8	32.71	6 500	677
Livonia	66.2	654	6.8	757	22.9	72.9	15.5	83.8	32.71	6 500	677
Madison Heights	NA	NA	NA	NA	24.7	74.2	18.7	83.3	32.09	6 167	805
Midland	33.0	825	42.3	423	22.0	72.2	14.7	84.1	29.51	6 763	599
Mount Pleasant	26.1	1 117	30.6	NA	NA	NA	NA	NA	NA	NA	NA
Muskegon	23.0	589	21.7	NA	23.3	70.3	17.7	80.3	32.56	6 924	431
Novi	83.3	1 862	0.0	NA	21.0	71.0	13.6	81.4	29.95	7 064	515
Oak Park	34.8	1 176	11.2	NA	24.7	74.2	18.7	83.3	32.09	6 167	805
Pontiac	136.2	1 976	2.4	2 309	22.2	72.4	14.8	83.8	30.56	6 653	647
Portage	49.0	1 120	1.3	NA	23.7	73.5	16.4	84.9	37.03	6 230	764
Port Huron	28.1	871	35.6	400	22.4	71.7	15.4	81.5	30.34	6 898	544
Rochester Hills	39.1	580	0.0	255	22.2	72.4	14.8	83.8	30.56	6 653	647
Roseville	9.7	188	0.0	NA	24.7	74.2	18.7	83.3	32.09	6 167	805
Royal Oak	38.5	598	0.0	446	24.7	74.2	18.7	83.3	32.09	6 167	805
Saginaw	192.8	3 037	5.7	728	22.7	73.0	15.7	84.4	30.89	6 538	675
St. Clair Shores	22.4	338	0.0	NA	24.7	73.5	17.4	83.7	33.23	6 185	737
Southfield	21.9	291	0.0	848	22.2	72.4	14.8	83.8	30.56	6 653	647
Southgate	NA	NA	NA	NA	22.9	72.3	15.6	83.3	32.62	6 569	626
Sterling Heights	38.3	308	0.0	676	23.1	71.3	16.7	81.3	31.36	6 777	526
Taylor	56.2	774	0.0	636	22.9	72.3	15.6	83.3	32.62	6 569	626
Troy	5.7	72	0.0	534	22.2	72.4	14.8	83.8	30.56	6 653	647
Warren	63.8	448	0.0	1 046	24.7	74.2	18.7	83.3	32.09	6 167	805
Westland	21.5	249	0.0	425	22.9	72.3	15.6	83.3	32.62	6 569	626
Wyandotte	139.2	4 367	42.6	NA	22.9	72.9	15.5	83.8	32.71	6 500	677
Wyoming	47.0	685	12.8	495	21.8	71.6	14.7	82.8	36.04	6 973	534
MINNESOTA	X	X	X	X	X	X	X	X	X	X	X
Andover	48.5	2 028	0.0	NA	NA	NA	NA	NA	NA	NA	NA
Apple Valley	59.3	1 306	2.1	200	11.3	72.4	0.9	84.5	32.42	8 048	590
Blaine	60.7	1 351	1.9	NA	11.8	73.6	2.8	84.0	28.32	7 981	682
Bloomington	81.6	946	0.0	572	11.8	73.6	2.8	84.0	28.32	7 981	682
Brooklyn Center	73.7	2 645	0.0	NA	11.8	73.6	2.8	84.0	28.32	7 981	682
Brooklyn Park	64.2	1 016	11.1	490	11.8	73.6	2.8	84.0	28.32	7 981	682
Burnsville	297.2	5 009	0.0	290	11.8	73.6	2.8	84.0	28.32	7 981	682
Coon Rapids	171.0	2 685	6.3	232	11.8	73.6	2.8	84.0	28.32	7 981	682
Cottage Grove	28.4	907	8.9	NA	NA	NA	NA	NA	NA	NA	NA
Duluth	250.4	3 082	0.0	1 156	7.0	66.1	-2.2	77.1	30.00	9 818	180
Eagan	119.1	1 984	14.1	249	11.8	73.6	2.8	84.0	28.32	7 981	682
Eden Prairie	164.1	3 264	14.5	285	11.8	73.6	2.8	84.0	28.32	7 981	682
Edina	83.4	1 817	0.2	283	11.8	73.6	2.8	84.0	28.32	7 981	682
Fridley	29.0	1 036	19.4	167	11.8	73.6	2.8	84.0	28.32	7 981	682
Inver Grove Heights	48.0	1 638	17.2	NA	NA	NA	NA	NA	NA	NA	NA
Lakeville	39.2	1 000	39.6	250	NA	NA	NA	NA	NA	NA	NA
Mankato	79.9	2 597	2.5	250	11.7	73.1	1.2	84.7	29.51	8 005	670
Maple Grove	82.4	1 756	4.2	261	11.8	73.6	2.8	84.0	28.32	7 981	682
Maplewood	128.9	3 686	0.0	337	11.8	73.6	2.8	84.0	28.32	7 981	682
Minneapolis	1 744.5	4 960	2.7	5 827	11.8	73.6	2.8	84.0	28.32	7 981	682
Minnetonka	18.7	368	0.0	225	11.8	73.6	2.8	84.0	28.32	7 981	682
Moorhead	100.5	3 038	38.8	331	5.9	71.1	-3.6	83.4	19.45	9 254	537
Oakdale	32.3	1 210	0.0	NA	NA	NA	NA	NA	NA	NA	NA
Plymouth	82.5	1 341	2.7	284	11.8	73.6	2.8	84.0	28.32	7 981	682
Richfield	44.6	1 309	0.0	347	11.8	73.6	2.8	84.0	28.32	7 981	682

1. Based on the population estimated as of July 1 of the year shown.   2. Represents normal values based on the 30-year period, 1961–1990.   3. Average daily minimum.   4. Average daily maximum.

Table D. Cities — **Land Area and Population**

STATE Place code / City	Land area, 2000¹ (sq km)	Population 2000: Total persons	Rank	Per square kilometer	Total persons 1990	Percent change 1990–2000	Total persons 1980	Percent change 1980–1990	White	Black	Am. Indian, Alaska Native	Asian and Pacific Islander	Other race	His-panic²	Non-His-panic White
	1	2	3	4	5	6	7	8	9	10	11	12	13	14	15
MINNESOTA—Cont'd															
27 54880 Rochester	102.6	85 806	292	836.3	70 729	21.3	57 890	22.2	88.7	4.3	0.6	6.4	1.9	3.0	85.8
27 55852 Roseville	34.3	33 690	936	982.2	33 485	0.6	35 820	-6.5	90.9	3.5	0.7	5.6	1.1	2.0	88.5
27 56896 St. Cloud	78.1	59 107	476	756.8	48 812	21.1	42 566	14.7	92.9	2.9	1.2	3.6	0.8	1.3	91.1
27 57220 St. Louis Park	27.7	44 126	695	1 593.0	43 787	0.8	42 931	2.0	90.3	5.2	0.9	3.8	1.7	2.9	87.5
27 58000 St. Paul	136.7	287 151	59	2 100.6	272 235	5.5	270 230	0.7	69.6	13.4	2.1	13.9	5.2	7.9	64.0
27 59998 Shoreview	29.0	25 924	1 200	893.9	24 587	5.4	17 300	42.1	94.5	1.2	0.6	4.3	0.8	1.3	92.5
27 71032 Winona	47.2	27 069	1 143	573.5	25 435	6.4	25 075	1.4	95.3	1.3	0.6	3.2	0.8	1.3	93.7
27 71428 Woodbury	90.6	46 463	655	512.8	20 075	131.4	10 297	95.0	91.4	3.1	0.6	5.7	0.9	2.1	88.8
28 00000 **MISSISSIPPI**	121 488.5	2 844 658	X	23.4	2 575 475	10.5	2 520 770	2.2	61.9	36.6	0.7	0.9	0.7	1.4	60.7
28 06220 Biloxi	98.5	50 644	590	514.2	46 319	9.3	49 311	-6.1	73.4	19.8	1.1	6.3	2.0	3.6	69.7
28 15380 Columbus	55.5	25 944	1 199	467.5	23 799	9.0	27 383	-13.1	44.1	54.9	0.3	0.9	0.7	1.1	43.3
28 29180 Greenville	69.6	41 633	736	598.2	45 226	-7.9	40 613	11.4	29.2	69.9	0.2	1.0	0.3	0.7	28.7
28 29700 Gulfport	147.4	71 127	376	482.5	64 045	11.1	39 676	61.4	63.5	34.1	1.0	1.9	1.3	2.6	60.9
28 31020 Hattiesburg	127.6	44 779	685	350.9	45 325	-1.2	40 829	11.0	50.6	47.7	0.4	1.5	0.7	1.4	49.3
28 36000 Jackson	271.7	184 256	109	678.2	202 062	-8.8	202 893	-0.4	28.2	71.1	0.4	0.8	0.3	0.8	27.5
28 46640 Meridian	116.9	39 968	775	341.9	41 036	-2.6	46 577	-11.9	44.4	54.7	0.4	0.8	0.4	1.1	43.5
28 55360 Pascagoula	39.3	26 200	1 187	666.7	25 899	1.2	29 318	-11.7	68.0	29.3	0.5	1.3	2.0	3.9	65.2
28 69280 Southaven	87.5	28 977	1 072	331.2	18 705	61.4	16 071	11.7	91.0	6.8	0.6	1.0	1.4	2.3	89.3
28 74840 Tupelo	132.4	34 211	916	258.4	30 685	11.5	23 905	28.4	70.1	28.7	0.3	1.0	0.7	1.4	68.7
28 76720 Vicksburg	85.2	26 407	1 172	309.9	26 886	-1.8	25 434	5.7	38.1	60.8	0.4	0.7	0.6	1.0	37.4
29 00000 **MISSOURI**	178 413.7	5 595 211	X	31.4	5 116 901	9.3	4 916 766	4.1	86.1	11.7	1.1	1.5	1.2	2.1	83.8
29 03160 Ballwin	23.2	31 283	1 001	1 348.4	27 054	46.1	12 656	69.1	94.4	1.7	0.5	3.8	0.8	1.9	92.2
29 06652 Blue Springs	47.1	48 080	629	1 020.8	40 103	19.9	25 927	54.7	94.6	3.4	1.0	1.4	1.2	2.8	91.6
29 11242 Cape Girardeau	62.9	35 349	882	562.0	34 475	2.5	34 361	0.3	88.5	9.9	0.9	1.5	0.6	1.1	86.7
29 13600 Chesterfield	81.6	46 802	649	573.6	42 325	10.6	NA	NA	92.0	2.0	0.3	5.9	0.5	1.6	90.1
29 15670 Columbia	137.4	84 531	300	615.2	69 133	22.3	62 061	11.4	83.3	11.7	0.9	4.9	1.3	2.1	80.4
29 24778 Florissant	29.4	50 497	593	1 717.6	51 038	-1.1	55 372	-7.8	86.9	12.2	0.6	1.0	0.9	1.5	84.8
29 27190 Gladstone	20.7	26 365	1 174	1 273.7	26 243	0.5	24 990	5.0	94.7	2.4	1.1	1.8	1.7	3.6	91.1
29 31276 Hazelwood	41.1	26 206	1 185	637.6	15 512	68.9	12 935	19.9	81.7	16.8	0.7	1.7	0.9	1.6	79.3
29 35000 Independence	202.9	113 288	198	558.3	112 301	0.9	111 806	0.4	94.0	3.2	1.6	1.6	2.0	3.7	90.1
29 37000 Jefferson City	70.6	39 636	782	561.4	35 517	11.6	33 618	5.6	82.7	15.4	1.0	1.7	0.9	1.6	80.7
29 37592 Joplin	81.4	45 504	671	559.0	41 175	11.3	38 869	5.1	93.9	3.3	3.0	1.1	1.4	2.5	90.2
29 38000 Kansas City	812.1	441 545	36	543.7	434 829	1.5	448 154	-3.0	62.5	32.3	1.2	2.5	4.1	6.9	57.6
29 39044 Kirkwood	23.9	27 324	1 134	1 143.3	28 318	-3.5	27 987	1.2	91.6	7.5	0.4	1.1	0.4	1.1	90.0
29 41348 Lee's Summit	154.1	70 700	379	458.8	46 418	52.3	28 742	61.5	94.5	3.9	0.8	1.4	0.9	2.0	91.9
29 42032 Liberty	69.8	26 232	1 181	375.8	20 459	28.2	16 217	26.2	95.3	3.0	1.1	1.0	1.4	2.7	92.4
29 46586 Maryland Heights	55.4	25 756	1 207	464.9	25 440	1.2	NA	NA	86.2	5.9	0.5	7.6	0.9	2.3	83.8
29 54074 O'Fallon	58.2	46 169	660	793.3	17 427	164.9	NA	NA	96.3	2.6	0.6	1.1	0.6	1.5	94.4
29 60788 Raytown	25.7	30 388	1 023	1 182.4	30 601	-0.7	31 759	-3.6	85.8	12.4	1.1	1.3	1.3	2.3	83.0
29 64082 St. Charles	52.7	60 321	461	1 144.6	50 634	19.1	37 379	35.5	94.4	3.9	0.7	1.4	1.0	2.0	92.1
29 64550 St. Joseph	113.5	73 990	360	651.9	71 852	3.0	76 691	-6.3	93.2	5.7	0.9	0.8	1.0	2.6	90.2
29 65000 St. Louis	160.4	348 189	49	2 170.8	396 685	-12.2	453 085	-12.4	45.2	52.1	0.8	2.4	1.5	2.0	42.9
29 65126 St. Peters	54.9	51 381	583	935.9	40 660	26.4	15 700	159.0	95.2	3.1	0.5	1.6	0.7	1.5	93.3
29 70000 Springfield	189.5	151 580	132	799.9	140 494	7.9	133 116	5.5	93.5	3.9	1.7	1.9	1.2	2.3	90.5
29 75220 University City	15.2	37 428	831	2 462.4	40 087	-6.6	42 738	-6.2	50.6	46.4	0.6	3.4	0.9	1.6	48.4
29 79820 Wildwood	171.0	32 884	953	192.3	16 527	99.0	NA	NA	95.5	1.8	0.4	2.7	0.5	1.4	93.8
30 00000 **MONTANA**	376 979.1	902 195	X	2.4	799 065	12.9	786 690	1.6	92.2	0.5	7.4	0.9	0.9	2.0	89.5
30 06550 Billings	87.3	89 847	275	1 029.2	81 125	10.8	66 798	21.4	93.7	0.9	4.5	1.0	1.9	4.2	89.9
30 08950 Bozeman	32.6	27 509	1 122	843.8	22 660	21.4	21 645	4.7	96.1	0.5	1.9	2.3	0.9	1.6	93.8
30 11390 Butte-Silver Bow	1 860.4	34 606	909	18.6	33 252	2.0	NA	NA	96.7	0.3	3.0	0.8	0.8	2.7	93.7
30 32800 Great Falls	50.5	56 690	506	1 122.6	55 125	2.8	56 725	-2.8	92.2	1.4	6.6	1.6	0.9	2.4	88.7
30 35600 Helena	36.3	25 780	1 206	710.2	24 609	4.8	23 938	2.8	96.4	0.4	3.0	1.2	0.7	1.7	93.8
30 50200 Missoula	61.6	57 053	502	926.2	42 918	32.9	33 387	28.5	95.3	0.6	3.4	1.8	0.8	1.8	92.6
31 00000 **NEBRASKA**	199 098.6	1 711 263	X	8.6	1 578 417	8.4	1 569 825	0.5	90.8	4.4	1.3	1.7	3.3	5.5	87.3
31 03950 Bellevue	34.4	44 382	691	1 290.2	39 240	13.1	21 813	79.9	88.0	7.0	1.1	3.2	3.4	5.9	83.2
31 17670 Fremont	19.2	25 174	1 231	1 311.1	23 680	6.3	23 979	-1.2	96.0	0.7	0.7	1.0	2.6	4.3	93.6
31 19595 Grand Island	55.6	42 940	713	772.3	39 487	8.7	33 180	19.0	88.0	0.6	0.6	1.7	10.5	15.9	81.4
31 25055 Kearney	28.4	27 431	1 126	965.9	24 396	12.4	21 158	15.3	96.2	1.0	0.7	1.3	2.1	4.1	93.1
31 28000 Lincoln	193.3	225 581	76	1 167.0	191 972	17.5	171 932	11.7	91.0	3.8	1.2	3.6	2.4	3.6	87.8
31 37000 Omaha	299.7	390 007	44	1 301.3	344 463	13.8	314 267	9.1	80.0	14.2	1.2	2.2	4.5	7.5	75.4
32 00000 **NEVADA**	284 448.0	1 998 257	X	7.0	1 201 675	66.3	800 508	50.1	78.4	7.5	2.1	6.4	9.7	19.7	65.2
32 09700 Carson City	371.3	52 457	570	141.3	40 443	29.7	32 022	26.3	87.2	2.1	3.3	2.5	7.2	14.2	78.5
32 31900 Henderson	206.4	175 381	116	849.7	64 948	170.0	NA	NA	87.5	4.4	1.4	6.2	4.4	10.7	78.2
32 40000 Las Vegas	293.5	478 434	32	1 630.1	258 877	85.3	164 674	56.8	73.2	11.3	1.5	6.9	11.6	23.6	58.0
32 51800 North Las Vegas	203.3	115 488	194	568.1	47 849	141.4	42 739	12.0	59.8	20.2	1.5	5.4	18.2	37.6	37.1

1. Dry land or land partially or temporarily covered by water.   2. Hispanic persons may be of any race.

Table D. Cities — Population and Households

	Population characteristics, 2000 (cont'd)										Households, 2000				
	Age of population (percent)													Percent	
City	Under 5 years	5 to 17 years	18 to 24 years	25 to 34 years	35 to 44 years	45 to 54 years	55 to 64 years	65 to 74 years	75 years and over	Percent female	Number	Percent change, 1990–2000	Persons per house-hold	Female family house-holder[1]	One-person
	16	17	18	19	20	21	22	23	24	25	26	27	28	29	30
MINNESOTA—Cont'd															
Rochester	7.5	18.3	9.1	16.2	17.2	12.5	7.7	5.5	6.0	51.4	34 116	22.2	2.43	8.5	29.7
Roseville	4.6	13.7	11.1	12.4	14.4	13.3	10.4	9.2	11.0	53.5	14 598	7.6	2.20	7.2	33.6
St. Cloud	5.5	15.2	24.1	14.2	13.4	11.1	6.2	5.2	5.1	49.6	22 652	26.4	2.40	9.4	30.2
St. Louis Park	6.0	12.7	8.7	21.2	16.5	12.8	7.4	6.1	8.6	52.5	20 782	4.3	2.08	8.6	37.9
St. Paul	7.6	19.5	12.5	16.8	15.3	11.9	6.2	4.6	5.7	51.6	112 109	1.7	2.46	13.9	35.9
Shoreview	5.5	20.6	6.9	10.3	18.2	18.8	9.9	5.9	3.8	51.5	10 125	12.6	2.54	7.9	24.1
Winona	4.5	13.5	27.5	10.5	11.7	11.0	7.0	5.8	8.4	53.0	10 301	10.4	2.27	8.4	35.2
Woodbury	9.6	21.0	5.9	16.8	20.2	13.8	6.6	3.6	2.5	51.5	16 676	140.7	2.76	6.9	18.8
MISSISSIPPI	7.2	20.1	10.9	13.4	15.0	12.7	8.6	6.5	5.5	51.7	1 046 434	14.8	2.63	17.3	24.6
Biloxi	7.3	16.9	14.3	15.1	15.2	11.5	7.7	6.7	5.3	49.5	19 588	17.7	2.42	14.0	30.1
Columbus	7.1	18.9	12.0	13.5	13.1	11.7	8.1	7.3	8.2	54.8	10 062	10.1	2.42	21.7	31.3
Greenville	8.6	22.8	10.1	12.6	13.6	12.6	7.8	6.0	5.8	53.9	14 784	-3.5	2.77	27.7	25.8
Gulfport	7.1	18.9	11.1	14.8	15.6	12.7	8.3	6.5	4.9	50.4	26 943	70.6	2.51	18.2	27.7
Hattiesburg	6.7	14.8	24.4	15.0	11.3	9.6	6.3	5.5	6.3	54.0	17 295	8.7	2.29	19.4	34.4
Jackson	7.8	20.7	12.4	14.5	14.6	12.1	7.0	5.5	5.4	53.5	67 841	-5.6	2.61	25.3	28.9
Meridian	7.6	19.6	9.9	13.3	13.3	11.8	8.0	7.8	8.7	54.3	15 966	-1.3	2.39	23.3	33.2
Pascagoula	7.8	19.0	12.0	14.2	14.7	12.0	8.3	6.5	5.4	49.6	9 878	1.1	2.52	18.8	27.0
Southaven	7.6	19.6	9.0	16.7	15.8	12.9	9.7	5.5	3.4	51.2	11 007	80.0	2.62	12.4	21.3
Tupelo	7.5	20.0	8.1	14.5	16.0	12.8	8.7	6.1	6.3	53.0	13 395	14.4	2.47	16.2	28.0
Vicksburg	7.9	20.4	9.3	13.3	14.6	12.0	7.6	6.9	7.9	54.7	10 364	25.4	2.49	24.2	32.0
MISSOURI	6.6	18.9	9.6	13.2	15.9	13.3	9.1	7.0	6.5	51.4	2 194 594	11.9	2.48	11.6	27.3
Ballwin	7.3	19.8	6.4	12.1	17.8	14.8	9.7	7.6	4.6	51.5	11 797	50.3	2.65	8.0	20.6
Blue Springs	7.4	22.1	8.7	14.8	17.2	15.1	7.7	3.9	3.2	51.1	17 286	27.8	2.77	10.5	18.1
Cape Girardeau	5.4	15.2	18.4	12.7	12.9	12.2	7.7	6.9	8.6	52.8	14 380	7.0	2.24	10.9	33.6
Chesterfield	5.6	19.1	5.9	8.9	16.2	18.0	11.7	7.3	7.4	52.2	18 060	37.7	2.53	5.4	23.6
Columbia	5.8	14.0	26.7	15.9	12.8	10.5	5.8	4.1	4.5	52.1	33 689	30.4	2.26	10.3	33.1
Florissant	6.5	18.1	8.2	13.5	16.5	11.7	8.4	9.0	8.1	52.8	20 399	6.4	2.44	13.2	28.8
Gladstone	5.4	15.6	8.6	13.1	15.1	15.3	11.1	8.8	7.0	51.9	11 484	9.0	2.27	10.3	29.9
Hazelwood	6.1	18.5	9.7	14.8	16.9	13.6	8.8	6.6	5.0	52.0	10 954	72.4	2.38	12.7	32.1
Independence	6.6	17.3	8.7	13.2	15.7	13.4	9.6	8.1	7.4	52.2	47 390	4.6	2.37	12.3	30.1
Jefferson City	5.8	15.0	11.0	15.6	16.4	14.2	7.8	6.7	7.3	48.7	15 794	11.5	2.21	10.8	36.1
Joplin	7.1	16.1	13.5	13.6	13.7	12.1	8.2	7.4	8.3	52.5	19 101	9.3	2.28	12.3	32.4
Kansas City	7.2	18.2	9.7	16.4	16.1	12.8	7.9	6.2	5.6	51.7	183 981	3.6	2.35	16.0	34.1
Kirkwood	6.0	17.4	5.9	11.9	15.7	15.7	9.2	8.1	10.1	54.3	11 763	4.9	2.29	9.0	33.5
Lee's Summit	8.0	21.1	6.6	14.1	19.0	13.6	7.3	4.7	5.6	52.1	26 417	49.8	2.65	8.9	22.0
Liberty	6.7	20.9	10.4	13.4	16.8	13.7	7.7	5.2	5.2	52.1	9 511	32.6	2.62	10.9	22.4
Maryland Heights	5.9	15.6	9.8	20.2	17.1	12.9	9.1	5.6	3.9	50.6	11 302	6.0	2.25	9.5	33.8
O'Fallon	10.5	22.9	6.4	18.6	20.2	9.7	5.6	3.8	2.3	50.7	15 389	141.1	2.98	8.6	14.1
Raytown	5.8	16.7	7.8	12.4	15.6	13.3	9.2	9.5	9.8	53.0	12 855	1.2	2.32	12.6	30.3
St. Charles	6.2	17.1	12.0	14.1	16.4	13.3	8.7	6.4	5.8	50.9	24 210	11.7	2.38	10.2	29.6
St. Joseph	6.4	17.7	11.6	13.4	15.1	12.2	8.1	7.2	8.2	51.1	29 026	2.2	2.39	12.8	30.4
St. Louis	6.7	19.0	10.6	15.6	15.3	11.8	7.2	6.6	7.1	53.0	147 076	-10.8	2.30	21.3	40.3
St. Peters	7.4	22.5	7.4	13.9	19.7	14.5	6.7	4.4	3.4	51.3	18 435	21.1	2.78	9.7	20.3
Springfield	5.9	14.0	17.4	14.5	13.5	11.8	7.9	7.0	7.9	51.8	64 691	12.8	2.17	10.9	35.3
University City	6.1	15.7	11.3	16.4	14.8	13.1	9.4	6.8	6.5	54.3	16 453	-0.6	2.25	16.3	34.2
Wildwood	8.2	25.0	4.8	10.0	21.5	17.6	7.6	3.4	2.1	50.8	10 837	NA	3.02	4.6	12.4
MONTANA	6.1	19.4	9.5	11.4	15.7	15.0	9.4	6.9	6.5	50.2	358 667	17.1	2.45	8.9	27.4
Billings	6.5	17.5	10.1	13.2	15.5	13.7	8.6	7.2	7.7	51.9	37 525	13.1	2.32	10.8	31.3
Bozeman	5.0	11.1	33.0	17.1	11.5	10.1	4.3	3.2	4.8	47.4	10 877	24.3	2.26	7.3	30.4
Butte-Silver Bow	5.8	17.9	9.6	11.2	15.4	14.2	9.8	7.7	8.3	50.6	14 432	3.8	2.32	10.5	32.8
Great Falls	6.4	18.5	9.0	12.0	15.8	13.2	9.5	7.7	8.0	51.5	23 834	5.3	2.31	11.1	31.9
Helena	5.8	16.6	11.1	11.4	15.2	16.7	9.3	6.4	7.5	52.4	11 541	10.7	2.14	10.4	37.5
Missoula	5.3	14.4	20.7	15.7	13.7	13.1	6.6	4.7	5.6	50.3	24 141	36.6	2.23	10.0	33.6
NEBRASKA	6.8	19.5	10.2	13.0	15.4	13.2	8.3	6.8	6.8	50.7	666 184	10.6	2.49	9.1	27.6
Bellevue	7.1	20.3	10.2	14.7	16.3	12.7	9.0	6.0	3.5	50.4	16 937	48.2	2.61	11.3	23.2
Fremont	6.3	17.9	11.0	11.9	14.8	12.3	8.4	8.4	9.1	52.4	10 171	7.9	2.38	9.4	29.1
Grand Island	7.8	19.1	9.5	13.8	14.9	12.9	7.8	6.9	7.3	50.5	16 426	7.8	2.55	10.4	27.1
Kearney	6.7	15.5	23.9	13.9	12.3	11.1	6.0	4.7	6.0	51.9	10 549	17.6	2.37	9.7	28.7
Lincoln	6.7	16.3	16.4	15.9	14.8	12.6	6.9	5.2	5.2	50.2	90 485	20.0	2.36	9.5	30.4
Omaha	7.2	18.4	11.0	15.5	15.4	12.9	7.8	6.1	5.7	51.3	156 738	17.1	2.42	13.0	31.9
NEVADA	7.3	18.3	9.0	15.3	16.1	13.5	9.5	6.6	4.4	49.1	751 165	61.1	2.62	11.1	24.9
Carson City	6.3	17.1	7.9	12.9	16.4	14.7	10.2	7.8	7.1	48.3	20 171	26.9	2.44	11.0	27.8
Henderson	6.8	18.3	7.9	15.4	17.1	14.4	10.0	6.4	3.7	50.4	66 331	185.5	2.63	10.0	20.3
Las Vegas	7.7	18.2	8.8	16.1	15.9	12.5	9.2	7.1	4.5	49.2	176 750	77.2	2.66	12.2	25.0
North Las Vegas	10.4	23.6	9.6	18.5	15.8	10.0	6.4	3.7	2.0	49.0	34 018	134.2	3.36	15.2	13.6

1. No spouse present.

City	Persons in group quarters, 2000				Serious crimes known to police, 2000[2]				Education, 1990				Money income, 1989		
		Institutional		Non-Institutional[1]	Total		Rate[3]		School enrollment		Attainment[4] (percent)			Households	
														Median	
	Total	Total	Persons in nursing homes		Number	Rate[3]	Violent	Property	Public	Private	High school graduate or more	Bachelor's degree or more	Per capita (dollars)[5]	Dollars	Percent change, 1979–1989 (constant 1989 dollars)
	31	32	33	34	35	36	37	38	39	40	41	42	43	44	45
MINNESOTA—Cont'd															
Rochester	2 879	1 559	531	1 320	2 604	3 035	302	2 733	14 746	3 275	89.1	33.2	16 533	34 922	6.0
Roseville	1 642	702	649	940	1 721	5 108	172	4 936	5 869	2 480	88.6	34.5	18 593	37 862	-9.8
St. Cloud	4 724	1 661	506	3 063	1 305	2 208	188	2 020	17 215	1 828	84.4	25.4	11 736	24 004	-6.8
St. Louis Park	914	541	541	373	1 547	3 506	168	3 338	6 788	1 714	90.6	35.3	19 212	34 778	-2.9
St. Paul	11 196	3 240	2 352	7 956	18 719	6 519	833	5 686	52 372	21 353	81.1	26.5	13 727	26 498	-1.4
Shoreview	171	0	0	171	474	1 828	123	1 705	5 498	1 326	95.0	42.1	20 714	48 828	10.0
Winona	3 653	566	537	3 087	1 073	3 964	207	3 757	7 844	1 962	76.9	22.6	10 756	22 497	-2.0
Woodbury	440	359	359	81	1 038	2 234	84	2 150	4 944	1 029	95.1	43.0	21 569	51 014	9.4
MISSISSIPPI	95 414	50 826	18 382	44 588	113 911	4 004	361	3 644	646 850	80 636	64.3	14.7	9 648	20 136	-0.7
Biloxi	3 270	520	219	2 750	5 160	10 189	624	9 565	9 631	1 458	75.2	18.0	10 036	19 824	-3.3
Columbus	1 574	903	491	671	1 780	6 861	254	6 607	5 942	790	64.9	18.9	10 188	19 030	2.0
Greenville	719	575	393	144	5 120	12 298	939	11 359	11 422	2 229	61.5	15.6	9 081	18 060	3.2
Gulfport	3 424	1 512	243	1 912	5 940	8 351	373	7 979	8 387	1 482	74.8	18.3	10 013	21 174	-0.6
Hattiesburg	5 136	1 409	601	3 727	3 451	7 707	351	7 356	14 774	1 303	74.0	27.0	10 013	15 576	-15.4
Jackson	7 201	2 485	1 100	4 716	19 688	10 685	1 040	9 645	47 579	11 800	75.0	26.9	12 216	23 270	-6.2
Meridian	1 855	1 356	408	499	2 094	5 239	490	4 749	9 418	965	68.6	15.8	10 670	18 004	-8.8
Pascagoula	1 327	455	120	872	2 360	9 008	622	8 385	6 437	767	73.9	16.3	11 778	24 986	-7.3
Southaven	125	121	121	4	1 977	6 823	248	6 574	4 178	858	79.8	12.1	13 965	36 469	-2.4
Tupelo	1 114	905	548	209	2 167	6 334	319	6 016	7 350	634	76.1	21.9	14 083	27 871	11.1
Vicksburg	601	502	379	99	1 900	7 195	1 038	6 157	4 961	605	62.7	16.5	9 566	17 206	-17.2
MISSOURI	162 058	90 430	48 708	71 628	253 338	4 528	490	4 038	1 060 947	231 676	73.9	17.8	12 989	26 362	1.0
Ballwin	1	0	0	1	318	1 017	35	981	4 216	1 840	90.4	36.3	19 716	46 654	13.9
Blue Springs	246	206	206	40	1 320	2 745	83	2 662	11 237	1 473	90.1	23.8	14 793	39 904	-3.9
Cape Girardeau	3 070	983	938	2 087	2 492	7 050	311	6 739	9 984	1 223	77.0	24.3	12 254	22 634	-4.0
Chesterfield	1 073	1 070	1 001	3	1 002	2 141	73	2 068	8 336	3 537	92.9	53.7	28 019	66 930	NA
Columbia	8 459	595	549	7 864	3 607	4 267	442	3 825	28 099	3 008	87.2	45.0	12 452	22 059	-3.6
Florissant	781	557	557	224	1 291	2 557	101	2 456	8 923	3 334	80.3	16.3	14 914	36 809	-5.9
Gladstone	279	230	230	49	879	3 334	152	3 182	5 215	1 003	87.9	23.0	17 786	37 302	-6.7
Hazelwood	132	3	0	129	822	3 137	237	2 900	2 968	743	82.4	20.2	15 992	35 197	-1.9
Independence	1 140	590	383	550	7 983	7 047	546	6 501	21 019	3 436	78.3	13.7	13 208	28 242	-12.5
Jefferson City	4 734	3 993	456	741	1 666	4 203	555	3 648	6 801	1 653	78.1	27.5	15 701	27 597	-4.7
Joplin	1 906	676	618	1 230	4 243	9 324	451	8 874	8 315	1 294	73.0	16.5	11 296	19 420	-1.4
Kansas City	9 096	4 958	2 418	4 138	47 125	10 673	1 626	9 046	85 407	20 508	78.8	22.0	13 799	26 713	0.5
Kirkwood	341	250	223	91	639	2 339	106	2 232	4 447	2 049	88.2	42.9	22 058	42 113	8.5
Lee's Summit	779	746	746	33	1 916	2 710	74	2 636	11 021	1 603	89.9	27.1	16 658	38 800	13.8
Liberty	1 280	430	233	850	811	3 092	164	2 928	4 453	1 659	87.6	25.5	15 873	36 388	1.3
Maryland Heights	344	324	263	20	1 326	5 148	210	4 939	4 672	1 268	86.4	33.5	17 785	39 211	NA
O'Fallon	368	105	105	263	1 687	3 654	106	3 548	3 950	885	79.7	12.4	13 336	36 547	NA
Raytown	552	518	471	34	1 099	3 617	270	3 347	5 705	904	84.8	18.1	14 914	32 002	-13.4
St. Charles	2 641	771	452	1 870	1 842	3 054	124	2 929	9 326	4 357	79.9	22.9	15 626	34 336	4.2
St. Joseph	4 618	3 159	740	1 459	3 927	5 307	303	5 005	15 759	1 651	71.5	13.3	11 044	22 303	-3.7
St. Louis	10 632	4 667	2 943	5 965	50 653	14 548	2 279	12 268	67 583	29 211	62.8	15.3	10 798	19 458	0.9
St. Peters	146	127	127	19	1 754	3 414	206	3 207	10 707	3 288	89.8	25.5	16 458	45 298	8.0
Springfield	11 019	3 122	1 376	7 897	13 351	8 808	555	8 252	32 620	7 043	77.0	20.7	11 878	21 577	-1.8
University City	409	238	214	171	2 457	6 565	406	6 158	7 138	4 369	83.6	41.2	17 260	32 150	6.4
Wildwood	148	69	52	79	NA	NA	NA	NA	NA	NA	NA	NA	NA	NA	NA
MONTANA	24 762	12 068	6 470	12 694	31 878	3 533	241	3 293	197 360	18 399	81.0	19.8	11 213	22 988	-11.1
Billings	2 683	1 572	971	1 111	6 202	6 903	322	6 581	18 669	2 487	84.2	23.5	12 834	25 639	-7.8
Bozeman	2 901	304	262	2 597	NA	NA	NA	NA	10 514	423	92.9	41.6	10 172	19 168	-8.2
Butte-Silver Bow	1 092	715	397	377	NA	NA	NA	NA	7 508	1 019	78.3	17.9	11 364	21 216	NA
Great Falls	1 531	1 272	449	259	4 158	7 335	557	6 777	11 351	1 764	82.2	19.3	12 603	23 113	-15.3
Helena	1 096	312	248	784	NA	NA	NA	NA	4 860	1 254	89.4	34.2	13 256	25 462	-7.6
Missoula	3 286	487	108	2 799	NA	NA	NA	NA	14 246	838	87.2	33.4	11 759	21 033	-10.0
NEBRASKA	50 818	26 011	16 195	24 807	70 085	4 096	328	3 768	368 874	64 535	81.8	18.9	12 452	26 016	-2.5
Bellevue	223	101	101	122	1 498	3 375	86	3 290	8 040	1 567	89.4	24.1	13 540	31 923	-2.5
Fremont	938	368	340	570	885	3 516	87	3 428	4 666	1 329	79.7	14.8	11 504	24 768	-10.1
Grand Island	1 091	770	631	321	2 995	6 975	366	6 609	8 677	862	79.0	14.6	11 246	25 019	-4.9
Kearney	2 411	391	279	2 020	1 480	5 395	277	5 118	9 366	449	84.7	28.9	11 350	23 310	-6.9
Lincoln	11 643	3 689	959	7 954	14 161	6 278	532	5 745	53 203	8 151	88.3	28.5	13 720	28 056	-2.1
Omaha	10 581	5 760	2 808	4 821	26 819	6 877	811	6 065	69 339	21 515	82.6	23.1	13 957	26 927	-1.9
NEVADA	33 675	22 173	4 895	11 502	85 297	4 269	524	3 744	256 041	24 370	78.8	15.3	15 214	31 011	1.6
Carson City	3 223	3 102	272	121	1 767	3 368	395	2 974	8 859	666	82.7	16.3	15 131	31 570	0.9
Henderson	1 026	741	492	285	5 587	3 186	265	2 920	15 309	1 190	82.5	17.3	16 427	38 802	NA
Las Vegas	8 185	5 416	1 258	2 769	47 408	4 470	599	3 872	51 242	6 457	76.3	13.4	14 737	30 590	4.5
North Las Vegas	1 338	1 223	577	115	6 864	5 943	1 036	4 907	12 338	584	58.3	4.0	8 565	23 917	-8.4

1. Persons in emergency shelters and persons visible in street locations. 2. Data for serious crimes have not been adjusted for underreporting. This may affect comparability between geographic areas and over time. 3. Per 100,000 population estimated by the FBI. 4. Persons 25 years old and older. 5. Based on population enumerated as of April 1, 1990.

City	Money income, 1989 (cont'd)				Housing units, 2000									
	House-holds (cont'd)	Percent below poverty, 1989					Vacant units				Occupied units			
		Persons		Fam-ilies										
	Percent with $100,000 or more	Total	Percent change in rate, 1979–1989	Total	Total	Percent change, 1990–2000	Vacant units for sale or rent[1]	For seasonal use (percent)	Home owner vacancy rate	Renter vacancy rate	Total	Percent owner occu-pied	Percent renter occu-pied	Average size owner occu-pied	Average size renter occu-pied
	46	47	48	49	50	51	52	53	54	55	56	57	58	59	60
MINNESOTA—Cont'd															
Rochester	4.7	7.8	14.7	4.8	35 346	22.0	1 230	0.5	0.7	4.0	34 116	71.0	29.0	2.64	1.93
Roseville	5.7	3.7	19.4	2.6	14 917	4.9	319	0.5	0.5	2.3	14 598	67.5	32.5	2.44	1.69
St. Cloud	2.0	19.6	39.0	9.3	23 249	23.5	597	0.3	0.6	2.8	22 652	55.9	44.1	2.66	2.07
St. Louis Park	4.4	5.1	15.9	3.1	21 140	2.2	358	0.3	0.4	1.7	20 782	63.6	36.4	2.26	1.77
St. Paul	2.5	16.7	53.2	12.4	115 713	-1.6	3 604	0.4	0.7	2.8	112 109	54.8	45.2	2.72	2.15
Shoreview	8.4	2.8	16.7	2.1	10 289	10.9	164	0.4	0.5	2.3	10 125	87.2	12.8	2.64	1.91
Winona	1.1	17.2	26.5	7.2	10 666	10.2	365	0.2	0.8	4.1	10 301	60.9	39.1	2.46	1.99
Woodbury	10.9	2.5	8.7	2.0	17 541	132.6	865	0.6	1.4	13.3	16 676	85.2	14.8	2.87	2.13
MISSISSIPPI	1.7	25.2	5.5	20.2	1 161 953	15.0	115 519	1.9	1.6	9.2	1 046 434	72.3	27.7	2.67	2.52
Biloxi	1.3	21.4	32.9	16.4	22 115	17.2	2 527	1.3	2.4	9.9	19 588	48.9	51.1	2.47	2.37
Columbus	1.5	28.6	7.9	24.7	11 112	12.2	1 050	0.5	2.2	9.2	10 062	54.3	45.7	2.48	2.35
Greenville	2.2	32.0	2.9	26.9	16 251	-1.5	1 467	0.1	1.9	8.6	14 784	55.8	44.2	2.72	2.83
Gulfport	2.1	20.3	18.7	17.1	29 559	62.1	2 616	1.1	2.0	10.3	26 943	58.7	41.3	2.57	2.43
Hattiesburg	2.4	35.9	44.8	28.3	19 258	9.0	1 963	0.5	2.4	9.9	17 295	44.6	55.4	2.47	2.15
Jackson	3.7	22.7	23.4	18.0	75 678	-4.7	7 837	0.4	2.2	11.7	67 841	58.0	42.0	2.68	2.51
Meridian	2.7	27.8	21.9	23.3	17 890	0.8	1 924	0.3	3.3	8.8	15 966	56.3	43.7	2.43	2.33
Pascagoula	1.9	19.7	60.2	17.5	10 931	-1.1	1 053	0.5	1.7	11.7	9 878	56.8	43.2	2.55	2.48
Southaven	2.0	6.9	27.8	6.3	11 462	81.6	455	0.2	1.6	5.4	11 007	72.3	27.7	2.65	2.54
Tupelo	3.9	12.6	-9.4	9.2	14 551	18.0	1 156	0.4	1.4	10.9	13 395	62.2	37.8	2.59	2.28
Vicksburg	1.2	33.2	32.3	27.3	11 654	26.0	1 290	0.4	2.0	12.3	10 364	56.4	43.6	2.50	2.48
MISSOURI	2.8	13.3	9.3	10.1	2 442 017	11.0	247 423	2.7	2.1	9.0	2 194 594	70.3	29.7	2.59	2.20
Ballwin	7.3	2.5	-30.6	1.4	12 062	47.9	265	0.2	0.5	5.6	11 797	82.9	17.1	2.76	2.11
Blue Springs	3.0	4.7	27.0	3.8	17 733	24.5	447	0.2	1.0	3.7	17 286	74.2	25.8	2.92	2.34
Cape Girardeau	2.5	18.0	29.5	12.3	15 827	8.2	1 447	0.5	2.9	11.3	14 380	57.3	42.7	2.42	2.01
Chesterfield	24.2	2.1	NA	1.4	18 738	33.7	678	0.7	0.9	6.3	18 060	77.9	22.1	2.75	1.77
Columbia	2.9	22.4	28.0	12.4	35 916	30.4	2 227	0.3	2.5	6.2	33 689	47.3	52.7	2.50	2.04
Florissant	1.4	3.3	32.0	2.2	21 027	6.2	628	0.2	1.0	5.8	20 399	76.8	23.2	2.56	2.05
Gladstone	3.7	3.5	29.6	2.2	11 919	7.6	435	0.2	1.2	5.8	11 484	68.6	31.4	2.43	1.92
Hazelwood	1.7	4.5	-4.3	2.5	11 433	69.0	479	0.4	1.5	5.5	10 954	64.6	35.4	2.62	1.95
Independence	1.4	9.5	43.9	6.9	50 213	4.0	2 823	0.2	1.6	7.2	47 390	67.8	32.2	2.47	2.15
Jefferson City	2.9	9.7	36.6	6.8	16 987	10.0	1 193	0.8	2.2	7.4	15 794	58.6	41.4	2.43	1.90
Joplin	1.8	17.0	13.3	12.7	21 328	10.1	2 227	0.3	3.5	10.8	19 101	57.6	42.4	2.36	2.18
Kansas City	2.9	15.3	15.9	11.7	202 334	0.3	18 353	0.3	1.9	9.6	183 981	57.7	42.3	2.52	2.11
Kirkwood	9.8	2.8	-9.7	1.3	12 306	5.2	543	0.4	1.3	6.2	11 763	77.1	22.9	2.44	1.81
Lee's Summit	4.6	4.8	-7.7	3.4	27 311	45.6	894	0.2	1.2	5.4	26 417	75.6	24.4	2.86	1.99
Liberty	4.2	5.2	18.2	3.5	9 973	30.5	462	0.3	1.8	6.4	9 511	73.5	26.5	2.76	2.24
Maryland Heights	2.2	3.6	NA	2.4	11 846	3.3	544	0.5	0.7	7.4	11 302	62.6	37.4	2.46	1.89
O'Fallon	1.6	5.1	NA	3.8	15 920	137.1	531	0.2	1.9	6.4	15 389	89.5	10.5	3.04	2.42
Raytown	1.5	4.8	92.0	3.4	13 309	0.7	454	0.1	1.1	5.5	12 855	73.9	26.1	2.42	2.05
St. Charles	2.5	6.5	8.3	4.4	25 283	8.8	1 073	0.4	0.9	6.2	24 210	64.6	35.4	2.63	1.93
St. Joseph	1.6	16.7	41.5	13.2	31 752	1.5	2 726	0.3	2.0	7.6	29 026	64.8	35.2	2.49	2.20
St. Louis	1.3	24.6	12.8	20.6	176 354	-9.5	29 278	0.3	3.5	11.8	147 076	46.9	53.1	2.49	2.12
St. Peters	1.9	2.6	73.3	2.2	18 776	19.0	341	0.2	0.8	3.8	18 435	85.4	14.6	2.89	2.13
Springfield	2.3	17.8	24.5	11.6	69 650	11.5	4 959	0.4	2.5	7.1	64 691	53.7	46.3	2.27	2.06
University City	6.8	12.8	24.3	8.8	17 485	-1.2	1 032	0.2	1.5	6.8	16 453	57.8	42.2	2.47	1.94
Wildwood	NA	NA	NA	NA	11 229	NA	392	0.3	0.8	11.4	10 837	90.4	9.6	3.13	1.98
MONTANA	1.7	16.1	30.7	12.0	412 633	14.3	53 966	5.9	2.2	7.6	358 667	69.1	30.9	2.55	2.22
Billings	2.4	12.5	23.8	9.2	39 293	9.3	1 768	0.4	1.2	5.3	37 525	64.0	36.0	2.48	2.04
Bozeman	1.4	25.2	30.6	13.2	11 577	27.0	700	0.9	2.1	4.9	10 877	42.9	57.1	2.43	2.13
Butte-Silver Bow	1.6	14.7	NA	11.3	16 176	4.5	1 744	1.1	3.1	12.6	14 432	70.4	29.6	2.46	1.99
Great Falls	2.3	14.7	53.1	11.2	25 250	4.5	1 416	0.3	1.4	7.0	23 834	63.0	37.0	2.48	2.03
Helena	1.3	11.6	11.5	8.7	12 133	9.8	592	0.5	1.4	5.3	11 541	57.3	42.7	2.35	1.86
Missoula	1.9	19.0	26.7	12.9	25 225	36.4	1 084	0.5	1.0	3.6	24 141	50.2	49.8	2.47	1.98
NEBRASKA	2.2	11.1	4.2	8.0	722 668	9.4	56 484	1.6	1.8	7.6	666 184	67.4	32.6	2.63	2.20
Bellevue	1.6	5.7	26.7	4.3	17 439	45.8	502	0.1	0.8	4.1	16 937	66.1	33.9	2.76	2.32
Fremont	1.2	9.4	17.5	6.3	10 576	7.4	405	0.2	0.9	4.4	10 171	63.4	36.6	2.51	2.16
Grand Island	1.2	11.2	62.3	7.8	17 421	9.9	995	0.1	2.0	7.4	16 426	62.7	37.3	2.71	2.28
Kearney	2.4	16.5	44.7	8.4	11 099	18.4	550	0.3	1.9	5.3	10 549	56.5	43.5	2.59	2.08
Lincoln	2.3	11.3	27.0	6.5	95 199	20.4	4 714	0.3	1.3	6.2	90 485	58.0	42.0	2.59	2.05
Omaha	3.3	12.6	10.5	9.6	165 731	15.4	8 993	0.3	1.0	7.2	156 738	59.6	40.4	2.64	2.10
NEVADA	3.8	10.2	16.7	7.3	827 457	59.5	76 292	2.0	2.6	9.7	751 165	60.9	39.1	2.71	2.47
Carson City	2.8	8.0	14.3	5.6	21 283	28.0	1 112	0.5	1.5	6.8	20 171	63.1	36.9	2.46	2.41
Henderson	5.2	7.1	NA	5.0	71 149	180.1	4 818	1.2	2.2	9.4	66 331	70.5	29.5	2.71	2.43
Las Vegas	3.5	11.5	9.5	8.2	190 724	73.9	13 974	0.9	2.5	8.4	176 750	59.1	40.9	2.76	2.52
North Las Vegas	1.0	21.4	48.6	18.6	36 600	131.1	2 582	0.2	2.1	12.0	34 018	70.1	29.9	3.27	3.56

1. Includes units rented or sold but not occupied.   2. Specified owner-occupied units.   3. Specified renter-occupied units.   4. Overcrowded or lacking complete plumbing facilities.

Table D. Cities — Labor Force, Employment, Disability, and Construction

City	Civilian labor force, 2001		Unemployment		Civilian employment, 1990[2]	Percent		Disability 1990	Value of residential construction authorized by building permits, 2000		
	Total	Percent change, 2000–2001	Total	Rate[1]	Total	Professional, managerial, and technical	Precision production, craft, and repair	Work disabled persons[3] (percent)	New construction ($1,000)	Number of housing units	Percent single family
	61	62	63	64	65	66	67	68	69	70	71
MINNESOTA—Cont'd											
Rochester	53 125	4.4	1 412	2.7	38 108	43.5	6.3	6.0	121 670	1 250	47.2
Roseville	21 595	2.9	530	2.5	18 546	43.4	7.4	4.7	6 829	57	47.4
St. Cloud	38 879	2.4	1 563	4.0	25 283	28.9	6.9	7.0	23 552	220	84.1
St. Louis Park	29 113	3.1	775	2.7	26 394	39.1	5.9	6.3	18 165	213	6.1
St. Paul	144 764	2.8	5 937	4.1	133 383	33.6	7.2	9.5	38 582	359	36.2
Shoreview	17 485	2.6	411	2.4	14 432	45.6	6.4	4.4	31 860	247	7.7
Winona	14 946	2.2	676	4.5	12 437	26.9	10.1	5.8	5 496	42	69.0
Woodbury	27 956	3.0	585	2.1	11 235	47.2	5.8	4.1	138 731	784	97.7
MISSISSIPPI	1 296 193	-2.3	71 542	5.5	1 028 773	24.6	12.9	11.0	917 764	11 270	67.6
Biloxi	19 551	-2.6	938	4.8	14 916	33.3	9.7	11.3	19 702	223	62.3
Columbus	11 481	-0.8	1 288	11.2	9 793	26.6	11.7	9.1	3 303	30	100.0
Greenville	17 495	-4.5	1 851	10.6	16 429	26.5	10.0	10.5	5 213	61	39.3
Gulfport	31 815	-3.3	1 349	4.2	15 870	30.4	9.8	13.5	74 482	1 293	26.8
Hattiesburg	22 613	-0.5	906	4.0	16 896	34.1	6.8	9.3	22 884	295	40.3
Jackson	101 359	0.3	4 805	4.7	87 485	31.7	8.6	9.3	18 186	132	85.6
Meridian	17 846	-3.2	1 023	5.7	15 769	27.8	10.6	10.3	5 229	83	51.8
Pascagoula	14 806	-4.2	771	5.2	11 039	32.7	15.1	10.0	5 939	45	46.7
Southaven	16 320	2.1	350	2.1	9 308	25.1	13.4	7.2	63 392	919	36.5
Tupelo	20 506	-2.3	726	3.5	14 994	31.3	8.3	7.8	10 339	112	82.1
Vicksburg	13 454	-2.3	663	4.9	7 547	29.0	9.1	10.7	2 729	42	42.9
MISSOURI	2 970 118	1.4	139 715	4.7	2 367 395	27.8	11.1	8.5	2 569 404	24 321	73.7
Ballwin	13 021	-0.3	250	1.9	11 959	42.3	6.8	4.0	10 374	82	100.0
Blue Springs	24 906	1.3	701	2.8	20 770	33.0	10.4	4.4	37 487	420	72.9
Cape Girardeau	21 191	0.9	973	4.6	16 549	30.6	8.4	7.5	17 502	217	29.0
Chesterfield	20 968	-0.3	407	1.9	19 254	52.4	3.1	3.0	NA	NA	NA
Columbia	52 388	3.4	1 002	1.9	34 748	41.7	4.9	5.7	71 221	862	59.9
Florissant	29 303	0.0	880	3.0	26 616	29.3	12.9	6.3	490	2	100.0
Gladstone	19 811	1.3	454	2.3	14 623	30.6	10.0	5.9	8 031	49	93.9
Hazelwood	15 875	0.1	540	3.4	8 832	35.4	10.0	7.2	1 560	17	100.0
Independence	68 286	1.6	2 791	4.1	56 200	24.2	12.8	8.7	40 453	376	100.0
Jefferson City	23 092	3.6	747	3.2	17 033	38.8	7.2	7.4	21 041	173	87.9
Joplin	25 396	1.8	1 153	4.5	18 536	26.7	9.8	11.4	18 179	232	74.1
Kansas City	270 568	2.0	14 477	5.4	211 817	30.4	8.5	8.2	198 968	1 868	59.8
Kirkwood	15 094	-0.1	403	2.7	13 757	46.7	6.2	5.2	12 131	111	42.3
Lee's Summit	28 897	1.3	765	2.6	24 084	35.0	10.1	5.2	117 488	1 044	74.3
Liberty	14 328	1.4	398	2.8	10 523	32.9	9.9	4.4	26 478	208	100.0
Maryland Heights	17 627	-0.2	402	2.3	16 130	41.2	7.9	4.9	NA	NA	NA
O'Fallon	14 307	0.4	535	3.7	9 810	24.9	16.9	4.6	163 487	2 238	64.6
Raytown	18 883	1.3	550	2.9	15 732	31.6	11.1	7.0	3 563	39	74.4
St. Charles	43 523	0.3	1 453	3.3	29 966	33.8	11.0	7.1	31 779	270	100.0
St. Joseph	37 192	4.2	2 071	5.6	30 501	23.8	11.1	9.8	19 365	186	78.5
St. Louis	157 690	0.8	12 944	8.2	161 434	27.3	7.7	11.1	37 265	397	40.8
St. Peters	35 141	0.2	1 033	2.9	24 295	36.3	11.7	3.8	22 818	313	27.2
Springfield	86 089	-1.2	3 161	3.7	67 529	27.0	9.5	8.1	66 025	944	39.9
University City	23 144	0.7	1 286	5.6	20 468	48.8	3.8	5.8	21 155	259	5.0
Wildwood	16 489	0.0	484	2.9	NA	NA	NA	NA	NA	NA	NA
MONTANA	465 223	-2.9	21 319	4.6	350 723	26.9	10.4	9.7	235 126	2 572	60.8
Billings	51 462	-1.4	1 664	3.2	39 632	30.6	9.0	9.2	52 870	448	90.2
Bozeman	20 039	-1.4	571	2.8	11 353	35.1	6.7	5.6	39 578	403	54.7
Butte-Silver Bow	16 359	-5.2	839	5.1	13 935	29.6	10.6	12.5	3 195	31	93.5
Great Falls	27 116	-1.7	1 270	4.7	23 273	29.7	9.6	11.5	11 989	99	81.8
Helena	14 654	-1.8	593	4.0	12 140	44.8	5.2	8.7	7 928	95	42.1
Missoula	29 799	-1.9	1 184	4.0	20 335	35.6	6.7	8.1	40 165	570	52.3
NEBRASKA	928 297	0.4	28 868	3.1	772 813	26.2	10.3	7.1	830 393	9 105	71.5
Bellevue	19 613	0.8	575	2.9	14 403	31.9	8.9	7.0	52 919	632	59.8
Fremont	14 179	0.9	588	4.1	11 417	21.7	13.3	8.8	9 160	116	58.6
Grand Island	24 845	-0.7	794	3.2	19 662	23.2	12.4	8.6	11 521	124	71.0
Kearney	17 424	0.9	605	3.5	13 338	25.2	9.5	5.4	28 066	195	72.3
Lincoln	131 896	1.1	3 931	3.0	106 117	33.3	9.2	6.5	174 215	1 585	75.8
Omaha	207 067	0.8	7 931	3.8	167 866	30.8	9.1	8.2	221 602	2 805	71.6
NEVADA	1 023 488	3.8	54 729	5.3	607 437	24.8	11.4	8.3	3 312 242	32 285	79.7
Carson City	23 838	4.4	1 308	5.5	19 360	30.6	12.4	8.4	32 884	276	100.0
Henderson	62 212	4.3	2 800	4.5	32 372	27.6	11.9	7.9	817 289	5 886	93.6
Las Vegas	254 299	4.6	13 876	5.5	131 001	23.5	11.2	8.6	513 444	5 884	80.7
North Las Vegas	39 548	5.7	3 742	9.5	19 510	11.5	12.6	11.1	259 129	3 024	82.8

1. Percent of civilian labor force. 2. Persons 16 years and older. 3. Persons 16 to 64 years old.

Table D. Cities — **Wholesale Trade, Retail Trade, and Real Estate**

City	Wholesale Trade, 1997				Retail Trade[1], 1997				Real Estate and Rental and Leasing, 1997			
	Number of Establish-ments	Number of Employees	Sales (mil dol)	Annual Payroll (mil dol)	Number of Establish-ments	Number of Employees	Sales (mil dol)	Annual Payroll (mil dol)	Number of Establish-ments	Number of Employees	Receipts (mil dol)	Annual Payroll (mil dol)
	72	73	74	75	76	77	78	79	80	81	82	83
MINNESOTA—Cont'd												
Rochester	88	843	443.4	28.6	502	8 675	1 311.7	126.4	111	617	71.2	9.4
Roseville	151	2 334	1 227.2	89.6	350	8 031	1 210.6	122.9	81	824	133.2	19.8
St. Cloud	98	2 835	985.2	100.4	373	6 530	1 065.3	99.1	101	568	52.6	9.6
St. Louis Park	229	2 817	2 204.8	118.5	232	3 851	671.5	69.7	155	1 346	180.9	26.8
St. Paul	456	7 746	4 075.5	323.5	872	12 246	1 907.3	225.7	304	2 507	235.6	53.0
Shoreview	40	798	221.1	34.6	37	810	117.0	9.7	20	106	15.2	1.7
Winona	57	508	360.7	13.4	173	2 135	313.6	30.4	35	D	D	D
Woodbury	30	180	129.6	7.0	144	2 530	341.2	31.6	28	181	26.6	3.6
MISSISSIPPI	3 173	36 520	18 445.2	1 012.1	12 791	138 372	20 774.5	1 935.3	2 125	8 354	794.2	132.1
Biloxi	44	551	175.3	14.0	259	3 162	403.2	44.9	61	281	26.9	3.9
Columbus	76	969	287.2	26.2	318	3 644	567.8	51.2	53	294	25.9	5.0
Greenville	55	610	333.9	19.9	252	3 048	413.2	41.6	63	264	23.4	3.6
Gulfport	98	1 147	286.1	27.6	395	4 958	861.5	77.8	101	418	39.5	7.3
Hattiesburg	93	1 266	1 119.3	28.4	385	5 542	818.7	78.7	89	364	32.9	5.5
Jackson	404	6 820	2 828.5	218.4	968	15 841	2 595.6	265.7	263	1 455	147.7	23.6
Meridian	94	1 770	942.1	48.0	434	5 009	753.0	72.8	66	242	22.5	3.5
Pascagoula	30	271	173.1	8.6	186	2 632	499.8	41.5	34	156	11.7	2.9
Southaven	25	D	D	D	109	2 377	295.4	28.2	23	118	19.2	2.6
Tupelo	156	1 721	670.7	46.5	431	5 785	895.2	84.7	58	268	23.1	4.5
Vicksburg	38	325	134.4	9.8	257	2 973	402.8	39.8	41	121	13.6	1.9
MISSOURI	9 522	125 929	91 411.9	4 639.8	24 181	297 556	51 269.9	4 945.0	5 500	31 301	3 991.1	698.1
Ballwin	58	201	164.0	7.3	117	1 889	433.5	32.0	28	130	30.5	3.2
Blue Springs	61	372	195.0	12.7	171	2 833	534.3	51.2	43	211	26.1	3.4
Cape Girardeau	111	1 183	539.0	31.9	359	4 893	780.6	73.0	73	238	26.1	4.6
Chesterfield	243	2 023	3 024.1	98.0	218	3 564	380.5	47.5	120	555	73.7	13.4
Columbia	106	1 466	596.4	44.5	491	7 836	1 270.8	116.7	147	566	69.9	10.0
Florissant	48	415	95.1	11.7	227	4 432	688.2	68.7	33	125	24.5	3.2
Gladstone	22	101	31.0	2.8	104	1 828	317.2	31.3	38	300	20.2	7.1
Hazelwood	47	1 539	2 653.9	65.9	78	1 036	252.1	27.5	18	104	19.7	2.6
Independence	106	981	410.8	30.2	507	8 120	1 278.4	128.0	114	425	48.9	7.9
Jefferson City	83	D	D	D	260	4 191	694.0	64.4	65	172	20.8	3.3
Joplin	142	1 495	651.9	38.6	438	6 287	970.6	89.8	85	394	32.4	6.2
Kansas City	898	18 053	12 630.3	702.2	1 843	27 774	5 773.0	511.0	516	4 660	816.0	126.5
Kirkwood	97	637	286.6	22.4	140	1 994	437.9	44.9	39	184	26.6	5.3
Lee's Summit	101	975	907.8	31.0	195	2 709	475.3	46.3	82	307	40.7	5.5
Liberty	26	D	D	D	102	1 215	197.3	19.2	30	229	33.2	5.2
Maryland Heights	258	4 975	2 687.7	187.6	127	3 459	717.3	80.0	31	454	55.7	16.2
O'Fallon	43	487	355.8	19.3	107	1 645	237.7	24.0	21	100	8.0	1.4
Raytown	53	487	342.5	22.6	137	2 804	498.7	49.2	28	121	12.0	1.8
St. Charles	109	1 055	354.2	31.2	300	3 815	650.0	61.3	76	624	254.7	15.8
St. Joseph	139	1 556	1 106.3	42.9	382	4 733	777.6	71.2	85	D	D	D
St. Louis	902	16 599	10 582.9	646.4	1 241	14 511	2 361.7	282.4	401	3 520	402.9	76.7
St. Peters	67	594	666.2	19.6	308	5 619	1 000.8	95.7	39	197	20.0	3.7
Springfield	488	8 326	4 908.2	249.7	1 106	16 060	2 937.4	266.7	283	1 570	136.4	29.6
University City	54	615	180.3	20.7	105	1 366	164.1	20.6	43	395	26.8	6.9
Wildwood	NA	NA	NA	NA	NA	NA	NA	NA	NA	NA	NA	NA
MONTANA	1 577	14 381	7 709.5	372.3	5 042	48 337	7 779.1	746.5	1 186	4 265	353.4	58.1
Billings	314	4 128	2 295.1	121.1	642	8 103	1 432.0	133.8	170	712	77.8	11.4
Bozeman	73	697	230.6	20.8	307	3 387	492.7	52.2	74	257	24.5	3.6
Butte-Silver Bow	55	534	192.0	10.7	220	2 147	333.1	32.0	39	134	11.3	2.0
Great Falls	111	1 030	1 039.8	27.8	389	4 895	782.9	79.8	90	357	26.8	4.2
Helena	62	692	193.1	16.5	248	2 603	456.6	42.4	70	353	24.1	4.8
Missoula	145	1 675	515.4	42.7	463	6 166	990.0	97.1	124	536	42.7	7.1
NEBRASKA	3 157	41 002	38 015.4	1 170.2	8 295	102 684	16 529.3	1 554.6	1 587	8 240	891.1	160.8
Bellevue	12	15	3.4	0.3	124	2 335	379.2	34.6	30	146	12.9	2.1
Fremont	30	329	306.4	10.3	149	2 093	441.1	34.8	34	169	13.1	2.4
Grand Island	94	D	D	D	307	4 256	658.5	63.6	56	170	19.6	2.9
Kearney	44	D	D	D	198	2 903	399.2	44.0	40	D	D	D
Lincoln	270	D	D	D	952	15 326	2 197.5	225.2	254	1 460	147.6	25.0
Omaha	932	15 973	10 907.3	533.0	1 786	33 724	5 479.3	572.3	511	4 278	524.0	103.2
NEVADA	2 253	27 251	12 806.9	918.5	6 222	89 452	18 220.8	1 798.2	2 460	16 890	2 276.5	381.5
Carson City	88	557	222.4	18.7	262	3 383	678.4	66.1	102	343	51.2	7.4
Henderson	85	729	301.2	21.7	321	5 824	1 252.6	113.6	111	1 335	161.1	31.9
Las Vegas	500	6 266	2 208.8	209.2	1 516	24 600	5 811.5	535.7	608	4 009	498.6	83.6
North Las Vegas	91	1 903	735.5	67.5	138	2 277	433.9	39.7	49	451	79.8	16.6

1. Establishments with payroll.

City	Professional, Scientific, and Technical Services, 1997[1]				Manufacturing, 1997				Accommodation and Foodservices, 1997			
	Number of Establishments	Number of Employees	Receipts (mil dol)	Annual Payroll (mil dol)	Number of Establishments	Number of Employees	Receipts (mil dol)	Annual Payroll (mil dol)	Number of Establishments	Number of Employees	Sales (mil dol)	Annual Payroll (mil dol)
	84	85	86	87	88	89	90	91	92	93	94	95
MINNESOTA—Cont'd												
Rochester	184	2 082	155.3	81.8	64	D	D	D	247	5 624	196.7	56.4
Roseville	217	2 022	222.0	71.0	88	5 238	604.9	196.0	103	3 362	102.3	31.1
St. Cloud	141	1 012	78.1	33.8	75	7 189	981.7	194.0	142	3 759	100.5	27.5
St. Louis Park	384	3 228	321.2	135.2	113	4 241	707.5	159.9	89	2 255	66.5	20.6
St. Paul	803	6 333	646.5	290.9	375	20 215	5 536.6	737.5	599	10 532	350.9	105.5
Shoreview	76	425	37.3	17.4	35	1 870	269.1	71.8	22	346	11.9	3.6
Winona	57	197	12.9	4.1	83	5 992	921.5	170.7	85	1 501	40.0	10.6
Woodbury	103	227	33.4	9.7	17	1 062	253.4	39.4	64	1 514	49.0	15.2
MISSISSIPPI	3 627	21 671	1 761.6	662.1	3 008	227 800	39 658.3	5 599.4	4 050	84 834	3 064.8	814.5
Biloxi	100	618	53.3	20.0	36	D	D	D	144	4 911	183.2	51.8
Columbus	77	383	27.2	10.1	57	D	D	D	95	1 995	56.4	14.3
Greenville	66	299	31.7	8.8	49	4 313	904.0	105.3	80	1 400	44.7	11.7
Gulfport	182	909	75.7	28.5	67	1 885	259.3	50.4	156	3 017	87.4	23.0
Hattiesburg	156	827	63.3	20.9	62	4 625	942.4	103.4	161	3 502	101.1	26.5
Jackson	619	5 424	552.0	219.2	173	9 337	1 709.3	236.9	396	9 427	293.3	85.0
Meridian	106	452	32.5	9.8	70	D	D	D	138	2 777	85.8	23.5
Pascagoula	81	648	72.4	31.1	39	D	D	D	59	1 272	36.0	9.9
Southaven	33	177	11.2	4.4	NA	NA	NA	NA	38	783	23.5	6.0
Tupelo	131	838	62.7	26.3	109	8 813	1 470.7	231.3	134	2 662	78.3	21.7
Vicksburg	67	565	33.3	17.0	32	2 813	748.9	76.3	88	3 193	156.9	37.2
MISSOURI	10 601	93 792	9 953.3	3 643.6	7 497	371 448	93 115.5	11 647.0	11 150	203 849	6 780.8	1 933.3
Ballwin	87	637	67.2	28.3	NA	NA	NA	NA	43	956	28.5	8.4
Blue Springs	94	344	21.7	9.2	41	978	127.5	28.2	83	1 868	52.0	14.9
Cape Girardeau	91	639	41.3	14.6	52	3 602	1 246.9	111.3	103	2 468	77.0	21.5
Chesterfield	252	2 513	252.1	116.2	42	1 489	207.7	47.8	78	D	D	D
Columbia	232	1 242	88.8	29.9	62	4 277	1 376.1	120.7	278	5 731	173.6	46.6
Florissant	61	579	24.2	10.2	NA	NA	NA	NA	131	D	D	D
Gladstone	71	305	25.8	13.0	NA	NA	NA	NA	52	D	D	D
Hazelwood	41	D	D	D	36	5 349	6 583.2	258.2	48	1 065	35.8	9.7
Independence	183	1 079	73.1	29.2	108	3 711	812.5	129.1	221	4 577	143.1	41.5
Jefferson City	157	881	73.1	29.5	39	3 603	1 046.8	114.9	118	2 619	80.6	23.6
Joplin	109	750	45.4	19.6	108	5 585	849.8	148.2	187	4 118	116.1	33.9
Kansas City	1 317	17 551	1 907.7	806.7	575	27 888	7 155.5	998.5	1 053	26 879	1 042.5	312.3
Kirkwood	111	482	48.9	20.4	41	1 272	136.5	41.1	55	1 113	30.2	9.6
Lee's Summit	156	691	65.3	27.1	77	2 577	456.7	72.1	89	1 798	53.6	15.6
Liberty	71	446	30.9	11.5	23	D	D	D	47	816	26.5	8.2
Maryland Heights	119	2 918	301.1	105.3	132	4 858	980.3	171.6	75	3 097	126.7	38.8
O'Fallon	37	173	12.4	5.0	54	D	D	D	48	D	D	D
Raytown	69	427	21.0	9.4	33	663	58.0	17.5	60	921	25.4	7.1
St. Charles	194	1 805	119.8	37.2	83	2 565	360.2	78.7	176	3 783	113.6	31.9
St. Joseph	130	D	D	D	91	D	D	D	189	3 133	94.2	26.1
St. Louis	963	13 915	1 819.8	663.7	802	33 836	8 605.5	1 243.6	954	18 843	686.6	195.8
St. Peters	64	607	37.2	16.5	69	3 822	1 489.7	126.4	111	2 492	65.0	19.2
Springfield	509	3 691	338.6	111.7	310	18 260	3 673.5	488.3	545	11 243	335.8	96.2
University City	98	452	49.3	20.2	NA	NA	NA	NA	67	D	D	D
Wildwood	NA	NA	NA	NA	NA	NA	NA	NA	NA	NA	NA	NA
MONTANA	2 082	10 735	769.4	297.7	1 160	19 611	4 866.3	560.1	3 278	38 533	1 198.9	325.4
Billings	367	2 502	186.2	69.9	141	D	D	D	303	6 137	186.2	53.7
Bozeman	181	833	69.2	27.8	75	906	101.3	20.4	137	2 339	64.0	18.1
Butte-Silver Bow	88	861	60.2	25.7	NA	NA	NA	NA	130	1 354	47.8	12.3
Great Falls	162	962	66.8	27.7	64	853	221.2	22.1	223	3 277	95.8	27.0
Helena	139	947	72.2	30.6	NA	NA	NA	NA	135	2 186	60.5	16.6
Missoula	250	1 553	103.7	43.7	94	1 103	151.0	28.1	259	4 322	129.7	36.4
NEBRASKA	3 076	25 720	2 273.4	838.0	1 960	106 690	27 859.2	3 040.5	4 070	61 048	1 726.6	488.2
Bellevue	61	1 166	128.7	48.7	10	1 070	146.1	20.9	78	1 196	35.1	10.1
Fremont	40	257	11.7	5.2	40	1 469	316.4	34.7	68	1 295	36.6	9.2
Grand Island	90	401	31.3	11.7	59	5 107	1 714.9	139.1	139	2 702	67.7	20.2
Kearney	58	331	20.7	7.9	21	1 518	214.8	40.9	100	2 225	62.8	18.0
Lincoln	464	D	D	D	234	D	D	D	518	10 856	309.7	89.2
Omaha	1 121	11 882	1 075.5	447.0	497	24 767	6 528.1	787.2	960	18 796	590.8	176.1
NEVADA	4 171	28 963	2 974.4	1 171.1	1 615	37 849	6 361.8	1 178.0	3 632	241 672	15 322.7	4 665.3
Carson City	233	806	86.2	30.2	186	4 157	514.5	120.8	133	2 404	93.1	27.7
Henderson	166	691	72.1	28.8	60	3 131	939.0	96.8	167	3 736	206.8	55.0
Las Vegas	1 344	13 489	1 308.4	563.5	274	3 884	493.8	114.1	872	43 124	2 283.7	836.1
North Las Vegas	35	580	73.6	19.4	74	2 071	363.6	63.0	53	2 276	127.6	37.4

1. Firms subject to federal tax.

Table D. Cities — **Entertainment, Health Care, and Other Services**

City	Arts, Entertainment, and Recreation[1], 1997				Health Care and Social Assistance[1], 1997				Other Services[1], 1997			
	Number of Establishments	Number of Employees	Receipts (mil dol)	Annual Payroll (mil dol)	Number of Establishments	Number of Employees	Receipts (mil dol)	Annual Payroll (mil dol)	Number of Establishments	Number of Employees	Receipts (mil dol)	Annual Payroll (mil dol)
	96	97	98	99	100	101	102	103	104	105	106	107
MINNESOTA—Cont'd												
Rochester	22	322	14.1	4.0	145	2 151	97.4	48.7	145	1 221	60.3	18.0
Roseville	12	152	10.3	1.7	97	1 407	66.0	33.8	100	1 166	89.1	29.3
St. Cloud	26	251	11.9	3.0	179	2 765	213.6	111.4	121	1 006	60.7	18.8
St. Louis Park	24	937	38.7	8.4	164	2 542	165.7	83.5	111	775	52.2	16.5
St. Paul	72	764	32.1	9.4	578	9 286	622.3	349.4	420	3 054	177.5	55.7
Shoreview	4	4	0.4	0.2	46	453	25.3	11.4	17	180	6.5	2.6
Winona	10	134	7.3	2.1	57	498	31.4	13.9	51	260	14.1	3.7
Woodbury	9	243	8.1	2.5	72	1 075	52.0	23.6	28	277	15.2	6.0
MISSISSIPPI	483	21 239	1 394.0	371.7	4 139	55 529	3 632.3	1 547.0	3 491	17 449	1 057.1	299.6
Biloxi	32	8 696	587.8	164.3	118	2 554	192.8	77.2	66	468	21.7	6.7
Columbus	17	0	0.0	0.0	113	986	74.7	27.6	88	501	29.8	8.5
Greenville	12	0	0.0	0.0	106	1 108	74.5	29.0	91	438	24.5	7.1
Gulfport	23	0	0.0	0.0	190	2 279	181.5	68.3	137	918	48.9	16.7
Hattiesburg	13	118	5.4	2.2	125	2 489	177.6	100.1	75	653	40.3	11.9
Jackson	22	312	21.7	4.4	506	7 381	584.0	263.4	342	2 848	166.8	52.3
Meridian	12	53	2.1	0.6	142	1 932	160.2	80.5	115	609	30.8	9.2
Pascagoula	4	8	0.3	0.1	103	821	65.0	29.5	60	349	19.9	5.3
Southaven	5	0	0.0	0.0	56	594	43.6	18.1	54	245	14.2	3.7
Tupelo	8	0	0.0	0.0	136	1 928	162.5	91.1	97	780	47.0	20.6
Vicksburg	11	0	0.0	0.0	59	1 856	142.8	54.6	59	244	13.1	3.8
MISSOURI	1 493	29 484	1 803.9	684.2	10 213	131 485	7 885.4	3 596.7	9 427	52 060	3 203.3	963.1
Ballwin	8	97	2.6	0.8	54	529	39.6	20.0	42	222	13.8	5.0
Blue Springs	14	178	4.1	1.7	111	1 126	64.5	24.4	102	662	25.9	9.3
Cape Girardeau	12	75	6.4	0.9	162	1 850	146.5	67.9	82	442	26.9	8.4
Chesterfield	23	161	9.4	2.5	197	2 562	183.9	88.4	67	517	20.6	8.0
Columbia	25	473	14.4	4.3	287	3 639	308.7	123.8	183	1 155	59.4	19.0
Florissant	11	159	4.4	1.6	160	1 701	94.4	44.6	106	582	32.7	11.3
Gladstone	4	72	2.0	0.6	79	898	51.8	23.0	68	311	19.5	5.8
Hazelwood	8	96	4.4	1.8	29	413	31.2	11.6	34	226	14.6	4.7
Independence	20	238	11.9	2.7	214	3 759	233.7	110.8	215	1 180	59.9	20.3
Jefferson City	9	100	9.2	1.6	149	1 863	122.2	69.6	84	498	23.9	7.4
Joplin	18	147	4.4	1.1	208	2 049	146.1	66.6	150	929	50.2	14.7
Kansas City	97	3 530	296.5	174.0	949	13 404	1 011.8	508.2	793	6 083	420.5	123.3
Kirkwood	10	79	2.4	0.9	109	776	70.4	31.8	46	294	20.1	6.8
Lee's Summit	19	202	5.8	1.8	98	872	49.9	22.3	94	507	27.1	9.1
Liberty	4	52	1.6	0.4	79	852	55.3	29.1	55	256	13.8	4.3
Maryland Heights	8	91	19.0	1.3	36	1 834	135.9	49.8	51	485	40.4	12.7
O'Fallon	6	72	3.1	0.9	38	385	15.5	5.9	71	486	32.6	11.2
Raytown	6	107	3.6	1.3	59	582	21.6	9.3	69	525	36.8	10.2
St. Charles	22	2 085	157.1	46.5	155	2 052	180.6	91.7	141	711	40.9	12.5
St. Joseph	17	0	0.0	0.0	173	0	0.0	0.0	151	755	44.4	12.7
St. Louis	68	3 603	378.4	209.4	581	9 806	612.5	263.9	673	4 693	334.1	101.2
St. Peters	21	262	7.3	2.2	121	1 339	82.0	34.9	111	816	38.0	13.6
Springfield	45	536	16.5	5.0	411	6 608	509.0	244.3	438	3 184	166.0	51.8
University City	5	0	0.0	0.0	64	676	23.1	10.5	66	680	37.2	14.1
Wildwood	NA	NA	NA	NA	NA	NA	NA	NA	NA	NA	NA	NA
MONTANA	639	5 638	306.5	62.2	2 034	15 673	928.6	412.6	1 612	6 986	449.1	117.0
Billings	75	882	57.1	9.5	310	2 685	216.0	109.3	238	1 477	94.4	26.8
Bozeman	28	325	27.3	4.2	127	1 009	58.9	25.4	76	443	20.9	6.1
Butte-Silver Bow	25	185	9.8	2.1	114	1 055	53.4	24.7	71	282	16.6	4.3
Great Falls	41	349	18.0	4.2	201	1 721	103.9	40.5	127	606	36.6	9.7
Helena	26	421	16.1	3.5	138	1 144	67.2	26.1	67	367	20.9	5.9
Missoula	48	505	34.2	7.7	251	2 112	143.4	67.2	155	805	49.9	14.5
NEBRASKA	517	5 957	258.6	58.1	3 057	34 763	2 027.7	970.3	3 288	16 940	1 039.2	297.1
Bellevue	9	136	6.6	1.4	42	531	21.2	10.5	58	268	15.8	5.0
Fremont	9	70	2.3	0.6	66	615	36.0	15.9	67	285	13.7	3.9
Grand Island	13	314	15.7	2.4	103	0	0.0	0.0	107	639	36.8	10.4
Kearney	12	118	3.6	1.0	82	745	64.0	35.1	67	398	25.0	7.3
Lincoln	51	1 035	36.3	9.7	531	6 264	373.5	182.5	395	2 466	130.8	41.3
Omaha	116	1 870	70.3	17.3	865	10 874	793.5	374.4	817	6 339	367.5	119.9
NEVADA	811	23 960	1 667.5	465.8	3 226	39 476	3 406.5	1 358.9	2 175	16 185	1 061.7	328.0
Carson City	39	1 001	51.0	13.7	172	1 274	86.7	39.8	104	634	42.2	13.5
Henderson	48	2 654	150.3	43.6	186	1 694	125.9	49.9	108	975	55.9	18.7
Las Vegas	193	4 384	374.3	84.0	1 021	17 184	1 624.8	605.1	594	5 323	328.7	105.8
North Las Vegas	10	1 636	62.1	25.8	47	1 937	110.6	36.8	56	843	55.7	19.5

1. Firms subject to federal tax.

Table D. Cities — Federal Funds and City Government Finances

City	Selected federal funds, fiscal 2001[1] (mil dol)									City government finances, 1999						
	Procurement contracts		Grants					Direct payments for individuals		General revenue						
										Intergovernmental			Taxes			
														Per capita[3] (dollars)		
	Defense	Other	Total[2]	Health and family welfare	Energy and environment	Education	Housing and community development	Educational assistance	Housing assistance	Total (mil dol)	Total (mil dol)	Percent from state government	Total (mil dol)	Total	Property	Sales and gross receipts
	108	109	110	111	112	113	114	115	116	117	118	119	120	121	122	123
MINNESOTA—Cont'd																
Rochester	6.2	2.9	135.5	126.3	0.0	1.4	0.6	2.9	9.3	93.5	30.0	90.8	30.6	391	250	114
Roseville	2.5	1.8	0.1	0.0	0.0	0.0	0.0	0.0	1.3	40.1	5.3	93.8	13.8	400	349	4
St. Cloud	0.2	2.2	6.7	1.8	0.0	2.0	0.4	8.1	5.4	71.7	15.2	89.7	18.4	362	269	64
St. Louis Park	0.9	0.9	0.0	0.0	0.0	0.0	0.0	0.0	3.6	60.1	8.9	88.1	14.9	351	314	6
St. Paul	207.1	28.3	799.9	213.4	55.9	148.9	39.8	41.1	95.8	463.3	161.5	82.8	112.5	437	286	118
Shoreview	9.6	0.4	1.7	0.0	0.0	0.0	0.0	0.0	0.3	18.7	3.5	85.0	6.0	230	210	4
Winona	0.6	0.2	1.9	0.6	0.1	0.8	0.0	4.9	1.3	23.9	9.0	96.0	6.6	271	212	43
Woodbury	0.0	0.0	0.0	0.0	0.0	0.0	0.0	0.0	0.0	48.8	3.9	97.1	15.8	392	296	0
MISSISSIPPI	1 355.3	507.5	4 246.5	2 529.1	51.3	386.5	52.0	189.3	266.4	X	X	X	X	X	X	X
Biloxi	0.6	2.7	9.1	4.3	0.1	2.7	0.2	0.1	7.8	52.9	24.8	98.1	16.9	357	303	40
Columbus	9.3	0.4	2.2	0.0	0.0	0.2	0.4	2.8	4.2	20.3	9.0	87.3	5.4	240	178	43
Greenville	0.7	0.4	6.9	1.5	0.0	2.0	0.0	0.4	6.8	30.0	13.0	96.8	9.1	216	167	19
Gulfport	54.7	15.3	13.6	1.6	0.0	1.5	0.5	0.6	7.1	222.9	18.4	85.9	22.8	352	251	33
Hattiesburg	11.2	1.4	29.0	6.0	0.9	2.7	0.7	17.4	10.2	41.6	16.9	80.4	14.0	287	207	74
Jackson	22.9	25.5	697.5	253.8	36.3	119.6	47.0	30.7	40.2	163.5	48.2	80.3	58.6	311	268	35
Meridian	27.2	3.1	5.4	1.9	0.0	0.2	0.0	4.0	4.2	35.0	15.1	89.2	9.4	233	191	37
Pascagoula	632.7	1.2	2.5	0.0	0.0	0.2	0.4	0.0	3.2	20.1	6.6	81.9	5.7	210	171	35
Southaven	0.0	0.1	0.0	0.0	0.0	0.0	0.0	0.0	5.4	10.3	4.2	100.0	3.8	160	118	26
Tupelo	0.5	1.1	9.3	3.8	1.3	1.5	0.0	8.4	5.7	40.2	21.9	77.7	9.1	255	232	7
Vicksburg	81.3	4.3	0.5	0.0	0.2	0.0	0.0	0.0	5.6	30.6	15.2	97.7	9.1	333	298	0
MISSOURI	5 021.1	1 719.5	6 865.2	4 415.6	115.6	535.3	123.1	279.3	449.8	X	X	X	X	X	X	X
Ballwin	1.3	1.8	0.0	0.0	0.0	0.0	0.0	0.0	0.0	NA	NA	NA	NA	NA	NA	NA
Blue Springs	0.3	0.2	0.0	0.0	0.0	0.0	0.0	0.0	1.6	28.2	3.0	40.4	14.1	318	76	235
Cape Girardeau	3.2	0.2	9.0	0.8	0.0	2.2	0.0	5.3	0.9	37.4	2.7	94.7	23.7	666	51	584
Chesterfield	0.6	3.5	0.6	0.5	0.0	0.0	0.0	29.3	0.0	23.2	13.3	14.3	6.7	145	35	94
Columbia	4.7	10.8	119.5	40.1	5.6	13.2	2.0	15.8	7.3	70.1	3.4	26.2	29.9	379	63	309
Florissant	0.1	0.1	2.1	0.1	0.0	1.8	0.2	0.2	0.0	20.6	9.7	22.5	6.1	129	8	96
Gladstone	0.0	0.0	0.2	0.0	0.0	0.0	0.0	0.0	0.0	26.0	0.6	91.6	20.7	739	54	297
Hazelwood	1.2	0.5	0.4	0.0	0.0	0.0	0.0	0.0	0.0	15.6	5.4	25.2	7.9	546	79	136
Independence	2.1	16.4	2.9	0.0	0.0	0.9	1.1	0.1	20.0	72.0	10.9	46.3	34.4	295	58	215
Jefferson City	0.5	2.8	831.7	303.0	80.1	151.9	0.6	3.1	7.7	NA	NA	NA	NA	NA	NA	NA
Joplin	15.9	322.3	6.8	3.0	1.9	0.4	0.5	5.9	4.1	41.1	4.2	62.3	21.0	471	18	440
Kansas City	112.3	584.4	101.1	55.1	3.4	4.9	0.0	64.3	105.8	757.4	81.9	28.0	444.1	1 006	165	471
Kirkwood	0.2	0.0	0.1	0.0	0.0	0.0	0.0	0.0	0.7	20.2	9.2	11.3	6.4	240	62	145
Lee's Summit	4.5	4.2	0.5	0.0	0.0	0.0	0.4	0.0	4.0	53.0	2.5	53.5	27.2	408	203	186
Liberty	0.0	0.0	0.0	0.0	0.0	0.0	0.0	0.0	2.5	19.5	2.1	70.8	9.9	387	135	231
Maryland Heights	24.2	9.1	0.6	0.0	0.0	0.0	0.0	0.0	0.0	NA	NA	NA	NA	NA	NA	NA
O'Fallon	0.1	0.0	0.0	0.0	0.0	0.0	0.0	0.0	0.0	22.1	1.4	61.8	14.6	416	120	275
Raytown	0.0	0.1	0.0	0.0	0.0	0.0	0.0	0.0	0.7	14.6	2.1	57.8	7.4	260	43	206
St. Charles	9.9	1.1	6.1	4.9	0.1	0.0	0.4	2.6	3.0	55.1	9.2	31.2	35.5	611	123	464
St. Joseph	0.4	0.0	9.6	3.2	0.0	0.0	2.6	4.4	10.5	55.6	11.5	60.0	29.6	426	113	293
St. Louis	4 511.2	245.9	421.3	90.3	13.1	12.9	83.1	53.2	98.2	643.4	91.0	30.7	324.8	957	488	510
St. Peters	2.8	1.5	0.0	0.0	0.0	0.0	0.0	1.4	0.0	42.7	4.3	26.7	24.5	488	122	359
Springfield	3.2	19.7	28.1	8.8	0.0	3.6	3.1	22.0	14.8	153.3	18.8	48.9	72.2	505	72	409
University City	0.0	0.0	0.3	0.2	0.0	0.0	0.0	0.0	1.9	23.6	10.1	48.7	8.5	231	100	113
Wildwood	NA	NA	NA	NA	NA	NA	NA	NA	NA	3.9	2.3	14.9	1.4	NA	NA	NA
MONTANA	127.3	243.3	1 665.1	660.5	51.5	190.9	17.5	48.1	94.2	X	X	X	X	X	X	X
Billings	1.6	16.6	30.4	12.4	3.0	3.1	1.0	5.4	12.4	76.2	10.0	77.8	19.1	208	170	0
Bozeman	2.1	2.2	70.7	13.4	4.4	1.9	0.0	8.2	2.1	21.5	3.3	79.4	7.1	237	198	5
Butte-Silver Bow	3.7	25.2	6.4	1.4	1.0	0.7	0.0	2.1	3.1	36.5	7.2	66.5	16.1	473	445	14
Great Falls	9.2	3.8	15.3	4.5	0.0	1.5	1.6	2.9	14.3	36.0	5.6	73.7	9.3	164	139	1
Helena	3.9	14.2	258.4	62.8	33.5	46.8	11.5	8.7	25.6	20.8	3.4	75.7	5.3	186	160	6
Missoula	5.6	12.1	41.8	11.9	0.6	6.6	0.8	9.8	8.6	27.4	4.6	90.8	13.8	265	227	4
NEBRASKA	189.6	257.3	2 054.3	1 158.4	41.8	192.7	29.1	69.8	121.6	X	X	X	X	X	X	X
Bellevue	26.8	0.2	14.8	0.0	0.0	14.3	0.0	1.5	4.7	20.8	4.3	82.5	11.2	254	122	117
Fremont	0.3	1.6	0.3	0.3	0.0	0.0	0.0	1.3	0.8	19.1	4.3	15.1	5.5	224	162	55
Grand Island	1.3	9.5	11.3	0.7	0.0	0.3	0.0	2.9	5.2	33.6	5.1	91.0	14.2	342	159	175
Kearney	0.0	0.0	2.3	0.9	0.0	0.6	0.0	4.0	3.0	24.5	7.6	65.1	5.4	195	26	162
Lincoln	27.0	13.2	386.7	137.5	38.3	64.2	21.2	25.4	22.1	189.7	36.7	72.5	83.8	393	148	180
Omaha	27.1	82.1	104.1	50.7	2.2	7.3	7.8	18.6	37.2	305.9	49.4	74.2	194.4	524	211	290
NEVADA	323.0	718.2	1 441.8	660.5	60.4	166.7	24.8	29.2	111.2	X	X	X	X	X	X	X
Carson City	17.8	2.8	272.3	80.2	25.4	70.0	0.0	1.2	11.7	147.0	22.9	92.0	18.3	372	195	126
Henderson	1.6	0.3	4.3	0.0	0.0	0.0	0.8	0.0	1.4	177.3	54.7	87.7	48.7	319	170	69
Las Vegas	23.8	568.8	100.5	26.0	16.5	9.3	9.1	14.1	27.1	466.2	193.0	76.3	121.2	300	147	72
North Las Vegas	1.5	1.5	1.6	0.0	0.0	0.4	0.0	6.8	24.2	108.4	38.6	70.5	32.9	349	219	59

1. October 1, 2000 to September 30, 2001.   2. Includes program categories not shown separately. State totals include additional categories not allocated by city.   3. Based on population estimated as of July 1 of the year shown.

City	Total (mil dol)	Per capita[1] (dollars)		General expenditure — Percent of total for —									
		Total	Capital outlays	Public welfare	Highways	Parking facilities	Education	Health and hospitals	Police protection	Sewerage and sanitation	Parks and recreation	Housing and community development	Interest on debt
	124	125	126	127	128	129	130	131	132	133	134	135	136
MINNESOTA—Cont'd													
Rochester	82.6	1 056	354	0.0	8.1	8.3	0.0	0.2	11.5	6.0	14.5	0.7	6.2
Roseville	31.9	925	239	0.0	13.8	0.0	0.0	0.0	11.7	11.1	18.6	4.6	23.7
St. Cloud	67.5	1 330	287	0.0	15.7	0.7	0.0	1.5	11.3	12.5	6.1	0.0	28.2
St. Louis Park	60.9	1 436	218	0.0	9.9	0.0	0.0	0.1	8.6	11.5	9.5	5.8	39.4
St. Paul	495.5	1 926	458	0.0	12.1	0.3	0.0	1.3	11.1	7.8	17.4	5.8	10.6
Shoreview	19.1	729	114	0.0	16.1	0.0	0.0	0.1	5.7	7.8	17.2	15.5	10.6
Winona	21.4	883	195	1.0	16.9	0.0	0.0	0.0	12.7	15.3	8.7	5.1	12.1
Woodbury	36.8	910	331	0.0	17.4	0.0	0.0	1.6	9.7	22.2	16.9	0.0	15.9
MISSISSIPPI	X	X	X	X	X	X	X	X	X	X	X	X	X
Biloxi	50.1	1 058	26	7.8	21.4	0.0	0.0	0.0	18.2	16.4	5.7	1.1	1.6
Columbus	21.2	949	59	0.0	6.6	0.0	0.0	0.3	18.9	21.5	0.8	6.5	2.0
Greenville	26.3	627	142	0.0	17.4	0.0	0.0	0.0	22.2	11.5	3.8	0.4	2.7
Gulfport	234.4	3 620	453	0.1	2.4	0.0	0.0	74.5	5.4	3.4	1.1	0.5	2.0
Hattiesburg	46.6	955	347	0.0	11.0	0.4	0.0	0.9	12.9	14.4	3.7	1.6	7.5
Jackson	163.9	870	212	2.1	7.4	0.2	0.0	0.4	14.5	18.8	4.8	2.3	5.3
Meridian	32.8	815	161	0.0	23.4	0.0	0.0	0.0	16.6	12.3	5.8	4.7	5.3
Pascagoula	21.8	803	37	1.0	15.1	0.0	0.0	0.0	17.7	21.5	4.3	1.0	4.1
Southaven	10.1	433	32	0.0	12.2	0.0	0.0	1.0	31.1	10.6	2.0	0.0	3.3
Tupelo	31.0	871	61	0.0	16.8	0.0	0.0	0.0	19.8	16.5	13.0	3.6	6.6
Vicksburg	29.2	1 073	271	0.2	9.0	0.0	0.0	0.2	20.9	8.2	7.2	0.6	4.5
MISSOURI	X	X	X	X	X	X	X	X	X	X	X	X	X
Ballwin	NA	NA	NA	NA	NA	NA	NA	NA	NA	NA	NA	NA	NA
Blue Springs	22.1	497	142	0.0	18.5	0.0	0.0	4.6	21.8	14.9	17.4	1.3	2.9
Cape Girardeau	40.8	1 145	525	0.0	18.7	0.0	0.0	0.5	10.9	39.0	7.2	0.4	3.9
Chesterfield	27.5	596	235	0.0	34.9	0.0	0.0	0.0	18.3	0.1	15.7	0.0	17.8
Columbia	74.2	941	162	1.0	9.5	6.4	0.0	3.8	12.7	22.0	9.6	1.2	4.5
Florissant	19.3	410	60	0.0	17.4	0.0	0.0	2.1	30.2	0.0	22.5	1.9	2.2
Gladstone	17.2	613	159	0.0	29.4	0.0	0.0	0.0	19.1	1.9	9.7	4.3	1.0
Hazelwood	16.3	1 135	68	0.0	12.1	0.0	0.0	0.0	29.2	0.0	12.3	0.4	6.6
Independence	79.1	677	114	0.0	13.1	0.0	0.0	1.6	19.5	13.5	3.5	1.9	8.2
Jefferson City	NA	NA	NA	NA	NA	NA	NA	NA	NA	NA	NA	NA	NA
Joplin	31.1	696	90	0.2	20.0	0.0	0.0	3.5	17.4	11.2	7.6	1.5	5.3
Kansas City	692.9	1 569	147	0.0	5.1	0.1	0.0	9.0	16.2	7.1	9.4	6.6	8.4
Kirkwood	19.8	738	168	0.0	16.8	0.0	0.0	0.0	20.9	7.5	10.1	0.0	3.0
Lee's Summit	55.5	833	164	0.0	21.2	0.0	0.0	0.0	22.3	12.9	4.0	2.0	5.5
Liberty	16.3	638	109	0.0	17.0	0.0	0.0	0.0	14.7	22.8	15.1	1.2	1.6
Maryland Heights	NA	NA	NA	NA	NA	NA	NA	NA	NA	NA	NA	NA	NA
O'Fallon	42.7	1 220	909	0.0	53.4	0.0	0.0	0.0	7.2	0.0	6.3	0.0	2.0
Raytown	13.7	483	61	0.0	15.3	0.0	0.0	5.2	28.7	18.2	7.7	0.0	4.3
St. Charles	63.2	1 087	555	0.0	22.4	0.6	0.0	0.2	15.7	8.1	6.2	1.1	2.7
St. Joseph	44.1	634	103	0.7	19.8	0.5	0.0	3.4	14.3	14.3	9.0	7.5	2.7
St. Louis	630.1	1 857	337	0.0	2.4	0.8	0.0	4.7	19.7	0.5	1.2	6.9	7.9
St. Peters	42.6	847	268	0.0	36.1	0.0	0.0	0.7	11.2	13.5	15.1	0.0	3.1
Springfield	131.2	918	152	2.9	13.8	0.0	0.0	4.1	13.5	16.1	6.3	2.2	5.1
University City	23.1	627	31	0.0	14.5	0.3	0.0	0.0	24.4	7.8	12.2	0.0	6.9
Wildwood	4.4	NA	NA	0.0	69.5	0.0	0.0	0.0	16.2	0.0	0.0	5.0	0.0
MONTANA	X	X	X	X	X	X	X	X	X	X	X	X	X
Billings	71.1	775	122	0.0	12.9	0.7	0.0	0.5	11.5	15.3	3.4	2.0	5.4
Bozeman	19.4	648	16	0.0	5.5	0.0	0.0	0.0	12.2	21.3	5.3	3.1	5.9
Butte-Silver Bow	33.8	994	33	2.3	6.9	0.4	0.0	3.2	14.4	11.2	3.9	4.4	14.1
Great Falls	30.0	532	63	0.0	16.3	1.4	0.7	0.9	0.7	20.8	13.1	9.9	4.7
Helena	19.8	700	101	0.0	11.6	0.0	0.0	0.5	17.9	30.2	9.4	0.7	3.8
Missoula	31.6	604	68	0.0	5.9	0.0	0.0	5.1	21.0	10.1	0.1	0.8	7.2
NEBRASKA	X	X	X	X	X	X	X	X	X	X	X	X	X
Bellevue	19.3	439	53	1.0	17.6	0.0	0.0	0.0	21.0	15.8	9.1	2.3	4.0
Fremont	21.9	897	273	0.0	8.7	0.1	0.0	0.3	7.9	34.7	7.6	0.0	1.2
Grand Island	34.2	827	107	1.0	9.2	0.3	0.0	1.0	14.2	10.6	9.7	2.1	3.3
Kearney	23.6	842	242	0.0	26.9	0.0	0.1	0.0	14.2	19.3	9.5	3.4	5.1
Lincoln	179.1	840	187	0.0	15.2	0.9	0.0	12.7	12.1	12.2	6.6	4.7	2.1
Omaha	290.9	783	141	0.0	14.3	2.0	0.0	0.0	17.5	14.8	10.4	2.7	4.6
NEVADA	X	X	X	X	X	X	X	X	X	X	X	X	X
Carson City	138.9	2 817	297	0.9	4.2	0.0	0.0	57.0	10.6	2.1	4.8	0.0	1.7
Henderson	166.5	1 090	250	0.0	6.0	0.0	0.0	0.0	13.3	6.1	14.5	1.3	12.7
Las Vegas	421.6	1 043	220	0.2	11.0	0.5	0.0	0.4	16.4	5.8	11.6	9.0	3.7
North Las Vegas	118.8	1 261	291	0.0	3.7	0.0	0.0	0.3	18.2	12.4	4.6	2.8	1.5

1. Based on population estimated as of July 1 of the year shown.

Table D. Cities — **City Government Finances, City Government Employment, and Climate**

City	City government finances, 1999 (cont'd) Debt outstanding Total (mil dol)	Per capita[1] (dollars)	Percent utility	City government employment, 2001	Climate[2] Mean January	July	Limits January[3]	July[4]	Annual precipitation (inches)	Heating degree days	Cooling degree days
	137	138	139	140	141	142	143	144	145	146	147
MINNESOTA—Cont'd											
Rochester	95.2	1 218	0.0	808	11.5	70.9	2.6	81.8	29.66	8 250	472
Roseville	104.6	3 035	0.0	199	11.8	73.6	2.8	84.0	28.32	7 981	682
St. Cloud	352.3	6 942	19.2	470	8.1	70.1	-2.4	82.6	27.43	8 928	415
St. Louis Park	337.9	7 972	0.0	283	11.8	73.6	2.8	84.0	28.32	7 981	682
St. Paul	661.5	2 571	3.7	3 018	11.8	73.6	2.8	84.0	28.32	7 981	682
Shoreview	36.4	1 391	5.3	NA	NA	NA	NA	NA	NA	NA	NA
Winona	45.1	1 865	5.6	202	14.1	73.2	4.0	85.0	32.57	7 694	662
Woodbury	120.0	2 968	2.0	NA	NA	NA	NA	NA	NA	NA	NA
MISSISSIPPI	X	X	X	X	X	X	X	X	X	X	X
Biloxi	11.6	246	3.8	545	51.0	82.3	42.3	90.0	61.76	1 507	2 666
Columbus	47.2	2 117	84.8	339	NA	NA	NA	NA	NA	NA	NA
Greenville	24.3	579	46.2	496	41.2	81.9	31.0	92.5	53.38	2 778	2 153
Gulfport	86.6	1 337	0.0	3 131	50.7	82.3	41.2	91.3	62.72	1 551	2 645
Hattiesburg	83.1	1 702	20.9	760	46.0	81.3	34.3	91.8	60.58	2 180	2 265
Jackson	349.2	1 854	25.5	2 267	44.1	81.5	32.7	92.4	55.37	2 467	2 215
Meridian	54.3	1 349	49.5	530	45.0	81.0	33.4	92.1	56.71	2 444	2 138
Pascagoula	13.9	510	2.6	320	48.9	82.1	39.3	90.3	63.72	1 761	2 617
Southaven	11.1	472	37.9	244	NA	NA	NA	NA	NA	NA	NA
Tupelo	37.3	1 048	23.9	502	39.9	80.6	30.9	90.7	55.87	3 079	1 908
Vicksburg	24.7	907	12.2	671	NA	NA	NA	NA	NA	NA	NA
MISSOURI	X	X	X	X	X	X	X	X	X	X	X
Ballwin	NA	NA	NA	NA	NA	NA	NA	NA	NA	NA	NA
Blue Springs	9.7	218	22.1	309	25.7	78.5	16.7	88.7	37.62	5 393	1 288
Cape Girardeau	57.3	1 610	20.1	537	31.7	79.6	22.6	90.2	46.31	4 386	1 543
Chesterfield	45.0	978	0.0	179	29.3	79.8	20.8	89.3	37.51	4 758	1 534
Columbia	121.6	1 541	56.4	1 131	27.6	77.4	18.5	88.6	39.05	5 212	1 189
Florissant	8.2	175	0.0	346	29.3	79.8	20.8	89.3	37.51	4 758	1 534
Gladstone	7.9	282	63.6	167	25.7	78.5	16.7	88.7	37.62	5 393	1 288
Hazelwood	20.2	1 402	0.0	195	NA	NA	NA	NA	NA	NA	NA
Independence	168.0	1 438	38.3	1 160	25.7	78.5	16.7	88.7	37.62	5 393	1 288
Jefferson City	NA	NA	NA	NA	27.4	77.4	15.3	90.1	38.43	5 302	1 175
Joplin	18.6	417	0.0	407	32.3	80.0	22.7	90.2	43.23	4 303	1 560
Kansas City	1 029.7	2 332	12.8	6 714	25.7	78.5	16.7	88.7	37.62	5 393	1 288
Kirkwood	17.5	652	6.3	278	29.3	79.8	20.8	89.3	37.51	4 758	1 534
Lee's Summit	93.6	1 404	30.4	591	28.0	78.3	17.5	90.2	39.84	4 993	1 316
Liberty	21.1	826	51.6	196	NA	NA	NA	NA	NA	NA	NA
Maryland Heights	NA	NA	NA	NA	29.3	79.8	20.8	89.3	37.51	4 758	1 534
O'Fallon	15.6	447	31.6	230	NA	NA	NA	NA	NA	NA	NA
Raytown	0.0	0.0	0.0	177	25.7	78.5	16.7	88.7	37.62	5 393	1 288
St. Charles	69.1	1 188	0.0	476	27.5	77.6	17.2	89.2	37.74	5 179	1 226
St. Joseph	20.9	300	0.0	623	24.6	78.1	14.7	88.9	35.69	5 590	1 254
St. Louis	931.4	2 745	4.9	7 834	28.4	78.4	18.9	89.6	37.86	5 001	1 329
St. Peters	33.5	667	30.7	492	27.5	77.6	17.2	89.2	37.74	5 179	1 226
Springfield	244.5	1 711	53.2	2 729	31.1	78.1	20.4	89.6	43.04	4 638	1 320
University City	22.4	607	0.0	429	29.3	79.8	20.8	89.3	37.51	4 758	1 534
Wildwood	0.0	NA	NA	NA	NA	NA	NA	NA	NA	NA	NA
MONTANA	X	X	X	X	X	X	X	X	X	X	X
Billings	77.4	844	13.3	765	22.8	72.5	13.7	86.7	15.08	7 164	652
Bozeman	17.1	572	20.3	257	NA	NA	NA	NA	NA	NA	NA
Butte-Silver Bow	83.5	2 457	29.9	NA	NA	NA	NA	NA	NA	NA	NA
Great Falls	38.2	678	52.0	487	21.2	68.2	11.6	83.3	15.21	7 741	388
Helena	17.5	618	46.4	267	NA	NA	NA	NA	NA	NA	NA
Missoula	36.4	697	0.0	365	22.7	66.8	15.4	83.4	13.46	7 792	280
NEBRASKA	X	X	X	X	X	X	X	X	X	X	X
Bellevue	21.5	487	0.0	238	21.1	76.9	10.9	87.9	29.86	6 300	1 072
Fremont	1.6	66	100.0	301	NA	NA	NA	NA	NA	NA	NA
Grand Island	36.0	869	39.6	562	21.9	76.7	11.1	88.5	24.90	6 421	997
Kearney	18.5	662	18.0	224	NA	NA	NA	NA	NA	NA	NA
Lincoln	403.1	1 892	77.3	2 579	21.3	78.2	10.1	90.0	28.26	6 278	1 134
Omaha	237.2	639	0.0	3 028	21.1	76.9	10.9	87.9	29.86	6 300	1 072
NEVADA	X	X	X	X	X	X	X	X	X	X	X
Carson City	63.9	1 295	25.5	1 475	33.6	69.9	20.7	89.5	10.87	5 691	401
Henderson	512.9	3 358	28.8	1 588	45.5	91.1	33.6	105.9	4.13	2 407	3 201
Las Vegas	278.1	688	0.0	2 573	45.5	91.1	33.6	105.9	4.13	2 407	3 201
North Las Vegas	79.3	842	57.8	1 157	45.5	91.1	33.6	105.9	4.13	2 407	3 201

1. Based on the population estimated as of July 1 of the year shown.   2. Represents normal values based on the 30-year period, 1961–1990.   3. Average daily minimum.   4. Average daily maximum.

Table D. Cities — **Land Area and Population**

STATE Place code	City	Land area, 2000[1] (sq km)	Population, 2000 Total persons	Rank	Per square kilometer	Total persons 1990	Percent change 1990–2000	Total persons 1980	Percent change 1980–1990	White	Black	Am. Indian, Alaska Native	Asian and Pacific Islander	Other race	His-panic[2]	Non-His-panic White
		1	2	3	4	5	6	7	8	9	10	11	12	13	14	15
	NEVADA—Cont'd															
32 60600	Reno	179.0	180 480	112	1 008.3	134 230	34.8	100 756	32.8	80.5	3.2	2.1	7.2	10.8	19.2	69.2
32 68400	Sparks	62.0	66 346	411	1 070.1	53 367	24.3	40 780	30.9	81.4	2.9	1.9	6.8	10.7	19.7	69.5
33 00000	NEW HAMPSHIRE	23 227.3	1 235 786	X	53.2	1 109 252	11.4	920 610	20.5	97.0	1.0	0.6	1.7	0.9	1.7	95.1
33 14200	Concord	166.5	40 687	756	244.4	36 006	13.0	30 400	18.4	96.7	1.4	0.8	1.9	0.7	1.5	94.6
33 18820	Dover	69.2	26 884	1 150	388.5	25 042	7.4	22 387	11.9	95.8	1.5	0.7	2.8	0.7	1.1	93.8
33 45140	Manchester	85.5	107 006	214	1 251.5	99 332	7.7	90 936	9.2	93.3	2.6	0.7	2.8	2.5	4.6	89.3
33 50260	Nashua	80.0	86 605	288	1 082.6	79 662	8.7	67 865	17.4	90.5	2.5	0.6	4.4	3.7	6.2	86.5
33 65140	Rochester	116.9	28 461	1 088	243.5	26 630	6.9	21 560	23.5	98.0	0.8	0.6	1.2	0.5	0.9	96.6
34 00000	NEW JERSEY	19 210.8	8 414 350	X	438.0	7 747 750	8.9	7 365 011	5.0	74.4	14.4	0.6	6.3	6.9	13.3	66.0
34 02080	Atlantic City	29.4	40 517	760	1 378.1	37 986	6.7	40 199	-5.5	29.2	45.9	1.2	11.7	16.7	24.9	19.4
34 03580	Bayonne	14.6	61 842	446	4 235.8	61 464	0.6	65 047	-5.5	82.0	6.3	0.5	5.0	10.4	17.8	69.9
34 05170	Bergenfield Borough	7.5	26 247	1 180	3 499.6	24 458	7.3	25 568	-4.3	64.9	7.8	0.7	21.5	8.3	17.0	54.0
34 10000	Camden	22.8	79 904	324	3 504.6	87 492	-8.7	84 910	3.0	19.0	55.3	1.2	3.3	25.4	38.8	7.1
34 13690	Clifton	29.3	78 672	332	2 685.1	71 984	9.3	74 388	-3.2	80.3	3.3	0.5	7.3	13.4	19.8	67.6
34 19390	East Orange	10.2	69 824	385	6 845.5	73 552	-5.1	77 690	-5.3	4.5	92.8	0.9	1.0	4.9	4.7	2.7
34 21000	Elizabeth	31.7	120 568	182	3 803.4	110 002	9.6	106 201	3.6	60.2	21.6	0.8	3.0	20.5	49.5	26.8
34 21480	Englewood	12.8	26 203	1 186	2 047.1	24 850	5.4	23 701	4.8	44.8	41.5	1.0	6.1	11.5	21.8	32.0
34 22470	Fair Lawn Borough	13.4	31 637	987	2 361.0	30 548	3.6	32 229	-5.2	92.7	1.0	0.2	5.5	2.1	5.5	87.7
34 24420	Fort Lee Borough	6.6	35 461	879	5 372.9	31 997	10.8	32 449	-1.4	64.6	2.1	0.2	32.4	2.9	7.9	57.4
34 25770	Garfield	5.5	29 786	1 045	5 415.6	26 727	11.4	26 803	-0.3	85.4	4.0	0.6	3.2	10.7	20.1	72.4
34 28680	Hackensack	10.7	42 677	717	3 988.5	37 049	15.2	36 039	2.8	56.3	26.5	1.1	8.2	13.3	25.9	39.9
34 32250	Hoboken	3.3	38 577	806	690.0[11]	33 397	15.5	42 460	-21.3	83.1	5.1	0.5	5.0	9.3	20.2	70.5
34 36000	Jersey City	38.6	240 055	72	6 219.0	228 517	5.0	223 532	2.2	37.7	30.0	1.0	17.9	19.6	28.3	23.6
34 36510	Kearny	23.7	40 513	761	1 709.4	34 874	16.2	35 735	-2.4	79.5	4.6	0.6	6.2	13.5	27.3	60.3
34 40350	Linden	28.0	39 394	787	1 406.9	36 701	7.3	37 836	-3.0	68.5	24.4	0.5	2.8	7.7	14.4	57.9
34 41310	Long Branch	13.5	31 340	997	2 321.5	28 658	9.4	29 819	-3.9	71.5	20.0	0.8	2.3	9.9	20.7	56.9
34 46680	Millville	109.7	26 847	1 152	244.7	25 992	3.3	24 815	4.7	77.9	16.2	1.2	1.1	6.1	11.2	71.6
34 51000	Newark	61.6	273 546	63	4 440.7	275 221	-0.6	329 248	-16.4	29.4	55.0	0.8	1.8	17.6	29.5	14.2
34 51210	New Brunswick	13.5	48 573	622	3 598.0	41 711	16.5	41 442	0.6	51.7	24.5	1.2	6.1	21.0	39.0	32.9
34 55950	Paramus Borough	27.1	25 737	1 209	949.7	25 004	2.9	26 474	-5.6	80.4	1.3	0.2	18.0	1.6	4.9	75.5
34 56550	Passaic	8.1	67 861	400	8 377.9	58 041	16.9	52 463	10.6	39.0	15.2	1.2	6.3	43.5	62.5	18.3
34 57000	Paterson	21.9	149 222	138	6 813.8	140 891	5.9	137 970	2.1	35.0	34.6	1.0	2.8	32.9	50.1	13.2
34 58200	Perth Amboy	12.4	47 303	642	3 814.8	41 967	12.7	38 951	7.7	50.9	11.4	1.1	2.0	40.3	69.8	18.9
34 59190	Plainfield	15.6	47 829	632	3 066.0	46 577	2.7	45 555	2.2	24.4	63.9	1.1	1.5	14.0	25.2	11.5
34 61530	Rahway	10.3	26 500	1 163	2 572.8	25 325	4.6	26 723	-5.2	62.3	28.7	0.8	4.1	7.6	13.9	53.2
34 65790	Sayreville Borough	41.2	40 377	765	980.0	34 998	15.4	29 969	16.8	78.0	9.1	0.4	11.4	3.3	7.3	72.0
34 74000	Trenton	19.8	85 403	297	4 313.3	88 675	-3.7	92 124	-3.7	34.5	53.6	0.8	1.6	12.9	21.5	24.6
34 74630	Union City	3.3	67 088	407	329.7[20]	58 012	15.6	55 593	4.4	64.2	5.3	1.2	2.8	33.7	82.3	13.3
34 76070	Vineland	177.9	56 271	515	316.3	54 780	2.7	53 753	1.9	69.8	14.8	1.1	1.6	16.1	30.0	54.8
34 79040	Westfield	17.4	29 644	1 051	1 703.7	28 870	2.7	30 447	-5.2	91.1	4.3	0.3	4.8	1.0	2.8	87.9
34 79610	West New York	2.6	45 768	667	603.1[17]	38 125	20.0	39 194	-2.7	66.7	4.8	1.1	3.5	31.8	78.7	15.5
35 00000	NEW MEXICO	314 309.4	1 819 046	X	5.8	1 515 069	20.1	1 303 302	16.2	69.9	2.3	10.5	1.7	19.4	42.1	44.7
35 01780	Alamogordo	50.1	35 582	876	710.2	27 596	28.9	24 024	14.9	79.1	6.4	1.8	2.7	14.5	32.0	57.8
35 02000	Albuquerque	467.9	448 607	35	958.8	384 915	16.5	331 767	16.0	75.3	3.8	4.9	3.1	17.5	39.9	49.9
35 12150	Carlsbad	73.5	25 625	1 212	348.6	24 952	2.7	25 457	-2.0	79.7	2.6	1.9	1.0	17.4	36.7	58.8
35 16420	Clovis	58.0	32 667	957	563.2	30 954	5.5	31 194	-0.8	74.3	8.3	1.8	2.4	17.0	33.4	55.6
35 25800	Farmington	68.8	37 844	821	550.1	33 997	11.3	31 222	8.9	73.4	1.3	18.4	0.9	9.2	17.7	62.8
35 32520	Hobbs	49.0	28 657	1 078	584.8	29 121	-1.6	29 153	0.1	66.9	7.4	1.8	0.6	27.2	42.2	48.9
35 39380	Las Cruces	134.9	74 267	358	550.5	62 360	19.1	45 060	38.4	72.6	2.9	2.7	1.9	24.2	51.7	42.0
35 63460	Rio Rancho	190.2	51 765	578	272.2	32 512	59.2	NA	NA	82.0	3.4	3.4	2.4	13.1	27.7	64.1
35 64930	Roswell	74.9	45 293	675	604.7	44 260	2.3	39 676	11.6	73.9	2.9	2.1	1.1	23.6	44.3	50.9
35 70500	Santa Fe	96.7	62 203	443	643.3	56 537	10.0	48 953	15.5	80.1	1.0	3.3	1.9	18.3	47.8	47.1
36 00000	NEW YORK	122 283.1	18 976 457	X	155.2	17 990 778	5.5	17 558 165	2.5	70.0	17.0	0.9	6.4	9.1	15.1	62.0
36 01000	Albany	55.4	95 658	248	1 726.7	100 031	-4.4	101 727	-1.7	65.1	29.9	1.0	4.0	3.2	5.6	61.1
36 03078	Auburn	21.7	28 574	1 085	1 316.8	31 258	-8.6	32 501	-3.8	89.9	8.6	0.8	0.8	1.7	2.8	87.4
36 06067	Binghamton	27.0	47 380	641	1 754.8	53 008	-10.6	55 860	-5.1	85.7	10.0	0.8	4.0	2.8	3.9	81.7
36 11000	Buffalo	105.2	292 648	58	2 781.8	328 175	-10.8	357 870	-8.3	56.2	38.6	1.4	1.8	4.7	7.5	51.8
36 24229	Elmira	18.9	30 940	1 009	1 637.0	33 724	-8.3	35 327	-4.5	84.4	14.9	0.9	0.8	1.9	3.1	80.8
36 27485	Freeport	11.9	43 783	700	3 679.2	39 894	9.7	38 272	4.2	46.8	34.7	1.2	2.0	21.1	33.5	31.6
36 29113	Glen Cove	17.2	26 622	1 160	1 547.8	24 149	10.2	24 618	-1.9	82.9	7.0	0.6	5.0	7.8	20.0	68.2
36 33139	Hempstead	9.5	56 554	508	5 953.1	45 982	23.0	40 404	13.8	28.5	54.7	1.4	2.0	18.4	31.8	13.2
36 38077	Ithaca	14.1	29 287	1 064	2 077.1	29 541	-0.9	28 732	2.8	76.4	7.8	1.0	15.6	2.8	5.3	71.3
36 38264	Jamestown	23.3	31 730	979	1 361.8	34 681	-8.5	35 775	-3.1	93.5	4.5	1.2	0.7	2.4	4.9	89.0
36 42554	Lindenhurst	9.7	27 819	1 112	2 867.9	26 879	3.5	26 919	0.1	95.8	1.1	0.4	1.8	2.8	6.5	89.8
36 43335	Long Beach	5.5	35 462	878	6 447.6	33 510	5.8	34 073	-1.7	85.9	6.8	0.5	3.0	6.2	12.8	77.1

1. Dry land or land partially or temporarily covered by water. 2. Hispanic persons may be of any race.

Table D. Cities — **Population and Households**

City	Population characteristics, 2000 (cont'd) Age of population (percent)										Households, 2000			Percent	
	Under 5 years	5 to 17 years	18 to 24 years	25 to 34 years	35 to 44 years	45 to 54 years	55 to 64 years	65 to 74 years	75 years and over	Percent female	Number	Percent change, 1990–2000	Persons per household	Female family householder[1]	One-person
	16	17	18	19	20	21	22	23	24	25	26	27	28	29	30
NEVADA—Cont'd															
Reno	7.0	16.2	11.8	15.9	15.6	13.6	8.5	6.1	5.3	48.9	73 904	29.0	2.38	10.6	32.6
Sparks	7.4	19.5	9.2	14.7	16.9	13.8	8.3	5.6	4.6	50.6	24 601	19.6	2.67	12.0	24.3
NEW HAMPSHIRE	6.1	18.9	8.4	13.0	17.9	14.9	8.9	6.3	5.6	50.8	474 606	15.4	2.53	9.1	24.4
Concord	5.8	17.3	8.3	15.2	17.8	14.3	7.7	5.8	7.9	50.5	16 281	14.5	2.30	11.4	32.7
Dover	5.7	15.2	11.2	17.2	16.7	12.6	7.7	6.5	7.3	52.0	11 573	11.9	2.26	10.3	31.0
Manchester	6.7	17.0	9.5	16.9	16.5	12.9	7.6	6.1	6.8	51.0	44 247	9.7	2.36	11.7	31.7
Nashua	6.5	18.1	8.1	15.9	17.6	13.6	8.5	6.1	5.5	50.6	34 614	11.5	2.46	10.4	28.3
Rochester	6.8	18.5	7.7	14.2	17.4	13.4	8.6	7.3	6.2	51.4	11 434	11.9	2.46	11.4	25.7
NEW JERSEY	6.7	18.1	8.0	14.1	17.1	13.8	9.0	6.8	6.4	51.5	3 064 645	9.7	2.68	12.6	24.5
Atlantic City	7.5	18.2	8.9	15.8	15.2	11.5	8.7	7.3	6.8	51.0	15 848	0.7	2.46	23.2	37.2
Bayonne	5.8	16.3	8.2	14.6	16.1	13.8	8.7	8.0	8.6	52.7	25 545	0.9	2.42	15.1	32.8
Bergenfield Borough	6.8	18.1	7.3	13.4	17.6	14.3	9.0	6.9	6.6	52.2	8 981	2.1	2.92	11.8	20.8
Camden	9.1	25.5	12.0	15.3	14.1	9.9	6.4	4.5	3.1	51.5	24 177	-9.2	3.12	37.7	22.5
Clifton	6.0	15.6	7.7	14.4	16.3	13.8	8.7	7.9	9.7	52.3	30 244	4.1	2.59	11.5	27.9
East Orange	7.9	20.2	9.8	15.2	14.9	12.1	8.7	6.3	5.0	55.0	26 024	-4.4	2.63	28.8	33.0
Elizabeth	7.7	18.6	10.8	17.2	16.5	11.6	7.7	5.2	4.8	50.5	40 482	3.5	2.91	19.1	24.6
Englewood	6.9	17.0	7.4	14.6	15.9	14.3	10.5	7.3	6.0	53.0	9 273	3.4	2.79	17.4	24.8
Fair Lawn Borough	5.3	17.5	6.0	10.3	16.5	16.3	9.3	8.9	9.8	52.5	11 806	2.7	2.67	9.0	21.3
Fort Lee Borough	5.3	12.2	5.1	15.3	17.2	13.9	10.9	10.2	10.0	53.3	16 544	8.6	2.14	7.4	39.0
Garfield	6.1	16.3	9.6	17.0	16.2	13.0	7.8	6.7	7.4	51.3	11 250	2.8	2.64	13.8	27.4
Hackensack	5.8	12.4	8.6	20.7	17.7	13.4	8.9	6.3	6.2	50.3	18 113	10.0	2.26	13.0	39.8
Hoboken	3.2	7.3	15.3	37.9	13.9	8.1	5.4	4.6	4.5	49.1	19 418	29.1	1.92	9.0	41.8
Jersey City	6.9	17.8	10.7	19.4	15.7	11.8	7.9	5.2	4.5	51.2	88 632	7.6	2.67	20.2	29.2
Kearny	5.7	15.7	10.7	18.5	17.2	13.1	8.2	5.6	5.2	48.4	13 539	8.6	2.81	13.2	21.8
Linden	6.0	16.5	8.2	14.6	15.8	13.5	9.1	7.5	8.8	52.5	15 052	4.8	2.60	15.3	27.9
Long Branch	7.0	16.8	10.2	16.5	15.9	12.6	8.2	6.6	6.3	51.5	12 594	9.1	2.47	15.9	34.1
Millville	7.0	21.0	8.6	13.4	15.4	13.2	8.5	6.5	6.4	52.8	10 043	4.2	2.65	17.9	25.1
Newark	7.8	20.2	12.1	16.9	15.1	10.9	7.8	5.3	4.0	51.5	91 382	-0.2	2.85	29.3	26.6
New Brunswick	7.0	13.1	34.0	17.6	10.6	7.1	4.2	3.2	3.3	50.4	13 057	2.7	3.23	18.0	24.3
Paramus Borough	5.2	18.1	5.5	9.0	15.7	14.4	10.7	10.5	11.0	51.4	8 082	3.9	3.00	8.0	14.4
Passaic	9.6	21.2	12.5	17.5	14.2	10.5	6.4	4.2	3.9	50.1	19 458	3.9	3.46	21.7	20.3
Paterson	8.4	21.4	11.2	16.5	15.5	11.3	7.5	4.6	3.7	51.4	44 710	1.7	3.25	26.8	20.4
Perth Amboy	8.0	20.4	11.4	16.5	15.1	11.3	7.0	5.1	5.1	50.4	14 562	2.5	3.20	21.0	20.6
Plainfield	7.9	19.6	10.2	15.9	16.7	12.2	8.3	5.0	4.2	51.1	15 137	0.1	3.10	24.5	21.1
Rahway	6.3	17.6	7.8	14.7	17.3	13.5	8.3	7.2	7.3	52.3	10 028	4.2	2.63	15.6	28.0
Sayreville Borough	6.7	16.8	7.3	16.3	18.0	13.8	8.7	6.5	5.9	51.0	14 955	17.3	2.68	11.1	22.3
Trenton	7.6	20.1	10.1	16.7	15.2	11.5	7.4	5.8	5.6	49.9	29 437	-4.3	2.75	27.1	29.7
Union City	7.4	17.9	11.0	18.0	16.3	11.4	8.0	5.9	4.1	49.9	22 872	11.0	2.92	19.3	23.0
Vineland	6.2	19.5	8.3	13.6	15.4	13.8	9.1	6.9	7.2	52.1	19 930	6.4	2.70	16.8	23.7
Westfield	8.0	20.4	4.0	11.2	18.4	15.7	8.8	6.6	6.9	52.1	10 622	3.2	2.77	7.1	19.3
West New York	6.7	15.6	10.9	18.6	15.5	11.1	8.8	7.3	5.4	50.9	16 719	16.0	2.74	16.9	27.5
NEW MEXICO	7.2	20.8	9.8	12.9	15.5	13.5	8.7	6.5	5.2	50.8	677 971	24.9	2.63	13.2	25.4
Alamogordo	7.6	21.0	9.2	14.2	15.5	11.5	8.3	7.4	5.3	50.6	13 704	30.7	2.57	11.7	25.2
Albuquerque	6.9	17.7	10.6	15.0	16.0	13.8	8.2	6.1	5.8	51.4	183 236	19.1	2.40	12.9	30.5
Carlsbad	7.3	19.8	8.4	11.1	13.6	13.5	9.1	8.1	9.1	51.8	9 957	7.4	2.51	13.1	26.6
Clovis	8.3	21.7	9.4	13.1	14.9	11.5	8.0	6.7	6.3	52.0	12 458	6.7	2.57	14.9	26.8
Farmington	7.6	21.7	9.9	12.5	16.0	13.7	7.9	5.8	4.9	51.0	13 982	16.7	2.67	12.4	22.6
Hobbs	8.1	22.3	10.3	13.1	14.9	11.5	7.8	6.7	5.2	50.0	10 040	-2.0	2.72	14.6	23.4
Las Cruces	7.0	18.1	16.0	13.4	13.4	11.1	7.8	7.1	6.0	51.5	29 184	22.6	2.46	15.1	27.9
Rio Rancho	7.5	21.7	7.0	13.7	18.4	13.1	7.0	5.7	6.0	51.5	18 995	62.9	2.70	10.3	20.8
Roswell	7.4	21.1	9.9	11.3	13.6	12.3	8.3	7.8	8.2	51.8	17 068	5.4	2.58	14.9	27.1
Santa Fe	5.4	14.9	8.9	13.7	15.3	17.3	10.7	7.3	6.6	52.2	27 569	21.0	2.20	12.1	36.4
NEW YORK	6.5	18.2	9.3	14.5	16.2	13.5	8.9	6.7	6.2	51.8	7 056 860	6.3	2.61	14.7	28.1
Albany	5.6	14.3	19.3	15.9	13.4	11.3	6.9	5.9	7.4	52.5	40 709	-3.4	2.11	16.1	41.9
Auburn	6.3	16.5	9.3	14.8	15.5	12.6	7.2	7.2	10.6	50.3	11 411	-4.4	2.27	14.7	36.3
Binghamton	6.1	15.5	13.2	13.0	13.7	12.5	8.5	7.7	9.9	52.7	21 089	-6.8	2.19	13.8	40.3
Buffalo	7.1	19.2	11.3	14.4	14.9	12.0	7.6	6.8	6.7	53.0	122 720	-10.1	2.29	22.3	37.7
Elmira	7.0	18.1	13.0	14.2	15.7	11.5	6.7	6.5	7.3	49.7	11 475	-7.7	2.37	18.4	34.5
Freeport	6.9	19.5	9.1	15.1	16.9	13.5	8.5	5.7	4.8	51.9	13 504	2.0	3.20	17.8	21.2
Glen Cove	6.2	15.0	8.1	14.7	15.9	13.0	9.5	8.1	9.4	51.9	9 461	11.8	2.72	12.7	24.1
Hempstead	7.9	18.4	16.3	17.1	14.4	10.5	7.1	4.3	4.1	52.2	15 188	4.1	3.41	27.0	20.8
Ithaca	2.5	6.8	53.8	12.6	7.4	7.1	3.5	2.8	3.5	49.4	10 287	7.0	2.13	7.8	43.3
Jamestown	7.6	18.3	9.1	13.5	14.7	12.9	8.0	7.5	8.5	52.3	13 558	-5.0	2.29	14.5	35.0
Lindenhurst	6.9	19.8	7.1	14.5	19.5	13.5	7.6	6.3	4.7	51.4	9 061	5.4	3.06	11.8	17.0
Long Beach	4.9	13.7	6.6	16.5	17.9	14.9	8.9	7.6	9.1	51.9	14 923	9.8	2.26	10.8	36.7

1. No spouse present.

City	Persons in group quarters, 2000 Total	Institutional Total	Persons in nursing homes	Non-Institutional[1]	Serious crimes known to police, 2000[2] Total Number	Rate[3]	Violent	Property	Education, 1990 School enrollment Public	Private	Attainment[4] (percent) High school graduate or more	Bachelor's degree or more	Money income, 1989 Per capita (dollars)[5]	Households Median Dollars	Percent change, 1979–1989 (constant 1989 dollars)
	31	32	33	34	35	36	37	38	39	40	41	42	43	44	45
NEVADA—Cont'd															
Reno	4 496	1 633	651	2 863	9 965	5 521	496	5 025	28 714	2 951	81.9	22.4	16 091	28 388	-3.4
Sparks	623	551	429	72	3 365	5 072	424	4 648	12 119	898	82.3	16.0	14 453	32 420	-7.8
NEW HAMPSHIRE	35 539	13 784	9 316	21 755	30 068	2 433	175	2 258	219 482	57 283	82.2	24.4	15 959	36 329	27.4
Concord	3 267	2 819	684	448	NA	NA	NA	NA	6 766	1 677	84.5	28.1	15 981	32 733	22.6
Dover	757	646	493	111	NA	NA	NA	NA	4 543	1 179	83.1	24.3	15 413	31 507	20.7
Manchester	2 692	1 442	883	1 250	3 935	3 677	226	3 451	15 971	5 932	74.9	19.6	15 111	31 911	22.0
Nashua	1 403	639	588	764	NA	NA	NA	NA	14 699	4 765	82.7	28.8	18 010	40 505	25.3
Rochester	293	221	201	72	925	3 250	285	2 965	4 845	1 017	75.0	14.1	13 395	30 807	14.4
NEW JERSEY	194 821	110 169	51 493	84 652	265 935	3 161	384	2 777	1 453 475	413 927	76.7	24.9	18 714	40 927	23.3
Atlantic City	1 475	332	332	1 143	7 063	17 432	1 308	16 124	6 257	997	58.3	9.5	12 017	20 309	23.6
Bayonne	142	0	0	142	1 356	2 193	277	1 916	9 090	3 502	70.1	16.6	16 159	31 954	12.9
Bergenfield Borough	56	8	0	48	280	1 067	84	983	3 924	1 103	82.3	23.8	18 713	45 713	19.4
Camden	4 375	3 454	420	921	6 504	8 140	2 086	6 054	22 739	3 405	49.7	6.4	7 276	17 386	11.7
Clifton	386	244	244	142	2 284	2 903	280	2 624	11 339	3 127	72.9	20.4	18 950	39 905	20.0
East Orange	1 304	925	553	379	5 050	7 232	1 754	5 478	14 771	4 573	69.3	14.7	12 376	26 810	19.6
Elizabeth	2 916	2 313	497	603	7 062	5 857	719	5 138	21 337	6 015	58.5	11.5	12 112	27 631	6.9
Englewood	286	156	156	130	719	2 744	218	2 526	3 557	2 118	80.1	34.7	25 820	46 758	32.8
Fair Lawn Borough	168	139	139	29	523	1 653	145	1 508	5 059	1 786	81.3	30.3	22 418	49 658	19.2
Fort Lee Borough	34	0	0	34	646	1 822	73	1 748	3 651	1 847	84.9	42.2	31 758	46 395	23.2
Garfield	70	0	0	70	677	2 273	191	2 082	3 790	1 261	60.1	11.5	14 963	31 649	19.8
Hackensack	1 662	990	306	672	1 385	3 245	368	2 877	5 178	1 603	74.4	25.7	20 217	38 976	29.2
Hoboken	1 288	158	0	1 130	1 435	3 720	366	3 354	4 539	2 763	69.8	39.7	20 020	34 873	78.8
Jersey City	3 377	1 563	1 326	1 814	12 437	5 062	1 162	3 900	38 426	18 260	65.7	21.4	13 060	29 054	35.6
Kearny	2 520	2 423	160	97	1 327	3 275	205	3 071	6 166	2 098	68.5	15.3	15 735	37 840	19.8
Linden	253	246	246	7	1 705	4 328	381	3 947	6 110	1 428	68.2	12.2	16 308	35 911	9.8
Long Branch	205	70	70	135	1 094	3 491	475	3 015	4 756	1 401	71.8	20.1	16 104	30 693	32.8
Millville	258	123	123	135	1 420	5 289	711	4 578	5 768	709	69.8	11.6	13 748	31 266	14.9
Newark	12 773	7 451	2 420	5 322	19 663	7 188	1 496	5 692	64 085	12 541	51.2	8.5	9 424	21 650	27.7
New Brunswick	6 446	109	90	6 337	2 997	6 170	681	5 489	16 133	1 514	66.0	23.4	11 252	28 289	24.2
Paramus Borough	1 507	1 244	651	263	2 473	9 609	528	9 080	4 598	1 440	85.4	31.2	22 202	58 995	18.2
Passaic	579	200	200	379	3 104	4 574	1 229	3 345	11 197	3 442	55.6	14.2	11 057	26 669	29.7
Paterson	3 821	2 139	201	1 682	6 443	4 318	807	3 511	28 935	8 211	54.9	8.7	10 518	26 960	34.1
Perth Amboy	702	379	358	323	1 606	3 395	452	2 943	8 811	1 672	50.2	8.2	11 351	28 377	17.1
Plainfield	907	550	399	357	2 774	5 800	1 413	4 386	9 386	2 979	71.4	18.9	14 742	38 463	25.8
Rahway	160	118	118	42	882	3 328	260	3 068	4 265	1 209	77.2	17.8	17 383	40 776	13.9
Sayreville Borough	246	194	194	52	897	2 222	233	1 989	5 981	1 446	78.3	17.0	18 297	46 057	11.3
Trenton	4 401	3 301	512	1 100	6 369	7 458	1 609	5 849	16 369	5 161	58.2	10.5	11 018	25 719	26.0
Union City	355	181	181	174	2 420	3 607	478	3 129	10 978	3 510	50.5	10.7	11 089	25 655	22.4
Vineland	2 402	1 052	606	1 350	3 067	5 450	722	4 729	10 891	2 241	61.3	12.6	12 963	30 733	14.9
Westfield	267	177	177	90	380	1 282	44	1 238	5 833	1 510	91.2	53.6	30 748	66 760	31.9
West New York	28	0	0	28	1 360	2 972	354	2 618	6 725	1 735	49.9	12.4	12 047	26 361	23.8
NEW MEXICO	36 307	19 178	6 810	17 129	100 391	5 519	758	4 761	400 077	35 912	75.1	20.4	11 246	24 087	-1.9
Alamogordo	426	364	182	62	1 289	3 623	261	3 361	6 917	664	82.0	16.7	11 255	24 579	2.8
Albuquerque	9 344	4 043	1 835	5 301	39 447	8 793	1 145	7 648	94 742	11 923	83.9	28.4	14 013	27 555	-0.4
Carlsbad	654	517	378	137	1 728	6 743	523	6 220	6 356	491	68.9	11.5	10 508	22 605	-5.2
Clovis	596	500	300	96	2 439	7 466	1 378	6 089	8 510	341	74.1	13.8	10 002	21 222	-5.8
Farmington	509	348	221	161	2 088	5 517	1 015	4 503	9 771	580	79.9	18.4	12 302	28 911	-13.8
Hobbs	1 333	1 226	176	107	1 530	5 339	956	4 383	8 103	650	66.4	13.4	10 230	22 807	-25.7
Las Cruces	2 399	1 147	243	1 252	6 765	9 109	619	8 490	19 862	1 078	79.1	29.2	11 175	23 648	3.8
Rio Rancho	418	257	257	161	1 570	3 033	388	2 645	7 475	648	87.4	19.6	12 345	31 512	NA
Roswell	1 192	554	322	638	3 517	7 765	1 104	6 661	11 187	1 077	69.3	15.1	10 830	21 870	4.4
Santa Fe	1 474	415	415	1 059	4 915	7 902	649	7 252	10 888	2 973	84.0	36.1	16 554	30 023	12.2
NEW YORK	580 461	262 262	123 852	318 199	588 189	3 100	554	2 546	3 538 249	1 117 969	74.8	23.1	16 501	32 965	18.2
Albany	9 902	2 046	1 418	7 856	7 092	7 414	1 165	6 249	22 598	8 263	77.7	29.5	13 742	25 152	20.0
Auburn	2 620	2 200	445	420	1 130	3 955	259	3 696	6 179	778	68.3	11.9	10 638	22 271	-1.0
Binghamton	1 244	911	632	333	2 364	4 989	376	4 614	11 617	1 685	73.9	19.8	12 106	20 891	2.3
Buffalo	11 126	5 203	2 767	5 923	20 248	6 919	1 250	5 669	73 144	15 883	67.3	16.0	10 445	18 482	-4.9
Elmira	3 732	2 514	331	1 218	1 576	5 094	381	4 712	6 828	1 872	71.4	11.1	9 489	18 548	-7.4
Freeport	637	375	375	262	1 037	2 368	448	1 921	8 330	1 812	77.2	21.4	17 018	43 948	31.3
Glen Cove	876	558	558	318	236	886	64	823	4 048	1 706	76.3	28.0	21 787	42 982	14.0
Hempstead	4 741	1 001	1 001	3 740	1 393	2 463	626	1 837	9 452	6 029	70.2	16.0	13 294	36 715	29.0
Ithaca	7 417	180	171	7 237	955	3 261	137	3 124	5 648	12 862	86.7	50.2	9 213	17 738	2.8
Jamestown	735	341	300	394	1 296	4 084	394	3 691	7 384	856	71.2	13.4	10 731	20 582	1.4
Lindenhurst	125	0	0	125	NA	NA	NA	NA	5 190	1 111	77.4	12.1	16 116	46 615	32.6
Long Beach	1 714	900	814	814	592	1 669	228	1 441	4 724	1 499	83.0	28.7	20 993	41 495	51.8

1. Persons in emergency shelters and persons visible in street locations. 2. Data for serious crimes have not been adjusted for underreporting. This may affect comparability between geographic areas and over time. 3. Per 100,000 population estimated by the FBI. 4. Persons 25 years old and older. 5. Based on population enumerated as of April 1, 1990.

Table D. Cities — Income, Poverty, and Housing

City	Money income, 1989 (cont'd)				Housing units, 2000										
	House-holds (cont'd)	Percent below poverty, 1989					Vacant units				Occupied units				
		Persons		Fam-ilies											
	Percent with $100,000 or more	Total	Percent change in rate, 1979–1989	Total	Total	Percent change, 1990–2000	Vacant units for sale or rent[1]	For seasonal use (percent)	Home owner vacancy rate	Renter vacancy rate	Total	Percent owner occu-pied	Percent renter occu-pied	Average size owner occu-pied	Average size renter occu-pied
	46	47	48	49	50	51	52	53	54	55	56	57	58	59	60
NEVADA—Cont'd															
Reno	4.1	11.5	42.0	7.6	79 453	29.4	5 549	0.5	2.2	7.9	73 904	47.5	52.5	2.53	2.25
Sparks	2.1	7.2	26.3	4.8	26 025	20.2	1 424	0.2	2.4	7.0	24 601	59.7	40.3	2.76	2.54
NEW HAMPSHIRE	4.5	6.4	-24.4	4.4	547 024	8.6	72 418	10.3	1.0	3.5	474 606	69.7	30.3	2.70	2.14
Concord	3.4	6.7	-25.6	4.2	16 881	7.5	600	0.7	0.8	2.9	16 281	51.4	48.6	2.62	1.96
Dover	2.4	9.4	-17.5	5.6	11 924	5.5	351	0.6	0.7	1.8	11 573	51.2	48.8	2.54	1.96
Manchester	2.5	9.0	-13.5	6.3	45 892	3.5	1 645	0.5	0.5	3.1	44 247	46.0	54.0	2.61	2.14
Nashua	5.3	6.5	0.0	4.7	35 387	6.0	773	0.5	0.4	1.6	34 614	56.9	43.1	2.66	2.20
Rochester	1.2	6.3	-16.0	5.0	11 836	6.9	402	0.7	0.9	2.8	11 434	66.8	33.2	2.56	2.26
NEW JERSEY	8.8	7.6	-20.2	5.6	3 310 275	7.6	245 630	3.3	1.2	4.5	3 064 645	65.6	34.4	2.81	2.43
Atlantic City	1.8	25.0	0.4	20.6	20 219	-6.5	4 371	9.6	6.2	7.3	15 848	28.9	71.1	2.66	2.38
Bayonne	4.2	8.8	-8.3	6.3	26 826	1.4	1 281	0.2	0.9	3.6	25 545	40.0	60.0	2.61	2.28
Bergenfield Borough	8.8	3.3	3.1	2.1	9 147	1.2	166	0.2	0.4	1.8	8 981	71.1	28.9	3.09	2.49
Camden	0.5	36.6	-0.8	34.1	29 769	-1.2	5 592	0.1	5.1	6.1	24 177	46.1	53.9	3.16	3.09
Clifton	6.3	4.7	6.8	3.1	31 060	3.5	816	0.2	0.7	2.4	30 244	60.9	39.1	2.75	2.33
East Orange	3.0	17.7	-11.9	15.6	28 485	-1.7	2 461	0.1	2.3	6.8	26 024	26.6	73.4	3.27	2.40
Elizabeth	2.1	16.1	1.9	13.7	42 838	3.7	2 356	0.3	1.5	3.4	40 482	29.7	70.3	3.25	2.76
Englewood	15.0	8.4	-9.7	5.5	9 614	2.2	341	0.4	1.0	2.5	9 273	59.4	40.6	2.91	2.63
Fair Lawn Borough	11.6	2.9	-17.1	2.3	12 006	2.1	200	0.2	0.4	1.9	11 806	80.0	20.0	2.80	2.11
Fort Lee Borough	16.9	6.0	30.4	3.9	17 446	3.6	902	1.5	1.3	3.9	16 544	56.2	43.8	2.13	2.15
Garfield	2.0	7.4	8.8	5.1	11 698	2.1	448	0.3	0.8	2.9	11 250	40.2	59.8	2.80	2.54
Hackensack	5.7	7.0	-19.5	4.8	18 945	7.0	832	0.6	1.3	3.8	18 113	32.4	67.6	2.49	2.15
Hoboken	7.2	16.4	-30.2	15.9	19 915	14.3	497	0.3	0.6	1.7	19 418	22.6	77.4	1.96	1.91
Jersey City	3.5	18.9	-10.8	16.6	93 648	3.2	5 016	0.3	1.9	3.3	88 632	28.2	71.8	2.98	2.55
Kearny	4.6	6.1	-24.7	4.0	13 872	3.3	333	0.2	0.6	2.1	13 539	48.0	52.0	3.00	2.63
Linden	3.2	5.6	-20.0	4.0	15 567	4.4	515	0.2	1.1	3.0	15 052	58.7	41.3	2.75	2.39
Long Branch	5.0	14.7	-25.8	10.8	13 983	2.6	1 389	5.0	1.3	3.6	12 594	42.4	57.6	2.61	2.37
Millville	2.2	11.5	3.6	9.2	10 652	4.9	609	0.5	2.0	5.8	10 043	63.9	36.1	2.71	2.54
Newark	1.5	26.3	-19.8	22.8	100 141	-2.3	8 759	0.1	2.0	5.6	91 382	23.8	76.2	3.22	2.74
New Brunswick	2.9	22.0	-6.4	15.7	13 893	2.5	836	0.3	2.0	3.4	13 057	26.3	73.7	3.01	3.30
Paramus Borough	17.8	3.0	0.0	1.6	8 209	4.0	127	0.2	0.5	2.2	8 082	90.7	9.3	3.00	2.94
Passaic	3.5	17.0	-27.7	14.6	20 194	2.9	736	0.2	2.0	1.9	19 458	27.0	73.0	3.63	3.40
Paterson	2.5	18.5	-26.6	15.7	47 169	2.2	2 459	0.1	1.7	3.8	44 710	31.5	68.5	3.59	3.10
Perth Amboy	1.8	15.2	-14.1	12.5	15 236	1.5	674	0.2	1.5	2.8	14 562	40.5	59.5	3.24	3.17
Plainfield	6.8	12.2	-6.2	9.5	16 180	0.7	1 043	0.1	2.3	5.0	15 137	50.1	49.9	3.16	3.04
Rahway	5.0	6.4	6.7	4.9	10 381	3.9	353	0.1	1.2	3.3	10 028	62.7	37.3	2.84	2.26
Sayreville Borough	7.6	3.1	0.0	2.4	15 235	14.1	280	0.1	0.6	1.6	14 955	67.7	32.3	2.84	2.35
Trenton	1.5	18.1	-14.6	15.1	33 843	0.8	4 406	0.1	4.0	8.4	29 437	45.5	54.5	2.83	2.69
Union City	2.0	18.2	-10.3	16.7	23 741	5.1	869	0.2	1.0	2.3	22 872	18.2	81.8	2.98	2.90
Vineland	3.5	10.9	-21.6	8.6	20 958	7.2	1 028	0.5	1.7	4.4	19 930	66.2	33.8	2.74	2.63
Westfield	27.9	1.8	-41.9	1.2	10 819	2.2	197	0.4	0.3	2.7	10 622	81.7	18.3	2.94	1.99
West New York	2.4	16.4	-10.4	12.8	17 360	9.9	641	0.3	1.4	2.5	16 719	19.9	80.1	2.70	2.74
NEW MEXICO	2.5	20.6	17.1	16.5	780 579	23.5	102 608	4.1	2.2	11.6	677 971	70.0	30.0	2.72	2.41
Alamogordo	0.9	13.5	-10.0	11.4	15 920	33.0	2 216	1.1	3.5	18.0	13 704	60.7	39.3	2.61	2.49
Albuquerque	3.3	14.0	12.9	10.3	198 465	18.9	15 229	0.4	1.9	11.8	183 236	60.4	39.6	2.55	2.16
Carlsbad	2.2	20.7	59.2	16.9	11 421	8.0	1 464	0.6	3.3	20.1	9 957	71.5	28.5	2.56	2.38
Clovis	1.1	21.4	31.3	17.1	14 269	9.9	1 811	0.5	5.1	12.2	12 458	62.3	37.7	2.58	2.57
Farmington	2.8	15.2	67.0	12.2	15 077	14.9	1 095	0.7	1.5	9.5	13 982	68.4	31.6	2.74	2.51
Hobbs	2.3	24.8	100.0	20.9	11 968	-2.9	1 928	0.3	4.0	21.1	10 040	67.9	32.1	2.76	2.64
Las Cruces	1.4	22.6	11.3	16.6	31 682	23.4	2 498	0.7	2.3	9.3	29 184	58.1	41.9	2.60	2.28
Rio Rancho	1.0	4.6	NA	3.4	20 209	64.0	1 214	0.5	2.3	12.2	18 995	81.5	18.5	2.75	2.51
Roswell	2.4	21.6	21.3	17.7	19 327	5.9	2 259	0.6	3.3	14.2	17 068	68.4	31.6	2.64	2.47
Santa Fe	5.3	12.3	-12.8	9.2	30 533	23.7	2 964	5.2	1.7	5.5	27 569	58.2	41.8	2.31	2.05
NEW YORK	6.8	13.0	-2.8	10.0	7 679 307	6.3	622 447	3.1	1.6	4.6	7 056 860	53.0	47.0	2.78	2.41
Albany	2.6	18.3	4.6	12.1	45 288	-2.0	4 579	0.2	3.3	7.0	40 709	37.6	62.4	2.31	1.98
Auburn	0.8	13.8	7.8	11.9	12 637	-0.4	1 226	0.2	2.7	11.4	11 411	51.9	48.1	2.48	2.05
Binghamton	1.8	20.0	29.0	12.0	23 971	-2.7	2 882	0.3	3.9	11.2	21 089	43.0	57.0	2.33	2.08
Buffalo	1.4	25.6	23.7	21.7	145 574	-4.2	22 854	0.2	4.2	11.1	122 720	43.5	56.5	2.47	2.16
Elmira	1.2	22.2	26.9	19.4	12 895	-3.1	1 420	0.3	3.2	10.9	11 475	48.3	51.7	2.49	2.26
Freeport	8.5	7.4	-40.8	5.4	13 819	1.2	315	0.3	1.1	1.1	13 504	65.2	34.8	3.23	3.14
Glen Cove	12.5	6.4	10.3	4.2	9 734	10.6	273	0.7	0.9	1.3	9 461	58.5	41.5	2.75	2.67
Hempstead	5.7	12.4	-13.9	10.4	15 579	3.1	391	0.1	1.1	1.7	15 188	43.2	56.8	3.70	3.19
Ithaca	2.5	39.4	22.0	15.0	10 736	6.6	449	0.4	2.1	2.7	10 287	26.0	74.0	2.30	2.07
Jamestown	1.1	18.7	37.5	14.6	15 027	-2.8	1 469	0.2	2.6	9.8	13 558	51.3	48.7	2.46	2.10
Lindenhurst	6.5	3.5	-18.6	2.6	9 277	4.9	216	0.3	0.7	2.6	9 061	80.6	19.4	3.21	2.43
Long Beach	9.9	8.3	-37.6	5.4	16 128	5.0	1 205	4.2	1.0	3.2	14 923	53.4	46.6	2.45	2.05

1. Includes units rented or sold but not occupied.   2. Specified owner-occupied units.   3. Specified renter-occupied units.   4. Overcrowded or lacking complete plumbing facilities.

Table D. Cities — Labor Force, Employment, Disability, and Construction

City	Civilian labor force, 2001		Unemployment		Civilian employment, 1990[2]	Percent		Disability 1990	Value of residential construction authorized by building permits, 2000		
	Total	Percent change, 2000–2001	Total	Rate[1]	Total	Professional, managerial, and technical	Precision production, craft, and repair	Work disabled persons[3] (percent)	New construction ($1,000)	Number of housing units	Percent single family
	61	62	63	64	65	66	67	68	69	70	71
NEVADA—Cont'd											
Reno	97 188	2.8	4 350	4.5	74 448	28.3	8.0	7.8	201 890	2 380	53.6
Sparks	38 872	2.6	1 464	3.8	29 998	25.6	8.9	7.3	118 244	1 125	77.0
NEW HAMPSHIRE	688 657	0.5	24 364	3.5	574 237	32.6	12.5	7.3	936 623	6 680	91.3
Concord	22 459	0.6	549	2.4	17 890	37.6	9.8	7.0	12 680	103	100.0
Dover	15 200	1.1	367	2.4	13 701	33.2	11.0	7.8	23 718	177	95.5
Manchester	59 227	1.6	2 100	3.5	51 828	28.0	11.2	8.9	25 238	240	65.0
Nashua	48 774	1.4	2 228	4.6	43 728	37.3	10.4	7.3	11 655	159	78.6
Rochester	14 710	1.4	535	3.6	12 967	25.1	15.3	9.8	8 945	113	84.1
NEW JERSEY	4 179 451	-0.2	175 650	4.2	3 868 698	34.0	10.0	6.2	3 375 977	34 585	73.0
Atlantic City	19 078	-0.9	1 782	9.3	16 812	17.0	5.2	10.9	2 848	26	100.0
Bayonne	29 954	-0.6	1 246	4.2	29 354	28.3	10.9	7.7	2 378	35	2.9
Bergenfield Borough	13 166	-1.2	546	4.1	13 293	33.4	10.9	5.4	425	4	100.0
Camden	31 291	-0.4	3 743	12.0	27 308	17.0	8.8	12.2	190	5	100.0
Clifton	36 813	-1.4	1 369	3.7	37 633	30.7	11.8	4.9	0	0	0.0
East Orange	34 450	-0.4	2 496	7.2	33 853	25.4	7.5	9.1	18	2	0.0
Elizabeth	54 661	-0.3	4 072	7.4	50 977	18.2	11.5	7.1	22 668	344	31.4
Englewood	13 105	-1.2	574	4.4	13 200	41.3	5.6	5.9	0	0	0.0
Fair Lawn Borough	15 177	-1.4	469	3.1	15 493	40.3	8.0	5.7	1 095	13	30.8
Fort Lee Borough	16 411	-1.3	644	3.9	16 608	50.2	5.3	3.6	78 360	590	1.7
Garfield	13 611	-1.1	712	5.2	13 587	21.5	14.0	6.2	958	18	0.0
Hackensack	21 066	-1.1	1 005	4.8	21 132	31.9	8.5	6.1	34 392	323	7.4
Hoboken	19 625	-0.6	850	4.3	19 197	44.4	5.1	5.5	28 355	319	0.0
Jersey City	110 860	-0.3	8 565	7.7	104 595	27.5	7.7	7.2	9 667	167	3.6
Kearny	18 437	-0.6	807	4.4	18 026	24.8	10.8	5.6	539	8	0.0
Linden	18 659	-0.7	929	5.0	17 866	23.8	12.0	7.2	3 562	67	9.0
Long Branch	16 112	1.5	980	6.1	13 759	30.1	10.9	8.8	5 439	62	100.0
Millville	12 296	-1.7	797	6.5	12 191	24.6	13.6	8.6	1 715	41	100.0
Newark	109 718	-0.1	10 086	9.2	105 553	16.7	10.3	10.7	51 582	861	12.8
New Brunswick	24 152	1.3	1 577	6.5	20 422	28.3	6.6	5.6	2 391	40	75.0
Paramus Borough	12 392	-1.4	374	3.0	12 659	38.7	8.6	4.7	10 939	57	100.0
Passaic	27 317	-0.8	2 394	8.8	26 463	18.6	9.7	7.2	1 562	30	3.3
Paterson	64 617	-0.8	5 713	8.8	62 543	16.0	10.9	8.0	4 105	71	91.5
Perth Amboy	23 527	1.6	1 902	8.1	19 563	17.5	10.9	7.5	582	10	40.0
Plainfield	25 187	-0.5	1 630	6.5	23 738	26.0	7.9	7.4	894	14	100.0
Rahway	13 712	-0.8	545	4.0	13 268	29.1	11.2	5.9	2 548	32	93.8
Sayreville Borough	21 794	0.7	639	2.9	19 137	28.6	12.1	5.2	6 718	134	88.1
Trenton	41 960	2.6	3 054	7.3	37 616	21.1	8.7	9.9	1 724	34	100.0
Union City	29 209	-0.3	2 265	7.8	27 550	17.2	10.1	6.1	0	0	0.0
Vineland	25 242	-1.7	1 839	7.3	24 812	24.9	11.9	9.7	9 941	107	88.8
Westfield	15 532	-1.0	343	2.2	15 306	52.9	5.1	3.4	4 036	25	100.0
West New York	19 526	-0.4	1 187	6.1	18 751	17.8	10.7	6.3	6 212	377	2.1
NEW MEXICO	837 780	0.6	39 802	4.8	629 272	31.6	12.0	8.8	1 072 810	8 869	92.3
Alamogordo	11 404	-0.7	518	4.5	10 377	31.0	15.5	9.3	14 948	144	66.7
Albuquerque	243 272	0.9	8 389	3.4	187 555	37.6	9.1	8.2	328 170	3 522	96.9
Carlsbad	11 372	-1.5	649	5.7	9 264	26.0	18.5	11.9	3 000	26	100.0
Clovis	14 885	-0.7	498	3.3	11 757	25.7	13.7	10.9	4 261	39	100.0
Farmington	22 097	2.4	817	3.7	14 691	31.5	14.3	6.9	14 146	104	100.0
Hobbs	13 355	4.2	452	3.4	11 071	24.8	18.5	9.7	312	2	100.0
Las Cruces	36 037	0.5	2 292	6.4	26 918	38.6	8.4	7.0	45 133	513	55.6
Rio Rancho	25 136	1.0	734	2.9	14 892	31.2	11.7	7.2	50 634	576	100.0
Roswell	18 699	0.2	1 138	6.1	17 322	26.7	11.5	10.8	3 682	30	100.0
Santa Fe	37 949	-0.2	896	2.4	29 117	39.7	7.9	6.4	49 056	395	89.6
NEW YORK	8 831 770	-1.2	429 339	4.9	8 370 718	33.5	9.4	7.4	4 991 529	44 105	54.1
Albany	51 681	-1.1	1 922	3.7	49 915	38.0	5.0	8.0	4 916	84	4.8
Auburn	13 148	-1.0	816	6.2	12 641	24.3	10.2	9.4	1 126	11	100.0
Binghamton	22 566	-0.4	1 369	6.1	22 939	31.8	8.9	11.4	572	4	100.0
Buffalo	136 057	-1.8	11 689	8.6	131 001	27.2	8.5	11.7	9 213	307	20.8
Elmira	13 206	-1.4	1 058	8.0	12 530	24.0	11.2	13.0	469	16	6.3
Freeport	22 356	-0.7	796	3.6	21 601	27.8	10.3	6.7	886	6	100.0
Glen Cove	12 765	-0.7	443	3.5	12 346	34.7	10.6	5.9	11 625	48	79.2
Hempstead	26 967	-0.5	1 373	5.1	25 643	24.0	7.3	6.3	3 870	60	5.0
Ithaca	14 586	0.3	436	3.0	13 088	47.6	3.4	3.7	25 605	350	0.6
Jamestown	15 256	-2.2	915	6.0	14 743	25.4	10.0	11.0	50	1	100.0
Lindenhurst	14 819	-0.7	578	3.9	13 815	23.3	15.1	6.5	394	4	100.0
Long Beach	17 729	-0.7	733	4.1	17 029	35.9	7.9	6.1	2 312	20	60.0

1. Percent of civilian labor force.　2. Persons 16 years and older.　3. Persons 16 to 64 years old.

Table D. Cities — **Wholesale Trade, Retail Trade, and Real Estate**

City	Wholesale Trade, 1997				Retail Trade[1], 1997				Real Estate and Rental and Leasing, 1997			
	Number of Establishments	Number of Employees	Sales (mil dol)	Annual Payroll (mil dol)	Number of Establishments	Number of Employees	Sales (mil dol)	Annual Payroll (mil dol)	Number of Establishments	Number of Employees	Receipts (mil dol)	Annual Payroll (mil dol)
	72	73	74	75	76	77	78	79	80	81	82	83
NEVADA—Cont'd												
Reno....................	286	3 487	3 043.4	118.6	928	14 619	2 865.8	294.2	419	2 266	342.9	47.6
Sparks..................	290	5 391	2 376.7	188.2	256	3 559	640.2	71.2	86	495	63.0	11.8
NEW HAMPSHIRE	2 033	22 631	11 371.1	875.0	6 645	84 170	15 890.1	1 428.2	1 399	6 639	719.4	151.1
Concord....................	63	848	268.7	28.8	331	4 578	943.6	75.7	62	D	D	D
Dover....................	44	329	114.9	9.2	119	1 603	270.1	27.6	36	114	15.6	1.9
Manchester....................	226	3 185	1 368.2	115.0	561	7 594	1 547.6	140.5	143	821	86.2	19.2
Nashua....................	160	2 028	1 527.4	102.3	492	9 611	1 848.8	161.2	119	541	62.9	14.0
Rochester....................	26	829	88.8	20.1	143	2 154	371.2	35.4	26	79	10.8	1.5
NEW JERSEY..................	17 812	266 944	227 366.7	11 886.1	34 837	420 724	79 914.9	7 926.0	8 292	47 558	8 881.9	1 376.5
Atlantic City	24	203	63.5	7.0	255	1 832	296.5	31.8	63	773	112.1	13.2
Bayonne....................	57	1 127	1 081.0	45.7	224	1 588	232.1	31.8	40	208	25.3	4.9
Bergenfield Borough	39	D	D	D	117	904	241.6	21.4	23	82	11.0	1.6
Camden....................	92	1 184	480.5	40.8	158	1 212	241.7	24.1	32	285	18.9	5.2
Clifton....................	215	2 474	2 579.4	104.8	286	4 075	767.8	79.0	94	346	46.7	10.1
East Orange....................	17	D	D	D	131	939	149.1	17.0	78	346	52.8	7.5
Elizabeth	158	3 181	2 119.1	120.3	396	3 947	723.8	65.1	129	505	58.1	9.2
Englewood	159	1 658	1 162.2	89.0	169	1 593	528.9	41.2	67	198	47.0	5.9
Fair Lawn Borough	83	715	1 264.7	31.1	116	1 199	241.7	24.1	30	99	14.6	2.5
Fort Lee Borough	250	1 942	4 352.2	119.2	158	1 588	300.7	28.9	139	462	112.2	12.6
Garfield....................	61	D	D	D	81	817	137.5	17.4	15	36	10.0	1.1
Hackensack....................	279	2 902	2 434.3	131.5	284	3 895	719.8	82.1	155	2 624	487.4	77.0
Hoboken	83	575	742.6	25.7	152	974	130.0	12.7	61	306	41.8	7.3
Jersey City	278	5 701	2 510.8	202.7	809	8 787	1 536.0	144.6	212	1 082	188.2	25.3
Kearny	98	1 231	539.9	56.3	131	1 550	237.3	28.5	32	320	62.1	13.1
Linden	131	1 475	1 861.5	56.8	195	2 303	502.4	50.3	44	279	36.8	6.5
Long Branch....................	41	394	523.2	14.7	73	785	147.5	15.1	31	72	14.7	1.5
Millville....................	25	D	D	D	100	1 621	257.7	26.4	10	27	3.4	0.5
Newark....................	426	5 393	2 319.3	192.0	832	5 920	912.8	101.5	193	3 108	502.7	75.5
New Brunswick	63	908	249.1	28.8	136	1 208	149.7	18.5	37	185	36.0	3.8
Paramus Borough	167	2 785	2 943.1	157.9	623	13 648	2 438.3	249.3	60	575	139.4	18.1
Passaic....................	95	919	296.4	29.4	218	1 961	440.1	38.5	50	215	34.8	5.4
Paterson....................	211	2 804	1 105.6	104.4	382	2 513	409.3	48.1	77	419	45.6	9.9
Perth Amboy	62	871	514.8	32.8	152	1 302	215.5	21.8	20	109	15.6	2.6
Plainfield....................	35	381	97.9	11.3	122	813	136.3	16.0	31	123	18.4	2.8
Rahway	56	912	444.9	38.1	86	609	166.1	13.3	21	117	15.8	2.5
Sayreville Borough	48	335	117.6	12.0	104	1 673	243.0	24.8	23	98	17.7	1.9
Trenton....................	81	987	317.6	32.9	240	2 039	353.9	41.1	56	447	56.2	8.8
Union City	88	509	166.2	15.8	319	1 504	265.0	25.5	47	135	17.5	1.9
Vineland	123	1 184	542.7	38.8	308	3 680	643.8	69.6	79	362	41.9	7.1
Westfield	53	280	327.2	20.4	170	1 338	234.3	25.8	39	137	53.7	7.6
West New York	64	413	160.7	14.8	217	1 028	150.4	17.0	45	185	34.6	4.2
NEW MEXICO	2 182	21 344	7 397.6	601.1	7 421	86 300	14 984.5	1 455.5	1 887	8 844	893.9	165.2
Alamogordo....................	17	94	25.2	2.0	164	1 996	287.6	28.5	34	140	9.9	1.8
Albuquerque....................	919	10 636	3 630.1	330.3	2 004	30 720	5 914.6	568.7	677	4 251	480.0	80.6
Carlsbad....................	33	202	53.9	6.0	151	1 599	250.8	28.4	36	132	9.0	2.5
Clovis....................	33	268	95.3	5.9	221	2 352	330.5	33.3	51	D	D	D
Farmington....................	115	1 002	276.8	28.5	359	4 854	806.9	79.0	62	403	29.4	14.0
Hobbs....................	85	708	253.8	20.6	175	1 914	336.1	34.8	38	279	34.3	8.2
Las Cruces....................	79	656	194.2	17.8	407	5 655	955.6	89.1	138	448	40.6	6.4
Rio Rancho	NA	NA	NA	NA	NA	NA	NA	NA	NA	NA	NA	NA
Roswell	61	514	196.9	12.0	243	2 542	384.3	37.7	72	D	D	D
Santa Fe	146	1 207	319.7	37.7	782	7 504	1 368.3	143.1	174	798	99.9	18.1
NEW YORK	37 499	414 249	319 697.6	17 185.8	75 241	805 208	139 303.9	14 329.8	27 214	145 326	27 770.1	4 447.8
Albany....................	164	2 401	1 438.6	90.4	492	6 830	1 074.2	113.2	124	1 000	142.7	22.4
Auburn....................	44	424	131.5	12.1	183	2 671	412.1	41.4	35	130	16.3	2.4
Binghamton	80	1 018	305.7	26.6	202	3 239	452.3	45.2	46	283	21.1	3.3
Buffalo....................	468	7 225	3 273.0	235.5	916	10 187	1 243.9	154.3	217	1 635	279.0	48.1
Elmira....................	46	552	136.6	15.1	119	1 685	234.8	23.8	24	D	D	D
Freeport....................	120	969	350.6	30.6	162	1 964	431.1	39.9	39	189	27.2	4.7
Glen Cove	50	519	186.6	23.8	114	1 167	251.5	24.3	30	87	14.6	2.6
Hempstead....................	58	547	191.9	21.0	208	1 584	570.3	43.1	40	203	40.8	5.4
Ithaca....................	42	268	166.9	9.2	273	3 581	491.0	52.8	50	357	29.9	6.3
Jamestown....................	65	583	172.1	15.3	149	2 638	425.1	39.0	34	148	18.4	3.0
Lindenhurst	65	389	310.4	12.2	102	991	170.4	20.4	12	43	5.5	0.7
Long Beach....................	26	23	29.3	1.1	93	549	88.4	10.0	42	99	19.0	2.4

1. Establishments with payroll.

City	Professional, Scientific, and Technical Services, 1997[1]				Manufacturing, 1997				Accommodation and Foodservices, 1997			
	Number of Establishments	Number of Employees	Receipts (mil dol)	Annual Payroll (mil dol)	Number of Establishments	Number of Employees	Receipts (mil dol)	Annual Payroll (mil dol)	Number of Establishments	Number of Employees	Sales (mil dol)	Annual Payroll (mil dol)
	84	85	86	87	88	89	90	91	92	93	94	95
NEVADA—Cont'd												
Reno	860	4 999	486.1	197.6	192	6 086	1 076.3	191.6	565	26 468	1 406.6	462.7
Sparks	111	881	86.2	33.8	182	4 477	684.6	136.2	117	5 118	253.5	71.8
NEW HAMPSHIRE	3 341	18 268	1 626.6	713.1	2 328	98 934	19 813.1	3 361.4	3 029	43 942	1 543.5	449.8
Concord	216	1 340	132.0	60.7	56	3 016	372.7	89.6	119	2 266	73.5	21.6
Dover	71	415	20.8	9.5	58	3 300	525.2	111.4	61	D	D	D
Manchester	339	3 297	314.8	144.4	191	8 952	1 394.5	289.7	230	4 115	140.2	38.4
Nashua	333	1 454	168.5	70.9	179	11 164	1 990.4	521.2	182	3 677	131.1	39.3
Rochester	35	354	29.4	12.6	38	2 694	1 218.0	74.8	61	761	24.6	6.7
NEW JERSEY	25 849	220 238	25 943.8	10 441.0	11 812	409 788	97 060.8	15 430.2	16 974	251 872	13 407.4	3 608.2
Atlantic City	82	758	74.4	37.7	NA	NA	NA	NA	205	48 506	4 717.1	1 246.0
Bayonne	66	278	13.7	4.8	52	1 747	556.1	60.6	114	D	D	D
Bergenfield Borough	39	103	11.9	4.5	NA	NA	NA	NA	49	583	25.2	5.8
Camden	42	308	30.7	13.0	81	2 757	557.8	117.6	84	583	25.2	5.8
Clifton	271	2 605	232.0	83.8	211	9 631	1 780.5	374.9	142	D	D	D
East Orange	66	1 368	187.4	60.2	NA	NA	NA	NA	59	955	37.2	9.4
Elizabeth	115	401	40.0	14.1	129	5 983	1 143.6	191.0	227	2 132	117.9	30.0
Englewood	126	690	116.8	40.1	83	2 143	425.6	78.8	46	496	25.9	7.0
Fair Lawn Borough	210	1 075	175.6	56.9	62	3 146	589.3	116.4	59	566	22.5	6.1
Fort Lee Borough	260	1 658	230.9	70.9	NA	NA	NA	NA	96	1 062	53.6	15.0
Garfield	37	122	11.8	3.3	105	3 293	521.4	90.8	48	305	12.2	3.1
Hackensack	512	3 354	367.9	142.3	140	2 551	391.7	85.2	108	D	D	D
Hoboken	146	871	126.0	53.6	69	1 655	311.0	47.5	132	1 150	46.9	12.6
Jersey City	353	3 553	522.8	184.9	190	5 770	1 039.2	179.8	345	2 789	121.3	32.5
Kearny	58	199	17.9	5.4	69	2 068	361.9	62.7	74	D	D	D
Linden	53	318	20.9	9.5	164	8 202	6 332.5	364.1	103	987	39.2	11.1
Long Branch	36	109	8.7	3.3	24	505	58.5	15.2	77	941	39.2	12.5
Millville	38	112	8.5	2.7	52	4 684	609.5	154.4	44	408	14.3	3.8
Newark	281	4 559	722.5	245.1	439	14 960	3 353.1	491.9	454	5 346	335.0	88.5
New Brunswick	127	634	74.6	29.6	78	2 689	689.9	114.0	131	1 614	67.3	19.5
Paramus Borough	211	2 181	273.1	115.2	32	1 541	238.2	70.8	128	2 306	98.4	25.4
Passaic	49	344	26.7	11.1	144	4 687	433.2	108.6	68	418	19.3	4.4
Paterson	75	477	34.7	11.7	340	8 436	1 748.4	277.2	154	861	39.9	10.3
Perth Amboy	35	146	11.7	3.9	53	2 408	865.6	85.9	71	448	18.9	3.8
Plainfield	40	247	21.5	8.7	42	1 128	154.9	30.9	46	D	D	D
Rahway	35	270	22.0	13.9	68	3 316	1 153.8	167.4	66	572	24.5	6.3
Sayreville Borough	71	217	19.7	10.8	24	2 272	860.7	101.2	45	414	15.5	3.8
Trenton	109	730	83.2	40.4	89	2 790	370.8	104.7	187	1 131	51.8	13.3
Union City	78	207	18.8	5.3	133	1 563	102.3	29.4	143	D	D	D
Vineland	112	718	64.1	24.5	105	6 223	913.0	186.9	100	1 531	44.8	12.3
Westfield	191	1 086	119.2	47.5	NA	NA	NA	NA	64	D	D	D
West New York	63	168	18.9	6.7	172	1 970	142.2	34.3	66	502	17.5	4.2
NEW MEXICO	3 702	31 535	3 243.4	1 307.3	1 593	39 664	17 906.1	1 135.8	3 825	67 134	2 144.9	599.1
Alamogordo	45	187	8.3	3.2	18	562	92.1	10.1	73	1 068	29.3	7.7
Albuquerque	1 746	D	D	D	592	D	D	D	1 082	24 747	813.2	228.8
Carlsbad	36	168	15.9	6.6	NA	NA	NA	NA	62	1 059	34.3	9.3
Clovis	60	210	11.6	4.4	NA	NA	NA	NA	79	1 605	45.7	13.0
Farmington	125	768	42.8	17.2	47	695	74.1	16.9	121	2 783	79.8	21.7
Hobbs	51	283	17.1	7.3	NA	NA	NA	NA	78	1 152	33.5	8.9
Las Cruces	184	970	66.1	27.1	65	1 433	253.4	28.6	208	3 396	103.2	27.2
Rio Rancho	NA	NA	NA	NA	30	D	D	D	NA	NA	NA	NA
Roswell	84	456	37.3	13.6	40	D	D	D	106	1 859	51.5	13.7
Santa Fe	408	1 864	194.8	81.9	136	1 155	95.2	23.7	329	7 045	288.9	84.5
NEW YORK	45 619	416 892	57 475.0	21 773.1	23 908	785 891	146 720.2	26 515.8	38 045	473 327	21 671.1	6 101.1
Albany	377	3 579	433.5	151.9	86	1 933	420.5	62.6	365	4 395	152.2	41.1
Auburn	61	458	32.0	14.0	64	3 087	556.3	92.6	94	1 266	34.3	10.0
Binghamton	138	909	76.2	26.3	79	5 994	1 266.4	199.6	157	2 278	64.8	18.9
Buffalo	592	5 811	608.6	217.4	466	20 307	4 527.2	748.4	678	8 280	252.3	70.5
Elmira	58	411	37.8	11.0	30	2 531	334.5	70.3	80	D	D	D
Freeport	98	345	33.5	13.2	122	3 330	392.4	92.7	71	586	27.2	8.1
Glen Cove	80	276	36.9	11.2	32	2 597	448.4	82.3	50	D	D	D
Hempstead	88	633	56.1	18.5	38	674	84.1	20.3	53	709	30.8	8.1
Ithaca	137	1 215	111.1	42.5	61	2 775	515.3	97.0	213	2 718	81.3	23.3
Jamestown	75	394	27.9	10.8	83	5 056	666.9	150.2	96	897	26.1	6.9
Lindenhurst	42	168	13.5	4.9	68	802	82.0	20.5	65	684	24.8	6.2
Long Beach	50	122	16.8	5.8	NA	NA	NA	NA	43	269	12.5	3.2

1. Firms subject to federal tax.

City	Arts, Entertainment, and Recreation[1], 1997				Health Care and Social Assistance[1], 1997				Other Services[1], 1997			
	Number of Establish-ments	Number of Employees	Receipts (mil dol)	Annual Payroll (mil dol)	Number of Establish-ments	Number of Employees	Receipts (mil dol)	Annual Payroll (mil dol)	Number of Establish-ments	Number of Employees	Receipts (mil dol)	Annual Payroll (mil dol)
	96	97	98	99	100	101	102	103	104	105	106	107
NEVADA—Cont'd												
Reno	80	2 854	139.7	44.3	589	5 514	509.3	234.4	326	2 230	137.3	45.9
Sparks	28	1 173	65.6	19.7	115	1 657	117.1	43.5	140	874	68.1	19.3
NEW HAMPSHIRE	460	6 545	365.0	99.6	2 373	28 889	1 734.1	836.3	2 159	11 379	794.5	236.6
Concord	17	0	0.0	0.0	136	2 141	156.5	84.4	103	589	50.4	12.9
Dover	4	14	1.1	0.1	102	1 425	73.1	34.7	40	226	16.0	4.8
Manchester	24	342	13.6	4.0	231	2 887	195.4	99.0	222	1 642	116.4	39.2
Nashua	19	252	19.0	6.9	197	2 922	197.4	93.0	153	1 197	90.9	28.8
Rochester	8	92	3.7	1.1	62	643	34.9	18.6	47	231	16.3	4.4
NEW JERSEY	2 393	27 187	1 981.2	602.2	18 905	172 723	13 702.4	5 900.2	15 077	78 644	5 434.8	1 665.1
Atlantic City	16	100	11.2	2.7	57	624	34.1	17.3	68	725	27.7	9.2
Bayonne	9	66	3.1	1.1	130	791	70.7	30.5	100	315	26.2	10.1
Bergenfield Borough	10	97	4.0	1.3	31	162	17.0	6.1	69	258	16.3	5.0
Camden	2	0	0.0	0.0	74	1 020	74.7	39.6	64	673	36.8	11.0
Clifton	19	123	7.9	1.8	271	2 248	355.8	98.4	160	661	57.4	18.7
East Orange	2	0	0.0	0.0	113	1 707	85.6	36.1	61	388	57.1	12.8
Elizabeth	7	30	9.5	5.4	174	1 037	80.6	34.7	175	1 114	84.3	25.8
Englewood	17	75	6.5	2.1	187	1 492	161.5	77.7	83	397	23.5	7.7
Fair Lawn Borough	11	68	3.4	0.8	171	1 203	124.0	54.6	77	840	55.6	23.3
Fort Lee Borough	14	70	16.2	4.1	162	1 724	96.8	44.6	94	469	26.3	8.2
Garfield	4	13	0.5	0.2	22	80	5.8	1.5	62	200	17.9	4.3
Hackensack	12	149	16.9	3.3	250	2 583	233.5	113.0	157	1 230	84.2	27.6
Hoboken	13	78	3.6	1.0	80	389	42.3	14.4	75	238	15.3	4.2
Jersey City	27	227	17.4	6.6	329	2 776	214.8	89.8	303	2 357	114.2	32.8
Kearny	2	0	0.0	0.0	62	266	19.6	8.4	80	245	15.3	4.1
Linden	3	0	0.0	0.0	54	543	38.4	15.0	113	699	60.2	19.5
Long Branch	7	41	2.8	0.8	88	650	61.3	29.2	63	287	16.3	5.0
Millville	2	0	0.0	0.0	41	452	32.1	13.0	40	270	14.2	4.8
Newark	5	59	2.2	0.6	310	2 971	198.3	91.9	400	2 826	185.4	60.6
New Brunswick	2	0	0.0	0.0	94	1 271	241.9	64.0	66	433	20.5	6.7
Paramus Borough	17	304	9.7	2.7	137	1 230	102.1	40.2	68	893	60.0	21.7
Passaic	4	9	1.4	0.2	82	718	55.5	24.5	73	395	24.9	8.4
Paterson	5	12	1.4	0.3	157	800	78.2	36.4	193	1 182	83.5	28.1
Perth Amboy	2	0	0.0	0.0	66	794	52.8	21.8	75	399	29.3	9.3
Plainfield	1	0	0.0	0.0	69	668	53.3	23.2	48	192	13.8	4.5
Rahway	4	0	0.0	0.0	41	281	28.7	16.5	62	251	22.8	7.2
Sayreville Borough	3	0	0.0	0.0	49	481	30.0	12.2	52	260	13.4	3.9
Trenton	3	0	0.0	0.0	100	1 298	83.0	40.6	102	552	40.6	11.0
Union City	7	22	2.8	0.6	136	1 186	59.7	24.7	106	341	20.5	5.5
Vineland	8	56	2.2	0.5	130	1 081	81.3	37.9	140	647	34.2	11.8
Westfield	5	13	1.4	0.3	151	1 423	106.3	50.4	80	426	24.4	8.4
West New York	6	15	3.8	1.2	75	493	31.3	11.6	71	227	12.1	3.0
NEW MEXICO	440	8 679	520.4	115.4	2 923	32 824	2 057.3	864.3	2 318	13 448	759.1	227.2
Alamogordo	10	80	1.4	0.5	61	491	27.0	11.6	46	215	10.3	2.7
Albuquerque	121	2 980	150.1	39.2	1 073	15 510	1 085.5	450.0	788	6 073	339.0	111.0
Carlsbad	6	18	0.4	0.1	64	969	64.9	24.1	54	241	19.2	4.1
Clovis	10	0	0.0	0.0	94	0	0.0	0.0	67	302	15.5	4.2
Farmington	10	108	2.3	0.7	143	1 122	75.4	34.5	122	900	54.6	15.6
Hobbs	9	0	0.0	0.0	68	966	64.5	20.3	68	432	34.4	9.7
Las Cruces	17	134	7.0	1.9	246	2 587	157.4	65.5	132	688	33.4	9.5
Rio Rancho	NA	NA	NA	NA	NA	NA	NA	NA	NA	NA	NA	NA
Roswell	5	46	1.4	0.3	112	772	44.8	21.3	67	309	17.4	4.6
Santa Fe	67	878	136.9	16.3	286	2 785	161.9	73.3	159	825	52.0	15.1
NEW YORK	7 311	77 057	7 029.0	2 284.6	36 054	358 075	26 008.3	10 970.9	30 104	146 365	10 014.6	2 858.7
Albany	23	600	11.9	5.0	239	3 154	263.9	134.2	147	1 060	98.5	27.8
Auburn	16	98	4.9	1.4	119	879	56.2	23.9	55	313	24.5	5.6
Binghamton	14	254	9.3	1.6	145	1 672	100.6	47.0	89	452	27.2	8.4
Buffalo	55	1 170	68.7	40.9	436	7 567	431.0	218.8	440	2 527	155.8	47.1
Elmira	4	28	2.2	0.6	92	813	70.5	36.2	37	195	16.3	4.1
Freeport	17	46	5.1	1.1	85	804	66.2	23.3	95	343	29.3	7.7
Glen Cove	12	96	4.1	1.0	98	980	72.0	28.8	78	255	20.6	5.4
Hempstead	9	0	0.0	0.0	109	3 294	167.8	75.5	91	1 284	72.7	26.9
Ithaca	20	210	6.6	2.0	95	681	52.1	21.5	62	382	20.6	5.7
Jamestown	8	56	2.8	0.7	114	1 335	61.6	29.7	55	256	18.8	4.5
Lindenhurst	9	0	0.0	0.0	44	259	21.6	8.9	92	345	28.6	7.7
Long Beach	11	104	5.3	1.8	104	1 180	85.0	32.1	51	203	9.4	2.7

1. Firms subject to federal tax.

Table D. Cities — Federal Funds and City Government Finances

City	Selected federal funds, fiscal 2001[1] (mil dol)									City government finances, 1999						
	Procurement contracts		Grants					Direct payments for individuals		General revenue						
										Intergovernmental			Taxes			
														Per capita[3] (dollars)		
	Defense	Other	Total[2]	Health and family welfare	Energy and environment	Education	Housing and community development	Educational assistance	Housing assistance	Total (mil dol)	Total (mil dol)	Percent from state government	Total (mil dol)	Total	Property	Sales and gross receipts
	108	109	110	111	112	113	114	115	116	117	118	119	120	121	122	123
NEVADA—Cont'd																
Reno	4.3	22.8	130.7	31.1	7.5	5.2	3.2	5.9	24.4	172.3	52.1	83.1	68.5	419	254	66
Sparks	23.2	1.6	2.3	0.0	0.0	0.8	0.6	0.0	0.6	62.3	21.0	90.1	25.7	412	242	40
NEW HAMPSHIRE	479.2	175.9	1 287.6	711.9	47.8	103.0	18.4	46.3	143.2	X	X	X	X	X	X	X
Concord	0.8	2.3	252.7	68.4	37.0	37.9	13.8	15.5	23.9	39.4	4.5	53.5	23.6	631	603	0
Dover	0.5	0.1	1.1	0.0	0.0	0.2	0.4	0.3	4.3	47.2	8.6	67.1	32.0	1 235	1 220	0
Manchester	7.8	1.8	31.8	2.2	0.0	0.2	2.5	5.7	16.8	229.5	45.7	65.5	131.8	1 285	1 255	0
Nashua	266.1	5.2	8.3	0.0	1.9	1.5	0.7	2.1	15.6	165.2	18.3	79.6	124.4	1 527	1 514	0
Rochester	2.3	0.2	1.1	0.7	0.0	0.0	0.3	0.1	2.0	50.0	10.6	88.0	35.2	1 265	1 216	0
NEW JERSEY	2 799.7	1 358.2	8 477.7	5 305.0	143.6	726.6	183.6	209.6	1 172.5	X	X	X	X	X	X	X
Atlantic City	0.0	0.6	15.0	1.3	0.0	0.0	3.3	0.1	36.3	185.2	27.1	66.5	125.8	3 304	3 206	0
Bayonne	1.7	0.6	6.2	0.8	0.0	0.0	2.6	0.0	8.9	158.1	40.2	85.5	100.1	1 639	1 630	0
Bergenfield Borough	0.1	0.1	0.4	0.0	0.0	0.0	0.0	0.0	1.1	NA	NA	NA	NA	NA	NA	NA
Camden	83.2	4.7	55.1	12.5	-0.4	0.8	15.2	0.1	36.0	138.4	92.4	78.5	23.4	280	271	0
Clifton	56.1	0.5	3.1	0.0	0.0	0.3	2.5	0.4	9.0	60.1	18.6	81.2	34.8	457	447	0
East Orange	0.9	6.2	8.4	4.6	0.0	0.0	3.2	0.0	40.2	237.3	136.3	98.0	72.7	1 044	1 039	0
Elizabeth	3.1	18.8	14.0	1.4	1.5	0.0	10.8	0.9	12.8	147.5	57.9	84.6	51.1	462	416	0
Englewood	0.9	22.3	1.9	0.5	0.4	1.0	0.0	0.1	10.9	75.0	13.4	92.4	56.9	2 247	2 242	0
Fair Lawn Borough	0.1	0.0	0.0	0.0	0.0	0.0	0.0	0.1	0.0	29.3	6.7	100.0	20.9	671	651	0
Fort Lee Borough	0.3	0.0	0.4	0.4	0.0	0.0	0.0	0.0	17.8	NA	NA	NA	NA	NA	NA	NA
Garfield	0.1	0.0	0.1	0.0	0.0	0.0	0.0	0.0	0.0	NA	NA	NA	NA	NA	NA	NA
Hackensack	0.4	0.3	19.9	3.4	0.0	0.4	15.9	0.9	5.1	55.6	8.9	75.0	41.1	1 087	1 062	0
Hoboken	8.7	0.5	5.0	1.5	0.3	0.7	0.7	1.5	18.9	57.6	22.2	71.5	20.3	607	585	7
Jersey City	4.5	3.1	41.3	8.9	0.0	3.9	24.5	18.6	82.4	434.9	202.9	75.1	115.9	499	460	0
Kearny	0.1	0.1	1.5	0.0	0.0	0.0	0.0	0.0	0.3	64.7	29.6	98.4	28.1	794	786	0
Linden	0.6	0.6	1.8	0.0	0.0	0.0	0.0	0.0	6.0	54.8	24.7	93.7	23.8	639	634	0
Long Branch	0.0	0.1	1.1	0.0	0.0	0.0	1.1	0.0	8.2	NA	NA	NA	NA	NA	NA	NA
Millville	1.3	0.0	1.1	0.0	0.0	0.3	0.4	0.0	7.9	21.7	5.6	100.0	8.8	334	318	0
Newark	23.6	37.6	579.1	85.4	6.6	11.1	34.6	13.1	181.3	644.5	289.9	56.6	179.7	671	510	48
New Brunswick	7.5	2.3	82.2	6.6	4.6	7.2	5.8	29.4	9.7	126.2	51.9	78.4	50.9	1 219	1 122	64
Paramus Borough	2.0	1.3	5.7	0.0	0.0	0.0	0.0	5.7	0.1	39.2	5.8	95.9	24.1	923	874	0
Passaic	6.9	0.0	4.9	0.7	0.0	1.0	3.0	0.0	16.7	81.0	35.2	53.0	38.4	631	624	0
Paterson	2.4	12.5	23.6	13.7	0.2	1.4	4.0	4.4	42.5	193.3	98.0	55.6	67.3	454	454	0
Perth Amboy	4.5	0.1	1.8	0.0	0.0	0.3	1.4	0.3	2.1	52.3	17.7	71.6	22.5	530	521	0
Plainfield	0.0	0.0	5.8	3.6	0.0	0.0	0.0	0.3	10.7	NA	NA	NA	NA	NA	NA	NA
Rahway	0.3	0.1	1.0	0.0	0.0	0.0	0.0	0.0	4.0	37.5	11.6	86.2	14.7	579	557	0
Sayreville Borough	0.0	0.0	0.2	0.0	0.0	0.0	0.1	0.0	5.0	30.6	13.3	98.8	10.5	276	267	0
Trenton	14.6	7.1	1 182.8	401.8	103.1	186.9	22.6	8.2	92.9	375.5	210.9	93.7	114.3	1 353	1 305	0
Union City	0.1	0.0	2.8	0.0	0.0	0.3	2.5	0.0	7.2	192.9	117.2	97.4	57.9	1 005	996	0
Vineland	18.7	2.7	7.4	0.0	0.0	1.7	1.1	3.4	10.1	47.9	18.2	92.6	15.0	271	263	0
Westfield	0.0	0.5	0.0	0.0	0.0	0.0	0.0	0.0	1.4	NA	NA	NA	NA	NA	NA	NA
West New York	0.2	0.0	3.3	3.2	0.0	0.0	0.0	0.5	8.4	120.9	71.5	96.7	37.0	972	948	0
NEW MEXICO	760.6	4 361.0	3 586.2	1 788.5	110.7	460.1	31.6	91.1	145.2	X	X	X	X	X	X	X
Alamogordo	20.9	1.1	3.0	0.0	0.0	2.6	0.0	0.2	0.4	25.0	9.2	91.4	8.6	302	72	216
Albuquerque	261.4	1 801.5	332.2	83.9	29.4	24.7	26.0	37.6	47.5	639.8	213.8	72.7	205.2	489	163	303
Carlsbad	3.8	133.8	3.6	1.5	0.2	0.0	0.0	0.2	3.4	23.1	9.7	79.0	7.4	282	15	262
Clovis	1.5	0.1	2.9	0.0	0.7	1.5	0.0	2.9	7.0	21.6	5.7	100.0	9.6	298	29	266
Farmington	0.0	19.9	5.7	0.0	0.1	2.8	0.1	3.2	3.6	109.1	23.6	95.9	16.9	432	20	397
Hobbs	0.0	0.1	2.0	0.7	0.0	1.2	0.0	3.2	7.3	26.4	9.6	94.8	9.5	350	33	316
Las Cruces	50.6	56.6	61.2	14.8	11.8	5.2	1.8	19.6	9.0	78.4	16.8	95.5	29.2	384	57	314
Rio Rancho	0.0	0.4	0.1	0.0	0.0	0.5	0.0	0.0	0.0	33.2	5.4	100.0	15.5	309	79	225
Roswell	13.3	7.2	6.2	0.0	0.8	3.7	0.0	0.6	7.2	38.8	11.2	88.2	12.8	268	49	214
Santa Fe	7.0	8.3	347.6	136.3	49.1	75.2	1.1	3.6	11.7	113.7	38.6	80.3	40.3	594	17	541
NEW YORK	3 245.6	2 922.3	32 896.6	24 127.0	368.2	2 259.3	647.0	1 176.9	2 911.6	X	X	X	X	X	X	X
Albany	6.6	45.9	2 906.1	598.2	212.0	617.3	56.8	126.6	61.3	99.7	42.8	37.4	37.2	395	342	27
Auburn	2.1	0.4	7.6	0.6	0.5	1.9	1.8	1.9	4.4	34.8	15.7	54.0	9.1	311	272	26
Binghamton	29.7	3.4	27.6	7.9	0.0	1.5	4.3	6.2	10.6	50.7	22.5	29.3	18.8	401	373	18
Buffalo	73.6	30.1	213.2	99.9	0.5	10.2	31.0	59.6	61.5	857.9	632.5	78.2	118.3	393	320	53
Elmira	1.0	0.2	8.9	0.8	0.0	1.8	1.9	1.9	9.3	NA	NA	NA	NA	NA	NA	NA
Freeport	1.0	0.7	2.0	0.0	0.0	1.9	0.0	0.0	3.1	35.4	4.6	81.4	19.4	485	451	8
Glen Cove	5.7	0.0	0.3	0.3	0.0	0.0	0.0	0.0	8.1	32.2	9.4	51.2	16.9	679	582	25
Hempstead	0.2	0.4	3.5	1.4	0.0	0.9	0.0	8.0	36.6	NA	NA	NA	NA	NA	NA	NA
Ithaca	6.1	6.9	195.5	63.2	6.7	3.9	0.8	17.3	4.1	NA	NA	NA	NA	NA	NA	NA
Jamestown	22.0	0.4	4.7	0.0	0.0	0.9	1.9	3.5	4.5	44.2	16.7	70.2	9.9	307	288	10
Lindenhurst	4.0	0.1	0.1	0.0	0.0	0.0	0.0	0.0	0.0	NA	NA	NA	NA	NA	NA	NA
Long Beach	0.1	0.2	1.5	0.0	0.0	0.6	0.0	0.1	9.6	NA	NA	NA	NA	NA	NA	NA

1. October 1, 2000 to September 30, 2001. 2. Includes program categories not shown separately. State totals include additional categories not allocated by city. 3. Based on population estimated as of July 1 of the year shown.

Table D. Cities — **City Government Finances**

	City government finances, 1999 (cont'd)												
	General expenditure												
City	Per capita[1] (dollars)			Percent of total for —									
	Total (mil dol)	Total	Capital outlays	Public welfare	Highways	Parking facilities	Education	Health and hospitals	Police protection	Sewerage and sanitation	Parks and recreation	Housing and community development	Interest on debt
	124	125	126	127	128	129	130	131	132	133	134	135	136
NEVADA—Cont'd													
Reno	181.4	1 111	171	0.0	5.5	1.4	0.0	0.6	23.4	11.8	6.8	4.9	7.3
Sparks	64.1	1 027	191	0.4	10.6	0.4	0.0	0.0	16.6	6.8	14.3	5.1	4.1
NEW HAMPSHIRE	X	X	X	X	X	X	X	X	X	X	X	X	X
Concord	37.0	989	102	2.9	11.7	1.9	0.0	1.1	14.0	15.3	5.4	0.0	2.6
Dover	51.4	1 982	183	1.2	3.5	0.4	45.2	0.3	7.1	8.4	2.8	0.6	1.9
Manchester	292.4	2 852	963	0.3	4.2	0.6	32.1	0.9	4.8	3.4	1.8	0.9	2.0
Nashua	165.9	2 019	105	0.3	4.2	0.2	49.9	1.2	6.4	8.4	1.1	0.6	1.6
Rochester	48.4	1 735	146	0.9	2.7	0.0	56.6	0.3	6.2	4.3	2.8	0.0	4.9
NEW JERSEY	X	X	X	X	X	X	X	X	X	X	X	X	X
Atlantic City	155.9	4 096	771	1.8	15.9	0.2	0.2	3.9	23.5	3.5	4.8	7.7	2.8
Bayonne	150.7	2 468	49	4.1	2.3	0.4	46.9	0.8	8.2	6.6	2.7	5.8	3.2
Bergenfield Borough	NA	NA	NA	NA	NA	NA	NA	NA	NA	NA	NA	NA	NA
Camden	134.4	1 609	242	1.8	12.5	0.0	0.0	0.3	19.1	8.7	2.6	17.0	3.5
Clifton	61.0	801	71	1.2	9.3	0.0	0.0	1.4	19.5	18.1	1.2	6.1	3.1
East Orange	217.7	3 128	121	2.6	0.9	0.0	59.1	1.7	7.0	4.6	1.2	1.8	2.2
Elizabeth	138.3	1 250	87	0.0	7.8	1.1	0.0	2.1	20.1	16.9	0.5	9.6	5.6
Englewood	71.9	2 838	73	1.1	2.3	0.5	50.0	0.9	10.1	3.4	1.0	6.8	0.8
Fair Lawn Borough	27.9	896	190	0.6	10.4	0.0	0.0	1.4	18.0	19.8	5.6	0.0	3.7
Fort Lee Borough	NA	NA	NA	NA	NA	NA	NA	NA	NA	NA	NA	NA	NA
Garfield	NA	NA	NA	NA	NA	NA	NA	NA	NA	NA	NA	NA	NA
Hackensack	67.1	1 774	513	0.2	9.6	0.7	0.0	0.8	15.1	13.1	1.2	24.2	2.1
Hoboken	66.6	1 995	283	1.5	1.0	7.5	0.0	0.9	22.6	5.5	2.9	10.5	8.0
Jersey City	337.5	1 452	219	1.4	3.1	0.8	0.0	1.2	20.8	18.1	2.5	13.9	6.7
Kearny	42.1	1 189	0	0.5	4.5	0.0	0.0	1.7	21.5	7.0	2.3	0.0	9.3
Linden	51.9	1 395	66	0.2	3.9	1.7	0.0	1.1	16.2	6.7	3.8	9.3	5.6
Long Branch	NA	NA	NA	NA	NA	NA	NA	NA	NA	NA	NA	NA	NA
Millville	23.5	891	73	0.0	4.7	0.0	0.7	0.2	21.7	20.4	2.1	13.6	3.7
Newark	657.5	2 455	287	3.0	2.3	0.0	0.0	2.7	15.5	11.5	2.4	27.4	4.0
New Brunswick	122.4	2 930	231	1.1	1.0	8.3	49.8	0.3	8.5	6.0	0.8	8.9	3.6
Paramus Borough	33.3	1 275	103	0.2	4.4	0.0	0.0	1.8	29.1	18.8	6.1	1.7	4.6
Passaic	71.7	1 179	76	0.3	4.7	0.0	0.2	4.2	15.9	11.5	0.5	18.6	3.2
Paterson	216.1	1 458	119	5.5	4.3	1.2	16.7	3.5	16.6	9.5	1.1	9.6	1.8
Perth Amboy	41.7	982	2	2.4	3.0	1.2	0.0	1.7	25.0	14.8	1.7	0.1	11.6
Plainfield	NA	NA	NA	NA	NA	NA	NA	NA	NA	NA	NA	NA	NA
Rahway	33.7	1 329	138	1.5	11.1	1.3	0.0	2.9	16.6	14.8	2.3	3.6	4.5
Sayreville Borough	30.7	807	164	0.4	5.5	0.0	0.0	4.8	28.0	20.5	4.0	0.7	5.5
Trenton	318.5	3 770	350	1.3	0.9	0.4	52.3	0.6	8.0	6.2	1.1	6.0	2.5
Union City	164.2	2 850	125	0.5	1.7	0.5	61.4	0.7	8.0	3.2	0.6	1.7	2.2
Vineland	48.0	865	88	0.4	10.0	0.0	0.0	7.0	19.1	13.3	2.8	8.1	1.3
Westfield	NA	NA	NA	NA	NA	NA	NA	NA	NA	NA	NA	NA	NA
West New York	110.1	2 896	269	0.3	1.9	0.5	58.3	0.3	10.4	4.2	1.0	1.7	2.1
NEW MEXICO	X	X	X	X	X	X	X	X	X	X	X	X	X
Alamogordo	22.6	798	139	0.0	17.8	0.0	0.0	0.9	18.1	12.5	12.7	3.6	2.7
Albuquerque	597.1	1 424	277	0.8	6.0	0.5	0.0	1.7	16.6	11.7	12.4	5.7	8.8
Carlsbad	20.9	795	155	0.0	10.5	0.0	0.0	0.3	18.7	11.3	12.9	3.4	1.8
Clovis	28.1	868	406	0.0	10.1	0.0	0.0	0.4	15.2	22.1	4.5	0.0	2.8
Farmington	111.3	2 851	343	0.0	10.3	0.0	0.0	0.1	5.5	5.3	8.6	0.0	50.8
Hobbs	30.5	1 122	236	0.0	8.5	0.0	0.0	1.4	20.7	21.7	10.6	0.0	3.8
Las Cruces	42.5	558	4	0.0	11.4	0.0	0.0	0.0	18.0	24.0	8.2	0.3	2.5
Rio Rancho	30.1	602	143	0.0	16.3	0.0	0.0	0.0	30.9	13.1	9.2	0.0	4.4
Roswell	40.7	854	209	0.0	2.5	0.0	0.0	0.1	12.9	22.9	7.8	0.8	7.3
Santa Fe	138.0	2 034	555	6.8	8.3	1.9	0.0	0.0	10.1	13.4	17.3	3.9	7.7
NEW YORK	X	X	X	X	X	X	X	X	X	X	X	X	X
Albany	108.0	1 145	79	0.0	7.3	0.0	0.0	0.1	24.1	4.5	6.1	0.0	10.3
Auburn	31.9	1 095	167	0.0	7.8	0.6	0.0	0.0	12.3	24.0	4.3	3.3	13.0
Binghamton	56.2	1 202	254	1.9	12.7	0.9	0.0	0.1	13.5	16.3	3.6	5.8	2.9
Buffalo	951.7	3 165	258	0.0	3.9	0.4	52.4	0.3	6.4	1.4	0.7	6.6	2.6
Elmira	NA	NA	NA	NA	NA	NA	NA	NA	NA	NA	NA	NA	NA
Freeport	39.3	983	141	0.0	14.0	0.0	0.0	0.0	23.9	9.1	6.4	1.8	4.7
Glen Cove	30.3	1 213	224	9.5	8.2	0.0	0.0	0.3	20.8	14.7	6.4	1.5	8.3
Hempstead	NA	NA	NA	NA	NA	NA	NA	NA	NA	NA	NA	NA	NA
Ithaca	NA	NA	NA	NA	NA	NA	NA	NA	NA	NA	NA	NA	NA
Jamestown	48.5	1 508	32	0.0	4.5	0.1	46.0	0.0	8.4	9.3	2.7	0.0	4.2
Lindenhurst	NA	NA	NA	NA	NA	NA	NA	NA	NA	NA	NA	NA	NA
Long Beach	NA	NA	NA	NA	NA	NA	NA	NA	NA	NA	NA	NA	NA

1. Based on population estimated as of July 1 of the year shown.

Table D. Cities — City Government Finances, City Government Employment, and Climate

City	City government finances, 1999 (cont'd) Debt outstanding — Total (mil dol)	Per capita[1] (dollars)	Percent utility	City government employment, 2001	Climate[2] — Average daily temperature (degrees Fahrenheit) — Mean January	July	Limits January[3]	July[4]	Annual precipitation (inches)	Heating degree days	Cooling degree days
	137	138	139	140	141	142	143	144	145	146	147
NEVADA—Cont'd											
Reno..................	210.5	1 289	0.0	1 448	32.9	71.6	20.7	91.9	7.53	5 674	508
Sparks.................	59.5	953	0.0	616	32.9	71.6	20.7	91.9	7.53	5 674	508
NEW HAMPSHIRE	X	X	X	X	X	X	X	X	X	X	X
Concord................	67.6	1 804	16.6	445	18.6	69.5	7.4	82.4	36.37	7 554	328
Dover.................	35.5	1 367	47.8	793	22.2	69.8	11.0	82.9	42.18	7 002	347
Manchester.............	319.9	3 120	10.1	3 325	18.6	69.5	7.4	82.4	36.37	7 554	328
Nashua................	57.5	699	0.0	2 737	21.4	70.2	10.0	82.4	43.00	7 110	382
Rochester..............	44.4	1 592	0.0	870	21.5	70.2	10.4	83.2	46.85	7 052	397
NEW JERSEY..................	X	X	X	X	X	X	X	X	X	X	X
Atlantic City	100.1	2 631	19.6	1 746	30.9	74.7	21.4	84.5	40.29	5 169	826
Bayonne...............	88.1	1 443	0.0	2 250	29.5	74.9	23.3	82.2	43.50	5 362	874
Bergenfield Borough	NA	NA	NA	NA	NA	NA	NA	NA	NA	NA	NA
Camden................	78.7	942	15.4	1 385	31.8	76.6	23.7	86.6	45.56	4 725	1 085
Clifton................	33.5	440	0.0	NA	28.3	74.9	19.4	85.9	49.79	5 486	838
East Orange..............	51.8	745	0.0	2 731	30.6	77.8	23.4	87.0	43.97	4 888	1 201
Elizabeth...............	125.4	1 134	0.0	1 474	30.6	77.8	23.4	87.0	43.97	4 888	1 201
Englewood..............	12.3	487	0.0	681	NA	NA	NA	NA	NA	NA	NA
Fair Lawn Borough	16.4	527	7.3	432	28.3	74.9	19.4	85.9	49.79	5 486	838
Fort Lee Borough.............	NA	NA	NA	NA	29.5	74.9	23.3	82.2	43.50	5 362	874
Garfield................	NA	NA	NA	NA	28.3	74.9	19.4	85.9	49.79	5 486	838
Hackensack..............	41.1	1 087	0.0	446	28.3	74.9	19.4	85.9	49.79	5 486	838
Hoboken...............	92.1	2 760	0.0	643	29.5	74.9	23.3	82.2	43.50	5 362	874
Jersey City	374.9	1 613	11.4	3 801	29.5	74.9	23.3	82.2	43.50	5 362	874
Kearny................	30.4	857	2.7	NA	30.6	77.8	23.4	87.0	43.97	4 888	1 201
Linden................	46.9	1 260	0.0	625	30.6	77.8	23.4	87.0	43.97	4 888	1 201
Long Branch	NA	NA	NA	NA	30.6	73.7	22.3	82.3	47.13	5 253	746
Millville................	15.4	583	0.8	NA	31.1	75.9	22.5	85.3	42.28	4 946	983
Newark................	412.6	1 541	11.3	5 513	30.6	77.8	23.4	87.0	43.97	4 888	1 201
New Brunswick	92.3	2 210	0.0	3 917	29.0	74.6	20.6	84.9	47.02	5 340	804
Paramus Borough	17.8	682	0.0	NA	28.3	74.9	19.4	85.9	49.79	5 486	838
Passaic................	12.8	211	0.0	657	28.3	74.9	19.4	85.9	49.79	5 486	838
Paterson...............	95.1	642	10.7	1 690	28.3	74.9	19.4	85.9	49.79	5 486	838
Perth Amboy	84.0	1 978	8.7	484	29.0	74.6	20.6	84.9	47.02	5 340	804
Plainfield...............	NA	NA	NA	NA	29.4	75.0	21.5	86.4	49.00	5 227	891
Rahway................	21.2	838	2.0	347	30.6	77.8	23.4	87.0	43.97	4 888	1 201
Sayreville Borough	37.7	992	19.0	NA	29.0	74.6	20.6	84.9	47.02	5 340	804
Trenton................	179.0	2 118	24.8	4 150	29.6	75.4	20.5	87.3	45.43	5 172	937
Union City	64.1	1 113	0.0	2 062	29.5	74.9	23.3	82.2	43.50	5 362	874
Vineland...............	51.7	931	35.5	924	31.1	75.9	22.5	85.3	42.28	4 946	983
Westfield...............	NA	NA	NA	NA	29.7	74.8	20.3	86.6	48.75	5 239	841
West New York	44.7	1 177	0.0	1 273	29.5	74.9	23.3	82.2	43.50	5 362	874
NEW MEXICO	X	X	X	X	X	X	X	X	X	X	X
Alamogordo............	22.3	788	51.7	340	42.6	80.4	28.3	94.9	12.74	2 908	1 764
Albuquerque............	1 051.9	2 509	28.0	6 781	34.2	78.5	21.7	92.5	8.88	4 425	1 244
Carlsbad...............	25.0	950	84.0	372	NA	NA	NA	NA	NA	NA	NA
Clovis.................	19.9	613	0.0	351	36.5	76.9	22.3	90.5	17.51	4 068	1 156
Farmington.............	934.1	23 935	9.8	747	28.6	75.0	15.7	92.3	8.26	5 495	803
Hobbs.................	23.1	852	27.3	480	42.5	79.8	28.0	92.8	16.78	2 851	1 790
Las Cruces	166.0	2 181	24.5	1 417	41.8	80.4	26.4	94.2	9.40	3 155	1 618
Rio Rancho	99.9	1 997	80.0	888	34.2	78.5	21.7	92.5	8.88	4 425	1 244
Roswell................	54.3	1 140	0.0	558	39.5	80.7	24.7	94.6	12.58	3 267	1 776
Santa Fe	254.8	3 754	29.4	1 258	30.4	69.0	13.7	84.9	16.37	6 138	324
NEW YORK	X	X	X	X	X	X	X	X	X	X	X
Albany................	175.0	1 856	0.0	1 589	20.6	71.8	11.0	84.0	36.17	6 894	507
Auburn................	73.4	2 518	0.8	NA	23.1	71.5	15.1	81.7	36.57	6 782	501
Binghamton.............	31.6	675	19.3	776	21.1	69.2	14.3	78.6	36.99	7 273	337
Buffalo................	522.5	1 738	19.9	11 826	23.6	71.1	17.0	80.2	38.58	6 747	477
Elmira.................	NA	NA	NA	NA	22.8	69.7	13.4	82.7	33.32	6 982	373
Freeport...............	46.0	1 152	7.8	398	31.2	75.5	24.9	82.8	41.59	5 027	921
Glen Cove	53.9	2 160	10.1	NA	NA	NA	NA	NA	NA	NA	NA
Hempstead..............	NA	NA	NA	NA	31.0	74.4	25.0	82.6	44.68	5 316	853
Ithaca.................	NA	NA	NA	NA	21.5	68.6	12.9	79.8	35.40	7 207	288
Jamestown..............	27.5	855	44.3	829	24.3	70.5	17.8	78.7	45.82	6 591	461
Lindenhurst.............	NA	NA	NA	NA	31.2	75.5	24.9	82.8	41.59	5 027	921
Long Beach.............	NA	NA	NA	NA	31.2	75.5	24.9	82.8	41.59	5 027	921

1. Based on the population estimated as of July 1 of the year shown.   2. Represents normal values based on the 30-year period, 1961–1990.   3. Average daily minimum.   4. Average daily maximum.

Table D. Cities — Land Area and Population

STATE Place code	City	Land area, 2000[1] (sq km)	Population, 2000			Population				Population characteristics, 2000 — Percent						
			Total persons	Rank	Per square kilometer	Total persons 1990	Percent change 1990–2000	Total persons 1980	Percent change 1980–1990	Race (alone or in combination) White	Black	Am. Indian, Alaska Native	Asian and Pacific Islander	Other race	His- panic[2]	Non-His- panic White
		1	2	3	4	5	6	7	8	9	10	11	12	13	14	15
	NEW YORK—Cont'd															
36 47042	Middletown	13.3	25 388	1 222	1 908.9	24 160	5.1	21 454	12.6	72.1	17.4	1.5	2.3	11.4	25.1	56.8
36 49121	Mount Vernon	11.3	68 381	396	6 051.4	67 153	1.8	66 713	0.7	30.9	62.2	0.9	3.0	7.8	10.4	24.4
36 50034	Newburgh	9.9	28 259	1 095	2 854.4	26 454	6.8	23 438	12.9	45.9	35.5	1.5	1.3	21.1	36.3	28.2
36 50617	New Rochelle	26.8	72 182	369	2 693.4 10	67 265	7.3	70 794	-5.0	70.2	20.3	0.6	3.9	8.4	20.1	55.8
36 51000	New York	785.6	8 008 278	1	193.8	7 322 564	9.4	7 071 639	3.5	47.5	28.4	1.1	11.1	17.0	27.0	35.0
36 51055	Niagara Falls	36.4	55 593	527	1 527.3	61 840	-10.1	71 384	-13.4	77.9	19.8	2.4	1.0	1.1	2.0	75.3
36 53682	North Tonawanda	26.2	33 262	944	1 269.5	34 989	-4.9	35 760	-2.2	98.5	0.5	0.6	0.7	0.4	1.1	97.1
36 59223	Port Chester	6.1	27 867	1 109	4 568.4	24 728	12.7	23 565	4.9	67.0	7.6	0.7	2.5	29.3	46.2	42.8
36 59641	Poughkeepsie	13.3	29 871	1 042	2 245.9	28 844	3.6	29 757	-3.1	55.3	38.5	1.2	2.0	7.2	10.6	49.2
36 63000	Rochester	92.8	219 773	79	2 368.2	230 356	-4.6	241 741	-4.7	50.9	40.7	1.3	2.9	8.4	12.8	44.3
36 63418	Rome	194.1	34 950	899	180.1	44 350	-21.2	43 826	1.2	89.7	8.5	0.6	1.3	2.1	4.7	85.5
36 65255	Saratoga Springs	73.6	26 186	1 188	355.8	25 001	4.7	23 906	4.6	94.8	3.8	0.7	1.3	0.9	1.9	92.6
36 65508	Schenectady	28.1	61 821	447	2 200.0	65 566	-5.7	67 972	-3.5	79.6	16.8	1.0	2.8	3.6	5.9	74.5
36 70420	Spring Valley	5.4	25 464	1 220	4 715.6	21 802	16.8	20 537	6.2	40.3	48.3	0.8	6.9	10.2	15.4	30.9
36 73000	Syracuse	65.0	147 306	141	2 266.2	163 860	-10.1	170 105	-3.7	67.1	27.5	2.2	3.9	3.2	5.3	62.4
36 75484	Troy	27.0	49 170	614	1 821.1	54 269	-9.4	56 638	-4.2	82.2	12.6	0.7	4.0	3.1	4.3	78.7
36 76540	Utica	42.3	60 651	455	1 433.8	68 637	-11.6	75 632	-9.2	82.0	14.0	0.7	2.7	3.7	5.8	76.5
36 76705	Valley Stream	8.9	36 368	853	4 086.3	33 946	7.1	35 769	-5.1	80.4	8.3	0.4	7.9	5.8	12.3	71.4
36 78608	Watertown	23.2	26 705	1 156	1 151.1	29 429	-9.3	27 861	5.6	91.2	6.1	1.2	1.9	2.3	3.6	87.8
36 81677	White Plains	25.4	53 077	557	2 089.6	48 718	8.9	46 999	3.7	67.5	17.1	0.8	5.5	13.2	23.5	54.2
36 84000	Yonkers	46.8	196 086	96	4 189.9	188 082	4.3	195 351	-3.7	63.2	18.1	0.9	5.7	16.8	25.9	50.7
37 00000	NORTH CAROLINA	126 160.6	8 049 313	X	63.8	6 632 448	21.4	5 880 095	12.8	73.1	22.1	1.6	1.8	2.8	4.7	70.2
37 02140	Asheville	106.0	68 889	389	649.9	63 379	8.7	53 583	18.3	79.3	18.2	0.8	1.3	2.1	3.8	76.0
37 09060	Burlington	55.1	44 917	681	815.2	39 498	13.7	37 324	5.8	67.3	25.6	0.7	2.1	5.8	10.1	62.0
37 10740	Cary	109.0	94 536	254	867.3	44 394	112.9	21 708	104.5	83.7	6.6	0.6	8.9	2.2	4.3	79.7
37 11800	Chapel Hill	51.2	48 715	620	951.5	38 711	25.8	32 461	19.3	79.4	12.1	0.9	8.0	1.6	3.2	76.1
37 12000	Charlotte	627.5	540 828	26	861.9	419 558	28.9	314 447	33.4	59.4	33.4	0.7	3.9	4.4	7.4	55.1
37 14100	Concord	133.6	55 977	520	419.0	29 591	89.2	16 942	74.7	79.8	15.5	0.6	1.5	3.9	7.8	75.0
37 19000	Durham	245.1	187 035	103	763.1	138 894	34.7	100 847	37.7	46.8	44.6	0.8	4.2	5.6	8.6	42.4
37 22920	Fayetteville	152.2	121 015	180	795.1	75 850	59.5	59 507	27.5	50.7	43.8	1.8	3.4	3.4	5.7	46.6
37 25580	Gastonia	119.3	66 277	413	555.5	54 725	21.1	47 285	15.7	71.0	26.1	0.5	1.5	2.1	5.5	67.3
37 26880	Goldsboro	64.2	39 043	794	608.1	40 736	-4.1	31 895	27.6	44.2	53.2	0.8	2.0	1.6	2.7	41.9
37 28000	Greensboro	271.2	223 891	77	825.6	185 125	21.8	155 684	18.1	56.6	38.2	0.9	3.3	2.8	4.4	53.6
37 28080	Greenville	66.2	60 476	458	913.5	46 274	30.6	35 740	29.6	62.4	34.7	0.6	2.3	1.5	2.1	60.6
37 31060	Hickory	72.7	37 222	836	512.0	28 474	30.7	20 753	37.2	78.3	14.6	0.5	4.5	3.8	7.7	73.2
37 31400	High Point	127.0	85 839	290	675.9	69 428	23.6	63 355	9.6	61.6	32.3	0.8	4.0	3.0	4.9	58.5
37 34200	Jacksonville	115.2	66 715	409	579.1	78 031	-14.5	17 056	357.5	66.6	25.5	1.6	3.7	6.6	10.0	60.8
37 35200	Kannapolis	77.3	36 910	839	477.5	31 592	16.8	34 564	-8.6	78.7	16.9	0.6	1.2	3.8	6.3	75.2
37 43920	Monroe	63.6	26 228	1 184	412.4	18 623	40.8	12 639	47.3	61.4	28.2	0.7	0.9	10.4	21.4	49.6
37 55000	Raleigh	296.8	276 093	62	930.2	218 859	30.2	150 255	41.2	64.7	28.6	0.8	3.9	4.0	7.0	60.3
37 57500	Rocky Mount	92.1	55 893	523	606.9	53 078	13.1	41 283	19.8	41.7	56.5	0.6	1.0	1.3	1.8	40.3
37 58860	Salisbury	46.0	26 462	1 167	575.3	23 626	12.0	22 677	4.2	58.4	38.2	0.7	1.8	2.4	4.3	55.4
37 74440	Wilmington	106.2	75 838	350	714.1	55 530	36.6	44 000	26.2	71.5	26.3	0.7	1.2	1.5	2.6	69.4
37 74540	Wilson	60.3	44 405	690	736.4	38 400	15.6	34 424	11.6	47.4	47.9	0.5	0.9	4.4	7.3	43.9
37 75000	Winston-Salem	281.9	185 776	107	659.0	162 292	23.1	131 885	14.5	56.7	37.9	0.6	1.5	4.9	8.6	52.4
38 00000	NORTH DAKOTA	178 646.8	642 200	X	3.6	638 800	0.5	652 717	-2.1	93.4	0.8	5.5	0.9	0.6	1.2	91.7
38 07200	Bismarck	69.6	55 532	529	797.9	49 272	12.7	44 485	10.8	95.6	0.4	3.9	0.7	0.3	0.7	94.3
38 25700	Fargo	98.3	90 599	270	921.7	74 084	22.3	61 383	20.7	95.4	1.4	1.7	2.1	0.9	1.3	93.4
38 32060	Grand Forks	49.8	49 321	610	990.4	49 417	-0.2	43 765	12.9	94.6	1.2	3.5	1.4	0.8	1.9	92.3
38 53380	Minot	37.7	36 567	847	969.9	34 544	5.9	32 843	5.2	94.6	1.8	3.5	1.0	0.7	1.5	92.4
39 00000	OHIO	106 055.8	11 353 140	X	107.0	10 847 115	4.7	10 797 603	0.5	86.1	12.1	0.7	1.5	1.1	1.9	84.0
39 01000	Akron	160.8	217 074	81	1 350.0	223 019	-2.7	237 177	-6.0	68.9	29.7	0.9	1.9	0.8	1.2	66.7
39 03828	Barberton	23.3	27 899	1 107	1 197.4	27 623	1.0	29 751	-7.2	93.7	5.9	0.8	0.5	0.4	0.6	92.0
39 04720	Beavercreek	68.4	37 984	820	555.3	33 626	13.0	31 589	6.4	94.5	1.6	0.5	4.1	0.5	1.1	92.6
39 07972	Bowling Green	26.3	29 636	1 052	1 126.8	28 303	4.7	25 728	10.0	93.1	3.2	0.6	2.3	2.3	3.5	90.6
39 09680	Brunswick	32.5	33 388	942	1 027.3	28 218	18.3	28 104	0.4	97.8	0.9	0.4	1.1	0.6	1.4	96.2
39 12000	Canton	53.2	80 806	319	1 518.9	84 161	-4.0	94 730	-11.2	77.1	22.9	1.5	0.6	1.2	1.2	73.8
39 15000	Cincinnati	201.9	331 285	54	1 640.8	364 114	-9.0	385 457	-5.5	54.2	44.0	0.8	1.9	1.0	1.3	52.5
39 16000	Cleveland	200.9	478 403	33	2 381.3	505 616	-5.4	573 822	-11.9	43.2	52.1	0.9	1.7	4.6	7.3	38.8
39 16014	Cleveland Heights	21.0	49 958	598	2 379.0	54 052	-7.6	56 438	-4.2	54.2	43.3	0.8	3.1	1.2	1.6	51.7
39 18000	Columbus	544.6	711 470	15	1 306.4	632 945	12.4	564 866	12.1	69.8	26.0	1.0	4.0	2.0	2.5	66.9
39 19778	Cuyahoga Falls	66.2	49 374	607	745.8	48 950	0.9	43 890	11.5	96.6	2.1	0.5	1.2	0.4	0.6	95.4
39 21000	Dayton	144.5	166 179	123	1 150.0	182 011	-8.7	203 371	-10.5	54.8	44.3	1.0	1.0	1.0	1.6	52.6
39 21434	Delaware	38.8	25 243	1 226	650.6	19 966	26.4	18 780	6.3	94.3	4.6	0.9	1.2	0.8	1.2	92.2
39 22694	Dublin	54.7	31 392	995	573.9	16 366	91.8	NA	NA	90.5	2.0	0.3	8.0	0.3	1.0	88.9
39 23380	East Cleveland	8.0	27 217	1 135	3 402.1	33 096	-17.8	36 957	-10.4	5.2	94.6	0.9	0.5	0.5	0.8	4.5
39 25256	Elyria	51.5	55 953	522	1 086.5	56 746	-1.4	57 538	-1.4	83.7	15.6	1.1	1.0	1.4	2.8	80.0

1. Dry land or land partially or temporarily covered by water.   2. Hispanic persons may be of any race.

Items 1—15

Table D. Cities — **Population and Households**

City	Under 5 years	5 to 17 years	18 to 24 years	25 to 34 years	35 to 44 years	45 to 54 years	55 to 64 years	65 to 74 years	75 years and over	Percent female	Number	Percent change, 1990–2000	Persons per household	Female family householder[1]	One-person
	16	17	18	19	20	21	22	23	24	25	26	27	28	29	30
NEW YORK—Cont'd															
Middletown	7.9	19.9	9.4	15.3	15.6	12.4	7.5	5.4	6.6	51.7	9 466	7.7	2.62	16.7	30.0
Mount Vernon	7.1	18.3	8.3	14.9	16.2	13.1	9.3	6.5	6.4	54.9	25 729	2.2	2.63	23.0	30.0
Newburgh	9.8	23.4	12.7	15.1	13.7	9.4	6.7	4.5	4.6	52.6	9 144	1.5	2.97	25.4	27.1
New Rochelle	6.8	17.3	8.7	14.0	15.5	13.1	9.2	7.6	7.9	52.5	26 189	3.4	2.68	12.5	28.0
New York	6.8	17.5	10.0	17.1	15.8	12.6	8.5	6.2	5.5	52.6	3 021 588	7.2	2.59	19.1	31.9
Niagara Falls	6.4	18.3	8.6	12.4	15.3	12.5	7.9	8.7	9.9	53.2	24 099	-7.2	2.27	18.3	35.9
North Tonawanda	5.7	18.1	8.6	12.3	16.7	14.8	8.3	8.2	7.5	51.4	13 671	0.3	2.43	11.1	29.5
Port Chester	7.0	15.5	10.8	18.5	16.7	11.5	7.1	6.3	6.6	49.4	9 531	4.7	2.89	13.6	26.7
Poughkeepsie	7.6	18.3	12.2	15.0	14.2	11.4	7.7	6.6	7.0	52.2	12 014	1.2	2.40	19.7	35.4
Rochester	7.8	20.3	11.6	17.1	15.0	11.4	6.7	4.5	5.5	52.2	88 999	-4.9	2.36	23.3	37.1
Rome	5.9	16.3	8.5	14.3	15.6	13.2	9.2	7.8	9.4	48.8	13 653	-13.3	2.30	13.9	33.2
Saratoga Springs	5.3	14.0	15.5	13.2	14.3	14.6	8.8	6.1	8.2	52.5	10 784	11.3	2.21	9.6	35.0
Schenectady	7.0	17.3	11.6	14.4	15.3	11.7	7.4	6.6	8.6	52.2	26 265	-5.3	2.23	16.7	38.6
Spring Valley	9.6	22.5	10.7	16.4	15.3	11.5	7.3	3.8	2.9	50.3	7 566	0.7	3.33	21.4	20.6
Syracuse	6.9	18.0	16.8	14.5	13.4	11.0	6.5	5.8	7.1	52.9	59 482	-8.4	2.29	19.3	38.2
Troy	6.4	15.7	17.6	14.9	13.6	10.9	7.2	6.5	7.2	50.5	19 996	-3.7	2.26	16.3	36.6
Utica	6.7	17.4	10.0	13.2	13.7	11.8	8.4	8.1	10.7	53.0	25 100	-11.5	2.28	16.9	37.4
Valley Stream	5.8	17.7	7.7	12.6	16.6	14.7	8.7	8.2	8.1	52.3	12 484	5.3	2.91	11.5	20.2
Watertown	7.8	18.2	10.4	15.1	14.5	11.4	7.1	6.8	8.7	52.5	11 036	-3.4	2.32	14.2	34.5
White Plains	6.2	15.0	7.5	16.0	16.5	13.9	9.7	7.6	7.5	52.7	20 921	7.7	2.47	11.3	33.4
Yonkers	7.0	17.3	8.8	15.4	15.2	12.3	8.9	7.7	7.3	53.0	74 351	3.1	2.61	17.2	29.2
NORTH CAROLINA	6.7	17.7	10.0	15.1	16.0	13.5	9.0	6.6	5.4	51.0	3 132 013	24.4	2.49	12.5	25.4
Asheville	5.4	14.2	10.3	14.3	14.4	14.0	9.1	8.6	9.7	53.2	30 690	13.6	2.14	13.0	36.8
Burlington	6.5	17.2	8.9	14.6	14.4	12.6	8.8	8.5	8.5	53.0	18 280	9.9	2.40	14.9	30.3
Cary	8.1	21.0	6.6	16.9	21.6	14.1	6.3	3.1	2.3	50.2	34 906	106.4	2.69	6.3	21.0
Chapel Hill	3.6	11.5	37.1	14.2	10.2	9.9	5.5	3.9	4.2	54.9	17 808	29.2	2.22	7.5	31.2
Charlotte	7.1	17.6	10.4	19.1	17.1	12.9	7.1	4.7	4.1	51.0	215 449	35.5	2.45	13.7	29.5
Concord	7.9	18.3	8.9	17.1	16.4	12.3	7.9	5.6	5.5	51.1	20 962	94.0	2.61	11.5	23.6
Durham	7.2	15.8	14.1	20.1	15.5	11.8	6.3	4.6	4.7	51.9	74 981	33.9	2.37	15.9	31.9
Fayetteville	7.5	17.9	12.7	16.4	14.8	11.7	8.0	6.5	4.5	52.1	48 414	63.3	2.42	17.1	28.2
Gastonia	7.0	17.9	8.8	15.4	15.1	13.4	8.6	7.3	6.5	52.7	25 945	23.6	2.50	16.3	26.5
Goldsboro	7.1	17.9	11.4	14.6	15.2	12.0	8.0	7.3	6.4	50.8	14 630	9.0	2.40	20.4	30.5
Greensboro	6.3	15.9	14.1	16.7	14.9	12.5	7.6	6.1	5.8	52.8	92 394	23.3	2.30	14.6	32.6
Greenville	5.6	13.3	28.7	16.6	11.6	9.9	5.6	4.6	4.2	53.7	25 204	48.1	2.18	13.8	35.4
Hickory	6.9	16.3	11.2	16.1	14.6	12.8	8.5	7.0	6.6	51.9	15 372	30.3	2.35	12.3	32.2
High Point	7.5	18.5	9.3	15.6	16.2	13.0	8.0	6.1	5.7	52.2	33 519	21.8	2.49	16.3	27.2
Jacksonville	9.6	14.6	36.3	15.8	10.1	5.6	3.1	2.8	2.0	39.0	17 175	57.3	2.83	12.3	16.6
Kannapolis	7.0	17.1	9.0	15.1	15.4	12.0	8.8	7.6	8.0	51.6	14 804	23.2	2.46	13.5	26.5
Monroe	8.8	18.1	11.6	18.2	14.4	10.6	7.4	5.7	5.2	49.4	9 029	52.1	2.83	15.9	23.3
Raleigh	6.3	14.5	15.9	20.7	15.9	11.9	6.4	4.4	4.0	50.5	112 608	31.2	2.30	11.4	33.1
Rocky Mount	7.0	20.7	8.9	13.1	15.4	13.8	8.1	6.7	6.3	54.0	21 435	13.6	2.55	20.9	27.4
Salisbury	6.4	15.4	13.1	12.4	12.7	11.9	8.2	8.3	11.6	52.6	10 276	12.2	2.29	17.4	34.3
Wilmington	5.3	13.1	17.2	15.5	13.0	12.1	8.5	7.7	7.6	53.3	34 359	45.9	2.10	14.0	36.6
Wilson	7.4	18.6	9.8	14.0	14.9	13.4	8.4	7.1	6.3	53.2	17 296	19.6	2.47	19.3	29.4
Winston-Salem	6.7	16.6	11.7	15.6	14.8	12.7	8.2	7.0	6.7	53.0	76 247	27.3	2.32	16.6	33.4
NORTH DAKOTA	6.1	18.9	11.4	12.0	15.3	13.3	8.3	7.1	7.6	50.1	257 152	6.8	2.41	7.8	29.3
Bismarck	6.0	17.5	11.1	13.2	15.9	14.1	8.3	7.0	6.8	51.6	23 185	20.0	2.32	9.3	31.0
Fargo	6.4	14.8	19.2	16.7	14.4	12.2	6.3	5.0	5.1	50.0	39 268	30.2	2.20	7.8	34.6
Grand Forks	5.9	15.5	22.9	14.2	13.5	11.9	6.4	4.7	5.1	49.5	19 677	6.2	2.31	10.0	31.4
Minot	6.6	16.6	13.3	13.4	14.0	12.7	7.9	7.2	8.1	51.8	15 520	11.1	2.27	10.0	32.5
OHIO	6.6	18.8	9.3	13.4	15.9	13.8	8.9	7.0	6.3	51.4	4 445 773	8.8	2.49	12.1	27.3
Akron	7.2	18.1	10.5	15.3	15.0	12.7	7.6	6.7	6.8	52.2	90 116	0.2	2.35	17.7	33.1
Barberton	7.7	17.1	8.4	13.7	14.6	12.8	8.4	8.5	8.8	53.3	11 523	4.0	2.39	15.4	30.1
Beavercreek	5.2	20.1	6.3	9.5	17.5	17.8	11.5	7.0	5.2	50.6	14 071	20.3	2.66	5.8	17.5
Bowling Green	3.7	9.4	46.6	11.0	8.5	8.4	4.8	3.7	4.0	53.2	10 266	20.7	2.21	7.5	34.3
Brunswick	7.3	20.5	8.1	14.9	17.8	14.4	8.8	4.9	3.4	50.9	11 883	31.6	2.79	9.3	17.7
Canton	7.8	18.8	9.8	14.4	14.8	12.5	7.6	6.8	7.5	53.3	32 489	-2.9	2.39	19.1	33.0
Cincinnati	7.2	17.3	12.9	16.9	14.7	11.7	7.0	6.0	6.3	52.8	148 095	-4.0	2.15	18.6	42.8
Cleveland	8.1	20.4	9.5	15.0	15.4	11.5	7.5	6.6	5.9	52.6	190 638	-4.6	2.44	24.8	35.2
Cleveland Heights	6.2	17.7	9.2	16.7	15.0	15.0	8.6	6.2	5.5	53.3	20 913	-0.5	2.38	14.1	32.6
Columbus	7.5	16.7	14.0	19.6	15.5	11.4	6.5	4.7	4.1	51.4	301 534	17.3	2.30	14.5	34.1
Cuyahoga Falls	6.5	15.9	7.9	15.9	16.1	13.2	8.4	8.1	8.0	52.5	21 655	6.2	2.26	10.1	32.6
Dayton	7.1	18.0	14.2	14.1	14.9	12.1	7.6	6.4	5.6	51.8	67 409	-7.2	2.30	20.6	36.8
Delaware	7.9	16.7	14.5	16.2	14.8	11.7	7.2	5.6	5.3	52.2	9 520	33.4	2.45	11.1	26.9
Dublin	8.2	23.9	4.8	12.2	21.2	17.6	6.7	3.1	2.3	50.5	11 209	103.0	2.80	5.0	18.5
East Cleveland	7.4	22.3	9.0	12.5	14.1	12.2	9.2	7.8	5.5	55.7	11 210	-16.1	2.39	30.3	38.0
Elyria	7.9	18.7	8.9	14.8	15.5	12.9	8.4	6.6	6.4	52.0	22 409	4.6	2.46	15.1	28.5

1. No spouse present.

Table D. Cities — Group Quarters, Crime, Education, and Income

City	Persons in group quarters, 2000				Serious crimes known to police, 2000[2]				Education, 1990				Money income, 1989		
		Institutional			Total		Rate[3]		School enrollment		Attainment[4] (percent)			Households	
														Median	
	Total	Total	Persons in nursing homes	Non-Institutional[1]	Number	Rate[3]	Violent	Property	Public	Private	High school graduate or more	Bachelor's degree or more	Per capita (dollars)[5]	Dollars	Percent change, 1979–1989 (constant 1989 dollars)
	31	32	33	34	35	36	37	38	39	40	41	42	43	44	45
NEW YORK—Cont'd															
Middletown	581	199	191	382	776	3 057	335	2 722	5 190	821	70.3	16.1	13 525	30 194	30.3
Mount Vernon	748	539	517	209	2 313	3 383	550	2 833	12 743	4 004	70.8	20.4	15 835	34 850	30.0
Newburgh	1 105	193	20	912	1 730	6 122	1 550	4 572	6 446	1 045	57.9	11.4	9 989	22 224	21.4
New Rochelle	2 116	1 108	1 108	1 008	1 861	2 578	294	2 285	9 476	5 836	78.2	33.3	23 745	43 482	24.1
New York	182 430	75 870	42 480	106 560	288 311	3 600	945	2 655	1 357 534	528 124	68.3	23.0	16 281	29 823	28.4
Niagara Falls	806	505	505	301	3 186	5 731	874	4 857	11 748	2 479	67.7	9.7	10 904	20 641	-16.8
North Tonawanda	99	79	79	20	680	2 044	123	1 921	7 031	1 366	79.8	15.2	12 722	29 576	0.3
Port Chester	275	218	208	57	658	2 361	208	2 153	3 977	1 675	66.6	18.6	15 901	35 216	27.3
Poughkeepsie	985	559	180	426	1 346	4 506	639	3 867	5 549	1 209	68.5	21.8	14 936	27 606	33.1
Rochester	9 422	3 991	2 556	5 431	17 250	7 849	743	7 106	42 973	17 061	68.8	19.0	11 704	22 785	-0.3
Rome	3 498	3 152	490	346	725	2 074	134	1 940	9 775	1 167	74.3	15.4	11 171	24 234	0.3
Saratoga Springs	2 300	442	379	1 858	759	2 898	107	2 792	4 285	2 980	83.5	30.8	15 876	30 938	19.7
Schenectady	3 265	1 128	706	2 137	3 177	5 139	747	4 392	10 770	4 361	74.8	17.3	12 569	24 316	10.7
Spring Valley	296	86	77	210	972	3 817	1 017	2 800	4 730	1 757	75.3	18.5	13 714	33 757	18.3
Syracuse	10 989	2 267	1 623	8 722	9 130	6 198	1 062	5 136	30 062	20 398	71.2	22.0	11 351	21 242	2.9
Troy	3 988	846	606	3 142	2 253	4 582	602	3 980	8 999	8 003	71.5	18.4	11 704	23 362	16.7
Utica	3 404	1 714	1 151	1 690	2 796	4 610	473	4 137	13 047	3 276	67.4	12.3	10 726	19 950	0.5
Valley Stream	55	0	0	55	NA	NA	NA	NA	5 753	2 081	81.8	19.2	19 089	47 287	19.6
Watertown	1 097	741	601	356	930	3 482	292	3 190	5 285	1 012	76.8	16.1	11 616	22 765	10.7
White Plains	1 414	651	644	763	2 380	4 484	364	4 120	7 567	3 342	80.3	37.5	24 330	44 004	30.5
Yonkers	2 320	869	801	1 451	5 680	2 897	500	2 396	27 270	16 321	73.6	21.9	17 484	36 376	15.9
NORTH CAROLINA	253 881	106 659	50 892	147 222	395 972	4 919	498	4 422	1 444 680	180 233	70.0	17.4	12 885	26 647	9.8
Asheville	3 211	1 363	743	1 848	5 172	7 508	708	6 799	11 961	1 545	75.1	23.0	13 079	22 267	10.5
Burlington	1 111	749	714	362	3 206	7 138	592	6 545	6 742	1 193	70.3	19.2	14 635	26 500	3.8
Cary	569	497	497	72	2 295	2 428	83	2 345	10 139	1 702	94.9	48.8	20 595	46 259	10.3
Chapel Hill	9 247	345	290	8 902	2 566	5 267	450	4 818	18 120	1 560	93.4	71.2	16 288	30 489	15.5
Charlotte	12 228	5 081	2 428	7 147	49 464	7 904	1 201	6 703	81 623	16 104	81.0	28.4	16 793	31 873	12.4
Concord	1 346	756	617	590	1 383	2 471	205	2 265	4 963	656	66.2	14.8	13 452	25 473	7.8
Durham	9 373	2 341	1 605	7 032	16 397	8 767	987	7 780	28 098	12 204	78.5	35.4	14 498	27 256	26.6
Fayetteville	3 962	1 481	1 052	2 481	9 197	7 600	614	6 986	17 968	2 408	79.1	23.8	12 825	24 354	12.8
Gastonia	1 479	1 176	921	303	6 646	10 028	1 359	8 668	11 601	1 260	62.4	16.0	12 684	25 910	4.8
Goldsboro	3 901	2 704	480	1 197	3 568	9 139	1 132	8 007	9 550	1 342	74.9	16.0	10 726	19 955	6.7
Greensboro	11 307	1 902	1 848	9 405	14 973	6 688	845	5 843	44 080	6 205	79.2	29.9	15 644	29 184	9.0
Greenville	5 590	413	381	5 177	6 231	10 303	871	9 432	17 981	1 138	79.0	33.7	12 206	22 661	0.4
Hickory	1 164	400	400	764	3 134	8 420	615	7 805	5 155	1 456	72.1	23.4	15 433	27 212	15.1
High Point	2 303	949	608	1 354	6 621	7 713	861	6 852	13 569	2 288	68.2	18.1	13 324	25 035	6.8
Jacksonville	18 053	383	197	17 670	3 006	4 506	382	4 124	7 284	891	84.5	18.2	11 566	25 698	2.2
Kannapolis	502	486	390	16	918	2 487	279	2 208	5 392	370	58.7	7.7	11 031	22 369	-5.7
Monroe	673	507	380	166	2 350	8 960	907	8 052	3 593	351	64.9	14.6	11 070	23 153	7.6
Raleigh	17 316	4 935	1 116	12 381	19 424	7 035	742	6 293	48 512	10 640	86.6	40.6	16 896	32 451	13.7
Rocky Mount	1 164	420	420	744	5 745	10 279	1 077	9 202	11 044	1 349	66.9	16.7	12 593	24 055	5.1
Salisbury	2 979	1 290	1 096	1 689	2 105	7 955	722	7 233	4 197	1 420	69.3	20.7	12 953	24 081	5.2
Wilmington	3 589	725	376	2 864	7 967	10 505	993	9 512	13 966	1 161	73.1	20.7	12 077	20 609	13.7
Wilson	1 645	992	792	653	3 054	6 878	788	6 089	8 501	1 658	63.1	18.4	12 028	21 881	-0.9
Winston-Salem	9 114	3 145	1 988	5 969	16 754	9 018	1 295	7 723	27 405	9 202	77.0	27.2	15 696	26 488	12.0
NORTH DAKOTA	23 631	9 688	7 254	13 943	14 694	2 288	81	2 207	164 233	13 310	76.7	18.1	11 051	23 213	-9.4
Bismarck	1 728	1 334	597	394	1 899	3 420	56	3 364	10 955	1 891	83.4	26.4	13 339	28 223	-12.9
Fargo	4 015	817	648	3 198	2 915	3 217	125	3 093	21 535	1 924	88.7	30.2	13 554	25 326	-11.5
Grand Forks	3 817	566	461	3 251	2 177	4 414	172	4 242	17 482	854	85.8	29.3	11 902	25 456	-5.1
Minot	1 310	518	387	792	1 241	3 394	112	3 282	9 440	675	81.6	21.1	11 934	23 727	-13.1
OHIO	299 121	172 368	93 157	126 753	458 874	4 042	334	3 708	2 338 126	460 100	75.7	17.0	13 461	28 706	-3.5
Akron	4 908	2 259	1 027	2 649	6 088	2 805	281	2 524	51 202	6 897	72.9	14.9	12 015	22 279	-9.6
Barberton	394	319	238	75	1 498	5 369	362	5 007	5 845	596	68.8	7.9	10 366	21 688	-11.7
Beavercreek	555	453	453	102	1 638	4 312	92	4 220	7 915	2 037	89.0	37.2	18 362	49 143	4.7
Bowling Green	6 951	356	268	6 595	1 177	3 972	121	3 850	16 517	532	88.6	41.6	10 354	21 766	-4.0
Brunswick	255	185	185	70	NA	NA	NA	NA	6 916	1 321	81.6	13.1	13 821	40 950	-3.4
Canton	3 042	1 555	1 124	1 487	6 422	7 947	1 428	6 519	16 943	2 915	67.0	9.7	10 133	19 807	-15.0
Cincinnati	13 436	6 502	3 325	6 934	22 212	6 705	840	5 865	75 004	20 862	69.6	22.2	12 547	21 006	-1.1
Cleveland	13 434	6 962	3 670	6 472	32 584	6 811	1 263	5 548	94 499	29 944	58.8	8.1	9 258	17 822	-13.4
Cleveland Heights	261	157	155	104	842	1 685	36	1 649	10 361	5 859	88.1	45.0	18 228	36 043	3.6
Columbus	17 659	5 412	3 797	12 247	63 094	8 868	843	8 025	151 248	25 510	78.7	24.6	13 151	26 651	7.2
Cuyahoga Falls	399	316	304	83	1 702	3 447	174	3 273	9 278	2 186	85.2	21.5	14 472	30 895	-5.3
Dayton	10 829	3 336	959	7 493	16 456	9 903	1 243	8 660	37 015	13 248	68.3	12.3	9 946	19 779	-2.8
Delaware	1 924	360	351	1 564	929	3 680	158	3 522	3 822	2 141	79.4	20.2	12 155	28 975	3.4
Dublin	50	50	50	0	784	2 497	51	2 446	4 009	832	97.9	58.4	30 737	71 996	NA
East Cleveland	449	339	290	110	NA	NA	NA	NA	8 399	967	62.6	7.1	9 020	16 378	-18.0
Elyria	934	864	407	70	NA	NA	NA	NA	12 560	1 987	75.2	11.0	11 980	26 923	-12.0

1. Persons in emergency shelters and persons visible in street locations. Persons in institutions and other group quarters are in group homes, etc. and other group quarters not shown separately.
2. Data for serious crimes have not been adjusted for underreporting. This may affect comparability between geographic areas and over time.
3. Per 100,000 population estimated by the FBI.
4. Persons 25 years old and older.
5. Based on population enumerated as of April 1, 1990.

	Money income, 1989 (cont'd)				Housing units, 2000										
	House-holds (cont'd)	Percent below poverty, 1989						Vacant units					Occupied units		
		Persons		Fam-ilies											
City	Percent with $100,000 or more	Total	Percent change in rate, 1979–1989	Total	Total	Percent change, 1990–2000	Vacant units for sale or rent[1]	For seasonal use (percent)	Home owner vacancy rate	Renter vacancy rate	Total	Percent owner occu-pied	Percent renter occu-pied	Average size owner occu-pied	Average size renter occu-pied
	46	47	48	49	50	51	52	53	54	55	56	57	58	59	60
NEW YORK—Cont'd															
Middletown	3.8	13.8	-2.1	10.1	10 124	6.8	658	0.2	2.0	4.2	9 466	45.7	54.3	2.68	2.57
Mount Vernon	5.8	11.8	-19.2	8.9	27 048	3.1	1 319	0.2	2.0	4.0	25 729	36.5	63.5	2.93	2.45
Newburgh	2.1	26.2	-1.9	23.6	10 476	4.8	1 332	0.3	6.8	7.6	9 144	30.7	69.3	2.88	3.01
New Rochelle	15.7	7.6	-5.0	4.7	26 995	2.3	806	0.6	0.6	2.3	26 189	50.3	49.7	2.87	2.48
New York	6.4	19.3	-3.5	16.3	3 200 912	7.0	179 324	0.9	1.7	3.2	3 021 588	30.2	69.8	2.81	2.50
Niagara Falls	0.7	18.6	35.8	15.5	27 837	-2.8	3 738	0.2	2.7	16.0	24 099	57.6	42.4	2.40	2.10
North Tonawanda	1.0	6.1	-12.9	4.8	14 425	3.0	754	0.3	1.3	7.8	13 671	68.7	31.3	2.65	1.93
Port Chester	5.5	8.1	-28.9	5.1	9 772	2.7	241	0.2	1.4	1.4	9 531	43.2	56.8	2.76	3.00
Poughkeepsie	3.8	14.7	-14.5	11.6	13 153	0.3	1 139	0.5	3.3	5.8	12 014	36.8	63.2	2.46	2.37
Rochester	1.4	23.5	34.3	21.1	99 789	-1.3	10 790	0.2	3.8	9.0	88 999	40.2	59.8	2.54	2.24
Rome	1.7	12.1	12.0	9.7	16 272	-2.3	2 619	0.2	3.3	14.6	13 653	57.1	42.9	2.45	2.11
Saratoga Springs	4.2	8.9	-21.2	6.0	11 584	7.7	800	2.9	1.2	3.6	10 784	55.8	44.2	2.49	1.87
Schenectady	1.3	14.9	3.5	11.4	30 272	0.1	4 007	0.3	4.6	9.3	26 265	44.7	55.3	2.37	2.12
Spring Valley	3.0	10.4	-12.6	8.5	7 812	-3.7	246	0.2	2.2	2.3	7 566	31.4	68.6	3.41	3.29
Syracuse	1.7	22.7	23.4	17.0	68 192	-4.6	8 710	0.3	4.8	11.8	59 482	40.3	59.7	2.48	2.16
Troy	1.6	17.2	-5.5	12.7	23 093	1.0	3 097	0.5	4.2	9.2	19 996	40.1	59.9	2.45	2.13
Utica	1.2	21.7	29.2	16.6	29 186	-6.2	4 086	0.3	3.6	12.9	25 100	48.8	51.2	2.41	2.15
Valley Stream	9.0	3.2	-13.5	2.2	12 688	4.3	204	0.2	0.6	1.8	12 484	80.3	19.7	3.06	2.27
Watertown	1.7	15.8	12.1	13.1	12 450	0.4	1 414	0.3	4.5	11.5	11 036	43.0	57.0	2.51	2.18
White Plains	14.6	7.7	-1.3	4.3	21 576	4.2	655	0.8	0.8	2.1	20 921	52.2	47.8	2.53	2.41
Yonkers	6.9	11.0	12.2	9.0	77 589	2.7	3 238	0.4	1.3	3.5	74 351	43.2	56.8	2.68	2.55
NORTH CAROLINA	2.6	13.0	-12.3	9.9	3 523 944	25.0	391 931	3.8	2.0	8.8	3 132 013	69.4	30.6	2.54	2.37
Asheville	2.2	15.9	-4.8	11.4	33 567	13.0	2 877	1.3	2.6	8.1	30 690	56.8	43.2	2.24	2.01
Burlington	3.2	9.9	-14.7	6.5	19 567	10.6	1 287	0.3	2.1	7.7	18 280	59.4	40.6	2.39	2.40
Cary	7.7	3.2	3.2	2.1	36 863	104.7	1 957	0.6	1.9	8.2	34 906	72.8	27.2	2.86	2.23
Chapel Hill	9.3	16.1	-1.2	5.8	18 976	27.8	1 168	0.7	1.4	6.5	17 808	42.9	57.1	2.49	2.01
Charlotte	5.1	10.8	-12.9	8.5	230 434	35.2	14 985	0.3	2.2	8.4	215 449	57.5	42.5	2.56	2.30
Concord	2.9	12.1	11.0	8.7	22 485	93.6	1 523	0.3	2.4	7.3	20 962	67.6	32.4	2.65	2.52
Durham	3.2	14.9	-22.0	11.3	80 797	33.3	5 816	0.6	2.6	6.7	74 981	48.9	51.1	2.44	2.30
Fayetteville	2.9	18.8	-13.8	15.3	53 565	68.9	5 151	0.3	2.8	10.4	48 414	53.3	46.7	2.50	2.32
Gastonia	2.6	14.2	4.4	11.5	27 857	25.5	1 912	0.2	2.1	7.4	25 945	56.7	43.3	2.54	2.44
Goldsboro	1.1	21.2	-1.4	17.4	16 372	14.1	1 742	0.2	2.5	6.8	14 630	42.5	57.5	2.37	2.42
Greensboro	4.4	11.6	-9.4	8.2	99 305	23.5	6 911	0.4	2.0	7.2	92 394	53.0	47.0	2.42	2.17
Greenville	3.0	26.6	8.6	15.9	28 145	55.9	2 941	0.4	3.0	5.6	25 204	39.3	60.7	2.39	2.04
Hickory	4.3	11.3	-8.1	7.7	16 571	30.5	1 199	0.4	2.1	8.0	15 372	55.0	45.0	2.39	2.30
High Point	3.3	12.7	-9.3	9.9	35 952	22.3	2 433	0.5	2.2	7.0	33 519	59.0	41.0	2.53	2.44
Jacksonville	1.8	11.9	-15.6	10.3	18 312	55.1	1 137	0.2	2.9	5.2	17 175	39.2	60.8	2.67	2.94
Kannapolis	0.6	11.8	9.3	9.4	15 941	25.4	1 137	0.2	1.8	7.9	14 804	66.7	33.3	2.43	2.52
Monroe	2.2	16.7	-10.7	12.5	9 621	51.6	592	0.3	3.3	4.3	9 029	56.1	43.9	2.66	3.04
Raleigh	4.7	11.8	-3.3	7.7	120 699	30.3	8 091	0.4	2.1	8.3	112 608	51.6	48.4	2.43	2.15
Rocky Mount	3.1	18.1	-8.1	15.6	24 167	19.8	2 732	0.3	2.2	6.3	21 435	55.0	45.0	2.56	2.54
Salisbury	3.2	15.6	7.6	10.6	11 288	14.0	1 012	0.5	3.1	7.0	10 276	53.5	46.5	2.29	2.28
Wilmington	2.3	22.1	-9.4	16.8	38 678	46.1	4 319	1.3	3.6	11.0	34 359	48.6	51.4	2.20	2.01
Wilson	2.8	23.5	19.3	19.4	18 660	21.3	1 364	0.3	2.4	4.8	17 296	51.0	49.0	2.50	2.44
Winston-Salem	4.8	15.2	-7.3	11.6	82 593	25.8	6 346	0.3	2.2	9.7	76 247	55.8	44.2	2.34	2.28
NORTH DAKOTA	1.6	14.4	14.1	10.9	289 677	4.8	32 525	2.9	2.7	8.2	257 057	66.6	33.4	2.60	2.02
Bismarck	2.5	9.7	47.0	7.4	24 217	20.9	1 032	0.4	1.1	5.5	23 185	63.4	36.6	2.59	1.86
Fargo	2.9	13.7	41.2	7.9	41 200	29.9	1 932	0.5	1.6	5.1	39 268	47.1	52.9	2.61	1.84
Grand Forks	2.0	14.5	20.8	9.9	20 838	6.4	1 161	0.4	2.4	6.7	19 677	50.7	49.3	2.68	1.94
Minot	1.8	14.3	53.8	11.0	16 475	9.5	955	0.6	1.7	6.2	15 520	62.4	37.6	2.51	1.87
OHIO	2.9	12.5	21.7	10.1	4 783 051	9.4	337 278	1.0	1.6	8.3	4 445 773	69.1	30.9	2.62	2.19
Akron	2.0	20.5	36.7	16.5	97 315	1.0	7 199	0.3	1.8	8.8	90 116	59.4	40.6	2.45	2.21
Barberton	0.6	16.9	55.0	14.9	12 163	3.7	640	0.2	1.5	5.4	11 523	65.1	34.9	2.44	2.29
Beavercreek	5.0	3.5	59.1	2.6	14 769	21.6	698	0.5	1.3	13.6	14 071	84.5	15.5	2.74	2.22
Bowling Green	3.5	27.0	3.8	6.2	10 667	19.0	401	0.3	1.1	3.8	10 266	42.2	57.8	2.44	2.03
Brunswick	2.0	4.2	44.8	3.2	12 251	29.7	368	0.1	0.9	7.0	11 883	80.6	19.4	2.92	2.23
Canton	0.9	21.9	41.3	18.8	35 502	-2.8	3 013	0.1	2.2	10.2	32 489	59.7	40.3	2.51	2.22
Cincinnati	2.6	24.3	23.4	20.7	166 012	-1.8	17 917	0.4	2.2	9.9	148 095	39.0	61.0	2.43	1.97
Cleveland	0.7	28.7	29.9	25.2	215 856	-3.8	25 218	0.4	2.1	10.8	190 638	48.5	51.5	2.56	2.32
Cleveland Heights	6.2	8.5	13.3	5.4	21 798	-0.3	885	0.2	1.2	5.0	20 913	62.1	37.9	2.63	1.95
Columbus	1.9	17.2	4.2	12.6	327 175	17.7	25 641	0.3	2.0	8.3	301 534	49.1	50.9	2.48	2.13
Cuyahoga Falls	2.0	6.6	53.5	5.5	22 727	6.9	1 072	0.3	1.2	6.7	21 655	65.7	34.3	2.46	1.89
Dayton	0.5	26.5	27.4	22.0	77 321	-3.8	9 912	0.2	3.0	12.7	67 409	52.8	47.2	2.36	2.24
Delaware	1.2	9.8	5.4	7.4	10 208	33.3	688	0.3	1.7	9.2	9 520	60.3	39.7	2.63	2.17
Dublin	28.7	1.0	NA	0.6	12 038	103.4	829	1.7	1.3	12.8	11 209	76.8	23.2	3.04	1.99
East Cleveland	0.7	27.8	23.0	25.9	13 491	-11.1	2 281	0.1	3.6	15.4	11 210	35.5	64.5	2.75	2.19
Elyria	1.4	13.7	35.6	11.7	23 841	5.8	1 432	0.3	1.5	8.8	22 409	64.6	35.4	2.57	2.25

1. Includes units rented or sold but not occupied.   2. Specified owner-occupied units.   3. Specified renter-occupied units.   4. Overcrowded or lacking complete plumbing facilities.

Table D. Cities — Labor Force, Employment, Disability, and Construction

City	Civilian labor force, 2001				Civilian employment, 1990[2]			Disability 1990	Value of residential construction authorized by building permits, 2000		
	Total	Percent change, 2000–2001	Unemployment Total	Rate[1]	Total	Percent Professional, managerial, and technical	Precision production, craft, and repair	Work disabled persons[3] (percent)	New construction ($1,000)	Number of housing units	Percent single family
	61	62	63	64	65	66	67	68	69	70	71
NEW YORK—Cont'd											
Middletown	12 768	-0.1	541	4.2	11 437	26.6	10.2	9.9	3 565	47	100.0
Mount Vernon	32 986	-0.2	1 777	5.4	32 498	30.9	9.1	8.0	2 402	28	28.6
Newburgh	12 311	0.2	948	7.7	10 628	21.7	9.0	11.7	98	1	100.0
New Rochelle	34 962	-0.5	1 300	3.7	35 052	40.0	8.1	5.6	4 899	37	89.2
New York	3 508 494	-1.5	212 320	6.1	3 257 637	33.7	7.5	8.0	1 063 781	15 050	10.7
Niagara Falls	26 973	-1.1	2 772	10.3	24 888	21.7	11.2	11.9	748	10	60.0
North Tonawanda	17 784	-1.7	951	5.3	17 310	26.4	12.7	7.2	1 209	9	100.0
Port Chester	13 289	-0.4	562	4.2	13 252	25.0	10.7	5.4	1 630	10	40.0
Poughkeepsie	12 943	0.8	702	5.4	13 443	34.7	9.1	9.8	785	5	100.0
Rochester	110 611	-0.8	8 585	7.8	101 942	29.4	10.4	11.2	4 904	82	35.4
Rome	16 355	-2.1	781	4.8	15 900	30.1	10.3	10.9	545	7	100.0
Saratoga Springs	13 433	-1.3	478	3.6	11 763	41.6	7.2	5.5	27 062	208	72.1
Schenectady	30 060	-1.5	1 322	4.4	29 832	28.2	10.0	10.8	405	6	100.0
Spring Valley	NA	NA	NA	NA	10 886	28.5	8.1	6.2	107	1	100.0
Syracuse	71 994	-0.7	4 790	6.7	70 288	32.6	7.6	10.4	2 308	78	6.4
Troy	25 397	-1.0	1 379	5.4	24 502	29.6	8.0	8.2	1 931	57	29.8
Utica	28 943	-1.8	1 877	6.5	27 634	26.0	10.4	12.5	255	5	60.0
Valley Stream	17 241	-0.7	597	3.5	16 676	30.6	13.4	4.7	300	4	25.0
Watertown	11 671	-2.3	990	8.5	11 286	30.0	9.5	9.3	685	9	100.0
White Plains	26 466	-0.5	958	3.6	26 561	44.2	5.9	5.7	19 828	299	5.7
Yonkers	90 143	-0.3	4 232	4.7	89 458	32.4	10.0	7.2	20 224	171	17.0
NORTH CAROLINA	3 994 789	0.9	221 300	5.5	3 238 414	25.7	13.3	8.7	8 643 193	78 376	75.4
Asheville	34 241	0.0	1 648	4.8	28 410	31.2	8.7	11.2	30 190	381	42.8
Burlington	23 888	0.2	1 453	6.1	20 579	26.6	12.9	8.7	27 046	265	85.3
Cary	39 231	1.3	920	2.3	26 644	52.4	5.9	3.1	172 654	1 149	72.8
Chapel Hill	24 499	1.1	633	2.6	19 269	54.9	3.1	3.0	76 199	433	93.5
Charlotte	293 369	0.7	13 148	4.5	216 696	32.5	8.8	6.5	NA	NA	NA
Concord	18 702	1.5	999	5.3	13 753	23.3	13.8	9.2	NA	NA	NA
Durham	87 235	1.8	3 770	4.3	71 211	41.0	7.5	6.8	233 622	2 265	56.6
Fayetteville	37 526	-0.2	2 050	5.5	30 060	33.1	8.6	10.8	40 723	839	25.1
Gastonia	31 073	1.3	2 774	8.9	26 232	24.2	12.4	10.5	35 183	260	83.8
Goldsboro	14 833	1.3	1 035	7.0	13 102	26.4	9.6	10.7	10 665	145	55.2
Greensboro	115 793	-0.9	5 936	5.1	100 100	31.7	8.2	6.7	118 608	1 224	82.9
Greenville	29 485	0.5	2 185	7.4	22 486	37.9	6.1	5.8	77 654	1 375	29.9
Hickory	18 564	5.5	1 712	9.2	15 448	26.3	9.0	7.4	47 304	433	71.4
High Point	41 275	-0.5	2 467	6.0	35 360	23.4	10.9	8.8	95 598	904	84.1
Jacksonville	13 349	-0.9	579	4.3	10 631	30.2	10.0	7.3	23 279	390	32.6
Kannapolis	18 940	2.5	1 565	8.3	13 850	19.3	15.8	10.0	NA	NA	NA
Monroe	11 548	2.1	888	7.7	7 643	22.7	13.7	8.7	NA	NA	NA
Raleigh	176 288	2.2	6 835	3.9	117 849	42.1	6.7	5.7	600 947	6 644	47.3
Rocky Mount	24 746	0.3	2 173	8.8	23 032	26.8	10.2	9.4	29 748	394	56.9
Salisbury	12 971	1.1	1 016	7.8	10 240	27.6	9.6	10.7	NA	NA	NA
Wilmington	35 828	1.3	2 059	5.7	25 805	27.9	10.8	9.8	NA	NA	NA
Wilson	19 861	1.9	2 076	10.5	16 203	26.9	8.9	10.6	34 107	491	58.0
Winston-Salem	77 851	-1.1	4 238	5.4	69 563	34.2	8.2	7.5	131 449	1 448	70.2
NORTH DAKOTA	338 768	0.0	9 550	2.8	287 558	26.4	9.8	7.0	190 196	2 128	59.1
Bismarck	33 475	1.1	730	2.2	25 729	36.2	7.6	7.2	29 046	231	53.2
Fargo	54 363	1.1	868	1.6	40 254	33.6	7.2	6.1	56 380	854	35.6
Grand Forks	28 265	0.2	712	2.5	25 076	34.1	7.8	6.0	7 471	52	96.2
Minot	18 941	0.1	532	2.8	15 535	29.0	7.8	6.8	8 524	110	58.2
OHIO	5 857 254	1.3	251 321	4.3	4 931 357	28.5	11.6	9.0	6 153 624	49 745	76.4
Akron	114 491	0.5	6 849	6.0	94 103	25.2	10.6	11.1	29 241	315	71.4
Barberton	13 385	0.5	769	5.7	11 029	18.6	15.7	12.5	6 814	58	89.7
Beavercreek	19 668	1.3	430	2.2	16 960	49.5	8.5	6.3	NA	NA	NA
Bowling Green	17 437	0.9	727	4.2	14 118	39.9	4.9	3.4	NA	NA	NA
Brunswick	19 337	0.8	805	4.2	14 521	23.5	16.7	7.2	41 945	449	49.7
Canton	38 743	1.2	2 490	6.4	32 336	22.2	9.6	12.1	12 282	177	88.1
Cincinnati	176 267	1.6	9 169	5.2	158 881	33.6	7.8	11.5	36 729	547	25.8
Cleveland	205 707	0.3	18 037	8.8	182 225	20.3	10.7	13.7	33 711	373	84.2
Cleveland Heights	28 998	0.3	839	2.9	27 634	50.4	5.0	6.5	4 053	31	100.0
Columbus	409 254	2.5	13 165	3.2	325 088	33.6	7.5	8.9	551 359	6 874	42.2
Cuyahoga Falls	28 886	0.3	858	3.0	24 503	33.5	10.3	7.5	14 934	101	100.0
Dayton	78 366	2.3	5 835	7.4	70 730	25.7	10.0	12.9	5 893	39	100.0
Delaware	17 865	2.6	484	2.7	9 847	28.3	8.8	7.6	43 594	316	96.8
Dublin	11 395	2.2	80	0.7	8 497	59.7	2.5	2.4	69 380	353	96.0
East Cleveland	14 315	0.3	1 456	10.2	12 486	19.0	5.4	14.5	0	0	0.0
Elyria	30 842	0.9	1 877	6.1	26 257	24.2	13.4	8.5	22 943	358	29.1

1. Percent of civilian labor force.   2. Persons 16 years and older.   3. Persons 16 to 64 years old.

Table D. Cities — Wholesale Trade, Retail Trade, and Real Estate

City	Wholesale Trade, 1997				Retail Trade[1], 1997				Real Estate and Rental and Leasing, 1997			
	Number of Establishments	Number of Employees	Sales (mil dol)	Annual Payroll (mil dol)	Number of Establishments	Number of Employees	Sales (mil dol)	Annual Payroll (mil dol)	Number of Establishments	Number of Employees	Receipts (mil dol)	Annual Payroll (mil dol)
	72	73	74	75	76	77	78	79	80	81	82	83
NEW YORK—Cont'd												
Middletown	41	400	111.0	10.5	304	4 504	751.2	67.5	38	146	23.7	2.2
Mount Vernon	123	1 708	673.5	65.0	240	1 739	303.5	38.0	109	504	85.5	16.1
Newburgh	57	683	199.7	21.5	121	1 277	197.7	21.8	34	142	19.3	2.8
New Rochelle	147	1 221	614.1	55.8	256	2 581	609.4	51.0	146	552	80.6	11.1
New York	18 482	185 407	182 107.1	8 614.3	28 456	232 494	41 912.2	4 731.1	16 530	90 795	19 526.3	3 086.7
Niagara Falls	60	708	204.4	16.8	255	3 437	438.9	45.0	37	226	23.4	4.4
North Tonawanda	38	D	D	D	103	1 159	134.6	15.3	8	46	4.2	0.4
Port Chester	60	960	306.8	33.8	130	1 704	237.7	26.7	38	221	47.0	7.9
Poughkeepsie	50	D	D	D	172	1 475	195.6	23.7	49	490	28.6	6.5
Rochester	441	7 329	5 193.4	308.2	756	8 251	1 140.8	131.9	203	1 511	188.9	34.8
Rome	24	146	31.4	3.5	164	2 177	321.6	29.9	36	162	14.6	2.7
Saratoga Springs	28	294	188.3	8.8	183	2 348	375.0	35.9	35	128	13.1	2.0
Schenectady	57	1 060	425.5	41.3	235	2 169	338.4	35.5	27	118	11.7	2.1
Spring Valley	49	D	D	D	111	1 102	294.1	23.7	23	66	13.5	1.1
Syracuse	262	3 569	1 529.4	124.9	708	8 860	1 346.8	147.4	167	2 595	172.7	59.6
Troy	55	482	201.7	13.5	168	2 258	330.2	34.3	39	166	20.3	3.7
Utica	94	1 341	448.8	37.7	218	2 461	346.5	36.0	54	193	26.0	3.4
Valley Stream	119	779	592.1	35.9	251	2 873	586.8	51.2	56	191	37.6	5.0
Watertown	52	554	168.3	15.4	273	3 743	519.4	52.6	44	222	27.2	3.5
White Plains	139	1 781	3 222.7	127.4	497	6 946	1 176.7	133.4	179	641	167.5	21.0
Yonkers	228	2 460	1 037.6	84.2	620	8 171	1 533.4	144.8	336	1 106	227.8	29.4
NORTH CAROLINA	12 284	157 774	98 080.1	5 574.1	35 563	416 287	72 356.8	6 697.4	7 346	39 349	5 026.0	900.6
Asheville	211	2 134	777.0	64.8	794	10 637	1 762.0	170.8	149	829	107.1	17.9
Burlington	89	1 080	332.4	35.6	419	5 403	829.4	82.3	58	292	60.6	5.7
Cary	132	1 260	1 728.9	57.9	410	7 311	1 218.3	108.2	99	397	74.4	12.8
Chapel Hill	33	123	254.9	5.2	223	3 347	480.6	58.4	83	D	D	D
Charlotte	2 150	32 325	30 244.7	1 319.9	2 306	35 463	6 830.3	662.5	859	8 677	1 285.6	272.3
Concord	74	1 000	691.7	28.7	228	3 734	667.0	61.3	51	297	38.7	6.4
Durham	182	2 736	1 652.9	80.4	909	12 206	1 833.1	195.7	213	1 162	146.0	27.8
Fayetteville	140	1 653	549.5	45.8	755	12 055	2 089.9	193.4	197	867	90.5	16.9
Gastonia	127	1 197	726.9	41.8	442	6 895	1 128.1	103.3	67	308	27.1	5.1
Goldsboro	101	1 799	738.2	47.8	371	4 996	812.4	70.5	69	242	18.1	4.3
Greensboro	783	14 701	9 531.0	629.7	1 294	19 942	3 390.0	350.0	361	2 807	324.3	63.6
Greenville	122	1 196	527.2	30.2	474	6 729	1 144.5	105.3	100	431	44.7	6.9
Hickory	194	4 048	1 990.6	127.8	493	7 484	1 291.3	122.2	100	489	65.5	10.5
High Point	315	2 996	1 885.3	102.7	501	6 575	1 173.9	117.6	90	500	51.6	9.6
Jacksonville	28	156	36.4	3.7	321	4 561	758.4	69.2	75	365	41.2	5.8
Kannapolis	16	D	D	D	189	2 223	350.9	33.3	29	156	15.3	3.3
Monroe	77	1 112	367.7	37.5	240	3 094	585.6	53.4	40	138	16.9	2.7
Raleigh	778	11 873	8 296.7	553.2	1 618	22 689	4 568.5	414.5	494	3 291	624.6	95.0
Rocky Mount	99	1 744	896.0	58.6	392	4 833	825.3	76.4	75	395	48.5	7.2
Salisbury	65	729	235.7	19.6	252	3 412	574.2	55.2	50	197	19.2	3.8
Wilmington	209	2 748	994.0	74.1	743	9 566	1 952.2	163.6	159	755	85.8	14.6
Wilson	93	1 075	422.1	29.1	319	3 975	663.1	60.4	52	181	17.5	2.7
Winston-Salem	331	4 649	2 543.7	149.8	1 101	15 734	2 769.2	260.4	280	1 527	252.2	34.5
NORTH DAKOTA	1 604	16 992	8 618.4	454.4	3 569	40 685	6 702.1	616.1	657	3 325	287.0	46.3
Bismarck	134	1 472	591.2	42.0	356	5 081	808.4	82.0	90	D	D	D
Fargo	246	4 603	2 168.8	148.5	486	9 166	1 588.9	153.0	144	1 017	107.3	16.6
Grand Forks	97	D	D	D	312	5 345	889.2	77.5	63	494	31.8	6.7
Minot	62	D	D	D	292	4 534	711.7	69.8	55	D	D	D
OHIO	17 322	254 226	158 310.2	9 192.2	44 521	630 098	102 938.8	9 924.5	9 692	62 628	7 243.7	1 334.6
Akron	334	4 956	2 808.5	175.7	908	11 912	1 731.7	192.5	163	1 276	112.6	27.8
Barberton	42	401	122.2	15.0	93	873	123.8	12.6	10	60	4.1	1.1
Beavercreek	41	289	287.2	12.0	230	4 947	707.4	64.8	31	138	26.4	3.1
Bowling Green	23	164	63.3	4.4	124	1 895	262.5	23.7	33	156	13.4	2.1
Brunswick	44	464	155.8	13.3	102	1 285	307.8	24.9	15	71	10.6	1.5
Canton	141	2 493	1 072.0	75.1	391	5 050	775.7	78.8	82	375	32.5	6.7
Cincinnati	705	15 388	10 660.8	671.6	1 334	18 093	3 017.0	308.7	512	3 571	431.5	99.0
Cleveland	921	16 936	7 155.4	622.5	1 607	15 454	2 378.3	276.7	346	3 159	328.8	76.0
Cleveland Heights	27	58	52.7	1.7	154	1 594	278.7	28.8	56	267	26.9	3.5
Columbus	1 092	24 483	13 539.2	1 002.5	2 717	51 028	8 595.5	897.7	788	7 701	770.2	179.2
Cuyahoga Falls	79	530	157.2	16.8	207	3 683	760.3	64.7	49	305	25.3	5.3
Dayton	287	5 256	3 296.5	209.5	529	6 801	1 045.2	113.7	155	1 017	115.7	25.7
Delaware	29	171	63.0	5.2	110	1 600	278.5	22.6	35	103	14.4	2.4
Dublin	123	1 514	1 568.1	72.0	150	2 181	611.5	48.7	72	514	84.2	20.4
East Cleveland	12	D	D	D	69	515	54.3	6.7	21	116	11.9	1.8
Elyria	65	647	183.1	19.0	272	4 415	705.6	66.1	46	233	26.7	3.7

1. Establishments with payroll.

City	Professional, Scientific, and Technical Services, 1997[1]				Manufacturing, 1997				Accommodation and Foodservices, 1997			
	Number of Establish-ments	Number of Employees	Receipts (mil dol)	Annual Payroll (mil dol)	Number of Establish-ments	Number of Employees	Receipts (mil dol)	Annual Payroll (mil dol)	Number of Establish-ments	Number of Employees	Sales (mil dol)	Annual Payroll (mil dol)
	84	85	86	87	88	89	90	91	92	93	94	95
NEW YORK—Cont'd												
Middletown	80	272	19.0	8.2	46	1 581	256.6	44.3	104	1 465	47.9	13.0
Mount Vernon	80	313	34.5	10.1	147	4 405	602.1	142.3	63	376	15.8	3.9
Newburgh	57	578	86.7	26.2	48	1 467	116.9	28.5	62	D	D	D
New Rochelle	175	1 416	61.5	22.9	61	1 167	138.9	36.8	123	D	D	D
New York	19 790	249 961	40 075.3	15 355.4	10 569	207 975	27 735.8	5 504.1	13 726	182 381	11 000.4	3 119.7
Niagara Falls	79	320	32.0	8.2	69	3 942	1 234.0	183.7	221	3 253	104.6	28.4
North Tonawanda	37	150	9.2	3.9	61	2 131	522.2	72.6	60	477	12.4	3.3
Port Chester	61	407	49.7	14.5	42	1 054	137.1	30.8	74	637	31.7	8.2
Poughkeepsie	121	858	91.1	36.9	38	D	D	D	91	894	39.8	9.7
Rochester	718	6 970	706.4	277.6	533	51 405	12 269.7	2 218.8	516	6 498	222.5	63.9
Rome	55	467	51.0	16.2	49	2 278	547.5	72.9	85	957	28.2	7.9
Saratoga Springs	97	508	26.9	8.8	28	1 782	374.0	59.5	121	2 107	87.7	26.4
Schenectady	130	1 112	136.9	44.9	66	3 401	1 302.9	154.9	182	1 453	51.5	14.3
Spring Valley	35	151	27.6	4.5	NA	NA	NA	NA	37	454	16.1	4.2
Syracuse	486	5 183	484.7	185.4	163	10 193	1 958.1	409.5	414	5 253	167.9	50.7
Troy	102	946	70.3	29.9	41	1 727	196.9	53.2	127	1 590	46.1	13.6
Utica	157	1 046	75.2	27.0	102	4 095	509.2	118.7	149	1 625	50.4	14.1
Valley Stream	139	781	73.2	32.6	NA	NA	NA	NA	89	1 133	41.7	10.4
Watertown	65	452	27.1	13.0	41	1 855	279.9	56.0	122	1 642	57.2	15.1
White Plains	579	3 165	450.5	169.2	NA	NA	NA	NA	180	2 103	113.8	29.2
Yonkers	217	948	96.3	30.3	131	4 074	742.6	132.6	249	2 103	102.2	25.2
NORTH CAROLINA	14 351	101 610	9 760.9	3 693.5	11 306	773 548	161 900.5	21 297.9	14 579	262 848	8 625.0	2 393.2
Asheville	353	2 115	152.3	70.5	142	6 168	1 405.3	164.7	356	7 242	268.0	81.4
Burlington	91	475	36.6	16.3	110	8 811	1 435.6	208.6	151	3 553	103.7	28.3
Cary	385	2 538	309.3	135.9	65	2 767	384.7	89.3	187	3 765	132.8	37.5
Chapel Hill	228	1 541	128.5	55.1	NA	NA	NA	NA	211	3 566	130.1	38.0
Charlotte	1 958	23 207	2 648.9	1 044.1	787	31 811	6 504.0	1 058.5	1 277	27 598	1 008.7	279.1
Concord	80	510	36.8	16.7	78	6 253	6 968.6	225.4	89	1 915	66.4	18.0
Durham	470	4 648	689.2	204.0	123	D	D	D	386	7 800	295.9	81.9
Fayetteville	272	1 849	122.9	42.9	78	9 100	2 170.0	295.1	354	8 134	246.8	67.2
Gastonia	139	648	52.1	20.6	211	12 666	2 385.8	360.0	166	3 346	107.0	29.1
Goldsboro	101	519	38.7	14.2	64	4 644	579.8	116.1	125	2 553	73.0	19.9
Greensboro	763	5 741	542.0	192.7	411	21 305	5 903.6	711.5	653	15 531	489.3	142.7
Greenville	177	1 131	75.6	30.9	60	4 006	1 827.2	143.5	198	4 854	138.7	38.1
Hickory	172	939	73.6	26.6	253	17 501	2 235.8	441.1	195	4 498	127.5	37.4
High Point	206	1 579	127.6	51.5	288	17 182	2 247.9	465.0	184	3 023	97.1	27.9
Jacksonville	92	590	26.6	9.1	NA	NA	NA	NA	137	2 729	76.7	20.4
Kannapolis	46	229	12.3	5.6	21	D	D	D	58	909	31.0	8.4
Monroe	80	587	51.1	16.1	105	9 686	1 829.3	269.5	95	1 909	57.7	14.0
Raleigh	1 465	12 856	1 424.1	566.8	328	7 954	2 147.1	241.5	780	16 886	606.2	171.3
Rocky Mount	89	610	52.6	19.1	65	7 886	1 475.0	220.3	118	2 549	81.2	22.1
Salisbury	81	340	35.8	11.5	100	5 790	984.3	166.7	103	2 104	61.9	17.1
Wilmington	347	2 508	198.9	81.7	139	5 257	1 241.1	202.0	289	6 562	203.5	56.9
Wilson	79	D	D	D	70	7 534	2 821.1	238.5	115	2 463	76.2	20.5
Winston-Salem	575	4 515	465.8	179.4	241	17 789	4 449.7	583.0	479	10 328	327.7	94.0
NORTH DAKOTA	1 077	7 076	418.0	175.7	704	21 956	5 115.9	604.8	1 827	26 330	684.9	189.0
Bismarck	174	D	D	D	48	D	D	D	149	3 444	95.7	27.6
Fargo	246	2 129	147.9	58.0	133	5 206	1 057.5	131.2	242	6 616	178.7	51.5
Grand Forks	102	710	48.4	23.2	43	1 536	231.9	33.7	152	3 941	88.4	26.1
Minot	80	797	37.0	17.1	41	D	D	D	131	2 678	68.0	19.8
OHIO	21 182	182 805	18 294.7	6 948.0	17 974	984 201	241 902.9	35 950.5	22 631	401 206	12 411.0	3 444.2
Akron	480	4 837	564.6	203.3	370	12 822	2 020.4	451.8	489	7 364	223.9	62.6
Barberton	27	112	7.3	2.5	77	4 140	535.5	122.5	57	692	22.5	5.8
Beavercreek	141	2 040	231.2	92.4	31	826	167.7	31.4	69	D	D	D
Bowling Green	48	331	34.0	8.8	41	3 107	429.8	96.6	87	1 808	39.7	11.0
Brunswick	41	228	18.2	5.9	29	658	93.6	21.0	48	824	21.4	6.0
Canton	198	1 160	105.8	42.3	182	13 120	3 233.5	461.9	208	3 620	100.1	27.0
Cincinnati	1 282	18 517	2 137.0	830.5	604	28 917	6 540.2	1 021.8	829	16 006	564.1	158.1
Cleveland	1 284	19 671	2 502.5	987.2	1 270	44 400	8 675.8	1 662.2	1 099	17 757	674.4	176.9
Cleveland Heights	109	235	19.9	7.1	NA	NA	NA	NA	83	D	D	D
Columbus	1 825	20 837	2 377.4	875.1	685	32 243	8 409.3	1 173.3	1 508	32 807	1 160.0	334.7
Cuyahoga Falls	109	964	44.7	20.5	88	3 220	531.9	111.4	123	2 695	79.8	23.5
Dayton	407	4 535	550.6	181.8	350	20 112	3 579.4	811.2	327	5 098	180.7	48.0
Delaware	50	225	15.7	6.5	38	2 370	832.1	99.7	67	1 258	34.5	9.9
Dublin	185	2 204	422.6	115.7	24	1 142	157.6	36.8	93	1 966	67.9	18.8
East Cleveland	4	10	0.7	0.1	NA	NA	NA	NA	29	454	14.1	3.8
Elyria	97	506	43.8	18.5	132	7 704	1 610.8	260.2	124	2 278	68.6	17.6

1. Firms subject to federal tax.

City	Arts, Entertainment, and Recreation[1], 1997				Health Care and Social Assistance[1], 1997				Other Services[1], 1997			
	Number of Establishments	Number of Employees	Receipts (mil dol)	Annual Payroll (mil dol)	Number of Establishments	Number of Employees	Receipts (mil dol)	Annual Payroll (mil dol)	Number of Establishments	Number of Employees	Receipts (mil dol)	Annual Payroll (mil dol)
	96	97	98	99	100	101	102	103	104	105	106	107
NEW YORK—Cont'd												
Middletown	14	94	4.4	1.0	102	1 207	83.3	37.0	91	519	28.3	8.7
Mount Vernon	13	43	4.9	1.9	109	951	53.8	22.3	133	674	48.7	15.7
Newburgh	3	0	0.0	0.0	80	822	52.9	24.8	49	194	14.3	4.1
New Rochelle	34	580	32.2	8.5	202	1 459	125.3	51.5	141	508	38.0	9.9
New York	3 332	32 475	4 458.9	1 527.7	13 210	125 076	9 746.8	3 988.2	11 623	56 487	3 779.9	1 088.6
Niagara Falls	9	108	3.5	0.9	101	1 341	49.7	21.4	81	329	19.7	5.1
North Tonawanda	11	100	3.5	0.8	54	214	13.4	5.3	57	186	12.5	3.4
Port Chester	5	73	4.8	1.1	40	376	29.2	12.1	81	310	26.5	6.9
Poughkeepsie	13	149	6.0	1.8	126	1 365	102.7	45.7	70	273	21.4	4.8
Rochester	53	703	40.8	10.2	396	6 278	415.2	186.7	387	2 530	184.8	55.0
Rome	13	48	1.9	0.5	87	1 003	57.0	27.7	50	237	13.7	3.7
Saratoga Springs	14	0	0.0	0.0	85	882	64.1	25.9	46	224	12.5	3.2
Schenectady	13	0	0.0	0.0	171	2 027	127.2	60.1	113	798	54.6	15.1
Spring Valley	5	37	1.1	0.3	33	449	17.7	7.0	45	115	9.7	2.4
Syracuse	28	290	18.9	3.6	356	4 374	375.4	196.5	260	1 995	129.8	42.1
Troy	14	50	2.9	0.4	152	1 924	110.4	49.4	75	367	25.3	6.8
Utica	10	79	2.9	0.6	172	1 534	119.3	50.0	98	713	33.5	10.7
Valley Stream	12	33	6.7	2.7	113	749	67.4	26.9	119	998	37.6	13.0
Watertown	13	97	3.9	1.0	100	888	67.8	37.6	59	323	21.3	6.2
White Plains	28	231	22.2	7.6	327	3 565	283.3	139.9	115	735	48.8	15.1
Yonkers	32	536	49.1	10.5	375	3 612	261.6	107.8	278	961	64.7	18.6
NORTH CAROLINA	2 090	23 481	1 632.6	470.5	12 582	173 770	10 708.8	4 859.6	11 483	64 802	4 060.6	1 204.0
Asheville	38	788	51.3	15.6	366	4 785	376.6	192.9	214	1 324	78.2	25.6
Burlington	11	114	3.8	1.1	143	3 022	261.9	94.6	109	744	38.7	12.5
Cary	25	472	22.1	7.0	206	2 223	138.9	62.2	151	1 114	76.4	22.9
Chapel Hill	20	165	5.1	1.4	157	1 694	98.5	48.5	65	429	20.2	7.0
Charlotte	154	1 896	341.5	123.0	1 001	15 218	1 208.9	543.4	1 045	8 575	557.9	177.1
Concord	19	248	34.7	6.8	104	1 710	118.0	61.0	96	489	26.4	8.4
Durham	31	363	17.3	4.8	341	5 018	276.0	137.4	294	2 088	111.5	39.6
Fayetteville	35	601	18.7	6.1	336	5 054	328.7	142.6	239	1 835	98.5	31.9
Gastonia	16	179	5.0	1.4	189	2 807	189.2	91.8	131	926	50.3	14.6
Goldsboro	11	111	3.4	1.0	144	1 798	98.1	48.2	108	844	49.6	16.0
Greensboro	76	727	29.0	9.0	567	8 420	596.2	293.4	476	3 853	270.4	77.9
Greenville	29	410	12.2	4.2	167	2 805	194.9	105.4	114	742	39.2	11.6
Hickory	18	194	9.0	2.1	169	3 752	296.4	125.9	138	919	51.1	17.6
High Point	23	347	47.7	4.5	180	1 913	170.1	75.5	154	813	42.7	13.7
Jacksonville	16	123	4.0	1.1	138	2 078	109.3	49.0	107	596	27.5	9.1
Kannapolis	10	155	7.5	2.6	37	422	19.4	7.2	65	295	19.6	5.8
Monroe	9	65	1.7	0.5	80	944	62.1	30.6	78	528	26.8	8.0
Raleigh	95	899	39.9	10.6	731	10 956	833.0	387.7	575	4 540	371.6	97.6
Rocky Mount	15	100	3.8	1.3	132	2 849	192.4	77.9	114	830	49.8	14.3
Salisbury	12	79	3.0	0.7	131	1 667	94.9	44.4	77	395	21.9	7.3
Wilmington	38	467	16.4	5.0	329	5 047	344.8	146.6	224	1 496	90.8	28.3
Wilson	11	89	2.9	0.8	110	1 740	93.3	46.0	75	614	28.2	9.6
Winston-Salem	45	451	18.0	5.6	446	6 048	555.7	225.7	352	2 623	135.0	47.3
NORTH DAKOTA	248	3 154	164.3	32.6	1 013	13 181	904.1	386.4	1 281	6 294	364.3	101.3
Bismarck	15	0	0.0	0.0	131	1 437	121.0	55.4	132	808	44.1	13.6
Fargo	29	452	18.8	4.0	205	5 753	466.9	187.7	206	1 813	98.9	31.0
Grand Forks	19	166	4.8	1.0	75	1 414	62.9	43.4	94	673	33.7	10.8
Minot	26	170	6.1	1.6	97	1 010	88.6	27.8	87	510	22.6	7.1
OHIO	2 902	37 210	2 308.6	706.6	20 399	261 520	15 440.1	7 477.0	17 314	116 165	7 087.5	2 165.7
Akron	48	777	47.8	10.9	415	5 418	410.5	229.6	368	2 522	138.9	45.3
Barberton	4	42	1.1	0.3	63	755	48.6	20.7	51	322	17.4	5.7
Beavercreek	9	177	9.0	2.7	72	948	64.1	31.7	63	351	21.4	6.2
Bowling Green	5	66	1.7	0.5	45	533	26.3	12.7	40	281	14.4	4.7
Brunswick	5	77	1.6	0.6	45	660	27.5	13.2	49	283	17.0	4.9
Canton	16	155	8.2	2.0	185	2 703	196.6	107.3	153	1 009	66.1	21.5
Cincinnati	84	1 340	181.4	100.3	862	12 504	869.7	469.4	609	4 476	297.6	92.4
Cleveland	84	2 738	354.1	143.9	531	9 272	590.9	300.6	749	5 448	377.6	103.4
Cleveland Heights	13	88	2.8	0.8	112	736	48.6	20.5	65	457	28.9	8.8
Columbus	133	2 316	93.4	23.3	1 325	18 567	1 299.0	675.2	998	8 317	509.7	163.0
Cuyahoga Falls	7	68	2.8	0.7	155	1 311	77.7	39.9	92	532	28.7	9.3
Dayton	27	329	14.4	3.8	319	4 624	307.4	167.5	279	2 613	171.8	56.8
Delaware	5	31	1.2	0.4	68	726	42.1	18.1	31	130	7.1	2.2
Dublin	20	374	28.0	8.4	96	1 894	151.7	67.7	49	581	33.8	11.7
East Cleveland	1	0	0.0	0.0	21	288	16.0	7.1	22	96	3.7	1.1
Elyria	9	120	4.3	1.2	124	1 188	91.7	49.0	75	479	28.8	8.0

1. Firms subject to federal tax.

Table D. Cities — **Federal Funds and City Government Finances**

	Selected federal funds, fiscal 2001[1] (mil dol)									City government finances, 1999						
										General revenue						
	Procurement contracts		Grants					Direct payments for individuals		Intergovernmental			Taxes			
														Per capita[3] (dollars)		
City	Defense	Other	Total[2]	Health and family welfare	Energy and environment	Education	Housing and community development	Educational assistance	Housing assistance	Total (mil dol)	Total (mil dol)	Percent from state government	Total (mil dol)	Total	Property	Sales and gross receipts
	108	109	110	111	112	113	114	115	116	117	118	119	120	121	122	123
NEW YORK—Cont'd																
Middletown	0.4	1.7	2.6	1.7	0.0	0.2	0.4	1.8	1.0	22.2	7.4	36.8	9.7	406	373	20
Mount Vernon	1.8	0.0	18.5	3.7	0.0	0.4	3.9	0.0	22.8	63.1	16.2	41.2	38.1	570	396	143
Newburgh	2.4	1.3	8.6	1.9	0.0	0.8	1.6	8.9	8.9	30.6	10.9	40.1	9.5	363	309	39
New Rochelle	1.2	0.5	5.3	0.5	0.0	1.4	3.1	16.7	24.2	87.9	21.0	31.1	54.6	812	479	290
New York	285.9	1 028.6	17 353.1	14 743.8	29.3	260.6	382.6	404.6	1 783.2	45 993.9	17 477.0	87.1	21 533.3	2 902	1 038	574
Niagara Falls	8.6	1.0	7.4	0.0	0.0	0.4	4.0	0.1	9.4	89.4	29.3	38.1	31.3	552	403	135
North Tonawanda	2.9	0.1	0.2	0.0	0.0	0.0	0.1	0.0	2.5	32.0	10.2	28.8	15.2	461	384	62
Port Chester	0.4	0.0	0.2	0.0	0.0	0.2	0.0	0.0	5.9	22.3	5.2	16.8	11.6	470	429	16
Poughkeepsie	0.0	0.8	8.4	1.4	0.0	0.0	4.3	6.5	17.7	NA	NA	NA	NA	NA	NA	NA
Rochester	119.6	24.3	288.7	147.0	39.8	39.7	20.3	30.6	49.8	757.3	469.2	77.0	195.4	901	825	59
Rome	64.0	0.0	3.0	0.0	0.0	0.0	1.3	0.1	4.3	45.7	18.4	87.7	19.1	479	295	176
Saratoga Springs	0.6	1.0	2.6	0.1	0.0	0.0	0.9	2.0	1.2	27.0	9.7	22.7	12.4	414	331	36
Schenectady	184.3	240.4	18.2	4.4	2.9	3.6	4.7	4.5	21.7	55.8	22.2	27.5	20.4	330	288	27
Spring Valley	0.0	0.0	1.1	1.0	0.0	0.0	0.0	0.1	13.5	NA	NA	NA	NA	NA	NA	NA
Syracuse	237.7	25.3	112.4	36.8	35.8	5.4	13.2	20.7	37.1	374.7	286.4	77.5	28.8	189	150	21
Troy	3.3	3.3	27.9	6.8	8.9	0.9	2.5	12.8	12.9	45.4	21.5	45.2	16.0	313	281	17
Utica	17.0	16.0	16.1	2.1	0.2	2.7	2.6	30.5	13.3	58.1	19.6	58.3	26.9	454	260	186
Valley Stream	0.0	0.4	0.0	0.0	0.0	0.0	0.0	0.6	0.9	19.5	1.5	70.0	15.4	455	420	16
Watertown	11.7	0.7	10.8	1.8	0.0	1.0	1.8	3.4	7.2	28.5	15.7	23.9	8.1	291	257	20
White Plains	1.9	2.0	32.4	7.2	0.2	0.6	11.5	3.0	11.3	100.8	11.0	48.3	64.5	1 291	561	674
Yonkers	26.6	0.8	16.6	1.7	0.0	5.6	7.2	0.1	39.0	626.6	343.8	97.0	244.5	1 286	847	227
NORTH CAROLINA	1 555.8	1 597.8	9 122.5	5 998.5	116.6	735.1	117.2	276.5	487.4	X	X	X	X	X	X	X
Asheville	11.4	22.9	24.6	6.5	2.8	0.3	2.6	4.2	12.5	76.8	24.8	36.6	29.2	463	398	9
Burlington	8.6	1.1	0.9	0.2	0.0	0.0	0.6	0.0	9.3	40.8	12.5	43.1	12.1	299	282	2
Cary	16.4	5.9	3.2	0.1	0.0	0.0	0.0	0.0	0.2	97.8	19.4	36.4	40.9	498	433	15
Chapel Hill	1.2	36.3	327.5	268.7	11.0	11.1	0.8	6.8	1.0	42.8	17.2	28.8	17.6	411	364	22
Charlotte	35.4	479.4	94.0	23.7	2.2	12.7	9.5	23.1	23.2	750.8	172.4	38.4	278.1	551	410	85
Concord	0.0	0.1	3.5	1.2	0.0	1.4	1.0	1.7	1.3	64.6	15.5	35.4	26.1	755	730	7
Durham	18.5	127.7	416.9	316.4	14.7	10.4	4.5	14.5	10.4	181.6	46.5	34.4	69.1	450	390	11
Fayetteville	12.8	11.3	26.5	4.8	0.2	10.0	5.4	12.2	15.0	121.1	32.4	29.6	31.5	407	374	5
Gastonia	1.8	0.1	1.7	0.0	0.0	0.0	0.8	0.0	3.5	65.1	21.3	38.3	17.9	314	282	13
Goldsboro	4.2	1.5	6.1	3.6	0.0	1.2	0.5	2.2	4.0	NA	NA	NA	NA	NA	NA	NA
Greensboro	75.1	11.9	69.5	9.1	0.2	17.7	3.9	18.0	13.9	260.7	68.4	38.2	97.5	493	436	25
Greenville	14.4	3.0	11.0	5.1	0.1	0.0	0.0	0.0	4.7	51.8	16.9	38.9	16.1	282	236	20
Hickory	1.9	1.2	1.5	0.1	0.0	0.0	0.0	2.2	2.4	49.3	15.9	40.2	18.9	598	523	34
High Point	0.8	18.3	1.0	0.0	0.0	0.0	0.0	3.2	13.2	94.6	25.0	41.3	35.0	460	403	20
Jacksonville	4.9	0.5	3.8	0.7	0.0	2.0	0.2	1.9	6.3	NA	NA	NA	NA	NA	NA	NA
Kannapolis	0.0	0.0	1.2	0.3	0.0	0.2	0.7	0.0	5.3	NA	NA	NA	NA	NA	NA	NA
Monroe	10.5	0.2	1.9	1.3	0.0	0.0	0.0	0.0	2.3	28.9	7.0	57.9	7.9	332	320	3
Raleigh	36.7	49.2	1 329.6	468.6	80.8	211.6	73.4	41.8	14.0	263.5	77.8	35.5	102.1	393	323	14
Rocky Mount	1.9	0.1	8.4	3.5	0.0	0.8	1.4	2.8	6.8	49.9	16.7	48.3	13.0	229	210	3
Salisbury	0.2	9.0	7.4	5.3	0.0	1.7	0.1	4.9	4.2	NA	NA	NA	NA	NA	NA	NA
Wilmington	11.7	19.7	29.0	14.6	0.0	0.4	2.0	8.1	14.8	71.6	19.8	36.5	21.7	319	289	6
Wilson	3.9	2.4	1.1	1.0	0.0	0.0	0.0	0.0	4.1	42.2	10.6	46.4	11.6	288	260	4
Winston-Salem	7.6	13.9	124.3	99.2	1.5	8.3	5.6	10.6	17.2	200.7	53.3	45.8	70.1	427	384	12
NORTH DAKOTA	158.8	121.2	1 284.1	468.7	34.1	133.1	11.3	46.4	62.8	X	X	X	X	X	X	X
Bismarck	1.4	3.2	201.7	49.4	17.2	44.4	7.8	15.9	7.7	57.1	10.8	33.9	18.8	348	174	156
Fargo	10.2	9.1	32.3	6.6	0.4	1.9	1.3	6.5	8.4	86.4	19.6	52.9	27.1	313	112	181
Grand Forks	8.1	7.0	45.0	10.5	12.3	8.8	1.4	8.2	11.2	143.7	89.7	28.1	23.8	503	203	273
Minot	0.6	9.0	18.1	2.3	0.0	10.7	0.0	3.4	4.5	25.6	3.1	97.7	14.6	414	172	226
OHIO	3 311.9	1 812.0	11 761.6	7 973.8	113.2	1 066.9	236.2	512.0	1 348.8	X	X	X	X	X	X	X
Akron	177.3	11.2	46.5	14.7	0.6	2.9	11.7	18.2	39.5	290.1	62.7	62.5	129.7	601	117	12
Barberton	0.0	0.0	1.6	0.0	0.0	0.0	1.4	0.2	0.0	26.1	5.6	98.7	11.2	413	34	0
Beavercreek	276.9	4.2	0.2	0.0	0.0	0.0	0.6	0.0	0.4	NA	NA	NA	NA	NA	NA	NA
Bowling Green	0.1	0.1	9.4	2.6	0.0	3.0	0.6	8.5	3.5	22.6	3.8	75.4	11.5	408	51	0
Brunswick	0.1	0.2	0.0	0.0	0.0	0.0	0.0	0.0	1.2	16.9	3.8	66.4	8.6	263	48	5
Canton	7.1	5.0	23.1	2.8	4.8	1.5	9.5	6.2	27.9	91.3	21.1	69.2	43.4	548	31	0
Cincinnati	1 040.5	385.8	241.1	156.0	6.4	9.5	23.6	97.0	186.4	614.7	167.9	29.5	329.4	979	166	25
Cleveland	138.2	167.2	442.7	269.3	6.6	15.3	26.3	116.0	122.3	812.2	172.7	65.4	363.6	733	121	54
Cleveland Heights	0.1	0.1	2.2	0.0	0.0	0.0	2.2	0.1	7.8	47.7	7.3	33.4	29.8	557	160	7
Columbus	245.3	153.4	1 793.7	882.6	79.0	351.2	93.7	67.5	172.4	874.7	130.4	60.4	451.8	674	44	15
Cuyahoga Falls	4.1	0.5	0.4	0.0	0.0	0.2	0.0	1.1	4.7	47.0	6.0	100.0	23.0	460	154	6
Dayton	312.8	53.9	86.8	26.7	1.8	8.5	16.8	25.0	58.3	281.6	43.7	52.6	125.0	746	98	3
Delaware	0.1	0.1	2.0	0.1	0.0	0.5	0.0	1.4	6.3	NA	NA	NA	NA	NA	NA	NA
Dublin	5.7	0.4	0.6	0.0	0.0	0.0	0.0	0.0	0.2	NA	NA	NA	NA	NA	NA	NA
East Cleveland	0.0	0.0	1.5	0.0	0.0	0.0	1.4	0.0	14.1	NA	NA	NA	NA	NA	NA	NA
Elyria	3.6	1.7	4.6	0.0	0.0	0.5	0.6	3.9	9.1	47.5	7.3	87.1	20.6	365	35	5

1. October 1, 2000 to September 30, 2001. 2. Includes program categories not shown separately. State totals include additional categories not allocated by city. 3. Based on population estimated as of July 1 of the year shown.

City	City government finances, 1999 (cont'd)												
	General expenditure												
	Per capita[1] (dollars)			Percent of total for —									
	Total (mil dol)	Total	Capital outlays	Public welfare	Highways	Parking facilities	Education	Health and hospitals	Police protection	Sewerage and sanitation	Parks and recreation	Housing and community develop-ment	Interest on debt
	124	125	126	127	128	129	130	131	132	133	134	135	136
NEW YORK—Cont'd													
Middletown	22.4	937	132	0.0	5.9	0.0	0.0	0.0	25.3	15.5	3.7	3.9	9.0
Mount Vernon	64.4	964	95	8.9	3.9	0.0	0.0	0.6	17.9	7.0	2.8	3.5	3.6
Newburgh	34.0	1 301	169	0.0	6.0	0.2	0.0	0.0	19.6	20.1	6.0	3.4	5.2
New Rochelle	108.4	1 612	440	7.5	4.4	0.5	0.0	1.1	36.5	4.0	2.6	1.9	6.6
New York	44 139.9	5 949	667	17.1	1.7	0.0	25.7	9.6	6.8	4.0	1.1	5.4	7.0
Niagara Falls	84.7	1 492	63	3.6	5.9	0.4	0.0	0.0	14.0	14.3	10.9	2.2	9.8
North Tonawanda	30.8	935	72	0.0	10.0	0.0	0.0	0.1	11.8	16.8	8.5	1.1	6.1
Port Chester	23.3	939	131	8.1	9.9	0.2	0.0	0.3	19.6	6.0	3.2	1.5	10.0
Poughkeepsie	NA	NA	NA	NA	NA	NA	NA	NA	NA	NA	NA	NA	NA
Rochester	735.6	3 392	314	0.2	2.9	0.3	56.8	0.0	6.9	2.5	3.5	1.8	2.3
Rome	35.4	889	120	0.0	15.6	2.0	0.0	0.1	13.4	10.4	2.8	3.6	7.6
Saratoga Springs	25.1	997	68	0.0	12.6	0.0	0.0	0.1	16.2	9.1	8.4	1.2	2.3
Schenectady	60.6	982	112	0.0	6.0	0.7	0.0	0.0	16.5	17.8	3.2	5.5	8.1
Spring Valley	NA	NA	NA	NA	NA	NA	NA	NA	NA	NA	NA	NA	NA
Syracuse	406.6	2 671	168	0.0	5.1	0.0	53.7	0.0	6.7	2.5	0.8	1.6	6.1
Troy	43.7	852	116	0.0	9.3	0.6	0.0	0.6	19.3	11.1	4.6	6.5	5.1
Utica	52.7	888	20	5.0	3.6	1.0	0.0	0.1	18.2	4.5	3.1	8.7	11.5
Valley Stream	20.4	603	62	0.0	16.4	0.9	0.0	0.1	1.0	21.1	9.9	0.0	2.3
Watertown	29.5	1 063	73	0.0	9.3	0.0	0.0	0.0	15.3	9.4	4.2	0.0	10.2
White Plains	94.7	1 896	103	4.7	7.2	7.6	0.0	0.0	19.9	6.7	6.1	1.6	3.0
Yonkers	564.8	2 970	244	0.0	0.8	0.4	56.8	0.0	8.8	2.9	1.4	0.0	2.9
NORTH CAROLINA	X	X	X	X	X	X	X	X	X	X	X	X	X
Asheville	80.9	1 283	250	0.0	9.5	0.7	0.0	0.1	18.4	12.5	13.5	3.8	3.5
Burlington	35.6	879	90	0.0	8.0	0.0	0.0	0.8	18.4	23.8	15.9	1.8	2.7
Cary	62.9	766	194	0.0	7.4	0.0	0.0	0.0	12.1	19.6	16.6	0.0	3.1
Chapel Hill	35.7	833	121	0.0	5.6	3.1	0.0	0.0	19.3	7.5	11.5	8.5	4.2
Charlotte	581.6	1 153	228	0.0	10.1	0.1	0.0	0.5	17.5	10.0	6.2	4.5	11.0
Concord	51.2	1 480	169	0.0	4.5	0.0	0.0	0.0	12.0	22.2	8.0	1.3	4.9
Durham	166.2	1 083	123	0.0	8.0	0.6	0.0	0.0	15.7	24.8	7.3	5.4	7.9
Fayetteville	104.2	1 348	273	0.0	13.6	0.3	0.0	0.0	21.8	19.9	9.2	2.5	7.2
Gastonia	67.9	1 192	188	0.0	14.8	0.0	0.0	0.0	15.2	19.9	4.8	3.3	8.6
Goldsboro	NA	NA	NA	NA	NA	NA	NA	NA	NA	NA	NA	NA	NA
Greensboro	231.4	1 169	81	0.0	6.2	0.4	0.0	0.0	16.9	16.2	15.6	5.0	5.3
Greenville	49.5	868	155	0.0	13.4	0.2	0.0	0.4	20.9	14.6	8.3	2.5	2.1
Hickory	48.3	1 531	304	0.0	7.6	0.0	0.0	0.1	12.2	16.9	6.0	1.9	1.7
High Point	78.5	1 032	101	0.0	10.5	0.4	0.0	0.2	15.4	21.9	9.4	1.5	2.7
Jacksonville	NA	NA	NA	NA	NA	NA	NA	NA	NA	NA	NA	NA	NA
Kannapolis	NA	NA	NA	NA	NA	NA	NA	NA	NA	NA	NA	NA	NA
Monroe	23.6	992	185	0.0	6.0	0.0	0.0	0.1	22.6	20.3	16.0	0.5	6.6
Raleigh	236.4	911	209	0.6	10.9	2.1	0.0	0.0	13.5	14.6	14.2	3.7	3.4
Rocky Mount	46.5	818	116	0.0	10.2	0.0	0.0	0.0	16.6	21.3	7.7	2.6	2.0
Salisbury	NA	NA	NA	NA	NA	NA	NA	NA	NA	NA	NA	NA	NA
Wilmington	69.2	1 017	256	0.0	6.8	0.3	0.0	0.0	17.6	16.9	9.9	2.5	3.3
Wilson	37.2	925	76	0.0	6.8	0.2	0.0	0.0	17.7	24.0	11.2	3.5	0.7
Winston-Salem	170.7	1 039	87	0.0	10.7	1.3	0.0	0.0	19.9	23.8	8.0	5.7	4.8
NORTH DAKOTA	X	X	X	X	X	X	X	X	X	X	X	X	X
Bismarck	53.2	985	349	0.0	21.4	1.5	0.0	1.3	10.3	7.2	8.6	1.1	7.4
Fargo	85.1	981	429	0.2	5.7	0.5	0.0	3.6	6.8	5.1	6.3	40.6	8.1
Grand Forks	145.4	3 071	271	0.0	2.3	0.2	0.0	1.0	3.2	3.1	4.9	44.1	5.1
Minot	24.6	696	206	1.3	7.3	0.4	0.0	0.0	12.2	9.2	19.0	0.0	3.9
OHIO	X	X	X	X	X	X	X	X	X	X	X	X	X
Akron	317.3	1 471	452	0.0	9.1	4.6	0.0	3.8	11.5	14.7	3.2	2.9	5.3
Barberton	25.9	954	193	0.0	17.6	0.0	0.0	4.8	15.0	15.8	6.1	3.4	7.2
Beavercreek	NA	NA	NA	NA	NA	NA	NA	NA	NA	NA	NA	NA	NA
Bowling Green	22.8	809	134	0.0	10.5	0.5	0.0	0.0	25.3	16.7	4.1	4.2	7.7
Brunswick	18.9	579	222	0.0	9.5	0.0	0.0	0.1	12.2	9.3	6.3	35.5	3.2
Canton	84.5	1 066	146	0.0	10.9	0.0	0.0	4.4	18.2	15.2	2.9	5.6	1.7
Cincinnati	637.7	1 896	491	0.0	12.5	0.8	0.0	4.7	12.1	19.1	5.5	7.1	1.7
Cleveland	777.6	1 568	295	0.2	5.6	0.2	0.0	4.0	20.4	5.7	6.7	8.2	6.8
Cleveland Heights	44.5	832	143	0.2	10.3	1.4	0.0	1.1	16.0	7.2	8.1	5.5	4.0
Columbus	883.3	1 318	293	0.0	9.1	0.1	0.0	3.8	19.0	15.9	7.7	2.9	7.0
Cuyahoga Falls	48.5	971	257	0.0	6.1	0.0	0.0	0.0	13.0	16.2	13.6	0.4	2.9
Dayton	268.8	1 605	150	0.2	10.5	0.7	0.0	0.0	17.9	9.4	5.3	5.0	6.9
Delaware	NA	NA	NA	NA	NA	NA	NA	NA	NA	NA	NA	NA	NA
Dublin	NA	NA	NA	NA	NA	NA	NA	NA	NA	NA	NA	NA	NA
East Cleveland	NA	NA	NA	NA	NA	NA	NA	NA	NA	NA	NA	NA	NA
Elyria	54.6	971	206	0.0	7.4	0.0	0.0	2.5	22.8	28.0	4.3	1.7	6.7

1. Based on population estimated as of July 1 of the year shown.

Table D. Cities — **City Government Finances, City Government Employment, and Climate**

City	City government finances, 1999 (cont'd)			City government employment, 2001	Climate[2]						
	Debt outstanding				Average daily temperature (degrees Fahrenheit)						
					Mean		Limits				
	Total (mil dol)	Per capita[1] (dollars)	Percent utility		January	July	January[3]	July[4]	Annual precipitation (inches)	Heating degree days	Cooling degree days
	137	138	139	140	141	142	143	144	145	146	147
NEW YORK—Cont'd											
Middletown	33.8	1 412	9.4	NA	NA	NA	NA	NA	NA	NA	NA
Mount Vernon	35.6	532	0.0	787	28.7	74.1	19.7	85.7	46.01	5 470	779
Newburgh	23.2	887	7.0	NA	27.4	75.2	19.3	86.5	47.51	5 550	896
New Rochelle	131.0	1 949	0.0	775	28.7	74.1	19.7	85.7	46.01	5 470	779
New York	53 044.9	7 149	25.8	415 635	31.5	76.8	25.3	85.2	47.25	4 805	1 096
Niagara Falls	120.0	2 113	56.3	850	23.6	71.1	17.0	80.2	38.58	6 747	477
North Tonawanda	18.4	558	11.3	358	23.6	71.1	17.0	80.2	38.58	6 747	477
Port Chester	35.9	1 449	0.0	NA	NA	NA	NA	NA	NA	NA	NA
Poughkeepsie	NA	NA	NA	NA	23.8	72.2	14.2	83.8	40.72	6 391	566
Rochester	357.6	1 649	9.3	10 672	23.6	70.2	16.3	80.7	31.96	6 734	425
Rome	48.4	1 216	7.1	445	20.1	70.2	12.7	80.3	45.09	7 305	423
Saratoga Springs	12.4	492	5.0	NA	20.1	71.1	9.3	84.1	40.88	6 998	452
Schenectady	76.1	1 234	24.0	733	21.8	71.7	13.2	82.6	36.46	6 881	537
Spring Valley	NA	NA	NA	NA	NA	NA	NA	NA	NA	NA	NA
Syracuse	360.7	2 370	2.5	6 623	22.4	70.4	14.2	81.7	38.93	6 834	438
Troy	65.9	1 283	1.2	629	21.3	73.0	11.6	83.8	36.18	6 758	599
Utica	72.2	1 216	0.0	833	20.1	70.2	12.7	80.3	45.09	7 305	423
Valley Stream	13.8	408	0.0	NA	31.2	75.5	24.9	82.8	41.59	5 027	921
Watertown	51.6	1 859	26.5	371	17.9	68.6	8.3	79.6	32.04	7 753	299
White Plains	46.4	929	10.4	1 026	27.2	73.3	20.2	82.1	48.92	5 832	691
Yonkers	317.7	1 671	7.2	5 266	28.7	74.1	19.7	85.7	46.01	5 470	779
NORTH CAROLINA	X	X	X	X	X	X	X	X	X	X	X
Asheville	103.2	1 636	52.7	993	35.7	72.8	24.8	83.0	47.59	4 308	787
Burlington	17.3	427	38.1	610	37.5	78.2	27.0	88.9	44.96	3 680	1 408
Cary	49.6	604	25.3	983	38.9	78.1	28.8	88.0	41.43	3 457	1 417
Chapel Hill	23.8	555	0.0	607	37.2	76.8	25.7	88.7	46.02	3 802	1 233
Charlotte	1 454.8	2 883	17.7	5 371	39.3	79.3	29.6	88.9	43.09	3 341	1 582
Concord	120.8	3 491	54.0	776	38.5	78.8	27.2	90.0	45.70	3 497	1 541
Durham	298.4	1 944	19.6	2 028	37.1	77.1	25.1	88.8	48.10	3 867	1 278
Fayetteville	252.5	3 267	47.5	1 677	40.3	79.4	29.1	89.7	46.72	3 169	1 623
Gastonia	102.1	1 793	18.4	1 014	39.8	78.2	29.1	88.9	46.63	3 338	1 464
Goldsboro	NA	NA	NA	NA	41.0	79.8	30.5	89.9	49.27	3 040	1 689
Greensboro	274.3	1 386	3.3	3 852	36.7	76.9	26.6	86.9	42.62	3 865	1 253
Greenville	83.3	1 461	38.1	1 126	40.6	78.8	29.6	89.5	49.00	3 129	1 561
Hickory	17.2	544	0.0	659	37.7	76.8	27.8	86.6	49.38	3 728	1 258
High Point	75.7	994	19.6	1 339	38.9	77.9	29.0	88.3	44.52	3 420	1 400
Jacksonville	NA	NA	NA	NA	44.9	79.5	35.0	86.8	54.75	2 506	1 815
Kannapolis	NA	NA	NA	NA	38.5	78.8	27.2	90.0	45.70	3 497	1 541
Monroe	44.1	1 855	47.8	386	NA	NA	NA	NA	NA	NA	NA
Raleigh	261.1	1 007	19.0	3 296	38.8	78.6	28.9	88.3	44.97	3 397	1 493
Rocky Mount	22.2	390	40.5	858	39.9	78.4	29.4	88.9	45.69	3 321	1 447
Salisbury	NA	NA	NA	NA	NA	NA	NA	NA	NA	NA	NA
Wilmington	122.0	1 793	50.1	1 024	44.9	80.1	34.4	88.5	54.27	2 470	1 926
Wilson	8.3	206	53.4	682	39.4	78.5	28.4	89.4	46.96	3 371	1 519
Winston-Salem	263.8	1 605	22.4	2 268	38.9	77.9	29.0	88.3	44.52	3 420	1 400
NORTH DAKOTA	X	X	X	X	X	X	X	X	X	X	X
Bismarck	81.5	1 509	1.5	534	9.2	70.4	-1.7	84.4	15.47	8 968	488
Fargo	165.7	1 911	33.2	672	5.9	71.1	-3.6	83.4	19.45	9 254	537
Grand Forks	230.4	4 867	0.8	511	4.3	69.1	-5.3	81.6	18.34	9 733	453
Minot	26.6	755	33.0	328	9.0	69.9	0.4	82.0	18.57	9 193	492
OHIO	X	X	X	X	X	X	X	X	X	X	X
Akron	325.2	1 508	20.9	2 715	24.8	71.9	16.9	82.3	36.82	6 160	625
Barberton	34.8	1 283	8.6	NA	24.8	71.9	16.9	82.3	36.82	6 160	625
Beavercreek	NA	NA	NA	NA	26.0	74.2	17.9	84.9	36.64	5 708	886
Bowling Green	9.3	331	0.0	NA	22.7	73.0	14.4	84.6	32.77	6 482	694
Brunswick	10.6	325	0.0	NA	24.8	71.9	17.6	82.4	36.63	6 201	621
Canton	27.6	348	41.5	1 123	24.8	71.9	16.9	82.3	36.82	6 160	625
Cincinnati	291.1	865	32.2	6 631	29.8	76.4	21.2	86.6	40.70	4 928	1 135
Cleveland	1 984.3	4 002	52.7	9 684	24.8	71.9	17.6	82.4	36.63	6 201	621
Cleveland Heights	29.3	547	0.0	524	24.8	71.9	17.6	82.4	36.63	6 201	621
Columbus	1 606.8	2 397	25.4	8 753	26.4	73.2	18.5	83.7	38.09	5 708	797
Cuyahoga Falls	34.6	694	29.2	772	24.8	71.9	16.9	82.3	36.82	6 160	625
Dayton	292.3	1 746	17.5	3 059	26.0	74.2	17.9	84.9	36.64	5 708	886
Delaware	NA	NA	NA	NA	NA	NA	NA	NA	NA	NA	NA
Dublin	NA	NA	NA	NA	NA	NA	NA	NA	NA	NA	NA
East Cleveland	NA	NA	NA	NA	24.8	71.9	17.6	82.4	36.63	6 201	621
Elyria	28.2	500	1.5	591	26.2	73.3	17.9	85.0	35.95	5 818	779

1. Based on the population estimated as of July 1 of the year shown. 2. Represents normal values based on the 30-year period, 1961–1990. 3. Average daily minimum. 4. Average daily maximum.

Table D. Cities — Land Area and Population

STATE Place code	City	Land area, 2000[1] (sq km)	Population, 2000			Population				Population characteristics, 2000 — Percent						
											Race (alone or in combination)					Non-His-panic[2] White
			Total persons	Rank	Per square kilo-meter	Total persons 1990	Percent change 1990–2000	Total persons 1980	Percent change 1980–1990	White	Black	Am. Indian, Alaska Native	Asian and Pacific Islander	Other race	His-panic[2]	
		1	2	3	4	5	6	7	8	9	10	11	12	13	14	15
	OHIO—Cont'd															
39 25704	Euclid	27.7	52 717	566	1 903.1	54 875	-3.9	59 999	-8.5	67.6	31.6	0.6	1.3	0.7	1.1	65.8
39 25914	Fairborn	33.8	32 052	973	948.3	31 300	2.4	29 702	5.4	89.2	7.1	1.0	4.1	0.9	1.7	86.3
39 25970	Fairfield	54.4	42 097	726	773.8	39 709	6.0	30 777	29.0	90.9	6.6	0.4	2.6	0.8	1.5	89.0
39 27048	Findlay	44.5	38 967	798	875.7	35 703	9.1	35 594	0.3	94.8	1.8	0.5	2.1	2.1	3.9	91.8
39 29106	Gahanna	32.1	32 636	959	1 016.7	23 898	36.6	18 001	32.8	87.7	8.8	0.6	3.8	0.7	1.3	85.7
39 29428	Garfield Heights	18.7	30 734	1 015	1 643.5	31 739	-3.2	34 938	-9.2	81.5	17.2	0.5	1.1	0.6	1.3	80.0
39 32592	Grove City	36.1	27 075	1 142	750.0	19 661	37.7	16 849	16.7	97.2	1.9	0.6	0.9	0.5	1.2	95.4
39 33012	Hamilton	56.0	60 690	454	1 083.8	61 438	-1.2	63 189	-2.8	90.1	8.0	0.8	0.7	1.7	2.6	88.0
39 36610	Huber Heights	54.5	38 212	815	701.1	38 696	-1.3	35 480	9.1	86.8	10.9	0.8	2.9	1.0	1.7	83.9
39 39872	Kent	22.5	27 906	1 105	1 240.3	28 835	-3.2	26 164	10.2	87.9	10.2	0.7	2.6	0.9	1.3	85.3
39 40040	Kettering	48.4	57 502	498	1 188.1	60 569	-5.1	61 186	-1.0	96.3	2.0	0.5	1.9	0.6	1.1	94.5
39 41664	Lakewood	14.4	56 646	507	3 933.8	59 718	-5.1	61 963	-3.6	95.6	2.5	0.7	1.9	2.1	2.2	91.7
39 41720	Lancaster	46.8	35 335	883	755.0	34 507	2.4	34 953	-1.3	98.3	1.0	0.8	0.7	0.3	0.8	96.8
39 43554	Lima	33.1	40 081	772	1 210.9	45 553	-12.0	47 381	-3.9	71.5	28.2	0.9	0.7	1.3	2.0	68.4
39 44856	Lorain	62.2	68 652	393	1 103.7	71 245	-3.6	75 416	-5.5	73.2	17.8	1.2	0.6	11.5	21.0	61.1
39 47138	Mansfield	77.5	49 346	608	636.7	50 627	-2.5	53 927	-6.1	78.5	20.9	1.0	0.9	0.8	1.2	76.1
39 47306	Maple Heights	13.4	26 156	1 189	1 951.9	27 089	-3.4	29 735	-8.9	52.8	45.4	0.6	2.1	0.9	1.2	51.2
39 47754	Marion	29.4	35 318	884	1 201.3	34 075	3.6	37 040	-8.0	91.4	7.6	0.6	0.7	0.9	1.3	89.6
39 48244	Massillon	43.4	31 325	998	721.8	30 969	1.1	30 557	1.3	89.6	10.4	0.8	0.4	0.5	1.0	87.5
39 48790	Medina	28.8	25 139	1 232	872.9	19 231	30.7	15 268	26.0	96.0	3.5	0.6	1.0	0.4	1.0	93.9
39 49056	Mentor	69.3	50 278	595	725.5	47 491	5.9	42 065	12.9	97.9	0.8	0.2	1.4	0.3	0.7	96.8
39 49840	Middletown	66.5	51 605	579	776.0	46 758	12.1	43 719	5.3	88.2	11.4	0.7	0.6	0.6	0.9	86.5
39 54040	Newark	50.6	46 279	658	914.6	44 396	4.2	41 200	7.8	95.6	3.9	0.8	0.9	0.5	0.8	93.6
39 56882	North Olmsted	30.1	34 113	917	1 133.3	34 204	-0.3	36 486	-6.3	95.6	1.2	0.4	3.2	1.4	1.7	92.8
39 57008	North Royalton	55.1	28 648	1 079	519.9	23 197	23.5	17 671	31.3	96.9	0.8	0.2	2.4	0.5	1.0	95.5
39 61000	Parma	51.7	85 655	295	1 656.8	87 876	-2.5	92 548	-5.0	96.7	1.3	0.3	2.0	0.9	1.5	94.7
39 66390	Reynoldsburg	27.4	32 069	971	1 170.4	25 748	24.5	20 661	24.6	86.6	11.2	0.7	2.3	1.1	1.8	84.0
39 70380	Sandusky	26.0	27 844	1 111	1 070.9	29 764	-6.5	31 360	-5.1	77.0	23.1	0.8	0.6	1.6	3.1	73.0
39 71682	Shaker Heights	16.3	29 405	1 058	1 804.0	30 955	-5.0	32 487	-4.7	61.7	35.4	0.7	3.9	1.0	1.2	59.3
39 74118	Springfield	58.2	65 358	418	1 123.0	70 487	-7.3	72 563	-2.9	79.9	19.6	1.1	1.0	0.8	1.2	77.5
39 74944	Stow	44.3	32 139	968	725.5	27 998	14.8	25 303	10.7	96.1	1.8	0.4	2.3	0.5	0.9	94.6
39 75098	Strongsville	63.8	43 858	698	687.4	35 308	24.2	28 577	23.6	95.1	1.5	0.2	3.6	0.6	1.3	93.3
39 77000	Toledo	208.8	313 619	56	1 502.0	332 943	-5.8	354 635	-6.1	72.4	24.8	0.9	1.4	3.2	5.5	67.8
39 77504	Trotwood city	79.1	27 420	1 128	346.6	8 816	211.0	NA	NA	40.1	59.8	1.0	0.5	0.8	0.8	38.3
39 79002	Upper Arlington	25.3	33 686	937	1 331.5	34 128	-1.3	35 648	-4.3	95.4	0.8	0.3	3.9	0.4	1.0	93.9
39 80892	Warren	41.7	46 832	648	1 123.1	50 793	-7.8	56 629	-10.3	73.6	26.5	0.7	0.7	0.6	1.0	71.4
39 83342	Westerville	32.1	35 318	884	1 100.2	30 269	16.7	23 416	29.3	94.6	3.7	0.4	1.9	0.6	1.1	92.9
39 83622	Westlake	41.2	31 719	981	769.9	27 018	17.4	19 483	38.7	94.4	1.1	0.2	4.7	1.1	1.3	92.1
39 88000	Youngstown	87.8	82 026	313	934.2	95 732	-14.3	115 435	-17.1	52.6	45.5	1.1	0.6	3.0	5.2	48.9
39 88084	Zanesville	29.1	25 586	1 214	879.2	26 778	-4.5	28 655	-6.6	88.0	12.7	1.3	0.4	0.6	0.8	85.0
40 00000	OKLAHOMA	177 846.9	3 450 654	X	19.4	3 145 576	9.7	3 025 487	4.0	80.3	8.3	11.4	1.8	3.0	5.2	74.1
40 04450	Bartlesville	54.7	34 748	904	635.2	34 256	1.4	34 568	-0.9	87.4	3.8	11.8	1.4	1.5	3.0	80.6
40 09050	Broken Arrow	116.5	74 859	355	642.6	58 082	29.0	35 761	62.3	88.8	4.2	6.6	2.4	1.8	3.6	83.5
40 23200	Edmond	220.5	68 315	398	309.8	52 310	30.6	34 637	51.0	89.2	4.5	4.0	4.0	1.4	2.8	85.1
40 23950	Enid	191.6	47 045	646	245.5	45 309	3.8	50 363	-10.0	89.7	4.5	3.7	2.1	2.9	4.7	85.3
40 41850	Lawton	194.6	92 757	261	476.7	80 561	15.1	80 054	0.6	65.2	25.0	5.5	4.5	5.2	9.4	57.8
40 48350	Midwest City	63.7	54 088	548	849.1	52 267	3.5	49 559	5.5	73.0	20.9	5.9	2.7	2.1	4.1	67.6
40 49200	Moore	56.3	41 138	747	730.7	40 318	2.0	35 063	15.0	89.2	3.6	7.5	2.4	2.4	5.1	82.1
40 50050	Muskogee	96.7	38 310	810	396.2	37 708	1.6	40 011	-5.8	66.3	19.3	17.8	1.2	1.9	3.3	60.0
40 52500	Norman	458.4	95 694	247	208.8	80 071	19.5	67 996	17.8	86.0	5.0	7.0	4.2	1.9	3.9	80.3
40 55000	Oklahoma City	1 572.1	506 132	29	321.9	444 724	13.8	403 243	10.3	71.7	16.4	5.7	4.2	6.2	10.1	64.7
40 59850	Ponca City	46.9	25 919	1 201	552.6	26 359	-1.7	26 238	0.5	87.7	3.3	9.2	1.1	2.5	4.4	82.5
40 66800	Shawnee	109.5	28 692	1 077	262.0	26 017	10.3	26 506	-1.8	80.9	4.8	16.3	1.4	1.2	2.7	75.8
40 70300	Stillwater	72.1	39 065	792	541.8	36 676	6.5	38 268	-4.2	85.5	4.8	5.8	5.8	1.5	2.5	81.3
40 75000	Tulsa	473.1	393 049	43	830.8	367 302	7.0	360 919	1.8	73.9	16.5	7.7	2.3	4.2	7.2	67.1
41 00000	OREGON	248 630.5	3 421 399	X	13.8	2 842 337	20.4	2 633 156	7.9	89.3	2.1	2.5	4.2	5.2	8.0	83.5
41 01000	Albany	41.1	40 852	752	994.0	33 523	21.9	26 544	26.3	94.0	0.8	2.4	2.2	3.4	6.1	89.0
41 05350	Beaverton	42.3	76 129	348	1 799.7	53 307	42.8	30 582	74.3	81.5	2.4	1.4	12.0	6.7	11.1	73.6
41 05800	Bend	82.9	52 029	573	627.6	23 740	119.2	17 263	37.5	96.0	0.5	1.7	1.8	2.2	4.6	91.6
41 15800	Corvallis	35.2	49 322	609	1 401.2	44 757	10.2	40 960	9.3	88.6	1.6	1.6	8.1	3.3	5.7	83.3
41 23850	Eugene	104.9	137 893	156	1 314.5	112 733	22.3	105 624	6.7	91.5	2.0	2.3	5.1	3.1	5.0	86.0
41 31250	Gresham	57.4	90 205	273	1 571.5	68 285	32.2	33 005	106.8	86.1	2.6	2.0	5.0	8.5	11.9	78.9
41 34100	Hillsboro	55.9	70 186	381	1 255.6	37 598	86.7	27 664	35.9	80.4	1.7	1.6	8.2	11.7	18.9	70.3
41 38500	Keizer	18.7	32 203	966	1 722.1	21 884	47.2	18 592	17.7	88.6	1.2	2.5	2.6	8.7	12.3	81.7
41 40550	Lake Oswego	26.8	35 278	886	1 316.3	30 576	15.4	22 909	33.5	93.4	0.9	0.8	6.2	1.3	2.3	89.7
41 45000	McMinnville	25.6	26 499	1 164	1 035.1	17 894	48.1	14 080	27.1	89.0	1.0	2.4	2.4	8.3	14.6	80.4
41 47000	Medford	56.2	63 154	436	1 123.7	47 021	34.3	39 603	18.7	93.0	0.8	2.2	2.1	5.1	9.2	86.0
41 55200	Oregon City	21.1	25 754	1 208	1 220.6	14 698	75.2	14 673	0.2	94.8	1.1	2.1	2.1	2.7	5.0	90.1
41 59000	Portland	347.9	529 121	28	1 520.9	485 975	14.1	366 423	26.5	81.3	7.9	2.3	8.2	4.9	6.8	75.5

1. Dry land or land partially or temporarily covered by water.   2. Hispanic persons may be of any race.

Table D. Cities — Population and Households

City	Under 5 years	5 to 17 years	18 to 24 years	25 to 34 years	35 to 44 years	45 to 54 years	55 to 64 years	65 to 74 years	75 years and over	Percent female	Number	Percent change, 1990–2000	Persons per house-hold	Female family house-holder[1]	One-person
	16	17	18	19	20	21	22	23	24	25	26	27	28	29	30
OHIO—Cont'd															
Euclid	6.3	16.0	6.8	14.5	16.2	12.7	8.3	8.3	10.8	54.3	24 353	-2.2	2.14	15.2	39.7
Fairborn	6.0	15.1	18.4	15.3	13.9	11.7	8.0	6.9	4.7	51.4	13 615	7.4	2.28	12.4	31.0
Fairfield	6.3	18.0	9.5	15.9	16.4	14.6	8.6	6.1	4.6	51.3	16 960	10.9	2.44	9.7	26.6
Findlay	7.0	16.8	11.9	14.1	14.6	12.8	8.6	6.7	7.4	52.3	15 905	12.7	2.36	9.9	30.2
Gahanna	6.8	22.1	6.5	12.0	19.7	16.1	8.2	4.9	3.8	51.5	11 990	26.8	2.70	9.2	20.9
Garfield Heights	6.3	17.7	7.3	13.5	15.8	12.7	8.0	8.3	10.3	53.3	12 452	-0.2	2.43	15.3	30.0
Grove City	7.7	20.5	7.4	14.4	17.2	13.5	8.2	6.3	4.8	51.4	10 265	39.1	2.61	10.3	22.4
Hamilton	7.5	18.3	9.8	14.6	15.3	12.5	7.7	7.5	6.8	51.9	24 188	0.8	2.45	15.3	29.3
Huber Heights	7.3	20.1	8.6	15.1	16.0	14.3	9.3	6.0	3.3	51.3	14 392	6.5	2.64	12.0	20.5
Kent	5.0	11.4	40.0	13.0	10.0	8.8	4.2	3.7	3.9	54.2	9 772	10.9	2.27	13.3	32.4
Kettering	5.8	16.7	7.5	14.2	14.2	13.1	9.2	9.3	9.0	52.5	25 657	-1.7	2.22	9.5	33.4
Lakewood	5.9	15.1	9.5	20.7	16.5	13.0	7.0	5.7	6.5	51.9	26 693	-1.1	2.09	9.7	43.6
Lancaster	7.7	16.9	9.3	14.7	14.3	12.2	9.0	8.0	8.0	52.7	14 852	6.2	2.35	12.9	30.3
Lima	8.1	19.0	11.5	14.1	14.6	11.8	7.6	6.6	6.7	49.8	15 410	-5.5	2.42	19.7	32.1
Lorain	8.0	20.4	9.0	13.5	14.7	12.5	8.0	7.2	6.7	51.4	26 434	0.9	2.57	19.2	27.4
Mansfield	7.2	16.7	9.3	14.8	14.9	12.9	8.7	7.7	7.7	50.4	20 182	0.1	2.28	15.2	34.8
Maple Heights	6.3	19.4	6.7	13.5	17.4	12.6	7.5	7.9	8.6	53.3	10 489	-0.6	2.47	17.0	29.9
Marion	7.0	18.2	9.3	15.1	15.7	13.2	8.2	6.9	6.4	49.4	13 551	2.8	2.44	14.1	29.3
Massillon	6.6	18.7	7.9	13.1	15.0	13.1	9.4	8.2	7.9	51.9	12 677	4.7	2.40	13.8	29.6
Medina	9.2	20.7	7.2	16.1	17.7	12.6	6.3	4.7	5.6	52.1	9 467	33.3	2.60	10.6	25.1
Mentor	6.0	19.9	6.5	11.1	17.8	16.5	9.9	6.6	5.6	51.5	18 797	12.4	2.65	8.9	20.5
Middletown	7.2	17.8	9.3	14.0	15.3	13.0	8.6	7.8	7.1	52.2	21 469	16.9	2.38	14.6	29.6
Newark	7.5	17.8	9.4	13.8	15.3	12.7	8.4	7.2	7.7	52.7	19 312	8.5	2.35	13.4	31.5
North Clmsted	5.5	18.2	7.3	11.5	16.1	15.6	10.9	8.2	6.8	51.7	13 517	6.8	2.50	8.6	26.5
North Royalton	5.4	18.9	7.7	12.2	18.5	16.7	8.7	6.4	5.6	51.2	11 250	28.3	2.51	7.4	26.7
Parma	5.8	16.5	7.0	13.8	15.9	12.6	8.9	9.0	10.6	52.3	35 126	1.3	2.40	10.2	29.2
Reynoldsburg	7.1	19.5	8.0	14.8	17.1	14.9	8.5	6.0	4.2	52.4	12 849	28.7	2.49	12.3	25.8
Sandusky	7.2	18.6	9.2	13.1	15.4	12.9	8.4	7.5	7.6	52.8	11 851	-1.7	2.31	16.4	34.9
Shaker Heights	6.2	20.0	5.3	11.7	15.7	15.7	9.8	7.9	7.7	54.5	12 220	-3.4	2.39	12.9	30.2
Springfield	7.5	18.0	11.5	13.5	13.5	12.5	8.2	7.1	8.1	52.8	26 254	-3.6	2.38	16.6	32.2
Stow	6.6	19.4	7.4	13.5	17.7	15.3	8.2	6.1	5.9	51.6	12 317	22.1	2.57	8.4	23.7
Strongsville	6.2	20.0	6.2	10.5	18.0	17.3	10.3	6.4	4.9	51.2	16 209	32.0	2.69	6.4	19.9
Toledo	7.3	18.9	11.0	15.2	14.6	12.2	7.6	6.6	6.5	52.1	128 925	-1.5	2.38	17.2	32.8
Trotwood city	6.2	20.1	7.5	11.8	14.8	14.0	9.8	7.7	8.2	54.4	11 110	208.3	2.40	21.5	29.8
Upper Arlington	5.5	19.4	4.4	9.6	15.5	16.9	10.2	9.0	9.6	52.8	13 985	0.2	2.39	6.9	28.2
Warren	7.9	18.4	8.6	13.3	13.9	12.2	8.9	8.3	8.5	53.5	19 288	-5.1	2.37	19.4	32.9
Westerville	6.1	20.8	9.1	10.1	17.0	17.8	8.8	5.4	5.0	52.6	12 663	24.4	2.67	8.3	20.9
Westlake	5.1	17.7	5.6	11.1	15.7	16.7	9.9	7.6	10.7	52.8	12 826	25.0	2.37	5.8	32.0
Youngstown	7.1	18.7	10.1	12.5	13.9	12.4	8.0	8.6	8.8	52.1	32 177	-13.1	2.39	22.9	34.0
Zanesville	8.1	18.6	9.5	14.0	13.7	12.1	8.4	7.4	8.1	54.0	10 572	-2.3	2.36	18.0	33.4
OKLAHOMA	6.8	19.0	10.3	13.1	15.2	13.1	9.2	7.0	6.2	50.9	1 342 293	11.3	2.49	11.4	26.7
Bartlesville	6.2	18.8	8.1	10.8	13.9	13.9	9.8	9.1	9.4	52.6	14 565	3.9	2.35	9.7	29.5
Broken Arrow	8.0	22.9	7.7	14.1	18.2	14.6	7.0	4.3	3.2	51.2	26 159	35.8	2.84	9.7	15.7
Edmond	7.0	20.5	11.3	12.8	16.8	14.8	8.0	4.7	4.1	51.6	25 256	34.7	2.63	9.1	20.6
Enid	6.9	17.8	9.6	12.6	15.0	12.6	8.9	7.9	8.5	51.8	18 955	4.1	2.39	11.2	29.1
Lawton	8.4	19.5	15.3	16.6	14.8	9.9	6.4	5.2	4.1	47.9	31 778	7.5	2.61	15.3	24.6
Midwest City	7.3	19.1	10.7	13.8	14.9	12.9	7.9	7.1	6.1	52.2	22 161	8.7	2.42	16.5	28.6
Moore	7.7	21.8	9.3	15.5	17.0	13.1	8.4	4.6	2.6	51.6	14 848	9.4	2.75	13.3	18.2
Muskogee	7.5	18.2	9.7	12.1	13.7	12.7	8.7	7.9	9.5	53.0	15 523	2.9	2.39	15.4	31.8
Norman	5.9	15.3	21.4	15.0	14.1	12.3	7.0	4.8	4.2	49.8	38 834	21.7	2.31	9.5	30.3
Oklahoma City	7.3	18.2	10.7	15.1	15.7	13.2	8.3	6.1	5.4	51.1	204 434	14.4	2.41	13.2	30.7
Ponca City	7.2	19.1	8.5	11.2	14.4	13.4	8.7	8.4	9.2	52.4	10 636	-0.9	2.38	11.1	30.0
Shawnee	7.4	16.9	15.2	12.5	13.0	11.3	8.3	7.5	7.8	51.9	11 311	9.4	2.38	14.4	30.4
Stillwater	4.7	10.5	38.2	14.4	10.0	8.2	5.3	3.7	4.9	49.3	15 604	10.1	2.13	7.7	34.6
Tulsa	7.2	17.6	10.9	14.9	15.0	13.3	8.2	6.6	6.2	51.7	165 743	6.6	2.31	12.9	33.9
OREGON	6.5	18.2	9.6	13.8	15.4	14.8	8.9	6.4	6.4	50.4	1 333 723	20.9	2.51	9.8	26.1
Albany	7.6	18.8	9.6	14.5	14.9	13.7	8.2	5.6	7.1	51.4	16 108	36.7	2.49	11.7	26.1
Beaverton	7.2	17.7	10.6	18.4	16.7	13.6	6.8	4.0	5.0	50.6	30 821	39.5	2.44	9.7	29.7
Bend	6.9	17.6	10.2	15.5	15.6	14.3	7.5	6.0	6.4	50.7	21 062	147.0	2.42	9.7	26.1
Corvallis	4.9	12.8	28.4	14.8	12.1	11.3	5.5	4.4	5.6	50.2	19 630	17.2	2.26	7.2	31.5
Eugene	5.3	15.0	17.3	14.9	13.5	14.6	7.2	5.3	6.8	51.0	58 110	25.6	2.27	9.7	31.7
Gresham	8.0	19.6	11.1	14.7	15.6	13.7	7.5	4.7	5.1	50.6	33 327	29.7	2.67	12.0	24.3
Hillsboro	9.3	19.0	11.4	21.2	15.8	11.3	5.7	3.1	3.1	48.6	25 079	95.2	2.76	9.0	23.4
Keizer	8.1	19.7	8.2	15.0	15.1	13.5	8.4	6.0	6.2	51.5	12 110	45.3	2.64	11.2	22.4
Lake Oswego	4.9	19.8	6.1	9.9	16.9	20.6	10.4	5.7	5.7	51.9	14 769	18.3	2.38	6.9	27.9
McMinnville	7.6	18.7	14.7	13.6	13.3	11.2	6.7	6.2	8.0	51.6	9 367	41.8	2.66	10.8	23.9
Medford	7.0	18.8	8.6	12.8	14.5	13.5	8.3	7.2	9.4	52.1	25 093	33.0	2.47	11.7	27.7
Oregon City	8.4	18.6	10.3	16.5	16.1	13.3	7.1	4.5	5.3	50.8	9 471	72.9	2.62	12.3	22.4
Portland	6.1	15.0	10.3	18.3	16.4	14.8	7.6	5.3	6.2	50.6	223 737	19.5	2.30	10.8	34.6

1. No spouse present.

Table D. Cities — Group Quarters, Crime, Education, and Income

City	Persons in group quarters, 2000				Serious crimes known to police, 2000[2]				Education, 1990				Money income, 1989		
		Institutional		Non-Institutional[1]	Total		Rate[3]		School enrollment		Attainment[4] (percent)			Households Median	
	Total	Total	Persons in nursing homes		Number	Rate[3]	Violent	Property	Public	Private	High school graduate or more	Bachelor's degree or more	Per capita (dollars)[5]	Dollars	Percent change, 1979–1989 (constant 1989 dollars)
	31	32	33	34	35	36	37	38	39	40	41	42	43	44	45
OHIO—Cont'd															
Euclid	626	507	445	119	2 309	4 380	256	4 124	8 578	2 856	74.8	17.3	14 447	26 904	-10.8
Fairborn	1 031	87	87	944	1 546	4 823	246	4 577	8 988	793	77.8	21.0	13 053	27 558	-2.9
Fairfield	654	411	411	243	2 297	5 456	347	5 110	7 501	2 008	85.2	25.9	16 789	38 531	-6.7
Findlay	1 505	636	559	869	NA	NA	NA	NA	6 796	1 749	82.0	22.1	14 814	30 445	5.2
Gahanna	221	211	208	10	956	2 929	138	2 791	6 548	1 508	84.3	28.6	15 713	42 015	7.5
Garfield Heights	421	268	245	153	NA	NA	NA	NA	4 983	1 808	71.7	8.5	12 491	28 694	-12.4
Grove City	281	180	180	101	1 183	4 369	185	4 185	4 210	450	81.2	15.0	14 147	34 350	-3.3
Hamilton	1 340	1 014	459	326	4 659	7 677	919	6 757	11 827	2 056	66.6	9.9	11 108	22 886	-10.9
Huber Heights	199	91	91	108	1 806	4 726	228	4 499	9 805	1 249	84.1	18.3	14 323	37 912	2.3
Kent	5 725	92	91	5 633	906	3 247	226	3 021	15 595	559	85.9	33.6	9 191	21 463	-7.8
Kettering	435	341	341	94	2 106	3 662	120	3 542	11 125	3 250	86.8	28.6	18 988	34 506	-0.5
Lakewood	772	411	406	361	1 570	2 772	277	2 494	11 180	3 845	84.1	29.0	16 258	28 791	-0.1
Lancaster	450	415	317	35	NA	NA	NA	NA	6 381	923	72.8	11.6	11 307	22 430	-12.3
Lima	2 741	2 177	327	564	3 304	8 243	898	7 345	9 919	2 036	69.3	8.4	9 535	21 061	-11.3
Lorain	723	529	499	194	2 490	3 627	406	3 221	16 225	2 299	67.5	7.7	10 676	24 123	-20.0
Mansfield	3 346	2 871	339	475	3 491	7 075	395	6 679	9 455	1 642	69.7	13.0	11 774	22 591	-2.4
Maple Heights	224	189	189	35	271	1 036	84	952	4 771	1 185	72.2	8.1	12 792	29 568	-11.7
Marion	2 204	2 112	201	92	1 739	4 924	133	4 791	7 519	699	67.9	9.4	10 365	22 439	-10.4
Massillon	853	697	284	156	NA	NA	NA	NA	5 776	1 027	69.4	8.2	10 952	23 819	-8.6
Medina	521	494	266	27	NA	NA	NA	NA	4 476	686	83.7	23.5	14 548	32 952	-0.6
Mentor	476	324	320	152	1 529	3 041	147	2 894	10 104	2 592	86.0	22.3	16 717	42 095	-0.8
Middletown	578	488	426	90	3 238	6 275	233	6 042	8 664	1 300	71.4	12.8	12 988	25 714	-6.3
Newark	926	808	611	118	2 198	4 749	229	4 520	8 581	1 011	72.8	11.3	11 680	23 062	-6.1
North Olmsted	316	272	272	44	NA	NA	NA	NA	6 848	2 203	85.9	25.0	16 567	39 657	-5.2
North Royalton	363	236	236	127	NA	NA	NA	NA	4 366	1 466	84.6	22.6	17 262	40 952	0.2
Parma	1 224	1 145	979	79	2 150	2 510	218	2 292	14 456	4 843	76.9	15.3	14 702	33 281	-8.9
Reynoldsburg	103	91	86	12	1 373	4 281	209	4 072	5 393	1 115	88.2	24.7	16 853	37 169	2.8
Sandusky	473	322	322	151	2 071	7 438	718	6 720	5 726	1 274	71.2	9.5	11 620	22 532	-16.2
Shaker Heights	198	133	93	65	777	2 642	201	2 442	6 069	2 576	92.6	61.0	32 708	51 128	7.7
Springfield	2 820	1 304	996	1 516	6 049	9 255	1 288	7 967	14 616	3 597	68.3	10.9	10 648	21 407	-5.7
Stow	540	463	463	77	771	2 399	84	2 315	6 254	1 229	86.0	30.4	16 310	39 638	-2.2
Strongsville	329	258	258	71	812	1 851	71	1 781	7 735	2 358	89.5	30.2	20 217	50 916	6.4
Toledo	6 895	2 636	2 031	4 259	24 027	7 661	759	6 902	70 649	18 325	73.2	14.1	11 894	24 819	-8.6
Trotwood city	724	619	582	105	1 958	7 141	766	6 375	NA	NA	NA	NA	NA	NA	NA
Upper Arlington	314	314	227	0	702	2 084	95	1 989	6 853	1 523	95.7	59.2	30 388	53 140	7.7
Warren	1 161	1 039	702	122	NA	NA	NA	NA	10 265	1 615	71.3	10.0	11 508	22 637	-17.9
Westerville	1 558	575	575	983	1 010	2 860	62	2 797	7 196	2 363	91.5	40.1	17 835	48 212	16.0
Westlake	1 266	1 091	960	175	466	1 469	76	1 393	5 062	1 865	89.9	37.7	24 000	47 629	5.5
Youngstown	4 994	3 498	723	1 496	6 296	7 676	1 179	6 497	20 621	4 137	65.6	8.3	8 544	17 060	-24.3
Zanesville	663	519	342	144	NA	NA	NA	NA	5 505	642	62.2	9.4	9 504	17 658	-3.3
OKLAHOMA	112 375	66 746	28 021	45 629	157 302	4 559	498	4 061	754 928	83 883	74.6	17.8	11 893	23 577	-4.6
Bartlesville	552	285	234	267	1 512	4 351	446	3 905	7 497	1 035	82.4	16.3	16 411	30 366	-10.8
Broken Arrow	517	476	430	41	2 224	2 971	174	2 797	15 539	3 001	89.6	24.7	13 931	37 601	-2.4
Edmond	1 869	460	386	1 409	1 581	2 314	75	2 240	15 678	2 147	90.3	43.5	17 215	37 644	2.7
Enid	1 725	1 221	937	504	2 695	5 729	459	5 269	9 045	1 714	75.8	17.8	11 812	22 746	-17.0
Lawton	9 784	3 082	788	6 702	5 090	5 487	584	4 903	21 442	1 574	81.5	19.0	10 772	24 200	5.4
Midwest City	478	436	407	42	2 257	4 173	305	3 868	13 054	1 121	82.3	16.8	11 268	27 042	-8.0
Moore	263	190	190	73	1 668	4 055	287	3 768	11 522	1 175	82.2	13.9	11 739	32 984	-5.7
Muskogee	1 274	922	615	352	2 669	6 967	804	6 163	8 327	786	68.9	16.0	10 436	19 507	-1.3
Norman	6 071	1 123	786	4 948	3 599	3 761	218	3 543	29 231	1 670	87.1	38.1	13 690	25 165	-3.5
Oklahoma City	13 133	8 455	2 790	4 678	47 845	9 453	781	8 672	96 535	16 593	78.2	21.6	13 528	25 741	-3.4
Ponca City	587	392	320	195	1 391	5 367	467	4 900	5 417	610	80.0	21.9	13 776	26 405	-5.9
Shawnee	1 753	379	307	1 374	1 722	6 002	293	5 709	5 105	1 700	69.5	14.0	10 301	19 002	-7.3
Stillwater	5 902	288	200	5 614	1 287	3 295	282	3 013	19 050	505	89.5	44.3	10 747	18 501	-0.6
Tulsa	10 433	4 722	2 476	5 711	26 853	6 832	1 122	5 710	71 945	22 270	82.3	25.8	15 434	25 708	-9.1
OREGON	77 491	37 901	14 677	39 590	165 780	4 845	351	4 495	639 167	85 066	81.5	20.6	13 418	27 250	-3.1
Albany	687	492	155	195	2 778	6 800	215	6 585	6 739	554	81.1	12.4	11 444	24 474	-7.6
Beaverton	917	287	233	630	2 912	3 825	214	3 611	11 487	2 141	91.5	36.0	17 107	33 951	-1.4
Bend	1 011	497	238	514	2 871	5 518	256	5 262	4 479	651	85.3	23.0	13 110	25 787	-0.4
Corvallis	4 887	322	253	4 565	2 267	4 596	152	4 444	20 972	971	92.1	49.0	11 921	23 212	1.7
Eugene	6 086	1 672	726	4 414	9 902	7 181	450	6 731	35 773	3 269	88.6	34.9	13 886	25 369	1.2
Gresham	1 128	714	605	414	5 625	6 236	428	5 808	15 782	1 973	83.6	15.9	13 526	31 833	-10.9
Hillsboro	950	796	192	154	1 516	2 160	144	2 016	9 352	1 132	81.7	19.3	13 125	33 125	-0.2
Keizer	280	233	233	47	1 315	4 083	93	3 990	4 834	509	81.9	17.5	13 120	31 063	3.4
Lake Oswego	163	76	0	87	782	2 217	79	2 137	6 626	1 551	96.6	53.9	27 946	51 499	6.6
McMinnville	1 602	572	327	1 030	1 232	4 649	109	4 540	3 566	1 554	80.7	19.2	12 434	25 878	1.3
Medford	1 285	670	432	615	3 995	6 326	329	5 996	8 533	1 333	81.7	17.9	13 791	25 677	-1.9
Oregon City	903	823	322	80	1 245	4 834	198	4 636	3 300	258	80.9	12.8	12 106	28 687	0.2
Portland	14 992	5 454	2 569	9 538	40 943	7 738	1 077	6 661	84 548	19 773	82.9	25.9	14 478	25 592	3.3

1. Persons in emergency shelters and persons visible in street locations. 2. Data for serious crimes have not been adjusted for underreporting. This may affect comparability between geographic areas and over time. 3. Per 100,000 population estimated by the FBI. 4. Persons 25 years old and older. 5. Based on population enumerated as of April 1, 1990.

Table D. Cities — **Income, Poverty, and Housing**

City	Money income, 1989 (cont'd) Households (cont'd) — Percent with $100,000 or more	Percent below poverty, 1989 Persons — Total	Persons — Percent change in rate, 1979–1989	Families — Total	Housing units, 2000 — Total	Percent change, 1990–2000	Vacant units for sale or rent[1]	For seasonal use (percent)	Home owner vacancy rate	Renter vacancy rate	Occupied units — Total	Percent owner occupied	Percent renter occupied	Average size owner occupied	Average size renter occupied
	46	47	48	49	50	51	52	53	54	55	56	57	58	59	60
OHIO—Cont'd															
Euclid	1.2	7.8	30.0	5.3	26 123	-1.7	1 770	0.1	1.4	9.8	24 353	59.5	40.5	2.34	1.84
Fairborn	1.9	15.4	33.9	10.9	14 419	8.5	804	0.4	1.7	6.6	13 615	51.7	48.3	2.39	2.15
Fairfield	3.6	3.8	31.0	2.7	17 789	9.3	829	0.4	0.9	7.6	16 960	65.4	34.6	2.63	2.09
Findlay	2.7	8.5	16.4	6.7	17 152	14.3	1 247	0.5	2.0	8.5	15 905	64.8	35.2	2.47	2.14
Gahanna	4.2	5.0	35.1	3.6	12 390	24.9	400	0.5	0.6	5.9	11 990	77.7	22.3	2.86	2.16
Garfield Heights	0.8	5.9	0.0	4.0	12 998	0.0	546	0.1	1.3	7.6	12 452	79.9	20.1	2.51	2.15
Grove City	1.7	5.8	28.9	4.4	10 712	39.6	447	0.3	1.9	5.5	10 265	72.5	27.5	2.73	2.29
Hamilton	1.1	16.8	25.4	14.0	25 913	2.2	1 725	0.3	1.5	7.1	24 188	60.7	39.3	2.52	2.35
Huber Heights	1.8	4.3	-15.7	3.2	14 938	4.4	546	0.2	1.3	5.8	14 392	72.0	28.0	2.64	2.64
Kent	2.1	27.5	28.5	17.2	10 435	12.5	663	0.2	1.8	6.4	9 772	37.8	62.2	2.58	2.08
Kettering	4.7	4.2	0.0	2.8	26 936	-0.6	1 279	0.5	1.3	6.9	25 657	66.6	33.4	2.39	1.90
Lakewood	3.3	8.5	34.9	6.1	28 416	-0.4	1 723	0.5	0.9	6.4	26 693	45.2	54.8	2.53	1.74
Lancaster	1.5	14.1	42.4	11.0	15 891	7.7	1 039	0.8	1.6	7.1	14 852	59.4	40.6	2.41	2.26
Lima	1.0	21.6	27.8	18.6	17 631	-5.5	2 221	0.4	2.5	12.9	15 410	56.8	43.2	2.44	2.40
Lorain	0.8	19.8	47.8	16.6	28 231	2.5	1 797	0.2	1.6	7.2	26 434	61.2	38.8	2.61	2.51
Mansfield	1.6	17.8	30.9	14.5	22 267	1.6	2 085	0.4	2.1	10.6	20 182	57.6	42.4	2.36	2.17
Maple Heights	1.2	4.0	-16.7	2.9	10 935	1.3	446	0.1	1.8	5.7	10 489	83.8	16.2	2.55	2.09
Marion	1.0	16.8	13.5	13.9	14 713	3.3	1 162	0.2	2.3	8.0	13 551	63.5	36.5	2.52	2.32
Massillon	0.9	14.4	44.0	12.2	13 567	5.9	890	0.2	1.8	7.2	12 677	69.0	31.0	2.50	2.20
Medina	2.7	8.4	50.0	7.7	9 924	34.9	457	0.2	1.4	6.4	9 467	66.3	33.7	2.86	2.09
Mentor	4.0	2.9	3.6	2.3	19 301	12.4	504	0.4	0.9	5.6	18 797	87.5	12.5	2.69	2.33
Middletown	2.4	15.4	20.3	13.1	23 144	19.4	1 675	0.2	2.2	8.5	21 469	60.1	39.9	2.47	2.24
Newark	1.6	15.6	34.5	13.3	20 625	8.7	1 313	0.3	2.1	6.8	19 312	58.2	41.8	2.47	2.18
North Olmsted	3.1	3.1	10.7	2.5	14 059	7.5	542	0.4	1.1	7.9	13 517	79.7	20.3	2.62	2.01
North Royalton	4.1	2.5	-32.4	1.7	11 754	29.0	504	0.4	1.5	7.0	11 250	74.9	25.1	2.75	1.80
Parma	1.9	4.1	36.7	3.1	36 414	2.3	1 288	0.2	0.8	7.2	35 126	77.5	22.5	2.52	2.00
Reynoldsburg	2.7	4.4	57.1	2.5	13 434	26.9	585	0.3	1.2	7.1	12 849	65.1	34.9	2.63	2.23
Sandusky	1.3	15.4	40.0	12.9	13 323	-0.7	1 472	3.5	2.0	9.6	11 851	56.5	43.5	2.42	2.17
Shaker Heights	21.5	3.5	2.9	2.3	12 982	-2.9	762	0.4	1.1	8.2	12 220	64.9	35.1	2.66	1.89
Springfield	1.3	20.9	18.8	16.6	29 309	-0.9	3 055	0.4	2.6	10.7	26 254	57.2	42.8	2.42	2.33
Stow	2.9	3.1	10.7	2.3	12 852	22.8	535	0.4	1.4	6.4	12 317	72.1	27.9	2.79	1.99
Strongsville	8.0	2.3	9.5	1.9	16 863	28.7	654	0.5	0.9	10.1	16 209	82.7	17.3	2.85	1.92
Toledo	1.6	19.1	40.4	15.4	139 871	-1.6	10 946	0.3	1.5	8.8	128 925	59.8	40.2	2.50	2.19
Trotwood city	NA	NA	NA	NA	12 020	220.6	910	0.2	2.1	9.6	11 110	62.6	37.4	2.46	2.30
Upper Arlington	18.5	1.4	-41.7	0.7	14 432	0.4	447	0.7	0.9	4.1	13 985	81.3	18.7	2.51	1.85
Warren	1.3	20.0	43.9	16.9	21 279	-2.3	1 991	0.2	2.5	11.5	19 288	58.4	41.6	2.39	2.33
Westerville	7.5	2.8	-26.3	1.8	13 143	24.9	480	0.3	1.0	8.4	12 663	79.2	20.8	2.82	2.09
Westlake	13.8	2.1	0.0	1.6	13 648	23.9	822	0.7	1.9	8.9	12 826	74.8	25.2	2.61	1.67
Youngstown	0.6	29.0	59.3	24.4	37 159	-8.9	4 982	0.2	2.3	11.5	32 177	64.0	36.0	2.40	2.28
Zanesville	1.6	25.9	38.5	22.7	11 662	-0.9	1 090	0.2	3.4	7.6	10 572	54.6	45.4	2.42	2.28
OKLAHOMA	2.3	16.7	24.7	13.0	1 514 400	7.7	172 107	2.1	2.5	10.6	1 342 293	68.4	31.6	2.55	2.36
Bartlesville	4.7	11.1	73.4	8.7	16 091	1.2	1 526	0.6	1.9	7.9	14 565	70.4	29.6	2.39	2.24
Broken Arrow	2.4	6.5	47.7	5.2	27 085	32.6	926	0.1	1.3	6.9	26 159	78.7	21.3	2.90	2.62
Edmond	7.0	7.3	0.0	5.2	26 380	28.1	1 124	0.2	1.4	6.3	25 256	72.8	27.2	2.78	2.23
Enid	2.3	14.3	68.2	11.1	21 255	-2.0	2 300	0.4	2.9	11.2	18 955	67.2	32.8	2.40	2.37
Lawton	1.3	15.9	4.6	13.4	36 433	5.2	4 655	0.2	4.9	13.5	31 778	54.7	45.3	2.58	2.65
Midwest City	1.3	11.2	51.4	8.9	23 853	4.4	1 692	0.3	2.1	9.1	22 161	61.2	38.8	2.43	2.40
Moore	0.7	8.0	37.9	6.7	15 801	6.6	953	0.8	1.7	9.3	14 848	75.8	24.2	2.75	2.76
Muskogee	1.4	22.5	16.0	18.0	17 517	-0.9	1 994	0.4	2.6	10.2	15 523	61.9	38.1	2.45	2.27
Norman	3.1	15.0	20.0	8.2	41 547	16.5	2 713	0.4	1.7	8.0	38 834	55.2	44.8	2.53	2.04
Oklahoma City	2.8	15.9	32.5	12.0	228 149	7.4	23 715	0.5	2.2	12.3	204 434	59.4	40.6	2.51	2.27
Ponca City	2.1	10.7	46.6	8.1	11 871	-3.4	1 235	0.8	2.3	11.0	10 636	68.1	31.9	2.41	2.33
Shawnee	1.1	21.2	17.8	16.5	12 651	7.4	1 340	1.1	2.4	9.1	11 311	59.9	40.1	2.40	2.36
Stillwater	1.7	26.4	27.5	12.5	16 827	6.7	1 223	0.4	2.2	5.8	15 604	41.8	58.2	2.38	1.94
Tulsa	4.6	15.0	44.2	11.5	179 405	1.8	13 662	0.5	1.6	8.7	165 743	55.6	44.4	2.41	2.18
OREGON	2.8	12.4	16.1	8.7	1 452 709	21.7	118 986	2.5	2.3	7.3	1 333 723	64.3	35.7	2.59	2.36
Albany	0.9	14.7	1.4	11.3	17 374	41.0	1 266	0.3	2.6	9.8	16 108	59.5	40.5	2.57	2.38
Beaverton	4.0	6.4	-12.3	5.2	32 500	34.9	1 679	0.3	2.0	6.0	30 821	47.7	52.3	2.67	2.23
Bend	2.1	13.2	20.0	9.2	22 507	150.0	1 445	1.5	2.6	5.5	21 062	62.9	37.1	2.48	2.32
Corvallis	2.6	21.0	18.6	10.0	20 909	20.8	1 279	0.3	2.2	7.1	19 630	44.9	55.1	2.50	2.07
Eugene	3.3	17.0	15.6	9.0	61 444	28.0	3 334	0.4	1.7	6.6	58 110	51.8	48.2	2.47	2.05
Gresham	1.7	8.3	29.7	6.0	35 309	30.9	1 982	0.3	2.4	6.9	33 327	54.9	45.1	2.78	2.54
Hillsboro	1.7	8.3	6.4	6.2	27 211	103.9	2 132	0.6	4.0	8.2	25 079	52.3	47.7	2.92	2.58
Keizer	2.0	7.1	-15.5	4.0	12 774	49.0	664	0.2	2.8	6.7	12 110	64.7	35.3	2.67	2.57
Lake Oswego	16.4	3.7	-19.6	1.8	15 741	20.1	972	0.8	3.0	7.8	14 769	70.6	29.4	2.58	1.89
McMinnville	2.5	12.9	24.0	8.7	9 834	45.1	467	0.2	1.8	6.0	9 367	60.4	39.6	2.71	2.58
Medford	2.9	14.4	19.0	11.5	26 297	33.6	1 204	0.3	1.8	4.9	25 093	57.3	42.7	2.52	2.39
Oregon City	0.8	9.2	21.1	7.0	10 110	78.1	639	0.2	3.4	7.7	9 471	59.8	40.2	2.74	2.45
Portland	3.0	14.5	11.5	9.7	237 307	19.6	13 570	0.4	2.3	6.2	223 737	55.8	44.2	2.47	2.08

1. Includes units rented or sold but not occupied. 2. Specified owner-occupied units. 3. Specified renter-occupied units. 4. Overcrowded or lacking complete plumbing facilities.

City	Civilian labor force, 2001				Civilian employment, 1990[2]			Disability 1990	Value of residential construction authorized by building permits, 2000		
			Unemployment			Percent					
	Total	Percent change, 2000–2001	Total	Rate[1]	Total	Professional, managerial, and technical	Precision production, craft, and repair	Work disabled persons[3] (percent)	New construction ($1,000)	Number of housing units	Percent single family
	61	62	63	64	65	66	67	68	69	70	71
OHIO—Cont'd											
Euclid	27 461	0.3	979	3.6	25 714	31.0	10.5	7.7	2 271	16	100.0
Fairborn	16 516	1.3	762	4.6	13 889	33.4	9.9	10.6	16 987	266	27.1
Fairfield	31 106	3.0	690	2.2	22 000	36.9	8.9	6.0	15 986	139	100.0
Findlay	23 953	1.2	859	3.6	17 483	31.0	11.0	7.8	18 981	165	62.4
Gahanna	17 616	2.4	358	2.0	14 167	38.9	8.7	7.2	22 682	138	89.9
Garfield Heights	15 445	0.3	550	3.6	14 463	23.7	14.2	7.8	919	9	100.0
Grove City	13 000	2.4	227	1.7	10 486	27.9	9.1	7.2	63 880	561	50.6
Hamilton	36 757	3.2	1 800	4.9	25 285	21.5	12.8	13.6	13 145	123	82.9
Huber Heights	20 685	1.7	694	3.4	19 495	31.4	11.3	8.0	NA	NA	NA
Kent	16 975	0.3	801	4.7	13 891	30.0	6.5	5.3	9 381	51	100.0
Kettering	32 625	1.6	702	2.2	31 130	40.7	8.9	7.0	4 710	21	90.5
Lakewood	33 628	0.3	986	2.9	31 695	38.1	8.0	6.7	0	0	0.0
Lancaster	22 255	2.4	817	3.7	15 362	24.4	12.2	10.6	17 619	126	98.4
Lima	19 037	-0.2	1 553	8.2	16 656	19.8	12.0	11.5	1 483	12	100.0
Lorain	33 365	1.1	2 739	8.2	27 762	21.4	12.9	10.1	8 548	85	100.0
Mansfield	22 857	0.5	1 516	6.6	20 519	23.7	11.8	11.9	8 986	158	24.1
Maple Heights	13 660	0.3	432	3.2	12 844	23.1	11.6	7.1	1 193	11	100.0
Marion	16 665	1.6	939	5.6	14 086	20.7	13.8	12.7	1 853	42	88.1
Massillon	14 797	1.2	751	5.1	12 528	22.5	11.0	10.9	15 949	136	84.6
Medina	12 252	0.8	536	4.4	9 180	31.3	9.9	6.7	33 964	264	96.2
Mentor	28 589	0.8	1 017	3.6	24 672	34.1	12.2	6.1	18 212	94	87.2
Middletown	NA	NA	NA	NA	19 913	24.9	12.5	11.5	8 799	94	93.6
Newark	24 443	2.4	1 185	4.8	19 187	27.0	10.8	9.0	151 767	1 077	92.3
North Olmsted	18 617	0.3	391	2.1	17 697	33.9	10.1	5.9	6 819	47	100.0
North Royalton	12 951	0.3	296	2.3	12 288	34.3	12.7	5.7	46 081	452	40.9
Parma	44 551	0.3	961	2.2	42 325	29.2	12.2	7.1	3 462	30	66.7
Reynoldsburg	18 260	2.3	306	1.7	14 742	34.5	9.2	6.0	36 964	277	92.4
Sandusky	16 438	2.0	1 120	6.8	13 137	21.3	11.1	10.9	8 310	59	100.0
Shaker Heights	16 669	0.3	394	2.4	15 803	61.6	2.8	4.9	415	1	100.0
Springfield	31 349	2.2	2 093	6.7	28 636	24.5	10.4	12.5	4 168	35	100.0
Stow	16 921	0.3	346	2.0	14 490	40.2	9.3	5.2	49 580	637	23.7
Strongsville	19 794	0.3	426	2.2	18 806	39.3	9.3	3.8	25 903	180	100.0
Toledo	161 506	0.7	9 436	5.8	141 298	26.6	10.7	10.2	20 811	318	29.2
Trotwood city	14 560	1.9	745	5.1	NA	NA	NA	NA	2 226	21	100.0
Upper Arlington	20 910	2.3	209	1.0	16 994	60.3	2.8	4.4	11 068	27	88.9
Warren	22 555	0.7	2 156	9.6	19 323	21.7	11.3	12.7	521	6	66.7
Westerville	19 787	2.3	269	1.4	15 802	43.0	4.7	3.6	21 969	172	90.1
Westlake	14 315	0.3	259	1.8	13 648	48.0	6.6	4.1	45 115	230	76.1
Youngstown	34 190	-0.5	3 560	10.4	30 086	20.8	10.4	14.7	847	9	100.0
Zanesville	13 311	2.1	1 158	8.7	9 860	22.6	10.5	13.9	1 887	11	100.0
OKLAHOMA	1 665 427	1.1	63 506	3.8	1 369 138	27.9	12.0	10.2	1 204 003	11 148	80.5
Bartlesville	13 680	3.1	445	3.3	15 068	40.2	9.9	7.0	6 454	32	100.0
Broken Arrow	35 551	0.2	787	2.2	29 037	34.8	10.1	6.0	82 857	622	100.0
Edmond	31 693	0.2	725	2.3	26 930	42.9	7.0	5.2	81 675	430	100.0
Enid	20 431	-1.9	651	3.2	19 100	25.7	12.1	9.3	8 960	53	92.5
Lawton	31 567	-0.6	1 069	3.4	29 197	32.2	7.9	10.6	14 026	125	92.0
Midwest City	28 140	0.9	1 171	4.2	23 453	28.4	11.9	9.1	8 862	81	100.0
Moore	26 466	0.5	711	2.7	20 364	25.3	14.1	8.7	31 476	344	95.3
Muskogee	17 170	-0.3	665	3.9	14 782	25.8	10.2	13.2	5 601	59	100.0
Norman	53 005	0.9	1 889	3.6	40 417	40.5	8.1	6.9	60 810	446	100.0
Oklahoma City	254 882	1.0	10 823	4.2	209 496	30.7	10.0	9.7	297 039	3 237	63.1
Ponca City	12 353	2.8	578	4.7	11 952	33.0	12.9	7.7	8 267	70	50.0
Shawnee	12 557	1.3	700	5.6	10 266	29.8	10.8	11.8	8 929	67	100.0
Stillwater	22 452	-3.2	351	1.6	17 425	39.6	5.7	4.5	15 369	183	67.2
Tulsa	221 095	0.4	8 100	3.7	179 327	34.1	10.4	8.3	107 462	852	74.2
OREGON	1 793 724	-0.5	113 855	6.3	1 319 960	28.8	10.7	10.0	2 533 332	19 877	78.6
Albany	17 406	-0.6	1 269	7.3	13 441	22.4	13.2	10.7	31 855	308	64.3
Beaverton	46 034	0.2	2 272	4.9	30 118	39.0	7.6	5.8	36 014	363	62.0
Bend	18 140	0.0	1 011	5.6	10 651	30.2	10.3	8.1	124 860	966	85.8
Corvallis	24 692	-0.1	775	3.1	20 306	45.1	4.9	5.6	30 461	176	78.4
Eugene	69 136	-1.1	4 210	6.1	54 654	36.7	7.4	7.8	103 045	744	83.2
Gresham	43 999	-0.2	2 091	4.8	34 938	25.4	11.7	8.6	47 462	503	63.4
Hillsboro	28 496	0.4	1 518	5.3	18 566	28.3	13.1	9.3	101 457	996	62.6
Keizer	14 901	-1.8	851	5.7	10 781	28.0	10.6	10.1	35 662	315	81.6
Lake Oswego	22 844	-0.8	744	3.3	16 632	52.7	3.2	4.3	16 424	96	100.0
McMinnville	11 949	-0.4	684	5.7	8 003	25.4	10.0	9.6	37 037	371	37.7
Medford	30 559	-0.1	1 809	5.9	20 922	26.3	8.8	11.2	32 053	359	74.9
Oregon City	10 140	-0.6	373	3.7	7 280	22.9	15.6	8.9	54 665	340	98.2
Portland	281 440	0.5	18 824	6.7	218 750	32.7	9.4	10.4	187 854	1 798	48.2

1. Percent of civilian labor force.   2. Persons 16 years and older.   3. Persons 16 to 64 years old.

Table D. Cities — Wholesale Trade, Retail Trade, and Real Estate

City	Wholesale Trade, 1997				Retail Trade[1], 1997				Real Estate and Rental and Leasing, 1997			
	Number of Establishments	Number of Employees	Sales (mil dol)	Annual Payroll (mil dol)	Number of Establishments	Number of Employees	Sales (mil dol)	Annual Payroll (mil dol)	Number of Establishments	Number of Employees	Receipts (mil dol)	Annual Payroll (mil dol)
	72	73	74	75	76	77	78	79	80	81	82	83
OHIO—Cont'd												
Euclid	72	2 532	1 342.3	174.3	169	2 418	314.7	32.5	49	358	29.4	6.5
Fairborn	15	253	138.1	8.3	101	1 326	224.4	19.0	27	121	14.3	1.9
Fairfield	93	1 683	1 279.8	60.5	182	3 254	710.6	60.6	45	387	38.1	8.2
Findlay	61	607	336.0	17.8	259	3 665	569.3	52.3	55	D	D	D
Gahanna	49	421	278.9	19.3	89	1 296	189.2	17.6	22	81	14.0	1.6
Garfield Heights	51	1 487	810.2	71.4	78	1 287	179.9	18.6	13	46	6.5	0.6
Grove City	34	712	349.1	22.3	77	1 173	161.3	15.2	21	81	9.3	1.2
Hamilton	75	1 404	890.5	51.2	233	2 755	375.3	40.3	55	303	23.7	5.6
Huber Heights	21	295	160.1	13.1	129	2 150	276.6	26.1	24	212	27.0	6.4
Kent	28	189	61.0	6.1	74	1 215	338.1	26.3	28	154	14.8	1.9
Kettering	73	924	595.4	43.1	228	4 821	756.0	71.2	66	348	38.3	6.1
Lakewood	62	617	255.7	22.8	155	1 767	300.6	30.9	47	282	31.4	5.3
Lancaster	40	364	97.7	12.2	270	3 868	540.0	57.9	47	200	18.5	3.0
Lima	89	1 197	436.2	32.8	188	2 143	361.9	33.5	48	201	15.3	3.1
Lorain	40	877	199.0	23.6	175	2 148	314.9	29.5	55	212	16.2	3.3
Mansfield	96	1 344	445.3	36.2	273	3 186	486.6	53.1	53	214	25.8	3.7
Maple Heights	27	709	250.5	20.3	135	1 750	197.9	23.0	18	79	5.4	1.2
Marion	32	287	84.7	8.8	156	2 482	397.7	37.4	38	150	12.9	3.1
Massillon	33	1 158	833.3	45.5	128	1 831	296.6	28.1	14	54	4.1	0.8
Medina	59	655	307.3	22.6	112	2 217	243.1	24.7	27	105	13.4	1.7
Mentor	138	1 828	477.5	56.8	401	7 492	1 316.3	120.6	48	308	29.9	5.4
Middletown	40	876	302.2	29.0	193	2 232	327.0	33.5	59	245	27.5	4.4
Newark	43	447	178.5	14.8	192	2 038	323.3	32.9	45	199	16.9	3.5
North Olmsted	57	D	D	D	324	5 444	935.6	76.9	27	127	19.9	3.4
North Royalton	70	459	220.9	17.0	74	754	137.7	12.2	15	65	5.4	1.0
Parma	73	981	290.8	34.1	366	5 440	794.1	80.8	55	438	47.3	7.9
Reynoldsburg	33	432	147.9	8.9	101	1 214	151.7	16.6	48	221	26.6	3.6
Sandusky	47	498	147.8	15.1	224	3 016	419.7	43.4	37	165	13.7	2.7
Shaker Heights	34	245	337.0	8.8	89	1 187	203.9	19.6	29	162	19.0	2.7
Springfield	69	1 126	657.6	30.5	328	4 983	724.2	70.6	49	223	21.2	3.8
Stow	46	727	451.2	23.7	99	1 971	266.4	29.2	27	144	16.3	2.1
Strongsville	85	1 516	632.2	62.8	226	4 434	511.3	57.4	39	199	18.7	3.3
Toledo	487	7 731	3 692.8	259.5	1 281	18 732	2 513.1	280.4	255	1 729	192.4	37.6
Trotwood city	NA	NA	NA	NA	NA	NA	NA	NA	NA	NA	NA	NA
Upper Arlington	48	366	242.9	12.3	124	1 511	156.7	21.3	48	D	D	D
Warren	62	728	265.2	19.2	281	4 639	761.2	82.1	57	267	28.4	5.0
Westerville	74	963	831.9	35.1	136	1 989	283.7	28.1	44	293	29.7	5.3
Westlake	174	2 482	2 050.2	123.6	148	2 532	401.0	41.4	55	592	76.8	15.4
Youngstown	153	2 251	702.1	69.5	347	3 442	487.4	56.3	60	436	32.3	6.4
Zanesville	41	813	337.3	22.0	266	3 226	506.9	46.6	46	172	20.1	3.5
OKLAHOMA	5 191	59 641	32 132.3	1 756.1	14 352	161 613	27 065.6	2 406.9	3 344	15 354	1 576.0	284.5
Bartlesville	28	112	24.1	2.4	183	2 431	409.8	36.6	41	D	D	D
Broken Arrow	113	1 218	420.4	42.5	217	2 956	616.0	48.5	52	189	21.3	3.4
Edmond	96	399	156.0	11.9	274	3 549	522.6	50.4	91	789	106.8	12.4
Enid	96	D	D	D	282	3 333	488.6	46.9	65	277	23.8	4.6
Lawton	80	751	173.1	15.9	392	5 005	664.4	65.5	123	500	47.1	7.9
Midwest City	28	D	D	D	220	4 401	742.7	60.8	60	257	25.6	3.7
Moore	40	350	93.5	6.7	114	1 592	237.5	22.3	25	84	6.2	1.1
Muskogee	65	830	231.7	21.2	281	3 221	505.6	48.0	50	208	16.0	3.1
Norman	79	987	397.6	27.0	399	5 268	968.0	82.5	132	514	40.7	7.8
Oklahoma City	1 307	19 128	14 323.2	572.8	2 145	28 167	5 337.0	490.8	705	4 136	464.1	87.2
Ponca City	32	226	145.7	6.3	158	1 963	280.5	27.0	30	78	9.4	1.2
Shawnee	25	D	D	D	221	2 535	358.3	33.9	47	165	17.4	2.3
Stillwater	30	399	135.1	8.8	193	2 639	370.6	34.2	55	236	12.1	2.7
Tulsa	1 237	16 094	8 372.1	577.7	1 905	28 474	5 100.5	484.1	684	3 904	451.4	84.0
OREGON	5 943	74 790	53 679.1	2 578.7	14 467	178 349	33 396.8	3 308.8	4 556	23 058	2 704.0	470.9
Albany	55	731	214.6	21.7	198	2 773	461.9	45.4	47	218	21.4	3.4
Beaverton	271	3 919	5 353.3	189.0	399	6 830	1 584.6	146.0	169	1 115	124.7	16.4
Bend	108	868	374.3	27.1	391	4 511	848.6	85.6	105	457	49.8	8.2
Corvallis	29	387	45.4	7.4	236	2 792	413.7	46.7	87	322	33.1	4.4
Eugene	356	3 977	1 687.8	125.2	826	11 203	2 036.4	209.4	276	1 408	165.7	24.9
Gresham	64	722	507.8	23.5	277	4 397	905.4	79.6	102	461	53.3	8.1
Hillsboro	83	1 007	325.5	41.7	225	3 704	884.3	78.6	60	203	28.6	3.6
Keizer	19	D	D	D	69	512	97.7	10.8	44	137	20.7	2.4
Lake Oswego	166	1 448	2 076.1	70.5	151	1 357	251.4	28.3	105	880	100.6	22.4
McMinnville	22	169	99.2	4.9	137	1 938	379.5	34.4	40	167	20.2	2.8
Medford	149	1 216	462.5	38.3	499	6 687	1 306.9	121.6	117	640	60.7	10.3
Oregon City	19	244	183.7	9.4	108	1 661	238.5	24.4	38	107	9.9	1.6
Portland	1 700	26 464	23 728.9	948.6	2 621	34 060	6 190.4	683.9	945	7 255	926.8	189.9

1. Establishments with payroll.

Table D. Cities — Professional Services, Manufacturing, Accommodation and Foodservices

City	Professional, Scientific, and Technical Services, 1997[1]				Manufacturing, 1997				Accommodation and Foodservices, 1997			
	Number of Establishments	Number of Employees	Receipts (mil dol)	Annual Payroll (mil dol)	Number of Establishments	Number of Employees	Receipts (mil dol)	Annual Payroll (mil dol)	Number of Establishments	Number of Employees	Sales (mil dol)	Annual Payroll (mil dol)
	84	85	86	87	88	89	90	91	92	93	94	95
OHIO—Cont'd												
Euclid	60	378	31.3	15.3	108	8 223	1 627.6	326.0	83	D	D	D
Fairborn	65	1 932	200.6	84.2	14	779	139.5	27.0	79	1 656	50.5	14.6
Fairfield	69	461	33.8	13.7	84	3 096	492.8	95.9	81	1 727	48.5	13.6
Findlay	91	445	31.8	12.7	66	7 559	1 397.3	271.5	143	2 766	74.7	22.3
Gahanna	70	568	53.0	23.9	28	517	74.4	16.1	64	1 272	38.2	11.5
Garfield Heights	42	435	42.6	19.4	48	1 502	189.3	48.1	54	D	D	D
Grove City	40	137	10.5	3.5	20	1 165	221.1	42.1	75	1 521	52.5	14.9
Hamilton	102	756	38.9	17.8	86	3 717	692.2	136.9	130	2 184	62.1	17.0
Huber Heights	26	246	14.7	7.0	34	D	D	D	79	1 524	45.2	12.5
Kent	41	145	8.8	2.6	72	2 412	343.0	70.2	84	1 328	33.3	9.9
Kettering	142	1 360	132.7	53.2	51	5 025	831.9	269.9	115	D	D	D
Lakewood	110	526	36.0	16.6	41	1 128	182.1	44.1	112	1 356	41.3	10.7
Lancaster	79	337	22.9	8.8	78	4 282	625.1	134.0	100	2 249	66.3	18.4
Lima	98	556	38.5	14.2	48	3 856	1 743.7	209.3	93	1 427	43.7	11.7
Lorain	66	782	39.2	20.8	64	7 745	6 669.5	340.4	99	D	D	D
Mansfield	111	673	42.7	17.4	126	7 844	1 256.5	265.4	143	2 289	74.0	20.3
Maple Heights	12	47	3.1	1.2	31	576	77.9	19.0	47	575	19.3	5.0
Marion	56	313	17.7	6.7	48	2 723	784.9	92.6	67	1 395	41.6	10.8
Massillon	42	253	15.0	6.6	64	4 737	975.6	144.7	79	1 107	31.0	7.5
Medina	90	380	29.0	11.3	87	3 813	759.5	123.9	54	1 394	40.4	11.9
Mentor	140	659	62.8	23.7	244	8 617	1 450.4	274.8	127	3 338	86.5	24.9
Middletown	73	557	92.8	20.6	71	7 187	3 662.9	353.0	97	2 370	69.5	20.0
Newark	88	821	40.5	16.6	49	4 017	770.2	133.4	102	1 335	40.6	11.1
North Olmsted	70	466	33.4	15.7	NA	NA	NA	NA	117	2 617	72.3	20.6
North Royalton	50	148	21.6	5.1	84	1 111	135.2	37.4	45	558	15.5	4.3
Parma	102	1 001	42.6	14.8	58	5 002	972.8	278.8	189	2 778	76.2	20.4
Reynoldsburg	80	497	42.9	21.3	15	591	213.0	16.0	75	1 043	33.6	9.0
Sandusky	62	336	26.9	13.6	66	5 206	799.0	223.4	123	2 853	104.9	28.8
Shaker Heights	97	489	56.5	18.8	NA	NA	NA	NA	38	779	22.6	6.1
Springfield	91	532	27.4	11.2	115	D	D	D	169	3 258	95.0	26.3
Stow	64	229	14.5	4.9	72	2 527	342.5	89.4	44	886	23.6	6.2
Strongsville	117	447	35.4	16.2	76	3 286	650.9	122.7	95	2 151	51.4	13.4
Toledo	584	5 500	569.5	183.3	462	25 446	9 282.3	1 101.0	737	13 187	424.0	112.3
Trotwood city	NA	NA	NA	NA	NA	NA	NA	NA	NA	NA	NA	NA
Upper Arlington	128	552	46.9	18.3	NA	NA	NA	NA	53	1 016	29.6	9.2
Warren	127	715	50.3	21.1	69	12 471	3 247.4	629.7	137	2 415	67.9	18.4
Westerville	148	864	68.2	30.3	37	1 206	191.5	49.8	62	D	D	D
Westlake	162	1 047	85.6	37.5	55	1 662	308.7	54.8	70	1 936	61.5	16.9
Youngstown	126	906	80.2	35.5	148	4 658	954.0	166.5	177	2 467	79.3	19.9
Zanesville	54	344	27.1	10.0	53	4 194	599.0	112.2	105	2 097	61.4	16.9
OKLAHOMA	7 009	40 633	3 543.0	1 323.7	4 087	164 060	37 453.2	4 963.2	6 534	105 934	3 151.3	856.8
Bartlesville	68	762	73.5	23.0	31	930	139.7	40.2	83	1 443	47.1	13.1
Broken Arrow	141	484	42.5	12.9	129	4 191	614.9	136.8	101	1 789	49.3	14.0
Edmond	219	687	68.6	19.9	39	929	91.0	23.2	124	2 603	76.9	22.2
Enid	89	D	D	D	54	D	D	D	117	1 889	51.6	14.6
Lawton	119	1 008	60.2	29.1	45	D	D	D	179	3 391	89.1	25.0
Midwest City	68	625	47.2	20.2	18	D	D	D	98	1 973	56.3	16.0
Moore	35	190	11.0	3.5	NA	NA	NA	NA	68	1 107	31.7	8.7
Muskogee	63	326	23.0	7.2	61	3 476	760.7	117.4	109	1 959	54.9	14.2
Norman	288	1 239	106.8	37.2	83	2 442	679.6	71.6	225	4 779	139.9	38.6
Oklahoma City	1 848	12 251	1 100.3	449.3	759	38 354	9 658.1	1 251.1	1 071	21 553	684.2	188.8
Ponca City	57	776	33.7	14.0	45	D	D	D	62	1 054	29.5	7.8
Shawnee	61	269	20.3	6.1	41	2 799	545.5	96.3	111	2 439	70.0	19.2
Stillwater	85	550	40.1	15.9	28	2 195	814.6	68.4	114	2 398	56.0	15.6
Tulsa	1 688	12 883	1 355.7	504.0	872	29 436	5 526.1	986.6	1 035	19 183	643.9	172.6
OREGON	8 117	52 514	4 734.6	1 925.0	5 768	213 111	47 666.0	7 095.3	8 363	124 425	4 385.7	1 236.6
Albany	82	431	30.1	13.6	68	3 538	630.7	124.2	98	1 633	50.9	14.6
Beaverton	280	1 804	195.5	75.6	135	9 717	2 310.1	383.4	200	3 738	146.2	41.7
Bend	192	846	72.9	25.1	119	3 422	496.3	87.4	161	2 136	79.1	22.2
Corvallis	149	1 051	80.9	39.8	51	6 510	895.8	420.5	177	2 545	78.8	22.0
Eugene	605	3 899	333.3	123.5	340	9 524	1 330.3	277.1	452	7 351	234.5	68.1
Gresham	106	262	19.1	6.6	82	5 338	795.6	183.2	166	3 321	105.0	30.3
Hillsboro	143	1 165	143.7	69.9	173	8 734	1 977.3	339.4	130	2 613	82.3	23.1
Keizer	36	62	5.2	1.6	NA	NA	NA	NA	28	930	21.8	6.4
Lake Oswego	253	1 559	185.0	74.1	54	1 083	127.8	36.3	88	1 404	47.0	12.8
McMinnville	54	242	18.9	7.0	51	2 318	491.4	66.9	63	947	28.3	8.2
Medford	212	1 377	76.5	26.4	74	2 007	344.8	61.9	213	3 634	119.0	35.3
Oregon City	79	250	23.0	8.1	31	964	200.2	36.8	56	862	27.6	7.5
Portland	2 478	22 439	2 245.3	931.2	1 144	39 059	7 385.1	1 310.6	1 679	28 839	1 134.9	322.8

1. Firms subject to federal tax.

Table D. Cities — **Entertainment, Health Care, and Other Services**

City	Arts, Entertainment, and Recreation[1], 1997				Health Care and Social Assistance[1], 1997				Other Services[1], 1997			
	Number of Establishments	Number of Employees	Receipts (mil dol)	Annual Payroll (mil dol)	Number of Establishments	Number of Employees	Receipts (mil dol)	Annual Payroll (mil dol)	Number of Establishments	Number of Employees	Receipts (mil dol)	Annual Payroll (mil dol)
	96	97	98	99	100	101	102	103	104	105	106	107
OHIO—Cont'd												
Euclid	9	90	2.1	0.6	95	1 712	97.0	56.3	98	566	34.8	10.3
Fairborn	5	39	0.7	0.2	33	276	15.8	5.5	60	524	24.7	11.7
Fairfield	15	195	6.2	1.7	110	1 602	96.2	44.0	102	616	42.5	13.1
Findlay	8	56	2.2	0.6	105	1 183	77.0	39.2	74	566	30.3	10.0
Gahanna	6	133	6.5	2.7	72	562	32.4	14.4	43	576	34.6	10.1
Garfield Heights	NA	NA	NA	NA	61	416	37.7	15.7	48	266	15.0	4.8
Grove City	6	503	22.8	5.1	56	625	38.7	18.8	43	307	17.3	5.4
Hamilton	10	93	2.4	0.6	115	1 128	70.0	37.5	83	421	27.3	6.9
Huber Heights	6	61	1.5	0.5	64	671	35.6	15.1	51	286	14.5	4.4
Kent	2	0	0.0	0.0	40	385	22.2	8.7	35	201	9.5	3.1
Kettering	16	213	7.1	2.5	177	2 267	149.1	76.6	88	707	31.9	11.6
Lakewood	8	43	1.9	0.5	138	1 479	100.2	58.4	72	431	26.5	8.5
Lancaster	12	84	9.8	1.7	141	1 458	84.7	41.5	73	437	23.8	8.0
Lima	4	29	0.7	0.2	142	1 633	122.7	67.6	75	489	21.9	6.4
Lorain	15	168	8.2	1.9	139	1 775	115.6	65.1	85	689	37.6	12.4
Mansfield	15	260	4.7	1.5	176	1 887	111.4	53.7	112	955	47.1	20.2
Maple Heights	7	51	2.5	0.5	57	504	31.6	12.1	49	270	22.8	5.2
Marion	8	66	2.2	0.4	106	1 678	96.8	48.6	62	298	15.3	4.8
Massillon	4	45	0.7	0.2	49	742	39.0	17.2	61	318	15.3	4.7
Medina	3	0	0.0	0.0	92	926	54.4	26.0	56	381	22.4	7.7
Mentor	19	166	9.1	2.3	106	1 248	65.1	27.3	138	1 002	67.1	21.7
Middletown	11	130	5.6	2.3	109	1 157	82.7	43.1	91	578	28.8	9.5
Newark	10	139	3.9	1.2	118	2 582	114.3	60.0	80	518	29.1	9.5
North Olmsted	9	86	1.9	0.6	77	760	42.5	19.1	99	634	29.1	10.8
North Royalton	1	0	0.0	0.0	41	773	29.0	13.4	64	353	23.9	6.5
Parma	16	355	4.5	1.3	209	2 058	161.8	69.5	160	1 313	67.3	22.2
Reynoldsburg	6	71	2.5	1.2	67	396	23.7	10.8	63	283	17.5	5.0
Sandusky	18	0	0.0	0.0	119	877	62.2	31.9	73	384	16.0	5.2
Shaker Heights	4	11	0.6	0.2	68	1 248	42.2	22.9	40	294	14.1	4.9
Springfield	8	80	3.2	0.9	190	2 001	130.6	64.6	125	1 053	50.4	14.8
Stow	11	114	4.2	1.3	59	747	47.7	20.0	48	350	13.5	5.1
Strongsville	8	91	3.2	0.8	72	468	29.0	12.3	64	524	44.6	13.6
Toledo	80	1 230	66.2	16.3	596	8 240	543.8	267.6	571	3 880	247.0	74.5
Trotwood city	NA	NA	NA	NA	78	714	39.9	17.8	36	237	11.0	3.6
Upper Arlington	6	10	0.3	0.1	211	1 996	122.0	53.0	104	481	30.0	7.5
Warren	13	110	5.3	1.7	140	1 904	121.1	56.2	50	321	17.5	5.9
Westerville	10	559	13.8	4.2	161	2 122	111.7	49.3	58	485	31.1	10.3
Westlake	14	155	4.3	1.3	216	2 964	190.2	91.1	144	1 145	70.6	24.4
Youngstown	12	161	4.1	1.0	116	1 203	96.1	45.4	79	750	40.7	13.8
Zanesville	5	73	1.6	0.4								
OKLAHOMA	746	8 904	531.4	110.3	6 991	91 803	5 061.4	2 244.0	4 572	26 308	1 599.4	458.5
Bartlesville	10	0	0.0	0.0	99	819	59.4	29.8	61	335	19.7	6.6
Broken Arrow	18	403	15.3	5.1	123	1 822	73.7	35.3	111	698	37.7	12.9
Edmond	25	263	13.0	4.5	186	2 148	120.0	53.7	102	598	30.0	9.6
Enid	14	0	0.0	0.0	143	0	0.0	0.0	91	446	23.2	6.5
Lawton	19	0	0.0	0.0	196	2 295	139.0	51.9	135	709	33.5	9.8
Midwest City	16	134	2.7	0.8	127	2 273	161.3	62.4	69	393	19.3	5.4
Moore	8	85	2.2	0.5	53	617	23.4	10.7	45	255	15.6	4.7
Muskogee	10	0	0.0	0.0	150	2 195	97.7	44.1	61	362	21.0	6.4
Norman	34	348	22.9	3.8	236	2 426	148.1	66.7	112	679	32.3	9.7
Oklahoma City	109	2 521	104.8	31.3	1 474	18 208	1 308.1	586.6	892	7 677	445.6	135.6
Ponca City	11	0	0.0	0.0	84	593	35.1	14.9	49	226	13.8	3.9
Shawnee	6	0	0.0	0.0	84	1 273	62.3	27.0	49	214	11.8	3.4
Stillwater	11	87	1.7	0.5	88	1 012	51.0	23.6	67	372	16.1	4.8
Tulsa	106	1 305	92.5	19.0	1 240	17 228	1 244.7	553.7	794	5 621	399.7	115.3
OREGON	968	16 098	875.8	260.6	7 328	68 285	4 431.4	1 899.6	4 794	28 185	1 897.5	561.9
Albany	13	169	6.1	1.3	92	887	53.7	25.1	64	397	22.3	7.8
Beaverton	29	575	34.9	8.7	184	1 521	103.3	36.6	140	924	62.5	17.8
Bend	29	1 313	34.2	10.1	167	1 593	116.5	45.3	96	694	41.9	14.4
Corvallis	14	213	7.1	2.5	129	1 925	137.8	51.3	66	371	18.7	5.9
Eugene	48	641	20.7	6.5	489	4 929	373.8	162.3	260	2 135	130.9	38.7
Gresham	20	300	10.9	3.6	176	1 477	92.0	37.9	117	732	45.5	14.8
Hillsboro	12	151	3.8	1.3	146	1 197	79.4	33.7	103	493	36.9	11.5
Keizer	11	133	6.9	1.6	41	397	17.6	7.4	35	117	7.2	1.9
Lake Oswego	16	89	6.3	1.9	138	1 006	58.0	22.4	76	387	33.9	8.8
McMinnville	6	90	2.9	1.0	78	1 018	69.0	25.4	32	185	12.6	3.7
Medford	17	207	12.6	3.3	219	2 920	196.6	92.9	118	798	52.8	14.8
Oregon City	6	16	1.3	0.2	80	632	46.5	19.5	34	187	13.5	4.2
Portland	167	2 453	179.1	72.9	1 430	15 676	1 098.2	489.0	1 094	8 597	621.8	189.4

1. Firms subject to federal tax.

Table D. Cities — Federal Funds and City Government Finances

City	Selected federal funds, fiscal 2001[1] (mil dol)									City government finances, 1999						
	Procurement contracts		Grants					Direct payments for individuals		General revenue						
										Intergovernmental			Taxes			
														Per capita[3] (dollars)		
	Defense	Other	Total[2]	Health and family welfare	Energy and environment	Education	Housing and community development	Educational assistance	Housing assistance	Total (mil dol)	Total (mil dol)	Percent from state government	Total (mil dol)	Total	Property	Sales and gross receipts
	108	109	110	111	112	113	114	115	116	117	118	119	120	121	122	123
OHIO—Cont'd																
Euclid	3.7	0.0	1.3	0.0	0.0	0.0	1.2	0.0	2.7	51.3	4.8	75.2	29.9	590	156	3
Fairborn	30.1	2.1	2.8	1.0	0.0	1.1	0.6	0.4	5.4	NA	NA	NA	NA	NA	NA	NA
Fairfield	35.1	1.0	2.6	2.5	0.0	0.0	0.0	0.1	1.6	36.6	4.7	98.7	19.0	454	68	22
Findlay	0.2	0.2	4.6	2.1	0.0	1.0	0.0	2.5	2.6	28.7	3.6	95.9	14.8	398	74	8
Gahanna	0.0	0.4	0.0	0.0	0.0	0.0	0.0	0.0	2.8	NA	NA	NA	NA	NA	NA	NA
Garfield Heights	0.0	0.0	0.1	0.1	0.0	0.0	0.0	0.0	0.2	21.5	4.5	99.3	14.4	495	217	0
Grove City	0.0	0.1	0.0	0.0	0.0	0.0	0.0	0.0	0.8	19.4	4.1	56.5	12.3	647	119	7
Hamilton	1.0	0.5	7.4	0.0	0.1	1.0	3.5	0.2	7.6	65.3	12.0	76.4	22.6	366	52	6
Huber Heights	0.1	0.0	0.3	0.0	0.0	0.0	0.0	0.0	0.0	NA	NA	NA	NA	NA	NA	NA
Kent	0.7	0.0	18.4	3.2	0.4	5.1	0.3	21.0	7.3	22.4	4.4	75.2	11.1	414	69	0
Kettering	2.3	0.0	0.9	0.6	0.0	0.0	0.2	0.0	3.8	50.6	7.6	73.2	29.6	517	100	0
Lakewood	0.0	0.2	1.9	0.0	0.0	0.0	1.8	0.2	4.2	46.6	11.7	60.7	25.0	449	271	0
Lancaster	0.0	0.2	1.8	1.0	0.0	0.0	0.7	0.0	8.0	31.7	6.1	79.0	12.0	319	33	0
Lima	5.7	1.2	5.2	1.9	0.0	0.0	1.5	3.6	14.1	32.3	5.2	61.3	15.3	361	25	7
Lorain	0.1	0.4	7.1	2.5	0.0	1.2	2.8	0.9	10.2	45.0	11.2	100.0	21.2	308	50	4
Mansfield	10.7	0.0	7.6	1.0	1.0	1.2	2.0	1.8	4.4	46.5	10.9	53.9	24.9	500	56	4
Maple Heights	0.1	0.0	0.1	0.0	0.0	0.0	0.0	0.1	0.0	NA	NA	NA	NA	NA	NA	NA
Marion	2.4	0.0	2.0	1.8	0.0	0.0	0.0	0.9	7.6	NA	NA	NA	NA	NA	NA	NA
Massillon	0.1	0.0	4.1	2.3	0.0	0.5	1.0	0.0	1.3	28.0	6.0	79.9	12.5	406	39	0
Medina	0.3	0.8	0.2	0.0	0.0	0.0	0.0	0.1	2.8	14.0	3.4	66.4	5.5	240	83	0
Mentor	2.3	2.1	0.9	0.5	0.0	0.0	0.3	0.0	0.0	46.6	6.8	95.3	30.6	622	110	7
Middletown	0.2	0.1	2.1	0.0	0.1	0.0	0.9	0.1	4.7	50.3	13.8	94.2	19.8	407	85	0
Newark	110.4	0.2	3.7	2.0	0.0	0.0	1.1	1.6	12.3	NA	NA	NA	NA	NA	NA	NA
North Olmsted	0.0	3.5	0.0	0.0	0.0	0.0	0.0	0.0	0.0	39.3	8.6	47.4	18.9	564	250	1
North Royalton	0.1	0.1	0.0	0.0	0.0	0.0	0.0	0.0	0.5	18.2	2.4	100.0	10.5	420	137	5
Parma	0.0	0.0	1.5	0.0	0.0	0.0	1.5	0.0	1.7	50.6	12.5	65.1	30.0	360	88	4
Reynoldsburg	0.4	0.4	1.9	0.0	0.6	0.3	0.0	0.0	0.0	NA	NA	NA	NA	NA	NA	NA
Sandusky	7.7	9.7	9.3	1.4	0.0	0.0	0.0	0.2	3.7	NA	NA	NA	NA	NA	NA	NA
Shaker Heights	0.0	0.0	1.1	0.9	0.0	0.0	0.0	0.0	1.3	NA	NA	NA	NA	NA	NA	NA
Springfield	24.5	0.4	9.3	0.0	0.0	2.6	4.8	3.9	18.7	58.7	15.6	65.7	28.1	429	29	3
Stow	0.0	0.1	0.2	0.0	0.0	0.0	0.0	0.0	1.4	NA	NA	NA	NA	NA	NA	NA
Strongsville	3.1	1.3	0.0	0.0	0.0	0.0	0.0	0.0	4.4	NA	NA	NA	NA	NA	NA	NA
Toledo	52.1	6.6	68.9	28.0	1.0	2.8	10.6	14.7	60.7	314.9	57.4	63.4	174.0	558	49	19
Trotwood city	0.0	0.0	0.0	0.0	0.0	0.0	0.0	0.0	2.9	NA	NA	NA	NA	NA	NA	NA
Upper Arlington	0.0	0.0	0.0	0.0	0.0	0.0	0.0	0.0	0.0	33.8	5.5	14.4	21.7	684	211	11
Warren	2.0	0.1	6.7	3.9	0.0	0.0	2.7	0.9	11.3	44.3	9.4	55.1	16.5	352	30	8
Westerville	1.7	2.1	1.2	0.1	0.5	0.0	0.0	1.5	2.8	40.2	6.3	100.0	19.3	578	210	10
Westlake	2.4	4.8	0.3	0.2	0.0	0.0	0.0	0.0	0.0	38.3	3.7	94.1	22.9	768	283	7
Youngstown	0.6	9.6	16.1	3.7	0.0	1.0	5.8	9.6	9.0	75.6	21.0	68.7	33.4	395	21	6
Zanesville	3.9	0.2	1.5	0.4	0.0	0.0	0.5	2.0	5.3	31.5	6.1	100.0	14.0	523	79	10
OKLAHOMA	1 567.5	645.0	4 119.1	2 318.2	75.4	477.5	62.4	157.9	264.9	X	X	X	X	X	X	X
Bartlesville	0.0	1.0	1.6	0.1	0.1	0.2	0.7	1.0	6.3	27.5	0.5	92.1	15.2	452	64	384
Broken Arrow	0.4	0.4	1.5	0.0	0.0	0.3	0.2	0.1	0.4	36.9	1.9	34.5	24.2	333	53	260
Edmond	4.2	15.7	2.9	0.0	0.0	1.5	0.3	7.3	3.7	44.3	1.1	51.6	23.0	355	0	317
Enid	0.6	0.6	2.4	0.0	0.0	0.3	0.8	0.2	5.4	41.8	11.0	84.2	18.4	407	0	390
Lawton	17.7	4.9	15.6	1.7	0.1	5.7	1.7	5.2	6.7	48.3	5.1	18.2	27.2	336	9	309
Midwest City	137.0	6.5	0.7	0.0	0.0	0.0	0.5	0.0	5.0	113.0	1.9	33.5	21.4	396	9	363
Moore	0.0	0.5	1.2	0.0	0.0	0.9	0.0	0.7	2.4	27.2	5.7	8.8	12.6	277	38	229
Muskogee	0.9	4.6	2.9	0.7	0.0	1.9	0.0	2.4	3.7	95.1	1.2	100.0	18.5	481	11	456
Norman	89.2	16.6	49.2	15.7	3.8	6.9	1.2	13.3	3.4	188.1	5.4	60.5	37.3	401	21	361
Oklahoma City	413.0	115.0	675.7	274.5	46.4	104.6	37.0	25.2	59.6	614.2	73.0	34.5	315.4	668	63	589
Ponca City	87.7	0.0	7.9	2.3	0.3	0.7	0.0	0.2	1.4	19.3	1.0	23.4	7.4	286	14	256
Shawnee	2.7	0.3	13.1	8.2	0.1	2.1	0.8	4.0	1.7	41.9	1.7	28.5	13.2	488	10	451
Stillwater	9.0	9.3	54.6	2.4	1.1	23.4	0.0	13.6	3.5	63.5	0.8	100.0	15.3	395	32	351
Tulsa	155.6	40.1	55.7	13.0	3.9	5.7	8.7	20.3	51.7	558.3	51.7	24.4	237.3	622	67	543
OREGON	388.8	570.6	4 307.6	2 589.4	67.0	360.3	52.2	118.7	263.6	X	X	X	X	X	X	X
Albany	0.1	0.6	0.8	0.0	0.0	0.0	0.0	4.0	1.7	31.9	4.0	71.7	16.8	434	283	70
Beaverton	15.3	3.8	6.8	1.0	0.2	0.9	0.5	0.0	2.7	43.2	8.6	47.3	22.2	357	236	49
Bend	0.6	4.9	6.2	1.7	0.1	0.1	0.0	2.5	2.0	27.9	6.2	61.2	13.1	383	221	107
Corvallis	2.6	5.8	89.1	13.3	7.7	2.1	0.6	11.6	2.4	56.4	14.6	85.1	19.3	385	294	74
Eugene	0.8	8.8	117.1	52.8	2.3	24.5	3.5	19.8	13.3	154.7	25.0	35.9	58.3	455	384	27
Gresham	0.0	0.0	3.0	1.2	0.0	0.2	0.8	3.5	1.3	63.1	13.5	39.4	31.1	365	206	52
Hillsboro	0.2	1.1	2.1	0.5	0.0	0.1	0.0	0.0	2.1	69.0	5.0	100.0	38.9	636	404	56
Keizer	0.0	0.0	0.0	0.0	0.0	0.0	0.0	0.0	0.1	11.3	2.9	100.0	4.2	146	65	47
Lake Oswego	0.3	0.1	1.6	0.0	1.3	0.0	0.0	0.5	0.2	37.9	3.7	100.0	24.1	694	550	42
McMinnville	0.0	3.6	2.4	1.2	0.0	0.6	0.0	1.9	0.8	27.0	2.6	74.4	9.5	396	242	59
Medford	0.2	7.8	8.4	2.4	0.0	0.0	0.7	0.2	7.6	44.4	5.7	96.5	23.8	416	296	58
Oregon City	0.0	0.0	6.4	2.4	0.0	1.3	0.0	2.2	1.5	23.1	2.8	100.0	11.0	524	333	88
Portland	136.8	156.0	369.3	148.1	42.9	24.3	10.0	34.6	56.3	712.8	110.8	30.0	347.7	690	441	93

1. October 1, 2000 to September 30, 2001. 2. Includes program categories not shown separately. State totals include additional categories not allocated by city. 3. Based on population estimated as of July 1 of the year shown.

Table D. Cities — **City Government Finances**

City	City government finances, 1999 (cont'd)												
	General expenditure												
	Per capita[1] (dollars)			Percent of total for —									
	Total (mil dol)	Total	Capital outlays	Public welfare	Highways	Parking facilities	Education	Health and hospitals	Police protection	Sewerage and sanitation	Parks and recreation	Housing and community development	Interest on debt
	124	125	126	127	128	129	130	131	132	133	134	135	136
OHIO—Cont'd													
Euclid	53.7	1 060	88	0.0	6.1	0.0	0.0	0.8	13.7	23.5	6.0	6.5	3.8
Fairborn	NA	NA	NA	NA	NA	NA	NA	NA	NA	NA	NA	NA	NA
Fairfield	41.8	1 001	475	0.0	17.2	0.0	0.0	1.9	11.9	31.8	14.1	0.0	4.5
Findlay	21.4	577	9	0.0	8.2	0.4	0.0	0.2	23.0	10.1	4.6	0.0	6.8
Gahanna	NA	NA	NA	NA	NA	NA	NA	NA	NA	NA	NA	NA	NA
Garfield Heights	20.4	700	16	0.0	7.0	0.0	0.0	0.4	21.6	9.2	4.4	1.1	4.5
Grove City	17.5	924	346	0.0	33.2	0.0	0.0	0.8	20.8	4.0	12.8	4.6	2.9
Hamilton	69.8	1 128	290	0.0	7.9	0.9	0.0	2.8	12.6	24.4	4.0	5.7	4.1
Huber Heights	NA	NA	NA	NA	NA	NA	NA	NA	NA	NA	NA	NA	NA
Kent	22.9	853	201	0.0	23.5	0.0	0.0	2.4	17.9	14.8	4.1	6.0	6.1
Kettering	45.8	801	149	0.0	20.3	0.0	0.0	0.0	17.8	0.1	21.2	2.1	1.7
Lakewood	45.8	823	97	0.0	3.9	0.5	0.0	8.5	15.8	18.9	8.0	8.5	3.6
Lancaster	28.4	753	18	0.0	9.2	0.0	0.0	3.2	16.8	27.4	4.4	4.4	1.2
Lima	30.4	716	36	0.0	3.6	0.2	0.0	1.0	21.8	31.9	3.7	1.0	2.4
Lorain	45.7	664	58	0.0	8.7	0.0	0.0	4.0	19.9	13.0	3.1	12.4	6.9
Mansfield	44.2	887	153	0.1	11.9	0.2	0.0	0.2	20.4	14.8	2.0	4.7	0.8
Maple Heights	NA	NA	NA	NA	NA	NA	NA	NA	NA	NA	NA	NA	NA
Marion	NA	NA	NA	NA	NA	NA	NA	NA	NA	NA	NA	NA	NA
Massillon	29.7	962	253	0.0	5.9	0.0	0.0	1.5	11.0	14.8	6.2	1.4	2.4
Medina	16.5	719	244	0.0	15.6	0.4	0.0	4.2	22.8	15.6	3.9	0.0	1.2
Mentor	46.8	950	223	0.0	17.2	0.0	0.0	0.7	18.0	5.3	17.3	1.0	4.9
Middletown	49.5	1 020	106	0.0	10.2	0.6	0.0	2.3	18.3	14.9	5.8	7.2	2.4
Newark	NA	NA	NA	NA	NA	NA	NA	NA	NA	NA	NA	NA	NA
North Olmsted	36.0	1 074	215	0.2	12.2	0.0	0.0	0.1	11.7	22.4	8.8	0.1	9.2
North Royalton	16.8	670	52	0.0	7.6	0.0	0.0	1.3	22.7	27.0	1.8	4.9	2.1
Parma	62.3	747	264	0.4	8.4	0.0	0.0	1.0	14.5	6.4	4.3	2.5	2.4
Reynoldsburg	NA	NA	NA	NA	NA	NA	NA	NA	NA	NA	NA	NA	NA
Sandusky	NA	NA	NA	NA	NA	NA	NA	NA	NA	NA	NA	NA	NA
Shaker Heights	NA	NA	NA	NA	NA	NA	NA	NA	NA	NA	NA	NA	NA
Springfield	55.7	850	126	0.1	4.3	0.0	0.0	1.4	17.4	8.9	10.9	8.6	2.9
Stow	NA	NA	NA	NA	NA	NA	NA	NA	NA	NA	NA	NA	NA
Strongsville	NA	NA	NA	NA	NA	NA	NA	NA	NA	NA	NA	NA	NA
Toledo	330.1	1 057	247	0.0	11.2	0.1	0.0	3.2	20.1	16.5	4.1	4.9	5.7
Trotwood city	NA	NA	NA	NA	NA	NA	NA	NA	NA	NA	NA	NA	NA
Upper Arlington	26.0	821	60	0.0	8.1	3.0	0.0	0.5	20.5	8.9	9.1	0.0	8.1
Warren	49.5	1 057	245	0.0	12.0	0.2	0.0	1.5	17.2	18.7	1.5	5.8	4.7
Westerville	42.9	1 284	462	0.0	30.6	0.0	0.0	0.1	12.2	14.5	3.7	0.0	2.0
Westlake	33.6	1 130	371	0.0	15.7	0.0	0.0	0.2	11.3	9.0	28.2	0.0	12.0
Youngstown	67.0	791	46	0.0	8.9	0.0	0.0	2.0	21.9	15.7	3.3	11.1	4.5
Zanesville	30.5	1 138	192	0.4	7.3	0.2	0.0	0.6	25.3	19.1	15.5	8.5	0.0
OKLAHOMA	X	X	X	X	X	X	X	X	X	X	X	X	X
Bartlesville	23.9	711	95	0.0	5.9	0.0	0.0	0.0	15.8	26.3	10.6	0.0	3.6
Broken Arrow	36.1	497	139	0.0	16.4	0.0	0.0	2.9	17.2	14.3	5.6	2.7	9.1
Edmond	49.4	760	114	2.6	10.6	0.0	0.0	0.0	14.4	12.4	8.6	0.0	6.7
Enid	31.0	684	84	0.0	8.5	0.0	0.0	0.0	16.6	19.5	5.0	3.4	0.8
Lawton	41.6	513	57	0.0	6.4	0.0	0.0	0.3	22.1	14.2	7.5	3.6	0.3
Midwest City	94.1	1 742	78	0.0	3.2	0.0	0.0	63.8	7.3	5.1	3.8	0.0	2.1
Moore	25.2	556	43	0.4	5.7	0.0	0.0	0.0	16.0	7.0	1.7	0.5	7.5
Muskogee	104.7	2 728	166	0.0	6.0	0.0	0.0	63.2	5.3	3.3	2.6	0.1	2.9
Norman	189.4	2 036	295	0.0	4.8	0.0	0.0	66.2	5.7	8.4	2.5	0.9	2.4
Oklahoma City	531.6	1 126	250	0.0	7.5	0.9	0.0	0.0	18.1	12.0	17.2	5.5	7.1
Ponca City	21.2	818	40	0.0	7.6	0.0	0.0	3.0	15.7	15.6	6.3	1.5	1.5
Shawnee	39.9	1 477	136	0.0	11.4	0.0	0.0	55.2	7.8	4.6	1.0	2.4	0.3
Stillwater	66.0	1 702	158	1.2	4.6	0.0	0.0	59.3	7.5	6.3	5.6	0.0	0.1
Tulsa	530.2	1 390	344	1.9	2.8	0.2	0.0	3.4	14.3	21.6	5.7	1.1	10.1
OREGON	X	X	X	X	X	X	X	X	X	X	X	X	X
Albany	30.8	794	200	0.0	13.7	0.0	0.0	3.8	16.3	11.7	13.0	1.2	3.3
Beaverton	36.6	590	128	0.3	20.6	0.0	0.0	0.0	25.6	10.0	0.4	2.9	0.8
Bend	33.8	984	321	0.0	26.2	0.3	0.0	6.3	18.5	9.9	0.0	5.2	3.0
Corvallis	59.7	1 189	358	0.0	6.7	0.5	0.0	0.0	11.9	30.5	5.0	4.2	1.1
Eugene	151.5	1 181	200	0.0	4.9	1.6	0.0	3.3	15.4	9.8	7.8	6.6	1.9
Gresham	64.4	757	227	0.0	3.6	0.0	0.0	0.0	22.6	33.9	6.0	3.9	2.4
Hillsboro	61.1	1 000	306	0.0	12.6	0.2	0.0	0.0	14.0	26.7	7.5	0.0	1.0
Keizer	14.0	485	161	0.0	17.6	0.0	0.0	0.0	18.9	29.4	1.2	0.4	3.5
Lake Oswego	38.5	1 110	356	0.8	3.4	0.0	0.0	0.0	13.4	8.2	18.1	8.4	4.5
McMinnville	19.5	810	185	0.0	10.3	0.0	0.0	8.0	14.0	13.5	10.0	3.3	10.9
Medford	40.5	709	184	0.0	18.1	0.4	0.0	0.0	23.8	9.7	6.9	1.2	1.7
Oregon City	23.2	1 110	361	0.0	4.3	1.1	0.0	0.0	12.2	18.4	5.8	14.4	3.9
Portland	783.8	1 556	448	0.3	13.4	0.4	0.0	0.0	13.1	22.3	10.4	7.4	8.1

1. Based on population estimated as of July 1 of the year shown.

City	City government finances, 1999 (cont'd) Debt outstanding Total (mil dol)	Per capita[1] (dollars)	Percent utility	City government employment, 2001	Climate[2] Average daily temperature (degrees Fahrenheit) Mean January	Mean July	Limits January[3]	Limits July[4]	Annual precipitation (inches)	Heating degree days	Cooling degree days
	137	138	139	140	141	142	143	144	145	146	147
OHIO—Cont'd											
Euclid	34.5	681	0.0	537	24.8	71.9	17.6	82.4	36.63	6 201	621
Fairborn	NA	NA	NA	NA	26.0	74.2	17.9	84.9	36.64	5 708	886
Fairfield	40.3	965	5.2	NA	26.1	73.9	15.8	86.2	41.79	5 791	830
Findlay	50.4	1 356	47.6	NA	23.6	72.8	16.5	82.7	34.26	6 302	720
Gahanna	NA	NA	NA	NA	26.4	73.2	18.5	83.7	38.09	5 708	797
Garfield Heights	21.7	744	0.0	NA	24.8	71.9	17.6	82.4	36.63	6 201	621
Grove City	11.4	602	11.1	NA	NA	NA	NA	NA	NA	NA	NA
Hamilton	353.3	5 716	81.9	737	26.1	73.9	15.8	86.2	41.79	5 791	830
Huber Heights	NA	NA	NA	NA	26.0	74.2	17.9	84.9	36.64	5 708	886
Kent	22.3	831	2.3	NA	24.8	71.9	16.9	82.3	36.82	6 160	625
Kettering	13.2	232	0.0	806	26.0	74.2	17.9	84.9	36.64	5 708	886
Lakewood	40.1	720	16.6	592	24.8	71.9	17.6	82.4	36.63	6 201	621
Lancaster	6.8	180	0.0	471	25.4	72.8	16.0	84.7	36.32	5 988	724
Lima	17.6	416	48.8	441	23.6	73.6	15.2	84.4	35.94	6 253	810
Lorain	63.9	928	18.5	576	26.2	73.3	17.9	85.0	35.95	5 818	779
Mansfield	9.4	188	49.8	642	24.5	72.1	16.8	82.1	39.66	6 258	666
Maple Heights	NA	NA	NA	NA	24.8	71.9	17.6	82.4	36.63	6 201	621
Marion	NA	NA	NA	NA	23.4	72.6	14.3	84.5	36.91	6 407	692
Massillon	11.7	379	0.0	NA	24.8	71.9	16.9	82.3	36.82	6 160	625
Medina	4.6	200	54.5	NA	NA	NA	NA	NA	NA	NA	NA
Mentor	40.8	829	0.0	456	26.6	71.9	19.3	81.2	35.93	5 929	636
Middletown	19.5	402	13.1	570	26.6	74.3	17.5	85.5	39.26	5 694	897
Newark	NA	NA	NA	NA	26.7	73.2	18.2	85.0	41.48	5 657	767
North Olmsted	57.9	1 725	0.0	367	24.8	71.9	17.6	82.4	36.63	6 201	621
North Royalton	3.8	151	2.9	NA	NA	NA	NA	NA	NA	NA	NA
Parma	18.4	221	0.0	568	24.8	71.9	17.6	82.4	36.63	6 201	621
Reynoldsburg	NA	NA	NA	NA	26.4	73.2	18.5	83.7	38.09	5 708	797
Sandusky	NA	NA	NA	NA	24.8	73.6	17.5	82.4	34.05	6 131	752
Shaker Heights	NA	NA	NA	NA	24.8	71.9	17.6	82.4	36.63	6 201	621
Springfield	22.1	336	32.4	678	24.3	72.2	15.3	83.7	38.31	6 254	649
Stow	NA	NA	NA	NA	24.8	71.9	16.9	82.3	36.82	6 160	625
Strongsville	NA	NA	NA	NA	24.8	71.9	17.6	82.4	36.63	6 201	621
Toledo	302.9	970	11.1	2 973	22.5	72.1	14.9	83.4	32.97	6 579	610
Trotwood city	NA	NA	NA	NA	NA	NA	NA	NA	NA	NA	NA
Upper Arlington	17.9	563	0.0	NA	26.4	73.2	18.5	83.7	38.09	5 708	797
Warren	37.1	793	30.2	437	24.4	70.5	15.3	83.2	36.11	6 402	491
Westerville	50.0	1 495	14.0	376	25.9	73.2	16.5	85.5	39.32	5 719	786
Westlake	69.6	2 341	0.0	NA	24.8	71.9	17.6	82.4	36.63	6 201	621
Youngstown	31.4	371	5.2	919	23.6	70.3	16.4	81.3	37.32	6 544	497
Zanesville	7.5	279	100.0	NA	26.8	72.7	18.3	83.5	39.42	5 714	716
OKLAHOMA	X	X	X	X	X	X	X	X	X	X	X
Bartlesville	17.8	529	9.4	335	34.7	82.1	22.5	94.7	35.91	3 777	1 868
Broken Arrow	88.3	1 216	2.5	769	35.2	83.3	24.9	93.7	40.59	3 691	2 017
Edmond	72.2	1 112	74.3	528	35.9	82.0	25.2	93.4	33.36	3 659	1 859
Enid	61.5	1 359	89.1	477	35.1	83.3	24.7	95.2	32.35	3 788	2 008
Lawton	29.1	358	70.3	836	36.8	83.5	23.7	95.8	29.27	3 457	2 069
Midwest City	38.2	707	0.0	477	35.9	82.0	25.2	93.4	33.36	3 659	1 859
Moore	32.5	717	5.8	229	35.9	82.0	25.2	93.4	33.36	3 659	1 859
Muskogee	50.1	1 305	0.0	470	37.3	82.2	26.6	93.8	41.74	3 413	1 937
Norman	94.4	1 015	2.8	2 196	37.8	82.2	25.6	94.8	35.41	3 295	1 967
Oklahoma City	854.0	1 808	20.5	4 886	35.9	82.0	25.2	93.4	33.36	3 659	1 859
Ponca City	44.7	1 722	87.5	448	32.4	82.5	22.1	93.8	34.24	4 226	1 865
Shawnee	27.5	1 018	82.9	276	38.3	82.0	25.9	94.9	38.27	3 222	1 954
Stillwater	21.2	547	97.0	1 061	33.6	81.6	21.4	93.1	33.85	4 028	1 755
Tulsa	1 358.1	3 561	8.6	4 382	35.2	83.3	24.9	93.7	40.59	3 691	2 017
OREGON	X	X	X	X	X	X	X	X	X	X	X
Albany	43.7	1 125	32.0	325	38.3	64.3	31.6	78.4	66.42	5 287	172
Beaverton	52.7	849	49.6	429	38.9	65.8	32.5	79.7	37.57	5 011	232
Bend	24.7	720	4.4	339	NA	NA	NA	NA	NA	NA	NA
Corvallis	50.0	996	64.4	424	39.3	65.6	33.0	80.2	42.70	4 923	203
Eugene	263.8	2 057	82.6	1 926	40.8	67.3	35.2	81.7	49.37	4 546	300
Gresham	65.9	775	28.3	572	39.6	68.2	33.7	79.9	36.30	4 522	371
Hillsboro	14.7	241	0.0	382	38.9	65.8	32.5	79.7	37.57	5 011	232
Keizer	8.6	297	8.7	NA	NA	NA	NA	NA	NA	NA	NA
Lake Oswego	33.1	954	0.0	326	39.6	68.2	33.7	79.9	36.30	4 522	371
McMinnville	42.1	1 747	0.0	232	NA	NA	NA	NA	NA	NA	NA
Medford	22.2	389	1.5	417	38.1	72.9	30.4	90.5	18.86	4 611	725
Oregon City	21.7	1 038	19.7	NA	NA	NA	NA	NA	NA	NA	NA
Portland	1 412.5	2 803	10.7	5 542	39.6	68.2	33.7	79.9	36.30	4 522	371

1. Based on the population estimated as of July 1 of the year shown.   2. Represents normal values based on the 30-year period, 1961–1990.   3. Average daily minimum.   4. Average daily maximum.

Table D. Cities — **Land Area and Population**

STATE Place code	City	Land area, 2000[1] (sq km)	Population, 2000 Total persons	Rank	Per square kilometer	Population Total persons 1990	Percent change 1990–2000	Total persons 1980	Percent change 1980–1990	White	Black	Am. Indian, Alaska Native	Asian and Pacific Islander	Other race	His-panic[2]	Non-His-panic White
			1	**2**	**3**	**4**	**5**	**6**	**7**	**8**	**9**	**10**	**11**	**12**	**13**	**14**
	OREGON—Cont'd															
41 64900	Salem	118.4	136 924	158	1 156.5	107 793	27.0	89 233	20.8	86.1	1.8	2.7	3.8	9.1	14.6	77.7
41 69600	Springfield	37.3	52 864	564	1 417.3	44 664	18.4	41 621	7.3	93.1	1.3	3.2	2.5	3.9	6.9	86.7
41 73650	Tigard	28.1	41 223	742	1 467.0	29 435	40.0	14 286	106.0	88.0	1.7	1.3	7.6	4.6	8.9	80.8
42 00000	PENNSYLVANIA	116 074.5	12 281 054	X	105.8	11 882 842	3.4	11 864 720	0.2	86.3	10.5	0.4	2.1	1.9	3.2	84.1
42 02000	Allentown	45.9	106 632	215	2 323.1	105 301	1.3	103 758	1.5	75.5	9.3	0.7	2.8	15.5	24.4	64.4
42 02184	Altoona	25.3	49 523	603	1 957.4	51 881	-4.5	57 078	-9.1	96.8	3.0	0.3	0.5	0.4	0.7	95.6
42 06064	Bethel Park Borough	30.3	33 556	938	1 107.5	33 823	-0.8	34 755	-2.7	97.6	1.2	0.2	1.5	0.2	0.5	96.7
42 06088	Bethlehem	49.9	71 329	375	1 429.4	71 427	0.1	70 419	1.4	83.9	4.5	0.6	2.6	11.0	18.2	74.9
42 13208	Chester	12.6	36 854	840	2 924.9	41 856	-12.0	45 794	-8.6	19.7	76.9	0.6	0.9	3.6	5.4	17.9
42 21648	Easton	11.0	26 263	1 179	2 387.5	26 276	0.0	26 027	1.0	81.0	14.4	0.9	2.2	4.8	9.8	73.5
42 24000	Erie	56.9	103 717	222	1 822.8	108 718	-4.6	119 123	-8.7	82.6	15.5	0.7	1.1	2.6	4.4	78.7
42 32800	Harrisburg	21.0	48 950	617	2 331.0	52 376	-6.5	53 264	-1.7	34.3	57.5	1.1	3.4	7.8	11.7	28.6
42 41216	Lancaster	19.2	56 348	511	2 934.8	55 551	1.4	54 725	1.5	64.5	16.3	1.0	3.0	19.4	30.8	51.8
42 52330	Monroeville Borough	51.3	29 349	1 062	572.1	29 169	0.6	NA	NA	86.5	9.0	0.4	4.9	0.5	0.8	85.1
42 53368	New Castle	22.1	26 309	1 176	1 190.5	28 334	-7.1	33 621	-15.7	88.5	12.0	0.5	0.3	0.6	0.8	86.4
42 54656	Norristown	9.1	31 282	1 002	3 437.6	30 754	1.7	34 684	-11.3	56.7	36.7	0.9	3.4	5.7	10.5	49.4
42 60000	Philadelphia	349.9	1 517 550	5	4 337.1	1 585 577	-4.3	1 688 210	-6.1	46.4	44.3	0.7	5.1	6.0	8.5	42.5
42 61000	Pittsburgh	144.0	334 563	52	2 323.4	369 879	-9.5	423 938	-12.8	68.8	28.1	0.7	3.2	1.1	1.3	66.9
42 61536	Plum Borough	74.1	26 940	1 148	363.6	25 609	5.2	25 390	0.9	96.0	3.0	0.2	1.0	0.2	0.6	95.1
42 63624	Reading	25.4	81 207	316	3 197.1	78 380	3.6	78 686	-0.4	62.4	14.1	1.0	2.1	24.8	37.3	48.1
42 69000	Scranton	65.3	76 415	347	1 170.2	81 805	-6.6	88 117	-7.2	94.5	3.6	0.3	1.3	1.5	2.6	92.3
42 73808	State College Borough	11.8	38 420	808	3 255.9	38 981	-1.4	36 130	7.9	85.4	4.1	0.4	9.9	1.9	3.0	82.9
42 85152	Wilkes-Barre	17.7	43 123	711	2 436.3	47 523	-9.3	51 551	-7.8	93.3	5.8	0.4	1.1	0.8	1.6	91.4
42 85312	Williamsport	23.0	30 706	1 017	1 335.0	31 933	-3.8	33 401	-4.4	85.7	13.9	0.7	0.7	0.7	1.1	83.6
42 87048	York	13.5	40 862	751	3 026.8	42 192	-3.2	44 619	-5.4	62.8	27.6	1.0	2.0	10.7	17.2	54.2
44 00000	RHODE ISLAND	2 706.3	1 048 319	X	387.4	1 003 464	4.5	947 154	5.9	86.9	5.5	1.0	2.9	6.6	8.7	81.9
44 19180	Cranston	74.0	79 269	331	1 071.2	76 060	4.2	71 992	5.7	90.4	4.2	0.6	3.8	2.7	4.6	87.2
44 22960	East Providence	34.7	48 688	621	1 403.1	50 380	-3.4	50 980	-1.2	89.2	6.9	1.3	1.6	5.3	1.9	85.5
44 49960	Newport	20.6	26 475	1 166	1 285.2	28 227	-6.2	29 258	-3.5	86.6	9.7	1.8	2.2	3.5	5.5	81.7
44 54640	Pawtucket	22.6	72 958	363	3 228.2	72 644	0.4	71 204	2.0	78.6	9.7	0.8	1.5	15.0	13.9	69.1
44 59000	Providence	47.8	173 618	119	3 632.2	160 728	8.0	156 804	2.5	58.1	17.1	2.2	7.4	21.7	30.0	45.8
44 74300	Warwick	91.9	85 808	291	933.7	85 427	0.4	87 123	-1.9	96.3	1.6	0.7	1.8	1.0	1.6	94.3
44 80780	Woonsocket	20.0	43 224	706	2 161.2	43 877	-1.5	45 914	-4.4	85.5	5.7	0.8	5.0	6.4	9.3	79.8
45 00000	SOUTH CAROLINA	77 983.2	4 012 012	X	51.4	3 486 310	15.1	3 120 729	11.7	68.0	29.9	0.7	1.2	1.3	2.4	66.1
45 00550	Aiken	41.9	25 337	1 224	604.7	20 386	24.3	14 978	36.1	67.5	30.8	0.7	1.7	0.7	1.5	65.9
45 01360	Anderson	35.8	25 514	1 218	712.7	26 385	-3.3	27 313	-3.4	64.0	34.6	0.6	1.1	1.0	1.5	62.5
45 13330	Charleston	251.2	96 650	244	384.8	88 256	20.9	69 510	15.0	63.8	34.4	0.4	1.6	0.8	1.5	62.3
45 16000	Columbia	324.3	116 278	191	358.6	110 734	5.0	101 208	9.4	50.1	46.7	0.6	2.3	1.8	3.0	48.2
45 25810	Florence	45.8	30 248	1 026	660.4	29 913	1.1	30 104	-0.6	53.5	45.0	0.4	1.3	0.4	0.8	52.7
45 29815	Goose Creek	82.1	29 208	1 066	355.8	24 692	18.3	17 811	38.6	80.5	15.0	1.2	3.9	2.0	4.0	76.6
45 30850	Greenville	67.5	56 002	519	829.7	58 256	-3.9	58 242	0.0	63.0	34.4	0.4	1.6	1.8	3.4	60.6
45 34045	Hilton Head Island	108.9	33 862	926	310.9	23 694	42.9	11 344	108.9	86.4	8.5	0.3	0.7	5.3	11.5	79.0
45 48535	Mount Pleasant	108.5	47 609	637	438.8	30 108	58.1	13 888	117.6	90.9	7.4	0.4	1.5	0.7	1.3	89.3
45 50875	North Charleston	151.6	79 641	325	525.3	70 304	13.3	62 534	12.4	46.2	50.3	1.0	2.3	2.3	4.0	43.2
45 61405	Rock Hill	80.4	49 765	600	619.0	42 112	19.6	35 386	17.6	59.5	37.7	0.8	1.7	1.3	2.5	57.6
45 68290	Spartanburg	49.6	39 673	780	799.9	43 479	-8.8	43 838	-0.8	47.8	50.1	0.4	1.7	1.1	1.8	46.5
45 70270	Summerville	39.8	27 752	1 114	697.3	22 519	23.2	NA	NA	78.2	19.9	0.9	1.4	1.0	2.0	76.1
45 70405	Sumter	68.9	39 643	781	575.4	40 977	-3.3	24 896	64.6	50.5	46.9	0.6	2.0	1.6	2.4	48.7
46 00000	SOUTH DAKOTA	196 540.3	754 844	X	3.8	696 004	8.5	690 768	0.8	89.9	0.9	9.0	0.9	0.7	1.4	88.0
46 52980	Rapid City	115.5	59 607	473	516.1	54 523	9.3	46 492	17.3	86.8	1.5	12.0	1.5	1.1	2.8	83.2
46 59020	Sioux Falls	145.9	123 975	174	849.7	100 836	22.9	81 341	24.0	93.4	2.4	2.6	1.6	1.8	2.5	90.9
47 00000	TENNESSEE	106 751.8	5 689 283	X	53.3	4 877 203	16.7	4 591 023	6.2	81.2	16.8	0.7	1.3	1.3	2.2	79.2
47 03440	Bartlett	49.4	40 543	759	820.7	27 038	50.2	17 170	57.2	93.1	5.0	0.5	1.6	0.5	1.1	91.7
47 14000	Chattanooga	350.2	155 554	129	444.2	152 393	2.1	169 550	-10.1	60.7	36.7	0.7	2.0	1.4	2.1	58.9
47 15160	Clarksville	245.7	103 455	224	421.1	75 542	37.0	54 777	37.9	70.5	24.7	1.3	3.7	3.5	6.0	65.3
47 15400	Cleveland	64.6	37 192	837	575.7	32 236	15.4	26 432	22.0	90.3	7.5	0.8	1.3	1.7	2.9	87.7
47 16420	Collierville	63.6	31 872	976	501.1	14 501	119.8	NA	NA	90.6	7.5	0.4	1.8	0.6	1.5	88.9
47 16540	Columbia	76.7	33 055	947	431.0	28 583	15.6	26 372	8.4	75.9	21.9	0.6	0.6	2.6	4.7	72.8
47 27740	Franklin	77.8	41 842	732	537.8	20 098	108.2	12 407	62.0	85.5	10.6	0.5	2.0	2.6	4.8	82.2
47 28960	Germantown	45.5	37 348	833	820.8	33 159	13.1	20 459	61.4	93.7	2.5	0.4	3.8	0.5	1.1	92.1
47 33280	Hendersonville	70.8	40 620	758	573.7	32 188	26.2	26 561	21.2	93.8	4.3	0.6	1.4	0.9	1.7	92.0
47 37640	Jackson	128.2	59 643	471	465.2	49 145	21.4	49 131	0.0	55.9	42.5	0.5	1.1	1.1	2.2	54.2
47 38320	Johnson City	101.7	55 469	531	545.4	50 354	10.2	39 738	26.7	91.3	7.0	0.7	1.4	1.0	1.9	89.0
47 39560	Kingsport	114.1	44 905	682	393.6	40 457	11.0	32 027	26.3	94.3	4.6	0.7	1.1	0.6	1.0	92.7
47 40000	Knoxville	240.0	173 890	117	724.5	169 761	2.4	175 030	-3.0	81.1	16.8	0.9	1.8	1.1	1.6	79.0

1. Dry land or land partially or temporarily covered by water.   2. Hispanic persons may be of any race.

Table D. Cities — Population and Households

City	Population characteristics, 2000 (cont'd) Age of population (percent)									Percent female	Households, 2000 Number	Percent change, 1990–2000	Persons per house-hold	Female family householder[1]	One-person
	Under 5 years	5 to 17 years	18 to 24 years	25 to 34 years	35 to 44 years	45 to 54 years	55 to 64 years	65 to 74 years	75 years and over						
	16	17	18	19	20	21	22	23	24	25	26	27	28	29	30
OREGON—Cont'd															
Salem	7.4	18.0	11.4	15.1	15.0	13.3	7.3	5.5	6.9	49.8	50 676	23.8	2.53	11.6	28.3
Springfield	8.2	19.0	11.1	15.9	15.5	12.7	7.2	4.9	5.4	51.1	20 514	17.6	2.55	14.3	25.4
Tigard	7.7	17.8	9.0	16.3	17.7	14.2	7.2	4.5	5.6	51.0	16 507	36.9	2.48	9.2	26.7
PENNSYLVANIA	5.9	17.9	8.9	12.7	15.9	13.9	9.2	7.9	7.7	51.7	4 777 003	6.3	2.48	11.6	27.7
Allentown	7.1	17.6	11.2	14.8	15.0	11.6	7.5	7.1	8.0	52.1	42 032	-1.7	2.42	15.1	33.1
Altoona	6.3	16.6	10.9	12.7	14.6	13.1	8.9	8.2	8.6	53.1	20 059	-3.0	2.37	13.8	31.6
Bethel Park Borough	5.3	18.4	5.0	9.9	16.8	15.6	10.9	9.6	8.5	52.1	13 362	5.3	2.48	7.2	26.1
Bethlehem	5.4	15.5	14.4	12.9	13.7	12.0	8.1	8.1	9.8	52.2	28 116	3.1	2.34	12.8	32.3
Chester	8.4	21.4	13.0	12.9	14.0	11.3	7.3	6.0	5.8	52.9	12 814	-11.9	2.64	32.1	31.2
Easton	6.2	17.1	16.3	15.0	14.9	11.6	7.0	5.8	6.2	50.7	9 544	1.6	2.46	16.6	31.6
Erie	7.2	18.2	11.6	14.3	14.2	11.7	7.5	7.1	8.2	52.4	40 938	-2.8	2.39	16.8	33.4
Harrisburg	8.1	20.1	9.2	15.5	15.4	13.2	7.6	5.7	5.1	53.0	20 561	-4.5	2.32	24.4	39.3
Lancaster	7.9	19.6	13.9	15.6	14.8	11.0	6.7	5.3	5.2	51.2	20 933	-1.2	2.52	19.0	33.1
Monroeville Borough	4.9	15.4	6.2	12.1	15.3	15.4	10.5	10.0	10.3	53.0	12 376	4.6	2.30	9.7	30.8
New Castle	6.7	17.1	8.1	12.5	13.6	12.4	8.9	9.2	11.5	54.0	10 727	-5.7	2.36	16.9	33.5
Norristown	6.9	18.2	10.5	16.5	16.1	12.0	8.1	6.2	5.6	51.3	12 028	-1.3	2.52	19.8	32.7
Philadelphia	6.5	18.8	11.1	14.8	14.5	12.0	8.3	7.1	7.0	53.5	590 071	-2.2	2.48	22.3	33.8
Pittsburgh	5.3	14.6	14.8	14.6	14.0	12.3	8.0	7.9	8.5	52.4	143 739	-6.3	2.17	16.5	39.4
Plum Borough	6.3	18.5	6.1	13.4	17.6	14.4	10.4	7.1	6.0	51.2	10 270	13.3	2.60	8.5	21.5
Reading	8.7	21.3	11.7	15.1	13.9	10.3	6.8	6.1	6.3	51.7	30 113	-4.1	2.63	20.2	31.7
Scranton	5.3	15.5	12.3	11.8	13.8	12.5	8.7	9.0	11.1	53.5	31 303	-4.1	2.29	13.8	36.7
State College Borough	1.8	3.9	65.5	11.3	4.9	4.1	2.6	2.5	3.3	47.9	12 024	9.9	2.30	3.4	33.5
Wilkes-Barre	4.9	15.0	12.6	12.3	13.8	12.1	8.7	9.5	11.1	51.8	17 961	-7.6	2.20	14.0	39.0
Williamsport	6.0	16.5	18.0	12.7	13.9	11.9	7.4	6.4	7.0	50.6	12 219	-2.9	2.30	15.5	35.1
York	8.0	20.4	11.4	15.5	14.6	11.6	7.5	5.5	5.4	51.8	16 137	-4.4	2.48	20.6	33.1
RHODE ISLAND	6.1	17.5	10.2	13.4	16.2	13.5	8.5	7.0	7.5	52.0	408 424	8.1	2.47	12.9	28.6
Cranston	5.3	16.3	7.7	14.0	17.4	13.7	8.3	8.0	9.3	51.1	30 954	5.5	2.41	12.5	29.4
East Providence	5.4	16.3	7.4	13.4	16.0	13.2	9.4	8.8	10.1	53.5	20 530	2.9	2.33	12.7	32.4
Newport	5.8	13.9	14.6	16.0	15.6	13.1	8.2	6.2	6.7	51.8	11 566	3.3	2.11	13.6	39.4
Pawtucket	6.7	18.1	9.1	15.3	16.0	12.0	7.9	7.2	7.7	52.6	30 047	1.1	2.41	16.8	32.3
Providence	7.3	18.8	18.9	15.6	13.0	10.0	6.0	4.9	5.6	52.2	62 389	5.9	2.56	20.5	32.3
Warwick	5.4	16.5	6.7	12.8	17.3	14.8	9.5	8.3	8.7	52.4	35 517	6.2	2.39	10.2	29.8
Woonsocket	7.6	18.2	9.2	15.3	14.7	12.0	7.7	7.0	8.2	52.3	17 750	1.0	2.37	16.2	32.7
SOUTH CAROLINA	6.6	18.6	10.2	14.0	15.6	13.7	9.3	6.7	5.4	51.4	1 533 854	21.9	2.53	14.8	25.0
Aiken	5.8	17.4	9.4	11.3	14.2	14.2	9.8	8.7	9.2	53.4	10 287	32.8	2.34	13.7	29.6
Anderson	6.7	15.5	10.7	13.2	13.1	12.1	8.3	8.8	11.7	54.8	10 641	1.3	2.22	18.7	36.0
Charleston	5.4	14.6	17.2	15.2	13.6	12.4	8.1	6.7	6.8	52.7	40 791	32.6	2.23	15.2	33.7
Columbia	5.6	14.5	22.9	16.8	13.3	10.6	6.0	5.3	5.0	51.0	42 245	24.5	2.21	17.6	37.0
Florence	6.4	18.6	8.7	13.6	14.6	14.2	8.9	7.4	7.7	54.7	11 925	7.7	2.44	20.7	29.5
Goose Creek	8.6	21.0	18.2	16.2	16.2	9.8	5.6	2.8	1.4	46.4	8 947	21.0	2.94	10.6	12.9
Greenville	5.6	14.3	13.8	16.8	14.5	12.5	7.9	6.4	8.0	52.7	24 382	1.2	2.11	15.5	40.8
Hilton Head Island	4.4	12.9	6.9	11.8	12.8	13.4	13.9	14.0	10.1	50.0	14 408	39.3	2.32	6.2	23.8
Mount Pleasant	7.5	17.6	6.5	16.7	18.6	14.8	8.0	5.3	5.0	52.1	19 025	61.4	2.47	8.3	24.1
North Charleston	8.0	19.8	13.4	16.8	15.2	10.9	6.8	5.0	4.0	50.5	29 783	26.7	2.51	22.8	28.6
Rock Hill	7.0	18.0	14.8	16.2	14.2	11.5	6.9	5.1	6.2	54.2	18 750	27.8	2.49	18.3	27.5
Spartanburg	6.5	18.7	12.2	13.0	13.6	12.5	8.0	7.1	8.4	55.7	15 989	-4.3	2.33	23.0	34.0
Summerville	7.0	21.8	7.8	14.6	16.6	14.2	7.5	5.4	5.2	52.6	10 391	28.2	2.61	14.0	23.0
Sumter	8.1	19.7	12.5	13.9	14.3	10.8	7.1	6.4	7.2	52.8	14 564	14.3	2.57	19.3	27.3
SOUTH DAKOTA	6.8	20.1	10.3	12.1	15.3	12.9	8.3	7.0	7.3	50.4	290 245	12.0	2.50	9.0	27.6
Rapid City	7.0	18.3	11.8	13.2	15.5	13.0	7.9	6.7	6.5	51.0	23 969	13.3	2.39	12.6	29.4
Sioux Falls	7.3	17.9	11.8	16.0	16.3	12.5	7.1	5.6	5.5	50.7	49 731	25.0	2.40	10.0	29.8
TENNESSEE	6.6	18.0	9.6	14.3	15.9	13.8	9.4	6.7	5.6	51.3	2 232 905	20.5	2.48	12.9	25.8
Bartlett	6.6	22.4	6.8	11.1	18.9	16.9	8.6	5.2	3.4	51.2	13 773	62.9	2.92	8.7	12.1
Chattanooga	6.1	16.3	10.8	14.3	14.5	13.6	9.1	7.8	7.4	52.8	65 499	5.3	2.29	17.3	33.5
Clarksville	9.0	19.8	13.6	19.0	15.7	9.8	5.8	4.2	3.1	49.8	36 969	45.3	2.69	13.1	21.1
Cleveland	6.5	15.5	15.4	13.9	13.6	11.9	9.3	7.2	6.7	52.8	15 037	25.4	2.33	13.0	30.4
Collierville	7.6	25.8	5.8	10.4	22.0	15.7	6.6	3.7	2.3	50.6	10 368	134.1	3.06	8.0	11.8
Columbia	7.5	18.3	9.8	13.3	15.3	12.8	8.2	7.4	7.4	52.6	13 059	15.9	2.46	16.3	27.8
Franklin	8.5	19.4	7.5	18.7	19.4	13.1	6.1	3.7	3.7	51.7	16 128	106.0	2.55	10.8	25.0
Germantown	5.2	22.8	5.8	6.6	16.9	21.7	11.7	5.7	3.5	51.3	13 220	23.4	2.82	6.1	14.6
Hendersonville	6.6	19.2	7.8	14.2	17.2	14.8	10.0	5.7	4.4	51.3	15 823	38.3	2.55	10.7	22.3
Jackson	7.2	18.6	12.8	14.3	14.4	12.0	7.5	6.4	6.8	53.4	23 053	22.4	2.40	19.4	30.3
Johnson City	5.5	14.3	13.7	13.9	14.2	13.2	9.3	7.9	8.0	52.3	23 720	20.6	2.20	11.6	33.9
Kingsport	5.7	16.0	6.5	12.1	14.1	14.1	11.2	9.5	10.8	54.3	19 662	25.8	2.22	12.7	32.5
Knoxville	5.9	13.7	16.8	15.7	13.8	11.9	7.7	6.9	7.5	52.6	76 650	9.5	2.12	13.7	38.3

1. No spouse present.

City	Persons in group quarters, 2000				Serious crimes known to police, 2000[2]				Education, 1990				Money income, 1989		
		Institutional		Non-Institutional[1]	Total		Rate[3]		School enrollment		Attainment[4] (percent)			Households	
														Median	
	Total	Total	Persons in nursing homes		Number	Rate[3]	Violent	Property	Public	Private	High school graduate or more	Bachelor's degree or more	Per capita (dollars)[5]	Dollars	Percent change, 1979–1989 (constant 1989 dollars)
	31	32	33	34	35	36	37	38	39	40	41	42	43	44	45
OREGON—Cont'd															
Salem	8 884	6 360	1 063	2 524	9 983	7 291	246	7 045	22 513	4 774	81.5	21.7	12 641	25 236	-0.1
Springfield	635	93	93	542	4 415	8 352	174	8 178	10 414	830	77.7	10.8	10 222	21 932	-11.9
Tigard	221	107	107	114	2 396	5 812	226	5 587	6 005	1 066	90.9	30.1	16 946	35 669	6.1
PENNSYLVANIA	433 301	213 790	114 113	219 511	367 858	2 995	420	2 575	2 161 247	668 306	74.7	17.9	14 068	29 069	2.8
Allentown	4 996	2 260	880	2 736	5 516	5 173	645	4 528	17 369	5 851	69.4	15.3	12 822	25 983	1.1
Altoona	1 930	439	390	1 491	1 876	3 788	388	3 400	9 865	1 818	73.3	9.5	10 398	20 695	-8.9
Bethel Park Borough	382	271	263	111	312	930	57	873	6 005	2 215	89.7	33.2	17 603	41 149	-5.1
Bethlehem	5 652	1 275	1 003	4 377	2 448	3 432	311	3 121	11 083	8 370	71.1	20.2	13 684	28 375	-1.5
Chester	2 977	1 364	387	1 613	2 836	7 695	3 020	4 675	7 617	3 741	62.2	7.7	9 115	20 864	8.1
Easton	2 760	927	306	1 833	1 210	4 607	674	3 933	4 748	2 511	68.6	12.7	11 319	26 365	23.0
Erie	5 854	2 356	1 160	3 498	3 837	3 699	450	3 249	15 980	11 501	72.3	14.0	10 715	22 032	-10.7
Harrisburg	1 252	565	351	687	2 499	5 105	919	4 186	10 667	1 701	67.2	14.0	11 037	20 329	1.4
Lancaster	3 690	1 666	596	2 024	3 841	6 817	1 081	5 736	10 943	2 931	61.4	13.5	10 693	22 210	6.0
Monroeville Borough	940	474	382	466	989	3 370	351	3 019	5 355	1 273	87.0	31.7	17 753	36 422	NA
New Castle	999	725	472	274	1 060	4 029	680	3 349	5 136	529	67.8	8.6	9 298	17 103	-22.9
Norristown	995	848	231	147	1 901	6 077	1 144	4 933	4 699	1 916	67.3	12.9	13 527	28 643	16.7
Philadelphia	54 731	20 411	10 164	34 320	98 000	6 458	1 503	4 955	251 843	143 190	64.3	15.2	12 091	24 603	11.5
Pittsburgh	22 814	8 191	2 580	14 623	19 456	5 701	957	4 744	67 147	29 963	72.4	20.1	12 580	20 747	-7.7
Plum Borough	233	44	44	189	NA	NA	NA	NA	5 548	1 120	86.8	22.8	14 413	36 782	-0.7
Reading	2 125	261	222	1 864	5 893	7 257	1 105	6 152	13 831	3 624	58.4	8.5	11 041	22 112	8.8
Scranton	4 876	1 560	883	3 316	509	666	64	602	11 828	7 380	70.4	13.6	11 108	21 060	0.4
State College Borough	10 725	198	198	10 527	1 437	2 787	101	2 686	28 108	1 283	96.0	68.2	8 694	18 257	11.5
Wilkes-Barre	3 674	2 212	721	1 462	NA	NA	NA	NA	7 318	3 633	69.5	12.9	10 513	19 525	-1.1
Williamsport	2 597	514	150	2 083	465	1 514	186	1 329	6 951	1 592	72.3	13.1	10 276	20 290	-0.1
York	887	167	119	720	NA	NA	NA	NA	7 573	1 550	62.8	9.9	10 485	21 812	8.8
RHODE ISLAND	38 816	13 801	9 222	25 015	36 444	3 476	298	3 179	191 802	62 833	72.0	21.3	14 981	32 181	19.3
Cranston	4 659	4 051	242	608	2 218	2 798	179	2 619	12 779	3 270	74.0	21.1	15 922	34 528	18.9
East Providence	755	659	639	96	1 010	2 074	230	1 844	8 500	2 338	66.9	16.0	14 387	31 007	10.6
Newport	2 082	245	245	1 837	1 583	5 979	574	5 405	5 103	2 407	84.1	32.2	16 358	30 534	28.3
Pawtucket	657	422	422	235	2 943	4 034	514	3 520	12 198	3 781	61.6	13.1	12 865	26 541	16.2
Providence	13 648	1 491	1 375	12 157	12 840	7 396	674	6 722	29 887	20 234	62.8	21.6	11 838	22 147	15.5
Warwick	991	650	634	341	2 787	3 248	197	3 051	15 203	3 661	77.8	21.3	16 371	35 786	13.9
Woonsocket	1 075	742	742	333	1 218	2 818	356	2 462	8 535	1 081	56.2	9.1	11 997	25 363	20.9
SOUTH CAROLINA	135 037	60 533	20 867	74 504	209 482	5 221	805	4 417	807 539	105 471	68.3	16.6	11 897	26 256	6.5
Aiken	1 263	754	534	509	1 282	5 060	616	4 444	4 107	912	79.4	33.1	15 619	33 273	38.3
Anderson	1 890	1 007	716	883	2 039	7 992	964	7 028	4 761	1 240	62.6	17.0	10 866	19 433	-7.1
Charleston	5 510	455	438	5 055	6 819	7 055	743	6 312	20 313	4 266	76.5	29.4	14 093	25 153	11.3
Columbia	22 990	6 053	578	16 937	10 069	8 689	1 304	7 385	27 583	4 420	76.0	31.7	12 210	23 216	11.8
Florence	1 155	779	362	376	4 474	14 791	2 142	12 649	6 826	815	69.1	22.5	12 831	24 906	2.8
Goose Creek	2 893	28	28	2 865	764	2 616	226	2 390	6 958	792	87.3	14.1	9 935	30 007	21.2
Greenville	4 495	1 121	244	3 374	5 624	10 042	1 552	8 491	9 860	5 723	72.5	29.3	14 708	23 963	12.8
Hilton Head Island	442	234	200	208	NA	NA	NA	NA	3 247	1 001	93.8	42.5	25 171	42 995	7.5
Mount Pleasant	665	569	496	96	2 148	4 512	225	4 287	5 835	1 733	90.3	41.8	18 931	38 605	2.2
North Charleston	4 958	2 282	457	2 676	8 748	10 984	1 601	9 383	13 770	2 177	73.9	11.4	10 315	21 824	6.4
Rock Hill	3 118	721	670	2 397	3 260	6 551	1 029	5 522	11 694	915	62.9	17.7	11 481	26 615	9.7
Spartanburg	2 428	409	295	2 019	5 024	12 664	2 445	10 219	8 701	2 683	65.9	23.4	12 142	22 423	4.8
Summerville	608	266	266	342	1 474	5 311	555	4 756	5 108	759	83.3	25.5	12 556	31 448	NA
Sumter	2 221	322	322	1 899	3 433	8 660	1 360	7 300	10 066	1 658	77.9	20.6	11 495	21 221	6.0
SOUTH DAKOTA	28 418	14 387	7 791	14 031	17 511	2 320	167	2 153	165 993	19 253	77.1	17.2	10 661	22 503	2.1
Rapid City	2 233	841	511	1 392	2 827	4 743	367	4 375	13 173	1 553	84.9	23.4	12 469	25 740	-1.4
Sioux Falls	4 802	2 746	952	2 056	4 287	3 458	323	3 135	18 482	6 481	83.4	22.9	13 677	27 286	-2.7
TENNESSEE	147 946	83 397	36 994	64 549	278 218	4 890	707	4 183	1 023 651	147 989	67.1	16.0	12 255	24 807	4.7
Bartlett	327	313	150	14	1 009	2 489	163	2 326	7 493	1 461	90.9	23.5	16 080	47 346	7.4
Chattanooga	5 826	2 763	1 225	3 063	18 001	11 572	1 760	9 813	29 855	6 383	69.0	18.2	12 332	22 197	-2.4
Clarksville	4 080	897	534	3 183	4 985	4 819	581	4 238	18 542	1 498	81.3	18.5	11 252	25 341	9.6
Cleveland	2 151	646	478	1 505	1 940	5 216	532	4 684	5 836	1 686	66.2	17.1	12 265	22 894	4.0
Collierville	107	107	107	0	509	1 597	147	1 450	4 113	465	83.1	25.6	16 529	47 517	NA
Columbia	928	863	653	65	2 344	7 091	1 243	5 848	5 612	619	66.7	14.2	12 558	29 228	4.0
Franklin	717	526	189	191	1 208	2 887	280	2 607	3 898	705	76.8	28.7	16 202	32 348	23.5
Germantown	34	29	29	5	1 104	2 956	155	2 801	8 084	3 084	97.2	53.5	28 087	69 019	12.5
Hendersonville	229	224	219	5	1 126	2 772	293	2 479	7 279	1 112	83.3	21.1	16 010	38 068	-1.1
Jackson	3 150	1 185	882	1 965	4 761	7 982	1 457	6 525	9 711	2 744	67.4	17.1	11 268	21 063	-4.3
Johnson City	3 373	1 176	708	2 197	3 888	7 009	669	6 340	12 861	862	71.1	25.9	13 071	23 053	10.9
Kingsport	1 167	923	900	244	2 487	5 538	724	4 815	6 525	625	67.9	20.3	13 825	22 750	-8.1
Knoxville	11 034	2 738	1 922	8 296	10 771	6 194	1 070	5 125	41 467	3 478	70.8	21.7	12 108	19 923	-0.7

1. Persons in emergency shelters and persons visible in street locations. 2. Data for serious crimes have not been adjusted for underreporting. This may affect comparability between geographic areas and over time. 3. Per 100,000 population estimated by the FBI. 4. Persons 25 years old and older. 5. Based on population enumerated as of April 1, 1990.

City	Percent with $100,000 or more (46)	Persons Total (47)	Persons Percent change in rate, 1979–1989 (48)	Families Total (49)	Total (50)	Percent change, 1990–2000 (51)	Vacant units for sale or rent[1] (52)	For seasonal use (percent) (53)	Home owner vacancy rate (54)	Renter vacancy rate (55)	Total (56)	Percent owner occupied (57)	Percent renter occupied (58)	Average size owner occupied (59)	Average size renter occupied (60)
OREGON—Cont'd															
Salem	2.2	14.5	22.9	10.5	53 817	26.3	3 141	0.3	2.5	7.0	50 676	57.1	42.9	2.59	2.44
Springfield	0.9	16.5	8.6	13.2	21 500	18.6	986	0.3	2.1	4.3	20 514	53.6	46.4	2.57	2.52
Tigard	3.0	4.8	-31.4	3.7	17 369	37.9	862	0.3	1.9	6.9	16 507	58.3	41.7	2.66	2.24
PENNSYLVANIA	3.6	11.1	6.0	8.2	5 249 750	6.3	472 747	2.8	1.6	7.2	4 777 003	71.3	28.7	2.62	2.12
Allentown	1.8	12.9	10.3	9.3	45 960	0.7	3 928	0.3	2.6	8.4	42 032	53.0	47.0	2.55	2.26
Altoona	1.1	18.0	46.3	14.0	21 681	-4.5	1 622	0.1	1.4	9.7	20 059	65.9	34.1	2.51	2.11
Bethel Park Borough	5.4	3.8	58.3	3.0	13 871	6.7	509	0.4	1.4	6.0	13 362	79.9	20.1	2.69	1.66
Bethlehem	3.2	13.0	17.1	8.8	29 631	4.0	1 515	0.3	1.7	5.2	28 116	58.1	41.9	2.44	2.19
Chester	0.7	25.2	-2.7	20.6	14 976	-9.3	2 162	0.2	3.2	7.4	12 814	47.7	52.3	2.69	2.60
Easton	1.2	13.7	-12.2	9.4	10 545	2.3	1 001	0.2	4.6	9.4	9 544	48.5	51.5	2.67	2.27
Erie	1.0	19.3	44.0	15.2	44 971	-1.0	4 033	0.3	2.1	9.6	40 938	56.2	43.8	2.51	2.24
Harrisburg	1.5	27.0	16.9	23.9	24 314	-1.1	3 753	0.8	5.4	12.0	20 561	42.3	57.7	2.44	2.23
Lancaster	1.1	20.9	23.7	16.3	23 024	2.5	2 091	0.2	4.3	8.5	20 933	46.6	53.4	2.58	2.46
Monroeville Borough	4.9	4.3	NA	3.2	13 159	4.1	783	0.5	0.9	11.2	12 376	69.7	30.3	2.52	1.78
New Castle	0.1	19.7	27.1	16.1	11 709	-6.0	982	0.2	2.5	9.3	10 727	64.6	35.4	2.47	2.15
Norristown	2.0	9.5	-19.5	7.0	13 531	3.4	1 503	0.2	4.6	10.1	12 028	48.1	51.9	2.70	2.35
Philadelphia	2.2	20.3	-1.5	16.1	661 958	-1.9	71 887	0.3	1.9	7.0	590 071	59.3	40.7	2.65	2.23
Pittsburgh	2.9	21.4	29.7	16.6	163 366	-4.0	19 627	0.5	2.8	8.8	143 739	52.1	47.9	2.37	1.95
Plum Borough	2.3	4.3	13.2	3.5	10 624	14.4	354	0.2	0.8	5.9	10 270	79.8	20.2	2.74	2.03
Reading	1.2	19.4	12.8	15.2	34 314	0.1	4 201	0.2	4.9	9.1	30 113	51.0	49.0	2.74	2.51
Scranton	1.6	15.2	17.8	11.1	35 336	0.1	4 033	0.3	2.8	10.1	31 303	54.5	45.5	2.49	2.04
State College Borough	2.8	45.4	15.8	7.9	12 488	7.4	464	0.7	0.8	2.9	12 024	22.8	77.2	2.32	2.30
Wilkes-Barre	1.0	15.4	14.1	10.4	20 294	-2.1	2 333	0.3	2.8	11.9	17 961	53.5	46.5	2.41	1.95
Williamsport	1.5	21.1	27.1	16.4	13 524	1.5	1 305	0.2	2.9	8.7	12 219	44.8	55.2	2.47	2.16
York	0.9	20.3	16.0	16.4	18 534	0.7	2 397	0.1	4.1	12.8	16 137	46.8	53.2	2.51	2.45
RHODE ISLAND	4.1	9.6	-6.7	6.8	439 837	6.1	31 413	3.0	1.0	5.0	408 424	60.0	40.0	2.66	2.19
Cranston	3.8	6.5	-11.0	4.9	32 068	5.1	1 114	0.3	0.9	4.1	30 954	66.9	33.1	2.64	1.96
East Providence	2.2	6.8	-4.2	5.0	21 309	2.4	779	0.3	0.7	3.5	20 530	58.9	41.1	2.63	1.92
Newport	4.7	12.5	-22.4	10.0	13 226	1.0	1 660	6.5	1.5	6.7	11 566	41.9	58.1	2.22	2.03
Pawtucket	1.6	10.6	-9.4	8.1	31 819	0.6	1 772	0.2	1.1	5.5	30 047	44.4	55.6	2.59	2.26
Providence	3.5	23.0	12.7	18.3	67 915	1.7	5 526	0.5	2.3	6.1	62 389	34.6	65.4	2.71	2.49
Warwick	4.6	4.8	-27.3	3.2	37 085	5.5	1 568	1.3	1.1	3.9	35 517	72.7	27.3	2.58	1.87
Woonsocket	1.4	13.9	-2.8	11.6	18 757	0.1	1 007	0.2	0.9	5.1	17 750	35.0	65.0	2.66	2.22
SOUTH CAROLINA	2.3	15.4	-7.4	11.9	1 753 670	23.1	219 816	4.0	1.9	12.0	1 533 854	72.2	27.8	2.59	2.37
Aiken	5.6	15.7	1.3	11.1	11 373	33.1	1 086	1.0	3.1	10.6	10 287	66.1	33.9	2.42	2.19
Anderson	1.7	19.9	0.5	14.8	12 068	4.9	1 427	0.3	3.4	13.5	10 641	53.4	46.6	2.27	2.16
Charleston	4.5	21.6	-0.9	16.3	44 563	29.8	3 772	1.1	1.8	6.5	40 791	51.1	48.9	2.43	2.03
Columbia	3.8	21.2	1.4	15.7	46 142	25.0	3 897	0.5	2.2	7.7	42 245	45.6	54.4	2.29	2.14
Florence	4.1	21.8	8.5	17.8	13 090	11.0	1 165	0.4	2.1	9.4	11 925	61.4	38.6	2.52	2.32
Goose Creek	0.5	9.0	-8.2	7.9	9 482	23.4	535	0.1	1.5	3.2	8 947	63.5	36.5	2.89	3.03
Greenville	4.6	17.7	-9.7	13.7	27 295	3.2	2 913	0.7	2.4	10.9	24 382	47.0	53.0	2.21	2.03
Hilton Head Island	12.2	7.0	4.5	5.4	24 647	14.6	10 239	29.9	1.5	40.6	14 408	77.7	22.3	2.21	2.70
Mount Pleasant	5.4	5.8	-14.7	4.2	20 197	62.3	1 172	0.8	1.5	8.7	19 025	74.0	26.0	2.61	2.05
North Charleston	0.5	21.7	7.4	19.2	33 631	26.4	3 848	0.3	2.1	10.6	29 783	46.4	53.6	2.52	2.50
Rock Hill	2.1	16.4	11.6	12.1	20 287	29.4	1 537	0.3	3.1	7.8	18 750	53.4	46.6	2.57	2.39
Spartanburg	3.3	21.8	4.3	17.1	17 696	-1.4	1 707	0.3	3.0	9.6	15 989	49.8	50.2	2.40	2.26
Summerville	1.4	9.8	NA	8.3	11 087	25.5	696	0.4	1.7	6.8	10 391	65.7	34.3	2.81	2.23
Sumter	2.5	20.7	-8.8	16.6	16 032	17.5	1 468	0.4	2.2	8.2	14 564	53.1	46.9	2.58	2.55
SOUTH DAKOTA	1.7	15.9	-6.2	11.6	323 208	10.5	32 963	3.0	1.8	8.0	290 245	68.2	31.8	2.64	2.22
Rapid City	2.5	13.6	22.5	10.6	25 096	11.4	1 127	0.4	0.9	5.7	23 969	59.3	40.7	2.53	2.20
Sioux Falls	2.7	8.5	-1.2	5.5	51 680	24.3	1 949	0.2	1.0	5.2	49 731	61.1	38.9	2.65	2.00
TENNESSEE	2.6	15.7	-4.8	12.4	2 439 443	20.4	206 538	1.5	2.0	8.8	2 232 905	69.9	30.1	2.57	2.29
Bartlett	4.0	2.3	-28.1	2.1	14 021	59.2	248	0.1	1.0	4.2	13 773	92.2	7.8	2.93	2.81
Chattanooga	2.7	18.2	1.7	14.4	72 108	3.6	6 609	0.4	2.5	8.9	65 499	54.9	45.1	2.40	2.15
Clarksville	1.5	13.3	3.9	11.0	40 041	44.9	3 072	0.2	3.0	7.3	36 969	57.5	42.5	2.79	2.55
Cleveland	2.3	17.4	4.8	13.8	16 431	25.9	1 394	0.3	2.2	9.8	15 037	51.8	48.2	2.48	2.17
Collierville	7.9	6.6	NA	5.4	10 770	133.5	402	0.6	2.1	4.7	10 368	86.4	13.6	3.15	2.51
Columbia	1.9	14.3	-6.5	11.6	14 322	18.0	1 263	0.2	2.6	11.5	13 059	63.5	36.5	2.50	2.38
Franklin	3.8	7.2	-36.3	5.2	17 296	97.7	1 168	0.3	3.7	6.2	16 128	63.5	36.5	2.78	2.15
Germantown	24.3	1.1	-31.3	1.0	13 676	22.9	456	0.4	1.2	10.3	13 220	89.0	11.0	2.89	2.25
Hendersonville	4.6	4.5	12.5	3.0	16 507	32.4	684	0.3	1.9	6.2	15 823	71.4	28.6	2.72	2.13
Jackson	2.3	21.0	16.0	17.9	25 501	23.0	1 998	0.4	2.2	9.1	23 503	56.7	43.3	2.50	2.28
Johnson City	3.4	17.3	3.0	11.7	25 730	21.1	2 010	0.4	2.9	8.5	23 720	57.2	42.8	2.36	1.98
Kingsport	3.5	18.1	26.6	14.3	21 796	30.2	2 134	0.4	3.5	12.8	19 662	64.8	35.2	2.31	2.08
Knoxville	2.3	20.8	6.1	15.3	84 981	11.2	8 331	0.3	2.9	10.5	76 650	51.2	48.8	2.29	1.95

1. Includes units rented or sold but not occupied.   2. Specified owner-occupied units.   3. Specified renter-occupied units.   4. Overcrowded or lacking complete plumbing facilities.

Table D. Cities — Labor Force, Employment, Disability, and Construction

City	Civilian labor force, 2001				Civilian employment, 1990[2]			Disability 1990	Value of residential construction authorized by building permits, 2000		
	Total	Percent change, 2000–2001	Unemployment Total	Rate[1]	Total	Percent Professional, managerial, and technical	Precision production, craft, and repair	Work disabled persons[3] (percent)	New construction ($1,000)	Number of housing units	Percent single family
	61	62	63	64	65	66	67	68	69	70	71
OREGON—Cont'd											
Salem	65 189	-1.7	4 231	6.5	46 474	33.1	8.7	10.8	66 540	661	78.1
Springfield	26 062	-0.7	1 969	7.6	20 281	18.1	11.8	13.1	31 190	274	81.0
Tigard	24 381	0.4	1 272	5.2	15 904	37.0	9.7	6.3	72 109	403	100.0
PENNSYLVANIA	6 072 613	1.7	286 934	4.7	5 434 532	28.9	11.6	8.3	4 616 181	41 076	84.0
Allentown	52 374	3.5	2 826	5.4	49 821	25.1	11.0	8.1	11 503	76	100.0
Altoona	23 341	1.0	1 409	6.0	21 061	22.5	12.9	11.9	1 925	27	100.0
Bethel Park Borough	18 430	1.4	504	2.7	16 761	41.2	9.3	5.1	5 245	36	61.1
Bethlehem	34 074	2.6	1 420	4.2	32 127	30.1	9.9	7.2	5 093	103	11.7
Chester	16 636	2.6	1 142	6.9	15 715	20.2	9.2	14.0	14 426	122	100.0
Easton	12 161	1.6	457	3.8	11 644	22.5	10.6	9.0	379	5	20.0
Erie	49 227	0.2	3 178	6.5	46 064	25.6	11.0	10.9	3 131	37	86.5
Harrisburg	24 260	2.0	1 329	5.5	22 901	26.2	7.8	12.3	3 308	45	73.3
Lancaster	25 876	2.2	1 244	4.8	25 188	21.9	10.5	10.2	724	14	100.0
Monroeville Borough	17 407	1.4	495	2.8	14 930	43.4	7.3	7.3	3 117	27	100.0
New Castle	9 921	-2.6	807	8.1	9 906	22.7	9.5	13.5	534	6	100.0
Norristown	15 822	2.2	774	4.9	15 384	24.7	10.1	9.8	0	0	0.0
Philadelphia	639 775	1.6	40 703	6.4	651 621	28.6	9.0	11.0	87 571	1 333	7.1
Pittsburgh	161 995	1.5	6 494	4.0	153 991	33.1	7.4	10.7	35 090	249	73.1
Plum Borough	16 015	1.9	507	3.2	13 535	34.0	12.0	5.9	9 310	96	87.5
Reading	34 785	2.6	2 724	7.8	34 188	19.0	10.8	10.3	175	7	14.3
Scranton	35 286	1.5	1 880	5.3	34 256	24.4	10.6	11.5	1 721	21	100.0
State College Borough	16 746	2.9	212	1.3	15 632	44.0	1.7	2.3	1 142	10	80.0
Wilkes-Barre	20 626	0.7	1 117	5.4	20 210	23.7	9.5	10.8	216	3	100.0
Williamsport	13 873	2.2	1 004	7.2	13 018	22.9	10.4	11.5	1 904	20	100.0
York	18 526	2.5	1 411	7.6	18 903	18.5	11.7	12.1	210	3	100.0
RHODE ISLAND	503 566	-0.2	23 736	4.7	487 913	30.1	12.0	8.6	296 393	2 596	86.9
Cranston	37 130	-0.6	1 634	4.4	36 461	32.2	11.9	7.7	12 545	131	100.0
East Providence	24 824	-0.7	1 236	5.0	25 166	24.9	12.5	10.3	4 282	55	96.4
Newport	12 159	0.9	485	4.0	12 899	35.2	9.2	7.0	3 112	15	100.0
Pawtucket	35 666	0.7	2 237	6.3	36 356	21.7	13.6	9.7	991	18	88.9
Providence	68 159	0.1	4 454	6.5	69 200	28.9	10.7	9.8	5 628	109	28.4
Warwick	44 263	-0.7	1 780	4.0	43 769	31.7	11.7	8.6	13 873	139	67.6
Woonsocket	19 721	0.7	1 198	6.1	19 882	20.3	14.1	12.1	1 501	25	92.0
SOUTH CAROLINA	1 949 210	-1.8	105 817	5.4	1 603 425	25.4	13.8	9.1	3 532 667	32 812	75.8
Aiken	9 800	-2.2	509	5.2	8 689	42.7	9.5	8.0	24 273	192	100.0
Anderson	14 247	1.7	1 160	8.1	11 321	26.0	10.1	10.5	9 811	102	98.0
Charleston	45 266	-2.0	1 628	3.6	36 988	35.9	8.6	6.6	118 930	1 411	56.0
Columbia	46 690	-2.6	2 212	4.7	40 661	38.3	6.6	7.9	69 896	836	49.8
Florence	15 635	-2.4	1 058	6.8	12 924	31.6	8.5	10.3	NA	NA	NA
Goose Creek	9 385	-1.8	297	3.2	7 559	26.7	16.3	5.4	30 635	216	100.0
Greenville	34 526	-1.2	1 383	4.0	28 677	33.6	7.3	8.0	27 866	405	21.2
Hilton Head Island	18 604	-0.6	272	1.5	11 766	35.8	9.1	3.9	122 662	629	72.5
Mount Pleasant	19 807	-2.3	266	1.3	16 563	46.8	9.3	4.3	259 993	1 557	71.2
North Charleston	31 748	-1.9	1 492	4.7	25 645	22.8	16.1	8.8	47 704	459	59.9
Rock Hill	27 991	0.0	1 941	6.9	20 140	25.2	11.2	6.7	107 259	1 532	43.1
Spartanburg	23 310	-0.3	1 660	7.1	19 079	29.2	7.7	10.3	3 224	22	100.0
Summerville	12 161	-1.5	459	3.8	9 859	32.3	13.2	7.7	37 877	405	57.8
Sumter	15 782	-2.4	1 216	7.7	12 665	28.3	10.6	9.7	NA	NA	NA
SOUTH DAKOTA	405 088	1.0	13 463	3.3	321 891	24.5	10.4	7.8	369 135	4 196	74.9
Rapid City	32 971	1.7	992	3.0	24 681	29.7	12.2	8.4	18 758	157	91.1
Sioux Falls	76 707	1.9	1 873	2.4	54 787	28.9	9.4	8.3	134 910	1 786	59.4
TENNESSEE	2 817 654	0.7	125 978	4.5	2 250 842	26.1	12.2	9.7	3 377 629	32 203	75.9
Bartlett	16 363	0.5	226	1.4	14 217	36.6	9.9	4.5	36 283	241	100.0
Chattanooga	77 046	0.5	2 846	3.7	67 875	28.2	9.1	11.1	79 151	649	74.0
Clarksville	42 750	1.5	1 778	4.2	26 694	27.5	10.7	8.7	51 691	1 005	62.5
Cleveland	16 359	-1.7	696	4.3	14 355	27.6	11.7	9.9	12 788	158	60.8
Collierville	8 084	0.5	121	1.5	7 016	32.6	9.3	4.7	95 076	347	100.0
Columbia	19 053	0.0	769	4.0	13 218	24.2	12.2	9.5	9 435	116	100.0
Franklin	18 368	1.3	458	2.5	10 779	36.7	9.1	6.1	106 277	541	100.0
Germantown	19 183	0.5	248	1.3	16 682	51.9	2.9	3.2	NA	NA	NA
Hendersonville	24 036	2.0	805	3.3	17 509	34.2	9.5	4.8	29 264	290	100.0
Jackson	31 296	-0.3	1 673	5.3	21 755	28.0	8.9	10.0	39 993	361	100.0
Johnson City	27 117	1.4	1 320	4.9	22 533	33.8	8.7	9.8	36 552	441	42.9
Kingsport	16 754	0.9	700	4.2	14 829	31.2	12.1	11.6	9 489	91	100.0
Knoxville	95 166	2.2	3 113	3.3	75 323	31.3	8.4	11.0	38 603	817	51.8

1. Percent of civilian labor force.   2. Persons 16 years and older.   3. Persons 16 to 64 years old.

Table D. Cities — Wholesale Trade, Retail Trade, and Real Estate

City	Wholesale Trade, 1997				Retail Trade[1], 1997				Real Estate and Rental and Leasing, 1997			
	Number of Establishments	Number of Employees	Sales (mil dol)	Annual Payroll (mil dol)	Number of Establishments	Number of Employees	Sales (mil dol)	Annual Payroll (mil dol)	Number of Establishments	Number of Employees	Receipts (mil dol)	Annual Payroll (mil dol)
	72	73	74	75	76	77	78	79	80	81	82	83
OREGON—Cont'd												
Salem	171	2 083	694.8	60.3	665	10 054	1 826.2	181.9	225	1 232	136.8	29.0
Springfield	53	642	242.0	15.7	248	3 141	504.6	47.6	65	282	28.2	4.5
Tigard	246	3 515	3 212.5	157.4	335	7 330	1 429.4	139.7	110	667	117.5	19.8
PENNSYLVANIA	17 138	237 567	159 354.2	8 588.2	50 208	650 144	109 948.5	10 561.9	8 684	57 519	7 668.6	1 360.5
Allentown	203	2 749	1 531.9	92.2	452	5 234	1 037.1	99.6	115	645	80.2	12.0
Altoona	85	2 011	1 090.2	61.7	326	5 126	814.4	71.5	48	244	20.4	4.8
Bethel Park Borough	56	483	157.2	15.7	122	2 087	335.8	31.4	25	116	17.4	2.6
Bethlehem	111	1 344	858.8	55.4	228	2 856	486.2	49.9	52	320	43.4	7.7
Chester	30	311	96.2	10.3	79	657	156.2	16.0	10	47	5.5	1.0
Easton	46	1 235	624.2	52.6	129	1 071	167.2	19.3	16	41	7.2	1.1
Erie	128	1 861	487.4	57.8	494	5 859	772.3	83.3	74	386	34.7	8.1
Harrisburg	91	3 726	2 544.3	110.2	229	2 977	591.3	57.6	52	348	52.5	8.4
Lancaster	97	953	420.9	29.4	311	4 582	750.2	82.5	60	586	39.4	13.5
Monroeville Borough	81	824	331.7	31.8	335	7 123	1 173.7	108.9	55	435	50.9	8.8
New Castle	51	515	231.5	14.3	176	2 650	379.3	38.8	26	167	17.3	3.7
Norristown	77	1 416	549.7	50.9	106	1 337	225.5	25.8	27	155	25.4	3.5
Philadelphia	1 403	22 298	12 004.0	848.4	4 782	51 398	8 118.2	887.1	964	9 550	1 158.1	253.5
Pittsburgh	742	12 740	12 543.4	517.2	1 544	19 790	2 734.1	311.3	492	3 974	786.2	107.1
Plum Borough	46	515	257.2	20.7	60	673	103.4	10.6	18	55	6.5	1.4
Reading	95	1 851	583.5	61.0	310	2 919	502.8	55.7	50	298	36.9	7.8
Scranton	130	1 835	464.3	44.8	473	6 503	902.8	91.5	55	339	31.0	5.4
State College Borough	29	384	69.0	10.0	271	3 665	424.5	43.2	65	442	54.3	8.7
Wilkes-Barre	77	1 379	417.8	35.9	319	5 659	894.0	80.8	54	330	36.5	8.4
Williamsport	58	1 181	238.7	28.8	175	2 081	321.0	34.4	28	D	D	D
York	98	1 612	549.1	48.1	190	1 861	338.4	38.8	36	238	27.0	4.8
RHODE ISLAND	1 590	18 762	7 602.7	635.2	4 169	45 747	7 505.8	752.1	922	4 649	573.4	105.4
Cranston	153	2 776	961.9	97.3	305	4 031	689.4	61.3	70	301	29.3	5.7
East Providence	128	1 981	966.3	75.6	189	2 134	393.1	39.2	49	251	36.0	5.4
Newport	31	119	89.5	4.3	247	1 442	200.5	21.3	40	184	21.1	4.7
Pawtucket	92	953	231.7	27.8	233	2 489	434.7	49.7	57	275	31.0	5.0
Providence	295	3 589	1 462.4	125.9	611	5 155	772.6	92.2	175	1 374	125.8	29.5
Warwick	206	1 924	782.6	66.6	519	8 920	1 446.6	137.5	100	1 030	152.0	27.2
Woonsocket	45	683	161.6	19.6	152	1 806	245.0	24.1	30	94	13.4	1.5
SOUTH CAROLINA	5 035	58 910	34 179.8	1 866.8	18 481	209 256	33 634.3	3 107.2	3 541	18 760	2 012.6	377.1
Aiken	42	261	82.4	6.3	259	3 137	424.3	41.1	48	139	14.2	2.9
Anderson	57	685	241.9	17.0	378	5 272	718.7	69.6	59	204	22.1	3.1
Charleston	111	1 064	455.5	34.9	793	9 394	1 351.2	137.8	195	D	D	D
Columbia	276	3 637	1 584.9	136.6	827	11 608	1 917.3	190.5	240	1 132	162.2	35.3
Florence	93	D	D	D	415	5 954	926.9	89.6	74	244	29.9	5.0
Goose Creek	10	D	D	D	60	768	121.0	10.7	20	407	54.4	7.4
Greenville	288	3 975	6 613.6	162.4	812	12 028	2 011.1	186.8	202	1 047	137.6	24.2
Hilton Head Island	67	208	64.4	6.8	333	3 386	540.9	61.4	155	1 071	150.4	27.0
Mount Pleasant	52	178	161.2	7.5	234	2 625	357.2	38.0	66	280	28.5	5.3
North Charleston	203	3 211	2 237.3	107.6	507	7 214	1 341.4	125.7	93	724	71.9	14.6
Rock Hill	100	1 137	415.4	41.5	330	4 249	699.1	64.1	68	267	25.8	5.7
Spartanburg	105	D	D	D	440	6 349	1 017.1	96.4	102	435	47.7	9.9
Summerville	35	372	115.5	7.7	182	2 976	440.0	38.3	40	151	25.1	3.0
Sumter	56	D	D	D	340	4 355	654.1	62.8	60	233	22.1	3.6
SOUTH DAKOTA	1 402	15 509	7 874.2	389.8	4 311	45 867	11 707.1	689.6	719	2 951	245.7	45.1
Rapid City	144	1 897	633.9	54.2	486	6 368	1 040.6	102.1	108	487	50.3	8.6
Sioux Falls	313	5 146	2 073.5	157.5	696	11 676	1 913.6	184.8	176	919	95.3	17.2
TENNESSEE	8 234	120 228	82 626.4	3 975.4	24 808	304 452	50 813.2	4 810.3	4 999	29 626	3 732.0	667.3
Bartlett	50	D	D	D	144	3 110	466.7	44.4	24	136	15.6	3.2
Chattanooga	602	8 378	3 688.8	255.1	1 150	16 191	2 707.0	268.0	264	1 740	209.6	52.7
Clarksville	86	D	D	D	485	6 674	1 143.3	105.4	100	370	49.6	5.9
Cleveland	73	2 213	1 616.1	47.1	355	3 937	721.6	63.9	65	248	25.4	3.8
Collierville	42	542	369.3	19.9	101	1 759	265.6	22.8	23	64	9.7	1.2
Columbia	43	556	205.2	16.1	247	3 119	528.0	51.7	63	248	27.5	4.3
Franklin	65	596	693.4	30.1	369	5 762	1 092.5	108.0	73	804	90.4	18.2
Germantown	66	472	1 417.2	28.3	186	3 200	368.0	37.7	55	205	32.6	4.2
Hendersonville	71	437	218.2	16.4	139	1 552	238.5	23.6	49	183	29.9	3.2
Jackson	143	1 975	702.1	55.1	547	7 771	1 152.3	110.0	78	394	38.0	6.8
Johnson City	126	1 843	1 086.4	47.4	435	6 118	1 012.9	91.9	103	459	45.5	8.1
Kingsport	102	1 167	464.7	31.1	415	5 841	996.0	92.4	71	320	32.2	5.1
Knoxville	671	8 791	4 595.8	309.0	1 431	22 302	4 031.1	386.5	332	2 227	243.7	51.7

1. Establishments with payroll.

Table D. Cities — Professional Services, Manufacturing, Accommodation and Foodservices

City	Professional, Scientific, and Technical Services, 1997[1]				Manufacturing, 1997				Accommodation and Foodservices, 1997			
	Number of Establishments	Number of Employees	Receipts (mil dol)	Annual Payroll (mil dol)	Number of Establishments	Number of Employees	Receipts (mil dol)	Annual Payroll (mil dol)	Number of Establishments	Number of Employees	Sales (mil dol)	Annual Payroll (mil dol)
	84	85	86	87	88	89	90	91	92	93	94	95
OREGON—Cont'd												
Salem	395	2 357	178.2	70.4	224	7 085	1 226.0	211.4	335	5 642	186.1	52.4
Springfield	44	347	13.7	6.1	87	3 334	915.3	123.3	136	2 369	82.0	22.2
Tigard	247	2 528	234.0	108.3	110	3 706	566.4	125.5	130	2 541	88.4	25.5
PENNSYLVANIA	23 184	235 025	26 240.3	10 448.3	17 128	826 521	172 193.2	27 641.3	24 465	365 158	12 227.2	3 364.1
Allentown	258	1 624	136.1	54.9	238	8 310	4 060.0	325.0	230	3 665	132.1	36.5
Altoona	100	1 149	104.9	35.6	68	2 622	424.7	62.7	152	2 419	65.8	17.6
Bethel Park Borough	71	275	33.4	9.6	49	527	71.3	15.7	64	D	D	D
Bethlehem	177	1 388	175.9	55.3	109	6 650	1 063.1	237.3	182	2 120	81.1	21.7
Chester	9	52	4.2	1.8	34	2 372	782.6	101.3	51	335	12.7	3.1
Easton	92	290	43.6	8.8	53	3 748	639.5	112.4	89	884	33.8	9.6
Erie	207	1 486	121.7	43.3	203	10 286	1 789.0	357.2	238	2 926	81.0	21.5
Harrisburg	265	2 426	290.6	99.4	58	2 299	478.9	69.9	174	1 958	71.1	18.5
Lancaster	179	1 502	145.2	59.6	108	9 758	2 038.5	382.2	129	1 932	68.4	19.2
Monroeville Borough	104	2 796	416.0	124.2	26	687	82.2	19.6	109	3 260	98.5	28.3
New Castle	57	358	23.9	9.6	89	2 483	436.9	76.0	86	1 333	34.3	9.2
Norristown	117	834	89.6	33.3	63	1 517	196.6	48.8	68	D	D	D
Philadelphia	2 444	49 894	6 317.4	2 690.5	1 342	47 928	11 098.1	1 582.4	2 989	38 521	1 691.6	461.1
Pittsburgh	1 488	21 926	2 700.8	1 091.7	479	13 924	2 395.0	471.6	1 065	19 012	677.3	188.2
Plum Borough	36	297	49.0	15.6	36	1 523	194.2	48.1	29	470	13.0	3.8
Reading	132	925	88.6	46.2	160	16 969	3 654.2	737.4	164	D	D	D
Scranton	188	1 235	118.7	42.9	124	4 567	591.2	114.1	201	2 913	86.6	22.4
State College Borough	100	1 160	84.6	38.6	38	2 140	251.8	66.0	139	2 908	84.1	22.2
Wilkes-Barre	148	982	93.1	39.5	69	3 390	422.4	81.3	143	2 487	73.7	20.2
Williamsport	76	593	41.9	17.5	72	6 023	1 284.3	182.7	98	854	24.7	6.4
York	177	1 390	122.6	50.4	123	9 253	1 924.0	332.3	111	D	D	D
RHODE ISLAND	2 349	14 866	1 418.1	541.5	2 535	75 599	10 482.0	2 288.6	2 617	34 162	1 220.9	340.6
Cranston	185	1 072	107.0	34.3	252	7 160	949.0	213.3	162	D	D	D
East Providence	123	1 161	113.6	42.5	133	4 397	555.5	129.2	108	D	D	D
Newport	91	432	46.1	15.1	NA	NA	NA	NA	182	2 938	144.4	43.1
Pawtucket	94	355	30.2	11.4	205	9 766	1 535.2	294.3	122	D	D	D
Providence	689	4 672	517.3	206.2	570	12 465	1 294.1	337.1	443	6 216	237.6	63.7
Warwick	277	1 266	121.0	43.4	260	6 751	1 154.8	206.0	232	4 899	155.0	43.7
Woonsocket	43	199	15.0	5.8	84	2 700	317.3	80.5	89	D	D	D
SOUTH CAROLINA	6 576	47 679	6 820.9	1 850.5	4 450	346 142	70 797.0	10 369.4	7 775	150 621	4 835.8	1 313.8
Aiken	112	D	D	D	38	4 692	1 009.2	139.6	116	2 090	63.1	16.4
Anderson	125	501	36.8	10.3	73	9 005	2 141.4	285.6	130	2 792	87.3	23.4
Charleston	482	4 132	412.8	185.0	84	1 985	602.9	65.7	388	9 484	346.4	97.6
Columbia	699	6 453	771.7	256.8	105	7 137	1 648.3	253.4	387	7 826	242.4	69.7
Florence	129	1 006	70.5	28.6	52	4 653	701.2	148.6	162	3 838	113.0	31.5
Goose Creek	18	63	3.3	1.4	12	2 621	1 205.2	107.2	43	D	D	D
Greenville	617	8 440	3 116.3	437.3	159	14 641	4 021.7	504.2	342	7 560	238.0	68.3
Hilton Head Island	204	1 259	132.0	62.1	NA	NA	NA	NA	185	4 759	228.0	63.8
Mount Pleasant	153	607	52.1	19.5	NA	NA	NA	NA	103	2 181	72.8	19.8
North Charleston	190	2 160	203.1	65.0	108	5 292	1 237.0	188.6	211	4 297	135.1	35.1
Rock Hill	144	721	50.6	20.6	75	4 658	901.1	151.9	134	3 179	92.2	24.4
Spartanburg	197	1 296	121.5	43.6	93	8 867	2 339.5	311.4	194	4 282	109.8	31.9
Summerville	53	390	21.7	8.7	40	1 654	284.1	45.2	96	2 077	55.4	16.2
Sumter	101	423	26.6	8.3	59	10 009	1 522.3	234.4	107	2 148	65.3	17.7
SOUTH DAKOTA	1 282	6 228	450.4	161.7	888	46 539	12 305.5	1 162.6	2 258	30 131	888.0	234.4
Rapid City	195	1 104	88.7	30.2	109	3 513	756.2	77.3	234	4 643	135.5	37.6
Sioux Falls	343	2 341	181.1	72.6	133	11 605	2 995.2	301.9	352	7 691	215.0	61.8
TENNESSEE	8 812	72 225	6 911.8	2 686.6	7 407	483 823	98 503.1	14 351.9	9 604	197 881	6 790.2	1 880.3
Bartlett	66	320	25.1	10.8	31	1 327	242.8	29.5	53	D	D	D
Chattanooga	529	4 252	370.0	151.8	389	23 272	4 091.4	739.9	528	10 682	366.7	103.6
Clarksville	113	736	39.7	11.7	70	6 047	1 190.7	169.5	221	D	D	D
Cleveland	108	678	47.0	17.5	122	11 978	2 618.5	322.0	130	2 476	80.2	21.3
Collierville	49	199	24.3	9.9	40	3 281	809.9	89.9	42	D	D	D
Columbia	74	350	27.9	9.8	42	D	D	D	81	1 836	48.3	13.1
Franklin	118	706	59.9	25.8	71	3 760	704.2	107.3	120	2 748	93.2	27.2
Germantown	97	509	62.6	25.0	NA	NA	NA	NA	61	D	D	D
Hendersonville	87	621	24.9	9.5	62	1 917	307.2	52.7	61	1 135	34.8	10.4
Jackson	136	974	76.9	36.6	123	D	D	D	177	4 079	137.1	36.9
Johnson City	166	1 231	66.9	24.2	101	8 801	1 074.1	211.5	160	4 131	125.2	36.0
Kingsport	123	734	70.2	39.8	61	D	D	D	155	3 545	115.0	33.0
Knoxville	650	6 376	551.0	209.5	318	14 827	2 429.9	394.5	586	12 873	405.9	117.2

1. Firms subject to federal tax.

City	Arts, Entertainment, and Recreation[1], 1997				Health Care and Social Assistance[1], 1997				Other Services[1], 1997			
	Number of Establish-ments	Number of Employees	Receipts (mil dol)	Annual Payroll (mil dol)	Number of Establish-ments	Number of Employees	Receipts (mil dol)	Annual Payroll (mil dol)	Number of Establish-ments	Number of Employees	Receipts (mil dol)	Annual Payroll (mil dol)
	96	97	98	99	100	101	102	103	104	105	106	107
OREGON—Cont'd												
Salem	43	646	37.6	8.3	442	4 213	269.5	120.0	230	1 433	81.6	26.9
Springfield	18	197	4.6	1.4	124	1 280	77.1	36.0	85	604	34.2	10.4
Tigard	12	129	5.9	1.7	139	1 413	112.6	40.2	91	607	48.5	15.8
PENNSYLVANIA	2 883	40 892	2 439.3	810.6	24 888	262 603	17 633.5	7 994.9	19 754	107 502	7 085.7	2 049.0
Allentown	25	225	10.5	3.1	268	2 036	145.4	66.5	216	1 528	97.0	31.0
Altoona	20	245	6.2	1.9	182	2 033	160.9	67.5	138	719	37.7	10.5
Bethel Park Borough	8	155	6.3	1.1	67	781	42.9	17.2	84	428	21.9	7.1
Bethlehem	8	84	2.8	0.8	196	1 642	133.8	53.5	108	947	51.8	20.1
Chester	NA	NA	NA	NA	43	568	36.1	15.6	29	110	6.6	2.2
Easton	8	87	4.1	1.3	51	639	31.1	15.3	69	440	31.7	11.0
Erie	25	225	13.4	3.5	301	3 261	286.6	138.2	193	936	64.8	17.6
Harrisburg	17	86	6.2	1.7	117	970	74.6	37.0	104	638	48.6	14.0
Lancaster	17	276	14.6	4.2	138	1 711	156.0	88.1	97	697	40.1	14.9
Monroeville Borough	15	265	9.2	3.0	168	2 369	186.6	78.0	87	594	29.9	10.0
New Castle	12	152	6.8	1.6	84	893	52.9	24.2	77	347	18.6	4.9
Norristown	5	31	3.2	1.1	90	2 402	243.1	102.2	41	258	20.4	6.4
Philadelphia	160	4 595	413.7	224.1	2 574	27 295	1 931.1	899.0	1 913	10 971	737.4	199.6
Pittsburgh	84	2 331	237.3	128.5	1 070	15 743	1 402.7	622.3	722	4 725	317.6	91.7
Plum Borough	6	64	2.3	0.6	26	144	8.2	3.5	35	176	9.4	2.7
Reading	13	180	32.0	6.8	120	1 168	65.7	30.9	106	943	52.6	16.0
Scranton	21	135	6.6	1.5	249	2 599	202.0	93.8	151	998	57.0	16.7
State College Borough	13	228	5.5	1.4	120	1 214	82.8	37.5	53	533	25.7	8.2
Wilkes-Barre	5	0	0.0	0.0	140	1 709	125.5	57.7	95	441	25.1	6.9
Williamsport	2	0	0.0	0.0	108	1 042	76.1	36.3	63	324	27.9	6.3
York	10	0	0.0	0.0	65	667	46.6	25.6	63	414	27.5	8.1
RHODE ISLAND	307	3 877	234.8	58.1	2 074	25 368	1 459.3	647.4	1 949	8 602	546.2	167.8
Cranston	23	219	16.5	3.7	198	1 735	113.4	49.0	177	838	51.5	17.3
East Providence	18	509	13.7	4.1	102	1 611	96.8	43.0	115	466	36.2	10.6
Newport	18	441	20.2	6.3	57	499	32.6	13.5	52	210	12.8	4.5
Pawtucket	13	90	7.2	2.3	112	1 167	72.3	32.1	132	822	51.2	16.2
Providence	29	274	25.8	5.5	401	4 950	336.8	160.2	284	1 466	107.9	32.3
Warwick	31	202	14.8	3.4	271	3 314	223.8	86.0	199	918	58.2	17.5
Woonsocket	5	76	2.1	0.7	68	1 287	60.5	28.2	81	275	14.0	4.2
SOUTH CAROLINA	1 325	18 499	1 107.1	251.9	6 261	78 888	5 318.5	2 361.3	5 672	32 166	1 901.0	563.8
Aiken	23	280	10.3	3.6	118	2 411	187.0	72.2	66	410	16.4	4.9
Anderson	14	108	4.2	0.8	169	2 358	154.2	81.7	83	563	29.4	10.2
Charleston	50	614	30.0	6.2	356	2 858	222.6	101.5	174	1 409	51.5	19.6
Columbia	44	662	33.7	7.8	490	7 599	621.7	288.1	235	2 020	103.6	34.8
Florence	20	379	13.9	2.4	206	4 637	360.9	175.9	84	746	37.7	11.8
Goose Creek	5	185	7.2	3.0	23	180	8.5	3.4	33	146	7.5	1.8
Greenville	43	601	31.5	8.3	297	2 931	237.8	113.5	233	2 135	123.3	37.8
Hilton Head Island	50	961	49.7	13.3	82	939	82.9	28.3	76	295	19.3	5.8
Mount Pleasant	18	244	14.2	3.5	139	1 710	94.6	41.7	90	537	35.2	10.6
North Charleston	29	262	27.4	3.9	233	4 631	321.2	122.9	211	1 976	139.8	45.0
Rock Hill	27	243	8.5	2.5	144	3 527	222.1	97.3	121	700	42.8	13.9
Spartanburg	18	155	8.0	2.4	166	2 617	209.1	94.3	119	772	44.4	13.2
Summerville	13	81	3.5	1.1	82	1 175	78.1	27.2	85	385	21.4	6.5
Sumter	16	136	6.0	1.6	115	1 165	75.4	37.4	87	676	38.3	11.4
SOUTH DAKOTA	432	4 647	299.2	60.2	1 314	14 080	881.6	414.3	1 356	5 828	344.7	90.7
Rapid City	63	485	23.9	5.1	217	2 295	162.4	65.3	170	940	49.1	15.7
Sioux Falls	67	746	48.1	10.0	269	4 275	351.5	194.4	246	1 786	95.6	30.4
TENNESSEE	1 755	18 263	1 228.7	394.3	10 113	155 667	10 753.0	4 659.9	7 767	49 204	2 996.7	918.7
Bartlett	4	84	3.2	1.0	74	646	45.7	17.2	65	345	17.6	6.3
Chattanooga	55	648	27.3	9.3	611	9 114	727.1	332.2	385	2 809	167.9	53.5
Clarksville	28	0	0.0	0.0	143	1 979	115.0	48.0	157	755	39.7	10.8
Cleveland	18	0	0.0	0.0	195	10 316	437.6	199.4	91	1 239	63.5	24.1
Collierville	2	0	0.0	0.0	38	383	19.8	7.4	33	183	8.9	3.0
Columbia	16	90	4.6	1.6	117	1 411	102.5	36.3	80	500	26.8	8.6
Franklin	44	319	20.2	8.1	125	1 617	106.6	48.8	103	640	58.9	14.7
Germantown	5	96	4.5	2.0	101	1 056	84.1	36.3	45	428	17.1	7.5
Hendersonville	22	241	16.6	5.8	108	1 526	101.1	40.2	83	451	22.7	6.6
Jackson	20	162	5.2	1.5	198	3 728	290.1	147.4	151	995	51.1	16.7
Johnson City	13	116	2.9	1.0	211	3 117	247.7	115.2	133	965	44.4	17.1
Kingsport	15	147	6.1	2.1	213	3 881	288.1	132.9	127	1 014	48.7	18.1
Knoxville	71	869	31.0	10.1	700	8 146	798.6	378.2	497	3 653	188.1	60.9

1. Firms subject to federal tax.

Table D. Cities — Federal Funds and City Government Finances

City	Selected federal funds, fiscal 2001[1] (mil dol)									City government finances, 1999						
	Procurement contracts		Grants					Direct payments for individuals		General revenue						
										Intergovernmental			Taxes			
														Per capita[3] (dollars)		
	Defense	Other	Total[2]	Health and family welfare	Energy and environment	Education	Housing and community development	Educational assistance	Housing assistance	Total (mil dol)	Total (mil dol)	Percent from state government	Total (mil dol)	Total	Property	Sales and gross receipts
	108	109	110	111	112	113	114	115	116	117	118	119	120	121	122	123
OREGON—Cont'd																
Salem	2.2	4.3	633.8	142.4	3.7	103.5	20.7	8.4	34.3	127.7	15.6	73.1	62.6	494	357	69
Springfield	0.0	0.2	5.5	1.3	0.2	2.5	0.8	0.1	1.6	54.4	7.1	99.7	13.4	265	217	30
Tigard	1.0	0.0	0.4	0.0	0.0	0.3	0.0	0.1	0.0	27.4	4.4	49.7	14.6	396	234	64
PENNSYLVANIA	4 214.2	2 573.8	14 847.3	9 761.1	291.9	1 136.5	346.7	535.0	1 262.4	X	X	X	X	X	X	X
Allentown	153.4	9.7	38.5	0.9	11.8	1.1	3.7	5.3	14.2	70.8	12.9	63.5	33.8	336	201	0
Altoona	0.0	1.6	10.1	2.3	0.4	0.9	3.0	0.8	11.4	26.2	8.3	76.7	14.1	286	161	0
Bethel Park Borough	12.6	0.0	0.0	0.0	0.0	0.0	0.0	0.0	0.9	NA	NA	NA	NA	NA	NA	NA
Bethlehem	0.5	1.3	14.9	6.6	1.4	1.6	2.1	6.3	15.8	58.8	7.4	68.3	21.8	315	202	0
Chester	6.5	0.3	9.7	2.3	0.0	1.9	2.8	3.2	17.4	NA	NA	NA	NA	NA	NA	NA
Easton	4.9	2.0	1.8	0.5	0.0	0.0	0.7	0.0	1.9	NA	NA	NA	NA	NA	NA	NA
Erie	35.7	2.8	16.7	3.6	0.0	1.5	5.0	7.0	18.7	75.0	19.7	50.0	30.3	295	222	0
Harrisburg	7.3	14.0	2 093.6	736.7	176.7	353.7	91.6	53.2	25.6	67.3	16.4	52.9	19.0	384	236	0
Lancaster	60.3	4.1	16.8	4.5	0.0	1.7	7.2	2.2	18.3	37.9	7.1	58.7	14.7	278	188	0
Monroeville Borough	NA	NA	NA	NA	NA	NA	NA	NA	NA	NA	NA	NA	NA	NA	NA	NA
New Castle	0.5	0.2	0.7	0.5	0.0	0.0	0.0	1.2	9.2	12.6	3.1	100.0	7.0	267	131	0
Norristown	2.2	0.5	7.9	0.0	0.0	0.0	6.3	0.0	1.6	15.7	3.2	39.6	10.1	339	125	0
Philadelphia	1 362.2	241.9	1 257.9	775.2	19.3	41.0	85.3	93.2	248.4	4 215.7	1 761.9	68.1	1 821.9	1 268	236	113
Pittsburgh	242.9	216.9	689.3	382.5	37.9	11.2	56.4	108.2	166.3	469.9	129.0	54.0	252.3	741	351	101
Plum Borough	0.0	0.0	0.0	0.0	0.0	0.0	0.0	0.0	0.4	NA	NA	NA	NA	NA	NA	NA
Reading	17.7	4.4	22.2	4.4	0.0	1.3	8.7	8.3	10.6	54.9	10.5	41.2	22.7	304	196	0
Scranton	11.4	2.5	20.2	5.3	6.3	0.4	6.0	7.3	19.4	59.1	21.1	84.7	30.9	413	127	0
State College Borough	59.2	1.1	97.8	44.6	4.2	12.4	1.2	44.6	1.4	20.0	3.0	46.5	6.5	165	50	0
Wilkes-Barre	12.0	12.0	20.2	7.0	1.4	1.6	7.8	6.0	11.1	30.9	7.6	49.9	17.3	404	113	0
Williamsport	14.1	8.1	4.2	1.4	0.1	0.5	1.5	7.8	9.0	NA	NA	NA	NA	NA	NA	NA
York	453.0	0.7	13.0	2.7	1.0	0.6	5.6	4.2	8.5	36.0	6.6	99.7	11.7	293	168	0
RHODE ISLAND	283.1	109.1	1 607.5	1 016.2	32.3	120.6	26.2	63.8	307.2	X	X	X	X	X	X	X
Cranston	0.5	0.5	42.3	29.8	0.0	0.8	1.3	0.0	17.3	141.3	16.5	71.8	101.7	1 365	1 347	0
East Providence	0.0	1.2	2.4	1.0	0.0	0.0	1.3	0.3	18.5	97.2	29.4	92.0	58.1	1 214	1 205	0
Newport	44.4	4.0	3.5	1.4	0.0	2.1	0.0	1.2	13.3	68.1	14.8	83.4	42.4	1 745	1 705	12
Pawtucket	0.4	5.5	12.0	7.2	0.0	1.3	3.3	1.6	17.6	129.5	59.7	93.4	64.6	948	937	0
Providence	5.3	12.5	377.6	143.6	31.3	50.7	17.4	27.8	106.1	391.7	155.5	93.9	192.6	1 276	1 260	0
Warwick	4.0	2.4	15.1	2.5	0.0	1.9	0.8	20.0	11.0	204.2	42.3	96.6	143.3	1 704	1 664	8
Woonsocket	1.8	1.3	5.9	3.3	0.0	0.0	2.2	0.0	33.0	88.8	44.1	93.2	36.8	896	884	0
SOUTH CAROLINA	1 063.7	2 091.5	4 729.9	2 984.0	88.7	433.4	64.0	175.2	319.2	X	X	X	X	X	X	X
Aiken	0.5	1 581.5	4.7	2.2	0.5	0.1	0.6	5.3	3.0	23.6	2.2	50.6	10.8	474	265	60
Anderson	0.8	0.1	4.3	0.2	0.0	2.4	1.0	1.6	14.6	23.0	2.4	67.0	12.0	461	285	44
Charleston	244.5	83.3	133.4	71.2	5.8	3.1	7.1	3.1	23.4	136.9	31.4	18.1	55.4	636	340	35
Columbia	64.3	59.8	677.0	256.5	60.8	131.9	42.9	69.1	28.0	121.9	17.7	31.8	44.7	404	225	57
Florence	1.6	0.8	11.7	4.8	1.0	1.4	0.5	8.3	5.2	22.5	6.7	21.2	7.7	260	61	60
Goose Creek	7.8	0.3	0.7	0.0	0.0	0.0	0.0	0.0	0.6	NA	NA	NA	NA	NA	NA	NA
Greenville	98.5	26.2	30.4	11.7	1.0	3.5	6.0	7.2	13.4	71.9	7.2	73.9	43.0	761	415	94
Hilton Head Island	2.7	0.2	0.2	0.0	0.0	0.0	0.0	0.0	0.5	NA	NA	NA	NA	NA	NA	NA
Mount Pleasant	1.0	0.2	0.2	0.0	0.0	0.0	0.0	0.0	0.4	32.9	5.8	28.6	15.8	383	175	61
North Charleston	180.2	22.3	22.7	0.8	0.3	0.0	0.2	0.2	17.1	61.8	19.2	25.1	26.1	384	205	59
Rock Hill	0.0	0.0	9.5	5.8	0.0	2.1	0.6	5.8	4.7	32.0	7.3	29.3	13.8	299	208	0
Spartanburg	1.3	4.4	10.5	3.3	0.3	3.0	1.9	8.9	10.5	30.8	6.2	55.9	16.1	393	208	0
Summerville	1.5	0.0	0.1	0.0	0.0	0.1	0.0	0.0	5.0	16.1	1.3	72.0	7.4	303	179	29
Sumter	2.7	2.4	14.5	6.4	0.0	4.6	1.9	6.5	6.3	24.1	7.8	19.1	9.8	241	133	36
SOUTH DAKOTA	116.8	184.3	1 254.3	523.3	35.4	163.2	12.7	151.1	78.7	X	X	X	X	X	X	X
Rapid City	5.1	21.0	16.5	7.9	3.4	1.8	0.5	5.9	14.9	58.3	4.3	27.4	32.9	572	122	430
Sioux Falls	6.7	35.5	14.3	3.4	0.3	1.3	1.3	104.7	17.6	116.3	9.2	37.8	75.9	650	403	226
TENNESSEE	1 028.4	4 782.5	7 026.7	4 737.0	50.3	547.8	78.8	222.2	502.9	X	X	X	X	X	X	X
Bartlett	0.1	0.1	0.4	0.0	0.0	0.0	0.0	0.0	0.0	28.9	9.3	43.3	10.1	285	209	51
Chattanooga	11.9	474.3	39.2	6.1	0.4	6.8	4.1	10.3	23.0	241.4	65.6	49.3	91.9	622	433	175
Clarksville	0.2	0.0	9.9	1.2	0.0	3.0	1.2	7.4	4.2	50.9	18.8	49.1	17.3	176	130	46
Cleveland	0.0	0.8	4.1	2.6	0.0	0.4	0.0	5.1	3.6	58.1	31.8	49.6	15.4	436	176	247
Collierville	0.0	1.0	0.1	0.1	0.0	0.0	0.0	0.0	0.0	28.1	7.3	48.5	11.6	490	318	90
Columbia	0.1	4.8	0.6	0.0	0.0	0.3	0.0	2.3	2.2	26.1	9.6	37.8	6.2	196	130	57
Franklin	0.8	1.2	0.2	0.1	0.0	0.1	0.0	0.1	0.3	NA	NA	NA	NA	NA	NA	NA
Germantown	2.3	0.1	0.3	0.2	0.0	0.0	0.0	0.0	0.0	34.2	10.0	51.6	13.6	361	306	52
Hendersonville	0.2	0.2	0.1	0.0	0.0	0.0	0.0	0.0	1.6	18.1	8.2	48.7	5.3	137	93	17
Jackson	0.6	2.3	5.9	0.1	0.0	2.6	1.3	8.0	10.0	80.3	31.5	31.7	24.0	470	364	89
Johnson City	0.2	20.0	4.9	0.1	0.1	2.1	0.9	10.4	8.9	109.4	52.0	44.5	26.9	471	386	72
Kingsport	0.9	2.0	7.9	6.0	0.0	0.2	0.9	0.0	11.2	101.0	53.9	39.5	26.5	643	570	67
Knoxville	9.8	293.2	101.3	16.9	10.5	14.8	3.6	45.8	47.1	244.6	48.0	48.5	118.3	715	402	303

1. October 1, 2000 to September 30, 2001.   2. Includes program categories not shown separately. State totals include additional categories not allocated by city.   3. Based on population estimated as of July 1 of the year shown.

Table D. Cities — **City Government Finances**

	City government finances, 1999 (cont'd)												
	General expenditure												
	Per capita[1] (dollars)			Percent of total for —									
City	Total (mil dol)	Total	Capital outlays	Public welfare	Highways	Parking facilities	Education	Health and hospitals	Police protection	Sewerage and sanitation	Parks and recreation	Housing and community development	Interest on debt
	124	125	126	127	128	129	130	131	132	133	134	135	136
OREGON—Cont'd													
Salem	133.4	1 053	296	0.0	9.1	0.8	0.0	2.3	14.2	11.6	4.8	2.6	3.4
Springfield	52.0	1 026	140	0.0	6.6	0.0	0.0	6.1	16.1	32.3	0.1	12.0	1.6
Tigard	21.4	580	136	0.5	14.9	0.0	0.0	0.0	26.1	5.1	7.0	0.0	1.4
PENNSYLVANIA	X	X	X	X	X	X	X	X	X	X	X	X	X
Allentown	96.2	955	211	0.0	9.7	0.0	0.0	3.6	15.6	32.1	4.1	6.6	7.9
Altoona	18.2	369	18	0.0	14.5	0.1	0.0	0.0	22.5	0.4	1.4	0.8	1.0
Bethel Park Borough	NA	NA	NA	NA	NA	NA	NA	NA	NA	NA	NA	NA	NA
Bethlehem	49.7	716	3	0.0	6.2	0.0	0.0	2.0	16.0	13.7	5.6	0.5	7.7
Chester	NA	NA	NA	NA	NA	NA	NA	NA	NA	NA	NA	NA	NA
Easton	NA	NA	NA	NA	NA	NA	NA	NA	NA	NA	NA	NA	NA
Erie	82.0	799	119	0.0	12.5	0.0	0.0	0.0	21.4	20.0	6.7	7.2	2.8
Harrisburg	78.3	1 581	59	0.0	5.8	0.0	0.0	0.0	15.3	15.4	5.6	21.2	7.3
Lancaster	41.5	784	21	0.0	10.6	0.0	0.0	0.0	21.2	23.6	2.5	10.5	3.1
Monroeville Borough	NA	NA	NA	NA	NA	NA	NA	NA	NA	NA	NA	NA	NA
New Castle	12.4	475	2	0.0	9.4	0.2	0.0	0.0	14.3	11.9	4.9	13.1	2.1
Norristown	20.5	688	84	0.0	16.6	0.0	0.0	1.4	25.8	10.7	1.2	5.8	3.6
Philadelphia	4 010.5	2 792	302	8.4	2.1	0.0	0.5	19.6	10.7	7.8	2.0	4.6	3.1
Pittsburgh	473.8	1 391	118	0.0	7.0	0.0	0.0	2.7	14.8	1.5	2.2	16.5	12.5
Plum Borough	NA	NA	NA	NA	NA	NA	NA	NA	NA	NA	NA	NA	NA
Reading	55.8	746	22	0.0	9.4	0.0	0.0	0.0	22.7	14.0	3.5	12.1	9.0
Scranton	55.7	745	0	0.0	6.6	1.6	0.0	7.5	18.9	5.9	2.1	6.0	0.9
State College Borough	19.3	487	59	0.0	10.5	6.2	0.0	0.0	24.7	27.5	1.9	5.9	2.8
Wilkes-Barre	41.5	969	216	0.0	11.5	0.9	0.0	1.8	11.6	18.6	4.1	6.5	0.7
Williamsport	NA	NA	NA	NA	NA	NA	NA	NA	NA	NA	NA	NA	NA
York	39.0	974	59	0.0	7.0	1.7	0.0	0.2	18.0	18.9	5.5	9.8	5.5
RHODE ISLAND	X	X	X	X	X	X	X	X	X	X	X	X	X
Cranston	166.1	2 228	66	0.1	3.4	0.0	52.2	0.0	9.0	10.0	0.8	0.8	2.5
East Providence	91.2	1 905	42	0.0	3.0	0.0	53.9	0.0	8.7	7.4	2.3	2.3	0.6
Newport	57.7	2 377	61	0.3	3.9	0.5	49.2	0.0	11.2	9.1	2.9	0.8	2.4
Pawtucket	125.1	1 835	55	1.1	3.1	0.0	57.1	0.5	9.5	0.7	1.7	5.3	2.9
Providence	400.9	2 657	102	0.1	0.9	0.0	57.0	0.0	7.7	1.6	3.0	3.5	2.0
Warwick	199.7	2 375	153	0.7	3.2	0.0	55.2	0.1	6.1	3.0	1.7	0.9	1.6
Woonsocket	88.0	2 144	122	0.3	2.8	0.0	56.0	0.0	6.9	7.2	0.6	2.5	0.7
SOUTH CAROLINA	X	X	X	X	X	X	X	X	X	X	X	X	X
Aiken	21.7	951	106	0.0	6.6	1.1	0.0	0.0	18.6	19.0	12.2	2.2	0.4
Anderson	23.2	890	182	0.0	7.6	0.0	0.0	0.1	20.1	14.1	5.3	11.2	5.1
Charleston	127.4	1 464	446	0.4	1.6	3.2	0.0	0.0	14.9	21.1	18.6	2.6	4.6
Columbia	102.0	920	126	0.3	4.7	1.4	0.0	0.5	20.4	18.9	10.3	1.6	1.5
Florence	20.6	699	65	0.0	7.8	0.0	0.0	0.4	21.0	14.7	12.5	4.4	6.3
Goose Creek	NA	NA	NA	NA	NA	NA	NA	NA	NA	NA	NA	NA	NA
Greenville	59.9	1 062	146	0.0	15.3	1.6	0.0	0.2	19.9	9.4	13.1	3.5	4.7
Hilton Head Island	NA	NA	NA	NA	NA	NA	NA	NA	NA	NA	NA	NA	NA
Mount Pleasant	29.2	706	117	0.0	0.9	0.0	0.0	0.0	18.4	25.7	16.4	0.0	1.4
North Charleston	67.6	994	322	0.0	3.1	0.5	0.0	0.0	23.3	3.8	23.2	2.2	6.1
Rock Hill	31.3	676	29	0.0	4.8	0.0	0.0	0.0	19.6	9.6	9.3	0.0	11.7
Spartanburg	23.0	561	25	0.0	7.6	0.2	0.0	0.7	27.4	15.8	0.3	1.0	0.6
Summerville	13.3	547	120	0.0	10.3	0.0	0.0	0.0	18.0	31.1	3.4	0.0	0.9
Sumter	17.5	432	18	0.0	4.8	2.2	0.0	0.0	30.1	20.1	5.9	0.0	0.3
SOUTH DAKOTA	X	X	X	X	X	X	X	X	X	X	X	X	X
Rapid City	46.9	816	129	0.0	6.5	0.6	0.0	0.6	15.9	12.1	15.3	2.7	6.9
Sioux Falls	111.3	953	238	0.0	28.4	0.8	0.0	3.4	10.1	6.3	19.3	1.3	5.4
TENNESSEE	X	X	X	X	X	X	X	X	X	X	X	X	X
Bartlett	28.8	814	150	0.0	15.1	0.0	0.0	3.3	20.6	17.7	10.7	0.0	3.7
Chattanooga	221.5	1 499	251	4.9	8.5	0.0	0.0	0.6	13.8	12.0	12.9	4.5	6.5
Clarksville	65.6	670	194	0.0	13.8	0.5	0.0	0.5	21.5	27.4	6.0	1.7	3.9
Cleveland	64.0	1 804	466	0.2	5.9	0.0	50.2	0.5	7.4	17.0	2.0	0.0	3.4
Collierville	21.5	907	148	0.0	11.1	0.0	0.0	0.8	19.9	14.0	7.7	0.0	4.2
Columbia	20.8	651	43	0.5	14.1	1.0	0.0	0.0	20.6	26.0	4.9	0.0	2.1
Franklin	NA	NA	NA	NA	NA	NA	NA	NA	NA	NA	NA	NA	NA
Germantown	34.7	922	173	0.0	8.1	0.0	0.0	0.4	15.9	16.9	15.5	4.0	5.6
Hendersonville	17.1	444	44	0.9	14.1	0.0	0.0	0.1	23.9	10.8	7.9	0.0	2.6
Jackson	72.1	1 411	272	0.2	7.4	0.2	0.0	1.7	12.9	30.6	10.2	2.1	4.2
Johnson City	95.5	1 673	35	0.0	4.8	0.0	41.0	0.0	10.4	13.0	5.3	1.4	5.8
Kingsport	88.6	2 154	127	0.0	4.6	0.0	46.0	0.0	7.2	10.4	3.9	0.3	6.2
Knoxville	255.7	1 544	364	1.2	9.4	0.4	1.5	0.0	7.8	10.2	3.9	5.8	5.8

1. Based on population estimated as of July 1 of the year shown.

Table D. Cities — City Government Finances, City Government Employment, and Climate

City	City government finances, 1999 (cont'd) Debt outstanding			City government employment, 2001	Climate[2] Average daily temperature (degrees Fahrenheit)						
					Mean		Limits				
	Total (mil dol)	Per capita[1] (dollars)	Percent utility		January	July	January[3]	July[4]	Annual precipitation (inches)	Heating degree days	Cooling degree days
	137	138	139	140	141	142	143	144	145	146	147
OREGON—Cont'd											
Salem	141.0	1 113	17.0	1 269	39.6	66.3	32.7	81.6	39.16	4 927	247
Springfield	12.6	249	5.4	507	40.8	67.3	35.2	81.7	49.37	4 546	300
Tigard	8.1	220	0.0	235	38.9	65.8	32.5	79.7	37.57	5 011	232
PENNSYLVANIA	X	X	X	X	X	X	X	X	X	X	X
Allentown	161.6	1 603	29.1	947	26.6	74.1	18.8	84.5	43.52	5 785	773
Altoona	12.8	261	0.0	288	26.0	71.3	19.1	81.5	36.81	6 140	582
Bethel Park Borough	NA	NA	NA	NA	26.1	72.1	18.5	82.6	36.85	5 968	654
Bethlehem	173.0	2 494	70.9	731	26.6	74.1	18.8	84.5	43.52	5 785	773
Chester	NA	NA	NA	NA	32.4	78.3	26.4	87.3	42.45	4 586	1 291
Easton	NA	NA	NA	NA	26.6	74.1	18.8	84.5	43.52	5 785	773
Erie	78.7	766	0.0	842	25.4	71.3	18.2	79.9	41.53	6 279	550
Harrisburg	109.8	2 218	0.0	768	28.6	75.7	21.2	85.8	40.50	5 347	962
Lancaster	83.2	1 570	0.0	563	27.9	74.1	19.2	84.9	41.22	5 584	780
Monroeville Borough	NA	NA	NA	NA	26.1	72.1	18.5	82.6	36.85	5 968	654
New Castle	15.0	574	0.0	149	24.1	70.6	15.0	83.2	37.38	6 542	489
Norristown	23.5	791	0.0	156	29.8	75.9	21.4	86.5	44.38	5 114	1 022
Philadelphia	4 782.9	3 330	47.6	30 284	30.4	76.7	22.8	86.1	41.41	4 954	1 101
Pittsburgh	1 187.7	3 488	0.0	4 263	26.1	72.1	18.5	82.6	36.85	5 968	654
Plum Borough	NA	NA	NA	NA	26.1	72.1	18.5	82.6	36.85	5 968	654
Reading	102.0	1 364	28.5	744	26.6	74.0	17.0	85.1	44.71	5 796	759
Scranton	10.1	135	0.0	609	24.7	71.7	17.5	81.8	36.18	6 291	539
State College Borough	9.8	248	0.0	209	24.7	71.3	16.7	82.0	37.48	6 364	529
Wilkes-Barre	39.2	914	0.0	333	24.7	71.7	17.5	81.8	36.18	6 291	539
Williamsport	NA	NA	NA	NA	25.2	72.3	17.1	83.1	40.72	6 087	622
York	31.3	782	0.0	411	29.0	74.5	19.4	86.9	40.40	5 256	860
RHODE ISLAND	X	X	X	X	X	X	X	X	X	X	X
Cranston	70.2	942	0.9	2 056	27.9	72.7	19.1	82.1	45.53	5 884	606
East Providence	10.9	227	0.0	1 700	27.9	72.7	19.1	82.1	45.53	5 884	606
Newport	27.0	1 114	51.2	847	30.3	70.7	22.6	78.3	44.81	5 659	464
Pawtucket	83.9	1 231	25.6	2 157	27.9	72.7	19.1	82.1	45.53	5 884	606
Providence	301.0	1 995	6.7	6 160	27.9	72.7	19.1	82.1	45.53	5 884	606
Warwick	71.1	845	2.1	2 652	27.9	72.7	19.1	82.1	45.53	5 884	606
Woonsocket	34.3	835	24.6	NA	27.9	72.7	19.1	82.1	45.53	5 884	606
SOUTH CAROLINA	X	X	X	X	X	X	X	X	X	X	X
Aiken	12.6	551	60.8	316	NA	NA	NA	NA	NA	NA	NA
Anderson	22.7	868	0.0	359	42.1	79.8	32.2	89.9	46.38	2 891	1 807
Charleston	457.4	5 255	77.3	1 913	47.8	81.5	37.7	90.2	51.53	2 013	2 266
Columbia	138.0	1 245	84.1	1 910	43.8	80.8	32.1	91.6	49.91	2 649	1 966
Florence	32.9	1 114	37.0	403	43.8	80.6	33.4	90.4	43.84	2 585	1 993
Goose Creek	NA	NA	NA	NA	NA	NA	NA	NA	NA	NA	NA
Greenville	116.7	2 067	61.6	981	40.1	78.2	30.0	88.2	51.27	3 272	1 473
Hilton Head Island	NA	NA	NA	NA	NA	NA	NA	NA	NA	NA	NA
Mount Pleasant	37.2	901	70.8	NA	47.8	81.5	37.7	90.2	51.53	2 013	2 266
North Charleston	83.1	1 221	0.0	834	47.8	81.5	37.7	90.2	51.53	2 013	2 266
Rock Hill	90.9	1 967	36.0	639	40.9	79.1	30.9	89.2	48.65	3 054	1 624
Spartanburg	106.8	2 607	98.6	712	41.9	79.4	31.5	90.6	49.87	2 887	1 688
Summerville	7.4	306	82.5	NA	NA	NA	NA	NA	NA	NA	NA
Sumter	12.8	317	90.3	463	44.0	80.0	32.4	91.1	48.14	2 609	1 888
SOUTH DAKOTA	X	X	X	X	X	X	X	X	X	X	X
Rapid City	59.4	1 034	9.5	904	22.3	72.2	10.7	86.2	16.64	7 301	611
Sioux Falls	126.2	1 081	9.1	983	13.8	74.3	3.3	86.3	23.86	7 809	744
TENNESSEE	X	X	X	X	X	X	X	X	X	X	X
Bartlett	36.6	1 033	32.7	NA	39.7	82.6	30.9	92.3	52.10	3 082	2 118
Chattanooga	302.9	2 050	0.0	3 257	37.4	78.7	28.0	89.0	53.46	3 587	1 544
Clarksville	106.4	1 086	32.1	1 022	34.0	78.1	23.3	90.0	50.75	4 159	1 417
Cleveland	64.8	1 829	63.1	1 486	36.5	76.6	25.8	88.0	54.65	3 884	1 236
Collierville	33.0	1 391	46.8	NA	NA	NA	NA	NA	NA	NA	NA
Columbia	19.8	621	54.7	NA	34.4	77.1	23.2	88.8	54.26	4 206	1 281
Franklin	NA	NA	NA	NA	NA	NA	NA	NA	NA	NA	NA
Germantown	36.9	981	1.4	NA	39.7	82.6	30.9	92.3	52.10	3 082	2 118
Hendersonville	8.1	209	0.0	NA	36.2	79.3	26.5	89.5	47.30	3 729	1 616
Jackson	89.2	1 744	83.2	1 143	37.0	80.1	27.3	90.9	52.88	3 540	1 744
Johnson City	211.8	3 711	36.3	1 906	34.0	74.4	24.3	84.6	40.72	4 406	972
Kingsport	106.8	2 596	14.6	1 696	36.1	75.8	26.4	87.1	43.79	3 901	1 167
Knoxville	278.5	1 683	53.1	2 748	36.0	76.6	26.0	87.1	47.14	3 937	1 266

1. Based on the population estimated as of July 1 of the year shown.   2. Represents normal values based on the 30-year period, 1961–1990.   3. Average daily minimum.   4. Average daily maximum.

Table D. Cities — **Land Area and Population**

STATE Place code	City	Land area, 2000[1] (sq km)	Population, 2000			Population				Population characteristics, 2000						
										Percent						
										Race (alone or in combination)						
			Total persons	Rank	Per square kilo-meter	Total persons 1990	Percent change 1990–2000	Total persons 1980	Percent change 1980–1990	White	Black	Am. Indian, Alaska Native	Asian and Pacific Islander	Other race	His-panic[2]	Non-His-panic White
		1	2	3	4	5	6	7	8	9	10	11	12	13	14	15
	TENNESSEE—Cont'd															
47 48000	Memphis	723.4	650 100	18	898.7	618 652	5.1	646 356	-4.3	35.2	61.9	0.5	1.8	1.8	3.0	33.3
47 51560	Murfreesboro	101.0	68 816	391	681.3	44 922	53.2	32 845	36.8	80.9	14.4	0.7	3.2	2.3	3.5	78.4
47 52004	Nashville-Davidson	1 300.9	569 891	22	438.1	488 188	11.6	NA	NA	68.5	26.6	0.7	2.9	3.3	4.6	65.1
47 55120	Oak Ridge	221.6	27 387	1 129	123.6	27 310	0.3	27 662	-1.3	88.5	8.9	0.9	2.5	0.9	1.9	85.9
47 69420	Smyrna	59.1	25 569	1 217	432.6	14 720	73.7	NA	NA	88.7	8.4	0.7	1.6	2.4	4.3	85.1
48 00000	TEXAS	678 051.4	20 851 820	X	30.8	16 986 335	22.8	14 225 513	19.4	73.1	12.0	1.0	3.2	13.3	32.0	52.4
48 01000	Abilene	272.3	115 930	193	425.7	106 707	8.6	98 312	8.5	80.1	9.5	1.1	2.0	9.8	19.4	68.8
48 01924	Allen	68.2	43 554	704	638.6	19 315	125.5	NA	NA	88.7	4.8	1.0	4.3	3.1	7.0	83.2
48 03000	Amarillo	232.7	173 627	118	746.1	157 571	10.2	149 230	5.6	79.5	6.4	1.4	2.4	12.6	21.9	68.4
48 04000	Arlington	248.2	332 969	53	1 341.5	261 717	27.2	160 113	63.5	70.1	14.5	1.2	6.8	10.4	18.3	59.6
48 05000	Austin	651.4	656 562	16	1 007.9	472 020	39.1	345 544	36.6	67.8	10.7	1.1	5.6	18.0	30.5	52.9
48 06128	Baytown	84.6	66 430	410	785.2	63 843	4.1	56 923	12.2	70.2	14.0	0.9	1.4	16.3	34.2	50.2
48 07000	Beaumont	220.2	113 866	196	517.1	114 323	-0.4	118 102	-3.2	47.5	46.4	0.6	2.9	4.2	7.9	42.7
48 07132	Bedford	25.9	47 152	645	1 820.5	43 762	7.7	20 821	110.2	89.3	4.0	1.1	4.5	3.1	7.2	83.4
48 08236	Big Spring	49.5	25 233	1 227	509.8	23 093	9.3	24 804	-6.9	78.8	5.7	1.2	1.0	16.0	44.6	48.4
48 10768	Brownsville	208.2	139 722	151	671.1	107 027	30.5	84 997	25.9	83.8	0.5	0.6	0.8	16.7	91.3	7.7
48 10912	Bryan	112.2	65 660	416	585.2	55 002	19.4	44 337	24.1	66.5	18.2	0.8	2.0	14.7	27.8	51.7
48 13024	Carrollton	94.5	109 576	205	1 159.5	82 169	33.4	40 587	102.5	74.1	6.7	0.9	11.9	9.2	19.5	61.2
48 13492	Cedar Hill	91.0	32 093	970	352.7	19 988	60.6	NA	NA	58.4	34.4	1.0	2.5	6.0	11.9	50.8
48 13552	Cedar Park	44.0	26 049	1 192	592.0	5 161	404.7	NA	NA	88.4	3.6	0.9	3.3	6.0	13.5	79.0
48 15364	Cleburne	72.0	26 005	1 194	361.2	22 205	17.1	19 218	15.5	87.9	4.8	1.0	0.8	7.3	19.9	73.9
48 15976	College Station	104.3	67 890	399	650.9	52 443	29.5	37 272	40.7	82.2	5.7	0.7	8.1	5.4	10.0	75.7
48 16432	Conroe	97.9	36 811	842	376.0	27 675	33.0	18 034	53.5	73.8	11.5	0.8	1.4	15.6	32.6	54.5
48 16612	Coppell	38.5	35 958	865	934.0	16 881	113.0	NA	NA	84.7	3.6	0.7	10.4	2.7	6.9	78.7
48 16624	Copperas Cove	36.1	29 592	1 053	819.7	24 079	22.9	19 469	23.7	69.4	22.3	1.8	5.3	6.8	11.7	60.6
48 17000	Corpus Christi	400.5	277 454	60	692.8	257 428	7.8	231 999	11.0	74.4	5.1	1.1	1.9	20.9	54.3	38.5
48 19000	Dallas	887.2	1 188 580	8	1 339.7	1 007 618	18.0	904 074	11.5	53.0	26.5	1.0	3.2	19.2	35.6	34.6
48 19624	Deer Park	26.8	28 520	1 087	1 064.2	27 424	4.0	22 648	21.1	91.6	1.4	0.9	1.7	6.1	15.2	80.8
48 19792	Del Rio	40.0	33 867	925	846.7	30 705	10.3	30 034	2.2	79.5	1.4	1.1	0.8	20.0	81.0	16.7
48 19972	Denton	159.3	80 537	320	505.6	66 270	21.5	48 063	37.9	77.7	9.6	1.2	4.0	10.0	16.4	69.0
48 20092	DeSoto	55.9	37 646	827	673.5	30 544	23.3	15 538	96.6	49.9	46.1	0.7	1.6	3.2	7.3	44.7
48 21628	Duncanville	29.2	36 081	863	1 235.7	35 008	3.1	27 781	26.0	65.6	25.4	0.8	2.5	7.9	15.3	56.5
48 22660	Edinburg	96.8	48 465	623	500.7	31 091	55.9	24 075	29.1	75.4	0.7	0.7	0.9	24.7	88.7	9.8
48 24000	El Paso	645.1	563 662	23	873.8	515 342	9.4	425 259	21.2	76.3	3.5	1.2	1.7	20.8	76.6	18.3
48 24768	Euless	42.1	46 005	662	1 092.8	38 149	20.6	24 002	58.9	77.7	7.1	1.2	10.2	6.9	13.3	68.4
48 25452	Farmers Branch	31.1	27 508	1 123	884.5	24 250	13.4	24 863	-2.5	80.8	2.7	1.0	3.4	14.8	37.2	55.8
48 26232	Flower Mound	105.9	50 702	589	478.8	15 527	226.5	NA	NA	91.7	3.2	0.9	3.7	2.3	5.6	86.9
48 27000	Fort Worth	757.7	534 694	27	705.7	447 619	19.5	385 166	16.2	62.0	20.8	1.1	3.2	15.7	29.8	45.8
48 27648	Friendswood	54.4	29 037	1 070	533.8	22 814	27.3	10 719	112.8	91.5	3.0	0.8	2.9	3.4	8.8	84.5
48 27684	Frisco	181.0	33 714	934	186.3	6 138	449.3	NA	NA	89.0	4.1	0.8	3.0	5.1	11.0	81.4
48 28068	Galveston	119.5	57 247	500	479.1	59 067	-3.1	61 902	-4.6	60.7	26.0	0.9	3.8	11.3	25.8	44.2
48 29000	Garland	147.9	215 768	82	1 458.9	180 635	19.4	138 857	30.1	67.7	12.4	1.1	8.0	13.7	25.6	53.3
48 29336	Georgetown	59.1	28 339	1 091	479.5	14 840	90.9	NA	NA	87.0	3.7	0.7	1.1	9.4	18.1	76.8
48 30464	Grand Prairie	184.9	127 427	168	689.2	99 606	27.9	71 457	39.4	64.8	14.1	1.3	5.1	18.1	33.0	47.2
48 30644	Grapevine	83.6	42 059	728	503.1	29 407	44.0	11 801	147.4	89.6	2.6	1.1	3.2	5.3	11.6	81.8
48 31928	Haltom City	32.1	39 018	795	1 215.5	32 856	18.8	29 014	13.2	78.9	3.1	1.3	8.6	10.7	19.9	67.4
48 32372	Harlingen	88.2	57 564	497	652.7	48 746	18.1	43 543	11.9	81.1	1.1	0.8	1.1	18.6	72.8	25.0
48 35000	Houston	1 500.7	1 953 631	4	1 301.8	1 654 348	19.3	1 595 167	2.7	51.8	25.9	0.8	5.9	18.8	37.4	30.8
48 35528	Huntsville	80.0	35 078	893	438.5	30 628	25.6	23 936	16.7	67.1	26.6	0.7	1.5	5.8	16.2	55.3
48 35576	Hurst	25.6	36 273	857	1 416.9	33 574	8.0	31 420	6.9	87.7	4.5	1.3	2.6	6.0	11.0	80.8
48 37000	Irving	174.1	191 615	100	1 100.6	155 037	23.6	109 943	41.0	66.8	10.8	1.2	9.1	15.4	31.2	48.2
48 38632	Keller	47.8	27 345	1 133	572.1	13 683	99.8	NA	NA	95.0	1.7	0.9	2.3	1.7	4.5	90.7
48 39148	Killeen	91.5	86 911	287	949.8	63 535	36.8	46 296	37.2	49.7	36.1	1.7	7.5	11.2	17.8	39.8
48 39352	Kingsville	35.8	25 575	1 216	714.4	25 276	1.2	28 808	-12.3	74.1	4.7	1.1	2.2	21.4	67.1	26.1
48 40588	Lake Jackson	49.3	26 386	1 173	535.2	22 771	15.9	19 102	19.2	87.9	4.2	0.8	2.8	6.1	14.7	77.6
48 41212	Lancaster	75.9	25 894	1 203	341.2	22 117	17.1	14 807	49.4	39.1	53.8	1.0	0.7	7.5	11.6	33.6
48 41440	La Porte	49.1	31 880	975	649.3	27 923	14.2	14 062	98.6	83.2	6.6	1.0	1.5	9.9	20.5	70.7
48 41464	Laredo	203.2	176 576	115	869.0	122 893	43.7	91 449	34.4	84.6	0.5	0.6	0.6	16.2	94.1	5.0
48 41980	League City	132.7	45 444	672	342.5	30 159	50.7	16 575	82.0	85.7	5.5	0.8	3.8	6.3	13.5	76.6
48 42508	Lewisville	95.3	77 737	339	815.7	46 521	67.1	24 273	91.7	79.3	7.9	1.3	4.5	9.6	17.8	69.1
48 43888	Longview	141.6	73 344	362	518.0	70 311	4.3	62 762	12.0	71.4	22.5	1.0	1.1	5.6	10.3	65.5
48 45000	Lubbock	297.4	199 564	90	671.0	186 206	7.2	173 979	7.0	74.6	9.1	1.0	1.9	15.6	27.5	61.3
48 45072	Lufkin	69.2	32 709	956	472.7	30 210	8.3	28 562	5.8	61.2	27.1	0.6	1.6	11.2	17.6	53.7
48 45384	McAllen	119.1	106 414	216	893.5	84 021	26.7	66 281	26.8	81.0	0.7	0.6	2.3	18.2	80.3	16.8
48 45744	McKinney	150.3	54 369	545	361.7	21 283	155.5	16 256	30.9	80.3	7.7	1.1	1.9	11.3	18.2	71.5
48 46452	Mansfield	94.5	28 031	1 101	296.6	15 615	79.5	NA	NA	87.9	4.8	1.0	1.6	6.6	12.8	80.3
48 47892	Mesquite	112.4	124 523	172	1 107.9	101 484	22.7	67 053	51.3	75.6	13.8	1.2	4.2	7.6	15.7	65.4
48 48072	Midland	172.5	94 996	250	550.7	89 343	6.2	70 525	26.8	77.2	8.7	1.0	1.3	13.7	29.0	60.6
48 48768	Mission	62.5	45 408	673	726.5	28 653	58.5	22 551	27.1	79.8	0.5	0.6	0.8	20.7	81.0	17.7

1. Dry land or land partially or temporarily covered by water. 2. Hispanic persons may be of any race.

City	Under 5 years	5 to 17 years	18 to 24 years	25 to 34 years	35 to 44 years	45 to 54 years	55 to 64 years	65 to 74 years	75 years and over	Percent female	Number	Percent change, 1990–2000	Persons per household	Female family householder[1]	One-person
	16	17	18	19	20	21	22	23	24	25	26	27	28	29	30
TENNESSEE—Cont'd															
Memphis	7.8	20.1	10.8	15.8	14.9	12.4	7.2	5.6	5.3	52.7	250 721	9.1	2.52	23.8	30.5
Murfreesboro	6.5	16.2	20.5	16.4	14.4	11.0	6.3	4.6	4.2	50.3	26 511	54.9	2.42	11.9	28.3
Nashville-Davidson	6.6	15.6	11.6	17.6	16.4	13.2	7.9	5.9	5.3	51.6	237 405	14.4	2.30	14.3	33.4
Oak Ridge	4.8	17.7	6.6	9.5	14.1	15.7	10.6	9.7	11.4	53.2	12 062	2.5	2.24	11.1	32.7
Smyrna	8.6	19.0	10.5	17.3	17.8	12.4	7.5	3.9	2.9	51.1	9 608	98.7	2.62	14.2	21.1
TEXAS	7.8	20.4	10.5	15.2	15.9	12.5	7.7	5.5	4.5	50.4	7 393 354	21.8	2.74	12.7	23.7
Abilene	7.1	18.5	15.3	14.1	14.7	10.9	7.3	6.3	5.7	49.5	41 570	8.3	2.53	11.9	26.6
Allen	10.7	24.3	5.4	17.4	23.2	11.7	4.5	1.7	1.1	50.1	14 205	140.9	3.07	7.4	11.9
Amarillo	8.0	19.9	10.2	13.9	14.9	12.5	8.0	6.7	5.9	52.0	67 699	10.7	2.53	12.8	27.7
Arlington	8.3	20.0	11.0	18.5	17.2	12.3	6.5	3.6	2.5	50.0	124 686	23.9	2.65	11.8	24.7
Austin	7.1	15.4	16.6	21.1	16.0	11.6	5.6	3.5	3.2	48.6	265 649	38.3	2.40	10.8	32.8
Baytown	8.7	21.3	11.2	15.2	14.2	12.4	7.0	4.9	5.0	51.5	23 483	4.7	2.80	14.2	23.0
Beaumont	7.1	20.0	10.4	13.2	14.8	13.0	8.2	6.8	6.6	52.5	44 361	2.3	2.50	18.1	29.5
Bedford	5.9	16.6	9.7	15.9	17.1	16.7	9.5	4.8	3.9	51.8	20 251	15.2	2.30	8.8	31.6
Big Spring	6.1	17.5	9.9	16.3	16.4	12.2	7.6	7.2	6.9	44.4	8 155	-1.2	2.51	14.1	29.2
Brownsville	9.9	24.8	11.2	14.6	12.9	10.6	6.6	5.4	4.1	52.9	38 174	45.0	3.62	20.9	13.7
Bryan	8.0	19.0	18.1	16.6	13.2	9.7	6.1	4.5	4.8	50.2	23 759	14.8	2.65	14.0	26.1
Carrollton	7.9	20.3	8.0	17.3	19.8	14.3	7.1	3.2	2.1	50.5	39 136	28.5	2.78	9.4	20.1
Cedar Hill	8.5	24.1	7.7	15.9	19.9	13.7	5.6	2.6	2.1	52.3	10 748	63.6	2.96	14.4	15.0
Cedar Park	11.0	22.6	6.0	19.2	21.1	11.0	4.8	2.4	1.9	50.6	8 621	417.5	3.00	9.6	12.5
Cleburne	8.2	19.7	9.7	14.7	13.9	12.3	7.8	6.5	7.3	51.5	9 335	14.5	2.71	11.9	24.0
College Station	4.5	10.0	51.2	13.0	8.3	6.0	3.4	1.9	1.7	48.9	24 691	38.1	2.32	6.8	27.1
Conroe	8.7	19.4	13.4	17.5	14.1	10.6	6.7	4.9	4.8	49.7	13 145	31.2	2.73	13.5	27.2
Coppell	9.5	25.2	4.5	13.7	25.3	14.5	4.7	1.6	1.0	50.7	12 211	103.6	2.94	8.1	16.1
Copperas Cove	10.2	21.8	14.2	17.8	15.5	9.2	6.1	3.3	1.7	50.5	10 273	27.2	2.85	12.7	16.7
Corpus Christi	7.8	20.4	10.6	13.6	15.6	13.2	7.8	6.1	5.0	51.1	98 791	10.4	2.75	15.4	23.2
Dallas	8.3	18.2	11.8	19.8	15.5	11.1	6.5	4.5	4.1	49.6	451 833	12.4	2.58	14.9	32.9
Deer Park	6.3	22.7	9.4	12.1	18.2	15.9	8.0	4.6	2.8	50.3	9 615	9.0	2.93	11.5	14.0
Del Rio	8.6	23.1	8.8	14.2	13.4	11.4	8.8	6.5	5.2	51.5	10 778	13.9	3.09	15.8	18.7
Denton	6.2	14.5	25.0	17.9	12.9	9.9	5.8	3.8	4.1	50.8	30 895	20.1	2.35	9.5	31.5
DeSoto	7.0	21.1	7.6	12.5	17.7	16.0	8.8	4.9	4.4	53.0	13 709	27.5	2.71	14.1	20.6
Duncanville	6.5	21.6	8.5	12.3	15.4	16.1	10.0	5.7	3.9	52.6	12 896	3.1	2.79	16.1	17.6
Edinburg	9.8	23.2	13.1	16.3	13.5	9.9	6.0	4.8	3.5	51.2	14 183	67.4	3.29	19.0	15.4
El Paso	8.5	22.6	10.0	14.3	14.8	11.7	7.5	6.2	4.4	52.5	182 063	13.4	3.07	18.5	19.2
Euless	7.4	17.5	9.8	20.5	19.2	12.5	7.3	3.8	2.0	50.4	19 218	24.3	2.38	10.9	31.0
Farmers Branch	7.3	18.4	9.5	15.4	16.0	12.0	9.3	7.5	4.6	49.7	9 766	11.3	2.80	9.8	22.9
Flower Mound	10.7	24.1	4.2	14.8	24.7	13.9	4.9	1.6	1.1	50.2	16 179	222.4	3.12	5.4	9.1
Fort Worth	8.5	19.8	11.3	17.0	15.7	11.5	6.7	5.0	4.6	50.7	195 078	15.9	2.67	14.7	28.6
Friendswood	6.6	23.5	6.2	10.4	19.0	16.5	9.2	4.8	3.8	51.6	10 107	30.3	2.85	8.7	17.0
Frisco	12.8	18.0	5.3	25.6	20.3	9.5	5.0	2.2	1.4	50.5	12 065	482.9	2.78	6.3	15.6
Galveston	6.6	16.7	11.3	14.5	15.3	13.1	8.7	7.5	6.2	51.7	23 842	-1.3	2.30	16.9	35.6
Garland	8.2	21.6	9.6	16.0	17.0	13.1	7.4	4.2	2.9	50.4	73 241	15.9	2.93	13.7	19.8
Georgetown	6.4	17.0	11.4	12.6	13.7	11.4	9.8	9.6	8.0	51.3	10 393	100.7	2.52	9.5	21.5
Grand Prairie	8.9	21.7	10.1	17.2	16.9	12.1	6.7	3.7	2.6	50.5	43 791	25.3	2.90	13.7	20.7
Grapevine	7.4	21.9	7.5	14.5	22.1	15.7	6.2	2.5	2.2	49.9	15 712	43.2	2.66	9.4	22.2
Haltom City	8.2	18.9	10.2	17.1	15.8	11.9	7.5	5.8	4.6	49.8	14 922	17.0	2.61	12.0	27.1
Harlingen	9.1	21.7	9.6	13.9	12.7	11.0	7.0	7.5	7.6	52.4	19 021	23.5	2.94	16.2	20.9
Houston	8.2	19.2	11.2	18.1	15.6	12.0	7.1	4.8	3.6	50.1	717 945	16.4	2.67	15.3	29.6
Huntsville	4.6	10.5	29.3	15.0	15.7	10.5	5.9	4.4	4.1	39.5	10 266	30.7	2.31	12.5	30.8
Hurst	7.2	18.2	8.3	13.6	16.7	13.3	10.3	7.4	5.0	51.4	14 076	10.1	2.56	11.6	22.4
Irving	8.1	17.9	11.9	22.8	16.7	10.8	6.5	3.7	2.4	49.0	76 241	20.6	2.59	11.2	31.3
Keller	8.6	25.1	4.7	11.6	23.1	15.6	7.0	2.8	1.6	50.3	8 827	96.7	3.09	5.6	8.9
Killeen	10.1	19.8	16.0	20.7	15.0	8.9	4.6	3.2	1.7	49.8	32 447	39.6	2.67	13.4	22.3
Kingsville	8.0	18.9	17.3	15.3	11.8	10.6	7.7	5.6	4.9	50.1	8 943	4.9	2.73	14.9	23.5
Lake Jackson	7.4	23.2	7.6	12.5	17.8	14.3	7.4	5.5	4.4	51.2	9 588	17.8	2.74	8.5	20.0
Lancaster	8.2	22.2	8.6	15.2	17.1	12.8	6.8	4.5	4.5	53.9	9 182	19.2	2.77	20.8	21.3
La Porte	7.9	21.8	8.9	15.1	17.6	14.7	7.1	3.9	3.0	50.4	10 928	19.5	2.90	11.4	17.4
Laredo	10.5	25.0	11.4	16.1	13.4	9.7	6.1	4.4	3.4	52.0	46 852	46.3	3.70	18.7	12.7
League City	8.1	21.3	6.6	15.1	20.7	14.8	7.4	3.4	2.5	50.2	16 189	52.9	2.78	8.2	18.4
Lewisville	9.1	17.5	11.8	23.4	17.8	10.6	5.5	2.5	1.8	50.0	30 043	69.9	2.58	9.6	25.2
Longview	7.4	19.4	10.8	13.7	15.0	12.4	8.1	6.9	6.4	51.8	28 363	4.3	2.50	14.5	27.9
Lubbock	7.2	17.8	17.9	14.2	13.5	11.3	7.1	5.9	5.2	51.4	77 527	12.1	2.47	12.9	28.3
Lufkin	8.0	19.0	10.6	13.6	13.7	11.8	8.3	7.1	8.1	52.9	12 247	9.1	2.58	14.7	27.9
McAllen	8.7	22.1	10.5	15.3	14.0	11.8	7.1	5.6	4.9	52.6	33 151	33.1	3.18	16.0	17.9
McKinney	10.1	20.9	9.3	18.1	18.3	10.7	5.8	3.5	3.3	49.4	18 186	139.4	2.89	9.5	19.0
Mansfield	8.4	23.4	7.8	14.9	19.7	13.2	6.9	3.4	2.3	49.3	8 881	73.1	3.08	8.3	10.9
Mesquite	7.7	22.8	9.2	15.2	18.7	12.4	6.9	4.3	2.8	51.8	43 926	22.5	2.82	14.0	20.6
Midland	7.5	22.4	9.0	12.2	16.0	13.1	7.4	6.9	5.4	52.0	35 674	7.6	2.62	11.9	25.8
Mission	9.2	22.9	9.8	13.8	13.0	10.1	6.9	7.4	6.8	52.3	13 766	65.6	3.29	14.5	15.3

1. No spouse present.

Table D. Cities — **Group Quarters, Crime, Education, and Income**

City	Persons in group quarters, 2000				Serious crimes known to police, 2000[2]				Education, 1990				Money income, 1989		
		Institutional			Total		Rate[3]		School enrollment		Attainment[4] (percent)			Households	
														Median	
	Total	Total	Persons in nursing homes	Non-Institutional[1]	Number	Rate[3]	Violent	Property	Public	Private	High school graduate or more	Bachelor's degree or more	Per capita (dollars)[5]	Dollars	Percent change, 1979–1989 (constant 1989 dollars)
	31	32	33	34	35	36	37	38	39	40	41	42	43	44	45
TENNESSEE—Cont'd															
Memphis	17 226	11 067	3 709	6 159	59 620	9 171	1 479	7 692	134 579	24 065	70.4	17.5	11 682	22 674	-3.6
Murfreesboro	4 648	1 280	647	3 368	3 872	5 627	655	4 971	14 856	693	77.0	27.2	12 983	26 394	10.2
Nashville-Davidson	24 165	10 298	2 335	13 867	48 716	8 807	1 623	7 184	86 713	34 707	75.9	24.4	15 195	28 377	NA
Oak Ridge	423	282	271	141	1 589	5 802	424	5 378	5 777	519	85.6	35.5	17 661	32 615	-1.6
Smyrna	367	342	185	25	1 353	5 292	422	4 869	3 312	298	70.4	11.2	11 864	31 155	NA
TEXAS	561 109	374 704	105 052	186 405	1 033 311	4 956	545	4 410	4 313 852	492 043	72.1	20.3	12 904	27 016	-3.5
Abilene	10 932	5 832	754	5 100	4 797	4 138	348	3 789	22 076	8 601	76.0	22.0	11 857	24 725	-2.3
Allen	13	1	0	12	1 139	2 615	145	2 470	5 519	647	93.7	31.9	16 040	47 869	NA
Amarillo	2 309	1 625	1 459	684	13 728	7 907	826	7 081	38 082	3 383	75.7	17.8	12 744	24 915	-11.7
Arlington	2 448	954	832	1 494	21 480	6 451	648	5 803	63 396	9 712	87.8	30.0	16 239	35 048	-1.1
Austin	20 130	6 799	1 892	13 331	38 979	5 937	472	5 465	136 404	15 087	82.3	34.4	14 295	25 414	3.1
Baytown	631	443	417	188	3 255	4 900	360	4 540	16 749	1 112	71.2	14.7	12 963	30 151	-16.7
Beaumont	3 069	2 045	771	1 024	8 243	7 239	942	6 297	27 247	4 513	75.2	19.7	12 751	24 495	-13.9
Bedford	533	519	491	14	1 607	3 408	244	3 164	10 534	1 441	93.0	34.3	19 847	42 453	-5.4
Big Spring	4 786	4 392	147	394	1 187	4 704	376	4 328	5 487	244	64.2	13.0	10 263	21 298	-8.7
Brownsville	1 691	1 454	688	237	11 420	8 173	653	7 521	34 454	2 204	45.5	12.2	6 284	15 890	-18.9
Bryan	2 622	2 241	387	381	4 484	6 829	670	6 159	16 906	1 454	73.7	26.9	11 691	22 577	-2.5
Carrollton	589	375	370	214	3 709	3 385	190	3 195	18 429	3 305	89.9	37.4	19 065	45 787	6.6
Cedar Hill	272	138	129	134	1 090	3 396	299	3 097	5 083	843	86.1	28.2	15 194	41 457	NA
Cedar Park	168	144	133	24	541	2 077	92	1 985	NA	NA	NA	NA	NA	NA	NA
Cleburne	700	644	341	56	1 811	6 964	350	6 614	4 995	385	68.8	13.2	12 064	26 037	1.0
College Station	10 703	217	217	10 486	2 666	3 927	197	3 730	35 207	1 269	93.8	58.9	9 262	14 481	-11.7
Conroe	862	774	187	88	2 593	7 044	834	6 210	6 562	661	69.8	18.3	11 477	23 634	-17.5
Coppell	4	1	0	3	177	492	31	462	3 837	577	94.7	47.0	22 512	58 815	NA
Copperas Cove	284	180	180	104	1 169	3 950	493	3 457	6 573	559	87.7	13.9	9 509	24 596	4.2
Corpus Christi	5 332	2 536	1 329	2 796	20 009	7 212	758	6 453	70 472	6 576	70.9	17.8	11 755	25 773	-8.5
Dallas	21 164	15 899	5 399	5 265	105 050	8 838	1 350	7 489	207 066	38 835	73.5	27.1	16 300	27 489	1.1
Deer Park	303	89	89	214	574	2 013	88	1 925	8 267	719	84.3	15.3	15 645	46 199	-4.0
Del Rio	528	433	185	95	1 522	4 494	428	4 066	8 824	629	52.8	11.1	7 522	17 394	-8.1
Denton	7 842	2 463	667	5 379	3 233	4 014	335	3 679	26 259	1 443	81.9	36.4	12 013	23 156	-4.7
DeSoto	434	423	423	11	1 579	4 194	505	3 690	7 572	1 388	88.0	29.4	18 093	45 550	-2.2
Duncanville	90	63	57	27	1 512	4 191	466	3 725	9 306	1 423	87.0	29.0	17 060	41 028	-4.8
Edinburg	1 779	1 525	82	254	4 692	9 681	675	9 006	10 025	744	56.2	19.4	7 474	18 956	-5.6
El Paso	5 129	3 248	1 329	1 881	34 672	6 151	780	5 371	160 046	12 978	65.3	16.2	9 603	23 460	-1.6
Euless	213	166	165	47	1 517	3 297	222	3 076	8 026	1 144	86.2	25.8	16 633	34 950	2.0
Farmers Branch	156	6	0	150	1 420	5 162	298	4 864	5 126	739	79.5	25.1	17 122	38 037	-10.5
Flower Mound	212	142	93	70	704	1 389	75	1 314	3 977	744	93.6	35.6	19 066	53 693	NA
Fort Worth	14 754	9 513	3 392	5 241	38 143	7 134	714	6 420	92 695	20 327	71.6	21.5	13 162	26 547	3.5
Friendswood	242	232	232	10	466	1 605	231	1 374	6 530	530	92.6	34.9	20 409	50 492	-5.7
Frisco	115	77	77	38	795	2 358	116	2 242	NA	NA	NA	NA	NA	NA	NA
Galveston	2 364	1 250	330	1 114	4 261	7 443	643	6 800	14 619	1 699	70.0	21.1	12 399	20 825	-14.0
Garland	1 037	557	517	480	8 673	4 020	218	3 801	44 069	6 388	82.6	24.3	15 056	37 274	-1.9
Georgetown	2 119	1 062	468	1 057	588	2 075	60	2 015	3 323	1 292	73.3	23.2	12 048	25 953	NA
Grand Prairie	420	377	377	43	6 521	5 117	350	4 767	24 379	3 092	76.3	19.4	13 752	34 507	5.0
Grapevine	212	211	211	1	1 765	4 196	105	4 092	6 557	833	89.4	35.1	19 526	48 901	29.6
Haltom City	126	126	125	0	1 347	3 452	325	3 127	6 333	771	69.6	9.8	11 764	25 392	-12.8
Harlingen	1 590	1 174	732	416	4 109	7 138	526	6 612	13 775	1 156	59.3	14.8	9 183	20 858	3.1
Houston	33 256	18 819	5 774	14 437	131 711	6 742	1 100	5 642	387 704	57 424	70.5	25.1	14 261	26 261	-15.2
Huntsville	11 377	8 904	249	2 473	1 399	3 988	439	3 549	10 930	747	73.4	21.4	9 273	17 876	-4.5
Hurst	231	217	216	14	2 174	5 993	369	5 624	7 400	945	86.1	22.4	16 621	37 473	-6.5
Irving	1 073	468	410	605	9 025	4 710	409	4 301	31 464	6 880	80.7	26.2	16 424	31 767	-6.1
Keller	28	28	28	0	531	1 942	293	1 649	3 336	420	90.1	29.9	20 231	55 050	NA
Killeen	310	255	230	55	5 203	5 987	662	5 325	15 510	1 084	85.8	14.4	9 582	22 468	13.3
Kingsville	1 180	279	143	901	1 233	4 821	450	4 371	8 871	516	64.2	20.4	9 338	22 053	-2.4
Lake Jackson	106	106	106	0	924	3 502	99	3 403	6 019	760	90.2	33.3	18 798	46 007	-0.2
Lancaster	497	497	247	0	1 546	5 970	761	5 210	5 749	693	75.8	16.8	12 553	31 489	-6.9
La Porte	235	38	38	197	688	2 158	238	1 920	7 960	472	81.6	14.4	14 349	41 733	2.4
Laredo	3 044	1 929	388	1 115	13 384	7 580	550	7 029	41 001	3 279	48.8	11.6	6 981	18 395	3.5
League City	390	357	261	33	1 067	2 348	108	2 240	8 090	877	89.2	32.3	17 932	45 043	3.6
Lewisville	361	127	115	234	3 316	4 266	216	4 050	11 127	1 490	84.7	25.5	15 316	36 006	-0.6
Longview	2 496	1 601	790	895	5 147	7 018	646	6 371	15 714	2 684	77.4	18.9	12 761	25 377	-12.4
Lubbock	8 456	2 653	1 054	5 803	14 493	7 262	1 257	6 006	58 505	5 047	75.6	26.0	12 322	24 130	-8.5
Lufkin	1 122	824	633	298	2 228	6 812	639	6 173	7 361	641	68.9	18.8	12 527	22 357	-11.8
McAllen	986	811	752	175	8 740	8 213	366	7 848	26 121	2 017	57.9	19.1	9 814	22 068	-9.2
McKinney	1 827	1 093	397	734	1 873	3 445	291	3 154	4 725	391	69.0	19.0	14 119	27 236	22.9
Mansfield	648	574	68	74	764	2 726	200	2 526	3 930	334	82.0	20.0	14 506	38 108	NA
Mesquite	700	643	615	57	6 059	4 866	343	4 523	25 110	3 195	81.2	18.3	14 115	35 934	-1.2
Midland	1 422	1 042	718	380	3 301	5 303	416	3 059	21 706	2 534	78.3	29.0	16 201	31 544	-11.4
Mission	110	105	105	5	2 843	6 261	121	6 140	9 069	472	52.6	12.2	6 887	17 489	-8.5

1. Persons in emergency shelters and persons visible in street locations. 2. Data for serious crimes have not been adjusted for underreporting. This may affect comparability between geographic areas and over time. 3. Per 100,000 population estimated by the FBI. 4. Persons 25 years old and older. 5. Based on population enumerated as of April 1, 1990.

Table D. Cities — Income, Poverty, and Housing

City	Money income, 1989 (cont'd) Households (cont'd) Percent with $100,000 or more	Percent below poverty, 1989 Persons Total	Percent change in rate, 1979–1989	Families Total	Housing units, 2000 Total	Percent change, 1990–2000	Vacant units for sale or rent[1]	For seasonal use (percent)	Home owner vacancy rate	Renter vacancy rate	Occupied units Total	Percent owner occupied	Percent renter occupied	Average size owner occupied	Average size renter occupied
	46	47	48	49	50	51	52	53	54	55	56	57	58	59	60
TENNESSEE—Cont'd															
Memphis	2.9	23.0	5.5	18.7	271 552	9.2	20 831	0.3	2.0	8.4	250 721	55.8	44.2	2.62	2.40
Murfreesboro	2.4	16.0	0.6	9.9	28 815	54.0	2 304	0.4	3.1	9.8	26 511	52.1	47.9	2.63	2.19
Nashville-Davidson	3.8	13.0	NA	10.0	252 977	10.4	15 572	0.4	2.0	6.5	237 405	55.3	44.7	2.43	2.13
Oak Ridge	4.1	9.5	13.1	7.0	13 417	5.7	1 355	0.4	2.3	18.3	12 062	68.4	31.6	2.33	2.03
Smyrna	1.0	11.0	NA	9.9	10 016	88.6	408	0.1	1.8	5.3	9 608	64.5	35.5	2.76	2.38
TEXAS	3.7	18.1	23.1	14.1	8 157 575	16.4	764 221	2.1	1.8	8.5	7 393 354	63.8	36.2	2.87	2.53
Abilene	2.3	15.3	26.4	11.0	45 618	2.7	4 048	0.4	2.3	10.4	41 570	58.6	41.4	2.61	2.40
Allen	2.9	3.1	NA	2.5	15 227	146.7	1 022	0.1	1.6	26.3	14 205	85.7	14.3	3.13	2.69
Amarillo	2.6	16.8	69.7	13.1	72 408	5.6	4 709	0.3	1.7	8.1	67 699	63.3	36.7	2.64	2.34
Arlington	4.4	8.2	39.0	5.7	130 628	15.8	5 942	0.3	1.4	6.1	124 686	54.7	45.3	2.87	2.38
Austin	3.5	17.9	13.3	11.5	276 842	27.5	11 193	0.5	1.0	3.5	265 649	44.8	55.2	2.65	2.19
Baytown	3.3	16.1	56.3	13.4	26 203	4.7	2 720	0.6	1.4	14.3	23 483	59.6	40.4	2.91	2.64
Beaumont	3.5	21.1	34.4	16.6	48 815	-0.4	4 454	0.4	1.7	9.9	44 361	59.9	40.1	2.58	2.37
Bedford	6.6	3.6	12.5	2.3	21 113	12.0	862	0.2	0.7	6.7	20 251	55.0	45.0	2.64	1.89
Big Spring	0.9	23.4	46.3	19.8	9 865	0.1	1 710	0.4	4.9	23.7	8 155	63.6	36.4	2.53	2.47
Brownsville	1.3	43.9	31.8	38.5	42 323	46.0	4 149	3.0	1.1	8.0	38 174	61.2	38.8	3.74	3.42
Bryan	2.2	22.0	17.6	16.1	25 703	11.7	1 944	0.6	2.0	7.7	23 759	50.8	49.2	2.80	2.51
Carrollton	6.8	4.5	55.2	3.2	40 458	22.6	1 322	0.4	1.0	5.0	39 136	65.7	34.3	2.90	2.56
Cedar Hill	4.0	3.7	NA	3.5	11 075	57.3	327	0.1	1.3	2.8	10 748	81.0	19.0	3.03	2.67
Cedar Park	NA	NA	NA	NA	8 914	385.2	293	0.1	1.5	4.6	8 621	84.4	15.6	3.04	2.80
Cleburne	2.9	14.9	40.6	10.3	9 910	7.3	575	0.3	1.9	4.6	9 335	66.8	33.2	2.71	2.70
College Station	2.4	38.0	17.6	16.6	26 054	31.3	1 363	0.4	1.4	5.0	24 691	30.6	69.4	2.78	2.11
Conroe	2.4	18.8	35.3	15.1	14 378	25.0	1 233	0.3	1.5	10.0	13 145	47.3	52.7	3.00	2.50
Coppell	11.7	2.5	NA	2.0	12 587	96.5	376	0.3	1.2	5.5	12 211	77.2	22.8	3.15	2.23
Copperas Cove	0.5	12.0	0.0	10.1	11 120	19.5	847	0.2	2.6	9.9	10 273	54.2	45.8	2.94	2.76
Corpus Christi	2.7	20.0	27.4	16.4	107 831	7.6	9 040	1.0	2.0	9.5	98 791	59.6	40.4	2.89	2.56
Dallas	6.2	18.0	26.8	14.7	484 117	4.0	32 284	0.3	1.4	7.0	451 833	43.2	56.8	2.78	2.44
Deer Park	3.9	5.2	40.5	3.6	9 921	8.7	306	0.2	0.4	8.3	9 615	79.3	20.7	2.97	2.79
Del Rio	0.9	38.3	18.9	31.3	11 895	11.3	1 117	0.7	1.9	8.4	10 778	64.6	35.4	3.17	2.96
Denton	2.4	20.7	46.8	9.9	32 716	13.6	1 821	0.2	2.0	5.5	30 895	41.9	58.1	2.67	2.12
DeSoto	6.7	4.0	100.0	2.7	14 069	20.8	360	0.2	1.2	2.6	13 709	72.2	27.8	2.88	2.30
Duncanville	5.5	3.8	18.8	2.6	13 290	-0.5	394	0.1	1.0	4.6	12 896	71.7	28.3	2.84	2.66
Edinburg	1.9	33.8	20.7	30.8	16 031	74.1	1 848	2.5	1.7	8.2	14 183	61.7	38.3	3.45	3.03
El Paso	2.4	25.3	19.3	21.2	193 663	14.8	11 600	0.4	1.6	7.9	182 063	61.4	38.6	3.20	2.86
Euless	3.2	5.4	3.8	4.0	20 136	17.6	918	0.3	1.0	5.9	19 218	43.8	56.2	2.66	2.17
Farmers Branch	6.9	6.7	63.4	4.2	10 115	9.8	349	0.3	1.1	4.8	9 766	68.0	32.0	2.70	3.02
Flower Mound	6.7	1.1	NA	0.7	16 833	213.7	654	0.1	1.6	17.2	16 179	92.9	7.1	3.15	2.74
Fort Worth	3.2	17.4	25.2	13.6	211 035	8.5	15 957	0.3	1.9	9.1	195 078	55.9	44.1	2.84	2.44
Friendswood	9.6	2.9	70.6	2.3	10 405	29.3	298	0.2	1.1	6.1	10 107	80.1	19.9	3.00	2.25
Frisco	NA	NA	NA	NA	13 683	504.6	1 618	0.2	2.0	34.9	12 065	81.3	18.7	2.86	2.44
Galveston	3.1	24.2	52.2	20.0	30 017	-2.9	6 175	7.5	3.2	15.9	23 842	43.6	56.4	2.43	2.20
Garland	3.6	7.8	52.9	5.8	75 300	8.2	2 059	0.1	1.1	3.5	73 241	65.6	34.4	2.98	2.84
Georgetown	2.2	17.9	NA	13.5	10 902	89.0	509	0.6	2.2	3.6	10 393	68.7	31.3	2.54	2.48
Grand Prairie	2.3	10.0	14.9	7.7	46 425	19.9	2 634	0.6	1.2	7.8	43 791	61.2	38.8	3.06	2.65
Grapevine	7.1	4.2	-12.5	2.5	16 486	38.5	774	0.3	0.6	9.2	15 712	65.0	35.0	2.88	2.26
Haltom City	1.4	12.1	28.7	9.3	15 716	12.0	794	0.4	1.1	5.4	14 922	59.5	40.5	2.77	2.37
Harlingen	1.6	29.9	13.3	25.3	23 008	29.3	3 987	8.9	2.3	13.1	19 021	61.1	38.9	2.94	2.94
Houston	4.8	20.7	63.0	17.2	782 009	7.7	64 064	0.5	1.6	8.7	717 945	45.8	54.2	2.84	2.54
Huntsville	2.0	30.0	22.4	17.4	11 508	26.0	1 242	0.5	2.3	11.5	10 266	43.5	56.5	2.54	2.13
Hurst	4.4	7.8	110.8	5.3	14 729	6.7	653	0.2	0.7	9.1	14 076	66.1	33.9	2.60	2.48
Irving	3.8	10.5	75.0	7.7	80 293	13.0	4 052	0.6	1.1	5.2	76 241	37.2	62.8	2.76	2.35
Keller	14.1	2.5	NA	1.8	9 216	92.3	389	0.1	2.9	6.9	8 827	92.7	7.3	3.12	2.74
Killeen	0.6	14.5	-19.0	11.8	35 343	33.7	2 896	0.2	3.0	13.6	32 447	46.4	53.6	2.92	2.45
Kingsville	1.6	27.3	25.8	21.9	10 427	3.2	1 484	0.4	2.3	17.1	8 943	55.0	45.0	2.85	2.58
Lake Jackson	6.8	3.4	-27.7	2.2	10 475	16.9	887	0.8	1.6	16.7	9 588	71.1	28.9	2.87	2.41
Lancaster	2.0	10.1	42.3	7.9	9 590	13.5	408	0.2	1.6	5.2	9 182	65.6	34.4	2.88	2.55
La Porte	2.9	8.8	4.8	7.1	11 720	17.6	792	0.4	1.9	11.4	10 928	77.2	22.8	2.98	2.61
Laredo	2.2	37.3	8.1	32.2	50 319	48.0	3 467	0.9	1.3	5.8	46 852	64.4	35.6	3.87	3.40
League City	5.3	4.9	36.1	3.6	17 280	51.8	1 091	0.6	2.3	11.5	16 189	77.0	23.0	2.92	2.32
Lewisville	2.1	6.0	46.3	3.9	31 764	61.0	1 721	0.2	1.5	7.7	30 043	53.9	46.1	2.92	2.18
Longview	2.6	17.0	44.1	13.7	30 726	1.4	2 363	0.4	2.0	10.1	28 363	58.3	41.7	2.61	2.34
Lubbock	3.1	19.6	36.1	13.3	84 066	8.0	6 539	0.2	1.7	10.1	77 527	55.8	44.2	2.64	2.25
Lufkin	3.0	20.9	28.2	15.4	13 402	7.3	1 155	0.5	2.2	8.3	12 247	60.0	40.0	2.64	2.49
McAllen	3.9	32.7	23.9	27.7	37 922	32.6	4 771	4.5	2.2	10.7	33 151	63.3	36.7	3.33	2.92
McKinney	4.8	17.5	-6.9	10.6	19 462	127.9	1 276	0.2	2.7	10.4	18 186	70.2	29.8	3.00	2.62
Mansfield	3.9	7.3	NA	6.0	9 172	66.2	291	0.2	1.4	5.0	8 881	86.6	13.4	3.08	3.08
Mesquite	1.8	7.7	48.1	6.3	46 245	17.8	2 319	0.2	1.4	8.5	43 926	65.5	34.5	2.99	2.50
Midland	5.7	14.4	65.5	11.3	39 855	3.6	4 181	0.3	2.3	17.7	35 674	66.1	33.9	2.81	2.25
Mission	1.2	37.3	18.8	30.3	17 723	66.3	3 957	15.0	1.7	7.9	13 766	74.9	25.1	3.27	3.36

1. Includes units rented or sold but not occupied. 2. Specified owner-occupied units. 3. Specified renter-occupied units. 4. Overcrowded or lacking complete plumbing facilities.

Table D. Cities — **Labor Force, Employment, Disability, and Construction**

City	Civilian labor force, 2001				Civilian employment, 1990[2]			Disability 1990	Value of residential construction authorized by building permits, 2000		
			Unemployment			Percent					
	Total	Percent change, 2000–2001	Total	Rate[1]	Total	Professional, managerial, and technical	Precision production, craft, and repair	Work disabled persons[3] (percent)	New construction ($1,000)	Number of housing units	Percent single family
	61	62	63	64	65	66	67	68	69	70	71
TENNESSEE—Cont'd											
Memphis	319 547	0.7	16 291	5.1	267 179	27.7	8.8	9.2	NA	NA	NA
Murfreesboro	38 287	1.7	1 739	4.5	23 249	31.2	8.5	7.6	125 153	1 731	55.5
Nashville-Davidson	308 184	1.1	9 498	3.1	264 680	33.4	8.6	7.3	440 545	3 005	76.3
Oak Ridge	14 788	1.8	458	3.1	12 673	50.0	8.5	8.8	8 214	56	100.0
Smyrna	11 249	1.6	429	3.8	6 883	21.4	13.2	9.1	38 564	652	60.6
TEXAS	10 462 712	1.3	507 442	4.9	7 634 279	30.0	11.7	7.6	15 418 411	141 231	76.9
Abilene	50 735	-3.3	2 049	4.0	44 317	31.9	10.0	8.3	33 191	363	42.1
Allen	20 254	2.4	758	3.7	10 079	40.6	10.6	3.9	421 709	1 885	87.9
Amarillo	93 124	-1.2	3 159	3.4	73 106	27.0	12.9	8.5	66 601	520	99.6
Arlington	195 549	1.5	7 132	3.6	146 327	35.4	9.8	5.1	239 583	2 375	93.6
Austin	400 217	2.3	17 310	4.3	244 056	39.8	7.5	5.9	694 396	8 528	39.4
Baytown	36 147	1.8	1 852	5.1	27 419	25.1	20.3	7.4	14 736	127	100.0
Beaumont	56 105	-1.4	4 302	7.7	48 706	31.6	9.9	9.5	32 868	290	98.3
Bedford	34 895	1.2	891	2.6	26 408	40.1	7.4	4.1	10 759	99	100.0
Big Spring	9 536	2.2	417	4.4	8 479	27.6	14.5	12.1	964	15	100.0
Brownsville	49 994	2.2	5 329	10.7	31 884	26.3	9.9	7.7	111 295	1 763	87.9
Bryan	36 811	1.1	611	1.7	26 749	33.8	10.1	6.8	39 656	663	43.9
Carrollton	73 098	1.4	2 112	2.9	48 713	41.1	7.9	3.6	106 678	790	65.8
Cedar Hill	13 306	1.5	405	3.0	10 360	37.0	11.4	3.4	113 160	994	79.1
Cedar Park	5 742	2.9	264	4.6	NA	NA	NA	NA	134 776	1 604	79.8
Cleburne	13 364	1.5	745	5.6	9 177	25.5	13.8	8.2	14 427	157	84.7
College Station	30 881	1.1	532	1.7	22 425	47.8	3.8	2.1	62 308	709	65.0
Conroe	22 275	1.7	783	3.5	12 575	26.3	12.8	7.8	4 247	44	100.0
Coppell	12 563	1.1	239	1.9	9 900	50.2	7.5	2.9	103 225	908	37.0
Copperas Cove	10 824	0.7	583	5.4	7 781	25.7	9.7	8.8	9 884	81	85.2
Corpus Christi	129 878	-0.2	7 379	5.7	109 555	28.4	14.1	8.6	78 251	794	82.0
Dallas	697 089	2.7	43 200	6.2	511 202	31.8	8.4	7.2	482 954	4 030	43.0
Deer Park	17 709	1.7	599	3.4	13 702	30.6	17.1	6.2	9 162	64	100.0
Del Rio	15 126	1.4	985	6.5	10 332	22.7	14.7	9.1	6 951	127	92.1
Denton	58 946	1.9	2 586	4.4	34 108	35.5	7.9	5.5	152 349	1 288	83.1
DeSoto	21 990	1.7	759	3.5	17 055	38.7	9.3	4.7	51 858	305	100.0
Duncanville	24 610	1.8	947	3.8	19 008	36.1	9.3	4.9	5 067	52	100.0
Edinburg	17 929	2.2	2 082	11.6	10 697	33.9	9.1	8.4	26 908	571	55.0
El Paso	255 370	-0.4	20 045	7.8	195 521	29.1	10.5	7.9	151 191	2 913	88.9
Euless	30 696	1.3	922	3.0	23 123	33.0	10.4	4.6	25 103	451	10.2
Farmers Branch	17 315	2.1	787	4.5	13 277	32.2	10.0	6.1	2 260	6	100.0
Flower Mound	14 124	1.3	358	2.5	8 331	46.4	7.2	3.0	274 842	1 105	100.0
Fort Worth	282 059	2.0	15 560	5.5	206 967	29.3	11.5	8.5	398 153	4 199	91.8
Friendswood	14 519	0.4	417	2.9	12 143	47.1	8.4	3.7	97 086	412	100.0
Frisco	6 543	3.0	316	4.8	NA	NA	NA	NA	380 314	2 463	99.4
Galveston	31 189	-0.4	2 421	7.8	25 889	34.0	7.9	9.4	26 478	164	93.9
Garland	127 621	1.9	5 256	4.1	98 295	32.0	12.0	5.9	67 491	527	100.0
Georgetown	15 119	2.5	612	4.0	6 772	34.4	11.3	5.8	116 488	935	81.9
Grand Prairie	66 955	2.2	3 287	4.9	50 781	27.8	12.5	6.4	136 634	1 370	65.4
Grapevine	22 001	1.1	492	2.2	16 704	41.6	9.5	4.3	54 285	962	14.0
Haltom City	21 764	1.6	887	4.1	16 213	18.2	16.8	9.6	9 677	105	100.0
Harlingen	27 471	2.0	1 812	6.6	18 317	29.3	10.7	7.0	24 386	383	70.2
Houston	1 045 913	1.8	55 316	5.3	788 520	32.1	10.4	7.0	983 088	9 506	49.2
Huntsville	12 251	-1.4	393	3.2	9 790	30.9	4.7	5.0	6 681	56	100.0
Hurst	24 549	1.6	975	4.0	18 308	32.8	10.6	5.9	9 159	68	100.0
Irving	119 031	2.0	5 243	4.4	91 405	31.4	10.1	5.3	153 052	744	66.8
Keller	9 644	1.1	202	2.1	7 333	39.8	10.3	3.8	141 690	807	73.2
Killeen	27 998	1.4	1 896	6.8	19 508	25.4	12.7	8.3	102 675	1 261	64.9
Kingsville	10 490	0.1	513	4.9	9 661	31.4	12.6	8.1	848	11	100.0
Lake Jackson	13 898	0.4	531	3.8	11 545	46.1	14.2	5.6	11 088	56	100.0
Lancaster	14 568	2.1	663	4.6	11 170	25.5	10.4	6.8	20 070	193	95.9
La Porte	17 678	1.7	590	3.3	13 685	28.6	18.7	5.9	30 907	258	100.0
Laredo	70 366	1.6	4 839	6.9	42 951	24.1	9.6	6.4	111 755	1 863	76.4
League City	18 381	-0.5	488	2.7	16 151	43.4	11.7	5.1	126 086	1 061	76.6
Lewisville	46 434	1.3	1 254	2.7	27 666	34.2	9.5	5.8	60 895	560	43.2
Longview	39 435	-0.4	2 207	5.6	31 711	26.9	12.8	7.8	16 960	118	100.0
Lubbock	107 104	2.4	2 752	2.6	86 820	32.5	9.1	7.3	85 713	865	87.3
Lufkin	15 784	0.8	875	5.5	12 633	28.4	7.5	8.8	13 294	127	92.9
McAllen	51 687	2.3	4 837	9.4	31 624	31.9	7.7	7.2	60 329	903	87.3
McKinney	20 215	4.2	1 425	7.0	9 714	27.5	12.9	7.1	313 078	2 243	99.8
Mansfield	10 220	1.5	386	3.8	7 604	31.7	14.2	4.9	67 847	490	96.7
Mesquite	70 535	1.9	2 811	4.0	54 402	29.7	12.8	6.5	86 411	766	89.6
Midland	50 938	1.2	1 708	3.4	41 080	36.1	10.5	7.2	17 182	158	100.0
Mission	14 758	2.2	1 636	11.1	8 857	21.1	10.4	9.1	61 108	873	94.3

1. Percent of civilian labor force.   2. Persons 16 years and older.   3. Persons 16 to 64 years old.

City	Wholesale Trade, 1997				Retail Trade[1], 1997				Real Estate and Rental and Leasing, 1997			
	Number of Establishments	Number of Employees	Sales (mil dol)	Annual Payroll (mil dol)	Number of Establishments	Number of Employees	Sales (mil dol)	Annual Payroll (mil dol)	Number of Establishments	Number of Employees	Receipts (mil dol)	Annual Payroll (mil dol)
	72	73	74	75	76	77	78	79	80	81	82	83
TENNESSEE—Cont'd												
Memphis	1 470	27 381	24 961.4	948.4	2 535	37 267	6 358.3	635.4	609	5 875	691.5	144.7
Murfreesboro	92	935	477.6	28.3	433	6 874	1 187.9	113.8	102	358	44.0	5.5
Nashville-Davidson	1 445	26 012	17 005.2	962.7	3 017	44 452	7 737.6	782.7	866	6 603	1 119.8	173.2
Oak Ridge	30	180	52.7	6.1	192	2 625	455.4	41.1	54	277	36.0	5.7
Smyrna	26	388	155.6	12.7	84	1 366	225.5	20.9	27	D	D	D
TEXAS	33 346	425 744	323 111.7	15 504.9	74 105	950 848	182 516.1	16 197.1	20 753	128 915	15 957.4	3 119.2
Abilene	200	1 861	653.2	50.5	586	6 820	1 223.1	112.4	165	867	88.2	16.6
Allen	29	171	77.2	5.9	57	615	100.1	11.0	20	55	6.0	0.8
Amarillo	307	3 565	1 466.5	115.7	910	11 528	2 196.0	195.4	232	1 113	125.1	20.5
Arlington	519	6 347	4 614.2	226.9	1 152	18 925	3 806.7	368.2	322	1 787	217.8	43.8
Austin	1 065	16 673	8 086.0	661.5	2 604	40 259	7 561.4	749.7	1 022	5 751	725.1	140.4
Baytown	46	D	D	D	268	4 289	755.0	69.2	67	474	46.1	7.3
Beaumont	271	3 246	1 379.4	107.6	656	9 662	1 674.4	150.7	182	1 113	139.3	24.2
Bedford	84	332	335.6	17.8	141	2 039	448.9	36.3	52	293	33.7	7.3
Big Spring	36	448	166.4	18.9	136	1 474	244.0	20.7	36	D	D	D
Brownsville	220	1 952	585.7	37.3	518	6 661	985.0	91.5	131	525	39.3	6.3
Bryan	90	1 097	278.4	28.8	281	3 555	657.5	58.5	77	582	33.6	9.5
Carrollton	431	7 788	14 382.2	312.8	320	5 405	1 230.5	124.8	129	1 198	128.7	29.4
Cedar Hill	17	D	D	D	47	726	93.5	10.5	8	33	3.3	0.5
Cedar Park	NA	NA	NA	NA	NA	NA	NA	NA	NA	NA	NA	NA
Cleburne	32	444	156.0	9.8	168	2 139	399.5	34.0	35	91	12.2	1.5
College Station	22	368	79.5	7.8	268	4 342	653.5	62.1	93	471	42.1	6.7
Conroe	103	D	D	D	360	5 170	1 146.7	92.0	59	273	36.5	5.3
Coppell	32	304	159.9	10.1	45	692	174.7	12.9	30	76	13.5	1.6
Copperas Cove	5	4	0.6	0.1	80	1 115	157.5	14.3	36	106	6.2	1.3
Corpus Christi	453	4 708	1 656.2	144.5	1 183	16 289	2 666.6	255.7	358	2 379	327.1	61.4
Dallas	3 470	49 621	35 859.7	2 128.0	4 365	60 881	12 436.0	1 266.1	2 139	19 869	2 751.0	670.4
Deer Park	31	529	157.0	24.1	73	768	112.0	11.4	21	163	21.2	4.8
Del Rio	30	291	54.5	5.1	166	1 777	275.5	25.0	31	105	8.5	1.4
Denton	101	1 152	796.3	32.0	374	5 476	966.8	87.2	110	543	51.0	10.0
DeSoto	42	194	68.0	6.3	88	1 287	256.3	22.3	37	291	22.7	6.0
Duncanville	51	309	132.6	9.9	126	2 015	365.8	34.9	38	161	20.7	3.0
Edinburg	45	1 145	204.9	15.9	99	1 699	254.1	22.2	39	144	13.8	2.3
El Paso	950	10 705	5 954.5	300.9	2 006	28 171	4 588.9	420.2	533	2 400	282.0	46.9
Euless	69	606	294.5	25.1	83	1 076	191.3	16.6	32	159	21.0	2.8
Farmers Branch	398	10 070	8 354.8	444.9	197	3 417	636.2	78.0	96	1 176	202.5	31.0
Flower Mound	34	117	283.2	6.5	42	792	136.5	13.7	23	61	11.2	1.3
Fort Worth	843	14 840	9 968.1	524.9	1 856	23 572	4 703.3	449.2	535	3 489	445.1	92.6
Friendswood	26	252	78.5	8.2	192	2 648	375.3	39.8	31	173	21.9	4.2
Frisco	NA	NA	NA	NA	NA	NA	NA	NA	NA	NA	NA	NA
Galveston	55	606	212.3	16.5	252	2 777	362.0	37.8	73	282	34.8	7.3
Garland	283	4 671	2 727.3	170.5	543	7 133	1 426.8	135.5	168	883	110.7	19.3
Georgetown	31	D	D	D	126	1 310	289.1	26.2	49	182	22.7	4.0
Grand Prairie	326	6 538	5 025.1	236.1	305	4 760	920.0	92.9	93	1 052	165.9	22.6
Grapevine	60	411	425.5	21.7	206	2 205	573.7	48.2	34	169	35.4	4.2
Haltom City	116	1 305	431.6	42.4	149	1 527	291.9	28.2	44	203	30.9	4.9
Harlingen	96	1 170	359.9	27.4	326	4 106	611.4	59.0	74	349	39.4	7.3
Houston	5 750	82 917	99 680.2	3 389.1	7 871	112 989	21 778.4	2 078.3	2 912	27 355	3 223.5	680.8
Huntsville	25	D	D	D	157	2 122	371.1	30.7	43	207	38.5	4.0
Hurst	63	416	183.4	14.6	282	4 233	685.2	69.8	52	215	26.2	3.9
Irving	522	16 189	22 890.4	741.9	651	13 102	3 255.9	277.4	276	3 529	532.3	87.7
Keller	11	39	21.6	1.0	33	335	48.7	5.0	17	43	4.8	0.8
Killeen	25	206	54.3	3.9	329	3 879	660.3	61.2	123	614	50.6	8.2
Kingsville	9	D	D	D	105	1 385	209.2	19.7	22	D	D	D
Lake Jackson	12	48	17.9	1.6	126	2 549	361.3	32.6	32	139	18.0	3.0
Lancaster	11	D	D	D	65	1 092	196.0	19.2	20	116	14.0	2.0
La Porte	38	378	144.4	16.5	72	977	212.0	18.3	30	230	20.4	5.2
Laredo	335	D	D	D	723	9 027	1 520.8	138.5	155	574	64.3	10.0
League City	31	161	49.9	4.5	116	1 339	279.8	25.5	34	202	17.5	3.6
Lewisville	95	1 348	773.7	43.6	402	6 554	1 412.4	125.0	72	300	35.8	5.6
Longview	245	2 772	847.9	87.5	583	7 436	1 252.4	121.7	107	452	56.1	10.5
Lubbock	446	6 118	3 705.7	170.6	992	13 893	2 519.8	226.6	285	1 883	132.4	30.5
Lufkin	59	919	193.3	22.6	291	3 824	626.6	57.9	65	229	18.5	4.0
McAllen	295	2 443	966.8	54.6	757	10 916	1 665.7	165.9	168	577	62.4	8.9
McKinney	70	690	344.4	22.1	144	1 893	414.7	40.1	55	200	23.1	4.9
Mansfield	44	600	214.3	17.6	49	795	106.6	11.3	15	25	2.9	0.7
Mesquite	88	1 505	1 384.1	48.8	476	8 899	1 572.8	147.3	99	670	55.5	11.4
Midland	223	1 921	1 304.9	67.5	516	6 500	1 199.4	105.6	171	821	77.5	14.5
Mission	36	264	96.7	6.0	136	1 963	314.9	28.8	28	161	8.5	1.6

1. Establishments with payroll.

Table D. Cities — **Professional Services, Manufacturing, Accommodation and Foodservices**

City	Professional, Scientific, and Technical Services, 1997[1]				Manufacturing, 1997				Accommodation and Foodservices, 1997			
	Number of Establishments	Number of Employees	Receipts (mil dol)	Annual Payroll (mil dol)	Number of Establishments	Number of Employees	Receipts (mil dol)	Annual Payroll (mil dol)	Number of Establishments	Number of Employees	Sales (mil dol)	Annual Payroll (mil dol)
	84	85	86	87	88	89	90	91	92	93	94	95
TENNESSEE—Cont'd												
Memphis	1 300	13 282	1 328.0	496.3	688	32 938	8 888.5	1 104.8	1 071	25 344	920.6	254.9
Murfreesboro	150	622	48.1	17.7	87	5 660	1 415.5	170.8	171	4 785	151.0	44.6
Nashville-Davidson	1 694	15 055	1 636.8	605.8	752	31 716	6 721.8	1 100.0	1 407	37 523	1 511.7	426.3
Oak Ridge	142	7 814	926.4	382.3	59	5 669	897.3	247.3	79	1 504	48.1	13.3
Smyrna	28	116	12.1	3.3	21	D	D	D	43	914	27.7	7.7
TEXAS	42 492	351 422	42 044.1	15 906.7	21 808	959 665	297 657.0	32 760.8	34 160	638 333	22 698.8	6 175.4
Abilene	223	1 116	92.7	30.2	106	2 798	977.5	74.0	246	5 225	143.9	39.5
Allen	70	182	20.0	8.2	16	509	81.3	19.1	28	372	12.3	2.9
Amarillo	344	2 794	194.5	83.6	176	D	D	D	442	7 732	247.9	67.1
Arlington	649	3 950	342.5	130.0	323	13 408	2 909.8	481.6	548	13 989	521.9	139.3
Austin	2 699	25 127	2 897.0	1 179.9	596	46 780	13 235.1	1 892.1	1 491	33 899	1 215.7	348.8
Baytown	83	652	53.3	28.0	44	D	D	D	124	1 960	72.3	18.8
Beaumont	336	3 370	432.1	181.8	131	5 882	5 041.5	250.9	265	5 794	182.0	49.1
Bedford	148	731	59.7	23.3	24	D	D	D	82	1 850	67.6	18.5
Big Spring	37	121	9.0	3.0	22	D	D	D	66	945	23.3	6.5
Brownsville	185	940	72.4	24.5	110	6 511	963.3	123.6	221	3 035	105.3	26.4
Bryan	157	814	52.8	21.9	73	2 527	309.3	63.4	115	1 743	53.1	14.4
Carrollton	278	1 963	195.8	79.7	227	13 714	2 502.0	532.5	164	2 974	106.0	28.8
Cedar Hill	27	66	6.1	2.5	NA	NA	NA	NA	35	D	D	D
Cedar Park	NA	NA	NA	NA	NA	NA	NA	NA	NA	NA	NA	NA
Cleburne	46	250	25.4	7.3	35	2 429	426.8	59.4	62	D	D	D
College Station	102	1 229	144.8	51.9	NA	NA	NA	NA	156	3 909	117.4	33.7
Conroe	127	478	39.2	15.0	91	2 544	806.8	86.4	98	1 963	73.7	19.6
Coppell	66	97	18.8	5.4	NA	NA	NA	NA	38	461	18.3	5.3
Copperas Cove	17	64	3.2	1.3	NA	NA	NA	NA	32	D	D	D
Corpus Christi	678	4 376	413.8	149.6	205	D	D	D	647	11 822	382.5	102.0
Dallas	5 564	68 907	8 686.8	3 694.5	1 762	77 920	15 722.9	2 884.1	2 374	58 031	2 354.8	663.2
Deer Park	35	440	37.0	14.8	31	4 364	7 583.0	260.7	30	485	17.1	4.3
Del Rio	34	111	7.0	1.8	NA	NA	NA	NA	80	1 010	31.8	8.2
Denton	163	1 115	62.7	25.0	73	4 187	1 350.0	143.7	171	3 395	110.9	30.6
DeSoto	54	207	12.0	4.8	NA	NA	NA	NA	47	1 109	40.2	11.6
Duncanville	59	151	18.1	4.8	40	2 452	237.3	50.3	57	1 231	40.8	11.5
Edinburg	66	469	32.3	12.5	26	2 134	471.5	32.5	78	1 034	34.4	8.3
El Paso	909	5 633	389.3	158.9	599	33 212	7 602.1	716.2	1 040	18 828	687.2	189.6
Euless	63	269	25.1	9.3	41	1 060	107.1	31.0	54	871	35.0	9.1
Farmers Branch	310	4 592	446.0	216.4	134	7 477	1 299.6	251.2	82	1 884	75.4	21.0
Flower Mound	75	193	22.0	6.3	NA	NA	NA	NA	27	D	D	D
Fort Worth	1 297	9 539	1 064.3	404.8	821	56 215	11 198.3	2 337.9	881	17 152	614.7	172.6
Friendswood	61	241	29.3	13.0	NA	NA	NA	NA	51	771	28.0	7.0
Frisco	NA	NA	NA	NA	NA	NA	NA	NA	NA	NA	NA	NA
Galveston	104	438	48.0	17.3	32	592	56.3	15.8	190	4 240	141.4	41.2
Garland	256	1 439	222.5	59.6	377	16 285	2 944.6	556.5	301	4 471	165.6	42.4
Georgetown	84	283	24.6	9.1	54	D	D	D	55	869	27.0	7.5
Grand Prairie	130	768	59.1	22.8	232	12 709	2 014.2	464.0	151	2 236	88.0	21.6
Grapevine	106	307	45.9	14.0	36	1 539	310.4	47.6	92	3 629	180.8	51.8
Haltom City	35	136	9.2	3.1	138	3 292	361.3	89.7	52	664	26.5	6.4
Harlingen	105	731	43.4	17.4	65	4 480	562.4	86.1	126	2 269	77.1	21.0
Houston	7 763	91 030	14 150.3	4 922.5	2 969	104 218	32 595.8	3 599.3	3 902	83 796	3 398.9	903.4
Huntsville	48	D	D	D	NA	NA	NA	NA	73	1 477	44.0	12.2
Hurst	150	1 666	102.3	52.0	43	716	104.7	17.5	84	1 262	39.4	10.6
Irving	542	9 262	1 086.1	415.1	240	11 146	2 590.9	435.9	397	11 448	575.3	140.2
Keller	29	50	7.2	2.9	NA	NA	NA	NA	20	218	8.1	2.1
Killeen	64	929	87.6	16.6	NA	NA	NA	NA	174	3 022	90.5	23.9
Kingsville	22	D	D	D	NA	NA	NA	NA	66	923	28.0	7.6
Lake Jackson	29	110	8.7	3.3	NA	NA	NA	NA	53	1 487	40.8	12.9
Lancaster	11	26	1.9	0.6	30	1 275	191.0	35.9	26	434	12.7	3.7
La Porte	43	553	63.7	21.7	35	2 442	1 819.1	132.5	46	660	19.5	5.2
Laredo	206	973	64.8	21.3	86	D	D	D	249	4 341	144.2	37.3
League City	58	176	15.9	5.6	NA	NA	NA	NA	46	966	34.2	9.4
Lewisville	106	640	62.7	20.9	85	5 347	930.8	219.5	134	3 713	122.2	35.0
Longview	246	1 416	110.8	43.0	135	10 208	3 074.3	374.8	213	3 927	128.0	37.0
Lubbock	474	2 495	197.1	67.2	210	6 357	1 465.0	182.3	488	10 760	321.1	84.3
Lufkin	99	487	43.0	14.2	52	5 006	763.2	120.1	102	1 781	56.8	16.4
McAllen	302	1 677	124.3	38.6	100	3 709	511.4	69.5	253	6 005	188.6	50.0
McKinney	93	412	42.8	14.7	48	4 537	1 327.9	204.0	61	1 156	36.7	10.9
Mansfield	39	152	16.1	4.2	70	2 715	434.5	77.9	26	426	13.0	3.3
Mesquite	121	514	36.2	13.0	72	3 338	1 147.3	111.1	168	4 278	148.4	40.5
Midland	323	1 898	228.7	70.7	73	901	119.1	32.4	225	D	D	D
Mission	16	52	3.9	1.3	27	1 176	177.9	22.1	70	923	30.8	8.0

1. Firms subject to federal tax.

Table D. Cities — Entertainment, Health Care, and Other Services

City	Arts, Entertainment, and Recreation[1], 1997				Health Care and Social Assistance[1], 1997				Other Services[1], 1997			
	Number of Establishments	Number of Employees	Receipts (mil dol)	Annual Payroll (mil dol)	Number of Establishments	Number of Employees	Receipts (mil dol)	Annual Payroll (mil dol)	Number of Establishments	Number of Employees	Receipts (mil dol)	Annual Payroll (mil dol)
	96	97	98	99	100	101	102	103	104	105	106	107
TENNESSEE—Cont'd												
Memphis	99	2 062	90.7	24.4	1 364	17 644	1 635.3	695.0	1 039	8 210	534.1	166.8
Murfreesboro	18	158	6.4	1.8	189	3 057	166.6	83.2	132	701	41.4	12.2
Nashville-Davidson	545	6 077	560.4	211.3	1 462	27 389	2 174.0	925.5	1 092	8 627	530.2	163.9
Oak Ridge	6	53	1.8	0.5	113	1 243	93.1	51.2	63	337	16.6	6.1
Smyrna	5	92	2.8	0.7	40	505	27.8	8.8	31	147	7.9	2.6
TEXAS	3 894	65 218	3 743.8	1 143.4	37 974	557 007	35 620.9	14 725.4	29 162	197 113	12 477.7	3 785.0
Abilene	41	312	19.2	4.2	305	5 117	306.6	121.2	208	1 767	98.3	32.3
Allen	7	160	4.5	1.4	63	558	30.6	12.4	32	207	11.2	3.9
Amarillo	40	403	15.3	4.3	476	6 338	506.8	215.0	336	2 310	133.7	39.8
Arlington	65	4 831	246.8	107.3	702	8 890	618.9	257.8	438	3 628	216.4	70.4
Austin	171	2 810	126.8	45.5	1 550	27 475	1 894.7	770.0	1 210	8 761	558.0	183.2
Baytown	14	135	5.5	1.5	178	1 905	124.8	53.0	115	1 151	59.8	21.8
Beaumont	28	232	10.4	2.4	450	7 396	426.4	193.3	286	2 024	123.7	34.7
Bedford	14	250	6.6	2.5	176	2 119	161.4	62.2	68	395	19.4	6.2
Big Spring	5	0	0.0	0.0	60	1 000	63.6	24.7	50	231	10.2	3.0
Brownsville	21	235	8.9	2.6	230	4 623	272.4	109.4	144	1 217	50.0	15.9
Bryan	10	0	0.0	0.0	166	1 402	102.8	46.5	126	782	45.3	12.5
Carrollton	29	306	11.6	2.9	203	2 265	156.4	65.5	201	1 592	101.3	34.6
Cedar Hill	3	0	0.0	0.0	34	345	17.2	6.0	26	96	7.5	1.7
Cedar Park	NA	NA	NA	NA	NA	NA	NA	NA	NA	NA	NA	NA
Cleburne	6	24	1.1	0.3	76	971	48.0	21.4	66	321	18.7	5.3
College Station	17	300	8.9	3.4	94	1 432	109.2	38.4	56	408	15.8	4.9
Conroe	15	122	6.1	1.7	152	2 793	219.6	83.0	113	822	41.6	12.1
Coppell	9	98	4.6	1.4	43	301	21.2	9.6	32	199	10.2	3.3
Copperas Cove	4	0	0.0	0.0	22	270	8.4	3.5	38	158	7.7	2.2
Corpus Christi	56	579	30.5	7.6	831	14 413	768.8	343.7	510	3 465	205.2	63.8
Dallas	313	4 772	393.1	123.6	3 009	40 422	3 923.9	1 567.6	1 973	16 667	1 070.5	341.7
Deer Park	4	31	0.5	0.2	36	216	13.8	4.2	55	516	30.4	11.7
Del Rio	8	0	0.0	0.0	53	0	0.0	0.0	47	0	0.0	0.0
Denton	18	211	5.3	1.7	216	3 437	247.9	99.7	137	806	83.9	15.5
DeSoto	6	100	3.4	1.0	138	1 837	97.5	42.4	49	317	19.3	5.2
Duncanville	8	107	3.0	0.9	124	1 399	68.5	30.5	85	489	38.4	10.7
Edinburg	4	69	1.4	0.3	97	3 396	320.8	95.0	56	182	11.7	2.1
El Paso	73	1 710	94.0	23.4	970	16 345	1 159.2	453.7	791	5 613	258.7	85.7
Euless	4	0	0.0	0.0	74	674	51.4	22.1	49	330	23.8	6.6
Farmers Branch	14	559	31.0	10.3	126	2 247	212.1	76.2	97	2 145	214.6	78.4
Flower Mound	7	0	0.0	0.0	37	457	25.9	11.9	24	147	5.5	2.1
Fort Worth	81	1 342	70.0	19.7	1 159	14 987	1 053.0	487.1	783	5 483	355.5	111.6
Friendswood	7	88	1.0	0.3	54	450	25.2	11.9	41	246	14.3	4.4
Frisco	NA	NA	NA	NA	NA	NA	NA	NA	NA	NA	NA	NA
Galveston	34	280	15.5	5.8	104	1 048	49.4	17.2	97	472	23.8	6.7
Garland	37	632	30.3	7.5	342	5 525	261.5	111.7	316	1 901	118.2	34.9
Georgetown	6	135	4.6	1.5	68	647	29.7	12.1	42	151	10.2	2.9
Grand Prairie	20	311	76.3	5.9	157	1 633	85.4	34.8	154	1 133	88.5	28.4
Grapevine	14	295	3.9	1.4	112	1 036	74.3	33.4	74	388	28.7	8.2
Haltom City	8	0	0.0	0.0	34	804	22.8	12.2	83	455	30.7	9.3
Harlingen	9	48	2.4	0.5	207	5 611	184.3	90.6	116	719	33.0	10.3
Houston	361	8 000	654.1	203.5	4 768	66 288	5 075.2	2 087.9	3 429	32 465	2 289.5	694.0
Huntsville	4	0	0.0	0.0	70	0	0.0	0.0	42	245	10.1	3.3
Hurst	8	128	5.4	1.1	98	856	55.2	23.0	102	549	29.0	10.0
Irving	36	1 182	271.6	102.8	382	4 602	347.3	148.3	306	2 356	146.5	50.5
Keller	4	6	0.7	0.0	34	296	14.7	6.4	24	120	5.5	1.8
Killeen	16	162	5.9	1.3	101	866	46.3	15.1	151	731	35.6	11.1
Kingsville	3	0	0.0	0.0	51	0	0.0	0.0	46	0	0.0	0.0
Lake Jackson	7	65	2.4	0.6	121	801	58.8	25.7	38	333	10.5	3.6
Lancaster	2	0	0.0	0.0	45	1 040	51.7	22.3	38	258	22.7	7.4
La Porte	3	0	0.0	0.0	24	323	14.0	6.6	46	913	109.6	36.8
Laredo	17	0	0.0	0.0	226	0	0.0	0.0	189	0	0.0	0.0
League City	16	188	10.9	2.6	69	843	42.4	19.1	77	697	40.7	13.9
Lewisville	14	163	8.0	2.6	142	2 024	151.4	57.4	122	816	57.9	16.8
Longview	22	266	8.8	2.8	288	4 662	285.4	120.5	176	1 336	85.5	23.5
Lubbock	56	503	29.8	6.6	586	8 074	556.8	235.6	354	2 842	163.8	48.8
Lufkin	9	0	0.0	0.0	170	2 914	162.7	69.7	115	594	40.5	11.1
McAllen	16	282	13.7	2.5	436	8 354	663.1	251.5	179	1 169	52.9	15.7
McKinney	9	250	10.2	3.1	110	1 876	120.8	47.6	50	375	13.7	4.4
Mansfield	2	0	0.0	0.0	29	518	26.2	10.7	25	342	38.3	8.5
Mesquite	25	514	17.3	4.9	235	3 408	238.2	90.9	167	1 020	65.0	19.6
Midland	28	0	0.0	0.0	238	2 931	248.9	101.2	186	1 226	84.8	21.7
Mission	5	172	5.5	1.5	83	1 148	54.6	26.5	62	320	13.9	3.9

1. Firms subject to federal tax.

Table D. Cities — Federal Funds and City Government Finances

	Selected federal funds, fiscal 2001[1] (mil dol)									City government finances, 1999						
	Procurement contracts		Grants					Direct payments for individuals		General revenue						
										Intergovernmental			Taxes			
														Per capita[3] (dollars)		
City	Defense	Other	Total[2]	Health and family welfare	Energy and environment	Education	Housing and community development	Educational assistance	Housing assistance	Total (mil dol)	Total (mil dol)	Percent from state government	Total (mil dol)	Total	Property	Sales and gross receipts
	108	109	110	111	112	113	114	115	116	117	118	119	120	121	122	123
TENNESSEE—Cont'd																
Memphis	119.7	433.6	222.5	112.6	0.6	7.7	17.9	30.4	98.6	1 307.5	872.9	53.1	255.8	424	341	79
Murfreesboro	3.2	280.0	5.7	0.0	0.1	1.3	0.9	14.9	8.7	93.7	50.0	44.4	24.3	416	345	54
Nashville-Davidson	32.4	265.9	1 079.7	500.4	33.8	187.4	45.5	29.0	91.9	1 438.2	292.6	95.3	783.3	1 535	876	530
Oak Ridge	17.5	2 071.4	6.9	1.4	2.7	0.1	0.2	0.0	4.1	60.2	35.1	51.8	13.6	502	416	81
Smyrna	2.4	0.0	0.0	0.0	0.0	0.0	0.0	0.0	3.3	NA	NA	NA	NA	NA	NA	NA
TEXAS	9 460.4	6 188.4	21 675.2	11 663.7	400.9	2 848.1	419.0	861.6	1 345.8	X	X	X	X	X	X	X
Abilene	40.1	1.5	74.2	3.0	0.1	1.8	1.6	8.7	6.1	73.1	5.0	46.0	45.4	420	196	217
Allen	0.0	0.0	2.2	0.0	0.0	2.0	0.0	0.0	0.0	27.1	0.0	**********	15.6	400	232	140
Amarillo	119.6	114.8	18.3	3.3	0.0	0.5	3.0	0.7	3.1	157.8	19.6	56.4	65.1	380	81	293
Arlington	131.1	5.2	18.8	1.6	0.8	1.7	2.7	12.9	12.3	227.0	26.0	80.2	116.8	381	179	193
Austin	320.1	127.5	3 409.2	1 076.4	245.8	776.1	151.3	54.5	40.9	628.0	56.5	43.4	297.8	539	269	242
Baytown	93.5	0.1	3.1	0.0	0.0	0.6	1.3	2.6	10.8	58.9	6.7	7.3	32.1	468	321	142
Beaumont	241.3	45.5	11.6	0.6	2.3	2.1	3.1	10.7	16.9	99.7	7.4	33.2	69.0	628	200	297
Bedford	0.9	0.4	0.0	0.0	0.0	0.0	0.0	0.0	0.0	NA	NA	NA	NA	NA	NA	NA
Big Spring	24.8	6.5	0.5	0.0	0.0	0.5	0.0	2.4	7.6	34.5	1.5	0.5	7.8	350	112	230
Brownsville	0.0	5.2	36.3	13.6	2.2	6.0	5.3	15.2	13.5	79.7	10.4	12.3	33.8	245	99	140
Bryan	0.8	1.6	8.6	3.5	0.1	0.2	1.5	15.1	3.7	49.7	3.3	100.0	20.5	348	176	163
Carrollton	4.3	21.4	0.5	0.0	0.0	0.0	0.4	0.1	0.0	91.7	3.7	72.8	56.1	558	324	221
Cedar Hill	0.0	0.0	0.0	0.0	0.0	0.0	0.0	0.0	0.8	NA	NA	NA	NA	NA	NA	NA
Cedar Park	0.0	0.0	0.0	0.0	0.0	0.0	0.0	0.0	0.0	14.4	0.2	0.0	6.4	NA	NA	NA
Cleburne	0.0	0.1	0.5	0.0	0.0	0.0	0.0	0.0	2.3	NA	NA	NA	NA	NA	NA	NA
College Station	11.2	15.8	194.2	42.7	9.7	5.6	1.9	16.4	6.6	42.7	1.7	26.2	21.8	365	133	232
Conroe	2.3	3.4	3.4	0.0	0.0	0.0	2.5	0.0	7.2	NA	NA	NA	NA	NA	NA	NA
Coppell	0.0	0.3	0.0	0.0	0.0	0.0	0.0	0.0	0.0	NA	NA	NA	NA	NA	NA	NA
Copperas Cove	0.0	0.3	9.9	0.0	0.0	8.9	0.0	0.0	0.0	NA	NA	NA	NA	NA	NA	NA
Corpus Christi	54.1	5.8	31.2	4.2	0.5	5.9	7.6	12.7	29.7	212.7	14.9	44.8	100.1	356	176	168
Dallas	357.9	116.9	364.0	196.3	1.2	7.7	28.1	29.6	96.8	1 555.5	93.9	34.9	674.3	627	323	291
Deer Park	383.4	0.2	0.0	0.0	0.0	0.0	0.0	0.0	0.0	NA	NA	NA	NA	NA	NA	NA
Del Rio	0.3	2.3	0.7	0.4	0.0	0.1	0.0	0.0	3.1	NA	NA	NA	NA	NA	NA	NA
Denton	1.7	3.0	14.8	1.9	0.2	7.2	2.1	18.0	5.5	74.5	3.9	100.0	37.2	484	191	283
DeSoto	2.0	1.0	0.0	0.0	0.0	0.0	0.0	0.5	0.6	28.8	0.4	69.3	17.2	481	264	213
Duncanville	0.0	0.3	0.1	0.0	0.0	0.0	0.0	0.1	1.3	24.2	0.2	100.0	16.1	445	238	190
Edinburg	0.0	0.1	38.9	16.6	0.0	14.0	0.8	19.7	8.5	NA	NA	NA	NA	NA	NA	NA
El Paso	267.3	54.2	113.8	24.8	14.5	11.5	19.0	49.3	32.9	353.7	33.6	30.7	177.0	288	157	121
Euless	5.1	0.5	0.1	0.1	0.0	0.0	0.0	0.0	0.2	32.7	0.5	100.0	17.5	387	139	236
Farmers Branch	0.3	0.3	0.3	0.0	0.0	0.0	0.0	0.2	0.0	52.5	2.3	0.2	34.8	1 331	562	748
Flower Mound	0.2	0.0	0.0	0.0	0.0	0.0	0.0	0.0	0.0	26.7	0.1	0.0	16.6	373	209	92
Fort Worth	1 601.2	231.8	101.1	34.0	1.2	6.6	12.2	34.8	46.4	439.9	32.3	100.0	255.2	519	286	163
Friendswood	0.2	0.3	0.0	0.0	0.0	0.0	0.0	0.0	0.0	13.5	0.3	25.8	9.0	312	206	90
Frisco	0.1	0.0	0.4	0.0	0.0	0.0	0.0	0.0	0.0	NA	NA	NA	NA	NA	NA	NA
Galveston	2.2	42.4	89.1	71.7	0.7	1.4	2.9	2.0	12.6	74.8	4.5	6.0	29.6	497	176	313
Garland	110.0	4.8	2.8	0.0	0.0	0.0	2.6	4.3	5.0	139.1	9.6	69.6	66.2	342	217	118
Georgetown	0.4	0.1	6.4	4.2	0.0	1.5	0.0	0.8	1.4	NA	NA	NA	NA	NA	NA	NA
Grand Prairie	798.5	65.2	3.6	0.0	0.0	0.4	1.4	1.6	6.6	111.1	9.9	100.0	60.2	531	267	254
Grapevine	0.3	0.1	0.0	0.0	0.0	0.0	0.0	0.0	0.2	64.7	1.0	100.0	32.7	813	347	434
Haltom City	0.1	0.1	0.1	0.0	0.0	0.0	0.0	0.0	0.3	NA	NA	NA	NA	NA	NA	NA
Harlingen	0.8	0.9	11.6	5.9	0.0	2.4	1.9	4.2	4.9	54.1	6.2	5.8	22.5	386	111	271
Houston	312.2	3 481.9	866.0	516.2	16.1	67.1	68.3	94.0	195.1	1 912.2	165.8	23.5	1 017.3	569	279	273
Huntsville	1.6	0.0	15.3	0.0	0.0	3.2	0.0	6.9	2.6	17.1	0.0	100.0	7.5	238	51	182
Hurst	4.0	1.3	1.7	0.0	0.0	0.2	0.0	1.1	0.0	NA	NA	NA	NA	NA	NA	NA
Irving	94.9	7.2	6.5	0.7	0.0	1.5	2.0	7.0	4.5	150.9	3.8	11.1	101.5	569	275	273
Keller	0.1	4.3	0.0	0.0	0.0	0.0	0.0	0.0	0.0	NA	NA	NA	NA	NA	NA	NA
Killeen	7.0	0.5	37.4	0.0	0.0	36.0	1.2	40.0	0.2	43.8	2.1	0.0	24.0	297	118	162
Kingsville	4.5	0.4	4.6	1.2	0.0	2.5	0.0	8.7	5.7	NA	NA	NA	NA	NA	NA	NA
Lake Jackson	0.0	0.0	0.4	0.0	0.0	0.4	0.0	0.9	0.0	17.3	0.1	100.0	10.9	415	168	241
Lancaster	0.0	5.3	0.0	0.0	0.0	0.0	0.0	2.6	1.5	27.3	1.7	11.2	19.1	789	178	605
La Porte	0.1	0.1	0.0	0.0	0.0	0.0	0.0	0.0	2.2	NA	NA	NA	NA	NA	NA	NA
Laredo	2.7	22.8	62.0	29.5	0.0	6.6	4.8	13.4	9.2	148.5	22.1	35.8	42.8	243	121	110
League City	0.3	0.3	0.6	0.2	0.0	0.3	0.0	0.0	0.0	30.2	0.4	100.0	19.4	445	273	153
Lewisville	40.5	7.6	0.6	0.0	0.0	0.3	0.2	0.0	1.9	48.1	1.3	29.0	31.3	432	128	270
Longview	1.6	-4.4	4.2	1.3	0.0	0.0	1.2	1.9	8.3	59.3	4.7	4.0	36.6	484	218	258
Lubbock	5.2	6.7	42.3	15.6	1.2	3.3	4.3	17.9	23.8	149.7	13.2	36.3	70.1	367	179	182
Lufkin	0.0	1.0	0.3	0.0	0.0	0.0	0.0	4.3	2.2	NA	NA	NA	NA	NA	NA	NA
McAllen	67.9	11.6	10.7	1.6	0.1	1.0	4.1	22.9	8.4	106.1	3.8	57.5	44.7	418	137	275
McKinney	219.1	28.3	1.1	0.0	0.0	0.0	0.0	0.0	4.5	NA	NA	NA	NA	NA	NA	NA
Mansfield	14.5	0.5	0.0	0.0	0.0	0.0	0.0	0.0	0.0	NA	NA	NA	NA	NA	NA	NA
Mesquite	0.3	0.0	7.7	0.0	0.0	5.9	1.3	2.7	5.7	86.2	4.9	5.5	52.7	460	192	259
Midland	5.6	0.8	11.4	0.5	0.1	2.7	1.0	2.6	1.1	74.9	2.5	100.0	41.5	416	197	211
Mission	0.0	0.5	4.0	0.0	0.0	2.8	0.9	0.0	5.2	NA	NA	NA	NA	NA	NA	NA

1. October 1, 2000 to September 30, 2001.   2. Includes program categories not shown separately. State totals include additional categories not allocated by city.   3. Based on population estimated as of July 1 of the year shown.

Table D. Cities — **City Government Finances**

	City government finances, 1999 (cont'd)												
	General expenditure												
	Per capita[1] (dollars)			Percent of total for —									
City	Total (mil dol)	Total	Capital outlays	Public welfare	Highways	Parking facilities	Education	Health and hospitals	Police protection	Sewerage and sanitation	Parks and recreation	Housing and community development	Interest on debt
	124	125	126	127	128	129	130	131	132	133	134	135	136
TENNESSEE—Cont'd													
Memphis	1 402.7	2 324	377	0.0	2.7	0.0	50.6	0.5	10.5	4.4	11.4	2.0	2.4
Murfreesboro	99.6	1 704	411	0.0	4.0	0.1	34.0	0.1	7.8	6.4	7.3	1.0	3.2
Nashville-Davidson	1 469.8	2 880	491	1.1	2.5	0.0	39.9	9.0	7.6	3.7	6.3	0.0	8.7
Oak Ridge	61.0	2 257	105	0.3	2.3	0.0	56.3	0.3	7.3	7.5	5.1	0.8	4.5
Smyrna	NA	NA	NA	NA	NA	NA	NA	NA	NA	NA	NA	NA	NA
TEXAS	X	X	X	X	X	X	X	X	X	X	X	X	X
Abilene	67.4	623	57	0.1	12.2	0.0	0.0	4.5	17.3	11.2	7.9	7.1	2.5
Allen	25.8	663	169	0.0	2.5	0.0	0.0	0.0	11.8	15.2	6.4	2.7	12.0
Amarillo	122.9	718	12	0.0	8.4	0.0	0.0	14.8	13.1	11.4	11.2	7.0	8.2
Arlington	251.2	819	226	1.3	10.5	0.0	0.0	0.7	16.4	12.8	19.0	12.5	6.7
Austin	903.9	1 636	504	0.9	2.5	0.0	0.0	7.0	10.1	10.1	6.0	1.5	9.6
Baytown	54.0	787	112	0.1	7.2	0.0	0.0	0.8	25.5	10.5	7.5	2.4	6.6
Beaumont	109.2	994	159	0.0	15.6	0.0	0.0	4.1	17.4	8.0	3.2	2.7	5.0
Bedford	NA	NA	NA	NA	NA	NA	NA	NA	NA	NA	NA	NA	NA
Big Spring	33.8	1 509	73	0.1	3.7	0.0	0.1	2.6	7.9	6.3	1.6	3.8	0.7
Brownsville	90.2	654	181	0.6	4.0	0.5	0.0	2.9	16.2	27.0	5.4	5.4	3.5
Bryan	50.8	864	119	0.0	8.0	0.0	0.0	0.0	13.4	15.4	7.5	4.6	5.7
Carrollton	68.1	678	128	0.0	14.3	0.0	0.0	2.0	17.0	16.8	9.9	0.0	6.1
Cedar Hill	NA	NA	NA	NA	NA	NA	NA	NA	NA	NA	NA	NA	NA
Cedar Park	15.1	NA	NA	0.0	28.9	0.0	0.0	0.8	10.2	19.2	5.6	0.0	5.8
Cleburne	NA	NA	NA	NA	NA	NA	NA	NA	NA	NA	NA	NA	NA
College Station	48.0	803	166	0.0	11.9	0.3	0.0	0.0	10.5	18.7	15.4	4.0	5.1
Conroe	NA	NA	NA	NA	NA	NA	NA	NA	NA	NA	NA	NA	NA
Coppell	NA	NA	NA	NA	NA	NA	NA	NA	NA	NA	NA	NA	NA
Copperas Cove	NA	NA	NA	NA	NA	NA	NA	NA	NA	NA	NA	NA	NA
Corpus Christi	188.8	671	71	0.0	9.2	0.1	0.0	5.9	20.1	13.7	9.3	0.3	8.2
Dallas	1 479.9	1 376	297	0.1	5.4	0.2	0.0	1.5	14.3	11.0	7.2	2.8	14.5
Deer Park	NA	NA	NA	NA	NA	NA	NA	NA	NA	NA	NA	NA	NA
Del Rio	NA	NA	NA	NA	NA	NA	NA	NA	NA	NA	NA	NA	NA
Denton	60.6	788	64	0.0	9.2	0.0	0.0	0.8	14.5	22.4	6.6	2.9	5.8
DeSoto	29.5	825	96	0.0	10.8	0.0	0.0	0.0	16.9	11.0	4.5	0.0	20.9
Duncanville	25.1	694	73	0.0	12.2	0.0	0.0	0.0	19.3	26.6	4.8	0.0	5.2
Edinburg	NA	NA	NA	NA	NA	NA	NA	NA	NA	NA	NA	NA	NA
El Paso	346.3	563	133	0.0	8.3	0.0	0.0	6.3	20.2	13.1	7.2	3.1	8.1
Euless	42.1	930	157	0.0	3.3	0.0	0.0	0.5	12.8	7.5	15.6	0.0	6.2
Farmers Branch	43.2	1 652	357	0.0	15.1	0.0	0.0	1.1	15.1	18.7	20.7	0.0	4.1
Flower Mound	19.0	428	0	0.0	8.3	0.0	0.0	0.0	20.9	22.5	6.0	0.0	8.2
Fort Worth	434.9	884	133	0.2	15.6	0.1	0.0	1.4	21.6	11.8	9.9	2.7	7.5
Friendswood	12.6	438	29	0.1	8.2	0.0	0.0	0.0	25.4	22.1	6.9	1.3	5.4
Frisco	NA	NA	NA	NA	NA	NA	NA	NA	NA	NA	NA	NA	NA
Galveston	68.3	1 146	92	0.0	4.8	0.2	0.0	0.0	12.4	14.2	10.1	5.3	20.5
Garland	130.5	675	77	0.0	11.1	0.0	0.0	1.3	20.1	18.0	5.9	7.0	3.7
Georgetown	NA	NA	NA	NA	NA	NA	NA	NA	NA	NA	NA	NA	NA
Grand Prairie	92.5	816	54	0.0	10.3	0.0	0.0	1.0	18.4	13.7	7.1	10.7	11.8
Grapevine	67.0	1 662	386	0.0	21.1	0.0	0.0	0.0	10.7	3.6	9.3	1.6	25.3
Haltom City	NA	NA	NA	NA	NA	NA	NA	NA	NA	NA	NA	NA	NA
Harlingen	53.1	913	103	0.8	5.9	0.0	0.0	5.1	10.8	19.4	7.6	2.2	5.5
Houston	2 100.0	1 175	296	0.0	9.3	0.0	0.0	4.2	18.6	20.8	4.4	2.9	9.5
Huntsville	13.8	435	20	0.0	13.9	0.0	0.0	0.0	18.9	24.2	6.0	0.0	6.8
Hurst	NA	NA	NA	NA	NA	NA	NA	NA	NA	NA	NA	NA	NA
Irving	155.8	874	103	0.0	10.4	0.0	0.0	3.3	16.5	12.3	8.0	0.6	3.6
Keller	NA	NA	NA	NA	NA	NA	NA	NA	NA	NA	NA	NA	NA
Killeen	36.3	449	31	0.5	8.8	0.0	0.0	0.7	23.6	22.4	8.0	0.7	3.6
Kingsville	NA	NA	NA	NA	NA	NA	NA	NA	NA	NA	NA	NA	NA
Lake Jackson	18.4	698	245	0.0	9.3	0.0	0.0	0.0	14.0	15.1	31.2	0.0	6.4
Lancaster	20.5	845	0	0.0	11.0	0.0	0.0	12.7	13.2	12.9	2.9	6.4	4.7
La Porte	NA	NA	NA	NA	NA	NA	NA	NA	NA	NA	NA	NA	NA
Laredo	140.2	798	89	0.5	12.8	0.1	0.0	5.3	11.1	10.8	2.4	4.0	5.6
League City	29.1	667	105	0.0	21.0	0.0	0.0	1.9	16.3	13.4	2.7	0.0	5.0
Lewisville	43.0	594	19	0.3	8.4	0.0	0.0	3.2	22.2	11.3	8.1	0.7	6.0
Longview	61.8	818	163	4.9	14.6	0.0	0.0	1.4	16.0	14.1	6.0	2.5	10.0
Lubbock	130.9	686	81	0.0	9.1	0.0	0.0	3.2	19.2	13.6	8.2	3.1	8.3
Lufkin	NA	NA	NA	NA	NA	NA	NA	NA	NA	NA	NA	NA	NA
McAllen	94.1	881	140	0.9	12.3	0.0	0.0	0.5	15.3	11.3	8.0	2.2	17.2
McKinney	NA	NA	NA	NA	NA	NA	NA	NA	NA	NA	NA	NA	NA
Mansfield	NA	NA	NA	NA	NA	NA	NA	NA	NA	NA	NA	NA	NA
Mesquite	82.8	722	107	0.0	6.8	0.0	0.0	1.1	19.1	10.5	12.9	1.3	7.5
Midland	97.5	979	304	0.0	5.0	0.0	0.0	2.6	13.9	15.9	6.6	2.2	2.4
Mission	NA	NA	NA	NA	NA	NA	NA	NA	NA	NA	NA	NA	NA

1. Based on population estimated as of July 1 of the year shown.

Table D. Cities — City Government Finances, City Government Employment, and Climate

City	City government finances, 1999 (cont'd) Debt outstanding — Total (mil dol)	Per capita[1] (dollars)	Percent utility	City government employment, 2001	Climate[2] Average daily temperature (degrees Fahrenheit) Mean — January	Mean July	Limits January[3]	Limits July[4]	Annual precipitation (inches)	Heating degree days	Cooling degree days
	137	138	139	140	141	142	143	144	145	146	147
TENNESSEE—Cont'd											
Memphis	959.9	1 591	22.8	25 070	39.7	82.6	30.9	92.3	52.10	3 082	2 118
Murfreesboro	132.6	2 270	43.0	1 729	35.2	77.9	24.5	89.3	53.17	3 992	1 406
Nashville-Davidson	3 151.5	6 176	29.2	NA	NA	NA	NA	NA	NA	NA	NA
Oak Ridge	78.5	2 902	31.2	994	35.0	75.8	25.1	86.7	53.77	4 183	1 156
Smyrna	NA	NA	NA	NA	NA	NA	NA	NA	NA	NA	NA
TEXAS	X	X	X	X	X	X	X	X	X	X	X
Abilene	34.7	321	40.6	1 143	42.8	84.0	30.8	95.2	24.40	2 584	2 451
Allen	38.7	994	25.4	NA	NA	NA	NA	NA	NA	NA	NA
Amarillo	181.6	1 061	13.2	1 818	35.1	78.6	21.2	91.7	19.56	4 258	1 354
Arlington	373.9	1 220	23.1	2 565	43.4	85.3	32.7	96.5	33.70	2 407	2 603
Austin	4 013.4	7 265	69.6	10 640	48.8	84.5	38.6	95.0	31.88	1 688	3 016
Baytown	112.2	1 636	36.9	606	50.5	83.1	40.6	91.4	51.85	1 550	2 809
Beaumont	139.1	1 266	28.7	1 368	49.6	82.3	39.5	91.9	55.58	1 677	2 581
Bedford	NA	NA	NA	NA	43.4	85.3	32.7	96.5	33.70	2 407	2 603
Big Spring	11.0	492	68.8	267	NA	NA	NA	NA	NA	NA	NA
Brownsville	266.7	1 934	71.6	1 349	59.4	84.5	49.9	93.3	26.61	635	3 888
Bryan	75.1	1 278	50.8	856	48.5	83.6	38.7	93.8	39.08	1 788	2 776
Carrollton	127.5	1 269	18.8	909	43.4	85.3	32.7	96.5	33.70	2 407	2 603
Cedar Hill	NA	NA	NA	NA	NA	NA	NA	NA	NA	NA	NA
Cedar Park	63.7	NA	71.7	246	NA	NA	NA	NA	NA	NA	NA
Cleburne	NA	NA	NA	NA	NA	NA	NA	NA	NA	NA	NA
College Station	74.2	1 242	25.4	715	48.5	83.6	38.7	93.8	39.08	1 788	2 776
Conroe	NA	NA	NA	NA	48.8	83.1	37.9	94.0	47.33	1 774	2 676
Coppell	NA	NA	NA	NA	NA	NA	NA	NA	NA	NA	NA
Copperas Cove	NA	NA	NA	NA	NA	NA	NA	NA	NA	NA	NA
Corpus Christi	544.0	1 933	24.9	2 953	55.1	84.1	45.3	93.3	30.13	1 016	3 439
Dallas	4 135.9	3 844	8.4	15 071	44.6	85.9	34.5	95.7	36.08	2 259	2 763
Deer Park	NA	NA	NA	NA	52.2	83.5	42.9	92.3	50.83	1 371	3 012
Del Rio	NA	NA	NA	NA	50.2	85.2	38.5	96.2	18.24	1 506	3 142
Denton	182.8	2 375	67.3	1 107	41.9	83.2	30.3	94.0	37.27	2 665	2 225
DeSoto	90.0	2 523	7.6	NA	44.6	85.9	34.5	95.7	36.08	2 259	2 763
Duncanville	30.9	854	3.0	NA	44.6	85.9	34.5	95.7	36.08	2 259	2 763
Edinburg	NA	NA	NA	NA	58.5	85.4	48.5	95.8	22.83	693	4 076
El Paso	662.9	1 078	24.5	5 913	42.8	82.3	29.4	96.1	8.81	2 708	2 094
Euless	50.5	1 116	8.0	376	43.4	85.3	32.7	96.5	33.70	2 407	2 603
Farmers Branch	39.3	1 504	28.6	485	NA	NA	NA	NA	NA	NA	NA
Flower Mound	36.9	833	17.0	NA	NA	NA	NA	NA	NA	NA	NA
Fort Worth	954.3	1 940	45.7	5 777	43.4	85.3	32.7	96.5	33.70	2 407	2 603
Friendswood	12.4	430	70.0	NA	NA	NA	NA	NA	NA	NA	NA
Frisco	NA	NA	NA	NA	NA	NA	NA	NA	NA	NA	NA
Galveston	185.1	3 108	0.8	811	52.7	83.3	47.1	87.3	42.28	1 263	2 994
Garland	251.1	1 298	12.4	1 952	44.6	85.9	34.5	95.7	36.08	2 259	2 763
Georgetown	NA	NA	NA	NA	NA	NA	NA	NA	NA	NA	NA
Grand Prairie	128.8	1 137	20.6	1 015	43.4	85.3	32.7	96.5	33.70	2 407	2 603
Grapevine	236.9	5 879	12.1	513	41.6	83.7	30.0	94.9	33.68	2 683	2 328
Haltom City	NA	NA	NA	NA	43.4	85.3	32.7	96.5	33.70	2 407	2 603
Harlingen	52.0	893	37.3	738	57.3	83.9	46.7	94.4	27.53	813	3 662
Houston	6 378.9	3 570	19.2	25 360	52.2	83.5	42.9	92.3	50.83	1 371	3 012
Huntsville	37.3	1 177	36.4	NA	47.6	83.3	37.6	94.4	44.96	1 862	2 654
Hurst	NA	NA	NA	NA	43.4	85.3	32.7	96.5	33.70	2 407	2 603
Irving	187.5	1 052	31.9	2 024	44.6	85.9	34.5	95.7	36.08	2 259	2 763
Keller	NA	NA	NA	NA	NA	NA	NA	NA	NA	NA	NA
Killeen	50.4	625	56.2	748	45.4	84.0	34.5	95.2	34.87	2 153	2 623
Kingsville	NA	NA	NA	NA	56.4	84.3	44.7	95.0	27.60	911	3 590
Lake Jackson	22.5	854	0.0	NA	NA	NA	NA	NA	NA	NA	NA
Lancaster	16.4	678	12.5	NA	NA	NA	NA	NA	NA	NA	NA
La Porte	NA	NA	NA	NA	52.2	83.5	42.9	92.3	50.83	1 371	3 012
Laredo	239.4	1 362	16.1	2 062	54.4	86.9	42.9	98.8	21.42	1 025	3 915
League City	23.9	548	0.0	NA	52.2	83.5	42.9	92.3	50.83	1 371	3 012
Lewisville	95.7	1 321	52.7	621	41.9	83.2	30.3	94.0	37.27	2 665	2 225
Longview	116.3	1 539	56.1	761	44.0	82.6	32.7	93.2	47.27	2 433	2 249
Lubbock	256.1	1 341	40.4	1 850	38.8	80.0	24.6	91.9	18.65	3 431	1 689
Lufkin	NA	NA	NA	NA	47.6	82.8	36.9	93.2	42.40	1 951	2 551
McAllen	238.0	2 228	3.4	1 246	58.5	85.4	48.5	95.8	22.83	693	4 076
McKinney	NA	NA	NA	NA	NA	NA	NA	NA	NA	NA	NA
Mansfield	NA	NA	NA	NA	NA	NA	NA	NA	NA	NA	NA
Mesquite	126.1	1 100	21.4	1 055	44.6	85.9	34.5	95.7	36.08	2 259	2 763
Midland	79.4	797	44.6	896	43.6	81.4	28.5	94.6	15.21	2 570	2 132
Mission	NA	NA	NA	NA	57.1	85.5	45.8	96.7	22.82	829	3 985

1. Based on the population estimated as of July 1 of the year shown. 2. Represents normal values based on the 30-year period, 1961–1990. 3. Average daily minimum. 4. Average daily maximum.

Table D. Cities — Land Area and Population

STATE Place code	City	Land area, 2000[1] (sq km)	Total persons (2000)	Rank	Per square kilometer	Total persons 1990	Percent change 1990–2000	Total persons 1980	Percent change 1980–1990	White	Black	Am. Indian, Alaska Native	Asian and Pacific Islander	Other race	Hispanic[2]	Non-Hispanic White
		1	2	3	4	5	6	7	8	9	10	11	12	13	14	15
	TEXAS—Cont'd															
48 48804	Missouri City	76.9	52 913	562	688.1	36 143	46.3	24 533	47.5	45.7	39.1	0.5	11.3	5.5	10.9	38.6
48 50256	Nacogdoches	65.3	29 914	1 040	458.1	30 872	-3.1	27 149	13.7	67.3	25.4	0.7	1.6	6.6	10.8	61.9
48 50820	New Braunfels	75.8	36 494	849	481.5	27 334	33.5	22 404	22.0	86.3	1.6	1.0	0.9	12.5	34.5	62.5
48 52356	North Richland Hills	47.2	55 635	526	1 178.7	45 895	21.2	30 592	50.0	90.3	2.9	1.2	3.3	4.3	9.5	83.1
48 53388	Odessa	95.3	90 943	269	954.3	89 699	1.4	90 027	-0.4	76.1	6.2	1.3	1.2	18.2	41.4	50.8
48 55080	Paris	110.7	25 898	1 202	233.9	24 799	4.4	25 498	-2.7	74.3	22.9	1.7	0.9	1.9	4.1	70.8
48 56000	Pasadena	114.4	141 674	149	1 238.4	119 604	18.5	112 560	6.3	74.2	1.9	1.1	2.2	23.8	48.2	47.2
48 56348	Pearland	101.9	37 640	828	369.4	18 927	98.9	13 219	43.2	84.3	5.6	0.8	4.2	7.0	16.2	73.4
48 57200	Pharr	53.9	46 660	651	865.7	32 921	41.7	21 381	54.0	81.4	0.3	0.8	0.3	19.2	90.6	8.9
48 58016	Plano	185.4	222 030	78	1 197.6	127 885	73.6	72 329	76.8	80.2	5.4	0.8	11.1	4.9	10.1	72.8
48 58820	Port Arthur	214.8	57 755	491	268.9	58 551	-1.4	61 251	-4.4	40.6	44.3	0.8	6.3	10.2	17.5	31.8
48 61796	Richardson	74.0	91 802	266	1 240.6	74 840	22.7	72 480	3.3	77.5	6.6	1.0	12.8	4.8	10.3	69.6
48 63500	Round Rock	67.7	61 136	453	903.0	30 923	97.7	11 762	162.9	78.9	8.4	0.9	3.8	10.7	22.1	65.6
48 63572	Rowlett	52.4	44 503	689	849.3	23 260	91.3	NA	NA	83.4	9.4	0.8	3.9	4.4	8.8	77.3
48 64472	San Angelo	144.8	88 439	280	610.8	84 462	4.7	73 240	15.3	79.2	5.2	1.2	1.5	15.5	33.2	59.9
48 65000	San Antonio	1 055.6	1 144 646	9	1 084.4	976 514	19.3	785 809	22.1	70.8	7.4	1.3	2.3	22.0	58.7	31.8
48 65516	San Juan	28.5	26 229	1 183	920.3	12 561	108.8	NA	NA	82.9	0.5	0.8	0.2	17.6	95.1	4.4
48 65600	San Marcos	47.2	34 733	905	735.9	28 738	20.9	23 420	22.7	75.0	6.0	1.2	1.9	18.8	36.5	55.2
48 67496	Socorro	45.3	27 152	1 137	599.4	22 995	18.1	NA	NA	76.1	0.5	1.5	0.1	24.6	96.4	2.7
48 68636	Sherman	99.8	35 082	891	351.5	31 584	11.1	30 413	3.9	80.8	11.9	2.4	1.6	6.1	12.1	72.6
48 70808	Sugar Land	62.4	63 328	434	1 014.9	33 712	87.9	NA	NA	67.8	5.5	0.5	25.2	3.5	8.0	60.8
48 72176	Temple	169.3	54 514	544	322.0	46 150	18.1	42 483	8.6	71.8	17.3	1.0	2.2	10.4	17.8	62.7
48 72368	Texarkana	66.4	34 782	903	523.8	32 294	7.7	31 271	3.3	60.1	37.6	0.8	1.1	1.7	2.9	58.1
48 72392	Texas City	161.5	41 521	737	257.1	40 822	1.7	41 403	-1.4	62.5	28.0	0.8	1.2	9.6	20.5	50.1
48 72530	The Colony	35.4	26 531	1 162	749.5	22 113	20.0	11 596	90.7	86.9	5.7	1.3	2.3	6.5	13.3	77.5
48 74144	Tyler	127.7	83 650	306	655.1	75 450	10.9	70 501	7.0	63.3	27.0	0.7	1.3	9.4	15.8	55.6
48 75428	Victoria	85.4	60 603	456	709.6	55 076	10.0	50 695	8.6	73.2	8.0	0.8	1.3	19.1	42.9	47.7
48 76000	Waco	218.1	113 726	197	521.4	103 590	9.8	101 262	2.3	62.6	23.3	1.0	1.8	13.7	23.6	51.1
48 77272	Weslaco	32.9	26 935	1 149	818.7	22 739	18.5	19 331	17.6	76.9	0.4	0.7	1.3	22.9	83.8	14.7
48 79000	Wichita Falls	183.1	104 197	221	569.1	96 259	8.2	94 201	2.2	77.6	13.2	1.7	3.0	7.7	14.0	68.9
49 00000	**UTAH**	212 751.1	2 233 169	X	10.5	1 722 850	29.6	1 461 037	17.9	91.1	1.1	1.8	3.2	5.1	9.0	85.3
49 07690	Bountiful	34.9	41 301	741	1 183.4	37 544	10.0	32 877	14.2	96.8	0.4	0.5	2.3	1.5	2.9	94.1
49 13850	Clearfield	20.1	25 974	1 196	1 292.2	21 435	21.2	17 982	19.2	86.2	4.5	2.4	4.8	6.1	10.6	79.0
49 20120	Draper	78.6	25 220	1 229	320.9	7 143	253.1	NA	NA	93.0	1.8	1.3	2.6	3.5	5.8	88.9
49 43660	Layton	53.6	58 474	485	1 090.9	41 784	39.9	22 862	82.8	92.1	2.1	1.1	3.6	3.9	7.0	86.9
49 45860	Logan	42.8	42 670	718	997.0	32 771	30.2	26 844	22.1	90.3	0.9	1.1	4.5	4.8	8.2	85.4
49 49710	Midvale	15.1	27 029	1 144	1 790.0	11 886	127.4	10 146	17.1	84.8	1.6	1.7	3.2	11.5	20.8	73.4
49 53230	Murray	24.9	34 024	921	1 366.4	31 274	8.8	25 750	21.5	93.3	1.4	0.9	2.9	3.5	7.5	87.6
49 55980	Ogden	69.0	77 226	343	1 119.2	63 943	20.8	64 407	-0.7	81.5	2.9	1.9	2.3	14.4	23.6	70.2
49 57300	Orem	47.8	84 324	301	1 764.1	67 561	24.8	52 399	28.9	92.7	0.6	1.2	3.3	4.5	8.6	86.7
49 62470	Provo	102.7	105 166	219	1 024.0	86 835	21.1	74 108	17.2	90.7	0.7	1.3	4.0	6.0	10.5	84.0
49 64340	Riverton	32.6	25 011	1 237	767.2	11 261	122.1	NA	NA	97.5	0.4	0.5	1.4	1.5	3.2	94.7
49 65110	Roy	19.7	32 885	952	1 669.3	24 560	33.7	19 694	24.9	92.6	1.5	0.9	2.6	4.4	7.7	87.5
49 65330	St. George	166.8	49 663	601	297.7	28 572	73.8	11 350	151.7	93.9	0.5	2.2	1.9	3.5	6.7	89.0
49 67000	Salt Lake City	282.5	181 743	111	643.3	159 928	13.6	163 033	-1.9	82.2	2.5	1.9	6.6	10.6	18.8	70.6
49 67440	Sandy	57.8	88 418	281	1 529.7	75 240	17.5	50 546	48.9	95.0	0.7	0.6	3.4	2.1	4.4	91.1
49 70850	South Jordan	54.0	29 437	1 057	545.1	12 215	141.0	NA	NA	96.7	0.4	0.4	2.3	1.7	3.3	93.8
49 75360	Taylorsville	27.7	57 439	499	2 073.6	51 426	11.6	NA	NA	87.7	1.3	1.4	5.6	6.6	12.2	79.9
49 82950	West Jordan	80.0	68 336	397	854.2	42 915	59.2	27 192	57.8	90.8	0.9	1.0	3.9	5.8	10.1	84.4
49 83470	West Valley City	91.7	108 896	207	1 187.5	86 969	25.2	72 378	20.2	81.1	1.6	1.7	8.5	10.7	18.5	70.3
50 00000	**VERMONT**	23 956.2	608 827	X	25.4	562 758	8.2	511 456	10.0	97.9	0.7	1.1	1.2	0.4	0.9	96.2
50 10675	Burlington	27.4	38 889	800	1 419.3	39 127	-0.6	37 712	3.8	94.2	2.4	1.3	3.3	1.2	1.4	91.5
51 00000	**VIRGINIA**	102 548.2	7 078 515	X	69.0	6 189 197	14.4	5 346 797	15.8	73.9	20.4	0.7	4.4	2.7	4.7	70.2
51 01000	Alexandria	39.3	128 283	166	3 264.2	111 182	15.4	103 217	7.7	62.7	24.0	0.7	6.9	10.1	14.7	53.7
51 07784	Blacksburg	50.1	39 573	785	789.9	34 590	14.4	30 638	12.9	86.2	4.9	0.5	9.0	1.9	2.3	83.1
51 14968	Charlottesville	26.6	45 049	679	1 693.6	40 475	11.3	39 916	1.4	71.2	23.2	0.5	5.9	1.5	2.4	68.4
51 16000	Chesapeake	882.5	199 184	91	225.7	151 982	31.1	114 486	32.8	68.1	29.2	0.9	2.5	1.0	2.0	65.9
51 21344	Danville	111.5	48 411	624	434.2	53 056	-8.8	45 642	16.2	54.5	44.5	0.4	0.8	0.7	1.3	53.3
51 35000	Hampton	134.1	146 437	143	1 092.0	133 811	9.4	122 617	9.1	51.1	46.1	1.1	2.7	1.6	2.8	48.5
51 35624	Harrisonburg	45.5	40 468	762	889.4	30 707	31.8	19 671	56.1	87.1	6.7	0.5	4.2	4.3	8.8	80.1
51 44984	Leesburg	30.0	28 311	1 093	943.7	16 202	74.7	NA	NA	85.2	10.0	0.5	3.3	3.3	5.9	80.4
51 47672	Lynchburg	127.9	65 269	419	510.3	66 049	-1.2	66 743	-1.0	67.8	30.6	0.7	1.6	0.9	1.3	66.0
51 48952	Manassas	25.7	35 135	888	1 367.1	27 957	25.7	15 438	81.1	74.8	13.9	0.8	4.2	9.7	15.1	66.3
51 56000	Newport News	176.9	180 150	113	1 018.4	171 439	5.1	144 903	18.3	55.4	40.6	1.1	3.4	2.6	4.2	52.0
51 57000	Norfolk	139.2	234 403	73	1 683.9	261 250	-10.3	266 979	-2.1	50.1	45.3	1.1	3.9	2.4	3.8	47.0
51 61832	Petersburg	59.3	33 740	933	569.0	37 027	-8.9	41 055	-9.8	19.1	79.6	0.5	1.0	0.8	1.4	18.2
51 64000	Portsmouth	85.9	100 565	237	1 170.7	103 910	-3.2	104 577	-0.6	47.0	51.5	1.1	1.3	0.9	1.7	45.1

1. Dry land or land partially or temporarily covered by water.   2. Hispanic persons may be of any race.

Table D. Cities — **Population and Households**

City	Under 5 years	5 to 17 years	18 to 24 years	25 to 34 years	35 to 44 years	45 to 54 years	55 to 64 years	65 to 74 years	75 years and over	Percent female	Number	Percent change, 1990–2000	Persons per household	Female family householder[1]	One-person
	16	17	18	19	20	21	22	23	24	25	26	27	28	29	30
TEXAS—Cont'd															
Missouri City	7.3	23.5	7.0	11.3	19.7	17.8	7.9	3.5	1.9	51.6	17 069	47.9	3.09	12.5	11.9
Nacogdoches	5.8	14.4	30.9	12.1	10.2	9.5	6.0	5.2	5.9	53.3	11 220	-0.8	2.30	13.7	33.5
New Braunfels	7.1	18.6	8.5	14.2	14.2	12.6	8.0	7.6	9.3	52.1	13 558	35.6	2.60	11.5	24.8
North Richland Hills	7.1	20.2	9.0	14.3	18.3	14.4	7.9	5.0	3.9	50.8	20 793	23.0	2.66	10.3	20.4
Odessa	8.0	21.8	10.6	12.9	14.9	12.3	7.7	6.5	5.2	51.8	33 661	2.5	2.65	14.5	25.7
Paris	7.4	17.9	10.0	12.7	13.1	11.6	9.2	7.7	10.3	53.7	10 570	7.8	2.35	17.0	32.5
Pasadena	9.3	22.3	11.4	15.8	15.4	11.4	6.5	4.5	3.4	50.0	47 031	11.9	2.99	13.1	20.4
Pearland	8.0	20.9	7.3	15.1	19.1	13.7	7.5	5.0	3.4	50.9	13 192	100.2	2.84	9.7	15.8
Pharr	10.6	24.2	11.3	14.6	11.7	9.2	6.7	6.8	5.1	52.4	12 798	47.8	3.64	16.9	13.3
Plano	8.3	20.4	7.0	16.0	20.5	15.4	7.5	2.9	2.1	50.2	80 875	82.3	2.73	7.5	20.2
Port Arthur	7.8	20.8	9.7	12.1	14.1	12.0	7.9	7.7	7.8	52.3	21 839	-2.2	2.61	19.7	29.4
Richardson	6.7	18.1	8.7	15.2	17.5	14.5	9.4	5.9	4.1	50.6	35 191	29.3	2.59	8.9	22.9
Round Rock	9.7	22.2	8.5	19.6	19.2	11.6	4.7	2.3	2.2	50.2	21 076	99.4	2.87	11.0	18.1
Rowlett	8.7	24.8	5.6	15.1	21.9	13.2	5.6	3.1	2.1	50.6	14 266	88.7	3.09	8.0	10.6
San Angelo	7.1	18.8	13.8	13.0	13.9	11.7	7.9	6.9	6.9	52.1	34 006	10.9	2.48	12.5	28.8
San Antonio	8.1	20.5	10.8	15.5	15.3	12.1	7.3	5.6	4.8	51.7	405 474	24.1	2.77	16.4	25.1
San Juan	10.5	26.9	11.9	15.1	12.3	10.0	5.5	4.4	3.3	51.7	6 606	137.3	3.95	17.1	8.6
San Marcos	4.9	10.4	41.9	16.0	8.8	6.5	4.2	3.3	3.9	50.8	12 660	28.5	2.31	10.1	31.0
Sherman	7.2	17.3	13.1	13.6	14.2	11.6	7.7	6.9	8.3	52.1	13 739	10.3	2.42	13.4	30.4
Socorro	9.2	26.9	11.5	13.6	14.3	11.5	6.7	4.2	2.1	51.6	6 756	29.0	4.02	17.0	7.1
Sugar Land	6.1	25.0	6.2	9.0	19.7	19.7	7.5	3.8	3.0	51.1	20 515	153.3	3.06	8.4	12.6
Temple	7.8	18.5	9.2	14.2	14.4	12.3	7.8	7.1	8.7	52.2	21 543	18.7	2.44	13.6	29.9
Texarkana	7.1	18.9	10.0	13.1	14.5	12.6	8.1	7.3	8.5	52.9	13 569	8.8	2.42	19.3	29.9
Texas City	6.8	19.9	9.6	12.9	14.9	14.1	8.3	7.3	6.1	51.7	15 479	2.4	2.62	17.3	24.8
The Colony	8.4	25.6	7.4	16.4	21.5	12.9	4.9	1.9	1.0	50.3	8 462	25.0	3.14	10.4	11.4
Tyler	7.4	18.7	11.7	13.3	13.6	12.0	8.0	7.3	7.9	53.2	32 525	10.7	2.48	14.5	30.2
Victoria	7.9	20.9	9.7	13.1	14.9	13.0	8.0	6.6	6.0	51.9	22 129	11.9	2.68	14.3	24.5
Waco	7.6	17.8	20.3	12.9	12.0	9.7	6.3	6.2	7.2	52.3	42 279	7.1	2.49	16.2	31.1
Weslaco	9.5	22.3	9.9	14.2	11.7	10.1	7.1	7.5	7.6	53.2	8 295	25.9	3.21	17.0	18.4
Wichita Falls	7.1	17.5	15.2	14.3	15.0	11.3	7.3	6.5	5.8	48.5	37 970	7.0	2.46	12.3	28.7
UTAH	9.4	22.8	14.2	14.6	13.4	10.6	6.4	4.5	4.0	49.9	701 281	30.5	3.13	9.4	17.8
Bountiful	8.0	21.7	11.6	11.3	12.6	11.2	9.4	7.8	6.5	51.4	13 341	19.6	3.05	8.9	16.7
Clearfield	12.2	24.0	16.0	18.0	12.6	7.6	3.8	2.8	2.9	49.3	7 921	28.4	3.12	13.9	16.3
Draper	10.5	21.5	11.2	20.5	17.8	10.0	4.8	2.2	1.5	43.5	6 305	359.2	3.40	5.6	10.6
Layton	10.3	24.7	12.1	15.3	14.9	11.2	5.6	3.5	2.2	49.6	18 282	43.6	3.19	9.7	15.2
Logan	9.5	13.9	34.3	17.6	7.9	6.1	3.6	3.1	4.0	52.1	13 902	26.0	2.92	7.7	17.9
Midvale	9.5	16.3	16.7	19.2	12.7	9.4	7.2	4.8	4.2	49.3	10 089	117.9	2.66	12.7	25.3
Murray	7.5	19.8	13.3	14.2	14.4	12.3	7.3	6.0	5.4	51.1	12 673	8.2	2.68	11.3	24.6
Ogden	9.8	18.9	14.6	15.9	13.2	10.1	6.2	5.3	6.0	49.4	27 384	13.0	2.73	13.1	26.2
Orem	10.6	24.8	17.4	14.8	11.0	9.2	5.3	3.6	3.3	50.3	23 382	33.0	3.57	9.5	12.4
Provo	8.7	13.6	40.2	16.5	6.7	5.1	3.5	2.8	2.9	51.9	29 192	22.6	3.34	7.8	11.8
Riverton	12.4	30.2	8.9	15.8	16.3	9.2	3.9	2.0	1.3	49.7	6 348	131.3	3.93	5.7	5.8
Roy	10.1	23.4	11.6	16.2	14.4	10.1	5.9	4.8	3.6	50.5	10 689	39.6	3.06	10.3	15.8
St. George	8.6	19.7	13.7	11.5	10.4	8.9	7.8	9.8	9.5	51.4	17 367	83.8	2.81	8.6	19.4
Salt Lake City	7.9	15.7	15.2	19.7	13.8	10.8	5.9	4.9	6.1	49.4	71 461	7.2	2.48	10.2	33.2
Sandy	7.9	26.5	11.1	11.4	16.0	14.9	6.9	2.8	2.4	49.8	25 737	32.5	3.42	8.6	11.6
South Jordan	8.4	30.8	10.5	10.6	16.5	12.5	6.0	2.7	2.0	49.8	7 507	165.4	3.92	5.0	7.9
Taylorsville	8.4	22.3	14.7	15.0	13.9	12.7	6.8	3.8	2.5	50.0	18 530	NA	3.09	11.9	17.6
West Jordan	11.3	26.5	12.2	17.0	15.1	10.4	4.4	1.9	1.3	49.8	18 897	69.6	3.60	10.0	10.2
West Valley City	10.6	23.1	12.9	16.9	13.8	10.8	6.6	3.4	2.0	49.4	32 253	24.4	3.36	13.2	14.7
VERMONT	5.6	18.6	9.3	12.2	16.7	15.4	9.3	6.7	6.0	51.0	240 634	14.2	2.44	9.3	26.2
Burlington	4.6	11.7	25.4	17.5	13.5	10.5	6.3	5.0	5.5	51.7	15 885	8.2	2.19	10.0	35.6
VIRGINIA	6.5	18.0	9.6	14.6	17.0	14.1	8.9	6.1	5.1	51.0	2 699 173	17.8	2.54	11.9	25.1
Alexandria	6.2	10.6	9.2	25.4	18.1	13.8	7.8	4.4	4.6	51.7	61 889	16.2	2.04	9.2	43.4
Blacksburg	2.9	6.7	57.4	12.3	6.6	5.7	3.5	2.6	2.4	44.1	13 162	17.8	2.37	5.3	26.6
Charlottesville	4.4	10.8	33.8	14.6	11.2	-9.3	5.9	5.1	5.0	53.3	16 851	5.3	2.27	13.1	34.9
Chesapeake	7.2	21.6	8.2	13.5	18.9	13.8	7.9	5.1	3.8	51.4	69 900	34.5	2.79	14.0	18.0
Danville	6.0	17.3	8.0	11.5	14.0	13.8	9.8	9.7	9.9	54.5	20 607	-5.1	2.27	19.6	33.9
Hampton	6.3	17.9	12.6	14.8	17.7	12.4	8.0	5.8	4.5	50.4	53 887	8.5	2.49	16.4	26.6
Harrisonburg	4.7	10.7	40.9	11.3	9.9	8.0	5.2	4.3	5.0	52.6	13 133	27.4	2.53	9.3	28.3
Leesburg	9.8	19.6	6.4	18.3	20.6	12.6	6.7	3.1	3.0	50.9	10 325	62.8	2.69	9.7	22.9
Lynchburg	5.8	16.3	15.5	12.2	13.1	12.4	8.4	7.5	8.8	54.3	25 477	1.3	2.30	16.0	32.7
Manassas	8.6	21.0	9.8	17.4	18.4	13.1	6.3	3.1	2.3	49.1	11 757	24.0	2.92	11.3	21.1
Newport News	7.9	19.6	11.5	15.8	16.4	11.5	7.3	5.4	5.4	48.9	86 210	-3.7	2.45	18.8	30.2
Norfolk	7.1	17.0	18.2	15.6	14.3	10.7	6.2	5.5	5.4	48.9	86 210	-6.3	2.38	26.1	32.2
Petersburg	6.4	18.7	8.9	13.0	14.5	13.2	9.7	8.0	7.6	54.3	13 799	-6.3	2.38	26.1	32.2
Portsmouth	7.1	18.6	11.1	14.0	15.1	12.3	8.0	6.8	6.9	51.7	38 170	-1.5	2.51	20.9	27.5

1. No spouse present.

Table D. Cities — Group Quarters, Crime, Education, and Income

City	Persons in group quarters, 2000				Serious crimes known to police, 2000[2]				Education, 1990				Money income, 1989		
	Institutional			Non-Institutional[1]	Total		Rate[3]		School enrollment		Attainment[4] (percent)		Per capita (dollars)[5]	Households Median	
	Total	Total	Persons in nursing homes		Number	Rate[3]	Violent	Property	Public	Private	High school graduate or more	Bachelor's degree or more		Dollars	Percent change, 1979–1989 (constant 1989 dollars)
	31	32	33	34	35	36	37	38	39	40	41	42	43	44	45
TEXAS—Cont'd															
Missouri City	141	14	14	127	1 279	2 417	183	2 234	10 253	1 713	92.3	39.8	18 764	51 984	-8.6
Nacogdoches	4 133	486	295	3 647	1 529	5 111	745	4 366	13 908	606	72.8	26.0	9 478	15 917	-18.9
New Braunfels	1 178	819	558	359	2 696	7 388	532	6 856	6 066	688	68.4	18.5	11 777	26 409	5.2
North Richland Hills	269	202	194	67	2 445	4 395	338	4 057	10 401	1 916	86.4	22.0	15 912	38 354	-2.4
Odessa	1 837	1 563	627	274	4 823	5 303	550	4 754	24 136	1 668	69.5	13.6	11 588	24 346	-23.0
Paris	1 050	732	502	318	2 939	11 348	2 023	9 325	5 750	248	65.3	14.4	10 038	18 743	-1.8
Pasadena	1 050	865	747	185	6 342	4 476	383	4 093	30 795	2 089	69.8	10.9	12 402	28 729	-20.7
Pearland	182	165	165	17	1 150	3 055	175	2 880	4 735	469	85.0	22.1	17 437	42 565	-7.2
Pharr	21	0	0	21	3 276	7 021	570	6 451	11 037	323	41.6	8.4	5 561	15 605	-11.6
Plano	1 124	531	496	593	7 870	3 545	281	3 264	33 450	5 413	93.2	46.6	21 820	53 905	11.5
Port Arthur	734	497	471	237	2 873	4 974	746	4 228	14 491	1 094	65.5	10.0	9 706	18 548	-28.9
Richardson	809	548	509	261	3 876	4 222	305	3 917	18 315	2 913	93.3	45.9	21 335	50 240	3.2
Round Rock	550	438	438	112	1 489	2 436	190	2 246	8 471	937	85.0	22.1	12 764	33 228	-14.5
Rowlett	356	295	283	61	1 032	2 319	144	2 175	5 617	860	90.6	27.4	17 237	48 121	NA
San Angelo	3 955	1 123	787	2 832	4 800	5 427	386	5 042	23 095	1 477	70.9	17.6	11 353	23 534	-1.0
San Antonio	23 180	11 682	5 641	11 498	86 332	7 542	691	6 851	236 083	34 802	69.1	17.8	10 884	23 584	2.2
San Juan	135	124	119	11	554	2 112	99	2 013	3 636	142	40.7	7.3	6 014	14 292	NA
San Marcos	5 528	793	337	4 735	1 581	4 552	521	4 031	14 937	482	67.8	27.5	8 103	14 816	-16.2
Sherman	1 770	940	552	830	2 178	6 208	564	5 644	6 920	1 598	75.1	19.2	12 929	24 763	-6.3
Socorro	1	0	0	1	563	2 074	140	1 934	8 490	236	34.3	2.3	4 382	15 846	NA
Sugar Land	491	270	270	221	1 798	2 839	150	2 689	6 225	1 129	90.7	43.1	24 200	56 571	NA
Temple	1 994	1 578	1 083	416	2 735	5 017	325	4 692	10 107	1 176	73.8	20.4	12 914	23 194	-2.6
Texarkana	1 911	1 597	656	314	2 548	7 326	909	6 417	7 550	453	70.2	17.5	11 931	21 745	2.5
Texas City	922	871	473	51	3 600	8 670	1 045	7 625	10 678	633	71.4	9.9	11 794	26 144	-26.5
The Colony	0	0	0	0	1 118	4 214	128	4 086	6 170	700	89.9	21.5	14 070	42 743	2.6
Tyler	3 053	1 811	967	1 242	6 262	7 486	763	6 723	19 461	2 109	77.1	24.7	13 400	23 661	-12.3
Victoria	1 222	951	478	271	3 703	6 110	729	5 381	14 265	1 639	70.7	15.8	12 355	25 576	-12.3
Waco	8 443	3 430	1 599	5 013	9 334	8 207	825	7 383	21 923	12 251	68.4	17.0	10 195	17 852	-11.3
Weslaco	341	339	323	2	2 272	8 435	449	7 986	6 787	210	51.5	12.5	7 597	17 645	1.7
Wichita Falls	10 951	5 273	765	5 678	6 271	6 018	562	5 456	22 298	2 267	75.5	18.0	11 686	23 560	-5.9
UTAH	40 480	19 467	6 853	21 013	99 958	4 476	256	4 220	543 194	67 502	85.1	22.3	11 029	29 470	-0.5
Bountiful	564	429	427	135	1 059	2 564	252	2 312	11 691	859	91.6	30.5	14 399	38 346	-5.4
Clearfield	1 271	111	93	1 160	900	3 465	169	3 296	7 477	454	86.5	12.2	8 672	26 875	-1.7
Draper	3 802	3 787	86	15	NA	NA	NA	NA	NA	NA	NA	NA	NA	NA	NA
Layton	99	6	4	93	2 366	4 046	186	3 860	13 578	881	88.2	19.7	11 545	34 466	3.0
Logan	2 138	372	306	1 766	1 024	2 400	63	2 337	14 662	379	90.4	36.8	9 394	21 312	0.2
Midvale	201	0	0	201	1 788	6 615	392	6 223	2 774	225	73.7	13.2	9 631	21 183	-19.8
Murray	90	84	67	6	3 251	9 555	409	9 146	8 158	931	84.2	20.4	13 216	28 950	-6.1
Ogden	2 356	1 011	367	1 345	5 526	7 156	574	6 582	16 644	1 211	75.1	16.2	10 754	23 487	-0.9
Orem	751	624	301	127	3 475	4 121	64	4 057	23 570	3 841	90.0	30.4	9 726	31 262	6.8
Provo	7 572	879	231	6 693	4 041	3 842	125	3 718	17 547	27 699	89.8	34.5	8 408	21 162	-0.2
Riverton	55	7	7	48	NA	NA	NA	NA	4 204	308	88.7	14.7	9 391	36 242	NA
Roy	172	170	126	2	983	2 989	271	2 719	7 982	498	88.7	15.6	11 602	35 018	2.7
St. George	859	399	372	460	1 451	2 922	250	2 672	8 736	332	86.3	19.9	10 520	25 947	14.2
Salt Lake City	4 573	1 134	735	3 439	16 831	9 261	716	8 545	42 020	5 084	83.0	30.4	12 482	22 697	2.5
Sandy	524	322	304	202	3 170	3 585	165	3 420	26 947	2 680	93.1	29.4	12 840	43 971	10.1
South Jordan	12	7	7	5	683	2 320	109	2 212	4 841	384	90.9	22.9	10 626	43 804	NA
Taylorsville	184	77	77	107	NA	NA	NA	NA	NA	NA	NA	NA	NA	NA	NA
West Jordan	396	237	129	159	2 747	4 020	187	3 833	15 733	1 221	86.3	15.9	9 434	33 273	-2.5
West Valley City	495	200	86	295	7 259	6 666	476	6 190	27 447	1 565	79.7	11.6	9 511	29 510	-11.4
VERMONT	20 760	5 663	4 037	15 097	18 185	2 987	114	2 873	120 725	25 263	80.8	24.3	13 527	29 792	20.2
Burlington	4 022	485	477	3 537	2 294	5 899	404	5 495	11 397	2 954	82.4	34.8	13 918	25 523	16.7
VIRGINIA	231 398	111 484	38 865	119 914	214 348	3 028	282	2 746	1 331 800	214 457	75.2	24.5	15 713	33 328	13.8
Alexandria	1 901	1 439	948	462	5 299	4 131	245	3 886	15 153	5 930	86.9	48.5	25 509	41 472	17.7
Blacksburg	8 444	188	188	8 256	717	1 812	149	1 663	22 450	835	91.8	61.6	9 750	18 592	-1.4
Charlottesville	6 832	374	374	6 458	2 335	5 183	890	4 293	13 659	1 088	75.5	34.1	12 928	24 190	3.5
Chesapeake	4 114	3 205	716	909	6 894	3 461	536	2 925	35 713	4 926	77.1	16.9	13 817	35 737	13.2
Danville	1 679	1 078	609	601	2 195	4 534	496	4 038	9 712	1 252	57.4	12.4	11 344	20 413	-11.2
Hampton	12 468	9 341	720	3 127	5 668	3 830	332	3 498	28 947	7 620	79.7	19.1	13 099	30 144	6.0
Harrisonburg	7 194	898	591	6 296	1 536	3 796	351	3 445	12 155	1 556	76.8	28.7	11 607	25 312	8.8
Leesburg	518	495	324	23	640	2 261	265	1 996	3 155	490	82.7	28.6	17 574	39 887	NA
Lynchburg	6 551	1 703	1 085	4 848	2 779	4 258	458	3 800	11 962	7 242	69.5	21.7	12 657	23 726	-7.5
Manassas	861	747	228	114	1 431	4 073	387	3 686	5 850	938	84.2	25.8	18 554	46 674	12.7
Newport News	5 833	2 064	1 122	3 769	9 995	5 548	748	4 800	38 723	5 279	79.3	18.4	12 711	27 469	2.6
Norfolk	23 289	3 000	1 095	20 289	15 985	6 819	712	6 108	52 797	7 731	72.7	16.8	11 643	23 563	12.4
Petersburg	906	589	330	317	2 631	7 798	1 091	6 707	8 028	903	62.2	13.5	10 547	21 309	-5.4
Portsmouth	4 814	1 798	356	3 016	6 537	6 500	980	5 520	22 950	2 727	66.6	11.6	11 158	24 601	3.4

1. Persons in emergency shelters and persons visible in street locations.   2. Data for serious crimes have not been adjusted for underreporting. This may affect comparability between geographic areas and over time.   3. Per 100,000 population estimated by the FBI.   4. Persons 25 years old and older.   5. Based on population enumerated as of April 1, 1990.

City		Money income, 1989 (cont'd)			Housing units, 2000										
	Households (cont'd)	Percent below poverty, 1989					Vacant units				Occupied units				
		Persons		Families											
	Percent with $100,000 or more	Total	Percent change in rate, 1979–1989	Total	Total	Percent change, 1990–2000	Vacant units for sale or rent[1]	For seasonal use (percent)	Home owner vacancy rate	Renter vacancy rate	Total	Percent owner occupied	Percent renter occupied	Average size owner occupied	Average size renter occupied
	46	47	48	49	50	51	52	53	54	55	56	57	58	59	60
TEXAS—Cont'd															
Missouri City	9.4	3.4	36.0	2.0	17 481	41.6	412	0.1	1.3	3.5	17 069	90.8	9.2	3.08	3.18
Nacogdoches	1.8	31.5	40.0	18.4	12 329	0.6	1 109	0.6	1.7	8.9	11 220	43.5	56.5	2.49	2.15
New Braunfels	2.6	14.9	40.6	11.6	14 896	34.6	1 338	1.7	1.4	11.2	13 558	64.4	35.6	2.69	2.45
North Richland Hills	3.2	5.1	24.4	3.8	21 600	19.2	807	0.2	0.8	7.0	20 793	67.1	32.9	2.81	2.36
Odessa	2.5	19.4	68.7	15.5	37 966	0.6	4 305	0.4	2.0	17.3	33 661	64.1	35.9	2.80	2.38
Paris	1.5	25.4	19.8	20.5	11 777	5.2	1 207	0.6	2.3	9.2	10 570	54.3	45.7	2.34	2.36
Pasadena	2.3	14.1	83.1	11.1	50 367	5.9	3 336	0.2	1.3	9.5	47 031	56.1	43.9	3.10	2.85
Pearland	6.2	4.7	62.1	3.2	13 922	103.9	730	0.1	1.9	10.8	13 192	79.4	20.6	2.95	2.41
Pharr	1.1	44.5	18.7	37.7	16 537	49.9	3 739	11.9	1.5	16.6	12 798	73.2	26.8	3.68	3.55
Plano	12.9	3.3	-13.2	2.2	86 078	81.7	5 203	0.3	1.4	12.6	80 875	68.8	31.2	2.97	2.21
Port Arthur	1.5	28.1	58.8	24.0	24 713	-4.0	2 874	0.6	1.8	8.4	21 839	62.2	37.8	2.69	2.48
Richardson	10.7	4.4	41.9	3.1	36 530	27.1	1 339	0.2	1.0	5.5	35 191	64.4	35.6	2.70	2.37
Round Rock	1.7	9.0	26.8	7.3	21 766	86.1	690	0.3	1.0	3.5	21 076	65.3	34.7	3.03	2.58
Rowlett	4.7	2.5	NA	1.7	14 580	78.8	314	0.1	1.1	4.9	14 266	92.2	7.8	3.09	3.16
San Angelo	2.3	18.5	42.3	13.7	37 699	8.9	3 693	0.7	2.2	11.2	34 006	60.8	39.2	2.62	2.27
San Antonio	2.4	22.6	8.1	18.7	433 122	18.5	27 648	0.5	1.4	6.9	405 474	58.1	41.9	2.95	2.51
San Juan	1.3	38.9	NA	37.0	7 719	144.4	1 113	7.0	1.2	6.9	6 606	76.7	23.3	4.03	3.69
San Marcos	0.8	37.1	19.3	21.7	13 340	22.1	680	0.3	1.3	4.5	12 660	30.2	69.8	2.75	2.12
Sherman	3.0	15.6	64.2	10.8	14 926	4.7	1 187	0.3	2.0	8.9	13 739	56.4	43.6	2.53	2.29
Socorro	0.3	41.7	NA	38.9	7 140	31.0	384	0.4	0.6	6.3	6 756	81.1	18.9	4.11	3.64
Sugar Land	16.2	2.5	NA	1.4	21 090	145.8	575	0.3	1.1	5.1	20 515	84.1	15.9	3.15	2.61
Temple	3.3	19.2	27.2	14.8	23 511	13.5	1 968	0.3	2.5	8.4	21 543	55.9	44.1	2.59	2.25
Texarkana	3.2	21.8	5.3	16.7	15 105	5.5	1 536	0.4	2.2	11.5	13 569	58.7	41.3	2.44	2.40
Texas City	1.6	16.8	64.7	14.6	16 715	0.2	1 236	0.3	1.6	9.5	15 479	63.3	36.7	2.72	2.45
The Colony	1.6	2.9	7.4	2.3	8 812	23.2	350	0.0	2.3	7.2	8 462	82.5	17.5	3.14	3.12
Tyler	3.7	19.5	44.4	15.2	35 337	7.5	2 812	0.4	1.9	9.4	32 525	56.2	43.8	2.63	2.28
Victoria	3.2	18.9	33.1	15.2	24 192	11.0	2 063	0.5	1.4	11.3	22 129	60.8	39.2	2.76	2.57
Waco	1.9	28.7	32.9	19.7	45 819	1.6	3 540	0.3	1.9	6.6	42 279	46.4	53.6	2.60	2.40
Weslaco	1.4	35.5	-2.2	29.8	10 230	15.6	1 935	10.2	1.5	9.2	8 295	65.4	34.6	3.29	3.06
Wichita Falls	2.4	16.6	28.7	13.2	41 916	3.8	3 946	0.4	2.6	11.2	37 970	57.8	42.2	2.54	2.34
UTAH	2.5	11.4	10.3	8.6	768 594	28.4	67 313	3.9	2.1	6.5	701 281	71.5	28.5	3.28	2.75
Bountiful	5.9	4.9	19.5	4.2	13 819	20.3	478	0.3	1.5	4.8	13 341	77.7	22.3	3.19	2.59
Clearfield	0.6	17.5	-2.8	10.6	8 374	28.5	453	0.2	3.3	5.8	7 921	55.1	44.9	3.19	3.04
Draper	NA	NA	NA	NA	6 588	348.8	283	0.4	2.2	4.9	6 305	83.8	16.2	3.54	2.63
Layton	2.0	7.1	34.0	6.1	19 145	42.2	863	0.3	2.4	6.5	18 282	74.5	25.5	3.42	2.52
Logan	1.4	21.6	19.3	12.7	14 692	28.4	790	0.6	2.3	4.6	13 902	44.0	56.0	3.05	2.81
Midvale	0.9	20.7	86.5	17.6	10 730	115.8	641	0.6	1.4	6.9	10 089	48.1	51.9	2.66	2.66
Murray	2.6	8.0	3.9	5.9	13 327	7.9	654	0.2	2.1	6.9	12 673	66.7	33.3	2.81	2.40
Ogden	1.3	16.8	28.2	13.1	29 763	9.4	2 379	0.3	3.2	9.9	27 384	61.2	38.8	2.84	2.57
Orem	2.9	9.0	-21.7	7.9	24 166	34.5	784	0.3	1.2	3.4	23 382	67.1	32.9	3.82	3.06
Provo	2.2	29.6	7.2	17.4	30 374	23.6	1 182	0.4	2.2	2.4	29 192	42.6	57.4	3.45	3.27
Riverton	0.8	4.5	NA	4.4	6 555	131.5	207	0.2	1.3	5.0	6 348	94.0	6.0	3.96	3.50
Roy	0.6	4.4	-26.7	3.3	11 053	39.3	364	0.2	2.0	5.6	10 689	84.3	15.7	3.11	2.81
St. George	2.3	12.7	-21.1	7.9	21 083	79.2	3 716	11.9	3.7	6.6	17 367	67.9	32.1	2.78	2.88
Salt Lake City	3.4	16.4	15.5	11.9	77 054	4.5	5 593	0.8	2.1	6.8	71 461	51.2	48.8	2.69	2.26
Sandy	4.7	4.2	-22.2	3.2	26 579	32.2	842	0.3	1.3	6.7	25 737	84.3	15.7	3.53	2.82
South Jordan	3.2	3.2	NA	2.4	7 721	167.6	214	0.1	1.0	8.8	7 507	89.7	10.3	4.09	2.44
Taylorsville	NA	NA	NA	NA	19 159	NA	629	0.3	1.3	4.8	18 530	71.2	28.8	3.25	2.70
West Jordan	1.2	7.0	2.9	6.6	19 597	68.4	700	0.1	1.7	6.4	18 897	81.9	18.1	3.72	3.05
West Valley City	0.6	11.5	66.7	10.1	33 488	22.4	1 235	0.1	1.7	5.1	32 253	72.6	27.4	3.48	3.05
VERMONT	2.8	9.9	-18.5	6.9	294 382	8.5	53 748	14.6	1.4	4.2	240 634	70.6	29.4	2.58	2.11
Burlington	3.7	19.3	19.1	11.2	16 395	5.9	510	1.1	0.6	1.6	15 885	41.5	58.5	2.39	2.06
VIRGINIA	5.2	10.2	-13.2	7.7	2 904 192	16.3	205 019	1.9	1.5	5.2	2 699 173	68.1	31.9	2.62	2.36
Alexandria	8.9	7.1	-21.1	4.7	64 251	10.3	2 362	0.8	1.0	2.4	61 889	40.0	60.0	2.03	2.05
Blacksburg	2.1	37.4	17.6	12.8	13 732	15.8	570	0.4	1.6	3.2	13 162	30.4	69.6	2.45	2.33
Charlottesville	2.6	23.7	12.9	10.0	17 591	4.8	740	0.4	1.1	2.4	16 851	40.8	59.2	2.27	2.26
Chesapeake	2.4	9.0	-19.6	7.0	72 672	30.4	2 772	0.3	1.4	3.6	69 900	74.9	25.1	2.87	2.56
Danville	1.3	19.0	37.7	15.0	23 108	-0.8	2 501	0.4	2.8	11.6	20 607	58.1	41.9	2.28	2.25
Hampton	1.6	10.8	-7.7	8.8	57 311	9.0	3 424	0.5	2.0	5.6	53 887	58.6	41.4	2.55	2.40
Harrisonburg	3.0	21.5	31.1	8.4	13 689	25.6	556	0.3	1.7	3.3	13 133	39.0	61.0	2.52	2.54
Leesburg	3.6	6.1	NA	3.8	10 671	52.6	346	0.4	0.6	3.4	10 325	67.9	32.1	2.88	2.30
Lynchburg	2.8	16.4	25.2	12.8	27 640	1.5	2 163	0.5	2.2	7.1	25 477	58.5	41.5	2.44	2.12
Manassas	6.6	3.8	-50.6	2.7	12 114	18.4	357	0.2	1.0	3.6	11 757	69.8	30.2	2.98	2.78
Newport News	2.0	14.0	3.7	12.2	74 117	6.3	4 431	0.3	1.9	6.2	69 686	52.4	47.6	2.61	2.39
Norfolk	2.2	19.3	-6.8	15.4	94 416	-4.4	8 206	0.3	3.2	6.8	86 210	45.5	54.5	2.51	2.40
Petersburg	1.2	20.3	0.0	15.4	15 955	-1.5	2 156	0.1	3.4	12.4	13 799	51.5	48.5	2.40	2.36
Portsmouth	1.3	17.7	-7.8	14.9	41 605	-1.6	3 435	0.3	2.6	6.9	38 170	58.6	41.4	2.52	2.49

1. Includes units rented or sold but not occupied.   2. Specified owner-occupied units.   3. Specified renter-occupied units.   4. Overcrowded or lacking complete plumbing facilities.

City	Civilian labor force, 2001				Civilian employment, 1990[2]			Disability 1990	Value of residential construction authorized by building permits, 2000		
			Unemployment			Percent					
	Total	Percent change, 2000–2001	Total	Rate[1]	Total	Professional, managerial, and technical	Precision production, craft, and repair	Work disabled persons[3] (percent)	New construction ($1,000)	Number of housing units	Percent single family
	61	62	63	64	65	66	67	68	69	70	71
TEXAS—Cont'd											
Missouri City	33 085	1.7	673	2.0	19 676	45.6	7.9	3.6	67 163	558	100.0
Nacogdoches	14 866	4.0	611	4.1	13 251	29.5	6.7	6.7	5 100	100	42.0
New Braunfels	20 640	2.2	712	3.4	11 759	29.3	10.6	8.3	34 833	463	85.7
North Richland Hills	33 924	1.4	1 080	3.2	25 507	33.3	11.2	5.1	57 365	498	58.2
Odessa	45 387	1.3	2 320	5.1	38 514	25.9	15.8	8.7	20 621	238	43.7
Paris	11 540	-0.4	851	7.4	9 480	24.9	10.5	10.7	6 672	88	78.4
Pasadena	71 357	1.8	3 400	4.8	54 423	22.2	18.9	7.7	41 335	389	99.5
Pearland	12 074	0.5	434	3.6	9 990	35.1	14.0	4.8	149 860	818	100.0
Pharr	16 550	2.0	2 580	15.6	9 430	19.4	10.5	9.0	25 984	572	93.2
Plano	144 248	2.3	5 031	3.5	71 973	48.2	5.9	3.4	417 299	2 204	89.0
Port Arthur	25 071	-1.3	3 144	12.5	20 616	20.4	14.3	11.0	11 930	131	100.0
Richardson	57 333	1.9	2 087	3.6	41 250	46.7	5.2	4.3	142 547	1 178	42.8
Round Rock	35 955	1.9	1 107	3.1	16 267	32.0	10.9	5.7	204 507	2 233	76.3
Rowlett	17 093	1.4	445	2.6	12 686	39.1	11.7	4.7	126 352	823	100.0
San Angelo	42 402	0.6	1 288	3.0	35 394	27.3	10.8	8.8	25 994	247	96.8
San Antonio	540 976	1.7	23 911	4.4	389 772	29.0	10.7	8.8	485 076	7 667	72.6
San Juan	5 886	2.2	716	12.2	3 490	19.9	13.1	9.1	7 479	202	100.0
San Marcos	23 657	1.5	1 124	4.8	12 844	29.3	6.9	4.4	52 803	1 079	7.6
Sherman	16 972	-0.5	1 007	5.9	14 195	32.2	10.8	9.8	8 506	64	93.8
Socorro	10 348	-0.5	1 362	13.2	7 466	8.9	18.5	9.3	5 210	72	100.0
Sugar Land	21 674	1.7	548	2.5	12 437	49.9	6.9	2.7	41 347	265	100.0
Temple	27 582	0.5	852	3.1	19 977	32.7	9.4	10.1	29 218	241	100.0
Texarkana	14 230	-0.3	782	5.5	12 543	28.2	10.8	10.2	11 369	237	34.2
Texas City	21 053	-0.4	1 477	7.0	17 617	25.0	18.9	9.1	32 139	575	63.8
The Colony	19 869	1.5	642	3.2	11 636	32.1	13.1	4.7	105 561	637	100.0
Tyler	45 999	1.0	2 242	4.9	33 307	31.3	8.2	8.0	57 035	379	79.9
Victoria	32 703	1.7	1 391	4.3	24 073	27.9	13.2	8.8	18 335	167	100.0
Waco	51 317	-0.2	2 616	5.1	41 429	27.4	9.7	8.6	39 715	373	53.9
Weslaco	12 152	2.0	1 967	16.2	6 875	27.2	10.8	8.3	12 609	269	100.0
Wichita Falls	45 788	0.4	1 664	3.6	39 448	28.6	10.6	10.3	22 157	187	94.7
UTAH	1 115 380	1.0	48 719	4.4	736 059	30.8	11.4	7.3	2 137 953	17 638	83.4
Bountiful	25 557	0.1	779	3.0	16 319	39.1	7.3	5.8	28 121	125	72.8
Clearfield	11 747	0.9	742	6.3	7 248	24.9	14.2	8.3	8 825	99	100.0
Draper	3 046	0.3	90	3.0	NA	NA	NA	NA	58 194	442	84.4
Layton	28 694	0.3	1 153	4.0	18 139	32.2	12.8	6.8	35 172	346	94.2
Logan	22 414	1.7	884	3.9	15 092	34.0	8.4	5.0	11 482	98	100.0
Midvale	8 351	1.5	539	6.5	5 595	20.4	12.3	9.0	12 499	139	69.8
Murray	22 252	0.3	656	2.9	15 467	30.9	11.2	6.6	24 220	155	100.0
Ogden	40 404	0.7	2 918	7.2	26 843	27.7	11.8	11.8	56 237	613	54.8
Orem	42 642	1.2	1 338	3.1	26 162	35.6	10.2	6.3	38 451	364	52.2
Provo	62 350	1.6	2 644	4.2	37 818	34.6	6.8	4.9	42 084	319	50.5
Riverton	6 610	0.4	210	3.2	4 584	24.8	14.2	4.7	34 605	271	89.3
Roy	16 433	0.0	594	3.6	11 342	30.0	13.9	6.4	38 878	429	100.0
St. George	25 702	5.3	1 061	4.1	10 723	26.0	10.4	7.3	87 299	767	81.2
Salt Lake City	111 307	1.0	5 614	5.0	75 698	37.4	7.4	9.5	44 787	462	45.2
Sandy	47 048	0.4	1 511	3.2	32 614	35.7	9.2	4.9	33 326	191	89.5
South Jordan	7 145	0.3	206	2.9	4 970	33.6	10.8	6.1	37 925	311	100.0
Taylorsville	35 638	0.6	1 343	3.8	NA	NA	NA	NA	NA	NA	NA
West Jordan	26 541	0.5	879	3.3	18 379	26.3	14.4	7.1	89 657	841	51.6
West Valley City	58 887	1.2	3 352	5.7	39 774	22.4	15.6	8.7	36 628	461	96.5
VERMONT	334 695	0.9	12 021	3.6	283 146	31.3	12.3	7.9	319 486	2 506	88.3
Burlington	23 550	1.2	686	2.9	20 862	36.2	7.8	7.0	2 298	26	34.6
VIRGINIA	3 675 345	1.8	127 298	3.5	3 028 362	33.8	11.5	7.5	5 051 601	48 402	82.1
Alexandria	79 614	2.5	2 226	2.8	70 756	53.1	4.9	4.9	109 267	1 100	35.1
Blacksburg	15 850	2.2	601	3.8	14 129	51.5	4.6	2.8	10 197	103	47.6
Charlottesville	18 803	0.4	482	2.6	20 198	38.2	8.4	5.6	5 331	64	75.0
Chesapeake	108 360	1.0	3 193	2.9	72 486	30.4	16.1	7.4	125 057	1 081	100.0
Danville	25 689	1.4	2 207	8.6	23 259	21.9	11.5	10.4	6 473	89	32.6
Hampton	67 271	1.2	2 550	3.8	58 561	30.0	15.1	8.4	21 041	324	100.0
Harrisonburg	19 449	4.2	380	2.0	14 735	32.0	8.2	5.0	13 343	193	74.6
Leesburg	18 615	3.1	527	2.8	9 606	39.4	10.0	5.8	NA	NA	NA
Lynchburg	30 021	-0.7	1 357	4.5	29 569	30.7	8.6	8.7	35 314	364	41.8
Manassas	20 355	3.4	677	3.3	15 808	37.0	10.5	4.7	3 529	54	100.0
Newport News	85 777	1.5	3 490	4.1	72 950	30.6	14.6	8.7	25 035	407	100.0
Norfolk	85 344	1.8	4 851	5.7	89 560	27.2	12.4	9.2	26 356	287	61.7
Petersburg	16 184	3.1	1 030	6.4	15 920	21.7	8.2	12.5	510	11	100.0
Portsmouth	45 118	1.5	2 434	5.4	42 053	25.1	16.6	10.7	15 660	213	100.0

1. Percent of civilian labor force.   2. Persons 16 years and older.   3. Persons 16 to 64 years old.

Table D. Cities — **Wholesale Trade, Retail Trade, and Real Estate**

City	Wholesale Trade, 1997				Retail Trade[1], 1997				Real Estate and Rental and Leasing, 1997			
	Number of Establish-ments	Number of Employees	Sales (mil dol)	Annual Payroll (mil dol)	Number of Establish-ments	Number of Employees	Sales (mil dol)	Annual Payroll (mil dol)	Number of Establish-ments	Number of Employees	Receipts (mil dol)	Annual Payroll (mil dol)
	72	73	74	75	76	77	78	79	80	81	82	83
TEXAS—Cont'd												
Missouri City	33	117	35.8	4.2	85	1 163	145.3	15.0	29	168	18.6	3.0
Nacogdoches	37	355	118.3	10.0	230	2 749	431.0	40.4	51	163	17.3	2.6
New Braunfels	65	506	301.5	16.8	262	2 979	584.0	51.9	62	285	20.3	4.2
North Richland Hills	57	270	218.4	11.0	236	4 647	993.9	87.3	41	165	26.3	3.3
Odessa	234	2 279	738.8	73.7	489	5 614	1 063.4	98.2	120	697	64.3	12.4
Paris	54	418	107.2	10.2	205	2 394	448.4	36.6	42	122	14.6	1.8
Pasadena	110	1 583	589.6	56.5	422	5 739	878.2	88.1	120	811	99.9	19.9
Pearland	47	767	178.2	29.0	89	1 663	276.1	24.8	34	280	45.1	8.4
Pharr	55	713	201.6	14.0	160	1 587	208.8	21.9	17	76	6.7	0.9
Plano	443	4 766	5 038.9	194.4	804	14 928	3 167.2	290.9	224	1 332	261.6	41.9
Port Arthur	33	1 053	355.0	34.5	215	2 585	399.6	39.0	22	205	22.1	4.5
Richardson	478	10 306	8 145.8	565.8	417	6 096	1 597.7	141.5	159	667	101.7	21.2
Round Rock	70	767	433.2	27.9	162	D	D	D	54	171	17.7	2.6
Rowlett	37	135	66.1	5.7	53	511	108.2	10.1	18	46	4.4	0.6
San Angelo	141	1 282	346.5	29.6	446	5 246	874.8	82.8	128	535	50.6	8.0
San Antonio	1 650	23 198	12 097.5	756.4	3 848	55 174	9 723.6	947.0	1 170	8 005	974.7	187.0
San Juan	17	143	39.5	3.2	43	241	44.5	3.3	6	16	1.2	0.2
San Marcos	35	D	D	D	285	3 449	599.1	50.5	55	208	28.3	3.5
Sherman	67	569	206.6	15.7	250	4 231	749.1	67.8	63	250	23.0	4.0
Socorro	9	D	D	D	37	196	30.6	2.4	3	D	D	D
Sugar Land	92	924	1 726.2	44.6	271	4 472	743.8	68.9	63	174	22.8	3.1
Temple	76	2 081	1 271.7	69.5	305	4 196	730.0	71.3	69	325	28.1	5.6
Texarkana	102	1 411	879.6	44.5	331	4 263	768.3	69.6	65	351	42.0	6.1
Texas City	40	223	109.0	9.0	184	3 127	460.0	42.5	37	318	26.0	6.2
The Colony	4	8	7.5	0.2	37	618	95.1	8.5	12	53	11.4	0.5
Tyler	186	2 189	990.8	71.3	643	8 822	1 692.9	154.3	142	690	73.5	15.5
Victoria	125	D	D	D	379	4 913	846.3	77.9	89	D	D	D
Waco	210	2 956	1 481.1	82.1	601	8 053	1 393.7	128.1	170	938	120.8	19.1
Weslaco	21	D	D	D	130	2 194	398.3	35.0	29	122	7.6	1.4
Wichita Falls	176	1 771	391.2	41.0	514	6 450	1 070.1	96.4	129	467	48.3	7.5
UTAH	3 278	44 319	21 115.5	1 420.5	7 656	114 474	19 964.6	1 856.9	2 169	12 318	1 342.6	236.0
Bountiful	51	221	95.9	6.7	142	2 425	510.2	45.7	46	153	18.5	3.2
Clearfield	32	815	306.1	23.0	49	517	76.3	6.8	15	99	26.8	2.2
Draper	NA	NA	NA	NA	NA	NA	NA	NA	NA	NA	NA	NA
Layton	41	401	121.1	8.3	208	3 631	676.9	58.0	56	322	28.3	4.6
Logan	53	409	74.9	8.1	248	3 895	500.8	53.8	55	401	22.3	6.4
Midvale	63	490	220.0	15.4	96	1 815	444.0	32.3	32	188	33.1	4.0
Murray	186	2 103	967.7	64.1	343	6 445	1 418.9	128.5	103	632	71.0	12.6
Ogden	127	1 654	504.5	45.5	408	6 090	922.8	94.7	96	479	44.9	8.9
Orem	103	1 047	481.7	31.4	420	7 352	1 170.3	116.2	77	349	36.9	5.7
Provo	91	3 704	1 748.9	114.1	252	3 782	638.1	60.9	99	489	49.9	7.6
Riverton	13	49	21.7	1.1	29	466	56.2	6.3	12	19	1.4	0.3
Roy	7	D	D	D	54	886	120.0	13.2	22	79	5.0	0.9
St. George	66	559	216.8	16.4	332	4 151	784.5	68.4	86	277	28.9	4.0
Salt Lake City	714	13 524	7 479.4	471.0	1 039	15 539	3 041.0	278.5	362	3 606	380.2	80.9
Sandy	NA	NA	NA	NA	NA	NA	NA	NA	NA	NA	NA	NA
South Jordan	13	D	D	D	25	215	44.8	4.1	18	31	4.5	0.7
Taylorsville	NA	NA	NA	NA	NA	NA	NA	NA	NA	NA	NA	NA
West Jordan	53	626	262.3	17.7	97	2 173	330.7	32.8	33	127	14.5	1.5
West Valley City	NA	NA	NA	NA	NA	NA	NA	NA	NA	NA	NA	NA
VERMONT	941	10 987	4 731.4	330.6	4 093	36 306	5 898.6	603.3	701	2 362	240.6	42.2
Burlington	58	678	331.5	24.6	261	3 041	354.9	42.6	62	323	42.0	7.7
VIRGINIA	7 868	106 365	61 046.7	3 784.4	29 032	379 039	62 569.9	6 202.6	6 717	43 976	5 749.2	1 028.4
Alexandria	137	1 830	899.6	75.1	593	7 746	1 507.6	160.0	202	2 023	354.1	57.9
Blacksburg	8	D	D	D	127	1 773	191.3	21.2	37	345	39.7	7.9
Charlottesville	81	954	265.9	29.7	360	4 345	730.3	73.2	97	458	50.1	9.8
Chesapeake	246	3 833	1 768.2	115.7	779	12 554	1 993.3	184.5	144	704	98.0	15.9
Danville	55	964	211.8	22.6	334	3 787	585.5	56.9	59	242	18.1	3.5
Hampton	94	1 073	370.7	31.3	514	9 930	1 638.9	150.5	113	1 241	89.2	20.6
Harrisonburg	62	971	749.2	25.5	308	4 161	690.8	64.0	48	263	30.8	5.5
Leesburg	22	D	D	D	143	1 807	326.2	32.4	48	241	41.0	6.8
Lynchburg	100	1 292	504.6	43.8	446	7 209	1 228.5	115.8	95	390	37.4	8.2
Manassas	59	1 008	626.3	41.0	230	3 355	647.5	64.9	51	302	41.1	5.5
Newport News	132	1 634	604.2	50.3	681	9 284	1 488.6	143.6	226	1 720	169.9	35.8
Norfolk	324	5 845	2 914.6	183.9	918	12 628	1 900.4	207.3	273	2 128	203.8	44.2
Petersburg	35	538	139.2	16.8	189	1 764	290.0	29.5	28	131	11.1	2.2
Portsmouth	63	712	167.3	23.6	295	3 291	468.4	51.2	84	457	37.8	7.4

1. Establishments with payroll.

City	Professional, Scientific, and Technical Services, 1997[1]				Manufacturing, 1997				Accommodation and Foodservices, 1997			
	Number of Establish-ments	Number of Employees	Receipts (mil dol)	Annual Payroll (mil dol)	Number of Establish-ments	Number of Employees	Receipts (mil dol)	Annual Payroll (mil dol)	Number of Establish-ments	Number of Employees	Sales (mil dol)	Annual Payroll (mil dol)
	84	85	86	87	88	89	90	91	92	93	94	95
TEXAS—Cont'd												
Missouri City	54	D	D	D	18	675	163.4	28.3	39	531	17.9	4.4
Nacogdoches	46	174	12.7	3.1	36	3 101	719.6	92.5	78	1 789	54.0	14.9
New Braunfels	89	302	23.5	7.3	59	3 525	449.9	86.2	128	2 162	72.7	20.7
North Richland Hills	81	573	38.1	18.0	33	1 980	405.3	59.4	91	2 570	76.8	21.3
Odessa	181	949	65.4	25.1	120	1 886	758.9	62.1	217	3 704	117.9	32.4
Paris	49	243	13.5	4.2	44	4 585	2 032.3	157.0	84	1 352	42.5	12.2
Pasadena	137	1 410	176.9	69.1	100	5 905	4 893.4	270.7	174	3 081	108.6	28.8
Pearland	69	188	20.5	5.4	57	793	76.5	21.8	48	843	28.4	7.8
Pharr	30	112	8.5	2.2	NA	NA	NA	NA	48	678	25.1	5.9
Plano	683	3 535	535.3	179.3	124	8 614	2 547.5	448.6	347	8 108	298.8	83.9
Port Arthur	50	355	27.5	10.2	33	3 915	6 712.2	234.9	86	1 265	44.5	12.2
Richardson	521	4 020	459.1	191.2	179	11 246	3 350.5	444.5	205	3 633	149.7	39.4
Round Rock	83	870	152.9	40.6	69	D	D	D	102	2 130	77.2	21.5
Rowlett	37	123	10.7	4.5	44	771	62.6	20.3	20	310	9.4	2.5
San Angelo	149	735	58.1	16.2	85	4 323	803.4	101.8	184	3 706	108.6	32.0
San Antonio	2 507	19 099	1 831.9	729.7	953	32 870	5 199.7	911.6	2 237	50 503	1 844.1	509.4
San Juan	2	D	D	D	NA	NA	NA	NA	14	149	5.2	1.0
San Marcos	61	251	20.5	6.1	42	1 972	245.7	54.0	131	2 444	74.6	20.6
Sherman	108	484	34.6	12.9	58	6 992	2 672.0	274.4	95	1 921	63.6	17.6
Socorro	2	D	D	D	NA	NA	NA	NA	7	D	D	D
Sugar Land	168	D	D	D	40	2 703	983.4	105.3	104	2 200	78.7	21.2
Temple	77	602	49.1	20.6	59	5 515	1 164.7	183.0	130	2 497	77.5	20.8
Texarkana	108	503	50.5	15.1	49	2 717	608.3	90.3	102	2 081	70.2	17.1
Texas City	53	304	20.9	9.3	27	5 408	8 922.0	327.2	82	1 471	42.8	11.5
The Colony	17	19	2.1	0.8	NA	NA	NA	NA	24	435	13.8	4.1
Tyler	325	2 173	256.0	83.9	115	9 228	2 068.8	339.0	228	5 027	152.5	41.6
Victoria	135	705	58.4	21.0	60	2 765	1 195.5	111.0	147	2 680	78.5	21.5
Waco	241	1 910	125.0	54.7	177	14 884	3 608.3	444.3	276	5 511	177.4	48.3
Weslaco	36	234	14.7	5.1	18	1 414	77.8	24.9	59	1 063	34.0	8.6
Wichita Falls	200	1 037	83.4	30.6	121	6 090	1 069.6	206.0	234	D	D	D
UTAH	4 282	36 468	3 306.1	1 303.1	2 860	119 140	24 014.4	3 726.1	3 780	74 390	2 309.0	648.8
Bountiful	115	516	31.3	12.1	37	504	54.1	12.3	57	1 026	26.6	7.6
Clearfield	17	208	14.8	8.0	49	3 745	603.2	103.6	34	454	12.9	3.2
Draper	NA	NA	NA	NA	NA	NA	NA	NA	NA	NA	NA	NA
Layton	56	340	21.4	10.5	NA	NA	NA	NA	94	2 520	66.1	18.6
Logan	101	777	42.4	16.9	79	5 455	909.8	124.5	85	1 561	41.9	10.5
Midvale	48	256	31.5	9.6	NA	NA	NA	NA	49	1 074	33.5	9.1
Murray	198	2 165	255.9	93.1	148	2 680	247.3	61.9	95	2 186	62.1	18.2
Ogden	200	1 932	123.4	53.2	130	13 226	2 696.5	410.9	183	3 153	84.0	24.2
Orem	188	2 031	112.8	46.3	99	2 359	272.6	61.3	103	2 253	59.3	15.8
Provo	199	2 966	268.1	114.6	93	3 367	346.7	79.8	142	3 759	105.8	31.6
Riverton	13	24	2.2	0.5	NA	NA	NA	NA	18	164	6.7	1.5
Roy	14	51	2.3	0.7	11	D	D	D	40	690	20.6	5.1
St. George	105	552	33.7	14.0	60	1 377	191.3	35.5	133	2 961	83.9	24.4
Salt Lake City	1 123	12 408	1 400.3	558.4	512	25 306	4 894.8	813.8	638	15 653	572.6	157.4
Sandy	NA	NA	NA	NA	92	2 662	309.5	82.1	NA	NA	NA	NA
South Jordan	34	181	12.2	3.7	12	D	D	D	13	D	D	D
Taylorsville	NA	NA	NA	NA	NA	NA	NA	NA	NA	NA	NA	NA
West Jordan	31	74	5.1	1.5	76	2 567	433.5	91.1	61	1 054	30.7	8.3
West Valley City	NA	NA	NA	NA	170	6 627	1 199.4	230.8	NA	NA	NA	NA
VERMONT	1 622	7 792	719.1	279.0	1 226	42 533	7 803.0	1 459.6	1 932	27 088	910.2	277.2
Burlington	203	1 597	147.9	62.4	55	D	D	D	136	1 862	66.4	19.1
VIRGINIA	17 539	212 632	24 151.7	9 729.8	5 986	370 595	83 814.0	11 557.8	12 343	233 639	8 281.2	2 320.7
Alexandria	894	12 710	1 456.2	634.2	114	1 907	328.1	59.4	310	6 616	308.3	92.3
Blacksburg	99	1 046	105.0	38.0	23	1 910	225.3	57.8	72	1 689	42.9	11.6
Charlottesville	206	1 448	118.7	49.7	67	D	D	D	179	3 521	121.5	34.7
Chesapeake	263	2 653	198.1	84.5	132	4 558	1 085.0	147.0	305	6 321	187.4	51.6
Danville	76	577	27.3	11.6	47	D	D	D	114	2 159	65.7	18.8
Hampton	211	3 190	270.9	120.4	80	4 636	971.0	123.4	229	5 002	149.9	41.1
Harrisonburg	95	618	50.9	19.6	38	3 687	725.8	102.6	109	2 318	70.2	19.0
Leesburg	154	768	77.1	29.8	NA	NA	NA	NA	55	1 071	43.9	13.6
Lynchburg	182	2 715	260.3	107.1	117	12 535	3 096.4	481.1	173	3 808	110.8	30.9
Manassas	153	1 058	126.9	44.8	34	2 822	791.6	188.5	74	D	D	D
Newport News	286	3 023	218.8	88.6	131	24 707	3 300.5	898.4	312	5 464	170.1	47.7
Norfolk	439	6 582	468.7	207.0	199	10 996	5 737.3	402.2	539	9 980	299.4	85.1
Petersburg	45	1 122	79.8	42.1	43	2 553	409.6	72.4	83	1 194	34.2	10.1
Portsmouth	105	1 023	82.1	31.5	71	1 812	368.7	52.0	137	2 040	58.7	15.8

1. Firms subject to federal tax.

City	Arts, Entertainment, and Recreation[1], 1997				Health Care and Social Assistance[1], 1997				Other Services[1], 1997			
	Number of Establishments	Number of Employees	Receipts (mil dol)	Annual Payroll (mil dol)	Number of Establishments	Number of Employees	Receipts (mil dol)	Annual Payroll (mil dol)	Number of Establishments	Number of Employees	Receipts (mil dol)	Annual Payroll (mil dol)
	96	97	98	99	100	101	102	103	104	105	106	107
TEXAS—Cont'd												
Missouri City	3	0	0.0	0.0	80	1 196	76.1	29.2	44	228	11.6	3.6
Nacogdoches	10	0	0.0	0.0	148	2 224	127.6	48.3	63	397	15.9	5.4
New Braunfels	20	111	3.5	1.0	128	1 220	63.5	26.3	88	455	25.2	7.2
North Richland Hills	13	277	7.1	2.5	91	1 616	109.9	44.2	95	525	30.1	9.7
Odessa	32	231	8.1	1.6	220	3 646	164.0	69.1	175	1 168	128.6	24.1
Paris	9	0	0.0	0.0	139	2 668	98.5	45.4	75	367	16.9	4.7
Pasadena	18	195	6.9	2.2	308	4 293	298.3	116.7	184	1 502	87.4	33.6
Pearland	8	93	4.1	1.1	49	438	17.3	6.7	64	255	18.4	4.7
Pharr	4	21	1.1	0.2	54	1 030	32.1	12.0	53	314	11.6	3.5
Plano	57	979	49.6	13.2	582	6 465	591.2	227.3	280	1 758	108.0	34.1
Port Arthur	7	79	2.8	0.9	126	1 934	153.4	59.0	63	396	21.3	6.0
Richardson	24	433	19.8	6.0	330	3 203	195.2	80.3	183	1 408	99.3	33.6
Round Rock	12	111	4.1	1.6	103	1 208	87.1	34.6	81	670	39.7	12.5
Rowlett	4	50	0.9	0.5	52	1 014	62.8	20.5	31	214	13.3	3.2
San Angelo	16	0	0.0	0.0	180	3 316	207.7	91.1	167	912	53.8	15.3
San Antonio	233	8 152	343.9	104.2	2 525	47 329	2 859.8	1 165.6	1 821	13 038	723.0	233.0
San Juan	NA	NA	NA	NA	12	90	3.8	2.0	15	41	1.9	0.5
San Marcos	10	72	2.9	0.8	101	1 129	66.8	29.2	64	343	14.0	4.2
Sherman	10	60	1.8	0.5	160	2 632	147.5	68.3	66	317	15.0	4.4
Socorro	NA	NA	NA	NA	2	0	0.0	0.0	11	22	1.1	0.3
Sugar Land	9	234	11.6	3.9	152	1 257	78.9	32.6	78	649	33.1	11.2
Temple	19	256	7.4	2.4	139	4 347	333.1	111.0	112	613	28.8	9.5
Texarkana	12	0	0.0	0.0	194	3 204	208.9	101.9	92	616	34.9	10.3
Texas City	9	53	2.0	0.5	82	1 712	77.9	40.7	56	248	13.3	3.6
The Colony	3	0	0.3	0.0	18	168	6.5	3.1	21	88	4.8	1.6
Tyler	23	386	33.3	6.2	374	4 539	375.6	176.6	194	1 722	90.1	28.7
Victoria	15	0	0.0	0.0	228	0	0.0	0.0	132	900	53.7	15.8
Waco	29	431	18.9	6.7	293	4 296	238.5	115.2	210	1 389	73.9	24.1
Weslaco	5	12	0.4	0.1	89	1 217	67.8	32.0	40	207	7.1	2.1
Wichita Falls	23	319	14.4	3.7	235	3 396	193.7	77.9	182	1 296	70.8	22.9
UTAH	480	9 444	412.4	137.7	3 851	46 989	2 988.8	1 226.7	2 728	17 612	1 090.5	312.6
Bountiful	10	98	2.7	0.9	157	1 892	108.3	46.9	67	372	17.5	5.2
Clearfield	4	0	0.0	0.0	20	503	28.7	12.8	20	113	7.9	2.4
Draper	NA	NA	NA	NA	NA	NA	NA	NA	NA	NA	NA	NA
Layton	7	79	2.8	0.9	68	1 164	103.1	43.3	44	341	16.0	4.5
Logan	13	190	4.3	1.8	139	1 207	77.1	26.6	83	425	23.4	6.3
Midvale	6	120	4.3	1.0	26	135	9.9	4.7	44	314	25.1	6.1
Murray	15	64	3.0	0.8	185	2 209	149.7	71.9	135	901	55.4	16.3
Ogden	24	471	9.5	3.2	216	2 855	197.0	76.6	156	1 097	58.0	17.8
Orem	24	258	7.9	2.3	143	2 013	97.0	39.2	107	849	37.3	10.7
Provo	21	609	11.8	4.4	233	2 874	177.7	82.2	121	863	36.7	11.0
Riverton	NA	NA	NA	NA	15	103	3.7	1.1	19	64	3.9	1.0
Roy	5	81	1.4	0.4	40	445	17.7	9.0	33	158	6.7	1.8
St. George	18	0	0.0	0.0	166	1 501	104.0	37.7	75	356	27.3	7.2
Salt Lake City	71	1 709	150.4	60.6	567	8 700	668.8	265.0	445	3 886	262.3	80.8
Sandy	NA	NA	NA	NA	NA	NA	NA	NA	NA	NA	NA	NA
South Jordan	3	47	2.4	0.6	23	202	12.7	5.3	7	35	2.5	0.8
Taylorsville	NA	NA	NA	NA	NA	NA	NA	NA	NA	NA	NA	NA
West Jordan	5	88	2.9	0.7	78	971	60.9	25.2	52	255	15.2	4.1
West Valley City	NA	NA	NA	NA	NA	NA	NA	NA	NA	NA	NA	NA
VERMONT	293	5 450	226.9	61.4	1 262	11 481	631.6	273.9	1 171	4 490	304.7	76.4
Burlington	15	96	21.3	4.3	112	1 937	120.0	55.7	74	469	34.4	11.3
VIRGINIA	1 613	26 624	1 397.9	392.9	12 014	150 797	9 859.6	4 417.9	11 301	68 807	4 397.2	1 360.3
Alexandria	35	357	32.1	13.4	323	2 788	216.5	105.2	267	1 919	122.4	42.9
Blacksburg	6	0	0.0	0.0	60	1 216	84.7	31.6	42	246	9.4	3.6
Charlottesville	21	292	27.9	9.6	162	2 092	138.9	54.6	133	827	41.6	14.5
Chesapeake	29	482	17.6	4.4	338	3 228	195.7	87.9	305	2 846	241.4	53.0
Danville	12	61	2.0	0.6	126	1 459	89.6	42.0	123	735	36.0	10.2
Hampton	29	251	10.6	2.6	192	1 976	106.4	51.9	178	1 129	64.8	20.9
Harrisonburg	12	147	3.5	1.3	116	1 538	90.7	41.6	84	434	28.1	7.5
Leesburg	11	147	8.3	2.1	85	927	64.0	25.2	45	235	17.6	5.7
Lynchburg	22	212	5.6	1.5	177	2 893	171.0	86.8	152	933	51.6	15.6
Manassas	10	174	5.7	1.7	106	1 161	67.1	34.9	108	832	60.2	22.2
Newport News	31	516	17.2	4.3	324	3 878	217.6	122.3	306	2 234	116.3	41.1
Norfolk	49	707	27.3	7.4	400	6 583	451.7	219.1	388	2 569	147.8	49.7
Petersburg	9	79	5.1	0.9	89	1 438	64.1	32.6	76	620	32.6	12.0
Portsmouth	17	108	7.1	1.3	170	2 393	134.8	71.8	163	1 364	74.6	27.2

1. Firms subject to federal tax.

Table D. Cities — Federal Funds and City Government Finances

City	Selected federal funds, fiscal 2001[1] (mil dol)									City government finances, 1999						
	Procurement contracts		Grants					Direct payments for individuals		General revenue						
										Intergovernmental			Taxes			
														Per capita[3] (dollars)		
	Defense	Other	Total[2]	Health and family welfare	Energy and environment	Education	Housing and community development	Educational assistance	Housing assistance	Total (mil dol)	Total (mil dol)	Percent from state government	Total (mil dol)	Total	Property	Sales and gross receipts
	108	109	110	111	112	113	114	115	116	117	118	119	120	121	122	123
TEXAS—Cont'd																
Missouri City	0.0	0.1	0.2	0.0	0.0	0.0	0.1	0.0	0.0	23.2	5.2	0.0	16.7	268	169	75
Nacogdoches	0.4	0.1	7.6	4.5	0.1	2.4	0.1	9.2	9.3	19.6	0.4	42.6	10.8	351	156	182
New Braunfels	0.8	0.6	0.5	0.0	0.0	0.0	0.2	0.0	2.8	NA	NA	NA	NA	NA	NA	NA
North Richland Hills	0.0	0.0	0.0	0.0	0.0	0.0	0.0	0.0	0.1	NA	NA	NA	NA	NA	NA	NA
Odessa	1.3	0.3	9.1	1.7	0.0	5.2	1.5	5.8	10.8	58.0	3.1	6.6	27.5	300	122	175
Paris	0.1	0.2	1.7	0.3	0.0	0.9	0.0	2.6	2.6	NA	NA	NA	NA	NA	NA	NA
Pasadena	52.2	0.4	2.4	0.0	0.0	0.1	2.0	8.8	12.6	78.7	8.0	7.3	47.5	355	143	206
Pearland	0.1	1.1	0.0	0.0	0.0	0.0	0.0	0.0	0.0	NA	NA	NA	NA	NA	NA	NA
Pharr	4.3	3.1	8.5	4.4	0.0	1.6	0.6	0.0	2.4	NA	NA	NA	NA	NA	NA	NA
Plano	63.1	22.7	2.8	1.0	0.0	0.4	1.1	1.8	1.6	191.4	2.1	18.6	116.9	533	270	231
Port Arthur	0.0	0.3	5.3	2.3	0.0	0.2	1.9	2.4	32.3	50.6	6.0	100.0	28.6	504	197	304
Richardson	24.1	13.0	11.2	3.8	0.5	2.2	0.0	3.5	0.2	105.2	5.8	100.0	54.7	636	325	268
Round Rock	194.4	101.5	2.4	0.0	0.0	1.9	0.4	0.2	1.0	NA	NA	NA	NA	NA	NA	NA
Rowlett	0.0	0.0	0.0	0.0	0.0	0.0	0.0	0.0	0.0	NA	NA	NA	NA	NA	NA	NA
San Angelo	6.9	0.3	11.0	4.8	0.0	0.7	1.9	5.9	8.8	52.3	6.3	19.4	30.3	343	194	144
San Antonio	1 137.1	457.6	450.7	207.4	91.3	45.2	29.3	81.9	97.6	843.4	116.6	71.9	361.4	324	155	157
San Juan	0.0	0.0	0.0	0.0	0.0	0.0	0.0	0.0	2.7	NA	NA	NA	NA	NA	NA	NA
San Marcos	3.1	60.2	12.7	5.7	0.2	4.8	0.6	12.9	2.0	31.5	2.0	51.7	15.2	386	45	334
Sherman	0.0	2.4	1.1	0.1	0.0	0.0	0.4	1.1	1.0	NA	NA	NA	NA	NA	NA	NA
Socorro	0.0	0.0	0.0	0.0	0.0	0.0	0.0	0.0	0.0	2.8	0.7	6.0	1.6	57	37	17
Sugar Land	1.3	0.5	1.4	0.6	0.0	0.0	0.0	0.0	0.0	56.6	5.0	4.4	36.7	710	286	405
Temple	10.2	27.2	9.1	1.6	5.1	0.2	0.6	2.0	8.1	48.3	3.9	86.9	26.2	530	234	291
Texarkana	4.1	2.0	2.8	0.4	0.0	0.5	0.4	2.7	7.1	30.8	2.8	35.9	16.7	532	172	347
Texas City	151.2	0.0	1.6	0.0	0.0	0.5	0.7	1.7	3.0	40.7	1.7	51.2	25.1	591	261	249
The Colony	0.0	0.0	0.0	0.0	0.0	0.0	0.0	0.0	0.0	NA	NA	NA	NA	NA	NA	NA
Tyler	0.6	2.8	11.9	3.4	0.0	1.5	1.8	8.5	12.2	71.8	7.0	3.2	35.9	428	154	266
Victoria	1.8	0.3	8.0	2.2	0.0	2.6	1.0	3.2	4.1	40.9	1.9	25.0	26.0	421	206	205
Waco	41.9	2.5	22.1	11.6	0.6	2.7	4.1	55.0	26.7	104.1	12.1	50.8	50.4	465	191	269
Weslaco	0.0	0.1	4.1	0.0	0.0	1.8	0.0	1.3	2.6	17.6	0.6	49.6	10.2	370	154	209
Wichita Falls	2.6	5.7	7.5	1.7	0.0	2.6	2.2	3.1	14.1	76.6	8.8	37.3	41.3	416	154	258
UTAH	1 275.1	808.9	2 244.2	1 153.5	41.3	225.6	32.2	130.4	92.3	X	X	X	X	X	X	X
Bountiful	0.3	0.0	0.0	0.0	0.0	0.0	0.0	0.0	0.4	19.5	2.5	52.7	9.4	232	59	158
Clearfield	576.5	55.6	0.2	0.0	0.0	0.0	0.2	0.0	3.2	14.4	1.4	47.6	7.2	278	76	186
Draper	25.9	0.0	15.4	0.0	0.0	0.0	0.0	0.0	0.0	NA	NA	NA	NA	NA	NA	NA
Layton	1.6	1.5	1.7	0.0	0.0	0.0	1.4	0.0	3.9	26.9	2.0	84.7	15.1	274	80	176
Logan	27.8	9.8	50.3	13.1	2.6	9.4	0.0	15.2	1.3	36.2	5.1	28.1	10.5	262	53	190
Midvale	0.9	0.1	0.1	0.0	0.0	0.0	0.0	0.0	0.8	11.8	1.5	59.4	8.4	725	128	554
Murray	0.4	0.8	6.1	1.1	0.0	0.0	0.0	0.0	0.3	28.5	4.0	30.2	16.8	507	122	359
Ogden	28.3	39.2	9.5	3.3	0.0	1.4	1.9	13.6	19.5	68.7	7.0	36.5	30.0	451	196	222
Orem	0.4	1.4	3.1	0.9	0.0	0.8	0.6	11.7	0.1	42.5	4.7	53.3	23.8	302	84	204
Provo	3.7	4.7	17.6	5.2	0.7	3.7	2.3	22.4	2.9	53.7	7.2	42.6	26.4	239	66	159
Riverton	0.5	0.0	0.0	0.0	0.0	0.0	0.0	0.0	0.1	NA	NA	NA	NA	NA	NA	NA
Roy	0.0	0.3	0.0	0.0	0.0	0.0	0.0	0.0	0.9	NA	NA	NA	NA	NA	NA	NA
St. George	0.0	0.0	1.8	0.0	0.0	1.0	0.0	3.4	2.4	43.4	3.4	50.0	16.5	358	120	216
Salt Lake City	190.9	93.9	686.0	276.0	32.7	77.8	21.8	52.7	23.1	369.3	59.4	13.5	130.7	750	390	319
Sandy	0.7	1.5	5.7	0.0	3.9	1.8	0.0	0.1	0.0	44.5	4.5	71.9	27.6	278	92	168
South Jordan	0.8	0.2	0.3	0.0	0.0	0.0	0.0	0.0	0.0	11.4	1.0	72.3	4.9	185	67	89
Taylorsville	1.0	0.0	0.4	0.0	0.0	0.0	0.4	0.0	0.0	13.7	2.0	88.0	10.2	NA	NA	NA
West Jordan	0.5	2.0	0.8	0.0	0.0	0.0	0.7	0.1	0.8	31.5	3.2	65.1	15.9	262	72	142
West Valley City	0.1	0.9	0.3	0.0	0.0	0.0	0.0	0.0	0.0	56.4	6.5	52.3	33.2	334	120	189
VERMONT	307.2	83.9	1 069.5	627.1	27.8	98.5	12.6	44.2	64.7	X	X	X	X	X	X	X
Burlington	266.8	5.9	99.6	67.2	2.5	5.0	1.3	7.5	11.4	70.9	4.4	17.2	41.6	1 083	919	20
VIRGINIA	18 596.8	8 338.4	5 908.5	2 839.5	124.5	665.9	79.4	657.3	557.4	X	X	X	X	X	X	X
Alexandria	832.5	352.1	106.0	19.4	9.2	24.1	1.0	0.7	24.4	396.4	85.1	81.0	246.7	2 086	1 475	422
Blacksburg	19.4	7.0	75.1	5.9	8.1	4.4	0.2	8.4	4.2	18.1	4.3	62.5	7.5	222	68	116
Charlottesville	23.1	8.7	189.7	126.6	3.8	4.3	1.0	5.4	3.6	97.6	32.7	77.8	50.4	1 319	826	464
Chesapeake	120.8	9.5	5.6	0.0	0.0	2.2	1.4	0.0	15.4	503.4	209.6	94.7	241.6	1 211	821	278
Danville	0.5	0.7	9.8	1.4	0.0	2.7	1.8	2.5	9.9	119.3	58.5	86.5	36.9	726	402	231
Hampton	55.3	205.2	56.1	3.6	1.6	6.7	2.2	9.9	22.3	322.8	138.3	95.0	133.2	973	646	252
Harrisonburg	0.4	0.9	5.1	0.4	0.0	0.5	0.0	4.8	4.0	64.9	15.8	99.5	36.1	1 079	494	434
Leesburg	10.7	2.0	4.0	0.5	0.0	0.1	0.1	0.0	3.2	32.6	10.4	37.5	12.4	458	204	174
Lynchburg	12.4	500.6	16.8	2.9	4.8	0.0	1.2	8.4	15.7	184.0	66.8	99.2	78.0	1 191	1 184	0
Manassas	379.1	62.8	11.9	5.3	0.5	0.9	0.0	0.1	4.7	91.2	28.9	92.7	48.2	1 364	1 079	213
Newport News	5 842.9	128.9	32.8	4.6	0.7	5.6	2.8	5.2	35.0	460.0	213.0	86.4	184.8	1 035	699	259
Norfolk	1 281.6	-6.3	81.3	18.0	4.4	16.6	5.7	19.0	28.3	807.7	399.7	65.8	260.7	1 211	693	421
Petersburg	16.6	12.9	14.7	0.6	0.0	3.2	1.2	6.4	11.4	84.3	50.4	87.2	29.1	839	560	214
Portsmouth	191.7	22.6	13.8	1.2	0.0	1.6	2.9	12.4	10.0	277.6	147.4	88.0	88.7	897	580	249

1. October 1, 2000 to September 30, 2001.   2. Includes program categories not shown separately. State totals include additional categories not allocated by city.   3. Based on population estimated as of July 1 of the year shown.

Table D. Cities — City Government Finances

City	City government finances, 1999 (cont'd)												
	General expenditure												
	Per capita[1] (dollars)			Percent of total for —									
	Total (mil dol)	Total	Capital outlays	Public welfare	Highways	Parking facilities	Education	Health and hospitals	Police protection	Sewerage and sanitation	Parks and recreation	Housing and community development	Interest on debt
	124	125	126	127	128	129	130	131	132	133	134	135	136
TEXAS—Cont'd													
Missouri City	24.1	386	129	0.0	11.7	0.0	0.0	0.0	20.1	22.9	7.2	0.4	6.0
Nacogdoches	16.4	532	57	0.1	11.1	1.2	0.0	0.9	17.4	18.0	5.7	1.5	9.3
New Braunfels	NA	NA	NA	NA	NA	NA	NA	NA	NA	NA	NA	NA	NA
North Richland Hills	NA	NA	NA	NA	NA	NA	NA	NA	NA	NA	NA	NA	NA
Odessa	55.1	602	58	0.0	12.2	0.0	0.0	0.0	22.2	17.1	6.1	5.6	5.1
Paris	NA	NA	NA	NA	NA	NA	NA	NA	NA	NA	NA	NA	NA
Pasadena	65.8	491	88	0.8	8.3	0.0	0.0	1.6	27.8	14.9	8.5	8.2	7.4
Pearland	NA	NA	NA	NA	NA	NA	NA	NA	NA	NA	NA	NA	NA
Pharr	NA	NA	NA	NA	NA	NA	NA	NA	NA	NA	NA	NA	NA
Plano	184.7	841	160	0.0	8.1	0.0	0.0	0.8	13.1	13.3	10.3	2.7	6.6
Port Arthur	48.3	849	66	2.1	12.6	0.0	0.0	2.6	18.3	15.8	1.3	5.2	13.4
Richardson	97.6	1 135	213	0.0	11.8	0.0	0.0	0.9	12.7	13.9	8.6	0.0	4.3
Round Rock	NA	NA	NA	NA	NA	NA	NA	NA	NA	NA	NA	NA	NA
Rowlett	NA	NA	NA	NA	NA	NA	NA	NA	NA	NA	NA	NA	NA
San Angelo	48.8	553	31	0.6	10.4	0.0	0.0	8.5	20.4	9.6	10.4	4.4	4.2
San Antonio	948.5	851	165	3.7	11.4	0.5	3.6	3.9	16.9	13.9	12.3	1.7	6.4
San Juan	NA	NA	NA	NA	NA	NA	NA	NA	NA	NA	NA	NA	NA
San Marcos	35.2	892	233	6.1	4.2	0.0	0.0	1.0	14.1	24.5	3.4	0.1	12.8
Sherman	NA	NA	NA	NA	NA	NA	NA	NA	NA	NA	NA	NA	NA
Socorro	2.3	85	1	0.0	0.0	0.0	0.0	4.9	16.7	0.0	13.5	16.6	4.4
Sugar Land	47.2	912	161	0.0	19.5	0.0	0.0	0.5	13.5	14.5	2.3	0.0	13.5
Temple	41.5	840	159	0.0	18.6	0.0	0.0	2.6	16.1	13.9	6.8	0.0	4.1
Texarkana	26.9	855	103	0.0	15.5	0.0	0.0	4.6	20.1	19.7	6.8	1.2	3.7
Texas City	44.3	1 042	224	0.0	8.6	0.0	0.0	3.2	14.0	20.7	9.2	8.7	11.7
The Colony	NA	NA	NA	NA	NA	NA	NA	NA	NA	NA	NA	NA	NA
Tyler	65.8	784	39	5.5	7.7	0.2	0.0	1.1	18.2	15.2	4.1	7.9	13.9
Victoria	36.9	596	21	0.0	11.1	0.0	0.0	1.5	18.9	15.5	4.1	0.7	9.3
Waco	105.2	972	149	2.0	1.8	0.0	0.0	4.2	16.2	18.7	10.0	2.2	12.1
Weslaco	16.3	590	98	0.0	7.1	2.7	0.0	0.3	15.1	14.5	5.4	0.0	9.6
Wichita Falls	71.8	723	69	0.0	7.8	0.0	0.0	5.0	17.1	17.1	5.3	6.5	1.4
UTAH	X	X	X	X	X	X	X	X	X	X	X	X	X
Bountiful	20.2	501	157	0.0	21.1	0.0	0.0	0.0	17.6	9.9	11.0	4.0	1.5
Clearfield	20.6	798	398	0.0	3.8	0.0	0.0	3.6	11.3	9.7	6.3	3.5	3.5
Draper	NA	NA	NA	NA	NA	NA	NA	NA	NA	NA	NA	NA	NA
Layton	22.5	409	65	0.0	10.4	0.0	0.0	0.0	22.2	20.9	15.6	0.1	1.9
Logan	41.1	1 021	276	0.0	8.3	0.0	0.0	0.0	11.1	16.0	7.8	6.8	2.4
Midvale	11.0	945	185	0.0	21.4	0.0	0.0	1.8	27.2	3.9	3.2	2.7	0.0
Murray	29.2	879	211	0.0	17.6	0.0	0.0	0.0	19.9	12.6	13.2	1.6	1.4
Ogden	72.2	1 086	267	0.0	8.3	0.0	0.0	3.0	13.4	8.8	8.1	6.9	4.7
Orem	46.3	586	112	0.0	10.8	0.0	0.0	0.0	15.4	11.8	8.6	3.7	3.6
Provo	56.8	514	96	0.0	5.8	0.0	0.0	0.0	17.3	10.0	6.9	7.5	6.2
Riverton	NA	NA	NA	NA	NA	NA	NA	NA	NA	NA	NA	NA	NA
Roy	NA	NA	NA	NA	NA	NA	NA	NA	NA	NA	NA	NA	NA
St. George	42.1	911	274	0.0	11.9	0.0	0.0	0.0	12.0	33.6	16.7	1.4	7.4
Salt Lake City	293.4	1 683	492	0.0	11.1	0.0	0.0	0.0	12.4	7.2	5.1	3.8	1.9
Sandy	42.0	424	78	0.0	17.7	0.0	0.0	0.0	20.4	6.7	7.2	4.3	6.6
South Jordan	9.6	362	147	0.0	28.5	0.0	0.0	0.0	14.0	5.9	13.4	0.7	1.0
Taylorsville	13.9	NA	NA	0.0	4.4	0.0	0.0	1.1	16.2	0.0	35.0	1.3	3.3
West Jordan	28.7	471	46	0.0	10.4	0.0	0.0	0.0	24.0	14.8	5.9	1.7	5.4
West Valley City	72.2	726	216	0.0	13.2	0.0	0.0	0.0	15.0	1.2	23.1	8.5	8.2
VERMONT	X	X	X	X	X	X	X	X	X	X	X	X	X
Burlington	48.2	1 253	184	0.0	14.1	7.8	1.8	0.0	13.0	12.8	5.1	7.0	7.3
VIRGINIA	X	X	X	X	X	X	X	X	X	X	X	X	X
Alexandria	401.0	3 390	420	9.0	6.7	0.5	31.0	6.1	7.9	5.8	3.1	2.7	2.9
Blacksburg	12.9	385	0	0.0	16.3	0.0	0.0	0.0	26.5	20.9	7.8	0.0	2.9
Charlottesville	107.7	2 818	206	5.5	5.2	0.1	37.5	5.6	8.7	5.8	5.0	3.2	2.2
Chesapeake	541.6	2 714	610	2.3	11.9	0.0	47.2	2.6	4.5	3.1	2.7	0.6	5.4
Danville	129.3	2 541	354	5.1	5.5	0.0	39.0	0.6	5.5	9.2	2.5	2.0	6.5
Hampton	309.0	2 256	233	5.3	2.4	0.6	46.3	0.0	6.1	5.7	5.7	3.3	3.4
Harrisonburg	62.3	1 864	176	1.4	7.8	0.2	43.4	1.0	5.9	12.0	3.9	0.5	4.2
Leesburg	30.5	1 128	406	0.0	7.5	0.5	6.7	0.0	11.2	24.2	7.7	0.0	7.9
Lynchburg	196.5	3 001	676	1.5	8.3	0.0	33.6	5.4	4.7	5.2	1.3	1.7	4.4
Manassas	97.6	2 763	465	2.7	4.6	0.0	57.7	2.9	7.1	7.8	2.0	0.6	4.5
Newport News	455.7	2 551	162	10.2	3.0	0.1	45.8	5.2	6.6	3.5	3.4	3.9	4.9
Norfolk	800.4	3 719	629	5.8	3.5	2.2	31.2	4.5	5.6	3.1	5.9	14.0	6.3
Petersburg	90.9	2 617	38	10.5	2.9	0.0	46.2	0.9	6.5	2.8	0.7	3.0	2.1
Portsmouth	262.1	2 650	169	5.8	2.7	0.3	43.0	4.1	5.8	3.4	3.1	7.9	3.8

1. Based on population estimated as of July 1 of the year shown.

Table D. Cities — City Government Finances, City Government Employment, and Climate

City	City government finances, 1999 (cont'd) Debt outstanding — Total (mil dol)	Per capita[1] (dollars)	Percent utility	City government employment, 2001	Climate[2] Average daily temperature (degrees Fahrenheit) — Mean January	July	Limits January[3]	July[4]	Annual precipitation (inches)	Heating degree days	Cooling degree days
	137	138	139	140	141	142	143	144	145	146	147
TEXAS—Cont'd											
Missouri City	28.3	454	0.0	NA	52.2	83.5	42.9	92.3	50.83	1 371	3 012
Nacogdoches	42.8	1 391	23.6	NA	47.6	82.8	36.9	93.2	42.40	1 951	2 551
New Braunfels	NA	NA	NA	NA	48.2	83.7	36.5	95.3	34.27	1 790	2 791
North Richland Hills	NA	NA	NA	NA	43.4	85.3	32.7	96.5	33.70	2 407	2 603
Odessa	114.4	1 250	62.9	840	42.5	82.0	28.5	95.4	14.96	2 751	2 163
Paris	NA	NA	NA	NA	NA	NA	NA	NA	NA	NA	NA
Pasadena	75.5	564	19.2	942	52.2	83.5	42.9	92.3	50.83	1 371	3 012
Pearland	NA	NA	NA	NA	NA	NA	NA	NA	NA	NA	NA
Pharr	NA	NA	NA	NA	58.5	85.4	48.5	95.8	22.83	693	4 076
Plano	273.2	1 245	14.2	1 964	43.4	85.3	32.7	96.5	33.70	2 407	2 603
Port Arthur	84.2	1 482	0.0	695	50.9	82.8	41.5	91.9	57.18	1 499	2 764
Richardson	93.7	1 089	8.4	1 054	44.6	85.9	34.5	95.7	36.08	2 259	2 763
Round Rock	NA	NA	NA	NA	48.8	84.5	38.6	95.0	31.88	1 688	3 016
Rowlett	NA	NA	NA	NA	NA	NA	NA	NA	NA	NA	NA
San Angelo	40.5	459	3.5	981	43.7	82.7	30.6	96.2	20.45	2 414	2 400
San Antonio	4 511.8	4 050	73.4	16 041	49.3	85.0	37.9	95.0	30.98	1 644	2 996
San Juan	NA	NA	NA	NA	NA	NA	NA	NA	NA	NA	NA
San Marcos	100.7	2 550	61.3	422	48.1	83.2	36.2	94.7	34.55	1 818	2 712
Sherman	NA	NA	NA	NA	40.5	83.3	29.8	94.6	40.39	2 890	2 209
Socorro	1.4	50	0.0	NA	NA	NA	NA	NA	NA	NA	NA
Sugar Land	148.4	2 869	13.4	403	NA	NA	NA	NA	NA	NA	NA
Temple	62.4	1 262	45.6	587	45.4	84.0	34.5	95.2	34.87	2 153	2 623
Texarkana	41.8	1 328	51.5	573	44.5	82.8	35.0	93.0	46.89	2 295	2 380
Texas City	82.2	1 934	0.0	509	52.7	83.3	47.1	87.3	42.28	1 263	2 994
The Colony	NA	NA	NA	NA	NA	NA	NA	NA	NA	NA	NA
Tyler	141.0	1 681	6.1	791	46.4	83.2	35.0	95.2	39.74	2 105	2 490
Victoria	92.7	1 498	54.6	701	52.7	84.1	42.5	93.5	37.41	1 296	3 118
Waco	213.6	1 973	18.5	1 519	45.2	85.6	34.2	96.8	31.96	2 179	2 816
Weslaco	38.9	1 407	33.1	NA	NA	NA	NA	NA	NA	NA	NA
Wichita Falls	76.6	772	75.6	1 163	39.8	85.0	27.6	97.2	28.90	3 042	2 340
UTAH	X	X	X	X	X	X	X	X	X	X	X
Bountiful	4.7	116	0.0	312	27.9	77.9	19.3	92.2	16.18	5 765	1 047
Clearfield	18.4	711	5.8	NA	NA	NA	NA	NA	NA	NA	NA
Draper	NA	NA	NA	NA	NA	NA	NA	NA	NA	NA	NA
Layton	8.2	148	3.7	272	28.6	76.2	19.6	92.0	22.09	5 799	927
Logan	23.0	571	53.2	462	23.6	73.0	15.5	86.7	19.52	6 854	623
Midvale	0.4	32	100.0	NA	NA	NA	NA	NA	NA	NA	NA
Murray	14.7	442	24.3	408	27.9	77.9	19.3	92.2	16.18	5 765	1 047
Ogden	50.6	761	10.8	623	28.9	77.8	19.8	92.3	22.59	5 557	1 096
Orem	17.6	223	0.0	490	28.0	74.5	18.3	90.2	17.04	5 907	745
Provo	113.5	1 028	45.0	676	28.0	74.5	18.3	90.2	17.04	5 907	745
Riverton	NA	NA	NA	NA	NA	NA	NA	NA	NA	NA	NA
Roy	NA	NA	NA	NA	NA	NA	NA	NA	NA	NA	NA
St. George	98.2	2 126	28.4	478	32.2	73.5	19.8	88.8	18.23	5 452	687
Salt Lake City	347.5	1 993	11.4	2 981	27.9	77.9	19.3	92.2	16.18	5 765	1 047
Sandy	54.6	551	18.1	555	27.9	77.9	19.3	92.2	16.18	5 765	1 047
South Jordan	1.3	49	20.4	NA	NA	NA	NA	NA	NA	NA	NA
Taylorsville	5.4	NA	0.0	20	NA	NA	NA	NA	NA	NA	NA
West Jordan	25.9	426	6.1	323	27.9	77.9	19.3	92.2	16.18	5 765	1 047
West Valley City	116.1	1 168	0.0	571	27.9	77.9	19.3	92.2	16.18	5 765	1 047
VERMONT	X	X	X	X	X	X	X	X	X	X	X
Burlington	163.1	4 243	65.5	688	16.3	70.5	7.5	81.2	34.47	7 771	388
VIRGINIA	X	X	X	X	X	X	X	X	X	X	X
Alexandria	206.1	1 742	0.0	4 463	34.6	80.0	26.8	88.5	38.63	4 047	1 549
Blacksburg	11.2	334	28.4	NA	29.6	70.6	19.0	82.3	40.91	5 574	514
Charlottesville	45.7	1 195	16.4	1 735	34.5	76.4	25.5	86.7	47.29	4 224	1 156
Chesapeake	545.9	2 736	19.0	8 427	39.1	78.2	30.9	86.4	44.64	3 495	1 422
Danville	193.0	3 793	18.1	2 329	36.1	78.0	25.4	89.6	43.18	3 944	1 381
Hampton	195.3	1 426	0.0	5 769	39.1	78.2	30.9	86.4	44.64	3 495	1 422
Harrisonburg	42.8	1 280	2.7	1 090	31.3	74.3	20.5	86.7	35.24	4 908	876
Leesburg	63.7	2 358	20.1	NA	NA	NA	NA	NA	NA	NA	NA
Lynchburg	194.0	2 963	12.2	2 769	34.2	75.6	24.7	86.0	40.88	4 340	1 048
Manassas	110.8	3 137	26.2	1 242	33.0	77.2	22.9	88.7	36.13	4 447	1 198
Newport News	622.0	3 483	20.7	8 574	39.1	78.2	30.9	86.4	44.64	3 495	1 422
Norfolk	1 212.8	5 635	26.8	10 712	39.1	78.2	30.9	86.4	44.64	3 495	1 422
Petersburg	30.4	877	29.7	1 653	38.6	78.9	27.8	90.3	43.53	3 408	1 533
Portsmouth	260.2	2 630	20.0	4 599	39.1	78.2	30.9	86.4	44.64	3 495	1 422

1. Based on the population estimated as of July 1 of the year shown.   2. Represents normal values based on the 30-year period, 1961–1990.   3. Average daily minimum.   4. Average daily maximum.

Table D. Cities — Land Area and Population

STATE Place code	City	Land area, 2000[1] (sq km)	Population, 2000 Total persons	Rank	Per square kilometer	Population Total persons 1990	Percent change 1990–2000	Total persons 1980	Percent change 1980–1990	White	Black	Am. Indian, Alaska Native	Asian and Pacific Islander	Other race	His-panic[2]	Non-His-panic White
		1	2	3	4	5	6	7	8	9	10	11	12	13	14	15
	VIRGINIA—Cont'd															
51 67000	Richmond	155.6	197 790	95	1 271.1	202 798	-2.5	219 214	-7.5	39.2	58.1	0.7	1.7	2.0	2.6	37.7
51 68000	Roanoke	111.1	94 911	251	854.3	96 509	-1.7	100 220	-3.7	70.8	27.7	0.7	1.5	1.3	1.5	68.8
51 76432	Suffolk	1 036.0	63 677	428	61.5	52 143	22.1	47 621	9.5	54.7	44.1	0.8	1.2	0.6	1.3	53.3
51 82000	Virginia Beach	643.1	425 257	38	661.3	393 089	8.2	262 199	49.9	73.6	20.0	1.0	6.3	2.2	4.2	69.5
53 00000	WASHINGTON	172 348.3	5 894 121	X	34.2	4 866 669	21.1	4 132 353	17.8	84.9	4.0	2.7	7.4	4.9	7.5	78.9
53 03180	Auburn	55.1	40 314	768	731.7	33 650	19.8	26 417	27.4	86.8	3.5	4.0	5.0	4.9	7.5	79.9
53 05210	Bellevue	79.6	109 569	206	1 376.5	95 213	26.1	73 883	17.6	77.0	2.6	0.8	19.5	3.5	5.3	71.8
53 05280	Bellingham	66.4	67 171	405	1 011.6	52 179	28.7	45 805	13.9	90.6	1.6	2.5	5.8	2.9	4.6	85.9
53 07380	Bothell	31.2	30 150	1 029	966.3	12 575	144.2	NA	NA	89.9	1.7	1.2	8.0	2.4	4.4	84.8
53 07695	Bremerton	58.7	37 259	834	634.7	38 142	-2.3	36 209	5.3	80.4	9.4	4.1	9.5	3.8	6.6	72.3
53 17635	Des Moines	16.4	29 267	1 065	1 784.6	20 830	69.3	NA	NA	78.0	8.7	2.1	11.9	4.6	6.6	71.7
53 20750	Edmonds	23.1	39 515	786	1 710.6	30 743	28.5	27 679	11.1	90.4	1.9	1.7	7.4	1.9	3.3	86.1
53 22640	Everett	84.2	91 488	268	1 086.6	70 937	29.0	54 413	30.4	84.7	4.3	2.8	8.3	4.4	7.1	77.9
53 35275	Kennewick	59.4	54 693	540	920.8	42 148	29.8	34 397	22.5	86.1	1.7	1.7	3.0	11.0	15.5	78.1
53 35415	Kent	72.6	79 524	326	1 095.4	37 960	109.5	23 152	64.0	75.0	9.9	2.2	12.7	6.3	8.1	67.9
53 35940	Kirkland	27.6	45 054	678	1 632.4	40 059	12.5	18 779	113.3	87.8	2.1	1.1	9.6	2.4	4.1	83.1
53 36745	Lacey	41.3	31 226	1 004	756.1	19 279	62.0	13 940	38.3	82.2	6.0	2.5	11.2	3.2	5.9	75.4
53 40245	Longview	35.5	34 660	907	976.3	31 499	10.0	31 041	1.5	92.0	1.2	3.1	3.2	3.6	5.8	87.2
53 40840	Lynnwood	19.8	33 847	929	1 709.4	28 637	18.2	22 641	26.5	78.0	4.2	2.0	16.2	4.3	7.0	70.9
53 43955	Marysville	24.8	25 315	1 225	1 020.8	12 248	106.7	NA	NA	90.9	1.5	2.3	5.8	2.7	4.8	86.0
53 47560	Mount Vernon	28.8	26 232	1 181	910.8	17 647	48.6	13 009	35.7	78.1	1.1	1.7	3.6	18.7	25.1	68.4
53 51300	Olympia	43.3	42 514	720	981.8	33 729	26.0	27 447	22.9	88.6	2.7	2.5	7.8	2.5	4.4	83.1
53 53545	Pasco	72.7	32 066	972	441.1	20 337	57.7	17 944	13.3	56.2	3.7	1.4	2.6	40.3	56.3	37.0
53 56695	Puyallup	31.4	33 011	949	1 051.3	23 878	38.2	18 239	30.9	91.5	2.3	2.1	5.7	2.9	4.7	85.8
53 57535	Redmond	41.1	45 256	676	1 101.1	35 800	26.4	23 318	53.5	81.8	2.1	1.1	15.1	3.4	5.6	76.4
53 57745	Renton	44.1	50 052	597	1 135.0	41 688	20.1	30 612	36.2	71.7	10.0	1.8	15.9	5.6	7.6	65.4
53 58235	Richland	90.2	38 708	804	429.1	32 315	19.8	33 578	-3.8	91.6	1.8	1.5	5.0	2.6	4.7	87.2
53 61115	Sammamish	46.8	34 104	918	728.7	NA	NA	NA	NA	90.1	1.2	0.7	9.5	1.0	2.5	86.1
53 63000	Seattle	217.2	563 374	24	2 593.8	516 259	9.1	493 846	4.5	73.4	9.9	2.1	15.9	3.7	5.3	67.9
53 63960	Shoreline	30.2	53 025	559	1 755.8	49 229	7.7	NA	NA	80.5	3.6	2.0	15.9	2.6	3.9	75.2
53 67000	Spokane	149.6	195 629	97	1 307.7	177 165	10.4	171 300	3.4	92.6	3.0	3.0	3.4	1.7	3.0	87.9
53 70000	Tacoma	129.7	193 556	99	1 492.3	176 664	9.6	158 501	11.5	74.1	13.7	3.6	11.2	4.4	6.9	66.5
53 74060	Vancouver	110.8	143 560	145	1 295.7	62 065	162.7	42 834	27.6	88.2	3.3	2.1	6.5	4.0	6.3	82.2
53 75775	Walla Walla	28.0	29 686	1 048	1 060.2	26 482	12.1	25 631	3.3	86.3	3.0	2.0	2.3	9.5	17.4	75.7
53 77105	Wenatchee	17.8	27 856	1 110	1 564.9	21 746	28.1	17 257	26.0	83.2	0.6	1.9	1.7	15.2	21.5	74.7
53 80010	Yakima	52.1	71 845	371	1 379.0	58 427	23.0	49 826	17.3	72.2	2.7	3.1	2.0	24.2	33.7	59.8
54 00000	WEST VIRGINIA	62 361.0	1 808 344	X	29.0	1 793 477	0.8	1 950 186	-8.0	95.9	3.5	0.6	0.7	0.3	0.7	94.6
54 14600	Charleston	81.9	53 421	554	652.3	57 287	-6.7	63 968	-10.4	82.3	16.2	0.9	2.2	0.6	0.8	80.1
54 39460	Huntington	41.2	51 475	581	1 249.4	54 844	-6.1	63 684	-13.9	91.0	8.2	0.8	1.2	0.5	0.8	89.1
54 55756	Morgantown	25.4	26 809	1 154	1 055.5	25 879	3.6	27 605	-6.3	90.8	4.7	0.5	4.9	0.8	1.5	88.6
54 62140	Parkersburg	30.6	33 099	946	1 081.7	33 862	-2.3	39 967	-15.3	97.3	2.2	0.6	0.6	0.3	0.8	95.8
54 86452	Wheeling	36.0	31 419	993	872.8	34 882	-9.9	43 067	-19.0	93.7	5.6	0.3	1.2	0.3	0.6	92.3
55 00000	WISCONSIN	140 662.5	5 363 675	X	38.1	4 891 769	9.6	4 705 642	4.0	90.0	6.1	1.3	2.0	2.0	3.6	87.3
55 02375	Appleton	54.1	70 087	382	1 295.5	65 695	6.7	59 040	11.3	92.5	1.3	1.0	5.3	1.4	2.5	90.2
55 06500	Beloit	42.6	35 775	871	839.8	35 571	0.6	35 207	1.0	78.1	16.8	0.9	1.6	5.5	9.1	71.9
55 10025	Brookfield	70.4	38 649	805	549.0	35 184	9.8	34 035	3.4	94.9	1.0	0.2	4.4	0.4	1.2	93.3
55 22300	Eau Claire	78.4	61 704	449	787.0	56 806	8.6	51 516	10.3	94.5	1.0	1.0	4.3	0.6	1.0	92.9
55 26275	Fond du Lac	43.7	42 203	725	965.7	37 755	11.8	35 863	5.3	94.7	2.2	1.0	1.8	1.6	2.9	92.2
55 27300	Franklin	89.7	29 494	1 056	328.8	21 855	35.0	16 871	29.5	91.6	5.4	0.6	2.4	1.0	2.6	89.1
55 31000	Green Bay	113.6	102 313	229	900.6	96 466	6.1	87 899	9.7	87.5	1.9	4.1	4.2	4.3	7.1	83.2
55 31175	Greenfield	29.9	35 476	877	1 186.5	33 403	6.2	31 467	6.2	94.9	1.3	0.7	2.6	1.9	3.9	91.6
55 37825	Janesville	71.3	59 498	474	834.5	52 210	14.0	51 071	2.2	96.4	1.7	0.6	1.3	1.3	2.6	93.9
55 39225	Kenosha	61.7	90 352	272	1 464.4	80 426	12.3	77 685	3.5	85.7	8.6	1.0	1.4	5.7	10.0	79.3
55 40775	La Crosse	52.2	51 818	577	992.7	51 140	1.3	48 347	5.8	92.6	2.0	0.9	5.3	0.6	1.1	91.0
55 48000	Madison	177.9	208 054	83	1 169.5	190 766	9.1	170 616	11.8	86.0	6.8	0.9	6.6	2.2	4.1	82.0
55 48500	Manitowoc	43.7	34 053	920	779.2	32 521	4.7	32 547	0.1	94.0	0.8	0.9	4.2	1.2	2.5	91.8
55 51000	Menomonee Falls	86.2	32 647	958	378.7	26 840	21.6	27 845	-3.6	97.2	1.7	0.4	1.0	0.3	1.2	95.6
55 53000	Milwaukee	248.8	596 974	19	2 399.4	628 088	-5.0	636 212	-1.3	52.1	38.6	1.5	3.5	7.2	12.0	45.4
55 56375	New Berlin	95.4	38 220	814	400.6	33 592	13.8	30 529	10.0	96.5	0.6	0.4	2.5	0.6	1.6	94.9
55 58800	Oak Creek	74.1	28 456	1 089	384.0	19 513	45.8	16 932	15.2	93.3	2.2	1.0	2.8	2.4	4.5	89.7
55 60500	Oshkosh	61.2	62 916	438	1 028.0	55 006	14.4	49 620	10.9	93.6	2.4	0.8	3.5	0.7	1.7	91.8
55 66000	Racine	40.2	81 855	315	2 036.2	84 298	-2.9	85 730	-1.7	71.1	21.6	0.9	0.9	8.2	14.0	63.5
55 72975	Sheboygan	36.0	50 792	586	1 410.9	49 587	2.4	48 085	3.1	88.8	1.1	0.9	7.3	3.5	6.0	85.0
55 78650	Superior	95.7	27 368	1 131	286.0	27 134	0.9	29 571	-8.2	95.8	1.1	3.2	1.2	0.5	0.8	93.8
55 84250	Waukesha	56.0	64 825	420	1 157.6	56 894	13.9	50 319	13.1	92.7	1.7	0.8	2.6	4.0	8.6	86.7
55 84475	Wausau	42.7	38 426	807	899.9	37 060	3.7	32 426	14.3	86.8	0.8	1.1	12.2	0.5	1.0	85.4
55 84675	Wauwatosa	34.3	47 271	644	1 378.2	49 366	-4.2	51 308	-3.8	95.0	2.5	0.5	2.4	0.8	1.7	92.9

1. Dry land or land partially or temporarily covered by water.   2. Hispanic persons may be of any race.

Table D. Cities — Population and Households

City	Population characteristics, 2000 (cont'd) Age of population (percent)										Households, 2000			Percent	
	Under 5 years	5 to 17 years	18 to 24 years	25 to 34 years	35 to 44 years	45 to 54 years	55 to 64 years	65 to 74 years	75 years and over	Percent female	Number	Percent change, 1990–2000	Persons per household	Female family householder[1]	One-person
	16	17	18	19	20	21	22	23	24	25	26	27	28	29	30
VIRGINIA—Cont'd															
Richmond	6.3	15.6	13.1	16.6	15.1	12.6	7.5	6.5	6.7	53.5	84 549	-0.9	2.21	20.4	37.6
Roanoke	6.5	16.1	8.2	15.2	15.3	13.8	8.5	7.8	8.6	53.1	42 003	2.4	2.20	16.5	35.9
Suffolk	7.3	20.6	7.1	13.4	17.8	13.4	9.2	6.3	5.2	52.2	23 283	25.7	2.69	16.8	20.2
Virginia Beach	7.2	20.3	10.0	16.4	17.8	12.7	7.1	4.9	3.6	50.5	154 455	13.9	2.70	12.4	20.4
WASHINGTON	6.7	19.0	9.5	14.3	16.5	14.4	8.4	5.7	5.5	50.2	2 271 398	21.3	2.53	9.9	26.2
Auburn	7.7	18.9	9.5	15.1	16.5	12.5	8.2	5.7	5.9	50.4	16 108	20.6	2.47	13.4	29.1
Bellevue	5.6	15.5	7.8	16.0	16.6	14.8	10.2	7.1	6.4	50.4	45 836	28.2	2.37	7.5	28.4
Bellingham	5.2	12.5	23.8	14.3	12.2	12.9	6.6	5.3	7.2	51.9	27 999	32.1	2.24	9.2	33.0
Bothell	6.0	19.2	8.1	14.8	18.4	15.8	8.1	4.6	5.0	51.0	11 923	142.4	2.51	8.9	25.7
Bremerton	8.1	16.4	15.5	16.1	14.3	10.8	6.4	5.1	7.4	49.1	15 096	2.6	2.30	13.3	35.4
Des Moines	6.6	17.2	8.3	14.5	16.6	13.5	8.5	6.0	8.9	51.8	11 337	60.7	2.47	12.2	27.8
Edmonds	5.0	15.6	7.0	11.5	15.9	16.8	11.5	8.8	7.8	52.7	16 904	33.9	2.32	8.7	29.0
Everett	7.8	17.3	12.3	17.0	16.3	12.3	6.7	4.7	5.6	49.1	36 325	26.7	2.40	12.5	31.7
Kennewick	8.4	21.2	10.3	13.8	15.5	13.3	7.3	5.2	5.0	50.4	20 786	29.3	2.60	12.2	26.1
Kent	8.4	19.3	10.3	17.4	17.5	12.7	7.0	4.0	3.3	50.4	31 113	91.5	2.53	12.8	28.5
Kirkland	5.5	13.0	9.3	19.9	18.2	15.3	8.6	5.0	5.2	51.3	20 736	20.5	2.13	8.1	35.6
Lacey	7.7	18.6	9.7	15.0	15.6	13.0	7.0	5.3	8.0	52.2	12 459	61.3	2.47	11.4	28.2
Longview	7.1	18.8	8.9	13.1	14.0	13.8	8.8	6.8	8.6	51.8	14 066	9.3	2.40	12.3	30.1
Lynnwood	7.1	17.3	10.4	15.4	16.7	13.1	8.1	6.0	5.8	51.3	13 328	17.6	2.50	11.5	29.3
Marysville	8.2	21.9	7.9	15.5	17.4	11.3	6.4	4.9	6.4	51.2	9 400	119.2	2.66	11.3	23.5
Mount Vernon	8.4	20.6	11.9	14.9	14.1	11.4	6.2	5.3	7.2	51.0	9 276	34.7	2.75	11.4	26.1
Olympia	5.4	16.0	11.9	15.2	15.1	15.1	7.8	5.8	7.6	52.2	18 670	24.9	2.21	10.4	35.2
Pasco	11.1	24.4	11.8	15.6	12.9	9.8	5.8	4.6	4.1	48.4	9 619	40.6	3.30	14.3	20.1
Puyallup	6.9	20.3	10.2	13.9	17.0	13.6	7.2	4.8	6.1	51.7	12 870	43.9	2.53	11.7	26.9
Redmond	6.4	15.1	9.5	20.8	17.1	14.1	7.8	3.9	5.4	49.9	19 102	35.0	2.33	7.6	30.4
Renton	7.0	14.8	10.2	19.8	17.1	12.9	7.9	4.9	5.4	50.3	21 708	19.2	2.29	10.8	34.0
Richland	6.6	20.6	7.5	11.5	15.6	15.4	10.0	6.7	6.1	51.0	15 549	18.1	2.48	9.3	27.2
Sammamish	8.4	25.0	4.8	11.2	22.0	18.0	6.7	2.4	1.6	49.6	11 131	NA	3.06	5.3	9.4
Seattle	4.7	10.9	11.9	21.7	16.9	14.5	7.5	5.2	6.8	50.1	258 499	9.2	2.08	8.1	40.8
Shoreline	5.2	17.3	7.7	12.8	17.6	16.3	8.5	6.8	7.8	51.8	20 716	NA	2.50	10.0	26.4
Spokane	7.0	17.8	11.1	14.5	15.1	13.1	7.4	6.2	7.8	51.8	81 512	8.5	2.32	12.4	33.9
Tacoma	7.0	18.8	10.4	15.4	16.2	12.9	7.4	5.4	6.5	51.2	76 152	8.9	2.45	13.9	31.7
Vancouver	8.0	18.7	9.8	16.3	15.8	13.1	7.5	5.2	5.5	50.8	56 628	181.2	2.50	12.1	27.6
Walla Walla	6.0	16.8	15.2	13.5	14.0	12.3	7.2	6.2	8.9	48.0	10 596	6.9	2.44	11.0	31.9
Wenatchee	8.0	19.4	10.0	14.0	14.3	12.2	7.1	6.8	8.2	51.1	10 741	19.5	2.53	10.2	30.1
Yakima	8.9	20.5	10.8	14.5	13.1	11.0	7.2	5.9	8.2	51.1	26 498	22.7	2.63	14.2	30.3
WEST VIRGINIA	5.6	16.6	9.5	12.7	15.1	15.0	10.2	8.2	7.1	51.4	736 481	7.0	2.40	10.7	27.1
Charleston	5.5	15.1	8.4	12.6	15.4	15.6	9.7	8.5	9.1	53.4	24 505	-3.2	2.11	13.5	38.9
Huntington	4.9	12.9	17.5	12.7	12.2	12.8	9.0	8.7	9.3	53.0	22 955	-2.0	2.12	13.1	37.6
Morgantown	3.0	8.1	44.7	11.9	8.5	8.4	5.0	4.8	5.6	48.9	10 782	12.5	2.08	7.0	37.3
Parkersburg	5.6	15.6	9.1	12.9	14.2	13.7	10.0	9.1	9.7	53.3	14 467	0.0	2.23	13.5	34.0
Wheeling	4.9	15.7	9.1	10.5	13.8	14.6	9.8	10.1	11.5	54.3	13 719	-8.8	2.17	12.2	38.3
WISCONSIN	6.4	19.1	9.7	13.2	16.3	13.7	8.5	6.6	6.5	50.6	2 084 544	14.4	2.50	9.6	26.8
Appleton	6.9	20.5	9.7	14.7	17.1	12.9	6.9	5.5	5.8	50.8	26 864	8.2	2.52	8.7	27.6
Beloit	7.7	20.0	11.5	14.1	14.5	11.9	7.5	6.3	6.6	52.1	13 370	0.5	2.57	16.6	27.5
Brookfield	5.4	21.4	4.6	6.8	16.4	16.9	10.9	9.6	8.0	51.6	13 891	16.3	2.74	5.5	16.7
Eau Claire	5.8	15.9	22.1	13.2	12.8	12.0	6.2	5.5	6.4	52.4	24 016	13.7	2.38	9.3	30.0
Fond du Lac	6.5	17.6	10.7	14.1	15.3	13.1	7.4	6.5	8.8	53.0	16 638	13.7	2.38	9.8	29.4
Franklin	5.6	17.8	8.4	13.1	19.7	16.9	8.7	6.0	3.9	47.8	10 602	42.6	2.58	6.6	22.5
Green Bay	7.2	18.3	11.6	15.7	16.0	12.5	7.0	5.7	6.1	50.7	41 591	8.4	2.40	10.8	31.6
Greenfield	4.5	14.4	8.1	13.1	15.2	14.4	9.9	9.3	11.1	53.1	15 697	13.9	2.20	8.0	34.6
Janesville	7.0	19.2	8.3	15.1	16.2	12.7	8.7	6.8	6.1	51.1	23 894	17.2	2.45	10.5	27.4
Kenosha	7.5	19.7	10.1	15.0	16.5	11.8	7.2	5.9	6.3	50.8	34 411	15.0	2.54	13.9	28.4
La Crosse	4.8	14.0	24.4	12.6	12.4	10.3	6.7	6.6	8.3	52.9	21 110	5.7	2.23	9.3	37.0
Madison	5.2	12.7	21.4	17.8	14.4	12.8	6.5	4.6	4.7	50.9	89 019	15.1	2.19	7.8	35.3
Manitowoc	6.2	18.0	8.2	12.2	15.7	12.9	8.5	8.2	10.2	51.6	14 235	8.3	2.32	9.1	32.5
Menomonee Falls	6.6	18.4	5.4	11.9	18.6	13.6	9.8	8.9	6.8	51.6	12 844	30.8	2.52	6.5	23.7
Milwaukee	8.0	20.7	12.2	15.8	14.4	11.4	6.6	5.5	5.4	52.2	232 188	-3.5	2.50	21.1	33.5
New Berlin	6.0	18.8	6.4	10.8	18.2	16.7	10.4	7.6	5.1	50.8	14 495	23.9	2.62	5.7	19.0
Oak Creek	6.7	18.3	9.3	16.7	18.7	13.7	7.8	5.3	3.5	50.2	11 239	58.7	2.52	7.1	25.3
Oshkosh	5.4	15.3	18.1	14.8	14.9	11.5	6.8	6.0	7.1	50.0	24 082	14.9	2.31	9.1	32.4
Racine	8.0	20.7	9.9	14.3	15.7	12.0	7.2	6.0	6.3	51.3	31 449	-1.0	2.54	17.9	29.4
Sheboygan	7.0	18.6	9.2	14.6	15.4	11.8	7.7	6.9	8.9	51.0	20 779	5.5	2.39	9.4	32.2
Superior	6.0	16.7	12.9	13.1	14.8	13.7	7.9	6.4	8.6	52.0	11 609	5.5	2.26	12.3	34.2
Waukesha	7.4	17.3	10.8	17.2	16.4	13.0	7.2	5.0	5.6	51.1	25 663	20.9	2.43	9.8	29.0
Wausau	6.2	19.2	9.6	13.0	14.5	12.5	7.9	7.3	9.8	52.0	15 678	6.5	2.37	9.5	33.6
Wauwatosa	6.5	16.8	5.5	14.5	16.7	14.2	7.6	7.4	10.8	53.7	20 388	2.7	2.27	7.9	33.9

1. No spouse present.

Table D. Cities — Group Quarters, Crime, Education, and Income

City	Persons in group quarters, 2000				Serious crimes known to police, 2000[2]				Education, 1990				Money income, 1989		
	Total	Institutional		Non-Institu-tional[1]	Total		Rate[3]		School enrollment		Attainment[4] (percent)		Per capita (dollars)[5]	Households Median	
		Total	Persons in nursing homes		Number	Rate[3]	Violent	Property	Public	Private	High school graduate or more	Bachelor's degree or more		Dollars	Percent change, 1979–1989 (constant 1989 dollars)
	31	32	33	34	35	36	37	38	39	40	41	42	43	44	45
VIRGINIA—Cont'd															
Richmond	11 236	3 179	1 365	8 057	17 322	8 758	1 276	7 482	40 511	8 832	68.1	24.2	13 993	23 551	3.3
Roanoke	2 538	1 698	1 055	840	4 742	4 996	567	4 429	17 074	2 124	68.0	15.6	12 513	22 591	1.6
Suffolk	979	874	417	105	2 905	4 562	554	4 008	11 145	1 857	63.9	12.3	11 831	26 125	2.5
Virginia Beach	7 683	2 794	1 753	4 889	17 893	4 208	222	3 986	90 065	15 293	88.0	25.5	15 242	36 271	7.1
WASHINGTON	136 382	57 218	23 275	79 164	300 932	5 106	370	4 736	1 091 450	160 862	83.8	22.9	14 923	31 183	1.3
Auburn	593	218	177	375	3 470	8 607	556	8 052	6 396	952	82.0	12.9	13 866	30 007	-3.1
Bellevue	791	209	209	582	4 511	4 117	127	3 990	17 391	3 831	94.2	45.7	23 816	43 800	1.2
Bellingham	4 593	1 071	696	3 522	4 149	6 177	199	5 977	16 420	1 148	85.2	28.2	13 698	24 714	9.0
Bothell	216	175	175	41	815	2 703	153	2 551	2 445	463	90.0	27.2	17 764	37 159	NA
Bremerton	2 586	401	348	2 185	2 938	7 885	1 039	6 847	6 978	790	82.0	12.6	11 418	22 610	-6.0
Des Moines	1 262	1 240	1 220	22	1 074	3 670	328	3 342	2 933	684	86.2	19.9	16 778	32 145	NA
Edmonds	352	174	169	178	1 015	2 569	76	2 493	5 776	1 271	90.2	31.0	20 868	40 515	1.0
Everett	4 203	882	211	3 321	6 228	6 807	620	6 188	13 420	1 694	81.0	14.2	13 829	28 415	6.7
Kennewick	594	490	162	104	3 008	5 500	351	5 149	10 920	1 041	82.5	19.8	12 767	28 261	-20.3
Kent	698	165	46	533	5 451	6 855	371	6 484	7 449	1 164	86.4	21.0	15 993	32 341	-5.4
Kirkland	848	279	266	569	1 491	3 309	133	3 176	7 464	1 955	91.9	36.6	21 200	38 437	9.2
Lacey	470	297	297	173	1 451	4 647	282	4 365	4 226	540	88.3	24.1	13 233	29 426	1.9
Longview	861	549	401	312	2 896	8 355	467	7 888	6 861	597	77.9	13.0	12 908	25 535	-14.0
Lynnwood	522	47	15	475	2 864	8 462	378	8 083	6 155	895	86.1	18.5	13 984	30 512	-7.7
Marysville	280	117	98	163	1 091	4 310	194	4 116	1 993	122	77.3	11.0	12 444	26 107	NA
Mount Vernon	764	505	334	259	2 203	8 398	168	8 230	3 794	390	81.8	17.6	13 486	27 022	0.7
Olympia	1 312	893	487	419	2 878	6 770	348	6 421	7 414	925	88.9	33.1	15 502	27 785	5.5
Pasco	352	256	116	96	1 610	5 021	377	4 644	5 408	298	57.7	8.8	8 016	17 897	-33.1
Puyallup	496	276	264	220	3 273	9 915	273	9 642	5 145	771	83.2	17.7	13 576	32 849	8.3
Redmond	833	347	251	486	1 679	3 710	210	3 500	8 007	1 379	94.0	40.9	20 037	42 299	-4.2
Renton	401	312	265	89	3 797	7 586	466	7 121	7 968	1 186	85.5	21.8	16 298	32 393	-3.1
Richland	135	80	62	55	1 300	3 358	163	3 196	7 830	934	90.3	34.7	17 085	36 626	-13.9
Sammamish	0	0	0	0	525	1 539	41	1 498	NA	NA	NA	NA	NA	NA	NA
Seattle	26 655	6 860	2 951	19 795	45 300	8 041	769	7 272	93 394	26 830	86.4	37.9	18 308	29 353	7.8
Shoreline	1 302	538	352	764	1 710	3 225	241	2 983	NA	NA	NA	NA	NA	NA	NA
Spokane	6 152	2 693	1 522	3 459	16 317	8 341	631	7 710	37 985	7 857	83.2	21.0	12 375	22 192	-4.4
Tacoma	6 731	3 033	1 195	3 698	18 605	9 612	1 238	8 374	35 474	8 010	79.3	15.8	12 272	25 333	3.9
Vancouver	2 082	1 345	597	737	7 721	5 378	413	4 965	9 242	947	80.0	15.0	12 606	21 552	-5.3
Walla Walla	3 829	2 825	373	1 004	1 875	6 316	590	5 727	6 052	1 797	78.9	16.3	11 247	21 301	-9.6
Wenatchee	677	477	197	200	1 941	6 968	395	6 573	4 592	457	74.6	17.1	12 215	22 806	-9.8
Yakima	2 139	1 669	732	470	6 637	9 238	523	8 715	12 197	1 219	70.9	16.5	11 593	22 189	-3.2
WEST VIRGINIA	43 147	24 009	11 601	19 138	47 067	2 603	317	2 286	403 602	32 911	66.0	12.3	10 520	20 795	-14.8
Charleston	1 670	833	432	837	4 633	8 673	990	7 682	10 603	1 894	77.2	28.6	16 067	23 584	-11.9
Huntington	2 866	977	470	1 889	4 074	7 915	686	7 229	13 996	1 235	72.4	20.8	12 005	18 276	-13.0
Morgantown	4 329	181	93	4 148	1 255	4 681	422	4 260	13 480	604	85.2	44.2	10 533	18 022	-2.2
Parkersburg	870	516	377	354	1 199	3 622	208	3 414	6 386	653	69.2	12.8	11 269	20 461	-11.9
Wheeling	1 622	584	476	1 038	1 074	3 418	283	3 135	5 395	2 337	74.7	18.4	12 665	21 053	-9.7
WISCONSIN	155 958	79 073	41 370	76 885	172 124	3 209	237	2 972	1 088 366	213 864	78.6	17.7	13 276	29 442	-0.6
Appleton	2 405	1 035	504	1 370	1 734	2 474	138	2 336	13 920	3 790	85.3	23.7	14 735	33 006	3.2
Beloit	1 410	349	349	1 061	1 644	4 595	302	4 294	7 875	1 640	72.4	11.3	11 435	25 859	-7.6
Brookfield	652	481	481	171	1 129	2 921	80	2 841	6 632	2 813	91.0	41.7	24 814	57 132	6.0
Eau Claire	4 641	862	391	3 779	2 575	4 173	222	3 951	18 887	1 526	84.8	23.3	11 426	24 735	2.1
Fond du Lac	2 686	1 974	846	712	1 600	3 791	123	3 668	7 587	1 981	78.2	14.1	12 472	26 826	-7.3
Franklin	2 103	1 879	0	224	642	2 177	108	2 068	4 327	1 396	85.2	23.8	16 301	43 686	2.4
Green Bay	2 695	1 164	825	1 531	3 478	3 399	305	3 094	20 116	4 192	80.9	16.7	12 969	26 770	-1.7
Greenfield	922	606	606	316	1 300	3 664	116	3 549	5 258	1 905	80.9	19.2	16 102	35 082	-5.4
Janesville	921	512	370	409	3 185	5 353	277	5 076	10 745	1 448	81.2	15.5	14 447	31 583	-4.7
Kenosha	2 980	1 457	781	1 523	3 152	3 489	571	2 917	17 341	4 022	73.2	12.2	12 284	27 770	-12.5
La Crosse	4 806	998	633	3 808	2 068	3 991	189	3 802	14 873	2 406	80.7	21.4	10 898	21 947	-2.7
Madison	12 833	2 456	978	10 377	7 985	3 838	327	3 511	63 473	5 938	90.6	42.0	15 143	29 420	6.3
Manitowoc	960	788	580	172	1 176	3 453	97	3 357	5 537	1 854	74.5	14.5	12 286	24 202	-10.4
Menomonee Falls	243	211	211	32	521	1 596	46	1 550	4 912	1 361	84.9	19.9	17 074	42 315	-5.8
Milwaukee	16 403	6 464	3 645	9 939	44 092	7 386	957	6 429	132 933	43 700	71.5	14.8	11 106	23 627	-12.0
New Berlin	219	130	130	89	529	1 384	84	1 300	6 588	2 234	90.3	28.7	18 245	49 394	3.2
Oak Creek	99	19	19	80	798	2 804	70	2 734	4 058	1 089	81.1	15.9	15 467	39 995	1.9
Oshkosh	7 342	3 516	599	3 826	2 029	3 225	226	2 999	15 619	1 675	78.6	19.6	11 843	25 168	-1.4
Racine	1 872	1 541	463	331	5 611	6 855	655	6 200	19 115	3 626	72.0	14.9	11 858	26 540	-14.1
Sheboygan	1 207	937	724	270	2 331	4 589	171	4 418	9 400	2 253	75.4	13.2	12 740	27 647	-3.5
Superior	1 125	419	298	706	1 486	5 430	205	5 225	6 780	571	77.3	15.9	10 769	20 905	-13.6
Waukesha	2 445	1 213	510	1 232	1 399	2 158	102	2 056	12 120	3 749	85.1	25.3	14 915	36 192	2.0
Wausau	1 290	847	598	443	1 534	3 992	268	3 724	7 456	1 257	75.4	17.4	13 169	25 505	-1.8
Wauwatosa	983	833	495	150	2 507	5 303	296	5 007	8 411	3 104	88.7	38.5	19 065	40 041	2.6

1. Persons in emergency shelters and persons visible in street locations. 2. Data for serious crimes have not been adjusted for underreporting. This may affect comparability between geographic areas and over time. 3. Per 100,000 population estimated by the FBI. 4. Persons 25 years old and older. 5. Based on population enumerated as of April 1, 1990.

Table D. Cities — Income, Poverty, and Housing

City	Money income, 1989 (cont'd) Households (cont'd) Percent with $100,000 or more	Percent below poverty, 1989 Persons Total	Persons Percent change in rate, 1979–1989	Families Total	Housing units, 2000 Total	Percent change, 1990–2000	Vacant units Vacant units for sale or rent[1]	For seasonal use (percent)	Home owner vacancy rate	Renter vacancy rate	Occupied units Total	Percent owner occupied	Percent renter occupied	Average size owner occupied	Average size renter occupied
	46	47	48	49	50	51	52	53	54	55	56	57	58	59	60
VIRGINIA—Cont'd															
Richmond	3.4	20.9	8.3	17.4	92 282	-2.0	7 733	0.3	2.4	6.4	84 549	46.1	53.9	2.30	2.12
Roanoke	2.3	16.1	-1.2	12.8	45 257	2.0	3 254	0.4	2.0	6.4	42 003	56.3	43.7	2.30	2.07
Suffolk	2.5	17.3	0.0	13.9	24 704	23.5	1 421	0.3	1.7	6.2	23 283	72.2	27.8	2.71	2.64
Virginia Beach	4.2	5.9	-33.7	4.3	162 277	10.4	7 822	1.4	1.5	4.0	154 455	65.6	34.4	2.79	2.54
WASHINGTON	3.7	10.9	11.5	7.8	2 451 075	20.6	179 677	2.5	1.8	5.9	2 271 398	64.6	35.4	2.65	2.32
Auburn	1.6	10.8	9.1	8.1	16 767	20.0	659	0.1	1.7	4.0	16 108	54.2	45.8	2.55	2.37
Bellevue	11.2	5.6	14.3	3.4	48 396	29.3	2 560	1.1	1.6	5.3	45 836	61.5	38.5	2.54	2.10
Bellingham	3.0	16.7	-1.8	8.0	29 474	33.3	1 475	0.5	2.3	4.6	27 999	48.2	51.8	2.36	2.12
Bothell	5.1	3.6	NA	2.3	12 303	139.1	380	0.2	1.0	4.6	11 923	68.0	32.0	2.69	2.14
Bremerton	0.7	18.1	40.3	15.5	16 631	6.0	1 535	0.4	4.3	7.8	15 096	41.4	58.6	2.34	2.27
Des Moines	3.2	7.4	NA	6.4	11 777	58.3	440	0.5	1.2	4.4	11 337	61.0	39.0	2.56	2.33
Edmonds	7.8	4.7	6.8	2.9	17 508	35.2	604	0.5	1.3	3.3	16 904	68.1	31.9	2.46	2.01
Everett	2.0	12.0	-0.8	9.9	38 512	25.1	2 187	0.2	1.9	6.2	36 325	46.0	54.0	2.51	2.32
Kennewick	1.3	13.9	51.1	12.1	22 043	28.1	1 257	0.3	1.3	8.1	20 786	59.7	40.3	2.75	2.38
Kent	1.9	8.8	20.5	6.6	32 488	85.8	1 375	0.3	1.1	4.9	31 113	48.8	51.2	2.70	2.38
Kirkland	6.4	5.7	18.8	3.6	21 831	20.9	1 095	0.7	1.7	5.2	20 736	57.0	43.0	2.30	1.91
Lacey	1.4	7.9	-8.1	6.2	13 160	62.9	701	0.3	2.5	6.0	12 459	55.5	44.5	2.59	2.31
Longview	2.1	16.0	36.8	13.0	15 225	13.3	1 159	0.3	2.5	10.6	14 066	57.8	42.2	2.45	2.34
Lynnwood	1.4	9.3	31.0	7.5	13 808	16.3	480	0.2	1.3	3.8	13 328	53.0	47.0	2.63	2.35
Marysville	0.5	7.0	NA	4.5	9 730	113.1	330	0.4	1.2	3.8	9 400	63.4	36.6	2.83	2.37
Mount Vernon	3.2	13.2	7.3	9.8	9 686	35.1	410	0.3	2.1	4.3	9 276	57.3	42.7	2.74	2.75
Olympia	2.4	13.0	13.0	8.4	19 738	23.9	1 068	0.4	1.6	6.4	18 670	50.3	49.7	2.43	1.98
Pasco	1.0	33.0	93.0	28.4	10 341	34.3	722	0.3	2.5	7.4	9 619	60.0	40.0	3.26	3.35
Puyallup	1.7	7.0	-28.6	4.7	13 467	43.6	597	0.2	0.9	6.1	12 870	54.9	45.1	2.83	2.23
Redmond	6.6	3.6	-26.5	1.9	20 248	35.2	1 146	1.1	1.5	5.7	19 102	55.1	44.9	2.53	2.07
Renton	2.1	7.0	-15.7	5.6	22 676	17.8	968	0.4	1.2	4.7	21 708	50.0	50.0	2.47	2.11
Richland	3.9	7.8	56.0	5.8	16 458	18.6	909	0.3	1.5	7.1	15 549	66.3	33.7	2.61	2.23
Sammamish	NA	NA	NA	NA	11 599	NA	468	0.6	2.1	6.5	11 131	90.1	9.9	3.12	2.52
Seattle	4.8	12.4	10.7	7.4	270 524	8.6	12 025	0.7	1.2	3.5	258 499	48.4	51.6	2.32	1.84
Shoreline	NA	NA	NA	NA	21 338	NA	622	0.3	1.1	3.2	20 716	68.0	32.0	2.60	2.27
Spokane	2.2	17.3	24.5	12.5	87 941	10.1	6 429	0.3	2.4	9.4	81 512	58.8	41.2	2.47	2.11
Tacoma	1.7	16.8	19.1	12.5	81 102	7.9	4 950	0.3	1.9	6.4	76 152	54.7	45.3	2.60	2.27
Vancouver	2.0	17.1	31.5	13.3	60 039	185.6	3 411	0.4	2.3	6.4	56 628	52.9	47.1	2.57	2.42
Walla Walla	2.0	19.3	54.4	14.3	11 400	7.1	804	0.4	2.2	7.6	10 596	59.1	40.9	2.56	2.27
Wenatchee	1.6	18.9	62.9	12.7	11 486	21.5	745	0.2	3.4	6.9	10 741	57.7	42.3	2.64	2.37
Yakima	2.2	20.2	33.8	15.7	28 643	24.7	2 145	0.4	2.0	8.7	26 498	53.2	46.8	2.67	2.58
WEST VIRGINIA	1.5	19.7	31.1	16.0	844 623	8.1	108 142	3.9	2.2	9.1	736 481	75.2	24.8	2.47	2.17
Charleston	5.3	18.8	49.2	15.0	27 131	-3.5	2 626	0.6	2.7	9.3	24 505	58.1	41.9	2.27	1.90
Huntington	3.0	23.2	51.6	16.7	25 888	-2.9	2 933	0.3	3.0	8.7	22 955	54.6	45.4	2.27	1.94
Morgantown	2.5	30.7	26.3	10.4	11 721	12.5	939	0.4	3.1	6.6	10 782	41.7	58.3	2.26	1.96
Parkersburg	1.4	19.0	33.8	15.2	16 100	-1.5	1 633	0.8	2.4	10.0	14 467	62.0	38.0	2.28	2.13
Wheeling	3.0	16.9	33.1	13.6	15 706	-8.3	1 987	0.3	2.5	14.7	13 719	62.7	37.3	2.36	1.85
WISCONSIN	2.6	10.7	23.0	7.6	2 321 144	12.9	236 600	6.1	1.2	5.6	2 084 544	68.4	31.6	2.66	2.15
Appleton	3.1	6.8	15.3	5.1	27 736	8.6	872	0.3	1.1	4.4	26 864	68.7	31.3	2.72	2.08
Beloit	1.2	17.5	50.9	14.5	14 262	1.6	892	0.1	1.9	8.2	13 370	61.9	38.1	2.60	2.53
Brookfield	18.0	1.1	-47.6	0.8	14 208	15.9	317	0.6	0.6	3.8	13 891	89.9	10.1	2.81	2.06
Eau Claire	1.7	18.6	25.7	10.1	24 895	13.8	879	0.3	1.0	3.5	24 016	57.3	42.7	2.57	2.12
Fond du Lac	1.5	9.6	39.1	7.1	17 519	15.4	881	0.2	1.4	7.5	16 638	61.7	38.3	2.59	2.03
Franklin	4.4	2.1	-38.2	1.3	10 936	41.1	334	0.2	0.8	6.0	10 602	78.4	21.6	2.75	1.97
Green Bay	1.8	13.4	39.6	10.0	43 123	8.6	1 532	0.3	0.9	4.1	41 591	56.0	44.0	2.56	2.19
Greenfield	1.8	3.4	25.9	2.4	16 203	13.3	506	0.3	0.9	3.4	15 697	59.5	40.5	2.49	1.78
Janesville	2.2	8.3	48.2	6.5	25 083	18.6	1 189	0.3	1.3	7.4	23 894	68.2	31.8	2.60	2.14
Kenosha	1.3	12.7	58.8	9.9	36 004	15.4	1 593	0.3	1.3	4.9	34 411	62.2	37.8	2.69	2.29
La Crosse	1.4	21.0	50.0	10.2	22 233	6.4	1 123	0.5	1.0	5.1	21 110	50.9	49.1	2.39	2.06
Madison	3.7	16.1	20.1	6.6	92 394	15.4	3 375	0.3	0.8	3.9	89 019	47.7	52.3	2.40	2.00
Manitowoc	1.9	10.7	67.2	7.2	15 007	9.3	772	0.4	1.1	7.7	14 235	67.6	32.4	2.51	1.93
Menomonee Falls	4.6	2.8	100.0	2.0	13 140	30.8	296	0.3	0.8	2.8	12 844	77.4	22.6	2.75	1.75
Milwaukee	1.0	22.2	60.9	18.5	249 225	-2.0	17 037	0.2	1.3	6.0	232 188	45.3	54.7	2.60	2.42
New Berlin	5.1	1.7	-5.6	1.3	14 921	23.3	426	0.2	1.1	4.8	14 495	81.3	18.7	2.79	1.91
Oak Creek	2.6	2.2	-31.3	0.9	11 897	63.8	658	0.1	1.2	8.7	11 239	60.9	39.1	2.89	1.95
Oshkosh	1.4	12.6	40.0	6.7	25 420	16.5	1 338	0.4	1.3	6.5	24 082	57.5	42.5	2.49	2.06
Racine	1.3	15.9	69.1	13.2	33 414	0.8	1 965	0.2	1.0	7.2	31 449	60.3	39.7	2.61	2.44
Sheboygan	1.5	9.3	63.2	6.5	21 762	5.7	983	0.4	1.2	5.1	20 779	61.1	38.9	2.55	2.13
Superior	1.0	17.1	61.3	12.9	12 196	4.4	587	0.3	0.6	6.2	11 609	61.7	38.3	2.47	1.93
Waukesha	2.2	6.1	19.6	4.5	26 856	21.7	1 193	0.2	0.7	6.3	25 663	56.5	43.5	2.71	2.06
Wausau	2.7	11.7	34.5	7.8	16 668	8.8	990	0.4	1.6	7.7	15 678	61.7	38.3	2.54	2.10
Wauwatosa	5.8	3.3	26.9	1.8	20 917	3.1	529	0.2	0.5	3.5	20 388	67.8	32.2	2.55	1.68

1. Includes units rented or sold but not occupied.   2. Specified owner-occupied units.   3. Specified renter-occupied units.   4. Overcrowded or lacking complete plumbing facilities.

Table D. Cities — **Labor Force, Employment, Disability, and Construction**

City	Civilian labor force, 2001				Civilian employment, 1990[2]			Disability 1990	Value of residential construction authorized by building permits, 2000		
			Unemployment			Percent					
	Total	Percent change, 2000–2001	Total	Rate[1]	Total	Professional, managerial, and technical	Precision production, craft, and repair	Work disabled persons[3] (percent)	New construction ($1,000)	Number of housing units	Percent single family
	61	62	63	64	65	66	67	68	69	70	71
VIRGINIA—Cont'd											
Richmond	97 422	2.5	4 891	5.0	96 229	31.0	7.3	9.3	21 230	270	63.0
Roanoke	49 940	0.9	1 811	3.6	45 400	24.6	10.4	11.2	21 002	310	54.2
Suffolk	31 226	1.1	1 079	3.5	22 463	26.1	15.8	10.8	83 013	773	82.7
Virginia Beach	216 083	1.1	6 546	3.0	174 616	35.0	11.2	6.0	181 594	1 464	89.6
WASHINGTON	2 995 696	-1.6	191 610	6.4	2 293 961	31.7	11.6	9.1	4 426 088	39 021	65.3
Auburn	20 676	-1.7	1 256	6.1	16 756	24.0	16.6	11.5	60 248	355	59.4
Bellevue	60 070	-2.4	2 258	3.8	49 880	44.3	6.2	5.2	41 565	407	46.2
Bellingham	34 362	-1.2	2 299	6.7	26 416	29.9	10.4	7.8	66 976	699	38.9
Bothell	8 094	-2.3	330	4.1	6 661	37.4	9.2	7.2	26 289	244	17.2
Bremerton	15 648	-1.0	1 466	9.4	12 887	26.0	17.0	13.4	2 918	33	100.0
Des Moines	10 946	-2.0	572	5.2	8 951	27.5	11.1	7.7	0	0	0.0
Edmonds	23 535	-2.6	1 001	4.3	16 760	38.3	9.6	5.8	28 708	169	43.2
Everett	47 790	-1.6	3 916	8.2	32 632	24.8	16.6	11.2	55 871	813	14.1
Kennewick	26 846	1.0	2 017	7.5	19 393	33.1	10.5	9.6	35 385	267	100.0
Kent	26 710	-1.9	1 427	5.3	21 814	30.4	12.6	7.6	59 989	553	54.6
Kirkland	29 182	-2.3	1 246	4.3	24 103	38.0	8.5	5.6	43 080	182	78.0
Lacey	10 995	-1.3	593	5.4	8 315	32.9	10.6	8.4	13 869	135	91.9
Longview	15 680	-2.1	1 789	11.4	13 337	24.6	13.1	11.9	18 037	255	38.4
Lynnwood	21 940	-2.2	1 291	5.9	15 358	26.5	15.5	10.2	5 583	35	100.0
Marysville	6 463	-2.5	293	4.5	4 589	20.5	19.5	10.7	36 900	404	94.8
Mount Vernon	12 020	-0.9	914	7.6	8 018	26.7	13.9	9.9	17 546	177	52.5
Olympia	21 745	-1.3	1 210	5.6	16 415	43.3	6.9	10.4	16 003	122	96.7
Pasco	11 612	0.6	1 528	13.2	7 726	16.9	12.1	12.0	25 763	228	100.0
Puyallup	14 048	-1.5	788	5.6	10 860	29.7	14.5	10.5	33 533	327	14.7
Redmond	25 352	-2.5	898	3.5	21 099	43.3	7.7	4.5	36 084	179	65.9
Renton	28 409	-1.8	1 610	5.7	23 122	34.5	12.7	7.3	84 636	885	47.1
Richland	21 675	1.0	1 177	5.4	16 010	50.4	7.7	7.4	53 822	277	83.4
Sammamish	7 478	-2.1	363	4.9	NA	NA	NA	NA	NA	NA	NA
Seattle	350 535	-1.7	21 188	6.0	284 160	41.1	7.0	8.4	343 182	4 732	9.5
Shoreline	31 300	-2.2	1 409	4.5	NA	NA	NA	NA	NA	NA	NA
Spokane	99 917	-0.9	7 449	7.5	75 112	30.9	8.9	13.1	32 020	300	81.7
Tacoma	98 606	-1.2	7 229	7.3	74 841	27.0	11.9	12.4	73 524	532	89.8
Vancouver	74 816	0.4	6 916	9.2	20 079	25.5	12.1	13.1	65 905	817	68.1
Walla Walla	13 048	-1.2	1 081	8.3	10 461	27.9	7.8	10.9	4 222	37	89.2
Wenatchee	14 058	-0.8	1 548	11.0	9 394	28.6	10.2	10.4	7 403	57	78.9
Yakima	30 921	-1.5	3 545	11.5	22 118	28.0	9.5	10.6	5 263	89	20.2
WEST VIRGINIA	833 315	1.1	40 948	4.9	671 085	25.4	14.5	12.6	359 559	3 763	87.6
Charleston	30 741	0.4	1 295	4.2	24 462	40.1	6.9	11.3	13 051	64	95.3
Huntington	23 659	1.1	1 370	5.8	20 534	35.9	7.6	13.6	2 928	19	100.0
Morgantown	13 713	3.8	326	2.4	10 705	45.7	4.9	4.2	2 837	71	15.5
Parkersburg	16 824	0.5	982	5.8	13 862	26.5	10.7	12.0	3 506	44	54.5
Wheeling	17 083	0.9	571	3.3	14 920	31.9	9.3	9.7	1 805	13	100.0
WISCONSIN	2 990 578	1.9	136 105	4.6	2 386 439	26.4	11.5	7.3	3 916 822	34 154	70.3
Appleton	44 772	2.3	2 048	4.6	33 379	32.4	10.1	6.1	47 902	391	51.2
Beloit	17 712	2.2	1 701	9.6	15 920	24.1	13.1	9.6	6 266	117	55.6
Brookfield	21 222	0.8	570	2.7	17 654	44.8	7.2	4.1	34 593	200	64.5
Eau Claire	35 137	1.4	1 656	4.7	26 961	30.4	7.8	7.1	45 350	472	39.8
Fond du Lac	23 225	3.7	1 273	5.5	17 928	24.4	11.5	7.6	16 819	153	60.8
Franklin	15 268	1.1	542	3.5	11 470	34.2	12.2	4.4	46 030	451	42.8
Green Bay	62 358	3.2	3 732	6.0	47 686	25.0	10.7	7.5	31 624	203	92.1
Greenfield	19 467	0.8	562	2.9	17 941	30.5	12.1	7.2	17 288	150	100.0
Janesville	32 307	0.7	2 051	6.3	26 143	23.8	11.9	7.9	33 377	318	75.5
Kenosha	48 487	0.7	2 983	6.2	35 935	23.6	12.7	9.1	36 492	522	44.6
La Crosse	28 316	1.9	1 320	4.7	24 796	28.1	7.4	7.0	8 445	102	28.4
Madison	134 099	3.5	2 952	2.2	108 284	42.3	5.5	5.6	172 776	1 781	35.8
Manitowoc	17 602	3.8	1 254	7.1	14 554	24.5	12.0	8.5	16 082	187	50.3
Menomonee Falls	19 472	1.2	573	2.9	14 781	31.2	13.9	5.1	26 148	183	54.1
Milwaukee	270 892	1.5	21 308	7.9	274 237	24.8	10.2	10.2	34 226	342	32.7
New Berlin	24 184	1.0	698	2.9	19 132	36.6	10.8	4.5	32 866	208	57.7
Oak Creek	16 295	1.7	708	4.3	10 801	26.5	14.6	5.8	37 580	542	38.9
Oshkosh	38 906	1.9	1 601	4.1	27 170	26.6	9.3	6.4	17 996	277	39.4
Racine	38 646	3.2	4 168	10.8	37 407	24.4	12.6	9.1	2 267	47	23.4
Sheboygan	27 974	2.0	1 341	4.8	24 283	22.9	11.0	7.7	6 168	64	60.9
Superior	14 510	0.2	703	4.8	11 492	25.5	8.8	9.6	3 689	55	50.9
Waukesha	39 328	1.4	1 840	4.7	31 399	32.6	10.6	7.2	42 253	416	59.9
Wausau	20 933	1.5	1 037	5.0	17 387	29.0	9.7	7.8	12 024	135	46.7
Wauwatosa	23 483	1.0	821	3.5	24 674	45.7	6.5	4.7	140	1	100.0

1. Percent of civilian labor force.   2. Persons 16 years and older.   3. Persons 16 to 64 years old.

Table D. Cities — **Wholesale Trade, Retail Trade, and Real Estate**

City	Wholesale Trade, 1997				Retail Trade[1], 1997				Real Estate and Rental and Leasing, 1997			
	Number of Establishments	Number of Employees	Sales (mil dol)	Annual Payroll (mil dol)	Number of Establishments	Number of Employees	Sales (mil dol)	Annual Payroll (mil dol)	Number of Establishments	Number of Employees	Receipts (mil dol)	Annual Payroll (mil dol)
	72	73	74	75	76	77	78	79	80	81	82	83
VIRGINIA—Cont'd												
Richmond	464	7 572	5 979.5	283.5	1 013	11 579	1 738.1	193.5	265	2 166	213.5	54.8
Roanoke	299	3 768	1 292.7	121.0	792	12 425	1 843.7	191.3	158	1 861	114.5	31.8
Suffolk	61	1 305	822.5	43.7	212	2 697	380.0	38.0	43	210	24.1	3.4
Virginia Beach	479	5 642	1 922.8	159.4	1 621	21 987	3 342.7	337.2	472	3 101	333.0	66.8
WASHINGTON	10 039	118 810	75 397.8	4 376.0	22 841	283 653	52 472.9	5 385.9	7 544	41 899	5 352.8	935.3
Auburn	135	2 935	1 409.5	90.0	297	4 494	931.4	92.9	57	264	32.7	6.1
Bellevue	579	6 532	11 707.9	316.2	789	13 580	2 745.9	266.2	458	4 723	685.5	151.0
Bellingham	154	1 264	570.4	38.9	502	6 902	1 126.8	115.3	134	529	60.7	8.1
Bothell	90	1 232	869.2	59.1	115	1 596	667.0	51.6	48	220	47.2	4.4
Bremerton	24	289	86.9	10.0	182	2 149	463.6	48.3	48	288	25.6	4.1
Des Moines	18	76	67.1	3.6	57	518	86.6	10.2	16	57	6.8	0.9
Edmonds	70	316	325.1	11.4	160	1 788	361.2	38.5	70	175	27.9	5.8
Everett	144	1 570	592.6	56.1	473	6 518	1 340.0	133.5	138	787	108.4	14.5
Kennewick	59	419	193.2	11.3	378	5 236	890.7	83.8	86	678	82.9	16.1
Kent	454	9 062	5 480.1	346.8	315	4 399	929.9	94.4	95	677	120.6	17.9
Kirkland	206	2 341	2 421.9	135.7	250	3 984	1 012.9	86.1	129	800	102.8	18.3
Lacey	25	155	28.6	4.7	135	2 180	352.1	37.7	34	110	13.6	1.7
Longview	46	488	108.0	12.9	224	3 019	554.5	56.4	66	315	35.9	5.7
Lynnwood	87	835	726.1	29.7	404	7 637	1 374.9	139.4	94	519	56.3	10.4
Marysville	21	207	96.9	6.9	123	1 788	313.7	32.3	33	81	11.7	1.6
Mount Vernon	27	274	79.4	8.7	161	1 716	291.0	32.3	44	175	18.0	2.6
Olympia	74	647	204.8	23.7	371	4 670	853.5	86.5	108	465	50.1	7.7
Pasco	70	862	345.4	25.5	158	1 959	438.2	41.6	33	195	20.3	3.9
Puyallup	29	145	74.5	4.8	262	4 512	955.6	90.0	63	712	38.8	8.3
Redmond	344	4 489	4 405.2	202.9	271	3 061	543.6	65.2	73	441	82.7	12.3
Renton	126	3 117	1 709.3	121.8	228	4 662	1 417.5	121.1	76	801	176.5	22.7
Richland	22	D	D	D	131	1 338	203.0	21.8	41	143	13.4	2.0
Sammamish	NA	NA	NA	NA	NA	NA	NA	NA	NA	NA	NA	NA
Seattle	1 860	23 635	16 085.6	978.1	2 698	34 886	6 146.2	717.7	1 391	8 567	1 302.0	228.0
Shoreline	NA	NA	NA	NA	NA	NA	NA	NA	NA	NA	NA	NA
Spokane	521	7 028	2 709.8	214.1	1 054	13 757	2 389.8	263.0	291	1 800	202.8	33.8
Tacoma	318	4 790	2 819.6	181.7	832	11 432	2 180.3	226.6	237	1 695	152.4	36.9
Vancouver	248	2 277	1 237.4	86.5	440	6 900	1 298.4	137.9	206	1 376	154.5	30.6
Walla Walla	56	D	D	D	190	2 233	348.4	38.9	40	170	14.9	2.4
Wenatchee	77	821	519.8	31.6	211	2 634	475.4	50.7	63	265	26.4	5.3
Yakima	152	2 984	1 047.5	87.5	443	6 123	1 053.7	107.1	115	659	72.8	11.9
WEST VIRGINIA	1 956	23 805	10 290.4	681.1	8 082	90 087	14 057.9	1 309.3	1 449	5 812	665.0	100.8
Charleston	179	2 738	1 386.6	84.0	466	7 135	961.8	102.2	172	907	118.7	17.5
Huntington	136	1 803	551.4	50.0	313	4 091	637.5	65.4	101	464	39.6	7.1
Morgantown	36	D	D	D	267	3 650	505.5	54.9	60	246	20.8	2.8
Parkersburg	78	917	350.0	23.9	291	3 667	617.1	58.5	61	363	36.6	7.3
Wheeling	89	1 694	1 361.1	47.1	223	2 342	354.3	39.2	58	D	D	D
WISCONSIN	8 025	110 309	57 192.9	3 764.9	21 717	305 255	50 520.5	4 826.2	4 598	23 924	2 637.5	464.1
Appleton	94	1 631	583.2	56.7	329	4 683	691.0	73.9	61	345	30.6	5.9
Beloit	17	288	185.9	13.7	141	1 994	385.6	32.3	24	82	17.9	1.3
Brookfield	226	3 092	1 541.1	141.5	349	6 557	939.4	94.0	118	796	92.6	22.0
Eau Claire	100	1 629	754.4	52.3	372	6 849	1 007.5	95.3	86	391	42.2	6.2
Fond du Lac	66	848	361.7	27.2	270	4 084	635.9	61.5	49	222	22.2	3.3
Franklin	41	357	192.4	12.1	61	1 347	258.5	21.4	14	49	6.6	0.7
Green Bay	201	2 733	1 316.0	88.9	515	8 419	1 395.5	135.8	107	618	61.0	10.5
Greenfield	36	D	D	D	184	4 012	707.8	65.8	35	160	39.1	3.1
Janesville	68	1 829	1 270.6	60.4	310	5 461	992.1	98.4	52	217	29.1	3.6
Kenosha	66	853	208.6	27.3	313	4 549	699.7	66.4	80	336	34.3	5.0
La Crosse	92	2 701	1 746.4	88.7	336	5 685	905.3	90.9	80	683	47.5	11.8
Madison	324	4 530	1 621.6	149.1	1 078	18 263	2 761.0	282.4	328	2 523	277.3	51.3
Manitowoc	34	370	192.3	15.3	162	2 411	357.3	34.4	27	114	8.1	1.5
Menomonee Falls	151	1 762	1 051.2	74.2	152	3 142	535.1	56.1	30	191	21.2	6.5
Milwaukee	753	14 029	8 379.2	531.4	1 700	22 655	3 381.2	360.6	484	3 899	462.3	90.6
New Berlin	166	2 918	1 064.5	107.1	92	1 481	213.6	24.3	25	123	40.9	4.4
Oak Creek	38	755	473.2	27.1	57	1 695	291.6	29.7	14	80	11.5	0.9
Oshkosh	72	1 078	323.1	32.7	332	4 744	841.5	83.3	87	485	41.6	7.5
Racine	101	1 974	2 300.4	67.7	362	5 297	710.0	70.1	68	388	31.0	6.8
Sheboygan	57	1 173	712.8	38.1	210	3 565	523.9	54.7	47	212	24.0	3.4
Superior	48	D	D	D	128	1 884	309.2	28.6	34	113	8.5	1.5
Waukesha	203	2 738	3 554.5	114.7	242	4 556	970.8	82.6	83	620	72.7	12.5
Wausau	71	873	306.1	27.8	251	5 060	745.9	77.5	33	174	14.2	2.9
Wauwatosa	140	2 622	1 773.5	89.9	289	6 903	942.9	121.4	76	510	65.9	11.6

1. Establishments with payroll.

Table D. Cities — Professional Services, Manufacturing, Accommodation and Foodservices

City	Professional, Scientific, and Technical Services, 1997[1]				Manufacturing, 1997				Accommodation and Foodservices, 1997			
	Number of Establishments	Number of Employees	Receipts (mil dol)	Annual Payroll (mil dol)	Number of Establishments	Number of Employees	Receipts (mil dol)	Annual Payroll (mil dol)	Number of Establishments	Number of Employees	Sales (mil dol)	Annual Payroll (mil dol)
	84	85	86	87	88	89	90	91	92	93	94	95
VIRGINIA—Cont'd												
Richmond	732	8 113	853.7	356.0	325	21 879	11 748.3	941.2	551	9 087	304.2	91.4
Roanoke	331	2 632	211.6	88.7	152	8 489	2 156.3	242.9	325	6 380	203.4	58.7
Suffolk	59	273	21.4	9.2	52	2 257	1 103.5	63.8	62	1 027	32.8	8.9
Virginia Beach	895	8 910	726.1	302.6	236	5 806	967.2	139.2	888	18 145	576.3	163.3
WASHINGTON	13 411	101 848	10 564.8	4 247.3	7 801	328 511	78 852.5	13 004.1	13 105	194 955	6 995.1	1 962.9
Auburn	73	310	18.9	8.3	167	13 946	1 875.8	605.2	112	1 894	55.3	15.5
Bellevue	1 073	12 563	1 645.8	651.9	163	2 740	681.8	93.3	332	6 369	272.5	73.9
Bellingham	254	1 909	187.7	80.7	130	3 457	583.9	91.5	264	3 793	112.0	31.9
Bothell	104	1 054	167.2	52.1	50	4 260	707.0	217.1	79	1 153	38.5	11.3
Bremerton	71	976	65.6	27.1	NA	NA	NA	NA	108	1 613	49.4	13.6
Des Moines	27	127	6.9	3.4	NA	NA	NA	NA	48	915	30.7	7.6
Edmonds	146	555	53.5	20.5	NA	NA	NA	NA	92	1 167	41.6	11.4
Everett	221	1 390	119.7	51.0	130	D	D	D	263	4 184	143.5	37.7
Kennewick	118	D	D	D	46	D	D	D	141	2 339	77.2	20.2
Kent	162	1 387	140.7	51.6	295	26 894	3 997.4	1 274.8	181	2 744	96.2	25.7
Kirkland	302	4 454	330.1	148.9	93	1 941	315.8	63.2	168	3 838	150.1	45.2
Lacey	44	1 035	84.1	36.7	NA	NA	NA	NA	77	1 253	41.5	11.3
Longview	79	466	29.1	12.8	46	2 556	824.3	115.2	94	1 642	45.7	13.3
Lynnwood	120	618	58.5	28.2	61	1 526	145.9	40.8	150	3 142	106.4	29.1
Marysville	29	98	5.9	2.2	53	1 374	199.8	47.4	65	D	D	D
Mount Vernon	86	355	25.1	8.6	27	527	75.8	13.2	78	1 419	43.3	11.5
Olympia	253	1 248	90.1	39.2	47	1 368	387.0	47.3	202	3 426	106.9	32.9
Pasco	35	112	11.7	4.3	34	D	D	D	70	931	30.9	8.2
Puyallup	66	296	15.4	5.8	38	2 482	320.5	83.1	119	2 251	71.9	20.4
Redmond	278	3 426	269.9	125.3	227	11 807	2 183.7	448.5	134	2 062	79.7	22.3
Renton	122	627	67.1	26.1	70	D	D	D	165	2 468	84.4	24.0
Richland	127	3 310	278.2	166.8	28	1 449	294.2	65.6	79	1 483	47.2	13.4
Sammamish	NA	NA	NA	NA	NA	NA	NA	NA	NA	NA	NA	NA
Seattle	3 235	31 669	3 703.6	1 489.6	1 213	33 935	5 021.1	1 132.7	2 105	34 197	1 550.6	445.9
Shoreline	NA	NA	NA	NA	NA	NA	NA	NA	NA	NA	NA	NA
Spokane	635	4 413	357.4	151.9	315	6 862	927.5	210.0	568	9 847	306.0	88.5
Tacoma	434	2 722	278.6	108.7	276	10 894	2 625.6	363.5	425	6 735	220.6	61.9
Vancouver	333	2 070	158.3	68.3	193	13 073	2 515.9	494.0	254	4 169	137.0	39.9
Walla Walla	59	265	17.5	6.8	43	1 137	154.7	31.2	96	1 287	38.2	10.7
Wenatchee	78	467	36.6	15.4	32	621	71.6	13.5	96	1 721	49.4	13.4
Yakima	158	1 038	102.6	37.0	102	4 624	747.7	124.0	219	3 445	115.8	31.9
WEST VIRGINIA	2 517	15 714	1 166.9	395.2	1 505	72 813	18 293.3	2 460.7	3 290	51 529	1 633.2	462.3
Charleston	371	3 413	326.8	103.7	44	2 152	278.2	85.5	210	3 967	147.6	38.9
Huntington	140	992	67.8	24.1	72	5 111	1 034.8	176.3	187	3 573	102.1	28.6
Morgantown	98	647	52.5	17.4	20	D	D	D	150	2 726	72.4	21.0
Parkersburg	97	668	44.0	15.0	30	1 103	113.6	31.6	129	2 367	69.1	19.6
Wheeling	107	836	74.4	20.9	53	D	D	D	130	1 837	51.6	15.0
WISCONSIN	9 281	70 689	6 398.9	2 542.3	9 936	562 479	117 383.0	18 766.4	13 252	190 411	5 641.0	1 548.5
Appleton	165	1 457	130.3	52.9	120	8 235	2 168.1	314.7	168	3 336	94.0	28.1
Beloit	41	185	9.4	3.5	52	4 896	1 257.5	198.9	91	1 360	37.8	10.9
Brookfield	314	3 071	321.0	139.2	90	2 873	456.6	102.5	99	2 519	93.9	24.5
Eau Claire	136	1 328	100.5	43.3	93	4 353	623.5	115.6	200	4 659	108.4	32.9
Fond du Lac	91	468	36.3	14.8	93	7 301	1 609.5	297.4	134	2 525	69.3	19.4
Franklin	31	195	38.2	6.5	37	2 479	367.2	95.8	36	D	D	D
Green Bay	209	1 763	140.9	66.2	200	16 692	4 634.5	695.3	286	5 153	137.9	40.1
Greenfield	65	676	38.4	18.0	NA	NA	NA	NA	74	2 176	58.4	17.3
Janesville	99	564	39.6	15.2	104	12 380	8 390.6	504.2	154	3 107	88.3	24.2
Kenosha	126	544	36.7	16.2	126	5 949	1 287.7	280.6	207	2 787	78.6	21.8
La Crosse	139	1 403	105.9	49.4	91	7 001	1 110.3	246.2	208	3 799	98.3	29.2
Madison	702	8 705	759.2	341.9	228	11 464	2 573.9	370.4	602	12 763	390.8	110.9
Manitowoc	53	441	35.9	9.5	88	9 202	1 478.9	280.1	92	1 480	38.2	10.6
Menomonee Falls	89	585	45.3	21.3	211	9 784	1 476.3	354.1	56	868	24.5	7.4
Milwaukee	1 092	14 871	1 570.3	628.8	848	46 467	8 392.4	1 643.5	1 143	17 743	606.5	170.4
New Berlin	91	1 062	215.1	45.7	150	6 647	1 299.8	259.0	54	D	D	D
Oak Creek	16	101	9.7	4.5	65	7 192	2 537.0	300.2	42	777	23.6	6.1
Oshkosh	94	774	85.7	20.9	114	8 692	1 860.5	291.8	177	3 591	93.5	27.3
Racine	139	898	59.3	24.8	219	9 065	1 845.0	322.3	166	2 653	78.4	21.8
Sheboygan	83	786	57.8	24.6	99	7 887	1 415.6	260.6	136	1 809	49.3	13.3
Superior	45	300	19.7	7.4	45	D	D	D	111	1 447	37.6	10.5
Waukesha	186	1 971	199.1	75.7	195	9 902	2 578.4	394.2	127	2 688	79.9	23.3
Wausau	103	727	64.5	27.9	83	8 190	1 192.1	228.8	101	1 496	39.7	11.5
Wauwatosa	281	1 880	196.1	70.9	81	7 766	1 388.8	342.8	114	2 559	82.0	23.1

1. Firms subject to federal tax.

Table D. Cities — **Entertainment, Health Care, and Other Services**

City	Arts, Entertainment, and Recreation[1], 1997				Health Care and Social Assistance[1], 1997				Other Services[1], 1997			
	Number of Establish-ments	Number of Employees	Receipts (mil dol)	Annual Payroll (mil dol)	Number of Establish-ments	Number of Employees	Receipts (mil dol)	Annual Payroll (mil dol)	Number of Establish-ments	Number of Employees	Receipts (mil dol)	Annual Payroll (mil dol)
	96	97	98	99	100	101	102	103	104	105	106	107
VIRGINIA—Cont'd												
Richmond	45	840	25.1	10.0	540	14 788	1 111.6	414.8	504	3 887	256.6	82.0
Roanoke	34	674	17.4	5.4	274	3 623	274.3	127.4	337	2 403	123.8	43.2
Suffolk	4	0	0.0	0.0	89	1 334	69.9	34.9	85	453	22.2	6.7
Virginia Beach	131	1 656	89.3	18.7	809	8 315	473.4	223.9	716	4 870	254.7	89.2
WASHINGTON	1 680	27 971	1 620.1	544.6	12 310	122 813	7 797.7	3 390.2	8 771	49 756	3 492.0	1 033.0
Auburn	19	1 406	106.7	32.1	126	2 433	125.2	60.5	115	653	50.4	15.8
Bellevue	59	1 186	62.5	18.1	560	4 476	340.0	147.2	320	2 011	173.5	48.4
Bellingham	32	225	11.1	3.7	305	3 076	176.5	72.4	133	770	49.7	13.4
Bothell	7	0	0.0	0.0	69	533	34.6	13.3	34	221	10.4	3.4
Bremerton	15	129	4.4	1.0	148	2 235	115.0	56.8	65	376	22.8	6.9
Des Moines	2	0	0.0	0.0	29	140	8.4	3.7	26	111	5.6	1.7
Edmonds	9	238	10.5	2.6	151	1 271	96.3	43.4	83	343	21.8	6.8
Everett	25	352	17.8	4.5	253	3 407	216.0	117.4	197	1 591	105.4	36.7
Kennewick	19	327	12.3	2.9	149	1 329	88.3	34.1	113	642	32.0	10.4
Kent	13	183	8.5	2.2	133	1 620	110.3	44.2	179	1 507	120.9	38.4
Kirkland	20	356	82.1	58.2	225	2 116	132.9	57.7	154	914	65.0	21.1
Lacey	6	66	1.5	0.7	55	454	20.5	9.6	60	395	19.4	6.2
Longview	11	79	2.3	0.6	131	1 564	93.8	41.6	76	402	24.4	7.6
Lynnwood	12	152	5.7	1.9	125	1 069	66.0	24.9	113	560	42.3	13.7
Marysville	6	43	1.4	0.3	65	525	30.4	14.3	57	358	20.3	6.3
Mount Vernon	8	166	6.1	2.1	89	1 222	84.6	42.9	39	221	16.2	4.8
Olympia	22	314	14.3	3.0	288	3 199	258.6	111.4	111	505	32.7	10.3
Pasco	3	0	0.0	0.0	71	623	38.0	15.0	55	321	26.8	7.3
Puyallup	14	176	10.2	2.4	155	1 862	116.3	49.9	64	344	24.6	8.0
Redmond	21	310	16.5	5.1	126	1 491	95.3	36.5	116	879	75.2	23.6
Renton	16	231	27.6	2.4	174	1 763	115.1	50.8	118	786	54.5	17.7
Richland	9	133	5.1	1.5	148	1 108	79.9	32.9	45	313	20.9	6.2
Sammamish	NA	NA	NA	NA	NA	NA	NA	NA	NA	NA	NA	NA
Seattle	263	3 786	308.8	151.4	1 643	17 217	1 318.7	574.4	1 266	9 352	756.9	207.1
Shoreline	NA	NA	NA	NA	NA	NA	NA	NA	NA	NA	NA	NA
Spokane	59	863	47.1	8.8	622	8 079	505.9	234.3	444	2 938	180.0	54.2
Tacoma	44	1 260	116.1	30.2	598	7 046	461.2	215.1	318	2 360	154.4	52.2
Vancouver	36	537	21.1	4.7	293	4 380	286.1	135.3	224	1 319	84.7	26.0
Walla Walla	8	0	0.0	0.0	81	958	59.7	26.3	49	240	16.5	4.6
Wenatchee	4	84	2.0	0.6	95	1 623	147.3	58.8	65	291	19.4	5.8
Yakima	24	419	18.9	5.3	243	3 102	209.0	96.9	153	918	59.3	18.5
WEST VIRGINIA	408	4 996	273.3	56.6	3 266	40 085	2 575.0	1 056.9	2 512	14 805	867.4	255.9
Charleston	24	252	11.6	3.0	314	3 898	365.3	151.4	141	1 196	64.5	20.1
Huntington	20	118	4.4	1.2	199	3 237	254.2	121.2	113	808	44.3	14.6
Morgantown	15	122	4.6	1.3	74	1 887	133.2	68.6	83	590	37.8	11.1
Parkersburg	10	113	3.8	1.3	145	1 819	118.3	51.8	109	1 365	106.1	24.6
Wheeling	17	328	34.7	4.3	175	1 572	105.7	44.6	96	755	39.7	13.8
WISCONSIN	1 730	22 339	1 327.5	384.3	9 315	114 562	6 917.4	3 447.3	8 648	49 101	2 991.3	886.4
Appleton	18	195	8.7	2.0	185	2 058	164.6	85.6	158	1 218	72.0	20.5
Beloit	4	57	2.6	0.7	54	1 153	55.7	30.6	55	222	11.2	2.9
Brookfield	17	429	10.7	3.6	162	1 696	115.7	53.9	110	1 153	86.9	29.4
Eau Claire	20	230	14.9	3.8	148	2 706	179.9	105.4	150	1 026	51.0	15.8
Fond du Lac	19	180	5.3	1.9	106	1 325	162.2	45.2	98	709	31.2	10.4
Franklin	7	100	2.1	0.6	33	225	15.6	7.7	43	271	14.4	4.3
Green Bay	31	0	0.0	0.0	223	3 256	240.5	131.0	191	1 332	76.5	24.8
Greenfield	13	163	6.1	1.7	94	2 414	103.1	55.5	78	537	26.1	9.0
Janesville	16	242	7.9	2.2	104	1 618	116.7	55.0	107	542	32.7	8.8
Kenosha	25	703	37.8	9.0	217	2 182	120.3	58.6	159	931	46.9	14.0
La Crosse	23	465	9.5	3.9	90	629	40.3	18.5	123	882	47.4	15.9
Madison	75	1 475	49.2	14.2	431	6 355	549.7	235.5	343	2 911	162.8	57.6
Manitowoc	10	86	3.8	0.7	91	1 058	61.7	32.4	55	257	14.1	4.3
Menomonee Falls	9	105	8.0	1.8	62	1 647	108.1	57.0	70	964	113.6	28.4
Milwaukee	90	1 781	368.8	90.7	915	11 854	781.1	426.7	755	5 080	307.4	97.3
New Berlin	10	184	4.3	1.5	70	674	39.8	18.2	61	741	71.0	19.9
Oak Creek	9	52	2.1	0.5	24	169	10.5	4.4	36	200	11.3	3.5
Oshkosh	22	212	8.6	1.9	143	1 518	99.6	47.1	101	711	31.6	9.4
Racine	14	150	6.1	1.4	123	1 629	150.1	69.4	141	979	52.7	18.5
Sheboygan	9	99	2.4	0.6	117	1 904	110.6	62.9	97	685	41.0	10.5
Superior	10	90	5.1	0.9	47	583	29.3	14.0	61	357	20.9	5.5
Waukesha	21	236	7.8	2.4	185	2 249	134.2	73.3	126	774	41.2	13.3
Wausau	14	289	6.4	1.5	118	1 795	147.9	85.2	84	477	19.9	5.9
Wauwatosa	12	184	5.6	1.6	436	4 766	378.0	216.5	89	822	43.9	14.1

1. Firms subject to federal tax.

Table D. Cities — Federal Funds and City Government Finances

City	Selected federal funds, fiscal 2001[1] (mil dol) Procurement contracts: Defense	Procurement contracts: Other	Grants: Total[2]	Grants: Health and family welfare	Grants: Energy and environment	Grants: Education	Grants: Housing and community development	Direct payments for individuals: Educational assistance	Direct payments for individuals: Housing assistance	City government finances, 1999 — General revenue — Intergovernmental: Total (mil dol)	Intergovernmental: Total (mil dol)	Intergovernmental: Percent from state government	Taxes: Total (mil dol)	Taxes Per capita[3] (dollars): Total	Per capita: Property	Per capita: Sales and gross receipts
	108	109	110	111	112	113	114	115	116	117	118	119	120	121	122	123
VIRGINIA—Cont'd																
Richmond	134.5	111.9	940.1	366.8	74.2	170.3	37.4	15.5	97.8	791.8	340.7	80.6	292.5	1 506	961	365
Roanoke	53.3	10.8	29.4	5.5	0.1	1.0	2.1	4.7	20.0	285.0	125.1	86.2	120.5	1 286	724	430
Suffolk	52.4	4.6	2.8	0.1	0.0	0.1	1.5	0.1	6.6	161.8	79.2	93.1	66.5	1 061	807	183
Virginia Beach	322.4	78.5	13.0	0.7	0.0	9.8	1.7	11.2	21.1	992.2	396.1	91.0	482.3	1 115	757	276
WASHINGTON	2 403.6	3 076.9	6 793.7	4 160.8	113.9	580.7	87.4	178.6	408.4	X	X	X	X	X	X	X
Auburn	1.2	6.7	3.7	1.2	0.2	1.7	0.5	2.1	3.4	NA	NA	NA	NA	NA	NA	NA
Bellevue	23.0	7.9	9.1	1.0	4.4	1.1	1.1	2.5	9.5	185.4	24.7	45.4	108.6	1 044	239	593
Bellingham	2.8	8.9	22.3	3.6	0.5	5.1	1.2	10.3	5.6	73.9	9.8	55.8	37.9	612	164	315
Bothell	12.3	10.3	2.9	2.5	0.0	0.0	0.0	0.0	0.4	NA	NA	NA	NA	NA	NA	NA
Bremerton	170.9	9.5	15.8	3.3	3.5	3.1	0.5	3.0	11.7	44.4	12.1	86.8	16.5	419	137	219
Des Moines	0.0	0.3	0.1	0.0	0.0	0.0	0.0	0.0	0.0	NA	NA	NA	NA	NA	NA	NA
Edmonds	0.7	0.8	1.0	0.7	0.0	0.3	0.0	0.2	2.4	NA	NA	NA	NA	NA	NA	NA
Everett	22.7	6.3	14.6	2.5	0.0	0.5	1.2	6.2	26.0	136.7	16.3	80.5	79.4	895	271	413
Kennewick	2.4	5.5	3.1	0.0	0.3	0.6	0.6	0.0	8.2	39.7	7.4	81.3	21.7	431	109	294
Kent	61.3	5.1	1.9	1.3	0.5	0.0	0.0	0.0	4.6	109.8	19.9	56.3	49.9	1 107	402	674
Kirkland	3.6	0.9	0.5	0.0	0.1	0.4	0.0	1.6	2.9	55.6	3.7	95.7	30.2	661	192	450
Lacey	0.6	0.8	0.4	0.0	0.0	0.0	0.0	0.0	2.8	NA	NA	NA	NA	NA	NA	NA
Longview	0.3	0.9	5.5	1.1	0.0	2.9	0.6	0.8	4.2	34.9	4.9	44.7	17.1	507	166	258
Lynnwood	6.2	1.4	9.8	1.1	0.0	0.7	0.0	2.6	1.6	48.8	13.2	87.6	22.0	669	207	433
Marysville	0.2	0.0	1.8	0.2	0.1	1.2	0.0	0.0	0.9	23.5	2.1	87.0	9.5	506	201	267
Mount Vernon	4.2	0.0	2.5	0.8	0.0	1.1	0.0	2.2	0.9	26.5	3.8	91.9	10.8	476	163	288
Olympia	1.5	4.8	790.3	288.5	49.6	167.9	13.9	7.6	5.8	67.2	10.5	29.4	28.8	736	225	410
Pasco	2.9	1.3	12.6	4.4	1.5	2.6	0.8	2.7	2.7	25.5	4.2	88.2	11.5	420	90	305
Puyallup	0.3	0.4	1.4	0.1	0.0	0.5	0.0	1.2	1.2	38.6	2.3	91.1	21.8	750	247	478
Redmond	66.7	11.6	2.6	1.9	0.2	0.0	0.0	0.0	1.2	73.2	6.9	45.5	41.9	952	260	559
Renton	25.1	11.5	2.0	0.1	0.0	0.6	0.0	0.6	11.4	91.6	9.3	84.0	45.9	967	311	531
Richland	11.7	1 998.5	7.4	4.1	0.1	0.1	1.1	0.1	3.0	46.8	9.1	69.0	17.8	477	164	290
Sammamish	NA	NA	NA	NA	NA	NA	NA	NA	NA	NA	NA	NA	NA	NA	NA	NA
Seattle	1 168.1	336.4	1 130.9	656.3	29.2	31.3	26.1	47.6	76.7	1 037.9	139.1	61.6	528.9	985	286	442
Shoreline	0.0	0.0	0.1	0.0	0.0	0.0	0.0	0.0	0.0	24.6	6.7	80.9	13.8	NA	NA	NA
Spokane	4.4	22.4	51.0	13.8	1.9	7.9	9.6	20.9	34.1	207.2	25.4	76.0	82.0	446	165	251
Tacoma	81.8	24.1	50.0	9.8	0.4	11.0	5.2	13.1	34.6	255.2	28.5	67.7	106.9	594	195	255
Vancouver	12.0	24.7	22.6	7.6	0.1	2.2	0.2	4.0	11.2	139.1	35.4	61.6	58.8	799	343	382
Walla Walla	3.0	2.9	3.2	0.1	0.0	1.0	0.0	2.8	3.5	33.8	9.5	72.2	9.3	323	80	194
Wenatchee	1.0	1.7	7.1	4.2	0.0	0.9	0.0	2.4	2.5	NA	NA	NA	NA	NA	NA	NA
Yakima	1.9	22.4	19.6	8.9	0.0	2.9	1.8	4.4	5.8	60.5	8.2	58.6	32.3	498	142	338
WEST VIRGINIA	104.6	422.8	2 970.8	1 650.0	80.3	242.9	40.1	79.9	161.4	X	X	X	X	X	X	X
Charleston	5.4	21.3	494.7	120.6	12.6	76.4	32.2	4.3	24.9	80.0	4.7	7.7	42.3	769	176	71
Huntington	2.5	10.4	55.8	35.7	0.0	1.1	3.6	11.5	14.8	43.0	7.2	26.6	20.1	382	99	58
Morgantown	0.7	74.6	93.2	44.3	14.7	4.2	0.0	13.4	3.5	23.2	1.7	21.8	8.5	318	60	39
Parkersburg	1.3	25.1	4.9	1.0	0.0	0.0	1.4	3.7	9.4	107.1	1.1	21.2	11.5	363	105	2
Wheeling	0.3	3.9	25.2	2.1	2.9	2.9	2.1	3.6	6.7	27.1	5.4	22.8	12.8	392	95	51
WISCONSIN	905.8	911.4	5 842.6	3 663.1	123.1	533.3	105.5	204.1	439.2	X	X	X	X	X	X	X
Appleton	6.3	8.5	10.9	0.0	0.1	2.0	0.9	3.8	4.6	78.5	25.0	79.7	26 8	409	381	3
Beloit	7.5	0.7	2.7	0.8	0.5	0.5	0.6	1.1	5.3	50.4	22.8	90.7	9.8	279	256	7
Brookfield	1.0	37.9	0.6	0.2	0.0	0.0	0.0	1.9	0.0	42.2	6.0	79.0	22.0	584	510	46
Eau Claire	5.2	0.4	8.7	0.5	0.0	1.6	1.1	9.1	4.9	56.2	20.8	76.4	17.7	298	254	15
Fond du Lac	1.6	0.3	2.8	1.6	0.0	0.4	0.0	1.7	7.3	40.4	13.7	89.6	14.4	362	332	8
Franklin	0.2	0.0	0.2	0.0	0.0	0.2	0.0	1.9	2.2	22.2	4.0	73.1	11.7	424	354	2
Green Bay	7.9	91.4	16.1	2.2	0.1	2.2	3.5	5.6	7.0	106.6	38.2	88.3	35.7	365	337	11
Greenfield	0.0	0.0	0.0	0.0	0.0	0.0	0.0	0.0	4.2	29.5	6.5	89.3	15.7	455	429	1
Janesville	33.1	2.2	1.4	0.0	0.0	0.5	0.6	1.5	3.6	48.8	16.4	74.6	16.4	278	254	10
Kenosha	5.9	9.9	8.3	2.1	0.0	0.2	3.3	6.6	16.6	85.7	32.2	83.3	32.4	369	343	5
La Crosse	22.0	2.1	18.0	2.3	0.0	3.2	1.8	8.4	2.4	62.2	21.3	82.5	20.6	419	376	23
Madison	12.7	64.9	1 297.0	512.9	109.0	175.1	47.7	63.7	32.3	255.8	90.7	79.5	102.2	488	435	25
Manitowoc	0.3	0.5	0.1	0.0	0.0	0.0	0.0	0.7	3.5	35.1	11.7	88.1	8.1	245	213	10
Menomonee Falls	0.2	0.0	0.0	0.0	0.0	0.0	0.0	1.9	0.9	38.0	4.6	100.0	15.8	505	459	1
Milwaukee	51.8	80.8	246.8	126.9	6.9	21.2	30.9	33.7	134.9	748.0	383.4	82.2	164.4	284	266	0
New Berlin	0.6	0.5	0.1	0.0	0.0	0.0	0.0	0.0	0.4	32.7	4.2	91.6	14.9	400	358	0
Oak Creek	23.7	0.5	0.1	0.0	0.0	0.0	0.0	0.0	8.6	26.5	6.1	96.1	14.3	526	470	9
Oshkosh	546.2	3.5	4.5	1.0	0.0	1.5	0.6	4.3	4.3	57.0	21.4	85.8	17.7	305	272	11
Racine	8.1	0.2	23.9	1.0	0.0	0.3	3.5	0.6	10.6	101.2	47.5	80.1	34.6	42.	411	2
Sheboygan	3.5	4.1	2.3	0.9	0.0	0.0	0.5	0.1	4.9	51.3	20.4	87.0	17.5	355	321	11
Superior	0.2	-0.7	6.3	2.6	0.5	0.8	1.4	2.2	8.0	34.9	14.2	88.0	9.4	347	290	11
Waukesha	34.2	2.0	7.0	1.1	0.7	0.0	2.9	1.6	5.6	62.1	13.3	90.6	29.5	475	439	12
Wausau	0.2	0.2	6.2	1.3	0.0	2.9	1.3	1.6	5.2	41.6	16.8	81.7	14.2	390	369	12
Wauwatosa	0.0	0.0	1.4	0.6	0.0	0.0	1.0	0.1	1.9	50.2	11.7	70.4	25.9	566	522	18

1. October 1, 2000 to September 30, 2001.   2. Includes program categories not shown separately. State totals include additional categories not allocated by city.   3. Based on population estimated as of July 1 of the year shown.

City	City government finances, 1999 (cont'd)												
	General expenditure												
	Per capita[1] (dollars)			Percent of total for —									
	Total (mil dol)	Total	Capital outlays	Public welfare	Highways	Parking facilities	Education	Health and hospitals	Police protection	Sewerage and sanitation	Parks and recreation	Housing and community development	Interest on debt
	124	125	126	127	128	129	130	131	132	133	134	135	136
VIRGINIA—Cont'd													
Richmond	788.3	4 060	483	8.2	3.1	0.0	32.7	6.9	7.4	5.2	2.6	7.7	2.4
Roanoke	278.5	2 971	296	8.6	3.4	0.4	35.3	1.2	5.3	8.5	2.7	6.3	8.5
Suffolk	167.2	2 666	721	4.8	3.2	0.0	43.1	2.0	3.9	7.3	1.3	3.2	4.8
Virginia Beach	960.3	2 221	265	2.4	2.9	0.2	50.3	2.7	6.2	5.4	3.3	1.4	4.4
WASHINGTON	X	X	X	X	X	X	X	X	X	X	X	X	X
Auburn	NA	NA	NA	NA	NA	NA	NA	NA	NA	NA	NA	NA	NA
Bellevue	167.0	1 605	470	0.0	21.7	0.0	0.0	4.3	9.9	13.2	16.1	3.4	2.3
Bellingham	66.9	1 081	234	0.0	12.7	0.7	0.0	1.1	12.7	8.2	14.2	3.7	4.0
Bothell	NA	NA	NA	NA	NA	NA	NA	NA	NA	NA	NA	NA	NA
Bremerton	45.7	1 155	335	0.0	23.1	0.3	0.0	3.0	13.4	18.1	8.2	3.3	4.7
Des Moines	NA	NA	NA	NA	NA	NA	NA	NA	NA	NA	NA	NA	NA
Edmonds	NA	NA	NA	NA	NA	NA	NA	NA	NA	NA	NA	NA	NA
Everett	134.3	1 516	268	0.2	12.8	0.3	0.0	2.4	14.2	13.3	8.5	1.1	3.9
Kennewick	38.9	772	252	0.0	14.5	0.0	0.0	3.1	16.1	9.9	8.9	0.7	2.1
Kent	104.1	2 310	576	0.2	17.4	0.0	0.0	1.9	12.6	18.5	12.5	0.4	5.3
Kirkland	57.8	1 264	259	0.1	9.9	1.0	0.0	0.9	9.0	19.2	9.7	0.3	3.0
Lacey	NA	NA	NA	NA	NA	NA	NA	NA	NA	NA	NA	NA	NA
Longview	35.0	1 035	204	0.5	19.9	0.0	0.0	0.0	20.1	19.7	8.5	2.1	1.8
Lynnwood	49.9	1 515	543	0.0	25.2	0.0	0.0	2.2	12.3	6.1	11.9	0.3	4.3
Marysville	24.8	1 324	269	0.0	16.1	0.0	0.0	2.4	11.2	27.0	12.4	0.0	7.3
Mount Vernon	31.8	1 404	525	0.0	10.7	0.0	0.0	0.1	20.2	31.7	7.0	1.2	2.5
Olympia	53.0	1 352	101	0.5	7.4	0.1	0.0	2.3	12.4	25.6	7.9	1.7	1.1
Pasco	27.0	987	401	0.0	5.5	0.0	0.0	2.6	15.2	30.6	6.7	0.6	4.2
Puyallup	59.2	2 040	1 122	0.0	24.9	0.0	0.0	1.7	9.7	36.9	2.8	0.5	2.2
Redmond	55.4	1 257	252	0.0	20.2	0.0	0.1	3.9	11.5	15.4	7.7	1.1	2.0
Renton	86.4	1 820	440	0.0	16.8	0.0	0.0	0.1	11.2	19.1	9.7	1.7	2.2
Richland	63.5	1 702	813	0.0	18.3	0.0	0.2	1.1	6.1	9.3	3.8	2.9	5.2
Sammamish	NA	NA	NA	NA	NA	NA	NA	NA	NA	NA	NA	NA	NA
Seattle	1 165.3	2 170	442	0.0	12.1	6.3	0.0	1.4	12.0	18.0	11.9	5.2	2.9
Shoreline	14.8	NA	NA	0.0	18.8	0.0	0.1	0.0	2.6	0.3	12.0	7.3	0.0
Spokane	212.0	1 152	205	0.0	6.7	0.2	0.0	1.4	12.6	31.3	9.3	1.5	7.2
Tacoma	264.4	1 470	192	1.2	9.2	0.5	0.0	3.3	15.2	25.9	2.5	1.3	5.8
Vancouver	116.8	1 588	442	0.0	21.7	0.6	0.0	0.9	12.4	11.5	11.6	0.6	7.1
Walla Walla	32.9	1 145	495	0.0	19.6	0.0	0.0	3.4	11.6	21.8	3.7	0.8	1.7
Wenatchee	NA	NA	NA	NA	NA	NA	NA	NA	NA	NA	NA	NA	NA
Yakima	54.3	835	108	0.0	7.9	0.0	0.0	0.7	18.3	17.6	5.5	2.4	3.6
WEST VIRGINIA	X	X	X	X	X	X	X	X	X	X	X	X	X
Charleston	76.7	1 392	144	0.0	5.7	4.7	0.0	0.6	15.8	10.2	18.9	3.5	7.2
Huntington	56.2	1 069	199	0.0	4.6	1.5	0.0	0.2	13.1	13.1	7.4	10.8	7.5
Morgantown	20.4	762	95	0.0	10.3	8.9	0.0	0.0	16.4	13.1	8.5	2.0	4.5
Parkersburg	102.6	3 234	7	2.2	3.2	0.0	0.0	82.9	3.4	2.7	0.5	0.1	0.1
Wheeling	23.2	713	86	0.0	7.8	2.9	0.0	0.5	15.2	23.3	4.2	0.7	0.3
WISCONSIN	X	X	X	X	X	X	X	X	X	X	X	X	X
Appleton	74.1	1 131	239	0.2	18.2	2.3	0.0	1.3	15.7	16.1	8.2	1.5	6.6
Beloit	52.4	1 490	156	0.0	12.3	0.2	0.0	5.4	15.5	14.6	5.0	11.4	5.4
Brookfield	39.7	1 052	104	0.0	15.1	0.0	0.0	2.4	14.6	24.7	5.1	0.0	10.1
Eau Claire	60.4	1 020	247	0.0	22.6	1.2	0.0	5.9	14.7	8.0	10.7	2.4	5.1
Fond du Lac	39.5	993	205	0.0	15.8	1.1	0.0	3.2	14.5	17.5	5.8	2.2	7.5
Franklin	25.5	924	259	0.0	12.4	0.0	0.0	4.1	18.1	16.2	3.4	0.2	12.6
Green Bay	105.8	1 082	192	0.0	20.8	2.1	0.0	0.1	16.7	19.9	7.8	0.7	6.0
Greenfield	26.0	752	110	0.0	21.6	0.0	0.0	6.5	23.7	11.8	3.1	0.0	4.2
Janesville	57.4	970	264	4.5	16.4	0.3	0.0	3.1	13.0	19.0	7.9	3.8	5.3
Kenosha	86.1	980	174	0.0	11.1	0.0	0.0	4.6	17.1	12.3	7.3	6.8	11.4
La Crosse	71.2	1 451	369	0.1	13.0	10.5	0.1	0.1	11.4	10.2	12.2	3.0	7.3
Madison	225.6	1 078	148	0.0	8.9	2.6	0.0	4.0	15.1	13.9	10.7	5.7	6.0
Manitowoc	38.1	1 152	247	0.0	17.0	0.2	0.0	1.0	12.0	13.3	6.0	0.9	7.7
Menomonee Falls	41.5	1 322	268	0.0	15.4	0.0	0.0	0.1	14.1	35.5	2.1	0.3	13.9
Milwaukee	761.6	1 317	196	0.0	7.7	1.1	0.0	3.6	21.4	15.2	1.3	11.3	3.4
New Berlin	36.0	967	208	0.0	14.9	0.0	0.0	0.0	18.6	27.0	6.7	0.0	9.3
Oak Creek	26.3	965	194	0.0	22.0	0.0	0.0	2.1	18.3	17.8	3.2	0.0	3.8
Oshkosh	54.5	941	182	0.0	18.1	0.3	0.0	2.6	14.2	13.4	9.6	1.6	9.4
Racine	94.1	1 161	116	0.0	13.4	0.9	0.0	3.2	23.6	13.3	7.9	2.0	5.7
Sheboygan	49.1	995	116	0.0	16.8	0.8	0.0	0.2	16.3	15.6	6.7	4.7	8.9
Superior	31.8	1 170	114	0.0	12.3	0.0	0.0	0.4	15.5	15.9	6.7	5.9	5.2
Waukesha	63.6	1 026	243	0.0	14.6	0.7	0.0	1.8	15.5	16.0	12.0	0.5	8.4
Wausau	39.6	1 088	207	0.0	21.7	1.5	0.0	3.7	16.8	12.1	5.8	10.5	5.4
Wauwatosa	54.3	1 184	163	0.0	17.9	0.0	0.0	7.3	18.0	14.8	1.3	3.0	8.5

1. Based on population estimated as of July 1 of the year shown.

Table D. Cities — City Government Finances, City Government Employment, and Climate

City	City government finances, 1999 (cont'd)			City government employment, 2001	Climate[2]						
	Debt outstanding				Average daily temperature (degrees Fahrenheit)						
					Mean		Limits				
	Total (mil dol)	Per capita[1] (dollars)	Percent utility		January	July	January[3]	July[4]	Annual precipitation (inches)	Heating degree days	Cooling degree days
	137	138	139	140	141	142	143	144	145	146	147
VIRGINIA—Cont'd											
Richmond	933.5	4 808	30.5	8 016	35.7	78.0	25.7	88.4	43.16	3 963	1 348
Roanoke	409.3	4 366	5.8	4 528	34.5	75.6	25.0	86.4	41.13	4 360	1 052
Suffolk	165.1	2 634	15.8	2 819	39.1	78.2	30.9	86.4	44.64	3 495	1 422
Virginia Beach	783.1	1 811	10.6	17 970	39.1	78.2	30.9	86.4	44.64	3 495	1 422
WASHINGTON	X	X	X	X	X	X	X	X	X	X	X
Auburn	NA	NA	NA	NA	39.7	64.7	33.1	78.0	39.39	4 996	139
Bellevue	110.0	1 057	0.4	1 570	40.1	65.2	35.2	75.2	37.19	4 908	190
Bellingham	48.3	781	50.8	802	37.6	62.2	31.8	70.9	36.17	5 609	51
Bothell	NA	NA	NA	NA	NA	NA	NA	NA	NA	NA	NA
Bremerton	44.7	1 130	6.3	NA	39.1	64.1	33.7	75.0	51.65	5 119	134
Des Moines	NA	NA	NA	NA	NA	NA	NA	NA	NA	NA	NA
Edmonds	NA	NA	NA	NA	40.1	65.2	35.2	75.2	37.19	4 908	190
Everett	174.6	1 970	36.7	1 216	39.1	62.9	33.3	72.2	36.51	5 311	80
Kennewick	37.1	737	17.3	NA	33.1	74.7	26.1	90.3	7.49	4 895	830
Kent	91.9	2 039	5.5	830	39.7	64.7	33.1	78.0	39.39	4 996	139
Kirkland	34.7	759	0.0	NA	40.1	65.2	35.2	75.2	37.19	4 908	190
Lacey	NA	NA	NA	NA	NA	NA	NA	NA	NA	NA	NA
Longview	27.7	820	25.1	NA	39.0	63.8	32.7	76.4	46.54	5 094	132
Lynnwood	39.6	1 202	31.9	NA	40.1	65.2	35.2	75.2	37.19	4 908	190
Marysville	33.5	1 791	67.1	186	NA	NA	NA	NA	NA	NA	NA
Mount Vernon	20.2	890	46.5	NA	NA	NA	NA	NA	NA	NA	NA
Olympia	48.7	1 244	84.0	602	38.0	62.9	31.6	76.5	50.59	5 655	101
Pasco	59.7	2 180	14.9	NA	NA	NA	NA	NA	NA	NA	NA
Puyallup	51.3	1 767	1.4	NA	NA	NA	NA	NA	NA	NA	NA
Redmond	39.0	884	11.2	540	40.1	65.2	35.2	75.2	37.19	4 908	190
Renton	91.5	1 928	25.8	626	40.1	65.2	35.2	75.2	37.19	4 908	190
Richland	116.4	3 121	36.8	NA	33.4	74.4	25.9	89.4	6.99	4 882	822
Sammamish	NA	NA	NA	NA	NA	NA	NA	NA	NA	NA	NA
Seattle	2 019.7	3 761	64.8	10 704	40.1	65.2	35.2	75.2	37.19	4 908	190
Shoreline	0.0	NA	0.0	NA	NA	NA	NA	NA	NA	NA	NA
Spokane	245.3	1 333	1.8	2 220	27.1	68.8	20.8	83.1	16.49	6 842	398
Tacoma	314.8	1 751	53.0	3 412	40.1	65.2	35.2	75.2	37.19	4 908	190
Vancouver	189.1	2 572	0.8	1 046	38.1	64.6	31.2	77.1	41.30	5 196	183
Walla Walla	44.9	1 564	88.6	NA	34.1	75.1	28.4	89.4	19.49	4 958	889
Wenatchee	NA	NA	NA	NA	NA	NA	NA	NA	NA	NA	NA
Yakima	51.6	795	17.7	635	29.7	69.9	21.8	86.7	7.97	5 967	458
WEST VIRGINIA	X	X	X	X	X	X	X	X	X	X	X
Charleston	86.2	1 566	0.0	808	32.1	75.1	23.0	85.7	42.53	4 646	1 031
Huntington	64.9	1 235	0.0	487	32.0	74.7	23.2	84.3	41.49	4 665	1 005
Morgantown	24.4	912	11.8	354	29.0	72.9	20.8	83.2	41.21	5 363	785
Parkersburg	31.8	1 001	91.0	380	29.9	74.4	21.7	84.2	41.51	5 063	953
Wheeling	20.7	635	94.6	850	27.7	73.3	17.6	85.4	40.81	5 598	788
WISCONSIN	X	X	X	X	X	X	X	X	X	X	X
Appleton	140.9	2 150	39.6	722	15.5	71.9	7.2	81.9	30.75	7 693	539
Beloit	55.2	1 571	0.4	482	17.6	72.7	8.8	83.7	33.05	7 161	636
Brookfield	78.1	2 069	16.0	343	19.9	73.6	12.3	84.3	31.11	6 804	725
Eau Claire	68.4	1 156	14.7	884	10.7	71.5	0.8	83.2	31.61	8 330	507
Fond du Lac	52.2	1 315	22.0	521	16.1	72.0	7.9	82.0	29.39	7 541	562
Franklin	40.8	1 481	7.3	200	NA	NA	NA	NA	NA	NA	NA
Green Bay	146.0	1 493	20.1	1 059	14.3	69.7	5.8	80.5	28.83	8 089	381
Greenfield	19.4	562	0.0	241	18.9	70.9	11.6	79.9	32.93	7 324	479
Janesville	55.1	932	15.1	NA	17.6	72.7	8.8	83.7	33.05	7 161	636
Kenosha	174.3	1 985	2.9	820	20.0	69.7	11.7	78.7	33.21	7 195	410
La Crosse	89.2	1 817	3.2	647	14.4	73.5	5.3	84.5	30.55	7 491	692
Madison	275.7	1 317	7.0	2 543	16.0	71.0	7.2	82.4	30.88	7 673	485
Manitowoc	53.6	1 619	59.3	442	17.9	69.8	9.7	80.1	29.11	7 597	374
Menomonee Falls	92.8	2 955	17.9	278	18.9	70.9	11.6	79.9	32.93	7 324	479
Milwaukee	535.0	925	0.0	7 872	19.9	73.6	12.3	84.3	31.11	6 804	725
New Berlin	60.4	1 623	8.7	251	19.8	73.6	12.3	83.0	32.33	6 795	708
Oak Creek	24.1	885	80.2	249	NA	NA	NA	NA	NA	NA	NA
Oshkosh	136.5	2 355	32.0	638	14.8	71.8	5.4	82.5	31.15	7 852	522
Racine	101.6	1 253	21.3	992	19.4	71.0	11.2	79.7	34.37	7 167	509
Sheboygan	63.3	1 281	2.8	550	20.3	70.9	12.8	80.4	31.19	7 087	472
Superior	83.3	3 070	0.0	294	10.0	65.9	0.1	77.5	28.91	9 483	206
Waukesha	101.6	1 639	9.3	573	18.6	72.3	10.8	82.8	32.55	7 117	600
Wausau	45.6	1 253	8.0	341	12.0	70.0	2.8	80.8	32.82	8 427	402
Wauwatosa	77.1	1 682	11.3	451	19.9	73.6	12.3	84.3	31.11	6 804	725

1. Based on the population estimated as of July 1 of the year shown.   2. Represents normal values based on the 30-year period, 1961–1990.   3. Average daily minimum.   4. Average daily maximum.

Table D. Cities — **Land Area and Population**

STATE Place code	City	Land area, 2000[1] (sq km)	Population, 2000			Population				Population characteristics, 2000						
										Percent						
												Race (alone or in combination)				
			Total persons	Rank	Per square kilo-meter	Total persons 1990	Percent change 1990–2000	Total persons 1980	Percent change 1980–1990	White	Black	Am. Indian, Alaska Native	Asian and Pacific Islander	Other race	His-panic[2]	Non-His-panic White
		1	2	3	4	5	6	7	8	9	10	11	12	13	14	15
	WISCONSIN—Cont'd															
55 85300	West Allis	29.4	61 254	452	2 083.5	63 221	-3.1	63 982	-1.2	95.3	1.8	1.2	1.7	1.6	3.5	92.1
55 85350	West Bend	32.9	28 152	1 097	855.7	24 470	15.0	21 484	13.9	98.0	0.5	0.8	0.7	0.8	1.8	96.2
56 00000	WYOMING	251 488.9	493 782	X	2.0	453 589	8.9	469 557	-3.4	93.7	1.0	3.0	0.9	3.2	6.4	88.9
56 13150	Casper	62.0	49 644	602	800.7	46 765	6.2	51 016	-8.3	95.5	1.2	1.6	0.8	2.6	5.4	91.3
56 13900	Cheyenne	54.7	53 011	560	969.1	50 008	6.0	47 283	5.8	90.4	3.4	1.6	1.9	5.5	12.5	81.4
56 45050	Laramie	28.8	27 204	1 136	944.6	26 687	1.9	24 410	9.3	92.9	1.5	1.7	2.5	3.7	7.9	86.8

1. Dry land or land partially or temporarily covered by water.   2. Hispanic persons may be of any race.

Table D. Cities — **Population and Households**

City	Under 5 years	5 to 17 years	18 to 24 years	25 to 34 years	35 to 44 years	45 to 54 years	55 to 64 years	65 to 74 years	75 years and over	Percent female	Number	Percent change, 1990–2000	Persons per house-hold	Female family house-holder[1]	One-person
				Age of population (percent)										Percent	
												Households, 2000			
	16	17	18	19	20	21	22	23	24	25	26	27	28	29	30
WISCONSIN—Cont'd															
West Allis	5.8	15.7	8.4	15.3	16.9	12.9	7.7	7.5	9.8	51.8	27 604	3.0	2.19	10.6	37.3
West Bend	7.2	18.3	8.6	15.4	15.7	12.6	7.7	6.4	8.0	51.8	11 375	31.0	2.44	9.4	27.5
WYOMING	6.3	19.8	10.1	12.1	16.0	15.0	9.0	6.3	5.3	49.7	193 608	14.7	2.48	8.7	26.3
Casper........................	6.6	19.3	10.5	12.3	15.4	14.1	8.2	7.3	6.3	51.3	20 343	9.9	2.38	11.1	29.1
Cheyenne....................	6.5	18.5	8.8	13.9	15.8	14.0	8.8	7.0	6.8	51.2	22 324	10.3	2.33	10.6	31.3
Laramie......................	5.1	12.4	31.8	15.0	10.9	11.1	5.7	4.0	4.1	48.3	11 336	9.0	2.19	8.0	33.2

1. No spouse present.

City	Persons in group quarters, 2000				Serious crimes known to police, 2000[2]				Education, 1990				Money income, 1989		
		Institutional			Total		Rate[3]		School enrollment		Attainment[4] (percent)			Households	
														Median	
	Total	Total	Persons in nursing homes	Non-Institutional[1]	Number	Rate[3]	Violent	Property	Public	Private	High school graduate or more	Bachelor's degree or more	Per capita (dollars)[5]	Dollars	Percent change, 1979–1989 (constant 1989 dollars)
	31	32	33	34	35	36	37	38	39	40	41	42	43	44	45
WISCONSIN—Cont'd															
West Allis	922	596	529	326	2 631	4 295	261	4 034	10 678	2 965	79.2	12.4	13 978	29 622	-5.4
West Bend	405	324	216	81	875	3 108	36	3 073	4 807	1 154	80.3	16.5	13 957	34 337	3.8
WYOMING	14 083	7 861	2 869	6 222	16 285	3 298	267	3 032	127 228	7 511	83.0	18.8	12 311	27 096	-19.1
Casper	1 226	554	470	672	2 182	4 395	348	4 047	12 529	767	86.4	23.0	13 424	27 698	-28.5
Cheyenne	991	651	472	340	2 182	4 116	194	3 922	12 385	1 133	84.6	22.1	13 351	28 117	-5.3
Laramie	2 362	133	101	2 229	822	3 022	276	2 746	12 463	743	90.0	40.4	11 652	19 642	-15.6

1. Persons in emergency shelters and persons visible in street locations. areas and over time. 3. Per 100,000 population estimated by the FBI.

2. Data for serious crimes have not been adjusted for underreporting. This may affect comparability between geographic 4. Persons 25 years old and older. 5. Based on population enumerated as of April 1, 1990.

Table D. Cities — **Income, Poverty, and Housing**

City	Money income, 1989 (cont'd) Households (cont'd) Percent with $100,000 or more	Percent below poverty, 1989 Persons Total	Persons Percent change in rate, 1979–1989	Families Total	Housing units, 2000 Total	Percent change, 1990–2000	Vacant units Vacant units for sale or rent[1]	For seasonal use (percent)	Home owner vacancy rate	Renter vacancy rate	Occupied units Total	Percent owner occu-pied	Percent renter occu-pied	Average size owner occu-pied	Average size renter occu-pied
	46	47	48	49	50	51	52	53	54	55	56	57	58	59	60
WISCONSIN—Cont'd															
West Allis	0.8	5.3	17.8	4.3	28 708	4.4	1 104	0.1	1.1	4.5	27 604	58.1	41.9	2.47	1.80
West Bend	2.4	4.4	-12.0	3.1	11 926	34.2	551	0.3	2.0	6.1	11 375	62.2	37.8	2.65	2.08
WYOMING	2.0	11.9	50.1	9.3	223 854	10.1	30 246	5.5	2.1	9.7	193 608	70.0	30.0	2.58	2.25
Casper	2.7	11.4	90.0	9.6	21 872	0.8	1 529	0.5	1.5	8.1	20 343	66.9	33.1	2.50	2.13
Cheyenne	1.6	10.3	32.1	8.6	23 782	8.8	1 458	0.4	1.3	7.9	22 324	66.0	34.0	2.47	2.06
Laramie	1.9	21.0	28.8	10.6	11 994	8.3	658	0.5	1.9	4.9	11 336	47.5	52.5	2.41	1.99

1. Includes units rented or sold but not occupied.   2. Specified owner-occupied units.   3. Specified renter-occupied units.   4. Overcrowded or lacking complete plumbing facilities.

City	Civilian labor force, 2001				Civilian employment, 1990[2]			Disability 1990	Value of residential construction authorized by building permits, 2000		
			Unemployment			Percent					
	Total	Percent change, 2000–2001	Total	Rate[1]	Total	Professional, managerial, and technical	Precision production, craft, and repair	Work disabled persons[3] (percent)	New construction ($1,000)	Number of housing units	Percent single family
	61	62	63	64	65	66	67	68	69	70	71
WISCONSIN—Cont'd											
West Allis	31 809	1.3	1 396	4.4	32 452	24.3	13.0	7.3	1 126	12	50.0
West Bend	16 386	1.6	863	5.3	12 150	25.2	14.5	6.1	15 717	162	55.6
WYOMING	271 262	1.6	10 666	3.9	207 868	27.2	13.2	7.3	313 653	1 582	90.3
Casper...............	26 843	2.7	1 008	3.8	21 694	33.5	10.8	7.0	10 125	72	100.0
Cheyenne...............	29 626	2.0	1 035	3.5	23 126	33.3	8.5	8.4	16 549	143	100.0
Laramie	16 515	2.8	316	1.9	12 856	40.0	6.7	4.6	5 168	41	95.1

1. Percent of civilian labor force.   2. Persons 16 years and older.   3. Persons 16 to 64 years old.

Table D. Cities — **Wholesale Trade, Retail Trade, and Real Estate**

City	Wholesale Trade, 1997				Retail Trade[1], 1997				Real Estate and Rental and Leasing, 1997			
	Number of Establish-ments	Number of Employees	Sales (mil dol)	Annual Payroll (mil dol)	Number of Establish-ments	Number of Employees	Sales (mil dol)	Annual Payroll (mil dol)	Number of Establish-ments	Number of Employees	Receipts (mil dol)	Annual Payroll (mil dol)
	72	73	74	75	76	77	78	79	80	81	82	83
WISCONSIN—Cont'd												
West Allis	128	1 797	578.4	66.2	311	5 485	1 013.5	93.2	66	1 011	113.6	21.4
West Bend	37	339	101.5	10.6	149	2 341	661.9	34.3	24	101	14.5	1.4
WYOMING	800	5 761	2 547.1	161.9	2 939	26 934	4 530.5	426.7	717	2 463	220.8	39.5
Casper..................................	122	921	687.1	25.6	346	3 702	595.2	59.6	91	329	29.3	5.6
Cheyenne..............................	56	457	178.2	13.4	308	4 496	761.4	71.9	77	300	26.1	5.0
Laramie................................	19	101	81.5	2.3	158	1 607	332.6	26.9	44	125	9.0	1.4

1. Establishments with payroll.

City	Professional, Scientific, and Technical Services, 1997[1]				Manufacturing, 1997				Accommodation and Foodservices, 1997			
	Number of Establish-ments	Number of Employees	Receipts (mil dol)	Annual Payroll (mil dol)	Number of Establish-ments	Number of Employees	Receipts (mil dol)	Annual Payroll (mil dol)	Number of Establish-ments	Number of Employees	Sales (mil dol)	Annual Payroll (mil dol)
	84	85	86	87	88	89	90	91	92	93	94	95
WISCONSIN—Cont'd												
West Allis	135	843	73.8	29.5	145	7 537	864.7	226.4	159	D	D	D
West Bend	59	321	22.8	9.7	65	4 972	586.5	150.9	65	1 285	32.0	8.8
WYOMING	1 264	5 274	388.8	146.9	503	8 448	2 955.1	256.4	1 751	24 950	808.9	219.0
Casper	182	798	66.6	23.9	NA	NA	NA	NA	138	2 644	69.9	19.7
Cheyenne	186	807	61.9	23.7	35	D	D	D	156	3 423	90.4	26.9
Laramie	98	527	39.2	16.8	NA	NA	NA	NA	92	1 866	42.5	12.0

1. Firms subject to federal tax.

Table D. Cities — **Entertainment, Health Care, and Other Services**

City	Arts, Entertainment, and Recreation[1], 1997				Health Care and Social Assistance[1], 1997				Other Services[1], 1997			
	Number of Establish-ments	Number of Employees	Receipts (mil dol)	Annual Payroll (mil dol)	Number of Establish-ments	Number of Employees	Receipts (mil dol)	Annual Payroll (mil dol)	Number of Establish-ments	Number of Employees	Receipts (mil dol)	Annual Payroll (mil dol)
	96	97	98	99	100	101	102	103	104	105	106	107
WISCONSIN—Cont'd												
West Allis	15	284	16.3	2.9	170	2 274	139.8	74.1	164	1 167	77.2	25.1
West Bend	7	31	1.5	0.3	68	516	24.6	10.3	66	418	23.1	6.6
WYOMING	262	2 108	93.3	23.3	1 006	7 875	493.6	210.3	980	4 866	422.8	94.8
Casper..................................	23	123	7.3	1.6	165	0	0.0	0.0	117	627	37.1	11.2
Cheyenne..............................	18	0	0.0	0.0	142	1 524	103.7	50.3	103	1 046	159.5	22.7
Laramie	14	0	0.0	0.0	70	0	0.0	0.0	56	338	15.5	4.9

1. Firms subject to federal tax.

Table D. Cities — **Federal Funds and City Government Finances**

	Selected federal funds, fiscal 2001[1] (mil dol)									City government finances, 1999						
										General revenue						
City	Procurement contracts		Grants					Direct payments for individuals			Intergovernmental		Taxes			
														Per capita[3] (dollars)		
	Defense	Other	Total[2]	Health and family welfare	Energy and environment	Education	Housing and community development	Educational assistance	Housing assistance	Total (mil dol)	Total (mil dol)	Percent from state government	Total (mil dol)	Total	Property	Sales and gross receipts
	108	109	110	111	112	113	114	115	116	117	118	119	120	121	122	123
WISCONSIN—Cont'd																
West Allis	0.0	0.0	1.4	0.0	0.0	0.0	1.4	0.1	6.0	64.5	21.6	75.1	26.0	433	400	1
West Bend	0.0	0.0	0.2	0.2	0.0	0.0	0.0	0.0	2.4	30.6	7.2	84.9	11.7	410	374	4
WYOMING	95.6	245.5	1 213.1	277.0	35.0	102.6	5.2	20.6	36.7	X	X	X	X	X	X	X
Casper	1.6	4.0	12.9	1.0	0.2	0.7	4.2	2.1	7.1	50.6	29.0	63.0	3.9	81	49	21
Cheyenne	44.1	12.1	181.8	38.5	27.7	36.7	0.5	4.9	7.5	47.1	23.1	63.0	5.8	109	49	41
Laramie	0.6	5.6	40.8	9.1	5.9	4.5	0.0	8.4	1.0	19.5	11.6	65.1	1.9	77	46	17

1. October 1, 2000 to September 30, 2001.   2. Includes program categories not shown separately. State totals include additional categories not allocated by city.   3. Based on population estimated as of July 1 of the year shown.

Table D. Cities — **City Government Finances**

City	City government finances, 1999 (cont'd)												
	General expenditure												
	Per capita[1] (dollars)			Percent of total for —									
	Total (mil dol)	Total	Capital outlays	Public welfare	Highways	Parking facilities	Education	Health and hospitals	Police protection	Sewerage and sanitation	Parks and recreation	Housing and community develop-ment	Interest on debt
	124	125	126	127	128	129	130	131	132	133	134	135	136
WISCONSIN—Cont'd													
West Allis	62.7	1 045	77	2.6	18.6	0.1	0.0	5.5	20.1	12.1	0.8	4.7	5.2
West Bend	32.5	1 141	436	0.0	20.0	0.3	0.0	1.0	14.9	13.8	5.6	0.6	6.9
WYOMING	X	X	X	X	X	X	X	X	X	X	X	X	X
Casper...................................	46.0	953	201	0.3	11.7	0.1	0.0	1.9	13.6	21.1	13.1	3.4	0.6
Cheyenne..............................	41.3	771	153	1.1	16.1	0.7	0.0	1.8	13.3	18.3	9.4	3.1	4.5
Laramie	18.8	752	124	2.9	14.3	0.0	0.0	0.3	16.2	14.2	6.6	0.0	0.2

1. Based on population estimated as of July 1 of the year shown.

Table D. Cities — City Government Finances, City Government Employment, and Climate

City	City government finances, 1999 (cont'd)			City government employment, 2001	Climate[2]						
	Debt outstanding				Average daily temperature (degrees Fahrenheit)						
					Mean		Limits				
	Total (mil dol)	Per capita[1] (dollars)	Percent utility		January	July	January[3]	July[4]	Annual precipitation (inches)	Heating degree days	Cooling degree days
	137	138	139	140	141	142	143	144	145	146	147
WISCONSIN—Cont'd											
West Allis	65.5	1 092	3.7	629	19.8	73.6	12.3	83.0	32.33	6 795	708
West Bend	38.6	1 354	12.6	274	NA	NA	NA	NA	NA	NA	NA
WYOMING	X	X	X	X	X	X	X	X	X	X	X
Casper.................................	4.0	82	8.0	544	22.4	70.8	12.0	87.6	12.52	7 682	445
Cheyenne.............................	67.4	1 257	62.5	584	26.5	68.4	15.2	82.2	14.40	7 326	285
Laramie	27.9	1 115	7.6	243	20.0	64.1	8.0	80.4	10.88	9 008	74

1. Based on the population estimated as of July 1 of the year shown.   2. Represents normal values based on the 30-year period, 1961–1990.   3. Average daily minimum.   4. Average daily maximum.

TABLE E:

Congressional Districts of the 107th Congress

(For explanation of symbols, see page xii)

Page

Table E. Congressional Districts 107th Congress — **Land Area and Population**

STATE District	Land area, 2000[1] (sq km)	Total persons	Per square kilometer	White	Black	Am. Indian, Alaska Native	Asian and Pacific Islander	Other race	Hispanic[2]	Non-Hispanic White	2 or more races	Under 5 years	5 to 17 years	18 to 24 years	25 to 34 years	35 to 44 years	45 to 54 years	55 to 64 years
	1	2	3	4	5	6	7	8	9	10	11	12	13	14	15	16	17	18
ALABAMA	131 426.0	4 447 100	33.8	72.0	26.3	1.0	1.0	0.9	1.7	70.3	1.0	6.7	18.6	9.9	13.6	15.4	13.5	9.3
District 1	17 572.1	646 181	36.8	68.8	28.9	1.5	1.3	0.6	1.3	67.3	1.0	7.0	19.7	9.3	13.0	15.3	13.3	9.4
District 2	26 235.3	650 321	24.8	70.2	28.3	0.9	1.0	0.7	1.5	68.5	1.1	6.6	18.8	9.6	13.8	15.5	13.4	9.2
District 3	22 582.4	643 525	28.5	73.3	25.6	0.7	0.8	0.6	1.3	71.9	0.8	6.4	18.1	11.7	13.5	14.7	13.2	9.4
District 4	23 668.5	643 275	27.2	91.3	6.5	1.3	0.4	1.7	3.0	89.0	1.1	6.4	17.8	8.6	13.4	14.9	13.6	10.5
District 5	11 418.3	654 886	57.4	81.2	16.6	1.5	1.3	0.9	2.0	78.8	1.5	6.5	18.3	9.1	13.7	16.6	13.7	9.8
District 6	7 370.6	664 795	90.2	82.8	15.1	0.6	1.5	0.9	1.8	81.2	0.8	6.5	17.3	10.1	15.1	16.2	14.1	8.5
District 7	22 579.0	544 117	24.1	29.1	70.3	0.4	0.5	0.5	1.0	28.3	0.6	7.2	20.5	11.1	12.1	14.4	13.0	8.4
ALASKA	1 481 347.0	626 932	0.4	74.0	4.3	19.0	6.1	2.4	4.1	67.6	5.4	7.6	22.8	9.1	14.3	18.2	15.1	7.1
At Large	1 481 346.9	626 932	0.4	74.0	4.3	19.0	6.1	2.4	4.1	67.6	5.4	7.6	22.8	9.1	14.3	18.2	15.1	7.1
ARIZONA	294 312.0	5 130 632	17.4	77.9	3.6	5.7	2.6	13.2	25.3	63.8	2.9	7.5	19.2	10.0	14.5	15.0	12.2	8.6
District 1	545.6	829 492	1 520.3	79.3	4.5	2.7	4.2	12.7	22.7	66.8	3.1	7.7	18.1	12.9	18.3	16.3	11.9	6.6
District 2	45 865.9	773 824	16.9	58.9	5.6	5.2	1.5	32.6	62.5	27.3	3.7	9.3	22.9	12.0	15.3	13.7	10.2	6.9
District 3	107 779.2	997 565	9.3	84.8	3.0	3.3	2.0	9.5	18.1	74.2	2.5	6.9	18.4	7.7	12.4	14.2	12.2	10.1
District 4	500.6	735 344	1 468.9	84.0	3.7	2.4	3.3	9.7	18.8	72.5	2.9	7.2	18.1	10.0	15.5	16.0	13.6	8.7
District 5	32 866.3	793 256	24.1	84.7	3.7	2.0	3.1	9.8	20.5	71.7	3.0	6.1	17.1	10.0	12.7	14.9	13.5	9.8
District 6	106 754.6	1 001 151	9.4	74.8	1.8	16.4	1.7	7.6	14.2	66.6	2.2	7.7	20.5	8.5	13.4	15.0	12.2	9.1
ARKANSAS	134 856.0	2 673 400	19.8	81.2	16.0	1.4	1.1	1.8	3.2	78.6	1.3	6.8	18.7	9.8	13.2	14.9	13.1	9.6
District 1	42 986.3	629 974	14.7	80.9	18.0	1.0	0.6	0.7	1.6	79.1	1.0	6.8	19.2	9.4	12.6	14.6	12.9	10.0
District 2	15 338.4	666 058	43.4	77.8	19.9	1.0	1.3	1.4	2.4	75.6	1.3	6.8	18.3	10.2	14.4	15.6	13.5	8.9
District 3	29 804.0	764 853	25.7	92.5	2.1	2.4	1.7	3.2	5.8	88.2	1.8	7.0	18.5	10.0	13.4	14.8	12.8	9.6
District 4	46 727.2	612 515	13.1	71.0	27.0	1.0	0.6	1.6	2.7	69.0	1.1	6.5	18.7	9.5	12.3	14.5	13.1	9.9
CALIFORNIA	403 933.0	33 871 648	83.9	63.4	7.4	1.9	13.0	19.4	32.4	46.7	4.7	7.3	20.0	9.9	15.4	16.2	12.8	7.7
District 1	27 977.8	644 525	23.0	80.6	5.3	4.5	5.5	9.1	16.5	69.5	4.6	6.2	19.1	9.4	12.7	15.7	14.9	9.0
District 2	73 589.3	633 808	8.6	89.6	2.0	4.2	3.4	4.5	8.5	82.3	3.7	5.7	19.2	9.7	10.8	14.7	14.8	9.9
District 3	19 828.2	675 618	34.1	77.5	4.7	2.7	8.7	12.1	19.5	65.7	5.1	7.1	20.8	11.3	13.4	15.6	12.6	7.9
District 4	27 988.1	725 180	25.9	90.7	1.9	2.3	4.0	4.5	9.2	83.0	3.3	5.9	19.2	7.3	11.6	17.2	15.8	9.8
District 5	391.4	669 412	1 710.3	57.2	15.3	2.6	19.3	12.6	19.9	45.4	6.5	7.4	20.6	10.1	15.3	15.6	12.7	7.3
District 6	4 120.1	644 600	156.5	86.0	2.7	1.9	5.4	8.2	14.4	76.3	3.9	5.7	16.9	7.7	12.9	17.0	17.0	9.7
District 7	906.2	636 367	702.2	55.1	18.0	1.9	18.5	13.2	21.6	41.9	6.1	7.2	19.7	9.0	14.5	16.7	14.3	8.1
District 8	89.1	617 094	6 925.9	52.8	10.0	1.3	31.0	9.7	16.1	42.8	4.4	4.1	10.2	9.1	24.5	17.4	13.5	8.2
District 9	188.8	597 205	3 163.6	45.1	27.9	1.7	20.0	11.2	17.3	34.8	5.2	6.3	16.2	11.3	17.6	15.8	14.1	7.8
District 10	2 650.2	713 341	269.2	81.0	4.3	1.4	11.7	6.4	12.1	71.2	4.4	6.8	19.7	6.5	12.7	18.5	15.6	9.2
District 11	4 730.2	684 178	144.6	65.0	7.5	2.3	13.9	17.7	27.8	50.4	6.0	7.9	22.7	9.6	13.4	15.6	12.4	7.7
District 12	277.3	615 370	2 219.1	57.1	3.4	1.0	35.0	9.3	15.9	45.6	5.2	5.5	14.9	8.2	16.5	17.0	14.8	9.2
District 13	619.0	678 177	1 095.6	49.2	8.3	1.5	34.5	13.1	22.1	35.1	6.2	7.3	18.6	8.9	16.7	17.7	13.2	7.7
District 14	1 236.0	615 917	498.3	68.1	3.7	0.9	21.7	9.8	17.2	57.1	3.8	6.6	15.8	8.2	17.6	17.8	13.8	8.5
District 15	1 172.3	612 416	522.5	73.4	2.7	1.3	20.1	7.4	13.3	63.1	4.6	6.5	16.9	8.0	16.0	18.6	14.4	9.0
District 16	2 450.3	689 817	281.5	45.2	4.2	1.7	29.5	24.8	39.8	26.7	5.1	8.0	19.7	10.9	18.3	16.6	12.0	7.0
District 17	12 655.2	653 209	51.6	65.3	3.3	2.0	7.2	27.4	42.6	46.6	4.9	7.4	19.9	11.3	15.6	15.7	13.0	7.1
District 18	10 715.6	683 642	63.8	69.5	3.7	2.4	6.8	23.3	36.4	51.7	5.4	8.2	23.9	10.0	13.6	15.2	11.7	7.3
District 19	19 786.1	709 622	35.9	67.5	5.1	2.9	8.7	20.8	32.9	51.8	4.8	7.9	22.2	10.2	13.4	15.0	12.7	7.7
District 20	17 763.1	711 574	40.1	46.7	6.3	2.4	5.6	43.7	63.7	23.8	4.5	9.3	25.0	12.0	15.7	14.8	9.8	5.8
District 21	23 091.1	666 684	28.9	71.8	5.1	2.8	4.1	20.7	31.4	57.8	4.3	8.1	23.0	9.7	13.3	15.2	12.2	7.8
District 22	15 633.9	631 659	40.4	80.8	2.7	2.2	5.0	13.6	27.0	64.5	4.0	5.9	17.7	13.5	12.9	15.2	13.1	8.1
District 23	4 613.9	642 427	139.2	70.5	2.6	1.9	6.9	22.5	37.7	52.4	4.2	7.6	21.2	9.4	14.2	16.6	13.2	7.7
District 24	786.2	629 832	801.1	79.3	3.5	1.1	9.4	11.3	19.8	66.2	4.4	6.5	17.6	7.8	14.6	17.5	14.8	9.2
District 25	5 328.1	699 526	131.3	71.3	8.8	1.7	9.3	13.9	25.0	56.2	4.6	7.5	22.5	9.1	13.7	18.1	13.2	7.4
District 26	181.0	660 224	3 647.6	51.3	5.7	1.6	7.6	39.8	65.4	20.6	5.7	9.2	22.3	11.4	18.1	15.4	10.5	5.8
District 27	789.5	600 986	761.2	68.7	7.3	1.1	14.9	15.1	23.1	51.8	6.9	6.1	17.5	8.0	15.3	17.4	14.2	8.8
District 28	1 202.4	609 233	506.7	60.4	5.4	1.4	21.2	16.3	31.6	41.7	4.4	6.5	20.1	9.5	13.2	16.1	14.1	8.6
District 29	305.3	584 823	1 915.6	80.5	4.0	0.9	11.5	8.0	12.1	70.7	4.6	4.1	9.8	9.9	21.5	17.7	13.9	8.7
District 30	96.5	582 745	6 038.8	39.2	3.6	1.7	21.0	40.3	64.3	11.4	5.5	8.4	19.8	11.4	19.4	15.6	11.0	6.5
District 31	195.6	600 376	3 069.4	38.2	1.6	1.7	29.6	33.3	59.4	9.9	4.2	8.3	21.1	11.2	16.9	14.7	11.0	6.9
District 32	121.9	586 031	4 807.5	35.5	34.6	1.5	9.2	24.8	37.1	19.6	5.0	7.3	18.5	10.8	17.6	15.8	11.9	7.4
District 33	123.8	600 695	4 852.1	41.8	4.2	1.7	5.1	52.2	86.0	5.1	4.9	9.9	23.1	13.8	18.8	13.9	9.2	5.0
District 34	234.1	617 343	2 637.1	51.0	2.3	1.9	10.1	39.8	72.4	15.4	4.9	8.3	22.6	10.8	15.8	14.5	11.0	7.1
District 35	112.8	607 944	5 389.6	26.2	35.7	1.4	5.5	36.0	54.2	5.6	4.5	10.0	24.6	11.2	16.9	14.6	9.9	6.0
District 36	599.7	591 448	986.2	71.4	4.6	1.2	17.9	9.8	18.8	58.3	4.7	6.0	15.7	7.3	16.6	18.4	14.5	9.3
District 37	187.0	616 103	3 294.7	27.9	26.8	1.5	10.9	37.8	57.2	6.1	4.6	9.8	26.4	11.5	15.6	14.0	9.7	6.0
District 38	196.3	634 392	3 231.7	56.1	11.7	1.7	11.4	24.6	40.1	36.8	5.1	8.2	20.2	10.3	17.2	15.9	11.9	6.8
District 39	271.1	622 921	2 297.8	62.9	3.5	1.4	20.5	16.2	30.4	45.3	4.3	6.9	20.1	9.7	14.3	15.9	13.0	8.7
District 40	77 476.1	674 431	8.7	76.0	7.5	2.8	5.1	13.8	23.8	62.1	4.8	7.3	22.3	9.9	12.4	15.5	12.7	8.2
District 41	595.4	666 225	1 119.0	56.5	6.5	1.5	16.4	23.9	40.9	36.1	4.5	8.0	22.9	10.3	14.7	16.8	13.4	7.1
District 42	543.5	700 491	1 288.9	53.1	13.5	2.1	5.2	31.7	50.8	30.4	5.3	9.3	26.0	10.6	15.2	15.8	10.9	5.7
District 43	1 939.6	736 634	379.8	68.7	7.0	2.0	6.3	21.1	35.5	50.6	4.8	8.2	23.5	10.1	14.2	16.9	11.9	6.8
District 44	16 464.0	742 718	45.1	68.6	7.3	2.1	3.8	22.4	38.5	49.8	4.0	7.5	21.2	8.5	12.2	14.1	10.9	8.4

1. Dry land or land partially or temporarily covered by water. 2. Hispanic persons may be of any race.

Table E. Congressional Districts 107th Congress — **Population, Households, Group Quarters, and Education**

STATE District	65 to 74 years	75 years and over	Percent female	Number	Persons per house-hold	Female family house-holder[1]	One person	Persons in correctional institutions, 2000	Persons in nursing homes, 2000	Persons in military quarters, 2000	Public	Private
	19	20	21	22	23	24	25	26	27	28	29	30
ALABAMA	7.1	5.9	51.7	1 737 080	2.49	14.2	26.1	33 542	26 697	5 370	940 143	116 259
District 1	7.1	5.8	51.8	245 355	2.58	15.6	24.5	3 825	3 181	61	130 928	24 463
District 2	6.9	6.1	51.4	252 944	2.47	14.3	26.4	11 423	3 959	4 715	133 381	17 952
District 3	7.1	5.8	51.3	251 525	2.48	13.7	26.1	6 518	4 230	4	145 948	12 298
District 4	8.1	6.6	51.3	255 047	2.49	10.7	24.6	2 178	4 988	0	122 944	6 690
District 5	7.0	5.3	51.2	260 271	2.46	11.4	26.0	4 186	3 099	587	132 398	14 574
District 6	6.6	5.7	51.7	267 020	2.44	10.2	27.2	1 731	3 741	0	128 956	22 950
District 7	7.0	6.2	53.8	204 918	2.56	26.1	28.4	3 681	3 499	3	145 588	17 332
ALASKA	3.6	2.1	48.3	221 600	2.74	10.8	23.5	3 331	803	3 970	141 933	14 424
At Large	3.6	2.1	48.3	221 600	2.74	10.8	23.5	3 331	803	3 970	141 933	14 424
ARIZONA	7.1	5.9	50.1	1 901 327	2.64	11.1	24.8	45 783	13 607	5 256	896 427	94 695
District 1	4.3	3.9	49.4	317 145	2.58	10.8	27.2	33	2 424	0	158 476	17 856
District 2	5.6	3.9	49.0	236 436	3.17	16.6	20.7	13 055	1 493	1 677	163 163	10 830
District 3	9.7	8.5	50.7	381 331	2.57	9.1	23.1	5 993	4 151	681	128 856	13 315
District 4	5.8	5.1	50.3	290 096	2.52	11.5	28.1	7	669	0	130 917	23 503
District 5	8.5	7.4	50.8	320 429	2.39	10.0	28.4	10 745	2 405	2 898	149 618	16 837
District 6	7.7	5.9	50.1	355 890	2.74	10.4	21.3	15 950	2 465	0	165 397	12 354
ARKANSAS	7.4	6.6	51.2	1 042 696	2.49	12.1	25.6	20 565	21 379	1 290	530 045	52 360
District 1	7.7	6.7	51.4	243 643	2.52	13.2	25.0	7 746	5 601	0	137 897	8 892
District 2	6.5	5.7	51.5	263 453	2.46	12.8	26.7	2 763	4 460	1 246	126 639	23 950
District 3	7.5	6.5	50.7	297 580	2.52	9.3	24.4	1 498	5 301	27	130 270	10 621
District 4	8.1	7.5	51.3	238 020	2.48	13.9	26.4	8 558	6 017	17	135 239	8 897
CALIFORNIA	5.6	5.0	50.2	11 502 870	2.87	12.6	23.5	248 516	120 724	58 810	7 177 045	1 123 001
District 1	6.6	6.3	49.4	234 984	2.61	11.6	24.8	14 686	3 134	2 017	141 281	15 223
District 2	7.9	7.4	50.0	245 147	2.50	10.9	25.6	10 798	2 631	512	146 553	11 082
District 3	6.0	5.4	51.1	242 105	2.73	12.5	23.0	1 569	3 575	237	152 376	14 398
District 4	7.3	6.0	49.6	272 937	2.57	9.4	22.1	11 864	2 693	104	130 707	15 478
District 5	5.5	5.4	51.5	249 892	2.63	15.1	29.5	2 104	2 833	104	144 846	18 983
District 6	6.2	6.7	50.7	251 423	2.48	9.8	27.8	7 730	3 201	331	118 862	22 489
District 7	5.4	5.0	51.1	223 309	2.81	15.2	23.5	1 464	2 383	26	132 051	21 511
District 8	6.7	6.3	48.6	268 026	2.24	8.7	41.3	1 369	1 582	36	108 929	29 675
District 9	5.3	5.5	51.7	237 212	2.46	14.8	33.7	979	1 991	224	138 801	26 478
District 10	5.6	5.4	50.9	261 663	2.68	8.7	21.4	5 456	2 054	15	127 426	23 447
District 11	5.6	5.0	50.3	225 687	2.96	13.7	20.7	4 540	2 998	3	143 398	18 398
District 12	7.0	6.8	51.1	226 199	2.69	10.2	25.3	20	2 435	0	117 876	29 648
District 13	5.3	4.6	50.2	220 965	3.04	12.0	18.5	40	2 535	0	134 510	19 992
District 14	5.9	5.9	49.4	234 612	2.56	7.9	26.5	1 933	2 786	281	110 734	41 810
District 15	5.7	5.0	50.1	226 831	2.66	9.2	22.3	106	2 715	0	129 080	27 549
District 16	4.3	3.2	48.7	194 697	3.47	12.7	16.9	4 347	1 388	0	155 284	17 494
District 17	5.2	4.8	49.0	206 835	3.02	11.3	22.3	12 888	2 106	2 478	145 568	16 303
District 18	5.4	4.7	50.3	215 784	3.10	13.7	18.8	5 473	2 611	0	152 875	12 256
District 19	5.8	5.1	51.4	240 272	2.89	13.8	21.6	7 283	2 381	0	157 759	13 495
District 20	4.1	3.5	46.0	180 223	3.66	16.5	14.3	42 503	2 310	1 085	164 046	7 916
District 21	5.7	4.9	50.3	225 835	2.88	14.0	21.7	8 090	2 302	742	147 377	12 895
District 22	6.7	6.7	49.5	224 371	2.67	9.6	25.0	11 408	2 419	470	153 080	18 518
District 23	5.3	4.8	49.9	203 699	3.10	11.3	18.9	2 325	1 732	1 451	137 882	21 842
District 24	6.3	5.7	51.0	236 137	2.63	10.1	25.0	104	2 307	0	111 175	36 752
District 25	4.8	3.7	49.8	226 900	2.99	12.4	18.7	12 367	1 745	0	130 990	27 888
District 26	3.9	3.4	49.5	189 181	3.45	15.5	19.9	132	2 240	0	139 415	22 546
District 27	6.4	6.3	51.7	228 095	2.59	11.7	28.6	32	4 307	0	117 406	35 243
District 28	6.1	5.8	51.8	199 315	2.99	13.3	19.7	173	4 230	0	134 410	33 286
District 29	6.8	7.6	50.3	290 778	1.94	6.6	45.8	148	2 936	0	95 817	35 631
District 30	4.5	3.5	49.5	187 303	3.07	16.5	24.8	22	1 508	0	150 278	23 524
District 31	5.4	4.5	50.8	162 708	3.64	17.4	15.2	110	2 718	0	156 835	20 202
District 32	5.4	5.2	52.2	217 323	2.66	18.7	31.3	117	1 899	0	131 294	30 735
District 33	3.4	2.9	48.1	151 990	3.77	17.7	19.2	12 136	1 971	0	166 671	15 978
District 34	5.6	4.2	50.6	166 460	3.67	16.9	14.2	35	1 757	0	151 796	22 076
District 35	4.0	3.0	51.4	178 561	3.38	24.7	21.3	261	1 229	0	152 935	20 363
District 36	6.6	5.5	50.5	241 826	2.41	9.6	30.3	2	2 103	158	108 621	29 419
District 37	4.1	2.9	50.8	156 506	3.89	23.6	14.6	1 229	1 238	0	162 935	17 288
District 38	4.7	5.1	51.0	223 510	2.79	15.5	27.4	1 307	3 027	5	130 772	20 280
District 39	6.3	5.0	50.9	201 697	3.05	12.2	18.3	0	2 454	0	143 061	24 737
District 40	6.4	5.4	50.0	233 208	2.80	13.2	22.3	4 144	2 590	7 111	135 036	19 737
District 41	4.0	2.9	49.9	192 901	3.37	13.0	14.2	9 714	986	0	153 316	22 104
District 42	3.7	2.8	50.4	200 503	3.44	17.2	16.1	3 119	1 646	0	151 431	17 026
District 43	4.7	3.8	50.1	226 619	3.18	12.4	17.1	5 844	2 087	1	143 130	19 040
District 44	8.8	8.5	50.3	258 703	2.80	11.9	24.4	10 405	2 415	0	124 652	13 310

1. No spouse present.

Table E. Congressional Districts 107th Congress — Education, Money Income, Poverty, and Housing

STATE District	Education, 1990 (cont'd) Attainment[1] (percent)		Money income, 1989			Percent below poverty level, 1989		Housing units, 1990					
				Households		Persons	Families		Occupied units				
											Owner-occupied		
												Owner cost as a percent of income	
	High school graduate or more	Bachelor's degree or more	Per capita[2]	Median	Percent with $100,000 or more	Total	Total	Total	Total	Percent	Median value[3] (dollars)	With a mortgage	Without a mortgage
	31	32	33	34	35	36	37	38	39	40	41	42	43
ALABAMA	66.9	15.7	11 486	23 597	2.3	18.3	14.3	1 670 379	1 506 790	70.5	53 700	18.4	12.8
District 1	68.9	14.7	10 961	22 881	2.2	20.9	16.7	242 227	209 370	70.9	53 000	19.1	12.8
District 2	68.2	16.7	11 636	24 374	2.2	17.0	13.0	238 839	215 137	70.5	54 200	18.3	12.6
District 3	61.5	12.3	10 204	21 594	1.4	19.3	14.2	238 911	212 651	71.9	47 400	18.5	12.9
District 4	57.7	8.1	10 170	20 877	1.3	17.6	14.2	243 265	220 788	77.0	43 000	19.0	12.8
District 5	71.6	20.4	13 268	28 364	2.7	12.9	10.0	236 764	219 452	70.4	63 500	17.5	12.2
District 6	78.9	26.3	16 033	31 864	5.1	9.4	6.5	238 873	223 443	69.7	73 100	17.3	12.1
District 7	60.5	10.6	8 135	16 560	0.8	31.2	26.2	231 500	205 949	62.4	40 700	20.9	14.1
ALASKA	86.6	23.0	17 610	41 408	7.7	9.0	6.8	232 608	188 915	56.1	94 400	21.5	12.2
At Large	86.6	23.0	17 610	41 408	7.7	9.0	6.8	232 608	188 915	56.1	94 400	21.5	12.2
ARIZONA	78.7	20.3	13 461	27 540	3.4	15.7	11.4	1 659 430	1 368 843	64.2	80 100	22.8	12.4
District 1	86.1	27.6	15 144	31 288	3.4	11.5	7.6	275 479	241 398	55.1	88 700	22.6	12.4
District 2	59.1	9.2	8 424	20 258	1.1	27.9	22.6	231 083	196 480	57.9	54 900	22.5	13.8
District 3	79.0	16.2	13 185	27 627	2.3	12.1	8.6	295 941	234 162	74.4	80 100	23.8	11.9
District 4	86.7	26.3	18 331	33 681	6.9	8.6	6.2	280 302	246 345	62.8	91 100	22.7	12.5
District 5	84.4	25.0	14 361	27 047	3.4	13.2	9.0	278 234	242 990	63.1	81 200	22.0	11.8
District 6	73.8	15.9	11 322	25 710	2.8	21.3	16.1	298 391	207 468	72.2	76 400	23.5	12.3
ARKANSAS	66.3	13.3	10 520	21 147	1.8	19.1	14.8	1 000 667	891 179	69.6	46 300	20.0	13.4
District 1	58.3	9.5	9 148	18 180	1.4	24.6	19.4	246 976	220 333	68.0	40 100	20.6	14.0
District 2	74.4	19.0	12 334	25 142	2.5	14.4	10.8	248 354	224 233	66.3	56 800	19.9	13.1
District 3	68.8	13.3	10 876	21 903	1.8	14.9	11.3	253 952	227 700	71.2	49 000	20.2	12.5
District 4	63.9	11.4	9 723	19 621	1.4	22.4	17.6	251 385	218 913	72.7	40 400	19.1	14.0
CALIFORNIA	76.2	23.4	16 409	35 798	7.1	12.5	9.3	11 182 882	10 381 206	55.6	195 500	24.9	11.8
District 1	79.6	18.2	14 298	30 943	3.7	11.4	8.6	231 913	208 711	63.2	136 400	23.9	12.0
District 2	78.3	16.4	12 458	24 807	2.5	15.1	11.1	248 607	219 020	64.4	94 300	22.7	12.2
District 3	79.0	19.9	13 786	30 296	3.2	12.9	9.3	221 030	209 586	59.1	118 400	22.7	11.7
District 4	85.1	21.1	16 263	35 772	5.3	7.5	5.7	264 760	210 045	69.3	152 400	24.6	12.2
District 5	79.5	24.0	14 661	29 974	3.4	15.7	12.4	237 135	223 134	53.0	122 500	22.8	11.7
District 6	87.8	33.0	21 699	40 564	10.0	6.7	4.2	242 255	226 960	62.0	257 400	25.9	11.7
District 7	82.0	23.2	16 006	38 608	4.1	9.6	7.5	219 422	208 202	62.0	168 100	24.9	11.8
District 8	76.3	33.8	19 377	31 659	6.9	14.1	11.5	266 127	245 820	29.0	274 700	25.3	12.0
District 9	80.2	35.4	16 833	30 067	6.6	16.5	13.4	242 284	227 756	43.0	223 900	25.2	12.3
District 10	90.1	35.8	23 972	52 378	14.5	4.4	3.2	224 187	213 366	71.5	275 100	26.0	11.6
District 11	71.5	14.7	13 299	31 605	3.9	14.7	11.3	202 059	192 038	58.1	124 000	23.2	11.8
District 12	84.4	31.6	20 984	44 720	9.8	6.0	4.0	224 724	215 787	59.4	324 100	25.2	11.5
District 13	80.6	22.4	17 335	43 877	6.4	6.4	4.7	206 484	198 910	62.0	223 700	25.1	11.5
District 14	88.0	44.2	26 047	50 078	15.8	6.1	3.6	233 781	223 976	54.7	404 400	24.5	11.5
District 15	88.3	34.8	22 833	50 823	12.4	5.0	3.2	223 320	214 252	63.2	291 500	24.6	11.6
District 16	69.7	19.4	14 614	42 223	6.5	11.6	8.4	174 940	168 563	60.9	234 500	26.9	12.0
District 17	74.5	23.0	15 006	33 911	5.5	11.7	8.0	204 376	189 099	52.8	220 800	25.5	11.6
District 18	66.4	12.5	12 013	28 324	3.3	16.0	12.7	196 560	186 489	58.7	114 800	23.1	11.8
District 19	74.4	20.2	13 516	29 153	4.1	16.4	12.6	219 589	202 858	58.9	90 800	22.4	12.1
District 20	47.9	6.4	8 097	21 140	1.8	27.9	23.2	167 455	158 379	51.3	64 000	22.9	12.4
District 21	72.7	15.0	12 983	29 943	3.4	15.1	12.1	218 942	199 642	61.3	85 000	22.3	12.3
District 22	81.4	25.3	16 458	33 680	6.2	13.0	7.3	222 918	205 198	56.7	230 100	26.0	11.3
District 23	77.1	20.5	16 617	42 989	7.5	7.9	5.5	193 300	183 312	63.3	235 600	25.9	11.3
District 24	86.2	33.4	25 767	48 433	16.2	6.2	4.0	232 664	219 354	62.5	305 700	26.3	11.9
District 25	82.8	22.9	18 849	46 480	10.0	7.2	5.1	205 124	190 996	71.5	214 100	26.5	12.1
District 26	60.6	15.4	12 198	32 134	3.6	15.8	12.1	187 617	177 447	44.5	186 600	26.1	11.8
District 27	80.2	31.4	20 344	37 929	10.4	11.5	8.8	230 676	219 623	49.3	296 000	24.7	11.6
District 28	82.5	25.6	18 064	43 508	9.0	7.1	4.9	200 651	192 695	67.4	233 700	25.1	11.4
District 29	86.3	43.5	34 253	37 540	16.8	11.7	7.3	300 369	278 690	35.3	500 001	24.3	11.9
District 30	52.8	16.1	9 637	23 435	2.4	24.1	20.7	190 029	177 284	24.4	189 000	25.2	11.5
District 31	56.4	13.3	10 264	30 667	2.9	18.1	14.7	165 006	158 775	48.2	180 100	24.7	11.5
District 32	69.9	23.3	14 520	28 332	5.6	19.2	15.8	226 524	212 744	36.4	234 800	25.1	12.1
District 33	33.6	5.3	6 997	20 708	1.2	28.0	24.9	153 629	145 328	24.7	156 200	28.2	11.6
District 34	61.7	12.0	12 012	36 224	4.2	11.6	9.1	167 247	162 272	62.8	174 400	23.9	11.1
District 35	57.1	10.1	9 761	25 481	1.9	24.6	21.4	186 648	174 747	36.4	150 500	25.8	12.5
District 36	86.7	36.8	25 534	48 522	14.8	6.8	4.5	247 623	233 720	52.8	371 100	24.5	11.4
District 37	54.8	9.2	9 104	27 127	2.3	23.3	20.6	161 398	153 884	50.4	142 800	25.8	12.1
District 38	76.5	21.0	16 497	34 364	5.6	12.5	9.5	228 531	215 601	45.7	224 700	24.4	11.3
District 39	81.6	25.4	18 190	46 196	9.5	7.0	4.6	198 048	190 832	64.6	239 000	23.0	11.2
District 40	78.3	16.0	13 568	30 408	3.7	12.5	10.2	259 542	201 282	64.1	110 300	24.2	12.5
District 41	76.8	21.4	16 002	44 607	8.5	9.9	7.2	182 332	172 941	67.8	204 600	26.6	11.7
District 42	72.2	12.7	12 308	33 737	2.9	14.2	11.8	196 432	181 408	62.1	127 000	25.4	11.7
District 43	76.4	15.7	14 449	37 806	5.0	10.2	7.2	200 134	182 767	66.5	153 700	26.6	11.9
District 44	71.3	13.2	14 417	29 049	4.2	13.1	9.7	272 645	209 956	68.3	121 800	26.4	12.5

1. Persons 25 years old and older. 2. Based on the population enumerated as of April 1, 1990. 3. Specified owner-occupied units.

STATE District	Median rent[1] (dollars)	Rent as a percent of income	Substandard units[2] (percent)	Total	Total	Rate[3]	Total	Professional, managerial, and technical	Precision production, craft, and repair	Work disabled persons[5] (percent)
	Housing units, 1990 (cont'd) Occupied units (cont'd) Renter-occupied			Civilian labor force, 1990	Unemployment		Civilian employment, 1990[4]	Percent		Disability, 1990
	44	45	46	47	48	49	50	51	52	53
ALABAMA	325	24.8	4.5	1 870 381	128 587	6.9	1 741 794	26.1	13.0	9.7
District 1	322	25.8	5.2	257 686	21 704	8.4	235 982	25.9	13.2	9.5
District 2	329	23.5	4.8	266 730	15 580	5.8	251 150	26.5	11.9	9.4
District 3	296	26.3	4.9	263 608	19 051	7.2	244 557	21.8	14.4	10.3
District 4	262	24.5	3.5	263 925	18 362	7.0	245 563	17.9	16.7	11.8
District 5	361	23.1	3.0	286 996	16 482	5.7	270 514	31.9	13.4	8.6
District 6	405	23.4	2.1	293 669	11 810	4.0	281 859	36.1	10.6	6.9
District 7	276	28.6	8.5	237 767	25 598	10.8	212 169	19.9	11.1	11.5
ALASKA	559	23.8	12.4	268 966	23 587	8.8	245 379	34.3	11.2	6.6
At Large	559	23.8	12.4	268 966	23 587	8.8	245 379	34.3	11.2	6.6
ARIZONA	438	27.5	7.8	1 727 798	123 902	7.2	1 603 896	30.8	11.4	8.3
District 1	478	27.4	5.4	344 059	18 082	5.3	325 977	36.1	9.8	6.4
District 2	366	29.7	17.0	256 524	29 410	11.5	227 114	19.3	13.7	10.0
District 3	457	27.7	5.7	258 645	16 502	6.4	242 143	25.9	13.7	9.4
District 4	473	26.9	3.4	338 605	17 744	5.2	320 861	35.7	9.6	6.9
District 5	404	27.6	3.9	283 981	18 856	6.6	265 125	35.4	10.0	8.8
District 6	426	25.0	14.1	245 984	23 308	9.5	222 676	27.7	13.0	8.9
ARKANSAS	328	26.5	4.9	1 066 368	72 079	6.8	994 289	23.3	12.5	11.2
District 1	290	27.6	5.8	253 428	21 349	8.4	232 079	19.6	12.9	12.6
District 2	383	26.4	3.8	286 980	16 691	5.8	270 289	28.9	11.0	9.7
District 3	328	24.9	4.2	275 250	14 541	5.3	260 709	22.6	13.5	10.9
District 4	299	27.4	5.7	250 710	19 498	7.8	231 212	21.5	12.9	11.6
CALIFORNIA	620	29.1	12.0	14 992 811	996 502	6.6	13 996 309	32.3	11.1	7.4
District 1	512	28.8	6.2	264 821	17 741	6.7	247 080	27.8	12.8	10.5
District 2	429	30.0	5.3	241 522	21 393	8.9	220 129	27.7	12.1	12.2
District 3	498	28.8	6.7	278 111	19 874	7.1	258 237	29.5	11.4	9.3
District 4	569	28.1	4.2	277 140	14 713	5.3	262 427	31.7	12.6	8.5
District 5	505	29.7	7.5	278 768	19 446	7.0	259 322	34.4	8.8	10.1
District 6	709	29.8	3.8	308 961	12 877	4.2	296 084	37.9	10.3	7.3
District 7	625	28.8	7.4	293 836	18 738	6.4	275 098	32.5	11.9	8.8
District 8	631	28.0	12.6	329 403	22 199	6.7	307 204	37.3	6.2	8.6
District 9	538	29.3	9.5	289 473	22 017	7.6	267 456	42.6	6.9	9.0
District 10	746	27.7	2.5	313 157	12 063	3.9	301 094	42.0	9.6	5.7
District 11	499	28.1	11.1	261 968	21 496	8.2	240 472	25.7	12.2	9.5
District 12	780	27.5	8.5	323 495	13 774	4.3	309 721	35.5	9.1	5.6
District 13	726	27.8	9.3	314 374	16 014	5.1	298 360	32.2	12.8	6.8
District 14	777	26.4	6.9	332 677	12 107	3.6	320 570	49.7	7.7	5.2
District 15	794	27.4	5.6	336 280	12 835	3.8	323 445	43.6	9.8	5.5
District 16	718	29.5	19.6	298 455	19 890	6.7	278 565	29.0	14.3	6.4
District 17	643	29.3	13.1	274 605	20 389	7.4	254 216	29.0	9.7	7.3
District 18	462	28.6	12.2	250 269	25 598	10.2	224 671	23.0	13.2	9.6
District 19	450	28.7	8.9	267 363	19 488	7.3	247 875	30.8	10.2	8.7
District 20	379	28.6	23.5	224 242	35 244	15.7	188 998	14.9	9.8	9.8
District 21	454	28.0	7.8	254 789	19 280	7.6	235 509	28.1	13.0	9.9
District 22	621	31.5	8.1	285 521	15 435	5.4	270 086	31.6	11.2	7.3
District 23	733	29.2	11.8	297 601	14 679	4.9	282 922	31.0	12.5	7.2
District 24	779	29.7	6.4	334 603	15 232	4.6	319 371	41.3	8.8	5.3
District 25	690	28.7	6.5	299 582	15 602	5.2	283 980	35.5	13.4	6.6
District 26	624	30.1	26.3	302 105	24 212	8.0	277 893	23.4	14.3	6.3
District 27	671	29.2	12.3	306 541	17 886	5.8	288 655	40.5	9.0	6.5
District 28	705	28.7	9.2	299 246	14 540	4.9	284 706	35.3	10.6	6.3
District 29	678	28.4	7.6	341 150	20 037	5.9	321 113	51.0	4.4	5.2
District 30	525	30.1	41.0	290 735	29 044	10.0	261 691	20.7	11.7	6.2
District 31	622	29.6	30.9	265 665	21 809	8.2	243 856	21.3	12.8	6.3
District 32	592	31.0	17.8	294 698	26 007	8.8	268 691	31.5	8.8	8.0
District 33	484	30.9	50.9	252 675	30 937	12.2	221 738	10.5	14.0	6.6
District 34	637	29.4	22.1	275 183	20 216	7.3	254 967	22.1	13.6	6.9
District 35	573	31.6	27.7	262 143	29 948	11.4	232 195	19.6	12.3	8.6
District 36	812	26.8	6.5	341 509	14 426	4.2	327 083	44.5	8.7	5.4
District 37	548	32.2	32.7	242 189	27 933	11.5	214 256	18.0	14.3	9.0
District 38	636	28.7	12.8	293 538	17 626	6.0	275 912	31.4	11.6	7.8
District 39	736	28.2	10.1	317 414	14 955	4.7	302 459	34.0	11.0	6.0
District 40	507	28.3	6.9	239 718	18 831	7.9	220 887	28.8	15.1	9.8
District 41	656	29.8	12.2	292 909	16 494	5.6	276 415	31.5	11.4	5.8
District 42	562	30.4	12.6	263 898	22 251	8.4	241 647	24.8	14.7	8.4
District 43	595	29.5	9.5	270 568	17 826	6.6	252 742	27.6	15.2	7.6
District 44	545	30.7	10.0	240 511	18 297	7.6	222 214	24.1	13.6	9.5

1. Specified renter-occupied units. 2. Overcrowded or lacking complete plumbing facilities. 3. Percent of total civilian labor force. 4. Persons 16 years old and older. 5. Persons 16 to 64 years of age.

Table E. Congressional Districts 107th Congress — **Land Area and Population**

STATE District	Land area, 2000[1] (sq km)	Total persons	Per square kilometer	White	Black	Am. Indian, Alaska Native	Asian and Pacific Islander	Other race	Hispanic[2]	Non-Hispanic White	2 or more races	Under 5 years	5 to 17 years	18 to 24 years	25 to 34 years	35 to 44 years	45 to 54 years	55 to 64 years
	1	2	3	4	5	6	7	8	9	10	11	12	13	14	15	16	17	18
CALIFORNIA—Cont'd																		
District 45	235.8	619 092	2 625.5	71.7	1.7	1.4	17.6	11.9	21.2	58.8	4.0	6.6	16.8	9.0	17.5	16.6	12.8	9.0
District 46	162.7	663 548	4 078.4	47.9	2.3	1.6	16.7	36.4	62.3	19.0	4.7	9.7	22.8	11.8	18.9	15.1	9.5	5.5
District 47	787.5	715 625	908.7	75.0	2.0	1.0	15.7	10.5	19.7	62.0	4.0	6.9	17.8	9.0	15.7	17.5	13.7	8.4
District 48	3 929.8	773 292	196.8	79.5	3.9	1.8	7.0	12.1	22.5	65.9	4.1	7.8	20.1	10.2	14.0	17.2	13.0	7.3
District 49	306.7	586 882	1 913.5	77.7	6.1	1.5	10.5	9.0	16.7	66.1	4.4	5.1	11.8	14.8	20.3	15.9	11.9	7.5
District 50	347.9	641 790	1 844.8	45.3	12.7	1.4	17.3	29.3	50.8	20.4	5.7	8.4	23.0	11.2	15.8	15.3	10.9	6.5
District 51	1 282.7	713 746	556.4	77.4	2.7	1.2	13.4	9.7	17.6	66.0	4.0	7.1	19.2	8.1	14.1	17.8	14.5	7.7
District 52	16 656.5	640 630	38.5	75.7	5.4	2.1	5.0	16.7	29.7	58.9	4.5	7.1	20.6	9.9	13.9	16.6	13.1	7.7
COLORADO	268 627.0	4 301 261	16.0	85.2	4.4	1.9	3.0	8.5	17.1	74.5	2.8	6.9	18.7	10.0	15.4	17.1	14.3	7.9
District 1	565.2	662 711	1 172.5	67.7	12.4	2.2	3.7	18.2	33.4	50.0	3.9	7.2	16.0	11.0	20.1	15.5	12.4	7.0
District 2	3 962.5	702 336	177.2	89.3	1.3	1.5	4.1	6.5	13.7	80.1	2.5	6.7	18.4	10.7	15.6	17.8	14.6	7.7
District 3	147 721.9	723 533	4.9	89.5	1.0	2.6	0.9	8.4	18.9	77.3	2.3	6.2	18.3	9.5	13.5	16.2	15.0	9.1
District 4	104 330.3	748 228	7.2	88.1	1.4	1.6	2.0	9.4	18.4	77.3	2.5	7.1	19.9	11.5	14.0	16.5	13.6	7.6
District 5	10 959.5	810 423	73.9	87.8	5.7	1.7	3.8	4.5	9.3	80.5	3.1	7.7	20.4	8.8	14.8	18.7	15.5	7.5
District 6	1 087.8	654 030	601.2	87.3	5.5	1.5	3.9	4.7	10.5	79.3	2.7	6.5	18.6	8.6	15.0	17.9	15.6	8.5
CONNECTICUT	12 548.0	3 405 565	271.4	83.3	10.0	0.7	2.9	5.5	9.4	77.5	2.2	6.6	18.2	8.0	13.3	17.1	14.1	9.1
District 1	1 223.2	552 127	451.4	72.8	16.7	0.7	3.4	9.2	13.1	67.1	2.6	6.5	18.3	8.3	13.0	16.3	14.1	9.0
District 2	4 413.5	568 007	128.7	90.8	5.1	1.3	2.4	2.7	4.7	87.0	2.1	6.2	17.7	9.5	13.5	17.5	14.1	8.9
District 3	1 100.9	561 576	510.1	80.3	13.7	0.7	3.1	4.4	8.0	75.1	2.0	6.2	17.6	9.0	13.5	16.2	13.9	9.0
District 4	656.7	574 101	874.2	76.2	14.4	0.5	4.1	7.8	14.8	66.6	2.8	7.4	18.1	7.4	14.0	17.0	13.3	9.0
District 5	1 518.7	581 903	383.2	87.0	6.4	0.6	2.7	5.6	10.0	80.4	2.1	7.0	19.1	7.0	13.0	17.7	14.4	9.0
District 6	3 635.0	567 851	156.2	92.3	3.7	0.5	1.9	3.2	5.8	88.4	1.5	6.0	18.2	6.7	12.5	17.6	14.8	9.5
DELAWARE	5 060.0	783 600	154.9	75.9	20.1	0.8	2.5	2.6	4.8	72.5	1.7	6.6	18.3	9.6	13.9	16.3	13.3	9.1
At Large	5 059.7	783 600	154.9	75.9	20.1	0.8	2.5	2.6	4.8	72.5	1.7	6.6	18.3	9.6	13.9	16.3	13.3	9.1
DISTRICT OF COLUMBIA	159.0	572 059	3 597.9	32.2	61.3	0.8	3.2	5.0	7.9	27.8	2.4	5.7	14.4	12.7	17.8	15.3	13.2	8.7
Delegate	159.0	572 059	3 597.9	32.2	61.3	0.8	3.2	5.0	7.9	27.8	2.4	5.7	14.4	12.7	17.8	15.3	13.2	8.7
FLORIDA	139 670.0	15 982 378	114.4	79.7	15.5	0.7	2.3	4.4	16.8	65.4	2.4	5.9	16.9	8.3	13.0	15.5	12.9	9.8
District 1	11 595.0	683 987	59.0	83.0	13.5	1.7	2.8	1.3	3.0	79.3	2.3	6.1	18.0	10.0	13.5	16.4	13.4	9.7
District 2	30 607.2	678 025	22.2	71.9	25.7	1.1	1.6	1.3	3.4	68.7	1.5	5.9	17.2	13.5	13.8	15.3	13.4	9.0
District 3	4 716.2	586 694	124.4	45.7	50.8	0.7	1.9	3.2	5.8	41.5	2.1	7.4	20.8	9.8	13.5	15.3	12.5	8.5
District 4	4 732.5	734 246	155.1	86.9	9.4	0.8	3.1	1.6	4.0	82.9	1.7	6.1	16.9	8.2	14.0	16.7	14.4	9.5
District 5	9 379.6	689 672	73.5	88.2	9.0	0.8	2.0	1.5	4.5	83.8	1.5	4.8	14.6	11.1	10.8	12.7	12.1	10.8
District 6	12 368.4	755 939	61.1	85.4	1..6	0.9	1.6	2.1	5.3	81.0	1.5	5.7	17.1	6.9	11.6	14.9	12.5	11.2
District 7	2 509.5	722 139	287.8	86.6	8.6	0.8	2.4	3.8	10.0	78.7	2.0	5.8	17.6	8.3	13.0	16.4	14.0	9.5
District 8	2 184.3	782 397	358.2	78.9	9.9	0.8	4.5	9.4	23.0	62.7	3.4	6.5	17.5	11.2	16.9	17.3	12.7	7.6
District 9	2 319.8	722 068	311.3	91.7	4.6	0.7	2.4	2.3	7.4	85.1	1.6	5.6	16.2	6.4	12.2	16.3	14.0	10.0
District 10	390.5	583 809	1 495.0	84.7	11.8	0.8	2.8	1.7	4.1	80.6	1.7	5.0	14.2	6.5	11.8	15.6	14.0	10.5
District 11	654.6	628 167	959.6	71.5	21.5	1.0	3.0	6.3	20.0	55.7	2.9	6.9	18.0	10.4	16.2	16.3	12.7	8.2
District 12	9 070.5	671 347	74.0	80.4	13.1	0.9	1.3	6.1	12.3	72.9	1.7	6.6	18.9	8.6	12.3	14.5	12.4	9.7
District 13	3 987.5	677 666	169.9	90.6	6.1	0.6	1.2	2.9	7.5	84.9	1.2	4.7	13.5	5.7	9.7	12.8	12.3	11.9
District 14	9 048.3	790 852	87.4	89.2	6.1	0.6	1.1	4.8	11.9	80.7	1.7	5.0	14.0	6.0	10.3	13.0	12.1	12.9
District 15	8 112.3	718 294	88.5	88.0	8.5	0.8	1.3	2.7	7.2	81.9	1.8	5.3	16.8	6.7	10.8	15.8	13.1	10.9
District 16	13 655.5	758 365	55.5	87.5	7.8	0.7	1.6	4.3	11.8	78.5	1.8	5.4	16.3	6.4	10.9	14.8	12.6	10.4
District 17	271.8	577 167	2 123.5	31.3	63.4	0.6	1.8	7.9	27.4	9.9	4.8	7.8	23.0	10.7	13.8	15.1	12.1	8.0
District 18	297.9	597 947	2 007.2	88.2	5.7	0.4	1.7	7.4	70.5	23.6	3.3	5.5	15.2	8.8	15.1	15.6	12.5	10.2
District 19	679.4	800 902	1 178.8	86.4	8.5	0.4	2.8	4.2	12.2	76.1	2.3	5.4	14.9	6.1	12.0	15.2	14.3	8.9
District 20	8 957.2	783 412	87.5	82.2	11.8	0.6	3.5	4.9	23.1	61.6	2.8	6.5	18.3	6.8	13.8	18.2	14.3	8.6
District 21	615.1	789 742	1 283.9	87.7	5.4	0.3	2.1	8.3	77.5	16.3	3.6	6.6	18.5	8.9	15.9	17.0	12.4	8.1
District 22	330.8	630 775	1 906.8	88.2	7.5	0.5	1.9	4.6	20.6	69.7	2.7	4.5	10.9	5.9	13.9	16.2	14.1	11.1
District 23	3 185.8	618 766	194.2	36.1	58.7	0.6	1.6	7.7	13.1	27.1	4.7	7.6	21.5	9.9	14.5	16.0	11.8	7.6
GEORGIA	149 976.0	8 186 453	54.6	66.1	29.2	0.6	2.5	2.9	5.3	62.6	1.4	7.3	19.2	10.2	15.9	16.5	13.2	8.1
District 1	21 133.6	692 199	32.8	65.4	31.7	0.7	1.6	2.1	3.6	63.0	1.3	7.3	19.6	12.1	14.5	15.3	12.3	8.1
District 2	29 678.7	650 392	21.9	56.6	40.8	0.6	0.9	2.0	3.3	54.8	0.9	7.3	20.2	11.1	13.9	14.7	12.5	8.5
District 3	7 944.2	781 694	98.4	64.9	31.3	0.7	2.5	2.2	4.1	62.0	1.5	7.5	20.9	9.2	14.8	16.8	13.5	8.1
District 4	771.9	744 717	964.8	39.1	50.6	0.7	5.9	6.1	11.0	32.5	2.3	7.4	17.5	11.3	20.2	17.3	12.4	6.6
District 5	1 033.0	646 184	625.5	31.9	63.7	0.6	2.5	2.9	5.2	28.9	1.4	6.9	17.2	12.4	19.4	15.6	12.4	7.1
District 6	1 526.9	943 373	617.8	81.0	11.4	0.6	5.3	3.6	6.6	76.1	1.8	7.6	19.2	7.9	17.8	19.6	14.9	7.1
District 7	9 585.7	752 161	78.5	77.9	18.7	0.7	1.2	2.9	5.0	74.7	1.3	7.5	19.4	9.7	15.9	16.6	12.7	8.2
District 8	29 785.3	662 811	22.3	65.1	32.7	0.6	1.1	1.6	2.8	63.3	0.9	7.0	19.7	9.9	13.8	15.6	13.2	8.9
District 9	15 088.0	814 305	54.0	91.5	3.4	0.8	1.0	4.5	8.4	86.6	1.1	7.4	18.2	9.2	14.9	16.1	13.3	9.6
District 10	25 107.0	662 201	26.4	59.0	39.0	0.6	1.6	1.0	2.0	57.2	1.1	6.8	20.0	9.9	13.5	15.8	13.5	9.0
District 11	8 322.0	836 416	100.5	80.0	15.0	0.6	3.3	2.6	5.0	76.3	1.4	7.1	19.6	11.0	15.2	17.0	13.6	7.9

1. Dry land or land partially or temporarily covered by water.   2. Hispanic persons may be of any race.

STATE District	Population and population characteristics, 2000 (cont'd) Percent (cont'd) Age (cont'd) 65 to 74 years	75 years and over	Percent female	Households, 2000 Number	Persons per house-hold	Percent Female family house-holder[1]	One person	Persons in correctional institutions, 2000	Persons in nursing homes, 2000	Persons in military quarters, 2000	Education, 1990 School enrollment Public	Private
	19	20	21	22	23	24	25	26	27	28	29	30
CALIFORNIA—Cont'd												
District 45	6.1	5.5	50.1	223 672	2.73	10.4	25.0	94	2 786	35	129 212	21 484
District 46	3.8	3.0	48.6	158 971	4.10	13.6	14.4	4 919	1 745	0	145 927	14 110
District 47	5.4	5.6	51.3	260 153	2.70	9.5	23.8	944	1 508	0	134 293	25 071
District 48	5.5	4.9	49.4	263 378	2.85	9.3	19.5	1 325	1 090	15 770	122 723	20 171
District 49	6.3	6.5	48.1	250 694	2.17	8.6	36.5	2 350	2 266	18 800	118 532	26 356
District 50	5.0	3.9	50.3	189 064	3.32	18.5	16.9	7 221	804	2 642	162 685	13 956
District 51	5.6	5.9	50.5	255 803	2.75	9.1	21.4	148	2 794	4 114	130 907	22 227
District 52	6.0	5.3	50.3	218 203	2.84	13.4	20.9	11 139	3 543	58	149 489	15 581
COLORADO	5.3	4.4	49.6	1 658 238	2.53	9.6	26.3	30 136	18 495	8 512	789 735	106 409
District 1	5.4	5.4	49.2	276 278	2.35	11.4	37.5	3 415	3 136	0	103 373	25 128
District 2	4.8	3.8	49.9	270 561	2.55	9.1	24.7	699	2 464	0	141 214	16 453
District 3	6.6	5.5	49.2	282 826	2.49	9.1	25.2	5 177	3 340	0	133 296	10 140
District 4	5.2	4.6	49.6	271 325	2.67	8.9	21.9	7 657	4 165	0	154 377	11 309
District 5	4.4	3.2	49.4	294 551	2.66	9.0	21.4	11 076	2 435	8 321	132 360	22 223
District 6	5.2	4.2	50.5	262 697	2.46	10.1	27.2	2 112	2 955	191	125 115	21 156
CONNECTICUT	6.8	7.0	51.6	1 301 670	2.53	12.1	26.4	20 023	32 223	2 097	626 637	178 849
District 1	6.9	7.6	52.4	214 887	2.48	14.8	28.4	1 055	7 570	0	108 930	26 157
District 2	6.4	6.2	50.8	218 951	2.47	10.4	26.4	4 723	4 602	2 081	117 463	24 803
District 3	7.1	7.6	52.2	218 716	2.48	13.1	28.4	1 365	4 805	16	99 326	37 858
District 4	6.9	6.7	51.9	212 711	2.64	13.0	25.5	880	4 498	0	91 527	37 542
District 5	6.3	6.5	51.2	215 500	2.64	11.6	23.9	4 827	5 322	0	103 010	29 976
District 6	7.2	7.5	50.9	220 905	2.49	9.8	26.0	7 173	5 426	0	106 381	22 513
DELAWARE	7.2	5.8	51.4	298 736	2.54	13.1	25.0	5 965	4 852	381	135 362	35 857
At Large	7.2	5.8	51.4	298 736	2.54	13.1	25.0	5 965	4 852	381	135 362	35 857
DISTRICT OF COLUMBIA	6.3	5.9	52.9	248 338	2.16	18.9	43.8	2 838	3 759	927	97 160	54 088
Delegate	6.3	5.9	52.9	248 338	2.16	18.9	43.8	2 838	3 759	927	97 160	54 088
FLORIDA	9.1	8.5	51.2	6 337 929	2.46	12.0	26.6	139 148	88 828	13 457	2 459 541	467 121
District 1	7.5	5.4	49.8	262 806	2.47	12.2	24.8	14 549	4 239	7 817	129 082	15 103
District 2	6.5	5.3	50.0	257 083	2.45	13.7	26.6	29 183	4 261	412	151 482	13 592
District 3	6.7	5.5	51.7	217 220	2.61	22.1	26.8	5 802	2 694	1 069	125 092	17 463
District 4	7.6	6.6	51.2	298 583	2.42	9.8	25.8	1 283	4 774	2 967	102 743	24 538
District 5	11.7	11.2	52.0	293 149	2.28	10.0	27.7	2 915	4 513	0	122 401	11 198
District 6	11.4	8.8	50.5	295 256	2.46	10.4	22.8	20 482	4 469	4	107 364	12 865
District 7	8.2	7.2	51.3	285 542	2.49	11.0	24.1	1 216	3 312	5	107 556	23 368
District 8	5.6	4.7	50.2	296 753	2.58	11.7	24.2	7 092	3 411	0	110 278	20 900
District 9	9.6	9.8	51.9	301 814	2.36	9.0	27.0	623	4 624	0	96 621	18 455
District 10	10.4	11.9	52.2	264 641	2.15	11.1	35.1	3 422	5 733	56	84 608	18 419
District 11	6.1	5.3	51.2	253 362	2.42	15.4	30.5	3 130	2 060	412	113 733	23 386
District 12	9.2	7.8	50.4	250 701	2.61	11.9	22.8	6 141	3 727	0	111 587	16 538
District 13	14.3	15.1	52.3	300 006	2.21	8.4	29.4	2 065	7 123	13	80 825	12 392
District 14	14.6	12.0	50.8	336 848	2.31	7.9	25.3	2 965	5 262	16	84 730	12 380
District 15	11.1	9.4	51.0	294 302	2.39	9.9	25.8	4 581	3 736	215	102 294	20 246
District 16	11.8	11.4	51.1	313 747	2.38	8.9	26.3	4 015	3 279	7	90 314	19 403
District 17	5.5	4.1	51.7	181 274	3.10	27.0	22.4	4 193	3 491	262	148 820	22 330
District 18	8.9	8.2	51.3	220 843	2.65	13.8	27.3	3 175	2 536	62	99 203	35 799
District 19	10.8	14.5	52.8	341 063	2.32	8.6	28.5	354	5 761	0	84 064	22 223
District 20	6.6	6.8	51.5	298 441	2.60	11.0	24.0	3 282	1 948	118	98 338	27 960
District 21	6.7	4.9	51.9	252 930	3.07	16.1	15.3	6 350	2 904	11	121 234	34 017
District 22	10.8	12.7	50.9	309 937	2.01	8.1	40.5	91	2 376	11	59 776	26 809
District 23	5.6	5.4	50.4	211 628	2.82	22.0	25.7	12 239	2 595	0	127 396	17 737
GEORGIA	5.3	4.3	50.8	3 006 369	2.65	14.5	23.6	81 773	34 812	25 461	1 433 862	209 997
District 1	5.9	4.9	50.5	254 736	2.61	14.8	24.0	9 653	2 971	7 909	133 708	18 076
District 2	6.3	5.6	51.4	234 942	2.64	18.8	24.4	11 940	4 662	5 606	145 566	13 658
District 3	5.3	3.9	51.1	278 057	2.75	15.5	20.4	4 922	2 851	5 570	130 897	15 908
District 4	4.0	3.3	50.9	274 954	2.66	16.8	26.4	3 181	2 166	0	119 734	30 347
District 5	4.6	4.4	51.1	256 317	2.40	20.9	35.2	7 676	2 193	88	124 151	27 503
District 6	3.5	2.4	50.3	352 341	2.66	8.5	22.0	1 945	739	0	120 706	27 610
District 7	5.5	4.5	50.8	271 642	2.70	13.1	21.3	7 099	3 967	159	125 421	15 074
District 8	6.5	5.4	51.3	245 698	2.58	16.4	24.8	14 559	5 260	1 483	132 407	17 971
District 9	6.6	4.7	50.1	298 794	2.68	9.7	20.3	4 094	3 505	0	119 177	12 059
District 10	6.4	5.1	51.2	241 693	2.62	17.7	24.2	13 333	3 330	4 404	134 957	16 350
District 11	4.8	3.7	50.6	297 195	2.76	11.3	19.3	3 371	3 168	242	147 138	15 441

1. No spouse present.

STATE District	Education, 1990 (cont'd) Attainment[1] (percent)		Money income, 1989			Percent below poverty level, 1989		Housing units, 1990					
			Households			Persons	Families		Occupied units				
										Owner-occupied			
												Owner cost as a percent of income	
	High school graduate or more	Bachelor's degree or more	Per capita[2]	Median	Percent with $100,000 or more	Total	Total	Total	Total	Percent	Median value[3] (dollars)	With a mortgage	Without a mortgage
	31	32	33	34	35	36	37	38	39	40	41	42	43
CALIFORNIA—Cont'd													
District 45	84.5	27.7	21 046	45 074	10.2	7.4	4.8	226 144	213 006	56.4	266 300	23.4	11.6
District 46	59.8	12.5	11 297	35 416	3.0	15.5	10.7	163 094	155 659	48.2	188 500	24.9	11.2
District 47	89.7	37.1	25 268	51 554	16.1	5.6	3.0	224 182	212 084	65.6	280 800	25.9	11.5
District 48	86.3	27.7	19 435	42 389	10.5	7.7	5.0	220 694	200 215	63.9	237 300	28.9	11.9
District 49	87.7	33.9	19 184	32 562	6.9	10.9	6.6	250 763	233 952	42.2	226 000	23.1	11.3
District 50	67.9	13.9	10 577	27 655	2.1	18.5	16.2	183 673	175 606	47.9	137 300	25.5	11.4
District 51	87.6	34.5	20 586	45 186	10.2	7.0	4.1	223 276	207 876	65.0	231 000	27.1	11.6
District 52	77.9	17.1	14 075	33 046	4.0	11.9	9.1	212 029	199 359	59.5	155 400	24.9	11.5
COLORADO	84.4	27.0	14 821	30 140	3.8	11.7	8.6	1 477 349	1 282 489	62.2	82 700	22.5	12.7
District 1	78.9	26.8	14 942	24 870	3.5	17.1	13.3	277 331	242 791	49.7	75 500	22.4	13.1
District 2	87.7	29.5	15 823	35 117	3.7	8.7	5.6	227 757	210 000	65.4	89 900	22.6	12.3
District 3	79.8	20.5	12 115	24 521	2.4	15.9	12.3	287 282	210 794	66.0	62 300	21.9	12.9
District 4	79.7	21.5	12 387	26 577	2.6	13.8	9.7	226 424	202 437	65.4	70 200	22.3	13.1
District 5	89.5	30.1	15 370	33 348	5.0	8.9	6.9	223 409	199 048	64.0	90 600	22.9	12.2
District 6	91.1	33.4	18 289	37 333	5.5	5.7	4.0	235 146	217 419	65.0	92 400	22.4	11.9
CONNECTICUT	79.2	27.2	20 189	41 721	9.2	6.8	5.0	1 320 850	1 230 479	65.6	177 800	22.9	13.7
District 1	77.9	26.6	18 644	39 961	7.3	9.3	7.3	220 374	208 723	61.0	172 000	22.3	13.3
District 2	79.7	23.2	16 964	38 524	4.8	6.2	4.4	222 167	200 769	65.8	151 300	22.9	13.0
District 3	79.7	26.8	18 243	39 815	6.9	7.7	5.5	223 071	207 515	64.7	173 800	22.9	14.3
District 4	79.3	34.0	27 130	47 636	17.7	7.5	5.6	217 000	204 373	63.5	277 400	23.2	14.6
District 5	79.2	26.9	20 316	44 056	10.6	5.6	4.5	214 744	201 115	68.7	183 900	23.5	13.8
District 6	79.5	25.3	19 863	42 817	7.8	4.6	3.1	223 494	207 984	70.1	166 400	22.8	13.5
DELAWARE	77.5	21.4	15 854	34 875	4.5	8.7	6.1	289 919	247 497	70.2	100 100	19.5	12.0
At Large	77.5	21.4	15 854	34 875	4.5	8.7	6.1	289 919	247 497	70.2	100 100	19.5	12.0
DISTRICT OF COLUMBIA	73.1	33.3	18 881	30 727	7.8	16.9	13.3	278 489	249 634	38.9	123 900	20.5	12.8
Delegate	73.1	33.3	18 881	30 727	7.8	16.9	13.3	278 489	249 634	38.9	123 900	20.5	12.8
FLORIDA	74.4	18.3	14 698	27 483	3.9	12.7	9.0	6 100 262	5 134 869	67.2	77 100	22.3	12.2
District 1	77.5	18.4	12 505	25 866	2.3	14.9	11.6	258 132	211 725	67.0	62 400	20.6	12.1
District 2	70.9	19.1	11 341	22 839	2.1	19.5	14.1	239 932	207 532	68.1	57 400	19.8	12.7
District 3	64.7	10.3	10 047	21 306	1.3	22.0	17.5	233 261	204 394	59.9	50 500	21.0	12.9
District 4	82.4	23.0	16 718	31 676	4.7	7.9	5.4	254 229	224 605	66.7	80 900	21.1	12.1
District 5	71.8	15.8	11 876	21 434	1.8	15.8	10.0	279 405	237 502	73.6	61 700	22.2	11.7
District 6	72.0	12.5	12 026	25 036	1.9	12.3	9.1	252 176	214 281	76.0	66 500	21.5	11.7
District 7	81.3	20.5	15 132	30 921	3.5	7.7	5.2	252 429	222 116	71.3	80 600	22.7	11.8
District 8	81.4	22.7	15 464	31 251	3.9	8.7	5.7	242 521	216 066	60.0	85 100	22.3	11.8
District 9	79.9	19.8	15 797	29 293	3.8	8.0	5.6	276 822	233 442	74.4	85 300	23.4	11.7
District 10	76.0	17.3	15 124	25 145	3.0	10.4	6.8	306 396	253 213	68.6	69 000	22.2	12.5
District 11	74.5	19.4	13 578	26 166	2.9	15.2	11.2	255 548	225 942	56.7	66 600	21.6	12.7
District 12	67.0	13.0	12 277	25 315	2.5	14.0	10.2	248 234	209 945	71.6	62 200	20.5	12.0
District 13	77.8	18.5	16 254	27 616	4.0	8.8	5.7	309 680	247 527	74.9	81 800	23.2	11.8
District 14	77.4	17.7	17 165	29 620	5.3	9.3	6.0	329 550	234 797	72.8	90 900	22.8	11.8
District 15	79.8	18.9	15 225	29 755	3.3	9.1	6.3	266 306	226 294	71.1	75 500	21.2	11.6
District 16	77.9	18.4	16 952	30 582	4.9	8.3	5.6	300 042	233 951	75.7	88 500	22.5	11.8
District 17	57.7	11.0	9 157	21 899	1.5	26.6	22.6	202 033	182 462	50.4	64 100	23.1	12.9
District 18	62.3	21.2	14 779	25 537	6.2	17.9	13.5	228 069	209 846	50.3	95 600	22.8	13.1
District 19	82.7	22.8	20 029	34 396	6.6	5.5	3.5	296 389	244 747	76.4	107 600	24.2	12.2
District 20	80.9	21.9	18 285	35 378	6.5	7.1	4.7	258 189	222 030	74.8	103 200	23.3	12.9
District 21	67.7	19.4	13 173	32 043	3.6	12.2	9.9	203 185	188 480	59.3	91 300	23.4	12.8
District 22	79.5	24.1	24 663	29 595	8.8	9.8	6.4	376 377	284 067	62.9	118 200	23.6	13.2
District 23	61.4	11.0	10 511	23 039	1.6	21.5	17.3	231 357	200 175	54.9	67 600	23.1	13.1
GEORGIA	70.9	19.3	13 631	29 021	3.8	14.7	11.5	2 638 418	2 366 615	64.9	71 300	20.9	12.8
District 1	70.1	15.0	11 429	24 779	2.2	18.4	14.3	236 195	209 008	63.4	59 400	20.9	13.2
District 2	61.5	12.3	9 804	20 938	1.7	24.2	19.5	226 367	203 783	64.8	47 700	19.4	13.5
District 3	71.4	14.9	13 217	30 672	3.0	12.5	9.8	225 222	208 344	67.5	70 100	20.9	12.4
District 4	85.5	33.1	17 461	36 523	5.4	8.1	5.8	253 656	228 142	56.0	91 800	21.3	12.1
District 5	72.8	24.9	15 003	25 547	5.3	22.0	19.1	269 275	231 179	45.5	73 600	22.1	13.8
District 6	90.2	39.5	22 297	46 148	10.9	4.1	2.6	249 786	226 407	65.9	118 100	22.1	12.0
District 7	64.6	12.4	12 446	28 898	2.2	11.7	8.9	233 609	214 189	70.4	64 800	20.1	12.7
District 8	63.7	12.2	11 038	23 577	2.0	19.3	15.7	235 779	214 046	67.6	50 000	18.5	13.1
District 9	60.9	11.4	12 062	26 631	2.3	11.8	9.2	247 670	217 009	75.5	62 700	20.5	12.5
District 10	64.8	13.8	11 159	24 666	2.3	18.5	15.0	235 187	206 840	68.5	55 600	20.1	12.8
District 11	72.7	20.8	14 001	32 761	3.7	11.4	7.6	225 672	207 668	71.7	83 500	21.6	12.4

1. Persons 25 years old and older.   2. Based on the population enumerated as of April 1, 1990.   3. Specified owner-occupied units.

STATE District	Housing units, 1990 (cont'd)			Civilian labor force, 1990			Civilian employment, 1990[4]			Disability, 1990
	Occupied units (cont'd)				Unemployment			Percent		
	Renter-occupied									
	Median rent[1] (dollars)	Rent as a percent of income	Substandard units[2] (percent)	Total	Total	Rate[3]	Total	Professional, managerial, and technical	Precision production, craft, and repair	Work disabled persons[5] (percent)
	44	45	46	47	48	49	50	51	52	53
CALIFORNIA—Cont'd										
District 45	815	28.3	7.6	338 389	15 191	4.5	323 198	36.4	10.7	5.7
District 46	719	31.0	28.1	298 519	22 785	7.6	275 734	19.8	14.0	6.2
District 47	845	28.4	5.4	323 619	11 702	3.6	311 917	43.0	7.4	4.5
District 48	696	29.9	6.8	280 497	13 599	4.8	266 898	35.7	10.6	5.9
District 49	607	29.1	5.9	300 179	16 123	5.4	284 056	41.3	8.4	7.2
District 50	540	31.7	20.0	246 477	21 805	8.8	224 672	24.4	13.3	8.5
District 51	730	28.9	6.0	306 434	14 427	4.7	292 007	41.1	9.3	5.6
District 52	566	29.6	8.4	275 286	19 471	7.1	255 815	29.6	13.5	8.7
COLORADO	418	26.1	3.0	1 732 719	99 438	5.7	1 633 281	34.3	9.8	7.8
District 1	382	26.4	4.3	290 621	20 548	7.1	270 073	33.5	7.9	9.4
District 2	477	26.9	2.4	313 860	15 458	4.9	298 402	36.8	10.3	6.5
District 3	361	26.2	3.9	267 934	18 036	6.7	249 898	28.0	11.9	9.1
District 4	379	26.8	3.3	277 284	15 215	5.5	262 069	28.4	11.5	7.6
District 5	432	25.9	2.4	266 620	16 662	6.2	249 958	38.6	8.9	8.1
District 6	473	24.5	1.8	316 400	13 519	4.3	302 881	39.1	8.6	6.5
CONNECTICUT	598	26.6	2.5	1 788 693	95 819	5.4	1 692 874	35.5	11.2	6.4
District 1	572	27.0	3.2	294 722	15 651	5.3	279 071	35.9	9.6	6.5
District 2	564	25.6	1.9	291 699	15 610	5.4	276 089	33.1	13.2	7.2
District 3	623	28.1	2.3	297 972	16 659	5.6	281 313	35.3	11.0	6.8
District 4	706	27.6	3.7	298 189	17 371	5.8	280 818	39.0	8.9	5.7
District 5	574	26.1	2.2	300 164	16 043	5.3	284 121	35.6	12.0	6.3
District 6	571	24.7	1.7	305 947	14 485	4.7	291 462	34.2	12.7	5.9
DELAWARE	495	24.7	2.5	349 092	13 945	4.0	335 147	31.0	11.9	7.7
At Large	495	24.7	2.5	349 092	13 945	4.0	335 147	31.0	11.9	7.7
DISTRICT OF COLUMBIA	479	25.4	8.2	327 436	23 442	7.2	303 994	44.0	4.5	8.4
Delegate	479	25.4	8.2	327 436	23 442	7.2	303 994	44.0	4.5	8.4
FLORIDA	481	28.0	5.7	6 167 236	356 769	5.8	5 810 467	28.8	11.5	8.7
District 1	390	25.6	3.5	249 851	16 569	6.6	233 282	29.2	12.9	11.0
District 2	373	27.9	5.4	264 289	15 740	6.0	248 549	30.6	10.0	10.2
District 3	389	28.3	7.4	255 498	19 880	7.8	235 618	20.7	11.7	12.0
District 4	481	25.6	2.4	283 222	12 441	4.4	270 781	33.1	11.1	8.0
District 5	398	30.2	3.0	224 822	13 909	6.2	210 913	30.9	11.7	10.9
District 6	400	25.4	3.8	236 437	13 800	5.8	222 637	24.1	13.1	11.2
District 7	529	26.8	2.3	290 119	14 411	5.0	275 708	31.8	11.4	7.8
District 8	531	26.9	4.1	311 293	13 491	4.3	297 802	30.4	10.4	7.0
District 9	485	26.5	1.9	268 022	12 559	4.7	255 463	31.9	10.7	8.3
District 10	448	28.2	2.4	263 277	11 940	4.5	251 337	29.8	11.4	10.3
District 11	439	26.6	5.0	299 580	17 375	5.8	282 205	29.2	10.0	9.7
District 12	381	25.6	5.1	255 685	17 489	6.8	238 196	23.8	12.7	10.1
District 13	512	27.9	2.4	237 154	10 307	4.3	226 847	27.3	12.5	9.1
District 14	519	26.1	3.5	248 732	10 664	4.3	238 068	25.8	13.2	9.0
District 15	485	26.4	2.5	266 793	15 265	5.7	251 528	31.8	13.0	9.0
District 16	575	25.8	3.1	258 165	12 321	4.8	245 844	29.4	13.3	8.1
District 17	426	30.7	22.0	260 046	28 131	10.8	231 915	20.9	11.0	8.3
District 18	460	31.9	17.5	290 069	20 399	7.0	269 670	29.2	11.1	6.4
District 19	672	27.8	2.2	262 333	11 455	4.4	250 878	33.4	10.3	6.2
District 20	624	28.3	4.2	293 791	12 525	4.3	281 266	33.3	11.5	6.8
District 21	592	30.1	19.3	308 196	19 292	6.3	288 904	28.4	11.4	4.9
District 22	545	30.6	4.2	268 636	13 337	5.0	255 299	34.3	9.5	7.1
District 23	486	30.6	13.3	271 226	23 469	8.7	247 757	20.4	12.6	8.8
GEORGIA	433	25.8	4.7	3 278 378	188 102	5.7	3 090 276	28.2	11.9	8.8
District 1	375	26.7	5.3	259 372	17 076	6.6	242 296	25.6	13.1	10.1
District 2	298	26.0	7.3	258 595	18 703	7.2	239 892	22.7	11.8	10.8
District 3	412	25.7	4.3	289 932	17 441	6.0	272 491	25.5	13.5	9.1
District 4	561	25.9	3.8	353 265	18 058	5.1	335 207	37.0	7.8	5.7
District 5	456	27.9	6.2	302 906	24 994	8.3	277 912	30.6	7.9	9.0
District 6	598	23.9	1.4	355 591	12 093	3.4	343 498	41.4	7.7	4.3
District 7	405	25.3	3.7	303 726	17 082	5.6	286 644	23.0	15.2	9.7
District 8	315	25.4	5.6	271 715	17 974	6.6	253 741	23.3	13.7	11.8
District 9	365	23.5	4.0	302 602	14 005	4.6	288 597	20.8	15.0	10.1
District 10	338	25.7	6.5	269 381	16 581	6.2	252 800	25.3	13.4	10.3
District 11	443	26.6	3.5	311 293	14 095	4.5	297 198	28.8	13.3	7.8

1. Specified renter-occupied units. 2. Overcrowded or lacking complete plumbing facilities. 3. Percent of total civilian labor force. 4. Persons 16 years old and older. 5. Persons 16 to 64 years of age.

Table E. Congressional Districts 107th Congress — **Land Area and Population**

Population and population characteristics, 2000

STATE District	Land area, 2000[1] (sq km)	Total persons	Per square kilometer	White	Black	Am. Indian, Alaska Native	Asian and Pacific Islander	Other race	Hispanic[2]	Non-Hispanic White	2 or more races	Under 5 years	5 to 17 years	18 to 24 years	25 to 34 years	35 to 44 years	45 to 54 years	55 to 64 years
	1	2	3	4	5	6	7	8	9	10	11	12	13	14	15	16	17	18
HAWAII	16 635.0	1 211 537	72.8	39.3	2.8	2.1	81.3	3.9	7.2	22.9	21.4	6.5	18.0	9.5	14.1	15.8	14.1	8.8
District 1	470.1	568 524	1 209.4	31.3	3.0	1.5	83.9	2.9	5.4	18.5	16.9	5.8	15.7	9.3	14.9	15.9	14.0	9.2
District 2	16 164.4	643 013	39.8	46.3	2.5	2.5	79.1	4.8	8.9	26.8	25.4	7.1	19.9	9.7	13.4	15.6	14.2	8.5
IDAHO	214 314.0	1 293 953	6.0	92.8	0.6	2.1	1.5	5.0	7.9	88.0	2.0	7.5	21.0	10.7	13.1	14.9	13.2	8.3
District 1	102 436.0	702 521	6.9	93.5	0.5	2.2	1.6	4.3	6.8	89.0	2.0	7.4	20.4	9.6	13.2	15.3	13.7	8.7
District 2	111 878.2	591 432	5.3	92.1	0.7	2.0	1.4	5.8	9.1	86.9	1.9	7.8	21.6	12.1	13.0	14.4	12.5	7.8
ILLINOIS	143 961.0	12 419 293	86.3	75.1	15.6	0.6	3.9	6.8	12.3	67.8	1.9	7.1	19.1	9.8	14.6	16.0	13.1	8.4
District 1	143.7	560 239	3 898.7	24.0	71.1	0.6	1.7	4.3	7.5	19.9	1.5	7.7	20.8	10.1	14.0	14.5	11.9	8.1
District 2	322.3	556 482	1 726.6	19.0	76.6	0.6	0.7	4.6	7.8	15.2	1.4	8.0	23.1	9.3	12.9	14.7	12.3	9.0
District 3	327.5	629 597	1 922.4	81.2	4.7	0.6	2.1	14.3	24.3	67.7	2.9	7.3	18.9	9.1	14.3	15.6	12.7	8.3
District 4	102.3	625 941	6 118.7	48.3	8.7	1.1	3.2	43.1	70.1	18.4	4.2	9.4	21.8	13.6	20.6	14.3	9.3	5.2
District 5	136.6	635 824	4 654.6	80.0	2.3	0.6	7.0	13.7	25.0	64.5	3.6	6.2	13.9	10.4	21.4	15.8	12.4	8.1
District 6	476.5	615 419	1 291.5	85.3	2.7	0.5	8.5	5.0	10.9	77.5	1.9	6.6	17.8	8.5	14.3	16.7	13.9	8.9
District 7	131.5	569 470	4 330.6	29.0	64.0	0.5	5.2	2.9	5.2	25.7	1.5	7.4	20.3	10.6	16.4	15.2	12.3	7.8
District 8	1 117.2	699 513	626.1	85.0	3.0	0.5	8.1	5.3	11.3	77.3	1.9	7.8	19.5	7.6	15.8	18.4	14.1	8.2
District 9	139.1	593 205	4 264.6	69.4	13.2	0.7	13.4	7.0	12.3	60.5	3.6	5.6	13.6	10.6	18.4	15.8	12.9	8.4
District 10	632.8	627 793	992.1	80.7	7.1	0.5	6.4	7.3	13.9	72.4	1.9	7.3	20.3	8.7	12.1	16.3	14.5	8.8
District 11	6 725.6	635 653	94.5	80.8	13.7	0.6	1.0	5.6	10.5	74.4	1.6	7.1	20.1	8.7	13.2	16.4	13.3	8.6
District 12	9 081.0	560 912	61.8	79.4	18.9	0.7	1.3	1.0	2.0	77.4	1.2	6.4	19.1	10.7	13.2	15.6	12.8	8.4
District 13	1 044.3	759 124	726.9	87.1	4.9	0.4	6.8	2.4	5.4	82.5	1.6	7.6	20.5	7.5	14.3	18.3	14.7	8.1
District 14	6 350.5	720 663	113.5	85.1	4.9	0.6	2.9	8.5	17.5	74.5	1.9	8.2	21.0	10.2	14.5	17.1	13.1	7.3
District 15	19 402.3	595 833	30.7	86.8	9.4	0.5	3.1	1.8	3.0	84.2	1.4	6.3	17.3	15.3	13.4	14.6	12.4	8.0
District 16	8 009.9	691 356	86.3	90.2	5.5	0.6	1.7	3.5	6.9	85.4	1.4	7.4	20.6	7.7	13.6	17.3	13.7	8.5
District 17	21 569.1	567 712	26.3	93.4	4.2	0.5	0.9	2.4	4.6	90.0	1.2	5.9	17.6	10.0	11.7	14.7	13.7	9.8
District 18	15 987.3	597 447	37.4	91.8	6.8	0.5	1.1	0.8	1.5	90.1	1.0	6.3	18.5	8.9	12.4	15.5	14.4	9.4
District 19	27 790.5	575 769	20.7	94.4	4.9	0.5	0.5	0.4	1.0	93.1	0.8	5.9	17.7	9.9	11.7	14.8	13.3	9.9
District 20	24 470.7	601 341	24.6	93.2	5.9	0.6	0.8	0.5	1.1	91.8	0.9	6.1	18.4	9.0	12.7	15.9	13.5	9.2
INDIANA	92 895.0	6 080 485	65.5	88.6	8.8	0.6	1.3	2.0	3.5	85.8	1.2	7.0	18.9	10.1	13.4	16.3	13.4	8.7
District 1	1 682.9	571 747	339.7	72.5	22.1	0.7	1.2	5.4	11.2	65.2	1.8	7.1	19.5	9.5	12.7	15.6	14.1	8.9
District 2	10 070.2	567 204	56.3	94.2	4.7	0.6	0.9	0.7	1.3	92.6	1.0	6.5	17.9	10.2	13.0	14.9	13.5	9.7
District 3	4 702.5	610 182	129.8	86.8	9.1	0.8	1.4	3.8	5.8	83.1	1.8	7.3	19.3	10.3	13.7	15.2	13.3	8.2
District 4	9 341.2	619 891	66.4	90.8	6.7	0.7	1.2	2.1	3.5	88.1	1.3	7.6	20.5	9.3	13.6	15.6	13.3	8.2
District 5	18 031.3	585 988	32.5	95.4	2.7	0.8	0.7	1.6	3.0	92.8	1.1	6.6	19.3	8.8	12.5	15.5	13.8	9.8
District 6	5 277.6	724 143	137.2	95.1	2.6	0.4	1.8	1.0	1.9	93.2	0.9	7.5	19.7	9.6	14.3	16.4	14.2	8.3
District 7	12 306.7	633 484	51.5	95.1	2.4	0.7	1.8	1.1	2.0	93.1	1.0	6.5	18.1	13.3	13.5	15.5	12.9	8.5
District 8	13 535.7	590 205	43.6	94.6	3.9	0.6	1.4	0.6	1.1	93.1	1.0	6.1	17.1	13.4	12.8	15.0	13.2	8.9
District 9	17 437.7	608 430	34.9	96.8	2.3	0.5	0.6	0.7	1.3	95.4	0.8	6.7	19.2	8.5	13.3	16.4	14.1	9.4
District 10	509.1	569 211	1 118.1	61.2	35.3	0.8	1.8	3.0	4.8	57.8	1.9	7.7	18.5	11.0	16.9	16.1	11.9	7.3
IOWA	144 701.0	2 926 324	20.2	94.9	2.5	0.6	1.6	1.6	2.8	92.6	1.1	6.4	18.6	10.2	12.4	15.4	13.4	8.8
District 1	11 603.8	603 837	52.0	93.3	3.8	0.6	2.1	1.7	3.2	90.4	1.5	6.6	18.2	11.9	14.1	15.6	13.6	8.3
District 2	31 753.7	568 857	17.9	96.3	2.4	0.6	0.8	0.8	1.4	94.9	0.8	6.1	18.9	10.2	11.1	14.8	13.3	9.2
District 3	35 822.4	573 674	16.0	96.3	1.4	0.5	1.6	1.2	2.0	94.6	0.9	6.0	18.0	11.4	11.5	14.6	13.5	9.1
District 4	19 418.7	621 351	32.0	92.9	3.5	0.6	2.1	2.2	3.7	90.1	1.3	7.1	18.8	8.7	14.3	16.2	13.6	8.5
District 5	46 102.3	558 605	12.1	95.9	1.1	0.8	1.2	2.0	3.7	93.5	0.9	6.2	19.4	8.8	10.8	14.8	13.2	8.9
KANSAS	211 900.0	2 688 418	12.7	87.9	6.3	1.8	2.2	4.0	7.0	83.1	2.1	7.0	19.5	10.3	13.0	15.6	13.2	8.2
District 1	145 669.0	637 670	4.4	91.2	1.8	1.1	1.2	6.4	11.1	85.2	1.6	6.7	19.7	9.5	11.3	14.9	12.8	8.7
District 2	36 185.2	641 387	17.7	89.8	6.6	2.2	1.5	2.2	4.1	86.1	2.2	6.6	18.8	11.7	12.3	15.1	13.0	8.6
District 3	4 016.6	733 606	182.6	85.2	9.0	1.4	3.0	3.5	6.4	80.6	2.0	7.3	19.2	10.7	14.8	16.6	13.7	7.5
District 4	26 028.7	675 755	26.0	85.9	7.5	2.4	2.9	4.0	6.5	81.1	2.6	7.4	20.3	9.1	13.1	15.8	13.2	8.0
KENTUCKY	102 896.0	4 041 769	39.3	91.0	7.7	0.6	1.0	0.8	1.5	89.3	1.1	6.6	18.0	9.9	14.1	15.9	13.8	9.2
District 1	29 086.5	652 338	22.4	91.1	7.9	0.6	0.6	0.8	1.5	89.5	1.0	6.5	17.6	9.9	13.2	14.8	13.4	10.1
District 2	20 095.4	706 978	35.2	93.0	5.6	0.6	1.0	0.9	1.5	91.2	1.1	6.8	18.9	9.8	13.6	16.3	13.7	9.2
District 3	618.4	626 676	1 013.4	76.9	21.2	0.6	1.8	1.1	1.8	74.7	1.5	6.7	17.3	9.1	14.2	16.1	13.9	8.7
District 4	14 255.8	691 720	48.5	96.1	2.9	0.5	0.8	0.7	1.3	94.6	0.9	6.9	18.9	9.3	14.2	16.6	13.8	9.3
District 5	26 744.1	648 751	24.3	98.3	1.2	0.6	0.3	0.2	0.7	97.1	0.6	6.5	18.5	9.3	13.8	15.4	14.3	9.9
District 6	12 095.3	715 306	59.1	89.8	8.4	0.6	1.5	1.1	2.0	87.7	1.2	6.4	16.8	12.2	15.3	15.9	13.6	8.6
LOUISIANA	112 825.0	4 468 976	39.6	64.8	32.9	1.0	1.5	1.1	2.4	62.5	1.1	7.1	20.2	10.6	13.5	15.5	13.1	8.5
District 1	6 175.5	666 747	108.0	82.8	14.0	0.7	2.1	1.9	4.8	78.5	1.4	6.5	18.4	8.8	13.4	16.3	14.6	9.1
District 2	697.5	590 824	847.1	28.7	67.5	0.7	2.9	1.7	3.6	26.1	1.3	7.3	21.0	11.4	14.3	14.9	13.0	7.8
District 3	17 891.2	637 359	35.6	71.2	25.6	2.1	1.5	1.0	2.1	68.9	1.2	7.3	21.6	9.2	13.2	16.3	13.0	8.4
District 4	26 404.7	616 120	23.3	63.5	34.4	1.4	1.1	1.0	2.1	61.4	1.3	7.2	20.0	10.5	13.1	14.7	12.7	8.9
District 5	33 942.9	610 398	18.0	65.9	32.9	0.7	0.7	0.6	1.2	64.7	0.7	7.0	20.0	11.2	12.7	14.5	12.5	8.9
District 6	10 119.2	683 536	67.5	64.2	33.8	0.5	1.6	0.7	1.6	62.6	0.8	7.1	19.8	12.4	14.2	15.7	13.2	7.9

1. Dry land or land partially or temporarily covered by water.   2. Hispanic persons may be of any race.

STATE District	65 to 74 years	75 years and over	Percent female	Number	Persons per house-hold	Female family house-holder[1]	One person	Persons in correctional institutions, 2000	Persons in nursing homes, 2000	Persons in military quarters, 2000	Public	Private
	19	20	21	22	23	24	25	26	27	28	29	30
HAWAII	7.0	6.2	49.8	403 240	2.92	12.4	21.9	3 233	2 949	13 992	233 972	56 606
District 1	7.8	7.4	50.1	199 979	2.75	11.8	25.3	2 302	1 774	5 063	110 167	31 711
District 2	6.3	5.2	49.5	203 261	3.08	13.0	18.5	931	1 175	8 929	123 805	24 895
IDAHO	5.9	5.4	49.9	469 645	2.69	8.7	22.4	7 401	5 735	673	268 404	27 234
District 1	6.1	5.5	49.9	258 947	2.65	8.8	21.9	5 616	3 815	0	125 535	12 577
District 2	5.6	5.2	49.8	210 698	2.74	8.5	22.9	1 785	1 920	673	142 869	14 657
ILLINOIS	6.2	5.9	51.0	4 591 779	2.63	12.3	26.8	67 820	91 887	10 865	2 440 505	591 168
District 1	6.8	6.1	54.2	206 431	2.66	27.0	31.8	0	3 029	0	115 893	44 975
District 2	6.3	4.4	53.7	183 180	3.01	29.0	22.6	81	2 112	0	141 490	26 853
District 3	6.8	7.0	51.2	224 008	2.79	12.1	25.6	0	3 636	0	90 948	39 716
District 4	3.3	2.5	47.7	184 540	3.32	16.6	21.7	10 565	1 010	0	134 500	32 138
District 5	5.9	5.9	50.9	257 076	2.44	9.6	34.4	0	3 209	0	72 418	47 205
District 6	6.6	6.6	51.0	227 495	2.65	8.7	25.2	718	5 888	0	107 651	34 041
District 7	5.5	4.4	53.3	213 996	2.58	23.9	34.9	1 022	2 809	0	133 073	32 324
District 8	4.8	3.7	50.2	253 199	2.75	8.1	22.3	0	2 533	0	121 377	26 743
District 9	6.8	7.7	51.1	254 817	2.24	9.2	39.6	35	8 004	0	83 762	55 974
District 10	6.4	5.6	50.4	217 949	2.78	8.7	22.1	846	4 562	10 432	114 762	32 749
District 11	6.4	6.2	51.0	231 272	2.69	11.8	23.8	3 623	4 890	0	119 295	27 332
District 12	7.2	6.7	51.1	216 943	2.49	14.2	27.9	7 089	4 988	427	142 993	19 274
District 13	4.8	4.3	50.7	268 835	2.78	7.7	20.8	2 691	4 322	0	124 678	36 129
District 14	4.5	4.0	49.8	241 604	2.91	9.1	19.7	3 192	3 951	0	142 639	25 434
District 15	6.4	6.3	50.8	230 288	2.43	9.9	28.9	5 937	5 706	0	163 016	14 983
District 16	5.9	5.3	50.5	255 764	2.67	9.6	22.9	1 290	4 362	0	123 118	21 750
District 17	8.1	8.5	51.1	225 434	2.41	9.6	28.2	5 472	7 201	0	130 850	18 213
District 18	7.3	7.3	51.4	233 363	2.47	9.9	26.6	6 399	6 084	6	124 593	25 584
District 19	8.3	8.6	51.3	231 235	2.39	9.6	28.5	6 819	7 290	0	132 299	10 356
District 20	7.5	7.6	50.5	234 350	2.46	9.9	27.1	12 041	6 301	0	121 150	19 395
INDIANA	6.5	5.9	51.0	2 336 306	2.53	11.1	25.9	34 676	48 745	7	1 233 973	202 215
District 1	6.8	5.9	51.8	214 620	2.63	15.6	25.3	224	3 524	0	129 239	24 866
District 2	7.5	6.7	51.3	224 019	2.45	10.6	26.2	3 955	5 062	0	128 116	12 726
District 3	6.4	6.2	50.6	226 778	2.58	11.4	25.4	6 615	4 869	4	109 890	32 012
District 4	6.1	5.7	50.6	233 944	2.60	10.3	25.3	1 501	4 766	0	118 376	24 487
District 5	7.3	6.4	50.6	223 852	2.55	9.3	24.3	3 250	4 769	0	121 805	15 570
District 6	5.7	5.1	51.1	278 176	2.57	8.0	23.6	862	5 211	0	114 881	22 308
District 7	6.1	5.6	50.0	237 174	2.52	9.0	24.7	8 040	5 476	0	146 172	16 048
District 8	7.0	6.6	51.1	232 639	2.41	9.5	28.3	3 487	5 690	3	136 877	17 801
District 9	6.8	5.7	50.6	232 808	2.57	10.0	23.1	2 381	5 233	0	120 627	12 971
District 10	5.6	5.0	51.7	232 296	2.38	18.1	33.4	4 361	4 145	0	107 990	23 426
IOWA	7.2	7.7	50.9	1 149 276	2.46	8.6	27.2	11 771	33 428	4	626 759	110 970
District 1	6.0	5.9	50.7	238 345	2.45	9.2	27.3	3 085	4 141	0	140 148	21 722
District 2	7.8	8.5	51.2	221 713	2.47	8.1	26.8	706	7 189	1	121 393	26 324
District 3	7.6	8.4	50.6	224 379	2.43	8.0	27.2	4 364	7 504	3	134 632	17 202
District 4	6.5	6.4	51.3	245 495	2.47	9.8	27.0	1 476	6 064	0	116 217	20 867
District 5	8.4	9.4	50.9	219 344	2.46	7.5	27.9	2 140	8 530	0	114 369	24 855
KANSAS	6.5	6.7	50.6	1 037 891	2.51	9.3	27.0	16 703	25 248	4 580	593 376	74 989
District 1	7.8	8.6	50.3	247 024	2.49	7.5	27.6	4 914	8 495	0	145 568	13 957
District 2	6.8	7.0	50.3	246 530	2.48	9.5	27.0	7 619	6 723	4 067	155 428	14 431
District 3	5.2	4.9	51.0	281 782	2.55	10.0	25.9	649	4 679	0	152 418	25 649
District 4	6.5	6.5	50.7	262 555	2.52	10.1	27.6	3 521	5 351	513	139 962	20 952
KENTUCKY	6.8	5.7	51.1	1 590 647	2.47	11.8	26.0	28 388	29 266	7 277	807 842	110 473
District 1	7.6	7.0	51.0	258 480	2.44	10.7	26.0	4 931	6 638	4 648	132 226	8 906
District 2	6.5	5.1	50.7	269 060	2.56	10.7	23.2	3 260	4 766	2 629	137 126	16 468
District 3	7.4	6.6	52.4	262 582	2.34	15.2	31.7	1 169	4 911	0	115 452	35 838
District 4	6.3	5.1	50.7	262 841	2.56	10.9	24.2	7 081	4 258	0	132 266	20 867
District 5	7.0	5.5	50.9	253 054	2.50	12.1	24.1	6 171	4 505	0	145 258	9 850
District 6	6.0	5.1	51.2	284 630	2.41	11.3	26.9	5 776	4 188	0	145 514	18 544
LOUISIANA	6.3	5.2	51.6	1 656 053	2.62	16.6	25.3	49 854	31 521	3 877	979 200	206 559
District 1	6.9	5.9	51.7	262 349	2.50	12.5	27.0	2 393	3 777	0	108 597	49 215
District 2	5.6	4.7	52.9	218 125	2.62	25.7	29.4	6 851	2 864	284	134 896	46 987
District 3	6.0	4.5	51.3	222 949	2.81	15.4	20.1	3 168	3 571	30	138 324	27 104
District 4	7.0	6.0	51.6	233 417	2.56	16.7	26.4	5 170	5 186	3 563	147 134	13 332
District 5	7.1	6.2	51.6	224 698	2.58	16.7	25.5	12 462	7 023	0	154 590	15 522
District 6	5.3	4.3	51.0	248 925	2.64	15.7	24.3	12 232	4 010	0	147 842	32 109

1. No spouse present.

Table E. Congressional Districts 107th Congress — Education, Money Income, Poverty, and Housing

STATE District	Education, 1990 (cont'd) Attainment[1] (percent) High school graduate or more	Bachelor's degree or more	Money income, 1989 Per capita[2]	Households Median	Percent with $100,000 or more	Percent below poverty level, 1989 Persons Total	Families Total	Housing units, 1990 Total	Occupied units Total	Owner-occupied Percent	Median value[3] (dollars)	Owner cost as a percent of income With a mortgage	Without a mortgage
	31	32	33	34	35	36	37	38	39	40	41	42	43
HAWAII	80.1	22.9	15 770	38 829	7.1	8.3	6.0	389 810	356 267	53.9	245 300	21.4	10.8
District 1	81.4	26.6	17 508	40 257	8.3	7.0	4.7	201 204	188 969	50.4	311 200	21.1	10.7
District 2	78.6	18.8	14 032	37 247	5.8	9.5	7.4	188 606	167 298	57.8	190 900	21.6	10.9
IDAHO	79.7	17.7	11 457	25 257	2.1	13.3	9.7	413 327	360 723	70.1	58 200	19.3	11.8
District 1	78.8	16.7	11 530	25 086	2.0	13.0	9.4	212 660	185 172	71.3	60 300	19.7	11.7
District 2	80.7	18.7	11 384	25 446	2.3	13.5	10.0	200 667	175 551	68.7	55 900	18.8	12.0
ILLINOIS	76.2	21.0	15 201	32 252	4.9	11.9	9.0	4 506 275	4 202 240	64.2	80 900	20.2	12.7
District 1	70.7	18.4	11 709	24 140	2.6	23.8	19.8	235 969	210 872	44.7	73 100	19.6	13.3
District 2	70.1	13.1	11 468	30 217	2.6	18.0	15.1	197 780	183 227	62.9	65 000	20.7	13.3
District 3	74.5	15.7	15 854	36 250	4.0	5.4	3.9	221 318	214 647	73.8	92 800	20.5	12.8
District 4	46.5	8.4	8 352	23 083	1.1	23.8	21.5	189 130	170 646	36.0	64 900	21.4	13.6
District 5	73.6	26.1	19 242	33 262	5.9	8.0	5.3	258 537	243 577	48.8	109 900	22.2	13.5
District 6	85.1	28.6	19 405	44 216	7.6	3.3	2.0	218 595	210 552	73.7	130 400	21.4	12.3
District 7	66.6	20.9	13 056	25 220	4.9	29.5	25.9	233 596	204 386	36.9	89 500	21.3	13.3
District 8	87.1	30.2	20 488	47 374	9.5	3.3	2.3	217 242	205 605	74.2	132 300	21.9	12.4
District 9	81.1	36.6	18 691	32 183	6.4	11.9	8.3	261 802	245 104	45.8	145 800	21.4	13.0
District 10	87.6	40.4	26 405	50 355	18.5	4.4	3.0	208 089	199 839	74.4	181 400	21.2	12.4
District 11	75.8	13.4	13 838	33 632	2.5	8.2	6.3	215 470	204 630	73.7	67 400	18.8	12.5
District 12	71.9	13.9	11 547	25 032	1.7	17.4	13.1	231 781	213 212	66.6	48 000	18.4	13.1
District 13	89.0	35.0	20 912	50 087	10.5	2.5	1.8	207 243	197 921	77.4	140 300	22.3	12.5
District 14	80.4	22.7	15 769	39 815	5.5	6.9	4.5	200 903	192 838	71.1	100 600	21.6	12.6
District 15	79.7	21.1	12 709	26 760	2.3	13.6	8.6	228 106	213 068	64.0	52 500	17.8	12.3
District 16	78.9	17.1	15 107	34 668	3.8	7.6	5.7	223 666	210 646	72.5	73 700	20.0	12.6
District 17	76.3	13.3	12 052	25 195	1.7	12.8	9.7	240 317	221 563	70.0	41 600	16.4	12.5
District 18	79.0	17.5	13 792	30 189	2.6	10.6	8.0	230 713	217 008	70.3	52 000	16.1	12.3
District 19	70.7	11.1	11 333	22 979	1.5	15.3	11.7	245 810	223 161	74.6	38 800	17.2	12.9
District 20	73.9	13.2	12 289	26 173	1.9	12.2	9.3	240 208	219 738	73.1	47 200	17.9	12.9
INDIANA	75.6	15.6	13 149	28 797	2.5	10.7	7.9	2 246 046	2 065 355	70.2	53 900	16.7	12.3
District 1	75.0	14.2	13 161	31 300	2.5	12.8	10.7	212 239	198 750	68.6	57 000	16.4	13.1
District 2	73.1	12.3	12 311	26 185	1.8	12.7	9.3	224 937	209 961	71.2	43 400	15.5	12.4
District 3	74.8	16.1	13 385	29 470	2.7	8.8	6.5	219 701	203 314	72.5	55 500	16.9	12.3
District 4	78.2	15.0	13 436	30 859	2.4	7.8	5.5	226 688	202 849	74.3	56 500	16.1	11.7
District 5	75.1	10.9	12 252	27 893	1.6	9.8	7.6	228 884	205 013	75.1	46 700	15.8	12.4
District 6	85.3	26.7	17 971	38 644	6.0	4.5	3.1	220 193	209 027	72.8	81 400	17.7	11.7
District 7	78.8	17.4	12 536	28 080	2.3	10.7	6.9	216 510	200 596	71.4	54 700	16.7	12.2
District 8	74.5	15.7	12 153	25 242	2.1	13.4	9.2	230 924	211 519	70.1	49 200	17.3	12.5
District 9	69.9	10.2	11 727	26 900	1.5	10.7	8.3	219 460	202 651	76.0	49 300	17.2	12.3
District 10	71.6	16.9	12 562	25 304	1.9	15.8	12.6	246 510	221 675	52.0	46 200	17.7	12.7
IOWA	80.1	16.9	12 422	26 229	2.1	11.5	8.4	1 143 669	1 064 325	70.0	45 900	17.3	12.8
District 1	82.8	22.7	13 660	29 544	2.7	11.5	7.8	223 842	211 466	66.7	55 800	17.0	12.5
District 2	77.9	13.8	11 611	25 010	1.7	12.3	9.4	226 600	209 760	72.2	42 600	16.3	12.9
District 3	79.3	15.7	11 567	24 767	1.6	12.7	9.1	229 322	212 356	71.2	41 400	16.9	12.7
District 4	82.5	18.9	13 813	28 591	2.7	9.8	7.4	230 124	216 874	68.3	52 900	19.2	13.2
District 5	78.0	13.4	11 461	24 150	1.8	11.3	8.3	233 781	213 869	71.7	37 200	16.8	12.8
KANSAS	81.3	21.1	13 300	27 291	2.8	11.5	8.3	1 044 112	944 726	67.9	52 200	19.1	12.6
District 1	77.9	15.2	11 328	23 433	1.6	12.3	9.0	273 364	239 568	71.2	38 200	17.7	12.6
District 2	80.7	18.4	11 662	24 903	1.7	13.4	9.8	255 015	230 344	67.7	44 500	18.6	12.6
District 3	85.9	31.5	16 585	34 275	5.6	9.4	6.4	252 929	235 450	65.7	75 800	20.1	12.7
District 4	80.6	19.6	13 623	28 308	2.5	10.9	8.2	262 804	239 364	67.0	52 500	19.3	12.7
KENTUCKY	64.6	13.6	11 153	22 534	2.0	19.0	16.0	1 506 845	1 379 782	69.6	50 500	18.0	12.3
District 1	62.0	9.5	10 238	20 331	1.3	19.0	15.4	258 606	232 764	73.4	40 500	17.6	12.6
District 2	65.1	11.2	10 609	23 212	1.5	16.8	14.0	243 599	222 235	72.8	48 200	18.1	12.2
District 3	74.1	19.7	14 072	26 614	3.3	14.3	11.4	264 057	246 351	63.3	57 000	16.9	12.3
District 4	68.0	13.5	11 935	26 569	2.3	14.6	12.2	238 483	220 240	71.8	57 300	17.5	12.1
District 5	48.1	7.6	7 725	15 061	1.0	32.7	29.2	249 968	225 010	74.5	35 500	21.1	12.5
District 6	70.0	19.9	12 413	25 364	2.7	16.3	12.8	252 132	233 182	62.7	61 900	18.5	12.1
LOUISIANA	68.3	16.1	10 635	21 949	2.4	23.6	19.4	1 716 241	1 499 269	65.9	58 500	20.6	13.3
District 1	76.4	22.2	13 755	27 413	4.1	15.2	11.9	253 541	228 470	67.3	75 500	20.7	12.7
District 2	65.9	17.6	9 918	18 585	2.4	31.0	27.0	259 749	217 170	46.6	62 400	23.1	14.4
District 3	61.4	9.4	9 614	22 948	1.5	22.6	18.7	225 323	200 349	75.1	56 700	20.2	12.9
District 4	71.2	14.7	10 218	20 920	1.9	23.7	19.1	255 542	217 133	67.1	51 000	20.8	13.6
District 5	63.8	13.7	9 153	18 258	1.8	27.9	22.8	242 121	211 252	70.3	44 100	21.0	13.8
District 6	74.2	20.6	11 790	26 001	2.9	20.0	15.8	239 278	210 773	66.6	65 000	18.5	12.7

1. Persons 25 years old and older. 2. Based on the population enumerated as of April 1, 1990. 3. Specified owner-occupied units.

Table E. Congressional Districts 107th Congress — Housing, Labor Force, and Employment

STATE District	Housing units, 1990 (cont'd) Occupied units (cont'd) Renter-occupied Median rent[1] (dollars)	Rent as a percent of income	Substandard units[2] (percent)	Civilian labor force, 1990 Total	Unemployment Total	Rate[3]	Civilian employment, 1990[4] Total	Percent Professional, managerial, and technical	Precision production, craft, and repair	Disability, 1990 Work disabled persons[5] (percent)
	44	45	46	47	48	49	50	51	52	53
HAWAII	650	27.4	15.6	548 347	19 288	3.5	529 059	29.9	10.5	6.6
District 1	659	27.4	15.2	284 477	8 520	3.0	275 957	33.1	9.0	5.7
District 2	633	27.3	16.0	263 870	10 768	4.1	253 102	26.3	12.1	7.5
IDAHO	330	23.8	4.5	472 773	29 070	6.1	443 703	27.1	11.3	9.0
District 1	332	24.3	4.2	238 745	16 266	6.8	222 479	26.7	11.8	9.9
District 2	327	23.2	4.9	234 028	12 804	5.5	221 224	27.4	10.9	8.1
ILLINOIS	445	25.9	4.2	5 803 007	385 040	6.6	5 417 967	30.0	10.7	6.9
District 1	425	29.5	6.7	259 745	35 334	13.6	224 411	30.2	7.7	10.0
District 2	449	28.2	7.8	273 582	36 478	13.3	237 104	24.5	9.1	9.0
District 3	489	24.0	3.0	296 879	15 121	5.1	281 758	26.2	13.2	6.3
District 4	393	25.3	18.1	258 181	30 076	11.6	228 105	14.6	12.4	7.5
District 5	514	24.3	4.3	332 958	18 538	5.6	314 420	32.3	10.6	5.6
District 6	605	25.3	2.5	326 767	10 872	3.3	315 895	35.2	10.3	4.3
District 7	449	29.3	9.3	259 036	36 625	14.1	222 411	32.5	6.7	9.7
District 8	667	24.7	2.3	333 760	10 669	3.2	323 091	35.5	10.5	4.3
District 9	508	27.1	6.0	323 326	17 631	5.5	305 695	40.6	6.7	6.1
District 10	605	25.7	2.7	300 033	9 761	3.3	290 272	41.9	7.4	4.3
District 11	414	23.7	2.8	282 360	17 879	6.3	264 481	24.8	14.1	6.8
District 12	360	28.8	3.7	259 924	24 269	9.3	235 655	25.6	11.5	9.8
District 13	619	23.7	1.4	316 857	10 206	3.2	306 651	40.2	9.7	3.8
District 14	484	24.4	3.8	304 148	13 112	4.3	291 036	29.7	12.3	5.3
District 15	372	26.7	2.2	286 446	15 319	5.3	271 127	29.3	9.6	6.7
District 16	392	23.6	2.1	301 095	13 933	4.6	287 162	26.8	14.1	6.4
District 17	309	24.6	1.7	272 048	17 235	6.3	254 813	22.9	12.0	7.8
District 18	352	22.8	1.7	281 996	14 028	5.0	267 968	28.8	10.8	7.4
District 19	295	26.1	2.5	258 530	20 309	7.9	238 221	22.0	13.3	9.4
District 20	337	24.7	2.6	275 336	17 645	6.4	257 691	25.1	11.9	8.4
INDIANA	374	24.3	2.6	2 788 838	160 143	5.7	2 628 695	25.6	12.9	7.9
District 1	399	24.7	3.7	263 391	20 854	7.9	242 537	25.6	14.1	8.5
District 2	331	24.6	2.0	273 968	18 463	6.7	255 505	22.6	13.2	8.9
District 3	395	24.1	2.3	282 049	14 037	5.0	268 012	25.3	12.5	7.2
District 4	373	23.1	2.6	289 381	13 914	4.8	275 467	24.7	13.1	7.0
District 5	335	23.2	2.1	270 180	16 031	5.9	254 149	20.2	15.2	8.3
District 6	452	23.2	1.2	300 474	9 257	3.1	291 217	34.4	10.8	5.6
District 7	358	24.9	2.9	275 124	13 471	4.9	261 653	27.1	12.9	7.2
District 8	341	26.7	2.6	271 217	16 901	6.2	254 316	26.6	12.6	8.0
District 9	325	23.6	3.4	273 762	17 437	6.4	256 325	20.6	14.5	9.0
District 10	394	24.5	3.3	289 292	19 778	6.8	269 514	27.2	10.4	9.4
IOWA	336	24.1	1.9	1 403 883	63 641	4.5	1 340 242	25.3	10.5	7.6
District 1	365	24.6	1.8	294 488	15 106	5.1	279 382	29.7	10.3	6.6
District 2	300	23.6	1.9	271 182	13 261	4.9	257 921	22.2	11.2	7.5
District 3	315	24.6	2.0	276 177	13 080	4.7	263 097	24.6	10.9	8.1
District 4	405	24.6	2.1	296 650	11 956	4.0	284 694	27.7	9.3	7.9
District 5	285	22.7	1.6	265 386	10 238	3.9	255 148	21.7	11.0	7.9
KANSAS	372	24.5	2.7	1 229 986	57 772	4.7	1 172 214	28.7	11.5	7.2
District 1	297	22.4	2.6	301 308	10 355	3.4	290 953	21.8	12.7	7.2
District 2	344	25.2	2.8	284 824	15 891	5.6	268 933	27.6	10.8	8.1
District 3	454	25.4	2.3	332 705	15 632	4.7	317 073	35.8	8.3	5.7
District 4	376	24.6	3.1	311 149	15 894	5.1	295 255	29.0	14.2	8.0
KENTUCKY	319	24.9	4.7	1 688 314	124 354	7.4	1 563 960	24.7	12.9	11.4
District 1	278	24.5	4.0	269 270	21 778	8.1	247 492	19.9	14.3	12.0
District 2	310	24.5	4.5	284 214	20 406	7.2	263 808	20.9	13.8	10.5
District 3	344	24.8	2.5	309 313	19 413	6.3	289 900	29.9	10.3	9.1
District 4	337	24.1	4.4	288 295	16 579	5.8	271 716	25.4	12.6	10.0
District 5	243	27.7	9.1	221 371	27 962	12.6	193 409	20.4	17.6	18.2
District 6	352	24.9	3.9	315 851	18 216	5.8	297 635	29.0	10.6	8.8
LOUISIANA	352	27.9	6.5	1 816 917	175 303	9.6	1 641 614	28.1	12.5	10.3
District 1	416	25.3	3.9	287 863	19 040	6.6	268 823	33.7	10.7	9.0
District 2	372	31.5	9.2	257 514	33 025	12.8	224 489	29.2	8.9	11.0
District 3	330	26.1	8.2	252 431	23 449	9.3	228 982	22.1	16.6	11.2
District 4	336	27.7	6.2	246 496	28 011	11.4	218 485	26.7	12.2	10.3
District 5	302	28.9	6.4	241 803	24 747	10.2	217 056	25.8	11.9	11.2
District 6	365	26.7	5.6	279 794	23 400	8.4	256 394	31.0	12.9	8.0

1. Specified renter-occupied units.   2. Overcrowded or lacking complete plumbing facilities.   3. Percent of total civilian labor force.   4. Persons 16 years old and older.   5. Persons 16 to 64 years of age.

STATE District	Land area, 2000[1] (sq km)	Total persons	Per square kilometer	Race alone or in combination White	Black	Am. Indian, Alaska Native	Asian and Pacific Islander	Other race	Hispanic[2]	Non-Hispanic White	2 or more races	Under 5 years	5 to 17 years	18 to 24 years	25 to 34 years	35 to 44 years	45 to 54 years	55 to 64 years
	1	2	3	4	5	6	7	8	9	10	11	12	13	14	15	16	17	18
LOUISIANA—Cont'd																		
District 7	17 593.6	663 992	37.7	73.4	25.4	0.6	1.0	0.6	1.5	71.8	0.8	7.4	20 7	10.3	13.2	15.8	12.6	8.3
MAINE	79 931.0	1 274 923	16.0	97.9	0.7	1.0	1.0	0.4	0.7	96.5	1.0	5.5	18.1	8.1	12.4	16.7	15.1	9.7
District 1	9 368.3	666 936	71.2	97.7	0.9	0.7	1.3	0.4	0.8	96.3	1.0	5.7	18.1	7.7	12.8	17.1	15.2	9.4
District 2	70 562.8	607 987	8.6	98.0	0.6	1.4	0.8	0.4	0.7	96.7	1.0	5.4	18.1	8.7	11.9	16.2	15.0	9.9
MARYLAND	25 314.0	5 296 486	209.2	65.4	28.8	0.7	4.6	2.5	4.3	62.1	2.0	6.7	18.9	8.5	14.1	17.3	14.3	8.9
District 1	9 003.0	682 770	75.8	82.1	15.7	0.7	1.9	1.1	2.2	79.8	1.3	6.3	18.1	8.6	13.2	16.7	14.2	9.9
District 2	2 341.0	652 938	278.9	88.3	8.7	0.6	2.8	0.9	1.7	86.3	1.3	6.2	18.7	7.9	12.5	17.2	14.7	9.4
District 3	552.3	643 935	1 165.9	68.0	27.8	0.8	3.8	1.8	2.8	65.1	2.0	6.7	17.9	8.5	16.0	16.7	13.7	8.3
District 4	499.7	648 764	1 298.3	23.7	66.5	1.0	5.7	6.5	10.0	18.3	3.1	7.4	19.8	9.3	16.5	17.1	13.9	8.2
District 5	4 058.9	714 886	176.1	64.5	30.2	1.0	4.4	2.3	3.9	61.2	2.2	6.8	19.3	9.5	14.8	18.4	14.1	8.6
District 6	7 387.9	723 196	97.9	90.5	6.6	0.5	2.9	0.8	1.6	88.5	1.2	6.6	19.7	7.5	13.0	18.1	14.7	8.9
District 7	282.0	539 439	1 912.9	22.1	75.5	0.7	2.4	0.9	1.3	20.9	1.4	6.4	19.0	11.1	13.6	15.8	13.0	8.4
District 8	1 189.3	690 558	580.6	72.8	11.5	0.7	12.6	5.8	10.5	65.1	3.2	6.9	18.8	6.3	13.7	17.9	15.4	9.2
MASSACHUSETTS	20 306.0	6 349 097	312.7	86.2	6.3	0.6	4.3	5.1	6.8	81.9	2.3	6.3	17.4	9.1	14.6	16.7	13.8	8.6
District 1	7 853.4	610 522	77.7	92.6	2.5	0.7	2.2	3.9	6.5	88.6	1.7	5.8	18.3	10.6	12.1	16.2	14.4	8.5
District 2	2 293.8	615 557	268.4	86.7	6.7	0.6	1.8	6.1	9.5	82.1	1.9	6.4	19.0	8.7	13.1	16.6	13.9	8.5
District 3	1 868.6	655 701	350.9	91.2	3.2	0.6	3.3	3.6	5.5	87.2	1.8	6.7	18.6	8.6	13.7	17.4	13.7	8.3
District 4	1 974.9	639 072	323.6	91.1	3.0	0.6	3.7	3.9	3.1	88.0	2.1	6.4	18.0	8.9	13.6	16.7	14.4	8.8
District 5	1 518.0	644 869	424.8	85.6	2.8	0.5	6.1	7.4	11.1	80.1	2.3	7.4	20.0	7.3	13.7	18.3	14.1	8.4
District 6	1 295.4	652 455	503.7	92.2	2.9	0.4	2.9	3.3	5.0	89.0	1.6	6.5	17.8	7.0	12.8	17.7	14.8	9.1
District 7	447.3	616 542	1 378.4	88.1	4.2	0.4	6.1	3.6	4.8	83.8	2.3	6.0	15.0	8.1	16.0	16.9	13.7	9.0
District 8	115.1	620 372	5 389.9	62.3	22.6	0.8	8.5	10.4	14.5	53.8	4.5	5.1	13.0	18.4	22.5	14.1	10.3	6.7
District 9	658.3	630 499	957.8	79.1	12.1	0.6	5.3	6.1	6.2	75.1	3.0	6.3	16.8	7.8	15.9	16.9	13.5	8.6
District 10	2 280.9	663 508	290.9	92.3	3.4	0.7	3.1	2.4	1.7	90.1	1.8	5.9	16.9	6.2	12.8	16.7	14.7	10.1
MICHIGAN	147 121.0	9 938 444	67.6	81.8	14.8	1.3	2.2	2.0	3.3	78.6	1.9	6.8	19.4	9.4	13.7	16.1	13.8	8.7
District 1	58 958.0	639 161	10.8	95.4	1.3	3.8	0.7	0.5	1.0	93.4	1.5	5.5	17.9	8.7	11.2	15.6	14.5	10.4
District 2	14 162.9	686 086	48.4	91.5	4.8	1.3	1.3	2.8	5.0	87.8	1.6	7.0	20.8	9.3	12.6	16.1	13.3	8.7
District 3	4 312.2	662 041	153.5	86.3	9.0	1.1	2.0	3.7	6.4	81.9	2.1	7.6	20.5	10.5	14.8	16.3	12.7	7.2
District 4	22 466.5	651 347	29.0	96.1	2.0	1.4	0.9	1.0	2.2	93.7	1.3	6.1	18.9	10.9	11.8	15.4	13.5	10.1
District 5	14 125.8	587 031	41.6	88.8	9.1	1.2	0.8	1.9	3.8	85.4	1.6	6.3	19.8	8.1	11.9	15.5	14.0	9.9
District 6	7 529.5	610 640	81.1	86.9	10.4	1.3	1.5	2.1	3.6	83.5	1.9	6.6	19.1	10.9	12.7	15.3	13.8	8.9
District 7	10 714.3	620 053	57.9	91.2	6.7	1.1	1.0	1.8	3.3	88.1	1.7	6.4	19.4	8.7	13.0	16.2	14.4	9.2
District 8	5 028.7	658 695	131.0	89.5	7.0	1.2	2.7	1.8	3.4	86.0	2.0	6.6	18.9	11.9	13.4	16.6	14.5	8.3
District 9	2 111.7	633 553	300.0	78.6	18.1	1.2	2.3	1.9	3.8	75.0	2.0	7.7	19.9	8.6	15.0	17.2	14.0	8.2
District 10	2 925.5	671 306	229.5	95.2	3.2	0.9	1.4	0.9	1.8	92.7	1.4	6.6	18.4	7.9	14.3	17.2	14.0	8.8
District 11	984.1	640 548	650.9	86.1	9.3	0.7	4.6	1.1	1.6	83.6	1.7	6.4	18.5	6.4	13.2	17.6	15.4	9.2
District 12	385.9	574 950	1 489.9	88.5	6.5	0.9	5.1	1.4	1.4	85.6	2.2	6.2	17.2	7.8	15.7	16.6	13.9	9.0
District 13	1 179.0	628 363	533.0	80.3	14.0	1.0	5.7	1.4	2.4	76.9	2.3	6.8	16.8	13.0	16.6	16.0	13.3	7.8
District 14	206.8	550 599	2 662.5	18.3	80.2	0.9	1.8	1.4	1.2	16.4	2.2	7.9	23.5	9.1	14.9	14.6	12.6	7.3
District 15	218.8	531 634	2 429.8	23.6	71.0	1.0	1.6	5.7	8.2	18.5	2.7	7.9	21.8	9.8	14.8	14.4	12.2	7.2
District 16	1 811.3	592 437	327.1	94.9	2.8	1.0	1.7	2.6	3.3	90.0	2.9	6.8	18.9	8.2	13.8	16.1	13.8	8.6
MINNESOTA	206 189.0	4 919 479	23.9	90.8	4.1	1.6	3.4	1.8	2.9	88.2	1.7	6.7	19.5	9.6	13.7	16.8	13.5	8.2
District 1	24 059.2	594 864	24.7	95.5	1.5	0.6	2.1	1.5	2.7	93.3	1.0	6.3	19.4	10.9	12.1	15.9	13.2	8.5
District 2	42 182.8	613 816	14.6	96.3	0.7	0.8	1.2	1.9	3.3	94.2	0.8	6.9	20.8	8.1	12.2	16.5	12.9	8.4
District 3	1 284.3	642 053	499.9	90.1	4.7	0.7	4.9	1.3	2.0	87.8	1.7	6.9	19.8	7.5	14.2	18.4	15.2	8.5
District 4	475.8	577 077	1 212.9	81.0	8.1	1.5	9.1	3.4	5.4	76.8	2.8	6.8	18.6	11.0	14.8	15.7	13.2	7.7
District 5	277.1	557 819	2 013.1	74.8	15.8	2.6	6.2	4.6	6.2	70.1	3.6	6.4	15.2	12.2	19.3	16.1	12.4	6.7
District 6	2 879.2	720 995	250.4	94.6	2.3	1.0	2.8	1.1	1.9	92.2	1.6	7.8	22.0	7.5	14.7	19.6	14.1	7.6
District 7	68 162.6	588 825	8.6	95.2	0.7	3.4	1.1	0.9	1.6	93.4	1.1	6.1	19.7	11.5	11.0	15.0	12.8	8.9
District 8	66 868.1	624 030	9.3	96.4	0.8	3.0	0.7	0.4	0.9	94.8	1.1	6.0	19.4	8.7	11.3	16.0	14.1	9.6
MISSISSIPPI	121 488.0	2 844 658	23.4	61.9	36.6	0.7	0.9	0.7	1.4	60.7	0.7	7.2	20.1	10.9	13.4	15.0	12.7	8.6
District 1	26 931.2	607 229	22.5	76.3	22.6	0.4	0.6	0.8	1.5	75.2	0.6	6.9	19.3	10.4	13.7	15.0	12.8	9.3
District 2	31 723.3	517 345	16.3	33.7	65.5	0.3	0.6	0.5	1.2	33.0	0.5	7.7	22.2	11.2	12.6	14.2	12.3	8.0
District 3	25 893.1	588 915	22.7	65.4	32.3	1.4	0.9	0.6	1.4	64.3	0.6	7.1	19.4	11.1	13.8	15.1	12.9	8.5
District 4	20 298.3	530 679	26.1	52.0	47.2	0.4	0.6	0.5	0.9	51.3	0.6	7.2	20.3	10.9	13.0	14.8	12.7	8.3
District 5	16 642.6	600 490	36.1	77.0	20.8	0.8	1.8	0.9	1.9	75.0	1.2	7.1	19.5	11.1	13.8	15.5	12.9	9.0
MISSOURI	178 414.0	5 595 211	31.4	86.1	11.7	1.1	1.5	1.2	2.1	83.8	1.5	6.6	18.9	9.6	13.2	15.9	13.3	9.1
District 1	377.3	514 264	1 363.0	37.6	60.8	0.6	1.8	0.8	1.2	36.0	1.6	6.6	20.1	10.9	14.0	15.0	12.5	7.9
District 2	1 391.3	610 984	439.1	91.4	5.4	0.5	3.1	0.8	1.6	89.4	1.1	6.5	19.3	7.6	12.5	17.3	15.1	9.3
District 3	3 263.7	596 066	182.6	91.2	6.8	0.7	1.8	1.0	1.7	89.0	1.4	6.4	18.4	8.5	13.9	16.8	13.5	8.6

1. Dry land or land partially or temporarily covered by water.   2. Hispanic persons may be of any race.

STATE District	Population and population characteristics, 2000 (cont'd) Percent (cont'd) Age (cont'd)			Households, 2000		Percent		Persons in correctional institutions, 2000	Persons in nursing homes, 2000	Persons in military quarters, 2000	Education, 1990 School enrollment	
	65 to 74 years	75 years and over	Percent female	Number	Persons per house-hold	Female family house-holder[1]	One person				Public	Private
	19	20	21	22	23	24	25	26	27	28	29	30
LOUISIANA—Cont'd												
District 7	6.5	5.1	51.2	245 590	2.63	14.8	24.4	7 578	5 090	0	147 817	22 290
MAINE	7.5	6.8	51.3	518 200	2.39	9.5	27.0	2 864	9 339	688	267 445	37 423
District 1	7.2	6.8	51.5	270 935	2.40	9.5	27.2	1 957	4 244	547	125 381	22 305
District 2	7.9	6.9	51.2	247 265	2.39	9.5	26.8	907	5 095	141	142 064	15 118
MARYLAND	6.1	5.2	51.7	1 980 859	2.61	14.1	25.0	35 698	26 716	7 412	982 507	229 826
District 1	7.2	5.8	51.0	261 214	2.53	12.1	24.0	5 153	4 001	3 712	122 228	21 549
District 2	7.2	6.3	51.7	250 863	2.56	10.8	24.1	1 537	2 386	282	116 671	27 909
District 3	6.1	6.1	52.3	256 468	2.45	14.5	29.2	3 638	3 025	1 266	108 060	37 227
District 4	4.5	3.3	52.8	236 537	2.71	21.1	25.3	1 283	1 950	892	130 430	30 266
District 5	4.9	3.6	50.8	252 640	2.74	12.4	21.1	4 256	3 027	612	136 510	26 994
District 6	6.1	5.4	50.3	261 822	2.66	9.1	21.4	11 740	4 663	254	126 395	21 506
District 7	6.7	6.0	53.5	206 339	2.49	26.6	32.9	7 441	4 104	0	127 649	26 366
District 8	6.0	5.8	51.9	254 976	2.68	9.4	23.6	650	3 560	394	114 564	38 009
MASSACHUSETTS	6.7	6.8	51.8	2 443 580	2.51	11.9	28.0	23 513	55 837	472	1 100 827	429 307
District 1	6.8	7.3	51.6	236 215	2.46	11.5	28.1	1 441	6 041	0	136 410	27 658
District 2	6.7	7.2	52.2	236 234	2.53	13.8	27.0	2 133	5 301	0	115 664	36 960
District 3	6.4	6.7	51.4	246 370	2.57	11.1	25.9	2 062	5 992	0	115 245	38 702
District 4	6.5	6.7	52.2	238 717	2.57	11.1	25.6	4 231	5 939	55	112 568	45 466
District 5	5.7	5.1	50.8	230 732	2.73	12.0	22.7	5 521	4 422	0	124 398	32 039
District 6	7.2	7.0	51.9	249 622	2.55	10.9	26.6	1 340	6 614	21	108 322	34 197
District 7	7.6	7.8	52.3	246 169	2.44	10.4	29.6	812	5 618	163	93 609	44 595
District 8	5.0	4.8	51.6	250 834	2.30	14.5	36.4	530	3 725	0	89 945	95 976
District 9	6.9	7.3	52.0	243 334	2.51	13.2	29.4	3 639	6 260	176	96 541	44 845
District 10	8.6	8.2	52.0	265 353	2.45	10.4	28.2	1 804	5 925	57	108 125	28 869
MICHIGAN	6.5	5.8	51.0	3 785 661	2.56	12.5	26.2	65 330	50 113	112	2 242 239	338 803
District 1	8.5	7.7	49.7	255 335	2.40	8.5	27.3	10 969	4 803	51	141 202	10 208
District 2	6.4	5.8	50.4	249 359	2.67	9.7	22.4	5 803	4 168	7	136 535	21 779
District 3	5.3	5.1	50.4	243 202	2.64	11.4	25.1	6 740	4 455	0	125 240	34 953
District 4	7.4	5.9	50.3	244 789	2.56	9.1	23.0	7 738	3 578	6	155 564	15 753
District 5	7.7	6.8	51.2	227 407	2.54	12.2	25.3	1 780	3 158	6	142 201	16 336
District 6	6.6	6.0	51.1	235 284	2.51	11.5	26.0	1 475	2 986	4	144 530	19 892
District 7	6.7	6.0	50.1	232 134	2.55	11.0	24.7	14 531	3 509	0	136 113	20 856
District 8	5.3	4.5	50.9	248 451	2.56	9.9	24.7	2 306	3 054	0	171 559	17 147
District 9	5.2	4.2	51.0	240 949	2.58	14.0	26.0	3 594	1 618	0	143 213	19 014
District 10	6.8	6.0	50.9	261 520	2.54	10.0	25.9	2 738	2 635	34	132 964	18 247
District 11	6.9	6.4	51.3	252 118	2.51	8.3	26.4	233	3 401	0	121 979	27 812
District 12	6.9	6.8	51.3	232 339	2.46	10.4	29.8	0	2 436	0	129 810	21 323
District 13	5.3	4.4	51.1	246 781	2.45	11.2	29.0	2 122	2 565	0	162 931	19 505
District 14	5.4	4.7	53.4	193 235	2.81	30.5	26.4	2 245	2 383	0	136 841	31 412
District 15	6.1	5.7	52.0	193 624	2.67	28.7	33.1	2 716	2 850	4	135 115	21 008
District 16	7.1	6.7	51.0	229 134	2.57	11.3	26.3	340	2 514	0	126 442	23 558
MINNESOTA	6.0	6.1	50.5	1 895 127	2.52	8.9	26.9	16 999	40 506	12	1 006 375	168 652
District 1	6.6	7.1	50.4	225 585	2.53	7.6	25.8	3 557	5 899	0	132 798	21 838
District 2	6.7	7.5	50.1	230 060	2.60	6.9	24.4	2 278	6 494	0	122 315	19 628
District 3	5.3	4.3	50.9	248 428	2.56	8.4	24.4	792	2 188	0	119 766	21 890
District 4	5.9	6.3	51.9	228 672	2.44	11.7	31.8	590	4 868	0	108 657	36 614
District 5	5.1	6.5	50.5	238 619	2.24	11.4	38.1	804	7 016	0	109 395	23 613
District 6	4.0	2.7	50.1	255 730	2.79	9.1	18.9	3 582	1 361	0	137 283	17 939
District 7	7.4	7.6	50.1	223 955	2.53	7.7	26.2	1 500	7 030	0	142 435	16 630
District 8	7.6	7.3	50.1	244 078	2.48	8.5	26.3	3 896	5 650	12	133 726	10 500
MISSISSIPPI	6.5	5.5	51.7	1 046 434	2.63	17.3	24.6	25 778	18 382	5 722	646 850	80 636
District 1	6.7	5.8	51.5	229 413	2.58	13.7	23.8	2 206	4 051	0	123 001	10 407
District 2	6.1	5.7	52.4	177 271	2.79	25.6	24.9	10 985	3 865	4	141 705	18 117
District 3	6.5	5.6	51.8	220 494	2.58	15.7	25.0	4 963	4 262	873	128 182	16 617
District 4	6.8	6.0	52.4	196 773	2.61	19.1	26.0	3 159	3 263	2	123 559	21 636
District 5	6.5	4.7	50.7	222 483	2.61	14.3	23.7	4 465	2 941	4 843	130 403	13 859
MISSOURI	7.0	6.5	51.4	2 194 594	2.48	11.6	27.3	35 206	48 708	5 435	1 060 947	231 676
District 1	6.7	6.3	53.8	205 933	2.42	23.1	34.3	2 277	3 638	0	115 400	39 729
District 2	6.6	5.8	51.6	236 472	2.54	9.1	25.0	1 355	5 156	0	107 468	44 375
District 3	7.0	7.0	51.7	239 965	2.45	11.2	29.3	219	5 093	6	88 946	43 811

1. No spouse present.

STATE District	Education, 1990 (cont'd) Attainment[1] (percent)		Money income, 1989			Percent below poverty level, 1989		Housing units, 1990					
				Households		Persons	Families		Occupied units				
											Owner-occupied		
												Owner cost as a percent of income	
	High school graduate or more	Bachelor's degree or more	Per capita[2]	Median	Percent with $100,000 or more	Total	Total	Total	Total	Percent	Median value[3] (dollars)	With a mortgage	Without a mortgage
	31	32	33	34	35	36	37	38	39	40	41	42	43
LOUISIANA—Cont'd													
District 7	64.6	14.1	9 999	20 595	2.2	24.7	21.2	240 687	214 122	69.0	49 400	19.5	13.4
MAINE	78.8	18.8	12 957	27 854	2.4	10.8	8.0	587 045	465 312	70.5	87 400	21.4	13.4
District 1	81.8	22.6	14 453	31 124	3.2	8.4	5.9	288 000	235 671	69.0	107 700	22.3	13.2
District 2	75.8	14.9	11 462	24 718	1.7	13.2	10.0	299 045	229 641	72.0	66 700	20.0	13.6
MARYLAND	78.4	26.5	17 730	39 386	6.9	8.3	6.0	1 891 917	1 748 991	65.0	116 500	21.1	12.4
District 1	74.7	19.9	16 104	35 115	5.2	8.4	6.1	269 162	221 366	70.3	101 300	21.0	12.9
District 2	78.1	22.3	17 931	40 120	6.1	5.2	3.9	233 772	222 476	70.5	110 900	20.3	12.0
District 3	75.1	27.2	17 779	35 970	5.8	9.0	6.5	247 292	232 681	63.3	91 000	20.3	13.0
District 4	83.0	27.7	17 251	41 081	5.7	6.5	4.8	228 160	216 758	52.8	124 000	22.1	11.7
District 5	83.2	25.4	18 178	46 936	6.9	4.9	2.9	215 948	204 414	71.9	132 100	21.6	11.9
District 6	77.6	20.9	15 979	36 883	5.2	7.0	5.3	230 013	214 745	71.9	113 700	21.4	12.3
District 7	64.0	16.1	11 718	25 684	2.1	21.4	17.4	237 408	216 574	46.9	60 100	19.4	13.3
District 8	91.3	51.1	26 900	56 789	18.2	3.7	2.3	230 162	219 977	72.8	207 200	22.0	11.5
MASSACHUSETTS	80.0	27.2	17 224	36 952	6.7	8.9	6.7	2 472 711	2 247 110	59.3	162 800	22.3	13.8
District 1	78.0	21.4	14 200	31 903	3.3	10.2	7.7	245 899	222 811	62.8	123 700	21.8	13.4
District 2	74.7	18.8	14 652	33 401	3.5	9.9	7.9	235 845	222 230	63.9	129 100	21.7	13.5
District 3	76.6	24.2	15 917	36 873	5.0	7.9	5.9	234 772	220 174	61.7	150 800	22.0	13.6
District 4	77.5	30.9	18 963	39 005	10.0	7.7	5.8	235 024	218 092	63.8	170 600	22.7	14.0
District 5	79.9	28.8	18 293	42 701	9.3	8.9	7.0	222 166	209 525	64.4	174 200	22.2	13.5
District 6	83.3	27.4	18 549	40 836	8.0	6.8	5.2	242 831	225 496	65.5	181 100	22.8	13.9
District 7	84.0	30.6	19 825	41 318	8.6	5.9	4.2	243 218	232 429	57.4	193 600	21.9	13.9
District 8	76.7	36.0	16 327	30 417	5.5	17.4	13.5	257 784	238 103	29.1	189 700	22.2	14.4
District 9	81.6	27.8	17 980	38 646	7.6	8.9	6.7	241 312	226 665	57.4	172 800	21.6	13.5
District 10	86.7	26.4	17 535	37 489	6.2	6.3	4.9	313 860	231 585	68.7	163 700	23.5	14.4
MICHIGAN	76.8	17.4	14 154	31 020	3.8	13.1	10.2	3 847 926	3 419 331	71.0	60 600	18.0	13.5
District 1	77.0	14.5	10 846	22 788	1.5	13.3	9.9	324 094	219 934	75.8	44 900	19.9	14.3
District 2	75.9	13.6	12 305	28 905	2.3	11.4	8.8	251 114	206 301	78.7	58 400	18.2	13.2
District 3	79.9	19.1	13 924	31 917	3.3	9.4	7.2	221 593	208 512	70.8	66 000	18.5	13.0
District 4	76.2	13.5	11 549	25 898	1.9	15.2	11.3	272 679	207 299	78.1	49 300	17.8	13.4
District 5	73.8	10.7	11 891	26 312	1.7	15.0	12.5	251 888	214 348	75.7	47 400	17.3	13.7
District 6	77.2	18.6	13 043	28 453	2.8	13.8	10.2	244 821	216 367	70.0	54 600	17.3	13.3
District 7	78.2	13.9	12 900	29 976	2.2	11.4	8.8	230 242	210 201	74.0	50 700	16.9	13.1
District 8	84.0	24.1	15 455	35 911	4.5	10.6	7.2	220 922	208 151	70.1	72 100	18.5	13.1
District 9	78.0	17.7	15 132	34 737	4.5	14.2	11.8	227 038	213 603	67.9	65 200	18.5	13.6
District 10	77.3	12.8	15 603	36 536	3.9	6.6	5.2	225 686	214 512	76.8	71 500	18.8	13.7
District 11	87.7	34.4	24 466	49 021	13.7	3.4	2.2	232 727	220 558	77.9	111 100	19.3	12.8
District 12	78.6	19.9	16 796	38 760	4.4	6.0	4.5	227 981	220 490	73.9	76 200	18.0	13.3
District 13	81.6	27.3	16 267	36 596	4.9	10.1	6.5	226 392	215 487	61.6	77 500	18.2	13.0
District 14	69.2	12.5	11 462	25 079	2.5	24.6	21.9	219 109	206 555	64.9	29 800	17.4	14.2
District 15	58.6	11.1	9 650	15 264	2.1	36.6	32.6	247 821	220 864	45.2	23 200	19.0	15.3
District 16	74.0	12.9	15 175	35 315	3.6	8.4	6.8	223 819	216 149	75.4	62 400	16.2	13.5
MINNESOTA	82.4	21.8	14 389	30 909	3.6	10.2	7.3	1 848 445	1 647 853	71.8	74 000	20.4	12.4
District 1	79.9	18.5	12 688	28 403	2.5	9.8	6.4	213 303	201 475	75.0	58 800	18.1	12.4
District 2	75.6	13.3	12 043	26 937	2.3	10.0	7.5	220 151	200 523	77.5	54 700	19.6	12.5
District 3	92.2	32.9	20 805	44 329	9.1	4.0	3.0	216 358	205 269	72.5	102 900	21.5	11.6
District 4	85.0	28.1	15 937	32 287	4.2	10.8	7.6	227 007	215 257	62.8	84 100	20.9	12.6
District 5	84.9	30.3	16 099	28 880	3.8	14.0	9.9	250 444	235 878	55.9	80 100	20.4	12.5
District 6	89.1	22.1	15 922	42 161	4.3	4.6	3.6	192 441	184 815	81.4	89 500	21.6	11.7
District 7	74.7	14.6	10 341	23 146	1.3	15.3	10.9	246 080	198 065	74.8	50 900	18.8	12.8
District 8	77.1	13.8	11 279	24 472	1.3	13.5	9.9	282 661	206 571	78.7	49 000	17.9	12.7
MISSISSIPPI	64.3	14.7	9 648	20 136	1.7	25.2	20.2	1 010 423	911 374	71.5	45 600	20.8	13.5
District 1	59.6	10.8	9 639	20 867	1.3	20.1	15.8	203 963	186 772	77.2	43 900	20.5	13.0
District 2	55.3	13.5	7 771	15 530	1.4	37.7	31.0	186 579	170 188	64.4	40 200	22.0	15.0
District 3	66.6	16.1	10 303	21 625	1.8	22.0	17.6	201 965	184 721	74.0	47 100	20.0	13.1
District 4	67.7	18.1	10 411	20 234	2.3	25.3	20.4	207 200	185 716	71.3	47 900	21.6	13.8
District 5	71.6	15.1	10 116	21 702	1.6	20.8	17.1	210 716	183 977	70.0	49 700	20.4	12.8
MISSOURI	73.9	17.8	12 989	26 362	2.8	13.3	10.1	2 199 129	1 961 206	68.8	59 900	18.4	12.3
District 1	70.6	19.5	12 632	24 963	2.7	19.1	15.1	250 456	220 470	56.6	55 800	18.5	12.8
District 2	86.4	33.6	20 654	43 957	9.3	3.7	2.5	222 053	210 097	75.5	95 300	18.3	11.5
District 3	73.1	17.2	14 272	30 863	2.4	7.9	6.0	243 430	225 237	70.0	72 100	18.2	12.2

1. Persons 25 years old and older. 2. Based on the population enumerated as of April 1, 1990. 3. Specified owner-occupied units.

Table E. Congressional Districts 107th Congress — Housing, Labor Force, and Employment

STATE District	Housing units, 1990 (cont'd) — Occupied units (cont'd) — Renter-occupied			Civilian labor force, 1990	Unemployment		Civilian employment, 1990[4]	Percent		Disability, 1990
	Median rent[1] (dollars)	Rent as a percent of income	Substandard units[2] (percent)	Total	Total	Rate[3]	Total	Professional, managerial, and technical	Precision production, craft, and repair	Work disabled persons[5] (percent)
	44	45	46	47	48	49	50	51	52	53
LOUISIANA—Cont'd										
District 7	299	27.1	6.4	251 016	23 631	9.4	227 385	26.5	14.8	11.6
MAINE	419	26.8	3.1	612 564	40 722	6.6	571 842	27.8	13.4	10.2
District 1	476	26.8	2.2	319 148	18 082	5.7	301 066	30.7	12.9	9.0
District 2	365	26.7	3.9	293 416	22 640	7.7	270 776	24.6	14.0	11.3
MARYLAND	548	25.4	3.3	2 592 878	111 536	4.3	2 481 342	37.0	10.3	7.0
District 1	487	25.0	2.9	316 881	12 955	4.1	303 926	29.9	12.9	7.6
District 2	507	23.4	1.7	321 422	11 456	3.6	309 966	34.4	12.6	6.8
District 3	506	25.1	2.2	318 100	13 866	4.4	304 234	38.8	9.4	7.4
District 4	643	26.3	6.9	350 723	16 220	4.6	334 503	36.8	8.2	6.0
District 5	674	25.0	3.4	339 228	10 991	3.2	328 237	37.5	12.2	6.5
District 6	448	23.7	1.9	313 112	11 234	3.6	301 878	33.1	13.2	6.6
District 7	432	27.1	5.2	287 190	26 314	9.2	260 876	28.5	8.3	11.2
District 8	777	26.0	2.6	346 222	8 500	2.5	337 722	53.9	6.2	4.6
MASSACHUSETTS	580	26.8	2.7	3 245 950	218 000	6.7	3 027 950	36.2	10.0	7.2
District 1	479	26.7	2.4	309 808	20 952	6.8	288 856	31.8	12.0	8.0
District 2	497	26.1	2.3	312 166	20 992	6.7	291 174	29.7	11.8	8.1
District 3	515	25.4	2.0	319 569	21 468	6.7	298 101	33.9	11.0	7.4
District 4	512	25.7	1.9	319 762	21 540	6.7	298 222	38.6	9.4	7.3
District 5	603	27.3	3.5	322 110	23 599	7.3	298 511	39.9	10.5	6.6
District 6	617	26.9	1.7	330 930	19 978	6.0	310 952	36.9	10.6	6.8
District 7	685	25.8	1.9	343 166	20 105	5.9	323 061	39.9	8.7	6.4
District 8	636	27.8	6.4	340 921	25 903	7.6	315 018	41.2	5.9	7.1
District 9	616	27.0	3.3	327 990	22 017	6.7	305 973	36.7	8.7	7.4
District 10	651	27.9	1.7	319 528	21 446	6.7	298 082	32.7	11.5	7.1
MICHIGAN	423	27.2	2.9	4 540 537	374 341	8.2	4 166 196	28.3	12.0	9.0
District 1	328	26.2	2.8	258 970	22 749	8.8	236 221	24.4	13.1	9.7
District 2	383	26.6	2.8	279 389	19 378	6.9	260 011	23.7	13.7	9.3
District 3	425	24.9	2.4	297 820	16 566	5.6	281 254	26.4	11.7	7.8
District 4	360	28.0	2.7	267 165	23 811	8.9	243 354	24.2	13.4	9.4
District 5	366	29.4	2.7	262 224	27 850	10.6	234 374	22.4	13.6	9.9
District 6	385	27.0	2.8	291 458	20 633	7.1	270 825	27.7	12.0	8.8
District 7	382	25.2	2.2	280 617	20 589	7.3	260 028	24.9	12.6	9.7
District 8	435	26.0	2.4	307 202	18 386	6.0	288 816	32.4	11.2	7.1
District 9	448	28.4	3.2	288 004	26 855	9.3	261 149	29.4	12.3	9.5
District 10	471	25.4	2.0	299 272	19 666	6.6	279 606	27.0	14.9	8.2
District 11	638	23.9	1.4	317 353	13 676	4.3	303 677	42.4	9.3	5.6
District 12	512	24.3	2.3	310 557	17 788	5.7	292 769	32.6	12.0	7.5
District 13	519	26.2	3.2	317 717	18 356	5.8	299 361	34.2	10.5	7.4
District 14	421	32.8	5.4	255 943	39 271	15.3	216 672	24.6	9.0	11.6
District 15	337	35.1	5.6	221 076	49 314	22.3	171 762	24.0	8.4	15.1
District 16	456	24.4	2.5	285 770	19 453	6.8	266 317	25.3	14.1	9.0
MINNESOTA	422	26.7	2.4	2 311 336	118 919	5.1	2 192 417	30.3	10.1	7.4
District 1	343	24.9	2.1	283 587	12 701	4.5	270 886	27.3	10.6	7.0
District 2	306	24.6	2.1	270 553	11 727	4.3	258 826	22.6	12.2	7.2
District 3	569	25.1	1.5	327 353	11 687	3.6	315 666	37.4	8.6	5.2
District 4	455	27.4	3.0	298 090	14 387	4.8	283 703	35.6	7.9	7.6
District 5	446	27.9	3.0	310 203	17 689	5.7	292 514	36.5	6.8	8.8
District 6	513	26.0	1.6	311 414	13 466	4.3	297 948	30.9	11.9	6.2
District 7	321	27.5	3.0	260 477	16 556	6.4	243 921	23.7	10.5	8.0
District 8	303	28.1	3.2	249 659	20 706	8.3	228 953	24.7	13.5	9.5
MISSISSIPPI	309	27.1	7.2	1 123 485	94 712	8.4	1 028 773	24.6	12.9	11.0
District 1	277	25.3	5.5	240 550	16 136	6.7	224 414	19.7	14.3	10.6
District 2	267	30.2	12.0	201 161	23 852	11.9	177 309	23.1	11.0	11.4
District 3	324	25.1	6.8	234 720	16 044	6.8	218 676	25.7	13.0	9.8
District 4	344	27.9	6.7	225 917	19 907	8.8	206 010	26.9	11.3	11.5
District 5	329	26.3	5.2	221 137	18 773	8.5	202 364	27.7	14.7	11.7
MISSOURI	368	25.2	3.0	2 522 783	155 388	6.2	2 367 395	27.8	11.1	8.5
District 1	391	28.3	4.8	274 940	26 323	9.6	248 617	31.1	7.9	9.0
District 2	519	22.8	1.2	312 487	10 326	3.3	302 161	40.3	8.5	5.1
District 3	390	24.2	2.3	292 360	15 899	5.4	276 461	28.5	12.2	7.5

1. Specified renter-occupied units. 2. Overcrowded or lacking complete plumbing facilities. 3. Percent of total civilian labor force. 4. Persons 16 years old and older. 5. Persons 16 to 64 years of age.

STATE District	Land area, 2000[1] (sq km)	Total persons	Per square kilometer	Race alone or in combination					Hispanic[2]	Non-Hispanic White	2 or more races	Age						
				White	Black	Am. Indian, Alaska Native	Asian and Pacific Islander	Other race				Under 5 years	5 to 17 years	18 to 24 years	25 to 34 years	35 to 44 years	45 to 54 years	55 to 64 years
	1	2	3	4	5	6	7	8	9	10	11	12	13	14	15	16	17	18
MISSOURI—Cont'd																		
District 4	36 518.7	659 533	18.1	94.8	3.5	1.2	0.9	1.1	2.0	92.4	1.4	6.6	19.1	9.5	12.6	15.5	12.9	9.8
District 5	968.2	577 050	596.0	68.6	27.1	1.3	2.0	3.4	5.8	64.3	2.4	7.0	18.4	9.3	14.9	16.1	12.9	8.3
District 6	35 145.8	635 835	18.1	95.1	3.2	1.0	1.1	1.1	2.3	92.5	1.3	6.5	18.9	9.3	13.2	16.2	13.6	9.1
District 7	24 050.4	695 069	28.9	96.1	1.4	2.0	0.9	1.3	2.4	93.2	1.7	6.6	17.9	10.7	12.8	14.8	13.1	9.7
District 8	45 243.3	611 537	13.5	94.2	4.6	1.3	0.7	0.5	1.0	92.4	1.2	6.3	18.9	9.3	12.0	14.7	13.0	10.2
District 9	31 455.0	694 873	22.1	94.2	4.4	0.8	1.2	0.6	1.2	92.5	1.2	6.9	19.5	11.1	13.3	16.4	12.8	8.4
MONTANA	376 979.0	902 195	2.4	92.2	0.5	7.4	0.9	0.9	2.0	89.5	1.7	6.1	19.4	9.5	11.4	15.7	15.0	9.4
At Large	376 979.1	902 195	2.4	92.2	0.5	7.4	0.9	0.9	2.0	89.5	1.7	6.1	19.4	9.5	11.4	15.7	15.0	9.4
NEBRASKA	199 099.0	1 711 263	8.6	90.8	4.4	1.3	1.7	3.3	5.5	87.3	1.4	6.8	19.5	10.2	13.0	15.4	13.2	8.3
District 1	34 701.1	581 488	16.8	93.3	1.8	1.7	1.9	2.7	4.2	90.5	1.3	6.5	18.7	11.9	12.8	15.2	13.0	8.1
District 2	1 550.6	594 207	383.2	84.4	10.6	1.1	2.3	3.6	6.1	80.3	1.8	7.6	19.8	10.1	15.3	16.3	13.2	7.6
District 3	162 846.9	535 568	3.3	95.2	0.4	1.2	0.7	3.5	6.2	91.7	1.0	6.4	19.9	8.4	10.8	14.7	13.4	9.2
NEVADA	284 448.0	1 998 257	7.0	78.4	7.5	2.1	6.4	9.7	19.7	65.2	3.8	7.3	18.3	9.0	15.3	16.1	13.5	9.5
District 1	597.2	936 104	1 567.5	72.5	10.5	1.5	7.5	12.7	26.6	55.1	4.4	7.6	18.2	9.8	16.2	15.7	12.8	9.1
District 2	283 850.8	1 062 153	3.7	83.5	4.9	2.6	5.5	7.0	13.6	74.1	3.3	7.0	18.4	8.3	14.6	16.4	14.0	9.9
NEW HAMPSHIRE	23 227.0	1 235 786	53.2	97.0	1.0	0.6	1.7	0.9	1.7	95.1	1.1	6.1	18.9	8.4	13.0	17.9	14.9	8.9
District 1	6 491.8	625 527	96.4	97.1	1.1	0.6	1.6	0.8	1.6	95.2	1.1	6.2	18.8	8.4	13.4	18.2	14.6	8.6
District 2	16 735.5	610 259	36.5	96.9	0.9	0.7	1.7	1.0	1.7	95.0	1.1	6.0	19.1	8.3	12.4	17.6	15.1	9.1
NEW JERSEY	19 211.0	8 414 350	438.0	74.4	14.4	0.6	6.3	6.9	13.3	66.0	2.5	6.7	18.1	8.0	14.1	17.1	13.8	9.0
District 1	831.8	609 847	733.2	74.7	18.2	0.6	3.2	5.2	8.5	70.5	1.9	6.7	19.9	8.4	14.3	17.0	13.5	8.2
District 2	4 951.9	652 730	131.8	76.8	15.7	0.9	2.9	5.9	10.3	71.3	2.1	6.3	18.8	8.3	13.0	16.7	13.6	9.2
District 3	2 502.5	647 095	258.6	87.5	9.0	0.5	3.2	1.5	3.6	84.1	1.5	5.9	18.2	6.5	11.8	16.6	14.3	10.0
District 4	1 810.4	674 193	372.4	81.7	13.2	0.5	2.6	3.9	7.8	76.4	1.8	7.1	18.3	7.3	13.0	16.6	13.0	8.6
District 5	2 787.3	638 669	229.1	90.8	1.8	0.4	6.7	1.6	4.4	86.7	1.3	6.8	19.3	5.8	11.2	18.2	15.4	9.8
District 6	521.7	632 202	1 211.8	73.6	13.0	0.6	10.1	5.2	10.6	66.3	2.4	6.6	16.7	10.2	15.8	17.0	13.4	8.5
District 7	708.0	642 715	907.8	75.7	12.3	0.4	9.4	4.3	9.3	68.9	2.1	6.9	17.6	6.6	14.0	18.0	14.3	8.9
District 8	270.6	640 015	2 365.2	66.0	14.9	0.6	5.9	16.5	25.8	53.4	3.8	7.1	17.9	8.8	14.8	16.2	13.2	8.5
District 9	239.6	647 240	2 701.3	73.7	7.9	0.6	12.1	9.4	18.9	60.7	3.5	5.9	15.3	7.9	16.1	16.8	13.8	9.4
District 10	142.2	597 384	4 201.0	27.3	63.2	0.8	3.6	9.3	15.8	18.1	4.0	7.5	19.8	10.4	15.7	15.6	12.1	8.3
District 11	1 651.2	665 932	403.3	88.8	3.0	0.3	7.0	2.4	6.8	83.0	1.5	7.1	18.0	6.1	13.2	18.5	15.3	9.9
District 12	2 645.5	709 867	268.3	85.3	5.8	0.4	8.4	1.7	4.1	81.5	1.5	6.5	18.9	7.5	13.5	18.1	15.3	9.1
District 13	148.0	656 461	4 435.5	60.3	14.2	0.9	6.9	23.8	47.2	32.2	5.8	6.7	16.8	11.1	19.4	15.9	11.5	7.8
NEW MEXICO	314 309.0	1 819 046	5.8	69.9	2.3	10.5	1.7	19.4	42.1	44.7	3.6	7.2	20.8	9.8	12.9	15.5	13.5	8.7
District 1	12 201.9	592 911	48.6	74.6	3.2	4.5	2.6	19.5	42.8	48.4	4.2	6.9	18.8	10.0	13.9	16.2	14.2	8.5
District 2	174 408.6	596 790	3.4	72.8	2.2	5.0	1.0	22.5	48.0	44.8	3.4	7.3	21.5	10.2	11.9	14.5	12.5	9.0
District 3	127 698.8	629 345	4.9	62.8	1.6	21.4	1.3	16.4	35.7	41.2	3.4	7.3	21.9	9.1	12.9	15.8	13.8	8.7
NEW YORK	122 283.0	18 976 457	155.2	70.0	17.0	0.9	6.4	9.1	15.1	62.0	3.1	6.5	18.2	9.3	14.5	16.2	13.5	8.9
District 1	1 653.1	642 032	388.4	90.5	4.9	0.7	2.9	2.9	7.6	84.3	1.7	6.8	18.8	8.1	13.3	17.4	14.3	9.2
District 2	491.0	612 961	1 248.4	79.3	12.1	0.7	3.0	7.7	15.4	69.8	2.7	7.2	19.5	7.7	14.3	17.9	13.2	9.1
District 3	400.9	588 611	1 468.2	90.9	2.9	0.3	4.4	3.0	6.9	85.6	1.5	6.5	17.8	6.4	11.8	17.5	15.0	9.7
District 4	217.7	611 953	2 811.0	69.8	19.8	0.6	5.7	7.0	13.3	61.5	2.7	6.6	18.7	8.4	12.8	16.2	14.0	10.2
District 5	393.3	615 731	1 565.6	74.1	3.9	0.4	19.8	4.5	9.2	66.8	2.5	6.1	16.1	6.8	13.1	16.7	14.9	10.2
District 6	97.0	664 941	6 855.1	20.2	56.5	2.1	13.2	16.6	18.1	11.5	8.1	7.2	20.1	10.0	15.0	16.2	12.6	8.7
District 7	57.7	684 573	11 864.4	55.4	10.1	1.1	18.4	21.3	39.1	32.8	6.0	6.4	15.5	10.2	18.6	16.3	12.2	8.4
District 8	36.9	618 987	16 774.7	77.7	7.2	0.6	11.4	6.4	11.5	69.3	3.2	5.3	11.9	9.5	20.5	16.5	13.8	8.8
District 9	94.8	652 370	6 881.5	73.0	5.2	0.6	14.7	10.2	17.0	62.5	3.6	6.2	15.8	8.6	15.3	15.4	13.7	9.1
District 10	43.0	621 305	14 449.0	22.6	66.2	0.9	3.2	11.4	17.1	15.8	4.0	7.9	21.6	10.5	15.5	15.0	11.8	8.0
District 11	27.8	586 819	21 108.6	20.6	71.1	0.8	4.5	7.2	10.8	16.5	3.9	7.7	20.6	10.6	15.7	15.5	12.7	8.2
District 12	41.4	620 677	14 992.2	40.9	14.2	1.4	17.7	32.0	48.6	21.1	6.0	7.3	18.9	11.6	18.4	15.4	11.7	7.5
District 13	168.6	670 006	3 973.9	78.8	7.4	0.5	10.5	6.1	11.1	70.4	3.2	6.4	17.2	8.5	15.2	16.3	13.9	9.2
District 14	32.1	608 017	18 941.3	80.3	5.3	0.5	10.5	7.3	12.2	71.0	3.7	4.3	8.1	9.0	24.3	16.8	13.8	10.2
District 15	24.9	607 324	24 390.5	28.1	39.4	1.7	3.6	33.7	50.5	12.2	6.1	6.5	18.3	12.1	17.3	15.6	11.7	7.9
District 16	40.0	647 437	16 185.9	24.8	39.1	1.9	2.8	38.3	62.9	2.4	6.6	9.4	24.9	11.2	15.4	14.7	10.4	7.1
District 17	55.7	627 566	11 266.9	31.6	46.2	1.3	4.5	22.1	35.9	16.9	5.5	7.8	20.2	10.2	15.4	15.1	11.6	8.1
District 18	243.3	620 213	2 549.2	73.3	9.3	0.5	12.2	8.5	15.3	62.6	3.6	6.3	15.9	7.8	14.3	16.3	13.9	9.7
District 19	2 796.0	626 776	224.2	85.9	8.2	0.6	3.3	4.1	9.0	79.5	2.0	6.8	18.8	7.9	12.5	18.3	14.8	9.1
District 20	3 336.0	635 820	190.6	82.5	9.9	0.7	4.9	4.4	9.6	75.7	2.3	7.3	20.4	7.4	12.3	16.7	14.6	9.5
District 21	2 814.8	573 294	203.7	87.1	9.6	0.6	2.8	1.8	3.4	84.1	1.8	5.9	17.3	10.4	13.1	15.5	14.0	8.5
District 22	16 858.9	619 548	36.7	95.7	2.8	0.6	1.1	1.0	2.1	93.5	1.1	5.8	18.7	7.7	12.5	17.0	15.0	9.8
District 23	15 503.0	563 385	36.3	95.1	3.4	0.6	1.0	1.1	2.1	92.9	1.2	5.6	18.6	9.6	11.6	15.4	13.8	9.7
District 24	32 092.7	582 371	18.1	94.2	3.3	1.4	0.9	1.3	2.3	92.3	1.0	5.9	19.0	11.0	13.2	16.3	13.2	8.7

1. Dry land or land partially or temporarily covered by water.   2. Hispanic persons may be of any race.

Table E. Congressional Districts 107th Congress — Population, Households, Group Quarters, and Education

	Population and population characteristics, 2000 (cont'd)			Households, 2000					Persons in correctional institutions, 2000	Persons in nursing homes, 2000	Persons in military quarters, 2000	Education, 1990	
	Percent (cont'd)					Percent						School enrollment	
	Age (cont'd)												
STATE District	65 to 74 years	75 years and over	Percent female	Number	Persons per house-hold	Female family house-holder[1]	One person					Public	Private
	19	20	21	22	23	24	25	26	27	28	29	30
MISSOURI—Cont'd												
District 4	7.6	6.5	50.1	252 056	2.52	8.9	24.5	7 039	6 098	5 429	123 315	14 345
District 5	6.8	6.3	52.0	238 137	2.38	15.3	32.8	1 602	3 860	0	112 021	24 521
District 6	6.7	6.6	50.8	246 761	2.49	9.3	25.7	8 042	5 848	0	127 126	15 818
District 7	7.6	6.8	51.2	275 745	2.44	9.3	26.0	1 962	5 766	0	121 800	17 539
District 8	8.2	7.4	51.2	240 840	2.46	10.8	26.2	4 495	7 404	0	127 929	9 638
District 9	6.1	5.6	50.8	258 685	2.58	9.3	23.8	8 215	5 845	0	136 942	21 900
MONTANA	6.9	6.5	50.2	358 667	2.45	8.9	27.4	4 124	6 470	404	197 360	18 399
At Large	6.9	6.5	50.2	358 667	2.45	8.9	27.4	4 124	6 470	404	197 360	18 399
NEBRASKA	6.8	6.8	50.7	666 184	2.49	9.1	27.6	6 060	16 195	590	368 874	64 535
District 1	6.7	7.0	50.4	225 518	2.48	8.2	27.5	3 357	5 439	0	126 322	21 364
District 2	5.4	4.7	50.9	228 650	2.54	11.6	27.6	1 847	3 676	590	120 640	31 272
District 3	8.3	8.9	50.8	212 016	2.46	7.3	27.6	856	7 080	0	121 912	11 899
NEVADA	6.6	4.4	49.1	751 165	2.62	11.1	24.9	15 940	4 895	1 312	256 041	24 370
District 1	6.3	4.2	48.8	346 095	2.67	12.6	26.2	5 037	2 046	0	122 181	12 717
District 2	6.9	4.5	49.2	405 070	2.57	9.8	23.7	10 903	2 849	1 312	133 860	11 653
NEW HAMPSHIRE	6.3	5.6	50.8	474 606	2.53	9.1	24.4	3 468	9 316	95	219 482	57 283
District 1	6.2	5.5	51.0	241 411	2.53	9.2	24.6	1 422	4 341	89	108 795	27 677
District 2	6.5	5.8	50.7	233 195	2.53	8.9	24.3	2 046	4 975	6	110 687	29 606
NEW JERSEY	6.8	6.4	51.5	3 064 645	2.68	12.6	24.5	47 941	51 493	3 291	1 453 475	413 927
District 1	6.3	5.7	51.7	223 274	2.68	15.2	25.1	3 610	3 633	0	121 179	27 161
District 2	7.4	6.8	51.1	240 615	2.60	14.0	25.7	10 556	4 555	355	118 911	20 237
District 3	8.7	8.0	51.4	243 308	2.60	9.9	23.4	5 637	4 243	1 229	118 014	25 163
District 4	7.9	8.3	51.8	251 121	2.62	11.6	25.9	5 541	5 737	199	105 910	31 063
District 5	7.0	6.4	51.4	226 297	2.77	8.2	19.4	267	5 941	0	114 256	32 717
District 6	6.3	5.6	51.2	232 127	2.65	11.7	25.8	945	3 505	23	119 669	29 649
District 7	6.9	6.7	51.4	230 184	2.75	10.4	21.5	2 640	3 543	0	105 574	31 184
District 8	6.6	6.8	52.0	223 271	2.81	14.8	24.2	1 921	3 653	0	107 175	32 572
District 9	7.5	7.4	51.8	250 958	2.55	11.7	28.6	980	1 838	0	87 249	37 900
District 10	5.7	5.0	53.1	211 052	2.76	25.8	28.3	4 594	3 038	0	118 547	33 831
District 11	6.3	5.5	51.1	240 063	2.72	7.8	21.2	1 669	4 464	10	110 964	36 420
District 12	6.4	5.8	51.2	253 157	2.69	7.5	21.6	5 755	3 522	1 465	115 923	40 755
District 13	5.7	5.0	50.3	239 218	2.69	17.6	28.1	3 826	3 821	10	110 104	35 325
NEW MEXICO	6.5	5.2	50.8	677 971	2.63	13.2	25.4	10 940	6 810	1 827	400 077	35 912
District 1	6.1	5.4	51.0	233 136	2.50	12.8	27.9	2 444	1 825	431	124 601	15 151
District 2	7.4	5.6	50.6	216 085	2.69	13.2	23.6	6 297	2 729	834	141 133	8 293
District 3	5.9	4.7	50.9	228 750	2.71	13.7	24.5	2 199	2 256	562	134 343	12 468
NEW YORK	6.7	6.2	51.8	7 056 860	2.61	14.7	28.1	108 088	123 852	8 598	3 538 249	1 117 969
District 1	6.3	5.8	50.9	219 884	2.84	10.0	20.1	1 471	3 968	21	133 496	23 533
District 2	6.3	4.7	51.2	193 187	3.13	12.5	16.9	0	3 059	7	121 559	27 597
District 3	8.4	6.9	51.6	202 955	2.87	9.3	18.2	0	2 476	4	100 484	39 607
District 4	7.4	7.0	52.1	197 315	3.05	13.2	19.0	1 423	2 642	0	102 986	43 339
District 5	8.2	7.8	52.0	224 804	2.69	9.7	23.0	0	4 915	11	99 371	39 835
District 6	5.7	4.5	53.1	203 282	3.22	24.3	19.0	0	4 034	0	126 323	37 043
District 7	6.4	6.0	50.8	244 921	2.77	15.9	27.1	0	3 647	0	86 113	39 436
District 8	6.9	6.7	50.7	293 017	2.03	7.7	47.1	3 938	2 383	0	65 486	59 934
District 9	7.9	8.0	51.9	249 227	2.59	11.5	30.1	467	3 064	0	80 709	44 746
District 10	5.4	4.2	54.5	220 120	2.75	29.2	28.5	695	2 710	0	133 230	38 274
District 11	5.2	3.8	54.9	207 586	2.79	29.1	26.8	141	2 198	0	143 756	41 960
District 12	5.3	3.9	51.1	211 800	2.89	22.3	26.2	0	1 515	0	138 501	27 828
District 13	6.9	6.4	51.8	246 735	2.67	12.9	26.4	944	4 081	230	95 709	45 244
District 14	7.0	6.6	53.2	327 513	1.81	6.0	51.3	620	2 323	0	44 272	53 840
District 15	5.6	4.9	52.2	221 894	2.57	27.8	34.7	13 642	3 176	0	122 630	42 579
District 16	4.2	2.8	53.5	210 892	3.01	37.5	23.7	843	1 786	0	157 515	26 041
District 17	5.8	5.8	54.4	228 250	2.67	27.0	29.5	121	8 271	0	114 575	42 483
District 18	7.9	8.0	52.5	234 476	2.59	11.2	27.7	0	5 708	0	85 083	49 269
District 19	6.3	5.4	50.4	219 247	2.72	9.3	22.7	8 991	4 293	3 695	110 589	39 430
District 20	6.4	5.3	50.8	215 170	2.87	10.1	21.2	3 471	3 892	0	111 535	45 346
District 21	7.3	8.0	52.0	233 665	2.34	12.5	32.1	1 417	6 486	0	110 479	38 735
District 22	7.2	6.3	50.0	236 726	2.51	9.4	25.0	11 883	4 431	0	120 436	23 835
District 23	7.7	8.1	50.8	216 196	2.46	10.7	27.7	7 451	5 512	13	133 239	20 197
District 24	6.7	5.9	49.1	214 911	2.52	10.4	25.6	15 723	3 976	4 616	138 790	17 759

1. No spouse present.

STATE District	Education, 1990 (cont'd) Attainment[1] (percent)		Money income, 1989			Percent below poverty level, 1989		Housing units, 1990					
				Households		Persons	Families		Occupied units				
										Owner-occupied			
												Owner cost as a percent of income	
	High school graduate or more	Bachelor's degree or more	Per capita[2]	Median	Percent with $100,000 or more	Total	Total	Total	Total	Percent	Median value[3] (dollars)	With a mortgage	Without a mortgage
	31	32	33	34	35	36	37	38	39	40	41	42	43
MISSOURI—Cont'd													
District 4	72.0	12.7	10 984	23 064	1.5	13.7	10.3	260 130	211 458	72.8	49 600	19.9	12.5
District 5	78.8	20.0	13 650	26 968	2.6	13.9	10.4	257 319	230 604	60.0	56 700	18.1	12.4
District 6	78.4	16.0	12 641	27 165	2.2	11.4	8.7	239 346	216 556	70.8	55 300	17.7	12.3
District 7	72.9	14.6	11 029	21 712	1.9	15.2	11.1	249 377	222 201	70.7	48 400	18.2	12.0
District 8	59.0	9.5	9 300	18 207	1.2	22.4	18.1	243 493	216 430	71.3	37 900	18.5	12.9
District 9	73.6	16.6	11 741	26 055	1.9	12.9	9.2	233 525	208 153	72.3	55 400	18.3	12.4
MONTANA	81.0	19.8	11 213	22 988	1.7	16.1	12.0	361 155	306 163	67.3	56 600	20.2	12.5
At Large	81.0	19.8	11 213	22 988	1.7	16.1	12.0	361 155	306 163	67.3	56 600	20.2	12.5
NEBRASKA	81.8	18.9	12 452	26 016	2.2	11.1	8.0	660 621	602 363	66.5	50 400	19.4	12.6
District 1	81.4	18.5	12 088	25 763	1.7	10.9	7.3	216 569	200 847	66.9	50 100	18.5	12.4
District 2	85.6	24.8	14 322	30 889	3.5	9.5	7.2	211 302	197 804	62.8	61 300	20.7	12.6
District 3	78.5	13.8	10 942	22 344	1.5	13.0	9.5	232 750	203 712	69.6	38 300	17.7	12.7
NEVADA	78.8	15.3	15 214	31 011	3.8	10.2	7.3	518 858	466 297	54.8	95 700	22.4	11.9
District 1	75.9	13.3	14 837	29 611	3.5	11.4	8.2	257 734	236 070	50.1	89 300	22.1	11.8
District 2	81.7	17.3	15 592	32 413	4.0	8.9	6.4	261 124	230 227	59.6	104 100	22.6	11.9
NEW HAMPSHIRE	82.2	24.4	15 959	36 329	4.5	6.4	4.4	503 904	411 186	68.2	129 400	24.4	14.7
District 1	82.4	23.8	16 044	36 511	4.2	6.3	4.3	256 621	206 495	66.3	132 500	24.8	14.6
District 2	81.9	24.9	15 874	36 145	4.8	6.5	4.4	247 283	204 691	70.1	125 800	24.0	14.9
NEW JERSEY	76.7	24.9	18 714	40 927	8.8	7.6	5.6	3 075 310	2 794 711	64.9	162 300	23.4	15.1
District 1	74.2	16.9	14 502	35 250	3.3	9.9	7.8	224 858	211 962	69.1	94 100	22.3	14.9
District 2	71.3	14.9	14 732	32 410	3.7	9.9	7.3	293 580	218 043	69.0	93 900	22.1	14.9
District 3	80.5	24.1	18 138	41 257	7.5	4.3	3.1	258 262	212 334	82.3	129 200	23.3	15.2
District 4	75.9	18.7	16 107	36 888	4.4	6.9	5.0	241 499	220 574	73.6	130 500	24.3	15.8
District 5	85.4	32.6	23 942	53 433	16.3	3.2	2.2	219 632	206 078	80.8	214 400	24.3	15.0
District 6	79.5	24.9	18 135	42 309	7.4	6.4	4.3	233 776	215 093	63.1	160 600	23.7	15.5
District 7	82.7	32.4	23 253	50 996	13.9	3.4	2.2	222 996	215 596	74.6	186 900	23.1	14.7
District 8	72.4	24.5	18 527	39 944	9.5	8.7	6.4	221 064	212 344	57.2	193 600	23.4	15.1
District 9	74.9	24.7	20 012	40 816	8.1	6.0	4.4	250 771	234 586	54.6	195 700	23.3	15.8
District 10	65.7	14.6	12 833	28 849	3.2	17.1	14.1	229 399	212 001	35.7	137 600	24.3	16.0
District 11	87.3	37.4	25 454	57 219	18.0	2.6	1.7	219 540	209 150	76.4	215 600	23.3	14.0
District 12	87.5	39.7	24 615	54 630	16.9	2.9	1.7	222 475	209 601	78.3	205 700	23.9	14.3
District 13	58.0	15.9	13 028	28 721	3.3	17.1	14.4	237 458	217 349	31.0	143 900	24.5	15.6
NEW MEXICO	75.1	20.4	11 246	24 087	2.5	20.6	16.5	632 058	542 709	67.4	70 100	21.6	12.5
District 1	81.6	26.0	13 373	27 074	3.3	14.8	11.2	211 995	194 425	61.9	84 600	22.4	12.4
District 2	69.5	15.0	9 672	21 456	1.6	23.5	18.9	212 793	175 354	69.4	52 700	20.2	12.4
District 3	73.7	19.7	10 689	23 610	2.4	23.6	19.3	207 270	172 930	71.7	68 600	21.6	12.7
NEW YORK	74.8	23.1	16 501	32 965	6.8	13.0	10.0	7 226 891	6 639 322	52.2	131 600	21.5	14.4
District 1	82.3	22.8	17 614	45 464	8.7	5.2	3.7	239 124	192 807	79.1	159 000	24.5	17.0
District 2	80.2	18.9	17 515	50 076	10.1	4.9	3.4	187 197	178 664	79.6	159 600	23.8	16.6
District 3	86.4	29.9	23 702	56 060	17.3	3.0	2.0	201 470	195 063	83.8	205 300	22.9	15.7
District 4	81.3	26.2	20 349	50 887	13.3	4.5	3.1	197 348	191 210	78.1	197 800	23.4	16.4
District 5	83.9	34.8	24 296	50 103	16.2	4.8	3.3	221 098	212 262	66.6	256 900	22.4	14.8
District 6	69.0	14.6	13 150	36 223	4.5	11.4	8.9	187 044	180 632	54.5	159 600	21.7	14.3
District 7	67.9	18.0	14 905	30 324	3.3	12.2	9.3	245 730	235 147	32.5	206 100	23.1	14.5
District 8	78.6	42.1	26 168	32 784	11.8	16.8	13.3	305 736	282 170	22.9	223 000	25.7	15.8
District 9	75.2	24.2	17 918	34 758	6.1	9.4	6.9	251 674	238 905	42.9	212 300	21.1	13.6
District 10	61.9	16.8	11 479	23 164	3.7	28.3	24.6	217 709	202 579	23.6	167 900	22.0	15.4
District 11	67.0	17.5	11 706	26 148	3.3	21.7	19.1	208 896	199 404	18.5	183 900	20.9	13.8
District 12	47.4	10.5	8 534	20 444	1.4	30.4	28.3	193 414	184 010	15.3	176 300	25.2	14.8
District 13	74.2	19.3	17 143	38 437	7.0	9.0	7.2	228 476	215 118	52.4	190 700	21.6	13.9
District 14	84.9	51.4	41 151	42 184	18.3	9.4	5.6	351 475	316 747	25.8	235 700	22.0	13.1
District 15	56.9	17.6	10 367	19 238	2.3	33.0	29.8	229 718	214 632	6.4	186 600	17.4	15.7
District 16	47.0	6.1	7 102	15 060	0.8	41.8	39.5	195 891	188 194	8.2	144 300	24.4	13.0
District 17	66.6	17.1	13 155	27 227	3.2	18.3	15.8	226 051	217 580	21.8	176 400	22.8	14.9
District 18	80.3	33.4	24 392	43 754	14.3	6.1	4.2	232 883	222 962	53.7	288 500	22.2	15.2
District 19	83.4	32.4	22 458	50 239	14.4	4.8	3.1	215 634	199 080	71.0	199 200	23.2	14.6
District 20	81.7	29.6	19 680	47 107	12.7	7.1	4.4	211 857	192 825	71.8	193 600	23.1	15.4
District 21	79.3	24.2	15 304	31 489	3.7	9.8	6.5	244 635	228 409	59.1	99 200	20.1	13.2
District 22	79.0	20.4	14 646	33 306	3.6	7.4	5.2	258 294	210 874	73.6	99 600	20.9	13.6
District 23	75.4	15.9	11 792	26 155	1.9	11.9	8.4	243 283	211 591	70.0	67 900	19.4	13.9
District 24	73.8	13.7	11 060	25 687	1.5	13.6	10.0	261 036	202 380	68.3	56 700	18.3	13.6

1. Persons 25 years old and older.   2. Based on the population enumerated as of April 1, 1990.   3. Specified owner-occupied units.

STATE District	Housing units, 1990 (cont'd) Occupied units (cont'd) Renter-occupied			Civilian labor force, 1990	Unemployment		Civilian employment, 1990[4]	Percent		Disability, 1990
	Median rent[1] (dollars)	Rent as a percent of income	Substandard units[2] (percent)	Total	Total	Rate[3]	Total	Professional, managerial, and technical	Precision production, craft, and repair	Work disabled persons[5] (percent)
	44	45	46	47	48	49	50	51	52	53
MISSOURI—Cont'd										
District 4	319	24.4	3.1	260 703	16 491	6.3	244 212	22.7	13.3	9.7
District 5	398	25.6	2.9	296 982	20 157	6.8	276 825	29.2	9.6	8.5
District 6	362	23.4	2.2	283 964	14 874	5.2	269 090	25.6	11.5	7.6
District 7	315	24.8	2.9	274 984	15 482	5.6	259 502	23.2	11.9	9.7
District 8	268	27.2	4.3	244 026	20 097	8.2	223 929	20.5	12.9	12.7
District 9	338	25.2	2.9	282 337	15 739	5.6	266 598	26.3	12.6	7.6
MONTANA	311	25.0	3.2	376 940	26 217	7.0	350 723	26.9	10.4	9.7
At Large	311	25.0	3.2	376 940	26 217	7.0	350 723	26.9	10.4	9.7
NEBRASKA	348	23.7	1.9	802 139	29 326	3.7	772 813	26.2	10.3	7.1
District 1	338	23.8	1.8	274 624	9 385	3.4	265 239	25.7	11.1	6.8
District 2	405	24.5	2.1	272 303	11 290	4.1	261 013	32.1	8.9	7.1
District 3	284	22.4	2.0	255 212	8 651	3.4	246 561	20.5	10.8	7.6
NEVADA	509	26.8	6.4	647 520	40 083	6.2	607 437	24.8	11.4	8.3
District 1	505	27.7	7.3	324 969	23 003	7.1	301 966	22.9	10.6	9.0
District 2	515	25.6	5.5	322 551	17 080	5.3	305 471	26.7	12.1	7.6
NEW HAMPSHIRE	549	26.4	2.1	612 345	38 108	6.2	574 237	32.6	12.5	7.3
District 1	555	26.3	1.9	307 846	19 587	6.4	288 259	32.1	12.7	7.4
District 2	541	26.5	2.3	304 499	18 521	6.1	285 978	33.1	12.4	7.1
NEW JERSEY	592	26.3	4.1	4 104 673	235 975	5.7	3 868 698	34.0	10.0	6.2
District 1	514	27.1	3.6	301 618	18 014	6.0	283 604	30.2	12.0	7.7
District 2	525	27.5	3.5	298 490	18 467	6.2	280 023	25.9	12.0	7.9
District 3	651	27.8	1.6	295 827	13 571	4.6	282 256	35.5	10.6	6.4
District 4	583	27.6	2.7	293 829	16 755	5.7	277 074	31.1	11.2	7.0
District 5	717	27.5	1.4	321 606	12 413	3.9	309 193	39.5	10.4	4.8
District 6	645	26.5	3.4	330 769	18 000	5.4	312 769	33.9	10.3	6.1
District 7	699	25.4	2.2	335 075	13 983	4.2	321 092	40.0	9.0	4.9
District 8	595	26.4	5.8	321 203	20 653	6.4	300 550	32.0	9.8	6.1
District 9	640	25.1	4.1	331 373	18 679	5.6	312 694	33.9	9.5	5.4
District 10	520	26.8	9.9	302 157	32 441	10.7	269 716	23.9	8.9	8.6
District 11	730	25.0	1.7	341 973	11 598	3.4	330 375	42.1	8.9	4.4
District 12	696	25.4	1.2	323 319	11 416	3.5	311 903	46.2	7.8	4.2
District 13	505	25.5	11.7	307 434	29 985	9.8	277 449	23.4	10.2	7.2
NEW MEXICO	372	26.5	8.8	684 160	54 888	8.0	629 272	31.6	12.0	8.8
District 1	400	27.4	5.4	254 244	17 144	6.7	237 100	35.7	10.2	8.5
District 2	325	26.1	8.3	208 524	18 671	9.0	189 853	26.4	13.8	9.4
District 3	372	25.5	13.2	221 392	19 073	8.6	202 319	31.8	12.5	8.6
NEW YORK	486	26.3	6.8	8 989 621	618 903	6.9	8 370 718	33.5	9.4	7.4
District 1	782	31.2	2.0	296 385	14 163	4.8	282 222	33.2	12.2	6.1
District 2	817	30.2	3.5	313 560	15 807	5.0	297 753	28.7	12.7	6.6
District 3	811	27.8	1.8	315 140	12 489	4.0	302 651	37.7	9.1	5.1
District 4	705	27.7	3.9	307 030	13 667	4.5	293 363	35.0	9.0	5.3
District 5	660	25.2	5.2	310 388	14 322	4.6	296 066	41.8	8.0	4.6
District 6	565	26.1	12.5	293 135	25 862	8.8	267 273	25.2	8.8	7.5
District 7	520	24.8	10.5	299 744	22 708	7.6	277 036	27.4	9.9	6.7
District 8	544	24.3	8.7	325 148	22 614	7.0	302 534	52.5	4.4	6.9
District 9	534	24.7	5.7	284 285	17 787	6.3	266 498	36.7	8.6	6.6
District 10	441	27.2	14.8	251 627	30 858	12.3	220 769	30.6	6.6	9.8
District 11	482	25.7	19.8	284 039	31 195	11.0	252 844	28.4	7.0	7.4
District 12	454	28.9	26.3	257 574	29 928	11.6	227 646	17.2	9.4	9.3
District 13	553	25.5	4.4	285 756	18 640	6.5	267 116	31.6	9.8	6.8
District 14	678	22.6	5.8	371 386	19 360	5.2	352 026	55.8	3.9	5.3
District 15	402	26.3	17.8	244 974	33 674	13.7	211 300	29.5	6.0	10.6
District 16	398	29.8	24.4	210 473	34 894	16.6	175 579	15.8	8.7	13.2
District 17	483	25.1	13.3	276 890	25 718	9.3	251 172	28.5	8.4	8.9
District 18	594	24.6	6.4	312 392	15 333	4.9	297 059	40.3	8.0	5.0
District 19	653	26.6	2.1	306 422	12 426	4.1	293 996	41.4	9.9	5.5
District 20	659	27.6	3.8	301 878	13 084	4.3	288 794	38.6	9.9	6.0
District 21	453	25.2	1.7	301 022	15 194	5.0	285 828	34.7	8.5	7.4
District 22	465	26.0	2.0	291 866	15 815	5.4	276 051	31.6	11.9	7.5
District 23	366	27.0	2.1	270 258	17 453	6.5	252 805	27.5	12.0	9.1
District 24	368	27.2	2.8	257 903	22 901	8.9	235 002	25.3	12.5	8.8

1. Specified renter-occupied units. 2. Overcrowded or lacking complete plumbing facilities. 3. Percent of total civilian labor force. 4. Persons 16 years old and older. 5. Persons 16 to 64 years of age.

Table E. Congressional Districts 107th Congress — **Land Area and Population**

STATE District	Land area, 2000[1] (sq km)	Total persons	Per square kilometer	White	Black	Am. Indian, Alaska Native	Asian and Pacific Islander	Other race	Hispanic[2]	Non-Hispanic White	2 or more races	Under 5 years	5 to 17 years	18 to 24 years	25 to 34 years	35 to 44 years	45 to 54 years	55 to 64 years
	1	2	3	4	5	6	7	8	9	10	11	12	13	14	15	16	17	18
NEW YORK—Cont'd																		
District 25	4 760.8	569 864	119.7	88.7	8.6	1.4	2.1	1.2	2.1	86.2	1.8	6.4	19.3	9.8	12.6	16.1	13.6	8.5
District 26	7 984.2	589 237	73.8	87.5	7.5	0.8	3.1	3.3	6.6	82.6	2.1	5.7	17.6	12.3	12.2	15.7	13.6	9.0
District 27	9 306.6	610 516	65.6	94.4	3.4	0.6	1.7	0.9	1.9	92.4	1.1	5.8	19.1	8.8	11.8	16.8	14.6	9.2
District 28	714.4	592 533	829.4	77.3	17.2	0.7	3.3	3.8	6.1	73.4	2.1	6.5	19.0	9.5	13.6	15.8	13.8	8.4
District 29	3 059.7	572 581	187.1	90.2	6.6	1.2	1.3	2.3	4.0	87.2	1.5	6.0	18.4	9.1	12.8	16.3	13.8	8.8
District 30	1 876.9	563 256	300.1	79.2	18.9	1.0	1.0	1.2	2.2	77.2	1.2	6.3	18.7	8.3	12.6	16.0	13.4	9.2
District 31	17 060.0	575 753	33.7	95.1	3.1	1.1	0.9	1.1	2.1	93.0	1.1	5.9	19.2	9.5	11.6	15.4	14.0	9.4
NORTH CAROLINA	126 161.0	8 049 313	63.8	73.1	22.1	1.6	1.8	2.8	4.7	70.2	1.3	6.7	17.7	10.0	15.1	16.0	13.5	9.0
District 1	18 881.3	587 830	31.1	46.5	50.9	1.0	0.6	1.9	3.0	44.9	0.8	6.6	19.3	8.7	12.8	15.2	13.8	9.5
District 2	9 790.0	730 266	74.6	67.4	27.5	0.9	1.4	4.2	6.5	64.1	1.3	7.2	18.0	10.5	16.5	16.8	13.0	8.0
District 3	15 952.7	615 614	38.6	76.4	20.1	0.9	1.7	2.6	4.2	73.6	1.6	6.8	17.2	14.3	13.8	15.1	12.4	8.8
District 4	4 975.4	765 876	153.9	73.2	20.5	0.7	4.2	3.1	5.3	69.5	1.6	6.7	17.1	11.6	17.5	17.4	13.8	7.3
District 5	8 995.6	637 158	70.8	82.0	14.7	0.6	1.0	2.8	4.7	79.2	1.0	6.3	16.9	8.5	14.2	16.0	14.2	9.8
District 6	7 955.5	689 529	86.7	85.0	11.3	0.8	1.6	2.5	4.4	82.2	1.1	6.4	17.2	8.7	14.6	16.2	14.0	9.5
District 7	16 574.5	690 054	41.6	66.6	23.5	7.4	1.0	2.9	4.4	64.1	1.3	6.7	18.1	9.7	14.2	15.4	13.7	9.8
District 8	10 214.4	661 112	64.7	66.4	27.1	3.2	1.8	3.3	5.9	62.6	1.7	7.8	19.5	10.9	15.8	15.8	12.2	8.0
District 9	2 960.4	693 042	234.1	80.8	15.2	0.6	2.6	2.1	4.1	77.7	1.2	6.9	17.7	7.9	16.7	17.2	14.2	8.6
District 10	10 922.2	655 413	60.0	90.3	6.3	0.5	1.7	2.1	4.0	87.6	0.9	6.2	17.1	9.4	14.2	15.8	14.1	10.2
District 11	16 743.8	656 619	39.2	92.0	5.1	2.0	0.7	1.3	2.6	89.7	1.0	5.6	15.9	8.1	12.5	14.6	14.4	11.2
District 12	2 194.7	666 800	303.8	48.7	45.3	0.8	2.8	4.2	6.8	45.0	1.6	7.3	18.5	11.7	16.9	15.9	12.1	7.5
NORTH DAKOTA	178 647.0	642 200	3.6	93.4	0.8	5.5	0.9	0.6	1.2	91.7	1.2	6.1	18.9	11.4	12.0	15.3	13.3	8.3
At Large	178 646.8	642 200	3.6	93.4	0.8	5.5	0.9	0.6	1.2	91.7	1.2	6.1	18.9	11.4	12.0	15.3	13.3	8.3
OHIO	106 056.0	11 353 140	107.0	86.1	12.1	0.7	1.5	1.1	1.9	84.0	1.4	6.6	18.8	9.3	13.4	15.9	13.8	8.9
District 1	457.9	542 618	1 185.0	63.6	34.9	0.7	1.6	0.8	1.1	62.1	1.5	6.9	19.2	10.9	14.2	15.4	12.3	7.9
District 2	5 043.8	634 061	125.7	95.3	2.9	0.6	1.6	0.5	1.0	93.8	0.9	7.0	19.7	7.6	13.6	17.1	14.4	8.7
District 3	1 116.9	556 039	497.8	77.7	20.7	0.7	1.8	0.8	1.3	75.7	1.5	6.6	18.0	9.7	13.6	15.4	13.7	9.2
District 4	11 737.9	591 795	50.4	93.4	5.7	0.6	0.7	0.7	1.2	91.8	1.1	6.5	19.0	9.2	12.7	15.6	13.9	9.4
District 5	13 468.6	589 716	43.8	95.3	2.7	0.6	0.5	2.0	3.7	92.6	1.2	6.5	19.7	8.6	12.1	15.9	14.3	9.3
District 6	16 499.9	620 901	37.6	96.6	2.6	0.9	0.7	0.3	0.7	95.1	1.1	6.4	18.2	11.0	13.2	15.5	13.4	9.4
District 7	8 993.5	620 156	69.0	93.2	5.8	0.8	1.2	0.5	1.0	91.4	1.3	6.6	19.0	9.6	12.9	16.0	14.3	9.4
District 8	7 065.0	625 445	88.5	94.9	3.7	0.6	1.4	0.6	1.1	93.4	1.0	6.9	19.6	10.0	12.9	16.1	13.7	8.8
District 9	2 845.2	569 053	200.0	82.7	14.6	0.8	1.5	2.6	4.5	79.0	2.0	6.7	19.2	11.1	13.5	15.2	13.4	8.2
District 10	403.2	573 874	1 423.3	89.7	5.7	0.7	2.3	3.9	6.3	85.2	2.1	6.5	17.5	7.9	14.8	16.4	13.5	8.6
District 11	270.2	532 337	1 970.2	32.7	65.7	0.7	1.8	1.0	1.5	31.1	1.6	7.2	20.1	9.0	13.4	14.9	12.6	8.3
District 12	2 647.3	661 049	249.7	73.3	24.2	0.8	2.6	1.5	1.8	71.0	2.2	7.6	19.7	9.3	15.0	16.9	13.9	8.0
District 13	4 369.7	645 068	147.6	92.8	5.3	0.6	0.9	1.8	3.4	89.9	1.4	6.9	19.9	7.7	12.3	17.1	14.8	9.4
District 14	1 292.6	586 402	453.7	85.7	13.0	0.7	1.7	0.6	0.9	84.0	1.4	6.5	18.0	10.0	13.3	15.7	14.1	8.6
District 15	2 262.1	649 980	287.3	87.4	8.5	0.8	3.8	1.5	2.3	84.8	1.8	6.8	16.4	13.1	18.1	16.2	12.4	7.2
District 16	5 527.5	605 661	109.6	94.0	5.5	0.6	0.7	0.4	0.9	92.3	1.2	6.8	19.3	9.2	12.2	15.3	13.9	9.3
District 17	3 483.5	563 164	161.7	87.8	11.3	0.6	0.6	0.9	1.9	85.8	1.2	6.0	17.9	8.0	12.0	15.2	14.6	9.6
District 18	15 723.6	586 247	37.3	96.6	3.1	0.7	0.4	0.3	0.6	95.3	1.0	6.2	18.5	8.3	12.2	15.6	14.1	9.9
District 19	2 847.4	599 574	210.6	94.7	3.3	0.4	1.8	0.8	1.5	92.9	1.0	5.8	17.9	6.9	12.0	16.2	14.7	9.8
OKLAHOMA	177 847.0	3 450 654	19.4	80.3	8.3	11.4	1.8	3.0	5.2	74.1	4.5	6.8	19.0	10.3	13.1	15.2	13.1	9.2
District 1	1 745.2	586 853	336.3	79.3	11.4	4.5	2.1	3.4	5.8	72.8	4.4	7.3	19.0	9.9	14.6	15.8	13.5	8.2
District 2	30 291.4	599 445	19.8	77.1	4.9	23.2	0.6	1.2	2.2	69.8	6.8	6.8	19.9	8.7	11.8	14.8	13.4	10.5
District 3	46 520.1	565 932	12.2	82.9	4.3	15.3	1.0	1.4	2.6	77.4	4.7	6.4	18.5	11.2	12.0	14.2	12.8	9.9
District 4	20 930.0	572 589	27.4	83.1	8.3	7.1	2.7	3.1	5.7	77.1	4.0	6.9	19.0	12.0	13.7	15.6	12.7	8.6
District 5	12 074.8	593 898	49.2	83.3	7.2	6.6	3.0	3.8	6.7	77.2	3.7	6.9	18.5	10.1	13.6	15.7	13.7	8.7
District 6	66 285.3	531 937	8.0	75.9	13.8	6.9	1.8	5.2	8.4	70.1	3.4	6.8	19.1	10.2	12.9	15.0	12.6	9.1
OREGON	248 631.0	3 421 399	13.8	89.3	2.1	2.5	4.2	5.2	8.0	83.5	3.1	6.5	18.2	9.6	13.8	15.4	14.8	8.9
District 1	7 662.7	743 195	97.0	88.0	1.6	1.6	6.6	5.4	8.9	81.7	2.9	6.9	18.2	9.4	16.1	16.6	14.8	7.9
District 2	182 830.5	701 847	3.8	91.6	0.7	3.3	1.5	5.5	8.6	86.2	2.5	6.3	19.1	8.3	11.5	14.6	14.9	10.1
District 3	2 108.8	650 092	308.3	82.7	6.6	2.3	7.3	5.5	7.7	76.6	4.1	6.8	17.0	10.0	16.5	16.3	14.6	7.7
District 4	41 649.3	633 335	15.2	94.8	0.9	3.0	2.3	2.3	4.2	89.9	3.0	5.7	17.7	9.8	11.8	14.4	15.3	10.0
District 5	14 379.2	692 930	48.2	89.7	1.1	2.4	3.1	6.9	10.4	83.4	2.9	6.7	19.0	10.6	12.7	15.0	14.6	8.9
PENNSYLVANIA	116 074.0	12 281 054	105.8	86.3	10.5	0.4	2.1	1.9	3.2	84.1	1.2	5.9	17.9	8.9	12.7	15.9	13.9	9.2
District 1	135.7	515 560	3 799.3	32.2	56.6	0.8	4.8	8.0	11.5	28.0	2.2	7.0	20.8	11.0	14.2	14.6	11.9	8.1
District 2	117.6	532 455	4 527.7	30.3	65.7	0.8	3.9	1.5	2.0	28.7	1.9	5.9	17.3	13.1	15.2	14.1	12.1	8.3
District 3	146.9	572 488	3 897.1	74.2	14.4	0.6	5.8	7.5	10.8	68.9	2.4	6.6	18.6	8.9	14.7	15.0	12.2	8.2
District 4	3 426.1	582 777	170.1	95.7	3.8	0.3	0.6	0.3	0.6	94.6	0.8	5.8	17.9	6.8	11.2	16.7	14.6	9.6
District 5	27 140.2	582 083	21.4	96.6	1.8	0.4	1.5	0.5	1.0	95.4	0.7	5.3	16.9	13.6	12.2	14.7	13.1	9.4
District 6	4 924.2	600 437	121.9	91.8	4.0	0.4	1.1	4.1	6.6	88.4	1.2	5.8	17.7	8.2	12.8	15.9	13.8	9.2
District 7	786.0	587 281	747.2	89.6	6.2	0.3	4.3	0.7	1.3	88.0	1.1	6.0	17.8	8.2	12.7	16.6	14.0	9.0

1. Dry land or land partially or temporarily covered by water.   2. Hispanic persons may be of any race.

STATE District	Population and population characteristics, 2000 (cont'd) Percent (cont'd) Age (cont'd) 65 to 74 years	75 years and over	Percent female	Households, 2000 Number	Persons per house-hold	Percent Female family house-holder[1]	One person	Persons in correctional institutions, 2000	Persons in nursing homes, 2000	Persons in military quarters, 2000	Education, 1990 School enrollment Public	Private
	19	20	21	22	23	24	25	26	27	28	29	30
NEW YORK—Cont'd												
District 25	7.0	6.7	52.0	223 335	2.47	12.4	28.6	900	3 583	0	122 707	36 605
District 26	7.0	6.7	50.9	224 952	2.45	11.4	29.4	6 268	4 858	1	127 068	35 531
District 27	7.0	6.8	50.7	226 542	2.57	9.3	24.0	8 917	5 647	0	129 008	23 859
District 28	6.4	7.0	52.0	234 324	2.43	14.3	30.2	1 370	5 823	0	108 608	41 717
District 29	7.5	7.3	51.8	229 815	2.42	12.3	30.2	3 331	4 107	0	123 226	23 985
District 30	8.0	7.6	52.2	223 660	2.45	15.5	29.8	5 183	4 285	0	119 465	27 468
District 31	7.7	7.3	50.6	220 459	2.48	10.7	27.1	8 878	5 003	0	131 301	20 914
NORTH CAROLINA	6.6	5.4	51.0	3 132 013	2.49	12.5	25.4	46 614	50 892	37 022	1 444 680	180 233
District 1	7.7	6.4	52.7	227 415	2.52	19.3	26.8	5 233	4 891	0	134 868	9 663
District 2	5.5	4.4	50.4	273 133	2.56	13.0	24.9	10 472	3 947	0	112 324	21 898
District 3	6.8	4.8	49.1	229 460	2.51	11.2	23.3	5 188	2 424	22 547	129 274	11 719
District 4	4.7	4.0	51.2	303 568	2.45	10.0	26.7	958	4 234	0	134 932	22 232
District 5	7.5	6.5	51.6	257 913	2.41	10.9	26.8	1 548	5 775	0	115 289	14 789
District 6	7.2	6.1	51.1	275 257	2.46	9.7	24.8	1 737	4 176	0	109 667	17 488
District 7	7.3	5.2	51.3	271 249	2.49	13.9	25.2	4 505	2 529	244	122 876	11 369
District 8	5.6	4.4	49.9	235 881	2.68	14.1	21.5	5 171	3 994	14 231	123 772	12 733
District 9	5.9	4.9	51.4	275 985	2.48	10.5	25.6	711	3 883	0	112 566	21 466
District 10	7.3	5.7	50.4	257 182	2.48	9.9	24.1	4 242	4 031	0	111 122	11 321
District 11	9.3	8.3	51.7	272 478	2.34	9.8	26.9	2 927	6 111	0	109 507	11 071
District 12	5.5	4.6	51.4	252 492	2.54	18.8	27.4	3 922	4 897	0	128 483	14 484
NORTH DAKOTA	7.1	7.6	50.1	257 152	2.41	7.8	29.3	1 518	7 254	1 244	164 233	13 310
At Large	7.1	7.6	50.1	257 152	2.41	7.8	29.3	1 518	7 254	1 244	164 233	13 310
OHIO	7.0	6.3	51.4	4 445 773	2.49	12.1	27.3	68 873	93 157	369	2 338 126	460 100
District 1	6.8	6.4	52.5	223 204	2.36	17.3	34.7	2 364	4 951	0	115 474	36 735
District 2	6.4	5.6	51.4	245 751	2.55	9.2	25.1	403	4 865	0	116 047	27 010
District 3	7.3	6.4	52.0	228 130	2.37	13.9	30.4	1 969	4 838	0	118 751	30 101
District 4	7.3	6.5	50.3	225 205	2.52	10.3	25.2	12 766	4 990	0	122 355	20 107
District 5	7.2	6.6	50.7	225 250	2.57	9.3	24.1	2 945	5 549	12	128 740	19 363
District 6	7.1	5.9	50.9	237 265	2.51	10.6	24.8	7 481	5 399	0	142 204	10 518
District 7	6.7	5.7	50.8	232 728	2.56	10.4	23.1	8 597	5 520	339	129 801	19 770
District 8	6.5	5.5	50.9	233 779	2.61	9.7	22.6	1 013	4 819	0	134 813	16 069
District 9	6.5	6.2	51.8	223 894	2.47	13.6	28.9	661	4 522	5	133 634	27 818
District 10	7.2	7.6	51.5	236 328	2.38	11.7	32.9	2 116	4 931	5	92 667	39 890
District 11	7.4	7.0	54.3	216 521	2.39	24.0	34.7	999	4 638	0	117 640	33 157
District 12	5.4	4.3	51.8	260 480	2.49	14.1	27.8	908	4 021	2	122 945	28 490
District 13	6.5	5.5	51.0	236 922	2.67	10.0	21.4	2 655	4 110	1	125 213	26 719
District 14	7.2	6.7	51.9	234 093	2.44	12.7	28.1	1 154	4 238	0	136 173	18 719
District 15	5.3	4.6	50.1	263 748	2.37	10.3	30.4	9 872	3 387	0	137 714	20 879
District 16	7.3	6.9	51.5	228 760	2.57	10.4	24.9	684	6 969	0	114 809	25 217
District 17	8.5	8.2	51.7	223 232	2.46	13.0	27.9	6 852	5 108	0	122 075	17 330
District 18	8.0	7.1	51.1	229 853	2.49	10.5	25.7	4 998	5 074	0	120 210	14 266
District 19	8.4	8.3	51.9	240 630	2.46	9.7	27.3	436	5 228	5	106 861	27 942
OKLAHOMA	7.0	6.2	50.9	1 342 293	2.49	11.4	26.7	33 919	28 021	7 616	754 928	83 883
District 1	6.2	5.5	51.5	235 245	2.44	12.0	29.1	1 215	3 649	0	111 763	27 971
District 2	7.8	6.4	50.9	227 511	2.57	10.9	23.8	4 788	4 995	2	124 837	8 422
District 3	7.9	7.1	50.7	218 611	2.48	11.0	26.2	8 056	5 979	2	135 126	7 125
District 4	6.3	5.2	50.1	216 057	2.54	11.0	24.3	5 631	4 313	7 392	140 823	10 035
District 5	6.6	6.2	51.6	239 228	2.43	10.6	28.4	781	4 036	0	118 145	19 701
District 6	7.4	6.8	50.3	205 641	2.47	12.8	28.3	13 448	5 049	220	124 234	10 629
OREGON	6.4	6.4	50.4	1 333 723	2.51	9.8	26.1	19 523	14 677	95	639 167	85 066
District 1	5.0	5.1	50.0	293 498	2.48	8.4	28.2	3 805	2 331	45	123 228	23 901
District 2	7.8	7.3	50.3	271 846	2.52	9.7	24.3	6 665	3 447	0	125 701	10 824
District 3	5.3	6.0	50.8	256 369	2.48	11.8	28.6	1 953	3 138	0	115 597	21 627
District 4	7.8	7.4	50.8	254 232	2.45	9.8	25.5	1 732	2 354	33	135 962	11 644
District 5	6.3	6.2	50.3	257 778	2.61	9.7	23.6	5 368	3 407	17	138 679	17 070
PENNSYLVANIA	7.9	7.7	51.7	4 777 003	2.48	11.6	27.7	76 553	114 113	758	2 161 247	668 306
District 1	6.6	5.7	53.7	192 395	2.59	27.8	32.2	1 332	1 792	531	111 794	35 826
District 2	7.0	7.0	54.7	217 640	2.32	23.0	38.4	231	4 914	0	94 112	56 504
District 3	7.4	8.2	52.2	218 382	2.55	16.8	30.1	6 506	4 529	0	64 818	59 711
District 4	8.8	8.5	52.0	229 541	2.49	10.1	25.5	706	5 178	0	110 439	19 718
District 5	7.8	7.1	50.0	221 140	2.46	8.2	26.3	9 494	4 970	0	142 367	16 431
District 6	8.3	8.2	50.9	233 266	2.48	10.1	26.5	5 859	6 202	0	99 996	21 176
District 7	7.9	7.7	52.0	224 353	2.52	9.8	27.4	1 320	5 388	0	81 651	58 663

1. No spouse present.

Table E. Congressional Districts 107th Congress — Education, Money Income, Poverty, and Housing

STATE District	Education, 1990 (cont'd) Attainment[1] (percent) High school graduate or more	Bachelor's degree or more	Money income, 1989 Per capita[2]	Households Median	Percent with $100,000 or more	Percent below poverty level, 1989 Persons Total	Families Total	Housing units, 1990 Total	Occupied units Total	Owner-occupied Percent	Median value[3] (dollars)	Owner cost as a percent of income With a mortgage	Without a mortgage
	31	32	33	34	35	36	37	38	39	40	41	42	43
NEW YORK—Cont'd													
District 25	79.9	22.7	14 148	31 080	3.2	10.3	7.1	234 546	217 749	64.9	78 100	20.5	13.9
District 26	77.4	22.5	13 786	30 335	3.3	12.2	7.4	245 650	213 391	63.9	94 500	20.8	13.6
District 27	80.3	22.0	14 934	34 573	4.3	6.9	4.6	223 052	206 855	75.8	81 300	20.3	13.7
District 28	79.5	27.4	16 205	33 899	4.9	11.7	9.0	237 546	225 411	62.3	90 700	21.1	13.9
District 29	77.2	17.8	13 350	28 951	2.1	10.9	8.2	240 237	225 954	64.5	71 600	19.7	13.8
District 30	72.7	14.6	12 176	26 263	1.6	13.7	10.7	240 455	223 708	63.5	68 300	19.0	14.1
District 31	75.5	15.0	11 382	25 124	1.7	13.1	9.6	249 732	213 009	70.9	48 500	18.1	13.6
NORTH CAROLINA	70.0	17.4	12 885	26 647	2.6	13.0	9.9	2 818 193	2 517 026	68.0	65 800	20.5	12.9
District 1	57.8	9.3	8 918	18 226	0.9	26.1	22.1	226 602	202 736	62.2	46 100	21.4	14.6
District 2	70.5	18.1	13 172	27 271	2.6	12.7	9.6	231 097	212 833	68.4	67 600	20.8	13.3
District 3	71.6	14.4	11 567	24 553	1.9	14.5	11.1	252 022	205 941	69.4	63 100	21.5	13.2
District 4	84.0	35.9	16 708	34 569	5.1	9.3	5.7	231 012	215 806	61.0	96 000	21.9	12.6
District 5	65.3	14.8	12 716	25 543	2.4	12.3	9.0	241 796	217 545	70.3	59 500	18.7	12.6
District 6	72.1	19.0	14 942	30 628	3.8	7.5	5.3	232 020	216 882	73.7	73 300	19.4	12.2
District 7	74.9	15.8	11 663	24 708	2.1	14.4	11.4	225 714	184 729	65.2	64 000	21.6	13.4
District 8	65.8	11.4	11 462	26 180	1.7	12.2	9.3	216 877	200 750	73.0	57 100	20.3	13.2
District 9	78.5	26.2	17 234	35 346	5.1	6.6	4.6	231 164	215 438	69.0	83 600	20.1	12.3
District 10	65.4	13.6	13 434	28 511	2.8	8.8	6.5	235 030	212 320	78.9	64 000	18.9	12.1
District 11	68.2	15.3	11 923	23 564	1.8	13.7	10.1	266 453	221 168	74.3	59 700	19.7	12.6
District 12	65.6	14.3	10 878	23 068	1.2	17.7	14.5	228 406	210 878	50.0	58 400	20.5	13.6
NORTH DAKOTA	76.7	18.1	11 051	23 213	1.6	14.4	10.9	276 340	240 878	65.6	50 800	20.3	13.0
At Large	76.7	18.1	11 051	23 213	1.6	14.4	10.9	276 340	240 878	65.6	50 800	20.3	13.0
OHIO	75.7	17.0	13 461	28 706	2.9	12.5	9.7	4 371 945	4 087 546	67.5	63 500	18.2	12.5
District 1	72.2	18.7	12 616	25 405	2.3	17.4	14.0	240 036	223 619	52.2	65 100	18.7	12.5
District 2	76.9	23.7	16 813	34 688	6.3	8.0	6.5	223 177	211 251	71.6	79 400	18.9	12.2
District 3	77.8	20.1	14 500	30 083	3.0	12.7	9.8	239 785	225 198	62.8	65 000	17.7	12.6
District 4	75.3	11.3	12 009	27 312	1.6	11.1	8.7	226 597	210 326	73.0	50 600	16.3	12.2
District 5	77.0	12.4	12 755	30 117	2.2	8.6	6.4	227 819	206 472	76.0	58 000	16.6	12.1
District 6	68.3	11.4	10 349	21 761	1.5	20.1	16.3	228 672	209 760	71.3	46 600	18.0	12.8
District 7	76.2	15.3	12 919	30 364	2.3	11.0	8.5	216 324	205 376	70.8	62 900	17.7	12.3
District 8	75.4	14.8	13 355	31 171	2.7	9.4	7.0	216 423	204 772	72.3	66 300	17.8	12.1
District 9	76.9	16.3	13 477	28 856	3.1	14.1	10.7	229 932	214 332	66.3	58 700	17.3	13.4
District 10	75.5	19.5	14 813	30 323	3.2	10.4	8.2	241 919	228 377	65.6	73 700	19.0	12.7
District 11	68.5	18.2	12 629	22 459	3.0	22.1	18.7	251 169	227 289	51.7	58 800	20.1	13.7
District 12	80.2	23.5	14 723	30 859	4.1	13.4	10.6	232 495	215 958	57.6	75 800	19.8	12.3
District 13	78.6	16.5	14 307	34 725	3.8	8.5	6.7	207 670	198 819	76.9	77 000	19.7	12.3
District 14	78.2	19.7	13 931	28 184	3.4	12.9	9.7	231 833	219 388	67.1	60 600	18.6	12.6
District 15	81.0	27.0	15 076	31 020	3.3	10.8	6.3	236 234	223 084	58.0	73 200	19.5	12.0
District 16	74.0	13.7	12 413	27 524	2.2	11.7	9.1	220 757	209 545	70.6	58 200	17.3	12.0
District 17	74.4	12.3	11 938	25 220	1.8	14.4	11.7	231 698	217 693	72.5	48 600	17.7	12.9
District 18	71.4	8.5	10 531	22 808	1.1	15.5	12.6	239 127	216 909	74.1	44 400	17.2	12.3
District 19	79.8	19.4	16 609	34 385	4.9	6.1	4.5	230 278	219 378	75.4	77 900	18.9	12.6
OKLAHOMA	74.6	17.8	11 893	23 577	2.3	16.7	13.0	1 406 499	1 206 135	68.1	48 100	20.0	12.8
District 1	81.7	23.4	14 695	27 472	3.9	13.0	9.9	235 405	209 563	61.3	61 100	20.1	12.7
District 2	67.9	11.6	9 914	20 633	1.3	19.7	15.9	233 834	196 048	75.3	41 300	20.1	12.9
District 3	66.7	13.3	9 635	18 394	1.3	22.4	17.8	233 844	199 724	71.7	36 100	20.3	13.3
District 4	77.5	18.7	11 554	25 391	1.8	14.6	11.2	218 365	192 106	66.6	51 200	20.4	12.6
District 5	81.8	26.4	15 024	28 348	3.8	11.9	8.8	241 632	209 157	65.7	58 700	19.5	12.2
District 6	71.8	13.3	10 540	21 797	1.5	18.8	14.7	243 419	199 537	68.4	40 000	19.5	12.9
OREGON	81.5	20.6	13 418	27 250	2.8	12.4	8.7	1 193 567	1 103 313	63.1	67 100	20.4	13.4
District 1	87.3	30.8	17 120	33 227	5.4	8.6	5.5	239 642	225 335	59.7	84 800	20.4	13.1
District 2	77.6	15.2	11 704	23 949	2.0	14.7	11.0	250 107	219 958	66.8	62 600	20.7	13.4
District 3	81.5	19.0	13 167	27 150	2.0	12.5	9.0	240 658	226 909	58.7	59 800	20.2	14.0
District 4	79.4	17.1	11 919	24 593	2.0	14.4	10.1	235 820	221 212	64.4	60 600	20.2	13.4
District 5	81.6	20.7	13 180	28 608	2.8	11.8	7.9	227 340	209 899	66.2	69 200	20.7	12.9
PENNSYLVANIA	74.7	17.9	14 068	29 069	3.6	11.1	8.2	4 938 140	4 495 966	70.6	69 700	20.2	13.3
District 1	58.1	10.4	9 703	20 372	1.3	28.0	23.6	233 392	202 744	59.4	37 600	20.2	15.7
District 2	69.2	21.9	13 121	24 880	3.0	20.9	16.1	252 645	222 487	55.6	42 800	19.6	15.2
District 3	66.6	12.7	13 429	29 157	2.1	10.9	8.4	232 906	218 642	71.1	65 800	19.0	14.0
District 4	77.5	15.3	12 684	26 792	2.1	10.6	8.6	228 328	215 984	76.0	55 700	19.6	13.2
District 5	75.7	15.3	10 946	23 934	1.8	14.6	9.5	256 769	205 789	72.2	47 900	18.3	12.7
District 6	69.8	12.6	13 349	28 766	2.4	8.9	6.1	232 771	218 537	74.1	66 500	19.1	13.0
District 7	84.6	31.0	20 175	41 710	9.3	4.6	3.0	219 919	211 077	74.3	134 500	21.3	13.6

1. Persons 25 years old and older.   2. Based on the population enumerated as of April 1, 1990.   3. Specified owner-occupied units.

Table E. Congressional Districts 107th Congress — Housing, Labor Force, and Employment

STATE District	Housing units, 1990 (cont'd) Occupied units (cont'd) Renter-occupied Median rent[1] (dollars)	Rent as a percent of income	Substandard units[2] (percent)	Civilian labor force, 1990 Total	Unemployment Total	Rate[3]	Civilian employment, 1990[4] Total	Percent Professional, managerial, and technical	Precision production, craft, and repair	Disability, 1990 Work disabled persons[5] (percent)
	44	45	46	47	48	49	50	51	52	53
NEW YORK—Cont'd										
District 25	433	27.1	1.8	295 657	16 051	5.4	279 606	33.1	9.9	7.7
District 26	449	28.6	2.6	287 824	16 557	5.8	271 267	35.2	10.6	7.7
District 27	434	25.6	1.4	295 849	14 218	4.8	281 631	31.6	12.1	6.7
District 28	477	28.9	1.7	299 372	15 925	5.3	283 447	37.1	9.6	7.6
District 29	383	27.4	1.7	289 569	18 917	6.5	270 652	28.5	11.8	8.2
District 30	374	29.3	1.8	280 120	21 909	7.8	258 211	26.0	11.6	8.7
District 31	341	27.4	2.3	271 955	19 434	7.1	252 521	26.2	12.4	9.2
NORTH CAROLINA	382	24.4	3.9	3 401 495	163 081	4.8	3 238 414	25.7	13.3	8.7
District 1	290	27.9	8.3	246 996	19 288	7.8	227 708	17.9	13.2	12.0
District 2	376	23.9	4.3	286 505	12 648	4.4	273 857	28.0	13.7	8.7
District 3	359	25.2	4.2	261 335	14 393	5.5	246 942	24.5	14.4	9.6
District 4	477	24.8	2.6	321 449	11 137	3.5	310 312	40.2	9.1	5.8
District 5	348	23.7	3.7	291 264	12 969	4.5	278 295	23.7	14.1	9.0
District 6	403	23.0	2.2	314 266	9 836	3.1	304 430	26.0	14.1	7.2
District 7	391	25.6	4.1	225 060	14 888	6.6	210 172	25.2	14.0	10.0
District 8	359	24.0	4.7	273 784	13 889	5.1	259 895	20.7	15.1	9.3
District 9	472	23.0	2.2	317 014	10 931	3.4	306 083	32.1	11.0	6.3
District 10	352	21.5	3.1	305 379	10 821	3.5	294 558	21.6	15.0	8.3
District 11	333	24.5	3.0	267 899	14 052	5.2	253 847	23.3	14.8	10.4
District 12	381	25.3	4.8	290 544	18 229	6.3	272 315	21.1	11.7	9.4
NORTH DAKOTA	313	23.9	2.5	303 641	16 083	5.3	287 558	26.4	9.8	7.0
At Large	313	23.9	2.5	303 641	16 083	5.3	287 558	26.4	9.8	7.0
OHIO	379	25.3	2.2	5 279 995	348 638	6.6	4 931 357	28.5	11.6	9.0
District 1	336	25.6	3.7	276 732	18 124	6.5	258 608	31.4	9.3	10.1
District 2	409	23.8	2.2	288 646	13 058	4.5	275 588	33.2	11.2	8.0
District 3	403	25.1	2.1	281 876	17 378	6.2	264 498	33.2	10.0	9.4
District 4	337	23.8	2.1	272 753	19 257	7.1	253 496	22.3	13.9	8.9
District 5	351	22.9	2.0	281 396	17 929	6.4	263 467	22.1	14.5	7.7
District 6	315	28.7	4.3	244 376	22 384	9.2	221 992	24.8	13.3	12.7
District 7	376	24.5	2.2	274 824	16 857	6.1	257 967	27.4	12.4	9.2
District 8	389	24.4	2.0	283 594	14 807	5.2	268 787	26.3	12.6	8.4
District 9	392	25.9	1.9	279 761	22 284	8.0	257 477	28.1	11.2	8.6
District 10	388	24.7	1.6	283 444	16 978	6.0	266 466	30.7	10.8	8.5
District 11	376	28.6	2.8	258 249	29 251	11.3	228 998	31.0	7.7	11.3
District 12	417	24.7	2.4	299 109	16 298	5.4	282 811	33.4	8.3	8.5
District 13	403	24.2	2.3	285 963	15 637	5.5	270 326	27.9	13.8	7.3
District 14	394	27.0	1.5	281 368	18 754	6.7	262 614	30.2	11.2	8.9
District 15	438	24.5	1.7	312 928	13 894	4.4	299 034	34.5	8.6	7.6
District 16	353	24.2	2.1	274 286	17 411	6.3	256 875	24.9	11.7	8.4
District 17	337	26.4	1.7	258 333	21 757	8.4	236 576	24.0	12.9	10.3
District 18	298	26.0	2.8	251 720	22 498	8.9	229 222	20.7	14.2	10.4
District 19	464	24.9	1.3	290 637	14 082	4.8	276 555	31.4	12.7	7.3
OKLAHOMA	340	25.4	3.7	1 470 069	100 931	6.9	1 369 138	27.9	12.0	10.2
District 1	366	24.4	2.9	270 670	15 413	5.7	255 257	32.6	11.2	8.0
District 2	289	27.2	4.5	227 519	16 708	7.3	210 811	22.3	14.7	12.5
District 3	294	27.8	4.1	224 304	19 054	8.5	205 250	24.3	12.8	12.6
District 4	364	25.5	3.5	238 390	17 348	7.3	221 042	29.4	11.7	9.7
District 5	370	24.4	3.0	268 490	14 305	5.3	254 185	33.9	9.9	7.9
District 6	323	25.5	4.2	240 696	18 103	7.5	222 593	22.5	12.5	10.6
OREGON	408	25.5	3.9	1 407 143	87 183	6.2	1 319 960	28.8	10.7	10.0
District 1	453	24.4	3.2	306 224	13 194	4.3	293 030	36.6	9.7	7.7
District 2	363	25.3	4.8	262 274	20 950	8.0	241 324	23.4	10.9	10.9
District 3	414	25.5	3.5	295 378	17 481	5.9	277 897	27.5	11.2	10.3
District 4	390	26.7	3.9	266 853	20 076	7.5	246 777	25.2	11.2	11.7
District 5	403	25.8	3.9	276 414	15 482	5.6	260 932	29.8	10.5	9.5
PENNSYLVANIA	404	26.1	2.3	5 779 327	344 795	6.0	5 434 532	28.9	11.6	8.3
District 1	404	31.3	7.3	238 775	30 373	12.7	208 402	24.1	9.0	13.0
District 2	479	29.3	4.6	268 681	26 161	9.7	242 520	34.4	6.6	10.3
District 3	472	28.5	3.1	268 148	17 763	6.6	250 385	26.0	11.9	9.4
District 4	332	26.0	1.4	259 398	17 211	6.6	242 187	28.6	12.5	8.7
District 5	334	27.2	2.5	258 701	18 374	7.1	240 327	25.4	11.9	8.2
District 6	367	24.4	2.0	281 279	13 826	4.9	267 453	23.0	13.5	8.0
District 7	568	25.5	1.4	298 825	10 298	3.4	288 527	39.5	10.1	5.8

1. Specified renter-occupied units.   2. Overcrowded or lacking complete plumbing facilities.   3. Percent of total civilian labor force.   4. Persons 16 years old and older.   5. Persons 16 to 64 years of age.

Table E. Congressional Districts 107th Congress — **Land Area and Population**

STATE District	Land area, 2000[1] (sq km)	Total persons	Per square kilometer	White	Black	Am. Indian, Alaska Native	Asian and Pacific Islander	Other race	Hispanic[2]	Non-Hispanic White	2 or more races	Under 5 years	5 to 17 years	18 to 24 years	25 to 34 years	35 to 44 years	45 to 54 years	55 to 64 years
	1	2	3	4	5	6	7	8	9	10	11	12	13	14	15	16	17	18
PENNSYLVANIA—Cont'd																		
District 8	1 620.9	624 248	385.1	93.2	3.6	0.4	2.8	1.1	2.3	91.1	1.0	6.4	19.3	7.0	12.7	18.1	15.0	9.2
District 9	17 261.0	588 138	34.1	97.6	1.8	0.3	0.5	0.5	0.9	96.5	0.6	5.9	17.6	8.3	12.7	15.3	13.9	10.1
District 10	14 403.5	613 459	42.6	95.7	3.0	0.5	0.8	1.1	2.1	93.7	0.9	5.5	18.3	8.3	11.4	15.7	14.1	10.0
District 11	6 147.5	579 470	94.3	96.8	2.1	0.3	0.8	0.7	1.7	95.2	0.7	5.1	16.8	8.4	12.0	15.4	14.0	9.9
District 12	10 915.4	556 856	51.0	97.7	1.9	0.3	0.4	0.3	0.6	96.8	0.5	5.2	16.6	9.3	11.6	15.1	14.4	9.8
District 13	946.7	628 203	663.6	86.8	8.5	0.4	4.6	1.1	2.0	84.7	1.1	6.3	17.8	7.1	13.2	16.9	14.4	9.2
District 14	501.3	529 299	1 055.9	78.3	19.2	0.5	2.7	0.8	1.1	76.7	1.3	5.4	15.5	11.7	13.7	15.0	13.4	8.6
District 15	2 045.9	612 265	299.3	90.8	3.6	0.4	2.0	4.8	8.2	86.2	1.6	5.9	18.0	8.5	12.4	16.5	14.1	9.0
District 16	3 313.9	647 575	195.4	89.8	6.0	0.4	1.9	3.2	5.9	86.2	1.3	7.0	20.0	9.1	12.5	16.4	13.8	8.6
District 17	3 847.6	608 390	158.1	89.0	8.3	0.4	1.8	1.9	3.4	86.5	1.3	6.2	18.3	7.8	13.1	16.5	14.6	9.1
District 18	685.1	535 432	781.5	87.7	11.1	0.4	1.4	0.5	0.7	86.4	1.0	5.5	16.5	6.4	11.9	15.7	14.5	9.7
District 19	4 964.1	632 862	127.5	94.4	3.6	0.4	1.2	1.5	2.7	92.3	1.0	5.9	18.0	8.9	12.9	16.7	14.4	9.3
District 20	5 534.0	570 336	103.1	95.6	3.8	0.3	0.8	0.3	0.6	94.5	0.8	5.5	16.7	7.5	11.9	15.0	15.0	9.9
District 21	7 210.9	581 440	80.6	94.3	4.9	0.4	0.8	0.7	1.4	92.6	1.0	6.0	18.2	10.2	12.1	15.2	13.8	9.1
RHODE ISLAND	2 706.0	1 048 319	387.4	86.9	5.5	1.0	2.9	6.6	8.7	81.9	2.7	6.1	17.5	10.2	13.4	16.2	13.5	8.5
District 1	838.0	510 287	608.9	88.4	5.4	0.8	2.4	6.1	7.0	83.4	2.9	5.9	16.8	10.7	13.5	15.9	13.3	8.5
District 2	1 868.3	538 032	288.0	85.4	5.7	1.2	3.4	7.0	10.2	80.4	2.5	6.3	18.3	9.7	13.3	16.6	13.8	8.4
SOUTH CAROLINA	77 983.0	4 012 012	51.4	68.0	29.9	0.7	1.2	1.3	2.4	66.1	1.0	6.6	18.6	10.2	14.0	15.6	13.7	9.3
District 1	8 168.8	684 765	83.8	76.0	21.4	0.8	1.7	1.4	2.5	73.8	1.3	6.4	17.9	10.3	14.7	15.8	13.6	9.5
District 2	12 973.1	731 022	56.3	69.1	28.2	0.7	1.6	1.7	3.2	66.7	1.2	6.7	18.4	10.7	14.8	16.0	13.5	8.7
District 3	14 512.1	670 139	46.2	77.4	21.2	0.6	0.8	1.0	1.9	75.8	0.8	6.4	17.9	10.3	13.2	15.1	13.6	9.3
District 4	5 660.0	670 335	118.4	77.1	20.2	0.5	1.7	1.7	3.2	74.6	1.1	6.7	18.0	9.4	14.7	16.0	13.9	9.3
District 5	17 687.2	655 525	37.1	68.2	31.0	1.0	0.8	1.0	1.8	65.7	0.8	6.9	19.5	9.1	13.8	15.7	13.9	9.3
District 6	18 982.0	600 226	31.6	37.7	61.3	0.5	0.7	0.7	1.4	36.7	0.7	6.5	19.9	11.2	12.5	14.7	13.8	9.1
SOUTH DAKOTA	196 540.0	754 844	3.8	89.9	0.9	9.0	0.9	0.7	1.4	88.0	1.3	6.8	20.1	10.3	12.1	15.3	12.9	8.3
At Large	196 540.3	754 844	3.8	89.9	0.9	9.0	0.9	0.7	1.4	88.0	1.3	6.8	20.1	10.3	12.1	15.3	12.9	8.3
TENNESSEE	106 752.0	5 689 283	53.3	81.2	16.8	0.7	1.3	1.3	2.2	79.2	1.1	6.6	18.0	9.6	14.3	15.9	13.8	9.4
District 1	10 923.4	628 443	57.5	97.0	2.2	0.6	0.5	0.5	1.0	95.6	0.8	5.8	16.3	8.6	13.8	15.4	14.5	11.2
District 2	6 443.0	636 383	98.8	91.7	6.6	0.8	1.3	0.8	1.4	90.0	1.1	6.1	16.7	10.3	14.0	15.8	14.2	9.8
District 3	11 171.7	595 855	53.3	86.2	12.3	0.8	1.2	0.8	1.5	84.4	1.1	6.0	17.1	9.3	13.4	15.3	14.6	10.2
District 4	24 192.7	635 355	26.3	95.0	3.6	0.7	0.5	1.1	2.1	93.1	0.9	6.2	17.6	8.7	13.3	15.0	13.7	10.9
District 5	2 278.0	607 853	266.8	69.8	25.6	0.7	2.7	3.1	4.5	66.4	1.9	6.7	15.9	11.5	17.3	16.4	13.1	7.9
District 6	13 898.4	738 663	53.1	91.9	6.0	0.6	1.3	1.2	2.2	89.9	0.9	6.9	19.2	9.6	14.1	17.0	14.2	8.9
District 7	17 115.7	728 956	42.6	81.4	16.0	0.7	1.9	1.4	2.5	79.0	1.4	7.2	19.6	9.1	14.9	16.9	13.9	8.4
District 8	20 096.8	604 894	30.1	74.9	23.8	0.6	0.8	0.9	1.6	73.4	0.9	6.8	19.1	9.4	13.2	15.5	13.4	9.4
District 9	632.2	512 881	811.3	30.8	66.6	0.5	1.5	1.7	2.8	29.1	0.9	7.6	20.3	10.8	15.2	14.9	12.5	7.3
TEXAS	678 051.0	20 851 820	30.8	73.1	12.0	1.0	3.2	13.3	32.0	52.4	2.5	7.8	20.4	10.5	15.2	15.9	12.5	7.7
District 1	29 949.4	622 475	20.8	78.2	17.3	1.1	0.6	4.1	7.3	73.9	1.3	6.5	18.8	10.0	12.1	14.5	13.1	9.9
District 2	36 763.4	669 591	18.2	78.4	15.8	1.0	0.7	5.2	10.1	72.8	1.3	6.7	19.0	10.1	13.1	15.1	12.8	9.5
District 3	945.0	835 040	883.6	75.0	10.1	1.0	8.8	7.7	15.4	65.0	2.5	8.2	20.3	8.6	17.6	19.0	13.4	7.0
District 4	17 670.7	707 329	40.0	86.6	8.0	1.4	0.9	4.8	8.8	81.1	1.7	6.9	19.9	8.9	12.9	15.9	13.3	9.3
District 5	17 026.4	657 495	38.6	66.9	17.8	1.1	1.8	12.7	23.0	56.7	2.2	7.5	18.5	9.9	17.0	16.1	11.9	7.6
District 6	2 157.5	759 418	352.0	83.6	8.5	1.1	4.5	4.6	9.6	76.6	2.1	7.4	20.2	8.4	15.7	18.6	14.5	7.8
District 7	1 206.9	772 147	639.8	74.8	8.0	0.8	8.2	11.4	23.6	59.8	3.0	7.8	19.7	9.6	17.6	18.3	14.0	7.0
District 8	7 990.4	776 623	97.2	87.2	5.6	0.8	3.0	5.2	11.3	79.4	1.8	7.0	20.5	12.4	13.2	16.5	14.2	8.2
District 9	5 316.5	636 960	119.8	68.9	22.1	0.8	3.2	7.0	14.4	59.8	1.9	7.0	19.5	9.5	14.1	16.6	13.7	8.3
District 10	2 068.5	791 117	382.5	69.9	10.1	1.1	5.4	16.6	28.8	55.4	2.9	7.3	16.5	15.0	20.1	16.6	12.1	5.8
District 11	29 261.8	663 275	22.7	72.4	17.3	1.2	2.5	9.4	16.4	63.6	2.7	7.7	19.7	13.1	14.6	14.5	11.2	7.6
District 12	4 462.9	661 753	148.3	76.6	9.0	1.3	2.7	13.0	25.0	62.5	2.5	7.8	20.0	10.3	15.5	16.1	12.1	7.7
District 13	82 231.1	597 401	7.3	76.3	9.0	1.5	1.8	13.9	24.6	63.8	2.3	7.2	19.5	12.3	13.2	14.4	11.6	8.3
District 14	39 824.0	688 604	17.3	77.5	9.5	1.0	1.1	13.1	27.9	61.2	2.1	7.0	20.2	10.8	12.2	15.2	13.2	8.7
District 15	21 887.9	780 310	35.7	78.9	1.9	0.7	0.8	20.0	78.9	18.4	2.2	9.4	23.8	11.3	14.7	13.3	10.4	6.8
District 16	1 256.4	620 847	494.1	77.2	3.4	1.1	1.6	20.0	78.0	17.2	3.2	8.5	22.9	10.7	14.2	14.6	11.5	7.3
District 17	72 843.1	618 958	8.5	85.8	4.3	1.2	0.9	9.8	20.7	73.4	1.9	6.4	19.3	10.1	12.2	14.8	12.5	9.4
District 18	406.4	606 441	1 492.2	40.9	40.9	0.8	3.5	16.6	33.4	22.3	2.6	7.6	19.3	11.2	17.0	15.7	12.2	7.5
District 19	52 282.1	607 535	11.6	82.8	3.3	1.1	1.3	13.6	26.1	68.7	2.0	7.2	20.3	12.1	13.0	15.1	12.5	8.0
District 20	753.3	624 384	828.9	69.9	6.5	1.5	2.2	24.3	67.0	24.6	4.2	8.4	20.2	12.6	16.6	14.7	10.8	6.7
District 21	44 845.1	801 078	17.9	88.3	3.6	1.0	2.2	7.1	18.3	75.4	2.1	6.8	19.2	7.8	13.2	16.7	14.0	9.0
District 22	4 334.0	784 759	181.1	65.0	15.2	0.8	10.9	11.0	22.3	51.2	2.8	7.6	21.7	8.4	14.7	18.6	14.5	7.4
District 23	151 274.6	762 627	5.0	79.4	3.0	1.0	1.4	18.0	66.3	29.2	2.7	8.7	23.8	9.8	14.1	14.9	12.0	7.4
District 24	5 319.2	680 808	128.0	57.6	21.7	1.2	3.1	19.4	34.5	40.2	2.9	8.9	22.0	11.3	16.1	15.4	11.5	6.8
District 25	748.7	662 264	884.6	55.8	24.4	0.8	6.1	16.0	31.1	38.5	2.9	8.9	20.5	10.9	17.3	15.9	12.4	6.5
District 26	1 771.2	845 541	477.4	81.6	6.4	0.9	5.3	8.1	17.1	70.5	2.2	8.1	18.5	9.1	18.5	18.8	13.2	7.0
District 27	10 554.9	664 428	62.9	78.7	2.5	0.9	1.1	19.5	70.5	25.8	2.7	8.6	22.5	10.5	13.6	14.1	11.9	7.6

1. Dry land or land partially or temporarily covered by water.   2. Hispanic persons may be of any race.

Table E. Congressional Districts 107th Congress — Population, Households, Group Quarters, and Education

STATE District	Population and population characteristics, 2000 (cont'd) — Percent (cont'd) — Age (cont'd) 65 to 74 years	75 years and over	Percent female	Households, 2000 Number	Persons per household	Percent Female family householder[1]	One person	Persons in correctional institutions, 2000	Persons in nursing homes, 2000	Persons in military quarters, 2000	Education, 1990 School enrollment Public	Private
	19	20	21	22	23	24	25	26	27	28	29	30
PENNSYLVANIA—Cont'd												
District 8	6.7	5.6	50.9	228 657	2.69	8.8	21.5	798	4 203	159	102 963	38 849
District 9	8.4	7.8	50.9	229 022	2.48	8.9	25.1	6 300	6 694	0	108 087	15 583
District 10	8.6	8.1	51.4	239 044	2.48	10.1	26.9	4 253	5 119	3	105 728	24 191
District 11	9.1	9.3	51.6	231 911	2.40	10.5	29.0	6 000	6 411	0	101 306	24 342
District 12	9.0	8.9	51.3	219 874	2.43	9.6	27.3	4 846	4 241	0	117 824	17 040
District 13	7.4	7.8	51.8	238 092	2.55	8.8	25.5	5 011	6 805	0	83 570	51 078
District 14	8.2	8.6	52.5	224 277	2.24	13.9	36.2	4 713	4 265	0	100 985	40 274
District 15	7.7	7.9	51.5	235 233	2.51	10.1	25.6	1 989	6 867	0	99 682	33 141
District 16	6.3	6.2	51.0	231 969	2.69	8.7	22.3	1 683	6 867	0	107 194	32 987
District 17	7.5	6.9	51.6	240 154	2.47	10.3	26.4	1 823	6 359	0	104 222	21 221
District 18	9.7	10.0	53.1	228 136	2.31	12.4	32.0	0	4 698	0	95 134	27 001
District 19	7.3	6.8	50.9	243 143	2.50	8.7	24.1	5 283	7 021	62	104 790	23 425
District 20	8.7	8.9	51.8	228 234	2.42	10.2	27.5	3 842	5 141	3	108 497	20 511
District 21	7.7	7.8	51.3	222 540	2.48	10.9	27.0	4 564	6 449	0	116 088	30 634
RHODE ISLAND	7.0	7.5	52.0	408 424	2.47	12.9	28.6	3 576	9 222	870	191 802	62 833
District 1	7.3	8.1	52.3	203 247	2.40	12.5	30.3	324	5 621	867	86 460	39 128
District 2	6.7	6.9	51.6	205 177	2.54	13.2	26.8	3 252	3 601	3	105 342	23 705
SOUTH CAROLINA	6.7	5.4	51.4	1 533 854	2.53	14.8	25.0	34 909	20 867	17 102	807 539	105 471
District 1	7.0	4.8	51.0	268 997	2.49	12.6	24.6	2 615	2 917	3 392	129 195	19 405
District 2	6.3	4.9	50.9	277 387	2.51	13.0	24.9	9 701	3 567	12 829	136 157	18 888
District 3	7.4	6.0	51.3	259 294	2.50	13.1	24.6	5 058	4 060	0	135 564	14 899
District 4	6.5	5.6	51.4	261 904	2.49	13.1	26.0	4 309	2 994	0	117 135	24 754
District 5	6.5	5.3	51.7	246 866	2.59	16.0	23.7	4 394	4 119	830	136 389	11 887
District 6	6.7	5.5	52.4	219 406	2.61	22.5	26.3	8 832	3 210	51	153 099	15 638
SOUTH DAKOTA	7.0	7.3	50.4	290 245	2.50	9.0	27.6	4 479	7 791	566	165 993	19 253
At Large	7.0	7.3	50.4	290 245	2.50	9.0	27.6	4 479	7 791	566	165 993	19 253
TENNESSEE	6.7	5.6	51.3	2 232 905	2.48	12.9	25.8	38 481	36 994	2 593	1 023 651	147 989
District 1	8.0	6.4	51.2	257 054	2.39	10.4	25.7	3 284	4 934	0	108 560	9 678
District 2	7.1	6.0	51.5	259 475	2.39	10.5	27.1	718	3 847	1	120 208	12 377
District 3	7.6	6.5	51.6	239 446	2.42	12.3	26.7	4 066	4 148	10	110 709	17 742
District 4	8.1	6.3	50.9	250 400	2.49	10.8	23.8	3 856	4 904	45	110 283	8 460
District 5	5.9	5.3	51.5	250 719	2.33	14.3	32.5	6 014	2 625	0	93 390	35 098
District 6	5.6	4.5	50.7	276 700	2.62	10.1	21.1	1 743	3 789	0	124 211	13 677
District 7	5.6	4.4	50.6	272 103	2.62	11.2	22.1	5 752	4 683	2 287	117 616	18 568
District 8	7.0	6.3	51.6	230 970	2.54	14.5	24.4	6 671	5 667	250	116 347	12 324
District 9	5.9	5.4	52.7	196 038	2.54	25.3	30.9	6 377	2 397	0	122 327	20 065
TEXAS	5.5	4.5	50.4	7 393 354	2.74	12.7	23.7	244 363	105 052	34 056	4 313 852	492 043
District 1	7.9	7.3	51.0	236 648	2.53	12.1	25.4	10 059	6 299	0	139 109	9 430
District 2	7.6	6.0	49.2	238 699	2.62	12.1	23.4	33 243	4 998	0	137 702	9 404
District 3	3.5	2.4	50.4	307 084	2.71	9.9	23.1	85	2 038	0	137 473	21 492
District 4	6.9	6.0	50.8	262 101	2.63	10.6	22.5	4 176	6 539	0	132 890	13 353
District 5	6.1	5.3	48.9	244 380	2.56	13.3	28.8	23 238	4 491	0	118 872	15 650
District 6	4.3	3.1	50.8	289 202	2.61	9.0	23.2	53	2 082	0	129 541	23 915
District 7	3.9	2.9	50.4	294 650	2.61	9.2	27.3	13	2 173	0	127 056	24 801
District 8	4.7	3.4	50.5	279 054	2.73	9.0	19.9	112	2 917	0	170 785	16 351
District 9	6.2	5.1	50.2	237 696	2.59	13.7	25.7	16 032	3 304	26	141 230	14 786
District 10	3.5	3.0	48.8	312 251	2.47	10.5	30.4	3 544	2 096	0	161 795	18 544
District 11	6.0	5.7	50.5	236 004	2.64	12.2	23.9	11 972	6 310	12 262	130 259	21 781
District 12	5.6	5.0	50.1	237 205	2.71	12.7	25.1	9 119	5 114	271	120 459	19 292
District 13	7.1	6.4	49.9	219 041	2.56	11.9	27.0	17 274	5 090	4 696	145 260	9 003
District 14	6.8	6.0	50.3	246 955	2.68	11.0	23.0	7 723	5 703	10	145 441	12 501
District 15	5.8	4.6	50.3	225 044	3.36	14.9	15.7	18 007	2 924	839	180 969	8 618
District 16	6.0	4.2	51.9	193 995	3.14	18.3	18.5	5 732	1 329	2 751	177 054	13 551
District 17	7.9	7.2	49.9	228 972	2.54	10.4	25.3	20 305	5 894	897	129 487	15 699
District 18	5.4	4.1	49.7	216 972	2.69	19.0	30.4	9 600	2 118	0	140 552	14 002
District 19	6.5	5.3	51.0	229 090	2.58	10.3	25.0	3 816	3 122	0	156 876	12 617
District 20	5.4	4.6	50.9	214 548	2.79	17.6	26.0	6 243	3 262	9 451	143 916	20 892
District 21	7.0	6.2	51.3	306 967	2.56	8.8	23.3	1 256	5 645	1 428	126 397	19 576
District 22	4.2	2.8	49.8	264 138	2.90	10.9	18.9	12 482	2 444	0	148 588	20 203
District 23	5.3	3.9	51.0	238 925	3.13	13.4	17.4	8 421	2 430	353	167 218	12 860
District 24	4.4	3.5	50.0	224 408	2.99	16.1	20.8	2 963	3 042	0	139 409	16 982
District 25	4.2	3.4	51.1	240 902	2.73	15.9	25.8	3	1 895	0	137 616	22 456
District 26	3.8	3.1	50.1	329 781	2.54	8.2	27.5	34	2 831	0	112 179	29 681
District 27	6.3	4.9	51.6	212 615	3.08	16.2	19.2	2 403	2 965	468	169 692	12 148

1. No spouse present.

Table E. Congressional Districts 107th Congress — Education, Money Income, Poverty, and Housing

STATE District	Education, 1990 (cont'd) Attainment[1] (percent) High school graduate or more	Bachelor's degree or more	Money income, 1989 Per capita[2]	Households Median	Percent with $100,000 or more	Percent below poverty level, 1989 Persons Total	Families Total	Housing units, 1990 Total	Occupied units Total	Owner-occupied Percent	Median value[3] (dollars)	Owner cost as a percent of income With a mortgage	Without a mortgage
	31	32	33	34	35	36	37	38	39	40	41	42	43
PENNSYLVANIA—Cont'd													
District 8	83.2	25.1	18 374	43 483	7.7	3.9	2.8	209 434	199 677	75.4	140 700	23.1	13.5
District 9	70.2	10.0	11 229	24 309	1.5	12.1	9.1	238 208	212 351	75.2	49 700	18.5	12.7
District 10	75.0	13.9	12 005	25 648	2.1	11.0	8.1	283 288	212 813	71.8	70 600	20.5	13.7
District 11	71.7	12.7	11 937	24 310	1.8	10.7	7.6	248 454	218 969	72.0	58 000	18.9	13.6
District 12	71.6	10.8	10 586	22 024	1.3	14.9	11.6	237 174	213 386	75.0	44 400	19.8	13.1
District 13	84.5	33.5	22 786	44 764	12.0	3.5	2.2	220 507	211 735	73.0	147 500	21.6	13.0
District 14	76.0	22.6	14 255	24 751	3.9	16.3	12.2	252 583	231 642	58.6	52 000	19.6	13.9
District 15	74.1	18.2	15 073	33 049	3.4	7.1	4.8	223 545	213 418	71.6	102 100	21.5	12.7
District 16	76.4	24.3	16 321	37 553	6.2	7.2	4.8	206 629	197 885	70.9	115 800	21.6	12.3
District 17	75.4	16.3	14 434	31 841	2.8	7.7	5.4	229 228	216 856	68.9	76 700	19.8	12.1
District 18	80.0	21.0	15 251	29 003	3.7	9.0	7.2	246 887	232 220	69.9	55 800	19.7	13.7
District 19	74.2	16.0	14 539	32 424	2.7	6.4	4.1	223 078	212 004	73.3	80 600	19.6	11.9
District 20	75.7	17.2	13 349	26 294	3.1	12.8	10.1	232 939	217 875	74.8	56 900	18.6	12.7
District 21	76.5	14.6	11 884	25 845	2.0	12.9	9.7	229 456	209 875	71.8	50 600	17.3	12.6
RHODE ISLAND	72.0	21.3	14 981	32 181	4.1	9.6	6.8	414 572	377 977	59.5	133 500	22.7	13.9
District 1	70.7	21.9	15 224	31 675	4.3	9.2	6.5	206 624	191 853	55.6	137 300	22.6	14.0
District 2	73.3	20.7	14 739	32 729	3.9	10.0	7.2	207 948	186 124	63.4	130 200	22.9	13.8
SOUTH CAROLINA	68.3	16.6	11 897	26 256	2.3	15.4	11.9	1 424 155	1 258 044	69.8	61 100	19.8	13.0
District 1	77.9	19.7	13 112	28 765	2.7	12.4	9.5	266 586	210 982	65.6	75 600	22.0	12.9
District 2	78.4	24.4	13 913	30 693	3.6	12.1	9.2	242 035	210 778	69.3	74 000	20.3	12.6
District 3	64.0	14.0	11 707	25 693	1.8	13.4	9.9	238 600	215 512	74.7	53 900	17.9	12.5
District 4	67.3	17.6	13 011	27 703	2.6	11.3	8.4	235 201	220 099	68.2	59 500	18.1	12.6
District 5	62.9	12.5	11 009	25 215	1.8	16.0	12.4	222 014	205 042	73.5	53 300	18.5	13.1
District 6	59.2	11.5	8 631	19 189	1.2	27.0	22.6	219 719	195 631	67.6	48 500	20.8	14.3
SOUTH DAKOTA	77.1	17.2	10 661	22 503	1.7	15.9	11.6	292 436	259 034	66.1	45 200	19.8	13.3
At Large	77.1	17.2	10 661	22 503	1.7	15.9	11.6	292 436	259 034	66.1	45 200	19.8	13.3
TENNESSEE	67.1	16.0	12 255	24 807	2.6	15.7	12.4	2 026 067	1 853 725	68.0	58 400	20.1	12.6
District 1	61.9	12.7	11 024	21 952	1.7	16.6	12.9	231 024	210 363	74.6	51 200	18.3	12.2
District 2	70.0	19.3	13 118	25 267	2.9	14.1	10.8	229 461	212 752	68.5	59 700	19.0	12.5
District 3	67.5	16.0	12 338	24 687	2.6	15.1	12.0	229 420	209 558	68.7	55 200	18.4	12.6
District 4	56.4	9.0	9 886	20 685	1.2	18.3	15.0	226 325	204 747	75.7	44 600	19.7	12.5
District 5	75.0	23.3	14 874	28 208	3.7	12.9	10.0	240 552	218 369	54.8	74 500	20.9	12.6
District 6	68.2	17.2	13 286	29 234	3.3	11.3	8.6	215 141	197 185	74.2	71 400	21.0	12.6
District 7	72.5	18.6	13 758	29 242	3.9	12.0	9.5	215 917	197 446	70.9	69 600	21.0	12.5
District 8	62.8	10.4	10 712	22 622	1.5	16.8	13.3	219 198	200 919	70.3	47 400	19.5	13.0
District 9	69.5	17.3	11 296	22 117	2.7	24.2	19.8	219 029	202 386	55.5	55 700	20.8	13.5
TEXAS	72.1	20.3	12 904	27 016	3.7	18.1	14.1	7 008 999	6 070 937	60.9	59 600	20.9	13.1
District 1	68.1	13.1	10 785	21 697	1.9	20.1	15.4	247 437	212 663	72.5	44 100	19.0	13.6
District 2	64.9	10.4	10 113	21 216	1.6	20.5	16.2	252 735	202 546	74.2	42 200	19.3	13.8
District 3	88.7	35.9	18 858	41 683	7.6	5.7	4.0	228 860	210 090	60.6	92 400	22.3	12.1
District 4	73.7	16.3	12 724	26 974	2.8	13.7	10.4	243 456	211 624	70.6	57 500	20.8	13.6
District 5	71.1	19.3	13 045	25 817	3.0	17.6	14.0	260 137	217 824	58.4	62 400	20.2	13.5
District 6	90.1	32.6	18 573	40 930	6.4	4.7	3.3	235 118	215 161	63.5	90 900	22.1	12.0
District 7	87.6	40.6	22 666	40 331	11.1	8.6	6.1	249 856	221 903	51.9	92 100	20.9	12.2
District 8	83.0	29.2	16 006	35 809	6.9	10.7	7.0	222 156	198 519	65.1	79 200	20.8	12.8
District 9	76.5	18.9	13 759	29 406	3.3	15.8	12.7	245 527	212 067	63.4	53 400	18.4	13.1
District 10	83.2	34.5	14 978	27 280	4.3	16.2	10.4	257 728	228 606	45.2	77 400	23.0	12.6
District 11	72.6	14.8	10 630	22 283	1.8	18.4	13.7	233 019	200 738	59.4	50 400	20.4	13.2
District 12	70.9	15.3	12 641	27 366	2.5	14.1	10.7	233 681	207 789	61.5	57 800	20.3	12.8
District 13	66.9	14.3	10 344	20 907	1.8	21.3	16.2	249 706	209 966	64.8	38 600	19.3	13.3
District 14	66.1	13.8	11 127	23 812	2.2	20.0	15.1	250 002	201 932	68.9	52 800	20.7	13.2
District 15	50.8	11.5	7 407	17 866	1.7	37.5	31.6	202 513	164 944	69.9	37 200	21.0	12.9
District 16	63.3	15.4	9 195	22 632	2.3	27.0	22.6	179 518	170 915	58.1	57 600	20.5	12.0
District 17	66.2	13.4	10 642	21 532	1.8	19.1	14.5	259 973	210 111	70.6	38 900	20.0	13.4
District 18	62.3	16.0	10 744	22 240	2.1	26.7	22.7	243 275	202 510	49.3	47 600	20.7	14.6
District 19	76.0	20.8	13 184	27 267	3.3	14.7	10.9	235 793	208 449	65.1	55 400	19.5	12.3
District 20	68.4	15.6	9 672	22 372	1.3	24.4	20.4	216 539	192 134	50.1	48 900	20.9	12.7
District 21	83.7	28.0	16 086	32 103	4.8	9.7	7.1	256 664	217 836	66.8	79 400	22.0	12.5
District 22	83.1	29.9	16 291	40 160	5.8	8.4	6.3	215 591	195 058	64.9	70 900	20.4	12.3
District 23	59.7	16.6	9 764	21 555	3.3	29.5	24.2	203 972	174 390	68.1	48 200	22.1	13.1
District 24	68.5	14.7	11 371	27 091	2.0	16.4	12.9	222 698	194 480	58.8	58 800	21.2	13.3
District 25	78.8	25.6	15 056	29 611	4.7	14.8	11.9	248 004	216 809	47.1	63 300	18.5	12.3
District 26	89.4	40.8	23 770	40 269	11.0	6.2	3.9	259 527	235 193	52.4	117 800	22.3	12.5
District 27	60.5	14.8	9 366	21 552	2.2	29.7	24.6	208 727	177 612	61.0	47 700	21.0	12.7

1. Persons 25 years old and older.   2. Based on the population enumerated as of April 1, 1990.   3. Specified owner-occupied units.

STATE District	Housing units, 1990 (cont'd)			Civilian labor force, 1990			Civilian employment, 1990[4]			Disability, 1990
	Occupied units (cont'd)				Unemployment			Percent		
	Renter-occupied									
	Median rent[1] (dollars)	Rent as a percent of income	Substandard units[2] (percent)	Total	Total	Rate[3]	Total	Professional, managerial, and technical	Precision production, craft, and repair	Work disabled persons[5] (percent)
	44	45	46	47	48	49	50	51	52	53
PENNSYLVANIA—Cont'd										
District 8	608	25.9	1.4	309 717	11 844	3.8	297 873	33.9	12.2	6.0
District 9	305	24.0	2.7	265 147	17 495	6.6	247 652	20.9	14.0	9.2
District 10	339	25.1	1.9	266 263	15 789	5.9	250 474	24.3	13.2	9.3
District 11	327	25.3	1.6	263 801	16 119	6.1	247 682	23.6	12.8	9.2
District 12	293	26.4	2.3	239 950	21 128	8.8	218 822	22.9	14.1	10.0
District 13	600	25.1	1.2	306 867	9 707	3.2	297 160	40.8	9.1	5.3
District 14	379	27.7	1.8	267 981	20 026	7.5	247 955	34.9	8.1	9.3
District 15	458	25.8	1.9	289 590	12 885	4.4	276 705	28.5	12.2	6.7
District 16	500	24.4	2.6	297 424	9 386	3.2	288 038	30.5	11.8	5.9
District 17	415	23.2	1.9	302 329	11 453	3.8	290 876	27.0	11.9	7.3
District 18	394	25.6	0.9	274 365	16 022	5.8	258 343	33.8	9.7	7.9
District 19	416	23.1	1.7	304 001	11 036	3.6	292 965	25.2	13.0	6.7
District 20	332	26.3	1.8	253 653	19 433	7.7	234 220	29.5	12.4	8.9
District 21	326	25.9	2.0	264 432	18 466	7.0	245 966	25.2	12.7	8.7
RHODE ISLAND	489	27.5	2.6	522 603	34 690	6.6	487 913	30.1	12.0	8.6
District 1	482	26.9	2.3	262 391	17 478	6.7	244 913	30.5	11.3	8.3
District 2	498	28.2	3.0	260 212	17 212	6.6	243 000	29.6	12.6	8.9
SOUTH CAROLINA	376	24.4	5.0	1 698 098	94 673	5.6	1 603 425	25.4	13.8	9.1
District 1	442	24.5	3.9	276 028	12 757	4.6	263 271	29.0	14.6	8.0
District 2	437	23.9	3.9	290 649	12 811	4.4	277 838	32.9	11.5	7.6
District 3	323	23.5	4.1	287 928	15 842	5.5	272 086	23.2	15.8	9.7
District 4	367	23.1	3.3	303 767	14 747	4.9	289 020	26.6	12.9	9.1
District 5	327	24.2	6.3	281 716	17 457	6.2	264 259	20.5	14.9	9.3
District 6	315	28.4	9.0	258 010	21 059	8.2	236 951	19.5	13.3	11.1
SOUTH DAKOTA	306	24.6	3.4	335 874	13 983	4.2	321 891	24.5	10.4	7.8
At Large	306	24.6	3.4	335 874	13 983	4.2	321 891	24.5	10.4	7.8
TENNESSEE	357	25.0	3.8	2 405 077	154 235	6.4	2 250 842	26.1	12.2	9.7
District 1	295	24.3	3.9	264 028	19 158	7.3	244 870	23.0	14.5	11.4
District 2	337	25.0	2.3	274 284	16 495	6.0	257 789	29.4	11.8	9.5
District 3	348	24.7	3.4	262 737	17 177	6.5	245 560	26.8	12.8	10.6
District 4	277	24.1	4.8	253 005	17 298	6.8	235 707	18.0	15.4	12.5
District 5	430	25.3	2.7	293 835	14 595	5.0	279 240	32.4	9.0	7.4
District 6	378	24.7	3.5	281 653	13 889	4.9	267 764	26.0	12.9	8.3
District 7	412	23.5	3.7	267 725	14 231	5.3	253 494	28.5	11.9	8.2
District 8	311	24.4	3.9	251 295	17 570	7.0	233 725	21.4	13.2	10.4
District 9	362	27.7	6.1	256 515	23 822	9.3	232 693	27.4	8.4	9.4
TEXAS	395	24.6	8.5	8 219 028	584 749	7.1	7 634 279	30.0	11.7	7.6
District 1	334	27.3	5.5	248 343	18 426	7.4	229 917	22.6	14.5	10.3
District 2	333	27.1	7.1	231 862	17 989	7.8	213 873	21.9	15.4	11.1
District 3	497	23.4	4.4	335 764	13 097	3.9	322 667	40.3	8.7	4.5
District 4	385	24.7	4.4	274 486	15 980	5.8	258 506	26.7	13.6	8.9
District 5	413	24.8	7.4	280 707	18 708	6.7	261 999	27.8	11.4	8.8
District 6	462	22.6	2.6	330 700	13 134	4.0	317 566	39.5	9.3	4.7
District 7	454	21.9	6.3	325 020	14 092	4.3	310 928	43.3	7.9	4.0
District 8	442	25.4	4.4	289 190	13 473	4.7	275 717	36.8	11.0	5.6
District 9	398	24.4	5.3	272 644	18 696	6.9	253 948	32.2	13.4	8.2
District 10	415	26.8	6.3	316 965	19 172	6.0	297 793	40.2	7.9	5.8
District 11	362	26.1	5.6	230 624	18 035	7.8	212 589	25.9	12.0	9.1
District 12	402	24.8	6.8	280 345	19 321	6.9	261 024	25.2	14.4	8.9
District 13	334	27.2	6.5	253 774	18 172	7.2	235 602	22.6	12.9	9.4
District 14	344	25.4	8.2	259 128	17 480	6.7	241 648	24.0	15.0	8.1
District 15	290	25.7	22.4	217 324	27 532	12.7	189 792	23.1	12.3	8.9
District 16	345	26.0	15.3	233 127	25 066	10.8	208 061	27.8	10.9	7.9
District 17	329	25.5	5.5	247 014	17 941	7.3	229 073	23.4	13.4	9.5
District 18	364	25.1	12.6	277 165	29 987	10.8	247 178	26.0	11.8	9.4
District 19	366	24.6	5.4	278 872	15 098	5.4	263 774	29.1	12.3	6.8
District 20	362	25.6	11.9	250 483	23 567	9.4	226 916	27.3	11.3	9.0
District 21	434	23.5	3.5	282 164	13 371	4.7	268 793	36.6	9.7	6.8
District 22	455	22.2	6.7	304 311	14 399	4.7	289 912	39.3	10.8	5.0
District 23	322	25.1	16.1	236 209	23 453	9.9	212 756	27.6	11.9	7.5
District 24	414	26.1	10.1	284 128	21 079	7.4	263 049	23.1	13.1	7.8
District 25	398	23.3	9.0	303 961	21 051	6.9	282 910	33.0	11.8	6.1
District 26	488	23.1	4.1	342 809	13 625	4.0	329 184	41.8	6.9	4.3
District 27	343	26.5	16.4	238 459	25 238	10.6	213 221	26.7	12.9	8.3

1. Specified renter-occupied units.　2. Overcrowded or lacking complete plumbing facilities.　3. Percent of total civilian labor force.　4. Persons 16 years old and older.　5. Persons 16 to 64 years of age.

STATE District	Land area, 2000[1] (sq km)	Total persons	Per square kilometer	Race alone or in combination					Hispanic[2]	Non-Hispanic White	2 or more races	Age						
				White	Black	Am. Indian, Alaska Native	Asian and Pacific Islander	Other race				Under 5 years	5 to 17 years	18 to 24 years	25 to 34 years	35 to 44 years	45 to 54 years	55 to 64 years
	1	2	3	4	5	6	7	8	9	10	11	12	13	14	15	16	17	18
TEXAS—Cont'd																		
District 28	31 537.2	646 161	20.5	69.5	8.6	1.2	1.2	22.9	65.0	25.3	3.2	8.3	23.0	9.8	13.7	14.6	11.9	7.9
District 29	678.0	672 591	992.0	53.8	16.1	1.0	2.7	30.0	60.9	20.4	3.5	9.8	23.3	12.4	17.0	14.7	10.6	5.9
District 30	685.0	633 860	925.3	39.9	39.8	0.9	2.9	19.0	34.7	22.5	2.6	8.5	20.8	12.0	18.0	15.1	11.0	6.9
UTAH	212 751.0	2 233 169	10.5	91.1	1.1	1.8	3.2	5.1	9.0	85.3	2.1	9.4	22.8	14.2	14.6	13.4	10.6	6.4
District 1	88 233.2	765 156	8.7	92.8	1.2	1.4	2.1	4.4	7.7	87.9	1.9	9.5	23.6	13.6	13.5	13.2	10.4	6.6
District 2	1 187.0	702 102	591.5	91.4	1.2	1.2	3.8	4.8	8.7	85.3	2.2	8.4	21.2	12.9	15.8	14.7	11.9	6.6
District 3	123 330.9	765 911	6.2	89.1	0.9	2.8	3.5	6.1	10.7	82.5	2.2	10.1	23.6	16.1	14.7	12.4	9.7	5.9
VERMONT	23 956.0	608 827	25.4	97.9	0.7	1.1	1.2	0.4	0.9	96.2	1.2	5.6	18.6	9.3	12.2	16.7	15.4	9.3
At Large	23 956.2	608 827	25.4	97.9	0.7	1.1	1.2	0.4	0.9	96.2	1.2	5.6	18.6	9.3	12.2	16.7	15.4	9.3
VIRGINIA	102 548.0	7 078 515	69.0	73.9	20.4	0.7	4.4	2.7	4.7	70.2	2.0	6.5	18.0	9.6	14.6	17.0	14.1	8.9
District 1	11 430.3	709 060	62.0	76.8	20.5	1.0	2.2	1.5	2.8	74.1	1.8	6.4	19.2	8.9	12.9	17.3	13.8	9.4
District 2	746.6	574 058	768.9	69.6	24.2	1.1	5.8	2.3	4.3	65.6	2.7	7.1	19.0	12.9	16.4	16.8	12.0	6.8
District 3	2 995.3	567 683	189.5	39.6	57.7	1.1	2.0	1.8	2.7	37.5	1.9	7.0	18.8	11.7	14.9	15.9	12.7	7.8
District 4	11 619.8	645 733	55.6	58.4	39.7	0.8	1.6	1.0	1.8	56.6	1.3	6.6	19.6	9.0	13.5	17.2	13.6	8.8
District 5	22 857.7	620 104	27.1	74.1	24.5	0.5	1.1	0.8	1.6	72.6	0.9	5.6	16.7	9.7	12.6	15.5	14.2	10.6
District 6	13 458.8	609 802	45.3	86.2	12.2	0.6	1.3	1.0	1.9	84.2	1.2	5.7	16.4	11.3	12.5	15.1	14.1	9.8
District 7	8 788.3	699 196	79.6	82.6	14.0	0.6	2.9	1.3	2.3	80.5	1.3	6.5	19.1	7.4	13.9	17.8	15.3	8.8
District 8	419.2	627 849	1 497.7	69.9	15.0	0.8	10.2	8.3	13.8	60.5	4.0	6.3	14.4	8.4	20.1	18.1	14.9	8.4
District 9	20 434.4	582 943	28.5	95.8	3.0	0.5	1.0	0.6	1.0	94.5	0.8	5.2	15.4	12.4	13.1	14.7	14.3	10.5
District 10	9 154.2	792 534	86.6	85.1	7.3	0.6	6.1	3.2	5.6	80.4	2.2	7.8	20.1	7.0	15.2	19.1	14.7	8.4
District 11	643.6	649 553	1 009.2	69.8	12.2	0.8	13.9	7.5	12.9	60.3	4.1	7.2	18.6	8.6	16.1	18.0	15.3	8.7
WASHINGTON	172 348.0	5 894 121	34.2	84.9	4.0	2.7	7.4	4.9	7.5	78.9	3.6	6.7	19.0	9.5	14.3	16.5	14.4	8.4
District 1	971.1	632 484	651.3	86.6	2.4	1.8	10.5	2.5	4.2	81.5	3.5	6.3	18.4	8.1	14.6	17.9	15.9	8.6
District 2	16 112.3	719 487	44.7	90.2	1.8	3.0	4.7	3.6	5.8	85.1	3.0	6.9	19.7	9.9	13.6	16.6	14.1	8.2
District 3	21 719.3	698 038	32.1	92.2	1.8	2.4	4.1	2.7	4.7	87.4	3.0	6.9	20.0	8.6	13.0	16.0	14.8	9.0
District 4	61 408.0	672 059	10.9	78.5	1.3	3.8	1.9	17.7	25.4	68.2	3.0	8.0	22.2	9.8	12.7	14.6	13.0	8.2
District 5	45 778.2	625 971	13.7	92.4	1.9	2.8	2.8	2.9	4.9	87.8	2.7	6.4	19.1	11.6	12.5	15.2	14.0	8.5
District 6	16 184.9	611 292	37.8	84.8	6.8	3.9	6.8	2.9	5.0	78.7	4.6	6.2	18.3	9.1	12.6	15.6	14.5	9.4
District 7	327.1	590 062	1 803.9	72.8	10.1	2.1	16.0	4.0	5.6	67.2	4.5	4.8	11.6	11.7	21.2	16.9	14.6	7.5
District 8	7 614.0	695 277	91.3	86.5	3.1	1.8	9.8	2.5	4.1	81.6	3.4	7.1	20.9	7.2	13.8	19.0	15.1	8.3
District 9	2 233.5	649 451	290.8	78.1	8.6	2.8	11.6	4.7	7.2	71.0	5.2	7.3	19.6	9.9	15.2	17.0	13.4	8.1
WEST VIRGINIA	62 361.0	1 808 344	29.0	95.9	3.5	0.6	0.7	0.3	0.7	94.6	0.9	5.6	16.6	9.5	12.7	15.1	15.0	10.2
District 1	15 400.6	595 385	38.7	97.1	2.1	0.5	0.9	0.3	0.7	95.8	0.8	5.4	16.4	10.5	12.4	14.7	14.6	10.2
District 2	24 470.1	635 965	26.0	95.5	3.8	0.6	0.6	0.4	0.8	94.1	1.0	5.9	17.2	8.5	12.8	15.7	15.0	10.3
District 3	22 490.3	576 994	25.7	94.9	4.6	0.6	0.5	0.2	0.6	93.7	0.8	5.6	16.2	9.6	12.8	14.7	15.3	10.2
WISCONSIN	140 663.0	5 363 675	38.1	90.0	6.1	1.3	2.0	2.0	3.6	87.3	1.2	6.4	19.1	9.7	13.2	16.3	13.7	8.5
District 1	5 717.5	612 814	107.2	90.2	6.3	0.7	1.1	3.4	6.3	85.9	1.6	6.7	19.8	9.4	13.2	16.7	13.5	8.5
District 2	13 849.9	624 959	45.1	92.9	3.5	0.8	2.9	1.5	2.7	90.3	1.4	6.1	17.5	12.1	14.9	16.6	14.1	7.8
District 3	27 552.0	600 914	21.8	97.2	0.7	0.9	1.6	0.4	0.9	96.0	0.8	6.0	19.0	12.5	12.1	15.3	13.3	8.4
District 4	759.7	578 409	761.4	88.5	2.6	1.3	2.5	7.2	12.5	81.5	2.0	6.7	17.7	9.1	14.7	16.6	13.5	8.2
District 5	261.2	507 636	1 943.5	51.4	44.6	1.0	3.4	1.9	3.3	48.5	2.1	7.6	20.9	11.3	14.9	14.5	12.3	6.9
District 6	17 396.5	606 416	34.9	96.9	0.9	0.8	1.4	0.8	1.8	95.2	0.8	6.0	19.1	8.7	12.4	16.6	13.7	9.1
District 7	43 309.9	582 884	13.5	96.0	0.4	2.1	2.0	0.4	0.9	94.7	0.9	6.0	19.4	8.7	11.7	16.0	13.9	9.4
District 8	25 498.1	617 575	24.2	93.8	0.9	3.5	1.8	1.2	2.2	91.9	1.1	6.2	19.4	8.6	12.9	16.6	13.6	9.1
District 9	6 317.7	632 068	100.0	96.7	1.0	0.5	1.7	0.9	2.1	94.9	0.8	6.4	19.8	7.1	12.0	17.7	14.7	9.2
WYOMING	251 489.0	493 782	2.0	93.7	1.0	3.0	0.9	3.2	6.4	88.9	1.8	6.3	19.8	10.1	12.1	16.0	15.0	9.0
At Large	251 488.9	493 782	2.0	93.7	1.0	3.0	0.9	3.2	6.4	88.9	1.8	6.3	19.8	10.1	12.1	16.0	15.0	9.0

1. Dry land or land partially or temporarily covered by water. 2. Hispanic persons may be of any race.

Table E. Congressional Districts 107th Congress — Population, Households, Group Quarters, and Education

STATE District	Population and population characteristics, 2000 (cont'd) — Percent (cont'd) — Age (cont'd) 65 to 74 years	75 years and over	Percent female	Households, 2000 Number	Persons per house-hold	Percent Female family house-holder[1]	One person	Persons in correctional institutions, 2000	Persons in nursing homes, 2000	Persons in military quarters, 2000	Education, 1990 School enrollment Public	Private
	19	20	21	22	23	24	25	26	27	28	29	30
TEXAS—Cont'd												
District 28	6.1	4.8	51.1	208 259	3.05	17.6	19.2	4 305	2 661	604	157 245	12 759
District 29	3.8	2.5	49.3	203 259	3.29	16.5	18.8	1 454	889	0	154 413	11 760
District 30	4.5	3.3	50.0	214 509	2.87	20.6	25.9	10 696	2 447	0	134 369	17 936
UTAH	4.5	4.0	49.9	701 281	3.13	9.4	17.8	9 921	6 853	1 760	543 194	67 502
District 1	5.2	4.4	50.0	240 475	3.13	9.0	16.6	2 036	2 680	1 760	192 724	9 821
District 2	4.4	4.2	49.7	236 899	2.91	9.7	21.9	5 564	2 401	0	172 177	18 004
District 3	4.1	3.3	49.9	223 907	3.36	9.5	14.7	2 321	1 772	0	178 293	39 677
VERMONT	6.7	6.0	51.0	240 634	2.44	9.3	26.2	1 219	4 037	22	120 725	25 263
At Large	6.7	6.0	51.0	240 634	2.44	9.3	26.2	1 219	4 037	22	120 725	25 263
VIRGINIA	6.1	5.1	51.0	2 699 173	2.54	11.9	25.1	64 036	38 865	33 752	1 331 800	214 457
District 1	6.7	5.4	50.8	262 613	2.60	11.0	22.2	11 199	3 970	1 659	126 100	17 380
District 2	5.0	4.0	49.6	207 877	2.63	13.1	22.9	1 064	2 339	20 573	119 067	20 609
District 3	5.9	5.3	52.7	224 993	2.43	21.7	30.2	4 198	3 596	2 686	131 237	15 601
District 4	6.3	5.4	50.9	233 963	2.62	16.4	22.7	17 042	3 163	5 508	122 066	16 907
District 5	8.3	6.8	51.5	246 757	2.41	12.4	26.6	7 934	3 968	0	121 572	14 065
District 6	7.8	7.2	52.0	241 584	2.39	11.4	27.7	4 505	5 798	0	112 661	24 049
District 7	6.1	5.1	51.4	267 736	2.55	9.8	23.6	6 521	4 543	0	117 788	20 941
District 8	4.8	4.5	50.6	263 688	2.34	8.7	33.8	3 481	2 573	1 859	95 485	30 708
District 9	7.8	6.5	50.7	234 526	2.38	9.9	26.0	5 562	3 890	2	141 235	8 184
District 10	4.5	3.2	50.3	284 781	2.76	8.5	19.4	1 325	2 699	77	118 191	20 590
District 11	4.3	3.1	50.3	230 655	2.78	9.6	21.3	1 205	2 326	1 388	126 398	25 423
WASHINGTON	5.7	5.5	50.2	2 271 398	2.53	9.9	26.2	28 871	23 275	13 868	1 091 450	160 862
District 1	5.2	5.1	50.6	247 257	2.52	8.5	24.8	1 887	1 944	879	116 357	21 367
District 2	5.7	5.5	50.0	270 983	2.60	9.5	23.6	2 911	2 210	3 365	122 300	14 039
District 3	6.1	5.8	50.5	267 260	2.58	10.2	24.0	2 306	2 970	22	125 222	12 971
District 4	5.9	5.5	49.9	236 177	2.80	10.6	22.5	2 594	2 697	9	136 004	10 557
District 5	6.3	6.5	50.5	241 248	2.48	10.3	27.4	6 026	3 646	698	139 265	20 396
District 6	7.3	6.9	50.5	243 494	2.43	11.2	27.8	8 576	2 886	2 040	112 644	17 036
District 7	5.2	6.5	50.0	266 272	2.12	8.4	39.8	3 394	2 847	232	100 187	27 234
District 8	4.7	4.0	50.1	255 125	2.71	8.6	20.2	143	1 311	0	123 575	19 386
District 9	5.1	4.3	49.9	243 582	2.61	12.0	24.7	1 034	2 764	6 623	115 896	17 876
WEST VIRGINIA	8.2	7.1	51.4	736 481	2.40	10.7	27.1	10 505	11 601	59	403 602	32 911
District 1	8.2	7.6	51.5	242 584	2.38	10.2	27.8	2 416	4 514	0	136 269	14 280
District 2	8.0	6.6	51.2	258 077	2.42	10.5	26.4	2 212	3 620	59	126 081	10 713
District 3	8.5	7.2	51.5	235 820	2.39	11.6	27.2	5 877	3 467	0	141 252	7 918
WISCONSIN	6.6	6.5	50.6	2 084 544	2.50	9.6	26.8	31 068	41 370	82	1 088 366	213 864
District 1	6.3	5.9	50.5	230 453	2.58	10.9	24.7	3 879	3 728	5	122 994	21 549
District 2	5.6	5.5	50.3	250 519	2.41	7.8	28.2	4 175	3 702	0	141 960	15 302
District 3	6.6	6.8	50.4	228 360	2.52	7.8	25.7	2 664	5 906	0	142 442	14 622
District 4	6.8	6.7	50.7	231 445	2.45	10.4	29.7	2 017	3 233	13	99 448	33 885
District 5	5.7	5.9	53.3	201 567	2.44	20.6	33.7	2 063	4 564	0	120 632	36 364
District 6	7.4	7.1	50.0	234 087	2.50	7.6	25.5	6 996	5 591	53	114 170	22 184
District 7	7.5	7.5	50.3	228 895	2.49	8.0	26.1	1 279	5 110	2	123 503	16 013
District 8	7.0	6.6	50.2	241 200	2.50	8.0	25.8	3 685	4 527	7	113 855	23 348
District 9	6.7	6.3	50.3	238 018	2.59	7.0	22.3	4 310	5 009	2	109 362	30 597
WYOMING	6.3	5.3	49.7	193 608	2.48	8.7	26.3	4 176	2 869	545	127 228	7 511
At Large	6.3	5.3	49.7	193 608	2.48	8.7	26.3	4 176	2 869	545	127 228	7 511

1. No spouse present.

STATE District	Education, 1990 (cont'd) Attainment[1] (percent)		Money income, 1989			Percent below poverty level, 1989		Housing units, 1990					
				Households		Persons	Families		Occupied units				
										Owner-occupied			
												Owner cost as a percent of income	
	High school graduate or more	Bachelor's degree or more	Per capita[2]	Median	Percent with $100,000 or more	Total	Total	Total	Total	Percent	Median value[3] (dollars)	With a mortgage	Without a mortgage
	31	32	33	34	35	36	37	38	39	40	41	42	43
TEXAS—Cont'd													
District 28	58.4	8.3	8 050	20 276	0.9	28.2	24.2	204 554	178 888	68.6	40 400	21.1	13.0
District 29	55.6	8.6	9 314	23 808	1.4	21.8	18.3	212 350	184 101	52.0	40 900	19.8	13.0
District 30	65.8	14.2	11 015	24 775	2.0	21.8	18.1	229 883	196 049	47.7	60 200	21.1	13.8
UTAH	85.1	22.3	11 029	29 470	2.5	11.4	8.6	598 388	537 273	68.1	68 900	20.9	12.1
District 1	85.6	20.5	10 856	30 563	1.9	10.1	7.4	196 470	176 881	71.5	69 000	20.3	11.9
District 2	87.4	27.1	12 971	30 960	3.9	8.9	6.7	206 429	193 316	64.9	76 900	21.4	12.1
District 3	82.1	18.6	9 259	26 570	1.6	15.2	11.7	195 489	167 076	68.3	60 100	20.9	12.3
VERMONT	80.8	24.3	13 527	29 792	2.8	9.9	6.9	271 214	210 650	69.0	95 500	21.9	14.7
At Large	80.8	24.3	13 527	29 792	2.8	9.9	6.9	271 214	210 650	69.0	95 500	21.9	14.7
VIRGINIA	75.2	24.5	15 713	33 328	5.2	10.2	7.7	2 496 334	2 291 830	66.3	91 000	21.9	12.5
District 1	77.0	21.3	14 872	33 743	3.7	8.2	5.9	231 932	205 434	71.9	93 600	22.3	12.7
District 2	85.3	23.6	14 492	32 576	3.7	8.1	5.7	210 018	192 765	57.0	93 100	24.5	12.4
District 3	64.2	12.4	10 357	22 351	1.1	21.8	18.8	231 754	209 435	49.1	62 100	22.3	14.5
District 4	69.3	14.1	12 887	30 425	2.3	11.4	8.9	215 276	199 069	71.2	73 200	21.9	13.0
District 5	60.7	13.3	11 675	24 807	1.9	14.1	10.4	237 017	212 145	72.0	56 000	17.4	12.3
District 6	69.8	16.7	13 017	27 155	2.4	11.1	7.8	232 223	215 001	68.1	65 100	17.9	12.2
District 7	81.9	30.5	18 360	38 865	5.9	5.3	3.5	232 273	217 794	70.4	91 800	20.5	12.3
District 8	88.6	48.0	24 799	48 839	11.8	5.4	3.3	249 112	232 754	54.8	209 900	22.3	11.8
District 9	57.6	11.7	10 097	20 857	1.3	19.1	14.7	231 442	210 961	73.9	49 100	18.2	12.1
District 10	81.2	30.3	20 065	46 205	10.3	4.9	3.3	216 181	197 675	74.2	155 400	24.4	12.5
District 11	90.4	44.3	22 202	54 369	12.8	3.9	2.5	209 106	198 797	67.6	191 000	23.6	11.6
WASHINGTON	83.8	22.9	14 923	31 183	3.7	10.9	7.8	2 032 378	1 872 431	62.6	93 400	20.4	11.8
District 1	90.7	31.2	18 687	40 390	6.3	5.1	3.4	214 896	205 181	66.8	148 200	21.7	11.5
District 2	83.4	17.7	14 419	31 305	3.2	9.4	6.6	227 215	202 215	65.7	100 500	21.0	11.9
District 3	81.5	16.9	13 328	29 154	2.4	11.3	8.6	225 971	206 863	64.9	70 400	18.5	11.7
District 4	73.0	16.1	11 578	25 055	2.1	17.6	13.4	221 456	196 812	63.2	60 300	17.3	11.7
District 5	83.0	20.3	12 177	25 107	2.2	15.3	10.7	227 492	207 264	63.8	57 700	18.8	12.0
District 6	82.3	17.8	13 403	27 882	2.4	12.7	9.6	238 327	211 878	61.5	74 700	20.2	12.2
District 7	86.4	37.0	18 021	29 707	4.6	12.2	7.4	257 878	244 606	49.7	133 300	20.9	11.7
District 8	88.7	29.0	18 432	42 379	7.0	5.3	3.8	205 496	195 943	72.1	142 200	21.5	11.5
District 9	84.6	18.2	14 264	32 194	2.7	9.6	7.5	213 647	201 669	58.3	93 300	20.8	11.7
WEST VIRGINIA	66.0	12.3	10 520	20 795	1.5	19.7	16.0	781 295	688 557	74.1	47 900	17.5	12.0
District 1	70.9	13.7	10 920	21 903	1.5	17.3	13.4	258 144	230 990	73.9	46 700	16.9	12.1
District 2	67.3	13.1	11 083	22 253	1.7	17.6	14.2	263 693	230 330	73.9	55 600	17.3	11.8
District 3	59.7	10.2	9 557	18 166	1.4	24.1	20.3	259 458	227 237	74.4	41 900	18.6	12.1
WISCONSIN	78.6	17.7	13 276	29 442	2.6	10.7	7.6	2 055 774	1 822 118	66.7	62 500	20.1	13.4
District 1	77.1	14.8	13 567	31 431	2.4	9.8	7.3	218 877	198 940	68.5	61 700	18.9	12.9
District 2	84.8	26.7	14 319	30 625	3.2	10.1	5.5	221 842	208 577	60.6	70 000	20.8	13.3
District 3	78.1	16.3	11 505	25 758	1.9	13.0	8.3	216 730	197 728	69.7	52 600	19.8	13.8
District 4	78.7	16.6	14 177	32 260	1.9	8.0	6.1	217 561	210 102	60.5	71 800	20.8	13.9
District 5	76.3	23.6	13 277	26 267	3.1	21.0	17.1	219 667	207 859	47.9	63 200	20.6	13.8
District 6	76.4	13.1	12 400	28 038	1.9	8.7	6.1	232 394	201 139	73.2	55 000	19.3	13.0
District 7	75.6	13.2	11 427	25 277	1.7	11.6	8.4	257 014	202 076	74.3	48 600	18.5	13.6
District 8	78.4	14.8	12 628	28 169	2.2	9.9	7.5	269 817	202 772	72.4	58 100	20.1	13.7
District 9	82.1	20.8	16 187	37 579	5.5	4.3	2.9	201 872	192 925	74.7	82 800	20.7	13.1
WYOMING	83.0	18.8	12 311	27 096	2.0	11.9	9.3	203 411	168 839	67.8	61 600	18.8	11.9
At Large	83.0	18.8	12 311	27 096	2.0	11.9	9.3	203 411	168 839	67.8	61 600	18.8	11.9

1. Persons 25 years old and older.   2. Based on the population enumerated as of April 1, 1990.   3. Specified owner-occupied units.

STATE District	Housing units, 1990 (cont'd) Occupied units (cont'd) Renter-occupied Median rent[1] (dollars)	Rent as a percent of income	Substandard units[2] (percent)	Civilian labor force, 1990 Total	Unemployment Total	Rate[3]	Civilian employment, 1990[4] Total	Percent Professional, managerial, and technical	Precision production, craft, and repair	Disability, 1990 Work disabled persons[5] (percent)
	44	45	46	47	48	49	50	51	52	53
TEXAS—Cont'd										
District 28	328	27.5	14.5	236 118	25 781	10.9	210 337	20.1	14.6	10.0
District 29	357	23.9	17.4	268 722	24 372	9.1	244 350	17.5	17.1	7.7
District 30	413	25.7	12.4	288 610	27 414	9.5	261 196	22.6	10.8	8.9
UTAH	369	23.8	5.4	777 448	41 389	5.3	736 059	30.8	11.4	7.3
District 1	364	22.8	5.1	251 977	13 524	5.4	238 453	30.5	12.0	7.3
District 2	379	23.7	3.8	278 409	12 163	4.4	266 246	34.1	9.6	6.8
District 3	358	24.8	7.7	247 062	15 702	6.4	231 360	27.4	12.8	7.8
VERMONT	446	27.1	2.5	300 746	17 600	5.9	283 146	31.3	12.3	7.9
At Large	446	27.1	2.5	300 746	17 600	5.9	283 146	31.3	12.3	7.9
VIRGINIA	495	25.8	4.1	3 170 410	142 048	4.5	3 028 362	33.8	11.5	7.5
District 1	493	25.1	4.2	278 919	12 261	4.4	266 658	32.1	13.9	7.1
District 2	528	27.3	3.0	244 505	13 336	5.5	231 169	33.7	11.7	6.5
District 3	401	27.6	5.1	256 505	21 111	8.2	235 394	22.1	12.2	10.4
District 4	424	25.8	5.0	270 943	14 187	5.2	256 756	26.2	15.5	8.7
District 5	325	23.0	6.0	283 066	13 267	4.7	269 799	21.8	13.3	9.0
District 6	358	23.6	2.9	284 592	11 948	4.2	272 644	25.8	11.8	8.4
District 7	520	24.5	2.1	314 480	9 016	2.9	305 464	37.2	10.9	5.8
District 8	729	26.1	4.3	338 394	10 174	3.0	328 220	52.5	6.0	4.8
District 9	315	26.8	5.3	250 636	17 841	7.1	232 795	23.1	15.0	12.6
District 10	657	24.9	3.1	317 049	9 985	3.1	307 064	38.5	11.8	5.7
District 11	797	26.3	3.8	331 321	8 922	2.7	322 399	47.9	7.4	4.5
WASHINGTON	445	25.7	4.1	2 433 177	139 216	5.7	2 293 961	31.7	11.6	9.1
District 1	587	25.6	2.5	297 349	10 541	3.5	286 808	37.2	11.3	6.6
District 2	468	25.7	4.1	260 820	13 052	5.0	247 768	25.9	16.0	9.2
District 3	414	24.9	3.5	257 075	17 337	6.7	239 738	27.9	12.2	10.5
District 4	333	24.1	7.4	252 252	21 016	8.3	231 236	25.7	10.2	9.7
District 5	345	26.8	3.3	249 711	18 589	7.4	231 122	30.0	9.8	10.5
District 6	415	26.1	4.2	240 079	17 254	7.2	222 825	29.3	12.6	11.3
District 7	462	26.9	4.3	312 107	15 483	5.0	296 624	40.4	7.3	8.4
District 8	550	24.9	2.8	292 610	11 004	3.8	281 606	36.4	12.0	6.7
District 9	478	24.9	4.4	271 174	14 940	5.5	256 234	28.4	13.6	9.3
WEST VIRGINIA	303	26.8	4.0	742 227	71 142	9.6	671 085	25.4	14.5	12.6
District 1	307	26.8	2.9	259 983	22 313	8.6	237 670	25.8	14.2	9.9
District 2	321	25.0	4.3	262 039	22 157	8.5	239 882	25.4	14.0	11.4
District 3	284	28.9	4.7	220 205	26 672	12.1	193 533	24.9	15.5	16.6
WISCONSIN	399	24.9	2.6	2 517 238	130 799	5.2	2 386 439	26.4	11.5	7.3
District 1	401	24.7	2.4	279 309	16 363	5.9	262 946	24.2	13.6	7.7
District 2	441	25.4	2.4	305 316	11 006	3.6	294 310	32.6	9.2	6.1
District 3	336	25.6	2.7	276 114	14 778	5.4	261 336	23.5	10.4	7.4
District 4	448	24.6	2.7	289 999	13 381	4.6	276 618	27.5	12.3	7.4
District 5	435	28.3	4.0	262 758	21 519	8.2	241 239	32.0	8.3	9.3
District 6	349	23.3	2.0	273 295	13 169	4.8	260 126	21.8	12.8	7.1
District 7	327	24.7	3.0	264 755	16 602	6.3	248 153	22.7	11.4	8.1
District 8	357	23.5	2.4	274 228	14 487	5.3	259 741	24.0	12.4	7.0
District 9	430	22.4	1.5	291 464	9 494	3.3	281 970	28.3	13.0	5.8
WYOMING	333	23.7	3.1	220 980	13 112	5.9	207 868	27.2	13.2	7.3
At Large	333	23.7	3.1	220 980	13 112	5.9	207 868	27.2	13.2	7.3

1. Specified renter-occupied units.   2. Overcrowded or lacking complete plumbing facilities.   3. Percent of total civilian labor force.   4. Persons 16 years old and older.   5. Persons 16 to 64 years of age.

Appendices

APPENDIX A
GEOGRAPHIC CONCEPTS AND CODES

AREAS FOR WHICH DATA ARE PRESENTED

County and City Extra presents data for States (Table A), States and Counties (Table B), Metropolitan Areas (Table C), Cities (Table D), and Congressional Districts (Table E).

STATES AND COUNTIES

Data are presented for each of the 50 states, the District of Columbia, and the United States as a whole. The states are arranged alphabetically, and in Table B counties are arranged alphabetically within each state.

Data are presented for 3,141 counties and county equivalents. Maps of each state, showing their counties and county equivalents and their metropolitan areas are contained in Appendix D.

County equivalents

In Louisiana, the primary divisions of the state are known as parishes rather than counties. In Alaska, the county equivalents are the organized boroughs, together with the census areas that were developed for general statistical purposes by the State of Alaska and the U.S. Bureau of the Census. Four states—Maryland, Missouri, Nevada, and Virginia—have one or more incorporated places that are legally independent of any county and thus constitute primary divisions of their states. Within each state, independent cities are listed alphabetically following the list of counties. A list of independent cities is given at the end of this appendix. The District of Columbia is not divided into counties or county equivalents—data for the entire District are presented as a county equivalent. New York City contains five counties—Bronx, Kings, New York, Queens, and Richmond.

County changes since the 1990 Census

- Dade County in Florida officially became Miami-Dade County.
- Denali Borough in Alaska was formed primarily from the Yukon-Koyukuk census area and a small part of the Southeast Fairbanks census area.
- The Skagway-Yakutat-Angoon census area in Alaska was dissolved and replaced by Yakutat Borough and the Skagway-Hoonah-Angoon census area.
- South Boston City in Virginia, formerly an independent city, became a town within Halifax County.
- Yellowstone Park in Montana, which had not been part of any county, was dissolved as a county equivalent and became part of Park and Gallatin Counties.
- The city of Takoma Park, Maryland, formerly split between Montgomery and Prince George's Counties, moved its boundary, and now lies completely within Montgomery County.

METROPOLITAN AREAS

Table C presents data for 335 metropolitan areas comprising 248 metropolitan statistical areas (MSAs), 17 consolidated metropolitan statistical areas (CMSAs), 58 primary metropolitan statistical areas (PMSAs), and 12 New England county metropolitan areas (NECMAs). The left-hand column of each page provides an alphabetical listing of MSAs, CMSAs, and NECMAs—PMSAs are listed alphabetically under the CMSAs of which they are components.

The metropolitan areas used in this edition of *County and City Extra* are those defined by the U.S. government based on 1990 census data. The U.S. Office of Management and Budget first issued these definitions in December 1992. Additional revisions occurred throughout the decade, with the final revisions dated June 30, 1999.

In general, a metropolitan area is a geographic area consisting of a large population nucleus together with adjacent communities that have a high degree of economic and social integration with that nucleus. The major purpose of defining these areas is to enable all U.S. government agencies to use the same geographic definitions in tabulating and publishing data.

Metropolitan complexes with populations of one million or more may be divided into primary metropolitan statistical areas (PMSAs) with the support of local opinion. When PMSAs are defined, the larger metropolitan area of which they are components is designated a consolidated metropolitan statistical area (CMSA).

For most of the United States, metropolitan areas are defined in terms of counties because counties are the smallest geographical units for which a wide variety of statistical data can be obtained. In New England, however, the metropolitan area definitions are in terms of cities and towns because these subcounty units are of great local significance. An alternative concept for the New England states is the New England county metropolitan area (NECMA). NECMAs, rather than MSAs, CMSAs, and PMSAs, are presented for New England in this volume to allow presentation of a variety of data that are available only for counties and groups of counties.

In recent years, the Office of Management and Budget has issued new standards that will eventually replace the current metropolitan statistical areas. These will be based on the 2000 census and will be defined in 2003. The criteria will be new, and there will be smaller areas called micropolitan areas in addition to metropolitan areas.

CITIES

Table D presents data for 1,237 cities with 2000 census populations of 25,000 or more. Corresponding data for states are also provided. The states are arranged alphabetically, and the cities are arranged alphabetically within each state.

As used in this volume, the term *city* refers to places that have been incorporated as cities, boroughs, towns, or villages under the laws of their respective states. Towns in the New England states and New York are treated as minor civil divisions (MCDs) and are not included in the cities database. For Hawaii, data for census designated places (CDPs) are included in the Cities table, since the U.S. Bureau of the Census does not recognize any incorporated places in Hawaii. CDPs are delineated by the U.S. Bureau of the Census, in cooperation with states and localities, as statistical counterparts of incorporated places for purposes of the decennial census. CDPs comprise densely settled concentrations of population that are identifiable by name but are not legally incorporated places.

A consolidated city is an incorporated place that has combined its governmental functions with a county or subcounty entity but contains one or more other semi-independent incorporated places that continue to function as local governments within the consolidated government. Consolidated cities included in this volume are Milford, CT; Athens-Clarke County, GA; Augusta-Richmond County, GA; Columbus, GA; Indianapolis, IN; Butte-Silver Bow, MT; and Nashville-Davidson, TN.

CONGRESSIONAL DISTRICTS

The congressional districts shown in this volume are the districts used for the election of the 107th Congress, which convened in January 2001. These are the districts that were established following the 1990 Census and are based on population data from that census. As a result of litigation, some boundaries have changed during the decade. The new data from the 2000 census are being used to draw boundaries for the 108th Congress. Data are shown for the 435 regular districts plus the District of Columbia, which has no representative. Corresponding data for each state also are included. States are listed alphabetically and districts numerically within each state. A map showing congressional districts of the 105th Congress is included in Appendix D. There have been no boundary changes since then.

GEOGRAPHIC CODES

Tables A, B, C, and D provide, in one or more columns at the beginning of the table, a geographic code or codes for each area.

In Table B (States and Counties), a five-digit state and county code is given for each state and county. The first two digits indicate the state; the remaining three represent the county. Within each state the counties are numbered in alphabetical order, beginning with 001, with even numbers usually omitted. Independent cities follow the counties and begin with the number 510. In the second column of Table B, a four-digit metropolitan area (MSA, PMSA, or NECMA) code is given for those counties that are within metropolitan areas. In Table A, a two-digit state code is provided. The state code is a sequential numbering, with some gaps, of the states and the District of Columbia in alphabetical order from Alabama (01) to Wyoming (56).

These codes have been established by the U.S. government as Federal Information Processing Standards and are often referred to as *FIPS codes*. They are used by U.S. government agencies and many other organizations for data presentation. The codes are provided in this volume for use in matching the data given here with other data sources in which counties may be identified by FIPS code. The metro area codes will also enable the user to

identify the metro area of which a county is a component. Table C (Metropolitan Areas) provides the same metro area codes for each metropolitan area.

Table D (Cities) provides, in the first column, a seven-digit state and place code. The first two digits identify the state and are the same as the state FIPS codes described above. The remaining five digits are the place FIPS codes established by the U.S. government.

INDEPENDENT CITIES

Independent cities are not included in any county; data are presented separately in this volume.

MARYLAND:
    Baltimore: (Separate from Baltimore County)

MISSOURI:
    St. Louis: (Separate from St. Louis County)

NEVADA:
    Carson City

VIRGINIA:

Alexandria	Lynchburg
Bedford	Manassas
Bristol	Manassas Park
Buena Vista	Martinsville
Charlottesville	Newport News
Chesapeake	Norfolk
Clifton Forge	Norton
Colonial Heights	Petersburg
Covington	Poquoson
Danville	Portsmouth
Emporia	Radford
Fairfax	Richmond
Falls Church	Roanoke
Franklin	Salem
Fredericksburg	Staunton
Galax	Suffolk
Hampton	Virginia Beach
Harrisonburg	Waynesboro
Hopewell	Williamsburg
Lexington	Winchester

COUNTY TYPE

Table B (States and Counties) provides, in the third column, a *county type* code that identifies each county by its metropolitan/nonmetropolitan status and its size. These codes were developed by the Economic Research Service (ERS) of the U.S. Department of Agriculture and are commonly referred to as *Beale* codes after their originator, Calvin Beale. The ERS county typology scheme goes beyond the Beale codes to a detailed typology of economic and land-use classifications. In this volume, only the basic Beale codes, based on the 1990 Census, are used:

Metropolitan Counties

0. Central county of a metropolitan area of 1 million population or more.
1. Fringe county of a metropolitan area of 1 million population or more.
2. County in a metropolitan area of 250,000 to 1,000,000 population.
3. County in a metropolitan area of less than 250,000 population.

Nonmetropolitan Counties

4. Urban population of 20,000 or more, adjacent to a metropolitan area.
5. Urban population of 20,000 or more, not adjacent to a metropolitan area.
6. Urban population of 2,500–19,999, adjacent to a metropolitan area.
7. Urban population of 2,500–19,999, not adjacent to a metropolitan area.
8. Completely rural (no places with a population of 2,500 or more), adjacent to a metropolitan area.
9. Completely rural (no places with a population of 2,500 or more), not adjacent to a metropolitan area.

APPENDIX B
METROPOLITAN STATISTICAL AREAS AND COMPONENTS

(MSA = metropolitan statistical area; CMSA = consolidated MSA; PMSA = primary MSA; and NECMA = New England county metropolitan area. For further information, see Appendix A.)

MSA/CMSA/PMSA/NECMA	State and County	Title and Geographic Components	2000 Population	MSA/CMSA/PMSA/NECMA	State and County	Title and Geographic Components	2000 Population
0040		Abilene, TX MSA...............................	126 555		13 063	Clayton County, GA..........................	236 517
	48 441	Taylor County, TX............................	126 555		13 067	Cobb County, GA	607 751
0080		Akron, OH PMSA	694 960		13 077	Coweta County, GA	89 215
		(See Cleveland-Akron, OH CMSA)			13 089	De Kalb County, GA	665 865
0120		Albany, GA MSA	120 822		13 097	Douglas County, GA	92 174
	13 095	Dougherty County, GA	96 065		13 113	Fayette County, GA	91 263
	13 177	Lee County, GA	24 757		13 117	Forsyth County, GA	98 407
0160		Albany-Schenectady-Troy, NY MSA	875 583		13 121	Fulton County, GA	816 006
	36 001	Albany County, NY	294 565		13 135	Gwinnett County, GA	588 448
	36 057	Montgomery County, NY	49 708		13 151	Henry County, GA	119 341
	36 083	Rensselaer County, NY	152 538		13 217	Newton County, GA	62 001
	36 091	Saratoga County, NY	200 635		13 223	Paulding County, GA	81 678
	36 093	Schenectady County, NY	146 555		13 227	Pickens County, GA	22 983
	36 095	Schoharie County, NY	31 582		13 247	Rockdale County, GA	70 111
0200		Albuquerque, NM MSA	712 738		13 255	Spalding County, GA	58 417
	35 001	Bernalillo County, NM	556 678		13 297	Walton County, GA	60 687
	35 043	Sandoval County, NM	89 908	0560		Atlantic-Cape May, NJ PMSA	354 878
	35 061	Valencia County, NM	66 152			(See Philadelphia-Wilmington-Atlantic City, PA-NJ-DE-MD CMSA)	
0220		Alexandria, LA MSA	126 337	0580		Auburn-Opelika, AL MSA	115 092
	22 079	Rapides Parish, LA	126 337		01 081	Lee County, AL	115 092
0240		Allentown-Bethlehem-Easton, PA MSA ...	637 958	0600		Augusta-Aiken, GA-SC MSA	477 441
	42 025	Carbon County, PA	58 802		13 073	Columbia County, GA	89 288
	42 077	Lehigh County, PA............................	312 090		13 189	McDuffie County, GA	21 231
	42 095	Northampton County, PA.....................	267 066		13 245	Richmond County, GA	199 775
					45 003	Aiken County, SC	142 552
0280		Altoona, PA MSA	129 144		45 037	Edgefield County, SC	24 595
	42 013	Blair County, PA	129 144	0640		Austin-San Marcos, TX MSA	1 249 763
0320		Amarillo, TX MSA	217 858		48 021	Bastrop County, TX	57 733
	48 375	Potter County, TX	113 546		48 055	Caldwell County, TX	32 194
	48 381	Randall County, TX	104 312		48 209	Hays County, TX	97 589
					48 453	Travis County, TX	812 280
0380		Anchorage, AK MSA	260 283		48 491	Williamson County, TX	249 967
	02 020	Anchorage Borough, AK	260 283	0680		Bakersfield, CA MSA	661 645
0440		Ann Arbor, MI PMSA..........................	578 736		06 029	Kern County, CA..............................	661 645
		(See Detroit-Ann Arbor-Flint, MI CMSA)		0720	08 872	Baltimore, MD PMSA	2 552 994
0450		Anniston, AL MSA	112 249			(See Washington-Baltimore, DC-MD-VA-WV CMSA)	
	01 015	Calhoun County, AL	112 249	0733		Bangor, ME NECMA	144 919
0460		Appleton-Oshkosh-Neenah, WI MSA......	358 365		23 019	Penobscot County, ME	144 919
	55 015	Calumet County, WI	40 631	0743		Barnstable-Yarmouth, MA NECMA	222 230
	55 087	Outagamie County, WI	160 971		25 001	Barnstable County, MA	222 230
	55 139	Winnebago County, WI.......................	156 763	0760		Baton Rouge, LA MSA	602 894
0480		Asheville, NC MSA............................	225 965		22 005	Ascension Parish, LA	76 627
	37 021	Buncombe County, NC.......................	206 330		22 033	East Baton Rouge Parish, LA	412 852
	37 115	Madison County, NC..........................	19 635		22 063	Livingston Parish, LA........................	91 814
0500		Athens, GA MSA	153 444		22 121	West Baton Rouge Parish, LA	21 601
	13 059	Clarke County, GA............................	101 489	0840		Beaumont-Port Arthur, TX MSA............	385 090
	13 195	Madison County, GA	25 730		48 199	Hardin County, TX	48 073
	13 219	Oconee County, GA	26 225		48 245	Jefferson County, TX	252 051
0520		Atlanta, GA MSA	4 112 198		48 361	Orange County, TX	84 966
	13 013	Barrow County, GA	46 144	0860		Bellingham, WA MSA	166 814
	13 015	Bartow County, GA	76 019		53 073	Whatcom County, WA	166 814
	13 045	Carroll County, GA	87 268				
	13 057	Cherokee County, GA	141 903				

(MSA = metropolitan statistical area; CMSA = consolidated MSA; PMSA = primary MSA; and NECMA = New England county metropolitan area. For further information, see Appendix A.)

Geographic Codes				Geographic Codes			
MSA/ CMSA/ PMSA/ NECMA	State and County	Title and Geographic Components	2000 Population	MSA/ CMSA/ PMSA/ NECMA	State and County	Title and Geographic Components	2000 Population
0870		Benton Harbor, MI MSA....................	162 453	1260		Bryan-College Station, TX MSA.................	152 415
	26 021	Berrien County, MI.........................	162 453		48 041	Brazos County, TX	152 415
0875		Bergen-Passaic, NJ PMSA	1 373 167	1280		Buffalo-Niagara Falls, NY MSA.................	1 170 111
		(See New York-Northern New Jersey-Long Island, NY-NJ-CT-PA CMSA)			36 029	Erie County, NY.........................	950 265
					36 063	Niagara County, NY	219 846
0880		Billings, MT MSA.............................	129 352	1303		Burlington, VT NECMA	198 889
	30 111	Yellowstone County, MT....................	129 352		50 077	Chittenden County, VT....................	146 571
0920		Biloxi-Gulfport-Pascagoula, MS MSA	363 988		50 011	Franklin County, VT	45 417
	28 045	Hancock County, MS......................	42 967		50 013	Grand Isle County, VT....................	6 901
	28 047	Harrison County, MS......................	189 601	1320		Canton-Massillon, OH MSA.................	406 934
	28 059	Jackson County, MS......................	131 420		39 019	Carroll County, OH	28 836
0960		Binghamton, NY MSA........................	252 320		39 151	Stark County, OH	378 098
	36 007	Broome County, NY......................	200 536	1350		Casper, WY MSA............................	66 533
	36 107	Tioga County, NY	51 784		56 025	Natrona County, WY......................	66 533
1000		Birmingham, AL MSA........................	921 106	1360		Cedar Rapids, IA MSA......................	191 701
	01 009	Blount County, AL.........................	51 024		19 113	Linn County, IA	191 701
	01 073	Jefferson County, AL......................	662 047				
	01 115	St. Clair County, AL......................	64 742	1400		Champaign-Urbana, IL MSA	179 669
	01 117	Shelby County, AL........................	143 293		17 019	Champaign County, IL....................	179 669
1010		Bismarck, ND MSA..........................	94 719	1480		Charleston, WV MSA........................	251 662
1010	38 015	Burleigh County, ND......................	69 416		54 039	Kanawha County, WV....................	200 073
1010	38 059	Morton County, ND.......................	25 303		54 079	Putnam County, WV......................	51 589
1020		Bloomington, IN MSA.......................	120 563	1440		Charleston-North Charleston, SC MSA	549 033
1020	18 105	Monroe County, IN	120 563		45 015	Berkeley County, SC.....................	142 651
1040		Bloomington-Normal, IL MSA.................	150 433		45 019	Charleston County, SC...................	309 969
1040	17 113	McLean County, IL	150 433		45 035	Dorchester County, SC...................	96 413
1080		Boise City, ID MSA..........................	432 345	1520		Charlotte-Gastonia-Rock Hill, NC-SC MSA	1 499 293
1080	16 001	Ada County, ID	300 904		37 025	Cabarrus County, NC.....................	131 063
1080	16 027	Canyon County, ID	131 441		37 071	Gaston County, NC	190 365
1123		Boston-Worcester-Lawrence-Lowell-Brockton, MA-NH NECMA	6 057 826		37 109	Lincoln County, NC	63 780
					37 119	Mecklenburg County, NC.................	695 454
	25 005	Bristol County, MA........................	534 678		37 159	Rowan County, NC	130 340
	25 009	Essex County, MA........................	723 419		37 179	Union County, NC	123 677
	25 017	Middlesex County, MA.....................	1 465 396		45 091	York County, SC.........................	164 614
	25 021	Norfolk County, MA.......................	650 308	1540		Charlottesville, VA MSA....................	159 576
	25 023	Plymouth County, MA.....................	472 822		51 003	Albemarle County, VA....................	79 236
	25 025	Suffolk County, MA.......................	689 807		51 065	Fluvanna County, VA.....................	20 047
	25 027	Worcester County, MA....................	750 963		51 079	Greene County, VA	15 244
	33 011	Hillsborough County, NH	380 841		51 540	Charlottesville City, VA...................	45 049
	33 015	Rockingham County, NH	277 359	1560		Chattanooga, TN-GA MSA..................	465 161
	33 017	Strafford County, NH	112 233		13 047	Catoosa County, GA.....................	53 282
1125		Boulder-Longmont, CO PMSA	291 288		13 083	Dade County, GA	15 154
		(See Denver-Boulder-Greeley, CO CMSA)			13 295	Walker County, GA	61 053
1145		Brazoria, TX PMSA	241 767		47 065	Hamilton County, TN.....................	307 896
		(See Houston-Galveston-Brazoria, TX CMSA)			47 115	Marion County, TN	27 776
				1580		Cheyenne, WY MSA........................	81 607
1150		Bremerton, WA PMSA	231 969		56 021	Laramie County, WY......................	81 607
		(See Seattle-Tacoma-Bremerton, WA CMSA)		14		Chicago-Gary-Kenosha, IL-IN-WI CMSA...........	9 157 540
1240		Brownsville-Harlingen-San Benito, TX MSA	335 227	1600		Chicago, IL PMSA..........................	8 272 768
	48 061	Cameron County, TX......................	335 227		17 031	Cook County, IL.........................	5 376 741
					17 037	De Kalb County, IL	88 969
					17 043	Du Page County, IL......................	904 161
					17 063	Grundy County, IL.......................	37 535

(MSA = metropolitan statistical area; CMSA = consolidated MSA; PMSA = primary MSA; and NECMA = New England county metropolitan area. For further information, see Appendix A.)

MSA/CMSA/PMSA/NECMA	State and County	Title and Geographic Components	2000 Population	MSA/CMSA/PMSA/NECMA	State and County	Title and Geographic Components	2000 Population
	17 089	Kane County, IL	404 119	1800		Columbus, GA-AL MSA	274 624
	17 093	Kendall County, IL	54 544		01 113	Russell County, AL	49 756
	17 097	Lake County, IL	644 356		13 053	Chattahoochee County, GA	14 882
	17 111	McHenry County, IL	260 077		13 145	Harris County, GA	23 695
	17 197	Will County, IL	502 266		13 215	Muscogee County, GA	186 291
2960		Gary, IN PMSA	631 362	1840		Columbus, OH MSA	1 540 157
	18 089	Lake County, IN	484 564		39 041	Delaware County, OH	109 989
	18 127	Porter County, IN	146 798		39 045	Fairfield County, OH	122 759
					39 049	Franklin County, OH	1 068 978
3740		Kankakee, IL PMSA	103 833		39 089	Licking County, OH	145 491
	17 091	Kankakee County, IL	103 833		39 097	Madison County, OH	40 213
					39 129	Pickaway County, OH	52 727
3800		Kenosha, WI PMSA	149 577				
	55 059	Kenosha County, WI	149 577	1880		Corpus Christi, TX MSA	380 783
					48 355	Nueces County, TX	313 645
1620		Chico-Paradise, CA MSA	203 171		48 409	San Patricio County, TX	67 138
	06 007	Butte County, CA	203 171	1890		Corvallis, OR MSA	78 153
21		Cincinnati-Hamilton, OH-KY-IN CMSA	1 979 202		41 003	Benton County, OR	78 153
1640		Cincinnati, OH-KY-IN PMSA	1 646 395	1900		Cumberland, MD-WV MSA	102 008
	18 029	Dearborn County, IN	46 109		24 001	Allegany County, MD	74 930
	18 115	Ohio County, IN	5 623		54 057	Mineral County, WV	27 078
	21 015	Boone County, KY	85 991				
	21 037	Campbell County, KY	88 616	31		Dallas-Fort Worth, TX CMSA	5 221 801
	21 077	Gallatin County, KY	7 870				
	21 081	Grant County, KY	22 384	1920		Dallas, TX PMSA	3 519 176
	21 117	Kenton County, KY	151 464		48 085	Collin County, TX	491 675
	21 191	Pendleton County, KY	14 390		48 113	Dallas County, TX	2 218 899
	39 015	Brown County, OH	42 285		48 121	Denton County, TX	432 976
	39 025	Clermont County, OH	177 977		48 139	Ellis County, TX	111 360
	39 061	Hamilton County, OH	845 303		48 213	Henderson County, TX	73 277
	39 165	Warren County, OH	158 383		48 231	Hunt County, TX	76 596
					48 257	Kaufman County, TX	71 313
3200		Hamilton-Middletown, OH PMSA	332 807		48 397	Rockwall County, TX	43 080
	39 017	Butler County, OH	332 807				
				2800		Fort Worth-Arlington, TX PMSA	1 702 625
1660		Clarksville-Hopkinsville, TN-KY MSA	207 033		48 221	Hood County, TX	41 100
	21 047	Christian County, KY	72 265		48 251	Johnson County, TX	126 811
	47 125	Montgomery County, TN	134 768		48 367	Parker County, TX	88 495
					48 439	Tarrant County, TX	1 446 219
28		Cleveland-Akron, OH CMSA	2 945 831				
				1950		Danville, VA MSA	110 156
80		Akron, OH PMSA	694 960		51 143	Pittsylvania County, VA	61 745
	39 133	Portage County, OH	152 061		51 590	Danville City, VA	48 411
	39 153	Summit County, OH	542 899	1960		Davenport-Moline-Rock Island, IA-IL MSA	359 062
1680		Cleveland-Lorain-Elyria, OH PMSA	2 250 871		17 073	Henry County, IL	51 020
	39 007	Ashtabula County, OH	102 728		17 161	Rock Island County, IL	149 374
	39 035	Cuyahoga County, OH	1 393 978		19 163	Scott County, IA	158 668
	39 055	Geauga County, OH	90 895				
	39 085	Lake County, OH	227 511	2000		Dayton-Springfield, OH MSA	950 558
	39 093	Lorain County, OH	284 664		39 023	Clark County, OH	144 742
	39 103	Medina County, OH	151 095		39 057	Greene County, OH	147 886
					39 109	Miami County, OH	98 868
1720		Colorado Springs, CO MSA	516 929		39 113	Montgomery County, OH	559 062
	08 041	El Paso County, CO	516 929				
				2020		Daytona Beach, FL MSA	493 175
1740		Columbia, MO MSA	135 454		12 035	Flagler County, FL	49 832
	29 019	Boone County, MO	135 454		12 127	Volusia County, FL	443 343
1760		Columbia, SC MSA	536 691	2030		Decatur, AL MSA	145 867
	45 063	Lexington County, SC	216 014		01 079	Lawrence County, AL	34 803
	45 079	Richland County, SC	320 677		01 103	Morgan County, AL	111 064

Metropolitan Statistical Areas and Components – Continued

(MSA = metropolitan statistical area; CMSA = consolidated MSA; PMSA = primary MSA; and
NECMA = New England county metropolitan area. For further information, see Appendix A.)

MSA/ CMSA/ PMSA/ NECMA	State and County	Title and Geographic Components	2000 Population	MSA/ CMSA/ PMSA/ NECMA	State and County	Title and Geographic Components	2000 Population
2040		Decatur, IL MSA	114 706	2330		Elkhart-Goshen, IN MSA	182 791
	17 115	Macon County, IL	114 706		18 039	Elkhart County, IN	182 791
34		Denver-Boulder-Greeley, CO CMSA	2 581 506	2335		Elmira, NY MSA	91 070
1125		Boulder-Longmont, CO PMSA	291 288		36 015	Chemung County, NY	91 070
	08 013	Boulder County, CO	291 288	2340		Enid, OK MSA	57 813
2080		Denver, CO PMSA	2 109 282		40 047	Garfield County, OK	57 813
	08 001	Adams County, CO	363 857	2360		Erie, PA MSA	280 843
	08 005	Arapahoe County, CO	487 967		42 049	Erie County, PA	280 843
	08 031	Denver County, CO	554 636				
	08 035	Douglas County, CO	175 766	2400		Eugene-Springfield, OR MSA	322 959
	08 059	Jefferson County, CO	527 056		41 039	Lane County, OR	322 959
3060		Greeley, CO PMSA	180 936	2440		Evansville-Henderson, IN-KY MSA	296 195
	08 123	Weld County, CO	180 936		18 129	Posey County, IN	27 061
2120		Des Moines, IA MSA	456 022		18 163	Vanderburgh County, IN	171 922
	19 049	Dallas County, IA	40 750		18 173	Warrick County, IN	52 383
	19 153	Polk County, IA	374 601		21 101	Henderson County, KY	44 829
	19 181	Warren County, IA	40 671	2520		Fargo-Moorhead, ND-MN MSA	174 367
2162		Detroit-Ann Arbor-Flint, MI CMSA	5 456 428		27 027	Clay County, MN	51 229
					38 017	Cass County, ND	123 138
0440		Ann Arbor, MI PMSA	578 736	2560		Fayetteville, NC MSA	302 963
	26 091	Lenawee County, MI	98 890		37 051	Cumberland County, NC	302 963
	26 093	Livingston County, MI	156 951				
	26 161	Washtenaw County, MI	322 895	2580		Fayetteville-Springdale-Rogers, AR MSA	311 121
2160		Detroit, MI PMSA	4 441 551		05 007	Benton County, AR	153 406
	26 087	Lapeer County, MI	87 904		05 143	Washington County, AR	157 715
	26 099	Macomb County, MI	788 149	2620		Flagstaff, AZ-UT MSA	122 366
	26 115	Monroe County, MI	145 945		04 005	Coconino County, AZ	116 320
	26 125	Oakland County, MI	1 194 156		49 025	Kane County, UT	6 046
	26 147	St. Clair County, MI	164 235	2640		Flint, MI PMSA	436 141
	26 163	Wayne County, MI	2 061 162			(See Detroit-Ann Arbor-Flint, MI CMSA)	
2640		Flint, MI PMSA	436 141	2650		Florence, AL MSA	142 950
	26 049	Genesee County, MI	436 141		01 033	Colbert County, AL	54 984
2180		Dothan, AL MSA	137 916		01 077	Lauderdale County, AL	87 966
	01 045	Dale County, AL	49 129	2655		Florence, SC MSA	125 761
	01 069	Houston County, AL	88 787		45 041	Florence County, SC	125 761
2190		Dover, DE MSA	126 697	2670		Fort Collins-Loveland, CO MSA	251 494
	10 001	Kent County, DE	126 697		08 069	Larimer County, CO	251 494
2200		Dubuque, IA MSA	89 143	2680		Fort Lauderdale, FL PMSA	1 623 018
	19 061	Dubuque County, IA	89 143			(See Miami-Fort Lauderdale, FL CMSA)	
2240		Duluth-Superior, MN-WI MSA	243 815	2700		Fort Myers-Cape Coral, FL MSA	440 888
	27 137	St. Louis County, MN	200 528		12 071	Lee County, FL	440 888
	55 031	Douglas County, WI	43 287	2710		Fort Pierce-Port St. Lucie, FL MSA	319 426
2281		Dutchess County, NY PMSA	280 150		12 085	Martin County, FL	126 731
		(See New York-Northern New Jersey-Long Island, NY-NJ-CT-PA CMSA)			12 111	St. Lucie County, FL	192 695
2290		Eau Claire, WI MSA	148 337	2720		Fort Smith, AR-OK MSA	207 290
	55 017	Chippewa County, WI	55 195		05 033	Crawford County, AR	53 247
	55 035	Eau Claire County, WI	93 142		05 131	Sebastian County, AR	115 071
2320		El Paso, TX MSA	679 622		40 135	Sequoyah County, OK	38 972
	48 141	El Paso County, TX	679 622	2750		Fort Walton Beach, FL MSA	170 498
					12 091	Okaloosa County, FL	170 498

Metropolitan Statistical Areas and Components – Continued

(MSA = metropolitan statistical area; CMSA = consolidated MSA; PMSA = primary MSA; and NECMA = New England county metropolitan area. For further information, see Appendix A.)

MSA/CMSA/PMSA/NECMA	State and County	Title and Geographic Components	2000 Population	MSA/CMSA/PMSA/NECMA	State and County	Title and Geographic Components	2000 Population
2760		Fort Wayne, IN MSA	502 141	3150		Greenville, NC MSA	133 798
	18 001	Adams County, IN	33 625		37 147	Pitt County, NC	133 798
	18 003	Allen County, IN	331 849	3160		Greenville-Spartanburg-Anderson, SC MSA	962 441
	18 033	De Kalb County, IN	40 285		45 007	Anderson County, SC	165 740
	18 069	Huntington County, IN	38 075		45 021	Cherokee County, SC	52 537
	18 179	Wells County, IN	27 600		45 045	Greenville County, SC	379 616
	18 183	Whitley County, IN	30 707		45 077	Pickens County, SC	110 757
2800		Fort Worth-Arlington, TX PMSA	1 702 625		45 083	Spartanburg County, SC	253 791
		(See Dallas-Fort Worth, TX CMSA)		3180		Hagerstown, MD PMSA	131 923
2840		Fresno, CA MSA	922 516			(See Washington-Baltimore, DC-MD-VA-WV CMSA)	
	06 019	Fresno County, CA	799 407				
	06 039	Madera County, CA	123 109	3240		Harrisburg-Lebanon-Carlisle, PA MSA	629 401
2880		Gadsden, AL MSA	103 459		42 041	Cumberland County, PA	213 674
	01 055	Etowah County, AL	103 459		42 043	Dauphin County, PA	251 798
2900		Gainesville, FL MSA	217 955		42 075	Lebanon County, PA	120 327
	12 001	Alachua County, FL	217 955		42 099	Perry County, PA	43 602
2920		Galveston-Texas City, TX PMSA	250 158	3280		Hartford, CT NECMA	1 148 618
		(See Houston-Galveston-Brazoria, TX CMSA)			09 003	Hartford County, CT	857 183
					09 007	Middlesex County, CT	155 071
2975		Glens Falls, NY MSA	124 345		09 013	Tolland County, CT	136 364
	36 113	Warren County, NY	63 303	3285		Hattiesburg, MS MSA	111 674
	36 115	Washington County, NY	61 042		28 035	Forrest County, MS	72 604
					28 073	Lamar County, MS	39 070
2980		Goldsboro, NC MSA	113 329	3290		Hickory-Morganton-Lenoir, NC MSA	341 851
	37 191	Wayne County, NC	113 329		37 003	Alexander County, NC	33 603
2985		Grand Forks, ND-MN MSA	97 478		37 023	Burke County, NC	89 148
	27 119	Polk County, MN	31 369		37 027	Caldwell County, NC	77 415
	38 035	Grand Forks County, ND	66 109		37 035	Catawba County, NC	141 685
2995		Grand Junction, CO MSA	116 255	3320		Honolulu, HI MSA	876 156
	08 077	Mesa County, CO	116 255		15 003	Honolulu County, HI	876 156
3000		Grand Rapids-Muskegon-Holland, MI MSA	1 088 514	3350		Houma, LA MSA	194 477
	26 005	Allegan County, MI	105 665		22 057	Lafourche Parish, LA	89 974
	26 081	Kent County, MI	574 335		22 109	Terrebonne Parish, LA	104 503
	26 121	Muskegon County, MI	170 200	3362		Houston-Galveston-Brazoria, TX CMSA	4 669 571
	26 139	Ottawa County, MI	238 314	1145		Brazoria, TX PMSA	241 767
3040		Great Falls, MT MSA	80 357		48 039	Brazoria County, TX	241 767
	30 013	Cascade County, MT	80 357	2920		Galveston-Texas City, TX PMSA	250 158
3060		Greeley, CO PMSA	180 936			Galveston County, TX	250 158
		(See Denver-Boulder-Greeley, CO CMSA)		3360		Houston, TX PMSA	4 177 646
3080		Green Bay, WI MSA	226 778		48 071	Chambers County, TX	26 031
	55 009	Brown County, WI	226 778		48 157	Fort Bend County, TX	354 452
3120		Greensboro-Winston-Salem-High Point, NC MSA	1 251 509		48 201	Harris County, TX	3 400 578
	37 001	Alamance County, NC	130 800		48 291	Liberty County, TX	70 154
	37 057	Davidson County, NC	147 246		48 339	Montgomery County, TX	293 768
	37 059	Davie County, NC	34 835		48 473	Waller County, TX	32 663
	37 067	Forsyth County, NC	306 067	3400		Huntington-Ashland, WV-KY-OH MSA	315 538
	37 081	Guilford County, NC	421 048		21 019	Boyd County, KY	49 752
	37 151	Randolph County, NC	130 454		21 043	Carter County, KY	26 889
	37 169	Stokes County, NC	44 711		21 089	Greenup County, KY	36 891
	37 197	Yadkin County, NC	36 348		39 087	Lawrence County, OH	62 319
					54 011	Cabell County, WV	96 784
					54 099	Wayne County, WV	42 903

(MSA = metropolitan statistical area; CMSA = consolidated MSA; PMSA = primary MSA; and NECMA = New England county metropolitan area. For further information, see Appendix A.)

MSA/ CMSA/ PMSA/ NECMA	State and County	Title and Geographic Components	2000 Population	MSA/ CMSA/ PMSA/ NECMA	State and County	Title and Geographic Components	2000 Population
3440		Huntsville, AL MSA	342 376	3710		Joplin, MO MSA	157 322
	01 083	Limestone County, AL	65 676		29 097	Jasper County, MO	104 686
	01 089	Madison County, AL	276 700		29 145	Newton County, MO	52 636
3480		Indianapolis, IN MSA	1 607 486	3720		Kalamazoo-Battle Creek, MI MSA	452 851
	18 011	Boone County, IN	46 107		26 025	Calhoun County, MI	137 985
	18 057	Hamilton County, IN	182 740		26 077	Kalamazoo County, MI	238 603
	18 059	Hancock County, IN	55 391		26 159	Van Buren County, MI	76 263
	18 063	Hendricks County, IN...................	104 093	3740		Kankakee, IL PMSA	103 833
	18 081	Johnson County, IN	115 209			(See Chicago-Gary-Kenosha, IL-IN-WI CMSA)	
	18 095	Madison County, IN	133 358				
	18 097	Marion County, IN	860 454	3760		Kansas City, MO-KS MSA	1 776 062
	18 109	Morgan County, IN	66 689		20 091	Johnson County, KS	451 086
	18 145	Shelby County, IN	43 445		20 103	Leavenworth County, KS................	68 691
3500		Iowa City, IA MSA	111 006		20 121	Miami County, KS	28 351
	19 103	Johnson County, IA	111 006		20 209	Wyandotte County, KS	157 882
3520		Jackson, MI MSA	158 422		29 037	Cass County, MO	82 092
	26 075	Jackson County, MI	158 422		29 047	Clay County, MO	184 006
3560		Jackson, MS MSA	440 801		29 049	Clinton County, MO	18 979
	28 049	Hinds County, MS	250 800		29 095	Jackson County, MO	654 880
	28 089	Madison County, MS	74 674		29 107	Lafayette County, MO...................	32 960
	28 121	Rankin County, MS	115 327		29 165	Platte County, MO	73 781
					29 177	Ray County, MO	23 354
3580		Jackson, TN MSA	107 377	3800		Kenosha, WI PMSA	149 577
	47 023	Chester County, TN	15 540			(See Chicago-Gary-Kenosha, IL-IN-WI CMSA)	
	47 113	Madison County, TN	91 837				
3600		Jacksonville, FL MSA	1 100 491	3810		Killeen-Temple, TX MSA................	312 952
	12 019	Clay County, FL	140 814		48 027	Bell County, TX	237 974
	12 031	Duval County, FL	778 879		48 099	Coryell County, TX	74 978
	12 089	Nassau County, FL	57 663	3840		Knoxville, TN MSA	687 249
	12 109	St. Johns County, FL	123 135		47 001	Anderson County, TN	71 330
3605		Jacksonville, NC MSA	150 355		47 009	Blount County, TN	105 823
	37 133	Onslow County, NC	150 355		47 093	Knox County, TN	382 032
3610		Jamestown, NY MSA	139 750		47 105	Loudon County, TN	39 086
	36 013	Chautauqua County, NY	139 750		47 155	Sevier County, TN	71 170
3620		Janesville-Beloit, WI MSA	152 307		47 173	Union County, TN	17 808
	55 105	Rock County, WI........................	152 307	3850		Kokomo, IN MSA	101 541
3640		Jersey City, NJ PMSA...................	608 975		18 067	Howard County, IN	84 964
		(See New York-Northern New Jersey-Long Island, NY-NJ-CT-PA CMSA)			18 159	Tipton County, IN	16 577
				3870		La Crosse, WI-MN MSA.................	126 838
3660		Johnson City-Kingsport-Bristol, TN-VA MSA	480 091		27 055	Houston County, MN	19 718
	47 019	Carter County, TN	56 742		55 063	La Crosse County, WI	107 120
	47 073	Hawkins County, TN.....................	53 563	3920		Lafayette, IN MSA	182 821
	47 163	Sullivan County, TN.....................	153 048		18 023	Clinton County, IN	33 866
	47 171	Unicoi County, TN	17 667		18 157	Tippecanoe County, IN..................	148 955
	47 179	Washington County, TN	107 198	3880		Lafayette, LA MSA	385 647
	51 169	Scott County, VA	23 403		22 001	Acadia Parish, LA	58 861
	51 191	Washington County, VA	51 103		22 055	Lafayette Parish, LA	190 503
	51 520	Bristol City, VA.........................	17 367		22 097	St. Landry Parish, LA	87 700
3680		Johnstown, PA MSA	232 621		22 099	St. Martin Parish, LA	48 583
	42 021	Cambria County, PA	152 598	3960		Lake Charles, LA MSA..................	183 577
	42 111	Somerset County, PA	80 023		22 019	Calcasieu Parish, LA	183 577
3700		Jonesboro, AR MSA	82 148	3980		Lakeland-Winter Haven, FL MSA	483 924
	5 031	Craighead County, AR...................	82 148		12 105	Polk County, FL.........................	483 924

Metropolitan Statistical Areas and Components – Continued

(MSA = metropolitan statistical area; CMSA = consolidated MSA; PMSA = primary MSA; and NECMA = New England county metropolitan area. For further information, see Appendix A.)

MSA/CMSA/PMSA/NECMA	State and County	Title and Geographic Components	2000 Population	MSA/CMSA/PMSA/NECMA	State and County	Title and Geographic Components	2000 Population
4000		Lancaster, PA MSA	470 658		18 043	Floyd County, IN	70 823
	42 071	Lancaster County, PA	470 658		18 061	Harrison County, IN	34 325
4040		Lansing-East Lansing, MI MSA	447 728		18 143	Scott County, IN	22 960
	26 037	Clinton County, MI	64 753		21 029	Bullitt County, KY	61 236
	26 045	Eaton County, MI	103 655		21 111	Jefferson County, KY	693 604
	26 065	Ingham County, MI	279 320		21 185	Oldham County, KY	46 178
4080		Laredo, TX MSA	193 117	4600		Lubbock, TX MSA	242 628
	48 479	Webb County, TX	193 117		48 303	Lubbock County, TX	242 628
4100		Las Cruces, NM MSA	174 682	4640		Lynchburg, VA MSA	214 911
	35 013	Dona Ana County, NM	174 682		51 009	Amherst County, VA	31 894
4120		Las Vegas, NV-AZ MSA	1 563 282		51 019	Bedford County, VA	60 371
	04 015	Mohave County, AZ	155 032		51 031	Campbell County, VA	51 078
	32 003	Clark County, NV	1 375 765		51 515	Bedford City, VA	6 299
	32 023	Nye County, NV	32 485		51 680	Lynchburg City, VA	65 269
4150		Lawrence, KS MSA	99 962	4680		Macon, GA MSA	322 549
	20 045	Douglas County, KS	99 962		13 021	Bibb County, GA	153 887
4200		Lawton, OK MSA	114 996		13 153	Houston County, GA	110 765
	40 031	Comanche County, OK	114 996		13 169	Jones County, GA	23 639
4240		Lewiston-Auburn, ME NECMA	103 793		13 225	Peach County, GA	23 668
	23 001	Androscoggin County, ME	103 793		13 289	Twiggs County, GA	10 590
4280		Lexington, KY MSA	479 198	4720		Madison, WI MSA	426 526
	21 017	Bourbon County, KY	19 360		55 025	Dane County, WI	426 526
	21 049	Clark County, KY	33 144	4800		Mansfield, OH MSA	175 818
	21 067	Fayette County, KY	260 512		39 033	Crawford County, OH	46 966
	21 113	Jessamine County, KY	39 041		39 139	Richland County, OH	128 852
	21 151	Madison County, KY	70 872	4880		McAllen-Edinburg-Mission, TX MSA	569 463
	21 209	Scott County, KY	33 061		48 215	Hidalgo County, TX	569 463
	21 239	Woodford County, KY	23 208	4890		Medford-Ashland, OR MSA	181 269
4320		Lima, OH MSA	155 084		41 029	Jackson County, OR	181 269
	39 003	Allen County, OH	108 473	4900		Melbourne-Titusville-Palm Bay, FL MSA	476 230
	39 011	Auglaize County, OH	46 611		12 009	Brevard County, FL	476 230
4360		Lincoln, NE MSA	250 291	4920		Memphis, TN-AR-MS MSA	1 135 614
	31 109	Lancaster County, NE	250 291		05 035	Crittenden County, AR	50 866
4400		Little Rock-North Little Rock, AR MSA	583 845		28 033	De Soto County, MS	107 199
	05 045	Faulkner County, AR	86 014		47 047	Fayette County, TN	28 806
	05 085	Lonoke County, AR	52 828		47 157	Shelby County, TN	897 472
	05 119	Pulaski County, AR	361 474		47 167	Tipton County, TN	51 271
	05 125	Saline County, AR	83 529	4940		Merced, CA MSA	210 554
4420		Longview-Marshall, TX MSA	208 780		06 047	Merced County, CA	210 554
	48 183	Gregg County, TX	111 379	4992		Miami-Fort Lauderdale, FL CMSA	3 876 380
	48 203	Harrison County, TX	62 110	2680		Fort Lauderdale, FL PMSA	1 623 018
	48 459	Upshur County, TX	35 291		12 011	Broward County, FL	1 623 018
4472		Los Angeles-Riverside-Orange County, CA CMSA	16 373 645	5000		Miami, FL PMSA	2 253 362
					12 086	Miami-Dade County, FL	2 253 362
4480		Los Angeles-Long Beach, CA PMSA	9 519 338	5082		Milwaukee-Racine, WI CMSA	1 689 572
	06 037	Los Angeles County, CA	9 519 338	5080		Milwaukee-Waukesha, WI PMSA	1 500 741
5945		Orange County, CA PMSA	2 846 289		55 079	Milwaukee County, WI	940 164
	06 059	Orange County, CA	2 846 289		55 089	Ozaukee County, WI	82 317
4520		Louisville, KY-IN MSA	1 025 598		55 131	Washington County, WI	117 493
	18 019	Clark County, IN	96 472		55 133	Waukesha County, WI	360 767

MSA/ CMSA/ PMSA/ NECMA	State and County	Title and Geographic Components	2000 Population	MSA/ CMSA/ PMSA/ NECMA	State and County	Title and Geographic Components	2000 Population
6600		Racine, WI PMSA	188 831	5560		New Orleans, LA MSA	1 337 726
	55 101	Racine County, WI	188 831		22 051	Jefferson Parish, LA	455 466
					22 071	Orleans Parish, LA	484 674
5120		Minneapolis-St. Paul, MN-WI MSA	2 968 806		22 075	Plaquemines Parish, LA	26 757
	27 003	Anoka County, MN	298 084		22 087	St. Bernard Parish, LA	67 229
	27 019	Carver County, MN	70 205		22 089	St. Charles Parish, LA	48 072
	27 025	Chisago County, MN	41 101		22 093	St. James Parish, LA	21 216
	27 037	Dakota County, MN	355 904		22 095	St. John the Baptist Parish, LA	43 044
	27 053	Hennepin County, MN	1 116 200		22 103	St. Tammany Parish, LA	191 268
	27 059	Isanti County, MN	31 287				
	27 123	Ramsey County, MN	511 035	5600		New York, NY PMSA	9 314 235
	27 139	Scott County, MN	89 498			(See New York-Northern New Jersey-Long Island, NY-NJ-CT-PA CMSA)	
	27 141	Sherburne County, MN	64 417				
	27 163	Washington County, MN	201 130	70		New York-Northern New Jersey-Long Island, NY-NJ-CT-PA CMSA	21 199 865
	27 171	Wright County, MN	89 986				
	55 093	Pierce County, WI	36 804				
	55 109	St. Croix County, WI	63 155	875		Bergen-Passaic, NJ PMSA	1 373 167
5140		Missoula, MT MSA	95 802		34 003	Bergen County, NJ	884 118
	30 063	Missoula County, MT	95 802		34 031	Passaic County, NJ	489 049
5160		Mobile, AL MSA	540 258	2281		Dutchess County, NY PMSA	280 150
	01 003	Baldwin County, AL	140 415		36 027	Dutchess County, NY	280 150
	01 097	Mobile County, AL	399 843				
5170		Modesto, CA MSA	446 997	3640		Jersey City, NJ PMSA	608 975
	06 099	Stanislaus County, CA	446 997		34 017	Hudson County, NJ	608 975
5190		Monmouth-Ocean, NJ PMSA	1 126 217	5015		Middlesex-Somerset-Hunterdon, NJ PMSA	1 169 641
		(See New York-Northern New Jersey-Long Island, NY-NJ-CT-PA CMSA)			34 019	Hunterdon County, NJ	121 989
					34 023	Middlesex County, NJ	750 162
					34 035	Somerset County, NJ	297 490
5200		Monroe, LA MSA	147 250	5190		Monmouth-Ocean, NJ PMSA	1 126 217
	22 073	Ouachita Parish, LA	147 250		34 025	Monmouth County, NJ	615 301
5240		Montgomery, AL MSA	333 055		34 029	Ocean County, NJ	510 916
	01 001	Autauga County, AL	43 671	5380		Nassau-Suffolk, NY PMSA	2 753 913
	01 051	Elmore County, AL	65 874		36 059	Nassau County, NY	1 334 544
	01 101	Montgomery County, AL	223 510		36 103	Suffolk County, NY	1 419 369
5280		Muncie, IN MSA	118 769	5483		New Haven-Bridgeport-Stamford-Danbury-Waterbury, CT NECMA	1 706 575
	18 035	Delaware County, IN	118 769				
					09 001	Fairfield County, CT	882 567
5330		Myrtle Beach, SC MSA	196 629		09 009	New Haven County, CT	824 008
	45 051	Horry County, SC	196 629				
				5600		New York, NY PMSA	9 314 235
5345		Naples, FL MSA	251 377		36 005	Bronx County, NY	1 332 650
	12 021	Collier County, FL	251 377		36 047	Kings County, NY	2 465 326
5360		Nashville, TN MSA	1 231 311		36 061	New York County, NY	1 537 195
	47 021	Cheatham County, TN	35 912		36 079	Putnam County, NY	95 745
	47 037	Davidson County, TN	569 891		36 081	Queens County, NY	2 229 379
	47 043	Dickson County, TN	43 156		36 085	Richmond County, NY	443 728
	47 147	Robertson County, TN	54 433		36 087	Rockland County, NY	286 753
	47 149	Rutherford County, TN	182 023		36 119	Westchester County, NY	923 459
	47 165	Sumner County, TN	130 449	5640		Newark, NJ PMSA	2 032 989
	47 187	Williamson County, TN	126 638		34 013	Essex County, NJ	793 633
	47 189	Wilson County, TN	88 809		34 027	Morris County, NJ	470 212
					34 037	Sussex County, NJ	144 166
5380		Nassau-Suffolk, NY PMSA	2 753 913		34 039	Union County, NJ	522 541
		(See New York-Northern New Jersey-Long Island, NY-NJ-CT-PA CMSA)			34 041	Warren County, NJ	102 437
				5660		Newburgh, NY-PA PMSA	387 669
5520		New London-Norwich, CT NECMA	259 088		36 071	Orange County, NY	341 367
	09 011	New London County, CT	259 088		42 103	Pike County, PA	46 302

(MSA = metropolitan statistical area; CMSA = consolidated MSA; PMSA = primary MSA; and NECMA = New England county metropolitan area. For further information, see Appendix A.)

MSA/CMSA/PMSA/NECMA	State and County	Title and Geographic Components	2000 Population	MSA/CMSA/PMSA/NECMA	State and County	Title and Geographic Components	2000 Population
8480		Trenton, NJ PMSA	350 761	6020		Parkersburg-Marietta, WV-OH MSA	151 237
	34 021	Mercer County, NJ..............................	350 761		39 167	Washington County, OH........................	63 251
					54 107	Wood County, WV..............................	87 986
5720		Norfolk-Virginia Beach-Newport News, VA-NC MSA..	1 569 541	6080		Pensacola, FL MSA.............................	412 153
	37 053	Currituck County, NC...........................	18 190		12 033	Escambia County, FL...........................	294 410
	51 073	Gloucester County, VA..........................	34 780		12 113	Santa Rosa County, FL.........................	117 743
	51 093	Isle of Wight County, VA........................	29 728	6120		Peoria-Pekin, IL MSA...........................	347 387
	51 095	James City, VA................................	48 102		17 143	Peoria County, IL..............................	183 433
	51 115	Mathews County, VA............................	9 207		17 179	Tazewell County, IL............................	128 485
	51 199	York County, VA...............................	56 297		17 203	Woodford County, IL...........................	35 469
	51 550	Chesapeake City, VA...........................	199 184	6162		Philadelphia-Wilmington-Atlantic City, PA-NJ-DE-MD CMSA	6 188 463
	51 650	Hampton City, VA..............................	146 437				
	51 700	Newport News City, VA.........................	180 150	560		Atlantic-Cape May, NJ PMSA....................	354 878
	51 710	Norfolk City, VA...............................	234 403		34 001	Atlantic County, NJ............................	252 552
	51 735	Poquoson City, VA.............................	11 566		34 009	Cape May County, NJ..........................	102 326
	51 740	Portsmouth City, VA............................	100 565	6160		Philadelphia, PA-NJ PMSA......................	5 100 931
	51 800	Suffolk City, VA...............................	63 677		34 005	Burlington County, NJ..........................	423 394
	51 810	Virginia Beach City, VA.........................	425 257		34 007	Camden County, NJ............................	508 932
	51 830	Williamsburg City, VA..........................	11 998		34 015	Gloucester County, NJ.........................	254 673
5775		Oakland, CA PMSA.............................	2 392 557		34 033	Salem County, NJ.............................	64 285
		(See San Francisco-Oakland-San Jose, CA CMSA)			42 017	Bucks County, PA.............................	597 635
					42 029	Chester County, PA............................	433 501
5790		Ocala, FL MSA................................	258 916		42 045	Delaware County, PA...........................	550 864
	12 083	Marion County, FL.............................	258 916		42 091	Montgomery County, PA.........................	750 097
5800		Odessa-Midland, TX MSA........................	237 132		42 101	Philadelphia County, PA........................	1 517 550
	48 135	Ector County, TX..............................	121 123	8760		Vineland-Millville-Bridgeton, NJ PMSA	146 438
	48 329	Midland County, TX............................	116 009		34 011	Cumberland County, NJ.........................	146 438
5880		Oklahoma City, OK MSA.........................	1 083 346	9160		Wilmington-Newark, DE-MD PMSA.................	586 216
	40 017	Canadian County, OK...........................	87 697		10 003	New Castle County, DE.........................	500 265
	40 027	Cleveland County, OK...........................	208 016		24 015	Cecil County, MD..............................	85 951
	40 083	Logan County, OK.............................	33 924	6200		Phoenix-Mesa, AZ MSA.........................	3 251 876
	40 087	McClain County, OK............................	27 740		04 013	Maricopa County, AZ...........................	3 072 149
	40 109	Oklahoma County, OK...........................	660 448		04 021	Pinal County, AZ..............................	179 727
	40 125	Pottawatomie County, OK........................	65 521	6240		Pine Bluff, AR MSA............................	84 278
5910		Olympia, WA PMSA.............................	207 355		05 069	Jefferson County, AR...........................	84 278
		(See Seattle-Tacoma-Bremerton, WA CMSA)		6280		Pittsburgh, PA MSA............................	2 358 695
5920		Omaha, NE-IA MSA.............................	716 998		42 003	Allegheny County, PA..........................	1 281 666
	19 155	Pottawattamie County, IA........................	87 704		42 007	Beaver County, PA............................	181 412
	31 025	Cass County, NE..............................	24 334		42 019	Butler County, PA.............................	174 083
	31 055	Douglas County, NE............................	463 585		42 051	Fayette County, PA............................	148 644
	31 153	Sarpy County, NE.............................	122 595		42 125	Washington County, PA.........................	202 897
	31 177	Washington County, NE.........................	18 780		42 129	Westmoreland County, PA.......................	369 993
5945		Orange County, CA PMSA........................	2 846 289	6323		Pittsfield, MA NECMA..........................	134 953
		(See Los Angeles-Long Beach, CA PMSA)			25 003	Berkshire County, MA..........................	134 953
5960		Orlando, FL MSA..............................	1 644 561	6340		Pocatello, ID MSA.............................	75 565
	12 069	Lake County, FL..............................	210 528		16 005	Bannock County, ID............................	75 565
	12 095	Orange County, FL............................	896 344	6403		Portland, ME NECMA...........................	265 612
	12 097	Osceola County, FL............................	172 493		23 005	Cumberland County, ME.........................	265 612
	12 117	Seminole County, FL...........................	365 196	6442		Portland-Salem, OR-WA CMSA....................	2 265 223
5990		Owensboro, KY MSA............................	91 545				
	21 059	Daviess County, KY............................	91 545	6440		Portland-Vancouver, OR-WA PMSA.................	1 918 009
6015		Panama City, FL MSA...........................	148 217		41 005	Clackamas County, OR.........................	338 391
	12 005	Bay County, FL...............................	148 217				

(MSA = metropolitan statistical area; CMSA = consolidated MSA; PMSA = primary MSA; and NECMA = New England county metropolitan area. For further information, see Appendix A.)

MSA/ CMSA/ PMSA/ NECMA	State and County	Title and Geographic Components	2000 Population
	41 009	Columbia County, OR	43 560
	41 051	Multnomah County, OR	660 486
	41 067	Washington County, OR	445 342
	41 071	Yamhill County, OR	84 992
	53 011	Clark County, WA	345 238
7080		Salem, OR PMSA	347 214
	41 047	Marion County, OR	284 834
	41 053	Polk County, OR	62 380
6483		Providence-Warwick-Pawtucket, RI NECMA	962 886
	44 001	Bristol County, RI	50 648
	44 003	Kent County, RI	167 090
	44 007	Providence County, RI	621 602
	44 009	Washington County, RI	123 546
6520		Provo-Orem, UT MSA	368 536
	49 049	Utah County, UT	368 536
6560		Pueblo, CO MSA	141 472
	08 101	Pueblo County, CO	141 472
6580		Punta Gorda, FL MSA	141 627
	12 015	Charlotte County, FL	141 627
6600		Racine, WI PMSA	188 831
		(See Milwaukee-Waukesha, WI PMSA)	
6640		Raleigh-Durham-Chapel Hill, NC MSA	1 187 941
	37 037	Chatham County, NC	49 329
	37 063	Durham County, NC	223 314
	37 069	Franklin County, NC	47 260
	37 101	Johnston County, NC	121 965
	37 135	Orange County, NC	118 227
	37 183	Wake County, NC	627 846
6660		Rapid City, SD MSA	88 565
	46 103	Pennington County, SD	88 565
6680		Reading, PA MSA	373 638
	42 011	Berks County, PA	373 638
6690		Redding, CA MSA	163 256
	06 089	Shasta County, CA	163 256
6720		Reno, NV MSA	339 486
	32 031	Washoe County, NV	339 486
6740		Richland-Kennewick-Pasco, WA MSA	191 822
	53 005	Benton County, WA	142 475
	53 021	Franklin County, WA	49 347
6760		Richmond-Petersburg, VA MSA	996 512
	51 036	Charles City, VA	6 926
	51 041	Chesterfield County, VA	259 903
	51 053	Dinwiddie County, VA	24 533
	51 075	Goochland County, VA	16 863
	51 085	Hanover County, VA	86 320
	51 087	Henrico County, VA	262 300
	51 127	New Kent County, VA	13 462
	51 145	Powhatan County, VA	22 377
	51 149	Prince George County, VA	33 047
	51 570	Colonial Heights City, VA	16 897
	51 670	Hopewell City, VA	22 354
	51 730	Petersburg City, VA	33 740
	51 760	Richmond City, VA	197 790
6780		Riverside-San Bernardino, CA PMSA	3 254 821
		(See Los Angeles-Riverside-Orange County, CA CMSA)	
6800		Roanoke, VA MSA	235 932
	51 023	Botetourt County, VA	30 496
	51 161	Roanoke County, VA	85 778
	51 770	Roanoke City, VA	94 911
	51 775	Salem City, VA	24 747
6820		Rochester, MN MSA	124 277
	27 109	Olmsted County, MN	124 277
6840		Rochester, NY MSA	1 098 201
	36 037	Genesee County, NY	60 370
	36 051	Livingston County, NY	64 328
	36 055	Monroe County, NY	735 343
	36 069	Ontario County, NY	100 224
	36 073	Orleans County, NY	44 171
	36 117	Wayne County, NY	93 765
6880		Rockford, IL MSA	371 236
	17 007	Boone County, IL	41 786
	17 141	Ogle County, IL	51 032
	17 201	Winnebago County, IL	278 418
6895		Rocky Mount, NC MSA	143 026
	37 065	Edgecombe County, NC	55 606
	37 127	Nash County, NC	87 420
6922		Sacramento-Yolo, CA CMSA	1 796 857
6920		Sacramento, CA PMSA	1 628 197
	06 017	El Dorado County, CA	156 299
	06 061	Placer County, CA	248 399
	06 067	Sacramento County, CA	1 223 499
9270		Yolo, CA PMSA	168 660
	06 113	Yolo County, CA	168 660
6960		Saginaw-Bay City-Midland, MI MSA	403 070
	26 017	Bay County, MI	110 157
	26 111	Midland County, MI	82 874
	26 145	Saginaw County, MI	210 039
6980		St. Cloud, MN MSA	167 392
	27 009	Benton County, MN	34 226
	27 145	Stearns County, MN	133 166
7000		St. Joseph, MO MSA	102 490
	29 003	Andrew County, MO	16 492
	29 021	Buchanan County, MO	85 998
7040		St. Louis, MO-IL MSA	2 603 607
	17 027	Clinton County, IL	35 535
	17 083	Jersey County, IL	21 668
	17 119	Madison County, IL	258 941
	17 133	Monroe County, IL	27 619
	17 163	St. Clair County, IL	256 082
	29 071	Franklin County, MO	93 807
	29 099	Jefferson County, MO	198 099
	29 113	Lincoln County, MO	38 944
	29 183	St. Charles County, MO	283 883
	29 189	St. Louis County, MO	1 016 315
	29 219	Warren County, MO	24 525

Geographic Codes MSA/CMSA/PMSA/NECMA	Geographic Codes State and County	Title and Geographic Components	2000 Population	Geographic Codes MSA/CMSA/PMSA/NECMA	Geographic Codes State and County	Title and Geographic Components	2000 Population
	29 510	St. Louis City, MO..........................	348 189		13 051	Chatham County, GA	232 048
7080		Salem, OR PMSA	347 214		13 103	Effingham County, GA	37 535
		(See Portland-Vancouver, OR-WA PMSA)		7560		Scranton-Wilkes-Barre-Hazleton, PA MSA	624 776
7120		Salinas, CA MSA..........................	401 762		42 037	Columbia County, PA	64 151
	06 053	Monterey County, CA	401 762		42 069	Lackawanna County, PA	213 295
7160		Salt Lake City-Ogden, UT MSA	1 333 914		42 079	Luzerne County, PA	319 250
	49 011	Davis County, UT	238 994		42 131	Wyoming County, PA	28 080
	49 035	Salt Lake County, UT	898 387	7602		Seattle-Tacoma-Bremerton, WA CMSA.............	3 554 760
	49 057	Weber County, UT	196 533			Bremerton, WA PMSA	231 969
7200		San Angelo, TX MSA....................	104 010	1150	53 035	Kitsap County, WA	231 969
	48 451	Tom Green County, TX	104 010	5910		Olympia, WA PMSA	207 355
7240		San Antonio, TX MSA....................	1 592 383		53 067	Thurston County, WA	207 355
	48 029	Bexar County, TX	1 392 931	7600		Seattle-Bellevue-Everett, WA PMSA	2 414 616
	48 091	Comal County, TX	78 021		53 029	Island County, WA	71 558
	48 187	Guadalupe County, TX	89 023		53 033	King County, WA	1 737 034
	48 493	Wilson County, TX	32 408		53 061	Snohomish County, WA	606 024
7320		San Diego, CA MSA....................	2 813 833	8200		Tacoma, WA PMSA	700 820
	06 073	San Diego County, CA	2 813 833		53 053	Pierce County, WA	700 820
7362		San Francisco-Oakland-San Jose, CA CMSA....	7 039 362	7610		Sharon, PA MSA	120 293
5775		Oakland, CA PMSA......................	2 392 557		42 085	Mercer County, PA	120 293
	06 001	Alameda County, CA	1 443 741	7620		Sheboygan, WI MSA	112 646
	06 013	Contra Costa County, CA...........	948 816		55 117	Sheboygan County, WI	112 646
7360		San Francisco, CA PMSA...............	1 731 183	7640		Sherman-Denison, TX MSA	110 595
	06 041	Marin County, CA	247 289		48 181	Grayson County, TX	110 595
	06 075	San Francisco County, CA	776 733	7680		Shreveport-Bossier City, LA MSA.................	392 302
	06 081	San Mateo County, CA	707 161		22 015	Bossier Parish, LA	98 310
7400		San Jose, CA PMSA....................	1 682 585		22 017	Caddo Parish, LA	252 161
	06 085	Santa Clara County, CA	1 682 585		22 119	Webster Parish, LA...............	41 831
7485		Santa Cruz-Watsonville, CA PMSA	255 602	7720		Sioux City, IA-NE MSA.............................	124 130
	06 087	Santa Cruz County, CA	255 602		19 193	Woodbury County, IA	103 877
7500		Santa Rosa, CA PMSA..................	458 614		31 043	Dakota County, NE................	20 253
	06 097	Sonoma County, CA	458 614	7760		Sioux Falls, SD MSA	172 412
8720		Vallejo-Fairfield-Napa, CA PMSA	518 821		46 083	Lincoln County, SD	24 131
	06 055	Napa County, CA	124 279		46 099	Minnehaha County, SD	148 281
	06 095	Solano County, CA	394 542	7800		South Bend, IN MSA	265 559
7460		San Luis Obispo-Atascadero-Paso Robles, CA MSA..........................	246 681		18 141	St. Joseph County, IN	265 559
	06 079	San Luis Obispo County, CA	246 681	7840		Spokane, WA MSA	417 939
7480		Santa Barbara-Santa Maria-Lompoc, CA MSA ..	399 347		53 063	Spokane County, WA	417 939
	06 083	Santa Barbara County, CA	399 347	7880		Springfield, IL MSA	201 437
7490		Santa Fe, NM MSA....................	147 635		17 129	Menard County, IL	12 486
	35 028	Los Alamos County, NM.............	18 343		17 167	Sangamon County, IL	188 951
	35 049	Santa Fe County, NM	129 292	8003		Springfield, MA NECMA	608 479
7510		Sarasota-Bradenton, FL MSA	589 959		25 013	Hampden County, MA	456 228
	12 081	Manatee County, FL	264 002		25 015	Hampshire County, MA	152 251
	12 115	Sarasota County, FL.................	325 957	7920		Springfield, MO MSA	325 721
7520		Savannah, GA MSA...................	293 000		29 043	Christian County, MO	54 285
	13 029	Bryan County, GA...................	23 417		29 077	Greene County, MO	240 391
					29 225	Webster County, MO	31 045

(MSA = metropolitan statistical area; CMSA = consolidated MSA; PMSA = primary MSA; and
NECMA = New England county metropolitan area. For further information, see Appendix A.)

Geographic Codes MSA/CMSA/PMSA/NECMA	Geographic Codes State and County	Title and Geographic Components	2000 Population	Geographic Codes MSA/CMSA/PMSA/NECMA	Geographic Codes State and County	Title and Geographic Components	2000 Population
8050		State College, PA MSA	135 758			Tyler, TX MSA	174 706
	42 027	Centre County, PA	135 758	8640	48 423	Smith County, TX	174 706
8080		Steubenville-Weirton, OH-WV MSA	132 008			Utica-Rome, NY MSA	299 896
	39 081	Jefferson County, OH	73 894	8680			
	54 009	Brooke County, WV	25 447		36 043	Herkimer County, NY	64 427
	54 029	Hancock County, WV	32 667		36 065	Oneida County, NY	235 469
8120		Stockton-Lodi, CA MSA	563 598	8720		Vallejo-Fairfield-Napa, CA PMSA	518 821
	06 077	San Joaquin County, CA	563 598			(See San Francisco-Oakland-San Jose, CA CMSA)	
8140		Sumter, SC MSA	104 646	8735		Ventura, CA PMSA	753 197
	45 085	Sumter County, SC	104 646			(See Los Angeles-Riverside-Orange County, CA CMSA)	753 197
8160		Syracuse, NY MSA	732 117				
	36 011	Cayuga County, NY	81 963	8750		Victoria, TX MSA	84 088
	36 053	Madison County, NY	69 441		48 469	Victoria County, TX	84 088
	36 067	Onondaga County, NY	458 336				
	36 075	Oswego County, NY	122 377	8760		Vineland-Millville-Bridgeton, NJ PMSA	146 438
8200		Tacoma, WA PMSA	700 820			(See Philadelphia-Wilmington-Atlantic City, PA-NJ-DE-MD CMSA)	
		(See Seattle-Tacoma-Bremerton, WA CMSA)					
8240		Tallahassee, FL MSA	284 539	8780		Visalia-Tulare-Porterville, CA MSA	368 021
	12 039	Gadsden County, FL	45 087		06 107	Tulare County, CA	368 021
	12 073	Leon County, FL	239 452				
				8800		Waco, TX MSA	213 517
8280		Tampa-St. Petersburg-Clearwater, FL MSA	2 395 997		48 309	McLennan County, TX	213 517
	12 053	Hernando County, FL	130 802				
	12 057	Hillsborough County, FL	998 948	8872		Washington-Baltimore, DC-MD-VA-WV CMSA	7 608 070
	12 101	Pasco County, FL	344 765				
	12 103	Pinellas County, FL	921 482	720		Baltimore, MD PMSA	2 552 994
					24 003	Anne Arundel County, MD	489 656
8320		Terre Haute, IN MSA	149 192		24 005	Baltimore County, MD	754 292
	18 021	Clay County, IN	26 556		24 013	Carroll County, MD	150 897
	18 165	Vermillion County, IN	16 788		24 025	Harford County, MD	218 590
	18 167	Vigo County, IN	105 848		24 027	Howard County, MD	247 842
					24 035	Queen Anne's County, MD	40 563
8360		Texarkana, TX-Texarkana, AR MSA	129 749		24 510	Baltimore City, MD	651 154
	05 091	Miller County, AR	40 443				
	48 037	Bowie County, TX	89 306	3180		Hagerstown, MD PMSA	131 923
					24 043	Washington County, MD	131 923
8400		Toledo, OH MSA	618 203				
	39 051	Fulton County, OH	42 084	8840		Washington, DC-MD-VA-WV PMSA	4 923 153
	39 095	Lucas County, OH	455 054		11 001	District of Columbia	572 059
	39 173	Wood County, OH	121 065		24 009	Calvert County, MD	74 563
					24 017	Charles County, MD	120 546
8440		Topeka, KS MSA	169 871		24 021	Frederick County, MD	195 277
	20 177	Shawnee County, KS	169 871		24 031	Montgomery County, MD	873 341
					24 033	Prince George's County, MD	801 515
8480		Trenton, NJ PMSA	350 761		51 013	Arlington County, VA	189 453
		(See New York-Northern New Jersey-Long Island, NY-NJ-CT-PA CMSA)			51 043	Clarke County, VA	12 652
					51 047	Culpeper County, VA	34 262
8520		Tucson, AZ MSA	843 746		51 059	Fairfax County, VA	969 749
	04 019	Pima County, AZ	843 746		51 061	Fauquier County, VA	55 139
					51 099	King George County, VA	16 803
8560		Tulsa, OK MSA	803 235		51 107	Loudoun County, VA	169 599
	40 037	Creek County, OK	67 367		51 153	Prince William County, VA	280 813
	40 113	Osage County, OK	44 437		51 177	Spotsylvania County, VA	90 395
	40 131	Rogers County, OK	70 641		51 179	Stafford County, VA	92 446
	40 143	Tulsa County, OK	563 299		51 187	Warren County, VA	31 584
	40 145	Wagoner County, OK	57 491		51 510	Alexandria City, VA	128 283
					51 600	Fairfax City, VA	21 498
8600		Tuscaloosa, AL MSA	164 875		51 610	Falls Church City, VA	10 377
	01 125	Tuscaloosa County, AL	164 875		51 630	Fredericksburg City, VA	19 279
					51 683	Manassas City, VA	35 135

(MSA = metropolitan statistical area; CMSA = consolidated MSA; PMSA = primary MSA; and
NECMA = New England county metropolitan area. For further information, see Appendix A.)

Geographic Codes		Title and Geographic Components	2000 Population	Geographic Codes		Title and Geographic Components	2000 Population
MSA/ CMSA/ PMSA/ NECMA	State and County			MSA/ CMSA/ PMSA/ NECMA	State and County		
	51 685	Manassas Park City, VA................................	10 290	9200		Wilmington, NC MSA	233 450
	54 003	Berkeley County, WV	75 905		37 019	Brunswick County, NC................................	73 143
	54 037	Jefferson County, WV	42 190		37 129	New Hanover County, NC	160 307
8920		Waterloo-Cedar Falls, IA MSA	128 012	9160		Wilmington-Newark, DE-MD PMSA	586 216
	19 013	Black Hawk County, IA	128 012			(See Philadelphia-Wilmington-Atlantic City, PA-NJ-DE-MD CMSA)	
8940		Wausau, WI MSA	125 834				
	55 073	Marathon County, WI	125 834	9260		Yakima, WA MSA................................	222 581
					53 077	Yakima County, WA	222 581
8960		West Palm Beach-Boca Raton, FL MSA	1 131 184	9270		Yolo, CA PMSA................................	168 660
	12 099	Palm Beach County, FL	1 131 184			(See Sacramento-Yolo, CA CMSA)	
9000		Wheeling, WV-OH MSA	153 172	9280		York, PA MSA	381 751
	39 013	Belmont County, OH	70 226	9280	42 133	York County, PA	381 751
	54 051	Marshall County, WV	35 519				
	54 069	Ohio County, WV	47 427	9320		Youngstown-Warren, OH MSA	594 746
9080		Wichita Falls, TX MSA	140 518	9320	39 029	Columbiana County, OH................................	112 075
	48 009	Archer County, TX	8 854	9320	39 099	Mahoning County, OH................................	257 555
	48 485	Wichita County, TX	131 664	9320	39 155	Trumbull County, OH................................	225 116
9040		Wichita, KS MSA	545 220	9340		Yuba City, CA MSA................................	139 149
	20 015	Butler County, KS	59 482	9340	06 101	Sutter County, CA................................	78 930
	20 079	Harvey County, KS	32 869	9340	06 115	Yuba County, CA................................	60 219
	20 173	Sedgwick County, KS	452 869				
				9360		Yuma, AZ MSA	160 026
9140		Williamsport, PA MSA	120 044	9360	04 027	Yuma County, AZ	160 026
	42 081	Lycoming County, PA	120 044				

APPENDIX C
METROPOLITAN STATISTICAL AREAS AND COMPONENTS BY STATE

The following table is arranged alphabetically by state. Under each state heading, all of the metropolitan areas that lie wholly or partly within that state are listed alphabetically along with their component counties, which are also listed alphabetically. For metropolitan areas that cross state lines, only the counties within a particular state are included under that state. However, the metropolitan area names include the two letter abbreviation for each state involved, and the remaining counties can be located under their respective state headings.

For states containing Consolidated Metropolitan Statistical Areas (CMSAs), or parts of such areas, the CMSAs appear first, followed by the Primary Metropolitan Statistical Areas (PMSAs) that make up the CMSA, and their component counties.

(MSA = metropolitan statistical area; CMSA = consolidated MSA; PMSA = primary MSA; and NECMA = New England county metropolitan area. For further information, see Appendix A.)

Geographic Codes MSA/CMSA/ PMSA/ NECMA	State and County	Title and Geographic Components	Geographic Codes MSA/CMSA/ PMSA/ NECMA	State and County	Title and Geographic Components
		ALABAMA	9360		YUMA, AZ MSA
0450		ANNISTON, AL MSA	9360	04 027	Yuma
	01 015	Calhoun			
0580		AUBURN-OPELIKA, AL MSA			**ARKANSAS**
	01 081	Lee	2580		FAYETTEVILLE-SPRINGDALE-ROGERS, AR MSA
1000		BIRMINGHAM, AL MSA		05 007	Benton
	01 009	Blount		05 143	Washington
	01 073	Jefferson	2720		FORT SMITH, AR-OK MSA
	01 115	St. Clair		05 033	Crawford
	01 117	Shelby		05 131	Sebastian
1800		COLUMBUS, GA-AL MSA	3700		JONESBORO, AR MSA
	01 113	Russell		5 031	Craighead
2030		DECATUR, AL MSA	4400		LITTLE ROCK-NORTH LITTLE ROCK, AR MSA
	01 079	Lawrence		05 045	Faulkner
	01 103	Morgan		05 085	Lonoke
2180		DOTHAN, AL MSA		05 119	Pulaski
	01 045	Dale		05 125	Saline
	01 069	Houston	4920		MEMPHIS, TN-AR-MS MSA
2650		FLORENCE, AL MSA		05 035	Crittenden
	01 033	Colbert	6240		PINE BLUFF, AR MSA
	01 077	Lauderdale		05 069	Jefferson
2880		GADSDEN, AL MSA	8360		TEXARKANA, TX-TEXARKANA, AR MSA
	01 055	Etowah		05 091	Miller
3440		HUNTSVILLE, AL MSA			
	01 083	Limestone			**CALIFORNIA**
	01 089	Madison	4472		LOS ANGELES-RIVERSIDE-ORANGE COUNTY, CA
5160		MOBILE, AL MSA			CMSA
	01 003	Baldwin	4480		LOS ANGELES-LONG BEACH, CA PMSA
	01 097	Mobile		06 037	Los Angeles
5240		MONTGOMERY, AL MSA	5945		ORANGE COUNTY, CA PMSA
	01 001	Autauga		06 059	Orange
	01 051	Elmore	6780		RIVERSIDE-SAN BERNARDINO, CA PMSA
	01 101	Montgomery			SAN BERNARDINO, CA
8600		TUSCALOOSA, AL MSA			RIVERSIDE, CA
	01 125	Tuscaloosa	6922		SACRAMENTO-YOLO, CA CMSA
			6920		SACRAMENTO, CA PMSA
		ALASKA		06 017	El Dorado
0380		ANCHORAGE, AK MSA		06 061	Placer
	02 020	Anchorage		06 067	Sacramento
			9270		YOLO, CA PMSA
		ARIZONA		06 113	Yolo
2620		FLAGSTAFF, AZ-UT MSA	7362		SAN FRANCISCO-OAKLAND-SAN JOSE, CA CMSA
	04 005	Coconino	5775		OAKLAND, CA PMSA
4120		LAS VEGAS, NV-AZ MSA		06 001	Alameda
	04 015	Mohave		06 013	Contra Costa
6200		PHOENIX-MESA, AZ MSA	7360		SAN FRANCISCO, CA PMSA
	04 013	Maricopa		06 041	Marin
	04 021	Pinal		06 075	San Francisco
8520		TUCSON, AZ MSA		06 081	San Mateo
	04 019	Pima	7400		SAN JOSE, CA PMSA
				06 085	Santa Clara

Metropolitan Statistical Areas and Components by State – Continued
(MSA = metropolitan statistical area; CMSA = consolidated MSA; PMSA = primary MSA; and
NECMA = New England county metropolitan area. For further information, see Appendix A.)

Geographic Codes MSA/CMSA/ PMSA/ NECMA	State and County	Title and Geographic Components	Geographic Codes MSA/CMSA/ PMSA/ NECMA	State and County	Title and Geographic Components
7485		SANTA CRUZ-WATSONVILLE, CA PMSA		09 007	Middlesex
	06 087	Santa Cruz		09 013	Tolland
7500		SANTA ROSA, CA PMSA	5520		NEW LONDON-NORWICH, CT NECMA
	06 097	Sonoma		09 011	New London
8720		VALLEJO-FAIRFIELD-NAPA, CA PMSA			
	06 055	Napa			**DELAWARE**
	06 095	Solano	6162		PHILADELPHIA-WILMINGTON-ATLANTIC CITY, PA-NJ-DE-MD CMSA
0680		BAKERSFIELD, CA MSA			
	06 029	Kern	9160		WILMINGTON-NEWARK, DE-MD PMSA
1620		CHICO-PARADISE, CA MSA		10 003	New Castle
	06 007	Butte	2190		DOVER, DE MSA
2840		FRESNO, CA MSA		10 001	Kent
	06 019	Fresno			
	06 039	Madera			**FLORIDA**
4940		MERCED, CA MSA	4992		MIAMI-FORT LAUDERDALE, FL CMSA
	06 047	Merced	2680		FORT LAUDERDALE, FL PMSA
5170		MODESTO, CA MSA		12 011	Broward
	06 099	Stanislaus	5000		MIAMI, FL PMSA
6690		REDDING, CA MSA		12 086	Miami-Dade
	06 089	Shasta	2020		DAYTONA BEACH, FL MSA
7120		SALINAS, CA MSA		12 035	Flagler
	06 053	Monterey		12 127	Volusia
7320		SAN DIEGO, CA MSA	2700		FORT MYERS-CAPE CORAL, FL MSA
	06 073	San Diego		12 071	Lee
7460		SAN LUIS OBISPO-ATASCADERO-PASO ROBLES, CA MSA	2710		FORT PIERCE-PORT ST. LUCIE, FL MSA
				12 085	Martin
	06 079	San Luis Obispo		12 111	St. Lucie
7480		SANTA BARBARA-SANTA MARIA-LOMPOC, CA MSA	2750		FORT WALTON BEACH, FL MSA
	06 083	Santa Barbara		12 091	Okaloosa
8120		STOCKTON-LODI, CA MSA	2900		GAINESVILLE, FL MSA
	06 077	San Joaquin		12 001	Alachua
8780		VISALIA-TULARE-PORTERVILLE, CA MSA	3600		JACKSONVILLE, FL MSA
	06 107	Tulare		12 019	Clay
9340		YUBA CITY, CA MSA		12 031	Duval
	06 101	Sutter		12 089	Nassau
	06 115	Yuba		12 109	St. Johns
			3980		LAKELAND-WINTER HAVEN, FL MSA
		COLORADO		12 105	Polk
34		DENVER-BOULDER-GREELEY, CO CMSA	4900		MELBOURNE-TITUSVILLE-PALM BAY, FL MSA
1125		BOULDER-LONGMONT, CO PMSA		12 009	Brevard
	08 013	Boulder	5345		NAPLES, FL MSA
2080		DENVER, CO PMSA		12 021	Collier
	08 001	Adams	5790		OCALA, FL MSA
	08 005	Arapahoe		12 083	Marion
	08 031	Denver	5960		ORLANDO, FL MSA
	08 035	Douglas		12 069	Lake
	08 059	Jefferson		12 095	Orange
3060		GREELEY, CO PMSA		12 097	Osceola
	08 123	Weld		12 117	Seminole
1720		COLORADO SPRINGS, CO MSA	6015		PANAMA CITY, FL MSA
	08 041	El Paso		12 005	Bay
2670		FORT COLLINS-LOVELAND, CO MSA	6080		PENSACOLA, FL MSA
	08 069	Larimer		12 033	Escambia
2995		GRAND JUNCTION, CO MSA		12 113	Santa Rosa
	08 077	Mesa	6580		PUNTA GORDA, FL MSA
6560		PUEBLO, CO MSA		12 015	Charlotte
	08 101	Pueblo	7510		SARASOTA-BRADENTON, FL MSA
				12 081	Manatee
		CONNECTICUT		12 115	Sarasota
70		NEW YORK-NORTHERN NEW JERSEY-LONG ISLAND, NY-NJ-CT-PA CMSA	8240		TALLAHASSEE, FL MSA
				12 039	Gadsden
5483		NEW HAVEN-BRIDGEPORT-STAMFORD-DANBURY-WATERBURY, CT NECMA		12 073	Leon
		FAIRFIELD COUNTY, CT	8280		TAMPA-ST. PETERSBURG-CLEARWATER, FL MSA
		NEW HAVEN COUNTY, CT		12 053	Hernando
3280		HARTFORD, CT NECMA		12 057	Hillsborough
	09 003	Hartford		12 101	Pasco
				12 103	Pinellas

Metropolitan Statistical Areas and Components by State – Continued

(MSA = metropolitan statistical area; CMSA = consolidated MSA; PMSA = primary MSA; and NECMA = New England county metropolitan area. For further information, see Appendix A.)

Geographic Codes MSA/CMSA/ PMSA/ NECMA	State and County	Title and Geographic Components	Geographic Codes MSA/CMSA/ PMSA/ NECMA	State and County	Title and Geographic Components
8960		WEST PALM BEACH-BOCA RATON, FL MSA			**ILLINOIS**
	12 099	Palm Beach	1040		BLOOMINGTON-NORMAL, IL MSA
			1040	17 113	McLean
		GEORGIA	1400		CHAMPAIGN-URBANA, IL MSA
0120		ALBANY, GA MSA		17 019	Champaign
	13 095	DOUGHERTY COUNTY, GA	14		CHICAGO-GARY-KENOSHA, IL-IN-WI CMSA
	13 177	LEE COUNTY, GA	1600		CHICAGO, IL PMSA
0500		ATHENS, GA MSA		17 031	Cook
	13 059	Clarke		17 037	De Kalb
	13 195	Madison		17 043	Du Page
	13 219	Oconee		17 063	Grundy
0520		ATLANTA, GA MSA		17 089	Kane
	13 013	Barrow		17 093	Kendall
	13 015	Bartow		17 097	Lake
	13 045	Carroll		17 111	McHenry
	13 057	Cherokee		17 197	Will
	13 063	Clayton	3740		KANKAKEE, IL PMSA
	13 067	Cobb		17 091	Kankakee
	13 077	Coweta	1960		DAVENPORT-MOLINE-ROCK ISLAND, IA-IL MSA
	13 089	De Kalb		17 073	Henry
	13 097	Douglas		17 161	Rock Island
	13 113	Fayette	2040		DECATUR, IL MSA
	13 117	Forsyth		17 115	Macon
	13 121	Fulton	6120		PEORIA-PEKIN, IL MSA
	13 135	Gwinnett		17 143	Peoria
	13 151	Henry		17 179	Tazewell
	13 217	Newton		17 203	Woodford
	13 223	Paulding	6880		ROCKFORD, IL MSA
	13 227	Pickens		17 007	Boone
	13 247	Rockdale		17 141	Ogle
	13 255	Spalding		17 201	Winnebago
	13 297	Walton	7040		ST. LOUIS, MO-IL MSA
0600		AUGUSTA-AIKEN, GA-SC MSA		17 027	Clinton
	13 073	Columbia		17 083	Jersey
	13 189	McDuffie		17 119	Madison
	13 245	Richmond		17 133	Monroe
1560		CHATTANOOGA, TN-GA MSA		17 163	St. Clair
	13 047	Catoosa	7880		SPRINGFIELD, IL MSA
	13 083	Dade		17 129	Menard
	13 295	Walker		17 167	Sangamon
1800		COLUMBUS, GA-AL MSA			
	13 053	Chattahoochee			**INDIANA**
	13 145	Harris	1020		BLOOMINGTON, IN MSA
	13 215	Muscogee	1020	18 105	Monroe
4680		MACON, GA MSA	14		CHICAGO-GARY-KENOSHA, IL-IN-WI CMSA
	13 021	Bibb	2960		GARY, IN PMSA
	13 153	Houston		18 089	Lake
	13 169	Jones		18 127	Porter
	13 225	Peach	21		CINCINNATI-HAMILTON, OH-KY-IN CMSA
	13 289	Twiggs	1640		CINCINNATI, OH-KY-IN PMSA
7520		SAVANNAH, GA MSA		18 029	Dearborn
	13 029	Bryan		18 115	Ohio
	13 051	Chatham	2330		ELKHART-GOSHEN, IN MSA
	13 103	Effingham		18 039	Elkhart
			2440		EVANSVILLE-HENDERSON, IN-KY MSA
		HAWAII		18 129	Posey
3320		HONOLULU, HI MSA		18 163	Vanderburgh
	15 003	Honolulu		18 173	Warrick
			2760		FORT WAYNE, IN MSA
		IDAHO		18 001	Adams
1080		BOISE CITY, ID MSA		18 003	Allen
1080	16 001	Ada		18 033	De Kalb
1080	16 027	Canyon		18 069	Huntington
6340		POCATELLO, ID MSA		18 179	Wells
	16 005	Bannock		18 183	Whitley
			3480		INDIANAPOLIS, IN MSA
				18 011	Boone

Metropolitan Statistical Areas and Components by State – Continued

(MSA = metropolitan statistical area; CMSA = consolidated MSA; PMSA = primary MSA; and NECMA = New England county metropolitan area. For further information, see Appendix A.)

Geographic Codes MSA/CMSA/ PMSA/ NECMA	State and County	Title and Geographic Components
	18 057	Hamilton
	18 059	Hancock
	18 063	Hendricks
	18 081	Johnson
	18 095	Madison
	18 097	Marion
	18 109	Morgan
	18 145	Shelby
3850		KOKOMO, IN MSA
	18 067	Howard
	18 159	Tipton
3920		LAFAYETTE, IN MSA
	18 023	Clinton
	18 157	Tippecanoe
4520		LOUISVILLE, KY-IN MSA
	18 019	Clark
	18 043	Floyd
	18 061	Harrison
	18 143	Scott
7800		SOUTH BEND, IN MSA
	18 141	St. Joseph
5280		MUNCIE, IN MSA
	18 035	Delaware
8320		TERRE HAUTE, IN MSA
	18 021	Clay
	18 165	Vermillion
	18 167	Vigo
		IOWA
1360		CEDAR RAPIDS, IA MSA
	19 113	Linn
1960		DAVENPORT-MOLINE-ROCK ISLAND, IA-IL MSA
	19 163	Scott
2120		DES MOINES, IA MSA
	19 049	Dallas
	19 153	Polk
	19 181	Warren
2200		DUBUQUE, IA MSA
	19 061	Dubuque
3500		IOWA CITY, IA MSA
	19 103	Johnson
5920		OMAHA, NE-IA MSA
	19 155	Pottawattamie
7720		SIOUX CITY, IA-NE MSA
	19 193	Woodbury
8920		WATERLOO-CEDAR FALLS, IA MSA
	19 013	Black Hawk
		KANSAS
3760		KANSAS CITY, MO-KS MSA
	20 091	Johnson
	20 103	Leavenworth
	20 121	Miami
	20 209	Wyandotte
4150		LAWRENCE, KS MSA
	20 045	Douglas
8440		TOPEKA, KS MSA
	20 177	Shawnee
9040		WICHITA, KS MSA
	20 015	Butler
	20 079	Harvey
	20 173	Sedgwick
		KENTUCKY
21		CINCINNATI-HAMILTON, OH-KY-IN CMSA
1640		CINCINNATI, OH-KY-IN PMSA
	21 015	Boone
	21 037	Campbell
	21 077	Gallatin
	21 081	Grant
	21 117	Kenton
	21 191	Pendleton
1660		CLARKSVILLE-HOPKINSVILLE, TN-KY MSA
	21 047	Christian
2440		EVANSVILLE-HENDERSON, IN-KY MSA
	21 101	Henderson
3400		HUNTINGTON-ASHLAND, WV-KY-OH MSA
	21 019	Boyd
	21 043	Carter
	21 089	Greenup
4280		LEXINGTON, KY MSA
	21 017	Bourbon
	21 049	Clark
	21 067	Fayette
	21 113	Jessamine
	21 151	Madison
	21 209	Scott
	21 239	Woodford
4520		LOUISVILLE, KY-IN MSA
	21 029	Bullitt
	21 111	Jefferson
	21 185	Oldham
5990		OWENSBORO, KY MSA
	21 059	Daviess
		LOUISIANA
0220		ALEXANDRIA, LA MSA
	22 079	Rapides
0760		BATON ROUGE, LA MSA
	22 005	Ascension
	22 033	East Baton Rouge
	22 063	Livingston
	22 121	West Baton Rouge
3350		HOUMA, LA MSA
	22 057	Lafourche
	22 109	Terrebonne
3880		LAFAYETTE, LA MSA
	22 001	Acadia
	22 055	Lafayette
	22 097	St. Landry
	22 099	St. Martin
3960		LAKE CHARLES, LA MSA
	22 019	Calcasieu
5200		MONROE, LA MSA
	22 073	Ouachita
5560		NEW ORLEANS, LA MSA
	22 051	Jefferson
	22 071	Orleans
	22 075	Plaquemines
	22 087	St. Bernard
	22 089	St. Charles
	22 093	St. James
	22 095	St. John the Baptist
	22 103	St. Tammany
7680		SHREVEPORT-BOSSIER CITY, LA MSA
	22 015	Bossier
	22 017	Caddo
	22 119	Webster
		MAINE
0733		BANGOR, ME NECMA
	23 019	Penobscot
4240		LEWISTON-AUBURN, ME NECMA
	23 001	Androscoggin

Metropolitan Statistical Areas and Components by State – Continued

(MSA = metropolitan statistical area; CMSA = consolidated MSA; PMSA = primary MSA; and
NECMA = New England county metropolitan area. For further information, see Appendix A.)

Geographic Codes MSA/CMSA/ PMSA/ NECMA	State and County	Title and Geographic Components	Geographic Codes MSA/CMSA/ PMSA/ NECMA	State and County	Title and Geographic Components
6403		PORTLAND, ME NECMA		26 139	Ottawa
	23 005	Cumberland	3520		JACKSON, MI MSA
				26 075	Jackson
		MARYLAND	3720		KALAMAZOO-BATTLE CREEK, MI MSA
6162		PHILADELPHIA-WILMINGTON-ATLANTIC CITY, PA-NJ-DE-MD CMSA		26 025	Calhoun
				26 077	Kalamazoo
9160		WILMINGTON-NEWARK, DE-MD PMSA		26 159	Van Buren
	24 015	Cecil	4040		LANSING-EAST LANSING, MI MSA
8872		WASHINGTON-BALTIMORE, DC-MD-VA-WV CMSA		26 037	Clinton
0720		BALTIMORE, MD PMSA		26 045	Eaton
	24 003	Anne Arundel		26 065	Ingham
	24 005	Baltimore	6960		SAGINAW-BAY CITY-MIDLAND, MI MSA
	24 013	Carroll		26 017	Bay
	24 025	Harford		26 111	Midland
	24 027	Howard		26 145	Saginaw
	24 035	Queen Anne's			
	24 510	BALTIMORE CITY, MD			**MINNESOTA**
3180		HAGERSTOWN, MD PMSA	2240		DULUTH-SUPERIOR, MN-WI MSA
	24 043	Washington		27 137	St. Louis
8840		WASHINGTON, DC-MD-VA-WV PMSA	2520		FARGO-MOORHEAD, ND-MN MSA
	24 009	Calvert		27 027	Clay
	24 017	Charles	2985		GRAND FORKS, ND-MN MSA
	24 021	Frederick		27 119	Polk
	24 031	Montgomery	3870		LA CROSSE, WI-MN MSA
	24 033	Prince George's		27 055	Houston
1900		CUMBERLAND, MD-WV MSA	5120		MINNEAPOLIS-ST. PAUL, MN-WI MSA
	24 001	Allegany		27 003	Anoka
				27 019	Carver
		MASSACHUSETTS		27 025	Chisago
0743		BARNSTABLE-YARMOUTH, MA NECMA		27 037	Dakota
	25 001	Barnstable		27 053	Hennepin
1123		BOSTON-WORCESTER-LAWRENCE-LOWELL-BROCKTON, MA-NH NECMA		27 059	Isanti
				27 123	Ramsey
	25 005	Bristol		27 139	Scott
	25 009	Essex		27 141	Sherburne
	25 017	Middlesex		27 163	Washington
	25 021	Norfolk		27 171	Wright
	25 023	Plymouth	6820		ROCHESTER, MN MSA
	25 025	Suffolk		27 109	Olmsted
	25 027	Worcester	6980		ST. CLOUD, MN MSA
6323		PITTSFIELD, MA NECMA		27 009	Benton
	25 003	Berkshire		27 145	Stearns
8003		SPRINGFIELD, MA NECMA			
	25 013	Hampden			**MISSISSIPPI**
	25 015	Hampshire	0920		BILOXI-GULFPORT-PASCAGOULA, MS MSA
				28 045	Hancock
		MICHIGAN		28 047	Harrison
2162		DETROIT-ANN ARBOR-FLINT, MI CMSA		28 059	Jackson
0440		ANN ARBOR, MI PMSA	3285		HATTIESBURG, MS MSA
	26 091	Lenawee		28 035	Forrest
	26 093	Livingston		28 073	Lamar
	26 161	Washtenaw	3560		JACKSON, MS MSA
2160		DETROIT, MI PMSA		28 049	Hinds
	26 087	Lapeer		28 089	Madison
	26 099	Macomb		28 121	Rankin
	26 115	Monroe	4920		MEMPHIS, TN-AR-MS MSA
	26 125	Oakland		28 033	De Soto
	26 147	St. Clair			
	26 163	Wayne			**MISSOURI**
2640		FLINT, MI PMSA	1740		COLUMBIA, MO MSA
	26 049	Genesee		29 019	Boone
0870		BENTON HARBOR, MI MSA	3710		JOPLIN, MO MSA
	26 021	Berrien		29 097	Jasper
3000		GRAND RAPIDS-MUSKEGON-HOLLAND, MI MSA		29 145	Newton
	26 005	Allegan	3760		KANSAS CITY, MO-KS MSA
	26 081	Kent		29 037	Cass
	26 121	Muskegon		29 047	Clay

Metropolitan Statistical Areas and Components by State – Continued

(MSA = metropolitan statistical area; CMSA = consolidated MSA; PMSA = primary MSA; and
NECMA = New England county metropolitan area. For further information, see Appendix A.)

Geographic Codes MSA/CMSA/ PMSA/ NECMA	State and County	Title and Geographic Components	Geographic Codes MSA/CMSA/ PMSA/ NECMA	State and County	Title and Geographic Components
	29 049	Clinton	5190		MONMOUTH-OCEAN, NJ PMSA
	29 095	Jackson		34 025	Monmouth
	29 107	Lafayette		34 029	Ocean
	29 165	Platte	5640		NEWARK, NJ PMSA
	29 177	Ray		34 013	Essex
7000		ST. JOSEPH, MO MSA		34 027	Morris
	29 003	Andrew		34 037	Sussex
	29 021	Buchanan		34 039	Union
7040		ST. LOUIS, MO-IL MSA		34 041	Warren
	29 071	Franklin	8480		TRENTON, NJ PMSA
	29 099	Jefferson		34 021	Mercer
	29 113	Lincoln	560		ATLANTIC-CAPE MAY, NJ PMSA
	29 183	St. Charles		34 001	Atlantic
	29 189	St. Louis		34 009	Cape May
	29 219	Warren	6160		PHILADELPHIA, PA-NJ PMSA
	29 510	St. Louis City		34 005	Burlington
7920		SPRINGFIELD, MO MSA		34 007	Camden
	29 043	Christian		34 015	Gloucester
	29 077	Greene		34 033	Salem
	29 225	Webster	8760		VINELAND-MILLVILLE-BRIDGETON, NJ PMSA
				34 011	Cumberland
		MONTANA			
0880		BILLINGS, MT MSA			**NEW MEXICO**
	30 111	Yellowstone	0200		ALBUQUERQUE, NM MSA
3040		GREAT FALLS, MT MSA		35 001	Bernalillo
	30 013	Cascade		35 043	Sandoval
5140		MISSOULA, MT MSA		35 061	Valencia
	30 063	Missoula	4100		LAS CRUCES, NM MSA
				35 013	Dona Ana
		NEBRASKA	7490		SANTA FE, NM MSA
4360		LINCOLN, NE MSA		35 028	Los Alamos
	31 109	Lancaster		35 049	Santa Fe
5920		OMAHA, NE-IA MSA			
	31 025	Cass			**NEW YORK**
	31 055	Douglas	70		NEW YORK-NORTHERN NEW JERSEY-LONG ISLAND, NY-NJ-CT-PA CMSA
	31 153	Sarpy	2281		DUTCHESS COUNTY, NY PMSA
	31 177	Washington		36 027	Dutchess
7720		SIOUX CITY, IA-NE MSA	5380		NASSAU-SUFFOLK, NY PMSA
	31 043	Dakota		36 059	Nassau
				36 103	Suffolk
		NEVADA	5600		NEW YORK, NY PMSA
4120		LAS VEGAS, NV-AZ MSA		36 005	Bronx
	32 003	Clark		36 047	Kings
	32 023	Nye		36 061	New York
6720		RENO, NV MSA		36 079	Putnam
	32 031	Washoe		36 081	Queens
				36 085	Richmond
		NEW HAMPSHIRE		36 087	Rockland
1123		BOSTON-WORCESTER-LAWRENCE-LOWELL-BROCKTON, MA-NH NECMA		36 119	Westchester
			5660		NEWBURGH, NY-PA PMSA
	33 011	Hillsborough		36 071	Orange
	33 015	Rockingham	0160		ALBANY-SCHENECTADY-TROY, NY MSA
	33 017	Strafford		36 001	ALBANY COUNTY, NY
				36 057	MONTGOMERY COUNTY, NY
		NEW JERSEY		36 083	RENSSELAER COUNTY, NY
70		NEW YORK-NORTHERN NEW JERSEY-LONG ISLAND, NY-NJ-CT-PA CMSA		36 091	SARATOGA COUNTY, NY
				36 093	SCHENECTADY COUNTY, NY
0875		BERGEN-PASSAIC, NJ PMSA		36 095	SCHOHARIE COUNTY, NY
	34 003	Bergen	0960		BINGHAMTON, NY MSA
	34 031	Passaic		36 007	Broome
3640		JERSEY CITY, NJ PMSA		36 107	Tioga
	34 017	HUDSON COUNTY, NJ	1280		BUFFALO-NIAGARA FALLS, NY MSA
5015		MIDDLESEX-SOMERSET-HUNTERDON, NJ PMSA		36 029	Erie
	34 019	Hunterdon		36 063	Niagara
	34 023	Middlesex	2335		ELMIRA, NY MSA
	34 035	Somerset		36 015	Chemung

(MSA = metropolitan statistical area; CMSA = consolidated MSA; PMSA = primary MSA; and
NECMA = New England county metropolitan area. For further information, see Appendix A.)

Geographic Codes MSA/CMSA/ PMSA/ NECMA	State and County	Title and Geographic Components	Geographic Codes MSA/CMSA/ PMSA/ NECMA	State and County	Title and Geographic Components
2281		DUTCHESS COUNTY, NY PMSA	6895		ROCKY MOUNT, NC MSA
2975		GLENS FALLS, NY MSA		37 065	Edgecombe
	36 113	Warren		37 127	Nash
	36 115	Washington	9200		WILMINGTON, NC MSA
3610		JAMESTOWN, NY MSA		37 019	Brunswick
	36 013	Chautauqua		37 129	New Hanover
6840		ROCHESTER, NY MSA			
	36 037	Genesee			**NORTH DAKOTA**
	36 051	Livingston	1010		BISMARCK, ND MSA
	36 055	Monroe	1010	38 015	Burleigh
	36 069	Ontario	1010	38 059	Morton
	36 073	Orleans	2520		FARGO-MOORHEAD, ND-MN MSA
	36 117	Wayne		38 017	Cass
8160		SYRACUSE, NY MSA	2985		GRAND FORKS, ND-MN MSA
	36 011	Cayuga		38 035	Grand Forks
	36 053	Madison			
	36 067	Onondaga			**OHIO**
	36 075	Oswego	21		CINCINNATI-HAMILTON, OH-KY-IN CMSA
8680		UTICA-ROME, NY MSA	1640		CINCINNATI, OH-KY-IN PMSA
	36 043	Herkimer		39 015	Brown
	36 065	Oneida		39 025	Clermont
				39 061	Hamilton
		NORTH CAROLINA		39 165	Warren
0480		ASHEVILLE, NC MSA	3200		HAMILTON-MIDDLETOWN, OH PMSA
	37 021	Buncombe		39 017	Butler
	37 115	Madison	28		CLEVELAND-AKRON, OH CMSA
1520		CHARLOTTE-GASTONIA-ROCK HILL, NC-SC MSA	0080		AKRON, OH PMSA
	37 025	Cabarrus		39 133	PORTAGE COUNTY, OH
	37 071	Gaston		39 153	SUMMIT COUNTY, OH
	37 109	Lincoln	1680		CLEVELAND-LORAIN-ELYRIA, OH PMSA
	37 119	Mecklenburg		39 007	Ashtabula
	37 159	Rowan		39 035	Cuyahoga
	37 179	Union		39 055	Geauga
2560		FAYETTEVILLE, NC MSA		39 085	Lake
	37 051	Cumberland		39 093	Lorain
2980		GOLDSBORO, NC MSA		39 103	Medina
	37 191	Wayne	1320		CANTON-MASSILLON, OH MSA
3120		GREENSBORO-WINSTON-SALEM-HIGH POINT, NC MSA		39 019	Carroll
	37 001	Alamance		39 151	Stark
	37 057	Davidson	1840		COLUMBUS, OH MSA
	37 059	Davie		39 041	Delaware
	37 067	Forsyth		39 045	Fairfield
	37 081	Guilford		39 049	Franklin
	37 151	Randolph		39 089	Licking
	37 169	Stokes		39 097	Madison
	37 197	Yadkin		39 129	Pickaway
3150		GREENVILLE, NC MSA	2000		DAYTON-SPRINGFIELD, OH MSA
	37 147	Pitt		39 023	Clark
3290		HICKORY-MORGANTON-LENOIR, NC MSA		39 057	Greene
	37 003	Alexander		39 109	Miami
	37 023	Burke		39 113	Montgomery
	37 027	Caldwell	3400		HUNTINGTON-ASHLAND, WV-KY-OH MSA
	37 035	Catawba		39 087	Lawrence
3605		JACKSONVILLE, NC MSA	4320		LIMA, OH MSA
	37 133	Onslow		39 003	Allen
5720		NORFOLK-VIRGINIA BEACH-NEWPORT NEWS, VA-NC MSA		39 011	Auglaize
			4800		MANSFIELD, OH MSA
	37 053	Currituck		39 033	Crawford
6640		RALEIGH-DURHAM-CHAPEL HILL, NC MSA		39 139	Richland
	37 037	Chatham	6020		PARKERSBURG-MARIETTA, WV-OH MSA
	37 063	Durham		39 167	Washington
	37 069	Franklin	8080		STEUBENVILLE-WEIRTON, OH-WV MSA
	37 101	Johnston		39 081	Jefferson
	37 135	Orange	8400		TOLEDO, OH MSA
	37 183	Wake		39 051	Fulton
				39 095	Lucas
				39 173	Wood

(MSA = metropolitan statistical area; CMSA = consolidated MSA; PMSA = primary MSA; and
NECMA = New England county metropolitan area. For further information, see Appendix A.)

Geographic Codes MSA/CMSA/ PMSA/ NECMA	State and County	Title and Geographic Components	Geographic Codes MSA/CMSA/ PMSA/ NECMA	State and County	Title and Geographic Components
9000		WHEELING, WV-OH MSA	3240		HARRISBURG-LEBANON-CARLISLE, PA MSA
	39 013	Belmont		42 041	Cumberland
9320		YOUNGSTOWN-WARREN, OH MSA		42 043	Dauphin
9320	39 029	Columbiana		42 075	Lebanon
9320	39 099	Mahoning		42 099	Perry
9320	39 155	Trumbull	3680		JOHNSTOWN, PA MSA
				42 021	Cambria
		OKLAHOMA		42 111	Somerset
2340		ENID, OK MSA	4000		LANCASTER, PA MSA
	40 047	Garfield		42 071	Lancaster
2720		FORT SMITH, AR-OK MSA	6280		PITTSBURGH, PA MSA
	40 135	Sequoyah		42 003	Allegheny
4200		LAWTON, OK MSA		42 007	Beaver
	40 031	Comanche		42 019	Butler
5880		OKLAHOMA CITY, OK MSA		42 051	Fayette
	40 017	Canadian		42 125	Washington
	40 027	Cleveland		42 129	Westmoreland
	40 083	Logan	6680		READING, PA MSA
	40 087	McClain		42 011	Berks
	40 109	Oklahoma	7560		SCRANTON-WILKES-BARRE-HAZLETON, PA MSA
	40 125	Pottawatomie		42 037	Columbia
8560		TULSA, OK MSA		42 069	Lackawanna
	40 037	Creek		42 079	Luzerne
	40 113	Osage		42 131	Wyoming
	40 131	Rogers	7610		SHARON, PA MSA
	40 143	Tulsa		42 085	Mercer
	40 145	Wagoner	8050		STATE COLLEGE, PA MSA
				42 027	Centre
		OREGON	9140		WILLIAMSPORT, PA MSA
1890		CORVALLIS, OR MSA		42 081	Lycoming
	41 003	Benton	9280		YORK, PA MSA
6442		PORTLAND-SALEM, OR-WA CMSA	9280	42 133	York
6440		PORTLAND-VANCOUVER, OR-WA PMSA			
	41 005	Clackamas			**RHODE ISLAND**
	41 009	Columbia	6483		PROVIDENCE-WARWICK-PAWTUCKET, RI NECMA
	41 051	Multnomah		44 001	Bristol
	41 067	Washington		44 003	Kent
	41 071	Yamhill		44 007	Providence
7080		SALEM, OR PMSA		44 009	Washington
	41 047	Marion			
	41 053	Polk			**SOUTH CAROLINA**
2400		EUGENE-SPRINGFIELD, OR MSA	0600		AUGUSTA-AIKEN, GA-SC MSA
	41 039	Lane		45 003	Aiken
4890		MEDFORD-ASHLAND, OR MSA		45 037	Edgefield
	41 029	Jackson	1440		CHARLESTON-NORTH CHARLESTON, SC MSA
				45 015	Berkeley
		PENNSYLVANIA		45 019	Charleston
70		NEW YORK-NORTHERN NEW JERSEY-LONG ISLAND, NY-NJ-CT-PA CMSA		45 035	Dorchester
5660		NEWBURGH, NY-PA PMSA	1520		CHARLOTTE-GASTONIA-ROCK HILL, NC-SC MSA
	42 103	Pike		45 091	York
6162		PHILADELPHIA-WILMINGTON-ATLANTIC CITY, PA-NJ-DE-MD CMSA	1760		COLUMBIA, SC MSA
6160		PHILADELPHIA, PA-NJ PMSA		45 063	Lexington
	42 017	Bucks		45 079	Richland
	42 029	Chester	2655		FLORENCE, SC MSA
	42 045	Delaware		45 041	Florence
	42 091	Montgomery	3160		GREENVILLE-SPARTANBURG-ANDERSON, SC MSA
	42 101	Philadelphia		45 007	Anderson
0240		ALLENTOWN-BETHLEHEM-EASTON, PA MSA		45 021	Cherokee
	42 025	CARBON COUNTY, PA		45 045	Greenville
	42 077	Lehigh		45 077	Pickens
	42 095	Northampton		45 083	Spartanburg
0280		ALTOONA, PA MSA	5330		MYRTLE BEACH, SC MSA
	42 013	Blair		45 051	Horry
2360		ERIE, PA MSA	8140		SUMTER, SC MSA
	42 049	Erie		45 085	Sumter

Metropolitan Statistical Areas and Components by State – Continued

(MSA = metropolitan statistical area; CMSA = consolidated MSA; PMSA = primary MSA; and NECMA = New England county metropolitan area. For further information, see Appendix A.)

Geographic Codes MSA/CMSA/ PMSA/ NECMA	State and County	Title and Geographic Components	Geographic Codes MSA/CMSA/ PMSA/ NECMA	State and County	Title and Geographic Components
		SOUTH DAKOTA	48 201		Harris
6660		RAPID CITY, SD MSA	48 291		Liberty
	46 103	PENNINGTON COUNTY, SD	48 339		Montgomery
7760		SIOUX FALLS, SD MSA	48 473		Waller
	46 083	LINCOLN COUNTY, SD	0040		ABILENE, TX MSA
	46 099	MINNEHAHA COUNTY, SD		48 441	TAYLOR COUNTY, TX
			0320		AMARILLO, TX MSA
		TENNESSEE		48 375	Potter
1560		CHATTANOOGA, TN-GA MSA		48 381	Randall
	47 065	Hamilton	0640		AUSTIN-SAN MARCOS, TX MSA
	47 115	Marion		48 021	Bastrop
1660		CLARKSVILLE-HOPKINSVILLE, TN-KY MSA		48 055	Caldwell
	47 125	Montgomery		48 209	Hays
3580		JACKSON, TN MSA		48 453	Travis
	47 023	Chester		48 491	Williamson
	47 113	Madison	0840		BEAUMONT-PORT ARTHUR, TX MSA
3660		JOHNSON CITY-KINGSPORT-BRISTOL, TN-VA MSA		48 199	Hardin
	47 019	Carter		48 245	Jefferson
	47 073	Hawkins		48 361	Orange
	47 163	Sullivan	1240		BROWNSVILLE-HARLINGEN-SAN BENITO, TX MSA
	47 171	Unicoi		48 061	Cameron
	47 179	Washington	1260		BRYAN-COLLEGE STATION, TX MSA
3840		KNOXVILLE, TN MSA		48 041	Brazos
	47 001	Anderson	1880		CORPUS CHRISTI, TX MSA
	47 009	Blount		48 355	Nueces
	47 093	Knox		48 409	San Patricio
	47 105	Loudon	2320		EL PASO, TX MSA
	47 155	Sevier		48 141	El Paso
	47 173	Union	3810		KILLEEN-TEMPLE, TX MSA
4920		MEMPHIS, TN-AR-MS MSA		48 027	Bell
	47 047	Fayette		48 099	Coryell
	47 157	Shelby	4080		LAREDO, TX MSA
	47 167	Tipton		48 479	Webb
5360		NASHVILLE, TN MSA	4420		LONGVIEW-MARSHALL, TX MSA
	47 021	Cheatham		48 183	Gregg
	47 037	Davidson		48 203	Harrison
	47 043	Dickson		48 459	Upshur
	47 147	Robertson	4600		LUBBOCK, TX MSA
	47 149	Rutherford		48 303	Lubbock
	47 165	Sumner	4880		MCALLEN-EDINBURG-MISSION, TX MSA
	47 187	Williamson		48 215	Hidalgo
	47 189	Wilson	5800		ODESSA-MIDLAND, TX MSA
				48 135	Ector
		TEXAS		48 329	Midland
31		DALLAS-FORT WORTH, TX CMSA	7200		SAN ANGELO, TX MSA
1920		DALLAS, TX PMSA		48 451	Tom Green
	48 085	Collin	7240		SAN ANTONIO, TX MSA
	48 113	Dallas		48 029	Bexar
	48 121	Denton		48 091	Comal
	48 139	Ellis		48 187	Guadalupe
	48 213	Henderson		48 493	Wilson
	48 231	Hunt	7640		SHERMAN-DENISON, TX MSA
	48 257	Kaufman		48 181	Grayson
	48 397	Rockwall	8360		TEXARKANA, TX-TEXARKANA, AR MSA
2800		FORT WORTH-ARLINGTON, TX PMSA		48 037	Bowie
	48 221	Hood	8640		TYLER, TX MSA
	48 251	Johnson		48 423	Smith
	48 367	Parker	8750		VICTORIA, TX MSA
	48 439	Tarrant		48 469	Victoria
3362		HOUSTON-GALVESTON-BRAZORIA, TX CMSA	8800		WACO, TX MSA
1145		BRAZORIA, TX PMSA		48 309	McLennan
	48 039	Brazoria	9080		WICHITA FALLS, TX MSA
2920		GALVESTON-TEXAS CITY, TX PMSA		48 009	Archer
		GALVESTON COUNTY, TX		48 485	Wichita
3360		HOUSTON, TX PMSA			
	48 071	Chambers			
	48 157	Fort Bend			

(MSA = metropolitan statistical area; CMSA = consolidated MSA; PMSA = primary MSA; and
NECMA = New England county metropolitan area. For further information, see Appendix A.)

Geographic Codes MSA/CMSA/ PMSA/ NECMA	State and County	Title and Geographic Components	Geographic Codes MSA/CMSA/ PMSA/ NECMA	State and County	Title and Geographic Components
		UTAH		51 800	Suffolk City
2620		FLAGSTAFF, AZ-UT MSA		51 810	Virginia Beach City
	49 025	Kane		51 830	Williamsburg City
6520		PROVO-OREM, UT MSA	6760		RICHMOND-PETERSBURG, VA MSA
	49 049	Utah		51 036	Charles City
7160		SALT LAKE CITY-OGDEN, UT MSA		51 041	Chesterfield
	49 011	Davis		51 053	Dinwiddie
	49 035	Salt Lake		51 075	Goochland
	49 057	Weber		51 085	Hanover
				51 087	Henrico
		VERMONT		51 127	New Kent
1303		BURLINGTON, VT NECMA		51 145	Powhatan
	50 077	Chittenden		51 149	Prince George
	50 011	Franklin		51 570	Colonial Heights City
	50 013	Grand Isle		51 670	Hopewell City
				51 730	Petersburg City
		VIRGINIA		51 760	Richmond City
8872		WASHINGTON-BALTIMORE, DC-MD-VA-WV CMSA	6800		ROANOKE, VA MSA
8840		WASHINGTON, DC-MD-VA-WV PMSA		51 023	Botetourt
	51 013	Arlington		51 161	Roanoke
	51 043	Clarke		51 770	Roanoke City
	51 047	Culpeper		51 775	Salem City
	51 059	Fairfax			
	51 061	Fauquier			**WASHINGTON**
	51 099	King George	6442		PORTLAND-SALEM, OR-WA CMSA
	51 107	Loudoun	6440		PORTLAND-VANCOUVER, OR-WA PMSA
	51 153	Prince William		53 011	Clark
	51 177	Spotsylvania	7602		SEATTLE-TACOMA-BREMERTON, WA CMSA
	51 179	Stafford	1150		BREMERTON, WA PMSA
	51 187	Warren		53 035	Kitsap
	51 510	Alexandria City	5910		OLYMPIA, WA PMSA
	51 600	Fairfax City		53 067	Thurston
	51 610	Falls Church City	7600		SEATTLE-BELLEVUE-EVERETT, WA PMSA
	51 630	Fredericksburg City		53 029	Island
	51 683	Manassas City		53 033	King
	51 685	Manassas Park City		53 061	Snohomish
1540		CHARLOTTESVILLE, VA MSA	8200		TACOMA, WA PMSA
	51 003	Albemarle		53 053	Pierce
	51 065	Fluvanna	0860		BELLINGHAM, WA MSA
	51 079	Greene		53 073	Whatcom
	51 540	Charlottesville City	6740		RICHLAND-KENNEWICK-PASCO, WA MSA
1950		DANVILLE, VA MSA		53 005	Benton
	51 143	Pittsylvania		53 021	Franklin
	51 590	Danville City	7840		SPOKANE, WA MSA
3660		JOHNSON CITY-KINGSPORT-BRISTOL, TN-VA MSA		53 063	Spokane
	51 169	Scott	9260		YAKIMA, WA MSA
	51 191	Washington		53 077	Yakima
	51 520	Bristol City			
4640		LYNCHBURG, VA MSA			**WEST VIRGINIA**
	51 009	Amherst	97		WASHINGTON-BALTIMORE, DC-MD-VA-WV CMSA
	51 019	Bedford	8840		WASHINGTON, DC-MD-VA-WV PMSA
	51 031	Campbell		54 003	Jefferson
	51 515	Bedford City		54 037	Berkeley
	51 680	Lynchburg City	1480		CHARLESTON, WV MSA
5720		NORFOLK-VIRGINIA BEACH-NEWPORT NEWS, VA-NC MSA		54 039	Kanawha
				54 079	Putnam
	51 073	Gloucester	1900		CUMBERLAND, MD-WV MSA
	51 093	Isle of Wight		54 057	Mineral
	51 095	James City	3400		HUNTINGTON-ASHLAND, WV-KY-OH MSA
	51 115	Mathews		54 011	Cabell
	51 199	York		54 099	Wayne
	51 550	Chesapeake City	6020		PARKERSBURG-MARIETTA, WV-OH MSA
	51 650	Hampton City		54 107	Wood
	51 700	Newport News City	8080		STEUBENVILLE-WEIRTON, OH-WV MSA
	51 710	Norfolk City		54 009	Brooke
	51 735	Poquoson City		54 029	Hancock
	51 740	Portsmouth City			

(MSA = metropolitan statistical area; CMSA = consolidated MSA; PMSA = primary MSA; and
NECMA = New England county metropolitan area. For further information, see Appendix A.)

Geographic Codes MSA/CMSA/ PMSA/ NECMA	State and County	Title and Geographic Components	Geographic Codes MSA/CMSA/ PMSA/ NECMA	State and County	Title and Geographic Components
9000		WHEELING, WV-OH MSA	3080		GREEN BAY, WI MSA
	54 051	Marshall		55 009	Brown
	54 069	Ohio	3620		JANESVILLE-BELOIT, WI MSA
				55 105	Rock
		WISCONSIN	3870		LA CROSSE, WI-MN MSA
14		CHICAGO-GARY-KENOSHA, IL-IN-WI CMSA		55 063	La Crosse
3800		KENOSHA, WI PMSA	4720		MADISON, WI MSA
	55 059	Kenosha		55 025	Dane
5082		MILWAUKEE-RACINE, WI CMSA	5120		MINNEAPOLIS-ST. PAUL, MN-WI MSA
5080		MILWAUKEE-WAUKESHA, WI PMSA		55 093	Pierce
	55 079	Milwaukee		55 109	St. Croix
	55 089	Ozaukee	7620		SHEBOYGAN, WI MSA
	55 131	Washington		55 117	Sheboygan
	55 133	Waukesha	8940		WAUSAU, WI MSA
6600		RACINE, WI PMSA		55 073	Marathon
	55 101	Racine			
0460		APPLETON-OSHKOSH-NEENAH, WI MSA			**WYOMING**
	55 015	Calumet	1350		CASPER, WY MSA
	55 087	Outagamie		56 025	Natrona
	55 139	Winnebago	1580		CHEYENNE, WY MSA
2240		DULUTH-SUPERIOR, MN-WI MSA		56 021	Laramie
	55 031	Douglas			
2290		EAU CLAIRE, WI MSA			
	55 017	Chippewa			
	55 035	Eau Claire			

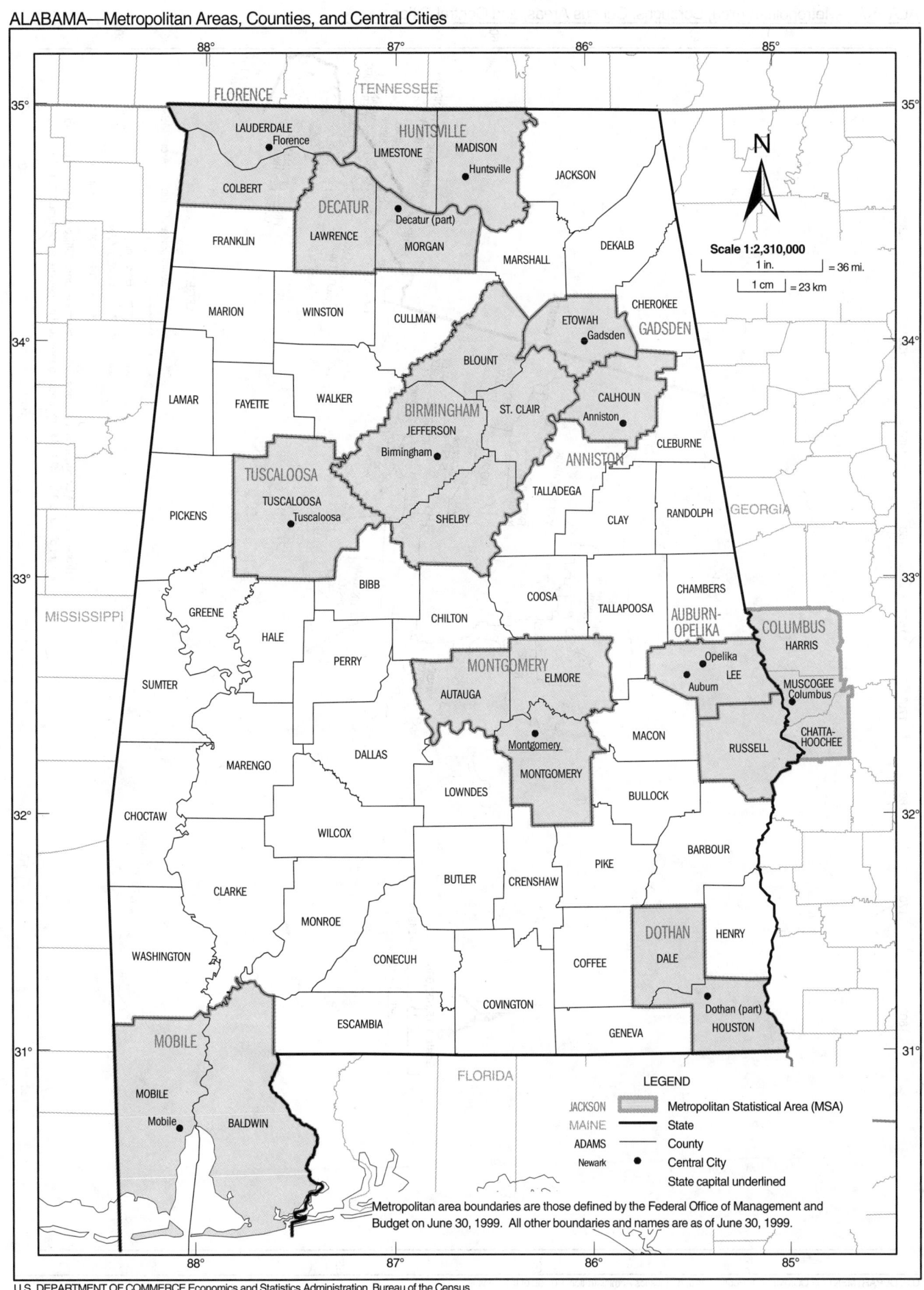

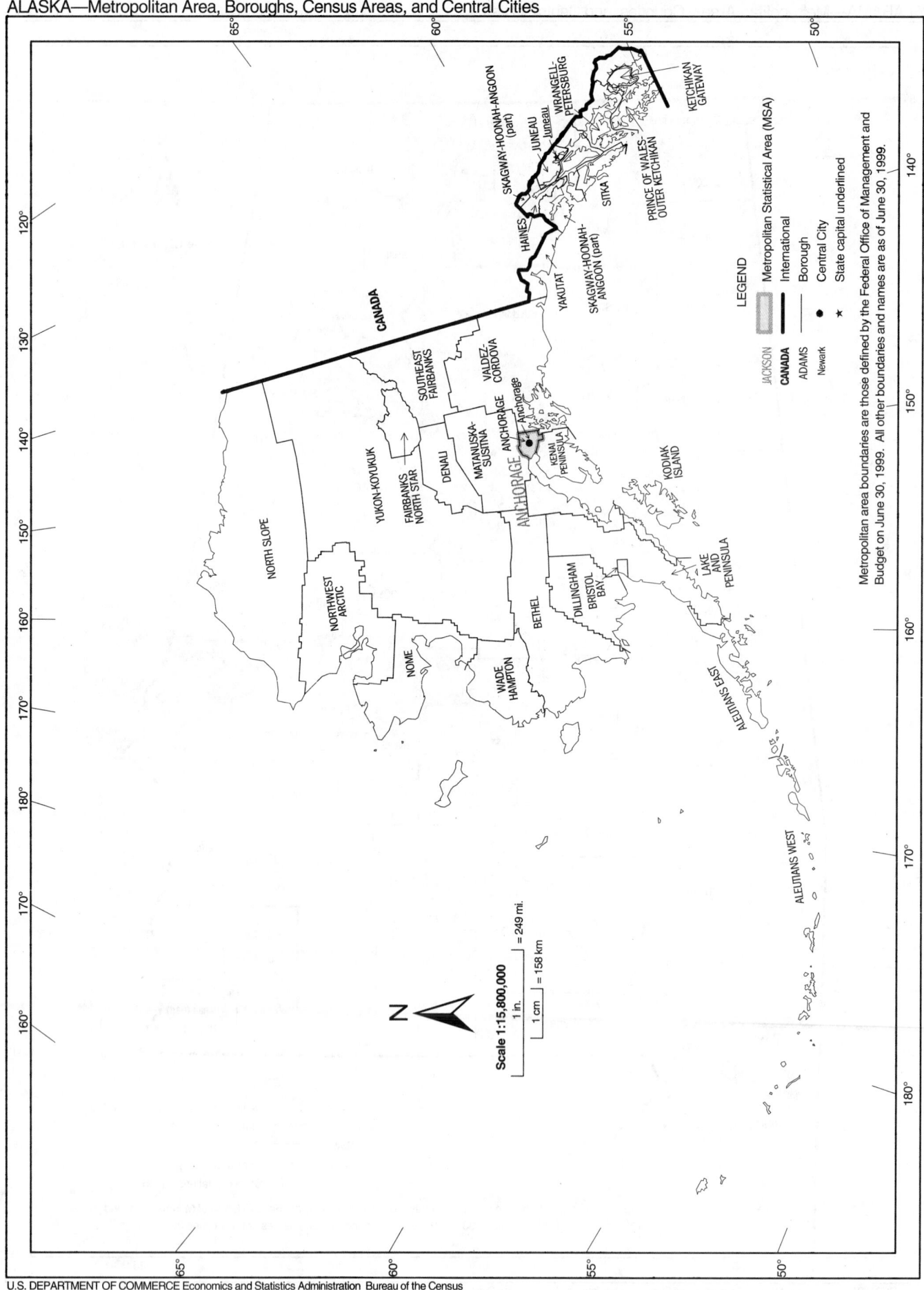

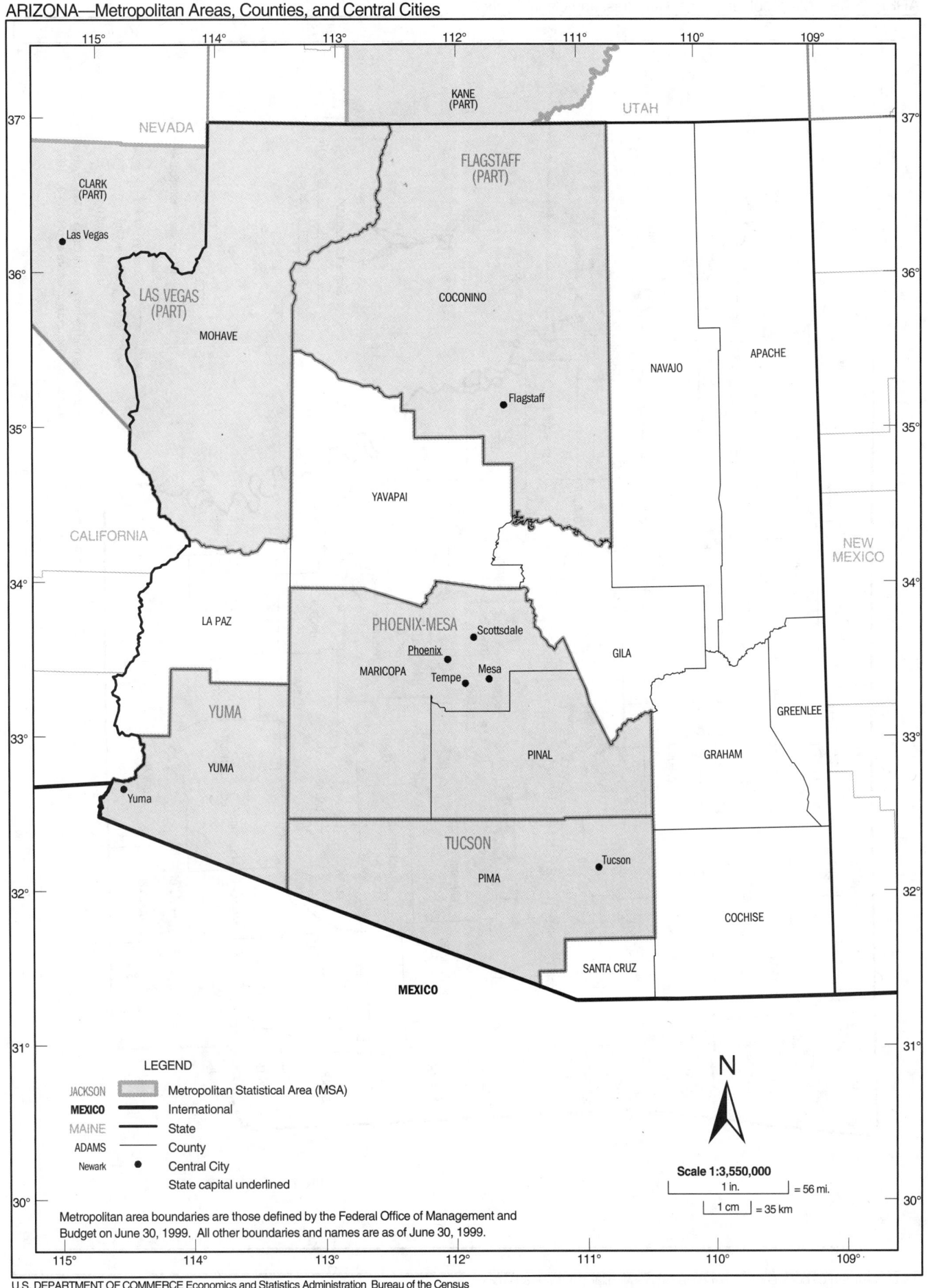

ARIZONA—Metropolitan Areas, Counties, and Central Cities

LEGEND

JACKSON   Metropolitan Statistical Area (MSA)
MEXICO   International
MAINE   State
ADAMS   County
Newark •   Central City
     State capital underlined

Metropolitan area boundaries are those defined by the Federal Office of Management and Budget on June 30, 1999. All other boundaries and names are as of June 30, 1999.

Scale 1:3,550,000

1 in. = 56 mi.

1 cm = 35 km

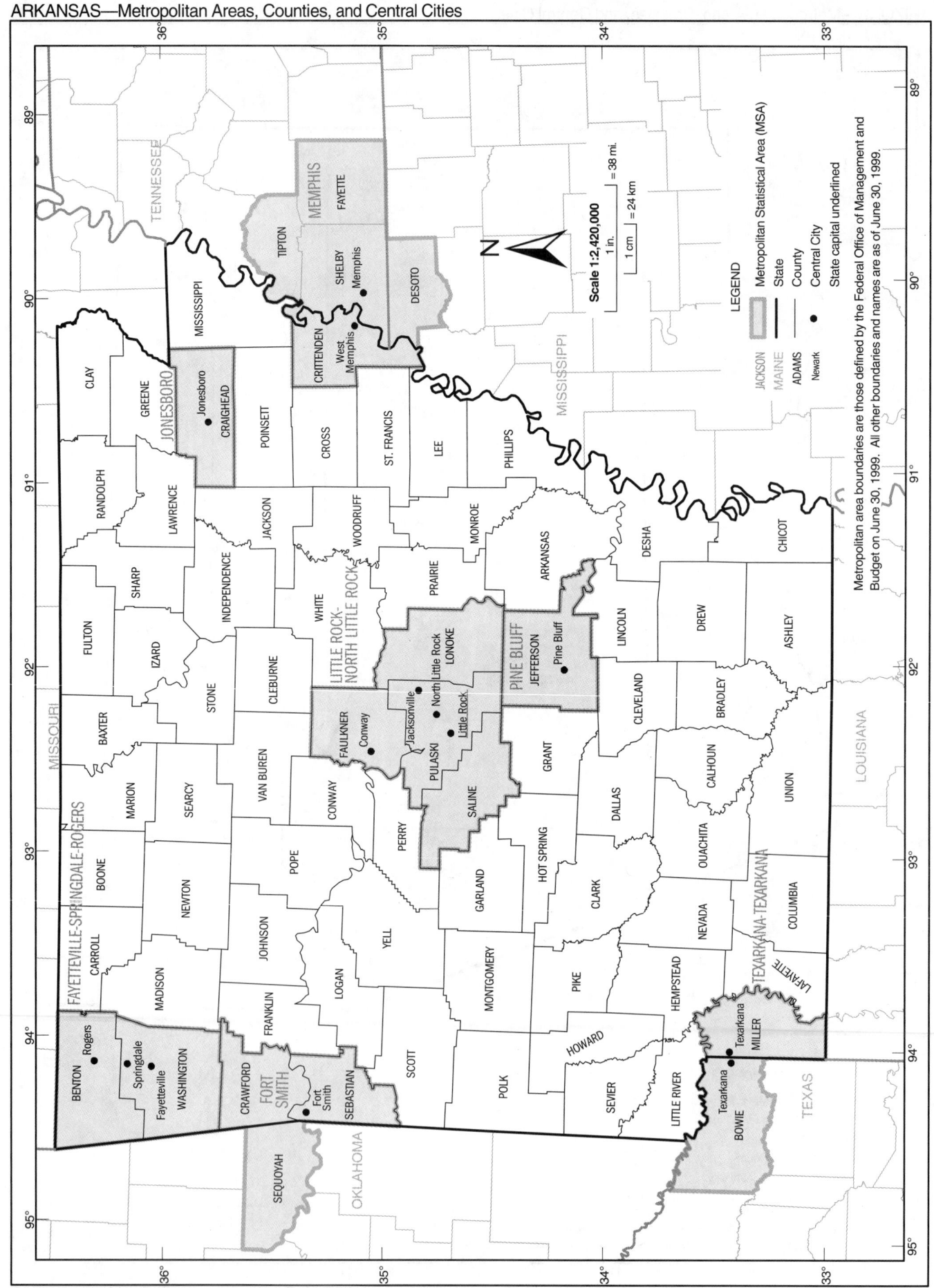

Scale 1:2,420,000

| 1 in. | = 38 mi. |
| 1 cm | = 24 km |

N

LEGEND

Metropolitan Statistical Area (MSA)
State
County
Central City
State capital underlined

JACKSON
MAINE
ADAMS
Newark

Metropolitan area boundaries are those defined by the Federal Office of Management and Budget on June 30, 1999. All other boundaries and names are as of June 30, 1999.

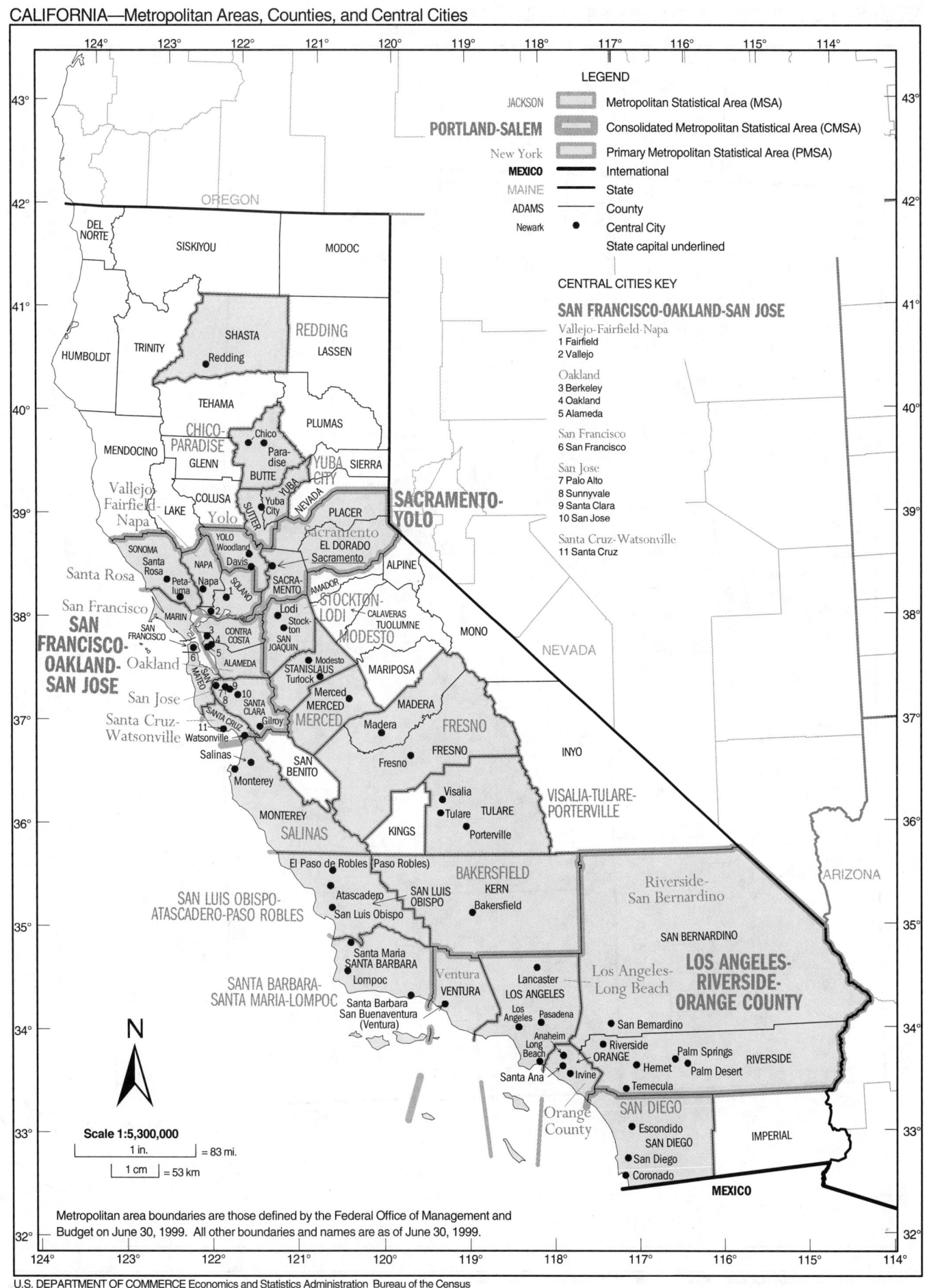

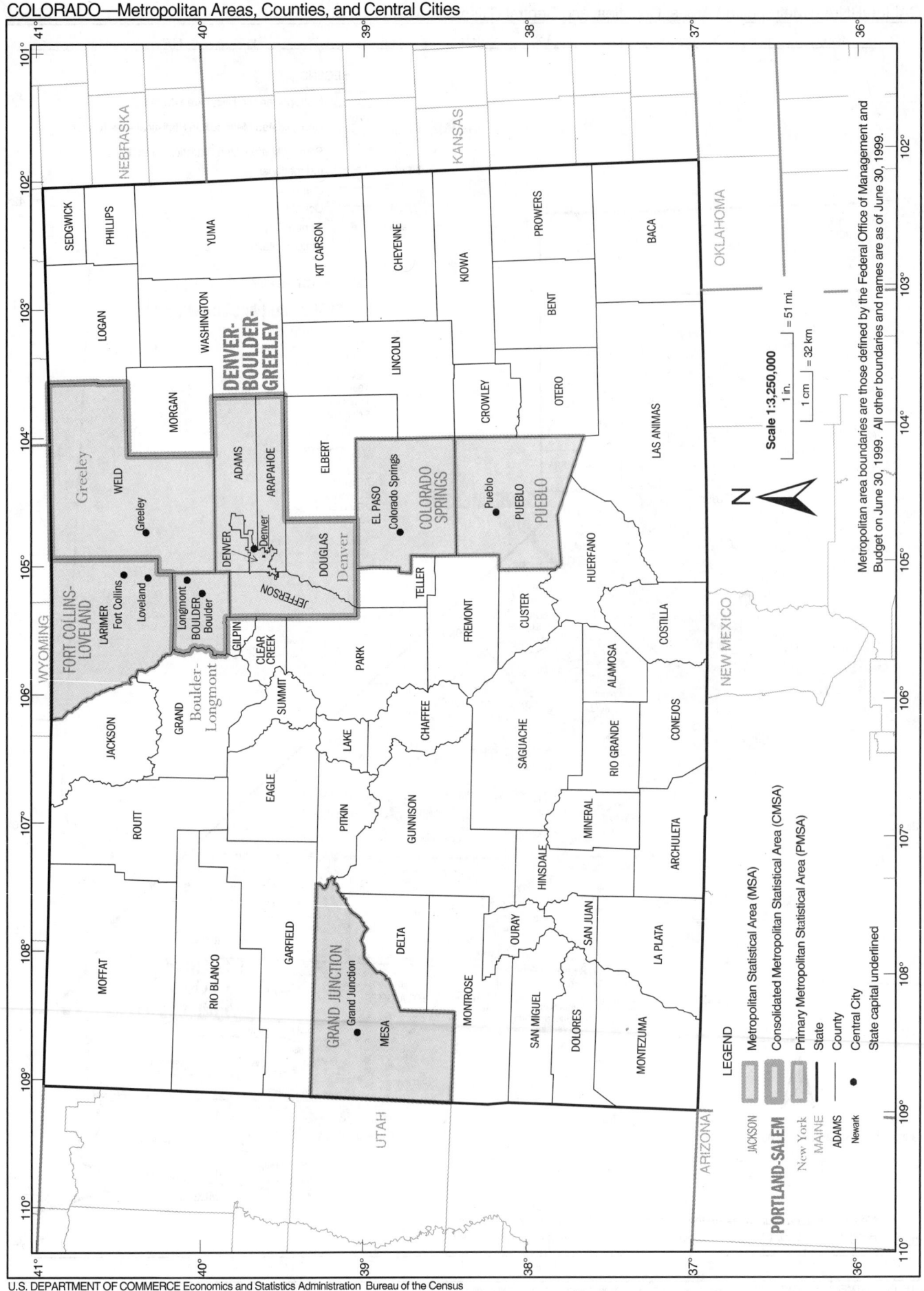

Scale 1:3,250,000

1 in. = 51 mi.

1 cm = 32 km

Metropolitan area boundaries are those defined by the Federal Office of Management and Budget on June 30, 1999. All other boundaries and names are as of June 30, 1999.

N

LEGEND

Metropolitan Statistical Area (MSA)

Consolidated Metropolitan Statistical Area (CMSA)

Primary Metropolitan Statistical Area (PMSA)

State

County

Central City

State capital underlined

JACKSON

PORTLAND-SALEM

New York

MAINE

ADAMS

Newark

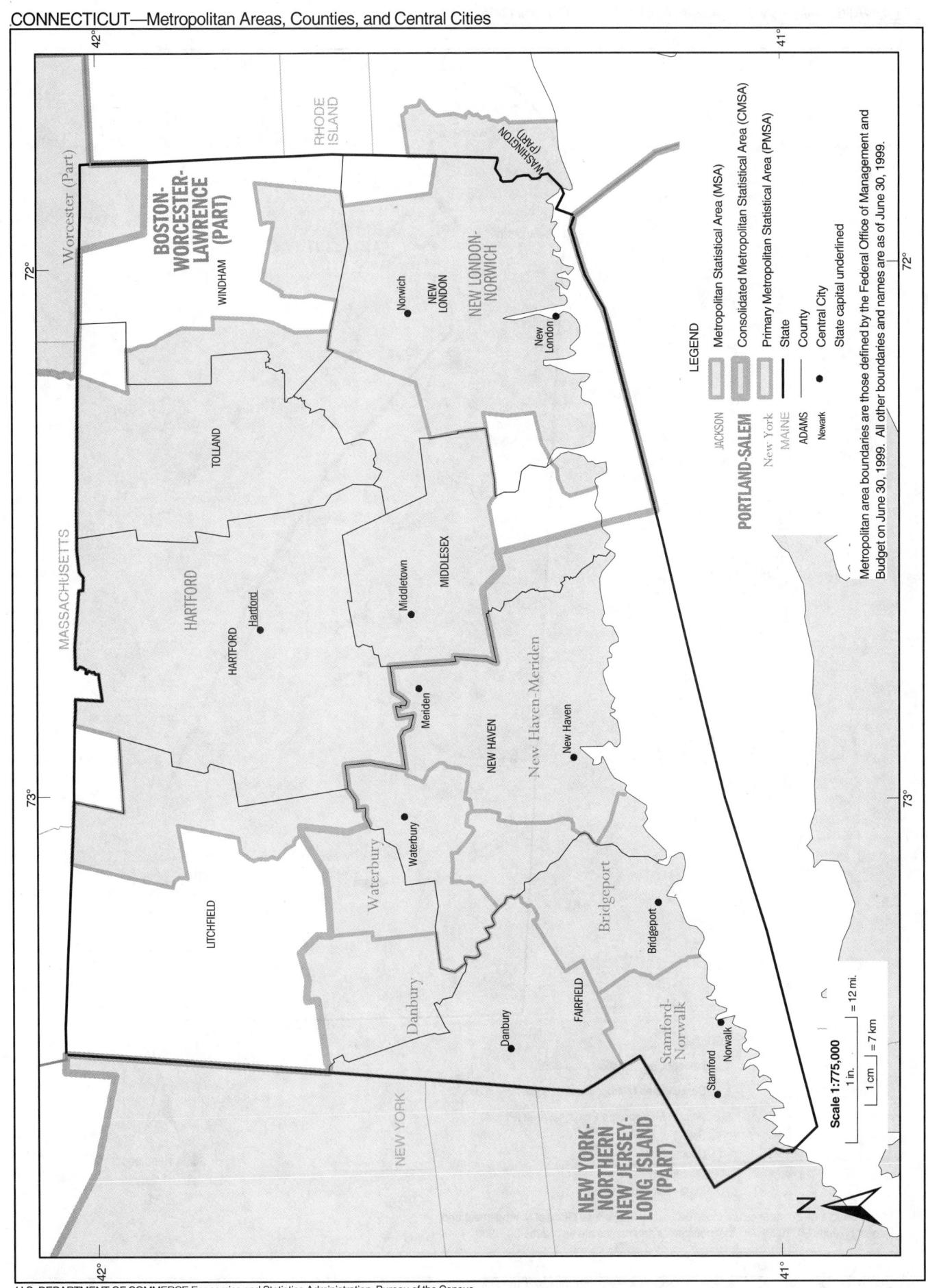

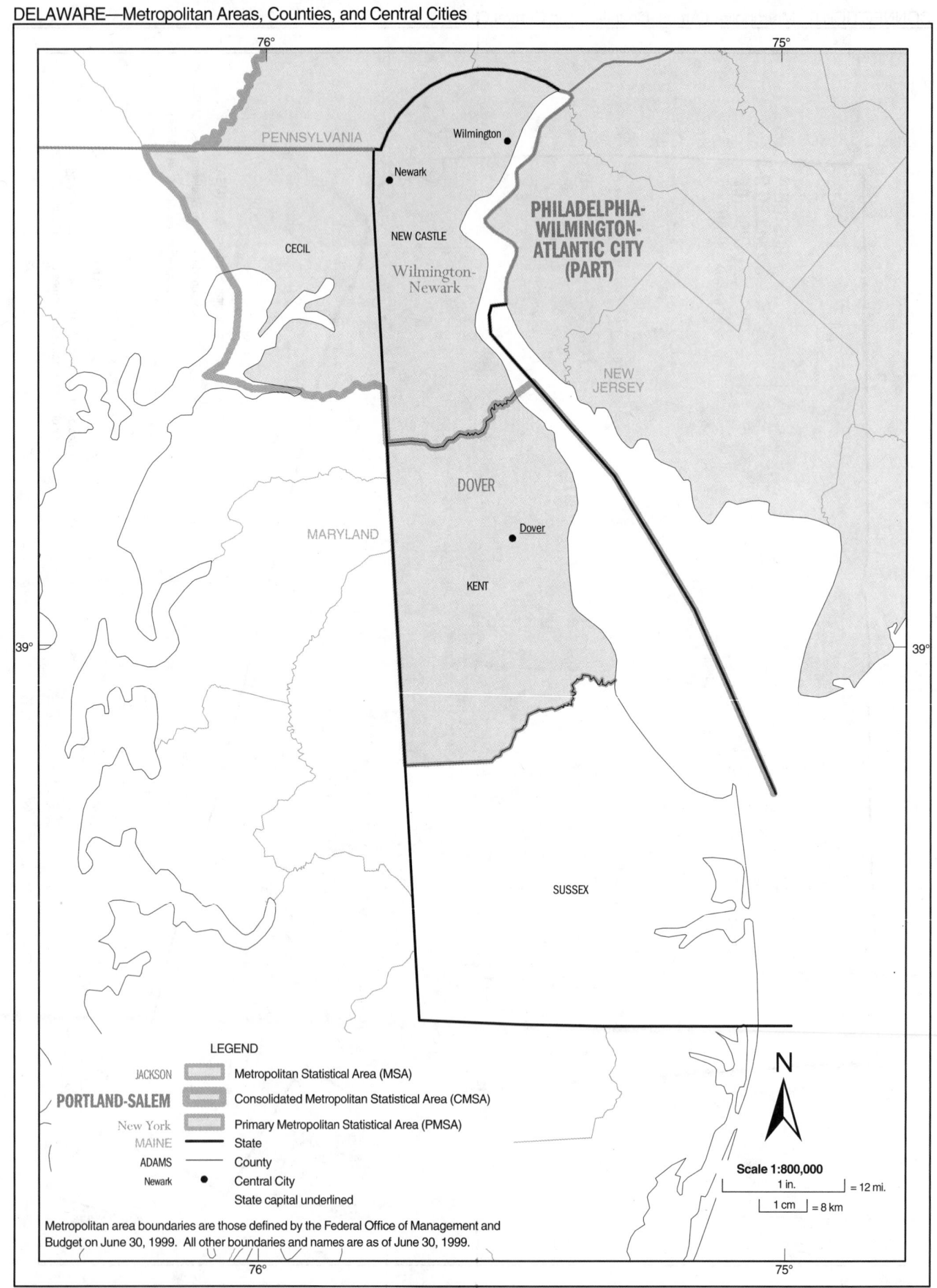

PENNSYLVANIA

CECIL

NEW CASTLE

Wilmington

Newark

Wilmington-Newark

PHILADELPHIA-WILMINGTON-ATLANTIC CITY (PART)

NEW JERSEY

MARYLAND

DOVER

Dover

KENT

SUSSEX

N

LEGEND

JACKSON		Metropolitan Statistical Area (MSA)
PORTLAND-SALEM		Consolidated Metropolitan Statistical Area (CMSA)
New York		Primary Metropolitan Statistical Area (PMSA)
MAINE		State
ADAMS		County
Newark	●	Central City
		State capital underlined

Scale 1:800,000

1 in. = 12 mi.

1 cm = 8 km

Metropolitan area boundaries are those defined by the Federal Office of Management and Budget on June 30, 1999. All other boundaries and names are as of June 30, 1999.

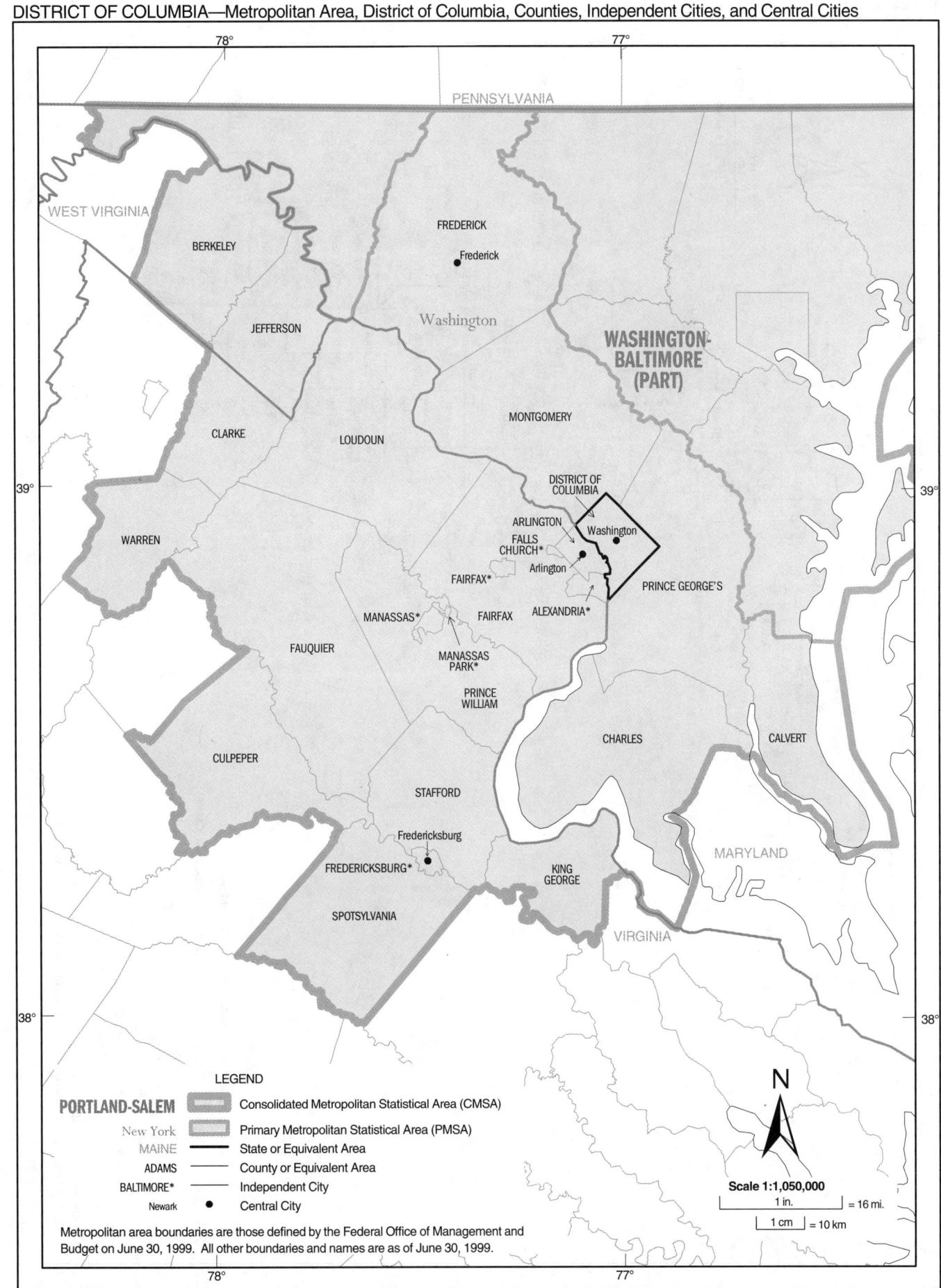

LEGEND

PORTLAND-SALEM	Consolidated Metropolitan Statistical Area (CMSA)
New York	Primary Metropolitan Statistical Area (PMSA)
MAINE	State or Equivalent Area
ADAMS	County or Equivalent Area
BALTIMORE*	Independent City
Newark ●	Central City

Metropolitan area boundaries are those defined by the Federal Office of Management and Budget on June 30, 1999. All other boundaries and names are as of June 30, 1999.

Scale 1:1,050,000

1 in. = 16 mi.

1 cm = 10 km

Scale 1:4,200,000

1 in. = 66 mi.
1 cm = 42 km

LEGEND

Metropolitan Statistical Area (MSA)

Consolidated Metropolitan Statistical Area (CMSA)

Primary Metropolitan Statistical Area (PMSA)

—— State

—— County

• Central City

State capital underlined

JACKSON

PORTLAND-SALEM

New York
MAINE

ADAMS

Newark

Metropolitan area boundaries are those defined by the Federal Office of Management and Budget on June 30, 1999. All other boundaries and names are as of June 30, 1999.

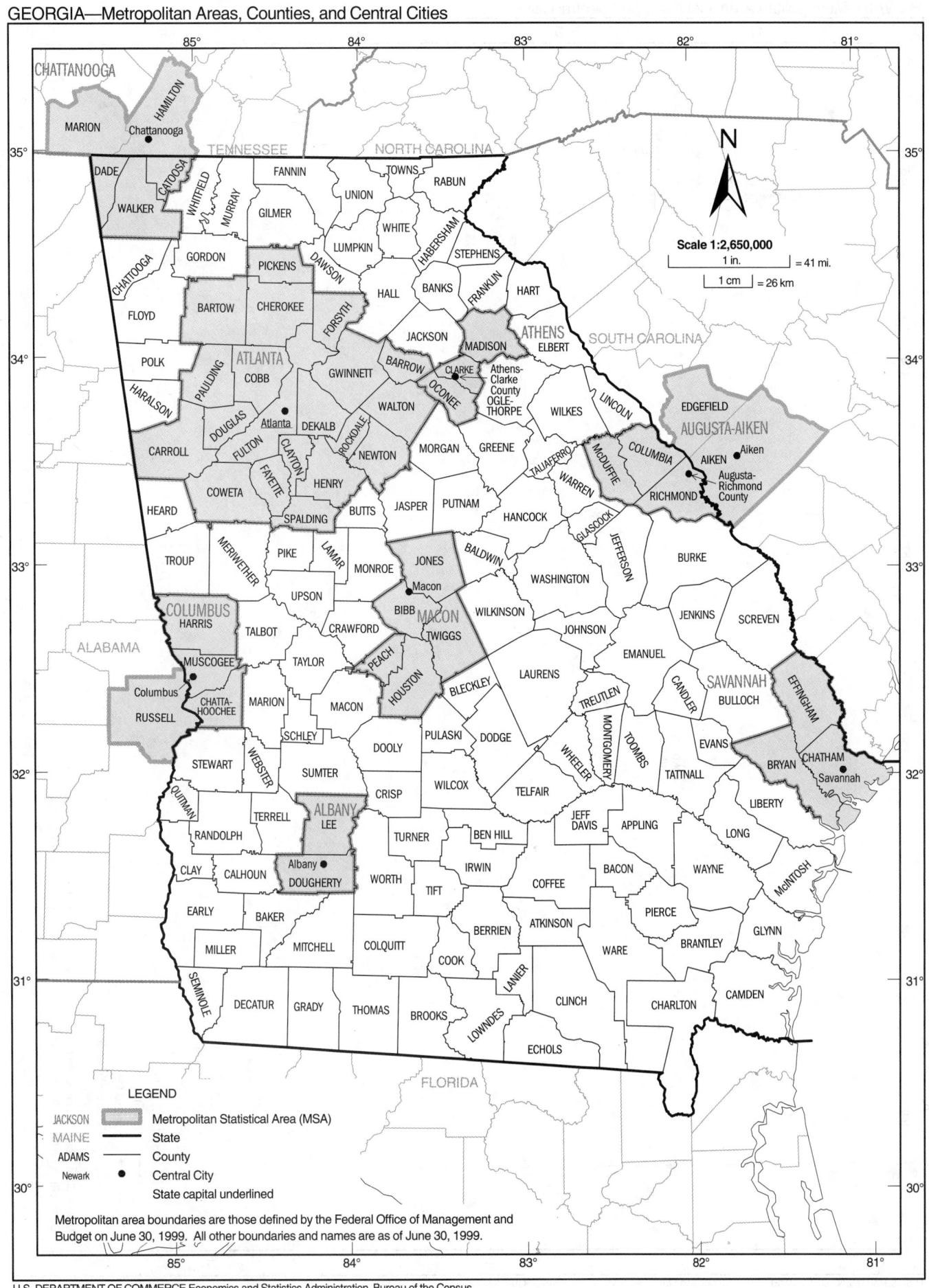

Scale 1:2,650,000

| 1 in. | = 41 mi. |
| 1 cm | = 26 km |

LEGEND

JACKSON
MAINE
ADAMS
Newark

- Metropolitan Statistical Area (MSA)
- State
- County
- Central City
State capital underlined

Metropolitan area boundaries are those defined by the Federal Office of Management and Budget on June 30, 1999. All other boundaries and names are as of June 30, 1999.

U.S. DEPARTMENT OF COMMERCE Economics and Statistics Administration Bureau of the Census

Scale 1:2,700,000
1 in. = 42 mi.
1 cm = 27 km

N

HAWAII

MAUI

KALAWAO

HONOLULU
(part)

HONOLULU

Honolulu

KAUAI

LEGEND

JACKSON

ADAMS   Metropolitan Statistical Area (MSA)

Newark   County

● Central City

State capital underlined

Metropolitan area boundaries are those defined by the Federal Office of Management and
Budget on June 30, 1999. All other boundaries and names are as of June 30, 1999.

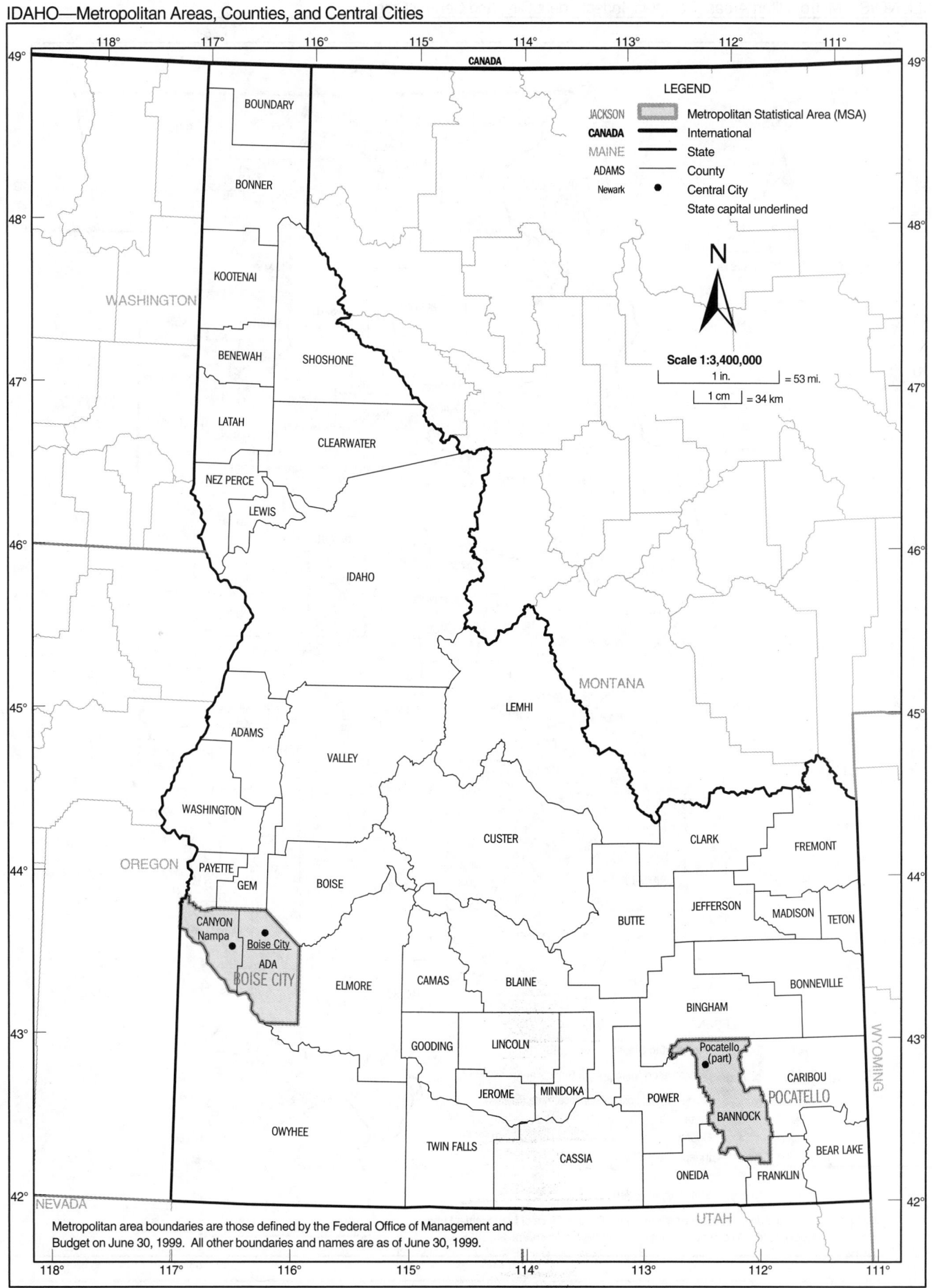

LEGEND

JACKSON   Metropolitan Statistical Area (MSA)
CANADA   International
MAINE   State
ADAMS   County
Newark   ● Central City
    State capital underlined

Scale 1:3,400,000

| 1 in. | = 53 mi. |
| 1 cm | = 34 km |

Metropolitan area boundaries are those defined by the Federal Office of Management and
Budget on June 30, 1999. All other boundaries and names are as of June 30, 1999.

ILLINOIS—Metropolitan Areas, Counties, Independent City, and Central Cities

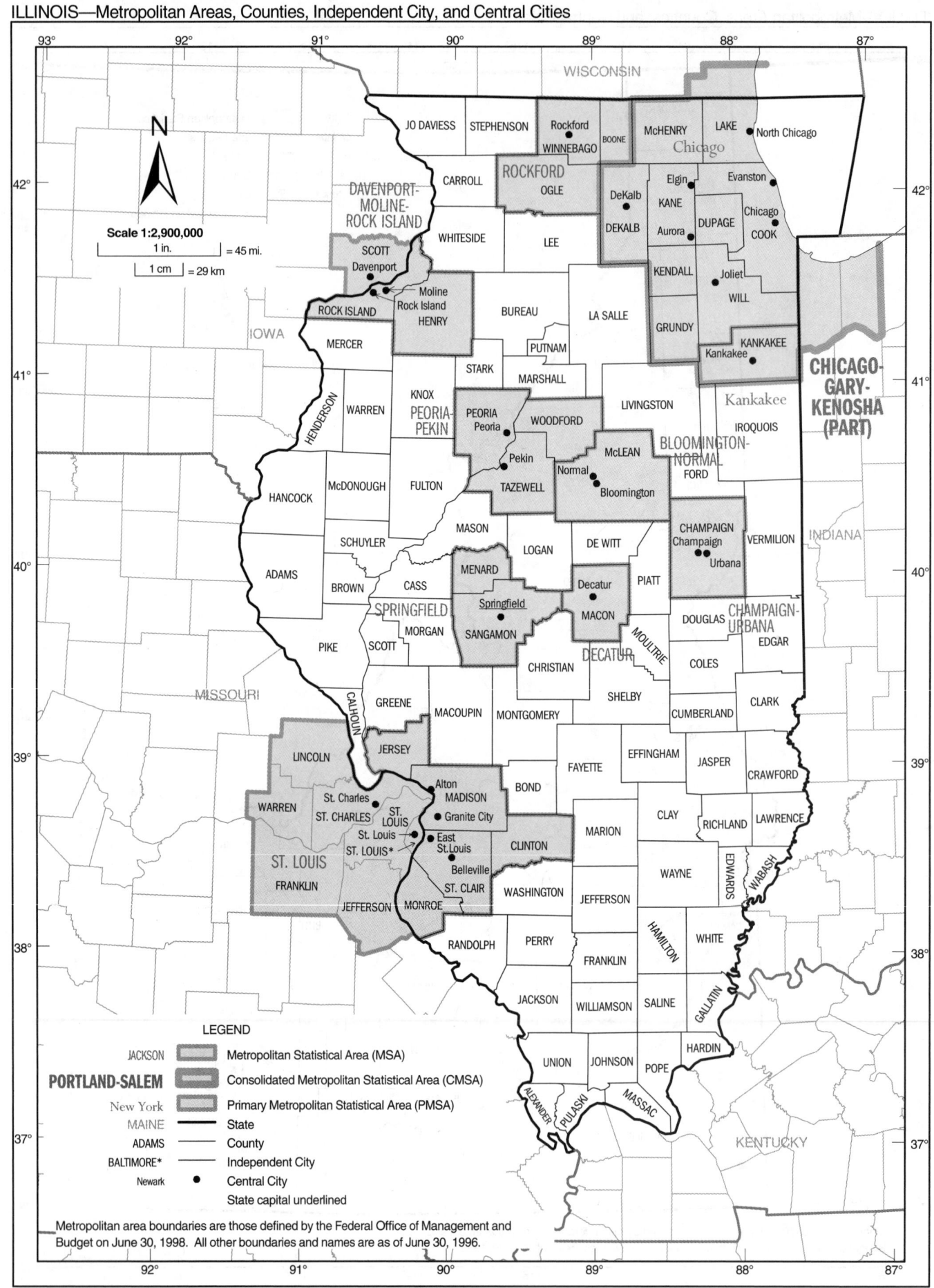

U.S. DEPARTMENT OF COMMERCE Economics and Statistics Administration Bureau of the Census

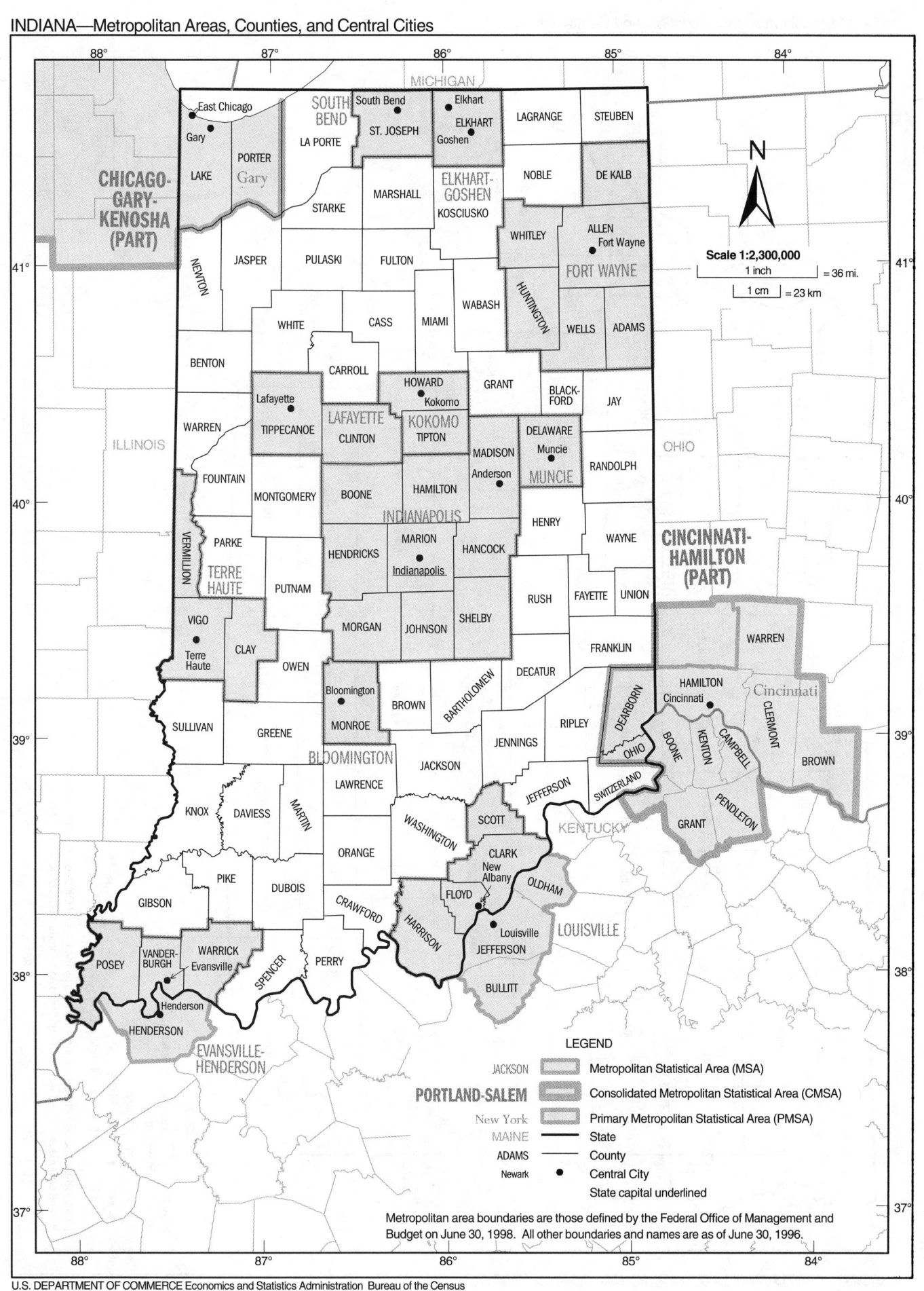

MICHIGAN

CHICAGO-GARY-KENOSHA (PART)

East Chicago
Gary
LAKE
PORTER
Gary
NEWTON
JASPER
PULASKI
WHITE
BENTON
WARREN
FOUNTAIN
VERMILLION
PARKE
TERRE HAUTE
VIGO
Terre Haute
CLAY
OWEN
SULLIVAN
GREENE
KNOX
DAVIESS
MARTIN
GIBSON
PIKE
DUBOIS
POSEY
VANDER-BURGH
Evansville
WARRICK
SPENCER
PERRY
Henderson
HENDERSON
EVANSVILLE-HENDERSON

SOUTH BEND
South Bend
ST. JOSEPH
LA PORTE
STARKE
MARSHALL
FULTON
CASS
CARROLL
Lafayette
LAFAYETTE
TIPPECANOE
CLINTON
MONTGOMERY
BOONE
HENDRICKS
PUTNAM
MORGAN
JOHNSON
BLOOMINGTON
Bloomington
MONROE
BROWN
LAWRENCE
ORANGE
WASHINGTON
CRAWFORD
HARRISON

Elkhart
ELKHART
Goshen
ELKHART-GOSHEN
KOSCIUSKO
MIAMI
WABASH
HOWARD
Kokomo
KOKOMO
TIPTON
HAMILTON
INDIANAPOLIS
MARION
Indianapolis
HANCOCK
SHELBY
BARTHOLOMEW
JACKSON
SCOTT
CLARK
New Albany
FLOYD

LAGRANGE
NOBLE
WHITLEY
GRANT
DELAWARE
Muncie
MUNCIE
MADISON
Anderson
HENRY
RUSH
DECATUR
JENNINGS
JEFFERSON
Louisville
JEFFERSON
BULLITT
LOUISVILLE
OLDHAM

STEUBEN
DE KALB
ALLEN
Fort Wayne
FORT WAYNE
HUNTINGTON
WELLS
ADAMS
BLACK-FORD
JAY
RANDOLPH
WAYNE
FAYETTE
UNION
FRANKLIN
RIPLEY
SWITZERLAND

OHIO

KENTUCKY

CINCINNATI-HAMILTON (PART)
WARREN
DEARBORN
HAMILTON
Cincinnati
Cincinnati
CLERMONT
BROWN
OHIO
BOONE
KENTON
CAMPBELL
SWITZERLAND
GRANT
PENDLETON

ILLINOIS

N

Scale 1:2,300,000
1 inch = 36 mi.
1 cm = 23 km

LEGEND

JACKSON   Metropolitan Statistical Area (MSA)

PORTLAND-SALEM   Consolidated Metropolitan Statistical Area (CMSA)

New York   Primary Metropolitan Statistical Area (PMSA)

MAINE ——— State

ADAMS ——— County

Newark ● Central City

State capital underlined

Metropolitan area boundaries are those defined by the Federal Office of Management and Budget on June 30, 1998. All other boundaries and names are as of June 30, 1996.

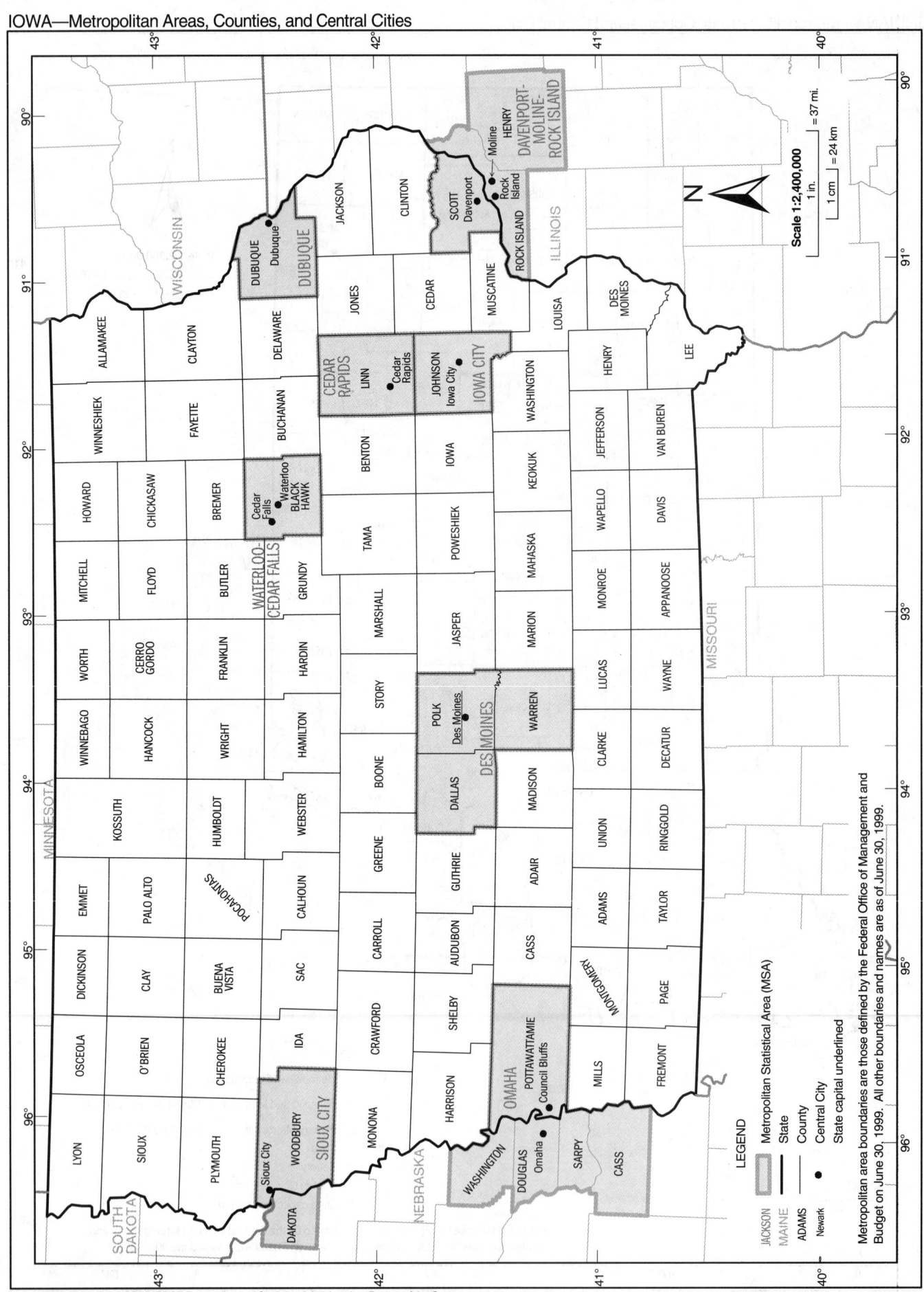

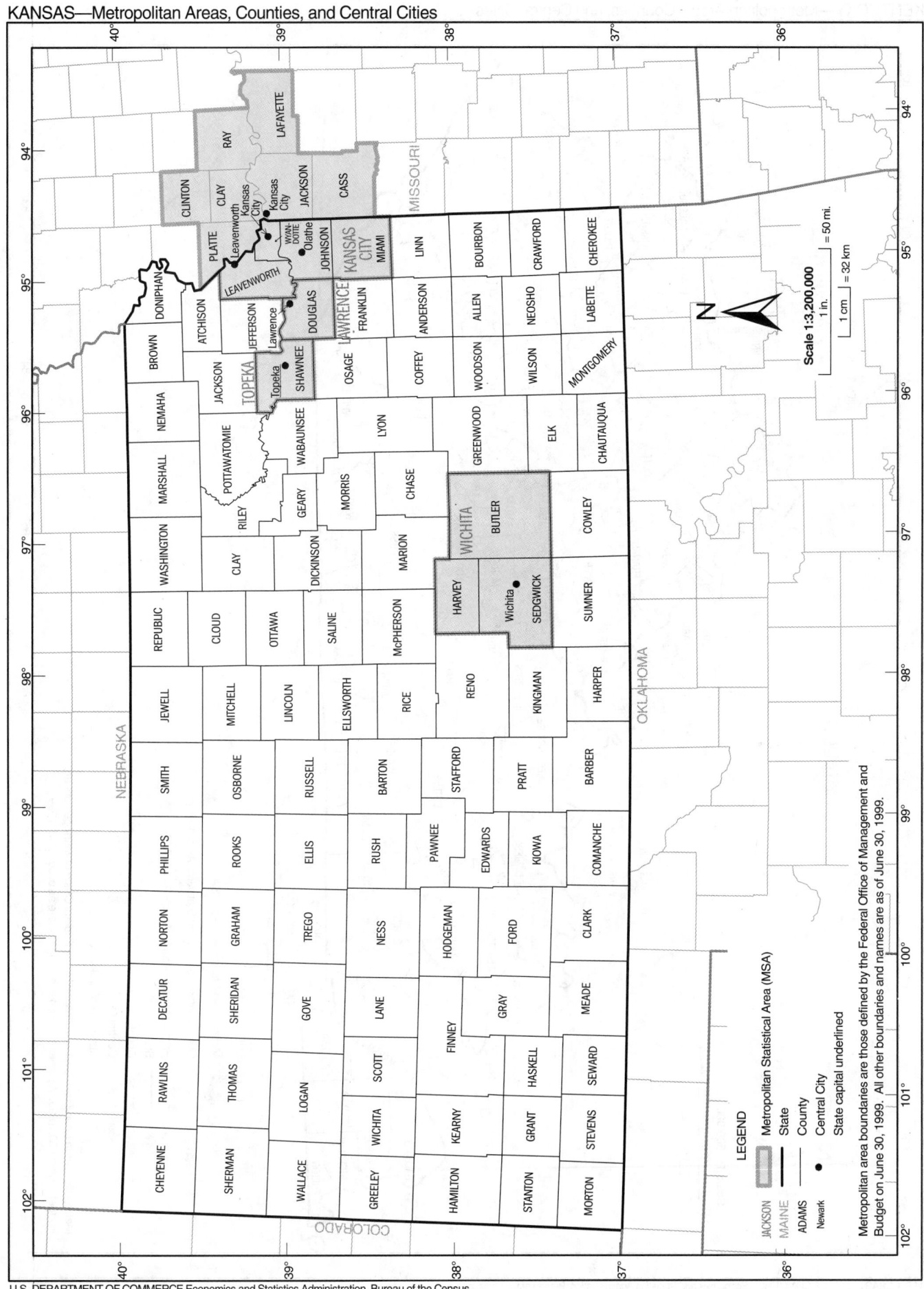

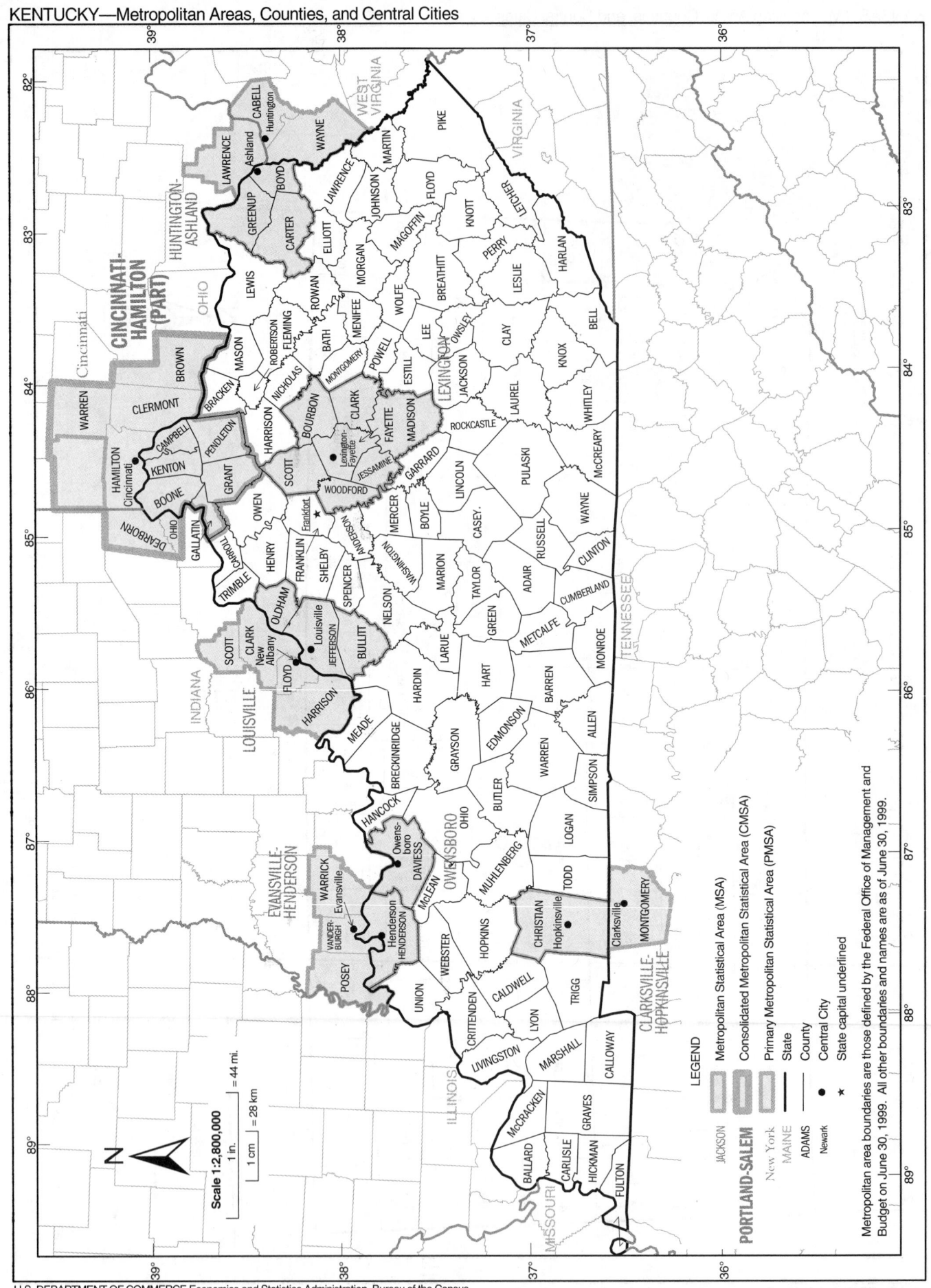

LOUISIANA—Metropolitan Areas, Parishes, and Central Cities

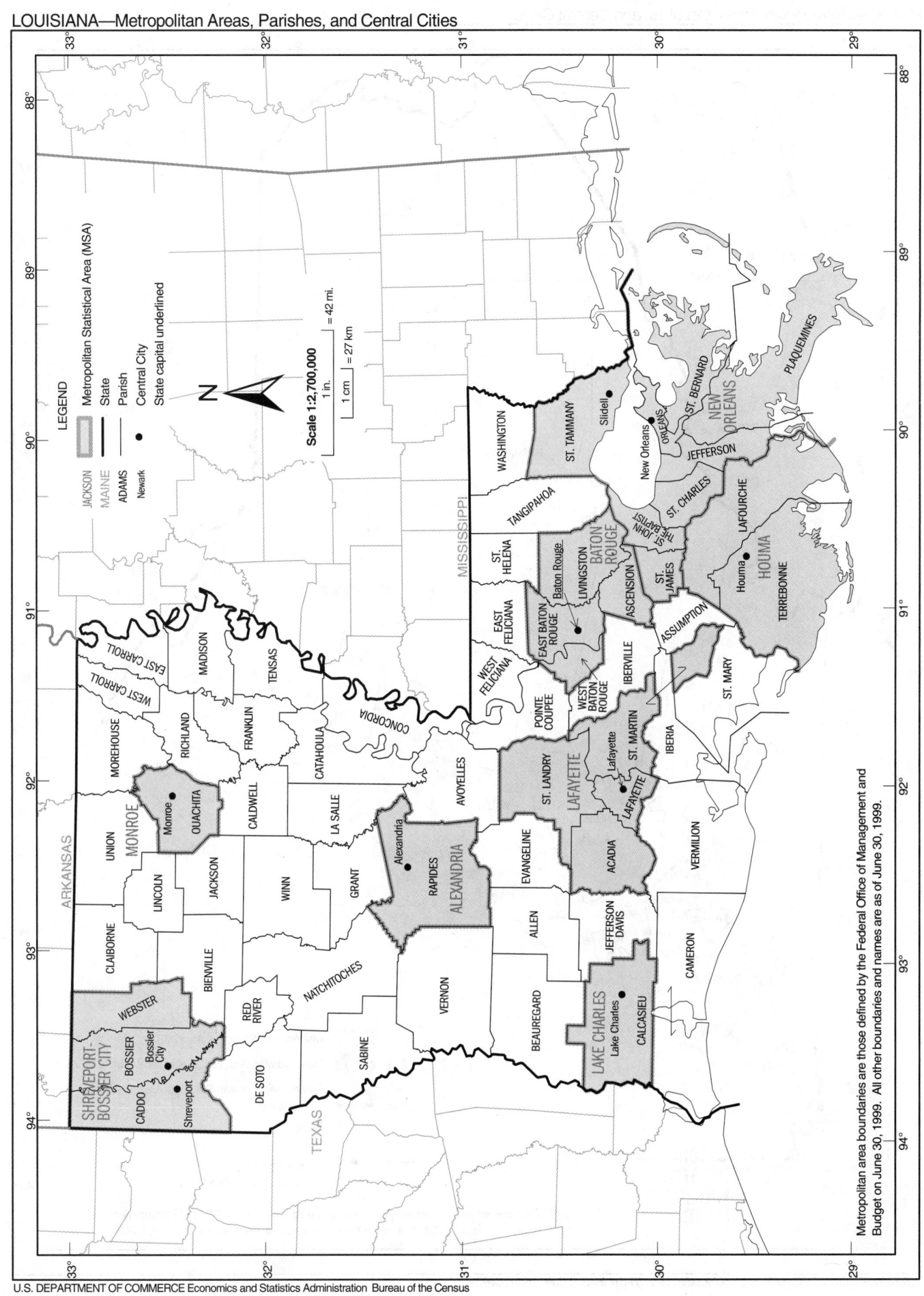

Metropolitan area boundaries are those defined by the Federal Office of Management and Budget on June 30, 1999. All other boundaries and names are as of June 30, 1999.

LEGEND

- Metropolitan Statistical Area (MSA)
- State
- Parish
- Central City
- State capital underlined

JACKSON
MAINE
ADAMS
Newark

Scale 1:2,700,000

1 in. = 42 mi.

1 cm = 27 km

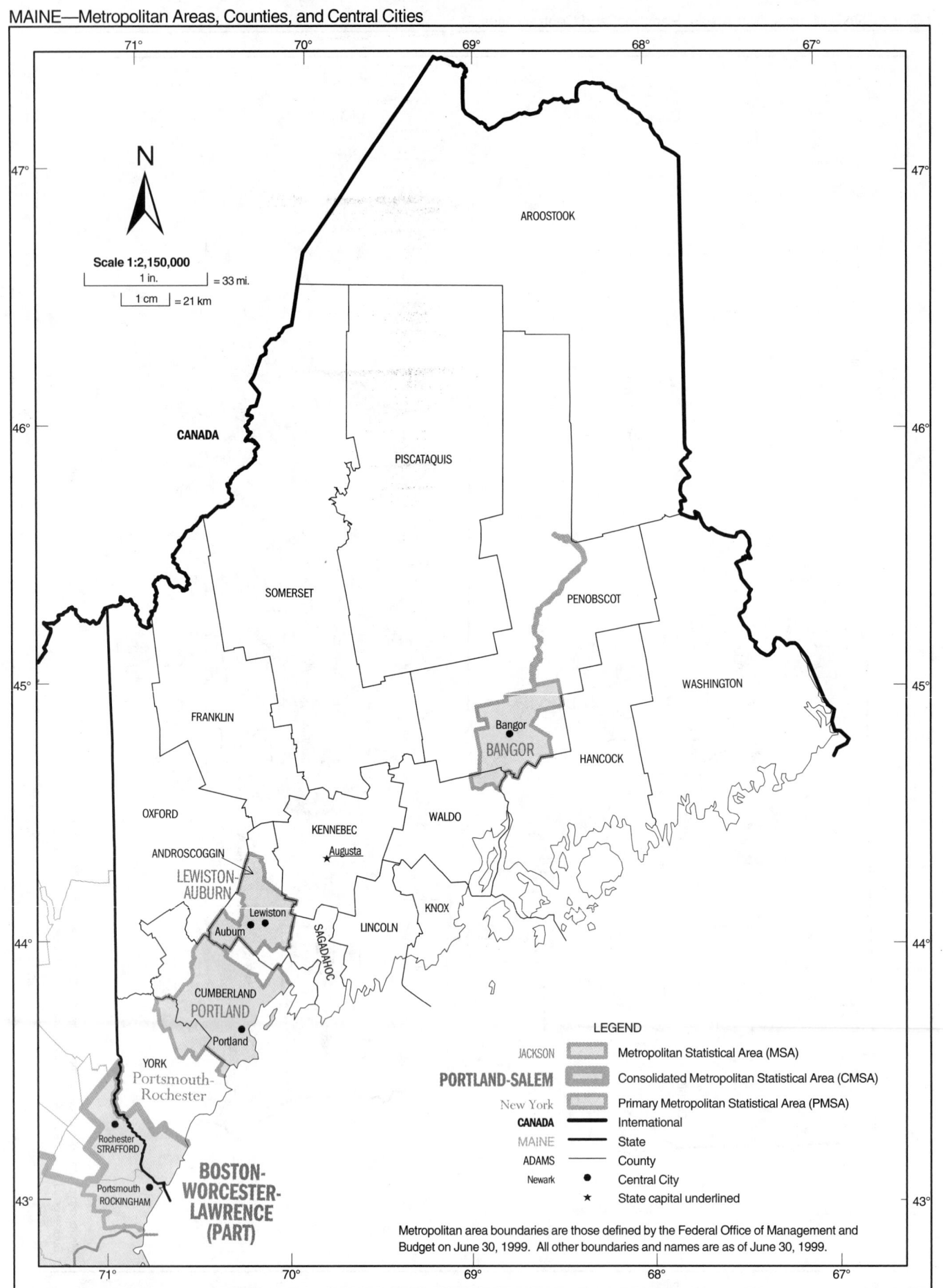

MAINE—Metropolitan Areas, Counties, and Central Cities

N

Scale 1:2,150,000
1 in. = 33 mi.
1 cm = 21 km

CANADA

AROOSTOOK

PISCATAQUIS

SOMERSET

PENOBSCOT

WASHINGTON

FRANKLIN

Bangor
BANGOR

HANCOCK

OXFORD

KENNEBEC

WALDO

ANDROSCOGGIN

Augusta

LEWISTON-
AUBURN

Lewiston

KNOX

Auburn

LINCOLN

SAGADAHOC

CUMBERLAND
PORTLAND

Portland

YORK
Portsmouth-
Rochester

Rochester
STRAFFORD

LEGEND

Portsmouth
ROCKINGHAM

BOSTON-
WORCESTER-
LAWRENCE
(PART)

JACKSON — Metropolitan Statistical Area (MSA)

PORTLAND-SALEM — Consolidated Metropolitan Statistical Area (CMSA)

New York — Primary Metropolitan Statistical Area (PMSA)

CANADA — International

MAINE — State

ADAMS — County

Newark ● Central City

★ State capital underlined

Metropolitan area boundaries are those defined by the Federal Office of Management and Budget on June 30, 1999. All other boundaries and names are as of June 30, 1999.

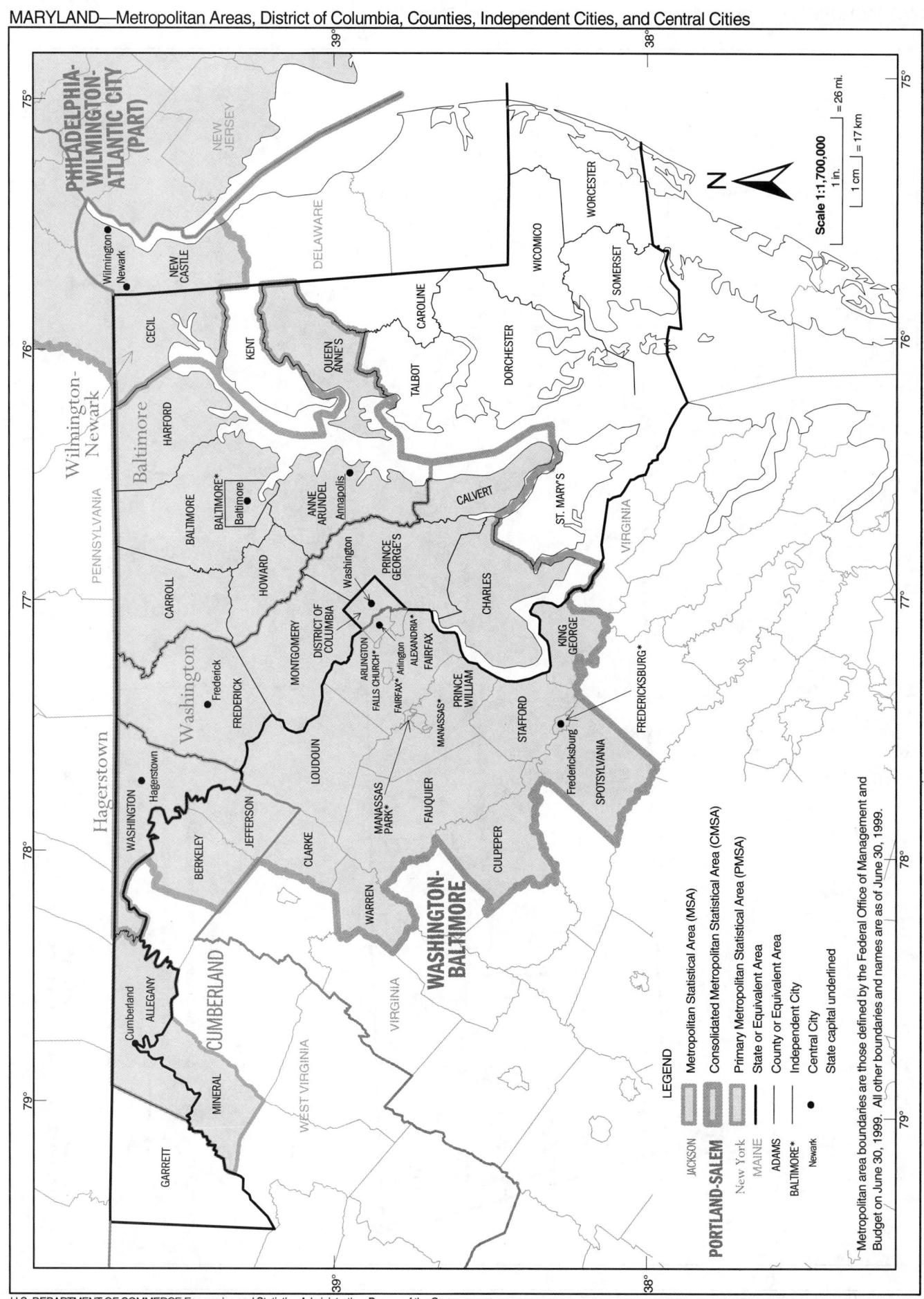

Scale 1:1,700,000

1 in. = 26 mi.

1 cm = 17 km

LEGEND

Metropolitan Statistical Area (MSA)

Consolidated Metropolitan Statistical Area (CMSA)

Primary Metropolitan Statistical Area (PMSA)

State or Equivalent Area

County or Equivalent Area

Independent City

● Central City

State capital underlined

JACKSON

PORTLAND-SALEM

New York

MAINE

ADAMS

BALTIMORE*

● Newark

Metropolitan area boundaries are those defined by the Federal Office of Management and Budget on June 30, 1999. All other boundaries and names are as of June 30, 1999.

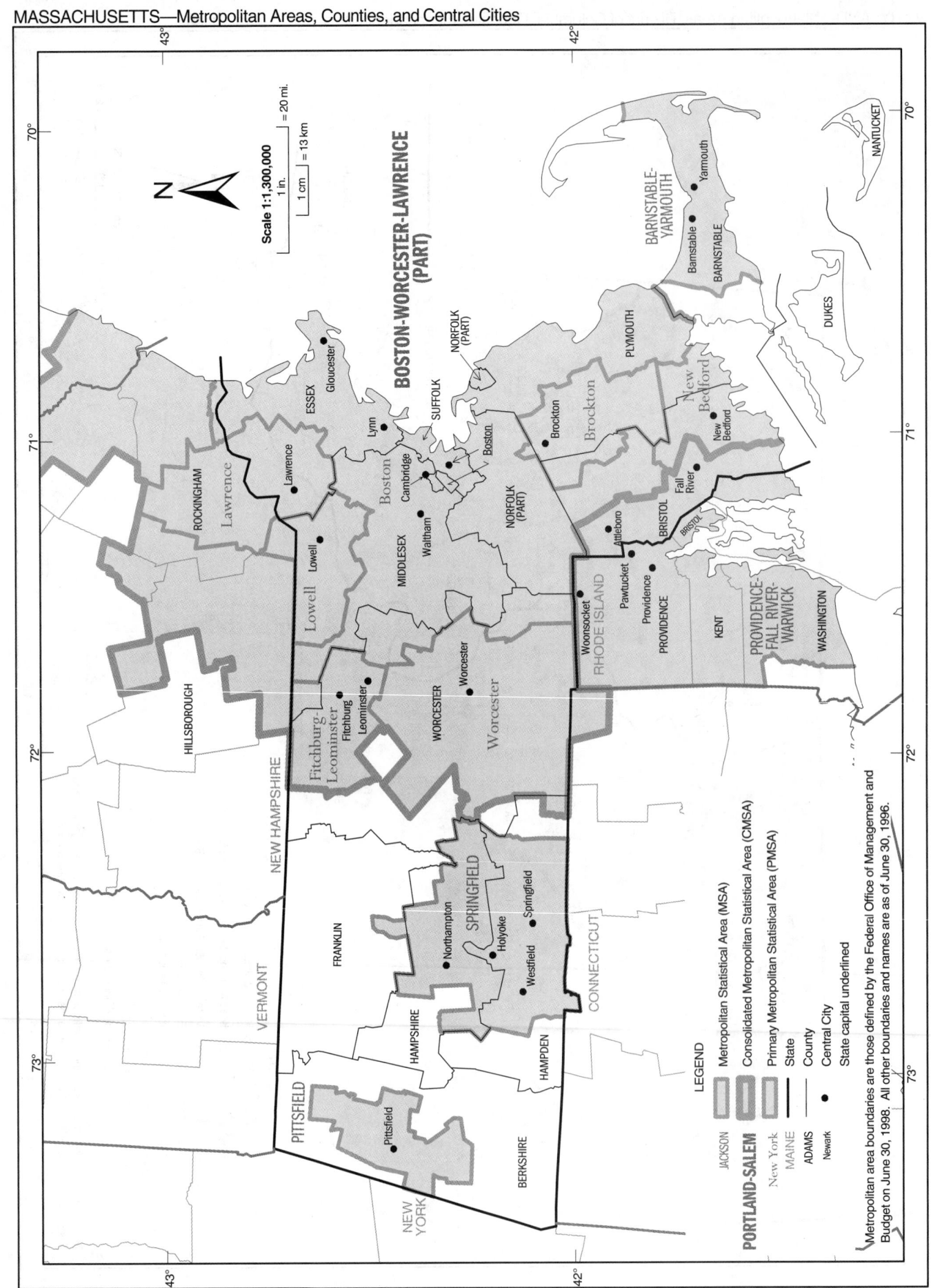

Scale 1:1,300,000

1 in. = 20 mi.

1 cm = 13 km

BOSTON-WORCESTER-LAWRENCE (PART)

BARNSTABLE-YARMOUTH

Yarmouth

Barnstable

BARNSTABLE

NANTUCKET

DUKES

NORFOLK (PART)

SUFFOLK

ESSEX

Gloucester

Lynn

PLYMOUTH

New Bedford

New Bedford

Brockton

Brockton

ROCKINGHAM

Lawrence

Lawrence

Boston

Cambridge

Boston

Fall River

Fall River

BRISTOL

BRISTOL

Waltham

MIDDLESEX

NORFOLK (PART)

Attleboro

Lowell

Lowell

Woonsocket

Pawtucket

Providence

Providence

PROVIDENCE-FALL RIVER-WARWICK

RHODE ISLAND

KENT

WASHINGTON

HILLSBOROUGH

Fitchburg-Leominster

Fitchburg

Leominster

Worcester

Worcester

WORCESTER

NEW HAMPSHIRE

VERMONT

FRANKLIN

SPRINGFIELD

Northampton

Holyoke

Springfield

Springfield

Westfield

HAMPSHIRE

HAMPDEN

CONNECTICUT

PITTSFIELD

Pittsfield

BERKSHIRE

NEW YORK

LEGEND

Metropolitan Statistical Area (MSA)

Consolidated Metropolitan Statistical Area (CMSA)

Primary Metropolitan Statistical Area (PMSA)

———— State

———— County

• Central City

State capital underlined

JACKSON

PORTLAND-SALEM

New York

MAINE

ADAMS

Newark

Metropolitan area boundaries are those defined by the Federal Office of Management and Budget on June 30, 1996. All other boundaries and names are as of June 30, 1998.

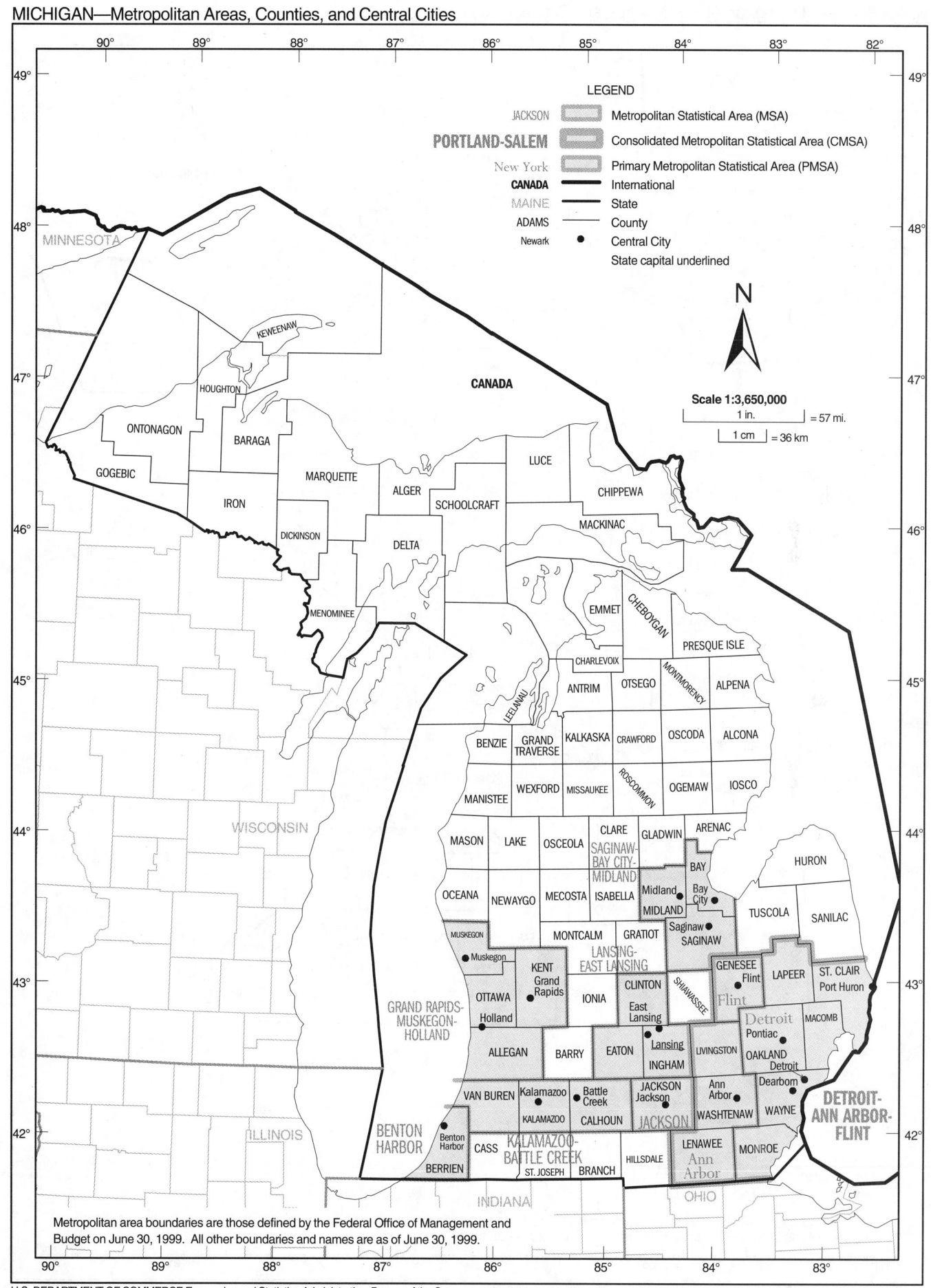

LEGEND

JACKSON	Metropolitan Statistical Area (MSA)
PORTLAND-SALEM	Consolidated Metropolitan Statistical Area (CMSA)
New York	Primary Metropolitan Statistical Area (PMSA)
CANADA	International
MAINE	State
ADAMS	County
• Newark	Central City
	State capital underlined

N

Scale 1:3,650,000

1 in. = 57 mi.

1 cm = 36 km

Metropolitan area boundaries are those defined by the Federal Office of Management and Budget on June 30, 1999. All other boundaries and names are as of June 30, 1999.

MINNESOTA—Metropolitan Areas, Counties, and Central Cities

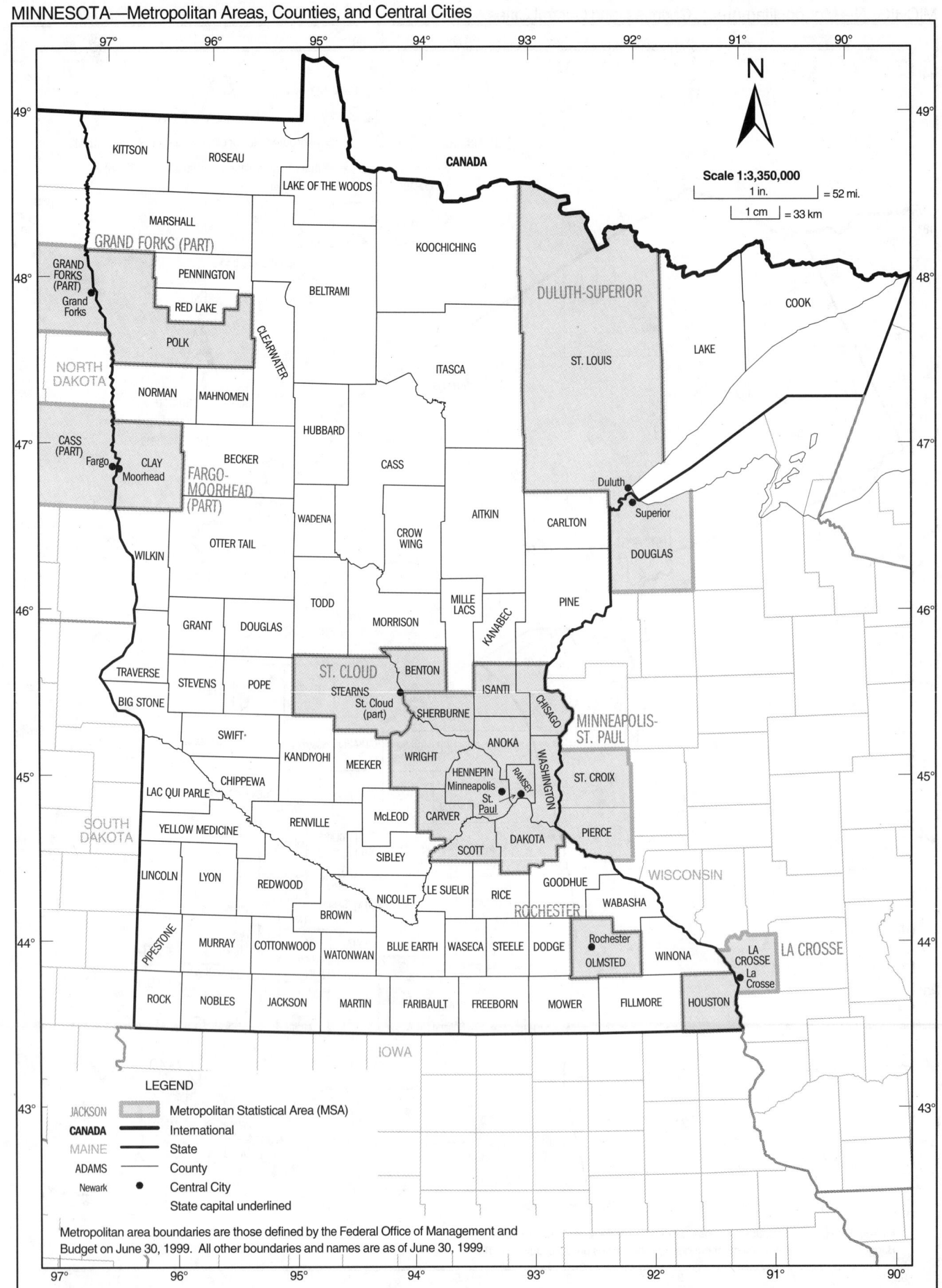

LEGEND

JACKSON	Metropolitan Statistical Area (MSA)
CANADA	International
MAINE	State
ADAMS	County
Newark ●	Central City
	State capital underlined

Metropolitan area boundaries are those defined by the Federal Office of Management and Budget on June 30, 1999. All other boundaries and names are as of June 30, 1999.

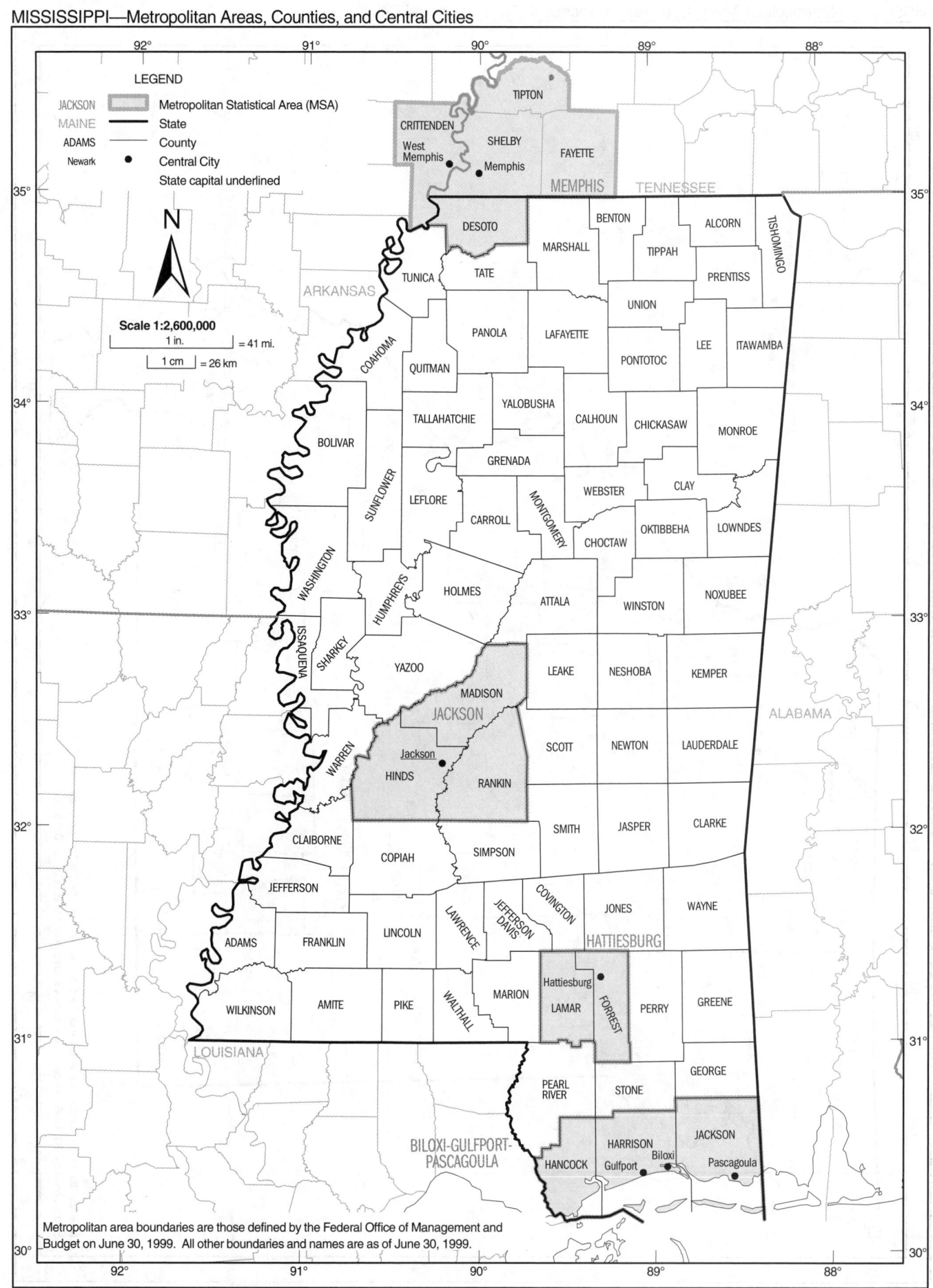

Metropolitan area boundaries are those defined by the Federal Office of Management and Budget on June 30, 1999. All other boundaries and names are as of June 30, 1999.

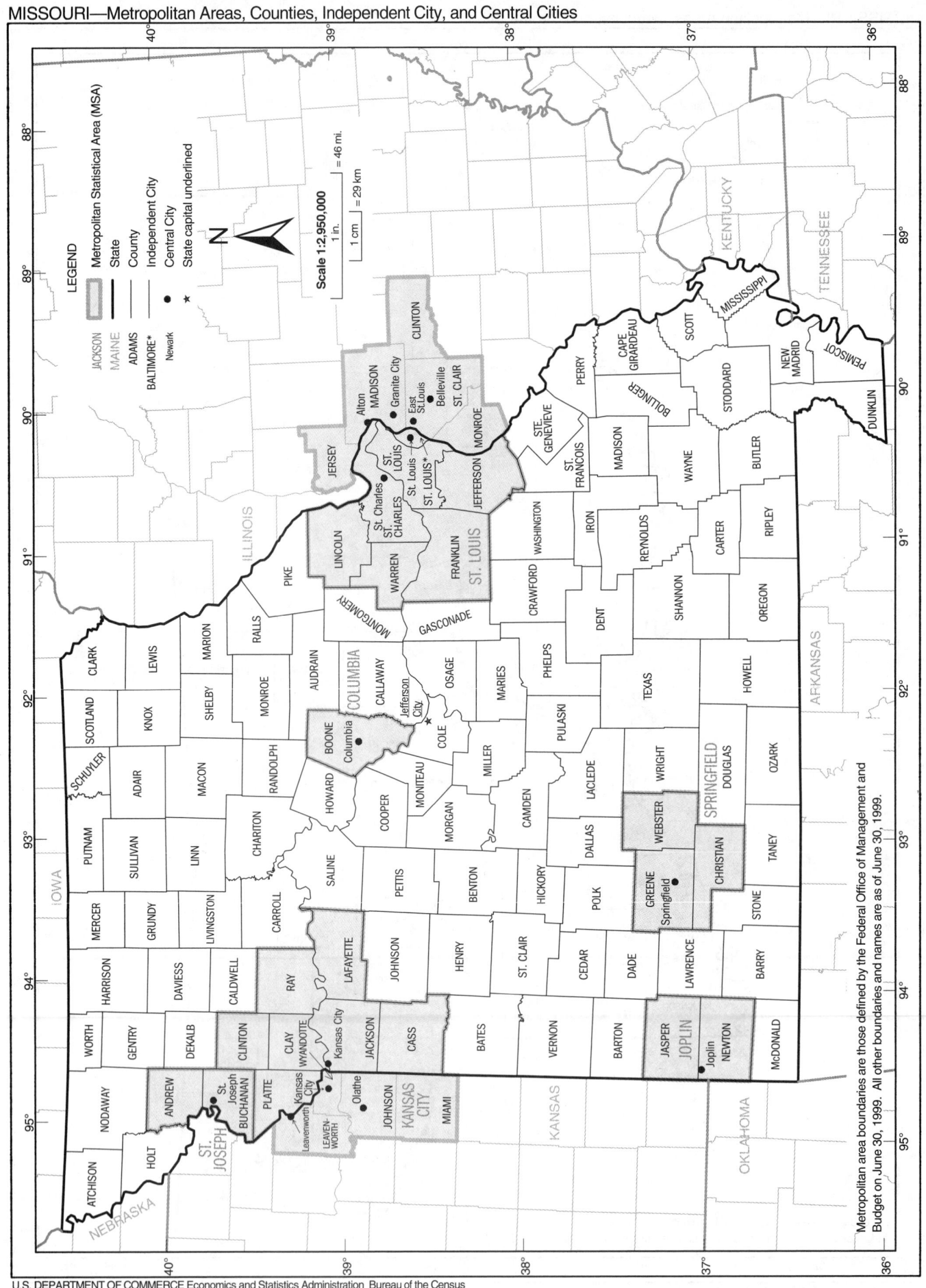

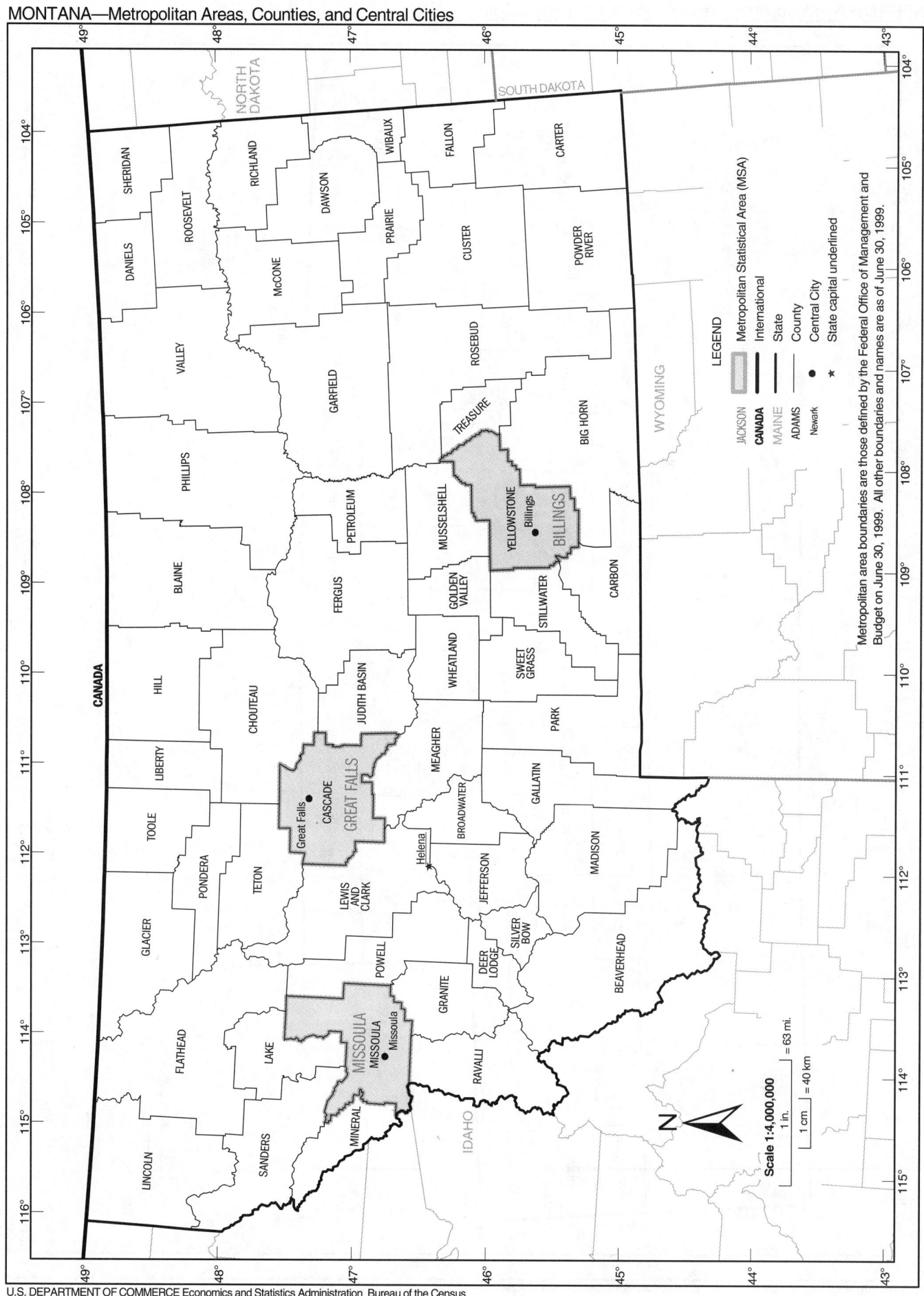

Scale 1:4,000,000

1 in. = 63 mi.

1 cm = 40 km

LEGEND

Metropolitan Statistical Area (MSA)
International
State
County
Central City
State capital underlined

JACKSON
CANADA
MAINE
ADAMS
Newark

Metropolitan area boundaries are those defined by the Federal Office of Management and Budget on June 30, 1999. All other boundaries and names are as of June 30, 1999.

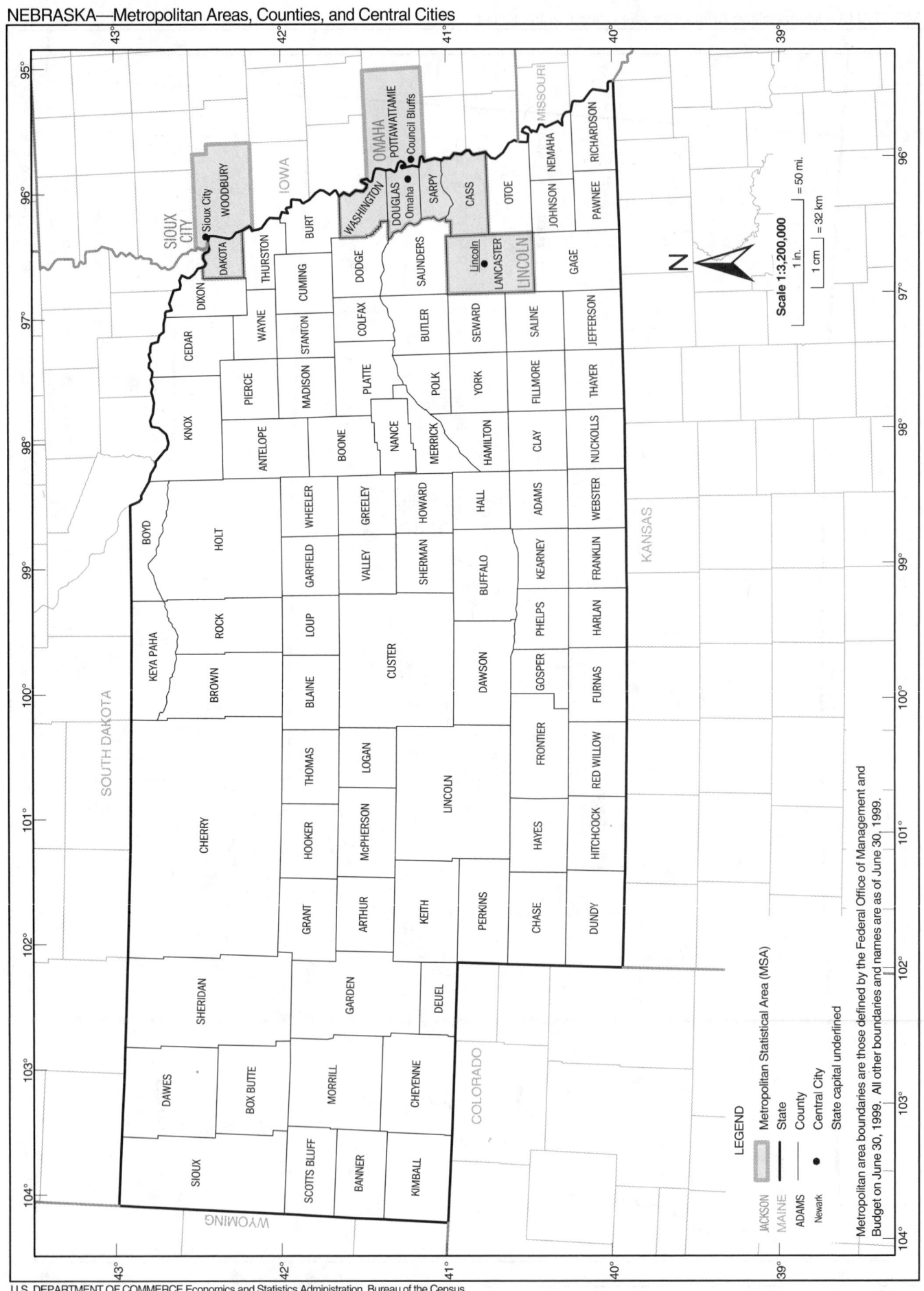

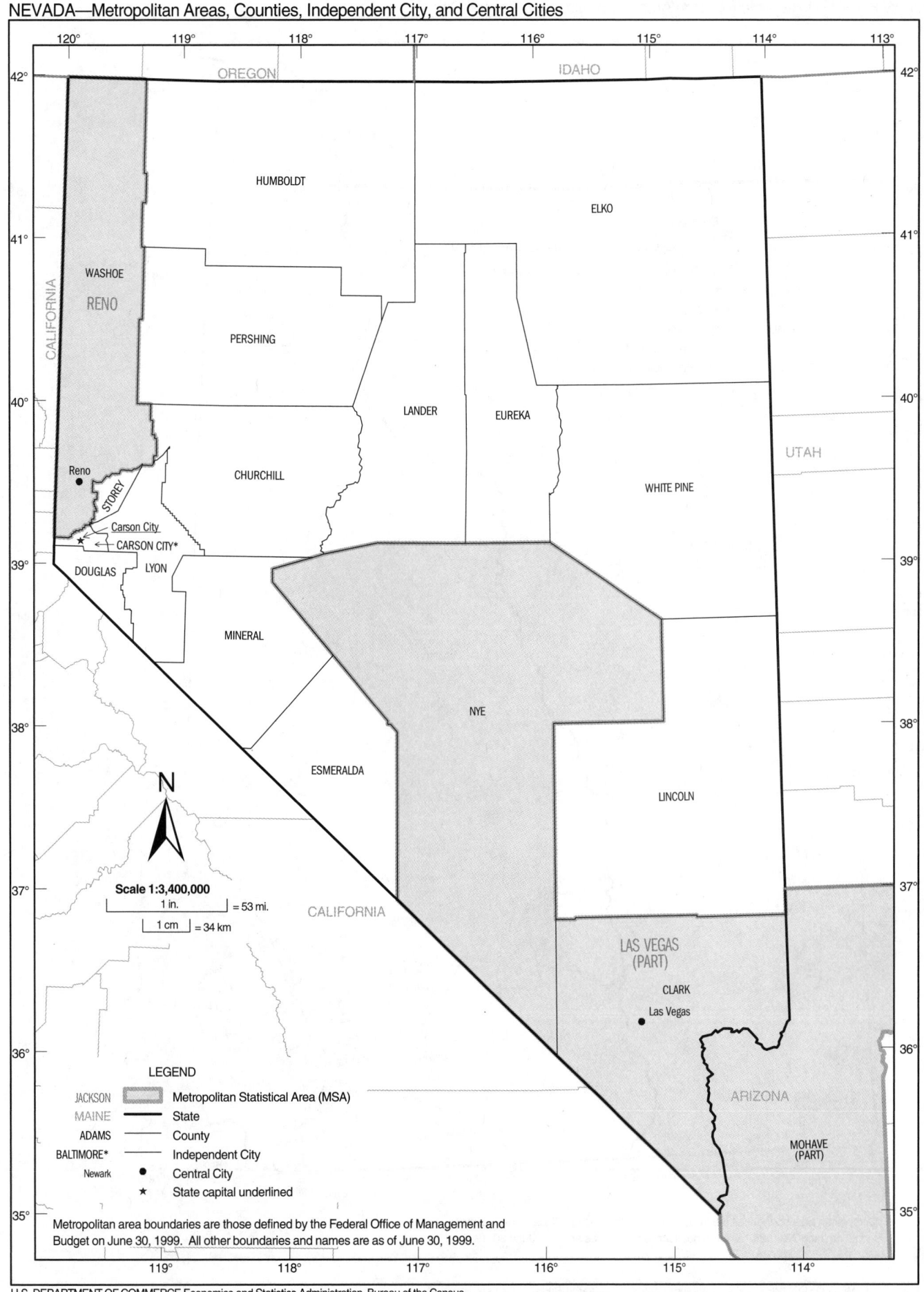

LEGEND

JACKSON	Metropolitan Statistical Area (MSA)
MAINE	State
ADAMS	County
BALTIMORE*	Independent City
Newark ●	Central City
★	State capital underlined

Scale 1:3,400,000
1 in. = 53 mi.
1 cm = 34 km

Metropolitan area boundaries are those defined by the Federal Office of Management and Budget on June 30, 1999. All other boundaries and names are as of June 30, 1999.

73° 72° 71°

CANADA

45° 45°

LEGEND

PORTLAND-SALEM ▨ Consolidated Metropolitan Statistical Area (CMSA)

New York ▨ Primary Metropolitan Statistical Area (PMSA)

CANADA ▬▬ International

MAINE ▬▬ State

ADAMS ── County

Newark ● Central City

★ State capital underlined

COOS

N

Scale 1:1,300,000

| 1 in. | = 20 mi.

| 1 cm | = 13 km

MAINE

44° 44°

VERMONT

GRAFTON

CARROLL

YORK
(PART)

BELKNAP

BOSTON-
WORCESTER-
LAWRENCE
(PART)

SULLIVAN

Rochester ●

MERRIMACK

STRAFFORD

Concord ★

Manchester

Portsmouth ●

43° Portsmouth-
Rochester 43°

HILLSBOROUGH Manchester ●

ROCKINGHAM

CHESHIRE Lawrence

Nashua

Nashua ●

Lawrence ●

ESSEX
(PART)

MASSACHUSETTS

MIDDLESEX
(PART) Lowell ●

Boston
(Part)

Lowell

Metropolitan area boundaries are those defined by the Federal Office of Management and
Budget on June 30, 1998. All other boundaries and names are as of June 30, 1996.

73° 72° 71°

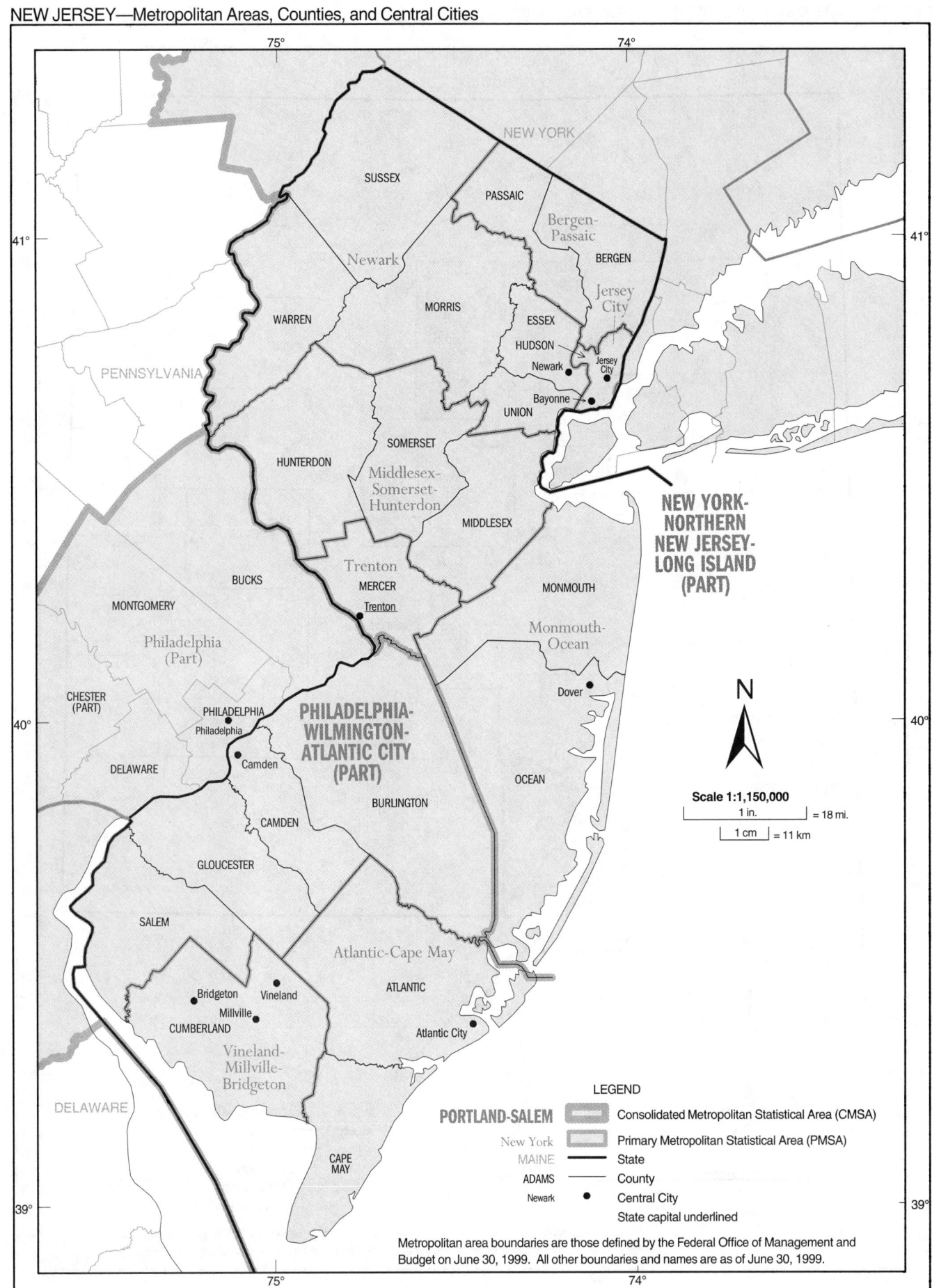

NEW YORK-
NORTHERN
NEW JERSEY-
LONG ISLAND
(PART)

PHILADELPHIA-
WILMINGTON-
ATLANTIC CITY
(PART)

N

Scale 1:1,150,000

| 1 in. | = 18 mi. |
| 1 cm | = 11 km |

LEGEND

PORTLAND-SALEM ▭ Consolidated Metropolitan Statistical Area (CMSA)

New York ▭ Primary Metropolitan Statistical Area (PMSA)

MAINE ▬▬▬ State

ADAMS ──── County

Newark ● Central City

State capital underlined

Metropolitan area boundaries are those defined by the Federal Office of Management and
Budget on June 30, 1999. All other boundaries and names are as of June 30, 1999.

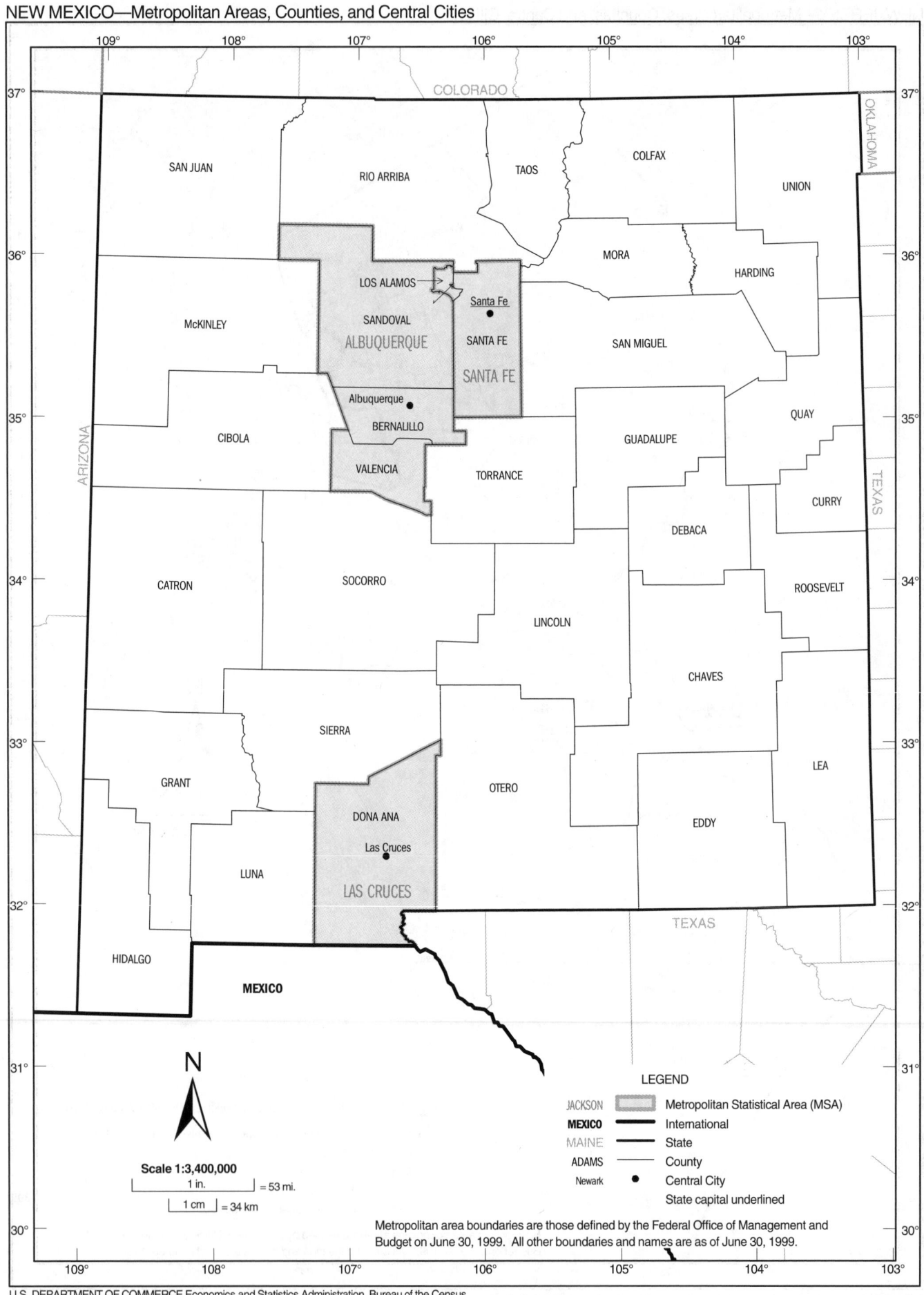

LEGEND

JACKSON	Metropolitan Statistical Area (MSA)
MEXICO	International
MAINE	State
ADAMS	County
Newark ●	Central City
	State capital underlined

Metropolitan area boundaries are those defined by the Federal Office of Management and Budget on June 30, 1999. All other boundaries and names are as of June 30, 1999.

Scale 1:3,400,000

1 in. = 53 mi.

1 cm = 34 km

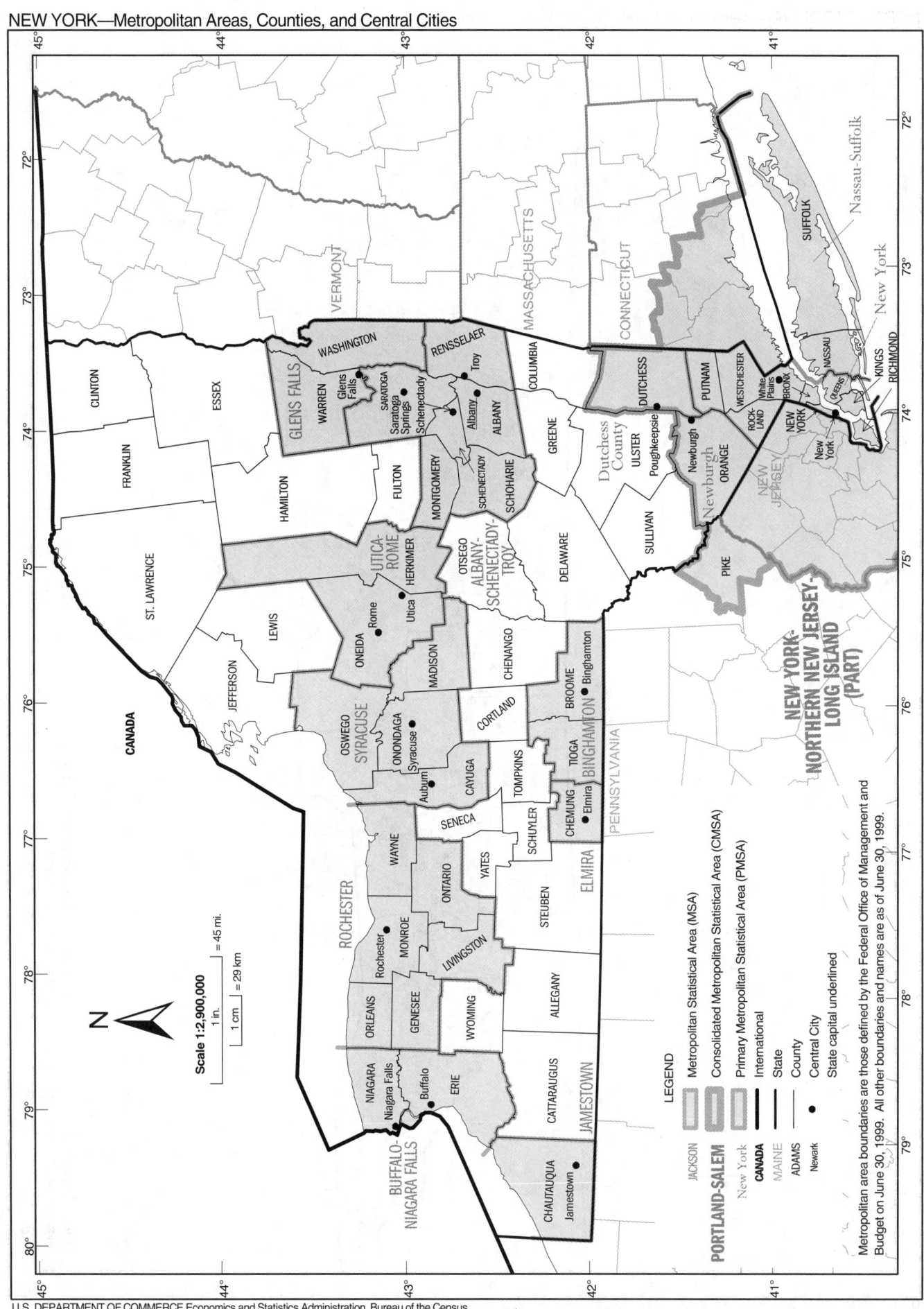

Scale 1:2,900,000

1 in. | = 45 mi.

1 cm | = 29 km

LEGEND

Metropolitan Statistical Area (MSA)

Consolidated Metropolitan Statistical Area (CMSA)

Primary Metropolitan Statistical Area (PMSA)

International

State

County

● Central City

State capital underlined

PORTLAND-SALEM

JACKSON   New York

CANADA

MAINE

ADAMS

Newark

Metropolitan area boundaries are those defined by the Federal Office of Management and Budget on June 30, 1999. All other boundaries and names are as of June 30, 1999.

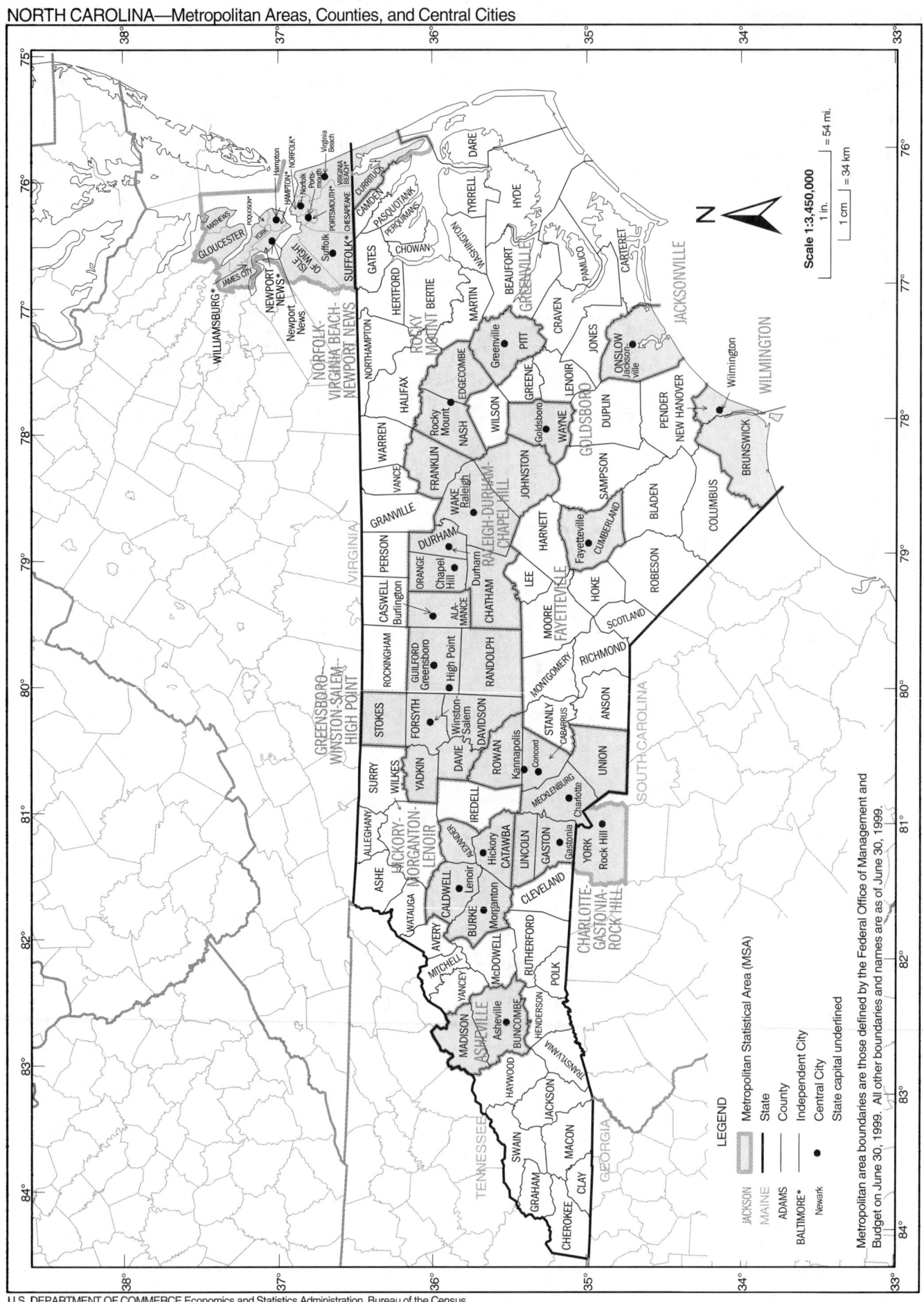

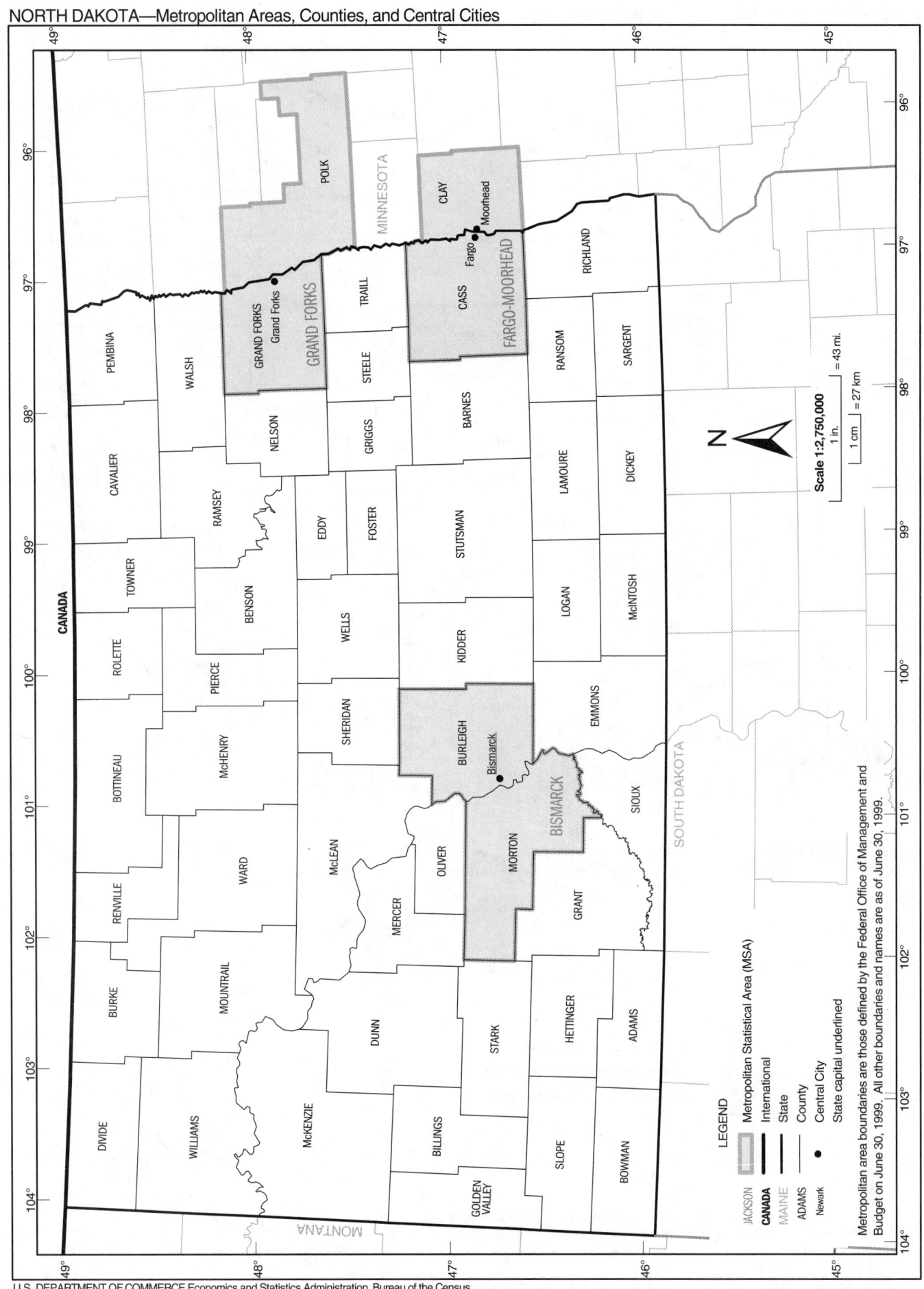

Scale 1:2,750,000

1 in. = 43 mi.

1 cm = 27 km

LEGEND

Metropolitan Statistical Area (MSA)

International

State

County

Central City

State capital underlined

JACKSON

CANADA

MAINE

ADAMS

Newark

Metropolitan area boundaries are those defined by the Federal Office of Management and Budget on June 30, 1999. All other boundaries and names are as of June 30, 1999.

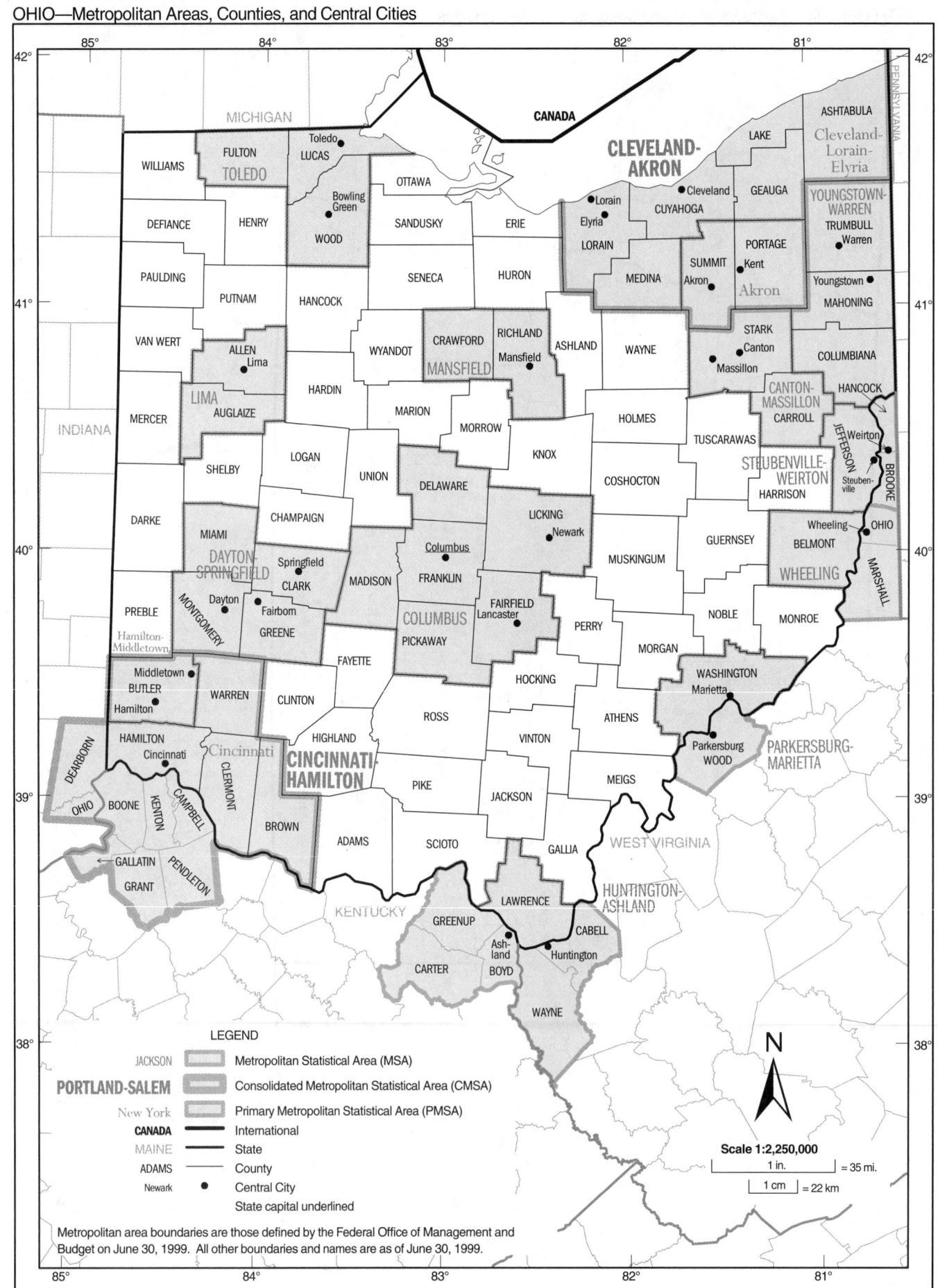

LEGEND

JACKSON	Metropolitan Statistical Area (MSA)
PORTLAND-SALEM	Consolidated Metropolitan Statistical Area (CMSA)
New York	Primary Metropolitan Statistical Area (PMSA)
CANADA	International
MAINE	State
ADAMS	County
● Newark	Central City
	State capital underlined

Scale 1:2,250,000

1 in. = 35 mi.

1 cm = 22 km

N

Metropolitan area boundaries are those defined by the Federal Office of Management and Budget on June 30, 1999. All other boundaries and names are as of June 30, 1999.

MISSOURI

ARKANSAS

KANSAS

TEXAS

COLORADO

TEXAS

FORT SMITH

CRAWFORD

SEBASTIAN

Fort Smith

OTTAWA

DELAWARE

ADAIR

SEQUOYAH

LE FLORE

McCURTAIN

CHEROKEE

HASKELL

LATIMER

PUSHMATAHA

CHOCTAW

CRAIG

MAYES

NOWATA

ROGERS

WAGONER

MUSKOGEE

McINTOSH

PITTSBURG

WASHINGTON

Tulsa

TULSA

OKMULGEE

ATOKA

BRYAN

TULSA

OSAGE

CREEK

OKFUSKEE

HUGHES

COAL

SEMINOLE

PONTOTOC

JOHNSTON

MARSHALL

PAWNEE

LINCOLN

Shawnee

POTTAWATOMIE

MURRAY

CARTER

LOVE

KAY

PAYNE

NOBLE

LOGAN

OKLAHOMA

Oklahoma City

CLEVELAND

Norman

McCLAIN

GARVIN

GRANT

ENID

Enid

GARFIELD

KINGFISHER

OKLAHOMA CITY

CANADIAN

GRADY

STEPHENS

JEFFERSON

ALFALFA

MAJOR

BLAINE

CADDO

LAWTON

COMANCHE

Lawton

COTTON

WOODS

DEWEY

CUSTER

WASHITA

KIOWA

TILLMAN

WOODWARD

HARPER

ELLIS

ROGER MILLS

BECKHAM

GREER

JACKSON

HARMON

BEAVER

TEXAS

CIMARRON

N

Scale 1:3,500,000

| 1 in. | = 55 mi. |
| 1 cm | = 35 km |

LEGEND

☐ Metropolitan Statistical Area (MSA)

— State

— County

• Central City

State capital underlined

JACKSON
MAINE
ADAMS
Newark

Metropolitan area boundaries are those defined by the Federal Office of Management and Budget on June 30, 1999. All other boundaries and names are as of June 30, 1999.

U.S. DEPARTMENT OF COMMERCE Economics and Statistics Administration Bureau of the Census

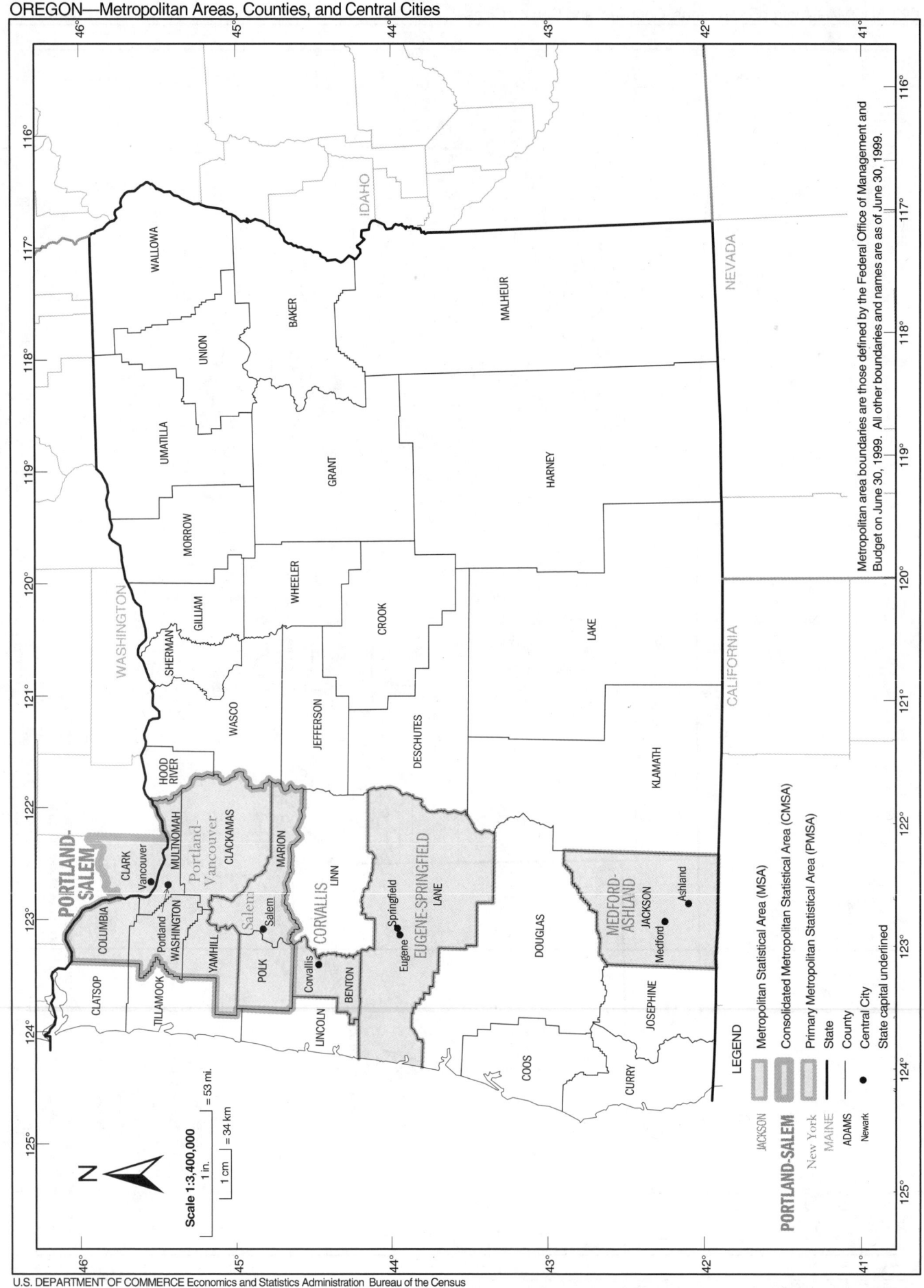

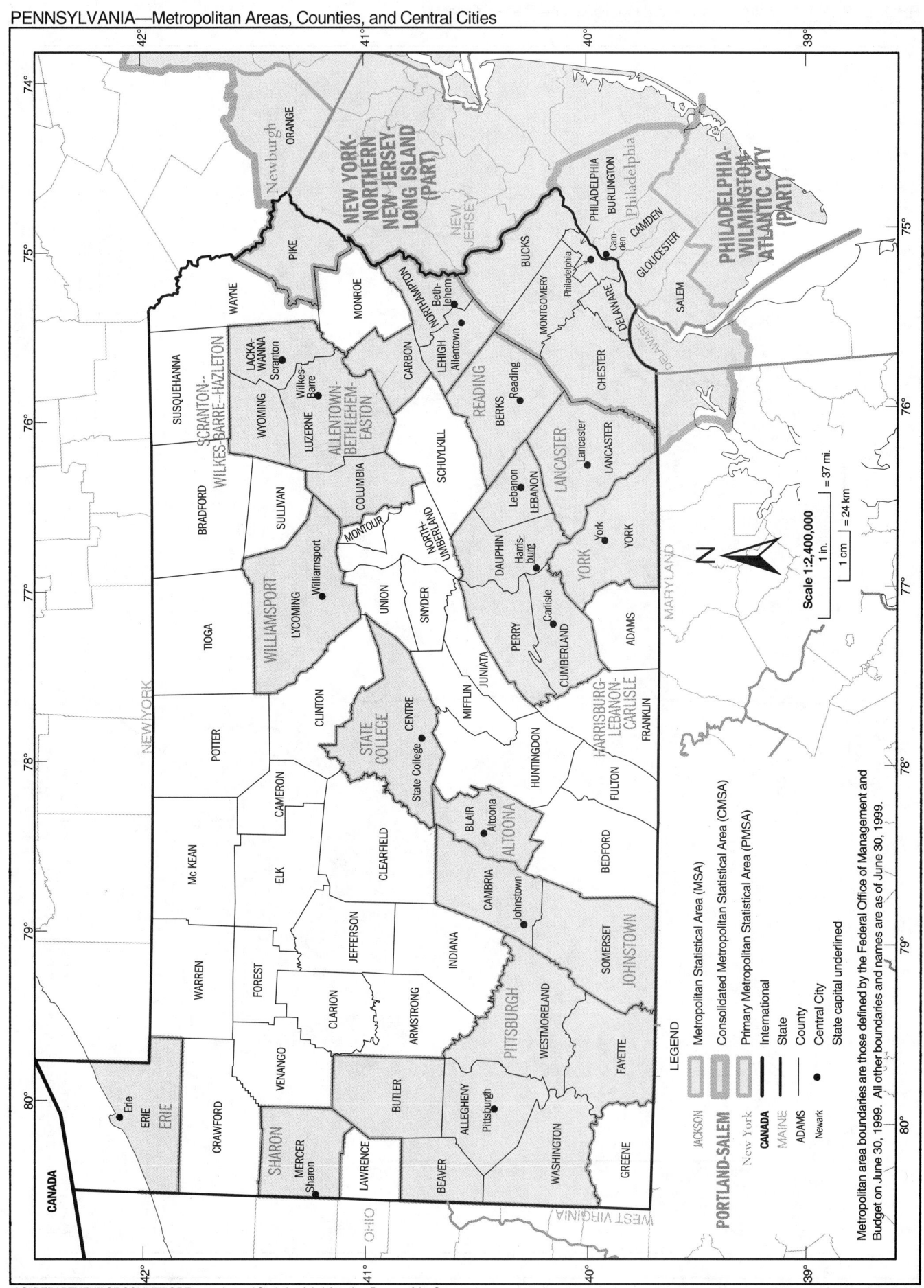

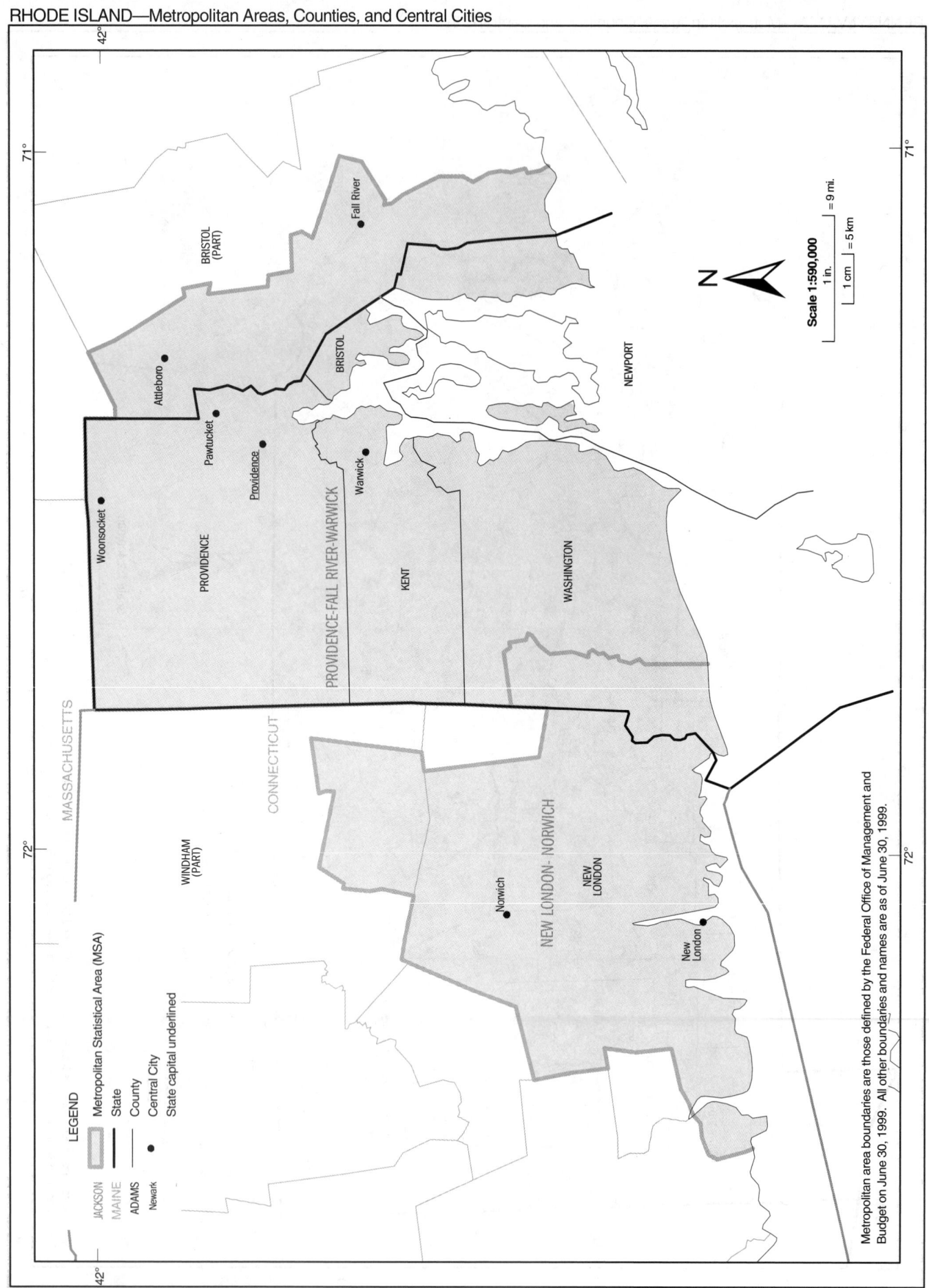

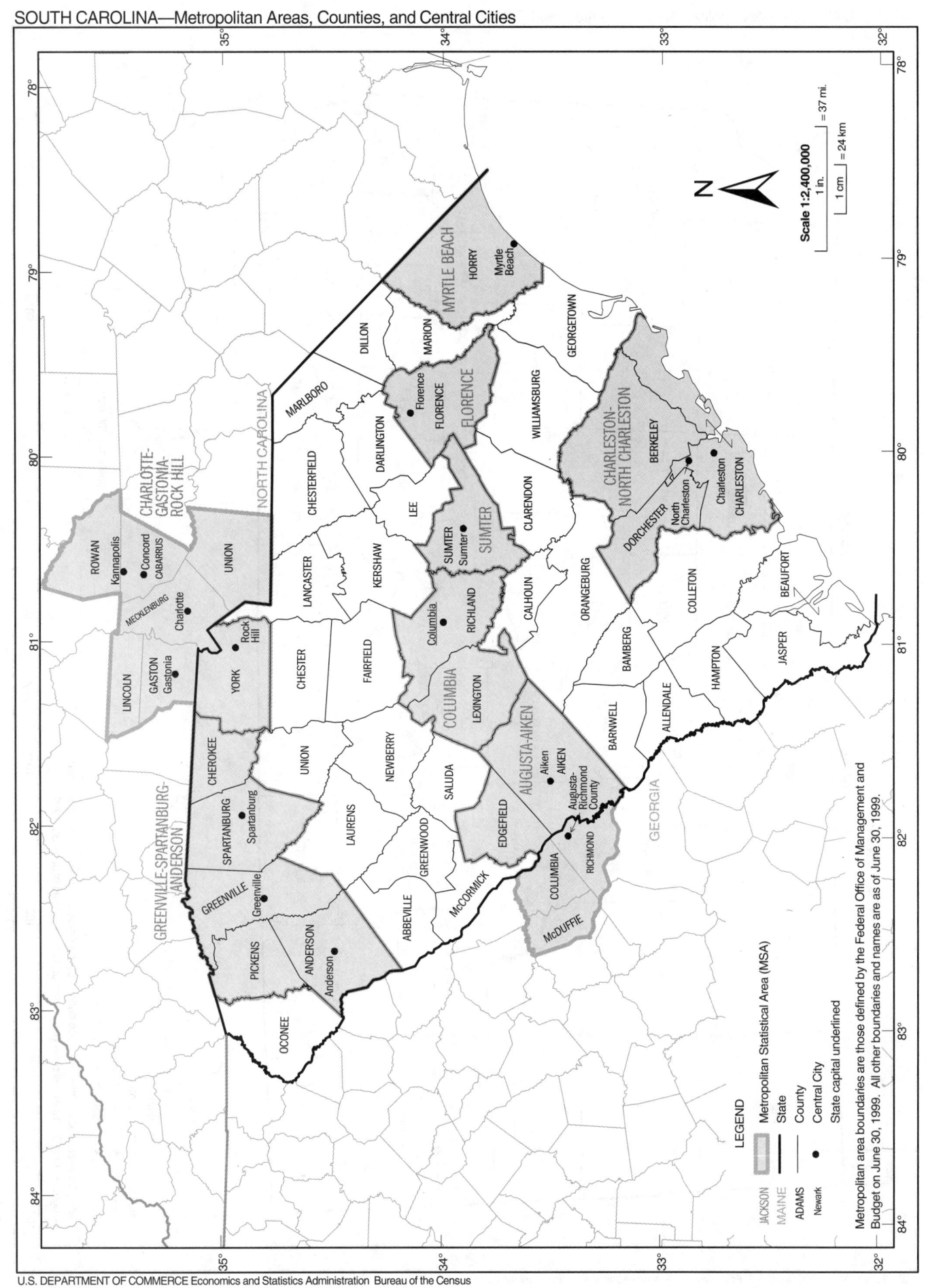

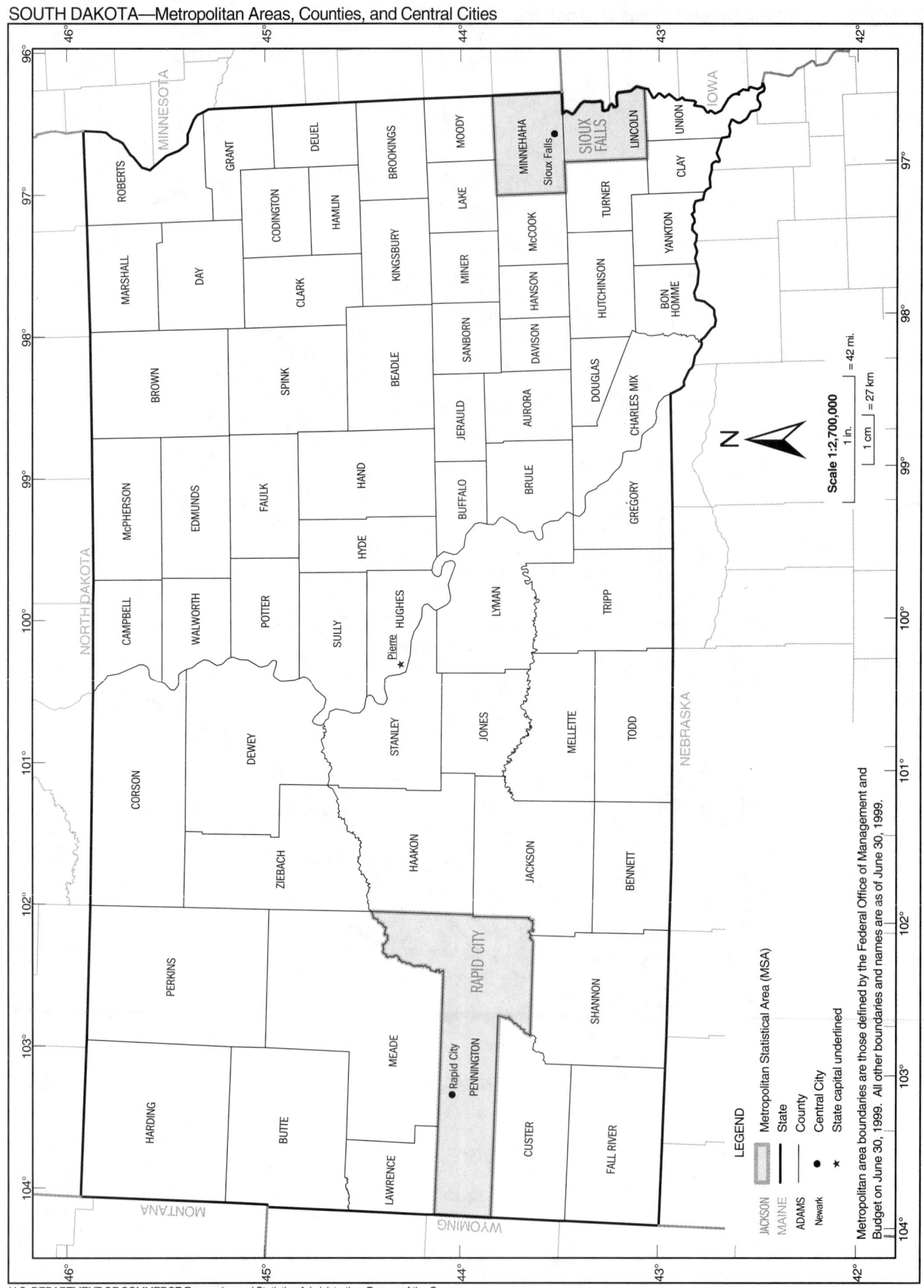

LEGEND

Metropolitan Statistical Area (MSA)

——— State

——— County

● Central City

★ State capital underlined

JACKSON
MAINE
ADAMS
Newark

Metropolitan area boundaries are those defined by the Federal Office of Management and Budget on June 30, 1999. All other boundaries and names are as of June 30, 1999.

Scale 1:2,700,000

1 in. = 42 mi.

1 cm = 27 km

N

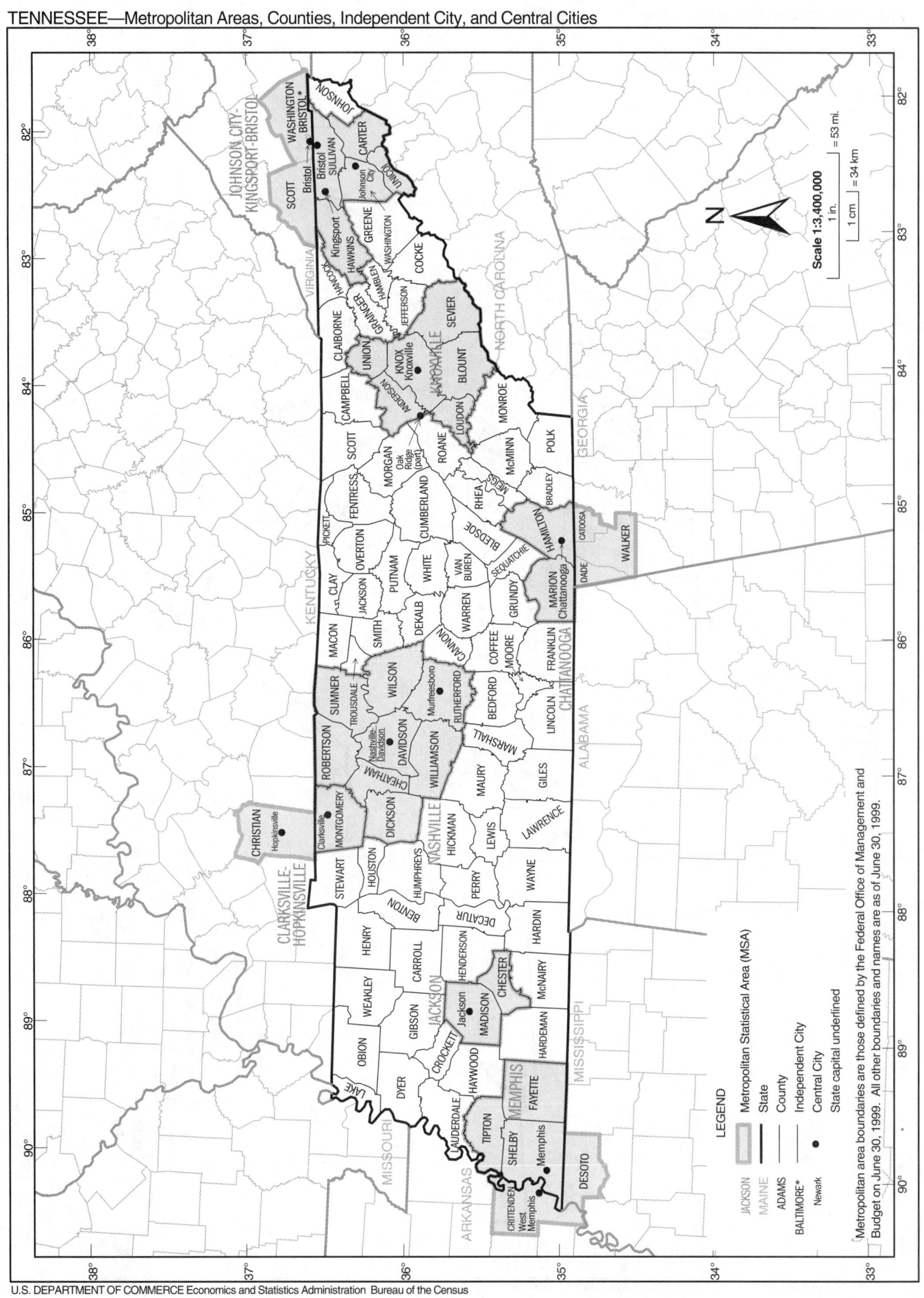

LEGEND

Metropolitan Statistical Area (MSA)
State
County
Independent City
• Central City
State capital underlined

JACKSON
MAINE
ADAMS
BALTIMORE*   Newark

Metropolitan area boundaries are those defined by the Federal Office of Management and Budget on June 30, 1999. All other boundaries and names are as of June 30, 1999.

Scale 1:3,400,000

1 in. = 53 mi.
1 cm = 34 km

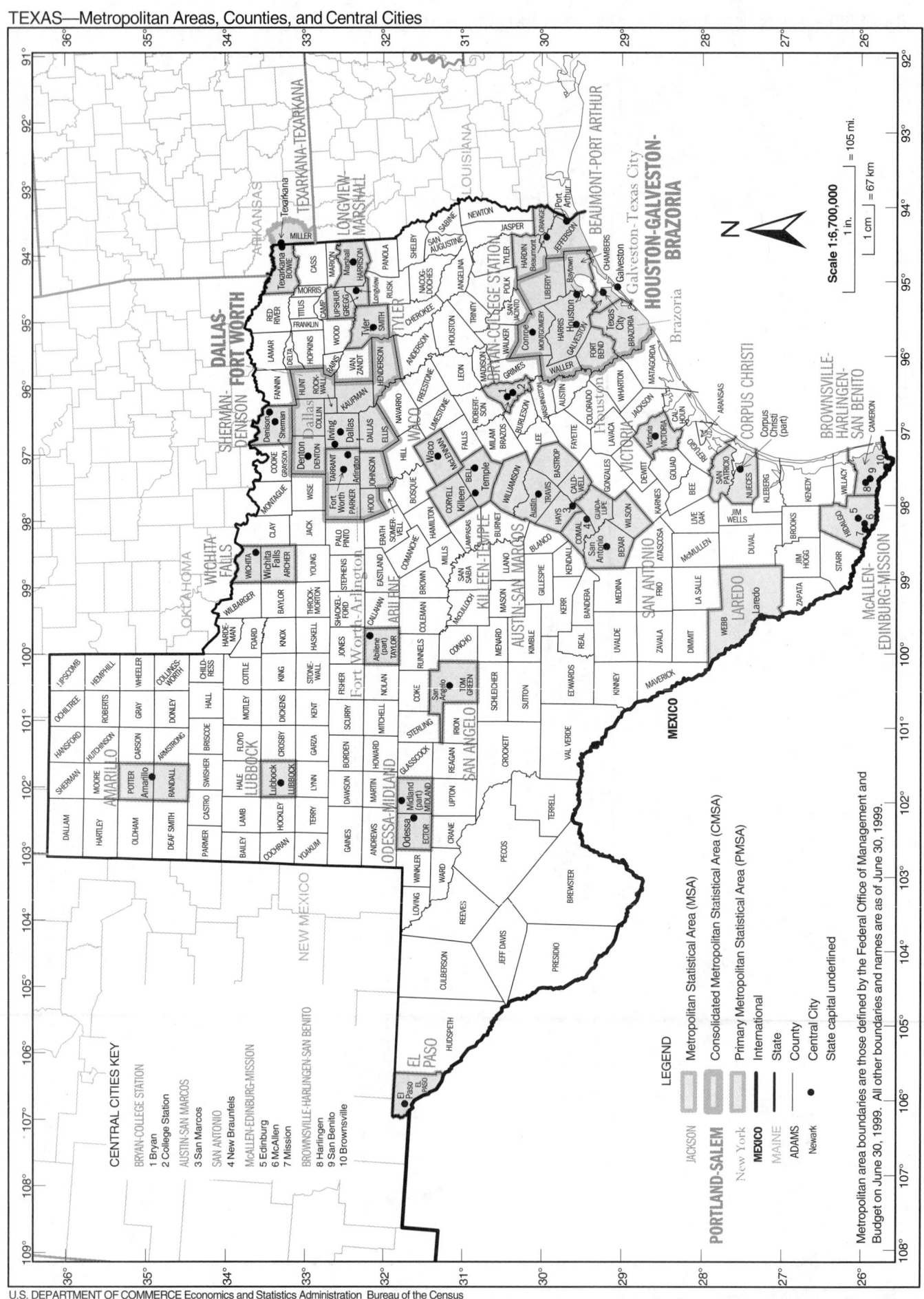

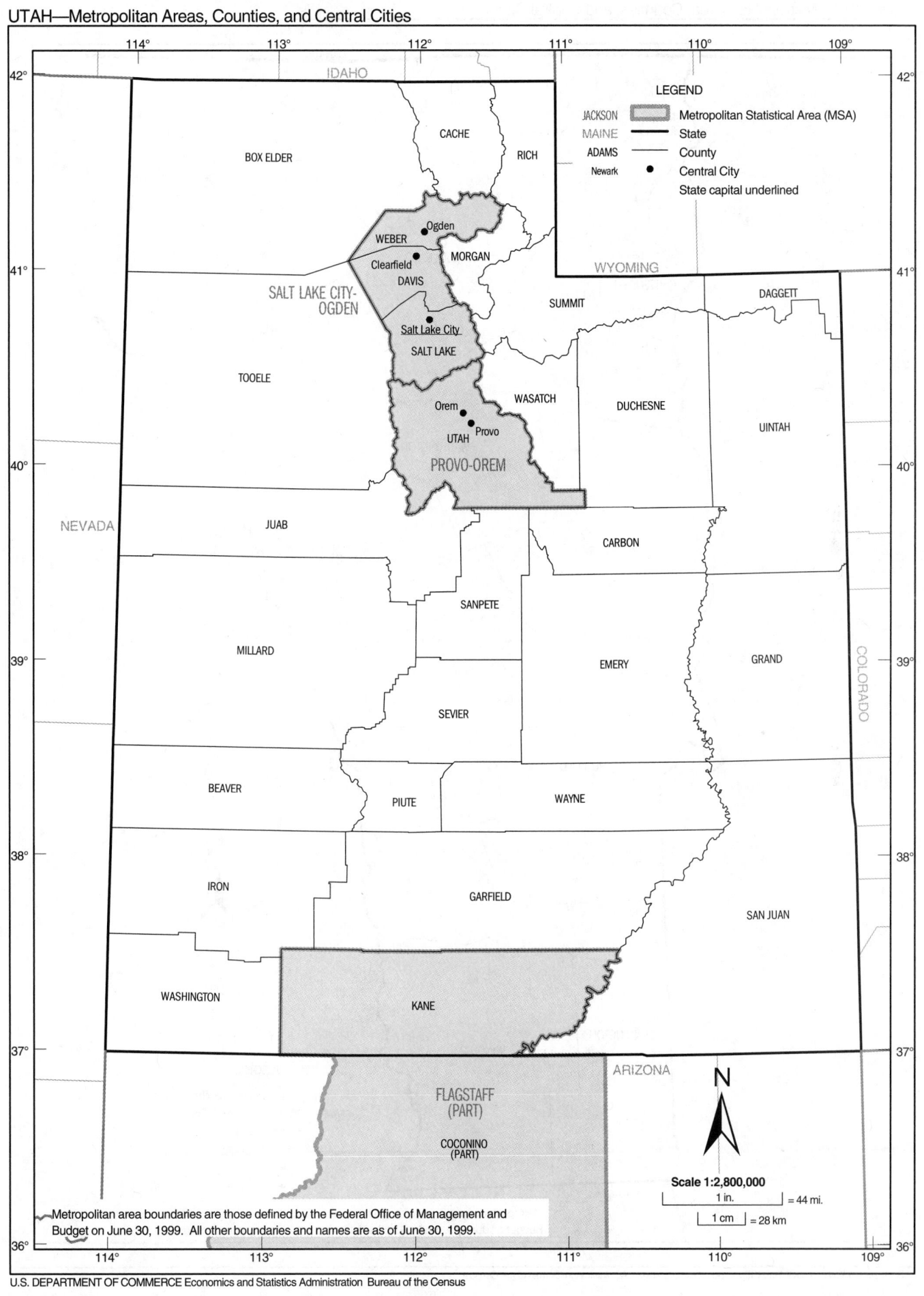

LEGEND

JACKSON   Metropolitan Statistical Area (MSA)
MAINE   State
ADAMS   County
Newark   ●   Central City
  State capital underlined

Metropolitan area boundaries are those defined by the Federal Office of Management and Budget on June 30, 1999. All other boundaries and names are as of June 30, 1999.

Scale 1:2,800,000

1 in. = 44 mi.

1 cm = 28 km

VERMONT—Metropolitan Area, Counties, and Central Cities

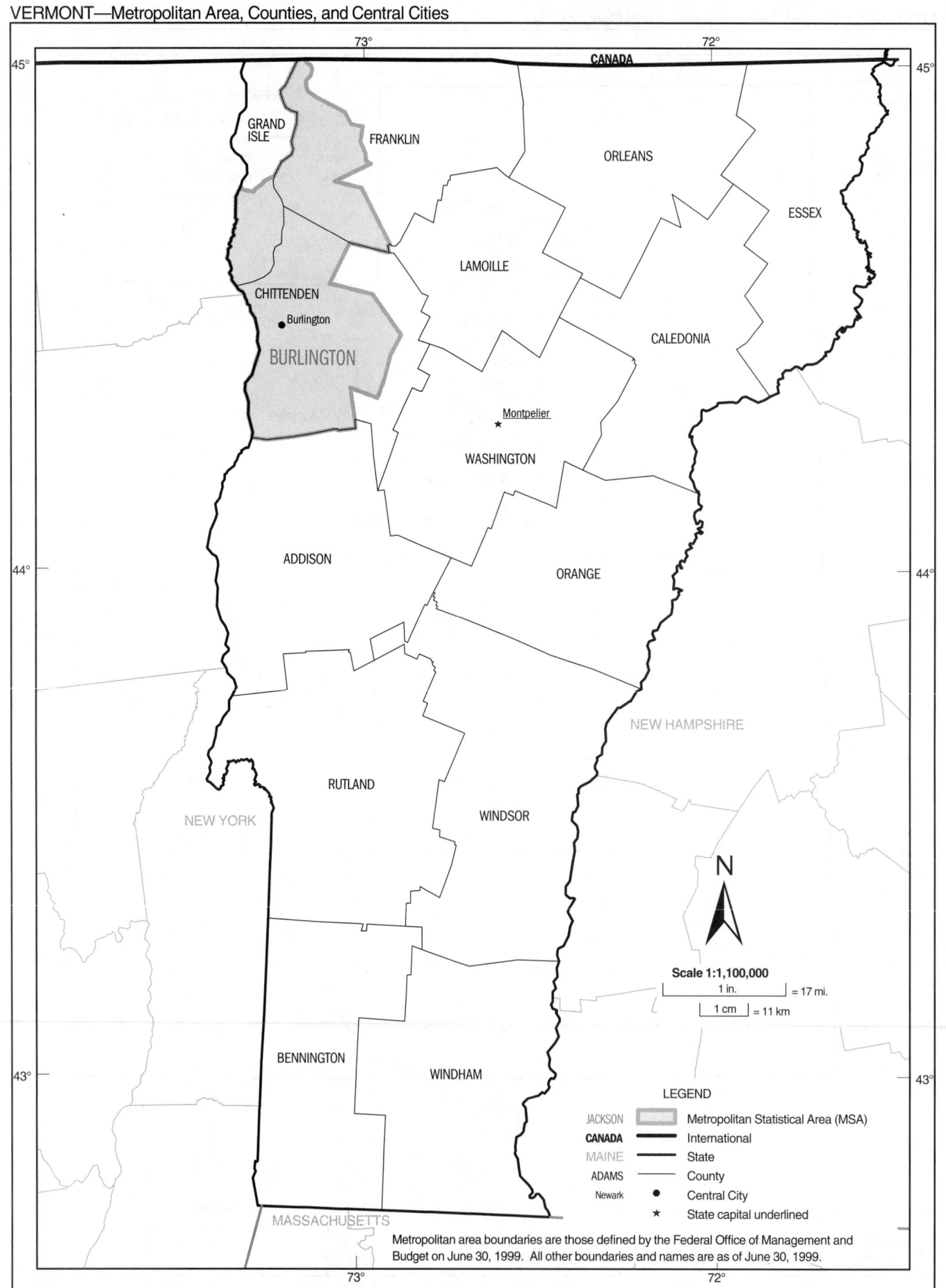

Scale 1:1,100,000

1 in. = 17 mi.

1 cm = 11 km

LEGEND

JACKSON	Metropolitan Statistical Area (MSA)
CANADA	International
MAINE	State
ADAMS	County
Newark ●	Central City
★	State capital underlined

Metropolitan area boundaries are those defined by the Federal Office of Management and Budget on June 30, 1999. All other boundaries and names are as of June 30, 1999.

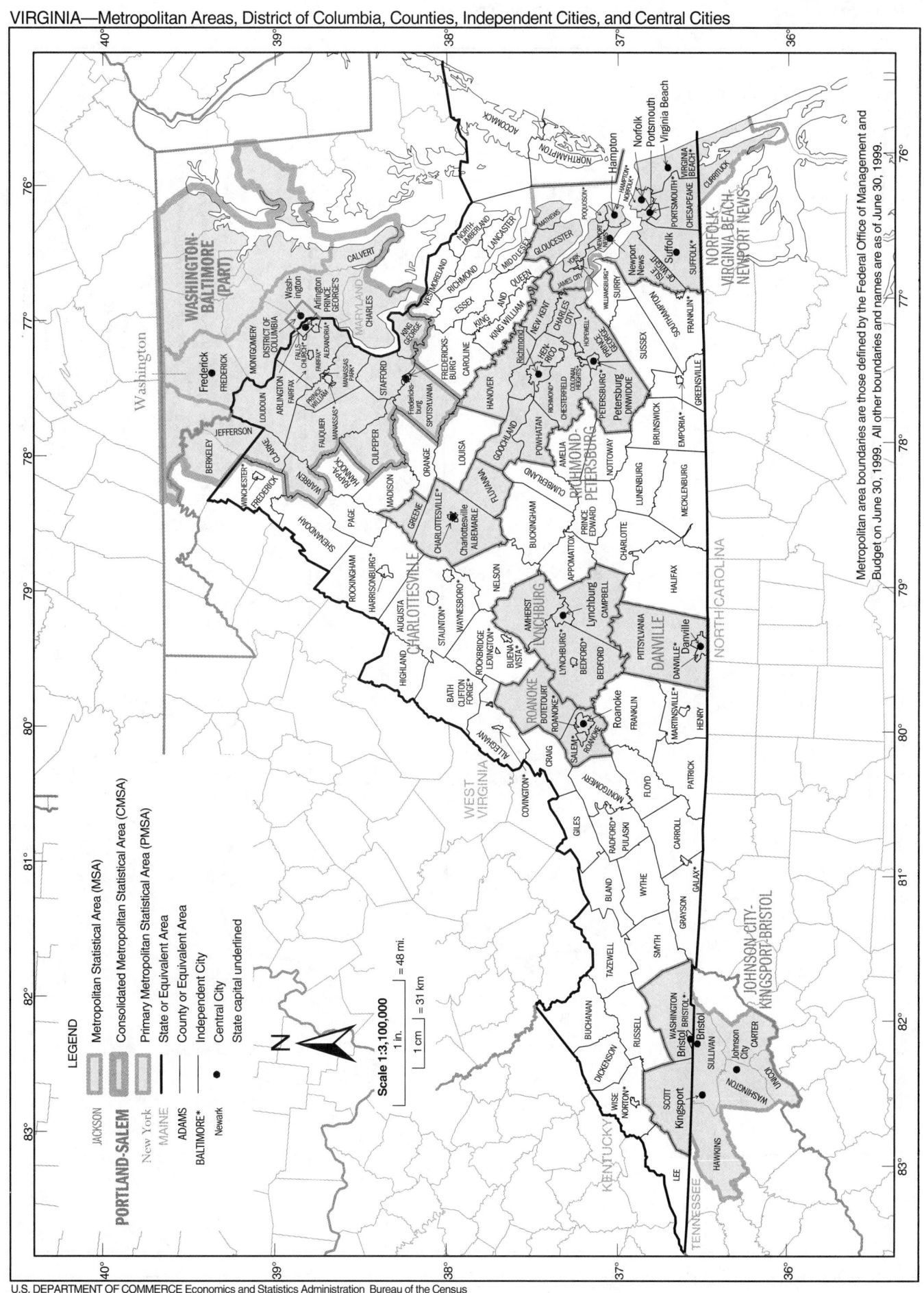

Metropolitan area boundaries are those defined by the Federal Office of Management and Budget on June 30, 1999. All other boundaries and names are as of June 30, 1999.

LEGEND

Metropolitan Statistical Area (MSA)

Consolidated Metropolitan Statistical Area (CMSA)

Primary Metropolitan Statistical Area (PMSA)

State or Equivalent Area

County or Equivalent Area

● Independent City

● Central City

State capital underlined

JACKSON

New York

MAINE

ADAMS

BALTIMORE*

Newark

PORTLAND-SALEM

Scale 1:3,100,000

1 in. = 48 mi.

1 cm = 31 km

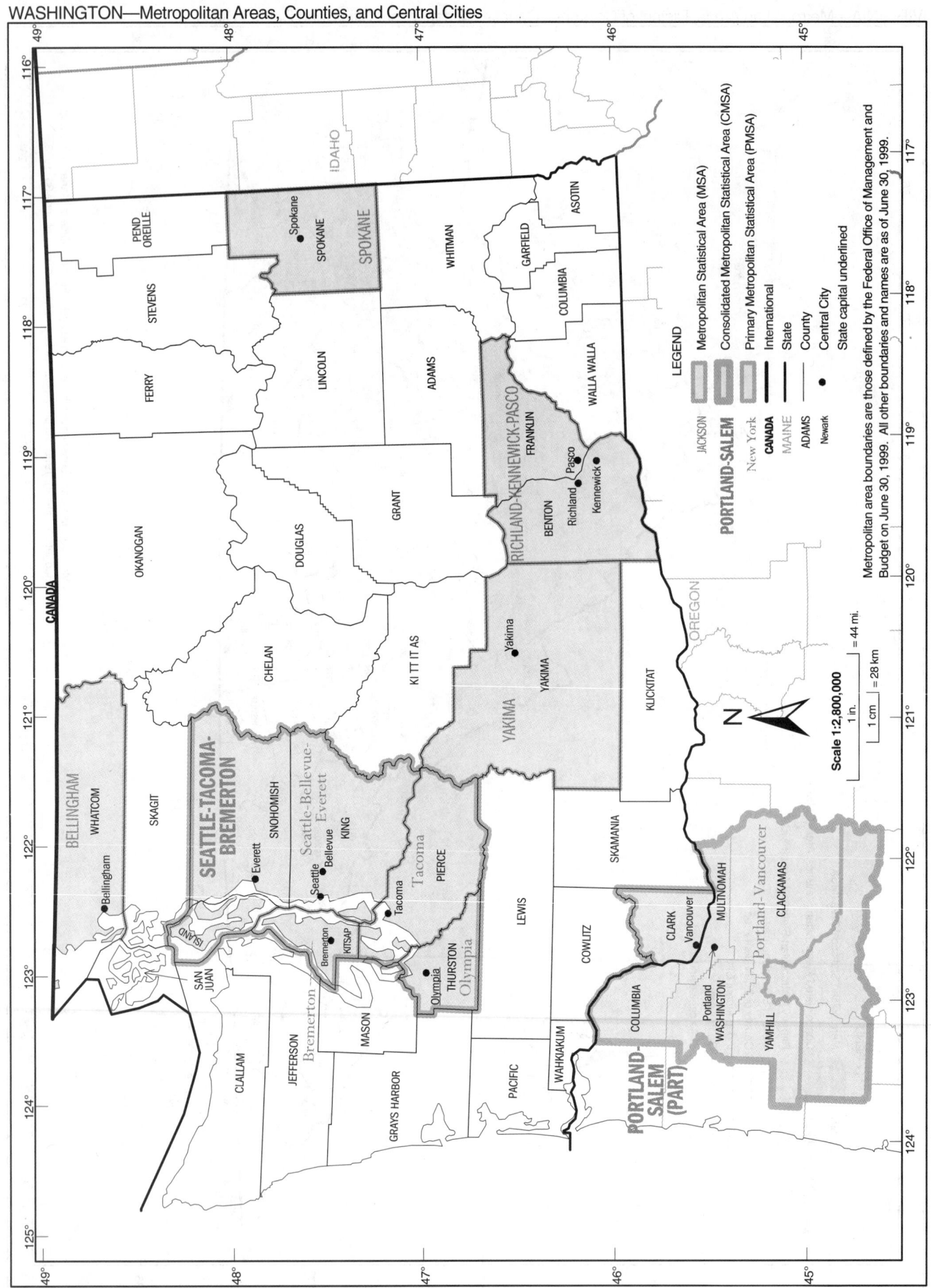

LEGEND

Metropolitan Statistical Area (MSA)

Consolidated Metropolitan Statistical Area (CMSA)

Primary Metropolitan Statistical Area (PMSA)

International
State
County
● Central City
State capital underlined

JACKSON
New York
CANADA
MAINE
ADAMS
● Newark
PORTLAND-SALEM

Metropolitan area boundaries are those defined by the Federal Office of Management and Budget on June 30, 1999. All other boundaries and names are as of June 30, 1999.

Scale 1:2,800,000

1 in. = 44 mi.
1 cm = 28 km

N

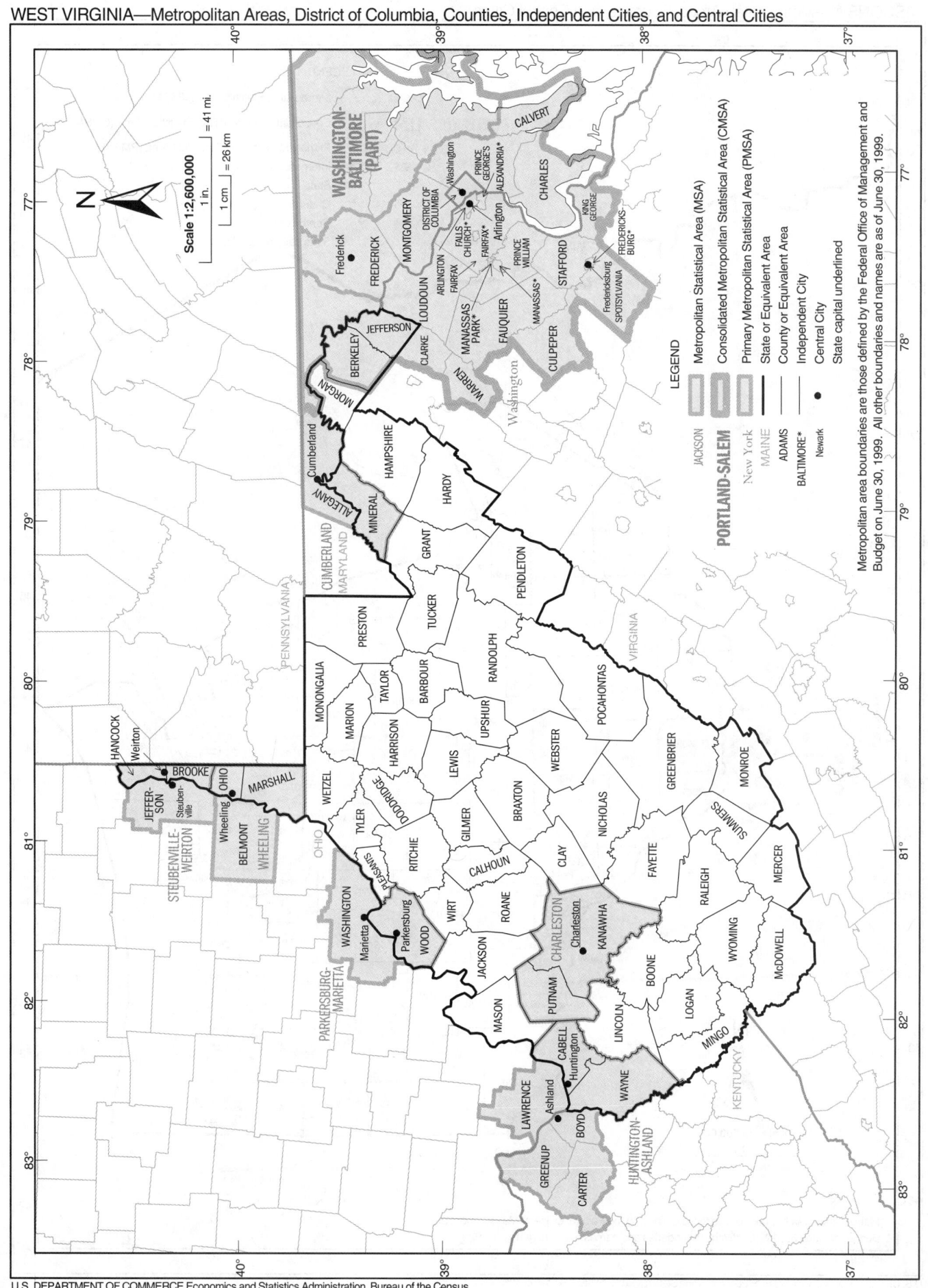

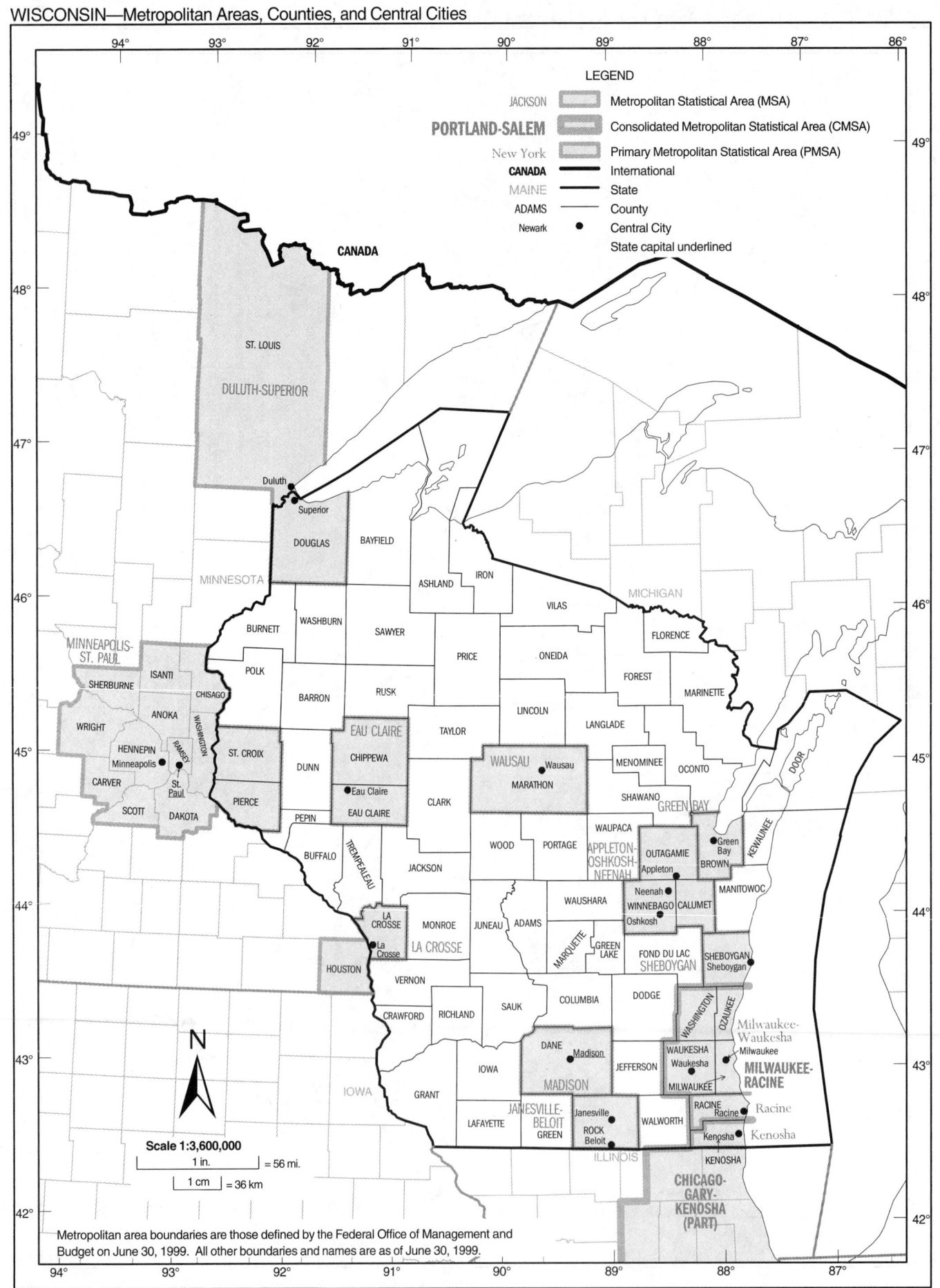

LEGEND

JACKSON — Metropolitan Statistical Area (MSA)

PORTLAND-SALEM — Consolidated Metropolitan Statistical Area (CMSA)

New York — Primary Metropolitan Statistical Area (PMSA)

CANADA — International

MAINE — State

ADAMS — County

Newark ● — Central City

State capital underlined

Scale 1:3,600,000

1 in. = 56 mi.

1 cm = 36 km

Metropolitan area boundaries are those defined by the Federal Office of Management and Budget on June 30, 1999. All other boundaries and names are as of June 30, 1999.

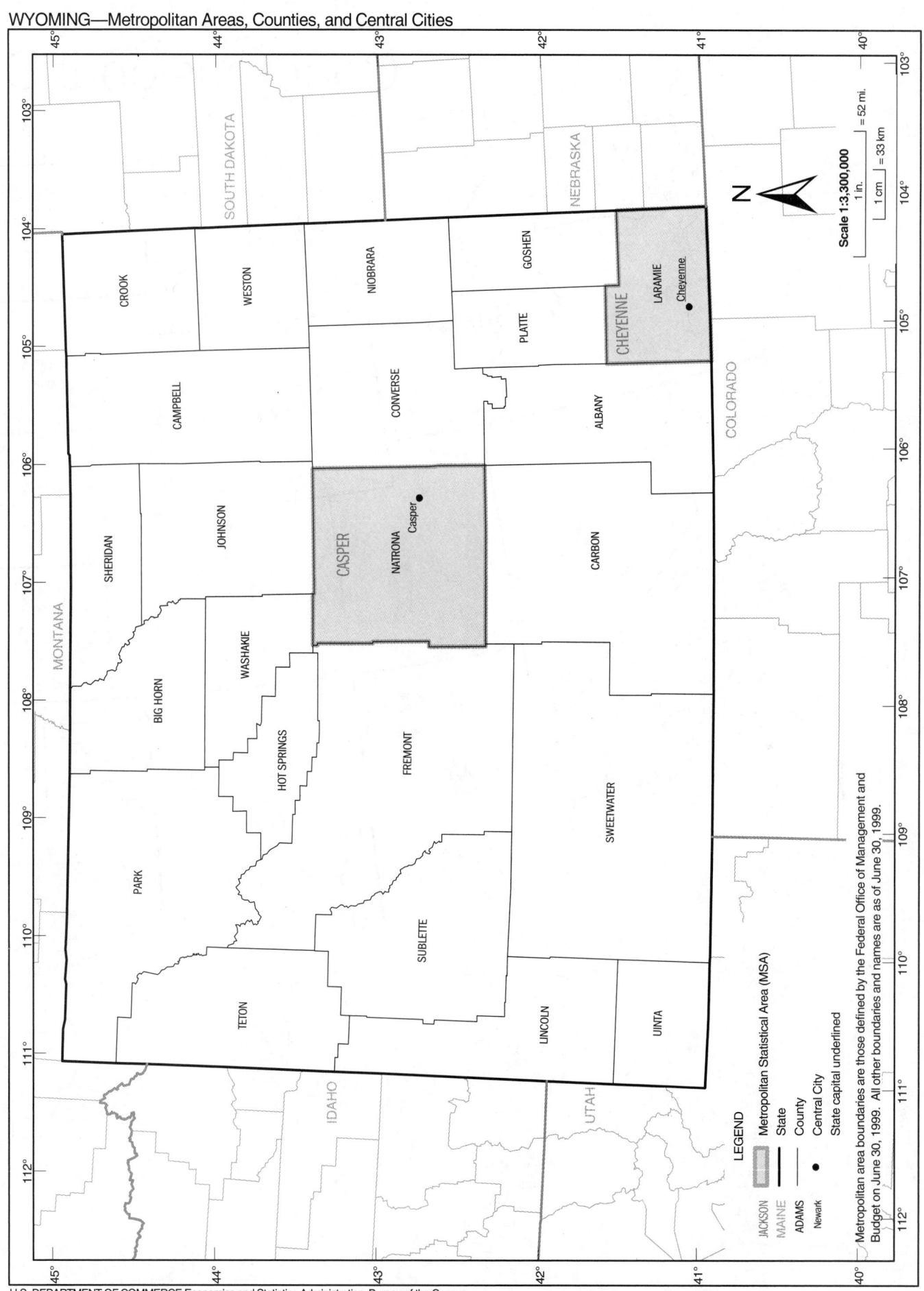

Scale 1:3,300,000

| 1 in. | = 52 mi. |
| 1 cm | = 33 km |

LEGEND

Metropolitan Statistical Area (MSA)
State
County
Central City
State capital underlined

JACKSON
MAINE
ADAMS
Newark

Metropolitan area boundaries are those defined by the Federal Office of Management and Budget on June 30, 1999. All other boundaries and names are as of June 30, 1999.

U.S. DEPARTMENT OF COMMERCE Economics and Statistics Administration Bureau of the Census

ts 105th Congress

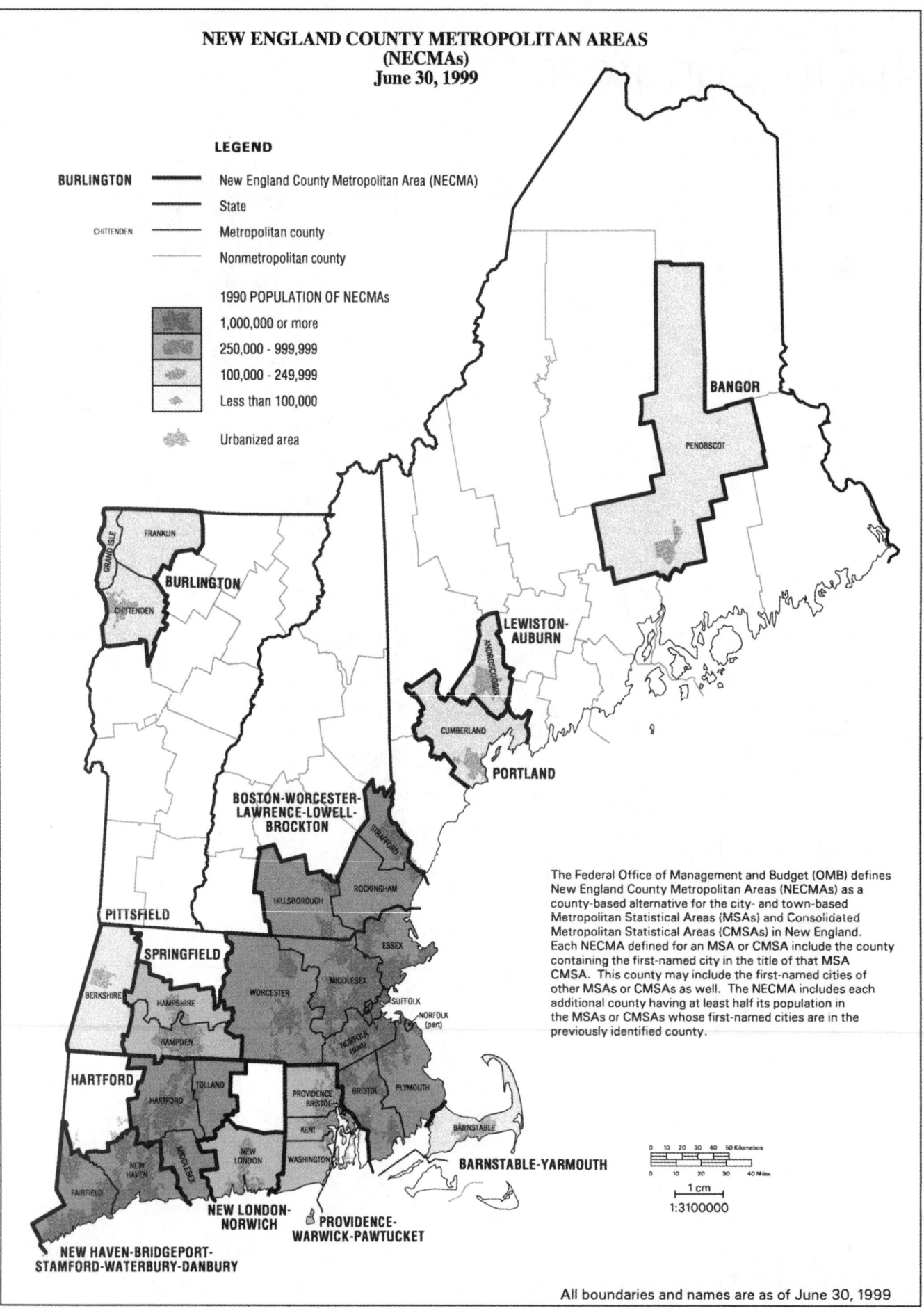

NEW ENGLAND COUNTY METROPOLITAN AREAS
(NECMAs)
June 30, 1999

LEGEND

BURLINGTON ———— New England County Metropolitan Area (NECMA)

———— State

CHITTENDEN ———— Metropolitan county

———— Nonmetropolitan county

1990 POPULATION OF NECMAs

1,000,000 or more

250,000 - 999,999

100,000 - 249,999

Less than 100,000

Urbanized area

BANGOR

PENOBSCOT

FRANKLIN

GRAND ISLE

BURLINGTON

CHITTENDEN

LEWISTON-AUBURN

ANDROSCOGGIN

CUMBERLAND

PORTLAND

BOSTON-WORCESTER-LAWRENCE-LOWELL-BROCKTON

STRAFFORD

ROCKINGHAM

HILLSBOROUGH

PITTSFIELD

SPRINGFIELD

ESSEX

MIDDLESEX

BERKSHIRE

HAMPSHIRE

WORCESTER

SUFFOLK

NORFOLK (part)

HAMPDEN

NORFOLK (bulk)

HARTFORD

TOLLAND

BRISTOL

PLYMOUTH

HARTFORD

PROVIDENCE BRISTOL

BARNSTABLE

KENT

NEW HAVEN

MIDDLESEX

NEW LONDON

WASHINGTON

BARNSTABLE-YARMOUTH

FAIRFIELD

NEW LONDON-NORWICH

PROVIDENCE-WARWICK-PAWTUCKET

NEW HAVEN-BRIDGEPORT-STAMFORD-WATERBURY-DANBURY

The Federal Office of Management and Budget (OMB) defines
New England County Metropolitan Areas (NECMAs) as a
county-based alternative for the city- and town-based
Metropolitan Statistical Areas (MSAs) and Consolidated
Metropolitan Statistical Areas (CMSAs) in New England.
Each NECMA defined for an MSA or CMSA include the county
containing the first-named city in the title of that MSA
CMSA. This county may include the first-named cities of
other MSAs or CMSAs as well. The NECMA includes each
additional county having at least half its population in
the MSAs or CMSAs whose first-named cities are in the
previously identified county.

0 10 20 30 40 50 Kilometers

0 10 20 30 40 Miles

1 cm

1:3100000

All boundaries and names are as of June 30, 1999

APPENDIX E
CITIES BY COUNTY

The following table is arranged alphabetically by state. Under each state heading are listed all cities with a 2000 Census population over 25,000 along with their component counties and the population in each component.

State Code	Place Code	County Code	Geographic Area Name	2000 Population	State Code	Place Code	County Code	Geographic Area Name	2000 Population
01			**ALABAMA**	4 447 100	04			**ARIZONA**	5 130 632
01	03076		Auburn city	42 987	04	02830		Apache Junction city	31 814
01	03076	081	Lee County	42 987	04	02830	013	Maricopa County	273
					04	02830	021	Pinal County	31 541
01	05980		Bessemer city	29 672					
01	05980	073	Jefferson County	29 672	04	04720		Avondale city	35 883
					04	04720	013	Maricopa County	35 883
01	07000		Birmingham city	242 820					
01	07000	073	Jefferson County	242 307	04	08220		Bullhead City city	33 769
01	07000	117	Shelby County	513	04	08220	015	Mohave County	33 769
01	20104		Decatur city	53 929	04	10530		Casa Grande city	25 224
01	20104	083	Limestone County	83	04	10530	021	Pinal County	25 224
01	20104	103	Morgan County	53 846					
					04	12000		Chandler city	176 581
01	21184		Dothan city	57 737	04	12000	013	Maricopa County	176 581
01	21184	045	Dale County	650					
01	21184	067	Henry County	5	04	23620		Flagstaff city	52 894
01	21184	069	Houston County	57 082	04	23620	005	Coconino County	52 894
01	26896		Florence city	36 264	04	27400		Gilbert town	109 697
01	26896	077	Lauderdale County	36 264	04	27400	013	Maricopa County	109 697
01	28696		Gadsden city	38 978	04	27820		Glendale city	218 812
01	28696	055	Etowah County	38 978	04	27820	013	Maricopa County	218 812
01	35800		Homewood city	25 043	04	39370		Lake Havasu City city	41 938
01	35800	073	Jefferson County	25 043	04	39370	015	Mohave County	41 938
01	35896		Hoover city	62 742	04	46000		Mesa city	396 375
01	35896	073	Jefferson County	46 868	04	46000	013	Maricopa County	396 375
01	35896	117	Shelby County	15 874					
					04	51600		Oro Valley town	29 700
01	37000		Huntsville city	158 216	04	51600	019	Pima County	29 700
01	37000	083	Limestone County	264					
01	37000	089	Madison County	157 952	04	54050		Peoria city	108 364
					04	54050	013	Maricopa County	108 363
01	45784		Madison city	29 329	04	54050	025	Yavapai County	1
01	45784	083	Limestone County	139					
01	45784	089	Madison County	29 190	04	55000		Phoenix city	1321 045
					04	55000	013	Maricopa County	1321 045
01	50000		Mobile city	198 915					
01	50000	097	Mobile County	198 915	04	57380		Prescott city	33 938
					04	57380	025	Yavapai County	33 938
01	51000		Montgomery city	201 568					
01	51000	101	Montgomery County	201 568	04	65000		Scottsdale city	202 705
					04	65000	013	Maricopa County	202 705
01	59472		Phenix City city	28 265					
01	59472	081	Lee County	1 980	04	66820		Sierra Vista city	37 775
01	59472	113	Russell County	26 285	04	66820	003	Cochise County	37 775
01	62496		Prichard city	28 633	04	71510		Surprise city	30 848
01	62496	097	Mobile County	28 633	04	71510	013	Maricopa County	30 848
01	77256		Tuscaloosa city	77 906	04	73000		Tempe city	158 625
01	77256	125	Tuscaloosa County	77 906	04	73000	013	Maricopa County	158 625
02			**ALASKA**	626 932	04	77000		Tucson city	486 699
02	03000		Anchorage municipality	260 283	04	77000	019	Pima County	486 699
02	03000	020	Anchorage Municipality	260 283					
					04	85540		Yuma city	77 515
02	24230		Fairbanks city	30 224	04	85540	027	Yuma County	77 515
02	24230	090	Fairbanks North Star Borough	30 224					
					05			**ARKANSAS**	2 673 400
02	36400		Juneau city and borough	30 711	05	15190		Conway city	43 167
02	36400	110	Juneau City and Borough	30 711	05	15190	045	Faulkner County	43 167

State Code	Place Code	County Code	Geographic Area Name	2000 Population	State Code	Place Code	County Code	Geographic Area Name	2000 Population
05	23290		Fayetteville city	58 047	06	04982		Bellflower city	72 878
05	23290	143	Washington County	58 047	06	04982	037	Los Angeles County	72 878
05	24550		Fort Smith city	80 268	06	04996		Bell Gardens city	44 054
05	24550	131	Sebastian County	80 268	06	04996	037	Los Angeles County	44 054
05	33400		Hot Springs city	35 750	06	05108		Belmont city	25 123
05	33400	051	Garland County	35 750	06	05108	081	San Mateo County	25 123
05	34750		Jacksonville city	29 916	06	05290		Benicia city	26 865
05	34750	119	Pulaski County	29 916	06	05290	095	Solano County	26 865
05	35710		Jonesboro city	55 515	06	06000		Berkeley city	102 743
05	35710	031	Craighead County	55 515	06	06000	001	Alameda County	102 743
05	41000		Little Rock city	183 133	06	06308		Beverly Hills city	33 784
05	41000	119	Pulaski County	183 133	06	06308	037	Los Angeles County	33 784
05	50450		North Little Rock city	60 433	06	08100		Brea city	35 410
05	50450	119	Pulaski County	60 433	06	08100	059	Orange County	35 410
05	55310		Pine Bluff city	55 085	06	08786		Buena Park city	78 282
05	55310	069	Jefferson County	55 085	06	08786	059	Orange County	78 282
05	60410		Rogers city	38 829	06	08954		Burbank city	100 316
05	60410	007	Benton County	38 829	06	08954	037	Los Angeles County	100 316
05	66080		Springdale city	45 798	06	09066		Burlingame city	28 158
05	66080	007	Benton County	2 011	06	09066	081	San Mateo County	28 158
05	66080	143	Washington County	43 787	06	09710		Calexico city	27 109
05	68810		Texarkana city	26 448	06	09710	025	Imperial County	27 109
05	68810	091	Miller County	26 448	06	10046		Camarillo city	57 077
05	74540		West Memphis city	27 666	06	10046	111	Ventura County	57 077
05	74540	035	Crittenden County	27 666	06	10345		Campbell city	38 138
06			**CALIFORNIA**	33 871 648	06	10345	085	Santa Clara County	38 138
06	00562		Alameda city	72 259	06	11194		Carlsbad city	78 247
06	00562	001	Alameda County	72 259	06	11194	073	San Diego County	78 247
06	00884		Alhambra city	85 804	06	11530		Carson city	89 730
06	00884	037	Los Angeles County	85 804	06	11530	037	Los Angeles County	89 730
06	02000		Anaheim city	328 014	06	12048		Cathedral City city	42 647
06	02000	059	Orange County	328 014	06	12048	065	Riverside County	42 647
06	02252		Antioch city	90 532	06	12524		Ceres city	34 609
06	02252	013	Contra Costa County	90 532	06	12524	099	Stanislaus County	34 609
06	02364		Apple Valley town	54 239	06	12552		Cerritos city	51 488
06	02364	071	San Bernardino County	54 239	06	12552	037	Los Angeles County	51 488
06	02462		Arcadia city	53 054	06	13014		Chico city	59 954
06	02462	037	Los Angeles County	53 054	06	13014	007	Butte County	59 954
06	03064		Atascadero city	26 411	06	13210		Chino city	67 168
06	03064	079	San Luis Obispo County	26 411	06	13210	071	San Bernardino County	67 168
06	03386		Azusa city	44 712	06	13392		Chula Vista city	173 556
06	03386	037	Los Angeles County	44 712	06	13392	073	San Diego County	173 556
06	03526		Bakersfield city	247 057	06	13756		Claremont city	33 998
06	03526	029	Kern County	247 057	06	13756	037	Los Angeles County	33 998
06	03666		Baldwin Park city	75 837	06	14218		Clovis city	68 468
06	03666	037	Los Angeles County	75 837	06	14218	019	Fresno County	68 468
06	04870		Bell city	36 664	06	14890		Colton city	47 662
06	04870	037	Los Angeles County	36 664	06	14890	071	San Bernardino County	47 662

State Code	Place Code	County Code	Geographic Area Name	2000 Population	State Code	Place Code	County Code	Geographic Area Name	2000 Population
06	15044		Compton city	93 493	06	24638		Folsom city	51 884
06	15044	037	Los Angeles County	93 493	06	24638	067	Sacramento County.................	51 884
06	16000		Concord city	121 780	06	24680		Fontana city.................	128 929
06	16000	013	Contra Costa County	121 780	06	24680	071	San Bernardino County	128 929
06	16350		Corona city	124 966	06	25338		Foster City city	28 803
06	16350	065	Riverside County	124 966	06	25338	081	San Mateo County....................	28 803
06	16532		Costa Mesa city	108 724	06	25380		Fountain Valley city	54 978
06	16532	059	Orange County	108 724	06	25380	059	Orange County	54 978
06	16742		Covina city....................	46 837	06	26000		Fremont city....................	203 413
06	16742	037	Los Angeles County	46 837	06	26000	001	Alameda County	203 413
06	17568		Culver City city	38 816	06	27000		Fresno city....................	427 652
06	17568	037	Los Angeles County	38 816	06	27000	019	Fresno County	427 652
06	17610		Cupertino city	50 546	06	28000		Fullerton city....................	126 003
06	17610	085	Santa Clara County	50 546	06	28000	059	Orange County	126 003
06	17750		Cypress city	46 229	06	28168		Gardena city	57 746
06	17750	059	Orange County	46 229	06	28168	037	Los Angeles County	57 746
06	17918		Daly City city	103 621	06	29000		Garden Grove city	165 196
06	17918	081	San Mateo County	103 621	06	29000	059	Orange County	165 196
06	17946		Dana Point city	35 110	06	29504		Gilroy city....................	41 464
06	17946	059	Orange County	35 110	06	29504	085	Santa Clara County	41 464
06	17988		Danville town	41 715	06	30000		Glendale city....................	194 973
06	17988	013	Contra Costa County	41 715	06	30000	037	Los Angeles County	194 973
06	18100		Davis city	60 308	06	30014		Glendora city	49 415
06	18100	113	Yolo County	60 308	06	30014	037	Los Angeles County	49 415
06	18394		Delano city....................	38 824	06	31960		Hanford city	41 686
06	18394	029	Kern County....................	38 824	06	31960	031	Kings County	41 686
06	19192		Diamond Bar city....................	56 287	06	32548		Hawthorne city....................	84 112
06	19192	037	Los Angeles County	56 287	06	32548	037	Los Angeles County	84 112
06	19766		Downey city....................	107 323	06	33000		Hayward city....................	140 030
06	19766	037	Los Angeles County	107 323	06	33000	001	Alameda County	140 030
06	20018		Dublin city....................	29 973	06	33182		Hemet city	58 812
06	20018	001	Alameda County	29 973	06	33182	065	Riverside County	58 812
06	20956		East Palo Alto city	29 506	06	33434		Hesperia city....................	62 582
06	20956	081	San Mateo County....................	29 506	06	33434	071	San Bernardino County	62 582
06	21712		El Cajon city	94 869	06	33588		Highland city....................	44 605
06	21712	073	San Diego County	94 869	06	33588	071	San Bernardino County	44 605
06	21782		El Centro city....................	37 835	06	34120		Hollister city....................	34 413
06	21782	025	Imperial County....................	37 835	06	34120	069	San Benito County....................	34 413
06	22230		El Monte city	115 965	06	36000		Huntington Beach city	189 594
06	22230	037	Los Angeles County	115 965	06	36000	059	Orange County	189 594
06	22678		Encinitas city	58 014	06	36056		Huntington Park city	61 348
06	22678	073	San Diego County	58 014	06	36056	037	Los Angeles County	61 348
06	22804		Escondido city	133 559	06	36294		Imperial Beach city	26 992
06	22804	073	San Diego County	133 559	06	36294	073	San Diego County	26 992
06	23042		Eureka city....................	26 128	06	36448		Indio city	49 116
06	23042	023	Humboldt County	26 128	06	36448	065	Riverside County	49 116
06	23182		Fairfield city	96 178	06	36546		Inglewood city....................	112 580
06	23182	095	Solano County	96 178	06	36546	037	Los Angeles County	112 580

State Code	Place Code	County Code	Geographic Area Name	2000 Population	State Code	Place Code	County Code	Geographic Area Name	2000 Population
06	36770		Irvine city	143 072	06	45778		Marina city	25 101
06	36770	059	Orange County	143 072	06	45778	053	Monterey County	25 101
06	39248		Laguna Niguel city	61 891	06	46114		Martinez city	35 866
06	39248	059	Orange County	61 891	06	46114	013	Contra Costa County	35 866
06	39290		La Habra city	58 974	06	46492		Maywood city	28 083
06	39290	059	Orange County	58 974	06	46492	037	Los Angeles County	28 083
06	39486		Lake Elsinore city	28 928	06	46870		Menlo Park city	30 785
06	39486	065	Riverside County	28 928	06	46870	081	San Mateo County	30 785
06	39496		Lake Forest city	58 707	06	46898		Merced city	63 893
06	39496	059	Orange County	58 707	06	46898	047	Merced County	63 893
06	39892		Lakewood city	79 345	06	47766		Milpitas city	62 698
06	39892	037	Los Angeles County	79 345	06	47766	085	Santa Clara County	62 698
06	40004		La Mesa city	54 749	06	48256		Mission Viejo city	93 102
06	40004	073	San Diego County	54 749	06	48256	059	Orange County	93 102
06	40032		La Mirada city	46 783	06	48354		Modesto city	188 856
06	40032	037	Los Angeles County	46 783	06	48354	099	Stanislaus County	188 856
06	40130		Lancaster city	118 718	06	48648		Monrovia city	36 929
06	40130	037	Los Angeles County	118 718	06	48648	037	Los Angeles County	36 929
06	40340		La Puente city	41 063	06	48788		Montclair city	33 049
06	40340	037	Los Angeles County	41 063	06	48788	071	San Bernardino County	33 049
06	40830		La Verne city	31 638	06	48816		Montebello city	62 150
06	40830	037	Los Angeles County	31 638	06	48816	037	Los Angeles County	62 150
06	40886		Lawndale city	31 711	06	48872		Monterey city	29 674
06	40886	037	Los Angeles County	31 711	06	48872	053	Monterey County	29 674
06	41992		Livermore city	73 345	06	48914		Monterey Park city	60 051
06	41992	001	Alameda County	73 345	06	48914	037	Los Angeles County	60 051
06	42202		Lodi city	56 999	06	49138		Moorpark city	31 415
06	42202	077	San Joaquin County	56 999	06	49138	111	Ventura County	31 415
06	42524		Lompoc city	41 103	06	49270		Moreno Valley city	142 381
06	42524	083	Santa Barbara County	41 103	06	49270	065	Riverside County	142 381
06	43000		Long Beach city	461 522	06	49278		Morgan Hill city	33 556
06	43000	037	Los Angeles County	461 522	06	49278	085	Santa Clara County	33 556
06	43280		Los Altos city	27 693	06	49670		Mountain View city	70 708
06	43280	085	Santa Clara County	27 693	06	49670	085	Santa Clara County	70 708
06	44000		Los Angeles city	3694 820	06	50076		Murrieta city	44 282
06	44000	037	Los Angeles County	3694 820	06	50076	065	Riverside County	44 282
06	44028		Los Banos city	25 869	06	50258		Napa city	72 585
06	44028	047	Merced County	25 869	06	50258	055	Napa County	72 585
06	44112		Los Gatos town	28 592	06	50398		National City city	54 260
06	44112	085	Santa Clara County	28 592	06	50398	073	San Diego County	54 260
06	44574		Lynwood city	69 845	06	50916		Newark city	42 471
06	44574	037	Los Angeles County	69 845	06	50916	001	Alameda County	42 471
06	45022		Madera city	43 207	06	51182		Newport Beach city	70 032
06	45022	039	Madera County	43 207	06	51182	059	Orange County	70 032
06	45400		Manhattan Beach city	33 852	06	52526		Norwalk city	103 298
06	45400	037	Los Angeles County	33 852	06	52526	037	Los Angeles County	103 298
06	45484		Manteca city	49 258	06	52582		Novato city	47 630
06	45484	077	San Joaquin County	49 258	06	52582	041	Marin County	47 630

State Code	Place Code	County Code	Geographic Area Name	2000 Population	State Code	Place Code	County Code	Geographic Area Name	2000 Population
06	53000		Oakland city	399 484	06	59514		Rancho Palos Verdes city	41 145
06	53000	001	Alameda County	399 484	06	59514	037	Los Angeles County	41 145
06	53322		Oceanside city	161 029	06	59920		Redding city	80 865
06	53322	073	San Diego County	161 029	06	59920	089	Shasta County	80 865
06	53896		Ontario city	158 007	06	59962		Redlands city	63 591
06	53896	071	San Bernardino County	158 007	06	59962	071	San Bernardino County	63 591
06	53980		Orange city	128 821	06	60018		Redondo Beach city	63 261
06	53980	059	Orange County	128 821	06	60018	037	Los Angeles County	63 261
06	54652		Oxnard city	170 358	06	60102		Redwood City city	75 402
06	54652	111	Ventura County	170 358	06	60102	081	San Mateo County	75 402
06	54806		Pacifica city	38 390	06	60466		Rialto city	91 873
06	54806	081	San Mateo County	38 390	06	60466	071	San Bernardino County	91 873
06	55156		Palmdale city	116 670	06	60620		Richmond city	99 216
06	55156	037	Los Angeles County	116 670	06	60620	013	Contra Costa County	99 216
06	55184		Palm Desert city	41 155	06	62000		Riverside city	255 166
06	55184	065	Riverside County	41 155	06	62000	065	Riverside County	255 166
06	55254		Palm Springs city	42 807	06	62364		Rocklin city	36 330
06	55254	065	Riverside County	42 807	06	62364	061	Placer County	36 330
06	55282		Palo Alto city	58 598	06	62546		Rohnert Park city	42 236
06	55282	085	Santa Clara County	58 598	06	62546	097	Sonoma County	42 236
06	55520		Paradise town	26 408	06	62896		Rosemead city	53 505
06	55520	007	Butte County	26 408	06	62896	037	Los Angeles County	53 505
06	55618		Paramount city	55 266	06	62938		Roseville city	79 921
06	55618	037	Los Angeles County	55 266	06	62938	061	Placer County	79 921
06	56000		Pasadena city	133 936	06	64000		Sacramento city	407 018
06	56000	037	Los Angeles County	133 936	06	64000	067	Sacramento County	407 018
06	56700		Perris city	36 189	06	64224		Salinas city	151 060
06	56700	065	Riverside County	36 189	06	64224	053	Monterey County	151 060
06	56784		Petaluma city	54 548	06	65000		San Bernardino city	185 401
06	56784	097	Sonoma County	54 548	06	65000	071	San Bernardino County	185 401
06	56924		Pico Rivera city	63 428	06	65028		San Bruno city	40 165
06	56924	037	Los Angeles County	63 428	06	65028	081	San Mateo County	40 165
06	57456		Pittsburg city	56 769	06	65042		San Buenaventura (Ventura) city	100 916
06	57456	013	Contra Costa County	56 769	06	65042	111	Ventura County	100 916
06	57526		Placentia city	46 488	06	65070		San Carlos city	27 718
06	57526	059	Orange County	46 488	06	65070	081	San Mateo County	27 718
06	57764		Pleasant Hill city	32 837	06	65084		San Clemente city	49 936
06	57764	013	Contra Costa County	32 837	06	65084	059	Orange County	49 936
06	57792		Pleasanton city	63 654	06	66000		San Diego city	1223 400
06	57792	001	Alameda County	63 654	06	66000	073	San Diego County	1223 400
06	58072		Pomona city	149 473	06	66070		San Dimas city	34 980
06	58072	037	Los Angeles County	149 473	06	66070	037	Los Angeles County	34 980
06	58240		Porterville city	39 615	06	67000		San Francisco city	776 733
06	58240	107	Tulare County	39 615	06	67000	075	San Francisco County	776 733
06	58520		Poway city	48 044	06	67042		San Gabriel city	39 804
06	58520	073	San Diego County	48 044	06	67042	037	Los Angeles County	39 804
06	59451		Rancho Cucamonga city	127 743	06	68000		San Jose city	894 943
06	59451	071	San Bernardino County	127 743	06	68000	085	Santa Clara County	894 943

Cities by County — Continued

State Code	Place Code	County Code	Geographic Area Name	2000 Population	State Code	Place Code	County Code	Geographic Area Name	2000 Population
06	68028		San Juan Capistrano city.............	33 826	06	75000		Stockton city.................................	243 771
06	68028	059	Orange County	33 826	06	75000	077	San Joaquin County	243 771
06	68084		San Leandro city.......................	79 452	06	75630		Suisun City city.............................	26 118
06	68084	001	Alameda County	79 452	06	75630	095	Solano County	26 118
06	68154		San Luis Obispo city	44 174	06	77000		Sunnyvale city	131 760
06	68154	079	San Luis Obispo County...........	44 174	06	77000	085	Santa Clara County	131 760
06	68196		San Marcos city..........................	54 977	06	78120		Temecula city................................	57 716
06	68196	073	San Diego County	54 977	06	78120	065	Riverside County	57 716
06	68252		San Mateo city............................	92 482	06	78148		Temple City city............................	33 377
06	68252	081	San Mateo County	92 482	06	78148	037	Los Angeles County	33 377
06	68294		San Pablo city.............................	30 215	06	78582		Thousand Oaks city	117 005
06	68294	013	Contra Costa County................	30 215	06	78582	111	Ventura County	117 005
06	68364		San Rafael city............................	56 063	06	80000		Torrance city.................................	137 946
06	68364	041	Marin County	56 063	06	80000	037	Los Angeles County	137 946
06	68378		San Ramon city...........................	44 722	06	80238		Tracy city......................................	56 929
06	68378	013	Contra Costa County................	44 722	06	80238	077	San Joaquin County	56 929
06	69000		Santa Ana city.............................	337 977	06	80644		Tulare city....................................	43 994
06	69000	059	Orange County	337 977	06	80644	107	Tulare County	43 994
06	69070		Santa Barbara city.......................	92 325	06	80812		Turlock city...................................	55 810
06	69070	083	Santa Barbara County..............	92 325	06	80812	099	Stanislaus County....................	55 810
06	69084		Santa Clara city...........................	102 361	06	80854		Tustin city.....................................	67 504
06	69084	085	Santa Clara County	102 361	06	80854	059	Orange County	67 504
06	69088		Santa Clarita city.........................	151 088	06	81204		Union City city	66 869
06	69088	037	Los Angeles County	151 088	06	81204	001	Alameda County	66 869
06	69112		Santa Cruz city............................	54 593	06	81344		Upland city....................................	68 393
06	69112	087	Santa Cruz County	54 593	06	81344	071	San Bernardino County	68 393
06	69196		Santa Maria city	77 423	06	81554		Vacaville city.................................	88 625
06	69196	083	Santa Barbara County..............	77 423	06	81554	095	Solano County	88 625
06	70000		Santa Monica city........................	84 084	06	81666		Vallejo city....................................	116 760
06	70000	037	Los Angeles County	84 084	06	81666	095	Solano County	116 760
06	70042		Santa Paula city	28 598	06	82590		Victorville city................................	64 029
06	70042	111	Ventura County	28 598	06	82590	071	San Bernardino County	64 029
06	70098		Santa Rosa city...........................	147 595	06	82954		Visalia city	91 565
06	70098	097	Sonoma County	147 595	06	82954	107	Tulare County	91 565
06	70224		Santee city...................................	52 975	06	82996		Vista city	89 857
06	70224	073	San Diego County	52 975	06	82996	073	San Diego County	89 857
06	70280		Saratoga city	29 843	06	83332		Walnut city....................................	30 004
06	70280	085	Santa Clara County	29 843	06	83332	037	Los Angeles County	30 004
06	70742		Seaside city.................................	31 696	06	83346		Walnut Creek city	64 296
06	70742	053	Monterey County	31 696	06	83346	013	Contra Costa County................	64 296
06	72016		Simi Valley city............................	111 351	06	83668		Watsonville city.............................	44 265
06	72016	111	Ventura County	111 351	06	83668	087	Santa Cruz County	44 265
06	73080		South Gate city............................	96 375	06	84200		West Covina city	105 080
06	73080	037	Los Angeles County	96 375	06	84200	037	Los Angeles County	105 080
06	73262		South San Francisco city	60 552	06	84410		West Hollywood city......................	35 716
06	73262	081	San Mateo County	60 552	06	84410	037	Los Angeles County	35 716
06	73962		Stanton city.................................	37 403	06	84550		Westminster city...........................	88 207
06	73962	059	Orange County	37 403	06	84550	059	Orange County	88 207

State Code	Place Code	County Code	Geographic Area Name	2000 Population	State Code	Place Code	County Code	Geographic Area Name	2000 Population
06	84816		West Sacramento city	31 615	08	54330		Northglenn city	31 575
06	84816	113	Yolo County	31 615	08	54330	001	Adams County	31 563
					08	54330	123	Weld County	12
06	85292		Whittier city	83 680					
06	85292	037	Los Angeles County	83 680	08	62000		Pueblo city	102 121
					08	62000	101	Pueblo County	102 121
06	86328		Woodland city	49 151					
06	86328	113	Yolo County	49 151	08	77290		Thornton city	82 384
					08	77290	001	Adams County	82 384
06	86832		Yorba Linda city	58 918	08	77290	123	Weld County	0
06	86832	059	Orange County	58 918					
					08	83835		Westminster city	100 940
06	86972		Yuba City city	36 758	08	83835	001	Adams County	57 419
06	86972	101	Sutter County	36 758	08	83835	059	Jefferson County	43 521
06	87042		Yucaipa city	41 207	08	84440		Wheat Ridge city	32 913
06	87042	071	San Bernardino County	41 207	08	84440	059	Jefferson County	32 913
08			**COLORADO**	4 301 261	09			**CONNECTICUT**	3 405 565
08	03455		Arvada city	102 153	09	08000		Bridgeport city	139 529
08	03455	001	Adams County	2 847	09	08000	001	Fairfield County	139 529
08	03455	059	Jefferson County	99 306					
					09	08420		Bristol city	60 062
08	04000		Aurora city	276 393	09	08420	003	Hartford County	60 062
08	04000	001	Adams County	40 249					
08	04000	005	Arapahoe County	236 144	09	18430		Danbury city	74 848
08	04000	035	Douglas County	0	09	18430	001	Fairfield County	74 848
08	07850		Boulder city	94 673	09	37000		Hartford city	121 578
08	07850	013	Boulder County	94 673	09	37000	003	Hartford County	121 578
08	09280		Broomfield city	38 272	09	46450		Meriden city	58 244
08	09280	001	Adams County	15 239	09	46450	009	New Haven County	58 244
08	09280	013	Boulder County	21 474					
08	09280	059	Jefferson County	1 549	09	47290		Middletown city	43 167
08	09280	123	Weld County	10	09	47290	007	Middlesex County	43 167
08	16000		Colorado Springs city	360 890	09	47500		Milford city	52 305
08	16000	041	El Paso County	360 890					
					09	49880		Naugatuck borough	30 989
08	20000		Denver city	554 636	09	49880	009	New Haven County	30 989
08	20000	031	Denver County	554 636					
					09	50370		New Britain city	71 538
08	24785		Englewood city	31 727	09	50370	003	Hartford County	71 538
08	24785	005	Arapahoe County	31 727					
					09	52000		New Haven city	123 626
08	27425		Fort Collins city	118 652	09	52000	009	New Haven County	123 626
08	27425	069	Larimer County	118 652					
					09	52280		New London city	25 671
08	31660		Grand Junction city	41 986	09	52280	011	New London County	25 671
08	31660	077	Mesa County	41 986					
					09	55990		Norwalk city	82 951
08	32155		Greeley city	76 930	09	55990	001	Fairfield County	82 951
08	32155	123	Weld County	76 930					
					09	56200		Norwich city	36 117
08	43000		Lakewood city	144 126	09	56200	011	New London County	36 117
08	43000	059	Jefferson County	144 126					
					09	68100		Shelton city	38 101
08	45255		Littleton city	40 340	09	68100	001	Fairfield County	38 101
08	45255	005	Arapahoe County	40 168					
08	45255	035	Douglas County	63	09	73000		Stamford city	117 083
08	45255	059	Jefferson County	109	09	73000	001	Fairfield County	117 083
08	45970		Longmont city	71 093	09	76500		Torrington city	35 202
08	45970	013	Boulder County	71 069	09	76500	005	Litchfield County	35 202
08	45970	123	Weld County	24					
					09	80000		Waterbury city	107 271
08	46465		Loveland city	50 608	09	80000	009	New Haven County	107 271
08	46465	069	Larimer County	50 608					
					09	82800		West Haven city	52 360
					09	82800	009	New Haven County	52 360

State Code	Place Code	County Code	Geographic Area Name	2000 Population	State Code	Place Code	County Code	Geographic Area Name	2000 Population
10			**DELAWARE**	783 600	12	25175		Gainesville city	95 447
10	21200		Dover city	32 135	12	25175	001	Alachua County	95 447
10	21200	001	Kent County	32 135					
					12	27322		Greenacres city	27 569
10	50670		Newark city...............	28 547	12	27322	099	Palm Beach County	27 569
10	50670	003	New Castle County	28 547					
					12	28450		Hallandale city	34 282
10	77580		Wilmington city	72 664	12	28450	011	Broward County	34 282
10	77580	003	New Castle County	72 664					
					12	30000		Hialeah city	226 419
11			**DISTRICT OF COLUMBIA**	572 059	12	30000	086	Miami-Dade County	226 419
11	50000		Washington city	572 059					
11	50000	001	District of Columbia	572 059	12	32000		Hollywood city	139 357
					12	32000	011	Broward County	139 357
12			**FLORIDA**	15 982 378					
12	00950		Altamonte Springs city	41 200	12	32275		Homestead city............	31 909
12	00950	117	Seminole County	41 200	12	32275	086	Miami-Dade County	31 909
12	01700		Apopka city...............	26 642	12	35000		Jacksonville city............	735 617
12	01700	095	Orange County	26 642	12	35000	031	Duval County	735 617
12	07300		Boca Raton city	74 764	12	35875		Jupiter town............	39 328
12	07300	099	Palm Beach County	74 764	12	35875	099	Palm Beach County	39 328
12	07875		Boynton Beach city	60 389	12	36550		Key West city	25 478
12	07875	099	Palm Beach County	60 389	12	36550	087	Monroe County	25 478
12	07950		Bradenton city	49 504	12	36950		Kissimmee city	47 814
12	07950	081	Manatee County	49 504	12	36950	097	Osceola County	47 814
12	10275		Cape Coral city	102 286	12	38250		Lakeland city	78 452
12	10275	071	Lee County	102 286	12	38250	105	Polk County	78 452
12	12875		Clearwater city............	108 787	12	39075		Lake Worth city	35 133
12	12875	103	Pinellas County	108 787	12	39075	099	Palm Beach County	35 133
12	13275		Coconut Creek city	43 566	12	39425		Largo city............	69 371
12	13275	011	Broward County	43 566	12	39425	103	Pinellas County	69 371
12	14125		Cooper City city............	27 939	12	39525		Lauderdale Lakes city	31 705
12	14125	011	Broward County	27 939	12	39525	011	Broward County	31 705
12	14250		Coral Gables city............	42 249	12	39550		Lauderhill city	57 585
12	14250	086	Miami-Dade County	42 249	12	39550	011	Broward County	57 585
12	14400		Coral Springs city	117 549	12	43125		Margate city............	53 909
12	14400	011	Broward County	117 549	12	43125	011	Broward County	53 909
12	16475		Davie town............	75 720	12	43975		Melbourne city	71 382
12	16475	011	Broward County	75 720	12	43975	009	Brevard County	71 382
12	16525		Daytona Beach city	64 112	12	45000		Miami city	362 470
12	16525	127	Volusia County	64 112	12	45000	086	Miami-Dade County	362 470
12	16725		Deerfield Beach city	64 583	12	45025		Miami Beach city	87 933
12	16725	011	Broward County	64 583	12	45025	086	Miami-Dade County	87 933
12	17100		Delray Beach city	60 020	12	45975		Miramar city	72 739
12	17100	099	Palm Beach County	60 020	12	45975	011	Broward County	72 739
12	18575		Dunedin city............	35 691	12	49425		North Lauderdale city	32 264
12	18575	103	Pinellas County	35 691	12	49425	011	Broward County	32 264
12	24000		Fort Lauderdale city	152 397	12	49450		North Miami city	59 880
12	24000	011	Broward County	152 397	12	49450	086	Miami-Dade County	59 880
12	24125		Fort Myers city............	48 208	12	49475		North Miami Beach city	40 786
12	24125	071	Lee County	48 208	12	49475	086	Miami-Dade County	40 786
12	24300		Fort Pierce city	37 516	12	50575		Oakland Park city	30 966
12	24300	111	St. Lucie County	37 516	12	50575	011	Broward County	30 966

Cities by County — Continued

State Code	Place Code	County Code	Geographic Area Name	2000 Population	State Code	Place Code	County Code	Geographic Area Name	2000 Population
12	50750		Ocala city....................................	45 943	12	76582		Weston city...............................	49 286
12	50750	083	Marion County	45 943	12	76582	011	Broward County	49 286
12	53000		Orlando city...............................	185 951	12	76600		West Palm Beach city	82 103
12	53000	095	Orange County	185 951	12	76600	099	Palm Beach County....................	82 103
12	53150		Ormond Beach city.....................	36 301	12	78275		Winter Haven city	26 487
12	53150	127	Volusia County	36 301	12	78275	105	Polk County	26 487
12	53575		Oviedo city.................................	26 316	12	78325		Winter Springs city	31 666
12	53575	117	Seminole County	26 316	12	78325	117	Seminole County	31 666
12	54000		Palm Bay city	79 413	13			**GEORGIA**	8 186 453
12	54000	009	Brevard County	79 413	13	01052		Albany city...............................	76 939
12	54075		Palm Beach Gardens city	35 058	13	01052	095	Dougherty County	76 939
12	54075	099	Palm Beach County...................	35 058	13	01696		Alpharetta city...........................	34 854
12	54700		Panama City city.........................	36 417	13	01696	121	Fulton County	34 854
12	54700	005	Bay County..............................	36 417	13	03436		Athens-Clarke County	101 489
12	55775		Pembroke Pines city	137 427	13	04000		Atlanta city................................	416 474
12	55775	011	Broward County	137 427	13	04000	089	DeKalb County	29 775
12	55925		Pensacola city	56 255	13	04000	121	Fulton County	386 699
12	55925	033	Escambia County......................	56 255	13	04200		Augusta-Richmond County	199 775
12	56975		Pinellas Park city	45 658	13	19000		Columbus city............................	186 291
12	56975	103	Pinellas County........................	45 658	13	21380		Dalton city.................................	27 912
12	57425		Plantation city	82 934	13	21380	313	Whitfield County......................	27 912
12	57425	011	Broward County	82 934	13	25720		East Point city	39 595
12	57550		Plant City city	29 915	13	25720	121	Fulton County	39 595
12	57550	057	Hillsborough County	29 915	13	31908		Gainesville city	25 578
12	58050		Pompano Beach city	78 191	13	31908	139	Hall County	25 578
12	58050	011	Broward County	78 191	13	38964		Hinesville city............................	30 392
12	58575		Port Orange city	45 823	13	38964	179	Liberty County.........................	30 392
12	58575	127	Volusia County	45 823	13	44340		LaGrange city............................	25 998
12	58715		Port St. Lucie city......................	88 769	13	44340	285	Troup County	25 998
12	58715	111	St. Lucie County	88 769	13	49000		Macon city	97 255
12	60975		Riviera Beach city	29 884	13	49000	021	Bibb County	96 777
12	60975	099	Palm Beach County...................	29 884	13	49000	169	Jones County	478
12	63000		St. Petersburg city......................	248 232	13	49756		Marietta city..............................	58 748
12	63000	103	Pinellas County........................	248 232	13	49756	067	Cobb County..........................	58 748
12	63650		Sanford city	38 291	13	59724		Peachtree City city	31 580
12	63650	117	Seminole County	38 291	13	59724	113	Fayette County.........................	31 580
12	64175		Sarasota city..............................	52 715	13	66668		Rome city	34 980
12	64175	115	Sarasota County	52 715	13	66668	115	Floyd County	34 980
12	69700		Sunrise city	85 779	13	67284		Roswell city	79 334
12	69700	011	Broward County	85 779	13	67284	121	Fulton County	79 334
12	70600		Tallahassee city..........................	150 624	13	69000		Savannah city............................	131 510
12	70600	073	Leon County	150 624	13	69000	051	Chatham County......................	131 510
12	70675		Tamarac city..............................	55 588	13	71492		Smyrna city...............................	40 999
12	70675	011	Broward County	55 588	13	71492	067	Cobb County..........................	40 999
12	71000		Tampa city.................................	303 447	13	78800		Valdosta city	43 724
12	71000	057	Hillsborough County	303 447	13	78800	185	Lowndes County	43 724
12	71900		Titusville city..............................	40 670	13	80508		Warner Robins city......................	48 804
12	71900	009	Brevard County	40 670	13	80508	153	Houston County	48 787
					13	80508	225	Peach County	17

Cities by County — Continued

State Code	Place Code	County Code	Geographic Area Name	2000 Population	State Code	Place Code	County Code	Geographic Area Name	2000 Population
					17	04013		Bartlett village	36 706
15			**HAWAII**	1 211 537	17	04013	031	Cook County	12 196
15	14650		Hilo CDP	40 759	17	04013	043	DuPage County	24 508
15	14650	001	Hawaii County	40 759	17	04013	089	Kane County	2
15	17000		Honolulu CDP	371 657	17	04845		Belleville city	41 410
15	17000	003	Honolulu County	371 657	17	04845	163	St. Clair County	41 410
15	23150		Kailua CDP	36 513	17	05573		Berwyn city	54 016
15	23150	003	Honolulu County	36 513	17	05573	031	Cook County	54 016
15	28250		Kaneohe CDP	34 970	17	06613		Bloomington city	64 808
15	28250	003	Honolulu County	34 970	17	06613	113	McLean County	64 808
15	51050		Mililani Town CDP	28 608	17	07133		Bolingbrook village	56 321
15	51050	003	Honolulu County	28 608	17	07133	043	DuPage County	1 748
15	62600		Pearl City CDP	30 976	17	07133	197	Will County	54 573
15	62600	003	Honolulu County	30 976	17	09447		Buffalo Grove village	42 909
15	77750		Waimalu CDP	29 371	17	09447	031	Cook County	14 418
15	77750	003	Honolulu County	29 371	17	09447	097	Lake County	28 491
15	79700		Waipahu CDP	33 108	17	09642		Burbank city	27 902
15	79700	003	Honolulu County	33 108	17	09642	031	Cook County	27 902
16			**IDAHO**	1 293 953	17	10487		Calumet City city	39 071
16	08830		Boise City city	185 787	17	10487	031	Cook County	39 071
16	08830	001	Ada County	185 787	17	11332		Carol Stream village	40 438
16	12250		Caldwell city	25 967	17	11332	043	DuPage County	40 438
16	12250	027	Canyon County	25 967	17	11358		Carpentersville village	30 586
16	16750		Coeur d'Alene city	34 514	17	11358	089	Kane County	30 586
16	16750	055	Kootenai County	34 514	17	12385		Champaign city	67 518
16	39700		Idaho Falls city	50 730	17	12385	019	Champaign County	67 518
16	39700	019	Bonneville County	50 730	17	14000		Chicago city	2 896 016
16	46540		Lewiston city	30 904	17	14000	031	Cook County	2 896 014
16	46540	069	Nez Perce County	30 904	17	14000	043	DuPage County	2
16	52120		Meridian city	34 919	17	14026		Chicago Heights city	32 776
16	52120	001	Ada County	34 919	17	14026	031	Cook County	32 776
16	56260		Nampa city	51 867	17	14351		Cicero town	85 616
16	56260	027	Canyon County	51 867	17	14351	031	Cook County	85 616
16	64090		Pocatello city	51 466	17	17887		Crystal Lake city	38 000
16	64090	005	Bannock County	51 442	17	17887	111	McHenry County	38 000
16	64090	077	Power County	24	17	18563		Danville city	33 904
16	82810		Twin Falls city	34 469	17	18563	183	Vermilion County	33 904
16	82810	083	Twin Falls County	34 469	17	18823		Decatur city	81 860
17			**ILLINOIS**	12 419 293	17	18823	115	Macon County	81 860
17	00243		Addison village	35 914	17	19161		DeKalb city	39 018
17	00243	043	DuPage County	35 914	17	19161	037	DeKalb County	39 018
17	01114		Alton city	30 496	17	19642		Des Plaines city	58 720
17	01114	119	Madison County	30 496	17	19642	031	Cook County	58 720
17	02154		Arlington Heights village	76 031	17	20292		Dolton village	25 614
17	02154	031	Cook County	76 031	17	20292	031	Cook County	25 614
17	02154	097	Lake County	0	17	20591		Downers Grove village	48 724
17	03012		Aurora city	142 990	17	20591	043	DuPage County	48 724
17	03012	043	DuPage County	38 905	17	22255		East St. Louis city	31 542
17	03012	089	Kane County	100 290	17	22255	163	St. Clair County	31 542
17	03012	093	Kendall County	840					
17	03012	197	Will County	2 955					

Cities by County — Continued

State Code	Place Code	County Code	Geographic Area Name	2000 Population	State Code	Place Code	County Code	Geographic Area Name	2000 Population
17	23074		Elgin city	94 487	17	51089		Mount Prospect village	56 265
17	23074	031	Cook County	20 474	17	51089	031	Cook County	56 265
17	23074	089	Kane County	74 013					
					17	51349		Mundelein village	30 935
17	23256		Elk Grove Village village	34 727	17	51349	097	Lake County	30 935
17	23256	031	Cook County	34 727					
17	23256	043	DuPage County	0	17	51622		Naperville city	128 358
					17	51622	043	DuPage County	90 984
17	23620		Elmhurst city	42 762	17	51622	197	Will County	37 374
17	23620	031	Cook County	0					
17	23620	043	DuPage County	42 762	17	53000		Niles village	30 068
					17	53000	031	Cook County	30 068
17	23724		Elmwood Park village	25 405					
17	23724	031	Cook County	25 405	17	53234		Normal town	45 386
					17	53234	113	McLean County	45 386
17	24582		Evanston city	74 239					
17	24582	031	Cook County	74 239	17	53481		Northbrook village	33 435
					17	53481	031	Cook County	33 435
17	27884		Freeport city	26 443					
17	27884	177	Stephenson County	26 443	17	53559		North Chicago city	35 918
					17	53559	097	Lake County	35 918
17	28326		Galesburg city	33 706					
17	28326	095	Knox County	33 706	17	54638		Oak Forest city	28 051
					17	54638	031	Cook County	28 051
17	29730		Glendale Heights village	31 765					
17	29730	043	DuPage County	31 765	17	54820		Oak Lawn village	55 245
					17	54820	031	Cook County	55 245
17	29756		Glen Ellyn village	26 999					
17	29756	043	DuPage County	26 999	17	54885		Oak Park village	52 524
					17	54885	031	Cook County	52 524
17	29938		Glenview village	41 847					
17	29938	031	Cook County	41 847	17	56640		Orland Park village	51 077
					17	56640	031	Cook County	51 071
17	30926		Granite City city	31 301	17	56640	197	Will County	6
17	30926	119	Madison County	31 301					
					17	57225		Palatine village	65 479
17	32018		Gurnee village	28 834	17	57225	031	Cook County	65 479
17	32018	097	Lake County	28 834					
					17	57875		Park Ridge city	37 775
17	32746		Hanover Park village	38 278	17	57875	031	Cook County	37 775
17	32746	031	Cook County	20 755					
17	32746	043	DuPage County	17 523	17	58447		Pekin city	33 857
					17	58447	143	Peoria County	0
17	33383		Harvey city	30 000	17	58447	179	Tazewell County	33 857
17	33383	031	Cook County	30 000					
					17	59000		Peoria city	112 936
17	34722		Highland Park city	31 365	17	59000	143	Peoria County	112 936
17	34722	097	Lake County	31 365					
					17	62367		Quincy city	40 366
17	35411		Hoffman Estates village	49 495	17	62367	001	Adams County	40 366
17	35411	031	Cook County	49 495					
17	35411	089	Kane County	0	17	65000		Rockford city	150 115
					17	65000	201	Winnebago County	150 115
17	38570		Joliet city	106 221					
17	38570	093	Kendall County	624	17	65078		Rock Island city	39 684
17	38570	197	Will County	105 597	17	65078	161	Rock Island County	39 684
17	38934		Kankakee city	27 491	17	66040		Round Lake Beach village	25 859
17	38934	091	Kankakee County	27 491	17	66040	097	Lake County	25 859
17	42028		Lansing village	28 332	17	66703		St. Charles city	27 896
17	42028	031	Cook County	28 332	17	66703	043	DuPage County	169
					17	66703	089	Kane County	27 727
17	44407		Lombard village	42 322					
17	44407	043	DuPage County	42 322	17	68003		Schaumburg village	75 386
					17	68003	031	Cook County	75 386
17	47774		Maywood village	26 987	17	68003	043	DuPage County	0
17	47774	031	Cook County	26 987					
					17	70122		Skokie village	63 348
17	49867		Moline city	43 768	17	70122	031	Cook County	63 348
17	49867	161	Rock Island County	43 768					

State Code	Place Code	County Code	Geographic Area Name	2000 Population	State Code	Place Code	County Code	Geographic Area Name	2000 Population
17	72000		Springfield city	111 454	18	34114		Hobart city	25 363
17	72000	167	Sangamon County	111 454	18	34114	089	Lake County	25 363
17	73157		Streamwood village	36 407	18	36000		Indianapolis city	791 926
17	73157	031	Cook County	36 407					
					18	38358		Jeffersonville city	27 362
17	75484		Tinley Park village	48 401	18	38358	019	Clark County	27 362
17	75484	031	Cook County	45 887					
17	75484	197	Will County	2 514	18	40392		Kokomo city	46 113
					18	40392	067	Howard County	46 113
17	77005		Urbana city	36 395					
17	77005	019	Champaign County	36 395	18	40788		Lafayette city	56 397
					18	40788	157	Tippecanoe County	56 397
17	79293		Waukegan city	87 901					
17	79293	097	Lake County	87 901	18	42426		Lawrence city	38 915
					18	42426	097	Marion County	38 915
17	81048		Wheaton city	55 416					
17	81048	043	DuPage County	55 416	18	46908		Marion city	31 320
					18	46908	053	Grant County	31 320
17	81087		Wheeling village	34 496					
17	81087	031	Cook County	34 496	18	48528		Merrillville town	30 560
17	81087	097	Lake County	0	18	48528	089	Lake County	30 560
17	82075		Wilmette village	27 651	18	48798		Michigan City city	32 900
17	82075	031	Cook County	27 651	18	48798	091	LaPorte County	32 900
17	83245		Woodridge village	30 934	18	49932		Mishawaka city	46 557
17	83245	031	Cook County	0	18	49932	141	St. Joseph County	46 557
17	83245	043	DuPage County	30 934					
17	83245	197	Will County	0	18	51876		Muncie city	67 430
					18	51876	035	Delaware County	67 430
18			**INDIANA**	6 080 485					
18	01468		Anderson city	59 734	18	52326		New Albany city	37 603
18	01468	095	Madison County	59 734	18	52326	043	Floyd County	37 603
18	05860		Bloomington city	69 291	18	54180		Noblesville city	28 590
18	05860	105	Monroe County	69 291	18	54180	057	Hamilton County	28 590
18	10342		Carmel city	37 733	18	61092		Portage city	33 496
18	10342	057	Hamilton County	37 733	18	61092	127	Porter County	33 496
18	14734		Columbus city	39 059	18	64260		Richmond city	39 124
18	14734	005	Bartholomew County	39 059	18	64260	177	Wayne County	39 124
18	19486		East Chicago city	32 414	18	71000		South Bend city	107 789
18	19486	089	Lake County	32 414	18	71000	141	St. Joseph County	107 789
18	20728		Elkhart city	51 874	18	75428		Terre Haute city	59 614
18	20728	039	Elkhart County	51 874	18	75428	167	Vigo County	59 614
18	22000		Evansville city	121 582	18	78326		Valparaiso city	27 428
18	22000	163	Vanderburgh County	121 582	18	78326	127	Porter County	27 428
18	23278		Fishers town	37 835	18	82862		West Lafayette city	28 778
18	23278	057	Hamilton County	37 835	18	82862	157	Tippecanoe County	28 778
18	25000		Fort Wayne city	205 727	19			**IOWA**	2 926 324
18	25000	003	Allen County	205 727	19	01855		Ames city	50 731
					19	01855	169	Story County	50 731
18	27000		Gary city	102 746					
18	27000	089	Lake County	102 746	19	02305		Ankeny city	27 117
					19	02305	153	Polk County	27 117
18	28386		Goshen city	29 383					
18	28386	039	Elkhart County	29 383	19	06355		Bettendorf city	31 275
					19	06355	163	Scott County	31 275
18	29898		Greenwood city	36 037					
18	29898	081	Johnson County	36 037	19	09550		Burlington city	26 839
					19	09550	057	Des Moines County	26 839
18	31000		Hammond city	83 048					
18	31000	089	Lake County	83 048	19	11755		Cedar Falls city	36 145
					19	11755	013	Black Hawk County	36 145

Cities by County — Continued

State Code	Place Code	County Code	Geographic Area Name	2000 Population	State Code	Place Code	County Code	Geographic Area Name	2000 Population
19	12000		Cedar Rapids city	120 758					
19	12000	113	Linn County	120 758	20	39350		Lenexa city	40 238
					20	39350	091	Johnson County	40 238
19	14430		Clinton city	27 772					
19	14430	045	Clinton County	27 772	20	44250		Manhattan city	44 831
					20	44250	149	Pottawatomie County	3
19	16860		Council Bluffs city	58 268	20	44250	161	Riley County	44 828
19	16860	155	Pottawattamie County	58 268					
					20	52575		Olathe city	92 962
19	19000		Davenport city	98 359	20	52575	091	Johnson County	92 962
19	19000	163	Scott County	98 359					
					20	53775		Overland Park city	149 080
19	21000		Des Moines city	198 682	20	53775	091	Johnson County	149 080
19	21000	153	Polk County	198 682					
					20	62700		Salina city	45 679
19	22395		Dubuque city	57 686	20	62700	169	Saline County	45 679
19	22395	061	Dubuque County	57 686					
					20	64500		Shawnee city	47 996
19	28515		Fort Dodge city	25 136	20	64500	091	Johnson County	47 996
19	28515	187	Webster County	25 136					
					20	71000		Topeka city	122 377
19	38595		Iowa City city	62 220	20	71000	177	Shawnee County	122 377
19	38595	103	Johnson County	62 220					
					20	79000		Wichita city	344 284
19	49485		Marion city	26 294	20	79000	173	Sedgwick County	344 284
19	49485	113	Linn County	26 294					
					21			**KENTUCKY**	4 041 769
19	49755		Marshalltown city	26 009	21	08902		Bowling Green city	49 296
19	49755	127	Marshall County	26 009	21	08902	227	Warren County	49 296
19	50160		Mason City city	29 172	21	17848		Covington city	43 370
19	50160	033	Cerro Gordo County	29 172	21	17848	117	Kenton County	43 370
19	73335		Sioux City city	85 013	21	28900		Frankfort city	27 741
19	73335	149	Plymouth County	0	21	28900	073	Franklin County	27 741
19	73335	193	Woodbury County	85 013					
					21	35866		Henderson city	27 373
19	79950		Urbandale city	29 072	21	35866	101	Henderson County	27 373
19	79950	049	Dallas County	327					
19	79950	153	Polk County	28 745	21	37918		Hopkinsville city	30 089
					21	37918	047	Christian County	30 089
19	82425		Waterloo city	68 747					
19	82425	013	Black Hawk County	68 747	21	40222		Jeffersontown city	26 633
					21	40222	111	Jefferson County	26 633
19	83910		West Des Moines city	46 403					
19	83910	049	Dallas County	3 878	21	46027		Lexington-Fayette	260 512
19	83910	153	Polk County	42 525	21	46027	067	Fayette County	260 512
20			**KANSAS**	2 688 418	21	48000		Louisville city	256 231
20	18250		Dodge City city	25 176	21	48000	111	Jefferson County	256 231
20	18250	057	Ford County	25 176					
					21	58620		Owensboro city	54 067
20	21275		Emporia city	26 760	21	58620	059	Daviess County	54 067
20	21275	111	Lyon County	26 760					
					21	58836		Paducah city	26 307
20	25325		Garden City city	28 451	21	58836	145	McCracken County	26 307
20	25325	055	Finney County	28 451					
					21	65226		Richmond city	27 152
20	33625		Hutchinson city	40 787	21	65226	151	Madison County	27 152
20	33625	155	Reno County	40 787					
					22			**LOUISIANA**	4 468 976
20	36000		Kansas City city	146 866	22	00975		Alexandria city	46 342
20	36000	209	Wyandotte County	146 866	22	00975	079	Rapides Parish	46 342
20	38900		Lawrence city	80 098	22	05000		Baton Rouge city	227 818
20	38900	045	Douglas County	80 098	22	05000	033	East Baton Rouge Parish	227 818
20	39000		Leavenworth city	35 420	22	08920		Bossier City city	56 461
20	39000	103	Leavenworth County	35 420	22	08920	015	Bossier Parish	56 461
20	39075		Leawood city	27 656	22	36255		Houma city	32 393
20	39075	091	Johnson County	27 656	22	36255	109	Terrebonne Parish	32 393

State Code	Place Code	County Code	Geographic Area Name	2000 Population	State Code	Place Code	County Code	Geographic Area Name	2000 Population
					25	07000		Boston city	589 141
22	39475		Kenner city	70 517	25	07000	025	Suffolk County	589 141
22	39475	051	Jefferson Parish	70 517					
					25	09000		Brockton city	94 304
22	40735		Lafayette city	110 257	25	09000	023	Plymouth County	94 304
22	40735	055	Lafayette Parish	110 257					
					25	11000		Cambridge city	101 355
22	41155		Lake Charles city	71 757	25	11000	017	Middlesex County	101 355
22	41155	019	Calcasieu Parish	71 757					
					25	13205		Chelsea city	35 080
22	51410		Monroe city	53 107	25	13205	025	Suffolk County	35 080
22	51410	073	Ouachita Parish	53 107					
					25	13660		Chicopee city	54 653
22	54035		New Iberia city	32 623	25	13660	013	Hampden County	54 653
22	54035	045	Iberia Parish	32 623					
					25	21990		Everett city	38 037
22	55000		New Orleans city	484 674	25	21990	017	Middlesex County	38 037
22	55000	071	Orleans Parish	484 674					
					25	23000		Fall River city	91 938
22	70000		Shreveport city	200 145	25	23000	005	Bristol County	91 938
22	70000	015	Bossier Parish	734					
22	70000	017	Caddo Parish	199 411	25	23875		Fitchburg city	39 102
					25	23875	027	Worcester County	39 102
22	70805		Slidell city	25 695					
22	70805	103	St. Tammany Parish	25 695	25	25100		Franklin city	29 560
					25	25100	021	Norfolk County	29 560
23			**MAINE**	1 274 923					
23	02795		Bangor city	31 473	25	26150		Gloucester city	30 273
23	02795	019	Penobscot County	31 473	25	26150	009	Essex County	30 273
23	38740		Lewiston city	35 690	25	29405		Haverhill city	58 969
23	38740	001	Androscoggin County	35 690	25	29405	009	Essex County	58 969
23	60545		Portland city	64 249	25	30840		Holyoke city	39 838
23	60545	005	Cumberland County	64 249	25	30840	013	Hampden County	39 838
24			**MARYLAND**	5 296 486	25	34550		Lawrence city	72 043
24	01600		Annapolis city	35 838	25	34550	009	Essex County	72 043
24	01600	003	Anne Arundel County	35 838					
					25	35075		Leominster city	41 303
24	04000		Baltimore city	651 154	25	35075	027	Worcester County	41 303
24	04000	510	Baltimore city	651 154					
					25	37000		Lowell city	105 167
24	08775		Bowie city	50 269	25	37000	017	Middlesex County	105 167
24	08775	033	Prince George's County	50 269					
					25	37490		Lynn city	89 050
24	30325		Frederick city	52 767	25	37490	009	Essex County	89 050
24	30325	021	Frederick County	52 767					
					25	37875		Malden city	56 340
24	31175		Gaithersburg city	52 613	25	37875	017	Middlesex County	56 340
24	31175	031	Montgomery County	52 613					
					25	38715		Marlborough city	36 255
24	36075		Hagerstown city	36 687	25	38715	017	Middlesex County	36 255
24	36075	043	Washington County	36 687					
					25	39835		Medford city	55 765
24	67675		Rockville city	47 388	25	39835	017	Middlesex County	55 765
24	67675	031	Montgomery County	47 388					
					25	40115		Melrose city	27 134
25			**MASSACHUSETTS**	6 349 097	25	40115	017	Middlesex County	27 134
25	00765		Agawam city	28 144					
25	00765	013	Hampden County	28 144	25	40710		Methuen city	43 789
					25	40710	009	Essex County	43 789
25	02690		Attleboro city	42 068					
25	02690	005	Bristol County	42 068	25	45000		New Bedford city	93 768
					25	45000	005	Bristol County	93 768
25	03600		Barnstable Town city	47 821					
25	03600	001	Barnstable County	47 821	25	45560		Newton city	83 829
					25	45560	017	Middlesex County	83 829
25	05595		Beverly city	39 862					
25	05595	009	Essex County	39 862	25	46330		Northampton city	28 978
					25	46330	015	Hampshire County	28 978

State Code	Place Code	County Code	Geographic Area Name	2000 Population	State Code	Place Code	County Code	Geographic Area Name	2000 Population
25	52490		Peabody city	48 129	26	29000		Flint city	124 943
25	52490	009	Essex County	48 129	26	29000	049	Genesee County	124 943
25	53960		Pittsfield city	45 793	26	31420		Garden City city	30 047
25	53960	003	Berkshire County	45 793	26	31420	163	Wayne County	30 047
25	55745		Quincy city	88 025	26	34000		Grand Rapids city	197 800
25	55745	021	Norfolk County	88 025	26	34000	081	Kent County	197 800
25	56585		Revere city	47 283	26	38640		Holland city	35 048
25	56585	025	Suffolk County	47 283	26	38640	005	Allegan County	7 202
					26	38640	139	Ottawa County	27 846
25	59105		Salem city	40 407					
25	59105	009	Essex County	40 407	26	40680		Inkster city	30 115
					26	40680	163	Wayne County	30 115
25	62535		Somerville city	77 478					
25	62535	017	Middlesex County	77 478	26	41420		Jackson city	36 316
					26	41420	075	Jackson County	36 316
25	67000		Springfield city	152 082					
25	67000	013	Hampden County	152 082	26	42160		Kalamazoo city	77 145
					26	42160	077	Kalamazoo County	77 145
25	69170		Taunton city	55 976					
25	69170	005	Bristol County	55 976	26	42820		Kentwood city	45 255
					26	42820	081	Kent County	45 255
25	72600		Waltham city	59 226					
25	72600	017	Middlesex County	59 226	26	46000		Lansing city	119 128
					26	46000	045	Eaton County	4 807
25	76030		Westfield city	40 072	26	46000	065	Ingham County	114 321
25	76030	013	Hampden County	40 072					
					26	47800		Lincoln Park city	40 008
25	81035		Woburn city	37 258	26	47800	163	Wayne County	40 008
25	81035	017	Middlesex County	37 258					
					26	49000		Livonia city	100 545
25	82000		Worcester city	172 648	26	49000	163	Wayne County	100 545
25	82000	027	Worcester County	172 648					
					26	50560		Madison Heights city	31 101
26			**MICHIGAN**	9 938 444	26	50560	125	Oakland County	31 101
26	01380		Allen Park city	29 376					
26	01380	163	Wayne County	29 376	26	53780		Midland city	41 685
					26	53780	017	Bay County	222
26	03000		Ann Arbor city	114 024	26	53780	111	Midland County	41 463
26	03000	161	Washtenaw County	114 024					
					26	56020		Mount Pleasant city	25 946
26	05920		Battle Creek city	53 364	26	56020	073	Isabella County	25 946
26	05920	025	Calhoun County	53 364					
					26	56320		Muskegon city	40 105
26	06020		Bay City city	36 817	26	56320	121	Muskegon County	40 105
26	06020	017	Bay County	36 817					
					26	59440		Novi city	47 386
26	12060		Burton city	30 308	26	59440	125	Oakland County	47 386
26	12060	049	Genesee County	30 308					
					26	59920		Oak Park city	29 793
26	21000		Dearborn city	97 775	26	59920	125	Oakland County	29 793
26	21000	163	Wayne County	97 775					
					26	65440		Pontiac city	66 337
26	21020		Dearborn Heights city	58 264	26	65440	125	Oakland County	66 337
26	21020	163	Wayne County	58 264					
					26	65560		Portage city	44 897
26	22000		Detroit city	951 270	26	65560	077	Kalamazoo County	44 897
26	22000	163	Wayne County	951 270					
					26	65820		Port Huron city	32 338
26	24120		East Lansing city	46 525	26	65820	147	St. Clair County	32 338
26	24120	037	Clinton County	34					
26	24120	065	Ingham County	46 491	26	69035		Rochester Hills city	68 825
					26	69035	125	Oakland County	68 825
26	24290		Eastpointe city	34 077					
26	24290	099	Macomb County	34 077	26	69800		Roseville city	48 129
					26	69800	099	Macomb County	48 129
26	27440		Farmington Hills city	82 111					
26	27440	125	Oakland County	82 111	26	70040		Royal Oak city	60 062
					26	70040	125	Oakland County	60 062

State Code	Place Code	County Code	Geographic Area Name	2000 Population	State Code	Place Code	County Code	Geographic Area Name	2000 Population
26	70520		Saginaw city	61 799	27	18188		Edina city	47 425
26	70520	145	Saginaw County	61 799	27	18188	053	Hennepin County	47 425
26	70760		St. Clair Shores city	63 096	27	22814		Fridley city	27 449
26	70760	099	Macomb County	63 096	27	22814	003	Anoka County	27 449
26	74900		Southfield city	78 296	27	31076		Inver Grove Heights city	29 751
26	74900	125	Oakland County	78 296	27	31076	037	Dakota County	29 751
26	74960		Southgate city	30 136	27	35180		Lakeville city	43 128
26	74960	163	Wayne County	30 136	27	35180	037	Dakota County	43 128
26	76460		Sterling Heights city	124 471	27	39878		Mankato city	32 427
26	76460	099	Macomb County	124 471	27	39878	013	Blue Earth County	32 427
					27	39878	079	Le Sueur County	0
26	79000		Taylor city	65 868	27	39878	103	Nicollet County	0
26	79000	163	Wayne County	65 868					
					27	40166		Maple Grove city	50 365
26	80700		Troy city	80 959	27	40166	053	Hennepin County	50 365
26	80700	125	Oakland County	80 959					
					27	40382		Maplewood city	34 947
26	84000		Warren city	138 247	27	40382	123	Ramsey County	34 947
26	84000	099	Macomb County	138 247					
					27	43000		Minneapolis city	382 618
26	86000		Westland city	86 602	27	43000	053	Hennepin County	382 618
26	86000	163	Wayne County	86 602					
					27	43252		Minnetonka city	51 301
26	88900		Wyandotte city	28 006	27	43252	053	Hennepin County	51 301
26	88900	163	Wayne County	28 006					
					27	43864		Moorhead city	32 177
26	88940		Wyoming city	69 368	27	43864	027	Clay County	32 177
26	88940	081	Kent County	69 368					
					27	47680		Oakdale city	26 653
27			**MINNESOTA**	4 919 479	27	47680	163	Washington County	26 653
27	01486		Andover city	26 588					
27	01486	003	Anoka County	26 588	27	51730		Plymouth city	65 894
					27	51730	053	Hennepin County	65 894
27	01900		Apple Valley city	45 527					
27	01900	037	Dakota County	45 527	27	54214		Richfield city	34 439
					27	54214	053	Hennepin County	34 439
27	06382		Blaine city	44 942					
27	06382	003	Anoka County	44 942	27	54880		Rochester city	85 806
27	06382	123	Ramsey County	0	27	54880	109	Olmsted County	85 806
27	06616		Bloomington city	85 172	27	55852		Roseville city	33 690
27	06616	053	Hennepin County	85 172	27	55852	123	Ramsey County	33 690
27	07948		Brooklyn Center city	29 172	27	56896		St. Cloud city	59 107
27	07948	053	Hennepin County	29 172	27	56896	009	Benton County	6 391
					27	56896	141	Sherburne County	5 982
27	07966		Brooklyn Park city	67 388	27	56896	145	Stearns County	46 734
27	07966	053	Hennepin County	67 388					
					27	57220		St. Louis Park city	44 126
27	08794		Burnsville city	60 220	27	57220	053	Hennepin County	44 126
27	08794	037	Dakota County	60 220					
					27	58000		St. Paul city	287 151
27	13114		Coon Rapids city	61 607	27	58000	123	Ramsey County	287 151
27	13114	003	Anoka County	61 607					
					27	59998		Shoreview city	25 924
27	13456		Cottage Grove city	30 582	27	59998	123	Ramsey County	25 924
27	13456	163	Washington County	30 582					
					27	71032		Winona city	27 069
27	17000		Duluth city	86 918	27	71032	169	Winona County	27 069
27	17000	137	St. Louis County	86 918					
					27	71428		Woodbury city	46 463
27	17288		Eagan city	63 557	27	71428	163	Washington County	46 463
27	17288	037	Dakota County	63 557					
					28			**MISSISSIPPI**	2 844 658
27	18116		Eden Prairie city	54 901	28	06220		Biloxi city	50 644
27	18116	053	Hennepin County	54 901	28	06220	047	Harrison County	50 644

State Code	Place Code	County Code	Geographic Area Name	2000 Population	State Code	Place Code	County Code	Geographic Area Name	2000 Population
28	15380		Columbus city	25 944	29	38000		Kansas City city	441 545
28	15380	087	Lowndes County	25 944	29	38000	037	Cass County	104
					29	38000	047	Clay County	84 009
28	29180		Greenville city	41 633	29	38000	095	Jackson County	322 806
28	29180	151	Washington County	41 633	29	38000	165	Platte County	34 626
28	29700		Gulfport city	71 127	29	39044		Kirkwood city	27 324
28	29700	047	Harrison County	71 127	29	39044	189	St. Louis County	27 324
28	31020		Hattiesburg city	44 779	29	41348		Lee's Summit city	70 700
28	31020	035	Forrest County	42 475	29	41348	037	Cass County	1 180
28	31020	073	Lamar County	2 304	29	41348	095	Jackson County	69 520
28	36000		Jackson city	184 256	29	42032		Liberty city	26 232
28	36000	049	Hinds County	183 723	29	42032	047	Clay County	26 232
28	36000	089	Madison County	533					
28	36000	121	Rankin County	0	29	46586		Maryland Heights city	25 756
					29	46586	189	St. Louis County	25 756
28	46640		Meridian city	39 968					
28	46640	075	Lauderdale County	39 968	29	54074		O'Fallon city	46 169
					29	54074	183	St. Charles County	46 169
28	55360		Pascagoula city	26 200					
28	55360	059	Jackson County	26 200	29	60788		Raytown city	30 388
					29	60788	095	Jackson County	30 388
28	69280		Southaven city	28 977					
28	69280	033	DeSoto County	28 977	29	64082		St. Charles city	60 321
					29	64082	183	St. Charles County	60 321
28	74840		Tupelo city	34 211					
28	74840	081	Lee County	34 211	29	64550		St. Joseph city	73 990
					29	64550	021	Buchanan County	73 990
28	76720		Vicksburg city	26 407					
28	76720	149	Warren County	26 407	29	65000		St. Louis city	348 189
					29	65000	510	St. Louis city	348 189
29			**MISSOURI**	5 595 211					
29	03160		Ballwin city	31 283	29	65126		St. Peters city	51 381
29	03160	189	St. Louis County	31 283	29	65126	183	St. Charles County	51 381
29	06652		Blue Springs city	48 080	29	70000		Springfield city	151 580
29	06652	095	Jackson County	48 080	29	70000	043	Christian County	4
					29	70000	077	Greene County	151 576
29	11242		Cape Girardeau city	35 349					
29	11242	031	Cape Girardeau County	35 349	29	75220		University City city	37 428
29	11242	201	Scott County	0	29	75220	189	St. Louis County	37 428
29	13600		Chesterfield city	46 802	29	79820		Wildwood city	32 884
29	13600	189	St. Louis County	46 802	29	79820	189	St. Louis County	32 884
29	15670		Columbia city	84 531	30			**MONTANA**	902 195
29	15670	019	Boone County	84 531	30	06550		Billings city	89 847
					30	06550	111	Yellowstone County	89 847
29	24778		Florissant city	50 497					
29	24778	189	St. Louis County	50 497	30	08950		Bozeman city	27 509
					30	08950	031	Gallatin County	27 509
29	27190		Gladstone city	26 365					
29	27190	047	Clay County	26 365	30	11390		Butte-Silver Bow	34 606
29	31276		Hazelwood city	26 206	30	32800		Great Falls city	56 690
29	31276	189	St. Louis County	26 206	30	32800	013	Cascade County	56 690
29	35000		Independence city	113 288	30	35600		Helena city	25 780
29	35000	047	Clay County	0	30	35600	049	Lewis and Clark County	25 780
29	35000	095	Jackson County	113 288					
					30	50200		Missoula city	57 053
29	37000		Jefferson City city	39 636	30	50200	063	Missoula County	57 053
29	37000	027	Callaway County	25					
29	37000	051	Cole County	39 611	31			**NEBRASKA**	1 711 263
					31	03950		Bellevue city	44 382
29	37592		Joplin city	45 504	31	03950	153	Sarpy County	44 382
29	37592	097	Jasper County	40 433					
29	37592	145	Newton County	5 071	31	17670		Fremont city	25 174
					31	17670	053	Dodge County	25 174

State Code	Place Code	County Code	Geographic Area Name	2000 Population	State Code	Place Code	County Code	Geographic Area Name	2000 Population
31	19595		Grand Island city	42 940	34	22470		Fair Lawn borough	31 637
31	19595	079	Hall County	42 940	34	22470	003	Bergen County	31 637
31	25055		Kearney city............................	27 431	34	24420		Fort Lee borough........................	35 461
31	25055	019	Buffalo County	27 431	34	24420	003	Bergen County	35 461
31	28000		Lincoln city............................	225 581	34	25770		Garfield city	29 786
31	28000	109	Lancaster County	225 581	34	25770	003	Bergen County	29 786
31	37000		Omaha city..............................	390 007	34	28680		Hackensack city	42 677
31	37000	055	Douglas County	390 007	34	28680	003	Bergen County	42 677
32			**NEVADA**.............................	1 998 257	34	32250		Hoboken city..............................	38 577
32	09700		Carson City.............................	52 457	34	32250	017	Hudson County	38 577
32	09700	510	Carson City	52 457	34	36000		Jersey City city	240 055
32	31900		Henderson city	175 381	34	36000	017	Hudson County	240 055
32	31900	003	Clark County...........................	175 381	34	36510		Kearny town	40 513
32	40000		Las Vegas city........................	478 434	34	36510	017	Hudson County	40 513
32	40000	003	Clark County...........................	478 434	34	40350		Linden city	39 394
32	51800		North Las Vegas city.................	115 488	34	40350	039	Union County	39 394
32	51800	003	Clark County...........................	115 488	34	41310		Long Branch city	31 340
32	60600		Reno city.................................	180 480	34	41310	025	Monmouth County	31 340
32	60600	031	Washoe County	180 480	34	46680		Millville city	26 847
32	68400		Sparks city..............................	66 346	34	46680	011	Cumberland County	26 847
32	68400	031	Washoe County	66 346	34	51000		Newark city...............................	273 546
33			**NEW HAMPSHiRE**..........................	1 235 786	34	51000	013	Essex County	273 546
33	14200		Concord city	40 687	34	51210		New Brunswick city	48 573
33	14200	013	Merrimack County	40 687	34	51210	023	Middlesex County	48 573
33	18820		Dover city	26 884	34	55950		Paramus borough	25 737
33	18820	017	Strafford County.......................	26 884	34	55950	003	Bergen County	25 737
33	45140		Manchester city	107 006	34	56550		Passaic city	67 861
33	45140	011	Hillsborough County	107 006	34	56550	031	Passaic County	67 861
33	50260		Nashua city.............................	86 605	34	57000		Paterson city.............................	149 222
33	50260	011	Hillsborough County	86 605	34	57000	031	Passaic County	149 222
33	65140		Rochester city...........................	28 461	34	58200		Perth Amboy city	47 303
33	65140	017	Strafford County.......................	28 461	34	58200	023	Middlesex County	47 303
34			**NEW JERSEY**	8 414 350	34	59190		Plainfield city	47 829
34	02080		Atlantic City city.........................	40 517	34	59190	039	Union County	47 829
34	02080	001	Atlantic County.........................	40 517	34	61530		Rahway city	26 500
34	03580		Bayonne city............................	61 842	34	61530	039	Union County	26 500
34	03580	017	Hudson County	61 842	34	65790		Sayreville borough......................	40 377
34	05170		Bergenfield borough....................	26 247	34	65790	023	Middlesex County	40 377
34	05170	003	Bergen County	26 247	34	74000		Trenton city...............................	85 403
34	10000		Camden city	79 904	34	74000	021	Mercer County	85 403
34	10000	007	Camden County.......................	79 904	34	74630		Union City city	67 088
34	13690		Clifton city................................	78 672	34	74630	017	Hudson County	67 088
34	13690	031	Passaic County	78 672	34	76070		Vineland city	56 271
34	19390		East Orange city........................	69 824	34	76070	011	Cumberland County	56 271
34	19390	013	Essex County..........................	69 824	34	79040		Westfield town	29 644
34	21000		Elizabeth city............................	120 568	34	79040	039	Union County	29 644
34	21000	039	Union County	120 568	34	79610		West New York town....................	45 768
34	21480		Englewood city.........................	26 203	34	79610	017	Hudson County	45 768
34	21480	003	Bergen County	26 203					

State Code	Place Code	County Code	Geographic Area Name	2000 Population	State Code	Place Code	County Code	Geographic Area Name	2000 Population
35			**NEW MEXICO**	1 819 046	36	49121		Mount Vernon city	68 381
35	01780		Alamogordo city..........................	35 582	36	49121	119	Westchester County	68 381
35	01780	035	Otero County	35 582					
					36	50034		Newburgh city...........................	28 259
35	02000		Albuquerque city........................	448 607	36	50034	071	Orange County	28 259
35	02000	001	Bernalillo County	448 607					
					36	50617		New Rochelle city......................	72 182
35	12150		Carlsbad city.............................	25 625	36	50617	119	Westchester County	72 182
35	12150	015	Eddy County	25 625					
					36	51000		New York city...........................	8008 278
35	16420		Clovis city	32 667	36	51000	005	Bronx County	1332 650
35	16420	009	Curry County	32 667	36	51000	047	Kings County	2465 326
					36	51000	061	New York County....................	1537 195
35	25800		Farmington city..........................	37 844	36	51000	081	Queens County	2229 379
35	25800	045	San Juan County	37 844	36	51000	085	Richmond County	443 728
35	32520		Hobbs city................................	28 657	36	51055		Niagara Falls city......................	55 593
35	32520	025	Lea County	28 657	36	51055	063	Niagara County	55 593
35	39380		Las Cruces city..........................	74 267	36	53682		North Tonawanda city	33 262
35	39380	013	Dona Ana County	74 267	36	53682	063	Niagara County	33 262
35	63460		Rio Rancho city	51 765	36	59223		Port Chester village....................	27 867
35	63460	001	Bernalillo County	0	36	59223	119	Westchester County	27 867
35	63460	043	Sandoval County	51 765					
					36	59641		Poughkeepsie city	29 871
35	64930		Roswell city..............................	45 293	36	59641	027	Dutchess County	29 871
35	64930	005	Chaves County	45 293					
					36	63000		Rochester city...........................	219 773
35	70500		Santa Fe city	62 203	36	63000	055	Monroe County	219 773
35	70500	049	Santa Fe County.....................	62 203					
					36	63418		Rome city	34 950
36			**NEW YORK**	18 976 457	36	63418	065	Oneida County	34 950
36	01000		Albany city...............................	95 658					
36	01000	001	Albany County	95 658	36	65255		Saratoga Springs city	26 186
					36	65255	091	Saratoga County	26 186
36	03078		Auburn city	28 574					
36	03078	011	Cayuga County	28 574	36	65508		Schenectady city	61 821
					36	65508	093	Schenectady County................	61 821
36	06607		Binghamton city	47 380					
36	06607	007	Broome County	47 380	36	70420		Spring Valley village...................	25 464
					36	70420	087	Rockland County	25 464
36	11000		Buffalo city	292 648					
36	11000	029	Erie County	292 648	36	73000		Syracuse city............................	147 306
					36	73000	067	Onondaga County...................	147 306
36	24229		Elmira city...............................	30 940					
36	24229	015	Chemung County	30 940	36	75484		Troy city...................................	49 170
					36	75484	083	Rensselaer County	49 170
36	27485		Freeport village..........................	43 783					
36	27485	059	Nassau County	43 783	36	76540		Utica city..................................	60 651
					36	76540	065	Oneida County	60 651
36	29113		Glen Cove city...........................	26 622					
36	29113	059	Nassau County	26 622	36	76705		Valley Stream village..................	36 368
					36	76705	059	Nassau County	36 368
36	33139		Hempstead village......................	56 554					
36	33139	059	Nassau County	56 554	36	78608		Watertown city	26 705
					36	78608	045	Jefferson County	26 705
36	38077		Ithaca city	29 287					
36	38077	109	Tompkins County....................	29 287	36	81677		White Plains city........................	53 077
					36	81677	119	Westchester County	53 077
36	38264		Jamestown city..........................	31 730					
36	38264	013	Chautauqua County.................	31 730	36	84000		Yonkers city..............................	196 086
					36	84000	119	Westchester County	196 086
36	42554		Lindenhurst village	27 819					
36	42554	103	Suffolk County	27 819	37			**NORTH CAROLINA**	8 049 313
					37	02140		Asheville city............................	68 889
36	43335		Long Beach city.........................	35 462	37	02140	021	Buncombe County	68 889
36	43335	059	Nassau County	35 462					
					37	09060		Burlington city............................	44 917
36	47042		Middletown city	25 388	37	09060	001	Alamance County	44 917
36	47042	071	Orange County	25 388					

State Code	Place Code	County Code	Geographic Area Name	2000 Population	State Code	Place Code	County Code	Geographic Area Name	2000 Population
37	10740		Cary town	94 536	37	75000		Winston-Salem city	185 776
37	10740	037	Chatham County	19	37	75000	067	Forsyth County	185 776
37	10740	183	Wake County	94 517	38			**NORTH DAKOTA**	642 200
37	11800		Chapel Hill town	48 715	38	07200		Bismarck city	55 532
37	11800	063	Durham County	1 917	38	07200	015	Burleigh County	55 532
37	11800	135	Orange County	46 798	38	25700		Fargo city	90 599
37	12000		Charlotte city	540 828	38	25700	017	Cass County	90 599
37	12000	119	Mecklenburg County	540 828	38	32060		Grand Forks city	49 321
37	14100		Concord city	55 977	38	32060	035	Grand Forks County	49 321
37	14100	025	Cabarrus County	55 977	38	53380		Minot city	36 567
37	19000		Durham city	187 035	38	53380	101	Ward County	36 567
37	19000	063	Durham County	186 996	39			**OHIO**	11 353 140
37	19000	135	Orange County	39	39	01000		Akron city	217 074
37	19000	183	Wake County	0	39	01000	153	Summit County	217 074
37	22920		Fayetteville city	121 015	39	03828		Barberton city	27 899
37	22920	051	Cumberland County	121 015	39	03828	153	Summit County	27 899
37	25580		Gastonia city	66 277	39	04720		Beavercreek city	37 984
37	25580	071	Gaston County	66 277	39	04720	057	Greene County	37 984
37	26880		Goldsboro city	39 043	39	07972		Bowling Green city	29 636
37	26880	191	Wayne County	39 043	39	07972	173	Wood County	29 636
37	28000		Greensboro city	223 891	39	09680		Brunswick city	33 388
37	28000	081	Guilford County	223 891	39	09680	103	Medina County	33 388
37	28080		Greenville city	60 476	39	12000		Canton city	80 806
37	28080	147	Pitt County	60 476	39	12000	151	Stark County	80 806
37	31060		Hickory city	37 222	39	15000		Cincinnati city	331 285
37	31060	023	Burke County	63	39	15000	061	Hamilton County	331 285
37	31060	027	Caldwell County	14	39	16000		Cleveland city	478 403
37	31060	035	Catawba County	37 145	39	16000	035	Cuyahoga County	478 403
37	31400		High Point city	85 839	39	16014		Cleveland Heights city	49 958
37	31400	057	Davidson County	1 163	39	16014	035	Cuyahoga County	49 958
37	31400	067	Forsyth County	6	39	18000		Columbus city	711 470
37	31400	081	Guilford County	84 656	39	18000	041	Delaware County	1 891
37	31400	151	Randolph County	14	39	18000	045	Fairfield County	7 447
37	34200		Jacksonville city	66 715	39	18000	049	Franklin County	702 132
37	34200	133	Onslow County	66 715	39	19778		Cuyahoga Falls city	49 374
37	35200		Kannapolis city	36 910	39	19778	153	Summit County	49 374
37	35200	025	Cabarrus County	27 890	39	21000		Dayton city	166 179
37	35200	159	Rowan County	9 020	39	21000	113	Montgomery County	166 179
37	43920		Monroe city	26 228	39	21434		Delaware city	25 243
37	43920	179	Union County	26 228	39	21434	041	Delaware County	25 243
37	55000		Raleigh city	276 093	39	22694		Dublin city	31 392
37	55000	063	Durham County	0	39	22694	041	Delaware County	4 283
37	55000	183	Wake County	276 093	39	22694	049	Franklin County	27 087
37	57500		Rocky Mount city	55 893	39	22694	159	Union County	22
37	57500	065	Edgecombe County	17 297	39	23380		East Cleveland city	27 217
37	57500	127	Nash County	38 596	39	23380	035	Cuyahoga County	27 217
37	58860		Salisbury city	26 462	39	25256		Elyria city	55 953
37	58860	159	Rowan County	26 462	39	25256	093	Lorain County	55 953
37	74440		Wilmington city	75 838	39	25704		Euclid city	52 717
37	74440	129	New Hanover County	75 838	39	25704	035	Cuyahoga County	52 717
37	74540		Wilson city	44 405					
37	74540	195	Wilson County	44 405					

State Code	Place Code	County Code	Geographic Area Name	2000 Population	State Code	Place Code	County Code	Geographic Area Name	2000 Population
39	25914		Fairborn city	32 052					
39	25914	057	Greene County	32 052	39	57008		North Royalton city	28 648
					39	57008	035	Cuyahoga County	28 648
39	25970		Fairfield city	42 097					
39	25970	017	Butler County	42 097	39	61000		Parma city	85 655
39	25970	061	Hamilton County	0	39	61000	035	Cuyahoga County	85 655
39	27048		Findlay city	38 967	39	66390		Reynoldsburg city	32 069
39	27048	063	Hancock County	38 967	39	66390	045	Fairfield County	0
					39	66390	049	Franklin County	26 388
39	29106		Gahanna city	32 636	39	66390	089	Licking County	5 681
39	29106	049	Franklin County	32 636					
					39	70380		Sandusky city	27 844
39	29428		Garfield Heights city	30 734	39	70380	043	Erie County	27 844
39	29428	035	Cuyahoga County	30 734					
					39	71682		Shaker Heights city	29 405
39	32592		Grove City city	27 075	39	71682	035	Cuyahoga County	29 405
39	32592	049	Franklin County	27 075					
					39	74118		Springfield city	65 358
39	33012		Hamilton city	60 690	39	74118	023	Clark County	65 358
39	33012	017	Butler County	60 690					
					39	74944		Stow city	32 139
39	36610		Huber Heights city	38 212	39	74944	153	Summit County	32 139
39	36610	109	Miami County	35					
39	36610	113	Montgomery County	38 177	39	75098		Strongsville city	43 858
					39	75098	035	Cuyahoga County	43 858
39	39872		Kent city	27 906					
39	39872	133	Portage County	27 906	39	77000		Toledo city	313 619
					39	77000	095	Lucas County	313 619
39	40040		Kettering city	57 502					
39	40040	057	Greene County	0	39	77504		Trotwood city	27 420
39	40040	113	Montgomery County	57 502	39	77504	113	Montgomery County	27 420
39	41664		Lakewood city	56 646	39	79002		Upper Arlington city	33 686
39	41664	035	Cuyahoga County	56 646	39	79002	049	Franklin County	33 686
39	41720		Lancaster city	35 335	39	80892		Warren city	46 832
39	41720	045	Fairfield County	35 335	39	80892	155	Trumbull County	46 832
39	43554		Lima city	40 081	39	83342		Westerville city	35 318
39	43554	003	Allen County	40 081	39	83342	041	Delaware County	5 900
					39	83342	049	Franklin County	29 418
39	44856		Lorain city	68 652					
39	44856	093	Lorain County	68 652	39	83622		Westlake city	31 719
					39	83622	035	Cuyahoga County	31 719
39	47138		Mansfield city	49 346					
39	47138	139	Richland County	49 346	39	88000		Youngstown city	82 026
					39	88000	099	Mahoning County	82 026
39	47306		Maple Heights city	26 156	39	88000	155	Trumbull County	0
39	47306	035	Cuyahoga County	26 156					
					39	88084		Zanesville city	25 586
39	47754		Marion city	35 318	39	88084	119	Muskingum County	25 586
39	47754	101	Marion County	35 318					
					40			**OKLAHOMA**	3 450 654
39	48244		Massillon city	31 325	40	04450		Bartlesville city	34 748
39	48244	151	Stark County	31 325	40	04450	113	Osage County	2
					40	04450	147	Washington County	34 746
39	48790		Medina city	25 139					
39	48790	103	Medina County	25 139	40	09050		Broken Arrow city	74 859
					40	09050	143	Tulsa County	67 791
39	49056		Mentor city	50 278	40	09050	145	Wagoner County	7 068
39	49056	085	Lake County	50 278					
					40	23200		Edmond city	68 315
39	49840		Middletown city	51 605	40	23200	109	Oklahoma County	68 315
39	49840	017	Butler County	49 574					
39	49840	165	Warren County	2 031	40	23950		Enid city	47 045
					40	23950	047	Garfield County	47 045
39	54040		Newark city	46 279					
39	54040	089	Licking County	46 279	40	41850		Lawton city	92 757
					40	41850	031	Comanche County	92 757
39	56882		North Olmsted city	34 113					
39	56882	035	Cuyahoga County	34 113					

State Code	Place Code	County Code	Geographic Area Name	2000 Population	State Code	Place Code	County Code	Geographic Area Name	2000 Population
40	48350		Midwest City city	54 088					
40	48350	109	Oklahoma County	54 088	41	59000		Portland city	529 121
					41	59000	005	Clackamas County	747
40	49200		Moore city	41 138	41	59000	051	Multnomah County	526 986
40	49200	027	Cleveland County	41 138	41	59000	067	Washington County	1 388
40	50050		Muskogee city	38 310	41	64900		Salem city	136 924
40	50050	101	Muskogee County	38 310	41	64900	047	Marion County	119 040
					41	64900	053	Polk County	17 884
40	52500		Norman city	95 694					
40	52500	027	Cleveland County	95 694	41	69600		Springfield city	52 864
					41	69600	039	Lane County	52 864
40	55000		Oklahoma City city	506 132					
40	55000	017	Canadian County	26 311	41	73650		Tigard city	41 223
40	55000	027	Cleveland County	47 271	41	73650	067	Washington County	41 223
40	55000	109	Oklahoma County	432 498					
40	55000	125	Pottawatomie County	52	42			**PENNSYLVANIA**	12 281 054
					42	02000		Allentown city	106 632
40	59850		Ponca City city	25 919	42	02000	077	Lehigh County	106 632
40	59850	071	Kay County	25 919					
40	59850	113	Osage County	0	42	02184		Altoona city	49 523
					42	02184	013	Blair County	49 523
40	66800		Shawnee city	28 692					
40	66800	125	Pottawatomie County	28 692	42	06064		Bethel Park borough	33 556
					42	06064	003	Allegheny County	33 556
40	70300		Stillwater city	39 065					
40	70300	119	Payne County	39 065	42	06088		Bethlehem city	71 329
					42	06088	077	Lehigh County	19 029
40	75000		Tulsa city	393 049	42	06088	095	Northampton County	52 300
40	75000	113	Osage County	5 630					
40	75000	131	Rogers County	0	42	13208		Chester city	36 854
40	75000	143	Tulsa County	387 419	42	13208	045	Delaware County	36 854
41			**OREGON**	3 421 399	42	21648		Easton city	26 263
41	01000		Albany city	40 852	42	21648	095	Northampton County	26 263
41	01000	003	Benton County	5 104					
41	01000	043	Linn County	35 748	42	24000		Erie city	103 717
					42	24000	049	Erie County	103 717
41	05350		Beaverton city	76 129					
41	05350	067	Washington County	76 129	42	32800		Harrisburg city	48 950
					42	32800	043	Dauphin County	48 950
41	05800		Bend city	52 029					
41	05800	017	Deschutes County	52 029	42	41216		Lancaster city	56 348
					42	41216	071	Lancaster County	56 348
41	15800		Corvallis city	49 322					
41	15800	003	Benton County	49 322	42	52330		Municipality of Monroeville borough	29 349
41	23850		Eugene city	137 893	42	52330	003	Allegheny County	29 349
41	23850	039	Lane County	137 893					
					42	53368		New Castle city	26 309
41	31250		Gresham city	90 205	42	53368	073	Lawrence County	26 309
41	31250	051	Multnomah County	90 205					
					42	54656		Norristown borough	31 282
41	34100		Hillsboro city	70 186	42	54656	091	Montgomery County	31 282
41	34100	067	Washington County	70 186					
					42	60000		Philadelphia city	1 517 550
41	38500		Keizer city	32 203	42	60000	101	Philadelphia County	1 517 550
41	38500	047	Marion County	32 203					
					42	61000		Pittsburgh city	334 563
41	40550		Lake Oswego city	35 278	42	61000	003	Allegheny County	334 563
41	40550	005	Clackamas County	32 989					
41	40550	051	Multnomah County	2 274	42	61536		Plum borough	26 940
41	40550	067	Washington County	15	42	61536	003	Allegheny County	26 940
41	45000		McMinnville city	26 499	42	63624		Reading city	81 207
41	45000	071	Yamhill County	26 499	42	63624	011	Berks County	81 207
41	47000		Medford city	63 154	42	69000		Scranton city	76 415
41	47000	029	Jackson County	63 154	42	69000	069	Lackawanna County	76 415
41	55200		Oregon City city	25 754	42	73808		State College borough	38 420
41	55200	005	Clackamas County	25 754	42	73808	027	Centre County	38 420

State Code	Place Code	County Code	Geographic Area Name	2000 Population	State Code	Place Code	County Code	Geographic Area Name	2000 Population
42	85152		Wilkes-Barre city	43 123	45	70270		Summerville town	27 752
42	85152	079	Luzerne County	43 123	45	70270	015	Berkeley County	945
					45	70270	019	Charleston County	20
42	85312		Williamsport city	30 706	45	70270	035	Dorchester County	26 787
42	85312	081	Lycoming County	30 706					
					45	70405		Sumter city	39 643
42	87048		York city	40 862	45	70405	085	Sumter County	39 643
42	87048	133	York County	40 862					
					46			**SOUTH DAKOTA**	754 844
44			**RHODE ISLAND**	1 048 319	46	52980		Rapid City city	59 607
44	19180		Cranston city	79 269	46	52980	103	Pennington County	59 607
44	19180	007	Providence County	79 269					
					46	59020		Sioux Falls city	123 975
44	22960		East Providence city....................	48 688	46	59020	083	Lincoln County	6 620
44	22960	007	Providence County	48 688	46	59020	099	Minnehaha County	117 355
44	49960		Newport city..................................	26 475	47			**TENNESSEE**	5 689 283
44	49960	005	Newport County	26 475	47	03440		Bartlett city	40 543
					47	03440	157	Shelby County	40 543
44	54640		Pawtucket city	72 958					
44	54640	007	Providence County	72 958	47	14000		Chattanooga city	155 554
					47	14000	065	Hamilton County	155 554
44	59000		Providence city	173 618	47	14000	115	Marion County	0
44	59000	007	Providence County	173 618					
					47	15160		Clarksville city.............................	103 455
44	74300		Warwick city	85 808	47	15160	125	Montgomery County	103 455
44	74300	003	Kent County	85 808					
					47	15400		Cleveland city	37 192
44	80780		Woonsocket city	43 224	47	15400	011	Bradley County	37 192
44	80780	007	Providence County	43 224					
					47	16420		Collierville town	31 872
45			**SOUTH CAROLINA**	4 012 012	47	16420	157	Shelby County	31 872
45	00550		Aiken city	25 337					
45	00550	003	Aiken County	25 337	47	16540		Columbia city	33 055
					47	16540	119	Maury County	33 055
45	01360		Anderson city................................	25 514					
45	01360	007	Anderson County	25 514	47	27740		Franklin city	41 842
					47	27740	187	Williamson County	41 842
45	13330		Charleston city.............................	96 650					
45	13330	015	Berkeley County	1 122	47	28960		Germantown city	37 348
45	13330	019	Charleston County	95 528	47	28960	157	Shelby County	37 348
45	16000		Columbia city	116 278	47	33280		Hendersonville city	40 620
45	16000	063	Lexington County	402	47	33280	165	Sumner County	40 620
45	16000	079	Richland County	115 876					
					47	37640		Jackson city	59 643
45	25810		Florence city	30 248	47	37640	113	Madison County	59 643
45	25810	041	Florence County	30 248					
					47	38320		Johnson City city	55 469
45	29815		Goose Creek city	29 208	47	38320	019	Carter County	1 138
45	29815	015	Berkeley County	29 208	47	38320	163	Sullivan County	240
45	29815	019	Charleston County	0	47	38320	179	Washington County	54 091
45	30850		Greenville city	56 002	47	39560		Kingsport city	44 905
45	30850	045	Greenville County	56 002	47	39560	073	Hawkins County	2 907
					47	39560	163	Sullivan County	41 998
45	34045		Hilton Head Island town	33 862					
45	34045	013	Beaufort County	33 862	47	40000		Knoxville city..............................	173 890
					47	40000	093	Knox County	173 890
45	48535		Mount Pleasant town....................	47 609					
45	48535	019	Charleston County	47 609	47	48000		Memphis city	650 100
					47	48000	157	Shelby County	650 100
45	50875		North Charleston city....................	79 641					
45	50875	019	Charleston County	76 244	47	51560		Murfreesboro city........................	68 816
45	50875	035	Dorchester County	3 397	47	51560	149	Rutherford County	68 816
45	61405		Rock Hill city	49 765	47	52004		Nashville-Davidson......................	569 891
45	61405	091	York County	49 765					
					47	55120		Oak Ridge city............................	27 387
45	68290		Spartanburg city	39 673	47	55120	001	Anderson County	24 610
45	68290	083	Spartanburg County..................	39 673	47	55120	145	Roane County	2 777

State Code	Place Code	County Code	Geographic Area Name	2000 Population	State Code	Place Code	County Code	Geographic Area Name	2000 Population
47	69420		Smyrna town	25 569	48	17000		Corpus Christi city	277 454
47	69420	149	Rutherford County	25 569	48	17000	273	Kleberg County	0
					48	17000	355	Nueces County	277 450
48			**TEXAS**	20 851 820	48	17000	409	San Patricio County	4
48	01000		Abilene city	115 930					
48	01000	253	Jones County	5 488	48	19000		Dallas city	1188 580
48	01000	441	Taylor County	110 442	48	19000	085	Collin County	45 155
					48	19000	113	Dallas County	1121 131
48	01924		Allen city	43 554	48	19000	121	Denton County	22 273
48	01924	085	Collin County	43 554	48	19000	257	Kaufman County	0
					48	19000	397	Rockwall County	21
48	03000		Amarillo city	173 627					
48	03000	375	Potter County	99 833	48	19624		Deer Park city	28 520
48	03000	381	Randall County	73 794	48	19624	201	Harris County	28 520
48	04000		Arlington city	332 969	48	19792		Del Rio city	33 867
48	04000	439	Tarrant County	332 969	48	19792	465	Val Verde County	33 867
48	05000		Austin city	656 562	48	19972		Denton city	80 537
48	05000	453	Travis County	644 752	48	19972	121	Denton County	80 537
48	05000	491	Williamson County	11 810					
					48	20092		DeSoto city	37 646
48	06128		Baytown city	66 430	48	20092	113	Dallas County	37 646
48	06128	071	Chambers County	3 081					
48	06128	201	Harris County	63 349	48	21628		Duncanville city	36 081
					48	21628	113	Dallas County	36 081
48	07000		Beaumont city	113 866					
48	07000	245	Jefferson County	113 866	48	22660		Edinburg city	48 465
					48	22660	215	Hidalgo County	48 465
48	07132		Bedford city	47 152					
48	07132	439	Tarrant County	47 152	48	24000		El Paso city	563 662
					48	24000	141	El Paso County	563 662
48	08236		Big Spring city	25 233					
48	08236	227	Howard County	25 233	48	24768		Euless city	46 005
					48	24768	439	Tarrant County	46 005
48	10768		Brownsville city	139 722					
48	10768	061	Cameron County	139 722	48	25452		Farmers Branch city	27 508
					48	25452	113	Dallas County	27 508
48	10912		Bryan city	65 660					
48	10912	041	Brazos County	65 660	48	26232		Flower Mound town	50 702
					48	26232	121	Denton County	50 702
48	13024		Carrollton city	109 576	48	26232	439	Tarrant County	0
48	13024	085	Collin County	0					
48	13024	113	Dallas County	49 822	48	27000		Fort Worth city	534 694
48	13024	121	Denton County	59 754	48	27000	121	Denton County	44
					48	27000	439	Tarrant County	534 650
48	13492		Cedar Hill city	32 093					
48	13492	113	Dallas County	32 044	48	27648		Friendswood city	29 037
48	13492	139	Ellis County	49	48	27648	167	Galveston County	21 237
					48	27648	201	Harris County	7 800
48	13552		Cedar Park city	26 049					
48	13552	453	Travis County	541	48	27684		Frisco city	33 714
48	13552	491	Williamson County	25 508	48	27684	085	Collin County	30 312
					48	27684	121	Denton County	3 402
48	15364		Cleburne city	26 005					
48	15364	251	Johnson County	26 005	48	28068		Galveston city	57 247
					48	28068	167	Galveston County	57 247
48	15976		College Station city	67 890					
48	15976	041	Brazos County	67 890	48	29000		Garland city	215 768
					48	29000	085	Collin County	0
48	16432		Conroe city	36 811	48	29000	113	Dallas County	215 768
48	16432	339	Montgomery County	36 811	48	29000	397	Rockwall County	0
48	16612		Coppell city	35 958	48	29336		Georgetown city	28 339
48	16612	113	Dallas County	35 734	48	29336	491	Williamson County	28 339
48	16612	121	Denton County	224					
					48	30464		Grand Prairie city	127 427
48	16624		Copperas Cove city	29 592	48	30464	113	Dallas County	99 760
48	16624	027	Bell County	0	48	30464	139	Ellis County	46
48	16624	099	Coryell County	29 455	48	30464	439	Tarrant County	27 621
48	16624	281	Lampasas County	137					

State Code	Place Code	County Code	Geographic Area Name	2000 Population
48	30644		Grapevine city	42 059
48	30644	113	Dallas County	0
48	30644	121	Denton County	2
48	30644	439	Tarrant County	42 057
48	31928		Haltom City city	39 018
48	31928	439	Tarrant County	39 018
48	32372		Harlingen city	57 564
48	32372	061	Cameron County	57 564
48	35000		Houston city	1953 631
48	35000	157	Fort Bend County	33 384
48	35000	201	Harris County	1919 789
48	35000	339	Montgomery County	458
48	35528		Huntsville city	35 078
48	35528	471	Walker County	35 078
48	35576		Hurst city	36 273
48	35576	439	Tarrant County	36 273
48	37000		Irving city	191 615
48	37000	113	Dallas County	191 615
48	38632		Keller city	27 345
48	38632	439	Tarrant County	27 345
48	39148		Killeen city	86 911
48	39148	027	Bell County	86 911
48	39352		Kingsville city	25 575
48	39352	273	Kleberg County	25 575
48	40588		Lake Jackson city	26 386
48	40588	039	Brazoria County	26 386
48	41212		Lancaster city	25 894
48	41212	113	Dallas County	25 894
48	41440		La Porte city	31 880
48	41440	201	Harris County	31 880
48	41464		Laredo city	176 576
48	41464	479	Webb County	176 576
48	41980		League City city	45 444
48	41980	167	Galveston County	45 306
48	41980	201	Harris County	138
48	42508		Lewisville city	77 737
48	42508	113	Dallas County	2
48	42508	121	Denton County	77 735
48	43888		Longview city	73 344
48	43888	183	Gregg County	71 746
48	43888	203	Harrison County	1 598
48	45000		Lubbock city	199 564
48	45000	303	Lubbock County	199 564
48	45072		Lufkin city	32 709
48	45072	005	Angelina County	32 709
48	45384		McAllen city	106 414
48	45384	215	Hidalgo County	106 414
48	45744		McKinney city	54 369
48	45744	085	Collin County	54 369
48	46452		Mansfield city	28 031
48	46452	139	Ellis County	129
48	46452	251	Johnson County	622
48	46452	439	Tarrant County	27 280
48	47892		Mesquite city	124 523
48	47892	113	Dallas County	124 522
48	47892	257	Kaufman County	1
48	48072		Midland city	94 996
48	48072	317	Martin County	0
48	48072	329	Midland County	94 996
48	48768		Mission city	45 408
48	48768	215	Hidalgo County	45 408
48	48804		Missouri City city	52 913
48	48804	157	Fort Bend County	47 419
48	48804	201	Harris County	5 494
48	50256		Nacogdoches city	29 914
48	50256	347	Nacogdoches County	29 914
48	50820		New Braunfels city	36 494
48	50820	091	Comal County	35 328
48	50820	187	Guadalupe County	1 166
48	52356		North Richland Hills city	55 635
48	52356	439	Tarrant County	55 635
48	53388		Odessa city	90 943
48	53388	135	Ector County	89 901
48	53388	329	Midland County	1 042
48	55080		Paris city	25 898
48	55080	277	Lamar County	25 898
48	56000		Pasadena city	141 674
48	56000	201	Harris County	141 674
48	56348		Pearland city	37 640
48	56348	039	Brazoria County	35 696
48	56348	157	Fort Bend County	0
48	56348	201	Harris County	1 944
48	57200		Pharr city	46 660
48	57200	215	Hidalgo County	46 660
48	58016		Plano city	222 030
48	58016	085	Collin County	219 890
48	58016	121	Denton County	2 140
48	58820		Port Arthur city	57 755
48	58820	245	Jefferson County	57 755
48	58820	361	Orange County	0
48	61796		Richardson city	91 802
48	61796	085	Collin County	20 873
48	61796	113	Dallas County	70 929
48	63500		Round Rock city	61 136
48	63500	453	Travis County	1 076
48	63500	491	Williamson County	60 060
48	63572		Rowlett city	44 503
48	63572	113	Dallas County	37 462
48	63572	397	Rockwall County	7 041
48	64472		San Angelo city	88 439
48	64472	451	Tom Green County	88 439
48	65000		San Antonio city	1144 646
48	65000	029	Bexar County	1144 646
48	65000	091	Comal County	0

State Code	Place Code	County Code	Geographic Area Name	2000 Population	State Code	Place Code	County Code	Geographic Area Name	2000 Population
					49	57300		Orem city	84 324
48	65516		San Juan city	26 229	49	57300	049	Utah County	84 324
48	65516	215	Hidalgo County	26 229					
					49	62470		Provo city	105 166
48	65600		San Marcos city	34 733	49	62470	049	Utah County	105 166
48	65600	055	Caldwell County	0					
48	65600	209	Hays County	34 733	49	64340		Riverton city	25 011
					49	64340	035	Salt Lake County	25 011
48	67496		Sherman city	35 082					
48	67496	181	Grayson County	35 082	49	65110		Roy city	32 885
					49	65110	057	Weber County	32 885
48	68636		Socorro city	27 152					
48	68636	141	El Paso County	27 152	49	65330		St. George city	49 663
					49	65330	053	Washington County	49 663
48	70808		Sugar Land city	63 328					
48	70808	157	Fort Bend County	63 328	49	67000		Salt Lake City city	181 743
					49	67000	035	Salt Lake County	181 743
48	72176		Temple city	54 514					
48	72176	027	Bell County	54 514	49	67440		Sandy city	88 418
					49	67440	035	Salt Lake County	88 418
48	72368		Texarkana city	34 782					
48	72368	037	Bowie County	34 782	49	70850		South Jordan city	29 437
					49	70850	035	Salt Lake County	29 437
48	72392		Texas City city	41 521					
48	72392	071	Chambers County	0	49	75360		Taylorsville city	57 439
48	72392	167	Galveston County	41 521	49	75360	035	Salt Lake County	57 439
48	72530		The Colony city	26 531	49	82950		West Jordan city	68 336
48	72530	121	Denton County	26 531	49	82950	035	Salt Lake County	68 336
48	74144		Tyler city	83 650	49	83470		West Valley City city	108 896
48	74144	423	Smith County	83 650	49	83470	035	Salt Lake County	108 896
48	75428		Victoria city	60 603	50			**VERMONT**	608 827
48	75428	469	Victoria County	60 603	50	10675		Burlington city	38 889
					50	10675	007	Chittenden County	38 889
48	76000		Waco city	113 726					
48	76000	309	McLennan County	113 726	51			**VIRGINIA**	7 078 515
					51	01000		Alexandria city	128 283
48	77272		Weslaco city	26 935	51	01000	510	Alexandria city	128 283
48	77272	215	Hidalgo County	26 935					
					51	07784		Blacksburg town	39 573
48	79000		Wichita Falls city	104 197	51	07784	121	Montgomery County	39 573
48	79000	485	Wichita County	104 197					
					51	14968		Charlottesville city	45 049
49			**UTAH**	2 233 169	51	14968	540	Charlottesville city	45 049
49	07690		Bountiful city	41 301					
49	07690	011	Davis County	41 301	51	16000		Chesapeake city	199 184
					51	16000	550	Chesapeake city	199 184
49	13850		Clearfield city	25 974					
49	13850	011	Davis County	25 974	51	21344		Danville city	48 411
					51	21344	590	Danville city	48 411
49	20120		Draper city	25 220					
49	20120	035	Salt Lake County	25 220	51	35000		Hampton city	146 437
49	20120	049	Utah County	0	51	35000	650	Hampton city	146 437
49	43660		Layton city	58 474	51	35624		Harrisonburg city	40 468
49	43660	011	Davis County	58 474	51	35624	660	Harrisonburg city	40 468
49	45860		Logan city	42 670	51	44984		Leesburg town	28 311
49	45860	005	Cache County	42 670	51	44984	107	Loudoun County	28 311
49	49710		Midvale city	27 029	51	47672		Lynchburg city	65 269
49	49710	035	Salt Lake County	27 029	51	47672	680	Lynchburg city	65 269
49	53230		Murray city	34 024	51	48952		Manassas city	35 135
49	53230	035	Salt Lake County	34 024	51	48952	683	Manassas city	35 135
49	55980		Ogden city	77 226	51	56000		Newport News city	180 150
49	55980	057	Weber County	77 226	51	56000	700	Newport News city	180 150

State Code	Place Code	County Code	Geographic Area Name	2000 Population	State Code	Place Code	County Code	Geographic Area Name	2000 Population
51	57000		Norfolk city............................	234 403	53	51300		Olympia city............................	42 514
51	57000	710	Norfolk city.............................	234 403	53	51300	067	Thurston County	42 514
51	61832		Petersburg city........................	33 740	53	53545		Pasco city...............................	32 066
51	61832	730	Petersburg city........................	33 740	53	53545	021	Franklin County	32 066
51	64000		Portsmouth city.......................	100 565	53	56695		Puyallup city............................	33 011
51	64000	740	Portsmouth city........................	100 565	53	56695	053	Pierce County	33 011
51	67000		Richmond city..........................	197 790	53	57535		Redmond city..........................	45 256
51	67000	760	Richmond city..........................	197 790	53	57535	033	King County	45 256
51	68000		Roanoke city...........................	94 911	53	57745		Renton city	50 052
51	68000	770	Roanoke city............................	94 911	53	57745	033	King County	50 052
51	76432		Suffolk city..............................	63 677	53	58235		Richland city	38 708
51	76432	800	Suffolk city..............................	63 677	53	58235	005	Benton County	38 708
51	82000		Virginia Beach city....................	425 257	53	61115		Sammamish city.......................	34 104
51	82000	810	Virginia Beach city....................	425 257	53	61115	033	King County	34 104
53			**WASHINGTON**	5 894 121	53	63000		Seattle city..............................	563 374
53	03180		Auburn city	40 314	53	63000	033	King County	563 374
53	03180	033	King County	40 168					
53	03180	053	Pierce County	146	53	63960		Shoreline city..........................	53 025
					53	63960	033	King County	53 025
53	05210		Bellevue city	109 569					
53	05210	033	King County	109 569	53	67000		Spokane city............................	195 629
					53	67000	063	Spokane County	195 629
53	05280		Bellingham city	67 171					
53	05280	073	Whatcom County	67 171	53	70000		Tacoma city.............................	193 556
					53	70000	053	Pierce County	193 556
53	07380		Bothell city..............................	30 150					
53	07380	033	King County	16 185	53	74060		Vancouver city.........................	143 560
53	07380	061	Snohomish County	13 965	53	74060	011	Clark County	143 560
53	07695		Bremerton city.........................	37 259	53	75775		Walla Walla city........................	29 686
53	07695	035	Kitsap County	37 259	53	75775	071	Walla Walla County	29 686
53	17635		Des Moines city........................	29 267	53	77105		Wenatchee city........................	27 856
53	17635	033	King County	29 267	53	77105	007	Chelan County	27 856
53	20750		Edmonds city...........................	39 515	53	80010		Yakima city..............................	71 845
53	20750	061	Snohomish County	39 515	53	80010	077	Yakima County	71 845
53	22640		Everett city..............................	91 488	54			**WEST VIRGINIA**	1 808 344
53	22640	061	Snohomish County	91 488	54	14600		Charleston city.........................	53 421
					54	14600	039	Kanawha County	53 421
53	35275		Kennewick city.........................	54 693					
53	35275	005	Benton County	54 693	54	39460		Huntington city.........................	51 475
					54	39460	011	Cabell County	47 341
53	35415		Kent city.................................	79 524	54	39460	099	Wayne County	4 134
53	35415	033	King County	79 524					
					54	55756		Morgantown city	26 809
53	35940		Kirkland city............................	45 054	54	55756	061	Monongalia County	26 809
53	35940	033	King County	45 054					
					54	62140		Parkersburg city	33 099
53	36745		Lacey city...............................	31 226	54	62140	107	Wood County	33 099
53	36745	067	Thurston County	31 226					
					54	86452		Wheeling city...........................	31 419
53	40245		Longview city...........................	34 660	54	86452	051	Marshall County	360
53	40245	015	Cowlitz County	34 660	54	86452	069	Ohio County	31 059
53	40840		Lynnwood city..........................	33 847	55			**WISCONSIN**	5 363 675
53	40840	061	Snohomish County	33 847	55	02375		Appleton city...........................	70 087
					55	02375	015	Calumet County	10 974
53	43955		Marysville city..........................	25 315	55	02375	087	Outagamie County	58 301
53	43955	061	Snohomish County	25 315	55	02375	139	Winnebago County	812
53	47560		Mount Vernon city	26 232	55	06500		Beloit city................................	35 775
53	47560	057	Skagit County	26 232	55	06500	105	Rock County	35 775

Cities by County — Continued

State Code	Place Code	County Code	Geographic Area Name	2000 Population	State Code	Place Code	County Code	Geographic Area Name	2000 Population
55	10025		Brookfield city	38 649	55	56375		New Berlin city	38 220
55	10025	133	Waukesha County	38 649	55	56375	133	Waukesha County	38 220
55	22300		Eau Claire city	61 704	55	58800		Oak Creek city	28 456
55	22300	017	Chippewa County	1 910	55	58800	079	Milwaukee County	28 456
55	22300	035	Eau Claire County	59 794	55	60500		Oshkosh city	62 916
55	26275		Fond du Lac city	42 203	55	60500	139	Winnebago County	62 916
55	26275	039	Fond du Lac County	42 203					
					55	66000		Racine city	81 855
55	27300		Franklin city	29 494	55	66000	101	Racine County	81 855
55	27300	079	Milwaukee County	29 494					
					55	72975		Sheboygan city	50 792
55	31000		Green Bay city	102 313	55	72975	117	Sheboygan County	50 792
55	31000	009	Brown County	102 313					
					55	78650		Superior city	27 368
55	31175		Greenfield city	35 476	55	78650	031	Douglas County	27 368
55	31175	079	Milwaukee County	35 476					
					55	84250		Waukesha city	64 825
55	37825		Janesville city	59 498	55	84250	133	Waukesha County	64 825
55	37825	105	Rock County	59 498					
					55	84475		Wausau city	38 426
55	39225		Kenosha city	90 352	55	84475	073	Marathon County	38 426
55	39225	059	Kenosha County	90 352					
					55	84675		Wauwatosa city	47 271
55	40775		La Crosse city	51 818	55	84675	079	Milwaukee County	47 271
55	40775	063	La Crosse County	51 818					
					55	85300		West Allis city	61 254
55	48000		Madison city	208 054	55	85300	079	Milwaukee County	61 254
55	48000	025	Dane County	208 054					
					55	85350		West Bend city	28 152
55	48500		Manitowoc city	34 053	55	85350	131	Washington County	28 152
55	48500	071	Manitowoc County	34 053					
					56			**WYOMING**	493 782
55	51000		Menomonee Falls village	32 647	56	13150		Casper city	49 644
55	51000	133	Waukesha County	32 647	56	13150	025	Natrona County	49 644
55	53000		Milwaukee city	596 974	56	13900		Cheyenne city	53 011
55	53000	079	Milwaukee County	596 974	56	13900	021	Laramie County	53 011
55	53000	131	Washington County	0					
55	53000	133	Waukesha County	0	56	45050		Laramie city	27 204
					56	45050	001	Albany County	27 204

APPENDIX F
SOURCE NOTES AND EXPLANATIONS

TABLE A—STATES

Table A presents 327 items for the United States as a whole, each state, and the District of Columbia. The states are presented in alphabetical order.

The following documentation is provided in the order in which the items appear in the databases.

LAND AREA, Items 1 and 5
Source: U.S. Bureau of the Census

Land area measurements are shown to the nearest square kilometer. Land area includes dry land and land temporarily or partially covered by water, such as marshlands, swamps, and river floodplains.

POPULATION AND POPULATION CHANGE, Items 2; 29–31; and 33–37
Source: U.S. Bureau of the Census

The population data for 2001 are U.S. Bureau of the Census estimates of the resident population as of July 1 of that year.

The population data for 1980, 1990, and 2000 are from the decennial censuses and represent the resident population as of April 1, 1980, 1990, and 2000 respectively. The change in population between 2000 and 2001 is composed of (a) natural increase—the excess of births over deaths, and (b) net migration—the difference between the number of persons moving into a particular state and the number of persons moving out.

POPULATION PROJECTIONS, Item 32
Source: U.S. Bureau of the Census

The projection of the population in the year 2025 is based on the 1990 census counts and the 1994 estimates of state population. Separate assumptions about future trends were developed for each component of population change: births; deaths; internal migration; and international migration. The state projections are consistent with the national population projection. The data in this volume are the Bureau of the Census' "preferred series" (series A). Three alternative projection series are available from the Bureau of the Census.

Detailed data and information on projection methodology may be found in the Bureau of the Census publication *PPL-47, Population Projections for States, by Age, Sex, Race, and Hispanic Origin: 1995 to 2025*, Paul R. Campbell, U.S. Bureau of the Census, Washington, DC, 1996.

POPULATION AND POPULATION CHARACTERISTICS, Items 3–20 and 38–54
Source: U.S. Bureau of the Census—1990 and 2000 Censuses of Population and Housing

The data on **race** were derived from answers to the question on race that was asked of all people. The concept of race, as used by the Census Bureau, reflects self-identification by people according to the race or races with which they most closely identify. These categories are socio-political constructs and should not be interpreted as being scientific or anthropological in nature. Furthermore, the race categories include both racial and national-origin groups.

In the 2000 Census, respondents were offered the option of selecting one or more races. This was not the case in prior censuses, so comparisons should be made with caution. In Table A, columns 6 through 9 refer to individuals who identified with only one race. Columns 38 through 42 include racial categories from 1990 when each person indicated only one race.

The **White** population is defined as persons who indicated their race as white, as well as persons who did not classify themselves in one of the specific race categories listed on the questionnaire but entered a nationality such as Irish, German, Italian, Lebanese, Near Easterner, Arab, or Polish.

The **Black** population includes persons who indicated their race as "Black, African Am., or Negro", as well as persons who did not classify themselves in one of the specific race categories but reported entries such as African American, Afro American, Kenyan, Nigerian, or Haitian.

The **American Indian or Alaska Native** population includes persons who indicated their race as American Indian or Alaska Native, as well as persons who did not classify themselves in one of the specific race categories but reported entries such as Canadian Indian, French American Indian, Spanish-American Indian, Eskimo, Aleut, Alaska Indian, or any of the American Indian or Alaska Native tribes.

The **Asian** population includes persons who indicated their race as Asian Indian, Chinese, Filipino, Japanese, Korean, Vietnamese, or "Other Asian", as well as persons who provided write-in entries of such Asian groups as Cambodian, Laotian, Hmong, Pakistani, or Taiwanese. Also, persons who wrote in an entry indicating one of the specific categories were classified accordingly. The **Native Hawaiian or Other Pacific Islander** population includes persons who indicated their race as "Native Hawaiian", "Guamanian or Chamorro", "Samoan" or "Other Pacific Islander", as well as persons who reported entries such as Part Hawaiian, American Samoan, Fijian, Melanesian, or Tahitian. Also, persons who wrote in an entry indicating one of the specific categories were classified accordingly. In 1990, the **Asian** and **Native Hawaiian or Other**

Pacific Islander categories were combined as **Asian and Pacific Islander**. This volume uses the 1990 combination.

The population of **Some other race** includes all persons who indicated "Some other race" as well as persons who wrote in a category not included in the race categories described above, including entries such as multiracial, mixed, interracial, or a Hispanic/Latino group such as Mexican, Puerto Rican, or Cuban in the "Some other race" write-in space.

Changes in specific listing of racial categories, the new practice of allowing more than one selection in 2000, and the order in which questions appeared on the questionnaire, could all affect comparability between the 2000 and 1990 censuses.

The Hispanic population is based on a complete-count question that asked respondents "Is this person Spanish/Hispanic/Latino?" Persons marking any one of the four Hispanic categories (i.e., Mexican, Puerto Rican, Cuban, or other Spanish) are collectively referred to as Hispanic.

In the 2000 Census, the Hispanic Origin question was placed before the race question and specific instructions indicated that both questions should be answered. These changes were designed to improve accuracy, and may affect comparability with 1990 data.

The **foreign-born population** is based on birthplace and citizenship questions asked of a sample of persons in the 1990 census. **Foreign-born** includes persons not born in the United States, Puerto Rico, or an outlying area of the United States. Persons who were born in a foreign country but who have at least one American parent are not included.

Age is defined as age at last birthday (i.e., number of completed years from birth to April 1, 2000 for the 2000 Census.

The 2000 Census also asked for the specific date of birth of the respondent, and 2000 census procedures used the birth date for deriving age data. For this reason, it is likely that the 2000 data have fewer problems than prior censuses, such as a tendency to round ages or report the person's age on the date the questionnaire was filled out rather than on April 1.

HOUSEHOLDS, Items 21–27 and 55–59
Source: U.S. Bureau of the Census—1990 and 2000 Census of Population and Housing

A household consists of persons occupying a single housing unit. A housing unit is a house, an apartment, a group of rooms, or a single room occupied as separate living quarters. The occupants may be a single family, one person living alone, two or more families living together, or any other group of related or unrelated persons who share a housing unit. The number of households is the same as the number of year-round occupied housing units.

A family household consists of two or more persons, including the householder, who are related by birth, marriage, or adoption and who live together as one household; all such persons are considered as members of one family. A married-couple family is one in which the householder and spouse are enumerated as members of the same household.

The measure of persons per household is obtained by dividing the number of persons in households by the number of households or householders. The category **Female family householder** includes only female-headed family households with no spouse present. One person in each household is designated as the householder. In most cases, this is the person, or one of the persons, in whose name the home is owned, being bought, or rented. If there is no such person in the household, any adult household member 15 years old and over could be designated as the householder.

IMMIGRANTS, Item 28
Source: U.S. Department of Justice, Immigration and Naturalization Service

The number of immigrants by their state of intended residence is summarized from the administrative records of the Immigration and Naturalization Service. This information is compiled from immigrant visas and forms granting legal permanent resident status.

An **immigrant** is an alien admitted to the United States as a lawful permanent resident. Immigrants are those persons lawfully accorded the privilege of residing permanently in the United States. They may be newly-arrived individuals who were issued immigrant visas by the Department of State overseas or they may be U.S. residents who were admitted to permanent resident status in 2000 by the Immigration and Naturalization Service in the United States.

BIRTHS AND DEATHS, Items 60–66
Source: U.S. Centers for Disease Control

The registration of births, deaths, and other vital events in the United States is primarily a state and local function. The civil laws of every state provide for a continuous and permanent birth and death registration system. Through the National Vital Statistics System, the National Center for Health Statistics (NCHS) obtains data on births and deaths from the registration offices of each state, New York City, and the District of Columbia.

Birth and death statistics are limited to events occurring during the year. The data are by place of residence and exclude events occurring to nonresidents of the United States. Births or deaths that occur outside the United States are excluded.

Birth and death rates represent the number of births and deaths per 1,000 resident population enumerated as of April 1 for decennial census years and estimated as of July 1 for other years.

Figures for infant deaths include deaths of children under 1 year of age—they exclude fetal deaths. The infant death rate is per 1,000 live births.

The rates of almost all causes of disease, injury, and death vary by age. Age adjustment is a technique for "removing" the effects of age from crude rates, so as to allow meaningful comparisons across populations with different underlying age structures. For example, comparing the crude death rate in Florida to that of California is misleading, since the relatively older population in Florida will lead to a higher crude death rate. For such a comparison, age-adjusted rates would be preferable.

Age-adjusted rates are calculated by applying the age-specific rates of various populations to a single standard population. In this volume, the standard population is 2000. After many years of using 1940 as the standard population for age-adjusted death rates, the CDC has recently switched to 2000. For this reason, the 1999 age-adjusted rates are almost identical to the actual death rates.

PHYSICIANS, Items 67–68
Source: Health Market Science, Inc., as published in Bernan's *Health and Healthcare in the United States*, copyright 1999 NationsHealth Corporation, LLC. Reprinted with permission.

Physicians are health practitioners having the degree of M.D. (Doctor of Medicine) or D.O. (Doctor of Osteopathy) primarily engaged in the practice of general or specialized medicine or surgery. The rate of physicians per 100,000 resident population is an indicator of the supply of physicians within a geographic area.

HOSPITALS, Items 69–71
Source: Health Market Science, Inc., as published in Bernan's *Health and Healthcare in the United States*, copyright 2001 NationsHealth Corporation, LLC. Reprinted with permission.

Hospitals are licensed institutions with at least six beds whose primary function is to provide diagnostic and therapeutic patient services for medical conditions by an organized physician staff, and have continuous nursing services under the supervision of registered nurses. Only short term general hospitals are included in these figures.

A hospital bed is any bed that is licensed for use by inpatients. The count of beds in a facility typically represents the count of beds at the end of reporting period (e.g., a year) regardless of whether it is operational or not. The number of hospitals beds per 100,000 population is a measure of the supply of hospitals beds within a geographic area.

MEDICARE ENROLLEES, Item 72
Source: Centers for Medicare and Medicaid Services (CMS)

The Centers for Medicare and Medicaid Services (CMS) administers Medicare which provides health insurance to people aged 65 and over and those who have permanent kidney failure and certain people with disabilities. Medicare has two parts: Hospital Insurance and Supplemental Medical Insurance. The numbers in this volume include persons enrolled in either or both parts of the program as of July 1, 2000, by their state of residence.

CRIME, Items 73–76
Source: U.S. Federal Bureau of Investigation— Uniform Crime Reports

Crime data are as reported to the FBI by law enforcement agencies and have not been adjusted for under-reporting. This may affect comparability between geographic areas or over time.

For some states, reporting by jurisdictions within the state is not sufficiently complete to be representative of the state as a whole, and state totals for these states have been estimated by the FBI.

Through the voluntary contribution of crime statistics by law enforcement agencies across the United States, the Uniform Crime Reporting (UCR) Program provides periodic assessments of crime in the nation as measured by offenses coming to the attention of the law enforcement community. The Committee on Uniform Crime Records of the International Association of Chiefs of Police initiated this voluntary national data-collection effort in 1930. UCR Program contributors compile and submit their crime data in 1 of 2 means: either directly to the FBI or through the state UCR Programs.

Seven offenses, because of their seriousness, frequency of occurrence, and likelihood of being reported to police, were initially selected to serve as an index for evaluating fluctuations in the volume of crime. These serious crimes were murder and nonnegligent manslaughter, forcible rape, robbery, aggravated assault, burglary, larceny/theft, and motor vehicle theft. By congressional mandate, arson was added as the eighth index offense in 1979. Arson is not included in the totals given in this volume.

Violent offenses include 4 crime categories: (1) Murder and nonnegligent manslaughter, as defined in the UCR Program, is the willful (nonnegligent) killing of one human being by another. This offense excludes deaths caused by negligence, suicide or accident; justifiable homicides; and attempts to murder or assaults to murder. (2) Forcible rape is the carnal knowledge of a female forcibly and against her will. Assaults or attempts to commit rape by force or threat of force are also included; however, statutory rape (without force) and other sex offenses are excluded. (3) Robbery is the taking or attempting to take anything of value from the care, custody, or control of a person or persons by force or threat of force or violence and/or by putting the victim in fear. (4) Aggravated assault is an unlawful attack by 1 person upon another for the purpose of inflicting severe or aggravated bodily injury. This type of assault is usually accompanied by the use of a weapon or by means likely to produce death or great bodily harm. Attempts are included since an injury does not necessarily have to result when a gun, knife, or other weapon is used, which could and probably would result in a serious personal injury if the crime were successfully completed.

Property crimes include 3 categories: (1) Burglary, or breaking and entering, is the unlawful entry of a structure to commit a felony or theft, even though no force was used to gain entrance. (2) Larceny/theft is the unauthorized taking of the personal property of another, without the use of force. (3) Motor vehicle theft is the unauthorized taking of any motor vehicle.

ELEMENTARY AND SECONDARY SCHOOL ENROLLMENT, Items 77–78
Source: U.S. Department of Education, National Center for Education Statistics; Common Core of Data for public schools, and Private School Survey for private schools.

Data on public school enrollment is from the *Common Core of Data* 1999–2000 survey while that for private elementary and secondary enrollment is from the *Private School Survey* of 1999–2000. The private school figures include grades kindergarten through grade 12, including special education, vocational/technical education and alternative schools. Excluded from private enrollment is prekindergarten enrollment or enrollment in schools that do not offer first grade or above. Public school enrollment includes prekindergarten through grade 12.

EDUCATIONAL ATTAINMENT, Items 79–82
Source: U.S. Bureau of the Census—1990 Census of Population and Housing for 1990 data and the Current Population Survey for 2000 data

The 1990 census data on educational attainment were obtained from a sample of the population.

Statistics for educational attainment are for persons 25 years old and over. The 1990 data were derived from a question on the 1990 census questionnaire that asked respondents for the highest level of school they had completed or the highest degree they had received. The 2000 data were derived from a similar question on the Current Population Survey. Persons who passed a high school equivalency examination were considered high school graduates. Schooling received in foreign schools was to be reported as the equivalent grade or years in the regular American school system.

LOCAL GOVERNMENT EDUCATION EXPENDITURES, Items 83–84
Source: U.S. Department of Education, National Center for Education Statistics, Common Core of Data

These data pertain to expenditures for public elementary and secondary education. Current expenditures includes expenditures for instruction, school administration, operation and maintenance, student transportation, food services, support services, adult education, and community services. Total expenditures also includes capital outlay and interest on debt. Current expenditures per pupil is the current expenditures divided by the number of students in membership as reported in the Common Core of Data Nonfiscal Survey for school year 1999–2000. Student membership is the count of students enrolled on or about October 1.

MONEY INCOME AND POVERTY, Items 85–95
Source: U.S. Bureau of the Census—2000 Census of Population and Housing for 1999 data and the Current Population Survey for 1998–2000 and 2000 data

The data on income and poverty are derived from the responses of a sample of persons 15 years and older. The data for 1999 are from the 2000 census "long form" sample—a sample large enough to permit publication of data for small geographic areas. The 1998–2000 and 2000 data were gathered each March from a national sample of about 60,000 households. These data are available for states but not for counties or cities.

Total money income is defined by the Bureau of the Census for statistical purposes as the sum of the following: wage or salary income; nonfarm self-employment income; net farm self-employment income; Social Security and railroad retirement income; public assistance income; and all other regularly received income such as interest, dividends, veterans payments, pensions, unemployment compensation, and alimony. Receipts not counted as income include various "lump sum" payments such as capital gains or inheritances.

The total represents the amount of income received before deductions for personal income taxes, Social Security, bond purchases, union dues, Medicare deductions, etc.

Per capita income for 1999 is based on resident population enumerated as of April 1, 2000.

Household income includes the income of the householder and all other persons 15 years and older in the household. Median household income is usually less than median family income because many households consist of only 1 person. The median divides the income distribution into 2 equal parts, 1 having incomes above the median, the other with incomes below.

The constant-dollar figures are based on an annual average Consumer Price Index from the Bureau of Labor Statistics. Constant-dollar figures are estimates representing an effort to remove the effects of price changes from statistical series reported in dollar terms. However, the estimates do not reflect the price and cost-of-living differences that may exist between areas.

Money income differs in definition from personal income (item 98). For example, money income does not include the pension rights, employer provided health insurance, food stamps, or Medicare payments that are included in personal income.

Poverty status is based on the definition prescribed by the U.S. Office of Management and Budget as the standard to be used by federal agencies for statistical purposes. Families and persons are classified as below the poverty level if their total family income or unrelated individual income was less than the poverty threshold specified for the applicable family size, age of householder, and number of related children under 18 present. The poverty threshold for a 4-person family was $17,209 in 1999 and $17,603 in 2000.

In the 2000 census, poverty status was determined for all families (and by implication all family members). For persons not in families, poverty status is determined by their income in relation to the appropriate poverty threshold. Inmates of institutions, persons in military group quarters or college dormitories, and unrelated individuals under age 15 are excluded.

PERSONS LACKING HEALTH INSURANCE, Items 96–97
Source: U.S. Bureau of the Census—Current Population Survey

The data on which these estimates are based were gathered in March 2001 from a national sample of about 60,000 households — the same sample from which the 2000 data on income and poverty were obtained. Data are available for states but not for counties or cities.

Those lacking coverage are the percent of the population of each state who were covered neither by private health plans nor by Medicaid, Medicare, or military health care.

PERSONAL INCOME AND EARNINGS, Items 98–122
Source: U.S. Bureau of Economic Analysis, Regional Economic Information System

Total personal income is the current income received by residents of an area from all sources. It is measured before deductions of income and other personal taxes but after deduction of personal contributions for Social Security, government retirement, and other social insurance programs. It consists of wage and salary disbursements (covering all employee earnings, including executive salaries, bonuses, commissions, payments-in-kind, incentive payments, and tips), various types of supplementary earnings, such as employers' contributions to pension funds, (termed "other labor income"); proprietors' income; rental income of persons; dividends; personal interest income; and government and business transfer payments.

Proprietors' income is the monetary income and income in-kind of proprietorships and partnerships, including the independent professions, and of tax-exempt cooperatives. **Dividends** are cash payments by corporations to stockholders who are U.S. residents. **Interest** is the monetary and imputed interest income of persons from all sources. **Rent** is the monetary income of persons from the rental of real property, except the income of persons primarily engaged in the real estate business, the imputed net rental income of owner-occupants of nonfarm dwellings, and the royalties received by persons.

Transfer payments are income for which services are not currently rendered. They consist of both government and business transfer payments. Government transfer payments include payments under the following programs: Federal Old-age, Survivors, and Disability Insurance ("Social Security"); Medicare and medical vendor payments; unemployment insurance, railroad and government retirement; federal and state government-insured workers' compensation; veterans benefits, including veterans life insurance; food stamps; black lung; Supplemental Security Income; and Aid to Families with Dependent Children. Government payments to nonprofit institutions, other than for work under research and development contracts, are also included. The principal business transfers are corporate gifts to nonprofit institutions and consumer bad debts.

Per capita personal income is based on resident population estimated as of July 1 of the year shown.

Personal tax payments includes taxes paid by individuals to federal, state, and local governments. Personal taxes include individual income taxes, estate and gift taxes, motor vehicle license taxes, and personal property taxes. Personal contributions to social insurance ("social security taxes") are not included, nor are sales taxes.

Disposable personal income equals personal income less personal tax payments. It is a measure of the income available to persons for spending or saving.

Earnings cover wage and salary disbursements, other labor income, and proprietors' income.

Data for earnings obtained from the Bureau of Economic Analysis (BEA) are based on place of work. In computing personal income, BEA makes an "adjustment for residence" to earnings, based on commuting patterns so that personal income is presented on a place of residence basis.

Farm earnings include the income of farm workers (wages and salaries and other labor income) and farm proprietors. Farm proprietors' income includes only the income of sole proprietorships and partnerships.

Farm earning estimates are benchmarked to data collected in the Census of Agriculture and the revised U.S. Department of Agriculture state totals of income and expense items.

Goods related industries include mining, construction, and manufacturing. Service-related and other include private sector earnings in agricultural services, forestry and fisheries; transportation and public utilities; wholesale trade; retail trade; finance, insurance, and real estate; and services. Government earnings include all levels of government.

GROSS STATE PRODUCT, Item 123
Source: Bureau of Economic Analysis, Regional Economic Information System

GSP for a state is derived as the sum of gross state product originating in all industries in the state. In concept, an industry's GSP, referred to as its "value added," is equivalent to its gross output (sales or receipts and other operating income, commodity taxes, and inventory change) minus its intermediate inputs (consumption of goods and services purchased from other industries or imported). As such, it is often referred to as the state counterpart of the nation's gross domestic product (GDP). In practice, GSP estimates are measured as the sum of distributions by industry of the components of gross domestic income—that is, the sum of the costs incurred (such as compensation of employees, net interest, and indirect business taxes) and the profits earned in production.

HOUSING, Items 124–137
Source: U.S. Bureau of the Census—1990 and 2000 Census of Population and Housing and Census 2000 Supplementary Survey

Housing data are from the **1990 or 2000 Census**, except for the housing value and rent items (132 through 136) which are from the **Census 2000 Supplementary Survey (C2SS)**. The C2SS was conducted as part of Census 2000 operations, to demonstrate the operational feasibility of collecting long form information at the same time as, but in a separate process, from the decennial census. It was conducted using the American Community Survey questionnaire, but it is separate from the Continuous Measurement Program, which is collecting data from larger samples, but only in the 31 sites. The C2SS covered 1,203 counties nationwide surveying 58,000 households monthly.

A **housing unit** is a house, apartment, mobile home or trailer, group of rooms, or single room occupied or, if vacant, intended for occupancy as separate living quarters. Separate living quarters are those in which the occupants do not live and eat with any other persons in the structure and which have direct access from the outside of the building through a common hall.

The occupants of a housing unit may be a single family, 1 person living alone, or 2 or more families living together, or any other group of related or unrelated persons who share living arrangements. Both occupied and vacant housing units are included in the housing inventory, with the exception that recreational vehicles, tents, caves, boats, railroad cars, and the like are included only if they are occupied as a person's usual place of residence.

A housing unit is classified as occupied if it is the usual place of residence of the person or group of persons living in it at the time of enumeration or if the occupants are only temporarily absent (e.g., away on vacation). A household consists of all persons who occupy a housing unit as their usual place of residence.

Median value is the dollar amount that divides the distribution of owner occupied housing units into 2 equal parts, one half of the units falling below this value and the other half exceeding it. Value is defined as the respondent's estimate of what the house would sell for if for sale. Data are presented for 1-family units on less than 10 acres and with no business or medical office on the property.

Median rent divides the distribution of renter-occupied housing units into 2 equal parts. The rent concept used in this volume is gross rent, which includes the amount of cash rent a renter pays (contract rent) plus the estimated average cost of utilities and fuels if paid by the renter. The rent is the amount of rent only for living quarters, not for any business or other space occupied. Single family houses on lots of 10 or more acres are excluded.

Housing cost as a percent of income is shown separately for owners with mortgages, owners without mortgages, and renters. Rent as a percent of income is a computed ratio of gross rent and monthly household income (total household income in 1989 divided by 12). Selected owner costs include utilities and fuels, as well as mortgage payments, insurance, taxes, etc. In each case, the ratio of housing cost to income is computed separately for each housing unit. The ratios for one-half of the units are above the median shown in this book, and one-half are below.

Substandard units are occupied units which are overcrowded or lack complete plumbing facilities. For the purposes of this item, "overcrowded" is defined as having 1.01 persons or more per room. Complete plumbing facilities include hot and cold piped water, a flush toilet, and a bathtub or shower. These facilities must be located inside the housing unit but not necessarily in the same room.

SOCIAL SECURITY AND SUPPLEMENTAL SECURITY INCOME, Items 138–140
Source: U.S. Social Security Administration

Social Security beneficiaries is the number of persons receiving benefits under the Old Age, Survivors, and Disability Insurance Program. These include retired or disabled workers covered by the program, their spouses and dependent children, and the surviving spouses and dependent children of deceased workers.

Supplemental Security Income (SSI) recipients is the number of persons receiving SSI payments. Data are as of December of the year shown.

CIVILIAN EMPLOYMENT, Items 141–143
Source: U.S. Bureau of the Census— Current Population Survey, March 2000

Total employment includes all civilians 16 years old and older who were either (1) "at work" — those who did any work at all during the reference week as paid employees, worked in their own business or profession, worked on their own farm, or worked 15 hours or more as unpaid workers in a family farm or business; or were (2) "with a job, but not at work" — those who had a job but were not at work that week due to illness, weather, industrial dispute, vacation, or other personal reasons. The "reference week" for these employment questions was during March.

The **occupational categories** shown are consistent with the 1980 edition of the *Standard Occupational Classification Manual (SOC)*, published by the Office of Federal Statistical Policy and Standards, U.S. Department of Commerce. Professional, managerial, and technical occupations include the following categories: executive, administrative, and managerial occupations (000-042); professional specialty occupations (043-202); and technicians and related support occupations (203-242). Precision production, craft, and repair include SOC codes 503-702.

CIVILIAN LABOR FORCE AND UNEMPLOYMENT, Items 144–148
Source: U.S. Bureau of Labor Statistics

Data for the civilian labor force are the product of a federal-state cooperative program in which state employment security agencies prepare labor force and unemployment estimates under concepts, definitions, and technical procedures established by the Bureau of Labor Statistics. The civilian labor force consists of all civilians 16 years and over who are either employed or unemployed.

Unemployment includes all persons who did not work during the survey week, made specific efforts to find a job in the prior 4 weeks, and were available for work during the survey week (except for temporary illness). Persons waiting to be called back to a job from which they had been laid off and those waiting to report to a new job within the next 30 days are included in unemployment figures.

PRIVATE NONFARM EMPLOYMENT AND EARNINGS, Items 149–159
Source: U.S. Bureau of Labor Statistics, Current Employment Survey

Data for private nonfarm employment and earnings are compiled from payroll information reported monthly on a voluntary basis to the BLS and its cooperating state agencies. More than 350,000 establishments represent all industries except agriculture.

Employment is the annual average of monthly totals of persons who received pay for any part of the pay period including the 12th day of the month. Included are all full-time and part-time workers in nonfarm establishments. Not covered are government employees, proprietors, the self-employed, unpaid volunteers or family workers, farm workers, and domestic workers in households. The data by industry conform to the definitions used in the 1987 Standard Industrial Classification (SIC).

Earnings of production workers in manufacturing industries are derived from reports of gross payrolls and corresponding paid hours. Payroll is reported before deductions of any kind. Total hours during the pay period include all hours worked (including overtime hours) and hours paid for holidays, vacations, and sick leave.

AGRICULTURE, Items 160–177
Source: U.S. Department of Agriculture, National Agricultural Statistics Service 1997 Census of Agriculture

Data for the 1997 Census of Agriculture were collected in 1998 and pertain to the year 1997.

The Bureau of the Census took a census of agriculture every 10 years from 1840 to 1920 and roughly every 5 years from 1925 to 1992. The 1997 Census of Agriculture was transferred to the National Agricultural Statistics Service of the U.S. Department of Agriculture. Over time, the definition of a farm has varied. For recent censuses, including the 1997 census, a farm has been defined as any place from which $1,000 or more of agricultural products were sold or normally would have been sold during the census year.

The term **operator** refers to a person who operates a farm, either doing the work or making day-to-day decisions about such things as planting, harvesting, feeding, marketing, etc. The operator may be the owner, a member of the owner's household, a salaried manager, a tenant, a renter, or a sharecropper. For partnerships, only 1 partner is counted as an operator. For census purposes, the number of operators is the same as the number of farms.

The acreage designated as **land in farms** consists primarily of agricultural land used for crops, pasture, or grazing. It also includes woodland and wasteland not actually under cultivation or used for pasture or grazing, provided it was part of the farm operator's total operation.

Land in farms is an operating-unit concept and includes land owned and operated, as well as land rented from others. Land used rent free is classified as land rented from others. All land in Indian reservations used for growing crops or grazing livestock is classified as land in farms.

Irrigated land covers any land in farms to which water was artificially applied in the census year. Land irrigated prior to but not in the census year is not included. Irrigation may have been used for producing a harvested crop, for pasture or grazing lands, for cultivated summer fallow, or for land planted with a crop intended for future harvest. Land flooded during high-water periods was included as irrigated only if water was diverted to agricultural lands by dams, canals, or other works.

Cropland consists of land from which crops were harvested and land that could have been used for crops without additional improvements. This includes land in nonbearing orchards and vineyards, land from which any hay was cut, land on which crops failed, idle or fallow land, and land used for grazing purposes.

Respondents were asked to report their estimate of the current market **value of land and buildings** owned, rented, or leased from others, and rented and leased to others. Market value refers to the respondent's estimate of what the land and buildings would sell for under current market conditions.

The **value of machinery and equipment** was estimated by the respondent as the current market value of all cars, trucks, tractors, combines, balers, irrigation equipment, etc., used on the farm. This value is an estimate of what the machinery and equipment would sell for in its present condition and not the replacement or depreciated value. Share interests are reported at full value at the farm where the equipment and machinery are usually kept. Only equipment that was actually used in 1996 and 1997, or newly purchased but not yet used, and physically located at the farm on December 31, 1997 is included.

The **value of farm products sold** by farms represent the gross market value before taxes and production expenses of all agricultural products sold or removed from the place in 1997 regardless of who received the payment. It includes sales by the operator as well as the value of any share received by partners, landlords, contractors, and others associated with the operation. It represents the sum of all crops, including nursery products, sold and livestock and poultry and their products sold.

The value of crops sold in 1997 does not necessarily represent the sales from crops harvested that year. The data include sales from crops produced in earlier years and exclude some crops produced in 1997 but held in storage and not sold in the census year. For crops sold through a co-op that made payments in several installments, only the total value received in the census year was to be reported.

LAND USE, Items 178–179
Source: U.S. Department of Agriculture, Natural Resources Conservation Service, 1997 National Resources Inventory

The National Resources Inventory has been conducted every five years since 1982. The 1997 NRI is based on a sample of about 800,000 locations throughout the United States (excluding Alaska and the District of Columbia.) Federally owned lands include military bases, national forests, wildlife refuges, parks, grassland game preserves, scenic waterways, wilderness areas, monuments, lakeshore, parkways, battlefields, Bureau of Land Management lands, and other federal lands. Developed land includes any built-up area greater than 1/4 acre. Built-up areas include residential, industrial, commercial, and institutional land; construction sites; public administrative sites; railroad yards; cemeteries; airports; golf courses; sanitary landfills; sewage treatment plants; water control structures and spillways; other land used for such purposes; small parks (less than 10 acres) within urban and built-up areas; and highways, railroads ,and other transportation facilities if they are surrounded by urban areas. Also included are tracts of less than 10 acres that do not meet the above definition but are completely surrounded by urban and built-up land and all highways, roads, railroads and associated rights-of-way outside urban and built-up areas (including private roads to farmsteads or ranch headquarters, logging roads, and other private roads).

WATER CONSUMPTION, Item 180
Source: U.S. Geological Survey, National Water Use Information Program, 1995 Water Use Data.

Every five years the U.S. Geological Survey compiles national water-use estimates. This volume includes the total freshwater withdrawals expressed as million gallons per day. Estimates of withdrawals of ground and surface water are given for the following categories of use: public water supplies, domestic, commercial, irrigation, livestock, industrial, mining, and thermoelectric power.

MANUFACTURES, Items 181–190
Source: U.S. Bureau of the Census— 2000 Annual Survey of Manufacturers

The Annual Survey of Manufacturers has been conducted every year since 1949.

The **all employees** number is the average number of production workers for the payroll periods including the 12th of March, May, August, and November plus the number of other employees in mid-March. Included are all persons on paid sick leave, paid holidays, and paid vacations during the pay period. Officers of corporations are included as employees—proprietors and partners of unincorporated firms are excluded.

Payroll figures include the gross annual earnings of all employees on the payroll of operating manufacturing establishments. The definition, which is the same as the one used for calculating the federal withholding tax, includes all forms of compensation, such as salaries, wages, commissions, dismissal pay, all bonuses, vacation and sick leave pay, and compensation-in-kind, prior to such deductions as employees' Social Security contributions, withholding taxes, group insurance, union dues, and savings bonds. The total includes salaries of officers of corporations but excludes payments to proprietors or partners of unincorporated concerns. Also excluded are payments to members of the Armed Forces and to pensioners carried on the active payroll of manufacturing establishments.

Production workers include workers (up through the line-supervisor level) engaged in fabricating; processing; assembling; inspecting; receiving; storing; handling; packing; warehousing; shipping (but not delivering); maintenance; repair; janitorial and guard services; product development; auxiliary production for plant's own use (e.g., power plant); record-keeping; and other services closely associated with these production operations. Employees above the working supervisor level are excluded.

The number of production workers is the average for the payroll periods including the 12th of March, May, August, and November. Not included in this classification are all other employees, defined as non-production employees, including those engaged in factory supervision above the line-supervisor level.

Production worker hours cover hours worked or paid for at the plant, including actual overtime hours (not straight-time-equivalent hours). The data exclude hours paid for vacations, holidays, or sick leave. Production wages represent all compensation paid to production workers.

Value added by manufacture is derived by subtracting the cost of materials, supplies, containers, fuel, purchased electricity, and contract work from the value of shipments (products manufactured plus receipts for services rendered). The result of this calculation is adjusted by the addition of value added by merchandising operations (i.e., the difference between the sales value and cost of merchandise sold without further manufacture, processing, or assembly) plus the net change in finished goods and work in process between the beginning-and end-of-year inventories.

Value of shipments covers the received or receivable net selling values; free on board plant (exclusive freight charges and taxes) of all products shipped, both primary and secondary; as well as miscellaneous receipts, such as receipts for contract work performed for others, installation and repair, sales of scrap, and sales of products bought and resold without further processing. Included are all items made by or for the establishment from materials owned by it, whether sold, transferred to other plants of the same company, or shipped on consignment. The net selling value of products made in 1 plant on a contract basis from materials owned by another was reported by the plant providing the materials.

In the case of multi-unit companies, the manufacturer was requested to report the value of products transferred to other establishments of the same company at full economic or commercial value, including not only the direct costs of production but also a reasonable proportion of "all other costs" (including company overhead) and profit.

The aggregate of the value of shipments figure for industry groups and for all manufacturing industries includes large amounts of duplication since the products of some industries are used as materials by others. Estimates as to the overall extent of this duplication indicate that the value of manufactured products exclusive of such duplication (the value of finished manufactures) tend to approximate two-thirds of the total value of products reported in the census of manufactures.

TOTAL CAPITAL EXPENDITURES (NEW AND USED)

For establishments in operation and any known plants under construction, manufacturers were asked to report their new and used expenditures for (1) permanent additions and major alterations to manufacturing establishments and (2) machinery and equipment used for replacement and additions to plant capacity if they were of the type for which depreciation accounts were ordinarily maintained.

Totals for expenditures include the costs of assets leased from nonmanufacturing concerns through capital leases. New facilities owned by the federal government but operated under contract by private companies and plant and equipment furnished to the manufacturer by communities and nonprofit organizations are excluded. Also excluded are expenditures for land and cost of maintenance and repairs charged as current operating expenses.

For any equipment or structure transferred for the use of the reporting establishment by the parent company or one of its subsidiaries, the value at which it was transferred to the establishment was to be reported.

If an establishment changed ownership during the year, the cost of the fixed assets (building and equipment) was to be reported.

1997 ECONOMIC CENSUS: OVERVIEW
Items 191–278
Source: U.S. Bureau of the Census

The Economic Census provides a detailed portrait of the nation's economy once every five years, from the national to the local level. The 1997 Economic Census covers nearly all of the U.S. economy in its basic collection of establishment statistics. It is the first major data source to use the new North American Industry Classification System (NAICS) and is therefore not comparable to economic data from prior years which were based on the Standard Industrial Classification (SIC) system.

NAICS, developed in cooperation with Canada and Mexico, classifies North America's economic activities at 2-, 3-, 4-, and 5-digit levels of detail, and the U.S. version of NAICS further defines industries to a sixth digit. The Economic Census takes advantage of this hierarchy to publish data at these successive levels of detail: sector (2-digit); subsector (3-digit); industry group (4-digit); industry(5-digit); and U.S. industry(6-digit.) Information in Table A is at the 2-digit level, with a few 3- and 4-digit items.

Several key statistics are tabulated for all industries included in this volume: number of establishments (or companies); number of employees; payroll; and a measure of output (sales, receipts, revenue, value of shipments, or value of construction work done.)

Number of Establishments. An establishment is a single physical location at which business is conducted. It is not necessarily identical with a company or enterprise, which may consist of one establishment or more. Economic Census figures represent a summary of reports for individual establishments rather than companies. For cases where a census report was received, separate information was obtained for each location where business was conducted. When administrative records of other Federal agencies were used instead of a census report, no information was available on the number of locations operated. Each Economic Census establishment was tabulated according to the physical location at which the business was conducted. The count of establishments represents those in business at any time during 1997.

When two activities or more were carried on at a single location under a single ownership, all activities generally were grouped together as a single establishment. The entire establishment was classified on the basis of its major activity and all data for it were included in that classification. However, when distinct and separate economic activities (for which different industry classification codes were appropriate) were conducted at a single location under a single ownership, separate establishment reports for each of the different activities were obtained in the census.

Number of Employees. Paid employees consist of the full-time and part-time employees, including salaried officers and executives of corporations. Included are employees on paid sick leave, paid holidays, and paid vacations; not included are proprietors and partners of unincorporated businesses. The definition of paid employees is the same as that used on IRS form 941.

Payroll. Payroll includes all forms of compensation such as salaries, wages, commissions, dismissal pay, bonuses, vacation allowances, sick-leave pay, and employee contributions to qualified pension plans paid during the year to all employees. For corporations, payroll includes amounts paid to officers and executives; for unincorporated businesses, it does not include profit or other compensation of proprietors or partners. Payroll is reported before deductions for social security, income tax, insurance, union dues, etc. This definition of payroll is the same as that used by the Internal Revenue Service (IRS) on form 941.

Sales, Shipments, Receipts, Revenue, or Business Done. This measure includes the total sales, shipments, receipts, revenue, or business done by establishments within the scope of the Economic Census. The definition of each of these items is specific to the economic sector measured.

CONSTRUCTION (Items 191–194)
Source: U.S. Bureau of the Census,
1997 Economic Census
(See Overview of 1997 Economic Census prior to Item 191)

The Construction sector (sector 23) comprises establishments primarily engaged in the construction of buildings and other structures, heavy construction (except buildings), additions, alterations, reconstruction, installation, and maintenance and repairs. Establishments engaged in demolition or wrecking of buildings and other structures, clearing of building sites, and sale of materials from demolished structures are also included. This sector also includes those establishments engaged in blasting, test drilling, landfill, leveling, earthmoving, excavating, land drainage, and other land preparation. The industries within this sector have been defined on the basis of their unique production processes. As with all industries, the production processes are distinguished by their use of specialized human resources and specialized physical capital. Construction activities are generally administered or managed at a relatively fixed place of business, but the actual construction work is performed at one or more different project sites. This sector is divided into three subsectors of construction activities: (1) building construction and land subdivision and land development; (2) heavy construction (except buildings), such as highways, power plants, and pipelines; and (3) construction activity by special trade contractors.

WHOLESALE TRADE, Items 195–198
**Source: U.S. Bureau of the Census,
1997 Economic Census
(See Overview of 1997 Economic Census
prior to Item 191)**

The Wholesale Trade sector (sector 42) comprises establishments engaged in wholesaling merchandise, generally without transformation, and rendering services incidental to the sale of merchandise. The wholesaling process is an intermediate step in the distribution of merchandise. Wholesalers are organized to sell or arrange the purchase or sale of (a) goods for resale (i.e., goods sold to other wholesalers or retailers), (b) capital or durable nonconsumer goods, and (c) raw and intermediate materials and supplies used in production.

Wholesalers sell merchandise to other businesses and normally operate from a warehouse or office. These warehouses and offices are characterized by having little or no display of merchandise. In addition, neither the design nor the location of the premises is intended to solicit walk-in traffic. Wholesalers do not normally use advertising directed to the general public. Customers are generally reached initially via telephone, in-person marketing, or by specialized advertising that may include Internet and other electronic means. Follow-up orders are either vendor-initiated or client-initiated, generally based on previous sales, and typically exhibit strong ties between sellers and buyers. In fact, transactions are often conducted between wholesalers and clients that have long-standing business relationships.

This sector comprises two main types of wholesalers: those that sell goods on their own account and those that arrange sales and purchases for others for a commission or fee.

(1) Establishments that sell goods on their own account are known as wholesale merchants, distributors, jobbers, drop shippers, import/export merchants, and sales branches. These establishments typically maintain their own warehouse, where they receive and handle goods for their customers. Goods are generally sold without transformation, but may include integral functions, such as sorting, packaging, labeling, and other marketing services.

(2) Establishments arranging for the purchase or sale of goods owned by others or purchasing goods on a commission basis are known as agents and brokers, commission merchants, import/export agents and brokers, auction companies, and manufacturers' representatives. These establishments operate from offices and generally do not own or handle the goods they sell.

Some wholesale establishments may be connected with a single manufacturer and promote and sell the particular manufacturer's products to a wide range of other wholesalers or retailers. Other wholesalers may be connected to a retail chain or a limited number of retail chains and only provide a variety of products needed by that particular retail operation(s). These wholesalers may obtain the products from a wide range of manufacturers. Still other wholesalers may not take title to the goods, but act as agents and brokers for a commission.

Although, in general, wholesaling normally denotes sales in large volumes, durable nonconsumer goods may be sold in single units. Sales of capital or durable nonconsumer goods used in the production of goods and services, such as farm machinery, medium and heavy duty trucks, and industrial machinery, are always included in wholesale trade.

RETAIL TRADE, Items 199–206
**Source: U.S. Bureau of the Census,
1997 Economic Census
(See Overview of 1997 Economic Census
prior to Item 191)**

The Retail Trade sector (44-45) comprises establishments engaged in retailing merchandise, generally without transformation, and rendering services incidental to the sale of merchandise.

The retailing process is the final step in the distribution of merchandise; retailers are, therefore, organized to sell merchandise in small quantities to the general public. This sector comprises two main types of retailers: store and nonstore retailers.

Store retailers operate fixed point-of-sale locations, located and designed to attract a high volume of walk-in customers. In general, retail stores have extensive displays of merchandise and use mass-media advertising to attract customers. They typically sell merchandise to the general public for personal or household consumption, but some also serve business and institutional clients. These include establishments, such as office supply stores, computer and software stores, building materials dealers, plumbing supply stores, and electrical supply stores. Catalog showrooms, gasoline service stations, automotive dealers, and mobile home dealers are treated as store retailers.

In addition to retailing merchandise, some types of store retailers are also engaged in the provision of after-sales services, such as repair and installation. For example, new automobile dealers, electronic and appliance stores, and musical instrument and supply stores often provide repair services. As a general rule, establishments engaged in retailing merchandise and providing after-sales services are classified in this sector.

Nonstore retailers, like store retailers, are organized to serve the general public, but their retailing methods differ. The establishments of this subsector reach customers and market merchandise with methods, such as the broadcasting of "infomercials," the broadcasting and publishing of direct-response advertising, the publishing of paper and electronic catalogs, door-to-door solicitation, in-home demonstration, selling from portable stalls (street vendors, except food), and distribution through vending machines. Establishments engaged in the direct sale (nonstore) of products, such as home heating oil dealers and home delivery newspaper routes.

The buying of goods for resale is a characteristic of retail trade establishments that particularly distinguishes them from establishments in the agriculture, manufacturing, and construction industries. For example, farms that sell their products at or from the point of production are not classified in retail, but rather in agriculture. Similarly, establishments that both manufacture and sell their products to the general public are not classified in retail, but rather in manufacturing. However, establishments that engage in processing activities incidental to retailing are classified in retail.

Industries in the **Motor Vehicle and Parts Dealers** subsector (441) retail motor vehicle and parts merchandise from fixed point-of-sale locations. Establishments in this subsector typically operate from a showroom and/or an open lot where the vehicles are on display. The display of vehicles and the related parts require little by way of display equipment. The personnel generally include both the sales and sales support staff familiar with the requirements for registering and financing a vehicle as well as a staff of parts experts and mechanics trained to provide repair and maintenance services for the vehicles. Specific industries have been included in this subsector to identify the type of vehicle being retailed. Sales of capital or durable nonconsumer goods, such as medium and heavy-duty trucks, are always included in wholesale trade. These goods are virtually never sold through retail methods.

Industries in the **Food and Beverage Stores** subsector (445) usually retail food and beverage merchandise from fixed point-of-sale locations. Establishments in this subsector have special equipment (e.g., freezers, refrigerated display cases, refrigerators) for displaying food and beverage goods. They have staff trained in the processing of food products to guarantee the proper storage and sanitary conditions required by regulatory authority.

Industries in the **Clothing and Clothing Accessories Stores** subsector (448) retail new clothing and clothing accessories merchandise from fixed point-of-sale locations. Establishments in this subsector have similar display equipment and staff that is knowledgeable regarding fashion trends and the proper match of styles, colors, and combinations of clothing and accessories to the characteristics and tastes of the customer.

Industries in the **General Merchandise Stores** subsector (452) retail new general merchandise from fixed point-of-sale locations. Establishments in this subsector are unique in that they have the equipment and staff capable of retailing a large variety of goods from a single location. This includes a variety of display equipment and staff trained to provide information on many lines of products.

TRANSPORTATION AND WAREHOUSING, Items 207–210
Source: U.S. Bureau of the Census, 1997 Economic Census
(See Overview of 1997 Economic Census prior to Item 191)

The Transportation and Warehousing sector (48-49) includes industries providing transportation of passengers and cargo, warehousing and storage for goods, scenic and sightseeing transportation, and support activities related to modes of transportation.

Establishments in these industries use transportation equipment or transportation related facilities as a productive asset. The type of equipment depends on the mode of transportation. The modes of transportation are air, rail, water, road, and pipeline.

The Transportation and Warehousing sector distinguishes three basic types of activities: subsectors for each mode of transportation, a subsector for warehousing and storage, and a subsector for establishments providing support activities for transportation. In addition, there are subsectors for establishments that provide passenger transportation for scenic and sightseeing purposes, postal services, and courier services.

FINANCE AND INSURANCE, Items 211–214
Source: U.S. Bureau of the Census, 1997 Economic Census
(See Overview of 1997 Economic Census prior to Item 191)

The Finance and Insurance sector (52) comprises establishments primarily engaged in financial transactions (transactions involving the creation, liquidation, or change in ownership of financial assets) and/or in facilitating financial transactions. Three principal types of activities are identified:

(1) Raising funds by taking deposits and/or issuing securities and, in the process, incurring liabilities. Establishments engaged in this activity use raised funds to acquire financial assets by making loans and/or purchasing securities. Putting themselves at risk, they channel funds from lenders to borrowers and transform or repackage the funds with respect to maturity, scale and risk. This activity is known as financial intermediation.

(2) Pooling of risk by underwriting insurance and annuities. Establishments engaged in this activity collect fees, insurance premiums, or annuity considerations; build up reserves; invest those reserves; and make contractual payments. Fees are based on the expected incidence of the insured risk and the expected return on investment.

(3) Providing specialized services facilitating or supporting financial intermediation, insurance, and employee benefit programs.

In addition, monetary authorities charged with monetary control are included in this sector.

REAL ESTATE AND RENTAL AND LEASING, Items 215–218
Source: U.S. Bureau of the Census, 1997 Economic Census
(See Overview of 1997 Economic Census prior to Item 191)

The Real Estate and Rental and Leasing sector (53) comprises establishments primarily engaged in renting, leasing, or otherwise allowing the use of tangible or intangible assets, and establishments providing related services. The major portion of this sector comprises establishments that rent, lease, or otherwise allow the use of their own assets by others. The assets may be tangible, as is the case of real estate and equipment, or intangible, as is the case with patents and trademarks.

This sector also includes establishments primarily engaged in managing real estate for others, selling, renting and/or buying real estate for others, and appraising real estate. These activities are closely related to this sector's main activity, and it was felt that from a production basis they would best be included here. In addition, a substantial proportion of property management is self-performed by lessors.

The main components of this sector are the real estate lessors industries; equipment lessors industries (including motor vehicles, computers, and consumer goods); and lessors of nonfinancial intangible assets (except copyrighted works).

INFORMATION, Items 219–226
Source: U.S. Bureau of the Census, 1997 Economic Census
(See Overview of 1997 Economic Census prior to Item 191)

The Information sector (51) comprises establishments engaged in the following processes: (a) producing and distributing information and cultural products, (b) providing the means to transmit or distribute these products as well as data or communications, and (c) processing data.

The main components of this sector are the publishing industries, including software publishing, the motion picture and sound recording industries, the broadcasting and telecommunications industries, and the information services and data processing industries.

For the purpose of NAICS, it is the transformation of information into a commodity that is produced and distributed by a number of growing industries that is at issue. The Information sector groups three types of establishments: (1) those engaged in producing and distributing information and cultural products; (2) those that provide the means to transmit or distribute these products as well as data or communications; and (3) those that process data. Cultural products are those that directly express attitudes, opinions, ideas, values, and artistic creativity; provide entertainment; or offer information and analysis concerning the past and present. Included in this definition are popular, mass-produced, products as well as cultural products that normally have a more limited audience, such as poetry books, literary magazines, or classical records. These activities were formerly classified throughout the existing national classifications. Traditional publishing was in manufacturing; broadcasting in communications; software production in business services; film production in amusement services; and so forth.

Industries in the **Publishing Industries** subsector (511) group establishments engaged in the publishing of newspapers, magazines, other periodicals, and books, as well as database and software publishing. In general, these establishments, which are known as publishers, issue copies of works for which they usually possess copyright. Works may be in one or more formats including traditional print form, CD-ROM, or on-line. Publishers may publish works originally created by others for which they have obtained the rights and/or works that they have created in-house. Software

publishing is included here because the activity, creation of a copyrighted product and bringing it to market, is equivalent to the creation process for other types of intellectual products.

In NAICS, publishing—the reporting, writing, editing, and other processes that are required to create an edition of a book or a newspaper—is treated as a major economic activity in its own right, rather than as a subsidiary activity to a manufacturing activity, printing. Thus, publishing is classified in the Information sector; whereas, printing remains in the NAICS Manufacturing sector. In part, the NAICS classification reflects the fact that publishing increasingly takes place in establishments that are physically separate from the associated printing establishments. More crucially, the NAICS classification of book and newspaper publishing is intended to portray their roles in a modern economy, in which they do not resemble manufacturing activities.

Music publishers are not included in the Publishing Industries subsector, but are included in the Motion Picture and Sound Recording Industries subsector. Reproduction of prepackaged software is treated in NAICS as a manufacturing activity; on-line distribution of software products is in the Information sector, and custom design of software to client specifications is included in the Professional, Scientific, and Technical Services sector. These distinctions arise because of the different ways that software is created, reproduced, and distributed.

The Information sector does not include products, such as manifold business forms. Information is not the essential component of these items. Establishments producing these items are included in Subsector 323, Printing and Related Support Activities.

Industries in the **Motion Picture and Sound Recording Industries** subsector (512) group establishments involved in the production and distribution of motion pictures and sound recordings. While producers and distributors of motion pictures and sound recordings issue works for sale as traditional publishers do, the processes are sufficiently different to warrant placing establishments engaged in these activities in a separate subsector. Production is typically a complex process that involves several distinct types of establishments that are engaged in activities, such as contracting with performers, creating the film or sound content, and providing technical postproduction services. Film distribution is often to exhibitors, such as theaters and broadcasters, rather than through the wholesale and retail distribution chain. When the product is in a mass-produced form, NAICS treats production and distribution as the major economic activity as it does in the Publishing Industries subsector, rather than as a subsidiary activity to the manufacture of such products.

This subsector does not include establishments primarily engaged in the wholesale distribution of video cassettes and sound recordings, such as compact discs and audio tapes; these establishments are included in the Wholesale Trade sector. Reproduction of video cassettes and sound recordings that is carried out separately from establishments engaged in production and distribution is treated in NAICS as a manufacturing activity.

Industries in the **Broadcasting and Telecommunications** subsector (513) include establishments providing point-to-point communications and the services related to that activity. The industry groups (Radio and Television Broadcasting, Cable Networks and Program Distribution, and Telecommunications) are based on differences in the methods of communication and in the nature of services provided. The Radio and Television Broadcasting industry group includes establishments that operate broadcasting studios and facilities for over the air or satellite delivery of radio and television programs of entertainment, news, talk, and the like. These establishments are often engaged in the production and purchase of programs and generating revenues from the sale of air time to advertisers and from donations, subsidies, and/or the sale of programs. The Cable Networks and Program Distribution industry group includes two types of establishments. Those in the Cable Networks industry operate studios and facilities for the broadcasting of programs that are typically narrowcast in nature (limited format, such as news, sports, education, and youth-oriented programming). The services of these establishments are typically sold on a subscription or fee basis. Delivery of the programs to customers is handled by other establishments, in the Cable and Other Program Distribution industry, that operate cable systems, direct-to-home satellite systems, or other similar systems. The Telecommunications industry group is primarily engaged in operating, maintaining, and/or providing access to facilities for the transmission of voice, data, text, sound, and full motion picture video between network termination points. A transmission facility may be based on a single technology or a combination of technologies. Establishments primarily engaged as independent contractors in the maintenance and installation of broadcasting and telecommunications systems are classified in Sector 23, Construction.

Industries in the **Information Services and Data Processing Services** subsector (514) group establishments providing information, storing information, providing access to information, and processing information. The main components of the subsector are news syndicates, libraries, archives, on-line information service providers, and data processors.

UTILITIES, Items 227–230
Source: U.S. Bureau of the Census,
1997 Economic Census
(See Overview of 1997 Economic Census
prior to Item 191)

The Utilities sector (22) comprises establishments engaged in the provision of the following utility services: electric power, natural gas, steam supply, water supply, and sewage removal. Within this sector, the specific activities associated with the utility services provided vary by utility: electric power includes generation, transmission, and distribution; natural gas includes distribution; steam supply includes provision and/or distribution; water supply includes treatment and distribution; and sewage removal includes collection, treatment, and disposal of waste through sewer systems and sewage treatment facilities.

Excluded from this sector are establishments primarily engaged in waste management services classified in Subsector 562, Waste Management and Remediation Services, which also collect, treat, and dispose of waste materials; however, they do not use sewer systems or sewage treatment facilities.

PROFESSIONAL, SCIENTIFIC, AND TECHNICAL SERVICES, Items 231–238
Source: U.S. Bureau of the Census,
1997 Economic Census
(See Overview of 1997 Economic Census
prior to Item 191)

The Professional, Scientific, and Technical Services sector (54) comprises establishments that specialize in performing professional, scientific, and technical activities for others. These activities require a high degree of expertise and training. The establishments in this sector specialize according to expertise and provide these services to clients in a variety of industries and, in some cases, to households. Activities performed include: legal advice and representation; accounting, bookkeeping, and payroll services; architectural, engineering, and specialized design services; computer services; consulting services; research services; advertising services; photographic services; translation and interpretation services; veterinary services; and other professional, scientific, and technical services.

This volume includes only those establishments subject to federal income tax.

This sector excludes establishments primarily engaged in providing a range of day-to-day office administrative services, such as financial planning, billing and recordkeeping, personnel, and physical distribution and logistics. These establishments are classified in Sector 56, Administrative and Support and Waste Management and Remediation Services.

Legal Services is a NAICS industry group (5411) that includes establishments classified in the following NAICS industries: 54111, Offices of Lawyers; and 54119, Other Legal Services.

Accounting, Tax Preparation, Bookkeeping, and Payroll Services is a NAICS industry group (5412) that comprises establishments primarily engaged in providing services, such as auditing of accounting records, designing accounting systems, preparing financial statements, developing budgets, preparing tax returns, processing payrolls, bookkeeping, and billing.

Architectural, Engineering, and Related Services is a NAICS industry group (5413) that includes establishments classified in the following NAICS industries: 54131, Architectural Services; 54133, Engineering Services; 54134, Drafting Services; 54135, Building Inspection Services; 54136, Geophysical Surveying and Mapping Services; 54137, Surveying and Mapping (Except Geophysical) Services; and 54138, Testing Laboratories.

Computer Systems Design and Related Services is a NAICS industry that comprises establishments primarily engaged in providing expertise in the field of information technologies through one or more of the following activities: (1) writing, modifying, testing, and supporting software to meet the needs of a particular customer; (2) planning and designing computer systems that integrate computer hardware, software, and communication technologies; (3) on-site management and operation of clients' computer systems and/or data processing facilities; and (4) other professional and technical computer-related advice and services.

ARTS, ENTERTAINMENT, AND RECREATION, Items 239–242
Source: U.S. Bureau of the Census,
1997 Economic Census
(See Overview of 1997 Economic Census
prior to Item 191)

The Arts, Entertainment, and Recreation sector (71) includes a wide range of establishments that operate facilities or provide services to meet varied cultural, entertainment, and recreational interests of their patrons. This sector comprises (1) establishments that are involved in producing, promoting, or participating in live performances, events, or exhibits intended for public viewing; (2) establishments that preserve and exhibit objects and sites of historical, cultural, or educational interest; and (3) establishments that operate facilities or provide services that enable patrons to participate in recreational activities or pursue amusement, hobby, and leisure time interests.

Some establishments that provide cultural, entertainment, or recreational facilities and services are classified in other sectors. Excluded from this sector are: (1) establishments that provide both accommodations and recreational facilities, such as hunting and fishing camps and resort and casino hotels are classified in Subsector 721, Accommodation; (2) restaurants and night clubs that provide live entertainment in addition to the sale of food and beverages are classified in Subsector 722, Food Services and Drinking Places; (3) motion picture theaters, libraries and archives, and publishers of newspapers, magazines, books, periodicals, and computer software are classified in Sector 51, Information; and (4) establishments using transportation equipment to provide recreational and entertainment services, such as those operating sightseeing buses, dinner cruises, or helicopter rides are classified in Subsector 487, Scenic and Sightseeing Transportation.

HEALTH CARE AND SOCIAL ASSISTANCE, Items 243–254
Source: U.S. Bureau of the Census,
1997 Economic Census
(See Overview of 1997 Economic Census
prior to Item 191)

The Health Care and Social Assistance sector (62) comprises establishments providing health care and social assistance for individuals. The sector includes both health care and social assistance because it is sometimes difficult to distinguish between the boundaries of these two activities. The industries in this sector are arranged on a continuum starting with those establishments providing medical care exclusively, continuing with those providing health care and social assistance, and finally finishing with those providing only social assistance. The services provided by establishments in this sector are delivered by trained professionals. All industries in the sector share this commonality of process, namely, labor inputs of health practitioners or social workers with the requisite expertise. Many of the industries in the sector are defined based on the educational degree held by the practitioners included in the industry.

In this volume, taxable and tax-exempt establishments are presented separately.

Excluded from this sector are aerobic classes in Subsector 713, Amusement, Gambling and Recreation Industries and nonmedical diet and weight reducing centers in Subsector 812, Personal and Laundry Services. Although these can be viewed as health services, these services are not typically delivered by health practitioners.

Industries in the **Ambulatory Health Care Services** subsector (621) provide health care services directly or indirectly to ambulatory patients and do not usually provide inpatient services. Health practitioners in this subsector provide outpatient services, with the facilities and equipment not usually being the most significant part of the production process.

Industries in the **Hospitals** subsector (622) provide medical, diagnostic, and treatment services that include physician, nursing, and other health services to inpatients and the specialized accommodation services required by inpatients. Hospitals may also provide outpatient services as a secondary activity. Establishments in the Hospitals subsector provide inpatient health services, many of which can only be provided using the specialized facilities and equipment that form a significant and integral part of the production process.

ACCOMMODATION AND FOOD SERVICES, Items 255–259
Source: U.S. Bureau of the Census,
1997 Economic Census
(See Overview of 1997 Economic Censu
prior to Item 191)

The Accommodation and Food Services sector (72) comprises establishments providing customers with lodging and/or preparing meals, snacks, and beverages for immediate consumption. The sector includes both accommodation and food services establishments because the two activities are often combined at the same establishment.

Excluded from this sector are civic and social organizations; amusement and recreation parks; theaters; and other recreation or entertainment facilities providing food and beverage services.

Industries in the **Food Services and Drinking Places** subsector (722) prepare meals, snacks, and beverages to customer order for immediate on-premises and off-premises consumption. There is a wide range of establishments in these industries. Some provide food and drink only; while others provide various combinations of seating space, waiter/waitress services and incidental amenities, such as limited entertainment. The industries in the subsector are grouped based on the type and level of services provided. The industry groups are full-service restaurants; limited-service eating places; special food services, such as food service contractors, caterers, and mobile food services, and drinking places.

Food services and drink activities at hotels and motels; amusement parks, theaters, casinos, country clubs, and similar recreational facilities; and civic and social organizations are included in this subsector only if these services are provided by a separate establishment primarily engaged in providing food and beverage services.

Excluded from this subsector are establishments operating dinner cruises. These establishments are classified in Subsector 487, Scenic and Sightseeing Transportation because those establishments utilize transportation equipment to provide scenic recreational entertainment.

OTHER SERVICES, Items 260–266
Source: U.S. Bureau of the Census,
1997 Economic Census
(See Overview of 1997 Economic Census
prior to Item 191)

The Other Services (except Public Administration) sector (81) comprises establishments engaged in providing services not specifically provided for elsewhere in the classification system. Establishments in this sector are primarily engaged in activities, such as equipment and machinery repairing, promoting or administering religious activities, grantmaking, advocacy, and providing drycleaning and laundry services, personal care services, death care services, pet care services, photofinishing services, temporary parking services, and dating services.

Private households that engage in employing workers on or about the premises in activities primarily concerned with the operation of the household are included in this sector.

In this volume, only firms subject to federal tax are included in the categories that include the full "other services" sector, as well as the number of employees in the "Repair and Maintenance" and "Personal and Laundry Services" subsectors. However, the number of employees in the "Religious, Civic, and Similar Services" subsector include only non-taxable establishments.

Excluded from this sector are establishments primarily engaged in retailing new equipment and also performing repairs and general maintenance on equipment. These establishments are classified in Sector 44-45, Retail Trade.

Industries in the **Repair and Maintenance** subsector (811) restore machinery, equipment, and other products to working order. These establishments also typically provide general or routine maintenance (i.e., servicing) on such products to ensure they work efficiently and to prevent breakdown and unnecessary repairs.

The NAICS structure for this subsector brings together most types of repair and maintenance establishments and categorizes them based on production processes (i.e., on the type of repair and maintenance activity performed, and the necessary skills, expertise, and processes that are found in different repair and maintenance establishments). This NAICS classification does not delineate between repair services provided to businesses versus those that serve households. Although some industries primarily serve either businesses or households, separation by class of customer is limited by the fact that many establishments serve both. Establishments repairing computers and consumer electronics products are two examples of such overlap.

The Repair and Maintenance subsector does not include all establishments that do repair and maintenance. For example, a substantial amount of repair is done by establishments that also manufacture machinery, equipment, and other goods. These establishments are included in the Manufacturing sector in NAICS. In addition, repair of transportation equipment is often provided by or based at transportation facilities, such as airports, seaports, and these activities are included in the Transportation and Warehousing sector. A particularly unique situation exists with repair of buildings. Plumbing, electrical installation and repair, painting and decorating, and other construction-related establishments are often involved in performing installation or other work on new construction as well as providing repair services on existing structures. While some specialize in repair, it is difficult to distinguish between the two types and all have been included in the Construction sector.

Excluded from this subsector are establishments primarily engaged in rebuilding or remanufacturing machinery and equipment. These are classified in Sector 31-33, Manufacturing. Also excluded are retail establishments that provide after-sale services and repair. These are classified in Sector 44-45, Retail Trade.

Industries in the **Personal and Laundry Services** subsector (812) group establishments that provide personal and laundry services to individuals, households, and businesses. Services performed include: personal care services; death care services; laundry and drycleaning services; and a wide range of other personal services, such as pet care (except veterinary) services, photofinishing services, temporary parking services, and dating services.

The Personal and Laundry Services subsector is by no means all-inclusive of the services that could be termed personal services (i.e., those provided to individuals rather than businesses). There are many other subsectors, as well as sectors, that provide services to persons. Establishments providing legal, accounting, tax preparation, architectural, portrait photography, and similar professional services are classified in Sector 54, Professional, Scientific, and Technical Services; those providing job placement, travel arrangement, home security, interior and exterior house cleaning, exterminating, lawn and garden care, and similar support services are classified in Sector 56, Administrative and Support, Waste Management and Remediation Services; those providing health and social services are classified in Sector 62, Health Care and Social Assistance; those providing amusement and recreation services are classified in Sector 71, Arts, Entertainment and Recreation; those providing educational instruction are classified in Sector 61, Educational Services; those providing repair services are classified in Subsector 811, Repair and Maintenance; and those providing spiritual, civic, and advocacy services are classified in Subsector 813, Religious, Grantmaking, Civic, Professional, and Similar Organizations.

Industries in the **Religious, Grantmaking, Civic, Professional, and Similar Organizations** subsector (813) group establishments that organize and promote religious activities; support various causes through grantmaking; advocate various social and political causes; and promote and defend the interests of their members. This category includes only tax-exempt establishments.

The industry groups within the subsector are defined in terms of their activities, such as establishments that provide funding for specific causes or for a variety of charitable causes; establishments that advocate and actively promote causes and beliefs for the public good; and establishments that have an active membership structure to promote causes and represent the interests of their members. Establishments in this subsector may publish newsletters, books, and periodicals, for distribution to their membership.

ECONOMIC CENSUS BY SIC CODE
(Items 267–278)
Source: U.S. Bureau of the Census, 1997 Economic Census
(See Overview of 1997 Economic Census prior to Item 191)

Because the 1997 Economic Census used the new North American Industry Classification System (NAICS), it is not directly comparable with Economic Census data from previous years. Because 1997 Economic Census records were assigned both SIC and NAICS codes, the Census Bureau was able to compile comparative statistics in which the 1997 data are compared with 1992 data using the Standard Industrial Classification (SIC) system. This volume includes the number of employees and the percent change from 1992 for six SIC sectors.

While many of the individual SIC industries correspond directly to industries as defined under the NAICS system, most of the higher level groupings do not. Particular care should be taken in comparing data for retail trade, wholesale trade, and manufacturing, which are sector titles used in both NAICS and SIC, but cover somewhat different groups of industries. The industry definitions discuss the relationships between NAICS and SIC industries. Where changes are significant, it will not be possible to construct time series that include data for points both before and after 1997.

For the SIC-based tables from the 1997 Economic Census, all auxiliaries are included in the category titled "Auxiliaries" and are not included in this volume. Note that in published reports from previous censuses for manufacturing and mining, auxiliary establishments were included in, or along with, data for the industries served; for other SIC divisions, auxiliary establishments were excluded from the detailed tables.

Construction. While some changes affecting construction were within the sector, this sector now includes industries that were previously classified in other sectors. Prominent among these industries are construction management and land subdividers and developers. In addition, although the construction sector is enumerated on an establishment basis, statistical information was obtained in the census by a survey which included all large employers and a sample of the smaller ones.

Manufacturing. While most of the changes affecting the manufacturing sector were within the sector, this sector now excludes industries which were previously within the scope of manufacturing and includes others that were not in manufacturing. Prominent among the industries that are excluded from manufacturing are logging and portions of publishing. Prominent among the industries that are now included in manufacturing are bakeries, candy stores where candy is made on the premises, custom tailors, makers of custom draperies, and tire retreading. The Information sector (new) includes publishing establishments that were classified in Manufacturing under the SIC.

Wholesale Trade. This sector includes most of what was classified in Wholesale Trade under the SIC system. Excluded from this sector, however, are establishments with retail selling characteristics; these establishments are now clasified in the Retail Trade sector. Prominent examples of these are auto parts, farm supplies, and building products dealers and lumber yards.

In addition, this sector now includes prerecorded video tape wholesalers; this industry was previously classified in Services Industries under the SIC system.

Retail Trade. This sector includes much of what was classified in Retail Trade under the SIC system. Excluded from this sector, however, are eating and drinking places and mobile foodservices (which are now in the Accommodation and Foodservices sector); pawn shops (which are now in the Finance and Insurance sector); and bakeries (which are now in the Manufacturing sector).

In addition, this sector now includes industries previously classified in Wholesale Trade that sold merchandise using facilities open to the general public. Prominent examples of these are automotive supplies dealers, computer and peripheral equipment merchants, office supplies dealers, farm supplies dealers, and building materials dealers.

Finance, Insurance, and Real Estate. The Finance and Insurance sector and the Real Estate Rental and Leasing sector were created from the SIC Finance, Insurance, and Real Estate sector. While most of the changes affecting finance and insurance were minor at the sector level, some industries left the finance part of this sector and other industries came into this sector. Prominent among those leaving are holding companies and patent owners and lessors. Prominent among the industries coming into the sector are pawnshops. Also, there are conceptual differences in what defines an establishment in this sector, since distinct activities have a less physical/geographical basis than industries in most other sectors. Note that funds, trusts, and other financial vehicles (except for REITs), although part of this sector, are not in scope of the 1997 Economic Census.

While most of the changes affecting real estate were minor at the sector level, some industries left the real estate part of this sector and other industries came into this sector. Prominent among those leaving are title abstract offices and land subdividers and developers. Prominent among the industries coming into the sector are patent owners and lessors, miniwarehouses, and most of the rental industries previously classified in the Services Division of the SIC, including video tape, motor vehicle, computer, and equipment rental and leasing. Rental of equipment with operators is classified elsewhere, depending on the services provided.

Service Industries. The Professional, Scientific, and Technical Services sector primarily includes professional and other highly specialized technical service establishments that were classified Services under the SIC. The Educational Services sector, the Health Care and Social Assistance sector, the Arts, Entertainment, and Recreation sector, and the Other Services Sector primarily include establishments that were classified as Services under the SIC.

BUILDING PERMITS, Items 279–281
Source: U.S. Bureau of the Census— Building Permits Survey

Figures represent private residential construction authorized by building permits in approximately 19,000 places in the United States. Valuation represents the expected cost of construction as recorded on the building permit. This figure usually excludes the cost of on-site and off-site development and improvements and the cost of heating, plumbing, electrical, and elevator installations.

County, state, and U.S. totals were obtained by adding the data for permit issuing places within each jurisdiction. These totals thus are limited to permits issued in the 19,000 place universe covered by the Census Bureau and may not include all permits issued within the state.

Residential building permits include buildings with any number of housing units. Apartment hotels, hotels, dormitories, fraternity houses, and other non-housekeeping residential buildings are not included.

MANUFACTURED HOUSING UNITS, Item 282
Source: U.S. Bureau of the Census, Survey of New Mobile Home Placements

The Survey of New Mobile Home Placements involves a monthly sample of new mobile homes shipped by manufacturers. The dealer to whom the sampled unit was shipped is contacted by

A mobile home, often referred to as a manufactured housing unit , is defined as a movable dwelling, 8 feet or more wide and 40 feet or more long, designed to be towed on its own chassis, with transportation gear integral to the unit when it leaves the factory, and without need of a permanent foundation. These mobile homes include multiwides, which are counted as single units, and expandable mobile homes. Excluded are travel trailers, motor homes, and modular housing.

EXPORTS, Items 283–285
Source: U.S. Bureau of the Census

The data on exports of goods by state of origin are based on the location of the exporter, that is, the principal party responsible for effecting export from the United States. Exporters often are intermediaries, so the data do not necessarily represent the states where the goods were actually produced. The total includes reexports of foreign goods.

FEDERAL FUNDS, Items 286–302
Source: U.S. Bureau of the Census— Consolidated Federal Funds Report

Data on federal expenditures and obligations are obtained from a report prepared by the Bureau of the Census in accordance with the Consolidated Federal Funds Report (CFFR) Act of 1982 (P.L. 97-326). The data are for federal fiscal years beginning on October 1 and ending the following September 30.

Direct payments for individuals include social security benefits, federal government retirement, medicare, supplemental security income, food stamps, educational and housing assistance, and other categories not shown separately. All data represent actual expenditures during the fiscal year.

Direct payments for educational assistance consist primarily of higher education grants and insured loans. Direct housing assistance includes primarily the Low Income Housing Assistance Program.

Grants data represent the federal obligations incurred at the time the grant is awarded. The amounts reported do not represent actual expenditures since obligations in one time period may not result in outlays during the same time period. Moreover, initial amounts obligated may be adjusted at a later date, either through enhancements or de-obligations.

Medicaid and other health-related grants include a variety of grants from the Department of Health and Human Services for health services and research.

Nutrition and family welfare grants include a variety of grants by the Department of Health and Human Services for child welfare, special programs for the aging, and related areas. The school lunch program and other nutritional assistance programs administered by the Department of Agriculture are also included.

Energy and environment grants include grants from the Department of Energy for energy development, energy conservation, and nuclear waste disposal, as well as from the Environmental Protection Agency for a variety of pollution control and waste management activities.

Education grants include a variety of grant programs relating to elementary, secondary, and post-secondary education; adult education; vocational education; faculty training; and related areas.

Housing and community development grants include Community Development Block Grants, housing demonstration programs, rental housing rehabilitation, and other housing programs.

Salaries and wages represent actual federal expenditures during the fiscal year; the geographic distribution of these amounts by state and county was estimated based upon place of employment.

Procurement contract awards cover awards by the United States Postal Service (USPS) as well as all other federal agencies. Amounts provided by the USPS represent actual outlays for contractual commitments, while amounts for other agencies represent the value of obligations for contract actions and do not reflect actual federal government expenditures. In general, only current-year contract actions are included—however, multiple-year obligations may be reported for contract actions of less than 3 years duration.

STATE GOVERNMENT FINANCES, Items 303–321
Source: U.S. Bureau of the Census

Data are from an annual survey conducted by the Bureau of the Census and pertain to state government fiscal years ending between July 1, 1999 and June 30, 2000.

Total general revenue includes all revenue except utility, liquor stores, and insurance trust revenue. All tax revenue and intergovernmental revenue, even if designated for employee-retirement or local utility purpose, are classified as general revenue.

Intergovernmental revenue covers amounts received from the federal government as fiscal aid, reimbursements for performance of general government functions and specific services for the paying government, or in lieu of taxes. It excludes any amounts received from other governments for sale of property, commodities, and utility services.

Taxes consist of compulsory contributions exacted by governments for public purposes. However, this category excludes employer and employee payments for retirement and social insurance purposes, which are classified as insurance trust revenue, and special assessments, which are classified as non-tax general revenue. Sales and gross receipts taxes, including "licenses" at more than normal rates, are based on volume or value of transfers of goods or services, on gross receipts, or on gross income, and related taxes based on use, storage, production, importation, or consumption of goods. Sales and gross receipts taxes exclude dealer discounts or "commissions" allowed to merchants for collection of taxes from consumers. General sales taxes and selected taxes on sales of motor fuels, tobacco products, and other particular commodities and services are included.

General government expenditure includes capital outlay, of which a major portion is commonly financed by borrowing, while governmental revenue does not include receipts from borrowing. Among other things, this distorts the relationship between totals of revenue and expenditure figures that are presented and renders it useless as a direct measure of the degree of budgetary "balance, as that term is generally applied.

Direct general expenditure comprises all expenditures of the state governments, excluding utility, liquor stores, insurance trust expenditures, and any intergovernmental payments.

State government expenditures for **education** are mainly for provision and support of schools and other educational facilities and services, including those for educational institutions beyond high school. They cover such related services as pupil transportation; school lunch and other cafeteria operations; school health, recreation, and library services; and dormitories, dining halls, and bookstores operated by public institutions of higher education.

Health and hospital expenditures include health research; clinics; nursing; immunization; and other categorical, environmental, and general health services provided by health agencies; establishment and operation of hospital facilities; provision of hospital care; and support of other public and private hospitals.

Highway expenditure is for provision and maintenance of highway facilities, including toll turnpikes, bridges, tunnels, and ferries, as well as regular roads, highways, and streets. Also included are expenditures for street lighting and for snow and ice removal.

Public safety expenditure includes police and correctional institution expenditure.

Public welfare expenditure covers support of and assistance to needy persons contingent upon their needs. Included are cash assistance paid directly to needy persons under categorical (Old Age Assistance, Aid to Families with Dependent Children, Aid to the Blind, and Aid to the Disabled) and other welfare programs; vendor payments made directly to private purveyors for medical care, burials, and other commodities and services provided under welfare programs; welfare institutions; and any intergovernmental or other direct expenditure for welfare purposes. Pensions to former employees and other benefits not contingent on need are excluded.

Debt outstanding includes all long-term debt obligations of the government and its agencies (exclusive of utility debt) and all interest-bearing short-term (i.e., repayable within 1 year) debt obligations remaining unpaid at the close of the fiscal year. It includes judgments, mortgages, and revenue bonds, as well as general obligation bonds, notes, and interest-bearing warrants. It includes non-interest-bearing short-term obligations; inter-fund obligations; amounts owed in a trust or agency capacity; advances and contingent loans from other governments; and rights of individuals to benefits from government-administered employee retirement funds.

GOVERNMENT EMPLOYMENT,
Items 322–324
Source: U.S. Bureau of Economic Analysis

Employment is measured as the average annual number of jobs, full-time plus part-time. The estimates are on a place-of-work basis. The data for federal civilian employment include civilian employees of the Department of Defense. Military employment includes all person on active duty status.

ELECTION STATISTICS, Items 325–327
Source: Election Data Services, Inc.
Washington, DC (copyright)

Election results show the percentage of the total vote cast for the Democratic and Republican candidates, as well as the combined percentage for all other candidates in the 2000 presidential election.

TABLES B AND C—STATES/COUNTIES and METRO AREAS

Table B presents 197 items for the United States as a whole; each state and the District of Columbia; and each county, county equivalent, or independent city. The counties are presented in alphabetical order within states, which are also in alphabetical order. Independent cities, which are found in Maryland, Missouri, Nevada, and Virginia, are placed in alphabetical order at the end of the list of counties for those states. The District of Columbia is included in Table B as both a county and a state (it is also included as a city in Table D).

Table C presents the same data for each of the 335 metropolitan areas.

LAND AREA, Items 1 and 4
Source: U.S. Bureau of the Census

Land area measurements are shown to the nearest square kilometer. Land area includes dry land and land temporarily or partially covered by water, such as marshland, swamps, and river floodplains.

POPULATION, Items 2–4
Source: U.S. Bureau of the Census, 2000 Census of Population and Housing

The population data are from the decennial census and represent the resident population as of April 1, 2000. The ranks are shown for counties (including independent cities and the District of Columbia) and separately, for metropolitan areas (including MSAs, PMSAs, and NECMAs but excluding CMSAs).

POPULATION BY AGE, RACE, SEX AND HISPANIC ORIGIN, Items 5–19
Source: U.S. Bureau of the Census—2000 Census of Population and Housing

The data on **race** were derived from answers to the question on race that was asked of all people. The concept of race, as used by the Census Bureau, reflects self-identification by people according to the race or races with which they most closely identify. These categories are socio-political constructs and should not be interpreted as being scientific or anthropological in nature. Furthermore, the race categories include both racial and national-origin groups.

In the 2000 Census, respondents were offered the option of selecting one or more races. This was not the case in prior censuses, so comparisons should be made with caution. In Table B and C, columns 5 through 8 refer to individuals who identified with each racial category, either alone or in combination with other races.

The **White** population is defined as persons who indicated their race as white, as well as persons who did not classify themselves in one of the specific race categories listed on the questionnaire but entered a nationality such as Irish, German, Italian, Lebanese, Near Easterner, Arab, or Polish.

The **Black** population includes persons who indicated their race as "Black, African Am., or Negro", as well as persons who did not classify themselves in one of the specific race categories but reported entries such as African American, Afro American, Kenyan, Nigerian, or Haitian.

The **American Indian or Alaska Native** population includes persons who indicated their race as American Indian or Alaska Native, as well as persons who did not classify themselves in one of the specific race categories but reported entries such as Canadian Indian, French American Indian, Spanish-American Indian, Eskimo, Aleut, Alaska Indian, or any of the American Indian or Alaska Native tribes.

The **Asian** population includes persons who indicated their race as Asian Indian, Chinese, Filipino, Japanese, Korean, Vietnamese, or "Other Asian", as well as persons who provided write-in entries of such Asian groups as Cambodian, Laotian, Hmong, Pakistani, or Taiwanese. Also, persons who wrote in an entry indicating one of the specific categories were classified accordingly. The **Native Hawaiian or Other Pacific Islander** population includes persons who indicated their race as "Native Hawaiian", "Guamanian or Chamorro", "Samoan" or "Other Pacific Islander", as well as persons who reported entries such as Part Hawaiian, American Samoan, Fijian, Melanesian, or Tahitian. Also, persons who wrote in an entry indicating one of the specific categories were classified accordingly. In 1990, the **Asian** and **Native Hawaiian or Other Pacific Islander** categories were combined as **Asian and Pacific Islander**. This volume uses the 1990 combination.

The population of **Some other race** includes all persons who indicated "Some other race" as well as persons who wrote in a category not included in the race categories described above, including entries such as multiracial, mixed, interracial, or a Hispanic/Latino group such as Mexican, Puerto Rican, or Cuban in the "Some other race" write-in space.

Changes in specific listing of racial categories, the new practice of allowing more than one selection in 2000, and the order in which questions appeared on the questionnaire, could all affect comparability between the 2000 and 1990 censuses.

The Hispanic population is based on a complete-count question that asked respondents "Is this person Spanish/Hispanic/Latino?" Persons marking any one of the four Hispanic categories (i.e., Mexican, Puerto Rican, Cuban, or other Spanish) are collectively referred to as Hispanic.

In the 2000 Census, the Hispanic Origin question was placed before the race question and specific instructions indicated that both questions should be answered. These changes were designed to improve accuracy, and may affect comparability with 1990 data.

Age derived from the census (1990) is classified as age at last birthday (i.e., number of completed years from birth to April 1). The percent figures are derived by dividing the number of persons in a specified age group by the total population of a given geographic area. Data on age are based on complete counts of resident population.

The 2000 Census also asked for the specific date of birth of the respondent, and 2000 census procedures used the birth date for deriving age data. For this reason, it is likely that the 2000 data have fewer problems than prior censuses, such as a tendency to round ages or report the person's age on the date the questionnaire was filled out rather than on April 1.

The female population of a geographic area is shown as a percent of the total population of the area.

POPULATION—COMPONENTS OF CHANGE, Items 20–26
Source: U.S. Bureau of the Census

Data on components of change cover an area's population for a specified number of years. Net change is the difference between the count of persons in the 1990 and 2000 census and the Census Bureau's estimate of the population on July 1, 2001. It is equal to natural change (the number of births minus the number of deaths) plus net migration. Natural change shows the total number of births and deaths in a particular area during the decade. Net migration represents the difference between the number of persons moving into a particular area and the number of persons moving away from the area. A positive figure indicates net immigration to the area; a negative figure indicates net out-migration from the area.

Because the 2001 population estimates are based on a model that begins with a national population estimate, the county components of change do not always exactly add up to the difference between the 2000 census population and the 2001 estimates.

HOUSEHOLDS, Items 27–31
Source: U.S. Bureau of the Census— 2000 Census of Population and Housing

A household consists of persons occupying a single housing unit. A housing unit is a house, an apartment, a group of rooms, or a single room occupied as separate living quarters. The occupants may be a single family, one person living alone, 2 or more families living together, or any other group of related or unrelated persons sharing a housing unit. The number of households is the same as the number of year-round occupied housing units.

A family household consists of 2 or more persons, including the householder, who are related by birth, marriage, or adoption and who live together as one household; all such persons are considered as members of 1 family.

The measure of persons per household is obtained by dividing the number of persons in households by the number of households or householders. The category **female family householder** includes only female-headed family households with no spouse present.

BIRTHS AND DEATHS, Items 32–37
Source: U.S. Centers for Disease Control (CDC)

The registration of births, deaths, and other vital events in the United States is primarily a state and local function. The civil laws of every state provide for a continuous and permanent birth and death registration system. Through the National Vital Statistics System, the National Center for Health Statistics (NCHS) obtains data on births and deaths from the registration offices of each state, New York City, and the District of Columbia.

Birth and death statistics are limited to events occurring during the year. The data are by place of residence and exclude events occurring to nonresidents of the United States. Births or deaths that occur outside the United States are excluded.

Birth and death rates represent the number of births and deaths per 1,000 resident population enumerated as of April 1 for decennial census years and estimated as of July 1 for other years.

Figures for infant deaths include deaths of children under 1 year of age; they exclude fetal deaths. The infant death rate is per 1,000 live births.

In order to protect the privacy of individuals, the Centers for Disease Control does not make county-level data available where the number of individual events falls below a threshold figure. Since a 3-year time span allows time for more events to occur, cumulative data covering 3 years tend to be more complete than data for a single year. Also, an average for a 3-year period may more accurately represent the trend level when the number of events each year is small. For these reasons, the county data in this volume are presented as an average computed from data covering a 3-year time span. State data in this table are presented on the same basis in order to maintain comparability. Even with the 3-year average, death rates based on fewer than 20 deaths should be considered unreliable.

Beginning with 1999 data, the CDC used a new revision of the International Classification of Diseases, preventing combinations of data from 1999 with prior years. In this volume, where only the total deaths are used, the separate data sets were combined, but accurate infant death rates at the county level were not possible in many cases.

PHYSICIANS, Items 38–39
Source: Health Market Science, Inc., as published in Bernan's *Health and Healthcare in the United States*, copyright 2001 NationsHealth Corporation, LLC. Reprinted with permission.

Physicians are health practitioners having the degree of M.D. (Doctor of Medicine) or D.O. (Doctor of Osteopathy) primarily engaged in the practice of general or specialized medicine or surgery. The rate of physicians per 100,000 resident population is an indicator of the supply of physicians within a geographic area.

HOSPITALS, Items 40–42
Source: Health Market Science, Inc., as published in Bernan's *Health and Healthcare in the United States*, copyright 1999 NationsHealth Corporation, LLC. Reprinted with permission.

Hospitals are licensed institutions with at least six beds whose primary function is to provide diagnostic and therapeutic patient services for medical conditions by an organized physician staff, and have continuous nursing services under the supervision of registered nurses. Only short term general hospitals are included in these figures.

A hospital bed is any bed that is licensed for use by inpatients. The count of beds in a facility typically represents the count of beds at the end of the reporting period (e.g., a year) regardless of whether it is operational or not. The number of hospital beds per 100,000 population is a measure of the supply of hospital beds within a geographic area.

MEDICARE ENROLLEES, Item 43
Source: Centers for Medicare and Medicaid Services (CMS)

The Centers for Medicare and Medicaid Services (CMS) administers Medicare which provides health insurance to people aged 65 and over and those who have permanent kidney failure and certain people with disabilities. Medicare has two parts: Hospital Insurance and Supplemental Medical Insurance. The numbers in this volume include persons enrolled in either or both parts of the program as of July 1, 2000, by their state of residence.

CRIME, Items 44–47
Source: U.S. Federal Bureau of Investigation— Uniform Crime Reports

Crime data are as reported to the FBI by law enforcement agencies and have not been adjusted for under-reporting. This may affect comparability between geographic areas or over time.

Through the voluntary contribution of crime statistics by law enforcement agencies across the United States, the Uniform Crime Reporting (UCR) Program provides periodic assessments of crime in the nation as measured by those offenses which come to the attention of the law enforcement community. The Committee on Uniform Crime Records of the International Association of Chiefs of Police initiated this voluntary national data-collection effort in 1930. UCR Program contributors compile and submit their crime data in 1 of 2 manners: either directly to the FBI or through the state UCR Programs.

Seven offenses, because of their seriousness, frequency of occurrence, and likelihood of being reported to police, were initially selected to serve as an index for evaluating fluctuations in the volume of crime. These serious crimes were murder and nonnegligent manslaughter, forcible rape, robbery, aggravated assault, burglary, larceny-theft, and motor vehicle theft. By congressional mandate, arson was added as the eighth index offense in 1979. The totals shown in this volume do not include arson.

Violent offenses include 4 crime categories: (1) Murder and nonnegligent manslaughter, as defined in the UCR Program, is the willful (nonnegligent) killing of 1 human being by another. This offense excludes deaths caused by negligence, suicide or accident; justifiable homicides; and attempts to murder or assaults to murder. (2) Forcible rape is the carnal knowledge of a female forcibly and against her will. Assaults or attempts to commit rape by force or threat of force are also included; however, statutory rape (without force) and other sex offenses are excluded. (3) Robbery is the taking or attempting to take anything of value from the care, custody, or control of a person or persons by force or threat of force

or violence and/or by putting the victim in fear. (4) Aggravated assault is an unlawful attack by 1 person upon another for the purpose of inflicting severe or aggravated bodily injury. This type of assault is usually accompanied by the use of a weapon or by means likely to produce death or great bodily harm. Attempts are included since an injury does not necessarily have to result when a gun, knife, or other weapon is used, which could and probably would result in a serious personal injury if the crime were successfully completed.

Property crimes include 3 categories: (1) Burglary, or breaking and entering, is the unlawful entry of a structure to commit a felony or theft, even though no force was used to gain entrance. (2) Larceny/theft is the unauthorized taking of the personal property of another, without the use of force. (3) Motor vehicle theft is the unauthorized taking of any motor vehicle.

Rates are based on population estimates provided by the FBI. The county totals published in this volume were obtained by aggregating individual reporting units within each county. If the population total for the units aggregated was less than 75 percent of the county's population (as estimated by the Bureau of the Census), the total was not considered representative of the county as a whole and is not published. State and US totals include FBI estimates for those areas.

EDUCATION—SCHOOL ENROLLMENT AND EDUCATIONAL ATTAINMENT, Items 48–51
Source: U.S. Bureau of the Census— 1990 Census of Population and Housing

Data on school enrollment and educational attainment were derived from a sample of the population. Persons were classified as enrolled in school if they reported attending a "regular" public or private school (or college) at any time between February 1, 1990 and the time of enumeration. The instructions were to "include only nursery school, kindergarten, elementary school, and schooling which would lead to a high school diploma or a college degree" as regular school. Public school is defined as "any school or college controlled and supported by a local, county, state, or federal government." Schools supported and controlled primarily by religious organizations or other private groups are defined as private.

Statistics for years of school completed are for persons 25 years old and over. The data were derived from a question on the 1990 census questionnaire that asked respondents for the highest level of school they had completed or the highest degree they had received. Persons who passed a high school equivalency examination were considered high school graduates. Schooling received in foreign schools was to be reported as the equivalent grade or years in the regular American school system.

LOCAL GOVERNMENT EDUCATION EXPENDITURES, Items 52–53
Source: U.S. National Center for Educational Statistics

Total expenditure for education includes provision or support of schools and facilities for elementary and secondary education. It encompasses instructional, support, and auxiliary services (school lunch, student activities, and community services) offered by public school systems. Retirement benefits paid to former education employees and interest payments are not included. Current expenditure includes all components of total expenditure except capital outlay. Expenditure data are obtained by the U.S. Bureau of the Census through its annual surveys of government finances and are supplied by the Bureau of the Census to the National Center for Education Statistics. Current expenditures per pupil is current expenditures divided by the number of students enrolled. The number of students enrolled is based on an annual "membership" count of students on or about October 1.

NCES uses the Common Core of Data (CCD) Survey to acquire and maintain statistical data from each of the 50 states, the District of Columbia, and the outlying areas. The state education agencies compile and submit data for approximately 85,000 schools and 15,000 local school districts. Typically this results in varying interpretation of NCES definitions and different record-keeping systems, leading to large amounts of missing data for several states in this volume. Schools and school districts are included in the county where the school district offices (the Local Education Agency) are located.

MONEY INCOME, Items 54–57
Source: U.S. Bureau of the Census—
1990 Census of Population and Housing

The data on income are derived from the responses of a sample of persons 15 years old and older. **Total money income** is defined by the Bureau of the Census for statistical purposes as the sum of the following: wage or salary income; nonfarm self-employment income; net farm self-employment income; Social Security and railroad retirement income; public assistance income; and all other regularly received income such as interest, dividends, veterans' payments, pensions, unemployment compensation, and alimony. Receipts not counted as income include various "lump sum" payments such as capital gains or inheritances.

The total represents the amount of income received before deductions for personal income taxes, Social Security, bond purchases, union dues, Medicare deductions, etc.

Per capita income is based on resident population enumerated as of April 1, 1990.

Income of households includes the income of the householder and all other persons 15 years old and older in the household. Median household income is usually less than median family income because many households consist of only 1 person. The median divides the income distribution into 2 equal parts, 1 having incomes above the median, the other with incomes below.

The constant-dollar figures are based on an annual average Consumer Price Index from the Bureau of Labor Statistics. Constant-dollar figures are estimates representing an effort to remove the effects of price changes from statistical series reported in dollar terms. However, the estimates do not reflect the price and cost-of-living differences that may exist between areas.

Money income differs in definition from personal income (item 62). For example, money income does not include the pension rights, employer provided health insurance, food stamps, or Medicare payments that are included in personal income.

INCOME AND POVERTY, Items 58–61
Source: U.S. Bureau of the Census—Small Area Income and Poverty Estimates Program

The 1998 income and poverty estimates by county are constructed from statistical models that relate income and poverty to indicators based on summary data from federal income tax returns, data about participation in the Food Stamp program, and the previous Census.

Poverty status is based on the definition prescribed by the Federal Office of Management and Budget as the standard to be used by federal agencies for statistical purposes. Families and persons are classified as being below the poverty level if their total family income or unrelated individual income was less than the poverty threshold specified for the applicable family size, age of householder, and number of related children present under 18. Poverty status is determined for all families (and by implication all family members). For persons not in families, poverty status is determined by their income in relation to the appropriate poverty threshold. Inmates of institutions, persons in military group quarters or college dormitories, and unrelated individuals under 15 are excluded.

The 1998 poverty thresholds are shown in Figure 1.

Figure 1.
Poverty Thresholds in 1998 by Size of Family

Size of Family Unit	Weighted average thresholds
One person (unrelated individual)	$8,316
Under 65 years	8,480
65 years and over	7,818
Two persons	10,634
Householder under 65 years	10,972
Householder 65 years and over	9,862
Three persons	13,003
Four persons	16,660
Five persons	19,680
Six persons	22,228
Seven persons	25,257
Eight persons	28,166
Nine or more persons	33,339

PERSONAL INCOME AND EARNINGS, Items 62–83
Source: U.S. Bureau of Economic Analysis

Total personal income is the current income received by residents of an area from all sources. It is measured before deductions of income and other personal taxes but after deduction of personal contributions for Social Security, government retirement, and other social insurance programs. It consists of **wage and salary disbursements** (covering all employee earnings, including executive salaries, bonuses, commissions, payments-in-kind, incentive payments, and tips), **other labor income** (primarily employer contributions to private pension funds), proprietors' income, rental income of persons, dividends, personal interest income, and government and business transfer payments.

Proprietors' income is the monetary income and income in-kind of proprietorships and partnerships, including the independent professions, and of tax-exempt cooperatives. **Dividends** are cash payments by for-profit corporations to stockholders who are U.S. residents. **Interest** is the monetary and imputed interest income of persons from all sources. **Rent** is the monetary income of persons from the rental of real property except the income of persons primarily engaged in the real estate business, the imputed net rental income of owner-occupants of nonfarm dwellings, and the royalties received by persons.

Transfer payments are income for which services are not currently rendered. They consist of both government and business transfer payments. Government transfer payments include payments under the following programs: Federal Old-age, Survivors, and Disability Insurance ("Social Security"); Medicare and medical vendor payments; unemployment insurance, railroad and government retirement; federal and state government-insured workers' compensation; veterans benefits, including veterans life insurance; food stamps; black lung; Supplemental Security Income; and Aid to Families with Dependent Children. Government payments to nonprofit institutions, other than for work under research and development contracts, are also included. The principal business transfers are corporate gifts to nonprofit institutions and consumer bad debts.

Per capita personal income is based on resident population estimated as of July 1 of the year shown.

Personal income differs in definition from money income (items 54-57). For example, personal income includes pension rights, employer provided health insurance, food stamps, and Medicare. These are not included in the definition of money income.

Earnings cover wage and salary disbursements, other labor income, and proprietors' income.

Data for earnings obtained from the Bureau of Economic Analysis (BEA) are based on place of work. In computing personal income, BEA makes an "adjustment for residence" to earnings based on commuting patterns, so that personal income is presented on a place of residence basis.

Farm earnings include the income of farm workers (wages and salaries and other labor income) and farm proprietors. Farm proprietors' income includes only the income of sole proprietorships and partnerships.

Farm earning estimates are benchmarked to data collected in the Census of Agriculture and the revised U.S. Department of Agriculture State totals of income and expense items.

"Goods-related" industries include mining, construction, and manufacturing. "Service-related and other" includes private sector earnings in agricultural services, forestry and fisheries; transportation and public utilities; wholesale trade; retail trade; finance, insurance, and real estate; and services. Government earnings include all levels of government.

SOCIAL SECURITY AND SUPPLEMENTAL SECURITY INCOME, Items 84–86
Source: U.S. Social Security Administration

Social Security beneficiaries is the number of persons receiving benefits under the Old-age, Survivors, and Disability Insurance Program. These include retired or disabled workers covered by the program, their spouses and dependent children, and the surviving spouses and dependent children of deceased workers.

Supplemental Security Income (SSI) recipients is the number of persons receiving SSI payments. Data are as of December of the year shown.

HOUSING, Items 87–96
Source: U.S. Bureau of the Census—
1990 Census of Population and Housing

A **housing unit** is a house, apartment, mobile home or trailer, group of rooms, or single room occupied or, if vacant, intended for occupancy as separate living quarters. Separate living quarters are those in which the occupants do not live and eat with any other persons in the structure and which have direct access from the outside of the building through a common hall.

The occupants of a housing unit may be a single family, 1 person living alone, 2 or more families living together, or a group of related or unrelated persons who share living arrangements. For vacant units, the criteria of separateness and direct access are applied to the intended occupants whenever possible. If that information cannot be obtained, the criteria are applied to the previous occupants. Both occupied and vacant housing units are included in the housing inventory, except that recreational vehicles, tents, caves, boats, railroad cars, and the like are included only if they are occupied as someone's usual place of residence.

A housing unit is classified as occupied if it is the usual place of residence of the person or group of persons living in it at the time of enumeration, or if the occupants are only temporarily absent (e.g., away on vacation). A household consists of all persons who occupy a housing unit as their usual place of residence.

The percent change represents the difference in the number of total housing units in a specified area over the decade 1980-1990.

Median value is the dollar amount that divides the distribution of owner-occupied housing units into 2 equal parts, with one half of the units falling below this value and the other half exceeding it. Value is defined as the respondent's estimate of what the house would sell for if it were for sale. Data are presented for 1-family units on less than 10 acres and with no business or medical office on the property.

Median rent divides the distribution of renter-occupied housing units into 2 equal parts. Median rent represents the amount of cash rent a renter pays (contract rent) plus the estimated average cost of utilities and fuels if paid by the renter (gross rent). Rent is to be reported only for living quarters, not for any business or other space occupied. Single family houses on lots of 10 or more acres are excluded.

Housing cost as a percent of income is shown separately for owners with mortgages, owners without mortgages, and renters.

Rent as a percentage of income is a computed ratio of gross rent and monthly household income (total household income in 1989 divided by 12). Selected owner costs include utilities and fuels, as well as mortgage payments, insurance, taxes, etc. In each case, the ratio of housing cost to income is computed separately for each housing unit. The ratios for one-half of the units are above the median shown in this book, and one-half are below.

Substandard units are occupied units which are overcrowded or lack complete plumbing facilities. For the purposes of this item "overcrowded" is defined as having 1.01 persons or more per room. Complete plumbing facilities include hot and cold piped water, a flush toilet, and a bathtub or shower. These facilities must be located inside the housing unit but not necessarily in the same room.

CIVILIAN LABOR FORCE AND UNEMPLOYMENT, Items 97–100
Source: U.S. Bureau of Labor Statistics

Data for the civilian labor force are the product of a federal-state cooperative program in which state employment security agencies prepare labor force and unemployment estimates under concepts, definitions, and technical procedures established by the Bureau of Labor Statistics. The civilian labor force consists of all civilians 16 years and over who are either employed in a civilian job or unemployed.

Unemployment includes all persons who did not work during the survey week, made specific efforts to find a job in the prior four weeks, and were available for work during the survey week (except for temporary illness). Persons waiting to be called back to a job from which they had been laid off and those waiting to report to a new job within the next 30 days are included in unemployment figures.

CIVILIAN EMPLOYMENT, 1990, Items 101–103
Source: U.S. Bureau of the Census— 1990 Census of Population and Housing

Total employment includes all civilians 16 years old or older who were either (1) "at work" — those who did any work at all during the reference week as paid employees, worked in their own business or profession, worked on their own farm, or worked 15 hours or more as unpaid workers in a family farm or business; or were (2) "with a job, but not at work" — those who had a job but were not at work that week due to illness, weather, industrial dispute, vacation, or other personal reasons.

The **occupation categories** shown are consistent with the 1980 edition of the *Standard Occupational Classification Manual (SOC)*, published by the Office of Federal Statistical Policy and Standards, U.S. Department of Commerce. Professional, managerial, and technical occupations include the following categories: executive, administrative, and managerial occupations (000-042); professional specialty occupations (043-202); and technicians and related support occupations (203-242). Precision production, craft and repair includes SOC codes 503-702.

PRIVATE NONFARM ESTABLISHMENTS AND EMPLOYMENT, Items 104–112
Source: U.S. Bureau of the Census— County Business Patterns

Data for private nonfarm establishments, employment, and payroll are reported in the U.S. Bureau of the Census publication *County Business Patterns*. The estimates are based on surveys conducted by the Bureau of the Census and administrative records from the Internal Revenue Service (IRS).

The following types of employment are excluded from the tables: government employment; self employed persons; farm workers; and domestic service workers. Railroad employment jointly covered by social security and railroad retirement programs, employment on oceanborne vessels, and employment in foreign countries are also excluded.

Annual payroll is the combined amount of wages paid, tips reported, and other compensation (including salaries, vacation allowances, bonuses, commissions, sick leave pay, and the value of payments-in-kind such as free meals and lodging) paid to employees before deductions for Social Security, income tax, insurance, union dues, etc. All forms of compensation are included, whether or not subject to income tax or Federal Insurance Contributions Act tax, with the exception of annuities, third-party sick pay, and supplemental unemployment compensation benefits (even if income tax was withheld). For corporations, total annual payroll includes compensation paid to officers and executives; for unincorporated businesses, it does not include profit or other compensation of proprietors or partners.

AGRICULTURE, Items 113–130
Source: U.S. Department of Agriculture, National Agricultural Statistics Service— 1997 Census of Agriculture

Data for the 1997 Census of Agriculture were collected in 1998 and pertain to the year 1997.

The Bureau of the Census took a census of agriculture every 10 years from 1840 to 1920 and roughly every 5 years from 1925 to 1992. The 1997 Census of Agriculture was transfered to the National Agricultural Statistics Service of the U.S. Department of Agriculture. Over time, the definition of a farm has varied. For recent censuses, including the 1997 census, a farm has been defined as any place from which $1,000 or more of agricultural products were sold or normally would have been sold during the census year.

The term **operator** refers to a person who operates a farm, either doing the work or making day-to-day decisions about such things as planting, harvesting, feeding, marketing, etc. The operator may be the owner, a member of the owner's household, a salaried manager, a tenant, a renter, or a sharecropper. For partnerships, only one partner is counted as an operator. For census purposes, the number of operators is the same as the number of farms.

The acreage designated as **land in farms** consists primarily of agricultural land used for crops, pasture, or grazing. It also includes woodland and wasteland not actually under cultivation or used for pasture or grazing, if it was part of the operator's total operation.

Land in farms is an operating-unit concept and includes land owned and operated, as well as land rented from others. Land used rent free was to be reported as land rented from others. All land in Indian reservations used for growing crops or grazing livestock was to be included as land in farms.

With few exceptions, the land in each farm was tabulated as being in the operator's principal county. The principal county was defined as the one where the largest value of agricultural products were raised or produced; it was usually the county containing all or the largest proportion of the land in the farm. For a limited number of Western states, this procedure resulted in the allocation of more land in farms to a county than the total land area of the county.

Irrigated land covers any land in farms to which water was artificially applied in the census year. Land irrigated prior to, but not in the census year, is not included. Irrigation may have been used for producing a harvested crop, for pasture or grazing lands, for cultivated summer fallow, or for land planted to a crop intended for future harvest. Land flooded during high-water periods was included as irrigated only if water was diverted to agricultural lands by dams, canals, or other works.

Cropland consists of land from which crops were harvested and land that could have been used for crops without additional improvements. This includes land in nonbearing orchards and vineyards, land from which any hay was cut, land on which crops failed, idle or fallow land, and land used for grazing purposes.

Respondents were asked to report their estimate of the current market value of land and buildings owned, rented, or leased from others, and rented and leased to others. Market value refers to the respondent's estimate of what the land and buildings would sell for under current market conditions. If the value of land and buildings was not reported, it was estimated during processing by using the average value of land and buildings from similar farms in the same geographic area.

The **value of machinery and equipment** was estimated by the respondent as the current market value of all cars, trucks, tractors, combines, balers, irrigation equipment, etc., used on the farm. This value is an estimate of what the machinery and equipment would sell for in its present condition and not the replacement or depreciated value. Share interests are reported at full value at the farm where the equipment and machinery are usually kept. Only equipment that was actually used in 1996 and 1997, or newly purchased but not yet used, and physically located at the farm on December 31, 1997 is included

The **value of farm products sold** by farms represents the gross market value before taxes and production expenses of all agricultural products sold or removed from the place in 1997 regardless of who received the payment. It includes sales by the operator as well as the value of any share received by partners, landlords, contractors, and others associated with the operation. It represents the sum of all crops, including nursery products sold and livestock and poultry and their products sold.

The value of crops sold in 1997 does not necessarily represent the sales from crops harvested that year. The data include sales from crops produced in earlier years and exclude some crops

produced in 1997 but held in storage and not sold in the census year. For crops sold through a co-op that made payments in several installments, only the total value received in the census year was to be reported.

LAND USE, Item 131
**Source: U.S. Department of Agriculture,
Natural Resources Conservation Service,
1997 National Resources Inventory**

The National Resources Inventory has been conducted every five years since 1982. The 1997 NRI is based on a sample of about 800,000 locations throughout the United States (excluding Alaska and the District of Columbia.) Federally owned lands include military bases, national forests, wildlife refuges, parks, grassland game preserves, scenic waterways, wilderness areas, monuments, lakeshore, parkways, battlefields, Bureau of Land Management lands, and other federal lands.

WATER CONSUMPTION, Item 132
Source: U.S. Geological Survey, National Water Use Information Program, 1995 Water Use Data.

Every five years the U.S. Geological Survey compiles national water-use estimates. This volume includes the total freshwater withdrawals expressed as million gallons per day. Estimates of withdrawals of ground and surface water are given for the following categories of use: public water supplies, domestic, commercial, irrigation, livestock, industrial, mining, and thermoelectric power.

CONSTRUCTION—BUILDING PERMITS, Items 133–134
Source: U.S. Bureau of the Census— Building Permits Survey

Figures represent private residential construction authorized by building permits in approximately 19,000 places in the United States. Valuation represents the cost of construction as recorded on the building permit. This figure usually excludes the cost of on-site and off-site development and improvements and the cost of heating, plumbing, electrical, and elevator installations.

County, state, and U.S. totals were obtained by summing the data for permit-issuing places within each jurisdiction. Thus, these totals are limited to permits issued in the 19,000 place universe covered by the Census Bureau and may not include all permits issued within the county. If a county does not contain permit-issuing places covered by the Census Bureau, an "NA" is shown. Counties with permit-issuing places that issued no permits during the period are represented by a "0."

Residential building permits include buildings with any number of housing units. Hotels, apartment hotels, dormitories, fraternity houses, and other non-housekeeping residential buildings are not included.

1997 ECONOMIC CENSUS: OVERVIEW
Items 135–166
Source: U.S. Bureau of the Census

The Economic Census provides a detailed portrait of the nation's economy once every five years, from the national to the local level. The 1997 Economic Census covers nearly all of the U.S. economy in its basic collection of establishment statistics. It is the first major data source to use the new North American Industry Classification System (NAICS) and is therefore not comparable to economic data from prior years which were based on the Standard Industrial Classification (SIC) system.

NAICS, developed in cooperation with Canada and Mexico, classifies North America's economic activities at 2-, 3-, 4-, and 5-digit levels of detail, and the U.S. version of NAICS further defines industries to a sixth digit. The Economic Census takes advantage of this hierarchy to publish data at these successive levels of detail: sector (2-digit); subsector (3-digit); industry group (4-digit); industry(5-digit); and U.S. industry(6-digit.)

This volume was published during the initial release of the 1997 Economic Census and therefore includes those sectors that were available at the time of publication. The information in Tables B and C is at the 2-digit level.

Several key statistics are tabulated for all industries included in this volume: number of establishments (or companies); number of employees; payroll; and a measure of output (sales, receipts, revenue, value of shipments, or value of construction work done.)

Number of Establishments. An establishment is a single physical location at which business is conducted. It is not necessarily identical with a company or enterprise, which may consist of one establishment or more. Economic Census figures represent a summary of reports for individual establishments rather than companies. For cases where a census report was received, separate information was obtained for each location where business was conducted. When administrative records of other Federal agencies were used instead of a census report, no information was available on the number of locations operated. Each Economic Census establishment was tabulated according to the physical location at which the business was conducted. The count of establishments represents those in business at any time during 1997.

When two activities or more were carried on at a single location under a single ownership, all activities generally were grouped together as a single establishment. The entire establishment was classified on the basis of its major activity and all data for it were included in that classification. However, when distinct and separate economic activities (for which different industry classification codes were appropriate) were conducted at a single location under a single ownership, separate establishment reports for each of the different activities were obtained in the census.

Number of Employees. Paid employees consist of the full-time and part-time employees, including salaried officers and executives of corporations. Included are employees on paid sick leave, paid holidays, and paid vacations; not included are proprietors and partners of unincorporated businesses. The definition of paid employees is the same as that used on IRS form 941.

Payroll. Payroll includes all forms of compensation such as salaries, wages, commissions, dismissal pay, bonuses, vacation allowances, sick-leave pay, and employee contributions to qualified pension plans paid during the year to all employees. For corporations, payroll includes amounts paid to officers and executives; for unincorporated businesses, it does not include profit or other compensation of proprietors or partners. Payroll is reported before deductions for social security, income tax, insurance, union dues, etc. This definition of payroll is the same as that used by the Internal Revenue Service (IRS) on form 941.

Sales, Shipments, Receipts, Revenue, or Business Done. This measure includes the total sales, shipments, receipts, revenue, or business done by establishments within the scope of the Economic Census. The definition of each of these items is specific to the economic sector measured.

WHOLESALE TRADE, Items 135–138
Source: U.S. Bureau of the Census,
1997 Economic Census
(See Overview of 1997 Economic Census
prior to Item 135)

The Wholesale Trade sector (sector 42) comprises establishments engaged in wholesaling merchandise, generally without transformation, and rendering services incidental to the sale of merchandise. The wholesaling process is an intermediate step in the distribution of merchandise.

Wholesalers are organized to sell or arrange the purchase or sale of (a) goods for resale (i.e., goods sold to other wholesalers or retailers), (b) capital or durable nonconsumer goods, and (c) raw and intermediate materials and supplies used in production.

Wholesalers sell merchandise to other businesses and normally operate from a warehouse or office. These warehouses and offices are characterized by having little or no display of merchandise. In addition, neither the design nor the location of the premises is intended to solicit walk-in traffic. Wholesalers do not normally use advertising directed to the general public. Customers are generally reached initially via telephone, in-person marketing, or by specialized advertising that may include Internet and other electronic means. Follow-up orders are either vendor-initiated or client-initiated, generally based on previous sales, and typically exhibit strong ties between sellers and buyers. In fact, transactions are often conducted between wholesalers and clients that have long-standing business relationships.

This sector comprises two main types of wholesalers: those that sell goods on their own account and those that arrange sales and purchases for others for a commission or fee.

(1) Establishments that sell goods on their own account are known as wholesale merchants, distributors, jobbers, drop shippers, import/export merchants, and sales branches. These establishments typically maintain their own warehouse, where they receive and handle goods for their customers. Goods are generally sold without transformation, but may include integral functions, such as sorting, packaging, labeling, and other marketing services.

(2) Establishments arranging for the purchase or sale of goods owned by others or purchasing goods on a commission basis are

known as agents and brokers, commission merchants, import/export agents and brokers, auction companies, and manufacturers' representatives. These establishments operate from offices and generally do not own or handle the goods they sell.

Some wholesale establishments may be connected with a single manufacturer and promote and sell the particular manufacturer=s products to a wide range of other wholesalers or retailers. Other wholesalers may be connected to a retail chain or a limited number of retail chains and only provide a variety of products needed by that particular retail operation(s). These wholesalers may obtain the products from a wide range of manufacturers. Still other wholesalers may not take title to the goods, but act as agents and brokers for a commission.

Although, in general, wholesaling normally denotes sales in large volumes, durable nonconsumer goods may be sold in single units. Sales of capital or durable nonconsumer goods used in the production of goods and services, such as farm machinery, medium and heavy duty trucks, and industrial machinery, are always included in wholesale trade.

RETAIL TRADE, Items 139–142
Source: U.S. Bureau of the Census, 1997 Economic Census
(See Overview of 1997 Economic Census prior to Item 135)

The Retail Trade sector (44-45) comprises establishments engaged in retailing merchandise, generally without transformation, and rendering services incidental to the sale of merchandise.

The retailing process is the final step in the distribution of merchandise; retailers are, therefore, organized to sell merchandise in small quantities to the general public. This sector comprises two main types of retailers: store and nonstore retailers.

Store retailers operate fixed point-of-sale locations, located and designed to attract a high volume of walk-in customers. In general, retail stores have extensive displays of merchandise and use mass-media advertising to attract customers. They typically sell merchandise to the general public for personal or household consumption, but some also serve business and institutional clients. These include establishments, such as office supply stores, computer and software stores, building materials dealers, plumbing supply stores, and electrical supply stores. Catalog showrooms, gasoline service stations, automotive dealers, and mobile home dealers are treated as store retailers.

In addition to retailing merchandise, some types of store retailers are also engaged in the provision of after-sales services, such as repair and installation. For example, new automobile dealers, electronic and appliance stores, and musical instrument and supply stores often provide repair services. As a general rule, establishments engaged in retailing merchandise and providing after-sales services are classified in this sector.

Nonstore retailers, like store retailers, are organized to serve the general public, but their retailing methods differ. The establishments of this subsector reach customers and market merchandise with methods, such as the broadcasting of "infomercials," the

broadcasting and publishing of direct-response advertising, the publishing of paper and electronic catalogs, door-to-door solicitation, in-home demonstration, selling from portable stalls (street vendors, except food), and distribution through vending machines. Establishments engaged in the direct sale (nonstore) of products, such as home heating oil dealers and home delivery newspaper routes.

The buying of goods for resale is a characteristic of retail trade establishments that particularly distinguishes them from establishments in the agriculture, manufacturing, and construction industries. For example, farms that sell their products at or from the point of production are not classified in retail, but rather in agriculture. Similarly, establishments that both manufacture and sell their products to the general public are not classified in retail, but rather in manufacturing. However, establishments that engage in processing activities incidental to retailing are classified in retail.

REAL ESTATE AND RENTAL AND LEASING, Items 143–146
Source: U.S. Bureau of the Census, 1997 Economic Census
(See Overview of 1997 Economic Census prior to Item 135)

The Real Estate and Rental and Leasing sector (53) comprises establishments primarily engaged in renting, leasing, or otherwise allowing the use of tangible or intangible assets, and establishments providing related services. The major portion of this sector comprises establishments that rent, lease, or otherwise allow the use of their own assets by others. The assets may be tangible, as is the case of real estate and equipment, or intangible, as is the case with patents and trademarks.

This sector also includes establishments primarily engaged in managing real estate for others, selling, renting and/or buying real estate for others, and appraising real estate. These activities are closely related to this sector's main activity, and it was felt that from a production basis they would best be included here. In addition, a substantial proportion of property management is self-performed by lessors.

The main components of this sector are the real estate lessors industries; equipment lessors industries (including motor vehicles, computers, and consumer goods); and lessors of nonfinancial intangible assets (except copyrighted works).

PROFESSIONAL, SCIENTIFIC, AND TECHNICAL SERVICES, Items 147–150
Source: U.S. Bureau of the Census, 1997 Economic Census
(See Overview of 1997 Economic Census prior to Item 135)

The Professional, Scientific, and Technical Services sector (54) comprises establishments that specialize in performing professional, scientific, and technical activities for others. These activities require a high degree of expertise and training. The establishments in this sector specialize according to expertise and provide these services to clients in a variety of industries and, in some cases, to households. Activities performed include: legal advice and representation; accounting, bookkeeping, and payroll services; architectural, engineering, and specialized design services; computer services; consulting services; research services; advertising services; photographic services; translation and interpretation services; veterinary services; and other professional, scientific, and technical services.

This volume includes only those establishments subject to federal income tax.

This sector excludes establishments primarily engaged in providing a range of day-to-day office administrative services, such as financial planning, billing and recordkeeping, personnel, and physical distribution and logistics. These establishments are classified in Sector 56, Administrative and Support and Waste Management and Remediation Services.

MANUFACTURING, Items 151–154
Source: U.S. Bureau of the Census,
1997 Economic Census
(See Overview of 1997 Economic Census prior to Item 135)

The Manufacturing sector comprises establishments engaged in the mechanical, physical, or chemical transformation of materials, substances, or components into new products. The assembling of component parts of manufactured products is considered manufacturing, except in cases where the activity is appropriately classified as Construction. Establishments in the Manufacturing sector are often described as plants, factories, or mills and characteristically use power-driven machines and materials-handling equipment. However, establishments that transform materials or substances into new products by hand or in the worker's home and those engaged in selling to the general public products made on the same premises from which they are sold, such as bakeries, candy stores, and custom tailors, may also be included in this sector. Manufacturing establishments may process materials or may contract with other establishments to process their materials for them. Both types of establishments are included in manufacturing. The materials, substances, or components transformed by manufacturing establishments are raw materials that are products of agriculture, forestry, fishing, mining, or quarrying as well as products of other manufacturing establishments. The materials used may be purchased directly from producers, obtained through customary trade channels, or secured without recourse to the market by transferring the product from one establishment to another, under the same ownership. The new product of a manufacturing establishment may be finished in the sense that it is ready for utilization or consumption, or it may be semifinished to become an input for an establishment engaged in further manufacturing. For example, the product of the alumina refinery is the input used in the primary production of aluminum; primary aluminum is the input to an aluminum wire drawing plant; and aluminum wire is the input for a fabricated wire product manufacturing establishment.

Data are included for counties with 500 or more employees in the manufacturing sector.

ACCOMMODATION AND FOOD SERVICES, Items 155–158
Source: U.S. Bureau of the Census,
1997 Economic Census
(See Overview of 1997 Economic Census prior to Item 135)

The Accommodation and Food Services sector (72) comprises establishments providing customers with lodging and/or preparing meals, snacks, and beverages for immediate consumption. The sector includes both accommodation and food services establishments because the two activities are often combined at the same establishment.

Excluded from this sector are civic and social organizations; amusement and recreation parks; theaters; and other recreation or entertainment facilities providing food and beverage services.

HEALTH CARE AND SOCIAL ASSISTANCE, Items 159–162
Source: U.S. Bureau of the Census,
1997 Economic Census
(See Overview of 1997 Economic Census prior to Item 135)

The Health Care and Social Assistance sector (62) comprises establishments providing health care and social assistance for individuals. The sector includes both health care and social assistance because it is sometimes difficult to distinguish between the boundaries of these two activities. The industries in this sector are arranged on a continuum starting with those establishments providing medical care exclusively, continuing with those providing health care and social assistance, and finally finishing with those providing only social assistance. The services provided by establishments in this sector are delivered by trained professionals. All industries in the sector share this commonality of process, namely, labor inputs of health practitioners or social workers with the requisite expertise. Many of the industries in the sector are defined based on the educational degree held by the practitioners included in the industry.

In this volume, only taxable establishments are included in Table B and Table C.

Excluded from this sector are aerobic classes in Subsector 713, Amusement, Gambling and Recreation Industries and nonmedical diet and weight reducing centers in Subsector 812, Personal and Laundry Services. Although these can be viewed as health services, these services are not typically delivered by health practitioners.

OTHER SERVICES, Items 163–166
Source: U.S. Bureau of the Census,
1997 Economic Census
(See Overview of 1997 Economic Census prior to Item 135)

The Other Services (except Public Administration) sector (81) comprises establishments engaged in providing services not specifically provided for elsewhere in the classification system. Establishments in this sector are primarily engaged in activities, such as equipment and machinery repairing, promoting or administering religious activities, grantmaking, advocacy, and providing drycleaning and laundry services, personal care services, death care services, pet care services, photofinishing services, temporary parking services, and dating services.

Private households that engage in employing workers on or about the premises in activities primarily concerned with the operation of the household are included in this sector.

In this volume, only firms subject to federal tax are included.

Excluded from this sector are establishments primarily engaged in retailing new equipment and also performing repairs and general maintenance on equipment. These establishments are classified in Sector 44-45, Retail Trade.

FEDERAL FUNDS, Items 167–177
Source: U.S. Bureau of the Census— Consolidated Federal Funds Report

Data on federal expenditures and obligations are obtained from a report prepared by the Bureau of the Census in accordance with the Consolidated Federal Funds Report (CFFR) Act of 1982 (P.L. 97-326). The data are for federal fiscal years beginning on October 1 and ending the following September 30. Dollar amounts reported can reflect expenditures or obligations. In some cases dollar amounts are negative representing deobligations of financial assistance that had been previously awarded. Such amounts generally appear in the grant categories.

Direct payments for individuals include social security benefits, federal government retirement, medicare, supplemental security income, food stamps, and certain other payments, including educational and housing assistance, not shown separately. All data represent actual expenditures during the fiscal year.

Salaries and wages represent actual federal expenditures during the fiscal year; the geographic distribution of these amounts by state and county was estimated based upon place of employment.

Procurement contract awards cover awards by the United States Postal Service (USPS) as well as all other federal agencies. Amounts provided by the USPS represent actual outlays for contractual commitments, while amounts for other agencies represent the value of obligations for contract actions and do not reflect actual federal government expenditures. In general, only current-year contract actions are included—however, multiple-year obligations may be reported for contract actions of less than 3 years duration.

Grants data represent the federal obligations incurred at the time the grant is awarded. The amounts reported do not represent actual expenditures since obligations in one time period may not result in outlays during the same time period. Moreover, initial amounts obligated may be adjusted at a later date, either through enhancements or de-obligations. All grant awards were reported by state, county, and city of the initial recipient. For many grants, this recipient is the state government even though the grant monies are subsequently distributed to county, municipal, or township governments.

Medicaid and other health-related grants include a variety of grants from the Department of Health and Human Services for health services and research.

Nutrition and family welfare grants include a variety of grants by the Department of Health and Human Services for child welfare, special programs for the aging, and related areas. The school lunch program and other nutritional assistance programs administered by the Department of Agriculture are also included.

Education grants include a variety of grant programs relating to elementary, secondary, and post-secondary education; adult education; vocational education; faculty training; and related areas.

LOCAL GOVERNMENT FINANCES, Items 178–191
Source: U.S. Bureau of the Census

Data on local government finances are based on results of the 1997 Census of Governments. For each county area, the financial data comprise amounts for all local governments—not only the county government but also any municipalities, townships, school districts, and special districts within the county. Statistics from governmental units located in two or more county areas are assigned to the county area containing the administrative office.

Revenue and expenditure items include all amounts of money received and paid out, respectively, by a government and its agencies (net of correcting transactions such as recoveries of refunds), with the exception of amounts for debt issuance and retirement and for loan and investment, agency, and private transactions.

Payments among the various funds and agencies of a particular government are excluded from revenue and expenditure items as representing internal transfers. Therefore, a government's contribution to a retirement fund that it administers is not counted as expenditure, nor is the receipt of this contribution by the retirement fund counted as revenue.

Total **general revenue** includes all revenue except utility, liquor stores, and insurance trust revenue. All tax revenue and intergovernmental revenue, even if designated for employee-retirement or local utility purpose, are classified as general revenue. However, to avoid duplication, revenue figures are net of reported transactions between local governments.

Intergovernmental revenue covers amounts received from the federal or state government as fiscal aid, reimbursements for performance of general government functions and specific services for the paying government, or amounts received in lieu of taxes. It excludes amounts received from other governments for sale of property, commodities, and utility services.

Taxes consist of compulsory contributions exacted by governments for public purposes. However, this category excludes employer and employee payments for retirement and social insurance purposes, which are classified as insurance trust revenue, and special assessments, which are classified as non-tax general revenue. Property taxes are taxes conditioned on ownership of property and assessed by its value.

Government expenditure includes all capital outlay, of which a major portion is commonly financed by borrowing, while governmental revenue does not include receipts from borrowing. Among other things, this distorts the relationship between totals of revenue and expenditure figures that are presented, and renders this relationship useless as a direct measure of the degree of budgetary "balance," as that term is generally applied.

Direct general expenditure comprises all expenditures of the local governments, excluding utility, liquor stores, insurance trust expenditures, and any intergovernmental payments.

Local government expenditures for **education** are mainly for provision and support of schools and other educational facilities and services, including those for educational institutions beyond the high school level operated by local governments. They cover such related services as pupil transportation; school lunch and other cafeteria operations; school health, recreation, and library services administered by local school systems; and dormitories, dining halls, and bookstores operated by public institutions of higher education.

Health and hospital expenditures include health research, clinics, nursing, immunization, and other categorical, environmental, and general health services provided by health agencies. It also includes establishment and operation of hospital facilities, provision of hospital care, and support of other public and private hospitals.

Police protection expenditure includes police activities such as patrols, communications, custody of persons awaiting trial, and vehicular inspection.

Public welfare expenditure covers support of and assistance to needy persons contingent upon their needs. Included are cash assistance paid directly to needy persons under categorical (Old Age Assistance, Aid to Families with Dependent Children, Aid to the Blind, and Aid to the Disabled) and other welfare programs; vendor payments made directly to private purveyors for medical care, burials, and other commodities and services provided under welfare programs; welfare institutions; and any intergovernmental or other direct expenditure for welfare purposes. Pensions to former employees and other benefits not contingent upon need are excluded.

Highway expenditure is for provision and maintenance of highway facilities, including toll turnpikes, bridges, tunnels, and ferries, as well as regular roads, highways, and streets. Also included are expenditures for street lighting and for snow and ice removal.

Debt outstanding includes all long-term debt obligations of the government and its agencies (exclusive of utility debt) and all interest-bearing short-term (i.e., repayable within one year) debt obligations remaining unpaid at the close of the fiscal year. It includes judgments, mortgages, and revenue bonds, as well as general obligation bonds, notes, and interest-bearing warrants. It includes non-interest-bearing short-term obligations, inter-fund obligations, amounts owed in a trust or agency capacity, advances and contingent loans from other governments, and rights of individuals to benefits from government-administered employee retirement funds.

GOVERNMENT EMPLOYMENT, Items 192–194
Source: U.S. Bureau of Economic Analysis

Employment is measured as the average annual number of jobs, full-time plus part-time. The estimates are on a place-of work basis. State and local government employment includes employment in all state and local government agencies and enterprises.

Federal civilian employment includes all civilian employees of the federal government, including civilian employees of the Department of Defense. Military employment includes all person on active duty status.

ELECTION STATISTICS, Items 195–197
Source: Election Data Services, Inc.
Washington, DC (copyright)

Election results show the percentage of the total vote cast for each of the Democratic and Republican candidates, as well as the combined percentage for all other candidates in the 1996 presidential election.

TABLE D—CITIES

Table D presents 147 items of data for cities that had a population of 25,000 or more at the time of the 2000 census.

LAND AREA, Items 1 and 4
Source: U.S. Bureau of the Census

Land area measurements are shown to the nearest square kilometer. Land area includes dry land and land temporarily or partially covered by water, such as marshland, swamps, and river floodplains.

POPULATION, Items 2–4
Source: U.S. Bureau of the Census

The population data are from the decennial census and represent the resident population as of April 1, 2000.

POPULATION AND POPULATION CHANGE, Items 5–8
Source: 1980, 1990, and 2000 Census of Population and Housing

These population counts are from the decennial census and represent resident population as of April 1, 1980, 1990, and 2000 respectively.

Population change 1980-1990 and 1990-2000 is calculated from census data based on city boundaries as they existed in 1980, 1990, and 2000 respectively. No attempt was made to adjust the data to reflect boundary changes.

POPULATION BY RACE AND HISPANIC ORIGIN, Items 9–15
Source: U.S. Bureau of the Census— 2000 Census of Population and Housing

The data on **race** were derived from answers to the question on race that was asked of all people. The concept of race, as used by the Census Bureau, reflects self-identification by people according to the race or races with which they most closely identify. These categories are socio-political constructs and should not be interpreted as being scientific or anthropological in nature. Furthermore, the race categories include both racial and national-origin groups.

In the 2000 Census, respondents were offered the option of selecting one or more races. This was not the case in prior censuses, so comparisons should be made with caution. In Table D, columns 9 through 13 refer to individuals who identified with each racial category, either alone or in combination with other races.

The **White** population is defined as persons who indicated their race as white, as well as persons who did not classify themselves in one of the specific race categories listed on the questionnaire but entered a nationality such as Irish, German, Italian, Lebanese, Near Easterner, Arab, or Polish.

The **Black** population includes persons who indicated their race as "Black, African Am., or Negro", as well as persons who did not classify themselves in one of the specific race categories but reported entries such as African American, Afro American, Kenyan, Nigerian, or Haitian.

The **American Indian or Alaska Native** population includes persons who indicated their race as American Indian or Alaska Native, as well as persons who did not classify themselves in one of the specific race categories but reported entries such as Canadian Indian, French American Indian, Spanish-American Indian, Eskimo, Aleut, Alaska Indian, or any of the American Indian or Alaska Native tribes.

The **Asian** population includes persons who indicated their race as Asian Indian, Chinese, Filipino, Japanese, Korean, Vietnamese, or "Other Asian", as well as persons who provided write-in entries of such Asian groups as Cambodian, Laotian, Hmong, Pakistani, or Taiwanese. Also, persons who wrote in an entry indicating one of the specific categories were classified accordingly. The **Native Hawaiian or Other Pacific Islander** population includes persons who indicated their race as "Native Hawaiian", "Guamanian or Chamorro", "Samoan" or "Other Pacific Islander", as well as persons who reported entries such as Part Hawaiian, American Samoan, Fijian, Melanesian, or Tahitian. Also, persons who wrote in an entry indicating one of the specific categories were classified accordingly. In 1990, the **Asian** and **Native Hawaiian or Other Pacific Islander** categories were combined as **Asian and Pacific Islander**. This volume uses the 1990 combination.

The population of **Some other race** includes all persons who indicated "Some other race" as well as persons who wrote in a category not included in the race categories described above, including entries such as multiracial, mixed, interracial, or a Hispanic/Latino group such as Mexican, Puerto Rican, or Cuban in the ''Some other race '' write-in space.

Changes in specific listing of racial categories, the new practice of allowing more than one selection in 2000, and the order in which questions appeared on the questionnaire, could all affect comparability between the 2000 and 1990 censuses.

The Hispanic population is based on a complete-count question that asked respondents "Is this person Spanish/Hispanic/Latino?" Persons marking any one of the four Hispanic categories (i.e., Mexican, Puerto Rican, Cuban, or other Spanish) are collectively referred to as Hispanic.

In the 2000 Census, the Hispanic Origin question was placed before the race question and specific instructions indicated that both questions should be answered. These changes were designed to improve accuracy, and may affect comparability with 1990 data.

POPULATION—AGE, Items 16–24
Source: U.S. Bureau of the Census— 2000 Census of Population and Housing

Age derived from the census (1990) is classified as age at last birthday (i.e., number of completed years from birth to April 1). The percent figures are derived by dividing the number of persons in a specified age group by the total population of a given geographic area. Data on age are based on complete counts of resident population.

The 2000 Census also asked for the specific date of birth of the respondent, and 2000 census procedures used the birth date for deriving age data. For this reason, it is likely that the 2000 data have fewer problems than prior censuses, such as a tendency to round ages or report the person's age on the date the questionnaire was filled out rather than on April 1.

POPULATION—PERCENT FEMALE, Item 25
Source: U.S. Bureau of the Census—
2000 Census of Population and Housing

The female population of a geographic area is shown as a percent of the total population of the area.

HOUSEHOLDS, 2000, Items 26–30
Source: U.S. Bureau of the Census—
2000 Census of Population and Housing

A household consists of persons occupying a single housing unit. A housing unit is a house, an apartment, a group of rooms, or a single room occupied as separate living quarters. The occupants may be a single family, 1 person living alone, 2 or more families living together, or any other group of related or unrelated persons who share a housing unit. The number of households is the same as the number of year-round occupied housing units.

A family household consists of 2 or more persons, including the householder, who are related by birth, marriage, or adoption and who live together as 1 household; all such persons are considered as members of one family.

The measure of persons per household is obtained by dividing the number of persons in households by the number of households or householders. The category **female family householder** includes only female-headed family households with no spouse present.

GROUP QUARTERS, Items 31–34
Source: U.S. Bureau of the Census—
1990 Census of Population and Housing

All persons not living in households are classified by the Census Bureau as living in group quarters. This volume includes the total number of persons in group quarters and in selected types of group quarters.

Institutionalized population includes people under formally authorized, supervised care or custody in institutions at the time of enumeration. These include correctional institutions, nursing homes, mental (psychiatric) hospitals, hospitals or wards for the chronically ill, schools, hospitals, or wards for the mentally retarded, the physically handicapped, or for drug/alcohol abuse, wards in general or military hospitals for patients who have no usual home elsewhere, and juvenile institutions.

Nursing homes comprise a heterogeneous group of places. The majority of patients are elderly, although persons who require nursing care because of chronic physical conditions may be found in these homes regardless of their age. Included in this category are

skilled-nursing facilities, intermediate-care facilities, long-term care rooms in wards or buildings on the grounds of hospitals, or long-term care rooms/nursing wings in congregate housing facilities. Also included are nursing, convalescent, and rest homes, such as soldiers', sailors', veterans', and fraternal or religious homes for the aged, with or without nursing care.

The **Noninstitutionalized population** includes people who live in group quarters other than institutions, such as college dormitories and military quarters.

CRIME, Items 35–38
Source: U.S. Federal Bureau of Investigation—
Uniform Crime Reports

Crime data are as reported to the FBI by law enforcement agencies and have not been adjusted for under-reporting. This may affect comparability between geographic areas or over time.

Through the voluntary contribution of crime statistics by law enforcement agencies across the United States, the Uniform Crime Reporting (UCR) Program provides periodic assessments of crime in the nation as measured by those offenses which come to the attention of the law enforcement community. The Committee on Uniform Crime Records of the International Association of Chiefs of Police initiated this voluntary national data-collection effort in 1930. UCR Program contributors compile and submit their crime data in 1 of 2 manners: either directly to the FBI or through the State UCR Programs.

Seven offenses, because of their seriousness, frequency of occurrence, and likelihood of being reported to police, were initially selected to serve as an index for evaluating fluctuations in the volume of crime. These serious crimes were murder and nonnegligent manslaughter, forcible rape, robbery, aggravated assault, burglary, larceny-theft, and motor vehicle theft. By congressional mandate, arson was added as the eighth index offense in 1979. The totals shown in this volume do not include arson.

Violent offenses include 4 crime categories: (1) Murder and nonnegligent manslaughter, as defined in the UCR Program, is the willful (nonnegligent) killing of 1 human being by another. This offense excludes deaths caused by negligence, suicide or accident; justifiable homicides; and attempts to murder or assaults to murder. (2) Forcible rape is the carnal knowledge of a female forcibly and against her will. Assaults or attempts to commit rape by force or threat of force are also included; however, statutory rape (without force) and other sex offenses are excluded. (3) Robbery is the taking or attempting to take anything of value from the care, custody, or control of a person or persons by force or threat of force or violence and/or by putting the victim in fear. (4) Aggravated assault is an unlawful attack by 1 person upon another for the purpose of inflicting severe or aggravated bodily injury. This type of assault is usually accompanied by the use of a weapon or by means likely to produce death or great bodily harm. Attempts are included since an injury does not necessarily have to result when a gun, knife, or other weapon is used, which could and probably would result in a serious personal injury if the crime were successfully completed.

Property crimes include 3 categories: (1) Burglary, or breaking and entering, is the unlawful entry of a structure to commit a felony or theft, even though no force was used to gain entrance. (2) Larceny/theft is the unauthorized taking of the personal property of another, without the use of force. (3) Motor vehicle theft is the unauthorized taking of any motor vehicle.

Rates are based on population estimates provided by the FBI.

EDUCATION—SCHOOL ENROLLMENT AND EDUCATIONAL ATTAINMENT, Items 39–42
Source: U.S. Bureau of the Census— 1990 Census of Population and Housing

Data on school enrollment and educational attainment were derived from a sample of the population. Persons were classified as enrolled in school if they reported attending a "regular" public or private school (or college) at any time between February 1, 1990 and the time of enumeration. The instructions were to "include only nursery school, kindergarten, elementary school, and schooling which would lead to a high school diploma or a college degree" as regular school. Public school is defined as "any school or college controlled and supported by a local, county, state, or federal government." Schools supported and controlled primarily by religious organizations or other private groups are defined as private.

Statistics for years of school completed are for persons 25 years old and over. The data were derived from a question on the 1990 census questionnaire that asked respondents for the highest level of school they had completed or the highest degree they had received. Persons who passed a high school equivalency examination were considered high school graduates. Schooling received in foreign schools was to be reported as the equivalent grade or years in the regular American school system.

MONEY INCOME, Items 43–46
Source: U.S. Bureau of the Census— 1990 Census of Population and Housing

The data on income are derived from the responses of a sample of persons 15 years old and older. **Total money income** is defined by the Bureau of the Census for statistical purposes as the sum of the following: wage or salary income; nonfarm self-employment income; net farm self-employment income; Social Security and railroad retirement income; public assistance income; and all other regularly received income such as interest, dividends, veterans' payments, pensions, unemployment compensation, and alimony. Receipts not counted as income include various "lump sum" payments such as capital gains or inheritances.

The total represents the amount of income received before deductions for personal income taxes, Social Security, bond purchases, union dues, Medicare deductions, etc.

Per capita income is based on resident population enumerated as of April 1, 1990.

Income of households includes the income of the householder and all other persons 15 years old and older in the household. Household income is usually less than family income because many households consist of only 1 person. The median divides the income distribution into 2 equal parts, 1 having incomes above the median, the other with incomes below. The constant-dollar figures are based on an annual average Consumer Price Index from the Bureau of Labor Statistics. Constant-dollar figures are estimates representing an effort to remove the effects of price changes from statistical series reported in dollar terms. However, the estimates do not reflect the price and cost-of-living differences that may exist between areas.

POVERTY, Items 47–49
Source: U.S. Bureau of the Census— 1990 Census of Population and Housing

The data on poverty are derived from the same questions as the data on money income. Poverty status is based on the definition prescribed by the Federal Office of Management and Budget as the standard to be used by federal agencies for statistical purposes. Families and persons are classified as below the poverty level if their total family income or unrelated individual income was less than the poverty threshold specified for the applicable family size, age of householder, and number of related children present under 18. Poverty status is determined for all families (and by implication all family members). For persons not in families, poverty status is determined by their income in relation to the appropriate poverty threshold. Inmates of institutions, persons in military group quarters or college dormitories, and unrelated individuals under 15 are excluded.

The 1989 poverty thresholds are shown in Figure 1.

Figure 1.
Poverty Thresholds in 1989 by Size of Family

Size of Family Unit	Weighted average thresholds
One person (unrelated individual)	$6,310
Under 65 years	6,451
65 years and over	5,947
Two persons	8,076
Householder under 65 years	8,343
Householder 65 years and over	7,501
Three persons	9,885
Four persons	12,674
Five persons	14,990
Six persons	16,921
Seven persons	19,162
Eight persons	21,328
Nine or more persons	25,480

HOUSING, Items 50–60
Source: U.S. Bureau of the Census—
2000 Census of Population and Housing

A **housing unit** is a house, apartment, mobile home or trailer, group of rooms, or single room occupied or, if vacant, intended for occupancy as separate living quarters. Separate living quarters are those in which the occupants do not live and eat with any other persons in the structure and which have direct access from the outside of the building through a common hall.

The occupants of a housing unit may be a single family, 1 person living alone, 2 or more families living together, or a group of related or unrelated persons who share living arrangements. For vacant units, the criteria of separateness and direct access are applied to the intended occupants whenever possible. If that information cannot be obtained, the criteria are applied to the previous occupants. Both occupied and vacant housing units are included in the housing inventory, except that recreational vehicles, tents, caves, boats, railroad cars, and the like are included only if they are occupied as someone's usual place of residence.

A housing unit is classified as occupied if it is the usual place of residence of the person or group of persons living in it at the time of enumeration or if the occupants are only temporarily absent (e.g., away on vacation). A household consists of all persons who occupy a housing unit as their usual place of residence. Vacant units for sale or rent include units rented or sold but not occupied and any other units held off the market.

The percent change represents the difference in the number of total housing units in a specified area over the decade 1980-1990.

Vacant housing units are considered for **seasonal, recreational, or occasional use** if they are used or intended for use only in certain seasons, for weekends, or other occasional use throughout the year. Seasonal units include those used for summer or winter sports or recreation, such as beach cottages and hunting cabins. Seasonal units also may include quarters for such workers as herders and loggers. Interval ownership units, sometimes called shared-ownership or time-sharing condominiums, also are included in this category.

The **homeowner vacancy rate** is the proportion of the homeowner housing inventory that is vacant for sale. It is computed by dividing the number of vacant units for sale only by the sum of the owner-occupied units and vacant units that are for sale only.

The **rental vacancy rate** is the proportion of the rental inventory that is vacant for rent. It is computed by dividing the number of vacant units for rent by the sum of the renter-occupied units and the number of vacant units for rent.

A housing unit is **owner occupied** if the owner or co-owner lives in the unit even if it is mortgaged or not fully paid for. The owner or co-owner must live in the unit and usually is Person 1 on the census questionnaire.

All occupied housing units that are not owner occupied, whether they are rented for cash rent or occupied without payment of cash rent, are classified as **renter occupied**.

Average Household Size of Owner-Occupied Units is a measure obtained by dividing the number of people living in owner-occupied housing units by the number of owner-occupied housing units.

Average Household Size of Renter-Occupied Units is a measure obtained by dividing the number of people living in renter-occupied housing units by the number of renter-occupied housing units.

CIVILIAN LABOR FORCE AND UNEMPLOYMENT, Items 61–64
Source: U.S. Bureau of Labor Statistics

Data for the civilian labor force are the product of a federal-state cooperative program in which state employment security agencies prepare labor force and unemployment estimates under concepts, definitions, and technical procedures established by the Bureau of Labor Statistics. The civilian labor force consists of all persons 16 years and over who are either employed in a civilian job or unemployed.

Unemployment includes all persons who did not work during the survey week, made specific efforts to find a job in the prior 4 weeks, and were available for work during the survey week (except for temporary illness). Persons waiting to be called back to a job from which they had been laid off and those waiting to report to a new job within the next 30 days are included in unemployment figures.

CIVILIAN EMPLOYMENT, 1990, Items 65–67
Source: U.S. Bureau of the Census—
1990 Census of Population and Housing

Total employment includes all civilians 16 years old or older who were either (1) "at work" — those who did any work at all during the reference week as paid employees, worked in their own business or profession, worked on their own farm, or worked 15 hours or more as unpaid workers in a family farm or business; or were (2) "with a job, but not at work"—those who had a job but were not at work that week due to illness, weather, industrial dispute, vacation, or other personal reasons.

The **occupation categories** shown are consistent with the 1980 edition of the *Standard Occupational Classification Manual (SOC)* published by the Office of Federal Statistical Policy and Standards, U.S. Department of Commerce. Professional, managerial, and technical occupations include the following categories: executive administrative, and managerial occupations (000-042); professional specialty occupations (043-202); and technicians and related support occupations (203-242). Precision production, craft, and repair includes SOC codes 503-702.

WORK DISABILITY, Item 68
Source: U.S. Bureau of the Census—
1990 Census of Population and Housing

Data are shown for persons 16 to 64 years old in 1990. Persons were identified as having a work disability if they reported a health condition that had lasted 6 months or more and which limited the kind or amount of work they could do at a job or business.

CONSTRUCTION—BUILDING PERMITS, Items 69–71
Source: U.S. Bureau of the Census— Building Permits Survey

Figures represent private residential construction authorized by building permits in approximately 19,000 places in the United States. Valuation represents the cost of construction as recorded on the building permit. This figure usually excludes the cost of on-site and off-site development and improvements and the cost of heating, plumbing, electrical, and elevator installations.

If a city is not a permit-issuing place covered by the Census Bureau, an "NA" is shown. Cities that are permit-issuing places but that issued no permits during the period are represented by a "0." State and U.S. totals were obtained by summing the data for permit issuing places within each jurisdiction.

Residential building permits include buildings with any number of housing units. Hotels, apartment hotels, dormitories, fraternity houses, and other non-housekeeping residential buildings are not included.

1997 ECONOMIC CENSUS: OVERVIEW
Items 72–107
Source: U.S. Bureau of the Census

The Economic Census provides a detailed portrait of the nation's economy once every five years, from the national to the local level. The 1997 Economic Census covers nearly all of the U.S. economy in its basic collection of establishment statistics. It is the first major data source to use the new North American Industry Classification System (NAICS) and is therefore not comparable to economic data from prior years which were based on the Standard Industrial Classification (SIC) system.

NAICS, developed in cooperation with Canada and Mexico, classifies North America's economic activities at 2-, 3-, 4-, and 5-digit levels of detail, and the U.S. version of NAICS further defines industries to a sixth digit. The Economic Census takes advantage of this hierarchy to publish data at these successive levels of detail: sector (2-digit); subsector (3-digit); industry group (4-digit); industry(5-digit); and U.S. industry(6-digit.)

This volume was published during the initial release of the 1997 Economic Census and therefore includes those sectors that were available at the time of publication. The information in Table D is at the 2-digit level.

Several key statistics are tabulated for all industries included in this volume: number of establishments (or companies); number of employees; payroll; and a measure of output (sales, receipts, revenue, value of shipments, or value of construction work done.)

Number of Establishments. An establishment is a single physical location at which business is conducted. It is not necessarily identical with a company or enterprise, which may consist of one establishment or more. Economic Census figures represent a summary of reports for individual establishments rather than companies. For cases where a census report was received, separate information was obtained for each location where business was conducted. When administrative records of other Federal agencies were used instead of a census report, no information was available on the number of locations operated. Each Economic Census establishment was tabulated according to the physical location at which the business was conducted. The count of establishments represents those in business at any time during 1997.

When two activities or more were carried on at a single location under a single ownership, all activities generally were grouped together as a single establishment. The entire establishment was classified on the basis of its major activity and all data for it were included in that classification. However, when distinct and separate economic activities (for which different industry classification codes were appropriate) were conducted at a single location under a single ownership, separate establishment reports for each of the different activities were obtained in the census.

Number of Employees. Paid employees consist of the full-time and part-time employees, including salaried officers and executives of corporations. Included are employees on paid sick leave, paid holidays, and paid vacations; not included are proprietors and partners of unincorporated businesses. The definition of paid employees is the same as that used on IRS form 941.

Payroll. Payroll includes all forms of compensation such as salaries, wages, commissions, dismissal pay, bonuses, vacation allowances, sick-leave pay, and employee contributions to qualified pension plans paid during the year to all employees. For corporations, payroll includes amounts paid to officers and executives; for unincorporated businesses, it does not include profit or other compensation of proprietors or partners. Payroll is reported before deductions for social security, income tax, insurance, union dues, etc. This definition of payroll is the same as that used by the Internal Revenue Service (IRS) on form 941.

Sales, Shipments, Receipts, Revenue, or Business Done. This measure includes the total sales, shipments, receipts, revenue, or business done by establishments within the scope of the Economic Census. The definition of each of these items is specific to the economic sector measured.

WHOLESALE TRADE, Items 72–75
Source: U.S. Bureau of the Census, 1997 Economic Census
(See Overview of 1997 Economic Census prior to Item 72)

The Wholesale Trade sector (sector 42) comprises establishments engaged in wholesaling merchandise, generally without transformation, and rendering services incidental to the sale of merchandise. The wholesaling process is an intermediate step in the distribution of merchandise.

Wholesalers are organized to sell or arrange the purchase or sale of (a) goods for resale (i.e., goods sold to other wholesalers or retailers), (b) capital or durable nonconsumer goods, and (c) raw and intermediate materials and supplies used in production.

Wholesalers sell merchandise to other businesses and normally operate from a warehouse or office. These warehouses and offices are characterized by having little or no display of merchandise. In addition, neither the design nor the location of the premises is intended to solicit walk-in traffic. Wholesalers do not normally use advertising directed to the general public. Customers are generally reached initially via telephone, in-person marketing, or by specialized advertising that may include Internet and other electronic means. Follow-up orders are either vendor-initiated or client-initiated, generally based on previous sales, and typically exhibit strong ties between sellers and buyers. In fact, transactions are often conducted between wholesalers and clients that have long-standing business relationships.

This sector comprises two main types of wholesalers: those that sell goods on their own account and those that arrange sales and purchases for others for a commission or fee.

(1) Establishments that sell goods on their own account are known as wholesale merchants, distributors, jobbers, drop shippers, import/export merchants, and sales branches. These establishments typically maintain their own warehouse, where they receive and handle goods for their customers. Goods are generally sold without transformation, but may include integral functions, such as sorting, packaging, labeling, and other marketing services.

(2) Establishments arranging for the purchase or sale of goods owned by others or purchasing goods on a commission basis are known as agents and brokers, commission merchants, import/export agents and brokers, auction companies, and manufacturers' representatives. These establishments operate from offices and generally do not own or handle the goods they sell.

Some wholesale establishments may be connected with a single manufacturer and promote and sell the particular manufacturer=s products to a wide range of other wholesalers or retailers. Other wholesalers may be connected to a retail chain or a limited number of retail chains and only provide a variety of products needed by that particular retail operation(s). These wholesalers may obtain the products from a wide range of manufacturers. Still other wholesalers may not take title to the goods, but act as agents and brokers for a commission.

Although, in general, wholesaling normally denotes sales in large volumes, durable nonconsumer goods may be sold in single units. Sales of capital or durable nonconsumer goods used in the production of goods and services, such as farm machinery, medium and heavy duty trucks, and industrial machinery, are always included in wholesale trade.

RETAIL TRADE, Items 76–79
Source: U.S. Bureau of the Census,
1997 Economic Census
(See Overview of 1997 Economic Census
prior to Item 72)

The Retail Trade sector (44-45) comprises establishments engaged in retailing merchandise, generally without transformation, and rendering services incidental to the sale of merchandise.

The retailing process is the final step in the distribution of merchandise; retailers are, therefore, organized to sell merchandise in small quantities to the general public. This sector comprises two main types of retailers: store and nonstore retailers.

Store retailers operate fixed point-of-sale locations, located and designed to attract a high volume of walk-in customers. In general, retail stores have extensive displays of merchandise and use

mass-media advertising to attract customers. They typically sell merchandise to the general public for personal or household consumption, but some also serve business and institutional clients. These include establishments, such as office supply stores, computer and software stores, building materials dealers, plumbing supply stores, and electrical supply stores. Catalog showrooms, gasoline service stations, automotive dealers, and mobile home dealers are treated as store retailers.

In addition to retailing merchandise, some types of store retailers are also engaged in the provision of after-sales services, such as repair and installation. For example, new automobile dealers, electronic and appliance stores, and musical instrument and supply stores often provide repair services. As a general rule, establishments engaged in retailing merchandise and providing after-sales services are classified in this sector.

Nonstore retailers, like store retailers, are organized to serve the general public, but their retailing methods differ. The establishments of this subsector reach customers and market merchandise with methods, such as the broadcasting of "infomercials," the broadcasting and publishing of direct-response advertising, the publishing of paper and electronic catalogs, door-to-door solicitation, in-home demonstration, selling from portable stalls (street vendors, except food), and distribution through vending machines. Establishments engaged in the direct sale (nonstore) of products, such as home heating oil dealers and home delivery newspaper routes.

The buying of goods for resale is a characteristic of retail trade establishments that particularly distinguishes them from establishments in the agriculture, manufacturing, and construction industries. For example, farms that sell their products at or from the point of production are not classified in retail, but rather in agriculture. Similarly, establishments that both manufacture and sell their products to the general public are not classified in retail, but rather in manufacturing. However, establishments that engage in processing activities incidental to retailing are classified in retail.

REAL ESTATE AND RENTAL AND LEASING, Items 80–83
Source: U.S. Bureau of the Census,
1997 Economic Census
(See Overview of 1997 Economic Census
prior to Item 72)

The Real Estate and Rental and Leasing sector (53) comprises establishments primarily engaged in renting, leasing, or otherwise allowing the use of tangible or intangible assets, and establishments providing related services. The major portion of this sector comprises establishments that rent, lease, or otherwise allow the use of their own assets by others. The assets may be tangible, as is the case of real estate and equipment, or intangible, as is the case with patents and trademarks.

This sector also includes establishments primarily engaged in managing real estate for others, selling, renting and/or buying real estate for others, and appraising real estate. These activities are closely related to this sector's main activity, and it was felt that from a production basis they would best be included here. In addition, a substantial proportion of property management is self-performed by lessors.

The main components of this sector are the real estate lessors industries; equipment lessors industries (including motor vehicles, computers, and consumer goods); and lessors of nonfinancial intangible assets (except copyrighted works).

PROFESSIONAL, SCIENTIFIC, AND TECHNICAL SERVICES, Items 84–87
Source: U.S. Bureau of the Census,
1997 Economic Census
(See Overview of 1997 Economic Census
prior to Item 72)

The Professional, Scientific, and Technical Services sector (54) comprises establishments that specialize in performing professional, scientific, and technical activities for others. These activities require a high degree of expertise and training. The establishments in this sector specialize according to expertise and provide these services to clients in a variety of industries and, in some cases, to households. Activities performed include: legal advice and representation; accounting, bookkeeping, and payroll services; architectural, engineering, and specialized design services; computer services; consulting services; research services; advertising services; photographic services; translation and interpretation services; veterinary services; and other professional, scientific, and technical services.

This volume includes only those establishments subject to federal income tax.

This sector excludes establishments primarily engaged in providing a range of day-to-day office administrative services, such as financial planning, billing and recordkeeping, personnel, and physical distribution and logistics. These establishments are classified in Sector 56, Administrative and Support and Waste Management and Remediation Services.

MANUFACTURING, Items 88-91
Source: U.S. Bureau of the Census,
1997 Economic Census
(See Overview of 1997 Economic Census prior to Item 72)

The Manufacturing sector comprises establishments engaged in the mechanical, physical, or chemical transformation of materials, substances, or components into new products. The assembling of component parts of manufactured products is considered manufacturing, except in cases where the activity is appropriately classified as Construction. Establishments in the Manufacturing sector are often described as plants, factories, or mills and characteristically use power-driven machines and materials-handling equipment. However, establishments that transform materials or substances into new products by hand or in the worker's home and those engaged in selling to the general public products made on the same premises from which they are sold, such as bakeries, candy stores, and custom tailors, may also be included in this sector. Manufacturing establishments may process materials or may contract with other establishments to process their materials for them. Both types of establishments are included in manufacturing. The materials, substances, or components transformed by manufacturing establishments are raw materials that are products of agriculture, forestry, fishing, mining, or quarrying as well as products of other manufacturing establishments. The materials used may be purchased directly from producers, obtained through customary trade channels, or secured without recourse to the market by transferring the product from one establishment to another, under the same ownership. The new product of a manufacturing establishment may be finished in the sense that it is ready for utilization or consumption, or it may be semifinished to become an input for an establishment engaged in further manufacturing. For example, the product of the alumina refinery is the input used in the primary production of aluminum; primary aluminum is the input to an aluminum wire drawing plant; and aluminum wire is the input for a fabricated wire product manufacturing establishment.

Data are included for cities with 500 or more employees in the manufacturing sector.

ACCOMMODATION AND FOOD SERVICES, Items 92–95
Source: U.S. Bureau of the Census,
1997 Economic Census
(See Overview of 1997 Economic Census
prior to Item 72)

The Accommodation and Food Services sector (72) comprises establishments providing customers with lodging and/or preparing meals, snacks, and beverages for immediate consumption. The sector includes both accommodation and food services establishments because the two activities are often combined at the same establishment.

Excluded from this sector are civic and social organizations; amusement and recreation parks; theaters; and other recreation or entertainment facilities providing food and beverage services.

ARTS, ENTERTAINMENT, AND RECREATION, Items 96–99
Source: U.S. Bureau of the Census,
1997 Economic Census
(See Overview of 1997 Economic Census
prior to Item 181)

The Arts, Entertainment, and Recreation sector (71) includes a wide range of establishments that operate facilities or provide services to meet varied cultural, entertainment, and recreational interests of their patrons. This sector comprises (1) establishments that are involved in producing, promoting, or participating in live performances, events, or exhibits intended for public viewing; (2) establishments that preserve and exhibit objects and sites of historical, cultural, or educational interest; and (3) establishments that operate facilities or provide services that enable patrons to participate in recreational activities or pursue amusement, hobby, and leisure time interests.

Some establishments that provide cultural, entertainment, or recreational facilities and services are classified in other sectors. Excluded from this sector are: (1) establishments that provide both accommodations and recreational facilities, such as hunting and fishing camps and resort and casino hotels are classified in Subsector 721, Accommodation; (2) restaurants and night clubs that provide live entertainment in addition to the sale of food and beverages are classified in Subsector 722, Food Services and Drinking Places; (3) motion picture theaters, libraries and archives, and publishers of newspapers, magazines, books, periodicals, and computer software are classified in Sector 51, Information; and (4) establishments using transportation equipment to provide recreational and entertainment services, such as those operating sightseeing buses, dinner cruises, or helicopter rides are classified in Subsector 487, Scenic and Sightseeing Transportation.

HEALTH CARE AND SOCIAL ASSISTANCE, Items 100–103
Source: U.S. Bureau of the Census, 1997 Economic Census (See Overview of 1997 Economic Census prior to Item 72)

The Health Care and Social Assistance sector (62) comprises establishments providing health care and social assistance for individuals. The sector includes both health care and social assistance because it is sometimes difficult to distinguish between the boundaries of these two activities. The industries in this sector are arranged on a continuum starting with those establishments providing medical care exclusively, continuing with those providing health care and social assistance, and finally finishing with those providing only social assistance. The services provided by establishments in this sector are delivered by trained professionals. All industries in the sector share this commonality of process, namely, labor inputs of health practitioners or social workers with the requisite expertise. Many of the industries in the sector are defined based on the educational degree held by the practitioners included in the industry.

In this volume, only taxable establishments are included in Table D.

Excluded from this sector are aerobic classes in Subsector 713, Amusement, Gambling and Recreation Industries and nonmedical diet and weight reducing centers in Subsector 812, Personal and Laundry Services. Although these can be viewed as health services, these services are not typically delivered by health practitioners.

OTHER SERVICES, Items 104–107
Source: U.S. Bureau of the Census, 1997 Economic Census (See Overview of 1997 Economic Census prior to Item 72)

The Other Services (except Public Administration) sector (81) comprises establishments engaged in providing services not specifically provided for elsewhere in the classification system. Estab-

lishments in this sector are primarily engaged in activities, such as equipment and machinery repairing, promoting or administering religious activities, grantmaking, advocacy, and providing drycleaning and laundry services, personal care services, death care services, pet care services, photofinishing services, temporary parking services, and dating services.

Private households that engage in employing workers on or about the premises in activities primarily concerned with the operation of the household are included in this sector.

In this volume, only firms subject to federal tax are included.

Excluded from this sector are establishments primarily engaged in retailing new equipment and also performing repairs and general maintenance on equipment. These establishments are classified in Sector 44–45, Retail Trade.

FEDERAL FUNDS, Items 108–116
Source: U.S. Bureau of the Census— Consolidated Federal Funds Report

Data on federal expenditures and obligations are obtained from a report prepared by the Bureau of the Census in accordance with the Consolidated Federal Funds Report (CFFR) Act of 1982 (P.L. 97-326). The data are for federal fiscal years beginning on October 1 and ending the following September 30.

Only selected categories of data from the CFFR can be allocated to the city level. The city items shown in this book are "selected" federal funds and do not represent all federal funds received by individuals and entities within the city.

Dollar amounts reported can reflect expenditure or obligations. In some cases, dollar amounts are negative, representing deobligations of financial assistance that had been previously awarded. Such amounts generally appear in the grant categories. Many categories are assigned only to state and county levels and never assigned to cities. Even the District of Columbia has funds assigned to "state undistributed" or "county undistributed," with the resulting "city" total enabling a more accurate comparison with other cities

Direct payments for individuals represent actual expenditures during the fiscal year. Direct payments data at the city level are limited largely to educational and housing assistance payments. Direct payments for educational assistance consist primarily of higher education grants and insured loans. Direct housing assistance includes primarily the Low Income Housing Assistance Program. Data on other types of direct payments, including food stamps, social security, and federal retirement, and data on federal wages and salaries are available for counties but not for cities.

Procurement contract awards cover awards by the United States Postal Service (USPS) as well as all other federal agencies. Amounts provided by the USPS represent actual outlays for contractual commitments, while amounts for other agencies represent the value of obligations for contract actions and do not reflect actual federal government expenditures. In general, only current-year contract actions are included—however, multiple-year obligations may be reported for contract actions of less than 3 years duration. The procurement contract data for cities are relatively complete.

Salaries and wages represent actual federal expenditures during the fiscal year; the geographic distribution of these amounts by state and county was estimated based upon place of employment.

Grants data represent the federal obligations incurred at the time the grant is awarded. The amounts reported do not represent actual expenditures since obligations in one time period may not result in outlays during the same time period. Moreover, initial amounts obligated may be adjusted at a later date, either through enhancements or de-obligations. All grant awards were reported by state, county, and city of the initial recipient. For many grants, this recipient is the state government even though the grant monies are subsequently distributed to county, municipal, or township governments. The grants for cities data exclude a number of large grant categories, such as grants made for the school lunch program.

Health and family welfare grants include a variety of grants by the U.S. Department of Health and Human Services for health research, child welfare, special programs for the aging, and related areas. The school lunch program and other nutritional assistance programs administered by the U.S. Department of Agriculture are also included.

Energy and environment grants include grants from the U.S. Department of Energy for energy development, energy conservation, and nuclear waste disposal, as well as from the Environmental Protection Agency for a variety of pollution control and waste management activities.

Education grants include a variety of grant programs relating to elementary, secondary, and post-secondary education; adult education; vocational education; faculty training; and related areas.

Housing and community development grants include Community Development Block Grants, housing demonstration programs, rental housing rehabilitation, and other housing programs.

CITY GOVERNMENT FINANCES,
Items 117–139
Source: U.S. Bureau of the Census—
Survey of Governments, 1999: Finance Statistics

Revenue and expenditure data for the city government only are included in this table. The numbers do not include funds of any special district governments located in the city.

Total **general revenue** includes all government revenue except utility, liquor store, and employee-retirement or other insurance trust revenue. It includes all tax collections and intergovernmental revenue, even if designated for employee-retirement or local utility purposes.

Intergovernmental revenue consists of amounts received from other governments as fiscal aid in the form of shared revenues and grants-in-aid, as reimbursements for performance of general expenditure functions and specific services for the paying government (e.g., care of prisoners or contractual research), or amounts in lieu of taxes. It excludes amounts received from other governments for sale of property, commodities, and utility services. All intergovernmental revenue is classified as general revenue. Intergovernmental revenue from the state government includes amounts originally from the federal government but channeled through the state.

Taxes are compulsory contributions exacted by a government for public purposes, and exclude employee and employer assessments for retirement and social insurance purposes, which are classified as insurance trust revenue. All tax revenue is classified as general revenue and comprises amounts received (including interest and penalties but excluding protested amounts and refunds) from all taxes imposed by a government. Note that local government tax revenue excludes any amounts from shares of state-imposed and collected taxes, which are classified as intergovernmental revenue.

Property taxes are based on ownership of property and measured by its value. They include general property taxes related to property as a whole—real and personal, tangible or intangible—whether taxed at a single rate or at classified rates. Also included are taxes on selected types of property, such as motor vehicles or certain or all intangibles.

Sales and gross receipts taxes include: "licenses" at more than nominal rates, based on volume or value of transfers of goods or services; taxes upon gross receipts, or upon gross income; and related taxes based upon use, storage, production (other than severance of natural resources), importation, or consumption of goods. Dealer discounts of "commissions" allowed to merchants for collection of taxes from consumers are excluded.

Total **general expenditure** includes all city expenditure other than the specifically enumerated kinds of expenditure classified as utility, liquor store, and employee retirement and other insurance trust expenditures.

Capital outlays are direct expenditures for contract or force account construction of buildings, roads, and other improvements, and for purchases of equipment, land, and existing structures. They include amounts for additions, replacements, and major alterations to fixed works and structures. Expenditure for repair to such works and structures, however, is classified as current operation expenditure.

A major portion of capital outlay is commonly financed by borrowing, while governmental revenue does not include receipts from borrowing. Among other things, this distorts the relationship between the totals presented for revenue and expenditure and renders this relationship useless as a direct measure of the degree of budgetary "balance," as that term is generally applied.

Public welfare is defined as support of and assistance to needy persons contingent upon their need. This excludes pensions to former employees and other benefits not contingent upon need. Health and hospital services provided directly by the government through its own hospitals and health agencies, as well as any payments to other governments for such purposes, are classified under those functional headings rather than being included as part of public welfare.

Highways includes construction, maintenance, and operation of highways, streets, and related structures, including toll highways, bridges, tunnels, ferries, street lighting, and snow and ice removal. Not included are highway policing and traffic control, which are considered as part of police protection.

Parking facilities include the construction, purchase, maintenance, and operation of public-use parking lots, garages, parking meters, and other distinctive parking facilities on a commercial basis.

Education includes provision or support of schools and facilities for elementary and secondary, higher, and other education. Elementary and secondary education includes the provision of public kindergarten through high school education by local governments. It encompasses instructional, support, and auxiliary services (school lunch, student activities, and community services) offered by public school systems. Higher education consists of all local institutions of higher education.

Health expenditures include outpatient health services other than hospital care, such as public health administration; research and education; categorical health programs; treatment and immunization clinics; nursing; environmental health activities such as air and water pollution control; ambulance service if provided separately from fire protection services; and other general public health activities such as mosquito abatement. School health services provided by health agencies (rather than school agencies) are included here. Not included are sewage treatment operations, which are classified as part of sewerage and sanitation. Hospital expenditures include financing, construction, acquisition, maintenance and operation of hospital facilities, provision of hospital care, and support of public or private hospitals.

Police protection encompasses expenditures for the preservation of law and order, as well as for traffic safety. It includes police patrols and communications, crime prevention activities, detention and custody of persons awaiting trial, traffic safety, and vehicular inspection.

Sewerage and sanitation includes sanitary and storm sewers, sewage disposal facilities and services, and other government activities for such purposes. Street cleaning and the collection and disposal of garbage and other waste are also included.

Parks and recreation includes cultural and scientific activities such as museums and art galleries; organized recreation, including playgrounds and playing fields, swimming pools, and bathing beaches; and municipal parks and special recreation facilities, such as auditoriums, stadiums, auto camps, recreation piers, and boat harbors.

Housing and community development includes city housing and redevelopment projects and the regulation, promotion, and support of private housing and redevelopment activities. Data from Arizona, Kentucky, Michigan, New Mexico, New York, and Virginia generally include municipal housing authorities. Housing authorities for other cities are usually classified as independent governments, and data for them are not included.

Interest on debt are the amounts paid for the use of borrowed money.

Total **debt** outstanding is the total of all debt obligations remaining unpaid on the date specified.

Utility debt is that portion of outstanding debt originally issued specifically to finance government owned and operated water, electric, gas, or transit utility facilities.

CITY GOVERNMENT EMPLOYMENT, Item 140
Source: U.S. Bureau of the Census— Survey of Governments, 1999: Employment Statistics

The data are from an annual survey conducted by the Bureau of the Census and represent paid employment by city governments during October 1999. Full-time equivalent employment is a computed statistic representing the number of full-time employees that would have been employed if the hours worked by the part-time employees were converted to full-time equivalents.

CLIMATE, Items 141–147
Source: National Oceanic and Atmospheric Administration

All climate data are average values for the 30-year period from 1961-1990.

Mean temperatures for January and July were determined by adding the average daily maximum temperatures and the average daily minimum temperatures and dividing by 2.

Temperature limits represent average daily minimum for January and average daily maximum for July.

Annual precipitation values are the average annual water equivalent of all precipitation for the 30-year period.

Heating and cooling degree days are used as relative measures of the energy required for heating and cooling buildings. One heating degree day is accumulated for each whole degree that the mean daily temperature is below 65 degrees Fahrenheit (i.e., a mean daily temperature of 62 degrees Fahrenheit will produce three heating degree days). Cooling degree days are accumulated in similar fashion for deviations of the mean daily temperature above 65 degrees Fahrenheit.

TABLE E—CONGRESSIONAL DISTRICTS OF THE 105TH CONGRESS

LAND AREA, Items 1–3
Source: U.S. Bureau of the Census

Land area measurements are shown to the nearest square kilometer. Land area includes dry land and land temporarily or partially covered by water, such as marshland, swamps, and river floodplains.

POPULATION, Items 2–3
Source: U.S. Bureau of the Census—
2000 Census of Population and Housing

The population data are based on the 100 percent count from the 1990 census.

POPULATION BY RACE AND HISPANIC ORIGIN, Items 4–11
Source: U.S. Bureau of the Census—
2000 Census of Population and Housing

The data on **race** were derived from answers to the question on race that was asked of all people. The concept of race, as used by the Census Bureau, reflects self-identification by people according to the race or races with which they most closely identify. These categories are socio-political constructs and should not be interpreted as being scientific or anthropological in nature. Furthermore, the race categories include both racial and national-origin groups.

In the 2000 Census, respondents were offered the option of selecting one or more races. This was not the case in prior censuses, so comparisons should be made with caution. In Table E, columns 4 through 11 refer to individuals who identified with each racial category, either alone or in combination with other races.

The **White** population is defined as persons who indicated their race as white, as well as persons who did not classify themselves in one of the specific race categories listed on the questionnaire but entered a nationality such as Irish, German, Italian, Lebanese, Near Easterner, Arab, or Polish.

The **Black** population includes persons who indicated their race as "Black, African Am., or Negro", as well as persons who did not classify themselves in one of the specific race categories but reported entries such as African American, Afro American, Kenyan, Nigerian, or Haitian.

The **American Indian or Alaska Native** population includes persons who indicated their race as American Indian or Alaska Native, as well as persons who did not classify themselves in one of the specific race categories but reported entries such as Canadian Indian, French American Indian, Spanish-American Indian, Eskimo, Aleut, Alaska Indian, or any of the American Indian or Alaska Native tribes.

The **Asian** population includes persons who indicated their race as Asian Indian, Chinese, Filipino, Japanese, Korean, Vietnamese, or "Other Asian", as well as persons who provided write-in entries of such Asian groups as Cambodian, Laotian, Hmong, Pakistani, or Taiwanese. Also, persons who wrote in an entry indicating one of the specific categories were classified accordingly. The **Native Hawaiian or Other Pacific Islander** population includes persons who indicated their race as "Native Hawaiian", "Guamanian or Chamorro", "Samoan" or "Other Pacific Islander", as well as persons who reported entries such as Part Hawaiian, American Samoan, Fijian, Melanesian, or Tahitian. Also, persons who wrote in an entry indicating one of the specific categories were classified accordingly. In 1990, the **Asian** and **Native Hawaiian or Other Pacific Islander** categories were combined as **Asian and Pacific Islander**. This volume uses the 1990 combination.

The population of **Some other race** includes all persons who indicated "Some other race" as well as persons who wrote in a category not included in the race categories described above, including entries such as multiracial, mixed, interracial, or a Hispanic/Latino group such as Mexican, Puerto Rican, or Cuban in the "Some other race" write-in space.

Changes in specific listing of racial categories, the new practice of allowing more than one selection in 2000, and the order in which questions appeared on the questionnaire, could all affect comparability between the 2000 and 1990 censuses.

The Hispanic population is based on a complete-count question that asked respondents "Is this person Spanish/Hispanic/Latino?" Persons marking any one of the four Hispanic categories (i.e., Mexican, Puerto Rican, Cuban, or other Spanish) are collectively referred to as Hispanic.

In the 2000 Census, the Hispanic Origin question was placed before the race question and specific instructions indicated that both questions should be answered. These changes were designed to improve accuracy, and may affect comparability with 1990 data.

POPULATION—AGE, Items 12–20
Source: U.S. Bureau of the Census—
2000 Census of Population and Housing

Age derived from the census (1990) is classified as age at last birthday (i.e., number of completed years from birth to April 1). The percent figures are derived by dividing the number of persons in a specified age group by the total population of a given geographic area.

The 2000 Census also asked for the specific date of birth of the respondent, and 2000 census procedures used the birth date for deriving age data. For this reason, it is likely that the 2000 data have fewer problems than prior censuses, such as a tendency to round ages or report the person's age on the date the questionnaire was filled out rather than on April 1.

POPULATION—PERCENT FEMALE, Item 21
Source: U.S. Bureau of the Census—
2000 Census of Population and Housing

The female population of a geographic area is shown as a percent of the total population of the area.

HOUSEHOLDS, Items 22–25
**Source: U.S. Bureau of the Census—
2000 Census of Population and Housing**

A household consists of persons occupying a single housing unit. A housing unit is a house, an apartment, a group of rooms, or a single room occupied as separate living quarters. The occupants may be a single family, 1 person living alone, 2 or more families living together, or any other group of related or unrelated persons sharing a housing unit. The number of households is the same as the number of year-round occupied housing units.

A family household consists of 2 or more persons, including the householder, who are related by birth, marriage, or adoption and who live together as 1 household; all such persons are considered as members of 1 family.

The measure of persons per household is obtained by dividing the number of persons in households by the number of households or householders. The category **female family householder** includes only female-headed family households with no spouse present.

PERSONS IN CORRECTIONAL INSTITUTIONS, Item 26
**Source: U.S. Bureau of the Census—
2000 Census of Population and Housing**

Correctional institutions includes prisons, federal detention centers, military disciplinary barracks and jails, police lockups, halfway houses used for correctional purposes, local jails, and other confinement facilities, including work farms.

PERSONS IN NURSING HOMES, Item 27
**Source: U.S. Bureau of the Census—
2000 Census of Population and Housing**

Nursing homes comprise a heterogeneous group of places. The majority of patients are elderly, although persons who require nursing care because of chronic physical conditions may be found in these homes regardless of their age. Included in this category are skilled-nursing facilities, intermediate-care facilities, long-term care rooms in wards or buildings on the grounds of hospitals, or long-term care rooms/nursing wings in congregate housing facilities. Also included are nursing, convalescent, and rest homes, such as soldiers', sailors', veterans', and fraternal or religious homes for the aged, with or without nursing care.

PERSONS IN MILITARY QUARTERS, Item 28
**Source: U.S. Bureau of the Census—
2000 Census of Population and Housing**

Military quarters includes military personnel living in barracks and dormitories on base, transient quarters on base for temporary residents (both civilian and military), and military ships. However, patients in military hospitals receiving treatment for chronic diseases or who had no usual home elsewhere, and people being held in military disciplinary barracks were included as part of the institutionalized population.

EDUCATION—SCHOOL ENROLLMENT AND EDUCATIONAL ATTAINMENT, Items 29–32
**Source: U.S. Bureau of the Census—
1990 Census of Population and Housing**

Data on school enrollment and educational attainment were derived from a sample of the population. Persons were classified as enrolled in school if they reported attending a "regular" public or private school (or college) at any time between February 1, 1990 and the time of enumeration. The instructions were to "include only nursery school, kindergarten, elementary school, and schooling which would lead to a high school diploma or a college degree" as regular school. Public school is defined as "any school or college controlled and supported by a local, county, state, or federal government." Schools supported and controlled primarily by religious organizations or other private groups are defined as private. Statistics for years of school completed are for persons 25 years old and over. The data were derived from a question on the 1990 census questionnaire that asked respondents for the highest level of school they had completed or the highest degree they had received. Persons who passed a high school equivalency examination were considered high school graduates. Schooling received in foreign schools was to be reported as the equivalent grade or years in the regular American school system.

MONEY INCOME, Items 33–35
**Source: U.S. Bureau of the Census—
1990 Census of Population and Housing**

The data on income are derived from the responses of a sample of persons 15 years old and older. **Total money income** is defined by the Bureau of the Census for statistical purposes as the sum of the following: wage or salary income; nonfarm self-employment income; net farm self-employment income; Social Security and railroad retirement income; public assistance income; and all other regularly received income such as interest, dividends, veterans' payments, pensions, unemployment compensation, and alimony. Receipts not counted as income include various "lump sum" payments such as capital gains or inheritances.

The total represents the amount of income received before deductions for personal income taxes, Social Security, bond purchases, union dues, Medicare deductions, etc.

Per capita income is based on resident population enumerated as of April 1, 1990.

Income of households includes the income of the householder and all other persons 15 years old and older in the household. Median household income is usually less than median family income because many households consist of only 1 person. The median divides the income distribution into 2 equal parts, 1 having incomes above the median, the other with incomes below.

The constant-dollar figures are based on an annual average Consumer Price Index from the Bureau of Labor Statistics. Constant-dollar figures are estimates representing an effort to remove the effects of price changes from statistical series reported in dollar terms. However, the estimates do not reflect the price and cost-of-living differences that may exist between areas.

POVERTY, Items 36–37
Source: U.S. Bureau of the Census—
1990 Census of Population and Housing

The data on poverty are derived from the same questions as the data on money income. Poverty status is based on the definition prescribed by the Federal Office of Management and Budget as the standard to be used by federal agencies for statistical purposes. Families and persons are classified as being below the poverty level if their total family income or unrelated individual income was less than the poverty threshold specified for the applicable family size, age of householder, and number of related children present under 18. Poverty status is determined for all families (and by implication all family members). For persons not in families, poverty status is determined by their income in relation to the appropriate poverty threshold. Inmates of institutions, persons in military group quarters or college dormitories, and unrelated individuals under 15 are excluded.

The 1989 poverty thresholds are shown in Figure 1.

Figure 1.
Poverty Thresholds in 1989 by Size of Family

Size of Family Unit	Weighted average thresholds
One person (unrelated individual)	$6,310
Under 65 years	6,451
65 years and over	5,947
Two persons	8,076
Householder under 65 years	8,343
Householder 65 years and over	7,501
Three persons	9,885
Four persons	12,674
Five persons	14,990
Six persons	16,921
Seven persons	19,162
Eight persons	21,328
Nine or more persons	25,480

HOUSING, Items 38–46
Source: U.S. Bureau of the Census—
1990 Census of Population and Housing

A **housing unit** is a house, apartment, mobile home or trailer, group of rooms, or single room occupied or, if vacant, intended for occupancy as separate living quarters. Separate living quarters are those in which the occupants do not live and eat with any other persons in the structure and which have direct access from the outside of the building through a common hall.

The occupants of a housing unit may be a single family, 1 person living alone, 2 or more families living together, or any other group of related or unrelated persons who share living arrangements (except as described in the definition for persons "living in group quarters"). For vacant units, the criteria of separateness and direct access are applied to the intended occupants whenever possible. If that information cannot be obtained, the criteria are applied to the previous occupants. Both occupied and vacant housing units are included in the housing inventory, except that recreational vehicles, tents, caves, boats, railroad cars, and the like are included only if they are occupied as someone's usual place of residence.

A housing unit is classified as occupied if it is the usual place of residence of the person or group of persons living in it at the time of enumeration, or if the occupants are only temporarily absent (e.g., away on vacation). A household consists of all persons who occupy a housing unit as their usual place of residence.

The percent change represents the difference in the number of total housing units in a specified area over the decade 1980-1990.

Median value is the dollar amount that divides the distribution of owner occupied housing units into 2 equal parts, with one half of the units falling below this value and the other half exceeding it. Value is defined as the respondent's estimate of what the house would sell for if it were for sale. Data are presented for 1-family units on less than 10 acres and with no business or medical office on the property.

Median rent divides the distribution of renter-occupied housing units into 2 equal parts. Median rent represents the amount of cash rent a renter pays (contract rent) plus the estimated average cost of utilities and fuels if paid by the renter (gross rent). Rent is to be reported only for living quarters, not for any business or other space occupied. Single family houses on lots of 10 or more acres are excluded.

Housing cost as a percent of income is shown separately for owners with mortgages, owners without mortgages, and renters. Rent as a percentage of income is a computed ratio of gross rent and monthly household income (total household income in 1989 divided by 12). Selected owner costs include utilities and fuels, as well as mortgage payments, insurance, taxes, etc. In each case, the ratio of housing cost to income is computed separately for each housing unit. The ratio for one-half of the units is above the median shown in this book, and one-half is below.

Substandard units are occupied units which are overcrowded or lack complete plumbing facilities. For the purposes of this item "overcrowded" is defined as having 1.01 persons or more per room. Complete plumbing facilities include hot and cold piped water, a flush toilet, and a bathtub or shower. These facilities must be located inside the housing unit but not necessarily in the same room.

CIVILIAN LABOR FORCE, UNEMPLOYMENT, EMPLOYMENT, Items 47–52
Source: U.S. Bureau of the Census—
1990 Census of Population and Housing

All data pertain to persons 16 years of age and over. The civilian labor force consists of persons classified as either employed or unemployed in accordance with the criteria described below.

Unemployment data include all persons who did not work during the survey week, made specific efforts to find a job in the prior 4 weeks, and were available for work during the survey week (except for temporary illness). Persons waiting to be called back to a job from which they had been laid off and those waiting to report to a new job within the next 30 days are included in unemployment figures.

Total employment includes all civilians who were either (1) "at work" — those who did any work at all during the reference week as paid employees, worked in their own business or profession, worked on their own farm, or worked 15 hours or more as unpaid workers in a family farm or business; or were (2) "with a job but not at work" — those who had a job but were not at work that week due to illness, weather, industrial dispute, vacation, or other personal reasons.

The occupation categories shown are consistent with the 1980 edition of the *Standard Occupational Classification Manual (SOC)*, published by the Office of Federal Statistical Policy and Standards, U.S. Department of Commerce. Professional, managerial, and technical occupations include the following categories: executive, administrative, and managerial occupations (000-042); professional specialty occupations (043-202); and technicians and related support occupations (203-242). Precision production, craft and repair includes SOC codes 503-702.

WORK DISABILITY, Item 53
Source: U.S. Bureau of the Census— 1990 Census of Population and Housing

Data are shown for persons 16 to 64 years old in 1990. Persons were identified as having a work disability if they reported a health condition that had lasted 6 months or more and which limited the kind or amount of work they could do at a job or business.